THE VIRGIN BOOK OF BRITISH HIT SINGLES

VOLUME 2

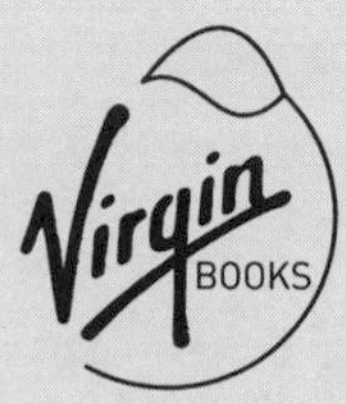

THE VIRGIN BOOK OF BRITISH HIT SINGLES

VOLUME 2

Entry biographies by Dave McAleer, Andy Gregory and Matthew White

OFFICIAL

1 2 3 4 5 6 7 8 9 10

Published in 2010 by Virgin Books, an imprint of Ebury Publishing
A Random House Group Company

The Random House Group Limited Reg. No. 954009

Addresses for companies within the Random House Group can be found at www.randomhouse.co.uk

A CIP catalogue record for this book is available from the British Library

The Random House Group Limited supports The Forest Stewardship Council [FSC], the leading international forest certification organisation. All our titles that are printed on Greenpeace-approved FSC-certified paper carry the FSC logo. Our paper procurement policy can be found at www.rbooks.co.uk/environment

ISBN 9780753522455

Text design: www.carrstudio.co.uk
Printed and bound in Italy by L.E.G.O.

45 RPM

Acknowledgements

The OCC would like to thank Matthew White, Dave McAleer, Andy Gregory, Elliot Costi, Efehan Gür, Colin Hughes, Lonnie Readioff and Graham Betts for all their invaluable help collating this book, as well as Louisa Joyner, Clare Wallis and the staff at Virgin Books.

Virgin Books would like to thank Phil Matcham at the OCC for all his friendly co-operation and tireless checking, Mary Tobin and Kelly Falconer for their editorial work, and last but not least, Rich Carr for the design.

Contents

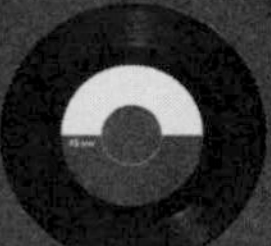

CHART LISTINGS

How To Use This Book

KEY TO ARTIST ENTRIES

TAKE THAT

UK, male vocal group – Gary Barlow*, Howard Donald, Jason Orange, Mark Owen* & Robbie Williams* (left 1995, rejoined 2010). Comeback kings who have sold 7.4 million singles in the UK. The boys, who came back for good – as a quartet – in 2006, were the first act to score four successive No.1s since The Beatles – a feat they've achieved twice. See Helping Haiti

Date	Title / Label	Peak Position	Weeks at No.1	Weeks on Chart (356)
23 Nov 91	**PROMISES** *RCA PB 45085*	38		2
8 Feb 92	**ONCE YOU'VE TASTED LOVE** *RCA PB 45257*	47		3
6 Jun 92	**IT ONLY TAKES A MINUTE** *RCA 74321101007*	7		8
15 Aug 92	**I FOUND HEAVEN** *RCA 74321108137*	15		6
10 Oct 92	**A MILLION LOVE SONGS** *RCA 74321116307*	7		9
12 Dec 92	**COULD IT BE MAGIC** *RCA 74321123137* ○	3		12
20 Feb 93	**WHY CAN'T I WAKE UP WITH YOU** *RCA 74321133102* ○	2		10
17 Jul 93	**PRAY** *RCA 74321154502* ●	1	4	11
9 Oct 93	**RELIGHT MY FIRE** *RCA 74321167722* FEATURING LULU ○	1	2	14
18 Dec 93	**BABE** *RCA 74321182122* ⊛	1	1	10
9 Apr 94	**EVERYTHING CHANGES** *RCA 74321167732* ○	1	2	10
9 Jul 94	**LOVE AIN'T HERE ANYMORE** *RCA 74321214832* ○	3		12
15 Oct 94	**SURE** *RCA 74321236622* ○	1	2	15
8 Apr 95	**BACK FOR GOOD** *RCA 74321271462* ⊛	1	4	13
5 Aug 95	**NEVER FORGET** *RCA 74321299572* ●	1	3	9
9 Mar 96	**HOW DEEP IS YOUR LOVE** *RCA 74321355592* ⊛	1	3	14
25 Nov 06	**PATIENCE** *Polydor 1714832* ●	1	4	39
10 Feb 07	**SHINE** *Polydor 1724294* ●	1	2	42
30 Jun 07	**I'D WAIT FOR LIFE** *Polydor 1736401*	17		2
27 Oct 07	**RULE THE WORLD** *Polydor 1746285* ●	2		66
6 Dec 08	**GREATEST DAY** *Polydor 1787445*	1	1	20
6 Dec 08	**PATIENCE** *Polydor 1714832*	59		1
6 Dec 08	**NEVER FORGET** *RCA GBARL9500200*	64		1
14 Feb 09	**UP ALL NIGHT** *Polydor 1796964*	14		11
13 Jun 09	**SAID IT ALL** *Polydor 2708717*	9		10
20 Jun 09	**RULE THE WORLD** *Polydor 1746285*	57		6
27 Jun 09	**GREATEST DAY** *Polydor 1787445*	73		1+

BIOGRAPHIES

Biographies include the nationality and category for every chart entrant.

Each entrant has at least a mini biography. The acts with the most weeks on the chart (see page 372 for the chart) each have extended biographies

Real names are included for all solo artists and, where applicable, dates of death and age of the artist at the time. "See..." links are included for soloists who also had singles chart entries in other acts.

The best known line-up is listed for every group that had a Top 10 single, with the vocalist/leader mentioned first and the others following in alphabetical order. In cases where later replacements had similar success both people are named and, where applicable, the dates of death are also shown for every group/duo member listed.

Certified Awards are given by the BPI to mark unit sales to retailers. They were introduced in April 1973. In January 1989 the levels of unit sales to the trade required to achieve each of the awards was amended to the following amounts:

Silver symbol ○ = 200,000 units
Gold symbol ● = 400,000 units
Platinum symbol ⊛ = 600,000 units

As from February 2005, download sales also count towards certified awards.

How To Use This Book

KEY TO EP ENTRIES

Weeks on Chart / Weeks at No.1 / Peak Position

Artist's Total Weeks On Chart

BEATLES

Date	Title / Label	Peak Position	Weeks at No.1	Weeks on Chart
				392
20 Jul 63	**TWIST AND SHOUT** *Parlophone GEP 8882*	1	21	64
21 Sep 63	**THE BEATLES' HITS** *Parlophone GEP 8880*	1	3	43
9 Nov 63	**THE BEATLES (NO. 1)** *Parlophone GEP 8883*	2		29
8 Feb 64	**ALL MY LOVING** *Parlophone GEP 8891*	1	8	44
4 Jul 64	**LONG TALL SALLY** *Parlophone GEP 8913*	1	7	37
14 Nov 64	**EXTRACTS FROM THE FILM 'A HARD DAY'S NIGHT'** *Parlophone GEP 8920*	1	6	30
9 Jan 65	**EXTRACTS FROM THE ALBUM 'A HARD DAY'S NIGHT'** *Parlophone GEP 8924*	8		17
10 Apr 65	**BEATLES FOR SALE** *Parlophone GEP 8931*	1	6	47
12 Jun 65	**BEATLES FOR SALE (NO. 2)** *Parlophone GEP 8938*	5		24
11 Dec 65	**THE BEATLES' MILLION SELLERS** *Parlophone GEP 8946*	1	4	26
12 Mar 66	**YESTERDAY** *Parlophone GEP 8948*	1	8	13
16 Jul 66	**NOWHERE MAN** *Parlophone GEP 8952*	4		18

Date of entry into chart — Title of EP — Label and Catalogue Number

KEY TO INDEX ENTRIES

Album Title — Artist/Group — Peak Position — Year of Release

	Peak Position	Year of Release
A BA NI BI IZHAR COHEN & ALPHABETA	20	1978
'A' BOMB IN WARDOUR STREET JAM	1	1978
A9 ARIEL	28	2000
THE A TEAM MIKE POST	45	1984
A&E GOLDFRAPP	10	2008
AAAH D YAAA GOATS	53	1993
AARON'S PARTY (COME GET IT) AARON CARTER	51	2000
ABACAB GENESIS	9	1981
ABACUS (WHEN I FALL IN LOVE) AXUS	62	1998
ABANDON [A] DARE	71	1989
ABANDON [B] THAT PETROL EMOTION	73	1990
ABANDON SHIP BLAGGERS I.T.A.	48	1994
ABBA-ESQUE EP ERASURE	1	1992
THE ABBEY ROAD EP SPIRITUALIZED	39	1998
ABC JACKSON 5	8	1970

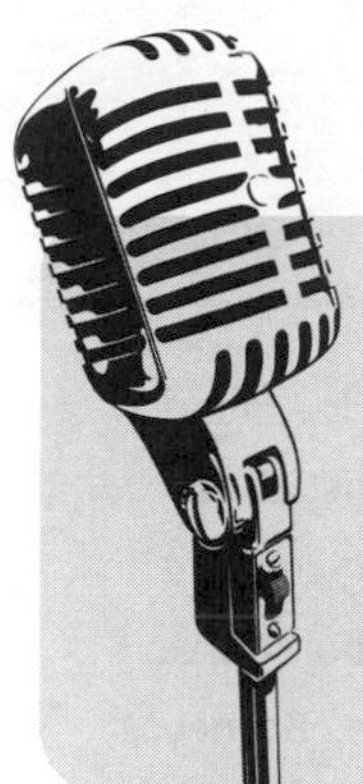

Introduction

There's never been a more exciting time to be a chart-watcher.

The birth of the 'digital age' has forever changed the way we buy music and the way we listen to it, but downloads have also shaken up the singles chart beyond recognition – and it happened almost overnight.

It's hard to imagine that when the first Top 12 was published back in the foggy days of November 1952, every record sold was made of heavy, breakable 10" shellac and cost the equivalent of a current full price album. At that time, most record-buyers played these 78 rpm singles on 'wind-up' gramophones – that is, non-electric record players that had to be wound by a handle to get the turntable to go round at the right speed. These winds would last for about two records, which was also how often you had to change the 'needle' (early stylus' that came in tiny tins of 200). It's a little different today, isn't it?

Over the 58 years covered in *Hit Singles*, we have seen the 78 followed by the 7" 45 rpm vinyl single, the cassette single, the CD single and, in this century, the digital single. In the second half of the 20th century, the gramophone was quickly replaced by the record player and radiogram, and then by the tape recorder, cassette and CD player. Today, while some people still prefer to listen to music on their earlier equipment, iPods, mobile phones and computers are the music players of choice for many people and, as hard to believe as it is, these will probably seem as obsolete to future generations as the gramophone does to us now.

In January 2007, when Official Charts Company rules were amended to allow *all* legally downloadable 'singles' to chart, even without a physical release, strange things started to happen to the weekly countdown. The trend for high debuts followed by rapid downward momentum was generally cast aside in favour of 'slow burners', hits that gained momentum over a number of weeks thanks to the power of radio, TV and the internet. Amazingly, the chart had come full circle and singles were actually climbing again – just like they used to.

One of the prime beneficiaries of the chart's new format has been Snow Patrol's indefatigable 2006 hit 'Chasing Cars', which, at the time of going to press, had stalled at an astonishing 96 chart weeks but was *still* hovering in the 100s purely on the strength of digital sales. Interestingly, several 'golden oldies' have also been given a new lease of life. Who'd have thought that Journey's soft rock ballad 'Don't Stop Believin'' – which peaked at a lowly No.62 in 1982 – would become a Top 10 smash in 2010 (albeit with a little help from the cast of *Glee*), that Rage Against The Machine would have Facebook to thank for spectacularly reviving 'Killing In The Name' or that adopted football anthems 'The Best' and 'You'll Never Walk Alone' would be thrown into the Top 40 mix with the young pretenders.

We have now come to expect the unexpected when the new chart is announced. No longer are retailers and

music fans looking at release schedules for an indication of the make-up of each week's chart; factor in a prime-time TV performance or a memorable TV advertising campaign, online support that has the potential to spread like wildfire, a savvy marketing and PR set-up or a crowd-pleasing tour or festival appearance and it matters little if you're Cheryl Cole or Nat King Cole when it comes to having a hit these days: the singles chart has become a window of opportunity for any musician you'd care to mention, past or present, dead or alive.

Since the last edition of *Hit Singles*, we've witnessed the untimely demise of Michael Jackson, the first global music superstar to die in the digital era. The old adage that death can do wonders for your career will never be better illustrated than when, in the weeks and months following his death on 25th June 2009, no less than 31 tracks from the 'King of Pop' flooded the Top 75. While the world was mourning, chart statisticians were frantically totting up his total weeks on chart and analysing the effect his death was having on his career-spanning UK singles sales. The pages of this book will reveal those figures and offer further irrefutable evidence of the exciting and unpredictable times in which we chart fans live.

The introduction of digital sales has meant that, for the first time, the chart truly reflects the musical mood of the public. A song can be heard on a TV show one day and be in the best-sellers list the next, making the terms 'overnight sensation' and 'instant hit' now actually true. If there's a downside, it's that the biggest hits sometimes do not sell in quite the same quantities as they have done in the past. However, the fact that music purchases are now spread over so many more tracks means that total, across-the-board sales more than make up for this.

Another interesting by-product of the download age is the pace with which an act's chart statistics can quickly be bolstered by just a couple of long-running singles or a series of rapid fire all-star collaborations. Contemporary superstars Take That, Rihanna, Britney Spears, Jay-Z, Kanye West, Beyoncé, Akon and Justin Timberlake have already spilt enough chart ink to be ranked among the top 50 hit-makers of all-time by weeks spent on the singles chart. You'll be flabbergasted when you find out just how many chart weeks Rihanna has amassed in her fledgling five-year career, and you can be sure she'll have amassed a whole lot more by the time you read this!

Despite what you may have read about 'the death of the single', sales of 'singles' – or should we say sales of single tracks – have never been higher. A record-shattering 152.7 million singles were sold in the UK in 2009, comparing favourably to 2008 (115.1 million), 1979 (89.1 million), the highest non-digital year on record, and, indeed, 2004's record low of 31.4 million. The 2009 figure also included a record 4.22 million sales in the last week of the year, beating 2008's benchmark of 4.03 million, and 2009 was also the first year since 1967 that singles sold more than albums in the UK.

With downloads now accounting for 98% of all singles sales and recordings more accessible than at any time in history, there's no doubt that more music is finding its way into more people's homes than ever before. This has naturally affected traditional record stores, which have relegated their CD singles section to a pitifully small shelf somewhere close to the specialist music aisles, done away with physical singles altogether or have had to shut up shop completely as a consequence of a difficult economic climate.

The evolving musical landscape has also, inevitably, brought with it a few more negative perspectives, the most prevalent being the ongoing fight against illegal file-sharing. It's been estimated that seven million people in the UK are locking themselves away in their bedrooms to 'steal' the latest hits, in varying quantities and from a dizzying array of P2P sites. The two sections of society reported to be suffering most at the hands of the file-sharers are the recording artists themselves and their record labels, which have been railroaded into making many redundancies.

Moves to encourage fans to purchase their music legitimately, shut down file-sharing sites, slap legal writs on offenders or threaten to cut off their broadband access have all, ultimately, fallen on deaf ears and perhaps irrevocably damaged the reputation of a music industry seemingly powerless to stop the trend and often perceived to be 'bullying' the public.

In simple terms, for as long as the internet is available, illegal downloading will survive, adapt and flourish. The industry and the government must deal with the problem upfront and start providing some viable solutions and alternatives for this and future generations of music-hungry consumers.

Conversely, some innovative musicians – among them Coldplay, Nine Inch Nails and Radiohead – have embraced the digital age head-on and actively encourage free downloading by offering individual tracks or whole albums. In one week in 2008, a staggering two million people downloaded Coldplay's 'Violet Hill' single free of charge from the band's website. If it had been eligible to chart, it would have outsold the entire Top 40 four times over! The move has stirred up a whole new hornet's nest in the legal vs. illegal debate, and it doesn't look like going away anytime soon.

Whatever the rights and wrongs or the successes and failings of the music industry in the 21st century, we should be thankful that we still have a singles chart to enjoy and scrutinise, and books such as *Hit Singles*, which handily bring all the information together in one mouth-watering edition.

New features in this edition, which spans every singles chart from 14th November 1952 to 10th April 2010, include the addition of informative mini-biographies for the many thousands of acts that have reached the Top 75, and these come complete with real names, death details and the full band line-up for every group or duo that has made the Top 10. There are also numerous fact-packed, never-seen-before listings scattered throughout the book, including the UK's best-selling downloads of all-time, the top singles artists based on career sales and the top-selling downloads from each year since 2004.

Regular chart book readers will also notice the changes that downloads continue to make to the chart: inflated weeks on chart totals for many singles, the large number of hits some artists have crammed into a very short period of time or those previously unrecognisable digital-only catalogue numbers.

Finally, if music charts are your thing, you may want to check out Virgin's *Hit Albums* and *Top 40 Charts* books. The latter is essential reading for anyone with a singles chart fetish as it lists every weekly Top 40 chart in full from 1960 to 2009, allowing you to find out not only what was perched at No.1 on special days in your life but also what the other 39 hits were at that time. It's a perfect companion to this, the No.1 pop singles chart book.

Dave McAleer and Matthew White
Chart Consultants

Every No.1 Single From 1952–2010

Includes the date of the first week at No.1 and the number of weeks at No.1

Chart Date	Title Artist	Weeks at No.1
14 Nov 52	**HERE IN MY HEART** AL MARTINO	9
16 Jan 53	**YOU BELONG TO ME** JO STAFFORD	1
23 Jan 53	**COMES A-LONG A-LOVE** KAY STARR	1
30 Jan 53	**OUTSIDE OF HEAVEN** EDDIE FISHER	1
6 Feb 53	**DON'T LET THE STARS GET IN YOUR EYES** PERRY COMO	5
13 Mar 53	**SHE WEARS RED FEATHERS** GUY MITCHELL	4
10 Apr 53	**BROKEN WINGS** STARGAZERS	1
17 Apr 53	**(HOW MUCH IS) THAT DOGGIE IN THE WINDOW** LITA ROZA	1
24 Apr 53	**I BELIEVE** FRANKIE LAINE	9
26 Jun 53	**I'M WALKING BEHIND YOU** EDDIE FISHER FT SALLY SWEETLAND	1
3 Jul 53	**I BELIEVE** FRANKIE LAINE	6
14 Aug 53	**SONG FROM 'THE MOULIN ROUGE'** MANTOVANI	1
21 Aug 53	**I BELIEVE** FRANKIE LAINE	3
11 Sep 53	**LOOK AT THAT GIRL** GUY MITCHELL	6
23 Oct 53	**HEY JOE** FRANKIE LAINE	2
6 Nov 53	**ANSWER ME** DAVID WHITFIELD	1
13 Nov 53	**ANSWER ME** FRANKIE LAINE	8*
11 Dec 53	**ANSWER ME** DAVID WHITFIELD	1
8 Jan 54	**OH MEIN PAPA** EDDIE CALVERT	9
12 Mar 54	**I SEE THE MOON** STARGAZERS	5
16 Apr 54	**SECRET LOVE** DORIS DAY	1
23 Apr 54	**I SEE THE MOON** STARGAZERS	1
30 Apr 54	**SUCH A NIGHT** JOHNNIE RAY	1
7 May 54	**SECRET LOVE** DORIS DAY	8
2 Jul 54	**CARA MIA** DAVID WHITFIELD	10
10 Sep 54	**LITTLE THINGS MEAN A LOT** KITTY KALLEN	1
17 Sep 54	**THREE COINS IN THE FOUNTAIN** FRANK SINATRA	3
8 Oct 54	**HOLD MY HAND** DON CORNELL	4
5 Nov 54	**MY SON MY SON** VERA LYNN	2
19 Nov 54	**HOLD MY HAND** DON CORNELL	1
26 Nov 54	**THIS OLE HOUSE** ROSEMARY CLOONEY	1
3 Dec 54	**LET'S HAVE ANOTHER PARTY** WINIFRED ATWELL	5
7 Jan 55	**FINGER OF SUSPICION** DICKIE VALENTINE	1
14 Jan 55	**MAMBO ITALIANO** ROSEMARY CLOONEY	1
21 Jan 55	**FINGER OF SUSPICION** DICKIE VALENTINE	2
4 Feb 55	**MAMBO ITALIANO** ROSEMARY CLOONEY	2
18 Feb 55	**SOFTLY, SOFTLY** RUBY MURRAY	3
11 Mar 55	**GIVE ME YOUR WORD** TENNESSEE ERNIE FORD	7
29 Apr 55	**CHERRY PINK AND APPLE BLOSSOM WHITE** PEREZ PREZ PRADO & HIS ORCHESTRA	2
13 May 55	**STRANGER IN PARADISE** TONY BENNETT	2
27 May 55	**CHERRY PINK AND APPLE BLOSSOM WHITE** EDDIE CALVERT	4
24 Jun 55	**UNCHAINED MELODY** JIMMY YOUNG	3
15 Jul 55	**DREAMBOAT** ALMA COGAN	2

*Equal No.1 on 11 Dec 1953 with ANSWER ME by DAVID WHITFIELD

Chart Date	Title Artist	Weeks at No.1
29 Jul 55	**ROSE MARIE** SLIM WHITMAN	11
14 Oct 55	**THE MAN FROM LARAMIE** JIMMY YOUNG	4
11 Nov 55	**HERNANDO'S HIDEAWAY** JOHNSTON BROTHERS	2
25 Nov 55	**ROCK AROUND THE CLOCK** BILL HALEY & HIS COMETS	3
16 Dec 55	**CHRISTMAS ALPHABET** DICKIE VALENTINE	3
6 Jan 56	**ROCK AROUND THE CLOCK** BILL HALEY & HIS COMETS	2
20 Jan 56	**SIXTEEN TONS** TENNESSEE ERNIE FORD	4
17 Feb 56	**MEMORIES ARE MADE OF THIS** DEAN MARTIN	4
16 Mar 56	**IT'S ALMOST TOMORROW** DREAM WEAVERS	2
30 Mar 56	**ROCK AND ROLL WALTZ** KAY STARR	1
6 Apr 56	**IT'S ALMOST TOMORROW** DREAM WEAVERS	1
13 Apr 56	**POOR PEOPLE OF PARIS** WINIFRED ATWELL	3
4 May 56	**NO OTHER LOVE** RONNIE HILTON	6
15 Jun 56	**I'LL BE HOME** PAT BOONE	5
20 Jul 56	**WHY DO FOOLS FALL IN LOVE** FRANKIE LYMON AND THE TEENAGERS	3
10 Aug 56	**WHATEVER WILL BE WILL BE (QUE SERA, SERA)** DORIS DAY	6
21 Sep 56	**LAY DOWN YOUR ARMS** ANNE SHELTON	4
19 Oct 56	**A WOMAN IN LOVE** FRANKIE LAINE	4
16 Nov 56	**JUST WALKIN' IN THE RAIN** JOHNNIE RAY	7
4 Jan 57	**SINGING THE BLUES** GUY MITCHELL	1
11 Jan 57	**SINGING THE BLUES** TOMMY STEELE	1
18 Jan 57	**SINGING THE BLUES** GUY MITCHELL	1
25 Jan 57	**THE GARDEN OF EDEN** FRANKIE VAUGHAN	4*
1 Feb 57	**SINGING THE BLUES** GUY MITCHELL	1
22 Feb 57	**YOUNG LOVE** TAB HUNTER	7
12 Apr 57	**CUMBERLAND GAP** LONNIE DONEGAN	5
17 May 57	**ROCK-A-BILLY** GUY MITCHELL	1
24 May 57	**BUTTERFLY** ANDY WILLIAMS	2
7 Jun 57	**YES TONIGHT JOSEPHINE** JOHNNIE RAY	3
28 Jun 57	**PUTTIN' ON THE STYLE / GAMBLIN' MAN** LONNIE DONEGAN	2
12 Jul 57	**ALL SHOOK UP** ELVIS PRESLEY	7
30 Aug 57	**DIANA** PAUL ANKA	9
1 Nov 57	**THAT'LL BE THE DAY** CRICKETS	3
22 Nov 57	**MARY'S BOY CHILD** HARRY BELAFONTE	7
10 Jan 58	**GREAT BALLS OF FIRE** JERRY LEE LEWIS	2
24 Jan 58	**JAILHOUSE ROCK** ELVIS PRESLEY	3
14 Feb 58	**THE STORY OF MY LIFE** MICHAEL HOLLIDAY	2
28 Feb 58	**MAGIC MOMENTS** PERRY COMO	8
25 Apr 58	**WHOLE LOTTA WOMAN** MARVIN RAINWATER	3
16 May 58	**WHO'S SORRY NOW** CONNIE FRANCIS	6
27 Jun 58	**ON THE STREET WHERE YOU LIVE** VIC DAMONE	2†
4 Jul 58	**ALL I HAVE TO DO IS DREAM / CLAUDETTE** EVERLY BROTHERS	7
22 Aug 58	**WHEN** KALIN TWINS	5
26 Sep 58	**CAROLINA MOON / STUPID CUPID** CONNIE FRANCIS	6

* Equal No.1 on 1 Feb 1957 with SINGING THE BLUES by GUY MITCHELL

† Equal No.1 on 4 July 1958 with ALL I HAVE TO DO IS DREAM / CLAUDETTE by EVERLY BROTHERS

Chart Date	Title	Artist	Weeks at No.1
7 Nov 58	**ALL IN THE GAME**	TOMMY EDWARDS	3
28 Nov 58	**HOOTS MON**	LORD ROCKINGHAM'S XI	3
19 Dec 58	**IT'S ONLY MAKE BELIEVE**	CONWAY TWITTY	5
23 Jan 59	**THE DAYS THE RAINS CAME**	JANE MORGAN	1
30 Jan 59	**I GOT STUNG / ONE NIGHT**	ELVIS PRESLEY	3
20 Feb 59	**AS I LOVE YOU**	SHIRLEY BASSEY	4
20 Mar 59	**SMOKE GETS IN YOUR EYES**	PLATTERS	1
27 Mar 59	**SIDE SADDLE**	RUSS CONWAY	4
24 Apr 59	**IT DOESN'T MATTER ANYMORE**	BUDDY HOLLY	3
15 May 59	**A FOOL SUCH AS I / I NEED YOUR LOVE TONIGHT**	ELVIS PRESLEY	5
19 Jun 59	**ROULETTE**	RUSS CONWAY	2
3 Jul 59	**DREAM LOVER**	BOBBY DARIN	4
31 Jul 59	**LIVING DOLL**	CLIFF RICHARD & THE DRIFTERS	6
11 Sep 59	**ONLY SIXTEEN**	CRAIG DOUGLAS	4
9 Oct 59	**HERE COMES SUMMER**	JERRY KELLER	1
16 Oct 59	**MACK THE KNIFE**	BOBBY DARIN	2
30 Oct 59	**TRAVELLIN' LIGHT**	CLIFF RICHARD & THE SHADOWS	5
4 Dec 59	**WHAT DO YOU WANT**	ADAM FAITH	3*
18 Dec 59	**WHAT DO YOU WANT TO MAKE THOSE EYES AT ME FOR**	EMILE FORD & THE CHECKMATES	6
29 Jan 60	**STARRY EYED**	MICHAEL HOLLIDAY	1
5 Feb 60	**WHY**	ANTHONY NEWLEY	4
10 Mar 60	**POOR ME**	ADAM FAITH	1
17 Mar 60	**RUNNING BEAR**	JOHNNY PRESTON	2
31 Mar 60	**MY OLD MAN'S A DUSTMAN**	LONNIE DONEGAN	4
28 Apr 60	**DO YOU MIND**	ANTHONY NEWLEY	1
5 May 60	**CATHY'S CLOWN**	EVERLY BROTHERS	7
23 Jun 60	**THREE STEPS TO HEAVEN**	EDDIE COCHRAN	2
7 Jul 60	**GOOD TIMIN'**	JIMMY JONES	3
28 Jul 60	**PLEASE DON'T TEASE**	CLIFF RICHARD & THE SHADOWS	1
4 Aug 60	**SHAKIN' ALL OVER**	JOHNNY KIDD & THE PIRATES	1
11 Aug 60	**PLEASE DON'T TEASE**	CLIFF RICHARD & THE SHADOWS	2
25 Aug 60	**APACHE**	SHADOWS	5
29 Sep 60	**TELL LAURA I LOVE HER**	RICKY VALANCE	3
20 Oct 60	**ONLY THE LONELY**	ROY ORBISON	2
3 Nov 60	**IT'S NOW OR NEVER**	ELVIS PRESLEY	8
29 Dec 60	**I LOVE YOU**	CLIFF RICHARD & THE SHADOWS	2
12 Jan 61	**POETRY IN MOTION**	JOHNNY TILLOTSON	2
26 Jan 61	**ARE YOU LONESOME TONIGHT**	ELVIS PRESLEY	4
23 Feb 61	**SAILOR**	PETULA CLARK	1
2 Mar 61	**WALK RIGHT BACK**	EVERLY BROTHERS	3
23 Mar 61	**WOODEN HEART**	ELVIS PRESLEY	6
4 May 61	**BLUE MOON**	MARCELS	2
18 May 61	**ON THE REBOUND**	FLOYD CRAMER	1
25 May 61	**YOU'RE DRIVING ME CRAZY**	TEMPERANCE SEVEN	1
1 Jun 61	**SURRENDER**	ELVIS PRESLEY	4
29 Jun 61	**RUNAWAY**	DEL SHANNON	3
20 Jul 61	**TEMPTATION**	EVERLY BROTHERS	2
3 Aug 61	**WELL I ASK YOU**	EDEN KANE	1
10 Aug 61	**YOU DON'T KNOW**	HELEN SHAPIRO	3
31 Aug 61	**JOHNNY REMEMBER ME**	JOHN LEYTON	3
21 Sep 61	**REACH FOR THE STARS / CLIMB EV'RY MOUNTAIN**	SHIRLEY BASSEY	1
28 Sep 61	**JOHNNY REMEMBER ME**	JOHN LEYTON	1
5 Oct 61	**KON TIKI**	SHADOWS	1
12 Oct 61	**MICHAEL**	HIGHWAYMEN	1
19 Oct 61	**WALKIN' BACK TO HAPPINESS**	HELEN SHAPIRO	3
9 Nov 61	**HIS LATEST FLAME**	ELVIS PRESLEY	4
7 Dec 61	**TOWER OF STRENGTH**	FRANKIE VAUGHAN	3
28 Dec 61	**MOON RIVER**	DANNY WILLIAMS	2
11 Jan 62	**THE YOUNG ONES**	CLIFF RICHARD & THE SHADOWS	6
22 Feb 62	**CAN'T HELP FALLING IN LOVE / ROCK-A-HULA BABY**	ELVIS PRESLEY	4
22 Mar 62	**WONDERFUL LAND**	SHADOWS	8
17 May 62	**NUT ROCKER**	B. BUMBLE & THE STINGERS	1
24 May 62	**GOOD LUCK CHARM**	ELVIS PRESLEY	5
28 Jun 62	**COME OUTSIDE**	MIKE SARNE WITH WENDY RICHARD	2
12 Jul 62	**I CAN'T STOP LOVING YOU**	RAY CHARLES	2
26 Jul 62	**I REMEMBER YOU**	FRANK IFIELD	7
13 Sep 62	**SHE'S NOT YOU**	ELVIS PRESLEY	3
4 Oct 62	**TELSTAR**	TORNADOS	5
8 Nov 62	**LOVESICK BLUES**	FRANK IFIELD	5
13 Dec 62	**RETURN TO SENDER**	ELVIS PRESLEY	3
3 Jan 63	**THE NEXT TIME / BACHELOR BOY**	CLIFF RICHARD & THE SHADOWS	3
24 Jan 63	**DANCE ON**	SHADOWS	1
31 Jan 63	**DIAMONDS**	JET HARRIS & TONY MEEHAN	3
21 Feb 63	**WAYWARD WIND**	FRANK IFIELD	3
14 Mar 63	**SUMMER HOLIDAY**	CLIFF RICHARD & THE SHADOWS	2
29 Mar 63	**FOOT TAPPER**	SHADOWS	1
4 Apr 63	**SUMMER HOLIDAY**	CLIFF RICHARD & THE SHADOWS	1
11 Apr 63	**HOW DO YOU DO IT?**	GERRY & THE PACEMAKERS	3
2 May 63	**FROM ME TO YOU**	BEATLES	7
20 Jun 63	**I LIKE IT**	GERRY & THE PACEMAKERS	4
18 Jul 63	**CONFESSIN' (THAT I LOVE YOU)**	FRANK IFIELD	2
1 Aug 63	**(YOU'RE THE) DEVIL IN DISGUISE**	ELVIS PRESLEY	1
8 Aug 63	**SWEETS FOR MY SWEET**	SEARCHERS	2
22 Aug 63	**BAD TO ME**	BILLY J KRAMER & THE DAKOTAS	3
12 Sep 63	**SHE LOVES YOU**	BEATLES	4
10 Oct 63	**DO YOU LOVE ME**	BRIAN POOLE & THE TREMELOES	3
31 Oct 63	**YOU'LL NEVER WALK ALONE**	GERRY & THE PACEMAKERS	4
28 Nov 63	**SHE LOVES YOU**	BEATLES	2
12 Dec 63	**I WANT TO HOLD YOUR HAND**	BEATLES	5
16 Jan 64	**GLAD ALL OVER**	DAVE CLARK FIVE	2
30 Jan 64	**NEEDLES & PINS**	SEARCHERS	3
20 Feb 64	**DIANE**	BACHELORS	1
27 Feb 64	**ANYONE WHO HAD A HEART**	CILLA BLACK	3
19 Mar 64	**LITTLE CHILDREN**	BILLY J KRAMER & THE DAKOTAS	2
2 Apr 64	**CAN'T BUY ME LOVE**	BEATLES	3
23 Apr 64	**A WORLD WITHOUT LOVE**	PETER & GORDON	2
7 May 64	**DON'T THROW YOUR LOVE AWAY**	SEARCHERS	2
21 May 64	**JULIET**	FOUR PENNIES	1
28 May 64	**YOU'RE MY WORLD**	CILLA BLACK	4
25 Jun 64	**IT'S OVER**	ROY ORBISON	2
9 Jul 64	**THE HOUSE OF THE RISING SUN**	ANIMALS	1
16 Jul 64	**IT'S ALL OVER NOW**	ROLLING STONES	1
23 Jul 64	**A HARD DAY'S NIGHT**	BEATLES	3
13 Aug 64	**DO WAH DIDDY DIDDY**	MANFRED MANN	2
27 Aug 64	**HAVE I THE RIGHT**	HONEYCOMBS	2
10 Sep 64	**YOU REALLY GOT ME**	KINKS	2

* Equal No.1 on 4 Dec 1959 with WHAT DO YOU WANT TO MAKE THOSE EYES AT ME FOR by EMILE FORD & THE CHECKMATES

Chart Date	Title	Artist	Weeks at No.1
24 Sep 64	I'M INTO SOMETHING GOOD	HERMAN'S HERMITS	2
8 Oct 64	OH PRETTY WOMAN	ROY ORBISON	2
22 Oct 64	(THERE'S) ALWAYS SOMETHING THERE TO REMIND ME	SANDIE SHAW	3
12 Nov 64	OH PRETTY WOMAN	ROY ORBISON	1
19 Nov 64	BABY LOVE	SUPREMES	2
3 Dec 64	LITTLE RED ROOSTER	ROLLING STONES	1
10 Dec 64	I FEEL FINE	BEATLES	5
14 Jan 65	YEH YEH	GEORGIE FAME & THE BLUE FLAMES	2
28 Jan 65	GO NOW!	MOODY BLUES	1
4 Feb 65	YOU'VE LOST THAT LOVIN' FEELIN'	RIGHTEOUS BROTHERS	2
18 Feb 65	TIRED OF WAITING FOR YOU	KINKS	1
25 Feb 65	I'LL NEVER FIND ANOTHER YOU	SEEKERS	2
11 Mar 65	IT'S NOT UNUSUAL	TOM JONES	1
18 Mar 65	THE LAST TIME	ROLLING STONES	3
8 Apr 65	CONCRETE & CLAY	UNIT FOUR PLUS TWO	1
15 Apr 65	THE MINUTE YOU'RE GONE	CLIFF RICHARD	1
22 Apr 65	TICKET TO RIDE	BEATLES	3
13 May 65	KING OF THE ROAD	ROGER MILLER	1
20 May 65	WHERE ARE YOU NOW (MY LOVE)	JACKIE TRENT	1
27 May 65	LONG LIVE LOVE	SANDIE SHAW	3
17 Jun 65	CRYING IN THE CHAPEL	ELVIS PRESLEY	1
24 Jun 65	I'M ALIVE	HOLLIES	1
1 Jul 65	CRYING IN THE CHAPEL	ELVIS PRESLEY	1
8 Jul 65	I'M ALIVE	HOLLIES	2
22 Jul 65	MR TAMBOURINE MAN	BYRDS	2
5 Aug 65	HELP!	BEATLES	3
26 Aug 65	I GOT YOU BABE	SONNY & CHER	2
9 Sep 65	(I CAN'T GET NO) SATISFACTION	ROLLING STONES	2
23 Sep 65	MAKE IT EASY ON YOURSELF	WALKER BROTHERS	1
30 Sep 65	TEARS	KEN DODD	5
4 Nov 65	GET OFF OF MY CLOUD	ROLLING STONES	3
25 Nov 65	THE CARNIVAL IS OVER	SEEKERS	3
16 Dec 65	DAY TRIPPER / WE CAN WORK IT OUT	BEATLES	5
20 Jan 66	KEEP ON RUNNING	SPENCER DAVIS GROUP	1
27 Jan 66	MICHELLE	OVERLANDERS	3
17 Feb 66	THESE BOOTS ARE MADE FOR WALKING	NANCY SINATRA	4
17 Mar 66	THE SUN AIN'T GONNA SHINE ANYMORE	WALKER BROTHERS	4
14 Apr 66	SOMEBODY HELP ME	SPENCER DAVIS GROUP	2
28 Apr 66	YOU DON'T HAVE TO SAY YOU LOVE ME	DUSTY SPRINGFIELD	1
5 May 66	PRETTY FLAMINGO	MANFRED MANN	3
26 May 66	PAINT IT BLACK	ROLLING STONES	1
2 Jun 66	STRANGERS IN THE NIGHT	FRANK SINATRA	3
23 Jun 66	PAPERBACK WRITER	BEATLES	2
7 Jul 66	SUNNY AFTERNOON	KINKS	2
21 Jul 66	GET AWAY	GEORGIE FAME & THE BLUE FLAMES	1
28 Jul 66	OUT OF TIME	CHRIS FARLOWE & THE THUNDERBIRDS	1
4 Aug 66	WITH A GIRL LIKE YOU	TROGGS	2
18 Aug 66	YELLOW SUBMARINE / ELEANOR RIGBY	BEATLES	4
15 Sep 66	ALL OR NOTHING	SMALL FACES	1
22 Sep 66	DISTANT DRUMS	JIM REEVES	5
27 Oct 66	REACH OUT I'LL BE THERE	FOUR TOPS	3
17 Nov 66	GOOD VIBRATIONS	BEACH BOYS	2
1 Dec 66	GREEN GREEN GRASS OF HOME	TOM JONES	7

Chart Date	Title	Artist	Weeks at No.1
19 Jan 67	I'M A BELIEVER	MONKEES	4
16 Feb 67	THIS IS MY SONG	PETULA CLARK	2
2 Mar 67	RELEASE ME (AND LET ME LOVE AGAIN)	ENGELBERT HUMPERDINCK	6
13 Apr 67	SOMETHIN' STUPID	FRANK SINATRA & NANCY SINATRA	2
27 Apr 67	PUPPET ON A STRING	SANDIE SHAW	3
18 May 67	SILENCE IS GOLDEN	TREMELOES	3
8 Jun 67	A WHITER SHADE OF PALE	PROCOL HARUM	6
19 Jul 67	ALL YOU NEED IS LOVE	BEATLES	3
9 Aug 67	SAN FRANCISCO (BE SURE TO WEAR SOME FLOWERS IN YOUR HAIR)	SCOTT MCKENZIE	4
6 Sep 67	THE LAST WALTZ	ENGELBERT HUMPERDINCK	5
11 Oct 67	MASSACHUSETTS	BEE GEES	4
8 Nov 67	BABY NOW THAT I'VE FOUND YOU	FOUNDATIONS	2
22 Nov 67	LET THE HEARTACHES BEGIN	LONG JOHN BALDRY	2
6 Dec 67	HELLO GOODBYE	BEATLES	7
24 Jan 68	THE BALLAD OF BONNIE & CLYDE	GEORGIE FAME	1
31 Jan 68	EVERLASTING LOVE	LOVE AFFAIR	2
14 Feb 68	THE MIGHTY QUINN	MANFRED MANN	2
28 Feb 68	CINDERELLA ROCKEFELLA	ESTHER & ABI OFARIM	3
20 Mar 68	LEGEND OF XANADU	DAVE DEE, DOZY, BEAKY, MICK & TICH	1
27 Mar 68	LADY MADONNA	BEATLES	2
10 Apr 68	CONGRATULATIONS	CLIFF RICHARD	2
24 Apr 68	WHAT A WONDERFUL WORLD / CABARET	LOUIS ARMSTRONG	4
22 May 68	YOUNG GIRL	UNION GAP FEATURING GARY PUCKETT	4
19 Jun 68	JUMPIN' JACK FLASH	ROLLING STONES	2
3 Jul 68	BABY COME BACK	EQUALS	3
24 Jul 68	I PRETEND	DES O'CONNOR	1
31 Jul 68	MONY MONY	TOMMY JAMES & THE SHONDELLS	2
14 Aug 68	FIRE	CRAZY WORLD OF ARTHUR BROWN	1
21 Aug 68	MONY MONY	TOMMY JAMES & THE SHONDELLS	1
28 Aug 68	DO IT AGAIN	BEACH BOYS	1
4 Sep 68	I'VE GOTTA GET A MESSAGE TO YOU	BEE GEES	1
11 Sep 68	HEY JUDE	BEATLES	2
25 Sep 68	THOSE WERE THE DAYS	MARY HOPKIN	6
6 Nov 68	WITH A LITTLE HELP FROM MY FRIENDS	JOE COCKER	1
13 Nov 68	THE GOOD THE BAD AND THE UGLY	HUGO MONTENEGRO ORCHESTRA	4
11 Dec 68	LILY THE PINK	SCAFFOLD	3
1 Jan 69	OB-LA-DI OB-LA-DA	MARMALADE	1
8 Jan 69	LILY THE PINK	SCAFFOLD	1
15 Jan 69	OB-LA-DI OB-LA-DA	MARMALADE	2
29 Jan 69	ALBATROSS	FLEETWOOD MAC	1
5 Feb 69	BLACKBERRY WAY	MOVE	1
12 Feb 69	(IF PARADISE IS) HALF AS NICE	AMEN CORNER	2
26 Feb 69	WHERE DO YOU GO TO MY LOVELY?	PETER SARSTEDT	4
26 Mar 69	I HEARD IT THROUGH THE GRAPEVINE	MARVIN GAYE	3
16 Apr 69	ISRAELITES	DESMOND DEKKER & THE ACES	1
23 Apr 69	GET BACK	BEATLES WITH BILLY PRESTON	6
4 Jun 69	DIZZY	TOMMY ROE	1
11 Jun 69	THE BALLAD OF JOHN & YOKO	BEATLES	3
2 Jul 69	SOMETHING IN THE AIR	THUNDERCLAP NEWMAN	3

Chart Date	Title Artist	Weeks at No.1
23 Jul 69	**HONKY TONK WOMEN** ROLLING STONES	5
30 Aug 69	**IN THE YEAR 2525 (EXORIUM & TERMINUS)** ZAGER & EVANS	3
20 Sep 69	**BAD MOON RISING** CREEDENCE CLEARWATER REVIVAL	3
11 Oct 69	**JE T'AIME... MOI NON PLUS** JANE BIRKIN & SERGE GAINSBOURG	1
18 Oct 69	**I'LL NEVER FALL IN LOVE AGAIN** BOBBY GENTRY	1
25 Oct 69	**SUGAR SUGAR** ARCHIES	8
20 Dec 69	**TWO LITTLE BOYS** ROLF HARRIS	6
31 Jan 70	**LOVE GROWS (WHERE MY ROSEMARY GOES)** EDISON LIGHTHOUSE	5
7 Mar 70	**WANDRIN' STAR** LEE MARVIN	3
28 Mar 70	**BRIDGE OVER TROUBLED WATER** SIMON & GARFUNKEL	3
18 Apr 70	**ALL KINDS OF EVERYTHING** DANA	2
2 May 70	**SPIRIT IN THE SKY** NORMAN GREENBAUM	2
16 May 70	**BACK HOME** ENGLAND WORLD CUP SQUAD	3
6 Jun 70	**YELLOW RIVER** CHRISTIE	1
13 Jun 70	**IN THE SUMMERTIME** MUNGO JERRY	7
1 Aug 70	**THE WONDER OF YOU** ELVIS PRESLEY	6
12 Sep 70	**TEARS OF A CLOWN** SMOKEY ROBINSON & THE MIRACLES	1
19 Sep 70	**BAND OF GOLD** FREDA PAYNE	6
31 Oct 70	**WOODSTOCK** MATTHEWS' SOUTHERN COMFORT	3
21 Nov 70	**VOODOO CHILE** JIMI HENDRIX EXPERIENCE	1
28 Nov 70	**I HEAR YOU KNOCKING** DAVE EDMUNDS	6
9 Jan 71	**GRANDAD** CLIVE DUNN	3
30 Jan 71	**MY SWEET LORD** GEORGE HARRISON	5
6 Mar 71	**BABY JUMP** MUNGO JERRY	2
20 Mar 71	**HOT LOVE** T REX	6
1 May 71	**DOUBLE BARREL** DAVE & ANSIL COLLINS	2
15 May 71	**KNOCK THREE TIMES** DAWN	5
19 Jun 71	**CHIRPY CHIRPY CHEEP CHEEP** MIDDLE OF THE ROAD	5
24 Jul 71	**GET IT ON** T REX	4
21 Aug 71	**I'M STILL WAITING** DIANA ROSS	4
18 Sep 71	**HEY GIRL DON'T BOTHER ME** TAMS	3
9 Oct 71	**MAGGIE MAY** ROD STEWART	5
13 Nov 71	**COZ I LUV YOU** SLADE	4
11 Dec 71	**ERNIE (THE FASTEST MILKMAN IN THE WEST)** BENNY HILL	4
8 Jan 72	**I'D LIKE TO TEACH THE WORLD TO SING** NEW SEEKERS	4
5 Feb 72	**TELEGRAM SAM** T REX	2
19 Feb 72	**SON OF MY FATHER** CHICORY TIP	3
11 Mar 72	**WITHOUT YOU** NILSSON	5
15 Apr 72	**AMAZING GRACE** PIPES & DRUMS & MILITARY BAND OF THE ROYAL SCOTS DRAGOON GUARDS	5
20 May 72	**METAL GURU** T REX	4
17 Jun 72	**VINCENT** DON MCLEAN	2
1 Jul 72	**TAKE ME BACK 'OME** SLADE	1
8 Jul 72	**PUPPY LOVE** DONNY OSMOND	5
12 Aug 72	**SCHOOL'S OUT** ALICE COOPER	3
2 Sep 72	**YOU WEAR IT WELL** ROD STEWART	1
9 Sep 72	**MAMA WEER ALL CRAZEE NOW** SLADE	3
30 Sep 72	**HOW CAN I BE SURE** DAVID CASSIDY	2
14 Oct 72	**MOULDY OLD DOUGH** LIEUTENANT PIGEON	4
11 Nov 72	**CLAIR** GILBERT O'SULLIVAN	2
25 Nov 72	**MY DING-A-LING** CHUCK BERRY	4

Chart Date	Title Artist	Weeks at No.1
23 Dec 72	**LONG HAIRED LOVER FROM LIVERPOOL** LITTLE JIMMY OSMOND	5
27 Jan 73	**BLOCKBUSTER** SWEET	5
3 Mar 73	**CUM ON FEEL THE NOIZE** SLADE	4
31 Mar 73	**THE TWELFTH OF NEVER** DONNY OSMOND	1
7 Apr 73	**GET DOWN** GILBERT O'SULLIVAN	2
21 Apr 73	**TIE A YELLOW RIBBON ROUND THE OLD OAK TREE** DAWN FT TONY ORLANDO	4
19 May 73	**SEE MY BABY JIVE** WIZZARD	4
16 Jun 73	**CAN THE CAN** SUZI QUATRO	1
23 Jun 73	**RUBBER BULLETS** 10 CC	1
30 Jun 73	**SKWEEZE ME PLEEZE ME** SLADE	3
21 Jul 73	**WELCOME HOME** PETERS & LEE	1
28 Jul 73	**I'M THE LEADER OF THE GANG (I AM)** GARY GLITTER	4
25 Aug 73	**YOUNG LOVE** DONNY OSMOND	4
22 Sep 73	**ANGEL FINGERS** WIZZARD	1
29 Sep 73	**EYE LEVEL** SIMON PARK ORCHESTRA	4
27 Oct 73	**DAYDREAMER / THE PUPPY SONG** DAVID CASSIDY	3
17 Nov 73	**I LOVE YOU LOVE ME LOVE** GARY GLITTER	4
15 Dec 73	**MERRY XMAS EVERYBODY** SLADE	5
19 Jan 74	**YOU WON'T FIND ANOTHER FOOL LIKE ME** NEW SEEKERS	1
26 Jan 74	**TIGER FEET** MUD	4
23 Feb 74	**DEVIL GATE DRIVE** SUZI QUATRO	2
9 Mar 74	**JEALOUS MIND** ALVIN STARDUST	1
16 Mar 74	**BILLY DON'T BE A HERO** PAPER LACE	3
6 Apr 74	**SEASONS IN THE SUN** TERRY JACKS	4
4 May 74	**WATERLOO** ABBA	2
18 May 74	**SUGAR BABY LOVE** RUBETTES	4
15 Jun 74	**THE STREAK** RAY STEVENS	1
22 Jun 74	**ALWAYS YOURS** GARY GLITTER	1
29 Jun 74	**SHE** CHARLES AZNAVOUR	4
27 Jul 74	**ROCK YOUR BABY** GEORGE MCCRAE	3
17 Aug 74	**WHEN WILL I SEE YOU AGAIN** THREE DEGREES	2
31 Aug 74	**LOVE ME FOR A REASON** OSMONDS	3
21 Sep 74	**KUNG FU FIGHTING** CARL DOUGLAS	3
12 Oct 74	**ANNIE'S SONG** JOHN DENVER	1
19 Oct 74	**SAD SWEET DREAMER** SWEET SENSATION	1
26 Oct 74	**EVERYTHING I OWN** KEN BOOTHE	3
16 Nov 74	**GONNA MAKE YOU A STAR** DAVID ESSEX	3
7 Dec 74	**YOU'RE THE FIRST, THE LAST, MY EVERYTHING** BARRY WHITE	2
21 Dec 74	**LONELY THIS CHRISTMAS** MUD	4
18 Jan 75	**DOWN DOWN** STATUS QUO	1
25 Jan 75	**MS GRACE** TYMES	1
1 Feb 75	**JANUARY** PILOT	3
22 Feb 75	**MAKE ME SMILE (COME UP AND SEE ME)** STEVE HARLEY & COCKNEY REBEL	2
8 Mar 75	**IF** TELLY SAVALAS	2
22 Mar 75	**BYE BYE BABY** BAY CITY ROLLERS	6
3 May 75	**OH BOY** MUD	2
17 May 75	**STAND BY YOUR MAN** TAMMY WYNETTE	3
7 Jun 75	**WHISPERING GRASS** WINDSOR DAVIES & DON ESTELLE	3
28 Jun 75	**I'M NOT IN LOVE** 10CC	2
12 Jul 75	**TEARS ON MY PILLOW** JOHNNY NASH	1
19 Jul 75	**GIVE A LITTLE LOVE** BAY CITY ROLLERS	3
9 Aug 75	**BARBADOS** TYPICALLY TROPICAL	1

Chart Date	Title Artist	Weeks at No.1
16 Aug 75	**CAN'T GIVE YOU ANYTHING (BUT MY LOVE)** STYLISTICS	3
6 Sep 75	**SAILING** ROD STEWART	4
4 Oct 75	**HOLD ME CLOSE** DAVID ESSEX	3
25 Oct 75	**I ONLY HAVE EYES FOR YOU** ART GARFUNKEL	2
8 Nov 75	**SPACE ODDITY** DAVID BOWIE	2
22 Nov 75	**D.I.V.O.R.C.E.** BILLY CONNOLLY	1
29 Nov 75	**BOHEMIAN RHAPSODY** QUEEN	9
31 Jan 76	**MAMMA MIA** ABBA	2
14 Feb 76	**FOREVER AND EVER** SLIK	1
21 Feb 76	**DECEMBER '63** FOUR SEASONS	2
6 Mar 76	**I LOVE TO LOVE (BUT MY BABY LOVES TO DANCE)** TINA CHARLES	3
27 Mar 76	**SAVE YOUR KISSES FOR ME** BROTHERHOOD OF MAN	6
8 May 76	**FERNANDO** ABBA	4
5 Jun 76	**NO CHARGE** J J BARRIE	1
12 Jun 76	**COMBINE HARVESTER (BRAND NEW KEY)** WURZELS	2
26 Jun 76	**YOU TO ME ARE EVERYTHING** REAL THING	3
17 Jul 76	**THE ROUSSOS PHENOMENON EP (MAIN TRACK: FOREVER AND EVER)** DEMIS ROUSSOS	1
24 Jul 76	**DON'T GO BREAKING MY HEART** ELTON JOHN & KIKI DEE	6
4 Sep 76	**DANCING QUEEN** ABBA	6
16 Oct 76	**MISSISSIPPI** PUSSYCAT	4
13 Nov 76	**IF YOU LEAVE ME NOW** CHICAGO	3
4 Dec 76	**UNDER THE MOON OF LOVE** SHOWADDYWADDY	3
25 Dec 76	**WHEN A CHILD IS BORN (SOLEADO)** JOHNNY MATHIS	3
15 Jan 77	**DON'T GIVE UP ON US** DAVID SOUL	4
12 Feb 77	**DON'T CRY FOR ME ARGENTINA** JULIE COVINGTON	1
19 Feb 77	**WHEN I NEED YOU** LEO SAYER	3
12 Mar 77	**CHANSON D'AMOUR** MANHATTAN TRANSFER	3
2 Apr 77	**KNOWING ME KNOWING YOU** ABBA	5
7 May 77	**FREE** DENIECE WILLIAMS	2
21 May 77	**I DON'T WANT TO TALK ABOUT IT / FIRST CUT IS THE DEEPEST** ROD STEWART	4
18 Jun 77	**LUCILLE** KENNY ROGERS	1
25 Jun 77	**SHOW YOU THE WAY TO GO** JACKSONS	1
2 Jul 77	**SO YOU WIN AGAIN** HOT CHOCOLATE	3
23 Jul 77	**I FEEL LOVE** DONNA SUMMER	4
20 Aug 77	**ANGELO** BROTHERHOOD OF MAN	1
27 Aug 77	**FLOAT ON** FLOATERS	1
3 Sep 77	**WAY DOWN** ELVIS PRESLEY	5
8 Oct 77	**SILVER LADY** DAVID SOUL	3
29 Oct 77	**YES SIR I CAN BOOGIE** BACCARA	1
5 Nov 77	**THE NAME OF THE GAME** ABBA	4
3 Dec 77	**MULL OF KINTYRE / GIRLS' SCHOOL** WINGS	9
4 Feb 78	**UP TOWN TOP RANKING** ALTHIA & DONNA	1
11 Feb 78	**FIGARO** BROTHERHOOD OF MAN	1
18 Feb 78	**TAKE A CHANCE ON ME** ABBA	3
11 Mar 78	**WUTHERING HEIGHTS** KATE BUSH	4
8 Apr 78	**MATCHSTALK MEN AND MATCHSTALK CATS AND DOGS** BRIAN & MICHAEL	3
29 Apr 78	**NIGHT FEVER** BEE GEES	2
13 May 78	**RIVERS OF BABYLON / BROWN GIRL IN THE GIRL** BONEY M	5
17 Jun 78	**YOU'RE THE ONE THAT I WANT** JOHN TRAVOLTA & OLIVIA NEWTON JOHN	9
19 Aug 78	**THREE TIMES A LADY** COMMODORES	5
23 Sep 78	**DREADLOCK HOLIDAY** 10CC	1
30 Sep 78	**SUMMER NIGHTS** JOHN TRAVOLTA & OLIVIA NEWTON JOHN	7
18 Nov 78	**RAT TRAP** BOOMTOWN RATS	2
2 Dec 78	**DA YA THINK I'M SEXY** ROD STEWART	1
9 Dec 78	**MARY'S BOY CHILD – OH MY LORD** BONEY M	4
6 Jan 79	**Y.M.C.A.** VILLAGE PEOPLE	3
27 Jan 79	**HIT ME WITH YOUR RHYTHM STICK** IAN DURY & THE BLOCKHEADS	1
3 Feb 79	**HEART OF GLASS** BLONDIE	4
3 Mar 79	**TRAGEDY** BEE GEES	2
17 Mar 79	**I WILL SURVIVE** GLORIA GAYNOR	4
14 Apr 79	**BRIGHT EYES** ART GARFUNKEL	6
26 May 79	**SUNDAY GIRL** BLONDIE	3
16 Jun 79	**RING MY BELL** ANITA WARD	2
30 Jun 79	**ARE 'FRIENDS' ELECTRIC** TUBEWAY ARMY	4
28 Jul 79	**I DON'T LIKE MONDAYS** BOOMTOWN RATS	4
25 Aug 79	**WE DON'T TALK ANYMORE** CLIFF RICHARD	4
22 Sep 79	**CARS** GARY NUMAN	1
29 Sep 79	**MESSAGE IN A BOTTLE** POLICE	3
20 Oct 79	**VIDEO KILLED THE RADIO STAR** BUGGLES	1
27 Oct 79	**ONE DAY AT A TIME** LENA MARTELL	3
17 Nov 79	**WHEN YOU'RE IN LOVE WITH A BEAUTIFUL WOMAN** DR HOOK	3
8 Dec 79	**WALKING ON THE MOON** POLICE	1
15 Dec 79	**ANOTHER BRICK IN THE WALL** PINK FLOYD	5
19 Jan 80	**BRASS IN POCKET** PRETENDERS	2
2 Feb 80	**THE SPECIALS LIVE EP (MAIN TRACK: TOO MUCH TOO YOUNG)** SPECIAL AKA	2
16 Feb 80	**COWARD OF THE COUNTY** KENNY ROGERS	2
1 Mar 80	**ATOMIC** BLONDIE	2
15 Mar 80	**TOGETHER WE ARE BEAUTIFUL** FERN KINNEY	1
22 Mar 80	**GOING UNDERGROUND / DREAMS OF CHILDREN** JAM	3
12 Apr 80	**WORKING MY WAY BACK TO YOU – FORGIVE ME GIRL** DETROIT SPINNERS	2
26 Apr 80	**CALL ME** BLONDIE	1
3 May 80	**GENO** DEXY'S MIDNIGHT RUNNERS	2
17 May 80	**WHAT'S ANOTHER YEAR** JOHNNY LOGAN	2
31 May 80	**SUICIDE IS PAINLESS (THEME FROM M*A*S*H)** MASH	3
21 Jun 80	**CRYING** DON MCLEAN	3
12 Jul 80	**XANADU** OLIVIA NEWTON-JOHN & ELECTRIC LIGHT ORCHESTRA	2
26 Jul 80	**USE IT UP AND WEAR IT OUT** ODYSSEY	2
9 Aug 80	**THE WINNER TAKES IT ALL** ABBA	2
23 Aug 80	**ASHES TO ASHES** DAVID BOWIE	2
6 Sep 80	**START** JAM	1
13 Sep 80	**FEELS LIKE I'M IN LOVE** KELLY MARIE	2
27 Sep 80	**DON'T STAND SO CLOSE TO ME** POLICE	4
25 Oct 80	**WOMAN IN LOVE** BARBRA STREISAND	3
15 Nov 80	**THE TIDE IS HIGH** BLONDIE	2
29 Nov 80	**SUPER TROUPER** ABBA	3
20 Dec 80	**(JUST LIKE) STARTING OVER** JOHN LENNON	1
27 Dec 80	**THERE'S NO ONE QUITE LIKE GRANDMA** ST WINIFRED'S SCHOOL CHOIR	2
10 Jan 81	**IMAGINE** JOHN LENNON	4
7 Feb 81	**WOMAN** JOHN LENNON	2
21 Feb 81	**SHADDAP YOU FACE** JOE DOLCE MUSIC THEATRE	3
14 Mar 81	**JEALOUS GUY** ROXY MUSIC	2

Chart Date	Title	Artist	Weeks at No.1
28 Mar 81	**THIS OLE HOUSE**	SHAKIN' STEVENS	3
18 Apr 81	**MAKING YOUR MIND UP**	BUCKS FIZZ	3
9 May 81	**STAND AND DELIVER**	ADAM & THE ANTS	5
13 Jun 81	**BEING WITH YOU**	SMOKEY ROBINSON	2
27 Jun 81	**ONE DAY IN YOUR LIFE**	MICHAEL JACKSON	2
11 Jul 81	**GHOST TOWN**	SPECIALS	3
1 Aug 81	**GREEN DOOR**	SHAKIN' STEVENS	4
29 Aug 81	**JAPANESE BOY**	ANEKA	1
5 Sep 81	**TAINTED LOVE**	SOFT CELL	2
19 Sep 81	**PRINCE CHARMING**	ADAM & THE ANTS	4
17 Oct 81	**IT'S MY PARTY**	DAVE STEWART WITH BARBARA GASKIN	4
14 Nov 81	**EVERY LITTLE THING SHE DOES IS MAGIC**	POLICE	1
21 Nov 81	**UNDER PRESSURE**	QUEEN & DAVID BOWIE	2
5 Dec 81	**BEGIN THE BEGUINE (VOLVER A EMPEZAR)**	JULIO IGLESIAS	1
12 Dec 81	**DON'T YOU WANT ME**	HUMAN LEAGUE	5
16 Jan 82	**LAND OF MAKE BELIEVE**	BUCKS FIZZ	2
30 Jan 82	**OH JULIE**	SHAKIN' STEVENS	1
6 Feb 82	**THE MODEL / COMPUTER LOVE**	KRAFTWERK	1
13 Feb 82	**A TOWN CALLED MALICE / PRECIOUS**	JAM	3
6 Mar 82	**THE LION SLEEPS TONIGHT**	TIGHT FIT	3
27 Mar 82	**SEVEN TEARS**	GOOMBAY DANCE BAND	3
17 Apr 82	**MY CAMERA NEVER LIES**	BUCKS FIZZ	1
24 Apr 82	**EBONY AND IVORY**	PAUL MCCARTNEY WITH STEVIE WONDER	3
15 May 82	**A LITTLE PEACE**	NICOLE	2
29 May 82	**HOUSE OF FUN**	MADNESS	2
12 Jun 82	**GOODY TWO SHOES**	ADAM ANT	2
26 Jun 82	**I'VE NEVER BEEN TO ME**	CHARLENE	1
3 Jul 82	**HAPPY TALK**	CAPTAIN SENSIBLE	2
17 Jul 82	**FAME**	IRENE CARA	3
7 Aug 82	**COME ON EILEEN**	DEXY'S MIDNIGHT RUNNERS & THE EMERALD EXPRESS	4
4 Sep 82	**EYE OF THE TIGER**	SURVIVOR	4
2 Oct 82	**PASS THE DUTCHIE**	MUSICAL YOUTH	3
23 Oct 82	**DO YOU REALLY WANT TO HURT ME**	CULTURE CLUB	3
13 Nov 82	**I DON'T WANNA DANCE**	EDDY GRANT	3
4 Dec 82	**BEAT SURRENDER**	JAM	2
18 Dec 82	**SAVE YOUR LOVE**	RENEE & RENATO	4
15 Jan 83	**YOU CAN'T HURRY LOVE**	PHIL COLLINS	2
29 Jan 83	**DOWN UNDER**	MEN AT WORK	3
19 Feb 83	**TOO SHY**	KAJAGOOGOO	2
5 Mar 83	**BILLIE JEAN**	MICHAEL JACKSON	1
12 Mar 83	**TOTAL ECLIPSE OF THE HEART**	BONNIE TYLER	2
26 Mar 83	**IS THERE SOMETHING I SHOULD KNOW**	DURAN DURAN	2
9 Apr 83	**LET'S DANCE**	DAVID BOWIE	3
30 Apr 83	**TRUE**	SPANDAU BALLET	4
28 May 83	**CANDY GIRL**	NEW EDITION	1
4 Jun 83	**EVERY BREATH YOU TAKE**	POLICE	4
2 Jul 83	**BABY JANE**	ROD STEWART	3
23 Jul 83	**WHEREVER I LAY MY HAT**	PAUL YOUNG	3
13 Aug 83	**GIVE IT UP**	KC & THE SUNSHINE BAND	3
3 Sep 83	**RED RED WINE**	UB40	3
24 Sep 83	**KARMA CHAMELEON**	CULTURE CLUB	6
5 Nov 83	**UPTOWN GIRL**	BILLY JOEL	5
10 Dec 83	**ONLY YOU**	FLYING PICKETS	5
14 Jan 84	**PIPES OF PEACE**	PAUL MCCARTNEY	2
28 Jan 84	**RELAX**	FRANKIE GOES TO HOLLYWOOD	5
3 Mar 84	**99 RED BALLOONS**	NENA	3
24 Mar 84	**HELLO**	LIONEL RICHIE	6
5 May 84	**THE REFLEX**	DURAN DURAN	4
2 Jun 84	**WAKE ME UP BEFORE YOU GO-GO**	WHAM!	2
16 Jun 84	**TWO TRIBES**	FRANKIE GOES TO HOLLYWOOD	9
18 Aug 84	**CARELESS WHISPER**	GEORGE MICHAEL	3
8 Sep 84	**I JUST CALLED TO SAY I LOVE YOU**	STEVIE WONDER	6
20 Oct 84	**FREEDOM**	WHAM!	3
10 Nov 84	**I FEEL FOR YOU**	CHAKA KHAN	3
1 Dec 84	**I SHOULD HAVE KNOWN BETTER**	JIM DIAMOND	1
8 Dec 84	**THE POWER OF LOVE**	FRANKIE GOES TO HOLLYWOOD	1
15 Dec 84	**DO THEY KNOW IT'S CHRISTMAS?**	BAND AID	5
19 Jan 85	**I WANT TO KNOW WHAT LOVE IS**	FOREIGNER	3
9 Feb 85	**I KNOW HIM SO WELL**	ELAINE PAIGE & BARBARA DICKSON	4
9 Mar 85	**YOU SPIN ME ROUND (LIKE A RECORD)**	DEAD OR ALIVE	2
23 Mar 85	**EASY LOVER**	PHILIP BAILEY & PHIL COLLINS	4
20 Apr 85	**WE ARE THE WORLD**	USA FOR AFRICA	2
4 May 85	**MOVE CLOSER**	PHYLLIS NELSON	1
11 May 85	**19**	PAUL HARDCASTLE	5
15 Jun 85	**YOU'LL NEVER WALK ALONE**	CROWD	2
29 Jun 85	**FRANKIE**	SISTER SLEDGE	4
27 Jul 85	**THERE MUST BE AN ANGEL (PLAYING WITH MY HEART)**	EURYTHMICS	1
3 Aug 85	**INTO THE GROOVE**	MADONNA	4
31 Aug 85	**I GOT YOU BABE**	UB40 & CHRISSIE HYNDE	1
7 Sep 85	**DANCING IN THE STREETS**	DAVID BOWIE & MICK JAGGER	4
5 Oct 85	**IF I WAS**	MIDGE URE	1
12 Oct 85	**THE POWER OF LOVE**	JENNIFER RUSH	5
16 Nov 85	**A GOOD HEART**	FEARGAL SHARKEY	2
30 Nov 85	**I'M YOUR MAN**	WHAM!	2
14 Dec 85	**SAVING ALL MY LOVE FOR YOU**	WHITNEY HOUSTON	2
28 Dec 85	**MERRY CHRISTMAS EVERYONE**	SHAKIN' STEVENS	2
11 Jan 86	**WEST END GIRLS**	PET SHOP BOYS	2
25 Jan 86	**THE SUN ALWAYS SHINES ON TV**	A-HA	2
8 Feb 86	**WHEN THE GOING GETS TOUGH, THE TOUGH GET GOING**	BILLY OCEAN	4
8 Mar 86	**CHAIN REACTION**	DIANA ROSS	3
29 Mar 86	**LIVING DOLL**	CLIFF RICHARD & THE YOUNG ONES	3
19 Apr 86	**A DIFFERENT CORNER**	GEORGE MICHAEL	3
10 May 86	**ROCK ME AMADEUS**	FALCO	1
17 May 86	**THE CHICKEN SONG**	SPITTING IMAGE	3
7 Jun 86	**SPIRIT IN THE SKY**	DOCTOR & THE MEDICS	3
28 Jun 86	**THE EDGE OF HEAVEN**	WHAM!	2
12 Jul 86	**PAPA DON'T PREACH**	MADONNA	3
2 Aug 86	**THE LADY IN RED**	CHRIS DE BURGH	3
23 Aug 86	**I WANT TO WAKE UP WITH YOU**	BORIS GARDINER	3
13 Sep 86	**DON'T LEAVE ME THIS WAY**	COMMUNARDS	4
11 Oct 86	**TRUE BLUE**	MADONNA	1
18 Oct 86	**EVERY LOSER WINS**	NICK BERRY	3
8 Nov 86	**TAKE MY BREATH AWAY**	BERLIN	4
6 Dec 86	**THE FINAL COUNTDOWN**	EUROPE	2
20 Dec 86	**CARAVAN OF LOVE**	HOUSEMARTINS	1

Chart Date	Title	Artist	Weeks at No.1
27 Dec 86	**REET PETITE**	JACKIE WILSON	4
24 Jan 87	**JACK YOUR BODY**	STEVE 'SILK' HURLEY	2
7 Feb 87	**I KNEW YOU WERE WAITING (FOR ME)**	GEORGE MICHAEL & ARETHA FRANKLIN	2
21 Feb 87	**STAND BY ME**	BEN E KING	3
14 Mar 87	**EVERYTHING I OWN**	BOY GEORGE	2
28 Mar 87	**RESPECTABLE**	MEL & KIM	1
4 Apr 87	**LET IT BE**	FERRY AID	3
25 Apr 87	**LA ISLA BONITA**	MADONNA	2
9 May 87	**NOTHING'S GONNA STOP US NOW**	STARSHIP	4
6 Jun 87	**I WANNA DANCE WITH SOMEBODY (WHO LOVES ME)**	WHITNEY HOUSTON	2
20 Jun 87	**STAR TREKKIN'**	FIRM	2
4 Jul 87	**IT'S A SIN**	PET SHOP BOYS	3
25 Jul 87	**WHO'S THAT GIRL**	MADONNA	1
1 Aug 87	**LA BAMBA**	LOS LOBOS	2
15 Aug 87	**I JUST CAN'T STOP LOVING YOU**	MICHAEL JACKSON	2
29 Aug 87	**NEVER GONNA GIVE YOU UP**	RICK ASTLEY	5
3 Oct 87	**PUMP UP THE VOLUME / ANITINA (THE FIRST TIME I SEE SHE DANCE)**	M/A/R/R/S	2
17 Oct 87	**YOU WIN AGAIN**	BEE GEES	4
14 Nov 87	**CHINA IN YOUR HAND**	T'PAU	5
19 Dec 87	**ALWAYS ON MY MIND**	PET SHOP BOYS	4
16 Jan 88	**HEAVEN IS A PLACE ON EARTH**	BELINDA CARLISLE	2
30 Jan 88	**I THINK WE'RE ALONE NOW**	TIFFANY	3
20 Feb 88	**I SHOULD BE SO LUCKY**	KYLIE MINOGUE	5
26 Mar 88	**DON'T TURN AROUND**	ASWAD	2
9 Apr 88	**HEART**	PET SHOP BOYS	3
30 Apr 88	**THEME FROM S'EXPRESS**	S'EXPRESS	2
14 May 88	**PERFECT**	FAIRGROUND ATTRACTION	1
21 May 88	**WITH A LITTLE HELP FROM MY FRIENDS / SHE'S LEAVING HOME**	WET WET WET / BILLY BRAGG	4
18 Jun 88	**DOCTORIN' THE TARDIS**	TIMELORDS	1
25 Jun 88	**I OWE YOU NOTHING**	BROS	2
9 Jul 88	**NOTHING'S GONNA CHANGE MY LOVE FOR YOU**	GLENN MEDEIROS	4
6 Aug 88	**THE ONLY WAY IS UP**	YAZZ & THE PLASTIC POPULATION	5
10 Sep 88	**A GROOVY KIND OF LOVE**	PHIL COLLINS	2
24 Sep 88	**HE AIN'T HEAVY HE'S MY BROTHER**	HOLLIES	2
8 Oct 88	**DESIRE**	U2	1
15 Oct 88	**ONE MOMENT IN TIME**	WHITNEY HOUSTON	2
29 Oct 88	**ORINOCO FLOW (SAIL AWAY)**	ENYA	3
19 Nov 88	**THE FIRST TIME**	ROBIN BECK	3
10 Dec 88	**MISTLETOE & WINE**	CLIFF RICHARD	4
7 Jan 89	**ESPECIALLY FOR YOU**	KYLIE MINOGUE & JASON DONOVAN	3
28 Jan 89	**SOMETHING'S GOTTEN HOLD OF MY HEART**	MARC ALMOND WITH GENE PITNEY	4
25 Feb 89	**BELFAST CHILD**	SIMPLE MINDS	2
11 Mar 89	**TOO MANY BROKEN HEARTS**	JASON DONOVAN	2
25 Mar 89	**LIKE A PRAYER**	MADONNA	3
15 Apr 89	**ETERNAL FLAME**	BANGLES	4
13 May 89	**HAND ON YOUR HEART**	KYLIE MINOGUE	1
20 May 89	**FERRY 'CROSS THE MERSEY**	GERRY MARSDEN, PAUL McCARTNEY, HOLLY JOHNSON & CHRISTIANS	3
10 Jun 89	**SEALED WITH A KISS**	JASON DONOVAN	2
24 Jun 89	**BACK TO LIFE**	SOUL II SOUL FT CARON WHEELER	4
22 Jul 89	**YOU'LL NEVER STOP ME LOVING YOU**	SONIA	2
5 Aug 89	**SWING THE MOOD**	JIVE BUNNY & THE MASTERMIXERS	5
9 Sep 89	**RIDE ON TIME**	BLACK BOX	6
21 Oct 89	**THAT'S WHAT I LIKE**	JIVE BUNNY & THE MASTERMIXERS	3
11 Nov 89	**ALL AROUND THE WORLD**	LISA STANSFIELD	2
25 Nov 89	**YOU GOT IT (THE RIGHT STUFF)**	NEW KIDS ON THE BLOCK	3
16 Dec 89	**LET'S PARTY**	JIVE BUNNY & THE MASTERMIXERS	1
23 Dec 89	**DO THEY KNOW IT'S CHRISTMAS?**	BAND AID II	3
13 Jan 90	**HANGIN' TOUGH**	NEW KIDS ON THE BLOCK	2
27 Jan 90	**TEARS ON MY PILLOW**	KYLIE MINOGUE	1
3 Feb 90	**NOTHING COMPARES 2 U**	SINEAD O'CONNOR	4
3 Mar 90	**DUB BE GOOD TO ME**	BEATS INTERNATIONAL	4
31 Mar 90	**THE POWER**	SNAP!	2
14 Apr 90	**VOGUE**	MADONNA	4
12 May 90	**KILLER**	ADAMSKI	4
9 Jun 90	**WORLD IN MOTION**	ENGLANDNEWORDER	2
23 Jun 90	**SACRIFICE / HEALING HANDS**	ELTON JOHN	5
28 Jul 90	**TURTLE POWER**	PARTNERS IN KRYME	4
25 Aug 90	**ITSY BITSY TEENY WEENY YELLOW POLKA DOT BIKINI**	BOMBALURINA	3
15 Sep 90	**THE JOKER**	STEVE MILLER BAND	2
29 Sep 90	**SHOW ME HEAVEN**	MARIA MCKEE	4
27 Oct 90	**A LITTLE TIME**	BEAUTIFUL SOUTH	1
3 Nov 90	**UNCHAINED MELODY**	RIGHTEOUS BROTHERS	4
1 Dec 90	**ICE ICE BABY**	VANILLA ICE	4
29 Dec 90	**SAVIOUR'S DAY**	CLIFF RICHARD	1
5 Jan 91	**BRING YOUR DAUGHTER TO THE SLAUGHTER**	IRON MAIDEN	2
19 Jan 91	**SADNESS PART 1**	ENIGMA	1
26 Jan 91	**INNUENDO**	QUEEN	1
2 Feb 91	**3 AM ETERNAL**	KLF	2
16 Feb 91	**DO THE BARTMAN**	SIMPSONS	3
9 Mar 91	**SHOULD I STAY OR SHOULD I GO**	CLASH	2
23 Mar 91	**THE STONK**	HALE & PACE	1
30 Mar 91	**THE ONE AND ONLY**	CHESNEY HAWKES	5
4 May 91	**SHOOP SHOOP SONG (IT'S IN HIS KISS)**	CHER	5
8 Jun 91	**I WANNA SEX YOU UP**	COLOR ME BADD	3
29 Jun 91	**ANY DREAM WILL DO**	JASON DONOVAN	2
13 Jul 91	**(EVERYTHING I DO) I DO IT FOR YOU**	BRYAN ADAMS	16
2 Nov 91	**THE FLY**	U2	1
9 Nov 91	**DIZZY**	VIC REEVES & THE WONDER STUFF	2
23 Nov 91	**BLACK OR WHITE**	MICHAEL JACKSON	2
7 Dec 91	**DON'T LET THE SUN GO DOWN ON ME**	GEORGE MICHAEL & ELTON JOHN	2
21 Dec 91	**BOHEMIAN RHAPSODY / THESE ARE THE DAYS OF OUR LIVES**	QUEEN	5
25 Jan 92	**GOODNIGHT GIRL**	WET WET WET	4
22 Feb 92	**STAY**	SHAKESPEAR'S SISTER	8
18 Apr 92	**DEEPLY DIPPY**	RIGHT SAID FRED	3
9 May 92	**PLEASE DON'T GO / GAME BOY**	KWS	5
13 Jun 92	**ABBA-ESQUE EP**	ERASURE	5
18 Jul 92	**AIN'T NO DOUBT**	JIMMY NAIL	3
8 Aug 92	**RHYTHM IS A DANCER**	SNAP!	6
19 Sep 92	**EBENEEZER GOODE**	SHAMEN	4
17 Oct 92	**SLEEPING SATELLITE**	TASMIN ARCHER	2
31 Oct 92	**END OF THE ROAD**	BOYZ II MEN	3
21 Nov 92	**WOULD I LIE TO YOU**	CHARLES & EDDIE	2

Chart Date	Title Artist	Weeks at No.1
5 Dec 92	**I WILL ALWAYS LOVE YOU** WHITNEY HOUSTON	10
13 Feb 93	**NO LIMIT** 2 UNLIMITED	5
20 Mar 93	**OH CAROLINA** SHAGGY	2
3 Apr 93	**YOUNG AT HEART** BLUEBELLS	4
1 May 93	**FIVE LIVE (EP)** GEORGE MICHAEL & QUEEN WITH LISA STANSFIELD	3
22 May 93	**ALL THAT SHE WANTS** ACE OF BASE	3
12 Jun 93	**(I CAN'T HELP) FALLING IN LOVE WITH YOU** UB40	2
26 Jun 93	**DREAMS** GABRIELLE	3
17 Jul 93	**PRAY** TAKE THAT	4
14 Aug 93	**LIVING ON MY OWN** FREDDIE MERCURY	2
28 Aug 93	**MR VAIN** CULTURE BEAT	4
25 Sep 93	**BOOM! SHAKE THE ROOM** JAZZY JEFF & THE FRESH PRINCE	2
9 Oct 93	**RELIGHT MY FIRE** TAKE THAT FT LULU	2
23 Oct 93	**I'D DO ANYTHING FOR LOVE (BUT I WON'T DO THAT)** MEAT LOAF	7
11 Dec 93	**MR BLOBBY** MR BLOBBY	1
18 Dec 93	**BABE** TAKE THAT	1
25 Dec 93	**MR BLOBBY** MR BLOBBY	2
8 Jan 94	**TWIST & SHOUT** CHAKA DEMUS & PLIERS	2
22 Jan 94	**THINGS CAN ONLY GET BETTER** D:REAM	4
19 Feb 94	**WITHOUT YOU** MARIAH CAREY	4
19 Mar 94	**DOOP** DOOP	3
9 Apr 94	**EVERYTHING CHANGES** TAKE THAT	2
23 Apr 94	**THE MOST BEAUTIFUL GIRL IN THE WORLD** PRINCE	2
7 May 94	**THE REAL THING** TONY DI BART	1
14 May 94	**INSIDE** STILTSKIN	1
21 May 94	**COME ON YOU REDS** MANCHESTER UNITED 1994 FOOTBALL SQUAD	2
4 Jun 94	**LOVE IS ALL AROUND** WET WET WET	15
17 Sep 94	**SATURDAY NIGHT** WHIGFIELD	4
15 Oct 94	**SURE** TAKE THAT	2
29 Oct 94	**BABY COME BACK** PATO BANTON	4
26 Nov 94	**LET ME BE YOUR FANTASY** BABY D	2
10 Dec 94	**STAY ANOTHER DAY** EAST 17	5
14 Jan 95	**COTTON EYE JOE** REDNEX	3
4 Feb 95	**THINK TWICE** CELINE DION	7
25 Mar 95	**LOVE CAN BUILD A BRIDGE** CHER, CHRISSIE HYNDE, NENEH CHERRY & ERIC CLAPTON	1
1 Apr 95	**DON'T STOP (WIGGLE WIGGLE)** OUTHERE BROTHERS	1
8 Apr 95	**BACK FOR GOOD** TAKE THAT	4
6 May 95	**SOME MIGHT SAY** OASIS	1
13 May 95	**DREAMER** LIVIN' JOY	1
20 May 95	**UNCHAINED MELODY / WHITE CLIFFS OF DOVER** ROBSON GREEN & JEROME FLYNN	7
8 Jul 95	**BOOM BOOM BOOM** OUTHERE BROTHERS	4
5 Aug 95	**NEVER FORGET** TAKE THAT	3
26 Aug 95	**COUNTRY HOUSE** BLUR	2
9 Sep 95	**YOU ARE NOT ALONE** MICHAEL JACKSON	2
23 Sep 95	**BOOMBASTIC** SHAGGY	1
30 Sep 95	**FAIRGROUND** SIMPLY RED	4
28 Oct 95	**GANGSTA'S PARADISE** COOLIO FT LV	2
11 Nov 95	**I BELIEVE / UP ON THE ROOF** ROBSON GREEN & JEROME FLYNN	4
9 Dec 95	**EARTH SONG** MICHAEL JACKSON	6
20 Jan 96	**JESUS TO A CHILD** GEORGE MICHAEL	1
27 Jan 96	**SPACEMAN** BABYLON ZOO	5
2 Mar 96	**DON'T LOOK BACK IN ANGER** OASIS	1

Chart Date	Title Artist	Weeks at No.1
9 Mar 96	**HOW DEEP IS YOUR LOVE** TAKE THAT	3
30 Mar 96	**FIRESTARTER** PRODIGY	3
20 Apr 96	**RETURN OF THE MACK** MARK MORRISON	2
4 May 96	**FASTLOVE** GEORGE MICHAEL	3
25 May 96	**OOH AAH... JUST A LITTLE BIT** GINA G	1
1 Jun 96	**THREE LIONS** BADDIEL, SKINNER & LIGHTNING SEEDS	1
8 Jun 96	**KILLING ME SOFTLY** FUGEES	4
6 Jul 96	**THREE LIONS** BADDIEL, SKINNER & LIGHTNING SEEDS	1
13 Jul 96	**KILLING ME SOFTLY** FUGEES	1
20 Jul 96	**FOREVER LOVE** GARY BARLOW	1
27 Jul 96	**WANNABE** SPICE GIRLS	7
14 Sep 96	**FLAVA** PETER ANDRE	1
21 Sep 96	**READY OR NOT** FUGEES	2
5 Oct 96	**BREAKFAST AT TIFFANY'S** DEEP BLUE SOMETHING	1
12 Oct 96	**SETTING SUN** CHEMICAL BROTHERS	1
19 Oct 96	**WORDS** BOYZONE	1
26 Oct 96	**SAY YOU'LL BE THERE** SPICE GIRLS	2
9 Nov 96	**WHAT BECOMES OF THE BROKEN HEARTED / SATURDAY NIGHT AT THE MOVIES / YOU'LL NEVER WALK ALONE** ROBSON & JEROME	2
23 Nov 96	**BREATHE** PRODIGY	2
7 Dec 96	**I FEEL YOU** PETER ANDRE	1
14 Dec 96	**A DIFFERENT BEAT** BOYZONE	1
21 Dec 96	**KNOCKIN' ON HEAVEN'S DOOR / THROW THESE GUNS AWAY** DUNBLANE	1
28 Dec 96	**2 BECOME 1** SPICE GIRLS	3
18 Jan 97	**PROFESSIONAL WIDOW (IT'S GOT TO BE BIG)** TORI AMOS	1
25 Jan 97	**YOUR WOMAN** WHITE TOWN	1
1 Feb 97	**BEETLEBUM** BLUR	1
8 Feb 97	**AIN'T NOBODY** LL COOL J	1
15 Feb 97	**DISCOTHEQUE** U2	1
22 Feb 97	**DON'T SPEAK** NO DOUBT	3
15 Mar 97	**MAMA / WHO DO YOU THINK YOU ARE** SPICE GIRLS	3
5 Apr 97	**BLOCK ROCKIN' BEATS** CHEMICAL BROTHERS	1
12 Apr 97	**I BELIEVE I CAN FLY** R KELLY	3
3 May 97	**BLOOD ON THE DANCE FLOOR** MICHAEL JACKSON	1
10 May 97	**LOVE WON'T WAIT** GARY BARLOW	1
17 May 97	**YOU'RE NOT ALONE** OLIVE	2
31 May 97	**I WANNA BE THE ONE** ETERNAL FT BEBE WINANS	1
7 Jun 97	**MMMBOP** HANSON	3
28 Jun 97	**I'LL BE MISSING YOU** PUFF DADDY & FAITH EVANS	3
19 Jul 97	**D'YOU KNOW WHAT I MEAN** OASIS	1
26 Jul 97	**I'LL BE MISSING YOU** PUFF DADDY & FAITH EVANS	3
16 Aug 97	**MEN IN BLACK** WILL SMITH	4
13 Sep 97	**THE DRUGS DON'T WORK** VERVE	1
20 Sep 97	**CANDLE IN THE WIND '97 / SOMETHING ABOUT THE WAY YOU LOOK TONIGHT** ELTON JOHN	5
25 Oct 97	**SPICE UP YOUR LIFE** SPICE GIRLS	1
1 Nov 97	**BARBIE GIRL** AQUA	4
29 Nov 97	**PERFECT DAY** VARIOUS ARTISTS	2
13 Dec 97	**TELETUBBIES SAY EH-OH!** TELETUBBIES	2
27 Dec 97	**TOO MUCH** SPICE GIRLS	2
10 Jan 98	**PERFECT DAY** VARIOUS ARTISTS	1
17 Jan 98	**NEVER EVER** ALL SAINTS	1
24 Jan 98	**ALL AROUND THE WORLD** OASIS	1
31 Jan 98	**YOU MAKE ME WANNA...** USHER	1
7 Feb 98	**DOCTOR JONES** AQUA	2

Chart Date	Title Artist	Weeks at No.1
21 Feb 98	**MY HEART WILL GO ON** CELINE DION	1
28 Feb 98	**BRIMFUL OF ASHA** CORNERSHOP	1
7 Mar 98	**FROZEN** MADONNA	1
14 Mar 98	**MY HEART WILL GO ON** CELINE DION	1
21 Mar 98	**IT'S LIKE THAT** RUN DMC VS JASON NEVINS	6
2 May 98	**ALL THAT I NEED** BOYZONE	1
9 May 98	**UNDER THE BRIDGE / LADY MARMALADE** ALL SAINTS	1
16 May 98	**TURN BACK TIME** AQUA	1
23 May 98	**UNDER THE BRIDGE / LADY MARMALADE** ALL SAINTS	1
30 May 98	**FEEL IT** TAMPERER FT MAYA	1
6 Jun 98	**C'EST LA VIE** B*WITCHED	2
20 Jun 98	**THREE LIONS '98** BADDIEL, SKINNER & LIGHTNING SEEDS	3
11 Jul 98	**BECAUSE WE WANT TO** BILLIE	1
18 Jul 98	**FREAK ME** ANOTHER LEVEL	1
25 Jul 98	**DEEPER UNDERGROUND** JAMIROQUAI	1
1 Aug 98	**VIVA FOREVER** SPICE GIRLS	2
15 Aug 98	**NO MATTER WHAT** BOYZONE	3
5 Sep 98	**IF YOU TOLERATE THIS YOUR CHILDREN WILL BE NEXT** MANIC STREET PREACHERS	1
12 Sep 98	**BOOTIE CALL** ALL SAINTS	1
19 Sep 98	**MILLENNIUM** ROBBIE WILLIAMS	1
26 Sep 98	**I WANT YOU BACK** MELANIE B FT MISSY ELLIOTT	1
3 Oct 98	**ROLLERCOASTER** B*WITCHED	2
17 Oct 98	**GIRLFRIEND** BILLIE	1
24 Oct 98	**GYM & TONIC** SPACEDUST	1
31 Oct 98	**BELIEVE** CHER	7
19 Dec 98	**TO YOU I BELONG** B*WITCHED	1
26 Dec 98	**GOODBYE** SPICE GIRLS	1
2 Jan 99	**CHOCOLATE SALTY BALLS (PS I LOVE YOU)** CHEF	1
9 Jan 99	**HEARTBEAT / TRAGEDY** STEPS	1
16 Jan 99	**PRAISE YOU** FATBOY SLIM	1
23 Jan 99	**A LITTLE BIT MORE** 911	1
30 Jan 99	**PRETTY FLY (FOR A WHITE GUY)** OFFSPRING	1
6 Feb 99	**YOU DON'T KNOW ME** ARMAND VAN HELDEN FT DUANE HARDEN	1
13 Feb 99	**MARIA** BLONDIE	1
20 Feb 99	**FLY AWAY** LENNY KRAVITZ	1
27 Feb 99	**...BABY ONE MORE TIME** BRITNEY SPEARS	2
13 Mar 99	**WHEN THE GOING GETS TOUGH** BOYZONE	2
27 Mar 99	**BLAME IT ON THE WEATHERMAN** B*WITCHED	1
3 Apr 99	**FLAT BEAT** MR OIZO	2
17 Apr 99	**PERFECT MOMENT** MARTINE MCCUTCHEON	2
1 May 99	**SWEAR IT AGAIN** WESTLIFE	2
15 May 99	**I WANT IT THAT WAY** BACKSTREET BOYS	1
22 May 99	**YOU NEEDED ME** BOYZONE	1
29 May 99	**SWEET LIKE CHOCOLATE** SHANKS & BIGFOOT	2
12 Jun 99	**EVERYBODY'S FREE (TO WEAR SUNSCREEN)** BAZ LUHRMANN	1
19 Jun 99	**BRING IT ALL BACK** S CLUB 7	1
26 Jun 99	**BOOM BOOM BOOM BOOM!!** VENGABOYS	1
3 Jul 99	**9PM (TILL I COME)** ATB	2
17 Jul 99	**LIVIN' LA VIDA LOCA** RICKY MARTIN	3
7 Aug 99	**WHEN YOU SAY NOTHING AT ALL** RONAN KEATING	2
21 Aug 99	**IF I LET YOU GO** WESTLIFE	1
28 Aug 99	**MI CHICO LATINO** GERI HALLIWELL	1
4 Sep 99	**MAMBO NO 5** LOU BEGA	2

Chart Date	Title Artist	Weeks at No.1
18 Sep 99	**WE'RE GOING TO IBIZA** VENGABOYS	1
25 Sep 99	**BLUE (DA BA DEE)** EIFFEL 65	3
16 Oct 99	**GENIE IN A BOTTLE** CHRISTINA AGUILERA	2
30 Oct 99	**FLYING WITHOUT WINGS** WESTLIFE	1
6 Nov 99	**KEEP ON MOVIN'** FIVE	1
13 Nov 99	**LIFT ME UP** GERI HALLIWELL	1
20 Nov 99	**SHE'S THE ONE / IT'S ONLY US** ROBBIE WILLIAMS	1
27 Nov 99	**KING OF MY CASTLE** WAMDUE PROJECT	1
4 Dec 99	**MILLENNIUM PRAYER** CLIFF RICHARD	3
25 Dec 99	**I HAVE A DREAM / SEASONS IN THE SUN** WESTLIFE	4
22 Jan 00	**THE MASSES AGAINST THE CLASSES** MANIC STREET PREACHERS	1
29 Jan 00	**BORN TO MAKE YOU HAPPY** BRITNEY SPEARS	1
5 Feb 00	**RISE** GABRIELLE	2
19 Feb 00	**GO LET IT OUT** OASIS	1
26 Feb 00	**PURE SHORES** ALL SAINTS	2
11 Mar 00	**AMERICAN PIE** MADONNA	1
18 Mar 00	**DON'T GIVE UP** CHICANE FT BRYAN ADAMS	1
25 Mar 00	**BAG IT UP** GERI HALLIWELL	1
1 Apr 00	**NEVER BE THE SAME AGAIN** MELANIE C WITH LISA 'LEFT EYE' LOPES	1
8 Apr 00	**FOOL AGAIN** WESTLIFE	1
15 Apr 00	**FILL ME IN** CRAIG DAVID	1
22 Apr 00	**TOCA'S MIRACLE** FRAGMA	2
6 May 00	**BOUND 4 DA RELOAD (CASUALTY)** OXIDE & NEUTRINO	1
13 May 00	**OOPS!... I DID IT AGAIN** BRITNEY SPEARS	1
20 May 00	**DON'T CALL ME BABY** MADISON AVENUE	1
27 May 00	**DAY & NIGHT** BILLIE PIPER	1
3 Jun 00	**IT FEELS SO GOOD** SONIQUE	3
24 Jun 00	**YOU SEE THE TROUBLE WITH ME** BLACK LEGEND	1
1 Jul 00	**SPINNING AROUND** KYLIE MINOGUE	1
8 Jul 00	**THE REAL SLIM SHADY** EMINEM	1
15 Jul 00	**BREATHLESS** CORRS	1
22 Jul 00	**LIFE IS A ROLLERCOASTER** RONAN KEATING	1
29 Jul 00	**WE WILL ROCK YOU** FIVE & QUEEN	1
5 Aug 00	**7 DAYS** CRAIG DAVID	1
12 Aug 00	**ROCK DJ** ROBBIE WILLIAMS	1
19 Aug 00	**I TURN TO YOU** MELANIE C	1
26 Aug 00	**GROOVEJET (IF THIS AIN'T LOVE)** SPILLER	1
2 Sep 00	**MUSIC** MADONNA	1
9 Sep 00	**TAKE ON ME** A1	1
16 Sep 00	**LADY (HEAR ME TONIGHT)** MODJO	2
30 Sep 00	**AGAINST ALL ODDS** MARIAH CAREY & WESTLIFE	2
14 Oct 00	**BLACK COFFEE** ALL SAINTS	1
21 Oct 00	**BEAUTIFUL DAY** U2	1
28 Oct 00	**STOMP** STEPS	1
4 Nov 00	**HOLLER / LET LOVE LEAD THE WAY** SPICE GIRLS	1
11 Nov 00	**MY LOVE** WESTLIFE	1
18 Nov 00	**SAME OLD BRAND NEW YOU** A1	1
25 Nov 00	**CAN'T FIGHT THE MOONLIGHT** LEANN RIMES	1
2 Dec 00	**INDEPENDENT WOMEN PART 1** DESTINY'S CHILD	1
9 Dec 00	**NEVER HAD A DREAM COME TRUE** S CLUB 7	1
16 Dec 00	**STAN** EMINEM	1
23 Dec 00	**CAN WE FIX IT** BOB THE BUILDER	3
13 Jan 01	**TOUCH ME** RUI DA SILVA FT CASSANDRA	1
20 Jan 01	**LOVE DON'T COST A THING** JENNIFER LOPEZ	1
27 Jan 01	**ROLLIN'** LIMP BIZKIT	2

Chart Date	Title Artist	Weeks at No.1
10 Feb 01	**WHOLE AGAIN** ATOMIC KITTEN	4
10 Mar 01	**IT WASN'T ME** SHAGGY FT RICARDO 'RIKROK' DUCENT	1
17 Mar 01	**UPTOWN GIRL** WESTLIFE	1
24 Mar 01	**PURE AND SIMPLE** HEAR'SAY	3
14 Apr 01	**WHAT TOOK YOU SO LONG** EMMA BUNTON	2
28 Apr 01	**SURVIVOR** DESTINY'S CHILD	1
5 May 01	**DON'T STOP MOVIN'** S CLUB 7	1
12 May 01	**IT'S RAINING MEN** GERI HALLIWELL	2
26 May 01	**DON'T STOP MOVIN'** S CLUB 7	1
2 Jun 01	**DO YOU REALLY LIKE IT** DJ PIED PIPER	1
9 Jun 01	**ANGEL** SHAGGY FT RAYVON	3
30 Jun 01	**LADY MARMALADE** CHRISTINA AGUILERA WITH LIL' KIM, MYA & P!NK	1
7 Jul 01	**THE WAY TO YOUR LOVE** HEAR'SAY	1
14 Jul 01	**ANOTHER CHANCE** ROGER SANCHEZ	1
21 Jul 01	**ETERNITY/THE ROAD TO MANDALAY** ROBBIE WILLIAMS	2
4 Aug 01	**ETERNAL FLAME** ATOMIC KITTEN	2
18 Aug 01	**21 SECONDS** SO SOLID CREW	1
25 Aug 01	**LET'S DANCE** FIVE	2
8 Sep 01	**TOO CLOSE** BLUE	1
15 Sep 01	**MAMBO NO 5** BOB THE BUILDER	1
22 Sep 01	**HEY BABY** DJ OTZI	1
29 Sep 01	**CAN'T GET YOU OUT OF MY HEAD** KYLIE MINOGUE	4
27 Oct 01	**BECAUSE I GOT HIGH** AFROMAN	3
17 Nov 01	**QUEEN OF MY HEART** WESTLIFE	1
24 Nov 01	**IF YOU COME BACK** BLUE	1
1 Dec 01	**HAVE YOU EVER** S CLUB 7	1
8 Dec 01	**GOTTA GET THRU THIS** DANIEL BEDINGFIELD	2
22 Dec 01	**SOMETHIN' STUPID** ROBBIE WILLIAMS & NICOLE KIDMAN	3
12 Jan 02	**GOTTA GET THRU THIS** DANIEL BEDINGFIELD	1
19 Jan 02	**MORE THAN A WOMAN** AALIYAH	1
26 Jan 02	**MY SWEET LORD** GEORGE HARRISON	1
2 Feb 02	**HERO** ENRIQUE IGLESIAS	4
2 Mar 02	**WORLD OF OUR OWN** WESTLIFE	1
9 Mar 02	**ANYTHING IS POSSIBLE / EVERGREEN** WILL YOUNG	3
30 Mar 02	**UNCHAINED MELODY** GARETH GATES	4
27 Apr 02	**THE HINDU TIMES** OASIS	1
4 May 02	**FREAK LIKE ME** SUGABABES	1
11 May 02	**KISS KISS** HOLLY VALANCE	1
18 May 02	**IF TOMORROW NEVER COMES** RONAN KEATING	1
25 May 02	**JUST A LITTLE** LIBERTY X	1
1 Jun 02	**WITHOUT ME** EMINEM	1
8 Jun 02	**LIGHT MY FIRE** WILL YOUNG	2
22 Jun 02	**A LITTLE LESS CONVERSATION** ELVIS VS JXL	4
20 Jul 02	**ANYONE OF US (STUPID MISTAKE)** GARETH GATES	3
10 Aug 02	**COLOURBLIND** DARIUS	2
24 Aug 02	**ROUND ROUND** SUGABABES	1
31 Aug 02	**CROSSROADS** BLAZIN' SQUAD	1
7 Sep 02	**THE TIDE IS HIGH (GET THE FEELING)** ATOMIC KITTEN	3
28 Sep 02	**JUST LIKE A PILL** P!NK	1
5 Oct 02	**THE LONG AND WINDING ROAD / SUSPICIOUS MINDS** WILL YOUNG & GARETH GATES	2
19 Oct 02	**THE KETCHUP SONG (ASEREJE)** LAS KETCHUP	1
26 Oct 02	**DILEMMA** NELLY FT KELLY ROWLAND	2
9 Nov 02	**HEAVEN** DJ SAMMY & YANOU FT DO	1

Chart Date	Title Artist	Weeks at No.1
16 Nov 02	**UNBREAKABLE** WESTLIFE	1
23 Nov 02	**DIRRTY** CHRISTINA AGUILERA FT REDMAN	2
7 Dec 02	**IF YOU'RE NOT THE ONE** DANIEL BEDINGFIELD	1
14 Dec 02	**LOSE YOURSELF** EMINEM	1
21 Dec 02	**SORRY SEEMS TO BE THE HARDEST WORD** BLUE FT ELTON JOHN	1
28 Dec 02	**SOUND OF THE UNDERGROUND** GIRLS ALOUD	4
25 Jan 03	**STOP LIVING THE LIE** DAVID SNEDDON	2
8 Feb 03	**ALL THE THINGS SHE SAID** t.A.T.u.	4
8 Mar 03	**BEAUTIFUL** CHRISTINA AGUILERA	2
22 Mar 03	**SPIRIT IN THE SKY** GARETH GATES	2
5 Apr 03	**MAKE LUV** ROOM 5 FT OLIVER CHEATHAM	4
3 May 03	**YOU SAID NO** BUSTED	1
10 May 03	**LONELINESS** TOMCRAFT	1
17 May 03	**IGNITION** R KELLY	4
14 Jun 03	**BRING ME TO LIFE** EVANESCENCE	4
12 Jul 03	**CRAZY IN LOVE** BEYONCE	3
2 Aug 03	**NEVER GONNA LEAVE YOUR SIDE** DANIEL BEDINGFIELD	1
9 Aug 03	**BREATHE** BLU CANTRELL FT SEAN PAUL	4
6 Sep 03	**ARE YOU READY FOR LOVE?** ELTON JOHN	1
13 Sep 03	**WHERE IS THE LOVE?** BLACK EYED PEAS	6
25 Oct 03	**HOLE IN THE HEAD** SUGABABES	1
1 Nov 03	**BE FAITHFUL** FATMAN SCOOP	2
15 Nov 03	**SLOW** KYLIE MINOGUE	1
22 Nov 03	**CRASHED THE WEDDING** BUSTED	1
29 Nov 03	**MANDY** WESTLIFE	1
6 Dec 03	**LEAVE RIGHT NOW** WILL YOUNG	2
20 Dec 03	**CHANGES** KELLY OSBOURNE & OZZY OSBOURNE	1
27 Dec 03	**MAD WORLD** MICHAEL ANDREWS FT GARY JULES	3
17 Jan 04	**ALL THIS TIME** MICHELLE	3
7 Feb 04	**TAKE ME TO THE CLOUDS ABOVE** LMC V U2	2
21 Feb 04	**WITH A LITTLE HELP FROM MY FRIENDS / MEASURE OF A MAN** SAM & MARK	1
28 Feb 04	**WHO'S DAVID** BUSTED	1
6 Mar 04	**MYSTERIOUS GIRL** PETER ANDRE	1
13 Mar 04	**TOXIC** BRITNEY SPEARS	1
20 Mar 04	**CHA CHA SLIDE** DJ CASPER	1
27 Mar 04	**YEAH** USHER	2
10 Apr 04	**FIVE COLOURS IN HER HAIR** MCFLY	2
24 Apr 04	**F**K IT (I DON'T WANT YOU BACK)** EAMON	4
22 May 04	**F.U.R.B (F U RIGHT BACK)** FRANKEE	3
12 Jun 04	**I DON'T WANNA KNOW** MARIO WINANS FT ENYA & P. DIDDY	2
26 Jun 04	**EVERYTIME** BRITNEY SPEARS	1
3 Jul 04	**OBVIOUSLY** MCFLY	1
10 Jul 04	**BURN** USHER	2
24 Jul 04	**LOLA'S THEME** SHAPESHIFTERS	1
31 Jul 04	**DRY YOUR EYES** & STREETS	1
7 Aug 04	**THUNDERBIRDS / 3AM** BUSTED	2
21 Aug 04	**BABYCAKES** 3 OF A KIND	1
28 Aug 04	**THESE WORDS** NATASHA BEDINGFIELD	2
11 Sep 04	**MY PLACE / FLAP YOUR WINGS** NELLY	1
18 Sep 04	**REAL TO ME** BRIAN MCFADDEN	1
25 Sep 04	**CALL ON ME** ERIC PRYDZ	3
16 Oct 04	**RADIO** ROBBIE WILLIAMS	1
23 Oct 04	**CALL ON ME** ERIC PRYDZ	2
6 Nov 04	**WONDERFUL** JA RULE FT R. KELLY & ASHANTI	1

Chart Date	Title Artist	Weeks at No.1
13 Nov 04	**JUST LOSE IT** EMINEM	1
20 Nov 04	**VERTIGO** U2	1
27 Nov 04	**I'LL STAND BY YOU** GIRLS ALOUD	2
11 Dec 04	**DO THEY KNOW IT'S CHRISTMAS?** BAND AID 20	4
8 Jan 05	**AGAINST ALL ODDS** STEVE BROOKSTEIN	1
15 Jan 05	**JAILHOUSE ROCK** ELVIS PRESLEY	1
22 Jan 05	**I GOT STUNG / ONE NIGHT** ELVIS PRESLEY	1
29 Jan 05	**GOODIES** CIARA FT PETEY PABLO	1
5 Feb 05	**IT'S NOW OR NEVER** ** ELVIS PRESLEY	1
12 Feb 05	**LIKE TOY SOLDIERS** EMINEM	1
19 Feb 05	**SOMETIMES YOU CAN'T MAKE IT ON YOUR OWN** U2	1
26 Feb 05	**GET RIGHT** JENNIFER LOPEZ	1
5 Mar 05	**OVER AND OVER** NELLY FT TIM MCGRAW	1
12 Mar 05	**DAKOTA** STEREOPHONICS	1
19 Mar 05	**ALL ABOUT YOU / YOU'VE GOT A FRIEND** MCFLY	1
26 Mar 05	**(IS THIS THE WAY TO) AMARILLO** TONY CHRISTIE FT PETER KAY	7
14 May 05	**LONELY** AKON	2
28 May 05	**LYLA** OASIS	1
4 Jun 05	**AXEL F** CRAZY FROG	4
2 Jul 05	**GHETTO GOSPEL** 2PAC FT ELTON JOHN	3
23 Jul 05	**YOU'RE BEAUTIFUL** JAMES BLUNT	5
27 Aug 05	**I'LL BE OK** MCFLY	1
3 Sep 05	**THE IMPORTANCE OF BEING IDLE** OASIS	1
10 Sep 05	**DARE** GORILLAZ	1
17 Sep 05	**DON'T CHA** PUSSYCAT DOLLS FT BUSTA RHYMES	3
8 Oct 05	**PUSH THE BUTTON** SUGABABES	3
29 Oct 05	**I BET YOU LOOK GOOD ON THE DANCEFLOOR** ARCTIC MONKEYS	1
11 Nov 05	**YOU RAISE ME UP** WESTLIFE	2
19 Nov 05	**HUNG UP** MADONNA	3
10 Dec 05	**STICKWITU** PUSSYCAT DOLLS	2
24 Dec 05	**JCB SONG** NIZLOPI	1
31 Dec 05	**THAT'S MY GOAL** SHAYNE WARD	4
28 Jan 06	**WHEN THE SUN GOES DOWN** ARCTIC MONKEYS	1
4 Feb 06	**NASTY GIRL** NOTORIOUS BIG FT DIDDY, NELLY, JAGGED EDGE & AVERY STORM	2
18 Feb 06	**THUNDER IN MY HEART AGAIN** MECK FT LEO SAYER	2
4 Mar 06	**SORRY** MADONNA	1
11 Mar 06	**IT'S CHICO TIME** CHICO	2
25 Mar 06	**NO TOMORROW** ORSON	1
1 Apr 06	**SO SICK** NE-YO	1
8 Apr 06	**CRAZY** GNARLS BARKLEY	9
10 Jun 06	**I WISH I WAS A PUNK ROCKER (WITH FLOWERS IN MY HAIR)** SANDI THOM	1
17 Jun 06	**MANEATER** NELLY FURTADO	3
8 Jul 06	**HIPS DON'T LIE** SHAKIRA FT WYCLEF JEAN	1
15 Jul 06	**SMILE** LILY ALLEN	2
29 Jul 06	**PLEASE PLEASE / DONT STOP ME NOW** MCFLY	1
5 Aug 06	**HIPS DON'T LIE** SHAKIRA FT WYCLEF JEAN	4
2 Sep 06	**DEJA VU** BEYONCE FT JAY-Z	1
9 Sep 06	**SEXYBACK** JUSTIN TIMBERLAKE	1
16 Sep 06	**I DON'T FEEL LIKE DANCIN'** SCISSOR SISTERS	4
14 Oct 06	**AMERICA** RAZORLIGHT	1
21 Oct 06	**WELCOME TO THE BLACK PARADE** MY CHEMICAL ROMANCE	2
4 Nov 06	**STAR GIRL** MCFLY	1
11 Nov 06	**PUT YOUR HANDS UP FOR DETROIT** FEDDE LE GRAND	1

Chart Date	Title Artist	Weeks at No.1
18 Nov 06	**THE ROSE** WESTLIFE	1
25 Nov 06	**SMACK THAT** AKON FT EMINEM	1
2 Dec 06	**PATIENCE** TAKE THAT	4
30 Dec 06	**A MOMENT LIKE THIS** LEONA LEWIS	4
27 Jan 07	**GRACE KELLY** MIKA	5
3 Mar 07	**RUBY** KAISER CHIEFS	1
10 Mar 07	**SHINE** TAKE THAT	2
24 Mar 07	**WALK THIS WAY** SUGABABES VS GIRLS ALOUD	1
31 Mar 07	**I'M GONNA BE (500 MILES)** THE PROCLAIMERS FT BRIAN POTTER & ANDY PIPKIN	3
21 Apr 07	**GIVE IT TO ME** TIMBALAND / NELLY FURTADO / JUSTIN TIMBERLAKE	1
28 Apr 07	**BEAUTIFUL LIAR** BEYONCE & SHAKIRA	3
19 May 07	**BABY'S COMING BACK / TRANSYLVANIA** MCFLY	1
26 May 07	**UMBRELLA** RIHANNA FT JAY-Z	10
4 Aug 07	**THE WAY I ARE** TIMBALAND FT DOE / KERI HILSON	2
18 Aug 07	**WITH EVERY HEARTBEAT** ROBYN FT KLEERUP	1
25 Aug 07	**STRONGER** KANYE WEST	2
8 Sep 07	**BEAUTIFUL GIRLS** SEAN KINGSTON	4
6 Oct 07	**ABOUT YOU NOW** SUGABABES	4
3 Nov 07	**BLEEDING LOVE** LEONA LEWIS	7
22 Dec 07	**WHAT A WONDERFUL WORLD** EVA CASSIDY & KATIE MELUA	1
29 Dec 07	**WHEN YOU BELIEVE** LEON JACKSON	3
19 Jan 08	**NOW YOU'RE GONE** BASSHUNTER FT DJ MENTAL THEO'S BAZZHEADZ	5
23 Feb 08	**MERCY** DUFFY	5
29 Mar 08	**AMERICAN BOY** ESTELLE FT KANYE WEST	4
26 Apr 08	**4 MINUTES** MADONNA FT JUSTIN TIMBERLAKE	4
24 May 08	**THAT'S NOT MY NAME** TING TINGS	1
31 May 08	**TAKE A BOW** RIHANNA	2
14 Jun 08	**SINGIN' IN THE RAIN** MINT ROYALE	2
28 Jun 08	**VIVA LA VIDA** COLDPLAY	1
5 Jul 08	**CLOSER** NE-YO	1
12 Jul 08	**DANCE WIV ME** DIZZEE RASCAL / CALVIN HARRIS / CHROME	4
9 Aug 08	**ALL SUMMER LONG** KID ROCK	1
16 Aug 08	**I KISSED A GIRL** KATY PERRY	5
20 Sep 08	**SEX ON FIRE** KINGS OF LEON	3
11 Oct 08	**SO WHAT** P!NK	3
1 Nov 08	**PROMISE** GIRLS ALOUD	1
8 Nov 08	**HERO** X FACTOR FINALISTS 2008	3
29 Nov 08	**IF I WERE A BOY** BEYONCE	1
6 Dec 08	**GREATEST DAY** TAKE THAT	1
13 Dec 08	**RUN** LEONA LEWIS	2
27 Dec 08	**HALLELUJAH** ALEXANDRA BURKE	3
17 Jan 09	**JUST DANCE** LADY GAGA / COLBY O'DONIS	3
7 Feb 09	**THE FEAR** LILY ALLEN	4
7 Mar 09	**MY LIFE WOULD SUCK WITHOUT YOU** KELLY CLARKSON	1
14 Mar 09	**RIGHT ROUND** FLO RIDA	1
21 Mar 09	**ISLANDS IN THE STREAM: BBC COMIC RELIEF 2009** JENKINS, WEST, JONES, GIBB	1
28 Mar 09	**POKER FACE** LADY GAGA	3
18 Apr 09	**I'M NOT ALONE** CALVIN HARRIS	2
2 May 09	**NUMBER 1** TINCHY STRYDER FT N-DUBZ	3
23 May 09	**BOOM BOOM POW** BLACK EYED PEAS	1
30 May 09	**BONKERS** DIZZEE RASCAL FT ARMAND VAN HELDEN	2
13 Jun 09	**BOOM BOOM POW** BLACK EYED PEAS	1

Chart Date	Title Artist	Weeks at No.1
20 Jun 09	**MAMA DO** PIXIE LOTT	1
27 Jun 09	**WHEN LOVE TAKES OVER** DAVID GUETTA FT KELLY ROWLAND	1
4 Jul 09	**BULLETPROOF** LA ROUX	1
11 Jul 09	**EVACUATE THE DANCEFLOOR** CASCADA	2
25 Jul 09	**BEAT AGAIN** JLS	2
8 Aug 09	**I GOTTA FEELING** BLACK EYED PEAS	1
15 Aug 09	**NEVER LEAVE YOU** TINCHY STRYDER FT AMELLE	1
22 Aug 09	**I GOTTA FEELING** BLACK EYED PEAS	1
29 Aug 09	**SEXY CHICK** DAVID GUETTA FT AKON	1
5 Sep 09	**HOLIDAY** DIZZEE RASCAL	1
12 Sep 09	**RUN THIS TOWN** JAY-Z FT RIHANNA & KANYE WEST	1
19 Sep 09	**GIRLS & BOYS** PIXIE LOTT	1
26 Sep 09	**BREAK YOUR HEART** TAIO CRUZ	3
17 Oct 09	**OOPSY DAISY** CHIPMUNK	1
24 Oct 09	**BAD BOYS** ALEXANDRA BURKE FT FLO RIDA	1
31 Oct 09	**FIGHT FOR THIS LOVE** CHERYL COLE	2

Chart Date	Title Artist	Weeks at No.1
14 Nov 09	**EVERYBODY IN LOVE** JLS	1
21 Nov 09	**MEET ME HALFWAY** BLACK EYED PEAS	1
28 Nov 09	**YOU ARE NOT ALONE** X FACTOR FINALISTS 2009	1
5 Dec 09	**THE OFFICIAL BBC CHILDREN IN NEED MEDLEY** PETER KAY'S ANIMATED ALL STAR BAND	2
19 Dec 09	**BAD ROMANCE** LADY GAGA	1
26 Dec 09	**KILLING IN THE NAME** RAGE AGAINST THE MACHINE	1
2 Jan 10	**THE CLIMB** JOE MCELDERRY	1
9 Jan 10	**BAD ROMANCE** LADY GAGA	1
16 Jan 10	**REPLAY** IYAZ	2
30 Jan 10	**FIREFLIES** OWL CITY	3
20 Feb 10	**EVERYBODY HURTS** HELPING HAITI	2
6 Mar 10	**IN MY HEAD** JASON DERULO	1
13 Mar 10	**PASS OUT** TINIE TEMPAH	2
27 Mar 10	**TELEPHONE** LADY GAGA FT BEYONCE	2
10 Apr 10	**THIS AIN'T A LOVE SONG** SCOUTING FOR GIRLS	1

BIOGRAPHIES

Biographies include the nationality and category for every chart entrant.

Each entrant has at least a mini biography. The acts with the most weeks on the chart (see page 372 for the chart) each have extended biographies.

Real names are included for all solo artists and, where applicable, dates of death and age of the artist at the time. "See..." links are included for soloists who also had singles chart entries in other acts.

The best known line-up is listed for every group that had a Top 10 single, with the vocalist/leader mentioned first and the others following in alphabetical order. In cases where later replacements had similar success both people are named and, where applicable, the dates of death are also shown for every group/duo member listed.

Certified Awards are given by the BPI to mark unit sales to retailers. They were introduced in April 1973. In January 1989 the levels of unit sales to the trade required to achieve each of the awards was amended to the following amounts:

Silver symbol	●	=	200,000 units
Gold symbol	●	=	400,000 units
Platinum symbol	⊛	=	600,000 units

As from February 2005, download sales also count towards certified awards.

A–D

KEY TO ARTIST ENTRIES

Artist/Group Name — Artist/Group Biography — Silver-selling — Gold-selling — Platinum-selling — US No.1 ★ — Peak Position — Weeks at No.1 — Weeks on Chart

Asterisks (*) indicate group members with hits in their own right that are listed elsewhere in this book

TAKE THAT

UK, male vocal group – Gary Barlow*, Howard Donald, Jason Orange, Mark Owen* & Robbie Williams* (left 1995, rejoined 2010). Comeback kings who have sold 7.4 million singles in the UK. The boys, who came back for good – as a quartet – in 2006, were the first act to score four successive No.1s since The Beatles – a feat they've achieved twice. See Helping Haiti

Artist's Total Weeks On Chart: 356

Date	Title / Label	Peak	Wks No.1	Wks
23 Nov 91	**PROMISES** *RCA PB 45085*	38		2
8 Feb 92	**ONCE YOU'VE TASTED LOVE** *RCA PB 45257*	47		3
6 Jun 92	**IT ONLY TAKES A MINUTE** *RCA 74321101007*	7		8
15 Aug 92	**I FOUND HEAVEN** *RCA 74321108137*	15		6
10 Oct 92	**A MILLION LOVE SONGS** *RCA 74321116307*	7		9
12 Dec 92	**COULD IT BE MAGIC** *RCA 74321123137* ●	3		12
20 Feb 93	**WHY CAN'T I WAKE UP WITH YOU** *RCA 74321133102* ●	2		10
17 Jul 93	**PRAY** *RCA 74321154502* ●	1	4	11
9 Oct 93	**RELIGHT MY FIRE** *RCA 74321167722* FEATURING LULU ●	1	2	14
18 Dec 93	**BABE** *RCA 74321182122* ⊛	1	1	10
9 Apr 94	**EVERYTHING CHANGES** *RCA 74321167732* ●	1	2	10
9 Jul 94	**LOVE AIN'T HERE ANYMORE** *RCA 74321214832* ●	3		12
15 Oct 94	**SURE** *RCA 74321236622* ●	1	2	15
8 Apr 95	**BACK FOR GOOD** *RCA 74321271462* ⊛	1	4	13
5 Aug 95	**NEVER FORGET** *RCA 74321299572* ●	1	3	9
9 Mar 96	**HOW DEEP IS YOUR LOVE** *RCA 74321355592* ⊛	1	3	14
25 Nov 06	**PATIENCE** *Polydor 1714832* ●	1	4	39
10 Feb 07	**SHINE** *Polydor 1724294* ●	1	2	42
30 Jun 07	**I'D WAIT FOR LIFE** *Polydor 1736401*	17		2
27 Oct 07	**RULE THE WORLD** *Polydor 1746285* ●	2		66
6 Dec 08	**GREATEST DAY** *Polydor 1787445*	1	1	20
6 Dec 08	**PATIENCE** *Polydor 1714832*	59		1
6 Dec 08	**NEVER FORGET** *RCA GBARL9500200*	64		1
14 Feb 09	**UP ALL NIGHT** *Polydor 1796964*	14		11
13 Jun 09	**SAID IT ALL** *Polydor 2708717*	9		10
20 Jun 09	**RULE THE WORLD** *Polydor 1746285*	57		6
27 Jun 09	**GREATEST DAY** *Polydor 1787445*	73		1+

Date of entry into chart

Artist collaboration or variation on artist's name

Title of Single — Label and Catalogue Number — BPI Certified Award

A cross (+) indicates that the single was still on chart in the final week of March 2010

A

UK, male vocal/instrumental group – Jason Perry, Daniel P Carter, Mark Chapman, Adam Perry & Giles Perry **21**

Date	Title / Label	Peak Position	Weeks at No.1	Weeks on Chart
7 Feb 98	**FOGHORN** *Tycoon TYCD 5*	63		1
11 Apr 98	**NUMBER ONE** *Tycoon TYCD 6*	47		1
27 Jun 98	**SING-A-LONG** *Tycoon TYCD 7*	57		1
24 Oct 98	**SUMMER ON THE UNDERGROUND** *Tycoon TYCD 8*	72		1
5 Jun 99	**OLD FOLKS** *Tycoon TYCD 9*	54		1
21 Aug 99	**I LOVE LAKE TAHOE** *Tycoon TYCD 10*	59		1
2 Mar 02	**NOTHING** *London LONCD 463*	9		6
1 Jun 02	**STARBUCKS** *London LONCD 467*	20		3
30 Nov 02	**SOMETHING'S GOING ON** *London LONCD 471*	51		1
13 Sep 03	**GOOD TIME** *London LONCD 480*	23		2
14 May 05	**RUSH SONG** *London LONCDP487*	35		2
30 Jul 05	**BETTER OFF WITH HIM** *London LONCD488*	52		1

A-STUDIO FEATURING POLINA

Kazakhstan/Russia, male/female vocal/instrumental/production group **1**

Date	Title / Label	Peak Position	Weeks at No.1	Weeks on Chart
8 Jul 06	**SOS** *Absolution CXABSOL7*	64		1

A*TEENS

Sweden, male/female vocal group – Dhani Lennevald, Sara Lumholdt, Amit Sebastian Paul & Marie Serneholt **19**

Date	Title / Label	Peak Position	Weeks at No.1	Weeks on Chart
4 Sep 99	**MAMMA MIA** *Stockholm 5613432*	12		5
11 Dec 99	**SUPER TROUPER** *Stockholm 5615002*	21		5
26 May 01	**UPSIDE DOWN** *Stockholm 1588492*	10		7
27 Oct 01	**HALFWAY AROUND THE WORLD** *Stockholm 0153612*	30		2

A VS B

UK, male production duo **1**

Date	Title / Label	Peak Position	Weeks at No.1	Weeks on Chart
9 May 98	**RIPPED IN 2 MINUTES** *Positiva CDTIV 89*	49		1

AALIYAH

US, female vocalist (Aaliyah Haughton), d. 25 Aug 2001 (age 22) **72**

Date	Title / Label	Peak Position	Weeks at No.1	Weeks on Chart
2 Jul 94	**BACK AND FORTH** *Jive JIVECD 357*	16		5
15 Oct 94	**(AT YOUR BEST) YOU ARE LOVE** *Jive JIVECD 359*	27		2
11 Mar 95	**AGE AIN'T NOTHING BUT A NUMBER** *Jive JIVECD 369*	32		2
13 May 95	**DOWN WITH THE CLIQUE** *Jive JIVECD 377*	33		2
9 Sep 95	**THE THING I LIKE** *Jive JIVECD 382*	33		2
3 Feb 96	**I NEED YOU TONIGHT** *Big Beat A 8130CD* JUNIOR M.A.F.I.A. FEATURING AALIYAH	66		1
24 Aug 96	**IF YOUR GIRL ONLY KNEW** *Atlantic A 5669CD*	21		2
23 Nov 96	**GOT TO GIVE IT UP** *Atlantic A 5632CD*	37		2
24 May 97	**IF YOUR GIRL ONLY KNEW/ONE IN A MILLION** *Atlantic A 5610CD*	15		3
30 Aug 97	**4 PAGE LETTER** *Atlantic AT 0010CD1*	24		2
22 Nov 97	**THE ONE I GAVE MY HEART TO/HOT LIKE FIRE** *Atlantic AT 0017CD*	30		2
18 Apr 98	**JOURNEY TO THE PAST** *Atlantic AT 0026CD*	22		3
12 Sep 98	**ARE YOU THAT SOMEBODY?** *Atlantic AT 0047CD*	11		4
22 Jul 00	**TRY AGAIN** *Virgin VUSCD 167* ★	5		12
21 Jul 01	**WE NEED A RESOLUTION** *Blackground VUSCD 206* FEATURING TIMBALAND	20		6
19 Jan 02	**MORE THAN A WOMAN** *Blackground VUSCD 230*	1	1	12
18 May 02	**ROCK THE BOAT** *Blackground VUSCD 243*	12		7
26 Apr 03	**DON'T KNOW WHAT TO TELL YA** *Independiente/Blackground/Unique ISOM 73MS*	22		3

ABBA

Sweden/Norway, male/female vocal group – Bjorn Ulvaeus, Benny Andersson, Agnetha Faltskog* & Anni-Frid Lyngstad (Frida*). The most successful act from outside the UK or US, who have sold 10.9 million singles in the UK and had 9 No.1s. Additionally, they have had eight successive UK No.1 albums and *Gold – The Greatest Hits* topped the chart in 1992, 1999 and 2008 – a record-shattering feat **260**

Date	Title / Label	Peak Position	Weeks at No.1	Weeks on Chart
20 Apr 74	**WATERLOO** *Epic EPC 2240*	1	2	9
13 Jul 74	**RING RING** *Epic EPC 2452*	32		5
12 Jul 75	**I DO I DO I DO I DO I DO** *Epic EPC 3229*	38		6
20 Sep 75	**S.O.S.** *Epic EPC 3576*	6		10
13 Dec 75	**MAMMA MIA** *Epic EPC 3790* ○	1	2	14
27 Mar 76	**FERNANDO** *Epic EPC 4036* ●	1	4	15
21 Aug 76	**DANCING QUEEN** *Epic EPC 4499* ● ★	1	6	15
20 Nov 76	**MONEY MONEY MONEY** *Epic EPC 4713* ●	3		12
26 Feb 77	**KNOWING ME KNOWING YOU** *Epic EPC 4955* ●	1	5	13
22 Oct 77	**THE NAME OF THE GAME** *Epic EPC 5750* ●	1	4	12
4 Feb 78	**TAKE A CHANCE ON ME** *Epic EPC 5950* ●	1	3	10
16 Sep 78	**SUMMER NIGHT CITY** *Epic EPC 6395* ○	5		9
3 Feb 79	**CHIQUITITA** *Epic EPC 7030* ●	2		9
5 May 79	**DOES YOUR MOTHER KNOW** *Epic EPC 7316* ○	4		9
21 Jul 79	**ANGELEYES/VOULEZ-VOUS** *Epic EPC 7499* ○	3		11
20 Oct 79	**GIMME GIMME GIMME (A MAN AFTER MIDNIGHT)** *Epic EPC 7914* ○	3		12
15 Dec 79	**I HAVE A DREAM** *Epic EPC 8088* ●	2		10
2 Aug 80	**THE WINNER TAKES IT ALL** *Epic EPC 8835*	1	2	10
15 Nov 80	**SUPER TROUPER** *Epic EPC 9089* ●	1	3	12
18 Jul 81	**LAY ALL YOUR LOVE ON ME** *Epic EPC A 1314*	7		7
12 Dec 81	**ONE OF US** *Epic EPC A 1740* ●	3		10
20 Feb 82	**HEAD OVER HEELS** *Epic EPC A 2037*	25		7
23 Oct 82	**THE DAY BEFORE YOU CAME** *Epic EPC A 2847*	32		6
11 Dec 82	**UNDER ATTACK** *Epic EPC A 2971*	26		8
12 Nov 83	**THANK YOU FOR THE MUSIC** *CBS A 3894*	33		6
5 Sep 92	**DANCING QUEEN** *Polydor PO231*	16		5
29 May 04	**WATERLOO** *Polydor 9820539*	20		3
26 Jul 08	**MAMMA MIA** *Polar SEAYD7590001*	56		5

Top 3 Best-Selling Singles

		Approximate Sales
1	DANCING QUEEN	1,020,000
2	KNOWING ME KNOWING YOU	845,000
3	SUPER TROUPER	810,000

ABBACADABRA

UK, male/female vocal/production group **1**

Date	Title / Label	Peak Position	Weeks at No.1	Weeks on Chart
5 Sep 92	**DANCING QUEEN** *PWL International PWL 246*	57		1

RUSS ABBOT

UK, male comedian/vocalist (Russell Roberts) **22**

Date	Title / Label	Peak Position	Weeks at No.1	Weeks on Chart
6 Feb 82	**A DAY IN THE LIFE OF VINCE PRINCE** *EMI 5249*	61		2
29 Dec 84	**ATMOSPHERE** *Spirit FIRE 4* ○	7		13
13 Jul 85	**ALL NIGHT HOLIDAY** *Spirit FIRE 6*	20		7

GREGORY ABBOTT

US, male vocalist **13**

Date	Title / Label	Peak Position	Weeks at No.1	Weeks on Chart
22 Nov 86	**SHAKE YOU DOWN** *CBS A 7326* ○ ★	6		13

ABC

UK, male vocal/instrumental group – Martin Fry, Mark Lickley, David Palmer, Stephen Singleton & Mark White **93**

Date	Title / Label	Peak Position	Weeks at No.1	Weeks on Chart
31 Oct 81	**TEARS ARE NOT ENOUGH** *Neutron NT 101*	19		8
20 Feb 82	**POISON ARROW** *Neutron NT 102* ○	6		11
15 May 82	**THE LOOK OF LOVE** *Neutron NT 103* ○	4		12
4 Sep 82	**ALL OF MY HEART** *Neutron NT 104*	5		8
5 Nov 83	**THAT WAS THEN BUT THIS IS NOW** *Neutron NT 105*	18		4
21 Jan 84	**S.O.S.** *Neutron NT 106*	39		5
10 Nov 84	**HOW TO BE A MILLIONAIRE** *Neutron NT 107*	49		4
6 Apr 85	**BE NEAR ME** *Neutron NT 108*	26		4
15 Jun 85	**VANITY KILLS** *Neutron NT 109*	70		1
18 Jan 86	**OCEAN BLUE** *Neutron NT 110*	51		3
6 Jun 87	**WHEN SMOKEY SINGS** *Neutron NT 111*	11		10
5 Sep 87	**THE NIGHT YOU MURDERED LOVE** *Neutron NT 112*	31		8
28 Nov 87	**KING WITHOUT A CROWN** *Neutron NT 113*	44		3
27 May 89	**ONE BETTER WORLD** *Neutron NT 114*	32		4
23 Sep 89	**THE REAL THING** *Neutron NT 115*	68		1
14 Apr 90	**THE LOOK OF LOVE (REMIX)** *Neutron NT 116*	68		1
27 Jul 91	**LOVE CONQUERS ALL** *Parlophone R 6292*	47		2
11 Jan 92	**SAY IT** *Parlophone R 6298*	42		3
22 Mar 97	**STRANGER THINGS** *Blatant/Deconstruction 453632*	57		1

PAULA ABDUL

US, female vocalist **67**

Date	Title / Label	Peak Position	Weeks at No.1	Weeks on Chart
4 Mar 89	**STRAIGHT UP** *Siren SRN 111* ○ ★	3		13
3 Jun 89	**FOREVER YOUR GIRL** *Siren SRN 112* ★	24		6
19 Aug 89	**KNOCKED OUT** *Siren SRN 92*	45		3
2 Dec 89	**(IT'S JUST) THE WAY THAT YOU LOVE ME** *Siren SRN 101*	74		1
7 Apr 90	**OPPOSITES ATTRACT** *Siren SRN 124* & THE WILD PAIR ○ ★	2		13
21 Jul 90	**KNOCKED OUT (REMIX)** *Virgin America VUS 23*	21		5
29 Sep 90	**COLD HEARTED** *Virgin America VUS 27* ★	46		3
22 Jun 91	**RUSH RUSH** *Virgin America VUS 38* ★	6		11
31 Aug 91	**THE PROMISE OF A NEW DAY** *Virgin America VUS 44* ★	52		2
18 Jan 92	**VIBEOLOGY** *Virgin America VUS 53*	19		6

Silver-selling ○ Gold-selling ● Platinum-selling (x multiples) ⊛ US No.1 ★ Peak Position · Weeks at No.1 · Weeks on Chart

Date	Title	Peak Position	Weeks at No.1	Weeks on Chart
8 Aug 92	**WILL YOU MARRY ME** *Virgin America VUS 58*	73		1
17 Jun 95	**MY LOVE IS FOR REAL** *Virgin VUSCD 91* FEATURING OFRA HAZA	28		3

ABERFELDY
UK, male/female vocal/instrumental group — 2

Date	Title	Peak Position	Weeks at No.1	Weeks on Chart
28 Aug 04	**HELIOPOLIS BY NIGHT** *Rough Trade RTRADSCD192*	66		1
26 Feb 05	**LOVE IS AN ARROW** *Rough Trade RTRADSCD218*	60		1

ABI
UK, male vocalist/producer — 2

Date	Title	Peak Position	Weeks at No.1	Weeks on Chart
13 Jun 98	**COUNTING THE DAYS** *Kuku CDKUKU 1*	44		2

ABIGAIL
UK, female vocalist (Abigail Zsiga) — 4

Date	Title	Peak Position	Weeks at No.1	Weeks on Chart
16 Jul 94	**SMELLS LIKE TEEN SPIRIT** *Klone CDKLONE 25*	29		4

ANDY ABRAHAM
UK, male vocalist — 4

Date	Title	Peak Position	Weeks at No.1	Weeks on Chart
8 Apr 06	**HANG UP** *Sony BMG 82876816722*	63		1
23 Dec 06	**DECEMBER BRINGS ME BACK TO YOU** *Sony BMG 88697045072* & MICHAEL UNDERWOOD	18		2
31 May 08	**EVEN IF** *B-Line BLINE001*	67		1

COLONEL ABRAMS
US, male vocalist — 35

Date	Title	Peak Position	Weeks at No.1	Weeks on Chart
17 Aug 85	**TRAPPED** *MCA 997* ●	3		23
7 Dec 85	**THE TRUTH** *MCA 1022*	53		3
8 Feb 86	**I'M NOT GONNA LET YOU (GET THE BEST OF ME)** *MCA 1031*	24		7
15 Aug 87	**HOW SOON WE FORGET** *MCA 1179*	75		2

ABS
UK, male vocalist/rapper (Richard Breen). See Five — 24

Date	Title	Peak Position	Weeks at No.1	Weeks on Chart
31 Aug 02	**WHAT YOU GOT** *S 74321957192*	4		8
7 Jun 03	**STOP SIGN** *BMG 82876530392*	10		9
6 Sep 03	**MISS PERFECT** *BMG 82876556742* FEATURING NODESHA	5		7

ABSOLUTE
US, male instrumental/production duo. See Basstoy, Sandstorm — 3

Date	Title	Peak Position	Weeks at No.1	Weeks on Chart
18 Jan 97	**I BELIEVE** *AM:PM 5820752* FEATURING SUZANNE PALMER	38		2
14 Mar 98	**CATCH ME** *AM:PM 5825032*	69		1

AC/DC
Australia/UK, male vocal/instrumental group – Bon Scott, d. 19 Feb 1980 (replaced by Brian Johnson), Phillip Rudd, Cliff Williams, Angus Young & Malcolm Young — 126

Date	Title	Peak Position	Weeks at No.1	Weeks on Chart
10 Jun 78	**ROCK 'N' ROLL DAMNATION** *Atlantic K 11142*	24		9
1 Sep 79	**HIGHWAY TO HELL** *Atlantic K 11321*	56		4
2 Feb 80	**TOUCH TOO MUCH** *Atlantic K 11435*	29		9
28 Jun 80	**DIRTY DEEDS DONE DIRT CHEAP** *Atlantic HM2*	47		3
28 Jun 80	**HIGH VOLTAGE (LIVE VERSION)** *Atlantic HM1*	48		3
28 Jun 80	**IT'S A LONG WAY TO THE TOP (IF YOU WANNA ROCK 'N' ROLL)** *Atlantic HM3*	55		3
28 Jun 80	**WHOLE LOTTA ROSIE** *Atlantic HM4*	36		8
13 Sep 80	**YOU SHOOK ME ALL NIGHT LONG** *Atlantic K 11600*	38		6
29 Nov 80	**ROCK 'N' ROLL AIN'T NOISE POLLUTION** *Atlantic K 11630*	15		8
6 Feb 82	**LET'S GET IT UP** *Atlantic K 11706*	13		6
3 Jul 82	**FOR THOSE ABOUT TO ROCK (WE SALUTE YOU)** *Atlantic K 11721*	15		6
29 Oct 83	**GUNS FOR HIRE** *Atlantic A 9774*	37		4
4 Aug 84	**NERVOUS SHAKEDOWN** *Atlantic A 9651*	35		5
6 Jul 85	**DANGER** *Atlantic A 9532*	48		4
18 Jan 86	**SHAKE YOUR FOUNDATIONS** *Atlantic A 9474*	24		5
24 May 86	**WHO MADE WHO** *Atlantic A 9425*	16		5
30 Aug 86	**YOU SHOOK ME ALL NIGHT LONG** *Atlantic A 9377*	46		4
16 Jan 88	**HEATSEEKER** *Atlantic A 9136*	12		6
2 Apr 88	**THAT'S THE WAY I WANNA ROCK 'N' ROLL** *Atlantic A 9098*	22		5
22 Sep 90	**THUNDERSTRUCK** *Atco B 8907*	13		5
24 Nov 90	**MONEYTALKS** *Atco B 8886*	36		3
27 Apr 91	**ARE YOU READY** *Atco B 8830*	34		3
17 Oct 92	**HIGHWAY TO HELL (LIVE)** *Atco B 8479*	14		4
6 Mar 93	**DIRTY DEEDS DONE DIRT CHEAP (LIVE)** *Atco B 6073CD*	68		1
10 Jul 93	**BIG GUN** *Atco B 8396CD*	23		3
30 Sep 95	**HARD AS A ROCK** *Atlantic A 4368CD*	33		2

Date	Title	Peak Position	Weeks at No.1	Weeks on Chart
11 May 96	**HAIL CAESAR** *East West 7559660512*	56		1
15 Apr 00	**STIFF UPPER LIP** *EMI CDSTIFF 100*	65		1

ACE
UK, male vocal/instrumental group — 10

Date	Title	Peak Position	Weeks at No.1	Weeks on Chart
9 Nov 74	**HOW LONG** *Anchor ANC 1002*	20		10

RICHARD ACE
Jamaica, male vocalist — 2

Date	Title	Peak Position	Weeks at No.1	Weeks on Chart
2 Dec 78	**STAYIN' ALIVE** *Blue Inc. INC 2*	66		2

ACE OF BASE
Sweden, female/male vocal/instrumental group – Malin, Jenny & Jonas Berggren & Ulf Ekberg — 100

Date	Title	Peak Position	Weeks at No.1	Weeks on Chart
8 May 93	**ALL THAT SHE WANTS** *London 8612702* ⊛	1	3	16
28 Aug 93	**WHEEL OF FORTUNE** *London 8615452*	20		6
13 Nov 93	**HAPPY NATION** *London 8619272*	42		3
26 Feb 94	**THE SIGN** *London ACECD 1* ● ★	2		16
11 Jun 94	**DON'T TURN AROUND** *London ACECD 2*	5		11
15 Oct 94	**HAPPY NATION** *London 8610972*	40		3
14 Jan 95	**LIVING IN DANGER** *Metronome ACECD 3*	18		4
11 Nov 95	**LUCKY LOVE** *London ACCDP 4*	20		5
27 Jan 96	**BEAUTIFUL LIFE** *Metronome ACECD 5*	15		6
25 Jul 98	**LIFE IS A FLOWER** *London ACECD 7* ○	5		11
10 Oct 98	**CRUEL SUMMER** *London ACECD 8*	8		5
19 Dec 98	**ALWAYS HAVE, ALWAYS WILL** *London ACECD 9*	12		10
17 Apr 99	**EVERY TIME IT RAINS** *London ACECD 10*	22		4

ACEN
UK, male producer (Syed Ahsen Razvi) — 4

Date	Title	Peak Position	Weeks at No.1	Weeks on Chart
8 Aug 92	**TRIP II THE MOON** *Production House PNT 042*	38		3
10 Oct 92	**TRIP II THE MOON (REMIX)** *Production House PNT 042RX*	71		1

ACT
UK/Germany, male/female vocal/instrumental duo — 2

Date	Title	Peak Position	Weeks at No.1	Weeks on Chart
23 May 87	**SNOBBERY AND DECAY** *ZTT ZTAS 28*	60		2

ACT ONE
US, male vocal/instrumental group — 6

Date	Title	Peak Position	Weeks at No.1	Weeks on Chart
18 May 74	**TOM THE PEEPER** *Mercury 6008 005*	40		6

ACZESS
UK, male producer (Dave Birchard) — 1

Date	Title	Peak Position	Weeks at No.1	Weeks on Chart
27 Oct 01	**DO WHAT WE WOULD** *INCredible 6719782*	65		1

ADAM & THE ANTS
UK, male vocal/instrumental group – Adam Ant* (Stuart Goddard), Chris Hughes, Terry Lee Miall, Kevin Mooney & Marco Pirroni — 130

Date	Title	Peak Position	Weeks at No.1	Weeks on Chart
2 Aug 80	**KINGS OF THE WILD FRONTIER** *CBS 8877*	48		5
11 Oct 80	**DOG EAT DOG** *CBS 9039* ○	4		16
6 Dec 80	**ANTMUSIC** *CBS 9352* ●	2		18
27 Dec 80	**YOUNG PARISIANS** *Decca F 13803* ○	9		13
24 Jan 81	**CARTROUBLE** *Do It DUN 10*	33		9
24 Jan 81	**ZEROX** *Do It DUN 8*	45		9
21 Feb 81	**KINGS OF THE WILD FRONTIER** *CBS 8877*	2		13
9 May 81	**STAND AND DELIVER** *CBS A 1065* ●	1	5	15
12 Sep 81	**PRINCE CHARMING** *CBS A 1408* ●	1	4	12
12 Dec 81	**ANT RAP** *CBS A 1738* ●	3		10
27 Feb 82	**DEUTSCHER GIRLS** *Ego 5*	13		6
13 Mar 82	**THE ANTMUSIC EP (THE B-SIDES)** *Do It DUN 20*	46		4

A.D.A.M. FEATURING AMY
France, male/female vocal/instrumental trio — 11

Date	Title	Peak Position	Weeks at No.1	Weeks on Chart
1 Jul 95	**ZOMBIE** *Eternal YZ 951CD*	16		11

ARTHUR ADAMS
US, male vocalist/guitarist — 5

Date	Title	Peak Position	Weeks at No.1	Weeks on Chart
24 Oct 81	**YOU GOT THE FLOOR** *RCA 146*	38		5

BEN ADAMS

UK, male vocalist. See A1 — 3

Date	Title	Peak Position	Weeks at No.1	Weeks on Chart
11 Jun 05	**SORRY** *Phonogenic 82876699392*	18		3

BRYAN ADAMS

Canada, male vocalist/multi-instrumentalist/producer. World-renowned singer/songwriter and now award-winning photographer who has won 18 Juno awards (the Canadian equivalent of the BRITs), sold more than 65 million records worldwide and 5.3 million UK singles. 'Everything I Do' spent a record 16 consecutive weeks at No.1 — 248

Date	Title	Peak Position	Weeks at No.1	Weeks on Chart
12 Jan 85	**RUN TO YOU** *A&M AM 224*	11		12
16 Mar 85	**SOMEBODY** *A&M AM 236*	35		7
25 May 85	**HEAVEN** *A&M AM 256* ★	38		5
10 Aug 85	**SUMMER OF '69** *A&M AM 267*	42		7
2 Nov 85	**IT'S ONLY LOVE** *A&M AM 285* & TINA TURNER	29		6
21 Dec 85	**CHRISTMAS TIME** *A&M AM 297*	55		2
22 Feb 86	**THIS TIME** *A&M AM 295*	41		7
12 Jul 86	**STRAIGHT FROM THE HEART** *A&M AM 322*	51		3
28 Mar 87	**HEAT OF THE NIGHT** *A&M ADAM 2*	50		2
20 Jun 87	**HEARTS ON FIRE** *A&M ADAM 3*	57		3
17 Oct 87	**VICTIM OF LOVE** *A&M AM 407*	68		2
29 Jun 91	**(EVERYTHING I DO) I DO IT FOR YOU** *A&M AM 789* ⊛x2 ★	1	16	25
14 Sep 91	**CAN'T STOP THIS THING WE STARTED** *A&M AM 612*	12		6
23 Nov 91	**THERE WILL NEVER BE ANOTHER TONIGHT** *A&M AM 838*	32		3
22 Feb 92	**THOUGHT I'D DIED AND GONE TO HEAVEN** *A&M AM 848*	8		7
18 Jul 92	**ALL I WANT IS YOU** *A&M AM 879*	22		5
26 Sep 92	**DO I HAVE TO SAY THE WORDS** *A&M AM 0068*	30		3
30 Oct 93	**PLEASE FORGIVE ME** *A&M 5804232* ●	2		16
15 Jan 94	**ALL FOR LOVE** *A&M 5804772* BRYAN ADAMS, ROD STEWART & STING ● ★	2		13
22 Apr 95	**HAVE YOU EVER REALLY LOVED A WOMAN?** *A&M 5810282* ● ★	4		9
11 Nov 95	**ROCK STEADY** *Capitol CDCL 763* BONNIE RAITT & BRYAN ADAMS	50		2
1 Jun 96	**THE ONLY THING THAT LOOKS GOOD ON ME IS YOU** *A&M 5813692*	6		7
24 Aug 96	**LET'S MAKE A NIGHT TO REMEMBER** *A&M 5815672*	10		8
23 Nov 96	**STAR** *A&M 5820252*	13		4
8 Feb 97	**I FINALLY FOUND SOMEONE** *A&M 5820832* BARBRA STREISAND & BRYAN ADAMS	10		7
19 Apr 97	**18 TIL I DIE** *A&M 5821852*	22		3
20 Dec 97	**BACK TO YOU** *A&M 5824752*	18		7
21 Mar 98	**I'M READY** *A&M 5825352*	20		4
10 Oct 98	**ON A DAY LIKE TODAY** *Mercury MERCD 516*	13		5
12 Dec 98	**WHEN YOU'RE GONE** *A&M 5828212* FEATURING MELANIE C ⊛	3		19
15 May 99	**CLOUD NUMBER 9** *A&M 5828492*	6		9
18 Dec 99	**THE BEST OF ME** *Mercury/A&M 4971952*	47		3
18 Mar 00	**DON'T GIVE UP** *Xtravaganza XTRAV 9CDS* CHICANE FEATURING BRYAN ADAMS ●	1	1	14
20 Jul 02	**HERE I AM** *A&M 4977442*	5		8
25 Sep 04	**OPEN ROAD** *Polydor 9868053*	21		3
11 Dec 04	**FLYING** *Polydor 9869276*	39		2

CLIFF ADAMS ORCHESTRA

UK, male/female vocal group – leader d. 22 Oct 2001 (age 78) — 2

Date	Title	Peak Position	Weeks at No.1	Weeks on Chart
28 Apr 60	**LONELY MAN THEME** *Pye International 7N 25056*	39		2

GAYLE ADAMS

US, female vocalist — 1

Date	Title	Peak Position	Weeks at No.1	Weeks on Chart
26 Jul 80	**STRETCHIN' OUT** *Epic EPC 8791*	64		1

OLETA ADAMS

US, female vocalist/keyboard player — 36

Date	Title	Peak Position	Weeks at No.1	Weeks on Chart
24 Mar 90	**RHYTHM OF LIFE** *Fontana OLETA 1*	52		2
3 Nov 90	**RHYTHM OF LIFE** *Fontana OLETA 1*	56		3
12 Jan 91	**GET HERE** *Fontana OLETA 3*	4		12
13 Apr 91	**YOU'VE GOT TO GIVE ME ROOM/RHYTHM OF LIFE** *Fontana OLETA 4*	49		3
29 Jun 91	**CIRCLE OF ONE** *Fontana OLETA 5*	73		1
28 Sep 91	**DON'T LET THE SUN GO DOWN ON ME** *Fontana TRIBO 1*	33		5
25 Apr 92	**WOMAN IN CHAINS** *Fontana IDEA 16* TEARS FOR FEARS FEATURING OLETA ADAMS	57		1
10 Jul 93	**I JUST HAD TO HEAR YOUR VOICE** *Fontana OLETA 6*	42		3
7 Oct 95	**NEVER KNEW LOVE** *Fontana OLECD 9*	22		3
16 Dec 95	**RHYTHM OF LIFE (REMIX)** *Fontana OLECD 10*	38		2
10 Feb 96	**WE WILL MEET AGAIN** *Mercury OLECD 11*	51		1

RYAN ADAMS

US, male vocalist/multi-instrumentalist — 8

Date	Title	Peak Position	Weeks at No.1	Weeks on Chart
8 Dec 01	**NEW YORK NEW YORK** *Mercury 1722232*	53		1
20 Apr 02	**ANSWERING BELL** *Lost Highway 1722402*	39		2
28 Sep 02	**NUCLEAR** *Lost Highway 1722592*	37		1
31 Jan 04	**SO ALIVE** *Lost Highway 9861611*	21		2
10 Jul 04	**WONDERWALL** *Lost Highway 9863098*	27		2

ADAMSKI

UK, male producer (Adam Tinley) — 39

Date	Title	Peak Position	Weeks at No.1	Weeks on Chart
20 Jan 90	**N-R-G** *MCA 1386*	12		6
7 Apr 90	**KILLER** *MCA 1400* ●	1	4	18
8 Sep 90	**THE SPACE JUNGLE** *MCA 1435*	7		8
17 Nov 90	**FLASHBACK JACK** *MCA 1459*	46		2
9 Nov 91	**NEVER GOIN' DOWN/BORN TO BE ALIVE** *MCA MCS 1578* FEATURING JIMI POLO/ADAMSKI FEATURING SOHO	51		2
4 Apr 92	**GET YOUR BODY** *MCA MCS 1613* FEATURING NINA HAGEN	68		1
4 Jul 92	**BACK TO FRONT** *MCA MCS 1644*	63		1
11 Jul 98	**ONE OF THE PEOPLE** *ZTT 101CD* 'S THING	56		1

ADDAMS & GEE

UK, male production duo — 1

Date	Title	Peak Position	Weeks at No.1	Weeks on Chart
20 Apr 91	**CHUNG KUO (REVISITED)** *Debut DEBT 3108*	72		1

ADDICTIVE FEATURING T2

UK, female/male vocal/production trio — 3

Date	Title	Peak Position	Weeks at No.1	Weeks on Chart
22 Mar 08	**GONNA BE MINE** *Gusto/2NV CDGUST59*	47		3

ADDIS BLACK WIDOW

US, male rap duo — 2

Date	Title	Peak Position	Weeks at No.1	Weeks on Chart
3 Feb 96	**INNOCENT** *Mercury Black Vinyl MBVCD 1*	42		2

ADDRISI BROTHERS

US, male vocal duo – Dick & Don, d. 13 Nov 1984, Addrisi — 3

Date	Title	Peak Position	Weeks at No.1	Weeks on Chart
6 Oct 79	**GHOST DANCER** *Scotti Brothers K 11361*	57		3

ADELE

UK, female vocalist/guitarist (Adele Adkins) — 53

Date	Title	Peak Position	Weeks at No.1	Weeks on Chart
26 Jan 08	**CHASING PAVEMENTS** *XL Recordings XLS321CD*	2		19
9 Feb 08	**HOMETOWN GLORY** *XL Recordings Pacemaker1*	19		20
19 Apr 08	**COLD SHOULDER** *XL Recordings XLS358CD*	18		9
1 Nov 08	**MAKE YOU FEEL MY LOVE** *XL Recordings XLT393CD*	26		5

ADEMA

US, male vocal/instrumental group — 3

Date	Title	Peak Position	Weeks at No.1	Weeks on Chart
16 Mar 02	**GIVING IN** *Arista 74321924022*	62		1
10 Aug 02	**THE WAY YOU LIKE IT** *Arista 74321954712*	61		1
23 Aug 03	**UNSTABLE** *Arista 82876550862*	46		1

ADEVA

US, female vocalist (Patricia Daniels) — 66

Date	Title	Peak Position	Weeks at No.1	Weeks on Chart
14 Jan 89	**RESPECT** *Cooltempo COOL 179*	17		9
25 Mar 89	**MUSICAL FREEDOM (MOVING ON UP)** *Cooltempo COOL 182* PAUL SIMPSON FEATURING ADEVA	22		8
12 Aug 89	**WARNING** *Cooltempo COOL 185*	17		8
21 Oct 89	**I THANK YOU** *Cooltempo COOL 192*	17		7
16 Dec 89	**BEAUTIFUL LOVE** *Cooltempo COOL 195*	57		5
28 Apr 90	**TREAT ME RIGHT** *Cooltempo COOL 200*	62		2
6 Apr 91	**RING MY BELL** *Cooltempo COOL 224* MONIE LOVE Vs ADEVA	20		5
19 Oct 91	**IT SHOULD'VE BEEN ME** *Cooltempo COOL 236*	48		3
29 Feb 92	**DON'T LET IT SHOW ON YOUR FACE** *Cooltempo COOL 248*	34		4
6 Jun 92	**UNTIL YOU COME BACK TO ME** *Cooltempo COOL 254*	45		3
17 Oct 92	**I'M THE ONE FOR YOU** *Cooltempo COOL 264*	51		2
11 Dec 93	**RESPECT (REMIX)** *Network NWKCD 79*	65		1
27 May 95	**TOO MANY FISH** *Virgin VUSCD 89* FRANKIE KNUCKLES FEATURING ADEVA	34		2
18 Nov 95	**WHADDA U WANT (FROM ME)** *Virgin VUSCD 98* FRANKIE KNUCKLES FEATURING ADEVA	36		2
6 Apr 96	**DO WATCHA DO** *Avex UK AVEXCD 24* HYPER GO GO & ADEVA	54		1
4 May 96	**I THANK YOU (REMIX)** *Cooltempo CDCOOLS 318*	37		2

Silver-selling ● Gold-selling ● Platinum-selling (x multiples) ★ US No.1 — Peak Position · Weeks at No.1 · Weeks on Chart

Date	Title / Label	Peak Position	Weeks at No.1	Weeks on Chart
12 Apr 97	**DO WATCHA DO (REMIX)** *Distinctive DISNCD 28* HYPER GO GO & ADEVA	60		1
26 Jul 97	**WHERE IS THE LOVE/THE WAY THAT YOU FEEL** *Distinctive DISNCD 31*	54		1

ADICTS
UK, male vocal/instrumental group — 1

Date	Title / Label	Peak Position	Weeks at No.1	Weeks on Chart
14 May 83	**BAD BOY** *Razor RZS 104*	75		1

ADIEMUS
UK, male/female vocal/instrumental group — 2

Date	Title / Label	Peak Position	Weeks at No.1	Weeks on Chart
14 Oct 95	**ADIEMUS** *Venture VEND 4*	48		2

ADONIS FEATURING 2 PUERTO RICANS, A BLACK MAN & A DOMINICAN
US, male production group — 4

Date	Title / Label	Peak Position	Weeks at No.1	Weeks on Chart
13 Jun 87	**DO IT PROPERLY ('NO WAY BACK')/NO WAY BACK** *London LON 136*	47		4

ADRENALIN M.O.D.
UK, male production trio — 5

Date	Title / Label	Peak Position	Weeks at No.1	Weeks on Chart
8 Oct 88	**O-O-O** *MCA RAGAT 2*	49		5

ADULT NET
US/UK, female/male vocal/instrumental group — 2

Date	Title / Label	Peak Position	Weeks at No.1	Weeks on Chart
10 Jun 89	**WHERE WERE YOU** *Fontana BRX 2*	66		2

ADVENTURES
UK, male/female vocal/instrumental group — 24

Date	Title / Label	Peak Position	Weeks at No.1	Weeks on Chart
15 Sep 84	**ANOTHER SILENT DAY** *Chrysalis CHS 2000*	71		2
1 Dec 84	**SEND MY HEART** *Chrysalis CHS 2001*	62		4
13 Jul 85	**FEEL THE RAINDROPS** *Chrysalis AD 1*	58		3
9 Apr 88	**BROKEN LAND** *Elektra EKR 69*	20		10
2 Jul 88	**DROWNING THE THE SEA OF LOVE** *Elektra EKR 76*	44		4
13 Jun 92	**RAINING ALL OVER THE WORLD** *Polydor PO 211*	68		1

ADVENTURES OF STEVIE V
UK, male/female production/vocal group – Stevie Vincent, Mick Walsh & Melodie Washington — 22

Date	Title / Label	Peak Position	Weeks at No.1	Weeks on Chart
21 Apr 90	**DIRTY CASH** *Mercury MER 311*	2		13
29 Sep 90	**BODY LANGUAGE** *Mercury MER 331*	29		5
2 Mar 91	**JEALOUSY** *Mercury MER 337*	58		3
27 Sep 97	**DIRTY CASH (REMIX)** *Avex Trax AVEXCDX 57*	69		1

ADVERTS
UK, male/female vocal/instrumental group — 11

Date	Title / Label	Peak Position	Weeks at No.1	Weeks on Chart
27 Aug 77	**GARY GILMORE'S EYES** *Anchor ANC 1043*	18		7
4 Feb 78	**NO TIME TO BE 21** *Bright BR1*	34		4

AEROSMITH
US, male vocal/instrumental group – Steven Tyler, Tom Hamilton, Joey Kramer, Joe Perry & Brad Whitford — 93

Date	Title / Label	Peak Position	Weeks at No.1	Weeks on Chart
17 Oct 87	**DUDE (LOOKS LIKE A LADY)** *Geffen GEF 29*	45		5
16 Apr 88	**ANGEL** *Geffen GEF 34*	69		2
9 Sep 89	**LOVE IN AN ELEVATOR** *Geffen GEF 63*	13		8
24 Feb 90	**DUDE (LOOKS LIKE A LADY)** *Geffen GEF 72*	20		5
14 Apr 90	**RAG DOLL** *Geffen GEF 76*	42		4
1 Sep 90	**THE OTHER SIDE** *Geffen GEF 79*	46		2
10 Apr 93	**LIVIN' ON THE EDGE** *Geffen GFSTD 35*	19		4
3 Jul 93	**EAT THE RICH** *Geffen GFSTD 46*	34		3
30 Oct 93	**CRYIN'** *Geffen GFSTD 56*	17		6
18 Dec 93	**AMAZING** *Geffen GFSTD 63*	57		3
2 Jul 94	**SHUT UP AND DANCE** *Geffen GFSTD 75*	24		4
20 Aug 94	**SWEET EMOTION** *Columbia 6604492*	74		1
5 Nov 94	**CRAZY/BLIND MAN** *Geffen GFSTD 80*	23		4
8 Mar 97	**FALLING IN LOVE (IS HARD ON THE KNEES)** *Columbia 6640752*	22		4
21 Jun 97	**HOLE IN MY SOUL** *Columbia 6645012*	29		2
27 Dec 97	**PINK** *Columbia 6648722*	38		2
12 Sep 98	**I DON'T WANT TO MISS A THING** *Columbia 6664082* ● ★	4		20
26 Jun 99	**PINK** *Columbia 6675342*	13		6
17 Mar 01	**JADED** *Columbia 6709312*	13		7
17 May 08	**I DON'T WANT TO MISS A THING** *Columbia 6664085*	68		1

AFI
US, male vocal/instrumental group — 6

Date	Title / Label	Peak Position	Weeks at No.1	Weeks on Chart
21 Jun 03	**GIRL'S NOT GREY** *DreamWorks 4504601*	22		3
20 Sep 03	**THE LEAVING SONG PART 2** *DreamWorks 4504625*	43		1
24 Jun 06	**MISS MURDER** *Interscope 9859439*	44		2

AFRICAN BUSINESS
Italy, male production/rap group — 1

Date	Title / Label	Peak Position	Weeks at No.1	Weeks on Chart
17 Nov 90	**IN ZAIRE** *Urban URB 64*	73		1

AFRO CELT SOUND SYSTEM
UK/Ireland/France/Guinea, male vocal/instrumental group — 1

Date	Title / Label	Peak Position	Weeks at No.1	Weeks on Chart
29 Apr 00	**RELEASE** *Realworld RWSCD 10*	71		1

AFRO MEDUSA
UK/Spain, male/female vocal/production trio — 2

Date	Title / Label	Peak Position	Weeks at No.1	Weeks on Chart
28 Oct 00	**PASILDA** *Rulin 6CDS*	31		2

AFTER 7
US, male vocal trio — 3

Date	Title / Label	Peak Position	Weeks at No.1	Weeks on Chart
3 Nov 90	**CAN'T STOP** *Virgin America VUS 31*	54		3

AFROMAN
US, male rapper/vocalist (Joseph Foreman) — 30

Date	Title / Label	Peak Position	Weeks at No.1	Weeks on Chart
6 Oct 01	**BECAUSE I GOT HIGH (IMPORT)** *Universal 0152822*	45		3
27 Oct 01	**BECAUSE I GOT HIGH** *Universal MCSTD 40266* ●	1	3	19
2 Feb 02	**CRAZY RAP** *Universal MCSTD 40273*	10		8

AFTER THE FIRE
UK, male vocal/instrumental group — 12

Date	Title / Label	Peak Position	Weeks at No.1	Weeks on Chart
9 Jun 79	**ONE RULE FOR YOU** *CBS 7025*	40		6
8 Sep 79	**LASER LOVE** *CBS 7769*	62		2
9 Apr 83	**DER KOMMISSAR** *CBS A 2399*	47		4

AFTERSHOCK
US, male vocal duo — 8

Date	Title / Label	Peak Position	Weeks at No.1	Weeks on Chart
21 Aug 93	**SLAVE TO THE VIBE** *Virgin America VUSCD 75*	11		8

AFX
UK, male producer (Richard James). See Aphex Twin, Polygon Window, Powerpill — 1

Date	Title / Label	Peak Position	Weeks at No.1	Weeks on Chart
11 Aug 01	**2 REMIXES BY AFX** *MEN 1 MEN1CD*	69		1

AGE OF CHANCE
UK, male/female vocal/instrumental group — 13

Date	Title / Label	Peak Position	Weeks at No.1	Weeks on Chart
17 Jan 87	**KISS** *Fon AGE 5*	50		6
30 May 87	**WHO'S AFRAID OF THE BIG BAD NOISE?** *Fon VS 962*	65		2
20 Jan 90	**HIGHER THAN HEAVEN** *Virgin VS 1228*	53		5

AGE OF LOVE
Italy, male instrumental/production duo — 6

Date	Title / Label	Peak Position	Weeks at No.1	Weeks on Chart
5 Jul 97	**AGE OF LOVE – THE REMIXES** *React CDREACT 100*	17		4
19 Sep 98	**AGE OF LOVE** *React CDREACT 135*	38		2

AGENT BLUE
UK, male vocal/instrumental/production duo — 3

Date	Title / Label	Peak Position	Weeks at No.1	Weeks on Chart
29 May 04	**SEX DRUGS AND ROCKS THROUGH YOUR WINDOW** *Fierce Panda NING153CD*	71		1
21 Aug 04	**SOMETHING ELSE** *Island TEMPTCD011*	59		1
19 Mar 05	**CHILDREN'S CHILDREN** *Universal MCSTD40401*	62		1

Silver-selling ● Gold-selling ● Platinum-selling (× multiples) ⊛ US No.1 ★ Peak Position · Weeks at No.1 · Weeks on Chart

AGENT OO
UK, male production duo — 1

Date	Title / Label	Peak	No.1	Weeks
7 Mar 98	**THE MAGNIFICENT** *Inferno CDFERN 002*	65		1

AGENT PROVOCATEUR
UK, male/female vocal/production group — 1

Date	Title / Label	Peak	No.1	Weeks
22 Mar 97	**AGENT DAN** *Epic AGENT 3CD*	49		1

AGENT SUMO
UK, male production duo — 4

Date	Title / Label	Peak	No.1	Weeks
9 Jun 01	**24 HOURS** *Virgin VSCDT 1806*	44		2
20 Apr 02	**WHY** *Virgin VSCDT 1819*	40		2

AGNELLI & NELSON
Ireland, male DJ/production duo — 17

Date	Title / Label	Peak	No.1	Weeks
15 Aug 98	**EL NINO** *Xtravaganza 0091575 EXT*	21		4
11 Sep 99	**EVERYDAY** *Xtravaganza XTRAV 2CDS*	17		4
17 Jun 00	**EMBRACE** *Xtravaganza XTRAV 11CDS*	35		2
9 Sep 00	**HUDSON STREET** *Xtravaganza XTRAV 13CDS*	29		2
7 Apr 01	**VEGAS** *Xtravaganza XTRAV 23CDS*	48		1
15 Jun 02	**EVERYDAY (ALEX GOLD 2002 MIXES)** *Xtravaganza XTRAV 31CDS*	33		2
3 Apr 04	**HOLDING ON TO NOTHING** *Xtravaganza XTRAV 43CX* FEATURING AUREUS	41		2

AGNES
Sweden, female vocalist (Agnes Carlsson) — 19

Date	Title / Label	Peak	No.1	Weeks
6 Jun 09	**RELEASE ME** *3 Beat/AATW GBD620901710*	3		17
28 Nov 09	**I NEED YOU NOW** *AATW/UMTV CDGLOBE1280*	40		2

CHRISTINA AGUILERA
US, female vocalist. Controversial singer/songwriter and former New Mickey Mouse Club member who successfully 'sexed up' her girl-next-door image in 2001. In her homeland since 2000, Mrs Jordan Bratman has sold more singles than anyone else except Madonna — 231

Date	Title / Label	Peak	No.1	Weeks
11 Sep 99	**GENIE IN A BOTTLE (IMPORT)** *RCA 701062*	50		5
16 Oct 99	**GENIE IN A BOTTLE** *RCA 74321705482* ★	1	2	19
26 Feb 00	**WHAT A GIRL WANTS** *RCA 74321737522* ★	3		13
22 Jul 00	**I TURN TO YOU** *RCA 74321765472*	19		6
11 Nov 00	**COME ON OVER BABY (ALL I WANT IS YOU)** *RCA 74321799912* ★	8		8
10 Mar 01	**NOBODY WANTS TO BE LONELY** *Columbia 6709462* RICKY MARTIN WITH CHRISTINA AGUILERA	4		12
30 Jun 01	**LADY MARMALADE** *Interscope 4975612* CHRISTINA AGUILERA/LIL' KIM/MYA/PINK ● ★	1	1	16
23 Nov 02	**DIRRTY** *RCA 74321962722* FEATURING REDMAN ⊛	1	2	9
22 Feb 03	**BEAUTIFUL (IMPORT)** *RCA 74321983652*	51		2
8 Mar 03	**BEAUTIFUL** *RCA 82876502462*	1	1	10
21 Jun 03	**FIGHTER** *RCA 82876524292*	3		13
20 Sep 03	**CAN'T HOLD US DOWN** *RCA 82876556332* FEATURING LIL' KIM	6		9
20 Dec 03	**THE VOICE WITHIN** *RCA 82876584292*	9		10
13 Nov 04	**CAR WASH** *DreamWorks 9864630* & MISSY ELLIOTT	4		14
4 Dec 04	**TILT YA HEAD BACK** *Universal MCSTD40396* NELLY & CHRISTINA AGUILERA	5		12
29 Jul 06	**AIN'T NO OTHER MAN** *RCA 82876860722*	2		16
18 Nov 06	**HURT** *RCA 88697013962*	11		12
16 Dec 06	**TELL ME** *Atlantic AT0268CD* P DIDDY FEATURING CHRISTINA AGUILERA	8		17
10 Mar 07	**CANDYMAN** *RCA USRC10600413*	17		20
8 Dec 07	**HURT** *RCA 88697013962*	39		1
15 Nov 08	**KEEPS GETTIN' BETTER** *RCA 88697386462*	14		5
31 Oct 09	**HURT** *RCA 88697013962*	25		2

A-HA
Norway, male vocal/instrumental group – Morten Harket*, Magna Furuholmen & Pal Waaktaar — 140

Date	Title / Label	Peak	No.1	Weeks
28 Sep 85	**TAKE ON ME** *Warner Brothers W 9006* ● ★	2		19
28 Dec 85	**THE SUN ALWAYS SHINES ON TV** *Warner Brothers W 8846* ●	1	2	12
5 Apr 86	**TRAIN OF THOUGHT** *Warner Brothers W 8736*	8		8
14 Jun 86	**HUNTING HIGH AND LOW** *Warner Brothers W 6663*	5		10
4 Oct 86	**I'VE BEEN LOSING YOU** *Warner Brothers W 8594*	8		7
6 Dec 86	**CRY WOLF** *Warner Brothers W 8500* ●	5		9
28 Feb 87	**MANHATTAN SKYLINE** *Warner Brothers W 8405*	13		6
4 Jul 87	**THE LIVING DAYLIGHTS** *Warner Brothers W 8305*	5		9
26 Mar 88	**STAY ON THESE ROADS** *Warner Brothers W 7936*	5		6
18 Jun 88	**THE BLOOD THAT MOVES THE BODY** *Warner Brothers W 7840*	25		4
27 Aug 88	**TOUCHY!** *Warner Brothers W 7749*	11		7
3 Dec 88	**YOU ARE THE ONE** *Warner Brothers W 7636*	13		10
13 Oct 90	**CRYING IN THE RAIN** *Warner Brothers W 9547*	13		7
15 Dec 90	**I CALL YOUR NAME** *Warner Brothers W 9462*	44		5
26 Oct 91	**MOVE TO MEMPHIS** *Warner Brothers W 0070*	47		2
5 Jun 93	**DARK IS THE NIGHT** *Warner Brothers W 0175CD*	19		4
18 Sep 93	**ANGEL** *Warner Brothers W 0195CD*	41		3
26 Mar 94	**SHAPES THAT GO TOGETHER** *Warner Brothers W 0236CD*	27		3
3 Jun 00	**SUMMER MOVED ON** *WEA 275CD*	33		2
4 Feb 06	**ANALOGUE (ALL I WANT)** *Polydor 9876840*	10		5
29 Apr 06	**COSY PRISONS** *Polydor 9856227*	39		1
8 Aug 09	**FOOT OF THE MOUNTAIN** *UMRL NOUM70900268*	66		1

AHMAD
US, male rapper (Ahmad Lewis) — 2

Date	Title / Label	Peak	No.1	Weeks
9 Jul 94	**BACK IN THE DAY** *Giant 74321212942*	64		2

AIDA
Holland, male production duo — 1

Date	Title / Label	Peak	No.1	Weeks
19 Feb 00	**FAR AND AWAY** *48K/Perfecto SPECT 03CDS*	58		1

AIR
France, male instrumental/production duo — 16

Date	Title / Label	Peak	No.1	Weeks
21 Feb 98	**SEXY BOY** *Virgin VSCDT 1672*	13		4
16 May 98	**KELLY WATCH THE STARS** *Virgin VSCDT 1690*	18		3
21 Nov 98	**ALL I NEED** *Virgin VSCDT 1702*	29		3
26 Feb 00	**PLAYGROUND LOVE** *Virgin VSCDT 1764*	25		2
2 Jun 01	**RADIO #1** *Virgin VSCDT 1803*	31		2
21 Aug 04	**ALPHA BETA GAGA** *Source VSCDX1880*	44		2

AIR SUPPLY
Australia, male vocal/instrumental duo — 17

Date	Title / Label	Peak	No.1	Weeks
27 Sep 80	**ALL OUT OF LOVE** *Arista ARIST 362*	11		11
2 Oct 82	**EVEN THE NIGHTS ARE BETTER** *Arista ARIST 474*	44		4
20 Nov 93	**GOODBYE** *Giant 74321153462*	66		2

AIR TRAFFIC
UK, male vocal/instrumental group — 3

Date	Title / Label	Peak	No.1	Weeks
7 Apr 07	**CHARLOTTE** *EMI CDEM720*	33		1
30 Jun 07	**SHOOTING STAR** *EMI CDEM724*	30		1
6 Oct 07	**NO MORE RUNNING AWAY** *EMI CDEM729*	45		1

AIRBORNE TOXIC EVENT
US, male/female vocal/instrumental group — 3

Date	Title / Label	Peak	No.1	Weeks
7 Feb 09	**SOMETIME AROUND MIDNIGHT** *Majordomo 82666311310*	33		3

AIRHEAD
UK, male vocal/instrumental group — 10

Date	Title / Label	Peak	No.1	Weeks
5 Oct 91	**FUNNY HOW** *Korova KOW 47*	57		3
28 Dec 91	**COUNTING SHEEP** *Korova KOW 48*	35		5
7 Mar 92	**RIGHT NOW** *Korova KOW 49*	50		2

AIRHEADZ
UK, male DJ/production duo. See Double Trouble — 2

Date	Title / Label	Peak	No.1	Weeks
28 Apr 01	**STANLEY (HERE I AM)** *AM:PM CDAMPM 145*	36		2

AIRSCAPE
Belgium/Holland, male production duo. See Balearic Bill, Blue Bamboo, Cubic 22, Johan Gielen presents Abnea, Svenson & Gielen, Transformer 2 — 5

Date	Title / Label	Peak	No.1	Weeks
9 Aug 97	**PACIFIC MELODY** *Xtravaganza 0091165*	27		2
29 Aug 98	**AMAZON CHANT** *Xtravaganza 0091605 EXT*	46		1
4 Dec 99	**L'ESPERANZA** *Xtravaganza XTRAV 7CD*	33		2

LAUREL AITKEN & THE UNITONE
Jamaica (b. Cuba), male vocalist, d. 17 Jul 2005 (age 78), & UK, male vocal/instrumental group — 3

Date	Title / Label	Peak	No.1	Weeks
17 May 80	**RUDI GOT MARRIED** *I-Spy SEE 6*	60		3

AKA

UK, male vocal group

Date	Title	Peak Position	Weeks at No.1	Weeks on Chart
				2
12 Oct 96	**WARNING** *RCA 74321360662*	43		2

AKABU FEATURING LINDA CLIFFORD

UK/US, male/female vocal/production duo. See Hed Boys, Il Padrinos featuring Jocelyn Brown, Jakatta, Li Kwan, Joey Negro, Phase II, Raven Maize

Date	Title	Peak Position	Weeks at No.1	Weeks on Chart
				1
15 Sep 01	**RIDE THE STORM** *NRK Sound Division NRKCD 053*	69		1

AKALA

UK, male rapper (Kingslee Daley)

Date	Title	Peak Position	Weeks at No.1	Weeks on Chart
				1
28 May 05	**ROLL WID US** *Illa State ILLA001CD2*	72		1

JEWEL AKENS

US, male vocalist

Date	Title	Peak Position	Weeks at No.1	Weeks on Chart
				8
25 Mar 65	**THE BIRDS AND THE BEES** *London HLN 9954*	29		8

AKIN

UK, female vocal duo

Date	Title	Peak Position	Weeks at No.1	Weeks on Chart
				1
14 Jun 97	**STAY RIGHT HERE** *WEA 117CD*	60		1

AKON

US, male vocalist/rapper/record label owner (Aliaune Thiam). Versatile St Louis, Missouri native who spent much of his childhood honing his musical skills in Senegal. This in-demand entertainer, a four-time World Music Award-winner, has collaborated with more than 20 different rap, R'n'B, pop and dance acts

Date	Title	Peak Position	Weeks at No.1	Weeks on Chart
				294
25 Dec 04	**LOCKED UP** *Universal E9864569* FEATURING STYLES P	61		3
5 Mar 05	**LOCKED UP** *Universal 9864570CD*	5		13
14 May 05	**LONELY** *Universal MCSTD40415*	1	2	16
20 Aug 05	**BELLY DANCER (BANANZA)** *Universal MCSXD40426*	5		8
4 Feb 06	**SOUL SURVIVOR** *Def Jam 9889047* YOUNG JEEZY FEATURING AKON	16		4
19 Aug 06	**GIRLS** *Virgin VUSCD328* BEENIE FEATURING AKON	47		2
16 Sep 06	**SNITCH** *Interscope 1705438* OBIE TRICE FEATURING AKON	44		2
18 Nov 06	**SMACK THAT** *Universal 1714412* FEATURING EMINEM	1	1	23
13 Jan 07	**I WANNA LOVE YOU** *Universal 1722994* FEATURING SNOOP DOGGY DOGG ★	3		20
3 Feb 07	**THE SWEET ESCAPE** *Interscope 1724450* GWEN STEFANI FEATURING AKON	2		28
14 Apr 07	**DON'T MATTER** *Universal 1734175* ★	3		19
2 Jun 07	**I TRIED** *Polydor USUM70701555* BONE THUGS-N-HARMONY FEATURING AKON	69		1
11 Aug 07	**MAMA AFRICA** *Universal 1743396*	47		2
15 Sep 07	**SORRY BLAME IT ON ME** *Universal 1752178*	22		13
1 Dec 07	**SWEETEST GIRL (DOLLAR BILL)** *Columbia USSM10703185* WYCLEF JEAN FEATURING AKON, LIL WAYNE & NIIA	66		1
1 Mar 08	**WANNA BE STARTIN' SOMETHING 2008** *EPIC USSM10800553* MICHAEL JACKSON WITH AKON	69		1
5 Apr 08	**HYPNOTIZED** *Atlantic AT0301CD* PLIES FEATURING AKON	66		2
9 Aug 08	**BODY ON ME** *Island 1781914* NELLY FEATURING AKON & ASHANTI	17		9
11 Oct 08	**DANGEROUS** *Polydor 1789479* KARDINAL OFFISHALL FEATURING AKON	16		20
25 Oct 08	**RIGHT NOW** *Island 1793596*	6		27
1 Nov 08	**I'M SO PAID** *Island USUM70842012* FEATURING LIL WAYNE	59		3
13 Dec 08	**BEAUTIFUL** *Universal 2700494* FEATURING KARDINAL OFFISHALL & COLBY O'DONIS	8		30
28 Feb 09	**SILVER & GOLD** *Dcypha GBPVV0800081* SWAY FEATURING AKON	61		1
11 Apr 09	**STUCK WITH EACH OTHER** *Universal USUM70900875* SHONTELLE FEATURING AKON	23		9
18 Jul 09	**WE DON'T CARE** *Island USUM70845929*	61		2
22 Aug 09	**SEXY CHICK** *Positiva/Virgin FRZID0900930* DAVID GUETTA FEATURING AKON ●	1	1	26
30 Jan 10	**SHUT IT DOWN** *J USJAY0900143* PITBULL FEATURING AKON	33		5
13 Feb 10	**OH AFRICA** *Universal USUM71000583*	56		2
27 Feb 10	**JUST DANCE** *Interscope USUM70807646* LADY GAGA FEATURING COLBY O'DONIS & AKON	62		2

ALABAMA 3

UK, male vocal/instrumental group

Date	Title	Peak Position	Weeks at No.1	Weeks on Chart
				3
22 Nov 97	**SPEED AT THE SOUND OF LONELINESS** *Elemental ELM 42CDS*	72		1
11 Apr 98	**AIN'T GOIN' TO GOA** *Elemental ELM 45CDS1*	40		2

ALARM

UK, male vocal/instrumental group

Date	Title	Peak Position	Weeks at No.1	Weeks on Chart
				66
24 Sep 83	**68 GUNS** *IRS PFP 1023*	17		7
21 Jan 84	**WHERE WERE YOU HIDING WHEN THE STORM BROKE** *IRS 101*	22		6
31 Mar 84	**THE DECEIVER** *IRS 103*	51		4
3 Nov 84	**THE CHANT HAS JUST BEGUN** *IRS 104*	48		4
2 Mar 85	**ABSOLUTE REALITY** *IRS ALARM 1*	35		6
28 Sep 85	**STRENGTH** *IRS IRM 104*	40		4
18 Jan 86	**SPIRIT OF '76** *IRS IRM 109*	22		5
26 Apr 86	**KNIFE EDGE** *IRS IRM 112*	43		3
17 Oct 87	**RAIN IN THE SUMMERTIME** *IRS IRM 144*	18		5
12 Dec 87	**RESCUE ME** *IRS IRM 150*	48		2
20 Feb 88	**PRESENCE OF LOVE (LAUGHERNE)** *IRS IRM 155*	44		3
16 Sep 89	**SOLD ME DOWN THE RIVER** *IRS EIRS 123*	43		3
4 Nov 89	**A NEW SOUTH WALES/THE ROCK** *IRS EIRS 129* FEATURING THE MORRISTON ORPHEUS MALE VOICE CHOIR	31		5
3 Feb 90	**LOVE DON'T COME EASY** *IRS EIRS 134*	48		3
27 Oct 90	**UNSAFE BUILDING 1990** *IRS ALARM 2*	54		2
13 Apr 91	**RAW** *IRS ALARM 3*	51		2
3 Jul 04	**NEW HOME NEW LIFE** *Snapper Music SMASCD062*	45		1
18 Feb 06	**SUPERCHANNEL** *Liberty 3535112* ALARM MMVI	24		1

MORRIS ALBERT

Brazil, male vocalist (Morris Kaisermann)

Date	Title	Peak Position	Weeks at No.1	Weeks on Chart
				10
27 Sep 75	**FEELINGS** *Decca F 13591* ●	4		10

ALBERTA

Sierra Leone, female vocalist (Alberta Sheriff)

Date	Title	Peak Position	Weeks at No.1	Weeks on Chart
				3
26 Dec 98	**YOYO BOY** *RCA 74321640602*	48		3

ALBERTO Y LOST TRIOS PARANOIAS

UK, male vocal/instrumental group

Date	Title	Peak Position	Weeks at No.1	Weeks on Chart
				5
23 Sep 78	**HEADS DOWN NO NONSENSE MINDLESS BOOGIE** *Logo GO 323*	47		5

ALBION

Holland, male DJ/producer (Ferry Corsten). See Gouryella, Moonman, Starparty, System F, Veracocha

Date	Title	Peak Position	Weeks at No.1	Weeks on Chart
				1
3 Jun 00	**AIR 2000** *Platipus PLATCD 73*	59		1

ALCATRAZ

US, male instrumental/production duo. See Lithium & Sonya Madan, Submerge featuring Jan Johnston

Date	Title	Peak Position	Weeks at No.1	Weeks on Chart
				4
17 Feb 96	**GIV ME LUV** *AM:PM 5814332*	12		4

ALCAZAR

Sweden, male/female vocal trio

Date	Title	Peak Position	Weeks at No.1	Weeks on Chart
				19
8 Dec 01	**CRYING AT THE DISCOTEQUE** *Arista 74321893432*	13		12
16 Mar 02	**SEXUAL GUARANTEE** *Arista 74321920252*	30		2
2 Oct 04	**THIS IS THE WORLD WE LIVE IN** *RCA 82876652372*	15		5

ALDA

Iceland, female vocalist (Alda Olafsdottir)

Date	Title	Peak Position	Weeks at No.1	Weeks on Chart
				14
29 Aug 98	**REAL GOOD TIME** *Wildstar CDWILD 7*	7		7
26 Dec 98	**GIRLS NIGHT OUT** *Wildstar CDWILD 10*	20		7

ALENA

Jamaica, female vocalist (Alena Lova)

Date	Title	Peak Position	Weeks at No.1	Weeks on Chart
				5
13 Nov 99	**TURN IT AROUND** *Wonderboy WBOYD 16*	14		5

ALESSI

US, male vocal duo – Billy & Bobby Alessi

Date	Title	Peak Position	Weeks at No.1	Weeks on Chart
				11
11 Jun 77	**OH LORI** *A&M AMS 7289*	8		11

ALEX PARTY

Italy/UK, male/female production/vocal group – Paolo & Gianni Visnadi, Shanie Campbell & Alex Natale

Date	Title	Peak Position	Weeks at No.1	Weeks on Chart
				28
18 Dec 93	**SATURDAY NIGHT PARTY (READ MY LIPS)** *Cleveland City Imports CCICD 17000*	49		6

Date	Title / Label	Peak Position	Weeks at No.1	Weeks on Chart
28 May 94	**SATURDAY NIGHT PARTY (READ MY LIPS)** *Cleveland City Imports CCICD 17000*	29		4
18 Feb 95	**DON'T GIVE ME YOUR LIFE** *Systematic SYSCD 7* ○	2		13
18 Nov 95	**WRAP ME UP** *Systematic SYSCD 22*	17		3
19 Oct 96	**READ MY LIPS (REMIX)** *Systematic SYSCD 30*	28		2

ALEXIA

Italy, female vocalist (Alessia Aquilani) — 15

Date	Title / Label	Peak Position	Weeks at No.1	Weeks on Chart
21 Mar 98	**UH LA LA LA** *Dance Pool ALEX 1CD*	10		9
13 Jun 98	**GIMME LOVE** *Dance Pool ALEX 2CDZ*	17		4
10 Oct 98	**THE MUSIC I LIKE** *Dance Pool ALEX 3CD*	31		2

ALEXIA

UK, female vocalist (Alexia Khadime) — 1

Date	Title / Label	Peak Position	Weeks at No.1	Weeks on Chart
22 Feb 03	**RING** *Virgin VSCDT 1836*	48		1

ALFI & HARRY

US, male vocalist/pianist (Ross Bagdasarian), d. 16 Jan 1972 (age 52). See Chipmunks, David Seville — 5

Date	Title / Label	Peak Position	Weeks at No.1	Weeks on Chart
23 Mar 56	**THE TROUBLE WITH HARRY** *London HLU 8242*	15		5

ALFIE

UK, male vocal/instrumental group — 6

Date	Title / Label	Peak Position	Weeks at No.1	Weeks on Chart
8 Sep 01	**YOU MAKE NO BONES** *Twisted Nerve TN 033CD*	61		1
16 Mar 02	**A WORD IN YOUR EAR** *Twisted Nerve TN 037CD*	66		1
21 Jun 03	**PEOPLE** *Regal Recordings REG 84CD*	53		1
13 Sep 03	**STUNTMAN** *Regal Recordings REG 87CDS*	51		1
28 Feb 04	**NO NEED** *Regal Recordings REG 99CD*	66		1
13 Aug 05	**YOUR OWN RELIGION** *Regal REG124CD*	61		1

JOHN ALFORD

UK, male actor/vocalist (John Shannon) — 12

Date	Title / Label	Peak Position	Weeks at No.1	Weeks on Chart
17 Feb 96	**SMOKE GETS IN YOUR EYES** *Love This LUVTHIS CD7*	13		5
25 May 96	**BLUE MOON/ONLY YOU** *Love This LUVTHISCDX 9*	9		4
23 Nov 96	**IF/KEEP ON RUNNING** *Love This LUVTHISCD 15*	24		3

ALI

UK, male vocalist (Ali Tennant) — 2

Date	Title / Label	Peak Position	Weeks at No.1	Weeks on Chart
23 May 98	**LOVE LETTERS** *Wild Card 5698092*	63		1
24 Oct 98	**FEELIN' YOU** *Wild Card 5676992*	63		1

TATYANA ALI

US, female vocalist — 18

Date	Title / Label	Peak Position	Weeks at No.1	Weeks on Chart
14 Nov 98	**DAYDREAMIN'** *Epic 6669372*	6		5
13 Feb 99	**BOY YOU KNOCK ME OUT** *MJJ 6674742* FEATURING WILL SMITH ○	3		9
19 Jun 99	**EVERYTIME** *Epic 6665462*	20		4

ALI & FRAZIER

UK, female vocal duo — 4

Date	Title / Label	Peak Position	Weeks at No.1	Weeks on Chart
7 Aug 93	**UPTOWN TOP RANKING** *Arista 74321158842*	33		4

ALIBI

UK, male vocal duo — 2

Date	Title / Label	Peak Position	Weeks at No.1	Weeks on Chart
15 Feb 97	**I'M NOT TO BLAME** *Urgent 74321434762*	51		1
7 Feb 98	**HOW MUCH I FEEL** *Urgent 74321548472*	58		1

ALIBI VS ROCKERFELLER

Holland, male production trio — 4

Date	Title / Label	Peak Position	Weeks at No.1	Weeks on Chart
7 Jul 07	**SEXUAL HEALING** *Gusto CDGUS48*	34		4

ALICE BAND

UK/Ireland/US, female vocal/instrumental group — 2

Date	Title / Label	Peak Position	Weeks at No.1	Weeks on Chart
23 Jun 01	**ONE DAY AT A TIME** *Instant Karma KARMA 5CD*	52		1
27 Apr 02	**NOW THAT YOU LOVE ME** *Instant Karma KARMA 17CD*	44		1

ALICE DEEJAY

Holland, female/male vocal/production group – Judith Pronk, Eelke Kalberg, Sebastiaan Molijn & Jurgen Rijkers (DJ Jurgen) — 50

Date	Title / Label	Peak Position	Weeks at No.1	Weeks on Chart
31 Jul 99	**BETTER OFF ALONE** *Positiva CDTIV 113* DJ JURGEN PRESENTS ALICE DEEJAY ⊛	2		16
4 Dec 99	**BACK IN MY LIFE** *Positiva CDTIV 121* ●	4		15
15 Jul 00	**WILL I EVER** *Positiva CDTIV 134*	7		10
21 Oct 00	**THE LONELY ONE** *Positiva CDTIV 145*	16		5
10 Feb 01	**CELEBRATE OUR LOVE** *Positiva CDTIV 149*	17		4

ALICE IN CHAINS

US, male vocal/instrumental group — 14

Date	Title / Label	Peak Position	Weeks at No.1	Weeks on Chart
23 Jan 93	**WOULD** *Columbia 6588882*	19		3
20 Mar 93	**THEM BONES** *Columbia 6590902*	26		3
5 Jun 93	**ANGRY CHAIR** *Columbia 6593652*	33		2
23 Oct 93	**DOWN IN A HOLE** *Columbia 6597512*	36		2
11 Nov 95	**GRIND** *Columbia 6626232*	23		2
10 Feb 96	**HEAVEN BESIDE YOU** *Columbia 6628935*	35		2

ALIEN ANT FARM

US, male vocal/instrumental group – Dryden Mitchell, Terry Corso, Mike Cosgrove & Tye Zamora — 25

Date	Title / Label	Peak Position	Weeks at No.1	Weeks on Chart
30 Jun 01	**MOVIES** *DreamWorks 4508992*	53		1
8 Sep 01	**SMOOTH CRIMINAL (IMPORT)** *DreamWorks 4508852CD*	74		2
29 Sep 01	**SMOOTH CRIMINAL** *DreamWorks DRMDM 50887*	3		13
16 Feb 02	**MOVIES** *DreamWorks 4508492*	5		8
25 May 02	**ATTITUDE** *DreamWorks 4508292*	66		1

ALIEN VOICES FEATURING THE THREE DEGREES

UK, male producer & US, female vocal trio. See Boogie Box High, Andy G's Starsky & Hutch All Stars — 2

Date	Title / Label	Peak Position	Weeks at No.1	Weeks on Chart
26 Dec 98	**LAST CHRISTMAS** *Wildstar CDWILD 15*	54		2

ALISHA

US, female vocalist (Alisha Itkin) — 2

Date	Title / Label	Peak Position	Weeks at No.1	Weeks on Chart
25 Jan 86	**BABY TALK** *Total Control TOCO 6*	67		2

ALISHA'S ATTIC

UK, female vocal duo — 47

Date	Title / Label	Peak Position	Weeks at No.1	Weeks on Chart
3 Aug 96	**I AM, I FEEL** *Mercury AATDD 1*	14		10
2 Nov 96	**ALISHA RULES THE WORLD** *Mercury AATCD 2*	12		6
15 Mar 97	**INDESTRUCTIBLE** *Mercury AATCD 3*	12		6
12 Jul 97	**AIR WE BREATHE** *Mercury AATCD 4*	12		6
19 Sep 98	**THE INCIDENTALS** *Mercury AATCD 5*	13		7
9 Jan 99	**WISH I WERE YOU** *Mercury AATDD 6*	29		5
17 Apr 99	**BARBARELLA** *Mercury AATCD 7*	34		2
24 Mar 01	**PUSH IT ALL ASIDE** *Mercury AATDD 8*	24		4
28 Jul 01	**PRETENDER GOT MY HEART** *Mercury AATDD 9*	43		1

ALIVE FEATURING D D KLEIN

Italy/Antigua, male/female vocal/production group — 1

Date	Title / Label	Peak Position	Weeks at No.1	Weeks on Chart
27 Jul 02	**ALIVE** *Serious CDAMPM 153*	49		1

ALIZEE

France, female vocalist (Alizee Jacotet) — 9

Date	Title / Label	Peak Position	Weeks at No.1	Weeks on Chart
23 Feb 02	**MOI LOLITA** *Polydor 5705952*	9		9

ALKALINE TRIO

US, male vocal/instrumental group — 9

Date	Title / Label	Peak Position	Weeks at No.1	Weeks on Chart
2 Feb 02	**PRIVATE EYE** *B Unique/Vagrant BUN 013CDX*	51		1
30 Mar 02	**STUPID KID** *B Unique/Vagrant BUN 016CD*	53		1
26 Jul 03	**WE'VE HAD ENOUGH** *Vagrant 9809023*	50		1
18 Oct 03	**ALL ON BLACK** *Interscope 9811506*	60		1
9 Jul 05	**TIME TO WASTE** *Vagrant VRUK013CDS*	32		2
3 Dec 05	**MERCY ME** *Vagrant VRUK024CDS*	30		2
4 Mar 06	**BURN** *Vagrant VRUK029CDS*	34		1

Silver-selling ○ Gold-selling ● Platinum-selling (x multiples) ⊛ US No.1 ★ Peak Position ⬆ Weeks at No.1 ✪ Weeks on Chart ♥

ALL ABOUT EVE

UK, female/male vocal/instrumental group – Julianne Regan, Tim Bricheno, Andy Cousin, Mark Price & Marty Willson-Piper

		⬆	✪	48
31 Oct 87	**IN THE CLOUDS** *Mercury EVEN 5*	47		5
23 Jan 88	**WILD HEARTED WOMAN** *Mercury EVEN 6*	33		4
9 Apr 88	**EVERY ANGEL** *Mercury EVEN 7*	30		5
30 Jul 88	**MARTHA'S HARBOUR** *Mercury EVEN 8*	10		8
12 Nov 88	**WHAT KIND OF FOOL** *Mercury EVEN 9*	29		4
30 Sep 89	**ROAD TO YOUR SOUL** *Mercury EVEN 10*	37		4
16 Dec 89	**DECEMBER** *Mercury EVEN 11*	34		5
28 Apr 90	**SCARLET** *Mercury EVEN 12*	34		2
15 Jun 91	**FAREWELL MR SORROW** *Mercury EVEN 14*	36		2
10 Aug 91	**STRANGE WAY** *Vertigo EVEN 15*	51		3
19 Oct 91	**THE DREAMER** *Vertigo EVEN 16*	41		2
10 Oct 92	**PHASED (EP)** *MCA MCS 1688*	38		2
28 Nov 92	**SOME FINER DAY** *MCA MCS 1706*	57		1
5 Jun 04	**LET ME GO HOME** *Voiceprint AAEVP 10CD2*	52		1

ALL-AMERICAN REJECTS

US, male vocal/instrumental group

		⬆	✪	34
2 Aug 03	**SWING SWING** *DreamWorks 4504616*	13		5
22 Nov 03	**THE LAST SONG** *DreamWorks 4504641*	69		1
11 Mar 06	**MOVE ALONG** *Interscope 9853100*	42		3
17 Jun 06	**DIRTY LITTLE SECRET** *DreamWorks 9858254*	18		9
7 Oct 06	**IT ENDS TONIGHT** *Interscope 1708086*	66		1
31 Jan 09	**GIVES YOU HELL** *Geffen 1797778*	18		15

ALL ANGELS

UK, female vocal group

		⬆	✪	1
30 Dec 06	**ANGELS** *UCJ 1717439*	48		1

ALL BLUE

UK, male vocal duo

		⬆	✪	1
21 Aug 99	**PRISONER** *WEA 213CD1*	73		1

ALL EYES

UK, male vocal group

		⬆	✪	1
13 Nov 04	**SHE'S A VISION** *Specsavers CXSPECS1*	65		1

ALL-4-ONE

US, male vocal group – Tony Borowiak, Jamie Jones, Delious Kennedy & Alfred Nevarez

		⬆	✪	23
2 Apr 94	**SO MUCH IN LOVE** *Atlantic A 7261CD*	60		1
18 Jun 94	**I SWEAR** *Atlantic A 7255CD* ⊛ ★	2		18
19 Nov 94	**SO MUCH IN LOVE (REMIX)** *Atlantic A 7216CD*	49		2
15 Jul 95	**I CAN LOVE YOU LIKE THAT** *Atlantic A 8193CD*	33		2

ALL SAINTS

UK/Canada, female vocal group – Natalie & Nicole Appleton (Appleton*), Melanie Blatt* & Shaznay Lewis*. See Artful Dodger, Outsidaz featuring Rah Digga & Melanie Blatt

		⬆	✪	119
6 Sep 97	**I KNOW WHERE IT'S AT** *London LONCD 398*	4		8
22 Nov 97	**NEVER EVER** *London LONCD 407* ⊛ x2	1	1	24
9 May 98	**UNDER THE BRIDGE/LADY MARMALADE** *London LONCD 408* ●	1	2	14
12 Sep 98	**BOOTIE CALL** *London LONCD 415*	1	1	11
5 Dec 98	**WAR OF NERVES** *London LONCD 421* ○	7		11
26 Feb 00	**PURE SHORES** *London LONCD 444* ⊛	1	2	16
14 Oct 00	**BLACK COFFEE** *London LONCD 454* ○	1	1	18
27 Jan 01	**ALL HOOKED UP** *London LONCD 456*	7		7
11 Nov 06	**ROCK STEADY** *Parlophone CDR6726*	3		10

ALL SEEING I

UK, male instrumental/production trio – Jason Buckle, DJ Parrot (Richard Barratt) & Dean Honer

		⬆	✪	17
28 Mar 98	**BEAT GOES ON** *ffrr FCD 334*	11		7
23 Jan 99	**WALK LIKE A PANTHER '98** *ffrr FCDP 351* FEATURING TONY CHRISTIE	10		7
18 Sep 99	**1ST MAN IN SPACE** *ffrr FCDP 370*	28		3

ALL SYSTEMS GO

UK, male vocal/production group

		⬆	✪	2
18 Jun 88	**POP MUZIK** *Unique NIQ 03*	63		2

RICHARD ALLAN

UK, male vocalist

		⬆	✪	1
24 Mar 60	**AS TIME GOES BY** *Parlophone R 4634*	43		1

STEVE ALLAN

UK, male vocalist

		⬆	✪	2
27 Jan 79	**TOGETHER WE ARE BEAUTIFUL** *Creole CR 164*	67		2

DONNA ALLEN

US, female vocalist

Date	Title	⬆	✪	27
18 Apr 87	**SERIOUS** *Portrait PRT 6507447*	8		12
3 Jun 89	**JOY AND PAIN** *BCM 257*	10		10
21 Jan 95	**REAL** *Epic 6610882*	34		2
11 Oct 97	**SATURDAY** *AM:PM 5823752* EAST 57TH STREET FEATURING DONNA ALLEN	29		3

LILY ALLEN

UK, female vocalist. See Fat Les

Date	Title	⬆	✪	123
8 Jul 06	**SMILE** *Regal REG135*	1	1	23
30 Sep 06	**LDN** *Regal CDREG137*	6		14
16 Dec 06	**LITTLEST THINGS** *Regal CDREG140*	21		7
17 Feb 07	**ALFIE** *Regal CDREG141*	15		9
7 Jul 07	**OH MY GOD** *Columbia 88697113172* MARK RONSON FEATURING LILY ALLEN	8		11
27 Oct 07	**DRIVIN' ME WILD** *Geffen 1750856* COMMON FEATURING LILY ALLEN	56		1
7 Feb 09	**THE FEAR** *Regal REG150CD*	1	4	20
4 Apr 09	**NOT FAIR** *Regal REG153CD*	5		24
8 Aug 09	**22** *Regal REG154CD*	14		10
28 Nov 09	**WHO'D HAVE KNOWN** *EMI GBAYE0802266*	39		4

DOT ALLISON

UK, female vocalist. See One Dove

		⬆	✪	1
17 Aug 02	**STRUNG OUT** *Mantra MNT 74CD*	67		1

ALLISONS

UK, male vocal/instrumental duo – Brian Alford & Colin Day

Date	Title	⬆	✪	27
23 Feb 61	**ARE YOU SURE** *Fontana H 294*	2		16
18 May 61	**WORDS** *Fontana H 304*	34		5
15 Feb 62	**LESSONS IN LOVE** *Fontana H 362*	30		6

ALLNIGHT BAND

UK, male instrumental group

Date	Title	⬆	✪	3
3 Feb 79	**THE JOKER (THE WIGAN JOKER)** *Casino Classics CC 6*	50		3

ALLSTARS

UK, female/male vocal group – Sam Bloom, Ashley Taylor Dawson, Sandi Lee Hughes, Rebecca Hunter & Thaila Zucchi

		⬆	✪	22
23 Jun 01	**BEST FRIENDS** *Island CID 775*	20		7
22 Sep 01	**THINGS THAT GO BUMP IN THE NIGHT/IS THERE SOMETHING I SHOULD KNOW** *Island CID 783*	12		4
26 Jan 02	**THE LAND OF MAKE BELIEVE** *Island CID 791*	9		8
11 May 02	**BACK WHEN/GOING ALL THE WAY** *Island CID 796*	19		3

ALLURE

US, female vocal group

		⬆	✪	8
14 Jun 97	**HEAD OVER HEELS** *Epic 6645942* FEATURING NAS	18		3
10 Jan 98	**ALL CRIED OUT** *Epic 6652715* FEATURING 112	12		5

ALMIGHTY

UK/Canada, male vocal/instrumental group

		⬆	✪	22
30 Jun 90	**WILD AND WONDERFUL** *Polydor PO 75*	50		2
2 Mar 91	**FREE 'N' EASY** *Polydor PO 127*	35		2
11 May 91	**DEVIL'S TOY** *Polydor PO 144*	36		2
29 Jun 91	**LITTLE LOST SOMETIMES** *Polydor PO 151*	42		2
3 Apr 93	**ADDICTION** *Polydor PZCD 261*	38		2
29 May 93	**OUT OF SEASON** *Polydor PZCD 266*	41		2
30 Oct 93	**OVER THE EDGE** *Polydor PZCD 298*	38		2
24 Sep 94	**WRENCH** *Chrysalis CDCHS 5014*	26		2
14 Jan 95	**JONESTOWN MIND** *Chrysalis CDCHSS 5017*	26		3
16 Mar 96	**ALL SUSSED OUT** *Chrysalis CDCHS 5030*	28		2

Date	Title	Peak	Wks at No.1	Wks on Chart
25 May 96	**DO YOU UNDERSTAND** *Raw Power RAWX 1022*	38		1

MARC ALMOND

UK, male vocalist (Peter Almond). See Soft Cell — Weeks on Chart: **112**

Date	Title	Peak	Wks at No.1	Wks on Chart
2 Jul 83	**BLACK HEART** *Some Bizzare BZS 19* MARC & THE MAMBAS	49		3
2 Jun 84	**THE BOY WHO CAME BACK** *Some Bizzare BZS 23*	52		5
1 Sep 84	**YOU HAVE** *Some Bizzare BZS 24*	57		3
20 Apr 85	**I FEEL LOVE (MEDLEY)** *Forbidden Fruit BITE 4* BRONSKI BEAT & MARC ALMOND	3		12
24 Aug 85	**STORIES OF JOHNNY** *Some Bizzare BONK 1*	23		5
26 Oct 85	**LOVE LETTER** *Some Bizzare BONK 2*	68		3
4 Jan 86	**THE HOUSE IS HAUNTED (BY THE ECHO OF YOUR LAST GOODBYE)** *Some Bizzare GLOW 1*	55		3
7 Jun 86	**A WOMAN'S STORY** *Some Bizzare GLOW 2* & THE WILLING SINNERS	41		5
18 Oct 86	**RUBY RED** *Some Bizzare GLOW 3*	47		3
14 Feb 87	**MELANCHOLY ROSE** *Some Bizzare GLOW 4*	71		1
3 Sep 88	**TEARS RUN RINGS** *Parlophone R 6186*	26		7
5 Nov 88	**BITTER SWEET** *Some Bizzare R 6194*	40		3
14 Jan 89	**SOMETHING'S GOTTEN HOLD OF MY HEART** *Parlophone R 6201* FEATURING SPECIAL GUEST STAR GENE PITNEY	1	4	12
8 Apr 89	**ONLY THE MOMENT** *Parlophone R 6210*	45		2
3 Mar 90	**A LOVER SPURNED** *Some Bizzare R 6229*	29		4
19 May 90	**THE DESPERATE HOURS** *Some Bizzare R 6252*	45		2
23 Mar 91	**SAY HELLO WAVE GOODBYE** *Mercury SOFT 1* SOFT CELL/MARC ALMOND	38		3
18 May 91	**TAINTED LOVE** *Mercury SOFT 2* SOFT CELL/MARC ALMOND	5		8
28 Sep 91	**JACKY** *Some Bizzare YZ 610*	17		6
11 Jan 92	**MY HAND OVER MY HEART** *Some Bizzare YZ 633*	33		5
25 Apr 92	**THE DAYS OF PEARLY SPENCER** *Some Bizzare YZ 638*	4		7
27 Mar 93	**WHAT MAKES A MAN A MAN (LIVE)** *Some Bizzare YZ 720CD*	60		2
13 May 95	**ADORED AND EXPLORED** *Some Bizzare MERCD 431*	25		3
29 Jul 95	**THE IDOL** *Some Bizzare MERCD 437*	44		2
30 Dec 95	**CHILD STAR** *Some Bizzare MERCD 450*	41		1
28 Dec 96	**YESTERDAY HAS GONE** *EMI Premier CDPRESX 13* PJ PROBY & MARC ALMOND FEATURING THE MY LIFE STORY ORCHESTRA	58		2

ALOOF

UK, male vocal/instrumental group — Weeks on Chart: **6**

Date	Title	Peak	Wks at No.1	Wks on Chart
19 Sep 92	**ON A MISSION** *Cowboy RODEO 5*	64		1
18 May 96	**WISH YOU WERE HERE** *East West EW 038CD*	61		1
30 Nov 96	**ONE NIGHT STAND** *East West EW 067CD*	30		2
1 Mar 97	**WISH YOU WERE HERE (REMIX)** *East West EW 083CD1*	43		1
29 Aug 98	**WHAT I MISS THE MOST** *East West EW 179CD1*	70		1

HERB ALPERT & THE TIJUANA BRASS

US, male instrumental group – Herb Alpert; members also included Nick Ceroli, Bob Edmondson, Tonni Kalash, Lou Pagani, John Pisano, Pat Senatore & Julius Wechter — Weeks on Chart: **106**

Date	Title	Peak	Wks at No.1	Wks on Chart
3 Jan 63	**THE LONELY BULL** *Stateside SS 138* TIJUANA BRASS	22		9
9 Dec 65	**SPANISH FLEA** *Pye International 7N 25335*	3		20
24 Mar 66	**TIJUANA TAXI** *Pye International 7N 25352*	37		4
27 Apr 67	**CASINO ROYALE** *A&M AMS 700*	27		14
3 Jul 68	**THIS GUY'S IN LOVE WITH YOU** *A&M AMS 727* HERB ALPERT ★	3		19
18 Jun 69	**WITHOUT HER** *A&M AMS 755*	36		5
12 Dec 70	**JERUSALEM** *A&M AMS 810*	42		3
13 Oct 79	**RISE** *A&M AMS 7465* HERB ALPERT ★	13		13
19 Jan 80	**ROTATION** *A&M AMS 7500* HERB ALPERT	46		3
21 Mar 87	**KEEP YOUR EYE ON ME** *Breakout USA 602* HERB ALPERT	19		9
6 Jun 87	**DIAMONDS** *Breakout USA 605* HERB ALPERT	27		7

ALPHABEAT

Denmark, female/male vocal/instrumental group – Stine Bramsen, Anders B, Troels Hansen, Rasmus Nagel, Anders Reinholdt & Anders SG — Weeks on Chart: **60**

Date	Title	Peak	Wks at No.1	Wks on Chart
1 Mar 08	**FASCINATION** *Charisma CASDX18*	6		30
31 May 08	**TEN THOUSAND NIGHTS** *Charisma CASDX25*	16		16
16 Aug 08	**BOYFRIEND** *Charisma CASD35*	15		9
31 Oct 09	**THE SPELL** *Polydor 2719471*	20		3
6 Mar 10	**HOLE IN MY HEART** *Fascination 2732864*	29		2

ALPHAVILLE

Germany, male vocal/instrumental trio – Marian Gold, Bernhard Lloyd & Frank Mertens — Weeks on Chart: **13**

Date	Title	Peak	Wks at No.1	Wks on Chart
18 Aug 84	**BIG IN JAPAN** *WEA International X9505*	8		13

ALPINESTARS FEATURING BRIAN MOLKO

UK/Belgium, male vocal/production trio — Weeks on Chart: **1**

Date	Title	Peak	Wks at No.1	Wks on Chart
22 Jun 02	**CARBON KID** *Riverman RMR 11VS*	63		1

ALSOU

Russia, female vocalist (Alsou Safina) — Weeks on Chart: **3**

Date	Title	Peak	Wks at No.1	Wks on Chart
12 May 01	**BEFORE YOU LOVE ME** *Mercury 1589142*	27		3

GERALD ALSTON

US, male vocalist. See Manhattans — Weeks on Chart: **1**

Date	Title	Peak	Wks at No.1	Wks on Chart
15 Apr 89	**ACTIVATED** *RCA ZB 42681*	73		1

ALTER EGO

Germany, male production duo — Weeks on Chart: **6**

Date	Title	Peak	Wks at No.1	Wks on Chart
11 Dec 04	**ROCKER** *Skint SKINT103CD*	32		6

ALTERED IMAGES

UK, female/male vocal/instrumental group – Clare Grogan, Michael Anderson, Tony McDaid, Johnny McElhone, Gerard McInulty & Jim McKinven (replaced by Steve Lironi) — Weeks on Chart: **60**

Date	Title	Peak	Wks at No.1	Wks on Chart
28 Mar 81	**DEAD POP STARS** *Epic EPC A 1023*	67		2
26 Sep 81	**HAPPY BIRTHDAY** *Epic EPC A 1522*	2		17
12 Dec 81	**I COULD BE HAPPY** *Epic EPC A 1834*	7		12
27 Mar 82	**SEE THOSE EYES** *Epic EPC A 2198*	11		7
22 May 82	**PINKY BLUE** *Epic EPC A 2426*	35		6
19 Mar 83	**DON'T TALK TO ME ABOUT LOVE** *Epic EPC A 3083*	7		7
28 May 83	**BRING ME CLOSER** *Epic EPC A 3398*	29		6
16 Jul 83	**LOVE TO STAY** *Epic EPC A 3582*	46		3

ALTERKICKS

UK, male vocal/instrumental group — Weeks on Chart: **1**

Date	Title	Peak	Wks at No.1	Wks on Chart
26 Mar 05	**DO EVERYTHING I TAUGHT YOU** *XL Recordings XLS212CD*	71		1

ALTERN 8

UK, male production duo – Mark Archer & Chris Peat — Weeks on Chart: **34**

Date	Title	Peak	Wks at No.1	Wks on Chart
13 Jul 91	**INFILTRATE 202** *Network NWK 24*	28		7
16 Nov 91	**ACTIV 8 (COME WITH ME)** *Network NWK 34*	3		9
8 Feb 92	**FREQUENCY** *Network NWK 37*	41		1
11 Apr 92	**EVAPOR 8** *Network NWK 38*	6		6
4 Jul 92	**HYPNOTIC ST-8** *Network NWK 49*	16		4
10 Oct 92	**SHAME** *Network NWKTEN 56* VS EVELYN KING	74		1
12 Dec 92	**BRUTAL-8-E** *Network NWK 59*	43		5
3 Jul 93	**EVERYBODY** *Network NWKCD 73*	58		1

ALTHEA & DONNA

Jamaica, female vocal duo – Althea Forrest & Donna Reid — Weeks on Chart: **11**

Date	Title	Peak	Wks at No.1	Wks on Chart
24 Dec 77	**UP TOWN TOP RANKING** *Lightning LIG 506*	1	1	11

ALY & AJ

US, female vocal/instrumental duo — Weeks on Chart: **5**

Date	Title	Peak	Wks at No.1	Wks on Chart
13 Oct 07	**POTENTIAL BREAK UP SONG** *Hollywood/Angel CASD10*	22		5

ALY-US

US, male production/vocal group — Weeks on Chart: **3**

Date	Title	Peak	Wks at No.1	Wks on Chart
21 Nov 92	**FOLLOW ME** *Cooltempo COOL 266*	43		2
25 May 02	**FOLLOW ME (REMIX)** *Strictly Rhythm SRUKCD 05*	54		1

SADIE AMA

UK, female vocalist (Mersadie Hall) — Weeks on Chart: **1**

Date	Title	Peak	Wks at No.1	Wks on Chart
10 Feb 07	**FALLIN'** *Ministry Of Sound MOSREC01T*	68		1

SHOLA AMA

UK, female vocalist (Mathurin Campbell) — Weeks on Chart: **58**

Date	Title	Peak	Wks at No.1	Wks on Chart
19 Apr 97	**YOU MIGHT NEED SOMEBODY** *WEA 097CD*	4		14
30 Aug 97	**YOU'RE THE ONE I LOVE** *Freakstreet WEA 121CD1*	3		8
29 Nov 97	**WHO'S LOVING MY BABY** *Freakstreet WEA 145 CD1*	13		7
21 Feb 98	**MUCH LOVE** *WEA 154CD1*	17		3

Date	Title	Peak Position	Weeks at No.1	Weeks on Chart
11 Apr 98	**SOMEDAY I'LL FIND YOU/I'VE BEEN TO A MARVELLOUS PARTY** *EMI CDTCB 001* & CRAIG ARMSTRONG/DIVINE COMEDY	28		3
17 Apr 99	**TABOO** *WEA 203CD* GLAMMA KID FEATURING SHOLA AMA	10		8
6 Nov 99	**STILL BELIEVE** *WEA 239CD1*	26		3
29 Apr 00	**IMAGINE** *WEA 252CD*	24		4
11 Sep 04	**YOU SHOULD REALLY KNOW** *Relentless RELCD9* PIRATES FEATURING ENYA, SHOLA AMA, NAILA BOSS & ISHANI	8		8

EDDIE AMADOR
US, male DJ/producer

Weeks on Chart: 5

Date	Title	Peak Position	Weeks at No.1	Weeks on Chart
24 Oct 98	**HOUSE MUSIC** *Pukka CDPUKKA 18*	37		2
22 Jan 00	**RISE** *Defected DEFECT 9CDS*	19		3

RUBY AMANFU
US (b. Ghana), female vocalist

Weeks on Chart: 2

Date	Title	Peak Position	Weeks at No.1	Weeks on Chart
15 Mar 03	**SUGAH** *Polydor 0658302*	32		2

AMAR
UK, female vocalist (Amar Dhanjan)

Weeks on Chart: 1

Date	Title	Peak Position	Weeks at No.1	Weeks on Chart
9 Sep 00	**SOMETIMES (IT SNOWS IN APRIL)** *Blanco Y Negro NEG 129CD*	48		1

AMAZULU
UK, female/male vocal/instrumental group – Annie Ruddock, Nardo & Sharon Bailey, Lesley Beach, Clare Kenny & Margo Sagov

Weeks on Chart: 57

Date	Title	Peak Position	Weeks at No.1	Weeks on Chart
6 Jul 85	**EXCITABLE** *Island IS 201*	12		13
23 Nov 85	**DON'T YOU JUST KNOW IT** *Island IS 233*	15		11
15 Mar 86	**THE THINGS THE LONELY DO** *Island IS 267*	43		6
31 May 86	**TOO GOOD TO BE FORGOTTEN** *Island IS 284* ●	5		13
13 Sep 86	**MONTEGO BAY** *Island IS 293*	16		9
10 Oct 87	**MONY MONY** *EMI EM 32*	38		5

AMBASSADOR
Holland, male DJ/producer

Weeks on Chart: 1

Date	Title	Peak Position	Weeks at No.1	Weeks on Chart
12 Feb 00	**ONE OF THESE DAYS** *Platipus PLATCD 69*	67		1

AMBASSADORS OF FUNK FEATURING MC MARIO
UK, male production/rap duo – Simon Harris* & Einstein*

Weeks on Chart: 8

Date	Title	Peak Position	Weeks at No.1	Weeks on Chart
31 Oct 92	**SUPERMARIOLAND** *Living Beat SMASH 23*	8		8

AMBER
Holland, female vocalist (Marie Cremers)

Weeks on Chart: 2

Date	Title	Peak Position	Weeks at No.1	Weeks on Chart
24 Jun 00	**SEXUAL** *Substance SUBS 2CDS*	34		2

AMBULANCE LTD
US, male vocal/instrumental group

Weeks on Chart: 2

Date	Title	Peak Position	Weeks at No.1	Weeks on Chart
12 Mar 05	**STAY WHERE YOU ARE** *TVT TVTUKCD5*	67		1
25 Jun 05	**PRIMITIVE (THE WAY I TREAT YOU)** *TVT TVTUKCD10*	72		1

AMEN
US, male vocal/instrumental group

Weeks on Chart: 3

Date	Title	Peak Position	Weeks at No.1	Weeks on Chart
17 Feb 01	**TOO HARD TO BE FREE** *Virgin VUSCD 191*	72		1
21 Jul 01	**THE WAITING 18** *Virgin VUSCD 207*	61		1
3 Apr 04	**CALIFORNIA'S BLEEDING** *Columbia 6746162*	52		1

AMEN CORNER
UK, male vocal/instrumental group – Andy Fairweather-Low, Dennis Bryon, Alan Jones, Neil Jones, Mike Smith, Clive Taylor & Derek Weaver

Weeks on Chart: 67

Date	Title	Peak Position	Weeks at No.1	Weeks on Chart
26 Jul 67	**GIN HOUSE BLUES** *Deram DM 136*	12		10
11 Oct 67	**WORLD OF BROKEN HEARTS** *Deram DM 151*	24		6
17 Jan 68	**BEND ME SHAPE ME** *Deram DM 172*	3		12
31 Jul 68	**HIGH IN THE SKY** *Deram DM 197*	6		13
29 Jan 69	**(IF PARADISE IS) HALF AS NICE** *Immediate IM 073*	1	2	11
25 Jun 69	**HELLO SUZIE** *Immediate IM 081*	4		10
14 Feb 76	**(IF PARADISE IS) HALF AS NICE** *Immediate IMS 103*	34		5

AMEN! UK
UK, male/female vocal/production group

Weeks on Chart: 8

Date	Title	Peak Position	Weeks at No.1	Weeks on Chart
8 Feb 97	**PASSION** *Feverpitch CDFVR 1015*	15		4
28 Jun 97	**PEOPLE OF LOVE** *Feverpitch CDFVR 18*	36		2
6 Sep 03	**PASSION** *Positiva CDTIV 195*	40		2

AMERICA
US, male vocal/instrumental trio – Dewey Bunnell, Gerry Beckley & Dan Peek. See One World Project

Weeks on Chart: 20

Date	Title	Peak Position	Weeks at No.1	Weeks on Chart
18 Dec 71	**HORSE WITH NO NAME/EVERYONE I MEET IS FROM CALIFORNIA** *Warner Brothers K 16128* ★	3		13
25 Nov 72	**VENTURA HIGHWAY** *Warner Brothers K 16219*	43		4
6 Nov 82	**YOU CAN DO MAGIC** *Capitol CL 264*	59		3

AMERICAN BREED
US, male/female vocal/instrumental group

Weeks on Chart: 6

Date	Title	Peak Position	Weeks at No.1	Weeks on Chart
7 Feb 68	**BEND ME SHAPE ME** *Stateside SS 2078*	24		6

AMERICAN HEAD CHARGE
US, male vocal/instrumental group

Weeks on Chart: 1

Date	Title	Peak Position	Weeks at No.1	Weeks on Chart
8 Jun 02	**JUST SO YOU KNOW** *Mercury 5829622*	52		1

AMERICAN HI-FI
US, male vocal/instrumental group

Weeks on Chart: 4

Date	Title	Peak Position	Weeks at No.1	Weeks on Chart
8 Sep 01	**FLAVOR OF THE WEAK** *Mercury 5886722*	31		3
26 Apr 03	**THE ART OF LOSING** *Mercury 0779152*	75		1

AMERICAN MUSIC CLUB
US, male vocal/instrumental group

Weeks on Chart: 4

Date	Title	Peak Position	Weeks at No.1	Weeks on Chart
24 Apr 93	**JOHNNY MATHIS' FEET** *Virgin VSCDG 1445*	58		2
10 Sep 94	**WISH THE WORLD AWAY** *Virgin VSCDX 1512*	46		2

AMERIE
US, female vocalist (Amerie Rogers)

Weeks on Chart: 38

Date	Title	Peak Position	Weeks at No.1	Weeks on Chart
9 Nov 02	**WHY DON'T WE FALL IN LOVE** *Columbia 6732212* FEATURING LUDACRIS	40		2
22 Feb 03	**PARADISE** *Def Jam 0637242* LL COOL J FEATURING AMERIE	18		5
4 Jun 05	**1 THING** *Columbia 6759402*	4		14
3 Sep 05	**TOUCH** *Columbia 6760612*	19		4
5 May 07	**TAKE CONTROL** *Columbia 88697085182*	10		7
21 Jul 07	**GOTTA WORK** *Columbia 88697138472*	21		6

AMERITZ
US, male/female session musicians

Weeks on Chart: 2

Date	Title	Peak Position	Weeks at No.1	Weeks on Chart
29 Nov 08	**RUN (IN THE STYLE OF LEONA LEWIS)** *Ameritz USA560756798*	52		2

AMES BROTHERS
US, male vocal group – Ed, Gene, d. 26 Apr 1997, Joe, d. 22 Dec 2007, & Vic, d. 23 Jan 1978, Urick

Weeks on Chart: 6

Date	Title	Peak Position	Weeks at No.1	Weeks on Chart
4 Feb 55	**NAUGHTY LADY OF SHADY LANE** *HMV 10800*	6		6

AMILLIONSONS
UK/US, male/female vocal/production group

Weeks on Chart: 2

Date	Title	Peak Position	Weeks at No.1	Weeks on Chart
24 Aug 02	**MISTI BLU** *London LONCD 468*	39		2

AMIRA
US, female vocalist (Amira McNiel)

Weeks on Chart: 7

Date	Title	Peak Position	Weeks at No.1	Weeks on Chart
13 Dec 97	**MY DESIRE** *VC Recordings VCRD 27*	51		1
8 Aug 98	**MY DESIRE (REMIX)** *VC Recordings VCRD 36*	46		2
10 Feb 01	**MY DESIRE** *VC Recordings VCRD 71*	20		4

CHERIE AMORE
France, female vocalist

Weeks on Chart: 2

Date	Title	Peak Position	Weeks at No.1	Weeks on Chart
15 Apr 00	**I DON'T WANT NOBODY (TELLIN' ME WHAT TO DO)** *Eternal WEA 262CD*	33		2

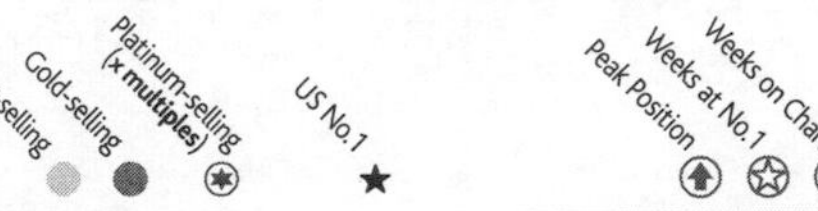

VANESSA AMOROSI
Australia, female vocalist — 10

Date	Title / Label	Peak	Wks at No.1	Wks
23 Sep 00	**ABSOLUTELY EVERYBODY** *Mercury 1582972*	7		10

AMOS
UK, male vocalist/producer (Amos Pizzey) — 12

Date	Title / Label	Peak	Wks at No.1	Wks
3 Sep 94	**ONLY SAW TODAY – INSTANT KARMA** *Positiva CDTIV 16*	48		2
25 Mar 95	**LET LOVE SHINE** *Positiva CDTIV 24*	31		2
7 Oct 95	**CHURCH OF FREEDOM** *Positiva CDTIV 38*	54		1
12 Oct 96	**STAMP!** *Positiva CDTIV 65* JEREMY HEALY & AMOS	11		5
31 May 97	**ARGENTINA** *Positiva CDTIV 74* JEREMY HEALY & AMOS	30		2

TORI AMOS
US, female vocalist/pianist (Myra Amos) — 66

Date	Title / Label	Peak	Wks at No.1	Wks
23 Nov 91	**SILENT ALL THESE YEARS** *East West YZ 618*	51		3
1 Feb 92	**CHINA** *East West YZ 7531*	51		2
21 Mar 92	**WINTER** *East West A 7504*	25		4
20 Jun 92	**CRUCIFY** *East West A 7479*	15		6
22 Aug 92	**SILENT ALL THESE YEARS** *East West A 7433*	26		4
22 Jan 94	**CORNFLAKE GIRL** *East West A 7281CD*	4		6
19 Mar 94	**PRETTY GOOD YEAR** *East West A 7263CD*	7		4
28 May 94	**PAST THE MISSION** *East West YZ 7257CD*	31		3
15 Oct 94	**GOD** *East West A 7251CD*	44		2
13 Jan 96	**CAUGHT A LITE SNEEZE** *East West A 5524CD2*	20		3
23 Mar 96	**TALULA** *East West A 8512CD*	22		2
3 Aug 96	**HEY JUPITER/PROFESSIONAL WIDOW (IT'S GOT TO BE BIG)** *East West A 5494CD*	20		9
9 Nov 96	**BLUE SKIES** *Perfecto PERF 130CD1* BT FEATURING TORI AMOS	26		2
11 Jan 97	**PROFESSIONAL WIDOW (IT'S GOT TO BE BIG)** *East West A 5450CD*	1	1	10
2 May 98	**SPARK** *East West AT 0031CD*	16		3
13 Nov 99	**GLORY OF THE 80'S** *Atlantic AT 0077CD1*	46		1
26 Oct 02	**A SORTA FAIRYTALE** *Epic 6730432*	41		2

AMOURE
UK, male production duo — 2

Date	Title / Label	Peak	Wks at No.1	Wks
27 May 00	**IS THAT YOUR FINAL ANSWER? (WHO WANTS TO BE A MILLIONAIRE – THE SINGLE)** *Celador MILLION 2*	33		2

AMP FIDDLER
US, male vocalist/producer/keyboard player (Joseph 'Amp' Fiddler) — 2

Date	Title / Label	Peak	Wks at No.1	Wks
20 Mar 04	**I BELIEVE IN YOU** *Genuine GEN022CD*	72		1
19 Jun 04	**DREAMIN'** *Genuine GEN025CDM*	71		1

AMPS
US, male/female vocal/instrumental group — 1

Date	Title / Label	Peak	Wks at No.1	Wks
21 Oct 95	**TIPP CITY** *4AD BAD 5015CD*	61		1

AMSTERDAM
UK, male/female vocal/instrumental group — 2

Date	Title / Label	Peak	Wks at No.1	Wks
5 Feb 05	**THE JOURNEY/STOP KNOCKING THE WALLS DOWN** *Beat Crazy BEAT001CD* AMSTERDAM/RICKY	32		1
11 Jun 05	**DOES THIS TRAIN STOP ON MERSEYSIDE** *Beat Crazy BEAT002CD1*	53		1

ANASTACIA
US, female vocalist (Anastacia Newkirk) — 100

Date	Title / Label	Peak	Wks at No.1	Wks
30 Sep 00	**I'M OUTTA LOVE** *Epic 6695782*	6		17
3 Feb 01	**NOT THAT KIND** *Epic 6707632*	11		8
2 Jun 01	**COWBOYS & KISSES** *Epic 6712622*	28		5
25 Aug 01	**MADE FOR LOVIN' YOU** *Epic 6717172*	27		3
1 Dec 01	**PAID MY DUES** *Epic 6721252*	14		9
6 Apr 02	**ONE DAY IN YOUR LIFE** *Epic 6724562*	11		9
21 Sep 02	**WHY'D YOU LIE TO ME** *Epic 6731112*	25		5
7 Dec 02	**YOU'LL NEVER BE ALONE** *Epic 6733802*	31		3
3 Apr 04	**LEFT OUTSIDE ALONE** *Epic 6746482*	3		20
14 Aug 04	**SICK AND TIRED** *Epic 6751092*	4		11
27 Nov 04	**WELCOME TO MY TRUTH** *Epic 6754922*	25		5
23 Apr 05	**HEAVY ON MY HEART** *Epic 6758402*	21		3
3 Dec 05	**PIECES OF A DREAM** *Epic 82876738082*	48		1
8 Nov 08	**I CAN FEEL YOU** *Mercury USUM70832275*	67		1

AND WHY NOT?
UK, male vocal/instrumental trio — 18

Date	Title / Label	Peak	Wks at No.1	Wks
14 Oct 89	**RESTLESS DAYS (SHE CRIES OUT LOUD)** *Island IS 426*	38		7
13 Jan 90	**THE FACE** *Island IS 444*	13		8
21 Apr 90	**SOMETHING YOU GOT** *Island 452*	39		3

...AND YOU WILL KNOW US BY THE TRAIL OF THE DEAD
US, male vocal/instrumental group — 2

Date	Title / Label	Peak	Wks at No.1	Wks
11 Nov 00	**MISTAKES AND REGRETS** *Domino RUG 114CD*	69		1
11 May 02	**ANOTHER MORNING STONER** *Interscope 4977162*	54		1

ANGRY ANDERSON
Australia, male vocalist (Gary Anderson). See Rose Tattoo — 13

Date	Title / Label	Peak	Wks at No.1	Wks
19 Nov 88	**SUDDENLY** *Food For Thought YUM 113*	3		13

BRETT ANDERSON
UK, male vocalist. See Suede, Tears — 1

Date	Title / Label	Peak	Wks at No.1	Wks
31 Mar 07	**LOVE IS DEAD** *Drowned In Sound DISO022CD2*	42		1

CARL ANDERSON
US, male vocalist/actor, d. 23 Feb 2004 (age 49) — 4

Date	Title / Label	Peak	Wks at No.1	Wks
8 Jun 85	**BUTTERCUP** *Streetwave KHAN 45*	49		4

CARLEEN ANDERSON
US, female vocalist. See Brand New Heavies, Young Disciples — 17

Date	Title / Label	Peak	Wks at No.1	Wks
12 Feb 94	**NERVOUS BREAKDOWN** *Circa YRCDG 112*	27		4
28 May 94	**MAMA SAID** *Circa YRCD 114*	26		4
13 Aug 94	**TRUE SPIRIT** *Circa YRCD 118*	24		3
14 Jan 95	**LET IT LAST** *Circa YRCDG 119*	16		3
7 Feb 98	**MAYBE I'M AMAZED** *Circa YRCD 128*	24		2
25 Apr 98	**WOMAN IN ME** *Circa YRCD 129*	74		1

LAURIE ANDERSON
US, female vocalist/instrumentalist — 6

Date	Title / Label	Peak	Wks at No.1	Wks
17 Oct 81	**O SUPERMAN** *Warner Brothers K 17870*	2		6

LC ANDERSON VS PSYCHO RADIO
UK/Italy, male vocal/production trio — 2

Date	Title / Label	Peak	Wks at No.1	Wks
26 Jul 03	**RIGHT STUFF** *Faith & Hope FHCD039*	45		2

LYNN ANDERSON
US, female vocalist — 20

Date	Title / Label	Peak	Wks at No.1	Wks
20 Feb 71	**ROSE GARDEN** *CBS 5360*	3		20

MOIRA ANDERSON
UK, female vocalist — 2

Date	Title / Label	Peak	Wks at No.1	Wks
27 Dec 69	**THE HOLY CITY** *Decca F 12989*	43		2

SUNSHINE ANDERSON
US, female vocalist — 8

Date	Title / Label	Peak	Wks at No.1	Wks
2 Jun 01	**HEARD IT ALL BEFORE** *Atlantic AT 0100CD*	9		7
22 Sep 01	**LUNCH OR DINNER** *Atlantic AT 0109CD*	57		1

JOHN ANDERSON BIG BAND
UK, big band — 5

Date	Title / Label	Peak	Wks at No.1	Wks
21 Dec 85	**GLENN MILLER MEDLEY** *Modern GLEN 1*	61		5

LEROY ANDERSON & HIS POPS CONCERT ORCHESTRA
US, orchestra – leader d. 18 May 1975 (age 66) — 4

Date	Title / Label	Peak	Wks at No.1	Wks
28 Jun 57	**FORGOTTEN DREAMS** *Brunswick 05485*	24		4

ANDERSON BRUFORD WAKEMAN HOWE

UK, male vocal/instrumental group. See Yes

Date	Title	Peak Position	Weeks at No.1	Weeks on Chart
				2
24 Jun 89	**BROTHER OF MINE** *Arista 112379*	63		2

PETER ANDRE

UK, male vocalist (Peter Andrea). See Childliners

Date	Title	Peak Position	Weeks at No.1	Weeks on Chart
				118
10 Jun 95	**TURN IT UP** *Mushroom D 1000*	64		1
16 Sep 95	**MYSTERIOUS GIRL** *Mushroom D 1192*	53		2
16 Mar 96	**ONLY ONE** *Mushroom D 1307*	16		4
1 Jun 96	**MYSTERIOUS GIRL** *Mushroom DX 2000* FEATURING BUBBLER RANX ⊛	2		18
14 Sep 96	**FLAVA** *Mushroom DX 2003* ●	1	1	9
7 Dec 96	**I FEEL YOU** *Mushroom D 1521* ●	1	1	11
8 Mar 97	**NATURAL** *Mushroom DX 1577*	6		11
9 Aug 97	**ALL ABOUT US** *Mushroom MUSH 5CD*	3		9
8 Nov 97	**LONELY** *Mushroom MUSH 16CD*	6		9
24 Jan 98	**ALL NIGHT ALL RIGHT** *Mushroom MUSH 21CD* FEATURING WARREN G	16		4
25 Jul 98	**KISS THE GIRL** *Mushroom MUSH 34CDSX*	9		5
6 Mar 04	**MYSTERIOUS GIRL** *Mushroom PA001CDX* FEATURING BUBBLER RANX	1	1	11
12 Jun 04	**INSANIA** *East West PA002CD*	3		7
18 Sep 04	**THE RIGHT WAY** *Atlantic ATUK001CD1*	14		5
16 Dec 06	**A WHOLE NEW WORLD** *K&P Recordings CDKANDP1* KATIE PRICE & PETER ANDRE	12		5
22 Aug 09	**BEHIND CLOSED DOORS** *Conehead GB4AA0900046*	4		6
21 Nov 09	**UNCONDITIONAL** *Conehead GB4AA0900057*	50		1

ANDRE 3000

US, male vocalist/rapper/multi-instrumentalist (Andre Benjamin). See Outkast

Date	Title	Peak Position	Weeks at No.1	Weeks on Chart
				17
30 Oct 04	**MILLIONAIRE** *Virgin VSCDX 1885* KELIS FEATURING ANDRE 3000	3		12
11 Oct 08	**GREEN LIGHT** *Columbia 88697378522* JOHN LEGEND FEATURING ANDRE 3000	35		5

CHRIS ANDREWS

UK, male vocalist

Date	Title	Peak Position	Weeks at No.1	Weeks on Chart
				36
7 Oct 65	**YESTERDAY MAN** *Decca F 12236*	3		15
2 Dec 65	**TO WHOM IT CONCERNS** *Decca F 22285*	13		10
14 Apr 66	**SOMETHING ON MY MIND** *Decca F 22365*	41		3
2 Jun 66	**WHATCHA GONNA DO NOW** *Decca F 22404*	40		4
25 Aug 66	**STOP THAT GIRL** *Decca F 22472*	36		4

EAMONN ANDREWS

UK, male TV presenter/vocalist, d. 5 Nov 1987 (age 64)

Date	Title	Peak Position	Weeks at No.1	Weeks on Chart
				3
20 Jan 56	**SHIFTING WHISPERING SANDS (PARTS 1 & 2)** *Parlophone R 4106* WITH RON GOODWIN & HIS ORCHESTRA	18		3

MICHAEL ANDREWS FEATURING GARY JULES

US, male vocal/production duo

Date	Title	Peak Position	Weeks at No.1	Weeks on Chart
				17
27 Dec 03	**MAD WORLD** *Adventure/Sanctuary SANXD 250X* ⊛	1	3	15
13 Jan 07	**MAD WORLD** *Adventure/Sanctuary SANXD 250X*	58		2

ANDROIDS

Australia, male vocal/instrumental group

Date	Title	Peak Position	Weeks at No.1	Weeks on Chart
				5
17 May 03	**DO IT WITH MADONNA** *Universal MCSTD 40321*	15		5

ANEKA

UK, female vocalist (Mary Sandeman)

Date	Title	Peak Position	Weeks at No.1	Weeks on Chart
				16
8 Aug 81	**JAPANESE BOY** *Hansa 5* ●	1	1	12
7 Nov 81	**LITTLE LADY** *Hansa 8*	50		4

DAVE ANGEL

UK, male DJ/producer (Dave Gooden)

Date	Title	Peak Position	Weeks at No.1	Weeks on Chart
				1
2 Aug 97	**TOKYO STEALTH FIGHTER** *Fourth & Broadway BRCD 355*	58		1

SIMONE ANGEL

Holland, female vocalist (Simone Engelen)

Date	Title	Peak Position	Weeks at No.1	Weeks on Chart
				1
13 Nov 93	**LET THIS FEELING** *A&M 5803652*	60		1

ANGEL CITY

Holland, male production duo – Aldwin Oomen & Hugo Zentveld. See Nightbreed

Date	Title	Peak Position	Weeks at No.1	Weeks on Chart
				23
8 Nov 03	**LOVE ME RIGHT (OH SHEILA)** *Data 59CDS* FEATURING LARA McALLEN	11		8
3 Jul 04	**TOUCH ME** *Data 73CDX*	18		4
16 Oct 04	**DO YOU KNOW (I GO CRAZY)** *Data 76CDS*	8		7
26 Feb 05	**SUNRISE** *Data 84CDS*	9		4

ANGELETTES

UK, female vocal group

Date	Title	Peak Position	Weeks at No.1	Weeks on Chart
				5
13 May 72	**DON'T LET HIM TOUCH YOU** *Decca F 13284*	35		5

ANGELHEART

UK, female DJ/producer (Angel Johnson)

Date	Title	Peak Position	Weeks at No.1	Weeks on Chart
				2
6 Apr 96	**COME BACK TO ME** *Hi-Life 5776312* FEATURING ROCHELLE HARRIS	68		1
22 Mar 97	**I'M STILL WAITING** *Hi-Life 5735452* FEATURING ALETIA BOURNE	74		1

ANGELIC

UK, male/female vocal/production duo. See Citizen Caned, DT8 Project, Orion, Jurgen Vries

Date	Title	Peak Position	Weeks at No.1	Weeks on Chart
				16
17 Jun 00	**IT'S MY TURN** *Serious MCSTD 40235*	11		10
24 Feb 01	**CAN'T KEEP ME SILENT** *Serious SERR 023CD*	12		4
10 Nov 01	**STAY WITH ME** *Serious SERR 35CD*	36		2

ANGELIC UPSTARTS

UK, male vocal/instrumental group

Date	Title	Peak Position	Weeks at No.1	Weeks on Chart
				30
21 Apr 79	**I'M AN UPSTART** *Warner Brothers K 17354*	31		8
11 Aug 79	**TEENAGE WARNING** *Warner Brothers K 17426*	29		6
3 Nov 79	**NEVER 'AD NOTHIN'** *Warner Brothers K 17476*	52		4
9 Feb 80	**OUT OF CONTROL** *Warner Brothers K 17558*	58		3
22 Mar 80	**WE GOTTA GET OUT OF THIS PLACE** *Warner Brothers K 17576*	65		2
2 Aug 80	**LAST NIGHT ANOTHER SOLDIER** *Zonophone Z 7*	51		4
7 Feb 81	**KIDS ON THE STREET** *Zonophone Z 16*	57		3

ANGELLE

UK, female vocalist (Sarah Davies)

Date	Title	Peak Position	Weeks at No.1	Weeks on Chart
				1
17 Aug 02	**JOY AND PAIN** *Innovation CXINNOV 1*	43		1

STEVE ANGELLO

Sweden, male DJ/producer (Steve Angello Josefsson Fragogiannis). See Supermode

Date	Title	Peak Position	Weeks at No.1	Weeks on Chart
				11
21 Aug 04	**WOZ NOT WOZ** *C2 CDC2002* ERIC PRYDZ & STEVE ANGELLO	55		1
4 Apr 09	**SHOW ME LOVE** *Data DATA212CDS* & LAIDBACK LUKE FEATURING ROBIN S	11		10

BOBBY ANGELO & THE TUXEDOS

UK, male vocal/instrumental group

Date	Title	Peak Position	Weeks at No.1	Weeks on Chart
				6
10 Aug 61	**BABY SITTIN'** *HMV POP 892*	30		6

ANGELS

US, female vocal group

Date	Title	Peak Position	Weeks at No.1	Weeks on Chart
				1
3 Oct 63	**MY BOYFRIEND'S BACK** *Mercury AMT 1211* ★	50		1

ANGELS & AIRWAVES

US, male vocal/instrumental group

Date	Title	Peak Position	Weeks at No.1	Weeks on Chart
				4
27 May 06	**THE ADVENTURE** *Geffen MCSTD40461*	20		3
5 Aug 06	**IT HURTS** *Geffen 1702863*	59		1

ANGELS REVERSE

Germany, male production duo

Date	Title	Peak Position	Weeks at No.1	Weeks on Chart
				1
31 Aug 02	**DON'T CARE** *Inferno CDFERN 46*	71		1

ANGELWITCH

UK, male vocal/instrumental group

Date	Title	Peak Position	Weeks at No.1	Weeks on Chart
				1
7 Jun 80	**SWEET DANGER** *EMI 5064*	75		1

ANIMAL

US, male drummer/vocalist/TV puppet (Frank Oz, b. UK,) — 3

Date	Title	Peak	Wks at No.1	Wks on Chart
23 Jul 94	**WIPE OUT** *BMG Kidz 74321219532*	38		3

ANIMAL NIGHTLIFE

UK, male vocal/instrumental group — 22

Date	Title	Peak	Wks at No.1	Wks on Chart
13 Aug 83	**NATIVE BOY (UPTOWN)** *Innervision A 3584*	60		3
18 Aug 84	**MR SOLITAIRE** *Island IS 193*	25		12
6 Jul 85	**LOVE IS JUST THE GREAT PRETENDER** *Island IS 200*	28		6
5 Oct 85	**PREACHER PREACHER** *Island IS 245*	67		1

ANIMALHOUSE

UK, male vocal/instrumental group — 1

Date	Title	Peak	Wks at No.1	Wks on Chart
15 Jul 00	**READY TO RECEIVE** *Boiler House! 74321771072*	61		1

ANIMALS

UK, male vocal/instrumental group – Eric Burdon*, Brian 'Chas' Chandler, Alan Price*, John Steel & Hilton Valentine — 147

Date	Title	Peak	Wks at No.1	Wks on Chart
16 Apr 64	**BABY LET ME TAKE YOU HOME** *Columbia DB 7247*	21		8
25 Jun 64	**THE HOUSE OF THE RISING SUN** *Columbia DB 7301* ★	1	1	12
17 Sep 64	**I'M CRYING** *Columbia DB 7354*	8		10
4 Feb 65	**DON'T LET ME BE MISUNDERSTOOD** *Columbia DB 7445*	3		9
8 Apr 65	**BRING IT ON HOME TO ME** *Columbia DB 7539*	7		11
15 Jul 65	**WE GOTTA GET OUT OF THIS PLACE** *Columbia DB 7639*	2		12
28 Oct 65	**IT'S MY LIFE** *Columbia DB 7741*	7		11
17 Feb 66	**INSIDE – LOOKING OUT** *Decca F 12332*	12		8
2 Jun 66	**DON'T BRING ME DOWN** *Decca F 12407*	6		8
27 Oct 66	**HELP ME GIRL** *Decca F 12502* ERIC BURDON & THE ANIMALS	14		10
15 Jun 67	**WHEN I WAS YOUNG** *MGM 1340* ERIC BURDON & THE ANIMALS	45		3
6 Sep 67	**GOOD TIMES** *MGM 1344* ERIC BURDON & THE ANIMALS	20		11
18 Oct 67	**SAN FRANCISCAN NIGHTS** *MGM 1359* ERIC BURDON & THE ANIMALS	7		10
14 Feb 68	**SKY PILOT** *MGM 1373* ERIC BURDON & THE ANIMALS	40		3
15 Jan 69	**RING OF FIRE** *MGM 1461* ERIC BURDON & THE ANIMALS	35		5
7 Oct 72	**THE HOUSE OF THE RISING SUN** *RAK RR 1*	25		6
18 Sep 82	**THE HOUSE OF THE RISING SUN** *RAK RR 1*	11		10

ANIMOTION

US, male/female vocal/instrumental group – Bill Wadhams, Astrid Plane, Don Kirkpatrick, Frenchy O'Brien, Charles Ottavio & Greg Smith — 12

Date	Title	Peak	Wks at No.1	Wks on Chart
11 May 85	**OBSESSION** *Mercury PH 34*	5		12

PAUL ANKA

Canada, male vocalist — 134

Date	Title	Peak	Wks at No.1	Wks on Chart
9 Aug 57	**DIANA** *Columbia DB 3980* ★	1	9	25
8 Nov 57	**I LOVE YOU BABY** *Columbia DB 4022*	3		15
8 Nov 57	**TELL ME THAT YOU LOVE ME** *Columbia DB 4022*	25		2
31 Jan 58	**YOU ARE MY DESTINY** *Columbia DB 4063*	6		13
30 May 58	**CRAZY LOVE** *Columbia DB 4110*	26		1
26 Sep 58	**MIDNIGHT** *Columbia DB 4172*	26		1
30 Jan 59	**(ALL OF A SUDDEN) MY HEART SINGS** *Columbia DB 4241*	10		13
10 Jul 59	**LONELY BOY** *Columbia DB 4324* ★	3		17
30 Oct 59	**PUT YOUR HEAD ON MY SHOULDER** *Columbia DB 4355*	7		12
26 Feb 60	**IT'S TIME TO CRY** *Columbia DB 4390*	28		2
21 Apr 60	**PUPPY LOVE** *Columbia DB 4434*	33		7
15 Sep 60	**HELLO YOUNG LOVERS** *Columbia DB 4504*	44		1
15 Mar 62	**LOVE ME WARM AND TENDER** *RCA 1276*	19		11
26 Jul 62	**A STEEL GUITAR AND A GLASS OF WINE** *RCA 1292*	41		4
28 Sep 74	**(YOU'RE) HAVING MY BABY** *United Artists UP 35713* FEATURING ODIA COATES ★	6		10

ANA ANN

UK, female vocalist (Ana Petrovic) — 3

Date	Title	Peak	Wks at No.1	Wks on Chart
23 Feb 02	**RIDE** *LL RIDELLR 100*	24		2
6 Mar 04	**CHILDREN OF THE WORLD** *Century Vista LLR104* & THE LONDON COMMUNITY CHOIR	44		1

ANNIE

Norway, female vocalist (Annie Lilia Berge Strand) — 5

Date	Title	Peak	Wks at No.1	Wks on Chart
25 Sep 04	**CHEWING GUM** *679 679L075CD1*	25		3
12 Mar 05	**HEARTBEAT** *679 679L091CD2*	50		1
26 Jul 08	**I KNOW UR GIRLFRIEND HATES ME** *Island 1779586*	54		1

ANOTHER CHANCE

UK, male/female vocal/production group. See Bodyrox — 1

Date	Title	Peak	Wks at No.1	Wks on Chart
28 Apr 07	**EVERYTIME I SEE HER (SOUND OF EDEN)** *Positiva CDTIVS253*	62		1

ANOTHER LEVEL

UK, male vocal group – Mark Baron, Dane Bowers*, Bobak Kianoush & Wayne Williams. See Upper Street — 81

Date	Title	Peak	Wks at No.1	Wks on Chart
28 Feb 98	**BE ALONE NO MORE** *Northwestside 74321551982* FEATURING JAY-Z	6		9
18 Jul 98	**FREAK ME** *Northwestside 74321582362* ●	1	1	12
7 Nov 98	**GUESS I WAS A FOOL** *Northwestside 74321621202*	5		13
23 Jan 99	**I WANT YOU FOR MYSELF** *Northwestside 74321643632* ANOTHER LEVEL/GHOSTFACE KILLAH	2		8
10 Apr 99	**BE ALONE NO MORE** *Northwestside 74321658482* FEATURING JAY-Z	11		9
12 Jun 99	**FROM THE HEART** *Northwestside 74321673012*	6		11
4 Sep 99	**SUMMERTIME** *Northwestside 74321694672* FEATURING TQ	7		7
13 Nov 99	**BOMB DIGGY** *Northwestside 74321712212*	6		12

ANOTHERSIDE

UK, female duo. See Honeyz — 1

Date	Title	Peak	Wks at No.1	Wks on Chart
5 Jul 03	**THIS IS YOUR NIGHT** *J-Did/V2 JAD 5023293*	41		1

ADAM ANT

UK, male vocalist/actor (Stuart Goddard). See Adam & The Ants — 69

Date	Title	Peak	Wks at No.1	Wks on Chart
22 May 82	**GOODY TWO SHOES** *CBS A 2367* ●	1	2	11
18 Sep 82	**FRIEND OR FOE** *CBS A 2736*	9		8
27 Nov 82	**DESPERATE BUT NOT SERIOUS** *CBS A 2892*	33		7
29 Oct 83	**PUSS 'N' BOOTS** *CBS A 3614* ●	5		11
10 Dec 83	**STRIP** *CBS A 3589*	41		6
22 Sep 84	**APOLLO 9** *CBS A 4719*	13		8
13 Jul 85	**VIVE LE ROCK** *CBS A 6367*	50		4
17 Feb 90	**ROOM AT THE TOP** *MCA 1387*	13		7
28 Apr 90	**CAN'T SET THE RULES ABOUT LOVE** *MCA 1404*	47		2
11 Feb 95	**WONDERFUL** *EMI CDEMS 366*	32		3
3 Jun 95	**GOTTA BE A SIN** *EMI CDEMS 379*	48		2

ANT & DEC

UK, male vocal/TV presenting/acting duo – Anthony McPartlin & Declan Donnelly. See Team Dec — 92

Date	Title	Peak	Wks at No.1	Wks on Chart
18 Dec 93	**TONIGHT I'M FREE** *Telstar CDSTAS 2706* PJ & DUNCAN	62		3
23 Apr 94	**WHY ME** *Telstar CDSTAS 2719* PJ & DUNCAN	27		4
23 Jul 94	**LET'S GET READY TO RHUMBLE** *XSrhythm CDDEC 1* PJ & DUNCAN	9		11
8 Oct 94	**IF I GIVE YOU MY NUMBER** *XSrhythm CDDEC 2* PJ & DUNCAN	15		7
3 Dec 94	**ETERNAL LOVE** *XSrhythm CDDEC 3* PJ & DUNCAN	12		9
25 Feb 95	**OUR RADIO ROCKS** *XSrhythm CDANT 4* PJ & DUNCAN	15		5
29 Jul 95	**STUCK ON U** *Telstar CDDEC 5* PJ & DUNCAN	12		5
14 Oct 95	**U KRAZY KATZ** *XSrhythm CDDEC 6* PJ & DUNCAN	15		4
2 Dec 95	**PERFECT** *Telstar CDANT 7* PJ & DUNCAN	16		7
30 Mar 96	**STEPPING STONE** *Telstar CDANT 8* PJ & DUNCAN	11		5
24 Aug 96	**BETTER WATCH OUT** *Telstar CDDEC 9*	10		4
23 Nov 96	**WHEN I FALL IN LOVE** *Telstar CDDEC 10*	12		8
15 Mar 97	**SHOUT** *Telstar CDDEC 11*	10		5
10 May 97	**FALLING** *Telstar CDDEC 12*	14		4
8 Jun 02	**WE'RE ON THE BALL** *Columbia 6727312*	3		11

ANTARCTICA

Australia, male producer (Steve Gibbs) — 2

Date	Title	Peak	Wks at No.1	Wks on Chart
29 Jan 00	**RETURN TO REALITY** *React CDREACT 173*	53		1
8 Jul 00	**ADRIFT (CAST YOUR MIND)** *React CDREACT 172*	72		1

BILLIE ANTHONY WITH ERIC JUPP & HIS ORCHESTRA

UK, female vocalist (Philomenia Brown), d. 5 Jan 1991 (age 58) — 16

Date	Title	Peak	Wks at No.1	Wks on Chart
15 Oct 54	**THIS OLE HOUSE** *Columbia DB 3519*	4		16

MARC ANTHONY

US, male vocalist (Marco Antonio Muniz) — 6

Date	Title	Peak	Wks at No.1	Wks on Chart
5 Oct 91	**RIDE ON THE RHYTHM** *Atlantic A 7602* LITTLE LOUIE VEGA & MARC ANTHONY	71		1
31 Jan 98	**RIDE ON THE RHYTHM** *Perfecto PERF 151CD1* LITTLE LOUIE & MARC ANTHONY	36		2
13 Nov 99	**I NEED TO KNOW** *Columbia 6683612*	28		3

MIKI ANTHONY

UK, male vocalist — 7

Date	Title	Peak Position	Weeks at No.1	Weeks on Chart
3 Feb 73	**IF IT WASN'T FOR THE REASON THAT I LOVE YOU** *Bell 1275*	27		7

RAY ANTHONY & HIS ORCHESTRA

US, orchestra – leader Raymond Antonini — 2

Date	Title	Peak Position	Weeks at No.1	Weeks on Chart
4 Dec 53	**DRAGNET** *Capitol CL 13983*	7		2

RICHARD ANTHONY

France, male vocalist (Richard Anthony Bush) — 15

Date	Title	Peak Position	Weeks at No.1	Weeks on Chart
12 Dec 63	**WALKING ALONE** *Columbia DB 7133*	37		5
23 Apr 64	**IF I LOVED YOU** *Columbia DB 7235*	18		10

ANTHRAX

US, male vocal/instrumental group — 37

Date	Title	Peak Position	Weeks at No.1	Weeks on Chart
28 Feb 87	**I AM THE LAW** *Island IS LAW 1*	32		5
27 Jun 87	**INDIANS** *Island IS 325*	44		4
5 Dec 87	**I'M THE MAN** *Island IS 338*	20		6
10 Sep 88	**MAKE ME LAUGH** *Island IS 379*	26		3
18 Mar 89	**ANTI-SOCIAL** *Island IS 409*	44		3
1 Sep 90	**IN MY WORLD** *Island IS 470*	29		2
5 Jan 91	**GOT THE TIME** *Island IS 476*	16		4
6 Jul 91	**BRING THE NOISE** *Island IS 490* FEATURING CHUCK D	14		5
8 May 93	**ONLY** *Elektra EKR 166CD*	36		3
11 Sep 93	**BLACK LODGE** *Elektra EKR 171CD*	53		2

ANTI-NOWHERE LEAGUE

UK, male vocal/instrumental group — 10

Date	Title	Peak Position	Weeks at No.1	Weeks on Chart
23 Jan 82	**STREETS OF LONDON** *WXYZ ABCD 1*	48		5
20 Mar 82	**I HATE…PEOPLE** *WXYZ ABCD 2*	46		3
3 Jul 82	**WOMAN** *WXYZ ABCD 4*	72		2

ANTICAPPELLA

Italy/UK, male/female production/vocal group — 12

Date	Title	Peak Position	Weeks at No.1	Weeks on Chart
16 Nov 91	**2v231** *PWL Continental PWL 205*	24		4
18 Apr 92	**EVERY DAY** *PWL Continental PWL 220*	45		2
25 Jun 94	**MOVE YOUR BODY** *Media MCSTD 1980* FEATURING MC FIXX IT	21		3
1 Apr 95	**EXPRESS YOUR FREEDOM** *Media MCSTD 2048*	31		2
25 May 96	**21231/MOVE YOUR BODY (REMIX)** *Media MCSTD 40037*	54		1

ANTONY & THE JOHNSONS

US, male/female vocal/instrumental group — 6

Date	Title	Peak Position	Weeks at No.1	Weeks on Chart
28 May 05	**HOPE THERE'S SOMEONE** *Rough Trade RTRADSCD229*	44		3
3 Dec 05	**YOU ARE MY SISTER** *Rough Trade RTRADSCDX276*	39		3

STEVE AOKI FEATURING ZUPER BLAHQ

US, male rap/DJ/production duo. See Black Eyed Peas, Will.I.Am — 3

Date	Title	Peak Position	Weeks at No.1	Weeks on Chart
20 Mar 10	**I'M IN THE HOUSE** *Data DATA228CDX*	29		3

A1

UK/Norway, male vocal group – Ben Adams*, Christian Ingebrigtsen, Paul Marazzi & Mark Read — 91

Date	Title	Peak Position	Weeks at No.1	Weeks on Chart
3 Jul 99	**BE THE FIRST TO BELIEVE** *Columbia 6674222*	6		9
11 Sep 99	**SUMMERTIME OF OUR LIVES** *Columbia 6678322*	5		8
20 Nov 99	**EVERYTIME/READY OR NOT** *Columbia 6681872*	3		11
4 Mar 00	**LIKE A ROSE** *Columbia 6689032*	6		12
9 Sep 00	**TAKE ON ME** *Columbia 6695902* ●	1	1	11
18 Nov 00	**SAME OLD BRAND NEW YOU** *Columbia 6705202*	1	1	10
3 Mar 01	**NO MORE** *Columbia 6708742*	6		13
2 Feb 02	**CAUGHT IN THE MIDDLE** *Columbia 6722322*	2		12
25 May 02	**MAKE IT GOOD** *Columbia 6726182*	11		5

APACHE INDIAN

UK, male vocalist (Steven Kapur) — 33

Date	Title	Peak Position	Weeks at No.1	Weeks on Chart
28 Nov 92	**JUST WANNA KNOW/FE' REAL** *10 TEN 416* MAXI PRIEST/MAXI PRIEST FEATURING APACHE INDIAN	33		3
2 Jan 93	**ARRANGED MARRIAGE** *Island CID 544*	16		6
27 Mar 93	**CHOK THERE** *Island CID 555*	30		4
14 Aug 93	**NUFF VIBES EP** *Island CID 560* ●	5		10
23 Oct 93	**MOVIN' ON** *Island CID 580*	48		2
7 May 94	**WRECKX SHOP** *MCA MCSTD 1969* WRECKX-N-EFFECT FEATURING APACHE INDIAN	26		2
11 Feb 95	**MAKE WAY FOR THE INDIAN** *Island CID 586* & TIM DOG	29		2
22 Apr 95	**RAGGAMUFFIN GIRL** *Island CID 606* FEATURING FRANKIE PAUL	31		2
29 Mar 97	**LOVIN' (LET ME LOVE YOU)** *Coalition COLA 002CD*	53		1
18 Oct 97	**REAL PEOPLE** *Coalition COLA 019CD*	66		1

APARTMENT

UK, male vocal/instrumental group — 1

Date	Title	Peak Position	Weeks at No.1	Weeks on Chart
19 Feb 05	**EVERYONE SAYS I'M PARANOID/JUNE JULY** *Fierce Panda NING160CD*	67		1

APHEX TWIN

UK, male producer (Richard James) — 12

Date	Title	Peak Position	Weeks at No.1	Weeks on Chart
9 May 92	**DIGERIDOO** *R&S RSUK 12*	55		2
27 Nov 93	**ON** *Warp WAP 39CD*	32		3
8 Apr 95	**VENTOLIN** *Warp WAP 60CD*	49		1
26 Oct 96	**GIRL/BOY (EP)** *Warp WAP 78CD*	64		1
18 Oct 97	**COME TO DADDY** *Warp WAP 94CD*	36		2
3 Apr 99	**WINDOWLICKER** *Warp WAP 105CD*	16		3

APHRODITE FEATURING WILDFLOWER

UK, male/female rap/vocal/production duo. See Urban Shakedown — 1

Date	Title	Peak Position	Weeks at No.1	Weeks on Chart
16 Nov 02	**SEE THRU IT** *V2 VVR 5020983*	68		1

APHRODITE'S CHILD

Greece, male vocal/instrumental group. See Demis Roussos/Vangelis (both in group) — 7

Date	Title	Peak Position	Weeks at No.1	Weeks on Chart
6 Nov 68	**RAIN AND TEARS** *Mercury MF 1039*	29		7

A+

US, male rapper (Andre Levins) — 9

Date	Title	Peak Position	Weeks at No.1	Weeks on Chart
13 Feb 99	**ENJOY YOURSELF** *Universal UND 56230*	5		9

APOLLO FOUR FORTY

UK, male production/vocal group – Norman Fisher-Jones & Trevor & Howard Gray with various collaborators — 53

Date	Title	Peak Position	Weeks at No.1	Weeks on Chart
22 Jan 94	**ASTRAL AMERICA** *Stealth Sonic SSXCD 2* APOLLO 440	36		2
5 Nov 94	**LIQUID COOL** *Stealth Sonic SSXCD 3* APOLLO 440	35		2
25 Mar 95	**(DON'T FEAR) THE REAPER** *Stealth Sonic SSXCD 4* APOLLO 440	35		2
27 Jul 96	**KRUPA** *Epic SSXCD 5* APOLLO 440	23		8
15 Feb 97	**AIN'T TALKIN' 'BOUT NO DUB** *Stealth Sonic SSXCDX 6* APOLLO 440	7		7
5 Jul 97	**RAW POWER** *Stealth Sonic SSXCD 7*	32		3
11 Jul 98	**RENDEZ-VOUS 98** *Epic 6661102* JEAN-MICHEL JARRE & APOLLO 440	12		6
8 Aug 98	**LOST IN SPACE** *Stealth Sonic SSX 9CD*	4		9
28 Aug 99	**STOP THE ROCK** *Epic SSX 10CD*	10		6
27 Nov 99	**HEART GO BOOM** *Epic SSX 11CD*	57		1
9 Dec 00	**CHARLIE'S ANGELS 2000** *Epic SSX 13CD*	29		6
21 Jun 03	**DUDE DESCENDING A STAIRCASE** *Sony Music SSX 14CDX* FEATURING THE BEATNUTS	58		1

APOLLO PRESENTS HOUSE OF VIRGINISM

Sweden, male vocalist/producer (Fredrik Asplund) — 1

Date	Title	Peak Position	Weeks at No.1	Weeks on Chart
17 Feb 96	**EXCLUSIVE** *Logic 74321324102*	67		1

FIONA APPLE

US, female vocalist (Fiona Apple Maggart) — 2

Date	Title	Peak Position	Weeks at No.1	Weeks on Chart
26 Feb 00	**FAST AS YOU CAN** *Columbia 6689962*	33		2

KIM APPLEBY

UK, female vocalist. See Mel & Kim — 31

Date	Title	Peak Position	Weeks at No.1	Weeks on Chart
3 Nov 90	**DON'T WORRY** *Parlophone R 6272* ●	2		10
9 Feb 91	**G.L.A.D.** *Parlophone R 6281*	10		6
29 Jun 91	**MAMA** *Parlophone R 6291*	19		8
19 Oct 91	**IF YOU CARED** *Parlophone R 6297*	44		3
31 Jul 93	**LIGHT OF THE WORLD** *Parlophone CDR 6352*	41		2
13 Nov 93	**BREAKAWAY** *Parlophone CDR 6362*	56		1
12 Nov 94	**FREE SPIRIT** *Parlophone CDR 6397*	51		1

APPLEJACKS
UK, male/female vocal/instrumental group – Megan Davies, Al Jackson, Martin Baggott, Philip Cash, Gerry Freeman & Don Gould — 29

Date	Title	Peak Position	Weeks at No.1	Weeks on Chart
5 Mar 64	**TELL ME WHEN** *Decca F 11833*	7		13
11 Jun 64	**LIKE DREAMERS DO** *Decca F 11916*	20		11
15 Oct 64	**THREE LITTLE WORDS (I LOVE YOU)** *Decca F 11981*	23		5

APPLES
UK, male vocal/instrumental trio — 1

Date	Title	Peak Position	Weeks at No.1	Weeks on Chart
23 Mar 91	**EYE WONDER** *Epic 6566717*	75		1

APPLETON
Canada, female vocal duo – Natalie & Nicole Appleton. See All Saints — 22

Date	Title	Peak Position	Weeks at No.1	Weeks on Chart
14 Sep 02	**FANTASY** *Polydor 5709852*	2		10
22 Feb 03	**DON'T WORRY** *Polydor 0658192*	5		10
26 Jul 03	**EVERYTHING EVENTUALLY** *Polydor 9808278*	38		2

STEVE APPLETON
UK, male vocalist/producer — 1

Date	Title	Peak Position	Weeks at No.1	Weeks on Chart
16 May 09	**DIRTY FUNK** *RCA 88697487992*	67		1

CHARLIE APPLEWHITE WITH VICTOR YOUNG & HIS ORCHESTRA & CHORUS
US, male vocalist, d. 27 Apr 2001 (age 67) — 1

Date	Title	Peak Position	Weeks at No.1	Weeks on Chart
23 Sep 55	**BLUE STAR (THE MEDIC THEME)** *Brunswick 05416*	20		1

APRIL WINE
Canada, male vocal/instrumental group — 9

Date	Title	Peak Position	Weeks at No.1	Weeks on Chart
15 Mar 80	**I LIKE TO ROCK** *Capitol CL 16121*	41		5
11 Apr 81	**JUST BETWEEN YOU AND ME** *Capitol CL 16184*	52		4

AQUA
Denmark/Norway, male/female vocal/production group – Lene & Soren Nystrom Rasted, René Dif & Claus Norreen. See Lazy B — 85

Date	Title	Peak Position	Weeks at No.1	Weeks on Chart
25 Oct 97	**BARBIE GIRL** *Universal UMD 80413* ㊉ x2	1	4	26
7 Feb 98	**DOCTOR JONES** *Universal UMD 80457* ●	1	2	14
16 May 98	**TURN BACK TIME** *Universal UMD 80490*	1	1	10
1 Aug 98	**MY OH MY** *Universal UMD 85058*	6		11
26 Dec 98	**GOOD MORNING SUNSHINE** *Universal UMD 85086*	18		7
26 Feb 00	**CARTOON HEROES** *Universal MCSTD 40226*	7		11
10 Jun 00	**AROUND THE WORLD** *Universal MCSXD 40234*	26		6

AQUAGEN
Germany, male production duo – Olaf Dieckman & Gino Montesano — 10

Date	Title	Peak Position	Weeks at No.1	Weeks on Chart
9 Dec 00	**PHATT BASS** *NuLife 74321817102* WARP BROTHERS VERSUS AQUAGEN	9		8
1 Mar 03	**HARD TO SAY I'M SORRY** *All Around The World CXGLOBE 265*	33		2

AQUALUNG
UK, male vocalist/producer/multi-instrumentalist (Matt Hales) — 10

Date	Title	Peak Position	Weeks at No.1	Weeks on Chart
28 Sep 02	**STRANGE AND BEAUTIFUL** *B Unique BUN 032CDX*	7		6
14 Dec 02	**GOOD TIMES GONNA COME** *B Unique BUN 043CDX*	71		1
25 Oct 03	**BRIGHTER THAN SUNSHINE** *B Unique BUN 072CDX*	37		2
27 Mar 04	**EASIER TO LIE** *B Unique WEA373CD2*	60		1

AQUANUTS
US/Argentina, male production/instrumental duo — 1

Date	Title	Peak Position	Weeks at No.1	Weeks on Chart
4 May 02	**DEEP SEA** *Data 34T*	75		1

AQUARIAN DREAM
US, male vocal/instrumental group — 1

Date	Title	Peak Position	Weeks at No.1	Weeks on Chart
24 Feb 79	**YOU'RE A STAR** *Elektra LV 7*	67		1

ARAB STRAP
UK, male vocal/instrumental duo. See Malcolm Middleton — 4

Date	Title	Peak Position	Weeks at No.1	Weeks on Chart
13 Sep 97	**THE GIRLS OF SUMMER (EP)** *Chemikal Underground CHEM 017CD*	74		1
4 Apr 98	**HERE WE GO/TRIPPY** *Chemikal Underground CHEM 20CD*	48		1
10 Oct 98	**(AFTERNOON) SOAPS** *Chemikal Underground CHEM 27CD*	74		1
10 Feb 01	**LOVE DETECTIVE** *Chemikal Underground CHEM 049CD*	66		1

ARCADE FIRE
Canada, male/female vocal/instrumental group — 13

Date	Title	Peak Position	Weeks at No.1	Weeks on Chart
9 Apr 05	**NEIGHBOURHOOD #2 (LAIKA)** *Rough Trade RTRADSCD225*	30		2
4 Jun 05	**POWER OUT** *Rough Trade RTRADSCD232*	26		2
13 Aug 05	**COLD WIND** *Rough Trade RTRADS254*	52		1
17 Sep 05	**REBELLION (LIES)** *Rough Trade RTRADSCD252*	19		2
26 Nov 05	**WAKE UP** *Rough Trade RTRADSCD286*	29		2
17 Mar 07	**KEEP THE CAR RUNNING** *Sonovox GBUM70607729*	56		4

ARCADIA
UK, male vocal/instrumental trio – Simon LeBon, Nick Rhodes & Roger Taylor. See Duran Duran — 13

Date	Title	Peak Position	Weeks at No.1	Weeks on Chart
26 Oct 85	**ELECTION DAY** *Odeon NSR 1*	7		7
25 Jan 86	**THE PROMISE** *Odeon NSR 2*	37		4
26 Jul 86	**THE FLAME** *Odeon NSR 3*	58		2

TASMIN ARCHER
UK, female vocalist — 37

Date	Title	Peak Position	Weeks at No.1	Weeks on Chart
12 Sep 92	**SLEEPING SATELLITE** *EMI EM 233* ●	1	2	17
20 Feb 93	**IN YOUR CARE** *EMI CDEMS 260*	16		6
29 May 93	**LORDS OF THE NEW CHURCH** *EMI CDEM 266*	26		4
21 Aug 93	**ARIENNE** *EMI CDEM 275*	30		4
8 Jan 94	**SHIPBUILDING** *EMI CDEM 302*	40		4
23 Mar 96	**ONE MORE GOOD NIGHT WITH THE BOYS** *EMI CDEM 401*	45		2

ARCHIES
US, male/female TV cartoon group featuring Ron Dante. See Cuff Links — 26

Date	Title	Peak Position	Weeks at No.1	Weeks on Chart
11 Oct 69	**SUGAR SUGAR** *RCA 1872* ★	1	8	26

ARCHITECHS
UK, male production trio – Ashley, Kevin (K-Warren*) & Paul — 19

Date	Title	Peak Position	Weeks at No.1	Weeks on Chart
7 Oct 00	**BODY GROOVE** *Go! Beat GOBCD 33* FEATURING NANA ●	3		14
7 Apr 01	**SHOW ME THE MONEY** *Go! Beat GOBCD 38*	20		5

ARCTIC MONKEYS
UK, male vocal/instrumental group – Alex Turner, Jamie Cook, Matt Helders & Andy Nicholson (replaced by Nick O'Malley) — 92

Date	Title	Peak Position	Weeks at No.1	Weeks on Chart
29 Oct 05	**I BET YOU LOOK GOOD ON THE DANCEFLOOR** *Domino RUG212CD*	1	1	25
28 Jan 06	**WHEN THE SUN GOES DOWN** *Domino RUG216CD*	1	1	15
26 Aug 06	**LEAVE BEFORE THE LIGHTS COME ON** *Domino RUG236CD*	4		9
14 Apr 07	**BRAINSTORM** *Domino RUG254CD*	2		10
5 May 07	**FLUORESCENT ADOLESCENT** *Domino RUG261CD*	5		17
5 May 07	**505** *Domino GBCEL0700074*	74		1
15 Dec 07	**TEDDY PICKER** *Domino RUG279CD*	20		7
18 Jul 09	**CRYING LIGHTNING** *Domino GBA320903290*	12		8

JANN ARDEN
Canada, female vocalist (Jann Arden Richards) — 2

Date	Title	Peak Position	Weeks at No.1	Weeks on Chart
13 Jul 96	**INSENSITIVE** *A&M 5812652*	40		2

A.R.E. WEAPONS
US, male vocal/instrumental group — 1

Date	Title	Peak Position	Weeks at No.1	Weeks on Chart
4 Aug 01	**STREET GANG** *Rough Trade RTRADESCD 022*	72		1

TINA ARENA
Australia, female vocalist (Filippina Arena) — 33

Date	Title	Peak Position	Weeks at No.1	Weeks on Chart
15 Apr 95	**CHAINS** *Columbia 6611255*	6		11
12 Aug 95	**HEAVEN HELP MY HEART** *Columbia 6620975*	25		5
2 Dec 95	**SHOW ME HEAVEN** *Columbia 6626975*	29		3
3 Aug 96	**SORRENTO MOON (I REMEMBER)** *Columbia 6635435*	22		4
27 Jun 98	**WHISTLE DOWN THE WIND** *Really Useful 5672192*	24		5
24 Oct 98	**IF I WAS A RIVER** *Columbia 6665605*	43		2
13 Mar 99	**BURN** *Columbia 6667442*	47		1
20 May 00	**LIVE FOR THE ONE I LOVE** *Columbia 6691332*	63		1
12 Apr 03	**NEVER (PAST TENSE)** *Illustrious CDILL 010* ROC PROFECT FEATURING TINA ARENA	42		1

Silver-selling ● Gold-selling ● Platinum-selling (x multiples) ⊛ US No.1 ★ Peak Position · Weeks at No.1 · Weeks on Chart

ARGENT
UK, male vocal/instrumental group – Rod Argent, Russ Ballard, Robert Henrit & Jim Rodford — 27

Date	Title	Peak	Wks at No.1	Wks on Chart
4 Mar 72	**HOLD YOUR HEAD UP** *Epic EPC 7786*	5		12
10 Jun 72	**TRAGEDY** *Epic EPC 8115*	34		7
24 Mar 73	**GOD GAVE ROCK AND ROLL TO YOU** *Epic EPC 1243*	18		8

INDIA.ARIE
US, female vocalist (India.Arie Simpson) — 7

Date	Title	Peak	Wks at No.1	Wks on Chart
30 Jun 01	**VIDEO** *Motown TMGCD 1505*	32		3
20 Oct 01	**BROWN SKIN** *Motown TMGCD 1507*	29		2
12 Apr 03	**LITTLE THINGS** *Motown TMGCD 1509*	62		1
24 Jun 06	**I AM NOT MY HAIR** *Motown/Uni-Island TMGCD1514*	65		1

ARIEL
UK, male/female vocal/production group — 2

Date	Title	Peak	Wks at No.1	Wks on Chart
27 Mar 93	**LET IT SLIDE** *Deconstruction 74321134512*	57		2

ARIEL
Argentina, male DJ/producer (Ariel Belloso) — 4

Date	Title	Peak	Wks at No.1	Wks on Chart
21 Jun 97	**DEEP (I'M FALLING DEEPER)** *Wonderboy WBOYD 005*	47		1
17 Jun 00	**A9** *Essential Recordings ESCD 15*	28		3

ARIZONA
UK, male production duo & female vocalist (b. Barbados) — 1

Date	Title	Peak	Wks at No.1	Wks on Chart
12 Mar 94	**I SPECIALIZE IN LOVE** *Union City UCRCD 27* FEATURING ZEITIA	74		1

SHIP'S COMPANY & ROYAL MARINE BAND OF HMS ARK ROYAL
UK, male choir & marine band — 6

Date	Title	Peak	Wks at No.1	Wks on Chart
23 Dec 78	**THE LAST FAREWELL** *BBC RESL 61*	46		6

ARKARNA
UK, male vocal/instrumental/production group — 3

Date	Title	Peak	Wks at No.1	Wks on Chart
25 Jan 97	**HOUSE ON FIRE** *WEA 088CD1*	33		2
2 Aug 97	**SO LITTLE TIME** *WEA 108CD1*	46		1

JOAN ARMATRADING
UK (b. St Kitts), female vocalist/guitarist — 53

Date	Title	Peak	Wks at No.1	Wks on Chart
16 Oct 76	**LOVE AND AFFECTION** *A&M AMS 7249*	10		9
23 Feb 80	**ROSIE** *A&M AMS 7506*	49		5
14 Jun 80	**ME MYSELF I** *A&M AMS 7527*	21		11
6 Sep 80	**ALL THE WAY FROM AMERICA** *A&M AMS 7552*	54		3
12 Sep 81	**I'M LUCKY** *A&M AMS 8163*	46		5
16 Jan 82	**NO LOVE** *A&M AMS 8179*	50		5
19 Feb 83	**DROP THE PILOT** *A&M AMS 8306*	11		10
16 Mar 85	**TEMPTATION** *A&M AM 238*	65		2
26 May 90	**MORE THAN ONE KIND OF LOVE** *A&M AM 561*	75		1
23 May 92	**WRAPPED AROUND HER** *A&M AM 877*	56		2

ARMOURY SHOW
UK, male vocal/instrumental group — 6

Date	Title	Peak	Wks at No.1	Wks on Chart
25 Aug 84	**CASTLES IN SPAIN** *Parlophone R 6079*	69		2
26 Jan 85	**WE CAN BE BRAVE AGAIN** *Parlophone R 6087*	66		1
17 Jan 87	**LOVE IN ANGER** *Parlophone R 6149*	63		3

DAVE ARMSTRONG & REDROCHE FEATURING H-BOOGIE
Canada/UK, male/female vocal/DJ/production trio — 3

Date	Title	Peak	Wks at No.1	Wks on Chart
19 Jan 08	**LOVE HAS GONE** *Hed Kandi HK50CDS*	43		3

LOUIS ARMSTRONG
US, male vocalist/trumpeter, d. 6 Jul 1971 (age 69) — 93

Date	Title	Peak	Wks at No.1	Wks on Chart
19 Dec 52	**TAKES TWO TO TANGO** *Brunswick 04995*	6		10
13 Apr 56	**THEME FROM THE 'THREEPENNY OPERA'** *Philips PB 574* WITH HIS ALL-STARS	8		11
15 Jun 56	**TAKE IT SATCH EP** *Philips BBE 12035* WITH HIS ALL-STARS	29		1
13 Jul 56	**THE FAITHFUL HUSSAR** *Philips PB 604* WITH HIS ALL-STARS	27		2
6 Nov 59	**MACK THE KNIFE** *Philips PB 967* WITH HIS ALL-STARS	24		1
4 Jun 64	**HELLO DOLLY** *London HLR 9878* ★	4		14
7 Feb 68	**WHAT A WONDERFUL WORLD/CABARET** *HMV POP 1615*	1	4	29
26 Jun 68	**THE SUNSHINE OF LOVE** *Stateside SS 2116*	41		7
16 Apr 88	**WHAT A WONDERFUL WORLD** *A&M AM 435*	53		5
19 Nov 94	**WE HAVE ALL THE TIME IN THE WORLD** *EMI CDEM 357* ●	3		13

ARMY OF LOVERS
Sweden, male/female vocal/instrumental trio — 10

Date	Title	Peak	Wks at No.1	Wks on Chart
17 Aug 91	**CRUCIFIED** *Ton Son Ton WOK 2007*	47		5
28 Dec 91	**OBSESSION** *Ton Son Ton WOK 2009*	67		1
15 Feb 92	**CRUCIFIED** *Ton Son Ton WOK 2017*	31		3
18 Apr 92	**RIDE THE BULLET** *Ton Son Ton WOK 2018*	67		1

ARNEE & THE TERMINATORS
UK, male vocal/instrumental/radio presenting posse – Richard Easter & Steve Wright — 7

Date	Title	Peak	Wks at No.1	Wks on Chart
24 Aug 91	**I'LL BE BACK** *Epic 6574177*	5		7

ARNIE'S LOVE
US, male/female vocal trio — 3

Date	Title	Peak	Wks at No.1	Wks on Chart
26 Nov 83	**I'M OUT OF YOUR LIFE** *Streetwave WAVE 9*	67		3

DAVID ARNOLD
UK, male composer/producer — 14

Date	Title	Peak	Wks at No.1	Wks on Chart
23 Oct 93	**PLAY DEAD** *Island CID 573* BJORK & DAVID ARNOLD	12		6
18 Oct 97	**ON HER MAJESTY'S SECRET SERVICE** *East West EW 136CD* PROPELLERHEADS & DAVID ARNOLD	7		5
22 Nov 97	**DIAMONDS ARE FOREVER** *East West EW 141CD* DAVID McALMONT & DAVID ARNOLD	39		2
29 Apr 00	**THEME FROM 'RANDALL & HOPKIRK (DECEASED)'** *Island CID 762* NINA PERSSON & DAVID ARNOLD	49		1

EDDY ARNOLD
US, male vocalist, d. 8 May 2008 (age 89) — 21

Date	Title	Peak	Wks at No.1	Wks on Chart
17 Feb 66	**MAKE THE WORLD GO AWAY** *RCA 1496*	8		17
26 May 66	**I WANT TO GO WITH YOU** *RCA 1519*	46		3
28 Jul 66	**IF YOU WERE MINE MARY** *RCA 1529*	49		1

PP ARNOLD
US, female vocalist (Patricia Arnold) — 37

Date	Title	Peak	Wks at No.1	Wks on Chart
4 May 67	**FIRST CUT IS THE DEEPEST** *Immediate IM 047*	18		10
2 Aug 67	**THE TIME HAS COME** *Immediate IM 055*	47		2
24 Jan 68	**(IF YOU THINK YOU'RE) GROOVY** *Immediate IM 061*	41		4
10 Jul 68	**ANGEL OF THE MORNING** *Immediate IM 067*	29		11
24 Sep 88	**BURN IT UP** *Rhythm King LEFT 27* BEATMASTERS WITH PP ARNOLD	14		10

ARPEGGIO
US, male/female vocal group — 3

Date	Title	Peak	Wks at No.1	Wks on Chart
31 Mar 79	**LOVE AND DESIRE (PART 1)** *Polydor POSP 40*	63		3

ARRESTED DEVELOPMENT
US, male/female vocal/instrumental group – Todd 'Speech' Thomas, Tim Barnwell, Montsho Eshe, Tasha LaRae, Spencer Love, Don Norris, Baba Oje', Jason Reichert, Nadirah Shakoor, Aerle Taree & Ike Williams — 39

Date	Title	Peak	Wks at No.1	Wks on Chart
16 May 92	**TENNESSEE** *Cooltempo COOL 253*	46		7
24 Oct 92	**PEOPLE EVERYDAY** *Cooltempo COOL 265* ●	2		14
9 Jan 93	**MR WENDAL/REVOLUTION** *Cooltempo CDCOOL 268*	4		9
3 Apr 93	**TENNESSEE** *Cooltempo CDCOOL 270*	18		6
28 May 94	**EASE MY MIND** *Cooltempo CDCOOL 293*	33		3

STEVE ARRINGTON
US, male vocalist — 19

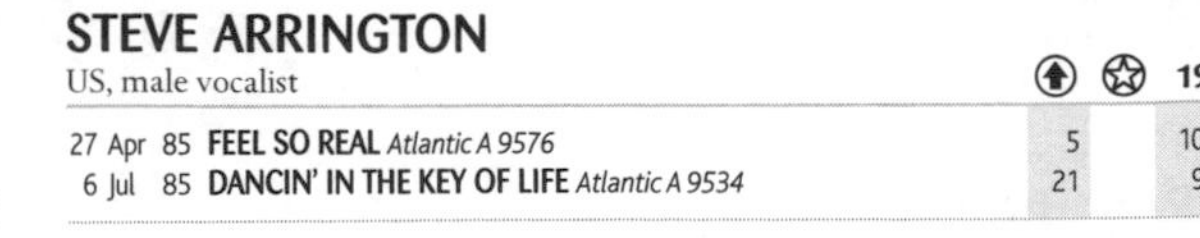

Date	Title	Peak	Wks at No.1	Wks on Chart
27 Apr 85	**FEEL SO REAL** *Atlantic A 9576*	5		10
6 Jul 85	**DANCIN' IN THE KEY OF LIFE** *Atlantic A 9534*	21		9

ARRIVAL

UK, male/female vocal/instrumental group – Dyan Birch, Carroll Carter, Frank Collins, Lloyd Courtney, Don Hume, Paddy McHugh & Tom O'Malley — 20

Date	Title	Peak Position	Weeks at No.1	Weeks on Chart
10 Jan 70	**FRIENDS** *Decca F 12986*	8		9
6 Jun 70	**I WILL SURVIVE** *Decca F 13026*	16		11

ARROW

Monserrat, male vocalist (Alphonsus Cassell) — 15

Date	Title	Peak Position	Weeks at No.1	Weeks on Chart
28 Jul 84	**HOT HOT HOT** *Cooltempo ARROW 1*	59		5
13 Jul 85	**LONG TIME** *London LON 70*	30		7
3 Sep 94	**HOT HOT HOT** *The Hit Label HLC 7*	38		3

ARROWS

US/UK, male vocal/instrumental trio – Alan Merrill, Jake Hooker & Paul Varley — 16

Date	Title	Peak Position	Weeks at No.1	Weeks on Chart
25 May 74	**A TOUCH TOO MUCH** *RAK 171*	8		9
1 Feb 75	**MY LAST NIGHT WITH YOU** *RAK 189*	25		7

ARSENAL FC

UK, male footballers/vocalists — 16

Date	Title	Peak Position	Weeks at No.1	Weeks on Chart
8 May 71	**GOOD OLD ARSENAL** *Pye 7N 45067* ARSENAL FC FIRST TEAM SQUAD	16		7
15 May 93	**SHOUTING FOR THE GUNNERS** *London LONCD 342* ARSENAL FA CUP SQUAD FEATURING TIPPA IRIE & PETER HUNNIGALE	34		3
23 May 98	**HOT STUFF** *Grapevine AFCCD 1*	9		5
3 Jun 00	**ARSENAL NUMBER ONE/OUR GOAL** *Grapevine CDGPS 280*	46		1

ART BRUT

UK, male vocal/instrumental group — 4

Date	Title	Peak Position	Weeks at No.1	Weeks on Chart
10 Apr 04	**FORMED A BAND** *Rough Trade RTRADSCD174*	52		1
18 Dec 04	**MODERN ART/MY LITTLE BROTHER** *Fierce Panda NING164CD*	49		1
14 May 05	**EMILY KANE** *Fierce Panda NING167CD*	41		1
8 Oct 05	**GOOD WEEKEND** *Fierce Panda NING173CD*	56		1

ART COMPANY

Holland, male vocal/instrumental group — 11

Date	Title	Peak Position	Weeks at No.1	Weeks on Chart
26 May 84	**SUSANNA** *Epic A 4174*	12		11

ART OF NOISE

UK, male/female instrumental/production group – Jonathan Jeczalik, Anne Dudley, Trevor Horn, Gary Langan & Paul Morley — 65

Date	Title	Peak Position	Weeks at No.1	Weeks on Chart
24 Nov 84	**CLOSE (TO THE EDIT)** *ZTT ZTPS 01*	8		19
13 Apr 85	**MOMENTS IN LOVE/BEAT BOX** *ZTT ZTPS 02*	51		4
9 Nov 85	**LEGS** *China WOK 5*	69		1
22 Mar 86	**PETER GUNN** *China WOK 6* FEATURING DUANE EDDY	8		9
21 Jun 86	**PARANOIMIA** *China WOK 9* FEATURING MAX HEADROOM	12		9
18 Jul 87	**DRAGNET** *China WOK 14*	60		4
29 Oct 88	**KISS** *China 11* FEATURING TOM JONES	5		7
12 Aug 89	**YEBO** *China 18*	63		3
16 Jun 90	**ART OF LOVE** *China 23*	67		1
11 Jan 92	**INSTRUMENTS OF DARKNESS (ALL OF US ARE ONE PEOPLE)** *China WOK 2012*	45		5
29 Feb 92	**SHADES OF PARANOIMIA** *China WOK 2014*	53		2
26 Jun 99	**METAFORCE** *ZTT 129CD*	53		1

ART OF TRANCE

UK, male producer/instrumentalist (Simon Berry). See Poltergeist, Vicious Circles — 6

Date	Title	Peak Position	Weeks at No.1	Weeks on Chart
31 Oct 98	**MADAGASCAR** *Platipus PLAT 43CD*	69		1
7 Aug 99	**MADAGASCAR (REMIX)** *Platipus PLAT 58CD*	48		2
15 Jun 02	**MADAGASCAR** *Platipus PLATCD 0102*	41		2
10 Aug 02	**LOVE WASHES OVER** *Platipus PLATCD 98*	60		1

ARTEMESIA

Holland, male producer (Patrick Prinz). See Ethics, Movin' Melodies, Subliminal Cuts — 4

Date	Title	Peak Position	Weeks at No.1	Weeks on Chart
15 Apr 95	**BITS + PIECES** *Hooj Choons HOOJ 31CD*	46		2
23 Sep 95	**BITS + PIECES** *Hooj Choons HOOJ 31CD*	75		1
12 Aug 00	**BITS + PIECES (REMIX)** *Tidy Trax TIDT 141CD*	51		1

ARTFUL DODGER

UK, male production/instrumental duo – Peter Devereux & Mark Hill — 71

Date	Title	Peak Position	Weeks at No.1	Weeks on Chart
11 Dec 99	**RE-REWIND THE CROWD SAY BO SELECTA** *Public Demand/Relentless RELENT 1CDS* FEATURING CRAIG DAVID ⊛	2		17
4 Mar 00	**MOVIN TOO FAST** *Locked On/XL Recordings LUX 117CD* & ROMINA JOHNSON ●	2		12
15 Jul 00	**WOMAN TROUBLE** *Public Demand/ffrr FCDP 380* FEATURING ROBBIE CRAIG & CRAIG DAVID	6		10
25 Nov 00	**PLEASE DON'T TURN ME ON** *ffrr FCD 388* FEATURING LIFFORD	4		10
17 Mar 01	**THINK ABOUT ME** *ffrr FCD 394* FEATURING MICHELLE ESCOFFERY	11		8
15 Sep 01	**TWENTYFOURSEVEN** *ffrr FCDP 400* FEATURING MELANIE BLATT	6		9
15 Dec 01	**IT AIN'T ENOUGH** *ffrr/Public Demand FCD 401* DREEM TEEM VERSUS ARTFUL DODGER	20		5

NEIL ARTHUR

UK, male vocalist. See Blancmange — 2

Date	Title	Peak Position	Weeks at No.1	Weeks on Chart
5 Feb 94	**I LOVE I HATE** *Chrysalis CDCHSS 5005*	50		2

ARTIFICIAL FUNK FEATURING NELLIE ETTISON

Denmark, male/female vocal/production duo — 2

Date	Title	Peak Position	Weeks at No.1	Weeks on Chart
22 Mar 03	**TOGETHER** *Skint 82CD*	40		2

ARTIFICIAL INTELLIGENCE

UK, male production duo — 1

Date	Title	Peak Position	Weeks at No.1	Weeks on Chart
21 Aug 04	**UPRISING/THROUGH THE GATE** *V Recordings VRECS001UK*	73		1

ARTISTS AGAINST AIDS WORLDWIDE

US/Ireland, male/female vocal charity ensemble — 12

Date	Title	Peak Position	Weeks at No.1	Weeks on Chart
17 Nov 01	**WHAT'S GOING ON** *Columbia 6721172*	6		12

ARTISTS FOR HAITI

International, male/female vocal charity ensemble — 1

Date	Title	Peak Position	Weeks at No.1	Weeks on Chart
27 Feb 10	**WE ARE THE WORLD 25 FOR HAITI** *We Are The World Foundation US25T9999982*	50		1

ARTISTS STAND UP TO CANCER

US/UK, female vocal charity ensemble — 3

Date	Title	Peak Position	Weeks at No.1	Weeks on Chart
13 Sep 08	**JUST STAND UP!** *Mercury USUG10800682*	26		3

ARTISTS UNITED AGAINST APARTHEID

International, male/female vocal/instrumental charity ensemble — 8

Date	Title	Peak Position	Weeks at No.1	Weeks on Chart
23 Nov 85	**SUN CITY** *Manhattan MT 7*	21		8

A.S.A.P.

UK, male vocal/instrumental group. See Childliners — 4

Date	Title	Peak Position	Weeks at No.1	Weeks on Chart
14 Oct 89	**SILVER AND GOLD** *EMI EM 107*	60		2
3 Feb 90	**DOWN THE WIRE** *EMI EM 131*	67		2

ASCENSION

UK, male production duo. See Chakra, Essence, Lustral, Oxygen featuring Andrea Britton, Space Brothers — 4

Date	Title	Peak Position	Weeks at No.1	Weeks on Chart
5 Jul 97	**SOMEONE** *Perfecto PERF 141CD*	55		1
15 Jul 00	**SOMEONE (REMIX)** *Code Blue BLU 011CD1*	43		2
23 Mar 02	**FOR A LIFETIME** *Xtravaganza XTRAV 20CDS* FEATURING ERIN LORDAN	45		1

ASH

UK, male vocal/instrumental trio – Tim Wheeler, Mark Hamilton & Rick McMurray — 73

Date	Title	Peak Position	Weeks at No.1	Weeks on Chart
1 Apr 95	**KUNG FU** *Infectious INFECT 21CD*	57		1
12 Aug 95	**GIRL FROM MARS** *Infectious INFECT 24CD*	11		5
21 Oct 95	**ANGEL INTERCEPTOR** *Infectious INFECT 27CD*	14		4
27 Apr 96	**GOLDFINGER** *Infectious INFECT 39CD*	5		5
6 Jul 96	**OH YEAH** *Infectious INFECT 41CD*	6		8
25 Oct 97	**A LIFE LESS ORDINARY** *Infectious INFECT 50CD*	10		5
3 Oct 98	**JESUS SAYS** *Infectious INFECT 59CD*	15		4
5 Dec 98	**WILD SURF** *Infectious INFECT 61CDS*	31		2
10 Feb 01	**SHINING LIGHT** *Infectious INFECT 98CDSX*	8		4
14 Apr 01	**BURN BABY BURN** *Infectious INFECT 99CDS*	13		6

Date	Title / Label	Peak Position	Weeks at No.1	Weeks on Chart
21 Jul 01	**SOMETIMES** *Infectious INFEC 101CDS*	21		6
13 Oct 01	**CANDY** *Infectious INFEC 106CDSX*	20		3
12 Jan 02	**THERE'S A STAR** *Infectious INFEC 112CDS*	13		3
7 Sep 02	**ENVY** *Infectious INFECT 119CDSX*	21		2
15 May 04	**ORPHEUS** *Infectious ASH01CD*	13		4
31 Jul 04	**STARCROSSED** *Infectious ASH02CD*	22		5
18 Dec 04	**RENEGADE CAVALCADE** *Atlantic ASH03CD*	33		2
28 Apr 07	**YOU CAN'T HAVE IT ALL** *Infectious ASH05CD*	16		2
30 Jun 07	**POLARIS** *Infectious ASH06CD*	32		1
22 Sep 07	**END OF THE WORLD** *Infectious ASH07CD*	62		1

ASHA
Italy, male/female vocal/production group — 2

Date	Title / Label	Peak Position	Weeks at No.1	Weeks on Chart
8 Jul 95	**JJ TRIBUTE** *ffrreedom TABCD 228*	38		2

ASHANTI
US, female vocalist (Ashanti Douglas) — 109

Date	Title / Label	Peak Position	Weeks at No.1	Weeks on Chart
2 Feb 02	**ALWAYS ON TIME** *Def Jam 5889462* JA RULE FEATURING ASHANTI ★	6		13
25 May 02	**WHAT'S LUV** *Atlantic AT 0128CD* FAT JOE FEATURING ASHANTI	4		8
8 Jun 02	**FOOLISH (IMPORT)** *Mercury 5829372*	68		3
20 Jul 02	**FOOLISH** *Murder Inc 0639942* ★	4		10
12 Oct 02	**DOWN 4 U** *Murder Inc 0639002* IRV GOTTI PRESENTS JA RULE, ASHANTI, CHARLI BALTIMORE & VITA	4		10
23 Nov 02	**HAPPY** *Def Jam 0638242*	13		8
29 Mar 03	**MESMERIZE** *Murder Inc 0779582* JA RULE FEATURING ASHANTI	12		8
28 Jun 03	**ROCK WIT U (AWWW BABY)** *Murder Inc 9808432*	7		10
1 Nov 03	**RAIN ON ME** *Murder Inc 9813177*	19		4
6 Nov 04	**WONDERFUL** *Def Jam 9864606* JA RULE FEATURING R KELLY & ASHANTI	1	1	10
5 Feb 05	**ONLY U** *The Inc 2103786*	2		8
18 Jun 05	**DON'T LET THEM** *The Inc 9882726*	38		2
27 Jan 07	**PAC'S LIFE** *Interscope 1723503* 2PAC FEATURING TI & ASHANTI	21		6
9 Aug 08	**BODY ON ME** *Island 1781914* NELLY FEATURING AKON & ASHANTI	17		9

ASHAYE
UK, male vocalist (Trevor Ashaye) — 3

Date	Title / Label	Peak Position	Weeks at No.1	Weeks on Chart
15 Oct 83	**MICHAEL JACKSON MEDLEY** *Record Shack SOHO 10*	45		3

RICHARD ASHCROFT
UK, male vocalist/multi-instrumentalist. See Verve — 43

Date	Title / Label	Peak Position	Weeks at No.1	Weeks on Chart
15 Apr 00	**A SONG FOR LOVERS** *Hut HUTCD 128*	3		11
24 Jun 00	**MONEY TO BURN** *Hut HUTCD 136*	17		4
23 Sep 00	**C'MON PEOPLE (WE'RE MAKING IT NOW)** *Hut HUTCD 138*	21		3
19 Oct 02	**CHECK THE MEANING** *Hut HUTCD 161*	11		6
18 Jan 03	**SCIENCE OF SILENCE** *Hut HUTCD 163*	14		4
19 Apr 03	**BUY IT IN BOTTLES** *Hut HUTCD 167*	26		2
21 Jan 06	**BREAK THE NIGHT WITH COLOUR** *Parlophone CDR6680*	3		8
29 Apr 06	**MUSIC IS POWER** *Parlophone CDR6688*	20		4
22 Jul 06	**WORDS JUST GET IN THE WAY** *Parlophone CDR6700*	40		1

JOHN ASHER
UK, male TV presenter/vocalist — 6

Date	Title / Label	Peak Position	Weeks at No.1	Weeks on Chart
15 Nov 75	**LET'S TWIST AGAIN** *Creole CR 112*	14		6

ASHFORD & SIMPSON
US, male/female vocal duo – Nickolas Ashford & Valerie Simpson — 22

Date	Title / Label	Peak Position	Weeks at No.1	Weeks on Chart
18 Nov 78	**IT SEEMS TO HANG ON** *Warner Brothers K 17237*	48		4
5 Jan 85	**SOLID** *Capitol CL 345* ●	3		15
20 Apr 85	**BABIES** *Capitol CL 355*	56		3

ASHTON, GARDNER & DYKE
UK, male vocal/instrumental trio – Tony Ashton, Kim Gardner & Roy Dyke — 14

Date	Title / Label	Peak Position	Weeks at No.1	Weeks on Chart
16 Jan 71	**RESURRECTION SHUFFLE** *Capitol CL 15665*	3		14

ASIA
UK, male vocal/instrumental group — 13

Date	Title / Label	Peak Position	Weeks at No.1	Weeks on Chart
3 Jul 82	**HEAT OF THE MOMENT** *Geffen GEF A 2494*	46		5
18 Sep 82	**ONLY TIME WILL TELL** *Geffen GEF A 2228*	54		3
13 Aug 83	**DON'T CRY** *Geffen A 3580*	33		5

ASIA BLUE
UK, female vocal trio — 2

Date	Title / Label	Peak Position	Weeks at No.1	Weeks on Chart
27 Jun 92	**ESCAPING** *Atomic WNR 882*	50		2

ASIAN DUB FOUNDATION
UK, male vocal/instrumental group — 8

Date	Title / Label	Peak Position	Weeks at No.1	Weeks on Chart
21 Feb 98	**FREE SATPAL RAM** *ffrr FCD 326*	56		1
2 May 98	**BUZZIN'** *ffrr FCDP 335*	31		2
4 Jul 98	**BLACK WHITE** *ffrr FCD 337*	52		1
18 Mar 00	**REAL GREAT BRITAIN** *ffrr FCD 376*	41		2
3 Jun 00	**NEW WAY, NEW LIFE** *ffrr FCD 378*	49		1
1 Feb 03	**FORTRESS EUROPE** *Virgin DINSDY 253*	57		1

ASSEMBLY
UK, male production/vocal group – Vince Clarke, Eric Radcliffe & Feargal Sharkey* — 10

Date	Title / Label	Peak Position	Weeks at No.1	Weeks on Chart
12 Nov 83	**NEVER NEVER** *Mute TINY 1* ●	4		10

ASSOCIATES
UK, male vocal/instrumental duo – Billy MacKenzie, d. 22 Jan 1997, & Alan Rankine — 47

Date	Title / Label	Peak Position	Weeks at No.1	Weeks on Chart
20 Feb 82	**PARTY FEARS TWO** *Associates ASC 1*	9		10
8 May 82	**CLUB COUNTRY** *Associates ASC 2*	13		10
7 Aug 82	**LOVE HANGOVER/18 CARAT LOVE AFFAIR** *Associates ASC 3*	21		8
16 Jun 84	**THOSE FIRST IMPRESSIONS** *WEA YZ 6*	43		6
1 Sep 84	**WAITING FOR THE LOVEBOAT** *WEA YZ 16*	53		4
19 Jan 85	**BREAKFAST** *WEA YX 28*	49		6
17 Sep 88	**HEART OF GLASS** *WEA YZ 310*	56		3

ASSOCIATION
US, male vocal/instrumental group — 8

Date	Title / Label	Peak Position	Weeks at No.1	Weeks on Chart
22 May 68	**TIME FOR LIVING** *Warner Brothers WB 7195*	23		8

RICK ASTLEY
UK, male vocalist — 92

Date	Title / Label	Peak Position	Weeks at No.1	Weeks on Chart
8 Aug 87	**NEVER GONNA GIVE YOU UP** *RCA PB 41447* ● ★	1	5	18
31 Oct 87	**WHENEVER YOU NEED SOMEBODY** *RCA PB 41567*	3		12
12 Dec 87	**WHEN I FALL IN LOVE/MY ARMS KEEP MISSING YOU** *RCA PB 41683* ●	2		10
27 Feb 88	**TOGETHER FOREVER** *RCA PB 41817* ★	2		9
24 Sep 88	**SHE WANTS TO DANCE WITH ME** *RCA PB 42189*	6		10
26 Nov 88	**TAKE ME TO YOUR HEART** *RCA PB 42573*	8		10
11 Feb 89	**HOLD ME IN YOUR ARMS** *RCA PB 42615*	10		8
26 Jan 91	**CRY FOR HELP** *RCA PB 44247*	7		7
30 Mar 91	**MOVE RIGHT OUT** *RCA PB 44407*	58		2
29 Jun 91	**NEVER KNEW LOVE** *RCA PB 44737*	70		1
4 Sep 93	**THE ONES YOU LOVE** *RCA 74321160142*	48		2
13 Nov 93	**HOPELESSLY** *RCA 74321175642*	33		2
27 Dec 08	**NEVER GONNA GIVE YOU UP** *RCA GBARL9300135*	73		1

ASTRO TRAX
UK, male/female vocal/production trio — 1

Date	Title / Label	Peak Position	Weeks at No.1	Weeks on Chart
24 Oct 98	**THE ENERGY (FEEL THE VIBE)** *Satellite 74321622052*	74		1

ASWAD
UK, male vocal/instrumental trio – Brinsley Forde, Angus 'Drummie Zeb' Gaye & Tony Robinson — 81

Date	Title / Label	Peak Position	Weeks at No.1	Weeks on Chart
3 Mar 84	**CHASING FOR THE BREEZE** *Island IS 160*	51		3
6 Oct 84	**54-66 (WAS MY NUMBER)** *Island IS 170*	70		3
27 Feb 88	**DON'T TURN AROUND** *Mango IS 341* ●	1	2	12
21 May 88	**GIVE A LITTLE LOVE** *Mango IS 358*	11		8
24 Sep 88	**SET THEM FREE** *Mango IS 383*	70		2
1 Apr 89	**BEAUTY'S ONLY SKIN DEEP** *Mango MNG 105*	31		6
22 Jul 89	**ON AND ON** *Mango MNG 708*	25		8
18 Aug 90	**NEXT TO YOU** *Mango MNG 753*	24		6
17 Nov 90	**SMILE** *Mango MNG 767* FEATURING SWEETIE IRIE	53		2
30 Mar 91	**TOO WICKED (EP)** *Mango MNG 771*	61		2
31 Jul 93	**HOW LONG** *Polydor PZCD 252* YAZZ & ASWAD	31		5
9 Oct 93	**DANCEHALL MOOD** *Bubblin' CDBUBB 1*	48		2
18 Jun 94	**SHINE** *Bubblin' CDBUBB 3* ●	5		14
17 Sep 94	**WARRIORS** *Bubblin' CDBUBB 4*	33		3
18 Feb 95	**YOU'RE NO GOOD** *Bubblin' CDBUBB 5*	35		3
5 Aug 95	**IF I WAS** *Bubblin' CDBUBB 6*	58		1

Silver-selling ○ · Gold-selling ● · Platinum-selling (x multiples) ⊛ · US No.1 ★ · Peak Position · Weeks at No.1 · Weeks on Chart

Date	Title / Label	Peak Position	Weeks at No.1	Weeks on Chart
31 Aug 02	**SHY GUY** *Universal Music TV 0192632*	62		1

AT THE DRIVE-IN
US, male vocal/instrumental group — 3

Date	Title / Label	Peak Position	Weeks at No.1	Weeks on Chart
19 Aug 00	**ONE ARMED SCISSOR** *Grand Royal GR 091CD*	64		1
16 Dec 00	**ROLODEX PROPAGANDA** *Grand Royal/Virgin VUSCD 189*	54		1
24 Mar 01	**INVALID LITTER DEPT** *Grand Royal/Virgin VUSCD 193*	50		1

ATARIS
US, male vocal/instrumental group — 1

Date	Title / Label	Peak Position	Weeks at No.1	Weeks on Chart
11 Oct 03	**THE BOYS OF SUMMER** *Columbia 6743402*	49		1

ATB
Germany, male producer (Andre Tanneberger) — 52

Date	Title / Label	Peak Position	Weeks at No.1	Weeks on Chart
13 Mar 99	**9PM (TILL I COME)** *Ministry Of Sound DATA 1*	68		1
22 May 99	**9PM (TILL I COME) (GERMAN IMPORT)** *Club Tools CLU 66066*	47		5
19 Jun 99	**9PM (TILL I COME) (AUSTRALIAN IMPORT)** *Dancenet DNET 131*	63		1
3 Jul 99	**9PM (TILL I COME)** *Sound Of Ministry MOSCDS 132* ⊛	1	2	15
9 Oct 99	**DON'T STOP (IMPORT)** *Club Tools CLU 66406*	61		2
23 Oct 99	**DON'T STOP** *Sound Of Ministry MOSCDS 134* ○	3		13
25 Mar 00	**KILLER** *Sound Of Ministry MOSCDS 138*	4		9
27 Jan 01	**THE FIELDS OF LOVE** *Club Tools 0124095 CLU* FEATURING YORK	16		4
30 Jun 01	**LET U GO** *Kontour 0117335 KTR*	34		2

ATC
Italy/New Zealand/UK/Australia, male/female vocal group — 4

Date	Title / Label	Peak Position	Weeks at No.1	Weeks on Chart
17 Aug 02	**AROUND THE WORLD (LA LA LA LA)** *Liberty CDATC 001*	15		4

ATEED
Germany, female vocalist — 1

Date	Title / Label	Peak Position	Weeks at No.1	Weeks on Chart
4 Oct 03	**COME TO ME** *Better The Devil BTD 4CD*	56		1

A.T.F.C. PRESENTS ONEPHATDEEVA
UK, male producer (Aydin Hasirci) — 10

Date	Title / Label	Peak Position	Weeks at No.1	Weeks on Chart
30 Oct 99	**IN AND OUT OF MY LIFE** *Defected DFECT 19CDX*	11		5
16 Sep 00	**BAD HABIT** *Defected DFECT 8CDS* FEATURING LISA MILLETT	17		3
9 Feb 02	**SLEEP TALK** *Defected DFECT 43CDS* FEATURING LISA MILLETT	33		2

A.T.G.O.C.
Italy, male instrumentalist/producer (Andrea Mazzali). See Flickman — 2

Date	Title / Label	Peak Position	Weeks at No.1	Weeks on Chart
21 Nov 98	**REPEATED LOVE** *Wonderboy WBOYD 012*	38		2

ATHLETE
UK, male vocal/instrumental group – Joel Pott, Steve Roberts, Tim Wanstall & Cary Willets — 40

Date	Title / Label	Peak Position	Weeks at No.1	Weeks on Chart
29 Jun 02	**YOU GOT THE STYLE** *Parlophone CDATH 001*	37		2
16 Nov 02	**BEAUTIFUL** *Parlophone CDATH 002*	41		1
5 Apr 03	**EL SALVADOR** *Parlophone CDATHS 003*	31		2
5 Jul 03	**WESTSIDE** *Parlophone CDATHS 005*	42		1
4 Oct 03	**YOU GOT THE STYLE** *Parlophone CDATH 006*	42		1
29 Jan 05	**WIRES** *Parlophone CDATHS007*	4		15
7 May 05	**HALF LIGHT** *Parlophone CDATHS008*	16		7
27 Aug 05	**TOURIST** *Parlophone CDATH009*	43		1
26 Nov 05	**TWENTY FOUR HOURS** *Parlophone CDATH010*	42		2
25 Aug 07	**HURRICANE** *Parlophone CDATH011*	31		6
29 Aug 09	**SUPERHUMAN TOUCH** *Fiction 2713982*	71		2

CHET ATKINS
US, male guitarist (Chester Atkins), d. 30 Jun 2001 (age 77) — 2

Date	Title / Label	Peak Position	Weeks at No.1	Weeks on Chart
17 Mar 60	**TEENSVILLE** *RCA 1174*	46		2

ATL
US, male vocal group — 9

Date	Title / Label	Peak Position	Weeks at No.1	Weeks on Chart
29 May 04	**CALLING ALL GIRLS** *Epic 6748272*	12		5
28 Aug 04	**MAKE IT UP WITH LOVE** *Epic 6751102*	21		4

ATLANTA RHYTHM SECTION
US, male vocal/instrumental group — 4

Date	Title / Label	Peak Position	Weeks at No.1	Weeks on Chart
27 Oct 79	**SPOOKY** *Polydor POSP 74*	48		4

ATLANTIC OCEAN
Holland, male production duo — 14

Date	Title / Label	Peak Position	Weeks at No.1	Weeks on Chart
19 Feb 94	**WATERFALL** *Eastern Bloc BLOCCD 001*	22		6
2 Jul 94	**BODY IN MOTION** *Eastern Bloc BLOCCD 009*	15		4
26 Nov 94	**MUSIC IS A PASSION** *Eastern Bloc BLOCCDX 017*	59		1
30 Nov 96	**WATERFALL (REMIX)** *Eastern Bloc BLOC 104CD*	21		3

ATLANTIC STARR
US, male/female vocal/instrumental group – Sharon Bryant, Clifford Archer, Porter Carroll, David, Jonathan & Wayne Lewis — 48

Date	Title / Label	Peak Position	Weeks at No.1	Weeks on Chart
9 Sep 78	**GIMME YOUR LOVIN'** *A&M AMS 7380*	66		3
29 Jun 85	**SILVER SHADOW** *A&M AM 260*	41		6
7 Sep 85	**ONE LOVE** *A&M AM 273*	58		4
15 Mar 86	**SECRET LOVERS** *A&M AM 307*	10		12
24 May 86	**IF YOUR HEART ISN'T IN IT** *A&M AM 319*	48		4
13 Jun 87	**ALWAYS** *Warner Brothers W 8455* ○ ★	3		14
12 Sep 87	**ONE LOVER AT A TIME** *Warner Brothers W 8327*	57		3
27 Aug 94	**EVERYBODY'S GOT SUMMER** *Arista 74321228072*	36		2

ATLANTIS VS AVATAR
UK, male production group — 2

Date	Title / Label	Peak Position	Weeks at No.1	Weeks on Chart
28 Oct 00	**FIJI** *Inferno CDFERN 34*	52		2

ATMOSFEAR
UK, male instrumental group — 7

Date	Title / Label	Peak Position	Weeks at No.1	Weeks on Chart
17 Nov 79	**DANCING IN OUTER SPACE** *MCA 543*	46		7

ATOMIC KITTEN
UK, female vocal group – Natasha Hamilton, Kerry Katona (replaced by Jenny Frost) & Liz McClarnon*. See Girls Of *FHM*, Route One featuring Jenny Frost — 152

Date	Title / Label	Peak Position	Weeks at No.1	Weeks on Chart
11 Dec 99	**RIGHT NOW** *Innocent SINCD 15*	10		9
8 Apr 00	**SEE YA** *Innocent SINCD 17*	6		7
15 Jul 00	**I WANT YOUR LOVE** *Innocent SINDX 18*	10		5
21 Oct 00	**FOLLOW ME** *Innocent SINDX 22*	20		5
10 Feb 01	**WHOLE AGAIN** *Innocent SINDX 24* ⊛	1	4	23
4 Aug 01	**ETERNAL FLAME** *Innocent SINCD 27* ●	1	2	19
1 Jun 02	**IT'S OK** *Innocent SINCD 36* ○	3		13
7 Sep 02	**THE TIDE IS HIGH (GET THE FEELING)** *Innocent SINDX 38* ●	1	3	16
7 Dec 02	**LAST GOODBYE/BE WITH YOU** *Innocent SINDX 42*	2		12
12 Apr 03	**LOVE DOESN'T HAVE TO HURT** *Innocent SINDX 45*	4		10
8 Nov 03	**IF YOU COME TO ME** *Innocent SINDX 50*	3		10
27 Dec 03	**LADIES NIGHT** *Innocent SINDX 53* FEATURING KOOL & THE GANG	8		11
10 Apr 04	**SOMEONE LIKE ME/RIGHT NOW 2004** *Innocent SINDX 60*	8		8
26 Feb 05	**CRADLE** *Innocent SINDX72*	10		4

ATOMIC ROOSTER
UK, male vocal/instrumental group – Vincent Crane, John Cann, Nick Graham, Paul Hammond & Carl Palmer — 25

Date	Title / Label	Peak Position	Weeks at No.1	Weeks on Chart
6 Feb 71	**TOMORROW NIGHT** *B&C CB 131*	11		12
10 Jul 71	**THE DEVIL'S ANSWER** *B&C CB 157*	4		13

WINIFRED ATWELL
Trinidad, female pianist, d. 28 Feb 1983 (age 68) — 117

Date	Title / Label	Peak Position	Weeks at No.1	Weeks on Chart
12 Dec 52	**BRITANNIA RAG** *Decca F 10015*	5		6
15 May 53	**CORONATION RAG** *Decca F 10110*	5		6
25 Sep 53	**FLIRTATION WALTZ** *Decca F 10161*	10		3
4 Dec 53	**LET'S HAVE A PARTY** *Philips PB 213*	2		9
23 Jul 54	**RACHMANINOFF'S 18TH VARIATION ON A THEME BY PAGANINI (THE STORY OF THREE LOVES)** *Philips PB 234*	9		9
26 Nov 54	**LET'S HAVE A PARTY** *Philips PB 213*	14		6
26 Nov 54	**LET'S HAVE ANOTHER PARTY** *Philips PB 268*	1	5	8
4 Nov 55	**LET'S HAVE A DING DONG** *Decca F 10634*	3		10
16 Mar 56	**POOR PEOPLE OF PARIS** *Decca F 10681*	1	3	16
18 May 56	**PORT AU PRINCE** *Decca F 10727* & FRANK CHACKSFIELD	18		6
20 Jul 56	**LEFT BANK** *Decca F 10762*	14		7
26 Oct 56	**MAKE IT A PARTY** *Decca F 10796*	7		12
22 Feb 57	**LET'S ROCK 'N' ROLL** *Decca F 10852*	24		4
6 Dec 57	**LET'S HAVE A BALL** *Decca F 10956*	4		6

Date	Title / Label	Peak Position	Weeks at No.1	Weeks on Chart
7 Aug 59	**THE SUMMER OF SEVENTEENTH DOLL** *Decca F 11143*	24		2
27 Nov 59	**PIANO PARTY** *Decca F 11183*	10		7

AUDIO BULLYS

UK, male vocal/production duo – Tom Dinsdale & Simon Franks — Weeks on Chart: 30

Date	Title / Label	Peak Position	Weeks at No.1	Weeks on Chart
18 Jan 03	**WE DON'T CARE** *Source SOURCD 061*	15		3
31 May 03	**THE THINGS/TURNED AWAY** *Source SOURCDX 084*	22		3
26 Jun 04	**BREAK DOWN THE DOORS** *Subliminal SUB124CD* MORILLO FEATURING THE AUDIO BULLYS	44		2
4 Jun 05	**SHOT YOU DOWN** *Source SOURCDX111* FEATURING NANCY SINATRA	3		17
5 Nov 05	**I'M IN LOVE** *Source SOURCD113*	27		3
3 Apr 10	**ONLY MAN** *Cooking Vinyl BULLYCDS2*	44		2+

AUDIOSLAVE

US, male vocal/instrumental group — Weeks on Chart: 4

Date	Title / Label	Peak Position	Weeks at No.1	Weeks on Chart
1 Feb 03	**COCHISE** *Epic/Interscope 6732762*	24		3
18 Jun 05	**BE YOURSELF** *Epic/Interscope 9882599*	40		1

AUDIOWEB

UK, male vocal/instrumental group — Weeks on Chart: 12

Date	Title / Label	Peak Position	Weeks at No.1	Weeks on Chart
14 Oct 95	**SLEEPER** *Mother MUMCD 69*	74		1
9 Mar 96	**YEAH** *Mother MUMCD 72*	73		1
15 Jun 96	**INTO MY WORLD** *Mother MUMCD 76*	42		1
19 Oct 96	**SLEEPER (REMIX)** *Mother MUMCD 78*	50		2
15 Feb 97	**BANKROBBER** *Mother MUMCD 85*	19		2
24 May 97	**FAKER** *Mother MUMCD 91*	70		1
25 Apr 98	**POLICEMAN SKANK...(THE STORY OF MY LIFE)** *Mother MUMCD 100*	21		2
4 Jul 98	**PERSONAL FEELING** *Mother MUMCD 104*	65		1
20 Feb 99	**TEST THE THEORY** *Mother MUMCD 110*	56		1

AUF DER MAUR

Canada, female vocalist/guitarist (Melissa Auf Der Maur). See Smashing Pumpkins — Weeks on Chart: 5

Date	Title / Label	Peak Position	Weeks at No.1	Weeks on Chart
28 Feb 04	**FOLLOWED THE WAVES** *EMI CDEM 635*	35		2
15 May 04	**REAL A LIE** *EMI CDEMS 642*	33		2
9 Oct 04	**TASTE YOU** *EMI CDEM 650*	51		1

AURORA

UK, male production duo. See Dive — Weeks on Chart: 19

Date	Title / Label	Peak Position	Weeks at No.1	Weeks on Chart
5 Jun 99	**HEAR YOU CALLING** *Addictive 12AD 040*	71		1
5 Feb 00	**HEAR YOU CALLING** *Positiva CDTIV 124*	17		4
23 Sep 00	**ORDINARY WORLD** *Positiva CDTIV 139* FEATURING NAIMEE COLEMAN	5		7
13 Apr 02	**DREAMING** *EMI CDEM 611*	24		4
6 Jul 02	**THE DAY IT RAINED FOREVER** *EMI CDEMS 613*	29		3

AURRA

US, male/female vocal duo — Weeks on Chart: 18

Date	Title / Label	Peak Position	Weeks at No.1	Weeks on Chart
4 May 85	**LIKE I LIKE IT** *10 TEN 45*	51		5
19 Apr 86	**YOU AND ME TONIGHT** *10 TEN 71*	12		8
21 Jun 86	**LIKE I LIKE IT** *10 TEN 126*	43		5

ADAM AUSTIN

UK, male vocalist — Weeks on Chart: 1

Date	Title / Label	Peak Position	Weeks at No.1	Weeks on Chart
13 Feb 99	**CENTERFOLD** *Media PSRCA 0107*	41		1

DAVID AUSTIN

UK, male vocalist — Weeks on Chart: 3

Date	Title / Label	Peak Position	Weeks at No.1	Weeks on Chart
21 Jul 84	**TURN TO GOLD** *Parlophone R 6068*	68		3

PATTI AUSTIN

US, female vocalist — Weeks on Chart: 20

Date	Title / Label	Peak Position	Weeks at No.1	Weeks on Chart
20 Jun 81	**RAZZAMATAZZ** *A&M 8140* QUINCY JONES FEATURING PATTI AUSTIN	11		9
12 Feb 83	**BABY COME TO ME** *Qwest K 15005* & JAMES INGRAM ★	11		10
5 Sep 92	**I'LL KEEP YOUR DREAMS ALIVE** *Ammi 101* GEORGE BENSON & PATTI AUSTIN	68		1

AUTECHRE

UK, male production duo — Weeks on Chart: 1

Date	Title / Label	Peak Position	Weeks at No.1	Weeks on Chart
7 May 94	**BASSCAD** *Warp WAP 44CD*	56		1

AUTEURS

UK, male/female vocal/instrumental group — Weeks on Chart: 9

Date	Title / Label	Peak Position	Weeks at No.1	Weeks on Chart
27 Nov 93	**LENNY VALENTINO** *Hut HUTCD 36*	41		2
23 Apr 94	**CHINESE BAKERY** *Hut HUTDX 41*	42		2
6 Jan 96	**BACK WITH THE KILLER AGAIN** *Hut HUTCD 65*	45		3
24 Feb 96	**LIGHT AIRCRAFT ON FIRE** *Hut HUTCD 66*	58		1
3 Jul 99	**THE RUBETTES** *Hut HUTCD 113*	66		1

AUTOMATIC

UK, male vocal/instrumental group – Robin Hawkins, James Frost, Iwan Griffiths & Alex Pennie (replaced by Paul Mullen) — Weeks on Chart: 28

Date	Title / Label	Peak Position	Weeks at No.1	Weeks on Chart
8 Apr 06	**RAOUL** *B Unique/Polydor BUN104CD*	32		1
10 Jun 06	**MONSTER** *B Unique/Polydor BUN106CD*	4		16
30 Sep 06	**RECOVER** *B Unique/Polydor BUN110CDX*	25		3
20 Jan 07	**RAOUL** *B Unique/Polydor BUN117CDX*	30		3
30 Aug 08	**STEVE McQUEEN** *B Unique/Polydor BUN139CD*	16		5

AUTUMN

UK, male vocal/instrumental group — Weeks on Chart: 6

Date	Title / Label	Peak Position	Weeks at No.1	Weeks on Chart
16 Oct 71	**MY LITTLE GIRL** *Pye 7N 45090*	37		6

PETER AUTY

UK, male vocalist & orchestra — Weeks on Chart: 9

Date	Title / Label	Peak Position	Weeks at No.1	Weeks on Chart
14 Dec 85	**WALKING IN THE AIR** *Stiff LAD 1* & THE SINFONIA OF LONDON	42		5
19 Dec 87	**WALKING IN THE AIR** *CBS GA 3950* & THE SINFONIA OF LONDON	37		4

AVALANCHES

Australia, male production group — Weeks on Chart: 12

Date	Title / Label	Peak Position	Weeks at No.1	Weeks on Chart
7 Apr 01	**SINCE I LEFT YOU** *XL Recordings XLS 128CD*	16		7
21 Jul 01	**FRONTIER PSYCHIATRIST** *XL Recordings XLS 134CD1*	18		5

FRANKIE AVALON

US, male vocalist (Francis Avallone) — Weeks on Chart: 15

Date	Title / Label	Peak Position	Weeks at No.1	Weeks on Chart
10 Oct 58	**GINGERBREAD** *HMV POP 517*	30		1
24 Apr 59	**VENUS** *HMV POP 603* ★	16		6
22 Jan 60	**WHY** *HMV POP 688* ★	20		4
28 Apr 60	**DON'T THROW AWAY ALL THOSE TEARDROPS** *HMV POP 727*	37		4

AVENGED SEVENFOLD

US, male vocal/instrumental group — Weeks on Chart: 2

Date	Title / Label	Peak Position	Weeks at No.1	Weeks on Chart
18 Mar 06	**BEAST AND THE HARLOT** *Warner Brothers W705CD1*	47		1
27 Oct 07	**ALMOST EASY** *Warner Brothers W785CD*	67		1

AVENUE

UK, male vocal group — Weeks on Chart: 1

Date	Title / Label	Peak Position	Weeks at No.1	Weeks on Chart
4 Oct 08	**LAST GOODBYE** *Island 1783187*	50		1

AVERAGE WHITE BAND

UK, male vocal/instrumental group – Onnie McIntyre, Roger Ball, Malcolm Duncan, Alan Gorrie, Robbie McIntosh, d. 23 Sep 1974 (replaced by Steve Ferrone), & Hamish Stuart — Weeks on Chart: 47

Date	Title / Label	Peak Position	Weeks at No.1	Weeks on Chart
22 Feb 75	**PICK UP THE PIECES** *Atlantic K 10489* ★	6		9
26 Apr 75	**CUT THE CAKE** *Atlantic K 10605*	31		4
9 Oct 76	**QUEEN OF MY SOUL** *Atlantic K 10825*	23		7
28 Apr 79	**WALK ON BY** *RCA XC 1087*	46		5
25 Aug 79	**WHEN WILL YOU BE MINE** *RCA XB 1096*	49		5
26 Apr 80	**LET'S GO ROUND AGAIN PART 1** *RCA AWB 1*	12		11
26 Jul 80	**FOR YOU FOR LOVE** *RCA AWB 2*	46		4
26 Mar 94	**LET'S GO ROUND AGAIN (REMIX)** *The Hit Label HLC 5*	56		2

KEVIN AVIANCE

US, male vocalist — Weeks on Chart: 1

Date	Title / Label	Peak Position	Weeks at No.1	Weeks on Chart
13 Jun 98	**DIN DA DA** *Distinctive DISNCD 42*	65		1

AVONS

UK, male/female vocal trio – Ray Adams, Valerie & Eileen Murtagh — 22

Date	Title	Peak Position	Weeks at No.1	Weeks on Chart
13 Nov 59	**SEVEN LITTLE GIRLS SITTING IN THE BACK SEAT** *Columbia DB 4363*	3		13
7 Jul 60	**WE'RE ONLY YOUNG ONCE** *Columbia DB 4461*	45		2
27 Oct 60	**FOUR LITTLE HEELS** *Columbia DB 4522*	45		3
26 Jan 61	**RUBBER BALL** *Columbia DB 4569*	30		4

AWESOME

UK, male vocal group — 2

Date	Title	Peak Position	Weeks at No.1	Weeks on Chart
8 Nov 97	**RUMOURS** *Universal MCSTD 40145*	58		1
21 Mar 98	**CRAZY** *Universal MCSTD 40195*	63		1

AWESOME 3

UK, male production group — 8

Date	Title	Peak Position	Weeks at No.1	Weeks on Chart
8 Sep 90	**HARD UP** *A&M AM 591*	55		3
3 Oct 92	**DON'T GO** *Citybeat CBE 1271*	75		1
4 Jun 94	**DON'T GO (REMIX)** *Citybeat CBX 771CD*	45		2
26 Oct 96	**DON'T GO (2ND REMIX)** *XL Recordings XLS 78CD* FEATURING JULIE McDERMOTT	27		2

HOYT AXTON

US, male vocalist, d. 26 Oct 1999 (age 61) — 4

Date	Title	Peak Position	Weeks at No.1	Weeks on Chart
7 Jun 80	**DELLA AND THE DEALER** *Young Blood YB 82*	48		4

AXUS

Canada, male DJ/producer (Austin Bascom) — 1

Date	Title	Peak Position	Weeks at No.1	Weeks on Chart
26 Sep 98	**ABACUS (WHEN I FELL IN LOVE)** *INCredible INCRL 8CD*	62		1

AXWELL

Sweden, male DJ/producer (Axel Hedfors). See Supermode — 14

Date	Title	Peak Position	Weeks at No.1	Weeks on Chart
20 Aug 05	**FEEL THE VIBE (TIL THE MORNING COMES)** *Data DATA85CDS*	16		4
30 Sep 06	**WATCH THE SUNRISE** *Positiva CDTIV243* FEATURING STEVE EDWARDS	70		1
18 Aug 07	**I FOUND U** *Positiva CDTIV261* FEATURING MAX C	6		8
11 Oct 08	**WHAT A WONDERFUL WORLD** *Defected/ Positiva CDTIV275* & BOB SINCLAR FEATURING RON CARROLL	48		1

ROY AYERS

US, male vocalist/vibraphone player — 13

Date	Title	Peak Position	Weeks at No.1	Weeks on Chart
21 Oct 78	**GET ON UP, GET ON DOWN** *Polydor AYERS 7*	41		4
13 Jan 79	**HEAT OF THE BEAT** *Polydor POSP 16* & WAYNE HENDERSON	43		5
2 Feb 80	**DON'T STOP THE FEELING** *Polydor STEP 6*	56		3
16 May 98	**EXPANSIONS** *Soma Recordings SOMA 65CDS* SCOTT GROOVES FEATURING ROY AYERS	68		1

AYLA

Germany, male producer (Ingo Kunzi) — 3

Date	Title	Peak Position	Weeks at No.1	Weeks on Chart
4 Sep 99	**AYLA** *Positiva CDTIV 117*	22		3

AZ

US, male rapper (Anthony Cruz) — 1

Date	Title	Peak Position	Weeks at No.1	Weeks on Chart
30 Mar 96	**SUGARHILL** *Cooltempo CDCOOL 315*	67		1

AZ YET

US, male vocal group – Dion Allen, Darryl Anthony, Marc Nelson (replaced by Tony Grant), Shawn Rivera & Kenny Terry — 10

Date	Title	Peak Position	Weeks at No.1	Weeks on Chart
1 Mar 97	**LAST NIGHT** *LaFace 74321423202*	21		3
21 Jun 97	**HARD TO SAY I'M SORRY** *LaFace 74321481482* FEATURING PETER CETERA	7		7

CHARLES AZNAVOUR

France, male vocalist (Shanaur Aznavourian) — 29

Date	Title	Peak Position	Weeks at No.1	Weeks on Chart
22 Sep 73	**THE OLD FASHIONED WAY** *Barclay BAR 20*	38		15
22 Jun 74	**SHE** *Barclay BAR 26* (silver)	1	4	14

AZTEC CAMERA

UK, male vocal/instrumental group – Roddy Frame* & various session musicians — 72

Date	Title	Peak Position	Weeks at No.1	Weeks on Chart
19 Feb 83	**OBLIVIOUS** *Rough Trade RT 122*	47		6
4 Jun 83	**WALK OUT TO WINTER** *Rough Trade RT 132*	64		4
5 Nov 83	**OBLIVIOUS** *WEA AZTEC 1*	18		11
1 Sep 84	**ALL I NEED IS EVERYTHING/JUMP** *WEA AC 1*	34		6
13 Feb 88	**HOW MEN ARE** *WEA YZ 168*	25		9
23 Apr 88	**SOMEWHERE IN MY HEART** *WEA YZ 181*	3		14
6 Aug 88	**WORKING IN A GOLDMINE** *WEA YZ 199*	31		5
8 Oct 88	**DEEP AND WIDE AND TALL** *WEA YZ 154*	55		3
7 Jul 90	**THE CRYING SCENE** *WEA YZ 492*	70		3
6 Oct 90	**GOOD MORNING BRITAIN** *WEA YZ 521* & MICK JONES	19		6
18 Jul 92	**SPANISH HORSES** *WEA YZ 688*	52		3
1 May 93	**DREAM SWEET DREAMS** *WEA YZ 740CD1*	67		2

AZURE

Italy/US, male/female vocal/DJ duo — 1

Date	Title	Peak Position	Weeks at No.1	Weeks on Chart
25 Apr 98	**MAMA USED TO SAY** *Inferno CDFERN 005*	56		1

AZYMUTH

Brazil, male instrumental trio — 8

Date	Title	Peak Position	Weeks at No.1	Weeks on Chart
12 Jan 80	**JAZZ CARNIVAL** *Milestone MRC 101*	19		8

BOB AZZAM & HIS ORCHESTRA

Egypt, orchestra – leader Bob Azzam (Wadih Azzam), d. 24 Jul 2004 (age 78) — 14

Date	Title	Peak Position	Weeks at No.1	Weeks on Chart
26 May 60	**MUSTAPHA** *Decca F 21235*	23		14

DEREK B

UK, male rapper (Derek Boland) — 15

Date	Title	Peak Position	Weeks at No.1	Weeks on Chart
27 Feb 88	**GOODGROOVE** *Music Of Life 7NOTE 12*	16		6
7 May 88	**BAD YOUNG BROTHER** *Tuff Audio DRKB 1*	16		6
2 Jul 88	**WE'VE GOT THE JUICE** *Tuff Audio DRKB 2*	56		3

ERIC B & RAKIM

US, male DJ/rap duo — 26

Date	Title	Peak Position	Weeks at No.1	Weeks on Chart
7 Nov 87	**PAID IN FULL** *Fourth & Broadway BRW 78*	15		6
20 Feb 88	**MOVE THE CROWD** *Fourth & Broadway BRW 88*	53		2
12 Mar 88	**I KNOW YOU GOT SOUL** *Cooltempo COOL 146*	13		6
2 Jul 88	**FOLLOW THE LEADER** *MCA 1256*	21		5
19 Nov 88	**THE MICROPHONE FIEND** *MCA 1300*	74		1
12 Aug 89	**FRIENDS** *MCA 1352* JODY WATLEY WITH ERIC B & RAKIM	21		6

HOWIE B

UK, male producer (Howard Bernstein) — 4

Date	Title	Peak Position	Weeks at No.1	Weeks on Chart
19 Jul 97	**ANGELS GO BALD: TOO** *Polydor 5711672*	36		2
18 Oct 97	**SWITCH** *Polydor 5717112*	62		1
11 Apr 98	**TAKE YOUR PARTNER BY THE HAND** *Polydor 5693272* FEATURING ROBBIE ROBERTSON	74		1

JOHN B

UK, male producer (John Bryn Williams) — 1

Date	Title	Peak Position	Weeks at No.1	Weeks on Chart
22 Jun 02	**UP ALL NIGHT/TAKE CONTROL** *Metalheadz METH 041CD*	58		1

JON B

US, male vocalist (Jonathan Buck) — 6

Date	Title	Peak Position	Weeks at No.1	Weeks on Chart
17 Oct 98	**THEY DON'T KNOW** *Epic 6663975*	32		2
26 May 01	**DON'T TALK** *Epic 6712792*	29		3
19 Mar 05	**LATELY** *Sanctuary Urban SANXS357*	68		1

LISA B

US, female vocalist/model (Lisa Barbuscia) — 9

Date	Title	Peak Position	Weeks at No.1	Weeks on Chart
12 Jun 93	**GLAM** *ffrr FCD 210*	49		2
25 Sep 93	**FASCINATED** *ffrr FCD 218*	35		3
8 Jan 94	**YOU AND ME** *ffrr FCD 226*	39		4

LORNA B

UK, female vocalist (Lorna Bannon) — Total weeks: 6

Date	Title	Peak Position	Weeks at No.1	Weeks on Chart
28 Jan 95	**DO YOU WANNA PARTY** *Steppin' Out SPONCD 2* DJ SCOTT FEATURING LORNA B	36		3
1 Apr 95	**SWEET DREAMS** *Steppin' Out SPONCD 3* DJ SCOTT FEATURING LORNA B	37		2
15 Mar 97	**FEELS SO GOOD** *Avex UK AVEXCD 53* ZERO VU FEATURING LORNA B	69		1

MARK B & BLADE

UK, male rap/production duo — Total weeks: 5

Date	Title	Peak Position	Weeks at No.1	Weeks on Chart
10 Feb 01	**THE UNKNOWN** *Wordplay WORDCDS 011*	49		1
26 May 01	**YA DON'T SEE THE SIGNS** *Wordplay WORDCDSE 019*	23		3
25 Sep 04	**MOVE NOW** *Genuine GEN033CD* MARK B FEATURING TOMMY EVANS	61		1

MELANIE B

UK, female vocalist (Melanie Brown). See Spice Girls — Total weeks: 37

Date	Title	Peak Position	Weeks at No.1	Weeks on Chart
26 Sep 98	**I WANT YOU BACK** *Virgin VSCDT 1716* FEATURING MISSY 'MISDEMEANOR' ELLIOTT ○	1	1	9
10 Jul 99	**WORD UP** *Virgin VSCDT 1748* MELANIE G	14		8
7 Oct 00	**TELL ME** *Virgin VSCDX 1777*	4		7
3 Mar 01	**FEELS SO GOOD** *Virgin VSCDT 1787*	5		8
16 Jun 01	**LULLABY** *Virgin VSCDT 1798*	13		4
25 Jun 05	**TODAY** *Amber Cafe AMBER003* MELANIE BROWN	41		1

SANDY B

US, female vocalist (Sandra Barber) — Total weeks: 11

Date	Title	Peak Position	Weeks at No.1	Weeks on Chart
20 Feb 93	**FEEL LIKE SINGIN'** *Nervous SANCD 1*	60		1
18 May 96	**MAKE THE WORLD GO ROUND** *Champion CHAMPCD 322*	73		1
24 May 97	**MAKE THE WORLD GO ROUND (REMIX)** *Champion CHAMPCD 327*	35		2
8 Nov 97	**AIN'T NO NEED TO HIDE** *Champion CHAMPCD 331*	60		1
28 Feb 98	**MAKE THE WORLD GO ROUND (2ND REMIX)** *Champion CHAMPCD 333*	20		3
1 May 04	**MAKE THE WORLD GO ROUND 2004** *Champion CHAMPCD 780*	51		3

STEVIE B

US, male vocalist (Steven Hill) — Total weeks: 9

Date	Title	Peak Position	Weeks at No.1	Weeks on Chart
23 Feb 91	**BECAUSE I LOVE YOU (THE POSTMAN SONG)** *Polydor PO 126* ★	6		9

TAIRRIE B

US, female rapper/vocalist (Theresa Beth) — Total weeks: 2

Date	Title	Peak Position	Weeks at No.1	Weeks on Chart
1 Dec 90	**MURDER SHE WROTE** *MCA 1455*	71		2

BB & Q BAND

US, male vocal/instrumental group — Total weeks: 15

Date	Title	Peak Position	Weeks at No.1	Weeks on Chart
18 Jul 81	**ON THE BEAT** *Capitol CL 202*	41		5
6 Jul 85	**GENIE** *Cooltempo COOL 110* BROOKLYN BRONX & QUEENS	40		4
20 Sep 86	**(I'M A) DREAMER** *Cooltempo COOL 132*	35		5
17 Oct 87	**RICOCHET** *Cooltempo COOL 154*	71		1

B. BUMBLE & THE STINGERS

US, male session musicians — Total weeks: 26

Date	Title	Peak Position	Weeks at No.1	Weeks on Chart
19 Apr 62	**NUT ROCKER** *Top Rank JAR 611*	1	1	15
3 Jun 72	**NUT ROCKER** *Stateside SS 2203*	19		11

B-CREW

US, female vocal group — Total weeks: 1

Date	Title	Peak Position	Weeks at No.1	Weeks on Chart
20 Sep 97	**PARTAY FEELING** *Positiva CDTIV 78*	45		1

B-15 PROJECT FEATURING CHRISSY D & LADY G

UK/Jamaica, male/female vocal/production group — Total weeks: 10

Date	Title	Peak Position	Weeks at No.1	Weeks on Chart
17 Jun 00	**GIRLS LIKE US** *Ministry Of Sound RELENT 3CDS*	7		10

B-52's

US, female/male vocal/instrumental group – Kate Pierson, Fred Schneider, Keith Strickland, Cindy Wilson & Ricky Wilson, d. 12 Oct 1985 — Total weeks: 61

Date	Title	Peak Position	Weeks at No.1	Weeks on Chart
11 Aug 79	**ROCK LOBSTER** *Island WIP 6506*	37		5
9 Aug 80	**GIVE ME BACK MY MAN** *Island WIP 6579*	61		3
7 May 83	**(SONG FOR A) FUTURE GENERATION** *Island IS 107*	63		2
10 May 86	**ROCK LOBSTER/PLANET CLAIRE** *Island BFT 1*	12		7
3 Mar 90	**LOVE SHACK** *Reprise W 9917* ○	2		13
19 May 90	**ROAM** *Reprise W 9827*	17		7
18 Aug 90	**CHANNEL Z** *Reprise W 9737*	61		2
20 Jun 92	**GOOD STUFF** *Reprise W 0109*	21		6
12 Sep 92	**TELL IT LIKE IT T-I-IS** *Reprise W 0130*	61		3
9 Jul 94	**(MEET) THE FLINTSTONES** *MCA MCSTD 1986* BC-52's	3		12
30 Jan 99	**LOVE SHACK 99** *Reprise W 0461CD*	66		1

B-MOVIE

UK, male vocal/instrumental group — Total weeks: 7

Date	Title	Peak Position	Weeks at No.1	Weeks on Chart
18 Apr 81	**REMEMBERANCE DAY** *Deram DM 437*	61		3
27 Mar 82	**NOWHERE GIRL** *Some Bizzare BZZ 8*	67		4

B REAL/BUSTA RHYMES/COOLIO/LL COOL J/ METHOD MAN

US, male rap group. See Cypress Hill — Total weeks: 6

Date	Title	Peak Position	Weeks at No.1	Weeks on Chart
5 Apr 97	**HIT 'EM HIGH (THE MONSTARS' ANTHEM)** *Atlantic A 5449CD*	8		6

B-TRIBE

Germany, male production trio. See NT Gang, Sacred Spirit — Total weeks: 4

Date	Title	Peak Position	Weeks at No.1	Weeks on Chart
25 Sep 93	**!FIESTA FATAL!** *East West YZ 770CD*	64		4

B*WITCHED

Ireland, female vocal group – Edele & Keavy Lynch, Lindsay Armaou & Sinéad O'Carroll — Total weeks: 85

Date	Title	Peak Position	Weeks at No.1	Weeks on Chart
6 Jun 98	**C'EST LA VIE** *Glow Worm 6660532* ⊛	1	2	19
3 Oct 98	**ROLLERCOASTER** *Glow Worm 6664752* ●	1	2	15
19 Dec 98	**TO YOU I BELONG** *Glow Worm 6667712* ●	1	1	14
27 Mar 99	**BLAME IT ON THE WEATHERMAN** *Glow Worm 6670335* ○	1	1	9
16 Oct 99	**JESSE HOLD ON** *Glow Worm 6679612*	4		12
18 Dec 99	**I SHALL BE THERE** *Glow Worm 6683332* FEATURING LADYSMITH BLACK MAMBAZO	13		9
8 Apr 00	**JUMP DOWN** *Glow Worm 6691285*	16		7

BABE INSTINCT

UK, female vocal group — Total weeks: 2

Date	Title	Peak Position	Weeks at No.1	Weeks on Chart
16 Jan 99	**DISCO BABES FROM OUTER SPACE** *Positiva CDTIV 103*	21		2

BABE TEAM

UK, female vocal group — Total weeks: 2

Date	Title	Peak Position	Weeks at No.1	Weeks on Chart
8 Jun 02	**OVER THERE** *Blacklist 0140695 ERE*	45		2

ALICE BABS

Sweden, female vocalist (Alice Nilsson) — Total weeks: 1

Date	Title	Peak Position	Weeks at No.1	Weeks on Chart
15 Aug 63	**AFTER YOU'VE GONE** *Fontana TF 409*	43		1

BABY BUMPS

UK, male/female vocal/instrumental duo — Total weeks: 6

Date	Title	Peak Position	Weeks at No.1	Weeks on Chart
8 Aug 98	**BURNING** *Delirious DELICD 10*	17		4
26 Feb 00	**I GOT THIS FEELING** *Sound Of Ministry MOSCDS 137*	22		2

BABY D

UK, male/female vocal/production group – Dee Galdes-Fearon, Floyd Dice, Claudio Galdes & Terry Jones — Total weeks: 45

Date	Title	Peak Position	Weeks at No.1	Weeks on Chart
18 Dec 93	**DESTINY** *Production House PNC 057*	69		1
23 Jul 94	**CASANOVA** *Production House PNC 065*	67		1
19 Nov 94	**LET ME BE YOUR FANTASY** *Systematic SYSCD 4* ●	1	2	14
3 Jun 95	**(EVERYBODY'S GOT TO LEARN SOMETIME) I NEED YOUR LOVING** *Systematic SYSCD 11* ○	3		12
13 Jan 96	**SO PURE** *Systematic SYSCD 21*	3		7
6 Apr 96	**TAKE ME TO HEAVEN** *Systematic SYSCD 26*	15		5
2 Sep 00	**LET ME BE YOUR FANTASY (REMIX)** *Systematic SYSCD 35*	16		5

BABY DC FEATURING IMAJIN

US, male vocal/rap group — Weeks on Chart: 1

Date	Title	Peak Position	Weeks at No.1	Weeks on Chart
24 Apr 99	**BOUNCE, ROCK, SKATE, ROLL** *Jive 0522142*	45		1

BABY FORD

UK, male producer/vocalist (Peter Ford) — Weeks on Chart: 16

Date	Title	Peak Position	Weeks at No.1	Weeks on Chart
10 Sep 88	**OOCHY KOOCHY (F.U. BABY YEAH YEAH)** *Rhythm King 7BFORD 1*	58		6
24 Dec 88	**CHIKKI CHIKKI AHH AHH** *Rhythm King 7BFORD 2*	54		4
17 Jun 89	**CHILDREN OF THE REVOLUTION** *Rhythm King 7BFORD 4*	53		4
17 Feb 90	**BEACH BUMP** *Rhythm King 7BFORD 6*	68		2

BABY JUNE

UK, male producer (Tim Hegarty) — Weeks on Chart: 1

Date	Title	Peak Position	Weeks at No.1	Weeks on Chart
15 Aug 92	**HEY! WHAT'S YOUR NAME** *Arista 115271*	75		1

BABY O

US, male/female vocal/instrumental group — Weeks on Chart: 5

Date	Title	Peak Position	Weeks at No.1	Weeks on Chart
26 Jul 80	**IN THE FOREST** *Calibre CAB 505*	46		5

BABYROOTS

UK, female vocalist (Sandra Chambers) — Weeks on Chart: 1

Date	Title	Peak Position	Weeks at No.1	Weeks on Chart
1 Aug 92	**ROCK ME BABY** *ZYX 68027*	71		1

BABYBIRD

UK, male vocal/instrumental group – Stephen Jones, Huw Chadbourn, Robert Gregory, John Pedder & Luke Scott — Weeks on Chart: 35

Date	Title	Peak Position	Weeks at No.1	Weeks on Chart
10 Aug 96	**GOODNIGHT** *Echo ECSCD 24*	28		2
12 Oct 96	**YOU'RE GORGEOUS** *Echo ECSCD 26* ●	3		16
1 Feb 97	**CANDY GIRL** *Echo ECSCD 31*	14		3
17 May 97	**CORNERSHOP** *Echo ECSCD 33*	37		2
9 May 98	**BAD OLD MAN** *Echo ECSCD 60*	31		2
22 Aug 98	**IF YOU'LL BE MINE** *Echo ECSCX 65*	28		4
27 Feb 99	**BACK TOGETHER** *Echo ECSCD 73*	22		3
25 Mar 00	**THE F-WORD** *Echo ECSCD 92*	35		2
3 Jun 00	**OUT OF SIGHT** *Echo ECSCD 97*	58		1

BABYFACE

US, male vocalist/producer (Kenneth Edmonds) — Weeks on Chart: 23

Date	Title	Peak Position	Weeks at No.1	Weeks on Chart
9 Jul 94	**ROCK BOTTOM** *Epic 6601832*	50		4
1 Oct 94	**WHEN CAN I SEE YOU** *Epic 6606592*	35		3
9 Nov 96	**THIS IS FOR THE LOVER IN YOU** *Epic 6639352*	12		5
8 Mar 97	**EVERYTIME I CLOSE MY EYES** *Epic 6642492*	13		4
19 Jul 97	**HOW COME, HOW LONG** *Epic 6646202* FEATURING STEVIE WONDER	10		5
25 Oct 97	**SUNSHINE** *Northwestside 74321528702* JAY-Z FEATURING BABYFACE & FOXY BROWN	25		2

BABYLON ZOO

UK, male vocalist/multi-instrumentalist (Jas Mann) — Weeks on Chart: 20

Date	Title	Peak Position	Weeks at No.1	Weeks on Chart
27 Jan 96	**SPACEMAN** *EMI CDEM 416* ⊛	1	5	14
27 Apr 96	**ANIMAL ARMY** *EMI CDEM 425*	17		3
5 Oct 96	**THE BOY WITH X-RAY EYES** *EMI CDEMS 440*	32		2
6 Feb 99	**ALL THE MONEY'S GONE** *EMI CDEM 519*	46		1

BABYS

UK, male/female vocal/instrumental group — Weeks on Chart: 3

Date	Title	Peak Position	Weeks at No.1	Weeks on Chart
21 Jan 78	**ISN'T IT TIME** *Chrysalis CHS 2173*	45		3

BABYSHAMBLES

UK, male vocal/instrumental group – Pete Doherty*, Adam Ficek, Drew McConnell & Mick Whitnall. See Libertines, Littl'ans featuring Pete Doherty, Wolfman — Weeks on Chart: 25

Date	Title	Peak Position	Weeks at No.1	Weeks on Chart
11 Dec 04	**KILLAMANGIRO** *Rough Trade RTRADSCD201*	8		8
27 Aug 05	**FUCK FOREVER** *Rough Trade RTRADSCDX210*	4		5
10 Dec 05	**ALBION** *Rough Trade TRADSCD260*	8		4
11 Nov 06	**JANIE JONES (STRUMMERVILLE)** *B Unique BUN116CD* & FRIENDS	17		3
29 Sep 07	**DELIVERY** *Parlophone CDRS6747*	6		4
15 Dec 07	**YOU TALK** *Parlophone CDRS6750*	54		1

BACCARA

Spain, female duo – Maria Mendiola & Mayte Mateos — Weeks on Chart: 25

Date	Title	Peak Position	Weeks at No.1	Weeks on Chart
17 Sep 77	**YES SIR I CAN BOOGIE** *RCA PB 5526* ●	1	1	16
14 Jan 78	**SORRY I'M A LADY** *RCA PB 5555* ○	8		9

BURT BACHARACH

US, male pianist — Weeks on Chart: 12

Date	Title	Peak Position	Weeks at No.1	Weeks on Chart
20 May 65	**TRAINS AND BOATS AND PLANES** *London HL 9968*	4		11
1 May 99	**TOLEDO** *Mercury 8709652* ELVIS COSTELLO/BURT BACHARACH	72		1

BACHELORS

Ireland, male vocal/instrumental trio – Con Cluskey, Declan Cluskey & John Stokes — Weeks on Chart: 187

Date	Title	Peak Position	Weeks at No.1	Weeks on Chart
24 Jan 63	**CHARMAINE** *Decca F 11559*	6		19
4 Jul 63	**FARAWAY PLACES** *Decca F 11666*	36		3
29 Aug 63	**WHISPERING** *Decca F 11712*	18		10
23 Jan 64	**DIANE** *Decca F 11799*	1	1	19
19 Mar 64	**I BELIEVE** *Decca F 11857*	2		17
4 Jun 64	**RAMONA** *Decca F 11910*	4		13
13 Aug 64	**I WOULDN'T TRADE YOU FOR THE WORLD** *Decca F 11949*	4		16
3 Dec 64	**NO ARMS CAN EVER HOLD YOU** *Decca F 12034*	7		12
1 Apr 65	**TRUE LOVE FOR EVER MORE** *Decca F 12108*	34		6
20 May 65	**MARIE** *Decca F 12156*	9		12
28 Oct 65	**IN THE CHAPEL IN THE MOONLIGHT** *Decca F 12256*	27		10
6 Jan 66	**HELLO DOLLY** *Decca F 12309*	38		4
17 Mar 66	**THE SOUND OF SILENCE** *Decca F 12351*	3		13
7 Jul 66	**CAN I TRUST YOU** *Decca F 12417*	26		7
1 Dec 66	**WALK WITH FAITH IN YOUR HEART** *Decca F 22523*	21		9
6 Apr 67	**OH HOW I MISS YOU** *Decca F 22592*	30		8
5 Jul 67	**MARTA** *Decca F 22634*	20		9

TAL BACHMAN

Canada, male vocalist/guitarist — Weeks on Chart: 2

Date	Title	Peak Position	Weeks at No.1	Weeks on Chart
30 Oct 99	**SHE'S SO HIGH** *Columbia 6679932*	30		2

BACHMAN-TURNER OVERDRIVE

Canada, male vocal/instrumental group – Randy Bachman, Robbie Bachman, Blair Thornton & C Fred Turner — Weeks on Chart: 18

Date	Title	Peak Position	Weeks at No.1	Weeks on Chart
16 Nov 74	**YOU AIN'T SEEN NOTHIN' YET** *Mercury 6167 025* ○ ★	2		12
1 Feb 75	**ROLL ON DOWN THE HIGHWAY** *Mercury 6167 071*	22		6

BACK TO THE PLANET

UK, female/male vocal/instrumental group — Weeks on Chart: 2

Date	Title	Peak Position	Weeks at No.1	Weeks on Chart
10 Apr 93	**TEENAGE TURTLES** *Parallel LLLCD 3*	52		1
4 Sep 93	**DAYDREAM** *Parallel LLLCD 8*	52		1

BACKBEAT BAND

US, male vocal/instrumental group — Weeks on Chart: 5

Date	Title	Peak Position	Weeks at No.1	Weeks on Chart
26 Mar 94	**MONEY** *Virgin VSCDX 1489*	48		4
14 May 94	**PLEASE MR POSTMAN** *Virgin VSCDX 1502*	69		1

BACKSTREET BOYS

US, male vocal/instrumental group – Nick Carter*, Howie Dorough, Brian Littrell, AJ McLean & Kevin Richardson (left 2006). See Childliners — Weeks on Chart: 175

Date	Title	Peak Position	Weeks at No.1	Weeks on Chart
28 Oct 95	**WE'VE GOT IT GOIN' ON** *Jive JIVECD 386*	54		1
16 Dec 95	**I'LL NEVER BREAK YOUR HEART** *Jive JIVECD 389*	42		3
1 Jun 96	**GET DOWN (YOU'RE THE ONE FOR ME)** *Jive JIVECD 394*	14		8
24 Aug 96	**WE'VE GOT IT GOIN' ON** *Jive JIVECD 400*	3		7
16 Nov 96	**I'LL NEVER BREAK YOUR HEART** *Jive JIVERCD 406*	8		8
18 Jan 97	**QUIT PLAYING GAMES (WITH MY HEART)** *Jive JIVECD 409* ○	2		10
29 Mar 97	**ANYWHERE FOR YOU** *Jive JIVECD 416*	4		8
2 Aug 97	**EVERYBODY (BACKSTREET'S BACK)** *Jive JIVECD 426* ○	3		11
11 Oct 97	**AS LONG AS YOU LOVE ME** *Jive JIVECD 434* ●	3		19
14 Feb 98	**ALL I HAVE TO GIVE** *Jive JIVECD 445* ○	2		12
15 May 99	**I WANT IT THAT WAY** *Jive 0523392* ●	1	1	14
30 Oct 99	**LARGER THAN LIFE** *Jive 0550562*	5		14
26 Feb 00	**SHOW ME THE MEANING OF BEING LONELY (IMPORT)** *Jive 9250002*	66		1
4 Mar 00	**SHOW ME THE MEANING OF BEING LONELY** *Jive 9250002* ○	3		11
24 Jun 00	**THE ONE** *Jive 9250662*	8		8
18 Nov 00	**SHAPE OF MY HEART** *Jive 9251442*	4		9
24 Feb 01	**THE CALL** *Jive 9251702*	8		5

Date	Title	Peak Position	Weeks at No.1	Weeks on Chart
7 Jul 01	**MORE THAN THAT** *Jive 9252342*	12		5
12 Jan 02	**DROWNING** *Jive 9253082*	4		7
9 Jul 05	**INCOMPLETE** *Jive 82876699282*	8		8
5 Nov 05	**JUST WANT YOU TO KNOW** *Jive 82876734282*	8		3
3 Nov 07	**INCONSOLABLE** *Jive 88697106602*	24		2
10 Oct 09	**STRAIGHT THROUGH MY HEART** *Jive 88697580142*	72		1

BACKYARD DOG

UK, male vocal/production group **6**

Date	Title	Peak Position	Weeks at No.1	Weeks on Chart
7 Jul 01	**BADDEST RUFFEST** *East West W 233CD*	15		6

BAD BOYS INC

UK, male vocal group – Ally Begg, Tony Dowding, David Ross & Matthew Pateman **31**

Date	Title	Peak Position	Weeks at No.1	Weeks on Chart
14 Aug 93	**DON'T TALK ABOUT LOVE** *A&M 5803412*	19		5
2 Oct 93	**WHENEVER YOU NEED SOMEONE** *A&M 5804032*	26		3
11 Dec 93	**WALKING ON AIR** *A&M 5804692*	24		6
21 May 94	**MORE TO THIS WORLD** *A&M 5806072*	8		7
23 Jul 94	**TAKE ME AWAY (I'LL FOLLOW YOU)** *A&M 5806912*	15		6
17 Sep 94	**LOVE HERE I COME** *A&M 5807752*	26		4

BAD COMPANY

UK, male vocal/instrumental group – Paul Rodgers*, Boz Burrell, Simon Kirke & Mick Ralphs **23**

Date	Title	Peak Position	Weeks at No.1	Weeks on Chart
1 Jun 74	**CAN'T GET ENOUGH** *Island WIP 6191*	15		8
22 Mar 75	**GOOD LOVIN' GONE BAD** *Island WIP 6223*	31		6
30 Aug 75	**FEEL LIKE MAKIN' LOVE** *Island WIP 6242*	20		9

BAD COMPANY

UK, male production group. See DJ Fresh, Fresh BC **5**

Date	Title	Peak Position	Weeks at No.1	Weeks on Chart
9 Mar 02	**SPACEHOPPER/TONIGHT** *Ram RAMM 37*	56		1
4 May 02	**RUSH HOUR/BLIND** *BC Recordings BCRUK 002CD*	59		1
15 Mar 03	**MO' FIRE** *BC Recordings BCRUK 003CD* BAD COMPANY UK/RAWHILL CRU	24		3

BAD ENGLISH

UK/US, male vocal/instrumental group **3**

Date	Title	Peak Position	Weeks at No.1	Weeks on Chart
25 Nov 89	**WHEN I SEE YOU SMILE** *Epic 6553471* ★	61		3

BAD HABIT BOYS

Germany, male production duo **1**

Date	Title	Peak Position	Weeks at No.1	Weeks on Chart
1 Jul 00	**WEEKEND** *Inferno CDFERN 28*	41		1

BAD MANNERS

UK, male vocal/instrumental group – Douglas 'Buster Bloodvessel' Trendle, Louis Cook, David Farren, Paul Hyman, Chris Kane, Andrew Marson, Alan Sayagg, Martin Stewart & Brian Tuitt **111**

Date	Title	Peak Position	Weeks at No.1	Weeks on Chart
1 Mar 80	**NE-NE-NA-NA-NA-NU-NU** *Magnet MAG 164*	28		14
14 Jun 80	**LIP UP FATTY** *Magnet MAG 175*	15		14
27 Sep 80	**SPECIAL BREW** *Magnet MAG 180* ○	3		13
6 Dec 80	**LORRAINE** *Magnet MAG 181*	21		12
28 Mar 81	**JUST A FEELING** *Magnet MAG 187*	13		9
27 Jun 81	**CAN CAN** *Magnet MAG 190* ○	3		13
26 Sep 81	**WALKING IN THE SUNSHINE** *Magnet MAG 197*	10		9
21 Nov 81	**BUONA SERA** *Magnet MAG 211*	34		9
1 May 82	**GOT NO BRAINS** *Magnet MAG 216*	44		5
31 Jul 82	**MY GIRL LOLLIPOP (MY BOY LOLLIPOP)** *Magnet MAG 232*	9		7
30 Oct 82	**SAMSON AND DELILAH** *Magnet MAG 236*	58		3
14 May 83	**THAT'LL DO NICELY** *Magnet MAG 243*	49		3

BAD MEETS EVIL FEATURING EMINEM & ROYCE DA 5' 9"

US, male rap/production group **1**

Date	Title	Peak Position	Weeks at No.1	Weeks on Chart
1 Sep 01	**SCARY MOVIES** *Mole UK MOLEUK 045*	63		1

BAD NEWS

UK, male vocal/acting group **5**

Date	Title	Peak Position	Weeks at No.1	Weeks on Chart
12 Sep 87	**BOHEMIAN RHAPSODY** *EMI EM 24*	44		5

BAD RELIGION

US, male vocal/instrumental group **3**

Date	Title	Peak Position	Weeks at No.1	Weeks on Chart
11 Feb 95	**21ST CENTURY (DIGITAL BOY)** *Columbia 6611435*	41		2
21 Aug 04	**LOS ANGELES IS BURNING** *Epitaph 11692*	67		1

WALLY BADAROU

Benin (b. France), male instrumentalist/producer **6**

Date	Title	Peak Position	Weeks at No.1	Weeks on Chart
19 Oct 85	**CHIEF INSPECTOR** *Fourth & Broadway BRW 37*	46		6

BADDIEL & SKINNER & LIGHTNING SEEDS

UK, male comedians/vocalists & vocal/instrumental group **40**

Date	Title	Peak Position	Weeks at No.1	Weeks on Chart
1 Jun 96	**THREE LIONS (THE OFFICIAL SONG OF THE ENGLAND FOOTBALL TEAM)** *Epic 6632732* ⊛	1	2	15
20 Jun 98	**THREE LIONS '98** *Epic 6660982* ⊛	1	3	13
15 Jun 02	**THREE LIONS** *Epic 6728152*	16		6
10 Jun 06	**THREE LIONS** *Epic 82876856672*	9		6

KLAUS BADELT

Germany, male composer/producer/arranger **3**

Date	Title	Peak Position	Weeks at No.1	Weeks on Chart
29 Jul 06	**HE'S A PIRATE** *Nebula NEBCD090*	40		3

BADFELLAS FEATURING CK

UK/Kenya, male/female vocal/production group **1**

Date	Title	Peak Position	Weeks at No.1	Weeks on Chart
15 Feb 03	**SOC IT TO ME** *Serious SER 053CD*	55		1

BADFINGER

UK, male vocal/instrumental group – Pete Ham, d. 23 Apr 1975, Tom Evans, d. 19 Nov 1983, Mike Gibbins & Joey Molland **34**

Date	Title	Peak Position	Weeks at No.1	Weeks on Chart
10 Jan 70	**COME AND GET IT** *Apple 20*	4		11
9 Jan 71	**NO MATTER WHAT** *Apple 31*	5		12
29 Jan 72	**DAY AFTER DAY** *Apple 40*	10		11

BADLY DRAWN BOY

UK, male vocalist/guitarist/pianist/producer (Damon Gough) **29**

Date	Title	Peak Position	Weeks at No.1	Weeks on Chart
4 Sep 99	**ONCE AROUND THE BLOCK** *Twisted Nerve TNXL 003CD*	46		2
17 Jun 00	**ANOTHER PEARL** *Twisted Nerve TNXL 004CD*	41		1
16 Sep 00	**DISILLUSION** *Twisted Nerve TNXL 005CD*	26		2
25 Nov 00	**ONCE AROUND THE BLOCK** *Twisted Nerve TNXL 009CD*	27		2
19 May 01	**PISSING IN THE WIND** *Twisted Nerve TNXL 010CD*	22		2
6 Apr 02	**SILENT SIGH** *Twisted Nerve TNXL 012CD1*	16		7
22 Jun 02	**SOMETHING TO TALK ABOUT** *Twisted Nerve TNXL 014CD*	28		2
26 Oct 02	**YOU WERE RIGHT** *Twisted Nerve TNXL 015CD*	9		3
18 Jan 03	**BORN AGAIN** *Twisted Nerve TNXL 016CD*	16		3
3 May 03	**ALL POSSIBILITIES** *Twisted Nerve TNXL 017CD*	24		2
31 Jul 04	**YEAR OF THE RAT** *XL Recordings TNXL018CD*	38		2
21 Oct 06	**NOTHING'S GONNA CHANGE YOUR MIND** *EMI CDEM701*	38		1

BADMAN

UK, male producer (Julian Brettle) **3**

Date	Title	Peak Position	Weeks at No.1	Weeks on Chart
2 Feb 91	**MAGIC STYLE** *Citybeat CBE 759*	61		3

ERYKAH BADU

US, female vocalist (Erica Wright) **17**

Date	Title	Peak Position	Weeks at No.1	Weeks on Chart
19 Apr 97	**ON & ON** *Universal UND 56117*	12		4
14 Jun 97	**NEXT LIFETIME** *Universal UND 56132*	30		3
29 Nov 97	**APPLE TREE** *Universal UND 56150*	47		1
11 Jul 98	**ONE** *Elektra E 3833CD1* BUSTA RHYMES FEATURING ERYKAH BADU	23		3
6 Mar 99	**YOU GOT ME** *MCA MCSTD 48110* ROOTS FEATURING ERYKAH BADU	31		2
15 Sep 01	**SWEET BABY** *Epic 6718822* MACY GRAY FEATURING ERYKAH BADU	23		4

JOAN BAEZ

US, female vocalist/guitarist **47**

Date	Title	Peak Position	Weeks at No.1	Weeks on Chart
6 May 65	**WE SHALL OVERCOME** *Fontana TF 564*	26		10
8 Jul 65	**THERE BUT FOR FORTUNE** *Fontana TF 587*	8		12
2 Sep 65	**IT'S ALL OVER NOW BABY BLUE** *Fontana TF 604*	22		8
23 Dec 65	**FAREWELL ANGELINA** *Fontana TF 639*	35		4
28 Jul 66	**PACK UP YOUR SORROWS** *Fontana TF 727*	50		1
9 Oct 71	**THE NIGHT THEY DROVE OLD DIXIE DOWN** *Vanguard VS 35138*	6		12

Peak Position · Weeks at No.1 · Weeks on Chart

BAHA MEN
Bahamas, male vocal group – Rik Carey, Leroy Butler, Patrick Carey, Jeffery Chea, Anthony Flowers, Colyn Grant, Dyson Knight & Isaiah Taylor **35**

Date	Title	Peak	No.1	Wks
14 Oct 00	**WHO LET THE DOGS OUT** *Edel 0115425 ERE* ⊛	2		23
3 Feb 01	**YOU ALL DAT** *Edel 0124855 ERE* GUEST VOCAL IMANI COPPOLA	14		5
13 Jul 02	**MOVE IT LIKE THIS** *EMI CDEM 615*	16		7

ABIGAIL BAILEY
UK, female vocalist **11**

Date	Title	Peak	No.1	Wks
17 Dec 05	**I JUST CAN'T GET ENOUGH** *All Around The World CDGLOBE473* HERD & FITZ FEATURING ABIGAIL BAILEY	11		10
22 Jul 06	**SOMETHING ON YOUR MIND** *Island APOLLO103CD* MYNC PROJECT FEATURING ABIGAIL BAILEY	71		1

CAROL BAILEY
UK, female vocalist **2**

Date	Title	Peak	No.1	Wks
25 Feb 95	**FEEL IT** *Multiply CDMULTY 3*	41		2

PHILIP BAILEY
US, male vocalist/percussionist. See Earth Wind & Fire **20**

Date	Title	Peak	No.1	Wks
9 Mar 85	**EASY LOVER** *CBS A 4915* (DUET WITH PHIL COLLINS) ●	1	4	12
18 May 85	**WALKING ON THE CHINESE WALL** *CBS A 6202*	34		8

MERRIL BAINBRIDGE
Australia, female vocalist **1**

Date	Title	Peak	No.1	Wks
7 Dec 96	**MOUTH** *Gotham 74321431012*	51		1

ADRIAN BAKER
UK, male vocalist/multi-instrumentalist **8**

Date	Title	Peak	No.1	Wks
19 Jul 75	**SHERRY** *Magnet MAG 34*	10		8

ANITA BAKER
US, female vocalist **22**

Date	Title	Peak	No.1	Wks
15 Nov 86	**SWEET LOVE** *Elektra EKR 44*	13		10
31 Jan 87	**CAUGHT UP IN THE RAPTURE** *Elektra EKR 49*	51		5
8 Oct 88	**GIVING YOU THE BEST THAT I GOT** *Elektra EKR 79*	55		3
30 Jun 90	**TALK TO ME** *Elektra EKR 111*	68		2
17 Sep 94	**BODY AND SOUL** *Elektra EKR 190CD*	48		2

ARTHUR BAKER
US, male producer **8**

Date	Title	Peak	No.1	Wks
20 May 89	**IT'S YOUR TIME** *Breakout USA 654* FEATURING SHIRLEY LEWIS	64		2
21 Oct 89	**THE MESSAGE IS LOVE** *Breakout USA 668* & THE BACKSTREET DISCIPLES FEATURING AL GREEN	38		5
30 Nov 02	**CONFUSION** *Whacked WACKT 002CD* VS NEW ORDER	64		1

HYLDA BAKER & ARTHUR MULLARD
UK, female/male actors/vocalists – Hylda Baker, d. 1 May 1986 & Arthur Mullard, d. 11 Dec 1995 **6**

Date	Title	Peak	No.1	Wks
9 Sep 78	**YOU'RE THE ONE THAT I WANT** *Pye 7N 46121*	22		6

GEORGE BAKER SELECTION
Holland, male vocal/instrumental group **10**

Date	Title	Peak	No.1	Wks
6 Sep 75	**PALOMA BLANCA** *Warner Brothers K 16541*	10		10

BAKSHELF DOG
UK, male bulldog vocalist (Churchill) **2**

Date	Title	Peak	No.1	Wks
21 Dec 02	**NO LIMITS** *WVC CDCHURCH 1*	51		2

BALAAM AND THE ANGEL
UK, male vocal/instrumental group **2**

Date	Title	Peak	No.1	Wks
29 Mar 86	**SHE KNOWS** *Virgin VS 842*	70		2

LONG JOHN BALDRY
UK, male vocalist, d. 21 Jul 2005 (age 64) **36**

Date	Title	Peak	No.1	Wks
8 Nov 67	**LET THE HEARTACHES BEGIN** *Pye 7N 17385*	1	5	13
28 Aug 68	**WHEN THE SUN COMES SHINING THRU'** *Pye 7N 17593*	29		7
23 Oct 68	**MEXICO** *Pye 7N 17563*	15		8
29 Jan 69	**IT'S TOO LATE NOW** *Pye 7N 17664*	21		8

BALEARIC BILL
Belgium/Holland, male production duo. See Airscape, Blue Bamboo, Cubic 22, Johan Gielen presents Abnea, Svenson & Gielen, Transformer 2 **2**

Date	Title	Peak	No.1	Wks
2 Oct 99	**DESTINATION SUNSHINE** *Xtravaganza XTRAV 3CDS*	36		2

EDWARD BALL
UK, male vocalist **2**

Date	Title	Peak	No.1	Wks
20 Jul 96	**THE MILL HILL SELF HATE CLUB** *Creation CRESCD 233*	57		1
22 Feb 97	**LOVE IS BLUE** *Creation CRESCD 244*	59		1

KENNY BALL & HIS JAZZMEN
UK, male trumpeter/vocalist & male instrumental group **136**

Date	Title	Peak	No.1	Wks
23 Feb 61	**SAMANTHA** *Pye Jazz Today 7NJ 2040*	13		15
11 May 61	**I STILL LOVE YOU ALL** *Pye Jazz 7NJ 2042*	24		6
31 Aug 61	**SOMEDAY (YOU'LL BE SORRY)** *Pye Jazz 7NJ 2047*	28		6
9 Nov 61	**MIDNIGHT IN MOSCOW** *Pye Jazz 7NJ 2049*	2		21
15 Feb 62	**MARCH OF THE SIAMESE CHILDREN** *Pye Jazz 7NJ 2051*	4		13
17 May 62	**THE GREEN LEAVES OF SUMMER** *Pye Jazz 7NJ 2054*	7		14
23 Aug 62	**SO DO I** *Pye Jazz 7NJ 2056*	14		8
18 Oct 62	**THE PAY OFF (AMOI DE PAYER)** *Pye Jazz 7NJ 2061*	23		6
17 Jan 63	**SUKIYAKI** *Pye Jazz 7NJ 2062*	10		13
25 Apr 63	**CASABLANCA** *Pye Jazz 7NJ 2064*	21		11
13 Jun 63	**RONDO** *Pye Jazz 7NJ 2065*	24		8
22 Aug 63	**ACAPULCO 1922** *Pye Jazz 7NJ 2067*	27		6
11 Jun 64	**HELLO DOLLY** *Pye Jazz 7NJ 2071*	30		7
19 Jul 67	**WHEN I'M SIXTY FOUR** *Pye 7N 17348*	43		2

MICHAEL BALL
UK, male vocalist/actor **39**

Date	Title	Peak	No.1	Wks
28 Jan 89	**LOVE CHANGES EVERYTHING** *Really Useful RUR 3* ●	2		14
28 Oct 89	**THE FIRST MAN YOU REMEMBER** *Really Useful RUR 6* & DIANA MORRISON	68		2
10 Aug 91	**IT'S STILL YOU** *Polydor PO 160*	58		2
25 Apr 92	**ONE STEP OUT OF TIME** *Polydor PO 206*	20		7
12 Dec 92	**IF I CAN DREAM (EP)** *Polydor PO 248*	51		2
11 Sep 93	**SUNSET BOULEVARD** *Polydor PZCD 293*	72		1
30 Jul 94	**FROM HERE TO ETERNITY** *Columbia 6606905*	36		3
17 Sep 94	**THE LOVERS WE WERE** *Columbia 6607972*	63		2
9 Dec 95	**THE ROSE** *Columbia 6614535*	42		4
17 Feb 96	**SOMETHING INSIDE SO STRONG** *Columbia 6629005*	40		2

STEVE BALSAMO
UK, male vocalist **2**

Date	Title	Peak	No.1	Wks
16 Mar 02	**SUGAR FOR THE SOUL** *Columbia 6718552*	32		2

BALTIMORA
Italy/UK, male vocal/instrumental group – Jimmy McShane, d. 29 Mar 1995, Maurizio Bassi, Claudio Bazzari, Giorgio Cocilovo, Gabriele Melotti & Pier Michelatti **12**

Date	Title	Peak	No.1	Wks
10 Aug 85	**TARZAN BOY** *Columbia DB 9102* ●	3		12

CHARLI BALTIMORE
US, female rapper (Tiffany Lane) **14**

Date	Title	Peak	No.1	Wks
1 Aug 98	**MONEY** *Epic 6662272*	12		4
12 Oct 02	**DOWN 4 U** *Murder Inc 0639002* IRV GOTTI PRESENTS JA RULE, ASHANTI, CHARLI BALTIMORE & VITA	4		10

BAM BAM
US, male producer/vocalist (Chris Westbrook) **2**

Date	Title	Peak	No.1	Wks
19 Mar 88	**GIVE IT TO ME** *Serious 7OUS 10*	65		2

Silver-selling ● Gold-selling ● Platinum-selling (x multiples) ⊛ US No.1 ★ Peak Position · Weeks at No.1 · Weeks on Chart

AFRIKA BAMBAATAA

US, male DJ/producer (Kevin Donovan) — 34

Date	Title	Peak Position	Weeks at No.1	Weeks on Chart
28 Aug 82	**PLANET ROCK** *Polydor POSP 497* & THE SONIC SOUL FORCE	53		3
10 Mar 84	**RENEGADES OF FUNK** *Tommy Boy AFR 1* & THE SONIC SOUL FORCE	30		4
1 Sep 84	**UNITY (PART 1 – THE THIRD COMING)** *Tommy Boy AFR 2* & JAMES BROWN	49		5
27 Feb 88	**RECKLESS** *EMI EM 41* FEATURING UB40 & FAMILY	17		8
12 Oct 91	**JUST GET UP AND DANCE** *EMI USA MT 100*	45		3
17 Oct 98	**GOT TO GET UP** *Multiply CDMULTY 42*	22		4
18 Sep 99	**AFRIKA SHOX** *Hard Hands HAND 057CD1* LEFTFIELD/BAMBAATAA	7		5
25 Aug 01	**PLANET ROCK** *Tommy Boy TBCD 2266* PAUL OAKENFOLD PRESENTS AFRIKA BAMBAATAA	47		1
13 Mar 04	**D-FUNKTIONAL** *Wall Of Sound WALLD092* MEKON FEATURING AFRIKA BAMBAATAA	72		1

BAMBOO

UK, male producer (Andrew Livingstone). See Hed Boys — 12

Date	Title	Peak Position	Weeks at No.1	Weeks on Chart
17 Jan 98	**BAMBOOGIE** *VC Recordings VCRD 29* ●	2		10
4 Jul 98	**THE STRUTT** *VC Recordings VCRD 35*	36		2

BANANARAMA

UK, female vocal trio – Sarah Dallin, Siobhan Fahey (replaced by Jacqui O'Sullivan) & Keren Woodward — 209

Date	Title	Peak Position	Weeks at No.1	Weeks on Chart
13 Feb 82	**IT AIN'T WHAT YOU DO IT'S THE WAY THAT YOU DO IT** *Chrysalis CHS 2570* FUN BOY THREE & BANANARAMA ●	4		10
10 Apr 82	**REALLY SAYING SOMETHING** *Deram NANA 1* WITH FUN BOY THREE ●	5		10
3 Jul 82	**SHY BOY** *London NANA 2* ●	4		11
4 Dec 82	**CHEERS THEN** *London NANA 3*	45		7
26 Feb 83	**NA NA HEY HEY KISS HIM GOODBYE** *London NANA 4*	5		10
9 Jul 83	**CRUEL SUMMER** *London NANA 5*	8		10
3 Mar 84	**ROBERT DE NIRO'S WAITING** *London NANA 6* ●	3		11
26 May 84	**ROUGH JUSTICE** *London NANA 7*	23		7
24 Nov 84	**HOTLINE TO HEAVEN** *London NANA 8*	58		2
24 Aug 85	**DO NOT DISTURB** *London NANA 9*	31		6
31 May 86	**VENUS** *London NANA 10* ★	8		13
16 Aug 86	**MORE THAN PHYSICAL** *London NANA 11*	41		5
14 Feb 87	**TRICK OF THE NIGHT** *London NANA 12*	32		5
11 Jul 87	**I HEARD A RUMOUR** *London NANA 13*	14		9
10 Oct 87	**LOVE IN THE FIRST DEGREE** *London NANA 14* ●	3		12
9 Jan 88	**I CAN'T HELP IT** *London NANA 15*	20		6
9 Apr 88	**I WANT YOU BACK** *London NANA 16*	5		10
24 Sep 88	**LOVE, TRUTH AND HONESTY** *London NANA 17*	23		8
19 Nov 88	**NATHAN JONES** *London NANA 18*	15		9
25 Feb 89	**HELP!** *London LON 222* BANANARAMA/LA NA NEE NEE NOO NOO ●	3		9
10 Jun 89	**CRUEL SUMMER (REMIX)** *London NANA 19*	19		6
28 Jul 90	**ONLY YOUR LOVE** *London NANA 21*	27		4
5 Jan 91	**PREACHER MAN** *London NANA 23*	20		6
20 Apr 91	**LONG TRAIN RUNNING** *London NANA 24*	30		5
29 Aug 92	**MOVIN' ON** *London NANA 25*	24		5
28 Nov 92	**LAST THING ON MY MIND** *London NANA 26*	71		2
20 Mar 93	**MORE MORE MORE** *London NACPD 27*	24		4
6 Aug 05	**MOVE IN MY DIRECTION** *A & G Productions CXAG003*	14		4
19 Nov 05	**LOOK ON THE FLOOR (HYPNOTIC TANGO)** *A & G Productions CXAG004*	26		2
19 Sep 09	**LOVE COMES** *Fascination 2714131*	44		1

Top 5 Downloads

By UK Sales 2004

Pos	Title Artist
1	**DO THEY KNOW IT'S CHRISTMAS?** BAND AID 20
2	**VERTIGO** U2
3	**WHAT YOU WAITING FOR** GWEN STEFANI
4	**LOSE MY BREATH** DESTINY'S CHILD
5	**I BELIEVE IN YOU** KYLIE MINOGUE

BAND

Canada, male vocal/instrumental group — 18

Date	Title	Peak Position	Weeks at No.1	Weeks on Chart
18 Sep 68	**THE WEIGHT** *Capitol CL 15559*	21		9
4 Apr 70	**RAG MAMA RAG** *Capitol CL 15629*	16		9

BAND AID

International, male/female vocal/instrumental charity assembly — 49

Date	Title	Peak Position	Weeks at No.1	Weeks on Chart
15 Dec 84	**DO THEY KNOW IT'S CHRISTMAS?** *Mercury FEED 1* ⊛	1	5	13
7 Dec 85	**DO THEY KNOW IT'S CHRISTMAS?** *Mercury FEED 1*	3		7
23 Dec 89	**DO THEY KNOW IT'S CHRISTMAS?** *PWL/Polydor FEED 2* BAND AID II ⊛	1	3	6
11 Dec 04	**DO THEY KNOW IT'S CHRISTMAS?** *Mercury 9869413* BAND AID 20 ⊛x2	1	4	10
10 Dec 05	**DO THEY KNOW IT'S CHRISTMAS?** *Mercury 9869413* BAND AID 20	52		1
15 Dec 07	**DO THEY KNOW IT'S CHRISTMAS?** *Mercury GBF088400001*	24		4
13 Dec 08	**DO THEY KNOW IT'S CHRISTMAS?** *Mercury GBF088400001*	54		4
12 Dec 09	**DO THEY KNOW IT'S CHRISTMAS?** *Mercury GBF088400001*	50		4

BAND AKA

US, male vocal/instrumental group — 12

Date	Title	Peak Position	Weeks at No.1	Weeks on Chart
15 May 82	**GRACE** *Epic EPC A 2376*	41		5
5 Mar 83	**JOY** *Epic EPC A 3145*	24		7

BAND OF GOLD

Holland, male/female vocal/instrumental group — 11

Date	Title	Peak Position	Weeks at No.1	Weeks on Chart
14 Jul 84	**LOVE SONGS ARE BACK AGAIN (MEDLEY)** *RCA 428*	24		11

BANDA SONORA

UK, male producer (Gerald Elms) — 3

Date	Title	Peak Position	Weeks at No.1	Weeks on Chart
6 Oct 01	**GUITARRA G** *Defected DFECT 36CDS*	50		2
19 Oct 02	**PRESSURE COOKER** *Defected DFTD 060CDS* G CLUB PRESENTS BANDA SONORA	46		1

BANDAGED

UK, male vocal charity duo – Aled Jones* & Sir Terry Wogan* — 3

Date	Title	Peak Position	Weeks at No.1	Weeks on Chart
20 Dec 08	**LITTLE DRUMMER BOY/PEACE ON EARTH** *Warner Brothers 2564692006*	3		3

BANDERAS

UK, female vocal/instrumental duo — 16

Date	Title	Peak Position	Weeks at No.1	Weeks on Chart
23 Feb 91	**THIS IS YOUR LIFE** *London LON 290*	16		10
15 Jun 91	**SHE SELLS** *London LON 298*	41		6

BANDITS

UK, male vocal/instrumental group — 2

Date	Title	Peak Position	Weeks at No.1	Weeks on Chart
28 Jun 03	**TAKE IT AND RUN** *B Unique BUN 055CDX*	32		1
20 Sep 03	**2 STEP ROCK** *B Unique BUN 065CDX*	35		1

HONEY BANE

UK, female vocalist (Donna Boylan) — 8

Date	Title	Peak Position	Weeks at No.1	Weeks on Chart
24 Jan 81	**TURN ME ON TURN ME OFF** *Zonophone Z 15*	37		5
18 Apr 81	**BABY LOVE** *Zonophone Z 19*	58		3

Peak Position
Weeks at No.1
Weeks on Chart

BANG
Greece, male vocal/instrumental duo — **2**

Date	Title	Peak	Wks No.1	Wks
6 May 89	**YOU'RE THE ONE** *RCA PB 42715*	74		2

THOMAS BANGALTER & DJ FALCON
France, male DJ/production duo. See Daft Punk — **1**

Date	Title	Peak	Wks No.1	Wks
4 Jan 03	**SO MUCH LOVE TO GIVE (IMPORT)** *Roule TOGETHER 2*	71		1

BANGLES
US, female vocal/instrumental group – Susanna Hoffs*, Debbi & Vicki Peterson & Michael Steele — **96**

Date	Title	Peak	Wks No.1	Wks
15 Feb 86	**MANIC MONDAY** *CBS A 6796* ○	2		12
26 Apr 86	**IF SHE KNEW WHAT SHE WANTS** *CBS A 7062*	31		7
5 Jul 86	**GOING DOWN TO LIVERPOOL** *CBS A 7255*	56		3
13 Sep 86	**WALK LIKE AN EGYPTIAN** *CBS 6500717* ○ ★	3		19
10 Jan 87	**WALKING DOWN YOUR STREET** *CBS BANGS 1*	16		6
18 Apr 87	**FOLLOWING** *CBS BANGS 2*	55		3
6 Feb 88	**HAZY SHADE OF WINTER** *Def Jam BANGS 3*	11		10
5 Nov 88	**IN YOUR ROOM** *CBS BANGS 4*	35		6
18 Feb 89	**ETERNAL FLAME** *CBS BANGS 5* ● ★	1	4	18
10 Jun 89	**BE WITH YOU** *CBS BANGS 6*	23		8
14 Oct 89	**I'LL SET YOU FREE** *CBS BANGS 7*	74		1
9 Jun 90	**WALK LIKE AN EGYPTIAN** *CBS BANGS 8*	73		1
15 Mar 03	**SOMETHING THAT YOU SAID** *Liberty BANGLES 003*	38		2

DEVENDRA BANHART
US, male vocalist/guitarist — **1**

Date	Title	Peak	Wks No.1	Wks
17 Sep 05	**I FEEL JUST LIKE A CHILD** *XL Recordings XLS217CD*	68		1

LLOYD BANK$
US, male rapper. See G-Unit — **12**

Date	Title	Peak	Wks No.1	Wks
21 Aug 04	**ON FIRE** *Interscope 9863485*	19		6
21 Oct 06	**HANDS UP** *Atlantic AT0253CD* FEATURING 50 CENT	43		3
13 Jan 07	**YOU DON'T KNOW** *Interscope USUM70613171* EMINEM, 50 CENT, LLOYD BANK$ & CA$HIS	32		3

BANNED
UK, male vocal/instrumental group — **6**

Date	Title	Peak	Wks No.1	Wks
17 Dec 77	**LITTLE GIRL** *Harvest HAR 5145*	36		6

BUJU BANTON
Jamaica, male vocalist (Mark Myrie) — **1**

Date	Title	Peak	Wks No.1	Wks
7 Aug 93	**MAKE MY DAY** *Mercury BUJCD 2*	72		1

PATO BANTON
UK, male vocalist (Patrick Murray) — **37**

Date	Title	Peak	Wks No.1	Wks
1 Oct 94	**BABY COME BACK** *Virgin VSCDT 1522* ⊛	1	4	18
11 Feb 95	**THIS COWBOY SONG** *A&M 5809652* STING FEATURING PATO BANTON	15		6
8 Apr 95	**BUBBLING HOT** *Virgin VSCDT 1530* WITH RANKING ROGER	15		7
20 Jan 96	**SPIRITS IN THE MATERIAL WORLD** *MCA MCSTD 2113* WITH STING	36		2
27 Jul 96	**GROOVIN'** *IRS CDEIRS 195* & THE REGGAE REVOLUTION	14		4

BAR-CODES FEATURING ALISON BROWN
UK, male/female production/vocal group — **1**

Date	Title	Peak	Wks No.1	Wks
17 Dec 94	**SUPERMARKET SWEEP (WILL YOU DANCE WITH ME)** *Blanca Casa BC 101CD*	72		1

BAR-KAYS
US, male vocal/instrumental group — **15**

Date	Title	Peak	Wks No.1	Wks
23 Aug 67	**SOUL FINGER** *Stax 601 014*	33		7
22 Jan 77	**SHAKE YOUR RUMP TO THE FUNK** *Mercury 6167 417*	41		4
12 Jan 85	**SEXOMATIC** *Club JAB 10*	51		4

CHRIS BARBER
UK, male trombone player & male instrumental group — **30**

Date	Title	Peak	Wks No.1	Wks
13 Feb 59	**PETITE FLEUR** *Pye Nixa 2026* CHRIS BARBER'S JAZZ BAND	3		24
9 Oct 59	**LONESOME (SI TU VOIS MA MERE)** *Columbia DB 4333* FEATURING MONTY SUNSHINE	27		2
4 Jan 62	**REVIVAL** *Columbia SCD 2166* CHRIS BARBER'S JAZZ BAND	43		4

BARCLAY JAMES HARVEST
UK, male vocal/instrumental group — **9**

Date	Title	Peak	Wks No.1	Wks
2 Apr 77	**LIVE (EP)** *Polydor 2229 198*	49		2
26 Jan 80	**LOVE ON THE LINE** *Polydor POSP 97*	63		2
22 Nov 80	**LIFE IS FOR LIVING** *Polydor POSP 195*	61		3
21 May 83	**JUST A DAY AWAY** *Polydor POSP 585*	68		2

BARDO
UK, vocal duo – Sally Ann Triplett & Stephen Fischer — **8**

Date	Title	Peak	Wks No.1	Wks
10 Apr 82	**ONE STEP FURTHER** *Epic EPC A 2265* ○	2		8

BARDOT
Australia, female vocal group — **1**

Date	Title	Peak	Wks No.1	Wks
14 Apr 01	**POISON** *East West EW 229CD*	45		1

BAREFOOT MAN
Germany, male vocalist (George Nowak) — **7**

Date	Title	Peak	Wks No.1	Wks
5 Dec 98	**BIG PANTY WOMAN** *Plaza PZACD 082*	21		7

SARA BAREILLES
US, female vocalist/guitarist/pianist — **19**

Date	Title	Peak	Wks No.1	Wks
10 May 08	**LOVE SONG** *Columbia 88697315932*	4		19

BARENAKED LADIES
Canada, male vocal/instrumental group – Steven Page, Ed Robertson, Jim Creeggan, Kevin Hearn & Tyler Stewart — **12**

Date	Title	Peak	Wks No.1	Wks
20 Feb 99	**ONE WEEK** *Reprise W 468CD* ★	5		8
15 May 99	**IT'S ALL BEEN DONE BEFORE** *Reprise W 476CD*	28		2
24 Jul 99	**CALL AND ANSWER** *Reprise W 498CD1*	52		1
11 Dec 99	**BRIAN WILSON** *Reprise W 511CD1*	73		1

BARKIN BROTHERS FEATURING JOHNNIE FIORI
UK/US, male/female vocal/production group — **2**

Date	Title	Peak	Wks No.1	Wks
15 Apr 00	**GONNA CATCH YOU** *Brothers Organisation BRUVCD 15*	51		2

GARY BARLOW
UK, male vocalist. See Take That — **47**

Date	Title	Peak	Wks No.1	Wks
20 Jul 96	**FOREVER LOVE** *RCA 74321397922* ●	1	1	16
10 May 97	**LOVE WON'T WAIT** *RCA 74321470842* ○	1	1	9
26 Jul 97	**SO HELP ME GIRL** *RCA 74321501202*	11		11
15 Nov 97	**OPEN ROAD** *RCA 74321518292*	7		5
17 Jul 99	**STRONGER** *RCA 74321682012*	16		4
9 Oct 99	**FOR ALL THAT YOU WANT** *RCA 74321701012*	24		2

BARNBRACK
UK, male vocal/instrumental trio — **7**

Date	Title	Peak	Wks No.1	Wks
16 Mar 85	**BELFAST** *Homespun HS 092*	45		7

BARNDANCE BOYS
UK, male production duo. See Bus Stop, Rikki & Daz featuring Glen Campbell, Uniting Nations — **2**

Date	Title	Peak	Wks No.1	Wks
13 Sep 03	**YIPPIE I OH** *Concept CDCON 41*	32		2

JIMMY BARNES & INXS
Australia (b. UK), male vocalist (James Swan) & vocal/instrumental group — **8**

Date	Title	Peak	Wks No.1	Wks
26 Jan 91	**GOOD TIMES** *Atlantic A 7751*	18		8

RICHARD BARNES

UK, male vocalist — 10

Date	Title / Label	Peak Position	Weeks at No.1	Weeks on Chart
23 May 70	**TAKE TO THE MOUNTAINS** *Philips BF 1840*	35		6
24 Oct 70	**GO NORTH** *Philips 6006 039*	38		4

BARON

UK, male producer (Piers Bailey) — 4

Date	Title / Label	Peak Position	Weeks at No.1	Weeks on Chart
7 Feb 04	**THE WAY IT WAS/REDHEAD** *Virus VRS012*	71		1
12 Feb 05	**SUPERNATURE** *Breakbeat Kaos BBK006* & FRESH	59		2
30 Apr 05	**GUNS AT DAWN** *Breakbeat Kaos BBK008* DJ BARON FEATURING PENDULUM	71		1

BARRACUDAS

Canada/UK, male vocal/instrumental group — 6

Date	Title / Label	Peak Position	Weeks at No.1	Weeks on Chart
16 Aug 80	**SUMMER FUN** *EMI-Wipe Out Z 5*	37		6

AMANDA BARRIE & JOHNNIE BRIGGS

UK, female/male actors/vocal duo — 3

Date	Title / Label	Peak Position	Weeks at No.1	Weeks on Chart
16 Dec 95	**SOMETHING STUPID** *EMI Premier CDEMS 411*	35		3

JJ BARRIE

Canada, male vocalist (Barrie Authors) — 11

Date	Title / Label	Peak Position	Weeks at No.1	Weeks on Chart
24 Apr 76	**NO CHARGE** *Power Exchange PX 209* ● (silver)	1	1	11

KEN BARRIE

UK, male vocalist — 15

Date	Title / Label	Peak Position	Weeks at No.1	Weeks on Chart
10 Jul 82	**POSTMAN PAT** *Post Music PP 001*	44		8
25 Dec 82	**POSTMAN PAT** *Post Music PP 001*	54		3
24 Dec 83	**POSTMAN PAT** *Post Music PP 001*	59		4

BARRON KNIGHTS

UK, male vocal/instrumental group – Duke D'Mond (Richard Palmer), Butch Baker, Dave Ballinger, Pet Langford & Barron Anthony Osmond — 95

Date	Title / Label	Peak Position	Weeks at No.1	Weeks on Chart
9 Jul 64	**CALL UP THE GROUPS** *Columbia DB 7317* WITH DUKE D'MOND	3		13
22 Oct 64	**COME TO THE DANCE** *Columbia DB 7375* WITH DUKE D'MOND	42		2
25 Mar 65	**POP GO THE WORKERS** *Columbia DB 7525* WITH DUKE D'MOND	5		13
16 Dec 65	**MERRY GENTLE POPS** *Columbia DB 7780* WITH DUKE D'MOND	9		7
1 Dec 66	**UNDER NEW MANAGEMENT** *Columbia DB 8071* WITH DUKE D'MOND	15		9
23 Oct 68	**AN OLYMPIC RECORD** *Columbia DB 8485*	35		4
29 Oct 77	**LIVE IN TROUBLE** *Epic EPC 5752* ● (silver)	7		11
2 Dec 78	**A TASTE OF AGGRO** *Epic EPC 6829* ● (gold)	3		10
8 Dec 79	**FOOD FOR THOUGHT** *Epic EPC 8011*	46		6
4 Oct 80	**THE SIT SONG** *Epic EPC 8994*	44		4
6 Dec 80	**NEVER MIND THE PRESENTS** *Epic EPC 9070*	17		8
5 Dec 81	**BLACKBOARD JUMBLE** *CBS A 1795*	52		5
19 Mar 83	**BUFFALO BILL'S LAST SCRATCH** *Epic EPC A 3208*	49		3

JOHN BARROWMAN

UK, male vocalist/actor/TV presenter — 1

Date	Title / Label	Peak Position	Weeks at No.1	Weeks on Chart
8 Aug 09	**I MADE IT THROUGH THE RAIN** *Epic GBARL0801065*	14		1

JOE BARRY

US, male vocalist (Joe Barrios) — 1

Date	Title / Label	Peak Position	Weeks at No.1	Weeks on Chart
24 Aug 61	**I'M A FOOL TO CARE** *Mercury AMT 1149*	49		1

LEN BARRY

US, male vocalist (Leonard Borisoff) — 24

Date	Title / Label	Peak Position	Weeks at No.1	Weeks on Chart
4 Nov 65	**1-2-3-** *Brunswick 05942*	3		14
13 Jan 66	**LIKE A BABY** *Brunswick 05949*	10		10

JOHN BARRY

UK, male composer/orchestra leader (John Prendergast) — 79

Date	Title / Label	Peak Position	Weeks at No.1	Weeks on Chart
5 Mar 60	**HIT AND MISS** *Columbia DB 4414* JOHN BARRY SEVEN	10		14
28 Apr 60	**BEAT FOR BEATNIKS** *Columbia DB 4446* JOHN BARRY ORCHESTRA	40		2
14 Jul 60	**NEVER LET GO** *Columbia DB 4480* JOHN BARRY ORCHESTRA	49		1
18 Aug 60	**BLUEBERRY HILL** *Columbia DB 4480* JOHN BARRY ORCHESTRA	34		3
8 Sep 60	**WALK DON'T RUN** *Columbia DB 4505* JOHN BARRY SEVEN	11		14
8 Dec 60	**BLACK STOCKINGS** *Columbia DB 4554* JOHN BARRY SEVEN	27		9
2 Mar 61	**THE MAGNIFICENT SEVEN** *Columbia DB 4598* JOHN BARRY SEVEN	45		5
26 Apr 62	**CUTTY SARK** *Columbia DB 4806* JOHN BARRY SEVEN	35		2
1 Nov 62	**THE JAMES BOND THEME** *Columbia DB 4898* JOHN BARRY ORCHESTRA	13		11
21 Nov 63	**FROM RUSSIA WITH LOVE** *Ember S 181* JOHN BARRY ORCHESTRA	39		3
11 Dec 71	**THE THEME FROM 'THE PERSUADERS'** *CBS 7469*	13		15

MICHAEL BARRYMORE

UK, male comedian/vocalist (Michael Parker). See Fat Les — 4

Date	Title / Label	Peak Position	Weeks at No.1	Weeks on Chart
16 Dec 95	**TOO MUCH FOR ONE HEART** *EMI CDEM 412*	25		4

LIONEL BART

UK, male composer/vocalist (Lionel Begleiter), d. 3 Apr 1999 (age 68) — 3

Date	Title / Label	Peak Position	Weeks at No.1	Weeks on Chart
25 Nov 89	**HAPPY ENDINGS (GIVE YOURSELF A PINCH)** *EMI EM 121*	68		3

BARTHEZZ

Holland, male producer (Bart Claessen) — 8

Date	Title / Label	Peak Position	Weeks at No.1	Weeks on Chart
22 Sep 01	**ON THE MOVE** *Positiva CDTIV 158*	18		4
20 Apr 02	**INFECTED** *Positiva CDTIVS 168*	25		4

BAS NOIR

US, female vocal duo — 1

Date	Title / Label	Peak Position	Weeks at No.1	Weeks on Chart
11 Feb 89	**MY LOVE IS MAGIC** *10 TEN 257*	73		1

ROB BASE & DJ E-Z ROCK

US, male rap/DJ duo — 19

Date	Title / Label	Peak Position	Weeks at No.1	Weeks on Chart
16 Apr 88	**IT TAKES TWO** *Citybeat CBE 724*	24		6
14 Jan 89	**GET ON THE DANCE FLOOR** *Supreme SUPE 139*	14		7
4 Mar 89	**IT TAKES TWO** *Citybeat CBE 724*	49		3
22 Apr 89	**JOY AND PAIN** *Supreme SUPE 143*	47		3

BASEMENT

UK, male vocal/instrumental group — 1

Date	Title / Label	Peak Position	Weeks at No.1	Weeks on Chart
14 Jun 03	**SLAIN THE TRUTH (AT THE ROADHOUSE)** *Deltasonic DLTCD 012*	48		1

BASEMENT BOYS PRESENT ULTRA NATE

US, male production group & female vocalist — 1

Date	Title / Label	Peak Position	Weeks at No.1	Weeks on Chart
23 Feb 91	**IS IT LOVE** *Eternal YZ 509*	71		1

BASEMENT JAXX

UK, male production duo – Felix Buxton & Simon Ratcliffe — 106

Date	Title / Label	Peak Position	Weeks at No.1	Weeks on Chart
31 May 97	**FLY LIFE** *Multiply CDMULTY 21*	19		3
1 May 99	**RED ALERT** *XL Recordings XLS 100CD*	5		10
14 Aug 99	**RENDEZ-VU** *XL Recordings XLS 110CD*	4		8
6 Nov 99	**JUMP N' SHOUT** *XL Recordings XLS 116CD*	12		5
15 Apr 00	**BINGO BANGO** *XL Recordings XLS 120CD*	13		4
16 Jun 01	**ROMEO** *XL Recordings XLS 132CD*	6		10
6 Oct 01	**JUS 1 KISS** *XL Recordings XLS 136CD1*	23		4
8 Dec 01	**WHERE'S YOUR HEAD AT** *XL Recordings XLS 140CD*	9		8
29 Jun 02	**GET ME OFF** *XL Recordings XLS 146CD*	22		3
22 Nov 03	**LUCKY STAR** *XL Recordings XLS 172CD* FEATURING DIZZEE RASCAL	23		4
17 Jan 04	**GOOD LUCK** *XL Recordings XLS 178CD* FEATURING LISA KEKAULA	12		8
10 Apr 04	**PLUG IT IN** *XL Recordings XLS 180CD* FEATURING JC CHASEZ	22		4
10 Jul 04	**GOOD LUCK** *XL Recordings XLS 190CD* FEATURING LISA KEKAULA	14		7
26 Mar 05	**OH MY GOSH** *XL Recordings XLS209CD1*	8		12
25 Jun 05	**U DON'T KNOW ME** *XL Recordings XLS215CD2* FEATURING LISA KEKAULA	26		3
8 Oct 05	**DO YOUR THING** *XL Recordings XLS220CD*	32		5
9 Sep 06	**HUSH BOY** *XL Recordings XLS241CD*	27		3
11 Nov 06	**TAKE ME BACK TO YOUR HOUSE** *XL Recordings XLS253CD1*	42		2
4 Jul 09	**RAINDROPS** *XL Recordings XLS444CD*	21		3

BASIA

Poland, female vocalist (Basia Trzetrzelewska). See Matt Bianco — 9

Date	Title / Label	Peak Position	Weeks at No.1	Weeks on Chart
23 Jan 88	**PROMISES** *Epic BASH 4*	48		4
28 May 88	**TIME AND TIDE** *Epic BASH 5*	61		3
14 Jan 95	**DRUNK ON LOVE** *Epic 6611582*	41		2

TONI BASIL
US, female vocalist (Antonia Basilotta) — 16

Date	Title	Peak Position	Weeks at No.1	Weeks on Chart
6 Feb 82	**MICKEY** *Radialchoice TIC 4* ● ★	2		12
1 May 82	**NOBODY** *Radialchoice TIC 2*	52		4

OLAV BASOSKI
Holland, male producer — 2

Date	Title	Peak Position	Weeks at No.1	Weeks on Chart
26 Aug 00	**OPIUM SCUMBAGZ** *Defected DFECT 20CDS*	56		1
29 Oct 05	**WATERMAN** *Positiva CDTIVS224* FEATURING MICHIE ONE	45		1

FONTELLA BASS
US, female vocalist — 15

Date	Title	Peak Position	Weeks at No.1	Weeks on Chart
2 Dec 65	**RESCUE ME** *Chess CRS 8023*	11		10
20 Jan 66	**RECOVERY** *Chess CRS 8027*	32		5

NORMAN BASS
Germany, male producer (Uwe Taubert) — 4

Date	Title	Peak Position	Weeks at No.1	Weeks on Chart
21 Apr 01	**HOW U LIKE BASS** *Substance SUBS 10CDS*	17		4

BASS BOYZ
UK, male producer (James Sammon). See Pianoman — 1

Date	Title	Peak Position	Weeks at No.1	Weeks on Chart
28 Sep 96	**GUNZ AND PIANOZ** *Polydor 5753432*	74		1

BASS BUMPERS
Germany, male production duo — 4

Date	Title	Peak Position	Weeks at No.1	Weeks on Chart
25 Sep 93	**RUNNIN'** *Vertigo VERCD 78*	68		1
5 Feb 94	**THE MUSIC'S GOT ME** *Vertigo VERCD 84*	25		3

BASS JUMPERS
Holland, male/female vocal/production trio — 1

Date	Title	Peak Position	Weeks at No.1	Weeks on Chart
13 Feb 99	**MAKE UP YOUR MIND** *Pepper 0530112*	44		1

BASS-O-MATIC
UK, male producer (William Orbit*) — 19

Date	Title	Peak Position	Weeks at No.1	Weeks on Chart
12 May 90	**IN THE REALM OF THE SENSES** *Virgin VS 1265*	66		3
1 Sep 90	**FASCINATING RHYTHM** *Virgin VS 1274*	9		11
22 Dec 90	**EASE ON BY** *Virgin VS 1295*	61		4
3 Aug 91	**FUNKY LOVE VIBRATIONS** *Virgin VS 1355*	71		1

SHIRLEY BASSEY
UK, female vocalist. Britain's most successful female chart artist, who has a 50-year Top 20 singles chart span and a Top 10 newly recorded albums chart span of over 46 years. The internationally acclaimed Welsh cabaret entertainer was made a dame in 2000 — 329

Date	Title	Peak Position	Weeks at No.1	Weeks on Chart
15 Feb 57	**BANANA BOAT SONG** *Philips PB 668*	8		10
23 Aug 57	**FIRE DOWN BELOW** *Philips PB 723*	30		1
6 Sep 57	**YOU YOU ROMEO** *Philips PB 723*	29		2
19 Dec 58	**AS I LOVE YOU** *Philips PB 845*	1	4	19
26 Dec 58	**KISS ME HONEY HONEY KISS ME** *Philips PB 860*	3		17
31 Mar 60	**WITH THESE HANDS** *Columbia DB 4421*	38		6
4 Aug 60	**AS LONG AS HE NEEDS ME** *Columbia DB 4490*	2		30
11 May 61	**YOU'LL NEVER KNOW** *Columbia DB 4643*	6		17
27 Jul 61	**REACH FOR THE STARS/CLIMB EV'RY MOUNTAIN** *Columbia DB 4685*	1	1	18
23 Nov 61	**I'LL GET BY** *Columbia DB 4737*	10		8
15 Feb 62	**TONIGHT** *Columbia DB 4777*	21		8
26 Apr 62	**AVE MARIA** *Columbia DB 4816*	31		4
31 May 62	**FAR AWAY** *Columbia DB 4836*	24		13
30 Aug 62	**WHAT NOW MY LOVE** *Columbia DB 4882*	5		17
28 Feb 63	**WHAT KIND OF FOOL AM I?** *Columbia DB 4974*	47		2
26 Sep 63	**I (WHO HAVE NOTHING)** *Columbia DB 7113*	6		20
23 Jan 64	**MY SPECIAL DREAM** *Columbia DB 7185*	32		7
9 Apr 64	**GONE** *Columbia DB 7248*	36		5
15 Oct 64	**GOLDFINGER** *Columbia DB 7360*	21		9
20 May 65	**NO REGRETS (NON JE NE REGRETTE RIEN)** *Columbia DB 7535*	39		4
11 Oct 67	**BIG SPENDER** *United Artists UP 1192*	21		15
20 Jun 70	**SOMETHING** *United Artists UP 35125*	4		22
2 Jan 71	**THE FOOL ON THE HILL** *United Artists UP 35156*	48		1
27 Mar 71	**(WHERE DO I BEGIN) LOVE STORY** *United Artists UP 35194*	34		9
7 Aug 71	**FOR ALL WE KNOW** *United Artists UP 35267*	6		24
15 Jan 72	**DIAMONDS ARE FOREVER** *United Artists UP 35293*	38		6
3 Mar 73	**NEVER NEVER NEVER** *United Artists UP 35490*	8		19
22 Aug 87	**THE RHYTHM DIVINE** *Mercury MER 253* YELLO FEATURING SHIRLEY BASSEY	54		2
16 Nov 96	**DISCO' LA PASSIONE** *East West EW 072CD* CHRIS REA & SHIRLEY BASSEY	41		1
20 Dec 97	**HISTORY REPEATING** *Wall Of Sound WALLD 036* PROPELLERHEADS & SHIRLEY BASSEY	19		7
23 Oct 99	**WORLD IN UNION** *Universal TV 4669402* SHIRLEY BASSEY/ BRYN TERFEL	35		3
5 May 07	**THE LIVING TREE** *Lock Stock & Barrel LSBRCD003*	37		2
4 Aug 07	**GET THE PARTY STARTED** *Lock Stock & Barrel LSBRCD006*	47		1

BASSHEADS
UK, male production duo – Eamonn Deery & Nick Murphy — 18

Date	Title	Peak Position	Weeks at No.1	Weeks on Chart
16 Nov 91	**IS THERE ANYBODY OUT THERE** *Deconstruction R 6303*	5		8
30 May 92	**BACK TO THE OLD SCHOOL** *Deconstruction R 6310*	12		4
28 Nov 92	**WHO CAN MAKE ME FEEL GOOD** *Deconstruction R 6326*	38		2
28 Aug 93	**START A BRAND NEW LIFE (SAVE ME)** *Deconstruction CDR 6353*	49		2
15 Jul 95	**IS THERE ANYBODY OUT THERE (REMIX)** *Deconstruction 74321293882*	24		2

BASSHUNTER
Sweden, male vocalist/DJ/producer (Jonas Altberg) — 73

Date	Title	Peak Position	Weeks at No.1	Weeks on Chart
12 Jan 08	**NOW YOU'RE GONE** *Hard2Beat H2B01CDS* FEATURING DJ MENTAL THEO'S BAZZHEADZ	1	5	32
12 Jul 08	**ALL I EVER WANTED** *Hard2Beat H2B08CDS*	2		16
13 Sep 08	**ANGEL IN THE NIGHT** *Hard2Beat H2B16CDS*	14		12
13 Dec 08	**JINGLE BELLS (BASS)** *HARD2BEAT SEPQA0651305*	35		4
27 Dec 08	**I MISS YOU** *Hard2Beat H2B20CDS*	32		5
3 Oct 09	**EVERY MORNING** *Hard2Beat H2B42CDS*	17		4

BASSTOY
US, male producer (Mark Picchiotti). See Absolute, Sandstorm — 6

Date	Title	Peak Position	Weeks at No.1	Weeks on Chart
27 May 00	**RUNNIN** *Neo NEOCD 029*	62		1
19 Jan 02	**RUNNIN'** *Black & Blue NEOCD 073* MARK PICCHIOTTI PRESENTS BASSTOY FEATURING DANA	13		5

BAT FOR LASHES
UK, female vocalist/multi-instrumentalist (Natasha Khan) — 6

Date	Title	Peak Position	Weeks at No.1	Weeks on Chart
11 Apr 09	**DANIEL** *Parlophone R6768*	36		6

BATES
Germany, male vocal/instrumental group — 1

Date	Title	Peak Position	Weeks at No.1	Weeks on Chart
3 Feb 96	**BILLIE JEAN** *Virgin International DINSD 151*	67		1

MIKE BATT WITH THE NEW EDITION
UK, male vocalist/producer — 8

Date	Title	Peak Position	Weeks at No.1	Weeks on Chart
16 Aug 75	**SUMMERTIME CITY** *Epic EPC 3460*	4		8

BATTLE
UK, male vocal/instrumental group — 3

Date	Title	Peak Position	Weeks at No.1	Weeks on Chart
25 Mar 06	**TENDENCY** *Transgressive TRANS022CD*	37		2
24 Jun 06	**CHILDREN** *Transgressive TRANS030CD*	60		1

BAUHAUS
UK, male vocal/instrumental group — 35

Date	Title	Peak Position	Weeks at No.1	Weeks on Chart
18 Apr 81	**KICK IN THE EYE** *Beggars Banquet BEG 54*	59		3
4 Jul 81	**THE PASSION OF LOVERS** *Beggars Banquet BEG 59*	56		2
6 Mar 82	**KICK IN THE EYE (EP)** *Beggars Banquet BEG 74*	45		4
19 Jun 82	**SPIRIT** *Beggars Banquet BEG 79*	42		5
9 Oct 82	**ZIGGY STARDUST** *Beggars Banquet BEG 83*	15		7
22 Jan 83	**LAGARTIJA NICK** *Beggars Banquet BEG 88*	44		4
9 Apr 83	**SHE'S IN PARTIES** *Beggars Banquet BEG 91*	26		6
29 Oct 83	**THE SINGLES 1981-83** *Beggars Banquet BEG 100E*	52		4

LES BAXTER
US, male orchestra leader, d. 15 Jan 1996 (age 73) — 9

Date	Title	Peak Position	Weeks at No.1	Weeks on Chart
13 May 55	**UNCHAINED MELODY** *Capitol CL 14257* ★	10		9

TOM BAXTER

UK, male vocalist/guitarist — 2

Date	Title / Label	Peak Position	Weeks at No.1	Weeks on Chart
31 Jul 04	THIS BOY *Sony Music 6751692*	65		1
15 Dec 07	BETTER *Charisma CASD8*	67		1

BAY CITY ROLLERS

UK, male vocal group – Leslie McKeown, Eric Faulkner, Alan & Derek Longmuir & Stuart Wood — 116

Date	Title / Label	Peak Position	Weeks at No.1	Weeks on Chart
18 Sep 71	KEEP ON DANCING *Bell 1164*	9		13
9 Feb 74	REMEMBER (SHA-LA-LA) *Bell 1338* ○	6		12
27 Apr 74	SHANG-A-LANG *Bell 1355* ○	2		10
27 Jul 74	SUMMERLOVE SENSATION *Bell 1369* ○	3		10
12 Oct 74	ALL OF ME LOVES ALL OF YOU *Bell 1382* ○	4		10
8 Mar 75	BYE BYE BABY *Bell 1409* ●	1	6	16
12 Jul 75	GIVE A LITTLE LOVE *Bell 1425* ●	1	3	9
22 Nov 75	MONEY HONEY *Bell 1461* ○	3		9
10 Apr 76	LOVE ME LIKE I LOVE YOU *Bell 1477*	4		9
11 Sep 76	I ONLY WANNA BE WITH YOU *Bell 1493* ○	4		9
7 May 77	IT'S A GAME *Arista 108*	16		6
30 Jul 77	YOU MADE ME BELIEVE IN MAGIC *Arista 127*	34		3

DUKE BAYSEE

UK, male vocalist (Kevin Rowe) — 6

Date	Title / Label	Peak Position	Weeks at No.1	Weeks on Chart
3 Sep 94	SUGAR SUGAR *Bell 74321228702*	30		4
21 Jan 95	DO YOU LOVE ME *Double Dekker CDDEK 1*	46		2

BAZ

UK, female vocalist (Baz Gooden) — 3

Date	Title / Label	Peak Position	Weeks at No.1	Weeks on Chart
15 Dec 01	BELIEVERS *One Little Indian 313 TP7CD*	36		2
30 Mar 02	SMILE TO SHINE *One Little Indian 316 TP7CD*	58		1

BBC CONCERT ORCHESTRA/BBC SYMPHONY CHORUS/STEPHEN JACKSON

UK, male/female orchestra & chorus & male conductor — 3

Date	Title / Label	Peak Position	Weeks at No.1	Weeks on Chart
22 Jun 96	ODE TO JOY (FROM BEETHOVEN'S SYMPHONY NO 9) *Virgin VSCDT 1591*	36		3

BBE

Italy/France, male vocal/instrumental/production trio – Bruno Quartier, Bruno Sanchioni & Emmanuel Top — 20

Date	Title / Label	Peak Position	Weeks at No.1	Weeks on Chart
28 Sep 96	SEVEN DAYS AND ONE WEEK *Positiva CDTIV 67* ○	3		9
29 Mar 97	FLASH *Positiva CDTIV 73*	5		5
14 Feb 98	DESIRE *Positiva CDTIV 87*	19		3
30 May 98	DEEPER LOVE (SYMPHONIC PARADISE) *Positiva CDTIV 93*	19		3

BBG

UK, male production trio — 10

Date	Title / Label	Peak Position	Weeks at No.1	Weeks on Chart
28 Apr 90	SNAPPINESS *Urban URB 54* FEATURING DINA TAYLOR	28		5
11 Aug 90	SOME KIND OF HEAVEN *Urban URB 59*	65		2
23 Mar 96	LET THE MUSIC PLAY *MCA MCSTD 40029* FEATURING ERIN	46		1
18 May 96	SNAPPINESS (REMIX) *Hi-Life 5762972*	50		1
5 Jul 97	JUST BE TONIGHT *Hi-Life 5738972*	45		1

BBM

UK, male vocal/instrumental trio — 2

Date	Title / Label	Peak Position	Weeks at No.1	Weeks on Chart
6 Aug 94	WHERE IN THE WORLD *Virgin VSCD 1495*	57		2

BBMAK

UK, male vocal trio – Mark Barry, Christian Burns & Stephen McNally — 18

Date	Title / Label	Peak Position	Weeks at No.1	Weeks on Chart
28 Aug 99	BACK HERE *Telstar CDSTAS 3053*	37		2
24 Feb 01	BACK HERE *Telstar CDSTAS 3166*	5		10
26 May 01	STILL ON YOUR SIDE *Telstar CXSTAS 3185*	8		4
16 Nov 02	OUT OF MY HEART *Telstar CDSTAS 3281*	36		2

BE BOP DELUXE

UK, male vocal/instrumental group — 13

Date	Title / Label	Peak Position	Weeks at No.1	Weeks on Chart
21 Feb 76	SHIPS IN THE NIGHT *Harvest HAR 5104*	23		8
13 Nov 76	HOT VALVES EP *Harvest HAR 5117*	36		5

BE YOUR OWN PET

US, male/female vocal/instrumental group — 5

Date	Title / Label	Peak Position	Weeks at No.1	Weeks on Chart
26 Mar 05	DAMN DAMN LEASH *XL Recordings XLS212CD*	68		1
2 Jul 05	FIRE DEPARTMENT *Rough Trade RTRADSCD238*	59		1
4 Feb 06	LET'S GET SANDY *XL Recordings XLS224CD*	51		1
25 Mar 06	ADVENTURE *XL Recordings XLS225CD*	36		2

BEACH BOYS

US, male vocal/instrumental group – Brian Wilson*, Al Jardine, Bruce Johnston, Mike Love, Carl Wilson, d. 6 Feb 1998, & Dennis Wilson*, d. 28 Dec 1983. Arguably the most popular US group of the rock 'n' roll era, whose hits span over 40 years and whose 'Good Vibrations' single and *Pet Sounds* album are regarded as among the greatest recordings ever — 281

Date	Title / Label	Peak Position	Weeks at No.1	Weeks on Chart
1 Aug 63	SURFIN' USA *Capitol CL 15305*	34		7
9 Jul 64	I GET AROUND *Capitol CL 15350* ★	7		13
29 Oct 64	WHEN I GROW UP TO BE A MAN *Capitol CL 15361*	27		7
21 Jan 65	DANCE DANCE DANCE *Capitol CL 15370*	24		6
3 Jun 65	HELP ME RHONDA *Capitol CL 15392* ★	27		10
2 Sep 65	CALIFORNIA GIRLS *Capitol CL 15409*	26		8
17 Feb 66	BARBARA ANN *Capitol CL 15432*	3		10
21 Apr 66	SLOOP JOHN B *Capitol CL 15441*	2		15
28 Jul 66	GOD ONLY KNOWS *Capitol CL 15459*	2		14
3 Nov 66	GOOD VIBRATIONS *Capitol CL 15475* ★	1	2	13
4 May 67	THEN I KISSED HER *Capitol CL 15502*	4		11
23 Aug 67	HEROES AND VILLAINS *Capitol CL 15510*	8		9
22 Nov 67	WILD HONEY *Capitol CL 15521*	29		6
17 Jan 68	DARLIN' *Capitol CL 15527*	11		14
8 May 68	FRIENDS *Capitol CL 15545*	25		7
24 Jul 68	DO IT AGAIN *Capitol CL 15554*	1	1	14
25 Dec 68	BLUEBIRDS OVER THE MOUNTAIN *Capitol CL 15572*	33		5
26 Feb 69	I CAN HEAR MUSIC *Capitol CL 15584*	10		13
11 Jun 69	BREAK AWAY *Capitol CL 15598*	6		11
16 May 70	COTTONFIELDS *Capitol CL 15640*	5		17
3 Mar 73	CALIFORNIA SAGA-CALIFORNIA *Reprise K 14232*	37		5
3 Jul 76	GOOD VIBRATIONS *Capitol CL 15875*	18		7
10 Jul 76	ROCK AND ROLL MUSIC *Reprise K 14440*	36		4
31 Mar 79	HERE COMES THE NIGHT *Caribou CRB 7204*	37		8
16 Jun 79	LADY LYNDA *Caribou CRB 7427*	6		11
29 Sep 79	SUMAHAMA *Caribou CRB 7846*	45		4
29 Aug 81	BEACH BOYS MEDLEY *Capitol CL 213*	47		4
22 Aug 87	WIPEOUT *Urban URB 5* FAT BOYS & THE BEACH BOYS ○	2		12
19 Nov 88	KOKOMO *Elektra EKR 85* ★	25		9
2 Jun 90	WOULDN'T IT BE NICE *Capitol CL 579*	58		1
29 Jun 91	DO IT AGAIN *Capitol EMCT 1*	61		2
2 Mar 96	FUN FUN FUN *Polygram TV 5762972* STATUS QUO WITH THE BEACH BOYS	24		4

WALTER BEASLEY

US, male vocalist/saxophonist — 3

Date	Title / Label	Peak Position	Weeks at No.1	Weeks on Chart
23 Jan 88	I'M SO HAPPY *Urban URB 14*	70		3

BEASTIE BOYS

US, male rap/vocal trio – Michael 'Mike D' Diamond, Adam 'Ad-Rock' Horowitz & Adam 'MCA' Yauch — 73

Date	Title / Label	Peak Position	Weeks at No.1	Weeks on Chart
28 Feb 87	(YOU GOTTA) FIGHT FOR YOUR RIGHT TO PARTY *Def Jam 6504187*	11		11
30 May 87	NO SLEEP TILL BROOKLYN *Def Jam BEAST 1*	14		7
18 Jul 87	SHE'S ON IT *Def Jam BEAST 2*	10		8
3 Oct 87	GIRLS/SHE'S CRAFTY *Def Jam BEAST 3*	34		4
11 Apr 92	PASS THE MIC *Capitol 12CL 653*	47		2
4 Jul 92	FROZEN METAL HEAD (EP) *Capitol 12CL 665*	55		1
9 Jul 94	GET IT TOGETHER/SABOTAGE *Capitol CDCL 716*	19		4
26 Nov 94	SURE SHOT *Capitol CDCLS 726*	27		3
4 Jul 98	INTERGALACTIC *Grand Royal CDCL 803*	5		7
7 Nov 98	BODY MOVIN' *Grand Royal CDCLS 809*	15		5
29 May 99	REMOTE CONTROL/3 MCS AND 1 DJ *Grand Royal CDCLS 812*	21		3
18 Dec 99	ALIVE *Grand Royal CDCL 818*	28		4
12 Jun 04	CH-CHECK IT OUT *Capitol CDCLS 857*	8		7
25 Sep 04	TRIPLE TROUBLE *Capitol CDCLS 859*	37		3
18 Dec 04	AN OPEN LETTER TO NYC *Capitol CDCLS867*	38		4

BEAT

UK, male vocal/instrumental group – Ranking Roger (Roger Charlery), Dave Wakeling, Andy Cox & David Steele — 92

Date	Title / Label	Peak Position	Weeks at No.1	Weeks on Chart
8 Dec 79	TEARS OF A CLOWN/RANKING FULL STOP *2 Tone CHSTT 6* ○	6		11
23 Feb 80	HANDS OFF – SHE'S MINE *Go Feet FEET 1*	9		9
3 May 80	MIRROR IN THE BATHROOM *Go Feet FEET 2*	4		9
16 Aug 80	BEST FRIEND/STAND DOWN MARGARET (DUB) *Go Feet FEET 3*	22		9

Silver-selling ● · Gold-selling ● · Platinum-selling (x multiples) ⊛ · US No.1 ★ · Peak Position · Weeks at No.1 · Weeks on Chart

Date	Title	Peak Position	Weeks at No.1	Weeks on Chart
13 Dec 80	**TOO NICE TO TALK TO** *Go Feet FEET 4* ●	7		11
18 Apr 81	**DROWNING/ALL OUT TO GET YOU** *Go Feet FEET 6*	22		8
20 Jun 81	**DOORS OF YOUR HEART** *Go Feet FEET 9*	33		6
5 Dec 81	**HIT IT** *Go Feet FEET 11*	70		2
17 Apr 82	**SAVE IT FOR LATER** *Go Feet FEET 333*	47		4
18 Sep 82	**JEANETTE** *Go Feet FEET 15*	45		3
4 Dec 82	**I CONFESS** *Go Feet FEET 16*	54		3
30 Apr 83	**CAN'T GET USED TO LOSING YOU** *Go Feet FEET 17* ●	3		11
2 Jul 83	**ACKEE 1-2-3** *Go Feet FEET 18*	54		4
27 Jan 96	**MIRROR IN THE BATHROOM (REMIX)** *Go Feet 74321232062*	44		2

BEAT RENEGADES

UK, male production duo. See Dream Frequency, Quake featuring Marcia Rae, Red — Weeks on Chart: 1

Date	Title	Peak Position	Weeks at No.1	Weeks on Chart
19 May 01	**AUTOMATIK** *Slinky Music SLINKY 014CD*	73		1

BEAT SYSTEM

UK, male producer (Derek Pierce) — Weeks on Chart: 3

Date	Title	Peak Position	Weeks at No.1	Weeks on Chart
3 Mar 90	**WALK ON THE WILD SIDE** *Fourth & Broadway BRW 163*	63		2
18 Sep 93	**TO A BRIGHTER DAY (O' HAPPY DAY)** *ffrr FCD 217*	70		1

BEAT UP

UK, male vocal/instrumental group — Weeks on Chart: 3

Date	Title	Peak Position	Weeks at No.1	Weeks on Chart
26 Oct 02	**BAD FEELINGS** *Fantastic Plastic FPS 034* BEATINGS	68		1
4 Dec 04	**MESSED UP** *Fantastic Plastic FPS043*	62		1
5 Mar 05	**ALRIGHT** *Fantastic Plastic FPS045*	58		1

BEATCHUGGERS FEATURING ERIC CLAPTON

Denmark, male producer & UK, male vocalist/guitarist — Weeks on Chart: 2

Date	Title	Peak Position	Weeks at No.1	Weeks on Chart
18 Nov 00	**FOREVER MAN (HOW MANY TIMES)** *ffrr FCD 386*	26		2

BEATFREAKZ

Holland, male production trio – Dennis Christopher, Dimitrie Siliakus & Mark Simmons — Weeks on Chart: 21

Date	Title	Peak Position	Weeks at No.1	Weeks on Chart
6 May 06	**SOMEBODY'S WATCHING ME** *Data DATA113CDS*	3		15
14 Oct 06	**SUPERFREAK** *Data DATA135CDS*	7		6

BEATLES

UK, male vocal/instrumental group – John Lennon*, d. 8 Dec 1980, Paul McCartney*, George Harrison*, d. 29 Nov 2001, & Ringo Starr*. The most popular group of all time with world sales of over one billion and UK singles sales of 20.8 million. No one has sold more albums around the globe than the act who had 11 successive (official) UK No.1 singles and once held the Top 5 places on the US chart — Weeks on Chart: 456

Date	Title	Peak Position	Weeks at No.1	Weeks on Chart
11 Oct 62	**LOVE ME DO** *Parlophone R 4949* ★	17		18
17 Jan 63	**PLEASE PLEASE ME** *Parlophone R 4983*	2		18
18 Apr 63	**FROM ME TO YOU** *Parlophone R 5015*	1	7	21
6 Jun 63	**MY BONNIE** *Polydor NH 66833* TONY SHERIDAN & THE BEATLES	48		1
29 Aug 63	**SHE LOVES YOU** *Parlophone R 5055* ★	1	6	33
5 Dec 63	**I WANT TO HOLD YOUR HAND** *Parlophone R 5084* ★	1	5	22
26 Mar 64	**CAN'T BUY ME LOVE** *Parlophone R 5114* ★	1	3	15
11 Jun 64	**AIN'T SHE SWEET** *Polydor 52 317*	29		6
16 Jul 64	**A HARD DAY'S NIGHT** *Parlophone R 5160* ★	1	3	13
3 Dec 64	**I FEEL FINE** *Parlophone R 5200* ★	1	5	13
15 Apr 65	**TICKET TO RIDE** *Parlophone R 5265* ★	1	3	12
29 Jul 65	**HELP!** *Parlophone R 5305* ★	1	3	14
9 Dec 65	**DAY TRIPPER/WE CAN WORK IT OUT** *Parlophone R 5389* ★	1	5	12
16 Jun 66	**PAPERBACK WRITER** *Parlophone R 5452* ★	1	2	11
11 Aug 66	**YELLOW SUBMARINE/ELEANOR RIGBY** *Parlophone R 5493*	1	4	13
23 Feb 67	**PENNY LANE/STRAWBERRY FIELDS FOREVER** *Parlophone R 5570* ★	2		11
12 Jul 67	**ALL YOU NEED IS LOVE** *Parlophone R 5620* ★	1	3	13
29 Nov 67	**HELLO GOODBYE** *Parlophone R 5655* ★	1	7	12
13 Dec 67	**MAGICAL MYSTERY TOUR (DOUBLE EP)** *Parlophone SMMTIMMT 1*	2		12
20 Mar 68	**LADY MADONNA** *Parlophone R 5675*	1	2	8
4 Sep 68	**HEY JUDE** *Apple R 5722* ★	1	2	16
23 Apr 69	**GET BACK** *Apple R 5777* WITH BILLY PRESTON ★	1	6	17
4 Jun 69	**THE BALLAD OF JOHN AND YOKO** *Apple R 5786*	1	3	14
8 Nov 69	**SOMETHING/COME TOGETHER** *Apple R 5814*	4		12
14 Mar 70	**LET IT BE** *Apple R 5833* ★	2		10
13 Mar 76	**YESTERDAY** *Apple R 6013* ★	8		7
27 Mar 76	**HEY JUDE** *Apple R 5722*	12		7
27 Mar 76	**PAPERBACK WRITER** *Parlophone R 5452*	23		5
3 Apr 76	**STRAWBERRY FIELDS FOREVER** *Parlophone R 5570*	32		3
3 Apr 76	**GET BACK** *Apple R 5777* WITH BILLY PRESTON	28		5

Acts With The Most Weeks At No.1

Pos	Artist	Weeks at No.1
1	ELVIS PRESLEY	80
2	BEATLES	69
3	CLIFF RICHARD	46
4	SHADOWS	44
5	FRANKIE LAINE	32
6	ABBA	31
7	MADONNA	29
8	TAKE THAT	28
9	ELTON JOHN	23
=	WET WET WET	23
11	SPICE GIRLS	22
12	QUEEN	21
13	SLADE	20
=	WESTLIFE	20
15	EVERLY BROTHERS	19
16	ROLLING STONES	18
=	ROD STEWART	18
=	OLIVIA NEWTON-JOHN	18
19	PAUL MCCARTNEY/WINGS	17
=	GEORGE MICHAEL	17
=	BRYAN ADAMS	17
=	FRANK IFIELD	17
23	MICHAEL JACKSON	16
=	T. REX	16
=	KYLIE MINOGUE	16
=	WHITNEY HOUSTON	16
=	JOHN TRAVOLTA	16
28	FRANKIE GOES TO HOLLYWOOD	15
=	DORIS DAY	15
30	GUY MITCHELL	14
31	DAVID BOWIE	13
=	POLICE	13
=	CHER	13
=	ROBSON & JEROME	13
=	PERRY COMO	13
=	BLONDIE	13
=	BEE GEES	13
=	RIHANNA	13
=	EDDIE CALVERT	13
=	LEONA LEWIS	13
41	CONNIE FRANCIS	12
=	DAVID WHITFIELD	12
=	JAY-Z	12
=	PETER KAY	12
=	PET SHOP BOYS	12

Date	Title / Label	Peak Position	Weeks at No.1	Weeks on Chart
10 Apr 76	**HELP!** *Parlophone R 5305*	37		3
10 Jul 76	**BACK IN THE U.S.S.R.** *Parlophone R 6016*	19		6
7 Oct 78	**SGT PEPPER'S LONELY HEARTS CLUB BAND – WITH A LITTLE HELP FROM MY FRIENDS** *Parlophone R 6022*	63		3
5 Jun 82	**BEATLES MOVIE MEDLEY** *Parlophone R 6055*	10		9
16 Oct 82	**LOVE ME DO** *Parlophone R 4949*	4		7
22 Jan 83	**PLEASE PLEASE ME** *Parlophone R 4983*	29		4
23 Apr 83	**FROM ME TO YOU** *Parlophone R 5015*	40		4
3 Sep 83	**SHE LOVES YOU** *Parlophone R 5055*	45		3
26 Nov 83	**I WANT TO HOLD YOUR HAND** *Parlophone R 5084*	62		2
31 Mar 84	**CAN'T BUY ME LOVE** *Parlophone R 5114*	53		2
21 Jul 84	**A HARD DAY'S NIGHT** *Parlophone R 5160*	52		2
8 Dec 84	**I FEEL FINE** *Parlophone R 5200*	65		1
20 Apr 85	**TICKET TO RIDE** *Parlophone R 5265*	70		2
30 Aug 86	**YELLOW SUBMARINE/ELEANOR RIGBY** *Parlophone R 5493*	63		1
28 Feb 87	**PENNY LANE/STRAWBERRY FIELDS FOREVER** *Parlophone R 5570*	65		2
18 Jul 87	**ALL YOU NEED IS LOVE** *Parlophone R 5620*	47		3
5 Dec 87	**HELLO GOODBYE** *Parlophone R 5655*	63		1
26 Mar 88	**LADY MADONNA** *Parlophone R 5675*	67		1
10 Sep 88	**HEY JUDE** *Apple R 5722*	52		2
22 Apr 89	**GET BACK** *Apple R 5777* WITH BILLY PRESTON	74		1
17 Oct 92	**LOVE ME DO** *Parlophone R 4949*	53		1
1 Apr 95	**BABY IT'S YOU** *Apple CDR 6406*	7		7
16 Dec 95	**FREE AS A BIRD** *Apple CDR 6422*	2		8
16 Mar 96	**REAL LOVE** *Apple CDR 6425*	4		7

Top 3 Best-Selling Singles

		Approximate Sales
1	SHE LOVES YOU	1,890,000
2	I WANT TO HOLD YOUR HAND	1,750,000
3	CAN'T BUY ME LOVE	1,520,000

BEATMASTERS

UK, male/female production trio – Paul Carter, Manda Glanfield & Richard Walmsley — 47

Date	Title / Label	Peak Position	Weeks at No.1	Weeks on Chart
9 Jan 88	**ROK DA HOUSE** *Rhythm King LEFT 11* FEATURING THE COOKIE CREW	5		11
24 Sep 88	**BURN IT UP** *Rhythm King LEFT 27* WITH PP ARNOLD	14		10
22 Apr 89	**WHO'S IN THE HOUSE** *Rhythm King LEFT 31* FEATURING MERLIN	8		9
12 Aug 89	**HEY DJ I CAN'T DANCE TO THAT MUSIC YOU'RE PLAYING/SKA TRAIN** *Rhythm King LEFT 34* FEATURING BETTY BOO	7		11
2 Dec 89	**WARM LOVE** *Rhythm King LEFT 37* FEATURING CLAUDIA FONTAINE	51		2
21 Sep 91	**BOULEVARD OF BROKEN DREAMS** *Rhythm King 6573617*	62		1
16 May 92	**DUNNO WHAT IT IS (ABOUT YOU)** *Rhythm King 6580017* FEATURING ELAINE VASSELL	43		3

BEATNUTS

US, male rap duo — 2

Date	Title / Label	Peak Position	Weeks at No.1	Weeks on Chart
14 Jul 01	**NO ESCAPIN' THIS** *Epic 6713412*	47		1
21 Jun 03	**DUDE DESCENDING A STAIRCASE** *Sony Music SSX 14CDX* APOLLO FOUR FORTY FEATURING THE BEATNUTS	58		1

BEATS INTERNATIONAL

UK, male production/vocal duo – Norman Cook* & Lester Noel – with various male/female vocal/rap/instrumental collaborators — 30

Date	Title / Label	Peak Position	Weeks at No.1	Weeks on Chart
10 Feb 90	**DUB BE GOOD TO ME** *Go! Beat GOD 39* FEATURING LINDY LAYTON ●	1	4	13
12 May 90	**WON'T TALK ABOUT IT** *Go! Beat GOD 43*	9		7
15 Sep 90	**BURUNDI BLUES** *Go! Beat GOD 45*	51		3
2 Mar 91	**ECHO CHAMBER** *Go! Beat GOD 51*	60		2
21 Sep 91	**THE SUN DOESN'T SHINE** *Go! Beat GOD 59*	66		2
23 Nov 91	**IN THE GHETTO** *Go! Beat GOD 64*	44		3

BEAUTIFUL PEOPLE

UK, male instrumental/production group — 1

Date	Title / Label	Peak Position	Weeks at No.1	Weeks on Chart
28 May 94	**IF 60S WERE 90S** *Essential ESSX 2037*	74		1

BEAUTIFUL SOUTH

UK, male/female vocal/instrumental group – Paul Heaton*, Briana Corrigan* (replaced by Jacqui Abbott, Abbott replaced by Alison Wheeler), Dave Hemingway, Dave Rotheray, Dave Stead & Sean Welch — 163

Date	Title / Label	Peak Position	Weeks at No.1	Weeks on Chart
3 Jun 89	**SONG FOR WHOEVER** *Go! Discs GOD 32* ●	2		11
23 Sep 89	**YOU KEEP IT ALL IN** *Go! Discs GOD 35*	8		8
2 Dec 89	**I'LL SAIL THIS SHIP ALONE** *Go! Discs GOD 38*	31		8
6 Oct 90	**A LITTLE TIME** *Go! Discs GOD 47* ●	1	1	14
8 Dec 90	**MY BOOK** *Go! Discs GOD 48*	43		6
16 Mar 91	**LET LOVE SPEAK UP ITSELF** *Go! Discs GOD 53*	51		2
11 Jan 92	**OLD RED EYES IS BACK** *Go! Discs GOD 66*	22		6
14 Mar 92	**WE ARE EACH OTHER** *Go! Discs GOD 71*	30		3
13 Jun 92	**BELL BOTTOMED TEAR** *Go! Discs GOD 78*	16		5
26 Sep 92	**36D** *Go! Discs GOD 88*	46		2
12 Mar 94	**GOOD AS GOLD** *Go! Discs GODCD 110*	23		5
4 Jun 94	**EVERYBODY'S TALKIN'** *Go! Discs GODCD 113*	12		8
3 Sep 94	**PRETTIEST EYES** *Go! Discs GODCD 119*	37		3
12 Nov 94	**ONE LAST LOVE SONG** *Go! Discs GODCD 122*	14		5
18 Nov 95	**PRETENDERS TO THE THRONE** *Go! Discs GODCD 134*	18		4
12 Oct 96	**ROTTERDAM** *Go! Discs GODCD 155*	6		9
14 Dec 96	**DON'T MARRY HER** *Go! Discs GOLCD 158*	8		10
29 Mar 97	**BLACKBIRD ON THE WIRE** *Go! Discs 5821252*	23		5
5 Jul 97	**LIARS' BAR** *Go! Discs 5822492*	43		1
3 Oct 98	**PERFECT 10** *Go! Discs 5664832* ●	2		14
19 Dec 98	**DUMB** *Go! Discs 5667532*	16		8
20 Mar 99	**HOW LONG'S A TEAR TAKE TO DRY?** *Go! Discs 8708232*	12		6
10 Jul 99	**THE TABLE** *Go! Discs 5621652*	47		2
7 Oct 00	**CLOSER THAN MOST** *Go! Discs 5629682*	22		4
23 Dec 00	**THE RIVER/JUST CHECKIN'** *Go! Discs 5727552*	59		1
17 Nov 01	**THE ROOT OF ALL EVIL** *Go! Discs 5888712*	50		1
25 Oct 03	**JUST A FEW THINGS THAT I AIN'T** *Go! Discs 9813039*	30		2
13 Dec 03	**LET GO WITH THE FLOW** *Go! Discs 9815084*	47		2
23 Oct 04	**LIVIN' THING** *Sony Music 6753712*	24		2
18 Dec 04	**THIS OLD SKIN** *Sony Music 6756842*	43		2
19 Feb 05	**THIS WILL BE OUR YEAR** *Sony Music 6757462*	36		2
20 May 06	**MANCHESTER** *Sony Music 82876831132*	41		2

GILBERT BECAUD

France, male vocalist (Francois Silly), d. 8 Dec 2001 (age 74) — 12

Date	Title / Label	Peak Position	Weeks at No.1	Weeks on Chart
29 Mar 75	**A LITTLE LOVE AND UNDERSTANDING** *Decca F 13537*	10		12

BECK

US, male vocalist/instrumentalist (David Campbell) — 31

Date	Title / Label	Peak Position	Weeks at No.1	Weeks on Chart
5 Mar 94	**LOSER** *Geffen GFSTD 67*	15		6
29 Jun 96	**WHERE IT'S AT** *Geffen GFSTD 22156*	35		2
16 Nov 96	**DEVILS HAIRCUT** *Geffen GFSTD 22183*	22		2
8 Mar 97	**THE NEW POLLUTION** *Geffen GFSTD 22205*	14		5
24 May 97	**SISSYNECK** *Geffen GFSTD 22253*	30		2
8 Nov 97	**DEADWEIGHT** *Geffen GFSTD 22293*	23		3
19 Dec 98	**TROPICALIA** *Geffen GFSTD 22365*	39		2
20 Nov 99	**SEXX LAWS** *Geffen 4971822*	27		3
8 Apr 00	**MIXED BIZNESS** *Geffen 4973012*	34		2
26 Mar 05	**E-PRO** *Interscope 9880052*	38		2
16 Jul 05	**GIRL** *Interscope 9882469*	45		2

JEFF BECK

UK, male vocalist/guitarist. See Yardbirds — 57

Date	Title / Label	Peak Position	Weeks at No.1	Weeks on Chart
23 Mar 67	**HI-HO SILVER LINING** *Columbia DB 8151*	14		14
2 Aug 67	**TALLYMAN** *Columbia DB 8227*	30		3
28 Feb 68	**LOVE IS BLUE** *Columbia DB 8359*	23		7
9 Jul 69	**GOO GOO BARABAJAGAL (LOVE IS HOT)** *Pye 7N 17778* DONOVAN WITH THE JEFF BECK GROUP	12		9
4 Nov 72	**HI-HO SILVER LINING** *RAK RR3*	17		11
5 May 73	**I'VE BEEN DRINKING** *RAK RR4* & ROD STEWART	27		6
9 Oct 82	**HI-HO SILVER LINING** *RAK RR3*	62		4
7 Mar 92	**PEOPLE GET READY** *Epic 6577567* & ROD STEWART	49		3

ROBIN BECK

US, female vocalist — 13

Date	Title / Label	Peak Position	Weeks at No.1	Weeks on Chart
22 Oct 88	**THE FIRST TIME** *Mercury MER 270* ●	1	3	13

VICTORIA BECKHAM

UK, female vocalist (Victoria Adams). See Spice Girls — 49

Date	Title / Label	Peak Position	Weeks at No.1	Weeks on Chart
26 Aug 00	**OUT OF YOUR MIND** *NuLife 74321782942* TRUE STEPPERS & DANE BOWERS FEATURING VICTORIA BECKHAM ●	2		20
29 Sep 01	**NOT SUCH AN INNOCENT GIRL** *Virgin VSCDT 1816*	6		14
23 Feb 02	**A MIND OF ITS OWN** *Virgin VSCDT 1824*	6		7
10 Jan 04	**THIS GROOVE/LET YOUR HEAD GO** *19 Recordings/Moody CXVB 1*	3		8

BEDAZZLED

UK, male vocal/instrumental group — 1

Date	Title / Label	Peak Position	Weeks at No.1	Weeks on Chart
4 Jul 92	**SUMMER SONG** *Columbia 6581627*	73		1

DANIEL BEDINGFIELD

UK (b. New Zealand), male vocalist/producer

Date	Title	Peak Position	Weeks at No.1	Weeks on Chart (87)
8 Dec 01	**GOTTA GET THRU THIS** *Relentless RELENT 27CD* ●	1	3	18
24 Aug 02	**JAMES DEAN (I WANNA KNOW)** *Polydor 5709342*	4		8
7 Dec 02	**IF YOU'RE NOT THE ONE** *Polydor 0658632* ●	1	1	21
19 Apr 03	**I CAN'T READ YOU** *Polydor 0657132*	6		11
2 Aug 03	**NEVER GONNA LEAVE YOUR SIDE** *Polydor 9809362*	1	1	11
1 Nov 03	**FRIDAY** *Polydor 9812920*	28		2
6 Nov 04	**NOTHING HURTS LIKE LOVE** *Polydor 9868820*	3		7
19 Feb 05	**WRAP MY WORDS AROUND YOU** *Polydor 9870179*	12		7
4 Jun 05	**THE WAY** *Polydor 9871535*	41		2

NATASHA BEDINGFIELD

UK, female vocalist

Date	Title	Peak Position	Weeks at No.1	Weeks on Chart (74)
15 May 04	**SINGLE** *Phonogenic 82876615232*	3		10
28 Aug 04	**THESE WORDS** *Phonogenic 82876639182*	1	2	13
11 Dec 04	**UNWRITTEN** *Phonogenic 82876663542*	6		12
16 Apr 05	**I BRUISE EASILY** *Phonogenic 82876681532*	12		7
14 Apr 07	**I WANNA HAVE YOUR BABIES** *Phonogenic 82876886422*	7		9
23 Jun 07	**SOULMATE** *Phonogenic 88697111992*	7		13
29 Mar 08	**LOVE LIKE THIS** *Phonogenic 88697287252* FEATURING SEAN KINGSTON	20		7
6 Sep 08	**BRUISED WATER** *Modena GBRDU0800032* CHICANE VERSUS NATASHA BEDINGFIELD	42		3

BEDLAM

UK, male DJ/production duo. See Diddy

Date	Title	Peak Position	Weeks at No.1	Weeks on Chart (1)
6 Feb 99	**DA-FORCE** *Playola 0091695 PLA*	68		1

BEDLAM AGO GO

UK, male vocal/instrumental group

Date	Title	Peak Position	Weeks at No.1	Weeks on Chart (1)
4 Apr 98	**SEASON NO. 5** *Sony S2 BDLM 2CD*	57		1

BEDOUIN SOUNDCLASH

Canada, male vocal/instrumental trio

Date	Title	Peak Position	Weeks at No.1	Weeks on Chart (15)
8 Oct 05	**WHEN THE NIGHT FEELS MY SONG** *B Unique/Polydor BUN098CD*	24		15

BEDROCK

UK, male vocal/instrumental duo

Date	Title	Peak Position	Weeks at No.1	Weeks on Chart (9)
1 Jun 96	**FOR WHAT YOU DREAM OF** *Stress CDSTR 23* FEATURING KYO	25		3
12 Jul 97	**SET IN STONE/FORBIDDEN ZONE** *Stress CDSTR 80*	71		1
6 Nov 99	**HEAVEN SCENT** *Bedrock BEDRCDS 001*	35		3
8 Jul 00	**VOICES** *Bedrock BEDRCDS 005*	44		2

BEDROCKS

UK, male vocal/instrumental group

Date	Title	Peak Position	Weeks at No.1	Weeks on Chart (7)
18 Dec 68	**OB-LA-DI OB-LA-DA** *Columbia DB 8516*	20		7

CELI BEE & THE BUZZY BUNCH

US, male/female vocal/instrumental group

Date	Title	Peak Position	Weeks at No.1	Weeks on Chart (1)
17 Jun 78	**HOLD YOUR HORSES BABE** *TK TKR 6032*	72		1

BEE GEES

UK, male vocal/instrumental group – Barry Gibb*, Maurice Gibb, d. 12 Jan 2003, & Robin Gibb*. The No.1 family act of all time have enjoyed Top 10 singles and albums in every decade since the '60s. They have written 10 No.1 singles and wrote and performed most tracks on the world's biggest-selling soundtrack (*Saturday Night Fever*). See One World Project, Vanessa Jenkins & Bryn West featuring Tom Jones & Robin Gibb

Date	Title	Peak Position	Weeks at No.1	Weeks on Chart (354)
27 Apr 67	**NEW YORK MINING DISASTER 1941** *Polydor 56 161*	12		10
12 Jul 67	**TO LOVE SOMEBODY** *Polydor 56 178*	41		5
20 Sep 67	**MASSACHUSETTS** *Polydor 56 192*	1	4	17
22 Nov 67	**WORLD** *Polydor 56 220*	9		16
31 Jan 68	**WORDS** *Polydor 56 229*	8		10
27 Mar 68	**JUMBO/THE SINGER SANG HIS SONG** *Polydor 56 242*	25		7
7 Aug 68	**I'VE GOTTA GET A MESSAGE TO YOU** *Polydor 56 273*	1	1	15
19 Feb 69	**FIRST OF MAY** *Polydor 56 304*	6		11
4 Jun 69	**TOMORROW TOMORROW** *Polydor 56 331*	23		8
16 Aug 69	**DON'T FORGET TO REMEMBER** *Polydor 56 343*	2		15
28 Mar 70	**I.O.I.O.** *Polydor 56 377*	49		1
5 Dec 70	**LONELY DAYS** *Polydor 2001 104*	33		9
29 Jan 72	**MY WORLD** *Polydor 2058 105*	16		9
22 Jul 72	**RUN TO ME** *Polydor 2058 255*	9		10
28 Jun 75	**JIVE TALKIN'** *RSO 2090 160* ○ ★	5		11
31 Jul 76	**YOU SHOULD BE DANCING** *RSO 2090 195* ★	5		10
13 Nov 76	**LOVE SO RIGHT** *RSO 2090 207*	41		4
29 Oct 77	**HOW DEEP IS YOUR LOVE** *RSO 2090 259* ● ★	3		15
4 Feb 78	**STAYIN' ALIVE** *RSO 2090 267* ○ ★	4		18
15 Apr 78	**NIGHT FEVER** *RSO 002* ● ★	1	2	20
25 Nov 78	**TOO MUCH HEAVEN** *RSO 25* ● ★	3		13
17 Feb 79	**TRAGEDY** *RSO 27* ● ★	1	2	10
14 Apr 79	**LOVE YOU INSIDE OUT** *RSO 31* ★	13		9
5 Jan 80	**SPIRITS (HAVING FLOWN)** *RSO 52*	16		7
17 Sep 83	**SOMEONE BELONGING TO SOMEONE** *RSO 96*	49		4
26 Sep 87	**YOU WIN AGAIN** *Warner Brothers W 8351* ●	1	4	15
12 Dec 87	**E.S.P.** *Warner Brothers W 8139*	51		5
15 Apr 89	**ORDINARY LIVES** *Warner Brothers W 7523*	54		3
24 Jun 89	**ONE** *Warner Brothers W 2916*	71		1
2 Mar 91	**SECRET LOVE** *Warner Brothers W 0014*	5		11
21 Aug 93	**PAYING THE PRICE OF LOVE** *Polydor PZCD 284*	23		5
27 Nov 93	**FOR WHOM THE BELL TOLLS** *Polydor PZCD 299* ○	4		14
16 Apr 94	**HOW TO FALL IN LOVE PART 1** *Polydor PZCD 311*	30		4
1 Mar 97	**ALONE** *Polydor 5735272* ○	5		9
21 Jun 97	**I COULD NOT LOVE YOU MORE** *Polydor 5712232*	14		3
8 Nov 97	**STILL WATERS (RUN DEEP)** *Polydor 5718892*	18		3
18 Jul 98	**IMMORTALITY** *Epic 6661682* CELINE DION WITH THE BEE GEES ○	5		12
7 Apr 01	**THIS IS WHERE I CAME IN** *Polydor 5879772*	18		5

BEENIE MAN

Jamaica, male rapper/vocalist (Anthony Moses David)

Date	Title	Peak Position	Weeks at No.1	Weeks on Chart (53)
20 Sep 97	**DANCEHALL QUEEN** *Island Jamaica IJCD 2018* CHEVELLE FRANKLYN/ BEENIE MAN	70		1
7 Mar 98	**WHO AM I** *Greensleeves GRECD 588*	10		5
8 Aug 98	**FOUNDATION** *Shocking Vibes SVJCDS1* & THE TAXI GANG	69		1
4 Mar 00	**MONEY** *Parlophone Rhythm CDRHYTHM 27* JAMELIA FEATURING BEENIE MAN	5		9
24 Mar 01	**GIRLS DEM SUGAR** *Virgin VUSCD 173* FEATURING MYA	13		5
28 Sep 02	**FEEL IT BOY** *Virgin VUSCD 258* FEATURING JANET JACKSON	9		7
14 Dec 02	**DIRTY HARRY'S REVENGE** *Kaos 004P* ADAM F FEATURING BEENIE MAN	50		2
8 Feb 03	**STREET LIFE** *Virgin VUSDX 260*	13		5
13 Mar 04	**DUDE** *Virgin VUSCDX 282* FEATURING MS THING	7		11
21 Aug 04	**KING OF THE DANCEHALL** *Virgin VUSCD 293*	14		5
19 Aug 06	**GIRLS** *Virgin VUSCD328* BEENIE FEATURING AKON	47		2

BEES

UK, male vocal/instrumental group

Date	Title	Peak Position	Weeks at No.1	Weeks on Chart (8)
1 May 04	**WASH IN THE RAIN** *Virgin VSCDT 1868*	31		3
26 Jun 04	**HORSEMEN** *Virgin VSCDX 1869*	41		2
16 Apr 05	**CHICKEN PAYBACK** *Virgin VSCDX1884*	28		3

SAM BEETON

UK, male vocalist/multi-instrumentalist

Date	Title	Peak Position	Weeks at No.1	Weeks on Chart (2)
20 Sep 08	**WHAT YOU LOOK FOR** *RCA 88697318862*	41		2

B.E.F. FEATURING LALAH HATHAWAY

UK, male production duo – Ian Craig Marsh & Martyn Ware – & US, female vocalist

Date	Title	Peak Position	Weeks at No.1	Weeks on Chart (5)
27 Jul 91	**FAMILY AFFAIR** *10 TEN 369*	37		5

LOU BEGA

Germany, male vocalist (David Lubega)

Date	Title	Peak Position	Weeks at No.1	Weeks on Chart (21)
7 Aug 99	**MAMBO NO 5 (A LITTLE BIT OF...) (IMPORT)** *Ariola 74321658012*	31		4
4 Sep 99	**MAMBO NO 5 (A LITTLE BIT OF...)** *RCA 74321696722* ⊛	1	2	15
18 Dec 99	**I GOT A GIRL** *RCA 74321720642*	55		2

BEGGAR & CO

UK, male vocal/instrumental group

Date	Title	Peak Position	Weeks at No.1	Weeks on Chart (15)
7 Feb 81	**(SOMEBODY) HELP ME OUT** *Ensign ENY 201*	15		10
12 Sep 81	**MULE (CHANT NO. 2)** *RCA 130*	37		5

BEGINERZ
UK, male production duo — 3

Date	Title	Peak	Wks at No.1	Wks
13 Jul 02	**RECKLESS GIRL** *Cheeky 74321942232*	28		3

BEGINNING OF THE END
US, male vocal/instrumental group — 6

Date	Title	Peak	Wks at No.1	Wks
23 Feb 74	**FUNKY NASSAU** *Atlantic K 10021*	31		6

BEIJING SPRING
UK, female vocal duo — 5

Date	Title	Peak	Wks at No.1	Wks
23 Jan 93	**I WANNA BE IN LOVE AGAIN** *MCA MCSTD 1709*	43		3
8 May 93	**SUMMERLANDS** *MCA MCSTD 1761*	53		2

BEL AMOUR
France, male/female vocal/production trio — 3

Date	Title	Peak	Wks at No.1	Wks
12 May 01	**BEL AMOUR** *Credence CDCRED 010*	23		3

BEL CANTO
UK, male vocal/instrumental group — 1

Date	Title	Peak	Wks at No.1	Wks
14 Oct 95	**WE'VE GOT TO WORK IT OUT** *Good Groove CDGG 2*	65		1

HARRY BELAFONTE
US, male vocalist/actor — 87

Date	Title	Peak	Wks at No.1	Wks
1 Mar 57	**BANANA BOAT SONG** *HMV POP 308* WITH TONY SCOTT'S ORCHESTRA & CHORUS & MILLARD THOMAS, GUITAR	2		18
14 Jun 57	**ISLAND IN THE SUN** *RCA 1007*	3		25
6 Sep 57	**SCARLET RIBBONS** *HMV POP 360* & MILLARD THOMAS	18		6
1 Nov 57	**MARY'S BOY CHILD** *RCA 1022* ★	1	7	12
22 Aug 58	**LITTLE BERNADETTE** *RCA 1072*	16		7
28 Nov 58	**MARY'S BOY CHILD** *RCA 1022*	10		6
12 Dec 58	**SON OF MARY** *RCA 1084*	18		4
11 Dec 59	**MARY'S BOY CHILD** *RCA 1022*	30		1
28 Sep 61	**HOLE IN THE BUCKET** *RCA 1247* & ODETTA	32		8

BELL & JAMES
US, male vocal duo — 3

Date	Title	Peak	Wks at No.1	Wks
31 Mar 79	**LIVIN' IT UP (FRIDAY NIGHT)** *A&M AMS 7424*	59		3

BELL & SPURLING
UK, male vocal duo – Martin Bellamy & John Spurling — 10

Date	Title	Peak	Wks at No.1	Wks
13 Oct 01	**SVEN SVEN SVEN** *Eternal WEA 336CD*	7		6
8 Jun 02	**GOLDENBALLS (MR BECKHAM TO YOU)** *Eternal WEA 350CD*	25		4

ANDY BELL
UK, male vocalist. See Erasure — 2

Date	Title	Peak	Wks at No.1	Wks
8 Oct 05	**CRAZY** *Sanctuary SANXS396*	35		2

ARCHIE BELL & THE DRELLS
US, male vocal/instrumental group — 33

Date	Title	Peak	Wks at No.1	Wks
7 Oct 72	**HERE I GO AGAIN** *Atlantic K 10210*	11		10
27 Jan 73	**THERE'S GONNA BE A SHOWDOWN** *Atlantic K 10263*	36		5
8 May 76	**SOUL CITY WALK** *Philadelphia International PIR 4250*	13		10
11 Jun 77	**EVERYBODY HAVE A GOOD TIME** *Philadelphia International PIR 5179*	43		4
28 Jun 86	**DON'T LET LOVE GET YOU DOWN** *Portrait A 7254*	49		4

BELL BIV DEVOE
US, male vocal/rap trio – Ricky Bell, Michael Bivins & Ronnie DeVoe — 36

Date	Title	Peak	Wks at No.1	Wks
30 Jun 90	**POISON** *MCA 1414*	19		11
22 Sep 90	**DO ME** *MCA 1440*	56		3
15 Aug 92	**THE BEST THINGS IN LIFE ARE FREE** *Perspective PERSS 7400* LUTHER VANDROSS & JANET JACKSON WITH SPECIAL GUESTS BBD & RALPH TRESVANT ●	2		13
9 Oct 93	**SOMETHING IN YOUR EYES** *MCA MCSTD 1934*	60		2
16 Dec 95	**THE BEST THINGS IN LIFE ARE FREE (REMIX)** *A&M 5813092* LUTHER VANDROSS & JANET JACKSON WITH SPECIAL GUESTS BBD & RALPH TRESVANT	7		7

BELL BOOK & CANDLE
Germany, male/female vocal/instrumental group — 1

Date	Title	Peak	Wks at No.1	Wks
17 Oct 98	**RESCUE ME** *Logic 74321616882*	63		1

BELL X1
Ireland, male vocal/instrumental group — 2

Date	Title	Peak	Wks at No.1	Wks
26 Jun 04	**EVE THE APPLE OF MY EYE** *Island CID 856*	65		1
25 Mar 06	**FLAME** *Island CID919*	65		1

FREDDIE BELL & THE BELLBOYS
US, male vocal/instrumental group – leader (Ferdinando Bello) d. 10 Feb 2008 (age 76) — 10

Date	Title	Peak	Wks at No.1	Wks
28 Sep 56	**GIDDY-UP-A-DING-DONG** *Mercury MT 122*	4		10

BELLAMY BROTHERS
US, male vocal duo – Howard & David Bellamy — 40

Date	Title	Peak	Wks at No.1	Wks
17 Apr 76	**LET YOUR LOVE FLOW** *Warner Brothers K 16690* ★	7		12
21 Aug 76	**SATIN SHEETS** *Warner Brothers K 16775*	43		3
11 Aug 79	**IF I SAID YOU HAD A BEAUTIFUL BODY WOULD YOU HOLD IT AGAINST ME** *Warner Brothers K 17405* ●	3		14
8 Nov 08	**LET YOUR LOVE FLOW** *Curb USBMG0300006*	21		11

MAGGIE BELL
UK, female vocalist. See Stone The Crows — 12

Date	Title	Peak	Wks at No.1	Wks
15 Apr 78	**HAZELL** *Swansong SSK 19412*	37		4
17 Oct 81	**HOLD ME** *Swansong BAM 1* B.A. ROBERTSON & MAGGIE BELL	11		8

WILLIAM BELL
US, male vocalist (William Yarbrough) — 22

Date	Title	Peak	Wks at No.1	Wks
29 May 68	**TRIBUTE TO A KING** *Stax 601 038*	31		7
20 Nov 68	**PRIVATE NUMBER** *Stax 101* JUDY CLAY & WILLIAM BELL	8		14
26 Apr 86	**HEADLINE NEWS** *Absolute LUTE 1*	70		1

BELLATRIX
Iceland, male/female vocal/instrumental group — 1

Date	Title	Peak	Wks at No.1	Wks
16 Sep 00	**JEDI WANNABE** *Fierce Panda NING 101CD*	65		1

BELLE & SEBASTIAN
UK, male/female vocal/instrumental group — 28

Date	Title	Peak	Wks at No.1	Wks
24 May 97	**DOG ON WHEELS** *Jeepster JPRCDS 001*	59		1
9 Aug 97	**LADY LINE PAINTER JANE** *Jeepster JPRCDS 002*	41		2
25 Oct 97	**3..6..9 SECONDS OF LIGHT (EP)** *Jeepster JPRCDS 003*	32		2
3 Jun 00	**LEGAL MAN** *Jeepster JPRCDS 018*	15		3
30 Jun 01	**JONATHAN DAVID** *Jeepster JPRCDS 022*	31		2
8 Dec 01	**I'M WAKING UP TO US** *Jeepster JPRCDS 023*	39		2
29 Nov 03	**STEP INTO MY OFFICE BABY** *Rough Trade RTRADESCD 128*	32		2
28 Feb 04	**I'M A CUCKOO** *Rough Trade RTRADSCD 157*	14		4
3 Jul 04	**BOOKS** *Rough Trade RTRADSCD 180*	20		3
28 Jan 06	**FUNNY LITTLE FROG** *Rough Trade RTRADSCD283*	13		4
15 Apr 06	**THE BLUES ARE STILL BLUE** *Rough Trade RTRADSCD313*	25		2
8 Jul 06	**THE WHITE COLLAR BOY** *Rough Trade RTRADSCD355*	45		1

BELLE & THE DEVOTIONS
UK, female vocal trio — 8

Date	Title	Peak	Wks at No.1	Wks
21 Apr 84	**LOVE GAMES** *CBS A 4332*	11		8

REGINA BELLE
US, female vocalist — 13

Date	Title	Peak	Wks at No.1	Wks
21 Oct 89	**GOOD LOVIN'** *CBS 6552307*	73		1
11 Dec 93	**A WHOLE NEW WORLD (ALADDIN'S THEME)** *Columbia 6599002* PEABO BRYSON & REGINA BELLE ★	12		12

BELLE STARS
UK, female vocal/instrumental group – Jennie Matthias, Stella Barker, Clare Hirst, Miranda Joyce, Sarah-Jane Owen, Judy Parsons & Lesley Shone — 42

Date	Title	Peak	Wks at No.1	Wks
5 Jun 82	**IKO IKO** *Stiff BUY 150*	35		6
17 Jul 82	**THE CLAPPING SONG** *Stiff BUY 155*	11		9

Silver-selling · Gold-selling · Platinum-selling (x multiples) · US No.1 · Peak Position · Weeks at No.1 · Weeks on Chart

Date	Title / Label	Peak Position	Weeks at No.1	Weeks on Chart
16 Oct 82	**MOCKINGBIRD** *Stiff BUY 159*	51		3
15 Jan 83	**SIGN OF THE TIMES** *Stiff BUY 167* (Silver)	3		11
16 Apr 83	**SWEET MEMORY** *Stiff BUY 174*	22		9
13 Aug 83	**INDIAN SUMMER** *Stiff BUY 185*	52		3
14 Jul 84	**80S ROMANCE** *Stiff BUY 200*	71		1

BELLEFIRE
Ireland, female vocal group — **12**

Date	Title / Label	Peak Position	Weeks at No.1	Weeks on Chart
14 Jul 01	**PERFECT BLISS** *Virgin VSCDT 1807*	18		4
18 May 02	**ALL I WANT IS YOU** *Virgin VSCDT 1820*	18		4
24 Apr 04	**SAY SOMETHING ANYWAY** *East West EW 287CD*	26		3
16 Oct 04	**SPIN THE WHEEL** *East West EW293CD*	67		1

BELLINI
Germany, male production duo – Gottfried Engels & Ramon Zenker. See E-Trax, Fragma, Hardfloor, Interactive, Paffendorf — **7**

Date	Title / Label	Peak Position	Weeks at No.1	Weeks on Chart
27 Sep 97	**SAMBA DE JANIERO** *Virgin DINSD 165*	8		7

BELLRAYS
US, male/female vocal/instrumental group — **1**

Date	Title / Label	Peak Position	Weeks at No.1	Weeks on Chart
20 Jul 02	**THEY GLUED YOUR HEAD ON UPSIDE DOWN** *Poptones MC 5073SCD*	75		1

BELLY
US, female/male vocal/instrumental group — **9**

Date	Title / Label	Peak Position	Weeks at No.1	Weeks on Chart
23 Jan 93	**FEED THE TREE** *4AD BAD 3001CD*	32		3
10 Apr 93	**GEPETTO** *4AD BAD 2018CD*	49		2
4 Feb 95	**NOW THEY'LL SLEEP** *4AD BAD 5003CD*	28		2
22 Jul 95	**SEAL MY FATE** *4AD BADD 5007CD*	35		2

BELOVED
UK, male vocal/production duo – Jon Marsh & Steve Waddington (replaced by Helena Marsh) — **47**

Date	Title / Label	Peak Position	Weeks at No.1	Weeks on Chart
21 Oct 89	**THE SUN RISING** *WEA YZ 414*	26		7
27 Jan 90	**HELLO** *WEA YZ 426*	19		7
24 Mar 90	**YOUR LOVE TAKES ME HIGHER** *East West YZ 463*	39		3
9 Jun 90	**TIME AFTER TIME** *East West YZ 482*	46		4
10 Nov 90	**IT'S ALRIGHT NOW** *East West YZ 541*	48		3
23 Jan 93	**SWEET HARMONY** *East West YZ 709CD*	8		10
10 Apr 93	**YOU'VE GOT ME THINKING** *East West YZ 738CD*	23		4
14 Aug 93	**OUTERSPACE GIRL** *East West YZ 726CD*	38		2
30 Mar 96	**SATELLITE** *East West EW 034CD*	19		3
10 Aug 96	**EASE THE PRESSURE** *East West EW 058CD*	43		2
30 Aug 97	**THE SUN RISING** *East West EW 122CD1*	31		2

BELTRAM
US, male producer (Joey Beltram) — **4**

Date	Title / Label	Peak Position	Weeks at No.1	Weeks on Chart
28 Sep 91	**ENERGY FLASH (EP)** *R&S RSUK 3*	52		2
7 Dec 91	**THE OMEN** *R&S RSUK 7* PROGRAM 2 BELTRAM	53		2

BEN'S BROTHER
UK, male vocal/instrumental group — **7**

Date	Title / Label	Peak Position	Weeks at No.1	Weeks on Chart
18 Aug 07	**LET ME OUT** *Relentless RELCD39*	38		3
26 Apr 08	**STUTTERING (KISS ME AGAIN)** *Relentless RELCD49*	41		4

BENNY BENASSI PRESENTS THE BIZ
UK/Italy, male/female vocal/DJ/production duo – Paul French & Violeta Bratu — **13**

Date	Title / Label	Peak Position	Weeks at No.1	Weeks on Chart
26 Jul 03	**SATISFACTION** *Data 58CDS*	2		11
14 Feb 04	**NO MATTER WHAT YOU DO** *Data 66CDS*	40		2

PAT BENATAR
US, female vocalist (Patricia Andrzejewski) — **53**

Date	Title / Label	Peak Position	Weeks at No.1	Weeks on Chart
21 Jan 84	**LOVE IS A BATTLEFIELD** *Chrysalis CHS 2747*	49		5
12 Jan 85	**WE BELONG** *Chrysalis CHS 2821*	22		9
23 Mar 85	**LOVE IS A BATTLEFIELD** *Chrysalis PAT 1*	17		10
15 Jun 85	**SHADOWS OF THE NIGHT** *Chrysalis PAT 2*	50		4
19 Oct 85	**INVINCIBLE (THEME FROM 'THE LEGEND OF BILLIE JEAN')** *Chrysalis PAT 3*	53		3
15 Feb 86	**SEX AS A WEAPON** *Chrysalis PAT 4*	67		3
2 Jul 88	**ALL FIRED UP** *Chrysalis PAT 5*	19		10
1 Oct 88	**DON'T WALK AWAY** *Chrysalis PAT 6*	42		5
14 Jan 89	**ONE LOVE** *Chrysalis PAT 7*	59		3
30 Oct 93	**SOMEBODY'S BABY** *Chrysalis CDCHS 5001*	48		1

DAVID BENDETH
Canada, male vocalist/multi-instrumentalist — **5**

Date	Title / Label	Peak Position	Weeks at No.1	Weeks on Chart
8 Sep 79	**FEEL THE REAL** *Sidewalk SID 113*	44		5

BENELUX & NANCY DEE
Belgium/Holland/Luxembourg, female vocal group — **4**

Date	Title / Label	Peak Position	Weeks at No.1	Weeks on Chart
25 Aug 79	**SWITCH** *Scope SC 4*	52		4

ERIC BENET
US, male vocalist (Eric Bennet Jordan) — **5**

Date	Title / Label	Peak Position	Weeks at No.1	Weeks on Chart
22 Mar 97	**SPIRITUAL THANG** *Warner Brothers W 0390CD*	62		1
1 May 99	**GEORGY PORGY** *Warner Brothers W 478CD1* FEATURING FAITH EVANS	28		3
5 Feb 00	**WHY YOU FOLLOW ME** *Warner Brothers W 491CD*	48		1

BENNETT
UK, male vocal/instrumental group — **3**

Date	Title / Label	Peak Position	Weeks at No.1	Weeks on Chart
22 Feb 97	**MUM'S GONE TO ICELAND** *Roadrunner RR 22853*	34		2
3 May 97	**SOMEONE ALWAYS GETS THERE FIRST** *Roadrunner RR 22983*	69		1

BOYD BENNETT & HIS ROCKETS
US, male vocal/instrumental group – leader d. 2 Jun 2002 (age 77) — **2**

Date	Title / Label	Peak Position	Weeks at No.1	Weeks on Chart
23 Dec 55	**SEVENTEEN** *Parlophone R 4063*	16		2

CLIFF BENNETT & THE REBEL ROUSERS
UK, male vocal/instrumental group — **23**

Date	Title / Label	Peak Position	Weeks at No.1	Weeks on Chart
1 Oct 64	**ONE WAY LOVE** *Parlophone R 5173*	9		9
4 Feb 65	**I'LL TAKE YOU HOME** *Parlophone R 5229*	42		3
11 Aug 66	**GOT TO GET YOU INTO MY LIFE** *Parlophone R 5489*	6		11

PETER E BENNETT WITH THE CO-OPERATION CHOIR
UK, male vocalist & choir — **1**

Date	Title / Label	Peak Position	Weeks at No.1	Weeks on Chart
7 Nov 70	**THE SEAGULL'S NAME WAS NELSON** *RCA 1991*	45		1

TONY BENNETT
US, male vocalist (Anthony Benedetto) — **61**

Date	Title / Label	Peak Position	Weeks at No.1	Weeks on Chart
15 Apr 55	**STRANGER IN PARADISE** *Philips PB 420*	1	2	16
16 Sep 55	**CLOSE YOUR EYES** *Philips PB 445*	18		1
13 Apr 56	**COME NEXT SPRING** *Philips PB 537*	29		1
5 Jan 61	**TILL** *Philips PB 1079*	35		2
18 Jul 63	**THE GOOD LIFE** *CBS AAG 153*	27		13
6 May 65	**IF I RULED THE WORLD** *CBS 201735*	40		5
27 May 65	**I LEFT MY HEART IN SAN FRANCISCO** *CBS 201730*	46		2
30 Sep 65	**I LEFT MY HEART IN SAN FRANCISCO** *CBS 201730*	25		12
23 Dec 65	**THE VERY THOUGHT OF YOU** *CBS 202021*	21		9

BRENDAN BENSON
US, male vocalist/guitarist — **1**

Date	Title / Label	Peak Position	Weeks at No.1	Weeks on Chart
9 Apr 05	**SPIT IT OUT** *V2 VVR5031203*	75		1

GARY BENSON
UK, male vocalist (Harry Hyams) — **8**

Date	Title / Label	Peak Position	Weeks at No.1	Weeks on Chart
9 Aug 75	**DON'T THROW IT ALL AWAY** *State STAT 10*	20		8

GEORGE BENSON
US, male vocalist/guitarist — **143**

Date	Title / Label	Peak Position	Weeks at No.1	Weeks on Chart
25 Oct 75	**SUPERSHIP** *CTI CTSP 002* GEORGE 'BAD' BENSON	30		6
4 Jun 77	**NATURE BOY** *Warner Brothers K 16921*	26		6
24 Sep 77	**THE GREATEST LOVE OF ALL** *Arista 133*	27		7
31 Mar 79	**LOVE BALLAD** *Warner Brothers K 17333*	29		9
26 Jul 80	**GIVE ME THE NIGHT** *Warner Brothers K 17673*	7		10
4 Oct 80	**LOVE X LOVE** *Warner Brothers K 17699*	10		8
7 Feb 81	**WHAT'S ON YOUR MIND** *Warner Brothers K 17748*	45		5

Silver-selling ● Gold-selling ● Platinum-selling (x multiples) ✱ US No.1 ★ Peak Position · Weeks at No.1 · Weeks on Chart

Date	Title	Peak Position	Weeks at No.1	Weeks on Chart
19 Sep 81	**LOVE ALL THE HURT AWAY** *Arista ARIST 428* ARETHA FRANKLIN & GEORGE BENSON	49		3
14 Nov 81	**TURN YOUR LOVE AROUND** *Warner Brothers K 17877*	29		11
23 Jan 82	**NEVER GIVE UP ON A GOOD THING** *Warner Brothers K 17902*	14		10
21 May 83	**LADY LOVE ME (ONE MORE TIME)** *Warner Brothers W 9614*	11		10
16 Jul 83	**FEEL LIKE MAKIN' LOVE** *Warner Brothers W 9551*	28		7
24 Sep 83	**IN YOUR EYES** *Warner Brothers W 9487*	7		10
17 Dec 83	**INSIDE LOVE (SO PERSONAL)** *Warner Brothers W 9427*	57		5
19 Jan 85	**20/20** *Warner Brothers W 9120*	29		9
20 Apr 85	**BEYOND THE SEA (LA MER)** *Warner Brothers W 9014*	60		3
16 Aug 86	**KISSES IN THE MOONLIGHT** *Warner Brothers W 8640*	60		4
29 Nov 86	**SHIVER** *Warner Brothers W 8523*	19		9
14 Feb 87	**TEASER** *Warner Brothers W 8437*	45		4
27 Aug 88	**LET'S DO IT AGAIN** *Warner Brothers W 7780*	56		3
5 Sep 92	**I'LL KEEP YOUR DREAMS ALIVE** *Ammi 101* & PATTI AUSTIN	68		1
11 Jul 98	**SEVEN DAYS** *MCA MCSTD 48083* MARY J BLIGE FEATURING GEORGE BENSON	22		3

RHIAN BENSON
Ghana, female vocalist — **2**

Date	Title	Peak Position	Weeks at No.1	Weeks on Chart
23 Oct 04	**SAY HOW I FEEL** *DKG DKG710071002*	27		2

BENT
UK, male production duo — **1**

Date	Title	Peak Position	Weeks at No.1	Weeks on Chart
12 Jul 03	**STAY THE SAME** *Sport 9CDX*	59		1

BENTLEY RHYTHM ACE
UK, male DJ/instrumental duo — **7**

Date	Title	Peak Position	Weeks at No.1	Weeks on Chart
6 Sep 97	**BENTLEY'S GONNA SORT YOU OUT!** *Skint CDRS 6476*	17		4
27 May 00	**THEME FROM 'GUTBUSTER'** *Parlophone CDRS 6537*	29		2
2 Sep 00	**HOW'D I DO DAT** *Parlophone CDRS 6543*	57		1

BROOK BENTON
US, male vocalist (Benjamin Peay), d. 9 Apr 1988 (age 56) — **18**

Date	Title	Peak Position	Weeks at No.1	Weeks on Chart
10 Jul 59	**ENDLESSLY** *Mercury AMT 1043*	28		2
6 Oct 60	**KIDDIO** *Mercury AMT 1109*	41		6
16 Feb 61	**FOOLS RUSH IN** *Mercury AMT 1121*	50		1
13 Jul 61	**BOLL WEEVIL SONG** *Mercury AMT 1148*	30		9

BENZ
UK, male vocal/rap group — **9**

Date	Title	Peak Position	Weeks at No.1	Weeks on Chart
16 Dec 95	**BOOM ROCK SOUL** *Hacktown 74321329652*	62		2
16 Mar 96	**URBAN CITY GIRL** *Hacktown 74321348732*	31		3
25 May 96	**MISS PARKER** *Hacktown 74321377292*	35		2
29 Mar 97	**IF I REMEMBER** *Hendricks CDBENZ 1*	59		1
9 Aug 97	**ON A SUN-DAY** *Hendricks CDBENZ 2*	73		1

BERLIN
US, female/male vocal/instrumental group – Terri Nunn, Rob Brill, John Crawford, David Diamond, Rick Olsen & Matt Reid — **39**

Date	Title	Peak Position	Weeks at No.1	Weeks on Chart
25 Oct 86	**TAKE MY BREATH AWAY (LOVE THEME FROM 'TOP GUN')** *CBS A 7320* ● ★	1	4	15
17 Jan 87	**YOU DON'T KNOW** *Mercury MER 237*	39		6
14 Mar 87	**LIKE FLAMES** *Mercury MER 240*	47		3
20 Feb 88	**TAKE MY BREATH AWAY (LOVE THEME FROM 'TOP GUN')** *CBS A 7320*	52		3
13 Oct 90	**TAKE MY BREATH AWAY (LOVE THEME FROM 'TOP GUN')** *CBS 6563617*	3		12

FRANCESCA BERLIN
UK, female vocalist — **1**

Date	Title	Peak Position	Weeks at No.1	Weeks on Chart
19 Aug 06	**COLOURS FADED** *Moon MNR001*	60		1

ELMER BERNSTEIN
US, male orchestra leader, d. 19 Aug 2004 (age 82) — **11**

Date	Title	Peak Position	Weeks at No.1	Weeks on Chart
18 Dec 59	**STACCATO'S THEME** *Capitol CL 15101*	4		11

LEONARD BERNSTEIN, ORCHESTRA & CHORUS
US, male conductor/composer/pianist, d. 14 Oct 1990 (age 72) — **4**

Date	Title	Peak Position	Weeks at No.1	Weeks on Chart
2 Jul 94	**AMERICA – WORLD CUP THEME 1994** *Deutsche Grammophon USACD 1*	44		4

BERRI
UK, female vocalist (Rebecca Sleight) — **22**

Date	Title	Peak Position	Weeks at No.1	Weeks on Chart
26 Nov 94	**THE SUNSHINE AFTER THE RAIN** *3 Beat TABCD 223* NEW ATLANTIC/U4EA FEATURING BERRI	26		6
2 Sep 95	**THE SUNSHINE AFTER THE RAIN** *ffrreedom TABCD 232* ●	4		11
2 Dec 95	**SHINE LIKE A STAR** *3 Beat TABCD 239*	20		5

LaKIESHA BERRI
US, female vocalist — **1**

Date	Title	Peak Position	Weeks at No.1	Weeks on Chart
5 Jul 97	**LIKE THIS AND LIKE THAT** *Adept ADPTCD 7*	54		1

CHUCK BERRY
US, male vocalist/guitarist — **91**

Date	Title	Peak Position	Weeks at No.1	Weeks on Chart
21 Jun 57	**SCHOOL DAY** *Columbia DB 3951*	24		4
25 Apr 58	**SWEET LITTLE SIXTEEN** *London HLM 8585*	16		5
11 Jul 63	**GO GO GO** *Pye International 7N 25209*	38		6
10 Oct 63	**LET IT ROCK/MEMPHIS TENNESSEE** *Pye International 7N 25218*	6		13
19 Dec 63	**RUN RUDOLPH RUN** *Pye International 7N 25228*	36		6
13 Feb 64	**NADINE (IS IT YOU)** *Pye International 7N 25236*	27		7
7 May 64	**NO PARTICULAR PLACE TO GO** *Pye International 7N 25242*	3		12
20 Aug 64	**YOU NEVER CAN TELL** *Pye International 7N 25257*	23		8
14 Jan 65	**PROMISED LAND** *Pye International 7N 25285*	26		6
28 Oct 72	**MY DING-A-LING** *Chess 6145 019* ★	1	4	17
3 Feb 73	**REELIN' AND ROCKIN'** *Chess 6145 020*	18		7

DAVE BERRY
UK, male vocalist (Dave Grundy) — **76**

Date	Title	Peak Position	Weeks at No.1	Weeks on Chart
19 Sep 63	**MEMPHIS TENNESSEE** *Decca F 11734* & THE CRUISERS	19		13
9 Jan 64	**MY BABY LEFT ME** *Decca F 11803* & THE CRUISERS	37		9
30 Apr 64	**BABY IT'S YOU** *Decca F 11876*	24		6
6 Aug 64	**THE CRYING GAME** *Decca F 11937*	5		12
26 Nov 64	**ONE HEART BETWEEN TWO** *Decca F 12020*	41		2
25 Mar 65	**LITTLE THINGS** *Decca F 12103*	5		12
22 Jul 65	**THIS STRANGE EFFECT** *Decca F 12188*	37		6
30 Jun 66	**MAMA** *Decca F 12435*	5		16

MIKE BERRY
UK, male vocalist (Michael Bourne) — **51**

Date	Title	Peak Position	Weeks at No.1	Weeks on Chart
12 Oct 61	**TRIBUTE TO BUDDY HOLLY** *HMV POP 912* WITH THE OUTLAWS	24		6
3 Jan 63	**DON'T YOU THINK IT'S TIME** *HMV POP 1105* WITH THE OUTLAWS	6		12
11 Apr 63	**MY LITTLE BABY** *HMV POP 1142* WITH THE OUTLAWS	34		7
2 Aug 80	**THE SUNSHINE OF YOUR SMILE** *Polydor 2059 261* ●	9		12
29 Nov 80	**IF I COULD ONLY MAKE YOU CARE** *Polydor POSP 202*	37		9
5 Sep 81	**MEMORIES** *Polydor POSP 287*	55		5

NICK BERRY
UK, male vocalist/actor — **24**

Date	Title	Peak Position	Weeks at No.1	Weeks on Chart
4 Oct 86	**EVERY LOSER WINS** *BBC RESL 204*	1	3	13
13 Jun 92	**HEARTBEAT** *Columbia 6581517*	2		8
31 Oct 92	**LONG LIVE LOVE** *Columbia 6587597*	47		3

BEST COMPANY
UK, male production/vocal duo — **1**

Date	Title	Peak Position	Weeks at No.1	Weeks on Chart
27 Mar 93	**DON'T YOU FORGET ABOUT ME** *ZYX 69468*	65		1

BEST SHOT
UK, male vocal/rap group — **2**

Date	Title	Peak Position	Weeks at No.1	Weeks on Chart
5 Feb 94	**UNITED COLOURS** *East West YZ 795CD*	64		2

BETA BAND
UK, male vocal/instrumental group — **7**

Date	Title	Peak Position	Weeks at No.1	Weeks on Chart
14 Jul 01	**BROKE/WON** *Regal Recordings REG 60CDDJ*	30		2
27 Oct 01	**HUMAN BEING** *Regal Recordings REG 65CD*	57		1
16 Feb 02	**SQUARES** *Regal Recordings REG 69CD*	42		1
24 Apr 04	**ASSESSMENT** *Regal Recordings REG 102CDS*	31		2
24 Jul 04	**OUT-SIDE** *Regal Recordings REG 110CDS*	54		1

BEVERLEY SISTERS
UK, female vocal trio – Joy, Babs & Teddie Beverley — 34

Date	Title	Peak Position	Weeks at No.1	Weeks on Chart
27 Nov 53	**I SAW MOMMY KISSING SANTA CLAUS** *Philips PB 188*	6		5
13 Apr 56	**WILLIE CAN** *Decca F 10705*	23		4
1 Feb 57	**I DREAMED** *Decca F 10832*	24		2
13 Feb 59	**LITTLE DRUMMER BOY** *Decca F 11107*	6		13
20 Nov 59	**LITTLE DONKEY** *Decca F 11172*	14		7
23 Jun 60	**GREEN FIELDS** *Columbia DB 4444*	29		3

BEYONCE
US, female vocalist/model/actor (Beyonce Knowles). Photogenic singer who received a record 64 gold and platinum single/album/video/ringtone certifications for the period 2000-2009 and bagged six Grammys in 2010 – a record for a female artist. See Destiny's Child — 318

Date	Title	Peak Position	Weeks at No.1	Weeks on Chart
27 Jul 02	**WORK IT OUT** *Columbia 6729822*	7		11
1 Feb 03	**03 BONNIE AND CLYDE** *Roc-A-Fella 0770102* JAY-Z FEATURING BEYONCE KNOWLES	2		12
12 Jul 03	**CRAZY IN LOVE** *Columbia 6740675* ★	1	3	15
18 Oct 03	**BABY BOY** *Columbia 6744082* FEATURING SEAN PAUL ★	2		11
24 Jan 04	**ME, MYSELF & I** *Columbia 6745445*	11		7
17 Apr 04	**NAUGHTY GIRL** *Columbia 6748282*	10		8
28 Jan 06	**CHECK ON IT** *Columbia 82876772532* FEATURING SLIM THUG ★	3		12
26 Aug 06	**DÉJÀ VU** *Columbia 82876884352* FEATURING JAY-Z	1	1	16
28 Oct 06	**IRREPLACEABLE** *Columbia 88697024472* ★	4		25
3 Feb 07	**LISTEN** *Columbia 88697059602*	16		8
14 Apr 07	**BEAUTIFUL LIAR** *Columbia 88697091242* & SHAKIRA ●	1	3	21
11 Aug 07	**GREEN LIGHT FREEMASONS EP** *Columbia USSM10603616*	12		6
15 Nov 08	**IF I WERE A BOY** *Columbia 88697401522* ●	1	1	27
29 Nov 08	**SINGLE LADIES (PUT A RING ON IT)** *Columbia 88697475032* ★	7		34
13 Dec 08	**LISTEN** *Columbia 88697059602*	8		9
14 Mar 09	**HALO** *Columbia 88697519782*	4		28
23 May 09	**DIVA** *Columbia USSM10804755*	72		2
18 Jul 09	**SWEET DREAMS** *Columbia 88697565722*	5		24
3 Oct 09	**BROKEN HEARTED GIRL** *Columbia 88697614332*	27		10
5 Dec 09	**TELEPHONE** *Interscope 2734706* LADY GAGA & BEYONCE	1	2	18+
2 Jan 10	**VIDEO PHONE** *Columbia USSM10804757* FEATURING LADY GAGA	58		3
6 Feb 10	**HALO** *Columbia 88697519782*	45		3
6 Feb 10	**SINGLE LADIES (PUT A RING ON IT)** *Columbia 88697475032*	45		8

BEYOND
UK, male vocal/instrumental group — 1

Date	Title	Peak Position	Weeks at No.1	Weeks on Chart
21 Sep 91	**RAGING EP** *Harvest HARS 530*	68		1

BG THE PRINCE OF RAP
Germany (b. US), male rapper (Bernard Greene) — 2

Date	Title	Peak Position	Weeks at No.1	Weeks on Chart
18 Jan 92	**TAKE CONTROL OF THE PARTY** *Columbia 6576330*	71		2

BHANGRA KNIGHTS VS HUSAN
UK/Holland, male vocal/production group – Jack Berry & Jules Spinner (Bhangra Knights) & Jeroen Den Hengst & Niels Zuiderhoek (Husan) — 7

Date	Title	Peak Position	Weeks at No.1	Weeks on Chart
17 May 03	**HUSAN** *Positiva CDTIV 188*	7		7

BHOYS FROM PARADISE
UK, football fans (Celtic)/vocal group. See Simple Minds — 2

Date	Title	Peak Position	Weeks at No.1	Weeks on Chart
3 Jul 04	**DIRTY OLD TOWN/THE ROAD TO PARADISE** *Lord Of The Wing LWSP7*	46		2

BIBLE
UK, male vocal/instrumental group — 8

Date	Title	Peak Position	Weeks at No.1	Weeks on Chart
20 May 89	**GRACELAND** *Chrysalis BIB 4*	51		4
26 Aug 89	**HONEY BE GOOD** *Chrysalis BIB 5*	54		4

BIDDU ORCHESTRA
India, male producer/orchestra leader (Biddu Appaiah) — 13

Date	Title	Peak Position	Weeks at No.1	Weeks on Chart
2 Aug 75	**SUMMER OF '42** *Epic EPC 3318*	14		8
17 Apr 76	**RAIN FOREST** *Epic EPC 4084*	39		4
11 Feb 78	**JOURNEY TO THE MOON** *Epic EPC 5910*	41		1

JUSTIN BIEBER
Canada, male vocalist — 18

Date	Title	Peak Position	Weeks at No.1	Weeks on Chart
16 Jan 10	**ONE TIME** *Def Jam USUV70901803*	11		12
30 Jan 10	**ONE LESS LONELY GIRL** *Def Jam USUM70996002*	62		1
30 Jan 10	**LOVE ME** *Def Jam USUM70902893*	71		1
20 Mar 10	**BABY** *Mercury USUM70919263* FEATURING LUDACRIS	3		4+

BIFFY CLYRO
UK, male vocal/instrumental trio – Simon Neil & Ben & James Johnston — 57

Date	Title	Peak Position	Weeks at No.1	Weeks on Chart
16 Feb 02	**57** *Beggars Banquet BBQ 358CD*	61		1
5 Apr 03	**THE IDEAL HEIGHT** *Beggars Banquet BBQ 365CD*	46		1
7 Jun 03	**QUESTIONS AND ANSWERS** *Beggars Banquet BBQ 368CD*	26		2
21 Aug 04	**GLITTER AND TRAUMA** *Beggars Banquet BBQ 377CD*	21		3
2 Oct 04	**MY RECOVERY INJECTION** *Beggars Banquet BBQ 379CD*	24		2
26 Feb 05	**ONLY ONE WORD COMES TO MIND** *Beggars Banquet BBQ384CD*	27		2
17 Mar 07	**SATURDAY SUPERHOUSE** *14th Floor 14FLR19CD*	13		3
19 May 07	**LIVING IS A PROBLEM BECAUSE EVERYTHING DIES** *Warner Brothers 14FLR21CD*	19		5
28 Jul 07	**FOLDING STARS** *14th Floor 14FLR24CD*	18		2
13 Oct 07	**MACHINES** *14th Floor 14FLR27CD*	29		5
9 Feb 08	**WHO'S GOT A MATCH** *14th Floor 14FLR29CD*	27		4
30 Aug 08	**MOUNTAINS** *14th Floor 14FLR32CD*	5		10
5 Sep 09	**THAT GOLDEN RULE** *14th Floor 14FLR38CD*	10		4
7 Nov 09	**THE CAPTAIN** *14th Floor 14FLR40CD*	17		4
23 Jan 10	**MANY OF HORROR (WHEN WE COLLIDE)** *14th Floor 14FLR41CD*	20		9

BIG ANG FEATURING SIOBHAN
UK, female vocal/production duo — 3

Date	Title	Peak Position	Weeks at No.1	Weeks on Chart
10 Sep 05	**IT'S OVER NOW** *All Around The World CDGLOBE298*	29		3

BIG AUDIO DYNAMITE
UK, male vocal/instrumental group — 27

Date	Title	Peak Position	Weeks at No.1	Weeks on Chart
22 Mar 86	**E = MC2** *CBS A 6963*	11		9
7 Jun 86	**MEDICINE SHOW** *CBS 7181*	29		5
18 Oct 86	**C'MON EVERY BEATBOX** *CBS 6501477*	51		3
21 Feb 87	**V THIRTEEN** *CBS BAAD 2*	49		5
28 May 88	**JUST PLAY MUSIC** *CBS BAAD 4*	51		3
12 Nov 94	**LOOKING FOR A SONG** *Columbia 6610182* BIG AUDIO	68		2

BIG BAM BOO
UK/US, male vocal/instrumental duo — 2

Date	Title	Peak Position	Weeks at No.1	Weeks on Chart
28 Jan 89	**SHOOTING FROM MY HEART** *MCA 1281*	61		2

BIG BANG THEORY
UK, male producer (Seamus Haji) — 1

Date	Title	Peak Position	Weeks at No.1	Weeks on Chart
2 Mar 02	**GOD'S CHILD** *Defected DFECT 45CDS*	51		1

BIG BASS VS MICHELLE NARINE
Canada, male/female vocal/production group — 6

Date	Title	Peak Position	Weeks at No.1	Weeks on Chart
2 Sep 00	**WHAT YOU DO** *Stonebridge/Edel 0110965 ERE*	67		1
6 Jan 07	**WHAT YOU DO (PLAYING WITH STONES)** *Apollo Recordings APOLLO106CDS*	27		5

BIG BEN
UK, clock — 2

Date	Title	Peak Position	Weeks at No.1	Weeks on Chart
1 Jan 00	**MILLENNIUM CHIMES** *London BIGONE 2000*	53		2

BIG BEN BANJO BAND
UK, male instrumental session band – leader Norrie Paramor, d. 9 Sep 1979 (age 65) — 6

Date	Title	Peak Position	Weeks at No.1	Weeks on Chart
10 Dec 54	**LET'S GET TOGETHER NO. 1** *Columbia DB 3549*	6		4
9 Dec 55	**LET'S GET TOGETHER AGAIN** *Columbia DB 3676*	18		2

BIG BOI
US, male vocalist/rapper (Antwan Patton). See Outkast — 5

Date	Title	Peak Position	Weeks at No.1	Weeks on Chart
10 May 03	**A.D.I.D.A.S.** *Columbia 6738652* KILLER MIKE FEATURING BIG BOI	22		3
16 Jul 05	**GIRLFIGHT** *Virgin VUSDX301* BROOKE VALENTINE FEATURING BIG BOI & LIL' JON	35		2

Silver-selling · Gold-selling · Platinum-selling (x multiples) · US No.1 · Peak Position · Weeks at No.1 · Weeks on Chart

BIG BOPPER

US, male vocalist (Jape Richardson), d. 3 Feb 1959 (age 28) — 8

Date	Title	Peak	Wks at No.1	Wks on Chart
26 Dec 58	**CHANTILLY LACE** *Mercury AMT 1002*	12		8

BIG BOSS STYLUS PRESENTS RED VENOM

UK, male rap/production trio — 1

Date	Title	Peak	Wks at No.1	Wks on Chart
31 Jul 99	**LET'S GET IT ON** *All Around The World CDGLOBE 195*	72		1

BIG BROVAZ

UK, male/female vocal/rap/production group – Dionne (Dionne Howell), Flawless (Tayo Aisida, b. Nigeria), J-Rock (John Horsley, b. US), Randy (Michael Brown), Cherise Roberts & Nadia Shepherd. See Booty Luv — 66

Date	Title	Peak	Wks at No.1	Wks on Chart
26 Oct 02	**NU FLOW** *Epic 6730282*	3		18
15 Feb 03	**OK** *Epic 6735212*	7		9
17 May 03	**FAVOURITE THINGS** *Epic 6738075*	2		11
13 Sep 03	**BABY BOY** *Epic 6743092*	4		12
20 Dec 03	**AIN'T WHAT YOU DO** *Epic 6745105*	15		7
17 Apr 04	**WE WANNA THANK YOU (THE THINGS YOU DO)** *Epic 6748602*	17		4
9 Oct 04	**YOURS FATALLY** *Epic 6753542*	15		4
13 May 06	**HANGIN' AROUND** *Genetic GENE500033*	57		1

BIG COUNTRY

UK, male vocal/instrumental group – Stuart Adamson, d. 16 Dec 2001 (age 43), Mark Brzezicki, Tony Butler & Bruce Watson — 103

Date	Title	Peak	Wks at No.1	Wks on Chart
26 Feb 83	**FIELDS OF FIRE (400 MILES)** *Mercury COUNT 2*	10		12
28 May 83	**IN A BIG COUNTRY** *Mercury COUNT 3*	17		7
3 Sep 83	**CHANCE** *Mercury COUNT 4*	9		9
21 Jan 84	**WONDERLAND** *Mercury COUNT 5*	8		8
29 Sep 84	**EAST OF EDEN** *Mercury MER 175*	17		6
1 Dec 84	**WHERE THE ROSE IS SOWN** *Mercury MER 185*	29		7
19 Jan 85	**JUST A SHADOW** *Mercury BCO 8*	26		4
12 Apr 86	**LOOK AWAY** *Mercury BIGC 1*	7		8
21 Jun 86	**THE TEACHER** *Mercury BIGC 2*	28		4
20 Sep 86	**ONE GREAT THING** *Mercury BIGC 3*	19		6
29 Nov 86	**HOLD THE HEART** *Mercury BIGC 4*	55		2
20 Aug 88	**KING OF EMOTION** *Mercury BIGC 5*	16		6
5 Nov 88	**BROKEN HEART (THIRTEEN VALLEYS)** *Mercury BIGC 6*	47		4
4 Feb 89	**PEACE IN OUR TIME** *Mercury BIGC 7*	39		3
12 May 90	**SAVE ME** *Mercury BIGC 8*	41		3
21 Jul 90	**HEART OF THE WORLD** *Mercury BIGC 9*	50		2
31 Aug 91	**REPUBLICAN PARTY REPTILE (EP)** *Vertigo BIC 1*	37		2
19 Oct 91	**BEAUTIFUL PEOPLE** *Vertigo BIC 2*	72		1
13 Mar 93	**ALONE** *Compulsion CDPULSS 4*	24		3
1 May 93	**SHIPS (WHERE WERE YOU)** *Compulsion CDPULSS 6*	29		3
10 Jun 95	**I'M NOT ASHAMED** *Transatlantic TRAX 1009*	69		1
9 Sep 95	**YOU DREAMER** *Transatlantic TRAX 1012*	68		1
21 Aug 99	**FRAGILE THING** *Track 0004A* FEATURING EDDI READER	69		1

BIG DADDY

US, male vocal/instrumental group — 8

Date	Title	Peak	Wks at No.1	Wks on Chart
9 Mar 85	**DANCING IN THE DARK EP** *Making Waves SURF 1033*	21		8

BIG DADDY KANE

US, male rapper (Antonio Hardy) — 6

Date	Title	Peak	Wks at No.1	Wks on Chart
13 May 89	**RAP SUMMARY/WRATH OF KANE** *Cold Chillin' W 2973*	52		2
26 Aug 89	**SMOOTHER OPERATOR** *Cold Chillin' W 2804*	65		1
13 Jan 90	**AIN'T NO STOPPIN' US NOW** *Cold Chillin' W 2605*	44		3

BIG DISH

UK, male vocal/instrumental group — 5

Date	Title	Peak	Wks at No.1	Wks on Chart
12 Jan 91	**MISS AMERICA** *East West YZ 529*	37		5

BIG FUN

UK, male vocal group – Phil Creswick, Mark Gillespie & Jason Herbert — 33

Date	Title	Peak	Wks at No.1	Wks on Chart
12 Aug 89	**BLAME IT ON THE BOOGIE** *Jive 217*	4		11
25 Nov 89	**CAN'T SHAKE THE FEELING** *Jive 234*	8		9
17 Mar 90	**HANDFUL OF PROMISES** *Jive 243*	21		6
23 Jun 90	**YOU'VE GOT A FRIEND** *Jive CHILD 90* & SONIA FEATURING GARY BARNACLE	14		6
4 Aug 90	**HEY THERE LONELY GIRL** *Jive 251*	62		1

BIG MOUNTAIN

US, male/female vocal/instrumental group – Joachin 'Quino' McWhinney, Gregory Blakney, Lynn Copeland, Jerome Cruz, Manfred Reinke & Lance Rhodes — 15

Date	Title	Peak	Wks at No.1	Wks on Chart
4 Jun 94	**BABY I LOVE YOUR WAY** *RCA 74321198062*	2		14
24 Sep 94	**SWEET SENSUAL LOVE** *Giant 74321234642*	51		1

BIG PINK

UK, male vocal/instrumental duo — 12

Date	Title	Peak	Wks at No.1	Wks on Chart
17 Oct 09	**DOMINOS** *4AD GBAFL0900085*	27		12

BIG RON

UK, male producer (Aaron Gilbert). See Big Time Charlie — 1

Date	Title	Peak	Wks at No.1	Wks on Chart
11 Mar 00	**LET THE FREAK** *48K SPECT 06CDS*	57		1

BIG ROOM GIRL FEATURING DARRYL PANDY

UK/US, male vocal/production/instrumental trio. See Rhythm Masters — 2

Date	Title	Peak	Wks at No.1	Wks on Chart
20 Feb 99	**RAISE YOUR HANDS** *VC Recordings VCRD 44*	40		2

BIG SOUND AUTHORITY

UK, male/female vocal/instrumental group — 12

Date	Title	Peak	Wks at No.1	Wks on Chart
19 Jan 85	**THIS HOUSE (IS WHERE YOUR LOVE STANDS)** *Source BSA 1*	21		9
8 Jun 85	**A BAD TOWN** *Source BSA 2*	54		3

BIG SUPREME

UK, male/female vocal trio — 5

Date	Title	Peak	Wks at No.1	Wks on Chart
20 Sep 86	**DON'T WALK** *Polydor POSP 809*	58		3
14 Mar 87	**PLEASE YOURSELF** *Polydor POSP 840*	64		2

BIG THREE

UK, male vocal/instrumental group — 17

Date	Title	Peak	Wks at No.1	Wks on Chart
11 Apr 63	**SOME OTHER GUY** *Decca F 11614*	37		7
11 Jul 63	**BY THE WAY** *Decca F 11689*	22		10

BIG TIME CHARLIE

UK, male DJ/production duo. See Big Ron — 4

Date	Title	Peak	Wks at No.1	Wks on Chart
23 Oct 99	**ON THE RUN** *Inferno CDFERN 18*	22		2
18 Mar 00	**MR DEVIL** *Inferno CDFERN 24* FEATURING SOOZY Q	39		2

BIGFELLA FEATURING NOEL McCALLA

US/UK, male vocal/production trio — 1

Date	Title	Peak	Wks at No.1	Wks on Chart
17 Aug 02	**BEAUTIFUL** *NuLife 74321954381*	52		1

BARRY BIGGS

Jamaica, male vocalist — 46

Date	Title	Peak	Wks at No.1	Wks on Chart
28 Aug 76	**WORK ALL DAY** *Dynamic DYN 101*	38		5
4 Dec 76	**SIDESHOW** *Dynamic DYN 118*	3		16
23 Apr 77	**YOU'RE MY LIFE** *Dynamic DYN 127*	36		4
9 Jul 77	**THREE RING CIRCUS** *Dynamic DYN 128*	22		8
15 Dec 79	**WHAT'S YOUR SIGN GIRL** *Dynamic DYN 150*	55		7
20 Jun 81	**WIDE AWAKE IN A DREAM** *Dynamic DYN 10*	44		6

IVOR BIGGUN

UK, male vocalist/comedian (Doc Cox) — 15

Date	Title	Peak	Wks at No.1	Wks on Chart
2 Sep 78	**WINKER'S SONG (MISPRINT)** *Beggars Banquet BOP 1* & THE RED NOSE BURGLARS	22		12
12 Sep 81	**BRAS ON 45 (FAMILY VERSION)** *Beggars Banquet BOP 6* & THE D CUPS	50		3

BILBO

UK, male vocal/instrumental group — 7

Date	Title	Peak	Wks at No.1	Wks on Chart
26 Aug 78	**SHE'S GONNA WIN** *Lightning LIG 548*	42		7

MR ACKER BILK
UK, male clarinettist/vocalist/band leader **172**

Date	Title	Peak Position	Weeks at No.1	Weeks on Chart
22 Jan 60	**SUMMER SET** *Columbia DB 4382* & HIS PARAMOUNT JAZZ BAND	5		20
9 Jun 60	**GOODNIGHT SWEET PRINCE** *Melodisc MEL 1547* & HIS PARAMOUNT JAZZ BAND	50		1
18 Aug 60	**WHITE CLIFFS OF DOVER** *Columbia DB 4492* & HIS PARAMOUNT JAZZ BAND	30		9
8 Dec 60	**BUONA SERA** *Columbia DB 4544* & HIS PARAMOUNT JAZZ BAND	7		18
13 Jul 61	**THAT'S MY HOME** *Columbia DB 4673* & HIS PARAMOUNT JAZZ BAND	7		17
2 Nov 61	**STARS AND STRIPES FOREVER/CREOLE JAZZ** *Columbia SCD 2155* & HIS PARAMOUNT JAZZ BAND	22		10
30 Nov 61	**STRANGER ON THE SHORE** *Columbia DB 4750* WITH THE LEON YOUNG STRING CHORALE ★	2		55
15 Mar 62	**FRANKIE AND JOHNNY** *Columbia DB 4795* & HIS PARAMOUNT JAZZ BAND	42		2
26 Jul 62	**GOTTA SEE BABY TONIGHT** *Columbia SCD 2176* & HIS PARAMOUNT JAZZ BAND	24		9
27 Sep 62	**LONELY** *Columbia DB 4897* WITH THE LEON YOUNG STRING CHORALE	14		11
24 Jan 63	**A TASTE OF HONEY** *Columbia DB 4949* WITH THE LEON YOUNG STRING CHORALE	16		9
21 Aug 76	**ARIA** *Pye 7N 45607* ACKER BILK, HIS CLARINET & STRINGS	5		11

BILL
UK, male vocalist/barman/radio show character **1**

Date	Title	Peak Position	Weeks at No.1	Weeks on Chart
23 Oct 93	**CAR BOOT SALE** *Mercury MINCD 1*	73		1

BILL & BEN
UK, male puppets (John Thomson) **4**

Date	Title	Peak Position	Weeks at No.1	Weeks on Chart
13 Jul 02	**FLOBBADANCE** *BBC WMSS 60552*	23		4

BILLIAM
UK, male vocal group **2**

Date	Title	Peak Position	Weeks at No.1	Weeks on Chart
29 Sep 07	**BEAUTIFUL ONES** *Nightingale 2*	32		1
28 Jun 08	**MY GENERATION** *Nightingale 4*	23		1

BILLY TALENT
Canada, male vocal/instrumental group **5**

Date	Title	Peak Position	Weeks at No.1	Weeks on Chart
13 Sep 03	**TRY HONESTY** *Atlantic AT 0160CD*	68		1
10 Apr 04	**THE EX** *Atlantic AT 0173CD*	61		1
17 Jul 04	**RIVER BELOW** *Atlantic AT 0178CD*	70		1
24 Jun 06	**DEVIL IN A MIDNIGHT MASS** *Atlantic AT0245CD*	66		1
23 Sep 06	**RED FLAG** *Atlantic AT0256CD*	49		1

BIMBO JET
France, male/female vocal/instrumental group **10**

Date	Title	Peak Position	Weeks at No.1	Weeks on Chart
26 Jul 75	**EL BIMBO** *EMI 2317*	12		10

BINARY FINARY
UK, male production duo **9**

Date	Title	Peak Position	Weeks at No.1	Weeks on Chart
10 Oct 98	**1998** *Positiva CDTIV 98*	24		3
28 Aug 99	**1999** *Positiva CDTIV 118*	11		6

UMBERTO BINDI
Italy, male vocalist, d. 24 May 2002 (age 70) **1**

Date	Title	Peak Position	Weeks at No.1	Weeks on Chart
10 Nov 60	**IL NOSTRO CONCERTO** *Oriole CD 1577*	47		1

BINI & MARTINI
Italy, male production duo. See Eclipse, Goodfellas featuring Lisa Millett, House Of Glass **2**

Date	Title	Peak Position	Weeks at No.1	Weeks on Chart
4 Mar 00	**HAPPINESS (MY VISION IS CLEAR)** *Azuli AZNYCDX 113*	53		1
10 Mar 01	**BURNING UP** *Azuli AZNY 137*	65		1

BIOHAZARD
US, male vocal/instrumental group **4**

Date	Title	Peak Position	Weeks at No.1	Weeks on Chart
9 Jul 94	**TALES FROM THE HARD SIDE** *Warner Brothers W 0254CD*	47		2
20 Aug 94	**HOW IT IS** *Warner Brothers W 0259CD*	62		2

BIOSPHERE
Norway, male producer/keyboard player (Ger Jenssen) **2**

Date	Title	Peak Position	Weeks at No.1	Weeks on Chart
29 Apr 95	**NOVELTY WAVES** *Apollo 20CDX*	51		2

BIRDLAND
UK, male vocal/instrumental group **7**

Date	Title	Peak Position	Weeks at No.1	Weeks on Chart
1 Apr 89	**HOLLOW HEART** *Lazy 13*	70		1
8 Jul 89	**PARADISE** *Lazy 14*	70		1
3 Feb 90	**SLEEP WITH ME** *Lazy 17*	32		3
22 Sep 90	**ROCK 'N' ROLL NIGGER** *Lazy 20*	47		1
2 Feb 91	**EVERYBODY NEEDS SOMEBODY** *Lazy 24*	44		1

BIRDS
UK, male vocal/instrumental group **1**

Date	Title	Peak Position	Weeks at No.1	Weeks on Chart
27 May 65	**LEAVING HERE** *Decca F 12140*	45		1

ZOE BIRKETT
UK, female vocalist **6**

Date	Title	Peak Position	Weeks at No.1	Weeks on Chart
25 Jan 03	**TREAT ME LIKE A LADY** *10/Universal 0196832*	12		6

JANE BIRKIN & SERGE GAINSBOURG
UK/France, male vocal duo – Serge Gainsbourg (Lucien Ginsberg), d. 2 Mar 1991 (age 62) **34**

Date	Title	Peak Position	Weeks at No.1	Weeks on Chart
30 Jul 69	**JE T'AIME...MOI NON PLUS** *Fontana TF 1042*	2		11
4 Oct 69	**JE T'AIME...MOI NON PLUS** *Major Minor MM 645*	1	1	14
7 Dec 74	**JE T'AIME...MOI NON PLUS** *Antic K 11511*	31		9

BIS
UK, male/female vocal/instrumental group **9**

Date	Title	Peak Position	Weeks at No.1	Weeks on Chart
30 Mar 96	**THE SECRET VAMPIRE SOUNDTRACK EP** *Chemikal Underground CHEM 003CD*	25		2
22 Jun 96	**BIS VS THE DIY CORPS (EP)** *Teen-C SKETCH 001CD*	45		1
9 Nov 96	**ATOM POWERED ACTION (EP)** *Wiiija WIJ 55CD*	54		1
15 Mar 97	**SWEET SHOP AVENGERZ** *Wiiija WIJ 67CD*	46		1
10 May 97	**EVERYBODY THINKS THEY'RE GOING TO GET THEIRS** *Wiiija WIJ 69CD*	64		1
14 Nov 98	**EURODISCO** *Wiiija WIJ 86CD*	37		2
27 Feb 99	**ACTION AND DRAMA** *Wiiija WIJ 95CD*	50		1

BISCUIT BOY
UK, male vocal/instrumental trio **1**

Date	Title	Peak Position	Weeks at No.1	Weeks on Chart
15 Sep 01	**MITCH** *Mercury 5887592*	75		1

ELVIN BISHOP
US, male guitarist **4**

Date	Title	Peak Position	Weeks at No.1	Weeks on Chart
15 May 76	**FOOLED AROUND AND FELL IN LOVE** *Capricorn 2089 024*	34		4

BIZARRE
US, male rapper (Rufus Johnson). See D12 **4**

Date	Title	Peak Position	Weeks at No.1	Weeks on Chart
2 Jul 05	**ROCKSTAR** *Sanctuary Urban SANXS379*	17		4

BIZARRE INC
UK, male production trio – Andrew Meecham, Dean Meredith & Carl Turner **49**

Date	Title	Peak Position	Weeks at No.1	Weeks on Chart
16 Mar 91	**PLAYING WITH KNIVES** *Vinyl Solution STORM 25R*	43		5
14 Sep 91	**SUCH A FEELING** *Vinyl Solution STORM 32S*	13		9
23 Nov 91	**PLAYING WITH KNIVES** *Vinyl Solution STORM 38S*	4		8
3 Oct 92	**I'M GONNA GET YOU** *Vinyl Solution STORM 46S* FEATURING ANGIE BROWN ●	3		13
27 Feb 93	**TOOK MY LOVE** *Vinyl Solution STORM 60CD* FEATURING ANGIE BROWN	19		5
23 Mar 96	**KEEP THE MUSIC STRONG** *Some Bizzare MERCD 451*	33		2
6 Jul 96	**SURPRISE** *Some Bizzare MERCD 462*	21		3
14 Sep 96	**GET UP SUNSHINE STREET** *Some Bizzare MERCD 471*	45		2
13 Mar 99	**PLAYING WITH KNIVES (REMIX)** *Vinyl Solution VC 01CD1*	30		2

Silver-selling ● Gold-selling ● Platinum-selling (x multiples) ⊛ US No.1 ★ Peak Position Weeks at No.1 Weeks on Chart

BIZZ NIZZ

Belgium, male producer (Jean-Paul de Coster) with various production/rap collaborators — 11

Date	Title / Label	Peak Position	Weeks at No.1	Weeks on Chart
31 Mar 90	**DON'T MISS THE PARTY LINE** *Cooltempo COOL 203*	7		11

BIZZI

UK, male vocalist (Basil Dixon) — 1

Date	Title / Label	Peak Position	Weeks at No.1	Weeks on Chart
6 Dec 97	**BIZZI'S PARTY** *Parlophone Rhythm CDRHYTHM 7*	62		1

BJORK

Iceland, female vocalist (Björk Gudmundsdóttir). See Sugarcubes — 80

Date	Title / Label	Peak Position	Weeks at No.1	Weeks on Chart
27 Apr 91	**OOOPS** *ZTT ZANG 19* 808 STATE FEATURING BJORK	42		3
19 Jun 93	**HUMAN BEHAVIOUR** *One Little Indian 112 TP7CD*	36		2
4 Sep 93	**VENUS AS A BOY** *One Little Indian 122 TP7CD*	29		4
23 Oct 93	**PLAY DEAD** *Island CID 573* & DAVID ARNOLD	12		6
4 Dec 93	**BIG TIME SENSUALITY** *One Little Indian 132 TP7CD*	17		8
19 Mar 94	**VIOLENTLY HAPPY** *One Little Indian 142 TP7CD*	13		4
6 May 95	**ARMY OF ME** *One Little Indian 162 TP7CD*	10		5
26 Aug 95	**ISOBEL** *One Little Indian 172 TP7CD*	23		3
25 Nov 95	**IT'S OH SO QUIET** *One Little Indian 182 TP7CD* ●	4		15
24 Feb 96	**HYPERBALLAD** *One Little Indian 192 TP7CD*	8		4
9 Nov 96	**POSSIBLY MAYBE** *One Little Indian 193 TP7CD*	13		3
1 Mar 97	**I MISS YOU** *One Little Indian 194 TP7CDL*	36		2
20 Dec 97	**BACHELORETTE** *One Little Indian 212 TP7CD*	21		5
17 Oct 98	**HUNTER** *One Little Indian 222 TP7CD*	44		1
12 Dec 98	**ALARM CALL** *One Little Indian 232 TP7CDL*	33		2
19 Jun 99	**ALL IS FULL OF LOVE** *One Little Indian 242 TP7CD*	24		2
18 Aug 01	**HIDDEN PLACE** *One Little Indian 332 TP7CD*	21		2
17 Nov 01	**PAGAN POETRY** *One Little Indian 352 TP7CD*	38		2
23 Mar 02	**COCOON** *One Little Indian 322 TP7CD*	35		1
7 Dec 02	**IT'S IN OUR HANDS** *One Little Indian 366 TP7CD*	37		2
30 Oct 04	**WHO IS IT** *One Little Indian 446 TP7CD*	26		2
12 Mar 05	**TRIUMPH OF A HEART** *One Little Indian 447TP7CD2*	31		2

BJORN AGAIN

Australia, male/female vocal/instrumental group — 8

Date	Title / Label	Peak Position	Weeks at No.1	Weeks on Chart
24 Oct 92	**ERASURE-ISH (A LITTLE RESPECT/STOP!)** *M&G MAGS 32*	25		3
12 Dec 92	**SANTA CLAUS IS COMING TO TOWN** *M&G MAGS 35*	55		4
27 Nov 93	**FLASHDANCE...WHAT A FEELING** *M&G MAGCD 50*	65		1

BK

UK, male producer (Ben Keen) — 11

Date	Title / Label	Peak Position	Weeks at No.1	Weeks on Chart
25 Nov 00	**HOOVERS & HORNS** *Nukleuz NUKC 0185* FERGIE & BK	57		2
8 Dec 01	**FLASH** *Nukleuz NUKPA 0361* & NICK SENTIENCE	67		1
26 Jan 02	**ERECTION (TAKE IT TO THE TOP)** *Nukleuz NUKCD 0352* CORTINA FEATURING BK & MADAM FRICTION	48		1
9 Feb 02	**FLASH** *Nukleuz NUKC 0361* & NICK SENTIENCE	61		1
7 Dec 02	**REVOLUTION** *Nukleuz NUKFB 0437*	42		2
16 Aug 03	**KLUB KOLLABORATIONS** *Nukleuz 0524 FNUK*	43		2
17 Jan 04	**KLUB KOLLABORATIONS** *Nukleuz 0524 FNUK*	59		2

BLACK

UK, male vocalist (Colin Vearncombe) — 35

Date	Title / Label	Peak Position	Weeks at No.1	Weeks on Chart
27 Sep 86	**WONDERFUL LIFE** *Ugly Man JACK 71*	72		1
27 Jun 87	**SWEETEST SMILE** *A&M AM 394*	8		10
22 Aug 87	**WONDERFUL LIFE** *A&M AM 402*	8		9
16 Jan 88	**PARADISE** *A&M AM 422*	38		3
24 Sep 88	**THE BIG ONE** *A&M AM 468*	54		4
21 Jan 89	**NOW YOU'RE GONE** *A&M AM 491*	66		2
4 May 91	**FEEL LIKE CHANGE** *A&M AM 780*	56		2
15 Jun 91	**HERE IT COMES AGAIN** *A&M AM 753*	70		1
5 Mar 94	**WONDERFUL LIFE** *Polygram TV 5805552*	42		3

CILLA BLACK

UK, female vocalist/TV presenter (Priscilla White) — 194

Date	Title / Label	Peak Position	Weeks at No.1	Weeks on Chart
17 Oct 63	**LOVE OF THE LOVED** *Parlophone R 5065*	35		6
6 Feb 64	**ANYONE WHO HAD A HEART** *Parlophone R 5101*	1	3	17
7 May 64	**YOU'RE MY WORLD** *Parlophone R 5133*	1	4	17
6 Aug 64	**IT'S FOR YOU** *Parlophone R 5162*	7		10
14 Jan 65	**YOU'VE LOST THAT LOVIN' FEELIN'** *Parlophone R 5225*	2		9
22 Apr 65	**I'VE BEEN WRONG BEFORE** *Parlophone R 5269*	17		8
13 Jan 66	**LOVE'S JUST A BROKEN HEART** *Parlophone R 5395*	5		11
31 Mar 66	**ALFIE** *Parlophone R 5427*	9		12
9 Jun 66	**DON'T ANSWER ME** *Parlophone R 5463*	6		10
20 Oct 66	**A FOOL AM I** *Parlophone R 5515*	13		9
8 Jun 67	**WHAT GOOD AM I** *Parlophone R 5608*	24		7
29 Nov 67	**I ONLY LIVE TO LOVE YOU** *Parlophone R 5652*	26		11
13 Mar 68	**STEP INSIDE LOVE** *Parlophone R 5674*	8		9
12 Jun 68	**WHERE IS TOMORROW** *Parlophone R 5706*	39		3
12 Feb 69	**SURROUND YOURSELF WITH SORROW** *Parlophone R 5759*	3		12
9 Jul 69	**CONVERSATIONS** *Parlophone R 5785*	7		12
13 Dec 69	**IF I THOUGHT YOU'D EVER CHANGE YOUR MIND** *Parlophone R 5820*	20		9
20 Nov 71	**SOMETHING TELLS ME (SOMETHING IS GONNA HAPPEN TONIGHT)** *Parlophone R 5924*	3		14
2 Feb 74	**BABY WE CAN'T GO WRONG** *EMI 2107*	36		6
18 Sep 93	**THROUGH THE YEARS** *Columbia 6596982*	54		1
30 Oct 93	**HEART AND SOUL** *Columbia 6598562* WITH DUSTY SPRINGFIELD	75		1

FRANK BLACK

US, male vocalist/guitarist (Charles Thompson). See Pixies — 4

Date	Title / Label	Peak Position	Weeks at No.1	Weeks on Chart
21 May 94	**HEADACHE** *4AD BAD 4007CD*	53		1
20 Jan 96	**MEN IN BLACK** *Dragnet 6627862*	37		2
27 Jul 96	**I DON'T WANT TO HURT YOU (EVERY SINGLE TIME)** *Dragnet 6634635*	63		1

JEANNE BLACK

US, female vocalist (Gloria Jeanne Black) — 4

Date	Title / Label	Peak Position	Weeks at No.1	Weeks on Chart
23 Jun 60	**HE'LL HAVE TO STAY** *Capitol CL 15131*	41		4

BLACK & WHITE ARMY

UK, football fans (Newcastle United)/vocal group — 2

Date	Title / Label	Peak Position	Weeks at No.1	Weeks on Chart
23 May 98	**BLACK & WHITE ARMY** *Toon 1CD*	26		2

BLACK BOX

Italy, male production trio – Daniele Davoli, Mirko Limono & Valerio Semplici – with various US, female vocalists. See Starlight — 74

Date	Title / Label	Peak Position	Weeks at No.1	Weeks on Chart
12 Aug 89	**RIDE ON TIME** *Deconstruction PB 43055* ⊛	1	6	22
17 Feb 90	**I DON'T KNOW ANYBODY ELSE** *Deconstruction PB 43479*	4		8
2 Jun 90	**EVERYBODY EVERYBODY** *Deconstruction PB 43715*	16		5
3 Nov 90	**FANTASY** *Deconstruction PB 43895* ●	5		11
15 Dec 90	**THE TOTAL MIX** *Deconstruction PB 44235*	12		8
6 Apr 91	**STRIKE IT UP/RIDE ON TIME (REMIX)** *Deconstruction PB 44459*	16		8
14 Dec 91	**OPEN YOUR EYES** *Deconstruction PB 45053*	48		4
14 Aug 93	**ROCKIN' TO THE MUSIC** *Deconstruction 74321158122*	39		2
24 Jun 95	**NOT ANYONE** *Mercury MERCD 434*	31		2
20 Apr 96	**I GOT THE VIBRATION/A POSITIVE VIBRATION** *Manifesto MERCD 459*	21		3
22 Feb 97	**NATIVE NEW YORKER** *Manifesto FESCD 18*	46		1

BLACK BOX RECORDER

UK, male/female vocal/instrumental group — 4

Date	Title / Label	Peak Position	Weeks at No.1	Weeks on Chart
22 Apr 00	**THE FACTS OF LIFE** *Nude NUD 48CD1*	20		3
15 Jul 00	**THE ART OF DRIVING** *Nude NUD 51CD1*	53		1

BLACK CONNECTION

Italy, male/female vocal/production group — 3

Date	Title / Label	Peak Position	Weeks at No.1	Weeks on Chart
14 Mar 98	**GIVE ME RHYTHM** *Xtravaganza 0091465 EXT*	32		2
24 Oct 98	**I'M GONNA GET YA BABY** *Xtravaganza 0091615 EXT*	62		1

BLACK CROWES

US, male vocal/instrumental group — 28

Date	Title / Label	Peak Position	Weeks at No.1	Weeks on Chart
1 Sep 90	**HARD TO HANDLE** *Def American DEFA 6*	45		5
12 Jan 91	**TWICE AS HARD** *Def American DEFA 7*	47		3
22 Jun 91	**JEALOUS AGAIN/SHE TALKS TO ANGELS** *Def American DEFA 8*	70		1
24 Aug 91	**HARD TO HANDLE** *Def American DEFA 10*	39		4
26 Oct 91	**SEEING THINGS** *Def American DEFA 13*	72		1
2 May 92	**REMEDY** *Def American DEFA 16*	24		3
26 Sep 92	**STING ME** *Def American DEFA 21*	42		2
28 Nov 92	**HOTEL ILLNESS** *Def American DEFA 23*	47		3
11 Feb 95	**HIGH HEAD BLUES/A CONSPIRACY** *American Recordings 74321258492*	25		2
22 Jul 95	**WISER TIME** *American Recordings 74321298272*	34		2
27 Jul 96	**ONE MIRROR TO MANY** *American Recordings 74321398572*	51		1
7 Nov 98	**KICKING MY HEART AROUND** *American Recordings 6666665*	55		1

BLACK DIAMOND

US, male vocalist (Charles Davis) — 1

Date	Title	Peak	Wks at No.1	Wks on Chart
17 Sep 94	**LET ME BE** *Systematic SYSCD 1*	56		1

BLACK DOG FEATURING OFRA HAZA

UK, male instrumentalist/producer & Israel, female vocalist, d. 23 Feb 2000 (age 40) — 1

Date	Title	Peak	Wks at No.1	Wks on Chart
3 Apr 99	**BABYLON** *warner.esp WESP 006 CD1*	65		1

BLACK DUCK

UK, male/female rap/vocal duo — 5

Date	Title	Peak	Wks at No.1	Wks on Chart
17 Dec 94	**WHIGGLE IN LINE** *Flying South CDDUCK 1*	33		5

BLACK EYED PEAS

US, male/female vocal/rap/instrumental group – Will Adams (Will.I.Am*), Stacy Ferguson (Fergie*), Jaime Gómez (Taboo) & Allan Pineda Lindo (apl.de.ap). World-conquering quartet who have sold more than 40 million singles. The group spent an unprecedented 26 consecutive weeks at the top of the US Billboard Hot 100 with 'Boom Boom Pow' and 'I Gotta Feeling'. See Steve Aoki featuring Zuper Blahq — 237

Date	Title	Peak	Wks at No.1	Wks on Chart
10 Oct 98	**JOINTS & JAMS** *Interscope IND 95604*	53		1
12 May 01	**REQUEST & LINE** *Interscope 4975032* FEATURING MACY GRAY	31		3
13 Sep 03	**WHERE IS THE LOVE** *A&M 9810996* ⊛	1	6	19
13 Dec 03	**SHUT UP** *A&M 9814501* ●	2		12
20 Mar 04	**HEY MAMA** *A&M 9861976*	6		10
10 Jul 04	**LET'S GET IT STARTED** *A&M 9863032*	11		10
28 May 05	**DON'T PHUNK WITH MY HEART** *Interscope 9882331*	3		16
3 Sep 05	**DON'T LIE** *A&M 9884438*	6		10
26 Nov 05	**MY HUMPS** *A&M 9887259*	3		15
18 Mar 06	**PUMP IT** *A&M 9850564*	3		24

Top 50 Downloads Of All Time

Based on UK Sales

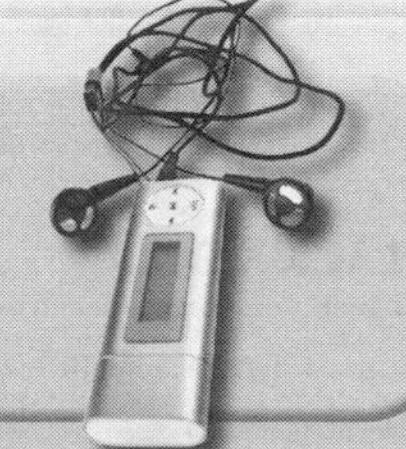

Pos	Title Artist	Approx Sales
1	**I GOTTA FEELING** BLACK EYED PEAS	945,000
2	**SEX ON FIRE** KINGS OF LEON	945,000
3	**POKER FACE** LADY GAGA	925,000
4	**JUST DANCE** LADY GAGA	790,000
5	**FIGHT FOR THIS LOVE** CHERYL COLE	780,000
6	**USE SOMEBODY** KINGS OF LEON	730,000
7	**IN FOR THE KILL** LA ROUX	710,000
8	**BAD ROMANCE** LADY GAGA	705,000
9	**MEET ME HALFWAY** BLACK EYED PEAS	680,000
10	**KILLING IN THE NAME** RAGE AGAINST THE MACHINE	680,000
11	**RUN** LEONA LEWIS	635,000
12	**BOOM BOOM POW** BLACK EYED PEAS	635,000
13	**CHASING CARS** SNOW PATROL	620,000
14	**BAD BOYS** ALEXANDRA BURKE FT FLO RIDA	615,000
15	**HALLELUJAH** ALEXANDRA BURKE	610,000
16	**RULE THE WORLD** TAKE THAT	600,000
17	**BLEEDING LOVE** LEONA LEWIS	590,000
18	**IF I WERE A BOY** BEYONCE	580,000
19	**BROKEN STRINGS** JAMES MORRISON FT NELLY FURTADO	575,000
20	**SEXY CHICK** DAVID GUETTA FT AKON	565,000
21	**DON'T STOP BELIEVIN'** JOURNEY	560,000
22	**I KISSED A GIRL** KATY PERRY	560,000
23	**ROCKSTAR** NICKELBACK	560,000
24	**UMBRELLA** RIHANNA FT JAY-Z	560,000
25	**NUMBER 1** TINCHY STRYDER FT N-DUBZ	555,000
26	**EMPIRE STATE OF MIND** JAY-Z FT ALICIA KEYS	550,000
27	**FIREFLIES** OWL CITY	540,000
28	**HOT N COLD** KATY PERRY	535,000
29	**MERCY** DUFFY	535,000
30	**HUMAN** KILLERS	530,000
31	**CRAZY** GNARLS BARKLEY	530,000
32	**DANCE WIV ME** DIZZEE RASCAL FT CALVIN HARRIS & CHROME	515,000
33	**BONKERS** DIZZEE RASCAL FT ARMAND VAN HELDEN	500,000
34	**THE FEAR** LILY ALLEN	495,000
35	**TIK TOK** KE$HA	490,000
36	**LOW** FLO RIDA FT T-PAIN	485,000
37	**SO WHAT** P!NK	485,000
38	**SINGLE LADIES (PUT A RING ON IT)** BEYONCE	480,000
39	**PAPARAZZI** LADY GAGA	475,000
40	**STARSTRUKK** 3OH!3 FT KATY PERRY	470,000
41	**AMERICAN BOY** ESTELLE FT KANYE WEST	470,000
42	**BLACK & GOLD** SAM SPARRO	465,000
43	**HALO** BEYONCE	465,000
44	**BEAT AGAIN** JLS	460,000
45	**APOLOGIZE** TIMBALAND PTS ONEREPUBLIC	460,000
46	**REPLAY** IYAZ	455,000
47	**WHEN LOVE TAKES OVER** DAVID GUETTA FT KELLY ROWLAND	455,000
48	**THE PROMISE** GIRLS ALOUD	455,000
49	**VIVA LA VIDA** COLDPLAY	450,000
50	**JAI HO (YOU ARE MY DESTINY)** AR RAHMAN FT PUSSYCAT DOLLS	445,000

Date	Title / Label / Credit	Peak Position	Weeks at No.1	Weeks on Chart
24 Jun 06	**MAS QUE NADA** *Concord/UCJ 9859631* SERGIO MENDES & THE BLACK EYED PEAS	6		10
23 May 09	**BOOM BOOM POW** *Interscope 2707191* [Platinum-selling] ★	1	2	32
20 Jun 09	**I GOTTA FEELING** *Interscope 2713158* [Platinum-selling] ★	1	2	42+
17 Oct 09	**MEET ME HALFWAY** *Interscope 2724544* [Gold-selling]	1	1	26+
6 Mar 10	**ROCK THAT BODY** *Interscope USUM70967623*	11		6+

BLACK GORILLA
UK, male/female vocal/instrumental group — Total weeks: 6

Date	Title / Label	Peak Position	Weeks at No.1	Weeks on Chart
27 Aug 77	**GIMME DAT BANANA** *Response SR 502*	29		6

BLACK GRAPE
UK, male vocal/instrumental group – Shaun Ryder, Bez (Mark Berry), Kermit, Jed Lynch & Psycho — Total weeks: 25

Date	Title / Label	Peak Position	Weeks at No.1	Weeks on Chart
10 Jun 95	**REVEREND BLACK GRAPE** *Radioactive RAXTD 16*	9		5
5 Aug 95	**IN THE NAME OF THE FATHER** *Radioactive RAXTD 19*	8		4
2 Dec 95	**KELLY'S HEROES** *Radioactive RAXDT 22*	17		5
25 May 96	**FAT NECK** *Radioactive RAXTD 24*	10		3
29 Jun 96	**ENGLAND'S IRIE** *Radioactive RAXTD 25* FEATURING JOE STRUMMER & KEITH ALLEN	6		4
1 Nov 97	**GET HIGHER** *Radioactive RAXTD 32*	24		3
7 Mar 98	**MARBLES** *Radioactive RAXTD 33*	46		1

BLACK KEYS
US, male vocal/instrumental duo — Total weeks: 2

Date	Title / Label	Peak Position	Weeks at No.1	Weeks on Chart
11 Sep 04	**10AM AUTOMATIC** *Epitah 11732*	66		1
11 Dec 04	**TILL I GET MY WAY/GIRL IS ON MY MIND** *Fat Possum 11832*	62		1

BLACK KIDS
US, male/female vocal/instrumental group — Total weeks: 15

Date	Title / Label	Peak Position	Weeks at No.1	Weeks on Chart
19 Apr 08	**I'M NOT GONNA TEACH YOUR BOYFRIEND HOW TO DANCE WITH YOU** *Mercury AGUK001CD*	11		12
5 Jul 08	**HURRICANE JANE** *Almost Gold AGUK002CDS*	36		3

BLACK LACE
UK, male vocal/instrumental duo – Alan Barton, d. 23 Mar 1995 & Colin Routh — Total weeks: 83

Date	Title / Label	Peak Position	Weeks at No.1	Weeks on Chart
31 Mar 79	**MARY ANN** *EMI 2919*	42		4
24 Sep 83	**SUPERMAN (GIOCA JOUER)** *Flair FLA 105* [Silver-selling]	9		18
30 Jun 84	**AGADOO** *Flair FLA 107* [Gold-selling]	2		30
24 Nov 84	**DO THE CONGA** *Flair FLA 108*	10		9
1 Jun 85	**EL VINO COLLAPSO** *Flair LACE 1*	42		5
7 Sep 85	**I SPEAKA DA LINGO** *Flair LACE 2*	49		4
7 Dec 85	**HOKEY COKEY** *Flair LACE 3*	31		6
20 Sep 86	**WIG WAM BAM** *Flair LACE 5*	63		3
26 Aug 89	**I AM THE MUSIC MAN** *Flair LACE 10*	52		3
22 Aug 98	**AGADOO** *Now CDWAG 260*	64		1

BLACK LEGEND
Italy, male production duo – Enrico Ferrari & Ciro Sasso — Total weeks: 22

Date	Title / Label	Peak Position	Weeks at No.1	Weeks on Chart
20 May 00	**YOU SEE THE TROUBLE WITH ME (IMPORT)** *Rise RISECD 072*	52		5
24 Jun 00	**YOU SEE THE TROUBLE WITH ME** *Eternal WEA 282CD* [Silver-selling]	1	1	15
4 Aug 01	**SOMEBODY** *WEA 328CDX* SHORTIE VS BLACK LEGEND	37		2

BLACK MACHINE
Italy/France/Nigeria, male production/rap group — Total weeks: 5

Date	Title / Label	Peak Position	Weeks at No.1	Weeks on Chart
9 Apr 94	**HOW GEE** *London LONCD 348*	17		5

BLACK MAGIC
US, male producer (Marvin Burns). See Lil' Louis — Total weeks: 2

Date	Title / Label	Peak Position	Weeks at No.1	Weeks on Chart
1 Jun 96	**FREEDOM (MAKE IT FUNKY)** *Positiva CDTIV 51*	41		2

BLACK REBEL MOTORCYCLE CLUB
US, male vocal/instrumental group — Total weeks: 14

Date	Title / Label	Peak Position	Weeks at No.1	Weeks on Chart
2 Feb 02	**LOVE BURNS** *Virgin VUSCD 234*	37		2
1 Jun 02	**SPREAD YOUR LOVE** *Virgin VUSCD 245*	27		2
28 Sep 02	**WHATEVER HAPPENED TO MY ROCK AND ROLL** *Virgin VUSCD 257*	46		2
30 Aug 03	**STOP** *Virgin VUSCD 273*	19		3
29 Nov 03	**WE'RE ALL IN LOVE** *Virgin VUSCDX 279*	45		1
27 Aug 05	**AIN'T NO EASY WAY** *Echo ECSCX175*	21		2
28 Apr 07	**WEAPON OF CHOICE** *Universal 1732965*	35		2

BLACK RIOT
US, male producer (Todd Terry*) — Total weeks: 3

Date	Title / Label	Peak Position	Weeks at No.1	Weeks on Chart
3 Dec 88	**WARLOCK/A DAY IN THE LIFE** *Champion CHAMP 75*	68		3

BLACK ROB
US, male rapper (Robert Ross) — Total weeks: 8

Date	Title / Label	Peak Position	Weeks at No.1	Weeks on Chart
12 Aug 00	**WHOA** *Puff Daddy 74321782732*	44		2
6 Oct 01	**BAD BOY FOR LIFE** *Arista 74321889982* P DIDDY FEATURING BLACK ROB & MARK CURRY	13		6

BLACK ROCK FEATURING DEBRA ANDREW
Germany/UK, male vocal/production duo — Total weeks: 2

Date	Title / Label	Peak Position	Weeks at No.1	Weeks on Chart
7 May 05	**BLUE WATER** *Positiva CDTIVS217*	36		2

BLACK SABBATH
UK, male vocal/instrumental group – Ozzy Osbourne*, Tommi Iommi, Terence 'Geezer' Butler & Bill Ward — Total weeks: 70

Date	Title / Label	Peak Position	Weeks at No.1	Weeks on Chart
29 Aug 70	**PARANOID** *Vertigo 6059 010*	4		18
3 Jun 78	**NEVER SAY DIE** *Vertigo SAB 001*	21		8
14 Oct 78	**HARD ROAD** *Vertigo SAB 002*	33		4
5 Jul 80	**NEON KNIGHTS** *Vertigo SAB 3*	22		9
16 Aug 80	**PARANOID** *Nems BSS 101*	14		12
6 Dec 80	**DIE YOUNG** *Vertigo SAB 4*	41		7
7 Nov 81	**MOB RULES** *Vertigo SAB 5*	46		4
13 Feb 82	**TURN UP THE NIGHT** *Vertigo SAB 6*	37		5
15 Apr 89	**HEADLESS CROSS** *IRS EIRS 107*	62		1
13 Jun 92	**TV CRIMES** *IRS EIRSP 178*	33		2

BLACK SHEEP
US, male rap duo — Total weeks: 1

Date	Title / Label	Peak Position	Weeks at No.1	Weeks on Chart
19 Nov 94	**WITHOUT A DOUBT** *Mercury MERCD 417*	60		1

BLACK SLATE
UK/Jamaica/Anguilla, male vocal/instrumental group – Keith Drummond, Elroy Bailey, Anthony Brightly, Chris Hanson, Desmond Mahoney & Cledwyn Rogers — Total weeks: 15

Date	Title / Label	Peak Position	Weeks at No.1	Weeks on Chart
20 Sep 80	**AMIGO** *Ensign ENY 42*	9		9
6 Dec 80	**BOOM BOOM** *Ensign ENY 47*	51		6

BLACK UHURU
Jamaica/US, male/female vocal trio — Total weeks: 9

Date	Title / Label	Peak Position	Weeks at No.1	Weeks on Chart
8 Sep 84	**WHAT IS LIFE?** *Island IS 150*	56		6
31 May 86	**THE GREAT TRAIN ROBBERY** *Real Authentic Sound RAS 7018*	62		3

BLACK VELVETS
UK, male vocal/instrumental group — Total weeks: 3

Date	Title / Label	Peak Position	Weeks at No.1	Weeks on Chart
26 Mar 05	**3345** *Vertigo 9870472*	34		2
17 Sep 05	**ONCE IN A WHILE** *Vertigo 9873237*	75		1

BAND OF THE BLACK WATCH
UK, male band — Total weeks: 22

Date	Title / Label	Peak Position	Weeks at No.1	Weeks on Chart
30 Aug 75	**SCOTCH ON THE ROCKS** *Spark SRL 1128*	8		14
13 Dec 75	**DANCE OF THE CUCKOOS (THE LAUREL AND HARDY THEME)** *Spark SRL 1135*	37		8

TONY BLACKBURN
UK, male vocalist/radio DJ (Kenneth Blackburn) — Total weeks: 7

Date	Title / Label	Peak Position	Weeks at No.1	Weeks on Chart
24 Jan 68	**SO MUCH LOVE** *MGM 1375*	31		4
26 Mar 69	**IT'S ONLY LOVE** *MGM 1467*	40		2
5 May 07	**I AM A CIDER DRINKER 2007** *EMI Gold 3926532* WURZELS FEATURING TONY BLACKBURN	57		1

BLACKBYRDS
US, male vocal/instrumental group — Total weeks: 6

Date	Title / Label	Peak Position	Weeks at No.1	Weeks on Chart
31 May 75	**WALKING IN RHYTHM** *Fantasy FTC 114*	23		6

BLACKFOOT
US/UK, male vocal/instrumental group — 5

Date	Title	Peak	Wks No.1	Wks
6 Mar 82	**DRY COUNTY** *Atco K 11686*	43		4
18 Jun 83	**SEND ME AN ANGEL** *Atco B 9880*	66		1

J BLACKFOOT
US, male vocalist (John Colbert) — 4

Date	Title	Peak	Wks No.1	Wks
17 Mar 84	**TAXI** *Allegiance ALES 2*	48		4

BLACKFOOT SUE
UK, male vocal/instrumental group – Tom Farmer, Dave Farmer, Eddie Galga & Alan Jones — 15

Date	Title	Peak	Wks No.1	Wks
12 Aug 72	**STANDING IN THE ROAD** *Jam 13*	4		10
16 Dec 72	**SING DON'T SPEAK** *Jam 29*	36		5

BLACKGIRL
US, female vocal trio — 3

Date	Title	Peak	Wks No.1	Wks
16 Jul 94	**90S GIRL** *RCA 74321217882*	23		3

BLACKNUSS
Sweden, male/female vocal/instrumental group — 1

Date	Title	Peak	Wks No.1	Wks
28 Jun 97	**DINAH** *Arista 74321479762*	56		1

BLACKOUT
UK, male/female vocal/rap group — 9

Date	Title	Peak	Wks No.1	Wks
27 Mar 99	**GOTTA HAVE HOPE** *Multiply CDMULTY 47*	46		1
31 Mar 01	**MR DJ** *Independiente ISOM 48MS*	19		7
6 Oct 01	**GET UP** *Independiente ISOM 52MS*	67		1

BILL BLACK'S COMBO
US, male instrumental group – Bill Black, d. 21 Oct 1965 (age 39) — 8

Date	Title	Peak	Wks No.1	Wks
8 Sep 60	**WHITE SILVER SANDS** *London HLU 9090*	50		1
3 Nov 60	**DON'T BE CRUEL** *London HLU 9212*	32		7

BLACKSTREET
US, male vocal group – Teddy Riley*, Chauncey 'Black' Hannibal, Levi Little (replaced by Eric Williams) & Joseph Stonestreet (replaced by Dave Hollister, then Mark Middleton) — 65

Date	Title	Peak	Wks No.1	Wks
19 Jun 93	**BABY BE MINE** *MCA MCSTD 1772* FEATURING TEDDY RILEY	37		3
13 Aug 94	**BOOTI CALL** *Interscope A 8250CD*	56		1
11 Feb 95	**U BLOW MY MIND** *Interscope A 8222CD*	39		2
27 May 95	**JOY** *Interscope A 8195CD*	56		2
19 Oct 96	**NO DIGGITY** *Interscope IND 95003* FEATURING DR DRE ★	9		7
8 Mar 97	**GET ME HOME** *Def Jam DEFCD 32* FOXY BROWN FEATURING BLACKstreet	11		5
26 Apr 97	**DON'T LEAVE ME** *Interscope IND 95534*	6		10
27 Sep 97	**FIX** *Interscope IND 97521*	7		5
13 Dec 97	**(MONEY CAN'T) BUY ME LOVE** *Interscope IND 95563*	18		6
27 Jun 98	**THE CITY IS MINE** *Northwestside 74321588012* JAY-Z FEATURING BLACKstreet	38		2
12 Dec 98	**TAKE ME THERE** *Interscope IND 95620* & MYA FEATURING MASE & BLINKY BLINK	7		9
17 Apr 99	**GIRLFRIEND/BOYFRIEND** *Interscope IND 95640* FEATURING JANET	11		7
10 Jul 99	**GET READY** *Puff Daddy 74321682612* MASE FEATURING BLACKstreet	32		4
8 Feb 03	**WIZZY WOW** *DreamWorks 4507902*	37		2

BLACKWELLS
US, male vocal duo — 2

Date	Title	Peak	Wks No.1	Wks
18 May 61	**LOVE OR MONEY** *London HLW 9334*	46		2

RICHARD BLACKWOOD
UK, male comedian/rapper — 16

Date	Title	Peak	Wks No.1	Wks
17 Jun 00	**MAMA – WHO DA MAN?** *East West MICKY 01CD1*	3		7
16 Sep 00	**1-2-3-4 GET WITH THE WICKED** *East West MICKY 05CD1*	10		6
25 Nov 00	**SOMEONE THERE FOR ME** *Hopefield MICKY 06CD*	23		3

BLAGGERS ITA
UK, male vocal/instrumental group — 7

Date	Title	Peak	Wks No.1	Wks
12 Jun 93	**STRESS** *Parlophone CDITA 1*	56		2
9 Oct 93	**OXYGEN** *Parlophone CDITA 2*	51		2
8 Jan 94	**ABANDON SHIP** *Parlophone CDITA 3*	48		3

BLAHZAY BLAHZAY
US, male rap/DJ/production duo — 1

Date	Title	Peak	Wks No.1	Wks
2 Mar 96	**DANGER** *Mercury Black Vinyl MBVCD 2*	56		1

VIVIAN BLAINE
US, female vocalist/actor (Vivienne Stapleton), d. 13 Dec 1995 (age 74) — 1

Date	Title	Peak	Wks No.1	Wks
10 Jul 53	**BUSHEL AND A PECK** *Brunswick 05100*	12		1

BLAIR
UK, male vocalist (Blair Mackichan) — 5

Date	Title	Peak	Wks No.1	Wks
2 Sep 95	**HAVE FUN, GO MAD!** *Mercury MERCD 443*	37		3
6 Jan 96	**LIFE** *Mercury MERCD 447*	44		2

BLAK TWANG
UK, male rapper (Tony Rotton) — 2

Date	Title	Peak	Wks No.1	Wks
29 Jun 02	**TRIXSTAR** *Bad Magic MAGIC24* FEATURING ESTELLE	54		1
26 Oct 02	**SO ROTTEN** *Bad Magic MAGICD 25* FEATURING JAHMALI	48		1

PETER BLAKE
UK, male vocalist — 4

Date	Title	Peak	Wks No.1	Wks
8 Oct 77	**LIPSMACKIN' ROCK 'N' ROLLIN'** *Pepper UP 36295*	40		4

BLAME
UK, male producer – Conrad Shafie — 2

Date	Title	Peak	Wks No.1	Wks
11 Apr 92	**MUSIC TAKES YOU** *Moving Shadow SHADOW 11*	48		2

BLAMELESS
UK, male vocal/instrumental group — 5

Date	Title	Peak	Wks No.1	Wks
4 Nov 95	**TOWN CLOWNS** *China WOKCD 2046*	56		1
23 Mar 96	**BREATHE (A LITTLE DEEPER)** *China WOKCD 2070*	27		3
1 Jun 96	**SIGNS...** *China WOKCD 2077*	49		1

BLANCMANGE
UK, male vocal/instrumental duo – Neil Arthur* & Stephen Luscombe — 71

Date	Title	Peak	Wks No.1	Wks
17 Apr 82	**GOD'S KITCHEN/I'VE SEEN THE WORD** *London BLANC 1*	65		2
31 Jul 82	**FEEL ME** *London BLANC 2*	46		5
30 Oct 82	**LIVING ON THE CEILING** *London BLANC 3* (silver)	7		14
19 Feb 83	**WAVES** *London BLANC 4*	19		9
7 May 83	**BLIND VISION** *London BLANC 5*	10		8
26 Nov 83	**THAT'S LOVE, THAT IS** *London BLANC 6*	33		8
14 Apr 84	**DON'T TELL ME** *London BLANC 7*	8		10
21 Jul 84	**THE DAY BEFORE YOU CAME** *London BLANC 8*	22		8
7 Sep 85	**WHAT'S YOUR PROBLEM?** *London BLANC 9*	40		5
10 May 86	**I CAN SEE IT** *London BLANC 11*	71		2

BOBBY BLANCO & MIKKI MOTO
UK, male production duo — 1

Date	Title	Peak	Wks No.1	Wks
29 May 04	**3AM** *Defected DFTD088*	70		1

BILLY BLAND
US, male vocalist — 10

Date	Title	Peak	Wks No.1	Wks
19 May 60	**LET THE LITTLE GIRL DANCE** *London HL 9096*	15		10

BLANK & JONES
Germany, male production duo — 9

Date	Title	Peak	Wks No.1	Wks
26 Jun 99	**CREAM** *Deviant DVNT 31CDS*	24		3
27 May 00	**AFTER LOVE** *Nebula NEBCDS 3*	57		1
30 Sep 00	**THE NIGHTFLY** *Nebula NEBCDS 010*	55		1
3 Mar 01	**BEYOND TIME** *Gang Go/Edel 01245115 GAG*	53		2
29 Jun 02	**DJS FANS AND FREAKS** *Incentive CENT 42CDS*	45		2

BLAQUE IVORY
US, female vocal group — 3

Date	Title	Peak	Wks No.1	Wks
3 Jul 99	**808** *Columbia 6674962*	31		3

BLAST FEATURING VDC
Italy, male production duo & male vocalist — 5

Date	Title	Peak	Wks No.1	Wks
18 Jun 94	**CRAYZY MAN** *UMM MCSTD 1982*	22		3
12 Nov 94	**PRINCES OF THE NIGHT** *UMM MCSTD 2011*	40		2

MEL BLATT
UK, female vocalist. See All Saints — 14

Date	Title	Peak	Wks No.1	Wks
15 Sep 01	**TWENTYFOURSEVEN** *ffrr FCDP 400* ARTFUL DODGER FEATURING MELANIE BLATT	6		9
2 Mar 02	**I'M LEAVIN'** *Rufflife RLCDM 03* OUTSIDAZ FEATURING RAH DIGGA & MELANIE BLATT	41		2
6 Sep 03	**DO ME WRONG** *London LONCD 479*	18		3

BLAZE
US, male vocal/production trio — 10

Date	Title	Peak	Wks No.1	Wks
10 Mar 01	**MY BEAT** *Black & Blue/Kickin NEOCD 053* FEATURING PALMER BROWN	53		2
21 Sep 02	**DO YOU REMEMBER HOUSE** *Slip N Slide SLIPCD 151* FEATURING PALMER BROWN	55		1
14 May 05	**MOST PRECIOUS LOVE** *Defected DFTD100CDS* PRESENTS UDA FEATURING BARBARA TUCKER	44		3
29 Apr 06	**MOST PRECIOUS LOVE** *Defected DFTD125CDX* FEATURING BARBARA TUCKER	17		4

BLAZIN' SQUAD
UK, male vocal/rap group – Tommy B (Tom Beasley), Flava (James Murray), Freek (Oliver Georgiou), Kenzie (James MacKenzie), Krazy (Lee Bailey), Melo-D (Chris Mackeckney), Plat'num (Marcel Sommerville), Reepa (Stuart Baker), Spike-E (Sam Foulkes) & Strider (Mus Omer). See Friday Hill — 60

Date	Title	Peak	Wks No.1	Wks
31 Aug 02	**CROSSROADS** *East West SQUAD 01CD*	1	1	13
23 Nov 02	**LOVE ON THE LINE** *East West SQUAD 02CD*	6		13
22 Feb 03	**REMINISCE/WHERE THE STORY ENDS** *East West SQUAD 03CD*	8		8
5 Jul 03	**WE JUST BE DREAMIN'** *East West SQUAD 04CD*	3		9
15 Nov 03	**FLIP REVERSE** *East West SQUAD 05CD*	2		10
14 Feb 04	**HERE 4 ONE** *East West SQUAD 06CD*	6		5
21 Oct 06	**ALL NIGHT LONG** *Peach Records PRL106*	54		1
27 Jun 09	**LET'S START AGAIN** *Naughty Boy NBREC1CDS*	51		1

BLEACHIN'
UK, male vocal/instrumental group — 4

Date	Title	Peak	Wks No.1	Wks
22 Jul 00	**PEAKIN'** *Boiler House! 74321774822*	32		4

BLESSID UNION OF SOULS
US, male vocal/instrumental group — 6

Date	Title	Peak	Wks No.1	Wks
27 May 95	**I BELIEVE** *EMI CDEM 374*	29		5
23 Mar 96	**LET ME BE THE ONE** *EMI CDEM 387*	74		1

BLESSING
UK, male vocal/instrumental group — 13

Date	Title	Peak	Wks No.1	Wks
11 May 91	**HIGHWAY 5** *MCA MCS 1509*	42		6
18 Jan 92	**HIGHWAY 5 (REMIX)** *MCA MCS 1603*	30		6
19 Feb 94	**SOUL LOVE** *MCA MCSTD 1940*	73		1

MARY J BLIGE
US, female vocalist — 202

Date	Title	Peak	Wks No.1	Wks
28 Nov 92	**REAL LOVE** *Uptown MCSTD 1721*	68		2
27 Feb 93	**REMINISCE** *Uptown MCSTD 1731*	31		4
12 Jun 93	**YOU REMIND ME** *Uptown MCSTD 1770*	48		3
28 Aug 93	**REAL LOVE (REMIX)** *Uptown MCSTD 1922*	26		4
4 Dec 93	**YOU DON'T HAVE TO WORRY** *Uptown MCSTD 1948*	36		2
14 May 94	**MY LOVE** *Uptown MCSTD 1972*	29		3
10 Dec 94	**BE HAPPY** *Uptown MCSTD 2033*	30		4
15 Apr 95	**I'M GOIN' DOWN** *Uptown MCSTD 2053*	12		4
29 Jul 95	**I'LL BE THERE FOR YOU-YOU'RE ALL I NEED TO GET BY** *Def Jam DEFDX11* METHOD MAN FEATURING MARY J BLIGE	10		5
30 Sep 95	**MARY JANE (ALL NIGHT LONG)** *Uptown MCSTD 2088*	17		4
16 Dec 95	**(YOU MAKE ME FEEL LIKE A) NATURAL WOMAN** *Uptown MCSTD 2108*	23		3
30 Mar 96	**NOT GON' CRY** *Arista 74321358252*	39		2
1 Mar 97	**CAN'T KNOCK THE HUSTLE** *Northwestside 74321447192* JAY-Z FEATURING MARY J BLIGE	30		2
17 May 97	**LOVE IS ALL WE NEED** *Uptown MCSTD 48053*	15		4
16 Aug 97	**EVERYTHING** *MCA MCSTD 48059*	6		9
29 Nov 97	**MISSING YOU** *MCA MCSTD 48071*	19		5
11 Jul 98	**SEVEN DAYS** *MCA MCSTD 48083* FEATURING GEORGE BENSON	22		3
13 Mar 99	**AS** *Epic 6670122* GEORGE MICHAEL & MARY J BLIGE ●	4		10
21 Aug 99	**ALL THAT I CAN SAY** *MCA MCSTD 40215*	29		3
11 Dec 99	**DEEP INSIDE** *MCA MCSTD 40224*	42		2
29 Apr 00	**GIVE ME YOU** *MCA MCSTD 40230*	19		4
16 Dec 00	**911** *Columbia 6706122* WYCLEF FEATURING MARY J BLIGE	9		10
6 Oct 01	**FAMILY AFFAIR** *MCA MCSTD 40267* ★	8		16
9 Feb 02	**DANCE FOR ME** *MCA MCSXD 40274* FEATURING COMMON	13		7
11 May 02	**NO MORE DRAMA** *MCA MCSXD 40281*	9		7
24 Aug 02	**RAINY DAYZ** *MCA MCSXD 40288* FEATURING JA RULE	17		5
27 Sep 03	**LOVE @ 1ST SIGHT** *MCA MCSTD 40338* FEATURING METHOD MAN	18		5
6 Dec 03	**NOT TODAY** *Geffen MCSTD 40349* FEATURING EVE	40		2
20 Dec 03	**WHENEVER I SAY YOUR NAME** *A&M 9815304* STING & MARY J BLIGE	60		1
18 Dec 04	**I TRY** *Island MCSTD40390* TALIB KWELI FEATURING MARY J BLIGE	59		1
31 Dec 05	**BE WITHOUT YOU** *Geffen MCSTD40445*	32		18
8 Apr 06	**ONE** *Geffen MCSTD40458* & U2	2		19
8 Jul 06	**ENOUGH CRYIN'** *Geffen MCSXD40465* FEATURING BROOK-LYNN	46		3
30 Dec 06	**MJB DA MVP** *Geffen 1720304*	33		6
27 Jan 07	**RUNAWAY LOVE** *Def Jam 1723705* LUDACRIS FEATURING MARY J BLIGE	52		5
26 Jan 08	**JUST FINE** *Geffen 1761580*	16		9
05 Sep 09	**REMEMBER ME** *Atlantic USAT20901697* TI FEATURING MARY J BLIGE	34		2
13 Mar 10	**I AM** *Geffen 2734850*	34		4

BLIND MELON
US, male vocal/instrumental group — 13

Date	Title	Peak	Wks No.1	Wks
12 Jun 93	**TONES OF HOME** *Capitol CDCL 687*	62		2
11 Dec 93	**NO RAIN** *Capitol CDCL 699*	17		6
9 Jul 94	**CHANGE** *Capitol CDCL 717*	35		3
5 Aug 95	**GALAXIE** *Capitol CDCLS 755*	37		2

BLINK
Ireland, male vocal/instrumental group — 1

Date	Title	Peak	Wks No.1	Wks
16 Jul 94	**HAPPY DAY** *Lime CDR 6385*	57		1

BLINK-182
US, male vocal/instrumental trio – Tom DeLonge, Travis Barker & Mark Hoppus — 53

Date	Title	Peak	Wks No.1	Wks
2 Oct 99	**WHAT'S MY AGE AGAIN?** *MCA MCSTD 40219*	38		2
25 Mar 00	**ALL THE SMALL THINGS** *MCA MCSTD 40223*	2		10
8 Jul 00	**WHAT'S MY AGE AGAIN?** *MCA MCSZD 40219*	17		6
14 Jul 01	**THE ROCK SHOW** *MCA MCSTD 40259*	14		7
6 Oct 01	**FIRST DATE** *MCA MCSTD 40264*	31		4
6 Dec 03	**FEELING THIS** *Geffen MCSTD 40347*	15		5
13 Mar 04	**I MISS YOU** *Geffen MCSTD 40359*	8		10
3 Jul 04	**DOWN** *Geffen MCSTD 40366*	24		3
25 Dec 04	**ALWAYS** *Geffen MCSTD 40400*	36		4
10 Dec 05	**NOT NOW** *Geffen MCSTD40440*	30		2

NICKI BLISS
UK, female vocalist — 1

Date	Title	Peak	Wks No.1	Wks
9 Aug 08	**I KISSED A GIRL** *NU NRG USCBK0812440*	50		1

BLOC PARTY
UK, male vocal/instrumental group – Kele Okereke, Russell Lissack, Gordon Moakes & Matt Tong — 58

Date	Title	Peak	Wks No.1	Wks
15 May 04	**BANQUET/STAYING FAT** *Moshi Moshi MOSHI10CD*	51		1
24 Jul 04	**LITTLE THOUGHT/TULIPS** *Wichita WEBB067SCD*	38		2
6 Nov 04	**HELICOPTER** *Wichita WEBB070SCD*	26		2
12 Feb 05	**SO HERE WE ARE/POSITIVE TENSION** *Wichita WEBB076SCD*	5		4
7 May 05	**BANQUET** *Wichita WEBB078SCD*	13		3
30 Jul 05	**THE PIONEERS** *Wichita WEBB088SCD*	18		2
15 Oct 05	**TWO MORE YEARS** *Wichita WEBB095SCD*	7		8
3 Feb 07	**THE PRAYER** *Wichita WEBB118SCD*	4		7
14 Apr 07	**I STILL REMEMBER** *Wichita WEBB125SCD*	20		4
21 Jul 07	**HUNTING FOR WITCHES** *Wichita WEBB130SCD*	22		2
24 Nov 07	**FLUX** *Wichita WEBB135SCD*	8		13
23 Aug 08	**MERCURY** *Wichita WEBB180SCD*	16		3
1 Nov 08	**TALONS** *Wichita WEBB190SCD*	39		2
22 Aug 09	**ONE MORE CHANCE** *Wichita WEBB215S*	15		5

BLOCKSTER
UK/Italy, male production trio – Brandon Block, Ricky Morrison & Fran Sidoli. See Mystic 3

Date	Title	Peak Position	Weeks at No.1	Weeks on Chart: 11
16 Jan 99	**YOU SHOULD BE…** *Sound Of Ministry MOSCDS 128*	3		9
24 Jul 99	**GROOVELINE** *Sound Of Ministry MOSCDS 131*	18		2

KRISTINE BLOND
Denmark, female vocalist

Date	Title	Peak Position	Weeks at No.1	Weeks on Chart: 7
11 Apr 98	**LOVE SHY** *Reverb BNOISE 1CD*	22		3
11 Nov 00	**LOVE SHY (REMIX)** *Relentless RELENT 4CDS*	28		2
4 May 02	**YOU MAKE ME GO OOH** *WEA 343CD1*	35		2

BLONDIE
US, female/male vocal/instrumental group – Deborah Harry*, Clem Burke, Jimmy Destri, Chris Stein & Gary Valentine

Date	Title	Peak Position	Weeks at No.1	Weeks on Chart: 172
18 Feb 78	**DENIS** *Chrysalis CHS 2204* ●	2		14
6 May 78	**(I'M ALWAYS TOUCHED BY YOUR) PRESENCE DEAR** *Chrysalis CHS 2217*	10		9
26 Aug 78	**PICTURE THIS** *Chrysalis CHS 2242* ○	12		11
11 Nov 78	**HANGING ON THE TELEPHONE** *Chrysalis CHS 2266* ○	5		12
27 Jan 79	**HEART OF GLASS** *Chrysalis CHS 2275* ⊛ ★	1	4	12
19 May 79	**SUNDAY GIRL** *Chrysalis CHS 2320* ●	1	3	13
29 Sep 79	**DREAMING** *Chrysalis CHS 2350* ○	2		8
24 Nov 79	**UNION CITY BLUES** *Chrysalis CHS 2400* ○	13		10
23 Feb 80	**ATOMIC** *Chrysalis CHS 2410* ●	1	2	9
12 Apr 80	**CALL ME** *Chrysalis CHS 2414* ○ ★	1	1	9
8 Nov 80	**THE TIDE IS HIGH** *Chrysalis CHS 2465* ● ★	1	2	12
24 Jan 81	**RAPTURE** *Chrysalis CHS 2485* ○ ★	5		8
8 May 82	**ISLAND OF LOST SOULS** *Chrysalis CHS 2608*	11		9
24 Jul 82	**WAR CHILD** *Chrysalis CHS 2624*	39		4
3 Dec 88	**DENIS (REMIX)** *Chrysalis CHS 3328*	50		3
11 Feb 89	**CALL ME (REMIX)** *Chrysalis CHS 3342*	61		2
10 Sep 94	**ATOMIC (REMIX)** *Chrysalis CDCHS 5013*	19		4
8 Jul 95	**HEART OF GLASS (REMIX)** *Chrysalis CDCHS 5023*	15		3
28 Oct 95	**UNION CITY BLUES** *Chrysalis CDCHSS 5027*	31		2
13 Feb 99	**MARIA** *Beyond 74321645632* ●	1	1	12
12 Jun 99	**NOTHING IS REAL BUT THE GIRL** *Beyond 74321669472*	26		3
18 Oct 03	**GOOD BOYS** *Epic 6743995*	12		3

NIKKI BLONSKY, ZAC EFRON & AMANDA BYNES
US, female/male actors/vocal trio

Date	Title	Peak Position	Weeks at No.1	Weeks on Chart: 1
18 Aug 07	**YOU CANT STOP THE BEAT (HAIRSPRAY)** *Decca/UMTV USNLR0700062*	71		1

BLOOD ARM
US, male vocal/instrumental group

Date	Title	Peak Position	Weeks at No.1	Weeks on Chart: 2
11 Jun 05	**SAY YES** *City Rockers ROCKERS29CD*	52		1
7 Oct 06	**SUSPICIOUS CHARACTER** *City Rockers ROCKERS34CD*	62		1

BLOOD RED SHOES
UK, male/female vocal/instrumental duo

Date	Title	Peak Position	Weeks at No.1	Weeks on Chart: 1
16 Feb 08	**YOU BRING ME DOWN** *V2 1756838*	64		1

BLOOD SWEAT & TEARS
US/Canada, male vocal/instrumental group

Date	Title	Peak Position	Weeks at No.1	Weeks on Chart: 6
30 Apr 69	**YOU'VE MADE ME SO VERY HAPPY** *CBS 4116*	35		6

BLOODHOUND GANG
US, male vocal/instrumental group – Jimmy Pop (James Franks), DJ Q-Ball (Harry Dean, Jr.), 'Evil' Jared Hasselhoff (Jared Hennegan), Lupus Thunder (Matthew Stigliano) & Willie The New Guy (William Brehony)

Date	Title	Peak Position	Weeks at No.1	Weeks on Chart: 22
23 Aug 97	**WHY'S EVERYBODY ALWAYS PICKIN' ON ME?** *Geffen GFSTD 22252*	56		1
15 Apr 00	**THE BAD TOUCH** *Geffen 4972682* ●	4		14
2 Sep 00	**THE BALLAD OF CHASEY LAIN** *Geffen 4973822*	15		6
1 Oct 05	**FOXTROT UNIFORM CHARLIE KILO** *Geffen 9885038*	47		1

BLOODSTONE
US, male vocal/instrumental group

Date	Title	Peak Position	Weeks at No.1	Weeks on Chart: 4
18 Aug 73	**NATURAL HIGH** *Decca F 13382*	40		4

BOBBY BLOOM
US, male vocalist, d. 28 Feb 1974 (age 28)

Date	Title	Peak Position	Weeks at No.1	Weeks on Chart: 24
29 Aug 70	**MONTEGO BAY** *Polydor 2058 051*	3		19
9 Jan 71	**HEAVY MAKES YOU HAPPY** *Polydor 2001 122*	31		5

BLOOMSBURY SET
UK, male vocal/instrumental group

Date	Title	Peak Position	Weeks at No.1	Weeks on Chart: 3
25 Jun 83	**HANGING AROUND WITH THE BIG BOYS** *Stiletto STL 13*	56		3

TANYA BLOUNT
US, female vocalist

Date	Title	Peak Position	Weeks at No.1	Weeks on Chart: 1
11 Jun 94	**I'M GONNA MAKE YOU MINE** *Polydor OZCD 315T*	69		1

KURTIS BLOW
US, male rapper (Kurtis Walker)

Date	Title	Peak Position	Weeks at No.1	Weeks on Chart: 23
15 Dec 79	**CHRISTMAS RAPPIN'** *Mercury BLOW 7*	30		6
11 Oct 80	**THE BREAKS** *Mercury BLOW 8*	47		4
16 Mar 85	**PARTY TIME (THE GO-GO EDIT)** *Club JAB 12*	67		1
15 Jun 85	**SAVE YOUR LOVE (FOR NUMBER 1)** *Club JAB 14* RENE & ANGELA FEATURING KURTIS BLOW	66		2
18 Jan 86	**IF I RULED THE WORLD** *Club JAB 26*	24		8
8 Nov 86	**I'M CHILLIN'** *Club JAB 42*	64		2

BLOW MONKEYS
UK, male vocal/instrumental group – Bruce 'Dr Robert' Howard, Mick Anker, Neville Henry & Tony Kiley

Date	Title	Peak Position	Weeks at No.1	Weeks on Chart: 46
1 Mar 86	**DIGGING YOUR SCENE** *RCA PB 40599*	12		10
17 May 86	**WICKED WAYS** *RCA MONK 2*	60		2
31 Jan 87	**IT DOESN'T HAVE TO BE THIS WAY** *RCA MONK 4*	5		8
28 Mar 87	**OUT WITH HER** *RCA MONK 5*	30		6
30 May 87	**(CELEBRATE) THE DAY AFTER YOU** *RCA MONK 6* WITH CURTIS MAYFIELD	52		2
15 Aug 87	**SOME KIND OF WONDERFUL** *RCA MONK 7*	67		1
6 Aug 88	**THIS IS YOUR LIFE** *RCA PB 42149*	70		2
8 Apr 89	**THIS IS YOUR LIFE (REMIX)** *RCA PB 42695*	32		5
15 Jul 89	**CHOICE?** *RCA PB 42885* FEATURING SYLVIA TELLA	22		6
14 Oct 89	**SLAVES NO MORE** *RCA PB 43201* FEATURING SYLVIA TELLA	73		2
26 May 90	**SPRINGTIME FOR THE WORLD** *RCA PB 43623*	69		2

BLU PETER
UK, male DJ/producer (Peter Harris)

Date	Title	Peak Position	Weeks at No.1	Weeks on Chart: 1
21 Mar 98	**TELL ME WHAT YOU WANT/JAMES HAS KITTENS** *React CDREACT 285*	70		1

BLUE
UK, male vocal/instrumental group

Date	Title	Peak Position	Weeks at No.1	Weeks on Chart: 8
30 Apr 77	**GONNA CAPTURE YOUR HEART** *Rocket ROKN 522*	18		8

BLUE
UK, male vocal group – Antony Costa*, Duncan James*, Lee Ryan* & Simon Webbe*

Date	Title	Peak Position	Weeks at No.1	Weeks on Chart: 142
2 Jun 01	**ALL RISE** *Innocent SINCD 28* ○	4		13
8 Sep 01	**TOO CLOSE** *Innocent SINCD 30* ○	1	1	13
24 Nov 01	**IF YOU COME BACK** *Innocent SINCD 32* ○	1	1	13
30 Mar 02	**FLY BY II** *Innocent SINCD 33*	6		12
2 Nov 02	**ONE LOVE** *Innocent SINCD 41* ○	3		12
21 Dec 02	**SORRY SEEMS TO BE THE HARDEST WORD** *Innocent SINCD 43* FEATURING ELTON JOHN ○	1	1	17
29 Mar 03	**U MAKE ME WANNA** *Innocent SINCD 44*	4		10
1 Nov 03	**GUILTY** *Innocent SINCD 51*	2		11
27 Dec 03	**SIGNED SEALED DELIVERED I'M YOURS** *Innocent SINCD 54* FEATURING STEVIE WONDER & ANGIE STONE	11		10
3 Apr 04	**BREATHE EASY** *Innocent SINDX 58*	4		12
10 Jul 04	**BUBBLIN'** *Innocent SINDX 64*	9		8
20 Nov 04	**CURTAIN FALLS** *Innocent SINDX 67*	4		11

BABBITY BLUE
US, female vocalist

Date	Title	Peak Position	Weeks at No.1	Weeks on Chart: 2
11 Feb 65	**DON'T MAKE ME (FALL IN LOVE WITH YOU)** *Decca F 12053*	48		2

Silver-selling · Gold-selling · Platinum-selling (x multiples) · US No.1 · Peak Position · Weeks at No.1 · Weeks on Chart

BARRY BLUE

UK, male vocalist (Barry Green). See Cry Sisco! — **48**

Date	Title	Label	Peak	Wks at No.1	Wks on Chart
28 Jul 73	(DANCING) ON A SATURDAY NIGHT	Bell 1295	2		15
3 Nov 73	DO YOU WANNA DANCE	Bell 1336	7		12
2 Mar 74	SCHOOL LOVE	Bell 1345	11		9
3 Aug 74	MISS HIT AND RUN	Bell 1364	26		7
26 Oct 74	HOT SHOT	Bell 1379	23		5

BLUE ADONIS FEATURING LIL' MISS MAX

Belgium, male/female vocal/production trio — **3**

Date	Title	Label	Peak	Wks at No.1	Wks on Chart
17 Oct 98	DISCO COP	Serious SERR 002CD	27		3

BLUE AEROPLANES

UK, male vocal/instrumental group — **3**

Date	Title	Label	Peak	Wks at No.1	Wks on Chart
17 Feb 90	JACKET HANGS	Ensign ENY 628	72		1
26 May 90	...AND STONES	Ensign ENY 632	63		2

BLUE AMAZON

UK, male/female vocal/production trio — **2**

Date	Title	Label	Peak	Wks at No.1	Wks on Chart
17 May 97	AND THEN THE RAIN FALLS	Sony S2 BAS 301 CD	53		1
1 Jul 00	BREATHE	Subversive SUB 61D	73		1

BLUE BAMBOO

Belgium, male production duo — **4**

Date	Title	Label	Peak	Wks at No.1	Wks on Chart
3 Dec 94	ABC AND D...	Escapade CDJAPE 6	23		4

BLUE BOY

UK, male producer (Alexis Blackmore) — **16**

Date	Title	Label	Peak	Wks at No.1	Wks on Chart
1 Feb 97	REMEMBER ME	Pharm CDPHARM 1	8		13
23 Aug 97	SANDMAN	Sidewalk CDSWALK 001	25		3

BLUE FEATHER

Holland, male vocal/instrumental group — **4**

Date	Title	Label	Peak	Wks at No.1	Wks on Chart
3 Jul 82	LET'S FUNK TONIGHT	Mercury MER 109	50		4

Top 5 Downloads

By UK Sales 2005

Pos	Title	Artist
1	YOU'RE BEAUTIFUL	JAMES BLUNT
2	PUSH THE BUTTON	SUGABABES
3	BAD DAY	DANIEL POWTER
4	FEEL GOOD INC	GORILLAZ
5	DON'T CHA	PUSSYCAT DOLLS FT BUSTA RHYMES

BLUE HAZE

UK, male vocal/instrumental group — **6**

Date	Title	Label	Peak	Wks at No.1	Wks on Chart
18 Mar 72	SMOKE GETS IN YOUR EYES	A&M AMS 891	32		6

BLUE MELONS

UK, male/female vocal/instrumental group — **1**

Date	Title	Label	Peak	Wks at No.1	Wks on Chart
8 Jun 96	DO WAH DIDDY DIDDY	Fundamental FUNDCD 1	70		1

BLUE MERCEDES

UK, male vocal/instrumental duo — **18**

Date	Title	Label	Peak	Wks at No.1	Wks on Chart
10 Oct 87	I WANT TO BE YOUR PROPERTY	MCA BONA 1	23		11
13 Feb 88	SEE WANT MUST HAVE	MCA BONA 2	57		2
23 Jul 88	LOVE IS THE GUN	MCA BONA 3	46		5

BLUE MINK

UK, male/female vocal/instrumental group – Madeline Bell, Roger Cook, Roger Coulam, Herbie Flowers, Barry Morgan & Alan Parker. See David & Jonathan, Pipkins — **83**

Date	Title	Label	Peak	Wks at No.1	Wks on Chart
15 Nov 69	MELTING POT	Philips BF 1818	3		15
28 Mar 70	GOOD MORNING FREEDOM	Philips BF 1838	10		10
19 Sep 70	OUR WORLD	Philips 6006 042	17		9
29 May 71	THE BANNER MAN	Regal Zonophone RZ 3034	3		14
11 Nov 72	STAY WITH ME	Regal Zonophone RZ 3064	11		15
3 Mar 73	BY THE DEVIL (I WAS TEMPTED)	EMI 2007	26		9
23 Jun 73	RANDY	EMI 2028	9		11

BLUE NILE

UK, male vocal/instrumental trio — **5**

Date	Title	Label	Peak	Wks at No.1	Wks on Chart
30 Sep 89	THE DOWNTOWN LIGHTS	Linn LKS 3	67		1
29 Sep 90	HEADLIGHTS ON PARADE	Linn LKS 4	72		1
19 Jan 91	SATURDAY NIGHT	Linn LKS 5	50		2
4 Sep 04	I WOULD NEVER	Sanctuary SANXD305	52		1

BLUE OYSTER CULT

US, male vocal/instrumental group — **14**

Date	Title	Label	Peak	Wks at No.1	Wks on Chart
20 May 78	(DON'T FEAR) THE REAPER	CBS 6333	16		14

BLUE PEARL

UK/US, male/female production/vocal duo – Martin 'Youth' Glover & Pamela 'Durga' McBroom — **29**

Date	Title	Label	Peak	Wks at No.1	Wks on Chart
7 Jul 90	NAKED IN THE RAIN	Big Life BLR 23	4		13
3 Nov 90	LITTLE BROTHER	Big Life BLR 32	31		5
11 Jan 92	(CAN YOU) FEEL THE PASSION	Big Life BLR 67	14		6
25 Jul 92	MOTHER DAWN	Big Life BLR 73	50		2
27 Nov 93	FIRE OF LOVE	Logic 74321170292 JUNGLE HIGH WITH BLUE PEARL	71		1
4 Jul 98	NAKED IN THE RAIN (REMIX)	Malarky MLKD 7	22		2

BLUE RONDO A LA TURK

UK male vocal/instrumental group — **9**

Date	Title	Label	Peak	Wks at No.1	Wks on Chart
14 Nov 81	ME AND MR SANCHEZ	Virgin VS 463	40		4
13 Mar 82	KLACTOVEESEDSTEIN	Diable Noir VS 476	50		5

BLUE ZOO

UK, male vocal/instrumental group — **17**

Date	Title	Label	Peak	Wks at No.1	Wks on Chart
12 Jun 82	I'M YOUR MAN	Magnet MAG 224	55		3
16 Oct 82	CRY BOY CRY	Magnet MAG 234	13		10
28 May 83	I JUST CAN'T (FORGIVE AND FORGET)	Magnet MAG 241	60		4

BLUEBELLS

UK, male vocal/instrumental group — **49**

Date	Title	Label	Peak	Wks at No.1	Wks on Chart
12 Mar 83	CATH/WILL SHE ALWAYS BE WAITING	London LON 20	62		2
9 Jul 83	SUGAR BRIDGE (IT WILL STAND)	London LON 27	72		1
24 Mar 84	I'M FALLING	London LON 45	11		12
23 Jun 84	YOUNG AT HEART	London LON 49	8		12
1 Sep 84	CATH	London LON 54	38		7
9 Feb 85	ALL I AM (IS LOVING YOU)	London LON 58	58		3
27 Mar 93	YOUNG AT HEART	London LONCD 338	1	4	12

Peak Position · Weeks at No.1 · Weeks on Chart

BLUES BAND
UK, male vocal/instrumental group — 2

Date	Title / Label	Peak	Wks at No.1	Wks on Chart
12 Jul 80	**BLUES BAND (EP)** *Arista BOOT 2*	68		2

BLUES BROTHERS
US/Canada, male vocal/acting duo – Jake (John Belushi, d. 5 Mar 1982) & Elwood (Dan Aykroyd) Blues – & US, male instrumental group — 8

Date	Title / Label	Peak	Wks at No.1	Wks on Chart
7 Apr 90	**EVERYBODY NEEDS SOMEBODY TO LOVE** *East West A 7591*	12		8

BLUESKINS
UK, male vocal/instrumental group — 2

Date	Title / Label	Peak	Wks at No.1	Wks on Chart
21 Feb 04	**CHANGE MY MIND/I WANNA KNOW** *Domino RUG174CD*	56		1
5 Jun 04	**THE STUPID ONES** *Domino RUG 175CD*	61		1

BLUETONES
UK, male vocal/instrumental group – Mark Morriss, Eds Chesters, Adam Devlin & Scott Morriss — 47

Date	Title / Label	Peak	Wks at No.1	Wks on Chart
17 Jun 95	**ARE YOU BLUE OR ARE YOU BLIND?** *Superior Quality BLUE 001CD*	31		2
14 Oct 95	**BLUETONIC** *Superior Quality BLUE 002CD*	19		3
3 Feb 96	**SLIGHT RETURN** *Superior Quality BLUE 003CD*	2		8
11 May 96	**CUT SOME RUG/CASTLE ROCK** *Superior Quality BLUE 005CD*	7		6
28 Sep 96	**MARBLEHEAD JOHNSON** *Superior Quality BLUE 006CD*	7		6
21 Feb 98	**SOLOMON BITES THE WORM** *Superior Quality BLUE 007CD*	10		3
9 May 98	**IF...** *Superior Quality BLUED 009*	13		5
8 Aug 98	**SLEAZY BED TRACK** *Superior Quality BLUED 010*	35		2
4 Mar 00	**KEEP THE HOME FIRES BURNING** *Superior Quality BLUED 012*	13		3
20 May 00	**AUTOPHILIA** *Superior Quality BLUEDD 013*	18		3
6 Apr 02	**AFTER HOURS** *Mercury BLUED 016*	26		2
3 May 03	**FAST BOY/LIQUID LIPS** *Superior Quality BLUE 18CDS*	25		2
23 Aug 03	**NEVER GOING NOWHERE** *Superior Quality BLUE 020CDS2*	40		1
30 Sep 06	**MY NEIGHBOUR'S HOUSE** *Cooking Vinyl FRYCD280*	68		1

COLIN BLUNSTONE
UK, male vocalist. See Neil MacArthur, Zombies — 29

Date	Title / Label	Peak	Wks at No.1	Wks on Chart
12 Feb 72	**SAY YOU DON'T MIND** *Epic EPC 7765*	15		9
11 Nov 72	**I DON'T BELIEVE IN MIRACLES** *Epic EPC 8434*	31		6
17 Feb 73	**HOW COULD WE DARE TO BE WRONG** *Epic EPC 1197*	45		2
14 Mar 81	**WHAT BECOMES OF THE BROKENHEARTED** *Stiff BROKEN 1* DAVE STEWART. GUEST VOCALS: COLIN BLUNSTONE	13		10
29 May 82	**TRACKS OF MY TEARS** *PRT 7P 236*	60		2

JAMES BLUNT
UK, male vocalist/guitarist (James Blount). See Helping Haiti — 112

Date	Title / Label	Peak	Wks at No.1	Wks on Chart
19 Mar 05	**WISEMEN** *Atlantic AT0198CD*	44		9
11 Jun 05	**YOU'RE BEAUTIFUL** *Atlantic AT0207CD* ○ ★	1	5	40
8 Oct 05	**HIGH** *Atlantic AT0184CD*	74		1
15 Oct 05	**HIGH** *Atlantic AT0222CDX*	16		11
31 Dec 05	**GOODBYE MY LOVER** *Atlantic AT0230CDX*	9		18
18 Mar 06	**WISEMEN** *Atlantic AT0236CD*	23		11
8 Sep 07	**1973** *Atlantic AT0285CDX*	4		16
15 Dec 07	**SAME MISTAKE** *Atlantic AT0294CD2*	57		1
29 Mar 08	**CARRY YOU HOME** *Atlantic AT0300CD*	20		5

BLUR
UK, male vocal/instrumental group – Damon Albarn, Graham Coxon*, Alex James & Dave Rowntree. See Fat Les, Gorillaz, Me Me Me — 146

Date	Title / Label	Peak	Wks at No.1	Wks on Chart
27 Oct 90	**SHE'S SO HIGH/I KNOW** *Food 26*	48		3
27 Apr 91	**THERE'S NO OTHER WAY** *Food 29*	8		8
10 Aug 91	**BANG** *Food 31*	24		4
11 Apr 92	**POPSCENE** *Food 37*	32		2
1 May 93	**FOR TOMORROW** *Food CDFOODS 40*	28		4
10 Jul 93	**CHEMICAL WORLD** *Food CDFOODS 45*	28		4
16 Oct 93	**SUNDAY SUNDAY** *Food CDFOODS 46*	26		3
19 Mar 94	**GIRLS AND BOYS** *Food CDFOODS 47*	5		7
11 Jun 94	**TO THE END** *Food CDFOODS 50*	16		5
3 Sep 94	**PARKLIFE** *Food CDFOODS 53*	10		7
19 Nov 94	**END OF A CENTURY** *Food CDFOODS 56*	19		3
26 Aug 95	**COUNTRY HOUSE** *Food CDFOODS 63* ●	1	2	11
9 Sep 95	**COUNTRY HOUSE** *Food 63*	57		1
25 Nov 95	**THE UNIVERSAL** *Food CDFOODS 69* ○	5		9
24 Feb 96	**STEREOTYPES** *Food CDFOOD 73*	7		5
11 May 96	**CHARMLESS MAN** *Food CDFOOD 77*	5		6
1 Feb 97	**BEETLEBUM** *Food CDFOODS 89*	1	1	7
19 Apr 97	**SONG 2** *Food CDFOODS 93*	2		5
28 Jun 97	**ON YOUR OWN** *Food CDFOOD 98*	5		5
27 Sep 97	**MOR** *Food CDFOOD 107*	15		3
6 Mar 99	**TENDER** *Food CDFOODS 117* ○	2		10
10 Jul 99	**COFFEE + TEA** *Food CDFOODS 122*	11		7
27 Nov 99	**NO DISTANCE LEFT TO RUN** *Food CDFOOD 123*	14		4
28 Oct 00	**MUSIC IS MY RADAR** *Food CDFOODS 135*	10		9
26 Apr 03	**OUT OF TIME** *Parlophone CDR 6606*	5		9
19 Jul 03	**CRAZY BEAT** *Parlophone CDR 6610*	18		3
18 Oct 03	**GOOD SONG** *Parlophone CDR 6619*	22		2

BM DUBS PRESENT MR RUMBLE FEATURING BRASS TOOTH & KEE
UK, male rap/production group — 2

Date	Title / Label	Peak	Wks at No.1	Wks on Chart
17 Mar 01	**WHOOMP THERE IT IS** *Incentive CENT 16CDS*	32		2

BMR FEATURING FELICIA
Germany, male/female vocal/production duo — 2

Date	Title / Label	Peak	Wks at No.1	Wks on Chart
1 May 99	**CHECK IT OUT (EVERYBODY)** *AM:PM CDAMPM 120*	29		2

BMU
US/UK, male vocal group — 2

Date	Title / Label	Peak	Wks at No.1	Wks on Chart
18 Feb 95	**U WILL KNOW** *Mercury MERCD 420*	23		2

BO SELECTA
UK, male comedian/vocalist (Avid Merrion). See Merrion, McCall & Kensit — 9

Date	Title / Label	Peak	Wks at No.1	Wks on Chart
27 Dec 03	**PROPER CRIMBO** *BMG 82876581412*	4		9

STAN BOARDMAN
UK, male comedian/vocalist — 5

Date	Title / Label	Peak	Wks at No.1	Wks on Chart
10 Jun 06	**STAN'S WORLD CUP SONG** *Harkit HRKCD8155*	15		5

BOB & EARL
US, male vocal duo – Bobby Relf, d. 20 Nov 2007, & Earl Nelson, d. 12 Jul 2008 — 13

Date	Title / Label	Peak	Wks at No.1	Wks on Chart
12 Mar 69	**HARLEM SHUFFLE** *Island WIP 6053*	7		13

BOB & MARCIA
Jamaica, male/female vocal duo – Bob Andy & Marcia Griffiths — 25

Date	Title / Label	Peak	Wks at No.1	Wks on Chart
14 Mar 70	**YOUNG GIFTED AND BLACK** *Harry J HJ 6605*	5		12
5 Jun 71	**PIED PIPER** *Trojan TR 7818*	11		13

BOB THE BUILDER
UK, male animated TV builder/vocalist (Neil Morrissey) — 41

Date	Title / Label	Peak	Wks at No.1	Wks on Chart
16 Dec 00	**CAN WE FIX IT** *BBC Music WMSS 60372* ⊛	1	3	22
15 Sep 01	**MAMBO NO 5** *BBC Music WMSS 60442* ●	1	1	19

BOBBYSOCKS
Norway/Sweden, female vocal duo — 4

Date	Title / Label	Peak	Wks at No.1	Wks on Chart
25 May 85	**LET IT SWING** *RCA PB 40127*	44		4

ANDREA BOCELLI
Italy, male vocalist — 27

Date	Title / Label	Peak	Wks at No.1	Wks on Chart
24 May 97	**TIME TO SAY GOODBYE** *Coalition COLA 003CD* SARAH BRIGHTMAN/ ANDREA BOCELLI ●	2		14
25 Sep 99	**CANTO DELLA TERRA** *Sugar 5613192*	25		4
18 Dec 99	**AVE MARIA** *Philips 4644852*	65		1
1 Jul 00	**CANTO DELLA TERRA** *Sugar 5613192*	24		5
3 Nov 07	**CON TE PARTIRO** *Polydor NLA319500035*	69		3

KAREN BODDINGTON & MARK WILLIAMS
Australia/New Zealand, female/male vocal duo — 1

Date	Title / Label	Peak	Wks at No.1	Wks on Chart
2 Sep 89	**HOME AND AWAY** *First Night SCORE 19*	73		1

Peak Position / Weeks at No.1 / Weeks on Chart

BODY COUNT
US, male rap/vocal/instrumental group — 4

Date	Title	Peak	Wks at No.1	Wks on Chart
8 Oct 94	**BORN DEAD** *Rhyme Syndicate SYNDG 4*	28		2
17 Dec 94	**NECESSARY EVIL** *Virgin VSCDX 1529*	45		2

BODYROCKERS
UK/Australia, male vocal/instrumental/production duo – Dylan Burns & Kaz James — 40

Date	Title	Peak	Wks at No.1	Wks on Chart
30 Apr 05	**I LIKE THE WAY** *Mercury 9871115*	3		40

BODYROX
UK, male production duo – Nick Bridges & Jon Pearn. See Another Chance — 22

Date	Title	Peak	Wks at No.1	Wks on Chart
14 Oct 06	**YEAH YEAH** *Eye Industries/UMTV 1702567*	45		3
4 Nov 06	**YEAH YEAH** *Eye Industries/UMTV 1712693* FEATURING LUCIANA	2		17
19 Jan 08	**WHAT PLANET YOU ON** *Phonetic 1754549* FEATURING LUCIANA	54		2

BODYSNATCHERS
UK, female vocal/instrumental group — 12

Date	Title	Peak	Wks at No.1	Wks on Chart
15 Mar 80	**LET'S DO ROCK STEADY** *2 Tone CHSTT 9*	22		9
19 Jul 80	**EASY LIFE** *2 Tone CHSTT 12*	50		3

HAMILTON BOHANNON
US, male vocalist/drummer — 38

Date	Title	Peak	Wks at No.1	Wks on Chart
15 Feb 75	**SOUTH AFRICAN MAN** *Brunswick BR 16*	22		8
24 May 75	**DISCO STOMP** *Brunswick BR 19*	6		12
5 Jul 75	**FOOT STOMPIN' MUSIC** *Brunswick BR 21*	23		6
6 Sep 75	**HAPPY FEELING** *Brunswick BR 24*	49		3
26 Aug 78	**LET'S START THE DANCE** *Mercury 6167 700*	56		4
13 Feb 82	**LET'S START TO DANCE AGAIN** *London HL 10582*	49		5

BOILING POINT
US, male vocal/instrumental group — 6

Date	Title	Peak	Wks at No.1	Wks on Chart
27 May 78	**LET'S GET FUNKTIFIED** *Bang 1312*	41		6

CJ BOLLAND
Belgium, male producer (Christian Jay Bolland). See Ravesignal III, Sonic Solution — 10

Date	Title	Peak	Wks at No.1	Wks on Chart
5 Oct 96	**SUGAR IS SWEETER** *Internal LIECD 35*	11		5
17 May 97	**THE PROPHET** *ffrr FCD 300*	19		3
3 Jul 99	**IT AIN'T GONNA BE ME** *Essential Recordings ESCDP 5*	35		2

MICHAEL BOLTON
US, male vocalist (Michael Bolotin) — 113

Date	Title	Peak	Wks at No.1	Wks on Chart
17 Feb 90	**HOW AM I SUPPOSED TO LIVE WITHOUT YOU** *CBS 6553977* ★	3		10
28 Apr 90	**HOW CAN WE BE LOVERS** *CBS 6559187*	10		10
21 Jul 90	**WHEN I'M BACK ON MY FEET AGAIN** *CBS 6560777*	44		5
20 Apr 91	**LOVE IS A WONDERFUL THING** *Columbia 6567717*	23		8
27 Jul 91	**TIME LOVE AND TENDERNESS** *Columbia 6569897*	28		7
9 Nov 91	**WHEN A MAN LOVES A WOMAN** *Columbia 6574887* ★	8		9
8 Feb 92	**STEEL BARS** *Columbia 6577257*	17		6
9 May 92	**MISSING YOU NOW** *Columbia 6579917* FEATURING KENNY G	28		4
31 Oct 92	**TO LOVE SOMEBODY** *Columbia 6584557*	16		6
26 Dec 92	**DRIFT AWAY** *Columbia 6588657*	18		5
13 Mar 93	**REACH OUT I'LL BE THERE** *Columbia 6588972*	37		4
13 Nov 93	**SAID I LOVED YOU BUT I LIED** *Columbia 6598762*	15		8
26 Feb 94	**SOUL OF MY SOUL** *Columbia 6601772*	32		3
14 May 94	**LEAN ON ME** *Columbia 6604132*	14		7
9 Sep 95	**CAN I TOUCH YOU...THERE?** *Columbia 6624385*	6		9
2 Dec 95	**A LOVE SO BEAUTIFUL** *Columbia 6627092*	27		5
16 Mar 96	**SOUL PROVIDER** *Columbia 6629812*	35		3
8 Nov 97	**THE BEST OF LOVE/GO THE DISTANCE** *Columbia 6652802*	14		4

BOMB THE BASS
UK, male producer (Tim Simenon) — 50

Date	Title	Peak	Wks at No.1	Wks on Chart
20 Feb 88	**BEAT DIS** *Mister-ron DOOD 1* ●	2		9
27 Aug 88	**MEGABLAST/DON'T MAKE ME WAIT** *Mister-ron DOOD 2* FEATURING MERLIN & ANTONIA/BOMB THE BASS FEATURING LORRAINE	6		9
26 Nov 88	**SAY A LITTLE PRAYER** *Rhythm King DOOD 3* FEATURING MAUREEN	10		10
27 Jul 91	**WINTER IN JULY** *Rhythm King 6572757*	7		9
9 Nov 91	**THE AIR YOU BREATHE** *Rhythm King 6575387*	52		3
2 May 92	**KEEP GIVING ME LOVE** *Rhythm King 6579887*	62		2
1 Oct 94	**BUG POWDER DUST** *Stoned Heights BRCD 300* FEATURING JUSTIN WARFIELD	24		3
17 Dec 94	**DARKHEART** *Stoned Heights BRCD 305* FEATURING SPIKEY TEE	35		3
1 Apr 95	**1 TO 1 RELIGION** *Stoned Heights BRCD 313* FEATURING CARLTON	53		1
16 Sep 95	**SANDCASTLES** *Fourth & Broadway BRCD 324* FEATURING BERNARD FOWLER	54		1

BOMBALURINA
UK, male/female vocal/dance group – Timmy Mallett, Dawn Andrews & Annie Dunkley — 20

Date	Title	Peak	Wks at No.1	Wks on Chart
28 Jul 90	**ITSY BITSY TEENY WEENY YELLOW POLKA DOT BIKINI** *Carpet CRPT 1* FEATURING TIMMY MALLETT ●	1	3	13
24 Nov 90	**SEVEN LITTLE GIRLS SITTING IN THE BACKSEAT** *Carpet CRPT 2*	18		7

BOMBERS
Canada, male/female vocal/instrumental group — 10

Date	Title	Peak	Wks at No.1	Wks on Chart
5 May 79	**(EVERYBODY) GET DANCIN'** *Flamingo FM 1*	37		7
18 Aug 79	**LET'S DANCE** *Flamingo FM 4*	58		3

BOMFUNK MC'S
Finland, male DJ/rap duo – B.O. Dubb (Raymond Ebanks) & DJ Gismo (Ismo Lappalainen) — 21

Date	Title	Peak	Wks at No.1	Wks on Chart
5 Aug 00	**FREESTYLER** *Dancepool DPS 2CD*	2		12
2 Dec 00	**UP ROCKING BEATS** *INCredible 6706132*	11		9

B.O.N.
Germany, male vocal duo — 5

Date	Title	Peak	Wks at No.1	Wks on Chart
3 Feb 01	**BOYS** *Epic 6707092*	15		5

BON GARCON
UK, male production/vocal/instrumental duo — 2

Date	Title	Peak	Wks at No.1	Wks on Chart
18 Jun 05	**FREEK U** *Eye Industries/UMTV 9871395*	42		2

BON JOVI
US, male vocal/instrumental group – Jon Bon Jovi*, David Bryan, Richie Sambora*, Alec John Such & Tico Torres. Stadium-packing New Jersey veterans who notched up a staggering 37th UK hit in 2009. Plans to use 'Always' in the film *Romeo Is Bleeding* were shelved by the band after they watched the cult cop comedy — 249

Date	Title	Peak	Wks at No.1	Wks on Chart
31 Aug 85	**HARDEST PART IS THE NIGHT** *Vertigo VER 22*	68		1
9 Aug 86	**YOU GIVE LOVE A BAD NAME** *Vertigo VER 26* ★	14		10
25 Oct 86	**LIVIN' ON A PRAYER** *Vertigo VER 28* ★	4		15
11 Apr 87	**WANTED DEAD OR ALIVE** *Vertigo JOV 1*	13		7
15 Aug 87	**NEVER SAY GOODBYE** *Vertigo JOV 2*	21		5
24 Sep 88	**BAD MEDICINE** *Vertigo JOV 3* ★	17		7
10 Dec 88	**BORN TO BE MY BABY** *Vertigo JOV 4*	22		7
29 Apr 89	**I'LL BE THERE FOR YOU** *Vertigo JOV 5* ★	18		7
26 Aug 89	**LAY YOUR HANDS ON ME** *Vertigo JOV 6*	18		6
9 Dec 89	**LIVING IN SIN** *Vertigo JOV 7*	35		6
24 Oct 92	**KEEP THE FAITH** *Jambco JOV 8*	5		6
23 Jan 93	**BED OF ROSES** *Jambco JOVCD 9*	13		6
15 May 93	**IN THESE ARMS** *Jambco JOVCD 10*	9		7
7 Aug 93	**I'LL SLEEP WHEN I'M DEAD** *Jambco JOVCD 11*	17		5
2 Oct 93	**I BELIEVE** *Jambco JOVCD 12*	11		6
26 Mar 94	**DRY COUNTY** *Jambco JOVCD 13*	9		6
24 Sep 94	**ALWAYS** *Jambco JOVCD 14*	2		18
17 Dec 94	**PLEASE COME HOME FOR CHRISTMAS** *Jambco JOVCD 16*	7		10
25 Feb 95	**SOMEDAY I'LL BE SATURDAY NIGHT** *Jambco JOVDD 15*	7		7
10 Jun 95	**THIS AIN'T A LOVE SONG** *Mercury JOVCX 17*	6		9
30 Sep 95	**SOMETHING FOR THE PAIN** *Mercury JOVCX 18*	8		7
25 Nov 95	**LIE TO ME** *Mercury JOVCD 19*	10		8
9 Mar 96	**THESE DAYS** *Mercury JOVCD 20*	7		6
6 Jul 96	**HEY GOD** *Mercury JOVCX 21*	13		5
10 Apr 99	**REAL LIFE** *Reprise W 479CD*	21		5
3 Jun 00	**IT'S MY LIFE** *Mercury 5627682*	3		13
9 Sep 00	**SAY IT ISN'T SO** *Mercury 5688982*	10		7
9 Dec 00	**THANK YOU FOR LOVING ME** *Mercury 5727312*	12		6
19 May 01	**ONE WILD NIGHT** *Mercury 5729502*	10		7
28 Sep 02	**EVERYDAY** *Mercury 0639372*	5		6
21 Dec 02	**MISUNDERSTOOD** *Mercury 0638162*	21		5
24 May 03	**ALL ABOUT LOVIN' YOU** *Mercury 9800242*	9		6
24 Sep 05	**HAVE A NICE DAY** *Mercury 9885841*	6		4
11 Feb 06	**WELCOME TO WHEREVER YOU ARE** *Mercury 9879526*	19		3
24 Jun 06	**WHO SAYS YOU CAN'T GO HOME** *Mercury 9858248*	5		3

Key: ○ Silver-selling · ● Gold-selling · ⊛ Platinum-selling (x multiples) · ★ US No.1 · Peak Position · Weeks at No.1 · Weeks on Chart

Date	Title / Label / Cat. No.	Peak Position	Weeks at No.1	Weeks on Chart
7 Jul 07	**(YOU WANT TO) MAKE A MEMORY** *Mercury 1737482*	33		1
22 Mar 08	**LIVIN' ON A PRAYER** *Mercury USPR38619998*	70		2
13 Dec 08	**ALWAYS** *Mercury USPR39402221*	67		1
14 Nov 09	**WE WEREN'T BORN TO FOLLOW** *Mercury USUV70902541*	25		2
14 Nov 09	**LIVIN' ON A PRAYER** *Mercury USPR38619998*	52		1

JON BON JOVI

US, male vocalist/guitarist (John Bongiovi). See Bon Jovi, Helping Haiti — **27**

Date	Title / Label / Cat. No.	Peak Position	Weeks at No.1	Weeks on Chart
4 Aug 90	**BLAZE OF GLORY** *Vertigo JBJ 1* ★	13		8
10 Nov 90	**MIRACLE** *Vertigo JBJ 2*	29		5
14 Jun 97	**MIDNIGHT IN CHELSEA** *Mercury MERCD 488*	4		7
30 Aug 97	**QUEEN OF NEW ORLEANS** *Mercury MERCD 493*	10		4
15 Nov 97	**JANIE, DON'T TAKE YOUR LOVE TO TOWN** *Mercury 5749872*	13		3

RONNIE BOND

UK, male vocalist — **5**

Date	Title / Label / Cat. No.	Peak Position	Weeks at No.1	Weeks on Chart
31 May 80	**IT'S WRITTEN ON YOUR BODY** *Mercury MER 13*	52		5

BONDE DO ROLE

Brazil, male/female vocal/instrumental/DJ group — **1**

Date	Title / Label / Cat. No.	Peak Position	Weeks at No.1	Weeks on Chart
2 Jun 07	**OFFICE BOY** *Domino RUG255CD*	75		1

GARY U.S. BONDS

US, male vocalist (Gary Anderson) — **39**

Date	Title / Label / Cat. No.	Peak Position	Weeks at No.1	Weeks on Chart
19 Jan 61	**NEW ORLEANS** *Top Rank JAR 527* U.S. BONDS	16		11
20 Jul 61	**QUARTER TO THREE** *Top Rank JAR 575* U.S. BONDS ★	7		13
30 May 81	**THIS LITTLE GIRL** *EMI America EA 122*	43		6
22 Aug 81	**JOLE BLON** *EMI America EA 127*	51		3
31 Oct 81	**IT'S ONLY LOVE** *EMI America EA 128*	43		3
17 Jul 82	**SOUL DEEP** *EMI America EA 140*	59		3

BONE

UK, male vocal/production duo — **1**

Date	Title / Label / Cat. No.	Peak Position	Weeks at No.1	Weeks on Chart
2 Apr 94	**WINGS OF LOVE** *Deconstruction 74321176282*	55		1

BONE THUGS-N-HARMONY

US, male rap group – Bizzy Bone (Bryon McCane II), Flesh-n-Bone (Stanley Howse), Krayzie Bone (Anthony Henderson), Layzie Bone (Steven Howse) & Wish Bone (Charles C Scruggs) — **27**

Date	Title / Label / Cat. No.	Peak Position	Weeks at No.1	Weeks on Chart
4 Nov 95	**1ST OF THA MONTH** *Epic 6625172*	32		2
10 Aug 96	**THA CROSSROADS** *Epic 6635502* ★	8		11
9 Nov 96	**1ST OF THA MONTH** *Epic 6638505*	15		4
15 Feb 97	**DAYS OF OUR LIVEZ** *East West A 3982CD*	37		2
26 Jul 97	**LOOK INTO MY EYES** *Epic 6647862*	16		3
24 May 03	**HOME** *Epic 6738305* FEATURING PHIL COLLINS	19		4
2 Jun 07	**I TRIED** *Polydor USUM70701555* FEATURING AKON	69		1

ELBOW BONES & THE RACKETEERS

US, male/female instrumental/vocal group — **9**

Date	Title / Label / Cat. No.	Peak Position	Weeks at No.1	Weeks on Chart
14 Jan 84	**A NIGHT IN NEW YORK** *EMI America EA 165*	33		9

BONEY M

Jamaica/Aruba/Montserrat, female/male vocal group – Liz Mitchell, Marcia Barrett, Bobby Farrell & Maizie Williams — **173**

Date	Title / Label / Cat. No.	Peak Position	Weeks at No.1	Weeks on Chart
18 Dec 76	**DADDY COOL** *Atlantic K 10827* ○	6		13
12 Mar 77	**SUNNY** *Atlantic K 10892*	3		10
25 Jun 77	**MA BAKER** *Atlantic K 10965*	2		13
29 Oct 77	**BELFAST** *Atlantic K 11020*	8		13
29 Apr 78	**RIVERS OF BABYLON/BROWN GIRL IN THE RING** *Atlantic/Hansa K 11120* ⊛	1	5	40
7 Oct 78	**RASPUTIN** *Atlantic/Hansa K 11192* ●	2		10
2 Dec 78	**MARY'S BOY CHILD – OH MY LORD** *Atlantic/Hansa K 11221* ⊛	1	4	8
3 Mar 79	**PAINTER MAN** *Atlantic/Hansa K 11255* ○	10		6
28 Apr 79	**HOORAY HOORAY IT'S A HOLI-HOLIDAY** *Atlantic/Hansa K 11279* ○	3		9
11 Aug 79	**GOTTA GO HOME/EL LUTE** *Atlantic/Hansa K 11351* ○	12		11
15 Dec 79	**I'M BORN AGAIN** *Atlantic/Hansa K 11410*	35		7
26 Apr 80	**MY FRIEND JACK** *Atlantic/Hansa K 11463*	57		5
14 Feb 81	**CHILDREN OF PARADISE** *Atlantic/Hansa K 11637*	66		2
21 Nov 81	**WE KILL THE WORLD (DON'T KILL THE WORLD)** *Atlantic/Hansa K 11689*	39		5
24 Dec 88	**MEGAMIX/MARY'S BOY CHILD (REMIX)** *Ariola 111947*	52		3
5 Dec 92	**BONEY M MEGAMIX** *Arista 74321125127*	7		9
17 Apr 93	**BROWN GIRL IN THE RING (REMIX)** *Arista 74321137052*	38		3
8 May 99	**MA BAKER – SOMEBODY SCREAM** *Logic 74321653872* VS HORNY UNITED	22		2
29 Dec 01	**DADDY COOL 2001** *BMG 74321913512*	47		2
22 Dec 07	**MARY'S BOY CHILD – OH MY LORD** *BMG DED168000015*	47		2

BONIFACE

Seychelles, male vocalist (Bruce Boniface) — **3**

Date	Title / Label / Cat. No.	Peak Position	Weeks at No.1	Weeks on Chart
31 Aug 02	**CHEEKY** *Columbia 6729902*	25		3

GRAHAM BONNET

UK, male vocalist. See Rainbow — **15**

Date	Title / Label / Cat. No.	Peak Position	Weeks at No.1	Weeks on Chart
21 Mar 81	**NIGHT GAMES** *Vertigo VER 1* ○	6		11
13 Jun 81	**LIAR** *Vertigo VER 2*	51		4

GRAHAM BONNEY

UK, male vocalist (Graham Bradley) — **8**

Date	Title / Label / Cat. No.	Peak Position	Weeks at No.1	Weeks on Chart
24 Mar 66	**SUPERGIRL** *Columbia DB 7843*	19		8

BONNIE 'PRINCE' BILLY

US, male vocalist/guitarist (Will Oldham) — **1**

Date	Title / Label / Cat. No.	Peak Position	Weeks at No.1	Weeks on Chart
4 Sep 04	**AGNES QUEEN OF SORROW** *Domino RUG185CD*	69		1

BONO

Ireland, male vocalist (Paul Hewson). See Passengers, U2 — **26**

Date	Title / Label / Cat. No.	Peak Position	Weeks at No.1	Weeks on Chart
25 Jan 86	**IN A LIFETIME** *RCA PB 40535* CLANNAD FEATURING BONO	20		5
10 Jun 89	**IN A LIFETIME** *RCA PB 42873* CLANNAD FEATURING BONO	17		7
4 Dec 93	**I'VE GOT YOU UNDER MY SKIN** *Island CID 578* FRANK SINATRA WITH BONO	4		9
9 Apr 94	**IN THE NAME OF THE FATHER** *Island CID 593* & GAVIN FRIDAY	46		2
23 Oct 99	**NEW DAY** *Columbia 6682122* WYCLEF JEAN FEATURING BONO	23		2
6 Feb 10	**STRANDED (HAITI MON AMOUR)** *MTV Networks USYP61000005* JAY-Z FEATURING BONO, THE EDGE & RIHANNA	41		1

BONZO DOG DOO-DAH BAND

UK, male vocal/instrumental group – Viv Stanshall, d. 5 Mar 1995, Martin Ashton, Dennis Cowan, Neil Innes, Rodney Slater, Larry Smith & Roger Ruskin Spear — **14**

Date	Title / Label / Cat. No.	Peak Position	Weeks at No.1	Weeks on Chart
6 Nov 68	**I'M THE URBAN SPACEMAN** *Liberty LBF 15144*	5		14

BETTY BOO

UK, female vocalist/rapper (Alison Clarkson) — **55**

Date	Title / Label / Cat. No.	Peak Position	Weeks at No.1	Weeks on Chart
12 Aug 89	**HEY DJ I CAN'T DANCE TO THAT MUSIC YOU'RE PLAYING/SKA TRAIN** *Rhythm King LEFT 34* BEATMASTERS FEATURING BETTY BOO	7		11
19 May 90	**DOIN' THE DO** *Rhythm King LEFT 39*	7		12
11 Aug 90	**WHERE ARE YOU BABY** *Rhythm King LEFT 43* ○	3		10
1 Dec 90	**24 HOURS** *Rhythm King LEFT 45*	25		8
8 Aug 92	**LET ME TAKE YOU THERE** *WEA YZ 677*	12		8
3 Oct 92	**I'M ON MY WAY** *WEA YZ 693*	44		3
10 Apr 93	**HANGOVER** *WEA YZ 719CD*	50		3

BOO RADLEYS

UK, male vocal/instrumental group – Simon 'Sice' Rowbottom, Timothy Brown, Martin Carr & Rob Cieka — **27**

Date	Title / Label / Cat. No.	Peak Position	Weeks at No.1	Weeks on Chart
20 Jun 92	**DOES THIS HURT/BOO! FOREVER** *Creation CRE 128*	67		1
23 Oct 93	**WISH I WAS SKINNY** *Creation CRESCD 169*	75		1
12 Feb 94	**BARNEY (...& ME)** *Creation CRESCD 178*	48		2
11 Jun 94	**LAZARUS** *Creation CRESCD 187*	50		2
11 Mar 95	**WAKE UP BOO!** *Creation CRESCD 191*	9		8
13 May 95	**FIND THE ANSWER WITHIN** *Creation CRESCD 202*	37		3
29 Jul 95	**IT'S LULU** *Creation CRESCD 211*	25		2
7 Oct 95	**FROM THE BENCH AT BELVIDERE** *Creation CRESCD 214*	24		2
17 Aug 96	**WHAT'S IN THE BOX? (SEE WHATCHA GOT)** *Creation CRESCD 220*	25		2
19 Oct 96	**C'MON KIDS** *Creation CRESCD 236*	18		2
1 Feb 97	**RIDE THE TIGER** *Creation CRESCD 248X*	38		1
17 Oct 98	**FREE HUEY** *Creation CRESCD 299X*	54		1

BOO-YAA T.R.I.B.E.
US, male rap group — 6

Date	Title	Peak Position	Weeks at No.1	Weeks on Chart
30 Jun 90	**PSYKO FUNK** *Fourth & Broadway BRW 179*	43		3
6 Nov 93	**ANOTHER BODY MURDERED** *Epic 6597942* FAITH NO MORE & BOO-YAA T.R.I.B.E.	26		3

BOOGIE BOX HIGH
UK, male producer – Andros Georgiou – with male/female vocal/instrumental collaborators including David Austin*, Chris Cameron, Deon Estus*, Nick Heyward*, Mick Talbot & (uncredited) George Michael* — 11

Date	Title	Peak Position	Weeks at No.1	Weeks on Chart
4 Jul 87	**JIVE TALKIN'** *Hardback 7BOSS 4*	7		11

BOOGIE DOWN PRODUCTIONS
US, male rap group — 2

Date	Title	Peak Position	Weeks at No.1	Weeks on Chart
4 Jun 88	**MY PHILOSOPHY/STOP THE VIOLENCE** *Jive JIVEX 170*	69		2

BOOGIE PIMPS
Germany, male DJ/production/instrumental duo – Mirko Jacob & Mark J Klak — 21

Date	Title	Peak Position	Weeks at No.1	Weeks on Chart
17 Jan 04	**SOMEBODY TO LOVE** *Data 61CDS*	3		15
8 May 04	**SUNNY** *Data 67CDX*	10		6

BOOKER T & THE MG's
US, male instrumental group – Booker T Jones, Steve Cropper, Donald Dunn & Al Jackson, d. 1 Oct 1975 — 43

Date	Title	Peak Position	Weeks at No.1	Weeks on Chart
11 Dec 68	**SOUL LIMBO** *Stax 102*	30		9
7 May 69	**TIME IS TIGHT** *Stax 119*	4		18
30 Aug 69	**SOUL CLAP '69** *Stax 127*	35		4
15 Dec 79	**GREEN ONIONS** *Atlantic K 10109*	7		12

BOOM!
UK, male/female vocal group — 5

Date	Title	Peak Position	Weeks at No.1	Weeks on Chart
27 Jan 01	**FALLING** *London LONCD 458*	11		5

TAKA BOOM
US, female vocalist (Yvonne Stevens) — 8

Date	Title	Peak Position	Weeks at No.1	Weeks on Chart
19 Feb 00	**MUST BE THE MUSIC** *Incentive CENT 4CDS* JOEY NEGRO FEATURING TAKA BOOM	8		5
16 Sep 00	**SATURDAY** *Yola CDX03* JOEY NEGRO FEATURING TAKA BOOM	41		1
9 Jun 01	**JUST CAN'T GET ENOUGH (NO NO NO NO)** *Xtravaganza XTRAV 25CD* EYE TO EYE FEATURING TAKA BOOM	36		2

BOOM BOOM ROOM
UK, male vocal/instrumental trio — 1

Date	Title	Peak Position	Weeks at No.1	Weeks on Chart
8 Mar 86	**HERE COMES THE MAN** *Fun After All FUN 101*	74		1

BOOMKAT
US, male/female vocal/instrumental/production duo — 2

Date	Title	Peak Position	Weeks at No.1	Weeks on Chart
31 May 03	**THE WRECKONING** *DreamWorks 4504580*	37		2

BOOMTOWN RATS
Ireland, male vocal/instrumental group – Bob Geldof*, Pete Briquette, Gerry Cott, Simon Crowe, Johnny Fingers (John Moylett) & Garry Roberts — 123

Date	Title	Peak Position	Weeks at No.1	Weeks on Chart
27 Aug 77	**LOOKING AFTER NO. 1** *Ensign ENY 4*	11		9
19 Nov 77	**MARY OF THE FOURTH FORM** *Ensign ENY 9*	15		9
15 Apr 78	**SHE'S SO MODERN** *Ensign ENY 13*	12		11
17 Jun 78	**LIKE CLOCKWORK** *Ensign ENY 14*	6		13
14 Oct 78	**RAT TRAP** *Ensign ENY 16*	1	2	15
21 Jul 79	**I DON'T LIKE MONDAYS** *Ensign ENY 30*	1	4	12
17 Nov 79	**DIAMOND SMILES** *Ensign ENY 33*	13		10
26 Jan 80	**SOMEONE'S LOOKING AT YOU** *Ensign ENY 34*	4		9
22 Nov 80	**BANANA REPUBLIC** *Ensign BONGO 1*	3		11
31 Jan 81	**THE ELEPHANT'S GRAVEYARD (GUILTY)** *Ensign BONGO 2*	26		6
12 Dec 81	**NEVER IN A MILLION YEARS** *Mercury MER 87*	62		4
20 Mar 82	**HOUSE ON FIRE** *Mercury MER 91*	24		8
18 Feb 84	**TONIGHT** *Mercury MER 154*	73		1
19 May 84	**DRAG ME DOWN** *Mercury MER 163*	50		3
2 Jul 94	**I DON'T LIKE MONDAYS** *Vertigo VERCD 87*	38		2

CLINT BOON EXPERIENCE
UK, male/female vocal/instrumental group — 3

Date	Title	Peak Position	Weeks at No.1	Weeks on Chart
6 Nov 99	**WHITE NO SUGAR** *Artful CDARTFUL 32*	61		1
5 Feb 00	**BIGGEST HORIZON** *Artful CDARTFUL 33*	70		1
5 Aug 00	**DO WHAT YOU DO (EARWORM SONG)** *Artful CDARTFUL 34*	63		1

DANIEL BOONE
UK, male vocalist (Peter Lee Stirling) — 25

Date	Title	Peak Position	Weeks at No.1	Weeks on Chart
14 Aug 71	**DADDY DON'T YOU WALK SO FAST** *Penny Farthing PEN 764*	17		15
1 Apr 72	**BEAUTIFUL SUNDAY** *Penny Farthing PEN 781*	21		10

DEBBY BOONE
US, female vocalist — 2

Date	Title	Peak Position	Weeks at No.1	Weeks on Chart
24 Dec 77	**YOU LIGHT UP MY LIFE** *Warner Brothers K 17043* ★	48		2

PAT BOONE
US, male vocalist (Charles Boone). The teen idol balladeer was the main rival to Elvis in the early rock 'n' roll years, during which time he was seldom off the UK or US charts. He was voted the 'World's No.1 Male Singer' in 1957 in the *NME* poll — 308

Date	Title	Peak Position	Weeks at No.1	Weeks on Chart
18 Nov 55	**AIN'T THAT A SHAME** *London HLD 8172* ★	7		9
27 Apr 56	**I'LL BE HOME** *London HLD 8253*	1	5	22
27 Jul 56	**LONG TALL SALLY** *London HLD 8291*	18		7
17 Aug 56	**I ALMOST LOST MY MIND** *London HLD 8303* ★	14		7
7 Dec 56	**FRIENDLY PERSUASION** *London HLD 8346*	3		21
11 Jan 57	**AIN'T THAT A SHAME** *London HLD 8172*	22		2
11 Jan 57	**I'LL BE HOME** *London HLD 8253*	19		2
1 Feb 57	**DON'T FORBID ME** *London HLD 8370* ★	2		16
26 Apr 57	**WHY BABY WHY** *London HLD 8404*	17		7
5 Jul 57	**LOVE LETTERS IN THE SAND** *London HLD 8445* ★	2		21
27 Sep 57	**REMEMBER YOU'RE MINE/THERE'S A GOLDMINE IN THE SKY** *London HLD 8479*	5		18
6 Dec 57	**APRIL LOVE** *London HLD 8512* ★	7		23
13 Dec 57	**WHITE CHRISTMAS** *London HLD 8520*	29		1
4 Apr 58	**A WONDERFUL TIME UP THERE** *London HLD 8574*	2		17
11 Apr 58	**IT'S TOO SOON TO KNOW** *London HLD 8574*	7		12
27 Jun 58	**SUGAR MOON** *London HLD 8640*	6		12
29 Aug 58	**IF DREAMS CAME TRUE** *London HLD 8675*	16		11
5 Dec 58	**GEE BUT IT'S LONELY** *London HLD 8739*	30		1
6 Feb 59	**I'LL REMEMBER TONIGHT** *London HLD 8775*	18		9
10 Apr 59	**WITH THE WIND AND THE RAIN IN YOUR HAIR** *London HLD 8824*	21		3
22 May 59	**FOR A PENNY** *London HLD 8855*	19		9
31 Jul 59	**'TWIXT TWELVE AND TWENTY** *London HLD 8910*	18		7
23 Jun 60	**WALKING THE FLOOR OVER YOU** *London HLD 9138*	39		5
6 Jul 61	**MOODY RIVER** *London HLD 9350* ★	18		10
7 Dec 61	**JOHNNY WILL** *London HLD 9461*	4		13
15 Feb 62	**I'LL SEE YOU IN MY DREAMS** *London HLD 9504*	27		9
24 May 62	**QUANDO QUANDO QUANDO** *London HLD 9543*	41		4
12 Jul 62	**SPEEDY GONZALES** *London HLD 9573*	2		19
15 Nov 62	**THE MAIN ATTRACTION** *London HLD 9620*	12		11

BOOTH & THE BAD ANGEL
UK/US, male vocal/composer/arranger duo. See James — 4

Date	Title	Peak Position	Weeks at No.1	Weeks on Chart
22 Jun 96	**I BELIEVE** *Fontana BBDD 1*	25		3
11 Jul 98	**FALL IN LOVE WITH ME** *Mercury MERCD 503*	57		1

TIM BOOTH
UK, male vocalist. See Booth & The Bad Angel, James — 1

Date	Title	Peak Position	Weeks at No.1	Weeks on Chart
10 Jul 04	**DOWN TO THE SEA** *Sanctuary SANXS279*	68		1

KEN BOOTHE
Jamaica, male vocalist — 22

Date	Title	Peak Position	Weeks at No.1	Weeks on Chart
21 Sep 74	**EVERYTHING I OWN** *Trojan TR 7920*	1	3	12
14 Dec 74	**CRYING OVER YOU** *Trojan TR 7944*	11		10

BOOTHILL FOOT-TAPPERS
UK, male/female vocal/instrumental group — 3

Date	Title	Peak Position	Weeks at No.1	Weeks on Chart
14 Jul 84	**GET YOUR FEET OUT OF MY SHOES** *Go! Discs TAP 1*	64		3

BOOTSY'S RUBBER BAND
US, male vocal/instrumental group

Date	Title	Peak Position	Weeks at No.1	Weeks on Chart
				3
8 Jul 78	**BOOTZILLA** *Warner Brothers K 17196*	43		3

BOOTY LUV
UK, female vocal duo – Cherise Roberts & Nadia Shepherd. See Big Brovaz

Date	Title	Peak Position	Weeks at No.1	Weeks on Chart
				56
2 Dec 06	**BOOGIE 2NITE** *Hed Kandi HK27CDS*	3		23
19 May 07	**SHINE** *Hed Kandi HK33CDX*	10		10
15 Sep 07	**DON'T MESS WITH MY MAN** *Hed Kandi HK38CDS*	11		6
8 Dec 07	**SOME KINDA RUSH** *Data HK46CDX*	19		13
12 Sep 09	**SAY IT** *Hed Kandi HK83CDX*	16		4

BOSS
US, male producer (David Morales)

Date	Title	Peak Position	Weeks at No.1	Weeks on Chart
				1
27 Aug 94	**CONGO** *Cooltempo CDCOOL 296*	54		1

NAILA BOSS
UK, female rapper/vocalist

Date	Title	Peak Position	Weeks at No.1	Weeks on Chart
				16
22 May 04	**IT CAN'T BE RIGHT** *2PSL/inferno 2PSLCD04* 2PLAY FEATURING RAGHAV & NAILA BOSS	8		7
10 Jul 04	**LA LA LA** *La Boss NBCD1*	65		1
11 Sep 04	**YOU SHOULD REALLY KNOW** *Relentless RELCD9* PIRATES FEATURING ENYA, SHOLA AMA, NAILA BOSS & ISHANI	8		8

BOSTON
US, male vocal/instrumental group

Date	Title	Peak Position	Weeks at No.1	Weeks on Chart
				16
29 Jan 77	**MORE THAN A FEELING** *Epic EPC 4658*	22		8
7 Oct 78	**DON'T LOOK BACK** *Epic EPC 6653*	43		5
6 Feb 10	**MORE THAN A FEELING** *Epic USSM17600639*	51		3

EVE BOSWELL
Hungary, female vocalist (Eva Keleti), d. 13 Aug 1998 (age 74)

Date	Title	Peak Position	Weeks at No.1	Weeks on Chart
				13
30 Dec 55	**PICKIN' A CHICKEN** *Parlophone R 4082*	9		13

JUDY BOUCHER
UK (b. St Vincent), female vocalist

Date	Title	Peak Position	Weeks at No.1	Weeks on Chart
				23
4 Apr 87	**CAN'T BE WITH YOU TONIGHT** *Orbitone OR 721*	2		14
4 Jul 87	**YOU CAUGHT MY EYE** *Orbitone OR 722*	18		9

BOUNCING CZECKS
UK, male vocal/instrumental group

Date	Title	Peak Position	Weeks at No.1	Weeks on Chart
				1
29 Dec 84	**I'M A LITTLE CHRISTMAS CRACKER** *RCA 463*	72		1

BOUNTY KILLER
Jamaica, male rapper (Rodney Price)

Date	Title	Peak Position	Weeks at No.1	Weeks on Chart
				1
27 Feb 99	**IT'S A PARTY** *Edel 0066135 BLA*	65		1

BOURGEOIS TAGG
US, male vocal/instrumental group

Date	Title	Peak Position	Weeks at No.1	Weeks on Chart
				6
6 Feb 88	**I DON'T MIND AT ALL** *Island IS 353*	35		6

BOURGIE BOURGIE
UK, male vocal/instrumental group

Date	Title	Peak Position	Weeks at No.1	Weeks on Chart
				4
3 Mar 84	**BREAKING POINT** *MCA BOU 1*	48		4

TOBY BOURKE/GEORGE MICHAEL
UK, male vocal duo

Date	Title	Peak Position	Weeks at No.1	Weeks on Chart
				4
7 Jun 97	**WALTZ AWAY DREAMING** *Aegean AECD 01*	10		4

BOW WOW
US, male rapper (Rashad Moss)

Date	Title	Peak Position	Weeks at No.1	Weeks on Chart
				31
14 Apr 01	**BOW WOW (THAT'S MY NAME)** *So So Def 6709832* LIL BOW WOW	6		9
27 Nov 04	**BABY IT'S YOU** *Mercury 9869056* JOJO FEATURING BOW WOW	8		9
8 Oct 05	**LET ME HOLD YOU (IMPORT)** *Sony BMG 6760602* FEATURING OMARION	64		2
22 Oct 05	**LET ME HOLD YOU** *Columbia 6760605* FEATURING OMARION	27		6
18 Mar 06	**LIKE YOU** *Columbia 82876779522* FEATURING CIARA	17		5

BOW WOW WOW
UK/Burma, female/male vocal/instrumental group – Annabella Lwin* (Myint Myint Aye), Matthew Ashman, d. 21 Nov 1995, David Barbarossa & Leigh Gorman

Date	Title	Peak Position	Weeks at No.1	Weeks on Chart
				54
26 Jul 80	**C30, C60, C90, GO** *EMI 5088*	34		7
6 Dec 80	**YOUR CASSETTE PET** *EMI WOW 1*	58		6
28 Mar 81	**W.O.R.K. (N.O. NAH NO NO MY DADDY DON'T)** *EMI 5153*	62		3
15 Aug 81	**PRINCE OF DARKNESS** *RCA 100*	58		4
7 Nov 81	**CHIHUAHUA** *RCA 144*	51		4
30 Jan 82	**GO WILD IN THE COUNTRY** *RCA 175*	7		13
1 May 82	**SEE JUNGLE (JUNGLE BOY)/TV SAVAGE** *RCA 220*	45		3
5 Jun 82	**I WANT CANDY** *RCA 238*	9		8
31 Jul 82	**LOUIS QUATORZE** *RCA 263*	66		2
12 Mar 83	**DO YOU WANNA HOLD ME?** *RCA 314*	47		4

BOWA FEATURING MALA
UK, male/female production/vocal group

Date	Title	Peak Position	Weeks at No.1	Weeks on Chart
				1
7 Dec 91	**DIFFERENT STORY** *Dead Dead Good 8*	64		1

DANE BOWERS
UK, male vocalist. See Another Level, Upper Street

Date	Title	Peak Position	Weeks at No.1	Weeks on Chart
				38
29 Apr 00	**BUGGIN'** *NuLife 74321753342* TRUE STEPPERS FEATURING DANE BOWERS	6		8
26 Aug 00	**OUT OF YOUR MIND** *NuLife 74321782942* TRUE STEPPERS & DANE BOWERS FEATURING VICTORIA BECKHAM	2		20
3 Mar 01	**SHUT UP AND FORGET ABOUT IT** *Arista 74321835342* DANE	9		5
7 Jul 01	**ANOTHER LOVER** *Arista 74321863412* DANE	9		5

DAVID BOWIE
UK, male vocalist/multi-instrumentalist/producer (David Jones). Groundbreaking musical chameleon who was recognised for his 'Outstanding Contribution to British Music' at the 1996 BRIT Awards. Despite an ongoing 17-year wait for his 25th Top 10 hit, this 'star man' has accumulated UK singles sales of 10.2 million. See Tin Machine

Date	Title	Peak Position	Weeks at No.1	Weeks on Chart
				457
6 Sep 69	**SPACE ODDITY** *Philips BF 1801*	5		14
24 Jun 72	**STARMAN** *RCA 2199*	10		11
16 Sep 72	**JOHN I'M ONLY DANCING** *RCA 2263*	12		10
9 Dec 72	**THE JEAN GENIE** *RCA 2302*	2		13
14 Apr 73	**DRIVE-IN SATURDAY** *RCA 2352*	3		10
30 Jun 73	**LIFE ON MARS** *RCA 2316*	3		13
15 Sep 73	**THE LAUGHING GNOME** *Deram DM 123*	6		12
20 Oct 73	**SORROW** *RCA 2424*	3		15
23 Feb 74	**REBEL REBEL** *RCA LPBO 5009*	5		7
20 Apr 74	**ROCK 'N' ROLL SUICIDE** *RCA LPBO 5021*	22		7
22 Jun 74	**DIAMOND DOGS** *RCA APBO 0293*	21		6
28 Sep 74	**KNOCK ON WOOD** *RCA 2466*	10		6
1 Mar 75	**YOUNG AMERICANS** *RCA 2523*	18		7
2 Aug 75	**FAME** *RCA 2579* ★	17		8
11 Oct 75	**SPACE ODDITY** *RCA 2593*	1	2	10
29 Nov 75	**GOLDEN YEARS** *RCA 2640*	8		10
22 May 76	**TVC 15** *RCA 2682*	33		4
19 Feb 77	**SOUND AND VISION** *RCA PB 0905*	3		11
15 Oct 77	**HEROES** *RCA PB 1121*	24		8
21 Jan 78	**BEAUTY AND THE BEAST** *RCA PB 1190*	39		3
2 Dec 78	**BREAKING GLASS (EP)** *RCA BOW 1*	54		7
5 May 79	**BOYS KEEP SWINGIN'** *RCA BOW 2*	7		10
21 Jul 79	**D.J.** *RCA BOW 3*	29		5
15 Dec 79	**JOHN I'M ONLY DANCING (AGAIN) (1975)/JOHN I'M ONLY DANCING (1972)** *RCA BOW 4*	12		8
1 Mar 80	**ALABAMA SONG** *RCA BOW 5*	23		5
16 Aug 80	**ASHES TO ASHES** *RCA BOW 6*	1	2	10
1 Nov 80	**FASHION** *RCA BOW 7*	5		12
10 Jan 81	**SCARY MONSTERS (AND SUPER CREEPS)** *RCA BOW 8*	20		6
28 Mar 81	**UP THE HILL BACKWARDS** *RCA BOW 9*	32		6
14 Nov 81	**UNDER PRESSURE** *EMI 5250* QUEEN & DAVID BOWIE	1	2	11
28 Nov 81	**WILD IS THE WIND** *RCA BOW 10*	24		10
6 Mar 82	**BAAL'S HYMN (EP)** *RCA BOW 11*	29		5
10 Apr 82	**CAT PEOPLE (PUTTING OUT THE FIRE)** *MCA 770*	26		6
27 Nov 82	**PEACE ON EARTH – LITTLE DRUMMER BOY** *RCA BOW 12* & BING CROSBY	3		8
26 Mar 83	**LET'S DANCE** *EMI America EA 152* ★	1	3	14
11 Jun 83	**CHINA GIRL** *EMI America EA 157*	2		8

Date	Title	Peak Position	Weeks at No.1	Weeks on Chart
24 Sep 83	**MODERN LOVE** *EMI America EA 158* ○	2		8
5 Nov 83	**WHITE LIGHT, WHITE HEAT** *RCA 372*	46		3
22 Sep 84	**BLUE JEAN** *EMI America EA 181*	6		8
8 Dec 84	**TONIGHT** *EMI America EA 187*	53		4
9 Feb 85	**THIS IS NOT AMERICA** *EMI America EA 190* & THE PAT METHENY GROUP	14		7
8 Jun 85	**LOVING THE ALIEN** *EMI America EA 195*	19		7
7 Sep 85	**DANCING IN THE STREET** *EMI America EA 204* & MICK JAGGER ●	1	4	12
15 Mar 86	**ABSOLUTE BEGINNERS** *Virgin VS 838* ○	2		9
21 Jun 86	**UNDERGROUND** *EMI America EA 216*	21		6
8 Nov 86	**WHEN THE WIND BLOWS** *Virgin VS 906*	44		4
4 Apr 87	**DAY-IN DAY-OUT** *EMI America EA 230*	17		6
27 Jun 87	**TIME WILL CRAWL** *EMI America EA 237*	33		4
29 Aug 87	**NEVER LET ME DOWN** *EMI America EA 239*	34		6
7 Apr 90	**FAME (REMIX)** *EMI-USA FAME 90*	28		4
22 Aug 92	**REAL COOL WORLD** *Warner Brothers W 0127*	53		1
27 Mar 93	**JUMP THEY SAY** *Arista 74321139422*	9		6
12 Jun 93	**BLACK TIE WHITE NOISE** *Arista 74321148682* FEATURING AL B. SURE!	36		2
23 Oct 93	**MIRACLE GOODNIGHT** *Arista 74321162262*	40		2
4 Dec 93	**BUDDHA OF SUBURBIA** *Arista 74321177052* FEATURING LENNY KRAVITZ	35		3
23 Sep 95	**THE HEART'S FILTHY LESSON** *RCA 74321307032*	35		2
2 Dec 95	**STRANGERS WHEN WE MEET/THE MAN WHO SOLD THE WORLD (LIVE)** *RCA 74321329402*	39		2
2 Mar 96	**HALLO SPACEBOY** *RCA 74321353842*	12		4
8 Feb 97	**LITTLE WONDER** *RCA 74321452072*	14		3
26 Apr 97	**DEAD MAN WALKING** *RCA 74321475852*	32		2
30 Aug 97	**SEVEN YEARS IN TIBET** *RCA 74321512542*	61		1
21 Feb 98	**I CAN'T READ** *Velvet ZYX 87578*	73		1
2 Oct 99	**THURSDAY'S CHILD** *Virgin VSCDT 1753*	16		3
18 Dec 99	**UNDER PRESSURE (REMIX)** *Parlophone CDQUEEN 28* QUEEN & DAVID BOWIE	14		7
5 Feb 00	**SURVIVE** *Virgin VSCDT 1767*	28		2
29 Jul 00	**SEVEN** *Virgin VSCDT 1776*	32		2
11 May 02	**LOVING THE ALIEN** *Positiva CDTIV 172* SCUMFROG VS BOWIE	41		1
28 Sep 02	**EVERYONE SAYS 'HI'** *Columbia 6731342*	20		3
12 Jul 03	**JUST FOR ONE DAY (HEROES)** *Virgin DINST 263* DAVID GUETTA VS DAVID BOWIE	73		1
26 Jun 04	**REBEL NEVER GETS OLD** *Columbia 6750406*	47		2
21 Apr 07	**LIFE ON MARS** *EMI USJT19900030*	55		2
29 Dec 07	**PEACE ON EARTH – LITTLE DRUMMER BOY** *Capitol ATS049735001* & BING CROSBY	73		1

BOWLING FOR SOUP

US, male vocal/instrumental group – Jaret Reddick, Chris Burney, Erik Chandler & Gary Wiseman — 16

Date	Title	Peak Position	Weeks at No.1	Weeks on Chart
17 Aug 02	**GIRL ALL THE BAD GUYS WANT** *Music For Nations CDXKUT 194*	8		8
16 Nov 02	**EMILY** *Music For Nations CDXKUT 198*	67		1
6 Sep 03	**PUNK ROCK 101** *Music For Nations CDKUT 203*	43		1
16 Oct 04	**1985** *Jive 82876647652*	35		2
3 Feb 07	**HIGH SCHOOL NEVER ENDS** *A & G Productions CDAG009*	40		4

GEORGE BOWYER

UK, male vocalist — 2

Date	Title	Peak Position	Weeks at No.1	Weeks on Chart
22 Aug 98	**GUARDIANS OF THE LAND** *Boys BYSCD 01*	33		2

BOX CAR RACER

US, male vocal/instrumental group — 1

Date	Title	Peak Position	Weeks at No.1	Weeks on Chart
6 Jul 02	**I FEEL SO** *MCA MCSTD 40290*	41		1

BOX TOPS

US, male vocal/instrumental group – Alex Chilton, d. 17 Mar 2010, Bill Cunningham, John Evans, Danny Smythe & Gary Talley — 33

Date	Title	Peak Position	Weeks at No.1	Weeks on Chart
13 Sep 67	**THE LETTER** *Stateside SS 2044* ★	5		12
20 Mar 68	**CRY LIKE A BABY** *Bell 1001*	15		12
23 Aug 69	**SOUL DEEP** *Bell 1068*	22		9

BOXER REBELLION

UK, male vocal/instrumental group — 2

Date	Title	Peak Position	Weeks at No.1	Weeks on Chart
10 Apr 04	**IN PURSUIT** *Poptones MC5088SCD*	57		1
9 Oct 04	**CODE RED** *Vertigo 9867001*	61		1

BOY GEORGE

UK, male vocalist (George O'Dowd). See Culture Club, Jesus Loves You, One World Project — 46

Date	Title	Peak Position	Weeks at No.1	Weeks on Chart
7 Mar 87	**EVERYTHING I OWN** *Virgin BOY 100* ○	1	2	9
6 Jun 87	**KEEP ME IN MIND** *Virgin BOY 101*	29		4
18 Jul 87	**SOLD** *Virgin BOY 102*	24		5
21 Nov 87	**TO BE REBORN** *Virgin BOY 103*	13		7
5 Mar 88	**LIVE MY LIFE** *Virgin BOY 105*	62		2
18 Jun 88	**NO CLAUSE 28** *Virgin BOY 106*	57		3
8 Oct 88	**DON'T CRY** *Virgin BOY 107*	60		2
4 Mar 89	**DON'T TAKE MY MIND ON A TRIP** *Virgin BOY 108*	68		2
19 Sep 92	**THE CRYING GAME** *Spaghetti CIAO 6*	22		4
12 Jun 93	**MORE THAN LIKELY** *Gee Street GESCD 49* PM DAWN FEATURING BOY GEORGE	40		3
1 Apr 95	**FUNTIME** *Virgin VSCDG 1538*	45		2
1 Jul 95	**IL ADORE** *Virgin VSCDX 1543*	50		2
21 Oct 95	**SAME THING IN REVERSE** *Virgin VSCDT 1561*	56		1

BOY KILL BOY

UK, male vocal/instrumental group — 9

Date	Title	Peak Position	Weeks at No.1	Weeks on Chart
25 Feb 06	**BACK AGAIN** *Vertigo 9876834*	26		2
20 May 06	**SUZIE** *Vertigo 9856256*	17		4
12 Aug 06	**CIVIL SIN** *Vertigo 1702238*	44		2
25 Nov 06	**SHOOT ME DOWN** *Vertigo 1709308*	63		1

BOY LEAST LIKELY TO

UK, male vocal/instrumental duo — 1

Date	Title	Peak Position	Weeks at No.1	Weeks on Chart
6 May 06	**BE GENTLE WITH ME** *Too Young To Die TYTD006CD*	62		1

BOY MEETS GIRL

US, male/female vocal duo – Shannon Rubicam & George Merrill — 13

Date	Title	Peak Position	Weeks at No.1	Weeks on Chart
3 Dec 88	**WAITING FOR A STAR TO FALL** *RCA PB 49519*	9		13

JIMMY BOYD

US, male vocalist, d. 7 Mar 2009 (age 70) — 22

Date	Title	Peak Position	Weeks at No.1	Weeks on Chart
8 May 53	**TELL ME A STORY** *Philips PB 126* FRANKIE LAINE & JIMMY BOYD	5		16
27 Nov 53	**I SAW MOMMY KISSING SANTA CLAUS** *Columbia DB 3365* ★	3		6

JACQUELINE BOYER

France, female vocalist — 2

Date	Title	Peak Position	Weeks at No.1	Weeks on Chart
28 Apr 60	**TOM PILLIBI** *Columbia DB 4452*	33		2

SUSAN BOYLE

UK, female vocalist. See Helping Haiti — 9

Date	Title	Peak Position	Weeks at No.1	Weeks on Chart
5 Dec 09	**WILD HORSES** *Syco Music GBHMU0900064*	9		5
5 Dec 09	**I DREAMED A DREAM** *Syco Music GBHMU0900087*	37		4

BOYS

US, male vocal group — 5

Date	Title	Peak Position	Weeks at No.1	Weeks on Chart
12 Nov 88	**DIAL MY HEART** *Motown ZB 42245*	61		2
29 Sep 90	**CRAZY** *Motown ZB 44037*	57		3

BOYS LIKE GIRLS

US, male vocal/instrumental group — 1

Date	Title	Peak Position	Weeks at No.1	Weeks on Chart
2 Aug 08	**THE GREAT ESCAPE** *RCA 88697271702*	72		1

BOYSTEROUS

UK, male vocal group — 1

Date	Title	Peak Position	Weeks at No.1	Weeks on Chart
22 Nov 03	**UP AND DOWN** *Square Biz SBR4*	53		1

BOYSTOWN GANG

US, female/male vocal group – Cynthia Manley (replaced by Jackson Moore), Bruce Carlton, Robin Charin, Phill Manganello, Tom Morley, Keith Stewart & Don Wood — 20

Date	Title	Peak Position	Weeks at No.1	Weeks on Chart
22 Aug 81	**AIN'T NO MOUNTAIN HIGH ENOUGH – REMEMBER ME (MEDLEY)** *WEA DICK 1*	46		6
31 Jul 82	**CAN'T TAKE MY EYES OFF YOU** *ERC 101* ○	4		11
9 Oct 82	**SIGNED SEALED DELIVERED (I'M YOURS)** *ERC 102*	50		3

BOYZ II MEN

US, male vocal group – Michael McCary, Nathan & Wanya Morris & Shawn Stockman

Date	Title	Peak Position	Weeks at No.1	83
5 Sep 92	**END OF THE ROAD** *Motown TMG 1411* ● ★	1	3	21
19 Dec 92	**MOTOWNPHILLY** *Motown TMG 1402*	23		6
27 Feb 93	**IN THE STILL OF THE NITE (I'LL REMEMBER)** *Motown TMGCD 1415*	27		4
3 Sep 94	**I'LL MAKE LOVE TO YOU** *Motown TMGCD 1431* ★	5		15
26 Nov 94	**ON BENDED KNEE** *Motown TMGCD 1433* ★	20		3
22 Apr 95	**THANK YOU** *Motown TMGCD 1438*	26		3
8 Jul 95	**WATER RUNS DRY** *Motown TMGCD 1443*	24		3
9 Dec 95	**ONE SWEET DAY** *Columbia 6626035* MARIAH CAREY & BOYZ II MEN ○ ★	6		11
20 Jan 96	**HEY LOVER** *Def Jam DEFCD 14* LL COOL J FEATURING BOYZ II MEN	17		4
20 Sep 97	**4 SEASONS OF LONELINESS** *Motown 8606992* ★	10		6
6 Dec 97	**A SONG FOR MAMA** *Motown 8607372*	34		2
25 Jul 98	**CAN'T LET HER GO** *Motown 8607952*	23		3
17 Nov 07	**END OF THE ROAD** *Motown USMO19200465*	43		2

BOYZONE

Ireland, male vocal group – Ronan Keating*, Keith Duffy, Stephen Gately*, d. 10 Oct 2009, Mikey Graham* & Shane Lynch. Main boy band rivals to Take That in the 1990s who amassed a career start record 17 consecutive Top 5 singles. Their latest Top 10 success was their first as a quartet following Gately's untimely death. See Childliners, Keith 'N' Shane

Date	Title	Peak Position	Weeks at No.1	234
10 Dec 94	**LOVE ME FOR A REASON** *Polydor 8512802* ●	2		13
29 Apr 95	**KEY TO MY LIFE** *Polydor PZCD 342* ○	3		8
12 Aug 95	**SO GOOD** *Polydor 5797732*	3		6
25 Nov 95	**FATHER AND SON** *Polydor 5775762* ⊛	2		16
9 Mar 96	**COMING HOME NOW** *Polydor 5775722* ○	4		9
19 Oct 96	**WORDS** *Polydor 5755372* ●	1	1	14
14 Dec 96	**A DIFFERENT BEAT** *Polydor 5732072*	1	1	15
22 Mar 97	**ISN'T IT A WONDER** *Polydor 5735472*	2		14
2 Aug 97	**PICTURE OF YOU** *Polydor 5713112*	2		18
6 Dec 97	**BABY CAN I HOLD YOU/SHOOTING STAR** *Polydor 5691652* ●	2		14
2 May 98	**ALL THAT I NEED** *Polydor 5698732*	1	1	14
15 Aug 98	**NO MATTER WHAT** *Polydor 5675672* ⊛	1	3	15
5 Dec 98	**I LOVE THE WAY YOU LOVE ME** *Polydor 5631992* ●	2		13
13 Mar 99	**WHEN THE GOING GETS TOUGH** *Polydor 5699132* ⊛	1	2	16
22 May 99	**YOU NEEDED ME** *Polydor 5639332* ○	1	1	15
4 Dec 99	**EVERY DAY I LOVE YOU** *Polydor 5615802* ○	3		13
11 Oct 08	**I LOVE YOU ANYWAY** *Polydor 1786297*	5		9
13 Dec 08	**BETTER** *Polydor 1793978*	22		6
13 Mar 10	**GAVE IT ALL AWAY** *Polydor 2733608*	9		5+
3 Apr 10	**LOVE IS A HURRICANE** *Polydor GBUM71000859*	72		1

BRAD

US, male vocal/instrumental group

Date	Title	Peak Position	Weeks at No.1	1
26 Jun 93	**20TH CENTURY** *Epic 6592482*	64		1

JAMES DEAN BRADFIELD

UK, male vocalist/guitarist. See Manic Street Preachers

Date	Title	Peak Position	Weeks at No.1	4
22 Jul 06	**THAT'S NO WAY TO TELL A LIE** *Columbia 82876861592*	18		3
7 Oct 06	**AN ENGLISH GENTLEMAN** *Columbia 88697003182*	31		1

SCOTT BRADLEY

UK, male vocalist (Scott Winter)

Date	Title	Peak Position	Weeks at No.1	1
15 Oct 94	**ZOOM** *Hidden Agenda HIDDCD 1*	61		1

PAUL BRADY

UK, male vocalist/guitarist

Date	Title	Peak Position	Weeks at No.1	1
13 Jan 96	**THE WORLD IS WHAT YOU MAKE IT** *Mercury PBCD 1*	67		1

BILLY BRAGG

UK, male vocalist/guitarist (Stephen William Bragg)

Date	Title	Peak Position	Weeks at No.1	58
16 Mar 85	**BETWEEN THE WARS (EP)** *Go! Discs AGOEP 1*	15		6
28 Dec 85	**DAYS LIKE THESE** *Go! Discs GOD 8*	43		5
28 Jun 86	**LEVI STUBBS TEARS** *Go! Discs GOD 12*	29		6
15 Nov 86	**GREETINGS TO THE NEW BRUNETTE** *Go! Discs GOD 15* WITH JOHNNY MARR & KIRSTY MacCOLL	58		2
14 May 88	**SHE'S LEAVING HOME** *Childline CHILD 1* WITH CARA TIVEY ○	1	4	11
10 Sep 88	**WAITING FOR THE GREAT LEAP FORWARDS** *Go! Discs GOD 23*	52		3
8 Jul 89	**WON'T TALK ABOUT IT/BLAME IT ON THE BASSLINE** *Go! Beat GOD 33* NORMAN COOK FEATURING BILLY BRAGG/NORMAN COOK FEATURING MC WILDSKI	29		6
6 Jul 91	**SEXUALITY** *Go! Discs GOD 56*	27		5
7 Sep 91	**YOU WOKE UP MY NEIGHBOURHOOD** *Go! Discs GOD 60*	54		2
29 Feb 92	**ACCIDENT WAITING TO HAPPEN (EP)** *Go! Discs GOD 67*	33		3
31 Aug 96	**UPFIELD** *Cooking Vinyl FRYCD 051*	46		1
17 May 97	**THE BOY DONE GOOD** *Cooking Vinyl FRYCD 064*	55		1
1 Jun 02	**TAKE DOWN THE UNION JACK** *Cooking Vinyl FRYCD 131XX* & THE BLOKES	22		2
12 Nov 05	**WE LAUGHED** *Cooking Vinyl FRYCD252* ROSETTA LIFE FEATURING BILLY BRAGG	11		5

BRAIDS

US, female vocal duo

Date	Title	Peak Position	Weeks at No.1	3
2 Nov 96	**BOHEMIAN RHAPSODY** *Atlantic A 5640CD*	21		3

BRAIN BASHERS

UK, male/female DJ/production duo

Date	Title	Peak Position	Weeks at No.1	1
1 Jul 00	**DO IT NOW** *Tidy Trax TIDY 137CD*	64		1

BRAINBUG

Italy, male producer (Alberto Bertapelle)

Date	Title	Peak Position	Weeks at No.1	8
3 May 97	**NIGHTMARE** *Positiva CDTIV 76*	11		5
22 Nov 97	**BENEDICTUS/NIGHTMARE** *Positiva CDTIV 86*	24		2
4 Sep 04	**NIGHTMARE** *Positiva 12TIV 200*	63		1

BRAINCHILD

Germany, male producer (Matthias Hoffmann). See Cygnus X, Vernon's Wonderland

Date	Title	Peak Position	Weeks at No.1	2
30 Oct 99	**SYMMETRY C** *Multiply CDMULTY 55*	31		2

BRAKES

UK, male vocal/instrumental group

Date	Title	Peak Position	Weeks at No.1	1
25 Jun 05	**ALL NIGHT DISCO PARTY** *Rough Trade RTRADSCD241*	67		1

WILFRID BRAMBELL & HARRY H CORBETT

UK, male vocal/TV comedy duo – Brambell, d. 18 Jan 1985, & Corbett, d. 21 Mar 1982

Date	Title	Peak Position	Weeks at No.1	12
28 Nov 63	**AT THE PALACE (PARTS 1 & 2)** *Pye 7N 15588*	25		12

BRAN VAN 3000

Canada, male/female vocal/instrumental/DJ collective – members include E.P. Bergen, James Di Salvio, Steve 'Liquid' Hawley, Jayne Hill, Sara Johnston, Jean Leloup & Stephane Moraille

Date	Title	Peak Position	Weeks at No.1	15
6 Jun 98	**DRINKING IN LA** *Capitol CDCL 802*	34		2
21 Aug 99	**DRINKING IN LA** *Capitol CDCL 811* ○	3		11
16 Jun 01	**ASTOUNDED** *Virgin VUSCD 194* FEATURING CURTIS MAYFIELD	40		2

BRANCACCIO & AISHER

UK, male production duo

Date	Title	Peak Position	Weeks at No.1	2
16 Mar 02	**IT'S GONNA BE (A LOVELY DAY)** *Credence CDCRED 017*	40		2

MICHELLE BRANCH

US, female vocalist/multi-instrumentalist

Date	Title	Peak Position	Weeks at No.1	18
13 Apr 02	**EVERYWHERE** *Maverick W 577CD*	18		6
3 Aug 02	**ALL YOU WANTED** *Maverick W 585CDX*	33		2
23 Nov 02	**THE GAME OF LOVE** *Arista 74321959442* SANTANA FEATURING MICHELLE BRANCH	16		8
12 Jul 03	**ARE YOU HAPPY NOW?** *Maverick W 613CD*	31		2

BRAND NEW

US, male vocal/instrumental group

Date	Title	Peak Position	Weeks at No.1	4
14 Feb 04	**SIC TRANSIT GLORIA GLORY FADES** *Sore Point SORE011CDS*	37		2
29 May 04	**THE QUIET THINGS THAT NO ONE EVER KNOWS** *Sore Point SORE014CDS*	39		2

BRAND NEW HEAVIES

UK/US, male/female vocal/instrumental group – N'Dea Davenport (replaced by Siedah Garrett, Carleen Anderson, then Nicole Russo), Simon Bartholomew, Jan Kincaid & Andrew Levy

Date	Title	Peak Position	Weeks at No.1	Weeks on Chart
				69
5 Oct 91	**NEVER STOP** *ffrr F 165* FEATURING N'DEA DAVENPORT	43		3
15 Feb 92	**DREAM COME TRUE** *ffrr F 180* FEATURING N'DEA DAVENPORT	24		4
18 Apr 92	**ULTIMATE TRUNK FUNK EP** *ffrr F 185* FEATURING N'DEA DAVENPORT	19		6
1 Aug 92	**DON'T LET IT GO TO YOUR HEAD** *ffrr BNH 1* FEATURING N'DEA DAVENPORT	24		4
19 Dec 92	**STAY THIS WAY** *ffrr BNH 2* FEATURING N'DEA DAVENPORT	40		5
26 Mar 94	**DREAM ON DREAMER** *ffrr BNHCD 3* FEATURING N'DEA DAVENPORT	15		4
11 Jun 94	**BACK TO LOVE** *ffrr BNHCD 4* FEATURING N'DEA DAVENPORT	23		4
13 Aug 94	**MIDNIGHT AT THE OASIS** *ffrr BNHCDP 5* FEATURING N'DEA DAVENPORT	13		6
5 Nov 94	**SPEND SOME TIME** *ffrr BNHCD 6* FEATURING N'DEA DAVENPORT	26		4
11 Mar 95	**CLOSE TO YOU** *ffrr BNCDP 7* FEATURING N'DEA DAVENPORT	38		3
12 Apr 97	**SOMETIMES** *ffrr BNHCD 8* ●	11		5
28 Jun 97	**YOU ARE THE UNIVERSE** *ffrr BNHCD 9*	21		4
18 Oct 97	**YOU'VE GOT A FRIEND** *ffrr BNHCD 10*	9		8
10 Jan 98	**SHELTER** *London BNHCD 11*	31		4
11 Sep 99	**SATURDAY NITE** *ffrr BNHCD 12*	35		2
29 Jan 00	**APPARENTLY NOTHING** *ffrr BNHCD 13*	32		2
23 Oct 04	**BOOGIE** *Onetwo TBNHCDS001* FEATURING NICOLE	66		1

JOHNNY BRANDON

UK, male vocalist & instrumental group

Date	Title	Peak Position	Weeks at No.1	Weeks on Chart
				12
11 Mar 55	**TOMORROW** *Polygon P 1131* & THE PHANTOMS & THE NORMAN WARREN MUSIC	8		8
1 Jul 55	**DON'T WORRY** *Polygon P 1163*	18		4

BRANDY

US, female vocalist/actor (Brandy Norwood)

Date	Title	Peak Position	Weeks at No.1	Weeks on Chart
				104
10 Dec 94	**I WANNA BE DOWN** *Atlantic A 7217CD*	44		3
3 Jun 95	**I WANNA BE DOWN (REMIX)** *Atlantic A 7186CD*	36		3
3 Feb 96	**SITTIN' UP IN MY ROOM** *Arista 74321344012*	30		4
6 Jun 98	**THE BOY IS MINE** *Atlantic AT 0036CD* & MONICA ● ★	2		20
10 Oct 98	**TOP OF THE WORLD** *Atlantic AT 0046CD* FEATURING MA$E ●	2		9
12 Dec 98	**HAVE YOU EVER?** *Atlantic AT 0058CD* ★	13		8
19 Jun 99	**ALMOST DOESN'T COUNT** *Atlantic AT 0068CD1*	15		5
16 Jun 01	**ANOTHER DAY IN PARADISE** *WEA 327CD1* & RAY J	5		10
23 Feb 02	**WHAT ABOUT US** *Atlantic AT 0125CD*	4		11
15 Jun 02	**FULL MOON (IMPORT)** *Atlantic 7567853092*	72		1
29 Jun 02	**FULL MOON** *Atlantic AT 0130CD*	15		9
26 Jun 04	**TALK ABOUT OUR LOVE** *Atlantic AT 0177CD* FEATURING KANYE WEST	6		10
16 Oct 04	**AFRODISIAC** *Atlantic AT0183CD*	11		8
2 Apr 05	**WHO IS SHE 2 U** *Atlantic AT0192CD*	50		3

LAURA BRANIGAN

US, female vocalist, d. 26 Aug 2004 (age 47)

Date	Title	Peak Position	Weeks at No.1	Weeks on Chart
				33
18 Dec 82	**GLORIA** *Atlantic K 11759*	6		13
7 Jul 84	**SELF CONTROL** *Atlantic A 9676* ●	5		17
6 Oct 84	**THE LUCKY ONE** *Atlantic A 9636*	56		3

BRASS CONSTRUCTION

US, male vocal/instrumental group

Date	Title	Peak Position	Weeks at No.1	Weeks on Chart
				35
3 Apr 76	**MOVIN'** *United Artists UP 36090*	23		6
5 Feb 77	**HA CHA CHA (FUNKTION)** *United Artists UP 36205*	37		5
26 Jan 80	**MUSIC MAKES YOU FEEL LIKE DANCING** *United Artists UP 615*	39		6
28 May 83	**WALKIN' THE LINE** *Capitol CL 292*	47		3
16 Jul 83	**WE CAN WORK IT OUT** *Capitol CL 299*	70		2
7 Jul 84	**PARTYLINE** *Capitol CL 335*	56		4
27 Oct 84	**INTERNATIONAL** *Capitol CL 341*	70		2
9 Nov 85	**GIVE AND TAKE** *Capitol CL 377*	62		3
28 May 88	**MOVIN' 1988 (REMIX)** *Syncopate SY 11*	24		4

BRAT

UK, male 'rapper' (Roger Kitter)

Date	Title	Peak Position	Weeks at No.1	Weeks on Chart
				8
10 Jul 82	**CHALK DUST-THE UMPIRE STRIKES BACK** *Hansa SMASH 1*	19		8

BRATZ ROCK ANGELZ

US, female cartoon dolls vocal/instrumental group

Date	Title	Peak Position	Weeks at No.1	Weeks on Chart
				7
15 Oct 05	**SO GOOD** *Universal 9885281*	23		7

BRAUND REYNOLDS

UK, male vocal/instrumental group

Date	Title	Peak Position	Weeks at No.1	Weeks on Chart
				3
17 Dec 05	**ROCKET (A NATURAL GAMBLER)** *Virgin TENCDX504*	27		3

BRAVADO

UK, male producer (Paul Riordan)

Date	Title	Peak Position	Weeks at No.1	Weeks on Chart
				3
18 Jun 94	**HARMONICA MAN** *Peach PEACHCD 5*	37		3

BRAVERY

US, male vocal/instrumental group – Sam Endicott, Anthony Burulcich, John Conway, Mike Hindert & Michael Zakarin

Date	Title	Peak Position	Weeks at No.1	Weeks on Chart
				12
12 Mar 05	**AN HONEST MISTAKE** *Loog 9880300*	7		10
4 Jun 05	**FEARLESS** *Loog 9882338*	43		1
10 Sep 05	**UNCONDITIONAL** *Loog 9885197*	49		1

BRAVO ALL STARS

UK/US, male/female vocal/instrumental group

Date	Title	Peak Position	Weeks at No.1	Weeks on Chart
				2
29 Aug 98	**LET THE MUSIC HEAL YOUR SOUL** *Edel 0039335 ERE*	36		2

ALAN BRAXE & FRED FALKE

France, male production duo

Date	Title	Peak Position	Weeks at No.1	Weeks on Chart
				3
25 Nov 00	**INTRO** *Vulture/Credence CDCRED 006*	35		3

DHAR BRAXTON

US, female vocalist

Date	Title	Peak Position	Weeks at No.1	Weeks on Chart
				8
31 May 86	**JUMP BACK (SET ME FREE)** *Fourth & Broadway BRW 47*	32		8

TONI BRAXTON

US, female vocalist

Date	Title	Peak Position	Weeks at No.1	Weeks on Chart
				86
18 Sep 93	**ANOTHER SAD LOVE SONG** *LaFace 74321163502*	51		2
15 Jan 94	**BREATHE AGAIN** *LaFace 74321163502* ●	2		12
2 Apr 94	**ANOTHER SAD LOVE SONG** *LaFace 74321196682*	15		8
9 Jul 94	**YOU MEAN THE WORLD TO ME** *LaFace 74321214702*	30		5
3 Dec 94	**LOVE SHOULDA BROUGHT YOU HOME** *LaFace 74321249412*	33		3
13 Jul 96	**YOU'RE MAKIN ME HIGH** *LaFace 74321395402* ★	7		11
2 Nov 96	**UN-BREAK MY HEART** *LaFace 74321410632* ⊛ ★	2		19
24 May 97	**I DON'T WANT TO** *LaFace 74321468612*	9		8
8 Nov 97	**HOW COULD AN ANGEL BREAK MY HEART** *LaFace 74321531982* WITH KENNY G	22		4
29 Apr 00	**HE WASN'T MAN ENOUGH** *LaFace 74321757852*	5		11
8 Mar 03	**HIT THE FREEWAY** *Arista 82876506372* FEATURING LOON	29		3

BRAXTONS

US, female vocal group

Date	Title	Peak Position	Weeks at No.1	Weeks on Chart
				7
1 Feb 97	**SO MANY WAYS** *Atlantic A 5469CD*	32		2
29 Mar 97	**THE BOSS** *Atlantic A 5441CD*	31		3
19 Jul 97	**SLOW FLOW** *Atlantic AT 0001CD*	26		2

BREAD

US, male vocal/instrumental group – David Gates, Jim Gordon (replaced by Mike Botts, d. 9 Dec 2005), James Griffin, d. 11 Jan 2005, & Robb Royer (replaced by Larry Knechtel)

Date	Title	Peak Position	Weeks at No.1	Weeks on Chart
				46
1 Aug 70	**MAKE IT WITH YOU** *Elektra 2101 010* ★	5		14
15 Jan 72	**BABY I'M A-WANT YOU** *Elektra K 12033*	14		10
29 Apr 72	**EVERYTHING I OWN** *Elektra K 12041*	32		6
30 Sep 72	**THE GUITAR MAN** *Elektra K 12066*	16		9
25 Dec 76	**LOST WITHOUT YOUR LOVE** *Elektra K 12241*	27		7

BREAK MACHINE

US, male vocalist (Keith Rodgers) fronted by male/female dance trio – Lindell & Lindsay Blake & Cortez Jordan

Date	Title	Peak Position	Weeks at No.1	Weeks on Chart
				32
4 Feb 84	**STREET DANCE** *Record Shack SOHO 13*	3		14
12 May 84	**BREAKDANCE PARTY** *Record Shack SOHO 20*	9		10
11 Aug 84	**ARE YOU READY?** *Record Shack SOHO 24*	27		8

BREAKBEAT ERA
UK, male/female instrumental/production trio — 5

Date	Title / Label	Peak	Wks at No.1	Wks on Chart
18 Jul 98	**BREAKBEAT ERA** *XL Recordings XLS 95CD*	38		2
21 Aug 99	**ULTRA-OBSCENE** *XL Recordings XLS 107CD*	48		2
11 Mar 00	**BULLITPROOF** *XL Recordings XLS 115CD*	65		1

BREAKFAST CLUB
US, male vocal/instrumental group — 3

Date	Title / Label	Peak	Wks at No.1	Wks on Chart
27 Jun 87	**RIGHT ON TRACK** *MCA 1146*	54		3

BREAKS CO-OP
New Zealand, male vocal/instrumental group — 2

Date	Title / Label	Peak	Wks at No.1	Wks on Chart
3 Jun 06	**THE OTHERSIDE** *Parlophone CDRS6689*	43		2

BREATHE
UK, male vocal/instrumental trio – David Glasper, Marcus Lillington & Ian Spice, d. 2000 — 27

Date	Title / Label	Peak	Wks at No.1	Wks on Chart
30 Jul 88	**HANDS TO HEAVEN** *Siren SRN 68*	4		12
22 Oct 88	**JONAH** *Siren SRN 95*	60		3
3 Dec 88	**HOW CAN I FALL** *Siren SRN 102*	48		7
11 Mar 89	**DON'T TELL ME LIES** *Siren SRN 109*	45		5

FREDDY BRECK
Germany, male vocalist (Gerhard Brecker), d. 17 Dec 2008 (age 66) — 4

Date	Title / Label	Peak	Wks at No.1	Wks on Chart
13 Apr 74	**SO IN LOVE WITH YOU** *Decca F 13481*	44		4

BRECKER BROTHERS
US, male vocal/instrumental duo – Michael, d.13 Jan 2007, & Randy Brecker — 5

Date	Title / Label	Peak	Wks at No.1	Wks on Chart
4 Nov 78	**EAST RIVER** *Arista ARIST 211*	34		5

BREED 77
Gibraltar, male vocal/instrumental group — 5

Date	Title / Label	Peak	Wks at No.1	Wks on Chart
1 May 04	**THE RIVER** *Albert Productions JASCDUKL007*	39		2
7 Aug 04	**WORLD'S ON FIRE** *Albert Productions JASCDUK011*	43		2
5 Feb 05	**SHADOWS** *Albert Productions JASCDVUK013*	42		1

BREEDERS
US/UK, female/male vocal/instrumental group — 7

Date	Title / Label	Peak	Wks at No.1	Wks on Chart
18 Apr 92	**SAFARI (EP)** *4AD BAD 2003*	69		1
21 Aug 93	**CANNONBALL (EP)** *4AD BAD 3011CD*	40		3
6 Nov 93	**DIVINE HAMMER** *4AD BAD 3017CD*	59		1
23 Jul 94	**HEAD TO TOE (EP)** *4AD BAD 4012CD*	68		1
14 Sep 02	**SON OF THREE** *4AD BAD 2213CD*	72		1

BREEKOUT CREW
US, male rap/vocal group — 3

Date	Title / Label	Peak	Wks at No.1	Wks on Chart
24 Nov 84	**MATT'S MOOD** *London LON 59*	51		3

ANN BREEN
Ireland, female vocalist — 2

Date	Title / Label	Peak	Wks at No.1	Wks on Chart
19 Mar 83	**PAL OF MY CRADLE DAYS** *Homespun HS 052*	69		1
7 Jan 84	**PAL OF MY CRADLE DAYS** *Homespun HS 052*	74		1

JO BREEZER
UK, female vocalist — 2

Date	Title / Label	Peak	Wks at No.1	Wks on Chart
13 Oct 01	**VENUS AND MARS** *Columbia 6717612*	27		2

BRENDON
UK, male vocalist (Brendon Dunning) — 9

Date	Title / Label	Peak	Wks at No.1	Wks on Chart
19 Mar 77	**GIMME SOME** *Magnet MAG 80*	14		9

MAIRE BRENNAN
Ireland, female vocalist. See Clannad — 12

Date	Title / Label	Peak	Wks at No.1	Wks on Chart
16 May 92	**AGAINST THE WIND** *RCA PB 45399*	64		2
5 Jun 99	**SALTWATER** *Xtravaganza XTRAV 1CDS* CHICANE FEATURING MAIRE BRENNAN OF CLANNAD	6		10

ROSE BRENNAN
Ireland, female vocalist — 9

Date	Title / Label	Peak	Wks at No.1	Wks on Chart
7 Dec 61	**TALL DARK STRANGER** *Philips PB 1193*	31		9

WALTER BRENNAN
US, male actor/vocalist, d. 21 Sep 1974 (age 80) — 3

Date	Title / Label	Peak	Wks at No.1	Wks on Chart
28 Jun 62	**OLD RIVERS** *Liberty LIB 55436*	38		3

TONY BRENT
UK, male vocalist (Reginald Bretagne), d. 19 Jun 1993 (age 65) — 52

Date	Title / Label	Peak	Wks at No.1	Wks on Chart
19 Dec 52	**WALKIN' TO MISSOURI** *Columbia DB 3147*	7		5
2 Jan 53	**MAKE IT SOON** *Columbia DB 3187*	9		9
23 Jan 53	**GOT YOU ON MY MIND** *Columbia DB 3226*	12		1
30 Nov 56	**CINDY OH CINDY** *Columbia DB 3844*	16		7
28 Jun 57	**DARK MOON** *Columbia DB 3950*	17		14
28 Feb 58	**THE CLOUDS WILL SOON ROLL BY** *Columbia DB 4066*	20		5
5 Sep 58	**GIRL OF MY DREAMS** *Columbia DB 4177*	16		7
24 Jul 59	**WHY SHOULD I BE LONELY** *Columbia DB 4304*	24		4

BERNARD BRESSLAW
UK, male actor/vocalist, d. 11 Jun 1993 (age 59) — 20

Date	Title / Label	Peak	Wks at No.1	Wks on Chart
30 May 58	**THE SIGNATURE TUNE OF 'THE ARMY GAME'** *HMV POP 490* MICHAEL MEDWIN, BERNARD BRESSLAW, ALFIE BASS & LESLIE FYSON	5		9
5 Sep 58	**MAD PASSIONATE LOVE** *HMV POP 522*	6		11

TERESA BREWER
US, female vocalist (Theresa Breuer), d. 17 Oct 2007 (age 76) — 19

Date	Title / Label	Peak	Wks at No.1	Wks on Chart
11 Feb 55	**LET ME GO LOVER** *Vogue Coral Q 72043* WITH THE LANCERS	9		10
13 Apr 56	**A TEAR FELL** *Vogue Coral Q 72146*	2		15
13 Jul 56	**SWEET OLD-FASHIONED GIRL** *Vogue Coral Q 72172*	3		15
10 May 57	**NORA MALONE** *Vogue Coral Q 72224*	26		2
23 Jun 60	**HOW DO YOU KNOW IT'S LOVE** *Coral Q 72396*	21		11
25 Feb 78	**MATCHSTALK MEN AND MATCHSTALK CATS AND DOGS** *Pye 7N 46035* BRIAN & MICHAEL ●	1	3	19

BRICK
US, male instrumental group — 4

Date	Title / Label	Peak	Wks at No.1	Wks on Chart
5 Feb 77	**DAZZ** *Bang 004*	36		4

EDIE BRICKELL & THE NEW BOHEMIANS
US, female/male vocal/instrumental group — 10

Date	Title / Label	Peak	Wks at No.1	Wks on Chart
4 Feb 89	**WHAT I AM** *Geffen GEF 49*	31		7
27 May 89	**CIRCLE** *Geffen GEF 51*	74		1
1 Oct 94	**GOOD TIMES** *Geffen GFSTD 78* EDIE BRICKELL	40		2

ALICIA BRIDGES
US, female vocalist — 11

Date	Title / Label	Peak	Wks at No.1	Wks on Chart
11 Nov 78	**I LOVE THE NIGHTLIFE (DISCO ROUND)** *Polydor 2066 936*	32		10
8 Oct 94	**I LOVE THE NIGHTLIFE (DISCO ROUND) (REMIX)** *Mother MUMCD 57*	61		1

BRIGHOUSE & RASTRICK BRASS BAND
UK, male brass band — 13

Date	Title / Label	Peak	Wks at No.1	Wks on Chart
12 Nov 77	**THE FLORAL DANCE** *Transatlantic BIG 548* ●	2		13

BETTE BRIGHT
UK, female vocalist (Anne Martin) — 5

Date	Title / Label	Peak	Wks at No.1	Wks on Chart
8 Mar 80	**HELLO I AM YOUR HEART** *Korova KOW 3*	50		5

Silver-selling ● Gold-selling ● Platinum-selling (x multiples) US No.1 ★ Peak Position · Weeks at No.1 · Weeks on Chart

BRIGHT EYES

US, male vocal/instrumental trio & various musicians. See Conor Oberst

Date	Title	Peak Position	Weeks at No.1	Weeks on Chart (5)
2 Apr 05	**FIRST DAY OF MY LIFE** *Saddle Creek SCE79CD*	37		3
6 Aug 05	**EASY/LUCKY/FREE** *Saddle Creek SCE84CD*	42		1
14 Apr 07	**FOUR WINDS** *Polydor 1725984*	57		1

SARAH BRIGHTMAN

UK, female vocalist

Date	Title	Peak Position	Weeks at No.1	Weeks on Chart (98)
11 Nov 78	**I LOST MY HEART TO A STARSHIP TROOPER** *Ariola/Hansa AHA 527* & HOT GOSSIP ●	6		14
7 Apr 79	**THE ADVENTURES OF THE LOVE CRUSADER** *Ariola/Hansa AHA 538* & THE STARSHIP TROOPERS	53		5
30 Jul 83	**HIM** *Polydor POSP 625* & THE LONDON PHILHARMONIC	55		4
23 Mar 85	**PIE JESU** *HMV WEBBER 1* & PAUL MILES-KINGSTON ●	3		8
11 Jan 86	**THE PHANTOM OF THE OPERA** *Polydor POSP 800* & STEVE HARLEY	7		10
4 Oct 86	**ALL I ASK OF YOU** *Polydor POSP 802* CLIFF RICHARD & SARAH BRIGHTMAN ●	3		16
10 Jan 87	**WISHING YOU WERE SOMEHOW HERE AGAIN** *Polydor POSP 803*	7		11
11 Jul 92	**AMIGOS PARA SIEMPRE (FRIENDS FOR LIFE)** *Really Useful RUR 10* JOSE CARRERAS & SARAH BRIGHTMAN	11		11
24 May 97	**TIME TO SAY GOODBYE** *Coalition COLA 003CD* SARAH BRIGHTMAN/ ANDREA BOCELLI ●	2		14
23 Aug 97	**WHO WANTS TO LIVE FOREVER** *Coalition COLA 014CD*	45		1
6 Dec 97	**JUST SHOW ME HOW TO LOVE YOU** *Coalition COLA 035CD* & THE LSO FEATURING JOSE CURA	54		2
14 Feb 98	**STARSHIP TROOPERS** *Coalition COLA 040CD* UNITED CITIZEN FEDERATION FEATURING SARAH BRIGHTMAN	58		1
13 Feb 99	**EDEN** *Coalition COLA 065CD*	68		1

BRIGHTON & HOVE ALBION FC

UK, male vocalists/footballers

Date	Title	Peak Position	Weeks at No.1	Weeks on Chart (2)
28 May 83	**THE BOYS IN THE OLD BRIGHTON BLUE** *Energy NRG 2*	65		2

BRILLIANT

UK, male/female vocal/instrumental group

Date	Title	Peak Position	Weeks at No.1	Weeks on Chart (13)
19 Oct 85	**IT'S A MAN'S MAN'S MAN'S WORLD** *Food 5*	58		5
22 Mar 86	**LOVE IS WAR** *Food 6*	64		4
2 Aug 86	**SOMEBODY** *Food 7*	67		4

DANIELLE BRISEBOIS

US, female actor/vocalist/multi-instrumentalist/producer. See New Radicals

Date	Title	Peak Position	Weeks at No.1	Weeks on Chart (1)
9 Sep 95	**GIMME LITTLE SIGN** *Epic 6610782*	75		1

JOHNNY BRISTOL

US, male vocalist, d. 21 Mar 2004 (age 65)

Date	Title	Peak Position	Weeks at No.1	Weeks on Chart (16)
24 Aug 74	**HANG ON IN THERE BABY** *MGM 2006 443*	3		11
19 Jul 80	**MY GUY – MY GIRL (MEDLEY)** *Atlantic/Hansa K 11550* AMII STEWART & JOHNNY BRISTOL	39		5

BRISTOL CITY & THE WURZELS

UK, male football fans/vocal group & vocal/instrumental group

Date	Title	Peak Position	Weeks at No.1	Weeks on Chart (1)
6 Oct 07	**ONE FOR THE BRISTOL CITY** *CIA CIA004*	66		1

BRIT & ALEX

US, female vocal duo

Date	Title	Peak Position	Weeks at No.1	Weeks on Chart (1)
26 Apr 08	**LET IT GO** *Hometown HOMETOWN2*	75		1

BRIT PACK

UK/Ireland, male vocal group

Date	Title	Peak Position	Weeks at No.1	Weeks on Chart (2)
12 Feb 00	**SET ME FREE** *When! WENX 2000*	41		2

BRITISH SEA POWER

UK, male vocal/instrumental group

Date	Title	Peak Position	Weeks at No.1	Weeks on Chart (8)
12 Jul 03	**CARRION/APOLOGIES TO INSECT LIFE** *Rough Trade RTRADES CD 92X*	36		1
1 Nov 03	**REMEMBER ME** *Rough Trade RTRADESCD 126*	30		2
2 Apr 05	**IT ENDED ON AN OILY STAGE** *Rough Trade RTRADSCDX220*	18		3
4 Jun 05	**PLEASE STAND UP** *Rough Trade RTRADSCDX242*	34		1
19 Jan 08	**WAVING FLAGS** *Rough Trade RTRADESCD416*	31		1

BRITISH WHALE

UK, male vocalist/guitarist (Justin Hawkins). See Darkness

Date	Title	Peak Position	Weeks at No.1	Weeks on Chart (4)
27 Aug 05	**THIS TOWN AIN'T BIG ENOUGH FOR THE BOTH OF US** *Atlantic ATUK011CD*	6		4

ANDREA BRITTON

UK, female vocalist

Date	Title	Peak Position	Weeks at No.1	Weeks on Chart (11)
11 Jan 03	**AM I ON YOUR MIND** *Innocent SINCD 40* OXYGEN FEATURING ANDREA BRITTON	30		3
19 Jun 04	**TAKE MY HAND** *Direction 6749932* JURGEN VRIES FEATURING ANDREA BRITTON	23		3
5 Mar 05	**WINTER** *Data 80CDS* DT8 PROJECT FEATURING ANDREA BRITTON	35		2
28 Jul 07	**COUNTING DOWN THE DAYS** *Positiva CDTIVS245* SUNFREAKZ FEATURING ANDREA BRITTON	37		3

BROCK LANDARS

UK, male vocal/production duo

Date	Title	Peak Position	Weeks at No.1	Weeks on Chart (2)
11 Jul 98	**S.M.D.U.** *Parlophone CDBLUE 001*	49		2

BROCKIE/ED SOLO

UK, male production duo

Date	Title	Peak Position	Weeks at No.1	Weeks on Chart (1)
24 Apr 04	**SYSTEM CHECK** *Undiluted UD010*	68		1

BROKEN ENGLISH

UK, male vocal/instrumental group

Date	Title	Peak Position	Weeks at No.1	Weeks on Chart (13)
30 May 87	**COMIN' ON STRONG** *EMI EM 5*	18		10
3 Oct 87	**LOVE ON THE SIDE** *EMI EM 55*	69		3

DIONNE BROMFIELD

UK, female vocalist

Date	Title	Peak Position	Weeks at No.1	Weeks on Chart (4)
24 Oct 09	**MAMA SAID** *Lioness GBUM70911972*	43		4

BRONSKI BEAT

UK, male vocal/instrumental group – Jimmy Somerville* (replaced by John Foster, then Jonathan Hellyer), Steve Bronski & Larry Steinbachek

Date	Title	Peak Position	Weeks at No.1	Weeks on Chart (78)
2 Jun 84	**SMALLTOWN BOY** *Forbidden Fruit BITE 1* ●	3		13
22 Sep 84	**WHY?** *Forbidden Fruit BITE 2* ●	6		10
1 Dec 84	**IT AIN'T NECESSARILY SO** *Forbidden Fruit BITE 3*	16		11
20 Apr 85	**I FEEL LOVE (MEDLEY)** *Forbidden Fruit BITE 4* & MARC ALMOND ●	3		12
30 Nov 85	**HIT THAT PERFECT BEAT** *Forbidden Fruit BITE 6* ●	3		14
29 Mar 86	**COME ON, COME ON** *Forbidden Fruit BITE 7*	20		7
1 Jul 89	**CHA CHA HEELS** *Arista 112331* EARTHA KITT & BRONSKI BEAT	32		7
2 Feb 91	**SMALLTOWN BOY (REMIX)** *London LON 287* JIMMY SOMERVILLE WITH BRONSKI BEAT	32		4

BRONX

US, male vocal/instrumental group

Date	Title	Peak Position	Weeks at No.1	Weeks on Chart (2)
24 Apr 04	**THEY WILL KILL US ALL (WITHOUT MERCY)** *Wichita WEBB060SCD*	65		1
17 Jul 04	**FALSE ALARM** *Wichita WEBB062SCD*	73		1

JET BRONX & THE FORBIDDEN

UK, male vocal/instrumental group

Date	Title	Peak Position	Weeks at No.1	Weeks on Chart (1)
17 Dec 77	**AIN'T DOIN' NOTHIN'** *Lightning LIG 50*	49		1

BROOK BROTHERS

UK, male vocal duo – Geoff & Ricky Brook

Date	Title	Peak Position	Weeks at No.1	Weeks on Chart (35)
30 Mar 61	**WARPAINT** *Pye 7N 15333*	5		14
24 Aug 61	**AIN'T GONNA WASH FOR A WEEK** *Pye 7N 15369*	13		10
25 Jan 62	**HE'S OLD ENOUGH TO KNOW BETTER** *Pye 7N 15409*	37		1
16 Aug 62	**WELCOME HOME BABY** *Pye 7N 15453*	33		6
21 Feb 63	**TROUBLE IS MY MIDDLE NAME** *Pye 7N 15498*	38		4

BROOKES BROTHERS

UK, male production duo

Date	Title	Peak Position	Weeks at No.1	Weeks on Chart (1)
15 Nov 08	**TEAR YOU DOWN** *Breakbeat Kaos BBK028*	56		1

BROOKLYN BOUNCE
Germany, male/female vocal/production group — 1

Date	Title / Label	Peak	Wks No.1	Wks
30 May 98	**THE MUSIC'S GOT ME** *Club Tools 0064795 CLU*	67		1

ELKIE BROOKS
UK, female vocalist (Elaine Bookbinder) — 91

Date	Title / Label	Peak	Wks No.1	Wks
2 Apr 77	**PEARL'S A SINGER** *A&M AMS 7275*	8		9
20 Aug 77	**SUNSHINE AFTER THE RAIN** *A&M AMS 7306*	10		9
25 Feb 78	**LILAC WINE** *A&M AMS 7333*	16		7
3 Jun 78	**ONLY LOVE CAN BREAK YOUR HEART** *A&M AMS 7353*	43		5
11 Nov 78	**DON'T CRY OUT LOUD** *A&M AMS 7395*	12		11
5 May 79	**THE RUNAWAY** *A&M AMS 7428*	50		5
16 Jan 82	**FOOL IF YOU THINK IT'S OVER** *A&M AMS 8187*	17		10
1 May 82	**OUR LOVE** *A&M AMS 8214*	43		5
17 Jul 82	**NIGHTS IN WHITE SATIN** *A&M AMS 8235*	33		5
22 Jan 83	**GASOLINE ALLEY** *A&M AMS 8305*	52		5
22 Nov 86	**NO MORE THE FOOL** *Legend LM 4*	5		16
4 Apr 87	**BREAK THE CHAIN** *Legend LM 8*	55		3
11 Jul 87	**WE'VE GOT TONIGHT** *Legend LM 9*	69		1

GARTH BROOKS
US, male vocalist/guitarist (Troyal Garth Brooks) — 15

Date	Title / Label	Peak	Wks No.1	Wks
1 Feb 92	**SHAMELESS** *Capitol CL 646*	71		1
22 Jan 94	**THE RED STROKES/AIN'T GOING DOWN (TILL THE SUN COMES UP)** *Liberty CDCLS 704*	13		5
16 Apr 94	**STANDING OUTSIDE THE FIRE** *Liberty CDCL 712*	28		4
18 Feb 95	**THE DANCE/FRIENDS IN LOW PLACES** *Capitol CDCL 735*	36		3
17 Feb 96	**SHE'S EVERY WOMAN** *Capitol CDCL 767*	55		1
13 Nov 99	**LOST IN YOU** *Capitol CDCL 814*	70		1

MEL BROOKS
US, male 'rapper'/actor (Melvin Kaminsky) — 10

Date	Title / Label	Peak	Wks No.1	Wks
18 Feb 84	**TO BE OR NOT TO BE (THE HITLER RAP)** *Island IS 158*	12		10

MEREDITH BROOKS
US, female vocalist/guitarist — 13

Date	Title / Label	Peak	Wks No.1	Wks
2 Aug 97	**BITCH** *Capitol CDCL 790* (silver)	6		10
6 Dec 97	**I NEED** *Capitol CDCLS 794*	28		2
7 Mar 98	**WHAT WOULD HAPPEN** *Capitol CDCL 798*	49		1

NORMAN BROOKS
Canada, male vocalist (Norman Arie), d. 14 Sep 2006 (age 78) — 1

Date	Title / Label	Peak	Wks No.1	Wks
12 Nov 54	**A SKY BLUE SHIRT AND A RAINBOW TIE** *London L 1228*	17		1

STEVE BROOKSTEIN
UK, male vocalist — 10

Date	Title / Label	Peak	Wks No.1	Wks
1 Jan 05	**AGAINST ALL ODDS** *Syco Music 82876672732*	1	1	10

BROS
UK, male vocal/instrumental trio – Matt & Luke Goss & Craig Logan (left 1989) — 84

Date	Title / Label	Peak	Wks No.1	Wks
5 Dec 87	**WHEN WILL I BE FAMOUS** *CBS ATOM 2*	2		15
19 Mar 88	**DROP THE BOY** *CBS ATOM 3* (silver)	2		10
18 Jun 88	**I OWE YOU NOTHING** *CBS ATOM 4*	1	2	11
17 Sep 88	**I QUIT** *CBS ATOM 5*	4		8
3 Dec 88	**CAT AMONG THE PIGEONS/SILENT NIGHT** *CBS ATOM 6* (silver)	2		8
29 Jul 89	**TOO MUCH** *CBS ATOM 7* (silver)	2		7
7 Oct 89	**CHOCOLATE BOX** *CBS ATOM 8*	9		6
16 Dec 89	**SISTER** *CBS ATOM 9*	10		6
10 Mar 90	**MADLY IN LOVE** *CBS ATOM 10*	14		4
13 Jul 91	**ARE YOU MINE** *Columbia 6568707*	12		5
21 Sep 91	**TRY** *Columbia 6574047*	27		4

BROTHER BEYOND
UK, male vocal/instrumental group – Nathan Moore, Carl Fysh, David Ben White & Francis 'Eg' White (replaced by Steve Alexander) — 58

Date	Title / Label	Peak	Wks No.1	Wks
4 Apr 87	**HOW MANY TIMES** *EMI 5591*	62		3
8 Aug 87	**CHAIN-GANG SMILE** *Parlophone R 6160*	57		3
23 Jan 88	**CAN YOU KEEP A SECRET** *Parlophone R 6174*	56		4
30 Jul 88	**THE HARDER I TRY** *Parlophone R 6184* (silver)	2		14
5 Nov 88	**HE AIN'T NO COMPETITION** *Parlophone R 6193*	6		10
21 Jan 89	**BE MY TWIN** *Parlophone R 6195*	14		6
1 Apr 89	**CAN YOU KEEP A SECRET (REMIX)** *Parlophone R 6197*	22		5
28 Oct 89	**DRIVE ON** *Parlophone R 6233*	39		4
9 Dec 89	**WHEN WILL I SEE YOU AGAIN** *Parlophone R 6239*	43		5
10 Mar 90	**TRUST** *Parlophone R 6245*	53		2
19 Jan 91	**THE GIRL I USED TO KNOW** *Parlophone R 6265*	48		2

BROTHER BROWN FEATURING FRANK'EE
Denmark, male/female vocal/DJ/production trio — 5

Date	Title / Label	Peak	Wks No.1	Wks
2 Oct 99	**UNDER THE WATER** *ffrr FCD 367*	18		4
24 Nov 01	**STAR CATCHING GIRL** *Rulin 21CDS*	51		1

BROTHERHOOD
UK, male rap group — 1

Date	Title / Label	Peak	Wks No.1	Wks
27 Jan 96	**ONE SHOT/NOTHING IN PARTICULAR** *Bite It BHOODD 3*	55		1

BROTHERHOOD OF MAN
UK, male/female vocal group – Martin Lee, Lee Sheriden, Nicky & Sandra Stevens — 97

Date	Title / Label	Peak	Wks No.1	Wks
14 Feb 70	**UNITED WE STAND** *Deram DM 284*	10		9
4 Jul 70	**WHERE ARE YOU GOING TO MY LOVE** *Deram DM 298*	22		10
13 Mar 76	**SAVE YOUR KISSES FOR ME** *Pye 7N 45569* (platinum)	1	6	16
19 Jun 76	**MY SWEET ROSALIE** *Pye 7N 45602*	30		7
26 Feb 77	**OH BOY (THE MOOD I'M IN)** *Pye 7N 45656*	8		12
9 Jul 77	**ANGELO** *Pye 7N 45699* (gold)	1	1	12
14 Jan 78	**FIGARO** *Pye 7N 46037* (gold)	1	1	11
27 May 78	**BEAUTIFUL LOVER** *Pye 7N 46071*	15		12
30 Sep 78	**MIDDLE OF THE NIGHT** *Pye 7N 46117*	41		6
3 Jul 82	**LIGHTNING FLASH** *EMI 5309*	67		2

BROTHERS
UK, male vocal group — 9

Date	Title / Label	Peak	Wks No.1	Wks
29 Jan 77	**SING ME** *Bus Stop Bus 1054*	8		9

BROTHERS FOUR
US, male vocal group — 2

Date	Title / Label	Peak	Wks No.1	Wks
23 Jun 60	**GREENFIELDS** *Philips PB 1009*	40		2

BROTHERS IN RHYTHM
UK, male production duo — 12

Date	Title / Label	Peak	Wks No.1	Wks
16 Mar 91	**SUCH A GOOD FEELING** *Fourth & Broadway BRW 228*	64		2
14 Sep 91	**SUCH A GOOD FEELING** *Fourth & Broadway BRW 228*	14		8
30 Apr 94	**FOREVER AND A DAY** *Stress CDSTR 36* PRESENT CHARVONI	51		2

BROTHERS JOHNSON
US, male vocal/instrumental duo — 34

Date	Title / Label	Peak	Wks No.1	Wks
9 Jul 77	**STRAWBERRY LETTER 23** *A&M AMS 7297*	35		5
2 Sep 78	**AIN'T WE FUNKIN' NOW** *A&M AMS 7379*	43		6
4 Nov 78	**RIDE-O-ROCKET** *A&M AMS 7400*	50		4
23 Feb 80	**STOMP** *A&M AMS 7509*	6		12
31 May 80	**LIGHT UP THE NIGHT** *A&M AMS 7526*	47		4
25 Jul 81	**THE REAL THING** *A&M AMS 8149*	50		3

BROTHERS LIKE OUTLAW FEATURING ALISON EVELYN
UK, male rap/production duo & female vocalist — 1

Date	Title / Label	Peak	Wks No.1	Wks
23 Jan 93	**GOOD VIBRATIONS** *Gee Street GESCD 44*	74		1

EDGAR BROUGHTON BAND
UK, male vocal/instrumental group — 10

Date	Title / Label	Peak	Wks No.1	Wks
18 Apr 70	**OUT DEMONS OUT** *Harvest HAR 5015*	39		5
23 Jan 71	**APACHE DROPOUT** *Harvest HAR 5032*	33		5

BOBBY BROWN
US, male vocalist. See New Edition — 131

Date	Title / Label	Peak	Wks No.1	Wks
6 Aug 88	**DON'T BE CRUEL** *MCA 1268*	42		7
17 Dec 88	**MY PREROGATIVE** *MCA 1299* ★	6		17
25 Mar 89	**DON'T BE CRUEL** *MCA 1310*	13		8
20 May 89	**EVERY LITTLE STEP** *MCA 1338*	6		9

Silver-selling ● Gold-selling ● Platinum-selling (x multiples) ⊛ US No.1 ★ Peak Position Weeks at No.1 Weeks on Chart

Date	Title	Peak Position	Weeks at No.1	Weeks on Chart
15 Jul 89	**ON OUR OWN (FROM GHOSTBUSTERS II)** *MCA 1350* ●	4		9
23 Sep 89	**ROCK WIT'CHA** *MCA 1367*	33		6
25 Nov 89	**RONI** *MCA 1384*	21		7
9 Jun 90	**THE FREE STYLE MEGA-MIX** *MCA 1421*	14		7
30 Jun 90	**SHE AIN'T WORTH IT** *London LON 265* GLENN MEDEIROS FEATURING BOBBY BROWN ★	12		9
22 Aug 92	**HUMPIN' AROUND** *MCA MCS 1680*	19		6
17 Oct 92	**GOOD ENOUGH** *MCA MCS 1704*	41		4
19 Jun 93	**THAT'S THE WAY LOVE IS** *MCA MCSTD 1783*	56		2
22 Jan 94	**SOMETHING IN COMMON** *MCA MCSTD 1957* & WHITNEY HOUSTON	16		5
25 Jun 94	**TWO CAN PLAY THAT GAME** *MCA MCSTD 1973*	38		3
1 Apr 95	**TWO CAN PLAY THAT GAME** *MCA MCSTD 1973* ●	3		12
8 Jul 95	**HUMPIN' AROUND** *MCA MCSTD 2073*	8		6
14 Oct 95	**MY PREROGATIVE** *MCA MCSTD 2094*	17		3
3 Feb 96	**EVERY LITTLE STEP** *MCA MCSTD 48004*	25		2
22 Nov 97	**FEELIN' INSIDE** *MCA MCSTD 48067*	40		1
21 Dec 02	**THUG LOVIN'** *Def Jam 637872* JA RULE FEATURING BOBBY BROWN	15		8

CRAZY WORLD OF ARTHUR BROWN

UK, male vocal/instrumental group – Arthur Wilton (Arthur Brown), Vincent Crane, d. 14 Feb 1989, Sean Nicholas, Carl Palmer & Drachen Theaker — Weeks at No.1: 1, Weeks on Chart: 14

Date	Title	Peak Position	Weeks at No.1	Weeks on Chart
26 Jun 68	**FIRE** *Track 604 022*	1	1	14

CHRIS BROWN

US, male vocalist/actor — Weeks on Chart: 151

Date	Title	Peak Position	Weeks at No.1	Weeks on Chart
11 Feb 06	**RUN IT!** *Jive 82876780532* FEATURING JUELZ SANTANA ★	2		14
29 Apr 06	**YO! (EXCUSE ME MISS)** *Jive 82876832192*	13		8
22 Jul 06	**GIMME THAT REMIX** *Jive 82876880762* FEATURING LIL' WAYNE	23		6
1 Sep 07	**WALL TO WALL** *Jive USZM20700174*	75		1
3 Nov 07	**KISS KISS** *Jive 88697385242* FEATURING T-PAIN ★	38		5
16 Feb 08	**WITH YOU** *Jive 88697269362* ●	8		30
26 Apr 08	**NO AIR** *Jive 88697296612* JORDIN SPARKS FEATURING CHRIS BROWN ●	3		27
17 May 08	**SHAWTY GET LOOSE** *Jive JIV7270821* LIL' MAMA FEATURING CHRIS BROWN & T-PAIN	57		3
7 Jun 08	**FOREVER** *Jive 88697330882*	4		22
27 Sep 08	**KISS KISS** *Jive 88697385242* FEATURING T-PAIN	39		2
1 Nov 08	**SUPERHUMAN** *Jive 88697416742* FEATURING KERI HILSON	32		9
1 Nov 08	**FREEZE** *Jive USJI10801038* T-PAIN FEATURING CHRIS BROWN	62		2
8 Aug 09	**FOREVER** *Jive 88697330882*	64		1
14 Nov 09	**I CAN TRANSFORM YA** *Jive USJI10900612* FEATURING LIL' WAYNE	26		13
20 Feb 10	**CRAWL** *Jive USJI10900689*	35		8+

DENNIS BROWN

Jamaica, male vocalist (Clarence Brown), d. 1 Jul 1999 (age 42) — Weeks on Chart: 18

Date	Title	Peak Position	Weeks at No.1	Weeks on Chart
3 Mar 79	**MONEY IN MY POCKET** *Lightning LV 5*	14		9
3 Jul 82	**LOVE HAS FOUND ITS WAY** *A&M AMS 8226*	47		6
11 Sep 82	**HALFWAY UP HALFWAY DOWN** *A&M AMS 8250*	56		3

DIANA BROWN & BARRIE K SHARPE

UK, female/male vocal duo — Weeks on Chart: 11

Date	Title	Peak Position	Weeks at No.1	Weeks on Chart
2 Jun 90	**THE MASTERPLAN** *ffrr F 133*	39		6
1 Sep 90	**SUN WORSHIPPERS (POSITIVE THINKING)** *ffrr F 144*	61		2
23 Mar 91	**LOVE OR NOTHING** *ffrr F 152*	71		1
27 Jun 92	**EATING ME ALIVE** *ffrr F 190*	53		2

ERROL BROWN

UK, male vocalist. See Hot Chocolate — Weeks on Chart: 13

Date	Title	Peak Position	Weeks at No.1	Weeks on Chart
4 Jul 87	**PERSONAL TOUCH** *WEA YZ 130*	25		8
28 Nov 87	**BODY ROCKIN'** *WEA YZ 162*	51		2
14 Feb 98	**IT STARTED WITH A KISS** *EMI CDHOT 101* HOT CHOCOLATE FEATURING ERROL BROWN	18		3

FOXY BROWN

US, female rapper (Inga Marchand) — Weeks on Chart: 25

Date	Title	Peak Position	Weeks at No.1	Weeks on Chart
21 Sep 96	**TOUCH ME TEASE ME** *Def Jam DEFCD 18* CASE FEATURING FOXXY BROWN	26		3
8 Mar 97	**GET ME HOME** *Def Jam DEFCD 32* FEATURING BLACKstreet	11		5
10 May 97	**AIN'T NO PLAYA** *Northwestside 74321474842* JAY-Z FEATURING FOXY BROWN	31		2
21 Jun 97	**I'LL BE** *Def Jam 5710432* FEATURING JAY-Z	9		5
11 Oct 97	**BIG BAD MAMMA** *Def Jam 5749792* FEATURING DRU HILL	12		3
25 Oct 97	**SUNSHINE** *Northwestside 74321528702* JAY-Z FEATURING BABYFACE & FOXY BROWN	25		2
13 Mar 99	**HOT SPOT** *Def Jam 8708352*	31		2
8 Sep 01	**OH YEAH** *Def Jam 5887312*	27		3

GLORIA D BROWN

US, female vocalist — Weeks on Chart: 3

Date	Title	Peak Position	Weeks at No.1	Weeks on Chart
8 Jun 85	**THE MORE THEY KNOCK, THE MORE I LOVE YOU** *10 TEN 52*	57		3

HORACE BROWN

US, male vocalist — Weeks on Chart: 7

Date	Title	Peak Position	Weeks at No.1	Weeks on Chart
25 Feb 95	**TASTE YOUR LOVE** *Uptown MCSTD 2026*	58		1
18 May 96	**ONE FOR THE MONEY** *Motown 8605232*	12		4
12 Oct 96	**THINGS WE DO FOR LOVE** *Motown 8605712*	27		2

HOWARD BROWN

UK, male vocalist — Weeks on Chart: 3

Date	Title	Peak Position	Weeks at No.1	Weeks on Chart
19 Mar 05	**YOU'RE THE FIRST THE LAST MY EVERYTHING** *HBOS CDHALIFAX1*	13		3

IAN BROWN

UK, male vocalist/guitarist. See Stone Roses — Weeks on Chart: 48

Date	Title	Peak Position	Weeks at No.1	Weeks on Chart
24 Jan 98	**MY STAR** *Polydor 5719872*	5		4
4 Apr 98	**CORPSES** *Polydor 5696552*	14		4
20 Jun 98	**CAN'T SEE ME** *Polydor 5440452*	21		3
20 Feb 99	**BE THERE** *Mo Wax MW 108CD1* UNKLE FEATURING IAN BROWN	8		6
6 Nov 99	**LOVE LIKE A FOUNTAIN** *Polydor 5615162*	23		3
19 Feb 00	**DOLPHINS WERE MONKEYS** *Polydor 5616372*	5		4
17 Jun 00	**GOLDEN GAZE** *Polydor 5618452*	29		2
29 Sep 01	**F.E.A.R.** *Polydor 5872842*	13		4
23 Feb 02	**WHISPERS** *Polydor 5705382*	33		2
2 Oct 04	**KEEP WHAT YA GOT** *Fiction 9868284*	18		3
27 Nov 04	**REIGN** *Mo Wax GUSIN007CDS* UNKLE FEATURING IAN BROWN	40		2
29 Jan 05	**TIME IS MY EVERYTHING** *Fiction 9869961*	15		4
17 Sep 05	**ALL ABLAZE** *Polydor 9873252*	20		2
29 Sep 07	**ILLEGAL ATTACKS** *Fiction 1724668* FEATURING SINEAD O'CONNOR	16		2
22 Aug 09	**STELLIFY** *Polydor GBUV70903416*	31		3

JAMES BROWN

US, male vocalist, d. 25 Dec 2006 (age 73) — Weeks on Chart: 104

Date	Title	Peak Position	Weeks at No.1	Weeks on Chart
23 Sep 65	**PAPA'S GOT A BRAND NEW BAG** *London HL 9990* & THE FAMOUS FLAMES	25		7
24 Feb 66	**I GOT YOU (I FEEL GOOD)** *Pye International 7N 25350* & THE FAMOUS FLAMES	29		6
16 Jun 66	**IT'S A MAN'S MAN'S MAN'S WORLD** *Pye International 7N 25371* & THE FAMOUS FLAMES	13		9
10 Oct 70	**GET UP I FEEL LIKE BEING A SEX MACHINE** *Polydor 2001 071*	32		7
27 Nov 71	**HEY AMERICA** *Mojo 2093 006*	47		3
18 Sep 76	**GET UP OFFA THAT THING** *Polydor 2066 687*	22		6
29 Jan 77	**BODY HEAT** *Polydor 2066 763*	36		4
10 Jan 81	**RAPP PAYBACK (WHERE IZ MOSES?)** *RCA 28*	39		5
2 Jul 83	**BRING IT ON…BRING IT ON** *Sonet SON 2258*	45		4
1 Sep 84	**UNITY (PART 1 – THE THIRD COMING)** *Tommy Boy AFR 2* AFRIKA BAAMBAATAA & JAMES BROWN	49		5
27 Apr 85	**FROGGY MIX** *Boiling Point FROG 1*	50		3
1 Jun 85	**GET UP I FEEL LIKE BEING A SEX MACHINE** *Boiling Point POSP 751*	47		5
25 Jan 86	**LIVING IN AMERICA** *Scotti Brothers A 6701*	5		10
1 Mar 86	**GET UP I FEEL LIKE BEING A SEX MACHINE** *Boiling Point POSP 751*	46		4
18 Oct 86	**GRAVITY** *Scotti Brothers 6500597*	65		2
30 Jan 88	**SHE'S THE ONE** *Urban URB 13*	45		3
23 Apr 88	**THE PAYBACK MIX** *Urban URB 17*	12		6
4 Jun 88	**I'M REAL** *Scotti Brothers JSB 1* FEATURING FULL FORCE	31		4
23 Jul 88	**I GOT YOU (I FEEL GOOD)** *A&M AM 444*	52		3
16 Nov 91	**GET UP I FEEL LIKE BEING A SEX MACHINE** *Polydor PO 185*	69		2
24 Oct 92	**I GOT YOU (I FEEL GOOD) (REMIX)** *FBI 9* VS DAKEYNE	72		1
17 Apr 93	**CAN'T GET ANY HARDER** *Polydor PZCD 262*	59		2
17 Apr 99	**FUNK ON AH ROLL** *Inferno/Eagle EAGXA 073*	40		2
22 Apr 00	**FUNK ON AH ROLL (REMIX)** *Eagle EAGXS 127*	63		1

JENNIFER BROWN

Sweden, female vocalist — Weeks on Chart: 1

Date	Title	Peak Position	Weeks at No.1	Weeks on Chart
1 May 99	**TUESDAY AFTERNOON** *RCA 74321604092*	57		1

JOCELYN BROWN
US, female vocalist. See Motiv 8 — 79

Date	Title	Peak Position	Weeks at No.1	Weeks on Chart
21 Apr 84	**SOMEBODY ELSE'S GUY** *Fourth & Broadway BRW 5*	13		9
22 Sep 84	**I WISH YOU WOULD** *Fourth & Broadway BRW 14*	51		3
15 Mar 86	**LOVE'S GONNA GET YOU** *Warner Brothers W 8889*	70		1
29 Jun 91	**ALWAYS THERE** *Talkin Loud TLK 10* INCOGNITO FEATURING JOCELYN BROWN	6		9
14 Sep 91	**SHE'S GOT SOUL** *A&M AM 819* JAMESTOWN FEATURING JOCELYN BROWN	57		3
7 Dec 91	**DON'T TALK JUST KISS** *Tug SNOG 2* RIGHT SAID FRED. GUEST VOCALS: JOCELYN BROWN	3		11
20 Mar 93	**TAKE ME UP** *A&M AMCD 210* SONIC SURFERS FEATURING JOCELYN BROWN	61		1
11 Jun 94	**NO MORE TEARS (ENOUGH IS ENOUGH)** *Ding Dong 74321209032* KYM MAZELLE & JOCELYN BROWN	13		7
8 Oct 94	**GIMME ALL YOUR LOVIN'** *Ding Dong 74321231322* KYM MAZELLE & JOCELYN BROWN	22		3
13 Jul 96	**KEEP ON JUMPIN'** *Manifesto FESCD 11* TODD TERRY FEATURING MARTHA WASH & JOCELYN BROWN	8		6
10 May 97	**IT'S ALRIGHT, I FEEL IT!** *Talkin Loud TLCD 22* NUYORICAN SOUL FEATURING JOCELYN BROWN	26		2
12 Jul 97	**SOMETHING GOIN' ON** *Manifesto FESCD 25* TODD TERRY FEATURING MARTHA WASH & JOCELYN BROWN	5		10
25 Oct 97	**I AM THE BLACK GOLD OF THE SUN** *Talkin Loud TLCD 26* NUYORICAN SOUL FEATURING JOCELYN BROWN	31		2
22 Nov 97	**HAPPINESS** *Sony S3 KAMCD 2* KAMASUTRA FEATURING JOCELYN BROWN	45		1
2 May 98	**FUN** *INCredible INCRL 2CD* DA MOB FEATURING JOCELYN BROWN	33		2
29 Aug 98	**AIN'T NO MOUNTAIN HIGH ENOUGH** *INCredible INCRL 7CD*	35		2
27 Mar 99	**I BELIEVE** *Playola 0091705 PLA* JAMESTOWN FEATURING JOCELYN BROWN	62		1
3 Jul 99	**IT'S ALL GOOD** *INCredible INCRL 14CD* DA MOB FEATURING JOCELYN BROWN	54		1
11 Mar 00	**BELIEVE** *Defected DFECT 14CDS* MINISTERS DE LA FUNK FEATURING JOCELYN BROWN	45		2
27 Jan 01	**BELIEVE (REMIX)** *Defected DFECT 26CDS* MINISTERS DE LA FUNK FEATURING JOCELYN BROWN	42		2
7 Sep 02	**THAT'S HOW GOOD YOUR LOVE IS** *Defected DFTD 057CDS* IL PADRINOS FEATURING JOCELYN BROWN	54		1

JOE BROWN & THE BRUVVERS
UK, male vocalist/guitarist — 92

Date	Title	Peak Position	Weeks at No.1	Weeks on Chart
17 Mar 60	**DARKTOWN STRUTTERS BALL** *Decca F 11207*	34		6
26 Jan 61	**SHINE** *Pye 7N 15322* JOE BROWN	33		6
11 Jan 62	**WHAT A CRAZY WORLD WE'RE LIVING IN** *Piccadilly 7N 35024*	37		2
17 May 62	**A PICTURE OF YOU** *Piccadilly 7N 35047*	2		19
13 Sep 62	**YOUR TENDER LOOK** *Piccadilly 7N 35058*	31		6
15 Nov 62	**IT ONLY TOOK A MINUTE** *Piccadilly 7N 35082*	6		14
7 Feb 63	**THAT'S WHAT LOVE WILL DO** *Piccadilly 7N 35106*	3		14
27 Jun 63	**NATURE'S TIME FOR LOVE** *Piccadilly 7N 35129*	26		6
26 Sep 63	**SALLY ANN** *Piccadilly 7N 35138*	28		9
29 Jun 67	**WITH A LITTLE HELP FROM MY FRIENDS** *Pye 7N 17339* JOE BROWN	32		4
14 Apr 73	**HEY MAMA** *Ammo AMO 101* JOE BROWN	33		6

KATHY BROWN
US, female vocalist — 16

Date	Title	Peak Position	Weeks at No.1	Weeks on Chart
25 Nov 95	**TURN ME OUT (TURN TO SUGAR)** *Stress CDSTR 40* PRAXIS FEATURING KATHY BROWN	44		2
20 Sep 97	**TURN ME OUT (TURN TO SUGAR) (REMIX)** *ffrr FCD 314* PRAXIS FEATURING KATHY BROWN	35		3
10 Apr 99	**JOY** *Azuli AZNYCDX 094*	63		1
5 May 01	**LOVE IS NOT A GAME** *Defected DFECT 31CDS* J MAJIK FEATURING KATHY BROWN	34		2
2 Jun 01	**OVER YOU** *Defected DFECT 28CDS* WARREN CLARKE FEATURING KATHY BROWN	42		1
22 Jan 05	**STRINGS OF LIFE (STRONGER ON MY OWN)** *Defected DFTD094CDS* SOUL CENTRAL FEATURING KATHY BROWN	6		7

MARK BROWN FEATURING SARAH CRACKNELL
UK, male/female vocal/production duo. See Saint Etienne — 5

Date	Title	Peak Position	Weeks at No.1	Weeks on Chart
9 Feb 08	**THE JOURNEY CONTINUES** *Positiva 12TIV267*	11		5

MIQUEL BROWN
Canada, female vocalist (Michael Brown) — 7

Date	Title	Peak Position	Weeks at No.1	Weeks on Chart
18 Feb 84	**HE'S A SAINT, HE'S A SINNER** *Record Shack SOHO 15*	68		4
24 Aug 85	**CLOSE TO PERFECTION** *Record Shack SOHO 48*	63		3

PETER BROWN
US, male vocalist — 9

Date	Title	Peak Position	Weeks at No.1	Weeks on Chart
11 Feb 78	**DO YA WANNA GET FUNKY WITH ME** *TK TKR 6009*	43		4
17 Jun 78	**DANCE WITH ME** *TK TKR 6027*	57		5

POLLY BROWN
UK, female vocalist. See Pickettywitch, Sweet Dreams — 5

Date	Title	Peak Position	Weeks at No.1	Weeks on Chart
14 Sep 74	**UP IN A PUFF OF SMOKE** *GTO GT 2*	43		5

ROY 'CHUBBY' BROWN
UK, male comedian/vocalist (Royston Vasey) — 22

Date	Title	Peak Position	Weeks at No.1	Weeks on Chart
13 May 95	**LIVING NEXT DOOR TO ALICE (WHO THE F**K IS ALICE)** *NOW CDWAG 245* SMOKIE FEATURING ROY CHUBBY BROWN	64		2
26 Aug 95	**LIVING NEXT DOOR TO ALICE (WHO THE F**K IS ALICE)** *NOW CDWAG 245* SMOKIE FEATURING ROY CHUBBY BROWN ●	3		17
21 Dec 96	**ROCKIN' GOOD CHRISTMAS** *Polystar 5732612*	51		3

SAM BROWN
UK, female vocalist — 35

Date	Title	Peak Position	Weeks at No.1	Weeks on Chart
11 Jun 88	**STOP** *A&M AM 440*	52		3
4 Feb 89	**STOP** *A&M AM 440* ●	4		12
13 May 89	**CAN I GET A WITNESS** *A&M AM 509*	15		7
3 Mar 90	**WITH A LITTLE LOVE** *A&M AM 539*	44		4
5 May 90	**KISSING GATE** *A&M AM 549*	23		8
26 Aug 95	**JUST GOOD FRIENDS** *Dick Bros. DDICK 014CD1* FISH FEATURING SAM BROWN	63		1

SHARON BROWN
US, female vocalist — 11

Date	Title	Peak Position	Weeks at No.1	Weeks on Chart
17 Apr 82	**I SPECIALIZE IN LOVE** *Virgin VS 494*	38		9
26 Feb 94	**I SPECIALIZE IN LOVE (REMIX)** *Deep Distraxion OILYCD 025*	62		2

SLEEPY BROWN
US, male rapper (Patrick Brown) — 11

Date	Title	Peak Position	Weeks at No.1	Weeks on Chart
27 Jul 02	**LAND OF A MILLION DRUMS** *Atlantic AT 0134CD* OUTKAST FEATURING KILLER MIKE & SLEEPY BROWN	46		1
3 Apr 04	**THE WAY YOU MOVE** *Arista 82876605672* OUTKAST FEATURING SLEEPY BROWN ★	7		10

VV BROWN
UK, female vocalist/producer (Vanessa Brown). See Young Soul Rebels — 5

Date	Title	Peak Position	Weeks at No.1	Weeks on Chart
18 Jul 09	**SHARK IN THE WATER** *Island 2711588*	34		5

BROWN SAUCE
UK, male/female vocal trio/TV presenters — 12

Date	Title	Peak Position	Weeks at No.1	Weeks on Chart
12 Dec 81	**I WANNA BE A WINNER** *BBC RESL 101*	15		12

DUNCAN BROWNE
UK, male vocalist — 8

Date	Title	Peak Position	Weeks at No.1	Weeks on Chart
19 Aug 72	**JOURNEY** *RAK 135*	23		6
22 Dec 84	**THEME FROM 'THE TRAVELLING MAN'** *Towerbell TOW 54*	68		2

JACKSON BROWNE
US, male vocalist — 14

Date	Title	Peak Position	Weeks at No.1	Weeks on Chart
1 Jul 78	**STAY** *Asylum K 13128*	12		11
18 Oct 86	**IN THE SHAPE OF A HEART** *Elektra EKR 42*	66		2
25 Jun 94	**EVERYWHERE I GO** *Elektra EKR 184CD1*	67		1

TOM BROWNE
US, male trumpeter — 24

Date	Title	Peak Position	Weeks at No.1	Weeks on Chart
19 Jul 80	**FUNKIN' FOR JAMAICA (NY)** *Arista ARIST 357*	10		11
25 Oct 80	**THIGHS HIGH (GRIP YOUR HIPS AND MOVE)** *Arista ARIST 367*	45		5
30 Jan 82	**FUNGI MAMA (BEBOPAFUNKADISCOLYPSO)** *Arista ARIST 450*	58		4
11 Jan 92	**FUNKIN' FOR JAMAICA (REMIX)** *Arista 114998*	45		4

BROWNS
US, male/female vocal trio – Jim Ed, Maxine & Bonnie Brown — **13**

Date	Title	Peak	Wks No.1	Wks
18 Sep 59	**THE THREE BELLS** *RCA 1140* ★	6		13

BROWNSTONE
US, female vocal trio – Kina Cosper, Nichole 'Nicci' Gilbert & Charmayne 'Maxee' Maxwell — **24**

Date	Title	Peak	Wks No.1	Wks
1 Apr 95	**IF YOU LOVE ME** *MJJ 6614135*	8		12
15 Jul 95	**GRAPEVYNE** *MJJ 6620942*	16		4
23 Sep 95	**I CAN'T TELL YOU WHY** *MJJ 6623775*	27		2
17 May 97	**5 MILES TO EMPTY** *MJJ 6640962*	12		4
27 Sep 97	**KISS AND TELL** *Epic 6649852*	21		2

BROWNSVILLE STATION
US, male vocal/instrumental group — **6**

Date	Title	Peak	Wks No.1	Wks
2 Mar 74	**SMOKIN' IN THE BOYS' ROOM** *Philips 6073 834*	27		6

DAVE BRUBECK QUARTET
US, male instrumental group – Dave Brubeck (Dave Warren), Paul Desmond, d. 30 May 1977, Joe Morello & Eugene Wright — **30**

Date	Title	Peak	Wks No.1	Wks
26 Oct 61	**TAKE FIVE** *Fontana H 339*	6		15
8 Feb 62	**IT'S A RAGGY WALTZ** *Fontana H 352*	36		3
17 May 62	**UNSQUARE DANCE** *CBS AAG 102*	14		12

TOMMY BRUCE & THE BRUISERS
UK, male vocalist & male vocal/instrumental group — **21**

Date	Title	Peak	Wks No.1	Wks
26 May 60	**AIN'T MISBEHAVIN'** *Columbia DB 4453*	3		16
8 Sep 60	**BROKEN DOLL** *Columbia DB 4498*	36		4
22 Feb 62	**BABETTE** *Columbia DB 4776* TOMMY BRUCE	50		1

CLAUDIA BRUCKEN
Germany, female vocalist. See Propaganda — **2**

Date	Title	Peak	Wks No.1	Wks
11 Aug 90	**ABSOLUT(E)** *Island IS 471*	71		1
16 Feb 91	**KISS LIKE ETHER** *Island IS 479*	63		1

BRUISERS
UK, male vocal/instrumental group. See Tommy Bruce — **7**

Date	Title	Peak	Wks No.1	Wks
8 Aug 63	**BLUE GIRL** *Parlophone R 5042*	31		7

FRANK BRUNO
UK, male boxer/vocalist — **4**

Date	Title	Peak	Wks No.1	Wks
23 Dec 95	**EYE OF THE TIGER** *RCA 74321336282*	28		4

TYRONE BRUNSON
US, male bassist — **5**

Date	Title	Peak	Wks No.1	Wks
25 Dec 82	**THE SMURF** *Epic EPC A 3024*	52		5

BASIL BRUSH FEATURING INDIA BEAU
UK, male fox puppet/vocalist & female vocalist — **3**

Date	Title	Peak	Wks No.1	Wks
27 Dec 03	**BOOM BOOM/CHRISTMAS SLIDE** *Right RRBB001*	44		3

DORA BRYAN
UK, female actor/vocalist (Dora Broadbent) — **4**

Date	Title	Peak	Wks No.1	Wks
5 Dec 63	**ALL I WANT FOR CHRISTMAS IS A BEATLE** *Fontana TF 427*	20		4

KELLE BRYAN
UK, female vocalist. See Eternal — **4**

Date	Title	Peak	Wks No.1	Wks
2 Oct 99	**HIGHER THAN HEAVEN** *1st Avenue MERCD 522*	14		4

ANITA BRYANT
US, female vocalist — **6**

Date	Title	Peak	Wks No.1	Wks
26 May 60	**PAPER ROSES** *London HLL 9144*	24		4
6 Oct 60	**MY LITTLE CORNER OF THE WORLD** *London HLL 9171*	48		2

PEABO BRYSON
US, male vocalist (Robert Peabo Bryson) — **35**

Date	Title	Peak	Wks No.1	Wks
20 Aug 83	**TONIGHT I CELEBRATE MY LOVE** *Capitol CL 302* & ROBERTA FLACK ●	2		13
16 May 92	**BEAUTY AND THE BEAST** *Epic 6576607* CELINE DION & PEABO BRYSON	9		7
17 Jul 93	**BY THE TIME THIS NIGHT IS OVER** *Arista 74321157142* KENNY G WITH PEABO BRYSON	56		3
11 Dec 93	**A WHOLE NEW WORLD (ALADDIN'S THEME)** *Columbia 6599002* & REGINA BELLE ★	12		12

BT
US, male producer (Brian Transeau). See Libra presents Taylor — **29**

Date	Title	Peak	Wks No.1	Wks
18 Mar 95	**EMBRACING THE SUNSHINE** *Perfecto YZ 895CD*	34		2
16 Sep 95	**LOVING YOU MORE** *Perfecto PERF 110CD* FEATURING VINCENT COVELLO	28		2
10 Feb 96	**LOVING YOU MORE (REMIX)** *Perfecto PERF 117CD* FEATURING VINCENT COVELLO	14		3
9 Nov 96	**BLUE SKIES** *Perfecto PERF 130CD1* FEATURING TORI AMOS	26		2
19 Jul 97	**FLAMING JUNE** *Perfecto PERF 145CD1*	19		4
29 Nov 97	**LOVE, PEACE & GREASE** *Perfecto PERF 153CD1*	41		1
10 Jan 98	**FLAMING JUNE (REMIX)** *Perfecto PERF 157CD1*	28		4
18 Apr 98	**REMEMBER** *Perfecto PERF 160CD1*	27		2
21 Nov 98	**GODSPEED** *Renaissance RENCD 002*	54		1
9 Oct 99	**MERCURY AND SOLACE** *Headspace HEDSCD 001*	38		2
24 Jun 00	**DREAMING** *Headspace HEDSCD 002* FEATURING KIRSTY HAWKSHAW	38		2
23 Jun 01	**NEVER GONNA COME BACK DOWN** *Ministry Of Sound MOSBT CDS1*	51		1
15 May 04	**LOVE COMES AGAIN** *Nebula NEBCD 058* TIESTO FEATURING BT	30		3

B.T. EXPRESS
US, male vocal/instrumental group — **11**

Date	Title	Peak	Wks No.1	Wks
29 Mar 75	**EXPRESS** *Pye International 7N 25674*	34		6
26 Jul 80	**DOES IT FEEL GOOD/GIVE UP THE FUNK (LET'S DANCE)** *Calibre CAB 503*	52		4
23 Apr 94	**EXPRESS (REMIX)** *PWL International PWCD 285*	67		1

B2K
US, male vocal group – Raz-B (De'Mario Thornton), J-Boog (Jarell Houston), Lil' Fizz (Dreux Frédéric) & Omarion* (Omari Grandberry) — **25**

Date	Title	Peak	Wks No.1	Wks
24 Aug 02	**UH HUH** *Epic 6729512*	35		2
29 Mar 03	**BUMP BUMP BUMP** *Epic 6736452* FEATURING P DIDDY ★	11		8
21 Jun 03	**GIRLFRIEND** *Epic 6739335*	10		8
18 Oct 03	**UH HUH 2003** *Epic 6744012*	31		2
20 Mar 04	**BADABOOM** *Epic 6747512* FEATURING FABOLOUS	26		5

MICHAEL BUBLE
Canada, male vocalist/pianist/actor. See Helping Haiti — **70**

Date	Title	Peak	Wks No.1	Wks
9 Apr 05	**HOME** *Reprise W668CD1*	31		4
3 Dec 05	**HOME/SONG FOR YOU** *Reprise W693CD*	63		3
28 Apr 07	**EVERYTHING** *Reprise W761CD1*	38		12
20 Oct 07	**EVERYTHING** *Reprise W761CD1*	52		2
27 Oct 07	**HOME/SONG FOR YOU** *Reprise W693CD*	45		8
1 Dec 07	**LOST** *Reprise W789CD*	19		15
24 Oct 09	**HAVEN'T MET YOU YET** *Reprise USRE10901437*	5		22
7 Nov 09	**CRY ME A RIVER** *Reprise USRE10901470*	34		3
26 Dec 09	**HOLD ON** *Reprise USRE10901475*	72		1

BUBBLEROCK
UK, male vocalist. See Jonathan King — **5**

Date	Title	Peak	Wks No.1	Wks
26 Jan 74	**(I CAN'T GET NO) SATISFACTION** *UK 53*	29		5

ROY BUCHANAN
US, male guitarist, d. 14 Aug 1988 (age 48) — **3**

Date	Title	Peak	Wks No.1	Wks
31 Mar 73	**SWEET DREAMS** *Polydor 2066 307*	40		3

BUCKETHEADS
US, male producer (Kenny Gonzalez) — **16**

Date	Title	Peak	Wks No.1	Wks
4 Mar 95	**THE BOMB! (THESE SOUNDS FALL INTO MY MIND)** *Positiva CDTIV 33* ●	5		13
20 Jan 96	**GOT MYSELF TOGETHER** *Positiva CDTIV 48*	12		3

Peak Position · Weeks at No.1 · Weeks on Chart

LINDSEY BUCKINGHAM
US, male vocalist/guitarist. See Fleetwood Mac — 7

Date	Title / Label	Peak	Wks No.1	Wks
16 Jan 82	**TROUBLE** *Mercury MER 85*	31		7

JEFF BUCKLEY
US, male vocalist/guitarist, d. 29 May 1997 (age 30) — 18

Date	Title / Label	Peak	Wks No.1	Wks
27 May 95	**LAST GOODBYE** *Columbia 6620422*	54		2
6 Jun 98	**EVERYBODY HERE WANTS YOU** *Columbia 6657912*	43		1
9 Jun 07	**HALLELUJAH** *Columbia 88697098847*	65		2
11 Oct 08	**HALLELUJAH** *Columbia 88697098847*	2		13

BUCKS FIZZ
UK, male/female vocal group – Jay Aston (replaced by Shelley Preston), Cheryl Baker, Robert Gubby (Bobby G) & Mike Nolan — 150

Date	Title / Label	Peak	Wks No.1	Wks
28 Mar 81	**MAKING YOUR MIND UP** *RCA 56* ●	1	3	12
6 Jun 81	**PIECE OF THE ACTION** *RCA 88* ○	12		9
15 Aug 81	**ONE OF THOSE NIGHTS** *RCA 114*	20		10
28 Nov 81	**THE LAND OF MAKE BELIEVE** *RCA 163*	1	2	16
27 Mar 82	**MY CAMERA NEVER LIES** *RCA 202* ○	1	2	8
19 Jun 82	**NOW THOSE DAYS ARE GONE** *RCA 241* ○	8		9
27 Nov 82	**IF YOU CAN'T STAND THE HEAT** *RCA 300* ○	10		11
12 Mar 83	**RUN FOR YOUR LIFE** *RCA FIZ 1*	14		7
18 Jun 83	**WHEN WE WERE YOUNG** *RCA 342*	10		8
1 Oct 83	**LONDON TOWN** *RCA 363*	34		6
17 Dec 83	**RULES OF THE GAME** *RCA 380*	57		6
25 Aug 84	**TALKING IN YOUR SLEEP** *RCA FIZ 2*	15		9
27 Oct 84	**GOLDEN DAYS** *RCA FIZ 3*	42		4
29 Dec 84	**I HEAR TALK** *RCA FIZ 4*	34		8
22 Jun 85	**YOU AND YOUR HEART SO BLUE** *RCA PB 40233*	43		4
14 Sep 85	**MAGICAL** *RCA PB 40367*	57		3
7 Jun 86	**NEW BEGINNING (MAMBA SEYRA)** *Polydor POSP 794*	8		10
30 Aug 86	**LOVE THE ONE YOU'RE WITH** *Polydor POSP 813*	47		3
15 Nov 86	**KEEP EACH OTHER WARM** *Polydor POSP 835*	45		4
5 Nov 88	**HEART OF STONE** *RCA PB 42035*	50		3

BUCKSHOT LEFONQUE
US, male vocal/instrumental group — 1

Date	Title / Label	Peak	Wks No.1	Wks
6 Dec 97	**ANOTHER DAY** *Columbia 6653762*	65		1

ROY BUDD
UK, male pianist — 1

Date	Title / Label	Peak	Wks No.1	Wks
10 Jul 99	**GET CARTER** *Cinephile CINX 1003*	68		1

JOE BUDDEN
US, male vocalist — 14

Date	Title / Label	Peak	Wks No.1	Wks
19 Jul 03	**PUMP IT UP** *Def Jam 9808879*	13		7
16 Oct 04	**WHATEVER U WANT** *Def Jam 9864266* CHRISTINA MILIAN FEATURING JOE BUDDEN	9		7

BUDGIE
UK, male vocal/instrumental group — 2

Date	Title / Label	Peak	Wks No.1	Wks
3 Oct 81	**KEEPING A RENDEZVOUS** *RCA BUDGIE 3*	71		2

MUTYA BUENA
UK, female vocalist (Rosa Isabel Mutya Buena). See Sugababes — 21

Date	Title / Label	Peak	Wks No.1	Wks
18 Nov 06	**THIS IS NOT REAL LOVE** *Aegean/Sony 88697019792* GEORGE MICHAEL & MUTYA	15		4
26 May 07	**REAL GIRL** *Fourth & Broadway 1734395*	2		13
3 Nov 07	**JUST A LITTLE BIT** *Fourth & Broadway 1748789*	65		2
12 Jan 08	**B BOY BABY** *Fourth & Broadway 1756344*	73		2

BUFFALO G
Ireland, female vocal/rap duo — 4

Date	Title / Label	Peak	Wks No.1	Wks
10 Jun 00	**WE'RE REALLY SAYING SOMETHING** *Epic 6694182*	17		4

BUFFALO TOM
US, male vocal/instrumental trio – Bill Janovitz, Chris Colbourn & Tom Maginnis — 5

Date	Title / Label	Peak	Wks No.1	Wks
23 Oct 99	**GOING UNDERGROUND** *Ignition IGNSCD 16*	6		5

BUG KAN & THE PLASTIC JAM
UK, male production group — 2

Date	Title / Label	Peak	Wks No.1	Wks
31 Aug 91	**MADE IN TWO MINUTES** *Optimum Dance BKPJ 1S* FEATURING PATTI LOW & DOOGIE	70		1
26 Feb 94	**MADE IN TWO MINUTES (REMIX)** *PWL International PWCD 286*	64		1

BUGGLES
UK, male vocal/instrumental duo – Trevor Horn & Geoff Downes — 28

Date	Title / Label	Peak	Wks No.1	Wks
22 Sep 79	**VIDEO KILLED THE RADIO STAR** *Island WIP 6524* ●	1	1	11
26 Jan 80	**THE PLASTIC AGE** *Island WIP 6540*	16		8
5 Apr 80	**CLEAN CLEAN** *Island WIP 6584*	38		5
8 Nov 80	**ELSTREE** *Island WIP 6624*	55		4

BUGZ IN THE ATTIC
UK, male/female vocal/instrumental/production group — 2

Date	Title / Label	Peak	Wks No.1	Wks
22 Jan 05	**BOOTY LA LA** *V2 VVR5030093*	44		2

JAMES BULLER
UK, male vocalist — 1

Date	Title / Label	Peak	Wks No.1	Wks
6 Mar 99	**CAN'T SMILE WITHOUT YOU** *BBC Music WMSS 60092*	51		1

BULLET FOR MY VALENTINE
UK, male vocal/instrumental group — 10

Date	Title / Label	Peak	Wks No.1	Wks
9 Apr 05	**4 WORDS (TO CHOKE UPON)** *Visible Noise TORMENT51*	40		2
1 Oct 05	**SUFFOCATING UNDER WORDS OF SORROW** *Visible Noise TORMENT58CD*	37		1
18 Feb 06	**ALL THESE THINGS I HATE** *Visible Noise TORMENT64CD*	29		2
29 Jul 06	**TEARS DON'T FALL** *Visible Noise TORMENT69CD*	37		2
2 Feb 08	**SCREAM AIM FIRE** *20-20 Recordings 88697222602*	34		2
12 Apr 08	**HEARTS BURST INTO FIRE** *20-20 Recordings 88697284192*	66		1

BULLETPROOF
UK, male producer (Paul Chambers) — 1

Date	Title / Label	Peak	Wks No.1	Wks
10 Mar 01	**SAY YEAH/DANCE TO THE RHYTHM** *Tidy Trax TIDY 148CD*	62		1

BUMP
UK, male production duo — 5

Date	Title / Label	Peak	Wks No.1	Wks
4 Jul 92	**I'M RUSHING** *Good Boy EDGE7 1*	40		4
11 Nov 95	**I'M RUSHING (REMIX)** *Deconstruction 74321320692*	45		1

BUMP & FLEX
UK, male/female vocal/production duo — 1

Date	Title / Label	Peak	Wks No.1	Wks
23 May 98	**LONG TIME COMING** *Heat Recordings HEATCD 014*	73		1

EMMA BUNTON
UK, female vocalist. See Spice Girls — 76

Date	Title / Label	Peak	Wks No.1	Wks
13 Nov 99	**WHAT I AM** *VC Recordings VCRD 53* TIN TIN OUT FEATURING EMMA BUNTON ○	2		12
14 Apr 01	**WHAT TOOK YOU SO LONG** *Virgin VSCDT 1796* ○	1	2	12
8 Sep 01	**TAKE MY BREATH AWAY** *Virgin VSCDT 1814*	5		9
22 Dec 01	**WE'RE NOT GONNA SLEEP TONIGHT** *Virgin VSCDT 1821*	20		5
7 Jun 03	**FREE ME** *19/Universal 9807473*	5		9
25 Oct 03	**MAYBE** *19/Universal 9812785*	6		9
7 Feb 04	**I'LL BE THERE** *19/Universal 9816268*	7		8
12 Jun 04	**CRICKETS SING FOR ANAMARIA** *19 9866856*	15		4
25 Nov 06	**DOWNTOWN** *19 1717347*	3		7
24 Feb 07	**ALL I NEED TO KNOW** *19 1723657*	60		1

TIM BURGESS
UK, male vocalist/harmonica player. See Charlatans, Chemical Brothers — 7

Date	Title / Label	Peak	Wks No.1	Wks
18 Dec 93	**I WAS BORN ON CHRISTMAS DAY** *Heavenly HVN 36CD* SAINT ETIENNE CO STARRING TIM BURGESS	37		5
6 Sep 03	**I BELIEVE IN THE SPIRIT** *PIAS PIASB109CD*	44		1
15 Nov 03	**ONLY A BOY** *PIAS PIASB119CD*	54		1

GEOFFREY BURGON
UK, male conductor — **4**

Date	Title	Peak	Wks at No.1	Wks on Chart
26 Dec 81	**BRIDESHEAD THEME** *Chrysalis CHS 2562*	48		4

ALEXANDRA BURKE
UK, female vocalist. See Helping Haiti, X Factor Finalists — **55**

Date	Title	Peak	Wks at No.1	Wks on Chart
27 Dec 08	**HALLELUJAH** *Syco Music 88697446252* ⊛	1	3	11
24 Oct 09	**BAD BOYS** *Syco Music 88697590932* FEATURING FLO RIDA ⊛	1	1	25+
31 Oct 09	**HALLELUJAH** *Syco Music 88697446252*	70		1
26 Dec 09	**BROKEN HEELS** *Syco Music 88697632832*	8		16+
3 Apr 10	**ALL NIGHT LONG** *Syco Music GBHMU0900055* FEATURING PITBULL	59		2+

KENI BURKE
US, male vocalist — **4**

Date	Title	Peak	Wks at No.1	Wks on Chart
27 Jun 81	**LET SOMEBODY LOVE YOU** *RCA 93*	59		3
18 Apr 92	**RISIN' TO THE TOP** *RCA PB 49103*	70		1

BURN
UK, male vocal/instrumental group — **2**

Date	Title	Peak	Wks at No.1	Wks on Chart
8 Jun 02	**THE SMILING FACE** *Hut HUTCD 155*	72		1
29 Mar 03	**DRUNKEN FOOL** *Hut HUTCD 166*	54		1

HANK C BURNETTE
Sweden, male multi-instrumentalist (Sven-Ake Hogberg) — **8**

Date	Title	Peak	Wks at No.1	Wks on Chart
30 Oct 76	**SPINNING ROCK BOOGIE** *Sonet SON 2094*	21		8

JOHNNY BURNETTE
US, male vocalist, d. 1 Aug 1964 (age 30) — **48**

Date	Title	Peak	Wks at No.1	Wks on Chart
29 Sep 60	**DREAMIN'** *London HLG 9172*	5		16
12 Jan 61	**YOU'RE SIXTEEN** *London HLG 9254*	3		12
13 Apr 61	**LITTLE BOY SAD** *London HLG 9315*	12		12
10 Aug 61	**GIRLS** *London HLG 9388*	37		5
17 May 62	**CLOWN SHOES** *Liberty LIB 55416*	35		3

ROCKY BURNETTE
US, male vocalist (Jonathan Burnette) — **7**

Date	Title	Peak	Wks at No.1	Wks on Chart
17 Nov 79	**TIRED OF TOEIN' THE LINE** *EMI 2992*	58		7

JERRY BURNS
UK, female vocalist — **1**

Date	Title	Peak	Wks at No.1	Wks on Chart
25 Apr 92	**PALE RED** *Columbia 6579467*	64		1

PETE BURNS
UK, male vocalist. See Dead Or Alive — **1**

Date	Title	Peak	Wks at No.1	Wks on Chart
19 Jun 04	**JACK AND JILL PARTY** *Olde English LKCD02*	75		1

RAY BURNS
UK, male vocalist — **19**

Date	Title	Peak	Wks at No.1	Wks on Chart
11 Feb 55	**MOBILE** *Columbia DB 3563*	4		13
26 Aug 55	**THAT'S HOW A LOVE SONG WAS BORN** *Columbia DB 3640* WITH THE CORONETS	14		6

MALANDRA BURROWS
UK, female vocalist/actor (Malandra Newman) — **10**

Date	Title	Peak	Wks at No.1	Wks on Chart
1 Dec 90	**JUST THIS SIDE OF LOVE** *Yorkshire Television DALE 1*	11		8
18 Oct 97	**CARNIVAL IN HEAVEN** *warner.esp WESP 001CD*	49		1
29 Aug 98	**DON'T LEAVE ME** *warner.esp WESP 004CD*	54		1

JENNY BURTON
US, female vocalist — **2**

Date	Title	Peak	Wks at No.1	Wks on Chart
30 Mar 85	**BAD HABITS** *Atlantic A 9583*	68		2

BURUNDI STEIPHENSON BLACK
Burundi/France, male instrumental group — **14**

Date	Title	Peak	Wks at No.1	Wks on Chart
13 Nov 71	**BURUNDI BLACK** *Barclay BAR 3*	31		14

BUS STOP
UK, male production group. See Barndance Boys, Flip & Fill, Rikki & Daz featuring Glen Campbell, Uniting Nations — **19**

Date	Title	Peak	Wks at No.1	Wks on Chart
23 May 98	**KUNG FU FIGHTING** *All Around The World CDGLOBE 173* FEATURING CARL DOUGLAS	8		11
24 Oct 98	**YOU AIN'T SEEN NOTHIN' YET** *All Around The World CDGLOBE 187* FEATURING RANDY BACHMAN	22		4
10 Apr 99	**JUMP** *All Around The World CXGLOBE 186*	23		3
7 Oct 00	**GET IT ON** *All Around The World CDGLOBE 225* FEATURING T REX	59		1

LOU BUSCH
US, male pianist (aka Joe 'Fingers' Carr), d. 19 Sep 1979 (age 69) — **17**

Date	Title	Peak	Wks at No.1	Wks on Chart
27 Jan 56	**ZAMBESI** *Capitol CL 14504*	2		17

BUSH
UK, male vocal/instrumental group – Gavin Rossdale, Robin Goodridge, Dave Parsons & Nigel Pulsford — **13**

Date	Title	Peak	Wks at No.1	Wks on Chart
8 Jun 96	**MACHINEHEAD** *Interscope IND 95505*	48		2
1 Mar 97	**SWALLOWED** *Interscope IND 95528*	7		5
7 Jun 97	**GREEDY FLY** *Interscope IND 95536*	22		2
1 Nov 97	**BONE DRIVEN** *Interscope IND 95553*	49		1
4 Dec 99	**THE CHEMICALS BETWEEN US** *Trauma/Polydor 4972222*	46		1
18 Mar 00	**WARM MACHINE** *Trauma/Polydor 4972752*	45		1
3 Jun 00	**LETTING THE CABLES SLEEP** *Trauma/Polydor 4973352*	51		1

KATE BUSH
UK, female vocalist/multi-instrumentalist/producer — **173**

Date	Title	Peak	Wks at No.1	Wks on Chart
11 Feb 78	**WUTHERING HEIGHTS** *EMI 2719* ●	1	4	13
10 Jun 78	**MAN WITH THE CHILD IN HIS EYES** *EMI 2806*	6		11
11 Nov 78	**HAMMER HORROR** *EMI 2887*	44		6
17 Mar 79	**WOW** *EMI 2911*	14		10
15 Sep 79	**KATE BUSH ON STAGE EP** *EMI MIEP 2991*	10		9
26 Apr 80	**BREATHING** *EMI 5058*	16		7
5 Jul 80	**BABOOSHKA** *EMI 5085* ○	5		10
4 Oct 80	**ARMY DREAMERS** *EMI 5106*	16		9
6 Dec 80	**DECEMBER WILL BE MAGIC AGAIN** *EMI 5121*	29		7
11 Jul 81	**SAT IN YOUR LAP** *EMI 5201*	11		7
7 Aug 82	**THE DREAMING** *EMI 5296*	48		3
17 Aug 85	**RUNNING UP THAT HILL** *EMI KB 1* ○	3		11
26 Oct 85	**CLOUDBURSTING** *EMI KB 2*	20		6
1 Mar 86	**HOUNDS OF LOVE** *EMI KB 3*	18		5
10 May 86	**THE BIG SKY** *EMI KB 4*	37		3
1 Nov 86	**DON'T GIVE UP** *Virgin PGS 2* PETER GABRIEL & KATE BUSH	9		11
8 Nov 86	**EXPERIMENT IV** *EMI KB 5*	23		4
30 Sep 89	**THE SENSUAL WORLD** *EMI EM 102*	12		5
2 Dec 89	**THIS WOMAN'S WORK** *EMI EM 119*	25		5
10 Mar 90	**LOVE AND ANGER** *EMI EM 134*	38		3
7 Dec 91	**ROCKET MAN (I THINK IT'S GOING TO BE A LONG LONG TIME)** *Mercury TRIBO 2*	12		8
18 Sep 93	**RUBBERBAND GIRL** *EMI CDEM 280*	12		5
27 Nov 93	**MOMENTS OF PLEASURE** *EMI CDEM 297*	26		3
16 Apr 94	**THE RED SHOES** *EMI CDEMS 316*	21		3
30 Jul 94	**THE MAN I LOVE** *Mercury MERCD 408* & LARRY ADLER	27		2
19 Nov 94	**AND SO IS LOVE** *EMI CDEMS 355*	26		2
5 Nov 05	**KING OF THE MOUNTAIN** *EMI CDEM674*	4		5

BUSTED
UK, male vocal/instrumental trio – Charlie Simpson, James Bourne & Mattie Jay — **92**

Date	Title	Peak	Wks at No.1	Wks on Chart
28 Sep 02	**WHAT I GO TO SCHOOL FOR** *Universal MCSXD 40294*	3		12
25 Jan 03	**YEAR 3000** *Universal MCSXD 40306*	2		15
3 May 03	**YOU SAID NO** *Universal MCSXD 40318*	1	1	10
23 Aug 03	**SLEEPING WITH THE LIGHT ON** *Universal MCSXD 40327*	3		10
22 Nov 03	**CRASHED THE WEDDING** *Universal MCSTD 40345*	1	1	12
28 Feb 04	**WHO'S DAVID** *Universal MCSXD 40355*	1	1	10
8 May 04	**AIR HOSTESS** *Universal MCSXD 40361*	2		10
7 Aug 04	**THUNDERBIRDS/3 AM** *Universal MCSXD 40375*	1	2	13

BUSTER
UK, male vocal/instrumental group — **1**

Date	Title	Peak	Wks at No.1	Wks on Chart
19 Jun 76	**SUNDAY** *RCA 2678*	49		1

BERNARD BUTLER
UK, male vocalist/guitarist. See McAlmont & Butler, Suede, Tears — **26**

Date	Title	Peak	Wks at No.1	Wks on Chart
27 May 95	**YES** *Hut HUTCD 53* McALMONT & BUTLER	8		8

Date	Title	Peak Position	Weeks at No.1	Weeks on Chart
4 Nov 95	**YOU DO** *Hut HUTDG 57* McALMONT & BUTLER	17		4
17 Jan 98	**STAY** *Creation CRESCD 281*	12		4
28 Mar 98	**NOT ALONE** *Creation CRESCD 289*	27		3
27 Jun 98	**A CHANGE OF HEART** *Creation CRESCD 297*	45		1
23 Oct 99	**YOU MUST GO ON** *Creation CRESCD 324*	44		1
10 Aug 02	**FALLING** *Chrysalis CDCHS 5141* McALMONT & BUTLER	23		3
9 Nov 02	**BRING IT BACK** *Chrysalis CDCHSS 5145* McALMONT & BUTLER	36		2

JONATHAN BUTLER
South Africa, male vocalist/guitarist — 18

Date	Title	Peak Position	Weeks at No.1	Weeks on Chart
25 Jan 86	**IF YOU'RE READY (COME GO WITH ME)** *Jive 109* RUBY TURNER FEATURING JONATHAN BUTLER	30		7
8 Aug 87	**LIES** *Jive 141*	18		11

BUTTERSCOTCH
UK, male vocal group — 11

Date	Title	Peak Position	Weeks at No.1	Weeks on Chart
2 May 70	**DON'T YOU KNOW** *RCA 1937*	17		11

BUTTHOLE SURFERS
US, male vocal/instrumental group — 1

Date	Title	Peak Position	Weeks at No.1	Weeks on Chart
5 Oct 96	**PEPPER** *Capitol CDCL 778*	59		1

BUY NOW!
Sweden, male production duo — 1

Date	Title	Peak Position	Weeks at No.1	Weeks on Chart
5 Jul 08	**BODYCRASH** *Positiva CDTIV271*	55		1

BUZZCOCKS
UK, male vocal/instrumental group — 53

Date	Title	Peak Position	Weeks at No.1	Weeks on Chart
18 Feb 78	**WHAT DO I GET** *United Artists UP 36348*	37		3
13 May 78	**I DON'T MIND** *United Artists UP 36386*	55		2
15 Jul 78	**LOVE YOU MORE** *United Artists UP 36433*	34		6
23 Sep 78	**EVER FALLEN IN LOVE (WITH SOMEONE YOU SHOULDN'T'VE)** *United Artists UP 36455*	12		11
25 Nov 78	**PROMISES** *United Artists UP 36471*	20		10
10 Mar 79	**EVERYBODY'S HAPPY NOWADAYS** *United Artists UP 36499*	29		6
21 Jul 79	**HARMONY IN MY HEAD** *United Artists UP 36541*	32		6
25 Aug 79	**SPIRAL SCRATCH EP** *New Hormones ORG 1*	31		6
6 Sep 80	**ARE EVERYTHING/WHY SHE'S A GIRL FROM THE CHAINSTORE** *United Artists BP 365*	61		3

B.V.S.M.P.
US, male vocal/rap trio – Frederick Byrd, Percy Rodgers & Calvin Williams — 12

Date	Title	Peak Position	Weeks at No.1	Weeks on Chart
23 Jul 88	**I NEED YOU** *Debut DEBT 3044*	3		12

BWO
Sweden, male/female vocal/instrumental group — 2

Date	Title	Peak Position	Weeks at No.1	Weeks on Chart
8 Mar 08	**SUNSHINE IN THE RAIN** *Shell GET11CDX*	69		1
9 Aug 08	**LAY YOUR LOVE ON ME** *Shell GET12CD*	69		1

BY ALL MEANS
US, male/female vocal/instrumental trio — 2

Date	Title	Peak Position	Weeks at No.1	Weeks on Chart
18 Jun 88	**I SURRENDER TO YOUR LOVE** *Fourth & Broadway BRW 102*	65		2

MAX BYGRAVES
UK, male vocalist/comedian (Walter Bygraves) — 131

Date	Title	Peak Position	Weeks at No.1	Weeks on Chart
14 Nov 52	**COWPUNCHER'S CANTATA** *HMV B 10250*	6		8
14 May 54	**(THE GANG THAT SANG) HEART OF MY HEART** *HMV B 10654*	7		8
10 Sep 54	**GILLY GILLY OSSENFEFFER KATZENELLEN BOGEN BY THE SEA** *HMV B 10734*	7		8
21 Jan 55	**MR SANDMAN** *HMV B 10801*	16		1
18 Nov 55	**MEET ME ON THE CORNER** *HMV POP 116*	2		11
17 Feb 56	**BALLAD OF DAVY CROCKETT** *HMV POP 153*	20		1
25 May 56	**OUT OF TOWN** *HMV POP 164*	18		7
5 Apr 57	**HEART** *Decca F 10862*	14		8
2 May 58	**YOU NEED HANDS/TULIPS FROM AMSTERDAM** *Decca F 11004*	3		25
22 Aug 58	**LITTLE TRAIN/GOTTA HAVE RAIN** *Decca F 11046*	28		2
2 Jan 59	**MY UKELELE** *Decca F 11077*	19		4
18 Dec 59	**JINGLE BELL ROCK** *Decca F 11176*	7		4
10 Mar 60	**FINGS AIN'T WOT THEY USED T'BE** *Decca F 11214*	5		15
28 Jul 60	**CONSIDER YOURSELF** *Decca F 11251*	50		1
1 Jun 61	**BELLS OF AVIGNON** *Decca F 11350*	36		5
19 Feb 69	**YOU'RE MY EVERYTHING** *Pye 7N 17705*	34		4
6 Oct 73	**DECK OF CARDS** *Pye 7N 45276*	13		15
9 Dec 89	**WHITE CHRISTMAS** *Parkfield PMS 5012*	71		4

BYKER GROOOVE!
UK, female vocal/acting trio — 3

Date	Title	Peak Position	Weeks at No.1	Weeks on Chart
24 Dec 94	**LOVE YOUR SEXY...!!** *Groove GROVD 01*	48		3

DANNY BYRD FEATURING LIQUID
UK, male DJ/production duo — 1

Date	Title	Peak Position	Weeks at No.1	Weeks on Chart
13 Feb 10	**SWEET HARMONY** *Hospital NHS160*	64		1

DONALD BYRD
US, male trumpeter. See Blackbyrds — 6

Date	Title	Peak Position	Weeks at No.1	Weeks on Chart
26 Sep 81	**LOVING YOU/LOVE HAS COME AROUND** *Elektra K 12559*	41		6

GARY BYRD & THE GB EXPERIENCE
US, male rapper with vocal/instrumental collaborators including Crystal Blake, Benjamin Bridges, Teena Marie*, Stevie Wonder* & Syreeta* Wright — 9

Date	Title	Peak Position	Weeks at No.1	Weeks on Chart
23 Jul 83	**THE CROWN** *Motown TMGT 1312*	6		9

BYRDS
US, male vocal/instrumental group – members included Roger McGuinn, Skip Battin, Gene Clark, d. 24 May 1991, Michael Clarke, d. 19 Dec 1993, David Crosby*, Chris Hillman, Gram Parsons, d. 19 Sep 1973, & Clarence White — 52

Date	Title	Peak Position	Weeks at No.1	Weeks on Chart
17 Jun 65	**MR TAMBOURINE MAN** *CBS 201765* ★	1	2	14
12 Aug 65	**ALL I REALLY WANT TO DO** *CBS 201796*	4		10
11 Nov 65	**TURN! TURN! TURN! (TO EVERYTHING THERE IS A SEASON)** *CBS 202008* ★	26		8
5 May 66	**EIGHT MILES HIGH** *CBS 202067*	24		9
5 Jun 68	**YOU AIN'T GOIN' NOWHERE** *CBS 3411*	45		3
13 Feb 71	**CHESTNUT MARE** *CBS 5322*	19		8

EDWARD BYRNES & CONNIE STEVENS
US, male/female actors/vocalists Edward Brietenberger & Concetta Ingolia — 8

Date	Title	Peak Position	Weeks at No.1	Weeks on Chart
5 May 60	**KOOKIE KOOKIE (LEND ME YOUR COMB)** *Warner Brothers WB 5*	27		8

BYSTANDERS
UK, male vocal/instrumental group — 1

Date	Title	Peak Position	Weeks at No.1	Weeks on Chart
9 Feb 67	**98.6** *Piccadilly 7N 35363*	45		1

MELANIE C
UK, female vocalist (Melanie Chisholm). See Spice Girls — 98

Date	Title	Peak Position	Weeks at No.1	Weeks on Chart
12 Dec 98	**WHEN YOU'RE GONE** *A&M 5828212* BRYAN ADAMS FEATURING MELANIE C ⊛	3		19
9 Oct 99	**GOIN' DOWN** *Virgin VSCDT 1744*	4		6
4 Dec 99	**NORTHERN STAR** *Virgin VSCDT 1762*	4		11
1 Apr 00	**NEVER BE THE SAME AGAIN** *Virgin VSCDT 1786* & LISA 'LEFT EYE' LOPES ●	1	1	16
19 Aug 00	**I TURN TO YOU** *Virgin VSCDT 1772* ●	1	1	12
9 Dec 00	**IF THAT WERE ME** *Virgin VSCDT 1786*	18		10
8 Mar 03	**HERE IT COMES AGAIN** *Virgin VSCDT 1842*	7		8
14 Jun 03	**ON THE HORIZON** *Virgin VSCDT 1851*	14		7
22 Nov 03	**MELT/YEH YEH YEH** *Virgin VSCDY 1858*	27		2
16 Apr 05	**NEXT BEST SUPERSTAR** *Red Girl CXREDG1*	10		4
7 Apr 07	**I WANT CANDY** *Red Girl CDREDG3*	24		2
30 Jun 07	**CAROLYNA** *Red Girl CDREDG4*	49		1

ROY C
US, male vocalist (Roy C Hammond) — 24

Date	Title	Peak Position	Weeks at No.1	Weeks on Chart
21 Apr 66	**SHOTGUN WEDDING** *Island WI 273*	6		11
25 Nov 72	**SHOTGUN WEDDING** *UK 19*	8		13

C & C MUSIC FACTORY
US, male production duo – Robert Clivilles & David Cole, d. 24 Jan 1995 (age 32) — 53

Date	Title	Peak Position	Weeks at No.1	Weeks on Chart
15 Dec 90	**GONNA MAKE YOU SWEAT (EVERYBODY DANCE NOW)** *CBS 6564540* (FEATURING FREEDOM WILLIAMS) ★	3		12
30 Mar 91	**HERE WE GO** *Columbia 6567557* (FEATURING FREEDOM WILLIAMS)	20		7
6 Jul 91	**THINGS THAT MAKE YOU GO HMMM** *Columbia 6566907* (FEATURING FREEDOM WILLIAMS)	4		11
23 Nov 91	**JUST A TOUCH OF LOVE EVERYDAY** *Columbia 6575247* FEATURING ZELMA DAVIS	31		3
18 Jan 92	**PRIDE (IN THE NAME OF LOVE)** *Columbia 6577017* CLIVILLES & COLE	15		5
14 Mar 92	**A DEEPER LOVE** *Columbia 6578497* CLIVILLES & COLE	15		5
3 Oct 92	**KEEP IT COMIN' (DANCE TILL YOU CAN'T DANCE NO MORE)** *Columbia 6584307* FEATURING Q UNIQUE & DEBORAH COOPER	34		3
27 Aug 94	**DO YOU WANNA GET FUNKY** *Columbia 6607622*	27		3
18 Feb 95	**I FOUND LOVE/TAKE A TOKE** *Columbia 6612112* FEATURING MARTHA WASH	26		2
11 Nov 95	**I'LL ALWAYS BE AROUND** *MCA MCSTD 40001*	42		2

CJ & CO
US, male vocal/instrumental group — 2

Date	Title	Peak Position	Weeks at No.1	Weeks on Chart
30 Jul 77	**DEVIL'S GUN** *Atlantic K 10956*	43		2

C-SIXTY FOUR
UK, male DJ/producer (Colin Hamilton) — 1

Date	Title	Peak Position	Weeks at No.1	Weeks on Chart
19 Mar 05	**ON A GOOD THING** *Manifesto 9870564*	54		1

CA VA CA VA
UK, male vocal/instrumental group — 8

Date	Title	Peak Position	Weeks at No.1	Weeks on Chart
18 Sep 82	**WHERE'S ROMEO** *Regard RG 103*	49		5
19 Feb 83	**BROTHER BRIGHT** *Regard RG 105*	65		3

MONTSERRAT CABALLE
Spain, female vocalist — 17

Date	Title	Peak Position	Weeks at No.1	Weeks on Chart
7 Nov 87	**BARCELONA** *Polydor POSP 887* FREDDIE MERCURY & MONTSERRAT CABALLE	8		9
8 Aug 92	**BARCELONA** *Polydor PO 221* FREDDIE MERCURY & MONTSERRAT CABALLE	2		8

CABANA
Brazil, male/female vocal/instrumental duo — 1

Date	Title	Peak Position	Weeks at No.1	Weeks on Chart
15 Jul 95	**BAILANDO CON LOBOS** *Hi-Life 5792512*	65		1

CABARET VOLTAIRE
UK, male vocal/instrumental duo — 8

Date	Title	Peak Position	Weeks at No.1	Weeks on Chart
18 Jul 87	**DON'T ARGUE** *Parlophone R 6157*	69		2
4 Nov 89	**HYPNOTISED** *Parlophone R 6227*	66		2
12 May 90	**KEEP ON** *Parlophone R 6250*	55		2
18 Aug 90	**EASY LIFE** *Parlophone R 6261*	61		2

CABIN CREW
Australia, male production duo – Ben Garden & Rob Kittler — 8

Date	Title	Peak Position	Weeks at No.1	Weeks on Chart
12 Mar 05	**STAR TO FALL** *Data DATA87CDX*	4		8

CABLE
UK, male vocal/instrumental group — 2

Date	Title	Peak Position	Weeks at No.1	Weeks on Chart
14 Jun 97	**FREEZE THE ATLANTIC** *Infectious INFECT 38CD*	44		2

CACIQUE
UK, male/female vocal/instrumental group — 1

Date	Title	Peak Position	Weeks at No.1	Weeks on Chart
1 Jun 85	**DEVOTED TO YOU** *Diamond Duel DISC 1*	69		1

CACTUS WORLD NEWS
Ireland, male vocal/instrumental group — 7

Date	Title	Peak Position	Weeks at No.1	Weeks on Chart
8 Feb 86	**YEARS LATER** *MCA 1024*	59		3
26 Apr 86	**WORLDS APART** *MCA 1040*	58		3
20 Sep 86	**THE BRIDGE** *MCA 1080*	74		1

CADETS WITH EILEEN READ
UK, male/female vocal/instrumental group — 1

Date	Title	Peak Position	Weeks at No.1	Weeks on Chart
3 Jun 65	**JEALOUS HEART** *Pye 7N 15852*	42		1

SUSAN CADOGAN
Jamaica, female vocalist (Alison Cadogan) — 19

Date	Title	Peak Position	Weeks at No.1	Weeks on Chart
5 Apr 75	**HURT SO GOOD** *Magnet MAG 23* ●	4		12
19 Jul 75	**LOVE ME BABY** *Magnet MAG 36*	22		7

CAESARS
Sweden, male vocal/instrumental group – Caesar Vidal, Joakim Ahlund, Nino Keller & David Lindquist — 11

Date	Title	Peak Position	Weeks at No.1	Weeks on Chart
19 Apr 03	**JERK IT OUT** *Virgin DINSD 244*	60		1
30 Apr 05	**JERK IT OUT** *Virgin DINSD274*	8		10

CAGE THE ELEPHANT
US, male vocal/instrumental group — 3

Date	Title	Peak Position	Weeks at No.1	Weeks on Chart
28 Jun 08	**AIN'T NO REST FOR THE WICKED** *Relentless RELCD52*	32		2
18 Oct 08	**IN ONE EAR** *Relentless RELCD57*	51		1

CAHILL FEATURING NIKKI BELLE
UK, male/female vocal/production group — 5

Date	Title	Peak Position	Weeks at No.1	Weeks on Chart
19 Apr 08	**TRIPPIN' ON YOU** *All Around The World CDGLOBE775*	25		5

COLBIE CAILLAT
US, female vocalist/guitarist — 6

Date	Title	Peak Position	Weeks at No.1	Weeks on Chart
6 Oct 07	**BUBBLY** *Island 1747525*	72		1
30 Aug 08	**BUBBLY** *Island 1747525*	58		5

AL CAIOLA
US, male guitarist/orchestra leader — 6

Date	Title	Peak Position	Weeks at No.1	Weeks on Chart
15 Jun 61	**THE MAGNIFICENT SEVEN** *HMV POP 889*	34		6

CAKE
US, male vocal/instrumental group — 7

Date	Title	Peak Position	Weeks at No.1	Weeks on Chart
22 Mar 97	**THE DISTANCE** *Capricorn 5742212*	22		3
31 May 97	**I WILL SURVIVE** *Capricorn 5744712*	29		2
1 May 99	**NEVER THERE** *Capricorn 8708112*	66		1
3 Nov 01	**SHORT SKIRT LONG JACKET** *Columbia 6720402*	63		1

CALIFORNIA SUNSHINE
Israel/Italy, male/female DJ/production group — 1

Date	Title	Peak Position	Weeks at No.1	Weeks on Chart
16 Aug 97	**SUMMER '89** *Perfecto PERF 143CD*	56		1

CALL
US, male vocal/instrumental group — 6

Date	Title	Peak Position	Weeks at No.1	Weeks on Chart
30 Sep 89	**LET THE DAY BEGIN** *MCA 1362*	42		6

TERRY CALLIER
US, male vocalist — 4

Date	Title	Peak Position	Weeks at No.1	Weeks on Chart
13 Dec 97	**BEST BIT EP** *Heavenly HVN 72CD* BETH ORTON FEATURING TERRY CALLIER	36		3
23 May 98	**LOVE THEME FROM SPARTACUS** *Talkin Loud TLCD 32*	57		1

CALLING
US, male vocal/instrumental trio – Alex Band, Aaron Kamin & Nate Wood — 21

Date	Title	Peak Position	Weeks at No.1	Weeks on Chart
29 Jun 02	**WHEREVER YOU WILL GO (IMPORT)** *RCA 74321912242*	64		1
6 Jul 02	**WHEREVER YOU WILL GO** *RCA 74321947652*	3		11
2 Nov 02	**ADRIENNE** *RCA 74321968352*	18		3
29 May 04	**OUR LIVES** *RCA 82876618652*	13		4
28 Aug 04	**THINGS WILL GO MY WAY** *RCA 82876637372*	34		2

EDDIE CALVERT

UK, male trumpeter, d. 7 Aug 1978 (age 56) — **80**

Date	Title / Label	Peak	Wks at No.1	Wks on Chart
18 Dec 53	**OH MEIN PAPA** *Columbia DB 3337*	1	9	21
8 Apr 55	**CHERRY PINK AND APPLE BLOSSOM WHITE** *Columbia DB 3581*	1	4	21
13 May 55	**STRANGER IN PARADISE** *Columbia DB 3594*	14		4
29 Jul 55	**JOHN AND JULIE** *Columbia DB 3624*	6		11
9 Mar 56	**ZAMBESI** *Columbia DB 3747*	13		7
7 Feb 58	**MANDY (LA PANSE)** *Columbia DB 3956*	9		14
20 Jun 58	**LITTLE SERENADE** *Columbia DB 4105*	28		2

CAMEO

US, male vocal/instrumental group – Larry Blackmon, Tomi Jenkins, Kevin Kendricks, Nathan Leftenant & Charles Singleton — **71**

Date	Title / Label	Peak	Wks at No.1	Wks on Chart
31 Mar 84	**SHE'S STRANGE** *Club JAB 2*	37		8
13 Jul 85	**ATTACK ME WITH YOUR LOVE** *Club JAB 16*	65		2
14 Sep 85	**SINGLE LIFE** *Club JAB 21*	15		10
7 Dec 85	**SHE'S STRANGE** *Club JAB 25*	22		8
22 Mar 86	**A GOODBYE** *Club JAB 28*	65		2
30 Aug 86	**WORD UP** *Club JAB 38* ●	3		13
29 Nov 86	**CANDY** *Club JAB 43*	27		9
25 Apr 87	**BACK AND FORTH** *Club JAB 49*	11		9
17 Oct 87	**SHE'S MINE** *Club JAB 57*	35		4
29 Oct 88	**YOU MAKE ME WORK** *Club JAB 70*	74		1
28 Jul 01	**LOVERBOY** *Virgin VUSCD 211* MARIAH CAREY FEATURING CAMEO	12		5

ANDY CAMERON

UK, male vocalist — **8**

Date	Title / Label	Peak	Wks at No.1	Wks on Chart
4 Mar 78	**ALLY'S TARTAN ARMY** *Klub 03*	6		8

CAM'RON

US, male rapper (Cameron Giles) — **30**

Date	Title / Label	Peak	Wks at No.1	Wks on Chart
19 Sep 98	**HORSE AND CARRIAGE** *Epic 6662612* FEATURING MA$E	12		4
17 Aug 02	**OH BOY** *Roc-A-Fella 0639642* FEATURING JUELZ SANTANA	13		7
8 Feb 03	**HEY MA** *Roc-A-Fella 0637242* FEATURING JUELZ SANTANA	8		10
5 Apr 03	**BOY (I NEED YOU)** *Def Jam 0779282* MARIAH CAREY FEATURING CAM'RON	17		6
12 Feb 05	**GIRLS** *Roc-A-Fella 2103990* FEATURING MONA LISA	25		3

TONY CAMILLO'S BAZUKA

US, male vocal/instrumental group — **5**

Date	Title / Label	Peak	Wks at No.1	Wks on Chart
31 May 75	**DYNOMITE (PART 1)** *A&M AMS 7168*	28		5

CAMISRA

UK, male DJ/producer ('Tall' Paul Newman). See Escrima, Grifters, Partizan, Tall Paul — **12**

Date	Title / Label	Peak	Wks at No.1	Wks on Chart
21 Feb 98	**LET ME SHOW YOU** *VC Recordings VCRD 31*	5		8
11 Jul 98	**FEEL THE BEAT** *VC Recordings VCRD 39*	32		2
22 May 99	**CLAP YOUR HANDS** *VC Recordings VCRD 49*	34		2

CAMOUFLAGE FEATURING MYSTI

US, male/female vocal/instrumental group — **3**

Date	Title / Label	Peak	Wks at No.1	Wks on Chart
24 Sep 77	**BEE STING** *State STAT 58*	48		3

A CAMP

Sweden/US, female/male vocal/instrumental group — **1**

Date	Title / Label	Peak	Wks at No.1	Wks on Chart
1 Sep 01	**I CAN BUY YOU** *Stockholm 0152162*	46		1

CAMP LO

US, male rap duo — **1**

Date	Title / Label	Peak	Wks at No.1	Wks on Chart
16 Aug 97	**LUCHINI AKA (THIS IS IT)** *ffrr FCD 305*	74		1

CAMPAG VELOCET

UK, male/female vocal/instrumental group — **1**

Date	Title / Label	Peak	Wks at No.1	Wks on Chart
19 Feb 00	**VITO SATAN** *Pias Recordings PIASX 010CD*	75		1

ALI CAMPBELL

UK, male vocalist. See Pato Banton, UB40 — **18**

Date	Title / Label	Peak	Wks at No.1	Wks on Chart
20 May 95	**THAT LOOK IN YOUR EYE** *Kuff KUFFDG 1*	5		10
26 Aug 95	**LET YOUR YEAH BE YEAH** *Kuff KUFFD 2*	25		4
9 Dec 95	**SOMETHIN' STUPID** *Kuff KUFFDG 5* ALI & KIBIBI CAMPBELL	30		4

DANNY CAMPBELL & SASHA

UK, male vocal/production duo — **1**

Date	Title / Label	Peak	Wks at No.1	Wks on Chart
31 Jul 93	**TOGETHER** *ffrr FCD 212*	57		1

ELLIE CAMPBELL

UK, female vocalist — **5**

Date	Title / Label	Peak	Wks at No.1	Wks on Chart
3 Apr 99	**SWEET LIES** *Eastern Bloc 0519222*	42		1
14 Aug 99	**SO MANY WAYS** *Eastern Bloc 0519362*	26		3
9 Jun 01	**DON'T WANT YOU BACK** *Jive 9201302*	50		1

ETHNA CAMPBELL

UK, female vocalist — **11**

Date	Title / Label	Peak	Wks at No.1	Wks on Chart
27 Dec 75	**THE OLD RUGGED CROSS** *Philips 6006 475*	33		11

GLEN CAMPBELL

US, male vocalist/guitarist — **106**

Date	Title / Label	Peak	Wks at No.1	Wks on Chart
29 Jan 69	**WICHITA LINEMAN** *Ember EMBS 261*	7		13
7 May 69	**GALVESTON** *Ember EMBS 263*	14		10
6 Dec 69	**ALL I HAVE TO DO IS DREAM** *Capitol CL 15619* BOBBIE GENTRY & GLEN CAMPBELL	3		14
7 Feb 70	**TRY A LITTLE KINDNESS** *Capitol CL 15622*	45		2
9 May 70	**HONEY COME BACK** *Capitol CL 15638*	4		19
26 Sep 70	**EVERYTHING A MAN COULD EVER NEED** *Capitol CL 15653*	32		5
21 Nov 70	**IT'S ONLY MAKE BELIEVE** *Capitol CL 15663*	4		14
27 Mar 71	**DREAM BABY** *Capitol CL 15674*	39		3
4 Oct 75	**RHINESTONE COWBOY** *Capitol CL 15824* ● ★	4		12
26 Mar 77	**SOUTHERN NIGHTS** *Capitol CL 15907* ★	28		6
30 Nov 02	**RHINESTONE COWBOY (GIDDY UP GIDDY UP)** *Serious SER 059CD* RIKKI & DAZ FEATURING GLEN CAMPBELL	12		8

IAN CAMPBELL FOLK GROUP

UK, male vocal/instrumental group — **5**

Date	Title / Label	Peak	Wks at No.1	Wks on Chart
11 Mar 65	**THE TIMES THEY ARE A-CHANGIN'** *Transatlantic SP 5*	42		5

JO ANN CAMPBELL

US, female vocalist — **3**

Date	Title / Label	Peak	Wks at No.1	Wks on Chart
8 Jun 61	**MOTORCYCLE MICHAEL** *HMV POP 873*	41		3

JUNIOR CAMPBELL

UK, male vocalist (William Campbell). See Marmalade — **18**

Date	Title / Label	Peak	Wks at No.1	Wks on Chart
14 Oct 72	**HALLELUJAH FREEDOM** *Deram DM 364*	10		9
2 Jun 73	**SWEET ILLUSION** *Deram DM 387*	15		9

NAOMI CAMPBELL

UK, female vocalist/model. See Girls Of *FHM* — **3**

Date	Title / Label	Peak	Wks at No.1	Wks on Chart
24 Sep 94	**LOVE AND TEARS** *Epic 6608352*	40		3

PAT CAMPBELL

Ireland, male vocalist — **5**

Date	Title / Label	Peak	Wks at No.1	Wks on Chart
15 Nov 69	**THE DEAL** *Major Minor MM 648*	31		5

STAN CAMPBELL

UK, male vocalist. See Specials — **3**

Date	Title / Label	Peak	Wks at No.1	Wks on Chart
6 Jun 87	**YEARS GO BY** *WEA YZ 127*	65		3

TEVIN CAMPBELL

US, male vocalist — **2**

Date	Title / Label	Peak	Wks at No.1	Wks on Chart
18 Apr 92	**TELL ME WHAT YOU WANT ME TO DO** *Qwest W 0102*	63		2

CAN

Germany, male vocal/instrumental group — **10**

Date	Title / Label	Peak	Wks at No.1	Wks on Chart
28 Aug 76	**I WANT MORE** *Virgin VS 153*	26		10

Silver-selling ● Gold-selling ● Platinum-selling (x multiples) ✪ US No.1 ★ Peak Position Weeks at No.1 Weeks on Chart

CANDIDO
Cuba, male percussionist (Candido Camero) **3**

Date	Title / Label	Peak Position	Weeks at No.1	Weeks on Chart
18 Jul 81	**JINGO** *Excalibur EXC 102*	55		3

CANDLEWICK GREEN
UK, male vocal/instrumental group **8**

Date	Title / Label	Peak Position	Weeks at No.1	Weeks on Chart
23 Feb 74	**WHO DO YOU THINK YOU ARE** *Decca F 13480*	21		8

CANDY FLIP
UK, male vocal/production duo – Daniel 'Dizzy Dee' Mould & Richard Anderson-Peet **14**

Date	Title / Label	Peak Position	Weeks at No.1	Weeks on Chart
17 Mar 90	**STRAWBERRY FIELDS FOREVER** *Debut DEBT 3092*	3		10
14 Jul 90	**THIS CAN BE REAL** *Debut DEBT 3099*	60		4

CANDY GIRLS
UK, male/female instrumental/production duo. See Clergy, Dorothy, Hi-Gate, Paul Masterson presents Sushi, Sleazesisters, Yomanda **10**

Date	Title / Label	Peak Position	Weeks at No.1	Weeks on Chart
30 Sep 95	**FEE FI FO FUM** *VC Recordings VCRD 1* FEATURING SWEET PUSSY PAULINE	23		4
24 Feb 96	**WHAM BAM** *VC Recordings VCRD 6* FEATURING SWEET PUSSY PAULINE	20		4
7 Dec 96	**I WANT CANDY** *Feverpitch CDFVR 1013* FEATURING VALERIE MALCOLM	30		2

CANDYLAND
UK, male vocal/instrumental group **1**

Date	Title / Label	Peak Position	Weeks at No.1	Weeks on Chart
9 Mar 91	**FOUNTAIN O' YOUTH** *Non Fiction YES 4*	72		1

CANDYSKINS
UK, male vocal/instrumental group **4**

Date	Title / Label	Peak Position	Weeks at No.1	Weeks on Chart
19 Oct 96	**MRS HOOVER** *Ultimate TOPP 051CD*	65		1
8 Feb 97	**MONDAY MORNING** *Ultimate TOPP 055CD*	34		2
3 May 97	**HANG MYSELF ON YOU** *Ultimate TOPP 059CD*	65		1

CANIBUS
US, male rapper (Germaine Williams) **3**

Date	Title / Label	Peak Position	Weeks at No.1	Weeks on Chart
27 Jun 98	**SECOND ROUND KO** *Universal UND 56198*	35		2
10 Oct 98	**HOW COME** *Interscope IND 95598* YOUSSOU N'DOUR & CANIBUS	52		1

CANNED HEAT
US, male vocal/instrumental group – Bob Hite, d. 6 Apr 1981, Adolfo De La Parra, Larry Taylor, Henry Vestine, d. 20 Oct 1997 (replaced by Harvey Mandel), & Alan Wilson, d. 3 Sep 1970 **41**

Date	Title / Label	Peak Position	Weeks at No.1	Weeks on Chart
24 Jul 68	**ON THE ROAD AGAIN** *Liberty LBS 15090*	8		15
1 Jan 69	**GOING UP THE COUNTRY** *Liberty LBF 15169*	19		10
17 Jan 70	**LET'S WORK TOGETHER** *Liberty LBF 15302*	2		15
11 Jul 70	**SUGAR BEE** *Liberty LBF 15350*	49		1

FREDDY CANNON
US, male vocalist (Freddy Picariello) **54**

Date	Title / Label	Peak Position	Weeks at No.1	Weeks on Chart
14 Aug 59	**TALLAHASSEE LASSIE** *Top Rank JAR 135*	17		8
1 Jan 60	**WAY DOWN YONDER IN NEW ORLEANS** *Top Rank JAR 247*	3		18
5 Mar 60	**CALIFORNIA HERE I COME** *Top Rank JAR 309*	25		3
17 Mar 60	**INDIANA** *Top Rank JAR 309*	42		1
19 May 60	**THE URGE** *Top Rank JAR 369*	18		10
20 Apr 61	**MUSKRAT RAMBLE** *Top Rank JAR 548*	32		5
28 Jun 62	**PALISADES PARK** *Stateside SS 101*	20		9

CANTAMUS GIRLS CHOIR
UK, female choir **1**

Date	Title / Label	Peak Position	Weeks at No.1	Weeks on Chart
31 Dec 05	**EVERYBODY'S GOTTA LEARN SOMETIME** *EMI Classics 3497582*	73		1

BLU CANTRELL
US, female vocalist (Tiffany Cantrell) **32**

Date	Title / Label	Peak Position	Weeks at No.1	Weeks on Chart
24 Nov 01	**HIT 'EM UP STYLE (OOPS)** *Arista 74321891632*	12		9
19 Jul 03	**BREATHE (IMPORT)** *Arista 82876534002* FEATURING SEAN PAUL	59		3
9 Aug 03	**BREATHE** *Arista 82876545722* FEATURING SEAN PAUL ●	1	4	18
13 Dec 03	**MAKE ME WANNA SCREAM** *Arista 82876583432*	24		2

JIM CAPALDI
UK, male vocalist, d. 28 Jan 2005 (age 60). See Traffic **17**

Date	Title / Label	Peak Position	Weeks at No.1	Weeks on Chart
27 Jul 74	**IT'S ALL UP TO YOU** *Island WIP 6198*	27		6
25 Oct 75	**LOVE HURTS** *Island WIP 6246* ●	4		11

CAPERCAILLIE
UK/Ireland, male/female vocal/instrumental group **3**

Date	Title / Label	Peak Position	Weeks at No.1	Weeks on Chart
23 May 92	**A PRINCE AMONG ISLANDS EP** *Survival ZB 45393*	39		2
17 Jun 95	**DARK ALAN (AILEIN DUNN)** *Survival SURCD 55*	65		1

CAPPELLA
Italy, male producer (Gianfranco Bortolotti) & UK, female/male vocal/rap duo – Rodney Bishop & Kelly Overett (replaced by Allison Jordan*) **68**

Date	Title / Label	Peak Position	Weeks at No.1	Weeks on Chart
9 Apr 88	**PUSH THE BEAT/BAUHAUS** *Fast Globe FGL 1*	60		2
6 May 89	**HELYOM HALIB** *Music Man MMPS 7004*	11		9
23 Sep 89	**HOUSE ENGERY REVENGE** *Music Man MMPS 7009*	73		1
27 Apr 91	**EVERYBODY** *ffrr F 158*	66		1
18 Jan 92	**TAKE ME AWAY** *PWL Continental PWL 210* FEATURING LOLEATTA HOLLOWAY	25		5
3 Apr 93	**U GOT 2 KNOW** *Internal Dance IDC 1*	6		11
14 Aug 93	**U GOT 2 KNOW (REMIX)** *Internal Dance IDCR 2*	43		3
23 Oct 93	**U GOT 2 LET THE MUSIC** *Internal Dance IDC 3* ●	2		12
19 Feb 94	**MOVE ON BABY** *Internal Dance IDC 4*	7		7
18 Jun 94	**U & ME** *Internal Dance IDCC 6*	10		7
15 Oct 94	**MOVE IT UP/BIG BEAT** *Internal Dance IDC 7*	16		6
16 Sep 95	**TELL ME THE WAY** *Systematic SYSCD 17*	17		3
6 Sep 97	**BE MY BABY** *Nukleuz PSNC 0072*	53		1

CAPRICCIO
UK, male production duo **2**

Date	Title / Label	Peak Position	Weeks at No.1	Weeks on Chart
27 Mar 99	**EVERYBODY GET UP** *Defected DFECT 2CDS*	44		2

CAPRICE
US, female model/vocalist (Caprice Bourret) **5**

Date	Title / Label	Peak Position	Weeks at No.1	Weeks on Chart
4 Sep 99	**OH YEAH** *Virgin VSCDT 1745*	24		3
10 Mar 01	**ONCE AROUND THE SUN** *Virgin VSCDT 1750*	24		2

CAPRICORN
Belgium, male DJ/producer (Hans Weekhout) **1**

Date	Title / Label	Peak Position	Weeks at No.1	Weeks on Chart
29 Nov 97	**20 HZ (NEW FREQUENCIES)** *R&S RS 97126CD*	73		1

TONY CAPSTICK & THE CARLTON MAIN/FRICKLEY COLLIERY BAND
UK, male vocalist/comedian (Joseph Anthony Capstick), d. 23 Oct 2003 (age 59), & instrumental band **8**

Date	Title / Label	Peak Position	Weeks at No.1	Weeks on Chart
21 Mar 81	**THE SHEFFIELD GRINDER/CAPSTICK COMES HOME** *Dingles SID 27* ●	3		8

CAPTAIN
UK, male/female vocal/instrumental group **8**

Date	Title / Label	Peak Position	Weeks at No.1	Weeks on Chart
13 May 06	**BROKE** *EMI CDEM689*	34		2
5 Aug 06	**GLORIOUS** *EMI CDEM700*	30		4
25 Nov 06	**FRONTLINE** *EMI CDEM708*	62		1
17 May 08	**KEEP AN OPEN MIND** *EMI CDEM746*	53		1

CAPTAIN HOLLYWOOD PROJECT
US, male rapper (Tony Dawson-Harrison) **31**

Date	Title / Label	Peak Position	Weeks at No.1	Weeks on Chart
22 Sep 90	**I CAN'T STAND IT** *BCM BCMR 395* TWENTY 4 SEVEN FEATURING CAPTAIN HOLLYWOOD	7		10
24 Nov 90	**ARE YOU DREAMING** *BCM 07504* TWENTY 4 SEVEN FEATURING CAPTAIN HOLLYWOOD	17		10
27 Mar 93	**ONLY WITH YOU** *Pulse 8 CDLOSE 40*	67		1
6 Nov 93	**MORE AND MORE** *Pulse 8 CDLOSE 50*	23		5
5 Feb 94	**IMPOSSIBLE** *Pulse 8 CDLOSE 54*	29		3
11 Jun 94	**ONLY WITH YOU** *Pulse 8 CDLOSE 62*	61		1
1 Apr 95	**FLYING HIGH** *Pulse 8 CDLOSE 82*	58		1

CAPTAIN SENSIBLE

UK, male vocalist/guitarist (Ray Burns). See Damned

Date	Title / Label	Peak Position	Weeks at No.1	Weeks on Chart (31)
26 Jun 82	HAPPY TALK *A&M CAP 1* ●	1	2	8
14 Aug 82	WOT *A&M CAP 2*	26		7
24 Mar 84	GLAD IT'S ALL OVER/DAMNED ON 45 *A&M CAP 6*	6		10
28 Jul 84	THERE ARE MORE SNAKES THAN LADDERS *A&M CAP 7*	57		5
10 Dec 94	THE HOKEY COKEY *Have A Nice Day CDHOKEY 1*	71		1

CAPTAIN & TENNILLE

US, male keyboard player (Daryl Dragon) & female vocalist (Toni Tennille)

Date	Title / Label	Peak Position	Weeks at No.1	Weeks on Chart (24)
2 Aug 75	LOVE WILL KEEP US TOGETHER *A&M AMS 7165* ★	32		5
24 Jan 76	THE WAY I WANT TO TOUCH YOU *A&M AMS 7203*	28		6
4 Nov 78	YOU NEVER DONE IT LIKE THAT *A&M AMS 7384*	63		3
16 Feb 80	DO THAT TO ME ONE MORE TIME *Casablanca CAN 175* ★	7		10

IRENE CARA

US, female vocalist

Date	Title / Label	Peak Position	Weeks at No.1	Weeks on Chart (33)
3 Jul 82	FAME *RSO 90* ●	1	3	16
4 Sep 82	OUT HERE ON MY OWN *RSO 66*	58		3
4 Jun 83	FLASHDANCE...WHAT A FEELING *Casablanca CAN 1016* ● ★	2		14

CARAMBA

Sweden, male vocal/instrumental/production group

Date	Title / Label	Peak Position	Weeks at No.1	Weeks on Chart (6)
12 Nov 83	FEDORA (I'LL BE YOUR DAWG) *Billco BILL 101*	56		6

CARAVELLES

UK, female vocal duo – Lois Wilkinson & Andrea Simpson

Date	Title / Label	Peak Position	Weeks at No.1	Weeks on Chart (13)
8 Aug 63	YOU DON'T HAVE TO BE A BABY TO CRY *Decca F 11697*	6		13

CARBON/SILICON

UK, male vocal/instrumental duo

Date	Title / Label	Peak Position	Weeks at No.1	Weeks on Chart (1)
16 Jun 07	THE NEWS *Carbon Silicon CS1001*	59		1

CARDIGANS

Sweden, female/male vocal/instrumental group – Nina Persson*, Lars-Olof Johansson, Bengt Lagerberg, Magnus Sveningsson & Peter Svensson

Date	Title / Label	Peak Position	Weeks at No.1	Weeks on Chart (70)
17 Jun 95	CARNIVAL *Trampolene PZCD 345*	72		1
30 Sep 95	SICK & TIRED *Stockholm 5773112*	34		3
2 Dec 95	CARNIVAL *Trampolene PZCD 345*	35		2
17 Feb 96	RISE & SHINE *Trampolene 5778252*	29		2
21 Sep 96	LOVEFOOL *Stockholm 5752952*	21		4
7 Dec 96	BEEN IT *Stockholm 5759672*	56		1
3 May 97	LOVEFOOL *Stockholm 5710502* ●	2		13
6 Sep 97	YOUR NEW CUCKOO *Stockholm 5716632*	35		2
17 Oct 98	MY FAVOURITE GAME *Stockholm 5679912*	14		18
6 Mar 99	ERASE/REWIND *Stockholm 5635352*	7		9
24 Jul 99	HANGING AROUND *Stockholm 5612692*	17		4
25 Sep 99	BURNING DOWN THE HOUSE *Gut CDGUT 26* TOM JONES & THE CARDIGANS	7		7
22 Mar 03	FOR WHAT IT'S WORTH *Stockholm 0657232*	31		2
26 Jul 03	YOU'RE THE STORM *Stockholm 9809673*	74		1
15 Oct 05	I NEED SOME FINE WINE AND YOU, YOU NEED TO BE NICER *Stockholm 9874124*	59		1

CARE

UK, male vocal/instrumental duo

Date	Title / Label	Peak Position	Weeks at No.1	Weeks on Chart (4)
12 Nov 83	FLAMING SWORD *Arista KBIRD 2*	48		4

IAN CAREY PROJECT

US, male DJ/producer/multi-instrumentalist

Date	Title / Label	Peak Position	Weeks at No.1	Weeks on Chart (15)
15 Aug 09	GET SHAKY *3 Beat CXGLOBE1131*	9		15

MARIAH CAREY

US, female vocalist. Diva with a dynamic vocal range who was named the top US artist of the 1990s by *Billboard* magazine. The songwriter has had more No.1 singles in her homeland (18) than any other solo act. In the UK, 'All I Want For Christmas Is You' has made the Top 20 four times. See Helping Haiti

Date	Title / Label	Peak Position	Weeks at No.1	Weeks on Chart (376)
4 Aug 90	VISION OF LOVE *CBS 6559320* ★	9		12
10 Nov 90	LOVE TAKES TIME *CBS 6563647* ★	37		8
26 Jan 91	SOMEDAY *Columbia 6565837* ★	38		5
1 Jun 91	THERE'S GOT TO BE A WAY *Columbia 6569317*	54		3
5 Oct 91	EMOTIONS *Columbia 6574037* ★	17		9
11 Jan 92	CAN'T LET GO *Columbia 6576627*	20		7
18 Apr 92	MAKE IT HAPPEN *Columbia 6579417*	17		5
27 Jun 92	I'LL BE THERE *Columbia 6581377* ★	2		9
21 Aug 93	DREAMLOVER *Columbia 6594445* ★	9		10
6 Nov 93	HERO *Columbia 6598122* ★	7		15
19 Feb 94	WITHOUT YOU *Columbia 6599192* ●	1	4	14
18 Jun 94	ANYTIME YOU NEED A FRIEND *Columbia 6603542*	8		10
17 Sep 94	ENDLESS LOVE *Epic 6608062* LUTHER VANDROSS & MARIAH CAREY	3		16
10 Dec 94	ALL I WANT FOR CHRISTMAS IS YOU *Columbia 6610702* ●	2		8
23 Sep 95	FANTASY *Columbia 6624952* ● ★	4		11
9 Dec 95	ONE SWEET DAY *Columbia 6626035* & BOYZ II MEN ● ★	6		11
17 Feb 96	OPEN ARMS *Columbia 6629772*	4		6
22 Jun 96	ALWAYS BE MY BABY *Columbia 6633345* ★	3		10
6 Sep 97	HONEY *Columbia 6650192* ★	3		8
13 Dec 97	BUTTERFLY *Columbia 6653365*	22		6
13 Jun 98	MY ALL *Columbia 6660592* ★	4		8
19 Dec 98	WHEN YOU BELIEVE *Columbia 6667522* & WHITNEY HOUSTON	4		13
10 Apr 99	I STILL BELIEVE *Columbia 6670735*	16		7
6 Nov 99	HEARTBREAKER *Columbia 6683012* FEATURING JAY-Z ★	5		13
11 Mar 00	THANK GOD I FOUND YOU *Columbia 6690582* FEATURING JOE & 98o ★	10		10
30 Sep 00	AGAINST ALL ODDS (TAKE A LOOK AT ME NOW) *Columbia 6698872* FEATURING WESTLIFE ●	1	2	12
28 Jul 01	LOVERBOY *Virgin VUSCD 211* FEATURING CAMEO	12		5
29 Dec 01	NEVER TOO FAR/DON'T STOP (FUNKIN' 4 JAMAICA) *Virgin VUSCD 228* MARIAH CAREY/MARIAH CAREY FEATURING MYSTIKAL	32		4
30 Nov 02	THROUGH THE RAIN *Mercury 0638072*	8		8
5 Apr 03	BOY (I NEED YOU) *Def Jam 0779282* FEATURING CAM'RON	17		6
7 Jun 03	I KNOW WHAT YOU WANT *J Records 82876528292* BUSTA RHYMES & MARIAH CAREY	3		13
9 Apr 05	IT'S LIKE THAT *Def Jam 9881337*	4		11
16 Jul 05	WE BELONG TOGETHER *Def Jam 9883483* ★	2		18
15 Oct 05	GET YOUR NUMBER/SHAKE IT OFF *Def Jam 9886375*	9		8
24 Dec 05	DON'T FORGET ABOUT US *Def Jam/Island 9889761* ★	11		7
10 Jun 06	SAY SOMETHIN' *Mercury 9885446*	27		4
1 Dec 07	ALL I WANT FOR CHRISTMAS IS YOU *Columbia 6610702*	4		6
29 Dec 07	WHEN YOU BELIEVE *Columbia 6667522* & WHITNEY HOUSTON	65		1
12 Apr 08	TOUCH MY BODY *Def Jam 1766285* ★	5		11
31 May 08	BYE BYE *Def Jam 1774467*	30		9
22 Nov 08	ALL I WANT FOR CHRISTMAS IS YOU *Columbia 6610702*	12		7
22 Nov 08	HERO *Columbia USSM19303171*	67		1
5 Sep 09	OBSESSED *Mercury USUM70973055*	52		2
5 Dec 09	I WANT TO KNOW WHAT LOVE IS *Mercury USUM70984045*	19		3
5 Dec 09	ALL I WANT FOR CHRISTMAS IS YOU *Columbia 6610702*	18		5
5 Dec 09	OBSESSED *Mercury USUM70973055*	62		1

Top 3 Best-Selling Singles

	Title	Approximate Sales
1	ALL I WANT FOR CHRISTMAS IS YOU	670,000
2	WITHOUT YOU	445,000
3	AGAINST ALL ODDS	370,000

BELINDA CARLISLE

US, female vocalist. See Go-Go's

Date	Title / Label	Peak Position	Weeks at No.1	Weeks on Chart (145)
12 Dec 87	HEAVEN IS A PLACE ON EARTH *Virgin VS 1036* ● ★	1	2	14
27 Feb 88	I GET WEAK *Virgin VS 1046*	10		9
7 May 88	CIRCLE IN THE SAND *Virgin VS 1074*	4		11
6 Aug 88	MAD ABOUT YOU *IRS IRM 118*	67		3
10 Sep 88	WORLD WITHOUT YOU *Virgin VS 1114*	34		6
10 Dec 88	LOVE NEVER DIES... *Virgin VS 1150*	54		5
7 Oct 89	LEAVE A LIGHT ON *Virgin VS 1210* ●	4		10
9 Dec 89	LA LUNA *Virgin VS 1230*	38		6
24 Feb 90	RUNAWAY HORSES *Virgin VS 1244*	40		5
26 May 90	VISION OF YOU *Virgin VS 1264*	41		4
13 Oct 90	(WE WANT) THE SAME THING *Virgin VS 1219*	6		10
22 Dec 90	SUMMER RAIN *Virgin VS 1323*	23		10
20 Apr 91	VISION OF YOU *Virgin VS 1264*	71		1
28 Sep 91	LIVE YOUR LIFE BE FREE *Virgin VS 1370*	12		7

Silver-selling ○ · Gold-selling ● · Platinum-selling (x multiples) · US No.1 ★ · Peak Position · Weeks at No.1 · Weeks on Chart

Date	Title	Peak Position	Weeks at No.1	Weeks on Chart
16 Nov 91	**DO YOU FEEL LIKE I FEEL** *Virgin VS 1383*	29		4
11 Jan 92	**HALF THE WORLD** *Virgin VS 1388*	35		4
29 Aug 92	**LITTLE BLACK BOOK** *Virgin VS 1428*	28		5
25 Sep 93	**BIG SCARY ANIMAL** *Virgin VSCDT 1472*	12		6
27 Nov 93	**LAY DOWN YOUR ARMS** *Virgin VSDG 1476*	27		6
13 Jul 96	**IN TOO DEEP** *Chrysalis CDCHS 5033*	6		7
21 Sep 96	**ALWAYS BREAKING MY HEART** *Chrysalis CDCHS 5037*	8		6
30 Nov 96	**LOVE IN THE KEY OF C** *Chrysalis CDCHS 5044*	20		3
1 Mar 97	**CALIFORNIA** *Chrysalis CDCHSS 5047*	31		2
27 Nov 99	**ALL GOD'S CHILDREN** *Virgin VSCDT 1756*	66		1

BOB CARLISLE
US, male vocalist — 2

Date	Title	Peak Position	Weeks at No.1	Weeks on Chart
30 Aug 97	**BUTTERFLY KISSES** *Jive JIVECD 249*	56		2

CARLTON
UK, male vocalist (Carlton McCarthy) — 3

Date	Title	Peak Position	Weeks at No.1	Weeks on Chart
16 Feb 91	**LOVE AND PAIN** *Smith & Mighty SNM 4*	56		2
1 Apr 95	**1 TO 1 RELIGION** *Stoned Heights BRCD 313* BOMB THE BASS FEATURING CARLTON	53		1

CARL CARLTON
US, male vocalist — 8

Date	Title	Peak Position	Weeks at No.1	Weeks on Chart
18 Jul 81	**SHE'S A BAD MAMA JAMA (SHE'S BUILT, SHE'S STACKED)** *20th Century TC 2488*	34		8

VANESSA CARLTON
US, female vocalist/pianist — 23

Date	Title	Peak Position	Weeks at No.1	Weeks on Chart
3 Aug 02	**A THOUSAND MILES** *A&M 4977542*	6		13
30 Nov 02	**ORDINARY DAY** *A&M 4978132*	53		1
15 Feb 03	**BIG YELLOW TAXI** *Geffen 4978492* COUNTING CROWS FEATURING VANESSA CARLTON	16		9

CARMEL
UK, female/male vocal/instrumental trio — 19

Date	Title	Peak Position	Weeks at No.1	Weeks on Chart
6 Aug 83	**BAD DAY** *London LON 29*	15		9
11 Feb 84	**MORE, MORE, MORE** *London LON 44*	23		7
14 Jun 86	**SALLY** *London LON 90*	60		3

ERIC CARMEN
US, male vocalist — 7

Date	Title	Peak Position	Weeks at No.1	Weeks on Chart
10 Apr 76	**ALL BY MYSELF** *Arista 42*	12		7

KIM CARNEGIE
UK, female vocalist — 1

Date	Title	Peak Position	Weeks at No.1	Weeks on Chart
19 Jan 91	**JAZZ RAP** *Best ZB 44085*	73		1

KIM CARNES
US, female vocalist — 15

Date	Title	Peak Position	Weeks at No.1	Weeks on Chart
9 May 81	**BETTE DAVIS' EYES** *EMI America EA 121* ★	10		9
8 Aug 81	**DRAW OF THE CARDS** *EMI America EA 125*	49		4
9 Oct 82	**VOYEUR** *EMI America EA 143*	68		2

CARNIVAL FEATURING RIP VS RED RAT
UK/Jamaica, male vocal/production trio — 1

Date	Title	Peak Position	Weeks at No.1	Weeks on Chart
12 Sep 98	**ALL OF THE GIRLS (ALL AI-DI-GIRL DEM)** *Pepper 0530072*	51		1

CAROLINA LIAR
US, male vocal/instrumental group — 3

Date	Title	Peak Position	Weeks at No.1	Weeks on Chart
13 Jun 09	**SHOW ME WHAT I'M LOOKING AT** *Atlantic AT0341CD*	31		3

RENATO CAROSONE & HIS SEXTET
Italy, male vocalist, d. 27 Apr 2001 (age 81) — 1

Date	Title	Peak Position	Weeks at No.1	Weeks on Chart
4 Jul 58	**TORERO – CHA CHA CHA** *Parlophone R 4433*	25		1

MARY CHAPIN CARPENTER
US, female vocalist/guitarist — 6

Date	Title	Peak Position	Weeks at No.1	Weeks on Chart
20 Nov 93	**HE THINKS HE'LL KEEP HER** *Columbia 6598632*	71		1
7 Jan 95	**ONE COOL REMOVE** *Columbia 6611342* SHAWN COLVIN WITH MARY CHAPIN CARPENTER	40		3
3 Jun 95	**SHUT UP AND KISS ME** *Columbia 6613675*	35		2

CARPENTERS
US, female/male vocal/instrumental duo – Karen Carpenter, d. 4 Feb 1983, & Richard Carpenter — 173

Date	Title	Peak Position	Weeks at No.1	Weeks on Chart
5 Sep 70	**(THEY LONG TO BE) CLOSE TO YOU** *A&M AMS 800* ★	6		18
9 Jan 71	**WE'VE ONLY JUST BEGUN** *A&M AMS 813*	28		7
18 Sep 71	**SUPERSTAR/FOR ALL WE KNOW** *A&M AMS 864*	18		13
1 Jan 72	**MERRY CHRISTMAS DARLING** *A&M AME 601*	45		1
23 Sep 72	**I WON'T LAST A DAY WITHOUT YOU/GOODBYE TO LOVE** *A&M AMS 7023*	9		16
7 Jul 73	**YESTERDAY ONCE MORE** *A&M AMS 7073* ○	2		17
20 Oct 73	**TOP OF THE WORLD** *A&M AMS 7086* ○ ★	5		18
2 Mar 74	**JAMBALAYA (ON THE BAYOU)/MR GUDER** *A&M AMS 7098*	12		11
8 Jun 74	**I WON'T LAST A DAY WITHOUT YOU** *A&M AMS 7111*	32		5
18 Jan 75	**PLEASE MR. POSTMAN** *A&M AMS 7141* ○ ★	2		12
19 Apr 75	**ONLY YESTERDAY** *A&M AMS 7159*	7		10
30 Aug 75	**SOLITAIRE** *A&M AMS 7187*	32		5
20 Dec 75	**SANTA CLAUS IS COMIN' TO TOWN** *A&M AMS 7144*	37		4
27 Mar 76	**THERE'S A KIND OF HUSH (ALL OVER THE WORLD)** *A&M AMS 7219*	22		6
3 Jul 76	**I NEED TO BE IN LOVE** *A&M AMS 7238*	36		5
8 Oct 77	**CALLING OCCUPANTS OF INTERPLANETARY CRAFT (THE RECOGNISED ANTHEM OF WORLD CONTACT DAY)** *A&M AMS 7318*	9		9
11 Feb 78	**SWEET SWEET SMILE** *A&M AMS 7327*	40		4
22 Oct 83	**MAKE BELIEVE IT'S YOUR FIRST TIME** *A&M AM 147*	60		3
8 Dec 90	**MERRY CHRISTMAS DARLING/(THEY LONG TO BE) CLOSE TO YOU** *A&M AM 716*	25		5
13 Feb 93	**RAINY DAYS AND MONDAYS** *A&M AMCD 0180*	63		2
24 Dec 94	**TRYIN' TO GET THE FEELING AGAIN** *A&M 5807612*	44		2

CARPET BOMBERS FOR PEACE
UK/US, male/female vocal/instrumental group — 1

Date	Title	Peak Position	Weeks at No.1	Weeks on Chart
5 Apr 03	**SALT IN THE WOUND** *Jungle JUNG 066CD*	67		1

JOE 'FINGERS' CARR
US, male pianist (Lou Busch), d. 19 Sep 1979 (age 69) — 5

Date	Title	Peak Position	Weeks at No.1	Weeks on Chart
29 Jun 56	**PORTUGUESE WASHERWOMAN** *Capitol CL 14587*	20		5

LINDA CARR
US, female vocalist — 12

Date	Title	Peak Position	Weeks at No.1	Weeks on Chart
12 Jul 75	**HIGHWIRE** *Chelsea 2005 025* & THE LOVE SQUAD	15		8
5 Jun 76	**SOLD MY ROCK 'N' ROLL (GAVE IT FOR FUNKY SOUL)** *Spark SRL 1139* LINDA & THE FUNKY BOYS	36		4

LUCY CARR
UK, female vocalist — 3

Date	Title	Peak Position	Weeks at No.1	Weeks on Chart
25 Jan 03	**MISSING YOU** *Lickin LICKINCD 001*	28		2
9 Aug 03	**THIS IS GOODBYE** *Lickin LICKINCX 002*	41		1

PEARL CARR & TEDDY JOHNSON
UK, male/female vocal duo — 19

Date	Title	Peak Position	Weeks at No.1	Weeks on Chart
20 Mar 59	**SING LITTLE BIRDIE** *Columbia DB 4275*	12		8
6 Apr 61	**HOW WONDERFUL TO KNOW** *Columbia DB 4603*	23		11

SUZI CARR
US, female vocalist — 1

Date	Title	Peak Position	Weeks at No.1	Weeks on Chart
8 Oct 94	**ALL OVER ME** *Cowboy RODEO 947CD*	45		1

VALERIE CARR
US, female vocalist — 2

Date	Title	Peak Position	Weeks at No.1	Weeks on Chart
4 Jul 58	**WHEN THE BOYS TALK ABOUT THE GIRLS** *Columbia DB 4131*	29		2

VIKKI CARR
US, female vocalist (Florencia Bisenta de Casillas Martinez Cardona) — 26

Date	Title	Peak	Wks at No.1	Wks
1 Jun 67	**IT MUST BE HIM (SEUL SUR SON ETOILE)** *Liberty LIB 55917*	2		20
30 Aug 67	**THERE I GO** *Liberty LBF 15022*	50		1
12 Mar 69	**WITH PEN IN HAND** *Liberty LBF 15166*	39		5

RAFFAELLA CARRA
Italy, female vocalist (Raffaella Pelloni) — 12

Date	Title	Peak	Wks at No.1	Wks
15 Apr 78	**DO IT DO IT AGAIN** *Epic EPC 6094*	9		12

PAUL CARRACK
UK, male vocalist. See Ace, Mike + The Mechanics, Squeeze — 18

Date	Title	Peak	Wks at No.1	Wks
16 May 87	**WHEN YOU WALK IN THE ROOM** *Chrysalis CHS 3109*	48		5
18 Mar 89	**DON'T SHED A TEAR** *Chrysalis CHS 3166*	60		3
6 Jan 96	**EYES OF BLUE** *IRS CDEIRS 192*	40		4
6 Apr 96	**HOW LONG?** *IRS CDEIRS 193*	32		5
24 Aug 96	**EYES OF BLUE (REMIX)** *IRS CDEIRS 194*	45		1

JOSE CARRERAS
Spain, male vocalist — 19

Date	Title	Peak	Wks at No.1	Wks
11 Jul 92	**AMIGOS PARA SIEMPRE (FRIENDS FOR LIFE)** *Really Useful RUR 10* & SARAH BRIGHTMAN	11		11
30 Jul 94	**LIBIAMO/LA DONNA E MOBILE** *Teldec YZ 843CD* JOSE CARRERAS, PLACIDO DOMINGO & LUCIANO PAVAROTTI	21		4
25 Jul 98	**YOU'LL NEVER WALK ALONE** *Decca 4607982* CARRERAS/DOMINGO/PAVAROTTI WITH MEHTA	35		4

TIA CARRERE
US, female vocalist/actor (Althea Janairo) — 6

Date	Title	Peak	Wks at No.1	Wks
30 May 92	**BALLROOM BLITZ** *Reprise W 0105*	26		6

JIM CARREY
Canada, male actor/vocalist — 3

Date	Title	Peak	Wks at No.1	Wks
21 Jan 95	**CUBAN PETE** *Columbia 6606625*	31		3

CARRIE
US/UK, male vocal/instrumental group — 2

Date	Title	Peak	Wks at No.1	Wks
14 Mar 98	**MOLLY** *Island CID 687*	56		1
9 May 98	**CALIFORNIA SCREAMIN'** *Island CID 694*	55		1

DINA CARROLL
UK, female vocalist (Geraldine Carroll) — 99

Date	Title	Peak	Wks at No.1	Wks
2 Feb 91	**IT'S TOO LATE** *Mercury ITM 3* QUARTZ INTRODUCING DINA CARROLL	8		14
15 Jun 91	**NAKED LOVE (JUST SAY YOU WANT ME)** *Mercury ITM 4* QUARTZ & DINA CARROLL	39		3
11 Jul 92	**AIN'T NO MAN** *A&M AM 0001*	16		8
10 Oct 92	**SPECIAL KIND OF LOVE** *A&M AM 0088*	16		5
5 Dec 92	**SO CLOSE** *A&M AM 0101*	20		8
27 Feb 93	**THIS TIME** *A&M AMCD 0184*	23		6
15 May 93	**EXPRESS** *A&M 5802632*	12		6
16 Oct 93	**DON'T BE A STRANGER** *A&M 5803892* ●	3		13
11 Dec 93	**THE PERFECT YEAR** *A&M 5804812* ●	5		11
28 Sep 96	**ESCAPING** *Mercury DCCD 1*	3		8
21 Dec 96	**ONLY HUMAN** *Mercury DCCD 2*	33		4
24 Oct 98	**ONE, TWO, THREE** *1st Avenue MERCD 514*	16		4
24 Jul 99	**WITHOUT LOVE** *1st Avenue FESCDD 57*	13		7
16 Jun 01	**SOMEONE LIKE YOU** *1st Avenue 5689072*	38		2

RON CARROLL
US, male vocalist/DJ/producer — 3

Date	Title	Peak	Wks at No.1	Wks
4 Mar 00	**LUCKY STAR** *Virgin DINSD 198* SUPERFUNK FEATURING RON CARROLL	42		1
28 Apr 01	**MY LOVE** *Scorpio Music 1928112* KLUSTER FEATURING RON CARROLL	73		1
11 Oct 08	**WHAT A WONDERFUL WORLD** *Defected/ Positiva CDTIV275* AXWELL & BOB SINCLAR FEATURING RON CARROLL	48		1

RONNIE CARROLL
UK, male vocalist (Ronald Cleghorn) — 50

Date	Title	Peak	Wks at No.1	Wks
27 Jul 56	**WALK HAND IN HAND** *Philips PB 605*	13		8
29 Mar 57	**THE WISDOM OF A FOOL** *Philips PB 667*	20		2
31 Mar 60	**FOOTSTEPS** *Philips PB 1004*	36		3
22 Feb 62	**RING A DING GIRL** *Philips PB 1222*	46		3
2 Aug 62	**ROSES ARE RED** *Philips 326532 BF*	3		16
15 Nov 62	**IF ONLY TOMORROW** *Philips 326550 BF*	33		4
7 Mar 63	**SAY WONDERFUL THINGS** *Philips 326574 BF*	6		14

JASPER CARROTT
UK, male comedian/vocalist (Bob Davies) — 15

Date	Title	Peak	Wks at No.1	Wks
16 Aug 75	**FUNKY MOPED/MAGIC ROUNDABOUT** *DJM DJS 388* ●	5		15

CARS
US, male vocal/instrumental group – Ric Okasek, Elliot Easton, Greg Hawkes, Benjamin Orr & David Robinson — 51

Date	Title	Peak	Wks at No.1	Wks
11 Nov 78	**MY BEST FRIEND'S GIRL** *Elektra K 12301*	3		10
17 Feb 79	**JUST WHAT I NEEDED** *Elektra K 12312*	17		10
28 Jul 79	**LET'S GO** *Elektra K 12371*	51		4
5 Jun 82	**SINCE YOU'RE GONE** *Elektra K 13177*	37		4
29 Sep 84	**DRIVE** *Elektra E 9706* ●	5		11
3 Aug 85	**DRIVE** *Elektra E 9706* ●	4		12

ALEX CARTANA
Spain, female vocalist (Alexandra Cartana-Marks) — 8

Date	Title	Peak	Wks at No.1	Wks
6 Sep 03	**SHAKE IT (MOVE A LITTLE CLOSER)** *Credence CDCRED 039* LEE CABRERA FEATURING ALEX CARTANA	16		6
8 May 04	**HEY PAPI** *EMI PAP1CDS*	34		2

AARON CARTER
US, male vocalist — 33

Date	Title	Peak	Wks at No.1	Wks
29 Nov 97	**CRUSH ON YOU** *Ultra Pop 6099605 ULT*	9		8
7 Feb 98	**CRAZY LITTLE PARTY GIRL** *Ultra Pop 0099645 ULT*	7		6
28 Mar 98	**I'M GONNA MISS YOU FOREVER** *Ultra Pop 0099725 ULT*	24		5
4 Jul 98	**SURFIN' USA** *Ultra Pop 0099805 ULT*	18		5
16 Sep 00	**I WANT CANDY** *Jive 9250892*	31		3
28 Oct 00	**AARON'S PARTY (COME GET IT)** *Jive 9251272*	51		2
13 Apr 02	**LEAVE IT UP TO ME** *Jive 9253262*	22		4

BRAD CARTER
UK, male vocalist/producer. See Ruff Driverz — 1

Date	Title	Peak	Wks at No.1	Wks
23 Oct 04	**MORNING ALWAYS COMES TOO SOON** *Positiva CDTIVS210*	48		1

CLARENCE CARTER
US, male vocalist — 13

Date	Title	Peak	Wks at No.1	Wks
10 Oct 70	**PATCHES** *Atlantic 2091 030*	2		13

NICK CARTER
US, male vocalist. See Backstreet Boys — 3

Date	Title	Peak	Wks at No.1	Wks
19 Oct 02	**HELP ME** *Jive 9254332*	17		3

CARTER – THE UNSTOPPABLE SEX MACHINE
UK, male vocal/instrumental duo – Leslie 'Fruitbat' Carter & James 'Jim Bob' Morrison — 46

Date	Title	Peak	Wks at No.1	Wks
26 Jan 91	**BLOODSPORTS FOR ALL** *Rough Trade R 20112687*	48		2
22 Jun 91	**SHERIFF FATMAN** *Big Cat USM 1*	23		7
26 Oct 91	**AFTER THE WATERSHED** *Big Cat USM 2*	11		5
11 Jan 92	**RUBBISH** *Big Cat USM 3*	14		5
25 Apr 92	**THE ONLY LIVING BOY IN NEW CROSS** *Big Cat USM 4*	7		5
4 Jul 92	**DO RE ME SO FAR SO GOOD** *Chrysalis USM 5*	22		3
28 Nov 92	**THE IMPOSSIBLE DREAM** *Chrysalis USM 6*	21		3
4 Sep 93	**LEAN ON ME I WON'T FALL OVER** *Chrysalis CDUSM 7*	16		3
16 Oct 93	**LENNY AND TERENCE** *Chrysalis CDUSM 8*	40		2
12 Mar 94	**GLAM ROCK COPS** *Chrysalis CDUSMS 10*	24		3
19 Nov 94	**LET'S GET TATTOOS** *Chrysalis CDUSMS 30*	30		3
4 Feb 95	**THE YOUNG OFFENDER'S MUM** *Chrysalis CDUSMS 12*	34		3
30 Sep 95	**BORN ON THE 5TH OF NOVEMBER** *Chrysalis CDUSM 13*	35		2

CARTER TWINS
Ireland, male vocal duo — 1

Date	Title	Peak	Wks at No.1	Wks
8 Mar 97	**THE TWELFTH OF NEVER/TOO RIGHT TO BE WRONG** *RCA 74321453082*	61		1

JUNIOR CARTIER
UK, male producer (Jon Carter) — 1

Date	Title	Peak Position	Weeks at No.1	Weeks on Chart
6 Nov 99	**WOMEN BEAT THEIR MEN** *Nucamp CAMPD 3X*	70		1

CARTOONS
Denmark, male/female vocal/instrumental group – Boop, Buzz, Puddy, Shooter, Sponge & Toonie — 30

Date	Title	Peak Position	Weeks at No.1	Weeks on Chart
3 Apr 99	**WITCH DOCTOR** *Flex TOONCD 1* ●	2		13
19 Jun 99	**DOODAH** *Flex CDTOON 002*	7		12
4 Sep 99	**AISY WAISY** *Flex CDTOONS 003*	16		5

RICHARD CARTRIDGE
UK, male vocalist — 1

Date	Title	Peak Position	Weeks at No.1	Weeks on Chart
25 Sep 04	**I'VE FOUND LOVE AGAIN** *Springboard Media SMCDSRC001*	50		1

CARVELLS
UK, male vocal/instrumental group — 4

Date	Title	Peak Position	Weeks at No.1	Weeks on Chart
26 Nov 77	**THE L.A. RUN** *Creole CR 143*	31		4

CASCADA
Germany, female/male vocal/production group – Natalie Horler, Yann Pfeiffer (Yanou) & Manuel Reuter (DJ Manian) — 110

Date	Title	Peak Position	Weeks at No.1	Weeks on Chart
5 Aug 06	**EVERYTIME WE TOUCH** *All Around The World CDGLOBE537*	2		39
16 Dec 06	**TRULY MADLY DEEPLY** *All Around The World CDGLOBE622*	4		16
17 Feb 07	**I NEED A MIRACLE** *Ministry Of Sound PDT20CDS*	8		12
7 Jul 07	**NEVER ENDING DREAM** *All Around The World CDGLOBE70*	46		2
15 Dec 07	**WHAT HURTS THE MOST** *All Around The World CDGLOBE790*	10		18
5 Apr 08	**WHAT DO YOU WANT FROM ME?** *All Around The World CDGLOBE797*	51		1
9 Aug 08	**BECAUSE THE NIGHT** *All Around The World CDGLOBE942*	28		4
11 Jul 09	**EVACUATE THE DANCEFLOOR** *All Around The World CDGLOBE1179*	1	2	17
24 Oct 09	**DANGEROUS** *All Around The World CDGLOBE1180*	67		1

CASCADES
US, male vocal/instrumental group – John Gummoe, Eddie Snyder, David Stevens, David Wilson, d. 14 Nov 2000, & David Zabo — 16

Date	Title	Peak Position	Weeks at No.1	Weeks on Chart
28 Feb 63	**RHYTHM OF THE RAIN** *Warner Brothers WB 88*	5		16

CASE
US, male rapper (Case Woodard) — 15

Date	Title	Peak Position	Weeks at No.1	Weeks on Chart
21 Sep 96	**TOUCH ME TEASE ME** *Def Jam DEFCD 18* FEATURING FOXXY BROWN	26		3
10 Nov 01	**LIVIN' IT UP** *Def Jam 5888142* JA RULE FEATURING CASE	27		4
3 Aug 02	**LIVIN' IT UP (REMIX)** *Def Jam 0639782* JA RULE FEATURING CASE	5		8

ED CASE
UK, male producer (Edward Makromallies) — 5

Date	Title	Peak Position	Weeks at No.1	Weeks on Chart
21 Oct 00	**SOMETHING IN YOUR EYES** *Red Rose CDROSE 003*	38		2
15 Sep 01	**WHO?** *Columbia 6718302* & SWEETIE IRIE	29		2
20 Jul 02	**GOOD TIMES** *Columbia 6727672* & SKIN	49		1

NATALIE CASEY
UK, female vocalist/actor — 1

Date	Title	Peak Position	Weeks at No.1	Weeks on Chart
7 Jan 84	**CHICK CHICK CHICKEN** *Polydor CHICK 1*	72		1

JOHNNY CASH
US, male vocalist/guitarist (J R Cash), d. 12 Sep 2003 (age 71) — 62

Date	Title	Peak Position	Weeks at No.1	Weeks on Chart
3 Jun 65	**IT AIN'T ME, BABE** *CBS 201760*	28		8
6 Sep 69	**A BOY NAMED SUE** *CBS 4460*	4		19
23 May 70	**WHAT IS TRUTH** *CBS 4934*	21		11
15 Apr 72	**A THING CALLED LOVE** *CBS 7797* WITH THE EVANGEL TEMPLE CHOIR	4		14
3 Jul 76	**ONE PIECE AT A TIME** *CBS 4087* WITH THE TENNESSEE THREE	32		7
10 May 03	**HURT/PERSONAL JESUS** *American/Lost Highway 0779982*	42		1
15 Nov 03	**HURT/PERSONAL JESUS** *American/Lost Highway 0779982*	39		2

CA$HFLOW
US, male vocal/instrumental group — 8

Date	Title	Peak Position	Weeks at No.1	Weeks on Chart
24 May 86	**MINE ALL MINE/PARTY FREAK** *Club JAB 30*	15		8

CASHMERE
US, male vocal/instrumental trio — 11

Date	Title	Peak Position	Weeks at No.1	Weeks on Chart
19 Jan 85	**CAN I** *Fourth & Broadway BRW 19*	29		8
23 Mar 85	**WE NEED LOVE** *Fourth & Broadway BRW 22*	52		3

CASINO
UK, male vocal/production group — 2

Date	Title	Peak Position	Weeks at No.1	Weeks on Chart
17 May 97	**SOUND OF EDEN** *Worx WORXCD 006*	52		1
10 Jul 99	**ONLY YOU** *Pow! CDPOW 006*	72		1

CASINOS
US, male vocal group — 7

Date	Title	Peak Position	Weeks at No.1	Weeks on Chart
23 Feb 67	**THEN YOU CAN TELL ME GOODBYE** *President PT 123*	28		7

CASSIDY
US, male rapper (Barry Reese) — 18

Date	Title	Peak Position	Weeks at No.1	Weeks on Chart
29 May 04	**HOTEL** *J Records 82876618612* FEATURING R KELLY	3		14
25 Sep 04	**GET NO BETTER** *J Records 82876649282* FEATURING MASHONDA	24		4

DAVID CASSIDY
US, male vocalist. See Partridge Family — 109

Date	Title	Peak Position	Weeks at No.1	Weeks on Chart
8 Apr 72	**COULD IT BE FOREVER/CHERISH** *Bell 1224*	2		17
16 Sep 72	**HOW CAN I BE SURE** *Bell 1258*	1	2	11
25 Nov 72	**ROCK ME BABY** *Bell 1268*	11		9
24 Mar 73	**I'M A CLOWN/SOME KIND OF A SUMMER** *Bell MABEL 4*	3		12
13 Oct 73	**DAYDREAMER/THE PUPPY SONG** *Bell 1334*	1	3	15
11 May 74	**IF I DIDN'T CARE** *Bell 1350*	9		8
27 Jul 74	**PLEASE PLEASE ME** *Bell 1371*	16		6
5 Jul 75	**I WRITE THE SONGS/GET IT UP FOR LOVE** *RCA 2571*	11		8
25 Oct 75	**DARLIN'** *RCA 2622*	16		8
23 Feb 85	**THE LAST KISS** *Arista ARIST 589*	6		9
11 May 85	**ROMANCE (LET YOUR HEART GO)** *Arista ARIST 620*	54		6

EVA CASSIDY
US, female vocalist/guitarist, d. 2 Nov 1996 (age 33) — 15

Date	Title	Peak Position	Weeks at No.1	Weeks on Chart
21 Apr 01	**OVER THE RAINBOW** *Blix Street/Hot HIT 16*	42		9
11 Oct 03	**YOU TAKE MY BREATH AWAY** *Blix Street/Hot HIT 27*	54		1
22 Dec 07	**WHAT A WONDERFUL WORLD** *Dramatico TD001* & KATIE MELUA	1	1	4
26 Sep 09	**SONGBIRD** *Blix Street USA449845005*	56		1

CASSIE
US, female vocalist/model (Cassandra Ventura) — 35

Date	Title	Peak Position	Weeks at No.1	Weeks on Chart
19 Aug 06	**ME & U** *Bad Boy AT0251CD*	6		15
28 Oct 06	**LONG WAY 2 GO** *Bad Boy AT0262CD*	12		12
5 Apr 08	**IS IT YOU** *Bad Boy AT0311CD*	52		8

CASSIUS
France, DJ/production duo – Hubert Blanc-Francart & Philippe Zdar — 13

Date	Title	Peak Position	Weeks at No.1	Weeks on Chart
23 Jan 99	**CASSIUS 1999** *Virgin DINSD 177*	7		7
15 May 99	**FEELING FOR YOU** *Virgin DINSD 181*	16		4
20 Nov 99	**LA MOUCHE** *Virgin DINSD 188*	53		1
5 Oct 02	**THE SOUND OF VIOLENCE** *Virgin DINSD 241*	49		1

CAST
UK, male vocal/instrumental group – John Power, Keith O'Neill, Liam Tyson & Peter Wilkinson — 55

Date	Title	Peak Position	Weeks at No.1	Weeks on Chart
15 Jul 95	**FINETIME** *Polydor 5795072*	17		4
30 Sep 95	**ALRIGHT** *Polydor 5799272*	13		4
20 Jan 96	**SANDSTORM** *Polydor 5778732*	8		5
30 Mar 96	**WALKAWAY** *Polydor 5762852*	9		7
26 Oct 96	**FLYING** *Polydor 5754772*	4		5
5 Apr 97	**FREE ME** *Polydor 5736512*	7		7
28 Jun 97	**GUIDING STAR** *Polydor 5711732*	9		6
13 Sep 97	**LIVE THE DREAM** *Polydor 5716852*	7		5
15 Nov 97	**I'M SO LONELY** *Polydor 5690592*	14		3
8 May 99	**BEAT MAMA** *Polydor 5635952*	9		5
7 Aug 99	**MAGIC HOUR** *Polydor 5612272*	28		3
28 Jul 01	**DESERT DROUGHT** *Polydor 5871762*	45		1

CAST FROM CASUALTY
UK, male/female actors/vocal group **6**

Date	Title / Label	Peak	No.1	Weeks
14 Mar 98	**EVERLASTING LOVE** *warner.esp WESP 003CD*	5		6

CAST OF HIGH SCHOOL MUSICAL
US, male/female actors/vocal group **37**

Date	Title / Label	Peak	No.1	Weeks
30 Sep 06	**BREAKING FREE** *Walt Disney HSMCD01*	9		19
9 Dec 06	**WE'RE ALL IN THIS TOGETHER** *Walt Disney 3814510*	40		6
13 Jan 07	**STICK TO THE STATUS QUO** *Walt Disney USWD10527739*	74		1
28 Jul 07	**WHAT TIME IS IT** *Walt Disney 5016470 2*	20		6
6 Oct 07	**YOU ARE THE MUSIC IN ME** *Walt Disney 5075640 2*	26		3
6 Oct 07	**EVERYDAY** *Walt Disney USWD10732100 2*	59		1
8 Nov 08	**NOW OR NEVER** *Walt Disney USWD10834644 3*	41		1

CAST OF THE NEW ROCKY HORROR SHOW
UK, male/female actors/vocal group **1**

Date	Title / Label	Peak	No.1	Weeks
12 Dec 98	**THE TIMEWARP** *Damn It Janet DAMJAN 1CD*	57		1

ROY CASTLE
UK, male vocalist/trumpeter, d. 2 Sep 1994 (age 62) **3**

Date	Title / Label	Peak	No.1	Weeks
22 Dec 60	**LITTLE WHITE BERRY** *Philips PB 1087*	40		3

CASUALS
UK, male vocal/instrumental group – Howard Newcomb, Bob O'Brien, Alan Taylor & John Tebb **26**

Date	Title / Label	Peak	No.1	Weeks
14 Aug 68	**JESAMINE** *Decca F 22784*	2		18
4 Dec 68	**TOY** *Decca F 22852*	30		8

CAT
UK, male vocalist/actor (Danny John-Jules) **4**

Date	Title / Label	Peak	No.1	Weeks
23 Oct 93	**TONGUE TIED** *EMI CDEM 286*	17		4

CATATONIA
UK, female/male vocal/instrumental group – Cerys Matthews*, Paul Jones, Owen Powell, Aled Richards & Mark Roberts **58**

Date	Title / Label	Peak	No.1	Weeks
3 Feb 96	**SWEET CATATONIA** *Blanco Y Negro NEG 85CD*	61		1
4 May 96	**LOST CAT** *Blanco Y Negro NEG 88CD1*	41		1
7 Sep 96	**YOU'VE GOT A LOT TO ANSWER FOR** *Blanco Y Negro NEG 93CD1*	35		2
30 Nov 96	**BLEED** *Blanco Y Negro NEG 97CD1*	46		1
18 Oct 97	**I AM THE MOB** *Blanco Y Negro NEG 107CD*	40		2
31 Jan 98	**MULDER AND SCULLY** *Blanco Y Negro NEG 109CD*	3		10
2 May 98	**ROAD RAGE** *Blanco Y Negro NEG 112CD*	5		8
1 Aug 98	**STRANGE GLUE** *Blanco Y Negro NEG 113CD*	11		6
7 Nov 98	**GAME ON** *WEA NEG 114CD*	33		2
10 Apr 99	**DEAD FROM THE WAIST DOWN** *Blanco Y Negro NEG 115CD*	7		8
24 Jul 99	**LONDINIUM** *Blanco Y Negro NEG 117CD*	20		3
13 Nov 99	**KARAOKE QUEEN** *Blanco Y Negro NEG 119CD*	36		2
4 Aug 01	**STONE BY STONE** *Blanco Y Negro NEG 134CD*	19		4

CATCH
UK, male vocal/instrumental trio **7**

Date	Title / Label	Peak	No.1	Weeks
17 Nov 90	**FREE (C'MON)** *ffrr F 147*	70		1
11 Oct 97	**BINGO** *Virgin VSCDT 1656*	23		4
21 Feb 98	**DIVE IN** *Virgin VSCDT 1665*	44		2

CATHERINE WHEEL
UK, male vocal/instrumental group **12**

Date	Title / Label	Peak	No.1	Weeks
23 Nov 91	**BLACK METALLIC (EP)** *Fontana CW 1*	68		1
8 Feb 92	**BALLOON** *Fontana CW 2*	59		1
18 Apr 92	**I WANT TO TOUCH YOU** *Fontana CW 3*	35		2
9 Jan 93	**30TH CENTURY MAN** *Fontana CWCD 4*	47		2
10 Jul 93	**CRANK** *Fontana CWCD 5*	66		1
16 Oct 93	**SHOW ME MARY** *Fontana CWCDA 6*	62		1
5 Aug 95	**WAYDOWN** *Fontana CWCD 7*	67		1
13 Dec 97	**DELICIOUS** *Chrysalis CDCHS 5071*	53		1
28 Feb 98	**MA SOLITUDA** *Chrysalis CDCHS 5077*	53		1
2 May 98	**BROKEN NOSE** *Chrysalis CDCHS 5086*	48		1

LORRAINE CATO
UK, female vocalist **3**

Date	Title / Label	Peak	No.1	Weeks
6 Feb 93	**HOW CAN YOU TELL ME IT'S OVER** *Columbia 6587662*	46		2
3 Aug 96	**I WAS MADE TO LOVE YOU** *MCA MCSTD 40055*	41		1

CATS
UK, male instrumental group **2**

Date	Title / Label	Peak	No.1	Weeks
9 Apr 69	**SWAN LAKE** *BAF 1*	48		2

CATS UK
UK, male instrumental group **8**

Date	Title / Label	Peak	No.1	Weeks
6 Oct 79	**LUTON AIRPORT** *WEA K 18075*	22		8

NICK CAVE & THE BAD SEEDS
Australia/Germany/UK/US, male/female vocal/instrumental group **18**

Date	Title / Label	Peak	No.1	Weeks
11 Apr 92	**STRAIGHT TO YOU/JACK THE RIPPER** *Mute 140*	68		1
12 Dec 92	**WHAT A WONDERFUL WORLD** *Mute 151* & SHANE McGOWAN	72		1
9 Apr 94	**DO YOU LOVE ME** *Mute CDMUTE 160*	68		1
14 Oct 95	**WHERE THE WILD ROSES GROW** *Mute CDMUTE 185* & KYLIE MINOGUE	11		4
9 Mar 96	**HENRY LEE** *Mute CDMUTE 189* & PJ HARVEY	36		1
22 Feb 97	**INTO MY ARMS** *Mute CDMUTE 192*	53		1
31 May 97	**(ARE YOU) THE ONE THAT I'VE BEEN...** *Mute CDMUTE 206*	67		1
31 Mar 01	**AS I SAT SADLY BY HER SIDE** *Mute CDMUTE 249*	42		1
2 Jun 01	**FIFTEEN FEET OF PURE WHITE SNOW** *Mute CDMUTE 262*	52		1
8 Mar 03	**BRING IT ON** *Mute CDMUTE 265*	58		1
18 Sep 04	**NATURE BOY** *Mute CDMUTE 324*	37		2
27 Nov 04	**BREATHLESS/THERE SHE GOES MY BEAUTIFUL WORLD** *Mute CDMUTE329*	45		1
26 Mar 05	**GET READY FOR LOVE** *Atlantic AT0196CD*	62		1
1 Mar 08	**DIG, LAZARUS, DIG** *Mute CDMUTE377*	66		1

CAVE IN
US, male vocal/instrumental group **1**

Date	Title / Label	Peak	No.1	Weeks
31 May 03	**ANCHOR** *RCA 82876522992*	53		1

CAVEMAN
UK, male rap/production trio **2**

Date	Title / Label	Peak	No.1	Weeks
9 Mar 91	**I'M READY** *Profile PROF 330*	65		2

C.C.S.
UK, male vocal/instrumental collective – members included Alexis Korner, d. 1 Jan 1984, John Cameron, Roger Coulam, Herbie Flowers, Barry Morgan & Peter Thorup, d. 3 Aug 2007 **55**

Date	Title / Label	Peak	No.1	Weeks
31 Oct 70	**WHOLE LOTTA LOVE** *RAK 104*	13		13
27 Feb 71	**WALKIN'** *RAK 109*	7		16
4 Sep 71	**TAP TURNS ON THE WATER** *RAK 119*	5		13
4 Mar 72	**BROTHER** *RAK 126*	25		8
4 Aug 73	**THE BAND PLAYED THE BOOGIE** *RAK 154*	36		5

CECIL
UK, male vocal/instrumental group **2**

Date	Title / Label	Peak	No.1	Weeks
25 Oct 97	**HOSTAGE IN A FROCK** *Parlophone CDRS 6471*	68		1
28 Mar 98	**THE MOST TIRING DAY** *Parlophone CDRS 6490*	69		1

CELEDA
US, female vocalist (Victoria Sharpe) **5**

Date	Title / Label	Peak	No.1	Weeks
5 Sep 98	**MUSIC IS THE ANSWER (DANCING' & PRANCIN')** *Twisted UK TWCD 10038* DANNY TENAGLIA & CELEDA	36		3
12 Jun 99	**BE YOURSELF** *Twisted UK TWCD 10049*	61		1
23 Oct 99	**MUSIC IS THE ANSWER (REMIX)** *Twisted UK TWCD 10052* DANNY TENAGLIA & CELEDA	50		1

CELETIA
UK, female vocalist (Celetia Martin) **3**

Date	Title / Label	Peak	No.1	Weeks
11 Apr 98	**REWIND** *Big Life BLRD 142*	29		2
8 Aug 98	**RUNAWAY SKIES** *Big Life BLRD 144*	66		1

Silver-selling ● Gold-selling ● Platinum-selling (× multiples) ✱ US No.1 ★ Peak Position · Weeks at No.1 · Weeks on Chart

CENOGINERZ
Holland, male producer (Michel Pollen) — Weeks on Chart: 1

Date	Title / Label	Peak Position	Weeks at No.1	Weeks on Chart
2 Feb 02	**GIT DOWN** *Tripoli Trax TTRAX 081CD*	75		1

CENTORY
US/Germany, male rap/vocal/production group — Weeks on Chart: 1

Date	Title / Label	Peak Position	Weeks at No.1	Weeks on Chart
17 Dec 94	**POINT OF NO RETURN** *EMI CDEM 354*	67		1

CENTRAL LINE
UK, male vocal/instrumental group — Weeks on Chart: 30

Date	Title / Label	Peak Position	Weeks at No.1	Weeks on Chart
31 Jan 81	**(YOU KNOW) YOU CAN DO IT** *Mercury LINE 7*	67		3
15 Aug 81	**WALKING INTO SUNSHINE** *Mercury MER 78*	42		10
30 Jan 82	**DON'T TELL ME** *Mercury MER 90*	55		3
20 Nov 82	**YOU'VE SAID ENOUGH** *Mercury MER 117*	58		3
22 Jan 83	**NATURE BOY** *Mercury MER 131*	21		8
11 Jun 83	**SURPRISE SURPRISE** *Mercury MER 133*	48		3

CERRONE
France, male producer/multi-instrumentalist (Jean-Marc Cerrone) — Weeks on Chart: 21

Date	Title / Label	Peak Position	Weeks at No.1	Weeks on Chart
5 Mar 77	**LOVE IN C MINOR** *Atlantic K 10895*	31		4
29 Jul 78	**SUPERNATURE** *Atlantic K 11089* ●	8		12
13 Jan 79	**JE SUIS MUSIC** *CBS 6918*	39		4
10 Aug 96	**SUPERNATURE (REMIX)** *Encore CDCOR 013*	66		1

A CERTAIN RATIO
UK, male vocal/instrumental group — Weeks on Chart: 3

Date	Title / Label	Peak Position	Weeks at No.1	Weeks on Chart
16 Jun 90	**WON'T STOP LOVING YOU** *A&M ACR 540*	55		3

PETER CETERA
US, male vocalist/bass player. See Chicago — Weeks on Chart: 20

Date	Title / Label	Peak Position	Weeks at No.1	Weeks on Chart
2 Aug 86	**GLORY OF LOVE** *Full Moon W 8662* ● ★	3		13
21 Jun 97	**HARD TO SAY I'M SORRY** *LaFace 74321481482* AZ YET FEATURING PETER CETERA	7		7

FRANK CHACKSFIELD
UK, male orchestra leader, d. 9 Jun 1995 (age 81) — Weeks on Chart: 41

Date	Title / Label	Peak Position	Weeks at No.1	Weeks on Chart
3 Apr 53	**LITTLE RED MONKEY** *Parlophone R 3658* FRANK CHACKSFIELD'S TUNESMITHS, FEATURING JACK JORDAN – CLAVIOLINE	10		3
22 May 53	**TERRY'S THEME FROM 'LIMELIGHT'** *Decca F 10106*	2		24
12 Feb 54	**EBB TIDE** *Decca F 10122*	9		2
24 Feb 56	**IN OLD LISBON** *Decca F 10689*	15		4
18 May 56	**PORT AU PRINCE** *Decca F 10727* WINIFRED ATWELL & FRANK CHACKSFIELD	18		6
31 Aug 56	**DONKEY CART** *Decca F 10743*	26		2

CHAD & RYAN
US, male actors/vocal duo — Weeks on Chart: 1

Date	Title / Label	Peak Position	Weeks at No.1	Weeks on Chart
6 Oct 07	**I DON'T DANCE** *Walt Disney USWD10732097*	57		1

CHAIRLIFT
US, male/female vocal/instrumental group — Weeks on Chart: 2

Date	Title / Label	Peak Position	Weeks at No.1	Weeks on Chart
18 Oct 08	**BRUISES** *Columbia US28E0834204*	50		2

CHAIRMEN OF THE BOARD
US, male vocal group – 'General' Norman Johnson, Eddie Curtis, Harrison Kennedy & Danny Woods — Weeks on Chart: 77

Date	Title / Label	Peak Position	Weeks at No.1	Weeks on Chart
22 Aug 70	**GIVE ME JUST A LITTLE MORE TIME** *Invictus INV 501*	3		13
14 Nov 70	**YOU'VE GOT ME DANGLING ON A STRING** *Invictus INV 504*	5		13
20 Feb 71	**EVERYTHING'S TUESDAY** *Invictus INV 507*	12		9
15 May 71	**PAY TO THE PIPER** *Invictus INV 511*	34		7
4 Sep 71	**CHAIRMAN OF THE BOARD** *Invictus INV 516*	48		2
15 Jul 72	**WORKING ON A BUILDING OF LOVE** *Invictus INV 519*	20		8
7 Oct 72	**ELMO JAMES** *Invictus INV 524*	21		7
16 Dec 72	**I'M ON MY WAY TO A BETTER PLACE** *Invictus INV 527*	30		6
23 Jun 73	**FINDERS KEEPERS** *Invictus INV 530*	21		9
13 Sep 86	**LOVERBOY** *EMI EM 5585* FEATURING GENERAL JOHNSON	56		3

CHAKACHAS
Belgium, male/female vocal/instrumental group — Weeks on Chart: 8

Date	Title / Label	Peak Position	Weeks at No.1	Weeks on Chart
11 Jan 62	**TWIST TWIST** *RCA 1264*	48		1
27 May 72	**JUNGLE FEVER** *Polydor 2121 064*	29		7

GEORGE CHAKIRIS
US, male vocalist — Weeks on Chart: 1

Date	Title / Label	Peak Position	Weeks at No.1	Weeks on Chart
2 Jun 60	**HEART OF A SINGLE GIRL** *Triumph ROM 1010*	49		1

CHAKKA BOOM BANG
Holland, male instrumental/production group — Weeks on Chart: 1

Date	Title / Label	Peak Position	Weeks at No.1	Weeks on Chart
20 Jan 96	**TOSSING AND TURNING** *Hooj Choons HOOJCD 39*	57		1

CHAKRA
UK, male/female vocal/production trio. See Ascension, Essence, Lustral, Oxygen featuring Andrea Britton, Space Brothers — Weeks on Chart: 5

Date	Title / Label	Peak Position	Weeks at No.1	Weeks on Chart
18 Jan 97	**I AM** *WEA 091CD*	24		2
23 Aug 97	**HOME** *WEA 116CD2*	46		1
23 Oct 99	**LOVE SHINES THROUGH** *WEA 227CD*	67		1
26 Aug 00	**HOME (REMIX)** *WEA 266CD*	47		1

SUE CHALONER
UK, female vocalist — Weeks on Chart: 1

Date	Title / Label	Peak Position	Weeks at No.1	Weeks on Chart
22 May 93	**MOVE ON UP** *Pulse 8 CDLOSE 41*	64		1

CHAM
Jamaica, male vocalist/producer (Damian Beckett) — Weeks on Chart: 1

Date	Title / Label	Peak Position	Weeks at No.1	Weeks on Chart
9 Sep 06	**GHETTO STORY** *Atlantic AT0254CD*	62		1

RICHARD CHAMBERLAIN
US, male vocalist (George Chamberlain) — Weeks on Chart: 36

Date	Title / Label	Peak Position	Weeks at No.1	Weeks on Chart
7 Jun 62	**THEME FROM 'DR KILDARE' (THREE STARS WILL SHINE TONIGHT)** *MGM 1160*	12		10
1 Nov 62	**LOVE ME TENDER** *MGM 1173*	15		11
21 Feb 63	**HI-LILI HI-LO** *MGM 1189*	20		9
18 Jul 63	**TRUE LOVE** *MGM 1205*	30		6

CHAMELEON
UK, male vocal/instrumental group — Weeks on Chart: 2

Date	Title / Label	Peak Position	Weeks at No.1	Weeks on Chart
18 May 96	**THE WAY IT IS** *Stress CDSTR 65*	34		2

CHAMILLIONAIRE
US, male rapper (Hakeem Seriki) — Weeks on Chart: 26

Date	Title / Label	Peak Position	Weeks at No.1	Weeks on Chart
19 Aug 06	**RIDIN'** *Universal 1705043* FEATURING KRAYZIE BONE ★	2		18
2 Dec 06	**GROWN AND SEXY** *Universal 1713495*	35		2
6 Oct 07	**HIP HOP POLICE** *Universal 1751125* FEATURING SLICK RICK	50		6

CHAMPAIGN
US, male/female vocal/instrumental group — Weeks on Chart: 13

Date	Title / Label	Peak Position	Weeks at No.1	Weeks on Chart
9 May 81	**HOW 'BOUT US** *CBS A 1046* ●	5		13

CHAMPS
US, male instrumental group – Danny Flores, d. 19 Sep 2006, Gene Alden, Buddy Bruce, Dave Burgess & Cliff Hills — Weeks on Chart: 10

Date	Title / Label	Peak Position	Weeks at No.1	Weeks on Chart
4 Apr 58	**TEQUILA** *London HLU 8580* ★	5		9
17 Mar 60	**TOO MUCH TEQUILA** *London HLH 9052*	49		1

CHAMPS BOYS
French, male instrumental group — Weeks on Chart: 6

Date	Title / Label	Peak Position	Weeks at No.1	Weeks on Chart
19 Jun 76	**TUBULAR BELLS** *Philips 6006 519*	41		6

GENE CHANDLER
US, male vocalist (Eugene Dixon) — Weeks on Chart: 29

Date	Title / Label	Peak Position	Weeks at No.1	Weeks on Chart
5 Jun 68	**NOTHING CAN STOP ME** *Soul City SC 102*	41		4
3 Feb 79	**GET DOWN** *20th Century BTC 1040* ●	11		11

Date	Title	Label	Peak	Wks at No.1	Wks on Chart
1 Sep 79	**WHEN YOU'RE NUMBER 1**	*20th Century TC 2411*	43		5
28 Jun 80	**DOES SHE HAVE A FRIEND**	*20th Century TC 2451*	28		9

CHANEL
US, female vocalist — 4

Date	Title	Label	Peak	Wks at No.1	Wks on Chart
30 Sep 06	**MY LIFE**	*Hed Kandi HK22CDS*	39		4

CHANELLE
US, female vocalist (Charlene Munford) — 9

Date	Title	Label	Peak	Wks at No.1	Wks on Chart
11 Mar 89	**ONE MAN**	*Cooltempo COOL 183*	16		8
10 Dec 94	**ONE MAN (REMIX)**	*Deep Distraxion OILYCD 031*	50		1

CHANGE
Italy/US, male/female vocal/instrumental/production group — 43

Date	Title	Label	Peak	Wks at No.1	Wks on Chart
28 Jun 80	**A LOVER'S HOLIDAY/GLOW OF LOVE**	*WEA K 79141*	14		8
6 Sep 80	**SEARCHING**	*WEA K 79156*	11		10
2 Jun 84	**CHANGE OF HEART**	*WEA YZ 7*	17		10
11 Aug 84	**YOU ARE MY MELODY**	*WEA YZ 14*	48		4
16 Mar 85	**LET'S GO TOGETHER**	*Cooltempo COOL 107*	37		7
25 May 85	**OH WHAT A FEELING**	*Cooltempo COOL 109*	56		2
13 Jul 85	**MUTUAL ATTRACTION**	*Cooltempo COOL 111*	60		2

CHANGING FACES
US, female vocal duo – Cassandra Lucas & Charisse Rose — 12

Date	Title	Label	Peak	Wks at No.1	Wks on Chart
24 Sep 94	**STROKE YOU UP**	*Big Beat A 8251CD*	43		3
26 Jul 97	**G.H.E.T.T.O.U.T.**	*Atlantic AT 0003CD*	10		5
1 Nov 97	**I GOT SOMEBODY ELSE**	*Atlantic AT 0014CD*	42		1
4 Apr 98	**TIME AFTER TIME**	*Atlantic AT 0027CD*	35		2
1 Aug 98	**SAME TEMPO**	*Atlantic 5826952*	53		1

BRUCE CHANNEL
US, male vocalist — 28

Date	Title	Label	Peak	Wks at No.1	Wks on Chart
22 Mar 62	**HEY! BABY**	*Mercury AMT 1171* ★	2		12
26 Jun 68	**KEEP ON**	*Bell 1010*	12		16

CHANNEL X
Belgium, male/female vocal/production group — 1

Date	Title	Label	Peak	Wks at No.1	Wks on Chart
14 Dec 91	**GROOVE TO MOVE**	*PWL Continental 209*	67		1

CHANSON
US, male/female vocal group — 7

Date	Title	Label	Peak	Wks at No.1	Wks on Chart
13 Jan 79	**DON'T HOLD BACK**	*Ariola ARO 140*	33		7

CHANTAYS
US, male instrumental group — 14

Date	Title	Label	Peak	Wks at No.1	Wks on Chart
18 Apr 63	**PIPELINE**	*London HLD 9696*	16		14

CHANTER SISTERS
UK, female vocal group — 5

Date	Title	Label	Peak	Wks at No.1	Wks on Chart
17 Jul 76	**SIDE SHOW**	*Polydor 2058 735*	43		5

CHAOS
UK, male vocal group. See Ultimate Kaos — 2

Date	Title	Label	Peak	Wks at No.1	Wks on Chart
3 Oct 92	**FAREWELL MY SUMMER LOVE**	*Arista 74321116397*	55		2

HARRY CHAPIN
US, male vocalist, d. 26 Jul 1981 (age 38) — 5

Date	Title	Label	Peak	Wks at No.1	Wks on Chart
11 May 74	**W.O.L.D.**	*Elektra K 12133*	34		5

TRACY CHAPMAN
US, female vocalist/guitarist — 16

Date	Title	Label	Peak	Wks at No.1	Wks on Chart
11 Jun 88	**FAST CAR**	*Elektra EKR 73*	5		12
30 Sep 89	**CROSSROADS**	*Elektra EKR 95*	61		3
20 Feb 10	**FAST CAR**	*Elektra GBAHS9701356*	57		1

CHAPTERHOUSE
UK, male vocal/instrumental group — 3

Date	Title	Label	Peak	Wks at No.1	Wks on Chart
30 Mar 91	**PEARL**	*Dedicated STONE 003*	67		1
12 Oct 91	**MESMERISE**	*Dedicated HOUSE 001*	60		2

CHAQUITO
UK, orchestra — 1

Date	Title	Label	Peak	Wks at No.1	Wks on Chart
27 Oct 60	**NEVER ON SUNDAY**	*Fontana H 265*	50		1

CHARTJACKERS
UK, male vocal/video blogging charity group — 1

Date	Title	Label	Peak	Wks at No.1	Wks on Chart
21 Nov 09	**I'VE GOT NOTHING**	*Swinging Mantis GB5WK0900001*	36		1

CHARLATANS
UK, male vocal/instrumental group – Tim Burgess*, Martin Blunt, Jon Brookes, Mark Collins & Rob Collins, d. 23 Jul 1996 (replaced by Tony Rogers) — 87

Date	Title	Label	Peak	Wks at No.1	Wks on Chart
2 Jun 90	**THE ONLY ONE I KNOW**	*Situation Two SIT 70T*	9		9
22 Sep 90	**THEN**	*Situation Two SIT 74T*	12		5
9 Mar 91	**OVER RISING**	*Situation Two SIT 76*	15		5
17 Aug 91	**INDIAN ROPE**	*Dead Dead Good GOOD 1T*	57		1
9 Nov 91	**ME. IN TIME**	*Situation Two SIT 84*	28		3
7 Mar 92	**WEIRDO**	*Situation Two SIT 88*	19		4
18 Jul 92	**TREMELO SONG (EP)**	*Situation Two SIT 97T*	44		2
5 Feb 94	**CAN'T GET OUT OF BED**	*Beggars Banquet BBQ 27CD*	24		3
19 Mar 94	**I NEVER WANT AN EASY LIFE IF ME AND HE WERE EVER TO GET THERE**	*Beggars Banquet BBQ 31CD*	38		1
2 Jul 94	**JESUS HAIRDO**	*Beggars Banquet BBQ 32CD*	48		2
7 Jan 95	**CRASHIN' IN**	*Beggars Banquet BBQ 44CD*	31		2
27 May 95	**JUST LOOKIN'/BULLET COMES**	*Beggars Banquet BBQ 55CD*	32		3
26 Aug 95	**JUST WHEN YOU'RE THINKING THINGS OVER**	*Beggars Banquet BBQ 60CD*	12		3
7 Sep 96	**ONE TO ANOTHER**	*Beggars Banquet BBQ 301CD*	3		6
5 Apr 97	**NORTH COUNTRY BOY**	*Beggars Banquet BBQ 309CD*	4		6
21 Jun 97	**HOW HIGH**	*Beggars Banquet BBQ 312CD*	6		5
1 Nov 97	**TELLIN' STORIES**	*Beggars Banquet BBQ 318CD*	16		3
16 Oct 99	**FOREVER**	*Universal MCSTD 40220*	12		3
18 Dec 99	**MY BEAUTIFUL FRIEND**	*Universal MCSTD 40225*	31		3
27 May 00	**IMPOSSIBLE**	*Universal MCSTXD 40231*	15		3
8 Sep 01	**LOVE IS THE KEY**	*Universal MCSTD 40262*	16		3
1 Dec 01	**A MAN NEEDS TO BE TOLD**	*Universal MCSTD 40271*	31		2
22 May 04	**UP AT THE LAKE**	*Universal MCSTD 40363*	23		3
7 Aug 04	**TRY AGAIN TODAY**	*Universal MCSTD 40370*	24		3
15 Apr 06	**BLACKENED BLUE EYES**	*Creole SANXS421*	28		2
15 Jul 06	**NYC (THERE'S NO NEED TO STOP)**	*Creole SANXS427*	53		1
25 Nov 06	**YOU'RE SO PRETTY WE'RE SO PRETTY**	*Universal 1712414*	56		1

CHARLENE
US, female vocalist (Charlene D'Angelo) — 12

Date	Title	Label	Peak	Wks at No.1	Wks on Chart
15 May 82	**I'VE NEVER BEEN TO ME**	*Motown TMG 1260* ●	1	1	12

DON CHARLES
UK, male vocalist (Walter Scuffham), d. 4 Dec 2005 (age 71) — 5

Date	Title	Label	Peak	Wks at No.1	Wks on Chart
22 Feb 62	**WALK WITH ME MY ANGEL**	*Decca F 11424*	39		5

RAY CHARLES
US, male vocalist/pianist/band leader (Ray Charles Robinson), d. 10 Jun 2004 (age 73) — 130

Date	Title	Label	Peak	Wks at No.1	Wks on Chart
1 Dec 60	**GEORGIA ON MY MIND**	*HMV POP 792* ★	24		8
19 Oct 61	**HIT THE ROAD JACK**	*HMV POP 935* ★	6		12
14 Jun 62	**I CAN'T STOP LOVING YOU**	*HMV POP 1034* ★	1	2	17
13 Sep 62	**YOU DON'T KNOW ME**	*HMV POP 1064*	9		13
13 Dec 62	**YOUR CHEATING HEART**	*HMV POP 1099*	13		8
28 Mar 63	**DON'T SET ME FREE**	*HMV POP 1133*	37		3
16 May 63	**TAKE THESE CHAINS FROM MY HEART**	*HMV POP 1161*	5		20
12 Sep 63	**NO ONE**	*HMV POP 1202*	35		7
31 Oct 63	**BUSTED**	*HMV POP 1221*	21		10
24 Sep 64	**NO ONE TO CRY TO**	*HMV POP 1333*	38		3
21 Jan 65	**MAKIN' WHOOPEE**	*HMV POP 1383*	42		4
10 Feb 66	**CRYIN' TIME**	*HMV POP 1502*	50		1
21 Apr 66	**TOGETHER AGAIN**	*HMV POP 1519*	48		1
5 Jul 67	**HERE WE GO AGAIN**	*HMV POP 1595*	38		3
20 Dec 67	**YESTERDAY**	*Stateside SS 2071*	44		4
31 Jul 68	**ELEANOR RIGBY**	*Stateside SS 2170*	36		9

Silver-selling ○ Gold-selling ● Platinum-selling (× multiples) ⊛ US No.1 ★

Peak Position · Weeks at No.1 · Weeks on Chart

Date	Title	Peak Position	Weeks at No.1	Weeks on Chart
13 Jan 90	**I'LL BE GOOD TO YOU** *Qwest W 2697* QUINCY JONES FEATURING RAY CHARLES & CHAKA KHAN	21		7

SUZETTE CHARLES
US, female vocalist (Suzette DeGaetano) — **2**

Date	Title	Peak Position	Weeks at No.1	Weeks on Chart
21 Aug 93	**FREE TO LOVE AGAIN** *RCA 74321158372*	58		2

TINA CHARLES
UK, female vocalist (Tina Hoskins). See 5000 Volts — **63**

Date	Title	Peak Position	Weeks at No.1	Weeks on Chart
7 Feb 76	**I LOVE TO LOVE (BUT MY BABY LOVES TO DANCE)** *CBS 3937* ●	1	3	12
1 May 76	**LOVE ME LIKE A LOVER** *CBS 4237*	31		7
21 Aug 76	**DANCE LITTLE LADY DANCE** *CBS 4480* ○	6		13
4 Dec 76	**DR LOVE** *CBS 4779* ○	4		10
14 May 77	**RENDEZVOUS** *CBS 5174*	27		6
29 Oct 77	**LOVE BUG – SWEETS FOR MY SWEET (MEDLEY)** *CBS 5680*	26		4
11 Mar 78	**I'LL GO WHERE YOUR MUSIC TAKES ME** *CBS 6062*	27		8
30 Aug 86	**I LOVE TO LOVE (REMIX)** *DMC DECK 1*	67		3

CHARLES & EDDIE
US, male vocal duo – Charles Pettigrew, d. 6 Apr 2001, & Eddie Chacon — **30**

Date	Title	Peak Position	Weeks at No.1	Weeks on Chart
31 Oct 92	**WOULD I LIE TO YOU** *Capitol CL 673* ⊛	1	2	17
20 Feb 93	**N.Y.C. (CAN YOU BELIEVE THIS CITY)** *Capitol CDCL 681*	33		5
22 May 93	**HOUSE IS NOT A HOME** *Capitol CDCLS 688*	29		4
13 May 95	**24-7-365** *Capitol CDCLS 747*	38		4

DICK CHARLESWORTH & HIS CITY GENTS
UK, male vocal/instrumental group – leader d. 15 Apr 2008 (age 76) — **1**

Date	Title	Peak Position	Weeks at No.1	Weeks on Chart
4 May 61	**BILLY BOY** *Top Rank JAR 558*	43		1

CHARLOTTE
UK, female vocalist (Charlotte Kelly) — **4**

Date	Title	Peak Position	Weeks at No.1	Weeks on Chart
12 Mar 94	**QUEEN OF HEARTS** *Big Life BLRD 106*	54		1
2 May 98	**BE MINE** *Parlophone Rhythm CDRHYTHM 10*	59		1
29 May 99	**SKIN** *Parlophone Rhythm CDRHYTHM 20*	56		1
4 Sep 99	**SOMEDAY** *Parlophone Rhythm CDRHYTHM 23*	74		1

CHARME
US, male/female vocal/production group — **2**

Date	Title	Peak Position	Weeks at No.1	Weeks on Chart
17 Nov 84	**GEORGY PORGY** *RCA 464*	68		2

CHARO & THE SALSOUL ORCHESTRA
US, female vocalist (Maria Martinez) & orchestra — **4**

Date	Title	Peak Position	Weeks at No.1	Weeks on Chart
29 Apr 78	**DANCE A LITTLE BIT CLOSER** *Salsoul SSOL 101*	44		4

CHAS & DAVE
UK, male vocal/instrumental duo – Chas Hodges & Dave Peacock — **66**

Date	Title	Peak Position	Weeks at No.1	Weeks on Chart
11 Nov 78	**STRUMMIN'** *EMI 2874* WITH ROCKNEY	52		3
26 May 79	**GERTCHA** *EMI 2947*	20		8
1 Sep 79	**THE SIDEBOARD SONG (GOT MY BEER IN THE SIDEBOARD HERE)** *EMI 2986*	55		3
29 Nov 80	**RABBIT** *Rockney 9* ○	8		11
12 Dec 81	**STARS OVER 45** *Rockney KOR 12*	21		8
13 Mar 82	**AIN'T NO PLEASING YOU** *Rockney KOR 14* ○	2		11
17 Jul 82	**MARGATE** *Rockney KOR 15*	46		4
19 Mar 83	**LONDON GIRLS** *Rockney KOR 17*	63		3
3 Dec 83	**MY MELANCHOLY BABY** *Rockney KOR 21*	51		6
3 May 86	**SNOOKER LOOPY** *Rockney POT 147* MATCHROOM MOB WITH CHAS & DAVE	6		9

CHASE & STATUS
UK, male DJ/production duo – Will Kennard & Saul Milton — **15**

Date	Title	Peak Position	Weeks at No.1	Weeks on Chart
11 Oct 08	**PIECES** *Ram RAMM73CD*	70		1
7 Mar 09	**AGAINST ALL ODDS** *Ram RAMM76CD* FEATURING KANO	45		1
14 Nov 09	**END CREDITS** *Vertigo 2723595* FEATURING PLAN B	9		13

JC CHASEZ
US, male vocalist. See *NSync — **10**

Date	Title	Peak Position	Weeks at No.1	Weeks on Chart
10 Apr 04	**PLUG IT IN** *XL Recordings XLS 180CD* BASEMENT JAXX FEATURING JC CHASEZ	22		4
24 Apr 04	**SOME GIRLS/BLOWIN' ME UP** *Jive 82876605442*	13		6

CHEAP TRICK
US, male vocal/instrumental group — **14**

Date	Title	Peak Position	Weeks at No.1	Weeks on Chart
5 May 79	**I WANT YOU TO WANT ME** *Epic EPC 7258*	29		9
2 Feb 80	**WAY OF THE WORLD** *Epic EPC 8114*	73		2
31 Jul 82	**IF YOU WANT MY LOVE** *Epic EPCA 2406*	57		3

OLIVER CHEATHAM
US, male vocalist — **22**

Date	Title	Peak Position	Weeks at No.1	Weeks on Chart
2 Jul 83	**GET DOWN SATURDAY NIGHT** *MCA 828*	38		5
5 Apr 03	**MAKE LUV** *Positiva CDTIV 187* ROOM 5 FEATURING OLIVER CHEATHAM ○	1	4	15
6 Dec 03	**MUSIC AND YOU** *Positiva CDTIVS 197* ROOM 5 FEATURING OLIVER CHEATHAM	38		2

CHUBBY CHECKER
US, male vocalist (Ernest Evans) — **112**

Date	Title	Peak Position	Weeks at No.1	Weeks on Chart
22 Sep 60	**THE TWIST** *Columbia DB 4503* ★	44		2
30 Mar 61	**PONY TIME** *Columbia DB 4591* ★	27		6
17 Aug 61	**LET'S TWIST AGAIN** *Columbia DB 4691*	37		3
28 Dec 61	**LET'S TWIST AGAIN** *Columbia DB 4691*	2		31
11 Jan 62	**THE TWIST** *Columbia DB 4503*	14		10
5 Apr 62	**SLOW TWISTIN'** *Columbia DB 4808*	23		8
19 Apr 62	**TEACH ME TO TWIST** *Columbia DB 4802* & BOBBY RYDELL	45		1
9 Aug 62	**DANCIN' PARTY** *Columbia DB 4876*	19		13
1 Nov 62	**LIMBO ROCK** *Cameo Parkway P 849*	32		10
20 Dec 62	**JINGLE BELL ROCK** *Cameo Parkway C 205* & BOBBY RYDELL	40		3
31 Oct 63	**WHAT DO YA SAY** *Cameo Parkway P 806*	37		4
29 Nov 75	**LET'S TWIST AGAIN/THE TWIST** *London HL 10512* ○	5		10
18 Jun 88	**THE TWIST (YO, TWIST)** *Urban URB 20* FAT BOYS & CHUBBY CHECKER	2		11

CHECKMATES LTD
US, male vocal/instrumental group — **8**

Date	Title	Peak Position	Weeks at No.1	Weeks on Chart
15 Nov 69	**PROUD MARY** *A&M AMS 769*	30		8

JUDY CHEEKS
US, female vocalist — **15**

Date	Title	Peak Position	Weeks at No.1	Weeks on Chart
13 Nov 93	**SO IN LOVE (THE REAL DEAL)** *Positiva CDTIV 6*	27		3
7 May 94	**REACH** *Positiva CDTIV 12*	17		4
4 Mar 95	**THIS TIME/RESPECT** *Positiva CDTIV 28*	23		2
17 Jun 95	**YOU'RE THE STORY OF MY LIFE/AS LONG AS YOU'RE GOOD TO ME** *Positiva CDTIV 34*	30		3
13 Jan 96	**REACH** *Positiva CDTIV 42*	22		3

CHEEKY GIRLS
Romania, female vocal duo – Gabriella & Monica Irimia — **41**

Date	Title	Peak Position	Weeks at No.1	Weeks on Chart
14 Dec 02	**CHEEKY SONG (TOUCH MY BUM)** *Multiply CDMULTY 97* ○	2		14
17 May 03	**TAKE YOUR SHOES OFF** *Multiply CXMULTY 101*	3		10
16 Aug 03	**HOORAY HOORAY (IT'S A CHEEKY HOLIDAY)** *Multiply CXMULTY 106*	3		7
20 Dec 03	**HAVE A CHEEKY CHRISTMAS** *Multiply CXMULTY 110*	10		5
9 Oct 04	**CHEEKY FLAMENCO** *XBN XBNCD1*	29		2
18 Dec 04	**BOYS AND GIRLS** *XBN XBNCDS3*	50		3

CHEETAH GIRLS
US, female vocal group — **2**

Date	Title	Peak Position	Weeks at No.1	Weeks on Chart
20 Jan 07	**THE PARTY'S JUST BEGUN** *Walt Disney 3844312*	53		2

CHEETAHS
UK, male vocal/instrumental group — **6**

Date	Title	Peak Position	Weeks at No.1	Weeks on Chart
1 Oct 64	**MECCA** *Philips BF 1362*	36		3
21 Jan 65	**SOLDIER BOY** *Philips BF 1383*	39		3

CHEF

US, male cartoon vocalist (Isaac Hayes) — 13

Date	Title	Peak Position	Weeks at No.1	Weeks on Chart
26 Dec 98	**CHOCOLATE SALTY BALLS (PS I LOVE YOU)** *Columbia 6667985* ⊛	1	1	13

CHELSEA FC

UK, male footballers/vocalists — 22

Date	Title	Peak Position	Weeks at No.1	Weeks on Chart
26 Feb 72	**BLUE IS THE COLOUR** *Penny Farthing PEN 782*	5		12
14 May 94	**NO ONE CAN STOP US NOW** *RCA 74321210452*	23		3
17 May 97	**BLUE DAY** *WEA 112CD* SUGGS & CO FEATURING CHELSEA TEAM	22		5
27 May 00	**BLUE TOMORROW** *Telstar TV CFCCD 2000* CHELSEA FOOTBALL CLUB	22		2

CHEMICAL BROTHERS

UK, male DJ/production duo – Tom Rowlands & Ed Simons — 104

Date	Title	Peak Position	Weeks at No.1	Weeks on Chart
17 Jun 95	**LEAVE HOME** *Junior Boy's Own CHEMSD 1*	17		4
9 Sep 95	**LIFE IS SWEET** *Junior Boy's Own CHEMSDX 2*	25		3
27 Jan 96	**LOOPS OF FURY EP** *Freestyle Dust CHEMSD 3*	13		1
12 Oct 96	**SETTING SUN** *Virgin CHEMSD 4* ●	1	1	7
5 Apr 97	**BLOCK ROCKIN' BEATS** *Virgin CHEMSD 5*	1	1	7
20 Sep 97	**ELEKTROBANK** *Virgin CHEMSD 6*	17		4
12 Jun 99	**HEY BOY HEY GIRL** *Virgin CHEMSD 8* ●	3		10
14 Aug 99	**LET FOREVER BE** *Virgin CHEMSD 9*	9		7
23 Oct 99	**OUT OF CONTROL** *Virgin CHEMSD 10*	21		4
22 Sep 01	**IT BEGAN IN AFRIKA** *Virgin CHEMSD 12*	8		6
26 Jan 02	**STAR GUITAR** *Virgin CHEMSD 14*	8		8
4 May 02	**COME WITH US/THE TEST** *Virgin CHEMSD 15*	14		3
27 Sep 03	**THE GOLDEN PATH** *Virgin CHEMSD 18* FEATURING THE FLAMING LIPS	17		4
29 Jan 05	**GALVANIZE** *Virgin CHEMSD21*	3		16
14 May 05	**BELIEVE** *Virgin CHEMSDX22*	18		4
23 Jul 05	**THE BOXER** *Freestyle Dust CHEMSDX23*	41		2
16 Jun 07	**DO IT AGAIN** *Virgin CHEMSD25*	12		9
15 Sep 07	**SALMON DANCE** *Virgin CHEMSD26*	27		5

CHEQUERS

UK, male vocal/instrumental group — 10

Date	Title	Peak Position	Weeks at No.1	Weeks on Chart
18 Oct 75	**ROCK ON BROTHER** *Creole CR 111*	21		5
28 Feb 76	**HEY MISS PAYNE** *Creole CR 116*	32		5

CHER

US, female vocalist (Cherilyn LaPierre). Indefatigable singer who continues to be a live attraction despite completing her 'Farewell Tour' in 2005. *Believe*, the biggest-selling album of her career, sold 20 million copies worldwide. See Sonny & Cher — 229

Date	Title	Peak Position	Weeks at No.1	Weeks on Chart
19 Aug 65	**ALL I REALLY WANT TO DO** *Liberty LIB 66114*	9		10
31 Mar 66	**BANG BANG (MY BABY SHOT ME DOWN)** *Liberty LIB 66160*	3		12
4 Aug 66	**I FEEL SOMETHING IN THE AIR** *Liberty LIB 12034*	43		2
22 Sep 66	**SUNNY** *Liberty LIB 12083*	32		5
6 Nov 71	**GYPSYS TRAMPS AND THIEVES** *MCA MU 1142* ★	4		13
16 Feb 74	**DARK LADY** *MCA 101* ★	36		4
19 Dec 87	**I FOUND SOMEONE** *Geffen GEF 31*	5		10
2 Apr 88	**WE ALL SLEEP ALONE** *Geffen GEF 35*	47		5
2 Sep 89	**IF I COULD TURN BACK TIME** *Geffen GEF 59*	6		14
13 Jan 90	**JUST LIKE JESSE JAMES** *Geffen GEF 69*	11		11
7 Apr 90	**HEART OF STONE** *Geffen GEF 75*	43		5
11 Aug 90	**YOU WOULDN'T KNOW LOVE** *Geffen GEF 77*	55		3
13 Apr 91	**THE SHOOP SHOOP SONG (IT'S IN HIS KISS)** *Epic 6566737* ●	1	5	15
13 Jul 91	**LOVE AND UNDERSTANDING** *Geffen GFS 5*	10		8
12 Oct 91	**SAVE UP ALL YOUR TEARS** *Geffen GFS 11*	37		5
7 Dec 91	**LOVE HURTS** *Geffen GFS 16*	43		5
18 Apr 92	**COULD'VE BEEN YOU** *Geffen GFS 19*	31		4
14 Nov 92	**OH NO NOT MY BABY** *Geffen GFS 29*	33		4
16 Jan 93	**MANY RIVERS TO CROSS** *Geffen GFSTD 31*	37		3
6 Mar 93	**WHENEVER YOU'RE NEAR** *Geffen GFSTD 32*	72		1
15 Jan 94	**I GOT YOU BABE** *Geffen GFSTD 64* WITH BEAVIS & BUTT-HEAD	35		3
18 Mar 95	**LOVE CAN BUILD A BRIDGE** *London COCD 1* CHER, CHRISSIE HYNDE & NENEH CHERRY WITH ERIC CLAPTON ●	1	1	8
28 Oct 95	**WALKING IN MEMPHIS** *WEA 021CD1*	11		7
20 Jan 96	**ONE BY ONE** *WEA 032CD*	7		9
27 Apr 96	**NOT ENOUGH LOVE IN THE WORLD** *WEA 052CD*	31		2
17 Aug 96	**THE SUN AIN'T GONNA SHINE ANYMORE** *WEA 071CD*	26		3
31 Oct 98	**BELIEVE** *WEA 175CD* ⊛x2 ★	1	7	28
6 Mar 99	**STRONG ENOUGH** *WEA 201CD* ●	5		10
19 Jun 99	**ALL OR NOTHING** *WEA 212CD1*	12		7
6 Nov 99	**DOV'E L'AMORE** *WEA 230CD1*	21		3
17 Nov 01	**THE MUSIC'S NO GOOD WITHOUT YOU** *WEA 337CD*	8		10

CHERI

Canada, female vocal duo — 9

Date	Title	Peak Position	Weeks at No.1	Weeks on Chart
19 Jun 82	**MURPHY'S LAW** *Polydor POSP 459*	13		9

CHERISH

US, female vocal group — 6

Date	Title	Peak Position	Weeks at No.1	Weeks on Chart
23 Sep 06	**DO IT TO IT** *Capitol CDCL878* FEATURING SEAN PAUL	30		4
12 Apr 08	**KILLA** *Parlophone USCA20706004* FEATURING YUNG JOC	52		2

CHEROKEES

UK, male vocal/instrumental group — 5

Date	Title	Peak Position	Weeks at No.1	Weeks on Chart
3 Sep 64	**SEVEN DAFFODILS** *Columbia DB 7341*	33		5

CHERRELLE

US, female vocalist (Cheryl Norton) — 26

Date	Title	Peak Position	Weeks at No.1	Weeks on Chart
28 Dec 85	**SATURDAY LOVE** *Tabu A 6829* WITH ALEXANDER O'NEAL	6		11
1 Mar 86	**WILL YOU SATISFY?** *Tabu A 6927*	57		3
6 Feb 88	**NEVER KNEW LOVE LIKE THIS** *Tabu 6513827* ALEXANDER O'NEAL FEATURING CHERRELLE	26		7
6 May 89	**AFFAIR** *Tabu 6546737*	67		2
24 Mar 90	**SATURDAY LOVE (REMIX)** *Tabu 6558007* WITH ALEXANDER O'NEAL	55		2
2 Aug 97	**BABY COME TO ME** *One World Entertainment OWECD 1* ALEXANDER O'NEAL FEATURING CHERRELLE	56		1

DON CHERRY

US, male vocalist, d. 19 Oct 1995 (age 71) — 11

Date	Title	Peak Position	Weeks at No.1	Weeks on Chart
10 Feb 56	**BAND OF GOLD** *Philips PB 549*	6		11

EAGLE-EYE CHERRY

Sweden, male vocalist/guitarist — 28

Date	Title	Peak Position	Weeks at No.1	Weeks on Chart
4 Jul 98	**SAVE TONIGHT** *Polydor 5695952* ●	6		13
14 Nov 98	**FALLING IN LOVE AGAIN** *Polydor 5630252*	8		8
20 Mar 99	**PERMANENT YEARS** *Polydor 5636752*	43		1
29 Apr 00	**ARE YOU STILL HAVING FUN?** *Polydor 5618032*	21		4
11 Nov 00	**LONG WAY AROUND** *Polydor 5677812* FEATURING NENEH CHERRY	48		2

NENEH CHERRY

UK (b. Sweden), female vocalist/rapper (Neneh Karlsson) — 98

Date	Title	Peak Position	Weeks at No.1	Weeks on Chart
10 Dec 88	**BUFFALO STANCE** *Circa YR 21* ●	3		13
20 May 89	**MANCHILD** *Circa YR 30*	5		10
12 Aug 89	**KISSES ON THE WIND** *Circa YR 33*	20		6
23 Dec 89	**INNA CITY MAMMA** *Circa YR 42*	31		7
29 Sep 90	**I'VE GOT YOU UNDER MY SKIN** *Circa YR 53*	25		5
3 Oct 92	**MONEY LOVE** *Circa YR 83*	23		4
19 Jun 93	**BUDDY X** *Circa YRCD 98*	35		3
25 Jun 94	**7 SECONDS** *Columbia 6605082* YOUSSOU N'DOUR (FEATURING NENEH CHERRY) ●	3		25
18 Mar 95	**LOVE CAN BUILD A BRIDGE** *London COCD 1* CHER, CHRISSIE HYNDE & NENEH CHERRY WITH ERIC CLAPTON ●	1	1	8
3 Aug 96	**WOMAN** *Hut HUTD 70*	9		7
14 Dec 96	**KOOTCHI** *Hut HUTCD 75*	38		2
22 Feb 97	**FEEL IT** *Hut HUTCD 79*	68		1
6 Nov 99	**BUDDY X 99** *4 Liberty LIBTCD33* DREEM TEEM VS NENEH CHERRY	15		5
11 Nov 00	**LONG WAY AROUND** *Polydor 5677812* EAGLE-EYE CHERRY FEATURING NENEH CHERRY	48		2

CHERRY GHOST

UK, male vocal/instrumental group — 7

Date	Title	Peak Position	Weeks at No.1	Weeks on Chart
21 Apr 07	**MATHEMATICS** *Heavenly HVN167CD*	57		1
23 Jun 07	**PEOPLE HELP THE PEOPLE** *EMI HVN168CD*	27		6

CHERRYFALLS

UK, male vocal/instrumental group — 2

Date	Title	Peak Position	Weeks at No.1	Weeks on Chart
14 Aug 04	**STANDING WATCHING** *Island CID 868*	64		1
9 Apr 05	**MY DRUG** *Island CID881*	71		1

Silver-selling ○ Gold-selling ● Platinum-selling (x multiples) ⊛ US No.1 ★ Peak Position ⬆ Weeks at No.1 ✪ Weeks on Chart ♥

CHI-LITES
US, male vocal group – Eugene Record, d. 22 Jul 2005, Creadel Jones, d. 25 Aug 1994, Robert Lester, d. 21 Jan 2010, & Marshall Thompson

Date	Title	⬆	✪	89
28 Aug 71	**(FOR GOD'S SAKE) GIVE MORE POWER TO THE PEOPLE** *MCA MU 1138*	32		6
15 Jan 72	**HAVE YOU SEEN HER** *MCA MU 1146*	3		12
27 May 72	**OH GIRL** *MCA MU 1156* ★	14		9
23 Mar 74	**HOMELY GIRL** *Brunswick BR 9*	5		13
20 Jul 74	**I FOUND SUNSHINE** *Brunswick BR 12*	35		5
2 Nov 74	**TOO GOOD TO BE FORGOTTEN** *Brunswick BR 13*	10		11
21 Jun 75	**HAVE YOU SEEN HER/OH GIRL** *Brunswick BR 20*	5		9
13 Sep 75	**IT'S TIME FOR LOVE** *Brunswick BR 25*	5		10
31 Jul 76	**YOU DON'T HAVE TO GO** *Brunswick BR 34*	3		11
13 Aug 83	**CHANGING FOR YOU** *R&B RBS 215*	61		3

CHIC
US, male/female vocal/instrumental group – Bernard Edwards, d. 18 Apr 1996, Nile Rodgers, Luci Martin, Tony Thompson & Norma Jean Wright (replaced by Alfa Anderson)

Date	Title	⬆	✪	92
26 Nov 77	**DANCE DANCE DANCE (YOWSAH YOWSAH YOWSAH)** *Atlantic K 11038* ○	6		12
1 Apr 78	**EVERYBODY DANCE** *Atlantic K 11097*	9		11
18 Nov 78	**LE FREAK** *Atlantic K 11209* ● ★	7		16
24 Feb 79	**I WANT YOUR LOVE** *Atlantic LV 16*	4		11
30 Jun 79	**GOOD TIMES** *Atlantic K 11310* ★	5		11
13 Oct 79	**MY FORBIDDEN LOVER** *Atlantic K 11385*	15		8
8 Dec 79	**MY FEET KEEP DANCING** *Atlantic K 11415*	21		9
12 Mar 83	**HANGIN'** *Atlantic A 9898*	64		1
19 Sep 87	**JACK LE FREAK** *Atlantic A 9198*	19		6
14 Jul 90	**MEGACHIC – CHIC MEDLEY** *East West A 7949*	58		2
15 Feb 92	**CHIC MYSTIQUE** *Warner Brothers W 0083*	48		3
5 Aug 06	**SENSITIVITY** *Positiva CDTIV238* SHAPESHIFTERS & CHIC	40		2

CHICAGO
US, male vocal/instrumental group – Peter Cetera*, Terry Kath, d. 23 Jan 1978 (replaced by Bill Champlin), Robert Lamm, Lee Loughnane, James Pankow, Walter Parazaider & Danny Seraphine

Date	Title	⬆	✪	81
10 Jan 70	**I'M A MAN** *CBS 4715*	8		11
18 Jul 70	**25 OR 6 TO 4** *CBS 5076*	7		13
9 Oct 76	**IF YOU LEAVE ME NOW** *CBS 4603* ● ★	1	3	16
5 Nov 77	**BABY WHAT A BIG SURPRISE** *CBS 5672*	41		3
21 Aug 82	**HARD TO SAY I'M SORRY** *Full Moon K 79301* ○ ★	4		15
27 Oct 84	**HARD HABIT TO BREAK** *Full Moon W 9214*	8		13
26 Jan 85	**YOU'RE THE INSPIRATION** *Warner Brothers W 9126*	14		10

CHICANE
UK, male producer/keyboard player/guitarist (Nick Bracegirdle). See Disco Citizens

Date	Title	⬆	✪	79
21 Dec 96	**OFFSHORE** *Xtravaganza 0091005 EXT*	14		7
14 Jun 97	**SUNSTROKE** *Xtravaganza 0091125 EXT*	21		3
13 Sep 97	**OFFSHORE 97** *Xtravaganza 0091255 EXT*	17		4
20 Dec 97	**LOST YOU SOMEWHERE** *Xtravaganza 0091415 EXT*	35		3
10 Oct 98	**STRONG IN LOVE** *Xtravaganza 0091675 EXT* FEATURING MASON	32		2
5 Jun 99	**SALTWATER** *Xtravaganza XTRAV 1CDS* FEATURING MAIRE BRENNAN OF CLANNAD	6		10
18 Mar 00	**DON'T GIVE UP** *Xtravaganza XTRAV 9CDS* FEATURING BRYAN ADAMS ○	1	1	14
22 Jul 00	**NO ORDINARY MORNING/HALCYON** *Xtravaganza XTRAV 12CDS*	28		3
28 Oct 00	**AUTUMN TACTICS** *Xtravaganza XTRAV 17CDS*	44		2
8 Feb 03	**SALTWATER** *Xtravaganza XTRAV 35CDS*	43		2
8 Mar 03	**LOVE ON THE RUN** *WEA 361CD1* FEATURING PETER CUNNAH	33		2
14 Feb 04	**DON'T GIVE UP 2004** *Xtravaganza XTRAV 44CDS*	43		1
29 Apr 06	**STONED IN LOVE** *Universal TV 9878360* FEATURING TOM JONES	7		13
6 Sep 08	**BRUISED WATER** *Modena GBRDU0800032* VERSUS NATASHA BEDINGFIELD	42		3
25 Jul 09	**POPPIHOLLA** *Modena CDMODENA4*	7		9
31 Oct 09	**HIDING ALL THE STARS** *Modena GBRDU0900007*	42		1

CHICKEN SHACK
UK, male/female vocal/instrumental group

Date	Title	⬆	✪	19
7 May 69	**I'D RATHER GO BLIND** *Blue Horizon 57-3153*	14		13
6 Sep 69	**TEARS IN THE WIND** *Blue Horizon 57-3160*	29		6

CHICKEN SHED
UK, male/female theatre company vocal group

Date	Title	⬆	✪	6
27 Dec 97	**I AM IN LOVE WITH THE WORLD** *Columbia 6654172*	15		6

CHICKS ON SPEED
Australia/Germany/US, female vocal/instrumental trio

Date	Title	⬆	✪	2
21 Feb 04	**WHAT WAS HER NAME** *Skint 94CD* DAVE CLARKE FEATURING CHICKS ON SPEED	50		1
13 Mar 04	**WORDY RAPPINGHOOD** *Labels 5478360*	66		1

CHICO
UK, male vocalist (Yousseph 'Chico' Slimani)

Date	Title	⬆	✪	14
11 Mar 06	**IT'S CHICO TIME** *Sony BMG 82876812132*	1	1	10
26 Aug 06	**DISCO** *Sony BMG 82876892752*	24		3
20 Oct 07	**CURVY COLA BOTTLE BODY** *Chico Enterprises CDCHIENT1*	45		1

CHICORY TIP
UK, male vocal/instrumental group – Peter Hewson, Rick Foster, Barry Mayger & Brian Shearer

Date	Title	⬆	✪	34
29 Jan 72	**SON OF MY FATHER** *CBS 7737*	1	3	13
20 May 72	**WHAT'S YOUR NAME** *CBS 8021*	13		8
31 Mar 73	**GOOD GRIEF CHRISTINA** *CBS 1258*	17		13

CHIDDY BANG
US, male vocal/instrumental duo

Date	Title	⬆	✪	6
6 Mar 10	**THE OPPOSITE OF ADULTS** *Regal REG156*	12		6+

CHIEFTAINS
Ireland, male vocal/instrumental group

Date	Title	⬆	✪	4
18 Mar 95	**HAVE I TOLD YOU LATELY THAT I LOVE YOU** *RCA 74321271702* WITH VAN MORRISON	71		1
12 Jun 99	**I KNOW MY LOVE** *RCA Victor 74321670622* FEATURING THE CORRS	37		3

CHIFFONS
US, female vocal group – Patricia Bennett, Judy Craig, Barbara Lee Jones, d. 15 May 1992, & Sylvia Peterson

Date	Title	⬆	✪	40
11 Apr 63	**HE'S SO FINE** *Stateside SS 172* ★	16		12
18 Jul 63	**ONE FINE DAY** *Stateside SS 202*	29		6
26 May 66	**SWEET TALKIN' GUY** *Stateside SS 512*	31		8
18 Mar 72	**SWEET TALKIN' GUY** *London HL 10271*	4		14

CHIKINKI
UK, male vocal/instrumental group

Date	Title	⬆	✪	4
29 Nov 03	**ASSASSINATOR 13** *Island CID 834*	72		1
27 Mar 04	**LIKE IT OR LEAVE IT** *Island CID 848*	65		1
19 Jun 04	**ETHER RADIO** *Island CID 860*	50		1
6 Nov 04	**ALL EYES** *Island CIDX 875*	74		1

CHILD
UK, male vocal/instrumental group – Graham Bilbrough, Keith & Tim Atack & Mike McKenzie

Date	Title	⬆	✪	22
29 Apr 78	**WHEN YOU WALK IN THE ROOM** *Ariola Hansa AHA 511*	38		5
22 Jul 78	**IT'S ONLY MAKE BELIEVE** *Ariola Hansa AHA 522* ○	10		12
28 Apr 79	**ONLY YOU (AND YOU ALONE)** *Ariola Hansa AHA 536*	33		5

JANE CHILD
Canada, female vocalist

Date	Title	⬆	✪	8
12 May 90	**DON'T WANNA FALL IN LOVE** *Warner Brothers W 9817*	22		8

CHILDLINERS
UK/Australia/Ireland, male/female vocal charity group – Peter Andre*, A.S.A.P.*, Backstreet Boys*, Boyzone*, China Black*, Deuce*, East 17*, E.Y.C.*, Flood, Michelle Gayle*, Gemini*, Let Loose*, CJ Lewis*, Sean Maguire*, Dannii Minogue*, MN8*, Nightcrawlers*, Ultimate Kaos* & West End*

Date	Title	⬆	✪	6
16 Dec 95	**THE GIFT OF CHRISTMAS** *London LONCD 376*	9		6

CHILDREN FOR RWANDA
International, male/female vocal/instrumental charity assembly

Date	Title	⬆	✪	2
10 Sep 94	**LOVE CAN BUILD A BRIDGE** *East West YZ 849CD*	57		2

CHILDREN OF THE NIGHT
UK, male production duo — 2

Date	Title	Peak	Wks at No.1	Wks on Chart
26 Nov 88	**IT'S A TRIP (TUNE IN, TURN ON, DROP OUT)** *Jive 189*	52		2

TONI CHILDS
US, female vocalist — 4

Date	Title	Peak	Wks at No.1	Wks on Chart
25 Mar 89	**DON'T WALK AWAY** *A&M AM 462*	53		4

CHILI HI FLY
Australia, male DJ/production duo — 2

Date	Title	Peak	Wks at No.1	Wks on Chart
18 Mar 00	**IS IT LOVE?** *Ministry Of Sound MOSCDS 141*	37		2

CHILL FAC-TORR
US, male vocal group — 8

Date	Title	Peak	Wks at No.1	Wks on Chart
2 Apr 83	**TWIST (ROUND 'N' ROUND)** *Phillyworld PWS 109*	37		8

CHILLI FEATURING CARRAPICHO
US/Ghana/Brazil, male/female vocal/instrumental group — 1

Date	Title	Peak	Wks at No.1	Wks on Chart
20 Sep 97	**TIC, TIC TAC** *Arista 74321511332*	59		1

CHIMES
UK, male/female vocal/instrumental trio – Pauline Henry, James Locke & Mike Peden — 28

Date	Title	Peak	Wks at No.1	Wks on Chart
19 Aug 89	**1-2-3-** *CBS 6551667*	60		3
2 Dec 89	**HEAVEN** *CBS 6554327*	66		5
19 May 90	**STILL HAVEN'T FOUND WHAT I'M LOOKING FOR** *CBS CHIM 1*	6		9
28 Jul 90	**TRUE LOVE** *CBS CHIM 2*	48		3
29 Sep 90	**HEAVEN** *CBS CHIM 3*	24		6
1 Dec 90	**LOVE COMES TO MIND** *CBS CHIM 4*	49		2

CHIMIRA
UK (b. South Africa), female vocalist (Miriam Stockley) — 1

Date	Title	Peak	Wks at No.1	Wks on Chart
6 Dec 97	**SHOW ME HEAVEN** *Neoteric NRDCD 11*	70		1

CHINA BLACK
UK, male vocal/instrumental duo – Simon Fung & Errol Reid. See Childliners — 35

Date	Title	Peak	Wks at No.1	Wks on Chart
16 Jul 94	**SEARCHING** *Wild Card CARDD 7* ●	4		20
29 Oct 94	**STARS** *Wild Card CARDD 9*	19		7
11 Feb 95	**ALMOST SEE YOU (SOMEWHERE)** *Wild Card CARDW 15*	31		2
3 Jun 95	**SWING LOW SWEET CHARIOT** *Polygram TV SWLDW 2* LADYSMITH BLACK MAMBAZO FEATURING CHINA BLACK	15		6

CHINA CRISIS
UK, male vocal/instrumental group – Gary Daly, Gazza Johnson, Eddie Lundon & Kevin Wilkinson, d. 17 Jul 1999 — 66

Date	Title	Peak	Wks at No.1	Wks on Chart
7 Aug 82	**AFRICAN AND WHITE** *Inevitable INEV 011*	45		5
22 Jan 83	**CHRISTIAN** *Virgin VS 562*	12		9
21 May 83	**TRAGEDY AND MYSTERY** *Virgin VS 587*	46		6
15 Oct 83	**WORKING WITH FIRE AND STEEL** *Virgin VS 620*	48		5
14 Jan 84	**WISHFUL THINKING** *Virgin VS 647*	9		8
10 Mar 84	**HANNA HANNA** *Virgin VS 665*	44		3
30 Mar 85	**BLACK MAN RAY** *Virgin VS 752*	14		9
1 Jun 85	**KING IN A CATHOLIC STYLE (WAKE UP)** *Virgin VS 765*	19		9
7 Sep 85	**YOU DID CUT ME** *Virgin VS 799*	54		3
8 Nov 86	**ARIZONA SKY** *Virgin VS 898*	47		4
24 Jan 87	**BEST KEPT SECRET** *Virgin VS 926*	36		5

CHINA DRUM
UK, male vocal/instrumental group — 4

Date	Title	Peak	Wks at No.1	Wks on Chart
2 Mar 96	**CAN'T STOP THESE THINGS** *Mantra MNT 8CD*	65		1
20 Apr 96	**LAST CHANCE** *Mantra MNT 10CD*	60		1
9 Aug 97	**FICTION OF LIFE** *Mantra MNT 21CD*	65		1
27 Sep 97	**SOMEWHERE ELSE** *Mantra MNT022CD1*	74		1

JONNY CHINGAS
US, male keyboard player (Raul Garcia), d. 18 Mar 1992 (age 52) — 6

Date	Title	Peak	Wks at No.1	Wks on Chart
19 Feb 83	**PHONE HOME** *CBS A 3121*	43		6

CHINGY
US, male rapper (Howard Bailey, Jr.) — 17

Date	Title	Peak	Wks at No.1	Wks on Chart
25 Oct 03	**RIGHT THURR** *Capitol CDCLS 849*	17		5
21 Feb 04	**HOLIDAE INN** *Capitol CDCLS 852*	35		3
29 May 04	**ONE CALL AWAY** *Capitol CDCL 856* FEATURING J WEAV	26		4
13 Nov 04	**BALLA BABY** *Parlophone CDCLS865*	34		3
23 Sep 06	**PULLIN' ME BACK** *Capitol CDR6710* FEATURING TYRESE	44		2

CHIPMUNK
UK, male vocalist/rapper (Jahmaal Fyffe). See Young Soul Rebels — 63

Date	Title	Peak	Wks at No.1	Wks on Chart
14 Mar 09	**CHIP DIDDY CHIP** *Alwayz ARCM002*	21		6
9 May 09	**TINY DANCER (HOLD ME CLOSER)** *Asylum ASYLUM9CD* IRONIK FEATURING CHIPMUNK & ELTON JOHN	3		9
18 Jul 09	**DIAMOND RINGS** *Jive 88697553162* FEATURING EMELI SANDE	6		12
17 Oct 09	**OOPSY DAISY** *Jive 88697588692*	1	1	15
28 Nov 09	**LOOK FOR ME** *Columbia 88697632322* FEATURING TALAY RILEY	7		16+
13 Mar 10	**NUMBER ONE ENEMY** *Jive GBARL0901628* DAISY DARES YOU FEATURING CHIPMUNK	13		5+

CHIPMUNKS
US, male sped-up vocalist (Ross Bagdasarian, later Ross Bagdasarian, Jr) — 12

Date	Title	Peak	Wks at No.1	Wks on Chart
24 Jul 59	**RAGTIME COWBOY JOE** *London HLU 8916* DAVID SEVILLE & THE CHIPMUNKS	11		8
19 Dec 92	**ACHY BREAKY HEART** *Epic 6588837* ALVIN & THE CHIPMUNKS FEATURING BILLY RAY CYRUS	53		3
14 Dec 96	**MACARENA** *Sony Wonder 6639981* LOS DEL CHIPMUNKS	65		1

CHIPPENDALES
UK/US, male vocal/erotic dance group — 4

Date	Title	Peak	Wks at No.1	Wks on Chart
31 Oct 92	**GIVE ME YOUR BODY** *XSrhythm XSR 3*	28		4

CHIPZ
Holland, male/female vocal group — 1

Date	Title	Peak	Wks at No.1	Wks on Chart
24 Feb 07	**COWBOY** *Sony BMG 88697060862*	44		1

!!!
US, male vocal/instrumental group — 1

Date	Title	Peak	Wks at No.1	Wks on Chart
21 Aug 04	**HELLO? IS THIS THING ON?** *Warp WAP176CD*	74		1

CHOCOLATE MONDAY
UK, female vocal group — 2

Date	Title	Peak	Wks at No.1	Wks on Chart
12 Feb 05	**YOUR PLACE OR MINE** *DPI DPIBD1*	49		1
29 Oct 05	**MODEL LIFE** *DPI CDDPIBD2*	61		1

CHOCOLATE PUMA
Holland, male production duo – Rene ter Horst (DJ Dobri) & Gaston Steenkist (DJ Zki). See Goodmen, Jark Prongo, Rhythmkillaz, Riva featuring Dannii Minogue, Tomba Vira — 12

Date	Title	Peak	Wks at No.1	Wks on Chart
24 Mar 01	**I WANNA BE U** *Cream 13CD*	6		9
19 Aug 06	**ALWAYS AND FOREVER** *Positiva CDTIV241*	43		3

CHOIRBOYS
UK, male choristers — 2

Date	Title	Peak	Wks at No.1	Wks on Chart
31 Dec 05	**TEARS IN HEAVEN** *UCJ 4763116*	22		2

CHOO CHOO PROJECT
US, male/female vocal/production/instrumental duo. See Harry 'Choo Choo' Romero, Jose Nunez featuring Octahvia — 3

Date	Title	Peak	Wks at No.1	Wks on Chart
15 Jan 00	**HAZIN' & PHAZIN'** *Defected DEFECT 10CDS*	21		3

CHOONG FAMILY
UK, male rap/vocal group — 1

Date	Title	Peak	Wks at No.1	Wks on Chart
11 Feb 06	**MEMORY LANE** *Grizlockaz GRICDSMF1001*	57		1

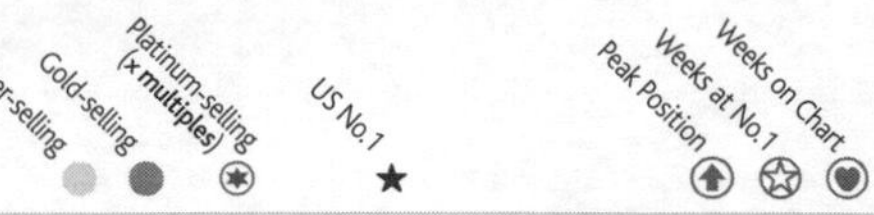

CHOPS-EMC + EXTENSIVE
UK, male production duo

Date	Title	Peak Position	Weeks at No.1	Weeks on Chart
				1
8 Aug 92	**ME ISRAELITES** *Faze 2 FAZE 6*	60		1

CHORDETTES
US, female vocal group – Janet Ertel, d. 22 Nov 1988, Carol Buschman, Lynn Evans & Margie Needham

Date	Title	Peak Position	Weeks at No.1	Weeks on Chart
				25
17 Dec 54	**MR SANDMAN** *Columbia DB 3553* ★	11		8
31 Aug 56	**BORN TO BE WITH YOU** *London HLA 8302*	8		9
18 Apr 58	**LOLLIPOP** *London HLD 8584*	6		8

CHORDS
UK, male vocal/instrumental group

Date	Title	Peak Position	Weeks at No.1	Weeks on Chart
				17
6 Oct 79	**NOW IT'S GONE** *Polydor 2059 141*	63		2
2 Feb 80	**MAYBE TOMORROW** *Polydor POSP 101*	40		5
26 Apr 80	**SOMETHING'S MISSING** *Polydor POSP 146*	55		3
12 Jul 80	**THE BRITISH WAY OF LIFE** *Polydor 2059 258*	54		3
18 Oct 80	**IN MY STREET** *Polydor POSP 185*	50		4

CHRIS & JAMES
UK, male instrumental/production duo

Date	Title	Peak Position	Weeks at No.1	Weeks on Chart
				17
17 Sep 94	**CALM DOWN (BASS KEEPS PUMPIN')** *Stress 12STR 38*	74		1
4 Nov 95	**FOX FORCE FIVE** *Stress CDSTR 61*	71		1
7 Nov 98	**CLUB FOR LIFE '98** *Stress CDSTR 85*	66		1

NEIL CHRISTIAN
UK, male vocalist (Christopher Tidmarsh), d. 4 Jan 2010 (age 66)

Date	Title	Peak Position	Weeks at No.1	Weeks on Chart
				10
7 Apr 66	**THAT'S NICE** *Strike JH 301*	14		10

ROGER CHRISTIAN
UK, male vocalist, d. 8 Mar 1998 (age 38). See Christians

Date	Title	Peak Position	Weeks at No.1	Weeks on Chart
				3
30 Sep 89	**TAKE IT FROM ME** *Island IS 427*	63		3

CHRISTIANS
UK, male vocal/instrumental group – Garry, Roger & Russell Christian & Henry Priestman

Date	Title	Peak Position	Weeks at No.1	Weeks on Chart
				84
31 Jan 87	**FORGOTTEN TOWN** *Island IS 291*	22		11
13 Jun 87	**HOOVERVILLE (THEY PROMISED US THE WORLD)** *Island IS 326*	21		10
26 Sep 87	**WHEN THE FINGERS POINT** *Island IS 335*	34		7
5 Dec 87	**IDEAL WORLD** *Island IS 347*	14		13
23 Apr 88	**BORN AGAIN** *Island IS 365*	25		7
15 Oct 88	**HARVEST FOR THE WORLD** *Island IS 395*	8		7
20 May 89	**FERRY 'CROSS THE MERSEY** *PWL 41* CHRISTIANS, HOLLY JOHNSON, PAUL McCARTNEY, GERRY MARSDEN & STOCK AITKEN WATERMAN	1	3	7
23 Dec 89	**WORDS** *Island IS 450*	18		8
7 Apr 90	**I FOUND OUT** *Island IS 453*	56		2
15 Sep 90	**GREENBANK DRIVE** *Island IS 466*	63		2
5 Sep 92	**WHAT'S IN A WORD** *Island IS 536*	33		5
14 Nov 92	**FATHER** *Island IS 543*	55		2
6 Mar 93	**THE BOTTLE** *Island CID 549*	39		3

CHRISTIE
UK, male vocal/instrumental trio – Jeff Christie, Mike Blakely & Vic Elmes

Date	Title	Peak Position	Weeks at No.1	Weeks on Chart
				37
2 May 70	**YELLOW RIVER** *CBS 4911*	1	1	22
10 Oct 70	**SAN BERNADINO** *CBS 5169*	7		14
25 Mar 72	**IRON HORSE** *CBS 7747*	47		1

DAVID CHRISTIE
France, male vocalist (Jacques Pepino)

Date	Title	Peak Position	Weeks at No.1	Weeks on Chart
				12
14 Aug 82	**SADDLE UP** *KR 9*	9		12

JOHN CHRISTIE
Australia, male vocalist

Date	Title	Peak Position	Weeks at No.1	Weeks on Chart
				6
25 Dec 76	**HERE'S TO LOVE (AULD LANG SYNE)** *EMI 2554*	24		6

LOU CHRISTIE
US, male vocalist (Lugee Sacco)

Date	Title	Peak Position	Weeks at No.1	Weeks on Chart
				35
24 Feb 66	**LIGHTNIN' STRIKES** *MGM 1297* ★	11		8
28 Apr 66	**RHAPSODY IN THE RAIN** *MGM 1308*	37		2
13 Sep 69	**I'M GONNA MAKE YOU MINE** *Buddah 201 057*	2		17
27 Dec 69	**SHE SOLD ME MAGIC** *Buddah 201 073*	25		8

TONY CHRISTIE
UK, male vocalist (Tony Fitzgerald)

Date	Title	Peak Position	Weeks at No.1	Weeks on Chart
				91
9 Jan 71	**LAS VEGAS** *MCA MK 5058*	21		9
8 May 71	**I DID WHAT I DID FOR MARIA** *MCA MK 5064*	2		17
20 Nov 71	**IS THIS THE WAY TO AMARILLO** *MCA MKS 5073*	18		13
10 Feb 73	**AVENUES AND ALLEYWAYS** *MCA MKS 5101*	37		4
17 Jan 76	**DRIVE SAFELY DARLIN'** *MCA 219*	35		4
23 Jan 99	**WALK LIKE A PANTHER '98** *ffrr FCDP 351* ALL SEEING I FEATURING TONY CHRISTIE	10		7
26 Mar 05	**(IS THIS THE WAY TO) AMARILLO** *Universal TV 9828606* FEATURING PETER KAY ⊛	1	7	25
6 Aug 05	**AVENUES AND ALLEYWAYS** *Universal TV 9831670*	26		3
17 Dec 05	**MERRY XMAS EVERYBODY** *Amarillo AMARILLOCD1*	49		1
31 Dec 05	**(IS THIS THE WAY TO) AMARILLO** *Universal TV 9828606* FEATURING PETER KAY	58		3
10 Jun 06	**(IS THIS THE WAY TO) THE WORLD CUP?** *Tug CDSNOG16*	8		5

BRYN CHRISTOPHER
UK, male vocalist

Date	Title	Peak Position	Weeks at No.1	Weeks on Chart
				4
21 Jun 08	**THE QUEST** *Polydor 1774810*	45		2
13 Sep 08	**SMILIN'** *Polydor 1779943*	31		2

SHAWN CHRISTOPHER
US, female vocalist

Date	Title	Peak Position	Weeks at No.1	Weeks on Chart
				10
4 May 91	**ANOTHER SLEEPLESS NIGHT** *Arista 114186*	50		4
21 Mar 92	**DON'T LOSE THE MAGIC** *Arista 115097*	30		5
2 Jul 94	**MAKE MY LOVE** *BTB BTBCD 502*	57		1

CHUCKIE & LMFAO
Suriname/US, male vocal/rap/DJ/production trio – Clyde Narain, Redfoo (Stefan Gordy) & Sky Blu (Skyler Gordy)

Date	Title	Peak Position	Weeks at No.1	Weeks on Chart
				9
19 Dec 09	**LET THE BASS KICK IN MIAMI GIRL** *Cr2 CDC2171*	9		9

CHUCKS
UK, male vocal/instrumental group

Date	Title	Peak Position	Weeks at No.1	Weeks on Chart
				7
24 Jan 63	**LOO-BE-LOO** *Decca F 11569*	22		7

CHUMBAWAMBA
UK, male/female vocal/instrumental group – Allan 'Boff' Whalley, Jude Abbott, Dunstan Bruce, Dave 'Mavis'" Dillon, Paul Greco, Harry 'Daz' Hamer, Anne 'Alice Nutter' Holden, Nigel 'Danbert Nobacon' Hunter & Lou Watts

Date	Title	Peak Position	Weeks at No.1	Weeks on Chart
				31
18 Sep 93	**ENOUGH IS ENOUGH** *One Little Indian 79 TP7CD* & CREDIT TO THE NATION	56		2
4 Dec 93	**TIMEBOMB** *One Little Indian 89 TP7CD*	59		1
23 Aug 97	**TUBTHUMPING** *EMI CDEM 486* ⊛	2		20
31 Jan 98	**AMNESIA** *EMI CDEM 498*	10		5
13 Jun 98	**TOP OF THE WORLD (OLÉ OLÉ OLÉ)** *EMI CDEM 511*	21		3

CHUBBY CHUNKS
UK, male producer (Scott Tinsley)

Date	Title	Peak Position	Weeks at No.1	Weeks on Chart
				2
4 Jun 94	**TESTAMENT 4** *Cleveland City CLECD 13017* VOLUME II	52		1
29 May 99	**I'M TELLIN' YOU** *Cleveland City CLECD 13052* FEATURING KIM RUFFIN	61		1

CHUPITO
Spain, male vocalist

Date	Title	Peak Position	Weeks at No.1	Weeks on Chart
				2
23 Sep 95	**AMERICAN PIE** *Eternal WEA 018CD*	54		2

CHARLOTTE CHURCH
UK, female vocalist (Charlotte Reed)

Date	Title	Peak Position	Weeks at No.1	Weeks on Chart
				51
25 Dec 99	**JUST WAVE HELLO** *Sony Classical 6685312*	34		4
1 Feb 03	**THE OPERA SONG (BRAVE NEW WORLD)** *Direction 6734642* JURGEN VRIES FEATURING CMC	3		10

Date	Title	Peak Position	Weeks at No.1	Weeks on Chart
9 Jul 05	**CRAZY CHICK** *Sony BMG 6759542*	2		18
8 Oct 05	**CALL MY NAME** *Sony BMG 82876727642*	10		9
17 Dec 05	**EVEN GOD CAN'T CHANGE THE PAST** *Sony BMG 82876767052*	17		5
11 Mar 06	**MOODSWINGS (TO COME AT ME LIKE THAT)** *Sony BMG 82876804482*	14		5

CIARA
US, female vocalist (Ciara Harris) — 87

Date	Title	Peak Position	Weeks at No.1	Weeks on Chart
15 Jan 05	**GOODIES (IMPORT)** *Jive 82876648252* FEATURING PETEY PABLO	68		1
29 Jan 05	**GOODIES** *LaFace 82876673132* FEATURING PETEY PABLO ★	1	1	9
23 Apr 05	**1 2 STEP** *LaFace 82876688342* FEATURING MISSY ELLIOTT	3		11
13 Aug 05	**OH** *LaFace 82876711372* FEATURING LUDACRIS	4		9
18 Mar 06	**LIKE YOU** *Columbia 82876779522* BOW WOW FEATURING CIARA	17		5
26 Aug 06	**SO WHAT** *Geffen 1705382* FIELD MOBB FEATURING CIARA	56		2
31 Mar 07	**LIKE A BOY** *LaFace 88697082882*	16		10
7 Mar 09	**TAKIN' BACK MY LOVE** *Interscope USUM70840861* ENRIQUE IGLESIAS FEATURING CIARA	12		20
18 Apr 09	**LOVE SEX MAGIC** *RCA 88697520672* FEATURING JUSTIN TIMBERLAKE	5		14
11 Jul 09	**WORK** *LaFace USLF20900040* FEATURING MISSY ELLIOTT	52		6

CICERO
UK (b. US), male vocalist (David Cicero) — 12

Date	Title	Peak Position	Weeks at No.1	Weeks on Chart
18 Jan 92	**LOVE IS EVERYWHERE** *Spaghetti CIAO 3*	19		8
18 Apr 92	**THAT LOVING FEELING** *Spaghetti CIAO 4*	46		3
1 Aug 92	**HEAVEN MUST HAVE SENT YOU BACK TO ME** *Spaghetti CIAO 5*	70		1

GABRIELLA CILMI
Australia, female vocalist — 48

Date	Title	Peak Position	Weeks at No.1	Weeks on Chart
15 Mar 08	**SWEET ABOUT ME** *Island 1764472*	6		37
30 Aug 08	**SAVE THE LIES (GOOD TO ME)** *Island 1781879*	33		2
13 Dec 08	**WARM THIS WINTER** *Island GBUM70815528*	22		5
20 Mar 10	**ON A MISSION** *Island 2732289*	9		4+

CINDERELLA
US, male vocal/instrumental group — 7

Date	Title	Peak Position	Weeks at No.1	Weeks on Chart
6 Aug 88	**GYPSY ROAD** *Vertigo VER 40*	54		2
4 Mar 89	**DON'T KNOW WHAT YOU GOT (TILL IT'S GONE)** *Vertigo VER 43*	54		2
17 Nov 90	**SHELTER ME** *Vertigo VER 51*	55		2
27 Apr 91	**HEARTBREAK STATION** *Vertigo VER 53*	63		1

CINDY & THE SAFFRONS
UK, female vocal trio — 3

Date	Title	Peak Position	Weeks at No.1	Weeks on Chart
15 Jan 83	**PAST, PRESENT AND FUTURE** *Stiletto STL 9*	56		3

CINERAMA
UK, male/female vocal/instrumental duo. See Wedding Present — 1

Date	Title	Peak Position	Weeks at No.1	Weeks on Chart
18 Jul 98	**KERRY KERRY** *Cooking Vinyl FRYCD 072*	71		1

GIGLIOLA CINQUETTI
Italy, female vocalist — 27

Date	Title	Peak Position	Weeks at No.1	Weeks on Chart
23 Apr 64	**NON HO L'ETA PER AMARTI** *Decca F 21882*	17		17
4 May 74	**GO (BEFORE YOU BREAK MY HEART)** *CBS 2294*	8		10

CIRCA FEATURING DESTRY
UK/US, male vocal/production group — 1

Date	Title	Peak Position	Weeks at No.1	Weeks on Chart
27 Nov 99	**SUN SHINING DOWN** *Inferno CDFERN 22*	70		1

CIRCUIT
UK, male/female production trio — 3

Date	Title	Peak Position	Weeks at No.1	Weeks on Chart
20 Jul 91	**SHELTER ME** *Cooltempo COOL 237*	44		2
1 Apr 95	**SHELTER ME** *Pukka CDPUKA 2*	50		1

CIRCULATION
UK, male production duo — 1

Date	Title	Peak Position	Weeks at No.1	Weeks on Chart
1 Sep 01	**TURQUOISE** *Hooj Choons HOOJ 109CD*	64		1

CIRRUS
UK, female vocal group — 1

Date	Title	Peak Position	Weeks at No.1	Weeks on Chart
30 Sep 78	**ROLLIN' ON** *Jet 123*	62		1

CITIZEN CANED
UK, male producer (Darren Tate). See Angelic, DT8 Project, Orion, Jurgen Vries — 2

Date	Title	Peak Position	Weeks at No.1	Weeks on Chart
7 Apr 01	**THE JOURNEY** *Serious SERR 029CD*	41		2

CITY BOY
UK, male vocal/instrumental group – Lol Mason, Steve Broughton, Chris Dunn, Mike Slamer, Max Thomas & Roy Ward — 20

Date	Title	Peak Position	Weeks at No.1	Weeks on Chart
8 Jul 78	**5-7-0-5** *Vertigo 6059 207* ●	8		12
28 Oct 78	**WHAT A NIGHT** *Vertigo 6059 211*	39		5
15 Sep 79	**THE DAY THE EARTH CAUGHT FIRE** *Vertigo 6059 238*	67		3

CITY HIGH
US, male/female vocal/rap trio – Ryan Toby, Claudette Ortiz & Robby Pardlo — 27

Date	Title	Peak Position	Weeks at No.1	Weeks on Chart
6 Oct 01	**WHAT WOULD YOU DO** *Interscope IND 97617*	3		17
16 Mar 02	**CARAMEL** *Interscope 4976742* FEATURING EVE	9		10

CK & SUPREME DREAM TEAM
Holland/Belgium/US, male production trio — 3

Date	Title	Peak Position	Weeks at No.1	Weeks on Chart
11 Jan 03	**DREAMER** *Multiply CDMULTY 96*	23		3

GARY CLAIL
UK, male vocal/production duo – Gary Clail & Adrian Sherwood – and vocal/production collaborators — 19

Date	Title	Peak Position	Weeks at No.1	Weeks on Chart
14 Jul 90	**BEEF** *RCA PB 49265*	64		2
30 Mar 91	**HUMAN NATURE** *Perfecto PB 44401* ON-U SOUND SYSTEM	10		9
8 Jun 91	**ESCAPE** *Perfecto PB 44563* ON-U SOUND SYSTEM	44		3
14 Nov 92	**WHO PAYS THE PIPER** *Perfecto 74321117017* ON-U SOUND SYSTEM	31		3
22 May 93	**THESE THINGS ARE WORTH FIGHTING FOR** *Perfecto 74321147222* ON-U SOUND SYSTEM	45		2

CLAIRE & FRIENDS
UK, female vocalist (Claire Usher) & male/female school friends — 11

Date	Title	Peak Position	Weeks at No.1	Weeks on Chart
7 Jun 86	**IT'S 'ORRIBLE BEING IN LOVE (WHEN YOU'RE 8XHALFX)** *BBC RESL 189*	13		11

CLANNAD
Ireland, female/male vocal/instrumental group – Máire Brennan*, Ciarán & Pól Brennan & Noel & Pádraig Duggan — 39

Date	Title	Peak Position	Weeks at No.1	Weeks on Chart
6 Nov 82	**THEME FROM HARRY'S GAME** *RCA 292* ●	5		10
2 Jul 83	**NEWGRANGE** *RCA 340*	65		1
12 May 84	**ROBIN (THE HOODED MAN)** *RCA HOOD 1*	42		5
25 Jan 86	**IN A LIFETIME** *RCA PB 40535* FEATURING BONO	20		5
10 Jun 89	**IN A LIFETIME** *RCA PB 42873* FEATURING BONO	17		7
10 Aug 91	**BOTH SIDES NOW** *MCA MCS 1546* & PAUL YOUNG	74		1
5 Jun 99	**SALTWATER** *Xtravaganza XTRAV 1CDS* CHICANE FEATURING MAIRE BRENNAN OF CLANNAD	6		10

JIMMY CLANTON
US, male vocalist — 1

Date	Title	Peak Position	Weeks at No.1	Weeks on Chart
21 Jul 60	**ANOTHER SLEEPLESS NIGHT** *Top Rank JAR 382*	50		1

CLAP YOUR HANDS SAY YEAH
US, male vocal/instrumental group — 2

Date	Title	Peak Position	Weeks at No.1	Weeks on Chart
17 Dec 05	**IS THIS LOVE** *Wichita WEBB101S*	74		1
11 Mar 06	**IN THIS HOME ON ICE** *Wichita WEBB102SCD*	68		1

ERIC CLAPTON
UK, male vocalist/guitarist. See Blind Faith, Cream, Yardbirds — 150

Date	Title	Peak Position	Weeks at No.1	Weeks on Chart
20 Dec 69	**COMIN' HOME** *Atlantic 584 308* DELANEY & BONNIE & FRIENDS FEATURING ERIC CLAPTON	16		9
12 Aug 72	**LAYLA** *Polydor 2058 130* DEREK & THE DOMINOES	7		11
27 Jul 74	**I SHOT THE SHERIFF** *RSO 2090 132* ★	9		9

Silver-selling ● Gold-selling ● Platinum-selling (x multiples) ✪ US No.1 ★ Peak Position | Weeks at No.1 | Weeks on Chart

Date	Title	Peak Position	Weeks at No.1	Weeks on Chart
10 May 75	**SWING LOW SWEET CHARIOT** *RSO 2090 158*	19		9
16 Aug 75	**KNOCKIN' ON HEAVEN'S DOOR** *RSO 2090 166*	38		4
24 Dec 77	**LAY DOWN SALLY** *RSO 2090 264*	39		6
21 Oct 78	**PROMISES** *RSO 21*	37		7
6 Mar 82	**LAYLA** *RSO 87* DEREK & THE DOMINOES	4		10
5 Jun 82	**I SHOT THE SHERIFF** *RSO 88*	64		2
23 Apr 83	**THE SHAPE YOU'RE IN** *Duck W 9701*	75		1
16 Mar 85	**FOREVER MAN** *Warner Brothers W 9069*	51		4
4 Jan 86	**EDGE OF DARKNESS** *BBC RESL 178* FEATURING MICHAEL KAMEN	65		3
17 Jan 87	**BEHIND THE MASK** *Duck W 8461*	15		11
20 Jun 87	**TEARING US APART** *Duck W 8299* & TINA TURNER	56		3
27 Jan 90	**BAD LOVE** *Duck W 2644*	25		7
14 Apr 90	**NO ALIBIS** *Duck W 3644*	53		3
16 Nov 91	**WONDERFUL TONIGHT (LIVE)** *Duck W 0069*	30		7
8 Feb 92	**TEARS IN HEAVEN** *Reprise W 0081*	5		12
1 Aug 92	**RUNAWAY TRAIN** *Rocket EJS 29* ELTON JOHN & ERIC CLAPTON	31		4
29 Aug 92	**IT'S PROBABLY ME** *A&M AM 883* STING WITH ERIC CLAPTON	30		5
3 Oct 92	**LAYLA (ACOUSTIC)** *Duck W 0134*	45		3
15 Oct 94	**MOTHERLESS CHILD** *Duck W 0271CD*	63		1
18 Mar 95	**LOVE CAN BUILD A BRIDGE** *London COCD 1* CHER, CHRISSIE HYNDE & NENEH CHERRY WITH ERIC CLAPTON ●	1	1	8
20 Jul 96	**CHANGE THE WORLD** *Reprise W 0358CD*	18		5
4 Apr 98	**MY FATHER'S EYES** *Duck W 0443CD*	33		2
4 Jul 98	**CIRCUS** *Duck W 0447CD*	39		2
18 Nov 00	**FOREVER MAN (HOW MANY TIMES)** *ffrr FCD 386* BEATCHUGGERS FEATURING ERIC CLAPTON	26		2

DAVE CLARK FIVE

UK, male vocal/instrumental group – Mike Smith, d. 28 Feb 2008, Dave Clark, Lenny Davidson, Rick Huxley & Denis Payton, d. 17 Dec 2006 — 174

Date	Title	Peak Position	Weeks at No.1	Weeks on Chart
3 Oct 63	**DO YOU LOVE ME** *Columbia DB 7112*	30		6
21 Nov 63	**GLAD ALL OVER** *Columbia DB 7154*	1	2	19
20 Feb 64	**BITS AND PIECES** *Columbia DB 7210*	2		11
28 May 64	**CAN'T YOU SEE THAT SHE'S MINE** *Columbia DB 7291*	10		11
13 Aug 64	**THINKING OF YOU BABY** *Columbia DB 7335*	26		4
22 Oct 64	**ANYWAY YOU WANT IT** *Columbia DB 7377*	25		5
14 Jan 65	**EVERYBODY KNOWS** *Columbia DB 7453*	37		4
11 Mar 65	**REELIN' AND ROCKIN'** *Columbia DB 7503*	24		8
27 May 65	**COME HOME** *Columbia DB 7580*	16		8
15 Jul 65	**CATCH US IF YOU CAN** *Columbia DB 7625*	5		11
11 Nov 65	**OVER AND OVER** *Columbia DB 7744* ★	45		4
19 May 66	**LOOK BEFORE YOU LEAP** *Columbia DB 7909*	50		1
16 Mar 67	**YOU GOT WHAT IT TAKES** *Columbia DB 8152*	28		8
1 Nov 67	**EVERYBODY KNOWS** *Columbia DB 8286*	2		14
28 Feb 68	**NO ONE CAN BREAK A HEART LIKE YOU** *Columbia DB 8342*	28		7
18 Sep 68	**RED BALLOON** *Columbia DB 8465*	7		11
27 Nov 68	**LIVE IN THE SKY** *Columbia DB 8505*	39		6
25 Oct 69	**PUT A LITTLE LOVE IN YOUR HEART** *Columbia DB 8624*	31		4
6 Dec 69	**GOOD OLD ROCK 'N' ROLL** *Columbia DB 8638*	7		12
7 Mar 70	**EVERYBODY GET TOGETHER** *Columbia DB 8660*	8		8
4 Jul 70	**HERE COMES SUMMER** *Columbia DB 8689*	44		3
7 Nov 70	**MORE GOOD OLD ROCK 'N' ROLL** *Columbia DB 8724*	34		6
1 May 93	**GLAD ALL OVER** *EMI CDEMCT 8*	37		3

DEE CLARK

US, male vocalist (Delecta Clark), d. 7 Dec 1990 (age 52) — 9

Date	Title	Peak Position	Weeks at No.1	Weeks on Chart
2 Oct 59	**JUST KEEP IT UP** *London HL 8915*	26		1
11 Oct 75	**RIDE A WILD HORSE** *Chelsea 2005 037*	16		8

GARY CLARK

UK, male vocalist. See Danny Wilson — 8

Date	Title	Peak Position	Weeks at No.1	Weeks on Chart
30 Jan 93	**WE SAIL ON THE STORMY WATERS** *Circa YRCDX 93*	34		4
3 Apr 93	**FREEFLOATING** *Circa YRCDX 94*	50		3
19 Jun 93	**MAKE A FAMILY** *Circa YRCDX 105*	70		1

LONI CLARK

US, female vocalist — 6

Date	Title	Peak Position	Weeks at No.1	Weeks on Chart
5 Jun 93	**RUSHING** *A&M 5802862*	37		2
22 Jan 94	**U** *A&M 5804752*	28		3
17 Dec 94	**LOVE'S GOT ME ON A TRIP SO HIGH** *A&M 5808872*	59		1

PETULA CLARK

UK, female vocalist. World War II child star who appeared in a string of films and was voted the UK's top TV personality before she had her first hit. She was also the first British female to win a Grammy and the first to be named 'Female Vocalist of the Year' in the US — 247

Date	Title	Peak Position	Weeks at No.1	Weeks on Chart
11 Jun 54	**THE LITTLE SHOEMAKER** *Polygon P 1117*	7		10
18 Feb 55	**MAJORCA** *Polygon P 1146*	12		5
25 Nov 55	**SUDDENLY THERE'S A VALLEY** *Pye Nixa N 15013*	7		10
26 Jul 57	**WITH ALL MY HEART** *Pye Nixa N 15096*	4		18
15 Nov 57	**ALONE** *Pye Nixa N 15112*	8		12
28 Feb 58	**BABY LOVER** *Pye Nixa N 15126*	12		7
26 Jan 61	**SAILOR** *Pye 7N 15324*	1	1	15
13 Apr 61	**SOMETHING MISSING** *Pye 7N 15337*	44		1
13 Jul 61	**ROMEO** *Pye 7N 15361*	3		15
16 Nov 61	**MY FRIEND THE SEA** *Pye 7N 15389*	7		13
8 Feb 62	**I'M COUNTING ON YOU** *Pye 7N 15407*	41		2
28 Jun 62	**YA YA TWIST** *Pye 7N 15448*	14		13
2 May 63	**CASANOVA/CHARIOT** *Pye 7N 15522*	39		7
12 Nov 64	**DOWNTOWN** *Pye 7N 15722* ★	2		15
11 Mar 65	**I KNOW A PLACE** *Pye 7N 15772*	17		8
12 Aug 65	**YOU BETTER COME HOME** *Pye 7N 15864*	44		3
14 Oct 65	**ROUND EVERY CORNER** *Pye 7N 15945*	43		3
4 Nov 65	**YOU'RE THE ONE** *Pye 7N 15991*	23		9
10 Feb 66	**MY LOVE** *Pye 7N 17038* ★	4		9
21 Apr 66	**A SIGN OF THE TIMES** *Pye 7N 17071*	49		1
30 Jun 66	**I COULDN'T LIVE WITHOUT YOUR LOVE** *Pye 7N 17133*	6		11
2 Feb 67	**THIS IS MY SONG** *Pye 7N 17258*	1	2	14
25 May 67	**DON'T SLEEP IN THE SUBWAY** *Pye 7N 17325*	12		11
13 Dec 67	**THE OTHER MAN'S GRASS (IS ALWAYS GREENER)** *Pye 7N 17416*	20		9
6 Mar 68	**KISS ME GOODBYE** *Pye 7N 17466*	50		1
30 Jan 71	**THE SONG OF MY LIFE** *Pye 7N 45026*	32		12
15 Jan 72	**I DON'T KNOW HOW TO LOVE HIM** *Pye 7N 45112*	47		2
19 Nov 88	**DOWNTOWN** *PRT PYS 19*	10		11

ROLAND CLARK

US, male vocalist/producer — 7

Date	Title	Peak Position	Weeks at No.1	Weeks on Chart
1 May 99	**FLOWERZ** *ffrr FCD 361* ARMAND VAN HELDEN FEATURING ROLAND CLARK	18		6
23 Mar 02	**SPEED (CAN YOU FEEL IT?)** *Club Tools 0135815 CLU* AZZIDO DA BASS FEATURING ROLAND CLARK	68		1

DAVE CLARKE

UK, male producer — 10

Date	Title	Peak Position	Weeks at No.1	Weeks on Chart
30 Sep 95	**RED THREE, THUNDER/STORM** *Deconstruction 74321306992*	45		2
3 Feb 96	**SOUTHSIDE** *Bush 74321335382*	34		2
15 Jun 96	**NO ONE'S DRIVING** *Bush 74321380162*	37		2
8 Dec 01	**THE COMPASS** *Skint 73CD*	46		1
28 Dec 02	**THE WOLF** *Skint 78*	66		1
25 Oct 03	**WAY OF LIFE** *Skint 93CD*	59		1
21 Feb 04	**WHAT WAS HER NAME** *Skint 94CD* FEATURING CHICKS ON SPEED	50		1

JOHN COOPER CLARKE

UK, male vocalist — 3

Date	Title	Peak Position	Weeks at No.1	Weeks on Chart
10 Mar 79	**GIMMIX! PLAY LOUD** *Epic EPC 7009*	39		3

RICK CLARKE

UK, male vocalist — 2

Date	Title	Peak Position	Weeks at No.1	Weeks on Chart
30 Apr 88	**I'LL SEE YOU ALONG THE WAY** *WA 1*	63		2

WARREN CLARKE FEATURING KATHY BROWN

UK/US, male/female vocal/production duo — 1

Date	Title	Peak Position	Weeks at No.1	Weeks on Chart
2 Jun 01	**OVER YOU** *Defected DFECT 28CDS*	42		1

KELLY CLARKSON

US, female vocalist — 140

Date	Title	Peak Position	Weeks at No.1	Weeks on Chart
6 Sep 03	**MISS INDEPENDENT** *S 82876553642*	6		10
29 Nov 03	**LOW/THE TROUBLE WITH LOVE IS** *S 82876570702*	35		3
16 Jul 05	**SINCE U BEEN GONE** *RCA 82876700852*	5		37
1 Oct 05	**BEHIND THESE HAZEL EYES** *RCA 82876730302*	9		15
10 Dec 05	**BECAUSE OF YOU** *RCA 82876764542*	7		25
25 Mar 06	**WALK AWAY** *RCA 82876809832*	21		8
1 Jul 06	**BREAKAWAY** *RCA 82876845702*	22		8
23 Jun 07	**NEVER AGAIN** *RCA 88697110252*	9		8
7 Mar 09	**MY LIFE WOULD SUCK WITHOUT YOU** *RCA 88697463372* ●	1	1	17

Date	Title / Label	Peak Position	Weeks at No.1	Weeks on Chart
16 May 09	**I DO NOT HOOK UP** *RCA 88697524492*	36		7
29 Aug 09	**ALREADY GONE** *RCA GBCTA0900011*	66		2

CLARKESVILLE
UK, male vocalist/guitarist (Michael Clarke) — **1**

Date	Title / Label	Peak Position	Weeks at No.1	Weeks on Chart
7 Feb 04	**SPINNING** *Wildstar CDWILD 53*	72		1

CLASH
UK, male vocal/instrumental group – Joe Strummer*, d. 23 Dec 2002, Topper Headon, Mick Jones & Paul Simonon — **135**

Date	Title / Label	Peak Position	Weeks at No.1	Weeks on Chart
2 Apr 77	**WHITE RIOT** *CBS 5058*	38		3
8 Oct 77	**COMPLETE CONTROL** *CBS 5664*	28		2
4 Mar 78	**CLASH CITY ROCKERS** *CBS 5834*	35		4
24 Jun 78	**(WHITE MAN) IN HAMMERSMITH PALAIS** *CBS 6383*	32		7
2 Dec 78	**TOMMY GUN** *CBS 6788*	19		10
3 Mar 79	**ENGLISH CIVIL WAR (JOHNNY COMES MARCHING HOME)** *CBS 7082*	25		6
19 May 79	**THE COST OF LIVING EP** *CBS 7324*	22		8
15 Dec 79	**LONDON CALLING** *CBS 8087*	11		10
9 Aug 80	**BANKROBBER** *CBS 8323*	12		10
6 Dec 80	**THE CALL UP** *CBS 9339*	40		6
24 Jan 81	**HITSVILLE UK** *CBS 9480*	56		4
25 Apr 81	**THE MAGNIFICENT SEVEN** *CBS 1133*	34		5
28 Nov 81	**THIS IS RADIO CLASH** *CBS A 1797*	47		6
1 May 82	**KNOW YOUR RIGHTS** *CBS A 2309*	43		3
26 Jun 82	**ROCK THE CASBAH** *CBS A 2429*	30		10
25 Sep 82	**SHOULD I STAY OR SHOULD I GO/STRAIGHT TO HELL** *CBS A 2646*	17		9
12 Oct 85	**THIS IS ENGLAND** *CBS A 6122*	24		5
12 Mar 88	**I FOUGHT THE LAW** *CBS CLASH 1*	29		5
7 May 88	**LONDON CALLING** *CBS CLASH 2*	46		3
21 Jul 90	**RETURN TO BRIXTON** *CBS 6560727*	57		2
2 Mar 91	**SHOULD I STAY OR SHOULD I GO** *Columbia 6566677*	1	2	9
13 Apr 91	**ROCK THE CASBAH** *Columbia 6568147*	15		6
8 Jun 91	**LONDON CALLING** *Columbia 6569467*	64		2

CLASS ACTION FEATURING CHRIS WILTSHIRE
US, female vocal trio — **3**

Date	Title / Label	Peak Position	Weeks at No.1	Weeks on Chart
7 May 83	**WEEKEND** *Jive 35*	49		3

CLASSICS IV
US, male vocal/instrumental group — **1**

Date	Title / Label	Peak Position	Weeks at No.1	Weeks on Chart
28 Feb 68	**SPOOKY** *Liberty LBS 15051*	46		1

CLASSIX NOUVEAUX
UK, male vocal/instrumental group — **34**

Date	Title / Label	Peak Position	Weeks at No.1	Weeks on Chart
28 Feb 81	**GUILTY** *Liberty BP 388*	43		7
16 May 81	**TOKYO** *Liberty BP 397*	67		3
8 Aug 81	**INSIDE OUTSIDE** *Liberty BP 403*	45		5
7 Nov 81	**NEVER AGAIN (THE DAYS TIME ERASED)** *Liberty BP 406*	44		4
13 Mar 82	**IS IT A DREAM** *Liberty BP 409*	11		9
29 May 82	**BECAUSE YOU'RE YOUNG** *Liberty BP 411*	43		4
30 Oct 82	**THE END...OR THE BEGINNING** *Liberty BP 414*	60		2

CLAWFINGER
Sweden/Norway, male vocal/instrumental group — **1**

Date	Title / Label	Peak Position	Weeks at No.1	Weeks on Chart
19 Mar 94	**WARFAIR** *East West YZ 804CD1*	54		1

ADAM CLAYTON & LARRY MULLEN
Ireland, male instrumental duo. See U2 — **12**

Date	Title / Label	Peak Position	Weeks at No.1	Weeks on Chart
15 Jun 96	**THEME FROM 'MISSION: IMPOSSIBLE'** *Mother MUMCD 75*	7		12

MERRY CLAYTON
US, female vocalist — **1**

Date	Title / Label	Peak Position	Weeks at No.1	Weeks on Chart
21 May 88	**YES** *RCA PB 49563*	70		1

CLAYTOWN TROUPE
UK, male vocal/instrumental group — **3**

Date	Title / Label	Peak Position	Weeks at No.1	Weeks on Chart
16 Jun 90	**WAYS OF LOVE** *Island IS 464*	57		2
14 Mar 92	**WANTED IT ALL** *EMI USA MT 102*	74		1

CLEA
UK, female vocal group — **8**

Date	Title / Label	Peak Position	Weeks at No.1	Weeks on Chart
4 Oct 03	**DOWNLOAD IT** *1967 CLEA01CD*	21		3
28 Feb 04	**STUCK IN THE MIDDLE** *1967 CLEA02CD*	23		2
29 Oct 05	**WE DON'T HAVE TO TAKE OUR CLOTHES OFF** *Upside UPSIDECD02* DA PLAYAZ VS CLEA	35		2
24 Apr 06	**LUCKY LIKE THAT** *Upside UPSIDECD04*	55		1

JOHNNY CLEGG & SAVUKA
South Africa (b. UK), male vocalist/instrumentalist & male/female vocal/instrumental group — **1**

Date	Title / Label	Peak Position	Weeks at No.1	Weeks on Chart
16 May 87	**SCATTERLINGS OF AFRICA** *EMI 5605*	75		1

CLEOPATRA
UK, female vocal trio – Cleo, Yonah & Zainam Higgins — **31**

Date	Title / Label	Peak Position	Weeks at No.1	Weeks on Chart
14 Feb 98	**CLEOPATRA'S THEME** *WEA 133CD*	3		10
16 May 98	**LIFE AIN'T EASY** *WEA 159CD1*	4		7
22 Aug 98	**I WANT YOU BACK** *WEA 172CD1*	4		7
6 Mar 99	**A TOUCH OF LOVE** *WEA 199CD*	24		4
29 Jul 00	**COME AND GET ME** *WEA 261CD1*	29		3

CLEPTOMANIACS FEATURING BRYAN CHAMBERS
UK, male vocal/production group — **3**

Date	Title / Label	Peak Position	Weeks at No.1	Weeks on Chart
3 Feb 01	**ALL I DO** *Defected DFECT 27CDS*	23		3

CLERGY
UK, male production duo. See Candy Girls, Dorothy, Hi-Gate, Paul Masterson presents Sushi, Precocious Brats featuring Kevin & Perry, Sleazesisters, Stix 'N' Stoned, Yomanda — **1**

Date	Title / Label	Peak Position	Weeks at No.1	Weeks on Chart
20 Jul 02	**THE OBOE SONG** *ffrr DFCD 005*	50		1

CLICK
US, male rap group — **1**

Date	Title / Label	Peak Position	Weeks at No.1	Weeks on Chart
29 Jun 96	**SCANDALOUS** *Jive JIVECD 393*	54		1

CLIENT
UK, female vocal/instrumental duo — **4**

Date	Title / Label	Peak Position	Weeks at No.1	Weeks on Chart
26 Jun 04	**IN IT FOR THE MONEY** *Toast Hawaii CDTH005*	51		1
2 Oct 04	**RADIO** *Toast Hawaii CDTH006*	68		1
22 Jan 05	**PORNOGRAPHY** *Toast Hawaii LCDTH008*	22		2

JIMMY CLIFF
Jamaica, male vocalist (James Chambers) — **33**

Date	Title / Label	Peak Position	Weeks at No.1	Weeks on Chart
25 Oct 69	**WONDERFUL WORLD BEAUTIFUL PEOPLE** *Trojan TR 690*	6		13
14 Feb 70	**VIETNAM** *Trojan TR 7722*	46		3
8 Aug 70	**WILD WORLD** *Island WIP 6087*	8		12
19 Mar 94	**I CAN SEE CLEARLY NOW** *Columbia 6601982*	23		5

BUZZ CLIFFORD
US, male vocalist (Reese Clifford III) — **13**

Date	Title / Label	Peak Position	Weeks at No.1	Weeks on Chart
2 Mar 61	**BABY SITTIN' BOOGIE** *Fontana H 297*	17		13

LINDA CLIFFORD
US, female vocalist — **13**

Date	Title / Label	Peak Position	Weeks at No.1	Weeks on Chart
10 Jun 78	**IF MY FRIENDS COULD SEE ME NOW** *Curtom K 17163*	50		5
5 May 79	**BRIDGE OVER TROUBLED WATER** *RSO 30*	28		7
15 Sep 01	**RIDE THE STORM** *NRK Sound Division NRKCD 053* AKABU FEATURING LINDA CLIFFORD	69		1

CLIMAX BLUES BAND
UK, male vocal/instrumental group – Colin Cooper, d. 3 Jul 2008, John Cuffley, Peter Haycock & Derek Holt — **9**

Date	Title / Label	Peak Position	Weeks at No.1	Weeks on Chart
9 Oct 76	**COULDN'T GET IT RIGHT** *BTM SBT 105*	10		9

Silver-selling ○ · Gold-selling ● · Platinum-selling (x multiples) · US No.1 ★ · Peak Position · Weeks at No.1 · Weeks on Chart

CLIMIE FISHER

UK, male vocal/instrumental duo – Simon Climie & Rob Fisher, d. 25 Aug 1999 — 44

Date	Title	Peak Position	Weeks at No.1	Weeks on Chart
5 Sep 87	**LOVE CHANGES (EVERYTHING)** *EMI EM 15*	67		2
12 Dec 87	**RISE TO THE OCCASION** *EMI EM 33*	10		11
12 Mar 88	**LOVE CHANGES EVERYTHING** *EMI EM 47*	2		12
21 May 88	**THIS IS ME** *EMI EM 58*	22		5
20 Aug 88	**I WON'T BLEED FOR YOU** *EMI EM 66*	35		4
24 Dec 88	**LOVE LIKE A RIVER** *EMI EM 81*	22		7
23 Sep 89	**FACTS OF LOVE** *EMI EM 103*	50		3

SIMON CLIMIE

UK, male vocalist. See Climie Fisher — 2

Date	Title	Peak Position	Weeks at No.1	Weeks on Chart
19 Sep 92	**SOUL INSPIRATION** *Epic 6582837*	60		2

PATSY CLINE

US, female vocalist (Virginia Hensley), d. 5 Mar 1963 (age 30) — 17

Date	Title	Peak Position	Weeks at No.1	Weeks on Chart
26 Apr 62	**SHE'S GOT YOU** *Brunswick 05866*	43		1
29 Nov 62	**HEARTACHES** *Brunswick 05878*	31		5
8 Dec 90	**CRAZY** *MCA 1465*	14		11

CLINIC

UK, male vocal/instrumental group — 3

Date	Title	Peak Position	Weeks at No.1	Weeks on Chart
22 Apr 00	**THE RETURN OF EVIL BILL** *Domino RUG 093CD*	70		1
4 Nov 00	**THE SECOND LINE** *Domino RUG 116CD*	56		1
2 Mar 02	**WALKING WITH THEE** *Domino Recordings RUG 134CD*	65		1

GEORGE CLINTON

US, male vocalist/producer. See Funkadelic — 10

Date	Title	Peak Position	Weeks at No.1	Weeks on Chart
4 Dec 82	**LOOPZILLA** *Capitol CL 271*	57		5
26 Apr 86	**DO FRIES GO WITH THAT SHAKE** *Capitol CL 402*	57		2
27 Aug 94	**BOP GUN (ONE NATION)** *Fourth & Broadway BRCD 308* ICE CUBE FEATURING GEORGE CLINTON	22		3

CLIPSE

US, male rap duo — 5

Date	Title	Peak Position	Weeks at No.1	Weeks on Chart
22 Feb 03	**WHEN THE LAST TIME** *Arista 82876502212*	41		2
24 May 03	**MA I DON'T LOVE HER** *Arista 82876526482* FEATURING FAITH EVANS	38		3

CLIPZ

UK, male DJ/producer (Hugh Pescod) — 2

Date	Title	Peak Position	Weeks at No.1	Weeks on Chart
6 Mar 04	**COCOA/JIGGY** *Full Cycle FCY064*	71		1
5 Mar 05	**SLIPPERY SLOPES/NASTY BREAKS** *Full Cycle FCY075*	72		1

CLOCK

UK, male production duo – Stu Allen & Pete Pritchard – with male/female vocal/rap duo – Marcus 'ODC MC' Thomas (replaced by Che-gun Peters) & Lorna Saunders — 70

Date	Title	Peak Position	Weeks at No.1	Weeks on Chart
30 Oct 93	**HOLDING ON** *Media MRLCD 007*	66		1
21 May 94	**THE RHYTHM** *Media MCSTD 1971*	28		2
10 Sep 94	**KEEP THE FIRES BURNING** *Media MCSTD 1998*	36		3
4 Mar 95	**AXEL F/KEEP PUSHIN'** *Media MCSXD 2041*	7		9
1 Jul 95	**WHOOMPH! (THERE IT IS)** *Media MCSTD 2059*	4		9
26 Aug 95	**EVERYBODY** *Media MCSTD 2077*	6		5
18 Nov 95	**IN THE HOUSE** *Media MCSTD 40005*	23		3
24 Feb 96	**HOLDING ON 4 U** *Media MCSTD 40019*	27		2
7 Sep 96	**OH WHAT A NIGHT** *Power Station MCSTD 40057*	13		10
22 Mar 97	**IT'S OVER** *Media MCSTD 40100*	10		5
18 Oct 97	**U SEXY THING** *Media MCSTD 40138*	11		9
17 Jan 98	**THAT'S THE WAY (I LIKE IT)** *Media MCSTD 40148*	11		4
11 Jul 98	**ROCK YOUR BODY** *Media MCSTD 40160*	30		3
28 Nov 98	**BLAME IT ON THE BOOGIE** *Media MCSTD 40191*	16		4
31 Jul 99	**SUNSHINE DAY** *Media MCSTD 40208*	58		1

ROSEMARY CLOONEY

US, female vocalist, d. 29 Jun 2002 (age 74) — 81

Date	Title	Peak Position	Weeks at No.1	Weeks on Chart
14 Nov 52	**HALF AS MUCH** *Columbia DB 3129* ★	3		9
5 Feb 54	**MAN (UH-HUH)** *Philips PB 220*	7		5
8 Oct 54	**THIS OLE HOUSE** *Philips PB 336* ★	1	1	18
17 Dec 54	**MAMBO ITALIANO** *Philips PB 382* WITH THE MELLOMEN	1	3	16
20 May 55	**WHERE WILL THE DIMPLE BE** *Philips PB 428* WITH THE MELLOMEN	6		13
30 Sep 55	**HEY THERE** *Philips PB 494* ★	4		11
29 Mar 57	**MANGOS** *Philips PB 671*	17		9

CLOR

UK, male vocal/instrumental group — 3

Date	Title	Peak Position	Weeks at No.1	Weeks on Chart
7 May 05	**LOVE & PAIN** *Regal REG120CD*	48		1
23 Jul 05	**OUTLINES** *Regal REG121CDS*	43		1
22 Oct 05	**GOOD STUFF** *Regal REG128CD*	50		1

CLOUD

UK, male instrumental group — 1

Date	Title	Peak Position	Weeks at No.1	Weeks on Chart
31 Jan 81	**ALL NIGHT LONG/TAKE IT TO THE TOP** *UK Champagne FUNK 1*	72		1

CLOUT

South Africa, female vocal/instrumental group – Cindi Alter, Ron Brettell, Jennie Garson, Ingrid Herbst, Sandy Robbie & Lee Tomlinson — 15

Date	Title	Peak Position	Weeks at No.1	Weeks on Chart
17 Jun 78	**SUBSTITUTE** *Carrere EMI 2788* ●	2		15

CLS

US, male vocal/production duo — 1

Date	Title	Peak Position	Weeks at No.1	Weeks on Chart
30 May 98	**CAN YOU FEEL IT** *Satellite 74321580162*	46		1

CLUB NOUVEAU

US, male/female vocal group – Denzil Foster, Thomas McElroy, Samuelle Prater & Valerie Watson — 12

Date	Title	Peak Position	Weeks at No.1	Weeks on Chart
21 Mar 87	**LEAN ON ME** *King Jay W 8430* ○ ★	3		12

CLUB 69

Austria, male producer (Peter Rauhofer) — 6

Date	Title	Peak Position	Weeks at No.1	Weeks on Chart
5 Dec 92	**LET ME BE YOUR UNDERWEAR** *ffrr F 204*	33		5
14 Nov 98	**ALRIGHT** *Twisted UK TWCD 10039* FEATURING SUZANNE PALMER	70		1

CLUBHOUSE

Italy, male production group – leader Gianfranco Bortolotti — 40

Date	Title	Peak Position	Weeks at No.1	Weeks on Chart
23 Jul 83	**DO IT AGAIN-BILLIE JEAN (MEDLEY)** *Island IS 132*	11		6
3 Dec 83	**SUPERSTITION – GOOD TIMES (MEDLEY)** *Island IS 147*	59		3
1 Jul 89	**I'M A MAN – YE KE YE KE (MEDLEY)** *Music Man MMPS 7003*	69		3
20 Apr 91	**DEEP IN MY HEART** *ffrr F 157*	55		4
4 Sep 93	**LIGHT MY FIRE** *PWL Continental PWCD 272* FEATURING CARL	45		12
30 Apr 94	**LIGHT MY FIRE (REMIX)** *PWL Continental PWCD 288* FEATURING CARL	7		8
23 Jul 94	**LIVING IN THE SUNSHINE** *PWL Continental PWCD 309* FEATURING CARL	21		3
11 Mar 95	**NOWHERE LAND** *PWL International PWCD 318* FEATURING CARL	56		1

CLUBZONE

UK, male producer – Mike Koglin — 1

Date	Title	Peak Position	Weeks at No.1	Weeks on Chart
19 Nov 94	**HANDS UP** *Logic 74321236982*	50		1

CLUELESS

US, male/female vocal/production group — 1

Date	Title	Peak Position	Weeks at No.1	Weeks on Chart
5 Apr 97	**DON'T SPEAK** *ZYX 660738*	61		1

CLYDE VALLEY STOMPERS

UK, male/female vocal/instrumental group — 8

Date	Title	Peak Position	Weeks at No.1	Weeks on Chart
9 Aug 62	**PETER AND THE WOLF** *Parlophone R 4928*	25		8

CM2 FEATURING LISA LAW

UK, male/female vocal/production group — 1

Date	Title	Peak Position	Weeks at No.1	Weeks on Chart
18 Jan 03	**FALL AT YOUR FEET** *INCredible 6732532*	66		1

CO-CO

UK, male/female vocal/instrumental group — 7

Date	Title	Peak Position	Weeks at No.1	Weeks on Chart
22 Apr 78	**BAD OLD DAYS** *Ariola Hansa AHA 513*	13		7

COAST TO COAST

UK, male/female vocal/instrumental group – Alan Mills (replaced by Sandy Fontaine), Earl Barton, Pattie Hem, Jamie Ling, Donna Page, Budd Smith & Eugene Torlot — 22

Date	Title	Peak Position	Weeks at No.1	Weeks on Chart
31 Jan 81	**(DO) THE HUCKLEBUCK** *Polydor POSP 214* ●	5		15
23 May 81	**LET'S JUMP THE BROOMSTICK** *Polydor POSP 249*	28		7

COAST 2 COAST FEATURING DISCOVERY

Ireland, male/female vocal/production trio — 1

Date	Title	Peak Position	Weeks at No.1	Weeks on Chart
16 Jun 01	**HOME** *Religion 0126955 RLG*	44		1

COASTERS

US, male vocal group – Carl Gardner, Billy Guy, Leon Hughes & Bobby Nunn — 32

Date	Title	Peak Position	Weeks at No.1	Weeks on Chart
27 Sep 57	**SEARCHIN'** *London HLE 8450*	30		1
15 Aug 58	**YAKETY YAK** *London HLE 8665* ★	12		8
27 Mar 59	**CHARLIE BROWN** *London HLE 8819*	6		12
30 Oct 59	**POISON IVY** *London HLE 8938*	15		7
9 Apr 94	**SORRY BUT I'M GONNA HAVE TO PASS** *Rhino A 4519CD*	41		4

LUIS COBOS FEATURING PLACIDO DOMINGO

Spain, male conductor & vocalist — 2

Date	Title	Peak Position	Weeks at No.1	Weeks on Chart
16 Jun 90	**NESSUN DORMA FROM 'TURANDOT'** *Epic 6560057*	59		2

COBRA STARSHIP

US, male vocal/instrumental group — 4

Date	Title	Peak Position	Weeks at No.1	Weeks on Chart
31 Oct 09	**GOOD GIRLS GO BAD** *Fueled By Ramen AT0349CD*	17		4

EDDIE COCHRAN

US, male vocalist/guitarist, d. 17 Apr 1960 (age 21) — 90

Date	Title	Peak Position	Weeks at No.1	Weeks on Chart
7 Nov 58	**SUMMERTIME BLUES** *London HLU 8702*	18		6
13 Mar 59	**C'MON EVERYBODY** *London HLU 8792*	6		13
16 Oct 59	**SOMETHIN' ELSE** *London HLU 8944*	22		3
22 Jan 60	**HALLELUJAH I LOVE HER SO** *London HLW 9022*	22		4
12 May 60	**THREE STEPS TO HEAVEN** *London HLG 9115*	1	2	15
6 Oct 60	**SWEETIE PIE** *London HLG 9196*	38		3
3 Nov 60	**LONELY** *London HLG 9196*	41		1
15 Jun 61	**WEEKEND** *London HLG 9362*	15		16
30 Nov 61	**JEANNIE, JEANNIE, JEANNIE** *London HLG 9460*	31		4
25 Apr 63	**MY WAY** *Liberty LIB 10088*	23		10
24 Apr 68	**SUMMERTIME BLUES** *Liberty LBF 15071*	34		8
13 Feb 88	**C'MON EVERYBODY** *Liberty EDDIE 501*	14		7

TOM COCHRANE

Canada, male vocalist/guitarist — 2

Date	Title	Peak Position	Weeks at No.1	Weeks on Chart
27 Jun 92	**LIFE IS A HIGHWAY** *Capitol CL 660*	62		2

COCK ROBIN

US, male/female vocal/instrumental group — 12

Date	Title	Peak Position	Weeks at No.1	Weeks on Chart
31 May 86	**THE PROMISE YOU MADE** *CBS A 6764*	28		12

JARVIS COCKER

UK, male vocalist/guitarist/keyboard player. See Pulp — 1

Date	Title	Peak Position	Weeks at No.1	Weeks on Chart
20 Jan 07	**DON'T LET HIM WASTE YOUR TIME** *Rough Trade RTRADSCD385*	36		1

JOE COCKER

UK, male vocalist/guitarist — 89

Date	Title	Peak Position	Weeks at No.1	Weeks on Chart
22 May 68	**MARJORINE** *Regal Zonophone RZ 3006*	48		1
2 Oct 68	**WITH A LITTLE HELP FROM MY FRIENDS** *Regal Zonophone RZ 3013*	1	1	13
27 Sep 69	**DELTA LADY** *Regal Zonophone RZ 3024*	10		11
4 Jul 70	**THE LETTER** *Regal Zonophone RZ 3027*	39		6
26 Sep 81	**I'M SO GLAD I'M STANDING HERE TODAY** *MCA 741* CRUSADERS, FEATURED VOCALIST JOE COCKER	61		3
15 Jan 83	**UP WHERE WE BELONG** *Island WIP 6830* & JENNIFER WARNES ● ★	7		13
14 Nov 87	**UNCHAIN MY HEART** *Capitol CL 465*	46		4
13 Jan 90	**WHEN THE NIGHT COMES** *Capitol CL 535*	65		2
7 Mar 92	**(ALL I KNOW) FEELS LIKE FOREVER** *Capitol CL 645*	25		5
9 May 92	**NOW THAT THE MAGIC HAS GONE** *Capitol CL 657*	28		6
4 Jul 92	**UNCHAIN MY HEART** *Capitol CL 664*	17		6
21 Nov 92	**WHEN THE NIGHT COMES** *Capitol CL 674*	61		3

Date	Title	Peak Position	Weeks at No.1	Weeks on Chart
13 Aug 94	**THE SIMPLE THINGS** *Capitol CDCLS 722*	17		5
22 Oct 94	**TAKE ME HOME** *Capitol CDCLS 729* FEATURING BEKKA BRAMLETT	41		3
17 Dec 94	**LET THE HEALING BEGIN** *Capitol CDCLS 727*	32		5
23 Sep 95	**HAVE A LITTLE FAITH** *Capitol CDCLS 744*	67		2
12 Oct 96	**DON'T LET ME BE MISUNDERSTOOD** *Parlophone CDCLS 779*	53		1

COCKEREL CHORUS

UK, football fans (Tottenham Hotspur) /vocal group — 12

Date	Title	Peak Position	Weeks at No.1	Weeks on Chart
24 Feb 73	**NICE ONE CYRIL** *Young Blood YB 1017*	14		12

COCKNEY REJECTS

UK, male vocal/instrumental group — 22

Date	Title	Peak Position	Weeks at No.1	Weeks on Chart
1 Dec 79	**I'M NOT A FOOL** *EMI 5008*	65		2
16 Feb 80	**BAD MAN** *EMI 5035*	65		3
26 Apr 80	**THE GREATEST COCKNEY RIPOFF** *Zonophone Z 2*	21		7
17 May 80	**I'M FOREVER BLOWING BUBBLES** *Zonophone Z 4*	35		5
12 Jul 80	**WE CAN DO ANYTHING** *Zonophone Z 6*	65		2
25 Oct 80	**WE ARE THE FIRM** *Zonophone Z 10*	54		3

COCO

UK, female vocalist (Sue Bryce). See Fragma — 2

Date	Title	Peak Position	Weeks at No.1	Weeks on Chart
8 Nov 97	**I NEED A MIRACLE** *Positiva CDTIV 81*	39		2

COCONUTS

US, female vocal trio. See Kid Creole & The Coconuts — 3

Date	Title	Peak Position	Weeks at No.1	Weeks on Chart
11 Jun 83	**DID YOU HAVE TO LOVE ME LIKE YOU DID** *EMI America EA 156*	60		3

COCTEAU TWINS

UK, female/male vocal/instrumental trio – Elizabeth Fraser, Robin Guthrie & Simon Raymonde — 25

Date	Title	Peak Position	Weeks at No.1	Weeks on Chart
28 Apr 84	**PEARLY-DEWDROPS' DROPS** *4AD 405*	29		5
30 Mar 85	**AIKEA-GUINEA** *4AD AD 501*	41		3
23 Nov 85	**TINY DYNAMITE (EP)** *4AD BAD 510*	52		2
7 Dec 85	**ECHOES IN A SHALLOW BAY (EP)** *4AD BAD 511*	65		1
25 Oct 86	**LOVE'S EASY TEARS** *4AD BAD 610*	53		1
8 Sep 90	**ICEBLINK LUCK** *4AD AD 0011*	38		3
2 Oct 93	**EVANGELINE** *Fontana CTCD 1*	34		2
18 Dec 93	**WINTER WONDERLAND/FROSTY THE SNOWMAN** *Fontana COCCD 1*	58		1
26 Feb 94	**BLUEBEARD** *Fontana CTCD 2*	33		2
7 Oct 95	**TWINLIGHTS (EP)** *Fontana CTCD 3*	59		1
4 Nov 95	**OTHERNESS (EP)** *Fontana CTCD 4*	59		1
30 Mar 96	**TISHBITE** *Fontana CTCD 5*	34		2
20 Jul 96	**VIOLAINE** *Fontana CTCD 6*	56		1

C.O.D.

US, male/female vocal group — 2

Date	Title	Peak Position	Weeks at No.1	Weeks on Chart
14 May 83	**IN THE BOTTLE** *Streetwave WAVE 2*	54		2

CODE RED

UK, male vocal group — 7

Date	Title	Peak Position	Weeks at No.1	Weeks on Chart
6 Jul 96	**I GAVE YOU EVERYTHING** *Polydor 5763992*	50		1
16 Nov 96	**THIS IS OUR SONG** *Polydor 5766332*	59		1
14 Jun 97	**CAN WE TALK...** *Polydor 5710992*	29		2
9 Aug 97	**IS THERE SOMEONE OUT THERE?** *Polydor 5714652*	34		2
4 Jul 98	**WHAT WOULD YOU DO IF...?** *Polydor 5673312*	55		1

COFFEE

US, female vocal trio — 13

Date	Title	Peak Position	Weeks at No.1	Weeks on Chart
27 Sep 80	**CASANOVA** *De-Lite MER 38*	13		10
6 Dec 80	**SLIP AND DIP/I WANNA BE WITH YOU** *De-Lite DE 1*	57		3

ALMA COGAN

UK, female vocalist, d. 26 Oct 1966 (age 34) — 110

Date	Title	Peak Position	Weeks at No.1	Weeks on Chart
19 Mar 54	**BELL BOTTOM BLUES** *HMV B 10653*	4		9
27 Aug 54	**LITTLE THINGS MEAN A LOT** *HMV B 10717*	11		5
3 Dec 54	**I CAN'T TELL A WALTZ FROM A TANGO** *HMV B 10786*	6		11
27 May 55	**DREAMBOAT** *HMV B 10872*	1	2	16
23 Sep 55	**BANJO'S BACK IN TOWN** *HMV B 10917*	17		1
14 Oct 55	**GO ON BY** *HMV B 10917*	16		4
16 Dec 55	**TWENTY TINY FINGERS** *HMV POP 129*	17		1

Silver-selling ● Gold-selling ● Platinum-selling (x multiples) ⊛ US No.1 ★ Peak Position · Weeks at No.1 · Weeks on Chart

Date	Title	Peak	Wks No.1	Wks
23 Dec 55	**NEVER DO A TANGO WITH AN ESKIMO** *HMV POP 129*	6		5
30 Mar 56	**WILLIE CAN** *HMV POP 187* WITH DESMOND LANE – PENNY WHISTLE	13		8
13 Jul 56	**THE BIRDS AND THE BEES** *HMV POP 223*	25		4
10 Aug 56	**WHY DO FOOLS FALL IN LOVE** *HMV POP 223*	22		3
2 Nov 56	**IN THE MIDDLE OF THE HOUSE** *HMV POP 261*	20		4
18 Jan 57	**YOU ME AND US** *HMV POP 284*	18		6
29 Mar 57	**WHATEVER LOLA WANTS** *HMV POP 317*	26		2
31 Jan 58	**THE STORY OF MY LIFE** *HMV POP 433*	25		2
14 Feb 58	**SUGARTIME** *HMV POP 450*	16		11
23 Jan 59	**LAST NIGHT ON THE BACK PORCH** *HMV POP 573*	27		2
18 Dec 59	**WE GOT LOVE** *HMV POP 670*	26		4
12 May 60	**DREAM TALK** *HMV POP 728*	48		1
11 Aug 60	**TRAIN OF LOVE** *HMV POP 760*	27		5
20 Apr 61	**COWBOY JIMMY JOE** *Columbia DB 4607*	37		6

SHAYE COGAN

US, female vocalist, d. 12 Jun 2009 (age 84) — 1

Date	Title	Peak	Wks No.1	Wks
24 Mar 60	**MEAN TO ME** *MGM 1063*	40		1

COHEED AND CAMBRIA

US, male vocal/instrumental group — 1

Date	Title	Peak	Wks No.1	Wks
18 Feb 06	**THE SUFFERING** *Columbia 82876766672*	60		1

COHEN VS DELUXE

Brazil/UK, male production duo. See Tim Deluxe, Double 99, RIP Productions, Saffron Hill featuring Ben Onono — 1

Date	Title	Peak	Wks No.1	Wks
13 Mar 04	**JUST KICK** *Intec INTEC024*	70		1

IZHAR COHEN & ALPHABETA

Israel, male/female vocal group — 7

Date	Title	Peak	Wks No.1	Wks
13 May 78	**A BA NI BI** *Polydor 2001 781*	20		7

LEONARD COHEN

Canada, male vocalist/guitarist — 1

Date	Title	Peak	Wks No.1	Wks
27 Dec 08	**HALLELUJAH** *Sony Music NLB638860001*	36		1

MARC COHN

US, male vocalist/pianist — 15

Date	Title	Peak	Wks No.1	Wks
25 May 91	**WALKING IN MEMPHIS** *Atlantic A 7747*	66		4
10 Aug 91	**SILVER THUNDERBIRD** *Atlantic A 7657*	54		3
12 Oct 91	**WALKING IN MEMPHIS** *Atlantic A 7585*	22		5
29 May 93	**WALK THROUGH THE WORLD** *Atlantic A 7340CD*	37		3

COLA BOY

UK, female/male vocal/instrumental duo – Janey Lee Grace & Andrew Midgely — 7

Date	Title	Peak	Wks No.1	Wks
6 Jul 91	**7 WAYS TO LOVE** *Arista 114526*	8		7

COLDJAM FEATURING GRACE

Italy, male/female production/vocal duo — 2

Date	Title	Peak	Wks No.1	Wks
28 Jul 90	**LAST NIGHT A DJ SAVED MY LIFE** *Big Wave BWR 39*	64		2

COLD WAR KIDS

US, male vocal/instrumental group — 2

Date	Title	Peak	Wks No.1	Wks
10 Feb 07	**HANG ME UP TO DRY** *V2 VVR5044633*	57		2

COLDCUT

UK, male production duo – Matthew 'Matt Black' Cohn & Jonathan More — 40

Date	Title	Peak	Wks No.1	Wks
20 Feb 88	**DOCTORIN' THE HOUSE** *Ahead Of Our Time CCUT 2* FEATURING YAZZ & THE PLASTIC POPULATION	6		9
10 Sep 88	**STOP THIS CRAZY THING** *Ahead Of Our Time CCUT 4* FEATURING JUNIOR REID & THE AHEAD OF OUR TIME ORCHESTRA	21		7
25 Mar 89	**PEOPLE HOLD ON** *Ahead Of Our Time CCUT 5* FEATURING LISA STANSFIELD	11		9
3 Jun 89	**MY TELEPHONE** *Ahead Of Our Time CCUT 6*	52		2
16 Dec 89	**COLDCUT'S CHRISTMAS BREAK** *Ahead Of Our Time CCUT 7*	67		3
26 May 90	**FIND A WAY** *Ahead Of Our Time CCUT 8* FEATURING QUEEN LATIFAH	52		2
4 Sep 93	**DREAMER** *Arista 74321156642*	54		2
22 Jan 94	**AUTUMN LEAVES** *Arista 74321171052*	50		2
16 Aug 97	**MORE BEATS & PIECES** *Ninja Tune ZENCDS 58*	37		2
16 Jun 01	**REVOLUTION** *Ninja Tune ZENCDS 88*	67		1
29 Apr 06	**TRUE SKOOL** *Ninja Tune ZENCDS178* FEATURING ROOTS MANUVA	61		1

COLDPLAY

UK, male vocal/instrumental group – Chris Martin, Guy Berryman, Jonny Buckland & Will Champion. See Kanye West — 170

Date	Title	Peak	Wks No.1	Wks
18 Mar 00	**SHIVER** *Parlophone CDR 6536*	35		3
8 Jul 00	**YELLOW** *Parlophone CDR 6538*	4		11
4 Nov 00	**TROUBLE** *Parlophone CDRS 6549*	10		9
17 Aug 02	**IN MY PLACE** *Parlophone CDR 6579*	2		10
23 Nov 02	**THE SCIENTIST** *Parlophone CDR 6588*	10		9
5 Apr 03	**CLOCKS** *Parlophone CDR 6594*	9		8
4 Jun 05	**SPEED OF SOUND** *Parlophone CDR6664*	2		17
17 Sep 05	**FIX YOU** *Parlophone CDRS6671*	4		25
31 Dec 05	**TALK** *Parlophone CDR6679*	10		10
17 May 08	**VIOLET HILL** *EMI GBAYE0800269*	8		15
21 Jun 08	**LOST** *Parlophone GBAYE0800255*	55		2
28 Jun 08	**VIVA LA VIDA** *Parlophone GBAYE0800265* ★	1	1	43
28 Jun 08	**FIX YOU** *Parlophone CDRS6671*	61		1
22 Nov 08	**LOST** *Parlophone GBAYE0800255*	54		2
7 Feb 09	**LIFE IN TECHNICOLOR II** *Parlophone R6766*	28		4
24 Oct 09	**THE SCIENTIST** *Parlophone CDR 6588*	59		1

ANDY COLE

UK, male footballer/vocalist — 1

Date	Title	Peak	Wks No.1	Wks
18 Sep 99	**OUTSTANDING** *WEA 224CD*	68		1

CHERYL COLE

UK, female vocalist. See Girls Aloud, Helping Haiti — 76

Date	Title	Peak	Wks No.1	Wks
29 Mar 08	**HEARTBREAKER** *A&M 1771789* WILL.I.AM FEATURING CHERYL COLE	4		24
31 Oct 09	**FIGHT FOR THIS LOVE** *Fascination 2721778*	1	2	24+
7 Nov 09	**3 WORDS** *Fascination 2729724* FEATURING WILL.I.AM	4		18
26 Dec 09	**PARACHUTE** *Fascination 2734193*	5		10+

COZY COLE

US, male drummer (William Cole), d. 9 Jan 1981 (age 71) — 1

Date	Title	Peak	Wks No.1	Wks
5 Dec 58	**TOPSY (PARTS 1 AND 2)** *London HL 8750*	29		1

KEYSHIA COLE

US, female vocalist — 23

Date	Title	Peak	Wks No.1	Wks
15 Apr 06	**I SHOULD HAVE CHEATED/I CHANGED MY MIND** *A&M/Polydor 9855074*	48		1
4 Nov 06	**(WHEN YOU GONNA) GIVE IT UP TO ME** *VP/Atlantic AT0265CD* SEAN PAUL FEATURING KEYSHIA COLE	31		6
3 Mar 07	**LAST NIGHT** *Atlantic AT0273CD* P DIDDY FEATURING KEYSHIA COLE	14		16

LLOYD COLE & THE COMMOTIONS

UK, male vocalist/guitarist — 62

Date	Title	Peak	Wks No.1	Wks
26 May 84	**PERFECT SKIN** *Polydor COLE 1*	26		9
25 Aug 84	**FOREST FIRE** *Polydor COLE 2*	41		6
17 Nov 84	**RATTLESNAKES** *Polydor COLE 3*	65		2
14 Sep 85	**BRAND NEW FRIEND** *Polydor COLE 4*	19		8
9 Nov 85	**LOST WEEKEND** *Polydor COLE 5*	17		7
18 Jan 86	**CUT ME DOWN** *Polydor COLE 6*	38		4
3 Oct 87	**MY BAG** *Polydor COLE 7*	46		4
9 Jan 88	**JENNIFER SHE SAID** *Polydor COLE 8*	31		5
23 Apr 88	**FROM THE HIP (EP)** *Polydor COLE 9*	59		2
3 Feb 90	**NO BLUE SKIES** *Polydor COLE 11* LLOYD COLE	42		4
7 Apr 90	**DON'T LOOK BACK** *Polydor COLE 12* LLOYD COLE	59		3
31 Aug 91	**SHE'S A GIRL AND I'M A MAN** *Polydor COLE 14* LLOYD COLE	55		2
25 Sep 93	**SO YOU'D LIKE TO SAVE THE WORLD** *Fontana VIBE D1* LLOYD COLE	72		2
16 Sep 95	**LIKE LOVERS DO** *Fontana LCDD 1* LLOYD COLE	24		3
2 Dec 95	**SENTIMENTAL FOOL** *Fontana LCDD 2* LLOYD COLE	73		1

MJ COLE

UK, male producer (Matt Coleman) — 19

Date	Title	Peak	Wks No.1	Wks
23 May 98	**SINCERE** *AM:PM 5826912*	38		2
6 May 00	**CRAZY LOVE** *Talkin Loud TLCD 59*	10		7
12 Aug 00	**SINCERE** *Talkin Loud TLCD 60*	13		5
2 Dec 00	**HOLD ON TO ME** *Talkin Loud TLCD 62* FEATURING ELISABETH TROY	35		2
29 Mar 03	**WONDERING WHY** *Talkin Loud 0779522*	30		3

NAT 'KING' COLE

US, male vocalist/pianist (Nathaniel Coles), d. 15 Feb 1965 (age 45). The jazzy song stylist is universally acclaimed as one of the greatest vocalists of the 20th century. His timeless recordings were still charting 30 years after his death

Date	Title	Peak Position	Weeks at No.1	Weeks on Chart (250)
14 Nov 52	**SOMEWHERE ALONG THE WAY** *Capitol CL 13774*	3		7
19 Dec 52	**BECAUSE YOU'RE MINE** *Capitol CL 13811*	6		4
2 Jan 53	**FAITH CAN MOVE MOUNTAINS** *Capitol CL 13811*	10		4
24 Apr 53	**PRETEND** *Capitol CL 13878*	2		18
14 Aug 53	**CAN'T I?** *Capitol CL 13937*	6		8
18 Sep 53	**MOTHER NATURE AND FATHER TIME** *Capitol CL 13912*	7		7
16 Apr 54	**TENDERLY** *Capitol CL 14061*	10		1
10 Sep 54	**SMILE** *Capitol CL 14149*	2		14
8 Oct 54	**MAKE HER MINE** *Capitol CL 14149*	11		2
25 Feb 55	**A BLOSSOM FELL** *Capitol CL 14235*	3		10
26 Aug 55	**MY ONE SIN** *Capitol CL 14327*	17		2
27 Jan 56	**DREAMS CAN TELL A LIE** *Capitol CL 14513*	10		9
11 May 56	**TOO YOUNG TO GO STEADY** *Capitol CL 14573*	8		14
14 Sep 56	**LOVE ME AS THOUGH THERE WERE NO TOMORROW** *Capitol CL 14621*	11		15
19 Apr 57	**WHEN I FALL IN LOVE** *Capitol CL 14709*	2		20
5 Jul 57	**WHEN ROCK 'N ROLL CAME TO TRINIDAD** *Capitol CL 14733*	28		1
18 Oct 57	**MY PERSONAL POSSESSION** *Capitol CL 14765* & THE FOUR KNIGHTS	21		2
25 Oct 57	**STARDUST** *Capitol CL 14787*	24		2
29 May 59	**YOU MADE ME LOVE YOU** *Capitol CL 15017*	22		3
4 Sep 59	**MIDNIGHT FLYER** *Capitol CL 15056*	23		4
12 Feb 60	**TIME AND THE RIVER** *Capitol CL 15111*	23		5
26 May 60	**THAT'S YOU** *Capitol CL 15129*	10		8
10 Nov 60	**JUST AS MUCH AS EVER** *Capitol CL 15163*	18		10
2 Feb 61	**THE WORLD IN MY ARMS** *Capitol CL 15178*	36		10
16 Nov 61	**LET TRUE LOVE BEGIN** *Capitol CL 15224*	29		10
22 Mar 62	**BRAZILIAN LOVE SONG** *Capitol CL 15241*	34		4
31 May 62	**THE RIGHT THING TO SAY** *Capitol CL 15250*	42		4
19 Jul 62	**LET THERE BE LOVE** *Capitol CL 15257* WITH GEORGE SHEARING	11		14
27 Sep 62	**RAMBLIN' ROSE** *Capitol CL 15270*	5		14
20 Dec 62	**DEAR LONELY HEARTS** *Capitol CL 15280*	37		3
12 Dec 87	**WHEN I FALL IN LOVE** *Capitol CL 15975*	4		7
22 Jun 91	**UNFORGETTABLE** *Elektra EKR 128* NATALIE COLE WITH NAT 'KING' COLE	19		8
14 Dec 91	**THE CHRISTMAS SONG** *Capitol CL 641*	69		2
19 Mar 94	**LET'S FACE THE MUSIC AND DANCE** *EMI CDEM 312*	30		3
29 Dec 07	**THE CHRISTMAS SONG** *Capitol EUEDD03067199*	51		1

NATALIE COLE

US, female vocalist

Date	Title	Peak Position	Weeks at No.1	Weeks on Chart (87)
11 Oct 75	**THIS WILL BE** *Capitol CL 15834*	32		5
8 Aug 87	**JUMP START** *Manhattan MT 22*	44		8
26 Mar 88	**PINK CADILLAC** *Manhattan MT 35*	5		12
25 Jun 88	**EVERLASTING** *Manhattan MT 46*	28		6
20 Aug 88	**JUMP START** *Manhattan MT 50*	36		5
26 Nov 88	**I LIVE FOR YOUR LOVE** *Manhattan MT 57*	23		14
15 Apr 89	**MISS YOU LIKE CRAZY** *EMI-USA MT 63* ○	2		15
22 Jul 89	**REST OF THE NIGHT** *EMI-USA MT 69*	56		2
16 Dec 89	**STARTING OVER AGAIN** *EMI-USA MT 77*	56		4
21 Apr 90	**WILD WOMEN DO** *EMI-USA MT 81*	16		7
22 Jun 91	**UNFORGETTABLE** *Elektra EKR 128* WITH NAT 'KING' COLE	19		8
16 May 92	**THE VERY THOUGHT OF YOU** *Elektra EKR 147*	71		1

PAULA COLE

US, female vocalist

Date	Title	Peak Position	Weeks at No.1	Weeks on Chart (9)
28 Jun 97	**WHERE HAVE ALL THE COWBOYS GONE?** *Warner Brothers W 0406CD*	15		8
1 Aug 98	**I DON'T WANT TO WAIT** *Warner Brothers W 0422CD*	43		1

COLLAGE

US, male vocal/instrumental group

Date	Title	Peak Position	Weeks at No.1	Weeks on Chart (5)
21 Sep 85	**ROMEO WHERE'S JULIET** *MCA 1006*	46		5

COLLAPSED LUNG

UK, male vocal/instrumental group

Date	Title	Peak Position	Weeks at No.1	Weeks on Chart (8)
22 Jun 96	**LONDON TONIGHT/EAT MY GOAL** *Deceptive BLUFF 029CD*	31		3
30 May 98	**EAT MY GOAL** *Deceptive BLUFF 060CD*	18		5

DAVE & ANSIL COLLINS

Jamaica, male vocal/instrumental duo – Dave Collins (Dave Barker) & Ansil Collins

Date	Title	Peak Position	Weeks at No.1	Weeks on Chart (27)
27 Mar 71	**DOUBLE BARREL** *Technique TE 901*	1	2	15
26 Jun 71	**MONKEY SPANNER** *Technique TE 914*	7		12

EDWYN COLLINS

UK, male vocalist/guitarist. See Orange Juice

Date	Title	Peak Position	Weeks at No.1	Weeks on Chart (25)
11 Aug 84	**PALE BLUE EYES** *Swamplands SWP 1* PAUL QUINN & EDWYN COLLINS	72		2
12 Nov 94	**EXPRESSLY (EP)** *Setanta ZOP 001CD1*	42		3
17 Jun 95	**A GIRL LIKE YOU** *Setanta ZOP 003CD* ○	4		14
2 Mar 96	**KEEP ON BURNING** *Setanta ZOP 004CD1*	45		2
2 Aug 97	**THE MAGIC PIPER (OF LOVE)** *Setanta SETCDA 041*	32		3
18 Oct 97	**ADIDAS WORLD** *Setanta SETCDA 045*	71		1

JEFF COLLINS

UK, male vocalist

Date	Title	Peak Position	Weeks at No.1	Weeks on Chart (8)
18 Nov 72	**ONLY YOU** *Polydor 2058 287*	40		8

JUDY COLLINS

US, female vocalist

Date	Title	Peak Position	Weeks at No.1	Weeks on Chart (86)
17 Jan 70	**BOTH SIDES NOW** *Elektra EKSN 45043*	14		11
5 Dec 70	**AMAZING GRACE** *Elektra 2101 020*	5		67
17 May 75	**SEND IN THE CLOWNS** *Elektra K 12177*	6		8

MICHELLE COLLINS

UK, female actor/vocalist

Date	Title	Peak Position	Weeks at No.1	Weeks on Chart (3)
27 Feb 99	**SUNBURN** *BBC Music WMSS 60082*	28		3

PHIL COLLINS

UK, male vocalist/drummer/actor. Award-winning singer/songwriter who successfully combined a solo career – in which he has sold 5.5 million singles – with fronting Genesis between 1981 and 1996. He was inducted into the Rock & Roll Hall of Fame (as a member of Genesis) in 2010

Date	Title	Peak Position	Weeks at No.1	Weeks on Chart (251)
17 Jan 81	**IN THE AIR TONIGHT** *Virgin VSK 102* ●	2		10
7 Mar 81	**I MISSED AGAIN** *Virgin VS 402*	14		8
30 May 81	**IF LEAVING ME IS EASY** *Virgin VS 423*	17		8
23 Oct 82	**THRU' THESE WALLS** *Virgin VS 524*	56		2
4 Dec 82	**YOU CAN'T HURRY LOVE** *Virgin VS 531* ●	1	2	16
19 Mar 83	**DON'T LET HIM STEAL YOUR HEART AWAY** *Virgin VS 572*	45		5
7 Apr 84	**AGAINST ALL ODDS (TAKE A LOOK AT ME NOW)** *Virgin VS 674* ● ★	2		14
26 Jan 85	**SUSSUDIO** *Virgin VS 736* ★	12		9
9 Mar 85	**EASY LOVER** *CBS A 4915* PHILIP BAILEY (DUET WITH PHIL COLLINS) ●	1	4	12
13 Apr 85	**ONE MORE NIGHT** *Virgin VS 755* ★	4		9
27 Jul 85	**TAKE ME HOME** *Virgin VS 777*	19		9
23 Nov 85	**SEPARATE LIVES** *Virgin VS 818* & MARILYN MARTIN ○ ★	4		13
18 Jun 88	**IN THE AIR TONIGHT (REMIX)** *Virgin VS 102*	4		9
3 Sep 88	**A GROOVY KIND OF LOVE** *Virgin VS 1117* ○ ★	1	2	13
26 Nov 88	**TWO HEARTS** *Virgin VS 1141* ○ ★	6		11
4 Nov 89	**ANOTHER DAY IN PARADISE** *Virgin VS 1234* ○ ★	2		11
27 Jan 90	**I WISH IT WOULD RAIN DOWN** *Virgin VS 1240*	7		9
28 Apr 90	**SOMETHING HAPPENED ON THE WAY TO HEAVEN** *Virgin VS 1251*	15		7
28 Jul 90	**THAT'S JUST THE WAY IT IS** *Virgin VS 1277*	26		5
6 Oct 90	**HANG IN LONG ENOUGH** *Virgin VS 1300*	34		3
8 Dec 90	**DO YOU REMEMBER (LIVE)** *Virgin VS 1305*	57		5
15 May 93	**HERO** *Atlantic A 7360* DAVID CROSBY FEATURING PHIL COLLINS	56		3
30 Oct 93	**BOTH SIDES OF THE STORY** *Virgin VSCDT 1500*	7		6
15 Jan 94	**EVERYDAY** *Virgin VSCDT 1505*	15		5
7 May 94	**WE WAIT AND WE WONDER** *Virgin VSCDT 1510*	45		2
5 Oct 96	**DANCE INTO THE LIGHT** *Face Value EW 066CD*	9		6
14 Dec 96	**IT'S IN YOUR EYES** *Face Value EW 076CD1*	30		4
12 Jul 97	**WEAR MY HAT** *Face Value EW 113CD*	43		2
7 Nov 98	**TRUE COLOURS** *Virgin VSCDT 1715*	26		4
6 Nov 99	**YOU'LL BE IN MY HEART** *Walt Disney 0100735 DNY*	17		6
22 Sep 01	**IN THE AIR TONITE** *WEA 331CD* LIL' KIM FEATURING PHIL COLLINS	26		2
16 Nov 02	**CAN'T STOP LOVING YOU** *Face Value EW 254CD*	28		2
24 May 03	**HOME** *Epic 6738305* BONE THUGS-N-HARMONY FEATURING PHIL COLLINS	19		4
29 Nov 03	**LOOK THROUGH MY EYES** *Walt Disney DISNEY001*	61		1
15 Sep 07	**IN THE AIR TONIGHT** *Virgin VS102*	14		16

RODGER COLLINS
US, male vocalist

Date	Title	Peak Position	Weeks at No.1	Weeks on Chart (6)
3 Apr 76	**YOU SEXY SUGAR PLUM (BUT I LIKE IT)** *Fantasy FTC 132*	22		6

WILLIE COLLINS
US, male vocalist

Date	Title	Peak Position	Weeks at No.1	Weeks on Chart (4)
28 Jun 86	**WHERE YOU GONNA BE TONIGHT?** *Capitol CL 410*	46		4

WILLIE COLON
US, male vocalist/brass player

Date	Title	Peak Position	Weeks at No.1	Weeks on Chart (7)
28 Jun 86	**SET FIRE TO ME** *A&M AM 330*	41		7

COLOR ME BADD
US, male vocal group – Bryan Abrams, Mark Calderon, Kevin Thornton & Sam Watters

Date	Title	Peak Position	Weeks at No.1	Weeks on Chart (31)
18 May 91	**I WANNA SEX YOU UP** *Giant W 0036* ○	1	3	14
3 Aug 91	**ALL 4 LOVE** *Giant W 0053* ★	5		10
12 Oct 91	**I ADORE MI AMOR** *Giant W 0067* ★	44		4
22 Feb 92	**HEARTBREAKER** *Giant W 0078*	58		1
20 Nov 93	**TIME AND CHANCE** *Giant 74321168992*	62		1
16 Apr 94	**CHOOSE** *Giant 74321199432*	65		1

COLORADO
UK, female vocal group

Date	Title	Peak Position	Weeks at No.1	Weeks on Chart (3)
21 Oct 78	**CALIFORNIA DREAMIN'** *Pinnacle PIN 67*	45		3

COLOUR FIELD
UK, male vocal/instrumental trio

Date	Title	Peak Position	Weeks at No.1	Weeks on Chart (18)
21 Jan 84	**THE COLOUR FIELD** *Chrysalis COLF 1*	43		4
28 Jul 84	**TAKE** *Chrysalis COLF 2*	70		1
26 Jan 85	**THINKING OF YOU** *Chrysalis COLF 3*	12		10
13 Apr 85	**CASTLES IN THE AIR** *Chrysalis COLF 4*	51		3

COLOUR GIRL
UK, female vocalist (Rebecca Skingley)

Date	Title	Peak Position	Weeks at No.1	Weeks on Chart (5)
11 Mar 00	**CAN'T GET USED TO LOSING YOU** *4 Liberty LIBTCD 037*	31		3
9 Sep 00	**JOYRIDER (YOU'RE PLAYING WITH FIRE)** *4 Liberty LIBTCD 039*	51		1
3 Feb 01	**MAS QUE NADA** *4 Liberty LIBTCD 040* FEATURING PSG	57		1

COLOURS FEATURING EMMANUEL & ESKA
UK, male/female vocal/instrumental/production group. See En-core featuring Stephen Emmanuel & Eska, Nitin Sawhney

Date	Title	Peak Position	Weeks at No.1	Weeks on Chart (1)
27 Feb 99	**WHAT U DO** *Inferno CDFERN 12*	51		1

COLOURSOUND
UK, male production duo

Date	Title	Peak Position	Weeks at No.1	Weeks on Chart (2)
28 Sep 02	**FLY WITH ME** *City Rockers ROCKERS 20CD*	49		2

COLUMBO FEATURING OOE
UK, male production duo

Date	Title	Peak Position	Weeks at No.1	Weeks on Chart (1)
15 May 99	**ROCKABILLY BOB** *V2/Milkgems VVR 5006903*	59		1

SHAWN COLVIN
US, female vocalist/guitarist

Date	Title	Peak Position	Weeks at No.1	Weeks on Chart (12)
27 Nov 93	**I DON'T KNOW WHY** *Columbia 6598272*	62		1
12 Feb 94	**ROUND OF BLUES** *Columbia 6594282*	73		1
3 Sep 94	**EVERY LITTLE THING HE DOES IS MAGIC** *Columbia 6607742*	65		2
7 Jan 95	**ONE COOL REMOVE** *Columbia 6611342* WITH MARY CHAPIN CARPENTER	40		3
12 Aug 95	**I DON'T KNOW WHY** *Columbia 6622725*	52		1
15 Mar 97	**GET OUT OF THIS HOUSE** *Columbia 6638522*	70		1
30 May 98	**SUNNY CAME HOME** *Columbia 6648022*	29		3

COMING OUT CREW
US, male/female vocal duo

Date	Title	Peak Position	Weeks at No.1	Weeks on Chart (1)
18 Mar 95	**FREE, GAY AND HAPPY** *Out On Vinyl CDOOV 002*	50		1

COMMANDER TOM
Germany, male producer (Tom Weyer)

Date	Title	Peak Position	Weeks at No.1	Weeks on Chart (5)
23 Dec 00	**EYE BEE M** *Tripoli Trax TTRAX 069CD*	75		1
5 Feb 05	**ATTENTION!** *Data 81CDS*	23		4

COMMENTATORS
UK, male impressionist (Rory Bremner)

Date	Title	Peak Position	Weeks at No.1	Weeks on Chart (7)
22 Jun 85	**N-N-NINETEEN NOT OUT** *Oval 100*	13		7

COMMITMENTS
Ireland, male/female vocal/instrumental/acting group

Date	Title	Peak Position	Weeks at No.1	Weeks on Chart (1)
30 Nov 91	**MUSTANG SALLY** *MCA MCS 1598*	63		1

COMMODORES
US, male vocal/instrumental group – Lionel Richie*, William King, Ronald LaPread, Thomas McClary, Walter Orange & Milan Williams, d. 9 Jul 2006

Date	Title	Peak Position	Weeks at No.1	Weeks on Chart (121)
24 Aug 74	**MACHINE GUN** *Tamla Motown TMG 902*	20		11
23 Nov 74	**THE ZOO (THE HUMAN ZOO)** *Tamla Motown TMG 924*	44		2
2 Jul 77	**EASY** *Motown TMG 1073*	9		10
8 Oct 77	**SWEET LOVE/BRICK HOUSE** *Motown TMG 1086*	32		6
11 Mar 78	**TOO HOT TO TROT/ZOOM** *Motown TMG 1096*	38		4
24 Jun 78	**FLYING HIGH** *Motown TMG 1111*	37		7
5 Aug 78	**THREE TIMES A LADY** *Motown TMG 1113* ● ★	1	5	14
25 Nov 78	**JUST TO BE CLOSE TO YOU** *Motown TMG 1127*	62		4
25 Aug 79	**SAIL ON** *Motown TMG 1155*	8		10
3 Nov 79	**STILL** *Motown TMG 1166* ○ ★	4		11
19 Jan 80	**WONDERLAND** *Motown TMG 1172*	40		4
2 Aug 80	**LADY (YOU BRING ME UP)** *Motown TMG 1238*	56		5
21 Nov 81	**OH NO** *Motown TMG 1245*	44		3
26 Jan 85	**NIGHTSHIFT** *Motown TMG 1371* ○	3		14
11 May 85	**ANIMAL INSTINCT** *Motown ZB 40097*	74		1
25 Oct 86	**GOIN' TO THE BANK** *Polydor POSPA 826*	43		4
13 Aug 88	**EASY** *Motown ZB 41793*	15		11

COMMON
US, male rapper (Rasheed Lynn)

Date	Title	Peak Position	Weeks at No.1	Weeks on Chart (13)
8 Nov 97	**REMINDING ME (OF SEF)** *Relativity 6560762* FEATURING CHANTAY SAVAGE	59		1
14 Oct 00	**THE LIGHT/THE 6TH SENSE** *MCA MCSTD 40237*	56		1
28 Apr 01	**GETO HEAVEN** *MCA MCSTD 40246* FEATURING MACY GRAY	48		1
9 Feb 02	**DANCE FOR ME** *MCA MCSXD 40274* MARY J BLIGE FEATURING COMMON	13		7
27 Oct 07	**DRIVIN' ME WILD** *Geffen 1750856* FEATURING LILY ALLEN	56		1
26 Sep 09	**MAKE HER SAY** *Island USUM70969614* KID CUDI FEATURING KANYE WEST, COMMON & LADY GAGA	67		2

COMMUNARDS
UK, male vocal/instrumental duo – Jimmy Somerville* & Richard Coles

Date	Title	Peak Position	Weeks at No.1	Weeks on Chart (76)
12 Oct 85	**YOU ARE MY WORLD** *London LON 77*	30		8
24 May 86	**DISENCHANTED** *London LON 89*	29		5
23 Aug 86	**DON'T LEAVE ME THIS WAY** *London LON 103* WITH SARAH-JANE MORRIS ●	1	4	14
29 Nov 86	**SO COLD THE NIGHT** *London LON 110*	8		10
21 Feb 87	**YOU ARE MY WORLD** *London LON 123*	21		6
12 Sep 87	**TOMORROW** *London LON 143*	23		7
7 Nov 87	**NEVER CAN SAY GOODBYE** *London LON 158* ○	4		11
20 Feb 88	**FOR A FRIEND** *London LON 166*	28		7
11 Jun 88	**THERE'S MORE TO LOVE** *London LON 173*	20		8

PERRY COMO
US, male vocalist, d. 12 May 2001 (age 88). The relaxed balladeer launched his career in the 1930s, was Frank Sinatra's No.1 rival in the 1940s, hosted a top-rated TV entertainment show in the 1950s and was still having hits in his sixties

Date	Title	Peak Position	Weeks at No.1	Weeks on Chart (329)
16 Jan 53	**DON'T LET THE STARS GET IN YOUR EYES** *HMV B 10400* WITH THE RAMBLERS ★	1	5	15
4 Jun 54	**WANTED** *HMV B 10667* ★	4		15
25 Jun 54	**IDLE GOSSIP** *HMV B 10710*	3		15
10 Dec 54	**PAPA LOVES MAMBO** *HMV B 10776*	16		1
30 Dec 55	**TINA MARIE** *HMV POP 103*	24		1
27 Apr 56	**JUKE BOX BABY** *HMV POP 191*	22		6
25 May 56	**HOT DIGGITY (DOG ZIGGITY BOOM)** *HMV POP 212* ★	4		13
21 Sep 56	**MORE** *HMV POP 240*	10		12

Date	Title	Peak Position	Weeks at No.1	Weeks on Chart
28 Sep 56	**GLENDORA** *HMV POP 240*	18		6
7 Feb 58	**MAGIC MOMENTS** *RCA 1036*	1	8	17
7 Mar 58	**CATCH A FALLING STAR** *RCA 1036* ★	9		10
9 May 58	**KEWPIE DOLL** *RCA 1055*	9		7
30 May 58	**I MAY NEVER PASS THIS WAY AGAIN** *RCA 1062*	15		8
5 Sep 58	**MOON TALK** *RCA 1071*	17		11
7 Nov 58	**LOVE MAKES THE WORLD GO ROUND** *RCA 1086*	6		14
21 Nov 58	**MANDOLINS IN THE MOONLIGHT** *RCA 1086*	13		12
27 Feb 59	**TOMBOY** *RCA 1111*	10		12
10 Jul 59	**I KNOW** *RCA 1126*	13		16
26 Feb 60	**DELAWARE** *RCA 1170*	3		14
10 May 62	**CATERINA** *RCA 1283*	37		6
30 Jan 71	**IT'S IMPOSSIBLE** *RCA 2043*	4		23
15 May 71	**I THINK OF YOU** *RCA 2075*	14		11
21 Apr 73	**AND I LOVE YOU SO** *RCA 2346*	3		35
25 Aug 73	**FOR THE GOOD TIMES** *RCA 2402* ●	7		27
8 Dec 73	**WALK RIGHT BACK** *RCA 2432*	33		10
25 May 74	**I WANT TO GIVE** *RCA LPBO 7518*	31		6
15 Dec 07	**IT'S BEGINNING TO LOOK A LOT LIKE CHRISTMAS** *RCA USRC15106173*	49		3
13 Dec 08	**IT'S BEGINNING TO LOOK A LOT LIKE CHRISTMAS** *RCA USRC15106173*	47		3

COMPAGNONS DE LA CHANSON
France, male/female vocal ensemble

Date	Title	Peak Position	Weeks at No.1	Weeks on Chart 3
9 Oct 59	**THE THREE BELLS (THE JIMMY BROWN SONG)** *Columbia DB 4358*	21		3

COMSAT ANGELS
UK, male vocal/instrumental group

Date	Title	Peak Position	Weeks at No.1	Weeks on Chart 2
21 Jan 84	**INDEPENDENCE DAY** *Jive 54*	71		2

CON FUNK SHUN
US, male vocal/instrumental group

Date	Title	Peak Position	Weeks at No.1	Weeks on Chart 2
19 Jul 86	**BURNIN' LOVE** *Club JAB 32*	68		2

CONCEPT
US, male/female vocal/production group

Date	Title	Peak Position	Weeks at No.1	Weeks on Chart 6
14 Dec 85	**MR DJ** *Fourth & Broadway BRW 40*	27		6

CONCRETES
Sweden, male/female vocal/instrumental group

Date	Title	Peak Position	Weeks at No.1	Weeks on Chart 3
26 Jun 04	**YOU CAN'T HURRY LOVE** *EMI LFS011*	55		1
2 Oct 04	**SEEMS FINE** *EMI LFSX013*	52		1
18 Mar 06	**CHOSEN ONE** *EMI LFCD019*	54		1

CONDUCTOR & THE COWBOY
UK, male production duo

Date	Title	Peak Position	Weeks at No.1	Weeks on Chart 2
20 May 00	**FEELING THIS WAY** *Serious SERR 016CD*	35		2

CONGREGATION
UK, male/female choir

Date	Title	Peak Position	Weeks at No.1	Weeks on Chart 14
27 Nov 71	**SOFTLY WHISPERING I LOVE YOU** *Columbia DB 8830*	4		14

CONGRESS
UK, male production duo

Date	Title	Peak Position	Weeks at No.1	Weeks on Chart 4
26 Oct 91	**40 MILES** *Inner Rhythm 7HEART 01*	26		4

CONJURE ONE
Canada, male producer (Rhys Fulber)

Date	Title	Peak Position	Weeks at No.1	Weeks on Chart 1
15 Feb 03	**SLEEP/TEARS FROM THE MOON** *Nettwerk 331792*	42		1

ARTHUR CONLEY
US, male vocalist, d. 17 Nov 2003 (age 57)

Date	Title	Peak Position	Weeks at No.1	Weeks on Chart 15
27 Apr 67	**SWEET SOUL MUSIC** *Atlantic 584 083*	7		14
10 Apr 68	**FUNKY STREET** *Atlantic 583 175*	46		1

CONNELLS
US, male vocal/instrumental group

Date	Title	Peak Position	Weeks at No.1	Weeks on Chart 11
12 Aug 95	**'74-'75** *TNT LONCD 369*	14		8
16 Mar 96	**'74-'75** *TNT LONCD 369*	21		3

HARRY CONNICK, JR
US, male vocalist/keyboard player

Date	Title	Peak Position	Weeks at No.1	Weeks on Chart 11
25 May 91	**RECIPE FOR LOVE/IT HAD TO BE YOU** *Columbia 6568907*	32		6
3 Aug 91	**WE ARE IN LOVE** *Columbia 6572847*	62		2
23 Nov 91	**BLUE LIGHT RED LIGHT (SOMEONE'S THERE)** *Columbia 6575367*	54		3

BILLY CONNOLLY
UK, male comedian/vocalist/instrumentalist

Date	Title	Peak Position	Weeks at No.1	Weeks on Chart 31
1 Nov 75	**D.I.V.O.R.C.E.** *Polydor 2058 652* ●	1	1	10
17 Jul 76	**NO CHANCE (NO CHARGE)** *Polydor 2058 748*	24		5
25 Aug 79	**IN THE BROWNIES** *Polydor 2059 160*	38		7
9 Mar 85	**SUPER GRAN** *Stiff BUY 218*	32		9

SARAH CONNOR
Germany, female vocalist (Sarah Lewe)

Date	Title	Peak Position	Weeks at No.1	Weeks on Chart 10
13 Oct 01	**LET'S GET BACK TO BED...BOY** *Epic 6718662* FEATURING TQ	16		5
5 Jun 04	**BOUNCE** *Epic 6749001*	14		5

CONQUERING LION
UK, male vocalist/rapper (Michael West). See Rebel MC

Date	Title	Peak Position	Weeks at No.1	Weeks on Chart 1
8 Oct 94	**CODE RED** *Mango CIDM 821*	53		1

LEENA CONQUEST & HIP HOP FINGER
US, female vocalist & male rap/instrumental trio

Date	Title	Peak Position	Weeks at No.1	Weeks on Chart 1
18 Jun 94	**BOUNDARIES** *Naturalresponse 74321208522*	67		1

JESS CONRAD
UK, male vocalist (Gerald James)

Date	Title	Peak Position	Weeks at No.1	Weeks on Chart 13
30 Jun 60	**CHERRY PIE** *Decca F 11236*	39		1
26 Jan 61	**MYSTERY GIRL** *Decca F 11315*	18		10
11 Oct 62	**PRETTY JENNY** *Decca F 11511*	50		2

CONSORTIUM
UK, male vocal group

Date	Title	Peak Position	Weeks at No.1	Weeks on Chart 9
12 Feb 69	**ALL THE LOVE IN THE WORLD** *Pye 7N 17635*	22		9

BILL CONTI
US, male film director/composer/conductor (William Conti)

Date	Title	Peak Position	Weeks at No.1	Weeks on Chart 3
27 Jan 07	**GONNA FLY NOW (THEME FROM ROCKY)** *Capitol USEM38800372* ★	52		3

CONTOURS
US, male vocal group

Date	Title	Peak Position	Weeks at No.1	Weeks on Chart 6
24 Jan 70	**JUST A LITTLE MISUNDERSTANDING** *Tamla Motown TMG 723*	31		6

CONTRABAND
US/Germany, male/female vocal/instrumental group

Date	Title	Peak Position	Weeks at No.1	Weeks on Chart 2
20 Jul 91	**ALL THE WAY FROM MEMPHIS** *Impact American EM 195*	65		2

CONTROL
UK, male/female production group

Date	Title	Peak Position	Weeks at No.1	Weeks on Chart 5
2 Nov 91	**DANCE WITH ME (I'M YOUR ECSTASY)** *All Around The World GLOBE 105*	17		5

CONVERT
Belgium, male production duo

Date	Title	Peak Position	Weeks at No.1	Weeks on Chart 7
11 Jan 92	**NIGHTBIRD** *A&M AM 845*	39		4
29 May 93	**ROCKIN' TO THE RHYTHM** *A&M 5802532*	42		2
31 Jan 98	**NIGHTBIRD** *Wonderboy WBOYD 008*	45		1

Silver-selling ● Gold-selling ● Platinum-selling (x multiples) ⊛ US No.1 ★ Peak Position Weeks at No.1 Weeks on Chart

CONWAY BROTHERS
US, male vocal/instrumental group — **10**

Date	Title	Peak	Wks at No.1	Wks
22 Jun 85	**TURN IT UP** *10 TEN 57*	11		10

RUSS CONWAY
UK, male pianist (Trevor Stanford), d. 16 Nov 2000 (age 75) — **179**

Date	Title	Peak	Wks at No.1	Wks
29 Nov 57	**PARTY POPS** *Columbia DB 4031*	24		5
29 Aug 58	**GOT A MATCH** *Columbia DB 4166*	30		1
28 Nov 58	**MORE PARTY POPS** *Columbia DB 4204*	10		7
23 Jan 59	**THE WORLD OUTSIDE** *Columbia DB 4234*	24		1
20 Feb 59	**SIDE SADDLE** *Columbia DB 4256*	1	4	30
6 Mar 59	**THE WORLD OUTSIDE** *Columbia DB 4234*	24		3
15 May 59	**ROULETTE** *Columbia DB 4298*	1	2	19
21 Aug 59	**CHINA TEA** *Columbia DB 4337*	5		13
13 Nov 59	**SNOW COACH** *Columbia DB 4368*	7		9
20 Nov 59	**MORE AND MORE PARTY POPS** *Columbia DB 4373*	5		8
5 Mar 60	**ROYAL EVENT** *Columbia DB 4418*	15		8
21 Apr 60	**FINGS AIN'T WOT THEY USED TO BE** *Columbia DB 4422*	47		1
19 May 60	**LUCKY FIVE** *Columbia DB 4457*	14		9
29 Sep 60	**PASSING BREEZE** *Columbia DB 4508*	16		10
24 Nov 60	**EVEN MORE PARTY POPS** *Columbia DB 4535*	27		9
19 Jan 61	**PEPE** *Columbia DB 4564*	19		9
25 May 61	**PABLO** *Columbia DB 4649*	45		2
24 Aug 61	**SAY IT WITH FLOWERS** *Columbia DB 4665* DOROTHY SQUIRES & RUSS CONWAY	23		10
30 Nov 61	**TOY BALLOONS** *Columbia DB 4738*	7		11
22 Feb 62	**LESSON ONE** *Columbia DB 4784*	21		7
29 Nov 62	**ALWAYS YOU AND ME** *Columbia DB 4934*	33		7

DAVID COOK
US, male vocalist — **1**

Date	Title	Peak	Wks at No.1	Wks
7 Jun 08	**THE TIME OF MY LIFE** *RCA GBCTA0800153*	61		1

NORMAN COOK
UK, male producer/DJ (Quentin Cook). See Beats International, Fatboy Slim, Freakpower, Housemartins, Mighty Dub Katz, Pizzaman, Urban All Stars — **10**

Date	Title	Peak	Wks at No.1	Wks
8 Jul 89	**WON'T TALK ABOUT IT/BLAME IT ON THE BASSLINE** *Go! Beat GOD 33* FEATURING BILLY BRAGG/NORMAN COOK FEATURING MC WILDSKI	29		6
21 Oct 89	**FOR SPACIOUS LIES** *Go! Beat GOD 37* FEATURING LESTER	48		4

PETER COOK
UK, male comedy/vocal duo – Peter Cook, d. 9 Jan 1995 & Dudley Moore, d. 28 Mar 2002 — **15**

Date	Title	Peak	Wks at No.1	Wks
17 Jun 65	**GOODBYE-EE** *Decca F 12158* & DUDLEY MOORE	18		10
15 Jul 65	**THE BALLAD OF SPOTTY MULDOON** *Decca F 12182*	34		5

BRANDON COOKE FEATURING ROXANNE SHANTE
US, male producer & female rapper — **3**

Date	Title	Peak	Wks at No.1	Wks
29 Oct 88	**SHARP AS A KNIFE** *Club JAB 73*	45		3

SAM COOKE
US, male vocalist, d. 11 Dec 1964 (age 33) — **82**

Date	Title	Peak	Wks at No.1	Wks
17 Jan 58	**YOU SEND ME** *London HLU 8506* ★	29		1
14 Aug 59	**ONLY SIXTEEN** *HMV POP 642*	23		4
7 Jul 60	**WONDERFUL WORLD** *HMV POP 754*	27		8
29 Sep 60	**CHAIN GANG** *RCA 1202*	9		11
27 Jul 61	**CUPID** *RCA 1242*	7		14
8 Mar 62	**TWISTIN' THE NIGHT AWAY** *RCA 1277*	6		14
16 May 63	**ANOTHER SATURDAY NIGHT** *RCA 1341*	23		12
5 Sep 63	**FRANKIE AND JOHNNY** *RCA 1361*	30		6
22 Mar 86	**WONDERFUL WORLD** *RCA PB 49871* ●	2		11
10 May 86	**ANOTHER SATURDAY NIGHT** *RCA PB 49849*	75		1

COOKIE
UK, female vocal group — **1**

Date	Title	Peak	Wks at No.1	Wks
16 Jul 05	**DO IT AGAIN** *The Bakery CXBAKERY1*	52		1

COOKIE CREW
UK, female rap duo – Susan 'Susie Q' Banfield & Debbie 'MC Remedee' Pryce — **31**

Date	Title	Peak	Wks at No.1	Wks
9 Jan 88	**ROK DA HOUSE** *Rhythm King LEFT 11* BEATMASTERS FEATURING THE COOKIE CREW	5		11
7 Jan 89	**BORN THIS WAY (LET'S DANCE)** *ffrr FFR 19*	23		5
1 Apr 89	**GOT TO KEEP ON** *ffrr FFR 25*	17		9
15 Jul 89	**COME AND GET SOME** *ffrr F 110*	42		3
27 Jul 91	**SECRETS (OF SUCCESS)** *ffrr F 159* FEATURING DANNY D	53		3

COOKIES
US, female vocal group — **1**

Date	Title	Peak	Wks at No.1	Wks
10 Jan 63	**CHAINS** *London HLU 9634*	50		1

COOL DOWN ZONE
UK, male/female vocal/instrumental trio — **4**

Date	Title	Peak	Wks at No.1	Wks
30 Jun 90	**HEAVEN KNOWS** *10 TEN 309*	52		4

COOL JACK
Italy, male instrumental/production duo — **1**

Date	Title	Peak	Wks at No.1	Wks
9 Nov 96	**JUS' COME** *AM:PM 5819892*	44		1

COOL NOTES
UK, male/female vocal/instrumental group — **28**

Date	Title	Peak	Wks at No.1	Wks
18 Aug 84	**YOU'RE NEVER TOO YOUNG** *Abstract Dance AD 1*	42		5
17 Nov 84	**I FORGOT** *Abstract Dance AD 2*	63		2
23 Mar 85	**SPEND THE NIGHT** *Abstract Dance AD 3*	11		9
13 Jul 85	**IN YOUR CAR** *Abstract Dance AD 4*	13		9
19 Oct 85	**HAVE A GOOD FOREVER** *Abstract Dance AD 5*	73		1
17 May 86	**INTO THE MOTION** *Abstract Dance AD 8*	66		2

COOL, THE FAB & THE GROOVY PRESENT QUINCY JONES
UK/US, male vocal/production/instrumental group — **1**

Date	Title	Peak	Wks at No.1	Wks
1 Aug 98	**SOUL BOSSA NOVA** *Manifesto FESCD 48*	47		1

RITA COOLIDGE
US, female vocalist — **24**

Date	Title	Peak	Wks at No.1	Wks
25 Jun 77	**WE'RE ALL ALONE** *A&M AMS 7295*	6		13
15 Oct 77	**(YOUR LOVE HAS LIFTED ME) HIGHER AND HIGHER** *A&M AMS 7315*	48		2
4 Feb 78	**WORDS** *A&M AMS 7330*	25		8
25 Jun 83	**ALL TIME HIGH** *A&M AM 007*	75		1

COOLIO
US, male rapper (Artis Ivey, Jr) — **68**

Date	Title	Peak	Wks at No.1	Wks
23 Jul 94	**FANTASTIC VOYAGE** *Tommy Boy TB 0617CD*	41		2
15 Oct 94	**I REMEMBER** *Tommy Boy TBXCD 635*	73		1
28 Oct 95	**GANGSTA'S PARADISE** *Tommy Boy MCSTD 2104* FEATURING LV ⊛ ★	1	2	20
20 Jan 96	**TOO HOT** *Tommy Boy TBCD 718*	9		6
6 Apr 96	**1,2,3,4 (SUMPIN' NEW)** *Tommy Boy TBCD 7721*	13		7
17 Aug 96	**IT'S ALL THE WAY LIVE (NOW)** *Tommy Boy TBCD 7731*	34		2
14 Sep 96	**STOMP – THE REMIXES** *Qwest W 0372CD* QUINCY JONES FEATURING MELLE MEL, COOLIO, YO-YO, SHAQUILLE O'NEAL & THE LUNIZ	28		2
5 Apr 97	**HIT 'EM HIGH (THE MONSTARS' ANTHEM)** *Atlantic A 5449CD* B REAL/BUSTA RHYMES/COOLIO/LL COOL J/METHOD MAN	8		6
7 Jun 97	**THE WINNER** *Atlantic A 5433CD*	53		1
19 Jul 97	**C U WHEN U GET THERE** *Tommy Boy TBCD 785* FEATURING 40 THEVZ ●	3		12
11 Oct 97	**OOH LA LA** *Tommy Boy TBCD 799*	14		5
28 Oct 06	**GANGSTA WALK** *All Around The World CDGLOBE565* FEATURING SNOOP DOGG	67		1
17 Jan 09	**GANGSTA'S PARADISE** *Tommy Boy 8122747781* FEATURING LV	31		3

COOPER
Holland, male production trio — **2**

Date	Title	Peak	Wks at No.1	Wks
11 Jan 03	**I BELIEVE IN LOVE** *Incentive PDT 05CDS*	50		2

ALICE COOPER
US, male vocalist (Vincent Furnier) — 104

Date	Title / Label	Peak Position	Weeks at No.1	Weeks on Chart
15 Jul 72	**SCHOOL'S OUT** *Warner Brothers K 16188*	1	3	12
7 Oct 72	**ELECTED** *Warner Brothers K 16214*	4		10
10 Feb 73	**HELLO HURRAY** *Warner Brothers K 16248*	6		12
21 Apr 73	**NO MORE MR. NICE GUY** *Warner Brothers K 16262*	10		10
19 Jan 74	**TEENAGE LAMENT '74** *Warner Brothers K 16345*	12		7
21 May 77	**(NO MORE) LOVE AT YOUR CONVENIENCE** *Warner Brothers K 16935*	44		2
23 Dec 78	**HOW YOU GONNA SEE ME NOW** *Warner Brothers K 17270*	61		6
6 Mar 82	**SEVEN AND SEVEN IS (LIVE)** *Warner Brothers K 17924*	62		3
8 May 82	**FOR BRITAIN ONLY/UNDER MY WHEELS** *Warner Brothers K 17940*	66		2
18 Oct 86	**HE'S BACK (THE MAN BEHIND THE MASK)** *MCA 1090*	61		2
9 Apr 88	**FREEDOM** *MCA 1241*	50		3
29 Jul 89	**POISON** *Epic 6550617*	2		11
7 Oct 89	**BED OF NAILS** *Epic ALICE 3*	38		5
2 Dec 89	**HOUSE OF FIRE** *Epic ALICE 4*	65		2
22 Jun 91	**HEY STOOPID** *Epic 6569837*	21		6
5 Oct 91	**LOVE'S A LOADED GUN** *Epic 6574387*	38		3
6 Jun 92	**FEED MY FRANKENSTEIN** *Epic 6580927*	27		3
28 May 94	**LOST IN AMERICA** *Epic 6603472*	22		3
23 Jul 94	**IT'S ME** *Epic 6605632*	34		2

TOMMY COOPER
UK, male comedian/vocalist, d. 15 Apr 1984 (age 61) — 3

Date	Title / Label	Peak Position	Weeks at No.1	Weeks on Chart
29 Jun 61	**DON'T JUMP OFF THE ROOF DAD** *Palette PG 9019*	40		3

COOPER TEMPLE CLAUSE
UK, male vocal/instrumental group — 12

Date	Title / Label	Peak Position	Weeks at No.1	Weeks on Chart
29 Sep 01	**LET'S KILL MUSIC** *Morning 9*	41		1
9 Feb 02	**FILM MAKER/BEEN TRAINING DOGS** *Morning 16*	20		3
18 May 02	**WHO NEEDS ENEMIES** *Morning 25*	22		2
13 Sep 03	**PROMISES PROMISES** *Morning 30*	19		2
22 Nov 03	**BLIND PILOTS** *Morning 38*	37		2
4 Nov 06	**HOMO SAPIENS** *Sequel SEQXS002*	36		1
20 Jan 07	**WAITING GAME** *Sequel SEQXD004*	41		1

JULIAN COPE
UK, male vocalist. See Teardrop Explodes — 59

Date	Title / Label	Peak Position	Weeks at No.1	Weeks on Chart
19 Nov 83	**SUNSHINE PLAYROOM** *Mercury COPE 1*	64		1
31 Mar 84	**THE GREATNESS AND PERFECTION OF LOVE** *Mercury MER 155*	52		5
27 Sep 86	**WORLD SHUT YOUR MOUTH** *Island IS 290*	19		8
17 Jan 87	**TRAMPOLENE** *Island IS 305*	31		6
11 Apr 87	**EVE'S VOLCANO (COVERED IN SIN)** *Island IS 318*	41		5
24 Sep 88	**CHARLOTTE ANNE** *Island IS 380*	35		6
21 Jan 89	**5 O'CLOCK WORLD** *Island IS 399*	42		4
24 Jun 89	**CHINA DOLL** *Island IS 406*	53		2
9 Feb 91	**BEAUTIFUL LOVE** *Island IS 483*	32		6
20 Apr 91	**EAST EASY RIDER** *Island IS 492*	51		3
3 Aug 91	**HEAD** *Island IS 497*	57		2
8 Aug 92	**WORLD SHUT YOUR MOUTH** *Island IS 534*	44		3
17 Oct 92	**FEAR LOVES THIS PLACE** *Island IS 545*	42		2
12 Aug 95	**TRY TRY TRY** *Echo ECSCD 11*	24		3
27 Jul 96	**I COME FROM ANOTHER PLANET, BABY** *Echo ECSCD 22*	34		2
5 Oct 96	**PLANETARY SIT-IN (EVERY GIRL HAS YOUR NAME)** *Echo ECSCD 25*	34		1

ROSS COPPERMAN
US, male vocalist/guitarist — 4

Date	Title / Label	Peak Position	Weeks at No.1	Weeks on Chart
12 May 07	**ALL SHE WROTE** *Phonogenic 88697048572*	39		3
25 Aug 07	**FOUND YOU** *Phonogenic 88697137592*	68		1

IMANI COPPOLA
US, female vocalist/producer. See Baha Men, Little Jackie — 8

Date	Title / Label	Peak Position	Weeks at No.1	Weeks on Chart
28 Feb 98	**LEGEND OF A COWGIRL** *Columbia 6656015*	32		3
3 Feb 01	**YOU ALL DAT** *Edel 0124855 ERE* BAHA MEN: GUEST VOCAL IMANI COPPOLA	14		5

CORAL
UK, male vocal/instrumental group – James Skelly, Paul Duffy, Nick Power, Bill Ryder-Jones, Ian Skelly & Lee Southall — 39

Date	Title / Label	Peak Position	Weeks at No.1	Weeks on Chart
27 Jul 02	**GOODBYE** *Deltasonic DLTCD 2005*	21		2
19 Oct 02	**DREAMING OF YOU** *Deltasonic DLTCD 2008*	13		5
15 Mar 03	**DON'T THINK YOU'RE THE FIRST** *Deltasonic DLTCDC 2010*	10		4
26 Jul 03	**PASS IT ON** *Deltasonic DLTCD 2013*	5		7
18 Oct 03	**SECRET KISS** *Deltasonic DLTCD 2015*	25		2
6 Dec 03	**BILL MCCAI** *Deltasonic DLTCD 2017*	23		2
21 May 05	**IN THE MORNING** *Deltasonic DLTCD2033*	6		12
3 Sep 05	**SOMETHING INSIDE OF ME** *Deltasonic DLTCD2039*	41		1
11 Aug 07	**WHO'S GONNA FIND ME** *Deltasonic DLTCD068*	25		2
13 Oct 07	**JACQUELINE** *Deltasonic DLTCD072*	44		1
23 Feb 08	**PUT THE SUN BACK** *Deltasonic DLTCD074*	64		1

CORD
UK, male vocal/instrumental trio — 2

Date	Title / Label	Peak Position	Weeks at No.1	Weeks on Chart
8 Jul 06	**WINTER** *Island CORDCD007*	34		1
30 Sep 06	**SEA OF TROUBLE** *Island CORDCD009*	50		1

FRANK CORDELL
UK, male orchestra leader, d. 6 Jul 1980 (age 62) — 4

Date	Title / Label	Peak Position	Weeks at No.1	Weeks on Chart
24 Aug 56	**SADIE'S SHAWL** *HMV POP 229*	29		2
16 Feb 61	**BLACK BEAR** *HMV POP 824*	44		2

LOUISE CORDET
UK, female vocalist (Louise Boisot) — 13

Date	Title / Label	Peak Position	Weeks at No.1	Weeks on Chart
5 Jul 62	**I'M JUST A BABY** *Decca F 11476*	13		13

CORENELL & LISA MARIE EXPERIENCE
Germany/UK, male DJ/production/instrumental trio — 2

Date	Title / Label	Peak Position	Weeks at No.1	Weeks on Chart
16 Jun 07	**KEEP ON JUMPIN'** *Gusto CDGUS46*	37		2

BILLY CORGAN
UK, male vocalist/guitarist. See Smashing Pumpkins, Zwan — 1

Date	Title / Label	Peak Position	Weeks at No.1	Weeks on Chart
18 Jun 05	**WALKING SHADE** *Reprise W673DVD*	74		1

CHRIS CORNELL
US, male vocalist/multi-instrumentalist (Christopher Boyle). See Audioslave, Soundgarden — 14

Date	Title / Label	Peak Position	Weeks at No.1	Weeks on Chart
23 Oct 99	**CAN'T CHANGE ME** *A&M 4971732*	62		1
16 Dec 06	**YOU KNOW MY NAME** *Interscope 1718880*	7		12
15 Nov 08	**YOU KNOW MY NAME** *Interscope 1718880*	74		1

DON CORNELL
US, male vocalist (Luigi Variaro), d. 23 Feb 2004 (age 84) — 23

Date	Title / Label	Peak Position	Weeks at No.1	Weeks on Chart
3 Sep 54	**HOLD MY HAND** *Vogue Q 2013*	1	5	21
22 Apr 55	**STRANGER IN PARADISE** *Vogue Q 72073*	19		2

LYNN CORNELL
UK, female vocalist. See Pearls — 9

Date	Title / Label	Peak Position	Weeks at No.1	Weeks on Chart
20 Oct 60	**NEVER ON SUNDAY** *Decca F 11277*	30		9

CORNERSHOP
UK, male vocal/instrumental group – Tjinder Singh, Ben Ayres, Pete Bengry, Anthony Saffery & Nick Simms — 19

Date	Title / Label	Peak Position	Weeks at No.1	Weeks on Chart
30 Aug 97	**BRIMFUL OF ASHA** *Wiiija WIJ 75CD*	60		1
28 Feb 98	**BRIMFUL OF ASHA (REMIX)** *Wiiija WIJ 81CD* ●	1	1	12
16 May 98	**SLEEP ON THE LEFT SIDE** *Wiiija WIJ 80CD*	23		3
16 Mar 02	**LESSONS LEARNT FROM ROCK I TO ROCKY III** *Wiiija WIJ 129CD*	37		2
7 Aug 04	**TOPKNOT** *Rough Trade RTRADSCD168*	53		1

HUGH CORNWELL
UK, male vocalist/guitarist. See Stranglers — 4

Date	Title / Label	Peak Position	Weeks at No.1	Weeks on Chart
24 Jan 87	**FACTS + FIGURES** *Virgin VS 922*	61		2
7 May 88	**ANOTHER KIND OF LOVE** *Virgin VS 945*	71		1
12 Feb 05	**(UNDER HER) SPELL** *Track TRACK00013B*	62		1

CO-RO FEATURING TARLISA
Italy, male production duo & female vocalist — 1

Date	Title / Label	Peak Position	Weeks at No.1	Weeks on Chart
12 Dec 92	**BECAUSE THE NIGHT** *ZYX 68227*	61		1

CORONA
Brazil, male producer (Francesco Bontempi) & female vocalist (Olga de Souza) — 44

10 Sep 94	**THE RHYTHM OF THE NIGHT** *WEA YZ 837CD1*	2		18
8 Apr 95	**BABY BABY** *Eternal YZ 919CD*	5		8
22 Jul 95	**TRY ME OUT** *Eternal YZ 955CD*	6		10
23 Dec 95	**I DON'T WANNA BE A STAR** *Eternal 029CD*	22		6
22 Feb 97	**MEGAMIX** *Eternal 092CD*	36		2

CORONATION STREET CAST FEATURING BILL WADDINGTON
UK, male/female actors/vocal group & male actor/vocalist, d. 11 Sep 2000 (age 84) — 3

16 Dec 95	**ALWAYS LOOK ON THE BRIGHT SIDE OF LIFE** *EMI Premier CDEMS 411*	35		3

CORONETS
UK, male/female vocal group — 7

26 Aug 55	**THAT'S HOW A LOVE SONG WAS BORN** *Columbia DB 3640* RAY BURNS WITH THE CORONETS	14		6
25 Nov 55	**TWENTY TINY FINGERS** *Columbia DB 3671*	20		1

BRIANA CORRIGAN
UK, female vocalist. See Beautiful South — 2

11 May 96	**LOVE ME NOW** *East West EW 041CD1*	48		2

CORRS
Ireland, female/male vocal/instrumental group – Andrea Corr*, Caroline, Jim & Sharon Corr — 108

17 Feb 96	**RUNAWAY** *Atlantic A 5727CD*	49		2
7 Dec 96	**RUNAWAY** *Atlantic A 5727CD*	60		1
1 Feb 97	**LOVE TO LOVE YOU/RUNAWAY** *Atlantic A 5621CD*	62		1
25 Oct 97	**ONLY WHEN I SLEEP** *Atlantic AT 0015CD*	58		1
20 Dec 97	**I NEVER LOVED YOU ANYWAY** *Atlantic AT 0018CD*	43		2
28 Mar 98	**WHAT CAN I DO** *Atlantic AT 0029CD*	53		1
16 May 98	**DREAMS** *Atlantic AT 0032CD*	6		10
29 Aug 98	**WHAT CAN I DO (REMIX)** *Atlantic AT 0044CD*	3		11
28 Nov 98	**SO YOUNG** *Atlantic AT 0057CD1*	6		13
27 Feb 99	**RUNAWAY (REMIX)** *Atlantic AT 0062CD*	2		11
12 Jun 99	**I KNOW MY LOVE** *RCA Victor 74321670622* CHIEFTAINS FEATURING THE CORRS	37		3
11 Dec 99	**RADIO** *Atlantic AT 0079CD*	18		9
15 Jul 00	**BREATHLESS** *Atlantic AT 0084CD*	1	1	13
11 Nov 00	**IRRESISTIBLE** *Atlantic AT 0089CD*	20		7
28 Apr 01	**GIVE ME A REASON** *Atlantic AT 0097CD*	27		2
10 Nov 01	**WOULD YOU BE HAPPIER** *Atlantic AT 0115CD*	14		5
29 May 04	**SUMMER SUNSHINE** *Atlantic AT 0179CD1*	6		8
25 Sep 04	**ANGEL** *Atlantic AT 0182CD*	16		4
18 Dec 04	**LONG NIGHT** *Atlantic AT 0190CD1*	31		3
5 Nov 05	**HEART LIKE A WHEEL/OLD TOWN** *Atlantic ATUK016CD*	68		1

CORRUPTED CRU FEATURING MC NEAT
UK, male rap/production trio. See Scott Garcia featuring MC Styles — 1

2 Mar 02	**GARAGE** *Red Rose CDRROSE 011*	59		1

FERRY CORSTEN
Holland, male DJ/producer. See Albion, Gouryella, Moonman, Starparty, System F, Veracocha — 15

8 Jun 02	**PUNK** *Positiva CDTIV 173*	29		3
21 Feb 04	**ROCK YOUR BODY ROCK** *Positiva CDTIVS 202*	11		6
10 Jul 04	**IT'S TIME** *Positiva CDTIVS 206*	51		2
4 Feb 06	**FIRE** *Positiva CDTIVS229*	40		3
15 Jul 06	**WATCH OUT** *Positiva CDTIVS239*	57		1

CORTINA
UK, male producer (Ben Keen) — 3

24 Mar 01	**MUSIC IS MOVING** *Nukleuz NUKC 0159*	42		2
26 Jan 02	**ERECTION (TAKE IT TO THE TOP)** *Nukleuz NUKCD 0352* FEATURING BK & MADAM FRICTION	48		1

VLADIMIR COSMA
Romania, orchestra — 1

14 Jul 79	**DAVID'S SONG (MAIN THEME FROM 'KIDNAPPED')** *Decca FR 13841*	64		1

COSMIC BABY
Germany, male producer (Harald Bluchel) — 1

26 Feb 94	**LOOPS OF INFINITY** *Logic 74321191432*	70		1

COSMIC GATE
Germany, male production duo – Stefan Bossems (DJ Bossi) & Claus Terhoeven (Nic Chagall) — 12

4 Aug 01	**FIREWIRE** *Data 24CDS*	9		7
11 May 02	**EXPLORATION OF SPACE** *Data 30CDS*	29		3
25 Jan 03	**THE WAVE/RAGING** *Nebula NEBCD 036*	48		2

COSMIC ROUGH RIDERS
UK, male vocal/instrumental group — 4

4 Aug 01	**REVOLUTION (IN THE SUMMERTIME)** *Poptones MC 5047SCX*	35		1
29 Sep 01	**THE PAIN INSIDE** *Poptones MC 5052SCX*	36		1
5 Jul 03	**BECAUSE YOU** *Measured MRCOSMIC 002SCX*	34		1
20 Sep 03	**JUSTIFY THE RAIN** *Measured MRCOSMIC 3SC*	39		1

COSMOS
UK, male DJ/producer/pianist/cellist (Tom Middleton). See Global Communication — 3

18 Sep 99	**SUMMER IN SPACE** *Island Blue PFACD 3*	49		1
5 Oct 02	**TAKE ME WITH YOU** *Polydor 0659952*	32		2

ANTONY COSTA
UK, male vocalist. See Blue — 2

18 Feb 06	**DO YOU EVER THINK OF ME?** *Globe Records 9877410*	19		2

DON COSTA
US, male orchestra leader/producer, d. 19 Jan 1983 (age 57) — 10

13 Oct 60	**NEVER ON SUNDAY** *London HLT 9195*	27		10

NIKKA COSTA
US, female vocalist — 1

11 Aug 01	**LIKE A FEATHER** *Virgin VUSCD 199*	53		1

ELVIS COSTELLO
UK, male vocalist/multi-instrumentalist (Declan MacManus) — 180

5 Nov 77	**WATCHING THE DETECTIVES** *Stiff BUY 20*	15		11
11 Mar 78	**(I DON'T WANNA GO TO) CHELSEA** *Radar ADA 3* & THE ATTRACTIONS	16		10
13 May 78	**PUMP IT UP** *Radar ADA 10* & THE ATTRACTIONS	24		10
28 Oct 78	**RADIO RADIO** *Radar ADA 24* & THE ATTRACTIONS	29		7
10 Feb 79	**OLIVER'S ARMY** *Radar ADA 31* & THE ATTRACTIONS	2		12
12 May 79	**ACCIDENTS WILL HAPPEN** *Radar ADA 35* & THE ATTRACTIONS	28		8
16 Feb 80	**I CAN'T STAND UP FOR FALLING DOWN** *F. Beat XX 1*	4		8
12 Apr 80	**HI FIDELITY** *F. Beat XX 3*	30		5
7 Jun 80	**NEW AMSTERDAM** *F. Beat XX 5*	36		6
20 Dec 80	**CLUBLAND** *F. Beat XX 12* & THE ATTRACTIONS	60		4
3 Oct 81	**A GOOD YEAR FOR THE ROSES** *F. Beat XX 17*	6		11
12 Dec 81	**SWEET DREAMS** *F. Beat XX 19*	42		8
10 Apr 82	**I'M YOUR TOY** *F. Beat XX 21* & THE ATTRACTIONS WITH THE ROYAL PHILHARMONIC ORCHESTRA	51		3
19 Jun 82	**YOU LITTLE FOOL** *F. Beat XX 26*	52		3
31 Jul 82	**MAN OUT OF TIME** *F. Beat XX 28*	58		2
25 Sep 82	**FROM HEAD TO TOE** *F. Beat XX 30*	43		4
11 Dec 82	**PARTY PARTY** *A&M AMS 8267* & THE ATTRACTIONS WITH THE ROYAL HORN GUARDS	48		6
11 Jun 83	**PILLS AND SOAP** *Imp 001* IMPOSTER	16		4
9 Jul 83	**EVERYDAY I WRITE THE BOOK** *F. Beat XX 32*	28		8
17 Sep 83	**LET THEM ALL TALK** *F. Beat XX 33*	59		2
28 Apr 84	**PEACE IN OUR TIME** *Imposter TRUCE 1* IMPOSTER	48		3
16 Jun 84	**I WANNA BE LOVED/TURNING THE TOWN RED** *F. Beat XX 35*	25		6
25 Aug 84	**THE ONLY FLAME IN TOWN** *F. Beat XX 37*	71		2
4 May 85	**GREEN SHIRT** *F. Beat ZB 40085*	68		2

Date	Title	Peak Position	Weeks at No.1	Weeks on Chart
1 Feb 86	**DON'T LET ME BE MISUNDERSTOOD** *F. Beat ZB 40555* COSTELLO SHOW FEATURING THE CONFEDERATES	33		4
30 Aug 86	**TOKYO STORM WARNING** *Imp 007*	73		1
4 Mar 89	**VERONICA** *Warner Brothers W 7558*	31		6
20 May 89	**BABY PLAYS AROUND (EP)** *Warner Brothers W 2949*	65		1
4 May 91	**THE OTHER SIDE OF SUMMER** *Warner Brothers W 0025*	43		4
5 Mar 94	**SULKY GIRL** *Warner Brothers W 0234CD* & THE ATTRACTIONS	22		3
30 Apr 94	**13 STEPS LEAD DOWN** *Warner Brothers W 0245CD* & THE ATTRACTIONS	59		1
26 Nov 94	**LONDON'S BRILLIANT PARADE** *Warner Brothers W 0270CD1* & THE ATTRACTIONS	48		2
11 May 96	**IT'S TIME** *Warner Brothers W 0348CD* & THE ATTRACTIONS	58		1
1 May 99	**TOLEDO** *Mercury 8709652* ELVIS COSTELLO/BURT BACHARACH	72		1
31 Jul 99	**SHE** *Mercury MERDD 521*	19		10
20 Apr 02	**TEAR OFF YOUR OWN HEAD** *Mercury 5828872*	58		1

BILLY COTTON & HIS BAND
UK, male band leader/vocalist, d. 25 Mar 1969 (age 69) — 25

Date	Title	Peak Position	Weeks at No.1	Weeks on Chart
1 May 53	**IN A GOLDEN COACH** *Decca F 10058* VOCALS BY DOREEN STEPHENS	3		10
18 Dec 53	**I SAW MOMMY KISSING SANTA CLAUS** *Decca F 10206* VOCALS BY THE MILL GIRLS & THE BANDITS	11		3
30 Apr 54	**FRIENDS AND NEIGHBOURS** *Decca F 10299* ,VOCALS BY THE BANDITS	3		12

MIKE COTTON'S JAZZMEN
UK, male vocal/instrumental group — 4

Date	Title	Peak Position	Weeks at No.1	Weeks on Chart
20 Jun 63	**SWING THAT HAMMER** *Columbia DB 7029*	36		4

COUGARS
UK, male vocal/instrumental group — 8

Date	Title	Peak Position	Weeks at No.1	Weeks on Chart
28 Feb 63	**SATURDAY NITE AT THE DUCK POND** *Parlophone R 4989*	33		8

COUNCIL COLLECTIVE
UK/US, male/female vocal/instrumental charity ensemble — 6

Date	Title	Peak Position	Weeks at No.1	Weeks on Chart
22 Dec 84	**SOUL DEEP (PART 1)** *Polydor MINE 1*	24		6

COUNT & SINDEN FEATURING KID SISTER
UK/US, male/female vocal/rap trio — 1

Date	Title	Peak Position	Weeks at No.1	Weeks on Chart
12 Apr 08	**BEEPER** *Domino RUG290CD*	69		1

COUNT INDIGO
UK, male vocalist (Bruce Marcus) — 1

Date	Title	Peak Position	Weeks at No.1	Weeks on Chart
9 Mar 96	**MY UNKNOWN LOVE** *Cowboy RODEO 952CD*	59		1

COUNTING CROWS
US, male vocal/instrumental group — 29

Date	Title	Peak Position	Weeks at No.1	Weeks on Chart
30 Apr 94	**MR JONES** *Geffen GFSTD 69*	28		2
9 Jul 94	**ROUND HERE** *Geffen GFSTD 74*	70		1
15 Oct 94	**RAIN KING** *Geffen GFSTD 82*	49		3
19 Oct 96	**ANGELS OF THE SILENCES** *Geffen GFSTD 22182*	41		1
14 Dec 96	**A LONG DECEMBER** *Geffen GFSTD 22190*	62		1
31 May 97	**DAYLIGHT FADING** *Geffen GFSTD 22247*	54		1
20 Dec 97	**A LONG DECEMBER** *Geffen GFSTD 22190*	68		1
30 Oct 99	**HANGINAROUND** *Geffen 4971842*	46		1
29 Jun 02	**AMERICAN GIRLS** *Geffen 4977452*	33		2
15 Feb 03	**BIG YELLOW TAXI** *Geffen 4978492* FEATURING VANESSA CARLTON	16		9
21 Jun 03	**IF I COULD GIVE YOU ALL MY LOVE** *Geffen GED 9806831*	50		1
27 Mar 04	**HANGINAROUND** *Geffen 9861994*	68		1
24 Jul 04	**ACCIDENTLY IN LOVE** *DreamWorks 9862881*	28		5

COUNTRYMEN
UK, male vocal/instrumental group — 2

Date	Title	Peak Position	Weeks at No.1	Weeks on Chart
3 May 62	**I KNOW WHERE I'M GOING** *Piccadilly 7N 35029*	45		2

COURSE
Holland, male/female vocal/instrumental duo – Vincent Hendrinks & Dewi Lopulalan — 15

Date	Title	Peak Position	Weeks at No.1	Weeks on Chart
19 Apr 97	**READY OR NOT** *The Brothers Organisation CDBRUV 2*	5		7
5 Jul 97	**AIN'T NOBODY** *The Brothers Organisation CDBRUV 3*	8		6
20 Dec 97	**BEST LOVE** *The Brothers Organisation CDBRUV 6*	51		2

COURTEENERS
UK, male vocal/instrumental group — 14

Date	Title	Peak Position	Weeks at No.1	Weeks on Chart
3 Nov 07	**ACRYLIC** *A&M 1749715*	44		2
26 Jan 08	**WHAT TOOK YOU SO LONG** *A&M 1756917*	20		3
12 Apr 08	**NOT NINETEEN FOREVER** *A&M 1764280*	19		4
5 Jul 08	**NO YOU DIDN'T, NO YOU DON'T** *A&M 1775075*	35		1
18 Oct 08	**THAT KISS** *A&M 1785867*	36		1
27 Feb 10	**YOU OVERDID IT DOLL** *A&M GBUM70915579*	28		3

TINA COUSINS
UK, female vocalist/model — 23

Date	Title	Peak Position	Weeks at No.1	Weeks on Chart
15 Aug 98	**MYSTERIOUS TIMES** *Multiply CDMULTY 40* SASH! FEATURING TINA COUSINS ●	2		12
21 Nov 98	**PRAY** *Jive 0519162*	20		3
27 Mar 99	**KILLIN' TIME** *Jive/Eastern Bloc 0519232*	15		4
10 Jul 99	**FOREVER** *Jive 0519332*	45		2
9 Oct 99	**ANGEL** *Ebul/Jive 0519432*	46		1
10 Dec 05	**WONDERFUL LIFE** *All Around The World CDGLOBE472*	58		1

DON COVAY
US, male vocalist — 6

Date	Title	Peak Position	Weeks at No.1	Weeks on Chart
7 Sep 74	**IT'S BETTER TO HAVE (AND DON'T NEED)** *Mercury 6052 634*	29		6

COVENTRY CITY CUP FINAL SQUAD
UK, male vocalists/footballers — 2

Date	Title	Peak Position	Weeks at No.1	Weeks on Chart
23 May 87	**GO FOR IT!** *Sky Blue SKB 1*	61		2

COVER GIRLS
US, female vocal trio — 4

Date	Title	Peak Position	Weeks at No.1	Weeks on Chart
1 Aug 92	**WISHING ON A STAR** *Epic 6581437*	38		4

DAVID COVERDALE
UK, male vocalist. See Coverdale Page, Deep Purple, Whitesnake — 4

Date	Title	Peak Position	Weeks at No.1	Weeks on Chart
24 Jun 78	**SNAKE BITE (EP)** *EMI International INEP 751* DAVID COVERDALE'S WHITESNAKE	61		3
7 Jun 97	**TOO MANY TEARS** *EMI CDEM 471* & WHITESNAKE	46		1

COVERDALE PAGE
UK, male vocal/instrumental duo – David Coverdale & Jimmy Page — 3

Date	Title	Peak Position	Weeks at No.1	Weeks on Chart
3 Jul 93	**TAKE ME FOR A LITTLE WHILE** *EMI CDEM 270*	29		2
23 Oct 93	**TAKE A LOOK AT YOURSELF** *EMI CDEM 279*	43		1

JULIE COVINGTON
UK, female actor/vocalist — 35

Date	Title	Peak Position	Weeks at No.1	Weeks on Chart
25 Dec 76	**DON'T CRY FOR ME ARGENTINA** *MCA 260* ●	1	1	15
3 Dec 77	**ONLY WOMEN BLEED** *Virgin VS 196*	12		11
15 Jul 78	**DON'T CRY FOR ME ARGENTINA** *MCA 260*	63		3
21 May 77	**O.K.?** *Polydor 2001 714* JULIE COVINGTON, RULA LENSKA, CHARLOTTE CORNWELL & SUE JONES-DAVIES	10		6

CARL COX
UK, male producer/DJ — 19

Date	Title	Peak Position	Weeks at No.1	Weeks on Chart
28 Sep 91	**I WANT YOU (FOREVER)** *Perfecto PB 44885* DJ CARL COX	23		7
8 Aug 92	**DOES IT FEEL GOOD TO YOU** *Perfecto 74321102877* DJ CARL COX	35		3
6 Nov 93	**THE PLANET OF LOVE** *Perfecto 74321161772*	44		2
9 Mar 96	**TWO PAINTINGS AND A DRUM EP** *Edel 0090715 COX*	24		2
8 Jun 96	**SENSUAL SOPHIS-TI-CAT/THE PLAYER** *Ultimatum 0090875 COX*	25		2
12 Dec 98	**THE LATIN THEME** *Edel 0091685 COX*	52		1
22 May 99	**PHUTURE 2000** *Worldwide Ultimatum 0091715 COX*	40		2

DEBORAH COX
Canada, female vocalist — 8

Date	Title	Peak Position	Weeks at No.1	Weeks on Chart
11 Nov 95	**SENTIMENTAL** *Arista 74321324962*	34		3
24 Feb 96	**WHO DO U LOVE** *Arista 74321337942*	31		3
31 Jul 99	**IT'S OVER NOW** *Arista 74321686942*	49		1
9 Oct 99	**NOBODY'S SUPPOSED TO BE HERE** *Arista 74321702102*	55		1

MICHAEL COX
UK, male vocalist — 15

Date	Title	Peak Position	Weeks at No.1	Weeks on Chart
9 Jun 60	**ANGELA JONES** *Triumph RGM 1011*	7		13
20 Oct 60	**ALONG CAME CAROLINE** *HMV POP 789*	41		2

PETER COX
UK, male vocalist/multi-instrumentalist. See Go West — 6

Date	Title	Peak Position	Weeks at No.1	Weeks on Chart
2 Aug 97	**AIN'T GONNA CRY AGAIN** *Chrysalis CDCHS 5056*	37		2
15 Nov 97	**IF YOU WALK AWAY** *Chrysalis CDCHSS 5069*	24		2
20 Jun 98	**WHAT A FOOL BELIEVES** *Chrysalis CDCHS 5089*	39		2

GRAHAM COXON
UK, male vocalist/guitarist. See Blur — 15

Date	Title	Peak Position	Weeks at No.1	Weeks on Chart
20 Mar 04	**FREAKIN' OUT** *Transcopic R 6632*	37		1
15 May 04	**BITTERSWEET BUNDLE OF MAN** *Transcopic CDRS 6637*	22		3
7 Aug 04	**SPECTACULAR** *Transcopic CDRS 6643*	32		2
6 Nov 04	**FREAKIN' OUT/ALL OVER ME** *Transcopic CDRS6652*	19		3
11 Mar 06	**STANDING ON MY OWN AGAIN** *Parlophone CDR6681*	20		2
20 May 06	**YOU & I** *Parlophone CDRS6691*	39		2
21 Jul 07	**THIS OLD TOWN** *Regal Recordings GB01A0700935* PAUL WELLER & GRAHAM COXON	39		2

CRACKER
US, male vocal/instrumental group — 9

Date	Title	Peak Position	Weeks at No.1	Weeks on Chart
28 May 94	**LOW** *Virgin America VUSDG 80*	43		4
23 Jul 94	**GET OFF THIS** *Virgin America VUSCD 83*	41		3
3 Dec 94	**LOW** *Virgin America VUSDG 80*	54		2

SARAH CRACKNELL
UK, female vocalist. See Saint Etienne — 6

Date	Title	Peak Position	Weeks at No.1	Weeks on Chart
14 Sep 96	**ANYMORE** *Gut CDGUT 3*	39		1
9 Feb 08	**THE JOURNEY CONTINUES** *Positiva 12TIV267* MARK BROWN FEATURING SARAH CRACKNELL	11		5

CRACKOUT
UK, male vocal/instrumental group — 3

Date	Title	Peak Position	Weeks at No.1	Weeks on Chart
22 Jun 02	**I AM THE ONE** *Hut HUTCD 156*	72		1
9 Aug 03	**OUT OF OUR MINDS** *Hut HUTCD 170*	63		1
13 Mar 04	**THIS IS WHAT WE DO** *Hut HUTCD174*	65		1

CRADLE OF FILTH
UK, male vocal/instrumental group — 2

Date	Title	Peak Position	Weeks at No.1	Weeks on Chart
15 Mar 03	**BABYLON A.D. (SO GLAD FOR THE MADNESS)** *Epic 6735549*	35		2

CRAIG
UK, male vocalist (Craig Phillips) — 6

Date	Title	Peak Position	Weeks at No.1	Weeks on Chart
23 Dec 00	**AT THIS TIME OF YEAR** *WEA 321CD* ●	14		6

FLOYD CRAMER
US, male pianist, d. 31 Dec 1997 (age 64) — 24

Date	Title	Peak Position	Weeks at No.1	Weeks on Chart
13 Apr 61	**ON THE REBOUND** *RCA 1231*	1	1	14
20 Jul 61	**SAN ANTONIO ROSE** *RCA 1241*	36		8
23 Aug 62	**HOT PEPPER** *RCA 1301*	46		2

CRAMPS
US, male/female vocal/instrumental group — 4

Date	Title	Peak Position	Weeks at No.1	Weeks on Chart
9 Nov 85	**CAN YOUR PUSSY DO THE DOG?** *Big Beat NS 110*	68		1
10 Feb 90	**BIKINI GIRLS WITH MACHINE GUNS** *Enigma ENV 17*	35		3

CRANBERRIES
Ireland, female/male vocal/instrumental group – Dolores O'Riordan*, Michael & Noel Hogan & Fergal Lawler — 50

Date	Title	Peak Position	Weeks at No.1	Weeks on Chart
27 Feb 93	**LINGER** *Island CID 556*	74		1
12 Feb 94	**LINGER** *Island CID 559*	14		11
7 May 94	**DREAMS** *Island CIDX 594*	27		5
1 Oct 94	**ZOMBIE** *Island CID 600*	14		6
3 Dec 94	**ODE TO MY FAMILY** *Island CIDX 601*	26		6
11 Mar 95	**I CAN'T BE WITH YOU** *Island CIDX 605*	23		5
12 Aug 95	**RIDICULOUS THOUGHTS** *Island CID 616*	20		3
20 Apr 96	**SALVATION** *Island CID 633*	13		5
13 Jul 96	**FREE TO DECIDE** *Instant CIDX 637*	33		3
17 Apr 99	**PROMISES** *Island US 5725912*	13		4
17 Jul 99	**ANIMAL INSTINCT** *Island US 5621972*	54		1

LES CRANE
US, male vocalist (Leslie Stein), d. 13 Jul 2008 (age 74) — 14

Date	Title	Peak Position	Weeks at No.1	Weeks on Chart
19 Feb 72	**DESIDERATA** *Warner Brothers K 16119*	7		14

CRANES
UK, male/female vocal/instrumental group — 2

Date	Title	Peak Position	Weeks at No.1	Weeks on Chart
25 Sep 93	**JEWEL** *Dedicated CRANE 007CD*	29		1
3 Sep 94	**SHINING ROAD** *Dedicated CRANE 008CD1*	57		1

CRASH TEST DUMMIES
Canada, male/female vocal/instrumental group – Brad Roberts, Benjamin Darvill, Mitch Dorge, Ellen Reid & Dan Roberts — 20

Date	Title	Peak Position	Weeks at No.1	Weeks on Chart
23 Apr 94	**MMM MMM MMM MMM** *RCA 74321201512* ●	2		11
16 Jul 94	**AFTERNOONS & COFFEESPOONS** *RCA 74321219622*	23		5
15 Apr 95	**THE BALLAD OF PETER PUMPKINHEAD** *RCA 74321276772* FEATURING ELLEN REID	30		4

BEVERLEY CRAVEN
UK, female vocalist/keyboard player — 33

Date	Title	Peak Position	Weeks at No.1	Weeks on Chart
20 Apr 91	**PROMISE ME** *Epic 6559437* ●	3		13
20 Jul 91	**HOLDING ON** *Epic 6565507*	32		7
5 Oct 91	**WOMAN TO WOMAN** *Epic 6574647*	40		5
7 Dec 91	**MEMORIES** *Epic 6576617*	68		2
25 Sep 93	**LOVE SCENES** *Epic 6595952*	34		4
20 Nov 93	**MOLLIE'S SONG** *Epic 6598132*	61		2

BILLY CRAWFORD
US, male vocalist — 6

Date	Title	Peak Position	Weeks at No.1	Weeks on Chart
10 Oct 98	**URGENTLY IN LOVE** *V2 VVR 5003063*	48		2
3 May 03	**YOU DIDN'T EXPECT THAT** *V2 VVR 5022083*	35		2
30 Aug 03	**TRACKIN'** *V2 VVR 5023108*	32		2

JIMMY CRAWFORD
UK, male vocalist (Ronald Lindsey) — 11

Date	Title	Peak Position	Weeks at No.1	Weeks on Chart
8 Jun 61	**LOVE OR MONEY** *Columbia DB 4633*	49		1
16 Nov 61	**I LOVE HOW YOU LOVE ME** *Columbia DB 4717*	18		10

MICHAEL CRAWFORD
UK, male vocalist/actor (Michael Dumble-Smith) — 14

Date	Title	Peak Position	Weeks at No.1	Weeks on Chart
10 Jan 87	**THE MUSIC OF THE NIGHT** *Polydor POSP 803*	7		11
15 Jan 94	**THE MUSIC OF THE NIGHT** *Columbia 6597382* BARBRA STREISAND (DUET WITH MICHAEL CRAWFORD)	54		3

RANDY CRAWFORD
US, female vocalist (Veronica Crawford) — 75

Date	Title	Peak Position	Weeks at No.1	Weeks on Chart
21 Jun 80	**LAST NIGHT AT DANCELAND** *Warner Brothers K 17631*	61		2
30 Aug 80	**ONE DAY I'LL FLY AWAY** *Warner Brothers K 17680* ●	2		11
20 May 81	**YOU MIGHT NEED SOMEBODY** *Warner Brothers K 17803*	11		13
8 Aug 81	**RAINY NIGHT IN GEORGIA** *Warner Brothers K 17840*	18		9
31 Oct 81	**SECRET COMBINATION** *Warner Brothers K 17872*	48		3
30 Jan 82	**IMAGINE** *Warner Brothers K 17906*	60		2
5 Jun 82	**ONE HELLO** *Warner Brothers K 17948*	48		4
19 Feb 83	**HE REMINDS ME** *Warner Brothers K 17970*	65		2
8 Oct 83	**NIGHT LINE** *Warner Brothers W 9530*	51		4
29 Nov 86	**ALMAZ** *Warner Brothers W 8583*	4		17
18 Jan 92	**DIAMANTE** *London LON 313* ZUCCHERO WITH RANDY CRAWFORD	44		7
15 Nov 97	**GIVE ME THE NIGHT** *WEA 142CD*	60		1

ROBERT CRAY BAND
US, male vocal/instrumental group — 5

Date	Title	Peak Position	Weeks at No.1	Weeks on Chart
20 Jun 87	**RIGHT NEXT DOOR (BECAUSE OF ME)** *Mercury CRAY 3*	50		4
20 Apr 96	**BABY LEE** *Silvertone ORECD 81* JOHN LEE HOOKER WITH ROBERT CRAY	65		1

CRAZY ELEPHANT
US, male vocal group — **13**

Date	Title / Label	Peak	Wks at No.1	Wks
21 May 69	**GIMME GIMME GOOD LOVIN'** *Major Minor MM 609*	12		13

CRAZY FROG
Sweden, computer animated frog/male production duo – Daniel Malmedahl & Erik Wernquist — **37**

Date	Title / Label	Peak	Wks at No.1	Wks
4 Jun 05	**AXEL F** *Gusto CDGUS17* ●	1	4	16
3 Sep 05	**POPCORN** *Gusto CDGUS21*	12		7
24 Dec 05	**JINGLE BELLS/U CAN'T TOUCH THIS** *Gut CDGUS27*	5		5
10 Jun 06	**WE ARE THE CHAMPIONS** *Gut CDGUS41*	11		6
23 Dec 06	**LAST CHRISTMAS** *Tug CDSNOG17*	16		3

CRAZY TOWN
US, male vocal/rap/instrumental group – Seth Binzer (Shifty* Shellshock), Bret Mazur (Epic), James Bradley, Jr (JBJ), Doug Miller (Faydoedeelay), Kraig Tyler (Squirrel) & Anthony 'Trouble' Valli — **19**

Date	Title / Label	Peak	Wks at No.1	Wks
7 Apr 01	**BUTTERFLY** *Columbia 6710012* ○ ★	3		13
11 Aug 01	**REVOLVING DOOR** *Columbia 6714942*	23		5
30 Nov 02	**DROWNING** *Columbia 6733262*	50		1

CRAZYHEAD
UK, male vocal/instrumental group — **4**

Date	Title / Label	Peak	Wks at No.1	Wks
16 Jul 88	**TIME HAS TAKEN ITS TOLL ON YOU** *Food 12*	65		2
25 Feb 89	**HAVE LOVE WILL TRAVEL (EP)** *Food SGE 2025*	68		2

CREAM
UK, male vocal/instrumental trio – Ginger Baker*, Jack Bruce* & Eric Clapton* — **61**

Date	Title / Label	Peak	Wks at No.1	Wks
20 Oct 66	**WRAPPING PAPER** *Reaction 591 007*	34		6
15 Dec 66	**I FEEL FREE** *Reaction 591 011*	11		12
8 Jun 67	**STRANGE BREW** *Reaction 591 015*	17		9
5 Jun 68	**ANYONE FOR TENNIS (THE SAVAGE SEVEN THEME)** *Polydor 56 258*	40		3
9 Oct 68	**SUNSHINE OF YOUR LOVE** *Polydor 56 286*	25		7
15 Jan 69	**WHITE ROOM** *Polydor 56 300*	28		8
9 Apr 69	**BADGE** *Polydor 56 315*	18		10
28 Oct 72	**BADGE** *Polydor 2058 285*	42		4
26 Nov 05	**SUNSHINE OF YOUR LOVE** *Manifesto 9874942* VS HOXTONS	46		2

CREATION
UK, male vocal/instrumental group — **3**

Date	Title / Label	Peak	Wks at No.1	Wks
7 Jul 66	**MAKING TIME** *Planet PLF 116*	49		1
3 Nov 66	**PAINTER MAN** *Planet PLF 119*	36		2

CREATURES
UK, male/female vocal/instrumental duo. See Siouxsie & The Banshees — **28**

Date	Title / Label	Peak	Wks at No.1	Wks
3 Oct 81	**MAD EYED SCREAMER** *Polydor POSPD 354*	24		7
23 Apr 83	**MISS THE GIRL** *Wonderland SHE 1*	21		7
16 Jul 83	**RIGHT NOW** *Wonderland SHE 2*	14		10
14 Oct 89	**STANDING HERE** *Wonderland SHE 17*	53		2
27 Mar 99	**SAY** *Sioux 6CD*	72		1
25 Oct 03	**GODZILLA** *Sioux 14CD3*	53		1

CREDIT TO THE NATION
UK, male rapper/vocalist (Matthew 'MC Fusion' Hanson) & male dance duo — **11**

Date	Title / Label	Peak	Wks at No.1	Wks
22 May 93	**CALL IT WHAT YOU WANT** *One Little Indian 94 TP7CD*	57		3
18 Sep 93	**ENOUGH IS ENOUGH** *One Little Indian 79 TP7CD* CHUMBAWAMBA & CREDIT TO THE NATION	56		2
12 Mar 94	**TEENAGE SENSATION** *One Little Indian 124 TP7DC*	24		3
14 May 94	**SOWING THE SEEDS OF HATRED** *One Little Indian 134 TP7DC*	72		1
22 Jul 95	**LIAR LIAR** *One Little Indian 144 TP7DC*	60		1
12 Sep 98	**TACKY LOVE SONG** *Chrysalis CDCHS 5097*	60		1

CREED
US, male vocal/instrumental group — **13**

Date	Title / Label	Peak	Wks at No.1	Wks
15 Jan 00	**HIGHER** *Epic 6683152*	47		1
20 Jan 01	**WITH ARMS WIDE OPEN** *Epic 6706952* ★	13		5
29 Sep 01	**HIGHER** *Epic 6710642*	64		1
16 Mar 02	**MY SACRIFICE** *Epic 6723162*	18		5
3 Aug 02	**ONE LAST BREATH/BULLETS** *Epic 6728262*	47		1

CREEDENCE CLEARWATER REVIVAL
US, male vocal/instrumental group – John Fogerty, Doug Clifford, Stu Cook & Tom Fogerty, d. 6 Sep 1990 — **94**

Date	Title / Label	Peak	Wks at No.1	Wks
28 May 69	**PROUD MARY** *Liberty LBF 15223*	8		13
16 Aug 69	**BAD MOON RISING** *Liberty LBF 15230*	1	3	15
15 Nov 69	**GREEN RIVER** *Liberty LBF 15250*	19		11
14 Feb 70	**DOWN ON THE CORNER** *Liberty LBF 15283*	31		6
4 Apr 70	**TRAVELLIN' BAND** *Liberty LBF 15310*	8		13
20 Jun 70	**UP AROUND THE BEND** *Liberty LBF 15354*	3		12
5 Sep 70	**LONG AS I CAN SEE THE LIGHT** *Liberty LBF 15384*	20		9
20 Mar 71	**HAVE YOU EVER SEEN THE RAIN** *Liberty LBF 15440*	36		6
24 Jul 71	**SWEET HITCH-HIKER** *United Artists UP 35261*	36		8
2 May 92	**BAD MOON RISING** *Epic 6580047*	71		1

KID CREOLE & THE COCONUTS
US, male/female vocal group – Thomas August Darnell Browder, Andy 'Coati Mundi' Hernandez, Taryn Hagey (replaced by Janique Svedberg), Adriana Kaegi & Cheryl Poirier — **58**

Date	Title / Label	Peak	Wks at No.1	Wks
13 Jun 81	**ME NO POP I** *Ze WIP 6711* PRESENTS COATI MUNDI	32		7
15 May 82	**I'M A WONDERFUL THING, BABY** *Ze WIP 6756*	4		11
24 Jul 82	**STOOL PIGEON** *Ze WIP 6793*	7		9
9 Oct 82	**ANNIE I'M NOT YOUR DADDY** *Ze WIP 6801*	2		8
11 Dec 82	**DEAR ADDY** *Ze WIP 6840*	29		7
10 Sep 83	**THERE'S SOMETHING WRONG IN PARADISE** *Island IS 130*	35		5
19 Nov 83	**THE LIFEBOAT PARTY** *Island IS 142*	49		4
14 Apr 90	**THE SEX OF IT** *CBS 6556987*	29		5
10 Apr 93	**I'M A WONDERFUL THING, BABY (REMIX)** *Island CID 551*	60		2

CRESCENDO
UK/US, male/female vocal/instrumental duo — **5**

Date	Title / Label	Peak	Wks at No.1	Wks
23 Dec 95	**ARE YOU OUT THERE** *ffrr FCD 270*	20		5

CRESCENT
UK, male vocal/instrumental group — **3**

Date	Title / Label	Peak	Wks at No.1	Wks
18 May 02	**ON THE RUN** *Hut HUTCD 153*	49		1
27 Jul 02	**TEST OF TIME** *Hut HUTCD 157*	60		1
28 Sep 02	**SPINNIN' WHEELS** *Hut HUTDX 160*	61		1

CREW CUTS
US, male vocal group – Pat Barrett, Rudi Maugeri, d. 7 May 2004, John & Ray Perkins — **29**

Date	Title / Label	Peak	Wks at No.1	Wks
1 Oct 54	**SH-BOOM** *Mercury MB 3140* ★	12		9
15 Apr 55	**EARTH ANGEL** *Mercury MB 3202*	4		20

BERNARD CRIBBINS
UK, male actor/vocalist — **29**

Date	Title / Label	Peak	Wks at No.1	Wks
15 Feb 62	**HOLE IN THE GROUND** *Parlophone R 4869*	9		13
5 Jul 62	**RIGHT SAID FRED** *Parlophone R 4923*	10		10
13 Dec 62	**GOSSIP CALYPSO** *Parlophone R 4961*	25		6

CRIBS
UK, male vocal/instrumental trio — **14**

Date	Title / Label	Peak	Wks at No.1	Wks
6 Mar 04	**YOU WERE ALWAYS THE ONE** *Wichita WEBB059SCD*	66		1
29 May 04	**WHAT ABOUT ME** *Wichita WEBB061SCD*	75		1
30 Apr 05	**HEY SCENESTERS!** *Wichita WEBB074SCD*	27		2
25 Jun 05	**MIRROR KISSERS** *Wichita WEBB080SCD*	27		2
3 Sep 05	**MARTELL** *Wichita WEBB092SCD*	39		1
17 Dec 05	**YOU'RE GONNA LOSE US** *Wichita WEBB097SCD*	30		2
26 May 07	**MEN'S NEEDS** *Wichita WEBB124SCD*	17		3
11 Aug 07	**MOVING PICTURES** *Wichita WEBB128SCD*	38		1
10 Nov 07	**DON'T YOU WANNA BE RELEVANT?** *Wichita WEBB156SCD*	39		1

CRICKETS
US, male vocal/instrumental group – Buddy Holly*, d. 3 Feb 1959, Jerry Allison, Sonny Curtis & Joe B Mauldin — **97**

Date	Title / Label	Peak	Wks at No.1	Wks
27 Sep 57	**THAT'LL BE THE DAY** *Vogue Coral Q 72279* ★	1	3	15
27 Dec 57	**OH BOY** *Coral Q 72298*	3		15
14 Mar 58	**MAYBE BABY** *Coral Q 72307*	4		10
25 Jul 58	**THINK IT OVER** *Coral Q 72329*	11		7

Silver-selling ○ Gold-selling ● Platinum-selling (x multiples) US No.1 ★ Peak Position · Weeks at No.1 · Weeks on Chart

Date	Title / Label	Peak Position	Weeks at No.1	Weeks on Chart
24 Apr 59	**LOVE'S MADE A FOOL OF YOU** *Coral Q 72365*	26		2
15 Jan 60	**WHEN YOU ASK ABOUT LOVE** *Coral Q 72382*	27		1
12 May 60	**MORE THAN I CAN SAY** *Coral Q 72395*	42		1
26 May 60	**BABY MY HEART** *Coral Q 72395*	33		4
21 Jun 62	**DON'T EVER CHANGE** *Liberty LIB 55441*	5		13
24 Jan 63	**MY LITTLE GIRL** *Liberty LIB 10067*	17		9
6 Jun 63	**DON'T TRY TO CHANGE ME** *Liberty LIB 10092*	37		4
14 May 64	**YOU'VE GOT LOVE** *Coral Q 72472* BUDDY HOLLY & THE CRICKETS	40		6
2 Jul 64	**(THEY CALL HER) LA BAMBA** *Liberty LIB 55696*	21		10

CRIMEA
Ireland, male vocal/instrumental group

Date	Title / Label	Peak Position	Weeks at No.1	Weeks on Chart
				3
21 Jan 06	**LOTTERY WINNERS ON ACID** *Warner Brothers W698CD1*	31		2
22 Apr 06	**WHITE RUSSIAN GALAXY** *Warner Brothers W708CD1*	51		1

CRISPY & COMPANY
US, male vocal/instrumental group

Date	Title / Label	Peak Position	Weeks at No.1	Weeks on Chart
				11
16 Aug 75	**BRAZIL** *Creole CR 109*	26		5
27 Dec 75	**GET IT TOGETHER** *Creole CR 114*	21		6

CRITTERS
US, male vocal/instrumental group

Date	Title / Label	Peak Position	Weeks at No.1	Weeks on Chart
				5
30 Jun 66	**YOUNGER GIRL** *London HL 10047*	38		5

TONY CROMBIE & HIS ROCKETS
UK, male vocal/instrumental group – leader d. 18 Oct 1999 (age 74)

Date	Title / Label	Peak Position	Weeks at No.1	Weeks on Chart
				2
19 Oct 56	**TEACH YOU TO ROCK/SHORT'NIN' BREAD** *Columbia DB 3822*	25		2

BING CROSBY
US, male vocalist/actor (Harry Crosby), d. 14 Oct 1977 (age 74)

Date	Title / Label	Peak Position	Weeks at No.1	Weeks on Chart
				101
14 Nov 52	**ISLE OF INNISFREE** *Brunswick 04900*	3		12
5 Dec 52	**ZING A LITTLE ZONG** *Brunswick 04981* & JANE WYMAN	10		2
19 Dec 52	**SILENT NIGHT** *Brunswick 03929*	8		2
19 Mar 54	**CHANGING PARTNERS** *Brunswick 05244*	9		3
7 Jan 55	**COUNT YOUR BLESSINGS** *Brunswick 05339*	11		3
29 Apr 55	**STRANGER IN PARADISE** *Brunswick 05410*	17		2
27 Apr 56	**IN A LITTLE SPANISH TOWN** *Brunswick 05543*	22		3
23 Nov 56	**TRUE LOVE** *Capitol CL 14645* & GRACE KELLY	4		27
24 May 57	**AROUND THE WORLD** *Brunswick 05674*	5		15
9 Aug 75	**THAT'S WHAT LIFE IS ALL ABOUT** *United Artists UP 35852*	41		4
3 Dec 77	**WHITE CHRISTMAS** *MCA 111* ○	5		7
27 Nov 82	**PEACE ON EARTH – LITTLE DRUMMER BOY** *RCA BOW 12* DAVID BOWIE & BING CROSBY ○	3		8
17 Dec 83	**TRUE LOVE** *Capitol CL 315* & GRACE KELLY	70		3
21 Dec 85	**WHITE CHRISTMAS** *MCA BING 1*	69		2
19 Dec 98	**WHITE CHRISTMAS** *MCA MCSTD 48105*	29		4
15 Dec 07	**WHITE CHRISTMAS** *MCA MCSTD 48105*	42		3
29 Dec 07	**PEACE ON EARTH – LITTLE DRUMMER BOY** *Capitol ATS049735001* DAVID BOWIE & BING CROSBY	73		1

DAVID CROSBY FEATURING PHIL COLLINS
UK, male vocal/instrumental duo

Date	Title / Label	Peak Position	Weeks at No.1	Weeks on Chart
				3
15 May 93	**HERO** *Atlantic A 7360*	56		3

CROSBY, STILLS & NASH
US/UK, male vocal/instrumental group

Date	Title / Label	Peak Position	Weeks at No.1	Weeks on Chart
				12
16 Aug 69	**MARRAKESH EXPRESS** *Atlantic 584 283*	17		9
21 Jan 89	**AMERICAN DREAM** *Atlantic A 9003* CROSBY, STILLS, NASH & YOUNG	55		3

CROSS
UK/US, male vocal/instrumental group

Date	Title / Label	Peak Position	Weeks at No.1	Weeks on Chart
				1
17 Oct 87	**COWBOYS AND INDIANS** *Virgin VS 1007*	74		1

CHRISTOPHER CROSS
US, male vocalist (Christopher Geppert)

Date	Title / Label	Peak Position	Weeks at No.1	Weeks on Chart
				27
19 Apr 80	**RIDE LIKE THE WIND** *Warner Brothers K 17582*	69		1
14 Feb 81	**SAILING** *Warner Brothers K 17695* ★	48		6
17 Oct 81	**ARTHUR'S THEME (BEST THAT YOU CAN DO)** *Warner Brothers K 17847*	56		4
9 Jan 82	**ARTHUR'S THEME (BEST THAT YOU CAN DO)** *Warner Brothers K 17847* ★	7		11
5 Feb 83	**ALL RIGHT** *Warner Brothers W 9843*	51		5

CROW
Germany, male production duo

Date	Title / Label	Peak Position	Weeks at No.1	Weeks on Chart
				1
19 May 01	**WHAT YA LOOKIN' AT** *Tidy Trax TIDY 153CD*	60		1

SHERYL CROW
US, female vocalist/guitarist

Date	Title / Label	Peak Position	Weeks at No.1	Weeks on Chart
				91
18 Jun 94	**LEAVING LAS VEGAS** *A&M 5806472*	66		1
5 Nov 94	**ALL I WANNA DO** *A&M 5808452* ○	4		13
11 Feb 95	**STRONG ENOUGH** *A&M 5809212*	33		4
27 May 95	**CAN'T CRY ANYMORE** *A&M 5810552*	33		3
29 Jul 95	**RUN, BABY, RUN** *A&M 5811492*	24		4
11 Nov 95	**WHAT I CAN DO FOR YOU** *A&M 5812292*	43		1
21 Sep 96	**IF IT MAKES YOU HAPPY** *A&M 5819032*	9		6
30 Nov 96	**EVERYDAY IS A WINDING ROAD** *A&M 5820232*	12		6
29 Mar 97	**HARD TO MAKE A STAND** *A&M 5821492*	22		3
12 Jul 97	**A CHANGE WOULD DO YOU GOOD** *A&M 5822092*	8		5
18 Oct 97	**HOME** *A&M 5823992*	25		2
13 Dec 97	**TOMORROW NEVER DIES** *A&M 5824572*	12		9
12 Sep 98	**MY FAVORITE MISTAKE** *A&M 5827632*	9		6
5 Dec 98	**THERE GOES THE NEIGHBORHOOD** *A&M 5828092*	19		7
6 Mar 99	**ANYTHING BUT DOWN** *A&M 5828292*	19		4
11 Sep 99	**SWEET CHILD O' MINE** *Columbia 6678882*	30		3
13 Apr 02	**SOAK UP THE SUN** *A&M 4977052*	16		8
13 Jul 02	**STEVE McQUEEN** *A&M 4977422*	44		1
1 Nov 03	**FIRST CUT IS THE DEEPEST** *A&M 9813556*	37		3
3 Jul 04	**LIGHT IN YOUR EYES** *A&M 9862700*	73		1
1 Oct 05	**GOOD IS GOOD** *A&M 9885348*	75		1

CROWD
International, male/female vocal/instrumental charity assembly

Date	Title / Label	Peak Position	Weeks at No.1	Weeks on Chart
				11
1 Jun 85	**YOU'LL NEVER WALK ALONE** *Spartan BRAD 1* ●	1	2	11

CROWDED HOUSE
New Zealand/Australia, male vocal/instrumental group – Neil Finn*, Tim Finn*, Mark Hart, Paul Hester, d. 26 Mar 2005 (replaced by Peter Jones), & Nick Seymour

Date	Title / Label	Peak Position	Weeks at No.1	Weeks on Chart
				67
6 Jun 87	**DON'T DREAM IT'S OVER** *Capitol CL 438*	27		8
22 Jun 91	**CHOCOLATE CAKE** *Capitol CL 618*	69		2
2 Nov 91	**FALL AT YOUR FEET** *Capitol CL 626*	17		7
29 Feb 92	**WEATHER WITH YOU** *Capitol CL 643*	7		9
20 Jun 92	**FOUR SEASONS IN ONE DAY** *Capitol CL 655*	26		5
26 Sep 92	**IT'S ONLY NATURAL** *Capitol CL 661*	24		4
2 Oct 93	**DISTANT SUN** *Capitol CDCLS 697*	19		6
20 Nov 93	**NAILS IN MY FEET** *Capitol CDCLS 701*	22		4
19 Feb 94	**LOCKED OUT** *Capitol CDCLS 707*	12		4
11 Jun 94	**FINGERS OF LOVE** *Capitol CDCL 715*	25		3
24 Sep 94	**PINEAPPLE HEAD** *Capitol CDCL 723*	27		3
22 Jun 96	**INSTINCT** *Capitol CDCLS 774*	12		4
17 Aug 96	**NOT THE GIRL YOU THINK YOU ARE** *Capitol CDCLS 776*	20		3
9 Nov 96	**DON'T DREAM IT'S OVER** *Capitol CDCL 780*	25		2
7 Jul 07	**DON'T STOP NOW** *Parlophone CDR6743*	41		1
22 Dec 07	**POUR LE MONDE** *EMI GBAYE0701724*	51		1
10 May 08	**FALL AT YOUR FEET** *Capitol USCA29100170*	75		1

CROWN HEIGHTS AFFAIR
US, male vocal/instrumental group – Phillip Thomas, William Anderson, James Baynard, Bert, d. 12 Dec 2004, & Raymond Reid, Raymond Rock, Arnold 'Muki' Wilson & Howard Young

Date	Title / Label	Peak Position	Weeks at No.1	Weeks on Chart
				34
19 Aug 78	**GALAXY OF LOVE** *Mercury 6168 801*	24		10
11 Nov 78	**I'M GONNA LOVE YOU FOREVER** *Mercury 6168 803*	47		4
14 Apr 79	**DANCE LADY DANCE** *Mercury 6168 804*	44		4
3 May 80	**YOU GAVE ME LOVE** *De-Lite MER 9*	10		12
9 Aug 80	**YOU'VE BEEN GONE** *De-Lite MER 28*	44		4

JULEE CRUISE
US, female vocalist

Date	Title / Label	Peak Position	Weeks at No.1	Weeks on Chart
				14
10 Nov 90	**FALLING** *Warner Brothers W 9544*	7		11
2 Mar 91	**ROCKIN' BACK INSIDE MY HEART** *Warner Brothers W 0004*	66		2
11 Sep 99	**IF I SURVIVE** *Distinctive DISNCD 55* HYBRID FEATURING JULEE CRUISE	52		1

Silver-selling ● Gold-selling ● Platinum-selling (x multiples) ✪ US No.1 ★ Peak Position Weeks at No.1 Weeks on Chart

CRUSADERS

US, male instrumental group – Wilton Felder*, Wayne Henderson, Stix Hooper & Joe Sample — 16

Date	Title	Peak	Wks No.1	Wks
18 Aug 79	**STREET LIFE** *MCA 513*	5		11
26 Sep 81	**I'M SO GLAD I'M STANDING HERE TODAY** *MCA 741* FEATURED VOCALIST JOE COCKER	61		3
7 Apr 84	**NIGHT LADIES** *MCA 853*	55		2

CRUSH

UK, female vocal duo — 3

Date	Title	Peak	Wks No.1	Wks
24 Feb 96	**JELLYHEAD** *Telstar CDSTAS 2809*	50		2
3 Aug 96	**LUV'D UP** *Telstar CDSTAS 2833*	45		1

BOBBY CRUSH

UK, male pianist — 4

Date	Title	Peak	Wks No.1	Wks
4 Nov 72	**BORSALINO** *Philips 6006 248*	37		4

TAIO CRUZ

UK, male vocalist/producer (Adetayo Onile-Ere) — 95

Date	Title	Peak	Wks No.1	Wks
11 Nov 06	**I JUST WANNA KNOW** *Universal 1713178*	29		6
15 Sep 07	**MOVING ON** *Island 1746784*	26		4
23 Feb 08	**COME ON GIRL** *Fourth & Broadway 1764408* FEATURING LUCIANA	5		17
17 May 08	**I CAN BE** *Fourth & Broadway 1772004*	18		12
16 Aug 08	**SHE'S LIKE A STAR** *Fourth & Broadway 1781907*	20		14
17 Jan 09	**TAKE ME BACK** *Fourth & Broadway 1797027* TINCHY STRYDER FEATURING TAIO CRUZ	3		19
26 Sep 09	**BREAK YOUR HEART** *Fourth & Broadway 2717453*	1	3	20
5 Dec 09	**NO OTHER ONE** *Fourth & Broadway GBUM70911468*	42		3

CRW

Italy, male producer (Mauro Picotto). See R.A.F. — 8

Date	Title	Peak	Wks No.1	Wks
26 Feb 00	**I FEEL LOVE** *VC Recordings VRCD 63*	15		4
25 Nov 00	**LOVIN'** *VC Recordings VRCD 77*	49		2
27 Apr 02	**LIKE A CAT** *BXR BXRC 0397* FEATURING VERONIKA	57		1
26 Oct 02	**PRECIOUS LIFE** *BXR BXRC 0395* PRESENTS VERONIKA	57		1

CRY BEFORE DAWN

Ireland, male vocal/instrumental group — 2

Date	Title	Peak	Wks No.1	Wks
17 Jun 89	**WITNESS FOR THE WORLD** *Epic GONE 3*	67		2

CRY OF LOVE

US, male vocal/instrumental group — 1

Date	Title	Peak	Wks No.1	Wks
15 Jan 94	**BAD THING** *Columbia 6600462*	60		1

CRY SISCO!

UK, male producer (Barry Blue) — 9

Date	Title	Peak	Wks No.1	Wks
2 Sep 89	**AFRO DIZZI ACT** *Escape AWOL 1*	42		9

CRYIN' SHAMES

UK, male vocal/instrumental group — 7

Date	Title	Peak	Wks No.1	Wks
31 Mar 66	**PLEASE STAY** *Decca F 12340*	26		7

CRYSTAL METHOD

US, male instrumental duo — 4

Date	Title	Peak	Wks No.1	Wks
11 Oct 97	**(CAN'T YOU) TRIP LIKE I DO** *Epic 6650862* FILTER & THE CRYSTAL METHOD	39		2
7 Mar 98	**KEEP HOPE ALIVE** *Sony S2 CM 3CD*	71		1
8 Aug 98	**COMIN' BACK** *Sony S2 CM 4CD*	73		1

CRYSTAL PALACE

UK, male vocalists/footballers & backing band — 2

Date	Title	Peak	Wks No.1	Wks
12 May 90	**GLAD ALL OVER/WHERE EAGLES FLY** *Parkfield PMS 5019*	50		2

CRYSTALS

US, female vocal group – Darlene Love, Barbara Alston, Delores Brooks, Myrna Gerrard, Dee Dee Kenniebrew, Mary Thomas & Patricia Wright — 54

Date	Title	Peak	Wks No.1	Wks
22 Nov 62	**HE'S A REBEL** *London HLU 9611* ★	19		13
20 Jun 63	**DA DOO RON RON** *London HLU 9732*	5		16
19 Sep 63	**THEN HE KISSED ME** *London HLU 9773*	2		14
5 Mar 64	**I WONDER** *London HLU 9852*	36		3
19 Oct 74	**DA DOO RON RON** *Warner Brothers K 19010*	15		8

CSILLA

Hungary, female vocalist (Csilla Domonkos) — 1

Date	Title	Peak	Wks No.1	Wks
13 Jul 96	**MAN IN THE MOON** *Worx WORXCD 001*	69		1

CSS

Brazil, female/male vocal/instrumental group — 4

Date	Title	Peak	Wks No.1	Wks
10 Mar 07	**OFF THE HOOK** *Warner Brothers WEA416CD*	43		1
19 May 07	**LET'S MAKE LOVE AND LISTEN TO DEATH FROM ABOVE** *Sire WEA418CD*	39		3

ALEX CUBA BAND FEATURING RON SEXSMITH

Cuba/Canada, male vocal/instrumental group — 1

Date	Title	Peak	Wks No.1	Wks
6 Nov 04	**LO MISMO QUE YO (IF ONLY)** *Shell GET2CD*	52		1

CUBAN BOYS

UK, male/female production group — 9

Date	Title	Peak	Wks No.1	Wks
25 Dec 99	**COGNOSCENTI VERSUS THE INTELLIGENTSIA** *EMI CDCUBAN 001* ●	4		9

CUBAN HEELS

UK, male vocal/instrumental group — 1

Date	Title	Peak	Wks No.1	Wks
19 Mar 05	**SHE'S ON FIRE** *Sugar Shack FOD062*	72		1

CUBIC 22

Belgium, male production duo — 7

Date	Title	Peak	Wks No.1	Wks
22 Jun 91	**NIGHT IN MOTION** *XL Recordings XLS 20*	15		7

CUD

UK, male vocal/instrumental group — 16

Date	Title	Peak	Wks No.1	Wks
19 Oct 91	**OH NO WON'T DO EP** *A&M AMB 829*	49		2
28 Mar 92	**THROUGH THE ROOF** *A&M AM 857*	44		2
30 May 92	**RICH AND STRANGE** *A&M AM 871*	24		3
15 Aug 92	**PURPLE LOVE BALLOON** *A&M AM 0024*	27		3
10 Oct 92	**ONCE AGAIN** *A&M AM 0081*	45		1
12 Feb 94	**NEUROTICA** *A&M 5805172*	37		2
2 Apr 94	**STICKS AND STONES** *A&M 5805472*	68		1
3 Sep 94	**ONE GIANT LOVE** *A&M 5807292*	52		2

CUFF LINKS

US, male vocalist (Ron Dante) multi-tracked. See Archies — 30

Date	Title	Peak	Wks No.1	Wks
29 Nov 69	**TRACY** *MCA MU 1101*	4		16
14 Mar 70	**WHEN JULIE COMES AROUND** *MCA MU 1112*	10		14

JAMIE CULLUM

UK, male vocalist/multi-instrumentalist — 18

Date	Title	Peak	Wks No.1	Wks
20 Mar 04	**THESE ARE THE DAYS/FRONTIN'** *UCJ 9866211*	12		5
20 Nov 04	**EVERLASTING LOVE** *UCJ 9868834*	20		9
1 Oct 05	**GET YOUR WAY** *UCJ 9873425*	44		1
10 Dec 05	**MIND TRICK** *UCJ 9875047*	32		1
14 Nov 09	**I'M ALL OVER IT** *Decca GBUM70907760*	55		2

CULT

UK, male vocal/instrumental duo – Ian Astbury & Billy Duffy – with various instrumental collaborators — 80

Date	Title	Peak	Wks No.1	Wks
22 Dec 84	**RESURRECTION JOE** *Beggars Banquet BEG 122*	74		2
25 May 85	**SHE SELLS SANCTUARY** *Beggars Banquet BEG 135*	15		19
5 Oct 85	**RAIN** *Beggars Banquet BEG 147*	17		8
30 Nov 85	**REVOLUTION** *Beggars Banquet BEG 152*	30		7

Silver-selling ● Gold-selling ● Platinum-selling (x multiples) ⊛ US No.1 ★ Peak Position · Weeks at No.1 · Weeks on Chart

Date	Title	Peak Position	Weeks at No.1	Weeks on Chart
28 Feb 87	**LOVE REMOVAL MACHINE** *Beggars Banquet BEG 182*	18		7
2 May 87	**LIL' DEVIL** *Beggars Banquet BEG 188*	11		7
22 Aug 87	**WILD FLOWER (DOUBLE SINGLE)** *Beggars Banquet BEG 195D*	24		2
29 Aug 87	**WILD FLOWER** *Beggars Banquet BEG 195*	30		4
1 Apr 89	**FIRE WOMAN** *Beggars Banquet BEG 228*	15		4
8 Jul 89	**EDIE (CIAO BABY)** *Beggars Banquet BEG 230*	32		5
18 Nov 89	**SUN KING/EDIE (CIAO BABY)** *Beggars Banquet BEG 235*	39		2
10 Mar 90	**SWEET SOUL SISTER** *Beggars Banquet BEG 241*	42		4
14 Sep 91	**WILD HEARTED SON** *Beggars Banquet BEG 255*	40		2
29 Feb 92	**HEART OF SOUL** *Beggars Banquet BEG 260*	51		1
30 Jan 93	**SHE SELLS SANCTUARY (REMIX)** *Beggars Banquet BEG 253CD*	15		4
8 Oct 94	**COMING DOWN** *Beggars Banquet BBQ 40CD*	50		1
7 Jan 95	**STAR** *Beggars Banquet BBQ 45CD*	65		1

CULTURE BEAT

Germany, male producer (Torsten Fenslau), d. 6 Nov 1993, & US/UK, male/female rap/vocal duo – Jay 'Supreme' Williams & Tania Evans

Date	Title	Peak Position	Weeks at No.1	Weeks on Chart (47)
3 Feb 90	**CHERRY LIPS (DER ERDBEERMUND)** *Epic 6556337*	55		3
7 Aug 93	**MR VAIN** *Epic 6594682* ● (Gold)	1	4	15
6 Nov 93	**GOT TO GET IT** *Epic 6597212*	4		11
15 Jan 94	**ANYTHING** *Epic 6600252*	5		8
2 Apr 94	**WORLD IN YOUR HANDS** *Epic 6602292*	20		4
27 Jan 96	**INSIDE OUT** *Epic 6626562*	32		2
15 Jun 96	**CRYING IN THE RAIN** *Epic 6633582*	29		2
28 Sep 96	**TAKE ME AWAY** *Epic 6637552*	52		1
20 Sep 03	**MR VAIN RECALL** *East West EW 270CD*	51		1

CULTURE CLUB

UK, male vocal/instrumental group – Boy George* (George O'Dowd), Mikey Craig, Roy Hay & Jon Moss

Date	Title	Peak Position	Weeks at No.1	Weeks on Chart (119)
18 Sep 82	**DO YOU REALLY WANT TO HURT ME** *Virgin VS 518* ● (Gold)	1	3	18
27 Nov 82	**TIME (CLOCK OF THE HEART)** *Virgin VS 558* ● (Gold)	3		12
9 Apr 83	**CHURCH OF THE POISON MIND** *Virgin VS 571* ● (Silver)	2		9
17 Sep 83	**KARMA CHAMELEON** *Virgin VS 612* ⊛ ★	1	6	20
10 Dec 83	**VICTIMS** *Virgin VS 641* ● (Gold)	3		10
24 Mar 84	**IT'S A MIRACLE** *Virgin VS 662*	4		9
6 Oct 84	**THE WAR SONG** *Virgin VS 694* ● (Silver)	2		8
1 Dec 84	**THE MEDAL SONG** *Virgin VS 730*	32		5
15 Mar 86	**MOVE AWAY** *Virgin VS 845*	7		7
31 May 86	**GOD THANK YOU WOMAN** *Virgin VS 861*	31		5
31 Oct 98	**I JUST WANNA BE LOVED** *Virgin VSCDT 1710*	4		10
7 Aug 99	**YOUR KISSES ARE CHARITY** *Virgin VSCDT 1736*	25		4
27 Nov 99	**COLD SHOULDER/STARMAN** *Virgin VSCDT 1758*	43		2

SMILEY CULTURE

UK, male vocalist (David Emmanuel)

Date	Title	Peak Position	Weeks at No.1	Weeks on Chart (13)
15 Dec 84	**POLICE OFFICER** *Fashion FAD 7012*	12		10
6 Apr 85	**COCKNEY TRANSLATION** *Fashion FAD 7028*	71		1
13 Sep 86	**SCHOOLTIME CHRONICLE** *Polydor POSP 815*	59		2

LARRY CUNNINGHAM & THE MIGHTY AVONS

Ireland, male vocalist & instrumental group

Date	Title	Peak Position	Weeks at No.1	Weeks on Chart (11)
10 Dec 64	**TRIBUTE TO JIM REEVES** *King KG 1016*	40		11

CUPID'S INSPIRATION

UK, male vocal/instrumental group – Terry Rice Milton, Wyndham George, Roger Gray, Laughton James & Garfield Tonkin

Date	Title	Peak Position	Weeks at No.1	Weeks on Chart (19)
19 Jun 68	**YESTERDAY HAS GONE** *Nems 56 3500*	4		11
2 Oct 68	**MY WORLD** *Nems 56 3702*	33		8

CURE

UK, male vocal/instrumental group – Robert Smith, Simon Gallup, Laurence 'Lol' Tolhurst, Porl Thompson & Boris Williams

Date	Title	Peak Position	Weeks at No.1	Weeks on Chart (151)
12 Apr 80	**A FOREST** *Fiction FICS 10*	31		8
4 Apr 81	**PRIMARY** *Fiction FICS 12*	43		6
17 Oct 81	**CHARLOTTE SOMETIMES** *Fiction FICS 14*	44		4
24 Jul 82	**HANGING GARDEN** *Fiction FICS 15*	34		4
27 Nov 82	**LET'S GO TO BED** *Fiction FICS 17*	44		5
9 Jul 83	**THE WALK** *Fiction FICS 18*	12		8
29 Oct 83	**THE LOVE CATS** *Fiction FICS 19*	7		11
7 Apr 84	**THE CATERPILLAR** *Fiction FICS 20*	14		7
27 Jul 85	**IN BETWEEN DAYS** *Fiction FICS 22*	15		10
21 Sep 85	**CLOSE TO ME** *Fiction FICS 23*	24		8
3 May 86	**BOYS DON'T CRY** *Fiction FICS 24*	22		6
18 Apr 87	**WHY CAN'T I BE YOU** *Fiction FICS 25*	21		5
4 Jul 87	**CATCH** *Fiction FICS 26*	27		6
17 Oct 87	**JUST LIKE HEAVEN** *Fiction FICS 27*	29		5
20 Feb 88	**HOT HOT HOT!!!** *Fiction FICSX 28*	45		3
22 Apr 89	**LULLABY** *Fiction FICS 29*	5		6
2 Sep 89	**LOVESONG** *Fiction FICS 30*	18		7
31 Mar 90	**PICTURES OF YOU** *Fiction FICS 34*	24		6
29 Sep 90	**NEVER ENOUGH** *Fiction FICS 35*	13		5
3 Nov 90	**CLOSE TO ME (REMIX)** *Fiction FICS 36*	13		5
28 Mar 92	**HIGH** *Fiction FICS 39*	8		3
11 Apr 92	**HIGH (REMIX)** *Fiction FICSX 41*	44		1
23 May 92	**FRIDAY I'M IN LOVE** *Fiction FICS 42*	6		7
17 Oct 92	**A LETTER TO ELSIE** *Fiction FICS 46*	28		2
4 May 96	**THE 13TH** *Fiction 5764692*	15		2
29 Jun 96	**MINT CAR** *Fiction FICSD 52*	31		2
14 Dec 96	**GONE** *Fiction FICD 53*	60		1
29 Nov 97	**WRONG NUMBER** *Fiction FICD 54*	62		1
10 Nov 01	**CUT HERE** *Fiction 5873892*	54		1
31 Jul 04	**THE END OF THE WORLD** *Geffen 9862976*	25		3
30 Oct 04	**TAKING OFF** *Geffen 9864491*	39		1
24 May 08	**THE ONLY ONE** *Geffen 1773237*	48		1
26 Jul 08	**SLEEP WHEN I'M DEAD** *Geffen 1778504*	68		1

CURIOSITY KILLED THE CAT

UK, male vocal/instrumental group – Ben Volpeliere-Pierrot, Julian Godfrey Brookhouse, Migi Drummond & Nick Thorpe

Date	Title	Peak Position	Weeks at No.1	Weeks on Chart (58)
13 Dec 86	**DOWN TO EARTH** *Mercury CAT 2*	3		18
4 Apr 87	**ORDINARY DAY** *Mercury CAT 3*	11		7
20 Jun 87	**MISFIT** *Mercury CAT 4*	7		9
19 Sep 87	**FREE** *Mercury CAT 5*	56		2
16 Sep 89	**NAME AND NUMBER** *Mercury CAT 6* CURIOSITY	14		9
25 Apr 92	**HANG ON IN THERE BABY** *RCA PB 45377* CURIOSITY	3		10
29 Aug 92	**I NEED YOUR LOVIN'** *RCA 74321111377* CURIOSITY	47		2
30 Oct 93	**GIMME THE SUNSHINE** *RCA 74321168602* CURIOSITY	73		1

CHANTAL CURTIS

France, female vocalist

Date	Title	Peak Position	Weeks at No.1	Weeks on Chart (3)
14 Jul 79	**GET ANOTHER LOVE** *Pye 7P 5003*	51		3

TC CURTIS

Jamaica, male vocalist

Date	Title	Peak Position	Weeks at No.1	Weeks on Chart (4)
23 Feb 85	**YOU SHOULD HAVE KNOWN BETTER** *Holt Melt VS 754*	50		4

CURVE

UK, male/female vocal/instrumental duo

Date	Title	Peak Position	Weeks at No.1	Weeks on Chart (14)
16 Mar 91	**THE BLINDFOLD (EP)** *AnXious ANX 27*	68		1
25 May 91	**COAST IS CLEAR** *AnXious ANX 30*	34		3
9 Nov 91	**CLIPPED** *AnXious ANX 35*	36		2
7 Mar 92	**FAIT ACCOMPLI** *AnXious ANX 36*	22		3
18 Jul 92	**HORROR HEAD (EP)** *AnXious ANXT 38*	31		2
4 Sep 93	**BLACKERTHREETRACKER EP** *AnXious ANXCD 42*	39		2
16 May 98	**COMING UP ROSES** *Universal UND 80489*	51		1

CURVED AIR

UK, female/male vocal/instrumental group – Sonja Kristina Linwood, Rob Martin, Francis Monkman, Florian Pilkington-Miksa & Darryl Way

Date	Title	Peak Position	Weeks at No.1	Weeks on Chart (12)
7 Aug 71	**BACK STREET LUV** *Warner Brothers K 16092*	4		12

CUSHH

Denmark, male vocal/instrumental group

Date	Title	Peak Position	Weeks at No.1	Weeks on Chart (1)
10 Mar 07	**DO IT 2 ME** *E-Park GBGGF0600003*	31		1

CUT 'N' MOVE

Denmark, male/female vocal/rap/production group

Date	Title	Peak Position	Weeks at No.1	Weeks on Chart (4)
2 Oct 93	**GIVE IT UP** *EMI CDEM 273*	61		2
9 Sep 95	**I'M ALIVE** *EMI CDEM 375*	49		2

FRANKIE CUTLASS

US, male rapper (Francis Parker)

Date	Title	Peak Position	Weeks at No.1	Weeks on Chart (1)
5 Apr 97	**THE CYPHER: PART 3** *Epic 6641445*	59		1

JON CUTLER FEATURING E-MAN
US, male vocal/production duo — 2

Date	Title	Peak Position	Weeks at No.1	Weeks on Chart
19 Jan 02	**IT'S YOURS** *Direction 6720532*	38		2

CUTTING CREW
UK/Canada, male vocal/instrumental group — 37

Date	Title	Peak Position	Weeks at No.1	Weeks on Chart
16 Aug 86	**(I JUST) DIED IN YOUR ARMS** *Siren 21* ● ★	4		12
25 Oct 86	**I'VE BEEN IN LOVE BEFORE** *Siren 29*	31		10
7 Mar 87	**ONE FOR THE MOCKINGBIRD** *Siren 40*	52		5
21 Nov 87	**I'VE BEEN IN LOVE BEFORE** *Siren SRN 29*	24		8
22 Jul 89	**(BETWEEN A) ROCK AND A HARD PLACE** *Siren SRN 108*	66		2

CYBERSONIK
UK/Canada, male production trio — 1

Date	Title	Peak Position	Weeks at No.1	Weeks on Chart
10 Nov 90	**TECHNARCHY** *Champion CHAMP 264*	73		1

CYCLEFLY
Ireland, male vocal/instrumental group — 1

Date	Title	Peak Position	Weeks at No.1	Weeks on Chart
6 Apr 02	**NO STRESS** *Radioactive RAXTD 41*	68		1

CYGNUS X
Germany, male producer (Matthias Hoffmann). See Brainchild, Vernon's Wonderland — 5

Date	Title	Peak Position	Weeks at No.1	Weeks on Chart
11 Mar 00	**THE ORANGE THEME** *Hooj Choons HOOJ 88CD*	43		2
18 Aug 01	**SUPERSTRING** *Xtravaganza XTRAV 28CDS*	33		3

JOHNNY CYMBAL
Canada (b. UK), male vocalist, d. 16 Mar 1993 (age 48) — 10

Date	Title	Peak Position	Weeks at No.1	Weeks on Chart
14 Mar 63	**MR BASS MAN** *London HLR 9682*	24		10

CYPRESS HILL
US, male rap/DJ group — 45

Date	Title	Peak Position	Weeks at No.1	Weeks on Chart
31 Jul 93	**INSANE IN THE BRAIN** *Ruffhouse 6595332*	32		4
2 Oct 93	**WHEN THE SH.. GOES DOWN** *Ruffhouse 6596702*	19		4
11 Dec 93	**I AIN'T GOIN' OUT LIKE THAT** *Ruffhouse 6596902*	15		7
26 Feb 94	**INSANE IN THE BRAIN** *Ruffhouse 6601762*	21		4
7 May 94	**LICK A SHOT** *Ruffhouse 6603192*	20		3
7 Oct 95	**THROW YOUR SET IN THE AIR** *Ruffhouse 6623542*	15		3
17 Feb 96	**ILLUSIONS** *Columbia 6629052*	23		2
10 Oct 98	**TEQUILA SUNRISE** *Columbia 6664935*	23		2
10 Apr 99	**DR GREENTHUMB** *Columbia 6671202*	34		2
26 Jun 99	**INSANE IN THE BRAIN** *INCredible INCRL 17CD* JASON NEVINS VERSUS CYPRESS HILL	19		3
29 Apr 00	**RAP SUPERSTAR/ROCK SUPERSTAR** *Columbia 6692645*	13		5
16 Sep 00	**HIGHLIFE/CAN'T GET THE BEST OF ME** *Columbia 6697895*	35		2
8 Dec 01	**LOWRIDER/TROUBLE** *Columbia 6721662*	33		2
27 Mar 04	**WHAT'S YOUR NUMBER?** *Columbia 6746172*	44		2

BILLY RAY CYRUS
US, male vocalist/guitarist — 18

Date	Title	Peak Position	Weeks at No.1	Weeks on Chart
25 Jul 92	**ACHY BREAKY HEART** *Mercury MER 373* ●	3		10
10 Oct 92	**COULD'VE BEEN ME** *Mercury MER 378*	24		4
28 Nov 92	**THESE BOOTS ARE MADE FOR WALKIN'** *Mercury MER 384*	63		1
19 Dec 92	**ACHY BREAKY HEART** *Epic 6588837* ALVIN & THE CHIPMUNKS FEATURING BILLY RAY CYRUS	53		3

MILEY CYRUS
US, female vocalist/actor (Destiny Cyrus). See Helping Haiti — 76

Date	Title	Peak Position	Weeks at No.1	Weeks on Chart
3 Mar 07	**THE BEST OF BOTH WORLDS** *Walt Disney 3879752* HANNAH MONTANA	43		1
30 Aug 08	**SEE YOU AGAIN** *Walt Disney D000264632*	11		12
18 Oct 08	**7 THINGS** *Polydor USHR10823877*	25		15
14 Feb 09	**FLY ON THE WALL** *Polydor USHR10823893*	16		6
4 Apr 09	**THE CLIMB** *Polydor USWD10935758*	11		14
18 Apr 09	**HOEDOWN THROWDOWN** *Polydor USWD10935873*	18		11
7 Nov 09	**PARTY IN THE USA** *Hollywood/Polydor D510832*	11		15
26 Dec 09	**THE CLIMB** *Polydor USWD10935758*	31		3

CZR FEATURING DELANO
US, male vocal/production duo — 1

Date	Title	Peak Position	Weeks at No.1	Weeks on Chart
30 Sep 00	**I WANT YOU** *Credence CDCRED 002*	57		1

ASHER D
UK, male rapper (Ashley Walters). See So Solid Crew — 2

Date	Title	Peak Position	Weeks at No.1	Weeks on Chart
4 Aug 01	**BABY, CAN I GET YOUR NUMBER** *East West EW 235CD* OBI PROJECT FEATURING HARRY, ASHER D & DJ WHAT?	75		1
8 Jun 02	**BACK IN THE DAY/WHY ME** *Independiente ISOM 57MS*	43		1

CHUCK D
US, male rapper (Carlton Ridenhour) — 9

Date	Title	Peak Position	Weeks at No.1	Weeks on Chart
6 Jul 91	**BRING THE NOISE** *Island IS 490* ANTHRAX FEATURING CHUCK D	14		5
26 Oct 96	**NO** *Mercury MERCD 476*	55		1
23 Jun 01	**ROCK DA FUNKY BEATS** *Xtrahard X2H3 CDS* PUBLIC DOMAIN FEATURING CHUCK D	19		3

DIMPLES D
US, female rapper (Crystal Smith) — 10

Date	Title	Peak Position	Weeks at No.1	Weeks on Chart
17 Nov 90	**SUCKER DJ** *FBI 11*	17		10

LONGSY D'S HOUSE SOUND
UK, male instrumentalist/producer (Andrew Long) — 7

Date	Title	Peak Position	Weeks at No.1	Weeks on Chart
4 Mar 89	**THIS IS SKA** *Big One VBIG 13*	56		7

MAXWELL D
UK, male rapper (Maxwell Donaldson) — 2

Date	Title	Peak Position	Weeks at No.1	Weeks on Chart
15 Sep 01	**SERIOUS** *4 Liberty LIBTCD 046*	38		2

NIKKI D
US, female rapper (Nichelle Strong) — 6

Date	Title	Peak Position	Weeks at No.1	Weeks on Chart
6 May 89	**MY LOVE IS SO RAW** *Def Jam 6548987* ALYSON WILLIAMS FEATURING NIKKI D	34		5
30 Mar 91	**DADDY'S LITTLE GIRL** *Def Jam 6567347*	75		1

VICKY D
US, female vocalist — 6

Date	Title	Peak Position	Weeks at No.1	Weeks on Chart
13 Mar 82	**THIS BEAT IS MINE** *Virgin VS 486*	42		6

D KAY & EPSILION FEATURING STAMINA MC
Austria/UK, male vocal/production trio — 5

Date	Title	Peak Position	Weeks at No.1	Weeks on Chart
30 Aug 03	**BARCELONA** *Alphamagic/BC/BMG BCAU001CD*	14		5

D'MENACE
UK, male production duo — 3

Date	Title	Peak Position	Weeks at No.1	Weeks on Chart
8 Aug 98	**DEEP MENACE (SPANK)** *Inferno CDFERN 8*	20		3

D MOB
UK, male producer (Daniel Poku) — 48

Date	Title	Peak Position	Weeks at No.1	Weeks on Chart
15 Oct 88	**WE CALL IT ACIEED** *ffrr FFR 13* FEATURING GARY HAISMAN	3		12
3 Jun 89	**IT IS TIME TO GET FUNKY** *ffrr F 107* FEATURING LRS	9		10
21 Oct 89	**C'MON AND GET MY LOVE** *ffrr F 117* WITH CATHY DENNIS	15		10
6 Jan 90	**PUT YOUR HANDS TOGETHER** *ffrr F 124* FEATURING NUFF JUICE	7		8
7 Apr 90	**THAT'S THE WAY OF THE WORLD** *ffrr F 132* WITH CATHY DENNIS	48		3
12 Feb 94	**WHY** *ffrr FCD 227* WITH CATHY DENNIS	23		3
3 Sep 94	**ONE DAY** *ffrr FCDP 239*	41		2

D*NOTE
UK, male producer (Matt Winn) — 3

Date	Title	Peak Position	Weeks at No.1	Weeks on Chart
12 Jul 97	**WAITING HOPEFULLY** *VC Recordings VCRD 21*	46		1
15 Nov 97	**LOST AND FOUND** *VC Recordings VCRD 25*	59		1
27 Apr 02	**SHED MY SKIN** *Channel 4 Music C4M 00182*	73		1

D.O.S.E. FEATURING MARK E SMITH

UK, male vocal/production group. See Fall			1
23 Mar 96 **PLUG MYSELF IN** *Coliseum TOGA 001CD1*	50		1

D-RAIL

UK, male vocal trio			1
5 Feb 05 **HOW DO I SAY GOODBYE** *Silverword ECPCDS1*	63		1

D:REAM

UK, male vocalist/production duo – Peter Cunnah & Al MacKenzie (left 1993)			74
4 Jul 92 **U R THE BEST THING** *FXU 3*	72		1
30 Jan 93 **THINGS CAN ONLY GET BETTER** *Magnet MAG 1010CD*	24		5
24 Apr 93 **U R THE BEST THING** *Magnet MAG 1011CD*	19		8
31 Jul 93 **UNFORGIVEN** *Magnet MAG 1016CD*	29		3
2 Oct 93 **STAR/I LIKE IT** *Magnet MAG 1019CD*	26		4
8 Jan 94 **THINGS CAN ONLY GET BETTER** *Magnet MAG 1020CD* ●	1	4	16
26 Mar 94 **U R THE BEST THING (REMIX)** *Magnet MAG 1021CD*	4		10
18 Jun 94 **TAKE ME AWAY** *Magnet MAG 1025CD*	18		5
10 Sep 94 **BLAME IT ON ME** *Magnet MAG 1027CD*	25		5
8 Jul 95 **SHOOT ME WITH YOUR LOVE** *Magnet MAG 1034CD*	7		7
9 Sep 95 **PARTY UP THE WORLD** *Magnet MAG 1037CD*	20		6
11 Nov 95 **THE POWER (OF ALL THE LOVE IN THE WORLD)** *Magnet MAG 1039CD*	40		1
3 May 97 **THINGS CAN ONLY GET BETTER** *Magnet MAG 1050CD*	19		3

D-SHAKE

Holland, male producer (Adrianus de Mooy)			8
2 Jun 90 **YAAH/TECHNO TRANCE** *Cooltempo COOL 213*	20		6
2 Feb 91 **MY HEART THE BEAT** *Cooltempo COOL 228*	42		2

D-SIDE

Ireland, male vocal trio – Ryan O'Rian, Shane Creevey & Derek Moran			25
26 Apr 03 **SPEECHLESS** *WEA 366CD*	9		8
26 Jul 03 **INVISIBLE** *WEA 369CD*	7		6
13 Dec 03 **REAL WORLD** *Blacklist/Edel 9814017*	9		8
12 Jun 04 **PUSHIN' ME OUT** *Blacklist/Edel 0155826ERE*	21		3

D-TEK

UK, male production group			1
6 Nov 93 **DROP THE ROCK (EP)** *Positiva 12TIV 5*	70		1

D TRAIN

US, male vocal/instrumental duo			36
6 Feb 82 **YOU'RE THE ONE FOR ME** *Epic EPC A 2016*	30		8
8 May 82 **WALK ON BY** *Epic EPC A 2298*	44		6
7 May 83 **MUSIC PART 1** *Prelude A 3332*	23		7
16 Jul 83 **KEEP GIVING ME LOVE** *Prelude A 3497*	65		2
27 Jul 85 **YOU'RE THE ONE FOR ME** *Prelude ZB 40302*	15		11
12 Oct 85 **MUSIC (REMIX)** *Prelude ZB 40431*	62		2

AZZIDO DA BASS

Germany, male DJ/producer (Ingo Martens)			13
4 Mar 00 **DOOMS NIGHT** *Club Tools 0067285 CLU*	58		1
24 Jun 00 **DOOMS NIGHT** *Club Tools 0067285 CLU*	46		2
21 Oct 00 **DOOMS NIGHT (REMIX)** *Club Tools 0120285 CLU*	8		9
23 Mar 02 **SPEED (CAN YOU FEEL IT?)** *Club Tools 0135815 CLU* FEATURING ROLAND CLARK	68		1

DA BRAT

US, female rapper (Shawntae Harris)			1
22 Oct 94 **FUNKDAFIED** *Columbia 6609212*	65		1

DA CLICK

UK, male/female rap/vocal group			8
16 Jan 99 **GOOD RHYMES** *ffrr FCD 353*	14		6
29 May 99 **WE ARE DA CLICK** *ffrr FCD 363*	38		2

DA FOOL

US, male DJ/producer (Mike Stewart)			2
16 Jan 99 **NO GOOD** *ffrr FCD 352*	38		2

RICARDO DA FORCE

UK, male rapper (Ricardo Lyte). See N-Trance			14
18 Mar 95 **PUMP UP THE VOLUME** *Stress CDSTR 49* GREED FEATURING RICARDO DA FORCE	51		2
16 Sep 95 **STAYIN' ALIVE** *All Around The World CDGLOBE 131* N-TRANCE FEATURING RICARDO DA FORCE ●	2		11
31 Aug 96 **WHY** *ffrr FCD 280*	58		1

DA HOOL

Germany, male instrumentalist/producer (Frank Tomiczek)			13
14 Feb 98 **MEET HER AT THE LOVE PARADE** *Manifesto FESCD 39*	15		4
22 Aug 98 **BORA BORA** *Manifesto FESCD 47*	35		3
28 Jul 01 **MEET HER AT THE LOVE PARADE 2001** *Manifesto FESCD 85*	11		6

DA LENCH MOB

US, male rap group			2
20 Mar 93 **FREEDOM GOT AN A.K.** *East West America A 8431CD*	51		2

DA MOB FEATURING JOCELYN BROWN

US, male/female vocal/instrumental group			3
2 May 98 **FUN** *INCredible INCRL 2CD*	33		2
3 Jul 99 **IT'S ALL GOOD** *INCredible INCRL 14CD*	54		1

DA MUTTZ

UK, male production duo. See Shaft			10
9 Dec 00 **WASSUUP** *Eternal WEA 319CD*	11		10

DA PLAYAZ VS CLEA

Sweden/UK, male/female vocal/production group			2
29 Oct 05 **WE DON'T HAVE TO TAKE OUR CLOTHES OFF** *Upside UPSIDECD02*	35		2

DA SLAMMIN' PHROGZ

France, male production duo			1
29 Apr 00 **SOMETHING ABOUT THE MUSIC** *WEA 251CD*	53		1

RUI DA SILVA FEATURING CASSANDRA

Portugal, male producer & UK, female vocalist (Cassandra Fox)			14
13 Jan 01 **TOUCH ME** *Kismet 74321823992* ●	1	1	14

DA TECHNO BOHEMIAN

Holland, male production trio. See Drunkenmunky, Hi_Tack, Itty Bitty Boozy Woozy, Klubbheads			1
25 Jan 97 **BANGIN' BASS** *Hi-Life 5731772*	63		1

PAUL DA VINCI

UK, male vocalist			8
20 Jul 74 **YOUR BABY AIN'T YOUR BABY ANYMORE** *Penny Farthing PEN 843*	20		8

TERRY DACTYL & THE DINOSAURS

UK, male vocal/instrumental group			16
15 Jul 72 **SEASIDE SHUFFLE** *UK 5*	2		12
13 Jan 73 **ON A SATURDAY NIGHT** *UK 21*	45		4

DADA

US, male vocal/instrumental trio			1
4 Dec 93 **DOG** *IRS CDEIRSS 185*	71		1

DADA FEATURING SANDY RIVERA & TRIX

Israel/US, male vocal/instrumental/production group			4
5 May 07 **LOLLIPOP** *Data DATA158CDS*	18		4

DADDY YANKEE

Puerto Rico, male rapper (Raymond Ayala) — 9

Date	Title	Label	Peak	Wks No.1	Wks
30 Jul 05	**GASOLINA**	*Machete 9883426*	5		9

DADDY'S FAVOURITE

UK, male DJ/producer (James Harrigan) — 3

Date	Title	Label	Peak	Wks No.1	Wks
21 Nov 98	**I FEEL GOOD THINGS FOR YOU**	*Go! Beat GONCD 12*	44		2
9 Oct 99	**I FEEL GOOD THINGS FOR YOU**	*Go! Beat GONCD 22*	50		1

DAFFY DUCK FEATURING THE GROOVE GANG

Germany, male/female production/vocal group — 3

Date	Title	Label	Peak	Wks No.1	Wks
6 Jul 91	**PARTY ZONE**	*East West YZ 592*	58		3

DAFT PUNK

France, male instrumental/production duo – Thomas Bangalter & Guy-Manuel de Homem-Christo. See Together — 40

Date	Title	Label	Peak	Wks No.1	Wks
22 Feb 97	**DA FUNK/MUSIQUE**	*Soma VSCDT 1625*	7		5
26 Apr 97	**AROUND THE WORLD**	*Virgin VSCDT 1633*	5		5
4 Oct 97	**BURNIN'**	*Virgin VSCDT 1649*	30		2
28 Feb 98	**REVOLUTION 909**	*Virgin VSCDT 1682*	47		1
25 Nov 00	**ONE MORE TIME**	*Virgin VSCDT 1791*	2		12
23 Jun 01	**DIGITAL LOVE**	*Virgin VSCDT 1810*	14		7
17 Nov 01	**HARDER BETTER FASTER STRONGER**	*Virgin VSCDT 1822*	25		3
23 Apr 05	**ROBOT ROCK**	*Virgin VSCDX1897*	32		3
16 Jul 05	**TECHNOLOGIC**	*Virgin VSCDX1900*	40		2

DAISY CHAINSAW

UK, male/female vocal/instrumental group — 6

Date	Title	Label	Peak	Wks No.1	Wks
18 Jan 92	**LOVE YOUR MONEY**	*Deva 001*	26		5
28 Mar 92	**PINK FLOWER/ROOM ELEVEN**	*Deva 82 TP7*	65		1

DAISY DARES YOU FEATURING CHIPMUNK

UK, female/male vocal/rap duo — 5

Date	Title	Label	Peak	Wks No.1	Wks
13 Mar 10	**NUMBER ONE ENEMY**	*Jive GBARL0901628*	13		5+

DAKOTAS

UK, male vocal/instrumental group. See Billy J. Kramer & The Dakotas — 13

Date	Title	Label	Peak	Wks No.1	Wks
11 Jul 63	**THE CRUEL SEA**	*Parlophone R 5044*	18		13

JIM DALE

UK, male vocalist (James Smith) — 22

Date	Title	Label	Peak	Wks No.1	Wks
11 Oct 57	**BE MY GIRL**	*Parlophone R 4343*	2		16
10 Jan 58	**JUST BORN**	*Parlophone R 4376*	27		1
17 Jan 58	**CRAZY DREAM**	*Parlophone R 4376*	24		2
7 Mar 58	**SUGARTIME**	*Parlophone R 4402*	25		3

DALE & GRACE

US, male/female vocal duo — 2

Date	Title	Label	Peak	Wks No.1	Wks
9 Jan 64	**I'M LEAVING IT UP TO YOU**	*London HL 9807* ★	42		2

DALE SISTERS

UK, female vocal group. See England Sisters — 6

Date	Title	Label	Peak	Wks No.1	Wks
23 Nov 61	**MY SUNDAY BABY**	*Ember S 140*	36		6

DALI'S CAR

UK, male vocal/instrumental duo — 2

Date	Title	Label	Peak	Wks No.1	Wks
3 Nov 84	**THE JUDGEMENT IS THE MIRROR**	*Paradox DOX 1*	66		2

DALLAS SUPERSTARS

Finland, male production duo — 1

Date	Title	Label	Peak	Wks No.1	Wks
27 Sep 03	**HELIUM**	*All Around The World CDGLOBE 289*	64		1

ROGER DALTREY

UK, male vocalist/guitarist. See High Numbers, John McEnroe & Pat Cash with the Full Metal Rackets, Who — 46

Date	Title	Label	Peak	Wks No.1	Wks
14 Apr 73	**GIVING IT ALL AWAY**	*Track 2094 110*	5		11
4 Aug 73	**I'M FREE**	*Ode ODS 66302*	13		10
14 May 77	**WRITTEN ON THE WIND**	*Polydor 2121 319*	46		2
2 Aug 80	**FREE ME**	*Polydor 2001 980*	39		6
11 Oct 80	**WITHOUT YOUR LOVE**	*Polydor POSP 181*	55		4
3 Mar 84	**WALKING IN MY SLEEP**	*WEA U 9686*	56		3
5 Oct 85	**AFTER THE FIRE**	*10 TEN 69*	50		5
8 Mar 86	**UNDER A RAGING MOON**	*10 TEN 81*	43		5

DAMAGE

UK, male vocal group – Andrez Harriott, Rahsaan J. Bromfield, Jade Jones, Coreé Richards & Noel Simpson — 59

Date	Title	Label	Peak	Wks No.1	Wks
20 Jul 96	**ANYTHING**	*Big Life BLRD 129*	68		1
12 Oct 96	**LOVE II LOVE**	*Big Life BLRD 131*	12		6
14 Dec 96	**FOREVER**	*Big Life BLRDB 132* ●	6		9
22 Mar 97	**LOVE GUARANTEED**	*Big Life BLRDA 133*	7		7
17 May 97	**WONDERFUL TONIGHT**	*Big Life BLRDA 134*	3		8
9 Aug 97	**LOVE LADY**	*Big Life BLRDB 137*	33		2
1 Jul 00	**GHETTO ROMANCE**	*Cooltempo CDCOOL 347*	7		7
28 Oct 00	**RUMOURS**	*Cooltempo CDCOOLS 352*	22		4
31 Mar 01	**STILL BE LOVIN' YOU**	*Cooltempo CDCOOLS 355*	11		7
14 Jul 01	**SO WHAT IF I**	*Cooltempo CDCOOLS 357*	12		6
15 Dec 01	**AFTER THE LOVE HAS GONE**	*Cooltempo CDCOOLS 360*	42		2

BOBBY D'AMBROSIO FEATURING MICHELLE WEEKS

US, male/female vocal/DJ/production duo — 3

Date	Title	Label	Peak	Wks No.1	Wks
2 Aug 97	**MOMENT OF MY LIFE**	*Ministry Of Sound MOSCDS 1*	23		3

DAMIAN

UK, male vocalist (Damian Davis) — 26

Date	Title	Label	Peak	Wks No.1	Wks
26 Dec 87	**THE TIME WARP 2**	*Jive 160*	51		6
27 Aug 88	**THE TIME WARP 2**	*Jive 182*	64		3
19 Aug 89	**THE TIME WARP 2 (REMIX)**	*Jive 209*	7		13
16 Dec 89	**WIG WAM BAM**	*Jive 236*	49		4

DAMNED

UK, male vocal/instrumental group – Dave Vanian (David Letts), Captain Sensible* (Raymond Burns), Roman Jugg, Rat Scabies (Chris Millar) & Algy Ward (replaced by Paul Gray, then Bryn Merrick) — 77

Date	Title	Label	Peak	Wks No.1	Wks
5 May 79	**LOVE SONG**	*Chiswick CHIS 112*	20		8
20 Oct 79	**SMASH IT UP**	*Chiswick CHIS 116*	35		5
1 Dec 79	**I JUST CAN'T BE HAPPY TODAY**	*Chiswick CHIS 120*	46		5
4 Oct 80	**HISTORY OF THE WORLD (PART 1)**	*Chiswick CHIS 135*	51		4
28 Nov 81	**FRIDAY 13TH (EP)**	*Stale One TRY 1*	50		4
10 Jul 82	**LOVELY MONEY**	*Bronze BRO 149*	42		4
9 Jun 84	**THANKS FOR THE NIGHT**	*Damned 1*	43		4
30 Mar 85	**GRIMLY FIENDISH**	*MCA GRIM 1*	21		7
22 Jun 85	**THE SHADOW OF LOVE (EDITION PREMIERE)**	*MCA GRIM 2*	25		8
21 Sep 85	**IS IT A DREAM**	*MCA GRIM 3*	34		4
8 Feb 86	**ELOISE**	*MCA GRIM 4* ●	3		10
22 Nov 86	**ANYTHING**	*MCA GRIM 5*	32		4
7 Feb 87	**GIGOLO**	*MCA GRIM 6*	29		3
25 Apr 87	**ALONE AGAIN OR**	*MCA GRIM 7*	27		6
28 Nov 87	**IN DULCE DECORUM**	*MCA GRIM 8*	72		1

KENNY DAMON

US, male vocalist — 1

Date	Title	Label	Peak	Wks No.1	Wks
19 May 66	**WHILE I LIVE**	*Mercury MF 907*	48		1

VIC DAMONE

US, male vocalist (Vito Farinola) — 22

Date	Title	Label	Peak	Wks No.1	Wks
6 Dec 57	**AN AFFAIR TO REMEMBER**	*Philips PB 745*	29		2
9 May 58	**ON THE STREET WHERE YOU LIVE**	*Philips PB 819*	1	2	17
1 Aug 58	**THE ONLY MAN ON THE ISLAND**	*Philips PB 837*	24		3

DAN-I

UK, male vocalist (Selmore Lewinson) — 9

Date	Title	Label	Peak	Wks No.1	Wks
10 Nov 79	**MONKEY CHOP**	*Island WIP 6520*	30		9

Legend: Silver-selling ● Gold-selling ● Platinum-selling (x multiples) ✪ US No.1 ★ | Peak Position | Weeks at No.1 | Weeks on Chart

RICHIE DAN
UK, male DJ/producer (Richard Gittens) — 3

Date	Title	Peak	No.1	Weeks
12 Aug 00	**CALL IT FATE** *Pure Silk CDPSR 1*	34		3

DANA
Ireland, female vocalist (Rosemary Brown) — 75

Date	Title	Peak	No.1	Weeks
4 Apr 70	**ALL KINDS OF EVERYTHING** *Rex R 11054*	1	2	16
13 Feb 71	**WHO PUT THE LIGHTS OUT** *Rex R 11062*	14		11
25 Jan 75	**PLEASE TELL HIM I SAID HELLO** *GTO GT 6*	8		14
13 Dec 75	**IT'S GONNA BE A COLD COLD CHRISTMAS** *GTO GT 45*	4		6
6 Mar 76	**NEVER GONNA FALL IN LOVE AGAIN** *GTO GT 55*	31		4
16 Oct 76	**FAIRYTALE** *GTO GT 66*	13		16
31 Mar 79	**SOMETHING'S COOKIN' IN THE KITCHEN** *GTO GT 243*	44		5
15 May 82	**I FEEL LOVE COMIN' ON** *Creole CR 32*	66		3

DANA INTERNATIONAL
Israel, female vocalist (Yaron Cohen) — 4

Date	Title	Peak	No.1	Weeks
27 Jun 98	**DIVA** *Dance Pool DANA 1CD*	11		4

CHARLEAN DANCE
UK, female vocalist/DJ — 1

Date	Title	Peak	No.1	Weeks
22 Sep 07	**MR DJ** *Positiva CDTIVS260*	51		1

DANCE CONSPIRACY
UK, male production trio — 1

Date	Title	Peak	No.1	Weeks
3 Oct 92	**DUB WAR** *XL Recordings XLT 34*	72		1

DANCE FLOOR VIRUS
Italy, male vocal/instrumental group — 2

Date	Title	Peak	No.1	Weeks
21 Oct 95	**MESSAGE IN A BOTTLE** *Epic 6623742*	49		2

DANCE TO TIPPERARY
UK, male vocal/instrumental group — 2

Date	Title	Peak	No.1	Weeks
24 May 03	**THE BHOYS ARE BACK IN TOWN** *Nede NRCD 2105*	44		2

DANCE 2 TRANCE
Germany, male production duo — 8

Date	Title	Peak	No.1	Weeks
24 Apr 93	**P.OWER OF A.MERICAN N.ATIVES** *Logic 74321139582*	25		4
24 Jul 93	**TAKE A FREE FALL** *Logic 74321153602*	36		3
4 Feb 95	**WARRIOR** *Logic 74321257722*	56		1

DANCING DJS VS ROXETTE
UK/Sweden, male/female vocal/instrumental/production group — 5

Date	Title	Peak	No.1	Weeks
6 Aug 05	**FADING LIKE A FLOWER** *All Around The World CDGLOBE426*	18		5

EVAN DANDO
US, male vocalist/guitarist. See Lemonheads — 3

Date	Title	Peak	No.1	Weeks
24 Jun 95	**PERFECT DAY** *Virgin VSCDT 1552* KIRSTY MacCOLL & EVAN DANDO	75		1
31 May 03	**STOP MY HEAD** *Setanta SETCDB 127*	38		1
13 Dec 03	**IT LOOKS LIKE YOU** *Setanta SETCDA 130*	68		1

DANDY WARHOLS
US, male/female vocal/instrumental group – Courtney Taylor-Taylor, Eric Hedford (replaced by Brent De Boer), Peter Holmstrom & Zia McCabe — 36

Date	Title	Peak	No.1	Weeks
28 Feb 98	**EVERY DAY SHOULD BE A HOLIDAY** *Capitol CDCL 797*	29		2
2 May 98	**NOT IF YOU WERE THE LAST JUNKIE ON EARTH** *Capitol CDCL 800*	13		4
8 Aug 98	**BOYS BETTER** *Capitol CDCLS 805*	36		2
10 Jun 00	**GET OFF** *Capitol CDCLS 821*	38		2
9 Sep 00	**BOHEMIAN LIKE YOU** *Capitol CDCLS 823*	42		1
7 Jul 01	**GODLESS** *Capitol CDCL 829*	66		1
10 Nov 01	**BOHEMIAN LIKE YOU** *Capitol CDCLX 823*	5		10
16 Mar 02	**GET OFF** *Capitol CDCL 835*	34		2
17 May 03	**WE USED TO BE FRIENDS** *Capitol CDCL 843*	18		3
9 Aug 03	**YOU WERE THE LAST HIGH** *Parlophone CDCLX 845*	34		2
6 Dec 03	**PLAN A** *Parlophone CDCLS 851*	66		1
10 Sep 05	**SMOKE IT** *Parlophone CDCLS871*	59		1
12 Aug 06	**HORNY AS A DANDY** *Feverpitch/Free2air CDFEV14* MOUSSE T VS DANDY WARHOLS	17		5

DANDYS
UK, male vocal/instrumental group — 2

Date	Title	Peak	No.1	Weeks
14 Mar 98	**YOU MAKE ME WANT TO SCREAM** *Artificial ATFCD 3*	71		1
30 May 98	**ENGLISH COUNTRY GARDEN** *Artificial ATFCD 4*	57		1

D'ANGELO
US, male vocalist (Michael D'Angelo) — 11

Date	Title	Peak	No.1	Weeks
28 Oct 95	**BROWN SUGAR** *Cooltempo CDCOOL 307*	24		3
2 Mar 96	**COLD WORLD** *Geffen GFSTD 22114* GENIUS/GZA FEATURING D'ANGELO	40		2
2 Mar 96	**CRUISIN'** *Cooltempo CDCOOL 316*	31		2
15 Jun 96	**LADY** *Cooltempo CDCOOLS 323*	21		2
22 May 99	**BREAK UPS 2 MAKE UPS** *Def Jam 8709272* METHOD MAN FEATURING D'ANGELO	33		2

DANGER DANGER
US, male vocal/instrumental group — 5

Date	Title	Peak	No.1	Weeks
8 Feb 92	**MONKEY BUSINESS** *Epic 6577517*	42		2
28 Mar 92	**I STILL THINK ABOUT YOU** *Epic 6578387*	46		2
13 Jun 92	**COMIN' HOME** *Epic 6581337*	75		1

CHARLIE DANIELS BAND
US, male vocal/instrumental group — 10

Date	Title	Peak	No.1	Weeks
22 Sep 79	**THE DEVIL WENT DOWN TO GEORGIA** *Epic EPC 7737*	14		10

JOHNNY DANKWORTH
UK, male band leader/saxophonist, d. 6 Feb 2010 (age 82) — 33

Date	Title	Peak	No.1	Weeks
22 Jun 56	**EXPERIMENTS WITH MICE** *Parlophone R 4185*	7		12
23 Feb 61	**AFRICAN WALTZ** *Columbia DB 4590*	9		21

DANNY & THE JUNIORS
US, male vocal group – Danny Rapp, d. 5 Apr 1983, Frank Maffei, Joe Terranova & David White — 19

Date	Title	Peak	No.1	Weeks
17 Jan 58	**AT THE HOP** *HMV POP 436* ★	3		14
10 Jul 76	**AT THE HOP** *ABC 4123*	39		5

DANNY WILSON
UK, male vocal/instrumental trio – Gary Clark*, Kit Clark & Ged Grimes — 28

Date	Title	Peak	No.1	Weeks
22 Aug 87	**MARY'S PRAYER** *Virgin VS 934*	42		7
2 Apr 88	**MARY'S PRAYER** *Virgin VS 934*	3		11
17 Jun 89	**THE SECOND SUMMER OF LOVE** *Virgin VS 1186*	23		9
16 Sep 89	**NEVER GONNA BE THE SAME** *Virgin VS 1203*	69		1

DANSE SOCIETY
UK, male vocal/instrumental group — 5

Date	Title	Peak	No.1	Weeks
27 Aug 83	**WAKE UP** *Society SOC 5*	61		3
5 Nov 83	**HEAVEN IS WAITING** *Society SOC 6*	60		2

STEVEN DANTE
UK, male vocalist (Steven Dennis) — 16

Date	Title	Peak	No.1	Weeks
26 Sep 87	**THE REAL THING** *Chrysalis CHS 3167* JELLYBEAN FEATURING STEVEN DANTE	13		10
9 Jul 88	**I'M TOO SCARED** *Cooltempo DANTE 1*	34		6

TONJA DANTZLER
US, female vocalist — 1

Date	Title	Peak	No.1	Weeks
17 Dec 94	**IN AND OUT OF MY LIFE** *ffrr FCD 246*	66		1

DANZEL
Belgium, male vocalist (Johan Waem) — 8

Date	Title	Peak	No.1	Weeks
6 Nov 04	**PUMP IT UP** *Data 75CDS*	11		8

DANZIG

US, male vocal/instrumental group — 1

Date	Title	Peak	Wks at No.1	Wks on Chart
14 May 94	**MOTHER** *American Recordings MOMDD 1*	62		1

DAPHNE

US, female vocalist — 1

Date	Title	Peak	Wks at No.1	Wks on Chart
9 Dec 95	**CHANGE** *Stress CDSTR 54*	71		1

DAPHNE & CELESTE

US, female vocal duo – Karen DeConcetto & Celeste Cruz — 28

Date	Title	Peak	Wks at No.1	Wks on Chart
5 Feb 00	**OOH STICK YOU!** *Universal MCSTD 40209*	8		12
17 Jun 00	**UGLY** *Universal MCSTD 40232*	18		12
2 Sep 00	**SCHOOL'S OUT** *Universal MCSTD 40238*	12		4

TERENCE TRENT D'ARBY

US, male vocalist (Sananda Maitreya, b. Terence Trent Howard) — 77

Date	Title	Peak	Wks at No.1	Wks on Chart
14 Mar 87	**IF YOU LET ME STAY** *CBS TRENT 1*	7		13
20 Jun 87	**WISHING WELL** *CBS TRENT 2* ★	4		11
10 Oct 87	**DANCE LITTLE SISTER (PART ONE)** *CBS TRENT 3*	20		7
9 Jan 88	**SIGN YOUR NAME** *CBS TRENT 4*	2		10
20 Jan 90	**TO KNOW SOMEONE DEEPLY IS TO KNOW SOMEONE SOFTLY** *CBS TRENT 6*	55		3
17 Apr 93	**DO YOU LOVE ME LIKE YOU SAY** *Columbia 6590732*	14		6
19 Jun 93	**DELICATE** *Columbia 6593312* FEATURING DES'REE	14		6
28 Aug 93	**SHE KISSED ME** *Columbia 6595922*	16		7
20 Nov 93	**LET HER DOWN EASY** *Columbia 6598642*	18		7
8 Apr 95	**HOLDING ON TO YOU** *Columbia 6614235*	20		6
5 Aug 95	**VIBRATOR** *Columbia 6622585*	57		1

RICHARD DARBYSHIRE

UK, male vocalist. See Living In A Box — 7

Date	Title	Peak	Wks at No.1	Wks on Chart
20 Aug 88	**COMING BACK FOR MORE** *Chrysalis JEL 4* JELLYBEAN FEATURING RICHARD DARBYSHIRE	41		3
24 Jul 93	**THIS I SWEAR** *Dome CDDOME 1003*	50		3
12 Feb 94	**WHEN ONLY LOVE WILL DO** *Dome CDDOME 1008*	54		1

DARE

UK, male vocal/instrumental group — 8

Date	Title	Peak	Wks at No.1	Wks on Chart
29 Apr 89	**THE RAINDANCE** *A&M AM 483*	62		2
29 Jul 89	**ABANDON** *A&M AM 519*	71		2
10 Aug 91	**WE DON'T NEED A REASON** *A&M AM 775*	52		2
5 Oct 91	**REAL LOVE** *A&M AM 824*	67		1
13 Sep 03	**CHIHUAHUA** *All Around The World CDGLOBE 311*	45		1

MATT DAREY

UK, male producer/instrumentalist. See Lost Tribe, MDM, M3, Melt featuring Little Ms Marcie, Space Baby, Sunburst — 17

Date	Title	Peak	Wks at No.1	Wks on Chart
9 Oct 99	**LIBERATION (TEMPTATION – FLY LIKE AN EAGLE)** *Incentive CENT 1CDS* PRESENTS MASH UP	19		3
22 Apr 00	**FROM RUSSIA WITH LOVE** *Liquid Asset ASSETCD 003* PRESENTS DSP	40		2
15 Jul 00	**BEAUTIFUL** *Incentive CENT 7CDS* MATT DAREY'S MASH UP PRESENTS MARCELLA WOODS	21		4
20 Apr 02	**BEAUTIFUL** *Incentive CENT 38CDS* FEATURING MARCELLA WOODS	10		6
14 Dec 02	**U SHINE ON** *Incentive CENT 50CDS* & MARCELLA WOODS	34		2

BOBBY DARIN

US, male vocalist/multi-instrumentalist (Walden Robert Cassotto), d. 20 Dec 1973 (age 37) — 162

Date	Title	Peak	Wks at No.1	Wks on Chart
1 Aug 58	**SPLISH SPLASH** *London HLE 8666*	18		7
9 Jan 59	**QUEEN OF THE HOP** *London HLE 8737*	24		2
29 May 59	**DREAM LOVER** *London HLE 8867*	1	4	19
25 Sep 59	**MACK THE KNIFE** *London HLK 8939* ★	1	2	18
29 Jan 60	**LA MER (BEYOND THE SEA)** *London HLK 9034*	8		13
31 Mar 60	**CLEMENTINE** *London HLK 9086*	8		12
30 Jun 60	**BILL BAILEY** *London HLK 9142*	34		2
16 Mar 61	**LAZY RIVER** *London HLK 9303*	2		13
6 Jul 61	**NATURE BOY** *London HLK 9375*	24		7
12 Oct 61	**YOU MUST HAVE BEEN A BEAUTIFUL BABY** *London HLK 9429*	10		11
26 Oct 61	**THEME FROM 'COME SEPTEMBER'** *London HLK 9407* ORCHESTRA	50		1
21 Dec 61	**MULTIPLICATION** *London HLK 9474*	5		13
19 Jul 62	**THINGS** *London HLK 9575*	2		17
4 Oct 62	**IF A MAN ANSWERS** *Capitol CL 15272*	24		6
29 Nov 62	**BABY FACE** *London HLK 9624*	40		4
25 Jul 63	**EIGHTEEN YELLOW ROSES** *Capitol CL 15306*	37		4
13 Oct 66	**IF I WERE A CARPENTER** *Atlantic 584 051*	9		12
14 Apr 79	**DREAM LOVER/MACK THE KNIFE** *Lightning LIG 9017*	64		1

DARIO G

UK, male DJ/production trio – Scott Rosser, Paul Spencer & Stephen Spencer (unrelated) — 44

Date	Title	Peak	Wks at No.1	Wks on Chart
27 Sep 97	**SUNCHYME** *Eternal 130CD*	2		18
20 Jun 98	**CARNAVAL DE PARIS** *Eternal 162CD*	5		9
12 Sep 98	**SUNMACHINE** *Eternal 173CD*	17		4
25 Mar 00	**VOICES** *Eternal 256CD1*	37		2
3 Feb 01	**DREAM TO ME** *Manifesto FESCD 79*	9		6
8 Jun 02	**CARNAVAL 2002** *Eternal WEA 349CD*	34		3
25 Jan 03	**HEAVEN IS CLOSER (FEELS LIKE HEAVEN)** *Serious SER 61CD*	39		2

DARIUS

UK, male vocalist (Darius Campbell, formerly Danesh) — 52

Date	Title	Peak	Wks at No.1	Wks on Chart
10 Aug 02	**COLOURBLIND** *Mercury 639662*	1	2	16
7 Dec 02	**RUSHES** *Mercury 0638052*	5		12
15 Mar 03	**INCREDIBLE (WHAT I MEANT TO SAY)** *Mercury 0779782*	9		8
21 Jun 03	**GIRL IN THE MOON** *Mercury 9808234*	21		3
30 Oct 04	**KINDA LOVE** *Mercury 9868350*	8		7
22 Jan 05	**LIVE TWICE** *Mercury 9869470*	7		6

DARK GLOBE FEATURING AMANDA GHOST

UK, male/female vocal/production trio — 1

Date	Title	Peak	Wks at No.1	Wks on Chart
1 May 04	**BREAK MY WORLD** *Island CID 853*	52		1

DARK MONKS

UK, male production duo — 1

Date	Title	Peak	Wks at No.1	Wks on Chart
14 Sep 02	**INSANE** *Incentive CENT 45CDS*	62		1

DARK STAR

UK, male vocal/instrumental group — 6

Date	Title	Peak	Wks at No.1	Wks on Chart
26 Jun 99	**ABOUT 3AM** *Harvest CDEM 545*	50		1
15 Jan 00	**GRACEADELICA** *Harvest CDEMS 556*	25		3
13 May 00	**I AM THE SUN** *Harvest CDEMS 566*	31		2

DARKMAN

UK, male rapper (Brian Mitchell) — 7

Date	Title	Peak	Wks at No.1	Wks on Chart
14 May 94	**YABBA DABBA DOO** *Wild Card CARDD 6*	49		2
20 Aug 94	**WHO'S THE DARKMAN** *Wild Card CARDD 8*	46		2
3 Dec 94	**YABBA DABBA DOO** *Wild Card CARDD 11*	37		2
21 Oct 95	**BRAND NEW DAY** *Wild Card 5771892*	74		1

DARKNESS

UK, male vocal/instrumental group – Justin Hawkins, Ed Graham, Dan Hawkins & Frankie Poullain (replaced by Richie Edwards) — 46

Date	Title	Peak	Wks at No.1	Wks on Chart
8 Mar 03	**GET YOUR HANDS OFF MY WOMAN** *Must Destroy DUSTY 006CD*	43		2
28 Jun 03	**GROWING ON ME** *Must Destroy DUSTY 010CD*	11		5
4 Oct 03	**I BELIEVE IN A THING CALLED LOVE** *Must Destroy DARK 01CD*	2		11
27 Dec 03	**CHRISTMAS TIME (DON'T LET THE BELLS END)** *Must Destroy DARK 02CD*	2		7
3 Apr 04	**LOVE IS ONLY A FEELING** *Must Destroy DARK 03CD*	5		8
1 Jan 05	**CHRISTMAS TIME (DON'T LET THE BELLS END)** *Must Destroy DARK 01CD*	58		1
26 Nov 05	**ONE WAY TICKET** *Atlantic DARK04CD*	8		7
4 Mar 06	**IS IT JUST ME?** *Atlantic DARK05CD*	8		3
3 Jun 06	**GIRLFRIEND** *Atlantic DARK06CD*	39		2

DARLING BUDS

UK, male/female vocal/instrumental group — 20

Date	Title	Peak	Wks at No.1	Wks on Chart
8 Oct 88	**BURST** *Epic BLOND 1*	50		5
7 Jan 89	**HIT THE GROUND** *CBS BLOND 2*	27		5
25 Mar 89	**LET'S GO ROUND THERE** *CBS BLOND 3*	49		4
22 Jul 89	**YOU'VE GOT TO CHOOSE** *CBS BLOND 4*	45		3
2 Jun 90	**TINY MACHINE** *CBS BLOND 5*	60		2
12 Sep 92	**SURE THING** *Epic 6582157*	71		1

GUY DARRELL
UK, male vocalist — 13

Date	Title / Label / Cat. No.	Peak	Wks at No.1	Wks on Chart
18 Aug 73	**I'VE BEEN HURT** *Santa Ponsa PNS 4*	12		13

JAMES DARREN
US, male vocalist (James Ercolani) — 25

Date	Title / Label / Cat. No.	Peak	Wks at No.1	Wks on Chart
11 Aug 60	**BECAUSE THEY'RE YOUNG** *Pye International 7N 25059*	29		7
14 Dec 61	**GOODBYE CRUEL WORLD** *Pye International 7N 25116*	28		9
29 Mar 62	**HER ROYAL MAJESTY** *Pye International 7N 25125*	36		3
21 Jun 62	**CONSCIENCE** *Pye International 7N 25138*	30		6

DARTS
UK, male/female vocal group – Ian Collier, George Currie, John Dummer, Bob Fish, Den Hegarty, Hammy Howell, d. 13 Jan 1999, Rita Ray, Thump Thomson & Nigel Trubridge — 117

Date	Title / Label / Cat. No.	Peak	Wks at No.1	Wks on Chart
5 Nov 77	**DADDY COOL/THE GIRL CAN'T HELP IT** *Magnet MAG 100* ○	6		13
28 Jan 78	**COME BACK MY LOVE** *Magnet MAG 110* ●	2		12
6 May 78	**BOY FROM NEW YORK CITY** *Magnet MAG 116* ○	2		13
5 Aug 78	**IT'S RAINING** *Magnet MAG 126* ●	2		11
11 Nov 78	**DON'T LET IT FADE AWAY** *Magnet MAG 134*	18		11
10 Feb 79	**GET IT** *Magnet MAG 140*	10		9
21 Jul 79	**DUKE OF EARL** *Magnet MAG 147* ○	6		11
20 Oct 79	**CAN'T GET ENOUGH OF YOUR LOVE** *Magnet MAG 156*	43		6
1 Dec 79	**REET PETITE** *Magnet MAG 160*	51		7
31 May 80	**LET'S HANG ON** *Magnet MAG 174*	11		14
6 Sep 80	**PEACHES** *Magnet MAG 179*	66		3
29 Nov 80	**WHITE CHRISTMAS/SH-BOOM (LIFE COULD BE A DREAM)** *Magnet MAG 184*	48		7

DARUDE
Finland, male producer (Ville Virtanen) — 29

Date	Title / Label / Cat. No.	Peak	Wks at No.1	Wks on Chart
24 Jun 00	**SANDSTORM** *Neo NEOCD 033* ○	3		15
25 Nov 00	**FEEL THE BEAT** *Neo NEOCD 045*	5		10
15 Sep 01	**OUT OF CONTROL (BACK FOR MORE)** *Neo NEOCD 067*	13		4

DAS EFX
US, male rap duo — 5

Date	Title / Label / Cat. No.	Peak	Wks at No.1	Wks on Chart
7 Aug 93	**CHECK YO SELF** *Fourth & Broadway BRCD 283* ICE CUBE FEATURING DAS EFX	36		4
25 Apr 98	**RAP SCHOLAR** *East West E 3853CD* FEATURING REDMAN	42		1

DASHBOARD CONFESSIONAL
US, male vocalist (Chris Carrabba) — 3

Date	Title / Label / Cat. No.	Peak	Wks at No.1	Wks on Chart
22 Nov 03	**HANDS DOWN** *Interscope 9813790*	60		1
27 Mar 04	**RAPID HOPE LOSS** *Vagrant 9861991*	75		1
2 Sep 06	**DON'T WAIT** *Vagrant VRUK037CDS*	68		1

DATSUNS
New Zealand, male vocal/instrumental group — 7

Date	Title / Label / Cat. No.	Peak	Wks at No.1	Wks on Chart
5 Oct 02	**IN LOVE** *V2 VVR 5020953*	25		2
22 Feb 03	**HARMONIC GENERATOR** *V2 VVR 5021228*	33		2
6 Sep 03	**MF FROM HELL** *V2 VVR 5021753*	55		1
12 Jun 04	**BLACKEN MY THUMB** *V2 VVR 5026953*	48		1
23 Oct 04	**GIRLS BEST FRIEND** *V2 VVR 5028893*	71		1

DAUGHTRY
US, male vocal/instrumental group — 7

Date	Title / Label / Cat. No.	Peak	Wks at No.1	Wks on Chart
5 Sep 09	**WHAT ABOUT NOW** *19/Epic GBCTA0600237*	11		7

N'DEA DAVENPORT
US, female vocalist. See Brand New Heavies — 50

Date	Title / Label / Cat. No.	Peak	Wks at No.1	Wks on Chart
5 Oct 91	**NEVER STOP** *ffrr F 165* BRAND NEW HEAVIES FEATURING N'DEA DAVENPORT	43		3
15 Feb 92	**DREAM COME TRUE** *ffrr F 180* BRAND NEW HEAVIES FEATURING N'DEA DAVENPORT	24		4
18 Apr 92	**ULTIMATE TRUNK FUNK EP** *ffrr F 185* BRAND NEW HEAVIES FEATURING N'DEA DAVENPORT	19		6
1 Aug 92	**DON'T LET IT GO TO YOUR HEAD** *ffrr BNH 1* BRAND NEW HEAVIES FEATURING N'DEA DAVENPORT	24		4
19 Dec 92	**STAY THIS WAY** *ffrr BNH 2* BRAND NEW HEAVIES FEATURING N'DEA DAVENPORT	40		5
11 Sep 93	**TRUST ME** *Cooltempo CDCOOL 278* GURU FEATURING N'DEA DAVENPORT	34		2
26 Mar 94	**DREAM ON DREAMER** *ffrr BNHCD 3* BRAND NEW HEAVIES FEATURING N'DEA DAVENPORT	15		4
11 Jun 94	**BACK TO LOVE** *ffrr BNHCD 4* BRAND NEW HEAVIES FEATURING N'DEA DAVENPORT	23		4
13 Aug 94	**MIDNIGHT AT THE OASIS** *ffrr BNHCDP 5* BRAND NEW HEAVIES FEATURING N'DEA DAVENPORT	13		6
5 Nov 94	**SPEND SOME TIME** *ffrr BNHCD 6* BRAND NEW HEAVIES FEATURING N'DEA DAVENPORT	26		4
11 Mar 95	**CLOSE TO YOU** *ffrr BNCDP 7* BRAND NEW HEAVIES FEATURING N'DEA DAVENPORT	38		3
20 Jun 98	**BRING IT ON** *Gee Street VVR 5002033*	52		1
15 Dec 01	**YOU CAN'T CHANGE ME** *Defected DFECT 41CDS* ROGER SANCHEZ FEATURING ARMAND VAN HELDEN & N'DEA DAVENPORT	25		4

ANNE-MARIE DAVID
Luxembourg, female vocalist — 9

Date	Title / Label / Cat. No.	Peak	Wks at No.1	Wks on Chart
28 Apr 73	**WONDERFUL DREAM** *Epic EPC 1446*	13		9

CRAIG DAVID
UK, male vocalist — 175

Date	Title / Label / Cat. No.	Peak	Wks at No.1	Wks on Chart
11 Dec 99	**RE-REWIND THE CROWD SAY BO SELECTA** *Public Demand/Relentless RELENT 1CDS* ARTFUL DODGER FEATURING CRAIG DAVID ⊛	2		17
15 Apr 00	**FILL ME IN** *Wildstar CDWILD 28* ●	1	1	14
15 Jul 00	**WOMAN TROUBLE** *Public Demand/ffrr FCDP 380* ARTFUL DODGER FEATURING ROBBIE CRAIG & CRAIG DAVID	6		10
5 Aug 00	**7 DAYS** *Wildstar CDWILD 30*	1	1	15
2 Dec 00	**WALKING AWAY** *Wildstar CDWILD 35* ○	3		13
31 Mar 01	**RENDEZVOUS** *Wildstar CDWILD 36*	8		10
9 Nov 02	**WHAT'S YOUR FLAVA?** *Wildstar CDWILD 43*	8		10
1 Feb 03	**HIDDEN AGENDA** *Wildstar CDWILD 44*	10		6
10 May 03	**RISE & FALL** *Wildstar CDWILD 45* & STING	2		10
9 Aug 03	**SPANISH** *Wildstar CXWILD 49*	8		6
25 Oct 03	**WORLD FILLED WITH LOVE** *Wildstar CDWILD 51*	15		4
10 Jan 04	**YOU DON'T MISS YOUR WATER** *Wildstar CDWILD 52*	43		2
20 Aug 05	**ALL THE WAY** *Warner Brothers WEA393CD1*	3		6
12 Nov 05	**DON'T LOVE YOU NO MORE** *Warner Brothers WEA396CD2*	4		15
18 Mar 06	**UNBELIEVABLE** *Warner Brothers WEA402CD1*	18		5
1 Sep 07	**THIS IS THE GIRL** *679 679L148CD* KANO FEATURING CRAIG DAVID	18		11
10 Nov 07	**HOT STUFF (LET'S DANCE)** *Warner Brothers WEA434CD2*	7		12
9 Feb 08	**6 OF 1 THING** *Warner Brothers WEA440CD*	39		6
22 Nov 08	**WHERE'S YOUR LOVE** *Warner Brothers GBAHT0800447* FEATURING TINCHY STRYDER	58		1
29 Nov 08	**INSOMNIA** *Warner Brothers GBAHT0800557*	43		2

F.R. DAVID
France (b. Tunisia), male vocalist (Elli Robert Fitoussi) — 13

Date	Title / Label / Cat. No.	Peak	Wks at No.1	Wks on Chart
2 Apr 83	**WORDS** *Carrere CAR 248*	2		12
18 Jun 83	**MUSIC** *Carrere CAR 282*	71		1

DAVID & JONATHAN
UK, male vocal duo – Roger Cook & Roger Greenaway. See Blue Mink, Pipkins — 22

Date	Title / Label / Cat. No.	Peak	Wks at No.1	Wks on Chart
13 Jan 66	**MICHELLE** *Columbia DB 7800*	11		6
7 Jul 66	**LOVERS OF THE WORLD UNITE** *Columbia DB 7950*	7		16

JIM DAVIDSON
UK, male vocalist/comedian — 4

Date	Title / Label / Cat. No.	Peak	Wks at No.1	Wks on Chart
27 Dec 80	**WHITE CHRISTMAS/TOO RISKY** *Scratch SCR 001*	52		4

PAUL DAVIDSON
Jamaica, male vocalist — 10

Date	Title / Label / Cat. No.	Peak	Wks at No.1	Wks on Chart
27 Dec 75	**MIDNIGHT RIDER** *Tropical ALO 56*	10		10

DAVE DAVIES
UK, male vocalist/guitarist. See Kinks — 17

Date	Title / Label / Cat. No.	Peak	Wks at No.1	Wks on Chart
19 Jul 67	**DEATH OF A CLOWN** *Pye 7N 17356*	3		10
6 Dec 67	**SUSANNAH'S STILL ALIVE** *Pye 7N 17429*	20		7

WINDSOR DAVIES & DON ESTELLE
UK, male actors/vocal duo

Date	Title	Peak Position	Weeks at No.1	Weeks on Chart
				16
17 May 75	**WHISPERING GRASS** *EMI 2290* ●	1	3	12
25 Oct 75	**PAPER DOLL** *EMI 2361*	41		4

BILLIE DAVIS
UK, female vocalist (Carol Hedges)

Date	Title	Peak Position	Weeks at No.1	Weeks on Chart
				33
30 Aug 62	**WILL I WHAT** *Parlophone R 4932* MIKE SARNE WITH BILLIE DAVIS	18		10
7 Feb 63	**TELL HIM** *Decca F 11572*	10		12
30 May 63	**HE'S THE ONE** *Decca F 11658*	40		3
9 Oct 68	**I WANT YOU TO BE MY BABY** *Decca F 12823*	33		8

DARLENE DAVIS
US, female vocalist

Date	Title	Peak Position	Weeks at No.1	Weeks on Chart
				5
7 Feb 87	**I FOUND LOVE** *Serious 7OUS 1*	55		5

JOHN DAVIS & THE MONSTER ORCHESTRA
US, male vocal/instrumental group

Date	Title	Peak Position	Weeks at No.1	Weeks on Chart
				2
10 Feb 79	**AIN'T THAT ENOUGH FOR YOU** *Miracle M 2*	70		2

MAC DAVIS
US, male vocalist

Date	Title	Peak Position	Weeks at No.1	Weeks on Chart
				22
4 Nov 72	**BABY DON'T GET HOOKED ON ME** *CBS 8250* ★	29		6
15 Nov 80	**IT'S HARD TO BE HUMBLE** *Casablanca CAN 210*	27		16

ROY DAVIS, JR
US, male producer

Date	Title	Peak Position	Weeks at No.1	Weeks on Chart
				5
1 Nov 97	**GABRIEL** *XL Recordings XLS 88CD* FEATURING PEVEN EVERETT	22		4
31 Jan 04	**ABOUT LOVE** *Classic CMC21*	70		1

SAMMY DAVIS, JR
US, male vocalist, d. 16 May 1990 (age 64)

Date	Title	Peak Position	Weeks at No.1	Weeks on Chart
				37
29 Jul 55	**SOMETHING'S GOTTA GIVE** *Brunswick 05428*	11		7
9 Sep 55	**LOVE ME OR LEAVE ME** *Brunswick 05428*	8		8
30 Sep 55	**THAT OLD BLACK MAGIC** *Brunswick 05450*	16		1
7 Oct 55	**HEY THERE** *Brunswick 05469*	19		1
20 Apr 56	**IN A PERSIAN MARKET** *Brunswick 05518*	28		1
28 Dec 56	**ALL OF YOU** *Brunswick 05629*	28		1
16 Jun 60	**HAPPY TO MAKE YOUR ACQUAINTANCE** *Brunswick 05830* & CARMEN McRAE	46		1
22 Mar 62	**WHAT KIND OF FOOL AM I?/GONNA BUILD A MOUNTAIN** *Reprise R 20048*	26		8
13 Dec 62	**ME AND MY SHADOW** *Reprise R 20128* FRANK SINATRA & SAMMY DAVIS, Jr	20		9

SKEETER DAVIS
US, female vocalist (Mary Penick), d. 19 Sep 2004 (age 72)

Date	Title	Peak Position	Weeks at No.1	Weeks on Chart
				13
14 Mar 63	**END OF THE WORLD** *RCA 1328*	18		13

SPENCER DAVIS GROUP
UK, male vocal/instrumental group – Spencer Davis, Muff Winwood, Steve Winwood* & Peter York

Date	Title	Peak Position	Weeks at No.1	Weeks on Chart
				73
5 Nov 64	**I CAN'T STAND IT** *Fontana TF 499*	47		3
25 Feb 65	**EVERY LITTLE BIT HURTS** *Fontana TF 530*	41		3
10 Jun 65	**STRONG LOVE** *Fontana TF 571*	44		4
2 Dec 65	**KEEP ON RUNNING** *Fontana TF 632*	1	1	14
24 Mar 66	**SOMEBODY HELP ME** *Fontana TF 679*	1	2	10
1 Sep 66	**WHEN I COME HOME** *Fontana TF 739*	12		9
3 Nov 66	**GIMME SOME LOVING** *Fontana TF 762*	2		12
26 Jan 67	**I'M A MAN** *Fontana TF 785*	9		7
9 Aug 67	**TIME SELLER** *Fontana TF 854*	30		5
10 Jan 68	**MR SECOND CLASS** *United Artists UP 1203*	35		4
5 Apr 08	**I'M A MAN** *Island GBAAN6700008*	54		2

TJ DAVIS
UK, female vocalist

Date	Title	Peak Position	Weeks at No.1	Weeks on Chart
				4
27 Jul 96	**BRILLIANT FEELING** *Arista 74321380902* FULL MONTY ALLSTARS FEATURING TJ DAVIS	72		1
29 Dec 01	**WONDERFUL LIFE** *Melting Pot MPRCD 20*	42		3

DAWN
US, male/female vocal trio – Tony Orlando*, Telma Hopkins & Joyce Vincent

Date	Title	Peak Position	Weeks at No.1	Weeks on Chart
				109
16 Jan 71	**CANDIDA** *Bell 1118*	9		11
10 Apr 71	**KNOCK THREE TIMES** *Bell 1146* ★	1	5	27
31 Jul 71	**WHAT ARE YOU DOING SUNDAY** *Bell 1169* FEATURING TONY ORLANDO	3		12
10 Mar 73	**TIE A YELLOW RIBBON ROUND THE OLD OAK TREE** *Bell 1287* FEATURING TONY ORLANDO ★	1	4	40
4 Aug 73	**SAY, HAS ANYBODY SEEN MY SWEET GYPSY ROSE** *Bell 1322* FEATURING TONY ORLANDO	12		15
9 Mar 74	**WHO'S IN THE STRAWBERRY PATCH WITH SALLY** *Bell 1343* TONY ORLAND & DAWN	37		4

DAWN OF THE REPLICANTS
UK, male vocal/instrumental group

Date	Title	Peak Position	Weeks at No.1	Weeks on Chart
				2
7 Feb 98	**CANDLEFIRE** *East West EW 147CD1*	52		1
4 Apr 98	**HOGWASH FARM (THE DIESEL HANDS EP)** *East West EW 157CD*	65		1

DANA DAWSON
US, female vocalist

Date	Title	Peak Position	Weeks at No.1	Weeks on Chart
				14
15 Jul 95	**3 IS FAMILY** *EMI CDEM 378*	9		8
28 Oct 95	**GOT TO GIVE ME LOVE** *EMI CDEM 392*	27		2
4 May 96	**SHOW ME** *EMI CDEMS 423*	28		3
20 Jul 96	**HOW I WANNA BE LOVED** *EMI CDEMS 432*	42		1

BOBBY DAY
US, male vocalist (Robert Byrd), d. 15 Jul 1990 (age 60)

Date	Title	Peak Position	Weeks at No.1	Weeks on Chart
				2
7 Nov 58	**ROCKIN' ROBIN** *London HL 8726*	29		2

DARREN DAY
UK, male vocalist

Date	Title	Peak Position	Weeks at No.1	Weeks on Chart
				7
8 Oct 94	**YOUNG GIRL** *Bell 74321231082*	42		2
8 Jun 96	**SUMMER HOLIDAY MEDLEY** *RCA 74321384472*	17		4
9 May 98	**HOW CAN I BE SURE?** *Eastcoast DDCD 001*	71		1

DORIS DAY
US, female vocalist/actor (Doris Kappelhoff)

Date	Title	Peak Position	Weeks at No.1	Weeks on Chart
				146
14 Nov 52	**SUGARBUSH** *Columbia DB 3123* & FRANKIE LAINE	8		8
21 Nov 52	**MY LOVE AND DEVOTION** *Columbia DB 3157*	10		2
3 Apr 53	**MA SAYS PA SAYS** *Columbia DB 3242* & JOHNNIE RAY	12		1
17 Apr 53	**FULL TIME JOB** *Columbia DB 3242* & JOHNNIE RAY	11		1
24 Jul 53	**LET'S WALK THATA-WAY** *Philips PB 157* & JOHNNIE RAY	4		14
2 Apr 54	**SECRET LOVE** *Philips PB 230* ★	1	9	29
27 Aug 54	**BLACK HILLS OF DAKOTA** *Philips PB 287*	7		8
1 Oct 54	**IF I GIVE MY HEART TO YOU** *Philips PB 325* WITH THE MELLOMAN	4		11
8 Apr 55	**READY WILLING AND ABLE** *Philips PB 402*	7		9
9 Sep 55	**LOVE ME OR LEAVE ME** *Philips PB 479*	20		1
21 Oct 55	**I'LL NEVER STOP LOVING YOU** *Philips PB 497*	17		3
29 Jun 56	**WHATEVER WILL BE WILL BE** *Philips PB 586*	1	6	22
13 Jun 58	**A VERY PRECIOUS LOVE** *Philips PB 799*	16		11
15 Aug 58	**EVERYBODY LOVES A LOVER** *Philips PB 843*	25		4
12 Mar 64	**MOVE OVER DARLING** *CBS AAG 183*	8		16
18 Apr 87	**MOVE OVER DARLING** *CBS LEGS 1*	45		6

INAYA DAY
US, female vocalist (Inaya Davis). See Boris Dlugosch

Date	Title	Peak Position	Weeks at No.1	Weeks on Chart
				11
22 May 99	**JUST CAN'T GET ENOUGH** *AM:PM CDAMPM 121* HARRY 'CHOO CHOO' ROMERO PRESENTS INAYA DAY	39		2
7 Oct 00	**FEEL IT** *Positiva CDTIV 141*	51		1
23 Jul 05	**NASTY GIRL** *All Around The World CDGLOBE449*	9		8

PATTI DAY
US, female vocalist

Date	Title	Peak Position	Weeks at No.1	Weeks on Chart
				1
9 Dec 89	**RIGHT BEFORE MY EYES** *Debut DEBT 3080*	69		1

DAY ONE
UK, male vocal/instrumental duo

Date	Title	Peak Position	Weeks at No.1	Weeks on Chart
				1
13 Nov 99	**I'M DOIN' FINE** *Melankolic/Virgin SADD6*	68		1

Silver-selling ● Gold-selling ● Platinum-selling (x multiples) ✪ US No.1 ★ Peak Position Weeks at No.1 Weeks on Chart

DAYEENE
Sweden, female vocal duo — Weeks on Chart: 1

Date	Title / Label	Peak Position	Weeks at No.1	Weeks on Chart
17 Jul 99	**AND IT HURTS** *Pukka CDPUKKA 20*	63		1

TAYLOR DAYNE
US, female vocalist (Leslie Wundermann) — Weeks on Chart: 54

Date	Title / Label	Peak Position	Weeks at No.1	Weeks on Chart
23 Jan 88	**TELL IT TO MY HEART** *Arista 109616*	3		13
19 Mar 88	**PROVE YOUR LOVE** *Arista 109830*	8		10
11 Jun 88	**I'LL ALWAYS LOVE YOU** *Arista 111536*	41		7
18 Nov 89	**WITH EVERY BEAT OF MY HEART** *Arista 112760*	53		2
14 Apr 90	**I'LL BE YOUR SHELTER** *Arista 112996*	43		5
4 Aug 90	**LOVE WILL LEAD YOU BACK** *Arista 113277* ★	69		1
3 Jul 93	**CAN'T GET ENOUGH OF YOUR LOVE** *Arista 74321147852*	14		8
16 Apr 94	**I'LL WAIT** *Arista 74321203472*	29		3
4 Feb 95	**ORIGINAL SIN (THEME FROM 'THE SHADOW')** *Arista 74321223462*	63		1
18 Nov 95	**SAY A PRAYER** *Arista 74321324292*	58		1
13 Jan 96	**TELL IT TO MY HEART (REMIX)** *Arista 74321335962*	23		3

DAYTON
US, male/female vocal/instrumental group — Weeks on Chart: 1

Date	Title / Label	Peak Position	Weeks at No.1	Weeks on Chart
10 Dec 83	**THE SOUND OF MUSIC** *Capitol CL 318*	75		1

DAZZ BAND
US, male vocal/instrumental group — Weeks on Chart: 12

Date	Title / Label	Peak Position	Weeks at No.1	Weeks on Chart
3 Nov 84	**LET IT ALL BLOW** *Motown TMG 1361*	12		12

DB BOULEVARD
Italy, male/female vocal/production group – Alfred Azzetto, Monica 'Moony' Bragato, Diego Broggio & Rossano 'Roxy' Palu. See Moony — Weeks on Chart: 12

Date	Title / Label	Peak Position	Weeks at No.1	Weeks on Chart
23 Feb 02	**POINT OF VIEW** *Illustrious CDILL 002*	3		12

DBM
Germany, male/female vocal/instrumental group — Weeks on Chart: 3

Date	Title / Label	Peak Position	Weeks at No.1	Weeks on Chart
12 Nov 77	**DISCO BEATLEMANIA** *Atlantic K 11027*	45		3

D, B, M & T
UK, male vocal/instrumental group. See Dave Dee, Dozy, Beaky, Mick & Tich — Weeks on Chart: 8

Date	Title / Label	Peak Position	Weeks at No.1	Weeks on Chart
1 Aug 70	**MR PRESIDENT** *Fontana 6007 022*	33		8

D'BORA
US, female vocalist (Deborah Walker) — Weeks on Chart: 4

Date	Title / Label	Peak Position	Weeks at No.1	Weeks on Chart
14 Sep 91	**DREAM ABOUT YOU** *Polydor PO 161*	75		1
1 Jul 95	**GOING ROUND** *Vibe MCSTD 2055*	40		2
30 Mar 96	**GOOD LOVE REAL LOVE** *Music Plant MCSTD 40023*	58		1

NINO DE ANGELO
Germany, male vocalist — Weeks on Chart: 5

Date	Title / Label	Peak Position	Weeks at No.1	Weeks on Chart
21 Jul 84	**GUARDIAN ANGEL** *Carrere CAR 335*	57		5

DE BOS
Holland, male DJ/producer (Andre Van Den Bosch). See Freakyman — Weeks on Chart: 1

Date	Title / Label	Peak Position	Weeks at No.1	Weeks on Chart
25 Oct 97	**ON THE RUN** *Jive JIVECD 433*	51		1

CHRIS DE BURGH
Ireland (b. Argentina), male vocalist/guitarist (Christopher Davidson) — Weeks on Chart: 71

Date	Title / Label	Peak Position	Weeks at No.1	Weeks on Chart
23 Oct 82	**DON'T PAY THE FERRYMAN** *A&M AMS 8256*	48		5
12 May 84	**HIGH ON EMOTION** *A&M AM 190*	44		5
12 Jul 86	**THE LADY IN RED** *A&M AM 331* ●	1	3	15
20 Sep 86	**FATAL HESITATION** *A&M AM 346*	44		4
13 Dec 86	**A SPACEMAN CAME TRAVELLING/THE BALLROOM OF ROMANCE** *A&M AM 365*	40		5
12 Dec 87	**THE SIMPLE TRUTH (A CHILD IS BORN)** *A&M AM 427*	55		3
29 Oct 88	**MISSING YOU** *A&M AM 474*	3		12
7 Jan 89	**TENDER HANDS** *A&M AM 486*	43		6
14 Oct 89	**THIS WAITING HEART** *A&M AM 528*	59		3
25 May 91	**THE SIMPLE TRUTH (A CHILD IS BORN)** *A&M RELF 1*	36		2
11 Apr 92	**SEPARATE TABLES** *A&M AM 863*	30		4
21 May 94	**BLONDE HAIR BLUE JEANS** *A&M 5805932*	51		1
9 Dec 95	**THE SNOWS OF NEW YORK** *A&M 5813132*	60		1
27 Sep 97	**SO BEAUTIFUL** *A&M 5823932*	29		4
18 Sep 99	**WHEN I THINK OF YOU** *A&M 4971302*	59		1

DE CASTRO SISTERS
Cuba, female vocal group — Weeks on Chart: 1

Date	Title / Label	Peak Position	Weeks at No.1	Weeks on Chart
11 Feb 55	**TEACH ME TONIGHT** *London HL 8104*	20		1

DE-CODE FEATURING BEVERLI SKEETE
UK, male/female vocal/instrumental group — Weeks on Chart: 1

Date	Title / Label	Peak Position	Weeks at No.1	Weeks on Chart
18 May 96	**WONDERWALL/SOME MIGHT SAY** *Neoteric NRCD 2*	69		1

ETIENNE DE CRECY
France, male DJ/producer — Weeks on Chart: 3

Date	Title / Label	Peak Position	Weeks at No.1	Weeks on Chart
28 Mar 98	**PRIX CHOC REMIXES** *Different DIF 007CD*	60		1
20 Jan 01	**AM I WRONG** *XL Recordings XLS 127CD*	44		2

DE FUNK FEATURING F45
Italy/UK, male vocal/production group — Weeks on Chart: 1

Date	Title / Label	Peak Position	Weeks at No.1	Weeks on Chart
25 Sep 99	**PLEASURE LOVE** *INCredible INCS 3CD*	49		1

LENNIE DE ICE
UK, male producer — Weeks on Chart: 1

Date	Title / Label	Peak Position	Weeks at No.1	Weeks on Chart
17 Apr 99	**WE ARE I. E.** *Distinctive DISNCD 50*	61		1

DE LA SOUL
US, male rap trio – Kelvin Mercer, Vincent Mason & David Jude Jolicoeur — Weeks on Chart: 63

Date	Title / Label	Peak Position	Weeks at No.1	Weeks on Chart
8 Apr 89	**ME MYSELF AND I** *Big Life BLR 7*	22		8
8 Jul 89	**SAY NO GO** *Big Life BLR 10*	18		7
21 Oct 89	**EYE KNOW** *Big Life BLR 13*	14		7
23 Dec 89	**THE MAGIC NUMBER/BUDDY** *Big Life BLR 14*	7		8
24 Mar 90	**MAMA GAVE BIRTH TO THE SOUL CHILDREN** *Gee Street GEE 26* QUEEN LATIFAH + DE LA SOUL	14		7
27 Apr 91	**RING RING RING (HA HA HEY)** *Big Life BLR 42*	10		7
3 Aug 91	**A ROLLER SKATING JAM NAMED 'SATURDAYS'** *Big Life BLR 55*	22		5
23 Nov 91	**KEEPIN' THE FAITH** *Big Life BLR 64*	50		2
18 Sep 93	**BREAKADAWN** *Big Life BLRD 103*	39		3
2 Apr 94	**FALLIN'** *Epic 6602622* TEENAGE FANCLUB & DE LA SOUL	59		1
29 Jun 96	**STAKES IS HIGH** *Tommy Boy TBCD 7730*	55		1
8 Mar 97	**4 MORE** *Tommy Boy TBCD 7779A* FEATURING ZHANE	52		1
22 Jul 00	**OOOH** *Tommy Boy TBCD 2102B* FEATURING REDMAN	29		2
11 Nov 00	**ALL GOOD** *Tommy Boy TBCD 2154B* FEATURING CHAKA KHAN	33		3
2 Mar 02	**BABY PHAT** *Tommy Boy TBCD 2359B*	55		1

DONNA DE LORY
US, female vocalist — Weeks on Chart: 1

Date	Title / Label	Peak Position	Weeks at No.1	Weeks on Chart
24 Jul 93	**JUST A DREAM** *MCA MCSTD 1750*	71		1

WALDO DE LOS RIOS
Argentina, male orchestra leader (Osvaldo Guiterrez), d. 28 Mar 1977 (age 42) — Weeks on Chart: 16

Date	Title / Label	Peak Position	Weeks at No.1	Weeks on Chart
10 Apr 71	**MOZART SYMPHONY NO. 40 IN G MINOR K550 1ST MOVEMENT (ALLEGRO MOLTO)** *A&M AMS 836*	5		16

VINCENT DE MOOR
Holland, male producer. See Veracocha — Weeks on Chart: 4

Date	Title / Label	Peak Position	Weeks at No.1	Weeks on Chart
16 Aug 97	**FLOWTATION** *XL Recordings XLS 89CD*	54		1
7 Apr 01	**FLY AWAY** *VC Recordings VCRD 87*	30		3

DE NADA
UK, male/female vocal/production group — Weeks on Chart: 7

Date	Title / Label	Peak Position	Weeks at No.1	Weeks on Chart
25 Aug 01	**LOVE YOU ANYWAY** *Wildstar CDWILD 37*	15		4
9 Feb 02	**BRING IT ON TO MY LOVE** *Wildstar CDWILD 39*	24		3

DE NUIT

Italy, male production duo — 2

Date	Title	Peak Position	Weeks at No.1	Weeks on Chart
23 Nov 02	**ALL THAT MATTERED (LOVE YOU DOWN)** *Credence CDCRED 029*	38		2

LYNSEY DE PAUL

UK, female vocalist/pianist (Lynsey Rubin) — 54

Date	Title	Peak Position	Weeks at No.1	Weeks on Chart
19 Aug 72	**SUGAR ME** *MAM 81*	5		11
2 Dec 72	**GETTING A DRAG** *MAM 88*	18		8
27 Oct 73	**WON'T SOMEBODY DANCE WITH ME** *MAM 109*	14		7
8 Jun 74	**OOH I DO** *Warner Brothers K 16401*	25		6
2 Nov 74	**NO HONESTLY** *Jet 747*	7		11
22 Mar 75	**MY MAN AND ME** *Jet 750*	40		4
26 Mar 77	**ROCK BOTTOM** *Polydor 2058 859* & MIKE MORAN	19		7

TULLIO DE PISCOPO

Italy, male vocalist/drummer — 4

Date	Title	Peak Position	Weeks at No.1	Weeks on Chart
28 Feb 87	**STOP BAJON...PRIMAVERA** *Greyhound GREY 9*	58		4

REBECCA DE RUVO

Sweden, female vocalist — 1

Date	Title	Peak Position	Weeks at No.1	Weeks on Chart
1 Oct 94	**I CAUGHT YOU OUT** *Arista 74321230782*	72		1

TERI DE SARIO

US, female vocalist — 5

Date	Title	Peak Position	Weeks at No.1	Weeks on Chart
2 Sep 78	**AIN'T NOTHING GONNA KEEP ME FROM YOU** *Casablanca CAN 128*	52		5

DE SOUZA FEATURING SHENA

UK, male/female vocal/production group — 2

Date	Title	Peak Position	Weeks at No.1	Weeks on Chart
14 Apr 07	**GUILTY** *Hed Kandi HK32CDS*	46		2

STEPHANIE DE SYKES

UK, female vocalist (Stephanie Ryton) — 17

Date	Title	Peak Position	Weeks at No.1	Weeks on Chart
20 Jul 74	**BORN WITH A SMILE ON MY FACE** *Bradley's BRAD 7409* WITH RAIN ●	2		10
19 Apr 75	**WE'LL FIND OUR DAY** *Bradley's BRAD 7509*	17		7

WILLIAM DE VAUGHN

US, male vocalist — 10

Date	Title	Peak Position	Weeks at No.1	Weeks on Chart
6 Jul 74	**BE THANKFUL FOR WHAT YOU'VE GOT** *Chelsea 2005 002*	31		5
20 Sep 80	**BE THANKFUL FOR WHAT YOU'VE GOT** *EMI 5101*	44		5

TONY DE VIT

UK, male DJ/producer, d. 2 Jul 1998 (age 40) — 13

Date	Title	Peak Position	Weeks at No.1	Weeks on Chart
4 Mar 95	**BURNING UP** *Icon ICONCD 001*	25		3
12 Aug 95	**HOOKED** *Labello Dance LAD 18CD* 99TH FLOOR ELEVATORS FEATURING TONY DE VIT	28		2
9 Sep 95	**TO THE LIMIT** *X:Plode BANG 1CD*	44		2
30 Mar 96	**I'LL BE THERE** *Labello Dance LAD 25CD2* 99TH FLOOR ELEVATORS FEATURING TONY DE VIT	37		2
28 Oct 00	**DAWN** *Tidy Trax TIDY 140CD*	56		2
21 Dec 02	**I DON'T CARE** *Tidy Trax TIDY 181T*	65		1
12 Jul 03	**GIVE ME A REASON** *Tidy Two 123C* FEATURING NIKI MAK	53		1

DEACON BLUE

UK, male/female vocal/instrumental group – Ricky Ross*, Graeme Kelling, d. 10 Jun 2004, Lorraine McIntosh, James Prime, Ewen Vernal & Dougie Vipond — 112

Date	Title	Peak Position	Weeks at No.1	Weeks on Chart
23 Jan 88	**DIGNITY** *CBS DEAC 4*	31		8
9 Apr 88	**WHEN WILL YOU MAKE MY TELEPHONE RING** *CBS DEAC 5*	34		7
16 Jul 88	**CHOCOLATE GIRL** *CBS DEAC 6*	43		7
15 Oct 88	**REAL GONE KID** *CBS DEAC 7*	8		13
4 Mar 89	**WAGES DAY** *CBS DEAC 8*	18		6
20 May 89	**FERGUS SINGS THE BLUES** *CBS DEAC 9*	14		6
16 Sep 89	**LOVE AND REGRET** *CBS DEAC 10*	28		5
6 Jan 90	**QUEEN OF THE NEW YEAR** *CBS DEAC 11*	21		5
25 Aug 90	**FOUR BACHARACH AND DAVID SONGS EP** *CBS DEAC 12*	2		9
25 May 91	**YOUR SWAYING ARMS** *Columbia 6568937*	23		4
27 Jul 91	**TWIST AND SHOUT** *Columbia 6573027*	10		9
12 Oct 91	**CLOSING TIME** *Columbia 6575027*	42		3
14 Dec 91	**COVER FROM THE SKY** *Columbia 6576737*	31		4
28 Nov 92	**YOUR TOWN** *Columbia 6587867*	14		8
13 Feb 93	**WILL WE BE LOVERS** *Columbia 6589732*	31		4
24 Apr 93	**ONLY TENDER LOVE** *Columbia 6591842*	22		4
17 Jul 93	**HANG YOUR HEAD** *Columbia 6594602*	21		3
2 Apr 94	**I WAS RIGHT AND YOU WERE WRONG** *Columbia 6602222*	32		3
28 May 94	**DIGNITY** *Columbia 6604485*	20		3
28 Apr 01	**EVERYTIME YOU SLEEP** *Papillon BTFLY 0011*	64		1

DEAD DRED

UK, male production duo — 2

Date	Title	Peak Position	Weeks at No.1	Weeks on Chart
5 Nov 94	**DRED BASS** *Moving Shadow SHADOW 50CD*	60		2

DEAD END KIDS

UK, male vocal group – Robbie Gray, Colin Ivory, Davey Johnston, Alistair Kerr & Ricky Squires — 10

Date	Title	Peak Position	Weeks at No.1	Weeks on Chart
26 Mar 77	**HAVE I THE RIGHT** *CBS 4972*	6		10

DEAD KENNEDYS

US, male vocal/instrumental group — 9

Date	Title	Peak Position	Weeks at No.1	Weeks on Chart
1 Nov 80	**KILL THE POOR** *Cherry Red CHERRY 16*	49		3
30 May 81	**TOO DRUNK TO FUCK** *Cherry Red CHERRY 24*	36		6

DEAD OR ALIVE

UK, male vocal/instrumental group – Pete Burns, Steve Coy, Timothy Lever & Mike Percy — 81

Date	Title	Peak Position	Weeks at No.1	Weeks on Chart
24 Mar 84	**THAT'S THE WAY (I LIKE IT)** *Epic A 4271*	22		9
1 Dec 84	**YOU SPIN ME ROUND (LIKE A RECORD)** *Epic A 4861* ●	1	2	23
20 Apr 85	**LOVER COME BACK TO ME** *Epic A 6086*	11		8
29 Jun 85	**IN TOO DEEP** *Epic A 6360*	14		8
21 Sep 85	**MY HEART GOES BANG (GET ME TO THE DOCTOR)** *Epic A 6571*	23		6
20 Sep 86	**BRAND NEW LOVER** *Epic 6500757*	31		4
10 Jan 87	**SOMETHING IN MY HOUSE** *Epic BURNS 1*	12		7
4 Apr 87	**HOOKED ON LOVE** *Epic BURNS 2*	69		2
3 Sep 88	**TURN AROUND AND COUNT 2 TEN** *Epic BURNS 4*	70		1
22 Jul 89	**COME HOME WITH ME BABY** *Epic BURNS 5*	62		2
17 May 03	**YOU SPIN ME ROUND** *Epic 6735785*	23		3
11 Feb 06	**YOU SPIN ME ROUND (LIKE A RECORD)** *Epic 82876806212*	5		8

DEAD PREZ

US, male rap duo — 2

Date	Title	Peak Position	Weeks at No.1	Weeks on Chart
11 Mar 00	**HIP HOP** *Epic 6689862*	41		2

DEAD 60S

UK, male vocal/instrumental group — 11

Date	Title	Peak Position	Weeks at No.1	Weeks on Chart
16 Oct 04	**RIOT RADIO** *Deltasonic DLTCD025*	30		2
9 Apr 05	**THE LAST RESORT** *Deltasonic DLTCD2032*	24		2
25 Jun 05	**LOADED GUN** *Deltasonic DLTCD2037*	28		2
24 Sep 05	**RIOT RADIO** *Deltasonic DLTCD2041*	30		2
3 Dec 05	**GHOSTFACED KILLER** *Deltasonic DLTCD042*	25		2
22 Sep 07	**STAND UP** *Deltasonic DLTCD067*	54		1

DEADLY SINS

Italy/UK, male vocal/production group — 2

Date	Title	Peak Position	Weeks at No.1	Weeks on Chart
30 Apr 94	**WE ARE GOING ON DOWN** *ffrreedom TABCD 220*	45		2

DEADMAU5

Canada, male DJ/producer (Joel Zimmerman) — 22

Date	Title	Peak Position	Weeks at No.1	Weeks on Chart
25 Apr 09	**I REMEMBER** *Virgin MAU5017X* & KASKADE	14		15
19 Sep 09	**GHOSTS 'N' STUFF** *Mau5trap/Virgin MAU5020T* FEATURING ROB SWIRE	12		7

HAZELL DEAN

UK, female vocalist (Hazel Dean Poole) — 71

Date	Title	Peak Position	Weeks at No.1	Weeks on Chart
18 Feb 84	**EVERGREEN/JEALOUS LOVE** *Proto ENA 114*	63		3
21 Apr 84	**SEARCHIN' (I GOTTA FIND A MAN)** *Proto ENA 109*	6		15
28 Jul 84	**WHATEVER I DO (WHEREVER I GO)** *Proto ENA 119*	4		11
3 Nov 84	**BACK IN MY ARMS (ONCE AGAIN)** *Proto ENA 122*	41		4
2 Mar 85	**NO FOOL (FOR LOVE)** *Proto ENA 123*	41		5
12 Oct 85	**THEY SAY IT'S GONNA RAIN** *Parlophone R 6107*	58		4
2 Apr 88	**WHO'S LEAVING WHO** *EMI EM 45*	4		11
25 Jun 88	**MAYBE (WE SHOULD CALL IT A DAY)** *EMI EM 62*	15		6

Date	Title	Peak Position	Weeks at No.1	Weeks on Chart
24 Sep 88	**TURN IT INTO LOVE** *EMI EM 71*	21		7
26 Aug 89	**LOVE PAINS** *Lisson DOLE 12*	48		4
23 Mar 91	**BETTER OFF WITHOUT YOU** *Lisson DOLE 19*	72		1

JIMMY DEAN

US, male vocalist, d. 13 Jun 2010 (age 81) — 17

Date	Title	Peak Position	Weeks at No.1	Weeks on Chart
26 Oct 61	**BIG BAD JOHN** *Philips PB 1187* ★	2		13
8 Nov 62	**LITTLE BLACK BOOK** *CBS AAG 122*	33		4

LETITIA DEAN & PAUL MEDFORD

UK, female/male vocal/acting duo — 7

Date	Title	Peak Position	Weeks at No.1	Weeks on Chart
25 Oct 86	**SOMETHING OUTA NOTHING** *BBC RESL 203*	12		7

DEAR JON

UK, female/male vocal/instrumental group — 1

Date	Title	Peak Position	Weeks at No.1	Weeks on Chart
22 Apr 95	**ONE GIFT OF LOVE** *MDMC DEVCS 2*	68		1

DEARS

Canada, male/female vocal/instrumental group — 2

Date	Title	Peak Position	Weeks at No.1	Weeks on Chart
20 Nov 04	**LOST IN THE PLOT** *Bella Union BELLACD86*	49		1
14 May 05	**22 – THE DEATH OF ALL THE ROMANCE** *Bella Union BELLACD100*	53		1

DEATH CAB FOR CUTIE

US, male vocal/instrumental group — 2

Date	Title	Peak Position	Weeks at No.1	Weeks on Chart
22 Apr 06	**CROOKED TEETH** *Atlantic AT0232CD*	69		1
29 Jul 06	**I WILL FOLLOW YOU INTO THE DARK** *Atlantic AT0246CD*	66		1

DEATH FROM ABOVE 1979

Canada, male vocal/instrumental duo — 4

Date	Title	Peak Position	Weeks at No.1	Weeks on Chart
13 Nov 04	**ROMANTIC RIGHTS** *679 679L090CD*	57		1
26 Feb 05	**BLOOD ON OUR HANDS** *679 679L078CD*	33		2
25 Jun 05	**BLACK HISTORY MONTH** *679 679L106CD*	48		1

DEATH IN VEGAS

UK, male instrumental/production duo – Richard Fearless & Tim Holmes — 17

Date	Title	Peak Position	Weeks at No.1	Weeks on Chart
2 Aug 97	**DIRT** *Concrete HARD 27CD*	61		1
1 Nov 97	**ROCCO** *Concrete HARD 29CD*	51		1
12 Feb 00	**AISHA** *Concrete HARD 43CD*	9		4
6 May 00	**DIRGE** *Concrete HARD 44CD*	24		2
21 Sep 02	**HANDS AROUND MY THROAT** *Concrete HARD 48CD*	36		1
28 Dec 02	**SCORPIO RISING** *Concrete HARD 54CD* FEATURING LIAM GALLAGHER	14		8

DeBARGE

US, male/female vocal group – El DeBarge*, Etterlene 'Bunny', James, Mark & Randy DeBarge — 17

Date	Title	Peak Position	Weeks at No.1	Weeks on Chart
6 Apr 85	**RHYTHM OF THE NIGHT** *Gordy TMG 1376*	4		14
21 Sep 85	**YOU WEAR IT WELL** *Gordy ZB 40345* EL DeBARGE WITH DeBARGE	54		3

CHICO DeBARGE

US, male vocalist. See DeBarge — 1

Date	Title	Peak Position	Weeks at No.1	Weeks on Chart
14 Mar 98	**IGGIN' ME** *Universal UND 56170*	50		1

EL DeBARGE

US, male vocalist (Eldra DeBarge). See DeBarge — 6

Date	Title	Peak Position	Weeks at No.1	Weeks on Chart
21 Sep 85	**YOU WEAR IT WELL** *Gordy ZB 40345* WITH DeBARGE	54		3
28 Jun 86	**WHO'S JOHNNY ('SHORT CIRCUIT' THEME)** *Gordy ELD 1*	60		2
31 Mar 90	**SECRET GARDEN** *Qwest W 9992* QUINCY JONES FEATURING AL B SURE!, JAMES INGRAM, EL DeBARGE & BARRY WHITE	67		1

DIANA DECKER

US, female actor/vocalist — 10

Date	Title	Peak Position	Weeks at No.1	Weeks on Chart
23 Oct 53	**POPPA PICCOLINO** *Columbia DB 3325*	2		10

DECLAN FEATURING THE YOUNG VOICES CHOIR

UK, male vocalist & male/female choir — 4

Date	Title	Peak Position	Weeks at No.1	Weeks on Chart
21 Dec 02	**TELL ME WHY** *Liberty CDDECS 004*	29		4

DECOY AND ROY

Belgium, male production duo. See Convert, Cubic 22 — 1

Date	Title	Peak Position	Weeks at No.1	Weeks on Chart
1 Feb 03	**INNER LIFE** *Data/Ministry Of Sound/Heat DATA 43CDS*	45		1

DAVE DEE

UK, male vocalist (Dave Harman), d. 9 Jan 2009 (age 67). See Dave Dee, Dozy, Beaky, Mick & Tich — 4

Date	Title	Peak Position	Weeks at No.1	Weeks on Chart
14 Mar 70	**MY WOMAN'S MAN** *Fontana TF 1074*	42		4

DAVE DEE, DOZY, BEAKY, MICK & TICH

UK, male vocal/instrumental group – Dave Dee*, d. 9 Jan 2009, Ian Amey, Trevor Davies, John Dymond & Michael Wilson — 141

Date	Title	Peak Position	Weeks at No.1	Weeks on Chart
23 Dec 65	**YOU MAKE IT MOVE** *Fontana TF 630*	26		8
3 Mar 66	**HOLD TIGHT** *Fontana TF 671*	4		17
9 Jun 66	**HIDEAWAY** *Fontana TF 711*	10		11
15 Sep 66	**BEND IT** *Fontana TF 746*	2		12
8 Dec 66	**SAVE ME** *Fontana TF 775*	3		10
9 Mar 67	**TOUCH ME TOUCH ME** *Fontana TF 798*	13		9
18 May 67	**OKAY!** *Fontana TF 830*	4		11
11 Oct 67	**ZABADAK!** *Fontana TF 873*	3		14
14 Feb 68	**THE LEGEND OF XANADU** *Fontana TF 903*	1	1	12
3 Jul 68	**LAST NIGHT IN SOHO** *Fontana TF 953*	8		11
2 Oct 68	**WRECK OF THE ANTOINETTE** *Fontana TF 971*	14		9
5 Mar 69	**DON JUAN** *Fontana TF 1000*	23		9
14 May 69	**SNAKE IN THE GRASS** *Fontana TF 1020*	23		8

DEE DEE

Belgium, male/female vocal/production group. See Ian Van Dahl — 9

Date	Title	Peak Position	Weeks at No.1	Weeks on Chart
20 Jul 02	**FOREVER** *Incentive CENT 43CDS*	12		7
1 Mar 03	**THE ONE** *Incentive CENT 52CDX*	28		2

JAZZY DEE

US, male rapper (Darren Williams) — 5

Date	Title	Peak Position	Weeks at No.1	Weeks on Chart
5 Mar 83	**GET ON UP** *Laurie LRS 101*	53		5

JOEY DEE & THE STARLITERS

US, male vocal/instrumental group — 8

Date	Title	Peak Position	Weeks at No.1	Weeks on Chart
8 Feb 62	**PEPPERMINT TWIST** *Columbia DB 4758* ★	33		8

KIKI DEE

UK, female vocalist (Pauline Matthews) — 79

Date	Title	Peak Position	Weeks at No.1	Weeks on Chart
10 Nov 73	**AMOUREUSE** *Rocket PIG 4*	13		13
7 Sep 74	**I GOT THE MUSIC IN ME** *Rocket PIG 12* BAND	19		8
12 Apr 75	**(YOU DON'T KNOW) HOW GLAD I AM** *Rocket PIG 16* BAND	33		4
3 Jul 76	**DON'T GO BREAKING MY HEART** *Rocket ROKN 512* ELTON JOHN & KIKI DEE ● ★	1	6	14
11 Sep 76	**LOVING AND FREE/AMOUREUSE** *Rocket ROKN 515*	13		8
19 Feb 77	**FIRST THING IN THE MORNING** *Rocket ROKN 520*	32		5
11 Jun 77	**CHICAGO** *Rocket ROKN 526*	28		4
21 Feb 81	**STAR** *Ariola ARO 251*	13		10
23 May 81	**PERFECT TIMING** *Ariola ARO 257*	66		3
20 Nov 93	**TRUE LOVE** *Rocket EJSCX 32* ELTON JOHN & KIKI DEE ●	2		10

DEEE-LITE

US/Russia/Japan, female/male vocal/DJ/production trio – Lady Miss Kier (Kierin Kirby), Super DJ Dmitri (Dmitri Brill) & Towa Tei (Dong-hwa Chung) — 30

Date	Title	Peak Position	Weeks at No.1	Weeks on Chart
18 Aug 90	**GROOVE IS IN THE HEART/WHAT IS LOVE** *Elektra EKR 114*	2		13
24 Nov 90	**DEEE-LITE THEME/POWER OF LOVE** *Elektra EKR 117*	25		7
23 Feb 91	**HOW DO YOU SAY...LOVE/GROOVE IS IN THE HEART (REMIX)** *Elektra EKR 118*	52		2
27 Apr 91	**GOOD BEAT** *Elektra EKR 122*	53		3
13 Jun 92	**RUNAWAY** *Elektra EKR 148*	45		3
30 Jul 94	**PICNIC IN THE SUMMERTIME** *Elektra EKR 186CD1*	43		2

DEEJAY PUNK-ROC
US, male DJ/producer (Charles Gettis)

Weeks on Chart: 5

Date	Title	Peak Position	Weeks at No.1	Weeks on Chart
21 Mar 98	DEAD HUSBAND *Independiente ISOM 9MS*	71		1
9 May 98	MY BEATBOX *Independiente ISOM 12MS*	43		1
8 Aug 98	FAR OUT *Independiente ISOM 17MS*	43		2
20 Feb 99	ROC-IN-IT *Independiente ISOM 21MS* VS ONYX	59		1

CAROL DEENE
UK, female vocalist (Carole Carver)

Weeks on Chart: 25

Date	Title	Peak Position	Weeks at No.1	Weeks on Chart
26 Oct 61	SAD MOVIES (MAKE ME CRY) *HMV POP 922*	44		3
25 Jan 62	NORMAN *HMV POP 973*	24		8
5 Jul 62	JOHNNY GET ANGRY *HMV POP 1027*	32		4
23 Aug 62	SOME PEOPLE *HMV POP 1058*	25		10

DEEP BLUE
UK, male producer (Sean O'Keeffe)

Weeks on Chart: 2

Date	Title	Peak Position	Weeks at No.1	Weeks on Chart
16 Apr 94	HELICOPTER TUNE *Moving Shadow SHADOW 41CD*	68		2

DEEP BLUE SOMETHING
US, male vocal/instrumental group – Todd Pipes, John Kirtland, Toby Pipes & Kirk Tatum

Weeks on Chart: 17

Date	Title	Peak Position	Weeks at No.1	Weeks on Chart
6 Jul 96	BREAKFAST AT TIFFANY'S *Interscope IND 80032*	55		2
21 Sep 96	BREAKFAST AT TIFFANY'S *Interscope IND 80032*	1	1	12
7 Dec 96	JOSEY *Interscope IND 95518*	27		3

DEEP C
UK, male production group

Weeks on Chart: 3

Date	Title	Peak Position	Weeks at No.1	Weeks on Chart
19 Jan 91	AFRICAN REIGN *M&G MAGS 4*	75		1
8 Jun 91	CHILL TO THE PANIC *M&G MAGS 10*	73		2

DEEP COVER
UK, male production group. See Scott & Leon, Tru Faith & Dub Conspiracy

Weeks on Chart: 1

Date	Title	Peak Position	Weeks at No.1	Weeks on Chart
11 May 02	SOUNDS OF EDEN (EVERYTIME I SEE THE) *Attitude 0158392*	63		1

DEEP CREED '94
US, male producer (Armand Van Helden)

Weeks on Chart: 1

Date	Title	Peak Position	Weeks at No.1	Weeks on Chart
7 May 94	CAN U FEEL IT *Eastern Bloc BLOCCD 005*	59		1

DEEP DISH
Iran, male/instrumental/production duo – Ali 'Dubfire' Shirazinia & Sharam Tayebi. See Sharam

Weeks on Chart: 31

Date	Title	Peak Position	Weeks at No.1	Weeks on Chart
26 Oct 96	STAY GOLD *Deconstruction 74321418222*	41		1
1 Nov 97	STRANDED *Deconstruction 74321512232*	60		1
3 Oct 98	THE FUTURE OF THE FUTURE (STAY GOLD) *Deconstruction 74321616252* WITH EVERYTHING BUT THE GIRL	31		2
9 Oct 04	FLASHDANCE *Positiva CDTIVS211*	3		16
23 Jul 05	SAY HELLO *Positiva CDTIVS220*	14		7
29 Apr 06	DREAMS *Positiva CDTIV232* FEATURING STEVIE NICKS	14		4

DEEP FEELING
UK, male vocal/instrumental group

Weeks on Chart: 5

Date	Title	Peak Position	Weeks at No.1	Weeks on Chart
25 Apr 70	DO YOU LOVE ME *Page One POF 165*	34		5

DEEP FOREST
France, male instrumental/production duo – Eric Mouquet & Michel Sanchez

Weeks on Chart: 14

Date	Title	Peak Position	Weeks at No.1	Weeks on Chart
5 Feb 94	SWEET LULLABY *Columbia 6599242*	10		6
21 May 94	DEEP FOREST *Columbia 6604115*	20		4
23 Jul 94	SAVANNA DANCE *Columbia 6606355*	28		2
24 Jun 95	MARTA'S SONG *Columbia 6621402*	26		2

DEEP PURPLE
UK, male vocal/instrumental group – Ian Gillan*, Ritchie Blackmore, Roger Glover, Jon Lord & Ian Paice; members also included David Coverdale* (1973-1976)

Weeks on Chart: 85

Date	Title	Peak Position	Weeks at No.1	Weeks on Chart
15 Aug 70	BLACK NIGHT *Harvest HAR 5020*	2		21
27 Feb 71	STRANGE KIND OF WOMAN *Harvest HAR 5033*	8		12
13 Nov 71	FIREBALL *Harvest HAR 5045*	15		13
1 Apr 72	NEVER BEFORE *Purple PUR 102*	35		6
16 Apr 77	SMOKE ON THE WATER *Purple PUR 132*	21		7
15 Oct 77	NEW LIVE AND RARE EP *Purple PUR 135*	31		4
7 Oct 78	NEW LIVE AND RARE II (EP) *Purple PUR 137*	45		3
2 Aug 80	BLACK NIGHT *Harvest PUR 5210*	43		6
1 Nov 80	NEW LIVE AND RARE VOLUME 3 EP *Harvest SHEP 101*	48		3
26 Jan 85	PERFECT STRANGERS *Polydor POSP 719*	48		3
15 Jun 85	KNOCKING AT YOUR BACK DOOR/PERFECT STRANGERS *Polydor POSP 749*	68		1
18 Jun 88	HUSH *Polydor PO 4*	62		2
20 Oct 90	KING OF DREAMS *RCA PB 49247*	70		1
2 Mar 91	LOVE CONQUERS ALL *RCA PB 49225*	57		2
24 Jun 95	BLACK NIGHT (REMIX) *EMI CDEM 382*	66		1

DEEP RIVER BOYS
US, male vocal group

Weeks on Chart: 1

Date	Title	Peak Position	Weeks at No.1	Weeks on Chart
7 Dec 56	THAT'S RIGHT *HMV POP 263*	29		1

DEEP SENSATION
UK, male production duo

Weeks on Chart: 1

Date	Title	Peak Position	Weeks at No.1	Weeks on Chart
4 Sep 04	SOMEHOW SOMEWHERE *In The House INTHS 07*	74		1

SCOTTI DEEP
US, male producer/instrumentalist (Scott Kinchen)

Weeks on Chart: 1

Date	Title	Peak Position	Weeks at No.1	Weeks on Chart
15 Mar 97	BROOKLYN BEATS *Xtravaganza 0090095*	67		1

DEEPEST BLUE
Israel/UK, male vocal/production duo – Joel Edwards & Matti Schwartz

Weeks on Chart: 19

Date	Title	Peak Position	Weeks at No.1	Weeks on Chart
2 Aug 03	DEEPEST BLUE *Data 55CDS*	7		8
28 Feb 04	GIVE IT AWAY *Data 65CDS*	9		8
5 Jun 04	IS IT A SIN? *Open OPEN3CDX*	24		2
4 Sep 04	SHOOTING STAR *Open OPEN05CDS*	57		1

RICK DEES & HIS CAST OF IDIOTS
US, male vocalist (Rigdon Dees) & male/female vocal/instrumental group

Weeks on Chart: 9

Date	Title	Peak Position	Weeks at No.1	Weeks on Chart
18 Sep 76	DISCO DUCK (PART ONE) *RSO 2090 204* ★	6		9

DEETAH
Chile, female vocalist (Claudia Ogalde)

Weeks on Chart: 10

Date	Title	Peak Position	Weeks at No.1	Weeks on Chart
26 Sep 98	RELAX *ffrr FCDP 345*	11		8
1 May 99	EL PARAISO RICO *ffrr FCD 356*	39		2

DEEYAH
Norway, female vocalist (Deepika Thathaal)

Weeks on Chart: 2

Date	Title	Peak Position	Weeks at No.1	Weeks on Chart
12 Feb 05	PLAN OF MY OWN *Brainwash BRNWSHCDXS1*	37		2

DEF LEPPARD
UK, male vocal/instrumental group – Joe Elliott, Rick Allen, Steve Clark, d. 8 Jan 1991 (replaced by Vivian Campbell), Phil Collen & Rick Savage

Weeks on Chart: 116

Date	Title	Peak Position	Weeks at No.1	Weeks on Chart
17 Nov 79	WASTED *Vertigo 6059 247*	61		3
23 Feb 80	HELLO AMERICA *Vertigo LEPP 1*	45		4
5 Feb 83	PHOTOGRAPH *Vertigo VER 5*	66		3
27 Aug 83	ROCK OF AGES *Vertigo VER 6*	41		4
1 Aug 87	ANIMAL *Bludgeon Riffola LEP 1*	6		9
19 Sep 87	POUR SOME SUGAR ON ME *Bludgeon Riffola LEP 2*	18		6
28 Nov 87	HYSTERIA *Bludgeon Riffola LEP 3*	26		6
9 Apr 88	ARMAGEDDON IT *Bludgeon Riffola LEP 4*	20		5
16 Jul 88	LOVE BITES *Bludgeon Riffola LEP 5* ★	11		8
11 Feb 89	ROCKET *Bludgeon Riffola LEP 6*	15		7
28 Mar 92	LET'S GET ROCKED *Bludgeon Riffola DEF 7*	2		7
27 Jun 92	MAKE LOVE LIKE A MAN *Bludgeon Riffola LEP 7*	12		5
12 Sep 92	HAVE YOU EVER NEEDED SOMEONE SO BAD *Bludgeon Riffola LEP 8*	16		5
30 Jan 93	HEAVEN IS *Bludgeon Riffola LEPCD 9*	13		5
1 May 93	TONIGHT *Bludgeon Riffola LEPCD 10*	34		3
18 Sep 93	TWO STEPS BEHIND *Bludgeon Riffola LEPCD 12*	32		4
15 Jan 94	ACTION *Bludgeon Riffola LEPCD 13*	14		5
14 Oct 95	WHEN LOVE & HATE COLLIDE *Bludgeon Riffola LEPCD 14* (Silver)	2		10
4 May 96	SLANG *Bludgeon Riffola LEPDD 15*	17		5

Date	Title	Peak Position	Weeks at No.1	Weeks on Chart
13 Jul 96	**WORK IT OUT** *Bludgeon Riffola LEPCD 16*	22		3
28 Sep 96	**ALL I WANT IS EVERYTHING** *Bludgeon Riffola LEPDD 17*	38		2
30 Nov 96	**BREATHE A SIGH** *Bludgeon Riffola LEPCD 18*	43		1
24 Jul 99	**PROMISES** *Bludgeon Riffola 5621362*	41		1
9 Oct 99	**GOODBYE** *Bludgeon Riffola 5622892*	54		1
17 Aug 02	**NOW** *Bludgeon Riffola 0639692*	23		2
26 Apr 03	**LONG LONG WAY TO GO** *Bludgeon Riffola 9800024*	40		2

DEFAULT

US, male vocal/instrumental group — 1

Date	Title	Peak Position	Weeks at No.1	Weeks on Chart
8 Feb 03	**WASTING MY TIME** *Island CID 809*	73		1

DEFINITION OF SOUND

UK, male rap duo — 25

Date	Title	Peak Position	Weeks at No.1	Weeks on Chart
9 Mar 91	**WEAR YOUR LOVE LIKE HEAVEN** *Circa YR 61*	17		9
1 Jun 91	**NOW IS TOMORROW** *Circa YR 66*	46		4
8 Feb 92	**MOIRA JANE'S CAFE** *Circa YR 80*	34		4
19 Sep 92	**WHAT ARE YOU UNDER** *Circa YR 95*	68		1
14 Nov 92	**CAN I GET OVER** *Circa YR 97*	61		2
20 May 95	**BOOM BOOM** *Fontana DOSCD 1*	59		1
2 Dec 95	**PASS THE VIBES** *Fontana DOSCD 2*	23		3
24 Feb 96	**CHILD** *Fontana DOSCD 3*	48		1

DEFTONES

US, male vocal/instrumental group — 10

Date	Title	Peak Position	Weeks at No.1	Weeks on Chart
21 Mar 98	**MY OWN SUMMER (SHOVE IT)** *Maverick W 0432CD*	29		2
11 Jul 98	**BE QUIET AND DRIVE (FAR AWAY)** *Maverick W 0445CD*	50		1
26 Aug 00	**CHANGE (IN THE HOUSE OF FLIES)** *Maverick W 531CD*	53		1
24 May 03	**MINERVA** *Maverick W 605CD*	15		3
4 Oct 03	**HEXAGRAM** *Maverick W 623CD*	68		2
28 Oct 06	**HOLE IN THE EARTH** *Maverick W741CD1*	69		1

GAVIN DEGRAW

US, male vocalist/guitarist — 3

Date	Title	Peak Position	Weeks at No.1	Weeks on Chart
2 Jul 05	**I DON'T WANT TO BE** *J Records 82876702222*	38		3

DEGREES OF MOTION

US, male/female vocal/production duo – Richie Jones & Biti Strauchn — 21

Date	Title	Peak Position	Weeks at No.1	Weeks on Chart
25 Apr 92	**DO YOU WANT IT RIGHT NOW** *ffrr F 184* FEATURING BITI	31		5
18 Jul 92	**SHINE ON** *ffrr F 192* FEATURING BITI WITH KIT WEST	43		3
7 Nov 92	**SOUL FREEDOM – FREE YOUR SOUL** *ffrr FX 201* FEATURING BITI	64		1
19 Mar 94	**SHINE ON (REMIX)** *ffrr FCD 229* FEATURING BITI	8		8
25 Jun 94	**DO YOU WANT IT RIGHT NOW** *ffrr FCD 236* FEATURING BITI	26		4

DEJA

US, male/female vocal duo — 1

Date	Title	Peak Position	Weeks at No.1	Weeks on Chart
29 Aug 87	**SERIOUS** *10 TEN 132*	75		1

DEJA VU

UK, male vocal/production duo — 1

Date	Title	Peak Position	Weeks at No.1	Weeks on Chart
5 Feb 94	**WHY WHY WHY** *Cowboy CDRODEO 941*	57		1

DEJURE

UK, male production duo. See Dream Frequency, Red — 1

Date	Title	Peak Position	Weeks at No.1	Weeks on Chart
23 Aug 03	**SANCTUARY** *Nebula NEBT 032*	62		1

DESMOND DEKKER

Jamaica, male vocalist (Desmond Dacres) — 71

Date	Title	Peak Position	Weeks at No.1	Weeks on Chart
12 Jul 67	**007 (SHANTY TOWN)** *Pyramid PYR 6004* & THE ACES	14		11
19 Mar 69	**ISRAELITES** *Pyramid PYR 6058* & THE ACES	1	1	15
25 Jun 69	**IT MEK** *Pyramid PYR 6068* & THE ACES	7		11
10 Jan 70	**PICKNEY GAL** *Pyramid PYR 6078* & THE ACES	42		3
22 Aug 70	**YOU CAN GET IT IF YOU REALLY WANT** *Trojan TR 7777*	2		15
10 May 75	**ISRAELITES** *Cactus CT 57*	10		9
30 Aug 75	**SING A LITTLE SONG** *Cactus CT 73*	16		7

DEL AMITRI

UK, male vocal/instrumental group – Justin Currie, Andy Alston, David Cummings, Iain Harvie & Brian McDermott (replaced by Ashley Soan) — 71

Date	Title	Peak Position	Weeks at No.1	Weeks on Chart
19 Aug 89	**KISS THIS THING GOODBYE** *A&M AM 515*	59		2
13 Jan 90	**NOTHING EVER HAPPENS** *A&M AM 536*	11		9
24 Mar 90	**KISS THIS THING GOODBYE** *A&M AM 551*	43		4
16 Jun 90	**MOVE AWAY JIMMY BLUE** *A&M AM 555*	36		6
3 Nov 90	**SPIT IN THE RAIN** *A&M AM 589*	21		6
9 May 92	**ALWAYS THE LAST TO KNOW** *A&M AM 870*	13		7
11 Jul 92	**BE MY DOWNFALL** *A&M AM 884*	30		4
12 Sep 92	**JUST LIKE A MAN** *A&M AM 0057*	25		4
23 Jan 93	**WHEN YOU WERE YOUNG** *A&M AMCD 0132*	20		3
18 Feb 95	**HERE AND NOW** *A&M 5809692*	21		4
29 Apr 95	**DRIVING WITH THE BRAKES ON** *A&M 5810072*	18		4
8 Jul 95	**ROLL TO ME** *A&M 5811312*	22		4
28 Oct 95	**TELL HER THIS** *A&M 5812172*	32		2
21 Jun 97	**NOT WHERE IT'S AT** *A&M 5822532*	21		3
6 Dec 97	**SOME OTHER SUCKER'S PARADE** *A&M 5824352*	46		1
13 Jun 98	**DON'T COME HOME TOO SOON** *A&M 5827052*	15		4
5 Sep 98	**CRY TO BE FOUND** *A&M MERCD 513*	40		2
13 Apr 02	**JUST BEFORE YOU LEAVE** *Mercury 4976972*	37		2

DE'LACY

US, male/female vocal/instrumental group – Rainie Lassiter, Glen Branch, De'Lacy Davis & Gary Griffin — 16

Date	Title	Peak Position	Weeks at No.1	Weeks on Chart
2 Sep 95	**HIDEAWAY** *Slip 'N' Slide 74321310472*	9		10
31 Aug 96	**THAT LOOK** *Slip 'N' Slide 74321398322*	19		4
14 Feb 98	**HIDEAWAY 1998 (REMIX)** *Slip 'N' Slide 74321561052*	21		2

DELAGE

UK, female vocal group — 2

Date	Title	Peak Position	Weeks at No.1	Weeks on Chart
15 Dec 90	**ROCK THE BOAT** *PWL/Polydor PO 113*	63		2

DELAKOTA

UK, male vocal/instrumental duo — 3

Date	Title	Peak Position	Weeks at No.1	Weeks on Chart
18 Jul 98	**THE ROCK** *Go! Beat GOBCD 10*	60		1
19 Sep 98	**C'MON CINCINNATI** *Go! Beat GOBCD 11* FEATURING ROSE SMITH	55		1
13 Feb 99	**555** *Go! Beat GOBCD 14*	42		1

DELANEY & BONNIE & FRIENDS FEATURING ERIC CLAPTON

US, male/female vocal duo – Delaney, d. 27 Dec 2008 (age 69), & Bonnie Bramlett — 9

Date	Title	Peak Position	Weeks at No.1	Weeks on Chart
20 Dec 69	**COMIN' HOME** *Atlantic 584 308*	16		9

DELAYS

UK, male vocal/instrumental group — 13

Date	Title	Peak Position	Weeks at No.1	Weeks on Chart
2 Aug 03	**HEY GIRL** *Rough Trade RTRADESCD103*	40		1
31 Jan 04	**LONG TIME COMING** *Rough Trade RTRADESCD136*	16		4
3 Apr 04	**NEARER THAN HEAVEN** *Rough Trade RTRADSCD175*	21		3
4 Dec 04	**LOST IN A MELODY/WANDERLUST** *Rough Trade RTRADSCD197*	28		2
4 Mar 06	**VALENTINE** *Rough Trade RTRADSCD265*	23		2
20 May 06	**HIDEAWAY** *Rough Trade RTRADSCDX336*	35		1

DELEGATION

UK, male vocal/instrumental group — 7

Date	Title	Peak Position	Weeks at No.1	Weeks on Chart
23 Apr 77	**WHERE IS THE LOVE (WE USED TO KNOW)** *State STAT 40*	22		6
20 Aug 77	**YOU'VE BEEN DOING ME WRONG** *State STAT 55*	49		1

DELERIUM

Canada, male production duo – Rhys Fulber & Bill Leeb — 34

Date	Title	Peak Position	Weeks at No.1	Weeks on Chart
12 Jun 99	**SILENCE** *Nettwerk 398152*	73		1
5 Feb 00	**HEAVEN'S EARTH** *Nettwerk 331032*	44		1
14 Oct 00	**SILENCE (REMIXES)** *Nettwerk 331082* FEATURING SARAH McLACHLAN ●	3		16
7 Jul 01	**INNOCENTE (FALLING IN LOVE)** *Nettwerk 331182* FEATURING LEIGH NASH	32		3
24 Nov 01	**UNDERWATER** *Nettwerk 331432* FEATURING RANI	33		2
12 Jul 03	**AFTER ALL** *Nettwerk 332012* FEATURING JAEL	46		1
28 Feb 04	**TRULY** *Nettwerk 332202*	54		2
27 Nov 04	**SILENCE 2004** *Nettwerk 332422* FEATURING SARAH McLACHLAN	38		8

Peak Position | Weeks at No.1 | Weeks on Chart

DELFONICS
US, male vocal group — Weeks on Chart: 23

Date	Title	Peak	Wks at No.1	Wks
10 Apr 71	**DIDN'T I (BLOW YOUR MIND THIS TIME)** *Bell 1099*	22		9
10 Jul 71	**LA-LA MEANS I LOVE YOU** *Bell 1165*	19		10
16 Oct 71	**READY OR NOT HERE I COME** *Bell 1175*	41		4

DELGADOS
UK, male/female vocal/instrumental group — Weeks on Chart: 4

Date	Title	Peak	Wks at No.1	Wks
23 May 98	**PULL THE WIRES FROM THE WALL** *Chemikal Underground CHEM 023CD*	69		1
3 Jun 00	**AMERICAN TRILOGY** *Chemikal Underground CHEM 039CD*	61		1
1 Mar 03	**ALL YOU NEED IS HATE** *Mantra MNT 79CD*	72		1
18 Sep 04	**EVERYBODY COME DOWN** *Chemikal Underground CHEM073CD*	67		1

DELINQUENT FEATURING K-CAT
UK, male/female vocal/production trio — Weeks on Chart: 6

Date	Title	Peak	Wks at No.1	Wks
8 Mar 08	**MY DESTINY** *M&B/AATW CDGLOBE823*	19		6

DELIRIOUS?
UK, male vocal/instrumental group – Martin Smith, Stuart 'Stu G' Garrard, Tim Jupp, Stew Smith (replaced by Paul Evans) & Jon Thatcher — Weeks on Chart: 20

Date	Title	Peak	Wks at No.1	Wks
1 Mar 97	**WHITE RIBBON DAY** *Furious? CDFURY 1*	41		2
17 May 97	**DEEPER** *Furious? CDFURY 2*	20		3
26 Jul 97	**PROMISE** *Furious? CDFURY 3*	20		2
15 Nov 97	**DEEPER (EP)** *Furious? CXFURY 4*	36		2
27 Mar 99	**SEE THE STAR** *Furious? CDFURY 5*	16		2
4 Mar 00	**IT'S OK** *Furious? CDFURY 6*	18		2
16 Jun 01	**WAITING FOR THE SUMMER** *Furious? CDFURY 7*	26		2
22 Dec 01	**I COULD SING OF YOUR LOVE FOREVER** *Furious? CDFURY 9*	40		2
22 Oct 05	**PAINT THE TOWN RED** *Furious? CDFURY10*	56		1
29 Nov 08	**LOVE WILL FIND A WAY** *Furious? CDFURY21*	55		1
10 Apr 10	**HISTORY MAKER** *Furious GBCRQ0100028*	4		1+

'DELIVERANCE' SOUNDTRACK
US, male instrumental duo – Eric Weissberg & Steve Mandell — Weeks on Chart: 7

Date	Title	Peak	Wks at No.1	Wks
31 Mar 73	**DUELLING BANJOS** *Warner Brothers K 16223*	17		7

DELLS
US, male vocal group — Weeks on Chart: 9

Date	Title	Peak	Wks at No.1	Wks
16 Jul 69	**I CAN SING A RAINBOW – LOVE IS BLUE (MEDLEY)** *Chess CRS 8099*	15		9

KAT DELUNA FEATURING BUSTA RHYMES
US, female/male vocal/rap duo — Weeks on Chart: 3

Date	Title	Peak	Wks at No.1	Wks
7 Jun 08	**RUN THE SHOW** *Epic USSM10800485*	41		3

DELUXE
UK, female/male vocal/production duo — Weeks on Chart: 1

Date	Title	Peak	Wks at No.1	Wks
18 Mar 89	**JUST A LITTLE MORE** *Unyque UNQ 5*	74		1

TIM DELUXE
UK, male DJ/producer (Tim Liken). See Cohen vs. Deluxe, Double 99, RIP Productions, Saffron Hill featuring Ben Onono — Weeks on Chart: 12

Date	Title	Peak	Wks at No.1	Wks
20 Jul 02	**IT JUST WON'T DO** *Underwater H2O 016CD* FEATURING SAM OBERNIK	14		7
4 Oct 03	**LESS TALK MORE ACTION** *Underwater H2O 028CD*	45		2
7 Feb 04	**MUNDAYA (THE BOY)** *Underwater H2O 040CD* FEATURING SHAHIN BADAR	61		1
13 Mar 04	**JUST KICK** *Intec INTEC024* COHEN VS DELUXE	70		1
2 Jun 07	**LET THE BEATS ROLL** *Skint SKINT133* FEATURING SIMON FRANKS	71		1

DEM FRANCHIZE BOYZ
US, male rap group — Weeks on Chart: 1

Date	Title	Peak	Wks at No.1	Wks
25 Mar 06	**I THINK THEY LIKE ME** *Virgin VUSDX321*	66		1

DEM 2
UK, male production duo — Weeks on Chart: 2

Date	Title	Peak	Wks at No.1	Wks
24 Oct 98	**DESTINY** *Locked On LOX 101CD*	58		2

MARCO DEMARK FEATURING CASEY BARNES
Italy/Australia, male vocal/production/DJ duo — Weeks on Chart: 3

Date	Title	Peak	Wks at No.1	Wks
8 Mar 08	**TINY DANCER** *All Around The World CDGLOBE808*	54		3

DEMON VS HEARTBREAKER
France, male production group — Weeks on Chart: 1

Date	Title	Peak	Wks at No.1	Wks
19 May 01	**YOU ARE MY HIGH** *Source SOURCDSE 1032*	70		1

CHAKA DEMUS & PLIERS
Jamaica, male vocal duo – Everton Bonner & John Taylor — Weeks on Chart: 55

Date	Title	Peak	Wks at No.1	Wks
12 Jun 93	**TEASE ME** *Mango CIDM 806* ●	3		15
18 Sep 93	**SHE DON'T LET NOBODY** *Mango CIDM 810* ○	4		10
18 Dec 93	**TWIST AND SHOUT** *Mango CIDM 814* FEATURING JACK RADICS & TAXI GANG ●	1	2	13
12 Mar 94	**MURDER SHE WROTE** *Mango CIDM 812*	27		4
18 Jun 94	**I WANNA BE YOUR MAN** *Mango CIDM 817*	19		6
27 Aug 94	**GAL WINE** *Mango CIDM 818*	20		4
1 Apr 95	**TWIST AND SHOUT** *Mango CIDM 814* FEATURING JACK RADICS & TAXI GANG	67		1
31 Aug 96	**EVERY KINDA PEOPLE** *Island Jamaica IJCD 2005*	47		1
30 Aug 97	**EVERY LITTLE THING SHE DOES IS MAGIC** *Virgin VSCDT 1654*	51		1

TERRY DENE
UK, male vocalist (Terry Williams) — Weeks on Chart: 20

Date	Title	Peak	Wks at No.1	Wks
7 Jun 57	**A WHITE SPORT COAT** *Decca F 10895*	18		7
19 Jul 57	**START MOVIN'** *Decca F 10914*	15		8
16 May 58	**STAIRWAY OF LOVE** *Decca F 11016*	16		5

CATHY DENNIS
UK, female vocalist — Weeks on Chart: 68

Date	Title	Peak	Wks at No.1	Wks
21 Oct 89	**C'MON AND GET MY LOVE** *ffrr F 117* D MOB WITH CATHY DENNIS	15		10
7 Apr 90	**THAT'S THE WAY OF THE WORLD** *ffrr F 132* D MOB WITH CATHY DENNIS	48		3
4 May 91	**TOUCH ME (ALL NIGHT LONG)** *Polydor CATH 3*	5		10
20 Jul 91	**JUST ANOTHER DREAM** *Polydor CATH 2*	13		7
5 Oct 91	**TOO MANY WALLS** *Polydor CATH 4*	17		7
7 Dec 91	**EVERYBODY MOVE** *Polydor CATH 5*	25		8
29 Aug 92	**YOU LIED TO ME** *Polydor CATH 6*	34		4
21 Nov 92	**IRRESISTIBLE** *Polydor CATH 7*	24		6
6 Feb 93	**FALLING** *Polydor CATHD 8*	32		2
12 Feb 94	**WHY** *ffrr FCD 227* D MOB WITH CATHY DENNIS	23		3
10 Aug 96	**WEST END PAD** *Polydor 5752812*	25		2
1 Mar 97	**WATERLOO SUNSET** *Polydor 5759612*	11		5
21 Jun 97	**WHEN DREAMS TURN TO DUST** *Polydor 5711852*	43		1

JACKIE DENNIS
UK, male vocalist (James Smith) — Weeks on Chart: 10

Date	Title	Peak	Wks at No.1	Wks
14 Mar 58	**LA DEE DAH** *Decca F 10992*	4		9
27 Jun 58	**PURPLE PEOPLE EATER** *Decca F 11033*	29		1

STEFAN DENNIS
Australia, male vocalist/actor — Weeks on Chart: 8

Date	Title	Peak	Wks at No.1	Wks
6 May 89	**DON'T IT MAKE YOU FEEL GOOD** *Sublime LIME 105*	16		7
7 Oct 89	**THIS LOVE AFFAIR** *Sublime LIME 113*	67		1

DENNISONS
UK, male vocal/instrumental group — Weeks on Chart: 13

Date	Title	Peak	Wks at No.1	Wks
15 Aug 63	**BE MY GIRL** *Decca F 11691*	46		6
7 May 64	**WALKIN' THE DOG** *Decca F 11880*	36		7

ESMEE DENTERS
Holland, female vocalist — Weeks on Chart: 13

Date	Title	Peak	Wks at No.1	Wks
29 Aug 09	**OUTTA HERE** *Polydor USUV70901065*	7		11
9 Jan 10	**ADMIT IT** *Interscope 2730087*	56		2

RICHARD DENTON & MARTIN COOK
UK, male instrumental duo — Weeks on Chart: 7

Date	Title	Peak	Wks at No.1	Wks
15 Apr 78	**THEME FROM 'THE HONG KONG BEAT'** *BBC RESL 52*	25		7

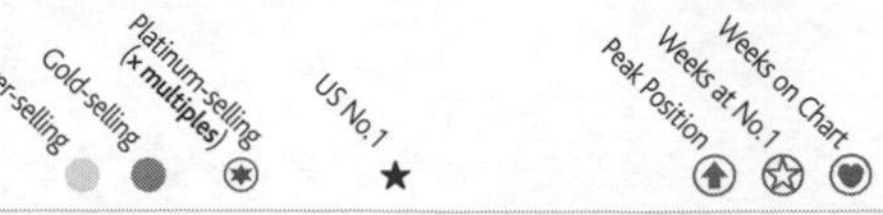

JOHN DENVER
US, male vocalist/guitarist (Henry John Deutschendorf), d. 12 Oct 1997 (age 53) — 22

Date	Title / Label	Peak Position	Weeks at No.1	Weeks on Chart
17 Aug 74	**ANNIE'S SONG** *RCA APBO 0295* ● ★	1	1	13
12 Dec 81	**PERHAPS LOVE** *CBS A 1905* PLACIDO DOMINGO WITH JOHN DENVER	46		9

KARL DENVER
UK, male vocalist (Angus McKenzie), d. 21 Dec 1998 (age 67) — 127

Date	Title / Label	Peak Position	Weeks at No.1	Weeks on Chart
22 Jun 61	**MARCHETA** *Decca F 11360*	8		20
19 Oct 61	**MEXICALI ROSE** *Decca F 11395*	8		11
25 Jan 62	**WIMOWEH** *Decca F 11420*	4		17
22 Feb 62	**NEVER GOODBYE** *Decca F 11431*	9		18
7 Jun 62	**A LITTLE LOVE A LITTLE KISS** *Decca F 11470*	19		10
20 Sep 62	**BLUE WEEKEND** *Decca F 11505*	33		5
21 Mar 63	**CAN YOU FORGIVE ME** *Decca F 11608*	32		8
13 Jun 63	**INDIAN LOVE CALL** *Decca F 11674*	32		8
22 Aug 63	**STILL** *Decca F 11720*	13		15
5 Mar 64	**MY WORLD OF BLUE** *Decca F 11828*	29		6
4 Jun 64	**LOVE ME WITH ALL YOUR HEART** *Decca F 11905*	37		6
9 Jun 90	**LAZYITIS – ONE ARMED BOXER** *Factory FAC 2227* HAPPY MONDAYS & KARL DENVER	46		3

DEODATO
Brazil, male multi-instrumentalist (Eumir Deodata) — 9

Date	Title / Label	Peak Position	Weeks at No.1	Weeks on Chart
5 May 73	**ALSO SPRACH ZARATHUSTRA (2001)** *CTI 4000*	7		9

DEPARTMENT S
UK, male vocal/instrumental group — 13

Date	Title / Label	Peak Position	Weeks at No.1	Weeks on Chart
4 Apr 81	**IS VIC THERE?** *Demon D 1003*	22		10
11 Jul 81	**GOING LEFT RIGHT** *Stiff BUY 118*	55		3

DEPARTURE
UK, male vocal/instrumental group — 5

Date	Title / Label	Peak Position	Weeks at No.1	Weeks on Chart
14 Aug 04	**ALL MAPPED OUT** *Parlophone CDR 6642*	30		2
30 Oct 04	**BE MY ENEMY** *Parlophone CDRS 6653*	41		1
16 Apr 05	**LUMP IN MY THROAT** *Parlophone CDRS6659*	30		1
18 Jun 05	**ALL MAPPED OUT** *Parlophone CDRS6665*	33		1

DEPECHE MODE
UK, male vocal/instrumental group – Dave Gahan*, Vince Clarke (replaced by Alan Wilder), Andy Fletcher & Martin Gore*. Enduring Essex outfit described by *Q* magazine as 'The most popular electronic band the world has ever known'. They have sold over 100 million records worldwide — 262

Date	Title / Label	Peak Position	Weeks at No.1	Weeks on Chart
4 Apr 81	**DREAMING OF ME** *Mute 013*	57		4
13 Jun 81	**NEW LIFE** *Mute 014*	11		15
19 Sep 81	**JUST CAN'T GET ENOUGH** *Mute 016* ●	8		10
13 Feb 82	**SEE YOU** *Mute 018* ●	6		10
8 May 82	**THE MEANING OF LOVE** *Mute 022*	12		8
28 Aug 82	**LEAVE IN SILENCE** *Mute BONG 1*	18		10
12 Feb 83	**GET THE BALANCE RIGHT** *Mute 7BONG 2*	13		8
23 Jul 83	**EVERYTHING COUNTS** *Mute 7BONG 3* ●	6		11
1 Oct 83	**LOVE IN ITSELF.2** *Mute 7BONG 4*	21		7
24 Mar 84	**PEOPLE ARE PEOPLE** *Mute 7BONG 5* ●	4		10
1 Sep 84	**MASTER AND SERVANT** *Mute 7BONG 6*	9		9
10 Nov 84	**SOMEBODY/BLASPHEMOUS RUMOURS** *Mute 7BONG 7*	16		6
11 May 85	**SHAKE THE DISEASE** *Mute BONG 8*	18		9
28 Sep 85	**IT'S CALLED A HEART** *Mute BONG 9*	18		4
22 Feb 86	**STRIPPED** *Mute BONG 10*	15		5
26 Apr 86	**A QUESTION OF LUST** *Mute BONG 11*	28		5
23 Aug 86	**A QUESTION OF TIME** *Mute BONG 12*	17		6
9 May 87	**STRANGELOVE** *Mute BONG 13*	16		5
5 Sep 87	**NEVER LET ME DOWN AGAIN** *Mute BONG 14*	22		4
9 Jan 88	**BEHIND THE WHEEL** *Mute BONG 15*	21		5
28 May 88	**LITTLE 15 (IMPORT)** *Mute LITTLE 15*	60		2
25 Feb 89	**EVERYTHING COUNTS** *Mute BONG 16*	22		7
9 Sep 89	**PERSONAL JESUS** *Mute BONG 17*	13		8
17 Feb 90	**ENJOY THE SILENCE** *Mute BONG 18*	6		9
19 May 90	**POLICY OF TRUTH** *Mute BONG 19*	16		6
29 Sep 90	**WORLD IN MY EYES** *Mute BONG 20*	17		6
27 Feb 93	**I FEEL YOU** *Mute CDBONG 21*	8		7
8 May 93	**WALKING IN MY SHOES** *Mute CDBONG 22*	14		4
25 Sep 93	**CONDEMNATION** *Mute CDBONG 23*	9		4
22 Jan 94	**IN YOUR ROOM** *Mute CDBONG 24*	8		4
15 Feb 97	**BARREL OF A GUN** *Mute CDBONG 25*	4		4
12 Apr 97	**IT'S NO GOOD** *Mute CDBONG 26*	5		5
28 Jun 97	**HOME** *Mute CDBONG 27*	23		4
1 Nov 97	**USELESS** *Mute CDBONG 28*	28		2
19 Sep 98	**ONLY WHEN I LOSE MYSELF** *Mute CDBONG 29*	17		3
5 May 01	**DREAM ON** *Mute LCDBONG 30*	6		5
11 Aug 01	**I FEEL LOVED** *Mute LCDBONG 31*	12		6
17 Nov 01	**FREELOVE** *Mute LCDBONG 32*	19		3
30 Oct 04	**ENJOY THE SILENCE 04** *Mute LCDBONG 34*	7		5
4 Dec 04	**SOMETHING TO DO** *Mute L12BONG34*	75		1
15 Oct 05	**PRECIOUS** *Mute LCDBONG35*	4		5
24 Dec 05	**A PAIN THAT I'M USED TO** *Mute LCDBONG36*	15		2
8 Apr 06	**SUFFER WELL** *Mute LCDBONG37*	12		2
17 Jun 06	**JOHN THE REVELATOR/LILIAN** *Mute LCDBONG38*	18		2
11 Nov 06	**MARTYR** *Mute CDBONG39*	13		3
18 Apr 09	**WRONG** *Mute LCDBONG40*	24		1
27 Jun 09	**PEACE** *Mute LCDBONG41*	57		1

DEPTH CHARGE
UK, male producer (Jonathan Kane) — 1

Date	Title / Label	Peak Position	Weeks at No.1	Weeks on Chart
29 Jul 95	**LEGEND OF THE GOLDEN SNAKE** *DC 01CD*	75		1

DER DRITTE RAUM
Germany, male producer (Andreas Kruger) — 1

Date	Title / Label	Peak Position	Weeks at No.1	Weeks on Chart
4 Sep 99	**HALE BOPP** *Addictive 12AD 042*	75		1

JASON DERULO
US, male vocalist/dancer (Jason Desrouleaux) — 27

Date	Title / Label	Peak Position	Weeks at No.1	Weeks on Chart
28 Nov 09	**WHATCHA SAY** *Warner Brothers USWB10901504* ★	3		18
6 Mar 10	**IN MY HEAD** *Warner Brothers USWB10904633*	1	1	6+
13 Mar 10	**RIDIN' SOLO** *Warner Brothers USWB10905329*	44		3+

YVES DERUYTER
Belgium, male DJ/producer — 3

Date	Title / Label	Peak Position	Weeks at No.1	Weeks on Chart
14 Apr 01	**BACK TO EARTH** *UK Bonzai UKBONZAICD 01*	63		1
19 Jan 02	**BACK TO EARTH (REMIX)** *UK Bonzai UKBONZA 109CD*	56		2

DESERT
UK, male production duo — 1

Date	Title / Label	Peak Position	Weeks at No.1	Weeks on Chart
20 Oct 01	**LETTIN' YA MIND GO** *Future Groove CDFGR 017*	74		1

DESERT EAGLE DISCS FEATURING KEISHA
UK, male/female vocal/production group — 1

Date	Title / Label	Peak Position	Weeks at No.1	Weeks on Chart
1 Mar 03	**BIGGER BETTER DEAL** *Echo ECSCD 129*	67		1

DESERT SESSIONS
US/UK, male/female vocal/instrumental group — 2

Date	Title / Label	Peak Position	Weeks at No.1	Weeks on Chart
15 Nov 03	**CRAWL HOME** *Island CID 835*	41		2

DESIDERIO
UK/Holland, male/female vocal/production trio — 1

Date	Title / Label	Peak Position	Weeks at No.1	Weeks on Chart
3 Jun 00	**STARLIGHT** *Code Blue BLU 010CD*	57		1

DESIRELESS
France, female vocalist (Claudie Fritsch-Mentrop) — 19

Date	Title / Label	Peak Position	Weeks at No.1	Weeks on Chart
31 Oct 87	**VOYAGE VOYAGE** *CBS DESI 1*	53		6
14 May 88	**VOYAGE VOYAGE (REMIX)** *CBS DESI 2*	5		13

DESIYA FEATURING MELISSA YIANNAKOU
UK, male producer (Matthew Parkhouse) & female vocalist — 1

Date	Title / Label	Peak Position	Weeks at No.1	Weeks on Chart
1 Feb 92	**COMIN' ON STRONG** *Black Market 12MKT 2*	74		1

DESKEE
Germany (b. US), male rapper (Derrick Crumpley) — 3

Date	Title / Label	Peak Position	Weeks at No.1	Weeks on Chart
3 Feb 90	**LET THERE BE HOUSE** *Big One VBIG 19*	52		2
8 Sep 90	**DANCE DANCE** *Big One VBIG 22*	74		1

DES'REE

UK, female vocalist (Desiree Weeks)

Date	Title	Peak Position	Weeks at No.1	Weeks on Chart (73)
31 Aug 91	**FEEL SO HIGH** *Dusted Sound 6573667*	51		5
11 Jan 92	**FEEL SO HIGH** *Dusted Sound 6576897*	13		7
21 Mar 92	**MIND ADVENTURES** *Dusted Sound 6578637*	43		3
27 Jun 92	**WHY SHOULD I LOVE YOU** *Dusted Sound 6580917*	44		3
19 Jun 93	**DELICATE** *Columbia 6593312* TERENCE TRENT D'ARBY FEATURING DES'REE	14		6
9 Apr 94	**YOU GOTTA BE** *Dusted Sound 6601342*	20		7
18 Jun 94	**I AN'T MOVIN'** *Dusted Sound 6604672*	44		3
3 Sep 94	**LITTLE CHILD** *Dusted Sound 6604515*	69		1
11 Mar 95	**YOU GOTTA BE (REMIX)** *Dusted Sound 6613215*	14		8
20 Jun 98	**LIFE** *Sony S2 6659302*	8		15
7 Nov 98	**WHAT'S YOUR SIGN** *Sony S2 6665165*	19		4
3 Apr 99	**YOU GOTTA BE** *Dusted Sound S2 6668935*	10		8
16 Oct 99	**AIN'T NO SUNSHINE** *Universal Music TV 1564332* LADYSMITH BLACK MAMBAZO FEATURING DES'REE	42		2
5 Apr 03	**IT'S OKAY** *Sony Music 6736495*	69		1

DESTINY'S CHILD

US, female vocal group – Beyoncé* Knowles, LeToya* Luckett (left 2000), Latavia Roberson (left 2000), Kelly Rowland* & Michelle Williams*

Date	Title	Peak Position	Weeks at No.1	Weeks on Chart (137)
28 Mar 98	**NO NO NO** *Columbia 6656592* FEATURING WYCLEF JEAN	5		8
11 Jul 98	**WITH ME** *Columbia 6661472*	19		3
7 Nov 98	**SHE'S GONE** *Columbia 6664915* MATTHEW MARSDEN FEATURING DESTINY'S CHILD	24		3
23 Jan 99	**GET ON THE BUS** *East West E 3780CD* FEATURING TIMBALAND	15		5
24 Jul 99	**BILLS, BILLS, BILLS** *Columbia 6676902* ★	6		9
30 Oct 99	**BUG A BOO** *Columbia 6681882*	9		7
8 Apr 00	**SAY MY NAME** *Columbia 6691882* ★	3		11
29 Jul 00	**JUMPIN' JUMPIN'** *Columbia 6696292*	5		11
2 Dec 00	**INDEPENDENT WOMEN PART 1** *Columbia 6705932* ● ★	1	1	15
28 Apr 01	**SURVIVOR** *Columbia 6711732* ○	1	1	13
4 Aug 01	**BOOTYLICIOUS** *Columbia 6717382* ★	2		11
24 Nov 01	**EMOTION** *Columbia 6721112*	3		14
13 Nov 04	**LOSE MY BREATH** *Columbia 6754912*	2		11
19 Feb 05	**SOLDIER** *Columbia 6757622* FEATURING TI & LIL' WAYNE	4		7
7 May 05	**GIRL** *Columbia 6758952*	6		9

MARCELLA DETROIT

US, female vocalist/guitarist (Marcella Levy). See Shakespear's Sister

Date	Title	Peak Position	Weeks at No.1	Weeks on Chart (16)
12 Mar 94	**I BELIEVE** *London LONCD 347*	11		8
14 May 94	**AIN'T NOTHING LIKE THE REAL THING** *London LONCD 350* & ELTON JOHN	24		4
16 Jul 94	**I'M NO ANGEL** *London LOCDP 351*	33		4

DETROIT COBRAS

US, male/female vocal/instrumental group

Date	Title	Peak Position	Weeks at No.1	Weeks on Chart (1)
25 Sep 04	**CHA CHA TWIST** *Rough Trade RTRADSCD189*	59		1

DETROIT EMERALDS

US, male vocal trio – Abe Tilmon, Ivory Tilmon & James Mitchell

Date	Title	Peak Position	Weeks at No.1	Weeks on Chart (44)
10 Feb 73	**FEEL THE NEED IN ME** *Janus 6146 020*	4		15
5 May 73	**YOU WANT IT YOU GOT IT** *Westbound 6146 103*	12		9
11 Aug 73	**I THINK OF YOU** *Westbound 6146 104*	27		9
18 Jun 77	**FEEL THE NEED IN ME** *Atlantic K 10945*	12		11

DETROIT GRAND PU BAHS

US, male vocal/production group

Date	Title	Peak Position	Weeks at No.1	Weeks on Chart (3)
8 Jul 00	**SANDWICHES** *Jive Electro 9230252*	29		3

DETROIT SPINNERS

US, male vocal group – Philippe Wynne, Henry Fambrough, Billy Henderson, Pervis Jackson & Bobbie Smith

Date	Title	Peak Position	Weeks at No.1	Weeks on Chart (93)
14 Nov 70	**IT'S A SHAME** *Tamla Motown TMG 755* MOTOWN SPINNERS	20		11
21 Apr 73	**COULD IT BE I'M FALLING IN LOVE** *Atlantic K 10283*	11		11
29 Sep 73	**GHETTO CHILD** *Atlantic K 10359*	7		10
19 Oct 74	**THEN CAME YOU** *Atlantic K 10495* DIONNE WARWICK & THE DETROIT SPINNERS ★	29		6
11 Sep 76	**THE RUBBERBAND MAN** *Atlantic K 10807*	16		11
29 Jan 77	**WAKE UP SUSAN** *Atlantic K 10799*	29		6
7 May 77	**COULD IT BE I'M FALLING IN LOVE EP** *Atlantic K 10935*	32		3
23 Feb 80	**WORKING MY WAY BACK TO YOU – FORGIVE ME GIRL (MEDLEY)** *Atlantic K 11432* ○	1	2	14
10 May 80	**BODY LANGUAGE** *Atlantic K 11392*	40		7
28 Jun 80	**CUPID-I'VE LOVED YOU FOR A LONG TIME (MEDLEY)** *Atlantic K 11498*	4		10
24 Jun 95	**I'LL BE AROUND** *Cooltempo CDCOOL 306* RAPPIN' 4-TAY FEATURING THE SPINNERS	30		4

DEUCE

UK, female/male vocal group – Kelly O'Keefe, Lisa Armstrong, Paul Holmes & Craig Robert Young. See Childliners

Date	Title	Peak Position	Weeks at No.1	Weeks on Chart (23)
21 Jan 95	**CALL IT LOVE** *London LONCD 355*	11		10
22 Apr 95	**I NEED YOU** *London LONCD 365*	10		5
19 Aug 95	**ON THE BIBLE** *London LONCD 368*	13		6
29 Jun 96	**NO SURRENDER** *Love This LUVTHISCD 10*	29		2

dEUS

Belgium, male vocal/instrumental group

Date	Title	Peak Position	Weeks at No.1	Weeks on Chart (7)
11 Feb 95	**HOTEL LOUNGE (BE THE DEATH OF ME)** *Island CID 603*	55		1
13 Jul 96	**THEME FROM TURNPIKE (EP)** *Island CID 630*	68		1
19 Oct 96	**LITTLE ARITHMETICS** *Island CID 643*	44		2
15 Mar 97	**ROSES** *Island CID 645*	56		1
24 Apr 99	**INSTANT STREET** *Island CID 742*	49		1
3 Jul 99	**SISTER DEW** *Island CID 750*	62		1

TERRA DEVA

US, female vocalist (Terra McNair)

Date	Title	Peak Position	Weeks at No.1	Weeks on Chart (3)
15 Feb 03	**STING ME RED (YOU THINK YOU'RE SO)** *Cream 19CDS* WHO DA FUNK FEATURING TERRA DEVA	32		2
12 Feb 05	**WHAT DO YOU WANT?** *Subliminal SUB138CD* MORILLO FEATURING TERRA DEVA	61		1

DAVID DEVANT & HIS SPIRIT WIFE

UK, male vocal/instrumental group

Date	Title	Peak Position	Weeks at No.1	Weeks on Chart (2)
5 Apr 97	**GINGER** *Rhythm King KIND 4CD*	54		1
21 Jun 97	**THIS IS FOR REAL** *Rhythm King KIND 5CD*	61		1

SIDNEY DEVINE

UK, male vocalist

Date	Title	Peak Position	Weeks at No.1	Weeks on Chart (1)
1 Apr 78	**SCOTLAND FOREVER** *Philips SCOT 1*	48		1

DEVO

US, male vocal/instrumental group

Date	Title	Peak Position	Weeks at No.1	Weeks on Chart (23)
22 Apr 78	**(I CAN'T GET ME NO) SATISFACTION** *Stiff BOY 1*	41		8
13 May 78	**JOCKO HOMO** *Stiff DEV 1*	62		3
12 Aug 78	**BE STIFF** *Stiff BOY 2*	71		1
2 Sep 78	**COME BACK JONEE** *Virgin VS 223*	60		4
22 Nov 80	**WHIP IT** *Virgin VS 383*	51		7

SHEILA B DEVOTION

France, female vocalist (Anny Chancel) & male vocal trio

Date	Title	Peak Position	Weeks at No.1	Weeks on Chart (33)
11 Mar 78	**SINGIN' IN THE RAIN PART 1** *Carrere EMI 2751*	11		13
22 Jul 78	**YOU LIGHT MY FIRE** *Carrere EMI 2828*	44		6
24 Nov 79	**SPACER** *Carrere CAR 128* SHEILA & B. DEVOTION	18		14

DEXY'S MIDNIGHT RUNNERS

UK, male/female vocal/instrumental group – Kevin Rowland, Billy Adams, Kevin 'Al' Archer, Helen O'Hara, Seb Shelton & various musicians

Date	Title	Peak Position	Weeks at No.1	Weeks on Chart (93)
19 Jan 80	**DANCE STANCE** *Oddball Productions R 6028*	40		6
22 Mar 80	**GENO** *Late Night Feelings R 6033* ○	1	2	14
12 Jul 80	**THERE THERE MY DEAR** *Late Night Feelings R 6038*	7		9
21 Mar 81	**PLAN B** *Parlophone R 6046*	58		2
11 Jul 81	**SHOW ME** *Mercury DEXYS 6*	16		9
20 Mar 82	**THE CELTIC SOUL BROTHERS** *Mercury DEXYS 8* WITH THE EMERALD EXPRESS	45		4
3 Jul 82	**COME ON EILEEN** *Mercury DEXYS 9* WITH THE EMERALD EXPRESS ⊛ ★	1	4	17
2 Oct 82	**JACKIE WILSON SAID** *Mercury DEXYS 10* KEVIN ROWLAND & DEXY'S MIDNIGHT RUNNERS	5		7
4 Dec 82	**LET'S GET THIS STRAIGHT (FROM THE START)/OLD** *Mercury DEXYS 11* KEVIN ROWLAND & DEXY'S MIDNIGHT RUNNERS	17		9
2 Apr 83	**THE CELTIC SOUL BROTHERS** *Mercury DEXYS 12* KEVIN ROWLAND & DEXY'S MIDNIGHT RUNNERS	20		6

Date	Title / Label / Catalogue	Peak Position	Weeks at No.1	Weeks on Chart
22 Nov 86	**BECAUSE OF YOU** *Mercury BRUSH 1*	13		10

D4
New Zealand, male vocal/instrumental group **3**

Date	Title / Label / Catalogue	Peak Position	Weeks at No.1	Weeks on Chart
28 Sep 02	**GET LOOSE** *Infectious INFEC 117CDSX*	64		1
7 Dec 02	**COME ON** *Infectious INFEC 121CDSX*	50		1
29 Mar 03	**LADIES MAN** *Infectious INFEC 122CDSX*	41		1

D4L
US, male vocal group **2**

Date	Title / Label / Catalogue	Peak Position	Weeks at No.1	Weeks on Chart
15 Apr 06	**LAFFY TAFFY** *Asylum AT0237CD* ★	29		2

DHS
UK, male producer (Ben Stokes) **1**

Date	Title / Label / Catalogue	Peak Position	Weeks at No.1	Weeks on Chart
9 Feb 02	**HOUSE OF GOD** *Club Tools 0135825 CLU*	72		1

DHT FEATURING EDMEE
Belgium, male/female vocal/production duo – Flor Theeuwes & Edmee Daenen **13**

Date	Title / Label / Catalogue	Peak Position	Weeks at No.1	Weeks on Chart
17 Dec 05	**LISTEN TO YOUR HEART** *Ministry Of Sound DATA109CDS*	7		13

TONY DI BART
UK, male vocalist (Antonio di Bartolomeo) **19**

Date	Title / Label / Catalogue	Peak Position	Weeks at No.1	Weeks on Chart
9 Apr 94	**THE REAL THING** *Cleveland City Blues CCBCD 15001* ●	1	1	12
20 Aug 94	**DO IT** *Cleveland City Blues CCBCD 15003*	21		4
20 May 95	**WHY DID YA** *Cleveland City Blues CCBCD 15004*	46		1
2 Mar 96	**TURN YOUR LOVE AROUND** *Cleveland City Blues CCBCD 15006*	66		1
17 Oct 98	**THE REAL THING (REMIX)** *Cleveland City CLECD 13050*	51		1

GREGG DIAMOND BIONIC BOOGIE
US, male/female vocal group – leader d. 14 Mar 1999 (age 49) **3**

Date	Title / Label / Catalogue	Peak Position	Weeks at No.1	Weeks on Chart
20 Jan 79	**CREAM (ALWAYS RISES TO THE TOP)** *Polydor POSP 18*	61		3

JIM DIAMOND
UK, male vocalist. See PhD **30**

Date	Title / Label / Catalogue	Peak Position	Weeks at No.1	Weeks on Chart
3 Nov 84	**I SHOULD HAVE KNOWN BETTER** *A&M AM 220*	1	1	13
2 Feb 85	**I SLEEP ALONE AT NIGHT** *A&M AM 229*	72		1
18 May 85	**REMEMBER I LOVE YOU** *A&M AM 247*	42		5
22 Feb 86	**HI HO SILVER** *A&M AM 296* ●	5		11

NEIL DIAMOND
US, male vocalist/guitarist **128**

Date	Title / Label / Catalogue	Peak Position	Weeks at No.1	Weeks on Chart
7 Nov 70	**CRACKLIN' ROSIE** *Uni UN 529* ★	3		17
20 Feb 71	**SWEET CAROLINE** *Uni UN 531*	8		11
8 May 71	**I AM...I SAID** *Uni UN 532*	4		12
13 May 72	**SONG SUNG BLUE** *Uni UN 538* ★	14		13
14 Aug 76	**IF YOU KNOW WHAT I MEAN** *CBS 4398*	35		4
23 Oct 76	**BEAUTIFUL NOISE** *CBS 4601*	13		9
24 Dec 77	**DESIREE** *CBS 5869*	39		6
25 Nov 78	**YOU DON'T BRING ME FLOWERS** *CBS 6803* BARBRA & NEIL ● ★	5		12
3 Mar 79	**FOREVER IN BLUE JEANS** *CBS 7047*	16		12
15 Nov 80	**LOVE ON THE ROCKS** *Capitol CL 16173*	17		12
14 Feb 81	**HELLO AGAIN** *Capitol CL 16176*	51		4
20 Nov 82	**HEARTLIGHT** *CBS A 2814*	47		7
21 Nov 92	**MORNING HAS BROKEN** *Columbia 6588267*	36		2
24 May 08	**PRETTY AMAZING GRACE** *Columbia USSM10800959*	49		4
14 Jun 08	**SWEET CAROLINE** *Columbia USSM10021421*	63		3

DIAMOND HEAD
UK, male vocal/instrumental group **2**

Date	Title / Label / Catalogue	Peak Position	Weeks at No.1	Weeks on Chart
11 Sep 82	**IN THE HEAT OF THE NIGHT** *MCA DHM 102*	67		2

DIAMONDS
Canada, male vocal group – Dave Somerville, Ted Kowalski, Phil Levitt & Bill Reed, d. 22 Oct 2004 **17**

Date	Title / Label / Catalogue	Peak Position	Weeks at No.1	Weeks on Chart
31 May 57	**LITTLE DARLIN'** *Mercury MT 148*	3		17

DICK & DEEDEE
US, male/female vocal duo **3**

Date	Title / Label / Catalogue	Peak Position	Weeks at No.1	Weeks on Chart
26 Oct 61	**THE MOUNTAIN'S HIGH** *London HLG 9408*	37		3

CHARLES DICKENS
UK, male vocalist (David Anthony) **8**

Date	Title / Label / Catalogue	Peak Position	Weeks at No.1	Weeks on Chart
1 Jul 65	**THAT'S THE WAY LOVE GOES** *Pye 7N 15887*	37		8

GWEN DICKEY
US, female vocalist. See Rose Royce **13**

Date	Title / Label / Catalogue	Peak Position	Weeks at No.1	Weeks on Chart
27 Jan 90	**CAR WASH** *Swanyard SYR 7*	72		2
2 Jul 94	**AIN'T NOBODY (LOVES ME BETTER)** *X-clusive XCLU 010CD* KWS & GWEN DICKEY	21		4
14 Feb 98	**WISHING ON A STAR** *Northwestside 74321554632* JAY-Z FEATURING GWEN DICKEY	13		4
31 Oct 98	**CAR WASH** *MCA MCSTD 48096* ROSE ROYCE FEATURING GWEN DICKEY	18		3

NEVILLE DICKIE
UK, male pianist **10**

Date	Title / Label / Catalogue	Peak Position	Weeks at No.1	Weeks on Chart
25 Oct 69	**ROBIN'S RETURN** *Major Minor MM 644*	33		10

DICKIES
US, male vocal/instrumental group – Leonard Graves Phillips, Greg Hanna, Stan Lee, Travis Johnson & Dylan Thomas **28**

Date	Title / Label / Catalogue	Peak Position	Weeks at No.1	Weeks on Chart
16 Dec 78	**SILENT NIGHT** *A&M AMS 7403*	47		4
21 Apr 79	**BANANA SPLITS (TRA LA LA SONG)** *A&M AMS 7431*	7		8
21 Jul 79	**PARANOID** *A&M AMS 7368*	45		6
15 Sep 79	**NIGHTS IN WHITE SATIN** *A&M AMS 7469*	39		5
16 Feb 80	**FAN MAIL** *A&M AMS 7504*	57		3
19 Jul 80	**GIGANTOR** *A&M AMS 7544*	72		2

BRUCE DICKINSON
UK, male vocalist/guitarist (Paul Bruce Dickinson). See Iron Maiden, Samson **23**

Date	Title / Label / Catalogue	Peak Position	Weeks at No.1	Weeks on Chart
28 Apr 90	**TATTOOED MILLIONAIRE** *EMI EM 138*	18		5
23 Jun 90	**ALL THE YOUNG DUDES** *EMI EM 142*	23		5
25 Aug 90	**DIVE! DIVE! DIVE!** *EMI EM 151*	45		2
4 Apr 92	**(I WANT TO BE) ELECTED** *London LON 319* MR BEAN & SMEAR CAMPAIGN FEATURING BRUCE DICKINSON	9		5
28 May 94	**TEARS OF THE DRAGON** *EMI CDEM 322*	28		2
8 Oct 94	**SHOOT ALL THE CLOWNS** *EMI CDEMS 341*	37		2
13 Apr 96	**BACK FROM THE EDGE** *Raw Power RAWX 1012*	68		1
3 May 97	**ACCIDENT OF BIRTH** *Raw Power RAWX 1042*	54		1

BARBARA DICKSON
UK, female vocalist/guitarist **49**

Date	Title / Label / Catalogue	Peak Position	Weeks at No.1	Weeks on Chart
17 Jan 76	**ANSWER ME** *RSO 2090 174*	9		7
26 Feb 77	**ANOTHER SUITCASE IN ANOTHER HALL** *MCA 266*	18		7
19 Jan 80	**CARAVAN SONG** *Epic EPC 8103*	41		7
15 Mar 80	**JANUARY FEBRUARY** *Epic EPC 8115*	11		10
14 Jun 80	**IN THE NIGHT** *Epic EPC 8593*	48		2
5 Jan 85	**I KNOW HIM SO WELL** *RCA CHESS 3* ELAINE PAIGE & BARBARA DICKSON ●	1	4	16

DICTATORS
US, male vocal/instrumental group **2**

Date	Title / Label / Catalogue	Peak Position	Weeks at No.1	Weeks on Chart
17 Sep 77	**SEARCH AND DESTORY** *Asylum K 13091*	49		2

BO DIDDLEY
US, male vocalist/guitarist (Ellas Bates, aka Ellas McDaniel), d. 2 Jun 2008 (age 79) **10**

Date	Title / Label / Catalogue	Peak Position	Weeks at No.1	Weeks on Chart
10 Oct 63	**PRETTY THING** *Pye International 7N 25217*	34		6
18 Mar 65	**HEY GOOD LOOKIN'** *Chess 8000*	39		4

DIDDY
UK, male producer (Richard Dearlove) **3**

Date	Title / Label / Catalogue	Peak Position	Weeks at No.1	Weeks on Chart
19 Feb 94	**GIVE ME LOVE** *Positiva CDTIV 8*	52		1
12 Jul 97	**GIVE ME LOVE (REMIX)** *Feverpitch CDFVR 19*	23		2

DIDO

UK, female vocalist/multi-instrumentalist (Florian Cloud de Bounevialle Armstrong) — 66

Date	Title	Peak Position	Weeks at No.1	Weeks on Chart
24 Feb 01	**HERE WITH ME** *Cheeky 74321832732* ●	4		12
2 Jun 01	**THANK YOU** *Cheeky 74321853042*	3		10
22 Sep 01	**HUNTER** *Cheeky 74321885722*	17		8
20 Apr 02	**ONE STEP TOO FAR** *Cheeky 74321926412* FAITHLESS FEATURING DIDO	6		3
4 May 02	**ONE STEP TOO FAR** *Cheeky 74321936742* FAITHLESS FEATURING DIDO	68		1
13 Sep 03	**WHITE FLAG** *Cheeky 82876546022*	2		13
13 Dec 03	**LIFE FOR RENT** *Cheeky 82876579472*	8		9
24 Apr 04	**DON'T LEAVE HOME** *Cheeky 82876611722*	25		6
25 Sep 04	**SAND IN MY SHOES** *Cheeky 82876626922*	29		3
8 Nov 08	**DON'T BELIEVE IN LOVE** *Cheeky 88697391362*	54		1

DIESEL PARK WEST

UK, male vocal/instrumental group — 15

Date	Title	Peak Position	Weeks at No.1	Weeks on Chart
4 Feb 89	**ALL THE MYTHS ON SUNDAY** *Food 17*	66		2
1 Apr 89	**LIKE PRINCES DO** *Food 19*	58		3
5 Aug 89	**WHEN THE HOODOO COMES** *Food 20*	62		2
18 Jan 92	**FALL TO LOVE** *Food 35*	48		3
21 Mar 92	**BOY ON TOP OF THE NEWS** *Food 36*	58		2
5 Sep 92	**GOD ONLY KNOWS** *Food 39*	57		3

DIFFERENT GEAR VERSUS THE POLICE

UK/Italy, male production group & UK/US, male vocal/instrumental trio. See Klark Kent, Sting — 3

Date	Title	Peak Position	Weeks at No.1	Weeks on Chart
5 Aug 00	**WHEN THE WORLD IS RUNNING DOWN** *Pagan 039CDS*	28		3

DIFFORD & TILBROOK

UK, male vocal/instrumental duo. See Squeeze — 2

Date	Title	Peak Position	Weeks at No.1	Weeks on Chart
30 Jun 84	**LOVE'S CRASHING WAVES** *A&M AM 193*	57		2

DIFF'RENT DARKNESS

UK, male vocal/instrumental group — 1

Date	Title	Peak Position	Weeks at No.1	Weeks on Chart
27 Dec 03	**ORCHESTRAL MANOEUVRES IN THE DARKNESS EP** *Guided Missile GUIDE49CD*	66		1

DIGABLE PLANETS

US, male/female rap trio — 2

Date	Title	Peak Position	Weeks at No.1	Weeks on Chart
13 Feb 93	**REBIRTH OF SLICK (COOL LIKE DAT)** *Pendulum EKR 159CD*	67		2

RAH DIGGA

US, male rapper (Rashia Fisher) — 4

Date	Title	Peak Position	Weeks at No.1	Weeks on Chart
2 Mar 02	**I'M LEAVIN'** *Rufflife RLCDM 03* OUTSIDAZ FEATURING RAH DIGGA & MELANIE BLATT	41		2
21 Jun 03	**BOUT** *Parlophone CDRS 6597* JAMELIA FEATURING RAH DIGGA	37		2

DIGITAL DREAM BABY

UK, male producer (Steven Teear) — 4

Date	Title	Peak Position	Weeks at No.1	Weeks on Chart
14 Dec 91	**WALKING IN THE AIR** *Columbia 6576067*	49		4

DIGITAL EXCITATION

Belgium, male production duo — 2

Date	Title	Peak Position	Weeks at No.1	Weeks on Chart
29 Feb 92	**PURE PLEASURE** *R&S RSUK 10*	37		2

DIGITAL ORGASM

Belgium, male production group — 14

Date	Title	Peak Position	Weeks at No.1	Weeks on Chart
7 Dec 91	**RUNNING OUT OF TIME** *Dead Dead Good GOOD 009*	16		9
18 Apr 92	**STARTOUCHERS** *DDG International GOOD 13*	31		3
25 Jul 92	**MOOG ERUPTION** *DDG International GOOD 17*	62		2

DIGITAL UNDERGROUND

US, male rap/instrumental/DJ group — 4

Date	Title	Peak Position	Weeks at No.1	Weeks on Chart
16 Mar 91	**SAME SONG** *Big Life BLR 40*	52		4

DILATED PEOPLES

US, male vocal/DJ/production group — 6

Date	Title	Peak Position	Weeks at No.1	Weeks on Chart
23 Feb 02	**WORST COMES TO THE WORST** *Capitol CDCL 834*	29		3
10 Apr 04	**THIS WAY** *Capitol CDCL 854*	35		3

DILEMMA

Italy, male instrumental/production group — 1

Date	Title	Peak Position	Weeks at No.1	Weeks on Chart
6 Apr 96	**IN SPIRIT** *ffrr FCDE 274*	42		1

DILLINJA

UK, male producer (Karl Francis) — 12

Date	Title	Peak Position	Weeks at No.1	Weeks on Chart
9 Nov 02	**TWIST 'EM OUT** *Renegade Hardware RH40*	50		1
21 Dec 02	**LIVE OR DIE/SOUTH MANZ** *Valve VLV007*	53		1
10 May 03	**THIS IS A WARNING/SUPER DJ** *Valve VLV008*	47		1
28 Jun 03	**TWIST 'EM OUT** *Trouble On Vinyl TOV 56CD* FEATURING SKIBADEE	35		3
27 Sep 03	**FAST CAR** *Valve VLV011*	56		2
12 Jun 04	**ALL THE THINGS/FORSAKEN DREAMS** *Valve VLV012*	71		1
10 Jul 04	**IN THE GRIND/ACID TRAK** *Valve VLV013*	71		1
8 Jan 05	**THUGGED OUT BITCH/RAINFOREST** *Valve VLV014*	54		2

DIMESTARS

UK, male/female vocal/instrumental group — 1

Date	Title	Peak Position	Weeks at No.1	Weeks on Chart
16 Jun 01	**MY SUPERSTAR** *Polydor 5870912*	72		1

D-INFLUENCE

UK, male/female vocal/instrumental group — 10

Date	Title	Peak Position	Weeks at No.1	Weeks on Chart
20 Jun 92	**GOOD LOVER** *East West A 8573*	46		2
27 Mar 93	**GOOD LOVER (REMIX)** *East West America A 8439CD*	61		1
24 Jun 95	**MIDNITE** *East West A 4418CD*	58		1
16 Aug 97	**HYPNOTIZE** *Echo ECSCD 41*	33		2
11 Oct 97	**MAGIC** *Echo ECSCD 45*	45		1
5 Sep 98	**ROCK WITH YOU** *Echo ECSCD 56*	30		3

MARK DINNING

US, male vocalist, d. 22 Mar 1986 (age 52) — 4

Date	Title	Peak Position	Weeks at No.1	Weeks on Chart
10 Mar 60	**TEEN ANGEL** *MGM 1053* ★	37		4

DINOSAUR JR

US, male vocal/instrumental group — 13

Date	Title	Peak Position	Weeks at No.1	Weeks on Chart
2 Feb 91	**THE WAGON** *Blanco Y Negro NEG 48*	49		2
14 Nov 92	**GET ME** *Blanco Y Negro NEG 60*	44		1
30 Jan 93	**START CHOPPIN** *Blanco Y Negro NEG 61CD*	20		3
12 Jun 93	**OUT THERE** *Blanco Y Negro NEG 63CD*	44		2
27 Aug 94	**FEEL THE PAIN** *Blanco Y Negro NEG 74CD*	25		3
11 Feb 95	**I DON'T THINK SO** *Blanco Y Negro NEG 77CD*	67		1
5 Apr 97	**TAKE A RUN AT THE SUN** *Blanco Y Negro NEG 103CD*	53		1

DIO

UK/US, male vocal/instrumental group — 22

Date	Title	Peak Position	Weeks at No.1	Weeks on Chart
20 Aug 83	**HOLY DIVER** *Vertigo DIO 1*	72		2
29 Oct 83	**RAINBOW IN THE DARK** *Vertigo DIO 2*	46		3
11 Aug 84	**WE ROCK** *Vertigo DIO 3*	42		3
29 Sep 84	**MYSTERY** *Vertigo DIO 4*	34		4
10 Aug 85	**ROCK 'N' ROLL CHILDREN** *Vertigo DIO 5*	26		6
2 Nov 85	**HUNGRY FOR HEAVEN** *Vertigo DIO 6*	72		1
17 May 86	**HUNGRY FOR HEAVEN** *Vertigo DIO 7*	56		2
1 Aug 87	**I COULD HAVE BEEN A DREAMER** *Vertigo DIO 8*	69		1

DION

US, male vocalist (Dion DiMucci). — 35

Date	Title	Peak Position	Weeks at No.1	Weeks on Chart
26 Jun 59	**A TEENAGER IN LOVE** *London HLU 8874* & THE BELMONTS	28		2
19 Jan 61	**LONELY TEENAGER** *Top Rank JAR 521*	47		1
2 Nov 61	**RUNAROUND SUE** *Top Rank JAR 586* ★	11		9
15 Feb 62	**THE WANDERER** *HMV POP 971*	10		12
22 May 76	**THE WANDERER** *Philips 6146 700*	16		9
19 Aug 89	**KING OF THE NEW YORK STREET** *Arista 112556*	74		2

CELINE DION

Canada, female vocalist. Award-winning entertainer from Quebec with worldwide record sales in excess of 200 million who won the Eurovision Song Contest for Switzerland in 1988. Mrs Rene Angelil is the only female solo singer with two UK million-sellers ('Think Twice' & 'My Heart Will Go On')

Weeks on Chart: 254

Date	Title	Peak Position	Weeks at No.1	Weeks on Chart
16 May 92	**BEAUTY AND THE BEAST** *Epic 6576607* & PEABO BRYSON	9		7
4 Jul 92	**IF YOU ASKED ME TO** *Epic 6581927*	60		2
14 Nov 92	**LOVE CAN MOVE MOUNTAINS** *Epic 6587787*	46		2
26 Dec 92	**IF YOU ASKED ME TO** *Epic 6581927*	57		3
3 Apr 93	**WHERE DOES MY HEART BEAT NOW** *Epic 6563265*	72		1
29 Jan 94	**THE POWER OF LOVE** *Epic 6597992* ★	4		10
23 Apr 94	**MISLED** *Epic 6602922*	40		3
22 Oct 94	**THINK TWICE** *Epic 6606422* ⊛	1	6	31
20 May 95	**ONLY ONE ROAD** *Epic 6613535*	8		8
9 Sep 95	**TU M'AIMES ENCORE (TO LOVE ME AGAIN)** *Epic 6624255*	7		9
2 Dec 95	**MISLED** *Epic 6626495*	15		6
2 Mar 96	**FALLING INTO YOU** *Epic 6629795*	10		10
1 Jun 96	**BECAUSE YOU LOVED ME (THEME FROM UP CLOSE AND PERSONAL)** *Epic 6632382* ○ ★	5		16
5 Oct 96	**IT'S ALL COMING BACK TO ME NOW** *Epic 6637112* ○	3		14
21 Dec 96	**ALL BY MYSELF** *Epic 6640622* ○	6		13
28 Jun 97	**CALL THE MAN** *Epic 6646922*	11		6
15 Nov 97	**TELL HIM** *Epic 6653052* BARBRA STREISAND & CELINE DION ●	3		15
20 Dec 97	**THE REASON** *Epic 6653812*	11		8
21 Feb 98	**MY HEART WILL GO ON** *Epic 6655472* ⊛x2 ★	1	2	20
18 Jul 98	**IMMORTALITY** *Epic 6661682* WITH THE BEE GEES ○	5		12
28 Nov 98	**I'M YOUR ANGEL** *Epic 6666282* & R KELLY ○ ★	3		13
10 Jul 99	**TREAT HER LIKE A LADY** *Epic 6675525*	29		3
11 Dec 99	**THAT'S THE WAY IT IS** *Epic 6684622*	12		11
8 Apr 00	**THE FIRST TIME EVER I SAW YOUR FACE** *Epic 6691942*	19		7
23 Mar 02	**A NEW DAY HAS COME** *Epic 6725032*	7		10
31 Aug 02	**I'M ALIVE** *Epic 6730652*	17		6
7 Dec 02	**GOODBYE'S (THE SADDEST WORD)** *Epic 6733732*	38		2
20 Sep 03	**ONE HEART** *Epic 6743482*	27		2
10 Nov 07	**TAKING CHANCES** *Columbia 88697170002*	40		4

DIONNE

Canada, female vocalist (Dionne Warren)

Weeks on Chart: 2

Date	Title	Peak Position	Weeks at No.1	Weeks on Chart
23 Sep 89	**COME GET MY LOVIN'** *Citybeat CBC 745*	69		2

WASIS DIOP FEATURING LENA FIAGBE

Senegal/UK, male/female vocal/production duo

Weeks on Chart: 2

Date	Title	Peak Position	Weeks at No.1	Weeks on Chart
10 Feb 96	**AFRICAN DREAM** *Mercury MERCD 453*	44		2

DIRE STRAITS

UK, male vocal/instrumental group – Mark Knopfler*, Alan Clark, Guy Fletcher, John Illsley, David Knopfler (replaced by Hal Lindes) & Pick Withers (replaced by Terry Williams)

Weeks on Chart: 119

Date	Title	Peak Position	Weeks at No.1	Weeks on Chart
10 Mar 79	**SULTANS OF SWING** *Vertigo 6059 206* ○	8		11
28 Jul 79	**LADY WRITER** *Vertigo 6059 230*	51		6
17 Jan 81	**ROMEO AND JULIET** *Vertigo MOVIE 1*	8		11
4 Apr 81	**SKATEAWAY** *Vertigo MOVIE 2*	37		5
10 Oct 81	**TUNNEL OF LOVE** *Vertigo MUSIC 3*	54		3
4 Sep 82	**PRIVATE INVESTIGATIONS** *Vertigo DSTR 1* ○	2		8
22 Jan 83	**TWISTING BY THE POOL** *Vertigo DSTR 2*	14		7
18 Feb 84	**LOVE OVER GOLD (LIVE)/SOLID ROCK (LIVE)** *Vertigo DSTR 6*	50		3
20 Apr 85	**SO FAR AWAY** *Vertigo DSTR 9*	20		6
6 Jul 85	**MONEY FOR NOTHING** *Vertigo DSTR 10* ○ ★	4		16
26 Oct 85	**BROTHERS IN ARMS** *Vertigo DSTR 11*	16		13
11 Jan 86	**WALK OF LIFE** *Vertigo DSTR 12*	2		11
3 May 86	**YOUR LATEST TRICK** *Vertigo DSTR 13*	26		6
5 Nov 88	**SULTANS OF SWING** *Vertigo DSTR 15*	62		1
31 Aug 91	**CALLING ELVIS** *Vertigo DSTR 16*	21		4
2 Nov 91	**HEAVY FUEL** *Vertigo DSTR 17*	55		2
29 Feb 92	**ON EVERY STREET** *Vertigo DSTR 18*	42		2
27 Jun 92	**THE BUG** *Vertigo DSTR 19*	67		1
22 May 93	**ENCORES EP** *Vertigo DSCD 20*	31		3

DIRECKT

UK, male production duo. See E-Lustrious

Weeks on Chart: 2

Date	Title	Peak Position	Weeks at No.1	Weeks on Chart
13 Aug 94	**TWO FATT GUITARS (REVISITED)** *UFG 7CD*	36		2

DIRECT DRIVE

UK, male/female vocal/instrumental group

Weeks on Chart: 3

Date	Title	Peak Position	Weeks at No.1	Weeks on Chart
26 Jan 85	**ANYTHING** *Polydor POSP 728*	67		2
4 May 85	**A.B.C. (FALLING IN LOVE'S NOT EASY)** *Boiling Point POSP 742*	75		1

DIRT DEVILS

UK/Finland, male production duo. See Oceanlab

Weeks on Chart: 8

Date	Title	Peak Position	Weeks at No.1	Weeks on Chart
2 Feb 02	**THE DRILL** *NuLife 74321915262*	15		6
6 Dec 03	**MUSIC IS LIFE** *NuLife 82876571412*	53		2

DIRTY PRETTY THINGS

UK, male vocal/instrumental group – Carl Barat, Didz Hammond, Gary Powell & Anthony Rossomando

Weeks on Chart: 15

Date	Title	Peak Position	Weeks at No.1	Weeks on Chart
29 Apr 06	**BANG BANG YOU'RE DEAD** *Vertigo 9854376*	5		10
22 Jul 06	**DEADWOOD** *Vertigo 1703653*	20		2
7 Oct 06	**WONDERING** *Vertigo 1705365*	34		2
5 Jul 08	**TIRED OF ENGLAND** *Vertigo 1774781*	54		1

DIRTY VEGAS

UK, male production trio

Weeks on Chart: 12

Date	Title	Peak Position	Weeks at No.1	Weeks on Chart
19 May 01	**DAYS GO BY** *Credence CDCRED 011*	27		4
3 Aug 02	**GHOSTS** *Credence CDCRED 028*	31		3
12 Oct 02	**DAYS GO BY** *Credence CDCREDS 030*	16		4
23 Oct 04	**WALK INTO THE SUN** *Parlophone CDRS6647*	54		1

DISCHARGE

UK, male vocal/instrumental group

Weeks on Chart: 3

Date	Title	Peak Position	Weeks at No.1	Weeks on Chart
24 Oct 81	**NEVER AGAIN** *Clay 6*	64		3

DISCO ANTHEM

Holland, male producer (Lex van Coeverden)

Weeks on Chart: 2

Date	Title	Peak Position	Weeks at No.1	Weeks on Chart
18 Jun 94	**SCREAM** *Sweat MCSTD 1977*	47		2

DISCO CITIZENS

UK, male producer (Nick Bracegirdle). See Chicane

Weeks on Chart: 5

Date	Title	Peak Position	Weeks at No.1	Weeks on Chart
22 Jul 95	**RIGHT HERE RIGHT NOW** *Deconstruction 74321293872*	40		2
12 Apr 97	**FOOTPRINT** *Xtravaganza 0091115*	34		2
4 Jul 98	**NAGASAKI BADGER** *Xtravaganza 0091595 EXT*	56		1

DISCO EVANGELISTS

UK, male production group

Weeks on Chart: 2

Date	Title	Peak Position	Weeks at No.1	Weeks on Chart
8 May 93	**DE NIRO** *Positiva CDTIV 2*	59		2

DISCO TEX & THE SEX-O-LETTES

US, male vocalist (Jospeh 'Sir Monti Rock III' Montanez) & female vocal group

Weeks on Chart: 22

Date	Title	Peak Position	Weeks at No.1	Weeks on Chart
23 Nov 74	**GET DANCING** *Chelsea 2005 013* ○	8		12
26 Apr 75	**I WANNA DANCE WIT CHOO** *Chelsea 2005 024* FEATURING SIR MONTI ROCK III	6		10

DISCO TEX PRESENTS CLOUDBURST

UK, male/femal vocal/production group. See Full Intention, Michael Gray, Hustlers Convention featuring Dave Laudat & Ondrea Duverney, Sex-O-Sonique

Weeks on Chart: 2

Date	Title	Peak Position	Weeks at No.1	Weeks on Chart
24 Mar 01	**I CAN CAST A SPELL** *Absolution CDABSOL 1*	35		2

DISPOSABLE HEROES OF HIPHOPRISY

US, male rap/instrumental duo

Weeks on Chart: 7

Date	Title	Peak Position	Weeks at No.1	Weeks on Chart
4 Apr 92	**TELEVISION THE DRUG OF THE NATION** *Fourth & Broadway BRW 241*	57		2
30 May 92	**LANGUAGE OF VIOLENCE** *Fourth & Broadway 12BRW 248*	68		1
19 Dec 92	**TELEVISION THE DRUG OF THE NATION** *Fourth & Broadway BRW 241*	44		4

DISTANT SOUNDZ

UK, male vocal/production trio

Weeks on Chart: 4

Date	Title	Peak Position	Weeks at No.1	Weeks on Chart
9 Mar 02	**TIME AFTER TIME** *W10/Incentive CENT 36CDS*	20		4

SACHA DISTEL

France, male vocalist, d. 22 Jul 2004 (age 71) — 27

Date	Title / Label	Peak Position	Weeks at No.1	Weeks on Chart
10 Jan 70	**RAINDROPS KEEP FALLING ON MY HEAD** *Warner Brothers WB 7345*	10		27

DISTILLERS

Australia/US, male/female vocal/instrumental group — 3

Date	Title / Label	Peak Position	Weeks at No.1	Weeks on Chart
15 Nov 03	**DRAIN THE BLOOD** *Sire W628CD*	51		1
10 Apr 04	**THE HUNGER** *Sire W636CD*	48		1
19 Jun 04	**BEAT YOUR HEART OUT** *Sire W644CD*	74		1

DISTORTED MINDS

UK, male production duo — 4

Date	Title / Label	Peak Position	Weeks at No.1	Weeks on Chart
29 Mar 03	**T-10/THE TENTH PLANET** *Kaos 006P*	43		2
24 Jan 04	**T-10/THE TENTH PLANET** *Kaos KAOS006*	45		2

DISTURBED

US, male vocal/instrumental group — 4

Date	Title / Label	Peak Position	Weeks at No.1	Weeks on Chart
7 Apr 01	**VOICES** *Giant 74321848962*	52		1
28 Sep 02	**PRAYER** *Reprise W591CD*	31		2
14 Dec 02	**REMEMBER** *Reprise W596CD*	56		1

DIVA

Norway, female vocal duo — 2

Date	Title / Label	Peak Position	Weeks at No.1	Weeks on Chart
7 Oct 95	**THE SUN ALWAYS SHINES ON TV** *East West YZ 947CD*	53		1
20 Jul 96	**EVERYBODY (MOVE YOUR BODY)** *East West YZ 035CD*	44		1

DIVA SURPRISE FEATURING GEORGIA JONES

US/Spain, male/female vocal/production trio. See Original — 2

Date	Title / Label	Peak Position	Weeks at No.1	Weeks on Chart
14 Nov 98	**ON THE TOP OF THE WORLD** *Positiva CDTIV 100*	29		2

DIVE

UK, male production duo. See Aurora — 1

Date	Title / Label	Peak Position	Weeks at No.1	Weeks on Chart
21 Feb 98	**BOOGIE** *WEA 147CD1*	35		1

DIVE DIVE

UK, male vocal/instrumental group — 2

Date	Title / Label	Peak Position	Weeks at No.1	Weeks on Chart
12 Mar 05	**555 FOR FILMSTARS** *Diablo DIACD006*	48		1
18 Jun 05	**THE SORRY SUITOR** *Diablo DIACD007*	54		1

DIVERSIONS

UK, male/female vocal/instrumental group — 3

Date	Title / Label	Peak Position	Weeks at No.1	Weeks on Chart
20 Sep 75	**FATTIE BUM BUM** *Gull GULS 18*	34		3

DIVINE

US, male vocalist/actor (Harris Glenn Milstead), d. 7 Mar 1988 (age 42) — 24

Date	Title / Label	Peak Position	Weeks at No.1	Weeks on Chart
15 Oct 83	**LOVE REACTION** *Design Communication DES 4*	65		2
14 Jul 84	**YOU THINK YOU'RE A MAN** *Proto ENA 118*	16		10
20 Oct 84	**I'M SO BEAUTIFUL** *Proto ENA 121*	52		2
27 Apr 85	**WALK LIKE A MAN** *Proto ENA 125*	23		7
20 Jul 85	**TWISTIN' THE NIGHT AWAY** *Proto ENA 127*	47		3

DIVINE

US, female vocal group — 1

Date	Title / Label	Peak Position	Weeks at No.1	Weeks on Chart
16 Oct 99	**LATELY** *Mushroom/Red Ant RA 002CDS* ★	52		1

DIVINE COMEDY

UK, male vocalist/guitarist (Neil Hannon) — 44

Date	Title / Label	Peak Position	Weeks at No.1	Weeks on Chart
29 Jun 96	**SOMETHING FOR THE WEEKEND** *Setanta SETCD 26*	14		5
24 Aug 96	**BECOMING MORE LIKE ALFIE** *Setanta SETCD 27*	27		2
16 Nov 96	**THE FROG PRINCESS** *Setanta SETCD 32*	15		2
22 Mar 97	**EVERYBODY KNOWS (EXCEPT YOU)** *Setanta SETCDA 038*	14		4
11 Apr 98	**I'VE BEEN TO A MARVELOUS PARTY** *EMI CDTCB 001*	28		3
26 Sep 98	**GENERATION SEX** *Setanta SETCDA 050*	19		3
28 Nov 98	**THE CERTAINTY OF CHANCE** *Setanta SETCDA 067*	49		1
6 Feb 99	**NATIONAL EXPRESS** *Setanta SETCDB 069*	8		7
21 Aug 99	**THE POP SINGER'S FEAR OF THE POLLEN COUNT** *Setanta SETCDB 070*	17		4
13 Nov 99	**GIN SOAKED BOY** *Setanta SETCD 071*	38		2
10 Mar 01	**LOVE WHAT YOU DO** *Parlophone CDRS 6554*	26		2
26 May 01	**BAD AMBASSADOR** *Parlophone CDRS 6558*	34		2
10 Nov 01	**PERFECT LOVESONG** *Parlophone CDRS 6561*	42		1
3 Apr 04	**COME HOME BILLY BIRD** *Parlophone CDRS 6630*	25		2
26 Jun 04	**ABSENT FRIENDS** *Parlophone CDRS 6641*	38		2
24 Jun 06	**DIVA LADY** *Parlophone CDRS6698*	52		1
26 Aug 06	**TO DIE A VIRGIN** *Parlophone CDRS6712*	67		1

DIVINE INSPIRATION

UK, female/male vocal/DJ/production group – Sarah-Jane Scott, Paul Crawley, Davin Lewin & Lee Robinson — 8

Date	Title / Label	Peak Position	Weeks at No.1	Weeks on Chart
18 Jan 03	**THE WAY (PUT YOUR HAND IN MY HAND)** *Data/Ministry Of Sound/ Heat DATA 42CDS*	5		7
15 Nov 03	**WHAT WILL BE WILL BE (DESTINY)** *Heat Recordings HEATCD036*	55		1

DIVINYLS

Australia, female/male vocal/instrumental duo – Christina Amphlett & Mark McEntee — 12

Date	Title / Label	Peak Position	Weeks at No.1	Weeks on Chart
18 May 91	**I TOUCH MYSELF** *Virgin America VUS 36*	10		12

DIXIE CHICKS

US, female vocal/instrumental trio — 9

Date	Title / Label	Peak Position	Weeks at No.1	Weeks on Chart
3 Jul 99	**THERE'S YOUR TROUBLE** *Epic 6675165*	26		5
6 Nov 99	**READY TO RUN** *Epic 6682472*	53		1
19 Apr 03	**LANDSLIDE** *Epic 6737392*	55		1
17 Jun 06	**NOT READY TO MAKE NICE** *Open Wide 82876861242*	70		2

DIXIE CUPS

US, female vocal group — 16

Date	Title / Label	Peak Position	Weeks at No.1	Weeks on Chart
18 Jun 64	**CHAPEL OF LOVE** *Pye International 7N 25245* ★	22		8
13 May 65	**IKO IKO** *Red Bird RB 10024*	23		8

ALESHA DIXON

UK, female vocalist/rapper. See Mis-Teeq — 65

Date	Title / Label	Peak Position	Weeks at No.1	Weeks on Chart
26 Aug 06	**LIPSTICK** *Polydor 1705458*	14		4
4 Nov 06	**KNOCKDOWN** *Polydor 1713036*	45		4
15 Nov 08	**THE BOY DOES NOTHING** *Asylum 6CDX*	5		24
17 Jan 09	**BREATHE SLOW** *Asylum 8CD*	3		21
2 May 09	**LET'S GET EXCITED** *Asylum 10C1*	13		9
28 Nov 09	**TO LOVE AGAIN** *Asylum 12CD*	15		3

DIZZEE RASCAL

UK, male rapper/producer (Dylan Mills) — 138

Date	Title / Label	Peak Position	Weeks at No.1	Weeks on Chart
7 Jun 03	**I LUV U** *XL Recordings XLS 165CD*	29		3
30 Aug 03	**FIX UP LOOK SHARP** *XL Recordings XLS 167CD*	17		5
22 Nov 03	**LUCKY STAR** *XL Recordings XLS 172CD* BASEMENT JAXX FEATURING DIZZEE RASCAL	23		4
6 Dec 03	**JUS' A RASCAL** *XL Recordings XLS 175CD*	30		3
4 Sep 04	**STAND UP TALL** *XL Recordings XLS 198CD*	10		6
20 Nov 04	**DREAM** *XL Recordings XLS 204CD1*	14		8
2 Apr 05	**OFF 2 WORK** *XL Recordings XLS208CD1*	44		2
2 Jun 07	**SIRENS** *XL Recordings XLS272CD*	20		3
11 Aug 07	**PUSSYOLE (OLD SKOOL)** *XL Recordings XLS285CD*	22		4
17 Nov 07	**FLEX** *XL Recordings XLS312CD*	23		6
12 Jul 08	**DANCE WIV ME** *Dirtee Stank STANK002CDS* FEATURING CALVIN HARRIS & CHROME (platinum-selling)	1	4	39
30 May 09	**BONKERS** *Dirtee Stank STANK005CDS* FEATURING ARMAND VAN HELDEN (gold-selling)	1	1	23
5 Sep 09	**HOLIDAY** *Dirtee Stank STANK006CDS* FEATURING CHROME (silver-selling)	1	1	13
3 Oct 09	**DIRTEE CASH** *Dirtee Stank GBPVV0900252*	10		12
27 Feb 10	**YOU GOT THE DIRTEE LOVE** *Dirtee Stank Island GB3CJ1000001* FLORENCE + THE MACHINE FEATURING DIZZEE RASCAL	2		7+

DIZZY HEIGHTS

UK, male rapper — 4

Date	Title / Label	Peak Position	Weeks at No.1	Weeks on Chart
18 Dec 82	**CHRISTMAS RAPPING** *Polydor WRAP 1*	49		4

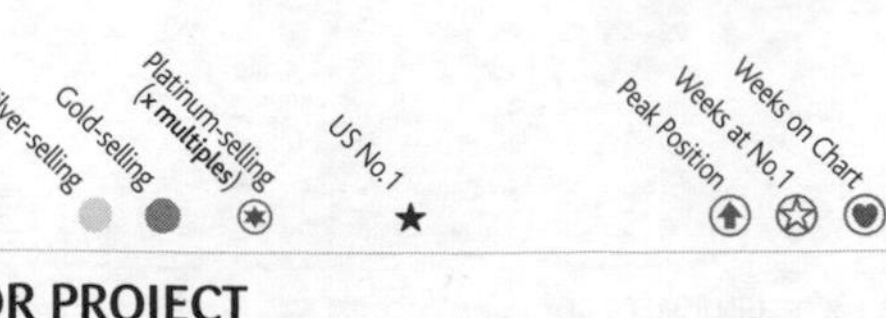

Peak Position
Weeks at No.1
Weeks on Chart

DJ ALIGATOR PROJECT
Denmark, male DJ/producer (Aliasghar Movasat) — 11

Date	Title	Peak Position	Weeks at No.1	Weeks on Chart
7 Oct 00	**THE WHISTLE SONG** *EMI CDBLOW 001*	57		1
19 Jan 02	**THE WHISTLE SONG (BLOW MY WHISTLE BITCH)** *All Around The World CDGLOBE 247*	5		10

DJ AMS & KHIZA FEATURING BINNS & TAFARI
UK, male vocal/DJ/production group — 1

Date	Title	Peak Position	Weeks at No.1	Weeks on Chart
12 Mar 05	**HOT LIKE FIRE** *Goldmind GM008CD*	72		1

DJ BADMARSH & SHRI FEATURING UK APACHE
India/Yemen, male rap/DJ/instrumental/production trio — 1

Date	Title	Peak Position	Weeks at No.1	Weeks on Chart
28 Jul 01	**SIGNS** *Outcaste OUT 38CD1*	63		1

DJ BOBO
Switzerland, male producer/vocalist (Peter Baumann) — 7

Date	Title	Peak Position	Weeks at No.1	Weeks on Chart
24 Sep 94	**EVERYBODY** *PWL Continental PWCD 312*	47		2
17 Jun 95	**LOVE IS ALL AROUND** *Avex UK AVEXCD 7*	49		2
25 Oct 03	**CHIHUAHUA** *Fuelin 82876559422*	36		3

DJ CASPER
US, male vocalist/DJ/producer (Willie Perry) — 24

Date	Title	Peak Position	Weeks at No.1	Weeks on Chart
13 Mar 04	**CHA CHA SLIDE** *All Around The World CDGLOBE329*	1	1	18
16 Oct 04	**OOPS UPSIDE YOUR HEAD** *All Around The World CDGLOBE376* FEATURING THE GAP BAND	16		6

DJ CHUS PRESENTS GROOVE FOUNDATION
Spain, male DJ/production duo — 1

Date	Title	Peak Position	Weeks at No.1	Weeks on Chart
2 Nov 02	**THAT FEELING** *Defected DFTD 055R2*	65		1

DJ DADO
Italy, male DJ/producer (Roberto Gallo) — 9

Date	Title	Peak Position	Weeks at No.1	Weeks on Chart
6 Apr 96	**X-FILES** *ZYX 8065R8*	8		6
14 Mar 98	**COMING BACK** *ffrr TABCD 247*	63		1
11 Jul 98	**GIVE ME LOVE** *VC Recordings VCRD 37* VS MICHELLE WEEKS	59		1
8 May 99	**READY OR NOT** *Chemistry CDKEM 006* & SIMONE JAY	51		1

DJ DAN PRESENTS NEEDLE DAMAGE
US, male DJ/production group — 1

Date	Title	Peak Position	Weeks at No.1	Weeks on Chart
5 May 01	**THAT ZIPPER TRACK** *Duty Free DF 213CD*	53		1

DJ DEE KLINE
UK, male DJ/producer (Nick Annand) — 6

Date	Title	Peak Position	Weeks at No.1	Weeks on Chart
3 Jun 00	**I DON'T SMOKE** *East West EW 213CD*	11		6

DJ DISCIPLE
US, male producer (David Banks) — 1

Date	Title	Peak Position	Weeks at No.1	Weeks on Chart
12 Nov 94	**ON THE DANCEFLOOR** *Mother MUMCD 55*	67		1

DJ DUKE
Denmark, male producer/DJ (Ken Larson) — 7

Date	Title	Peak Position	Weeks at No.1	Weeks on Chart
8 Jan 94	**BLOW YOUR WHISTLE** *ffrr FCD 228*	15		5
16 Jul 94	**TURN IT UP (SAY YEAH)** *ffrr FCD 235*	31		2

DJ EMPIRE PRESENTS GIORGIO MORODER
Germany/Italy, male DJ/production/instrumental duo — 1

Date	Title	Peak Position	Weeks at No.1	Weeks on Chart
12 Feb 00	**THE CHASE** *Logic 74321732112*	46		1

DJ ERIC
UK, male vocal/DJ/production trio — 3

Date	Title	Peak Position	Weeks at No.1	Weeks on Chart
13 Feb 99	**WE ARE LOVE** *Distinctive DISNCD 49*	37		2
10 Jun 00	**DESIRE** *Distinctive DISNCD 56*	67		1

DJ 'FAST' EDDIE
US, male producer (Eddie Smith) — 15

Date	Title	Peak Position	Weeks at No.1	Weeks on Chart
11 Apr 87	**CAN U DANCE** *Champion CHAMP 41* KENNY 'JAMMIN' JASON & 'FAST' EDDIE SMITH	71		2
14 Nov 87	**CAN U DANCE** *Champion CHAMP 41* KENNY 'JAMMIN' JASON & 'FAST' EDDIE SMITH	67		2
21 Jan 89	**HIP HOUSE/I CAN DANCE** *DJ International DJIN 5*	47		4
11 Mar 89	**YO YO GET FUNKY** *DJ International DJIN 7*	54		3
28 Oct 89	**GIT ON UP** *DJ International 6553667* FEATURING SUNDANCE	49		4

DJ FLAVOURS
UK, male DJ/producer (Neil Rumney). See NRG, Smokin Beats featuring Lyn Eden — 4

Date	Title	Peak Position	Weeks at No.1	Weeks on Chart
11 Oct 97	**YOUR CARESS (ALL I NEED)** *All Around The World CDGLOBE 160*	19		4

DJ FORMAT FEATURING CHALI 2NA & AKIL
UK/US, male rap/DJ/production trio — 1

Date	Title	Peak Position	Weeks at No.1	Weeks on Chart
22 Mar 03	**WE KNOW SOMETHING YOU DON'T KNOW** *Genuine GEN 004CDX*	73		1

DJ FRESH
UK, male DJ/producer (Dan Stein). See Bad Company, Fresh BC — 6

Date	Title	Peak Position	Weeks at No.1	Weeks on Chart
1 Nov 03	**DA LICKS/TEMPLE OF DOOM** *Breakbeat Kaos BBK001P*	60		1
31 Jul 04	**SUBMARINES** *Breakbeat Kaos BBK004*	73		1
30 Oct 04	**WHEN THE SUN GOES DOWN** *Breakbeat Kaos BBK005SCD* FEATURING ADAM F	68		1
12 Feb 05	**SUPERNATURE** *Breakbeat Kaos BBK006* BARON & FRESH	59		2
9 Jul 05	**TARANTULA/FASTEN YOUR SEATBELT** *Breakbeat Kaos BBK009SCD* PENDULUM & FRESH FEATURING SPYDA	60		1

DJ GARRY
Belgium, male DJ/producer (Marino Stephano) — 2

Date	Title	Peak Position	Weeks at No.1	Weeks on Chart
19 Jan 02	**DREAM UNIVERSE** *Xtravaganza XTRAV 32CDS*	36		2

DJ GERT
Belgium, male DJ/producer (Gert Rossenbacker) — 1

Date	Title	Peak Position	Weeks at No.1	Weeks on Chart
26 May 01	**GIVE ME SOME MORE** *Mostika 23200253*	50		1

DJ GREGORY
France, male DJ/producer (Gregory Darsa) — 2

Date	Title	Peak Position	Weeks at No.1	Weeks on Chart
9 Nov 02	**TROPICAL SOUNDCLASH** *Defected DFTD 061CDS*	59		1
11 Oct 03	**ELLE/TROPICAL SOUNDCLASH** *Defected DFTD 077CDX*	73		1

DJ HYPE
UK, male producer (Kevin Ford) — 2

Date	Title	Peak Position	Weeks at No.1	Weeks on Chart
20 Mar 93	**SHOT IN THE DARK** *Suburban Base SUBBASE 20CD*	63		1
2 Jun 01	**CASINO ROYALE/DEAD A'S** *True Playaz TPRCD 004* DJ ZINC/DJ HYPE	58		1

DJ INNOCENCE FEATURING ALEX CHARLES
UK, male/female vocal/DJ/production duo — 1

Date	Title	Peak Position	Weeks at No.1	Weeks on Chart
6 Apr 02	**SO BEAUTIFUL** *Echo ECSCD 119*	51		1

DJ JEAN
Holland, male DJ/producer (Jan Engelaar) — 11

Date	Title	Peak Position	Weeks at No.1	Weeks on Chart
11 Sep 99	**THE LAUNCH** *AM:PM CDAMPM 123* ●	2		11

DJ JURGEN PRESENTS ALICE DEEJAY
Holland, male/female vocal/DJ/production group – Jurgen Rijkers, Judith Pronk, Kalmani (Eelke Kalberg) & Pronti (Sebastiaan Molijn) — 16

Date	Title	Peak Position	Weeks at No.1	Weeks on Chart
31 Jul 99	**BETTER OFF ALONE** *Positiva CDTIV 113* ⊛	2		16

DJ KOOL
US, male rapper/DJ/producer (John Bowman) — 7

Date	Title	Peak Position	Weeks at No.1	Weeks on Chart
22 Feb 97	**LET ME CLEAR MY THROAT** *American Recordings 74321452092*	8		7

○ Silver-selling · ● Gold-selling · ⊛ Platinum-selling (x multiples) · ★ US No.1 · Peak Position · Weeks at No.1 · Weeks on Chart

DJ KRUSH

	Japan, male DJ/producer (Hideaki Ishi)	Peak Position	Weeks at No.1	2
16 Mar 96	**MEISO** *Mo Wax MW 042CD*	52		1
12 Oct 96	**ONLY THE STRONG SURVIVE** *Mo Wax MW 060CD*	71		1

DJ LUCK & MC NEAT

	UK, male rap/DJ/production duo – Michael Rose & Joel Samuels	Peak Position	Weeks at No.1	44
25 Dec 99	**A LITTLE BIT OF LUCK** *Red Rose CDRROSE 1*	9		15
27 May 00	**MASTERBLASTER 2000** *Red Rose RROSE 002CD* FEATURING JJ	5		8
7 Oct 00	**AIN'T NO STOPPIN US** *Red Rose CDRROSE 004* FEATURING JJ	8		6
17 Mar 01	**PIANO LOCO** *Island CID 773*	12		8
8 Sep 01	**I'M ALL ABOUT YOU** *Island CID 781* FEATURING ARI GOLD	18		5
25 May 02	**IRIE** *Island CID 795* LUCK & NEAT	31		2

DJ MANTA

	Holland, male/female DJ/production trio	Peak Position	Weeks at No.1	1
9 Oct 99	**HOLDING ON** *AM:PM CDAMPM 125*	47		1

DJ MARKY & XRS FEATURING STAMINA MC

	Brazil/UK, male rap/vocal/DJ/production trio	Peak Position	Weeks at No.1	7
20 Jul 02	**LK (CAROLINA CAROL BELA)** *V Recordings V 035*	17		6
16 Nov 02	**LK (REMIX)** *V Recordings V 038*	45		1

DJ MIKO

	Italy, male producer (Monier Gagliardo)	Peak Position	Weeks at No.1	10
13 Aug 94	**WHAT'S UP** *Systematic SYSCD 2*	6		10

DJ MILANO FEATURING SAMANTHA FOX

	Italy/UK, male/female vocal/DJ/production duo	Peak Position	Weeks at No.1	2
28 Mar 98	**SANTA MARIA** *All Around The World CDGLOBE 163*	31		2

DJ MISJAH & DJ TIM

	Holland, male DJ/production/instrumental duo	Peak Position	Weeks at No.1	4
23 Mar 96	**ACCESS** *ffrreedom TABCD 240*	16		3
27 May 00	**ACCESS (REMIX)** *Tripoli Trax TTRAXCD 063*	45		1

DJ OTZI

	Austria, male DJ/producer (Gerry Friedle)	Peak Position	Weeks at No.1	48
18 Aug 01	**HEY BABY (IMPORT)** *EMI 8892462*	41		5
22 Sep 01	**HEY BABY** *EMI CDOTZI 001* ⊛	1	1	24
1 Dec 01	**DO WAH DIDDY** *EMI CDOTZI 002*	9		9
29 Dec 01	**X-MAS TIME** *EMI CDOTZI 003*	51		2
8 Jun 02	**HEY BABY (UNOFFICIAL WORLD CUP REMIX)** *EMI CDOTZI 004*	10		7
28 Dec 02	**LIVE IS LIFE** *Liberty CDLIVE001* HERMES HOUSE BAND & DJ OTZI	50		1

DJ PIED PIPER & THE MASTERS OF CEREMONIES

	UK, male rap/DJ/production group	Peak Position	Weeks at No.1	14
2 Jun 01	**DO YOU REALLY LIKE IT** *Relentless RELMOS 1* ●	1	1	14

DJ POWER

	Italy, male producer (Stefano Gambarelli)	Peak Position	Weeks at No.1	2
7 Mar 92	**EVERYBODY PUMP** *Cooltempo COOL 252*	46		2

DJ PROFESSOR

	Italy, male producer (Luca Lauri)	Peak Position	Weeks at No.1	6
10 Aug 91	**WE GOTTA DO IT** *Fourth & Broadway BRW 225* FEATURING FRANCESCO ZAPPALA	57		2
28 Mar 92	**ROCK ME STEADY** *PWL Continental PWL 219*	49		2
8 Oct 94	**ROCKIN' ME** *Citra 1CD* PROFESSOR	56		1
1 Mar 97	**WALKIN' ON UP** *Nukleuz MCSTD 40098* DJ PROF-X-OR	64		1

DJ Q FEATURING MC BONEZ

	UK, male DJ/production duo	Peak Position	Weeks at No.1	2
2 Aug 08	**YOU WOT?** *Maximum Bass MAXB001CDS*	50		2

DJ QUICKSILVER

	Turkey, male DJ/producer (Orhan Terzi). See Watergate	Peak Position	Weeks at No.1	29
5 Apr 97	**BELLISSIMA** *Positiva CDTIV 72* ●	4		17
6 Sep 97	**FREE** *Positiva CDTIVS 77*	7		7
21 Feb 98	**PLANET LOVE** *Positiva CDTIV 88*	12		5

DJ RAP

	UK, female vocalist/DJ/producer (Charissa Saverio)	Peak Position	Weeks at No.1	5
4 Jul 98	**BAD GIRL** *Higher Ground HIGHS 8CD*	32		2
17 Oct 98	**GOOD TO BE ALIVE** *Higher Ground HIGHS 14CD*	36		2
3 Apr 99	**EVERYDAY GIRL** *Higher Ground HIGHS 19CD*	47		1

DJ ROLANDO AKA AZTEC MYSTIC

	US, male DJ/producer (Rolando Rocha)	Peak Position	Weeks at No.1	2
21 Oct 00	**JAGUAR** *430 West 430 WUKTCD1*	43		2

DJ SAKIN & FRIENDS

	Germany, male DJ/producer (Sakin Botzkurt)	Peak Position	Weeks at No.1	18
20 Feb 99	**PROTECT YOUR MIND (FOR THE LOVE OF A PRINCESS)** *Positiva CDTIV 107* ○	4		11
5 Jun 99	**NOMANSLAND (DAVID'S SONG)** *Positiva CDTIV 112*	14		7

DJ SAMMY

	Spain, male DJ/producer (Samuel Bouriah)	Peak Position	Weeks at No.1	53
9 Nov 02	**HEAVEN** *Data 45CDS* & YANOU FEATURING DO ○	1	1	20
8 Mar 03	**THE BOYS OF SUMMER** *Data 49CDS*	2		13
21 Jun 03	**SUNLIGHT** *Data 54CDS*	8		9
25 Jun 05	**WHY** *Data 89CDS*	7		6
17 Nov 07	**HEAVEN** *Data/MOS DEN120110195* & YANOU FEATURING DO	69		1
7 Jun 08	**HEAVEN** *Data/MOS DEN120110195* & YANOU FEATURING DO	63		4

DJ SANDY VS HOUSETRAP

	Germany, male/female vocal/production duo	Peak Position	Weeks at No.1	2
1 Jul 00	**OVERDRIVE** *Positiva CDTIV 133*	32		2

DJ SCOT PROJECT

	Germany, male DJ/producer (Frank Zenker)	Peak Position	Weeks at No.1	2
27 Jul 96	**U (I GOT THE FEELING)** *Positiva CDTIV 55*	66		1
14 Feb 98	**Y (HOW DEEP IS YOUR LOVE)** *Perfecto PERF 158CD1*	57		1

DJ SCOTT FEATURING LORNA B

	UK, male/female vocal/DJ/production duo	Peak Position	Weeks at No.1	5
28 Jan 95	**DO YOU WANNA PARTY** *Steppin' Out SPONCD 2*	36		3
1 Apr 95	**SWEET DREAMS** *Steppin' Out SPONCD 3*	37		2

DJ DOC SCOTT

	UK, male producer (Scott McIlroy)	Peak Position	Weeks at No.1	2
1 Feb 92	**NHS (EP)** *Absolute 2 ABS 001DJ*	64		2

DJ SEDUCTION

	UK, male producer (John Kalkan)	Peak Position	Weeks at No.1	8
22 Feb 92	**HARDCORE HEAVEN/YOU AND ME** *ffrreedom TAB 103*	26		5
11 Jul 92	**COME ON** *ffrreedom TAB 111*	37		3

DJ SHADOW

	US, male producer (Josh Davis). See Unkle	Peak Position	Weeks at No.1	12
25 Mar 95	**WHAT DOES YOUR SOUL LOOK LIKE** *Mo Wax MW 027CD*	59		1
14 Sep 96	**MIDNIGHT IN A PERFECT WORLD** *Mo Wax MW 057CD*	54		1
9 Nov 96	**STEM** *Mo Wax MW 058CD*	74		1
11 Oct 97	**HIGH NOON** *Mo Wax MW 063CD*	22		2
20 Dec 97	**CAMEL BOBSLED RACE** *Mo Wax MW 084CD*	62		1
24 Jan 98	**WHAT DOES YOUR SOUL LOOK LIKE (PART 1)** *Mo Wax MW 087*	54		1
1 Jun 02	**YOU CAN'T GO HOME AGAIN** *Island CID 797*	30		2
2 Nov 02	**SIX DAYS** *Island CID 807*	28		2
20 Jan 07	**THIS TIME (I'M GONNA TRY IT MY WAY)** *Island 1716789*	54		1

Silver-selling ● Gold-selling ● Platinum-selling (x multiples) ✱ US No.1 ★ Peak Position · Weeks at No.1 · Weeks on Chart

DJ SHOG
Germany, male DJ/producer (Sven Greiner) — 2

Date	Title	Peak Position	Weeks at No.1	Weeks on Chart
20 Jul 02	**THIS IS MY SOUND** *NuLife 74321942272*	40		2

DJ SNEAK FEATURING BEAR WHO?
Puerto Rico/US, male DJ/production duo — 3

Date	Title	Peak Position	Weeks at No.1	Weeks on Chart
1 Feb 03	**FIX MY SINK** *Credence CDCREDS 033*	26		3

DJ SS
UK, male DJ/producer (Leroy Small) — 1

Date	Title	Peak Position	Weeks at No.1	Weeks on Chart
20 Apr 02	**THE LIGHTER** *Formation FORM 12093*	63		1

DJ SUPREME
UK, male DJ/producer (Nick Destri) — 11

Date	Title	Peak Position	Weeks at No.1	Weeks on Chart
5 Oct 96	**THA WILD STYLE** *Distinctive DISNCD 19*	39		2
3 May 97	**THA WILD STYLE** *Distinctive DISNCD 29*	24		2
6 Dec 97	**ENTER THE SCENE** *Distinctive DISNCD 40* VS THE RHYTHM MASTERS	49		1
21 Feb 98	**THA HORNS OF JERICHO** *All Around The World CDGLOBE 164*	29		2
16 Jan 99	**UP TO THE WILDSTYLE** *All Around The World CDGLOBE 170* PORN KINGS VERSUS DJ SUPREME	10		4

DJ TAUCHER
Germany, male DJ/producer (Ralf Armand Beck) — 1

Date	Title	Peak Position	Weeks at No.1	Weeks on Chart
8 May 99	**CHILD OF THE UNIVERSE** *Addictive 12AD 037*	74		1

DJ TIESTO
Holland, male DJ/producer (Tijs Verwest). See Gouryella — 32

Date	Title	Peak Position	Weeks at No.1	Weeks on Chart
12 May 01	**FLIGHT 643** *Nebula NEBCD 016*	56		1
29 Sep 01	**URBAN TRAIN** *VC Recordings/Nebula VCRD 95* FEATURING KIRSTY HAWKSHAW	22		3
13 Apr 02	**LETHAL INDUSTRY** *Nebula VCRD 103*	25		3
29 Jun 02	**643 (LOVE'S ON FIRE)** *Nebula VCRD 106* FEATURING SUZANNE PALMER	36		2
30 Nov 02	**OBSESSION** *Nebula NEBCD 029* TIESTO & JUNKIE XL	56		1
11 Oct 03	**TRAFFIC** *Nebula NEBCD 052* TIESTO	48		2
15 May 04	**LOVE COMES AGAIN** *Nebula NEBCD 058* TIESTO FEATURING BT	30		3
23 Oct 04	**JUST BE** *Nebula NEBCD062* TIESTO FEATURING KIRSTY HAWKSHAW	43		2
23 Apr 05	**ADAGIO FOR STRINGS** *Nebula NEBCD068* TIESTO	37		12
11 Nov 06	**DANCE4LIFE** *Nebula NEBCD100* TIESTO FEATURING MAXI JAZZ	67		1
10 Oct 09	**I WILL BE HERE** *14th Floor 14FLR39CD* TIESTO & SNEAKY SOUNDSYSTEM	44		2

DJ TOUCHE
UK, male DJ/producer (Theo Keating). See Wiseguys — 1

Date	Title	Peak Position	Weeks at No.1	Weeks on Chart
31 Jan 04	**THE PADDLE/THE GIRL'S A FREAK** *Southern Fried ECB60*	65		1

DJ VISAGE FEATURING CLARISSA
Denmark/Germany, male/female vocal/DJ/production duo — 1

Date	Title	Peak Position	Weeks at No.1	Weeks on Chart
10 Jun 00	**THE RETURN (TIME TO SAY GOODBYE)** *One Step Music OSMCDS 13*	58		1

DJ ZINC
UK, male DJ/producer (Benjamin Pettit) — 12

Date	Title	Peak Position	Weeks at No.1	Weeks on Chart
18 Nov 00	**138 TREK** *Phaze One CDX033*	27		3
2 Jun 01	**CASINO ROYALE/DEAD A'S** *True Playaz TPRCD 004* DJ ZINC/DJ HYPE	58		1
13 Apr 02	**REACHOUT** *True Playaz TPR 12039*	73		1
21 Sep 02	**FAIR FIGHT/AS WE DO** *BinGo! Beats BINGO 008*	72		1
13 Mar 04	**SKA** *True Playaz TPR12051*	54		1
15 May 04	**STEPPIN STONES/SOUTH PACIFIC** *BinGo! Beats BINGO 012*	62		1
8 Jan 05	**DRIVE BY CAR/INS** *BinGo! Beats BINGO023* FEATURING EKSMAN	66		1
20 Feb 10	**WILE OUT** *Zinc/Essential EAST001* ZINC FEATURING MS DYNAMITE	38		3

DJAIMIN
Switzerland (b. Germany), male producer (Dario Mancini) — 2

Date	Title	Peak Position	Weeks at No.1	Weeks on Chart
19 Sep 92	**GIVE YOU** *Cooltempo COOL 262*	45		2

DJD PRESENTS HYDRAULIC DOGS
UK, male producer (Dominic Dawson) — 1

Date	Title	Peak Position	Weeks at No.1	Weeks on Chart
8 Jun 02	**SHAKE IT BABY** *Direction 6721812*	56		1

DJH FEATURING STEFY
Italy, male production duo — 14

Date	Title	Peak Position	Weeks at No.1	Weeks on Chart
16 Feb 91	**THINK ABOUT...** *RCA PB 44385*	22		6
13 Jul 91	**I LIKE IT** *RCA PB 44741*	16		7
19 Oct 91	**MOVE YOUR LOVE** *RCA PB 44965*	73		1

DJPC
Belgium, male producer (Patrick Cools) — 5

Date	Title	Peak Position	Weeks at No.1	Weeks on Chart
26 Oct 91	**INSSOMNIAK** *Hype 7PUM 005*	62		4
29 Feb 92	**INSSOMNIAK** *Hype PUMR 005*	64		1

DJ'S RULE
Canada, male instrumental/production duo — 2

Date	Title	Peak Position	Weeks at No.1	Weeks on Chart
2 Mar 96	**GET INTO THE MUSIC** *Distinctive DISNCD 9*	72		1
5 Apr 97	**GET INTO THE MUSIC (REMIX)** *Distinctive DISNCDD 27* FEATURING KAREN BROWN	65		1

BORIS DLUGOSCH
Germany, male producer — 8

Date	Title	Peak Position	Weeks at No.1	Weeks on Chart
7 Dec 96	**KEEP PUSHIN'** *Manifesto FESCD 17* PRESENTS BOOOM!	41		2
13 Sep 97	**HOLD YOUR HEAD UP HIGH** *Positiva CDTIV 79* PRESENTS BOOOM!	23		2
16 Jun 01	**NEVER ENOUGH** *Positiva CDTIV 156* FEATURING ROISIN MURPHY	16		4

D'LUX
UK, male/female vocal/instrumental group — 1

Date	Title	Peak Position	Weeks at No.1	Weeks on Chart
22 Jun 96	**LOVE RESURRECTION** *Logic 74321371012*	58		1

DMAC
UK, male vocalist (Derek McDonald) — 2

Date	Title	Peak Position	Weeks at No.1	Weeks on Chart
27 Jul 02	**THE WORLD SHE KNOWS** *Chrysalis CDCHS 5140*	33		2

DMX
US, male rapper (Earl Simmons) — 27

Date	Title	Peak Position	Weeks at No.1	Weeks on Chart
15 May 99	**SLIPPIN'** *Def Jam 8707552*	30		2
15 Dec 01	**WHO WE BE** *Def Jam 5888512*	34		3
3 May 03	**X GON GIVE IT TO YA** *Def Jam 0779042*	6		12
11 Oct 03	**WHERE THE HOOD AT?** *Def Jam 9811251*	16		5
10 Jan 04	**GET IT ON THE FLOOR** *Def Jam 9815206* FEATURING SWIZZ BEATZ	34		4
22 Apr 06	**INNOCENT MAN** *Mona MONASP5CDS* MARK MORRISON FEATURING DMX	46		1

DNA
UK, male production duo – Neal Slateford & Nick Batt — 29

Date	Title	Peak Position	Weeks at No.1	Weeks on Chart
28 Jul 90	**TOM'S DINER** *A&M AM 592* FEATURING SUZANNE VEGA ●	2		10
18 Aug 90	**LA SERENISSIMA** *Raw Bass RBASS 006*	34		8
3 Aug 91	**REBEL WOMAN** *DNA 7DNA 001* FEATURING JAZZI P	42		4
1 Feb 92	**CAN YOU HANDLE IT** *EMI EM 219* FEATURING SHARON REDD	17		5
9 May 92	**BLUE LOVE (CALL MY NAME)** *EMI EM 226* FEATURING JOE NYE	66		2

DO ME BAD THINGS
UK, male/female vocal/instrumental group — 4

Date	Title	Peak Position	Weeks at No.1	Weeks on Chart
6 Nov 04	**TIME FOR DELIVERANCE** *Must Destroy MDA002CD*	57		1
9 Apr 05	**WHAT'S HIDEOUS** *Must Destroy MDA003CD*	33		2
25 Jun 05	**MOVE IN STEREO (LIV ULLMAN ON DRUMS)** *Must Destroy MDA004CD*	49		1

CARL DOBKINS, JR
US, male vocalist — 1

Date	Title	Peak Position	Weeks at No.1	Weeks on Chart
31 Mar 60	**LUCKY DEVIL** *Brunswick 05817*	44		1

ANITA DOBSON
UK, female vocalist/actor — 13

Date	Title	Peak Position	Weeks at No.1	Weeks on Chart
9 Aug 86	**ANYONE CAN FALL IN LOVE** *BBC RESL 191* FEATURING THE SIMON MAY ORCHESTRA ●	4		9
18 Jul 87	**TALKING OF LOVE** *Parlophone R 6159*	43		4

FEFE DOBSON

US, female vocalist — 2

Date	Title	Peak Position	Weeks at No.1	Weeks on Chart
8 May 04	**EVERYTHING** *Mercury 9862501*	42		2

DR ALBAN

Nigeria, male vocalist/producer (Alban Nwapa) — 28

Date	Title	Peak Position	Weeks at No.1	Weeks on Chart
5 Sep 92	**IT'S MY LIFE** *Logic 74321153307*	2		12
14 Nov 92	**ONE LOVE** *Logic 74321108727*	45		2
10 Apr 93	**SING HALLELUJAH!** *Logic 74321136202*	16		8
26 Mar 94	**LOOK WHO'S TALKING** *Logic 74321195342*	55		3
13 Aug 94	**AWAY FROM HOME** *Logic 74321222682*	42		2
29 Apr 95	**SWEET DREAMS** *Logic 74321251552* SWING FEATURING DR ALBAN	59		1

DOCTOR & THE MEDICS

UK, male/female vocal/instrumental group – Clive 'The Doctor' Jackson, 'Anadin Brothers' (Colette Appleby & Wendi West), Steve McGuire, Steve 'Vom' Ritchie & Richard Searle — 25

Date	Title	Peak Position	Weeks at No.1	Weeks on Chart
10 May 86	**SPIRIT IN THE SKY** *IRS IRM 113* ●	1	3	15
9 Aug 86	**BURN** *IRS IRM 119*	29		6
22 Nov 86	**WATERLOO** *IRS IRM 125* FEATURING ROY WOOD	45		4

DR DRE

US, male rapper/producer (Andre Young). See NWA — 96

Date	Title	Peak Position	Weeks at No.1	Weeks on Chart
22 Jan 94	**NUTHIN' BUT A 'G' THANG/LET ME RIDE** *Death Row A 8328CD*	31		3
3 Sep 94	**DRE DAY** *Death Row A 8292CD*	59		2
15 Apr 95	**NATURAL BORN KILLAZ** *Death Row A 8197CD* & ICE CUBE	45		2
10 Jun 95	**KEEP THEIR HEADS RINGIN'** *Priority PTYCD 103*	25		4
13 Apr 96	**CALIFORNIA LOVE** *Death Row DRWCD 3* 2PAC FEATURING DR DRE	6		8
19 Oct 96	**NO DIGGITY** *Interscope IND 95003* BLACKstreet FEATURING DR DRE ★	9		7
11 Jul 98	**ZOOM** *Interscope IND 95594* & LL COOL J	15		3
14 Aug 99	**GUILTY CONSCIENCE** *Interscope IND 4971282* EMINEM FEATURING DR DRE	5		8
25 Mar 00	**STILL DRE** *Interscope 4972862* FEATURING SNOOP DOGGY DOGG	6		10
10 Jun 00	**FORGOT ABOUT DRE** *Interscope 4973422* FEATURING EMINEM	7		9
3 Feb 01	**THE NEXT EPISODE** *Interscope 4974762* FEATURING SNOOP DOGGY DOGG	3		10
19 Jan 02	**BAD INTENTIONS** *Interscope 4973932* FEATURING KNOC-TURN'AL	4		10
14 Feb 04	**THE NEXT EPISODE** *Interscope 4974762* FEATURING SNOOP DOGGY DOGG	58		2
14 Feb 04	**BAD INTENTIONS** *Interscope 4973932* FEATURING KNOC-TURN'AL	67		1
14 Feb 09	**CRACK A BOTTLE** *Interscope USUM70951735* EMINEM, DR DRE & 50 CENT ★	4		17

DR FEELGOOD

UK, male vocal/instrumental group – Lee Brilleaux, d. 7 Apr 1994, The Big Figure (John Martin), Wilko Johnson & John B Sparks — 29

Date	Title	Peak Position	Weeks at No.1	Weeks on Chart
11 Jun 77	**SNEAKIN' SUSPICION** *United Artists UP 36255*	47		3
24 Sep 77	**SHE'S A WIND UP** *United Artists UP 36304*	34		5
30 Sep 78	**DOWN AT THE DOCTOR'S** *United Artists UP 36444*	48		5
20 Jan 79	**MILK AND ALCOHOL** *United Artists UP 36468* ●	9		9
5 May 79	**AS LONG AS THE PRICE IS RIGHT** *United Artists YUP 36506*	40		6
8 Dec 79	**PUT HIM OUT OF YOUR MIND** *United Artists BP 306*	73		1

DR HOOK

US, male vocal/instrumental group – Dennis Locorriere, Rik Elswit, Billy Francis, Bob Henke & Ray Sawyer — 104

Date	Title	Peak Position	Weeks at No.1	Weeks on Chart
24 Jun 72	**SYLVIA'S MOTHER** *CBS 7929* & THE MEDICINE SHOW	2		13
26 Jun 76	**A LITTLE BIT MORE** *Capitol CL 15871* ●	2		14
30 Oct 76	**IF NOT YOU** *Capitol CL 15885*	5		10
25 Mar 78	**MORE LIKE THE MOVIES** *Capitol CL 15967*	14		10
22 Sep 79	**WHEN YOU'RE IN LOVE WITH A BEAUTIFUL WOMAN** *Capitol CL 16039* ●	1	3	17
5 Jan 80	**BETTER LOVE NEXT TIME** *Capitol CL 16112*	8		8
29 Mar 80	**SEXY EYES** *Capitol CL 16127*	4		9
23 Aug 80	**YEARS FROM NOW** *Capitol CL 16154*	47		6
8 Nov 80	**SHARING THE NIGHT TOGETHER** *Capitol CL 16171*	43		4
22 Nov 80	**GIRLS CAN GET IT** *Mercury MER 51*	40		5
1 Feb 92	**WHEN YOU'RE IN LOVE WITH A BEAUTIFUL WOMAN** *Capitol EMCT 4*	44		4
6 Jun 92	**A LITTLE BIT MORE** *EMI EMCT 6*	47		4

DR OCTAGON

US, male producer (Keith Thornton) — 1

Date	Title	Peak Position	Weeks at No.1	Weeks on Chart
7 Sep 96	**BLUE FLOWERS** *Mo Wax MW055CD*	66		1

DOCTOR SPIN

UK, male instrumental/production duo – Andrew Lloyd Webber & Nigel Wright — 8

Date	Title	Peak Position	Weeks at No.1	Weeks on Chart
3 Oct 92	**TETRIS** *Carpet CRPT 4*	6		8

KEN DODD

UK, male vocalist/comedian. Veteran comic and balladeer from Knotty Ash who was one of Liverpool's top-selling acts of the 1960s. Ironically, the man who has made millions laugh in his 56-year career is best known for 'Tears', which sold over 1.5 million copies — 233

Date	Title	Peak Position	Weeks at No.1	Weeks on Chart
7 Jul 60	**LOVE IS LIKE A VIOLIN** *Decca F 11248*	8		18
15 Jun 61	**ONCE IN EVERY LIFETIME** *Decca F 11355*	28		18
1 Feb 62	**PIANISSIMO** *Decca F 11422*	21		15
29 Aug 63	**STILL** *Columbia DB 7094*	35		10
6 Feb 64	**EIGHT BY TEN** *Columbia DB 7191*	22		11
23 Jul 64	**HAPPINESS** *Columbia DB 7325*	31		13
26 Nov 64	**SO DEEP IS THE NIGHT** *Columbia DB 7398*	31		7
2 Sep 65	**TEARS** *Columbia DB 7659*	1	5	24
18 Nov 65	**THE RIVER (LE COLLINE SONO IN FIORO)** *Columbia DB 7750*	3		14
12 May 66	**PROMISES** *Columbia DB 7914*	6		14
4 Aug 66	**MORE THAN LOVE** *Columbia DB 7976*	14		11
27 Oct 66	**IT'S LOVE** *Columbia DB 8031*	36		7
19 Jan 67	**LET ME CRY ON YOUR SHOULDER** *Columbia DB 8101*	11		10
30 Jul 69	**TEARS WON'T WASH AWAY THESE HEARTACHES** *Columbia DB 8600*	22		11
5 Dec 70	**BROKEN HEARTED** *Columbia DB 8725*	15		10
10 Jul 71	**WHEN LOVE COMES ROUND AGAIN (L'ARCA DI NOE)** *Columbia DB 8796*	19		16
18 Nov 72	**JUST OUT OF REACH (OF MY TWO EMPTY ARMS)** *Columbia DB 8947*	29		11
29 Nov 75	**(THINK OF ME) WHEREVER YOU ARE** *EMI 2342*	21		8
26 Dec 81	**HOLD MY HAND** *Images IMGS 0002*	44		5

DODGY

UK, male vocal/instrumental trio – Nigel Clark, Andy Miller & Mathew Priest — 41

Date	Title	Peak Position	Weeks at No.1	Weeks on Chart
8 May 93	**LOVEBIRDS** *A&M AMCD 0177*	65		2
3 Jul 93	**I NEED ANOTHER (EP)** *A&M 5803172*	67		2
6 Aug 94	**THE MELOD-EP** *Bostin 5806772*	53		1
1 Oct 94	**STAYING OUT FOR THE SUMMER** *Bostin 5807972*	38		2
7 Jan 95	**SO LET ME GO FAR** *Bostin 5809032*	30		3
11 Mar 95	**MAKING THE MOST OF** *Bostin 5809892* WITH THE KICK HORNS	22		3
10 Jun 95	**STAYING OUT FOR THE SUMMER (REMIX)** *Bostin 5810952*	19		5
8 Jun 96	**IN A ROOM** *A&M 5816252*	12		6
10 Aug 96	**GOOD ENOUGH** *A&M 5818152*	4		8
16 Nov 96	**IF YOU'RE THINKING OF ME** *A&M 5819992*	11		4
15 Mar 97	**FOUND YOU** *A&M 5821332*	19		3
26 Sep 98	**EVERY SINGLE DAY** *A&M MERCD 512*	32		2

DOES IT OFFEND YOU, YEAH?

UK, male vocal/instrumental group — 1

Date	Title	Peak Position	Weeks at No.1	Weeks on Chart
6 Sep 08	**DAWN OF THE DEAD** *Virgin GBAAA0701972*	41		1

TIM DOG

US, male rapper (Timothy Blair) — 3

Date	Title	Peak Position	Weeks at No.1	Weeks on Chart
29 Oct 94	**BITCH WITH A PERM** *Dis-stress DISCD 1*	49		1
11 Feb 95	**MAKE WAY FOR THE INDIAN** *Island CID 586* APACHE INDIAN & TIM DOG	29		2

DOG EAT DOG

US, male vocal/instrumental group – John Connor, Brandon Finley, Scott Mueller, Dan Nastasi (replaced by Sean Kilkenny) & Dave Neabore — 7

Date	Title	Peak Position	Weeks at No.1	Weeks on Chart
19 Aug 95	**NO FRONTS** *Roadrunner RR 23312*	64		1
3 Feb 96	**NO FRONTS – THE REMIXES** *Roadrunner RR 23313*	9		5
13 Jul 96	**ISMS** *Roadrunner RR 23083*	43		1

NATE DOGG

US, male vocalist (Nathaniel Hale) — 41

Date	Title	Peak Position	Weeks at No.1	Weeks on Chart
23 Jul 94	**REGULATE** *Death Row A 8290CD* WARREN G & NATE DOGG ●	5		14
3 Feb 01	**OH NO** *Rawkus RWK 302* MOS DEF & NATE DOGG FEATURING PHAROAHE MONCH	24		4
25 Aug 01	**WHERE I WANNA BE** *London LONCD 461* SHADE SHEIST FEATURING NATE DOGG & KURUPT	14		7
29 Sep 01	**AREA CODES** *Def Jam 5887722* LUDACRIS FEATURING NATE DOGG	25		3

Silver-selling ● Gold-selling ● Platinum-selling (x multiples) ⊛ US No.1 ★ Peak Position · Weeks at No.1 · Weeks on Chart

Date	Title	Peak	Wks at No.1	Wks on Chart
1 Mar 03	**THE STREETS** *Def Jam 0779852* WC FEATURING SNOOP DOGG & NATE DOGG	48		2
12 Jul 03	**21 QUESTIONS** *Interscope 9807195* 50 CENT FEATURING NATE DOGG ★	6		8
14 Feb 04	**THE SET UP (YOU DON'T KNOW)** *Interscope 9815333* OBIE TRICE FEATURING NATE DOGG	32		3

DOGS

UK, male vocal/instrumental group — 5

Date	Title	Peak	Wks at No.1	Wks on Chart
5 Mar 05	**SHE'S GOT A REASON** *Island/Uni-Island CID882*	36		1
14 May 05	**TUNED TO A DIFFERENT STATION** *Island CID891*	29		2
30 Jul 05	**SELFISH WAYS** *Island CID901*	45		1
10 Dec 05	**TARRED & FEATHERED (WHAT A BAD BOY)** *Island CID908*	64		1

DOGS D'AMOUR

UK, male vocal/instrumental group — 15

Date	Title	Peak	Wks at No.1	Wks on Chart
4 Feb 89	**HOW COME IT NEVER RAINS** *China 13*	44		3
5 Aug 89	**SATELLITE KID** *China 17*	26		3
14 Oct 89	**TRAIL OF TEARS** *China 20*	47		3
23 Jun 90	**VICTIMS OF SUCCESS** *China 24*	36		3
15 Sep 90	**EMPTY WORLD** *China 27*	61		2
19 Jun 93	**ALL OR NOTHING** *China WOKCD 2033*	53		1

DOGS DIE IN HOT CARS

UK, male/female vocal/instrumental group — 5

Date	Title	Peak	Wks at No.1	Wks on Chart
8 May 04	**GODHOPPING** *V2 VVR 5025868*	24		2
17 Jul 04	**I LOVE YOU 'CAUSE I HAVE TO** *V2 VVR 5025878*	32		2
16 Oct 04	**LOUNGER** *V2 VVR5028213*	43		1

KEN DOH

UK, male producer (Michael Devlin) — 7

Date	Title	Peak	Wks at No.1	Wks on Chart
30 Mar 96	**NAKASAKI EP (I NEED A LOVER TONIGHT)** *ffrr FCD 272*	7		7

PETE DOHERTY

UK, male vocalist/multi-instrumentalist. See Babyshambles, Libertines — 14

Date	Title	Peak	Wks at No.1	Wks on Chart
24 Apr 04	**FOR LOVERS** *Rough Trade RTRADSCD177* WOLFMAN FEATURING PETE DOHERTY	7		6
22 May 04	**BABYSHAMBLES** *High Society HSCDS003*	32		1
29 Oct 05	**THEIR WAY** *Rough Trade RTRADSCD267* LITTL'ANS FEATURING PETER DOHERTY	22		2
30 Sep 06	**PRANGIN' OUT** *Locked On/679 679L141CD1* STREETS FEATURING PETE DOHERTY	25		4
21 Mar 09	**LAST OF THE ENGLISH ROSES** *Parlophone CDR6770*	67		1

JOE DOLAN

Ireland, male vocalist — 40

Date	Title	Peak	Wks at No.1	Wks on Chart
25 Jun 69	**MAKE ME AN ISLAND** *Pye 7N 17738*	3		19
1 Nov 69	**TERESA** *Pye 7N 17833*	20		7
28 Feb 70	**YOU'RE SUCH A GOOD LOOKING WOMAN** *Pye 7N 17891*	17		13
17 Sep 77	**I NEED YOU** *Pye 7N 45702*	43		1

THOMAS DOLBY

UK, male vocalist/producer (Thomas Robertson) — 51

Date	Title	Peak	Wks at No.1	Wks on Chart
3 Oct 81	**EUROPA AND THE PIRATE TWINS** *Parlophone R 6051*	48		3
14 Aug 82	**WINDPOWER** *Venice In Peril VIPS 103*	31		8
6 Nov 82	**SHE BLINDED ME WITH SCIENCE** *Venice In Peril VIPS 104*	49		4
16 Jul 83	**SHE BLINDED ME WITH SCIENCE** *Venice In Peril VIPS 105*	56		4
21 Jan 84	**HYPERACTIVE** *Parlophone Odeon R 6065*	17		9
31 Mar 84	**I SCARE MYSELF** *Parlophone Odeon R 6067*	46		5
16 Apr 88	**AIRHEAD** *Manhattan MT 38*	53		3
9 May 92	**CLOSE BUT NO CIGAR** *Virgin VS 1410*	22		5
11 Jul 92	**I LOVE YOU GOODBYE** *Virgin VS 1417*	36		4
26 Sep 92	**SILK PYJAMAS** *Virgin VS 1430*	62		2
22 Jan 94	**HYPERACTIVE** *Parlophone CDEMCTS 10*	23		4

JOE DOLCE MUSIC THEATRE

Australia (b. US), male vocalist — 10

Date	Title	Peak	Wks at No.1	Wks on Chart
7 Feb 81	**SHADDAP YOU FACE** *Epic EPC 9518* ●	1	3	10

DOLL

UK, male/female vocal/instrumental group — 8

Date	Title	Peak	Wks at No.1	Wks on Chart
13 Jan 79	**DESIRE ME** *Beggars Banquet BEG 11*	28		8

DOLLAR

UK, male/female vocal duo – David Van Day & Thereze Bazar — 128

Date	Title	Peak	Wks at No.1	Wks on Chart
11 Nov 78	**SHOOTING STAR** *Carrere 2871* ●	14		12
19 May 79	**WHO WERE YOU WITH IN THE MOONLIGHT** *Carrere CAR 110*	14		12
18 Aug 79	**LOVE'S GOTTA HOLD ON ME** *Carrere CAR 122* ●	4		13
24 Nov 79	**I WANNA HOLD YOUR HAND** *Carrere CAR 131*	9		14
25 Oct 80	**TAKIN' A CHANCE ON YOU** *WEA K 18353*	62		3
15 Aug 81	**HAND HELD IN BLACK AND WHITE** *WEA BUCK 1*	19		12
14 Nov 81	**MIRROR MIRROR (MON AMOUR)** *WEA BUCK 2* ●	4		17
20 Mar 82	**RING RING** *Carrere CAR 225*	61		2
27 Mar 82	**GIVE ME BACK MY HEART** *WEA BUCK 3* ●	4		9
19 Jun 82	**VIDEOTHEQUE** *WEA BUCK 4*	17		10
18 Sep 82	**GIVE ME SOME KINDA MAGIC** *WEA BUCK 5*	34		6
16 Aug 86	**WE WALKED IN LOVE** *Arista DIME 1*	61		4
26 Dec 87	**O L'AMOUR** *London LON 146*	7		11
16 Jul 88	**IT'S NATURE'S WAY (NO PROBLEM)** *London LON 179*	58		3

DOLLY ROCKERS

UK, female vocal group — 1

Date	Title	Peak	Wks at No.1	Wks on Chart
12 Sep 09	**GOLD DIGGER** *Parlophone CDR6775*	46		1

JAMES DOMAN

Canada, male DJ/producer — 4

Date	Title	Peak	Wks at No.1	Wks on Chart
27 Sep 08	**ALRIGHT** *Positiva CDTIVX273*	50		1
21 Mar 09	**RUNNIN'** *Positiva 12TIV281* DOMAN & GOODING	56		3

PLACIDO DOMINGO

Spain, male vocalist (Jose Placido Domingo Embil) — 28

Date	Title	Peak	Wks at No.1	Wks on Chart
12 Dec 81	**PERHAPS LOVE** *CBS A 1905* WITH JOHN DENVER	46		9
27 May 89	**TILL I LOVED YOU** *CBS 6548437* & JENNIFER RUSH	24		9
16 Jun 90	**NESSUN DORMA FROM 'TURANDOT'** *Epic 6560057* LUIS COBOS FEATURING PLACIDO DOMINGO	59		2
30 Jul 94	**LIBIAMO/LA DONNA E MOBILE** *Teldec YZ 843CD* JOSE CARRERAS, PLACIDO DOMINGO & LUCIANO PAVAROTTI	21		4
25 Jul 98	**YOU'LL NEVER WALK ALONE** *Decca 4607982* CARRERAS/DOMINGO/ PAVAROTTI WITH MEHTA	35		4

DOMINO

US, male rapper (Shawn Ivy) — 6

Date	Title	Peak	Wks at No.1	Wks on Chart
22 Jan 94	**GETTO JAM** *Chaos 6600402*	33		4
14 May 94	**SWEET POTATO PIE** *Chaos 6603292*	42		2

FATS DOMINO

US, male vocalist/pianist (Antoine Domino) — 110

Date	Title	Peak	Wks at No.1	Wks on Chart
27 Jul 56	**I'M IN LOVE AGAIN** *London HLU 8280*	12		14
30 Nov 56	**BLUEBERRY HILL** *London HLU 8330*	6		15
25 Jan 57	**AIN'T THAT A SHAME** *London HLU 8173*	23		2
1 Feb 57	**HONEY CHILE** *London HLU 8356*	29		1
29 Mar 57	**BLUE MONDAY** *London HLP 8377*	23		2
19 Apr 57	**I'M WALKIN'** *London HLP 8407*	19		7
19 Jul 57	**VALLEY OF TEARS** *London HLP 8449*	25		1
28 Mar 58	**THE BIG BEAT** *London HLP 8575*	20		4
4 Jul 58	**SICK AND TIRED** *London HLP 8628*	26		1
22 May 59	**MARGIE** *London HLP 8865*	18		5
16 Oct 59	**I WANT TO WALK YOU HOME** *London HLP 8942*	14		5
18 Dec 59	**BE MY GUEST** *London HLP 9005*	11		12
17 Mar 60	**COUNTRY BOY** *London HLP 9073*	19		11
21 Jul 60	**WALKING TO NEW ORLEANS** *London HLP 9163*	19		10
10 Nov 60	**THREE NIGHTS A WEEK** *London HLP 9198*	45		2
5 Jan 61	**MY GIRL JOSEPHINE** *London HLP 9244*	32		4
27 Jul 61	**IT KEEPS RAININ** *London HLP 9374*	49		1
30 Nov 61	**WHAT A PARTY** *London HLP 9456*	43		1
29 Mar 62	**JAMBALAYA** *London HLP 9520*	41		1
31 Oct 63	**RED SAILS IN THE SUNSET** *HMV POP 1219*	34		6
24 Apr 76	**BLUEBERRY HILL** *United Artists UP 35797*	41		5

DON PABLO'S ANIMALS

Italy, male production trio – Paul Bisiach, Mauro Ferucci & Christian Hornbostel

Date	Title / Label	Peak	Wks at No.1	Wks on Chart: 10
19 May 90	**VENUS** *Rumour RUMA 18*	4		10

DON-E

UK, male vocalist (Donald McLean)

Date	Title / Label	Peak	Wks at No.1	Wks on Chart: 8
9 May 92	**LOVE MAKES THE WORLD GO ROUND** *Fourth & Broadway BRW 242*	18		6
25 Jul 92	**PEACE IN THE WORLD** *Fourth & Broadway BRW 256*	41		1
28 Feb 98	**DELICIOUS** *Mushroom MUSH 20CD* DENI HINES FEATURING DON-E	52		1

SIOBHAN DONAGHY

UK, female vocalist. See Sugababes

Date	Title / Label	Peak	Wks at No.1	Wks on Chart: 7
5 Jul 03	**OVERRATED** *London LONCD 476*	19		4
27 Sep 03	**TWIST OF FATE** *London LONCD 481*	52		1
21 Apr 07	**DON'T GIVE IT UP** *Parlophone CDR6729*	45		2

LONNIE DONEGAN

UK, male vocalist/guitarist/banjo player (Anthony Donegan), d. 4 Nov 2002 (age 71). Britain's most influential and successful act before The Beatles led the skiffle craze that convinced numerous '60s stars to take up music. He had an unprecedented 31 successive Top 30 hits and was the first UK male to score two US Top 10s

Date	Title / Label	Peak	Wks at No.1	Wks on Chart: 321
6 Jan 56	**ROCK ISLAND LINE** *Decca F 10647*	8		22
20 Apr 56	**STEWBALL** *Pye Nixa N 15036*	27		1
27 Apr 56	**LOST JOHN** *Pye Nixa N 15036*	2		17
6 Jul 56	**SKIFFLE SESSION EP** *Pye Nixa NJE 1017*	20		2
7 Sep 56	**BRING A LITTLE WATER SYLVIE/DEAD OR ALIVE** *Pye Nixa N 15071*	7		13
21 Dec 56	**LONNIE DONEGAN SHOWCASE (LP)** *Pye Nixa NPT 19012*	26		3
18 Jan 57	**DON'T YOU ROCK ME DADDY-O** *Pye Nixa N 15080*	4		17
5 Apr 57	**CUMBERLAND GAP** *Pye Nixa N 15087*	1	5	12
7 Jun 57	**GAMBLIN' MAN/PUTTING ON THE STYLE** *Pye Nixa N 15093*	1	2	19
11 Oct 57	**MY DIXIE DARLING** *Pye Nixa N 15108*	10		15
20 Dec 57	**JACK O' DIAMONDS** *Pye Nixa 7N 15116*	14		7
11 Apr 58	**GRAND COOLIE DAM** *Pye Nixa 7N 15129*	6		15
11 Jul 58	**SALLY DON'T YOU GRIEVE/BETTY BETTY BETTY** *Pye Nixa 7N 15148*	11		7
26 Sep 58	**LONESOME TRAVELLER** *Pye Nixa 7N 15158*	28		1
14 Nov 58	**LONNIE'S SKIFFLE PARTY** *Pye Nixa 7N 15165*	23		5
21 Nov 58	**TOM DOOLEY** *Pye Nixa 7N 15172*	3		14
6 Feb 59	**DOES YOUR CHEWING GUM LOSE IT'S FLAVOUR** *Pye 7N 15181*	3		12
8 May 59	**FORT WORTH JAIL** *Pye Nixa 7N 15198*	14		5
26 Jun 59	**THE BATTLE OF NEW ORLEANS** *Pye 7N 15206*	2		16
11 Sep 59	**SAL'S GOT A SUGAR LIP** *Pye 7N 15223*	13		4
4 Dec 59	**SAN MIGUEL** *Pye 7N 15237*	19		4
24 Mar 60	**MY OLD MAN'S A DUSTMAN** *Pye 7N 15256*	1	4	13
26 May 60	**I WANNA GO HOME** *Pye 7N 15267*	5		17
25 Aug 60	**LORELEI** *Pye 7N 15275*	10		8
24 Nov 60	**LIVELY** *Pye 7N 15312*	13		9
8 Dec 60	**VIRGIN MARY** *Pye 7N 15315*	27		5
11 May 61	**HAVE A DRINK ON ME** *Pye 7N 15354*	8		15
31 Aug 61	**MICHAEL ROW THE BOAT/LUMBERED** *Pye 7N 15371*	6		11
18 Jan 62	**THE COMANCHEROS** *Pye 7N 15410*	14		10
5 Apr 62	**THE PARTY'S OVER** *Pye 7N 15424*	9		12
16 Aug 62	**PICK A BALE OF COTTON** *Pye 7N 15455*	11		10

TANYA DONELLY

US, female vocalist/guitarist. See Belly, Throwing Muses

Date	Title / Label	Peak	Wks at No.1	Wks on Chart: 2
30 Aug 97	**PRETTY DEEP** *4AD BAD 7007CD*	55		1
6 Dec 97	**THE BRIGHT LIGHT** *4AD BAD 7012CD*	64		1

DONNAS

US, female vocal/instrumental group

Date	Title / Label	Peak	Wks at No.1	Wks on Chart: 5
12 Apr 03	**TAKE IT OFF** *Atlantic AT 0148CD*	38		2
5 Jul 03	**WHO INVITED YOU** *Atlantic AT 0156CD*	61		1
23 Oct 04	**FALL BEHIND ME** *Atlantic AT 0186CD*	55		1
19 Mar 05	**I DON'T WANT TO KNOW** *Atlantic AT0197CD*	55		1

RAL DONNER

US, male vocalist, d. 6 Apr 1984 (age 41)

Date	Title / Label	Peak	Wks at No.1	Wks on Chart: 10
21 Sep 61	**YOU DON'T KNOW WHAT YOU'VE GOT** *Parlophone R 4820*	25		10

DONOVAN

UK, male vocalist/guitarist (Donovan Leitch)

Date	Title / Label	Peak	Wks at No.1	Wks on Chart: 100
25 Mar 65	**CATCH THE WIND** *Pye 7N 15801*	4		13
3 Jun 65	**COLOURS** *Pye 7N 15866*	4		12
11 Nov 65	**TURQUOISE** *Pye 7N 15984*	30		6
8 Dec 66	**SUNSHINE SUPERMAN** *Pye 7N 17241* ★	2		11
9 Feb 67	**MELLOW YELLOW** *Pye 7N 17267*	8		8
25 Oct 67	**THERE IS A MOUNTAIN** *Pye 7N 17403*	8		11
21 Feb 68	**JENNIFER JUNIPER** *Pye 7N 17457*	5		11
29 May 68	**HURDY GURDY MAN** *Pye 7N 17537*	4		10
4 Dec 68	**ATLANTIS** *Pye 7N 17660*	23		8
9 Jul 69	**GOO GOO BARABAJAGAL (LOVE IS HOT)** *Pye 7N 17778* WITH THE JEFF BECK GROUP	12		9
1 Dec 90	**JENNIFER JUNIPER** *Fontana SYP 1* SINGING CORNER MEETS DONOVAN	68		1

JASON DONOVAN

Australia, male vocalist/actor

Date	Title / Label	Peak	Wks at No.1	Wks on Chart: 137
10 Sep 88	**NOTHING CAN DIVIDE US** *PWL 17* ○	5		12
10 Dec 88	**ESPECIALLY FOR YOU** *PWL 24* KYLIE MINOGUE & JASON DONOVAN ●	1	3	14
4 Mar 89	**TOO MANY BROKEN HEARTS** *PWL 32* ●	1	2	13
10 Jun 89	**SEALED WITH A KISS** *PWL 39*	1	2	10
9 Sep 89	**EVERY DAY (I LOVE YOU MORE)** *PWL 43*	2		9
9 Dec 89	**WHEN YOU COME BACK TO ME** *PWL 46* ●	2		11
7 Apr 90	**HANG ON TO YOUR LOVE** *PWL 51*	8		7
30 Jun 90	**ANOTHER NIGHT** *PWL 58*	18		5
1 Sep 90	**RHYTHM OF THE RAIN** *PWL 60*	9		6
27 Oct 90	**I'M DOING FINE** *PWL 69*	22		6
18 May 91	**RSVP** *PWL 80*	17		5
22 Jun 91	**ANY DREAM WILL DO** *Really Useful RUR 7* ●	1	2	12
24 Aug 91	**HAPPY TOGETHER** *PWL 203*	10		6
7 Dec 91	**JOSEPH MEGA REMIX** *Really Useful RUR 9* & ORIGINAL LONDON CAST FEATURING LINZI HATELY, DAVID EASTER & JOHNNY AMOBI	13		8
18 Jul 92	**MISSION OF LOVE** *Polydor PO 222*	26		4
28 Nov 92	**AS TIME GOES BY** *Polydor PO 245*	26		6
7 Aug 93	**ALL AROUND THE WORLD** *Polydor PZCD 278*	41		3

DONS FEATURING TECHNOTRONIC

Germany/Belgium, male production trio

Date	Title / Label	Peak	Wks at No.1	Wks on Chart: 3
5 Nov 05	**PUMP UP THE JAM** *Data DATA94CDS*	22		3

DOOBIE BROTHERS

US, male vocal/instrumental group – Patrick Simmons, Jeff 'Skunk' Baxter (replaced by John McFee), Cornelius Bumpus, d. 3 Feb 2004, John Hartman (replaced by Chet McCracken), Tom Johnston, Keith Knudsen d. 8 Feb 2005 (replaced by Mike Hossack), Bobby LaKind, d. 24 Dec 1992, Michael McDonald & Tiran Porter

Date	Title / Label	Peak	Wks at No.1	Wks on Chart: 45
9 Mar 74	**LISTEN TO THE MUSIC** *Warner Brothers K 16208*	29		7
7 Jun 75	**TAKE ME IN YOUR ARMS** *Warner Brothers K 16559*	29		5
17 Feb 79	**WHAT A FOOL BELIEVES** *Warner Brothers K 17314* ★	31		11
14 Jul 79	**MINUTE BY MINUTE** *Warner Brothers K 17411*	47		4
24 Jan 87	**WHAT A FOOL BELIEVES** *Warner Brothers W 8451* FEATURING MICHAEL McDONALD	57		3
29 Jul 89	**THE DOCTOR** *Capitol CL 536*	73		2
27 Nov 93	**LONG TRAIN RUNNIN'** *Warner Brothers W 0217CD*	7		10
14 May 94	**LISTEN TO THE MUSIC** *Warner Brothers W 0228CD*	37		3

DOOLALLY

UK, male production duo – Daniel Langsman & Stephen Meade. See Shanks & Bigfoot

Date	Title / Label	Peak	Wks at No.1	Wks on Chart: 16
14 Nov 98	**STRAIGHT FROM THE HEART** *Locked On LOX 104CD*	20		10
7 Aug 99	**STRAIGHT FROM THE HEART** *Chocolate Boy LOX 112CD*	9		6

DOOLEYS

UK, male vocal/instrumental group – Jim Dooley, Al Bogan, Anne, Frank, Helen, John & Kathy Dooley & Bob Walsh

Date	Title / Label	Peak	Wks at No.1	Wks on Chart: 83
13 Aug 77	**THINK I'M GONNA FALL IN LOVE WITH YOU** *GTO GT 95*	13		10
12 Nov 77	**LOVE OF MY LIFE** *GTO GT 110* ○	9		11
13 May 78	**DON'T TAKE IT LYIN' DOWN** *GTO GT 220*	60		3
2 Sep 78	**A ROSE HAS TO DIE** *GTO GT 229*	11		11
10 Feb 79	**HONEY I'M LOST** *GTO GT 242*	24		9
16 Jun 79	**WANTED** *GTO GT 249* ○	3		14
22 Sep 79	**THE CHOSEN FEW** *GTO GT 258* ○	7		11
8 Mar 80	**LOVE PATROL** *GTO GT 260*	29		7
6 Sep 80	**BODY LANGUAGE** *GTO GT 276*	46		4
10 Oct 81	**AND I WISH** *GTO GT 300*	52		3

VAL DOONICAN
Ireland, male vocalist/guitarist (Michael Doonican) — 143

Date	Title	Peak	Wks at No.1	Wks on Chart
15 Oct 64	**WALK TALL** *Decca F 11982*	3		21
21 Jan 65	**THE SPECIAL YEARS** *Decca F 12049*	7		13
8 Apr 65	**I'M GONNA GET THERE SOMEHOW** *Decca F 12118*	25		5
17 Mar 66	**ELUSIVE BUTTERFLY** *Decca F 12358*	5		12
3 Nov 66	**WHAT WOULD I BE** *Decca F 12505*	2		17
23 Feb 67	**MEMORIES ARE MADE OF THIS** *Decca F 12566*	11		12
25 May 67	**TWO STREETS** *Decca F 12608*	39		4
18 Oct 67	**IF THE WHOLE WORLD STOPPED LOVING** *Pye 7N 17396*	3		19
21 Feb 68	**YOU'RE THE ONLY ONE** *Pye 7N 17465*	37		4
12 Jun 68	**NOW** *Pye 7N 17534*	43		2
23 Oct 68	**IF I KNEW THEN WHAT I KNOW NOW** *Pye 7N 17616*	14		13
23 Apr 69	**RING OF BRIGHT WATER** *Pye 7N 17713*	48		1
4 Dec 71	**MORNING** *Philips 6006 177*	12		13
10 Mar 73	**HEAVEN IS MY WOMAN'S LOVE** *Philips 6028 031*	34		7

DOOP
Holland, male production duo – Fredrik 'Ferry' Ridderhof & Peter Garnefski — 12

Date	Title	Peak	Wks at No.1	Wks on Chart
12 Mar 94	**DOOP** *Citybeat CBE 774CD* ●	1	3	12

DOORS
US, male vocal/instrumental group – Jim Morrison, d. 3 Jul 1971, John Densmore, Robby Krieger & Ray Manzarek — 42

Date	Title	Peak	Wks at No.1	Wks on Chart
16 Aug 67	**LIGHT MY FIRE** *Elektra EKSN 45014* ★	49		1
28 Aug 68	**HELLO I LOVE YOU** *Elektra EKSN 45037* ★	15		12
16 Oct 71	**RIDERS ON THE STORM** *Elektra K 12021*	22		11
20 Mar 76	**RIDERS ON THE STORM** *Elektra K 12203*	33		5
3 Feb 79	**HELLO I LOVE YOU** *Elektra K 12215*	71		2
27 Apr 91	**BREAK ON THROUGH** *Elektra EKR 121*	64		2
1 Jun 91	**LIGHT MY FIRE** *Elektra EKR 125*	7		8
10 Aug 91	**RIDERS ON THE STORM** *Elektra EKR 131*	68		1

D.O.P.
UK, male instrumental/production duo — 2

Date	Title	Peak	Wks at No.1	Wks on Chart
3 Feb 96	**STOP STARTING TO START STOPPING (EP)** *Hi-Life 5779472*	58		1
13 Jul 96	**GROOVY BEAT** *Hi-Life 5750652*	54		1

DOPE SMUGGLAZ
UK, male DJ/production trio — 5

Date	Title	Peak	Wks at No.1	Wks on Chart
5 Dec 98	**THE WORD** *Mushroom PERFCDS 1*	62		1
7 Aug 99	**DOUBLE DOUBLE DUTCH** *Perfecto PERF 2CDS*	15		4

CHARLIE DORE
UK, female vocalist — 2

Date	Title	Peak	Wks at No.1	Wks on Chart
17 Nov 79	**PILOT OF THE AIRWAVES** *Island WIP 6526*	66		2

ANDREA DORIA
Italy, male producer/instrumentalist — 1

Date	Title	Peak	Wks at No.1	Wks on Chart
26 Apr 03	**BUCCI BAG** *Southern Fried ECB 38CDS*	57		1

DOROTHY
UK, male DJ/producer/instrumentalist (Paul Masterson). See Candy Girls, Clergy, Hi-Gate, Sleazesisters, Yomanda — 5

Date	Title	Peak	Wks at No.1	Wks on Chart
9 Dec 95	**WHAT'S THAT TUNE (DOO-DOO-DOO-DOO-DOO-DOO-DOO-DOO-DOO-DOO)** *RCA 74321330912*	31		5

LEE DORSEY
US, male vocalist (Irving Dorsey), d. 1 Dec 1986 (age 61) — 36

Date	Title	Peak	Wks at No.1	Wks on Chart
3 Feb 66	**GET OUT OF MY LIFE WOMAN** *Stateside SS 485*	22		7
5 May 66	**CONFUSION** *Stateside SS 506*	38		6
11 Aug 66	**WORKING IN THE COALMINE** *Stateside SS 528*	8		11
27 Oct 66	**HOLY COW** *Stateside SS 552*	6		12

MARC DORSEY
US, male vocalist — 1

Date	Title	Peak	Wks at No.1	Wks on Chart
19 Jun 99	**IF YOU REALLY WANNA KNOW** *Jive 0522592*	58		1

TOMMY DORSEY ORCHESTRA STARRING WARREN COVINGTON
US, male orchestra – leader d. 26 Nov 1956 (age 51) — 19

Date	Title	Peak	Wks at No.1	Wks on Chart
17 Oct 58	**TEA FOR TWO CHA CHA** *Brunswick 05757*	3		19

DOUBLE
Switzerland, male vocal/instrumental duo – Kurt 'Maloo' Meier & Felix Haug — 10

Date	Title	Peak	Wks at No.1	Wks on Chart
25 Jan 86	**THE CAPTAIN OF HER HEART** *Polydor POSP 779*	8		9
5 Dec 87	**DEVIL'S BALL** *Polydor POSP 888*	71		1

DOUBLE DEE FEATURING DANY
Italy, male vocal/production duo — 5

Date	Title	Peak	Wks at No.1	Wks on Chart
1 Dec 90	**FOUND LOVE** *Epic 6563766*	63		2
25 Nov 95	**FOUND LOVE (REMIX)** *Sony S2 DANUCD 1*	33		2
27 Sep 03	**SHINING** *Positiva CDTIV 194* DOUBLE DEE	58		1

DOUBLE 99
UK, male instrumental/production duo. See Cohen vs. Deluxe, Tim Deluxe, RIP Productions, Saffron Hill featuring Ben Onono — 9

Date	Title	Peak	Wks at No.1	Wks on Chart
31 May 97	**RIPGROOVE** *Satellite 74321485132*	31		3
1 Nov 97	**RIPGROOVE** *Satellite 74321529322*	14		6

DOUBLE SIX
UK, male vocal/instrumental group — 2

Date	Title	Peak	Wks at No.1	Wks on Chart
19 Sep 98	**REAL GOOD** *Multiply CDMULTY 39*	66		1
12 Jun 99	**BREAKDOWN** *Multiply CDMULTY 50*	59		1

DOUBLE TROUBLE & THE REBEL MC
UK, male production duo – Michael Menson, d. 13 Feb 1997, & Leigh Guest — 35

Date	Title	Peak	Wks at No.1	Wks on Chart
27 May 89	**JUST KEEP ROCKIN'** *Desire WANT 9*	11		12
7 Oct 89	**STREET TUFF** *Desire WANT 18*	3		14
12 May 90	**TALK BACK** *Desire WANT 27* DOUBLE TROUBLE FEATURING JANETTE SEWELL	71		1
30 Jun 90	**LOVE DON'T LIVE HERE ANYMORE** *Desire WANT 32* DOUBLE TROUBLE FEATURING JANETTE SEWELL & CARL BROWN	21		6
15 Jun 91	**RUB-A-DUB** *Desire WANT 41* DOUBLE TROUBLE	66		2

DOUBLE YOU?
Italy, male vocalist (William Naraine) — 3

Date	Title	Peak	Wks at No.1	Wks on Chart
2 May 92	**PLEASE DON'T GO** *ZYX 67488*	41		3

ROB DOUGAN
Australia, male vocalist/producer. See Our Tribe/One Tribe, Sphinx — 4

Date	Title	Peak	Wks at No.1	Wks on Chart
4 Apr 98	**FURIOUS ANGELS** *Cheeky CHEKCD 025*	42		1
6 Jul 02	**CLUBBED TO DEATH** *Cheeky 74321941702*	24		3

CARL DOUGLAS
Jamaica, male vocalist — 39

Date	Title	Peak	Wks at No.1	Wks on Chart
17 Aug 74	**KUNG FU FIGHTING** *Pye 7N 45377* ● ★	1	3	13
30 Nov 74	**DANCE THE KUNG FU** *Pye 7N 45418*	35		5
3 Dec 77	**RUN BACK** *Pye 7N 46018*	25		10
23 May 98	**KUNG FU FIGHTING** *All Around The World CDGLOBE 173* BUS STOP FEATURING CARL DOUGLAS	8		11

CAROL DOUGLAS
US, female vocalist — 4

Date	Title	Peak	Wks at No.1	Wks on Chart
22 Jul 78	**NIGHT FEVER** *Gull GULS 61*	66		4

CRAIG DOUGLAS
UK, male vocalist (Terence Perkins) — 112

Date	Title	Peak	Wks at No.1	Wks on Chart
12 Jun 59	**A TEENAGER IN LOVE** *Top Rank JAR 133*	13		11
7 Aug 59	**ONLY SIXTEEN** *Top Rank JAR 159*	1	4	15
22 Jan 60	**PRETTY BLUE EYES** *Top Rank JAR 268*	4		14
28 Apr 60	**THE HEART OF A TEENAGE GIRL** *Top Rank JAR 340*	10		9
11 Aug 60	**OH! WHAT A DAY** *Top Rank JAR 406*	43		1
20 Apr 61	**A HUNDRED POUNDS OF CLAY** *Top Rank JAR 555*	9		9

Date	Title	Peak Position	Weeks at No.1	Weeks on Chart
29 Jun 61	**TIME** *Top Rank JAR 569*	9		14
22 Mar 62	**WHEN MY LITTLE GIRL IS SMILING** *Top Rank JAR 610*	9		13
28 Jun 62	**OUR FAVOURITE MELODIES** *Columbia DB 4854*	9		10
18 Oct 62	**OH LONESOME ME** *Decca F 11523*	15		12
28 Feb 63	**TOWN CRIER** *Decca F 11575*	36		4

DOVE

Ireland, male/female vocal group — 2

Date	Title	Peak Position	Weeks at No.1	Weeks on Chart
11 Sep 99	**DON'T DREAM** *ZTT 135CD*	37		2

DOVES

UK, male vocal/instrumental trio – Jimi Goodwin & Andy & Jez Williams — 26

Date	Title	Peak Position	Weeks at No.1	Weeks on Chart
14 Aug 99	**HERE IT COMES** *Casino CHIP 003CD*	73		1
1 Apr 00	**THE CEDAR ROOM** *Heavenly HVN 95CD*	33		2
10 Jun 00	**CATCH THE SUN** *Heavenly HVN 96CDS*	32		2
11 Nov 00	**THE MAN WHO TOLD EVERYTHING** *Heavenly HVN 98CDS*	32		2
27 Apr 02	**THERE GOES THE FEAR** *Heavenly HVN 111CD*	3		3
3 Aug 02	**POUNDING** *Heavenly HVN 116CD*	21		3
26 Oct 02	**CAUGHT BY THE RIVER** *Heavenly HVN 126CDS*	29		2
19 Feb 05	**BLACK AND WHITE TOWN** *Heavenly HVN145CDS*	6		4
21 May 05	**SNOWDEN** *Heavenly HVN150CDS*	17		2
24 Sep 05	**SKY STARTS FALLING** *Heavenly HVN152CD*	45		1
11 Apr 09	**KINGDOM OF RUST** *Heavenly HVN188CD*	28		4

DOWLANDS

UK, male vocal/instrumental duo — 7

Date	Title	Peak Position	Weeks at No.1	Weeks on Chart
9 Jan 64	**ALL MY LOVING** *Oriole CB 1897*	33		7

ROBERT DOWNEY, JR

US, male vocalist/actor — 1

Date	Title	Peak Position	Weeks at No.1	Weeks on Chart
30 Jan 93	**SMILE** *Epic 6589052*	68		1

DON DOWNING

US, male vocalist — 10

Date	Title	Peak Position	Weeks at No.1	Weeks on Chart
10 Nov 73	**LONELY DAYS, LONELY NIGHTS** *People PEO 102*	32		10

WILL DOWNING

US, male vocalist — 35

Date	Title	Peak Position	Weeks at No.1	Weeks on Chart
2 Apr 88	**A LOVE SUPREME** *Fourth & Broadway BRW 90*	14		10
25 Jun 88	**IN MY DREAMS** *Fourth & Broadway BRW 104*	34		6
1 Oct 88	**FREE** *Fourth & Broadway BRW 112*	58		5
21 Jan 89	**WHERE IS THE LOVE** *Fourth & Broadway BRW 122* MICA PARIS & WILL DOWNING	19		7
28 Oct 89	**TEST OF TIME** *Fourth & Broadway BRW 146*	67		2
24 Feb 90	**COME TOGETHER AS ONE** *Fourth & Broadway BRW 159*	48		4
18 Sep 93	**THERE'S NO LIVING WITHOUT YOU** *Fourth & Broadway BRCD 278*	67		1

JASON DOWNS FEATURING MILK

US, male vocal/rap/production duo — 6

Date	Title	Peak Position	Weeks at No.1	Weeks on Chart
12 May 01	**WHITE BOY WITH A FEATHER** *Pepper 9230412*	19		5
14 Jul 01	**CAT'S IN THE CRADLE** *Pepper 9230442*	65		1

DRAGONHEART

UK, female vocal group — 1

Date	Title	Peak Position	Weeks at No.1	Weeks on Chart
27 Nov 04	**VIDEO KILLED THE RADIO STAR** *Lipstick 6150304*	74		1

DRAKE FEATURING KANYE WEST, LIL WAYNE & EMINEM

Canada, male rapper/actor (Aubrey Graham) & US, male rappers – Kanye West, Dwayne Carter, Jr. & Marshall Mathers III. See Young Money featuring Lloyd — 12

Date	Title	Peak Position	Weeks at No.1	Weeks on Chart
19 Dec 09	**FOREVER** *Interscope USUM70985104*	42		12

CHARLIE DRAKE

UK, male comedian/vocalist (Charles Sprigall), d. 23 Dec 2006 (age 81) — 37

Date	Title	Peak Position	Weeks at No.1	Weeks on Chart
8 Aug 58	**SPLISH SPLASH** *Parlophone R 4461*	7		11
24 Oct 58	**VOLARE** *Parlophone R 4478*	28		2
27 Oct 60	**MR CUSTER** *Parlophone R 4701*	12		12
5 Oct 61	**MY BOOMERANG WON'T COME BACK** *Parlophone R 4824*	14		11
1 Jan 72	**PUCKWUDGIE** *Columbia DB 8829*	47		1

NICK DRAKE

UK, male vocalist, d. 25 Nov 1974 (age 26) — 3

Date	Title	Peak Position	Weeks at No.1	Weeks on Chart
29 May 04	**MAGIC** *Island CID 854*	32		2
25 Sep 04	**RIVER MAN** *Island CID 871*	48		1

DRAMATIS

UK, male vocal/instrumental group — 8

Date	Title	Peak Position	Weeks at No.1	Weeks on Chart
5 Dec 81	**LOVE NEEDS NO DISGUISE** *Beggars Banquet BEG 33* GARY NUMAN & DRAMATIS	33		7
13 Nov 82	**I CAN SEE HER NOW** *Rocket XPRES 83*	57		1

RUSTY DRAPER

US, male vocalist (Farrell H. Draper), d. 29 Mar 2003 (age 80) — 4

Date	Title	Peak Position	Weeks at No.1	Weeks on Chart
11 Aug 60	**MULE SKINNER BLUES** *Mercury AMT 1101*	39		4

DREAD FLIMSTONE & THE NEW TONE AGE FAMILY

US, male producer (Rex Morgan) & male vocalists — 1

Date	Title	Peak Position	Weeks at No.1	Weeks on Chart
30 Nov 91	**FROM THE GHETTO** *Urban URB 87*	66		1

DREAD ZEPPELIN

US, male vocal/instrumental group — 3

Date	Title	Peak Position	Weeks at No.1	Weeks on Chart
1 Dec 90	**YOUR TIME IS GONNA COME** *IRS DREAD 1*	59		1
13 Jul 91	**STAIRWAY TO HEAVEN** *IRS DREAD 2*	62		2

DREADZONE

UK, male vocal/instrumental group — 15

Date	Title	Peak Position	Weeks at No.1	Weeks on Chart
6 May 95	**ZION YOUTH** *Virgin VSCDG 1537*	49		2
29 Jul 95	**CAPTAIN DREAD** *Virgin VSCDG 1541*	49		2
23 Sep 95	**MAXIMUM (EP)** *Virgin VSCDT 1555*	56		2
6 Jan 96	**LITTLE BRITAIN** *Virgin VSCDG 1565*	20		6
30 Mar 96	**LIFE LOVE AND UNITY** *Virgin VSCDT 1583*	56		1
10 May 97	**EARTH ANGEL** *Virgin VSCDT 1593*	51		1
26 Jul 97	**MOVING ON** *Virgin VSCDT 1635*	58		1

DREAM

US, female vocal group — 7

Date	Title	Peak Position	Weeks at No.1	Weeks on Chart
17 Mar 01	**HE LOVES U NOT** *Bad Boy 74321823542*	17		7

DREAM ACADEMY

UK, male/female vocal/instrumental trio — 10

Date	Title	Peak Position	Weeks at No.1	Weeks on Chart
30 Mar 85	**LIFE IN A NORTHERN TOWN** *Blanco Y Negro NEG 10*	15		8
14 Sep 85	**THE LOVE PARADE** *Blanco Y Negro NEG 16*	68		2

DREAM FREQUENCY

UK, male producer (Ian Bland) — 12

Date	Title	Peak Position	Weeks at No.1	Weeks on Chart
12 Jan 91	**LOVE PEACE AND UNDERSTANDING** *Citybeat CBE 756*	71		2
25 Jan 92	**FEEL SO REAL** *Citybeat CBE 763* FEATURING DEBBIE SHARP	23		5
25 Apr 92	**TAKE ME** *Citybeat CBE 768*	39		3
21 May 94	**GOOD TIMES/THE DREAM** *Citybeat CBE 773CD*	67		1
10 Sep 94	**YOU MAKE ME FEEL MIGHTY REAL** *Citybeat CBE 775CD*	65		1

DREAM WARRIORS

Canada, male rap/production duo — 19

Date	Title	Peak Position	Weeks at No.1	Weeks on Chart
14 Jul 90	**WASH YOUR FACE IN MY SINK** *Fourth & Broadway BRW 183*	16		8
24 Nov 90	**MY DEFINITION OF A BOOMBASTIC JAZZ STYLE** *Fourth & Broadway BRW 197*	13		8
2 Mar 91	**LUDI** *Fourth & Broadway BRW 206*	39		3

DREAMCATCHER

UK, male/female vocal/production trio — 4

Date	Title	Peak Position	Weeks at No.1	Weeks on Chart
12 Jan 02	**I DON'T WANT TO LOSE MY WAY** *Positiva CDTIVS 157*	14		4

DREAMHOUSE
UK, male vocal/instrumental group — **2**

Date	Title	Peak Position	Weeks at No.1	Weeks on Chart
3 Jun 95	**STAY** *Chase CDPALACE 1*	62		2

DREAMWEAVERS
US, male/female vocal trio – Wade Bluff, Gene Adkinson & Mary Rude — **18**

Date	Title	Peak Position	Weeks at No.1	Weeks on Chart
10 Feb 56	**IT'S ALMOST TOMORROW** *Brunswick 05515*	1	2	18

DREEM TEEM
UK, male DJ/production trio — **14**

Date	Title	Peak Position	Weeks at No.1	Weeks on Chart
13 Dec 97	**THE THEME** *4 Liberty 74321542032*	34		4
6 Nov 99	**BUDDY X 99** *4 Liberty LIBTCD33* VS NENEH CHERRY	15		5
15 Dec 01	**IT AIN'T ENOUGH** *ffrr/Public Demand FCD 401* VS ARTFUL DODGER	20		5

EDDIE DRENNON & B.B.S. UNLIMITED
US, male vocal/instrumental group — **6**

Date	Title	Peak Position	Weeks at No.1	Weeks on Chart
28 Feb 76	**LET'S DO THE LATIN HUSTLE** *Pye International 7N 25702*	20		6

ALAN DREW
UK, male vocalist — **2**

Date	Title	Peak Position	Weeks at No.1	Weeks on Chart
26 Sep 63	**ALWAYS THE LONELY ONE** *Columbia DB 7090*	48		2

DRIFTERS
US, male vocal group – members included Ben E. King*, Rudy Lewis, d. 20 May 1964, Clyde McPhatter, d. 13 Jun 1972, Johnny Moore, d. 30 Dec 1998, Bill Pinkney, d. 4 Jul 2007, & Charlie Thomas — **176**

Date	Title	Peak Position	Weeks at No.1	Weeks on Chart
8 Jan 60	**DANCE WITH ME** *London HLE 8988*	17		5
3 Nov 60	**SAVE THE LAST DANCE FOR ME** *London HLK 9201* ★	2		18
16 Mar 61	**I COUNT THE TEARS** *London HLK 9287*	28		6
5 Apr 62	**WHEN MY LITTLE GIRL IS SMILING** *London HLK 9522*	31		3
10 Oct 63	**I'LL TAKE YOU HOME** *London HLK 9785*	37		5
24 Sep 64	**UNDER THE BOARDWALK** *Atlantic AT 9785*	45		4
8 Apr 65	**AT THE CLUB** *Atlantic AT 4019*	35		7
29 Apr 65	**COME ON OVER TO MY PLACE** *Atlantic AT 4023*	40		5
2 Feb 67	**BABY WHAT I MEAN** *Atlantic 584 065*	49		1
25 Mar 72	**AT THE CLUB/SATURDAY NIGHT AT THE MOVIES** *Atlantic K 10148*	3		20
26 Aug 72	**COME ON OVER TO MY PLACE** *Atlantic K 10216*	9		11
4 Aug 73	**LIKE SISTER AND BROTHER** *Bell 1313*	7		12
15 Jun 74	**KISSIN' IN THE BACK ROW OF THE MOVIES** *Bell 1358* ○	2		13
12 Oct 74	**DOWN ON THE BEACH TONIGHT** *Bell 1381*	7		9
8 Feb 75	**LOVE GAMES** *Bell 1396*	33		6
6 Sep 75	**THERE GOES MY FIRST LOVE** *Bell 1433* ○	3		12
29 Nov 75	**CAN I TAKE YOU HOME LITTLE GIRL** *Bell 1462*	10		10
13 Mar 76	**HELLO HAPPINESS** *Bell 1469*	12		8
11 Sep 76	**EVERY NITE'S A SATURDAY NIGHT WITH YOU** *Bell 1491*	29		7
18 Dec 76	**YOU'RE MORE THAN A NUMBER IN MY LITTLE RED BOOK** *Arista 78* ○	5		12
14 Apr 79	**SAVE THE LAST DANCE FOR ME/WHEN MY LITTLE GIRL IS SMILING** *Lightning LIG 9014*	69		2

DRIFTWOOD
Holland, male production trio — **2**

Date	Title	Peak Position	Weeks at No.1	Weeks on Chart
1 Feb 03	**FREELOADER** *Positiva CDTIV 185*	32		2

JULIE DRISCOLL, BRIAN AUGER & THE TRINITY
UK, female vocalist & male instrumental group — **16**

Date	Title	Peak Position	Weeks at No.1	Weeks on Chart
17 Apr 68	**THIS WHEEL'S ON FIRE** *Marmalade 598 006*	5		16

MINNIE DRIVER
UK, female actor/vocalist — **3**

Date	Title	Peak Position	Weeks at No.1	Weeks on Chart
9 Oct 04	**EVERYTHING I'VE GOT IN MY POCKET** *Liberty 8674202*	34		2
22 Jan 05	**INVISIBLE GIRL** *Liberty 8703422*	68		1

DRIVER 67
UK, male vocalist (Paul Phillips) — **12**

Date	Title	Peak Position	Weeks at No.1	Weeks on Chart
23 Dec 78	**CAR 67** *Logo GO 336* ○	7		12

DRIZABONE
UK/US, male/female vocal/instrumental group — **18**

Date	Title	Peak Position	Weeks at No.1	Weeks on Chart
22 Jun 91	**REAL LOVE** *Fourth & Broadway BRW 223*	16		8
26 Oct 91	**CATCH THE FIRE** *Fourth & Broadway BRW 232*	54		2
23 Apr 94	**PRESSURE** *Fourth & Broadway BRCD 264*	33		2
15 Oct 94	**BRIGHTEST STAR** *Fourth & Broadway BRCD 293*	45		2
4 Mar 95	**REAL LOVE** *Fourth & Broadway BRCD 311*	24		4

FRANK D'RONE
US, male vocalist — **6**

Date	Title	Peak Position	Weeks at No.1	Weeks on Chart
22 Dec 60	**STRAWBERRY BLONDE (THE BAND PLAYED ON)** *Mercury AMT 1123*	24		6

DROWNING POOL
US, male vocal/instrumental group — **3**

Date	Title	Peak Position	Weeks at No.1	Weeks on Chart
27 Apr 02	**BODIES** *Epic 6723172*	34		2
10 Aug 02	**TEAR AWAY** *Epic 6729832*	65		1

DRU HILL
US, male vocal group – Sisqo* (Mark Andrews), Jazz (Larry Anthony, Jr), Woody (James Green) & Nokio (Tamir Ruffin) — **42**

Date	Title	Peak Position	Weeks at No.1	Weeks on Chart
15 Feb 97	**TELL ME** *Fourth & Broadway BRCD 342*	30		3
10 May 97	**IN MY BED** *Fourth & Broadway BRCD 353*	16		3
11 Oct 97	**BIG BAD MAMMA** *Def Jam 5749792* FOXY BROWN FEATURING DRU HILL	12		3
6 Dec 97	**5 STEPS** *Island Black Music CID 675*	22		3
24 Oct 98	**HOW DEEP IS YOUR LOVE** *Island Black Music CID 725* FEATURING REDMAN	9		8
6 Feb 99	**THESE ARE THE TIMES** *Island Black Music CID 733*	4		6
10 Jul 99	**WILD WILD WEST** *Columbia 6675962* WILL SMITH FEATURING DRU HILL ● ★	2		16

DRUGSTORE
UK/US/Brazil, male/female vocal/instrumental group — **5**

Date	Title	Peak Position	Weeks at No.1	Weeks on Chart
10 Jun 95	**FADER** *Honey HONCD 7*	72		1
2 May 98	**EL PRESIDENT** *Roadrunner RR 22369*	20		3
4 Jul 98	**SOBER** *Roadrunner RR 22303*	68		1

DRUM CLUB
UK, male production/instrumental duo — **1**

Date	Title	Peak Position	Weeks at No.1	Weeks on Chart
6 Nov 93	**SOUND SYSTEM** *Butterfly BFLD 10*	62		1

DRUM THEATRE
UK, male vocal/instrumental group — **8**

Date	Title	Peak Position	Weeks at No.1	Weeks on Chart
15 Feb 86	**LIVING IN THE PAST** *Epic A 6798*	67		2
17 Jan 87	**ELDORADO** *Epic EMU 1*	44		6

DRUMSOUND/SIMON BASSLINE SMITH
UK, male production duo — **2**

Date	Title	Peak Position	Weeks at No.1	Weeks on Chart
26 Jul 03	**JUNGLIST** *Technique TECH021*	67		1
12 Jun 04	**THE ODYSSEY/BODY MOVIN** *Prototype PROUK004*	66		1

DRUNKENMUNKY
Holland, male production group. See Da Techno Bohemian, Hi_Tack, Itty Bitty Boozy Woozy, Klubbheads — **2**

Date	Title	Peak Position	Weeks at No.1	Weeks on Chart
4 Oct 03	**E** *All Around The World CDGLOBE 285*	41		2

DRUPI
Italy, male vocalist (Giampiero Anelli) — **12**

Date	Title	Peak Position	Weeks at No.1	Weeks on Chart
1 Dec 73	**VADO VIA** *A&M AMS 7083*	17		12

DSK
UK, male production trio — **4**

Date	Title	Peak Position	Weeks at No.1	Weeks on Chart
31 Aug 91	**WHAT WOULD WE DO/READ MY LIPS** *Boy's Own BOI 6*	46		3
22 Nov 97	**WHAT WOULD WE DO (REMIX)** *Fresh FRSHD 63*	55		1

DSM
UK, male DJ/production group

Date	Title / Label	Peak Position	Weeks at No.1	Weeks on Chart
				4
7 Dec 85	**WARRIOR GROOVE** *10 DAZZ 45-7*	68		4

DT8 PROJECT
UK, male producer (Darren Tate). See Angelic, Citizen Caned, Orion, Jurgen Vries

Date	Title / Label	Peak Position	Weeks at No.1	Weeks on Chart
				8
3 May 03	**DESTINATION** *ffrr DFCD 007* DT8 FEATURING ROXANNE WILDE	23		3
14 Aug 04	**THE SUN IS SHINING (DOWN ON ME)** *Mondo MND019CD*	17		3
5 Mar 05	**WINTER** *Data 80CDS* FEATURING ANDREA BRITTON	35		2

DTI
UK, male producer (Paul Hardcastle)

Date	Title / Label	Peak Position	Weeks at No.1	Weeks on Chart
				1
16 Apr 88	**KEEP THIS FREQUENCY CLEAR** *Premiere UK ERE 501*	73		1

DTOX
UK, male/female vocal/production group

Date	Title / Label	Peak Position	Weeks at No.1	Weeks on Chart
				1
21 Nov 92	**SHATTERED GLASS** *Vitality VITal 1*	75		1

D12
US, male rap group – Eminem* (Marshall Mathers III), Bizarre* (Rufus Johnson), Bugz (Karnail Pitts), d. 21 May 1999 (replaced by Swift (Ondre Moore), Kon Artis (Denaun Porter), Kuniva (Von Carlisle) & Proof (DeShaun Holton), d. 11 Apr 2006

Date	Title / Label	Peak Position	Weeks at No.1	Weeks on Chart
				46
17 Mar 01	**SHIT ON YOU** *Interscope 4974962*	10		7
21 Jul 01	**PURPLE PILLS** *Interscope 4975692* ●	2		12
17 Nov 01	**FIGHT MUSIC** *Shady/Interscope 4976522*	11		5
14 Feb 04	**SHIT ON YOU** *Interscope 4974962*	71		1
24 Apr 04	**MY BAND** *Interscope 9862352*	2		13
7 Aug 04	**HOW COME** *Interscope 9863318*	4		8

JOHN DU CANN
UK, male vocalist

Date	Title / Label	Peak Position	Weeks at No.1	Weeks on Chart
				6
22 Sep 79	**DON'T BE A DUMMY** *Vertigo 6059 241*	33		6

DUALERS
UK, male vocal/instrumental duo

Date	Title / Label	Peak Position	Weeks at No.1	Weeks on Chart
				4
30 Oct 04	**KISS ON THE LIPS** *Galley Music GALLEY10003*	21		2
19 Nov 05	**TRULY MADLY DEEPLY** *Gut CDGUT73*	23		1
24 Jun 06	**DON'T GO** *Galley Music GALLEY104CDX*	61		1

DUB PISTOLS
UK, male vocal/instrumental/production group

Date	Title / Label	Peak Position	Weeks at No.1	Weeks on Chart
				2
10 Oct 98	**CYCLONE** *Concrete HARD 36CD*	63		1
18 Oct 03	**PROBLEM IS** *Distinctive DISNCD 107* FEATURING TERRY HALL	66		1

DUB WAR
UK, male vocal/instrumental group

Date	Title / Label	Peak Position	Weeks at No.1	Weeks on Chart
				5
3 Jun 95	**STRIKE IT** *Earache MOSH 138CD*	70		1
27 Jan 96	**ENEMY MAKER** *Earache MOSH 147CD*	41		2
24 Aug 96	**CRY DIGNITY** *Earache MOSH 163CD*	59		1
29 Mar 97	**MILLION DOLLAR LOVE** *Earache MOSH 170CD1*	73		1

DUBLINERS
Ireland, male vocal/instrumental group – Ronnie Drew, d. 16 Aug 2008, Ciaran Bourke, d. 10 May 1988, Luke Kelly, d. 30 Jan 1984, Barney McKenna & John Sheahan

Date	Title / Label	Peak Position	Weeks at No.1	Weeks on Chart
				45
30 Mar 67	**SEVEN DRUNKEN NIGHTS** *Major Minor MM 506*	7		17
30 Aug 67	**BLACK VELVET BAND** *Major Minor MM 530*	15		15
20 Dec 67	**MAIDS WHEN YOU'RE YOUNG NEVER WED AN OLD MAN** *Major Minor MM 551*	43		3
28 Mar 87	**THE IRISH ROVER** *Stiff BUY 258* POGUES & THE DUBLINERS	8		8
16 Jun 90	**JACK'S HEROES/WHISKEY IN THE JAR** *Pogue Mahone YZ 500* POGUES & THE DUBLINERS	63		2

DUBSTAR
UK, female/male vocal/instrumental group

Date	Title / Label	Peak Position	Weeks at No.1	Weeks on Chart
				26
8 Jul 95	**STARS** *Food CDFOOD 61*	40		3
30 Sep 95	**ANYWHERE** *Food CDFOOD 67*	37		3
6 Jan 96	**NOT SO MANIC NOW** *Food CDFOODS 71*	18		5
30 Mar 96	**STARS** *Food CDFOODS 75*	15		6
3 Aug 96	**ELEVATOR SONG** *Food CDFOOD 80*	25		2
19 Jul 97	**NO MORE TALK** *Food CDFOOD 96*	20		3
20 Sep 97	**CATHEDRAL PARK** *Food CDFOOD 104*	41		1
7 Feb 98	**I WILL BE YOUR GIRLFRIEND** *Food CDFOODS 108*	28		2
27 May 00	**I (FRIDAY NIGHT)** *Food CDFOODS 128*	37		1

DUCK SAUCE
US/Canada, male vocal/DJ/production duo. See Armand Van Helden

Date	Title / Label	Peak Position	Weeks at No.1	Weeks on Chart
				4
7 Nov 09	**ANYWAY** *Data DATA224CDX*	22		4

DUELS
UK, male vocal/instrumental group

Date	Title / Label	Peak Position	Weeks at No.1	Weeks on Chart
				1
22 Apr 06	**ANIMAL** *Nude NUDCDS62*	47		1

HILARY DUFF
US, female vocalist/actor

Date	Title / Label	Peak Position	Weeks at No.1	Weeks on Chart
				29
1 Nov 03	**SO YESTERDAY** *Hollywood HOL003CD1*	9		8
24 Apr 04	**COME CLEAN** *Hollywood HOL005CD1*	18		4
5 Nov 05	**WAKE UP** *Angel ANGEDX5*	7		8
25 Mar 06	**FLY** *Angel ANGEDX13*	20		5
24 Mar 07	**WITH LOVE** *Angel ANGECD32*	29		4

MARY DUFF
Ireland, female vocalist

Date	Title / Label	Peak Position	Weeks at No.1	Weeks on Chart
				6
10 Jun 95	**SECRET LOVE** *Ritz RITZCD 285* DANIEL O'DONNELL & MARY DUFF	28		3
9 Mar 96	**TIMELESS** *Ritz RITZCD 293* DANIEL O'DONNELL & MARY DUFF	32		3

DUFFO
Australia, male vocal group

Date	Title / Label	Peak Position	Weeks at No.1	Weeks on Chart
				2
24 Mar 79	**GIVE ME BACK ME BRAIN** *Beggars Banquet BEG 15*	60		2

DUFFY
UK, female vocalist (Aimee Duffy)

Date	Title / Label	Peak Position	Weeks at No.1	Weeks on Chart
				103
19 Jan 08	**ROCKFERRY** *A&M 1754106*	45		10
23 Feb 08	**MERCY** *A&M 1761794*	1	5	44
3 May 08	**WARWICK AVENUE** *A&M 1766149*	3		29
30 Aug 08	**STEPPING STONE** *A&M 1780731*	21		9
22 Nov 08	**RAIN ON YOUR PARADE** *A&M 1789249*	15		11

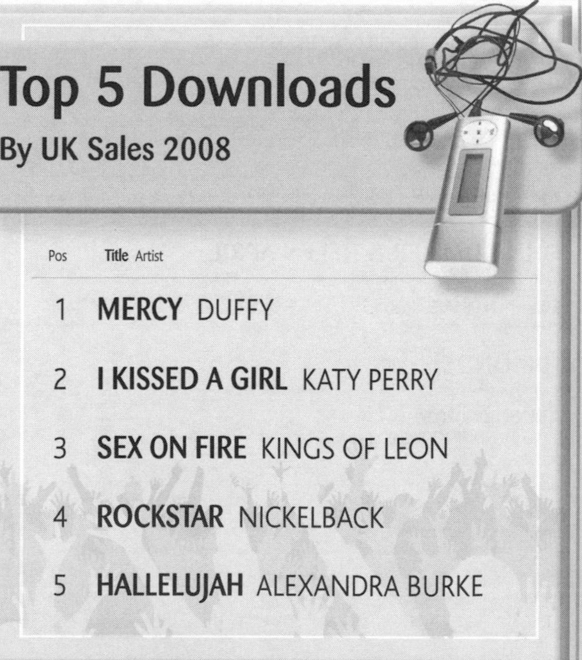

Top 5 Downloads

By UK Sales 2008

Pos	Title Artist
1	**MERCY** DUFFY
2	**I KISSED A GIRL** KATY PERRY
3	**SEX ON FIRE** KINGS OF LEON
4	**ROCKSTAR** NICKELBACK
5	**HALLELUJAH** ALEXANDRA BURKE

STEPHEN 'TIN TIN' DUFFY
UK, male vocalist

Date	Title	Peak Position	Weeks at No.1	Weeks on Chart
				24
9 Jul 83	**HOLD IT** *Curve X 9763*	55		4
2 Mar 85	**KISS ME** *10 TIN 2* ○	4		11
18 May 85	**ICING ON THE CAKE** *10 TIN 3*	14		9

DUKE
UK, male vocalist (Mark Adams)

Date	Title	Peak Position	Weeks at No.1	Weeks on Chart
				6
25 May 96	**SO IN LOVE WITH YOU** *Encore CDCOR 009*	66		1
26 Oct 96	**SO IN LOVE WITH YOU** *Pukka CDPUKKA 11*	22		4
11 Nov 00	**SO IN LOVE WITH YOU (REMIX)** *48k/Perfecto SPECT 08CDS*	65		1

GEORGE DUKE
US, male keyboard player/vocalist

Date	Title	Peak Position	Weeks at No.1	Weeks on Chart
				6
12 Jul 80	**BRAZILIAN LOVE AFFAIR** *Epic EPC 8751*	36		6

DUKE SPIRIT
UK, male/female vocal/instrumental group

Date	Title	Peak Position	Weeks at No.1	Weeks on Chart
				7
12 Jun 04	**DARK IS LIGHT ENOUGH** *Loog 9866673*	55		1
16 Oct 04	**CUTS ACROSS THE LAND** *Loog 9868119*	45		1
19 Feb 05	**LION RIP** *Loog 9870092*	25		2
14 May 05	**LOVE IS AN UNFAMILIAR NAME** *Loog 9871175*	33		2
1 Oct 05	**CUTS ACROSS THE LAND** *Loog 9873986*	66		1

DUKES
UK, male vocal/instrumental duo

Date	Title	Peak Position	Weeks at No.1	Weeks on Chart
				7
17 Oct 81	**MYSTERY GIRL** *WEA K 18867*	47		7

DUKES
UK, male vocal/instrumental duo

Date	Title	Peak Position	Weeks at No.1	Weeks on Chart
				6
1 May 82	**THANK YOU FOR THE PARTY** *WEA K 19136*	53		6

CANDY DULFER
Holland, female saxophonist

Date	Title	Peak Position	Weeks at No.1	Weeks on Chart
				14
24 Feb 90	**LILY WAS HERE** *RCA ZB 43045* DAVID A STEWART FEATURING CANDY DULFER	6		12
4 Aug 90	**SAXUALITY** *RCA PB 43769*	60		2

DUM DUMS
UK, male vocal/instrumental group

Date	Title	Peak Position	Weeks at No.1	Weeks on Chart
				15
11 Mar 00	**EVERYTHING** *Good Behaviour CDGOOD1*	21		5
8 Jul 00	**CAN'T GET YOU OUT OF MY THOUGHTS** *Good Behaviour CDGOOD2*	18		5
23 Sep 00	**YOU DO SOMETHING TO ME** *Good Behaviour CXGOOD3*	27		3
17 Feb 01	**ARMY OF TWO** *Good Behaviour CXGOOD5*	27		2

THULI DUMAKUDE
South Africa, female vocalist

Date	Title	Peak Position	Weeks at No.1	Weeks on Chart
				1
2 Jan 88	**THE FUNERAL (SEPTEMBER 25TH, 1977)** *MCA 1228*	75		1

JOHN DUMMER & HELEN APRIL
UK, male/female vocal/instrumental duo

Date	Title	Peak Position	Weeks at No.1	Weeks on Chart
				3
28 Aug 82	**BLUE SKIES** *Speed 8*	54		3

DUMONDE
Germany, male production duo. See JamX & DeLeon

Date	Title	Peak Position	Weeks at No.1	Weeks on Chart
				3
27 Jan 01	**TOMORROW** *Variation VART 6*	60		1
19 May 01	**NEVER LOOK BACK** *Manifesto FESCD 83*	36		2

DUNBLANE
UK, male/female vocal/instrumental charity group – Ted Christopher, Mark Knopfler & children's chorus

Date	Title	Peak Position	Weeks at No.1	Weeks on Chart
				15
21 Dec 96	**KNOCKIN' ON HEAVEN'S DOOR/THROW THESE GUNS AWAY** *BMG 74321442182* ●	1	1	15

JOHNNY DUNCAN & THE BLUE GRASS BOYS
US, male vocalist, d. 15 Jul 2000 (age 68), & UK, male instrumental group

Date	Title	Peak Position	Weeks at No.1	Weeks on Chart
				20
26 Jul 57	**LAST TRAIN TO SAN FERNANDO** *Columbia DB 3959*	2		17
25 Oct 57	**BLUE BLUE HEARTACHES** *Columbia DB 3996*	27		1
29 Nov 57	**FOOTPRINTS IN THE SNOW** *Columbia DB 4029*	27		2

DAVID DUNDAS
UK, male vocalist

Date	Title	Peak Position	Weeks at No.1	Weeks on Chart
				14
24 Jul 76	**JEANS ON** *Air CHS 2094* ○	3		9
9 Apr 77	**ANOTHER FUNNY HONEYMOON** *Air CHS 2136*	29		5

ERROL DUNKLEY
Jamaica, male vocalist

Date	Title	Peak Position	Weeks at No.1	Weeks on Chart
				14
22 Sep 79	**O.K. FRED** *Scope SC 6*	11		11
2 Feb 80	**SIT DOWN AND CRY** *Scope SC 11*	52		3

CLIVE DUNN
UK, male vocalist/actor

Date	Title	Peak Position	Weeks at No.1	Weeks on Chart
				28
28 Nov 70	**GRANDAD** *Columbia DB 8726*	1	3	28

SIMON DUPREE & THE BIG SOUND
UK, male vocalist (Derek Shulman) & male instrumental group

Date	Title	Peak Position	Weeks at No.1	Weeks on Chart
				16
22 Nov 67	**KITES** *Parlophone R 5646*	9		13
3 Apr 68	**FOR WHOM THE BELL TOLLS** *Parlophone R 5670*	43		3

JERMAINE DUPRI
US, male rapper/vocalist. See Marques Houston

Date	Title	Peak Position	Weeks at No.1	Weeks on Chart
				2
1 Oct 05	**GOTTA GETCHA** *Virgin VUSDX309*	54		2

DURAN DURAN
UK, male vocal/instrumental group – Simon Le Bon, Nick Rhodes & Andy, John & Roger Taylor. The BRITs' 2004 'Outstanding Contribution to British Music' award-winners went from New Romantics to pop idols with their catchy melodies and stylish videos. 'A View To A Kill' remains the UK's top-selling James Bond theme

Date	Title	Peak Position	Weeks at No.1	Weeks on Chart
				230
21 Feb 81	**PLANET EARTH** *EMI 5137*	12		11
16 May 81	**CARELESS MEMORIES** *EMI 5168*	37		7
25 Jul 81	**GIRLS ON FILM** *EMI 5206*	5		11
28 Nov 81	**MY OWN WAY** *EMI 5254*	14		11
15 May 82	**HUNGRY LIKE THE WOLF** *EMI 5295* ○	5		12
21 Aug 82	**SAVE A PRAYER** *EMI 5327* ○	2		9
13 Nov 82	**RIO** *EMI 5346* ○	9		11
26 Mar 83	**IS THERE SOMETHING I SHOULD KNOW** *EMI 5371* ●	1	2	9
29 Oct 83	**UNION OF THE SNAKE** *EMI 5429* ○	3		11
4 Feb 84	**NEW MOON ON MONDAY** *EMI DURAN 1*	9		7
28 Apr 84	**THE REFLEX** *EMI DURAN 2* ○ ★	1	4	14
3 Nov 84	**WILD BOYS** *EMI DURAN 3* ○	2		14
18 May 85	**A VIEW TO A KILL** *EMI DURAN 007* ○ ★	2		16
1 Nov 86	**NOTORIOUS** *EMI DDN 45*	7		7
21 Feb 87	**SKIN TRADE** *EMI TRADE 1*	22		6
25 Apr 87	**MEET EL PRESIDENTE** *EMI TOUR 1*	24		5
1 Oct 88	**I DON'T WANT YOUR LOVE** *EMI YOUR 1*	14		5
7 Jan 89	**ALL SHE WANTS IS** *EMI DD 11*	9		5
22 Apr 89	**DO YOU BELIEVE IN SHAME** *EMI DD 12*	30		4
16 Dec 89	**BURNING THE GROUND** *EMI DD 13*	31		5
4 Aug 90	**VIOLENCE OF SUMMER (LOVE'S TAKING OVER)** *Parlophone DD 14*	20		4
17 Nov 90	**SERIOUS** *Parlophone DD 15*	48		3
30 Jan 93	**ORDINARY WORLD** *Parlophone CDDDS 16*	6		9
10 Apr 93	**COME UNDONE** *Parlophone CDDDS 17*	13		8
4 Sep 93	**TOO MUCH INFORMATION** *Parlophone CDDDS 18*	35		3
25 Mar 95	**PERFECT DAY** *Parlophone CDDDS 20*	28		4
17 Jun 95	**WHITE LINES (DON'T DO IT)** *Parlophone CDDD 19* FEATURING MELLE MEL & GRANDMASTER FLASH & THE FURIOUS FIVE	17		5

Date	Title / Label	Peak Position	Weeks at No.1	Weeks on Chart
24 May 97	**OUT OF MY MIND** *Virgin VSCDT 1639*	21		2
30 Jan 99	**ELECTRIC BARBARELLA** *EMI CDELEC 2000*	23		3
10 Jun 00	**SOMEONE ELSE NOT ME** *Hollywood 0108845 HWR*	53		1
16 Oct 04	**(REACH UP FOR THE) SUNRISE** *Epic 6753532*	5		4
12 Feb 05	**WHAT HAPPENS TOMORROW** *Epic 6756502*	11		3
24 Nov 07	**FALLING DOWN** *Epic 88697191302*	52		1

Top 3 Best-Selling Singles

		Approximate Sales
1	THE REFLEX	590,000
2	IS THERE SOMETHING I SHOULD KNOW	550,000
3	SAVE A PRAYER	510,000

JIMMY DURANTE

US, male vocalist/comedian/actor, d. 29 Jan 1980 (age 86) — **1**

Date	Title / Label	Peak Position	Weeks at No.1	Weeks on Chart
14 Dec 96	**MAKE SOMEONE HAPPY** *Warner Brothers W0385CD*	69		1

JUDITH DURHAM

Australia, female vocalist. See Seekers — **5**

Date	Title / Label	Peak Position	Weeks at No.1	Weeks on Chart
15 Jun 67	**OLIVE TREE** *Columbia DB 8207*	33		5

IAN DURY & THE BLOCKHEADS

UK, male vocal/instrumental group – Ian Dury, d. 27 Mar 2000 (age 57), Charley Charles, Mickey Gallagher, Chaz Jankel, Davey Payne, John Turnbull & Norman Watt-Roy — **56**

Date	Title / Label	Peak Position	Weeks at No.1	Weeks on Chart
29 Apr 78	**WHAT A WASTE** *Stiff BUY 27*	9		12
9 Dec 78	**HIT ME WITH YOUR RHYTHM STICK** *Stiff BUY 38* ●	1	1	15
11 Aug 79	**REASONS TO BE CHEERFUL (PART 3)** *Stiff BUY 50* ●	3		8
30 Aug 80	**I WANT TO BE STRAIGHT** *Stiff BUY 90*	22		7
15 Nov 80	**SUPERMAN'S BIG SISTER** *Stiff BUY 100*	51		3
25 May 85	**HIT ME WITH YOUR RHYTHM STICK (REMIX)** *Stiff BUY 214*	55		4
26 Oct 85	**PROFOUNDLY IN LOVE WITH PANDORA** *EMI EM 5534* IAN & THE BLOCKHEADS	45		5
27 Jul 91	**HIT ME WITH YOU RHYTHM STICK (REMIX)** *Flying FLYR 1*	73		1
11 Mar 00	**DRIP FED FRED** *Virgin VSCDT 1768* MADNESS FEATURING IAN DURY	55		1

DUST BROTHERS

US, male production duo — **1**

Date	Title / Label	Peak Position	Weeks at No.1	Weeks on Chart
11 Dec 99	**THIS IS YOUR LIFE** *Restless 74321713962*	60		1

DUST JUNKYS

UK, male vocal/instrumental group — **5**

Date	Title / Label	Peak Position	Weeks at No.1	Weeks on Chart
15 Nov 97	**(NONSTOPOPERATION)** *Polydor 5719732*	47		2
28 Feb 98	**WHAT TIME IS IT?** *Polydor 5694912*	39		2
16 May 98	**NOTHIN' PERSONAL** *Polydor 5699092*	62		1

DUSTED

UK, male production/instrumental duo. See Faithless, Our Tribe/One Tribe, Rollo, Sphinx — **2**

Date	Title / Label	Peak Position	Weeks at No.1	Weeks on Chart
20 Jan 01	**ALWAYS REMEMBER TO RESPECT AND HONOUR YOUR MOTHER** *Go! Beat GOLCD 36*	31		2

SLIM DUSTY WITH DICK CARR & HIS BUSHLANDERS

Australia, male vocalist (David Kirkpatrick), d. 19 Sep 2003 (age 76) — **15**

Date	Title / Label	Peak Position	Weeks at No.1	Weeks on Chart
30 Jan 59	**A PUB WITH NO BEER** *Columbia DB 4212*	3		15

DUTCH FEATURING CRYSTAL WATERS

Holland/US, male/female vocal/production duo. See Scumfrog — **4**

Date	Title / Label	Peak Position	Weeks at No.1	Weeks on Chart
20 Sep 03	**MY TIME** *Illustrious/Epic CDILL 018*	22		4

DUTCH FORCE

Holland, male producer (Benno De Goeij) — **2**

Date	Title / Label	Peak Position	Weeks at No.1	Weeks on Chart
6 May 00	**DEADLINE** *Inferno CDFERN 27*	35		2

DWEEB

UK, male/female vocal/instrumental trio — **2**

Date	Title / Label	Peak Position	Weeks at No.1	Weeks on Chart
22 Feb 97	**SCOOBY DOO** *Blanco Y Negro NEG 100CD*	63		1
7 Jun 97	**OH YEAH, BABY** *Blanco Y Negro NEG 102CD*	70		1

DYKEENIES

UK, male vocal/instrumental group — **3**

Date	Title / Label	Peak Position	Weeks at No.1	Weeks on Chart
21 Apr 07	**NEW IDEAS** *Lavolta LAVOLTA012*	54		1
21 Jul 07	**CLEAN UP YOUR EYES** *Lavolta LAVOLTA015*	53		1
22 Sep 07	**STITCHES** *Lavolta LAVOLTA016*	61		1

BOB DYLAN

US, male vocalist/multi-instrumentalist (Robert Zimmerman) — **139**

Date	Title / Label	Peak Position	Weeks at No.1	Weeks on Chart
25 Mar 65	**TIMES THEY ARE A-CHANGIN'** *CBS 201751*	9		11
29 Apr 65	**SUBTERRANEAN HOMESICK BLUES** *CBS 201753*	9		9
17 Jun 65	**MAGGIE'S FARM** *CBS 201781*	22		8
19 Aug 65	**LIKE A ROLLING STONE** *CBS 201811*	4		12
28 Oct 65	**POSITIVELY FOURTH STREET** *CBS 201824*	8		12
27 Jan 66	**CAN YOU PLEASE CRAWL OUT YOUR WINDOW** *CBS 201900*	17		5
14 Apr 66	**ONE OF US MUST KNOW (SOONER OR LATER)** *CBS 202053*	33		5
12 May 66	**RAINY DAY WOMEN NOS. 12 & 35** *CBS 202307*	7		8
21 Jul 66	**I WANT YOU** *CBS 202258*	16		9
14 May 69	**I THREW IT ALL AWAY** *CBS 4219*	30		6
13 Sep 69	**LAY LADY LAY** *CBS 4434*	5		12
10 Jul 71	**WATCHING THE RIVER FLOW** *CBS 7329*	24		9
6 Oct 73	**KNOCKIN' ON HEAVEN'S DOOR** *CBS 1762*	14		9
7 Feb 76	**HURRICANE** *CBS 3878*	43		4
29 Jul 78	**BABY STOP CRYING** *CBS 6499*	13		11
28 Oct 78	**IS YOUR LOVE IN VAIN** *CBS 6718*	56		3
20 May 95	**DIGNITY** *Columbia 6620762*	33		2
11 Jul 98	**LOVE SICK** *Columbia 6659972*	64		1
14 Oct 00	**THINGS HAVE CHANGED** *Columbia 6693792*	58		1
6 Oct 07	**MOST LIKELY YOU GO YOUR OWN WAY** *Columbia 88697163192*	51		1
2 Jan 10	**MUST BE SANTA** *Columbia USSM10904557*	41		1

DYNAMITE MC

UK, male rapper (Dominic Smith) — **2**

Date	Title / Label	Peak Position	Weeks at No.1	Weeks on Chart
20 Sep 03	**HOTNESS** *Ram RAMM 45* & ORIGIN UNKNOWN	66		1
5 Jun 04	**RIDE** *Utlimate Dilemma EW 288CD*	54		1

DYNAMIX II FEATURING TOO TOUGH TEE

US, male instrumental/production duo & male rapper — **4**

Date	Title / Label	Peak Position	Weeks at No.1	Weeks on Chart
8 Aug 87	**JUST GIVE THE DJ A BREAK** *Cooltempo COOL 151*	50		4

DYNASTY

US, male/female vocal/instrumental group — **20**

Date	Title / Label	Peak Position	Weeks at No.1	Weeks on Chart
13 Oct 79	**I DON'T WANT TO BE A FREAK (BUT I CAN'T HELP MYSELF)** *Solar FB 1694*	20		13
9 Aug 80	**I'VE JUST BEGUN TO LOVE YOU** *Solar SO 10*	51		4
21 May 83	**DOES THAT RING A BELL** *Solar E 9911*	53		3

DYVERSE

UK, female vocal group — **1**

Date	Title / Label	Peak Position	Weeks at No.1	Weeks on Chart
31 Jan 04	**MISGUIDED** *Chilli Discs CCHIL 002*	71		1

RONNIE DYSON

US, male vocalist, d. 10 Nov 1990 (age 40) — **6**

Date	Title / Label	Peak Position	Weeks at No.1	Weeks on Chart
4 Dec 71	**WHEN YOU GET RIGHT DOWN TO IT** *CBS 7449*	34		6

BIOGRAPHIES

Biographies include the nationality and category for every chart entrant.

Each entrant has at least a mini biography. The acts with the most weeks on the chart (see page 372 for the chart) each have extended biographies.

Real names are included for all solo artists and, where applicable, dates of death and age of the artist at the time. "See..." links are included for soloists who also had singles chart entries in other acts.

The best known line-up is listed for every group that had a Top 10 single, with the vocalist/leader mentioned first and the others following in alphabetical order. In cases where later replacements had similar success both people are named and, where applicable, the dates of death are also shown for every group/duo member listed.

Certified Awards are given by the BPI to mark unit sales to retailers. They were introduced in April 1973. In January 1989 the levels of unit sales to the trade required to achieve each of the awards was amended to the following amounts:

Silver symbol ● = 200,000 units

Gold symbol ● = 400,000 units

Platinum symbol ⊛ = 600,000 units

As from February 2005, download sales also count towards certified awards.

E–H

KEY TO ARTIST ENTRIES

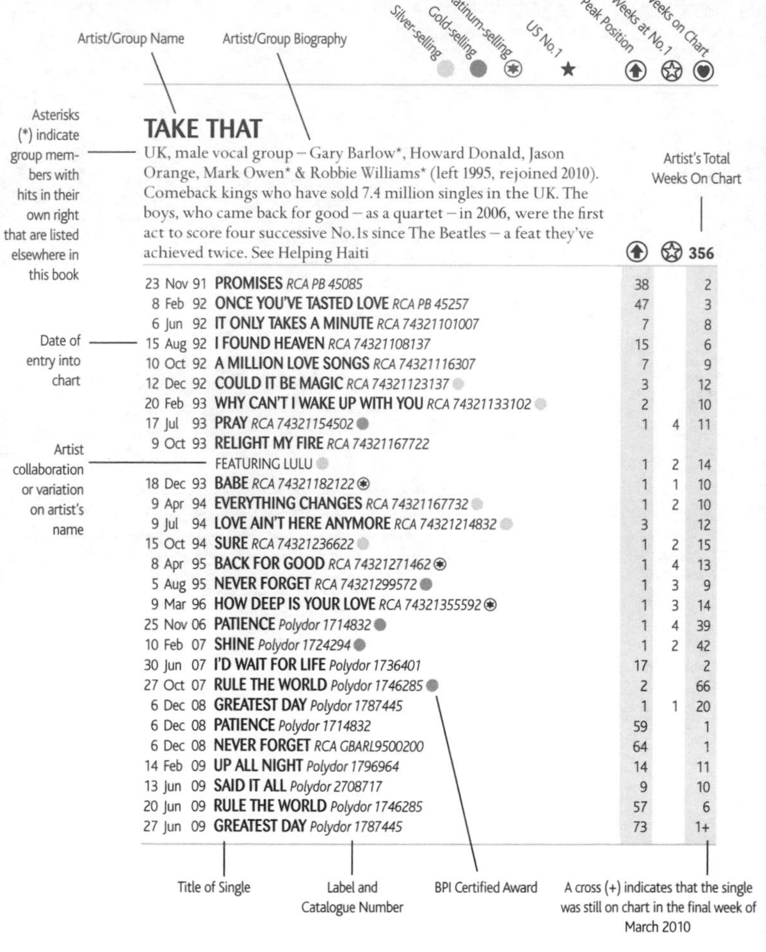

TAKE THAT

UK, male vocal group – Gary Barlow*, Howard Donald, Jason Orange, Mark Owen* & Robbie Williams* (left 1995, rejoined 2010). Comeback kings who have sold 7.4 million singles in the UK. The boys, who came back for good – as a quartet – in 2006, were the first act to score four successive No.1s since The Beatles – a feat they've achieved twice. See Helping Haiti

Date	Title / Label	Peak Position	Weeks at No.1	Weeks on Chart (356)
23 Nov 91	**PROMISES** *RCA PB 45085*	38		2
8 Feb 92	**ONCE YOU'VE TASTED LOVE** *RCA PB 45257*	47		3
6 Jun 92	**IT ONLY TAKES A MINUTE** *RCA 74321101007*	7		8
15 Aug 92	**I FOUND HEAVEN** *RCA 74321108137*	15		6
10 Oct 92	**A MILLION LOVE SONGS** *RCA 74321116307*	7		9
12 Dec 92	**COULD IT BE MAGIC** *RCA 74321123137* ●	3		12
20 Feb 93	**WHY CAN'T I WAKE UP WITH YOU** *RCA 74321133102* ●	2		10
17 Jul 93	**PRAY** *RCA 74321154502* ●	1	4	11
9 Oct 93	**RELIGHT MY FIRE** *RCA 74321167722* FEATURING LULU ●	1	2	14
18 Dec 93	**BABE** *RCA 74321182122* ●	1	1	10
9 Apr 94	**EVERYTHING CHANGES** *RCA 74321167732* ●	1	2	10
9 Jul 94	**LOVE AIN'T HERE ANYMORE** *RCA 74321214832* ●	3		12
15 Oct 94	**SURE** *RCA 74321236622* ●	1	2	15
8 Apr 95	**BACK FOR GOOD** *RCA 74321271462* ●	1	4	13
5 Aug 95	**NEVER FORGET** *RCA 74321299572* ●	1	3	9
9 Mar 96	**HOW DEEP IS YOUR LOVE** *RCA 74321355592* ●	1	3	14
25 Nov 06	**PATIENCE** *Polydor 1714832* ●	1	4	39
10 Feb 07	**SHINE** *Polydor 1724294* ●	1	2	42
30 Jun 07	**I'D WAIT FOR LIFE** *Polydor 1736401*	17		2
27 Oct 07	**RULE THE WORLD** *Polydor 1746285* ●	2		66
6 Dec 08	**GREATEST DAY** *Polydor 1787445*	1	1	20
6 Dec 08	**PATIENCE** *Polydor 1714832*	59		1
6 Dec 08	**NEVER FORGET** *RCA GBARL9500200*	64		1
14 Feb 09	**UP ALL NIGHT** *Polydor 1796964*	14		11
13 Jun 09	**SAID IT ALL** *Polydor 2708717*	9		10
20 Jun 09	**RULE THE WORLD** *Polydor 1746285*	57		6
27 Jun 09	**GREATEST DAY** *Polydor 1787445*	73		1+

ERICK E
Holland, male DJ/producer (Erick Eerdhuizen) — 6

Date	Title	Peak Position	Weeks at No.1	Weeks on Chart
10 Feb 07	**THE BEAT IS ROCKIN'** *Gusto CDGUS44*	25		6

KATHERINE E
US, female vocalist — 7

Date	Title	Peak Position	Weeks at No.1	Weeks on Chart
6 Apr 91	**I'M ALRIGHT** *Dead Dead Good GOOD 2*	41		5
18 Jan 92	**THEN I FEEL GOOD** *PWL Continental PWL 13*	56		2

KATHERINE ELLIS
UK, female vocalist — 9

Date	Title	Peak Position	Weeks at No.1	Weeks on Chart
29 Jan 05	**SALTY** *Kingsize KS093D1* DYLAN RHYMES FEATURING KATHERINE ELLIS	70		1
28 Jun 08	**WHEN YOU TOUCH ME** *Loaded LOAD130CD* FREEMASONS FEATURING KATHERINE ELLIS	23		8

SHEILA E
US, female vocalist/drummer (Sheila Escovedo) — 9

Date	Title	Peak Position	Weeks at No.1	Weeks on Chart
23 Feb 85	**THE BELLE OF ST MARK** *Warner Brothers W 9180*	18		9

E-LUSTRIOUS
UK, male production duo. See Direckt — 2

Date	Title	Peak Position	Weeks at No.1	Weeks on Chart
15 Feb 92	**DANCE NO MORE** *MOS 001T* FEATURING DEBORAH FRENCH	58		1
2 Jul 94	**IN YOUR DANCE** *UFG 6CD*	69		1

E-MALE
UK, male vocal/instrumental group — 1

Date	Title	Peak Position	Weeks at No.1	Weeks on Chart
31 Jan 98	**WE ARE E-MALE** *East West EW 137CD*	44		1

E-MOTION
UK, male vocal/instrumental duo — 7

Date	Title	Peak Position	Weeks at No.1	Weeks on Chart
3 Feb 96	**THE NAUGHTY NORTH & THE SEXY SOUTH** *Soundproof MCSTD 40017*	20		3
17 Aug 96	**I STAND ALONE** *Soundproof MCSTD 40061*	60		1
26 Oct 96	**THE NAUGHTY NORTH & THE SEXY SOUTH** *Soundproof MCSTD 40076*	17		3

E-ROTIC
Germany/US, male/female vocal/instrumental group — 2

Date	Title	Peak Position	Weeks at No.1	Weeks on Chart
3 Jun 95	**MAX DON'T HAVE SEX WITH YOUR EX** *Stip CDSTIP 2*	45		2

E-SMOOVE FEATURING LATANZA WATERS
US, male/female vocal/production duo. See Praise Cats, Thick D — 1

Date	Title	Peak Position	Weeks at No.1	Weeks on Chart
15 Aug 98	**DÉJÀ VU** *AM:PM 5827671*	63		1

E-TRAX
Germany, male production duo. See Bellini, Fragma, Hardfloor, Interactive, Paffendorf — 1

Date	Title	Peak Position	Weeks at No.1	Weeks on Chart
9 Jun 01	**LET'S ROCK** *Tidy Trax TIDY 155CD*	60		1

E-TYPE
Sweden, male vocalist (Bo Eriksson) — 2

Date	Title	Peak Position	Weeks at No.1	Weeks on Chart
23 Sep 95	**THIS IS THE WAY** *ffrreedom TABCD 237*	53		1
24 Jun 00	**CAMPIONE 2000** *Polydor 1580822*	58		1

E-Z ROLLERS
UK, male/female vocal/instrumental group — 4

Date	Title	Peak Position	Weeks at No.1	Weeks on Chart
24 Apr 99	**WALK THIS LAND** *Moving Shadow 130CD1*	18		3
8 Feb 03	**BACK TO LOVE** *Moving Shadow 159CD*	61		1

E-ZEE POSSEE
UK, female/male rap/vocal/production group — 16

Date	Title	Peak Position	Weeks at No.1	Weeks on Chart
26 Aug 89	**EVERYTHING STARTS WITH AN 'E'** *More Protein PROT 1*	69		1
20 Jan 90	**LOVE ON LOVE** *More Protein PROT 3*	59		3
17 Mar 90	**EVERYTHING STARTS WITH AN 'E'** *More Protein PROT 1*	15		8
30 Jun 90	**THE SUN MACHINE** *More Protein PROT 4*	62		3
21 Sep 91	**BREATHING IS E-ZEE** *More Protein PROT 12* FEATURING TARA NEWLEY	72		1

EAGLES
US, male vocal/instrumental group – Glenn Frey*, Don Henley*, Don Felder, Bernie Leadon (replaced by Joe Walsh) & Randy Meisner (replaced by Timothy B Schmit) — 52

Date	Title	Peak Position	Weeks at No.1	Weeks on Chart
9 Aug 75	**ONE OF THESE NIGHTS** *Asylum AYM 543* ★	23		7
1 Nov 75	**LYIN' EYES** *Asylum AYM 548*	23		7
6 Mar 76	**TAKE IT TO THE LIMIT** *Asylum K 13029*	12		7
15 Jan 77	**NEW KID IN TOWN** *Asylum K 13069* ★	20		7
16 Apr 77	**HOTEL CALIFORNIA** *Asylum K 13079* ★	8		10
16 Dec 78	**PLEASE COME HOME FOR CHRISTMAS** *Asylum K 13145*	30		5
13 Oct 79	**HEARTACHE TONIGHT** *Asylum K 12394* ★	40		5
1 Dec 79	**THE LONG RUN** *Elektra K 12404*	66		2
13 Jul 96	**LOVE WILL KEEP US ALIVE** *Geffen GFSTD 21980*	52		1
25 Oct 03	**HOLE IN THE WORLD** *Eagles 8122745472*	69		1

EAGLES OF DEATH METAL
US, male vocal/instrumental group — 1

Date	Title	Peak Position	Weeks at No.1	Weeks on Chart
9 Sep 06	**I WANT YOU SO HARD (BOY'S BAD NEWS)** *20-20 Recordings 82876886682*	73		1

EAMON
US, male vocalist (Eamon Doyle) — 27

Date	Title	Peak Position	Weeks at No.1	Weeks on Chart
3 Apr 04	**F**K IT (I DON'T WANT YOU BACK) (IMPORT)** *Jive 82876604852*	46		3
24 Apr 04	**F**K IT (I DON'T WANT YOU BACK)** *Jive 82876608522* ○	1	4	19
16 Oct 04	**LOVE THEM** *Jive 82876639212* FEATURING GHOSTFACE	27		4
25 Aug 07	**(HOW COULD YOU) BRING HIM HOME** *Jive USJI10700498*	61		1

ROBERT EARL
UK, male vocalist (Monty Leigh) — 27

Date	Title	Peak Position	Weeks at No.1	Weeks on Chart
25 Apr 58	**I MAY NEVER PASS THIS WAY AGAIN** *Philips PB 805*	14		13
24 Oct 58	**MORE THAN EVER (COME PRIMA)** *Philips PB 867*	26		4
13 Feb 59	**THE WONDERFUL SECRET OF LOVE** *Philips PB 891*	17		10

CHARLES EARLAND
US, male keyboard player , d. 11 Dec 1999 (age 58) — 5

Date	Title	Peak Position	Weeks at No.1	Weeks on Chart
19 Aug 78	**LET THE MUSIC PLAY** *Mercury 6167 703*	46		5

STEVE EARLE
US, male vocalist/guitarist — 10

Date	Title	Peak Position	Weeks at No.1	Weeks on Chart
15 Oct 88	**COPPERHEAD ROAD** *MCA 1280*	45		6
31 Dec 88	**JOHNNY COME LATELY** *MCA 1301*	75		1
7 Jun 08	**THE GALWAY GIRL** *The Daisy Label LRLCDS020* SHARON SHANNON & STEVE EARLE	67		3

EARLIES
US/UK, male vocal/instrumental group — 2

Date	Title	Peak Position	Weeks at No.1	Weeks on Chart
6 Nov 04	**MORNING WONDER** *WEA IAMNAMES07*	67		1
12 Mar 05	**BRING IT BACK AGAIN** *WEA IAMNAMES09*	61		1

EARLY MUSIC CONSORT DIRECTED BY DAVID MUNROW
UK, male/female instrumental group — 1

Date	Title	Peak Position	Weeks at No.1	Weeks on Chart
3 Apr 71	**HENRY VIII SUITE (EP)** *BBC RESL 1*	49		1

EARTH WIND & FIRE
US, male vocal/instrumental group – Philip Bailey*; members also included Larry Dunn, Ralph Johnson & Fred, Maurice & Verdine White — 128

Date	Title	Peak Position	Weeks at No.1	Weeks on Chart
12 Feb 77	**SATURDAY NITE** *CBS 4835*	17		9
11 Feb 78	**FANTASY** *CBS 6056*	14		10
13 May 78	**JUPITER** *CBS 6267*	41		5
29 Jul 78	**MAGIC MIND** *CBS 6490*	54		5
7 Oct 78	**GOT TO GET YOU INTO MY LIFE** *CBS 6553*	33		7
9 Dec 78	**SEPTEMBER** *CBS 6922* ○	3		13
12 May 79	**BOOGIE WONDERLAND** *CBS 7292* WITH THE EMOTIONS ●	4		13
28 Jul 79	**AFTER THE LOVE HAS GONE** *CBS 7721* ○	4		10
6 Oct 79	**STAR** *CBS 7092*	16		8
15 Dec 79	**CAN'T LET GO** *CBS 8077*	46		7
8 Mar 80	**IN THE STONE** *CBS 8252*	53		3

Silver-selling ○ · Gold-selling ● · Platinum-selling (x multiples) ⊛ · US No.1 ★ · Peak Position · Weeks at No.1 · Weeks on Chart

Date	Title	Peak Position	Weeks at No.1	Weeks on Chart
11 Oct 80	**LET ME TALK** *CBS 8982*	29		5
20 Dec 80	**BACK ON THE ROAD** *CBS 9377*	63		4
7 Nov 81	**LET'S GROOVE** *CBS A 1679* ○	3		13
6 Feb 82	**I'VE HAD ENOUGH** *CBS A 1959*	29		6
5 Feb 83	**FALL IN LOVE WITH ME** *CBS A 2927*	47		4
7 Nov 87	**SYSTEM OF SURVIVAL** *CBS EWF 1*	54		3
31 Jul 99	**SEPTEMBER 99 (REMIX)** *INCredible INCR 24CD*	25		3

EARTHLING

UK, male vocal/instrumental duo — 2

Date	Title	Peak Position	Weeks at No.1	Weeks on Chart
14 Oct 95	**ECHO ON MY MIND PART II** *Cooltempo CDCOOL 312*	61		1
1 Jun 96	**BLOOD MUSIC (EP)** *Cooltempo CDCOOL 319*	69		1

EAST 57TH STREET FEATURING DONNA ALLEN

UK/US, male/female vocal/production group — 3

Date	Title	Peak Position	Weeks at No.1	Weeks on Chart
11 Oct 97	**SATURDAY** *AM:PM 5823752*	29		3

EAST OF EDEN

UK, male instrumental group – Dave Arbus, Geoff Britton, Ron Gaines, Geoff Nicholson & Andy Sneddon — 12

Date	Title	Peak Position	Weeks at No.1	Weeks on Chart
17 Apr 71	**JIG A JIG** *Deram DM 297*	7		12

EAST 17

UK, male vocal group – Brian Harvey, Terry Coldwell, John Hendy & Tony Mortimer. See Childliners — 170

Date	Title	Peak Position	Weeks at No.1	Weeks on Chart
29 Aug 92	**HOUSE OF LOVE** *London LON 325*	10		9
14 Nov 92	**GOLD** *London LON 331*	28		8
30 Jan 93	**DEEP** *London LOCDP 334* ○	5		10
10 Apr 93	**SLOW IT DOWN** *London LONCD 339*	13		7
26 Jun 93	**WEST END GIRLS** *London LONCD 344*	11		7
4 Dec 93	**IT'S ALRIGHT** *London LONCD 345* ○	3		14
14 May 94	**AROUND THE WORLD** *London LONCD 349* ○	3		13
1 Oct 94	**STEAM** *London LONCD 353*	7		8
3 Dec 94	**STAY ANOTHER DAY** *London LONCD 354* ⊛	1	5	16
25 Mar 95	**LET IT RAIN** *London LOCDP 363*	10		7
17 Jun 95	**HOLD MY BODY TIGHT** *London LOCDP 367*	12		7
4 Nov 95	**THUNDER** *London LOCDP 373* ○	4		14
10 Feb 96	**DO U STILL?** *London LOCDP 379*	7		7
10 Aug 96	**SOMEONE TO LOVE** *London LONCD 385*	16		8
2 Nov 96	**IF YOU EVER** *London LONCD 388* FEATURING GABRIELLE ●	2		15
18 Jan 97	**HEY CHILD** *London LONCD 390*	3		5
14 Nov 98	**EACH TIME** *Telstar CDSTAS 3017* E-17	2		10
13 Mar 99	**BETCHA CAN'T WAIT** *Telstar CDSTAS 3031* E-17	12		5

EAST SIDE BEAT

Italy, male vocal/production duo – Carl Fanini & Francesco Petrocchi — 18

Date	Title	Peak Position	Weeks at No.1	Weeks on Chart
30 Nov 91	**RIDE LIKE THE WIND** *ffrr F 176*	3		11
19 Dec 92	**ALIVE AND KICKING** *ffrr F 206*	26		6
29 May 93	**YOU'RE MY EVERYTHING** *ffrr FCD 207*	65		1

EASTERN LANE

UK, male vocal/instrumental group — 3

Date	Title	Peak Position	Weeks at No.1	Weeks on Chart
15 Nov 03	**FEED YOUR ADDICTION** *Rough Trade RTRADESCD132*	72		1
13 Mar 04	**SAFFRON** *Rough Trade RTRADSCD156*	55		1
6 Nov 04	**I SAID PIG ON FRIDAY** *Rough Trade RTRADSCD199*	65		1

SHEENA EASTON

UK, female vocalist (Sheena Orr) — 104

Date	Title	Peak Position	Weeks at No.1	Weeks on Chart
5 Apr 80	**MODERN GIRL** *EMI 5042*	56		3
19 Jul 80	**9 TO 5** *EMI 5066* ● ★	3		15
9 Aug 80	**MODERN GIRL** *EMI 5042* ○	8		12
25 Oct 80	**ONE MAN WOMAN** *EMI 5114*	14		6
14 Feb 81	**TAKE MY TIME** *EMI 5135*	44		5
2 May 81	**WHEN HE SHINES** *EMI 5166*	12		8
27 Jun 81	**FOR YOUR EYES ONLY** *EMI 5195*	8		13
12 Sep 81	**JUST ANOTHER BROKEN HEART** *EMI 5232*	33		8
5 Dec 81	**YOU COULD HAVE BEEN WITH ME** *EMI 5252*	54		3
31 Jul 82	**MACHINERY** *EMI 5326*	38		5
12 Feb 83	**WE'VE GOT TONIGHT** *Liberty UP 658* KENNY ROGERS & SHEENA EASTON	28		7
21 Jan 89	**THE LOVER IN ME** *MCA 1289*	15		8
18 Mar 89	**DAYS LIKE THIS** *MCA 1325*	43		3
15 Jul 89	**101** *MCA 1348*	54		2
18 Nov 89	**THE ARMS OF ORION** *Warner Brothers W 2757* PRINCE WITH SHEENA EASTON	27		5
9 Dec 00	**GIVING UP GIVING IN** *Universal MCSTD 40244*	54		1

EASTSIDE CONNECTION

US, disco aggregation — 3

Date	Title	Peak Position	Weeks at No.1	Weeks on Chart
8 Apr 78	**YOU'RE SO RIGHT FOR ME** *Creole CR 149*	44		3

CLINT EASTWOOD

US, male actor/vocalist — 2

Date	Title	Peak Position	Weeks at No.1	Weeks on Chart
7 Feb 70	**I TALK TO THE TREES** *Paramount PARA 3004*	18		2

CLINT EASTWOOD & GENERAL SAINT

Jamaica/UK, male vocal duo — 8

Date	Title	Peak Position	Weeks at No.1	Weeks on Chart
29 Sep 84	**LAST PLANE (ONE WAY TICKET)** *MCA 910*	51		3
2 Apr 94	**OH CAROL!** *Copasetic COPCD 0009*	54		5

EASYBEATS

Australia, male vocal/instrumental group — 24

Date	Title	Peak Position	Weeks at No.1	Weeks on Chart
27 Oct 66	**FRIDAY ON MY MIND** *United Artists UP 1157*	6		15
10 Apr 68	**HELLO, HOW ARE YOU** *United Artists UP 2209*	20		9

EASYWORLD

UK, male vocal/instrumental trio — 7

Date	Title	Peak Position	Weeks at No.1	Weeks on Chart
1 Jun 02	**BLEACH** *Jive 9253552*	67		1
21 Sep 02	**YOU AND ME** *Jive 9254102*	57		1
8 Feb 03	**JUNKIES** *Jive 9254522*	40		1
18 Oct 03	**2ND AMENDMENT** *Jive 82876554692*	42		1
31 Jan 04	**TIL THE DAY** *Jive 82876585372*	27		2
11 Sep 04	**HOW DID IT EVER COME TO THIS?** *Jive 82876632102*	50		1

EAT

UK/US, male/female vocal/instrumental group — 1

Date	Title	Peak Position	Weeks at No.1	Weeks on Chart
12 Jun 93	**BLEED ME WHITE** *Fiction FICCD 48*	73		1

EAT STATIC

UK, male production duo — 3

Date	Title	Peak Position	Weeks at No.1	Weeks on Chart
22 Feb 97	**HYBRID** *Planet Dog BARK 024CD*	41		1
27 Sep 97	**INTERCEPTOR** *Planet Dog BARK 030CD*	44		1
27 Jun 98	**CONTACT...** *Planet Dog BARK 033CD*	67		1

CLEVELAND EATON

US, male keyboard player — 6

Date	Title	Peak Position	Weeks at No.1	Weeks on Chart
23 Sep 78	**BAMA BOOGIE WOOGIE** *Gull GULS 63*	35		6

EAV

Austria, male vocal/instrumental group — 4

Date	Title	Peak Position	Weeks at No.1	Weeks on Chart
27 Sep 86	**BA-BA-BANKROBBERY (ENGLISH VERSION)** *Columbia DB 9139*	63		4

EAZY-E

US, male rapper (Eric Wright), d. 26 Mar 1995 (age 31). See N.W.A. — 3

Date	Title	Peak Position	Weeks at No.1	Weeks on Chart
6 Jan 96	**JUST TAH LET U KNOW** *Ruthless 6628162*	30		3

EBONY DUBSTERS

UK, male production duo. See Shy FX — 3

Date	Title	Peak Position	Weeks at No.1	Weeks on Chart
24 Jan 04	**MURDERATION** *Ebony EBR029*	59		2
22 May 04	**NUMBER 1/THE RITUAL** *Ebony EBR030*	58		1

ECHELON

UK, male vocal/instrumental group — 1

Date	Title	Peak Position	Weeks at No.1	Weeks on Chart
20 Nov 04	**PLUS** *Poptones MC5095SCD*	57		1

ECHO & THE BUNNYMEN

UK, male vocal/instrumental group – Ian McCulloch*, Pete de Freitas, Les Pattinson & Will Sergeant. See England United — 87

Date	Title	Peak	Wks at No.1	Wks
17 May 80	**RESCUE** *Korova KOW 1*	62		1
18 Apr 81	**SHINE SO HARD (EP)** *Korova ECHO 1*	37		4
18 Jul 81	**A PROMISE** *Korova KOW 15*	49		4
29 May 82	**THE BACK OF LOVE** *Korova KOW 24*	19		7
22 Jan 83	**THE CUTTER** *Korova KOW 26*	8		8
16 Jul 83	**NEVER STOP** *Korova KOW 28*	15		7
28 Jan 84	**THE KILLING MOON** *Korova KOW 32*	9		6
21 Apr 84	**SILVER** *Korova KOW 34*	30		5
14 Jul 84	**SEVEN SEAS** *Korova KOW 35*	16		7
19 Oct 85	**BRING ON THE DANCING HORSES** *Korova KOW 43*	21		7
13 Jun 87	**THE GAME** *WEA YZ 134*	28		4
1 Aug 87	**LIPS LIKE SUGAR** *WEA YZ 144*	36		4
20 Feb 88	**PEOPLE ARE STRANGE** *WEA YZ 175*	29		5
2 Mar 91	**PEOPLE ARE STRANGE** *East West YZ 567*	34		4
28 Jun 97	**NOTHING LASTS FOREVER** *London LOCDP 396*	8		6
13 Sep 97	**I WANT TO BE THERE WHEN YOU COME** *London LONCD 399*	30		2
8 Nov 97	**DON'T LET IT GET YOU DOWN** *London LOCDP 406*	50		1
27 Mar 99	**RUST** *London LONCD 424*	22		3
5 May 01	**IT'S ALRIGHT** *Cooking Vinyl FRY CD104*	41		1
17 Sep 05	**STORMY WEATHER** *Cooking Vinyl FRYCD246*	55		1

ECHOBASS

UK, male producer (Simon Woodgate) — 1

Date	Title	Peak	Wks at No.1	Wks
14 Jul 01	**YOU ARE THE WEAKEST LINK** *House Of Bush CDANNE 001*	53		1

ECHOBEATZ

UK, male DJ/production duo – Dave De Braie & Paul Moody — 5

Date	Title	Peak	Wks at No.1	Wks
25 Jul 98	**MAS QUE NADA** *Eternal WEA 176CD*	10		5

ECHOBELLY

UK/Sweden, female/male vocal/instrumental group — 16

Date	Title	Peak	Wks at No.1	Wks
2 Apr 94	**INSOMNIAC** *Fauve FAUV 1CS*	47		1
2 Jul 94	**I CAN'T IMAGINE THE WORLD WITHOUT ME** *Fauve FAUV 2CD*	39		2
5 Nov 94	**CLOSE...BUT** *Fauve FAUV 4CD*	59		1
2 Sep 95	**GREAT THINGS** *Fauve FAUV 5CD*	13		3
4 Nov 95	**KING OF THE KERB** *Fauve FAUV 7CD*	25		3
2 Mar 96	**DARK THERAPY** *Fauve FAUV 8CD*	20		3
23 Aug 97	**THE WORLD IS FLAT** *Epic 6648152*	31		2
8 Nov 97	**HERE COMES THE BIG RUSH** *Epic 6652452*	56		1

BILLY ECKSTINE

US, male vocalist, d. 8 Mar 1993 (age 78) — 48

Date	Title	Peak	Wks at No.1	Wks
12 Nov 54	**NO ONE BUT YOU** *MGM 763*	3		17
27 Sep 57	**PASSING STRANGERS** *Mercury MT 164* & SARAH VAUGHAN	22		2
13 Feb 59	**GIGI** *Mercury AMT 1018*	8		14
12 Mar 69	**PASSING STRANGERS** *Mercury MF 1082* & SARAH VAUGHAN	20		15

ECLIPSE

Italy, male producer/instrumentalist (Gianni Bini). See Bini & Martini, Goodfellas featuring Lisa Millett, House Of Glass — 4

Date	Title	Peak	Wks at No.1	Wks
14 Aug 99	**MAKES ME LOVE YOU** *Azuli AZNYCDX 100*	25		4

SILVIO ECOMO

Holland, male producer — 1

Date	Title	Peak	Wks at No.1	Wks
15 Jul 00	**STANDING** *Hooj Choons HOOJ 098CD*	70		1

EDDIE & THE HOT RODS

UK, male vocal/instrumental group – Barrie Masters, Graeme Douglas, Paul Gray, Dave Higgs & Steve Nicol — 26

Date	Title	Peak	Wks at No.1	Wks
11 Sep 76	**LIVE AT THE MARQUEE (EP)** *Island IEP 2*	43		5
13 Nov 76	**TEENAGE DEPRESSION** *Island WIP 6354*	35		4
23 Apr 77	**I MIGHT BE LYING** *Island WIP 6388*	44		3
13 Aug 77	**DO ANYTHING YOU WANT TO DO** *Island WIP 6401* RODS	9		10
21 Jan 78	**QUIT THIS TOWN** *Island WIP 6411*	36		4

EDDY

UK, female vocalist (Edith Emenike) — 2

Date	Title	Peak	Wks at No.1	Wks
9 Jul 94	**SOMEDAY** *Positiva CDTIV 14*	49		2

DUANE EDDY & THE REBELS

US, male guitarist — 202

Date	Title	Peak	Wks at No.1	Wks
5 Sep 58	**REBEL ROUSER** *London HL 8669*	19		10
2 Jan 59	**CANNONBALL** *London HL 8764*	22		4
19 Jun 59	**PETER GUNN THEME** *London HLW 8879*	6		11
24 Jul 59	**YEP** *London HLW 8879*	17		5
4 Sep 59	**FORTY MILES OF BAD ROAD** *London HLW 8929*	11		9
18 Dec 59	**SOME KINDA EARTHQUAKE** *London HLW 9007*	12		5
19 Feb 60	**BONNIE CAME BACK** *London HLW 9050*	12		11
28 Apr 60	**SHAZAM!** *London HLW 9104*	4		13
21 Jul 60	**BECAUSE THEY'RE YOUNG** *London HLW 9162*	2		18
10 Nov 60	**KOMMOTION** *London HLW 9225*	13		10
12 Jan 61	**PEPE** *London HLW 9257*	2		14
20 Apr 61	**THEME FROM 'DIXIE'** *London HLW 9324*	7		10
22 Jun 61	**RING OF FIRE** *London HLW 9370*	17		10
14 Sep 61	**DRIVIN' HOME** *London HLW 9406*	30		4
5 Oct 61	**CARAVAN** *Parlophone R 4826*	42		3
24 May 62	**DEEP IN THE HEART OF TEXAS** *RCA 1288*	19		8
23 Aug 62	**BALLAD OF PALADIN** *RCA 1300*	10		10
8 Nov 62	**DANCE WITH THE GUITAR MAN** *RCA 1316* DUANE EDDY & THE REBELETTES	4		16
14 Feb 63	**BOSS GUITAR** *RCA 1329* DUANE EDDY & THE REBELETTES	27		8
30 May 63	**LONELY BOY LONELY GUITAR** *RCA 1344* DUANE EDDY & THE REBELETTES	35		4
29 Aug 63	**YOUR BABY'S GONE SURFIN'** *RCA 1357* DUANE EDDY & THE REBELETTES	49		1
8 Mar 75	**PLAY ME LIKE YOU PLAY YOUR GUITAR** *GTO GT 11* DUANE EDDY & THE REBELETTES	9		9
22 Mar 86	**PETER GUNN** *China WOK 6* ART OF NOISE FEATURING DUANE EDDY	8		9

EDDY & THE SOUL BAND

Holland/US, male production/vocal group — 7

Date	Title	Peak	Wks at No.1	Wks
23 Feb 85	**THE THEME FROM 'SHAFT'** *Club JAB 11*	13		7

RANDY EDELMAN

US, male vocalist/pianist — 18

Date	Title	Peak	Wks at No.1	Wks
6 Mar 76	**CONCRETE AND CLAY** *20th Century BTC 2261*	11		7
18 Sep 76	**UPTOWN UPTEMPO WOMAN** *20th Century BTC 2225*	25		7
15 Jan 77	**YOU** *20th Century BTC 2253*	49		2
17 Jul 82	**NOBODY MADE ME** *Rocket XPRES 81*	60		2

EDELWEISS

Austria, male production duo – Walter Werzowa & Martin Gletschermayer — 10

Date	Title	Peak	Wks at No.1	Wks
29 Apr 89	**BRING ME EDELWEISS** *WEA YZ 353*	5		10

EDEN

UK/Australia, male/female vocal/production duo — 2

Date	Title	Peak	Wks at No.1	Wks
6 Mar 93	**DO U FEEL 4 ME** *Logic 74321135422*	51		2

EDISON LIGHTHOUSE

UK, male session vocal/instrumental group featuring Tony Burrows* — 13

Date	Title	Peak	Wks at No.1	Wks
24 Jan 70	**LOVE GROWS (WHERE MY ROSEMARY GOES)** *Bell 1091*	1	5	12
30 Jan 71	**IT'S UP TO YOU PETULA** *Bell 1136*	49		1

EDITORS

UK, male vocal/instrumental group – Tom Smith, Edward Lay, Russell Leetch & Chris Urbanowicz — 35

Date	Title	Peak	Wks at No.1	Wks
5 Feb 05	**BULLETS** *Kitchenware SKCD77*	54		1
30 Apr 05	**MUNICH** *Kitchenware SKCD782*	22		3
23 Jul 05	**BLOOD** *Kitchenware SKCD792*	18		3
8 Oct 05	**BULLETS** *Kitchenware SKCD802*	27		2
14 Jan 06	**MUNICH** *Kitchenware SKCD832*	10		7
8 Apr 06	**ALL SPARKS** *Kitchenware SKCD84*	21		3
1 Jul 06	**BLOOD** *Kitchenware SKCD87*	39		1
23 Jun 07	**SMOKERS OUTSIDE THE HOSPITAL DOORS** *Columbia SKCD93*	7		7
8 Sep 07	**THE END HAS A START** *Kitchenware SKCD952*	27		4
8 Dec 07	**THE RACING RATS** *Kitchenware SKCD97*	26		1
24 Oct 09	**PAPILLON** *Kitchenware SKCD106*	23		3

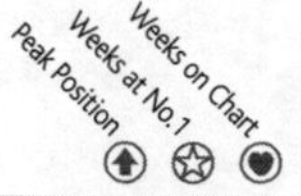

DAVE EDMUNDS
UK, male vocalist/guitarist — 93

Date	Title	Peak	Wks at No.1	Wks on Chart
21 Nov 70	**I HEAR YOU KNOCKING** *MAM 1*	1	6	14
20 Jan 73	**BABY I LOVE YOU** *Rockfield ROC 1*	8		13
9 Jun 73	**BORN TO BE WITH YOU** *Rockfield ROC 2*	5		12
2 Jul 77	**I KNEW THE BRIDE** *Swansong SSK 19411*	26		8
30 Jun 79	**GIRLS TALK** *Swansong SSK 19418* ●	4		11
22 Sep 79	**QUEEN OF HEARTS** *Swansong SSK 19419*	11		9
24 Nov 79	**CRAWLING FROM THE WRECKAGE** *Swansong SSK 19420*	59		4
9 Feb 80	**SINGING THE BLUES** *Swansong SSK 19422*	28		8
28 Mar 81	**ALMOST SATURDAY NIGHT** *Swansong SSK 19424*	58		3
20 Jun 81	**THE RACE IS ON** *Swansong SSK 19425* & THE STRAY CATS	34		6
26 Mar 83	**SLIPPING AWAY** *Arista ARIST 522*	60		4
7 Apr 90	**KING OF LOVE** *Capitol CL 568*	68		1

ALTON EDWARDS
Zimbabwe, male vocalist — 9

Date	Title	Peak	Wks at No.1	Wks on Chart
9 Jan 82	**I JUST WANNA (SPEND SOME TIME WITH YOU)** *Streetwave STRA 1897*	20		9

DENNIS EDWARDS FEATURING SIEDAH GARRETT
US, male/female vocal duo — 10

Date	Title	Peak	Wks at No.1	Wks on Chart
24 Mar 84	**DON'T LOOK ANY FURTHER** *Gordy TMG 1334*	45		5
20 Jun 87	**DON'T LOOK ANY FURTHER** *Gordy TMG 1334*	55		5

RUPIE EDWARDS
Jamaica, male vocalist — 16

Date	Title	Peak	Wks at No.1	Wks on Chart
23 Nov 74	**IRE FEELINGS (SKANGA)** *Cactus CT 38*	9		10
8 Feb 75	**LEGGO SKANGA** *Cactus CT 51*	32		6

STEVE EDWARDS
UK, male vocalist — 12

Date	Title	Peak	Wks at No.1	Wks on Chart
15 Jul 06	**WORLD, HOLD ON (CHILDREN OF THE SKY)** *Defected DFTD132CDX* BOB SINCLAR FEATURING STEVE EDWARDS	9		11
30 Sep 06	**WATCH THE SUNRISE** *Positiva CDTIV243* AXWELL FEATURING STEVE EDWARDS	70		1

TOMMY EDWARDS
US, male vocalist, d. 23 Oct 69 (age 57) — 18

Date	Title	Peak	Wks at No.1	Wks on Chart
3 Oct 58	**IT'S ALL IN THE GAME** *MGM 989* ★	1	3	17
7 Aug 59	**MY MELANCHOLY BABY** *MGM 1020*	29		1

EELS
US, male vocal/instrumental group – Mark Everett, Jonathan 'Butch' Norton & Tommy Walter — 24

Date	Title	Peak	Wks at No.1	Wks on Chart
15 Feb 97	**NOVOCAINE FOR THE SOUL** *DreamWorks DRMCD 22174*	10		5
17 May 97	**SUSAN'S HOUSE** *DreamWorks DRMCD 22238*	9		5
13 Sep 97	**YOUR LUCKY DAY IN HELL** *DreamWorks DRMCD 22277*	35		2
26 Sep 98	**LAST STOP THIS TOWN** *DreamWorks DRMCD 22346*	23		3
12 Dec 98	**CANCER FOR THE CURE** *DreamWorks DRMCD 22373*	60		1
26 Feb 00	**MR E'S BEAUTIFUL BLUES** *DreamWorks DRMCD 4509772*	11		4
24 Jun 00	**FLYSWATER** *DreamWorks DRMCD 4509462*	55		1
22 Sep 01	**SOULJACKER PART 1** *DreamWorks 4508932*	30		2
28 May 05	**HEY MAN (NOW YOU'RE REALLY LIVING)** *Vagrant 9881879*	45		1

EFUA
UK, female vocalist (Efua Baker) — 5

Date	Title	Peak	Wks at No.1	Wks on Chart
3 Jul 93	**SOMEWHERE** *Virgin VSCDT 1463*	42		5

EGG
UK, male vocal/instrumental group — 1

Date	Title	Peak	Wks at No.1	Wks on Chart
30 Jan 99	**GETTING AWAY WITH IT** *Indochina ID 079CD*	58		1

EGG VERSUS DAVID GUETTA
UK/France, male vocal/instrumental/production group — 24

Date	Title	Peak	Wks at No.1	Wks on Chart
15 Jul 06	**WALKING AWAY** *Gusto CDGUS37*	56		4
19 Aug 06	**LOVE DON'T LET ME GO (WALKING AWAY)** *Gusto CDGUS42* DAVID GUETTA VS THE EGG	3		20

EGGS ON LEGS
UK, male TV producer/vocalist — 1

Date	Title	Peak	Wks at No.1	Wks on Chart
23 Sep 95	**COCK A DOODLE DO IT** *Avex UKAVEXCD 18*	42		1

EGYPTIAN EMPIRE
UK, male producer (Tim Taylor) — 2

Date	Title	Peak	Wks at No.1	Wks on Chart
24 Oct 92	**THE HORN TRACK** *ffrreedom TAB 115*	61		2

EIFFEL 65
Italy, male vocal/DJ/instrumental/production trio – Jeffrey Jey, Maurizio Lobina & Gabriele 'Gabry' Ponte — 36

Date	Title	Peak	Wks at No.1	Wks on Chart
21 Aug 99	**BLUE (DA BA DEE) (IMPORT)** *Logic 74321688212*	39		5
25 Sep 99	**BLUE (DA BA DEE)** *Eternal WEA 226CD1* ●	1	3	21
19 Feb 00	**MOVE YOUR BODY** *Eternal WEA 255CD1*	3		10

808 STATE
UK, male production group – Andrew Barker, Graham Massey, Darren Partington, Martin Price & Gerald Simpson (A Guy Called Gerald*, left 1989) — 70

Date	Title	Peak	Wks at No.1	Wks on Chart
18 Nov 89	**PACIFIC – 707** *ZTT ZANG 1*	10		9
31 Mar 90	**THE EXTENDED PLEASURE OF DANCE (EP)** *ZTT ZANG 2T*	56		1
2 Jun 90	**THE ONLY RHYME THAT BITES** *ZTT ZANG 3* MC TUNES VERSUS 808 STATE	10		10
15 Sep 90	**TUNES SPLITS THE ATOM** *ZTT ZANG 6* MC TUNES VERSUS 808 STATE	18		7
10 Nov 90	**CUBIK/OLYMPIC** *ZTT ZANG 5*	10		10
16 Feb 91	**IN YER FACE** *ZTT ZANG 14*	9		6
27 Apr 91	**OOOPS** *ZTT ZANG 19* FEATURING BJORK	42		3
17 Aug 91	**LIFT/OPEN YOUR MIND** *ZTT ZANG 20*	38		4
29 Aug 92	**TIMB BOMB/NIMBUS** *ZTT ZANG 33*	59		1
12 Dec 92	**ONE IN TEN** *ZTT ZANG 39* VS UB40	17		8
30 Jan 93	**PLAN 9** *ZTT ZANG 38CD*	50		2
26 Jun 93	**10 X 10** *ZTT ZANG 42CD*	67		1
13 Aug 94	**BOMBADIN** *ZTT ZANG 54CD*	67		1
29 Jun 96	**BOND** *ZTT ZANG 80CD*	57		1
8 Feb 97	**LOPEZ** *ZTT ZANG 87CD*	20		2
16 May 98	**PACIFIC/CUBIK** *ZTT ZANG 98CD1*	21		3
6 Mar 99	**THE ONLY RHYME THAT BITES 99** *ZTT 125CD* MC TUNES VERSUS 808 STATE	53		1

18 WHEELER
UK, male vocal/instrumental group — 1

Date	Title	Peak	Wks at No.1	Wks on Chart
15 Mar 97	**STAY** *Creation CRESCD 249*	59		1

EIGHTH WONDER
UK, female/male vocal/instrumental group – Patsy Kensit, Geoff Beauchamp, Alex Godson (replaced by Steve Grantley) & Jamie Kensit — 25

Date	Title	Peak	Wks at No.1	Wks on Chart
2 Nov 85	**STAY WITH ME** *CBS A 6594*	65		2
20 Feb 88	**I'M NOT SCARED** *CBS SCARE 1*	7		13
25 Jun 88	**CROSS MY HEART** *CBS 6515527*	13		8
1 Oct 88	**BABY BABY** *CBS BABE 1*	65		2

EIGHTIES MATCHBOX B-LINE DISASTER
UK, male vocal/instrumental group — 11

Date	Title	Peak	Wks at No.1	Wks on Chart
28 Sep 02	**CELEBRATE YOUR MOTHER** *Universal MCSTD 40296*	66		1
18 Jan 03	**PSYCHOSIS SAFARI** *Universal MCSTD 40308*	26		2
24 May 03	**CHICKEN** *Island MCSXD 40317*	30		2
24 Jan 04	**MISTER MENTAL** *Universal MCSXD 40353*	25		2
10 Jul 04	**I COULD BE AN ANGLE** *Island MCSTD 40368*	35		2
23 Oct 04	**RISE OF THE EAGLES** *Universal MCSTD 40382*	40		2

EINSTEIN
UK, male rapper (Colin Case) — 6

Date	Title	Peak	Wks at No.1	Wks on Chart
18 Nov 89	**ANOTHER MONSTERJAM** *ffrr F 116* SIMON HARRIS FEATURING EINSTEIN	65		1
15 Dec 90	**TURN IT UP** *Swanyard SYD 9* TECHNOTRONIC FEATURING MELISSA & EINSTEIN	42		4
24 Aug 96	**THE POWER 96** *Arista 74321398672* SNAP! FEATURING EINSTEIN	42		1

EL CHOMBO
Panama (b. US), male vocalist/producer (Rodney Clark) — 4

Date	Title	Peak	Wks at No.1	Wks on Chart
16 Dec 06	**CHACARRON** *Substance SUBS21CDX*	20		4

EL COCO

US, male vocal/instrumental group — Weeks on Chart: 4

Date	Title / Label	Peak	Wks No.1	Wks
14 Jan 78	**COCOMOTION** *Pye International 7N 25761*	31		4

EL MARIACHI

US, male producer (Roger Sanchez). See Funk Junkeez — Weeks on Chart: 2

Date	Title / Label	Peak	Wks No.1	Wks
9 Nov 96	**CUBA** *ffrr FCD 286*	38		2

EL PRESIDENTE

UK, male/female vocal/instrumental group — Weeks on Chart: 6

Date	Title / Label	Peak	Wks No.1	Wks
14 May 05	**100MPH** *One 82876692142*	37		2
6 Aug 05	**WITHOUT YOU** *One 82876710782*	30		2
22 Oct 05	**ROCKET** *One 82876743032*	48		1
18 Feb 06	**TURN THIS THING AROUND** *One 82876781382*	39		1

ELASTICA

UK, female/male vocal/instrumental group – Justine Frischmann, Annie Holland, Donna Matthews & Justin Welch — Weeks on Chart: 12

Date	Title / Label	Peak	Wks No.1	Wks
12 Feb 94	**LINE UP** *Deceptive BLUFF 004CD*	20		3
22 Oct 94	**CONNECTION** *Deceptive BLUFF 010CD*	17		4
25 Feb 95	**WAKING UP** *Deceptive BLUFF 011CD*	13		4
24 Jun 00	**MAD DOG** *Deceptive BLUFF 077CD*	44		1

ELATE

UK, male/female vocal/instrumental trio — Weeks on Chart: 2

Date	Title / Label	Peak	Wks No.1	Wks
26 Jul 97	**SOMEBODY LIKE YOU** *VC Recordings VCRD 22*	38		2

DONNIE ELBERT

US, male vocalist, d. 26 Jan 1989 (age 52) — Weeks on Chart: 29

Date	Title / Label	Peak	Wks No.1	Wks
8 Jan 72	**WHERE DID OUR LOVE GO** *London HL 10352*	8		10
26 Feb 72	**I CAN'T HELP MYSELF** *Avco 6105 009*	11		10
29 Apr 72	**LITTLE PIECE OF LEATHER** *London HL 10370*	27		9

ELBOW

UK, male vocal/instrumental group — Weeks on Chart: 39

Date	Title / Label	Peak	Wks No.1	Wks
5 May 01	**RED** *V2 VVR 5016158*	36		1
21 Jul 01	**POWDER BLUE** *V2 VVR 5016163*	41		1
20 Oct 01	**NEWBORN** *V2 VVR 5016173*	42		1
16 Feb 02	**ASLEEP IN THE BACK** *V2 VVR 5018703*	19		3
16 Aug 03	**FALLEN ANGEL** *V2 VVR 5021808*	19		3
8 Nov 03	**FUGITIVE MOTEL** *V2 VVR 5021828*	44		1
6 Mar 04	**NOT A JOB** *V2 VVR 5024678*	26		2
10 Sep 05	**FORGET MYSELF** *V2 VVR5032548*	22		2
19 Nov 05	**LEADERS OF THE FREE WORLD** *V2 VVR5035628*	53		1
22 Mar 08	**GROUNDS FOR DIVORCE** *Fiction 1761656*	19		4
14 Jun 08	**ONE DAY LIKE THIS** *Fiction 1767730*	35		12
14 Feb 09	**ONE DAY LIKE THIS** *Fiction 1767730*	35		8

ELECTRA

UK, male production group — Weeks on Chart: 7

Date	Title / Label	Peak	Wks No.1	Wks
6 Aug 88	**JIBARO** *ffrr F 9*	54		3
30 Dec 89	**IT'S YOUR DESTINY/AUTUMN LOVE** *London F 121*	51		4

ELECTRAFIXION

UK, male vocal/instrumental group — Weeks on Chart: 6

Date	Title / Label	Peak	Wks No.1	Wks
19 Nov 94	**ZEPHYR** *WEA YZ 865CD*	47		2
9 Sep 95	**LOWDOWN** *WEA YZ 977CD*	54		2
4 Nov 95	**NEVER** *Spacejunk 022CD*	58		1
16 Mar 96	**SISTER PAIN** *Spacejunk 037CD*	27		1

ELECTRASY

UK, male vocal/instrumental group — Weeks on Chart: 7

Date	Title / Label	Peak	Wks No.1	Wks
13 Jun 98	**LOST IN SPACE** *MCA MCSTD 40171*	60		1
5 Sep 98	**MORNING AFTERGLOW** *MCA MCSTD 40184*	19		4
28 Nov 98	**BEST FRIEND'S GIRL** *MCA MCSXD 40195*	41		2

ELECTRIBE 101

UK/Germany, male/female vocal/production group — Weeks on Chart: 15

Date	Title / Label	Peak	Wks No.1	Wks
28 Oct 89	**TELL ME WHEN THE FEVER ENDED** *Mercury MER 310*	32		5
24 Feb 90	**TALKING WITH MYSELF** *Mercury MER 316*	23		5
22 Sep 90	**YOU'RE WALKING** *Mercury MER 328*	50		3
10 Oct 98	**TALKING WITH MYSELF '98 (REMIX)** *Manifesto FESDD 49*	39		2

ELECTRIC LIGHT ORCHESTRA

UK, male vocal/instrumental group – Jeff Lynne*, Bev Bevan, Kelly Groucutt, Richard Tandy & Roy Wood* (left 1972). The distinctive-sounding and innovative group, masterminded by the multi-talented Lynne, proved to be one of the biggest-selling UK acts on both sides of the Atlantic in the 1970s — Weeks on Chart: 255

Date	Title / Label	Peak	Wks No.1	Wks
29 Jul 72	**10538 OVERTURE** *Harvest HAR 5053*	9		8
27 Jan 73	**ROLL OVER BEETHOVEN** *Harvest HAR 5063*	6		10
6 Oct 73	**SHOWDOWN** *Harvest HAR 5077*	12		10
9 Mar 74	**MA-MA-MA-BELLE** *Warner Brothers K 16349*	22		8
10 Jan 76	**EVIL WOMAN** *Jet 764*	10		8
3 Jul 76	**STRANGE MAGIC** *Jet 779*	38		3
13 Nov 76	**LIVIN' THING** *Jet UP 36184* ●	4		12
19 Feb 77	**ROCKARIA!** *Jet UP 36209*	9		9
21 May 77	**TELEPHONE LINE** *Jet UP 36254*	8		10
29 Oct 77	**TURN TO STONE** *Jet UP 36313*	18		12
28 Jan 78	**MR BLUE SKY** *Jet UP 36342* ●	6		11
10 Jun 78	**WILD WEST HERO** *Jet 109* ●	6		14
7 Oct 78	**SWEET TALKIN' WOMAN** *Jet 121* ●	6		9
9 Dec 78	**ELO EP** *Jet ELO 1*	34		8
19 May 79	**SHINE A LITTLE LOVE** *Jet 144* ●	6		10
21 Jul 79	**THE DIARY OF HORACE WIMP** *Jet 150* ●	8		9
1 Sep 79	**DON'T BRING ME DOWN** *Jet 153* ●	3		9
17 Nov 79	**CONFUSION/LAST TRAIN TO LONDON** *Jet 166* ●	8		10
24 May 80	**I'M ALIVE** *Jet 179*	20		9
21 Jun 80	**XANADU** *Jet 185* OLIVIA NEWTON-JOHN & ELECTRIC LIGHT ORCHESTRA ●	1	2	11
2 Aug 80	**ALL OVER THE WORLD** *Jet 195*	11		8
22 Nov 80	**DON'T WALK AWAY** *Jet 7004*	21		10
1 Aug 81	**HOLD ON TIGHT** *Jet 7011* ●	4		12
24 Oct 81	**TWILIGHT** *Jet 7015*	30		7
9 Jan 82	**TICKET TO THE MOON/HERE IS THE NEWS** *Jet 7018*	24		8
18 Jun 83	**ROCK 'N' ROLL IS KING** *Jet A 3500*	13		9
3 Sep 83	**SECRET MESSAGES** *Jet A 3720*	48		3
1 Mar 86	**CALLING AMERICA** *Epic A 6844*	28		7
11 May 91	**HONEST MEN** *Telstar ELO 100 PART 2*	60		1

ELECTRIC PRUNES

US, male vocal/instrumental group — Weeks on Chart: 5

Date	Title / Label	Peak	Wks No.1	Wks
9 Feb 67	**I HAD TOO MUCH TO DREAM LAST NIGHT** *Reprise RS 20532*	49		1
11 May 67	**GET ME TO THE WORLD ON TIME** *Reprise RS 20564*	42		4

ELECTRIC SIX

US, male vocal/instrumental group – Tyler Spencer, Joe Frezza, Cory Martin, Steve Nawara & Christopher Tait — Weeks on Chart: 27

Date	Title / Label	Peak	Wks No.1	Wks
18 Jan 03	**DANGER HIGH VOLTAGE** *XL Recordings XLS 151CD*	2		11
14 Jun 03	**GAY BAR** *XL Recordings XLS 158CD*	5		10
25 Oct 03	**DANCE COMMANDER** *XL Recordings XLS 170CD*	40		1
25 Dec 04	**RADIO GAGA** *WEA WEA381CD1*	21		5

ELECTRIC SOFT PARADE

UK, male vocal/instrumental group — Weeks on Chart: 5

Date	Title / Label	Peak	Wks No.1	Wks
4 Aug 01	**EMPTY AT THE END/SUMATRAN** *DB 0067JC* SOFT PARADE	65		1
10 Nov 01	**THERE'S A SILENCE** *DB 007CD7JC*	52		1
16 Mar 02	**SILENT TO THE DARK II** *DB DB008 CDE7*	23		2
1 Jun 02	**EMPTY AT THE END** *DB DB009 ECD7*	39		1

ELECTRIQUE BOUTIQUE

UK/France, male production group — Weeks on Chart: 2

Date	Title / Label	Peak	Wks No.1	Wks
26 Aug 00	**REVELATION** *Data 14CDS*	37		2

ELECTRONIC

UK, male vocal/instrumental duo – Bernard Sumner & Johnny Marr — Weeks on Chart: 36

Date	Title / Label	Peak	Wks No.1	Wks
16 Dec 89	**GETTING AWAY WITH IT** *Factory FAC 2577*	12		9
27 Apr 91	**GET THE MESSAGE** *Factory FAC 2877*	8		7
21 Sep 91	**FEEL EVERY BEAT** *Factory FAC 3287*	39		4
4 Jul 92	**DISAPPOINTED** *Parlophone R 6311*	6		5
6 Jul 96	**FORBIDDEN CITY** *Parlophone CDR 6436*	14		4

Silver-selling ● Gold-selling ● Platinum-selling (× multiples) ⊛ US No.1 ★ | Peak Position | Weeks at No.1 | Weeks on Chart

Date	Title	Peak Position	Weeks at No.1	Weeks on Chart
28 Sep 96	**FOR YOU** *Parlophone CDR 6445*	16		2
15 Feb 97	**SECOND NATURE** *Parlophone CDR 6455*	35		2
24 Apr 99	**VIVID** *Parlophone CDR 6514*	17		3

ELECTRONICAS

Holland, male instrumental group — 8

Date	Title	Peak Position	Weeks at No.1	Weeks on Chart
19 Sep 81	**ORIGINAL BIRD DANCE** *Polydor POSP 360*	22		8

ELECTROSET

UK, male production duo — 4

Date	Title	Peak Position	Weeks at No.1	Weeks on Chart
21 Nov 92	**HOW DOES IT FEEL** *ffrr F 203*	27		3
15 Jul 95	**SENSATION** *ffrreedom TABCD 231*	69		1

ELEGANTS

US, male vocal group — 2

Date	Title	Peak Position	Weeks at No.1	Weeks on Chart
26 Sep 58	**LITTLE STAR** *HMV POP 520* ★	25		2

ELEMENTFOUR

UK, male production duo – Andy Gray & Paul Oakenfold. See Oakenfold, Perfecto Allstarz, Virus — 11

Date	Title	Peak Position	Weeks at No.1	Weeks on Chart
9 Sep 00	**BIG BROTHER UK TV THEME** *Channel 4 Music C4M 00072*	4		9
4 Aug 01	**BIG BROTHER UK TV THEME** *Channel 4 Music C4M 00072*	63		2

ELEPHANT MAN

Jamaica, male vocalist (O'Neil Bryan) — 5

Date	Title	Peak Position	Weeks at No.1	Weeks on Chart
22 Nov 03	**PON DE RIVER, PON DE BANK** *Atlantic AT 0168CD*	29		3
4 Sep 04	**JOOK GAL** *VP VPCD6416*	41		2

ELEVATION

UK, male producer (Shaun Imrei) — 1

Date	Title	Peak Position	Weeks at No.1	Weeks on Chart
23 May 92	**CAN YOU FEEL IT** *Nova Mute 12NOMU 3*	62		1

ELEVATOR SUITE

UK, male instrumental/production trio — 1

Date	Title	Peak Position	Weeks at No.1	Weeks on Chart
12 Aug 00	**BACK AROUND** *Infectious INFECT 85CDS*	71		1

ELEVATORMAN

UK, male instrumental/production group — 4

Date	Title	Peak Position	Weeks at No.1	Weeks on Chart
14 Jan 95	**FUNK AND DRIVE** *Wired 211*	37		3
1 Jul 95	**FIRED UP** *Wired 216*	44		1

ELGINS

US, male/female vocal group – Saundra Mallett Edwards, Johnny Dawson, Robert Fleming, Norbert McClean & Cleotha Miller — 20

Date	Title	Peak Position	Weeks at No.1	Weeks on Chart
1 May 71	**HEAVEN MUST HAVE SENT YOU** *Tamla Motown TMG 771*	3		13
9 Oct 71	**PUT YOURSELF IN MY PLACE** *Tamla Motown TMG 787*	28		7

ELIAS & HIS ZIGZAG JIVE FLUTES

South Africa, male instrumental group led by Elias & Aaron, d. 12 Mar 2003, Lerole — 14

Date	Title	Peak Position	Weeks at No.1	Weeks on Chart
25 Apr 58	**TOM HARK** *Columbia DB 4109*	2		14

YVONNE ELLIMAN

US, female vocalist — 44

Date	Title	Peak Position	Weeks at No.1	Weeks on Chart
29 Jan 72	**I DON'T KNOW HOW TO LOVE HIM** *MCA MMKS 5077*	47		1
6 Nov 76	**LOVE ME** *RSO 2090 205*	6		13
7 May 77	**HELLO STRANGER** *RSO 2090 236*	26		5
13 Aug 77	**I CAN'T GET YOU OUT OF MY MIND** *RSO 2090 251*	17		13
6 May 78	**IF I CAN'T HAVE YOU** *RSO 2090 266* ● ★	4		12

DUKE ELLINGTON WITH LOUIS BELLSON (DRUMS)

US, orchestra leader (Edward Ellington), d. 24 May 1974 (age 75) — 4

Date	Title	Peak Position	Weeks at No.1	Weeks on Chart
5 Mar 54	**SKIN DEEP** *Philips PB 243*	7		4

LANCE ELLINGTON

UK, male vocalist — 1

Date	Title	Peak Position	Weeks at No.1	Weeks on Chart
21 Aug 93	**LONELY (HAVE WE LOST OUR LOVE)** *RCA 74321158332*	57		1

RAY ELLINGTON

UK, band leader, d. 27 Feb 1985 (age 69) — 4

Date	Title	Peak Position	Weeks at No.1	Weeks on Chart
15 Nov 62	**THE MADISON** *Ember S 102*	36		4

ELLIOT MINOR

UK, male vocal/instrumental group — 13

Date	Title	Peak Position	Weeks at No.1	Weeks on Chart
21 Apr 07	**PARALLEL WORLDS** *Repossession REPO5CDS*	31		2
18 Aug 07	**JESSICA** *Repossession REPO7CDS*	19		2
10 Nov 07	**WHITE ONE IS EVIL** *Warner Brothers WEA432CD2*	27		2
9 Feb 08	**STILL FIGURING OUT** *Repossession WEA468CD*	17		3
19 Apr 08	**PARALLEL WORLDS** *Warner Brothers WEA444CD*	22		3
5 Jul 08	**TIME AFTER TIME** *Repossession WEA448CD*	47		1

BERN ELLIOTT & THE FENMEN

UK, male vocal/instrumental group — 22

Date	Title	Peak Position	Weeks at No.1	Weeks on Chart
21 Nov 63	**MONEY** *Decca F 11770*	14		13
19 Mar 64	**NEW ORLEANS** *Decca F 11852*	24		9

MISSY ELLIOTT

US, female rapper/producer (Melissa Elliott) — 177

Date	Title	Peak Position	Weeks at No.1	Weeks on Chart
30 Aug 97	**THE RAIN (SUPA DUPA FLY)** *East West E 3919CD* MISSY 'MISDEMEANOR' ELLIOT	16		3
29 Nov 97	**SOCK IT 2 ME** *East West E 3890CD* MISSY 'MISDEMEANOR' ELLIOT FEATURING DA BEAT	33		2
25 Apr 98	**BEEP ME 911** *East West E 3859CD*	14		3
22 Aug 98	**HIT 'EM WIT DA HEE** *East West E 3824CD1* MISSY 'MISDEMEANOR' ELLIOTT FEATURING LIL' KIM	25		3
22 Aug 98	**MAKE IT HOT** *East West E 3821CD* NICOLE FEATURING MISSY 'MISDEMEANOR' ELLIOTT	22		4
26 Sep 98	**I WANT YOU BACK** *Virgin VSCDT 1716* MELANIE B FEATURING MISSY 'MISDEMEANOR' ELLIOTT ●	1	1	9
21 Nov 98	**5 MINUTES** *Elektra E 3803CD* LIL' MO FEATURING MISSY 'MISDEMEANOR' ELLIOTT	72		1
13 Mar 99	**HERE WE COME** *Virgin DINSD 179* TIMBALAND/MISSY ELLIOTT & MAGOO	43		1
25 Sep 99	**ALL N MY GRILL** *Elektra E 3742CD* MISSY 'MISDEMEANOR' ELLIOTT FEATURING MC SOLAAR	20		4
22 Jan 00	**HOT BOYZ** *Elektra E 7002CD* MISSY 'MISDEMEANOR' ELLIOTT FEATURING NAS, EVE & Q-TIP	18		3
28 Apr 01	**GET UR FREAK ON** *Elektra E 7206CD*	4		11
18 Aug 01	**ONE MINUTE MAN** *The Gold Mind/Elektra E 7245CD* FEATURING LUDACRIS	10		8
13 Oct 01	**SUPERFREAKON** *Elektra 7559672550*	72		1
22 Dec 01	**SON OF A GUN (BETCHA THINK THIS SONG)** *Virgin VUSCDX 232* JANET JACKSON WITH CARLY SIMON FEATURING MISSY ELLIOTT	13		9
6 Apr 02	**4 MY PEOPLE** *Elektra E 7286CD*	5		13
16 Nov 02	**WORK IT** *Elektra E 7344CD*	6		9
22 Mar 03	**GOSSIP FOLKS** *Elektra E 7380CD* FEATURING LUDACRIS	9		9
22 Nov 03	**PASS THAT DUTCH** *Elektra E 7509CD*	10		11
13 Mar 04	**COP THAT SHIT** *Unique Corp TIMBACD001* TIMBALAND/MAGOO/MISSY ELLIOTT	22		3
3 Apr 04	**I'M REALLY HOT** *Elektra E 7552CD*	22		4
17 Jul 04	**TUSH** *Def Jam 9862837* GHOSTFACE FEATURING MISSY ELLIOTT	34		3
13 Nov 04	**CAR WASH** *DreamWorks 9864630* CHRISTINA AGUILERA & MISSY ELLIOTT	4		14
19 Mar 05	**TURN DA LIGHTS OFF** *Atlantic AT0200CD* TWEET FEATURING MISSY ELLIOTT	29		3
23 Apr 05	**1 2 STEP** *LaFace 82876688342* CIARA FEATURING MISSY ELLIOTT	3		11
2 Jul 05	**LOSE CONTROL** *Atlantic AT0209CD*	7		11
8 Oct 05	**TEARY EYED** *Atlantic AT0215CD*	47		2
26 Aug 06	**WE RUN THIS** *Atlantic AT0255CD*	38		4
7 Feb 09	**WHATCHA THINK ABOUT THAT** *Interscope 1799050* PUSSYCAT DOLLS & MISSY ELLIOTT	9		12
11 Jul 09	**WORK** *LaFace USLF20900040* CIARA FEATURING MISSY ELLIOTT	52		6

JOEY B ELLIS

US, male rapper/vocalist — 10

Date	Title	Peak Position	Weeks at No.1	Weeks on Chart
16 Feb 91	**GO FOR IT (HEART AND SOUL)** *Capitol CL 601* ROCKY V FEATURING JOEY B ELLIS & TYNETTA HARE	20		8
18 May 91	**THOUGHT U WERE THE ONE FOR ME** *Capitol CL 614*	58		2

SHIRLEY ELLIS
US, female vocalist (Shirley Elliston)

Date	Title	Peak Position	Weeks at No.1	Weeks on Chart (17)
6 May 65	**THE CLAPPING SONG** *London HLR 9961*	6		13
8 Jul 78	**THE CLAPPING SONG (EP)** *MCA MCEP 1*	59		4

SOPHIE ELLIS-BEXTOR
UK, female vocalist. See Spiller, Theaudience

Date	Title	Peak Position	Weeks at No.1	Weeks on Chart (86)
25 Aug 01	**TAKE ME HOME (A GIRL LIKE ME)** *Polydor 5872312* ○	2		12
15 Dec 01	**MURDER ON THE DANCEFLOOR** *Polydor 5704942*	2		16
22 Jun 02	**GET OVER YOU/MOVE THIS MOUNTAIN** *Polydor 5708342*	3		13
16 Nov 02	**MUSIC GETS THE BEST OF ME** *Polydor 0659232*	14		10
25 Oct 03	**MIXED UP WORLD** *Polydor 9812108*	7		6
10 Jan 04	**I WON'T CHANGE YOU** *Polydor 9815124*	9		6
10 Feb 07	**CATCH YOU** *Fascination 1724021*	8		8
26 May 07	**ME AND MY IMAGINATION** *Fascination 1733077*	23		4
25 Aug 07	**TODAY THE SUN'S ON US** *Fascination 1741966*	64		1
27 Jun 09	**HEARTBREAK (MAKE ME A DANCER)** *Loaded LOAD132CD* FREEMASONS FEATURING SOPHIE ELLIS-BEXTOR	13		10

ELLIS, BEGGS & HOWARD
UK, male vocal/instrumental trio

Date	Title	Peak Position	Weeks at No.1	Weeks on Chart (8)
2 Jul 88	**BIG BUBBLES, NO TROUBLES** *RCA PB 42089*	59		3
11 Mar 89	**BIG BUBBLES, NO TROUBLES** *RCA PB 42089*	41		5

JENNIFER ELLISON
UK, female actor/vocalist

Date	Title	Peak Position	Weeks at No.1	Weeks on Chart (14)
28 Jun 03	**BABY I DON'T CARE** *East West EW 268CD*	6		10
7 Aug 04	**BYE BYE BOY** *Sky-rocket CDSKYCON1*	13		4

ELWOOD
US, male rapper/vocalist (Elwood Strickland)

Date	Title	Peak Position	Weeks at No.1	Weeks on Chart (1)
26 Aug 00	**SUNDOWN** *Palm Pictures PPCD 70342*	72		1

EMBRACE
UK, male vocal/instrumental group – Danny McNamara, Mickey Dale, Steve Firth, Mike Heaton & Richard McNamara

Date	Title	Peak Position	Weeks at No.1	Weeks on Chart (76)
17 May 97	**FIREWORKS EP** *Hut HUTCD 84*	34		2
19 Jul 97	**ONE BIG FAMILY EP** *Hut HUTCD 86*	21		3
8 Nov 97	**ALL YOU GOOD GOOD PEOPLE EP** *Hut HUTCD 90*	8		4
6 Jun 98	**COME BACK TO WHAT YOU KNOW** *Hut HUTCD 93*	6		8
29 Aug 98	**MY WEAKNESS IS NONE OF YOUR BUSINESS** *Hut HUTCD 103*	9		4
13 Nov 99	**HOOLIGAN** *Hut HUTCD 123*	18		3
25 Mar 00	**YOU'RE NOT ALONE** *Hut HUTCD 126*	14		3
10 Jun 00	**SAVE ME** *Hut HUTCD 133*	29		3
19 Aug 00	**I WOULDN'T WANNA HAPPEN TO YOU** *Hut HUTDX 137*	23		2
1 Sep 01	**WONDER** *Hut HUTDX 142*	14		4
17 Nov 01	**MAKE IT LAST** *Hut HUTCD 144*	35		2
11 Sep 04	**GRAVITY** *Independiente ISOM87SMS*	7		7
27 Nov 04	**ASHES** *Independiente ISOM89SMS*	11		8
26 Feb 05	**LOOKING AS YOU ARE** *Independiente ISOM91SMS*	11		3
11 Jun 05	**A GLORIOUS DAY** *Independiente ISOM94SMS*	28		2
1 Apr 06	**NATURE'S LAW** *Independiente ISOM103SMS*	2		10
10 Jun 06	**WORLD AT YOUR FEET** *Independiente ISOM107SMS*	3		6
23 Sep 06	**TARGET** *Independiente ISOM110MSST*	29		1
16 Dec 06	**I CAN'T COME DOWN** *Independiente ISOM115MS*	54		1

KEITH EMERSON
UK, male keyboard player. See Emerson, Lake & Palmer, Nice

Date	Title	Peak Position	Weeks at No.1	Weeks on Chart (5)
10 Apr 76	**HONKY TONK TRAIN BLUES** *Manticore K 13513*	21		5

EMERSON, LAKE & PALMER
UK, male vocal/instrumental group – Keith Emerson*, Greg Lake* & Carl Palmer

Date	Title	Peak Position	Weeks at No.1	Weeks on Chart (13)
4 Jun 77	**FANFARE FOR THE COMMON MAN** *Atlantic K 10946* ○	2		13

DICK EMERY
UK, male comedian/vocalist, d. 2 Jan 1983 (age 65)

Date	Title	Peak Position	Weeks at No.1	Weeks on Chart (8)
26 Feb 69	**IF YOU LOVE HER** *Pye 7N 17644*	32		4
13 Jan 73	**YOU ARE AWFUL** *Pye 7N 45202*	43		4

EMF
UK, male vocal/instrumental group – James Atkin, Derry Brownson, Mark Decloedt, Ian Dench & Zac Foley, d. 2 Jan 2002

Date	Title	Peak Position	Weeks at No.1	Weeks on Chart (50)
3 Nov 90	**UNBELIEVABLE** *Parlophone R 6273* ○ ★	3		13
2 Feb 91	**I BELIEVE** *Parlophone R 6279*	6		7
27 Apr 91	**CHILDREN** *Parlophone R 6288*	19		5
31 Aug 91	**LIES** *Parlophone R 6295*	28		3
2 May 92	**UNEXPLAINED EP** *Parlophone SGE 2026*	18		4
19 Sep 92	**THEY'RE HERE** *Parlophone R 6321*	29		3
21 Nov 92	**IT'S YOU** *Parlophone R 6327*	23		3
25 Feb 95	**PERFECT DAY** *Parlophone CDRS 6401*	27		3
8 Jul 95	**I'M A BELIEVER** *Parlophone CDR 6412* EMF/REEVES & MORTIMER	3		8
28 Oct 95	**AFRO KING** *Parlophone CDRS 6416*	51		1

EMILIA
Sweden, female vocalist (Emilia Rydberg)

Date	Title	Peak Position	Weeks at No.1	Weeks on Chart (14)
12 Dec 98	**BIG BIG WORLD** *Universal UMD 87190* ○	5		13
1 May 99	**GOOD SIGN** *Universal UMD 87206*	54		1

EMINEM
US, male rapper/producer (Marshall Mathers III). 'Slim Shady' became the most successful rap artist in UK chart history with 16 Top 10 hits before announcing his short-lived retirement. He is credited with launching the career of Dido, whose 'Thank You' he sampled on 'Stan'. His UK singles sales have reached 5.7 million. See D12

Date	Title	Peak Position	Weeks at No.1	Weeks on Chart (284)
10 Apr 99	**MY NAME IS** *Interscope IND 95639*	2		12
14 Aug 99	**GUILTY CONSCIENCE** *Interscope IND 4971282* FEATURING DR DRE	5		8
10 Jun 00	**FORGOT ABOUT DRE** *Interscope 4973422* DR DRE FEATURING EMINEM	7		9
8 Jul 00	**THE REAL SLIM SHADY** *Interscope 4973792* ○	1	1	15
14 Oct 00	**THE WAY I AM** *Interscope 4974252*	8		9
16 Dec 00	**STAN** *Interscope 4974702* ⊛	1	1	17
1 Sep 01	**SCARY MOVIES** *Mole UK MOLEUK 045* BAD MEETS EVIL FEATURING EMINEM & ROCE DA 5' 9"	63		1
1 Jun 02	**WITHOUT ME** *Interscope 4977282* ●	1	1	16
28 Sep 02	**CLEANIN' OUT MY CLOSET** *Interscope 4973942*	4		13
14 Dec 02	**LOSE YOURSELF** *Interscope 4978282* ○ ★	1	1	21
15 Mar 03	**SING FOR THE MOMENT** *Interscope 4978612*	6		10
19 Jul 03	**BUSINESS** *Interscope 9809382*	6		9
14 Feb 04	**THE REAL SLIM SHADY** *Interscope 4973792*	72		1
13 Nov 04	**JUST LOSE IT** *Interscope 2103242*	1	1	12
12 Feb 05	**LIKE TOY SOLDIERS** *Aftermath 2103964*	1	1	12
14 May 05	**MOCKINGBIRD** *Interscope9882073*	4		12
6 Aug 05	**ASS LIKE THAT** *Interscope 9883904*	4		9
31 Dec 05	**WHEN I'M GONE** *Interscope 9889581*	4		9
18 Nov 06	**SMACK THAT** *Universal 1714412* AKON FEATURING EMINEM	1	1	23
13 Jan 07	**YOU DON'T KNOW** *Interscope USUM70613171* EMINEM, 50 CENT, LLOYD BANK$ & CA$HIS	32		3
14 Feb 09	**CRACK A BOTTLE** *Interscope USUM70951735* EMINEM, DR DRE & 50 CENT ★	4		17
25 Apr 09	**WE MADE YOU** *Interscope 2706416*	4		14
9 May 09	**3AM** *Polydor USUM70963051*	56		2
23 May 09	**BEAUTIFUL** *Polydor USUM70964089*	12		11
23 May 09	**OLD TIME'S SAKE** *Polydor USUM70964391*	61		1
30 May 09	**LOSE YOURSELF** *Interscope 4978282*	67		1
21 Nov 09	**TILL I COLLAPSE** *Interscope USIR10211109*	73		1
19 Dec 09	**FOREVER** *Interscope USUM70985104* DRAKE FEATURING KANYE WEST, LIL WAYNE & EMINEM	42		12
23 Jan 10	**DROP THE WORLD** *Cash Money USCM50901210* LIL WAYNE FEATURING EMINEM	51		4+

EMMA
UK, female vocalist (Emma Booth)

Date	Title	Peak Position	Weeks at No.1	Weeks on Chart (6)
28 Apr 90	**GIVE A LITTLE LOVE BACK TO THE WORLD** *Big Wave BWR 33*	33		6

EMMIE
UK, female vocalist (Emma Morton-Smith). See Indien

Date	Title	Peak Position	Weeks at No.1	Weeks on Chart (8)
23 Jan 99	**MORE THAN THIS** *Indirect FESCD 52*	5		8

AN EMOTIONAL FISH
Ireland, male vocal/instrumental group

Date	Title	Peak Position	Weeks at No.1	Weeks on Chart (5)
23 Jun 90	**CELEBRATE** *East West YZ 489*	46		5

Silver-selling ○ · Gold-selling ● · Platinum-selling (x multiples) · US No.1 ★ · Peak Position · Weeks at No.1 · Weeks on Chart

EMOTIONS
US, female vocal group – Wanda, Jeanette & Sheila Hutchinson

Date	Title	Peak Position	Weeks at No.1	Weeks on Chart
				28
10 Sep 77	BEST OF MY LOVE *CBS 5555* ○ ★	4		10
24 Dec 77	I DON'T WANNA TO LOSE YOUR LOVE *CBS 5819*	40		5
12 May 79	BOOGIE WONDERLAND *CBS 7292* EARTH WIND & FIRE WITH THE EMOTIONS ●	4		13

ALEC EMPIRE
Germany, male producer

Date	Title	Peak Position	Weeks at No.1	Weeks on Chart
				1
13 Apr 02	ADDICTED TO YOU *Digital Empire DHRMCD 38CD1*	64		1

EMPIRE OF THE SUN
Australia, male vocal/instrumental duo

Date	Title	Peak Position	Weeks at No.1	Weeks on Chart
				19
7 Mar 09	WALKING ON A DREAM *Virgin DIN283*	64		4
23 May 09	WE ARE THE PEOPLE *Virgin DINS284*	14		15

EMPIRION
UK, male instrumental/production group

Date	Title	Peak Position	Weeks at No.1	Weeks on Chart
				2
6 Jul 96	NARCOTIC INFLUENCE *XL Recordings XLS 72CD*	64		1
21 Jun 97	BETA *XL Recordings XLS 77CD*	75		1

EN VOGUE
US, female vocal group – Terry Ellis, Cindy Herron, Maxine Jones & Dawn Robinson

Date	Title	Peak Position	Weeks at No.1	Weeks on Chart
				83
5 May 90	HOLD ON *East West America 7908*	5		11
21 Jul 90	LIES *East West America 7893*	44		4
4 Apr 92	MY LOVIN' *East West America A 8578*	4		12
15 Aug 92	GIVING HIM SOMETHING HE CAN FEEL *East West America A 8524*	44		3
7 Nov 92	FREE YOUR MIND/GIVING HIM SOMETHING HE CAN FEEL *East West America A 8524*	16		8
16 Jan 93	GIVE IT UP TURN IT LOOSE *East West America A 8445CD*	22		4
10 Apr 93	LOVE DON'T LOVE YOU *East West America A 8424CD*	64		1
9 Oct 93	RUNAWAY LOVE *East West America A 8359CD*	36		3
19 Mar 94	WHATTA MAN *ffrr FCD 222* SALT-N-PEPA WITH EN VOGUE	7		10
11 Jan 97	DON'T LET GO (LOVE) *East West A 3976CD* ○	5		16
14 Jun 97	WHATEVER *East West E 3642CD*	14		5
6 Sep 97	TOO GONE, TOO LONG *East West E 3908CD*	20		3
28 Nov 98	HOLD ON (REMIX) *East West E 3796CD*	53		1
1 Jul 00	RIDDLE *Elektra E7053CD*	33		2

EN-CORE FEATURING STEPHEN EMMANUEL & ESKA
UK, male/female vocal/production duo

Date	Title	Peak Position	Weeks at No.1	Weeks on Chart
				2
9 Sep 00	COOCHY COO *VC Recordings VCRD 72*	32		2

ENCORE
France, female vocalist (Sabine Ohmes)

Date	Title	Peak Position	Weeks at No.1	Weeks on Chart
				4
14 Feb 98	LE DISC JOCKEY *Sum CDSUM 2*	12		4

ENEMY
US, male vocal/instrumental trio – Troy Van Leeuwen, Alan Cage (replaced by Kelli Scott) & Eddie Nappi

Date	Title	Peak Position	Weeks at No.1	Weeks on Chart
				28
21 Apr 07	AWAY FROM HERE *Warner Brothers WEA419CD*	8		9
30 Jun 07	HAD ENOUGH *Warner Brothers WEA423CD*	4		8
29 Sep 07	YOU'RE NOT ALONE *Warner Brothers WEA427CD*	18		4
15 Dec 07	WE'LL LIVE AND DIE IN THESE TOWNS *Warner Brothers WEA437CD*	21		2
29 Mar 08	THIS SONG IS ABOUT YOU *Warner Brothers WEA442CD*	41		1
25 Apr 09	NO TIME FOR TEARS *Warner Brothers WEA455CD*	16		4

ENERGISE
UK, male producer (Dave Lee)

Date	Title	Peak Position	Weeks at No.1	Weeks on Chart
				1
16 Feb 91	REPORT TO THE DANCEFLOOR *Network NWKT 16*	69		1

ENERGY 52
Germany, male DJ/producer (Paul Schmitz-Moormann)

Date	Title	Peak Position	Weeks at No.1	Weeks on Chart
				11
8 Mar 97	CAFÉ DEL MAR *Hooj Choons HOOJCD 51*	51		1
25 Jul 98	CAFE DEL MAR '98 (REMIX) *Hooj Choons HOOJ 64CD*	12		6
12 Oct 02	CAFÉ DEL MAR (2ND REMIX) *Lost Language LOST 019CD*	24		4

ENERGY ORCHARD
Ireland, male vocal/instrumental group

Date	Title	Peak Position	Weeks at No.1	Weeks on Chart
				6
27 Jan 90	BELFAST *MCA 1392*	52		4
7 Apr 90	SAILORTOWN *MCA 1402*	73		2

HARRY ENFIELD
UK, male 'rapper'/comedian

Date	Title	Peak Position	Weeks at No.1	Weeks on Chart
				7
7 May 88	LOADSAMONEY (DOIN' UP THE HOUSE) *Mercury DOSH 1*	4		7

ENGINEERS
UK, male vocal/instrumental group

Date	Title	Peak Position	Weeks at No.1	Weeks on Chart
				1
5 Mar 05	FORGIVENESS *Echo ECSCD159*	48		1

ENGLAND DAN & JOHN FORD COLEY
US, male vocal/instrumental duo

Date	Title	Peak Position	Weeks at No.1	Weeks on Chart
				12
25 Sep 76	I'D REALLY LOVE TO SEE YOU TONIGHT *Atlantic K 10810*	26		7
23 Jun 79	LOVE IS THE ANSWER *Big Tree K 11296*	45		5

ENGLAND BOYS
UK, football fans/vocal group

Date	Title	Peak Position	Weeks at No.1	Weeks on Chart
				3
8 Jun 02	GO ENGLAND *Mercury 5829592*	26		3

ENGLAND SISTERS
UK, female vocal group. See Dale Sisters

Date	Title	Peak Position	Weeks at No.1	Weeks on Chart
				1
17 Mar 60	HEARTBEAT *HMV POP 710*	33		1

ENGLAND SUPPORTERS' BAND
UK, football fans/instrumental group

Date	Title	Peak Position	Weeks at No.1	Weeks on Chart
				4
27 Jun 98	THE GREAT ESCAPE *V2 VVR 5002163*	46		2
24 Jun 00	THE GREAT ESCAPE 2000 *V2 VVR 5014293*	26		2

ENGLAND UNITED
UK, male/female vocal/instrumental group – Echo & The Bunnymen, Simon Fowler, Space & Spice Girls. See Ocean Colour Scene

Date	Title	Peak Position	Weeks at No.1	Weeks on Chart
				11
13 Jun 98	(HOW DOES IT FEEL TO BE) ON TOP OF THE WORLD *London LONCD 414*	9		11

ENGLAND WORLD CUP SQUAD
UK, male football team/vocalists

Date	Title	Peak Position	Weeks at No.1	Weeks on Chart
				48
18 Apr 70	BACK HOME *Pye 7N 17920*	1	3	17
10 Apr 82	THIS TIME (WE'LL GET IT RIGHT)/ENGLAND WE'LL FLY THE FLAG *England ER 1*	2		13
19 Apr 86	WE'VE GOT THE WHOLE WORLD AT OUR FEET/WHEN WE ARE FAR FROM HOME *Columbia DB 9128*	66		2
21 May 88	ALL THE WAY *MCA GOAL 1* ENGLAND FOOTBALL TEAM & THE SOUND OF STOCK, AITKEN & WATERMAN	64		2
2 Jun 90	WORLD IN MOTION... *Factory/MCA FAC 2937* ENGLANDNEWORDER ●	1	2	12
15 Jun 02	WORLD IN MOTION... *London NUOCD 12* ENGLANDNEWORDER	43		2

ENGLAND'S BARMY ARMY
UK, cricket fans/vocal group

Date	Title	Peak Position	Weeks at No.1	Weeks on Chart
				1
12 Jun 99	COME ON ENGLAND! *Wildstar CDWILD 20*	45		1

KIM ENGLISH
US, female vocalist

Date	Title	Peak Position	Weeks at No.1	Weeks on Chart
				7
23 Jul 94	NITE LIFE *Hi-Life PZCD 323*	35		2
4 Mar 95	TIME FOR LOVE *Hi-Life HICD 8*	48		1
9 Sep 95	I KNOW A PLACE *Hi-Life 5798072*	52		1
30 Nov 96	NITE LIFE (REMIX) *Hi-Life 5755332*	35		2
26 Apr 97	SUPERNATURAL *Hi-Life 5736972*	50		1

SCOTT ENGLISH
US, male vocalist

Date	Title	Peak Position	Weeks at No.1	Weeks on Chart
				10
9 Oct 71	BRANDY *Horse HOSS 7*	12		10

ENIGMA

UK, male/female vocal/instrumental group

Date	Title / Label	Peak Position	Weeks at No.1	Weeks on Chart (15)
23 May 81	**AIN'T NO STOPPING** *Creole CR 9*	11		8
8 Aug 81	**I LOVE MUSIC** *Creole CR 14*	25		7

ENIGMA

Romania/Germany, male vocal/production group – Michael Cretu & various musicians including Peter Cornelius, Sandra Cretu, David Fairstein, Jens Gad & Frank Peterson

Date	Title / Label	Peak Position	Weeks at No.1	Weeks on Chart (45)
15 Dec 90	**SADNESS PART 1** *Virgin International DINS 101*	1	1	12
30 Mar 91	**MEA CULPA PART II** *Virgin International DINS 104*	55		3
10 Aug 91	**PRINCIPLES OF LUST** *Virgin International DINS 110*	59		2
11 Jan 92	**THE RIVERS OF BELIEF** *Virgin International DINS 112*	68		2
29 Jan 94	**RETURN TO INNOCENCE** *Virgin International DINSD 123*	3		14
14 May 94	**THE EYES OF TRUTH** *Virgin International DINSD 126*	21		4
20 Aug 94	**AGE OF LONELINESS** *Virgin International DINSD 135*	21		5
25 Jan 97	**BEYOND THE INVISIBLE** *Virgin International DINSD 155*	26		2
19 Apr 97	**TNT FOR THE BRAIN** *Virgin International DINSD 161*	60		1

ENTER SHIKARI

UK, male vocal/instrumental group

Date	Title / Label	Peak Position	Weeks at No.1	Weeks on Chart (9)
10 Mar 07	**ANYTHING CAN HAPPEN IN THE NEXT HALF HOUR** *Ambush Reality AMBR003CD*	27		4
30 Jun 07	**JONNY SNIPER** *Ambush Reality AMBR004CD*	75		1
13 Jun 09	**JUGGERNAUTS** *Ambush Reality AMBR007CD*	28		3
29 Aug 09	**NO SLEEP TONIGHT** *Ambush Reality AMBR008CD*	63		1

ENVY & OTHER SINS

UK, male vocal/instrumental group

Date	Title / Label	Peak Position	Weeks at No.1	Weeks on Chart (1)
15 Mar 08	**HIGHNESS** *A&M 1762714*	65		1

ENYA

Ireland, female vocalist/multi-instrumentalist (Eithne Ni Bhraonáin). See Clannad

Date	Title / Label	Peak Position	Weeks at No.1	Weeks on Chart (89)
15 Oct 88	**ORINOCO FLOW** *WEA YZ 312*	1	3	13
24 Dec 88	**EVENING FALLS...** *WEA YZ 356*	20		4
10 Jun 89	**STORMS IN AFRICA (PART II)** *WEA YZ 368*	41		4
19 Oct 91	**CARIBBEAN BLUE** *WEA YZ 604*	13		7
7 Dec 91	**HOW CAN I KEEP FROM SINGING** *WEA YZ 365*	32		5
1 Aug 92	**BOOK OF DAYS** *WEA YZ 640*	10		6
14 Nov 92	**THE CELTS** *WEA YZ 705*	29		4
18 Nov 95	**ANYWHERE IS** *WEA 023CD*	7		12
7 Dec 96	**ON MY WAY HOME** *WEA 047CD*	26		2
13 Dec 97	**ONLY IF...** *WEA 143CD*	43		2
25 Nov 00	**ONLY TIME** *WEA 316CD*	32		3
31 Mar 01	**WILD CHILD** *WEA 324CD*	72		1
2 Feb 02	**MAY IT BE** *WEA W 578CD*	50		2
5 Jun 04	**I DON'T WANNA KNOW (IMPORT)** *Universal 9862372PMI* MARIO WINANS FEATURING ENYA & P DIDDY	71		1
12 Jun 04	**I DON'T WANNA KNOW** *Bad Boy MCSTD40369* MARIO WINANS FEATURING ENYA & P DIDDY	1	1	14
11 Sep 04	**YOU SHOULD REALLY KNOW** *Relentless RELCD9* PIRATES FEATURING ENYA, SHOLA AMA, NAILA BOSS & ISHANI	8		8
17 Dec 05	**AMARANTINE** *Warner Brothers WEA397CD1*	53		1

EON

UK, male producer (Ian Loveday), d. 17 Jun 2009 (age 54)

Date	Title / Label	Peak Position	Weeks at No.1	Weeks on Chart (1)
17 Aug 91	**FEAR, THE MINDKILLER** *Vinyl Solution STORM 33*	63		1
15 Aug 98	**STRICTLY BUSINESS** *Parlophone CDR 6502* MANTRONIK VS EPMD	43		1

EQUALS

UK, male vocal/instrumental group – Eddy Grant*, Derv & Lincoln Gordon, John Hall & Pat Lloyd

Date	Title / Label	Peak Position	Weeks at No.1	Weeks on Chart (69)
21 Feb 68	**I GET SO EXCITED** *President PT 180*	44		4
1 May 68	**BABY COME BACK** *President PT 135*	1	3	18
21 Aug 68	**LAUREL AND HARDY** *President PT 200*	35		5
27 Nov 68	**SOFTLY SOFTLY** *President PT 222*	48		3
2 Apr 69	**MICHAEL AND THE SLIPPER TREE** *President PT 240*	24		7
30 Jul 69	**VIVA BOBBY JOE** *President PT 260*	6		14
27 Dec 69	**RUB A DUB DUB** *President PT 275*	34		7
19 Dec 70	**BLACK SKIN BLUE EYED BOYS** *President PT 325*	9		11

ERASURE

UK, male vocal/instrumental/production duo – Andy Bell* & Vince Clarke. Prolific synthpop pioneers whose 36 hits in a glittering 25-year career included 15 consecutive Top 15 singles between 1986 and 1991 and five successive albums that debuted at No.1. See Assembly, Depeche Mode, Yazoo

Date	Title / Label	Peak Position	Weeks at No.1	Weeks on Chart (226)
5 Oct 85	**WHO NEEDS LOVE LIKE THAT** *Mute 40*	55		2
25 Oct 86	**SOMETIMES** *Mute 51*	2		17
28 Feb 87	**IT DOESN'T HAVE TO BE** *Mute 56*	12		9
30 May 87	**VICTIM OF LOVE** *Mute 61*	7		9
3 Oct 87	**THE CIRCUS** *Mute 66*	6		10
5 Mar 88	**SHIP OF FOOLS** *Mute 74*	6		8
11 Jun 88	**CHAINS OF LOVE** *Mute 83*	11		7
1 Oct 88	**A LITTLE RESPECT** *Mute 85*	4		10
10 Dec 88	**CRACKERS INTERNATIONAL EP** *Mute 93*	2		13
30 Sep 89	**DRAMA!** *Mute 89*	4		8
9 Dec 89	**YOU SURROUND ME** *Mute 99*	15		9
10 Mar 90	**BLUE SAVANNAH** *Mute 109*	3		10
2 Jun 90	**STAR** *Mute 111*	11		7
29 Jun 91	**CHORUS** *Mute 125*	3		9
21 Sep 91	**LOVE TO HATE YOU** *Mute 131*	4		9
7 Dec 91	**AM I RIGHT (EP)** *Mute 134*	15		6
11 Jan 92	**AM I RIGHT (EP) (REMIX)** *Mute L12MUTE 134*	22		3
28 Mar 92	**BREATH OF LIFE** *Mute 142*	8		6
13 Jun 92	**ABBA-ESQUE EP** *Mute 144*	1	5	12
7 Nov 92	**WHO NEEDS LOVE LIKE THAT** *Mute 150*	10		4
23 Apr 94	**ALWAYS** *Mute CDMUTE 152*	4		9
30 Jul 94	**RUN TO THE SUN** *Mute CDMUTE 153*	6		5
3 Dec 94	**I LOVE SATURDAY** *Mute CDMUTE 166*	20		6
23 Sep 95	**STAY WITH ME** *Mute LDMUTE 174*	15		4
9 Dec 95	**FINGERS AND THUMBS (COLD SUMMER'S DAY)** *Mute CDMUTE 178*	20		3
18 Jan 97	**IN MY ARMS** *Mute CDMUTE 190*	13		4
8 Mar 97	**DON'T SAY YOUR LOVE IS KILLING ME** *Mute CDMUTE 195*	23		2
21 Oct 00	**FREEDOM** *Mute LCDMUTE 244*	27		2
18 Jan 03	**SOLSBURY HILL** *Mute LCDMUTE 275*	10		3
19 Apr 03	**MAKE ME SMILE (COME UP AND SEE ME)** *Mute LCDMUTE 292*	14		3
25 Oct 03	**OH L'AMOUR** *Mute LCDMUTE 213*	13		3
15 Jan 05	**BREATHE** *Mute LCDMUTE 330*	4		6
2 Apr 05	**DON'T SAY YOU LOVE ME** *Mute LCDMUTE337*	15		3
2 Jul 05	**HERE I GO IMPOSSIBLE AGAIN** *Mute LCDMUTE344*	25		2
14 Apr 07	**I COULD FALL IN LOVE WITH YOU** *Mute LCDMUTE366*	21		2
23 Jun 07	**SUNDAY GIRL** *Mute LCDMUTE376*	33		1

ERCOLA FEATURING DANIELLA

Finland/Canada, male/female vocal/production duo

Date	Title / Label	Peak Position	Weeks at No.1	Weeks on Chart (2)
18 Apr 09	**EVERY WORD** *Cayenne SPICY023*	47		2

ERIC & THE GOOD GOOD FEELING

UK, male vocalist (Eric Robinson)

Date	Title / Label	Peak Position	Weeks at No.1	Weeks on Chart (1)
3 Jun 89	**GOOD GOOD FEELING** *Equinox EQN 1*	73		1

ERIK

UK, female vocalist (Erica Maggs)

Date	Title / Label	Peak Position	Weeks at No.1	Weeks on Chart (5)
10 Apr 93	**LOOKS LIKE I'M IN LOVE AGAIN** *PWL Sanctuary PWCD 252* KEY WEST FEATURING ERIK	46		2
29 Jan 94	**GOT TO BE REAL** *PWL International PWCD 278*	42		2
1 Oct 94	**WE GOT THE LOVE** *PWL International PWCD 305*	55		1

ERIN LORDAN

UK, female vocalist

Date	Title / Label	Peak Position	Weeks at No.1	Weeks on Chart (3)
15 Aug 92	**THE ART OF MOVING BUTTS** *Shut Up And Dance SUAD 34S* SHUT UP & DANCE FEATURING ERIN	69		1
23 Mar 96	**LET THE MUSIC PLAY** *MCA MCSTD 40029* BBG FEATURING ERIN	46		1
23 Mar 02	**FOR A LIFETIME** *Xtravaganza XTRAV 20CDS* ASCENSION FEATURING ERIN LORDAN	45		1

ERNESTO VS BASTIAN

Holland, male DJ/production duo

Date	Title / Label	Peak Position	Weeks at No.1	Weeks on Chart (1)
24 Sep 05	**DARK SIDE OF THE MOON** *Nebula NEBCD080*	48		1

EROTIC DRUM BAND

Canada, male/female vocal/instrumental group

Date	Title / Label	Peak Position	Weeks at No.1	Weeks on Chart (3)
9 Jun 79	**LOVE DISCO STYLE** *Scope SC 1*	47		3

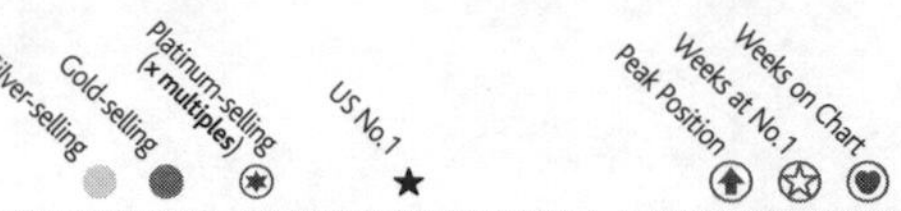

ERUPTION

Jamaica, male/female vocal/instrumental group – Precious Wilson, Leslie Johnson, Eric Kingsley, Horatio McKay, Gregory & Morgan Petrineau

Date	Title	Peak Position	Weeks at No.1	Weeks on Chart (21)
18 Feb 78	**I CAN'T STAND THE RAIN** *Atlantic K 11068* FEATURING PRECIOUS WILSON	5		11
21 Apr 79	**ONE WAY TICKET** *Atlantic/Hansa K 11266*	9		10

ESCALA

UK, female instrumental group

Date	Title	Peak Position	Weeks at No.1	Weeks on Chart (2)
6 Jun 09	**PALLADIO** *Syco Music GBHMU0900003*	39		2

SHAUN ESCOFFERY

UK, male vocalist

Date	Title	Peak Position	Weeks at No.1	Weeks on Chart (2)
10 Mar 01	**SPACE RIDER** *Oyster Music OYSCD 4*	52		1
20 Jul 02	**DAYS LIKE THIS** *Oyster Music OYSCDS 8*	53		1

ESCORTS

UK, male vocal/instrumental group

Date	Title	Peak Position	Weeks at No.1	Weeks on Chart (2)
2 Jul 64	**THE ONE TO CRY** *Fontana TF 474*	49		2

ESCRIMA

UK, male producer ('Tall' Paul Newman). See Camisra, Grifters, Partizan, Tall Paul

Date	Title	Peak Position	Weeks at No.1	Weeks on Chart (4)
11 Feb 95	**TRAIN OF THOUGHT** *ffrreedom TABCD 225*	36		2
7 Oct 95	**DEEPER** *Hooj Choons TABCD 236*	27		2

COLOURS FEATURING EMMANUEL & ESKA

UK, female vocalist (Eska Mtungwazi)

Date	Title	Peak Position	Weeks at No.1	Weeks on Chart (4)
27 Feb 99	**WHAT U DO** *Inferno CDFERN 12*	51		1
9 Sep 00	**COOCHY COO** *VC Recordings VCRD 72* EN-CORE FEATURING STEPHEN EMMANUEL & ESKA	32		2
28 Jul 01	**SUNSET** *V2 VVR 5016768* NITIN SAWHNEY FEATURING ESKA	65		1

ESKIMOS & EGYPT

UK, male vocal/instrumental group

Date	Title	Peak Position	Weeks at No.1	Weeks on Chart (4)
13 Feb 93	**FALL FROM GRACE** *One Little Indian EEF 96CD*	51		2
29 May 93	**UK-USA** *One Little Indian 99 TP7CD*	52		2

ESPIRITU

France/UK, female/male vocal/instrumental duo

Date	Title	Peak Position	Weeks at No.1	Weeks on Chart (10)
6 Mar 93	**CONQUISTADOR** *Heavenly HVN 28CD*	47		2
7 Aug 93	**LOS AMERICANOS** *Heavenly HVN 33CD*	45		2
20 Aug 94	**BONITA MANANA** *Columbia 6606925*	50		1
25 Mar 95	**ALWAYS SOMETHING THERE TO REMIND ME** *WEA YZ 911CD* TIN TIN OUT FEATURING ESPIRITU	14		5

ESSENCE

UK, male/female vocal/production group. See Ascension, Chakra, Lustral, Oxygen featuring Andrea Britton, Space Brothers

Date	Title	Peak Position	Weeks at No.1	Weeks on Chart (2)
21 Mar 98	**THE PROMISE** *Innocent SINCD 1*	27		2

ESSEX

US, male/female vocal group

Date	Title	Peak Position	Weeks at No.1	Weeks on Chart (5)
8 Aug 63	**EASIER SAID THAN DONE** *Columbia DB 7077* ★	41		5

DAVID ESSEX

UK, male vocalist/actor (David Cook)

Date	Title	Peak Position	Weeks at No.1	Weeks on Chart (199)
18 Aug 73	**ROCK ON** *CBS 1693*	3		11
10 Nov 73	**LAMPLIGHT** *CBS 1902*	7		15
11 May 74	**AMERICA** *CBS 2176*	32		5
12 Oct 74	**GONNA MAKE YOU A STAR** *CBS 2492*	1	3	17
14 Dec 74	**STARDUST** *CBS 2828*	7		10
5 Jul 75	**ROLLIN' STONE** *CBS 3425*	5		7
13 Sep 75	**HOLD ME CLOSE** *CBS 3572*	1	3	10
6 Dec 75	**IF I COULD** *CBS 3776*	13		8
20 Mar 76	**CITY LIGHTS** *CBS 4050*	24		4
16 Oct 76	**COMING HOME** *CBS 4486*	24		6
17 Sep 77	**COOL OUT TONIGHT** *CBS 5495*	23		6
11 Mar 78	**STAY WITH ME BABY** *CBS 6063*	45		5
19 Aug 78	**OH WHAT A CIRCUS** *Mercury 6007 185*	3		11
21 Oct 78	**BRAVE NEW WORLD** *CBS 6705*	55		3
3 Mar 79	**IMPERIAL WIZARD** *Mercury 6007 202*	32		8
5 Apr 80	**SILVER DREAM MACHINE (PART 1)** *Mercury BIKE 1*	4		11
14 Jun 80	**HOT LOVE** *Mercury HOT 11*	57		4
26 Jun 82	**ME AND MY GIRL (NIGHT-CLUBBING)** *Mercury MER 107*	13		10
11 Dec 82	**A WINTER'S TALE** *Mercury MER 127*	2		10
4 Jun 83	**THE SMILE** *Mercury ESSEX 1*	52		4
27 Aug 83	**TAHITI** *Mercury BOUNT 1*	8		11
26 Nov 83	**YOU'RE IN MY HEART** *Mercury ESSEX 2*	59		6
23 Feb 85	**FALLING ANGELS RIDING (MUTINY)** *Mercury ESSEX 5*	29		7
18 Apr 87	**MYFANWY** *Arista RIS 11*	41		7
26 Nov 94	**TRUE LOVE WAYS** *Polygram TV TLWCD 2* & CATHERINE ZETA JONES	38		3

GLORIA ESTEFAN

Cuba, female vocalist (Gloria Fajardo). See Miami Sound Machine

Date	Title	Peak Position	Weeks at No.1	Weeks on Chart (182)
16 Jul 88	**ANYTHING FOR YOU** *Epic 6516737* & MIAMI SOUND MACHINE ★	10		16
22 Oct 88	**1-2-3-** *Epic 6529587* & MIAMI SOUND MACHINE	9		10
17 Dec 88	**RHYTHM IS GONNA GET YOU** *Epic 6545147* & MIAMI SOUND MACHINE	16		9
11 Feb 89	**CAN'T STAY AWAY FROM YOU** *Epic 6514447* & MIAMI SOUND MACHINE	7		12
15 Jul 89	**DON'T WANNA LOSE YOU** *Epic 6550540* ★	6		10
16 Sep 89	**OYE MI CANTO (HEAR MY VOICE)** *Epic 6552877*	16		8
25 Nov 89	**GET ON YOUR FEET** *Epic 6554507*	23		7
3 Mar 90	**HERE WE ARE** *Epic 6554737*	23		6
26 May 90	**CUTS BOTH WAYS** *Epic 6559827*	49		5
26 Jan 91	**COMING OUT OF THE DARK** *Epic 6565747* ★	25		5
6 Apr 91	**SEAL OUR FATE** *Epic 6567737*	24		7
8 Jun 91	**REMEMBER ME WITH LOVE** *Epic 6569687*	22		6
21 Sep 91	**LIVE FOR LOVING YOU** *Epic 6573837*	33		5
24 Oct 92	**ALWAYS TOMORROW** *Epic 6583977*	24		4
12 Dec 92	**MIAMI HIT MIX/CHRISTMAS THROUGH YOUR EYES** *Epic 6588377*	8		9
13 Feb 93	**I SEE YOUR SMILE** *Epic 6589612*	48		2
3 Apr 93	**GO AWAY** *Epic 6590952*	13		6
3 Jul 93	**MI TIERRA** *Epic 6593512*	36		3
14 Aug 93	**IF WE WERE LOVERS/CON LOS ANOS QUE ME QUEDAN** *Epic 6595702*	40		3
18 Dec 93	**MONTUNO** *Epic 6599972*	55		2
15 Oct 94	**TURN THE BEAT AROUND** *Epic 6606822*	21		6
3 Dec 94	**HOLD ME THRILL ME KISS ME** *Epic 6610802*	11		11
18 Feb 95	**EVERLASTING LOVE** *Epic 6611595*	19		5
25 May 96	**REACH** *Epic 6632642*	15		8
24 Aug 96	**YOU'LL BE MINE (PARTY TIME)** *Epic 6636505*	18		3
14 Dec 96	**I'M NOT GIVING YOU UP** *Epic 6640225*	28		3
6 Jun 98	**HEAVEN'S WHAT I FEEL** *Epic 6660042*	17		4
10 Oct 98	**OYE** *Epic 6664645*	33		2
16 Jan 99	**DON'T LET THIS MOMENT END** *Epic 6667472*	28		2
8 Jan 00	**MUSIC OF MY HEART** *Epic 6678052* *NSYNC & GLORIA ESTEFAN	34		3

ESTELLE

UK, female vocalist/rapper (Estelle Swaray)

Date	Title	Peak Position	Weeks at No.1	Weeks on Chart (62)
29 Jun 02	**TRIXSTAR** *Bad Magic MAGIC24* BLAK TWANG FEATURING ESTELLE	54		1
31 Jul 04	**1980** *V2/J-Did JAD5027813*	14		7
16 Oct 04	**FREE** *V2/J-Did JAD5027848*	15		6
12 Feb 05	**OUTSPOKEN – PART 1** *Buzzin Fly 010BUZZCD* BEN WATT FEATURING ESTELLE & BABY BLAK	74		1
9 Apr 05	**GO GONE** *V2 JAD5030948*	32		3
11 Jun 05	**WHY GO?** *Cheeky 82876699292* FAITHLESS FEATURING ESTELLE	49		1
15 Mar 08	**AMERICAN BOY** *Atlantic AT0304CD* FEATURING KANYE WEST	1	4	32
28 Jun 08	**NO SUBSTITUTE LOVE** *Atlantic AT0318CD*	30		6
15 Aug 09	**WORLD GO ROUND** *Island USUM70852215* BUSTA RHYMES FEATURING ESTELLE	66		1
21 Nov 09	**ONE LOVE** *Positiva/Virgin FRZID0900980* DAVID GUETTA FEATURING ESTELLE	46		4

DEON ESTUS

US, male vocalist/bass guitarist

Date	Title	Peak Position	Weeks at No.1	Weeks on Chart (7)
25 Jan 86	**MY GUY – MY GIRL (MEDLEY)** *Sedition EDIT 3310* AMII STEWART & DEON ESTUS	63		3
29 Apr 89	**HEAVEN HELP ME** *Mika 2*	41		4

ETA

Denmark, male instrumental/production group

Date	Title	Peak Position	Weeks at No.1	Weeks on Chart (5)
28 Jun 97	**CASUAL SUB (BURNING SPEAR)** *East West EW 110CD*	28		3
31 Jan 98	**CASUAL SUB (BURNING SPEAR) (REMIX)** *East West Dance EW 145CD*	28		2

ETERNAL

UK, female vocal group – Easther & Vernie Bennett, Kéllé Bryan* & Louise* Nurding — 134

Date	Title	Peak	Wks No.1	Wks
2 Oct 93	**STAY** *EMI CDEM 284*	4		9
15 Jan 94	**SAVE OUR LOVE** *EMI CDEM 296*	8		7
30 Apr 94	**JUST A STEP FROM HEAVEN** *EMI CDEM 311*	8		10
20 Aug 94	**SO GOOD** *EMI CDEMS 339*	13		7
5 Nov 94	**OH BABY I...** *EMI CDEM 353* ●	4		13
24 Dec 94	**CRAZY** *EMI CDEMX 364*	15		7
21 Oct 95	**POWER OF A WOMAN** *EMI CDEM 396*	5		8
9 Dec 95	**I AM BLESSED** *EMI CDEMS 408*	7		12
9 Mar 96	**GOOD THING** *EMI CDEM 419*	8		6
17 Aug 96	**SOMEDAY** *EMI CDEMS 439*	4		9
7 Dec 96	**SECRETS** *EMI CDEM 459*	9		7
8 Mar 97	**DON'T YOU LOVE ME** *EMI CDEMS 465*	3		7
31 May 97	**I WANNA BE THE ONLY ONE** *EMI CDEM 472* FEATURING BEBE WINANS ●	1	1	15
11 Oct 97	**ANGEL OF MINE** *EMI CDEM 493* ●	4		13
30 Oct 99	**WHAT'CHA GONNA DO** *EMI CDEM 552*	16		4

ETHAN

France/Sweden, male production duo. See Fused — 1

Date	Title	Peak	Wks No.1	Wks
12 Mar 05	**IN MY HEART** *Back Yard BACK13CSC01*	49		1

ETHER

UK, male vocal/instrumental group — 1

Date	Title	Peak	Wks No.1	Wks
28 Mar 98	**WATCHING YOU** *Parlophone CDR 6491*	74		1

ETHICS

Holland, male producer (Patrick Prinz). See Artemesia, Movin' Melodies, Subliminal Cuts — 5

Date	Title	Peak	Wks No.1	Wks
25 Nov 95	**TO THE BEAT OF THE DRUM (LA LUNA)** *VC Recordings VCRD 5*	13		5

ETHIOPIANS

Jamaica, male vocal/instrumental group — 6

Date	Title	Peak	Wks No.1	Wks
13 Sep 67	**TRAIN TO SKAVILLE** *Rio 130*	40		6

TONY ETORIA

UK, male vocalist — 8

Date	Title	Peak	Wks No.1	Wks
4 Jun 77	**I CAN PROVE IT** *GTO GT 89*	21		8

EUROGROOVE

UK, male/female vocal group — 7

Date	Title	Peak	Wks No.1	Wks
20 May 95	**MOVE YOUR BODY** *Avex UK AVEXCD 4*	29		2
5 Aug 95	**DIVE TO PARADISE** *Avex UK AVEXCD 10*	31		2
21 Oct 95	**IT'S ON YOU (SCAN ME)** *Avex UK AVEXCD 17*	25		2
3 Feb 96	**MOVE YOUR BODY (REMIX)** *Avex UK AVEXCD 22*	44		1

EUROPE

Sweden, male vocal/instrumental group – Joey Tempest (Rolf Larsson), Ian Haugland, John Levén, Mic Michaeli & John Norum (replaced by Kee Marcello) — 50

Date	Title	Peak	Wks No.1	Wks
1 Nov 86	**THE FINAL COUNTDOWN** *Epic A 7127* ●	1	2	15
31 Jan 87	**ROCK THE NIGHT** *Epic EUR 1*	12		9
18 Apr 87	**CARRIE** *Epic EUR 2*	22		8
20 Aug 88	**SUPERSTITIOUS** *Epic EUR 3*	34		5
1 Feb 92	**I'LL CRY FOR YOU** *Epic 6576977*	28		5
21 Mar 92	**HALFWAY TO HEAVEN** *Epic 6578517*	42		4
25 Dec 99	**THE FINAL COUNTDOWN** *Epic 6685042*	36		4

EURYTHMICS

UK, female/male vocal/instrumental duo – Annie Lennox* & David A Stewart*. Distinctive tunesmiths who are the most prolific male/female duo in UK-chart history. Lennox has won more BRIT awards (8) than any other female and the duo received the 'Outstanding Contribution to British Music' award in 1999. See Tourists — 212

Date	Title	Peak	Wks No.1	Wks
4 Jul 81	**NEVER GONNA CRY AGAIN** *RCA 68*	63		3
20 Nov 82	**LOVE IS A STRANGER** *RCA DA 1*	54		5
12 Feb 83	**SWEET DREAMS (ARE MADE OF THIS)** *RCA DA 2* ● ★	2		14
9 Apr 83	**LOVE IS A STRANGER** *RCA DA 1*	6		8
9 Jul 83	**WHO'S THAT GIRL?** *RCA DA 3*	3		10
5 Nov 83	**RIGHT BY YOUR SIDE** *RCA DA 4*	10		11
21 Jan 84	**HERE COMES THE RAIN AGAIN** *RCA DA 5* ●	8		8
3 Nov 84	**SEXCRIME (NINETEEN EIGHTY FOUR)** *Virgin VS 728* ●	4		13
19 Jan 85	**JULIA** *Virgin VS 734*	44		4
20 Apr 85	**WOULD I LIE TO YOU?** *RCA PB 40101*	17		8
6 Jul 85	**THERE MUST BE AN ANGEL (PLAYING WITH MY HEART)** *RCA PB 40247*	1	1	13
2 Nov 85	**SISTERS ARE DOING IT FOR THEMSELVES** *RCA PB 40339* & ARETHA FRANKLIN	9		11
11 Jan 86	**IT'S ALRIGHT (BABY'S COMING BACK)** *RCA PB 40375*	12		8
14 Jun 86	**WHEN TOMORROW COMES** *RCA DA 7*	30		6
6 Sep 86	**THORN IN MY SIDE** *RCA DA 8*	5		11
29 Nov 86	**THE MIRACLE OF LOVE** *RCA DA 9*	23		9
28 Feb 87	**MISSIONARY MAN** *RCA DA 10*	31		4
24 Oct 87	**BEETHOVEN (I LOVE TO LISTEN TO)** *RCA DA 11*	25		5
26 Dec 87	**SHAME** *RCA DA 12*	41		6
9 Apr 88	**I NEED A MAN** *RCA DA 15*	26		5
11 Jun 88	**YOU HAVE PLACED A CHILL IN MY HEART** *RCA DA 16*	16		8
26 Aug 89	**REVIVAL** *RCA DA 17*	26		6
4 Nov 89	**DON'T ASK ME WHY** *RCA DA 19*	25		6
3 Feb 90	**THE KING AND QUEEN OF AMERICA** *RCA DA 20*	29		5
12 May 90	**ANGEL** *RCA DA 21*	23		6
9 Mar 91	**LOVE IS A STRANGER** *RCA PB 44265*	46		3
16 Nov 91	**SWEET DREAMS (ARE MADE OF THIS)** *RCA PB 45031*	48		2
16 Oct 99	**I SAVED THE WORLD TODAY** *RCA 74321695632*	11		6
5 Feb 00	**17 AGAIN** *RCA 74321726262*	27		4
12 Nov 05	**I'VE GOT A LIFE** *RCA 82876748352*	14		4

Top 3 Best-Selling Singles

	Title	Approximate Sales
1	THERE MUST BE AN ANGEL (PLAYING WITH MY HEART)	570,000
2	SWEET DREAMS (ARE MADE OF THIS)	530,000
3	WHO'S THAT GIRL?	380,000

EUSEBE

UK, male/female rap/vocal group — 3

Date	Title	Peak	Wks No.1	Wks
26 Aug 95	**SUMMERTIME HEALING** *Mama's Yard CDMAMA 4*	32		3

EVANESCENCE

US, female/male vocal/instrumental group – Amy Lee, Will Boyd, Rocky Gray, John LeCompt & Ben Moody (replaced by Terry Balsamo) — 47

Date	Title	Peak	Wks No.1	Wks
31 May 03	**BRING ME TO LIFE (IMPORT)** *Epic 8734881CD*	60		2
14 Jun 03	**BRING ME TO LIFE** *Epic 6739762*	1	4	17
4 Oct 03	**GOING UNDER** *Epic 6743522*	8		6
20 Dec 03	**MY IMMORTAL** *Epic 6745422*	7		9
12 Jun 04	**EVERYBODY'S FOOL** *Epic 6747992*	24		3
30 Sep 06	**CALL ME WHEN YOU'RE SOBER** *Columbia 82876894152*	4		8
20 Jan 07	**LITHIUM** *Wind Up 88697042082*	32		2

FAITH EVANS

US, female vocalist/producer/actor — 59

Date	Title	Peak	Wks No.1	Wks
14 Oct 95	**YOU USED TO LOVE ME** *Puff Daddy 74321299812*	42		2
23 Nov 96	**STRESSED OUT** *Jive JIVECD 404* A TRIBE CALLED QUEST FEATURING FAITH EVANS & RAPHAEL SAADIQ	33		2
28 Jun 97	**I'LL BE MISSING YOU** *Puff Daddy 74321499102* PUFF DADDY & FAITH EVANS FEATURING 112 ⊛x2 ★	1	6	21
14 Nov 98	**LOVE LIKE THIS** *Puff Daddy 74321665692*	24		4
1 May 99	**ALL NIGHT LONG** *Puff Daddy 74321625592* FEATURING PUFF DADDY	23		3
1 May 99	**GEORGY PORGY** *Warner Brothers W 478CD1* ERIC BENET FEATURING FAITH EVANS	28		3
30 Dec 00	**HEARTBREAK HOTEL** *Arista 74321820572* WHITNEY HOUSTON FEATURING FAITH EVANS & KELLY PRICE	25		5
24 May 03	**MA I DON'T LOVE HER** *Arista 82876526482* CLIPSE FEATURING FAITH EVANS	38		3
9 Apr 05	**HOPE** *Capitol 8694660* TWISTA FEATURING FAITH EVANS	25		5
14 May 05	**AGAIN** *EMI CDEMS658*	12		6
20 Aug 05	**MESMERIZED** *EMI CDEMS665*	48		1
14 Jul 07	**I'LL BE MISSING YOU** *Bad Boy USBB40300019* PUFF DADDY FEATURING FAITH EVANS	32		2
14 Feb 09	**I'LL BE MISSING YOU** *Bad Boy USBB40300019* PUFF DADDY FEATURING FAITH EVANS	68		2

MAUREEN EVANS
UK, female vocalist

Date	Title	Peak Position	Weeks at No.1	Weeks on Chart (37)
22 Jan 60	**THE BIG HURT** *Oriole CB 1533*	26		2
17 Mar 60	**LOVE KISSES AND HEARTACHES** *Oriole CB 1540*	44		1
2 Jun 60	**PAPER ROSES** *Oriole CB 1550*	40		5
29 Nov 62	**LIKE I DO** *Oriole CB 1763*	3		18
27 Feb 64	**I LOVE HOW YOU LOVE ME** *Oriole CB 1906*	34		11

PAUL EVANS
US, male vocalist

Date	Title	Peak Position	Weeks at No.1	Weeks on Chart (14)
27 Nov 59	**SEVEN LITTLE GIRLS SITTING IN THE BACK SEAT** *London HLL 8968* & THE CURLS	25		1
31 Mar 60	**MIDNITE SPECIAL** *London HLL 9045*	41		1
16 Dec 78	**HELLO THIS IS JOANNIE (THE TELEPHONE ANSWERING MACHINE SONG)** *Spring 2066 932* ●	6		12

EVASIONS
UK/Ireland, 'rap'/vocal/instrumental group

Date	Title	Peak Position	Weeks at No.1	Weeks on Chart (8)
13 Jun 81	**WIKKA WRAP** *Groove GP 107*	20		8

E.V.E.
UK/US, female vocal group

Date	Title	Peak Position	Weeks at No.1	Weeks on Chart (5)
1 Oct 94	**GROOVE OF LOVE** *Gasoline Alley MCSTD 2007*	30		3
28 Jan 95	**GOOD LIFE** *Gasoline Alley MCSTD 2038*	39		2

EVE
US, female rapper (Eve Jeffers)

Date	Title	Peak Position	Weeks at No.1	Weeks on Chart (80)
22 Jan 00	**HOT BOYZ** *Elektra E 7002CD* MISSY MISDEMEANOR ELLIOTT FEATURING NAS, EVE & Q-TIP	18		3
19 May 01	**WHO'S THAT GIRL** *Interscope 4975572*	6		8
25 Aug 01	**LET ME BLOW YA MIND** *Interscope 4976052* FEATURING GWEN STEFANI	4		12
9 Mar 02	**BROTHA PART II** *J Records 74321922142* ANGIE STONE FEATURING ALICIA KEYS & EVE	37		2
16 Mar 02	**CARAMEL** *Interscope 4976742* CITY HIGH FEATURING EVE	9		10
5 Oct 02	**GANGSTA LOVIN'** *Interscope 4978042* FEATURING ALICIA KEYS	6		8
12 Apr 03	**SATISFACTION** *Interscope 4978262*	20		4
6 Dec 03	**NOT TODAY** *Geffen MCSTD 40349* MARY J BLIGE FEATURING EVE	40		2
26 Mar 05	**RICH GIRL** *Interscope 9880219* GWEN STEFANI FEATURING EVE	4		12
16 Jun 07	**LIKE THIS** *Columbia 88697110322* KELLY ROWLAND FEATURING EVE	4		12
18 Aug 07	**TAMBOURINE** *Interscope 1745307*	19		7

EVERCLEAR
US, male vocal/instrumental group

Date	Title	Peak Position	Weeks at No.1	Weeks on Chart (7)
1 Jun 96	**HEARTSPARK DOLLARSIGN** *Capitol CDCLS 773*	48		2
31 Aug 96	**SANTA MONICA (WATCH THE WORLD DIE)** *Capitol CDCL 775*	40		2
9 May 98	**EVERYTHING TO EVERYONE** *Capitol CDCL 799*	41		1
14 Oct 00	**WONDERFUL** *Capitol CDCLS 824*	36		2

BETTY EVERETT
US, female vocalist, d. 18 Aug 2001 (age 61)

Date	Title	Peak Position	Weeks at No.1	Weeks on Chart (14)
14 Jan 65	**GETTING MIGHTY CROWDED** *Fontana TF 520*	29		7
30 Oct 68	**IT'S IN HIS KISS** *President PT 215*	34		7

JACE EVERETT
US, male vocalist

Date	Title	Peak Position	Weeks at No.1	Weeks on Chart (4)
7 Nov 09	**BAD THINGS** *Epic USSM10507166*	49		4

KENNY EVERETT
UK, male radio DJ/vocalist (Maurice Cole), d. 4 Apr 1995 (age 46)

Date	Title	Peak Position	Weeks at No.1	Weeks on Chart (12)
12 Nov 77	**CAPTAIN KREMMEN (RETRIBUTION)** *DJM DJS 10810* & MIKE VICKERS	32		4
26 Mar 83	**SNOT RAP** *RCA KEN 1*	9		8

EVERLAST
US, male vocalist (Erik Schrody)

Date	Title	Peak Position	Weeks at No.1	Weeks on Chart (5)
27 Feb 99	**WHAT IT'S LIKE** *Tommy Boy TBCD 7470*	34		2
3 Jul 99	**ENDS** *Tommy Boy TBCD 346*	47		1
20 Jan 01	**BLACK JESUS** *Tommy Boy TBCD 2180B*	37		2

EVERLY BROTHERS
US, male vocal/instrumental duo – Don & Phil* Everly. The most successful duo of the rock 'N' roll era, whose distinctive harmony sound influenced many later acts, including The Beatles. The Lifetime Grammy winners were the first group inducted into the Rock & Roll Hall of Fame

Date	Title	Peak Position	Weeks at No.1	Weeks on Chart (345)
12 Jul 57	**BYE BYE LOVE** *London HLA 8440*	6		16
8 Nov 57	**WAKE UP LITTLE SUSIE** *London HLA 8498* ★	2		13
23 May 58	**ALL I HAVE TO DO IS DREAM/CLAUDETTE** *London HLA 8618* ★	1	7	21
12 Sep 58	**BIRD DOG** *London HLA 8685* ★	2		16
23 Jan 59	**PROBLEMS** *London HLA 8781*	6		12
22 May 59	**TAKE A MESSAGE TO MARY** *London HLA 8863*	20		10
29 May 59	**POOR JENNY** *London HLA 8863*	14		11
11 Sep 59	**('TIL) I KISSED YOU** *London HLA 8934*	2		15
12 Feb 60	**LET IT BE ME** *London HLA 9039*	13		10
14 Apr 60	**CATHY'S CLOWN** *Warner Brothers WB 1* ★	1	7	18
14 Jul 60	**WHEN WILL I BE LOVED** *London HLA 9157*	4		16
22 Sep 60	**LUCILLE/SO SAD (TO WATCH GOOD LOVE GO BAD)** *Warner Brothers WB 19*	4		15
15 Dec 60	**LIKE STRANGERS** *London HLA 9250*	11		10
9 Feb 61	**WALK RIGHT BACK/EBONY EYES** *Warner Brothers WB 33*	1	3	16
15 Jun 61	**TEMPTATION** *Warner Brothers WB 42*	1	2	15
5 Oct 61	**MUSKRAT/DON'T BLAME ME** *Warner Brothers WB 50*	20		6
18 Jan 62	**CRYIN' IN THE RAIN** *Warner Brothers WB 56*	6		15
17 May 62	**HOW CAN I MEET HER** *Warner Brothers WB 67*	12		10
25 Oct 62	**NO ONE CAN MAKE MY SUNSHINE SMILE** *Warner Brothers WB 79*	11		11
21 Mar 63	**SO IT WILL ALWAYS BE** *Warner Brothers WB 94*	23		11
13 Jun 63	**IT'S BEEN NICE** *Warner Brothers WB 99*	26		5
17 Oct 63	**THE GIRL SANG THE BLUES** *Warner Brothers WB 109*	25		9
16 Jul 64	**FERRIS WHEEL** *Warner Brothers WB 135*	22		10
3 Dec 64	**GONE GONE GONE** *Warner Brothers WB 146*	36		7
6 May 65	**THAT'LL BE THE DAY** *Warner Brothers WB 158*	30		4
20 May 65	**THE PRICE OF LOVE** *Warner Brothers WB 161*	2		14
26 Aug 65	**I'LL NEVER GET OVER YOU** *Warner Brothers WB 5639*	35		5
21 Oct 65	**LOVE IS STRANGE** *Warner Brothers WB 5649*	11		9
8 May 68	**IT'S MY TIME** *Warner Brothers WB 7192*	39		6
22 Sep 84	**ON THE WINGS OF A NIGHTINGALE** *Mercury MER 170*	41		9

PHIL EVERLY
US, male vocalist. See Everly Brothers

Date	Title	Peak Position	Weeks at No.1	Weeks on Chart (24)
6 Nov 82	**LOUISE** *Capitol CL 266*	47		6
19 Feb 83	**SHE MEANS NOTHING TO ME** *Capitol CL 276* & CLIFF RICHARD	9		9
10 Dec 94	**ALL I HAVE TO DO IS DREAM/MISS YOU NIGHTS** *EMI CDEMS 359* & CLIFF RICHARD/CLIFF RICHARD	14		9

EVERSTRONG
UK, male vocal/instrumental group

Date	Title	Peak Position	Weeks at No.1	Weeks on Chart (1)
23 Apr 05	**TAKE ME HOME (WOMBLE 'TIL I DIE)** *Cornish Blue Music CBMCD02*	73		1

EVERTON FC
UK, male footballers/vocal group

Date	Title	Peak Position	Weeks at No.1	Weeks on Chart (8)
11 May 85	**HERE WE GO** *Columbia DB 9106*	14		5
20 May 95	**ALL TOGETHER NOW** *MDMC DEVCS 3*	24		3

EVERYTHING BUT THE GIRL
UK, female/male vocal/instrumental duo – Tracey Thorn & Ben Watt

Date	Title	Peak Position	Weeks at No.1	Weeks on Chart (96)
12 May 84	**EACH AND EVERYONE** *Blanco Y Negro NEG 1*	28		7
21 Jul 84	**MINE** *Blanco Y Negro NEG 3*	58		2
6 Oct 84	**NATIVE LAND** *Blanco Y Negro NEG 6*	73		2
2 Aug 86	**COME ON HOME** *Blanco Y Negro NEG 21*	44		7
11 Oct 86	**DON'T LEAVE ME BEHIND** *Blanco Y Negro NEG 23*	72		2
13 Feb 88	**THESE EARLY DAYS** *Blanco Y Negro NEG 30*	75		1
9 Jul 88	**I DON'T WANT TO TALK ABOUT IT** *Blanco Y Negro NEG 34*	3		9
27 Jan 90	**DRIVING** *Blanco Y Negro NEG 40*	54		2
22 Feb 92	**COVERS EP** *Blanco Y Negro NEG 54*	13		6
24 Apr 93	**THE ONLY LIVING BOY IN NEW YORK (EP)** *Blanco Y Negro NEG 62CD*	42		5
19 Jun 93	**I DIDN'T KNOW I WAS LOOKING FOR LOVE (EP)** *Blanco Y Negro NEG 64CD*	72		1
4 Jun 94	**ROLLERCOASTER (EP)** *Blanco Y Negro NEG 69CD*	65		1
20 Aug 94	**MISSING** *Blanco Y Negro NEG 71CD*	69		1
28 Oct 95	**MISSING (REMIX)** *Blanco Y Negro NEG 84CD* ⊛	3		22
20 Apr 96	**WALKING WOUNDED** *Virgin VSCDT 1577*	6		6
29 Jun 96	**WRONG** *Virgin VSCDT 1589*	8		7
5 Oct 96	**SINGLE** *Virgin VSCDT 1600*	20		3
7 Dec 96	**DRIVING (REMIX)** *Blanco Y Negro NEG 99CD1*	36		2
1 Mar 97	**BEFORE TODAY** *Virgin VSCDT 1624*	25		2

Silver-selling ● | Gold-selling ● | Platinum-selling (x multiples) ⊛ | US No.1 ★ | Peak Position | Weeks at No.1 | Weeks on Chart

Date	Title	Peak	Wks at No.1	Wks on Chart
3 Oct 98	**THE FUTURE OF THE FUTURE (STAY GOLD)** *Deconstruction 74321616252* DEEP DISH WITH EVERYTHING BUT THE GIRL	31		2
25 Sep 99	**FIVE FATHOMS** *Virgin VSCDT 1742*	27		3
4 Mar 00	**TEMPERAMENTAL** *Virgin VSCDT 1761*	72		1
27 Jan 01	**TRACEY IN MY ROOM** *VC Recordings VCRD 78* EBTG VS SOUL VISION	34		2

E'VOKE
UK, female vocal duo — 9

Date	Title	Peak	Wks at No.1	Wks on Chart
25 Nov 95	**RUNAWAY** *ffrreedom TABCD 238*	30		3
24 Aug 96	**ARMS OF LOREN** *Manifesto FESCD 10*	25		3
2 Feb 02	**ARMS OF LOREN 2001** *Inferno CDFERN 001*	31		3

EVOLUTION
UK, male production duo — 12

Date	Title	Peak	Wks at No.1	Wks on Chart
20 Mar 93	**LOVE THING** *Deconstruction 74321134272*	32		2
3 Jul 93	**EVERYBODY DANCE** *Deconstruction 74321152012*	19		5
8 Jan 94	**EVOLUTIONDANCE PART ONE (EP)** *Deconstruction 74321171912*	52		3
4 Nov 95	**LOOK UP TO THE LIGHT** *Deconstruction 74321318042*	55		1
19 Oct 96	**YOUR LOVE IS CALLING** *Deconstruction 74321422872*	60		1

JADE EWEN
UK, female vocalist. See Sugababes — 3

Date	Title	Peak	Wks at No.1	Wks on Chart
23 May 09	**IT'S MY TIME** *Geffen 2703204*	27		2
3 Oct 09	**MY MAN** *Geffen 2718154*	35		1

EX PISTOLS
UK, male vocal/instrumental group — 2

Date	Title	Peak	Wks at No.1	Wks on Chart
2 Feb 85	**LAND OF HOPE AND GLORY** *Virginia PISTOL 76*	69		2

EXAMPLE
UK, male rapper/vocalist (Elliot Gleave) — 18

Date	Title	Peak	Wks at No.1	Wks on Chart
3 Oct 09	**WATCH THE SUN COME UP** *Data DATA221CDX*	19		7
30 Jan 10	**WON'T GO QUIETLY** *Data DATA226CDX*	6		11+

EXCITERS
US, male/female vocal group — 7

Date	Title	Peak	Wks at No.1	Wks on Chart
21 Feb 63	**TELL HIM** *United Artists UP 1011*	46		1
4 Oct 75	**REACHING FOR THE BEST** *20th Century BTC 1005*	31		6

EXETER BRAMDEAN BOYS' CHOIR
UK, male choir — 3

Date	Title	Peak	Wks at No.1	Wks on Chart
18 Dec 93	**REMEMBERING CHRISTMAS** *Golden Sounds DSCC 1*	46		3

EXILE
US, male vocal/instrumental group – JP Pennington, Buzz Cornelison, Steve Goetzman, Sonny Lemaire & Jimmy Stokley — 18

Date	Title	Peak	Wks at No.1	Wks on Chart
19 Aug 78	**KISS YOU ALL OVER** *RAK 279* ● ★	6		12
12 May 79	**HOW COULD THIS GO WRONG** *RAK 293*	67		2
12 Sep 81	**HEART AND SOUL** *RAK 333*	54		4

EXOTERIX
UK, male producer (Duncan Millar) — 2

Date	Title	Peak	Wks at No.1	Wks on Chart
24 Apr 93	**VOID** *Positiva CDTIV 1*	58		1
5 Feb 94	**SATISFY MY LOVE** *Union City UCRCD 26*	62		1

EXOTICA FEATURING ITSY FOSTER
UK/Italy, male/female vocal/instrumental group — 1

Date	Title	Peak	Wks at No.1	Wks on Chart
16 Sep 95	**THE SUMMER IS MAGIC** *Polydor 5798392*	68		1

EXPLOSION
US, male vocal/instrumental group — 1

Date	Title	Peak	Wks at No.1	Wks on Chart
26 Mar 05	**HERE I AM** *Virgin VUSDX298*	75		1

EXPLOITED
UK, male vocal/instrumental group — 13

Date	Title	Peak	Wks at No.1	Wks on Chart
18 Apr 81	**DOGS OF WAR** *Secret SHH 110*	63		4
17 Oct 81	**DEAD CITIES** *Secret SHH 120*	31		5
5 Dec 81	**DON'T LET 'EM GRIND YOU DOWN** *Superville EXP 1003* & ANTI-PASTI	70		1
8 May 82	**ATTACK** *Secret SHH 130*	50		3

EXPOSE
US, female vocal trio — 1

Date	Title	Peak	Wks at No.1	Wks on Chart
28 Aug 93	**I'LL NEVER GET OVER YOU (GETTING OVER ME)** *Arista 74321158962*	75		1

EXPRESS OF SOUND
Italy, male instrumental/production group — 1

Date	Title	Peak	Wks at No.1	Wks on Chart
2 Nov 96	**REAL VIBRATION** *Positiva CDTIV 66*	45		1

EXPRESSOS
UK, male/female vocal/instrumental group — 5

Date	Title	Peak	Wks at No.1	Wks on Chart
21 Jun 80	**HEY GIRL** *WEA K 18246*	60		3
14 Mar 81	**TANGO IN MONO** *WEA K 18431*	70		2

EXTREME
US, male vocal/instrumental group – Gary Cherone, Pat Badger, Nuno Bettencourt & Paul Geary (replaced by Michael Mangini) — 46

Date	Title	Peak	Wks at No.1	Wks on Chart
8 Jun 91	**GET THE FUNK OUT** *A&M AM 737*	19		7
27 Jul 91	**MORE THAN WORDS** *A&M AM 792* ● ★	2		11
12 Oct 91	**DECADENCE DANCE** *A&M AM 773*	36		3
23 Nov 91	**HOLE HEARTED** *A&M AM 839*	12		7
2 May 92	**SONG FOR LOVE** *A&M AM 698*	12		6
5 Sep 92	**REST IN PEACE** *A&M AM 0055*	13		5
14 Nov 92	**STOP THE WORLD** *A&M AM 0096*	22		2
6 Feb 93	**TRAGIC COMIC** *A&M AMCD 0156*	15		4
11 Mar 95	**HIP TODAY** *A&M 5809932*	44		1

E.Y.C.
US, male vocal group. See Childliners — 36

Date	Title	Peak	Wks at No.1	Wks on Chart
11 Dec 93	**FEELIN' ALRIGHT** *MCA MCSTD 1952*	16		8
5 Mar 94	**THE WAY YOU WORK IT** *MCA MCSTD 1963*	14		7
14 May 94	**NUMBER ONE** *MCA MCSTD 1976*	27		5
30 Jul 94	**BLACK BOOK** *MCA MCSTD 1987*	13		6
10 Dec 94	**ONE MORE CHANCE** *MCA MCSTD 2025*	25		6
23 Sep 95	**OOH-AH-AA (I FEEL IT)** *Gasoline Alley MCSTD 2096*	33		2
2 Dec 95	**IN THE BEGINNING** *Gasoline Alley MCSTD 2107*	41		2

EYE TO EYE FEATURING TAKA BOOM
UK/US, male vocal/production duo. See Mukkaa, Umboza — 2

Date	Title	Peak	Wks at No.1	Wks on Chart
9 Jun 01	**JUST CAN'T GET ENOUGH (NO NO NO NO)** *Xtravaganza XTRAV 25CD*	36		2

EYEOPENER
UK, male/female vocal/production group. See Flip & Fill, Rezonance Q — 6

Date	Title	Peak	Wks at No.1	Wks on Chart
20 Nov 04	**HUNGRY EYES** *All Around The World CDGLOBE362*	16		6

EYES CREAM
Italy, male producer (Agostino Carollo) — 1

Date	Title	Peak	Wks at No.1	Wks on Chart
16 Oct 99	**FLY AWAY (BYE BYE)** *Accolade CDAC 001*	53		1

ADAM F
UK, male producer (Adam Fenton) — 23

Date	Title	Peak	Wks at No.1	Wks on Chart
27 Sep 97	**CIRCLES** *Positiva CDFJ 002*	20		3
7 Mar 98	**MUSIC IN MY MIND** *Positiva CDFJ 003*	27		3
15 Sep 01	**SMASH SUMTHIN'** *Def Jam 5886932* FEATURING REDMAN	11		7
1 Dec 01	**STAND CLEAR** *Chrysalis CDEM 597* FEATURING M.O.P.	43		1
6 Apr 02	**WHERE'S MY** *EMI CDEMS 598* FEATURING LIL' MO	37		2
27 Apr 02	**METROSOUND** *Kaos 001P* & J MAJIK	54		1
8 Jun 02	**STAND CLEAR** *Kaos KAOSCD 002* FEATURING M.O.P.	50		1
31 Aug 02	**SMASH SUMTHIN'** *Kaos KOASCD 003* FEATURING REDMAN	47		2
14 Dec 02	**DIRTY HARRY'S REVENGE** *Kaos 004P* FEATURING BEENIE MAN	50		2
30 Oct 04	**WHEN THE SUN GOES DOWN** *Breakbeat Kaos BBK005SCD* DJ FRESH FEATURING ADAM F	68		1

FAB

UK, male production group led by TV/film producer Gary Shoefield

Date	Title	Peak Position	Weeks at No.1	Weeks on Chart
				11
7 Jul 90	**THUNDERBIRDS ARE GO** *Brothers Organisation FAB 1* FEATURING MC PARKER	5		8
20 Oct 90	**THE PRISONER** *Brothers Organisation FAB 6* FEATURING MC NUMBER 6	56		2
1 Dec 90	**THE STINGRAY MEGAMIX** *Brothers Organisation FAB 2* FEATURING AQUA MARINA	66		1

FAB!

Ireland, female vocal group

Date	Title	Peak Position	Weeks at No.1	Weeks on Chart
				1
1 Aug 98	**TURN AROUND** *Break Records BRCX 107*	59		1

FAB FOR FEATURING ROBERT OWENS

Germany/Italy/US, male vocal/production trio

Date	Title	Peak Position	Weeks at No.1	Weeks on Chart
				1
15 Feb 03	**LAST NIGHT A DJ BLEW MY MIND** *Illustrious CDILL 013*	34		1

SHELLEY FABARES

US, female vocalist (Michelle Fabares)

Date	Title	Peak Position	Weeks at No.1	Weeks on Chart
				4
26 Apr 62	**JOHNNY ANGEL** *Pye International 7N 25132* ★	41		4

FABIAN

US, male vocalist (Fabiano Forte)

Date	Title	Peak Position	Weeks at No.1	Weeks on Chart
				1
10 Mar 60	**HOUND DOG MAN** *HMV POP 695*	46		1

LARA FABIAN

Canada (b. Belgium), female vocalist

Date	Title	Peak Position	Weeks at No.1	Weeks on Chart
				1
28 Oct 00	**I WILL LOVE AGAIN** *Columbia 6694062*	63		1

FABOLOUS

US, male rapper (John Jackson)

Date	Title	Peak Position	Weeks at No.1	Weeks on Chart
				27
16 Aug 03	**CAN'T LET YOU GO** *Elektra E 7408CD* FEATURING MIKE SHOREY & LIL' MO	14		5
1 Nov 03	**INTO YOU** *Elektra E 7470CD* FEATURING TAMIA	18		6
20 Mar 04	**BADABOOM** *Epic 6747512* B2K FEATURING FABOLOUS	26		5
27 Nov 04	**BREATHE** *Atlantic AT0189CD*	28		8
2 Apr 05	**BABY** *Atlantic AT0199CDX* FEATURING MIKE SHOREY	41		3

FABULOUS BAKER BOYS

UK, male DJ/production trio

Date	Title	Peak Position	Weeks at No.1	Weeks on Chart
				2
15 Nov 97	**OH BOY** *Multiply CDMULTY 28*	34		2

FACES

UK, male vocal/instrumental group – Rod Stewart*, Kenney Jones, Ronnie Lane*, d. 4 Jun 1997 (replaced by Tetsu Yamauchi), Ian McLagan & Ronnie Wood

Date	Title	Peak Position	Weeks at No.1	Weeks on Chart
				46
18 Dec 71	**STAY WITH ME** *Warner Brothers K 16136*	6		14
17 Feb 73	**CINDY INCIDENTALLY** *Warner Brothers K 16247*	2		9
8 Dec 73	**POOL HALL RICHARD/I WISH IT WOULD RAIN** *Warner Brothers K 16341*	8		11
7 Dec 74	**YOU CAN MAKE ME DANCE SING OR ANYTHING (EVEN TAKE THE DOG FOR A WALK, MEND A FUSE, FOLD AWAY THE IRONING BOARD, OR ANY OTHER DOMESTIC SHORTCOMINGS)** *Warner Brothers K 16494* ROD STEWART & THE FACES	12		9
4 Jun 77	**THE FACES (EP)** *Riva 8*	41		3

FACTORY OF UNLIMITED RHYTHM

Jamaica, male/female vocal/instrumental group

Date	Title	Peak Position	Weeks at No.1	Weeks on Chart
				1
1 Jun 96	**THE SWEETEST SURRENDER** *Kuff KUFFD 6*	59		1

FADERS

UK, female vocal/instrumental group

Date	Title	Peak Position	Weeks at No.1	Weeks on Chart
				9
2 Apr 05	**NO SLEEP TONIGHT** *Polydor 9870597*	13		6
9 Jul 05	**JUMP** *Polydor 9872017*	21		3

DONALD FAGEN

US, male vocalist/keyboard player. See Steely Dan

Date	Title	Peak Position	Weeks at No.1	Weeks on Chart
				2
3 Jul 93	**TOMORROW'S GIRLS** *Reprise W 0180CDX*	46		2

JOE FAGIN

UK, male vocalist

Date	Title	Peak Position	Weeks at No.1	Weeks on Chart
				20
7 Jan 84	**THAT'S LIVIN' ALRIGHT** *Towerbell TOW 46* ●	3		11
5 Apr 86	**BACK WITH THE BOYS AGAIN/GET IT RIGHT** *Towerbell TOW 84*	53		9

YVONNE FAIR

US, female vocalist, d. 6 Mar 1994 (age 51)

Date	Title	Peak Position	Weeks at No.1	Weeks on Chart
				11
24 Jan 76	**IT SHOULD HAVE BEEN ME** *Tamla Motown TMG 1013*	5		11

FAIR WEATHER

UK, male vocal/instrumental group – Andy Fairweather-Low*, Dennis Bryon, Neil Jones, Clive Taylor & Derek Weaver. See Amen Corner

Date	Title	Peak Position	Weeks at No.1	Weeks on Chart
				12
18 Jul 70	**NATURAL SINNER** *RCA 1977*	6		12

FAIRGROUND ATTRACTION

UK, female/male vocal/instrumental group – Eddi Reader*, Roy Dodds, Simon Edwards & Mark E Nevin

Date	Title	Peak Position	Weeks at No.1	Weeks on Chart
				27
16 Apr 88	**PERFECT** *RCA PB 41845* ●	1	1	13
30 Jul 88	**FIND MY LOVE** *RCA PB 42079*	7		10
19 Nov 88	**A SMILE IN A WHISPER** *RCA PB 42249*	75		1
28 Jan 89	**CLARE** *RCA PB 42607*	49		3

FAIRPORT CONVENTION

UK, male/female vocal/instrumental group

Date	Title	Peak Position	Weeks at No.1	Weeks on Chart
				9
23 Jul 69	**SI TU DOIS PARTIR** *Island WIP 6064*	21		9

ANDY FAIRWEATHER-LOW

UK, male vocalist. See Amen Corner, Fair Weather

Date	Title	Peak Position	Weeks at No.1	Weeks on Chart
				18
21 Sep 74	**REGGAE TUNE** *A&M AMS 7129*	10		8
6 Dec 75	**WIDE EYED AND LEGLESS** *A&M AMS 7202*	6		10

ADAM FAITH

UK, male vocalist (Terence Nelhams-Wright), d. 8 Mar 2003 (age 62). The first teen idol of the 1960s was the first UK artist to see their initial seven hits all reach the Top 5 (and, unlike his contemporaries, they were all original songs). Faith later found fame in both acting and in the financial world

Date	Title	Peak Position	Weeks at No.1	Weeks on Chart
				251
20 Nov 59	**WHAT DO YOU WANT** *Parlophone R 4591*	1	3	19
22 Jan 60	**POOR ME** *Parlophone R 4623*	1	1	17
14 Apr 60	**SOMEONE ELSE'S BABY** *Parlophone R 4643*	2		13
30 Jun 60	**WHEN JOHNNY COMES MARCHING HOME/MADE YOU** *Parlophone R 4665*	5		13
15 Sep 60	**HOW ABOUT THAT** *Parlophone R 4689*	4		14
17 Nov 60	**LONELY PUP (IN A CHRISTMAS SHOP)** *Parlophone R 4708*	4		11
9 Feb 61	**WHO AM I/THIS IS IT!** *Parlophone R 4735*	5		14
27 Apr 61	**EASY GOING ME** *Parlophone R 4766*	12		10
20 Jul 61	**DON'T YOU KNOW IT** *Parlophone R 4807*	12		10
26 Oct 61	**THE TIME HAS COME** *Parlophone R 4837*	4		14
18 Jan 62	**LONESOME** *Parlophone R 4864*	12		9
3 May 62	**AS YOU LIKE IT** *Parlophone R 4896*	5		15
30 Aug 62	**DON'T THAT BEAT ALL** *Parlophone R 4930* WITH JOHNNY KEATING & HIS ORCHESTRA	8		11
13 Dec 62	**BABY TAKE A BOW** *Parlophone R 4964*	22		6
31 Jan 63	**WHAT NOW** *Parlophone R 4990* WITH JOHNNY KEATING & HIS ORCHESTRA	31		5
11 Jul 63	**WALKIN' TALL** *Parlophone R 5039*	23		6
19 Sep 63	**THE FIRST TIME** *Parlophone R 5061* & THE ROULETTES	5		13
12 Dec 63	**WE ARE IN LOVE** *Parlophone R 5091* & THE ROULETTES	11		12
12 Mar 64	**IF HE TELLS YOU** *Parlophone R 5109* & THE ROULETTES	25		9
28 May 64	**I LOVE BEING IN LOVE WITH YOU** *Parlophone R 5138* & THE ROULETTES	33		6
26 Nov 64	**MESSAGE TO MARTHA (KENTUCKY BLUEBIRD)** *Parlophone R 5201*	12		11
11 Feb 65	**STOP FEELING SORRY FOR YOURSELF** *Parlophone R 5235*	23		6
17 Jun 65	**SOMEONE'S TAKEN MARIA AWAY** *Parlophone R 5289*	34		5
20 Oct 66	**CHERYL'S GOIN' HOME** *Parlophone R 5516*	46		2

HORACE FAITH

Jamaica, male vocalist (Horace Smith)

Date	Title	Peak Position	Weeks at No.1	Weeks on Chart
				10
12 Sep 70	**BLACK PEARL** *Trojan TR 7790*	13		10

PALOMA FAITH

UK, female vocalist/actor (Paloma Blomfield) — 17

Date	Title	Peak Position	Weeks at No.1	Weeks on Chart
27 Jun 09	**STONE COLD SOBER** *Epic 88697529352*	17		3
26 Sep 09	**NEW YORK** *Epic 88697562142*	15		11
23 Jan 10	**DO YOU WANT THE TRUTH OR SOMETHING BEAUTIFUL** *Epic GBARL0900489*	64		1
27 Mar 10	**UPSIDE DOWN** *Epic GB1100900205*	55		2

PERCY FAITH

Canada, male orchestra leader, d. 9 Feb 1976 (age 67) — 31

Date	Title	Peak Position	Weeks at No.1	Weeks on Chart
5 Mar 60	**THEME FROM 'A SUMMER PLACE'** *Philips PB 989* ★	2		31

FAITH BROTHERS

UK, male vocal/instrumental group — 6

Date	Title	Peak Position	Weeks at No.1	Weeks on Chart
13 Apr 85	**THE COUNTRY OF THE BLIND** *Siren 2*	63		3
6 Jul 85	**A STRANGER ON HOME GROUND** *Siren 4*	69		3

FAITH, HOPE & CHARITY

US, male/female vocal group — 4

Date	Title	Peak Position	Weeks at No.1	Weeks on Chart
31 Jan 76	**JUST ONE LOOK** *RCA 2632*	38		4

FAITH, HOPE & CHARITY

UK, female vocal trio — 3

Date	Title	Peak Position	Weeks at No.1	Weeks on Chart
23 Jun 90	**BATTLE OF THE SEXES** *WEA YZ 4801*	53		3

FAITH NO MORE

US, male vocal/instrumental group – Mike Patton, Mike Bordin, Roddy Bottum, Bill Gould & Jim Martin — 65

Date	Title	Peak Position	Weeks at No.1	Weeks on Chart
6 Feb 88	**WE CARE A LOT** *Slash LASH 17*	53		3
10 Feb 90	**EPIC** *Slash LASH 21*	37		4
14 Apr 90	**FROM OUT OF NOWHERE** *Slash LASH 24*	23		6
14 Jul 90	**FALLING TO PIECES** *Slash LASH 25*	41		3
8 Sep 90	**EPIC** *Slash LASH 26*	25		5
6 Jun 92	**MIDLIFE CRISIS** *Slash LASH 37*	10		5
15 Aug 92	**A SMALL VICTORY** *Slash LASH 39*	29		5
12 Sep 92	**A SMALL VICTORY (REMIX)** *Slash LASHX 40*	55		1
21 Nov 92	**EVERYTHING'S RUINED** *Slash LASH 43*	28		3
16 Jan 93	**I'M EASY/BE AGGRESSIVE** *Slash LACDP 44*	3		8
6 Nov 93	**ANOTHER BODY MURDERED** *Epic 6597942* & BOO-YAA T.R.I.B.E.	26		3
11 Mar 95	**DIGGING THE GRAVE** *Slash LACDP 51*	16		4
27 May 95	**RICOCHET** *Slash LASCD 53*	27		2
29 Jul 95	**EVIDENCE** *Slash LACDP 54*	32		3
31 May 97	**ASHES TO ASHES** *Slash LASCD 61*	15		3
16 Aug 97	**LAST CUP OF SORROW** *Slash LASCD 62*	51		1
13 Dec 97	**THIS TOWN AIN'T BIG ENOUGH FOR THE BOTH OF US** *Roadrunner RR 22513* SPARKS VERSUS FAITH NO MORE	40		2
17 Jan 98	**ASHES TO ASHES** *Slash LASCD 63*	29		3
7 Nov 98	**I STARTED A JOKE** *Slash LASCD 65*	49		1

MARIANNE FAITHFULL

UK, female vocalist — 59

Date	Title	Peak Position	Weeks at No.1	Weeks on Chart
13 Aug 64	**AS TEARS GO BY** *Decca F 11923*	9		13
18 Feb 65	**COME AND STAY WITH ME** *Decca F 12075*	4		13
6 May 65	**THIS LITTLE BIRD** *Decca F 12162*	6		11
22 Jul 65	**SUMMER NIGHTS** *Decca F 12193*	10		10
4 Nov 65	**YESTERDAY** *Decca F 12268*	36		4
9 Mar 67	**IS THIS WHAT I GET FOR LOVING YOU** *Decca F 22524*	43		2
24 Nov 79	**THE BALLAD OF LUCY JORDAN** *Island WIP 6491*	48		6

FAITHLESS

UK, male/female vocal/instrumental/production trio – Maxi Jazz (Maxwell Frazer), Rollo Armstrong & Sister Bliss (Alayah Bentovim). See Dido, Dusted, 1 Giant Leap featuring Maxi Jazz & Robbie Williams, Our Tribe/One Tribe, Rollo, Sister Bliss, Sphinx — 130

Date	Title	Peak Position	Weeks at No.1	Weeks on Chart
5 Aug 95	**SALVA MEA (SAVE ME)** *Cheeky CHEKCD 008*	30		2
9 Dec 95	**INSOMNIA** *Cheeky CHEKCD 010*	27		2
23 Mar 96	**DON'T LEAVE** *Cheeky CHEKCD 012*	34		2
26 Oct 96	**INSOMNIA** *Cheeky CHEKCD 017* ●	3		13
21 Dec 96	**SALVA MEA (SAVE ME) (REMIX)** *Cheeky CHEKXCD 018*	9		7
26 Apr 97	**REVERENCE** *Cheeky CHEKCD 019*	10		3
15 Nov 97	**DON'T LEAVE** *Cheeky CHEKXCD 024*	21		2
5 Sep 98	**GOD IS A DJ** *Cheeky CHEKCD 028*	6		8
5 Dec 98	**TAKE THE LONG WAY HOME** *Cheeky CHEKCD 031*	15		6
1 May 99	**BRING MY FAMILY BACK** *Cheeky CHEKCD 035*	14		5
16 Jun 01	**WE COME 1** *Cheeky 74321858352*	3		10
29 Sep 01	**MUHAMMAD ALI** *Cheeky 74321886452*	29		4
29 Dec 01	**TARANTULA** *Cheeky 74321903592*	29		5
20 Apr 02	**ONE STEP TOO FAR** *Cheeky 74321926412* FEATURING DIDO	6		3
4 May 02	**ONE STEP TOO FAR** *Cheeky 74321936742* FEATURING DIDO	68		1
12 Jun 04	**MASS DESTRUCTION** *Cheeky 82876614922*	7		8
4 Sep 04	**I WANT MORE** *BMG 82876641902*	22		3
30 Apr 05	**INSOMNIA** *Cheeky 82876690301*	48		19
11 Jun 05	**WHY GO?** *Cheeky 82876699292* FEATURING ESTELLE	49		1
13 Aug 05	**GOD IS A DJ** *Cheeky 82876719861*	66		2
13 Aug 05	**WE COME 1** *Cheeky 82876719871*	73		1
17 Sep 05	**INSOMNIA 2005** *Cheeky 82876724692*	17		19
2 Dec 06	**BOMBS** *Columbia 88697027602* FEATURING HARRY COLLIER	26		3
7 Apr 07	**MUSIC MATTERS** *Cheeky GBBXH0600040* FEATURING CASS FOX	38		1

FALCO

Austria, male vocalist (Johann Holzel), d. 6 Feb 1988 (age 40) — 26

Date	Title	Peak Position	Weeks at No.1	Weeks on Chart
22 Mar 86	**ROCK ME AMADEUS** *A&M AM 278* ● ★	1	1	15
31 May 86	**VIENNA CALLING** *A&M AM 318*	10		8
2 Aug 86	**JEANNY** *A&M AM 333*	68		1
27 Sep 86	**THE SOUND OF MUSIK** *WEA U 8591*	61		2

CHRISTIAN FALK

Sweden, male producer — 5

Date	Title	Peak Position	Weeks at No.1	Weeks on Chart
26 Aug 00	**MAKE IT RIGHT** *London LONCD 452* FEATURING DEMETREUS	22		3
29 Nov 08	**DREAM ON** *Data DATA208CDS* FEATURING ROBYN	29		2

THOMAS FALKE

Germany, male DJ/producer — 1

Date	Title	Peak Position	Weeks at No.1	Weeks on Chart
13 Aug 05	**HIGH AGAIN (HIGH ON EMOTION)** *Manifesto 9871558*	55		1

FALL

UK, male/female vocal/instrumental group — 27

Date	Title	Peak Position	Weeks at No.1	Weeks on Chart
13 Sep 86	**MR PHARMACIST** *Beggars Banquet BEG 168*	75		1
20 Dec 86	**HEY! LUCIANI** *Beggars Banquet BEG 176*	59		1
9 May 87	**THERE'S A GHOST IN MY HOUSE** *Beggars Banquet BEG 187*	30		4
31 Oct 87	**HIT THE NORTH** *Beggars Banquet BEG 200*	57		5
30 Jan 88	**VICTORIA** *Beggars Banquet BEG 206*	35		3
26 Nov 88	**BIG NEW PRINZ/JERUSALEM** *Beggars Banquet FALL 2/3*	59		2
27 Jan 90	**TELEPHONE THING** *Cog Sinister SIN 4*	58		1
8 Sep 90	**WHITE LIGHTNING** *Cog Sinister SIN 6*	56		2
14 Mar 92	**FREE RANGE** *Cog Sinister SINS 8*	40		1
17 Apr 93	**WHY ARE PEOPLE GRUDGEFUL** *Permanent CDSPERM 9*	43		1
25 Dec 93	**BEHIND THE COUNTER** *Permanent CDSPERM 13*	75		1
30 Apr 94	**15 WAYS** *Permanent CDSPERM 14*	65		1
17 Feb 96	**THE CHISELERS** *Jet JETSCD 500*	60		1
21 Feb 98	**MASQUERADE** *Artful CDARTFUYL 1*	69		1
14 Dec 02	**THE FALL VS 2003** *Action TAKE 020CD*	64		1
10 Jul 04	**THEME FROM SPARTA FC** *Action TAKE23CD*	66		1

FALL OUT BOY

US, male vocal/instrumental group – Patrick Stump, Andy Hurley, Joe Trohman & Pete Wentz — 100

Date	Title	Peak Position	Weeks at No.1	Weeks on Chart
21 Jan 06	**SUGAR WE'RE GOIN' DOWN** *Mercury 9884652*	24		4
18 Feb 06	**SUGAR WE'RE GOIN' DOWN** *Mercury 9850371*	8		17
22 Apr 06	**DANCE DANCE** *Mercury 9878031*	8		15
15 Jul 06	**A LITTLE LESS 16 CANDLES, A LITTLE MORE 'TOUCH ME'** *Mercury 1701063*	38		2
3 Feb 07	**THIS AIN'T A SCENE IT'S AN ARMS RACE** *Mercury 1718545*	2		18
14 Apr 07	**THNKS FR TH MMRS** *Mercury 1732074*	12		12
14 Jul 07	**THE TAKE OVER THE BREAKS OVER** *Mercury 1739377*	48		6
26 Apr 08	**BEAT IT** *Mercury USUM70808144* FEATURING JOHN MAYER	21		18
27 Sep 08	**I DON'T CARE** *Mercury 1788723*	33		8

FALLACY

UK, male producer (Daniel Fahey) — 4

Date	Title	Peak Position	Weeks at No.1	Weeks on Chart
22 Jun 02	**THE GROUNDBREAKER** *Wordplay WORCD 036* & FUSION	47		2
24 May 03	**BIG N BASHY** *Virgin VSCDT 1847* FEATURING TUBBY T	45		2

FALLOUT TRUST

UK, male vocal/instrumental group — 2

Date	Title	Peak Position	Weeks at No.1	Weeks on Chart
25 Jun 05	**WHEN WE ARE GONE** *At Large FUGCD007*	73		1
25 Feb 06	**WASHOUT** *At Large FUGCD014*	75		1

HAROLD FALTERMEYER
Germany, male keyboard player/producer (Harald Faltermeier) — 23

Date	Title	Peak Position	Weeks at No.1	Weeks on Chart
23 Mar 85	**AXEL F** *MCA 949* ●	2		22
24 Aug 85	**FLETCH THEME** *MCA 991*	74		1

AGNETHA FALTSKOG
Sweden, female vocalist. See Abba — 19

Date	Title	Peak Position	Weeks at No.1	Weeks on Chart
28 May 83	**THE HEAT IS ON** *Epic A 3436*	35		6
13 Aug 83	**WRAP YOUR ARMS AROUND ME** *Epic A 3622*	44		5
22 Oct 83	**CAN'T SHAKE LOOSE** *Epic A 3812*	63		1
24 Apr 04	**IF I THOUGHT YOU'D EVER CHANGE YOUR MIND** *WEA 375CD*	11		5
26 Jun 04	**WHEN YOU WALK IN THE ROOM** *WEA 378CD*	34		2

GEORGIE FAME
UK, male vocalist/keyboard player (Clive Powell) — 115

Date	Title	Peak Position	Weeks at No.1	Weeks on Chart
17 Dec 64	**YEH YEH** *Columbia DB 7428* & THE BLUE FLAMES	1	2	12
4 Mar 65	**IN THE MEANTIME** *Columbia DB 7494* & THE BLUE FLAMES	22		8
29 Jul 65	**LIKE WE USED TO BE** *Columbia DB 7633* & THE BLUE FLAMES	33		7
28 Oct 65	**SOMETHING** *Columbia DB 7727* & THE BLUE FLAMES	23		7
23 Jun 66	**GET AWAY** *Columbia DB 7946* & THE BLUE FLAMES	1	1	11
22 Sep 66	**SUNNY** *Columbia DB 8015*	13		8
22 Dec 66	**SITTING IN THE PARK** *Columbia DB 8096* & THE BLUE FLAMES	12		10
23 Mar 67	**BECAUSE I LOVE YOU** *CBS 202587*	15		8
13 Sep 67	**TRY MY WORLD** *CBS 2945*	37		5
13 Dec 67	**THE BALLAD OF BONNIE AND CLYDE** *CBS 3124*	1	1	13
9 Jul 69	**PEACEFUL** *CBS 4295*	16		9
13 Dec 69	**SEVENTH SON** *CBS 4659*	25		7
10 Apr 71	**ROSETTA** *CBS 7108* FAME & PRICE TOGETHER	11		10

FAMILY
UK, male vocal/instrumental group – Roger Chapman, Rick Grech, d. 16 Mar 1990, John Palmer, Rob Townsend, John Weider & John Whitney — 44

Date	Title	Peak Position	Weeks at No.1	Weeks on Chart
1 Nov 69	**NO MULE'S FOOL** *Reprise RS 27001*	29		7
22 Aug 70	**STRANGE BAND** *Reprise RS 27009*	11		12
17 Jul 71	**IN MY OWN TIME** *Reprise K 14090*	4		13
23 Sep 72	**BURLESQUE** *Reprise K 14196*	13		12

FAMILY CAT
UK, male vocal/instrumental group — 4

Date	Title	Peak Position	Weeks at No.1	Weeks on Chart
28 Aug 93	**AIRPLANE GARDENSATMOSPHERIC ROAD** *Dedicated FCUK 00CD*	69		1
21 May 94	**WONDERFUL EXCUSE** *Dedicated 74321208432*	48		1
30 Jul 94	**GOLDENBOOK** *Dedicated 74321220072*	42		2

FAMILY DOGG
UK, male/female vocal group – Steve Rowland, Doreen De Veuve, Albert Hammond*, Mike Hazlewood & Pam Quinn — 14

Date	Title	Peak Position	Weeks at No.1	Weeks on Chart
28 May 69	**A WAY OF LIFE** *Bell 1055*	6		14

FAMILY FOUNDATION
UK, male/female production/rap/vocal group — 4

Date	Title	Peak Position	Weeks at No.1	Weeks on Chart
13 Jun 92	**XPRESS YOURSELF** *380 PEW 1*	42		4

FAMILY STAND
US, female/male vocal/instrumental trio – Sandra St Victor (Sandra Matthews), Peter Lord Moreland & Vernon 'V' Jeffrey Smith — 13

Date	Title	Peak Position	Weeks at No.1	Weeks on Chart
31 Mar 90	**GHETTO HEAVEN** *East West A 7997*	10		11
17 Jan 98	**GHETTO HEAVEN (REMIX)** *Perfecto PERD 156CD1*	30		2

FANTASTIC FOUR
US, male vocal group — 4

Date	Title	Peak Position	Weeks at No.1	Weeks on Chart
24 Feb 79	**B.Y.O.F. (BRING YOUR OWN FUNK)** *Atlantic LV 14*	62		4

FANTASTICS
US, male vocal group – John Cheatdom, Donald Haywoode, Richard Pitts & Jerome Ramos — 12

Date	Title	Peak Position	Weeks at No.1	Weeks on Chart
27 Mar 71	**SOMETHING OLD, SOMETHING NEW** *Bell 1141*	9		12

FANTASY UFO
UK, male producer (Mark Ryder) — 6

Date	Title	Peak Position	Weeks at No.1	Weeks on Chart
29 Sep 90	**FANTASY** *XL Recordings XLT 15*	56		3
10 Aug 91	**MIND BODY SOUL** *Strictly Underground YZ 591* FEATURING JAY GROOVE	50		3

FAR CORPORATION
Germany, male producer – Frank Farian (Franz Reuther) – with international male/female vocal/instrumental collaborators David Barreto, Bernd Berwanger, Peter Bischof, Mats Bjorklund, Curt Cress, Johan Daansen, Bertl Gebhard, Bobby Kimball, Pit Low, Steve Lukather, Robin McAuley, Bimey Oberreit, David Paich & the Jackson Singers — 11

Date	Title	Peak Position	Weeks at No.1	Weeks on Chart
26 Oct 85	**STAIRWAY TO HEAVEN** *Arista ARIST 639*	8		11

DON FARDON
UK, male vocalist (Donald Maughn) — 22

Date	Title	Peak Position	Weeks at No.1	Weeks on Chart
18 Apr 70	**BELFAST BOY** *Young Blood YB 1010*	32		5
10 Oct 70	**INDIAN RESERVATION** *Young Blood YB 1015*	3		17

FARGETTA
Italy, male producer (Mario Fargetta). See Tamperer — 3

Date	Title	Peak Position	Weeks at No.1	Weeks on Chart
23 Jan 93	**MUSIC** *Synthetic CDR 6334* & ANNE-MARIE SMITH	34		2
10 Aug 96	**THE MUSIC IS MOVING** *Arista 74321381572*	74		1

CHRIS FARLOWE
UK, male vocalist (John Deighton) — 36

Date	Title	Peak Position	Weeks at No.1	Weeks on Chart
27 Jan 66	**THINK** *Immediate IM 023*	37		3
23 Jun 66	**OUT OF TIME** *Immediate IM 035*	1	1	13
27 Oct 66	**RIDE ON BABY** *Immediate IM 038*	31		7
16 Feb 67	**MY WAY OF GIVING IN** *Immediate IM 041*	48		1
29 Jun 67	**MOANIN'** *Immediate IM 056*	46		2
13 Dec 67	**HANDBAGS AND GLADRAGS** *Immediate IM 065*	33		6
27 Sep 75	**OUT OF TIME** *Immediate IMS 101*	44		4

FARM
UK, male vocal/instrumental group – Peter Hooton, Roy Boulter, Steve Grimes, Carl Hunter, Ben Leach & Keith Mullin — 59

Date	Title	Peak Position	Weeks at No.1	Weeks on Chart
5 May 90	**STEPPING STONE/FAMILY OF MAN** *Produce MILK 101*	58		4
1 Sep 90	**GROOVY TRAIN** *Produce MILK 102*	6		10
8 Dec 90	**ALL TOGETHER NOW** *Produce MILK 103* ●	4		12
13 Apr 91	**SINFUL! (SCARY JIGGIN' WITH DOCTOR LOVE)** *Siren SRN 138* PETE WYLIE WITH THE FARM	28		5
4 May 91	**DON'T LET ME DOWN** *Produce MILK 104*	36		3
24 Aug 91	**MIND** *Produce MILK 105*	31		4
14 Dec 91	**LOVE SEE NO COLOUR** *Produce MILK 106*	58		4
4 Jul 92	**RISING SUN** *End Product 6581737*	48		3
17 Oct 92	**DON'T YOU WANT ME** *End Product 6584687*	18		5
2 Jan 93	**LOVE SEE NO COLOUR (REMIX)** *End Product 6588682*	35		4
12 Jun 04	**ALL TOGETHER NOW 2004** *DMG ENGLCD2004* FEATURING SFX BOYS' CHOIR	5		5

FARMERS BOYS
UK, male vocal/instrumental group — 17

Date	Title	Peak Position	Weeks at No.1	Weeks on Chart
9 Apr 83	**MUCK IT OUT** *EMI 5380*	48		6
30 Jul 83	**FOR YOU** *EMI 5401*	66		3
4 Aug 84	**IN THE COUNTRY** *EMI FAB 2*	44		5
3 Nov 84	**PHEW WOW** *EMI FAB 3*	59		3

JOHN FARNHAM
Australia (b. UK), male vocalist — 17

Date	Title	Peak Position	Weeks at No.1	Weeks on Chart
25 Apr 87	**YOU'RE THE VOICE** *Wheatley PB 41093*	6		17

JOANNE FARRELL
US, female vocalist — 2

Date	Title	Peak Position	Weeks at No.1	Weeks on Chart
24 Jun 95	**ALL I WANNA DO** *Big Beat A 8194CD*	40		2

JOE FARRELL
US, male saxophonist, d. 10 Jan 1986 (age 48) — 4

Date	Title	Peak Position	Weeks at No.1	Weeks on Chart
16 Dec 78	**NIGHT DANCING** *Warner Brothers LV 2*	57		4

DIONNE FARRIS

US, female vocalist

Date	Title	Peak Position	Weeks at No.1	Weeks on Chart
				6
18 Mar 95	**I KNOW** *Columbia 6613542*	47		2
27 May 95	**I KNOW** *Columbia 6613542*	41		3
7 Jun 97	**HOPELESS** *Columbia 6645165*	42		1

GENE FARRIS

US, male DJ/producer

Date	Title	Peak Position	Weeks at No.1	Weeks on Chart
				1
20 Dec 03	**WELCOME TO CHICAGO EP** *Defected DFTD081R*	74		1

GENE FARROW & GF BAND

UK, male vocal/instrumental group

Date	Title	Peak Position	Weeks at No.1	Weeks on Chart
				8
1 Apr 78	**MOVE YOUR BODY** *Magnet MAG 109*	33		6
5 Aug 78	**DON'T STOP NOW** *Magnet MAG 125*	71		2

FASCINATIONS

US, female vocal group

Date	Title	Peak Position	Weeks at No.1	Weeks on Chart
				6
3 Jul 71	**GIRLS ARE OUT TO GET YOU** *Mojo 2092 004*	32		6

FASHION

UK, male vocal/instrumental group

Date	Title	Peak Position	Weeks at No.1	Weeks on Chart
				12
3 Apr 82	**STREETPLAYER (MECHANIK)** *Arista ARIST 456*	46		5
21 Aug 82	**LOVE SHADOW** *Arista ARIST 483*	51		5
18 Feb 84	**EYE TALK** *De Stijl A 4106*	69		2

SUSAN FASSBENDER

UK, female vocalist (Susan Whincup), d. 1991 (age 32)

Date	Title	Peak Position	Weeks at No.1	Weeks on Chart
				8
17 Jan 81	**TWILIGHT CAFE** *CBS 9468*	21		8

FAST FOOD ROCKERS

UK, female/male vocal trio – Lucy Meggitt, Martin Rycroft & Ria Scott

Date	Title	Peak Position	Weeks at No.1	Weeks on Chart
				24
28 Jun 03	**FAST FOOD SONG** *Better The Devil BTD1CD*	2		14
18 Oct 03	**SAY CHEESE (SMILE PLEASE)** *Better The Devil BTD5CD*	10		7
27 Dec 03	**I LOVE CHRISTMAS** *Better The Devil BTD6CDX*	25		3

FASTBALL

US, male vocal/instrumental trio

Date	Title	Peak Position	Weeks at No.1	Weeks on Chart
				5
3 Oct 98	**THE WAY** *Polydor 5689472*	21		5

FASTWAY

UK, male vocal/instrumental group

Date	Title	Peak Position	Weeks at No.1	Weeks on Chart
				1
2 Apr 83	**EASY LIVIN'** *CBS A 3196*	74		1

FAT BOYS

US, male rap trio – Mark 'Prince Markie Dee' Morales, Darren 'Buff Love – The Human Beat Box' Robinson, d. 10 Dec 1995, & Damon 'Kool Rock-ski' Wimbley

Date	Title	Peak Position	Weeks at No.1	Weeks on Chart
				29
4 May 85	**JAIL HOUSE RAP** *Sultra U 9123*	63		2
22 Aug 87	**WIPEOUT** *Urban URB 5* & THE BEACH BOYS ○	2		12
18 Jun 88	**THE TWIST (YO, TWIST)** *Urban URB 20* & CHUBBY CHECKER	2		11
5 Nov 88	**LOUIE LOUIE** *Urban URB 26*	46		4

FAT JOE

US, male rapper (Joseph Cartagena)

Date	Title	Peak Position	Weeks at No.1	Weeks on Chart
				34
1 Apr 00	**FEELIN' SO GOOD** *Columbia 6691972* JENNIFER LOPEZ FEATURING BIG PUN & FAT JOE	15		6
30 Mar 02	**WE THUGGIN'** *Atlantic AT 0124CD*	48		1
25 May 02	**WHAT'S LUV** *Atlantic AT 0128CD* FEATURING ASHANTI	4		8
14 Dec 02	**CRUSH TONIGHT** *Atlantic AT 0142CD* FEATURING GINUWINE	42		2
16 Oct 04	**LEAN BACK** *Universal MCSTD 40385* TERROR SQUAD FEATURING FAT JOE & REMY ★	24		5
28 May 05	**HOLD YOU DOWN** *Epic 6759342* JENNIFER LOPEZ FEATURING FAT JOE	6		9
16 Jul 05	**GET IT POPPIN'** *Atlantic AT0210CD* FEATURING NELLY	34		3

FAT LADY SINGS

Ireland, male vocal/instrumental group

Date	Title	Peak Position	Weeks at No.1	Weeks on Chart
				2
17 Jul 93	**DRUNKARD LOGIC** *East West YZ 756CD*	56		2

FAT LARRY'S BAND

US, male vocal/instrumental group – leader Larry James, d. 5 Dec 1987 (age 38)

Date	Title	Peak Position	Weeks at No.1	Weeks on Chart
				26
2 Jul 77	**CENTER CITY** *Atlantic K 10951*	31		5
10 Mar 79	**BOOGIE TOWN** *Fantasy FTC 168* F.L.B.	46		4
18 Aug 79	**LOOKING FOR LOVE TONIGHT** *Fantasy FTC 179*	46		6
18 Sep 82	**ZOOM** *Virgin VS 546* ○	2		11

FAT LES

UK, male/female vocal/comedy/actor ensemble – members included Keith Allen, Damien Hirst, Alex James, Lily Allen*, Michael Barrymore* (Michael Parker), Paul Kaye, Matt Lucas, Lisa Moorish* (Lisa Morrish), Rowland Rivron, Edward Tudor-Pole & David Walliams

Date	Title	Peak Position	Weeks at No.1	Weeks on Chart
				22
20 Jun 98	**VINDALOO** *Telstar CDSTAS 2982* ●	2		12
19 Dec 98	**NAUGHTY CHRISTMAS (GOBLIN IN THE OFFICE)** *Turtleneck NECKCD 001*	21		5
17 Jun 00	**JERUSALEM** *Parlophone CDRS 6540 2000*	10		5

FATBACK BAND

US, male vocal/instrumental group – Bill Curtis, George Adams, Kenny Ballard, John Flippin, Johnny King, Earl Shelton, Gerry Thomas & George Williams

Date	Title	Peak Position	Weeks at No.1	Weeks on Chart
				67
6 Sep 75	**YUM YUM (GIMME SOME)** *Polydor 2066 590*	40		6
6 Dec 75	**(ARE YOU READY) DO THE BUS STOP** *Polydor 2066 637*	18		10
21 Feb 76	**(DO THE) SPANISH HUSTLE** *Polydor 2066 656*	10		7
29 May 76	**PARTY TIME** *Polydor 2066 682*	41		4
14 Aug 76	**NIGHT FEVER** *Spring 2066 706*	38		4
12 Mar 77	**DOUBLE DUTCH** *Spring 2066 777*	31		4
9 Aug 80	**BACKSTROKIN'** *Spring POSP 149* FATBACK	41		9
23 Jun 84	**I FOUND LOVIN'** *Master Mix CHE 8401* FATBACK	49		4
4 May 85	**GIRLS ON MY MIND** *Atlantic/Cotillion FBACK 1* FATBACK	69		2
6 Sep 86	**I FOUND LOVIN'** *Important TAN 10*	55		5
5 Sep 87	**I FOUND LOVIN'** *Master Mix CHE 8401*	7		12

FATBOY SLIM

UK, male DJ/producer (Norman Cook, aka Quentin Cook). See Beats International, Freakpower, Housemartins, Pizzaman, Urban All Stars

Date	Title	Peak Position	Weeks at No.1	Weeks on Chart
				82
3 May 97	**GOING OUT OF MY HEAD** *Skint 19CD*	57		1
1 Nov 97	**EVERYBODY NEEDS A 303** *Skint 31CD*	34		2
20 Jun 98	**THE ROCKAFELLER SKANK** *Skint 35CD*	6		10
17 Oct 98	**GANGSTER TRIPPIN** *Skint 39CD*	3		8
16 Jan 99	**PRAISE YOU** *Skint 42CD* ○	1	1	12
1 May 99	**BADDER BADDER SCHWING** *Eye-Q EYEUK 040CD* FREDDY FRESH FEATURING FATBOY SLIM	34		2
1 May 99	**RIGHT HERE RIGHT NOW** *Skint 46CD*	2		10
28 Oct 00	**SUNSET (BIRD OF PREY)** *Skint 58CD*	9		13
20 Jan 01	**DEMONS** *Skint 60CD* FEATURING MACY GRAY	16		5
5 May 01	**STAR 69** *Skint 64XCD*	10		7
15 Sep 01	**A SONG FOR SHELTER/YA MAMA** *Skint 71CD*	30		2
26 Jan 02	**RETOX** *Skint FAT 18*	73		1
2 Oct 04	**SLASH DOT DASH** *Skint SKINT100CDX*	12		3
11 Dec 04	**WONDERFUL NIGHT** *Skint SKINT104CD*	51		2
12 Mar 05	**THE JOKER** *Skint SKINT106CD*	32		2
8 Jul 06	**THAT OLD PAIR OF JEANS** *Skint SKINT123CD*	39		2

FATHER ABRAPHART & THE SMURPS

UK, male vocalist (Jonathan King)

Date	Title	Peak Position	Weeks at No.1	Weeks on Chart
				4
16 Dec 78	**LICK A SMURP FOR CHRISTMAS (ALL FALL DOWN)** *Petrol GAS 1/ Magnet MAG 139*	58		4

FATIMA MANSIONS

Ireland, male vocal/instrumental group – Cathal Coughlan, Nicholas Tiompan Allum, Hugh Bunker, Andrias 'Sister Mary' O'Gruama & Duke O'Malaithe

Date	Title	Peak Position	Weeks at No.1	Weeks on Chart
				11
23 May 92	**EVIL MAN** *Radioactive SKX 56*	59		1
1 Aug 92	**1000%** *Radioactive SKX 59*	61		3
19 Sep 92	**(EVERYTHING I DO) I DO IT FOR YOU** *Columbia 6583827*	7		6
6 Aug 94	**THE LOYALISER** *Kitchenware SKCD 67*	58		1

FATMAN SCOOP FEATURING THE CROOKLYN CLAN

US, male DJ/rapper (Isaac Freeman III)

Date	Title	Peak Position	Weeks at No.1	Weeks on Chart
				22
1 Nov 03	**BE FAITHFUL** *Def Jam 9812716* ○	1	2	16
21 Feb 04	**IT TAKES SCOOP** *Def Jam 9816983*	9		6

Legend: Silver-selling ● Gold-selling ● Platinum-selling (x multiples) ⊛ US No.1 ★ Peak Position Weeks at No.1 Weeks on Chart

NEWTON FAULKNER
UK, male vocalist/guitarist (Sam Faulkner) — 52

Date	Title	Peak	No.1	Weeks
4 Aug 07	**DREAM CATCH ME** *Ugly Truth 88697117762*	7		35
11 Aug 07	**TEARDROP** *Ugly Truth GBHKB0600089*	57		11
3 Nov 07	**ALL I GOT** *Ugly Truth 88697189852*	59		2
12 Apr 08	**I NEED SOMETHING** *Ugly Truth 88697075922*	70		2
3 Oct 09	**IF THIS IS IT** *Ugly Truth GB1100900187*	56		2

FC KAHUNA
UK, male production duo — 3

Date	Title	Peak	No.1	Weeks
6 Apr 02	**GLITTERBALL** *City Rockers ROCKERS 11CD*	64		1
20 Jul 02	**MACHINE SAYS YES** *City Rockers ROCKERS 18CD*	58		1
22 Mar 03	**HAYLING** *Skint 84CD*	49		1

FEAR FACTORY
US, male vocal/instrumental group — 1

Date	Title	Peak	No.1	Weeks
9 Oct 99	**CARS** *Roadrunner RR 21893*	57		1

PHIL FEARON
UK, male vocalist/producer — 63

Date	Title	Peak	No.1	Weeks
23 Apr 83	**DANCING TIGHT** *Ensign ENY 501* GALAXY FEATURING PHIL FEARON	4		11
30 Jul 83	**WAIT UNTIL TONIGHT (MY LOVE)** *Ensign ENY 503* GALAXY FEATURING PHIL FEARON	20		8
22 Oct 83	**FANTASY REAL** *Ensign ENY 507* GALAXY FEATURING PHIL FEARON	41		6
10 Mar 84	**WHAT DO I DO** *Ensign ENY 510* & GALAXY ●	5		10
14 Jul 84	**EVERYBODY'S LAUGHING** *Ensign ENY 514* & GALAXY	10		10
15 Jun 85	**YOU DON'T NEED A REASON** *Ensign ENY 517* & GALAXY	42		4
27 Jul 85	**THIS KIND OF LOVE** *Ensign ENY 521* & GALAXY	70		3
2 Aug 86	**I CAN PROVE IT** *Ensign PF 1*	8		9
15 Nov 86	**AIN'T NOTHING BUT A HOUSEPARTY** *Ensign PF 2*	60		2

FEEDER
UK/Japan, male vocal/instrumental trio – Grant Nicholas, Taka Hirose & Jon Lee, d. 7 Jan 2002 (replaced by Mark Richardson) — 77

Date	Title	Peak	No.1	Weeks
8 Mar 97	**TANGERINE** *Echo ECSCD 32*	60		1
10 May 97	**CEMENT** *Echo ECSCX 36*	53		1
23 Aug 97	**CRASH** *Echo ECSCD 42*	48		1
18 Oct 97	**HIGH** *Echo ECSCD 44*	24		2
28 Feb 98	**SUFFOCATE** *Echo ECSCX 52*	37		1
3 Apr 99	**DAY IN DAY OUT** *Echo ECSCD 75*	31		2
12 Jun 99	**INSOMNIA** *Echo ECSCD 77*	22		3
21 Aug 99	**YESTERDAY WENT TOO SOON** *Echo ECSCD 79*	20		3
20 Nov 99	**PAPERFACES** *Echo ECSCD 85*	41		2
20 Jan 01	**BUCK ROGERS** *Echo ECSCX 106*	5		6
14 Apr 01	**SEVEN DAYS IN THE SUN** *Echo ECSCD 107*	14		6
14 Jul 01	**TURN** *Echo ECSCD 116*	27		2
22 Dec 01	**JUST A DAY EP** *Echo ECSCX 121*	12		7
12 Oct 02	**COME BACK AROUND** *Echo ECSCX 130*	14		5
25 Jan 03	**JUST THE WAY I'M FEELING** *Echo ECSCX 133*	10		8
17 May 03	**FORGET ABOUT TOMORROW** *Echo ECSCX 135*	12		4
4 Oct 03	**FIND THE COLOUR** *Echo ECSCD 145*	24		2
29 Jan 05	**TUMBLE AND FALL** *Echo ECSCX157*	5		5
16 Apr 05	**FEELING A MOMENT** *Echo ECSCX163*	13		4
9 Jul 05	**PUSHING THE SENSES** *Echo ECSCX173*	30		2
22 Oct 05	**SHATTER/TENDER** *Echo ECSCX180*	11		3
13 May 06	**LOST & FOUND** *Echo ECSCX184*	12		4
5 Aug 06	**SAVE US** *EMI ECSCD186*	34		2
21 Jun 08	**WE ARE THE PEOPLE** *Echo ECSCD199*	25		1

FEELING
UK, male vocal/instrumental group – Dan Gillespie Sells, Ciaran & Kevin Jeremiah, Richard Jones & Paul Stewart — 95

Date	Title	Peak	No.1	Weeks
11 Mar 06	**SEWN** *Island CID920*	7		18
27 May 06	**FILL MY LITTLE WORLD** *Island MCSTD40464*	10		24
2 Sep 06	**NEVER BE LONELY** *Island/Uni-Island 1705007*	9		21
25 Nov 06	**LOVE IT WHEN YOU CALL** *Island 1713050*	18		18
17 Feb 07	**ROSE** *Island/Uni-Island 1723753*	38		3
16 Feb 08	**I THOUGHT IT WAS OVER** *Island 1761837*	9		8
3 May 08	**WITHOUT YOU** *Island 1767553*	53		1
26 Jul 08	**TURN IT UP** *Island 1777562*	67		2

FEIST
Canada, female vocalist/guitarist (Leslie Feist) — 12

Date	Title	Peak	No.1	Weeks
29 Sep 07	**1234** *Polydor 5300680*	8		12

WILTON FELDER
US, male saxophonist — 7

Date	Title	Peak	No.1	Weeks
1 Nov 80	**INHERIT THE WIND** *MCA 646*	39		5
16 Feb 85	**(NO MATTER HOW HIGH I GET) I'LL STILL BE LOOKIN' UP TO YOU** *MCA 919* FEATURING BOBBY WOMACK & INTRODUCING ALLTRINA GRAYSON	63		2

JOSE FELICIANO
US (b. Puerto Rico), male vocalist/guitarist — 23

Date	Title	Peak	No.1	Weeks
18 Sep 68	**LIGHT MY FIRE** *RCA 1715*	6		16
18 Oct 69	**AND THE SUN WILL SHINE** *RCA 1871*	25		7

FELIX
UK, male producer (Francis Wright) — 29

Date	Title	Peak	No.1	Weeks
8 Aug 92	**DON'T YOU WANT ME** *Deconstruction 74321110507*	6		11
24 Oct 92	**IT WILL MAKE ME CRAZY** *Deconstruction 74321118137*	11		6
22 May 93	**STARS** *Deconstruction 74321147102*	29		3
12 Aug 95	**DON'T YOU WANT ME (REMIX)** *Deconstruction 74321293972*	10		5
19 Oct 96	**DON'T YOU WANT ME (2ND REMIX)** *Deconstruction 74321418142*	17		4

FELIX DA HOUSECAT
US, male producer (Felix Stallings, Jr) — 9

Date	Title	Peak	No.1	Weeks
6 Sep 97	**DIRTY MOTHA** *Manifesto FESCD 29* QWILO & FELIX DA HOUSECAT	66		1
14 Jul 01	**SILVER SCREEN SHOWER SCENE** *City Rockers ROCKERS 1CD*	55		1
2 Mar 02	**WHAT DOES IT FEEL LIKE?** *City Rockers ROCKERS 8CD*	66		1
5 Oct 02	**SILVER SCREEN SHOWER SCENE** *City Rockers ROCKERS 19CD*	39		2
14 Aug 04	**ROCKET RIDE** *Rykodisc ENR522*	55		1
27 Nov 04	**WATCHING CARS GO BY** *Emperor Norton ENR532*	49		2
26 Feb 05	**READY2WEAR** *Emperor Norton ENR562*	62		1

JULIE FELIX
US, female vocalist/guitarist — 19

Date	Title	Peak	No.1	Weeks
18 Apr 70	**IF I COULD (EL CONDOR PASA)** *RAK 101*	19		11
17 Oct 70	**HEAVEN IS HERE** *RAK 105*	22		8

FELON
UK, female vocalist (Simone Locker) — 2

Date	Title	Peak	No.1	Weeks
23 Mar 02	**GET OUT** *Serious SERR 32CD*	31		2

FE-M@IL
UK, female vocal group — 2

Date	Title	Peak	No.1	Weeks
5 Aug 00	**FLEE FLY FLO** *Jive 9250592*	46		2

FEMME FATALE
US, female/male vocal/instrumental group — 2

Date	Title	Peak	No.1	Weeks
11 Feb 89	**FALLING IN AND OUT OF LOVE** *MCA 1309*	69		2

FENDERMEN
US, male vocal/instrumental duo — 9

Date	Title	Peak	No.1	Weeks
18 Aug 60	**MULE SKINNER BLUES** *Top Rank JAR 395*	32		9

FENIX TX
US, male vocal/instrumental group — 1

Date	Title	Peak	No.1	Weeks
11 May 02	**THREESOME** *MCA MCSTD 40279*	66		1

GEORGE FENTON & JONAS GWANGWA
UK/South Africa, male conductor/vocal duo — 1

Date	Title	Peak	No.1	Weeks
2 Jan 88	**CRY FREEDOM** *MCA 1228*	75		1

PETER FENTON
UK, male vocalist — 3

Date	Title	Peak	No.1	Weeks
10 Nov 66	**MARBLE BREAKS IRON BENDS** *Fontana TF 748*	46		3

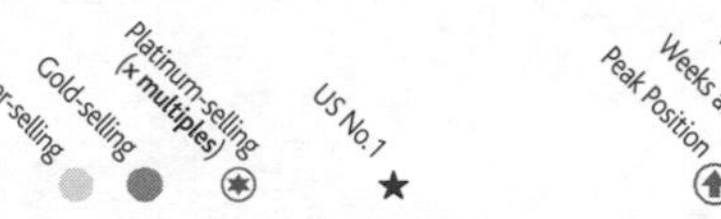

SHANE FENTON & THE FENTONES
UK, male vocal/instrumental group. See Alvin Stardust — 28

Date	Title	Peak	Wks at No.1	Wks on Chart
26 Oct 61	**I'M A MOODY GUY** *Parlophone R 4827*	22		8
1 Feb 62	**WALK AWAY** *Parlophone R 4866*	38		5
5 Apr 62	**IT'S ALL OVER NOW** *Parlophone R 4883*	29		7
12 Jul 62	**CINDY'S BIRTHDAY** *Parlophone R 4921*	19		8

FENTONES
UK, male vocal/instrumental group — 4

Date	Title	Peak	Wks at No.1	Wks on Chart
19 Apr 62	**THE MEXICAN** *Parlophone R 4899*	41		3
27 Sep 62	**THE BREEZE AND I** *Parlophone R 4937*	48		1

FERGIE
Ireland, male DJ/producer (Robert Ferguson) — 5

Date	Title	Peak	Wks at No.1	Wks on Chart
9 Sep 00	**DECEPTION** *Duty Free DF 020CD*	47		1
25 Nov 00	**HOOVERS & HORNS** *Nukleuz NUKC 0185* & BK	57		2
10 Aug 02	**THE BASS EP** *Duty Free DFTELCDX 004*	47		2

FERGIE
US, female vocalist (Stacy Ferguson). See Black Eyed Peas — 77

Date	Title	Peak	Wks at No.1	Wks on Chart
16 Sep 06	**LONDON BRIDGE** *A&M/Polydor 1707129* ★	3		8
24 Feb 07	**GLAMOROUS** *A&M 1730081* FEATURING LUDACRIS ★	6		26
23 Jun 07	**BIG GIRLS DON'T CRY (PERSONAL)** *Interscope 1741332* ★	2		28
17 Nov 07	**CLUMSY** *A&M USUM70609116*	62		3
26 Apr 08	**PARTY PEOPLE** *Island 1771901* NELLY & FERGIE	14		11
14 Jun 08	**LABELS OF LOVE** *A&M USUM70811028*	56		1

SHEILA FERGUSON
US, female vocalist. See Three Degrees — 1

Date	Title	Peak	Wks at No.1	Wks on Chart
5 Feb 94	**WHEN WILL I SEE YOU AGAIN** *XSrhythm CDSTAS 2711*	60		1

FERKO STRING BAND
US, male instrumental band — 2

Date	Title	Peak	Wks at No.1	Wks on Chart
12 Aug 55	**ALABAMA JUBILEE** *London HL 8140*	20		2

LUISA FERNANDEZ
Spain, female vocalist — 8

Date	Title	Peak	Wks at No.1	Wks on Chart
11 Nov 78	**LAY LOVE ON YOU** *Warner Brothers K 17061*	31		8

PAMELA FERNANDEZ
US, female vocalist — 3

Date	Title	Peak	Wks at No.1	Wks on Chart
17 Sep 94	**KICKIN' IN THE BEAT** *Ore AG 5CD*	43		2
3 Jun 95	**LET'S START OVER/KICKIN' IN THE BEAT (REMIX)** *Ore AG 9CD*	59		1

FERRANTE & TEICHER
US, male pianist duo – Arthur Ferrante, d. 19 Sep 2009 (age 88), & Louis Teicher, d. 3 Aug 2008 (age 83) — 18

Date	Title	Peak	Wks at No.1	Wks on Chart
18 Aug 60	**THEME FROM 'THE APARTMENT'** *London HLT 9164*	44		1
9 Mar 61	**THEME FROM 'EXODUS'** *London HLT 9298/HMV POP 881*	6		17

JOSE FERRER
US, male actor/vocalist (Jose Vincenti Ferrer Y Centron), d. 26 Jan 1992 (age 80) — 3

Date	Title	Peak	Wks at No.1	Wks on Chart
19 Feb 54	**WOMAN (UH-HUH)** *Philips PB 220*	7		3

TONY FERRINO
UK, male comedian/vocalist (Steve Coogan) — 2

Date	Title	Peak	Wks at No.1	Wks on Chart
23 Nov 96	**HELP YOURSELF/BIGAMY AT CHRISTMAS** *RCA 74321430302*	42		2

FERRY AID
International, male/female vocal/instrumental charity ensemble — 7

Date	Title	Peak	Wks at No.1	Wks on Chart
4 Apr 87	**LET IT BE** *The Sun AID 1* ●	1	3	7

BRYAN FERRY
UK, male vocalist/guitarist/keyboard player. See Roxy Music — 133

Date	Title	Peak	Wks at No.1	Wks on Chart
29 Sep 73	**A HARD RAIN'S GONNA FALL** *Island WIP 6170*	10		9
25 May 74	**THE IN CROWD** *Island WIP 6196*	13		6
31 Aug 74	**SMOKE GETS IN YOUR EYES** *Island WIP 6205*	17		8
5 Jul 75	**YOU GO TO MY HEAD** *Island WIP 6234*	33		3
12 Jun 76	**LET'S STICK TOGETHER** *Island WIP 6307* ●	4		10
7 Aug 76	**EXTENDED PLAY EP** *Island IEP 1*	7		9
5 Feb 77	**THIS IS TOMORROW** *Polydor 2001 704*	9		9
14 May 77	**TOKYO JOE** *Polydor 2001 711*	15		7
13 May 78	**WHAT GOES ON** *Polydor POSP 3*	67		2
5 Aug 78	**SIGN OF THE TIMES** *Polydor 2001 798*	37		8
11 May 85	**SLAVE TO LOVE** *EG FERRY 1*	10		9
31 Aug 85	**DON'T STOP THE DANCE** *EG FERRY 2*	21		7
7 Dec 85	**WINDSWEPT** *EG FERRY 3*	46		3
29 Mar 86	**IS YOUR LOVE STRONG ENOUGH** *EG FERRY 4*	22		7
10 Oct 87	**THE RIGHT STUFF** *Virgin VS 940*	37		6
13 Feb 88	**KISS AND TELL** *Virgin VS 1034*	41		5
29 Oct 88	**LET'S STICK TOGETHER (REMIX)** *EG EGO 44*	12		7
11 Feb 89	**THE PRICE OF LOVE (REMIX)** *EG EGO 46*	49		3
22 Apr 89	**HE'LL HAVE TO GO** *EG EGO 48*	63		1
6 Mar 93	**I PUT A SPELL ON YOU** *Virgin VSCDG 1400*	18		5
29 May 93	**WILL YOU LOVE ME TOMORROW** *Virgin VSCDG 1455*	23		5
4 Sep 93	**GIRL OF MY BEST FRIEND** *Virgin VSCDG 1468*	57		2
29 Oct 94	**YOUR PAINTED SMILE** *Virgin VSCDG 1508*	52		1
11 Feb 95	**MAMOUNA** *Virgin VSCDG 1528*	57		1

FEVER FEATURING TIPPA IRIE
UK, male vocal/instrumental/production group — 1

Date	Title	Peak	Wks at No.1	Wks on Chart
8 Jul 95	**STAYING ALIVE 95** *Telstar CDSTAS 2776*	48		1

LENA FIAGBE
UK, female vocalist — 13

Date	Title	Peak	Wks at No.1	Wks on Chart
24 Jul 93	**YOU COME FROM EARTH** *Mother MUMCD 42* LENA	69		1
23 Oct 93	**GOTTA GET IT RIGHT** *Mother MUMCD 44*	20		5
16 Apr 94	**WHAT'S IT LIKE TO BE BEAUTIFUL** *Mother MUMCD 49*	52		3
25 Jun 94	**VISIONS** *Mother MUMCD 53*	48		2
10 Feb 96	**AFRICAN DREAM** *Mercury MERCD 453* WASIS DIOP FEATURING LENA FIAGBE	44		2

KAREL FIALKA
UK (b. India), male vocalist — 12

Date	Title	Peak	Wks at No.1	Wks on Chart
17 May 80	**THE EYES HAVE IT** *Blueprint BLU 2005*	52		4
5 Sep 87	**HEY MATTHEW** *IRS IRM 140*	9		8

LUPE FIASCO
US, male rapper (Wasalu Jaco) — 37

Date	Title	Peak	Wks at No.1	Wks on Chart
18 Mar 06	**TOUCH THE SKY** *Roc-A-Fella 9852115* KANYE WEST FEATURING LUPE FIASCO	6		12
1 Jul 06	**KICK PUSH** *Atlantic AT0243CDX*	27		5
16 Sep 06	**DAYDREAMIN'** *Atlantic AT0252CD* FEATURING JILL SCOTT	25		6
19 Jan 08	**SUPERSTAR** *Atlantic ATO298CD2* FEATURING MATTHEW SANTOS	4		14

FIAT LUX
UK, male vocal/instrumental trio — 4

Date	Title	Peak	Wks at No.1	Wks on Chart
28 Jan 84	**SECRETS** *Polydor FIAT 2*	65		3
17 Mar 84	**BLUE EMOTION** *Polydor FIAT 3*	59		1

FICTION FACTORY
UK, male vocal/instrumental group – Kevin Patterson, Eddie Jordan, Graham McGregor, Chic Medley & Mike Ogletree — 11

Date	Title	Peak	Wks at No.1	Wks on Chart
14 Jan 84	**(FEELS LIKE) HEAVEN** *CBS A 3996*	6		9
17 Mar 84	**GHOST OF LOVE** *CBS A 3819*	64		2

FIDDLER'S DRAM
UK, male/female vocal/instrumental group – Cathy Lesurf, Alan Prosser, Chris Taylor, Ian Telfer & Will Ward — 9

Date	Title	Peak	Wks at No.1	Wks on Chart
15 Dec 79	**DAY TRIP TO BANGOR (DIDN'T WE HAVE A LOVELY TIME)** *Dingles SID 211*	3		9

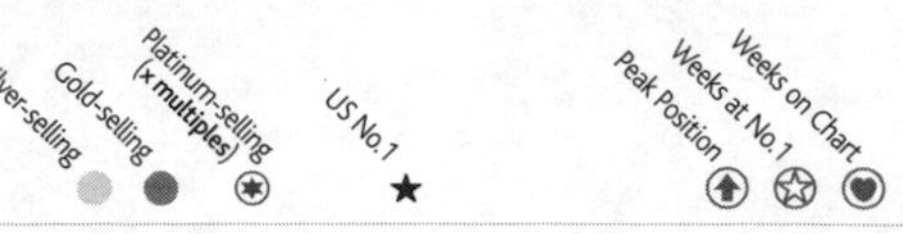

FIDELFATTI FEATURING RONETTE
Italy, male producer (Piero Fidelfatti) & female vocalist — 1

Date	Title	Peak	Wks at No.1	Wks
27 Jan 90	**JUST WANNA TOUCH ME** *Urban URB 46*	65		1

FIELD MOBB FEATURING CIARA
US, male/female vocal/rap trio — 2

Date	Title	Peak	Wks at No.1	Wks
26 Aug 06	**SO WHAT** *Geffen 1705382*	56		2

BILLY FIELD
Australia, male vocalist — 3

Date	Title	Peak	Wks at No.1	Wks
12 Jun 82	**YOU WEREN'T IN LOVE WITH ME** *CBS A 2344*	67		3

ERNIE FIELDS
US, male band leader, d. 11 May 1997 (age 91) — 8

Date	Title	Peak	Wks at No.1	Wks
25 Dec 59	**IN THE MOOD** *London HL 8985*	13		8

GRACIE FIELDS
UK, female vocalist (Grace Stansfield), d. 27 Sep 1979 (age 81) — 15

Date	Title	Peak	Wks at No.1	Wks
31 May 57	**AROUND THE WORLD** *Columbia DB 3953*	8		9
6 Nov 59	**LITTLE DONKEY** *Columbia DB 4360*	21		6

RICHARD 'DIMPLES' FIELDS
US, male vocalist, d. 12 Jan 2000 (age 58) — 4

Date	Title	Peak	Wks at No.1	Wks
20 Feb 82	**I'VE GOT TO LEARN TO SAY NO** *Epic EPC A 1918*	56		4

FIELDS OF THE NEPHILIM
UK, male vocal/instrumental group — 10

Date	Title	Peak	Wks at No.1	Wks
24 Oct 87	**BLUE WATER** *Situation Two SIT 48*	75		1
4 Jun 88	**MOONCHILD** *Situation Two SIT 52*	28		3
27 May 89	**PSYCHONAUT** *Situation Two ST 57*	35		3
4 Aug 90	**FOR HER LIGHT** *Beggars Banquet BEG 244T*	54		1
24 Nov 90	**SUMERLAND (DREAMED)** *Beggars Banquet BEG 250*	37		1
28 Sep 02	**FROM THE FIRE** *Jungle JUNG 65CD*	62		1

FIERCE
UK, female vocal trio – Chantal Alleyne, Aisha Peters & Sabrina Weathers — 23

Date	Title	Peak	Wks at No.1	Wks
9 Jan 99	**RIGHT HERE RIGHT NOW** *Wildstar CXWILD 13*	25		5
15 May 99	**DAYZ LIKE THAT** *Wildstar CDWILD 19*	11		5
14 Aug 99	**SO LONG** *Wildstar CDWILD 27*	15		5
12 Feb 00	**SWEET LOVE 2K** *Wildstar CDWILD 34*	3		8

FIERCE GIRL
UK, male vocal/rap duo — 2

Date	Title	Peak	Wks at No.1	Wks
11 Sep 04	**DOUBLE DROP** *Red Flag RF012CDS*	74		1
19 Feb 05	**WHAT MAKES A GIRL FIERCE** *Red Flag RF013CDS*	52		1

FIERY FURNACES
US, male/female vocal/production duo — 2

Date	Title	Peak	Wks at No.1	Wks
6 Mar 04	**TROPICAL ICE-LAND** *Rough Trade RTRADESCD152*	52		1
17 Jul 04	**SINGLE AGAIN** *Rough Trade RTRADSCD 190*	49		1

FIFTH DIMENSION
US, male/female vocal group — 21

Date	Title	Peak	Wks at No.1	Wks
16 Apr 69	**AQUARIUS/LET THE SUNSHINE IN (MEDLEY)** *Liberty LBF 15193* ★	11		12
17 Jan 70	**WEDDING BELL BLUES** *Liberty LBF 15288* ★	16		9

50 CENT
US, male rapper (Curtis Jackson). See G-Unit — 209

Date	Title	Peak	Wks at No.1	Wks
22 Mar 03	**IN DA CLUB** *Interscope 4978742* ● ★	3		24
12 Jul 03	**21 QUESTIONS** *Interscope 9807195* FEATURING NATE DOGG ★	6		8
18 Oct 03	**PIMP (IMPORT)** *Interscope 9811812CD*	74		1
25 Oct 03	**PIMP** *Interscope 9812333*	5		11
6 Mar 04	**IF I CAN'T/THEM THANGS** *Interscope 9815279* 50 CENT/G-UNIT	10		8
26 Feb 05	**HOW WE DO** *Interscope 9880361* GAME FEATURING 50 CENT	5		12
2 Apr 05	**CANDY SHOP** *Interscope 9881293* ★	4		25
21 May 05	**HATE IT OR LOVE IT** *Interscope 9882205* GAME FEATURING 50 CENT	4		13
2 Jul 05	**JUST A LIL BIT** *Interscope 9882950*	10		9
24 Sep 05	**OUTTA CONTROL** *Interscope 9885436* FEATURING MOBB DEEP	7		11
24 Sep 05	**SO SEDUCTIVE** *Interscope 9884360* TONY YAYO FEATURING 50 CENT	28		3
3 Dec 05	**WINDOW SHOPPER** *Interscope 9888358*	11		11
11 Feb 06	**HUSTLER'S AMBITION** *Interscope 9879772*	13		5
21 Oct 06	**HANDS UP** *Atlantic AT0253CD* LLOYD BANKS FEATURING 50 CENT	43		3
13 Jan 07	**YOU DON'T KNOW** *Interscope USUM70613171* EMINEM, 50 CENT, LLOYD BANK$ & CA$HIS	32		3
25 Aug 07	**AYO TECHNOLOGY** *Interscope 1746158* FEATURING JUSTIN TIMBERLAKE & TIMBALAND	2		27
3 Jan 09	**GET UP** *Polydor USUM70840464*	24		8
14 Feb 09	**CRACK A BOTTLE** *Interscope USUM70951735* EMINEM, DR DRE & 50 CENT ★	4		17
7 Mar 09	**I GET IT IN** *Polydor USUM70951284*	75		1
28 Nov 09	**BABY BY ME** *Interscope 2727064* FEATURING NE-YO	17		9

5050
UK, male production duo — 2

Date	Title	Peak	Wks at No.1	Wks
13 Oct 01	**WHO'S COMING ROUND** *Obsessive FIFTYCD 01*	54		1
23 Mar 02	**BAD BOYS HOLLER BOO** *Logic 74321910202*	73		1

50 GRIND FEATURING POKEMON ALLSTARS
UK, male vocal/instrumental group & cartoon vocalists — 1

Date	Title	Peak	Wks at No.1	Wks
22 Dec 01	**GOTTA CATCH 'EM ALL** *Recognition CDREC 21*	57		1

56K FEATURING BEJAY
UK, male/female vocal/production group — 1

Date	Title	Peak	Wks at No.1	Wks
19 Apr 03	**SAVE A PRAYER** *Kontor 0146495 KON*	46		1

53RD & A 3RD FEATURING THE SOUND OF SHAG
UK, male vocalist (Jonathan King) — 4

Date	Title	Peak	Wks at No.1	Wks
20 Sep 75	**CHICK-A-BOOM (DON'T YA JES LOVE IT)** *UK 2012 002*	36		4

52ND STREET
UK, male/female vocal/instrumental group — 13

Date	Title	Peak	Wks at No.1	Wks
2 Nov 85	**TELL ME (HOW IT FEELS)** *10 TEN 74*	54		5
11 Jan 86	**YOU'RE MY LAST CHANCE** *10 TEN 89*	49		4
8 Mar 86	**I CAN'T LET YOU GO** *10 TEN 114*	57		4

FIGHT CLUB FEATURING LAURENT KONRAD
France, male vocal/production duo — 1

Date	Title	Peak	Wks at No.1	Wks
7 Feb 04	**SPREAD LOVE** *Nebula NEBCD054*	70		1

FIGHTSTAR
UK, male vocal/instrumental group – Charlie Simpson, Omar Abidi, Dan Haigh & Alex Westaway. See Busted — 14

Date	Title	Peak	Wks at No.1	Wks
25 Jun 05	**PAINT YOUR TARGET** *Island CID897*	9		4
12 Nov 05	**GRAND UNIFICATION (PART 1)** *Island CID916*	20		2
18 Mar 06	**WASTE A MOMENT** *Island CID921*	29		2
17 Jun 06	**HAZY EYES** *Island/Uni-Island CIDX929*	47		1
29 Sep 07	**WE APOLOGISE FOR NOTHING** *Institute CDINSREC06*	63		1
15 Nov 08	**THE ENGLISH WAY** *Search & Destroy SADCDS002*	62		1
18 Apr 09	**MERCURY SUMMER** *Search & Destroy SADCDS004*	46		3

FILO & PERI FEATURING ERIC LUMIERE
US, male vocal/production trio — 7

Date	Title	Peak	Wks at No.1	Wks
22 Dec 07	**ANTHEM** *Positiva CDTIVS264*	39		7

FILTER & THE CRYSTAL METHOD
US, male vocal/instrumental duo — 5

Date	Title	Peak	Wks at No.1	Wks
11 Oct 97	**(CAN'T YOU) TRIP LIKE I DO** *Epic 6650862*	39		2
18 Mar 00	**TAKE A PICTURE** *Reprise W 515CD* FILTER	25		3

FILTERFUNK
Holland, male DJ/producer (Sander van Doorn, b. Sander Ketelaars) — 1

Date	Title	Peak	Wks at No.1	Wks
22 Apr 06	**SOS (MESSAGE IN A BOTTLE)** *Gusto CDGUS28*	60		1

PERCY FILTH

UK, male production duo. See Lil' Devious — 1

Date	Title	Peak	Wks No.1	Wks
9 Aug 03	**SHOW ME YOUR MONKEY** *Southern Fried ECB 53CDS*	72		1

FINCH

US, male vocal/instrumental group — 2

Date	Title	Peak	Wks No.1	Wks
5 Apr 03	**LETTERS TO YOU** *MCA MCSXD 40310*	39		2

FINE YOUNG CANNIBALS

UK, male vocal/instrumental trio – Roland Gift, Andy Cox & David Steele — 81

Date	Title	Peak	Wks No.1	Wks
8 Jun 85	**JOHNNY COME HOME** *London LON 68*	8		13
9 Nov 85	**BLUE** *London LON 79*	41		6
11 Jan 86	**SUSPICIOUS MINDS** *London LON 82*	8		9
12 Apr 86	**FUNNY HOW LOVE IS** *London LON 88*	58		4
21 Mar 87	**EVER FALLEN IN LOVE** *London LON 121*	9		10
7 Jan 89	**SHE DRIVES ME CRAZY** *London LON 199* ★	5		11
15 Apr 89	**GOOD THING** *London LON 218* ★	7		8
19 Aug 89	**DON'T LOOK BACK** *London LON 220*	34		4
18 Nov 89	**I'M NOT THE MAN I USED TO BE** *London LON 244*	20		8
24 Feb 90	**I'M NOT SATISFIED** *London LON 252*	46		3
16 Nov 96	**THE FLAME** *ffrr LONCD 389*	17		3
11 Jan 97	**SHE DRIVES ME CRAZY** *ffrr LONCD 391*	36		2

FINITRIBE

UK, male production/vocal group — 2

Date	Title	Peak	Wks No.1	Wks
11 Jul 92	**FOREVERGREEN** *One Little Indian 74 TP12F*	51		1
19 Nov 94	**BRAND NEW** *ffrr FCD 247*	69		1

FINK BROTHERS

UK, male vocal/instrumental duo — 4

Date	Title	Peak	Wks No.1	Wks
9 Feb 85	**MUTANTS IN MEGA CITY ONE** *Zarjazz JAZZ 2*	50		4

FINN BROTHERS

New Zealand, male vocal/instrumental duo. See Crowded House, Neil Finn, Tim Finn, Split Enz — 10

Date	Title	Peak	Wks No.1	Wks
14 Oct 95	**SUFFER NEVER** *Parlophone CDRS 6417* FINN	29		3
9 Dec 95	**ANGEL'S HEAP** *Parlophone CDRS 6421* FINN	41		2
21 Aug 04	**WON'T GIVE IN** *Parlophone CDRS 6644*	26		2
20 Nov 04	**NOTHING WRONG WITH YOU** *Parlophone CDRS 6655*	31		1
2 Apr 05	**EDIBLE FLOWERS** *Parlophone CDRS 6660*	32		2

NEIL FINN

New Zealand, male vocalist/guitarist. See Crowded House, Finn Brothers, Split Enz — 6

Date	Title	Peak	Wks No.1	Wks
13 Jun 98	**SHE WILL HAVE HER WAY** *Parlophone CDR 6495*	26		2
17 Oct 98	**SINNER** *Parlophone CDR 6505*	39		1
7 Apr 01	**WHEREVER YOU ARE** *Parlophone CDRS 6557*	32		2
22 Sep 01	**HOLE IN THE ICE** *Parlophone CDRS 6563*	43		1

TIM FINN

New Zealand, male vocalist/guitarist. See Crowded House, Finn Brothers, Split Enz — 6

Date	Title	Peak	Wks No.1	Wks
26 Jun 93	**PERSUASION** *Capitol CDCLS 692*	43		3
18 Sep 93	**HIT THE GROUND RUNNING** *Capitol CDCLS 694*	50		3

MELANIE FIONA

Canada, female vocalist (Melanie Fiona Hallim) — 2

Date	Title	Peak	Wks No.1	Wks
25 Jul 09	**GIVE IT TO ME RIGHT** *Island USUV70807339*	41		2

ELISA FIORILLO

US, female vocalist — 14

Date	Title	Peak	Wks No.1	Wks
28 Nov 87	**WHO FOUND WHO** *Chrysalis CHS JEL 1* JELLYBEAN FEATURING ELISA FIORILLO	10		10
13 Feb 88	**HOW CAN I FORGET YOU** *Chrysalis ELISA 1*	50		4

FIRE ISLAND

UK, male production duo — 7

Date	Title	Peak	Wks No.1	Wks
8 Aug 92	**FIRE ISLAND/IN YOUR BONES** *Boy's Own BOIX 11*	66		1
12 Mar 94	**THERE BUT FOR THE GRACE OF GOD** *Junior Boy's Own JBO 1BCD* FEATURING LOVE NELSON	32		3
4 Mar 95	**IF YOU SHOULD NEED A FRIEND** *Junior Boy's Own JBO 26CDS* FEATURING MARK ANTHONI	51		1
11 Apr 98	**SHOUT TO THE TOP** *JBO JNR 5001573* FEATURING LOLEATTA HOLLOWAY	23		2

FIREBALLS

US, male vocal/instrumental group — 17

Date	Title	Peak	Wks No.1	Wks
27 Jul 61	**QUITE A PARTY** *Pye International 7N 25092*	29		9
14 Nov 63	**SUGAR SHACK** *London HLD 9789* JIMMY GILMER & THE FIREBALLS ★	45		8

FIREHOUSE

US, male vocal/instrumental group — 2

Date	Title	Peak	Wks No.1	Wks
13 Jul 91	**DON'T TREAT ME BAD** *Epic 6567807*	71		1
19 Dec 92	**WHEN I LOOK INTO YOUR EYES** *Epic 6588347*	65		1

FIRM

UK, male vocal/instrumental duo – Grahame Lister & John O'Connor — 21

Date	Title	Peak	Wks No.1	Wks
17 Jul 82	**ARTHUR DALEY ('E'S ALRIGHT)** *Bark HID 1*	14		9
6 Jun 87	**STAR TREKKIN'** *Bark TREK 1* ●	1	2	12

FIRM FEATURING DAWN ROBINSON

US, male/female vocal/rap group — 3

Date	Title	Peak	Wks No.1	Wks
29 Nov 97	**FIRM BIZZ** *Columbia 6651612*	18		3

FIRST CHOICE

US, female vocal group – Rochelle Fleming, Annette Guest & Joyce Jones — 21

Date	Title	Peak	Wks No.1	Wks
19 May 73	**ARMED AND EXTREMELY DANGEROUS** *Bell 1297*	16		10
4 Aug 73	**SMARTY PANTS** *Bell 1324*	9		11

FIRST CLASS

UK, male vocal group – Tony Burrows*, John Carter, Del John & Chas Mills — 10

Date	Title	Peak	Wks No.1	Wks
15 Jun 74	**BEACH BABY** *UK 66*	13		10

FIRST LIGHT

UK, male vocal/instrumental duo — 5

Date	Title	Peak	Wks No.1	Wks
21 May 83	**EXPLAIN THE REASONS** *London LON 26*	65		3
28 Jan 84	**WISH YOU WERE HERE** *London LON 43*	71		2

FIRSTBORN

Ireland, male producer (Oisin Lunny) — 1

Date	Title	Peak	Wks No.1	Wks
19 Jun 99	**THE MOOD CLUB** *Independiente ISOM 28MS*	69		1

FISCHER-Z

UK, male vocal/instrumental group — 7

Date	Title	Peak	Wks No.1	Wks
26 May 79	**THE WORKER** *United Artists UP 36509*	53		5
3 May 80	**SO LONG** *United Artists BP 342*	72		2

FISCHERSPOONER

US, male vocal/instrumental duo — 4

Date	Title	Peak	Wks No.1	Wks
20 Jul 02	**EMERGE** *Ministry Of Sound FSMOS 1CDS*	25		3
27 Aug 05	**NEVER WIN** *EMI FSCD3*	55		1

FISH

UK, male vocalist (Derek Dick). See Marillion — 20

Date	Title	Peak	Wks No.1	Wks
18 Oct 86	**SHORT CUT TO SOMEWHERE** *Charisma CB 426* & TONY BANKS	75		1
28 Oct 89	**STATE OF MIND** *EMI EM 109*	32		3
6 Jan 90	**BIG WEDGE** *EMI EM 125*	25		4
17 Mar 90	**A GENTLEMAN'S EXCUSE ME** *EMI EM 135*	30		3
28 Sep 91	**INTERNAL EXILE** *Polydor FISHY 1*	37		2
11 Jan 92	**CREDO** *Polydor FISHY 2*	38		2

Silver-selling ● Gold-selling ● Platinum-selling (x multiples) ⊛ US No.1 ★ Peak Position · Weeks at No.1 · Weeks on Chart

Date	Title	Peak Position	Weeks at No.1	Weeks on Chart
4 Jul 92	**SOMETHING IN THE AIR** *Polydor FISHY 3*	51		2
16 Apr 94	**LADY LET IT LIE** *Dick Bros. DDICK 3CD1*	46		1
1 Oct 94	**FORTUNES OF WAR** *Dick Bros. DDICK 008CD1*	67		1
26 Aug 95	**JUST GOOD FRIENDS** *Dick Bros. DDICK 014CD1* FEATURING SAM BROWN	63		1

FISH GO DEEP FEATURING TRACEY K

Ireland, male/female vocal/production trio — 6

Date	Title	Peak Position	Weeks at No.1	Weeks on Chart
2 Dec 06	**THE CURE & THE CAUSE** *Defected DFTD145CDS*	23		6

FISHBONE

US, male vocal/instrumental group — 3

Date	Title	Peak Position	Weeks at No.1	Weeks on Chart
1 Aug 92	**EVERYDAY SUNSHINE/FIGHT THE YOUTH** *Columbia 6581937*	60		2
28 Aug 93	**SWIM** *Columbia 6596252*	54		1

CEVIN FISHER

US, male DJ/producer — 9

Date	Title	Peak Position	Weeks at No.1	Weeks on Chart
3 Oct 98	**THE FREAKS COME OUT** *Sound Of Ministry MOSCDS 127* CEVIN FISHER'S BIG BREAK	34		2
20 Feb 99	**(YOU GOT ME) BURNING UP** *Wonderboy BOYD 013* FEATURING LOLEATTA HOLLOWAY	14		4
7 Aug 99	**MUSIC SAVED MY LIFE** *Sm:)e Communications SM 90982*	67		1
20 Jan 01	**IT'S A GOOD LIFE** *Wonderboy BOYD 022* FEATURING RAMONA KELLY	54		1
24 Feb 01	**LOVE YOU SOME MORE** *Subversive SUB 68D* FEATURING SHEILA SMITH	60		1

EDDIE FISHER

US, male vocalist — 105

Date	Title	Peak Position	Weeks at No.1	Weeks on Chart
2 Jan 53	**OUTSIDE OF HEAVEN** *HMV B 10362*	1	1	17
23 Jan 53	**EVERYTHING I HAVE IS YOURS** *HMV B 10398*	8		5
1 May 53	**DOWNHEARTED** *HMV B 10450*	3		15
22 May 53	**I'M WALKING BEHIND YOU** *HMV B 10489* WITH SALLY SWEETLAND (SOPRANO) ★	1	1	18
6 Nov 53	**WISH YOU WERE HERE** *HMV B 10564* ★	8		9
22 Jan 54	**OH MY PAPA** *HMV B 10614* ★	9		4
29 Oct 54	**I NEED YOU NOW** *HMV B 10755* ★	13		10
18 Mar 55	**WEDDING BELLS** *HMV B 10839*	5		11
23 Nov 56	**CINDY OH CINDY** *HMV POP 273*	5		16

MARK FISHER FEATURING DOTTY GREEN

UK, male producer & female vocalist — 2

Date	Title	Peak Position	Weeks at No.1	Weeks on Chart
29 Jun 85	**LOVE SITUATION** *Total Control TOCO 3*	59		2

TONI FISHER

US, female vocalist, d. 12 Feb 1999 (age 67) — 1

Date	Title	Peak Position	Weeks at No.1	Weeks on Chart
12 Feb 60	**THE BIG HURT** *Top Rank JAR 261*	30		1

FITS OF GLOOM

Italy, male production group — 4

Date	Title	Peak Position	Weeks at No.1	Weeks on Chart
4 Jun 94	**HEAVEN** *Media MCSTD 1981*	47		2
5 Nov 94	**THE POWER OF LOVE** *Media MCSTD 2016* FEATURING LIZZY MACK	49		2

ELLA FITZGERALD

US, female vocalist, d. 15 Jun 1996 (age 79) — 29

Date	Title	Peak Position	Weeks at No.1	Weeks on Chart
23 May 58	**SWINGIN' SHEPHERD BLUES** *HMV POP 486*	15		5
16 Oct 59	**BUT NOT FOR ME** *HMV POP 657*	25		3
21 Apr 60	**MACK THE KNIFE** *HMV POP 736*	19		9
6 Oct 60	**HOW HIGH THE MOON** *HMV POP 782*	46		1
22 Nov 62	**DESAFINADO** *Verve VS 502*	38		6
30 Apr 64	**CAN'T BUY ME LOVE** *Verve VS 519*	34		5

SCOTT FITZGERALD

UK, male vocalist (William McPhail) — 12

Date	Title	Peak Position	Weeks at No.1	Weeks on Chart
14 Jan 78	**IF I HAD WORDS** *Pepper UP 36333* & YVONNE KEELEY & THE ST THOMAS MORE SCHOOL CHOIR ○	3		10
7 May 88	**GO** *PRT PYS 10*	52		2

FIVE

UK, male vocal group – Richard Breen (Abs*), Jason Brown, Sean Conlon, Ritchie Neville & Scott Robinson — 133

Date	Title	Peak Position	Weeks at No.1	Weeks on Chart
13 Dec 97	**SLAM DUNK (DA FUNK)** *RCA 74321537352*	10		9
14 Mar 98	**WHEN THE LIGHTS GO OUT** *RCA 74321562312*	4		9
20 Jun 98	**GOT THE FEELIN'** *RCA 74321584892* ○	3		13
12 Sep 98	**EVERYBODY GET UP** *RCA 74321613752*	2		12
28 Nov 98	**UNTIL THE TIME IS THROUGH** *RCA 74321632602* ○	2		12
31 Jul 99	**IF YA GETTING' DOWN** *RCA 74321689692* ○	2		12
6 Nov 99	**KEEP ON MOVIN'** *RCA 74321709862* ●	1	1	17
18 Mar 00	**DON'T WANNA LET YOU GO** *RCA 74321745302*	9		12
29 Jul 00	**WE WILL ROCK YOU** *RCA 74321774022* & QUEEN	1	1	13
25 Aug 01	**LET'S DANCE** *RCA 74321875962*	1	2	12
3 Nov 01	**CLOSER TO ME** *RCA 74321900742*	4		12

FIVE FOR FIGHTING

US, male vocalist/guitarist (John Ondrasik) — 1

Date	Title	Peak Position	Weeks at No.1	Weeks on Chart
1 Jun 02	**SUPERMAN (IT'S NOT EASY)** *Columbia 6727202*	48		1

5,6,7,8'S

Japan, female vocal/instrumental group — 3

Date	Title	Peak Position	Weeks at No.1	Weeks on Chart
17 Jul 04	**WOO HOO** *Sweet Nothing CSSN028*	28		2
18 Sep 04	**I'M BLUE** *Sweet Nothing CSSN029*	71		1

FIVE SMITH BROTHERS

US, male vocal group — 1

Date	Title	Peak Position	Weeks at No.1	Weeks on Chart
22 Jul 55	**I'M IN FAVOUR OF FRIENDSHIP** *Decca F 10527*	20		1

FIVE STAR

UK, female/male vocal/instrumental group – Denise, Delroy, Doris, Lorraine & Stedman Pearson — 140

Date	Title	Peak Position	Weeks at No.1	Weeks on Chart
4 May 85	**ALL FALL DOWN** *Tent PB 40039*	15		12
20 Jul 85	**LET ME BE THE ONE** *Tent PB 40193*	18		9
14 Sep 85	**LOVE TAKE OVER** *Tent PB 40353*	25		9
16 Nov 85	**RSVP** *Tent PB 40445*	45		5
11 Jan 86	**SYSTEM ADDICT** *Tent PB 40515* ○	3		11
12 Apr 86	**CAN'T WAIT ANOTHER MINUTE** *Tent PB 40697*	7		10
26 Jul 86	**FIND THE TIME** *Tent PB 40799*	7		10
13 Sep 86	**RAIN OR SHINE** *Tent PB 40901* ○	2		11
22 Nov 86	**IF I SAY YES** *Tent PB 40981*	15		9
7 Feb 87	**STAY OUT OF MY LIFE** *Tent PB 41131*	9		8
18 Apr 87	**THE SLIGHTEST TOUCH** *Tent PB 41265*	4		9
22 Aug 87	**WHENEVER YOU'RE READY** *Tent PB 41477*	11		6
10 Oct 87	**STRONG AS STEEL** *Tent PB 41565*	16		7
5 Dec 87	**SOMEWHERE SOMEBODY** *Tent PB 41661*	23		6
4 Jun 88	**ANOTHER WEEKEND** *Tent PB 42081*	18		4
6 Aug 88	**ROCK MY WORLD** *Tent PB 42145*	28		4
17 Sep 88	**THERE'S A BRAND NEW WORLD** *Tent PB 42235*	61		2
19 Nov 88	**LET ME BE YOURS** *Tent PB 42343*	51		3
8 Apr 89	**WITH EVERY HEARTBEAT** *Tent PB 42693*	49		2
10 Mar 90	**TREAT ME LIKE A LADY** *Tent FIVE 1*	54		2
7 Jul 90	**HOT LOVE** *Tent FIVE 2*	68		1

FIVE THIRTY

UK, male vocal/instrumental trio — 4

Date	Title	Peak Position	Weeks at No.1	Weeks on Chart
4 Aug 90	**ABSTAIN** *East West YZ 530*	75		1
25 May 91	**13TH DISCIPLE** *East West YZ 577*	67		1
3 Aug 91	**SUPERNOVA** *East West YZ 594*	75		1
2 Nov 91	**YOU (EP)** *East West YZ 624*	72		1

5000 VOLTS

UK, male/female vocal/instrumental group – Tina Charles*, Tony Eyeres, Martin Jay & Roger O'Dell — 18

Date	Title	Peak Position	Weeks at No.1	Weeks on Chart
6 Sep 75	**I'M ON FIRE** *Philips 6006 464*	4		9
24 Jul 76	**DR KISS KISS** *Philips 6006 533*	8		9

FIXATE

UK, male vocal group — 1

Date	Title	Peak Position	Weeks at No.1	Weeks on Chart
14 Jul 01	**24-Jul** *Epark EPKFIX CD1*	42		1

FIXX

UK, male vocal/instrumental group — Weeks on Chart: 8

Date	Title / Label	Peak Position	Weeks at No.1	Weeks on Chart
24 Apr 82	**STAND OR FALL** *MCA FIXX 2*	54		4
17 Jul 82	**RED SKIES** *MCA FIXX 3*	57		4

F.K.W.

UK, male production trio — Weeks on Chart: 8

Date	Title / Label	Peak Position	Weeks at No.1	Weeks on Chart
2 Oct 93	**NEVER GONNA (GIVE YOU UP)** *PWL International PWCD 273*	48		2
11 Dec 93	**SEIZE THE DAY** *PWL International PWCD 279*	45		2
5 Mar 94	**JINGO** *PWL International PWCD 283*	30		3
4 Jun 94	**THIS IS THE WAY** *PWL International PWCD 307*	63		1

ROBERTA FLACK

US, female vocalist/pianist — Weeks on Chart: 79

Date	Title / Label	Peak Position	Weeks at No.1	Weeks on Chart
27 May 72	**THE FIRST TIME EVER I SAW YOUR FACE** *Atlantic K 10161* ★	14		14
5 Aug 72	**WHERE IS THE LOVE** *Atlantic K 10202* & DONNY HATHAWAY	29		7
17 Feb 73	**KILLING ME SOFTLY WITH HIS SONG** *Atlantic K 10282* ★	6		14
24 Aug 74	**FEEL LIKE MAKING LOVE** *Atlantic K 10467* ★	34		7
6 May 78	**THE CLOSER I GET TO YOU** *Atlantic K 11099* & DONNY HATHAWAY	42		4
17 May 80	**BACK TOGETHER AGAIN** *Atlantic K 11481* & DONNY HATHAWAY	3		11
30 Aug 80	**DON'T MAKE ME WAIT TOO LONG** *Atlantic K 11555*	44		7
20 Aug 83	**TONIGHT I CELEBRATE MY LOVE** *Capitol CL 302* PEABO BRYSON & ROBERTA FLACK ●	2		13
29 Jul 89	**UH-UH OOH OOH LOOK OUT (HERE IT COMES)** *Atlantic A 8491*	72		2

FLAMING LIPS

US, male vocal/instrumental group — Weeks on Chart: 20

Date	Title / Label	Peak Position	Weeks at No.1	Weeks on Chart
9 Mar 96	**THIS HERE GIRAFFE** *Warner Brothers W 0335CD*	72		1
26 Jun 99	**RACE FOR THE PRIZE** *Warner Brothers W 494CD*	39		2
20 Nov 99	**WAITIN' FOR A SUPERMAN** *Warner Brothers W 505CD*	73		1
31 Aug 02	**DO YOU REALISE** *Warner Brothers W 586CD*	32		2
25 Jan 03	**YOSHIMI BATTLES THE PINK ROBOTS PART 1** *Warner Brothers W 595CD*	18		3
5 Jul 03	**FIGHT TEST** *Warner Brothers W 611CD*	28		2
27 Sep 03	**THE GOLDEN PATH** *Virgin CHEMSD18* CHEMICAL BROTHERS FEATURING THE FLAMING LIPS	17		4
22 Apr 06	**THE YEAH YEAH YEAH SONG** *Warner Brothers W711CD1*	16		4
29 Jul 06	**THE WAND** *Warner Brothers W706CD1*	41		1

FLAMINGOS

US, male vocal group — Weeks on Chart: 5

Date	Title / Label	Peak Position	Weeks at No.1	Weeks on Chart
4 Jun 69	**BOOGALOO PARTY** *Philips BF 1786*	26		5

MICHAEL FLANDERS WITH THE MICHAEL SAMMES SINGERS

UK, male vocalist, d. 14 Apr 1975 (age 53), & male/female vocal group – leader d. 19 May 2001 (age 73) — Weeks on Chart: 3

Date	Title / Label	Peak Position	Weeks at No.1	Weeks on Chart
27 Feb 59	**LITTLE DRUMMER BOY** *Parlophone R 4528*	20		3

FLASH & THE PAN

Australia, male vocal/production duo – Harry Vanda & George Young (Alfred Young) — Weeks on Chart: 15

Date	Title / Label	Peak Position	Weeks at No.1	Weeks on Chart
23 Sep 78	**AND THE BAND PLAYED ON (DOWN AMONG THE DEAD MEN)** *Ensign ENY 15*	54		4
21 May 83	**WAITING FOR A TRAIN** *Easybeat EASY 1*	7		11

FLASH BROTHERS

Israel, male production trio — Weeks on Chart: 1

Date	Title / Label	Peak Position	Weeks at No.1	Weeks on Chart
6 Nov 04	**AMEN (DON'T BE AFRAID)** *Direction 6754362*	75		1

LESTER FLATT & EARL SCRUGGS

US, male vocal/instrumental duo – Lester Flatt, d. 11 May 1979 — Weeks on Chart: 6

Date	Title / Label	Peak Position	Weeks at No.1	Weeks on Chart
15 Nov 67	**FOGGY MOUNTAIN BREAKDOWN** *CBS 3038/Mercury MF 1007*	39		6

FOGWELL FLAX & THE ANKLEBITERS FROM FREEHOLD JUNIOR SCHOOL

UK, male vocalist/comedian & school choir — Weeks on Chart: 2

Date	Title / Label	Peak Position	Weeks at No.1	Weeks on Chart
26 Dec 81	**ONE NINE FOR SANTA** *EMI 5255*	68		2

FLEE-REKKERS

UK, male instrumental group — Weeks on Chart: 13

Date	Title / Label	Peak Position	Weeks at No.1	Weeks on Chart
19 May 60	**GREEN JEANS** *Triumph RGM 1008*	23		13

FLEET

UK, male/female vocal/instrumental group — Weeks on Chart: 1

Date	Title / Label	Peak Position	Weeks at No.1	Weeks on Chart
15 Oct 05	**GET DOWN** *Cosmos FLEET01CD*	71		1

FLEET FOXES

US, male vocal/instrumental group — Weeks on Chart: 4

Date	Title / Label	Peak Position	Weeks at No.1	Weeks on Chart
31 Jan 09	**MYKONOS** *Bella Union GBBRP0816504*	53		4

FLEETWOOD MAC

UK/US, male/female vocal/instrumental group – members included Peter Green* (left 1970), Lindsey Buckingham*, Mick Fleetwood, Danny Kirwan, Christine McVie* (Christine Perfect), John McVie, Stevie Nicks* & Jeremy Spencer. Acclaimed British blues band turned Anglo/American rock superstars. The Rumours are true: their 1977 classic has spent more weeks on the UK chart (478) than any other LP — Weeks on Chart: 223

Date	Title / Label	Peak Position	Weeks at No.1	Weeks on Chart
10 Apr 68	**BLACK MAGIC WOMAN** *Blue Horizon 57 3138*	37		7
17 Jul 68	**NEED YOUR LOVE SO BAD** *Blue Horizon 57 3139*	31		13
4 Dec 68	**ALBATROSS** *Blue Horizon 57 3145*	1	1	20
16 Apr 69	**MAN OF THE WORLD** *Immediate IM 080*	2		14
23 Jul 69	**NEED YOUR LOVE SO BAD** *Blue Horizon 57 3157*	32		9
4 Oct 69	**OH WELL** *Reprise RS 27000*	2		16
23 May 70	**THE GREEN MANALISHI (WITH THE TWO-PRONG CROWN)** *Reprise RS 27007*	10		12
12 May 73	**ALBATROSS** *CBS 8306* ●	2		15
13 Nov 76	**SAY YOU LOVE ME** *Reprise K 14447*	40		4
19 Feb 77	**GO YOUR OWN WAY** *Warner Brothers K 16872*	38		4
30 Apr 77	**DON'T STOP** *Warner Brothers K 16930*	32		5
9 Jul 77	**DREAMS** *Warner Brothers K 16969* ★	24		9
22 Oct 77	**YOU MAKE LOVING FUN** *Warner Brothers K 17013*	45		2
11 Mar 78	**RHIANNON** *Warner Brothers K 14430*	46		3
6 Oct 79	**TUSK** *Warner Brothers K 17468* ●	6		10
22 Dec 79	**SARA** *Warner Brothers K 17533*	37		8
25 Sep 82	**GYPSY** *Warner Brothers K 17997*	46		3
18 Dec 82	**OH DIANE** *Warner Brothers FLEET 1*	9		15
4 Apr 87	**BIG LOVE** *Warner Brothers W 8398*	9		12
11 Jul 87	**SEVEN WONDERS** *Warner Brothers W 8317*	56		4
26 Sep 87	**LITTLE LIES** *Warner Brothers W 8291*	5		12
26 Dec 87	**FAMILY MAN** *Warner Brothers W 8114*	54		5
2 Apr 88	**EVERYWHERE** *Warner Brothers W 8143*	4		10
18 Jun 88	**ISN'T IT MIDNIGHT** *Warner Brothers W 7860*	60		2
17 Dec 88	**AS LONG AS YOU FOLLOW** *Warner Brothers W 7644*	66		3
5 May 90	**SAVE ME** *Warner Brothers W 9866*	53		3
25 Aug 90	**IN THE BACK OF MY MIND** *Warner Brothers W 9739*	58		3

FLEETWOODS

US, male/female vocal group – Gary Troxel, Gretchen Christopher & Barbara Ellis — Weeks on Chart: 8

Date	Title / Label	Peak Position	Weeks at No.1	Weeks on Chart
24 Apr 59	**COME SOFTLY TO ME** *London HLU 8841* ★	6		8

JOHN 'OO' FLEMING

UK, male DJ/producer — Weeks on Chart: 3

Date	Title / Label	Peak Position	Weeks at No.1	Weeks on Chart
25 Dec 99	**LOST IN EMOTION** *React CDREACT 170*	74		1
12 Aug 00	**FREE** *React CDREACT 186*	61		1
2 Feb 02	**BELFAST TRANCE** *Nebula BELFCD 001* VS SIMPLE MINDS	74		1

FLESH & BONES

Belgium, male/female vocal/production trio — Weeks on Chart: 1

Date	Title / Label	Peak Position	Weeks at No.1	Weeks on Chart
10 Aug 02	**I LOVE YOU** *Multiply CDMULTY 86*	70		1

FLICKMAN

Italy, male production duo. See A.T.G.O.C. — Weeks on Chart: 6

Date	Title / Label	Peak Position	Weeks at No.1	Weeks on Chart
4 Mar 00	**THE SOUND OF BAMBOO** *Inferno CDFERN 25*	11		5
28 Apr 01	**HEY! PARADISE** *Inferno CDFERN 37*	69		1

KC FLIGHTT
US, male rapper (Frank Toson)

Weeks on chart: 5

Date	Title	Peak	Wks at No.1	Wks on chart
1 Apr 89	**PLANET E** *RCA PT 49404*	48		4
12 May 01	**VOICES** *Hooj Choons HOOJ 106CD* VS FUNKY JUNCTION	59		1

BERNI FLINT
UK, male vocalist

Weeks on chart: 11

Date	Title	Peak	Wks at No.1	Wks on chart
19 Mar 77	**I DON'T WANT TO PUT A HOLD ON YOU** *EMI 2599* ●	3		10
23 Jul 77	**SOUTHERN COMFORT** *EMI 2621*	48		1

FLINTLOCK
UK, male vocal/instrumental group

Weeks on chart: 5

Date	Title	Peak	Wks at No.1	Wks on chart
29 May 76	**DAWN** *Pinnacle P 8419*	30		5

FLIP & FILL
UK, male DJ/production duo – Mark Hall & Graham Turner. See Bus Stop, Eyeopener, Open Arms featuring Rowetta

Weeks on chart: 45

Date	Title	Peak	Wks at No.1	Wks on chart
24 Mar 01	**TRUE LOVE NEVER DIES** *All Around The World CDGLOBE 240* FEATURING KELLY LLORENNA	34		3
2 Feb 02	**TRUE LOVE NEVER DIES (REMIX)** *All Around The World CDGLOBE 248* FEATURING KELLY LLORENNA	7		10
27 Jul 02	**SHOOTING STAR** *All Around The World CDGLOBE 258*	3		10
18 Jan 03	**I WANNA DANCE WITH SOMEBODY** *All Around The World CDGLOBE 275*	13		7
22 Mar 03	**SHAKE YA SHIMMY** *All Around The World CXGLOBE 213* PORN KINGS VERSUS FLIP & FILL FEATURING 740 BOYZ	28		2
28 Jun 03	**FIELD OF DREAMS** *All Around The World CDGLOBE 273* FEATURING JO JAMES	28		2
17 Jan 04	**IRISH BLUE** *All Around The World CXGLOBE 309* FEATURING JUNIOR	20		4
24 Jul 04	**DISCOLAND** *All Around The World CDGLOBE 346* FEATURING KAREN PARRY	11		7

FLIPMODE SQUAD
US, male/female rap/production group

Weeks on chart: 1

Date	Title	Peak	Wks at No.1	Wks on chart
31 Oct 98	**CHA CHA CHA** *Elektra E 3810CD*	54		1

FLO RIDA
US, male rapper (Tramar Dillard)

Weeks on chart: 147

Date	Title	Peak	Wks at No.1	Wks on chart
16 Feb 08	**LOW** *Atlantic AT0302CD* FEATURING T-PAIN ★	2		48
12 Apr 08	**ELEVATOR** *Atlantic AT0317CD* FEATURING TIMBALAND	20		14
23 Aug 08	**IN THE AYER** *Atlantic AT0322CD1* FEATURING WILL.I.AM	29		9
14 Mar 09	**RIGHT ROUND** *Atlantic AT0334CD* ★	1	1	19
4 Apr 09	**BE ON YOU** *Atlantic USAT20900455*	51		2
11 Apr 09	**SUGA** *Atlantic AT0338CD*	19		17
30 May 09	**LOW** *Atlantic AT0302CD* FEATURING T-PAIN	44		5
8 Aug 09	**JUMP** *Atlantic AT0344CD* FEATURING NELLY FURTADO	21		8
24 Oct 09	**BAD BOYS** *Syco Music 88697590932* ALEXANDRA BURKE FEATURING FLO RIDA ⊛	1	1	25+

FLOATERS
US, male vocal group – Charles Clarke, Larry Cunningham, Paul & Ralph Mitchell

Weeks on chart: 11

Date	Title	Peak	Wks at No.1	Wks on chart
23 Jul 77	**FLOAT ON** *ABC 4187* ●	1	1	11

FLOBOTS
US, male vocal/rap/instrumental group

Weeks on chart: 10

Date	Title	Peak	Wks at No.1	Wks on chart
30 Aug 08	**HANDLEBARS** *Island USUM70810498*	14		10

A FLOCK OF SEAGULLS
UK, male vocal/instrumental group – Michael & Alister Score, Frank Maudsley & Paul Reynolds

Weeks on chart: 46

Date	Title	Peak	Wks at No.1	Wks on chart
27 Mar 82	**I RAN** *Jive 14*	43		6
12 Jun 82	**SPACE AGE LOVE SONG** *Jive 17*	34		6
6 Nov 82	**WISHING (IF I HAD A PHOTOGRAPH OF YOU)** *Jive 25* ●	10		12
23 Apr 83	**NIGHTMARES** *Jive 33*	53		3
25 Jun 83	**TRANSFER AFFECTION** *Jive 41*	38		5
14 Jul 84	**THE MORE YOU LIVE, THE MORE YOU LOVE** *Jive 62*	26		11
19 Oct 85	**WHO'S THAT GIRL (SHE'S GOT IT)** *Jive 106*	66		3

FLOETRY
UK, female vocal duo

Weeks on chart: 1

Date	Title	Peak	Wks at No.1	Wks on chart
26 Apr 03	**FLOETIC** *DreamWorks 4507752*	73		1

FLOORPLAY
UK, male instrumental/production duo

Weeks on chart: 1

Date	Title	Peak	Wks at No.1	Wks on chart
27 Jan 96	**AUTOMATIC** *Perfecto PERF 115CD*	50		1

FLORENCE + THE MACHINE
UK, female vocalist (Florence Welch) & various musicians

Weeks on chart: 72

Date	Title	Peak	Wks at No.1	Wks on chart
16 Aug 08	**KISS WITH A FIST** *Moshi Moshi MOMO15*	51		2
4 Jul 09	**RABBIT HEART (RAISE IT UP)** *Island 2710011*	12		15
1 Aug 09	**YOU'VE GOT THE LOVE** *Island 2726059*	5		31+
26 Sep 09	**DRUMMING SONG** *Island 2718884*	54		2
16 Jan 10	**DOG DAYS ARE OVER** *Island MOSHI71*	23		13+
16 Jan 10	**RABBIT HEART (RAISE IT UP)** *Island 2710011*	60		2
27 Feb 10	**YOU GOT THE DIRTEE LOVE** *Dirtee Stank Island GB3CJ1000001* FEATURING DIZZEE RASCAL	2		7+

FLOWERED UP
UK, male vocal/instrumental group

Weeks on chart: 17

Date	Title	Peak	Wks at No.1	Wks on chart
28 Jul 90	**IT'S ON** *Heavenly HVN 3*	54		4
24 Nov 90	**PHOBIA** *Heavenly HVN 7*	75		1
11 May 91	**TAKE IT** *London FUP 1*	34		4
17 Aug 91	**IT'S ON/EGG RUSH** *London FUP 2*	38		3
2 May 92	**WEEKENDER** *Heavenly HVN 16*	20		5

FLOWERPOT MEN
US, male vocal group – Tony Burrows*, Perry Ford, Neil Landon & Robin Shaw

Weeks on chart: 12

Date	Title	Peak	Wks at No.1	Wks on chart
23 Aug 67	**LET'S GO TO SAN FRANCISCO** *Deram DM 142*	4		12

MIKE FLOWERS POPS
UK, male/female vocal/instrumental ensemble – Mike Flowers (Mike Roberts), the 'Sounds Superb Singers' & the 'Super Stereo Brass'

Weeks on chart: 14

Date	Title	Peak	Wks at No.1	Wks on chart
30 Dec 95	**WONDERWALL** *London LONCD 378* ●	2		9
8 Jun 96	**LIGHT MY FIRE/PLEASE RELEASE ME** *London LONCD 384*	39		2
28 Dec 96	**DON'T CRY FOR ME ARGENTINA** *Love This LUVTHISCD 16*	30		3

EDDIE FLOYD
US, male vocalist

Weeks on chart: 29

Date	Title	Peak	Wks at No.1	Wks on chart
2 Feb 67	**KNOCK ON WOOD** *Atlantic 584 041*	19		18
16 Mar 67	**RAISE YOUR HAND** *Stax 601 001*	42		3
9 Aug 67	**THINGS GET BETTER** *Stax 601 016*	31		8

FLUFFY
UK, female vocal/instrumental group

Weeks on chart: 2

Date	Title	Peak	Wks at No.1	Wks on chart
17 Feb 96	**HUSBAND** *Parkway PARK 006CD*	58		1
5 Oct 96	**NOTHING** *Virgin VSCDT 1614*	52		1

FLUKE
UK, male production/instrumental group

Weeks on chart: 20

Date	Title	Peak	Wks at No.1	Wks on chart
20 Mar 93	**SLID** *Circa YRCD 103*	59		1
19 Jun 93	**ELECTRIC GUITAR** *Circa YRCD 104*	58		2
11 Sep 93	**GROOVY FEELING** *Circa YRCD 106*	45		3
23 Apr 94	**BUBBLE** *Circa YRCD 110*	37		2
29 Jul 95	**BULLET** *Circa YRCD 121*	23		3
16 Dec 95	**TOSH** *Circa YRCD 122*	32		3
16 Nov 96	**ATOM BOMB** *Virgin YRCD 125*	20		3
31 May 97	**ABSURD** *Virgin YRCD 126*	25		2
27 Sep 97	**SQUIRT** *Circa YRCD 127*	46		1

FLYING LIZARDS
UK, male/female vocal/instrumental ensemble featuring Deborah Evans & David Cunningham

Weeks on chart: 16

Date	Title	Peak	Wks at No.1	Wks on chart
4 Aug 79	**MONEY** *Virgin VS 276* ●	5		10
9 Feb 80	**TV** *Virgin VS 325*	43		6

FLYING PICKETS
UK, male vocal group — 20

Date	Title / Label	Peak	Wks at No.1	Wks on Chart
26 Nov 83	**ONLY YOU** *10TEN 14* ●	1	5	11
21 Apr 84	**WHEN YOU'RE YOUNG AND IN LOVE** *10TEN 20*	7		8
8 Dec 84	**WHO'S THAT GIRL** *10GIRL 1*	71		1

FM
UK, male vocal/instrumental group — 11

Date	Title / Label	Peak	Wks at No.1	Wks on Chart
31 Jan 87	**FROZEN HEART** *Portrait DIDGE 1*	64		2
20 Jun 87	**LET LOVE BE THE LEADER** *Portrait MERV 1*	71		2
5 Aug 89	**BAD LUCK** *Epic 6550317*	54		4
7 Oct 89	**SOMEDAY (YOU'LL COME RUNNING)** *CBS DINK 1*	64		2
10 Feb 90	**EVERYTIME I THINK OF YOU** *Epic DINK 2*	73		1

FOALS
UK, male vocal/instrumental group — 8

Date	Title / Label	Peak	Wks at No.1	Wks on Chart
22 Dec 07	**BALLOONS** *Transgressive TRANS065CD*	39		1
1 Mar 08	**CASSIUS** *Transgressive TRANS069*	26		7

FOCUS
Holland, male instrumental group – Thijs van Leer, Jan Akkerman, Cyril Havermans (replaced by Bert Ruiter) & Pierre van der Linden (replaced by Colin Allen) — 21

Date	Title / Label	Peak	Wks at No.1	Wks on Chart
20 Jan 73	**HOCUS POCUS** *Polydor 2001 211*	20		10
27 Jan 73	**SYLVIA** *Polydor 2001 422*	4		11

FOG
US, male producer (Ralph Falcon) — 4

Date	Title / Label	Peak	Wks at No.1	Wks on Chart
19 Feb 94	**BEEN A LONG TIME** *Columbia 6601212*	44		2
6 Jun 98	**BEEN A LONG TIME (REMIX)** *Pukka CDPUKKA 16*	27		2

DAN FOGELBERG
US, male vocalist/guitarist, d. 16 Dec 2007 (age 56) — 4

Date	Title / Label	Peak	Wks at No.1	Wks on Chart
15 Mar 80	**LONGER** *Epic EPC 8230*	59		4

BEN FOLDS FIVE
US, male vocal/instrumental group — 13

Date	Title / Label	Peak	Wks at No.1	Wks on Chart
14 Sep 96	**UNDERGROUND** *Caroline CDCAR 008*	37		2
1 Mar 97	**BATTLE OF WHO COULD CARE LESS** *Epic 6642302*	26		3
7 Jun 97	**KATE** *Epic 6645365*	39		2
18 Apr 98	**BRICK** *Epic 6656612*	26		3
24 Apr 99	**ARMY** *Epic 6672182*	28		2
29 Sep 01	**ROCKIN' THE SUBURBS** *Epic 6718492* BEN FOLDS	53		1

FOLK IMPLOSION
US, male vocal/instrumental duo — 1

Date	Title / Label	Peak	Wks at No.1	Wks on Chart
15 Jun 96	**NATURAL ONE** *London LONCD 382*	45		1

LENNY FONTANA
US/Germany, male production duo — 3

Date	Title / Label	Peak	Wks at No.1	Wks on Chart
4 Mar 00	**CHOCOLATE SENSATION** *ffrr FCD 375* & DJ SHORTY	39		2
24 Mar 01	**POW WOW WOW** *Strictly Rhythm SRUKCD 01* FONTANA FEATURING DARRYL D'BONNEAU	62		1

WAYNE FONTANA & THE MINDBENDERS
UK, male vocalist (Glyn Ellis) & vocal/instrumental group — 76

Date	Title / Label	Peak	Wks at No.1	Wks on Chart
11 Jul 63	**HELLO JOSEPHINE** *Fontana TF 404*	46		2
28 May 64	**STOP LOOK AND LISTEN** *Fontana TF 451*	37		4
8 Oct 64	**UM UM UM UM UM UM** *Fontana TF 497*	5		15
4 Feb 65	**GAME OF LOVE** *Fontana TF 535* ★	2		11
17 Jun 65	**JUST A LITTLE BIT TOO LATE** *Fontana TF 579*	20		7
30 Sep 65	**SHE NEEDS LOVE** *Fontana TF 611*	32		6
9 Dec 65	**IT WAS EASIER TO HURT HER** *Fontana TF 642* WAYNE FONTANA	36		6
21 Apr 66	**COME ON HOME** *Fontana TF 684* WAYNE FONTANA	16		12
25 Aug 66	**GOODBYE BLUEBIRD** *Fontana TF 737* WAYNE FONTANA	49		1
8 Dec 66	**PAMELA PAMELA** *Fontana TF 770* WAYNE FONTANA	11		12

FOO FIGHTERS
US, male vocal/instrumental group – Dave Grohl, William Goldsmith (replaced by Taylor Hawkins), Nate Mendel & Pat Smear (replaced by Franz Stahl; Stahl replaced by Chris Shiflett) — 116

Date	Title / Label	Peak	Wks at No.1	Wks on Chart
1 Jul 95	**THIS IS A CALL** *Roswell CDCL 753*	5		4
16 Sep 95	**I'LL STICK AROUND** *Roswell CDCL 757*	18		3
2 Dec 95	**FOR ALL THE COWS** *Roswell CDCL 762*	28		2
6 Apr 96	**BIG ME** *Roswell CDCL 768*	19		3
10 May 97	**MONKEY WRENCH** *Roswell CDCLS 788*	12		4
30 Aug 97	**EVERLONG** *Roswell CDCL 792*	18		3
31 Jan 98	**MY HERO** *Roswell CDCL 796*	21		2
29 Aug 98	**WALKING AFTER YOU** *Elektra E 4100CD*	20		3
30 Oct 99	**LEARN TO FLY** *RCA 74321706622*	21		3
30 Sep 00	**BREAKOUT** *RCA 74321790112*	29		3
16 Dec 00	**NEXT YEAR** *RCA 74321809262*	42		2
19 Oct 02	**ALL MY LIFE** *RCA 74321973152*	5		9
18 Jan 03	**TIMES LIKE THESE** *RCA 74321989562*	12		6
5 Jul 03	**LOW** *RCA 82876522572*	21		2
4 Oct 03	**HAVE IT ALL** *RCA 82876563702*	37		2
11 Jun 05	**BEST OF YOU** *RCA 82876701212*	4		16
17 Sep 05	**DOA** *RCA 82876735392*	25		3
3 Dec 05	**RESOLVE** *RCA 82876738912*	32		2
25 Mar 06	**NO WAY BACK/COLD DAY IN THE SUN** *RCA 82876804732*	64		1
25 Aug 07	**THE PRETENDER** *RCA 88697160702*	8		27
15 Dec 07	**LONG ROAD TO RUIN** *RCA 88697190382*	35		10
21 Jun 08	**BEST OF YOU** *RCA 82876701212*	59		1
21 Jun 08	**THE PRETENDER** *RCA 88697160702*	65		1
31 Oct 09	**WHEELS** *RCA USRC10900528*	22		4

FOOL BOONA
UK, male DJ/producer (Colin Tevendale) — 1

Date	Title / Label	Peak	Wks at No.1	Wks on Chart
10 Apr 99	**POPPED!** *Virgin/VC Recordings/Uber Disko VCRD 46*	52		1

FOOL'S GARDEN
Germany, male vocal/instrumental group — 4

Date	Title / Label	Peak	Wks at No.1	Wks on Chart
25 May 96	**LEMON TREE** *Encore CDCOR 014*	61		1
3 Aug 96	**LEMON TREE (REMIX)** *Encore CDCOR 018*	26		3

FOOLPROOF
US, male vocal/instrumental group — 1

Date	Title / Label	Peak	Wks at No.1	Wks on Chart
26 Jun 04	**PAPER HOUSE** *Island CID 863*	53		1

FOR REAL
US, female vocal group — 2

Date	Title / Label	Peak	Wks at No.1	Wks on Chart
1 Jul 95	**YOU DON'T KNOW NOTHIN'** *A&M 5811232*	54		1
12 Jul 97	**LIKE I DO** *Rowdy 74321486582*	45		1

BILL FORBES
UK, male vocalist — 1

Date	Title / Label	Peak	Wks at No.1	Wks on Chart
15 Jan 60	**TOO YOUNG** *Columbia DB 4386*	29		1

DAVID FORBES
UK (b. Singapore), male producer — 1

Date	Title / Label	Peak	Wks at No.1	Wks on Chart
25 Aug 01	**QUESTIONS (MUST BE ASKED)** *Serious SERR 031CD*	57		1

FORCE & STYLES FEATURING KELLY LLORENNA
UK, male/female vocal/DJ duo. See Darren Styles & Mark Breeze — 1

Date	Title / Label	Peak	Wks at No.1	Wks on Chart
25 Jul 98	**HEART OF GOLD** *Diverse VERSE 2CD*	55		1

FORCE MDs
US, male vocal group — 9

Date	Title / Label	Peak	Wks at No.1	Wks on Chart
12 Apr 86	**TENDER LOVE** *Tommy Boy IS 269*	23		9

CLINTON FORD
UK, male vocalist (Ian Stopford Harrison), d. 21 Oct 2009 (age 77) — 25

Date	Title / Label	Peak	Wks at No.1	Wks on Chart
23 Oct 59	**OLD SHEP** *Oriole CB 1500*	27		1
17 Aug 61	**TOO MANY BEAUTIFUL GIRLS** *Oriole CB 1623*	48		1
8 Mar 62	**FANLIGHT FANNY** *Oriole CB 1706*	22		10
5 Jan 67	**RUN TO THE DOOR** *Piccadilly 7N 35361*	25		13

EMILE FORD & THE CHECKMATES

Bahamas/UK, male vocalist (Emile Sweatman) & UK, male vocal/instrumental group

Date	Title	Peak	Wks at No.1	Wks (89)
30 Oct 59	**WHAT DO YOU WANT TO MAKE THOSE EYES AT ME FOR** *Pye 7N 15225*	1	6	26
5 Feb 60	**ON A SLOW BOAT TO CHINA** *Pye 7N 15245*	3		15
26 May 60	**YOU'LL NEVER KNOW WHAT YOU'RE MISSING ('TIL YOU TRY)** *Pye 7N 15268*	12		9
1 Sep 60	**THEM THERE EYES** *Pye 7N 15282* EMILE FORD	18		16
8 Dec 60	**COUNTING TEARDROPS** *Pye 7N 15314*	4		12
2 Mar 61	**WHAT AM I GONNA DO** *Pye 7N 15331*	33		6
18 May 61	**HALF OF MY HEART** *Piccadilly 7N 35003* EMILE FORD	42		4
8 Mar 62	**I WONDER WHO'S KISSING HER NOW** *Piccadilly 7N 35033* EMILE FORD	43		1

LITA FORD

US (b. UK), female vocalist/guitarist

Date	Title	Peak	Wks at No.1	Wks (7)
17 Dec 88	**KISS ME DEADLY** *RCA PB 49575*	75		1
20 May 89	**CLOSE MY EYES FOREVER** *Dreamland PB 49409* DUET WITH OZZY OSBOURNE	47		3
11 Jan 92	**SHOT OF POISON** *RCA PB 49145*	63		3

MARTYN FORD ORCHESTRA

UK, orchestra

Date	Title	Peak	Wks at No.1	Wks (3)
14 May 77	**LET YOUR BODY GO DOWNTOWN** *Mountain TOP 26*	38		3

PENNYE FORD

US, female vocalist

Date	Title	Peak	Wks at No.1	Wks (7)
4 May 85	**DANGEROUS** *Total Experience FB 49975*	43		5
29 May 93	**DAYDREAMING** *Columbia 6590592* PENNY FORD	43		2

TENNESSEE ERNIE FORD

US, male vocalist, d. 17 Oct 1991 (age 72)

Date	Title	Peak	Wks at No.1	Wks (42)
21 Jan 55	**GIVE ME YOUR WORD** *Capitol CL 14005*	1	7	24
6 Jan 56	**SIXTEEN TONS** *Capitol CL 14500* ★	1	4	11
13 Jan 56	**THE BALLAD OF DAVY CROCKETT** *Capitol CL 14506*	3		7

JULIA FORDHAM

UK, female vocalist

Date	Title	Peak	Wks at No.1	Wks (32)
2 Jul 88	**HAPPY EVER AFTER** *Circa YR 15*	27		9
25 Feb 89	**WHERE DOES TIME GO** *Circa YR 23*	41		5
31 Aug 91	**I THOUGHT IT WAS YOU** *Circa YR 69*	64		2
18 Jan 92	**LOVE MOVES IN MYSTERIOUS WAYS** *Circa YR 73*	19		9
30 May 92	**I THOUGHT IT WAS YOU (REMIX)** *Circa YR 90*	45		3
30 Apr 94	**DIFFERENT TIME DIFFERENT PLACE** *Circa YRCD 111*	41		3
23 Jul 94	**I CAN'T HELP MYSELF** *Circa YRCD 116*	62		1

FOREIGNER

UK/US, male vocal/instrumental group – Lou Gramm, Dennis Elliott, Al Greenwood (replaced by Bob Mayo), Mick Jones, Ian McDonald, Mark Rivera & Rick Wills

Date	Title	Peak	Wks at No.1	Wks (78)
6 May 78	**FEELS LIKE THE FIRST TIME** *Atlantic K 11086*	39		6
15 Jul 78	**COLD AS ICE** *Atlantic K 10986*	24		10
28 Oct 78	**HOT BLOODED** *Atlantic K 11167*	42		3
24 Feb 79	**BLUE MORNING BLUE DAY** *Atlantic K 11236*	45		4
29 Aug 81	**URGENT** *Atlantic K 11664*	54		4
10 Oct 81	**JUKE BOX HERO** *Atlantic K 11678*	48		4
12 Dec 81	**WAITING FOR A GIRL LIKE YOU** *Atlantic K 11696*	8		13
8 May 82	**URGENT** *Atlantic K 11728*	45		5
8 Dec 84	**I WANT TO KNOW WHAT LOVE IS** *Atlantic A 9596* ● ★	1	3	16
6 Apr 85	**THAT WAS YESTERDAY** *Atlantic A 9571*	28		6
22 Jun 85	**COLD AS ICE (REMIX)** *Atlantic A 9539*	64		2
19 Dec 87	**SAY YOU WILL** *Atlantic A 9169*	71		4
22 Oct 94	**WHITE LIE** *Arista 74321232862*	58		1

FORMATIONS

US, male vocal group

Date	Title	Peak	Wks at No.1	Wks (11)
31 Jul 71	**AT THE TOP OF THE STAIRS** *Mojo 2027 001*	28		11

GEORGE FORMBY

UK, male vocalist/ukulele player (George Hoy Booth), d. 6 Mar 1961 (age 56). See 2 In A Tent

Date	Title	Peak	Wks at No.1	Wks (3)
21 Jul 60	**HAPPY GO LUCKY ME/BANJO BOY** *Pye 7N 15269*	40		3

FORREST

US, male vocalist (Forrest Thomas)

Date	Title	Peak	Wks at No.1	Wks (20)
26 Feb 83	**ROCK THE BOAT** *CBS A 3163* ○	4		10
14 May 83	**FEEL THE NEED IN ME** *CBS A 3411*	17		8
17 Sep 83	**ONE LOVER (DON'T STOP THE SHOW)** *CBS A 3734*	67		2

SHARON FORRESTER

Jamaica, female vocalist

Date	Title	Peak	Wks at No.1	Wks (1)
11 Feb 95	**LOVE INSIDE** *ffrr FCD 253*	50		1

LANCE FORTUNE

UK, male vocalist (Chris Morris)

Date	Title	Peak	Wks at No.1	Wks (18)
19 Feb 60	**BE MINE** *Pye 7N 15240*	4		13
5 May 60	**THIS LOVE I HAVE FOR YOU** *Pye 7N 15260*	26		5

FORTUNES

UK, male vocal/instrumental group – Rod Allen, d. 10 Jan 2008, Andy Brown, David Carr, Glen Dale & Barry Pritchard

Date	Title	Peak	Wks at No.1	Wks (65)
8 Jul 65	**YOU'VE GOT YOUR TROUBLES** *Decca F 12173*	2		14
7 Oct 65	**HERE IT COMES AGAIN** *Decca F 12243*	4		14
3 Feb 66	**THIS GOLDEN RING** *Decca F 12321*	15		9
11 Sep 71	**FREEDOM COME FREEDOM GO** *Capitol CL 15693*	6		17
29 Jan 72	**STORM IN A TEACUP** *Capitol CL 15707*	7		11

45 KING

UK, male DJ/producer (Mark James)

Date	Title	Peak	Wks at No.1	Wks (6)
28 Oct 89	**THE KING IS HERE/THE 900 NUMBER** *Dance Trax DRX 9*	60		5
11 Aug 90	**THE KING IS HERE/THE 900 NUMBER** *Dance Trax DRX 9*	73		1

49ERS

Italy, male producer (Gianfranco Bortolotti)

Date	Title	Peak	Wks at No.1	Wks (27)
16 Dec 89	**TOUCH ME** *Fourth & Broadway BRW 157*	3		13
17 Mar 90	**DON'T YOU LOVE ME** *Fourth & Broadway BRW 167*	12		6
9 Jun 90	**GIRL TO GIRL** *Fourth & Broadway BRW 174*	31		3
6 Jun 92	**GIRL TO GIRL** *Fourth & Broadway BRW 255*	46		2
29 Aug 92	**THE MESSAGE** *Fourth & Broadway BRW 257*	68		1
18 Mar 95	**ROCKIN' MY BODY** *Media MCSTD 2021* FEATURING ANN-MARIE SMITH	31		2

FORWARD, RUSSIA!

UK, male/female vocal/instrumental group

Date	Title	Peak	Wks at No.1	Wks (5)
27 Aug 05	**THIRTEEN/FOURTEEN** *Drowned In Sound OPE002CDS*	74		1
28 Jan 06	**TWELVE** *Dance To The Radio DTTR006CD*	36		1
13 May 06	**NINE** *Dance To The Radio DTTR011CD*	40		1
5 Aug 06	**EIGHTEEN** *Dance To The Radio DTTR016CD*	44		1
25 Nov 06	**NINETEEN** *Dance To The Radio DTTR021CD*	67		1

FOSTER & ALLEN

Ireland, male vocal/instrumental duo

Date	Title	Peak	Wks at No.1	Wks (47)
27 Feb 82	**A BUNCH OF THYME** *Ritz 5*	18		11
30 Oct 82	**OLD FLAMES** *Ritz 028*	51		8
19 Feb 83	**MAGGIE** *Ritz 025*	27		9
29 Oct 83	**I WILL LOVE YOU ALL MY LIFE** *Ritz 056*	49		6
30 Jun 84	**JUST FOR OLD TIME'S SAKE** *Ritz 066*	47		6
29 Mar 86	**AFTER ALL THESE YEARS** *Ritz 106*	43		7

FOUNDATION FEATURING NATALIE ROSSI

Holland/UK, male/female vocal/production trio

Date	Title	Peak	Wks at No.1	Wks (2)
12 Jul 03	**ALL OUT OF LOVE** *Arista 82876513292*	40		2

FOUNDATIONS

West Indies/UK/Sri Lanka, male vocal/instrumental group – Clem Curtis, Eric Allendale, Pat Burke, Michael Elliott, Anthony Gomez, Tim Harris & Peter McBeth — 57

Date	Title	Peak	Wks at No.1	Wks on Chart
27 Sep 67	**BABY NOW THAT I'VE FOUND YOU** *Pye 7N 17366*	1	2	16
24 Jan 68	**BACK ON MY FEET AGAIN** *Pye 7N 17417*	18		10
1 May 68	**ANY OLD TIME (YOU'RE LONELY AND SAD)** *Pye 7N 17503*	48		2
20 Nov 68	**BUILD ME UP BUTTERCUP** *Pye 7N 17636*	2		15
12 Mar 69	**IN THE BAD BAD OLD DAYS** *Pye 7N 17702*	8		10
13 Sep 69	**BORN TO LIVE AND BORN TO DIE** *Pye 7N 17809*	46		3
12 Dec 98	**BUILD ME UP BUTTERCUP** *Castle NEEX 1001*	71		1

FOUNTAINS OF WAYNE

US, male vocal/instrumental group — 15

Date	Title	Peak	Wks at No.1	Wks on Chart
22 Mar 97	**RADIATION VIBE** *Atlantic 7567956262*	32		2
10 May 97	**SINK TO THE BOTTOM** *Atlantic A 5612CD*	42		1
26 Jul 97	**SURVIVAL CAR** *Atlantic AT 0004CD*	53		1
27 Dec 97	**I WANT AN ALIEN FOR CHRISTMAS** *Atlantic AT 0020CD*	36		2
20 Mar 99	**DENISE** *Atlantic AT 0053CD*	57		1
20 Mar 04	**STACY'S MUM** *Virgin VSCDX 1860*	11		7
18 Sep 04	**HEY JULIE** *Virgin VSCDX 1881*	57		1

FOUR ACES

US, male vocal group – Al Alberts, d. 27 Nov 2009, Dave Mahoney, Lou Silvestri & Rosario Vaccaro — 40

Date	Title	Peak	Wks at No.1	Wks on Chart
30 Jul 54	**THREE COINS IN THE FOUNTAIN** *Brunswick 05308* FEATURING AL ALBERTS ★	5		6
7 Jan 55	**MR SANDMAN** *Brunswick 05355* FEATURING AL ALBERTS	9		5
20 May 55	**STRANGER IN PARADISE** *Brunswick 05418*	6		6
18 Nov 55	**LOVE IS A MANY SPLENDOURED THING** *Brunswick 05480* FEATURING AL ALBERTS ★	2		13
19 Oct 56	**WOMAN IN LOVE** *Brunswick 05589* FEATURING AL ALBERTS	19		3
4 Jan 57	**FRIENDLY PERSUASION** *Brunswick 05623* FEATURING AL ALBERTS	29		1
23 Jan 59	**THE WORLD OUTSIDE** *Brunswick 05773*	18		6

FOUR BUCKETEERS

UK, male/female vocal/TV presenting group — 6

Date	Title	Peak	Wks at No.1	Wks on Chart
3 May 80	**THE BUCKET OF WATER SONG** *CBS 8393*	26		6

4CLUBBERS

Germany, male production group. See Future Breeze — 1

Date	Title	Peak	Wks at No.1	Wks on Chart
14 Sep 02	**CHILDREN** *Code Blue BLU O26CD*	45		1

FOUR ESQUIRES

US, male vocal group — 2

Date	Title	Peak	Wks at No.1	Wks on Chart
31 Jan 58	**LOVE ME FOREVER** *London HLO 8533*	23		2

4-4-2

UK, TalkSport presenters/football fans/vocal ensemble — 5

Date	Title	Peak	Wks at No.1	Wks on Chart
19 Jun 04	**COME ON ENGLAND** *Gut CDGUT58*	2		5

4 HERO

UK, male production duo — 6

Date	Title	Peak	Wks at No.1	Wks on Chart
24 Nov 90	**MR KIRK'S NIGHTMARE** *Reinforced RIVET 1203*	73		2
9 May 92	**COOKIN' UP YAH BRAIN** *Reinforced RIVET 1216*	59		2
15 Aug 98	**STAR CHASERS** *Talkin Loud TLCD 36*	41		1
3 Nov 01	**LES FLEUR** *Talkin Loud TLCD 66*	53		1

400 BLOWS

UK, male/female vocal/production group — 4

Date	Title	Peak	Wks at No.1	Wks on Chart
29 Jun 85	**MOVIN'** *Illuminated ILL 61*	54		4

FOUR KNIGHTS

US, male vocal group – Gene Alford, d. 1960, Oscar Broadway, Clarence Dixon & John Wallace, d. 1978 — 13

Date	Title	Peak	Wks at No.1	Wks on Chart
4 Jun 54	**(OH BABY MINE) I GET SO LONELY** *Capitol CL 14076*	5		11
18 Oct 57	**MY PERSONAL POSSESSION** *Capitol CL 14765* NAT 'KING' COLE & THE FOUR KNIGHTS	21		2

FOUR LADS

Canada, male vocal group – Bernie Toorish, Jimmie Arnold, d. 15 Jun 2004, Frankie Busseri & Corrado Codarini, d. 28 Apr 2010 — 23

Date	Title	Peak	Wks at No.1	Wks on Chart
19 Dec 52	**FAITH CAN MOVE MOUNTAINS** *Columbia DB 3154* JOHNNIE RAY & THE FOUR LADS	7		3
22 Oct 54	**RAIN RAIN RAIN** *Philips PB 311* FRANKIE LAINE & THE FOUR LADS	8		16
28 Apr 60	**STANDING ON THE CORNER** *Philips PB 1000*	34		4

4 NON BLONDES

US, female/male vocal/instrumental group – Linda Perry, Christa Hillhouse, Dawn Richardson & Roger Rocha — 19

Date	Title	Peak	Wks at No.1	Wks on Chart
19 Jun 93	**WHAT'S UP** *Interscope A 8412CD* ○	2		17
16 Oct 93	**SPACEMAN** *Interscope A 8349CD*	53		2

4 OF US

Ireland, male vocal/instrumental group — 6

Date	Title	Peak	Wks at No.1	Wks on Chart
27 Feb 93	**SHE HITS ME** *Columbia 6589192*	35		4
1 May 93	**I MISS YOU** *Columbia 6591722*	62		2

411

UK, female vocal group – Carolyn Barratt, Tanya Boniface, Suzie Furlonger & Tisha Martin — 26

Date	Title	Peak	Wks at No.1	Wks on Chart
29 May 04	**ON MY KNEES** *Sony Music 6749382* FEATURING GHOSTFACE KILLAH	4		11
4 Sep 04	**DUMB** *Sony/Streetside 6752622*	3		10
27 Nov 04	**TEARDROPS** *Sony/Streetside 6754812*	23		5

FOUR PENNIES

UK, male vocal/instrumental group – Lionel Morton, Alan Buck, d. 1994, Fritz Fryer, d. 2 Sep 2007, & Mike Wilsh — 56

Date	Title	Peak	Wks at No.1	Wks on Chart
16 Jan 64	**DO YOU WANT ME TO** *Philips BF 1296*	47		2
2 Apr 64	**JULIET** *Philips BF 1322*	1	1	15
16 Jul 64	**I FOUND OUT THE HARD WAY** *Philips BF 1349*	14		11
29 Oct 64	**BLACK GIRL** *Philips BF 1366*	20		12
7 Oct 65	**UNTIL IT'S TIME FOR YOU TO GO** *Philips BF 1435*	19		11
17 Feb 66	**TROUBLE IS MY MIDDLE NAME** *Philips BF 1469*	32		5

FOUR PREPS

US, male vocal group – Bruce Belland, Ed Cobb, d. 19 Sep 1999, Marvin Inabnett, d. 7 Mar 1999, & Glen Larson — 23

Date	Title	Peak	Wks at No.1	Wks on Chart
13 Jun 58	**BIG MAN** *Capitol CL 14873*	2		14
26 May 60	**GOT A GIRL** *Capitol CL 15128*	28		7
9 Nov 61	**MORE MONEY FOR YOU AND ME (MEDLEY)** *Capitol CL 15217*	39		2

FOUR SEASONS

US, male vocal/instrumental group – Frankie Valli*, Tommy DeVito, Bob Gaudio & Nick Massi, d. 24 Dec 2000 (replaced by Joe Long) — 157

Date	Title	Peak	Wks at No.1	Wks on Chart
4 Oct 62	**SHERRY** *Stateside SS 122* ★	8		16
17 Jan 63	**BIG GIRLS DON'T CRY** *Stateside SS 145* ★	13		10
28 Mar 63	**WALK LIKE A MAN** *Stateside SS 169* ★	12		12
27 Jun 63	**AIN'T THAT A SHAME** *Stateside SS 194*	38		3
27 Aug 64	**RAG DOLL** *Philips BF 1347* WITH THE SOUND OF FRANKIE VALLI ★	2		13
18 Nov 65	**LET'S HANG ON** *Philips BF 1439* WITH THE SOUND OF FRANKIE VALLI	4		16
31 Mar 66	**WORKING MY WAY BACK TO YOU** *Philips BF 1474* WITH FRANKIE VALLI	50		3
2 Jun 66	**OPUS 17 (DON'T YOU WORRY 'BOUT ME)** *Philips BF 1493* WITH FRANKIE VALLI	20		9
29 Sep 66	**I'VE GOT YOU UNDER MY SKIN** *Philips BF 1511* WITH FRANKIE VALLI	12		11
12 Jan 67	**TELL IT TO THE RAIN** *Philips BF 1538* WITH FRANKIE VALLI	37		5
19 Apr 75	**THE NIGHT** *Mowest MW 3024* FRANKIE VALLI & THE FOUR SEASONS	7		9
20 Sep 75	**WHO LOVES YOU** *Warner Brothers K 16602*	6		9
31 Jan 76	**DECEMBER '63 (OH WHAT A NIGHT)** *Warner Brothers K 16688* ● ★	1	2	10
24 Apr 76	**SILVER STAR** *Warner Brothers K 16742*	3		9
27 Nov 76	**WE CAN WORK IT OUT** *Warner Brothers K 16845*	34		4
18 Jun 77	**RHAPSODY** *Warner Brothers K 16932*	37		3
20 Aug 77	**DOWN THE HALL** *Warner Brothers K 16982*	34		5
29 Oct 88	**DECEMBER '63 (OH WHAT A NIGHT) (REMIX)** *BR 45277* FRANKIE VALLI & THE FOUR SEASONS	49		4
14 Jul 07	**BEGGIN'** *679 679L146CD* FRANKIE VALLI & THE FOUR SEASONS	32		4
7 Mar 09	**BEGGIN'** *679 679L146CD* FRANKIE VALLI & THE FOUR SEASONS	46		2

4 STRINGS

Holland, male/female vocal/production duo. See Madelyne — 17

Date	Title	Peak	Wks at No.1	Wks on Chart
23 Dec 00	**DAY TIME** *A&M CDAMPM 139*	48		3
11 May 02	**TAKE ME AWAY INTO THE NIGHT** *Nebula VCRD 107*	15		7
14 Sep 02	**DIVING** *Nebula VCRD 108*	38		2

Silver-selling ● Gold-selling ● Platinum-selling (x multiples) ✱ US No.1 ★ Peak Position · Weeks at No.1 · Weeks on Chart

Date	Title / Label	Peak	Wks at No.1	Wks on Chart
13 Sep 03	**LET IT RAIN** *Nebula NEBTCD 049*	49		1
31 Jul 04	**TURN IT AROUND** *Nebula NEBCD059*	50		2
19 Sep 09	**TAKE ME AWAY INTO THE NIGHT** *Nebula VCRD 107*	59		2

4 THE CAUSE

US, male/female vocal group — 9

Date	Title / Label	Peak	Wks at No.1	Wks on Chart
10 Oct 98	**STAND BY ME** *RCA 74321622442*	12		9

FOUR TOPS

US, male vocal group – Levi Stubbs, d. 17 Oct 2008, Renaldo Benson, d. 1 Jul 2005, Abdul Fakir & Lawrence Payton, d. 20 Jun 1997. Unmistakable Detroit-based R&B act who performed together for a record-breaking 44 years and were among the first groups inducted into the Rock & Roll Hall of Fame — 318

Date	Title / Label	Peak	Wks at No.1	Wks on Chart
1 Jul 65	**I CAN'T HELP MYSELF** *Tamla Motown TMG 515* ★	23		9
2 Sep 65	**IT'S THE SAME OLD SONG** *Tamla Motown TMG 528*	34		8
21 Jul 66	**LOVING YOU IS SWEETER THAN EVER** *Tamla Motown TMG 568*	21		12
13 Oct 66	**REACH OUT I'LL BE THERE** *Tamla Motown TMG 579* ★	1	3	16
12 Jan 67	**STANDING IN THE SHADOWS OF LOVE** *Tamla Motown TMG 589*	6		8
30 Mar 67	**BERNADETTE** *Tamla Motown TMG 601*	8		10
15 Jun 67	**SEVEN ROOMS OF GLOOM** *Tamla Motown TMG 612*	12		9
11 Oct 67	**YOU KEEP RUNNING AWAY** *Tamla Motown TMG 623*	26		7
13 Dec 67	**WALK AWAY RENEE** *Tamla Motown TMG 634*	3		11
13 Mar 68	**IF I WERE A CARPENTER** *Tamla Motown TMG 647*	7		11
21 Aug 68	**YESTERDAY'S DREAMS** *Tamla Motown TMG 665*	23		15
13 Nov 68	**I'M IN A DIFFERENT WORLD** *Tamla Motown TMG 675*	27		13
28 May 69	**WHAT IS A MAN** *Tamla Motown TMG 698*	16		11
27 Sep 69	**DO WHAT YOU GOTTA DO** *Tamla Motown TMG 710*	11		11
21 Mar 70	**I CAN'T HELP MYSELF** *Tamla Motown TMG 732*	10		11
30 May 70	**IT'S ALL IN THE GAME** *Tamla Motown TMG 736*	5		16
3 Oct 70	**STILL WATER (LOVE)** *Tamla Motown TMG 752*	10		12
1 May 71	**JUST SEVEN NUMBERS (CAN STRAIGHTEN OUT MY LIFE)** *Tamla Motown TMG 770*	36		5
26 Jun 71	**RIVER DEEP MOUNTAIN HIGH** *Tamla Motown TMG 777* SUPREMES & THE FOUR TOPS	11		10
25 Sep 71	**SIMPLE GAME** *Tamla Motown TMG 785*	3		11
20 Nov 71	**YOU GOTTA HAVE LOVE IN YOUR HEART** *Tamla Motown TMG 793* SUPREMES & THE FOUR TOPS	25		10
11 Mar 72	**BERNADETTE** *Tamla Motown TMG 803*	23		7
5 Aug 72	**WALK WITH ME TALK WITH ME DARLING** *Tamla Motown TMG 823*	32		6
18 Nov 72	**KEEPER OF THE CASTLE** *Probe PRO 575*	18		9
10 Nov 73	**SWEET UNDERSTANDING LOVE** *Probe PRO 604*	29		10
17 Oct 81	**WHEN SHE WAS MY GIRL** *Casablanca CAN 1005* ●	3		10
19 Dec 81	**DON'T WALK AWAY** *Casablanca CAN 1006*	16		11
6 Mar 82	**TONIGHT I'M GONNA LOVE YOU ALL OVER** *Casablanca CAN 1008*	43		4
26 Jun 82	**BACK TO SCHOOL AGAIN** *RSO 89*	62		2
23 Jul 88	**REACH OUT I'LL BE THERE** *Motown ZB 41943*	11		9
17 Sep 88	**INDESTRUCTIBLE** *Arista 111717* FEATURING SMOKEY ROBINSON	55		4
3 Dec 88	**LOCO IN ACAPULCO** *Arista 111850*	7		13
25 Feb 89	**INDESTRUCTIBLE** *Arista 112074* FEATURING SMOKEY ROBINSON	30		7

Top 3 Best-Selling Singles

		Approximate Sales
1	REACH OUT I'LL BE THERE	470,000
2	WHEN SHE WAS MY GIRL	390,000
3	WALK AWAY RENEE	245,000

4TUNE 500

UK, male/female production group — 1

Date	Title / Label	Peak	Wks at No.1	Wks on Chart
16 Aug 03	**DANCING IN THE DARK** *Black Gold BLGD04CSC 01*	75		1

4 VINI FEATURING ELISABETH TROY

UK, male/female vocal/production group — 1

Date	Title / Label	Peak	Wks at No.1	Wks on Chart
18 May 02	**FOREVER YOUNG** *Botchit & Scarper BOS2CD 033*	75		1

4MANDU

UK, male vocal group — 6

Date	Title / Label	Peak	Wks at No.1	Wks on Chart
29 Jul 95	**THIS IS IT** *Final Vinyl 74321291222*	45		3
17 Feb 96	**DO IT FOR LOVE** *Final Vinyl 74321343902*	45		2
15 Jun 96	**BABY DON'T GO** *Final Vinyl 74321375912*	47		1

FOURMOST

UK, male vocal/instrumental group – Billy Hatton, Dave Lovelady, Mike Millward, d. 3 Jul 1966, & Brian O'Hara, d. 27 Jun 1999 — 64

Date	Title / Label	Peak	Wks at No.1	Wks on Chart
12 Sep 63	**HELLO LITTLE GIRL** *Parlophone R 5056*	9		17
26 Dec 63	**I'M IN LOVE** *Parlophone R 5078*	17		12
23 Apr 64	**A LITTLE LOVING** *Parlophone R 5128*	6		13
13 Aug 64	**HOW CAN I TELL HER** *Parlophone R 5157*	33		4
26 Nov 64	**BABY I NEED YOUR LOVIN'** *Parlophone R 5194*	24		12
9 Dec 65	**GIRLS GIRLS GIRLS** *Parlophone R 5379*	33		6

14-18

UK, male producer/vocalist (Pete Waterman). See Stock Aitken Waterman — 4

Date	Title / Label	Peak	Wks at No.1	Wks on Chart
1 Nov 75	**GOODBYE-EE** *Magnet MAG 48*	33		4

FOX

UK/US/Australia, male/female vocal/instrumental group – Noosha Fox*, Herbie Armstrong, Jim Frank, Jim Gannon, Mike Lavender, Pete Solley, Gary Taylor & Kenny Young — 29

Date	Title / Label	Peak	Wks at No.1	Wks on Chart
15 Feb 75	**ONLY YOU CAN** *GTO GT 8* ●	3		11
10 May 75	**IMAGINE ME IMAGINE YOU** *GTO GT 21*	15		8
10 Apr 76	**S-S-S-SINGLE BED** *GTO GT 57*	4		10

CASS FOX

UK, female vocalist (Cassandra Fox) — 4

Date	Title / Label	Peak	Wks at No.1	Wks on Chart
4 Nov 06	**TOUCH ME** *Universal 1712211*	52		3
7 Apr 07	**MUSIC MATTERS** *Cheeky GBBXH0600040* FAITHLESS FEATURING CASS FOX	38		1

GEMMA FOX FEATURING MC LYTE

UK/US, female vocal/rap duo — 3

Date	Title / Label	Peak	Wks at No.1	Wks on Chart
8 May 04	**GIRLFRIEND'S STORY** *Polydor 9866362*	38		3

JAMES FOX

UK, male vocalist — 9

Date	Title / Label	Peak	Wks at No.1	Wks on Chart
1 May 04	**HOLD ON TO OUR LOVE** *Sony Music 6748732*	13		7
17 May 08	**BLUEBIRDS FLYING HIGH** *Plastic Tomato PLT02*	15		2

NOOSHA FOX

UK, female vocalist. See Fox — 6

Date	Title / Label	Peak	Wks at No.1	Wks on Chart
12 Nov 77	**GEORGINA BAILEY** *GTO GT 106*	31		6

SAMANTHA FOX

UK, female vocalist/model. See Sox — 73

Date	Title / Label	Peak	Wks at No.1	Wks on Chart
22 Mar 86	**TOUCH ME (I WANT YOUR BODY)** *Jive FOXY 1* ●	3		10
28 Jun 86	**DO YA DO YA (WANNA PLEASE ME)** *Jive FOXY 2*	10		7
6 Sep 86	**HOLD ON TIGHT** *Jive FOXY 3*	26		5
13 Dec 86	**I'M ALL YOU NEED** *Jive FOXY 4*	41		6
30 May 87	**NOTHING'S GONNA STOP ME NOW** *Jive FOXY 5*	8		9
25 Jul 87	**I SURRENDER (TO THE SPIRIT OF THE NIGHT)** *Jive FOXY 6*	25		7
17 Oct 87	**I PROMISE YOU (GET READY)** *Jive FOXY 7*	58		3
19 Dec 87	**TRUE DEVOTION** *Jive FOXY 8*	62		3
21 May 88	**NAUGHTY GIRLS** *Jive FOXY 9* FEATURING FULL FORCE	31		5
19 Nov 88	**LOVE HOUSE** *Jive FOXY 10*	32		6
28 Jan 89	**I ONLY WANNA BE WITH YOU** *Jive FOXY 11*	16		8
17 Jun 89	**I WANNA HAVE SOME FUN** *Jive FOXY 12*	63		2
28 Mar 98	**SANTA MARIA** *All Around The World CDGLOBE 163* DJ MILANO FEATURING SAMANTHA FOX	31		2

BRUCE FOXTON

UK, male vocalist/bass player. See Jam — 9

Date	Title / Label	Peak	Wks at No.1	Wks on Chart
30 Jul 83	**FREAK** *Arista BFOX 1*	23		5
29 Oct 83	**THIS IS THE WAY** *Arista BFOX 2*	56		3
21 Apr 84	**IT MAKES ME WONDER** *Arista BFOX 3*	74		1

INEZ FOXX

US, female vocalist — 8

Date	Title / Label	Peak	Wks at No.1	Wks on Chart
23 Jul 64	**HURT BY LOVE** *Sue WI 323*	40		3
19 Feb 69	**MOCKINGBIRD** *United Artists UP 2269* INEZ & CHARLIE FOXX	33		5

Silver-selling ○ Gold-selling ● Platinum-selling (x multiples) ⊛ US No.1 ★ Peak Position Weeks at No.1 Weeks on Chart

JAMIE FOXX
US, male actor/comedian/vocalist (Eric Bishop) — 52

Date	Title / Label	Peak	Wks at No.1	Wks on Chart
1 Oct 05	**GOLD DIGGER** *Roc-A-Fella 9885699* KANYE WEST FEATURING JAMIE FOXX ○ ★	2		44
22 Apr 06	**UNPREDICTABLE** *J Records 82876804772* FEATURING LUDACRIS	16		6
1 Jul 06	**EXTRAVAGANZA** *J Records 82876869422* FEATURING KANYE WEST	43		2

JOHN FOXX
UK, male vocalist (Dennis Leigh) — 31

Date	Title / Label	Peak	Wks at No.1	Wks on Chart
26 Jan 80	**UNDERPASS** *Virgin VS 318*	31		8
29 Mar 80	**NO-ONE DRIVING (DOUBLE SINGLE)** *Virgin VS 338*	32		4
19 Jul 80	**BURNING CAR** *Virgin VS 360*	35		7
8 Nov 80	**MILES AWAY** *Virgin VS 382*	51		3
29 Aug 81	**EUROPE (AFTER THE RAIN)** *Virgin VS 393*	40		5
2 Jul 83	**ENDLESSLY** *Virgin VS 543*	66		3
17 Sep 83	**YOUR DRESS** *Virgin VS 615*	61		1

FPI PROJECT
Italy, male production trio – Marco Frattini, Corrado Presti & Roberto Intrallazzi – with Luciano Bericchia & various Italy/UK, male/female vocalists — 17

Date	Title / Label	Peak	Wks at No.1	Wks on Chart
9 Dec 89	**GOING BACK TO MY ROOTS/RICH IN PARADISE** *Rumour RUMAT 9*	9		12
9 Mar 91	**EVERYBODY (ALL OVER THE WORLD)** *Rumour RUMA 29*	65		3
7 Aug 93	**COME ON (AND DO IT)** *Synthetic SYNTH 006CD*	59		1
13 Mar 99	**EVERYBODY (ALL OVER)** *99 North CDNTH 14*	67		1

FRAGGLES
UK/US, male/female TV puppet creatures — 8

Date	Title / Label	Peak	Wks at No.1	Wks on Chart
18 Feb 84	**'FRAGGLE ROCK' THEME** *RCA 389*	33		8

FRAGMA
Germany/UK, male production trio & female vocalists – Damae (Damae Klein), Maria Rubia*, Dirk & Marco Duderstadt & Ramon Zenker. See Bellini, E-Trax, Hardfloor, Interactive, Paffendorf — 51

Date	Title / Label	Peak	Wks at No.1	Wks on Chart
25 Sep 99	**TOCA ME** *Positiva CDTIV 120*	11		6
22 Apr 00	**TOCA'S MIRACLE** *Positiva CDTIV 128* ●	1	2	17
13 Jan 01	**EVERYTIME YOU NEED ME** *Positiva CDTIVS 147* FEATURING MARIA RUBIA ○	3		11
19 May 01	**YOU ARE ALIVE** *Positiva CDTIVS 153*	4		9
8 Dec 01	**SAY THAT YOU'RE HERE** *Illustrious CD1LL*	25		2
12 Apr 08	**TOCA'S MIRACLE 2008** *Positiva CDTIV 128*	16		6

RODDY FRAME
UK, male vocalist/guitarist. See Aztec Camera — 2

Date	Title / Label	Peak	Wks at No.1	Wks on Chart
19 Sep 98	**REASON FOR LIVING** *Independiente ISOM 18MS*	45		2

PETER FRAMPTON
UK, male vocalist. See Herd, Humble Pie — 24

Date	Title / Label	Peak	Wks at No.1	Wks on Chart
1 May 76	**SHOW ME THE WAY** *A&M AMS 7218*	10		12
11 Sep 76	**BABY I LOVE YOUR WAY** *A&M AMS 7246*	43		5
6 Nov 76	**DO YOU FEEL LIKE WE DO** *A&M AMS 7260*	39		4
23 Jul 77	**I'M IN YOU** *A&M AMS 7298*	41		3

LIVVI FRANC FEATURING PITBULL
UK/US, female vocal/rap duo — 3

Date	Title / Label	Peak	Wks at No.1	Wks on Chart
19 Sep 09	**NOW I'M THAT CHICK** *Jive USJI10900435*	40		3

CONNIE FRANCIS
US, female vocalist (Concetta Franconero). Even though her first 9 singles flopped, the New Jersey native became the most successful female vocalist of the early rock years. She was the first teenage female artist to top the singles chart and the first to have a No.1 album — 244

Date	Title / Label	Peak	Wks at No.1	Wks on Chart
4 Apr 58	**WHO'S SORRY NOW** *MGM 975*	1	6	25
27 Jun 58	**I'M SORRY I MADE YOU CRY** *MGM 982*	11		10
22 Aug 58	**CAROLINA MOON/STUPID CUPID** *MGM 985*	1	6	19
31 Oct 58	**I'LL GET BY** *MGM 993*	19		6
21 Nov 58	**FALLIN'** *MGM 993*	20		5
26 Dec 58	**YOU ALWAYS HURT THE ONE YOU LOVE** *MGM 998*	13		7
13 Feb 59	**MY HAPPINESS** *MGM 1001*	4		15
3 Jul 59	**LIPSTICK ON YOUR COLLAR** *MGM 1018*	3		16
11 Sep 59	**PLENTY GOOD LOVIN'** *MGM 1036*	18		6
4 Dec 59	**AMONG MY SOUVENIRS** *MGM 1046*	11		10
17 Mar 60	**VALENTINO** *MGM 1060*	27		8
19 May 60	**MAMA/ROBOT MAN** *MGM 1076*	2		19
18 Aug 60	**EVERYBODY'S SOMEBODY'S FOOL** *MGM 1086* ★	5		13
3 Nov 60	**MY HEART HAS A MIND OF ITS OWN** *MGM 1100* ★	3		15
12 Jan 61	**MANY TEARS AGO** *MGM 1111*	12		9
16 Mar 61	**WHERE THE BOYS ARE/BABY ROO** *MGM 1121*	5		14
15 Jun 61	**BREAKIN' IN A BRAND NEW BROKEN HEART** *MGM 1136*	12		11
14 Sep 61	**TOGETHER** *MGM 1138*	6		11
14 Dec 61	**BABY'S FIRST CHRISTMAS** *MGM 1145*	30		4
26 Apr 62	**DON'T BREAK THE HEART THAT LOVES YOU** *MGM 1157* ★	39		3
2 Aug 62	**VACATION** *MGM 1165*	10		9
20 Dec 62	**I'M GONNA BE WARM THIS WINTER** *MGM 1185*	48		1
10 Jun 65	**MY CHILD** *MGM 1271*	26		6
20 Jan 66	**JEALOUS HEART** *MGM 1293*	44		2

JILL FRANCIS
UK, female vocalist — 1

Date	Title / Label	Peak	Wks at No.1	Wks on Chart
3 Jul 93	**MAKE LOVE TO ME** *Glady Wax GW 003CD*	70		1

CLAUDE FRANCOIS
France (b. Egypt), male vocalist, d. 11 Mar 1978 (age 39) — 4

Date	Title / Label	Peak	Wks at No.1	Wks on Chart
10 Jan 76	**TEARS ON THE TELEPHONE** *Bradley's BRAD 7528*	35		4

FRANK
UK, female vocal group — 2

Date	Title / Label	Peak	Wks at No.1	Wks on Chart
12 Aug 06	**I'M NOT SHY** *Polydor FIMS170*	40		2

FRANK & WALTERS
Ireland, male vocal/instrumental trio — 13

Date	Title / Label	Peak	Wks at No.1	Wks on Chart
21 Mar 92	**HAPPY BUSMAN** *Setanta HOO 2*	49		2
12 Sep 92	**THIS IS NOT A SONG** *Setanta HOO 3*	46		3
9 Jan 93	**AFTER ALL** *Setanta HOOCD 4*	11		5
17 Apr 93	**FASHION CRISIS HITS NEW YORK** *Setanta HOOCD 5*	42		3

FRANKE
UK, male vocalist (Franke Howard) — 3

Date	Title / Label	Peak	Wks at No.1	Wks on Chart
7 Nov 92	**UNDERSTAND THIS GROOVE** *China WOK 2028*	60		2
21 May 94	**LOVE COME HOME** *Triangle BLUESCD 001* OUR TRIBE WITH FRANKE PHAROAH & KRISTINE W	73		1

FRANKEE
US, female vocalist (Nicole Francine Aiello) — 19

Date	Title / Label	Peak	Wks at No.1	Wks on Chart
1 May 04	**F.U.R.B. – F U RIGHT BACK (IMPORT)** *All Around The World 5603242CD*	43		3
22 May 04	**F.U.R.B. (F U RIGHT BACK)** *All Around The World CDGLOBE 355*	1	3	16

FRANKIE GOES TO HOLLYWOOD
UK, male vocal/instrumental group – Holly Johnson*, Peter Gill, Brian Nash, Mark O'Toole & Paul Rutherford* — 147

Date	Title / Label	Peak	Wks at No.1	Wks on Chart
26 Nov 83	**RELAX** *ZTT ZTAS 1* ⊛	1	5	52
16 Jun 84	**TWO TRIBES** *ZTT ZTAS 3* ⊛	1	9	21
1 Dec 84	**THE POWER OF LOVE** *ZTT ZTAS 5* ●	1	1	12
30 Mar 85	**WELCOME TO THE PLEASURE DOME** *ZTT ZTAS 7* ○	2		11
6 Sep 86	**RAGE HARD** *ZTT ZTAS 22* ○	4		7
22 Nov 86	**WARRIORS (OF THE WASTELAND)** *ZTT ZTAS 25*	19		8
7 Mar 87	**WATCHING THE WILDLIFE** *ZTT ZTAS 26*	28		6
2 Oct 93	**RELAX** *ZTT FGTH 1CD*	5		7
20 Nov 93	**WELCOME TO THE PLEASURE DOME (REMIX)** *ZTT FGTH 2CD*	18		3
18 Dec 93	**THE POWER OF LOVE** *ZTT FGTH 3CD*	10		7
26 Feb 94	**TWO TRIBES (REMIX)** *ZTT FGTH 4CD*	16		3
1 Jul 00	**THE POWER OF LOVE (REMIX)** *ZTT ZTT150CD*	6		6
9 Sep 00	**TWO TRIBES (REMIX)** *ZTT 154CD*	17		3
18 Nov 00	**WELCOME TO THE PLEASURE DOME (REMIX)** *ZTT 166CD*	45		1

ARETHA FRANKLIN
US, female vocalist/pianist — 182

Date	Title / Label	Peak	Wks at No.1	Wks on Chart
8 Jun 67	**RESPECT** *Atlantic 584 115* ★	10		14
23 Aug 67	**BABY I LOVE YOU** *Atlantic 584 127*	39		4
20 Dec 67	**CHAIN OF FOOLS/SATISFACTION** *Atlantic 584 157*	43		2
10 Jan 68	**SATISFACTION** *Atlantic 584 157*	37		5
13 Mar 68	**SINCE YOU'VE BEEN GONE** *Atlantic 584 172*	47		1

Date	Title	Peak Position	Weeks at No.1	Weeks on Chart
22 May 68	**THINK** *Atlantic 584 186*	26		9
7 Aug 68	**I SAY A LITTLE PRAYER FOR YOU** *Atlantic 584 206*	4		14
22 Aug 70	**DON'T PLAY THAT SONG** *Atlantic 2091 027*	13		11
2 Oct 71	**SPANISH HARLEM** *Atlantic 2091 138*	14		9
8 Sep 73	**ANGEL** *Atlantic K 10346*	37		5
16 Feb 74	**UNTIL YOU COME BACK TO ME (THAT'S WHAT I'M GONNA DO)** *Atlantic K 10399*	26		8
6 Dec 80	**WHAT A FOOL BELIEVES** *Arista ARIST 377*	46		7
19 Sep 81	**LOVE ALL THE HURT AWAY** *Arista ARIST 428* & GEORGE BENSON	49		3
4 Sep 82	**JUMP TO IT** *Arista ARIST 479*	42		5
23 Jul 83	**GET IT RIGHT** *Arista ARIST 537*	74		2
13 Jul 85	**FREEWAY OF LOVE** *Arista ARIST 624*	68		3
2 Nov 85	**SISTERS ARE DOING IT FOR THEMSELVES** *RCA PB 40339* EURYTHMICS & ARETHA FRANKLIN	9		11
23 Nov 85	**WHO'S ZOOMIN' WHO** *Arista ARIST 633*	11		14
22 Feb 86	**ANOTHER NIGHT** *Arista ARIST 657*	54		6
10 May 86	**FREEWAY OF LOVE** *Arista ARIST 624*	51		3
25 Oct 86	**JUMPIN' JACK FLASH** *Arista ARIST 678*	58		3
31 Jan 87	**I KNEW YOU WERE WAITING (FOR ME)** *Epic DUET 2* & GEORGE MICHAEL ● ★	1	2	9
14 Mar 87	**JIMMY LEE** *Arista RIS 6*	46		4
6 May 89	**THROUGH THE STORM** *Arista 112185* & ELTON JOHN	41		3
9 Sep 89	**IT ISN'T, IT WASN'T, IT AIN'T NEVER GONNA BE** *Arista 112545* & WHITNEY HOUSTON	29		5
7 Apr 90	**THINK** *East West A 7951*	31		2
27 Jul 91	**EVERYDAY PEOPLE** *Arista 114420*	69		1
12 Feb 94	**A DEEPER LOVE** *Arista 74321187022*	5		7
25 Jun 94	**WILLING TO FORGIVE** *Arista 74321213342*	17		7
9 May 98	**A ROSE IS STILL A ROSE** *Arista 74321569742*	22		4
26 Sep 98	**HERE WE GO AGAIN** *Arista 74321612742*	68		1

ERMA FRANKLIN

US, female vocalist, d. 7 September 2002 (age 64) — 10

Date	Title	Peak Position	Weeks at No.1	Weeks on Chart
10 Oct 92	**(TAKE A LITTLE) PIECE OF MY HEART** *Epic 6583847*	9		10

RODNEY FRANKLIN

US, male pianist — 9

Date	Title	Peak Position	Weeks at No.1	Weeks on Chart
19 Apr 80	**THE GROOVE** *CBS 8529*	7		9

CHEVELLE FRANKLYN/BEENIE MAN

Jamaica, female/male vocal duo — 1

Date	Title	Peak Position	Weeks at No.1	Weeks on Chart
20 Sep 97	**DANCEHALL QUEEN** *Island Jamaica IJCD 2018*	70		1

FRANKMUSIK

UK, male vocalist/multi-instrumentalist/producer (Vincent Frank, b. Vincent Turner). See Young Soul Rebels — 8

Date	Title	Peak Position	Weeks at No.1	Weeks on Chart
25 Apr 09	**BETTER OFF AS TWO** *Island 1799614*	26		2
1 Aug 09	**CONFUSION GIRL (SHAME SHAME SHAME)** *Island 2711959*	27		6

FRANTIQUE

UK, female session vocal group featuring Vivienne Savoie — 12

Date	Title	Peak Position	Weeks at No.1	Weeks on Chart
11 Aug 79	**STRUT YOUR FUNKY STUFF** *Philadelphia International PIR 7728*	10		12

FRANZ FERDINAND

UK, male vocal/instrumental group – Alex Kapranos, Bob Hardy, Nick McCarthy & Paul Thomson — 56

Date	Title	Peak Position	Weeks at No.1	Weeks on Chart
20 Sep 03	**DARTS OF PLEASURE** *Domino RUG 164CD*	44		1
24 Jan 04	**TAKE ME OUT** *Domino RUG 172CD*	3		9
1 May 04	**MATINEE** *Domino RUG 176CD*	8		6
28 Aug 04	**MICHAEL** *Domino RUG184CD1*	17		4
1 Oct 05	**DO YOU WANT TO** *Domino RUG211CDX*	4		14
17 Dec 05	**WALK AWAY** *Domino RUG215CD*	13		6
15 Apr 06	**THE FALLEN/L WELLS** *Domino RUG219CD*	14		2
29 Jul 06	**ELEANOR PUT YOUR BOOTS ON** *Domino RUG234CD*	30		2
31 Jan 09	**ULYSSES** *Domino RUG314CD*	20		3
21 Mar 09	**NO YOU GIRLS** *Domino RUG325CD*	22		9

ELIZABETH FRASER

UK, female vocalist. See Cocteau Twins — 4

Date	Title	Peak Position	Weeks at No.1	Weeks on Chart
12 May 90	**CANDLELAND (THE SECOND COMING)** *East West YZ 452* IAN McCULLOCH FEATURING ELIZABETH FRASER	75		1
13 Aug 94	**LIFEFORMS** *Virgin VSCD 1484* F.S.O.L. VOCALS BY ELIZABETH FRASER	14		3

FRASH

UK, male vocal/instrumental group — 1

Date	Title	Peak Position	Weeks at No.1	Weeks on Chart
18 Feb 95	**HERE I GO AGAIN** *PWL International FLIPCD 1*	69		1

FRATELLIS

UK, male vocal/instrumental trio – Jon Fratelli (John Lawler), Barry Fratelli (Barry Wallace) & Mince Fratelli (Gordon McRory) — 55

Date	Title	Peak Position	Weeks at No.1	Weeks on Chart
17 Jun 06	**HENRIETTA** *Island/Uni-Island CID938*	19		9
2 Sep 06	**CHELSEA DAGGER** *Fallout FALLOUTCD12*	5		23
2 Dec 06	**WHISTLE FOR THE CHOIR** *Fallout 1709876*	9		11
17 Mar 07	**FLATHEAD** *Island GBUM70601746*	67		1
24 Mar 07	**BABY FRATELLI** *Fallout 1723831*	24		4
31 May 08	**MISTRESS MABEL** *Fallout 1773039*	23		6
30 Aug 08	**LOOK OUT SUNSHINE!** *Fallout 1782024*	70		1

FRAY

US, male vocal/instrumental group – Isaac Slade, Joe King, Dave Welsh & Ben Wysocki — 64

Date	Title	Peak Position	Weeks at No.1	Weeks on Chart
27 Jan 07	**HOW TO SAVE A LIFE** *Epic 88697072302*	4		42
28 Apr 07	**OVER MY HEAD (CABLE CAR)** *Epic 88697012832*	19		16
24 Jan 09	**YOU FOUND ME** *Epic 88697453612*	35		6

FRAZIER CHORUS

UK, male/female vocal/instrumental group — 14

Date	Title	Peak Position	Weeks at No.1	Weeks on Chart
4 Feb 89	**DREAM KITCHEN** *Virgin VS 1145*	57		3
15 Apr 89	**TYPICAL!** *Virgin VS 1174*	53		2
15 Jul 89	**SLOPPY HEART** *Virgin VS 1192*	73		1
9 Jun 90	**CLOUD 8** *Virgin VS 1252*	52		3
25 Aug 90	**NOTHING** *Virgin VS 1284*	51		3
16 Feb 91	**WALKING ON AIR** *Virgin VS 1330*	60		2

FREAKPOWER

UK/Canada, male vocal/instrumental/production group – Norman Cook, Ashley Slater, Jim Carmichael, Dale Davies, Pete Eckford & Cyril McCammon — 20

Date	Title	Peak Position	Weeks at No.1	Weeks on Chart
16 Oct 93	**TURN ON, TUNE IN, COP OUT** *Fourth & Broadway BRCD 284*	29		5
26 Feb 94	**RUSH** *Fourth & Broadway BRCD 291*	62		2
18 Mar 95	**TURN ON, TUNE IN, COP OUT** *Fourth & Broadway BRCD 317* ●	3		9
8 Jun 96	**NEW DIRECTION** *Fourth & Broadway BRCD 331*	60		1
9 May 98	**NO WAY** *Deconstruction 74321578572*	29		3

FREAKS

UK, male vocal/production duo – Justin Harris & Luke Solomon — 10

Date	Title	Peak Position	Weeks at No.1	Weeks on Chart
28 May 07	**THE CREEPS (YOU'RE GIVING ME)** *Azuli AZNY237*	9		10

FREAKY REALISTIC

UK/Japan, male/female vocal/rap/instrumental trio — 3

Date	Title	Peak Position	Weeks at No.1	Weeks on Chart
3 Apr 93	**KOOCHIE RYDER** *Frealism FRESCD 2*	52		2
3 Jul 93	**LEONARD NIMOY** *Frealism FRESCD 3*	71		1

FREAKYMAN

Holland, male DJ/producer (Andre Van Den Bosch). See De Bos — 1

Date	Title	Peak Position	Weeks at No.1	Weeks on Chart
27 Sep 97	**DISCOBUG '97** *Xtravaganza 0091285 EXT*	68		1

STAN FREBERG

US, male comedian/vocalist — 5

Date	Title	Peak Position	Weeks at No.1	Weeks on Chart
19 Nov 54	**SH-BOOM** *Capitol CL 14187* WITH THE TOADS	15		2
27 Jul 56	**ROCK ISLAND LINE/HEARTBREAK HOTEL** *Capitol CL 14608* & HIS SKIFFLE GROUP	24		2
12 May 60	**THE OLD PAYOLA ROLL BLUES** *Capitol CL 15122* WITH JESSIE WHITE	40		1

FRED & ROXY

UK, female vocal duo — 2

Date	Title	Peak Position	Weeks at No.1	Weeks on Chart
5 Feb 00	**SOMETHING FOR THE WEEKEND** *Echo ECSCD 81*	36		2

JOHN FRED & THE PLAYBOY BAND

US, male vocal/instrumental group – John Fred Gourrier, d. 15 Apr 2005, Andrew Bernard, Howard Cowart, Tommy Degeneres, Ronnie Goodson, John Miceli, Jimmy O'Rourke & Charlie Spin — 12

Date	Title / Label	Peak	Wks at No.1	Wks on Chart
3 Jan 68	**JUDY IN DISGUISE (WITH GLASSES)** *Pye International 7N 25442* ★	3		12

FREDDIE & THE DREAMERS

UK, male vocal/instrumental group – Freddie Garrity, d. 19 May 2006, Peter Birrell, Roy Crewdson, Bernie Dwyer, d. 4 Dec 2002, & Derek Quinn — 85

Date	Title / Label	Peak	Wks at No.1	Wks on Chart
9 May 63	**IF YOU GOTTA MAKE A FOOL OF SOMEBODY** *Columbia DB 7032*	3		14
8 Aug 63	**I'M TELLING YOU NOW** *Columbia DB 7086* ★	2		11
7 Nov 63	**YOU WERE MADE FOR ME** *Columbia DB 7147*	3		15
20 Feb 64	**OVER YOU** *Columbia DB 7214*	13		11
14 May 64	**I LOVE YOU BABY** *Columbia DB 7286*	16		8
16 Jul 64	**JUST FOR YOU** *Columbia DB 7322*	41		3
5 Nov 64	**I UNDERSTAND** *Columbia DB 7381*	5		15
22 Apr 65	**A LITTLE YOU** *Columbia DB 7526*	26		5
4 Nov 65	**THOU SHALT NOT STEAL** *Columbia DB 7720*	44		3

DEE FREDRIX

UK, female vocalist — 5

Date	Title / Label	Peak	Wks at No.1	Wks on Chart
27 Feb 93	**AND SO I WILL WAIT FOR YOU** *East West YZ 725CD*	56		4
3 Jul 93	**DIRTY MONEY** *East West YZ 750CD*	74		1

FREE

UK, male vocal/instrumental group – Paul Rodgers*, John Bundrick, Andy Fraser (replaced by Tetsu Yamauchi), Simon Kirke & Paul Kossoff, d. 19 Mar 1976 — 75

Date	Title / Label	Peak	Wks at No.1	Wks on Chart
6 Jun 70	**ALL RIGHT NOW** *Island WIP 6082*	2		16
1 May 71	**MY BROTHER JAKE** *Island WIP 6100*	4		11
27 May 72	**LITTLE BIT OF LOVE** *Island WIP 6129*	13		10
13 Jan 73	**WISHING WELL** *Island WIP 6146*	7		10
21 Jul 73	**ALL RIGHT NOW** *Island WIP 6082*	15		9
18 Feb 78	**FREE EP** *Island IEP 6*	11		7
23 Oct 82	**FREE EP** *Island IEP 6*	56		3
9 Feb 91	**ALL RIGHT NOW** *Island IS 486*	8		9

FREE

US, female/male vocal/rap group — 8

Date	Title / Label	Peak	Wks at No.1	Wks on Chart
12 Apr 97	**MR BIG STUFF** *Motown 5736572* QUEEN LATIFAH, SHADES & FREE	31		2
14 Nov 98	**ANOTHER ONE BITES THE DUST** *DreamWorks DRMCD 22364* QUEEN WITH WYCLEF JEAN FEATURING PRAS MICHEL/FREE	5		6

FREE ASSOCIATION

UK, male/female vocal/instrumental group — 2

Date	Title / Label	Peak	Wks at No.1	Wks on Chart
12 Apr 03	**EVERYBODY KNOWS** *Ramp 001CDS*	74		1
13 Sep 03	**SUGARMAN** *13 Amp 9809471*	53		1

FREE SPIRIT

UK, male/female vocal duo — 1

Date	Title / Label	Peak	Wks at No.1	Wks on Chart
13 May 95	**NO MORE RAINY DAYS** *Columbia 6612822*	68		1

FREEEZ

UK, male vocal/instrumental group – John Rocca, Peter Maas, Paul Morgan (replaced by Everton McCalla) & Andy Stennet — 48

Date	Title / Label	Peak	Wks at No.1	Wks on Chart
7 Jun 80	**KEEP IN TOUCH** *Calibre CAB 103*	49		3
7 Feb 81	**SOUTHERN FREEEZ** *Beggars Banquet BEG 51* FEATURING INGRID MANSFIELD ALLMAN ●	8		11
18 Apr 81	**FLYING HIGH** *Beggars Banquet BEG 55*	35		5
18 Jun 83	**I.O.U.** *Beggars Banquet BEG 96* ●	2		15
1 Oct 83	**POP GOES MY LOVE** *Beggars Banquet BEG 98*	26		6
17 Jan 87	**I.O.U. (REMIX)** *Citybeat CBE 709* FEATURING JOHN ROCCA	23		6
30 May 87	**SOUTHERN FREEEZ (REMIX)** *Total Control TOCO 14* FEATURING INGRID MANSFIELD ALLMAN	63		2

FREEFALL FEATURING JAN JOHNSTON

UK/Australia, male/female vocal/DJ/production trio — 5

Date	Title / Label	Peak	Wks at No.1	Wks on Chart
28 Nov 98	**SKYDIVE** *Stress CDSTR 89*	75		1
22 Jul 00	**SKYDIVE (REMIX)** *Renaissance Recordings RENCDS 002*	43		2
8 Sep 01	**SKYDIVE (I FEEL WONDERFUL)** *Incentive CENT 22CDS*	35		2

FREEFALL FEATURING PSYCHOTROPIC

UK, male production duo — 1

Date	Title / Label	Peak	Wks at No.1	Wks on Chart
27 Jul 91	**FEEL SURREAL** *ffrr FX 160*	63		1

FREEFALLER

UK, male vocal/instrumental group – David Oliver, Rich Joy, Gary Mahon & Dean Robers — 8

Date	Title / Label	Peak	Wks at No.1	Wks on Chart
5 Feb 05	**DO THIS! DO THAT!** *Velocity VELOCD2*	8		5
14 May 05	**GOOD ENOUGH FOR YOU** *Emap VELOCD3*	21		2
3 Dec 05	**SHE'S MY EVERYTHING/BASKET CASE** *Velocity VELOCDX05*	36		1

FREELAND

UK/Chile, male/female vocal/production/instrumental group — 3

Date	Title / Label	Peak	Wks at No.1	Wks on Chart
13 Sep 03	**WE WANT YOUR SOUL** *Maximise Profit FREECDS01*	35		2
7 Feb 04	**SUPERNATURAL THING** *Marine Parade MAPACDS024*	65		1

CLAIRE FREELAND

UK, female vocalist — 1

Date	Title / Label	Peak	Wks at No.1	Wks on Chart
21 Jul 01	**FREE** *Statuesque CDSTATU 1*	44		1

FREELOADERS FEATURING THE REAL THING

UK, male production duo – Dale Longworth & Kevin O'Toole – & vocal group – Chris & Eddie Amoo, Ray Lake & Dave Smith — 7

Date	Title / Label	Peak	Wks at No.1	Wks on Chart
23 Apr 05	**SO MUCH LOVE TO GIVE** *All Around The World CDGLOBE412*	9		7

FREEMASONS

UK, male production duo – Russell Small & James Wiltshire — 54

Date	Title / Label	Peak	Wks at No.1	Wks on Chart
3 Sep 05	**LOVE ON MY MIND** *Loaded LOAD108CD* FEATURING AMANDA WILSON	11		5
11 Mar 06	**WATCHIN'** *Loaded LOAD111CD* FEATURING AMANDA WILSON	19		4
13 Jan 07	**RAIN DOWN LOVE** *Loaded LOAD116CD* FEATURING SIEDAH GARRETT	12		9
20 Oct 07	**UNINVITED** *Loaded LOAD118CD* FEATURING BAILEY TZUKE	8		18
28 Jun 08	**WHEN YOU TOUCH ME** *Loaded LOAD130CD* FEATURING KATHERINE ELLIS	23		8
27 Jun 09	**HEARTBREAK (MAKE ME A DANCER)** *Loaded LOAD132CD* FEATURING SOPHIE ELLIS-BEXTOR	13		10

FREESTYLE

US, male vocal/production group — 2

Date	Title / Label	Peak	Wks at No.1	Wks on Chart
14 Feb 09	**DON'T STOP THE ROCK** *Southern Fried GBEFR0801610*	73		2

FREESTYLERS

UK, male vocal/instrumental group — 11

Date	Title / Label	Peak	Wks at No.1	Wks on Chart
7 Feb 98	**B-BOY STANCE** *Freskanova FND 7* FEATURING TENOR FLY	23		3
14 Nov 98	**WARNING** *Freskanova FND 14* FEATURING NAVIGATOR	68		1
24 Jul 99	**HERE WE GO** *Freskanova FND 19*	45		1
20 Mar 04	**GET A LIFE** *Against The Grain ATG008*	66		1
26 Jun 04	**PUSH UP** *Against The Grain ATG009CD*	22		4
12 Feb 05	**BOOM BLAST** *Against The Grain ATG010R* FEATURING MILLION DAN	75		1

FREIHEIT

Germany, male vocal/instrumental group — 9

Date	Title / Label	Peak	Wks at No.1	Wks on Chart
17 Dec 88	**KEEPING THE DREAM ALIVE** *CBS 6529897*	14		9

FRENCH AFFAIR

France, male/female vocal/production trio — 3

Date	Title / Label	Peak	Wks at No.1	Wks on Chart
16 Sep 00	**MY HEART GOES BOOM** *Arista 74321780562*	44		3

Silver-selling ● Gold-selling ● Platinum-selling (× multiples) ✪ US No.1 ★ Peak Position · Weeks at No.1 · Weeks on Chart

NICKI FRENCH
UK, female vocalist — 18

Date	Title / Label	Peak	Wks at No.1	Wks
15 Oct 94	**TOTAL ECLIPSE OF THE HEART** *Bags Of Fun BAGSCD 1*	54		1
14 Jan 95	**TOTAL ECLIPSE OF THE HEART** *Bags Of Fun BAGSCD 1* ●	5		12
22 Apr 95	**FOR ALL WE KNOW** *Bags Of Fun BAGSCD 4*	42		2
15 Jul 95	**DID YOU EVER REALLY LOVE ME** *Love This LUVTHISCD 2*	55		1
27 May 00	**DON'T PLAY THAT SONG AGAIN** *RCA 74321764572*	34		2

FRESH
UK, male production group. See Bad Company, DJ Fresh — 3

Date	Title / Label	Peak	Wks at No.1	Wks
25 Oct 03	**SIGNAL/BIG LOVE** *Ram RAMM 46*	58		1
18 Sep 04	**COLOSSUS/HOODED** *Ram RAMM 51 BC*	74		1
25 Dec 04	**CAPTURE THE FLAG** *Ram RAMM 53 BC*	70		1

DOUG E FRESH & THE GET FRESH CREW
US, male rap/DJ group – Douglas Davis, Barry 'Bee' Moody & Willie 'Chill Will' Finch – with Richard 'Slick Rick' Walters — 11

Date	Title / Label	Peak	Wks at No.1	Wks
9 Nov 85	**THE SHOW** *Cooltempo COOL 116* ●	7		11

FRESH 4 FEATURING LIZZ E
UK, male DJ/production group – Paul 'Suv' Southey, Judge RNE, J 'Flyn' & Keith 'Krust' Thompson – & female vocalist — 9

Date	Title / Label	Peak	Wks at No.1	Wks
7 Oct 89	**WISHING ON A STAR** *10 TEN 287*	10		9

FREDDY FRESH
US, male producer (Frederick Schmid) — 3

Date	Title / Label	Peak	Wks at No.1	Wks
1 May 99	**BADDER BADDER SCHWING** *Eye-Q EYEUK 040CD* FEATURING FATBOY SLIM	34		2
31 Jul 99	**WHAT IT IS** *Eye-Q EYEUK 043CD*	63		1

FRESHIES
UK, male vocal/instrumental group — 3

Date	Title / Label	Peak	Wks at No.1	Wks
14 Feb 81	**I'M IN LOVE WITH THE GIRL ON A CERTAIN MANCHESTER VIRGIN MEGASTORE CHECKOUT DESK** *MCA 670*	54		3

MATT FRETTON
UK, male vocalist — 5

Date	Title / Label	Peak	Wks at No.1	Wks
11 Jun 83	**IT'S SO HIGH** *Chrysalis MATT 1*	50		5

STEPHEN FRETWELL
UK, male vocalist/guitarist — 4

Date	Title / Label	Peak	Wks at No.1	Wks
30 Jul 05	**EMILY** *Fiction 9871977*	42		4

FREUR
UK, male vocal/instrumental group — 4

Date	Title / Label	Peak	Wks at No.1	Wks
23 Apr 83	**DOOT DOOT** *CBS A 3141*	59		4

GLENN FREY
US, male vocalist/guitarist. See Eagles — 20

Date	Title / Label	Peak	Wks at No.1	Wks
2 Mar 85	**THE HEAT IS ON** *MCA 941*	12		12
22 Jun 85	**SMUGGLER'S BLUES** *BBC RESL 170*	22		8

FRIDA
Norway, female vocalist (Anni-Frid Lyngstad). See Abba — 12

Date	Title / Label	Peak	Wks at No.1	Wks
21 Aug 82	**I KNOW THERE'S SOMETHING GOING ON** *Epic EPC A 2603*	43		7
17 Dec 83	**TIME** *Epic A 3983* & BA ROBERTSON	45		5

FRIDAY HILL
UK, male vocal/rap trio – James Victor MacKenzie (Kenzie), James Murray & Mustafa Omer (Mus). See Blazin' Squad — 11

Date	Title / Label	Peak	Wks at No.1	Wks
22 Oct 05	**BABY GOODBYE** *Longside LONG1CDX*	5		8
25 Feb 06	**ONE MORE NIGHT ALONE** *Longside LONG2CDX*	13		3

RALPH FRIDGE
Germany, male producer (Ralf Fritsch) — 4

Date	Title / Label	Peak	Wks at No.1	Wks
24 Apr 99	**PARADISE** *Addictive 12AD 036*	68		1
8 Apr 00	**ANGEL** *Incentive CENT 6CDS*	20		3

DEAN FRIEDMAN
US, male vocalist/keyboard player — 22

Date	Title / Label	Peak	Wks at No.1	Wks
3 Jun 78	**WOMAN OF MINE** *Lifesong LS 401*	52		5
23 Sep 78	**LUCKY STARS** *Lifesong LS 402* ●	3		10
18 Nov 78	**LYDIA** *Lifesong LS 403*	31		7

FRIENDLY FIRES
UK, male vocal/instrumental group — 8

Date	Title / Label	Peak	Wks at No.1	Wks
14 Mar 09	**SKELETON BOY** *XL Recordings GBBKS0800402*	48		2
23 May 09	**JUMP IN THE POOL** *XL Recordings GBBKS0800398*	57		4
12 Sep 09	**KISS OF LIFE** *XL Recordings GBBKS0900288*	30		2

FRIENDS AGAIN
UK, male vocal/instrumental group — 3

Date	Title / Label	Peak	Wks at No.1	Wks
4 Aug 84	**THE FRIENDS AGAIN EP** *Mercury FA 1*	59		3

FRIENDS OF MATTHEW
UK, male/female vocal/instrumental group — 1

Date	Title / Label	Peak	Wks at No.1	Wks
10 Jul 99	**OUT THERE** *Serious SERR 007CD*	61		1

FRIGID VINEGAR
UK, male rap/production duo — 1

Date	Title / Label	Peak	Wks at No.1	Wks
21 Aug 99	**DOGMONAUT 2000 (IS THERE ANYONE OUT THERE)** *Gut CDGUT 27*	53		1

FRIJID PINK
US, male vocal/instrumental group – Kelly Green, Tom Beaudry, Rich Stevens & Gary Thompson — 16

Date	Title / Label	Peak	Wks at No.1	Wks
28 Mar 70	**HOUSE OF THE RISING SUN** *Deram DM 288*	4		16

JANE FROMAN
US, female vocalist (Ellen Froman), d. 22 Apr 1980 (age 72) — 4

Date	Title / Label	Peak	Wks at No.1	Wks
17 Jun 55	**I WONDER** *Capitol CL 14254*	14		4

FRON MALE VOICE CHOIR
UK, male choir — 1

Date	Title / Label	Peak	Wks at No.1	Wks
22 Nov 08	**TWO LITTLE BOYS** *Universal Jazz GBUM70811826*	57		1

FRONT 242
Belgium/US, male vocal/instrumental group — 1

Date	Title / Label	Peak	Wks at No.1	Wks
1 May 93	**RELIGION** *RRE 106CD*	46		1

LIAM FROST & SLOWDOWN FAMILY
UK, male vocal/instrumental group — 1

Date	Title / Label	Peak	Wks at No.1	Wks
9 Sep 06	**THE CITY IS AT STANDSTILL** *Lavolta LAVOLTA006*	74		1

FROU FROU
UK, male/female vocal/production duo — 1

Date	Title / Label	Peak	Wks at No.1	Wks
6 Jul 02	**BREATHE IN** *Island CID 799*	44		1

CHRISTIAN FRY
UK, male vocalist — 3

Date	Title / Label	Peak	Wks at No.1	Wks
14 Nov 98	**YOU GOT ME** *Mushroom MUSH 33CDS*	45		2
3 Apr 99	**WON'T YOU SAY** *Mushroom MUSH 46CDS*	48		1

FUGATIVE
US, male rapper/producer (Harry Byart) — 1

Date	Title / Label	Peak	Wks at No.1	Wks
30 Jan 10	**SUPAFLY** *Hard2beat GBCEN0901564*	48		1

FUGAZI
US, male vocal/instrumental group **1**

Date	Title	Peak	Wks at No.1	Wks on Chart
20 Oct 01	**FURNITURE** *Dischord DIS 129CD*	61		1

FUGEES
US/Haiti, female/male vocal/rap/production trio – Lauryn Hill*, Wyclef Jean* & Pras Michel* **68**

Date	Title	Peak	Wks at No.1	Wks on Chart
6 Apr 96	**FU-GEE-LA** *Columbia 6630662*	21		5
8 Jun 96	**KILLING ME SOFTLY** *Columbia 6633435* ⊛ x2	1	5	20
14 Sep 96	**READY OR NOT** *Columbia 6637215* ●	1	2	12
30 Nov 96	**NO WOMAN NO CRY** *Columbia 6639925*	2		9
15 Mar 97	**RUMBLE IN THE JUNGLE** *Mercury 5740692*	3		8
28 Jun 97	**WE TRYING TO STAY ALIVE** *Columbia 6646815* WYCLEF JEAN & THE REFUGEE ALLSTARS	13		5
6 Sep 97	**THE SWEETEST THING** *Columbia 6649785* REFUGEE ALLSTARS FEATURING LAURYN HILL	18		4
27 Sep 97	**GUANTANAMERA** *Columbia 6650852* WYCLEF JEAN & THE REFUGEE ALLSTARS	25		2
27 Oct 01	**LOVING YOU (OLE OLE OLE)** *Blacklist 0133045 ERE* BRIAN HARVEY & THE REFUGEE CREW	20		3

FULL CIRCLE
US, male vocal group **5**

Date	Title	Peak	Wks at No.1	Wks on Chart
7 Mar 87	**WORKIN' UP A SWEAT** *EMI America EA 229*	41		5

FULL FORCE
US, male vocal/instrumental group – Brian, Lucien & Paul George, Curt Bedeau, Gerry Charles & Junior Clark **37**

Date	Title	Peak	Wks at No.1	Wks on Chart
4 May 85	**I WONDER IF I TAKE YOU HOME** *CBS A 6057* LISA LISA & CULT JAM WITH FULL FORCE	12		17
21 Dec 85	**ALICE I WANT YOU JUST FOR ME** *CBS A 6640*	9		11
21 May 88	**NAUGHTY GIRLS** *Jive FOXY 9* SAMANTHA FOX FEATURING FULL FORCE	31		5
4 Jun 88	**I'M REAL** *Scotti Brothers JSB 1* JAMES BROWN FEATURING FULL FORCE	31		4

FULL INTENTION
UK, male instrumental/production group. See Disco Tex presents Cloudburst, Michael Gray, Hustlers Convention featuring Dave Laudat & Ondrea Duverney, Ronaldo's Revenge, Sex-O-Sonique **8**

Date	Title	Peak	Wks at No.1	Wks on Chart
6 Apr 96	**AMERICA (I LOVE AMERICA)** *Stress CDSTR 56*	32		2
10 Aug 96	**UPTOWN DOWNTOWN** *Stress CDSTR 67*	61		1
26 Jul 97	**SHAKE YOUR BODY (DOWN TO THE GROUND)** *Sugar Daddy CDSTR 82*	34		2
22 Nov 97	**AMERICA (I LOVE AMERICA) (REMIX)** *Sugar Daddy CDSTR 56*	56		1
6 Jun 98	**YOU ARE SOMEBODY** *Sugar Daddy CDSD 001*	75		1
1 Sep 01	**I'LL BE WAITING** *Rulin 17CDS* PRESENTS SHENA	44		1

FULL MONTY ALLSTARS FEATURING TJ DAVIS
UK, male/female vocal/instrumental group **1**

Date	Title	Peak	Wks at No.1	Wks on Chart
27 Jul 96	**BRILLIANT FEELING** *Arista 74321380902*	72		1

BOBBY FULLER FOUR
US, male vocal/instrumental group – leader d. 18 Jul 1966 (age 22) **4**

Date	Title	Peak	Wks at No.1	Wks on Chart
14 Apr 66	**I FOUGHT THE LAW** *London HL 10030*	33		4

FUN BOY THREE
UK, male vocal/instrumental trio – Terry Hall*, Lynval Golding & Neville Staple. See Specials **70**

Date	Title	Peak	Wks at No.1	Wks on Chart
7 Nov 81	**THE LUNATICS (HAVE TAKEN OVER THE ASYLUM)** *Chrysalis CHS 2563*	20		12
13 Feb 82	**IT AIN'T WHAT YOU DO IT'S THE WAY THAT YOU DO IT** *Chrysalis CHS 2570* & BANANARAMA ●	4		10
10 Apr 82	**REALLY SAYING SOMETHING** *Deram NANA 1* BANANARAMA WITH FUN BOY THREE ●	5		10
8 May 82	**THE TELEPHONE ALWAYS RINGS** *Chrysalis CHS 2609*	17		9
31 Jul 82	**SUMMERTIME** *Chrysalis CHS 2629*	18		8
15 Jan 83	**THE MORE I SEE (THE LESS I BELIEVE)** *Chrysalis CHS 2664*	68		1
5 Feb 83	**TUNNEL OF LOVE** *Chrysalis CHS 2678*	10		10
30 Apr 83	**OUR LIPS ARE SEALED** *Chrysalis FUNB 1*	7		10

FUN DMENTAL 03
UK, male vocal group **1**

Date	Title	Peak	Wks at No.1	Wks on Chart
25 Mar 06	**JUMP/PLAYGROUND** *Da Works FUND002X*	44		1

FUN LOVIN' CRIMINALS
US, male vocal/instrumental trio – Huey Morgan, Steve Borgovini (replaced by Maxwell Jayson) & Brian Leiser **32**

Date	Title	Peak	Wks at No.1	Wks on Chart
8 Jun 96	**THE GRAVE AND THE CONSTANT** *Chrysalis CDCHS 5031*	72		1
17 Aug 96	**SCOOBY SNACKS** *Chrysalis CDCHSS 5034*	22		3
16 Nov 96	**THE FUN LOVIN' CRIMINAL** *Chrysalis CDCHS 5040*	26		3
29 Mar 97	**KING OF NEW YORK** *Chrysalis CDCHS 5049*	28		3
5 Jul 97	**I'M NOT IN LOVE/SCOOBY SNACKS** *Chrysalis CDCHS 5060*	12		5
15 Aug 98	**LOVE UNLIMITED** *Chrysalis CDCHS 5096*	18		4
17 Oct 98	**BIG NIGHT OUT** *Chrysalis CDCHSS 5101*	29		2
8 May 99	**KOREAN BODEGA** *Chrysalis CDCHSS 5108*	15		3
17 Feb 01	**LOCO** *Chrysalis CDCHSS 5121*	5		6
1 Sep 01	**BUMP/RUN DADDY RUN** *Chrysalis CDHSS 5128*	50		1
13 Sep 03	**TOO HOT** *Sanctuary SANXD 205X*	61		1

FUNERAL FOR A FRIEND
UK, male vocal/instrumental group **21**

Date	Title	Peak	Wks at No.1	Wks on Chart
9 Aug 03	**JUNEAU** *Infectious EW 269CD1*	19		3
18 Oct 03	**SHE DROVE ME TO DAYTIME TELEVISION** *Infectious EW 274CD2*	20		2
14 Feb 04	**ESCAPE ARTISTS NEVER DIE** *Infectious EW 283CD*	19		3
11 Jun 05	**STREETCAR** *Atlantic ATUK009CDX*	15		3
10 Sep 05	**MONSTERS** *IHT/Atlantic ATUK012CD*	36		1
26 Nov 05	**HISTORY** *Atlantic ATUK017CD*	21		2
4 Mar 06	**ROSES FOR THE DEAD** *Atlantic ATUK022*	39		1
12 May 07	**INTO OBLIVION (REUNION)** *Atlantic ATUK058CD*	16		5
4 Aug 07	**WALK AWAY** *Atlantic ATUK068CD*	40		1

FARLEY 'JACKMASTER' FUNK
US, male producer (Farley Williams) **16**

Date	Title	Peak	Wks at No.1	Wks on Chart
23 Aug 86	**LOVE CAN'T TURN AROUND** *DJ International LON 105*	10		12
11 Feb 89	**AS ALWAYS** *Champion CHAMP 90* FEATURING RICKY DILLARD	49		2
14 Dec 96	**LOVE CAN'T TURN AROUND** *4 Liberty LIBTCD 27R* FEATURING DARRYL PANDY	40		2

FUNK D'VOID
Sweden, male producer (Lars Sandberg) **2**

Date	Title	Peak	Wks at No.1	Wks on Chart
20 Oct 01	**DIABLA** *Soma 112*	70		1
31 Jan 04	**EMOTIONAL CONTENT** *Soma 139R*	74		1

FUNK JUNKEEZ
US, male DJ/producer (Roger Sanchez). See El Mariachi **1**

Date	Title	Peak	Wks at No.1	Wks on Chart
21 Feb 98	**GOT FUNK** *Evocative EVOKE 1CDS*	57		1

FUNK MASTERS
UK, male producer – Tony Williams – with male/female vocal/instrumental collaborators **12**

Date	Title	Peak	Wks at No.1	Wks on Chart
18 Jun 83	**IT'S OVER** *Master Funk Records 7MP 004*	8		12

FUNKADELIC
US, male vocal/instrumental ensemble led by George Clinton **13**

Date	Title	Peak	Wks at No.1	Wks on Chart
9 Dec 78	**ONE NATION UNDER A GROOVE (PART 1)** *Warner Brothers K 17246*	9		12
21 Aug 99	**MOTHERSHIP RECONNECTION** *Virgin DINSD 185* SCOTT GROOVES FEATURING PARLIAMENT/FUNKADELIC	55		1

FUNKAPOLITAN
UK, male vocal/instrumental group **7**

Date	Title	Peak	Wks at No.1	Wks on Chart
22 Aug 81	**AS THE TIME GOES BY** *London LON 001*	41		7

FUNKDOOBIEST
US, male rap trio **6**

Date	Title	Peak	Wks at No.1	Wks on Chart
11 Dec 93	**WOPBABALUBOP** *Immortal 6597112*	37		4
5 Mar 94	**BOW WOW WOW** *Immortal 6594052*	34		2

FUNKERMAN

Holland, male DJ/producer (Ardie van Beek) — 1

Date	Title	Peak Position	Weeks at No.1	Weeks on Chart
3 May 08	**SPEED UP** *Defected DTTD180CDX*	55		1

FUNKSTAR DE LUXE

Denmark, male producer/instrumentalist (Matt Ottesen) — 18

Date	Title	Peak Position	Weeks at No.1	Weeks on Chart
25 Sep 99	**SUN IS SHINING** *Club Tools 0066895 CLU* BOB MARLEY VERSUS FUNKSTAR DE LUXE ●	3		10
22 Jan 00	**RAINBOW COUNTRY** *Club Tools 0067225 CLU* BOB MARLEY VERSUS FUNKSTAR DE LUXE	11		6
13 May 00	**WALKING IN THE NAME** *Club Tools 0067375 CLU* VS TERRY MAXX	42		1
25 Nov 00	**PULL UP TO THE BUMPER** *Club Tools 0120375 CLU* GRACE JONES VS FUNKSTAR DE LUXE	60		1

FUNKY CHOAD FEATURING NICK SKITZ

Australia/Italy, male vocal/production trio — 1

Date	Title	Peak Position	Weeks at No.1	Weeks on Chart
29 Aug 98	**THE ULTIMATE** *ffrr FCD 341*	51		1

FUNKY GREEN DOGS

US, male/female vocal/production trio. See Fog — 6

Date	Title	Peak Position	Weeks at No.1	Weeks on Chart
12 Apr 97	**FIRED UP!** *Twisted UK TWCD 10016*	17		3
28 Jun 97	**THE WAY** *Twisted UK TWCD 10026*	43		1
20 Jun 98	**UNTIL THE DAY** *Twisted UK TWCD 10034*	75		1
27 Feb 99	**BODY** *Twisted UK TWCD 110041*	46		1

FUNKY POETS

US, male vocal group — 1

Date	Title	Peak Position	Weeks at No.1	Weeks on Chart
7 May 94	**BORN IN THE GHETTO** *Epic 6603522*	72		1

FUNKY WORM

UK, vocal/instrumental/production group — 14

Date	Title	Peak Position	Weeks at No.1	Weeks on Chart
30 Jul 88	**HUSTLE! (TO THE MUSIC...)** *Fon 15*	13		8
26 Nov 88	**THE SPELL!** *Fon 16*	61		3
20 May 89	**U + ME = LOVE** *Fon 19*	46		3

FUREYS

Ireland, male vocal duo — 14

Date	Title	Peak Position	Weeks at No.1	Weeks on Chart
10 Oct 81	**WHEN YOU WERE SWEET SIXTEEN** *Ritz 003* WITH DAVEY ARTHUR	14		11
3 Apr 82	**I WILL LOVE YOU (EV'RY TIME WHEN WE ARE GONE)** *Ritz 012*	54		3

FURNITURE

UK, male/female vocal/instrumental group — 10

Date	Title	Peak Position	Weeks at No.1	Weeks on Chart
14 Jun 86	**BRILLIANT MIND** *Stiff BUY 251*	21		10

NELLY FURTADO

Canada, female vocalist/producer — 209

Date	Title	Peak Position	Weeks at No.1	Weeks on Chart
10 Mar 01	**I'M LIKE A BIRD** *DreamWorks 4509192* ●	5		16
1 Sep 01	**TURN OFF THE LIGHT** *DreamWorks DRMDM 50891*	4		10
19 Jan 02	**...ON THE RADIO (REMEMBER THE DAYS)** *DreamWorks DRMDM 50856*	18		6
20 Dec 03	**POWERLESS (SAY WHAT YOU WANT)** *DreamWorks 4504645*	13		10
27 Mar 04	**TRY** *DreamWorks 4505113*	15		7
24 Jul 04	**FORCA** *DreamWorks 9862823*	40		3
10 Jun 06	**MANEATER** *DreamWorks 9859585*	1	3	13
9 Sep 06	**PROMISCUOUS** *Geffen 1706030* FEATURING TIMBALAND ★	3		14
2 Dec 06	**ALL GOOD THINGS (COME TO AN END)** *Geffen 1714378*	4		19
10 Feb 07	**SAY IT RIGHT** *Polydor USUM70603368* ★	10		31
14 Apr 07	**GIVE IT TO ME** *Interscope 1732199* TIMBALAND FEATURING NELLY FURTADO & JUSTIN TIMBERLAKE ★	1	1	26
1 Dec 07	**DO IT** *Polydor USUM70603369*	75		1
29 Nov 08	**BROKEN STRINGS** *Polydor 1792152* JAMES MORRISON FEATURING NELLY FURTADO ●	2		31
8 Aug 09	**JUMP** *Atlantic AT0344CD* FLO RIDA FEATURING NELLY FURTADO	21		8
12 Dec 09	**MORNING AFTER DARK** *Interscope 2728036* TIMBALAND FEATURING SO SHY & NELLY FURTADO	6		14

BILLY FURY

UK, male vocalist/actor (Ronald Wycherley), d. 28 Jan 1983 (age 41). No Liverpool act had more hits in the 1960s than the early British rock 'n' roll idol, who spent longer on the chart without a No.1 than any other act — 281

Date	Title	Peak Position	Weeks at No.1	Weeks on Chart
27 Feb 59	**MAYBE TOMORROW** *Decca F 11102*	18		9
26 Jun 59	**MARGO** *Decca F 11128*	28		1
10 Mar 60	**COLETTE** *Decca F 11200*	9		10
26 May 60	**THAT'S LOVE** *Decca F 11237* WITH THE FOUR JAYS	19		11
22 Sep 60	**WONDROUS PLACE** *Decca F 11267*	25		9
19 Jan 61	**A THOUSAND STARS** *Decca F 11311*	14		10
27 Apr 61	**DON'T WORRY** *Decca F 11334* WITH THE FOUR KESTRELS	40		2
11 May 61	**HALFWAY TO PARADISE** *Decca F 11349*	3		23
7 Sep 61	**JEALOUSY** *Decca F 11384*	2		12
14 Dec 61	**I'D NEVER FIND ANOTHER YOU** *Decca F 11409*	5		15
15 Mar 62	**LETTER FULL OF TEARS** *Decca F 11437*	32		6
3 May 62	**LAST NIGHT WAS MADE FOR LOVE** *Decca F 11458*	4		16
19 Jul 62	**ONCE UPON A DREAM** *Decca F 11485*	7		13
25 Oct 62	**BECAUSE OF LOVE** *Decca F 11508*	18		14
14 Feb 63	**LIKE I'VE NEVER BEEN GONE** *Decca F 11582*	3		15
16 May 63	**WHEN WILL YOU SAY I LOVE YOU** *Decca F 11655*	3		12
25 Jul 63	**IN SUMMER** *Decca F 11701*	5		11
3 Oct 63	**SOMEBODY ELSE'S GIRL** *Decca F 11744*	18		7
2 Jan 64	**DO YOU REALLY LOVE ME TOO** *Decca F 11792*	13		10
30 Apr 64	**I WILL** *Decca F 11888*	14		12
23 Jul 64	**IT'S ONLY MAKE BELIEVE** *Decca F 11939*	10		10
14 Jan 65	**I'M LOST WITHOUT YOU** *Decca F 12048*	16		10
22 Jul 65	**IN THOUGHTS OF YOU** *Decca F 12178*	9		11
16 Sep 65	**RUN TO MY LOVIN' ARMS** *Decca F 12230*	25		7
10 Feb 66	**I'LL NEVER QUITE GET OVER YOU** *Decca F 12325*	35		5
4 Aug 66	**GIVE ME YOUR WORD** *Decca F 12459*	27		7
4 Sep 82	**LOVE OR MONEY** *Polydor POSP 488*	57		5
13 Nov 82	**DEVIL OR ANGEL** *Polydor POSP 528*	58		4
4 Jun 83	**FORGET HIM** *Polydor POSP 558*	59		4

FUSED

Sweden, male/female vocal/instrumental/production trio — 1

Date	Title	Peak Position	Weeks at No.1	Weeks on Chart
20 Mar 99	**THIS PARTY SUCKS!** *Columbia 6669302*	64		1

FUTURE BREEZE

Germany, male production duo. See 4Clubbers — 11

Date	Title	Peak Position	Weeks at No.1	Weeks on Chart
6 Sep 97	**WHY DON'T YOU DANCE WITH ME** *AM:PM 5823312*	50		1
20 Jan 01	**SMILE** *Nebula NEBCD 014*	67		1
13 Apr 02	**TEMPLE OF DREAMS** *Data 31CDS*	21		6
28 Dec 02	**OCEAN OF ETERNITY** *Data 44CD*	46		3

FUTURE FORCE

UK/US, male/female vocal/instrumental duo — 1

Date	Title	Peak Position	Weeks at No.1	Weeks on Chart
17 Aug 96	**WHAT YOU WANT** *AM:PM 5816592*	47		1

FUTURE SOUND OF LONDON

UK, male production/instrumental duo – Gary Cobain & Brian Dougans — 25

Date	Title	Peak Position	Weeks at No.1	Weeks on Chart
23 May 92	**PAPUA NEW GUINEA** *Jumpin' & Pumpin' TOT 17*	22		6
6 Nov 93	**CASCADE** *Virgin VSCDT 1478*	27		3
30 Jul 94	**EXPANDER** *Jumpin' & Pumpin' CDSTOR 37*	72		1
13 Aug 94	**LIFEFORMS** *Virgin VSCD 1484* F.S.O.L. VOCALS BY ELIZABETH FRASER	14		3
27 May 95	**FAR-OUT SON OF LUNG & THE RAMBLINGS OF A MADMAN** *Virgin VSCDT 1540*	22		3
26 Oct 96	**MY KINGDOM** *Virgin VSCDT 1605*	13		3
12 Apr 97	**WE HAVE EXPLOSIVE** *Virgin VSCDX 1616*	12		3
29 Sep 01	**PAPUA NEW GUINEA 2001** *Jumpin' & Pumpin' CDSTOT 44*	28		3

FUTUREHEADS

UK, male vocal/instrumental group – Barry & Dave Hyde, David 'Jaff' Craig & Ross Millard — 23

Date	Title	Peak Position	Weeks at No.1	Weeks on Chart
9 Aug 03	**FIRST DAY** *Fantastic Plastic FPS 036*	58		1
7 Aug 04	**DECENT DAYS AND NIGHTS** *679 679L080CD*	26		2
30 Oct 04	**MEANTIME** *679 Recordings 679L088CD*	49		1
5 Mar 05	**HOUNDS OF LOVE** *679 679L099CD2*	8		4
21 May 05	**DECENT DAYS AND NIGHTS** *679 Recordings 679L104CD2*	26		2
10 Dec 05	**AREA** *679 Recordings 679L117CD1*	18		3
3 Jun 06	**SKIP TO THE END** *679 679L128CD*	24		2
26 Aug 06	**WORRY ABOUT IT LATER** *679 679L137CD*	52		1
15 Mar 08	**THE BEGINNING OF THE TWIST** *Nul NUL101CD*	20		6
31 May 08	**RADIO HEART** *Nul NUL102CD*	65		1

FUTURESHOCK

UK, male vocal/production trio — Weeks on Chart: 3

Date	Title	Peak	Wks at No.1	Wks on Chart
15 Mar 03	**ON MY MIND** *Junior/Parlophone CDR 6595* FEATURING BEN ONONO	51		1
16 Aug 03	**PRIDE'S PARANOIA** *Parlophone CDR 6616*	60		1
1 Nov 03	**LATE AT NIGHT** *Parlophone CDR 6617*	73		1

FYA

UK, female vocal trio — Weeks on Chart: 9

Date	Title	Peak	Wks at No.1	Wks on Chart
13 Mar 04	**MUST BE LOVE** *Def Jam UK 9817508* FEATURING SMUJJI	13		7
24 Jul 04	**TOO HOT** *Def Jam 9867145*	49		2

ALI G & SHAGGY

UK, male comedian/rapper (Sacha Baron Cohen) & Jamaica, male vocalist (Orville Burrell) — Weeks on Chart: 14

Date	Title	Peak	Wks at No.1	Wks on Chart
23 Mar 02	**ME JULIE** *Island CID 793* ◯	2		14

ANDY G'S STARSKY & HUTCH ALL STARS

UK, male producer (Andros Georgiou) — Weeks on Chart: 1

Date	Title	Peak	Wks at No.1	Wks on Chart
3 Oct 98	**STARSKY & HUTCH – THE THEME** *Virgin VSCDT 1708*	51		1

BOBBY G

UK, male vocalist (Robert Gubby). See Bucks Fizz — Weeks on Chart: 12

Date	Title	Peak	Wks at No.1	Wks on Chart
1 Dec 84	**BIG DEAL** *BBC RESL 151*	65		6
19 Oct 85	**BIG DEAL** *BBC RESL 151*	46		6

GINA G

Australia, female vocalist (Gina Gardiner) — Weeks on Chart: 52

Date	Title	Peak	Wks at No.1	Wks on Chart
6 Apr 96	**OOH AAH...JUST A LITTLE BIT** *Eternal 041CD* ⊛	1	1	25
9 Nov 96	**I BELONG TO YOU** *Eternal 081CD*	6		11
22 Mar 97	**FRESH!** *Eternal 095CD*	6		7
7 Jun 97	**TI AMO** *Eternal 107CD1*	11		5
6 Sep 97	**GIMME SOME LOVE** *Eternal 101CD1*	25		2
15 Nov 97	**EVERY TIME I FALL** *Eternal 134CD*	52		1
14 Oct 06	**TONIGHT'S THE NIGHT** *Stuntgirl Music CDSTNT1*	57		1

KENNY G

US, male saxophonist (Kenny Gorelick) — Weeks on Chart: 26

Date	Title	Peak	Wks at No.1	Wks on Chart
21 Apr 84	**HI! HOW YA DOIN'?** *Arista ARIST 561*	70		3
30 Aug 86	**WHAT DOES IT TAKE (TO WIN YOUR LOVE)** *Arista ARIST 672*	64		2
4 Jul 87	**SONGBIRD** *Arista RIS 18*	22		7
9 May 92	**MISSING YOU NOW** *Columbia 6579917* MICHAEL BOLTON FEATURING KENNY G	28		4
24 Apr 93	**FOREVER IN LOVE** *Arista 74321145552*	47		3
17 Jul 93	**BY THE TIME THIS NIGHT IS OVER** *Arista 74321157142* WITH PEABO BRYSON	56		3
8 Nov 97	**HOW COULD AN ANGEL BREAK MY HEART** *LaFace 74321531982* TONI BRAXTON WITH KENNY G	22		4

WARREN G

US, male rapper (Warren Griffin) — Weeks on Chart: 60

Date	Title	Peak	Wks at No.1	Wks on Chart
23 Jul 94	**REGULATE** *Death Row A 8290CD* & NATE DOGG ◯	5		14
12 Nov 94	**THIS DJ** *RAL RALCD 1*	12		7
25 Mar 95	**DO YOU SEE** *RAL RALCD 3*	29		2
23 Nov 96	**WHAT'S LOVE GOT TO DO WITH IT** *Interscope IND 97008* FEATURING ADINA HOWARD	2		12
22 Feb 97	**I SHOT THE SHERIFF** *Def Jam DEFCD 31*	2		8
31 May 97	**SMOKIN' ME OUT** *Def Jam 5744432* FEATURING RONALD ISLEY	14		5
10 Jan 98	**PRINCE IGOR** *Def Jam 5749652* RHAPSODY FEATURING WARREN G & SISSEL	15		7
24 Jan 98	**ALL NIGHT ALL RIGHT** *Mushroom MUSH 21CD* PETER ANDRE FEATURING WARREN G	16		4
16 Mar 02	**LOOKIN' AT YOU** *Universal MCSTD 40275* FEATURING TOI	60		1

G-CLEFS

US, male vocal group — Weeks on Chart: 12

Date	Title	Peak	Wks at No.1	Wks on Chart
30 Nov 61	**I UNDERSTAND** *London HLU 9433*	17		12

G NATION FEATURING ROSIE

UK, male/female vocal/production trio — Weeks on Chart: 1

Date	Title	Peak	Wks at No.1	Wks on Chart
9 Aug 97	**FEEL THE NEED** *Cooltempo CDCOOL 327*	58		1

G-UNIT

US, male rap trio – 50 Cent* (Curtis Jackson), Lloyd Banks* (Christopher Lloyd) & Tony Yayo* (Marvin Bernard) — Weeks on Chart: 27

Date	Title	Peak	Wks at No.1	Wks on Chart
27 Dec 03	**STUNT 101** *Interscope 9815335*	25		7
6 Mar 04	**IF I CAN'T/THEM THANGS** *Interscope 9815279* 50 CENT/G-UNIT	10		8
17 Apr 04	**WANNA GET TO KNOW YA** *Interscope 9862268*	27		5
24 Apr 04	**RIDE WIT U/MORE & MORE** *Jive 82876609392* JOE FEATURING G-UNIT	12		7

G.O.S.H.

UK, male/female vocal charity ensemble — Weeks on Chart: 11

Date	Title	Peak	Wks at No.1	Wks on Chart
28 Nov 87	**THE WISHING WELL** *MBS GOSH 1*	22		11

GA GAS

UK, male vocal/instrumental group — Weeks on Chart: 1

Date	Title	Peak	Wks at No.1	Wks on Chart
12 Feb 05	**SEX** *Sanctuary SANXS328*	71		1

ERIC GABLE

US, male vocalist — Weeks on Chart: 1

Date	Title	Peak	Wks at No.1	Wks on Chart
19 Mar 94	**PROCESS OF ELMINATION** *Epic 6602282*	63		1

PETER GABRIEL

UK, male vocalist/multi-instrumentalist. See Genesis — Weeks on Chart: 114

Date	Title	Peak	Wks at No.1	Wks on Chart
9 Apr 77	**SOLSBURY HILL** *Charisma CB 301*	13		9
9 Feb 80	**GAMES WITHOUT FRONTIERS** *Charisma CB 354* ◯	4		11
10 May 80	**NO SELF CONTROL** *Charisma CB 360*	33		6
23 Aug 80	**BIKO** *Charisma CB 370*	38		3
25 Sep 82	**SHOCK THE MONKEY** *Charisma SHOCK 1*	58		5
9 Jul 83	**I DON'T REMEMBER** *Charisma GAB 1*	62		3
2 Jun 84	**WALK THROUGH THE FIRE** *Virgin VS 689*	69		3
26 Apr 86	**SLEDGEHAMMER** *Virgin PGS 1* ◯ ★	4		16
1 Nov 86	**DON'T GIVE UP** *Virgin PGS 2* & KATE BUSH	9		11
28 Mar 87	**BIG TIME** *Virgin PGS 3*	13		7
11 Jul 87	**RED RAIN** *Virgin PGS 4*	46		3
21 Nov 87	**BIKO (LIVE)** *Virgin PGS 6*	49		6
3 Jun 89	**SHAKING THE TREE** *Virgin VS 1167* YOUSSOU N'DOUR & PETER GABRIEL	61		3
22 Dec 90	**SOLSBURY HILL/SHAKING THE TREE** *Virgin VS 1322*	57		4
19 Sep 92	**DIGGING THE DIRT** *Realworld PGS 7*	24		4
16 Jan 93	**STEAM** *Realworld PGSDG 8*	10		7
3 Apr 93	**BLOOD OF EDEN** *Realworld PGSDG 9*	43		4
25 Sep 93	**KISS THAT FROG** *Realworld PGSDG 10*	46		3
25 Jun 94	**LOVETOWN** *Epic 6604802*	49		2
3 Sep 94	**SW LIVE EP** *Realworld PGSCD 11*	39		2
11 Jan 03	**MORE THAN THIS** *Realworld PGSCD 14*	47		2

GABRIELLA & TROY

US, female/male actors/vocal duo — Weeks on Chart: 2

Date	Title	Peak	Wks at No.1	Wks on Chart
6 Oct 07	**GOTTA GO MY OWN WAY** *Walt Disney USWD10732098*	40		2

GABRIELLE

UK, female vocalist (Louisa Gabrielle Bobb) — Weeks on Chart: 150

Date	Title	Peak	Wks at No.1	Wks on Chart
19 Jun 93	**DREAMS** *Go! Beat GODCD 99* ●	1	3	15
2 Oct 93	**GOING NOWHERE** *Go! Beat GODCD 106*	9		7
11 Dec 93	**I WISH** *Go! Beat GODCD 108*	26		5
26 Feb 94	**BECAUSE OF YOU** *Go! Beat GOLCD 109*	24		5
24 Feb 96	**GIVE ME A LITTLE MORE TIME** *Go! Beat GODCD 139* ◯	5		18
22 Jun 96	**FORGET ABOUT THE WORLD** *Go! Beat GOLCD 146*	23		5
5 Oct 96	**IF YOU REALLY CARED** *Go! Beat GODCD 153*	15		5
2 Nov 96	**IF YOU EVER** *London LONCD 388* EAST 17 FEATURING GABRIELLE ●	2		15
1 Feb 97	**WALK ON BY** *Go! Beat GODCD 159*	7		8
9 Oct 99	**SUNSHINE** *Go! Beat GOBCD 23*	9		8
5 Feb 00	**RISE** *Go! Beat GOLCD 25* ●	1	2	15
17 Jun 00	**WHEN A WOMAN** *Go! Beat GOLCD 27*	6		8
4 Nov 00	**SHOULD I STAY** *Go! Beat GOLCD 32*	13		7
21 Apr 01	**OUT OF REACH** *Go! Beat GOLCD 39* ◯	4		16
3 Nov 01	**DON'T NEED THE SUN TO SHINE (TO MAKE ME SMILE)** *Go! Beat GOLCD 47*	9		7
15 May 04	**STAY THE SAME** *Go! Beat 9866529*	20		3
14 Aug 04	**TEN YEARS TIME** *Go! Beat 9867550*	43		1
6 Oct 07	**WHY** *Polydor 1747463*	42		2

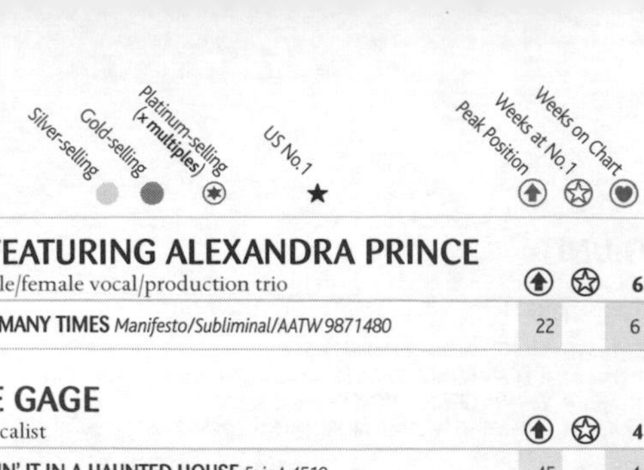

GADJO FEATURING ALEXANDRA PRINCE
Germany, male/female vocal/production trio

Date	Title	Peak Position	Weeks at No.1	Weeks on Chart
				6
28 May 05	**SO MANY TIMES** *Manifesto/Subliminal/AATW 9871480*	22		6

YVONNE GAGE
US, female vocalist

Date	Title	Peak Position	Weeks at No.1	Weeks on Chart
				4
16 Jun 84	**DOIN' IT IN A HAUNTED HOUSE** *Epic A 4519*	45		4

DANNI'ELLE GAHA
Australia, female vocalist

Date	Title	Peak Position	Weeks at No.1	Weeks on Chart
				7
1 Aug 92	**STUCK IN THE MIDDLE** *Epic 6581247*	68		2
27 Feb 93	**DO IT FOR LOVE** *Epic 6584612*	52		2
12 Jun 93	**SECRET LOVE** *Epic 6592212*	41		3

DAVE GAHAN
UK, male vocalist. See Depeche Mode

Date	Title	Peak Position	Weeks at No.1	Weeks on Chart
				7
7 Jun 03	**DIRTY STICKY FLOORS** *Mute LCDMUTE 294*	18		2
30 Aug 03	**I NEED YOU** *Mute LCDMUTE 301*	27		2
8 Nov 03	**BOTTLE LIVING** *Mute LCDMUTE 310*	36		2
20 Oct 07	**KINGDOM** *Mute LCDMUTE393*	44		1

BILLY & SARAH GAINES
US, male/female vocal duo

Date	Title	Peak Position	Weeks at No.1	Weeks on Chart
				1
14 Jun 97	**I FOUND SOMEONE** *Expansion CDEXP 27*	48		1

ROSIE GAINES
US, female vocalist. See Prince

Date	Title	Peak Position	Weeks at No.1	Weeks on Chart
				15
11 Nov 95	**I WANT U** *Motown 8604852*	70		1
31 May 97	**CLOSER THAN CLOSE** *Big Bang CDBBANG 1* ●	4		12
29 Nov 97	**I SURRENDER** *Big Bang CDBBANG 2*	39		2

GALA
Italy, female vocalist (Gala Rizzatto)

Date	Title	Peak Position	Weeks at No.1	Weeks on Chart
				24
19 Jul 97	**FREED FROM DESIRE** *Big Life BLRD 135* ●	2		14
6 Dec 97	**LET A BOY CRY** *Big Life BLRD 140*	11		8
22 Aug 98	**COME INTO MY LIFE** *Big Life BLRD 147*	38		2

EVE GALLAGHER
UK, female vocalist

Date	Title	Peak Position	Weeks at No.1	Weeks on Chart
				8
1 Dec 90	**LOVE COME DOWN** *More Protein PROT 6*	61		4
15 Apr 95	**YOU CAN HAVE IT ALL** *Cleveland City CLECD 13023*	43		2
28 Oct 95	**LOVE COME DOWN** *Cleveland City CLECD 13028*	57		1
6 Jul 96	**HEARTBREAK** *React CDREACT 78* MRS WOOD FEATURING EVE GALLAGHER	44		1

LIAM GALLAGHER
UK, male vocalist. See Oasis

Date	Title	Peak Position	Weeks at No.1	Weeks on Chart
				13
23 Oct 99	**CARNATION** *Ignition IGNSCD 16* & STEVE CRADDOCK	6		5
28 Dec 02	**SCORPIO RISING** *Concrete HARD 54CD* DEATH IN VEGAS FEATURING LIAM GALLAGHER	14		8

GALLAGHER & LYLE
UK, male vocal/instrumental duo – Benny Gallagher & Graham Lyle

Date	Title	Peak Position	Weeks at No.1	Weeks on Chart
				27
28 Feb 76	**I WANNA STAY WITH YOU** *A&M AMS 7211*	6		9
22 May 76	**HEART ON MY SLEEVE** *A&M AMS 7227*	6		10
11 Sep 76	**BREAKAWAY** *A&M AMS 7245*	35		4
29 Jan 77	**EVERY LITTLE TEARDROP** *A&M AMS 7274*	32		4

PATSY GALLANT
Canada, female vocalist

Date	Title	Peak Position	Weeks at No.1	Weeks on Chart
				9
10 Sep 77	**FROM NEW YORK TO LA** *EMI 2620*	6		9

GALLEON
France, male vocal/production trio

Date	Title	Peak Position	Weeks at No.1	Weeks on Chart
				2
20 Apr 02	**SO I BEGIN** *Epic 6724102*	36		2

LUKE GALLIANA
UK, male vocalist

Date	Title	Peak Position	Weeks at No.1	Weeks on Chart
				1
12 May 01	**TO DIE FOR** *Jive 9201272*	42		1

GALLIANO
UK, male/female vocal/instrumental group

Date	Title	Peak Position	Weeks at No.1	Weeks on Chart
				14
30 May 92	**SKUNK FUNK** *Talkin Loud TLK 23*	41		2
1 Aug 92	**PRINCE OF PEACE** *Talkin Loud TLK 24*	47		3
10 Oct 92	**JUS' REACH (RECYCLED)** *Talkin Loud TLK 29*	66		2
28 May 94	**LONG TIME GONE** *Talkin Loud TLKCD 48*	15		3
30 Jul 94	**TWYFORD DOWN** *Talkin Loud TLKDD 49*	37		2
27 Jul 96	**EASE YOUR MIND** *Talkin Loud TLKDD 10*	45		2

GALLOWS
UK, male vocal/instrumental group

Date	Title	Peak Position	Weeks at No.1	Weeks on Chart
				3
29 Sep 07	**IN THE BELLY OF A SHARK** *Warner Brothers WEA425CD*	56		1
1 Dec 07	**STARING AT THE RUDE BOIS** *Warner Brothers WEA435CD*	31		2

JAMES GALWAY
UK, male flautist

Date	Title	Peak Position	Weeks at No.1	Weeks on Chart
				13
27 May 78	**ANNIE'S SONG** *RCA Red Seal RB 5085*	3		13

GAMBAFREAKS
Italy, male production duo

Date	Title	Peak Position	Weeks at No.1	Weeks on Chart
				2
12 Sep 98	**INSTANT REPLAY** *Evocative EVOKE 7CDS* FEATURING PACO RIVAZ	57		1
13 May 00	**DOWN DOWN DOWN** *Azuli AZNYCDX 116*	57		1

GAME
US, male rapper (Jayceon Taylor). See G-Unit

Date	Title	Peak Position	Weeks at No.1	Weeks on Chart
				55
26 Feb 05	**HOW WE DO** *Interscope 9880361* FEATURING 50 CENT	5		12
21 May 05	**HATE IT OR LOVE IT** *Interscope 9882205* FEATURING 50 CENT	4		13
13 Aug 05	**DREAMS** *Interscope 9883713*	8		8
10 Sep 05	**PLAYA'S ONLY** *Jive 82876725552* R KELLY FEATURING GAME	33		2
19 Nov 05	**PUT YOU ON THE GAME** *Interscope 9887827*	46		2
4 Nov 06	**IT'S OKAY** *Geffen 1713921* FEATURING JUNIOR REID	26		6
20 Jan 07	**LET'S RIDE** *Geffen 1718917*	42		2
27 Sep 08	**MY LIFE** *Geffen 1788570* FEATURING LIL WAYNE	34		7
24 Jan 09	**CAMERA PHONE** *Geffen 1795606* FEATURING NE-YO	48		3

GANG OF FOUR
UK, male vocal/instrumental group

Date	Title	Peak Position	Weeks at No.1	Weeks on Chart
				5
16 Jun 79	**AT HOME HE'S A TOURIST** *EMI 2956*	58		3
22 May 82	**I LOVE A MAN IN UNIFORM** *EMI 5299*	65		2

GANG STARR
US, male rap/production duo

Date	Title	Peak Position	Weeks at No.1	Weeks on Chart
				8
13 Oct 90	**JAZZ THING** *CBS 6563777*	66		2
23 Feb 91	**TAKE A REST** *Cooltempo COOL 230*	63		1
25 May 91	**LOVESICK** *Cooltempo COOL 234*	50		3
13 Jun 92	**2 DEEP** *Cooltempo COOL 256*	67		2

GANT
UK, male production duo

Date	Title	Peak Position	Weeks at No.1	Weeks on Chart
				1
27 Dec 97	**SOUND BWOY BURIAL/ALL NIGHT LONG** *Positiva CDTIV 85*	67		1

GAP BAND
US, male vocal/instrumental trio – Charlie, Robert, d. 16 Aug 2010, & Ronnie Wilson

Date	Title	Peak Position	Weeks at No.1	Weeks on Chart
				88
12 Jul 80	**OOPS UPSIDE YOUR HEAD** *Mercury MER 22* ●	6		14
27 Sep 80	**PARTY LIGHTS** *Mercury MER 37*	30		8
27 Dec 80	**BURN RUBBER ON ME (WHY YOU WANNA HURT ME)** *Mercury MER 52*	22		11
11 Apr 81	**HUMPIN'** *Mercury MER 63*	36		6
27 Jun 81	**YEARNING FOR YOUR LOVE** *Mercury MER 73*	47		4
5 Jun 82	**EARLY IN THE MORNING** *Mercury MER 97*	55		3
19 Feb 83	**OUTSTANDING** *Total Experience TE 001*	68		2
31 Mar 84	**SOMEDAY** *Total Experience TE 5*	17		8
23 Jun 84	**JAMMIN' IN AMERICA** *Total Experience TE 6*	64		2
13 Dec 86	**BIG FUN** *Total Experience FB 49779*	4		12

Legend: ○ Silver-selling · ● Gold-selling · ⊛ Platinum-selling (x multiples) · ★ US No.1 · Peak Position · Weeks at No.1 · Weeks on Chart

Date	Title	Peak Position	Weeks at No.1	Weeks on Chart
14 Mar 87	**HOW MUSIC CAME ABOUT (BOP B DA B DA DA)** *Total Experience FB 49755*	61		2
11 Jul 87	**OOPS UPSIDE YOUR HEAD (REMIX)** *Club JAB 54*	20		8
18 Feb 89	**I'M GONNA GET YOU SUCKA** *Arista 112016*	63		2
16 Oct 04	**OOPS UPSIDE YOUR HEAD** *All Around The World CDGLOBE376* DJ CASPER FEATURING THE GAP BAND	16		6

GARBAGE

UK/US, female/male vocal/instrumental group – Shirley Manson, Duke Erikson, Steve Marker & Butch Vig — **75**

Date	Title	Peak Position	Weeks at No.1	Weeks on Chart
19 Aug 95	**SUBHUMAN** *Mushroom D 1138*	50		1
30 Sep 95	**ONLY HAPPY WHEN IT RAINS** *Mushroom D 1199*	29		3
2 Dec 95	**QUEER** *Mushroom D 1237*	13		4
23 Mar 96	**STUPID GIRL** *Mushroom D 1271*	4		7
23 Nov 96	**MILK** *Mushroom D 1494* FEATURING TRICKY	10		8
9 May 98	**PUSH IT** *Mushroom MUSH 28CDS*	9		5
18 Jul 98	**I THINK I'M PARANOID** *Mushroom MUSH 35CDS*	9		5
17 Oct 98	**SPECIAL** *Mushroom MUSH 39CDS*	15		4
6 Feb 99	**WHEN I GROW UP** *Mushroom MUSH 43CDS*	9		7
5 Jun 99	**YOU LOOK SO FINE** *Mushroom MUSH 49CDS*	19		4
27 Nov 99	**THE WORLD IS NOT ENOUGH** *Radioactive RAXTD 40*	11		9
6 Oct 01	**ANDROGYNY** *Mushroom MUSH 94CDSX*	24		2
2 Feb 02	**CHERRY LIPS (GO BABY GO)** *Mushroom MUSH 98CDS*	22		4
20 Apr 02	**BREAKING UP THE GIRL** *Mushroom MUSH 101CDS*	27		2
5 Oct 02	**SHUT YOUR MOUTH** *Mushroom MUSH 106CDSXX*	20		1
16 Apr 05	**WHY DO YOU LOVE ME** *Warner Brothers WEA385CD*	7		6
25 Jun 05	**SEX IS NOT THE ENEMY** *Mushroom WEA391CD*	24		2
28 Jul 07	**TELL ME WHERE IT HURTS** *Warner Brothers WEA424CD*	50		1

ADAM GARCIA

Australia, male vocalist — **5**

Date	Title	Peak Position	Weeks at No.1	Weeks on Chart
16 May 98	**NIGHT FEVER** *Polydor 5697972*	15		5

SCOTT GARCIA FEATURING MC STYLES

UK, male rap/production duo. See Corrupted Cru featuring MC Neat — **3**

Date	Title	Peak Position	Weeks at No.1	Weeks on Chart
1 Nov 97	**A LONDON THING** *Connected CDCONNECT 1*	29		3

BORIS GARDINER

Jamaica, male vocalist/bass guitarist — **38**

Date	Title	Peak Position	Weeks at No.1	Weeks on Chart
17 Jan 70	**ELIZABETHAN REGGAE** *Duke DU 39*	14		14
26 Jul 86	**I WANT TO WAKE UP WITH YOU** *Revue REV 733* ●	1	3	15
4 Oct 86	**YOU'RE EVERYTHING TO ME** *Revue REV 735*	11		8
27 Dec 86	**THE MEANING OF CHRISTMAS** *Revue REV 740*	69		1

PAUL GARDINER

UK, male bass player, d. 4 Feb 1984 (age 25) — **4**

Date	Title	Peak Position	Weeks at No.1	Weeks on Chart
25 Jul 81	**STORMTROOPER IN DRAG** *Beggars Banquet BEG 61*	49		4

ALEX GARDNER

UK, male vocalist — **1**

Date	Title	Peak Position	Weeks at No.1	Weeks on Chart
10 Apr 10	**I'M NOT MAD** *A&M 2734950*	44		1+

ART GARFUNKEL

US, male vocalist/guitarist. See Simon & Garfunkel — **37**

Date	Title	Peak Position	Weeks at No.1	Weeks on Chart
13 Sep 75	**I ONLY HAVE EYES FOR YOU** *CBS 3575* ○	1	2	11
3 Mar 79	**BRIGHT EYES** *CBS 6947* ⊛	1	6	19
7 Jul 79	**SINCE I DON'T HAVE YOU** *CBS 7371*	38		7

JUDY GARLAND

US, female vocalist/actor (Frances Gumm), d. 22 Jun 1969 (age 47) — **2**

Date	Title	Peak Position	Weeks at No.1	Weeks on Chart
10 Jun 55	**THE MAN THAT GOT AWAY** *Philips PB 366*	18		2

JESSICA GARLICK

UK, female vocalist — **6**

Date	Title	Peak Position	Weeks at No.1	Weeks on Chart
25 May 02	**COME BACK** *Columbia 6725662*	13		6

LAURENT GARNIER

France, male DJ/producer — **4**

Date	Title	Peak Position	Weeks at No.1	Weeks on Chart
15 Feb 97	**CRISPY BACON** *F Communications F 055CD*	60		1
22 Apr 00	**MAN WITH THE RED FACE** *F Communications F 119CD*	65		1
11 Nov 00	**GREED/THE MAN WITH THE RED FACE** *F Communications F127 CDUK*	36		2

LEE GARRETT

US, male vocalist — **7**

Date	Title	Peak Position	Weeks at No.1	Weeks on Chart
29 May 76	**YOU'RE MY EVERYTHING** *Chrysalis CHS 2087*	15		7

LEIF GARRETT

US, male vocalist — **14**

Date	Title	Peak Position	Weeks at No.1	Weeks on Chart
20 Jan 79	**I WAS MADE FOR DANCIN'** *Scotti Brothers K 11202* ○	4		10
21 Apr 79	**FEEL THE NEED** *Scotti Brothers K 11274*	38		4

LESLEY GARRETT & AMANDA THOMPSON

UK, female vocal/instrumental duo — **10**

Date	Title	Peak Position	Weeks at No.1	Weeks on Chart
6 Nov 93	**AVE MARIA** *Internal Affairs KGBD 012*	16		10

SIEDAH GARRETT

US, female vocalist. See Brand New Heavies, Michael Jackson — **19**

Date	Title	Peak Position	Weeks at No.1	Weeks on Chart
24 Mar 84	**DON'T LOOK ANY FURTHER** *Gordy TMG 1334* DENNIS EDWARDS FEATURING SIEDAH GARRETT	45		5
20 Jun 87	**DON'T LOOK ANY FURTHER** *Gordy TMG 1334* DENNIS EDWARDS FEATURING SIEDAH GARRETT	55		5
13 Jan 07	**RAIN DOWN LOVE** *Loaded LOAD116CD* FREEMASONS FEATURING SIEDAH GARRETT	12		9

DAVID GARRICK

UK, male vocalist (Philip Core) — **16**

Date	Title	Peak Position	Weeks at No.1	Weeks on Chart
9 Jun 66	**LADY JANE** *Piccadilly 7N 35317*	28		7
22 Sep 66	**DEAR MRS APPLEBEE** *Piccadilly 7N 35335*	22		9

GARY GO

UK, male vocalist/producer (Gary Baker) — **3**

Date	Title	Peak Position	Weeks at No.1	Weeks on Chart
28 Feb 09	**WONDERFUL** *Decca 4781659*	25		3

GARY'S GANG

US, male vocal/instrumental group – Eric Matthews, Bill Catalano, Bob Forman, Al Lauricella, Jay Leon, Rino Minetti & Gary Turnier — **18**

Date	Title	Peak Position	Weeks at No.1	Weeks on Chart
24 Feb 79	**KEEP ON DANCIN'** *CBS 7109*	8		10
2 Jun 79	**LET'S LOVE DANCE TONIGHT** *CBS 7328*	49		4
6 Nov 82	**KNOCK ME OUT** *Arista ARIST 499*	45		4

GAT DECOR

UK, male producer (Simon Slater) — **10**

Date	Title	Peak Position	Weeks at No.1	Weeks on Chart
16 May 92	**PASSION** *Effective EFFS 1*	29		4
9 Mar 96	**PASSION** *Way Of Life WAYDA 1*	6		6

STEPHEN GATELY

Ireland, male vocalist, d. 10 Oct 2009 (age 33). See Boyzone — **19**

Date	Title	Peak Position	Weeks at No.1	Weeks on Chart
10 Jun 00	**NEW BEGINNING/BRIGHT EYES** *A&M 5618202* ○	3		11
14 Oct 00	**I BELIEVE** *Polydor 5877482*	11		4
12 May 01	**STAY** *A&M 5870672*	13		4

DAVID GATES

US, male vocalist. See Bread — **2**

Date	Title	Peak Position	Weeks at No.1	Weeks on Chart
22 Jul 78	**TOOK THE LAST TRAIN** *Elektra K 12307*	50		2

GARETH GATES

UK, male vocalist — **113**

Date	Title	Peak Position	Weeks at No.1	Weeks on Chart
30 Mar 02	**UNCHAINED MELODY** *S 74321930882* ⊛x2	1	4	30
20 Jul 02	**ANYONE OF US (STUPID MISTAKE)** *S 74321950602* ●	1	3	15
5 Oct 02	**THE LONG AND WINDING ROAD/SUSPICIOUS MINDS** *S 74321965972* WILL YOUNG & GARETH GATES/GARETH GATES ●	1	2	18
21 Dec 02	**WHAT MY HEART WANTS TO SAY** *S 74321985602*	5		13
22 Mar 03	**SPIRIT IN THE SKY** *S 82876511202* FEATURING THE KUMARS ⊛	1	2	15
20 Sep 03	**SUNSHINE** *S 82876560042*	3		10
13 Dec 03	**SAY IT ISN'T SO** *S 82876583422*	4		8
21 Apr 07	**CHANGES** *19 1721080*	14		2
30 Jun 07	**ANGEL ON MY SHOULDER** *19 1736009*	22		2

ALEX GAUDINO

Italy, male DJ/producer (Alessandro Gaudino) — Weeks on Chart: 25

Date	Title	Peak Position	Weeks at No.1	Weeks on Chart
24 Mar 07	**DESTINATION CALABRIA** *Data DATA153CDS* FEATURING CRYSTAL WATERS	4		20
14 Jun 08	**WATCH OUT** *Data DATA190CDS* FEATURING SHENA	16		5

GAY DAD

UK, male/female vocal/instrumental group – Cliff Jones, Nicholas 'Baz' Crowe, Nigel Hoyle, James Riseboro & Charley Stone — Weeks on Chart: 10

Date	Title	Peak Position	Weeks at No.1	Weeks on Chart
30 Jan 99	**TO EARTH WITH LOVE** *London LONCD 413*	10		4
5 Jun 99	**JOY!** *London LONCD 428*	22		3
14 Aug 99	**OH JIM** *London LONCD 437*	47		1
31 Mar 01	**NOW ALWAYS AND FOREVER** *B Unique BUN 004CD*	41		1
22 Sep 01	**TRANSMISSION** *B Unique BUN 009CDX*	58		1

GAY GORDON & THE MINCE PIES

UK, male/female vocal/production group — Weeks on Chart: 5

Date	Title	Peak Position	Weeks at No.1	Weeks on Chart
6 Dec 86	**THE ESSENTIAL WALLY PARTY MEDLEY** *Lifestyle XY 2*	60		5

MARVIN GAYE

US, male vocalist, d. 1 Apr 1984 (age 44) — Weeks on Chart: 202

Date	Title	Peak Position	Weeks at No.1	Weeks on Chart
30 Jul 64	**ONCE UPON A TIME** *Stateside SS 316* & MARY WELLS	50		1
10 Dec 64	**HOW SWEET IT IS** *Stateside SS 360*	49		1
29 Sep 66	**LITTLE DARLIN'** *Tamla Motown TMG 574*	50		1
26 Jan 67	**IT TAKES TWO** *Tamla Motown TMG 590* & KIM WESTON	16		11
17 Jan 68	**IF I COULD BUILD MY WHOLE WORLD AROUND YOU** *Tamla Motown TMG 635* & TAMMI TERRELL	41		7
12 Jun 68	**AIN'T NOTHING LIKE THE REAL THING** *Tamla Motown TMG 655* & TAMMI TERRELL	34		7
2 Oct 68	**YOU'RE ALL I NEED TO GET BY** *Tamla Motown TMG 668* & TAMMI TERRELL	19		19
22 Jan 69	**YOU AIN'T LIVIN' TILL YOU'RE LOVIN'** *Tamla Motown TMG 681* & TAMMI TERRELL	21		8
12 Feb 69	**I HEARD IT THROUGH THE GRAPEVINE** *Tamla Motown TMG 686* ★	1	3	15
4 Jun 69	**GOOD LOVIN' AIN'T EASY TO COME BY** *Tamla Motown TMG 697* & TAMMI TERRELL	26		8
23 Jul 69	**TOO BUSY THINKING ABOUT MY BABY** *Tamla Motown TMG 705*	5		16
15 Nov 69	**ONION SONG** *Tamla Motown TMG 715* & TAMMI TERRELL	9		12
9 May 70	**ABRAHAM MARTIN AND JOHN** *Tamla Motown TMG 734*	9		14
11 Dec 71	**SAVE THE CHILDREN** *Tamla Motown TMG 796*	41		6
22 Sep 73	**LET'S GET IT ON** *Tamla Motown TMG 868* ★	31		7
23 Mar 74	**YOU ARE EVERYTHING** *Tamla Motown TMG 890* DIANA ROSS & MARVIN GAYE ○	5		12
20 Jul 74	**STOP LOOK LISTEN (TO YOUR HEART)** *Tamla Motown TMG 906* DIANA ROSS & MARVIN GAYE	25		8
7 May 77	**GOT TO GIVE IT UP** *Motown TMG 1069* ★	7		10
24 Feb 79	**POPS WE LOVE YOU** *Motown TMG 1136* DIANA ROSS, MARVIN GAYE, SMOKEY ROBINSON & STEVIE WONDER	66		5
30 Oct 82	**(SEXUAL) HEALING** *CBS A 2855* ○	4		14
8 Jan 83	**MY LOVE IS WAITING** *CBS A 3048*	34		5
18 May 85	**SANCTIFIED LADY** *CBS A 4894*	51		4
26 Apr 86	**I HEARD IT THROUGH THE GRAPEVINE** *Tamla Motown ZB 40701*	8		8
14 May 94	**LUCKY LUCKY ME** *Motown TMGCD 1426*	67		1
6 Oct 01	**MUSIC** *Polydor 4976222* ERICK SERMON FEATURING MARVIN GAYE	36		2

GAYE BYKERS ON ACID

UK, male vocal/instrumental group — Weeks on Chart: 2

Date	Title	Peak Position	Weeks at No.1	Weeks on Chart
31 Oct 87	**GIT DOWN (SHAKE YOUR THANG)** *Purple Fluid VS 1008*	54		2

CRYSTAL GAYLE

US, female vocalist (Brenda Gail Webb) — Weeks on Chart: 28

Date	Title	Peak Position	Weeks at No.1	Weeks on Chart
12 Nov 77	**DON'T IT MAKE MY BROWN EYES BLUE** *United Artists UP 36307* ○	5		14
26 Aug 78	**TALKING IN YOUR SLEEP** *United Artists UP 36422* ○	11		14

MICHELLE GAYLE

UK, female vocalist/actor. See Childliners — Weeks on Chart: 52

Date	Title	Peak Position	Weeks at No.1	Weeks on Chart
7 Aug 93	**LOOKING UP** *RCA 74321154532*	11		6
24 Sep 94	**SWEETNESS** *RCA 74321230192* ○	4		16
17 Dec 94	**I'LL FIND YOU** *RCA 74321247762*	26		7
27 May 95	**FREEDOM** *RCA 74321284692*	16		6
26 Aug 95	**HAPPY JUST TO BE WITH YOU** *RCA 74321302692*	11		7
8 Feb 97	**DO YOU KNOW** *RCA 74321419282*	6		6
26 Apr 97	**SENSATIONAL** *RCA 74321419302*	14		4

GAYLE & GILLIAN

Australia, female vocal/acting duo — Weeks on Chart: 2

Date	Title	Peak Position	Weeks at No.1	Weeks on Chart
3 Jul 93	**MAD IF YA DON'T** *Mushroom CDMUSH 1*	75		1
19 Mar 94	**WANNA BE YOUR LOVER** *Mushroom D 11598*	62		1

GLORIA GAYNOR

US, female vocalist (Gloria Fowles) — Weeks on Chart: 73

Date	Title	Peak Position	Weeks at No.1	Weeks on Chart
7 Dec 74	**NEVER CAN SAY GOODBYE** *MGM 2006 463* ○	2		13
8 Mar 75	**REACH OUT I'LL BE THERE** *MGM 2006 499*	14		8
9 Aug 75	**ALL I NEED IS YOUR SWEET LOVIN'** *MGM 2006 531*	44		3
17 Jan 76	**HOW HIGH THE MOON** *MGM 2006 558*	33		4
3 Feb 79	**I WILL SURVIVE** *Polydor 2095 017* ● ★	1	4	15
6 Oct 79	**LET ME KNOW (I HAVE THE RIGHT)** *Polydor STEP 5*	32		7
24 Dec 83	**I AM WHAT I AM (FROM 'LA CAGE AUX FOLLES')** *Chrysalis CHS 2765*	13		12
26 Jun 93	**I WILL SURVIVE (REMIX)** *Polydor PZCD 270*	5		10
3 Jun 00	**LAST NIGHT** *Logic 74321738082*	67		1

GAZ

US, male vocal/instrumental group — Weeks on Chart: 4

Date	Title	Peak Position	Weeks at No.1	Weeks on Chart
24 Feb 79	**SING SING** *Salsoul SSOL 116*	60		4

GAZZA

UK, male vocalist/footballer (Paul Gascoigne) — Weeks on Chart: 14

Date	Title	Peak Position	Weeks at No.1	Weeks on Chart
10 Nov 90	**FOG ON THE TYNE (REVISITED)** *Best ZB 44083* & LINDISFARNE	2		9
22 Dec 90	**GEORDIE BOYS (GAZZA RAP)** *Best ZB 44229*	31		5

GBH

UK, male vocal/instrumental group — Weeks on Chart: 5

Date	Title	Peak Position	Weeks at No.1	Weeks on Chart
6 Feb 82	**NO SURVIVORS** *Clay 8*	63		2
20 Nov 82	**GIVE ME FIRE** *Clay 16*	69		3

NIGEL GEE

UK, male producer — Weeks on Chart: 1

Date	Title	Peak Position	Weeks at No.1	Weeks on Chart
27 Jan 01	**HOOTIN'** *Neo NEOCD 040*	57		1

J GEILS BAND

US, male vocal/instrumental group – Peter Wolf, Stephen Jo Bladd, Jerome Geils, Seth Justman, Danny Klein & Richard Salwitz — Weeks on Chart: 20

Date	Title	Peak Position	Weeks at No.1	Weeks on Chart
9 Jun 79	**ONE LAST KISS** *EMI America AM 507*	74		1
13 Feb 82	**CENTERFOLD** *EMI America EA 135* ○ ★	3		9
10 Apr 82	**FREEZE-FRAME** *EMI America EA 134*	27		7
26 Jun 82	**ANGEL IN BLUE** *EMI America EA 138*	55		3

PETER GELDERBLOM

Holland, male DJ/producer — Weeks on Chart: 3

Date	Title	Peak Position	Weeks at No.1	Weeks on Chart
8 Dec 07	**WAITING 4** *Data DATA171CDS*	29		3

BOB GELDOF

Ireland, male vocalist. See Boomtown Rats — Weeks on Chart: 15

Date	Title	Peak Position	Weeks at No.1	Weeks on Chart
1 Nov 86	**THIS IS THE WORLD CALLING** *Mercury BOB 101*	25		5
21 Feb 87	**LOVE LIKE A ROCKET** *Mercury BOB 102*	61		3
23 Jun 90	**THE GREAT SONG OF INDIFFERENCE** *Mercury BOB 104*	15		6
7 May 94	**CRAZY** *Vertigo VERCX 85*	65		1

GEMINI

UK, male vocal duo. See Childliners — Weeks on Chart: 7

Date	Title	Peak Position	Weeks at No.1	Weeks on Chart
30 Sep 95	**EVEN THOUGH YOU BROKE MY HEART** *EMI CDEMS 391*	40		3
10 Feb 96	**STEAL YOUR LOVE AWAY** *EMI CDEMS 407*	37		2
29 Jun 96	**COULD IT BE FOREVER** *EMI CDEM 426*	38		2

GEMS FOR JEM

UK, male instrumental/production duo. See JDS — Weeks on Chart: 2

Date	Title	Peak Position	Weeks at No.1	Weeks on Chart
6 May 95	**LIFTING ME HIGHER** *Box 21 CDSBOK 3*	28		2

GENE
UK, male vocal/instrumental group — 23

Date	Title	Peak Position	Weeks at No.1	Weeks on Chart
13 Aug 94	**BE MY LIGHT BE MY GUIDE** *Costermonger COST 002CD*	54		1
12 Nov 94	**SLEEP WELL TONIGHT** *Costermonger COST 003CD*	36		2
4 Mar 95	**HAUNTED BY YOU** *Costermonger COST 004CD*	32		2
22 Jul 95	**OLYMPIAN** *Costermonger COST 005CD*	18		2
13 Jan 96	**FOR THE DEAD** *Costermonger COST 006CD*	14		3
2 Nov 96	**FIGHTING FIT** *Polydor COST 9CD*	22		2
1 Feb 97	**WE COULD BE KINGS** *Polydor COSCD 10*	17		2
10 May 97	**WHERE ARE THEY NOW?** *Polydor COSCD 11*	22		2
9 Aug 97	**SPEAK TO ME SOMEONE** *Polydor COSCD 12*	30		2
27 Feb 99	**AS GOOD AS IT GETS** *Polydor COSCD 14*	23		2
24 Apr 99	**FILL HER UP** *Polydor COSCD 15*	36		2
25 Dec 04	**LET ME MOVE ON** *Costermonger COST10CD1*	69		1

GENE AND JIM ARE INTO SHAKES
UK, male production/vocal duo — 2

Date	Title	Peak Position	Weeks at No.1	Weeks on Chart
19 Mar 88	**SHAKE! (HOW ABOUT A SAMPLING GENE)** *Rough Trade RT 216*	68		2

GENE LOVES JEZEBEL
UK, male vocal/instrumental group — 7

Date	Title	Peak Position	Weeks at No.1	Weeks on Chart
29 Mar 86	**SWEETEST THING** *Beggars Banquet BEG 156*	75		1
14 Jun 86	**HEARTACHE** *Beggars Banquet BEG 161*	71		2
5 Sep 87	**THE MOTION OF LOVE** *Beggars Banquet BEG 192*	56		3
5 Dec 87	**GORGEOUS** *Beggars Banquet BEG 202*	68		1

GENERAL LEVY
UK, male vocalist (Paul Levy) — 14

Date	Title	Peak Position	Weeks at No.1	Weeks on Chart
4 Sep 93	**MONKEY MAN** *ffrr FCD 214*	75		1
18 Jun 94	**INCREDIBLE** *Renk 42CD* M-BEAT FEATURING GENERAL LEVY	39		3
10 Sep 94	**INCREDIBLE (REMIX)** *Renk CDRENK 44* M-BEAT FEATURING GENERAL LEVY	8		9
13 Mar 04	**SHAKE (WHAT YA MAMA GAVE YA)** *East West EW281CD* VS ZEUS	51		1

GENERAL PUBLIC
UK, male vocal/instrumental group. See Beat — 4

Date	Title	Peak Position	Weeks at No.1	Weeks on Chart
10 Mar 84	**GENERAL PUBLIC** *Virgin VS 659*	60		3
2 Jul 94	**I'LL TAKE YOU THERE** *Epic 6605532*	73		1

GENERAL SAINT
UK, male vocalist (Winston Hislop) — 9

Date	Title	Peak Position	Weeks at No.1	Weeks on Chart
29 Sep 84	**LAST PLANE (ONE WAY TICKET)** *MCA 910* CLINT EASTWOOD & GENERAL SAINT	51		3
2 Apr 94	**OH CAROL!** *Copasetic COPCD 0009* CLINT EASTWOOD & GENERAL SAINT	54		5
6 Aug 94	**SAVE THE LAST DANCE FOR ME** *Copasetic COPCD 12* FEATURING DON CAMPBELL	75		1

GENERATION X
UK, male vocal/instrumental group — 31

Date	Title	Peak Position	Weeks at No.1	Weeks on Chart
17 Sep 77	**YOUR GENERATION** *Chrysalis CHS 2165*	36		4
11 Mar 78	**READY STEADY GO** *Chrysalis CHS 2207*	47		3
20 Jan 79	**KING ROCKER** *Chrysalis CHS 2261*	11		9
7 Apr 79	**VALLEY OF THE DOLLS** *Chrysalis CHS 2310*	23		7
30 Jun 79	**FRIDAY'S ANGELS** *Chrysalis CHS 2330*	62		2
18 Oct 80	**DANCING WITH MYSELF** *Chrysalis CHS 2444* GEN X	62		2
24 Jan 81	**DANCING WITH MYSELF (EP)** *Chrysalis CHS 2488* GEN X	60		4

GENERATOR
Holland, male producer (Robert Smit). See Starparty — 1

Date	Title	Peak Position	Weeks at No.1	Weeks on Chart
23 Oct 99	**WHERE ARE YOU NOW?** *Tidy Trax TIDY 130CD*	60		1

GENESIS
UK, male vocal/instrumental group – Peter Gabriel* (replaced by Phil Collins*, left 1996), Tony Banks*, Steve Hackett* & Mike Rutherford — 187

Date	Title	Peak Position	Weeks at No.1	Weeks on Chart
6 Apr 74	**I KNOW WHAT I LIKE (IN YOUR WARDROBE)** *Charisma CB 224*	21		7
26 Feb 77	**YOUR OWN SPECIAL WAY** *Charisma CB 300*	43		3
28 May 77	**SPOT THE PIGEON EP** *Charisma GEN 001*	14		7
11 Mar 78	**FOLLOW YOU FOLLOW ME** *Charisma CB 309* ●	7		13
8 Jul 78	**MANY TOO MANY** *Charisma CB 315*	43		5
15 Mar 80	**TURN IT ON AGAIN** *Charisma CB 356*	8		10
17 May 80	**DUCHESS** *Charisma CB 363*	46		5
13 Sep 80	**MISUNDERSTANDING** *Charisma CB 369*	42		5
22 Aug 81	**ABACAB** *Charisma CB 388*	9		8
31 Oct 81	**KEEP IT DARK** *Charisma CB 391*	33		4
13 Mar 82	**MAN ON THE CORNER** *Charisma CB 393*	41		5
22 May 82	**3 X 3 EP** *Charisma GEN 1*	10		8
3 Sep 83	**MAMA** *Virgin/Charisma MAMA 1* ●	4		10
12 Nov 83	**THAT'S ALL** *Charisma/Virgin TATA 1*	16		11
11 Feb 84	**ILLEGAL ALIEN** *Charisma/Virgin AL 1*	46		4
31 May 86	**INVISIBLE TOUCH** *Virgin GENS 1*	15		8
30 Aug 86	**IN TOO DEEP** *Virgin GENS 2*	19		9
22 Nov 86	**LAND OF CONFUSION** *Virgin GENS 3*	14		12
14 Mar 87	**TONIGHT TONIGHT TONIGHT** *Virgin GENS 4*	18		6
20 Jun 87	**THROWING IT ALL AWAY** *Virgin GENS 5*	22		8
2 Nov 91	**NO SON OF MINE** *Virgin GENS 6*	6		7
11 Jan 92	**I CAN'T DANCE** *Virgin GENS 7*	7		9
18 Apr 92	**HOLD ON MY HEART** *Virgin GENS 8*	16		5
25 Jul 92	**JESUS HE KNOWS ME** *Virgin GENS 9*	20		7
21 Nov 92	**INVISIBLE TOUCH (LIVE)** *Virgin GENS 10* ★	7		4
20 Feb 93	**TELL ME WHY** *Virgin GENDG 11*	40		3
27 Sep 97	**CONGO** *Virgin GENSD 12*	29		2
13 Dec 97	**SHIPWRECKED** *Virgin GENDX 14*	54		1
7 Mar 98	**NOT ABOUT US** *Virgin GENSD 15*	66		1

GENEVA
UK, male vocal/instrumental group — 9

Date	Title	Peak Position	Weeks at No.1	Weeks on Chart
26 Oct 96	**NO ONE SPEAKS** *Nude NUD 22CD*	32		2
8 Feb 97	**INTO THE BLUE** *Nude NUD 25CD*	26		2
31 May 97	**TRANQUILLIZER** *Nude NUD 28CD1*	24		2
16 Aug 97	**BEST REGRETS** *Nude NUD 31CD1*	38		1
27 Nov 99	**DOLLARS IN THE HEAVENS** *Nude NUD 46CD1*	59		1
11 Mar 00	**IF YOU HAVE TO GO** *Nude NUD 49CD1*	69		1

GENEVEVE
UK, female vocalist (Susan Hunt) — 1

Date	Title	Peak Position	Weeks at No.1	Weeks on Chart
5 May 66	**ONCE** *CBS 202061*	43		1

GENIUS CRU
UK, male rap/production group — 7

Date	Title	Peak Position	Weeks at No.1	Weeks on Chart
3 Feb 01	**BOOM SELECTION** *Incentive CENT 17CDS*	12		5
27 Oct 01	**COURSE BRUV** *Incentive CENT 28CDS*	39		2

GENIUS/GZA FEATURING D'ANGELO
US, male rap/vocal duo. See Wu-Tang Clan — 2

Date	Title	Peak Position	Weeks at No.1	Weeks on Chart
2 Mar 96	**COLD WORLD** *Geffen GFSTD 22114*	40		2

BOBBIE GENTRY
US, female vocalist (Roberta Streeter) — 48

Date	Title	Peak Position	Weeks at No.1	Weeks on Chart
13 Sep 67	**ODE TO BILLY JOE** *Capitol CL 15511* ★	13		11
30 Aug 69	**I'LL NEVER FALL IN LOVE AGAIN** *Capitol CL 15606*	1	1	19
6 Dec 69	**ALL I HAVE TO DO IS DREAM** *Capitol CL 15619* & GLEN CAMPBELL	3		14
21 Feb 70	**RAINDROPS KEEP FALLIN' ON MY HEAD** *Capitol CL 15626*	40		4

GEORDIE
UK, male vocal/instrumental group – Brian Johnson, Brian Gibson, Tom Hill & Vic Malcolm — 35

Date	Title	Peak Position	Weeks at No.1	Weeks on Chart
2 Dec 72	**DON'T DO THAT** *Regal Zonophone RZ 3067*	32		7
17 Mar 73	**ALL BECAUSE OF YOU** *EMI 2008*	6		13
16 Jun 73	**CAN YOU DO IT** *EMI 2031*	13		9
25 Aug 73	**ELECTRIC LADY** *EMI 2048*	32		6

ROBIN GEORGE
UK, male vocalist — 2

Date	Title	Peak Position	Weeks at No.1	Weeks on Chart
27 Apr 85	**HEARTLINE** *Bronze BRO 191*	68		2

SOPHIA GEORGE
Jamaica, female vocalist — 11

Date	Title	Peak Position	Weeks at No.1	Weeks on Chart
7 Dec 85	**GIRLIE GIRLIE** *Winner WIN 01*	7		11

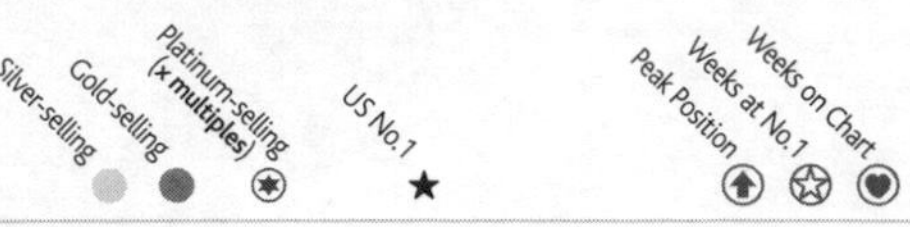

GEORGIA SATELLITES
US, male vocal/instrumental group — 8

Date	Title	Peak Position	Weeks at No.1	Weeks on Chart
7 Feb 87	**KEEP YOUR HANDS TO YOURSELF** *Elektra EKR 50*	69		1
16 May 87	**BATTLESHIP CHAINS** *Elektra EKR 58*	44		4
21 Jan 89	**HIPPY HIPPY SHAKE** *Elektra EKR 86*	63		3

GEORGIE PORGIE
US, male producer (George Andros) — 3

Date	Title	Peak Position	Weeks at No.1	Weeks on Chart
12 Aug 95	**EVERYBODY MUST PARTY** *Vibe MCSTD 2068*	61		1
4 May 96	**TAKE ME HIGHER** *Music Plant MCSTD 40031*	61		1
26 Aug 00	**LIFE GOES ON** *Neo NEOCD 039*	54		1

GEORGIO
US, male vocalist (Georgio Allentini) — 3

Date	Title	Peak Position	Weeks at No.1	Weeks on Chart
20 Feb 88	**LOVER'S LANE** *Motown ZB 41611*	54		3

GERALDINE
UK, male comedian/vocalist (Peter Kay) — 10

Date	Title	Peak Position	Weeks at No.1	Weeks on Chart
25 Oct 08	**THE WINNER'S SONG** *Polydor 1789241*	2		7
27 Dec 08	**ONCE UPON A CHRISTMAS SONG** *Polydor 1793980*	5		3

DANYEL GERARD
France, male vocalist (Gerard Daniel Kherlakian) — 12

Date	Title	Peak Position	Weeks at No.1	Weeks on Chart
18 Sep 71	**BUTTERFLY** *CBS 7454*	11		12

GERIDEAU
US, male vocalist (Theo Gerideau) — 2

Date	Title	Peak Position	Weeks at No.1	Weeks on Chart
27 Aug 94	**BRING IT BACK 2 LUV** *Fruittree FTREE 10CD* PROJECT FEATURING GERIDEAU	65		1
4 Jul 98	**MASQUERADE** *Inferno CDFERN 7*	63		1

GERRY & THE PACEMAKERS
UK, male vocal/instrumental group – Gerry Marsden, Les Chadwick, Les Maguire & Freddie Marsden, d. 9 Dec 2006 — 114

Date	Title	Peak Position	Weeks at No.1	Weeks on Chart
14 Mar 63	**HOW DO YOU DO IT?** *Columbia DB 4987*	1	3	18
30 May 63	**I LIKE IT** *Columbia DB 7041*	1	4	15
10 Oct 63	**YOU'LL NEVER WALK ALONE** *Columbia DB 7126*	1	4	19
16 Jan 64	**I'M THE ONE** *Columbia DB 7189*	2		15
16 Apr 64	**DON'T LET THE SUN CATCH YOU CRYING** *Columbia DB 7268*	6		11
3 Sep 64	**IT'S GONNA BE ALL RIGHT** *Columbia DB 7353*	24		7
17 Dec 64	**FERRY ACROSS THE MERSEY** *Columbia DB 7437*	8		13
25 Mar 65	**I'LL BE THERE** *Columbia DB 7504*	15		9
18 Nov 65	**WALK HAND IN HAND** *Columbia DB 7738*	29		7

GET CAPE. WEAR CAPE. FLY.
UK, male vocalist/guitarist (Sam Duckworth) — 5

Date	Title	Peak Position	Weeks at No.1	Weeks on Chart
23 Sep 06	**THE CHRONICLES OF A BOHEMIAN TEENAGER** *Atlantic ATUK042CD*	38		2
9 Dec 06	**WAR OF THE WORLDS** *Atlantic ATUK049CD*	39		1
17 Mar 07	**I SPY** *Atlantic ATUK056CDH*	37		1
15 Mar 08	**FIND THE TIME** *Atlantic ATUK073CD*	33		1

GET READY
UK, male vocal group — 1

Date	Title	Peak Position	Weeks at No.1	Weeks on Chart
3 Jun 95	**WILD WILD WEST** *Mega GACXCD 2698*	65		1

GETO BOYS FEATURING FLAJ
US, male rap group — 1

Date	Title	Peak Position	Weeks at No.1	Weeks on Chart
11 May 96	**THE WORLD IS A GHETTO** *Virgin America VUSCD 104*	49		1

STAN GETZ
US, male saxophonist (Stanley Gayetzsky), d. 6 Jun 1991 — 23

Date	Title	Peak Position	Weeks at No.1	Weeks on Chart
8 Nov 62	**DESAFINADO** *HMV POP 1061* & CHARLIE BYRD	11		13
23 Jul 64	**THE GIRL FROM IPANEMA (GAROTA DE IPANEMA)** *Verve VS 520* & JOAO GILBERTO	29		10

ASTRUD GILBERTO
Brazil, female vocalist (Astrud Weinert) — 6

Date	Title	Peak Position	Weeks at No.1	Weeks on Chart
25 Aug 84	**THE GIRL FROM IPANEMA** *Verve IPA 1*	55		6

G4
UK, male vocal group – Jonathan Ansell, Mike Christie, Matthew Stiff & Ben Thapa — 6

Date	Title	Peak Position	Weeks at No.1	Weeks on Chart
26 Mar 05	**BOHEMIAN RHAPSODY** *Sony Music 6758062*	9		6

GG
Czech Republic, male DJ — 1

Date	Title	Peak Position	Weeks at No.1	Weeks on Chart
22 Aug 09	**SEXY BITCH** *Power Music USCBK0911102*	60		1

AMANDA GHOST
UK, female vocalist (Amanda Gosein) — 2

Date	Title	Peak Position	Weeks at No.1	Weeks on Chart
8 Apr 00	**IDOL** *Warner Brothers W 518CD*	63		1
1 May 04	**BREAK MY WORLD** *Island CID 853* DARK GLOBE FEATURING AMANDA GHOST	52		1

GHOST DANCE
UK, male/female vocal/instrumental group — 2

Date	Title	Peak Position	Weeks at No.1	Weeks on Chart
17 Jun 89	**DOWN TO THE WIRE** *Chrysalis CHS 3376*	66		2

GHOSTFACE KILLAH
US, male rapper (Dennis Coles). See Wu-Tang Clan — 33

Date	Title	Peak Position	Weeks at No.1	Weeks on Chart
12 Jul 97	**ALL THAT I GOT IS YOU** *Epic 6646842*	11		4
23 Jan 99	**I WANT YOU FOR MYSELF** *Northwestside 74321643632* ANOTHER LEVEL/GHOSTFACE KILLAH	2		8
4 Nov 00	**MISS FAT BOOTY – PART II** *Rawkus RWK 282CD* MOS DEF FEATURING GHOSTFACE KILLAH	64		1
29 May 04	**ON MY KNEES** *Sony Music 6749382* 411 FEATURING GHOSTFACE KILLAH	4		11
17 Jul 04	**TUSH** *Def Jam 9862837* GHOSTFACE FEATURING MISSY ELLIOTT	34		3
16 Oct 04	**LOVE THEM** *Jive 82876639212* EAMON FEATURING GHOSTFACE	27		4
26 Aug 06	**BACK LIKE THAT** *Def Jam 1705586* FEATURING NE-YO & KANYE WEST	46		2

GHOSTS
UK, male vocal/instrumental group — 8

Date	Title	Peak Position	Weeks at No.1	Weeks on Chart
10 Mar 07	**STAY THE NIGHT** *Atlantic ATUK055CD*	25		6
16 Jun 07	**THE WORLD IS OUTSIDE** *Atlantic ATUK064CD*	35		2

ANDY GIBB
UK, male vocalist, d. 10 Mar 1988 (age 30) — 30

Date	Title	Peak Position	Weeks at No.1	Weeks on Chart
25 Jun 77	**I JUST WANNA BE YOUR EVERYTHING** *RSO 2090 237* ★	26		7
13 May 78	**SHADOW DANCING** *RSO 001* ★	42		6
12 Aug 78	**AN EVERLASTING LOVE** *RSO 015*	10		10
27 Jan 79	**(OUR LOVE) DON'T THROW IT ALL AWAY** *RSO 26*	32		7

ROBIN GIBB
UK, male vocalist. See Bee Gees, One World Project — 29

Date	Title	Peak Position	Weeks at No.1	Weeks on Chart
9 Jul 69	**SAVED BY THE BELL** *Polydor 56 337*	2		17
7 Feb 70	**AUGUST OCTOBER** *Polydor 56 371*	45		3
11 Feb 84	**ANOTHER LONELY NIGHT IN NEW YORK** *Polydor POSP 668*	71		1
1 Feb 03	**PLEASE** *SPV Recordings 05571463*	23		4
21 Mar 09	**ISLANDS IN THE STREAM** *Mercury 1799919* VANESSA JENKINS & BRYN WEST FEATURING TOM JONES & ROBIN GIBB	1	1	4

BETH GIBBONS & RUSTIN MAN
UK, female/male vocal/instrumental/production duo. See Portishead, Talk Talk — 1

Date	Title	Peak Position	Weeks at No.1	Weeks on Chart
15 Mar 03	**TOM THE MODEL** *Go! Beat GOBCD 55*	70		1

STEVE GIBBONS BAND
UK, male vocal/instrumental group — 14

Date	Title	Peak Position	Weeks at No.1	Weeks on Chart
6 Aug 77	**TULANE** *Polydor 2058 889*	12		10
13 May 78	**EDDY VORTEX** *Polydor 2059 017*	56		4

GEORGIA GIBBS
US, female vocalist (Freda Gibbons), d. 9 Dec 2006 (age 87) — **2**

Date	Title / Label	Peak Position	Weeks at No.1	Weeks on Chart
22 Apr 55	**TWEEDLE DEE** *Mercury MB 3196*	20		1
13 Jul 56	**KISS ME ANOTHER** *Mercury MT 110*	24		1

DEBBIE GIBSON
US, female vocalist — **70**

Date	Title / Label	Peak Position	Weeks at No.1	Weeks on Chart
26 Sep 87	**ONLY IN MY DREAMS** *Atlantic A 9322*	54		5
23 Jan 88	**SHAKE YOUR LOVE** *Atlantic A 9187*	7		8
19 Mar 88	**ONLY IN MY DREAMS** *Atlantic A 9322*	11		7
7 May 88	**OUT OF THE BLUE** *Atlantic A 9091*	19		7
9 Jul 88	**FOOLISH BEAT** *Atlantic A 9059* ★	9		9
15 Oct 88	**STAYING TOGETHER** *Atlantic A 9020*	53		2
28 Jan 89	**LOST IN YOUR EYES** *Atlantic A 8970* ★	34		7
29 Apr 89	**ELECTRIC YOUTH** *Atlantic A 8919*	14		8
19 Aug 89	**WE COULD BE TOGETHER** *Atlantic A 8896*	22		8
9 Mar 91	**ANYTHING IS POSSIBLE** *Atlantic A 7735*	51		2
3 Apr 93	**SHOCK YOUR MAMA** *Atlantic A 7386CD*	74		1
24 Jul 93	**YOU'RE THE ONE THAT I WANT** *Epic 6595222* CRAIG McLACHLAN & DEBBIE GIBSON	13		6

DON GIBSON
US, male vocalist/guitarist, d. 17 Nov 2003 (age 75) — **16**

Date	Title / Label	Peak Position	Weeks at No.1	Weeks on Chart
31 Aug 61	**SEA OF HEARTBREAK** *RCA 1243*	14		13
1 Feb 62	**LONESOME NUMBER ONE** *RCA 1272*	47		3

WAYNE GIBSON
UK, male vocalist — **13**

Date	Title / Label	Peak Position	Weeks at No.1	Weeks on Chart
3 Sep 64	**KELLY** *Pye 7N 15680*	48		2
23 Nov 74	**UNDER MY THUMB** *Pye Disco Demand DDS 2001*	17		11

GIBSON BROTHERS
Martinique, male vocal/instrumental group – Chris, Alex & Patrick Gibson — **54**

Date	Title / Label	Peak Position	Weeks at No.1	Weeks on Chart
10 Mar 79	**CUBA** *Island WIP 6483*	41		9
21 Jul 79	**OOH! WHAT A LIFE** *Island WIP 6503*	10		12
17 Nov 79	**QUE SERA MI VIDA (IF YOU SHOULD GO)** *Island WIP 6525* ●	5		11
23 Feb 80	**CUBA/BETTER DO IT SALSA** *Island WIP 6561*	12		9
12 Jul 80	**MARIANA** *Island WIP 6617*	11		10
9 Jul 83	**MY HEART'S BEATING WILD (TIC TAC TIC TAC)** *Stiff BUY 184*	56		3

GIDEA PARK
UK, male vocal/instrumental group — **19**

Date	Title / Label	Peak Position	Weeks at No.1	Weeks on Chart
4 Jul 81	**BEACHBOY GOLD** *Stone SON 2162*	11		13
12 Sep 81	**SEASONS OF GOLD** *Polo 14*	28		6

JOHAN GIELEN
Belgium, male producer. See Airscape, Balearic Bill, Blue Bamboo — **3**

Date	Title / Label	Peak Position	Weeks at No.1	Weeks on Chart
18 Aug 01	**VELVET MOODS** *Data 17T* PRESENTS ABNEA	74		1
22 Sep 01	**THE BEAUTY OF SILENCE** *Xtrahard/Xtravaganza X2H 5CDS* SVENSON & GIELEN	41		2

GIFTED
UK, male vocal/instrumental duo — **1**

Date	Title / Label	Peak Position	Weeks at No.1	Weeks on Chart
23 Aug 97	**DO I** *Perfecto PERF 140CD*	60		1

GIGGS FEATURING B.o.B.
UK/US, male rap/instrumental/production duo — **1**

Date	Title / Label	Peak Position	Weeks at No.1	Weeks on Chart
6 Mar 10	**DON'T GO THERE** *SN1 Entertainment GBBKS0900579*	60		1

GIGOLO AUNTS
US, male vocal/instrumental group — **4**

Date	Title / Label	Peak Position	Weeks at No.1	Weeks on Chart
23 Apr 94	**MRS WASHINGTON** *Fire BLAZE 68CD*	74		1
13 May 95	**WHERE I FIND MY HEAVEN** *Fire BLAZE 87CD*	29		3

DONNA GILES
US, female vocalist — **4**

Date	Title / Label	Peak Position	Weeks at No.1	Weeks on Chart
13 Aug 94	**AND I'M TELLING YOU I'M NOT GOING** *Ore AG 4CD*	43		2
10 Feb 96	**AND I'M TELLING YOU I'M NOT GOING** *Ore/XL Recordings AGR 4CD*	27		2

JOHNNY GILL
US, male vocalist. See New Edition — **12**

Date	Title / Label	Peak Position	Weeks at No.1	Weeks on Chart
23 Feb 91	**WRAP MY BODY TIGHT** *Motown ZB 44271*	57		2
28 Nov 92	**SLOW AND SEXY** *Epic 6587727* SHABBA RANKS FEATURING JOHNNY GILL	17		7
17 Jul 93	**THE FLOOR** *Motown TMGCD 1416*	53		1
29 Jan 94	**A CUTE SWEET LOVE ADDICTION** *Motown TMGCD 1420*	46		2

VINCE GILL
US, male vocalist/multi-instrumentalist — **5**

Date	Title / Label	Peak Position	Weeks at No.1	Weeks on Chart
14 Oct 95	**HOUSE OF LOVE** *A&M 5812332* AMY GRANT WITH VINCE GILL	46		2
30 Oct 99	**IF YOU EVER LEAVE ME** *Columbia 6681242* BARBRA STREISAND/VINCE GILL	26		3

GILLAN
UK, male vocal/instrumental group — **46**

Date	Title / Label	Peak Position	Weeks at No.1	Weeks on Chart
14 Jun 80	**SLEEPIN' ON THE JOB** *Virgin VS 355*	55		3
4 Oct 80	**TROUBLE** *Virgin VS 377*	14		6
14 Feb 81	**MUTUALLY ASSURED DESTRUCTION** *Virgin VS 103*	32		5
21 Mar 81	**NEW ORLEANS** *Virgin VS 406*	17		10
20 Jun 81	**NO LAUGHING IN HEAVEN** *Virgin VS 425*	31		6
10 Oct 81	**NIGHTMARE** *Virgin VS 441*	36		6
23 Jan 82	**RESTLESS** *Virgin VS 465*	25		7
4 Sep 82	**LIVING FOR THE CITY** *Virgin VS 519*	50		3

STUART GILLIES
UK, male vocalist — **10**

Date	Title / Label	Peak Position	Weeks at No.1	Weeks on Chart
31 Mar 73	**AMANDA** *Philips 6006 293*	13		10

THEA GILMORE
UK, female vocalist/guitarist — **2**

Date	Title / Label	Peak Position	Weeks at No.1	Weeks on Chart
16 Aug 03	**JULIET (KEEP THAT IN MIND)** *Hungry Dog YRGNUHS 2*	35		1
8 Nov 03	**MAINSTREAM** *Hungry Dog YRGNUHS 4*	50		1

DAVID GILMOUR
UK, male vocalist/guitarist. See Pink Floyd — **4**

Date	Title / Label	Peak Position	Weeks at No.1	Weeks on Chart
17 Jun 06	**SMILE** *EMI CDEM696*	72		1
6 Jan 07	**ARNOLD LAYNE** *EMI CDEM717*	19		3

JAMES GILREATH
US, male vocalist — **10**

Date	Title / Label	Peak Position	Weeks at No.1	Weeks on Chart
2 May 63	**LITTLE BAND OF GOLD** *Pye International 7N 25190*	29		10

JIM GILSTRAP
US, male vocalist — **11**

Date	Title / Label	Peak Position	Weeks at No.1	Weeks on Chart
15 Mar 75	**SWING YOUR DADDY** *Chelsea 2005 021*	4		11

GORDON GILTRAP
UK, male guitarist — **10**

Date	Title / Label	Peak Position	Weeks at No.1	Weeks on Chart
14 Jan 78	**HEARTSONG** *Electric WOT 19*	21		7
28 Apr 79	**FEAR OF THE DARK** *Electric WOT 29* BAND	58		3

GIN BLOSSOMS
US, male vocal/instrumental group — **12**

Date	Title / Label	Peak Position	Weeks at No.1	Weeks on Chart
5 Feb 94	**HEY JEALOUSY** *Fontana GINCD 3*	24		5
16 Apr 94	**FOUND OUT ABOUT YOU** *Fontana GINCD 4*	40		3
10 Feb 96	**TIL I HEAR IT FROM YOU** *A&M 5812272*	39		2
27 Apr 96	**FOLLOW YOU DOWN** *A&M 5815512*	30		2

Silver-selling ● Gold-selling ● Platinum-selling (x multiples) ⊛ US No.1 ★ Peak Position Weeks at No.1 Weeks on Chart

GINUWINE

US, male vocalist (Elgin Lumpkin) — 27

Date	Title / Label	Peak Position	Weeks at No.1	Weeks on Chart
25 Jan 97	**PONY** *Epic 6641282*	16		6
24 May 97	**TELL ME DO U WANNA** *Epic 6645272*	16		3
6 Sep 97	**WHEN DOVES CRY** *Epic 6649245*	10		5
14 Mar 98	**HOLLER** *Epic 6653372*	13		4
13 Mar 99	**WHAT'S SO DIFFERENT?** *Epic 6670522*	10		4
14 Dec 02	**CRUSH TONIGHT** *Atlantic AT0142CD* FAT JOE FEATURING GINUWINE	42		2
7 Jun 03	**HELL YEAH** *Epic 6739245*	27		3

GIPSY KINGS

France, male vocal/instrumental group — 2

Date	Title / Label	Peak Position	Weeks at No.1	Weeks on Chart
3 Sep 94	**HITS MEDLEY** *Columbia 6606022*	53		2

MARTINE GIRAULT

UK (b. US), female vocalist — 7

Date	Title / Label	Peak Position	Weeks at No.1	Weeks on Chart
29 Aug 92	**REVIVAL** *ffrr FX 195*	53		2
30 Jan 93	**REVIVAL** *ffrr FCD 205*	37		3
28 Oct 95	**BEEN THINKING ABOUT YOU** *RCA 74321316142*	63		1
1 Feb 97	**REVIVAL (REMIX)** *RCA 74321432162*	61		1

GIRESSE

UK, male DJ/production duo — 1

Date	Title / Label	Peak Position	Weeks at No.1	Weeks on Chart
14 Apr 01	**MON AMI** *Inferno CDFERN 36*	61		1

GIRL

UK, male vocal/instrumental group — 3

Date	Title / Label	Peak Position	Weeks at No.1	Weeks on Chart
12 Apr 80	**HOLLYWOOD TEASE** *Jet 176*	50		3

GIRL THING

UK/Holland, female vocal group – Jodi Albert, Michelle Barber, Anika Bostelaar, Linzi Martin & Nikki Stuart — 13

Date	Title / Label	Peak Position	Weeks at No.1	Weeks on Chart
1 Jul 00	**LAST ONE STANDING** *RCA 74321762422*	8		10
18 Nov 00	**GIRLS ON TOP** *RCA 74321801172*	25		3

GIRLFRIEND

Australia, female vocal group — 6

Date	Title / Label	Peak Position	Weeks at No.1	Weeks on Chart
30 Jan 93	**TAKE IT FROM ME** *Arista 74321142252*	47		4
15 May 93	**GIRL'S LIFE** *Arista 74321138452*	68		2

GIRLS ALOUD

UK/Ireland, female vocal group – Cheryl Cole*, Nadine Coyle, Sarah Harding, Nicola Roberts & Kimberley Walsh. The most successful female reality TV act clocked up 17 consecutive Top 10 singles (a record for a female group) after winning *Popstars: The Rivals*. The group won their first BRIT award in 2009 for 'The Promise' ('Best Single') — 255

Date	Title / Label	Peak Position	Weeks at No.1	Weeks on Chart
28 Dec 02	**SOUND OF THE UNDERGROUND** *Polydor 0658272* ⊛	1	4	21
24 May 03	**NO GOOD ADVICE** *Polydor 9800051*	2		14
30 Aug 03	**LIFE GOT COLD** *Polydor 9810656*	3		9
29 Nov 03	**JUMP** *Polydor 9814104*	2		14
10 Jul 04	**THE SHOW** *Polydor 9867041*	2		10
25 Sep 04	**LOVE MACHINE** *Polydor 9867984*	2		10
27 Nov 04	**I'LL STAND BY YOU** *Polydor 9869130*	1	2	14
5 Mar 05	**WAKE ME UP** *Polydor 9870426*	4		9
3 Sep 05	**LONG HOT SUMMER** *Polydor 9873589*	7		8
26 Nov 05	**BIOLOGY** *Polydor 9875297*	4		10
31 Dec 05	**SEE THE DAY** *Polydor 9875965*	9		6
25 Mar 06	**WHOLE LOTTA HISTORY** *Polydor 9877402*	6		5
28 Oct 06	**SOMETHING KINDA OOOOH** *Fascination FASC4*	3		15
23 Dec 06	**I THINK WE'RE ALONE NOW** *Fascination 1714586*	4		7
24 Mar 07	**WALK THIS WAY** *Fascination/Island 1724331* SUGABABES VS GIRLS ALOUD	1	1	6
8 Sep 07	**SEXY! NO NO NO** *Fascination 1744981*	5		10
1 Dec 07	**CALL THE SHOTS** *Fascination 1753047*	3		21
12 Jan 08	**THEME TO 'ST TRINIAN'S'** *Fascination GBUM70711532*	51		1
1 Mar 08	**CAN'T SPEAK FRENCH** *Fascination 1764167*	9		20
1 Nov 08	**THE PROMISE** *Fascination 1788035* ●	1	1	23
27 Dec 08	**THE LOVING KIND** *Fascination 1794885*	10		12
4 Apr 09	**UNTOUCHABLE** *Fascination 2704479*	11		10

GIRLS@PLAY

UK, female vocal group — 7

Date	Title / Label	Peak Position	Weeks at No.1	Weeks on Chart
24 Feb 01	**AIRHEAD** *GSM GSMCDR 1*	18		5
13 Oct 01	**RESPECTABLE** *Redbus Music RBMCD 101*	29		2

GIRLS CAN'T CATCH

UK, female vocal group — 5

Date	Title / Label	Peak Position	Weeks at No.1	Weeks on Chart
15 Aug 09	**KEEP YOUR HEAD UP** *Fascination 2715798*	26		2
30 Jan 10	**ECHO** *Fascination 2728244*	19		3

GIRLS OF FHM

International, female models/vocalists – members included Tina Barrett (S Club 7), Naomi Campbell, Myleene Klass (Hear'Say), Liberty X, Liz McClarnon (Atomic Kitten), Lisa Scott-Lee (Steps) & *FHM*'s 'High Street Honeys' — 7

Date	Title / Label	Peak Position	Weeks at No.1	Weeks on Chart
3 Jul 04	**DA YA THINK I'M SEXY?** *2PSL 2PSLCD5*	10		5
17 Feb 07	**I TOUCH MYSELF** *All Around The World CDGLOBE654* FHM HIGH STREET HONEYS	34		2

GIRLSCHOOL

UK, female vocal/instrumental group – Kim McAuliffe, Denise Dufort, Bernadette 'Kelly' Johnson, d. 15 Jul 2007, & Enid Williams (replaced by Gil Weston) — 25

Date	Title / Label	Peak Position	Weeks at No.1	Weeks on Chart
2 Aug 80	**RACE WITH THE DEVIL** *Bronze BRO 100*	49		6
21 Feb 81	**ST VALENTINE'S DAY MASSACRE EP** *Bronze BRO 116* MOTORHEAD & GIRLSCHOOL ●	5		8
11 Apr 81	**HIT AND RUN** *Bronze BRO 118*	32		6
11 Jul 81	**C'MON LET'S GO** *Bronze BRO 126*	42		3
3 Apr 82	**WILDLIFE (EP)** *Bronze BRO 144*	58		2

GITTA

Denmark/Italy, male/female vocal/instrumental group — 1

Date	Title / Label	Peak Position	Weeks at No.1	Weeks on Chart
19 Aug 00	**NO MORE TURNING BACK** *Pepper 9230302*	54		1

GLADIATOR FEATURING IZZY

UK, male/female vocal/DJ/production trio — 4

Date	Title / Label	Peak Position	Weeks at No.1	Weeks on Chart
29 May 04	**NOW WE ARE FREE** *Universal TV 9866813*	19		4

GLADIATORS

UK, male/female vocal group (TV gladiators) — 1

Date	Title / Label	Peak Position	Weeks at No.1	Weeks on Chart
30 Nov 96	**THE BOYS ARE BACK IN TOWN** *RCA 74321417002*	70		1

GLAM

Italy, male production group — 2

Date	Title / Label	Peak Position	Weeks at No.1	Weeks on Chart
1 May 93	**HELL'S PARTY** *Six6 SIXCD 001*	42		2

GLAM METAL DETECTIVES

UK, male/female vocal group — 2

Date	Title / Label	Peak Position	Weeks at No.1	Weeks on Chart
11 Mar 95	**EVERYBODY UP!** *ZTT ZANG 62CD*	29		2

GLAMMA KID

UK, male vocalist/rapper (Lyael Constable) — 25

Date	Title / Label	Peak Position	Weeks at No.1	Weeks on Chart
21 Nov 98	**FASHION '98** *WEA 179CD*	49		1
17 Apr 99	**TABOO** *WEA 203CD* FEATURING SHOLA AMA	10		8
27 Nov 99	**WHY** *WEA 229CD1*	10		10
2 Sep 00	**BILLS 2 PAY** *WEA 268CD1*	17		6

GLASS TIGER

Canada, male vocal/instrumental group — 18

Date	Title / Label	Peak Position	Weeks at No.1	Weeks on Chart
18 Oct 86	**DON'T FORGET ME (WHEN I'M GONE)** *Manhattan MT 13*	29		9
31 Jan 87	**SOMEDAY** *Manhattan MT 17*	66		2
26 Oct 91	**MY TOWN** *EMI EM 212*	33		7

GLASVEGAS

UK, male/female vocal/instrumental group — 9

Date	Title / Label	Peak Position	Weeks at No.1	Weeks on Chart
5 Jul 08	**GERALDINE** *Columbia GOWOW002*	16		5
6 Sep 08	**DADDY'S GONE** *Columbia GOWOW007*	12		4

GLEE CAST

US, male/female actors/vocalists – members include Dianna Agron, Chris Colfer, Jessalyn Gilsig, Jane Lynch, Jayma Mays, Kevin McHale, Lea Michele Sarfati, Cory Monteith, Matthew Morrison, Amber Riley, Mark Salling & Jenna Ushkowitz — Weeks on Chart: 58

Date	Title / Label	Peak	Wks at No.1	Wks on Chart
26 Dec 09	**DON'T STOP BELIEVIN'** *Epic USQX90900224*	2		13+
23 Jan 10	**TAKE A BOW** *Epic USQX90900497*	36		4
23 Jan 10	**GOLD DIGGER** *Epic USQX90900412*	44		3
23 Jan 10	**REHAB** *Epic USQX90900223*	62		2
23 Jan 10	**ON MY OWN** *Epic USQX90900458*	73		1
30 Jan 10	**BUST YOUR WINDOWS** *Epic USQX90900413*	57		2
13 Feb 10	**SOMEBODY TO LOVE** *Epic USQX90900303*	26		3
13 Feb 10	**ALONE** *Epic USQX90900569*	47		2
20 Feb 10	**HALO/WALKING ON SUNSHINE** *Epic USQX90900648*	9		8+
20 Feb 10	**IT'S MY LIFE/CONFESSIONS PART II** *Epic USQX90900647*	14		4
27 Feb 10	**KEEP HOLDING ON** *Epic USQX90900576*	47		2
27 Feb 10	**NO AIR** *Epic USQX90900574*	52		1
6 Mar 10	**SWEET CAROLINE** *Epic USQX90900578*	59		1
13 Mar 10	**DEFYING GRAVITY** *Epic USQX90900580*	38		3
20 Mar 10	**LEAN ON ME** *Epic USQX90900701*	43		2
20 Mar 10	**DON'T STAND SO CLOSE TO ME/YOUNG GIRL** *Epic USQX90900698*	62		2
27 Mar 10	**TRUE COLORS** *Epic USQX90900704*	35		3+
27 Mar 10	**IMAGINE** *Epic USQX90900703*	57		1
10 Apr 10	**MY LIFE WOULD SUCK WITHOUT YOU** *Epic USQX90900711*	53		1+

GLENN & CHRIS

UK, male vocal/footballing duo — Weeks on Chart: 8

Date	Title / Label	Peak	Wks at No.1	Wks on Chart
18 Apr 87	**DIAMOND LIGHTS** *Record Shack Records KICK 1*	12		8

GLITTER BAND

UK, male vocal/instrumental group – Harvey Ellison, Tony Leonard, Pete Phipps, John Rossall, Gerry Shephard, d. 29 May 2003, & John Springate. See Gary Glitter — Weeks on Chart: 60

Date	Title / Label	Peak	Wks at No.1	Wks on Chart
23 Mar 74	**ANGEL FACE** *Bell 1348* ◯	4		10
3 Aug 74	**JUST FOR YOU** *Bell 1368*	10		8
19 Oct 74	**LET'S GET TOGETHER AGAIN** *Bell 1383*	8		8
18 Jan 75	**GOODBYE MY LOVE** *Bell 1395*	2		9
12 Apr 75	**THE TEARS I CRIED** *Bell 1416*	8		8
9 Aug 75	**LOVE IN THE SUN** *Bell 1437*	15		8
28 Feb 76	**PEOPLE LIKE YOU PEOPLE LIKE ME** *Bell 1471*	5		9

GARY GLITTER

UK, male vocalist (Paul Gadd) — Weeks on Chart: 170

Date	Title / Label	Peak	Wks at No.1	Wks on Chart
10 Jun 72	**ROCK AND ROLL (PARTS 1 & 2)** *Bell 1216*	2		15
23 Sep 72	**I DIDN'T KNOW I LOVED YOU (TILL I SAW YOU ROCK 'N' ROLL)** *Bell 1259*	4		11
20 Jan 73	**DO YOU WANNA TOUCH ME (OH YEAH!)** *Bell 1280*	2		11
7 Apr 73	**HELLO! HELLO! I'M BACK AGAIN** *Bell 1299* ◯	2		14
21 Jul 73	**I'M THE LEADER OF THE GANG (I AM)** *Bell 1321* ●	1	4	12
17 Nov 73	**I LOVE YOU LOVE ME LOVE** *Bell 1337* ⊛	1	4	14
30 Mar 74	**REMEMBER ME THIS WAY** *Bell 1349* ◯	3		8
15 Jun 74	**ALWAYS YOURS** *Bell 1359* ◯	1	1	9
23 Nov 74	**OH YES! YOU'RE BEAUTIFUL** *Bell 1391* ◯	2		10
3 May 75	**LOVE LIKE YOU AND ME** *Bell 1423*	10		6
21 Jun 75	**DOING ALRIGHT WITH THE BOYS** *Bell 1429*	6		7
8 Nov 75	**PAPA OOM MOW MOW** *Bell 1451*	38		5
13 Mar 76	**YOU BELONG TO ME** *Bell 1473*	40		5
22 Jan 77	**IT TAKES ALL NIGHT LONG** *Arista 85*	25		6
16 Jul 77	**A LITTLE BOOGIE WOOGIE IN THE BACK OF MY MIND** *Arista 112*	31		5
20 Sep 80	**GARY GLITTER (EP)** *GTO GT 282*	57		3
10 Oct 81	**AND THEN SHE KISSED ME** *Bell 1497*	39		5
5 Dec 81	**ALL THAT GLITTERS** *Bell 1498*	48		5
23 Jun 84	**DANCE ME UP** *Arista ARIST 570*	25		5
1 Dec 84	**ANOTHER ROCK AND ROLL CHRISTMAS** *Arista ARIST 592* ◯	7		7
10 Oct 92	**AND THE LEADER ROCKS ON** *EMI EM 252*	58		2
21 Nov 92	**THROUGH THE YEARS** *EMI EM 256*	49		3
16 Dec 95	**HELLO! HELLO! I'M BACK AGAIN (AGAIN)** *Carlton Sounds 3036000192*	50		2

GLITTERATI

UK, male vocal/instrumental group — Weeks on Chart: 3

Date	Title / Label	Peak	Wks at No.1	Wks on Chart
26 Mar 05	**YOU GOT NOTHING ON ME** *Atlantic ATUK005CD*	36		1
4 Jun 05	**HEARTBREAKER** *Atlantic ATUK008CD*	45		1
5 Nov 05	**BACK IN POWER** *Atlantic ATUK015CD*	62		1

GLOBAL COMMUNICATION

UK, male instrumental/production duo. See Cosmos — Weeks on Chart: 1

Date	Title / Label	Peak	Wks at No.1	Wks on Chart
11 Jan 97	**THE WAY/THE DEEP** *Dedicated GLOBA 002CD*	51		1

GLOVE

UK, male vocal/instrumental group — Weeks on Chart: 3

Date	Title / Label	Peak	Wks at No.1	Wks on Chart
20 Aug 83	**LIKE AN ANIMAL** *Wonderland SHE 3*	52		3

DANA GLOVER

US, female vocalist/pianist — Weeks on Chart: 1

Date	Title / Label	Peak	Wks at No.1	Wks on Chart
10 May 03	**THINKING OVER** *DreamWorks 4507762*	38		1

GLOWORM

UK/US, male vocal/production duo – Will Mount & Sedric Johnson — Weeks on Chart: 17

Date	Title / Label	Peak	Wks at No.1	Wks on Chart
6 Feb 93	**I LIFT MY CUP** *Pulse 8 CDLOSE 37*	20		4
14 May 94	**CARRY ME HOME** *Go! Beat GODCD 112*	9		11
6 Aug 94	**I LIFT MY CUP** *Pulse 8 CDLOSE 67*	46		2

GNARLS BARKLEY

US, male vocal/rap/production/instrumental duo – Danger Mouse (Brian Burton) & Cee-Lo Green (Thomas Callaway) — Weeks on Chart: 41

Date	Title / Label	Peak	Wks at No.1	Wks on Chart
8 Apr 06	**CRAZY** *Warner Brothers WEA401CD* ⊛	1	9	18
22 Jul 06	**SMILEY FACES** *Warner Brothers WEA410CD1*	10		14
18 Nov 06	**WHO CARES** *Warner Brothers WEA413CD1*	60		1
23 Feb 08	**RUN** *Warner Brothers USAT20801097*	32		8

GO:AUDIO

UK, male vocal/instrumental group — Weeks on Chart: 3

Date	Title / Label	Peak	Wks at No.1	Wks on Chart
7 Jun 08	**MADE UP STORIES** *Epic 88697293022*	33		2
23 Aug 08	**SHE LEFT ME** *Epic 88697346472*	41		1

GO GO LORENZO & THE DAVIS PINCKNEY PROJECT

US, male rapper (Lorenzo Queen) & production duo — Weeks on Chart: 8

Date	Title / Label	Peak	Wks at No.1	Wks on Chart
6 Dec 86	**YOU CAN DANCE (IF YOU WANT TO)** *Boiling Point POSP 836*	46		8

Top 5 Downloads

By UK Sales 2006

Pos	Title	Artist
1	**CRAZY**	GNARLS BARKLEY
2	**HIPS DON'T LIE**	SHAKIRA FT WYCLEF JEAN
3	**I DON'T FEEL LIKE DANCIN'**	SCISSOR SISTERS
4	**MANEATER**	NELLY FURTADO
5	**CHASING CARS**	SNOW PATROL

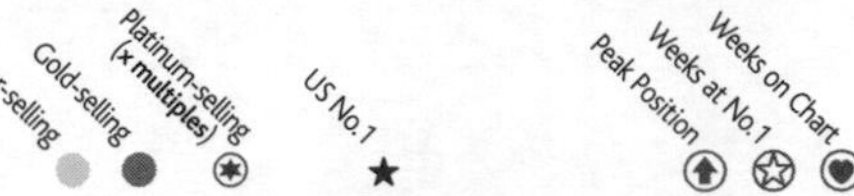

GO-GOS
US, female vocal/instrumental group — 10

Date	Title / Label	Peak Position	Weeks at No.1	Weeks on Chart
15 May 82	**OUR LIPS ARE SEALED** *IRS GDN 102*	47		6
26 Jan 91	**COOL JERK** *IRS AM 712*	60		1
18 Feb 95	**THE WHOLE WORLD LOST ITS HEAD** *IRS CDEIRS 190*	29		3

GO! TEAM
UK, male/female vocal/instrumental group — 7

Date	Title / Label	Peak Position	Weeks at No.1	Weeks on Chart
4 Dec 04	**LADYFLASH** *Memphis Industries MI041CDS*	68		1
8 Oct 05	**BOTTLE ROCKET** *Memphis Industries MI048CDS*	64		1
11 Feb 06	**LADYFLASH** *Memphis Industries MI054CDS*	26		3
14 Jul 07	**GRIP LIKE A VICE** *Memphis Industries MI092CDS*	57		1
15 Sep 07	**DOING IT RIGHT** *Memphis Industries MI098CDS*	55		1

GO WEST
UK, male vocal/instrumental duo – Peter Cox* & Richard Drummie — 85

Date	Title / Label	Peak Position	Weeks at No.1	Weeks on Chart
23 Feb 85	**WE CLOSE OUR EYES** *Chrysalis CHS 2850*	5		14
11 May 85	**CALL ME** *Chrysalis GOW 1*	12		10
3 Aug 85	**GOODBYE GIRL** *Chrysalis GOW 2*	25		7
23 Nov 85	**DON'T LOOK DOWN – THE SEQUEL** *Chrysalis GOW 3*	13		10
29 Nov 86	**TRUE COLOURS** *Chrysalis GOW 4*	48		7
9 May 87	**I WANT TO HEAR IT FROM YOU** *Chrysalis GOW 5*	43		3
12 Sep 87	**THE KING IS DEAD** *Chrysalis GOW 6*	67		2
28 Jul 90	**THE KING OF WISHFUL THINKING** *Chrysalis GOW 8*	18		10
17 Oct 92	**FAITHFUL** *Chrysalis GOW 9*	13		6
16 Jan 93	**WHAT YOU WON'T DO FOR LOVE** *Chrysalis CDGOWS 10*	15		5
27 Mar 93	**STILL IN LOVE** *Chrysalis CDGOWS 11*	43		3
2 Oct 93	**TRACKS OF MY TEARS** *Chrysalis CDGOWS 12*	16		5
4 Dec 93	**WE CLOSE OUR EYES (REMIX)** *Chrysalis CDGOWS 13*	40		3

GOATS
US, male rap group — 2

Date	Title / Label	Peak Position	Weeks at No.1	Weeks on Chart
29 May 93	**AAAH D YAAA/TYPICAL AMERICAN** *Ruffhouse 6593032*	53		2

GOD MACHINE
US, male vocal/instrumental group — 2

Date	Title / Label	Peak Position	Weeks at No.1	Weeks on Chart
30 Jan 93	**HOME** *Fiction FICCD 47*	65		2

GODIEGO
Japan/US, male vocal/instrumental group — 11

Date	Title / Label	Peak Position	Weeks at No.1	Weeks on Chart
15 Oct 77	**THE WATER MARGIN** *BBC RESL 50*	37		4
16 Feb 80	**GHANDARA** *BBC RESL 66*	56		7

GODLEY & CREME
UK, male vocal/instrumental duo – Kevin Godley & Lawrence 'Lol' Crème. See 10cc — 36

Date	Title / Label	Peak Position	Weeks at No.1	Weeks on Chart
12 Sep 81	**UNDER YOUR THUMB** *Polydor POSP 322*	3		11
21 Nov 81	**WEDDING BELLS** *Polydor POSP 369*	7		11
30 Mar 85	**CRY** *Polydor POSP 732*	19		14

GOD'S PROPERTY
US, male/female gospel choir — 1

Date	Title / Label	Peak Position	Weeks at No.1	Weeks on Chart
22 Nov 97	**STOMP** *B-rite Music IND 95559*	60		1

ALEX GOLD FEATURING PHILIP OAKEY
UK, male vocal/production duo. See Human League — 1

Date	Title / Label	Peak Position	Weeks at No.1	Weeks on Chart
26 Apr 03	**LA TODAY** *Xtravaganza XTRAV 37CDS*	68		1

ANDREW GOLD
US, male vocalist/pianist — 36

Date	Title / Label	Peak Position	Weeks at No.1	Weeks on Chart
2 Apr 77	**LONELY BOY** *Asylum K 13076*	11		9
25 Mar 78	**NEVER LET HER SLIP AWAY** *Asylum K 13112*	5		13
24 Jun 78	**HOW CAN THIS BE LOVE** *Asylum K 13126*	19		10
14 Oct 78	**THANK YOU FOR BEING A FRIEND** *Asylum K 13135*	42		4

BRIAN & TONY GOLD
Jamaica, male vocal duo – Patrick Morrison & Brian Thompson — 22

Date	Title / Label	Peak Position	Weeks at No.1	Weeks on Chart
30 Jul 94	**COMPLIMENTS ON YOUR KISS** *Mango CIDM 820* RED DRAGON WITH BRIAN & TONY GOLD	2		15
9 Nov 02	**HEY SEXY LADY** *MCA MCSTD 40304* SHAGGY FEATURING BRIAN AND TONY GOLD	10		7

GOLD BLADE
UK, male vocal/instrumental group — 1

Date	Title / Label	Peak Position	Weeks at No.1	Weeks on Chart
22 Mar 97	**STRICTLY HARDCORE** *Ultimate TOPP 056CD*	64		1

GOLDBUG
UK, male/female vocal/production duo – Sandi McKenzie & Richard Walmsley — 5

Date	Title / Label	Peak Position	Weeks at No.1	Weeks on Chart
27 Jan 96	**WHOLE LOTTA LOVE** *Make Dust JAZID 125CD*	3		5

GOLDEN BOY WITH MISS KITTIN
Germany/France, male/female vocal/production duo — 1

Date	Title / Label	Peak Position	Weeks at No.1	Weeks on Chart
7 Sep 02	**RIPPIN KITTIN** *Illustrious CDILL 007*	67		1

GOLDEN EARRING
Holland, male vocal/instrumental group – Barry Hay, Rinus Gerritsen, George Kooymans & Cesar Zuiderwijk — 16

Date	Title / Label	Peak Position	Weeks at No.1	Weeks on Chart
8 Dec 73	**RADAR LOVE** *Track 2094 116*	7		13
8 Oct 77	**RADAR LOVE** *Polydor 2121 335*	44		3

GOLDEN GIRLS
UK, male producer/instrumentalist (Mike Hazell) — 3

Date	Title / Label	Peak Position	Weeks at No.1	Weeks on Chart
3 Oct 98	**KINETIC** *Distinctive DISNCD 46*	38		2
4 Dec 99	**KINETIC '99** *Distinctive DISNCD 59*	56		1

GOLDENSCAN
UK, male DJ/production duo — 1

Date	Title / Label	Peak Position	Weeks at No.1	Weeks on Chart
11 Nov 00	**SUNRISE** *VC Recordings VCRD 79*	52		1

GOLDFINGER
US, male vocal/instrumental group — 1

Date	Title / Label	Peak Position	Weeks at No.1	Weeks on Chart
22 Jun 02	**OPEN YOUR EYES** *Jive 9270052*	75		1

GOLDFRAPP
UK, female/male vocal/instrumental duo – Alison Goldfrapp & Will Gregory — 50

Date	Title / Label	Peak Position	Weeks at No.1	Weeks on Chart
23 Jun 01	**UTOPIA** *Mute CDMUTE 264*	62		1
17 Nov 01	**PILOTS** *Mute LCDMUTE 267*	68		1
26 Apr 03	**TRAIN** *Mute LCDMUTE 291*	23		3
2 Aug 03	**STRICT MACHINE** *Mute LCDMUTE 295*	25		3
15 Nov 03	**TWIST** *Mute LCDMUTE 311*	31		2
13 Mar 04	**BLACK CHERRY** *Mute LCDMUTE 320*	28		2
22 May 04	**STRICT MACHINE** *Mute LCDMUTE 335*	20		3
20 Aug 05	**OOH LA LA** *Mute LCDMUTE342*	4		13
12 Nov 05	**NUMBER 1** *Mute LCDMUTE351*	9		4
25 Feb 06	**RIDE A WHITE HORSE** *Mute LCDMUTE356*	15		3
13 May 06	**FLY ME AWAY** *Mute LCDMUTE361*	26		2
16 Feb 08	**A&E** *Mute LCDMUTE389*	10		8
26 Apr 08	**HAPPINESS** *Mute CDMUTE392*	25		2
12 Jul 08	**CARAVAN GIRL** *Mute LCDMUTE401*	54		1
20 Mar 10	**ROCKET** *Mute CDMUTE430*	47		2

GOLDIE
UK, male vocal/instrumental group featuring Peter McDonald & Dave Black — 11

Date	Title / Label	Peak Position	Weeks at No.1	Weeks on Chart
27 May 78	**MAKING UP AGAIN** *Bronze BRO 50*	7		11

GOLDIE
UK, male producer (Clifford Price) — 16

Date	Title / Label	Peak Position	Weeks at No.1	Weeks on Chart
3 Dec 94	**INNER CITY LIFE** *ffrr FCD 251* PRESENTS METALHEADS	49		2
9 Sep 95	**ANGEL** *ffrr FCD 266*	41		3
11 Nov 95	**INNER CITY LIFE (REMIX)** *ffrr FCD 267* PRESENTS METALHEADS	39		2

Date	Title	Peak Position	Weeks at No.1	Weeks on Chart
1 Nov 97	**DIGITAL** *ffrr FCD 316* FEATURING KRS ONE	13		3
24 Jan 98	**TEMPERTEMPER** *ffrr FCD 325*	13		4
18 Apr 98	**BELIEVE** *ffrr FCD 332*	36		2

GOLDIE & THE GINGERBREADS

US, female vocal/instrumental group — **5**

Date	Title	Peak Position	Weeks at No.1	Weeks on Chart
25 Feb 65	**CAN'T YOU HEAR MY HEART BEAT?** *Decca F 12070*	25		5

GOLDIE LOOKIN CHAIN

UK, male rap/production group – Maggot (Andrew Major), Mike Balls, Eggsy (John Routledge), Adam Hussain, Mystikal (Christopher Edge), 2Hats (Andrew David), Billy Webb & Dwain Xain Zedong — **29**

Date	Title	Peak Position	Weeks at No.1	Weeks on Chart
1 May 04	**HALF MAN HALF MACHINE/SELF SUICIDE** *Must Destroy DUSTY019CD*	32		4
28 Aug 04	**GUNS DON'T KILL PEOPLE RAPPERS DO** *Atlantic GLC01CD*	3		9
6 Nov 04	**YOUR MOTHER'S GOT A PENIS** *East West GLC02CD*	14		3
25 Dec 04	**YOU KNOWS I LOVES YOU** *Atlantic GLC03CD*	22		5
17 Sep 05	**YOUR MISSUS IS A NUTTER** *Atlantic ATUK014CDX*	14		5
3 Dec 05	**R 'N' B** *Atlantic ATUK021CD*	26		3

GOLDRUSH

UK, male vocal/instrumental group — **2**

Date	Title	Peak Position	Weeks at No.1	Weeks on Chart
22 Jun 02	**SAME PICTURE** *Virgin VSCDT 1833*	64		1
7 Sep 02	**WIDE OPEN SKY** *Virgin VSCDT 1834*	70		1

BOBBY GOLDSBORO

US, male vocalist — **47**

Date	Title	Peak Position	Weeks at No.1	Weeks on Chart
17 Apr 68	**HONEY** *United Artists UP 2215* ★	2		15
4 Aug 73	**SUMMER (THE FIRST TIME)** *United Artists UP 35558*	9		10
3 Aug 74	**HELLO SUMMERTIME** *United Artists UP 35705*	14		10
29 Mar 75	**HONEY** *United Artists UP 35633*	2		12

GLEN GOLDSMITH

UK, male vocalist — **24**

Date	Title	Peak Position	Weeks at No.1	Weeks on Chart
7 Nov 87	**I WON'T CRY** *Reproduction PB 41493*	34		7
12 Mar 88	**DREAMING** *Reproduction PB 41711*	12		11
11 Jun 88	**WHAT YOU SEE IS WHAT YOU GET** *Reproduction PB 42075*	33		5
3 Sep 88	**SAVE A LITTLE BIT** *Reproduction PB 42147*	73		1

GOLDTRIX PRESENTS ANDREA BROWN

UK/US, male/female vocal/production/instrumental trio — **9**

Date	Title	Peak Position	Weeks at No.1	Weeks on Chart
19 Jan 02	**IT'S LOVE (TRIPPIN')** *AM:PM/Serious/Evolve CDAMPM 152*	6		9

GOMEZ

UK, male vocal/instrumental group — **20**

Date	Title	Peak Position	Weeks at No.1	Weeks on Chart
11 Apr 98	**78 STONE WOBBLE** *Hut HUTCD 95*	44		1
13 Jun 98	**GET MYSELF ARRESTED** *Hut HUTCD 97*	45		1
12 Sep 98	**WHIPPIN' PICCADILLY** *Hut HUTCD 105*	35		3
10 Jul 99	**BRING IT ON** *Hut HUTCD 112*	21		3
11 Sep 99	**RHYTHM & BLUES ALIBI** *Hut HUTCD 114*	18		3
27 Nov 99	**WE HAVEN'T TURNED AROUND** *Hut HUTCD 117*	38		2
16 Mar 02	**SHOT SHOT** *Hut HUTCDX 149*	28		2
15 Jun 02	**SOUND OF SOUNDS/PING ONE DOWN** *Hut HUTDX 154*	48		1
20 Mar 04	**CATCH ME UP** *Hut HUTDX 175*	36		2
22 May 04	**SILENCE** *Hut HUTDX 178*	41		1
10 Jun 06	**GIRLSHAPEDLOVEDRUG** *Independiente ISOM105SMS*	66		1

GOMPIE

Holland, male vocal/instrumental group — **12**

Date	Title	Peak Position	Weeks at No.1	Weeks on Chart
20 May 95	**ALICE (WHO THE X IS ALICE?) (LIVING NEXT DOOR TO ALICE)** *Habana HABSCD 5*	34		5
2 Sep 95	**ALICE (WHO THE X IS ALICE?) (LIVING NEXT DOOR TO ALICE)** *Habana HABSCD 5*	17		7

GONZALEZ

UK/US, male vocal/instrumental group — **11**

Date	Title	Peak Position	Weeks at No.1	Weeks on Chart
31 Mar 79	**HAVEN'T STOPPED DANCING YET** *Sidewalk SID 102*	15		11

JOSE GONZALEZ

Sweden, male vocalist/guitarist — **36**

Date	Title	Peak Position	Weeks at No.1	Weeks on Chart
21 Jan 06	**HEARTBEATS** *Peacefrog PFG076CD*	9		33
15 Jul 06	**HAND ON YOUR HEART** *Peacefrog PFG083CD*	29		3

GOO GOO DOLLS

US, male vocal/instrumental trio — **20**

Date	Title	Peak Position	Weeks at No.1	Weeks on Chart
1 Aug 98	**IRIS** *Reprise W0449CD*	50		1
27 Mar 99	**SLIDE** *Edel/Hollywood/Third Rail 0102035 HWR*	43		1
17 Jul 99	**IRIS** *Hollywood 0102485 HWR*	26		2
21 Oct 06	**IRIS/STAY WITH YOU** *Warner Brothers W736CD1*	39		14
19 Jul 08	**IRIS/STAY WITH YOU** *Warner Brothers W736CD1*	66		2

GOOD CHARLOTTE

US, male vocal/instrumental group – Joel & Benji Madden, Billy Martin, Paul Thomas & Chris Wilson (replaced by Dean Butterworth) — **43**

Date	Title	Peak Position	Weeks at No.1	Weeks on Chart
15 Feb 03	**LIFESTYLES OF THE RICH AND FAMOUS** *Epic 6735562*	8		10
17 May 03	**GIRLS AND BOYS** *Epic 6738775*	6		9
30 Aug 03	**THE ANTHEM** *Epic 6742552*	10		4
20 Dec 03	**THE YOUNG AND THE HOPELESS/HOLD ON** *Epic 6745435*	34		4
16 Oct 04	**PREDICTABLE** *Epic 6753882*	12		4
12 Feb 05	**I JUST WANNA LIVE** *Epic 6756492*	9		4
18 Jun 05	**THE CHRONICLES OF LIFE AND DEATH** *Epic 6759432*	30		2
10 Mar 07	**KEEP YOUR HANDS OFF MY GIRL** *Epic 88697063432*	23		6

GOOD GIRLS

US, female vocal trio — **1**

Date	Title	Peak Position	Weeks at No.1	Weeks on Chart
24 Jul 93	**JUST CALL ME** *Motown TMGCD 1417*	75		1

GOOD SHOES

UK, male vocal/instrumental group — **2**

Date	Title	Peak Position	Weeks at No.1	Weeks on Chart
6 Jan 07	**THE PHOTOS ON MY WALL** *Brille BRILS15CD*	48		1
24 Mar 07	**NEVER MEANT TO HURT YOU** *Brille BRILS20CD*	34		1

GOOD, THE BAD & THE QUEEN

UK/Nigeria, male vocal/instrumental group — **5**

Date	Title	Peak Position	Weeks at No.1	Weeks on Chart
11 Nov 06	**HERCULEAN** *Honest Jons CDR6722*	22		2
27 Jan 07	**KINGDOM OF DOOM** *Honest Jons CDR6732*	20		2
14 Apr 07	**GREEN FIELDS** *Honest Jons CDRS6738*	51		1

GOODBOOKS

UK, male vocal/instrumental group — **1**

Date	Title	Peak Position	Weeks at No.1	Weeks on Chart
28 Jul 07	**PASSCHENDAELE** *Columbia LIBRARY006*	73		1

GOODBYE MR MACKENZIE

UK, male/female vocal/instrumental group — **13**

Date	Title	Peak Position	Weeks at No.1	Weeks on Chart
20 Aug 88	**GOODBYE MR MACKENZIE** *Capitol CL 501*	62		2
11 Mar 89	**THE RATTLER** *Capitol CL 522*	37		6
29 Jul 89	**GOODWILL CITY/I'M SICK OF YOU** *Capitol CL 538*	49		2
21 Apr 90	**LOVE CHILD** *Parlophone R 6247*	52		2
23 Jun 90	**BLACKER THAN BLACK** *Parlophone R 6257*	61		1

ROGER GOODE FEATURING TASHA BAXTER

South Africa, male/female vocal/DJ/production duo — **2**

Date	Title	Peak Position	Weeks at No.1	Weeks on Chart
13 Apr 02	**IN THE BEGINNING** *ffrr DFCDP 004*	33		2

GOODFELLAS FEATURING LISA MILLETT

Italy/UK, male/female vocal/production trio. See Bini & Martini, Eclipse, House Of Glass — **2**

Date	Title	Peak Position	Weeks at No.1	Weeks on Chart
21 Jul 01	**SOUL HEAVEN** *Direction 6713852*	27		2

GOODFELLAZ

US, male vocal trio — **2**

Date	Title	Peak Position	Weeks at No.1	Weeks on Chart
10 May 97	**SUGAR HONEY ICE TEA** *Wild Card 5736132*	25		2

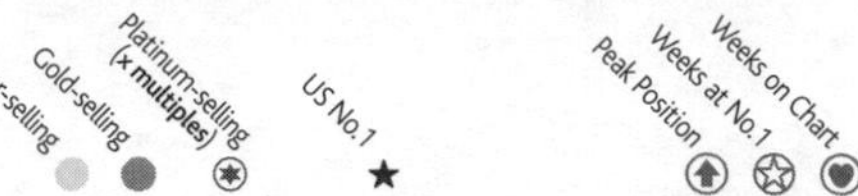

GOODIES

UK, male comedy/vocal trio – Bill Oddie, Graeme Garden & Tom Brooke-Taylor — **38**

Date	Title	Peak	Wks at No.1	Wks on Chart
7 Dec 74	**THE IN BETWEENIES/FATHER CHRISTMAS DO NOT TOUCH ME** *Bradley's BRAD 7421*	7		9
15 Mar 75	**FUNKY GIBBON/SICK MAN BLUES** *Bradley's BRAD 7504*	4		10
21 Jun 75	**BLACK PUDDING BERTHA (THE QUEEN OF NORTHERN SOUL)** *Bradley's BRAD 7517*	19		7
27 Sep 75	**NAPPY LOVE/WILD THING** *Bradley's BRAD 7524*	21		6
13 Dec 75	**MAKE A DAFT NOISE FOR CHRISTMAS** *Bradley's BRAD 7533*	20		6

CUBA GOODING

US, male vocalist. See Main Ingredient — **2**

Date	Title	Peak	Wks at No.1	Wks on Chart
19 Nov 83	**HAPPINESS IS JUST AROUND THE BEND** *London LON 41*	72		2

GOODMEN

Holland, male production duo – Rene ter Horst & Gaston Steenkist — **19**

Date	Title	Peak	Wks at No.1	Wks on Chart
7 Aug 93	**GIVE IT UP** *Fresh Fruit TABCD 118*	5		19

DELTA GOODREM

Australia, female vocalist/actor — **58**

Date	Title	Peak	Wks at No.1	Wks on Chart
22 Mar 03	**BORN TO TRY** *Epic 6736342*	3		13
28 Jun 03	**LOST WITHOUT YOU** *Epic 6739555*	4		11
4 Oct 03	**INNOCENT EYES** *Epic 6743155*	9		9
13 Dec 03	**NOT ME NOT I** *Epic 6745372*	18		6
20 Nov 04	**OUT OF THE BLUE** *Epic 6754732*	9		9
12 Feb 05	**ALMOST HERE** *Sony Music 6757352* BRIAN McFADDEN & DELTA GOODREM	3		10

RON GOODWIN

UK, male orchestra leader, d. 8 Jan 2003 (age 77) — **27**

Date	Title	Peak	Wks at No.1	Wks on Chart
15 May 53	**TERRY'S THEME FROM 'LIMELIGHT'** *Parlophone R 3686*	3		23
28 Oct 55	**BLUE STAR (THE MEDIC THEME)** *Parlophone R 4074*	20		1
20 Jan 56	**SHIFTING WHISPERING SANDS (PARTS 1 & 2)** *Parlophone R 4106* EAMONN ANDREWS WITH RON GOODWIN & HIS ORCHESTRA	18		3

GOODY GOODY

US, female vocal duo — **5**

Date	Title	Peak	Wks at No.1	Wks on Chart
2 Dec 78	**NUMBER ONE DEE JAY** *Atlantic LV 3*	55		5

GOOMBAY DANCE BAND

Germany/Montserrat, male/female vocal/instrumental group – Oliver Bendt (Jorg Knoch), Wendy Doorsen, Dorothy Hellings & Mario Slijngaard — **16**

Date	Title	Peak	Wks at No.1	Wks on Chart
27 Feb 82	**SEVEN TEARS** *Epic EPC A 1242*	1	3	12
15 May 82	**SUN OF JAMAICA** *Epic EPC A 2345*	50		4

GOONS

UK, male comedy/vocal group – Spike Milligan, d. 27 Feb 2002, Harry Secombe*, d. 11 Apr 2001, & Peter Sellers*, d. 24 Jul 1980 — **30**

Date	Title	Peak	Wks at No.1	Wks on Chart
29 Jun 56	**I'M WALKING BACKWARDS FOR CHRISTMAS/BLUEBOTTLE BLUES** *Decca F 10756*	4		10
14 Sep 56	**BLOODNOK'S ROCK 'N' ROLL CALL/YING TONG SONG** *Decca F 10780*	3		10
21 Jul 73	**YING TONG SONG** *Decca F 13414*	9		10

LONNIE GORDON

US, female vocalist — **23**

Date	Title	Peak	Wks at No.1	Wks on Chart
24 Jun 89	**(I'VE GOT YOUR) PLEASURE CONTROL** *ffrr F 106* SIMON HARRIS FEATURING LONNIE GORDON	60		3
27 Jan 90	**HAPPENIN' ALL OVER AGAIN** *Supreme SUPE 159*	4		10
11 Aug 90	**BEYOND YOUR WILDEST DREAMS** *Supreme SUPE 167*	48		2
17 Nov 90	**IF I HAVE TO STAND ALONE** *Supreme SUPE 181*	68		1
4 May 91	**GONNA CATCH YOU** *Supreme SUPE 185*	32		5
7 Oct 95	**LOVE EVICTION** *X:Plode BANG 2CD* QUARTZ LOCK FEATURING LONNIE GORDON	32		2

LESLEY GORE

US, female vocalist (Lesley Goldstein) — **20**

Date	Title	Peak	Wks at No.1	Wks on Chart
20 Jun 63	**IT'S MY PARTY** *Mercury AMT 1205* ★	9		12
24 Sep 64	**MAYBE I KNOW** *Mercury MF 829*	20		8

MARTIN L GORE

UK, male vocalist/guitarist. See Depeche Mode — **1**

Date	Title	Peak	Wks at No.1	Wks on Chart
26 Apr 03	**STARDUST** *Mute CDMUTE 296*	44		1

GORILLAZ

UK/US/Japan, male/female virtual cartoon group – 2D (Stuart Pot), Murdoc (Murdoc Niccals), Noodle & Russel (Russel Hobbs); all characters created by Damon Albarn & Jamie Hewlett. See Blur — **126**

Date	Title	Peak	Wks at No.1	Wks on Chart
17 Mar 01	**CLINT EASTWOOD** *Parlophone CDR 6552*	4		17
7 Jul 01	**19/2000** *Parlophone CDR 6559*	6		10
3 Nov 01	**ROCK THE HOUSE** *Parlophone CDRS 6565*	18		8
9 Mar 02	**TOMORROW COMES TODAY** *Parlophone CDR 6573*	33		3
3 Aug 02	**LIL' DUB CHEFIN'** *Parlophone CDR 6584* SPACE MONKEY VS GORILLAZ	73		1
23 Apr 05	**FEEL GOOD INC** *Parlophone CDR6663*	2		39
10 Sep 05	**DARE** *Parlophone CDRS6668*	1	1	27
3 Dec 05	**DIRTY HARRY** *Parlophone CDRS6676*	6		19
22 Apr 06	**KIDS WITH GUNS/EL MANANA** *Parlophone CDR6685*	27		2

GORKY'S ZYGOTIC MYNCI

UK, male/female vocal/instrumental group — **8**

Date	Title	Peak	Wks at No.1	Wks on Chart
9 Nov 96	**PATIO SONG** *Fontana GZMCD 1*	41		1
29 Mar 97	**DIAMOND DEW** *Fontana GZMCD 2*	42		1
21 Jun 97	**YOUNG GIRLS & HAPPY ENDINGS/DARK NIGHT** *Fontana GZMCD 3*	49		1
6 Jun 98	**SWEET JOHNNY** *Fontana GZMCD 4*	60		1
29 Aug 98	**LET'S GET TOGETHER (IN OUR MINDS)** *Fontana GZMCD 5*	43		1
2 Oct 99	**SPANISH DANCE TROUPE** *Mantra/Beggars Banquet MNT 47CD*	47		1
4 Mar 00	**POODLE ROCKIN'** *Mantra/Beggars Banquet MNT 52CD*	52		1
15 Sep 01	**STOOD ON GOLD** *Mantra MNT 64CD*	65		1

EYDIE GORME

US, female vocalist — **33**

Date	Title	Peak	Wks at No.1	Wks on Chart
24 Jan 58	**LOVE ME FOREVER** *HMV POP 432*	21		5
21 Jun 62	**YES MY DARLING DAUGHTER** *CBS AAG 105*	10		9
31 Jan 63	**BLAME IT ON THE BOSSA NOVA** *CBS AAG 131*	32		6
22 Aug 63	**I WANT TO STAY HERE** *CBS AAG 163* STEVE & EYDIE	3		13

LUKE GOSS & THE BAND OF THIEVES

UK, male vocal/instrumental group. See Bros — **3**

Date	Title	Peak	Wks at No.1	Wks on Chart
12 Jun 93	**SWEETER THAN THE MIDNIGHT RAIN** *Sabre CDSAB 1*	52		2
21 Aug 93	**GIVE ME ONE MORE CHANCE** *Sabre CDSAB 2*	68		1

MATT GOSS

UK, male vocalist. See Bros — **10**

Date	Title	Peak	Wks at No.1	Wks on Chart
26 Aug 95	**THE KEY** *Atlas 5811532*	40		2
27 Apr 96	**IF YOU WERE HERE TONIGHT** *Atlas 5762932*	23		3
15 Nov 03	**I'M COMING WITH YA** *Concept CDCON 49*	22		2
31 Jul 04	**FLY** *Concept CDCON57*	31		2
2 Oct 04	**I NEED THE KEY** *Inferno CDFERN63* MINIMAL CHIC FEATURING MATT GOSS	54		1

GOSSIP

US, female/male vocal/instrumental trio – Beth Ditto (Mary Patterson), Hannah Blilie & Brace Paine (Nathan Howdeshell) — **34**

Date	Title	Peak	Wks at No.1	Wks on Chart
11 Nov 06	**STANDING IN THE WAY OF CONTROL** *Back Yard Recordings BACK19CSC1*	7		28
23 Jun 07	**LISTEN UP** *Back Yard Recordings BACK18CSC2*	39		1
13 Jun 09	**HEAVY CROSS** *Columbia 88697536832*	37		5

IRV GOTTI PRESENTS JA RULE, ASHANTI, CHARLI BALTIMORE & VITA

US, male rapper/producer (Irving Lorenzo) & male/female rap/vocal group — **10**

Date	Title	Peak	Wks at No.1	Wks on Chart
12 Oct 02	**DOWN 4 U** *Murder Inc 0639002*	4		10

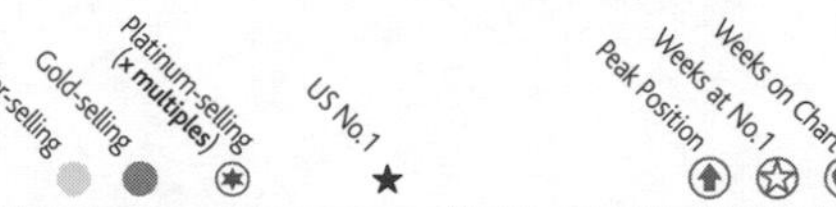

Peak Position / Weeks at No.1 / Weeks on Chart

ELLIE GOULDING
UK, female vocalist/guitarist (Elena Goulding) — 9

Date	Title / Label	Peak Position	Weeks at No.1	Weeks on Chart
28 Nov 09	**UNDER THE SHEETS** *Polydor GBUV70904692*	53		3
6 Mar 10	**STARRY EYED** *Polydor 2732866*	4		6+

GRAHAM GOULDMAN
UK, male vocalist/guitarist. See 10cc, Wax — 4

Date	Title / Label	Peak Position	Weeks at No.1	Weeks on Chart
23 Jun 79	**SUNBURN** *Mercury SUNNY 1*	52		4

GOURYELLA
Holland, male production duo. See Albion, Moonman, Starparty, System F, Veracocha — 11

Date	Title / Label	Peak Position	Weeks at No.1	Weeks on Chart
10 Jul 99	**GOURYELLA** *Code Blue BLU 001CD*	15		7
4 Dec 99	**WALHALLA** *Code Blue BLU 006CD*	27		2
23 Dec 00	**TENSHI** *Code Blue BLU 017CD*	45		2

GQ
US, male vocal/instrumental group — 6

Date	Title / Label	Peak Position	Weeks at No.1	Weeks on Chart
10 Mar 79	**DISCO NIGHTS (ROCK FREAK)** *Arista ARIST 245*	42		6

GRACE
UK, female vocalist (Dominique Atkins) — 24

Date	Title / Label	Peak Position	Weeks at No.1	Weeks on Chart
8 Apr 95	**NOT OVER YET** *Perfecto PERF 104CD*	6		8
23 Sep 95	**I WANT TO LIVE** *Perfecto PERF 109CD*	30		2
24 Feb 96	**SKIN ON SKIN** *Perfecto PERF 116CD*	21		3
1 Jun 96	**DOWN TO EARTH** *Perfecto PERF 120CD*	20		2
28 Sep 96	**IF I COULD FLY** *Perfecto PERF 127CD*	29		2
3 May 97	**HAND IN HAND** *Perfecto PERF 129CD*	38		1
26 Jul 97	**DOWN TO EARTH** *Perfecto PERF 142CD1*	29		2
14 Aug 99	**NOT OVER YET 99** *Code Blue BLU 004CD* PLANET PERFECTO FEATURING GRACE	16		4

GRACE BROTHERS
UK, male instrumental duo — 1

Date	Title / Label	Peak Position	Weeks at No.1	Weeks on Chart
20 Apr 96	**ARE YOU BEING SERVED** *EMI Premier PRESCD 1*	51		1

CHARLIE GRACIE
US, male vocalist (Charles Graci) — 43

Date	Title / Label	Peak Position	Weeks at No.1	Weeks on Chart
19 Apr 57	**BUTTERFLY** *Parlophone R 4290* ★	12		8
14 Jun 57	**FABULOUS** *Parlophone R 4313*	8		16
23 Aug 57	**I LOVE YOU SO MUCH IT HURTS** *London HLU 8467*	14		4
23 Aug 57	**WANDERIN' EYES** *London HLU 8467*	6		14
10 Jan 58	**COOL BABY** *London HLU 8521*	26		1

GRACIOUS K
UK, male rapper (Lance Gracious) — 1

Date	Title / Label	Peak Position	Weeks at No.1	Weeks on Chart
24 Oct 09	**MIGRAINE SKANK** *RCA 88697599582*	53		1

GRAFITI
UK, male producer (Mike Skinner). See Streets — 2

Date	Title / Label	Peak Position	Weeks at No.1	Weeks on Chart
30 Aug 03	**WHAT IS THE PROBLEM?** *679 Recordings 679L 021CD*	37		2

JAKI GRAHAM
UK, female vocalist — 75

Date	Title / Label	Peak Position	Weeks at No.1	Weeks on Chart
23 Mar 85	**COULD IT BE I'M FALLING IN LOVE** *Chrysalis GRAN 6* DAVID GRANT & JAKI GRAHAM	5		11
29 Jun 85	**ROUND AND ROUND** *EMI JAKI 4*	9		11
31 Aug 85	**HEAVEN KNOWS** *EMI JAKI 5*	59		3
16 Nov 85	**MATED** *EMI JAKI 6* DAVID GRANT & JAKI GRAHAM	20		10
3 May 86	**SET ME FREE** *EMI JAKI 7*	7		12
9 Aug 86	**BREAKING AWAY** *EMI JAKI 8*	16		8
15 Nov 86	**STEP RIGHT UP** *EMI JAKI 9*	15		12
9 Jul 88	**NO MORE TEARS** *EMI JAKI 12*	60		2
24 Jun 89	**FROM NOW ON** *EMI JAKI 15*	73		2
16 Jul 94	**AIN'T NOBODY** *Pulse 8 CDLOSE 64*	44		2
4 Feb 95	**YOU CAN COUNT ON ME** *Avex UK AVEXCD 1*	62		1
8 Jul 95	**ABSOLUTE E-SENSUAL** *Avex UK AVEXCD 5*	69		1

LARRY GRAHAM
US, male vocalist/bass player. See Sly & The Family Stone — 4

Date	Title / Label	Peak Position	Weeks at No.1	Weeks on Chart
3 Jul 82	**SOONER OR LATER** *Warner Brothers K 17925*	54		4

MAX GRAHAM VS YES
Canada/UK, male vocal/DJ/instrumental/production group — 8

Date	Title / Label	Peak Position	Weeks at No.1	Weeks on Chart
28 May 05	**OWNER OF A LONELY HEART** *Data DATA92CDS*	9		8

MIKEY GRAHAM
Ireland, male vocalist. See Boyzone — 6

Date	Title / Label	Peak Position	Weeks at No.1	Weeks on Chart
10 Jun 00	**YOU'RE MY ANGEL** *Public PR 001CDS*	13		5
14 Apr 01	**YOU COULD BE MY EVERYTHING** *Public PR 003CDS*	62		1

RON GRAINER ORCHESTRA
UK, male orchestra leader, d. 21 Feb 1981 (age 58) — 7

Date	Title / Label	Peak Position	Weeks at No.1	Weeks on Chart
9 Dec 78	**A TOUCH OF VELVET A STING OF BRASS** *Casino Classics CC 5*	60		7

GRAM'MA FUNK
US, male/female vocal/rap duo — 7

Date	Title / Label	Peak Position	Weeks at No.1	Weeks on Chart
27 Nov 99	**I SEE YOU BABY** *Pepper 9230002* GROOVE ARMADA FEATURING GRAM'MA FUNK	17		6
2 Sep 00	**CHEEKY ARMADA** *Yola YOLACDX 01* ILLICIT FEATURING GRAM'MA FUNK	72		1

GRAMOPHONEDZIE
Serbia, male DJ (Marko Milicevic) — 5

Date	Title / Label	Peak Position	Weeks at No.1	Weeks on Chart
13 Mar 10	**WHY DON'T YOU** *Positiva/Virgin CDTIV294*	12		5+

GRAND FUNK RAILROAD
US, male vocal/instrumental group — 1

Date	Title / Label	Peak Position	Weeks at No.1	Weeks on Chart
6 Feb 71	**INSIDE LOOKING OUT** *Capitol CL 15668*	40		1

GRAND PLAZ
UK, male production group — 4

Date	Title / Label	Peak Position	Weeks at No.1	Weeks on Chart
8 Sep 90	**WOW WOW – NA NA** *Urban URB 60*	41		4

GRAND PRIX
UK, male vocal/instrumental group — 1

Date	Title / Label	Peak Position	Weeks at No.1	Weeks on Chart
27 Feb 82	**KEEP ON BELIEVING** *RCA 162*	75		1

GRAND PUBA
US, male rapper (Maxwell Dixon) — 6

Date	Title / Label	Peak Position	Weeks at No.1	Weeks on Chart
13 Jan 96	**WHY YOU TREAT ME SO BAD** *Virgin VSCDT 1566* SHAGGY FEATURING GRAND PUBA	11		5
30 Mar 96	**WILL YOU BE MY BABY** *GHQ 74321339092* INFINITI FEATURING GRAND PUBA	53		1

GRAND THEFT AUDIO
UK, male vocal/instrumental group — 1

Date	Title / Label	Peak Position	Weeks at No.1	Weeks on Chart
24 Mar 01	**WE LUV U** *Sci-Fi SCIFI 1CD*	70		1

GRANDAD ROBERTS & HIS SON ELVIS
UK, male vocal duo — 1

Date	Title / Label	Peak Position	Weeks at No.1	Weeks on Chart
20 Jun 98	**MEAT PIE SAUSAGE ROLL** *WEA 160CD*	67		1

GRANDADDY
US, male vocal/instrumental group — 6

Date	Title / Label	Peak Position	Weeks at No.1	Weeks on Chart
2 Sep 00	**HEWLETT'S DAUGHTER** *V2 VVR 5014333*	71		1
10 Feb 01	**THE CRYSTAL LAKE** *V2 VVR 5015158*	38		2
14 Jun 03	**NOW IT'S ON** *V2 VVR 5022248*	23		2
6 Sep 03	**EL CAMINOS IN THE WEST** *V2 VVR 5023663*	48		1

GRANDMASTER FLASH
US (b. Barbados), male DJ/producer (Joseph Saddler) — 87

Date	Title	Peak	Wks No.1	Wks
28 Aug 82	**THE MESSAGE** *Sugarhill SHL 117* & THE FURIOUS FIVE	8		9
22 Jan 83	**MESSAGE II (SURVIVAL)** *Sugarhill SHL 119* MELLE MEL & DUKE BOOTEE	74		2
19 Nov 83	**WHITE LINES (DON'T DON'T DO IT)** *Sugarhill SHL 130* & MELLE MEL ●	7		43
30 Jun 84	**BEAT STREET BREAKDOWN** *Atlantic A 9659* GRANDMASTER MELLE MEL & THE FURIOUS FIVE	42		7
22 Sep 84	**WE DON'T WORK FOR FREE** *Sugarhill SH 136* GRANDMASTER MELLE MEL & THE FURIOUS FIVE	45		4
15 Dec 84	**STEP OFF (PART 1)** *Sugarhill SHL 139* GRANDMASTER MELLE MEL & THE FURIOUS FIVE	8		12
16 Feb 85	**SIGN OF THE TIMES** *Elektra E 9677*	72		1
16 Mar 85	**PUMP ME UP** *Sugarhill SH 141* GRANDMASTER MELLE MEL & THE FURIOUS FIVE	45		6
8 Jan 94	**WHITE LINES (DON'T DON'T DO IT) (REMIX)** *WGAF WGAFCD 103* & MELLE MEL	59		3

GRANDMIXER DST
US, male DJ/producer (Derek Showard) — 3

Date	Title	Peak	Wks No.1	Wks
24 Dec 83	**CRAZY CUTS** *Island IS 146*	71		3

GRANGE HILL CAST
UK, male/female actors/vocal group — 6

Date	Title	Peak	Wks No.1	Wks
19 Apr 86	**JUST SAY NO** *BBC RESL 183*	5		6

GERRI GRANGER
US, female vocalist — 3

Date	Title	Peak	Wks No.1	Wks
30 Sep 78	**I GO TO PIECES (EVERYTIME)** *Casino Classics CC 3*	50		3

AMY GRANT
US, female vocalist — 39

Date	Title	Peak	Wks No.1	Wks
11 May 91	**BABY BABY** *A&M AM 727* ● ★	2		13
3 Aug 91	**EVERY HEARTBEAT** *A&M AM 783*	25		7
2 Nov 91	**THAT'S WHAT LOVE IS FOR** *A&M AM 666*	60		3
15 Feb 92	**GOOD FOR ME** *A&M AM 810*	60		1
13 Aug 94	**LUCKY ONE** *A&M 5807322*	60		1
22 Oct 94	**SAY YOU'LL BE MINE** *A&M 5808292*	41		2
24 Jun 95	**BIG YELLOW TAXI** *A&M 5809972*	20		10
14 Oct 95	**HOUSE OF LOVE** *A&M 5812332* WITH VINCE GILL	46		2

ANDREA GRANT
UK, female vocalist — 1

Date	Title	Peak	Wks No.1	Wks
14 Nov 98	**REPUTATIONS (JUST BE GOOD TO ME)** *WEA 192CD*	75		1

DAVID GRANT
UK, male vocalist. See Linx — 59

Date	Title	Peak	Wks No.1	Wks
30 Apr 83	**STOP AND GO** *Chrysalis GRAN 1*	19		9
16 Jul 83	**WATCHING YOU WATCHING ME** *Chrysalis GRAN 2*	10		13
8 Oct 83	**LOVE WILL FIND A WAY** *Chrysalis GRAN 3*	24		6
26 Nov 83	**ROCK THE MIDNIGHT** *Chrysalis GRAN 4*	46		4
23 Mar 85	**COULD IT BE I'M FALLING IN LOVE** *Chrysalis GRAN 6* & JAKI GRAHAM	5		11
16 Nov 85	**MATED** *EMI JAKI 6* & JAKI GRAHAM	20		10
1 Aug 87	**CHANGE** *Polydor POSP 871*	55		4
12 May 90	**KEEP IT TOGETHER** *Fourth & Broadway BRW 169*	56		2

EDDY GRANT
Guyana, male vocalist/guitarist. See Equals — 107

Date	Title	Peak	Wks No.1	Wks
2 Jun 79	**LIVING ON THE FRONT LINE** *Ensign ENY 26*	11		11
15 Nov 80	**DO YOU FEEL MY LOVE** *Ensign ENY 45* ●	8		11
4 Apr 81	**CAN'T GET ENOUGH OF YOU** *Ensign ENY 207*	13		10
25 Jul 81	**I LOVE YOU, YES I LOVE YOU** *Ensign ENY 216*	37		6
16 Oct 82	**I DON'T WANNA DANCE** *Ice 56* ●	1	3	15
15 Jan 83	**ELECTRIC AVENUE** *Ice 57* ●	2		9
19 Mar 83	**LIVING ON THE FRONT LINE/DO YOU FEEL MY LOVE** *Mercury MER 135*	47		4
23 Apr 83	**WAR PARTY** *Ice 58*	42		4
29 Oct 83	**TILL I CAN'T TAKE LOVE NO MORE** *Ice 60*	42		7
19 May 84	**ROMANCING THE STONE** *Ice 61*	52		3
23 Jan 88	**GIMME HOPE JO'ANNA** *Ice 78701*	7		12
27 May 89	**WALKING ON SUNSHINE** *Blue Wave R 6217*	63		2
9 Jun 01	**ELECTRIC AVENUE** *Ice EW 232CD* ●	5		12
24 Nov 01	**WALKING ON SUNSHINE** *Ice EW 242CD*	57		1

GOGI GRANT
US, female vocalist (Audrey Arinsberg) — 11

Date	Title	Peak	Wks No.1	Wks
29 Jun 56	**WAYWARD WIND** *London HLB 8282* ★	9		11

JULIE GRANT
UK, female vocalist (Vivienne Foreman) — 17

Date	Title	Peak	Wks No.1	Wks
3 Jan 63	**UP ON THE ROOF** *Pye 7N 15483*	33		3
28 Mar 63	**COUNT ON ME** *Pye 7N 15508*	24		9
24 Sep 64	**COME TO ME** *Pye 7N 15684*	31		5

RUDY GRANT
Guyana, male vocalist — 3

Date	Title	Peak	Wks No.1	Wks
14 Feb 81	**LATELY** *Ensign ENY 202*	58		3

GRAPEFRUIT
UK, male vocal/instrumental group — 19

Date	Title	Peak	Wks No.1	Wks
14 Feb 68	**DEAR DELILAH** *RCA 1656*	21		9
14 Aug 68	**C'MON MARIANNE** *RCA 1716*	31		10

GRASS-SHOW
Sweden, male vocal/instrumental group — 2

Date	Title	Peak	Wks No.1	Wks
22 Mar 97	**1962** *Food CDFOOD 90*	53		1
23 Aug 97	**OUT OF THE VOID** *Food CDFOOD 103*	75		1

GRAVEDIGGAZ
US, male rap group. See RZA, Wu-Tang Clan — 6

Date	Title	Peak	Wks No.1	Wks
11 Mar 95	**SIX FEET DEEP (EP)** *Gee Street GESCD 62*	64		1
5 Aug 95	**THE HELL EP** *Fourth & Broadway BRCD 326* TRICKY VS THE GRAVEDIGGAZ	12		3
24 Jan 98	**THE NIGHT THE EARTH CRIED** *Gee Street GEE 5001013*	44		1
25 Apr 98	**UNEXPLAINED** *Gee Street GEE 5001623*	48		1

DAVID GRAY
UK, male vocalist/guitarist/pianist — 54

Date	Title	Peak	Wks No.1	Wks
4 Dec 99	**PLEASE FORGIVE ME** *IHT IHTCDS 003*	72		1
1 Jul 00	**BABYLON** *IHT/East West EW 215CD1*	5		12
28 Oct 00	**PLEASE FORGIVE ME** *IHT/East West EW 219CD*	18		6
17 Mar 01	**THIS YEAR'S LOVE** *IHT/East West EW 228CD1*	20		5
28 Jul 01	**SAIL AWAY** *IHT/East West EW 234CD*	26		6
29 Dec 01	**SAY HELLO WAVE GOODBYE** *IHT/East West EW 243CD*	26		4
21 Dec 02	**THE OTHER SIDE** *IHT/East West EW 259CD*	35		3
19 Apr 03	**BE MINE** *IHT/East West EW 264CD*	23		3
10 Sep 05	**THE ONE I LOVE** *IHT/Atlantic ATUK013CD*	8		10
10 Dec 05	**HOSPITAL FOOD** *Atlantic ATUK018CD*	34		2
8 Apr 06	**ALIBI** *Atlantic ATUK027CDX*	71		1
17 Nov 07	**YOU'RE THE WORLD TO ME** *Atlantic ATUK071CD2*	53		1

DOBIE GRAY
US, female vocalist (Lawrence Brown) — 11

Date	Title	Peak	Wks No.1	Wks
25 Feb 65	**THE IN CROWD** *London HL 9953*	25		7
27 Sep 75	**OUT ON THE FLOOR** *Black Magic BM 107*	42		4

DORIAN GRAY
UK, male vocalist — 7

Date	Title	Peak	Wks No.1	Wks
27 Mar 68	**I'VE GOT YOU ON MY MIND** *Parlophone R 5667*	36		7

LES GRAY
UK, male vocalist, d. 21 Feb 2004 (age 57). See Mud — 5

Date	Title	Peak	Wks No.1	Wks
26 Feb 77	**A GROOVY KIND OF LOVE** *Warner Brothers K 16883*	32		5

MACY GRAY
US, female vocalist (Natalie McIntyre) — 52

Date	Title	Peak	Wks No.1	Wks
3 Jul 99	**DO SOMETHING** *Epic 6675932*	51		1
9 Oct 99	**I TRY** *Epic 6681832* ●	6		22
25 Mar 00	**STILL** *Epic 6689622*	18		9
5 Aug 00	**WHY DIDN'T YOU CALL ME** *Epic 6696682*	38		3
20 Jan 01	**DEMONS** *Skint 60CD* FATBOY SLIM FEATURING MACY GRAY	16		5
28 Apr 01	**GETO HEAVEN** *MCA MCSTD 40246* COMMON FEATURING MACY GRAY	48		1

Date	Title	Peak Position	Weeks at No.1	Weeks on Chart
12 May 01	**REQUEST & LINE** *Interscope 4975032* BLACK EYED PEAS FEATURING MACY GRAY	31		3
15 Sep 01	**SWEET BABY** *Epic 6718822* FEATURING ERYKAH BADU	23		4
8 Dec 01	**SEXUAL REVOLUTION** *Epic 6721462*	45		1
3 May 03	**WHEN I SEE YOU** *Epic 6738405*	26		3

MICHAEL GRAY

UK, male producer. See Disco Tex presents Cloudburst, Full Intention, Hustlers Convention featuring Dave Laudat & Ondrea Duverney, Sex-O-Sonique — **20**

Date	Title	Peak Position	Weeks at No.1	Weeks on Chart
13 Nov 04	**THE WEEKEND** *Eye Industries/UMTV 9868865*	7		14
12 Aug 06	**BORDERLINE** *Eye Industries/UMTV 1703606* FEATURING SHELLEY POOLE	12		6

BARRY GRAY ORCHESTRA

UK, male orchestra leader, d. 26 Apr 1984 (age 75) — **8**

Date	Title	Peak Position	Weeks at No.1	Weeks on Chart
11 Jul 81	**THUNDERBIRDS** *PRT 7P 216*	61		2
14 Jun 86	**JOE 90 (THEME)/CAPTAIN SCARLET THEME** *PRT 7PX 354* WITH PETER BECKETT – KEYBOARDS	53		6

GREAT WHITE

US, male vocal/instrumental group — **5**

Date	Title	Peak Position	Weeks at No.1	Weeks on Chart
24 Feb 90	**HOUSE OF BROKEN LOVE** *Capitol CL 562*	44		2
16 Feb 91	**CONGO SQUARE** *Capitol CL 605*	62		1
7 Sep 91	**CALL IT ROCK 'N' ROLL** *Capitol CL 625*	67		2

MARTIN GRECH

UK, male vocalist/guitarist — **1**

Date	Title	Peak Position	Weeks at No.1	Weeks on Chart
12 Oct 02	**OPEN HEART ZOO** *Island CID 811*	68		1

BUDDY GRECO

US, male vocalist (Armando Greco) — **8**

Date	Title	Peak Position	Weeks at No.1	Weeks on Chart
7 Jul 60	**LADY IS A TRAMP** *Fontana H 225*	26		8

GREED FEATURING RICARDO DA FORCE

UK, male rap/instrumental trio — **2**

Date	Title	Peak Position	Weeks at No.1	Weeks on Chart
18 Mar 95	**PUMP UP THE VOLUME** *Stress CDSTR 49*	51		2

GREEDIES

Ireland/UK/US, male vocal/instrumental group — **5**

Date	Title	Peak Position	Weeks at No.1	Weeks on Chart
15 Dec 79	**A MERRY JINGLE** *Vertigo GREED 1*	28		5

ADAM GREEN

US, male vocalist/multi-instrumentalist — **2**

Date	Title	Peak Position	Weeks at No.1	Weeks on Chart
3 Apr 04	**JESSICA/KOKOMO** *Rough Trade RTRADESCD112*	63		1
19 Feb 05	**EMILY** *Rough Trade RTRADSCD213*	53		1

AL GREEN

US, male vocalist (Al Greene) — **68**

Date	Title	Peak Position	Weeks at No.1	Weeks on Chart
9 Oct 71	**TIRED OF BEING ALONE** *London HL 10337*	4		13
8 Jan 72	**LET'S STAY TOGETHER** *London HL 10348* ★	7		12
20 May 72	**LOOK WHAT YOU DONE FOR ME** *London HL 10369*	44		4
19 Aug 72	**I'M STILL IN LOVE WITH YOU** *London HL 10382*	35		5
16 Nov 74	**SHA-LA-LA (MAKES ME HAPPY)** *London HL 10470*	20		11
15 Mar 75	**L.O.V.E.** *London HL 10482*	24		8
3 Dec 88	**PUT A LITTLE LOVE IN YOUR HEART** *A&M AM 484* ANNIE LENNOX & AL GREEN	28		8
21 Oct 89	**THE MESSAGE IS LOVE** *Breakout USA 668* ARTHUR BAKER & THE BACKSTREET DISCIPLES FEATURING AL GREEN	38		5
2 Oct 93	**LOVE IS A BEAUTIFUL THING** *Arista 74321162692*	56		2

JESSE GREEN

Jamaica, male vocalist — **26**

Date	Title	Peak Position	Weeks at No.1	Weeks on Chart
7 Aug 76	**NICE AND SLOW** *EMI 2492*	17		12
18 Dec 76	**FLIP** *EMI 2564*	26		8
11 Jun 77	**COME WITH ME** *EMI 2615*	29		6

GREEN DAY

US, male vocal/instrumental trio – Billie Joe Armstrong, Tré Cool (Frank Wright III) & Mike Dirnt (Michael Pritchard) — **129**

Date	Title	Peak Position	Weeks at No.1	Weeks on Chart
20 Aug 94	**BASKET CASE** *Reprise W0257CD*	55		2
29 Oct 94	**WELCOME TO PARADISE** *Reprise W0269CDX*	20		3
28 Jan 95	**BASKET CASE** *Reprise W0279CDX*	7		6
18 Mar 95	**LONGVIEW** *Reprise W0287CDX*	30		3
20 May 95	**WHEN I COME AROUND** *Reprise W0294CD*	27		3
7 Oct 95	**GEEK STINK BREATH** *Reprise W0320CD*	16		3
6 Jan 96	**STUCK WITH ME** *Reprise W0327CD1*	24		3
6 Jul 96	**BRAIN STEW/JADED** *Reprise W0339CD*	28		2
11 Oct 97	**HITCHIN' A RIDE** *Reprise W0424CD*	25		2
31 Jan 98	**TIME OF YOUR LIFE (GOOD RIDDANCE)** *Reprise W0430CD1*	11		5
9 May 98	**REDUNDANT** *Reprise W0438CD1*	27		2
30 Sep 00	**MINORITY** *Reprise W532CD*	18		3
23 Dec 00	**WARNING** *Reprise W548CD1*	27		4
10 Nov 01	**WAITING** *Reprise W570CD*	34		2
25 Sep 04	**AMERICAN IDIOT** *Reprise W652CD*	3		8
11 Dec 04	**BOULEVARD OF BROKEN DREAMS** *Reprise W659CD1*	5		21
26 Mar 05	**HOLIDAY** *Reprise W664CD1*	11		7
25 Jun 05	**WAKE ME UP WHEN SEPTEMBER ENDS** *Reprise W674CD2*	8		20
26 Nov 05	**JESUS OF SUBURBIA** *Reprise W691CD*	17		3
11 Nov 06	**THE SAINTS ARE COMING** *Mercury 1713137* U2 & GREEN DAY	2		6
24 Mar 07	**TIME OF YOUR LIFE (GOOD RIDDANCE)** *Reprise W0430CD1*	67		1
4 Aug 07	**THE SIMPSONS THEME** *Warner Brothers USRE10701021*	19		3
25 Apr 09	**KNOW YOUR ENEMY** *Reprise W816CD*	21		9
18 Jul 09	**21 GUNS** *Reprise W817CD*	36		8

Top 3 Best-Selling Singles

	Title	Approximate Sales
1	TIME OF YOUR LIFE (GOOD RIDDANCE)	245,000
2	BOULEVARD OF BROKEN DREAMS	220,000
3	AMERICAN IDIOT	190,000

GREEN JELLY

US, male vocal/instrumental group — **15**

Date	Title	Peak Position	Weeks at No.1	Weeks on Chart
5 Jun 93	**THREE LITTLE PIGS** *Zoo 74321151422*	5		8
14 Aug 93	**ANARCHY IN THE UK** *Zoo 74321174892*	27		3
25 Dec 93	**I'M THE LEADER OF THE GANG** *Arista 74321174892* HULK HOGAN WITH GREEN JELLY	25		4

GREEN VELVET

US, male DJ/producer (Curtis Jones) — **2**

Date	Title	Peak Position	Weeks at No.1	Weeks on Chart
25 May 02	**LA LA LAND** *Credence CDCRED 025*	29		2

NORMAN GREENBAUM

US, male vocalist — **20**

Date	Title	Peak Position	Weeks at No.1	Weeks on Chart
21 Mar 70	**SPIRIT IN THE SKY** *Reprise RS 20885*	1	2	20

LORNE GREENE

Canada, male actor/vocalist, d. 11 Sep 1987 (age 73) — **8**

Date	Title	Peak Position	Weeks at No.1	Weeks on Chart
17 Dec 64	**RINGO** *RCA 1428* ★	22		8

LEE GREENWOOD

US, male vocalist — **6**

Date	Title	Peak Position	Weeks at No.1	Weeks on Chart
19 May 84	**THE WIND BENEATH MY WINGS** *MCA 877*	49		6

IAIN GREGORY

UK, male vocalist — **2**

Date	Title	Peak Position	Weeks at No.1	Weeks on Chart
4 Jan 62	**CAN'T YOU HEAR THE BEAT OF A BROKEN HEART** *Pye 7N 15397*	39		2

RICHARD GREY

France, male DJ/producer (Richard Jacquin) — **1**

Date	Title	Peak Position	Weeks at No.1	Weeks on Chart
23 Jun 07	**TAINTED LOVE** *Apollo Recordings APOLLO112CDX*	52		1

Silver-selling ● Gold-selling ● Platinum-selling (x multiples) ✪ US No.1 ★ Peak Position Weeks at No.1 Weeks on Chart

GREYHOUND

Jamaica, male vocal/instrumental group – Danny Smith, Sonny Binns, Glenroy Oakley & Ardley White — **33**

Date	Title / Label	Peak Position	Weeks at No.1	Weeks on Chart
26 Jun 71	**BLACK AND WHITE** *Trojan TR 7820*	6		13
8 Jan 72	**MOON RIVER** *Trojan TR 7848*	12		11
25 Mar 72	**I AM WHAT I AM** *Trojan TR 7853*	20		9

GRID

UK, male production/instrumental duo – Dave Ball & Richard Norris — **47**

Date	Title / Label	Peak Position	Weeks at No.1	Weeks on Chart
7 Jul 90	**FLOATATION** *East West YZ 475*	60		2
29 Sep 90	**A BEAT CALLED LOVE** *East West YZ 498*	64		4
25 Jul 92	**FIGURE OF 8** *Virgin VSCDT 1421*	50		3
3 Oct 92	**HEARTBEAT** *Virgin VSCDT 1427*	72		2
13 Mar 93	**CRYSTAL CLEAR** *Virgin VSCDT 1442*	27		4
30 Oct 93	**TEXAS COWBOYS** *Deconstruction 74321167762*	21		3
4 Jun 94	**SWAMP THING** *Deconstruction 74321205842* ●	3		17
17 Sep 94	**ROLLERCOASTER** *Deconstruction 74321230772*	19		4
3 Dec 94	**TEXAS COWBOYS** *Deconstruction 74321244032*	17		6
23 Sep 95	**DIABLO** *Deconstruction 74321308402*	32		2

ZAINE GRIFF

New Zealand, male vocalist — **6**

Date	Title / Label	Peak Position	Weeks at No.1	Weeks on Chart
16 Feb 80	**TONIGHT** *Automatic K 17547*	54		3
31 May 80	**ASHES AND DIAMONDS** *Automatic K 17619*	68		3

ALISTAIR GRIFFIN

UK, male vocalist — **9**

Date	Title / Label	Peak Position	Weeks at No.1	Weeks on Chart
10 Jan 04	**BRING IT ON/MY LOVER'S PRAYER** *Pro TV 9814926*	5		6
27 Mar 04	**YOU AND ME (TONIGHT)** *Universal TV 9817777*	18		3

BILLY GRIFFIN

US, male vocalist. See Miracles — **12**

Date	Title / Label	Peak Position	Weeks at No.1	Weeks on Chart
8 Jan 83	**HOLD ME TIGHTER IN THE RAIN** *CBS A 2935*	17		9
14 Jan 84	**SERIOUS** *CBS A 4053*	64		3

CLIVE GRIFFIN

UK, male vocalist — **5**

Date	Title / Label	Peak Position	Weeks at No.1	Weeks on Chart
24 Jun 89	**HEAD ABOVE WATER** *Mercury STEP 4*	60		2
11 May 91	**I'LL BE WAITING** *Mercury STEP 6*	56		3

RONI GRIFFITH

US, female vocalist — **4**

Date	Title / Label	Peak Position	Weeks at No.1	Weeks on Chart
30 Jun 84	**(THE BEST PART OF) BREAKING UP** *Making Waves SURF 101*	63		4

GRIFTERS

UK, male production duo. See Camisra, Escrima, Partizan, Tall Paul — **1**

Date	Title / Label	Peak Position	Weeks at No.1	Weeks on Chart
20 Feb 99	**FLASH** *Duty Free DF 004CD*	63		1

GRIM NORTHERN SOCIAL

UK, male vocal/instrumental group — **1**

Date	Title / Label	Peak Position	Weeks at No.1	Weeks on Chart
6 Sep 03	**URBAN PRESSURE** *One Little Indian 353 TP7CD*	60		1

GRINDERMAN

Australia/UK, male vocal/instrumental group — **1**

Date	Title / Label	Peak Position	Weeks at No.1	Weeks on Chart
3 Mar 07	**NO PUSSY BLUES** *Mute ICDMUTE373*	64		1

JOSH GROBAN

US, male vocalist/pianist/actor — **1**

Date	Title / Label	Peak Position	Weeks at No.1	Weeks on Chart
9 Jun 07	**YOU RAISE ME UP** *Warner Brothers USRE10301532*	74		1

GROOVE ARMADA

UK, male production/instrumental duo – Andy Cato & Tom Findlay — **49**

Date	Title / Label	Peak Position	Weeks at No.1	Weeks on Chart
8 May 99	**IF EVERYBODY LOOKED THE SAME** *Pepper 0530292*	25		2
7 Aug 99	**AT THE RIVER** *Pepper 0530062*	19		5
27 Nov 99	**I SEE YOU BABY** *Pepper 9230002* FEATURING GRAM'MA FUNK	17		6
25 Aug 01	**SUPERSTYLIN'** *Pepper 9230472*	12		7
17 Nov 01	**MY FRIEND** *Pepper 9230532*	36		2
2 Nov 02	**PURPLE HAZE** *Pepper 9230652*	36		2
17 May 03	**EASY** *Pepper 9230712*	31		2
6 Sep 03	**BUT I FEEL GOOD** *Pepper 82876556812*	50		1
2 Oct 04	**I SEE YOU BABY** *Jive 82876649982*	11		4
5 May 07	**GET DOWN** *Columbia 88697074402* FEATURING STUSH	9		7
14 Jul 07	**SONG 4 MUTYA (OUT OF CONTROL)** *Columbia 88697114322*	8		11

GROOVE CONNEKTION 2

UK, male producer/instrumentalist (Jeremy Sylvester) — **1**

Date	Title / Label	Peak Position	Weeks at No.1	Weeks on Chart
11 Apr 98	**CLUB LONELY** *XL Recordings XLT 94CD*	54		1

GROOVE CORPORATION

UK, male production group — **1**

Date	Title / Label	Peak Position	Weeks at No.1	Weeks on Chart
16 Apr 94	**RAIN** *Six6 SIXCD 109*	71		1

GROOVE COVERAGE

Germany, male/female vocal/DJ/production group — **3**

Date	Title / Label	Peak Position	Weeks at No.1	Weeks on Chart
11 Jun 05	**POISON** *All Around The World CDGLOBE361*	32		3

GROOVE CUTTERS

UK, male production duo — **2**

Date	Title / Label	Peak Position	Weeks at No.1	Weeks on Chart
5 Mar 05	**WE CLOSE OUR EYES** *Nebula NEBCD066*	33		2

GROOVE GENERATION FEATURING LEO SAYER

UK, male vocal/production group — **3**

Date	Title / Label	Peak Position	Weeks at No.1	Weeks on Chart
8 Aug 98	**YOU MAKE ME FEEL LIKE DANCING** *Brothers Organisation CDBRUV 8*	32		3

GROOVE THEORY

US, male/female vocal/production duo. See Mantronix — **3**

Date	Title / Label	Peak Position	Weeks at No.1	Weeks on Chart
18 Nov 95	**TELL ME** *Epic 6623882*	31		3

GROOVERIDER

UK, male DJ/producer (Ray Bingham) — **3**

Date	Title / Label	Peak Position	Weeks at No.1	Weeks on Chart
26 Sep 98	**RAINBOWS OF COLOUR** *Higher Ground HIGHS 13CD*	40		2
19 Jun 99	**WHERE'S JACK THE RIPPER** *Higher Ground HIGHS 20CD*	61		1

SCOTT GROOVES

US, male DJ/producer (Patrick Scott) — **3**

Date	Title / Label	Peak Position	Weeks at No.1	Weeks on Chart
16 May 98	**EXPANSIONS** *Soma Recordings SOMA 65CDS* FEATURING ROY AYERS	68		1
28 Nov 98	**MOTHERSHIP RECONNECTION** *Soma Recordings SOMA 71CDS*	55		1
21 Aug 99	**MOTHERSHIP RECONNECTION** *Virgin DINSD 185* FEATURING PARLIAMENT/FUNKADELIC	55		1

HENRY GROSS

US, male vocalist — **4**

Date	Title / Label	Peak Position	Weeks at No.1	Weeks on Chart
28 Aug 76	**SHANNON** *Life Song ELS 45002*	32		4

GROUND LEVEL

Australia, male production duo — **2**

Date	Title / Label	Peak Position	Weeks at No.1	Weeks on Chart
30 Jan 93	**DREAMS OF HEAVEN** *Faze 2 CDFAZE 14*	54		2

GROUNDED

UK, male vocal group — **1**

Date	Title / Label	Peak Position	Weeks at No.1	Weeks on Chart
26 Feb 05	**I NEED A GIRL** *Platinum PLATGROUND1A*	43		1

GROUP THERAPY

US, male rap group — **1**

Date	Title / Label	Peak Position	Weeks at No.1	Weeks on Chart
30 Nov 96	**EAST COAST/WEST COAST KILLAS** *Interscope IND 95516*	51		1

GSP

UK, male production duo — **3**

Date	Title / Label	Peak Position	Weeks at No.1	Weeks on Chart
3 Oct 92	**THE BANANA SONG** *Yoyo 1*	38		3

Silver-selling ○ | Gold-selling ● | Platinum-selling (× multiples) | US No.1 ★ | Peak Position | Weeks at No.1 | Weeks on Chart

GTO
UK, male production duo — 7

Date	Title	Peak	Wks at No.1	Wks on Chart
4 Aug 90	**PURE** *Cooltempo COOL 218*	57		3
7 Sep 91	**LISTEN TO THE RHYTHM FLOW/BULLFROG** *React 7001*	72		2
2 May 92	**ELEVATION** *React 4*	59		2

GUESS WHO
Canada, male vocal/instrumental group — 14

Date	Title	Peak	Wks at No.1	Wks on Chart
16 Feb 67	**HIS GIRL** *King KG 1044*	45		1
9 May 70	**AMERICAN WOMAN** *RCA 1943* ★	19		13

DAVID GUETTA
France, male producer — 103

Date	Title	Peak	Wks at No.1	Wks on Chart
31 Aug 02	**LOVE DON'T LET ME GO** *Virgin DINSD 243* FEATURING CHRIS WILLIS	46		1
12 Jul 03	**JUST FOR ONE DAY (HEROES)** *Virgin DINST 263* VS DAVID BOWIE	73		1
25 Oct 03	**JUST A LITTLE MORE LOVE** *Virgin DINSD 250* FEATURING CHRIS WILLIS	19		4
5 Mar 05	**THE WORLD IS MINE** *Virgin DINSDX271* FEATURING JD DAVIS	49		2
15 Jul 06	**WALKING AWAY** *Gusto CDGUS37* EGG VERSUS DAVID GUETTA	56		4
19 Aug 06	**LOVE DON'T LET ME GO (WALKING AWAY)** *Gusto CDGUS42* VS THE EGG	3		20
28 Jul 07	**LOVE IS GONE** *Angel ANGECD49*	9		12
8 Dec 07	**BABY WHEN THE LIGHT** *Charisma CASDX13* FEATURING COZI	50		3
31 Jan 09	**EVERYTIME WE TOUCH** *Positiva 12TIV279* FEATURING CHRIS WILLIS	68		1
20 Jun 09	**WHEN LOVE TAKES OVER** *Positiva CDTIV287* FEATURING KELLY ROWLAND ●	1	1	20
22 Aug 09	**SEXY CHICK** *Positiva/Virgin FRZID0900930* FEATURING AKON ●	1	1	26
21 Nov 09	**ONE LOVE** *Positiva/Virgin FRZID0900980* FEATURING ESTELLE	46		4
13 Mar 10	**MEMORIES** *Positiva/Virgin FRZID0900950* FEATURING KID CUDI	30		5+

GUILLEMOTS
UK/Canada/Brazil, male/female vocal/instrumental group — 13

Date	Title	Peak	Wks at No.1	Wks on Chart
8 Jul 06	**MADE-UP LOVE SONG #43** *Polydor 1700946*	23		4
23 Sep 06	**TRAINS TO BRAZIL** *Polydor 1705998*	36		2
27 Jan 07	**ANNIE LET'S NOT WAIT** *Polydor 1717323*	27		2
29 Mar 08	**GET OVER IT** *Polydor 1760834*	20		4
7 Jun 08	**FALLING OUT OF REACH** *Polydor 1767721*	49		1

GUN
UK, male vocal/instrumental trio – Adrian Gurvitz*, Brian Farrell & Paul Gurvitz — 11

Date	Title	Peak	Wks at No.1	Wks on Chart
20 Nov 68	**RACE WITH THE DEVIL** *CBS 3734*	8		11

GUN
UK, male vocal/instrumental group – Mark Rankin, Dante & Guiliano Gizzi, Scott Shields & Baby Stafford — 46

Date	Title	Peak	Wks at No.1	Wks on Chart
1 Jul 89	**BETTER DAYS** *A&M AM 505*	33		9
16 Sep 89	**MONEY (EVERYBODY LOVES HER)** *A&M AM 520*	73		2
11 Nov 89	**INSIDE OUT** *A&M AM 531*	57		2
10 Feb 90	**TAKING ON THE WORLD** *A&M AM 541*	50		3
14 Jul 90	**SHAME ON YOU** *A&M AM 573*	33		4
14 Mar 92	**STEAL YOUR FIRE** *A&M AM 851*	24		4
2 May 92	**HIGHER GROUND** *A&M AM 869*	48		2
4 Jul 92	**WELCOME TO THE REAL WORLD** *A&M AM 885*	43		2
9 Jul 94	**WORD UP** *A&M 5806672*	8		7
24 Sep 94	**DON'T SAY IT'S OVER** *A&M 5807572*	19		3
25 Feb 95	**THE ONLY ONE** *A&M 5809552*	29		3
15 Apr 95	**SOMETHING WORTHWHILE** *A&M 5810452*	39		2
26 Apr 97	**CRAZY YOU** *A&M 5821932* G.U.N.	21		2
12 Jul 97	**MY SWEET JANE** *A&M 5822792* G.U.N.	51		1

GUNS N' ROSES
US, male vocal/instrumental group – Axl Rose (William Bailey); members also included Steven Adler (replaced by Matt Sorum), Gilby Clarke*, Duff McKagan, Dizzy Reed, Slash (Saul Hudson) (Slash's Snakepit*) & Izzy Stradlin'* — 113

Date	Title	Peak	Wks at No.1	Wks on Chart
3 Oct 87	**WELCOME TO THE JUNGLE** *Geffen GEF 30*	67		2
20 Aug 88	**SWEET CHILD O' MINE** *Geffen GEF 43*	24		8
29 Oct 88	**WELCOME TO THE JUNGLE/NIGHTRAIN** *Geffen GEF 47*	24		5
18 Mar 89	**PARADISE CITY** *Geffen GEF 50*	6		9
3 Jun 89	**SWEET CHILD O' MINE** *Geffen GEF 55* ★	6		9
1 Jul 89	**PATIENCE** *Geffen GEF 56*	10		7
2 Sep 89	**NIGHTRAIN** *Geffen GEF 60*	17		5
13 Jul 91	**YOU COULD BE MINE** *Geffen GFS 6*	3		10
21 Sep 91	**DON'T CRY** *Geffen GFS 9*	8		4
21 Dec 91	**LIVE AND LET DIE** *Geffen GFS 17*	5		7
7 Mar 92	**NOVEMBER RAIN** *Geffen GFS 18*	4		5
23 May 92	**KNOCKIN' ON HEAVEN'S DOOR** *Geffen GFS 21*	2		9
21 Nov 92	**YESTERDAYS/NOVEMBER RAIN** *Geffen GFS 27*	8		9
29 May 93	**THE CIVIL WAR EP** *Geffen GEFSTD 43*	11		3
20 Nov 93	**AIN'T IT FUN** *Geffen GFSTD 62*	9		3
4 Jun 94	**SINCE I DON'T HAVE YOU** *Geffen GFSTD 70*	10		6
14 Jan 95	**SYMPATHY FOR THE DEVIL** *Geffen GFSTD 86*	9		6
19 Apr 08	**SWEET CHILD O' MINE** *Geffen USGF18714809*	57		2
22 Nov 08	**CHINESE DEMOCRACY** *Black Frog/Geffen USUM70842892*	27		3
14 Nov 09	**SWEET CHILD O' MINE** *Geffen USGF18714809*	75		1

GUNTHER & THE SUNSHINE GIRLS
Sweden, male/female vocal group — 4

Date	Title	Peak	Wks at No.1	Wks on Chart
15 May 04	**DING DONG SONG** *WEA 376CD*	14		4

GURU
US, male rapper/producer (Keith Elam), d. 19 Apr 2010 (age 48). See Gang Starr — 12

Date	Title	Peak	Wks at No.1	Wks on Chart
11 Sep 93	**TRUST ME** *Cooltempo CDCOOL 278* FEATURING N'DEA DAVENPORT	34		2
13 Nov 93	**NO TIME TO PLAY** *Cooltempo CDCOOL 282* FEATURING DEE C LEE	25		3
19 Aug 95	**WATCH WHAT YOU SAY** *Cooltempo CDCOOL 308* FEATURING CHAKA KHAN	28		3
18 Nov 95	**FEEL THE MUSIC** *Cooltempo CDCOOLS 313*	34		2
13 Jul 96	**LIVIN' IN THIS WORLD/LIFESAVER** *Cooltempo CDCOOL 320*	61		1
16 Dec 00	**KEEP YOUR WORRIES** *Virgin VUSCD 177* 'S JAZZAMATAZZ FEATURING ANGIE STONE	57		1

GURU JOSH
UK, male producer (Paul Walden) — 42

Date	Title	Peak	Wks at No.1	Wks on Chart
24 Feb 90	**INFINITY** *Deconstruction PB 43475*	5		10
16 Jun 90	**WHOSE LAW (IS IT ANYWAY)** *Deconstruction PB 43647*	26		4
25 Oct 08	**INFINITY** *COLUMBIA GBARL9100013*	50		4
1 Nov 08	**INFINITY 2008** *Maelstrom MAELCD100* GURU JOSH PROJECT	3		24

ADRIAN GURVITZ
UK, male vocalist. See Gun — 16

Date	Title	Peak	Wks at No.1	Wks on Chart
30 Jan 82	**CLASSIC** *RAK 339* ○	8		13
12 Jun 82	**YOUR DREAM** *RAK 343*	61		3

GUSGUS
Iceland, male/female vocal/instrumental group — 6

Date	Title	Peak	Wks at No.1	Wks on Chart
21 Feb 98	**POLYESTERDAY** *4AD BAD 8002CD*	55		1
13 Mar 99	**LADYSHAVE** *4AD BAD 9001CD*	64		1
24 Apr 99	**STARLOVERS** *4AD BADD 9004CD*	62		1
8 Feb 03	**DAVID** *Underwater H2O 022CD*	52		1
28 Jun 03	**CALL OF THE WILD** *Underwater H2O 032CD*	75		1
10 Apr 04	**DAVID (REMIX)** *Underwater H2O 042P*	72		1

GUSTO
US, male producer (Edward Green) — 11

Date	Title	Peak	Wks at No.1	Wks on Chart
2 Mar 96	**DISCO'S REVENGE** *Manifesto FESCD 6*	9		5
7 Sep 96	**LET'S ALL CHANT** *Manifesto FESCD 13*	21		3
24 May 08	**DISCO'S REVENGE 2008** *All Around The World CDGLOBE891*	34		3

GWEN GUTHRIE
US, female vocalist, d. 3 Feb 1999 (age 48) — 25

Date	Title	Peak	Wks at No.1	Wks on Chart
19 Jul 86	**AIN'T NOTHING GOIN' ON BUT THE RENT** *Boiling Point POSP 807* ○	5		12
11 Oct 86	**(THEY LONG TO BE) CLOSE TO YOU** *Boiling Point POSP 822*	25		7
14 Feb 87	**GOOD TO GO LOVER/OUTSIDE IN THE RAIN** *Boiling Point POSP 841*	37		4
4 Sep 93	**AIN'T NOTHING GOIN' ON BUT THE RENT (REMIX)** *Polydor PZCD 276*	42		2

GUY
US, male vocal trio — 4

Date	Title	Peak	Wks at No.1	Wks on Chart
4 May 91	**HER** *MCA MCS 1575*	58		4

A GUY CALLED GERALD
UK, male producer (Gerald Simpson). See 808 State — 23

Date	Title	Peak	Wks at No.1	Wks on Chart
8 Apr 89	**VOODOO RAY** *Rham! RS 804*	12		18
16 Dec 89	**FX/EYES OF SORROW** *Subscape AGCG 1*	52		5

Silver-selling ● Gold-selling ● Platinum-selling (x multiples) ⊛ US No.1 ★ Peak Position Weeks at No.1 Weeks on Chart

GUYS & DOLLS

UK, male/female vocal group – Thereze Bazar, Julie Forsythe, Dominic Grant, Paul Griggs, Martine Howard & David Van Day* **33**

Date	Title / Label	Peak Position	Weeks at No.1	Weeks on Chart
1 Mar 75	**THERE'S A WHOLE LOT OF LOVING** *Magnet MAG 20* ●	2		11
17 May 75	**HERE I GO AGAIN** *Magnet MAG 30*	33		5
21 Feb 76	**YOU DON'T HAVE TO SAY YOU LOVE ME** *Magnet MAG 50*	5		8
6 Nov 76	**STONEY GROUND** *Magnet MAG 76*	38		4
13 May 78	**ONLY LOVING DOES IT** *Magnet MAG 115*	42		5

GUYVER

UK, male producer (Guy Mearns) **1**

Date	Title / Label	Peak Position	Weeks at No.1	Weeks on Chart
29 Mar 03	**TRAPPED/DIFFERENCES** *Tidy Two 118*	72		1

GYM CLASS HEROES

US, male vocal/rap/instrumental group – Travie 'Schleprok' McCoy, Disashi Lumumba-Kasongo, Matt McGinley & Eric Roberts **48**

Date	Title / Label	Peak Position	Weeks at No.1	Weeks on Chart
21 Apr 07	**CUPID'S CHOKEHOLD/BREAKFAST IN AMERICA** *Decaydance/Fueled By Ramen AT0271CD*	3		21
25 Aug 07	**CLOTHES OFF** *Decaydance/Fueled By Ramen AT0282CDX*	5		12
13 Sep 08	**COOKIE JAR** *Decaydance/Fueled By Ramen AT0321CDX*	6		15

GYPSYMEN

US, male producer (Todd Terry). See Black Riot, Royal House, Swan Lake **2**

Date	Title / Label	Peak Position	Weeks at No.1	Weeks on Chart
11 Aug 01	**BABARABATIRI** *Sound Design SDES 09CDS*	32		2

GYRES

UK, male vocal/instrumental group **2**

Date	Title / Label	Peak Position	Weeks at No.1	Weeks on Chart
13 Apr 96	**POP COP** *Sugar SUGA 9CD*	71		1
6 Jul 96	**ARE YOU READY** *Sugar SUGA 11CD*	71		1

H & CLAIRE

UK, male/female vocal duo – Ian 'H' Watkins & Claire Richards. See Steps **25**

Date	Title / Label	Peak Position	Weeks at No.1	Weeks on Chart
18 May 02	**DJ** *WEA 347CD*	3		11
24 Aug 02	**HALF A HEART** *WEA 359CDX*	8		6
16 Nov 02	**ALL OUT OF LOVE** *WEA 360CDX*	10		8

HABIT

UK, male vocal/instrumental trio **2**

Date	Title / Label	Peak Position	Weeks at No.1	Weeks on Chart
30 Apr 88	**LUCY** *Virgin VS 1063*	56		2

STEVE HACKETT

UK, male vocalist/guitarist. See Genesis **2**

Date	Title / Label	Peak Position	Weeks at No.1	Weeks on Chart
2 Apr 83	**CELL 151** *Charisma CELL 1*	66		2

HADDAWAY

Trinidad & Tobago, male vocalist (Alexander Haddaway) **52**

Date	Title / Label	Peak Position	Weeks at No.1	Weeks on Chart
5 Jun 93	**WHAT IS LOVE** *Logic 74321148502* ●	2		15
25 Sep 93	**LIFE** *Logic 74321164212*	6		9
18 Dec 93	**I MISS YOU** *Logic 74321181522*	9		14
2 Apr 94	**ROCK MY HEART** *Logic 74321194122*	9		9
24 Jun 95	**FLY AWAY** *Logic 74321286942*	20		3
23 Sep 95	**CATCH A FIRE** *Logic 74321306652*	39		2

TONY HADLEY

UK, male vocalist. See Spandau Ballet **9**

Date	Title / Label	Peak Position	Weeks at No.1	Weeks on Chart
7 Mar 92	**LOST IN YOUR LOVE** *EMI EM 222*	42		4
29 Aug 92	**FOR YOUR BLUE EYES ONLY** *EMI EM 234*	67		2
16 Jan 93	**GAME OF LOVE** *EMI CDEM 254*	72		1
10 May 97	**DANCE WITH ME** *VC Recordings VCRD 17* TIN TIN OUT FEATURING TONY HADLEY	35		2

HADOUKEN

UK, male/female vocal/instrumental/production group **2**

Date	Title / Label	Peak Position	Weeks at No.1	Weeks on Chart
7 Jul 07	**LIQUID LIVES** *Surface Noise ATUK066CD*	36		1
10 May 08	**DECLARATION OF WAR** *Surface Noise ATUK077CD*	66		1

SAMMY HAGAR

US, male vocalist/guitarist. See Montrose, Van Halen **15**

Date	Title / Label	Peak Position	Weeks at No.1	Weeks on Chart
15 Dec 79	**THIS PLANET'S ON FIRE/SPACE STATION NO. 5** *Capitol CL 16114*	52		5
16 Feb 80	**I'VE DONE EVERYTHING FOR YOU** *Capitol CL 16120*	36		5
24 May 80	**HEARTBEAT/LOVE OR MONEY** *Capitol RED 1*	67		2
16 Jan 82	**PIECE OF MY HEART** *Geffen GEF A 1884*	67		3

PAUL HAIG

UK, male vocalist **3**

Date	Title / Label	Peak Position	Weeks at No.1	Weeks on Chart
28 May 83	**HEAVEN SENT** *Island IS 111*	74		3

HAIRCUT 100

UK, male vocal/instrumental group – Nick Heyward*, Blair Cunningham, Mark Fox, Graham Jones, Les Nemes & Phil Smith **47**

Date	Title / Label	Peak Position	Weeks at No.1	Weeks on Chart
24 Oct 81	**FAVOURITE SHIRTS (BOY MEETS GIRL)** *Arista CLIP 1* ●	4		14
30 Jan 82	**LOVE PLUS ONE** *Arista CLIP 2* ●	3		12
10 Apr 82	**FANTASTIC DAY** *Arista CLIP 3*	9		9
21 Aug 82	**NOBODY'S FOOL** *Arista CLIP 4*	9		7
6 Aug 83	**PRIME TIME** *Polydor HC 1*	46		5

CURTIS HAIRSTON

US, male vocalist, d. 18 Jan 1996 (age 34) **16**

Date	Title / Label	Peak Position	Weeks at No.1	Weeks on Chart
15 Oct 83	**I WANT YOU (ALL TONIGHT)** *RCA 368*	44		5
27 Apr 85	**I WANT YOUR LOVIN' (JUST A LITTLE BIT)** *London LON 66*	13		7
6 Dec 86	**CHILLIN' OUT** *Atlantic A 9335*	57		4

SEAMUS HAJI

UK, male producer **9**

Date	Title / Label	Peak Position	Weeks at No.1	Weeks on Chart
18 Dec 04	**LAST NIGHT A DJ SAVED MY LIFE (BIG LOVE)** *Big Love BL013*	69		1
4 Feb 06	**TAKE ME AWAY** *Big Love BL024CD* HAJI & EMANUEL	73		1
31 Mar 07	**LAST NIGHT A DJ SAVED MY LIFE** *Apollo Recordings APOLLO110CDS*	13		7

HAL

Ireland, male vocal/instrumental group **4**

Date	Title / Label	Peak Position	Weeks at No.1	Weeks on Chart
8 May 04	**WORRY ABOUT THE WIND** *Rough Trade RTRADESCD172*	53		1
5 Feb 05	**WHAT A LOVELY DANCE** *Rough Trade RTRADSCD212*	36		2
23 Apr 05	**PLAY THE HITS** *Rough Trade RTRADSCD226*	38		1

HAL FEATURING GILLIAN ANDERSON

UK, male/female vocal/production group **3**

Date	Title / Label	Peak Position	Weeks at No.1	Weeks on Chart
24 May 97	**EXTREMIS** *Virgin VSCDT 1636*	23		3

HALE & PACE & THE STONKERS

UK, male vocal/comedy duo – Gareth Hale & Norman Pace – & male/female vocal/instrumental charity ensemble **7**

Date	Title / Label	Peak Position	Weeks at No.1	Weeks on Chart
9 Mar 91	**THE STONK** *London LON 296*	1	1	7

BILL HALEY & HIS COMETS

US, male vocalist/guitarist, d. 9 Feb 1981, & male vocal/instrumental group **199**

Date	Title / Label	Peak Position	Weeks at No.1	Weeks on Chart
17 Dec 54	**SHAKE RATTLE AND ROLL** *Brunswick 05338*	4		14
7 Jan 55	**ROCK AROUND THE CLOCK** *Brunswick 05317*	17		2
15 Apr 55	**MAMBO ROCK** *Brunswick 05405*	14		2
14 Oct 55	**ROCK AROUND THE CLOCK** *Brunswick 05317* ★	1	5	17
30 Dec 55	**ROCK-A-BEATIN' BOOGIE** *Brunswick 05509*	4		9
9 Mar 56	**SEE YOU LATER ALLIGATOR** *Brunswick 05530*	7		13
25 May 56	**THE SAINTS ROCK 'N' ROLL** *Brunswick 05565*	5		24
17 Aug 56	**ROCKIN' THROUGH THE RYE** *Brunswick 05582*	3		23
14 Sep 56	**RAZZLE DAZZLE** *Brunswick 05453*	13		8
21 Sep 56	**ROCK AROUND THE CLOCK** *Brunswick 05317*	5		17
21 Sep 56	**SEE YOU LATER ALLIGATOR** *Brunswick 05530*	12		8
9 Nov 56	**RIP IT UP** *Brunswick 05615*	4		18
9 Nov 56	**ROCK 'N' ROLL STAGE SHOW (LP)** *Brunswick LAT 8139*	30		1
23 Nov 56	**RUDY'S ROCK** *Brunswick 05616*	26		5
1 Feb 57	**ROCK THE JOINT** *London HLF 8371*	20		4
8 Feb 57	**DON'T KNOCK THE ROCK** *Brunswick 05640*	7		8
3 Apr 68	**ROCK AROUND THE CLOCK** *MCA MU 1013*	20		11
16 Mar 74	**ROCK AROUND THE CLOCK** *MCA 128*	12		10
25 Apr 81	**HALEY'S GOLDEN MEDLEY** *MCA 694*	50		5

Silver-selling ○ · Gold-selling ● · Platinum-selling (x multiples) ⊛ · US No.1 ★ · Peak Position · Weeks at No.1 · Weeks on Chart

AARON HALL

US, male vocalist. See Guy — 3

Date	Title	Peak	No.1	Wks
13 Jun 92	**DON'T BE AFRAID** *MCA MCS 1632*	56		2
23 Oct 93	**GET A LITTLE FREAKY WITH ME** *MCA MCSTD 1936*	66		1

AUDREY HALL

Jamaica, female vocalist — 20

Date	Title	Peak	No.1	Wks
25 Jan 86	**ONE DANCE WON'T DO** *Germain DG7-1985*	20		11
5 Jul 86	**SMILE** *Germain DG 15*	14		9

DARYL HALL

US, male vocalist (Daryl Hohl). See Daryl Hall & John Oates — 26

Date	Title	Peak	No.1	Wks
2 Aug 86	**DREAMTIME** *RCA HALL 1*	28		8
25 Sep 93	**I'M IN A PHILLY MOOD** *Epic 6595555*	59		2
8 Jan 94	**STOP LOVING ME LOVING YOU** *Epic 6599982*	30		6
26 Mar 94	**I'M IN A PHILLY MOOD** *Epic 6595555*	52		2
14 May 94	**HELP ME FIND A WAY TO YOUR HEART** *Epic 6604102*	70		1
2 Jul 94	**GLORYLAND** *Mercury MERCD 404* & THE SOUNDS OF BLACKNESS	36		4
10 Jun 95	**WHEREVER WOULD I BE** *Columbia 6620592* DUSTY SPRINGFIELD & DARYL HALL	44		3

DARYL HALL & JOHN OATES

US, male vocal/instrumental duo – Daryl Hall* & John Oates — 84

Date	Title	Peak	No.1	Wks
16 Oct 76	**SHE'S GONE** *Atlantic K 10828*	42		4
14 Jun 80	**RUNNING FROM PARADISE** *RCA RUN 1*	41		6
20 Sep 80	**YOU'VE LOST THAT LOVIN' FEELIN'** *RCA 1*	55		3
15 Nov 80	**KISS ON MY LIST** *RCA 15* ★	33		8
23 Jan 82	**I CAN'T GO FOR THAT (NO CAN DO)** *RCA 172* ○ ★	8		10
10 Apr 82	**PRIVATE EYES** *RCA 134* ★	32		7
30 Oct 82	**MANEATER** *RCA 290* ★	6		11
22 Jan 83	**ONE ON ONE** *RCA 305*	63		3
30 Apr 83	**FAMILY MAN** *RCA 323*	15		7
12 Nov 83	**SAY IT ISN'T SO** *RCA 375*	69		3
10 Mar 84	**ADULT EDUCATION** *RCA 396*	63		2
20 Oct 84	**OUT OF TOUCH** *RCA 449* ★	48		5
9 Feb 85	**METHOD OF MODERN LOVE** *RCA 472*	21		8
22 Jun 85	**OUT OF TOUCH** *RCA PB 49967* ★	62		3
21 Sep 85	**A NIGHT AT THE APOLLO LIVE!** *RCA PB 49935* FEATURING DAVID RUFFIN & EDDIE KENDRICK	58		2
29 Sep 90	**SO CLOSE** *Arista 113600* HALL & OATES	69		1
26 Jan 91	**EVERYWHERE I LOOK** *Arista 113980*	74		1

LYNDEN DAVID HALL

UK, male vocalist/guitarist, d. 14 Feb 2006 (age 31) — 12

Date	Title	Peak	No.1	Wks
25 Oct 97	**SEXY CINDERELLA** *Cooltempo CDCOOL 328*	45		2
14 Mar 98	**DO I QUALIFY?** *Cooltempo CDCOOLS 331*	26		2
4 Jul 98	**CRESCENT MOON** *Cooltempo CDCOOL 333*	45		1
31 Oct 98	**SEXY CINDERELLA** *Cooltempo CDCOOLS 340*	17		3
11 Mar 00	**FORGIVE ME** *Cooltempo CDCOOLS 346*	30		2
27 May 00	**SLEEPING WITH VICTOR** *Cooltempo CDCOOL 348*	49		1
23 Sep 00	**LET'S DO IT AGAIN** *Cooltempo CDCOOL 351*	69		1

PAM HALL

Jamaica, female vocalist — 4

Date	Title	Peak	No.1	Wks
16 Aug 86	**DEAR BOOPSIE** *Bluemountain BM 027*	54		4

TERRY HALL

UK, male vocalist. See Colourfield, Fun Boy Three, Specials, Starving Souls, Vegas — 7

Date	Title	Peak	No.1	Wks
11 Nov 89	**MISSING** *Chrysalis CHS 3381*	75		1
27 Aug 94	**FOREVER J** *AnXious ANX 1024CDX*	67		1
12 Nov 94	**SENSE** *AnXious ANX 1027CD*	54		2
28 Oct 95	**RAINBOWS (EP)** *AnXious ANX 1033CD1*	62		1
14 Jun 97	**BALLAD OF A LANDLORD** *Southsea Bubble CDBUBBLE 1*	50		1
18 Oct 03	**PROBLEM IS** *Distinctive DISNCD 107* DUB PISTOLS FEATURING TERRY HALL	66		1

GERI HALLIWELL

UK, female vocalist. See Spice Girls — 104

Date	Title	Peak	No.1	Wks
22 May 99	**LOOK AT ME** *EMI CDEM 542* ●	2		14
28 Aug 99	**MI CHICO LATINO** *EMI CDEMS 548* ○	1	1	13
13 Nov 99	**LIFT ME UP** *EMI CDEM 554* ○	1	1	17
25 Mar 00	**BAG IT UP** *EMI CDEMS 560* ○	1	1	13
12 May 01	**IT'S RAINING MEN** *EMI CDEMS 584* ●	1	2	15
11 Aug 01	**SCREAM IF YOU WANNA GO FASTER** *EMI CDEM 595*	8		11
8 Dec 01	**CALLING** *EMI CDEMS 606*	7		10
4 Dec 04	**RIDE IT** *Innocent SINDX69*	4		9
11 Jun 05	**DESIRE** *Innocent SINDX75*	22		2

HALO

UK, male vocal/instrumental group — 3

Date	Title	Peak	No.1	Wks
16 Feb 02	**COLD LIGHT OF DAY** *Sony S2 6723072*	49		1
1 Jun 02	**SANCTIMONIOUS** *Sony S2 6725965*	44		1
7 Sep 02	**NEVER ENDING** *Sony S2 6730125*	56		1

HALO JAMES

UK, male vocal/instrumental trio – Christian James, Neil Palmer & Ray St John — 24

Date	Title	Peak	No.1	Wks
7 Oct 89	**WANTED** *Epic HALO 1*	45		5
23 Dec 89	**COULD HAVE TOLD YOU SO** *Epic HALO 2*	6		12
17 Mar 90	**BABY** *Epic HALO 3*	43		4
19 May 90	**MAGIC HOUR** *Epic HALO 4*	59		3

HAMFATTER

UK, male vocal/instrumental group — 2

Date	Title	Peak	No.1	Wks
21 Jul 07	**SZIGET (WE GET WRECKED)** *Pink Hedgehog SMILE24*	54		1
2 Aug 08	**THE GIRL I LOVE** *Hamfatter HAM1*	71		1

ASHLEY HAMILTON

US, male vocalist/actor — 4

Date	Title	Peak	No.1	Wks
14 Jun 03	**WIMMIN'** *Columbia 6739305*	27		4

GEORGE HAMILTON IV

US, male vocalist — 13

Date	Title	Peak	No.1	Wks
7 Mar 58	**WHY DON'T THEY UNDERSTAND** *HMV POP 429*	22		9
18 Jul 58	**I KNOW WHERE I'M GOING** *HMV POP 505*	23		4

LYNNE HAMILTON

Australia (b. UK), female vocalist — 11

Date	Title	Peak	No.1	Wks
29 Apr 89	**ON THE INSIDE (THEME FROM 'PRISONER CELL BLOCK H')** *A1 311*	3		11

RUSS HAMILTON

UK, male vocalist (Ronald Hume), d. 12 Oct 2008 (age 76) — 26

Date	Title	Peak	No.1	Wks
24 May 57	**WE WILL MAKE LOVE** *Oriole CB 1359*	2		20
27 Sep 57	**WEDDING RING** *Oriole CB 1388* WITH JOHNNY GREGORY & HIS ORCHESTRA WITH THE TONETTES	20		6

HAMILTON, JOE FRANK & REYNOLDS

US, male vocal/instrumental group — 6

Date	Title	Peak	No.1	Wks
13 Sep 75	**FALLIN' IN LOVE** *Pye International 7N 25690* ★	33		6

MARVIN HAMLISCH

US, male pianist — 13

Date	Title	Peak	No.1	Wks
30 Mar 74	**THE ENTERTAINER** *MCA 121*	25		13

MC HAMMER

US, male rapper (Stanley Burrell) — 68

Date	Title	Peak	No.1	Wks
9 Jun 90	**U CAN'T TOUCH THIS** *Capitol CL 578* ○	3		16
6 Oct 90	**HAVE YOU SEEN HER** *Capitol CL 590*	8		7
8 Dec 90	**PRAY** *Capitol CL 599*	8		10
23 Feb 91	**HERE COMES THE HAMMER** *Capitol CL 610*	15		5
1 Jun 91	**YO! SWEETNESS** *Capitol CL 616*	16		5
20 Jul 91	**(HAMMER HAMMER) THEY PUT ME IN THE MIX** *Capitol CL 607*	20		4
26 Oct 91	**2 LEGIT 2 QUIT** *Capitol CL 636* HAMMER	60		2
21 Dec 91	**ADDAMS GROOVE** *Capitol CL 642* HAMMER	4		9
21 Mar 92	**DO NOT PASS ME BY** *Capitol CL 650* HAMMER	14		6
12 Mar 94	**IT'S ALL GOOD** *RCA 74321188612* HAMMER	52		2
13 Aug 94	**DON'T STOP** *RCA 74321220012* HAMMER	72		1
3 Jun 95	**STRAIGHT TO MY FEET** *Priority PTYCD 102* HAMMER FEATURING DEION SAUNDERS	57		1

Peak Position | Weeks at No.1 | Weeks on Chart

JAN HAMMER
Czech Republic, male keyboard player — 26

Date	Title	Peak	Wks at No.1	Wks
12 Oct 85	**MIAMI VICE THEME** *MCA 1000* ● ★	5		8
19 Sep 87	**CROCKETT'S THEME** *MCA 1193* ●	2		12
1 Jun 91	**CROCKETT'S THEME** *MCA MCS 1541*	47		6

ALBERT HAMMOND
Gibraltar, male vocalist. See Family Dogg — 11

Date	Title	Peak	Wks at No.1	Wks
30 Jun 73	**FREE ELECTRIC BAND** *Mums 1494*	19		11

HAMPENBERG
Denmark, male/female vocal/instrumental/production trio — 2

Date	Title	Peak	Wks at No.1	Wks
21 Sep 02	**DUCK TOY** *Serious SERR 49CD*	30		2

HERBIE HANCOCK
US, male vocalist/keyboard player — 41

Date	Title	Peak	Wks at No.1	Wks
26 Aug 78	**I THOUGHT IT WAS YOU** *CBS 6530*	15		9
3 Feb 79	**YOU BET YOUR LOVE** *CBS 7010*	18		10
30 Jul 83	**ROCKIT** *CBS A 3577*	8		12
8 Oct 83	**AUTO DRIVE** *CBS A 3802*	33		4
21 Jan 84	**FUTURE SHOCK** *CBS A 4075*	54		3
4 Aug 84	**HARDROCK** *CBS A 4616*	65		3

HANDBAGGERS
UK, male/female vocal/instrumental group — 1

Date	Title	Peak	Wks at No.1	Wks
15 Jun 96	**U FOUND OUT** *Tidy Trax TIDY 104CD*	55		1

HANDLEY FAMILY
UK, male/female vocal/instrumental group — 7

Date	Title	Peak	Wks at No.1	Wks
7 Apr 73	**WAM BAM** *GL 100*	30		7

HANI
US, male DJ/producer (Hani Adnan Al-Bader) — 1

Date	Title	Peak	Wks at No.1	Wks
11 Mar 00	**BABY WANTS TO RIDE** *Neo CD025*	70		1

JAYN HANNA
UK, female vocalist — 2

Date	Title	Peak	Wks at No.1	Wks
13 Apr 96	**LOVELIGHT (RIDE ON A LOVE TRAIN)** *VC Recordings VCRD 10*	42		1
1 Feb 97	**LOST WITHOUT YOU** *VC Recordings VCRD 16*	44		1

HANNAH
UK, female vocalist (Hannah Waddingham) — 2

Date	Title	Peak	Wks at No.1	Wks
21 Oct 00	**OUR KIND OF LOVE** *Telstar CDSTAS 3149*	41		2

HANOI ROCKS
Finland/UK, male vocal/instrumental group — 2

Date	Title	Peak	Wks at No.1	Wks
7 Jul 84	**UP AROUND THE BEND** *CBS A 4513*	61		2

HANSON
US, male vocal/instrumental trio – Isaac, Taylor & Zac Hanson — 55

Date	Title	Peak	Wks at No.1	Wks
7 Jun 97	**MMMBOP** *Mercury 5745012* ⊛ ★	1	3	13
13 Sep 97	**WHERE'S THE LOVE** *Mercury 5749032* ●	4		9
22 Nov 97	**I WILL COME TO YOU** *Mercury 5680072*	5		9
28 Mar 98	**WEIRD** *Mercury 5685412*	19		5
4 Jul 98	**THINKING OF YOU** *Mercury 5688132*	23		7
29 Apr 00	**IF ONLY** *Mercury 5627502*	15		4
5 Feb 05	**PENNY AND ME** *Cooking Vinyl FRYCD220X*	10		5
9 Apr 05	**LOST WITHOUT EACH OTHER** *Cooking Vinyl FRYCD224X*	39		2
28 Apr 07	**GO** *Cooking Vinyl FRYCD291X*	44		1

HAPPENINGS
US, male vocal group — 14

Date	Title	Peak	Wks at No.1	Wks
18 May 67	**I GOT RHYTHM** *Stateside SS 2013*	28		9
16 Aug 67	**MY MAMMY** *Pye International 25501/BT Puppy BTS 45530*	34		5

HAPPY CLAPPERS
UK, female/male vocal/instrumental group – Sandra Edwards, Martin Knotts, Graeme Ripley, Chris Scott & Mark Topham — 19

Date	Title	Peak	Wks at No.1	Wks
3 Jun 95	**I BELIEVE** *Shindig SHIN 4CD*	21		3
26 Aug 95	**HOLD ON** *Shindig SHIN 7CD*	27		2
18 Nov 95	**I BELIEVE** *Shindig SHIN 9CD*	7		8
15 Jun 96	**CAN'T HELP IT** *Coliseum TOGA 004CD*	18		3
21 Dec 96	**NEVER AGAIN** *Coliseum TOGA 012CD*	49		1
22 Nov 97	**I BELIEVE** *Coliseum COLA 027CD*	28		2

HAPPY MONDAYS
UK, male vocal/instrumental group – Shaun Ryder, Mark 'Bez' Berry, Paul Davis, Mark Day, Paul Ryder & Gary Whelan — 54

Date	Title	Peak	Wks at No.1	Wks
30 Sep 89	**WFL** *Factory FAC 2327*	68		2
25 Nov 89	**MADCHESTER RAVE ON EP** *Factory FAC 2427*	19		14
7 Apr 90	**STEP ON** *Factory FAC 2727*	5		11
9 Jun 90	**LAZYITIS – ONE ARMED BOXER** *Factory FAC 2227* & KARL DENVER	46		3
20 Oct 90	**KINKY AFRO** *Factory FAC 3027*	5		7
9 Mar 91	**LOOSE FIT** *Factory FAC 3127*	17		7
30 Nov 91	**JUDGE FUDGE** *Factory FAC 3327*	24		3
19 Sep 92	**STINKIN THINKIN** *Factory FAC 3627*	31		3
21 Nov 92	**SUNSHINE AND LOVE** *Factory FAC 3727*	62		1
22 May 99	**THE BOYS ARE BACK IN TOWN** *London LONCD 432*	24		2
29 Oct 05	**PLAYGROUND SUPERSTAR** *Big Brother RKIDSCD34*	51		1

HAPPYLIFE
UK, male vocal/instrumental group — 1

Date	Title	Peak	Wks at No.1	Wks
9 Oct 04	**SILENCE WHEN YOU'RE BURNING** *Albert Productions JASCDUK012*	73		1

HAR MAR SUPERSTAR
US, male vocalist (Sean Tillman) — 3

Date	Title	Peak	Wks at No.1	Wks
5 Jul 03	**EZ PASS** *B Unique BUN 054CDS*	59		1
4 Sep 04	**DUI** *Record Collection W651CD*	46		2

ED HARCOURT
UK, male vocalist/multi-instrumentalist — 5

Date	Title	Peak	Wks at No.1	Wks
2 Feb 02	**APPLE OF MY EYE** *Heavenly HVN 107CDS*	61		1
15 Feb 03	**ALL OF YOUR DAYS WILL BE BLESSED** *Heavenly HVN 127CDS*	35		1
11 Sep 04	**THIS ONE'S FOR YOU** *Heavenly HVN 140CD*	41		1
13 Nov 04	**BORN IN THE 70'S** *Heavenly HVN 146CD*	61		1
26 Feb 05	**LONELINESS** *Heavenly HVN149CD*	59		1

HARD-FI
UK, male vocal/instrumental group – Richard Archer, Steve Kemp, Ross Phillips & Kai Stephens — 55

Date	Title	Peak	Wks at No.1	Wks
30 Apr 05	**TIED UP TOO TIGHT** *Necessary HARDFI02CD*	15		3
2 Jul 05	**HARD TO BEAT** *Necessary HARD03CD*	9		18
1 Oct 05	**LIVING FOR THE WEEKEND** *Necessary HARD04CD*	15		6
7 Jan 06	**CASH MACHINE** *Necessary HARD05CDX*	14		12
22 Apr 06	**BETTER DO BETTER** *Necessary/Atlantic HARD06CD*	14		4
25 Aug 07	**SUBURBAN KNIGHTS** *Necessary/Atlantic HARD07CD*	7		9
24 Nov 07	**CAN'T GET ALONG (WITHOUT YOU)** *Necessary/Atlantic HARD08CD*	45		2
22 Mar 08	**I SHALL OVERCOME** *Necessary/Atlantic HARD09CD*	36		1

PAUL HARDCASTLE
UK, male producer/keyboard player. See Direct Drive, First Light — 66

Date	Title	Peak	Wks at No.1	Wks
7 Apr 84	**YOU'RE THE ONE FOR ME – DAYBREAK – AM** *Total Control TOCO 1*	41		4
28 Jul 84	**GUILTY** *Total Control TOCO 2*	55		3
22 Sep 84	**RAIN FOREST** *Bluebird BR 8*	41		5
17 Nov 84	**EAT YOUR HEART OUT** *Cooltempo COOL 102*	59		4
4 May 85	**19** *Chrysalis CHS 2860* ●	1	5	16
15 Jun 85	**RAIN FOREST** *Bluebird/10 BR 15*	53		4
9 Nov 85	**JUST FOR MONEY** *Chrysalis CASH 1*	19		5
1 Feb 86	**DON'T WASTE MY TIME** *Chrysalis PAUL 1* FEATURING CAROL KENYON	8		11
21 Jun 86	**FOOLIN' YOURSELF** *Chrysalis PAUL 2*	51		3
11 Oct 86	**THE WIZARD** *Chrysalis PAUL 3*	15		6
9 Apr 88	**WALK IN THE NIGHT** *Chrysalis PAUL 4*	54		3
4 Jun 88	**40 YEARS** *Chrysalis PAUL 5*	53		2

HARDCORE RHYTHM TEAM
UK, male production duo — 1

Date	Title	Peak	Wks at No.1	Wks
14 Mar 92	**HARDCORE – THE FINAL CONFLICT** *Furious FRUT 001*	69		1

Silver-selling ● Gold-selling ● Platinum-selling (x multiples) ⊛ US No.1 ★ Peak Position · Weeks at No.1 · Weeks on Chart

DUANE HARDEN
US, male vocalist **16**

Date	Title	Peak Position	Weeks at No.1	Weeks on Chart
6 Feb 99	**YOU DON'T KNOW ME** *ffrr FCD 357* ARMAND VAN HELDEN FEATURING DUANE HARDEN ●	1	1	11
22 May 99	**WHAT YOU NEED** *Defected DEFECT 3CDS* POWERHOUSE FEATURING DUANE HARDEN	13		5

HARDFLOOR
Germany, male production duo. See Bellini, E-Trax, Fragma, Interactive, Paffendorf **6**

Date	Title	Peak Position	Weeks at No.1	Weeks on Chart
26 Dec 92	**HARDTRANCE ACPERIENCE** *Harthouse UK HARTUK 1*	56		4
10 Apr 93	**TRANCESCRIPT** *Harthouse UK HARTUK 5CD*	72		1
25 Oct 97	**ACPERIENCE** *Eye-Q EYEUK 018CD1*	60		1

TIM HARDIN
US, male vocalist/guitarist, d. 29 Dec 1980 (age 39) **1**

Date	Title	Peak Position	Weeks at No.1	Weeks on Chart
5 Jan 67	**HANG ON TO A DREAM** *Verve VS 1504*	50		1

MIKE HARDING
UK, male vocalist/comedian/radio DJ **8**

Date	Title	Peak Position	Weeks at No.1	Weeks on Chart
2 Aug 75	**ROCHDALE COWBOY** *Rubber ADUB 3*	22		8

HARDSOUL FEATURING RON CARROLL
Holland/US, male vocal/DJ/production trio **1**

Date	Title	Peak Position	Weeks at No.1	Weeks on Chart
12 Jun 04	**BACK TOGETHER** *In The House ITH02CDS*	60		1

FRANCOISE HARDY
France, female vocalist **26**

Date	Title	Peak Position	Weeks at No.1	Weeks on Chart
25 Jun 64	**TOUS LES GARCONS ET LES FILLES** *Pye 7N 15653*	36		7
7 Jan 65	**HOWEVER MUCH (ET MEME)** *Pye 7N 15740*	31		4
25 Mar 65	**ALL OVER THE WORLD** *Pye 7N 15802*	16		15

MORTEN HARKET
Norway, male vocalist/multi-instrumentalist. See A-ha **1**

Date	Title	Peak Position	Weeks at No.1	Weeks on Chart
19 Aug 95	**A KIND OF CHRISTMAS CARD** *Warner Brothers 0304CD*	53		1

HARLEQUIN 4S/BUNKER KRU
US, male/female production/vocal group & UK, male production duo **4**

Date	Title	Peak Position	Weeks at No.1	Weeks on Chart
19 Mar 88	**SET IT OFF** *Champion CHAMP 64*	55		4

STEVE HARLEY & COCKNEY REBEL
UK, male vocal/instrumental group – Steve Harley (Stephen Nice), John Crocker (replaced by Jim Cregan), Stuart Elliott, Paul Jeffreys, d. 21 Dec 1988 (replaced by George Ford), & Milton Reame-James (replaced by Duncan MacKay) **71**

Date	Title	Peak Position	Weeks at No.1	Weeks on Chart
11 May 74	**JUDY TEEN** *EMI 2128* COCKNEY REBEL	5		11
10 Aug 74	**MR SOFT** *EMI 2191* COCKNEY REBEL	8		9
8 Feb 75	**MAKE ME SMILE (COME UP AND SEE ME)** *EMI 2263* ●	1	2	9
7 Jun 75	**MR RAFFLES (MAN IT WAS MEAN)** *EMI 2299*	13		6
31 Jul 76	**HERE COMES THE SUN** *EMI 2505* STEVE HARLEY	10		7
6 Nov 76	**LOVE'S A PRIMA DONNA** *EMI 2539* STEVE HARLEY	41		4
20 Oct 79	**FREEDOM'S PRISONER** *EMI 2994* STEVE HARLEY	58		3
13 Aug 83	**BALLERINA (PRIMA DONNA)** *Stiletto STL 14* STEVE HARLEY	51		5
11 Jan 86	**THE PHANTOM OF THE OPERA** *Polydor POSP 800* SARAH BRIGHTMAN & STEVE HARLEY	7		10
25 Apr 92	**MAKE ME SMILE (COME UP AND SEE ME)** *EMI EMCT 5* STEVE HARLEY	46		2
30 Dec 95	**MAKE ME SMILE (COME UP AND SEE ME)** *EMI CDHARLEY 1*	33		3
2 Jul 05	**MAKE ME SMILE (COME UP AND SEE ME)** *Gott Discs GOTTCD030*	55		2

HARLEY QUINNE
UK, male vocal/instrumental group **8**

Date	Title	Peak Position	Weeks at No.1	Weeks on Chart
14 Oct 72	**NEW ORLEANS** *Bell 1255*	19		8

HARMONIX
UK, male producer (Hamish Brown) **2**

Date	Title	Peak Position	Weeks at No.1	Weeks on Chart
30 Mar 96	**LANDSLIDE** *Deconstruction 74321330762*	28		2

HARMONY GRASS
UK, male vocal/instrumental group **7**

Date	Title	Peak Position	Weeks at No.1	Weeks on Chart
29 Jan 69	**MOVE IN A LITTLE CLOSER** *RCA 1772*	24		7

BEN HARPER
US, male vocalist/guitarist **1**

Date	Title	Peak Position	Weeks at No.1	Weeks on Chart
4 Apr 98	**FADED** *Virgin VUSCD 134*	54		1

CHARLIE HARPER
UK, male vocalist (David Perez). See UK Subs **1**

Date	Title	Peak Position	Weeks at No.1	Weeks on Chart
19 Jul 80	**BARMY LONDON ARMY** *Gem GEMS 35*	68		1

HARPERS BIZARRE
US, male vocal/instrumental group **13**

Date	Title	Peak Position	Weeks at No.1	Weeks on Chart
30 Mar 67	**59TH STREET BRIDGE SONG (FEELING GROOVY)** *Warner Brothers WB 5890*	34		7
4 Oct 67	**ANYTHING GOES** *Warner Brothers WB 7063*	33		6

HARPO
Sweden, male vocalist (Jan Svensson) **6**

Date	Title	Peak Position	Weeks at No.1	Weeks on Chart
17 Apr 76	**MOVIE STAR** *DJM DJS 400*	24		6

ANITA HARRIS
UK, female vocalist **50**

Date	Title	Peak Position	Weeks at No.1	Weeks on Chart
29 Jun 67	**JUST LOVING YOU** *CBS 2724*	6		30
11 Oct 67	**PLAYGROUND** *CBS 2991*	46		3
24 Jan 68	**ANNIVERSARY WALTZ** *CBS 3211*	21		9
14 Aug 68	**DREAM A LITTLE DREAM OF ME** *CBS 3637*	33		8

CALVIN HARRIS
UK, male vocalist/DJ/producer (Adam Wiles) **124**

Date	Title	Peak Position	Weeks at No.1	Weeks on Chart
10 Mar 07	**ACCEPTABLE IN THE 80S** *Columbia 88697063932*	10		21
9 Jun 07	**THE GIRLS** *Sony BMG 88697072212*	3		13
25 Aug 07	**MERRYMAKING AT MY PLACE** *Columbia FLYEYE011*	43		3
12 Jul 08	**DANCE WIV ME** *Dirtee Stank STANK002CDS* DIZZEE RASCAL FEATURING CALVIN HARRIS & CHROME ⊛	1	4	39
18 Apr 09	**I'M NOT ALONE** *Columbia 88697513252*	1	2	23
22 Aug 09	**READY FOR THE WEEKEND** *Columbia 88697549322*	3		10
24 Oct 09	**FLASH BACK** *Columbia 88697606782*	18		8
30 Jan 10	**YOU USED TO HOLD ME** *Columbia 88697629202*	27		7

EMMYLOU HARRIS
US, female vocalist/guitarist **6**

Date	Title	Peak Position	Weeks at No.1	Weeks on Chart
6 Mar 76	**HERE THERE AND EVERYWHERE** *Reprise K 14415*	30		6

JET HARRIS
UK, male bass player (Terence Hawkins). See Shadows **57**

Date	Title	Peak Position	Weeks at No.1	Weeks on Chart
24 May 62	**BESAME MUCHO** *Decca F 11466*	22		7
16 Aug 62	**MAIN TITLE THEME FROM 'MAN WITH THE GOLDEN ARM'** *Decca F 11488*	12		11
10 Jan 63	**DIAMONDS** *Decca F 11563* & TONY MEEHAN	1	3	13
25 Apr 63	**SCARLETT O'HARA** *Decca F 11644* & TONY MEEHAN	2		13
5 Sep 63	**APPLEJACK** *Decca F 11710* & TONY MEEHAN	4		13

KEITH HARRIS & ORVILLE
UK, male vocalist/ventriloquist & duckling puppet **20**

Date	Title	Peak Position	Weeks at No.1	Weeks on Chart
18 Dec 82	**ORVILLE'S SONG** *BBC RESL 124* ●	4		11
24 Dec 83	**COME TO MY PARTY** *BBC RESL 138* WITH DIPPY	44		4
14 Dec 85	**WHITE CHRISTMAS** *Columbia DB 9121*	40		5

MAJOR HARRIS
US, male vocalist **9**

Date	Title	Peak Position	Weeks at No.1	Weeks on Chart
9 Aug 75	**LOVE WON'T LET ME WAIT** *Atlantic K 10585*	37		7
5 Nov 83	**ALL MY LIFE** *London LON 37*	61		2

MAX HARRIS

UK, male orchestra leader, d. 13 Mar 2004 (age 85) — Weeks on Chart: 10

Date	Title / Label	Peak Position	Weeks at No.1	Weeks on Chart
1 Dec 60	**GURNEY SLADE** *Fontana H 282*	11		10

RAHNI HARRIS & F.L.O.

US, male instrumental group — Weeks on Chart: 7

Date	Title / Label	Peak Position	Weeks at No.1	Weeks on Chart
16 Dec 78	**SIX MILLION STEPS (WEST RUNS SOUTH)** *Mercury 6007 198*	43		7

RICHARD HARRIS

Ireland, male actor/vocalist, d. 25 Oct 2002 (age 72) — Weeks on Chart: 18

Date	Title / Label	Peak Position	Weeks at No.1	Weeks on Chart
26 Jun 68	**MACARTHUR PARK** *RCA 1699*	4		12
8 Jul 72	**MACARTHUR PARK** *Probe GFF 101*	38		6

ROLF HARRIS

Australia, male vocalist/wobble board player/TV presenter — Weeks on Chart: 77

Date	Title / Label	Peak Position	Weeks at No.1	Weeks on Chart
21 Jul 60	**TIE ME KANGAROO DOWN SPORT** *Columbia DB 4483* WITH HIS WOBBLE BOARD & THE RHYTHM SPINNERS	9		13
25 Oct 62	**SUN ARISE** *Columbia DB 4888*	3		16
28 Feb 63	**JOHNNY DAY** *Columbia DB 8553*	44		2
16 Apr 69	**BLUER THAN BLUE** *Columbia DB 8553*	30		8
22 Nov 69	**TWO LITTLE BOYS** *Columbia DB 8630*	1	6	25
13 Feb 93	**STAIRWAY TO HEAVEN** *Vertigo VERCD 73*	7		6
1 Jun 96	**BOHEMIAN RHAPSODY** *Living Beat LBECD 41*	50		1
25 Oct 97	**SUN ARISE** *EMI CDROO 001*	26		3
14 Oct 00	**FINE DAY** *Tommy Boy TBCD 2155*	24		3

RONNIE HARRIS

UK, male vocalist — Weeks on Chart: 3

Date	Title / Label	Peak Position	Weeks at No.1	Weeks on Chart
24 Sep 54	**STORY OF TINA** *Columbia DB 3499*	12		3

SAM HARRIS

US, male vocalist/actor — Weeks on Chart: 2

Date	Title / Label	Peak Position	Weeks at No.1	Weeks on Chart
9 Feb 85	**HEARTS ON FIRE/OVER THE RAINBOW** *Motown TMG 1370*	67		2

SIMON HARRIS

UK, male producer. See Ambassadors Of Funk featuring MC Mario, World Warrior — Weeks on Chart: 17

Date	Title / Label	Peak Position	Weeks at No.1	Weeks on Chart
19 Mar 88	**BASS (HOW LOW CAN YOU GO)** *ffrr FFR 4*	12		6
29 Oct 88	**HERE COMES THAT SOUND** *ffrr FFR 12*	38		4
24 Jun 89	**(I'VE GOT YOUR) PLEASURE CONTROL** *ffrr F 106* FEATURING LONNIE GORDON	60		3
18 Nov 89	**ANOTHER MONSTERJAM** *ffrr F 116* FEATURING EINSTEIN	65		1
10 Mar 90	**RAGGA HOUSE (ALL NIGHT LONG)** *Living Beat 7SMASH 9* FEATURING DADDY FREDDY	56		3

GEORGE HARRISON

UK, male vocalist/guitarist, d. 29 Nov 2001 (age 58). See Beatles, Traveling Wilburys — Weeks on Chart: 94

Date	Title / Label	Peak Position	Weeks at No.1	Weeks on Chart
23 Jan 71	**MY SWEET LORD** *Apple R 5884* ★	1	5	17
14 Aug 71	**BANGLA DESH** *Apple R 5912*	10		9
2 Jun 73	**GIVE ME LOVE (GIVE ME PEACE ON EARTH)** *Apple R 5988* ★	8		10
21 Dec 74	**DING DONG** *Apple R 6002*	38		5
11 Oct 75	**YOU** *Apple R 6007*	38		5
10 Mar 79	**BLOW AWAY** *Dark Horse K 17327*	51		5
23 May 81	**ALL THOSE YEARS AGO** *Dark Horse K 17807*	13		7
24 Oct 87	**GOT MY MIND SET ON YOU** *Dark Horse W 8178* ● ★	2		14
6 Feb 88	**WHEN WE WAS FAB** *Dark Horse W 8131*	25		7
25 Jun 88	**THIS IS LOVE** *Dark Horse W 7913*	55		3
26 Jan 02	**MY SWEET LORD** *Parlophone CDR 6571*	1	1	10
24 May 03	**ANY ROAD** *Parlophone CDRS 6601*	37		2

NOEL HARRISON

UK, male vocalist — Weeks on Chart: 14

Date	Title / Label	Peak Position	Weeks at No.1	Weeks on Chart
26 Feb 69	**WINDMILLS OF YOUR MIND** *Reprise RS 20758*	8		14

HARRISONS

UK, male vocal/instrumental group — Weeks on Chart: 1

Date	Title / Label	Peak Position	Weeks at No.1	Weeks on Chart
25 Feb 06	**BLUE NOTE** *Melodic MELO036CD*	69		1

HARRY

UK, female vocalist (Victoria Harrison) — Weeks on Chart: 2

Date	Title / Label	Peak Position	Weeks at No.1	Weeks on Chart
2 Nov 02	**SO REAL** *Dirty World DWRCD 003*	53		1
19 Apr 03	**UNDER THE COVERS EP** *Dirty World DWRCD 005*	43		1

DEBBIE HARRY

US, female vocalist. See Blondie — Weeks on Chart: 53

Date	Title / Label	Peak Position	Weeks at No.1	Weeks on Chart
1 Aug 81	**BACKFIRED** *Chrysalis CHS 2526*	32		6
15 Nov 86	**FRENCH KISSIN' IN THE USA** *Chrysalis CHS 3066*	8		10
28 Feb 87	**FREE TO FALL** *Chrysalis CHS 3093*	46		4
9 May 87	**IN LOVE WITH LOVE** *Chrysalis CHS 3128*	45		5
7 Oct 89	**I WANT THAT MAN** *Chrysalis CHS 3369* DEBORAH HARRY	13		10
2 Dec 89	**BRITE SIDE** *Chrysalis CHS 3452* DEBORAH HARRY	59		4
31 Mar 90	**SWEET AND LOW** *Chrysalis CHS 3491* DEBORAH HARRY	57		3
5 Jan 91	**WELL DID YOU EVAH!** *Chrysalis CHS 3646* DEBORAH HARRY & IGGY POP	42		4
3 Jul 93	**I CAN SEE CLEARLY** *Chrysalis CDCHSS 4900* DEBORAH HARRY	23		4
18 Sep 93	**STRIKE ME PINK** *Chrysalis CDCHSS 5000* DEBORAH HARRY	46		2
11 Nov 06	**NEW YORK NEW YORK** *Mute CDMUTE371* MOBY FEATURING DEBBIE HARRY	43		1

RICHARD HARTLEY/MICHAEL REED ORCHESTRA

UK, male synthesizer player & orchestra — Weeks on Chart: 10

Date	Title / Label	Peak Position	Weeks at No.1	Weeks on Chart
25 Feb 84	**THE MUSIC OF TORVILL AND DEAN EP** *Safari SKATE 1* ●	9		10

DAN HARTMAN

US, male vocalist, d. 22 Mar 1994 (age 43) — Weeks on Chart: 34

Date	Title / Label	Peak Position	Weeks at No.1	Weeks on Chart
21 Oct 78	**INSTANT REPLAY** *Blue Sky 6706* ●	8		15
13 Jan 79	**THIS IS IT** *Blue Sky 6999*	17		8
18 May 85	**SECOND NATURE** *MCA 957*	66		2
24 Aug 85	**I CAN DREAM ABOUT YOU** *MCA 988*	12		8
1 Apr 95	**KEEP THE FIRE BURNIN'** *Columbia 6611552* STARRING LOLEATTA HOLLOWAY	49		1

HARVEY

UK, male rapper (Michael Harvey). See So Solid Crew — Weeks on Chart: 2

Date	Title / Label	Peak Position	Weeks at No.1	Weeks on Chart
7 Sep 02	**GET UP AND MOVE** *Go! Beat GOBCD 52*	24		2

SENSATIONAL ALEX HARVEY BAND

UK, male vocal/instrumental group – Alex Harvey, d. 4 Feb 1982, Zal Cleminson, Chris Glen & Hugh & Ted McKenna — Weeks on Chart: 25

Date	Title / Label	Peak Position	Weeks at No.1	Weeks on Chart
26 Jul 75	**DELILAH** *Vertigo ALEX 001*	7		7
22 Nov 75	**GAMBLIN' BAR ROOM BLUES** *Vertigo ALEX 002*	38		8
19 Jun 76	**THE BOSTON TEA PARTY** *Mountain TOP 12*	13		10

BRIAN HARVEY

UK, male vocalist. See East 17 — Weeks on Chart: 8

Date	Title / Label	Peak Position	Weeks at No.1	Weeks on Chart
2 Dec 00	**TRUE STEP TONIGHT** *NuLife 74321811312* TRUE STEPPERS FEATURING BRIAN HARVEY & DONELL JONES	25		3
28 Apr 01	**STRAIGHT UP NO BENDS** *Edel 0126605ERE*	26		2
27 Oct 01	**LOVING YOU (OLE OLE OLE)** *Blacklist 0133045 ERE* & THE REFUGEE CREW	20		3

PJ HARVEY

UK, female vocalist/guitarist (Polly Jean Harvey) & male instrumentalists (for 1992–3 hits) — Weeks on Chart: 27

Date	Title / Label	Peak Position	Weeks at No.1	Weeks on Chart
29 Feb 92	**SHEELA-NA-GIG** *Too Pure PURE 008*	69		1
1 May 93	**50FT QUEENIE** *Island CID 538*	27		2
17 Jul 93	**MAN-SIZE** *Island CID 569*	42		2
18 Feb 95	**DOWN BY THE WATER** *Island CID 607*	38		2
22 Jul 95	**C'MON BILLY** *Island CIDX 614*	29		2
28 Oct 95	**SEND HIS LOVE TO ME** *Island CID 610*	34		2
9 Mar 96	**HENRY LEE** *Mute CDMUTE 189* NICK CAVE & THE BAD SEEDS & PJ HARVEY	36		1
23 Nov 96	**THAT WAS MY VEIL** *Island CID 648* JOHN PARISH & POLLY JEAN HARVEY	75		1
26 Sep 98	**A PERFECT DAY ELISE** *Island CID 718*	25		2
23 Jan 99	**THE WIND** *Island CID 730*	29		2
25 Nov 00	**GOOD FORTUNE** *Island CID 769*	41		2
10 Mar 01	**A PLACE CALLED HOME** *Island CID 771*	43		2
20 Oct 01	**THIS IS LOVE** *Island CID 785*	41		1
29 May 04	**THE LETTER** *Island CIDX 861*	28		2
31 Jul 04	**YOU COME THROUGH** *Island CIDX 869*	41		2
2 Oct 04	**SHAME** *Island CID 873*	45		1

STEVE HARVEY
UK, male producer/vocalist — 6

Date	Title	Peak Position	Weeks at No.1	Weeks on Chart
28 May 83	**SOMETHING SPECIAL** *London LON 25*	46		4
29 Oct 83	**TONIGHT** *London LON 36*	63		2

HARVEY DANGER
US, male vocal/instrumental group — 1

Date	Title	Peak Position	Weeks at No.1	Weeks on Chart
1 Aug 98	**FLAGPOLE SITTA** *Slash LASCD 64*	57		1

GORDON HASKELL
UK, male vocalist/guitarist — 6

Date	Title	Peak Position	Weeks at No.1	Weeks on Chart
29 Dec 01	**HOW WONDERFUL YOU ARE** *Flying Sparks TDBCDS 04* ○	2		6

LEE HASLAM
UK, male DJ/producer — 1

Date	Title	Peak Position	Weeks at No.1	Weeks on Chart
14 Aug 04	**LIBERATE/HERE COMES THE PAIN** *Tidy Trax TIDYTWO135*	71		1

DAVID HASSELHOFF
US, male vocalist/actor — 6

Date	Title	Peak Position	Weeks at No.1	Weeks on Chart
13 Nov 93	**IF I COULD ONLY SAY GOODBYE** *Arista 74321172262*	35		2
14 Oct 06	**JUMP IN MY CAR** *Skintight CDHOFF1*	3		4

ERIK HASSLE
Sweden, male vocalist — 1

Date	Title	Peak Position	Weeks at No.1	Weeks on Chart
20 Feb 10	**HURTFUL** *Island 2719793*	59		1

TONY HATCH
UK, male orchestra leader/producer — 1

Date	Title	Peak Position	Weeks at No.1	Weeks on Chart
4 Oct 62	**OUT OF THIS WORLD** *Pye 7N 15460*	50		1

JULIANA HATFIELD THREE
US, female vocalist/guitarist — 2

Date	Title	Peak Position	Weeks at No.1	Weeks on Chart
11 Sep 93	**MY SISTER** *Mammoth YZ 767CD*	71		1
18 Mar 95	**UNIVERSAL HEART-BEAT** *East West YZ 916CD* JULIANA HATFIELD	65		1

LALAH HATHAWAY
US, female vocalist (Eulaulah Hathaway) — 10

Date	Title	Peak Position	Weeks at No.1	Weeks on Chart
1 Sep 90	**HEAVEN KNOWS** *Virgin America VUS 28*	66		2
2 Feb 91	**BABY DON'T CRY** *Virgin America VUS 35*	54		3
27 Jul 91	**FAMILY AFFAIR** *10 TEN 369* B.E.F. FEATURING LALAH HATHAWAY	37		5

CHARLOTTE HATHERLEY
UK, female vocalist/guitarist. See Ash — 4

Date	Title	Peak Position	Weeks at No.1	Weeks on Chart
21 Aug 04	**SUMMER** *Double Dragon DD2014CD*	31		2
5 Mar 05	**BASTARDO** *Double Dragon DD2019CD*	31		2

HATIRAS FEATURING SLARTA JOHN
Canada/UK, male rap/production duo — 5

Date	Title	Peak Position	Weeks at No.1	Weeks on Chart
27 Jan 01	**SPACED INVADER** *Defected DFECT 25CDS*	14		5

HAVANA
UK, male production trio — 1

Date	Title	Peak Position	Weeks at No.1	Weeks on Chart
6 Mar 93	**ETHNIC PRAYER** *Limbo 007CD*	71		1

HAVEN
UK, male vocal/instrumental group — 7

Date	Title	Peak Position	Weeks at No.1	Weeks on Chart
22 Sep 01	**LET IT LIVE** *Radiate RDT 3*	72		1
2 Feb 02	**SAY SOMETHING** *Radiate RDTX 4*	24		3
4 May 02	**TIL THE END** *Radiate RDTX 6*	28		2
27 Mar 04	**WOULDN'T CHANGE A THING** *Radiate RDTCD14*	57		1

NIC HAVERSON
UK, male vocalist/actor — 3

Date	Title	Peak Position	Weeks at No.1	Weeks on Chart
30 Jan 93	**HEAD OVER HEELS** *Telstar CDHOH 1*	48		3

CHESNEY HAWKES
UK, male vocalist — 27

Date	Title	Peak Position	Weeks at No.1	Weeks on Chart
23 Feb 91	**THE ONE AND ONLY** *Chrysalis CHS 3627* ●	1	5	16
22 Jun 91	**I'M A MAN NOT A BOY** *Chrysalis CHS 3708*	27		5
28 Sep 91	**SECRETS OF THE HEART** *Chrysalis CHS 3681*	57		3
29 May 93	**WHAT'S WRONG WITH THIS PICTURE** *Chrysalis CDCHS 3969*	63		1
12 Jan 02	**STAY AWAY BABY JANE** *ARC DSART 13*	74		1
4 Jun 05	**ANOTHER FINE MESS** *Right Track CHESCD001*	48		1

SCREAMIN' JAY HAWKINS
US, male vocalist (Jalacy Hawkins), d. 2 Feb 2000 (age 70) — 3

Date	Title	Peak Position	Weeks at No.1	Weeks on Chart
3 Apr 93	**HEART ATTACK AND VINE** *Columbia 6591092*	42		3

SOPHIE B HAWKINS
US, female vocalist — 37

Date	Title	Peak Position	Weeks at No.1	Weeks on Chart
4 Jul 92	**DAMN I WISH I WAS YOUR LOVER** *Columbia 6581077*	14		9
12 Sep 92	**CALIFORNIA HERE I COME** *Columbia 6583177*	53		3
6 Feb 93	**I WANT YOU** *Columbia 6587772*	49		2
13 Aug 94	**RIGHT BESIDE YOU** *Columbia 6606915*	13		12
26 Nov 94	**DON'T DON'T TELL ME NO** *Columbia 6610152*	36		5
11 Mar 95	**AS I LAY ME DOWN** *Columbia 6612125*	24		6

EDWIN HAWKINS SINGERS FEATURING DOROTHY COMBS MORRISON
US, male/female vocal ensemble — 13

Date	Title	Peak Position	Weeks at No.1	Weeks on Chart
21 May 69	**OH HAPPY DAY** *Buddah 201 048*	2		13

KIRSTY HAWKSHAW
UK, female vocalist. See Opus III — 9

Date	Title	Peak Position	Weeks at No.1	Weeks on Chart
24 Jun 00	**DREAMING** *Headspace HEDSCD 002* BT FEATURING KIRSTY HAWKSHAW	38		2
29 Sep 01	**URBAN TRAIN** *VC Recordings/Nebula VCRD 95* DJ TIESTO FEATURING KIRSTY HAWKSHAW	22		3
21 Sep 02	**STEALTH** *Distinctive Breaks DISNCD 90* WAY OUT WEST FEATURING KIRSTY HAWKSHAW	67		1
23 Nov 02	**FINE DAY** *Mainline CDMAIN002*	62		1
23 Oct 04	**JUST BE** *Nebula NEBCD062* TIESTO FEATURING KIRSTY HAWKSHAW	43		2

HAWKWIND
UK, male vocal/instrumental group – Dave Brock & various musicians; members also included Harvey Bainbridge, Robert Calvert, Simon King, Lemmy (Ian Willis/Kilmister), Huw Lloyd-Langton & Nik Turner — 28

Date	Title	Peak Position	Weeks at No.1	Weeks on Chart
1 Jul 72	**SILVER MACHINE** *United Artists UP 35381*	3		15
11 Aug 73	**URBAN GUERRILLA** *United Artists UP 35566*	39		3
21 Oct 78	**SILVER MACHINE** *United Artists UP 35381*	34		5
19 Jul 80	**SHOT DOWN IN THE NIGHT** *Bronze BRO 98*	59		3
15 Jan 83	**SILVER MACHINE** *United Artists UP 35381*	67		2

RICHARD HAWLEY
UK, male vocalist/guitarist. See Longpigs — 3

Date	Title	Peak Position	Weeks at No.1	Weeks on Chart
16 Sep 06	**HOTEL ROOM** *Mute CDMUTE379*	64		1
18 Aug 07	**TONIGHT THE STREETS ARE OURS** *Mute CDMUTE382*	40		2

BILL HAYES WITH ARCHIE BLEYER'S ORCHESTRA
US, male vocalist & orchestra — 9

Date	Title	Peak Position	Weeks at No.1	Weeks on Chart
6 Jan 56	**BALLAD OF DAVY CROCKETT** *London HLA 8220* ★	2		9

CHANELLE HAYES
UK, female vocalist — 1

Date	Title	Peak Position	Weeks at No.1	Weeks on Chart
24 May 08	**I WANT IT** *Emminence CHAN001*	63		1

DARREN HAYES
Australia, male vocalist. See Savage Garden — 41

Date	Title	Peak Position	Weeks at No.1	Weeks on Chart
30 Mar 02	**INSATIABLE** *Columbia 6723992*	8		14
20 Jul 02	**STRANGE RELATIONSHIP** *Columbia 6728685*	15		8
16 Nov 02	**I MISS YOU** *Columbia 6733315*	20		5
1 Feb 03	**CRUSH** *Columbia 6734905*	19		3
11 Sep 04	**POP!ULAR** *Columbia 6751112*	12		5
12 Nov 05	**SO BEAUTIFUL** *Columbia 82876739402*	15		3

Silver-selling ● Gold-selling ● Platinum-selling (x multiples) ⊛ US No.1 ★ | Peak Position | Weeks at No.1 | Weeks on Chart

Date	Title / Label	Peak Position	Weeks at No.1	Weeks on Chart
18 Aug 07	**ON THE VERGE OF SOMETHING WONDERFUL** *Powdered Sugar CXPOWSUG2*	20		2
24 Nov 07	**ME MYSELF AND I** *Powdered Sugar CXPOWSUG3*	59		1

GEMMA HAYES
Ireland, female vocalist/guitarist — Weeks on Chart: **3**

Date	Title / Label	Peak Position	Weeks at No.1	Weeks on Chart
25 May 02	**HANGING AROUND** *Source SOURCD 046*	62		1
10 Aug 02	**LET A GOOD THING GO** *Source SOURCDX 051*	54		1
18 Mar 06	**UNDERCOVER** *Source SOURDX119*	63		1

ISAAC HAYES
US, male vocalist/multi-instrumentalist, d. 10 Aug 2008 (age 65) — Weeks on Chart: **35**

Date	Title / Label	Peak Position	Weeks at No.1	Weeks on Chart
4 Dec 71	**THEME FROM 'SHAFT'** *Stax 2025 069* ★	4		12
3 Apr 76	**DISCO CONNECTION** *ABC 4100* MOVEMENT	10		9
26 Dec 98	**CHOCOLATE SALTY BALLS (PS I LOVE YOU)** *Columbia 6667985* CHEF ⊛	1	1	13
30 Sep 00	**THEME FROM 'SHAFT'** *LaFace 74321792582*	53		1

HAYSI FANTAYZEE
UK, male/female vocal/instrumental trio — Weeks on Chart: **25**

Date	Title / Label	Peak Position	Weeks at No.1	Weeks on Chart
24 Jul 82	**JOHN WAYNE IS BIG LEGGY** *Regard RG 100*	11		10
13 Nov 82	**HOLY JOE** *Regard RG 104*	51		3
22 Jan 83	**SHINY SHINY** *Regard RG 106*	16		10
25 Jun 83	**SISTER FRICTION** *Regard RG 108*	62		2

JUSTIN HAYWARD
UK, male vocalist/guitarist (David Hayward). See Moody Blues — Weeks on Chart: **20**

Date	Title / Label	Peak Position	Weeks at No.1	Weeks on Chart
25 Oct 75	**BLUE GUITAR** *Threshold TH 21* & JOHN LODGE	8		7
8 Jul 78	**FOREVER AUTUMN** *CBS 6368* ●	5		13

LEON HAYWOOD
US, male vocalist — Weeks on Chart: **11**

Date	Title / Label	Peak Position	Weeks at No.1	Weeks on Chart
15 Mar 80	**DON'T PUSH IT, DON'T FORCE IT** *20th Century TC 2443*	12		11

HAYWOODE
UK, female vocalist (Sidney Haywoode) — Weeks on Chart: **31**

Date	Title / Label	Peak Position	Weeks at No.1	Weeks on Chart
17 Sep 83	**A TIME LIKE THIS** *CBS A 3651*	48		7
29 Sep 84	**I CAN'T LET YOU GO** *CBS A 4664*	63		4
13 Apr 85	**ROSES** *CBS A 6069*	65		3
5 Oct 85	**GETTING CLOSER** *CBS A 6582*	67		2
21 Jun 86	**ROSES** *CBS A 7224*	11		11
13 Sep 86	**I CAN'T LET YOU GO** *CBS 6500767*	50		4

OFRA HAZA
Israel, female vocalist, d. 23 Feb 2000 (age 42) — Weeks on Chart: **12**

Date	Title / Label	Peak Position	Weeks at No.1	Weeks on Chart
30 Apr 88	**IM NIN'ALU** *WEA YZ 190*	15		8
17 Jun 95	**MY LOVE IS FOR REAL** *Virgin VUSCD 91* PAULA ABDUL FEATURING OFRA HAZA	28		3
3 Apr 99	**BABYLON** *warner.esp WESP 006 CD1* BLACK DOG FEATURING OFRA HAZA	65		1

HAZE
Malaysia, male vocalist/producer (Harikrish Ramachandran) — Weeks on Chart: **4**

Date	Title / Label	Peak Position	Weeks at No.1	Weeks on Chart
18 Jan 03	**CHANGES** *Defected DFTD 059R* SANDY RIVERA FEATURING HAZE	48		2
31 Jul 04	**DREAMS** *Defected DFTD 090CDS* KINGS OF TOMORROW FEATURING HAZE	69		1
26 Feb 05	**THRU** *Defected DFTD099CDS* KINGS OF TOMORROW FEATURING HAZE	55		1

HAZIZA
Sweden, male production duo — Weeks on Chart: **1**

Date	Title / Label	Peak Position	Weeks at No.1	Weeks on Chart
28 Apr 01	**ONE MORE** *Tidy Trax TIDY 152T*	75		1

LEE HAZLEWOOD
US, male vocalist/producer, d. 4 Aug 2007 (age 78) — Weeks on Chart: **39**

Date	Title / Label	Peak Position	Weeks at No.1	Weeks on Chart
5 Jul 67	**YOU ONLY LIVE TWICE/JACKSON** *Reprise RS 20595* NANCY SINATRA/NANCY SINATRA & LEE HAZLEWOOD	11		19
8 Nov 67	**LADYBIRD** *Reprise RS 20629* NANCY SINATRA & LEE HAZLEWOOD	47		1
21 Aug 71	**DID YOU EVER** *Reprise K 14093* NANCY & LEE	2		19

HAZZARDS
US, female vocal duo — Weeks on Chart: **1**

Date	Title / Label	Peak Position	Weeks at No.1	Weeks on Chart
22 Nov 03	**GAY BOYFRIEND** *Better The Devil BTD3CD*	67		1

MURRAY HEAD
UK, male vocalist — Weeks on Chart: **15**

Date	Title / Label	Peak Position	Weeks at No.1	Weeks on Chart
29 Jan 72	**SUPERSTAR** *MCA MMKS 5077*	47		1
10 Nov 84	**ONE NIGHT IN BANGKOK** *RCA CHESS 1*	12		14

ROY HEAD
US, male vocalist — Weeks on Chart: **5**

Date	Title / Label	Peak Position	Weeks at No.1	Weeks on Chart
4 Nov 65	**TREAT HER RIGHT** *Vocalion V-P 928*	30		5

HEAD AUTOMATICA
US, male vocal/instrumental group — Weeks on Chart: **2**

Date	Title / Label	Peak Position	Weeks at No.1	Weeks on Chart
12 Feb 05	**BEATING HEART BABY** *WEA W663CD*	44		2

HEADBANGERS
UK, male vocal/instrumental group — Weeks on Chart: **3**

Date	Title / Label	Peak Position	Weeks at No.1	Weeks on Chart
10 Oct 81	**STATUS ROCK** *Magnet MAG 206*	60		3

HEADBOYS
UK, male vocal/instrumental group — Weeks on Chart: **8**

Date	Title / Label	Peak Position	Weeks at No.1	Weeks on Chart
22 Sep 79	**THE SHAPE OF THINGS TO COME** *RSO 40*	45		8

HEADS
UK, male producer (Paul Hart) — Weeks on Chart: **4**

Date	Title / Label	Peak Position	Weeks at No.1	Weeks on Chart
21 Jun 86	**AZTEC LIGHTNING (THEME FROM BBC WORLD CUP GRANDSTAND)** *BBC RESL 184*	45		4

HEADS WITH SHAUN RYDER
US/UK, male/female vocal/instrumental group. See Happy Mondays, Talking Heads — Weeks on Chart: **1**

Date	Title / Label	Peak Position	Weeks at No.1	Weeks on Chart
9 Nov 96	**DON'T TAKE MY KINDNESS FOR WEAKNESS** *Radioactive MCSTD 48024*	60		1

HEADSWIM
UK, male vocal/instrumental group — Weeks on Chart: **5**

Date	Title / Label	Peak Position	Weeks at No.1	Weeks on Chart
25 Feb 95	**CRAWL** *Epic 6612252*	64		1
14 Feb 98	**TOURNIQUET** *Epic 6656442*	30		3
16 May 98	**BETTER MADE** *Epic 6658402*	42		1

JEREMY HEALY & AMOS
UK, male vocal/production duo. See HWA featuring Sonic The Hedgehog, Hayzi Fantayzee — Weeks on Chart: **7**

Date	Title / Label	Peak Position	Weeks at No.1	Weeks on Chart
12 Oct 96	**STAMP!** *Positiva CDTIV 65*	11		5
31 May 97	**ARGENTINA** *Positiva CDTIV 74*	30		2

IMOGEN HEAP
UK, female vocalist/multi-instrumentalist — Weeks on Chart: **3**

Date	Title / Label	Peak Position	Weeks at No.1	Weeks on Chart
6 Mar 99	**BLANKET** *Talkin Loud TLDD 39* URBAN SPECIES FEATURING IMOGEN HEAP	56		1
20 May 06	**GOODNIGHT AND GO** *Megaphonic/White 82876822842*	56		1
28 Oct 06	**HEADLOCK** *Megaphonic MEGACD004*	74		1

HEAR 'N AID
International, male/female vocal/instrumental charity assembly — Weeks on Chart: **6**

Date	Title / Label	Peak Position	Weeks at No.1	Weeks on Chart
19 Apr 86	**STARS** *Vertigo HEAR 1*	26		6

HEAR'SAY
UK, female/male vocal group – Danny Foster, Myleene Klass, Kym Marsh*, Suzanne Shaw & Noel Sullivan. See Girls Of FHM — Weeks on Chart: **60**

Date	Title / Label	Peak Position	Weeks at No.1	Weeks on Chart
24 Mar 01	**PURE AND SIMPLE** *Polydor 5870069* ⊛ x2	1	3	25
7 Jul 01	**THE WAY TO YOUR LOVE** *Polydor 5871492*	1	1	17
8 Dec 01	**EVERYBODY** *Polydor 5705122*	4		11
24 Aug 02	**LOVIN' IS EASY** *Polydor 5708552*	6		7

HEART

US, female/male vocal/instrumental group – Ann Wilson, Mark Andes, Denny Carmassi, Howard Leese & Nancy Wilson — 76

Date	Title / Label	Peak Position	Weeks at No.1	Weeks on Chart
29 Mar 86	**THESE DREAMS** *Capitol CL 394* ★	62		4
13 Jun 87	**ALONE** *Capitol CL 448* ● ★	3		16
19 Sep 87	**WHO WILL YOU RUN TO** *Capitol CL 457*	30		7
12 Dec 87	**THERE'S THE GIRL** *Capitol CL 473*	34		7
5 Mar 88	**NEVER/THESE DREAMS** *Capitol CL 482*	8		9
14 May 88	**WHAT ABOUT LOVE** *Capitol CL 487*	14		6
22 Oct 88	**NOTHIN' AT ALL** *Capitol CL 507*	38		3
24 Mar 90	**ALL I WANNA DO IS MAKE LOVE TO YOU** *Capitol CL 569*	8		13
28 Jul 90	**I DIDN'T WANT TO NEED YOU** *Capitol CL 580*	47		3
17 Nov 90	**STRANDED** *Capitol CL 595*	60		2
14 Sep 91	**YOU'RE THE VOICE** *Capitol CL 624*	56		2
20 Nov 93	**WILL YOU BE THERE (IN THE MORNING)** *Capitol CDCLS 700*	19		4

HEARTBEAT

UK, male/female vocal/instrumental group — 5

Date	Title / Label	Peak Position	Weeks at No.1	Weeks on Chart
24 Oct 87	**TEARS FROM HEAVEN** *Priority P 17*	32		4
23 Apr 88	**THE WINNER** *Priority P 19*	70		1

HEARTBEAT COUNTRY

UK, male vocalist/actor (Bill Maynard) — 1

Date	Title / Label	Peak Position	Weeks at No.1	Weeks on Chart
31 Dec 94	**HEARTBEAT** *MMM 01CD*	75		1

HEARTISTS

Italy, male DJ/production trio — 5

Date	Title / Label	Peak Position	Weeks at No.1	Weeks on Chart
9 Aug 97	**BELO HORIZONTI** *VC Recordings VCRD 23*	42		3
31 Jan 98	**BELO HORIZONTI (REMIX)** *VC Recordings VCRD 28*	40		2

HEARTLESS CREW

UK, male DJ/production trio — 4

Date	Title / Label	Peak Position	Weeks at No.1	Weeks on Chart
25 May 02	**THE HEARTLESS CREW THEME** *East West HEART 02CD*	21		3
28 Jun 03	**WHY (LOOKING BACK)** *East West HEART 03CD*	50		1

TED HEATH

UK, male band leader (George Heath), d. 18 Nov 1969 (age 67), & orchestra — 56

Date	Title / Label	Peak Position	Weeks at No.1	Weeks on Chart
16 Jan 53	**VANESSA** *Decca F 9983*	11		1
3 Jul 53	**HOT TODDY** *Decca F 10093*	6		11
23 Oct 53	**DRAGNET** *Decca F 10176*	9		5
12 Feb 54	**SKIN DEEP** *Decca F 10246*	9		3
6 Jul 56	**THE FAITHFUL HUSSAR** *Decca F 10746*	18		9
14 Mar 58	**SWINGIN' SHEPHERD BLUES** *Decca F 11000*	3		14
11 Apr 58	**TEQUILA** *Decca F 11003*	21		6
4 Jul 58	**TOM HARK** *Decca F 11025*	24		2
5 Oct 61	**SUCU SUCU** *Decca F 11392*	36		5

HEATWAVE

UK/US, male vocal/instrumental group – Johnnie, d. 23 May 2006, & Keith Wilder, Ernest Berger, Derek Brambiz, Calvin Duke, Eric Johns, William Jones & Rod Temperton — 80

Date	Title / Label	Peak Position	Weeks at No.1	Weeks on Chart
22 Jan 77	**BOOGIE NIGHTS** *GTO GT 77* ●	2		14
7 May 77	**TOO HOT TO HANDLE/SLIP YOUR DISC TO THIS** *GTO GT 91*	15		11
14 Jan 78	**THE GROOVE LINE** *GTO GT 115*	12		8
3 Jun 78	**MIND BLOWING DECISIONS** *GTO GT 226*	12		11
4 Nov 78	**ALWAYS AND FOREVER/MIND BLOWING DECISIONS** *GTO GT 236* ●	9		14
26 May 79	**RAZZLE DAZZLE** *GTO GT 248*	43		5
17 Jan 81	**GANGSTER OF THE GROOVE** *GTO GT 285*	19		8
21 Mar 81	**JITTERBUGGIN'** *GTO GT 290*	34		7
1 Sep 90	**MIND BLOWING DECISIONS** *Brothers Organisation HW 1*	65		2

HEAVEN 17

UK, male vocal/instrumental trio – Glenn Gregory, Ian Craig Marsh & Martyn Ware — 87

Date	Title / Label	Peak Position	Weeks at No.1	Weeks on Chart
21 Mar 81	**(WE DON'T NEED THIS) FASCIST GROOVE THANG** *Virgin VS 400*	45		5
5 Sep 81	**PLAY TO WIN** *Virgin VS 433*	46		7
14 Nov 81	**PENTHOUSE AND PAVEMENT** *Virgin VS 455*	57		3
30 Oct 82	**LET ME GO** *Virgin VS 532*	41		6
16 Apr 83	**TEMPTATION** *Virgin VS 570* ●	2		13
25 Jun 83	**COME LIVE WITH ME** *Virgin VS 607*	5		11
10 Sep 83	**CRUSHED BY THE WHEELS OF INDUSTRY** *Virgin VS 628*	17		7
1 Sep 84	**SUNSET NOW** *Virgin VS 708*	24		6
27 Oct 84	**THIS IS MINE** *Virgin VS 722*	23		7
19 Jan 85	**...(AND THAT'S NO LIE)** *Virgin VS 740*	52		5
17 Jan 87	**TROUBLE** *Virgin VS 920*	51		3
21 Nov 92	**TEMPTATION (REMIX)** *Virgin VS 1446* ●	4		11
27 Feb 93	**(WE DON'T NEED THIS) FASCIST GROOVE THANG** *Virgin VSCDT 1451*	40		2
10 Apr 93	**PENTHOUSE AND PAVEMENT (REMIX)** *Virgin VSCDT 1457*	54		1

HEAVENS CRY

Holland, male production duo — 2

Date	Title / Label	Peak Position	Weeks at No.1	Weeks on Chart
6 Oct 01	**TILL TEARS DO US PART** *Tidy Trax TIDY 158CD*	68		1
19 Jan 02	**TILL TEARS DO US PART** *Tidy Trax TIDY 158CD*	71		1

HEAVY D & THE BOYZ

US (b. Jamaica), male rapper (Dwight Myers) & DJ/backing dancers – Troy 'Trouble T Roy' Dixon, d. 15 Jul 1990, Edward "Eddie F" Ferrell & Glen 'G-Whiz' Parrish — 28

Date	Title / Label	Peak Position	Weeks at No.1	Weeks on Chart
6 Dec 86	**MR BIG STUFF** *MCA 1106*	61		8
15 Jul 89	**WE GOT OUR OWN THANG** *MCA 23942*	69		2
6 Jul 91	**NOW THAT WE FOUND LOVE** *MCA 1550*	2		12
28 Sep 91	**IS IT GOOD TO YOU** *MCA MCS 1564*	46		3
8 Oct 94	**THIS IS YOUR NIGHT** *MCA MCSTD 2010*	30		3

HEAVY PETTIN'

UK, male vocal/instrumental group — 2

Date	Title / Label	Peak Position	Weeks at No.1	Weeks on Chart
17 Mar 84	**LOVE TIMES LOVE** *Polydor HEP 3*	69		2

HEAVY STEREO

UK, male vocal/instrumental group — 4

Date	Title / Label	Peak Position	Weeks at No.1	Weeks on Chart
22 Jul 95	**SLEEP FREAK** *Creation CRESCD 203*	46		1
28 Oct 95	**SMILER** *Creation CRESCD 213*	46		1
10 Feb 96	**CHINESE BURN** *Creation CRESCD 218*	45		1
24 Aug 96	**MOUSE IN A HOLE** *Creation CRESCD 230*	53		1

HEAVY WEATHER

US, male vocalist (Peter Lee) — 1

Date	Title / Label	Peak Position	Weeks at No.1	Weeks on Chart
29 Jun 96	**LOVE CAN'T TURN AROUND** *Pukka CDPUKKA 6*	56		1

BOBBY HEBB

US, male vocalist, d. 3 Aug 2010 (age 72) — 15

Date	Title / Label	Peak Position	Weeks at No.1	Weeks on Chart
8 Sep 66	**SUNNY** *Philips BF 1503*	12		9
19 Aug 72	**LOVE LOVE LOVE** *Philips 6051 023*	32		6

SHARLENE HECTOR WITH THE NEW INSPIRATIONAL CHOIR

UK, female vocalist & choir — 4

Date	Title / Label	Peak Position	Weeks at No.1	Weeks on Chart
17 Apr 04	**I WISH I KNEW HOW IT WOULD FEEL** *Radar RAD0006CD*	28		4

HED BOYS

UK, male production duo — 6

Date	Title / Label	Peak Position	Weeks at No.1	Weeks on Chart
6 Aug 94	**GIRLS & BOYS** *Deconstruction 74321223322*	21		4
4 Nov 95	**GIRLS & BOYS (REMIX)** *Deconstruction 74321322032*	36		2

HEDGEHOPPERS ANONYMOUS

UK, male vocal/instrumental group – Mick Tinsley, Leslie Dash, Ray Honeybull, Alan Laud & John Stewart — 12

Date	Title / Label	Peak Position	Weeks at No.1	Weeks on Chart
30 Sep 65	**IT'S GOOD NEWS WEEK** *Decca F 12241*	5		12

HEFNER

UK, male vocal/instrumental group — 3

Date	Title / Label	Peak Position	Weeks at No.1	Weeks on Chart
26 Aug 00	**GOOD FRUIT** *Too Pure PURE 108CDS*	50		1
14 Oct 00	**THE GREEDY UGLY PEOPLE** *Too Pure PURE 111CDS*	64		1
8 Sep 01	**ALAN BEAN** *Too Pure PURE 118CDS*	58		1

NEAL HEFTI

US, male orchestra leader/composer, d. 11 Oct 2008 (age 85) — **4**

Date	Title	Peak	Wks at No.1	Wks
9 Apr 88	**BATMAN THEME** *RCA PB 49571*	55		4

DEN HEGARTY

UK, male vocalist. See Darts — **2**

Date	Title	Peak	Wks at No.1	Wks
31 Mar 79	**VOODOO VOODOO** *Magnet MAG 143*	73		2

HEINZ

UK (b. Germany), male vocalist/guitarist (Heinz Burt), d. 7 Apr 2000 (age 57). See Tornados — **35**

Date	Title	Peak	Wks at No.1	Wks
8 Aug 63	**JUST LIKE EDDIE** *Decca F 11693*	5		15
28 Nov 63	**COUNTRY BOY** *Decca F 11768*	26		9
27 Feb 64	**YOU WERE THERE** *Decca F 11831*	26		8
15 Oct 64	**QUESTIONS I CAN'T ANSWER** *Columbia DB 7374*	39		2
18 Mar 65	**DIGGIN' MY POTATOES** *Columbia DB 7482* & THE WILD BOYS	49		1

HELICOPTER

UK, male production duo — **4**

Date	Title	Peak	Wks at No.1	Wks
27 Aug 94	**ON YA WAY** *Helicopter TIG 007CD*	32		2
22 Jun 96	**ON YA WAY (REMIX)** *Systematic SYSCD 27*	37		2

HELIOCENTRIC WORLD

UK, male/female vocal/instrumental group — **2**

Date	Title	Peak	Wks at No.1	Wks
14 Jan 95	**WHERE'S YOUR LOVE BEEN** *Talkin Loud TLKCD 51*	71		2

HELIOTROPIC FEATURING VERNA V

UK, male/female vocal/production group — **2**

Date	Title	Peak	Wks at No.1	Wks
16 Oct 99	**ALIVE** *Multiply CDMULTY 52*	33		2

HELL IS FOR HEROES

UK, male vocal/instrumental group. See Symposium — **10**

Date	Title	Peak	Wks at No.1	Wks
9 Feb 02	**YOU DROVE ME TO IT** *Wishakismo CDWISH 003*	63		1
17 Aug 02	**I CAN CLIMB MOUNTAINS** *Chrysalis CDCHS 5143*	41		2
2 Nov 02	**NIGHT VISION** *Chrysalis CDCHSS 5147*	38		1
1 Feb 03	**YOU DROVE ME TO IT** *EMI CDCHSS 5149*	28		2
17 May 03	**RETREAT** *EMI CDEMS 619*	39		1
28 Aug 04	**ONE OF US** *Captains Of Industry CAPT008*	71		1
27 Nov 04	**KAMICHI** *Factotum TUM001CD*	72		1
12 Mar 05	**MODELS FOR THE PROGRAMME** *Factotum TUM002CD2*	56		1

HELLER & FARLEY PROJECT

UK, male instrumental/production duo. See Fire Island, Pete Heller, Stylus Trouble — **14**

Date	Title	Peak	Wks at No.1	Wks
24 Feb 96	**ULTRA FLAVA** *AM:PM 5814372*	22		3
28 Dec 96	**ULTRA FLAVA (REMIX)** *AM:PM 5820551*	32		4
15 May 99	**BIG LOVE** *Essential Recordings ESCD 4* PETE HELLER'S BIG LOVE	12		7

HELLO

UK, male vocal/instrumental group – Bob Bradbury, Jeff Allen, Vic Faulkner, Keith Marshall — **21**

Date	Title	Peak	Wks at No.1	Wks
9 Nov 74	**TELL HIM** *Bell 1377*	6		12
18 Oct 75	**NEW YORK GROOVE** *Bell 1438*	9		9

HELLOGOODBYE

US, male vocal/instrumental group – Forrest Kline, Marcus Cole (replaced by Travis Head), Jesse Kurvink, Joseph Marro, Chris Profeta & Andrew Richards — **16**

Date	Title	Peak	Wks at No.1	Wks
12 May 07	**HERE (IN YOUR ARMS)** *Drive Thru 88697098462*	4		16

HELLOWEEN

Germany, male vocal/instrumental group — **7**

Date	Title	Peak	Wks at No.1	Wks
27 Aug 88	**DR STEIN** *Noise International 7HELLO 1*	57		3
12 Nov 88	**I WANT OUT** *Noise International 7HELLO 2*	69		2
2 Mar 91	**KIDS OF THE CENTURY** *EMI EM 178*	56		2

BOBBY HELMS

US, male vocalist, d. 19 Jul 1997 (age 61) — **7**

Date	Title	Peak	Wks at No.1	Wks
29 Nov 57	**MY SPECIAL ANGEL** *Brunswick 05271* WITH THE ANITA KERR SINGERS	22		3
21 Feb 58	**NO OTHER BABY** *Brunswick 05730*	30		1
1 Aug 58	**JACQUELINE** *Brunswick 05748* WITH THE ANITA KERR SINGERS	20		3

JIMMY HELMS

US, male vocalist — **10**

Date	Title	Peak	Wks at No.1	Wks
24 Feb 73	**GONNA MAKE YOU AN OFFER YOU CAN'T REFUSE** *Cube BUG 27*	8		10

HELPING HAITI

International, male/female charity ensemble – James Blunt*, Jon Bon Jovi*, Susan Boyle*, Michael Buble*, Alexandra Burke*, Mariah Carey*, Cheryl Cole*, Miley Cyrus*, JLS*, Leona Lewis*, Joe McElderry*, Mika*, Kylie Minogue*, James Morrison*, Rod Stewart*, Take That*, Westlife* & Robbie Williams* — **5**

Date	Title	Peak	Wks at No.1	Wks
20 Feb 10	**EVERYBODY HURTS** *Syco Music 88697661102*	1	2	5

HELTAH SKELTAH & ORIGINOO GUNN CLAPPAZ AS THE FABULOUS FIVE

US, male rap group — **1**

Date	Title	Peak	Wks at No.1	Wks
1 Jun 96	**BLAH** *Priority PTYCD 117*	60		1

AINSLIE HENDERSON

UK, male vocalist — **7**

Date	Title	Peak	Wks at No.1	Wks
8 Mar 03	**KEEP ME A SECRET** *Mercury 0779812*	5		7

EDDIE HENDERSON

US, male trumpeter — **6**

Date	Title	Peak	Wks at No.1	Wks
28 Oct 78	**PRANCE ON** *Capitol CL 16015*	44		6

JOE 'MR PIANO' HENDERSON

UK, male pianist, d. 4 May 1980 (age 60) — **23**

Date	Title	Peak	Wks at No.1	Wks
3 Jun 55	**SING IT WITH JOE** *Polygon P 1167*	14		4
2 Sep 55	**SING IT AGAIN WITH JOE** *Polygon P 1184*	18		3
25 Jul 58	**TRUDIE** *Pye Nixa N 15147*	14		14
23 Oct 59	**TREBLE CHANCE** *Pye 7N 15224*	28		1
24 Mar 60	**OOH! LA! LA!** *Pye 7N 15257*	44		1

BILLY HENDRIX

Germany, male producer (Sharam Khososi). See Three 'n One — **2**

Date	Title	Peak	Wks at No.1	Wks
12 Sep 98	**THE BODY SHINE (EP)** *Hooj Choons HOOJ 65CD*	55		2

JIMI HENDRIX

US, male vocalist/guitarist (Johnny/James Hendrix), d. 18 Sep 1970 (age 27) — **88**

Date	Title	Peak	Wks at No.1	Wks
29 Dec 66	**HEY JOE** *Polydor 56 139*	6		11
23 Mar 67	**PURPLE HAZE** *Track 604 001* JIMI HENDRIX EXPERIENCE	3		14
11 May 67	**THE WIND CRIES MARY** *Track 604 004* JIMI HENDRIX EXPERIENCE	6		11
30 Aug 67	**BURNING OF THE MIDNIGHT LAMP** *Track 604 007* EXPERIENCE	18		9
23 Oct 68	**ALL ALONG THE WATCHTOWER** *Track 604 025* JIMI HENDRIX EXPERIENCE	5		11
16 Apr 69	**CROSSTOWN TRAFFIC** *Track 604 029* JIMI HENDRIX EXPERIENCE	37		3
7 Nov 70	**VOODOO CHILE** *Track 2095 001* JIMI HENDRIX EXPERIENCE	1	1	13
30 Oct 71	**GYPSY EYES/REMEMBER** *Track 2094 010* JIMI HENDRIX EXPERIENCE	35		5
12 Feb 72	**JOHNNY B. GOODE** *Track 2001 277*	35		5
21 Apr 90	**CROSSTOWN TRAFFIC** *Polydor PO 71*	61		3
20 Oct 90	**ALL ALONG THE WATCHTOWER (EP)** *Polydor PO 100*	52		3

NONA HENDRYX

US, female vocalist. See LaBelle — **2**

Date	Title	Peak	Wks at No.1	Wks
16 May 87	**WHY SHOULD I CRY** *EMI America EA 234*	60		2

DON HENLEY

US, male vocalist/drummer. See Eagles — **30**

Date	Title	Peak	Wks at No.1	Wks
12 Feb 83	**DIRTY LAUNDRY** *Asylum E 9894*	59		3
9 Feb 85	**THE BOYS OF SUMMER** *Geffen A 4945*	12		10
27 Jul 89	**THE END OF THE INNOCENCE** *Geffen GEF 57*	48		5

Date	Title / Label	Peak Position	Weeks at No.1	Weeks on Chart
3 Oct 92	**SOMETIMES LOVE JUST AIN'T ENOUGH** *MCA MCS 1692* PATTY SMYTH WITH DON HENLEY	22		6
18 Jul 98	**THE BOYS OF SUMMER** *Geffen GFSTD 22350*	12		6

CASSIUS HENRY
UK, male vocalist — 3

Date	Title / Label	Peak Position	Weeks at No.1	Weeks on Chart
30 Mar 02	**BROKE** *Blacklist 0130265 ERE*	31		2
3 Jul 04	**THE ONE** *Universal MCSTD 40334* FEATURING FREEWAY	56		1

CLARENCE 'FROGMAN' HENRY
US, male vocalist/pianist — 35

Date	Title / Label	Peak Position	Weeks at No.1	Weeks on Chart
4 May 61	**(I DON'T KNOW WHY) BUT I DO** *Pye International 7N 25078*	3		19
13 Jul 61	**YOU ALWAYS HURT THE ONE YOU LOVE** *Pye International 7N 25089*	6		12
21 Sep 61	**LONELY STREET/WHY CAN'T YOU** *Pye International 7N 25108*	42		2
17 Jul 93	**(I DON'T KNOW WHY) BUT I DO** *MCA MCSTD 1797*	65		2

PAUL HENRY & MAYSON GLEN ORCHESTRA
Uk, male actor/vocalist & orchestra — 2

Date	Title / Label	Peak Position	Weeks at No.1	Weeks on Chart
14 Jan 78	**BENNY'S THEME** *Pye 7N 46027*	39		2

PAULINE HENRY
UK, female vocalist. See Chimes — 21

Date	Title / Label	Peak Position	Weeks at No.1	Weeks on Chart
18 Sep 93	**TOO MANY PEOPLE** *Sony S2 6595942*	38		2
6 Nov 93	**FEEL LIKE MAKING LOVE** *Sony S2 6597972*	12		7
29 Jan 94	**CAN'T TAKE YOUR LOVE** *Sony S2 6599902*	30		3
21 May 94	**WATCH THE MIRACLE START** *Sony S2 6602772*	54		1
30 Sep 95	**SUGAR FREE** *Sony S2 6624362*	57		2
23 Dec 95	**LOVE HANGOVER** *Sony S2 6626132*	37		3
24 Feb 96	**NEVER KNEW LOVE LIKE THIS** *Sony S2 6629382* FEATURING WAYNE MARSHALL	40		2
1 Jun 96	**HAPPY** *Sony S2 6630692*	46		1

PIERRE HENRY
France, male composer/instrumentalist — 1

Date	Title / Label	Peak Position	Weeks at No.1	Weeks on Chart
4 Oct 97	**PSYCHE ROCK** *Hi-Life 4620312*	58		1

HEPBURN
UK, female vocal/instrumental group – Jamie Benson, Sarah Davies, Beverley Fullen (replaced by Tasha Bayliss) & Lisa Lister — 15

Date	Title / Label	Peak Position	Weeks at No.1	Weeks on Chart
29 May 99	**I QUIT** *Columbia 6674012*	8		7
28 Aug 99	**BUGS** *Columbia 6677385*	14		5
19 Feb 00	**DEEP DEEP DOWN** *Columbia 6683382*	16		3

HERCULES & LOVE AFFAIR
US, male/female vocal/instrumental group — 2

Date	Title / Label	Peak Position	Weeks at No.1	Weeks on Chart
15 Mar 08	**BLIND** *DFA/EMI DFAEMI2192CD*	40		2

HERD
UK, male vocal/instrumental group – Peter Frampton*, Andy Bown, Andrew Steele & Gary Taylor — 35

Date	Title / Label	Peak Position	Weeks at No.1	Weeks on Chart
13 Sep 67	**FROM THE UNDERWORLD** *Fontana TF 856*	6		13
20 Dec 67	**PARADISE LOST** *Fontana TF 887*	15		9
10 Apr 68	**I DON'T WANT OUR LOVING TO DIE** *Fontana TF 925*	5		13

HERD & FITZ FEATURING ABIGAIL BAILEY
UK, male/female vocal/production trio — 10

Date	Title / Label	Peak Position	Weeks at No.1	Weeks on Chart
17 Dec 05	**I JUST CAN'T GET ENOUGH** *All Around The World CDGLOBE473*	11		10

HERMAN'S HERMITS
UK, male vocal/instrumental group – Peter Noone*, Karl Green, Keith Hopwood, Derek Leckenby, d. 4 Jun 1994, & Barry Whitwam. Other than The Beatles, this Manchester band were the top-selling UK act in the US during the 1960s and Noone (aged 16 at the time) is still the youngest UK male singer to top the US chart — 211

Date	Title / Label	Peak Position	Weeks at No.1	Weeks on Chart
20 Aug 64	**I'M INTO SOMETHING GOOD** *Columbia DB 7338*	1	2	15
19 Nov 64	**SHOW ME GIRL** *Columbia DB 7408*	19		9
18 Feb 65	**SILHOUETTES** *Columbia DB 7475*	3		12
29 Apr 65	**WONDERFUL WORLD** *Columbia DB 7546*	7		9
2 Sep 65	**JUST A LITTLE BIT BETTER** *Columbia DB 7670*	15		9
23 Dec 65	**A MUST TO AVOID** *Columbia DB 7791*	6		11
24 Mar 66	**YOU WON'T BE LEAVING** *Columbia DB 7861*	20		7
23 Jun 66	**THIS DOOR SWINGS BOTH WAYS** *Columbia DB 7947*	18		7
6 Oct 66	**NO MILK TODAY** *Columbia DB 8012*	7		11
1 Dec 66	**EAST WEST** *Columbia DB 8076*	33		7
9 Feb 67	**THERE'S A KIND OF HUSH** *Columbia DB 8123*	7		11
17 Jan 68	**I CAN TAKE OR LEAVE YOUR LOVING** *Columbia DB 8327*	11		9
1 May 68	**SLEEPY JOE** *Columbia DB 8404*	12		10
17 Jul 68	**SUNSHINE GIRL** *Columbia DB 8446*	8		14
18 Dec 68	**SOMETHING'S HAPPENING** *Columbia DB 8504*	6		15
23 Apr 69	**MY SENTIMENTAL FRIEND** *Columbia DB 8563*	2		12
8 Nov 69	**HERE COMES THE STAR** *Columbia DB 8626*	33		9
7 Feb 70	**YEARS MAY COME, YEARS MAY GO** *Columbia DB 8556*	7		12
23 May 70	**BET YER LIFE I DO** *RAK 102*	22		10
14 Nov 70	**LADY BARBARA** *RAK 106* PETER NOONE & HERMAN'S HERMITS	13		12

HERMES HOUSE BAND
Holland, male/female vocal/instrumental group – revolving door of musicians; members included Judith Ansems, Robin Maas, Jaap van Reesema & Jop Wijlacker — 14

Date	Title / Label	Peak Position	Weeks at No.1	Weeks on Chart
15 Dec 01	**COUNTRY ROADS** *Liberty CDHHB 001*	7		12
13 Apr 02	**QUE SERA SERA** *EMI CDHHB 002*	53		1
28 Dec 02	**LIVE IS LIFE** *Liberty CDLIVE001* & DJ OTZI	50		1

HERNANDEZ
UK, male vocalist — 3

Date	Title / Label	Peak Position	Weeks at No.1	Weeks on Chart
15 Apr 89	**ALL MY LOVE** *Epic HER 1*	58		3

MARCOS HERNANDEZ
US, male vocalist — 1

Date	Title / Label	Peak Position	Weeks at No.1	Weeks on Chart
25 Feb 06	**IF YOU WERE MINE** *TVT TVTUKCD0019*	41		1

PATRICK HERNANDEZ
Guadeloupe, male vocalist — 14

Date	Title / Label	Peak Position	Weeks at No.1	Weeks on Chart
16 Jun 79	**BORN TO BE ALIVE** *Gem 4* (silver)	10		14

HERREYS
Sweden, male vocal trio — 3

Date	Title / Label	Peak Position	Weeks at No.1	Weeks on Chart
26 May 84	**DIGGI LOO-DIGGI LEY** *Panther PAN 5*	46		3

KRISTIN HERSH
US, female vocalist/guitarist. See Throwing Muses — 3

Date	Title / Label	Peak Position	Weeks at No.1	Weeks on Chart
22 Jan 94	**YOUR GHOST** *4AD BAD 4001CD*	45		2
16 Apr 94	**STRINGS** *4AD BAD 4006CD*	60		1

NICK HEYWARD
UK, male vocalist/guitarist. See Haircut 100 — 65

Date	Title / Label	Peak Position	Weeks at No.1	Weeks on Chart
19 Mar 83	**WHISTLE DOWN THE WIND** *Arista HEY 1*	13		8
4 Jun 83	**TAKE THAT SITUATION** *Arista HEY 2*	11		10
24 Sep 83	**BLUE HAT FOR A BLUE DAY** *Arista HEY 3*	14		8
3 Dec 83	**ON A SUNDAY** *Arista HEY 4*	52		5
2 Jun 84	**LOVE ALL DAY** *Arista HEY 5*	31		6
3 Nov 84	**WARNING SIGN** *Arista HEY 6*	25		9
8 Jun 85	**LAURA** *Arista HEY 8*	45		4
10 May 86	**OVER THE WEEKEND** *Arista HEY 9*	43		5
10 Sep 88	**YOU'RE MY WORLD** *Warner Brothers W 7758*	67		2
21 Aug 93	**KITE** *Epic 6594882*	44		2
16 Oct 93	**HE DOESN'T LOVE YOU LIKE I DO** *Epic 6597282*	58		2
30 Sep 95	**THE WORLD** *Epic 6623845*	47		2
13 Jan 96	**ROLLERBLADE** *Epic 6627915*	37		2

HHC
UK, male DJ/production duo — 1

Date	Title / Label	Peak Position	Weeks at No.1	Weeks on Chart
19 Apr 97	**WE'RE NOT ALONE** *Perfecto PERF 138CD*	44		1

HI-FIVE
US, male vocal group — 8

Date	Title / Label	Peak Position	Weeks at No.1	Weeks on Chart
1 Jun 91	**I LIKE THE WAY (THE KISSING GAME)** *Jive 271* ★	43		6
24 Oct 92	**SHE'S PLAYING HARD TO GET** *Jive 316*	55		2

Silver-selling · Gold-selling · Platinum-selling (× multiples) · US No.1 ★ · Peak Position · Weeks at No.1 · Weeks on Chart

HI-GATE

UK, male production duo – Paul Masterson & Julius 'Judge Jules' O'Riordan. See Candy Girls, Clergy, Dorothy, Precocious Brats featuring Kevin & Perry, Sleazesisters, Stix 'N' Stoned, Yomanda — 14

Date	Title	Label	Peak	Wks at No.1	Wks on Chart
29 Jan 00	**PITCHIN' (IN EVERY DIRECTION)**	*Incentive CENT 3CD*	6		6
26 Aug 00	**I CAN HEAR VOICES/CANED AND UNABLE**	*Incentive CENT 9CDS*	12		5
7 Apr 01	**GONNA WORK IT OUT**	*Incentive CENT 20CDS*	25		3

HI GLOSS

US, male producer (Guiliano Salerni) & various male/female vocal/instrumental collaborators — 13

Date	Title	Label	Peak	Wks at No.1	Wks on Chart
8 Aug 81	**YOU'LL NEVER KNOW**	*Epic EPC A 1387*	12		13

HI-LUX

UK, male instrumental/production duo — 3

Date	Title	Label	Peak	Wks at No.1	Wks on Chart
18 Feb 95	**FEEL IT**	*Cheeky CHEKCD 006*	41		2
2 Sep 95	**NEVER FELT THIS WAY/FEEL IT**	*Champion CHAMPCD 319*	58		1

HI POWER

Italy, male production group — 1

Date	Title	Label	Peak	Wks at No.1	Wks on Chart
1 Sep 90	**CULT OF SNAP/SIMBA GROOVE**	*Rumour RUMAT 34*	73		1

HI_TACK

Holland, male production duo – Koen Groeneveld & Addy Van Der Zwan. See Da Techno Bohemian, Drunkenmunky, Itty Bitty Boozy Woozy, Klubbheads — 18

Date	Title	Label	Peak	Wks at No.1	Wks on Chart
28 Jan 06	**SAY SAY SAY (WAITING 4 U)**	*Gusto CDGUS26*	4		16
22 Sep 07	**LET'S DANCE**	*Gusto CDGUS34*	38		2

HI-TEK FEATURING JONELL

US, male vocal/production duo — 1

Date	Title	Label	Peak	Wks at No.1	Wks on Chart
20 Oct 01	**ROUND & ROUND**	*Rawkus RWK 3432*	73		1

HI-TEK 3 FEATURING YA KID K

Belgium, male production trio & female rapper/vocalist — 10

Date	Title	Label	Peak	Wks at No.1	Wks on Chart
3 Feb 90	**SPIN THAT WHEEL**	*Brothers Organisation BORG 1*	69		3
29 Sep 90	**SPIN THAT WHEEL (TURTLES GET REAL)**	*Brothers Organisation BORG 16*	15		7

HI TENSION

UK, male vocal/instrumental group – David Joseph, Guy Barker, Ray Alan Eko, Jeff Guishard, Ken Joseph, Patrick & Paul McLean, Paapa Mensah, Paul Phillips, David Reid, Bob Sydor, Peter Thomas & Leroy Williams — 23

Date	Title	Label	Peak	Wks at No.1	Wks on Chart
6 May 78	**HI TENSION**	*Island WIP 6422*	13		12
12 Aug 78	**BRITISH HUSTLE/PEACE ON EARTH**	*Island WIP 6446*	8		11

AL HIBBLER

US, male vocalist, d. 24 Apr 2001 (age 85) — 17

Date	Title	Label	Peak	Wks at No.1	Wks on Chart
13 May 55	**UNCHAINED MELODY**	*Brunswick 05420*	2		17

HINDA HICKS

UK, female vocalist — 15

Date	Title	Label	Peak	Wks at No.1	Wks on Chart
7 Mar 98	**IF YOU WANT ME**	*Island CID 689*	25		3
16 May 98	**YOU THINK YOU OWN ME**	*Island CID 700*	19		4
15 Aug 98	**I WANNA BE YOUR LADY**	*Island CID 709*	14		5
24 Oct 98	**TRULY**	*Island CID 721*	31		2
14 Oct 00	**MY REMEDY**	*Island CID 765*	61		1

HIDDEN CAMERAS

Canada, male vocal ensemble — 1

Date	Title	Label	Peak	Wks at No.1	Wks on Chart
14 Jun 03	**A MIRACLE**	*Rough Trade RTRADESCD 105*	70		1

BERTIE HIGGINS

US, male vocalist (Elbert Higgins) — 4

Date	Title	Label	Peak	Wks at No.1	Wks on Chart
5 Jun 82	**KEY LARGO**	*Epic EPC A 2168*	60		4

HIGH

UK, male vocal/instrumental group — 11

Date	Title	Label	Peak	Wks at No.1	Wks on Chart
25 Aug 90	**UP AND DOWN**	*London LON 272*	53		4
27 Oct 90	**TAKE YOUR TIME**	*London LON 280*	56		2
12 Jan 91	**BOX SET GO**	*London LONG 286*	28		3
6 Apr 91	**MORE...**	*London LON 297*	67		2

HIGH CONTRAST

UK, male producer (Lincoln Barrett) — 4

Date	Title	Label	Peak	Wks at No.1	Wks on Chart
1 Jun 02	**GLOBAL LOVE**	*Hospital NHS 44CD*	68		1
9 Aug 03	**BASEMENT TRACK**	*Hospital NHS 60*	65		1
26 Jun 04	**TWILIGHTS LAST GLEAMING/MADE IT LAST**	*Hospital NHS 73*	74		1
18 Sep 04	**RACING GREEN**	*Hospital NHS 76*	73		1

HIGH FIDELITY

UK, male vocal/instrumental group — 1

Date	Title	Label	Peak	Wks at No.1	Wks on Chart
25 Jul 98	**LUV DUP**	*Plastique FAKE 03CDS*	70		1

HIGH NUMBERS

UK, male vocal/instrumental group. See Who — 4

Date	Title	Label	Peak	Wks at No.1	Wks on Chart
5 Apr 80	**I'M THE FACE**	*Back Door DOOR 4*	49		4

HIGH SOCIETY

UK, male vocal/instrumental group — 4

Date	Title	Label	Peak	Wks at No.1	Wks on Chart
15 Nov 80	**I NEVER GO OUT IN THE RAIN**	*Eagle ERS 002*	53		4

HIGHLY LIKELY

UK, male vocal/instrumental group — 4

Date	Title	Label	Peak	Wks at No.1	Wks on Chart
21 Apr 73	**WHATEVER HAPPENED TO YOU ('LIKELY LADS' THEME)**	*BBC RESL 10*	35		4

HIGHWAYMEN

US, male vocal/instrumental group – Dave Fisher, d. 7 May 2010, Bob Burnett, Steve Butts, Chan Daniels, d. 2 Aug 1975, & Steve Trott — 18

Date	Title	Label	Peak	Wks at No.1	Wks on Chart
7 Sep 61	**MICHAEL**	*HMV POP 910* ★	1	1	14
7 Dec 61	**GYPSY ROVER**	*HMV POP 948*	41		4

HIJACK

UK, male rap/DJ/production group — 3

Date	Title	Label	Peak	Wks at No.1	Wks on Chart
6 Jan 90	**THE BADMAN IS ROBBIN'**	*Rhyme Syndicate 6555177*	56		3

BENNY HILL

UK, male comedian/vocalist (Alfred Hill), d. 20 Apr 1992 (age 68) — 43

Date	Title	Label	Peak	Wks at No.1	Wks on Chart
16 Feb 61	**GATHER IN THE MUSHROOMS**	*Pye 7N 15327*	12		8
1 Jun 61	**TRANSISTOR RADIO**	*Pye 7N 15359*	24		6
16 May 63	**HARVEST OF LOVE**	*Pye 7N 15520*	20		8
13 Nov 71	**ERNIE (THE FASTEST MILKMAN IN THE WEST)**	*Columbia DB 8833*	1	4	17
30 May 92	**ERNIE (THE FASTEST MILKMAN IN THE WEST)**	*EMI ERN 1*	29		4

CHRIS HILL

UK, male DJ/producer — 14

Date	Title	Label	Peak	Wks at No.1	Wks on Chart
6 Dec 75	**RENTA SANTA**	*Philips 6006 491*	10		7
4 Dec 76	**BIONIC SANTA**	*Philips 6006 551*	10		7

DAN HILL

Canada, male vocalist/guitarist — 13

Date	Title	Label	Peak	Wks at No.1	Wks on Chart
18 Feb 78	**SOMETIMES WHEN WE TOUCH**	*20th Century BTC 2355*	13		13

FAITH HILL

US, female vocalist (Audrey Hill) — 37

Date	Title	Label	Peak	Wks at No.1	Wks on Chart
14 Nov 98	**THIS KISS**	*Warner Brothers W 463CD*	13		11
17 Apr 99	**LET ME LET GO**	*Warner Brothers W 473CD*	72		1
20 May 00	**BREATHE**	*WEA W 520CDX*	33		2
21 Apr 01	**THE WAY YOU LOVE ME**	*WEA W 541CD1*	15		5
30 Jun 01	**THERE YOU'LL BE**	*Warner Brothers W 563CD*	3		11
13 Oct 01	**BREATHE (REMIX)**	*Warner Brothers W 572CD*	36		2

Silver-selling ● Gold-selling ● Platinum-selling (x multiples) ✪ US No.1 ★ | Peak Position | Weeks at No.1 | Weeks on Chart

Date	Title	Peak Position	Weeks at No.1	Weeks on Chart
26 Oct 02	**CRY** *Warner Brothers W593CD*	25		2
4 Oct 08	**THERE YOU'LL BE** *Warner Brothers W563CD*	10		3

LAURYN HILL

US, female vocalist/rapper/guitarist/producer. See Fugees **35**

Date	Title	Peak Position	Weeks at No.1	Weeks on Chart
6 Sep 97	**THE SWEETEST THING** *Columbia 6649785* REFUGEE ALLSTARS FEATURING LAURYN HILL	18		4
27 Dec 97	**ALL MY TIME** *One World Entertainment OWECD 2* PAID + LIVE FEATURING LAURYN HILL	57		1
3 Oct 98	**DOO WOP (THAT THING)** *Ruffhouse 6665152* ● ★	3		7
27 Feb 99	**EX-FACTOR** *Columbia/Ruffhouse 6669452*	4		10
10 Jul 99	**EVERYTHING IS EVERYTHING** *Columbia/Ruffhouse 6675745*	19		6
11 Dec 99	**TURN YOUR LIGHTS DOWN LOW** *Columbia 6684362* BOB MARLEY FEATURING LAURYN HILL	15		7

LONNIE HILL

US, male vocalist/guitarist **4**

Date	Title	Peak Position	Weeks at No.1	Weeks on Chart
22 Mar 86	**GALVESTON BAY** *10 TEN 111*	51		4

RONI HILL

US, female vocalist **4**

Date	Title	Peak Position	Weeks at No.1	Weeks on Chart
7 May 77	**YOU KEEP ME HANGIN' ON – STOP IN THE NAME OF LOVE (MEDLEY)** *Creole CR 138*	36		4

VINCE HILL

UK, male vocalist **91**

Date	Title	Peak Position	Weeks at No.1	Weeks on Chart
7 Jun 62	**THE RIVER'S RUN DRY** *Piccadilly 7N 35043*	41		2
6 Jan 66	**TAKE ME TO YOUR HEART AGAIN** *Columbia DB 7781*	13		11
17 Mar 66	**HEARTACHES** *Columbia DB 7852*	28		5
2 Jun 66	**MERCI CHERI** *Columbia DB 7924*	36		6
9 Feb 67	**EDELWEISS** *Columbia DB 8127*	2		17
11 May 67	**ROSES OF PICARDY** *Columbia DB 8185*	13		11
27 Sep 67	**LOVE LETTERS IN THE SAND** *Columbia DB 8268*	23		9
26 Jun 68	**IMPORTANCE OF YOUR LOVE** *Columbia DB 8414*	32		12
12 Feb 69	**DOESN'T ANYBODY KNOW MY NAME?** *Columbia DB 8515*	50		1
25 Oct 69	**LITTLE BLUE BIRD** *Columbia DB 8616*	42		1
25 Sep 71	**LOOK AROUND (AND YOU'LL FIND ME THERE)** *Columbia DB 8804*	12		16

HILLMAN MINX

UK/France, male/female vocal/instrumental group **1**

Date	Title	Peak Position	Weeks at No.1	Weeks on Chart
5 Sep 98	**I'VE HAD ENOUGH** *Mercury MERCD 509*	72		1

HILLTOPPERS

US, male vocal group – Jimmy Sacca, Don McGuire, Seymour Spiegelman, d. 13 Feb 1987, & Billy Vaughn, d. 26 Sep 1991 **30**

Date	Title	Peak Position	Weeks at No.1	Weeks on Chart
27 Jan 56	**ONLY YOU** *London HLD 8221*	3		23
14 Sep 56	**TRYIN'** *London HLD 8298*	30		1
5 Apr 57	**MARIANNE** *London HLD 8381*	20		6

KERI HILSON

US, female vocalist **98**

Date	Title	Peak Position	Weeks at No.1	Weeks on Chart
7 Jul 07	**THE WAY I ARE** *Interscope 1742316* TIMBALAND FEATURING DOE & KERI HILSON	1	2	36
16 Feb 08	**SCREAM** *Interscope 1764136* TIMBALAND FEATURING KERI HILSON & NICOLE SCHERZINGER	12		14
23 Aug 08	**HERO** *Mercury USUM70821210* NAS FEATURING KERI HILSON	70		2
1 Nov 08	**SUPERHUMAN** *Jive 88697416742* CHRIS BROWN FEATURING KERI HILSON	32		9
2 May 09	**RETURN THE FAVOUR** *Polydor USUM70804618* FEATURING TIMBALAND	19		7
23 May 09	**KNOCK YOU DOWN** *Interscope 2711463* FEATURING KANYE WEST & NE-YO	5		21
22 Aug 09	**ENERGY** *Polydor USUM70818261*	43		9

PARIS HILTON

US, female socialite/model/vocalist **9**

Date	Title	Peak Position	Weeks at No.1	Weeks on Chart
5 Aug 06	**STARS ARE BLIND** *Warner Brothers W723CD1* PARIS	5		8
18 Nov 06	**NOTHING IN THIS WORLD** *Warner Brothers W746CD1*	55		1

RONNIE HILTON

UK, male vocalist (Adrian Hill), d. 21 Feb 2001 (age 75) **136**

Date	Title	Peak Position	Weeks at No.1	Weeks on Chart
26 Nov 54	**I STILL BELIEVE** *HMV B 10785*	3		14
10 Dec 54	**VENI VIDI VICI** *HMV B 10785*	12		8
11 Mar 55	**A BLOSSOM FELL** *HMV B 10808*	10		5
26 Aug 55	**STARS SHINE IN YOUR EYES** *HMV B 10901*	13		7
11 Nov 55	**YELLOW ROSE OF TEXAS** *HMV B 10924*	15		2
10 Feb 56	**YOUNG AND FOOLISH** *HMV POP 154*	17		3
20 Apr 56	**NO OTHER LOVE** *HMV POP 198*	1	6	14
29 Jun 56	**WHO ARE WE** *HMV POP 221*	6		12
21 Sep 56	**WOMAN IN LOVE** *HMV POP 248*	30		1
9 Nov 56	**TWO DIFFERENT WORLDS** *HMV POP 274*	13		13
24 May 57	**AROUND THE WORLD** *HMV POP 338*	4		18
2 Aug 57	**WONDERFUL WONDERFUL** *HMV POP 364*	27		2
21 Feb 58	**MAGIC MOMENTS** *HMV POP 446*	22		2
18 Apr 58	**I MAY NEVER PASS THIS WAY AGAIN** *HMV POP 468* WITH THE MICHAEL SAMMES SINGERS	27		3
9 Jan 59	**THE WORLD OUTSIDE** *HMV POP 559* WITH THE MICHAEL SAMMES SINGERS	18		6
21 Aug 59	**THE WONDER OF YOU** *HMV POP 638*	22		3
21 May 64	**DON'T LET THE RAIN COME DOWN** *HMV POP 1291*	21		10
11 Feb 65	**A WINDMILL IN OLD AMSTERDAM** *HMV POP 1378*	23		13

H.I.M.

Finland, male vocal/instrumental group – Ville Valo, Mika 'Gas Lipstick' Karppinen, Mikko 'Linde' Lindstrom, Mikko 'Mige' Paananen & Janne 'Burton' Puurtinen **19**

Date	Title	Peak Position	Weeks at No.1	Weeks on Chart
17 May 03	**BURIED ALIVE BY LOVE** *RCA 82876523182*	30		2
20 Sep 03	**THE SACREMENT** *RCA 82876558892*	23		2
24 Jan 04	**THE FUNERAL OF HEARTS** *RCA 82876585792*	15		4
8 May 04	**SOLITARY MAN** *RCA 82876610652*	9		4
24 Sep 05	**WINGS OF A BUTTERFLY** *Sire W686CD1*	10		4
6 May 06	**KILLING LONELINESS** *Sire W699CD2*	26		2
22 Sep 07	**THE KISS OF DAWN** *Sire W779CD*	59		1

HINDSIGHT

UK, male vocal/instrumental duo **3**

Date	Title	Peak Position	Weeks at No.1	Weeks on Chart
5 Sep 87	**LOWDOWN** *Circa YR 5*	62		3

DENI HINES

Australia, female vocalist **6**

Date	Title	Peak Position	Weeks at No.1	Weeks on Chart
14 Jun 97	**IT'S ALRIGHT** *Mushroom D 1593*	35		2
20 Sep 97	**I LIKE THE WAY** *Mushroom MUSH 7CDX*	37		2
28 Feb 98	**DELICIOUS** *Mushroom MUSH 20CD* FEATURING DON-E	52		1
23 May 98	**JOY** *Mushroom MUSH 30CDS*	47		1

HIPSWAY

UK, male vocal/instrumental group **21**

Date	Title	Peak Position	Weeks at No.1	Weeks on Chart
13 Jul 85	**THE BROKEN YEARS** *Mercury MER 193*	72		3
14 Sep 85	**ASK THE LORD** *Mercury MER 195*	72		1
22 Feb 86	**THE HONEYTHIEF** *Mercury MER 212*	17		9
10 May 86	**ASK THE LORD** *Mercury LORD 1*	50		5
20 Sep 86	**LONG WHITE CAR** *Mercury MER 230*	55		2
1 Apr 89	**YOUR LOVE** *Mercury MER 279*	66		1

HISS

US, male vocal/instrumental group **3**

Date	Title	Peak Position	Weeks at No.1	Weeks on Chart
1 Mar 03	**TRIUMPH** *Polydor 0657782*	53		1
9 Aug 03	**CLEVER KICKS** *Polydor 9809462*	49		1
15 Nov 03	**BACK ON THE RADIO** *Polydor 9813415*	65		1

HISTORY FEATURING Q-TEE

UK, male production duo & female rapper **5**

Date	Title	Peak Position	Weeks at No.1	Weeks on Chart
21 Apr 90	**AFRIKA** *SBK 7008*	42		5

CAROL HITCHCOCK

Australia, female vocalist **5**

Date	Title	Peak Position	Weeks at No.1	Weeks on Chart
30 May 87	**GET READY** *A&M AM 391*	56		5

Peak Position · Weeks at No.1 · Weeks on Chart

HITHOUSE
Holland, male producer (Peter Slaghuis), d. 5 Sep 1991 (age 30). See Video Kids

				13
5 Nov 88	**JACK TO THE SOUND OF THE UNDERGROUND** *Supreme SUPE 137*	14		12
19 Aug 89	**MOVE YOUR FEET TO THE RHYTHM OF THE BEAT** *Supreme SUPE 149*	69		1

HIVES
Sweden, male vocal/instrumental group

				18
23 Feb 02	**HATE TO SAY I TOLD YOU SO** *Burning Heart BHR 1059*	23		3
18 May 02	**MAIN OFFENDER** *Poptones MC 5076SCD*	24		2
17 Jul 04	**WALK IDIOT WALK** *Polydor 9867038*	13		9
30 Oct 04	**TWO TIMING TOUCH AND BROKEN BONES** *Polydor 9868351*	44		1
13 Oct 07	**TICK TICK BOOM** *Polydor 1748909*	41		3

HOCKEY
US, male vocal/instrumental group

				4
26 Sep 09	**SONG AWAY** *Capitol USCA20902269*	49		4

EDMUND HOCKRIDGE
Canada, male vocalist, d. 15 Mar 2009 (age 89)

				18
17 Feb 56	**YOUNG AND FOOLISH** *Nixa N 15039*	10		9
11 May 56	**NO OTHER LOVE** *Nixa N 15048*	24		4
31 Aug 56	**BY THE FOUNTAINS OF ROME** *Pye Nixa N 15063*	17		5

EDDIE HODGES
US, male actor/vocalist

				10
28 Sep 61	**I'M GONNA KNOCK ON YOUR DOOR** *London HLA 9369*	37		6
9 Aug 62	**MADE TO LOVE (GIRLS GIRLS GIRLS)** *London HLA 9576*	37		4

SUSANNA HOFFS
US, female vocalist/guitarist. See Bangles

				8
2 Mar 91	**MY SIDE OF THE BED** *Columbia 6565547*	44		4
11 May 91	**UNCONDITIONAL LOVE** *Columbia 6567827*	65		2
19 Oct 96	**ALL I WANT** *London LONCD 387*	32		2

HULK HOGAN WITH GREEN JELLY
US, male wrestler/vocalist (Terry Bollea) & vocal/instrumental group

				4
25 Dec 93	**I'M THE LEADER OF THE GANG** *Arista 74321174892*	25		4

HOGGBOY
UK, male vocal/instrumental group

				1
27 Apr 02	**SHOULDN'T LET THE SIDE DOWN** *Sobriety SOB 4CDA*	74		1

DEMI HOLBORN
UK, female vocalist

				2
27 Jul 02	**I'D LIKE TO TEACH THE WORLD TO SING** *Universal Classics & Jazz 0190982*	27		2

HOLDEN & THOMPSON
UK, male/female vocal/production duo

				1
17 May 03	**NOTHING** *Loaded LOAD 98CD*	51		1

HOLE
US/Canada, female/male vocal/instrumental group

				15
17 Apr 93	**BEAUTIFUL SON** *City Slang EFA 0491603*	54		1
9 Apr 94	**MISS WORLD** *City Slang EFA 049362*	64		1
15 Apr 95	**DOLL PARTS** *Geffen GFSXD 91*	16		3
29 Jul 95	**VIOLET** *Geffen GFSTD 94*	17		2
12 Sep 98	**CELEBRITY SKIN** *Geffen GFSTD 22345*	19		4
30 Jan 99	**MALIBU** *Geffen GFSTD 22369*	22		2
10 Jul 99	**AWFUL** *Geffen INTDE 97098*	42		2

HOLE IN ONE
Holland, male DJ/producer (Marcel Hol)

				2
15 Feb 97	**LIFE'S TOO SHORT** *Manifesto FESCD 21*	36		2

J HOLIDAY
US, male vocalist (Nahum Grymes)

				5
17 Nov 07	**BED** *Charisma CASDX16*	32		5

HOLIDAY PLAN
UK, male vocal/instrumental group

				1
26 Jun 04	**STORIES/SUNSHINE** *Island CID 858*	58		1

JOOLS HOLLAND & JAMIROQUAI
UK, male vocal/instrumental duo

				3
24 Feb 01	**I'M IN THE MOOD FOR LOVE** *warner.esp WSMS 001CD*	29		3

HOLLAND-DOZIER FEATURING LAMONT DOZIER
US, male production/vocal duo

				5
28 Oct 72	**WHY CAN'T WE BE LOVERS** *Invictus INV 525*	29		5

JENNIFER HOLLIDAY
US, female vocalist

				6
4 Sep 82	**AND I'M TELLING YOU I'M NOT GOING** *Geffen GEF A 2644*	32		6

MICHAEL HOLLIDAY
UK, male vocalist (Norman Milne), d. 29 Oct 1963 (age 37)

				69
30 Mar 56	**NOTHIN' TO DO** *Columbia DB 3746*	20		3
15 Jun 56	**GAL WITH THE YALLER SHOES** *Columbia DB 3783*	13		6
22 Jun 56	**HOT DIGGITY (DOG ZIGGITY BOOM)** *Columbia DB 3783*	14		8
5 Oct 56	**TEN THOUSAND MILES** *Columbia DB 3813*	24		3
17 Jan 58	**THE STORY OF MY LIFE** *Columbia DB 4058*	1	2	15
14 Mar 58	**IN LOVE** *Columbia DB 4087*	26		3
16 May 58	**STAIRWAY OF LOVE** *Columbia DB 4121*	3		13
11 Jul 58	**I'LL ALWAYS BE IN LOVE WITH YOU** *Columbia DB 4155*	27		1
1 Jan 60	**STARRY EYED** *Columbia DB 4378* WITH THE MICHAEL SAMMES SINGERS	1	1	13
14 Apr 60	**SKYLARK** *Columbia DB 4437*	39		3
1 Sep 60	**LITTLE BOY LOST** *Columbia DB 4475*	50		1

HOLLIES
UK, male vocal/instrumental group – Allan Clarke, Bobby Elliott, Eric Haydock (replaced by Bernie Calvert), Tony Hicks & Graham Nash (replaced by Terry Sylvester). One of the most popular, influential and well-respected acts of the 1960s, who have a 23-year span of No.1 singles

				318
30 May 63	**(AIN'T THAT) JUST LIKE ME** *Parlophone R 5030*	25		10
29 Aug 63	**SEARCHIN'** *Parlophone R 5052*	12		14
21 Nov 63	**STAY** *Parlophone R 5077*	8		16
27 Feb 64	**JUST ONE LOOK** *Parlophone R 5104*	2		13
21 May 64	**HERE I GO AGAIN** *Parlophone R 5137*	4		12
17 Sep 64	**WE'RE THROUGH** *Parlophone R 5178*	7		11
28 Jan 65	**YES I WILL** *Parlophone R 5232*	9		13
27 May 65	**I'M ALIVE** *Parlophone R 5287*	1	3	14
2 Sep 65	**LOOK THROUGH ANY WINDOW** *Parlophone R 5322*	4		11
9 Dec 65	**IF I NEEDED SOMEONE** *Parlophone R 5392*	20		9
24 Feb 66	**I CAN'T LET GO** *Parlophone R 5409*	2		10
23 Jun 66	**BUS STOP** *Parlophone R 5469*	5		9
13 Oct 66	**STOP STOP STOP** *Parlophone R 5508*	2		12
16 Feb 67	**ON A CAROUSEL** *Parlophone R 5562*	4		11
1 Jun 67	**CARRIE-ANNE** *Parlophone R 5602*	3		11
27 Sep 67	**KING MIDAS IN REVERSE** *Parlophone R 5637*	18		8
27 Mar 68	**JENNIFER ECCLES** *Parlophone R 5680*	7		11
2 Oct 68	**LISTEN TO ME** *Parlophone R 5733*	11		11
5 Mar 69	**SORRY SUZANNE** *Parlophone R 5765*	3		12
4 Oct 69	**HE AIN'T HEAVY, HE'S MY BROTHER** *Parlophone R 5806*	3		15
18 Apr 70	**I CAN'T TELL THE BOTTOM FROM THE TOP** *Parlophone R 5837*	7		10
3 Oct 70	**GASOLINE ALLEY BRED** *Parlophone R 5862*	14		7
22 May 71	**HEY WILLY** *Parlophone R 5905*	22		7
26 Feb 72	**THE BABY** *Polydor 2058 199*	26		6
2 Sep 72	**LONG COOL WOMAN IN A BLACK DRESS** *Parlophone R 5939*	32		8
13 Oct 73	**THE DAY THAT CURLY BILLY SHOT DOWN CRAZY SAM MCGHEE** *Polydor 2058 403*	24		6
9 Feb 74	**THE AIR THAT I BREATHE** *Polydor 2058 435* ●	2		13

Date	Title	Peak Position	Weeks at No.1	Weeks on Chart
14 Jun 80	**SOLDIER'S SONG** *Polydor 2059 246*	58		3
29 Aug 81	**HOLLIEDAZE (MEDLEY)** *EMI 5229*	28		7
3 Sep 88	**HE AIN'T HEAVY, HE'S MY BROTHER** *EMI EM 74* ●	1	2	11
3 Dec 88	**THE AIR THAT I BREATHE** *EMI EM 80*	60		5
20 Mar 93	**THE WOMAN I LOVE** *EMI CDEM 264*	42		2

Top 3 Best-Selling Singles

		Approximate Sales
1	HE AIN'T HEAVY HE'S MY BROTHER	790,000
2	THE AIR THAT I BREATHE	390,000
3	I'M ALIVE	350,000

LOLEATTA HOLLOWAY

US, female vocalist — 23

Date	Title	Peak Position	Weeks at No.1	Weeks on Chart
31 Aug 91	**GOOD VIBRATIONS** *Interscope A 8764* MARKY MARK & THE FUNKY BUNCH FEATURING LOLEATTA HOLLOWAY ★	14		7
18 Jan 92	**TAKE ME AWAY** *PWL Continental PWL 210* CAPPELLA FEATURING LOLEATTA HOLLOWAY	25		5
26 Mar 94	**STAND UP** *Six6 SIXCD 111*	68		1
1 Apr 95	**KEEP THE FIRE BURNIN'** *Columbia 6611552* DAN HARTMAN STARRING LOLEATTA HOLLOWAY	49		1
11 Apr 98	**SHOUT TO THE TOP** *JBO JNR 5001573* FIRE ISLAND FEATURING LOLEATTA HOLLOWAY	23		2
20 Feb 99	**(YOU GOT ME) BURNING UP** *Wonderboy BOYD 013* CEVIN FISHER FEATURING LOLEATTA HOLLOWAY	14		4
25 Nov 00	**DREAMIN'** *Defected DFECT 22CDS*	59		1
10 Jun 06	**LOVE SENSATION '06** *Gusto CDGUS40*	37		2

HOLLOWAY & CO

UK, male producer (Nicky Holloway) — 1

Date	Title	Peak Position	Weeks at No.1	Weeks on Chart
21 Aug 99	**I'LL DO ANYTHING – TO MAKE YOU MINE** *INCredible INCS 2CD*	58		1

HOLLOWAYS

UK, male vocal/instrumental group — 15

Date	Title	Peak Position	Weeks at No.1	Weeks on Chart
12 Aug 06	**TWO LEFT FEET** *TVT HOLLOCD1*	33		2
28 Oct 06	**GENERATOR** *TVT HOLLOCD2*	30		4
7 Apr 07	**DANCEFLOOR** *TVT HOLLOCD3*	41		1
23 Jun 07	**GENERATOR** *TVT TV61362*	14		7
6 Oct 07	**TWO LEFT FEET** *TVT TV61392*	74		1

BUDDY HOLLY

US, male vocalist/guitarist (Charles Hardin Holley), d. 3 Feb 1959 (age 22). See Crickets — 190

Date	Title	Peak Position	Weeks at No.1	Weeks on Chart
6 Dec 57	**PEGGY SUE** *Coral Q 72293*	6		17
14 Mar 58	**LISTEN TO ME** *Coral Q 72288*	16		2
20 Jun 58	**RAVE ON** *Coral Q 72325*	5		14
29 Aug 58	**EARLY IN THE MORNING** *Coral Q 72333*	17		4
16 Jan 59	**HEARTBEAT** *Coral Q 72346*	30		1
27 Feb 59	**IT DOESN'T MATTER ANYMORE** *Coral Q 72360*	1	3	21
31 Jul 59	**MIDNIGHT SHIFT** *Brunswick 05800*	26		3
11 Sep 59	**PEGGY SUE GOT MARRIED** *Coral Q 72376*	13		10
28 Apr 60	**HEARTBEAT** *Coral Q 72392*	30		3
26 May 60	**TRUE LOVE WAYS** *Coral Q 72397*	25		7
20 Oct 60	**LEARNIN' THE GAME** *Coral Q 72411*	36		3
9 Feb 61	**WHAT TO DO** *Coral Q 72419*	34		6
6 Jul 61	**BABY I DON'T CARE/VALLEY OF TEARS** *Coral Q 72432*	12		14
15 Mar 62	**LISTEN TO ME** *Coral Q 72449*	48		1
13 Sep 62	**REMINISCING** *Coral Q 72455*	17		11
14 Mar 63	**BROWN-EYED HANDSOME MAN** *Coral Q 72459*	3		17
6 Jun 63	**BO DIDDLEY** *Coral Q 72463*	4		12
5 Sep 63	**WISHING** *Coral Q 72466*	10		11
19 Dec 63	**WHAT TO DO** *Coral Q 72469*	27		8
14 May 64	**YOU'VE GOT LOVE** *Coral Q 72472* & THE CRICKETS	40		6
10 Sep 64	**LOVE'S MADE A FOOL OF YOU** *Coral Q 72475*	39		6
3 Apr 68	**PEGGY SUE/RAVE ON** *MCA MU 1012*	32		9
10 Dec 88	**TRUE LOVE WAYS** *MCA 1302*	65		4

HOLLY & THE IVYS

UK, male/female vocal/instrumental group — 4

Date	Title	Peak Position	Weeks at No.1	Weeks on Chart
19 Dec 81	**CHRISTMAS ON 45** *Decca SANTA 1*	40		4

HOLLYWOOD ARGYLES

US, male vocal/instrumental group — 10

Date	Title	Peak Position	Weeks at No.1	Weeks on Chart
21 Jul 60	**ALLEY OOP** *London HLU 9146* ★	24		10

HOLLYWOOD BEYOND

UK, male vocalist (Mark Rogers) & various vocal/instrumental collaborators — 14

Date	Title	Peak Position	Weeks at No.1	Weeks on Chart
12 Jul 86	**WHAT'S THE COLOUR OF MONEY?** *WEA YZ 76*	7		10
20 Sep 86	**NO MORE TEARS** *WEA YZ 81*	47		4

EDDIE HOLMAN

US, male vocalist — 13

Date	Title	Peak Position	Weeks at No.1	Weeks on Chart
19 Oct 74	**(HEY THERE) LONELY GIRL** *ABC 4012* ●	4		13

DAVE HOLMES

UK, male DJ/producer — 1

Date	Title	Peak Position	Weeks at No.1	Weeks on Chart
26 May 01	**DEVOTION** *Tidy Trax TIDY 154CD*	66		1

DAVID HOLMES

UK, male DJ/producer — 8

Date	Title	Peak Position	Weeks at No.1	Weeks on Chart
6 Apr 96	**GONE** *Go! Discs GODCD 140*	75		1
23 Aug 97	**GRITTY SHAKER** *Go! Beat GOBCD 2*	53		1
10 Jan 98	**DON'T DIE JUST YET** *Go! Beat GOLCD 6*	33		3
4 Apr 98	**MY MATE PAUL** *Go! Beat GOBCD 8*	39		2
19 Aug 00	**69 POLICE** *Go! Beat GOBCD 30*	53		1

RUPERT HOLMES

US (b. UK), male vocalist — 14

Date	Title	Peak Position	Weeks at No.1	Weeks on Chart
12 Jan 80	**ESCAPE (THE PINA COLADA SONG)** *Infinity INF 120* ★	23		7
22 Mar 80	**HIM** *MCA 565*	31		7

JOHN HOLT

Jamaica, male vocalist — 14

Date	Title	Peak Position	Weeks at No.1	Weeks on Chart
14 Dec 74	**HELP ME MAKE IT THROUGH THE NIGHT** *Trojan TR 7909*	6		14

NICHOLA HOLT

UK, female vocalist — 1

Date	Title	Peak Position	Weeks at No.1	Weeks on Chart
21 Oct 00	**THE GAME** *RCA 74321798992*	72		1

PAUL HOLT

UK, male vocalist — 3

Date	Title	Peak Position	Weeks at No.1	Weeks on Chart
18 Dec 04	**FIFTY GRAND FOR CHRISTMAS** *Sanctuary SANXS348*	35		3

A HOMEBOY, A HIPPIE & A FUNKI DREDD

UK, male production trio — 9

Date	Title	Peak Position	Weeks at No.1	Weeks on Chart
13 Oct 90	**TOTAL CONFUSION** *Tam Tam 7TTT 031*	56		3
29 Dec 90	**FREEDOM** *Tam Tam 7TTT 039*	68		4
8 Jan 94	**HERE WE GO AGAIN** *Polydor PZCD 302*	57		2

HONDY

Italy, male/female vocal/production group — 2

Date	Title	Peak Position	Weeks at No.1	Weeks on Chart
12 Apr 97	**HONDY (NO ACCESS)** *Manifesto FESCD 20*	26		2

HONEY RYDER

UK, female/male vocal/instrumental duo — 2

Date	Title	Peak Position	Weeks at No.1	Weeks on Chart
9 Aug 08	**NUMB** *Honey Ryder Music GBNUM0600016*	32		1
28 Feb 09	**FLY AWAY** *Honey Ryder Music GBWLF0800047*	31		1

HONEYBUS

UK, male vocal/instrumental group – Pete Dello, Roy Cane, Colin Hare & Pete Kircher — 12

Date	Title	Peak Position	Weeks at No.1	Weeks on Chart
20 Mar 68	**I CAN'T LET MAGGIE GO** *Deram DM 182*	8		12

Silver-selling ● Gold-selling ● Platinum-selling (x multiples) ✪ US No.1 ★ Peak Position · Weeks at No.1 · Weeks on Chart

HONEYCOMBS
UK, male/female vocal/instrumental group – Dennis Dalziel, d. 6 Jul 2005, Ann & John Lantree, Martin Murray & Alan Ward — **39**

Date	Title	Label	Peak	Wks at No.1	Wks on Chart
23 Jul 64	**HAVE I THE RIGHT**	*Pye 7N 15664*	1	2	15
22 Oct 64	**IS IT BECAUSE**	*Pye 7N 15705*	38		6
29 Apr 65	**SOMETHING BETTER BEGINNING**	*Pye 7N 15827*	39		4
5 Aug 65	**THAT'S THE WAY**	*Pye 7N 15890*	12		14

HONEYCRACK
UK, male vocal/instrumental group — **9**

Date	Title	Label	Peak	Wks at No.1	Wks on Chart
4 Nov 95	**SITTING AT HOME**	*Epic 6625382*	42		2
24 Feb 96	**GO AWAY**	*Epic 6628642*	41		2
11 May 96	**KING OF MISERY**	*Epic 6631475*	32		2
20 Jul 96	**SITTING AT HOME**	*Epic 6635032*	32		2
16 Nov 96	**ANYWAY**	*EG EGO 52A*	67		1

HONEYDRIPPERS
UK/US, male vocal/instrumental group — **3**

Date	Title	Label	Peak	Wks at No.1	Wks on Chart
2 Feb 85	**SEA OF LOVE**	*Es Paranza YZ 33*	56		3

HONEYMOON MACHINE
UK, male vocal/instrumental group — **2**

Date	Title	Label	Peak	Wks at No.1	Wks on Chart
21 May 05	**INTO YOUR HEAD**	*Easy Street EASYST009CD*	66		1
22 Oct 05	**FAITH IN PEOPLE**	*Easy Street EASYST011CD*	64		1

HONEYROOT
UK, male vocal/instrumental/production duo. See Heaven 17 — **1**

Date	Title	Label	Peak	Wks at No.1	Wks on Chart
7 May 05	**LOVE WILL TEAR US APART**	*Just Music TAOS003*	70		1

HONEYZ
UK/France, female vocal trio – Heavenli Abdi (replaced by Mariama Goodman in 1999; Goodman replaced by Abdi in 2000), Naima Belkhiati & Celena Cherry. See Anotherside, Solid Harmonie — **57**

Date	Title	Label	Peak	Wks at No.1	Wks on Chart
5 Sep 98	**FINALLY FOUND**	*1st Avenue HNZCD 1* ●	4		12
19 Dec 98	**END OF THE LINE**	*1st Avenue HNZCD 2* ●	5		14
24 Apr 99	**LOVE OF A LIFETIME**	*1st Avenue HNZCD 3*	9		9
23 Oct 99	**NEVER LET YOU DOWN**	*1st Avenue HNZCD 4*	7		6
11 Mar 00	**WON'T TAKE IT LYING DOWN**	*1st Avenue HNZCD 5*	7		8
28 Oct 00	**NOT EVEN GONNA TRIP**	*1st Avenue HNZDD 7*	24		5
18 Aug 01	**I DON'T KNOW**	*1st Avenue HNZDD 8*	28		3

HONKY
UK, male vocal/instrumental group — **5**

Date	Title	Label	Peak	Wks at No.1	Wks on Chart
28 May 77	**JOIN THE PARTY**	*Creole CR 137*	28		5

HONKY
UK, male rap/production duo — **5**

Date	Title	Label	Peak	Wks at No.1	Wks on Chart
30 Oct 93	**THE HONKY DOODLE DAY EP**	*ZTT ZANG 45CD*	61		1
19 Feb 94	**THE WHISTLER**	*ZTT ZANG 48CD*	41		2
20 Apr 96	**HIP HOP DON'T YA DROP**	*Higher Ground HIGHS 1CD*	70		1
10 Aug 96	**WHAT'S GOIN' DOWN**	*Higher Ground HIGHS 2CD*	49		1

HOOBASTANK
US, male vocal/instrumental group — **9**

Date	Title	Label	Peak	Wks at No.1	Wks on Chart
13 Apr 02	**CRAWLING IN THE DARK**	*Mercury 5828622*	47		2
12 Jun 04	**THE REASON**	*Mercury 9862567*	12		7

FRANK HOOKER & POSITIVE PEOPLE
US, male/female vocal/instrumental group — **4**

Date	Title	Label	Peak	Wks at No.1	Wks on Chart
5 Jul 80	**THIS FEELIN'**	*DJM DJS 10947*	48		4

JOHN LEE HOOKER
US, male vocalist/guitarist, d. 21 Jun 2001 (age 83) — **23**

Date	Title	Label	Peak	Wks at No.1	Wks on Chart
11 Jun 64	**DIMPLES**	*Stateside SS 297*	23		10
24 Oct 92	**BOOM BOOM**	*Pointblank POB 3*	16		5
16 Jan 93	**BOOGIE AT RUSSIAN HILL**	*Pointblank POBDX 4*	53		2
15 May 93	**GLORIA**	*Exile VANCD 11* VAN MORRISON & JOHN LEE HOOKER	31		3
11 Feb 95	**CHILL OUT (THINGS GONNA CHANGE)**	*Pointblank POBD 10*	45		2
20 Apr 96	**BABY LEE**	*Silvertone ORECD 81* WITH ROBERT CRAY	65		1

HOOSIERS
UK/Sweden, male vocal/instrumental trio – Irwin Sparkes, Alphonso Sharland & Martin Skarendahl — **64**

Date	Title	Label	Peak	Wks at No.1	Wks on Chart
30 Jun 07	**WORRIED ABOUT RAY**	*RCA 88697116512*	5		33
20 Oct 07	**GOODBYE MR A**	*RCA 88697156892*	4		23
26 Apr 08	**COPS AND ROBBERS**	*RCA 88697300752*	24		8

HOOTERS
US, male vocal/instrumental group — **9**

Date	Title	Label	Peak	Wks at No.1	Wks on Chart
21 Nov 87	**SATELLITE**	*CBS 6511687*	22		9

HOOTIE & THE BLOWFISH
US, male vocal/instrumental group — **6**

Date	Title	Label	Peak	Wks at No.1	Wks on Chart
25 Feb 95	**HOLD MY HAND**	*Atlantic A 7230CD*	50		3
27 May 95	**LET HER CRY**	*Atlantic A 7188CD*	75		1
4 May 96	**OLD MAN AND ME (WHEN I GET TO HEAVEN)**	*Atlantic A 5513CD*	57		1
7 Nov 98	**I WILL WAIT**	*Atlantic AT 0048CD*	57		1

HOPE A.D.
UK, male producer (David Hope). See Mind Of Kane — **1**

Date	Title	Label	Peak	Wks at No.1	Wks on Chart
4 Jun 94	**TREE FROG**	*Sun-Up SUN 003CD*	73		1

HOPE OF THE STATES
UK, male vocal/instrumental group — **9**

Date	Title	Label	Peak	Wks at No.1	Wks on Chart
11 Oct 03	**ENEMIES FRIENDS**	*Sony Music 6742572*	25		2
5 Jun 04	**THE RED, THE WHITE, THE BLUE**	*Sony Music 6749922*	15		3
28 Aug 04	**NEHEMIAH**	*Sony Music 6752472*	30		2
17 Jun 06	**SING IT OUT**	*Columbia LEFTCD003*	39		1
2 Sep 06	**LEFT**	*Columbia LEFTCD06*	63		1

MARY HOPKIN
UK, female vocalist/guitarist — **74**

Date	Title	Label	Peak	Wks at No.1	Wks on Chart
4 Sep 68	**THOSE WERE THE DAYS**	*Apple 2*	1	6	21
2 Apr 69	**GOODBYE**	*Apple 10*	2		14
31 Jan 70	**TEMMA HARBOUR**	*Apple 22*	6		11
28 Mar 70	**KNOCK KNOCK WHO'S THERE**	*Apple 26*	2		14
31 Oct 70	**THINK ABOUT YOUR CHILDREN**	*Apple 30*	19		9
31 Jul 71	**LET MY NAME BE SORROW**	*Apple 34*	46		1
20 Mar 76	**IF YOU LOVE ME**	*Good Earth GD 2*	32		4

ANTHONY HOPKINS
UK, male vocalist/actor (Philip Anthony Hopkins) — **1**

Date	Title	Label	Peak	Wks at No.1	Wks on Chart
27 Dec 86	**DISTANT STAR**	*Juice AA 5*	75		1

BRUCE HORNSBY & THE RANGE
US, male vocal/instrumental group — **15**

Date	Title	Label	Peak	Wks at No.1	Wks on Chart
2 Aug 86	**THE WAY IT IS**	*RCA PB 49805* ★	15		10
25 Apr 87	**MANDOLIN RAIN**	*RCA PB 49769*	70		1
28 May 88	**THE VALLEY ROAD**	*RCA PB 49561*	44		4

HORRORS
UK, male vocal/instrumental group — **1**

Date	Title	Label	Peak	Wks at No.1	Wks on Chart
10 Mar 07	**GLOVES**	*Loog 1725532*	34		1

HORSE
UK, female/male vocal/instrumental group — **10**

Date	Title	Label	Peak	Wks at No.1	Wks on Chart
24 Nov 90	**CAREFUL**	*Capitol CL 587*	52		3
21 Aug 93	**SHAKE THIS MOUNTAIN**	*Oxygen GASPD 7*	52		2
23 Oct 93	**GOD'S HOME MOVIE**	*Oxygen GASXD 10*	56		1
15 Jan 94	**CELEBRATE**	*Oxygen GASPD 11*	49		2
5 Apr 97	**CAREFUL (STRESS)**	*Stress CDSTRX 79*	44		2

JOHNNY HORTON
US, male vocalist, d. 5 Nov 1960 (age 35) — **15**

Date	Title	Label	Peak	Wks at No.1	Wks on Chart
26 Jun 59	**THE BATTLE OF NEW ORLEANS**	*Philips PB 932* ★	16		4
19 Jan 61	**NORTH TO ALASKA**	*Philips PB 1062*	23		11

HOT ACTION COP
US, male vocal/instrumental group — 1

Date	Title	Peak Position	Weeks at No.1	Weeks on Chart
14 Jun 03	**FEVER FOR THE FLAVA** *Lava AT 0152CD*	41		1

HOT BLOOD
France, male instrumental group — 5

Date	Title	Peak Position	Weeks at No.1	Weeks on Chart
9 Oct 76	**SOUL DRACULA** *Creole CR 132*	32		5

HOT BUTTER
US, male production duo – Steve & Bill Jerome – & moog player Stan Free, d. 17 Aug 1995 — 19

Date	Title	Peak Position	Weeks at No.1	Weeks on Chart
22 Jul 72	**POPCORN** *Pye International 7N 25583*	5		19

HOT CHIP
UK, male vocal/instrumental group – Alexis Taylor, Owen Clarke, Al Doyle, Joe Goddard & Felix Martin — 22

Date	Title	Peak Position	Weeks at No.1	Weeks on Chart
11 Mar 06	**OVER AND OVER** *EMI CDEM682*	32		2
20 May 06	**BOY FROM SCHOOL** *EMI CDEM690*	40		2
14 Oct 06	**OVER AND OVER** *EMI CDEMS707*	27		6
9 Feb 08	**READY FOR THE FLOOR** *EMI CDEM738*	6		9
24 May 08	**ONE PURE THOUGHT** *EMI CDEM748*	53		1
13 Feb 10	**ONE LIFE STAND** *EMI GBAYE0902866*	41		2

HOT CHOCOLATE
UK/Bahamas/Jamaica/Trinidad & Tobago, male vocal/instrumental group – Errol Brown*, Larry Ferguson, Harvey Hinsley, Ian King (replaced by Tony Connor) & Tony Wilson (replaced by Patrick Olive). 'You Sexy Thing' was a Top 10 hit in three different decades for the act who had a hit every year from 1970 to 1984 — 283

Date	Title	Peak Position	Weeks at No.1	Weeks on Chart
15 Aug 70	**LOVE IS LIFE** *RAK 103*	6		12
6 Mar 71	**YOU COULD HAVE BEEN A LADY** *RAK 110*	22		9
28 Aug 71	**I BELIEVE (IN LOVE)** *RAK 118*	8		11
28 Oct 72	**YOU'LL ALWAYS BE A FRIEND** *RAK 139*	23		8
14 Apr 73	**BROTHER LOUIE** *RAK 149*	7		10
18 Aug 73	**RUMOURS** *RAK 157*	44		3
16 Mar 74	**EMMA** *RAK 168*	3		10
30 Nov 74	**CHERI BABE** *RAK 188*	31		9
24 May 75	**DISCO QUEEN** *RAK 202*	11		7
9 Aug 75	**A CHILD'S PRAYER** *RAK 212*	7		10
8 Nov 75	**YOU SEXY THING** *RAK 221*	2		12
20 Mar 76	**DON'T STOP IT NOW** *RAK 230*	11		8
26 Jun 76	**MAN TO MAN** *RAK 238*	14		8
21 Aug 76	**HEAVEN IS IN THE BACK SEAT OF MY CADILLAC** *RAK 240*	25		8
18 Jun 77	**SO YOU WIN AGAIN** *RAK 259*	1	3	11
26 Nov 77	**PUT YOUR LOVE IN ME** *RAK 266*	10		9
4 Mar 78	**EVERY 1'S A WINNER** *RAK 270*	12		11
2 Dec 78	**I'LL PUT YOU TOGETHER AGAIN** *RAK 286*	13		11
19 May 79	**MINDLESS BOOGIE** *RAK 292*	46		5
28 Jul 79	**GOING THROUGH THE MOTIONS** *RAK 296*	53		4
3 May 80	**NO DOUBT ABOUT IT** *RAK 310*	2		11
19 Jul 80	**ARE YOU GETTING ENOUGH OF WHAT MAKES YOU HAPPY** *RAK 318*	17		7
13 Dec 80	**LOVE ME TO SLEEP** *RAK 324*	50		5
30 May 81	**YOU'LL NEVER BE SO WRONG** *RAK 331*	52		4
17 Apr 82	**GIRL CRAZY** *RAK 341*	7		11
10 Jul 82	**IT STARTED WITH A KISS** *RAK 344*	5		12
25 Sep 82	**CHANCES** *RAK 350*	32		5
7 May 83	**WHAT KINDA BOY YOU LOOKING FOR (GIRL)** *RAK 357*	10		9
17 Sep 83	**TEARS ON THE TELEPHONE** *RAK 363*	37		5
4 Feb 84	**I GAVE YOU MY HEART (DIDN'T I)** *RAK 369*	13		10
17 Jan 87	**YOU SEXY THING (REMIX)** *EMI 5592*	10		10
4 Apr 87	**EVERY 1'S A WINNER (REMIX)** *EMI 5607*	69		2
6 Mar 93	**IT STARTED WITH A KISS** *EMI CDEMCTS 7*	31		5
22 Nov 97	**YOU SEXY THING** *EMI CDHOT 100*	6		8
14 Feb 98	**IT STARTED WITH A KISS** *EMI CDHOT 101* FEATURING ERROL BROWN	18		3

HOT HOT HEAT
Canada, male vocal/instrumental group — 7

Date	Title	Peak Position	Weeks at No.1	Weeks on Chart
5 Apr 03	**BANDAGES** *B Unique BUN 045CDS*	25		3
9 Aug 03	**NO, NOT NOW** *Sub Pop W 615CD*	38		1
28 May 05	**GOODNIGHT GOODNIGHT** *Sire W670CD1*	36		2
30 Jul 05	**MIDDLE OF NOWHERE** *Sire W677CD1*	47		1

HOT HOUSE
UK, male/female vocal/instrumental trio — 3

Date	Title	Peak Position	Weeks at No.1	Weeks on Chart
14 Feb 87	**DON'T COME TO STAY** *Deconstruction CHEZ 1*	74		1
24 Sep 88	**DON'T COME TO STAY** *Deconstruction PB 42233*	70		2

HOT PANTZ
UK, female vocal duo — 1

Date	Title	Peak Position	Weeks at No.1	Weeks on Chart
25 Dec 04	**GIVE U ONE 4 CHRISTMAS** *Tug CDSNOG13*	64		1

HOT STREAK
US, male vocal/instrumental group — 8

Date	Title	Peak Position	Weeks at No.1	Weeks on Chart
10 Sep 83	**BODY WORK** *Polydor POSP 642*	19		8

HOTHOUSE FLOWERS
Ireland, male vocal/instrumental group — 36

Date	Title	Peak Position	Weeks at No.1	Weeks on Chart
14 May 88	**DON'T GO** *London LON 174*	11		8
23 Jul 88	**I'M SORRY** *London LON 187*	53		3
12 May 90	**GIVE IT UP** *London LON 258*	30		5
28 Jul 90	**I CAN SEE CLEARLY NOW** *London LON 269*	23		7
20 Oct 90	**MOVIES** *London LON 276*	68		2
13 Feb 93	**EMOTIONAL TIME** *London LONCD 335*	38		4
8 May 93	**ONE TONGUE** *London LOCDP 340*	45		3
19 Jun 93	**ISN'T IT AMAZING** *London LOCDP 343*	46		2
27 Nov 93	**THIS IS IT (YOUR SOUL)** *London LONCD 346*	67		1
16 May 98	**YOU CAN LEAVE ME NOW** *London LONCD 410*	65		1

HOTLEGS
UK, male vocal/instrumental group – Lol Crème, Kevin Goldey* & Eric Stewart. See 10cc — 14

Date	Title	Peak Position	Weeks at No.1	Weeks on Chart
4 Jul 70	**NEANDERTHAL MAN** *Fontana 6007 019*	2		14

HOTSHOTS
UK, male vocal group – members included Clive Crawley, Sonny Binns, Lloyd Donaldson, Franklyn Dunn, Maurice Ellis, Locksley Gichie, Carl Levy & Winston Reid — 15

Date	Title	Peak Position	Weeks at No.1	Weeks on Chart
2 Jun 73	**SNOOPY VS THE RED BARON** *Mooncrest MOON 5*	4		15

STEVEN HOUGHTON
UK, male actor/vocalist — 22

Date	Title	Peak Position	Weeks at No.1	Weeks on Chart
29 Nov 97	**WIND BENEATH MY WINGS** *RCA 74321529272*	3		15
7 Mar 98	**TRULY** *RCA 74321558552*	23		7

HOUND DOGS
UK/Italy, male vocal/production group — 7

Date	Title	Peak Position	Weeks at No.1	Weeks on Chart
31 Dec 05	**I LIKE GIRLS** *Direction 82876777032*	26		7

A HOUSE
Ireland, male/female vocal/instrumental group — 8

Date	Title	Peak Position	Weeks at No.1	Weeks on Chart
13 Jun 92	**ENDLESS ART** *Setanta AHOU 1*	46		3
8 Aug 92	**TAKE IT EASY ON ME** *Setanta AHOU 2*	55		2
25 Jun 94	**WHY ME** *Setanta CDAHOU 4*	52		1
1 Oct 94	**HERE COME THE GOOD TIMES** *Setanta CDAHOUS 5*	37		2

HOUSE ENGINEERS
UK, male production duo — 2

Date	Title	Peak Position	Weeks at No.1	Weeks on Chart
5 Dec 87	**GHOST HOUSE** *Syncopate SY 8*	69		2

HOUSE OF GLASS
Italy, male production duo. See Bini & Martini, Eclipse, Goodfellas featuring Lisa Millett — 1

Date	Title	Peak Position	Weeks at No.1	Weeks on Chart
14 Apr 01	**DISCO DOWN** *Azuli AZNY 138*	72		1

HOUSE OF LOVE
UK, male vocal/instrumental group — 22

Date	Title	Peak Position	Weeks at No.1	Weeks on Chart
22 Apr 89	**NEVER** *Fontana HOL 1*	41		2
18 Nov 89	**I DON'T KNOW WHY** *Fontana HOL 2*	41		3
3 Feb 90	**SHINE ON** *Fontana HOL 3*	20		4

Date	Title	Peak	Wks No.1	Wks
7 Apr 90	**BEATLES AND THE STONES** *Fontana HOL 4*	36		4
26 Oct 91	**THE GIRL WITH THE LONELIEST EYES** *Fontana HOL 5*	58		1
2 May 92	**FEEL** *Fontana HOL 6*	45		3
27 Jun 92	**YOU DON'T UNDERSTAND** *Fontana HOL 7*	46		3
5 Dec 92	**CRUSH ME** *Fontana HOL 810*	67		1
26 Feb 05	**LOVE YOU TOO MUCH** *Art And Industry 2ARTCD*	73		1

HOUSE OF PAIN

US/Latvia, male rap/DJ/production trio – Everlast* (Erik Schrody), Danny Boy (Daniel O'Connor) & DJ Lethal (Leor DiMant) **37**

Date	Title	Peak	Wks No.1	Wks
10 Oct 92	**JUMP AROUND** *Ruffness XLS 32*	32		4
22 May 93	**JUMP AROUND/TOP O' THE MORNING TO YA** *Ruffness XLS 43CD*	8		7
23 Oct 93	**SHAMROCKS AND SHENIGANS/WHO'S THE MAN** *Ruffness XLS 46CD*	23		4
16 Jul 94	**ON POINT** *Ruffness XLS 52CD*	19		3
12 Nov 94	**IT AIN'T A CRIME** *Ruffness XLS 55CD1*	37		2
1 Jul 95	**OVER THERE (I DON'T CARE)** *Ruffness XLS 61CD2*	20		3
5 Oct 96	**FED UP** *Tommy Boy TBCD 7744*	68		1
20 Nov 04	**JUMP AROUND** *Tommy Boy 5046760110*	44		11
22 Mar 08	**JUMP AROUND** *Tommy Boy 5046760110*	67		2

HOUSE OF VIRGINISM

Sweden, male vocalist (Fredrik 'Apollo' Asplund) **6**

Date	Title	Peak	Wks No.1	Wks
20 Nov 93	**I'LL BE THERE FOR YOU (DOYA DODODO DOYA)** *ffrr FCD 221*	29		3
30 Jul 94	**REACHIN** *ffrr FCD 238*	35		2
17 Feb 96	**EXCLUSIVE** *Logic 74321324102* APOLLO PRESENTS HOUSE OF VIRGINISM	67		1

HOUSE TRAFFIC

Italy/UK, male/female vocal/production group **3**

Date	Title	Peak	Wks No.1	Wks
4 Oct 97	**EVERYDAY OF MY LIFE** *Logic 74321249442*	24		3

HOUSEMARTINS

UK, male vocal/instrumental group – Paul Heaton*, Norman Cook*, Ian 'Stan' Cullimore & Hugh Whitaker (replaced by Dave Hemingway) **60**

Date	Title	Peak	Wks No.1	Wks
8 Mar 86	**SHEEP** *Go! Discs GOD 9*	56		4
7 Jun 86	**HAPPY HOUR** *Go! Discs GOD 11* ●	3		13
4 Oct 86	**THINK FOR A MINUTE** *Go! Discs GOD 13*	18		8
6 Dec 86	**CARAVAN OF LOVE** *Go! Discs GOD 16* ●	1	1	11
23 May 87	**FIVE GET OVER EXCITED** *Go! Discs GOD 18*	11		6
5 Sep 87	**ME AND THE FARMER** *Go! Discs GOD 19*	15		5
21 Nov 87	**BUILD** *Go! Discs GOD 21*	15		8
23 Apr 88	**THERE IS ALWAYS SOMETHING THERE TO REMIND ME** *Go! Discs GOD 22*	35		4
10 May 03	**CHANGE THE WORLD** *Free 2 Air 0146685 F2A* DINO LENNY VS THE HOUSEMARTINS	51		1

HOUSEMASTER BOYZ & THE RUDE BOY OF HOUSE

US, male production/vocal group **14**

Date	Title	Peak	Wks No.1	Wks
9 May 87	**HOUSE NATION** *Magnetic Dance MAGD 1*	48		6
12 Sep 87	**HOUSE NATION** *Magnetic Dance MAGD 1*	8		8

HOUSTON

US, male rapper (Houston Summers) **9**

Date	Title	Peak	Wks No.1	Wks
18 Sep 04	**I LIKE THAT** *Capitol CDCL 861*	11		6
5 Feb 05	**AIN'T NOTHING WRONG** *Capitol CDCL866*	33		3

MARQUES HOUSTON

US, male vocalist/actor **12**

Date	Title	Peak	Wks No.1	Wks
20 Mar 04	**CLUBBIN'** *Elektra E 7544CD*	15		6
31 Jul 04	**POP THAT BOOTY** *East West E7609CD* FEATURING JERMAINE	23		5
27 Nov 04	**BECAUSE OF YOU** *Atlantic AT0188CD*	51		1

THELMA HOUSTON

US, female vocalist **22**

Date	Title	Peak	Wks No.1	Wks
5 Feb 77	**DON'T LEAVE ME THIS WAY** *Motown TMG 1060* ★	13		8
27 Jun 81	**IF YOU FEEL IT** *RCA 77*	48		4
1 Dec 84	**YOU USED TO HOLD ME SO TIGHT** *MCA 932*	49		8
21 Jan 95	**DON'T LEAVE ME THIS WAY** *Dynamo DYND 001*	35		2

WHITNEY HOUSTON

US, female vocalist/actor. 'The Voice' had a string of hit singles from the soundtrack to the film *The Bodyguard* (in which she starred, alongside Kevin Costner), the biggest of which, Dolly Parton's 'I Will Always Love You', sold 1.3 million copies in the UK **331**

Date	Title	Peak	Wks No.1	Wks
16 Nov 85	**SAVING ALL MY LOVE FOR YOU** *Arista ARIST 640* ● ★	1	2	16
25 Jan 86	**HOLD ME** *Asylum EKR 32* TEDDY PENDERGRASS & WHITNEY HOUSTON	44		5
25 Jan 86	**HOW WILL I KNOW** *Arista ARIST 656* ● ★	5		12
12 Apr 86	**GREATEST LOVE OF ALL** *Arista ARIST 658* ★	8		11
23 May 87	**I WANNA DANCE WITH SOMEBODY (WHO LOVES ME)** *Arista RIS 1* ● ★	1	2	16
22 Aug 87	**DIDN'T WE ALMOST HAVE IT ALL** *Arista RIS 31* ★	14		8
14 Nov 87	**SO EMOTIONAL** *Arista RIS 43* ★	5		11
12 Mar 88	**WHERE DO BROKEN HEARTS GO** *Arista 109793* ★	14		8
28 May 88	**LOVE WILL SAVE THE DAY** *Arista 111516*	10		7
24 Sep 88	**ONE MOMENT IN TIME** *Arista 111613* ●	1	2	12
9 Sep 89	**IT ISN'T, IT WASN'T, IT AIN'T NEVER GONNA BE** *Arista 112545* ARETHA FRANKLIN & WHITNEY HOUSTON	29		5
20 Oct 90	**I'M YOUR BABY TONIGHT** *Arista 113594* ★	5		10
22 Dec 90	**ALL THE MAN THAT I NEED** *Arista 114000* ★	13		10
6 Jul 91	**MY NAME IS NOT SUSAN** *Arista 114510*	29		5
28 Sep 91	**I BELONG TO YOU** *Arista 114727*	54		2
14 Nov 92	**I WILL ALWAYS LOVE YOU** *Arista 74321120657* ⊛ x2 ★	1	10	23
20 Feb 93	**I'M EVERY WOMAN** *Arista 74321131502*	4		11
24 Apr 93	**I HAVE NOTHING** *Arista 74321146142*	3		10
31 Jul 93	**RUN TO YOU** *Arista 74321153332*	15		6
6 Nov 93	**QUEEN OF THE NIGHT** *Arista 74321169302*	14		5
25 Dec 93	**I WILL ALWAYS LOVE YOU** *Arista 74321120657*	25		6
22 Jan 94	**SOMETHING IN COMMON** *MCA MCSTD 1957* BOBBY BROWN & WHITNEY HOUSTON	16		5
18 Nov 95	**EXHALE (SHOOP SHOOP)** *Arista 74321332472* ★	11		9
24 Feb 96	**COUNT ON ME** *Arista 74321345842*	12		6
21 Dec 96	**STEP BY STEP** *Arista 74321449332*	13		13
29 Mar 97	**I BELIEVE IN YOU AND ME** *Arista 74321468602*	16		5
19 Dec 98	**WHEN YOU BELIEVE** *Columbia 6667522* MARIAH CAREY & WHITNEY HOUSTON	4		13
6 Mar 99	**IT'S NOT RIGHT BUT IT'S OKAY** *Arista 74321652412* ●	3		15
3 Jul 99	**MY LOVE IS YOUR LOVE** *Arista 74321672872*	2		12
11 Dec 99	**I LEARNED FROM THE BEST** *Arista 74321723992*	19		11
17 Jun 00	**IF I TOLD YOU THAT** *Arista 74321766282* & GEORGE MICHAEL	9		11
14 Oct 00	**COULD I HAVE THIS KISS FOREVER** *Arista 74321795992* & ENRIQUE IGLESIAS	7		8
30 Dec 00	**HEARTBREAK HOTEL** *Arista 74321820572* FEATURING FAITH EVANS & KELLY PRICE	25		5
9 Nov 02	**WHATCHULOOKINAT** *Arista 74321975732*	13		3
29 Dec 07	**WHEN YOU BELIEVE** *Columbia 6667522* MARIAH CAREY & WHITNEY HOUSTON	65		1
17 Oct 09	**MILLION DOLLAR BILL** *Arista 88697599082*	5		14
31 Oct 09	**I DIDN'T KNOW MY OWN STRENGTH** *Arista USAR10900288*	44		1

ADINA HOWARD

US, female vocalist **16**

Date	Title	Peak	Wks No.1	Wks
4 Mar 95	**FREAK LIKE ME** *East West A 4473CD*	33		4
23 Nov 96	**WHAT'S LOVE GOT TO DO WITH IT** *Interscope IND 97008* WARREN G FEATURING ADINA HOWARD	2		12

BILLY HOWARD

UK, male comedian/vocalist **12**

Date	Title	Peak	Wks No.1	Wks
13 Dec 75	**KING OF THE COPS** *Penny Farthing PEN 892*	6		12

MIKI HOWARD

US, female vocalist (Alicia Michelle Howard) **2**

Date	Title	Peak	Wks No.1	Wks
26 May 90	**UNTIL YOU COME BACK (THAT'S WHAT I'M GONNA DO)** *East West 7935*	67		2

NICK HOWARD

Australia, male vocalist **1**

Date	Title	Peak	Wks No.1	Wks
21 Jan 95	**EVERYBODY NEEDS SOMEBODY** *Bell 74321220942*	64		1

DANNY HOWELLS & DICK TREVOR FEATURING ERIRE

UK, male/female vocal/production trio. See Science Department featuring Erire **2**

Date	Title	Peak	Wks No.1	Wks
9 Oct 04	**DUSK TIL DAWN** *C2 CDC2004*	37		2

HOWLIN' WOLF
US, male vocalist/guitarist (Chester Burnette), d. 10 Jan 1976 (age 65) — 5

Date	Title	Peak	Wks at No.1	Wks on Chart
4 Jun 64	**SMOKESTACK LIGHTNIN'** *Pye International 7N 25244*	42		5

H20
UK, male vocal/instrumental group — 16

Date	Title	Peak	Wks at No.1	Wks on Chart
21 May 83	**DREAM TO SLEEP** *RCA 330*	17		10
13 Aug 83	**JUST OUTSIDE OF HEAVEN** *RCA 349*	38		6

H20
US/Switzerland, male/female vocal/instrumental group — 4

Date	Title	Peak	Wks at No.1	Wks on Chart
14 Sep 96	**NOBODY'S BUSINESS** *AM:PM 5818832* FEATURING BILLIE	19		3
30 Aug 97	**SATISFIED (TAKE ME HIGHER)** *AM:PM 5853252*	66		1

H TWO O FEATURING PLATNUM
UK, male/female vocal/DJ/production group – Selim Ben Rabha & Simon McDevitt (H Two O) & Aaron Evers, Michelle McKenna & Mina Poli (Platnum) — 16

Date	Title	Peak	Wks at No.1	Wks on Chart
23 Feb 08	**WHAT'S IT GONNA BE** *Hard2Beat H2B02CDS* ●	2		16

AL HUDSON
US, male vocalist — 20

Date	Title	Peak	Wks at No.1	Wks on Chart
9 Sep 78	**DANCE, GET DOWN (FEEL THE GROOVE)/HOW DO YOU DO** *ABC 4229*	57		4
15 Sep 79	**YOU CAN DO IT** *MCA 511* & THE PARTNERS	15		10
8 Dec 79	**MUSIC** *MCA 542* ONE WAY FEATURING AL HUDSON	56		6

JENNIFER HUDSON
US, female vocalist/actor — 39

Date	Title	Peak	Wks at No.1	Wks on Chart
14 Jun 08	**ALL DRESSED IN LOVE** *Decca USNLR0800015*	72		1
27 Sep 08	**SPOTLIGHT** *RCA USAV70800057*	11		24
7 Mar 09	**IF THIS ISN'T LOVE** *Arista USAR10800320*	37		10
19 Sep 09	**AND I'M TELLING YOU I'M NOT GOING** *RCA USLIC0602215*	32		4

LAVINE HUDSON
UK, female vocalist — 3

Date	Title	Peak	Wks at No.1	Wks on Chart
21 May 88	**INTERVENTION** *Virgin VS 1067*	57		3

HUDSON-FORD
UK, male vocal/instrumental duo – Richard Hudson & John Ford. See Monks, Strawbs — 20

Date	Title	Peak	Wks at No.1	Wks on Chart
18 Aug 73	**PICK UP THE PIECES** *A&M AMS 7078*	8		9
16 Feb 74	**BURN BABY BURN** *A&M AMS 7096*	15		9
29 Jun 74	**FLOATING IN THE WIND** *A&M AMS 7116*	35		2

HUE & CRY
UK, male vocal/instrumental duo – Greg & Pat Kane — 59

Date	Title	Peak	Wks at No.1	Wks on Chart
13 Jun 87	**LABOUR OF LOVE** *Circa YR 4*	6		16
19 Sep 87	**STRENGTH TO STRENGTH** *Circa YR 6*	46		5
30 Jan 88	**I REFUSE** *Circa YR 8*	47		3
22 Oct 88	**ORDINARY ANGEL** *Circa YR 18*	42		6
28 Jan 89	**LOOKING FOR LINDA** *Circa YR 24*	15		9
6 May 89	**VIOLENTLY (EP)** *Circa YR 29*	21		6
30 Sep 89	**SWEET INVISIBILITY** *Circa YR 37*	55		3
25 May 91	**MY SALT HEART** *Circa YR 64*	47		3
3 Aug 91	**LONG TERM LOVERS OF PAIN (EP)** *Circa YR 71*	48		3
11 Jul 92	**PROFOUNDLY YOURS** *Fidelity FIDEL 1*	74		1
13 Mar 93	**LABOUR OF LOVE (REMIX)** *Circa HUESCD 1*	25		4

HUES CORPORATION
US, male/female vocal trio – Ann Kelley, St Clair Lee & Fleming Williams, d. 15 Feb 1998 — 16

Date	Title	Peak	Wks at No.1	Wks on Chart
27 Jul 74	**ROCK THE BOAT** *RCA APBO 0232* ● ★	6		10
19 Oct 74	**ROCKIN' SOUL** *RCA PB 10066*	24		6

HUFF & HERB
UK, male DJ/production duo. See Huff & Puff — 4

Date	Title	Peak	Wks at No.1	Wks on Chart
6 Dec 97	**FEELING GOOD** *Planet 3 GXY 2018CD*	31		3
7 Nov 98	**FEELING GOOD '98 (REMIX)** *Planet 3 GXY 2020CD*	69		1

HUFF & PUFF
UK, male instrumental/production duo. See Dusted, Faithless, Huff & Herb, Our Tribe/One Tribe, Rollo — 4

Date	Title	Peak	Wks at No.1	Wks on Chart
2 Nov 96	**HELP ME MAKE IT** *Skyway SKYWCD 4*	31		2
21 Jun 97	**HELP ME MAKE IT** *Skyway SKYWCD 8*	37		2

DAVID HUGHES
UK, male vocalist (Geoffrey Paddison), d. 19 Oct 1972 (age 43) — 1

Date	Title	Peak	Wks at No.1	Wks on Chart
21 Sep 56	**BY THE FOUNTAINS OF ROME** *Philips PB 606*	27		1

HUGO & LUIGI
US, male producers/orchestra leaders – Hugo Peretti, d. 1 May 1986, & Luigi Creatore — 2

Date	Title	Peak	Wks at No.1	Wks on Chart
24 Jul 59	**LA PLUME DE MA TANTE** *RCA 1127*	29		2

HUMAN LEAGUE
UK, male/female vocal/instrumental group – Philip Oakey*, Joanne Catherall & Susanne Sulley; members also included Ian Burden, Jo Callis & Philip Wright — 156

Date	Title	Peak	Wks at No.1	Wks on Chart
3 May 80	**HOLIDAY 80 (DOUBLE SINGLE)** *Virgin SV 105*	56		5
21 Jun 80	**EMPIRE STATE HUMAN** *Virgin VS 351*	62		2
28 Feb 81	**BOYS AND GIRLS** *Virgin VS 395*	48		4
2 May 81	**THE SOUND OF THE CROWD** *Virgin VS 416*	12		10
8 Aug 81	**LOVE ACTION (I BELIEVE IN LOVE)** *Virgin VS 435* ●	3		13
10 Oct 81	**OPEN YOUR HEART** *Virgin VS 453* ●	6		9
5 Dec 81	**DON'T YOU WANT ME** *Virgin VS 466* ⊛ ★	1	5	13
9 Jan 82	**BEING BOILED** *EMI FAST 4*	6		9
6 Feb 82	**HOLIDAY 80 (DOUBLE SINGLE)** *Virgin SV 105*	46		5
20 Nov 82	**MIRROR MAN** *Virgin VS 522* ●	2		10
23 Apr 83	**(KEEP FEELING) FASCINATION** *Virgin VS 569* ●	2		9
5 May 84	**THE LEBANON** *Virgin VS 672*	11		7
30 Jun 84	**LIFE ON YOUR OWN** *Virgin VS 688*	16		6
17 Nov 84	**LOUISE** *Virgin VS 723*	13		10
23 Aug 86	**HUMAN** *Virgin VS 880* ★	8		8
22 Nov 86	**I NEED YOUR LOVING** *Virgin VS 900*	72		1
15 Oct 88	**LOVE IS ALL THAT MATTERS** *Virgin VS 1025*	41		5
18 Aug 90	**HEART LIKE A WHEEL** *Virgin VS 1262*	29		5
7 Jan 95	**TELL ME WHEN** *East West YZ 882CD1*	6		9
18 Mar 95	**ONE MAN IN MY HEART** *East West YZ 904CD1*	13		8
17 Jun 95	**FILLING UP WITH HEAVEN** *East West YZ 944CD*	36		2
28 Oct 95	**DON'T YOU WANT ME (REMIX)** *Virgin VSCDT 1557*	16		3
20 Jan 96	**STAY WITH ME TONIGHT** *East West EW 020CD*	40		2
11 Aug 01	**ALL I EVER WANTED** *Papillon BTFLYS 0012*	47		1

HUMAN MOVEMENT FEATURING SOPHIE MOLET
UK/Australia, male/female vocal/production trio — 1

Date	Title	Peak	Wks at No.1	Wks on Chart
3 Feb 01	**LOVE HAS COME AGAIN** *Renaissance Recordings RENCDS 005*	53		1

HUMAN NATURE
Australia, male vocal group — 7

Date	Title	Peak	Wks at No.1	Wks on Chart
10 May 97	**WISHES** *Epic 6644485*	44		1
30 Aug 97	**WHISPER YOUR NAME** *Epic 6649465*	53		1
10 Mar 01	**HE DON'T LOVE YOU** *Epic 6708922*	18		4
30 Jun 01	**WHEN WE WERE YOUNG** *Epic 6713792*	43		1

HUMAN RESOURCE
Holland/US, male production/rap group — 14

Date	Title	Peak	Wks at No.1	Wks on Chart
14 Sep 91	**DOMINATOR** *R&S RSUK 4*	36		7
21 Dec 91	**THE COMPLETE DOMINATOR** *R&S RSUK 4X*	18		7

HUMANOID
UK, male producer (Brian Dougans) — 14

Date	Title	Peak	Wks at No.1	Wks on Chart
26 Nov 88	**STAKKER HUMANOID** *Westside WSR 12*	17		8
22 Apr 89	**SLAM** *Westside WSR 14*	54		2
8 Aug 92	**STAKKER HUMANOID** *Jumpin' & Pumpin' TOT 27*	40		3
3 Mar 01	**STAKKER HUMANOID (REMIX)** *Jumpin' & Pumpin' CDSTOT 43*	65		1

Silver-selling ● Gold-selling ● Platinum-selling (x multiples) ● US No.1 ★ Peak Position · Weeks at No.1 · Weeks on Chart

HUMATE
Germany, male production trio **4**

Date	Title	Peak Position	Weeks at No.1	Weeks on Chart
30 Jan 99	**LOVE STIMULATION** *Deviant DVNT 22CDS*	18		4

HUMBLE PIE
UK, male vocal/instrumental group – Peter Frampton*, Steve Marriott*, d. 20 Apr 1991, Greg Ridley, d. 19 Nov 2003, & Jerry Shirley **10**

Date	Title	Peak Position	Weeks at No.1	Weeks on Chart
23 Aug 69	**NATURAL BORN BUGIE** *Immediate IM 082*	4		10

ENGELBERT HUMPERDINCK
UK (b. India), male vocalist (Arnold Dorsey). After a slow start, and after borrowing a noted German composer's name, the ever-popular Vegas veteran's career really took off. The top singles act of 1967 is now one of the world's richest entertainers **240**

Date	Title	Peak Position	Weeks at No.1	Weeks on Chart
26 Jan 67	**RELEASE ME** *Decca F 12541*	1	6	56
25 May 67	**THERE GOES MY EVERYTHING** *Decca F 12610*	2		29
23 Aug 67	**THE LAST WALTZ** *Decca F 12655*	1	5	27
10 Jan 68	**AM I THAT EASY TO FORGET** *Decca F 12722*	3		13
24 Apr 68	**A MAN WITHOUT LOVE** *Decca F 12770*	2		15
25 Sep 68	**LES BICYCLETTES DE BELSIZE** *Decca F 12834*	5		15
5 Feb 69	**THE WAY IT USED TO BE** *Decca F 12879*	3		14
9 Aug 69	**I'M A BETTER MAN (FOR HAVING LOVED YOU)** *Decca F 12957*	15		13
15 Nov 69	**WINTER WORLD OF LOVE** *Decca F 12980*	7		13
30 May 70	**MY MARIE** *Decca F 13032*	31		7
12 Sep 70	**SWEETHEART** *Decca F 13068*	22		7
11 Sep 71	**ANOTHER TIME ANOTHER PLACE** *Decca F 13212*	13		12
4 Mar 72	**TOO BEAUTIFUL TO LAST** *Decca F 13281*	14		10
20 Oct 73	**LOVE IS ALL** *Decca F 13443*	44		4
30 Jan 99	**QUANDO QUANDO QUANDO** *The Hit Label HLC 15*	40		3
6 May 00	**HOW TO WIN YOUR LOVE** *Universal TV 8822682*	59		1
12 Jun 04	**RELEASE ME** *Universal TV 9819567*	51		1

HUNDRED REASONS
UK, male vocal/instrumental group **16**

Date	Title	Peak Position	Weeks at No.1	Weeks on Chart
18 Aug 01	**EP TWO** *Columbia 6713922*	47		1
15 Dec 01	**EP THREE** *Columbia 6720782*	37		2
16 Mar 02	**IF I COULD** *Columbia 6724402*	19		3
18 May 02	**SILVER** *Columbia 6726642*	15		3
28 Sep 02	**FALTER** *Columbia 6731455*	38		1
15 Nov 03	**THE GREAT TEST** *Columbia 6743762*	29		2
28 Feb 04	**WHAT YOU GET** *Columbia 6745495*	30		2
16 Oct 04	**HOW SOON IS NOW** *Sore Point SORE029CDS*	47		1
18 Mar 06	**KILL YOUR OWN** *V2 VVR5036428*	48		1

GERALDINE HUNT
US, female vocalist **5**

Date	Title	Peak Position	Weeks at No.1	Weeks on Chart
25 Oct 80	**CAN'T FAKE THE FEELING** *Champagne FIZZ 501*	44		5

MARSHA HUNT
US, female vocalist **3**

Date	Title	Peak Position	Weeks at No.1	Weeks on Chart
21 May 69	**WALK ON GILDED SPLINTERS** *Track 604 030*	46		2
2 May 70	**KEEP THE CUSTOMER SATISFIED** *Track 604 037*	41		1

TOMMY HUNT
US, male vocalist (Charles Hunt) **17**

Date	Title	Peak Position	Weeks at No.1	Weeks on Chart
11 Oct 75	**CRACKIN' UP** *Spark SRL 1132*	39		5
21 Aug 76	**LOVING ON THE LOSING SIDE** *Spark SRL 1146*	28		9
4 Dec 76	**ONE FINE MORNING** *Spark SRL 1148*	44		3

ALFONZO HUNTER
US, male rapper/instrumentalist **2**

Date	Title	Peak Position	Weeks at No.1	Weeks on Chart
22 Feb 97	**JUST THE WAY** *Cooltempo CDCOOL 326*	38		2

HUNTER FEATURING RUBY TURNER
UK, male TV gladiator/vocalist & female vocalist **1**

Date	Title	Peak Position	Weeks at No.1	Weeks on Chart
9 Dec 95	**SHAKABOOM!** *Telstar HUNTCD 1*	64		1

IAN HUNTER
UK, male vocalist/guitarist/keyboard player (Ian Patterson). See Mott The Hoople **10**

Date	Title	Peak Position	Weeks at No.1	Weeks on Chart
3 May 75	**ONCE BITTEN TWICE SHY** *CBS 3194*	14		10

TAB HUNTER
US, male vocalist (Arthur Kelm) **30**

Date	Title	Peak Position	Weeks at No.1	Weeks on Chart
8 Feb 57	**YOUNG LOVE** *London HLD 8380* ★	1	7	18
12 Apr 57	**99 WAYS** *London HLD 8410*	5		12

TERRY HUNTER
US, male DJ/producer **1**

Date	Title	Peak Position	Weeks at No.1	Weeks on Chart
26 Jul 97	**HARVEST FOR THE WORLD** *Delirious DELICD 4*	48		1

HURLEY & TODD
UK/South Africa, male production duo **2**

Date	Title	Peak Position	Weeks at No.1	Weeks on Chart
29 Apr 00	**SUNSTORM** *Multiply CDMULTY 58*	38		2

STEVE 'SILK' HURLEY
US, male DJ/producer. See JM Silk, Voices Of Life **9**

Date	Title	Peak Position	Weeks at No.1	Weeks on Chart
10 Jan 87	**JACK YOUR BODY** *DJ International LON 117* ●	1	2	9

HURRICANE #1
UK, male vocal/instrumental group **17**

Date	Title	Peak Position	Weeks at No.1	Weeks on Chart
10 May 97	**STEP INTO MY WORLD** *Creation CRESCD 253*	29		2
5 Jul 97	**JUST ANOTHER ILLUSION** *Creation CRESCD 264*	35		2
6 Sep 97	**CHAIN REACTION** *Creation CRESCD 271*	30		2
1 Nov 97	**STEP INTO MY WORLD** *Creation CRESCD 276*	19		3
21 Feb 98	**ONLY THE STRONGEST WILL SURVIVE** *Creation CRESCD 285*	19		6
24 Oct 98	**RISING SIGN** *Creation CRESCD 303*	47		1
3 Apr 99	**THE GREATEST HIGH** *Creation CRESCD 309*	43		1

PHIL HURTT
US, male vocalist **5**

Date	Title	Peak Position	Weeks at No.1	Weeks on Chart
11 Nov 78	**GIVING IT BACK** *Fantasy FTC 161*	36		5

HUSTLERS CONVENTION FEATURING DAVE LAUDAT & ONDREA DUVERNEY
UK/US, male/female vocal/production group. See Disco Tex presents Cloudburst, Full Intention, Michael Gray, Sex-O-Sonique **1**

Date	Title	Peak Position	Weeks at No.1	Weeks on Chart
20 May 95	**DANCE TO THE MUSIC** *Stress CDSTR 53*	71		1

WILLIE HUTCH
US, male vocalist (Willie Hutchinson), d. 19 Sep 2005 (age 60) **8**

Date	Title	Peak Position	Weeks at No.1	Weeks on Chart
4 Dec 82	**IN AND OUT** *Motown TMG 1285*	51		7
6 Jul 85	**KEEP ON JAMMIN'** *Motown ZB 40173*	73		1

JUNE HUTTON & AXEL STORDAHL & THE BOYS NEXT DOOR
US, female vocalist, d. 2 May 1973 (age 51) **7**

Date	Title	Peak Position	Weeks at No.1	Weeks on Chart
7 Aug 53	**SAY YOU'RE MINE AGAIN** *Capitol CL 13918*	6		7

HWA FEATURING SONIC THE HEDGEHOG
UK, male production duo & video game character **6**

Date	Title	Peak Position	Weeks at No.1	Weeks on Chart
5 Dec 92	**SUPERSONIC** *Internal Affairs KGB 008*	33		6

HYBRID
UK, male production trio **5**

Date	Title	Peak Position	Weeks at No.1	Weeks on Chart
10 Jul 99	**FINISHED SYMPHONY** *Distinctive DISNCD 52*	58		1
11 Sep 99	**IF I SURVIVE** *Distinctive DISNCD 55* FEATURING JULEE CRUISE	52		1
3 Jun 00	**KID 2000** *Virgin VTS CD2* FEATURING CHRISSIE HYNDE	32		2
20 Sep 03	**TRUE TO FORM** *Distinctive DISNCD 111* FEATURING PETER HOOK	59		1

BRIAN HYLAND

US, male vocalist — 72

Date	Title	Peak Position	Weeks at No.1	Weeks on Chart
7 Jul 60	**ITSY BITSY TEENY WEENY YELLOW POLKA DOT BIKINI** *London HLR 9161* ★	8		13
20 Oct 60	**FOUR LITTLE HEELS** *London HLR 9203*	29		6
10 May 62	**GINNY COME LATELY** *HMV POP 1013*	5		15
2 Aug 62	**SEALED WITH A KISS** *HMV POP 1051*	3		15
8 Nov 62	**WARMED OVER KISSES** *HMV POP 1079*	28		6
27 Mar 71	**GYPSY WOMAN** *Uni UN 530*	42		6
28 Jun 75	**SEALED WITH A KISS** *ABC 4059*	7		11

SHEILA HYLTON

Jamaica, female vocalist — 12

Date	Title	Peak Position	Weeks at No.1	Weeks on Chart
15 Sep 79	**BREAKFAST IN BED** *United Artists BP 304*	57		5
17 Jan 81	**THE BED'S TOO BIG WITHOUT YOU** *Island WIP 6671*	35		7

PHYLLIS HYMAN

US, female vocalist, d. 30 Jun 1995 (age 45) — 9

Date	Title	Peak Position	Weeks at No.1	Weeks on Chart
16 Feb 80	**YOU KNOW HOW TO LOVE ME** *Arista ARIST 323*	47		6
12 Sep 81	**YOU SURE LOOK GOOD TO ME** *Arista ARIST 424*	56		3

DICK HYMAN TRIO

US, male instrumental trio — 10

Date	Title	Peak Position	Weeks at No.1	Weeks on Chart
16 Mar 56	**THEME FROM 'THE THREEPENNY OPERA'** *MGM 890*	9		10

CHRISSIE HYNDE

US, female vocalist/guitarist — 41

Date	Title	Peak Position	Weeks at No.1	Weeks on Chart
3 Aug 85	**I GOT YOU BABE** *DEP International DEP 20* UB40 FEATURING CHRISSIE HYNDE ●	1	1	13
18 Jun 88	**BREAKFAST IN BED** *DEP International DEP 29* UB40 FEATURING CHRISSIE HYNDE	6		11
12 Oct 91	**SPIRITUAL HIGH (STATE OF INDEPENDENCE)** *Arista 114528* MOODSWINGS FEATURING CHRISSIE HYNDE	66		2
23 Jan 93	**SPIRITUAL HIGH (STATE OF INDEPENDENCE) (REMIX)** *Arista 74321127712* MOODSWINGS FEATURING CHRISSIE HYNDE	47		2
18 Mar 95	**LOVE CAN BUILD A BRIDGE** *London COCD 1* CHER, CHRISSIE HYNDE & NENEH CHERRY WITH ERIC CLAPTON ●	1	1	8
3 Jun 00	**KID 2000** *Virgin VTS CD2* HYBRID FEATURING CHRISSIE HYNDE	32		2
7 Feb 04	**STRAIGHT AHEAD** *Direction 6746222* TUBE & BERGER FEATURING CHRISSIE HYNDE	29		3

HYPER GO GO

UK, male production duo — 15

Date	Title	Peak Position	Weeks at No.1	Weeks on Chart
22 Aug 92	**HIGH** *Deconstruction 74321110497*	30		5
31 Jul 93	**NEVER LET GO** *Positiva CDTIV 3*	45		3
5 Feb 94	**RAISE** *Positiva CDTIV 9*	36		2
26 Nov 94	**IT'S ALRIGHT** *Positiva CDTIV 20*	49		1
6 Apr 96	**DO WATCHA DO** *Avex UK AVEXCD 24* & ADEVA	54		1
12 Oct 96	**HIGH (REMIX)** *Distinctive DISNCD 24*	32		2
12 Apr 97	**DO WATCHA DO (REMIX)** *Distinctive DISNCD 28* & ADEVA	60		1

HYPERLOGIC

UK, male instrumental/production trio — 3

Date	Title	Peak Position	Weeks at No.1	Weeks on Chart
29 Jul 95	**ONLY ME** *Systematic SYSCD 15*	35		2
9 May 98	**ONLY ME (REMIX)** *Tidy Trax TIDY 113CD1*	48		1

HYPERSTATE

UK, male/female production/vocal duo — 1

Date	Title	Peak Position	Weeks at No.1	Weeks on Chart
6 Feb 93	**TIME AFTER TIME** *M&G MAGCD 34*	71		1

HYPNOTIST

UK, male production duo — 5

Date	Title	Peak Position	Weeks at No.1	Weeks on Chart
28 Sep 91	**THE HOUSE IS MINE** *Rising High RSN 4*	65		2
21 Dec 91	**THE HARDCORE EP** *Rising High RSN 13*	68		3

HYPO PSYCHO

UK/US, male vocal/instrumental group — 1

Date	Title	Peak Position	Weeks at No.1	Weeks on Chart
24 Jul 04	**PUBLIC ENEMY NO 1** *Believe Music SMASCD059*	53		1

HYSTERIC EGO

UK, male producer (Rob White) — 8

Date	Title	Peak Position	Weeks at No.1	Weeks on Chart
31 Aug 96	**WANT LOVE** *WEA 070CD*	28		4
21 Jun 97	**MINISTRY OF LOVE** *WEA 094CD*	39		2
28 Feb 98	**WANT LOVE – THE REMIXES** *WEA 150CD*	46		1
13 Feb 99	**TIME TO GET BACK** *WEA 198CD*	50		1

HYSTERICS

US, male laughter/instrumental group — 5

Date	Title	Peak Position	Weeks at No.1	Weeks on Chart
12 Dec 81	**JINGLE BELLS LAUGHING ALL THE WAY/GESUNDHEIT** *Record Delivery KA 5*	44		5

HYSTERIX

UK, male production duo — 4

Date	Title	Peak Position	Weeks at No.1	Weeks on Chart
7 May 94	**MUST BE THE MUSIC** *Deconstruction 74321207362*	40		3
18 Feb 95	**EVERYTHING** *Deconstruction 74321236882*	65		1

BIOGRAPHIES

Biographies include the nationality and category for every chart entrant.

Each entrant has at least a mini biography. The acts with the most weeks on the chart (see page 372 for the chart) each have extended biographies.

Real names are included for all solo artists and, where applicable, dates of death and age of the artist at the time. "See..." links are included for soloists who also had singles chart entries in other acts.

The best known line-up is listed for every group that had a Top 10 single, with the vocalist/leader mentioned first and the others following in alphabetical order. In cases where later replacements had similar success both people are named and, where applicable, the dates of death are also shown for every group/duo member listed.

Certified Awards are given by the BPI to mark unit sales to retailers. They were introduced in April 1973. In January 1989 the levels of unit sales to the trade required to achieve each of the awards was amended to the following amounts:

Silver symbol	●	=	200,000 units
Gold symbol	●	=	400,000 units
Platinum symbol	⊛	=	600,000 units

As from February 2005, download sales also count towards certified awards.

I–L

KEY TO ARTIST ENTRIES

Artist/Group Name
Artist/Group Biography
Silver-selling
Gold-selling
Platinum-selling
US No.1
Peak Position
Weeks at No.1
Weeks on Chart
Asterisks (*) indicate group members with hits in their own right that are listed elsewhere in this book
TAKE THAT
UK, male vocal group – Gary Barlow*, Howard Donald, Jason Orange, Mark Owen* & Robbie Williams* (left 1995, rejoined 2010). Comeback kings who have sold 7.4 million singles in the UK. The boys, who came back for good – as a quartet – in 2006, were the first act to score four successive No.1s since The Beatles – a feat they've achieved twice. See Helping Haiti
Artist's Total Weeks On Chart
356
Date of entry into chart
Artist collaboration or variation on artist's name
23 Nov 91 PROMISES RCA PB 45085 38 2
8 Feb 92 ONCE YOU'VE TASTED LOVE RCA PB 45257 47 3
6 Jun 92 IT ONLY TAKES A MINUTE RCA 74321101007 7 8
15 Aug 92 I FOUND HEAVEN RCA 74321108137 15 6
10 Oct 92 A MILLION LOVE SONGS RCA 74321116307 7 9
12 Dec 92 COULD IT BE MAGIC RCA 74321123137 3 12
20 Feb 93 WHY CAN'T I WAKE UP WITH YOU RCA 74321133102 2 10
17 Jul 93 PRAY RCA 74321154502 1 4 11
9 Oct 93 RELIGHT MY FIRE RCA 74321167722 FEATURING LULU 1 2 14
18 Dec 93 BABE RCA 74321182122 1 1 10
9 Apr 94 EVERYTHING CHANGES RCA 74321167732 1 2 10
9 Jul 94 LOVE AIN'T HERE ANYMORE RCA 74321214832 3 12
15 Oct 94 SURE RCA 74321236622 1 2 15
8 Apr 95 BACK FOR GOOD RCA 74321271462 1 4 13
5 Aug 95 NEVER FORGET RCA 74321299572 1 3 9
9 Mar 96 HOW DEEP IS YOUR LOVE RCA 74321355592 1 3 14
25 Nov 06 PATIENCE Polydor 1714832 1 4 39
10 Feb 07 SHINE Polydor 1724294 1 2 42
30 Jun 07 I'D WAIT FOR LIFE Polydor 1736401 17 2
27 Oct 07 RULE THE WORLD Polydor 1746285 2 66
6 Dec 08 GREATEST DAY Polydor 1787445 1 1 20
6 Dec 08 PATIENCE Polydor 1714832 59 1
6 Dec 08 NEVER FORGET RCA GBARL9500200 64 1
14 Feb 09 UP ALL NIGHT Polydor 1796964 14 11
13 Jun 09 SAID IT ALL Polydor 2708717 9 10
20 Jun 09 RULE THE WORLD Polydor 1746285 57 6
27 Jun 09 GREATEST DAY Polydor 1787445 73 1+
Title of Single
Label and Catalogue Number
BPI Certified Award
A cross (+) indicates that the single was still on chart in the final week of March 2010

Silver-selling ● Gold-selling ● Platinum-selling (× multiples) ✪ US No.1 ★ Peak Position Weeks at No.1 Weeks on Chart

I AM KLOOT

UK, male vocal/instrumental group — Weeks on Chart: 3

Date	Title	Peak Position	Weeks at No.1	Weeks on Chart
21 Jun 03	**LIFE IN A DAY** *Echo ECSCX 140*	43		1
20 Sep 03	**3 FEET TALL** *Echo ECSCX 143*	46		1
2 Apr 05	**OVER MY SHOULDER** *Echo ECSCD160*	38		1

I DREAM FEATURING FRANKIE & CALVIN

UK, male/female actors/vocal group. See S Club Juniors — Weeks on Chart: 7

Date	Title	Peak Position	Weeks at No.1	Weeks on Chart
27 Nov 04	**DREAMING** *19/UMTV 9868872*	19		7

I KAMANCHI

UK, male production duo — Weeks on Chart: 1

Date	Title	Peak Position	Weeks at No.1	Weeks on Chart
14 Jun 03	**NEVER CAN TELL/SOUL BEAT CALLING** *Full Cycle FCY052*	69		1

I-LEVEL

UK/Sierra Leone, male vocal/production trio — Weeks on Chart: 9

Date	Title	Peak Position	Weeks at No.1	Weeks on Chart
16 Apr 83	**MINEFIELD** *Virgin VS 563*	52		6
18 Jun 83	**TEACHER** *Virgin VS 595*	56		3

I MONSTER

UK, male vocal/production duo — Weeks on Chart: 6

Date	Title	Peak Position	Weeks at No.1	Weeks on Chart
16 Jun 01	**DAYDREAM IN BLUE** *Instant Karma KARMA 7CD*	20		6

JANIS IAN

US, female vocalist (Janis Fink) — Weeks on Chart: 10

Date	Title	Peak Position	Weeks at No.1	Weeks on Chart
17 Nov 79	**FLY TOO HIGH** *CBS 7936*	44		7
28 Jun 80	**THE OTHER SIDE OF THE SUN** *CBS 8611*	44		3

IAN VAN DAHL

Belgium, female/male vocal/production group – Annemie Coenen, Christophe Chantzis, Peter Luts, Erik Vanspauwen & David Vervoort. See Dee Dee — Weeks on Chart: 49

Date	Title	Peak Position	Weeks at No.1	Weeks on Chart
21 Jul 01	**CASTLES IN THE SKY** *NuLife 74321867142* ●	3		16
22 Dec 01	**WILL I?** *NuLife 74321903402*	5		13
1 Jun 02	**REASON** *NuLife 74321938722*	8		8
12 Oct 02	**TRY** *NuLife 74321967942*	15		5
1 Nov 03	**I CAN'T LET YOU GO** *NuLife 82876570712*	20		4
17 Jul 04	**BELIEVE** *NuLife 82876626542*	27		3

ICE CUBE

US, male rapper/producer/actor (O'Shea Jackson) — Weeks on Chart: 36

Date	Title	Peak Position	Weeks at No.1	Weeks on Chart
27 Mar 93	**IT WAS A GOOD DAY** *Fourth & Broadway BRCD 270*	27		4
7 Aug 93	**CHECK YO SELF** *Fourth & Broadway BRCD 283* FEATURING DAS EFX	36		4
11 Sep 93	**WICKED** *Fourth & Broadway BRCD 282*	62		1
18 Dec 93	**REALLY DOE** *Fourth & Broadway BRCD 302*	66		1
26 Mar 94	**YOU KNOW HOW WE DO IT** *Fourth & Broadway BRCD 303*	41		3
27 Aug 94	**BOP GUN (ONE NATION)** *Fourth & Broadway BRCD 308* FEATURING GEORGE CLINTON	22		3
24 Dec 94	**YOU KNOW HOW WE DO IT** *Fourth & Broadway BRCD 303*	46		2
11 Mar 95	**HAND OF THE DEAD BODY** *Virgin America VUSCD 88* SCARFACE FEATURING ICE CUBE	41		2
15 Apr 95	**NATURAL BORN KILLAZ** *Death Row A 8197CD* DR DRE & ICE CUBE	45		2
22 Mar 97	**THE WORLD IS MINE** *Jive JIVECD 419*	60		1
11 Dec 04	**YOU CAN DO IT** *All Around The World CDGLOBE396* FEATURING MACK 10 & MS TOI	2		13

ICE MC

UK, male rapper (Ian Campbell) — Weeks on Chart: 5

Date	Title	Peak Position	Weeks at No.1	Weeks on Chart
6 Aug 94	**THINK ABOUT THE WAY (BOM DIGI DIGI BOM...)** *WEA YZ 829CD*	42		2
8 Apr 95	**IT'S A RAINY DAY** *Eternal YZ 902CD*	73		1
14 Sep 96	**BOM DIGI BOM (THINK ABOUT THE WAY)** *Eternal 073CD*	38		2

ICE-T

US, male rapper/actor (Tracy Marrow) — Weeks on Chart: 29

Date	Title	Peak Position	Weeks at No.1	Weeks on Chart
18 Mar 89	**HIGH ROLLERS** *Sire W 7574*	63		2
17 Feb 90	**YOU PLAYED YOURSELF** *Sire W 9994*	64		2
29 Sep 90	**SUPERFLY 1990** *Capitol CL 586* CURTIS MAYFIELD & ICE-T	48		3
8 May 93	**I AIN'T NEW TA THIS** *Rhyme Syndicate SYNDD 1*	62		2
18 Dec 93	**THAT'S HOW I'M LIVIN'** *Rhyme Syndicate SYNDD 2*	21		6
9 Apr 94	**GOTTA LOTTA LOVE** *Rhyme Syndicate SYNDD 3*	24		4
10 Dec 94	**BORN TO RAISE HELL** *Fox 74321230152* MOTORHEAD/ICE-T/ WHITFIELD CRANE	47		2
1 Jun 96	**I MUST STAND** *Rhyme Syndicate SYNDD 5*	23		3
7 Dec 96	**THE LANE** *Virgin SYNDD 6*	18		5

ICEBERG SLIMM

UK, male rapper (Duane Dyer) — Weeks on Chart: 3

Date	Title	Peak Position	Weeks at No.1	Weeks on Chart
7 Oct 00	**NURSERY RHYMES** *Polydor 5877632*	37		2
6 Nov 04	**STARSHIP** *V2 ARV5029063* FEATURING COREE	73		1

ICEHOUSE

Australia, male vocal/instrumental group — Weeks on Chart: 28

Date	Title	Peak Position	Weeks at No.1	Weeks on Chart
5 Feb 83	**HEY LITTLE GIRL** *Chrysalis CHS 2670*	17		10
23 Apr 83	**STREET CAFÉ** *Chrysalis COOL 1*	62		4
3 May 86	**NO PROMISES** *Chrysalis CHS 2978*	72		1
29 Aug 87	**CRAZY** *Chrysalis CHS 3156*	74		1
13 Feb 88	**CRAZY** *Chrysalis CHS 3156*	38		8
14 May 88	**ELECTRIC BLUE** *Chrysalis CHS 3239*	53		4

ICICLE WORKS

UK, male vocal/instrumental group — Weeks on Chart: 28

Date	Title	Peak Position	Weeks at No.1	Weeks on Chart
24 Dec 83	**LOVE IS A WONDERFUL COLOUR** *Beggars Banquet BEG 99*	15		8
10 Mar 84	**BIRDS FLY (WHISPER TO A SCREAM)/IN THE CAULDRON OF LOVE** *Beggars Banquet BEG 108*	53		4
26 Jul 86	**UNDERSTANDING JANE** *Beggars Banquet BEG 160*	52		3
4 Oct 86	**WHO DO YOU WANT FOR YOUR LOVE** *Beggars Banquet BEG 172*	54		4
14 Feb 87	**EVANGELINE** *Beggars Banquet BEG 181*	53		4
30 Apr 88	**LITTLE GIRL LOST** *Beggars Banquet BEG 215*	59		4
17 Mar 90	**MOTORCYCLE RIDER** *Epic WORKS 100*	73		1

ICON

UK, male/female vocal/instrumental duo — Weeks on Chart: 1

Date	Title	Peak Position	Weeks at No.1	Weeks on Chart
15 Jun 96	**TAINTED LOVE** *Eternal WEA 057CD*	51		1

IDEAL

UK, male producer (Jon da Silva) — Weeks on Chart: 2

Date	Title	Peak Position	Weeks at No.1	Weeks on Chart
6 Aug 94	**HOT** *Cleveland City CLECD 13019*	49		2

IDEAL US FEATURING LIL' MO

US, male/female vocal group — Weeks on Chart: 3

Date	Title	Peak Position	Weeks at No.1	Weeks on Chart
23 Sep 00	**WHATEVER** *Virgin VUSCD 172*	31		3

IDES OF MARCH

US, male vocal/instrumental group — Weeks on Chart: 9

Date	Title	Peak Position	Weeks at No.1	Weeks on Chart
6 Jun 70	**VEHICLE** *Warner Brothers WB 7378*	31		9

ERIC IDLE FEATURING RICHARD WILSON

UK, male vocal/comedy/acting duo — Weeks on Chart: 3

Date	Title	Peak Position	Weeks at No.1	Weeks on Chart
17 Dec 94	**ONE FOOT IN THE GRAVE** *Victa CDVICTA 1*	50		3

IDLEWILD

UK, male vocal/instrumental group – Roddy Woomble, Bob Fairfoull (replaced by Gareth Russell), Rod Jones, Jeremy Mills (replaced by Allan Stewart) & Colin Newton — Weeks on Chart: 37

Date	Title	Peak Position	Weeks at No.1	Weeks on Chart
9 May 98	**A FILM FOR THE FUTURE** *Food CDFOOD 111*	53		1
25 Jul 98	**EVERYONE SAYS YOU'RE SO FRAGILE** *Food CDFOOD 113*	47		1
24 Oct 98	**I'M A MESSAGE** *Food CDFOOD 114*	41		1
13 Feb 99	**WHEN I ARGUE I SEE SHAPES** *Food CDFOODS 116*	19		2
2 Oct 99	**LITTLE DISCOURAGE** *Food CDFOODS 124*	24		2
8 Apr 00	**ACTUALLY IT'S DARKNESS** *Food CDFOODS 127*	23		3
24 Jun 00	**THESE WOODEN IDEAS** *Food CDFOODS 132*	32		3
28 Oct 00	**ROSEABILITY** *Food CDFOODS 134*	38		2
4 May 02	**YOU HELD THE WORLD IN YOUR ARMS** *Parlophone CDRS 6575*	9		4
13 Jul 02	**AMERICAN ENGLISH** *Parlophone CDRS 6582*	15		7
2 Nov 02	**LIVE IN A HIDING PLACE** *Parlophone CDRS 6587*	26		2
22 Feb 03	**A MODERN WAY OF LETTING GO** *Parlophone CDR 6598*	28		2
5 Mar 05	**LOVE STEALS US FROM LONELINESS** *Parlophone CDRS6658*	16		3
14 May 05	**I UNDERSTAND IT** *Parlophone CDRS6662*	32		2
23 Jul 05	**EL CAPITAN** *Parlophone CDRS6667*	39		1
10 Mar 07	**NO EMOTION** *Sequel SEQXD008*	36		1

BILLY IDOL

UK, male vocalist/guitarist (William Broad). See Generation X — 106

Date	Title	Peak Position	Weeks at No.1	Weeks on Chart
11 Sep 82	**HOT IN THE CITY** *Chrysalis CHS 2625*	58		4
24 Mar 84	**REBEL YELL** *Chrysalis IDOL 2*	62		2
30 Jun 84	**EYES WITHOUT A FACE** *Chrysalis IDOL 3*	18		11
29 Sep 84	**FLESH FOR FANTASY** *Chrysalis IDOL 4*	54		3
13 Jul 85	**WHITE WEDDING** *Chrysalis IDOL 5* ○	6		15
14 Sep 85	**REBEL YELL** *Chrysalis IDOL 6*	6		12
4 Oct 86	**TO BE A LOVER** *Chrysalis IDOL 8*	22		8
7 Mar 87	**DON'T NEED A GUN** *Chrysalis IDOL 9*	26		5
13 Jun 87	**SWEET SIXTEEN** *Chrysalis IDOL 10*	17		9
3 Oct 87	**MONY MONY** *Chrysalis IDOL 11* ★	7		10
16 Jan 88	**HOT IN THE CITY (REMIX)** *Chrysalis IDOL 12*	13		9
13 Aug 88	**CATCH MY FALL** *Chrysalis IDOL 13*	63		3
28 Apr 90	**CRADLE OF LOVE** *Chrysalis IDOL 14*	34		4
11 Aug 90	**L.A. WOMAN** *Chrysalis IDOL 15*	70		2
22 Dec 90	**PRODIGAL BLUES** *Chrysalis IDOL 16*	47		4
26 Jun 93	**SHOCK TO THE SYSTEM** *Chrysalis CDCHS 3994*	30		3
10 Sep 94	**SPEED** *Fox 74321223472*	47		2

IDOLS

UK, male/female vocal ensemble – members included series 2 *Pop Idol* finalists Michelle* McManus, Sam Nixon & Mark Rhodes (Sam & Mark*) & Andy Scott-Lee (3SL*) — 5

Date	Title	Peak Position	Weeks at No.1	Weeks on Chart
27 Dec 03	**HAPPY XMAS (WAR IS OVER)** *S 82876583822*	5		5

FRANK IFIELD

Australia (b. UK), male vocalist — 163

Date	Title	Peak Position	Weeks at No.1	Weeks on Chart
19 Feb 60	**LUCKY DEVIL** *Columbia DB 4399*	22		8
29 Sep 60	**GOTTA GET A DATE** *Columbia DB 4496*	49		1
5 Jul 62	**I REMEMBER YOU** *Columbia DB 4856*	1	7	28
25 Oct 62	**LOVESICK BLUES** *Columbia DB 4913*	1	5	17
24 Jan 63	**THE WAYWARD WIND** *Columbia DB 4960*	1	3	13
11 Apr 63	**NOBODY'S DARLIN' BUT MINE** *Columbia DB 7007*	4		16
27 Jun 63	**CONFESSIN' (THAT I LOVE YOU)** *Columbia DB 7062*	1	2	16
17 Oct 63	**MULE TRAIN** *Columbia DB 7131*	22		6
9 Jan 64	**DON'T BLAME ME** *Columbia DB 7184*	8		13
23 Apr 64	**ANGRY AT THE BIG OAK TREE** *Columbia DB 7263*	25		8
23 Jul 64	**I SHOULD CARE** *Columbia DB 7319*	33		3
1 Oct 64	**SUMMER IS OVER** *Columbia DB 7355*	25		6
19 Aug 65	**PARADISE** *Columbia DB 7655*	26		9
23 Jun 66	**NO ONE WILL EVER KNOW** *Columbia DB 7940*	25		4
8 Dec 66	**CALL HER YOUR SWEETHEART** *Columbia DB 8078*	24		11
7 Dec 91	**THE YODELLING SONG** *EMI 7YODEL 1* FEATURING THE BACKROOM BOYS	40		4

ENRIQUE IGLESIAS

Spain, male vocalist (Enrique Miguel Iglesias Preysler) — 138

Date	Title	Peak Position	Weeks at No.1	Weeks on Chart
11 Sep 99	**BAILAMOS** *Interscope IND 97131* ○ ★	4		9
18 Dec 99	**RHYTHM DIVINE** *Interscope 4972242*	45		2
14 Oct 00	**COULD I HAVE THIS KISS FOREVER** *Arista 74321795992* WHITNEY HOUSTON & ENRIQUE IGLESIAS	7		8
2 Feb 02	**HERO** *Interscope IND 97671* ENRIQUE ●	1	4	20
27 Apr 02	**ESCAPE** *Interscope 4976922 (import)* ENRIQUE	71		2
25 May 02	**ESCAPE** *Interscope 4977232* ENRIQUE ○	3		14
7 Sep 02	**LOVE TO SEE YOU CRY** *Interscope IND 97760*	12		7
7 Dec 02	**MAYBE** *Interscope 4978232* ENRIQUE	12		9
26 Apr 03	**TO LOVE A WOMAN** *Mercury 0779082* LIONEL RICHIE FEATURING ENRIQUE IGLESIAS	19		4
29 Nov 03	**ADDICTED** *Interscope 9814328*	11		6
20 Mar 04	**NOT IN LOVE** *Interscope 9862023* ENRIQUE FEATURING KELIS	5		9
9 Jun 07	**DO YOU KNOW (THE PING PONG SONG)** *Interscope 1735807*	3		21
29 Sep 07	**TIRED OF BEING SORRY** *Interscope 1747082*	20		7
7 Mar 09	**TAKIN' BACK MY LOVE** *Interscope USUM70840861* FEATURING CIARA	12		20

JULIO IGLESIAS

Spain, male vocalist (Julio Iglesias de la Cueva) — 75

Date	Title	Peak Position	Weeks at No.1	Weeks on Chart
24 Oct 81	**BEGIN THE BEGUINE (VOLVER A EMPEZAR)** *CBS A 1612* ○	1	1	14
6 Mar 82	**QUIEREME MUCHO (YOURS)** *CBS A 1939* ○	3		9
9 Oct 82	**AMOR** *CBS A 2801*	32		7
9 Apr 83	**HEY!** *CBS JULIO 1*	31		7
7 Apr 84	**TO ALL THE GIRLS I'VE LOVED BEFORE** *CBS A 4252* & WILLIE NELSON	17		10
7 Jul 84	**ALL OF YOU** *CBS A 4522* & DIANA ROSS	43		8
6 Aug 88	**MY LOVE** *CBS JULIO 2* FEATURING STEVIE WONDER	5		11
4 Jun 94	**CRAZY** *Columbia 6603695*	43		5
26 Nov 94	**FRAGILE** *Columbia 6610192*	53		4

IGLU & HARTLY

US, male vocal/instrumental group – Jarvis Anderson, Michael Bucher, Simon Katz, Sam Martin & Luis Rosiles — 11

Date	Title	Peak Position	Weeks at No.1	Weeks on Chart
20 Sep 08	**IN THIS CITY** *Mercury 1778767*	5		11

IGNORANTS

UK, male rap duo — 3

Date	Title	Peak Position	Weeks at No.1	Weeks on Chart
25 Dec 93	**PHAT GIRLS** *Spaghetti CIOCD 8*	59		3

IL PADRINOS FEATURING JOCELYN BROWN

UK/US, male/female vocal/production trio. See Akabu featuring Linda Clifford, Hed Boys, Jakatta, Li Kwan, Joey Negro, Phase II, Raven Maize, Z Factor — 1

Date	Title	Peak Position	Weeks at No.1	Weeks on Chart
7 Sep 02	**THAT'S HOW GOOD YOUR LOVE IS** *Defected DFTD 057CDS*	54		1

ILLEGAL MOTION FEATURING SIMONE CHAPMAN

UK, male/female production/vocal duo — 1

Date	Title	Peak Position	Weeks at No.1	Weeks on Chart
9 Oct 93	**SATURDAY LOVE** *Arista 74321163032*	67		1

ILLICIT FEATURING GRAM'MA FUNK

UK/US, male/female vocal/production trio — 1

Date	Title	Peak Position	Weeks at No.1	Weeks on Chart
2 Sep 00	**CHEEKY ARMADA** *Yola YOLACDX 01*	72		1

IIO

US, female/male vocal/production duo – Nadia Ali & Markus Moser — 15

Date	Title	Peak Position	Weeks at No.1	Weeks on Chart
10 Nov 01	**RAPTURE** *Made/Data/MoS 27CDS* ○	2		12
14 Jun 03	**AT THE END** *Free 2 Air 0148065 F2A*	20		3

IKARA COLT

UK, male/female vocal/instrumental group — 4

Date	Title	Peak Position	Weeks at No.1	Weeks on Chart
2 Mar 02	**RUDD** *Fantastic Plastic FPS 029*	72		1
28 Feb 04	**WANNA BE THAT WAY** *Fantastic Plastic FPS 038X*	49		1
5 Jun 04	**WAKE IN THE CITY** *Fantastic Plastic FPS 040X*	55		1
23 Oct 04	**MODERN FEELING** *Fantastic Plastic FPS 042*	61		1

ILS

UK, male DJ/producer (Illian Walker) — 1

Date	Title	Peak Position	Weeks at No.1	Weeks on Chart
23 Feb 02	**NEXT LEVEL** *Marine Parade MAPA 012*	75		1

IMAANI

UK, female vocalist (Imaani Saleem). See Tru Faith & Dub Conspiracy — 7

Date	Title	Peak Position	Weeks at No.1	Weeks on Chart
9 May 98	**WHERE ARE YOU** *EMI CDEM 510*	15		7

IMAGINATION

UK/Jamaica, male vocal/instrumental trio – Leee John (John McGregor), Ashley Ingram & Errol Kennedy — 105

Date	Title	Peak Position	Weeks at No.1	Weeks on Chart
16 May 81	**BODY TALK** *R&B RBS 201* ○	4		18
5 Sep 81	**IN AND OUT OF LOVE** *R&B RBS 202*	16		9
14 Nov 81	**FLASHBACK** *R&B RBS 206*	16		13
6 Mar 82	**JUST AN ILLUSION** *R&B RBS 208* ○	2		11
26 Jun 82	**MUSIC AND LIGHTS** *R&B RBS 210* ●	5		9
25 Sep 82	**IN THE HEAT OF THE NIGHT** *R&B RBS 211*	22		8
11 Dec 82	**CHANGES** *R&B RBS 213*	31		8
4 Jun 83	**LOOKING AT MIDNIGHT** *R&B RBS 214*	29		7
5 Nov 83	**NEW DIMENSIONS** *R&B RBS 216*	56		3
26 May 84	**STATE OF LOVE** *R&B RBS 218*	67		2
24 Nov 84	**THANK YOU MY LOVE** *R&B RBS 219*	22		15
16 Jan 88	**INSTINCTUAL** *RCA PB 41697*	62		2

IMAJIN

US, male vocal group — 7

Date	Title	Peak Position	Weeks at No.1	Weeks on Chart
27 Jun 98	**SHORTY (YOU KEEP PLAYIN' WITH MY MIND)** *Jive 0521212* FEATURING KEITH MURRAY	22		3
20 Feb 99	**NO DOUBT** *Jive 0521772*	42		2
24 Apr 99	**BOUNCE, ROCK, SKATE, ROLL** *Jive 0522142* BABY DC FEATURING IMAJIN	45		1
12 Feb 00	**FLAVA** *Jive 9250012*	64		1

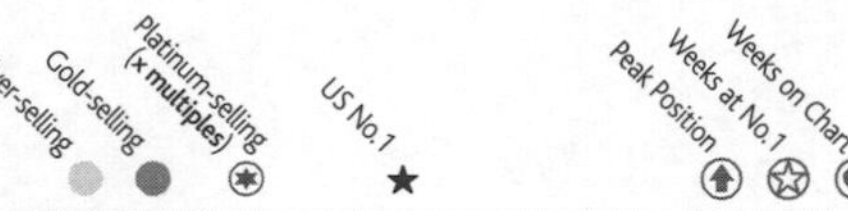

NATALIE IMBRUGLIA
Australia, female vocalist/actor — 75

Date	Title	Peak	Wks at No.1	Wks on Chart
8 Nov 97	**TORN** *RCA 74321527982* ⊛	2		17
14 Mar 98	**BIG MISTAKE** *RCA 74321566782*	2		10
6 Jun 98	**WISHING I WAS HERE** *RCA 74321585062*	19		5
17 Oct 98	**SMOKE** *RCA 74321621942*	5		7
10 Nov 01	**THAT DAY** *RCA 74321896792*	11		5
23 Mar 02	**WRONG IMPRESSION** *RCA 74321928352*	10		7
3 Aug 02	**BEAUTY ON THE FIRE** *RCA 74321950362*	26		2
2 Apr 05	**SHIVER** *Brightside 82876686882*	8		12
6 Aug 05	**COUNTING DOWN THE DAYS** *Brightside 82876715592*	23		5
8 Sep 07	**GLORIOUS** *Brightside 88697137112*	23		4
29 Sep 07	**TORN** *Brightside 74321527982*	70		1

IMMACULATE FOOLS
UK, male vocal/instrumental group — 4

Date	Title	Peak	Wks at No.1	Wks on Chart
26 Jan 85	**IMMACULATE FOOLS** *A&M AM 227*	51		4

IMMATURE FEATURING SMOOTH
US, male/female vocal group — 2

Date	Title	Peak	Wks at No.1	Wks on Chart
16 Mar 96	**WE GOT IT** *MCA MCSTD 48009*	26		2

IMPALAS
US, male vocal group — 1

Date	Title	Peak	Wks at No.1	Wks on Chart
21 Aug 59	**SORRY (I RAN ALL THE WAY HOME)** *MGM 1015*	28		1

IMPEDANCE
UK, male producer (Daniel Haydon) — 4

Date	Title	Peak	Wks at No.1	Wks on Chart
11 Nov 89	**TAINTED LOVE** *Jumpin' & Pumpin' TOT 4*	54		4

IMPERIAL DRAG
UK, male vocal/instrumental group — 1

Date	Title	Peak	Wks at No.1	Wks on Chart
12 Oct 96	**BOY OR A GIRL** *Columbia 6632992*	54		1

IMPERIAL TEEN
US, male/female vocal/instrumental group — 1

Date	Title	Peak	Wks at No.1	Wks on Chart
7 Sep 96	**YOU'RE ONE** *Slash LASCD 57*	69		1

IMPERIALS
US, male vocal group — 9

Date	Title	Peak	Wks at No.1	Wks on Chart
24 Dec 77	**WHO'S GONNA LOVE ME** *Power Exchange PX 266*	17		9

IMPRESSIONS
US, male vocal group — 10

Date	Title	Peak	Wks at No.1	Wks on Chart
22 Nov 75	**FIRST IMPRESSIONS** *Curtom K 16638*	16		10

IN CROWD
UK, male vocal/instrumental group — 1

Date	Title	Peak	Wks at No.1	Wks on Chart
20 May 65	**THAT'S HOW STRONG MY LOVE IS** *Parlophone R 5276*	48		1

IN TUA NUA
Ireland, male/female vocal/instrumental group — 2

Date	Title	Peak	Wks at No.1	Wks on Chart
14 May 88	**ALL I WANTED** *Virgin VS 1072*	69		2

INAURA
UK, male vocal/instrumental group — 1

Date	Title	Peak	Wks at No.1	Wks on Chart
18 May 96	**COMA AROMA** *EMI CDEM 421*	57		1

INCANTATION
UK/Ireland/Chile, male/female instrumental group — 12

Date	Title	Peak	Wks at No.1	Wks on Chart
4 Dec 82	**CACHARPAYA (ANDES PUMPSA DAESI)** *Beggars Banquet BEG 84*	12		12

INCOGNITO
UK, male/female vocal/instrumental group – Jean-Paul 'Bluey' Maunick with male/female vocal/instrumental collaborators including Pam Anderson, Mark Anthoni, Richard Bailey, Ganiyu 'Gee' Bello, Richard Bull, Ray Carless, Patrick Clahar, Jeff Dunn, Peter Hinds, Maysa Leak, Joy Malcolm, Randy Hope Taylor & Paul 'Tubbs' Williams — 38

Date	Title	Peak	Wks at No.1	Wks on Chart
15 Nov 80	**PARISIENNE GIRL** *Ensign ENY 44*	73		2
29 Jun 91	**ALWAYS THERE** *Talkin Loud TLK 10* FEATURING JOCELYN BROWN	6		9
14 Sep 91	**CRAZY FOR YOU** *Talkin Loud TLK 14* FEATURING CHYNA	59		2
6 Jun 92	**DON'T YOU WORRY 'BOUT A THING** *Talkin Loud TLK 21*	19		6
15 Aug 92	**CHANGE** *Talkin Loud TLK 26*	52		2
21 Aug 93	**STILL A FRIEND OF MINE** *Talkin Loud TLKCD 42*	47		2
20 Nov 93	**GIVIN' IT UP** *Talkin Loud TLKCD 44*	43		2
12 Mar 94	**PIECES OF A DREAM** *Talkin Loud TLKCD 46*	35		2
27 May 95	**EVERYDAY** *Talkin Loud TLKCD 55*	23		3
5 Aug 95	**I HEAR YOUR NAME** *Talkin Loud TLKCD 56*	42		3
11 May 96	**JUMP TO MY LOVE/ALWAYS THERE** *Talkin Loud TLCD 7* INCOGNITO/ INCOGNITO FEATURING JOCELYN BROWN	29		3
26 Oct 96	**OUT OF THE STORM** *Talkin Loud TLCD 14*	57		1
10 Apr 99	**NIGHTS OVER EGYPT** *Talkin Loud TLCD 40*	56		1

INCUBUS
US, male vocal/instrumental group — 12

Date	Title	Peak	Wks at No.1	Wks on Chart
20 May 00	**PARDON ME** *Epic 6693462*	61		1
23 Jun 01	**DRIVE** *Epic 6713782*	40		2
2 Feb 02	**WISH YOU WERE HERE** *Epic 6722552*	27		3
14 Sep 02	**ARE YOU IN** *Epic 6728485*	34		2
7 Feb 04	**MEGLOMANIAC** *Epic 6746465*	23		3
19 Jun 04	**TALK SHOWS ON MUTE** *Epic 6749022*	43		1

INDEEP
US, male/female production/vocal/rap trio — 11

Date	Title	Peak	Wks at No.1	Wks on Chart
22 Jan 83	**LAST NIGHT A DJ SAVED MY LIFE** *Sound Of New York SNY 1*	13		9
14 May 83	**WHEN BOYS TALK** *Sound of New York SNY 3*	67		2

INDIA
US (b. Puerto Rico), female vocalist (Linda Caballero) — 17

Date	Title	Peak	Wks at No.1	Wks on Chart
26 Feb 94	**LOVE AND HAPPINESS (YEMAYA Y OCHUN)** *Cooltempo CDCOOL 287* RIVER OCEAN FEATURING INDIA	50		2
5 Aug 95	**I CAN'T GET NO SLEEP** *A&M 5811412* MASTERS AT WORK PRESENT INDIA	44		2
16 Mar 96	**OYE COMO VA** *Media MCSTD 40013* TITO PUENTE Jr & THE LATIN RHYTHM FEATURING TITO PUENTE, INDIA & CALI ALEMAN	36		2
8 Feb 97	**RUNAWAY** *Talkin Loud TLCD 20* NUYORICAN SOUL FEATURING INDIA	24		6
19 Jul 97	**OYE COMO VA (REMIX)** *Nukleuz MCSTD 40120* TITO PUENTE Jr & THE LATIN RHYTHM FEATURING TITO PUENTE, INDIA & CALI ALEMAN	56		1
31 Jul 99	**TO BE IN LOVE** *Defected DEFECT 5CD* MAW PRESENTS INDIA	23		3
6 Jul 02	**BACKFIRED** *Susu CDSUSU 4* MASTERS AT WORK FEATURING INDIA	62		1

INDIAN VIBES
UK, male instrumental group — 2

Date	Title	Peak	Wks at No.1	Wks on Chart
24 Sep 94	**MATHAR** *Virgin International DINSD 136*	68		1
2 May 98	**MATHAR (REMIX)** *VC Recordings VCRD 32*	52		1

INDIEN
UK, male/female vocal/production duo. See Emmie — 1

Date	Title	Peak	Wks at No.1	Wks on Chart
9 Aug 03	**SHOW ME LOVE** *Concept CDCON 40*	69		1

INDO
US, female vocal duo — 3

Date	Title	Peak	Wks at No.1	Wks on Chart
18 Apr 98	**R U SLEEPING** *Satellite 74321568212*	31		3

INDUSTRY STANDARD
UK, male DJ/production duo — 3

Date	Title	Peak	Wks at No.1	Wks on Chart
10 Jan 98	**VOLUME 1 (WHAT YOU WANT WHAT YOU NEED)** *Satellite 74321543742*	34		3

INFADELS

UK, male vocal/instrumental group — 3

Date	Title / Label	Peak	Wks at No.1	Wks on Chart
4 Feb 06	**CAN'T GET ENOUGH** *Wall Of Sound WALLD110*	43		1
28 Jun 08	**FREE THINGS FOR POOR PEOPLE** *Wall Of Sound WOS033CD*	52		2

INFARED VS GIL FELIX

UK/Switzerland/Brazil, male vocal/instrumental/production trio — 1

Date	Title / Label	Peak	Wks at No.1	Wks on Chart
4 Oct 03	**CAPOIERA** *Infrared INFRA 24CD*	67		1

INFERNAL

Denmark, female/male vocal/production duo – Lina Rafn & Paw Lagermann — 28

Date	Title / Label	Peak	Wks at No.1	Wks on Chart
22 Apr 06	**FROM PARIS TO BERLIN** *Apollo APOLLO102CD*	2		23
11 Nov 06	**SELF CONTROL** *Europa EUROPA101CDS*	18		5

INGRAM

US, male/female vocal/instrumental group — 2

Date	Title / Label	Peak	Wks at No.1	Wks on Chart
11 Jun 83	**SMOOTHIN' GROOVIN'** *Streetwave WAVE 3*	56		2

JAMES INGRAM

US, male vocalist — 42

Date	Title / Label	Peak	Wks at No.1	Wks on Chart
12 Feb 83	**BABY COME TO ME** *Qwest K 15005* PATTI AUSTIN & JAMES INGRAM ★	11		10
18 Feb 84	**YAH MO B THERE** *Qwest W 9394* WITH MICHAEL McDONALD	44		8
12 Jan 85	**YAH MO B THERE** *Qwest W 9394* WITH MICHAEL McDONALD	12		8
11 Jul 87	**SOMEWHERE OUT THERE** *MCA 1132* LINDA RONSTADT & JAMES INGRAM	8		13
31 Mar 90	**SECRET GARDEN** *Qwest W 9992* QUINCY JONES FEATURING AL B SURE!, JAMES INGRAM, EL DeBARGE & BARRY WHITE	67		1
16 Apr 94	**THE DAY I FALL IN LOVE** *Columbia 6600282* DOLLY PARTON & JAMES INGRAM	64		2

INK SPOTS

US, male vocal group fronted by Bill Kenny — 4

Date	Title / Label	Peak	Wks at No.1	Wks on Chart
29 Apr 55	**MELODY OF LOVE** *Parlophone R 3977*	10		4

JOHN INMAN

UK, male actor/vocalist, d. 8 March 2007 (age 71) — 6

Date	Title / Label	Peak	Wks at No.1	Wks on Chart
25 Oct 75	**ARE YOU BEING SERVED SIR** *DJM DJS 602*	39		6

INMATES

UK, male vocal/instrumental group — 9

Date	Title / Label	Peak	Wks at No.1	Wks on Chart
8 Dec 79	**THE WALK** *Radar ADA 47*	36		9

INME

UK, male vocal/instrumental group — 10

Date	Title / Label	Peak	Wks at No.1	Wks on Chart
27 Jul 02	**UNDERDOSE** *Music For Nations CDKUT 195*	66		1
28 Sep 02	**FIREFLY** *Music For Nations CDKUT 197*	43		1
18 Jan 03	**CRUSHED LIKE FRUIT** *Music For Nations CDKUT 200*	25		2
26 Apr 03	**NEPTUNE** *Music For Nations CDXKUT 201*	46		1
5 Jun 04	**FASTER THE CHASE** *Music For Nations CDXKUT 210*	31		2
30 Jul 05	**7 WEEKS** *Pandora's Box PB002NMECD*	36		2
22 Oct 05	**SO YOU KNOW** *Pandora's Box PB003NMECD*	33		1

INNA

Romania, female vocalist (Elena Apostoleanu) — 3

Date	Title / Label	Peak	Wks at No.1	Wks on Chart
27 Mar 10	**HOT** *3 Beat GBSXS1000005*	6		3+

INNER CIRCLE

Jamaica, male vocal/instrumental group – Jacob Miller, d. 23 Mar 1980 (replaced by Calton Coffie), Lester Adderly, Lancelot Hall, Bernard 'Touter' Harvey & Ian & Roger Lewis — 35

Date	Title / Label	Peak	Wks at No.1	Wks on Chart
24 Feb 79	**EVERYTHING IS GREAT** *Island WIP 6472*	37		8
12 May 79	**STOP BREAKING MY HEART** *Island WIP 6488*	50		3
31 Oct 92	**SWEAT (A LA LA LA LA LONG)** *Magnet 9031776802*	43		5
1 May 93	**SWEAT (A LA LA LA LA LONG)** *Magnet 9031776802* ●	3		14
31 Jul 93	**BAD BOYS** *Magnet MAG 1017CD*	52		3
10 Sep 94	**GAMES PEOPLE PLAY** *Magnet MAG 1026CD*	67		2

INNER CITY

US, male/female production/vocal duo – Kevin Saunderson & Paris Grey (Shanna Jackson) — 81

Date	Title / Label	Peak	Wks at No.1	Wks on Chart
3 Sep 88	**BIG FUN** *10 TEN 240* FEATURING KEVIN SAUNDERSON	8		14
10 Dec 88	**GOOD LIFE** *10 TEN 249* ●	4		12
22 Apr 89	**AIN'T NOBODY BETTER** *10 TEN 252*	10		7
29 Jul 89	**DO YOU LOVE WHAT YOU FEEL** *10 TEN 237*	16		7
18 Nov 89	**WATCHA GONNA DO WITH MY LOVIN'** *10 TEN 290*	12		9
13 Oct 90	**THAT MAN (HE'S ALL MINE)** *10 TEN 334*	42		4
23 Feb 91	**TILL WE MEET AGAIN** *10 TEN 337*	47		2
7 Dec 91	**LET IT REIGN** *10 TEN 392*	51		2
4 Apr 92	**HALLELUJAH '92** *10 TEN 398*	22		4
13 Jun 92	**PENNIES FROM HEAVEN** *10 TEN 405*	24		4
12 Sep 92	**PRAISE** *10 TENX 408*	59		2
27 Feb 93	**TILL WE MEET AGAIN (REMIX)** *10 TENCD 414*	55		1
14 Aug 93	**BACK TOGETHER AGAIN** *Six6 SIXCD 104*	49		1
5 Feb 94	**DO YA** *Six6 SIXCD 107*	44		2
9 Jul 94	**SHARE MY LIFE** *Six6 SIXCD 114*	62		1
10 Feb 96	**YOUR LOVE** *Six6 SIXCD 127*	28		2
5 Oct 96	**DO ME RIGHT** *Six6 SIXXCD 2*	47		1
6 Feb 99	**GOOD LIFE (BUENA VIDA)** *Pias Recordings PIASX 002CD*	10		6

INNER SANCTUM

Canada, male producer (Steve Bolton) — 1

Date	Title / Label	Peak	Wks at No.1	Wks on Chart
23 May 98	**HOW SOON IS NOW** *Malarky MLKD 6*	75		1

INNERZONE ORCHESTRA

US, male producer (Carl Craig) — 1

Date	Title / Label	Peak	Wks at No.1	Wks on Chart
28 Sep 96	**BUG IN THE BASSBIN** *Mo Wax MW 049CD*	68		1

INNOCENCE

UK, male/female vocal/production group — 33

Date	Title / Label	Peak	Wks at No.1	Wks on Chart
3 Mar 90	**NATURAL THING** *Cooltempo COOL 201*	16		7
21 Jul 90	**SILENT VOICE** *Cooltempo COOL 212*	37		5
13 Oct 90	**LET'S PUSH IT** *Cooltempo COOL 220*	25		6
8 Dec 90	**A MATTER OF FACT** *Cooltempo COOL 223*	37		7
30 Mar 91	**REMEMBER THE DAY** *Cooltempo COOL 226*	56		2
20 Jun 92	**I'LL BE THERE** *Cooltempo COOL 255*	26		3
3 Oct 92	**ONE LOVE IN MY LIFETIME** *Cooltempo COOL 263*	40		2
21 Nov 92	**BUILD** *Cooltempo COOL 267*	72		1

INSANE CLOWN POSSE

US, male rap duo — 2

Date	Title / Label	Peak	Wks at No.1	Wks on Chart
17 Jan 98	**HALLS OF ILLUSION** *Island CID 685*	56		1
6 Jun 98	**HOKUS POKUS** *Island CIDX 705*	53		1

INSPIRAL CARPETS

UK, male vocal/instrumental group — 51

Date	Title / Label	Peak	Wks at No.1	Wks on Chart
18 Nov 89	**MOVE** *Cow DUNG 6*	49		2
17 Mar 90	**THIS IS HOW IT FEELS** *Cow DUNG 7*	14		8
30 Jun 90	**SHE COMES IN THE FALL** *Cow DUNG 10*	27		6
17 Nov 90	**ISLAND HEAD (EP)** *Cow DUNG 11*	21		4
30 Mar 91	**CARAVAN** *Cow DUNG 13*	30		5
22 Jun 91	**PLEASE BE CRUEL** *Cow DUNG 15*	50		2
29 Feb 92	**DRAGGING ME DOWN** *Cow DUNG 16*	12		5
30 May 92	**TWO WORLDS COLLIDE** *Cow DUNG 17*	32		2
19 Sep 92	**GENERATIONS** *Cow DUNG 18T*	28		3
14 Nov 92	**BITCHES BREW** *Cow DUNG 20T*	36		2
5 Jun 93	**HOW IT SHOULD BE** *Cow DUNG 22CD*	49		1
22 Jan 94	**SATURN 5** *Cow DUNG 23CD*	20		4
5 Mar 94	**I WANT YOU** *Cow DUNG 24CD* FEATURING MARK E SMITH	18		3
7 May 94	**UNIFORM** *Cow DUNG 26CD*	51		1
16 Sep 95	**JOE** *Cow DUNG 27CD*	37		2
26 Jul 03	**COME BACK TOMORROW** *Mute DUNG 31CD*	43		1

INSPIRATIONAL CHOIR

US, male/female choir/instrumental group — 11

Date	Title / Label	Peak	Wks at No.1	Wks on Chart
22 Dec 84	**ABIDE WITH ME** *Epic A 4997*	44		5
14 Dec 85	**ABIDE WITH ME** *Portrait A 4997*	36		6

INSTANT FUNK

US, male vocal/instrumental group — 5

Date	Title / Label	Peak	Wks at No.1	Wks on Chart
20 Jan 79	**GOT MY MIND MADE UP** *Salsoul SSOL 114*	46		5

INTASTELLA

UK, male/female vocal/instrumental group — 6

Date	Title	Peak Position	Weeks at No.1	Weeks on Chart
25 May 91	**DREAM SOME PARADISE** *MCA MCS 1520*	69		1
24 Aug 91	**PEOPLE** *MCA MCS 1559*	74		2
16 Nov 91	**CENTURY** *MCA MCS 1585*	70		2
23 Sep 95	**THE NIGHT** *Planet 3 GXY 2005CD*	60		1

INTELLIGENT HOODLUM

US, male rapper (Percy Chapman) — 3

Date	Title	Peak Position	Weeks at No.1	Weeks on Chart
6 Oct 90	**BACK TO REALITY** *A&M AM 598*	55		3

INTENSO PROJECT

UK, male vocal/production group — 7

Date	Title	Peak Position	Weeks at No.1	Weeks on Chart
17 Aug 02	**LUV DA SUNSHINE** *Inferno CDFERN 47*	22		2
26 Jul 03	**YOUR MUSIC** *Concept CDCON 43* FEATURING LAURA JAYE	32		2
4 Dec 04	**GET IT ON** *Inspired INSPMOS1CDS* FEATURING LISA SCOTT-LEE	23		3

INTERACTIVE

Germany, male instrumental/production group. See Bellini, E-Trax, Fragma, Hardfloor, Paffendorf — 6

Date	Title	Peak Position	Weeks at No.1	Weeks on Chart
13 Apr 96	**FOREVER YOUNG** *ffrreedom TABCD 235*	28		4
8 Mar 03	**FOREVER YOUNG** *All Around The World CDGLOBE 253*	37		2

INTERPOL

US, male vocal/instrumental group — 13

Date	Title	Peak Position	Weeks at No.1	Weeks on Chart
23 Nov 02	**OBSTACLE 1** *Matador OLE 5702*	72		1
26 Apr 03	**SAY HELLO TO THE ANGELS/NYC** *Matador OLE 5822*	65		1
27 Sep 03	**OBSTACLE 1** *Matador OLE 5942*	41		1
25 Sep 04	**SLOW HANDS** *Matador OLE 6362*	36		2
15 Jan 05	**EVIL** *Matador OLE 6376*	18		3
23 Apr 05	**C'MERE** *Matador OLE6642*	19		2
9 Jul 05	**SLOW HANDS** *Matador OLE6692*	44		1
14 Jul 07	**THE HEINRICH MANEUVER** *Parlophone CLCD894*	31		1
15 Sep 07	**MAMMOTH** *Parlophone CDCLS896*	44		1

INTRUDERS

US, male vocal group — 21

Date	Title	Peak Position	Weeks at No.1	Weeks on Chart
13 Apr 74	**I'LL ALWAYS LOVE MY MAMA** *Philadelphia International PIR 2149*	32		7
6 Jul 74	**(WIN PLACE OR SHOW) SHE'S A WINNER** *Philadelphia International PIR 2212*	14		9
22 Dec 84	**WHO DO YOU LOVE?** *Streetwave KHAN 34*	65		5

INVISIBLE MAN

UK, male producer (Graham Mew) — 1

Date	Title	Peak Position	Weeks at No.1	Weeks on Chart
17 Apr 99	**GIVE A LITTLE LOVE** *Serious SERR 006CD*	48		1

INXS

Australia, male vocal/instrumental group – Michael Hutchence, d. 22 Nov 1997, Garry Beers, Andrew, Jon & Tim Farriss & Kirk Pengilly — 132

Date	Title	Peak Position	Weeks at No.1	Weeks on Chart
19 Apr 86	**WHAT YOU NEED** *Mercury INXS 5*	51		6
28 Jun 86	**LISTEN LIKE THIEVES** *Mercury INXS 6*	46		7
30 Aug 86	**KISS THE DIRT (FALLING DOWN THE MOUNTAIN)** *Mercury INXS 7*	54		3
24 Oct 87	**NEED YOU TONIGHT** *Mercury INXS 8* ★	58		3
9 Jan 88	**NEW SENSATION** *Mercury INXS 9*	25		6
12 Mar 88	**DEVIL INSIDE** *Mercury INXS 10*	47		5
25 Jun 88	**NEVER TEAR US APART** *Mercury INXS 11*	24		7
12 Nov 88	**NEED YOU TONIGHT** *Mercury INXS 12*	2		11
8 Apr 89	**MYSTIFY** *Mercury INXS 13*	14		7
15 Sep 90	**SUICIDE BLONDE** *Mercury INXS 14*	11		6
8 Dec 90	**DISAPPEAR** *Mercury INXS 15*	21		8
26 Jan 91	**GOOD TIMES** *Atlantic A 7751* JIMMY BARNES & INXS	18		8
30 Mar 91	**BY MY SIDE** *Mercury INXS 16*	42		4
13 Jul 91	**BITTER TEARS** *Mercury INXS 17*	30		3
2 Nov 91	**SHINING STAR (EP)** *Mercury INXS 18*	27		3
18 Jul 92	**HEAVEN SENT** *Mercury INXS 19*	31		3
5 Sep 92	**BABY DON'T CRY** *Mercury INXS 20*	20		5
14 Nov 92	**TASTE IT** *Mercury INXS 23*	21		4
13 Feb 93	**BEAUTIFUL GIRL** *Mercury INXCD 24*	23		5
23 Oct 93	**THE GIFT** *Mercury INXCD 25*	11		4
11 Dec 93	**PLEASE (YOU GOT THAT...)** *Mercury INXCD 26*	50		3
22 Oct 94	**THE STRANGEST PARTY (THESE ARE THE TIMES)** *Mercury INXCD 27*	15		5
22 Mar 97	**ELEGANTLY WASTED** *Mercury INXCD 28*	20		4
7 Jun 97	**EVERYTHING** *Mercury INXDD 29*	71		1
18 Aug 01	**PRECIOUS HEART** *Duty Freee/Decode DFTELCD 001* TALL PAUL VS INXS	14		5
3 Nov 01	**I'M SO CRAZY** *Credence CDCRED 016* PAR-T-ONE VS INXS	19		6

SWEETIE IRIE

UK, male vocalist (Derrick Bent) — 7

Date	Title	Peak Position	Weeks at No.1	Weeks on Chart
17 Nov 90	**SMILE** *Mango MNG 767* ASWAD FEATURING SWEETIE IRIE	53		2
3 Aug 91	**TAKE ME IN YOUR ARMS AND LOVE ME** *Virgin VS 1346* SCRITTI POLITTI & SWEETIE IRIE	47		3
15 Sep 01	**WHO?** *Columbia 6718302* ED CASE & SWEETIE IRIE	29		2

TIPPA IRIE

UK, male vocalist (Anthony Henry) — 14

Date	Title	Peak Position	Weeks at No.1	Weeks on Chart
22 Mar 86	**HELLO DARLING** *UK Bubblers TIPPA 4*	22		7
19 Jul 86	**HEARTBEAT** *UK Bubblers TIPPA 5*	59		3
15 May 93	**SHOUTING FOR THE GUNNERS** *London LONCD 342* ARSENAL FA CUP SQUAD FEATURING TIPPA IRIE & PETER HUNNIGALE	34		3
8 Jul 95	**STAYING ALIVE 95** *Telstar CDSTAS 2776* FEVER FEATURING TIPPA IRIE	48		1

IRON MAIDEN

UK, male vocal/instrumental group – Bruce Dickinson*, Janick Gers, Steve Harris, Nicko McBrain*, Dave Murray & Adrian Smith; members also included Blaze Bayley, Clive Burr & Paul Di'Anno — 181

Date	Title	Peak Position	Weeks at No.1	Weeks on Chart
23 Feb 80	**RUNNING FREE** *EMI 5032*	34		5
7 Jun 80	**SANCTUARY** *EMI 5065*	29		5
8 Nov 80	**WOMEN IN UNIFORM** *EMI 5105*	35		4
14 Mar 81	**TWILIGHT ZONE/WRATH CHILD** *EMI 5145*	31		5
27 Jun 81	**PURGATORY** *EMI 5184*	52		3
26 Sep 81	**MAIDEN JAPAN** *EMI 5219*	43		4
20 Feb 82	**RUN TO THE HILLS** *EMI 5263*	7		10
15 May 82	**THE NUMBER OF THE BEAST** *EMI 5287*	18		8
23 Apr 83	**FLIGHT OF ICARUS** *EMI 5378*	11		6
2 Jul 83	**THE TROOPER** *EMI 5397*	12		7
18 Aug 84	**2 MINUTES TO MIDNIGHT** *EMI 5849*	11		6
3 Nov 84	**ACES HIGH** *EMI 5502*	20		5
5 Oct 85	**RUNNING FREE (LIVE)** *EMI 5532*	19		5
14 Dec 85	**RUN TO THE HILLS (LIVE)** *EMI 5542*	26		6
6 Sep 86	**WASTED YEARS** *EMI 5583*	18		4
22 Nov 86	**STRANGER IN A STRANGE LAND** *EMI 5589*	22		6
26 Mar 88	**CAN I PLAY WITH MADNESS** *EMI EM 49*	3		6
13 Aug 88	**THE EVIL THAT MEN DO** *EMI EM 64*	5		6
19 Nov 88	**THE CLAIRVOYANT** *EMI EM 79*	6		8
18 Nov 89	**INFINITE DREAMS** *EMI EM 117*	6		6
22 Sep 90	**HOLY SMOKE** *EMI EM 153*	3		4
5 Jan 91	**BRING YOUR DAUGHTER...TO THE SLAUGHTER** *EMI EMPD 171*	1	2	5
25 Apr 92	**BE QUICK OR BE DEAD** *EMI EM 229*	2		4
11 Jul 92	**FROM HERE TO ETERNITY** *EMI EMS 240*	21		4
13 Mar 93	**FEAR OF THE DARK (LIVE)** *EMI CDEMS 263*	8		3
16 Oct 93	**HALLOWED BE THY NAME (LIVE)** *EMI CDEM 288*	9		3
7 Oct 95	**MAN ON THE EDGE** *EMI CDEMS 398*	10		3
21 Sep 96	**VIRUS** *EMI CDEM 443*	16		3
21 Mar 98	**THE ANGEL AND THE GAMBLER** *EMI CDEM 507*	18		3
20 May 00	**THE WICKER MAN** *EMI CDEMS 568*	9		4
4 Nov 00	**OUT OF THE SILENT PLANET** *EMI CDEM 576*	20		3
23 Mar 02	**RUN TO THE HILLS** *EMI CDEMS 612*	9		4
13 Sep 03	**WILDEST DREAMS** *EMI CDEM 627*	6		6
6 Dec 03	**RAINMAKER** *EMI CDEM 633*	13		5
15 Jan 05	**THE NUMBER OF THE BEAST** *EMI CDEMS 666*	3		6
27 Aug 05	**THE TROOPER** *EMI CDEM662*	5		3
6 Jan 07	**DIFFERENT WORLD** *EMI CDEM714*	3		3

IRONHORSE

Canada, male vocal/instrumental group. See Randy Bachman — 1

Date	Title	Peak Position	Weeks at No.1	Weeks on Chart
5 May 79	**SWEET LUI-LOUISE** *Scotti Brothers K 11271*	64		1

IRONIK

UK, male vocalist/rapper/DJ (Michael Laurence). See Young Soul Rebels — 24

Date	Title	Peak Position	Weeks at No.1	Weeks on Chart
5 Jul 08	**STAY WITH ME** *Asylum ASYLUM3CD2*	5		13
4 Oct 08	**I WANNA BE YOUR MAN** *Asylum GBAHS0800371*	35		2
9 May 09	**TINY DANCER (HOLD ME CLOSER)** *Asylum ASYLUM9CD* FEATURING CHIPMUNK & ELTON JOHN	3		9

IRRITANT

UK, male vocal/instrumental group — 1

Date	Title	Peak Position	Weeks at No.1	Weeks on Chart
7 Jul 07	**VOICE OF THE SIREN** *Smackjaw GBLFP0783307*	70		1

Silver-selling ● Gold-selling ● Platinum-selling (x multiples) ⊛ US No.1 ★ Peak Position · Weeks at No.1 · Weeks on Chart

BIG DEE IRWIN

US, male vocalist (Difosco Erwin), d. 27 Aug 1995 (age 56) — 17

Date	Title / Label	Peak Position	Weeks at No.1	Weeks on Chart
21 Nov 63	**SWINGING ON A STAR** *Colpix PX 11010*	7		17

CHRIS ISAAK

US, male vocalist/guitarist — 22

Date	Title / Label	Peak Position	Weeks at No.1	Weeks on Chart
24 Nov 90	**WICKED GAME** *London LON 279*	10		10
2 Feb 91	**BLUE HOTEL** *Reprise W 0005*	17		7
3 Apr 93	**CAN'T DO A THING (TO STOP ME)** *Reprise W 0161CD*	36		3
10 Jul 93	**SAN FRANCISCO DAYS** *Reprise W 0182CD*	62		1
2 Oct 99	**BABY DID A BAD BAD THING** *Reprise W 503CD*	44		1

ISHA-D

UK, male/female vocal/instrumental duo — 4

Date	Title / Label	Peak Position	Weeks at No.1	Weeks on Chart
22 Jul 95	**STAY (TONIGHT)** *Cleveland City Blues CCBCD 15005*	28		3
5 Jul 97	**STAY** *Satellite 74321498212*	58		1

ISLEY BROTHERS

US, male vocal group – nucleus Ronald, Rudolph, O'Kelly, d. 31 Mar 1986, & Ernie Isley — 108

Date	Title / Label	Peak Position	Weeks at No.1	Weeks on Chart
25 Jul 63	**TWIST AND SHOUT** *Stateside SS 112*	42		1
28 Apr 66	**THIS OLD HEART OF MINE** *Tamla Motown TMG 555*	47		1
1 Sep 66	**I GUESS I'LL ALWAYS LOVE YOU** *Tamla Motown TMG 572*	45		2
23 Oct 68	**THIS OLD HEART OF MINE** *Tamla Motown TMG 555*	3		16
15 Jan 69	**I GUESS I'LL ALWAYS LOVE YOU** *Tamla Motown TMG 683*	11		9
16 Apr 69	**BEHIND A PAINTED SMILE** *Tamla Motown TMG 693*	5		12
25 Jun 69	**IT'S YOUR THING** *Major Minor MM 621*	30		5
30 Aug 69	**PUT YOURSELF IN MY PLACE** *Tamla Motown TMG 708*	13		11
22 Sep 73	**THAT LADY** *Epic EPC 1704*	14		9
19 Jan 74	**HIGHWAYS OF MY LIFE** *Epic EPC 1980*	25		8
25 May 74	**SUMMER BREEZE** *Epic EPC 2244*	16		8
10 Jul 76	**HARVEST FOR THE WORLD** *Epic EPC 4369*	10		8
13 May 78	**TAKE ME TO THE NEXT PHASE** *Epic EPC 6292*	50		4
3 Nov 79	**IT'S A DISCO NIGHT (ROCK DON'T STOP)** *Epic EPC 7911*	14		11
16 Jul 83	**BETWEEN THE SHEETS** *Epic A 3513*	52		3

ISLEY JASPER ISLEY

US, male vocal/instrumental trio — 5

Date	Title / Label	Peak Position	Weeks at No.1	Weeks on Chart
23 Nov 85	**CARAVAN OF LOVE** *Epic A 6612*	52		5

ISOTONIK

UK, male producer (Chris Paul) — 9

Date	Title / Label	Peak Position	Weeks at No.1	Weeks on Chart
11 Jan 92	**DIFFERENT STROKES** *ffrreedom TAB 101*	12		5
2 May 92	**EVERYWHERE I GO/LET'S GET DOWN** *ffrreedom TAB 108*	25		4

IT BITES

UK, male vocal/instrumental group — 21

Date	Title / Label	Peak Position	Weeks at No.1	Weeks on Chart
12 Jul 86	**CALLING ALL THE HEROES** *Virgin VS 872*	6		12
18 Oct 86	**WHOLE NEW WORLD** *Virgin VS 896*	54		3
23 May 87	**THE OLD MAN AND THE ANGEL** *Virgin VS 941*	72		1
13 May 89	**STILL TOO YOUNG TO REMEMBER** *Virgin VS 1184*	66		3
24 Feb 90	**STILL TOO YOUNG TO REMEMBER** *Virgin VS 1238*	60		2

IT'S IMMATERIAL

UK, male vocal/instrumental duo — 10

Date	Title / Label	Peak Position	Weeks at No.1	Weeks on Chart
12 Apr 86	**DRIVING AWAY FROM HOME (JIM'S TUNE)** *Siren 15*	18		7
2 Aug 86	**ED'S FUNKY DINER (FRIDAY NIGHT, SATURDAY MORNING)** *Siren 24*	65		3

ITTY BITTY BOOZY WOOZY

Holland, male instrumental/production duo. See Da Techno Bohemian, Drunkenmunky, Hi_Tack, Klubbheads — 2

Date	Title / Label	Peak Position	Weeks at No.1	Weeks on Chart
25 Nov 95	**TEMPO FIESTA (PARTY TIME)** *Systematic SYSCD 23*	34		2

BON IVER

US, male vocal/instrumental group — 2

Date	Title / Label	Peak Position	Weeks at No.1	Weeks on Chart
31 Jan 09	**BLOOD BANK** *Jagjaguwar JAG134CD*	37		2

BURL IVES

US, male vocalist, d. 14 Apr 1995 (age 85) — 25

Date	Title / Label	Peak Position	Weeks at No.1	Weeks on Chart
25 Jan 62	**A LITTLE BITTY TEAR** *Brunswick 05863*	9		15
17 May 62	**FUNNY WAY OF LAUGHIN'** *Brunswick 05868*	29		10

IVY LEAGUE

UK, male vocal trio – John Carter, Perry Ford & Ken Lewis — 31

Date	Title / Label	Peak Position	Weeks at No.1	Weeks on Chart
4 Feb 65	**FUNNY HOW LOVE CAN BE** *Piccadilly 7N 35222*	8		9
6 May 65	**THAT'S WHY I'M CRYING** *Piccadilly 7N 35228*	22		8
24 Jun 65	**TOSSING AND TURNING** *Piccadilly 7N 35251*	3		13
14 Jul 66	**WILLOW TREE** *Piccadilly 7N 35326*	50		1

IWASACUBSCOUT

UK, male vocal/instrumental duo — 1

Date	Title / Label	Peak Position	Weeks at No.1	Weeks on Chart
16 Feb 08	**PINK SQUARES** *Abeano AX1330A*	71		1

IYAZ

British Virgin Islands, male vocalist (Keidran Jones) — 13

Date	Title / Label	Peak Position	Weeks at No.1	Weeks on Chart
16 Jan 10	**REPLAY** *Reprise USRE10901936*	1	1	13+

IZIT

UK, male vocal/instrumental group — 3

Date	Title / Label	Peak Position	Weeks at No.1	Weeks on Chart
2 Dec 89	**STORIES** *ffrr F 122*	52		3

FRANKIE J

Mexico, male vocalist/pianist (Francisco Javier Bautista, Jr) — 2

Date	Title / Label	Peak Position	Weeks at No.1	Weeks on Chart
20 Aug 05	**OBSESSION (NO ES AMOR)** *Columbia 6760212*	38		2

HARRY J ALL STARS

Jamaica, male vocal/instrumental session group fronted by Harry Johnson — 25

Date	Title / Label	Peak Position	Weeks at No.1	Weeks on Chart
25 Oct 69	**THE LIQUIDATOR** *Trojan TR 675*	9		20
29 Mar 80	**THE LIQUIDATOR** *Trojan TRO 9063*	42		5

RAY J

US, male vocalist (Willie Ray Norwood, Jr.) — 22

Date	Title / Label	Peak Position	Weeks at No.1	Weeks on Chart
17 Oct 98	**THAT'S WHY I LIE** *Atlantic AT 0049CD*	71		1
16 Jun 01	**ANOTHER DAY IN PARADISE** *WEA 327CD1* BRANDY & RAY J	5		10
11 Aug 01	**WAIT A MINUTE** *Atlantic AT 0106CD* FEATURING LIL' KIM	54		1
12 Nov 05	**ONE WISH** *Sanctuary Urban SANXD397*	26		2
25 Mar 06	**ONE WISH** *Sanctuary SANXS424*	13		7
23 Aug 08	**SEXY CAN I** *UMTV USKO10702948* FEATURING YUNG BERG	66		1

SONNY J

UK, male vocalist (Sonnington James III) — 4

Date	Title / Label	Peak Position	Weeks at No.1	Weeks on Chart
6 Sep 08	**CAN'T STOP MOVING** *Stateside CDSSX2237*	40		4

J-KWON

US, male rapper (Jerrell Jones) — 12

Date	Title / Label	Peak Position	Weeks at No.1	Weeks on Chart
24 Jul 04	**TIPSY** *LaFace 82876634162*	4		12

J PAC

UK, male vocal/instrumental duo — 2

Date	Title / Label	Peak Position	Weeks at No.1	Weeks on Chart
22 Jul 95	**ROCK 'N' ROLL (DOLE)** *East West YZ 953CD*	51		2

JA RULE

US, male rapper/actor (Jeffrey Atkins) — 109

Date	Title / Label	Peak Position	Weeks at No.1	Weeks on Chart
13 Mar 99	**CAN I GET A...** *Def Jam 5668472* JAY-Z FEATURING AMIL & JA RULE	24		3
3 Mar 01	**BETWEEN YOU AND ME** *Def Jam 5727402* FEATURING CHRISTINA MILIAN	26		3
18 Aug 01	**AIN'T IT FUNNY** *Epic 6717592* JENNIFER LOPEZ FEATURING JA RULE & CADILLAC TAH ★	3		9
10 Nov 01	**I'M REAL** *Epic 6720322* JENNIFER LOPEZ FEATURING JA RULE ★	4		15
10 Nov 01	**LIVIN' IT UP** *Def Jam 5888142* FEATURING CASE	27		4
2 Feb 02	**ALWAYS ON TIME** *Def Jam 5889462* FEATURING ASHANTI ★	6		13
3 Aug 02	**LIVIN' IT UP** *Def Jam 0639782* FEATURING CASE	5		8
24 Aug 02	**RAINY DAYZ** *MCA MCSXD 40288* MARY J BLIGE FEATURING JA RULE	17		5

Date	Title	Peak Position	Weeks at No.1	Weeks on Chart
12 Oct 02	**DOWN 4 U** *Murder Inc 0639002* IRV GOTTI PRESENTS JA RULE, ASHANTI, CHARLI BALTIMORE & VITA	4		10
21 Dec 02	**THUG LOVIN'** *Def Jam 0637872* FEATURING BOBBY BROWN	15		8
29 Mar 03	**MESMERIZE** *Murder Inc 0779582* FEATURING ASHANTI	12		8
6 Dec 03	**CLAP BACK/REIGNS** *Def Jam 9861552*	9		9
6 Nov 04	**WONDERFUL** *Def Jam 9864606* FEATURING R KELLY & ASHANTI	1	1	10
30 Apr 05	**CAUGHT UP** *The Inc 9881232* FEATURING LLOYD	20		4

JACK 'N' CHILL

UK, male production duo

Date	Title	Peak Position	Weeks at No.1	21
6 Jun 87	**THE JACK THAT HOUSE BUILT** *Oval TEN 174*	48		5
9 Jan 88	**THE JACK THAT HOUSE BUILT** *Oval TEN 174*	6		11
9 Jul 88	**BEATIN' THE HEAT** *10 TEN 234*	42		5

TERRY JACKS

Canada, male vocalist. See Poppy Family

Date	Title	Peak Position	Weeks at No.1	21
23 Mar 74	**SEASONS IN THE SUN** *Bell 1344* ● ★	1	4	12
29 Jun 74	**IF YOU GO AWAY** *Bell 1362*	8		9

CHAD JACKSON

UK, male DJ/producer (Mark Chadwick)

Date	Title	Peak Position	Weeks at No.1	10
2 Jun 90	**HEAR THE DRUMMER (GET WICKED)** *Big Wave BWR 36*	3		10

DEE D JACKSON

UK, female vocalist (Deirdre Cozier)

Date	Title	Peak Position	Weeks at No.1	14
22 Apr 78	**AUTOMATIC LOVER** *Mercury 6007 171* ●	4		9
2 Sep 78	**METEOR MAN** *Mercury 6007 182*	48		5

FREDDIE JACKSON

US, male vocalist

Date	Title	Peak Position	Weeks at No.1	31
23 Nov 85	**YOU ARE MY LADY** *Capitol CL 379*	49		4
22 Feb 86	**ROCK ME TONIGHT (FOR OLD TIME'S SAKE)** *Capitol CL 358*	18		9
11 Oct 86	**TASTY LOVE** *Capitol CL 428*	73		1
7 Feb 87	**HAVE YOU EVER LOVED SOMEBODY** *Capitol CL 437*	33		6
9 Jul 88	**NICE 'N' SLOW** *Capitol CL 502*	56		2
15 Oct 88	**CRAZY (FOR ME)** *Capitol CL 510*	41		3
5 Sep 92	**ME AND MRS JONES** *Capitol CL 668*	32		5
15 Jan 94	**MAKE LOVE EASY** *RCA 74321179162*	70		1

GISELE JACKSON

US, female vocalist

Date	Title	Peak Position	Weeks at No.1	1
30 Aug 97	**LOVE COMMANDMENTS** *Manifesto FESCD 28*	54		1

JANET JACKSON

US, female vocalist/producer/actor/dancer. Multi-talented entertainer who has been a regular fixture at the top of the US Hot 100, R'n'B/hip hop and dance charts since the mid-1980s. In the UK, her best-selling single is 'Together Again', which shifted 750,000 copies

Date	Title	Peak Position	Weeks at No.1	304
22 Mar 86	**WHAT HAVE YOU DONE FOR ME LATELY** *A&M AM 308* ●	3		14
31 May 86	**NASTY** *A&M AM 316*	19		9
9 Aug 86	**WHEN I THINK OF YOU** *A&M AM 337* ★	10		10
1 Nov 86	**CONTROL** *A&M AM 359*	42		5
21 Mar 87	**LET'S WAIT AWHILE** *Breakout USA 601* ●	3		10
13 Jun 87	**PLEASURE PRINCIPLE** *Breakout USA 604*	24		5
14 Nov 87	**FUNNY HOW TIME FLIES (WHEN YOU'RE HAVING FUN)** *Breakout USA 613*	59		2
2 Sep 89	**MISS YOU MUCH** *Breakout USA 663* ★	22		7
4 Nov 89	**RHYTHM NATION** *Breakout USA 673*	23		5
27 Jan 90	**COME BACK TO ME** *Breakout USA 681*	20		7
31 Mar 90	**ESCAPADE** *Breakout USA 684* ★	17		7
7 Jul 90	**ALRIGHT** *A&M USA 693*	20		5
8 Sep 90	**BLACK CAT** *A&M EM 587* ★	15		6
27 Oct 90	**LOVE WILL NEVER DO (WITHOUT YOU)** *A&M EM 700* ★	34		4
15 Aug 92	**THE BEST THINGS IN LIFE ARE FREE** *Perspective PERSS 7400* LUTHER VANDROSS & JANET JACKSON WITH SPECIAL GUESTS BBD & RALPH TRESVANT ●	2		13
8 May 93	**THAT'S THE WAY LOVE GOES** *Virgin VSCDG 1460* ● ★	2		10
31 Jul 93	**IF** *Virgin VSCDT 1474*	14		7
20 Nov 93	**AGAIN** *Virgin VSCDG 1481* ★	6		11
12 Mar 94	**BECAUSE OF LOVE** *Virgin VSCDG 1488*	19		4
18 Jun 94	**ANY TIME ANY PLACE** *Virgin VSCDT 1501*	13		5
26 Nov 94	**YOU WANT THIS** *Virgin VSCDT 1519*	14		3
18 Mar 95	**WHOOPS NOW/WHAT'LL I DO** *Virgin VSCDT 1533*	9		8
10 Jun 95	**SCREAM** *Epic 6620222* MICHAEL JACKSON & JANET JACKSON	3		13
24 Jun 95	**SCREAM (REMIX)** *Epic 6621277* MICHAEL JACKSON & JANET JACKSON	43		2
23 Sep 95	**RUNAWAY** *A&M 5811972*	6		7
16 Dec 95	**THE BEST THINGS IN LIFE ARE FREE (REMIX)** *A&M 5813092* LUTHER VANDROSS & JANET JACKSON WITH SPECIAL GUESTS BBD & RALPH TRESVANT	7		7
6 Apr 96	**TWENTY FOREPLAY** *A&M 5815112*	22		4
4 Oct 97	**GOT 'TIL IT'S GONE** *Virgin VSCDG 1666* JANET FEATURING Q-TIP & JONI ●	6		9
13 Dec 97	**TOGETHER AGAIN** *Virgin VSCDG 1670* ⊛ ★	4		19
4 Apr 98	**I GET LONELY** *Virgin VSCDT 1683*	5		7
27 Jun 98	**GO DEEP** *Virgin VSCDT 1680*	13		5
19 Dec 98	**EVERY TIME** *Virgin VSCDT 1720*	46		1
17 Apr 99	**GIRLFRIEND/BOYFRIEND** *Interscope IND 95640* BLACKstreet FEATURING JANET	11		7
1 May 99	**WHAT'S IT GONNA BE?!** *Elektra E 3762CD1* BUSTA RHYMES FEATURING JANET	6		7
19 Aug 00	**DOESN'T REALLY MATTER** *Def Soul 5629152* ● ★	5		11
21 Apr 01	**ALL FOR YOU** *Virgin VSCDT 1801* ★	3		11
11 Aug 01	**SOMEONE TO CALL MY LOVER** *Virgin VSCDT 1813*	11		5
22 Dec 01	**SON OF A GUN (BETCHA THINK THIS SONG)** *Virgin VUSCDX 232* WITH CARLY SIMON FEATURING MISSY ELLIOTT	13		9
28 Sep 02	**FEEL IT BOY** *Virgin VUSCD 258* BEENIE MAN FEATURING JANET JACKSON	9		7
24 Apr 04	**JUST A LITTLE WHILE** *Virgin VUSDX 285*	15		5
19 Jun 04	**ALL NITE (DON'T STOP)/I WANT YOU** *Virgin VUSDX 292*	19		4
30 Sep 06	**CALL ON ME** *Virgin VUSCD330* JANET & NELLY	18		5
11 Jul 09	**SCREAM** *Epic 6620222* MICHAEL JACKSON & JANET JACKSON	70		1
19 Dec 09	**MAKE ME** *Polydor USUG10910919*	73		1

JERMAINE JACKSON

US, male vocalist. See Jacksons

Date	Title	Peak Position	Weeks at No.1	43
10 May 80	**LET'S GET SERIOUS** *Motown TMG 1183*	8		11
26 Jul 80	**BURNIN' HOT** *Motown TMG 1194*	32		6
30 May 81	**YOU LIKE ME DON'T YOU** *Motown TMG 1222*	41		5
12 May 84	**SWEETEST SWEETEST** *Arista JJK 1*	52		4
27 Oct 84	**WHEN THE RAIN BEGINS TO FALL** *Arista ARIST 584* & PIA ZADORA	68		2
16 Feb 85	**DO WHAT YOU DO** *Arista ARIST 609* ●	6		13
21 Oct 89	**DON'T TAKE IT PERSONAL** *Arista 112634*	69		2

JOE JACKSON

UK, male vocalist/pianist

Date	Title	Peak Position	Weeks at No.1	49
4 Aug 79	**IS SHE REALLY GOING OUT WITH HIM?** *A&M AMS 7459*	13		9
12 Jan 80	**IT'S DIFFERENT FOR GIRLS** *A&M AMS 7493* ●	5		9
4 Jul 81	**JUMPIN' JIVE** *A&M AMS 8145* JOE JACKSON'S JUMPIN' JIVE	43		5
8 Jan 83	**STEPPIN' OUT** *A&M AMS 8262*	6		8
12 Mar 83	**BREAKING US IN TWO** *A&M AM 101*	59		4
28 Apr 84	**HAPPY ENDING** *A&M AM 186*	58		3
7 Jul 84	**BE MY NUMBER TWO** *A&M AM 200*	70		2
7 Jun 86	**LEFT OF CENTER** *A&M AM 320* SUZANNE VEGA FEATURING JOE JACKSON	32		9

LEON JACKSON

UK, male vocalist

Date	Title	Peak Position	Weeks at No.1	13
29 Dec 07	**WHEN YOU BELIEVE** *Syco Music 88697220162*	1	3	9
25 Oct 08	**DON'T CALL THIS LOVE** *Syco Music 88697395232*	3		4

MICHAEL JACKSON

US, male vocalist/producer/dancer, d. 25 Jun 2009 (age 50). Among his numerous chart achievements, the 'King of Pop' was the first US act to enter the UK chart at No.1 since Elvis Presley with 'Black Or White' and, at $7 million, 'Scream' remains the most expensive music video of all time. In the weeks after his death, 50 of his songs flooded the UK Top 200, boosting his total UK singles sales to 14.3 million. See Jacksons

Date	Title	Peak Position	Weeks at No.1	662
12 Feb 72	**GOT TO BE THERE** *Tamla Motown TMG 797*	5		11
20 May 72	**ROCKIN' ROBIN** *Tamla Motown TMG 816*	3		14
19 Aug 72	**AIN'T NO SUNSHINE** *Tamla Motown TMG 826*	8		11
25 Nov 72	**BEN** *Tamla Motown TMG 834* ★	7		14
18 Nov 78	**EASE ON DOWN THE ROAD** *MCA 396* DIANA ROSS & MICHAEL JACKSON	45		4
15 Sep 79	**DON'T STOP 'TIL YOU GET ENOUGH** *Epic EPC 7763* ● ★	3		12
24 Nov 79	**OFF THE WALL** *Epic EPC 8045*	7		10
9 Feb 80	**ROCK WITH YOU** *Epic EPC 8206* ★	7		9
3 May 80	**SHE'S OUT OF MY LIFE** *Epic EPC 8384*	3		9
26 Jul 80	**GIRLFRIEND** *Epic EPC 8782*	41		5
23 May 81	**ONE DAY IN YOUR LIFE** *Motown TMG 976* ●	1	2	14
1 Aug 81	**WE'RE ALMOST THERE** *Motown TMG 977*	46		4
6 Nov 82	**THE GIRL IS MINE** *Epic A 2729* & PAUL McCARTNEY	8		10
29 Jan 83	**BILLIE JEAN** *Epic EPC A 3084* ● ★	1	1	15
9 Apr 83	**BEAT IT** *Epic EPC A 3258* ● ★	3		12

Acts With The Most Top 40 Hits

Pos	Artist	No. Top 40 Hits
1	ELVIS PRESLEY	146
2	CLIFF RICHARD	124
3	MICHAEL JACKSON	85
4	MADONNA	71
5	ELTON JOHN	69
6	SHADOWS	61
7	DAVID BOWIE	60
8	DIANA ROSS	58
9	STATUS QUO	56
10	QUEEN	54
11	PAUL McCARTNEY/WINGS	48
12	ROD STEWART	47
13	PET SHOP BOYS	45
14	DEPECHE MODE	43
=	KYLIE MINOGUE	43
=	PRINCE	43
=	ROLLING STONES	43
18	U2	42
19	MARIAH CAREY	41
=	STEVIE WONDER	41
21	UB40	40
22	BEATLES	38
=	JANET JACKSON	38
24	TOM JONES	37
25	BON JOVI	36
26	ERASURE	35
=	IRON MAIDEN	35
=	SHAKIN' STEVENS	35
29	R KELLY	34
=	GEORGE MICHAEL	34
=	FRANK SINATRA	34
32	WHITNEY HOUSTON	33
=	JAY-Z	33
=	MANIC STREET PREACHERS	33
=	MORRISSEY	33
36	NAT 'KING' COLE	32
=	SIMPLY RED	32
38	BEE GEES	31
=	LONNIE DONEGAN	31
=	ROY ORBISON	31
=	R.E.M.	31
=	SLADE	31
=	PAUL WELLER	31
=	ROBBIE WILLIAMS	31
45	MARY J BLIGE	30
=	DURAN DURAN	30
=	FOUR TOPS	30
=	MADNESS	30
=	SUPREMES	30
=	TINA TURNER	30

Silver-selling ○ Gold-selling ● Platinum-selling (x multiples) ⊛ US No.1 ★

Date	Title	Peak Position	Weeks at No.1	Weeks on Chart
11 Jun 83	**WANNA BE STARTIN' SOMETHING** *Epic A 3427*	8		9
23 Jul 83	**HAPPY (LOVE THEME FROM 'LADY SINGS THE BLUES')** *Tamla Motown TMG 986*	52		3
15 Oct 83	**SAY SAY SAY** *Parlophone R 6062* PAUL McCARTNEY & MICHAEL JACKSON ○ ★	2		15
19 Nov 83	**THRILLER** *Epic A 3643* ○	10		18
31 Mar 84	**P.Y.T. (PRETTY YOUNG THING)** *Epic A 4136*	11		8
2 Jun 84	**FAREWELL MY SUMMER LOVE** *Motown TMG 1342*	7		12
7 Jul 84	**STATE OF SHOCK** *Epic A 4431* JACKSONS, LEAD VOCALS MICK JAGGER & MICHAEL JACKSON	14		8
11 Aug 84	**GIRL YOU'RE SO TOGETHER** *Motown TMG 1355*	33		8
8 Aug 87	**I JUST CAN'T STOP LOVING YOU** *Epic 6502027* ★	1	2	9
26 Sep 87	**BAD** *Epic 6511557* ★	3		11
5 Dec 87	**THE WAY YOU MAKE ME FEEL** *Epic 6512757* ★	3		10
20 Feb 88	**MAN IN THE MIRROR** *Epic 6513887* ★	21		5
16 Apr 88	**I WANT YOU BACK** *Motown ZB 41913* & THE JACKSON 5	8		9
28 May 88	**GET IT** *Motown ZB 41883* STEVIE WONDER & MICHAEL JACKSON	37		4
16 Jul 88	**DIRTY DIANA** *Epic 6515467* ★	4		8
10 Sep 88	**ANOTHER PART OF ME** *Epic 6528447*	15		6
26 Nov 88	**SMOOTH CRIMINAL** *Epic 6530267*	8		10
25 Feb 89	**LEAVE ME ALONE** *Epic 6546727*	2		9
15 Jul 89	**LIBERIAN GIRL** *Epic 6549470*	13		6
23 Nov 91	**BLACK OR WHITE** *Epic 6575987* ○ ★	1	2	10
18 Jan 92	**BLACK OR WHITE** *Epic 6577316*	14		4
15 Feb 92	**REMEMBER THE TIME/COME TOGETHER** *Epic 6577747*	3		8
2 May 92	**IN THE CLOSET** *Epic 6580187*	8		6
25 Jul 92	**WHO IS IT** *Epic 6581797*	10		7
12 Sep 92	**JAM** *Epic 6583607*	13		5
5 Dec 92	**HEAL THE WORLD** *Epic 6584887* ●	2		15
27 Feb 93	**GIVE IN TO ME** *Epic 6590692*	2		9
10 Jul 93	**WILL YOU BE THERE** *Epic 6592222*	9		8
18 Dec 93	**GONE TOO SOON** *Epic 6599762*	33		5
10 Jun 95	**SCREAM** *Epic 6620222* & JANET JACKSON	3		13
24 Jun 95	**SCREAM (REMIX)** *Epic 6621277* & JANET JACKSON	43		2
2 Sep 95	**YOU ARE NOT ALONE** *Epic 6623102* ● ★	1	2	15
9 Dec 95	**EARTH SONG** *Epic 6626955* ⊛	1	6	17
20 Apr 96	**THEY DON'T CARE ABOUT US** *Epic 6629502* ○	4		14
24 Aug 96	**WHY** *Epic 6636482* 3T FEATURING MICHAEL JACKSON	2		9
16 Nov 96	**STRANGER IN MOSCOW** *Epic 6637872*	4		11
3 May 97	**BLOOD ON THE DANCE FLOOR** *Epic 6644625*	1	1	9
19 Jul 97	**HISTORY/GHOSTS** *Epic 6647962*	5		8
20 Oct 01	**YOU ROCK MY WORLD** *Epic 6720292*	2		15
22 Dec 01	**CRY** *Epic 6721822*	25		4
6 Dec 03	**ONE MORE CHANCE** *Epic 6744805*	5		7
4 Mar 06	**DON'T STOP 'TIL YOU GET ENOUGH** *Epic 82876725112*	17		2
11 Mar 06	**ROCK WITH YOU** *Epic 82876725132*	15		2
18 Mar 06	**BILLIE JEAN** *Epic 82876725172*	11		5
25 Mar 06	**BEAT IT** *Epic 82876725182*	15		2
1 Apr 06	**BAD** *Epic 82876725242*	16		2
8 Apr 06	**THE WAY YOU MAKE ME FEEL** *Epic 82876725252*	17		2
15 Apr 06	**DIRTY DIANA** *Epic 82876725272*	17		2
22 Apr 06	**SMOOTH CRIMINAL** *Epic 82876725292*	19		3
29 Apr 06	**LEAVE ME ALONE** *Epic 82876725302*	15		2
6 May 06	**BLACK OR WHITE** *Epic 82876773302*	18		2
13 May 06	**REMEMBER THE TIME** *Epic 82876773322*	22		2
20 May 06	**IN THE CLOSET** *Epic 82876773342*	20		2
27 May 06	**JAM** *Epic 82876773362*	22		1
3 Jun 06	**HEAL THE WORLD** *Epic 82876773382*	27		1
10 Jun 06	**YOU ARE NOT ALONE** *Epic 82876773402*	30		1
17 Jun 06	**EARTH SONG** *Epic 82876773422*	34		1
24 Jun 06	**THEY DON'T CARE ABOUT US** *Epic 82876773442*	26		1
1 Jul 06	**STRANGER IN MOSCOW** *Epic 82876773462*	22		1
8 Jul 06	**BLOOD ON THE DANCE FLOOR** *Epic 82876773482*	19		1
10 Nov 07	**THRILLER** *Epic USSM19902989*	57		1
2 Feb 08	**THE GIRL IS MINE** *Epic 88697226202* FEATURING WILL.I.AM	32		5
1 Mar 08	**WANNA BE STARTIN' SOMETHING 2008** *Epic USSM10800553* WITH AKON	69		1
1 Nov 08	**MAN IN THE MIRROR** *Epic 6513886*	55		1
8 Nov 08	**THRILLER** *Epic USSM19902989*	35		1
4 Jul 09	**MAN IN THE MIRROR** *Epic 6513886*	2		15
4 Jul 09	**THRILLER** *Epic USSM19902989*	12		7
4 Jul 09	**BILLIE JEAN** *Epic 82876725172*	10		8
4 Jul 09	**SMOOTH CRIMINAL** *Epic 82876725292*	13		7
4 Jul 09	**BEAT IT** *Epic 82876725182*	19		6
4 Jul 09	**EARTH SONG** *Epic 82876773422*	33		4
4 Jul 09	**YOU ARE NOT ALONE** *Epic 82876773402*	35		4
4 Jul 09	**BLACK OR WHITE** *Epic 82876773302*	25		5
4 Jul 09	**THE WAY YOU MAKE ME FEEL** *Epic 82876725252*	34		4
4 Jul 09	**DON'T STOP 'TIL YOU GET ENOUGH** *Epic 82876725112*	38		4
4 Jul 09	**DIRTY DIANA** *Epic 82876725272*	26		5
4 Jul 09	**BAD** *Epic 82876725242*	40		4
4 Jul 09	**BEN** *Motown USMO17200267*	46		3
4 Jul 09	**THEY DON'T CARE ABOUT US** *Epic 82876773442*	28		5
4 Jul 09	**WANNA BE STARTIN' SOMETHIN'** *Epic USSM19902986*	57		2
4 Jul 09	**ROCK WITH YOU** *Epic 82876725132*	54		2

Date	Title	Peak Position	Weeks at No.1	Weeks on Chart
11 Jul 09	**YOU ROCK MY WORLD** *Epic 6720292*	60		1
11 Jul 09	**HEAL THE WORLD** *Epic 82876773382*	44		2
11 Jul 09	**LEAVE ME ALONE** *Epic 82876725302*	66		1
11 Jul 09	**SCREAM** *Epic 6620222* & JANET JACKSON	70		1
11 Jul 09	**OFF THE WALL** *Epic USSM17900820*	73		1
11 Jul 09	**GIVE IN TO ME** *Epic 6590692*	74		1
18 Jul 09	**WILL YOU BE THERE** *Epic USSM10020712*	51		1
18 Jul 09	**HUMAN NATURE** *Epic USSM19902992*	62		1
18 Jul 09	**SMILE** *Epic USSM19500015*	74		1

Top 3 Best-Selling Singles

		Approximate Sales
1	EARTH SONG	1,140,000
2	BILLIE JEAN	870,000
3	ONE DAY IN YOUR LIFE	810,000

MICK JACKSON
UK, male vocalist — 16

Date	Title	Peak Position	Weeks at No.1	Weeks on Chart
30 Sep 78	**BLAME IT ON THE BOOGIE** *Atlantic K 11102*	15		8
3 Feb 79	**WEEKEND** *Atlantic K 11224*	38		8

MILLIE JACKSON
US, female vocalist — 8

Date	Title	Peak Position	Weeks at No.1	Weeks on Chart
18 Nov 72	**MY MAN A SWEET MAN** *Mojo 2093 022*	50		1
10 Mar 84	**I FEEL LIKE WALKIN' IN THE RAIN** *Sire W 9348*	55		2
15 Jun 85	**ACT OF WAR** *Rocket EJS 8* ELTON JOHN & MILLIE JACKSON	32		5

PAUL JACKSON & STEVE SMITH
UK, male vocal/production duo — 2

Date	Title	Peak Position	Weeks at No.1	Weeks on Chart
24 Jan 04	**THE PUSH (FAR FROM HERE)** *Underwater H2O041CD*	51		2

JACKSON SISTERS
US, female vocal group — 2

Date	Title	Peak Position	Weeks at No.1	Weeks on Chart
20 Jun 87	**I BELIEVE IN MIRACLES** *Urban URB 4*	72		2

STONEWALL JACKSON
US, male vocalist — 2

Date	Title	Peak Position	Weeks at No.1	Weeks on Chart
17 Jul 59	**WATERLOO** *Philips PB 941*	24		2

TONY JACKSON & THE VIBRATIONS
UK, male vocal/instrumental group – leader d. 18 Aug 2003. See Searchers — 3

Date	Title	Peak Position	Weeks at No.1	Weeks on Chart
8 Oct 64	**BYE BYE BABY** *Pye 7N 15685*	38		3

WANDA JACKSON
US, female vocalist — 11

Date	Title	Peak Position	Weeks at No.1	Weeks on Chart
1 Sep 60	**LET'S HAVE A PARTY** *Capitol CL 15147*	32		8
26 Jan 61	**MEAN MEAN MAN** *Capitol CL 15176*	40		3

JACKSON 5
US, male vocal group – Michael (Michael Jackson*), d. 25 Jun 2009, Jackie, Jermaine (Jermaine Jackson*), Marlon, Randy (joined 1977) & Tito Jackson. The group that introduced the world to Michael Jackson sold a reported 100 million records and saw their first four singles all top the US chart — 253

Date	Title	Peak Position	Weeks at No.1	Weeks on Chart
31 Jan 70	**I WANT YOU BACK** *Tamla Motown TMG 724* ★	2		13
16 May 70	**ABC** *Tamla Motown TMG 738* ★	8		11
1 Aug 70	**THE LOVE YOU SAVE** *Tamla Motown TMG 746* ★	7		9
21 Nov 70	**I'LL BE THERE** *Tamla Motown TMG 758* ★	4		16
10 Apr 71	**MAMA'S PEARL** *Tamla Motown TMG 769*	25		7
17 Jul 71	**NEVER CAN SAY GOODBYE** *Tamla Motown TMG 778*	33		7
11 Nov 72	**LOOKIN' THROUGH THE WINDOWS** *Tamla Motown TMG 833*	9		11
23 Dec 72	**SANTA CLAUS IS COMING TO TOWN** *Tamla Motown TMG 837*	43		3
17 Feb 73	**DOCTOR MY EYES** *Tamla Motown TMG 842*	9		10
9 Jun 73	**HALLELUJAH DAY** *Tamla Motown TMG 856*	20		9
8 Sep 73	**SKYWRITER** *Tamla Motown TMG 865*	25		8
9 Apr 77	**ENJOY YOURSELF** *Epic EPC 5063* JACKSONS	42		4
4 Jun 77	**SHOW YOU THE WAY TO GO** *Epic EPC 5266* JACKSONS ●	1	1	10
13 Aug 77	**DREAMER** *Epic EPC 5458* JACKSONS	22		9
5 Nov 77	**GOIN' PLACES** *Epic EPC 5732* JACKSONS	26		7
11 Feb 78	**EVEN THOUGH YOU'VE GONE** *Epic EPC 5919* JACKSONS	31		4
23 Sep 78	**BLAME IT ON THE BOOGIE** *Epic EPC 6683* JACKSONS ●	8		12
3 Feb 79	**DESTINY** *Epic EPC 6983* JACKSONS	39		6
24 Mar 79	**SHAKE YOUR BODY (DOWN TO THE GROUND)** *Epic EPC 7181* JACKSONS ●	4		12
25 Oct 80	**LOVELY ONE** *Epic EPC 9302* JACKSONS	29		6
13 Dec 80	**HEARTBREAK HOTEL** *Epic EPC 9391* JACKSONS	44		6
28 Feb 81	**CAN YOU FEEL IT** *Epic EPC 9554* JACKSONS ●	6		15
4 Jul 81	**WALK RIGHT NOW** *Epic EPC A 1294* JACKSONS	7		11
7 Jul 84	**STATE OF SHOCK** *Epic A 4431* JACKSONS, LEAD VOCALS MICK JAGGER & MICHAEL JACKSON	14		8
8 Sep 84	**TORTURE** *Epic A 4675* JACKSONS	26		6
16 Apr 88	**I WANT YOU BACK** *Motown ZB 41913* MICHAEL JACKSON & THE JACKSON 5	8		9
13 May 89	**NOTHIN' (THAT COMPARES 2 U)** *Epic 6548087* JACKSONS	33		6
27 Jan 07	**I WANT YOU BACK** *Motown USMO16900464*	53		2
2 May 09	**WHO'S LOVIN' YOU** *Motown USMO16982624*	54		1
4 Jul 09	**I WANT YOU BACK** *Motown USMO16900464*	43		3
4 Jul 09	**ABC** *Motown USMO17082628*	50		4
4 Jul 09	**I'LL BE THERE** *Motown USM017000497*	65		3
4 Jul 09	**BLAME IT ON THE BOOGIE** *Sony Music USSM17800445* JACKSONS	55		2
11 Jul 09	**CAN YOU FEEL IT** *Sony Music USSM19803304* JACKSONS	59		1
18 Jul 09	**WHO'S LOVIN' YOU** *Motown USMO16982624*	36		2

JADE
US, female vocal trio — 28

Date	Title	Peak Position	Weeks at No.1	Weeks on Chart
20 Mar 93	**DON'T WALK AWAY** *Giant W 0160CD*	7		8
3 Jul 93	**I WANNA LOVE YOU** *Giant 74321151662*	13		7
18 Sep 93	**ONE WOMAN** *Giant 74321165122*	22		5
5 Feb 94	**ALL THRU THE NITE** *Giant 74321187552* P.O.V. FEATURING JADE	32		3
11 Feb 95	**EVERY DAY OF THE WEEK** *Giant 74321260242*	19		5

JAGGED EDGE
UK, male vocal/instrumental group — 2

Date	Title	Peak Position	Weeks at No.1	Weeks on Chart
15 Sep 90	**YOU DON'T LOVE ME** *Polydor PO 97*	66		2

JAGGED EDGE
US, male vocal group – Brandon & Brian Casey, Kyle Norman & Richard Wingo. See Nivea — 27

Date	Title	Peak Position	Weeks at No.1	Weeks on Chart
27 Oct 01	**WHERE'S THE PARTY AT** *Columbia 6719012* FEATURING NELLY	25		3
21 Feb 04	**WALKED OUTTA HEAVEN** *Columbia 6745452*	21		5
28 Jan 06	**NASTY GIRL** *Bad Boy AT0229CDX* NOTORIOUS B.I.G. FEATURING DIDDY, NELLY, JAGGED EDGE AND AVERY STORM	1	2	19

MICK JAGGER
UK, male vocalist. See Rolling Stones — 45

Date	Title	Peak Position	Weeks at No.1	Weeks on Chart
14 Nov 70	**MEMO FROM TURNER** *Decca F 13067*	32		5
7 Jul 84	**STATE OF SHOCK** *Epic A 4431* JACKSONS, LEAD VOCALS MICK JAGGER & MICHAEL JACKSON	14		8
16 Feb 85	**JUST ANOTHER NIGHT** *CBS A 4722*	32		6
7 Sep 85	**DANCING IN THE STREET** *EMI America EA 204* DAVID BOWIE & MICK JAGGER ●	1	4	12
12 Sep 87	**LET'S WORK** *CBS 6510287*	31		7
6 Feb 93	**SWEET THING** *Atlantic A 7410CD*	24		4
23 Mar 02	**VISIONS OF PARADISE** *Virgin VUSCD 240*	43		1
6 Nov 04	**OLD HABITS DIE HARD** *Virgin VSCDX1887* & DAVE STEWART	45		2

JAGS
UK, male vocal/instrumental group — 11

Date	Title	Peak Position	Weeks at No.1	Weeks on Chart
8 Sep 79	**BACK OF MY HAND** *Island WIP 6501*	17		10
2 Feb 80	**WOMAN'S WORLD** *Island WIP 6531*	75		1

JAHEIM
US, male rapper (Jaheim Hoagland) — 10

Date	Title	Peak Position	Weeks at No.1	Weeks on Chart
24 Mar 01	**COULD IT BE** *Warner Brothers W 551CDX*	33		3
11 Aug 01	**JUST IN CASE** *Warner Brothers W 564CDX*	34		2
29 Jun 02	**JUST IN CASE** *Warner Brothers W 581CD*	38		3
8 Mar 03	**FABULOUS** *Warner Brothers W 598CD*	41		2

JAIMESON
UK, male producer (Jamie Williams) — 24

Date	Title	Peak Position	Weeks at No.1	Weeks on Chart
14 Sep 02	**SELECTA (URBAN HEROES)** *Soundproof SPR 1CD* JAMESON & VIPER	51		1
25 Jan 03	**TRUE** *V2/J-Did JAD 5021363* FEATURING ANGEL BLU	4		10

Silver-selling | Gold-selling | Platinum-selling (x multiples) | US No.1 | Peak Position | Weeks at No.1 | Weeks on Chart

Date	Title	Peak Position	Weeks at No.1	Weeks on Chart
23 Aug 03	**COMPLETE** *V2/J-Did JAD 5021713*	4		8
7 Feb 04	**TAKE CONTROL** *V2/J-Did JAD 5021738* & CK	16		5

JAKATTA

UK, male producer (Dave Lee). See Li Kwan, Joey Negro, Phase II — 30

Date	Title	Peak Position	Weeks at No.1	Weeks on Chart
24 Feb 01	**AMERICAN DREAM** *Rulin 15CDS*	3		14
11 Aug 01	**AMERICAN DREAM (REMIX)** *Rulin 20CDS*	63		1
16 Feb 02	**SO LONELY** *Rulin 25CDS*	8		5
12 Oct 02	**MY VISION** *Rulin 26CDS* FEATURING SEAL	6		8
1 Mar 03	**ONE FINE DAY** *Rulin 29CDX*	39		2

J.A.L.N. BAND

UK, male vocal/instrumental group — 17

Date	Title	Peak Position	Weeks at No.1	Weeks on Chart
11 Sep 76	**DISCO MUSIC (I LIKE IT)** *Magnet MAG 73*	21		9
27 Aug 77	**I GOT TO SING** *Magnet MAG 97*	40		4
1 Jul 78	**GET UP** *Magnet MAG 118*	53		4

JAM

UK, male vocal/instrumental trio – Paul Weller*, Rick Buckler & Bruce Foxton* — 204

Date	Title	Peak Position	Weeks at No.1	Weeks on Chart
7 May 77	**IN THE CITY** *Polydor 2058 866*	40		6
23 Jul 77	**ALL AROUND THE WORLD** *Polydor 2058 903*	13		8
5 Nov 77	**THE MODERN WORLD** *Polydor 2058 945*	36		4
11 Mar 78	**NEWS OF THE WORLD** *Polydor 2058 995*	27		5
26 Aug 78	**DAVID WATTS/'A' BOMB IN WARDOUR STREET** *Polydor 2059 054*	25		8
21 Oct 78	**DOWN IN THE TUBE STATION AT MIDNIGHT** *Polydor POSP 8*	15		7
17 Mar 79	**STRANGE TOWN** *Polydor POSP 34*	15		9
25 Aug 79	**WHEN YOU'RE YOUNG** *Polydor POSP 69*	17		7
3 Nov 79	**THE ETON RIFLES** *Polydor POSP 83*	3		12
22 Mar 80	**GOING UNDERGROUND/DREAMS OF CHILDREN** *Polydor POSP 113*	1	3	9
26 Apr 80	**ALL AROUND THE WORLD** *Polydor 2058 903*	43		3
26 Apr 80	**DAVID WATTS/'A' BOMB IN WARDOUR STREET** *Polydor 2059 054*	54		3
26 Apr 80	**IN THE CITY** *Polydor 2058 866*	40		4
26 Apr 80	**NEWS OF THE WORLD** *Polydor 2058 995*	53		3
26 Apr 80	**STRANGE TOWN** *Polydor POSP 34*	44		4
26 Apr 80	**THE MODERN WORLD** *Polydor 2058 945*	52		3
23 Aug 80	**START** *Polydor 2059 266*	1	1	8
7 Feb 81	**THAT'S ENTERTAINMENT** *Metronome 0030 364*	21		7
6 Jun 81	**FUNERAL PYRE** *Polydor POSP 257*	4		6
24 Oct 81	**ABSOLUTE BEGINNERS** *Polydor POSP 350*	4		6
13 Feb 82	**A TOWN CALLED MALICE/PRECIOUS** *Polydor POSP 400*	1	3	8
3 Jul 82	**JUST WHO IS THE FIVE O'CLOCK HERO** *Polydor 2059 504*	8		5
18 Sep 82	**THE BITTEREST PILL (I EVER HAD TO SWALLOW)** *Polydor POSP 505*	2		7
4 Dec 82	**BEAT SURRENDER** *Polydor POSP 540*	1	2	9
22 Jan 83	**ALL AROUND THE WORLD** *Polydor 2058 903*	38		4
22 Jan 83	**DAVID WATTS/'A' BOMB IN WARDOUR STREET** *Polydor 2059 054*	50		4
22 Jan 83	**DOWN IN THE TUBE STATION AT MIDNIGHT** *Polydor POSP 8*	30		6
22 Jan 83	**GOING UNDERGROUND/DREAMS OF CHILDREN** *Polydor POSP 113*	21		4
22 Jan 83	**IN THE CITY** *Polydor 2058 866*	47		4
22 Jan 83	**STRANGE TOWN** *Polydor POSP 34*	42		5
22 Jan 83	**NEWS OF THE WORLD** *Polydor 2058 995*	39		4
22 Jan 83	**THE MODERN WORLD** *Polydor 2058 945*	51		4
22 Jan 83	**WHEN YOU'RE YOUNG** *Polydor POSP 69*	53		4
29 Jan 83	**THAT'S ENTERTAINMENT** *Polydor POSP 482*	60		3
5 Feb 83	**START** *Polydor 2059 266*	62		2
5 Feb 83	**THE ETON RIFLES** *Polydor POSP 83*	54		3
5 Feb 83	**A TOWN CALLED MALICE/PRECIOUS** *Polydor POSP 400*	73		1
29 Jun 91	**THAT'S ENTERTAINMENT** *Polydor PO 155*	57		2
11 Oct 97	**THE BITTEREST PILL (I EVER HAD TO SWALLOW)** *Polydor 5715992*	30		2
11 May 02	**IN THE CITY** *Polydor 5876117*	36		1

JAM & SPOON

Germany, male production duo – Ralf 'Jam El Mar' Ellmer & Markus 'Mark Spoon' Loeffel, d. 11 Jan 2006 – & US, female vocalist (Plavka Lonich) — 26

Date	Title	Peak Position	Weeks at No.1	Weeks on Chart
2 May 92	**TALES FROM A DANCEOGRAPHIC OCEAN (EP)** *R&S RSUK 14*	49		1
6 Jun 92	**THE COMPLETE STELLA (REMIX)** *R&S RSUK 14X*	66		2
26 Feb 94	**RIGHT IN THE NIGHT (FALL IN LOVE WITH MUSIC)** *Epic 6600822* FEATURING PLAVKA	31		4
24 Sep 94	**FIND ME (ODYSSEY TO ANYOONA)** *Epic 6608082* FEATURING PLAVKA	37		3
10 Jun 95	**RIGHT IN THE NIGHT (FALL IN LOVE WITH MUSIC)** *Epic 6620182* FEATURING PLAVKA	10		8
16 Sep 95	**FIND ME (ODYSSEY TO ANYOONA)** *Epic 6623242* FEATURING PLAVKA	22		3
25 Nov 95	**ANGEL (LADADI O-HEYO)** *Epic 6626382* FEATURING PLAVKA	26		2
30 Aug 97	**KALEIDOSCOPE SKIES** *Epic 6647612* FEATURING PLAVKA	48		1
2 Mar 02	**BE ANGLED** *NuLife 74321878992* FEATURING REA	31		2

JAM MACHINE

Italy, male production group — 1

Date	Title	Peak Position	Weeks at No.1	Weeks on Chart
23 Dec 89	**EVERYDAY** *Deconstruction PB 43299*	68		1

JAM ON THE MUTHA

UK, male vocal/production group — 2

Date	Title	Peak Position	Weeks at No.1	Weeks on Chart
11 Aug 90	**HOTEL CALIFORNIA** *M&G MAGS 3*	62		2

JAM TRONIK

Germany, male/female production/vocal duo — 7

Date	Title	Peak Position	Weeks at No.1	Weeks on Chart
24 Mar 90	**ANOTHER DAY IN PARADISE** *Debut DEBT 3093*	19		7

JAMAICA UNITED

Jamaica, male vocal ensemble — 1

Date	Title	Peak Position	Weeks at No.1	Weeks on Chart
4 Jul 98	**RISE UP** *Columbia 6660522*	54		1

JAMELIA

UK, female vocalist (Jamelia Davis) — 97

Date	Title	Peak Position	Weeks at No.1	Weeks on Chart
31 Jul 99	**I DO** *Parlophone Rhythm CDRHYTHM 21*	36		2
4 Mar 00	**MONEY** *Parlophone Rhythm CDRHYTHM 27* FEATURING BEENIE MAN	5		9
24 Jun 00	**CALL ME** *Parlophone Rhythm CDRHYTHS 28*	11		5
21 Oct 00	**BOY NEXT DOOR** *Parlophone Rhythm CDRHYTHS 29*	42		2
21 Jun 03	**BOUT** *Parlophone CDRS 6597* FEATURING RAH DIGGA	37		2
27 Sep 03	**SUPERSTAR** *Parlophone CDRS 6615*	3		20
6 Mar 04	**THANK YOU** *Parlophone CDRS 6621*	2		14
24 Jul 04	**SEE IT IN A BOY'S EYES** *Parlophone CDRS 6635*	5		11
13 Nov 04	**DJ/STOP** *Parlophone CDR 6646*	9		12
16 Sep 06	**SOMETHING ABOUT YOU** *Parlophone CDR6713*	9		10
9 Dec 06	**BEWARE OF THE DOG** *Parlophone CDR6727*	10		8
31 Mar 07	**NO MORE** *Parlophone CDR6736*	43		2

JAMES

UK, male vocal/instrumental group – Tim Booth*, David Baynton-Power, Saul Davies, Andy Diagram, Jim Glennie, Larry Gott & Mark Hunter — 89

Date	Title	Peak Position	Weeks at No.1	Weeks on Chart
12 May 90	**HOW WAS IT FOR YOU** *Fontana JIM 5*	32		3
7 Jul 90	**COME HOME** *Fontana JIM 6*	32		4
8 Dec 90	**LOSE CONTROL** *Fontana JIM 7*	38		5
30 Mar 91	**SIT DOWN** *Fontana JIM 8*	2		10
30 Nov 91	**SOUND** *Fontana JIM 9*	9		7
1 Feb 92	**BORN OF FRUSTRATION** *Fontana JIM 10*	13		6
4 Apr 92	**RING THE BELLS** *Fontana JIM 11*	37		2
18 Jul 92	**SEVEN (EP)** *Fontana JIM 12*	46		2
11 Sep 93	**SOMETIMES** *Fontana JIMCD 13*	18		4
13 Nov 93	**LAID** *Fontana JIMCD 14*	25		4
2 Apr 94	**JAM J/SAY SOMETHING** *Fontana JIMCD 152*	24		4
22 Feb 97	**SHE'S A STAR** *Fontana JIMCD 16*	9		5
3 May 97	**TOMORROW** *Fontana JIMCD 17*	12		3
5 Jul 97	**WALTZING ALONG** *Fontana JIMCD 18*	23		4
21 Mar 98	**DESTINY CALLING** *Fontana JIMCD 19*	17		4
6 Jun 98	**RUNAGROUND** *Fontana JIMCD 20*	29		2
21 Nov 98	**SIT DOWN** *Fontana JIMCD 21*	7		7
31 Jul 99	**I KNOW WHAT I'M HERE FOR** *Fontana JIMDD 22*	22		5
16 Oct 99	**JUST LIKE FRED ASTAIRE** *Mercury JIMCD 23*	17		3
25 Dec 99	**WE'RE GOING TO MISS YOU** *Mercury JIMCD 24*	48		2
7 Jul 01	**GETTING AWAY WITH IT (ALL MESSED UP)** *Mercury JIMDD 25*	22		3

DAVID JAMES

UK, male DJ/producer — 1

Date	Title	Peak Position	Weeks at No.1	Weeks on Chart
11 Aug 01	**ALWAYS A PERMANENT STATE** *Hooj Choons HOOJ 108CD*	60		1

DICK JAMES

UK, male vocalist (Isaac Vapnic), d. 1 Feb 1986 (age 65) — 13

Date	Title	Peak Position	Weeks at No.1	Weeks on Chart
20 Jan 56	**ROBIN HOOD** *Parlophone R 4117*	14		8
18 May 56	**ROBIN HOOD/BALLAD OF DAVY CROCKETT** *Parlophone R 4117*	29		1
11 Jan 57	**GARDEN OF EDEN** *Parlophone R 4255*	18		4

DUNCAN JAMES

UK, male vocalist. See Blue — 10

Date	Title	Peak Position	Weeks at No.1	Weeks on Chart
23 Oct 04	**I BELIEVE MY HEART** *Innocent 8677122* & KEEDIE	2		7
17 Jun 06	**SOONER OR LATER** *Innocent SINCD78*	35		2

Date	Title	Peak Position	Weeks at No.1	Weeks on Chart
2 Sep 06	**CAN'T STOP A RIVER** *Innocent ANGEDX17*	59		1

ETTA JAMES
US, female vocalist (Jamesetta Hawkins) — 7

Date	Title	Peak Position	Weeks at No.1	Weeks on Chart
10 Feb 96	**I JUST WANT TO MAKE LOVE TO YOU** *Chess MCSTD 48003*	5		7

FREDDIE JAMES
Canada, male vocalist — 3

Date	Title	Peak Position	Weeks at No.1	Weeks on Chart
24 Nov 79	**GET UP AND BOOGIE** *Warner Brothers K 17478*	54		3

JONI JAMES
US, female vocalist (Joan Babbo) — 2

Date	Title	Peak Position	Weeks at No.1	Weeks on Chart
6 Mar 53	**WHY DON'T YOU BELIEVE ME** *MGM 582* ★	11		1
30 Jan 59	**THERE MUST BE A WAY** *MGM 1002*	24		1

NATE JAMES
UK, male vocalist — 3

Date	Title	Peak Position	Weeks at No.1	Weeks on Chart
19 Mar 05	**SET THE TONE** *4/Onetwo ONETCDS001*	69		1
25 Jun 05	**LOVIN' YOU** *Positiva CDTIVS218* POKER PETS FEATURING NATE JAMES	43		1
30 May 05	**UNIVERSAL** *4/Onetwo ONETCDX002*	72		1

RICK JAMES
US, male vocalist (James Johnson), d. 6 Aug 2004 (age 56) — 30

Date	Title	Peak Position	Weeks at No.1	Weeks on Chart
8 Jul 78	**YOU AND I** *Motown TMG 1110*	46		7
7 Jul 79	**I'M A SUCKER FOR YOUR LOVE** *Motown TMG 1146* TEENA MARIE, CO-LEAD VOCALS RICK JAMES	43		8
6 Sep 80	**BIG TIME** *Motown TMG 1198*	41		6
4 Jul 81	**GIVE IT TO ME BABY** *Motown TMG 1229*	47		3
12 Jun 82	**STANDING ON THE TOP (PART 1)** *Motown TMG 1263* TEMPTATIONS FEATURING RICK JAMES	53		3
3 Jul 82	**DANCE WIT ME** *Motown TMG 1266*	53		3

SONNY JAMES
US, male vocalist (James Loden) — 8

Date	Title	Peak Position	Weeks at No.1	Weeks on Chart
30 Nov 56	**THE CAT CAME BACK** *Capitol CL 14635*	30		1
8 Feb 57	**YOUNG LOVE** *Capitol CL 14683* ★	11		7

TYLER JAMES
UK, male vocalist — 9

Date	Title	Peak Position	Weeks at No.1	Weeks on Chart
13 Nov 04	**WHY DO I DO** *Island/Uni-Island CID872*	25		4
19 Mar 05	**FOOLISH** *Island CID884*	16		4
3 Sep 05	**YOUR WOMAN** *Island CIDX900*	60		1

WENDY JAMES
UK, female vocalist. See Transvision Vamp — 4

Date	Title	Peak Position	Weeks at No.1	Weeks on Chart
20 Feb 93	**THE NAMELESS ONE** *MCA MCSTD 1732*	34		3
17 Apr 93	**LONDON'S BRILLIANT** *MCA MCSTD 1763*	62		1

JAMES BOYS
UK, male vocal duo — 6

Date	Title	Peak Position	Weeks at No.1	Weeks on Chart
19 May 73	**OVER AND OVER** *Penny Farthing PEN 806*	39		6

JIMMY JAMES & THE VAGABONDS
UK, male vocal/instrumental group — 25

Date	Title	Peak Position	Weeks at No.1	Weeks on Chart
11 Sep 68	**RED RED WINE** *Pye 7N 17579*	36		8
24 Apr 76	**I'LL GO WHERE YOUR MUSIC TAKES ME** *Pye 7N 45585*	23		8
17 Jul 76	**NOW IS THE TIME** *Pye 7N 45606*	5		9

TOMMY JAMES & THE SHONDELLS
US, male vocal/instrumental group – Tommy James (Thomas Jackson), Eddie Gray, Pete Lucia, Ronnie Rosman & Mike Vale — 25

Date	Title	Peak Position	Weeks at No.1	Weeks on Chart
21 Jul 66	**HANKY PANKY** *Roulette RK 7000* ★	38		7
5 Jun 68	**MONY MONY** *Major Minor MM 567*	1	1	18

JAMESTOWN FEATURING JOCELYN BROWN
UK (b. US), male producer (Kent Brainerd) & US, female vocalist — 4

Date	Title	Peak Position	Weeks at No.1	Weeks on Chart
14 Sep 91	**SHE'S GOT SOUL** *A&M AM 819*	57		3
27 Mar 99	**I BELIEVE** *Playola 0091705 PLA*	62		1

JAMIROQUAI
UK, male vocal/instrumental group – Jay Kay (Jason Cheetham), Derrick McKenzie & various musicians; members also included Wallis Buchanan, Nick Fyffe, Matt Johnson, Mike & Toby Smith & Stuart Zender — 164

Date	Title	Peak Position	Weeks at No.1	Weeks on Chart
31 Oct 92	**WHEN YOU GONNA LEARN** *Acid Jazz JAZID 46*	52		2
20 Feb 93	**WHEN YOU GONNA LEARN** *Acid Jazz JAZID 46*	69		1
13 Mar 93	**TOO YOUNG TO DIE** *Sony S2 6590112*	10		7
5 Jun 93	**BLOW YOUR MIND** *Sony S2 6592972*	12		6
14 Aug 93	**EMERGENCY ON PLANET EARTH** *Sony S2 6595782*	32		3
25 Sep 93	**WHEN YOU GONNA LEARN** *Sony S2 6596952*	28		3
8 Oct 94	**SPACE COWBOY** *Sony S2 6608512*	17		5
19 Nov 94	**HALF THE MAN** *Sony S2 6610032*	15		8
1 Jul 95	**STILLNESS IN TIME** *Sony S2 6620255*	9		5
1 Jun 96	**DO U KNOW WHERE YOU'RE COMING FROM** *Renk CDRENK 63* M-BEAT FEATURING JAMIROQUAI	12		5
31 Aug 96	**VIRTUAL INSANITY** *Sony S2 6636132*	3		11
7 Dec 96	**COSMIC GIRL** *Sony S2 6638292*	6		10
10 May 97	**ALRIGHT** *Sony S2 6642352*	6		5
13 Dec 97	**HIGH TIMES** *Sony S2 6653702*	20		6
25 Jul 98	**DEEPER UNDERGROUND** *Sony S2 6662182*	1	1	11
5 Jun 99	**CANNED HEAT** *Sony S2 6673022*	4		10
25 Sep 99	**SUPERSONIC** *Sony S2 6678392*	22		4
11 Dec 99	**KING FOR A DAY** *Sony S2 6679732*	20		7
24 Feb 01	**I'M IN THE MOOD FOR LOVE** *warner.esp WSMS 001CD* JOOLS HOLLAND & JAMIROQUAI	29		3
25 Aug 01	**LITTLE L** *Sony S2 6717182*	5		11
1 Dec 01	**YOU GIVE ME SOMETHING** *Sony S2 6720072*	16		9
9 Mar 02	**LOVE FOOLOSOPHY** *Sony S2 6723255*	14		6
20 Jul 02	**CORNER OF THE EARTH** *Sony S2 6727885*	31		3
18 Jun 05	**FEELS JUST LIKE IT SHOULD** *Sony Music 6759682*	8		9
27 Aug 05	**SEVEN DAYS IN SUNNY JUNE** *Sony Music 6760642*	14		5
19 Nov 05	**(DON'T) GIVE HATE A CHANCE** *Sony Music 82876750652*	27		3
10 Jun 06	**SPACE COWBOY** *Sony Music 82876846001*	71		1
4 Nov 06	**RUNAWAY** *Columbia 88697016002*	18		5

JAMMERS
US, male/female vocal/instrumental group — 2

Date	Title	Peak Position	Weeks at No.1	Weeks on Chart
29 Jan 83	**BE MINE TONIGHT** *Salsoul SAL 101*	65		2

JAMX & DELEON
Germany, male production duo. See Dumonde — 2

Date	Title	Peak Position	Weeks at No.1	Weeks on Chart
7 Sep 02	**CAN U DIG IT** *Serious SERR 052CD*	40		2

JAN & DEAN
US, male vocal duo – Jan Berry, d. 27 Mar 2004, & Dean Torrence — 18

Date	Title	Peak Position	Weeks at No.1	Weeks on Chart
24 Aug 61	**HEART AND SOUL** *London HLH 9395*	24		8
15 Aug 63	**SURF CITY** *London LIB 55580* ★	26		10

JAN & KJELD
Denmark, male vocal duo — 4

Date	Title	Peak Position	Weeks at No.1	Weeks on Chart
21 Jul 60	**BANJO BOY** *Ember S 101*	36		4

JANE'S ADDICTION
US, male vocal/instrumental group — 10

Date	Title	Peak Position	Weeks at No.1	Weeks on Chart
23 Mar 91	**BEEN CAUGHT STEALING** *Warner Brothers W 0011*	34		3
1 Jun 91	**CLASSIC GIRL** *Warner Brothers W 0031*	60		1
26 Jul 03	**JUST BECAUSE** *Capitol CDCL 847*	14		4
8 Nov 03	**TRUE NATURE** *Parlophone CDCLS 850*	41		2

HORST JANKOWSKI
Germany, male pianist, d. 29 Jun 1998 (age 62) — 18

Date	Title	Peak Position	Weeks at No.1	Weeks on Chart
29 Jul 65	**A WALK IN THE BLACK FOREST** *Mercury MF 861*	3		18

Silver-selling ● Gold-selling ● Platinum-selling (x multiples) ⊛ US No.1 ★ Peak Position Weeks at No.1 Weeks on Chart

SAMANTHA JANUS
UK, female vocalist/actor — 3

Date	Title / Label	Peak	Wks at No.1	Wks on Chart
11 May 91	**A MESSAGE TO YOUR HEART** *Hollywood HWD 104*	30		3

PHILIP JAP
UK, male vocalist (Philip Gayle) — 8

Date	Title / Label	Peak	Wks at No.1	Wks on Chart
31 Jul 82	**SAVE US** *A&M AMS 8217*	53		4
25 Sep 82	**TOTAL ERASURE** *A&M JAP 1*	41		4

JAPAN
UK, male vocal/instrumental group – David Sylvian*, Richard Barbieri, Rob Dean, Steve Jansen & Mick Karn* — 81

Date	Title / Label	Peak	Wks at No.1	Wks on Chart
18 Oct 80	**GENTLEMEN TAKE POLAROIDS** *Virgin VS 379*	60		2
9 May 81	**THE ART OF PARTIES** *Virgin VS 409*	48		5
19 Sep 81	**QUIET LIFE** *Hansa 6*	19		9
7 Nov 81	**VISIONS OF CHINA** *Virgin VS 436*	32		12
23 Jan 82	**EUROPEAN SON** *Hansa 10*	31		6
20 Mar 82	**GHOSTS** *Virgin VS 472*	5		8
22 May 82	**CANTONESE BOY** *Virgin VS 502*	24		6
3 Jul 82	**I SECOND THAT EMOTION** *Hansa 12*	9		11
9 Oct 82	**LIFE IN TOKYO** *Hansa 17*	28		6
20 Nov 82	**NIGHT PORTER** *Virgin VS 554*	29		9
12 Mar 83	**ALL TOMORROW'S PARTIES** *Hansa 18*	38		4
21 May 83	**CANTON (LIVE)** *Virgin VS 581*	42		3

JARK PRONGO
Holland, male production duo. See Chocolate Puma, Goodmen, Rhythmkillaz, Riva featuring Dannii Minogue, Tomba Vira — 1

Date	Title / Label	Peak	Wks at No.1	Wks on Chart
3 Apr 99	**MOVIN' THRU YOUR SYSTEM** *Hooj Choons HOOJ 72CD*	58		1

JEAN-MICHEL JARRE
France, male synthesizer player/composer/producer — 40

Date	Title / Label	Peak	Wks at No.1	Wks on Chart
27 Aug 77	**OXYGENE PART IV** *Polydor 2001 721* ●	4		9
20 Jan 79	**EQUINOXE PART 5** *Polydor POSP 20*	45		5
23 Aug 86	**FOURTH RENDEZ-VOUS** *Polydor POSP 788*	65		4
5 Nov 88	**REVOLUTIONS** *Polydor PO 25*	52		2
7 Jan 89	**LONDON KID** *Polydor 32* FEATURING HANK MARVIN	52		3
7 Oct 89	**OXYGENE PART IV (REMIX)** *Polydor PO 55*	65		2
26 Jun 93	**CHRONOLOGIE PART 4** *Polydor PZCD 274*	55		2
30 Oct 93	**CHRONOLOGIE PART 4 (REMIX)** *Polydor PZ 274*	56		1
22 Mar 97	**OXYGENE 8** *Epic 6643232*	17		3
5 Jul 97	**OXYGENE 10** *Epic 6647152*	21		2
11 Jul 98	**RENDEZ-VOUS 98** *Epic 6661102* & APOLLO 440	12		6
26 Feb 00	**C'EST LA VIE** *Epic 6689302* FEATURING NATACHA ATLAS	40		1

AL JARREAU
US, male vocalist (Alwyn Jarreau) — 30

Date	Title / Label	Peak	Wks at No.1	Wks on Chart
26 Sep 81	**WE'RE IN THIS LOVE TOGETHER** *Warner Brothers K 17849*	55		4
14 May 83	**MORNIN'** *WEA U9929*	28		6
16 Jul 83	**TROUBLE IN PARADISE** *WEA International U9871*	36		5
24 Sep 83	**BOOGIE DOWN** *WEA U9814*	63		3
16 Nov 85	**DAY BY DAY** *Polydor POSP 770* SHAKATAK FEATURING AL JARREAU	53		3
5 Apr 86	**THE MUSIC OF GOODBYE (LOVE THEME FROM 'OUT OF AFRICA')** *MCA 1038*	75		1
7 Mar 87	**'MOONLIGHTING' THEME** *WEA U8407*	8		8

KENNY 'JAMMIN' JASON & DJ 'FAST' EDDIE SMITH
US, male production/DJ duo — 4

Date	Title / Label	Peak	Wks at No.1	Wks on Chart
11 Apr 87	**CAN U DANCE** *Champion CHAMP 41*	71		2
14 Nov 87	**CAN U DANCE** *Champion CHAMP 41*	67		2

JAVELLS FEATURING NOSMO KING
UK, male vocalist (Stephen Gold). See Truth — 8

Date	Title / Label	Peak	Wks at No.1	Wks on Chart
9 Nov 74	**GOODBYE NOTHING TO SAY** *Pye Disco Demand DDS 2003*	26		8

JAVINE
UK, female vocalist (Javine Hylton) — 27

Date	Title / Label	Peak	Wks at No.1	Wks on Chart
19 Jul 03	**REAL THINGS** *Innocent SINCD 46*	4		9
22 Nov 03	**SURRENDER (YOUR LOVE)** *Innocent SINDX 52*	15		5
26 Jun 04	**BEST OF MY LOVE** *Innocent SINDX 63*	18		4
21 Aug 04	**DON'T WALK AWAY** *Innocent SINDX 65*	16		4
28 May 05	**TOUCH MY FIRE** *Shalit Productions 9871694*	18		4
14 Oct 06	**DON'T LET THE MORNING COME** *Positiva CDTIVS244* SOUL AVENGERZ FEATURING JAVINE	49		1

CANDEE JAY
Holland, female vocalist (Ilze Lankhaar) — 8

Date	Title / Label	Peak	Wks at No.1	Wks on Chart
19 Jun 04	**IF I WERE YOU** *Incentive CENT 58CDX*	14		6
13 Nov 04	**BACK FOR ME** *Incentive CENT 67CDS*	23		2

ORIS JAY PRESENTS DELSENA
Holland/UK, male/female vocal/production duo. See Peran — 2

Date	Title / Label	Peak	Wks at No.1	Wks on Chart
23 Mar 02	**TRIPPIN'** *Gusto CDGUS 3*	42		2

PETER JAY & THE JAYWALKERS
UK, male vocal/instrumental group — 11

Date	Title / Label	Peak	Wks at No.1	Wks on Chart
8 Nov 62	**CAN CAN 62** *Decca F 11531*	31		11

JAYDEE
Holland, male DJ/producer (Robin Albers) — 7

Date	Title / Label	Peak	Wks at No.1	Wks on Chart
20 Sep 97	**PLASTIC DREAMS** *R&S RS 97117CD*	18		3
10 Jan 04	**PLASTIC DREAMS (REMIX)** *Positiva CDTIVS 198*	35		4

JAYHAWKS
US, male/female vocal/instrumental group — 1

Date	Title / Label	Peak	Wks at No.1	Wks on Chart
15 Jul 95	**BAD TIME** *American Recordings 74321291632*	70		1

JAY-Z
US, male rapper/entrepreneur/record label owner (Shawn Carter). World-renowned entertainer and king of the collaboration, Mr Beyonce Knowles, a multiple Grammy-winner, has racked up 25 hits with some of the biggest names in the game — 329

Date	Title / Label	Peak	Wks at No.1	Wks on Chart
1 Mar 97	**CAN'T KNOCK THE HUSTLE** *Northwestside 74321447192* FEATURING MARY J BLIGE	30		2
10 May 97	**AIN'T NO PLAYA** *Northwestside 74321474842* FEATURING FOXY BROWN	31		2
21 Jun 97	**I'LL BE** *Def Jam 5710432* FOXY BROWN FEATURING JAY-Z	9		5
23 Aug 97	**WHO YOU WIT** *Qwest W0411CD*	65		1
25 Oct 97	**SUNSHINE** *Northwestside 74321528702* FEATURING BABYFACE & FOXY BROWN	25		2
14 Feb 98	**WISHING ON A STAR** *Northwestside 74321554632* FEATURING GWEN DICKEY	13		4
28 Feb 98	**BE ALONE NO MORE** *Northwestside 74321551982* ANOTHER LEVEL FEATURING JAY-Z	6		9
27 Jun 98	**THE CITY IS MINE** *Northwestside 74321588012* FEATURING BLACKstreet	38		2
12 Dec 98	**HARD KNOCK LIFE (GHETTO ANTHEM)** *Northwestside 74321635332* ●	2		11
13 Mar 99	**CAN I GET A...** *Def Jam 5668472* FEATURING AMIL & JA RULE	24		3
10 Apr 99	**BE ALONE NO MORE** *Northwestside 74321658482* ANOTHER LEVEL FEATURING JAY-Z	11		9
19 Jun 99	**LOBSTER & SCRIMP** *Virgin DINSD 186* TIMBALAND FEATURING JAY-Z	48		1
6 Nov 99	**HEARTBREAKER** *Columbia 6683012* MARIAH CAREY FEATURING JAY-Z ★	5		13
4 Dec 99	**WHAT YOU THINK OF THAT** *Def Jam 8708292* MEMPHIS BLEEK FEATURING JAY-Z	58		1
26 Feb 00	**ANYTHING** *Def Jam 5626502*	18		4
24 Jun 00	**BIG PIMPIN'** *Def Jam 5627742*	29		3
16 Dec 00	**I JUST WANNA LOVE U (GIVE IT TO ME)** *Def Jam 5727462*	17		8
23 Jun 01	**FIESTA** *Jive 9252142* R KELLY FEATURING JAY-Z	23		3
27 Oct 01	**IZZO (H.O.V.A.)** *Roc-A-Fella 5888152*	21		4
19 Jan 02	**GIRLS GIRLS GIRLS** *Roc-A-Fella/Def Jam 5889062*	11		7
25 May 02	**HONEY** *Jive 9253662* R KELLY & JAY-Z	35		2
1 Feb 03	**03 BONNIE AND CLYDE** *Roc-A-Fella 0770102* FEATURING BEYONCE KNOWLES	2		12
26 Apr 03	**EXCUSE ME MISS** *Roc-A-Fella 0779122*	17		7
5 Jul 03	**JOGI/BEWARE OF THE BOYS** *Showbiz/Dharma DHARMA 1CDS* PANJABI MC FEATURING JAY-Z	25		3
16 Aug 03	**FRONTIN'** *Arista 82876553332* PHARRELL WILLIAMS FEATURING JAY-Z	6		10
20 Dec 03	**CHANGE CLOTHES** *Roc-A-Fella 9815226*	32		7
22 May 04	**99 PROBLEMS/DIRT OFF YOUR SHOULDER** *Roc-A-Fella 9862392*	12		10
4 Dec 04	**NUMB/ENCORE** *WEA W660CD* VS LINKIN PARK	14		43
26 Aug 06	**DÉJÀ VU** *Columbia 82876884352* BEYONCE FEATURING JAY-Z	1	1	16
9 Dec 06	**SHOW ME WHAT YOU GOT** *Mercury 1717945*	38		5
26 May 07	**UMBRELLA** *Def Jam 1735491* RIHANNA FEATURING JAY-Z ● ★	1	10	51
12 Jul 08	**99 PROBLEMS** *Roc-A-Fella 9862392*	35		2

Silver-selling ● | Gold-selling ● | Platinum-selling (x multiples) | US No.1 ★ | Peak Position | Weeks at No.1 | Weeks on Chart

Date	Title	Peak Position	Weeks at No.1	Weeks on Chart
27 Sep 08	**SWAGGA LIKE US** *Mercury USUM70835786* FEATURING KANYE WEST & LIL WAYNE	33		2
12 Sep 09	**RUN THIS TOWN** *Roc Nation USJZ10900011* FEATURING RIHANNA AND KANYE WEST	1	1	12
26 Sep 09	**EMPIRE STATE OF MIND** *Roc Nation USJZ10900031* FEATURING ALICIA KEYS ★	2		29+
26 Sep 09	**YOUNG FOREVER** *Roc Nation USJZ10900041* FEATURING MR HUDSON	10		23+
6 Feb 10	**STRANDED (HAITI MON AMOUR)** *MTV Networks USYP61000005* FEATURING BONO, THE EDGE & RIHANNA	41		1

MAXI JAZZ
UK, male rapper (Maxwell Frazer). See Faithless **7**

Date	Title	Peak Position	Weeks at No.1	Weeks on Chart
20 Apr 02	**MY CULTURE** *Palm Pictures PPCD 70732* 1 GIANT LEAP FEATURING MAXI JAZZ & ROBBIE WILLIAMS	9		6
11 Nov 06	**DANCE4LIFE** *Nebula NEBCD100* TIESTO FEATURING MAXI JAZZ	67		1

JAZZ & THE BROTHERS GRIMM
UK, male vocal/rap/production trio **2**

Date	Title	Peak Position	Weeks at No.1	Weeks on Chart
9 Jul 88	**(LET'S ALL GO BACK) DISCO NIGHTS** *Ensign ENY 616*	57		2

DJ JAZZY JEFF & THE FRESH PRINCE
US, male rap/DJ/production duo – Will Smith & Jeff Townes **49**

Date	Title	Peak Position	Weeks at No.1	Weeks on Chart
4 Oct 86	**GIRLS AIN'T NOTHING BUT TROUBLE** *Champion CHAMP 18*	21		8
3 Aug 91	**SUMMERTIME** *Jive 279*	8		8
9 Nov 91	**RING MY BELL** *Jive JIVECD 288*	53		2
11 Sep 93	**BOOM! SHAKE THE ROOM** *Jive JIVECD 335* JAZZY JEFF & THE FRESH PRINCE ●	1	2	13
20 Nov 93	**I'M LOOKING FOR THE ONE (TO BE WITH ME)** *Jive JIVECD 345* JAZZY JEFF & THE FRESH PRINCE	24		4
19 Feb 94	**CAN'T WAIT TO BE WITH YOU** *Jive JIVECD 348* JAZZY JEFF & THE FRESH PRINCE	29		4
4 Jun 94	**TWINKLE TWINKLE (I'M NOT A STAR)** *Jive JIVECD 354* JAZZY JEFF & THE FRESH PRINCE	62		2
6 Aug 94	**SUMMERTIME** *Jive JIVECD 279*	29		4
2 Dec 95	**BOOM! SHAKE THE ROOM** *Jive JIVECD 387* JAZZY JEFF & THE FRESH PRINCE	40		2
11 Jul 98	**LOVELY DAZE** *Jive 0518902*	37		2

JAZZY M
UK, male DJ/producer (Michael Connelly) **2**

Date	Title	Peak Position	Weeks at No.1	Weeks on Chart
21 Oct 00	**JAZZIN' THE WAY YOU KNOW** *Perfecto PERF 08CDS*	47		2

JB'S ALL STARS
UK, male/female vocal/instrumental group **4**

Date	Title	Peak Position	Weeks at No.1	Weeks on Chart
11 Feb 84	**BACKFIELD IN MOTION** *RCA Victor 384*	48		4

JC
UK, male producer (Jonathan Dennis) **1**

Date	Title	Peak Position	Weeks at No.1	Weeks on Chart
7 Feb 98	**SO HOT** *East West EW 146CD*	74		1

JC 001
UK, male rapper (Jonathan Chandra Pandy) **4**

Date	Title	Peak Position	Weeks at No.1	Weeks on Chart
24 Apr 93	**NEVER AGAIN** *AnXious ANX 1012CD*	67		2
26 Jun 93	**CUPID** *AnXious ANX 1014CD*	56		2

JD AKA DREADY
UK, male vocalist (Karl Jairzhino Daniel) **1**

Date	Title	Peak Position	Weeks at No.1	Weeks on Chart
2 Aug 03	**SIGNAL** *Independiente SSB2MS*	64		1

JDS
Italy/UK, male DJ/production duo. See Gems For Jem **3**

Date	Title	Peak Position	Weeks at No.1	Weeks on Chart
27 Sep 97	**NINE WAYS** *ffrr FCD 310*	61		1
23 May 98	**LONDON TOWN** *Jive 0530042*	49		1
3 Mar 01	**NINE WAYS (REMIX)** *ffrr FCD 391*	47		1

JEALOUSY
France, male vocal/instrumental group **4**

Date	Title	Peak Position	Weeks at No.1	Weeks on Chart
16 Sep 06	**LUCY** *Purple City CDPCTY105*	30		4

WYCLEF JEAN
Haiti, male vocalist/rapper/producer. See Fugees **115**

Date	Title	Peak Position	Weeks at No.1	Weeks on Chart
28 Jun 97	**WE TRYING TO STAY ALIVE** *Columbia 6646815* & THE REFUGEE ALLSTARS	13		5
27 Sep 97	**GUANTANAMERA** *Columbia 6650852* & THE REFUGEE ALLSTARS	25		2
28 Mar 98	**NO NO NO** *Columbia 6656592* DESTINY'S CHILD FEATURING WYCLEF JEAN	5		8
16 May 98	**GONE TILL NOVEMBER** *Columbia 6658712* ●	3		9
14 Nov 98	**ANOTHER ONE BITES THE DUST** *DreamWorks DRMCD 22364* QUEEN WITH WYCLEF JEAN FEATURING PRAS MICHEL/FREE	5		6
23 Oct 99	**NEW DAY** *Columbia 6682122* FEATURING BONO	23		2
16 Sep 00	**IT DOESN'T MATTER** *Columbia 6697782* FEATURING THE ROCK & MELKY SEDECK	3		8
16 Dec 00	**911** *Columbia 6706122* WYCLEF FEATURING MARY J BLIGE	9		10
21 Jul 01	**PERFECT GENTLEMAN** *Columbia 6710522* ●	4		14
8 Dec 01	**WISH YOU WERE HERE** *Columbia 6721562*	28		6
6 Jul 02	**TWO WRONGS (DON'T MAKE A RIGHT)** *Columbia 6728902* FEATURING CLAUDETTE ORTIZ	14		6
17 Jun 06	**HIPS DON'T LIE** *Epic 82876842702* SHAKIRA FEATURING WYCLEF JEAN ★	1	2	38
1 Dec 07	**SWEETEST GIRL (DOLLAR BILL)** *Columbia USSM10703185* FEATURING AKON, LIL WAYNE & NIIA	66		1

JEDWARD FEATURING VANILLA ICE
Ireland, male vocal duo – John & Edward Grimes & US, male rapper (Robert Van Winkle). See *X Factor* Finalists **7**

Date	Title	Peak Position	Weeks at No.1	Weeks on Chart
13 Feb 10	**UNDER PRESSURE (ICE ICE BABY)** *Sony BMG 88697658992*	2		7

JEEVAS
UK, male vocal/instrumental group **2**

Date	Title	Peak Position	Weeks at No.1	Weeks on Chart
22 Mar 03	**ONCE UPON A TIME IN AMERICA** *Cowboy Music COWCDB 005*	61		1
28 Feb 04	**HAVE YOU EVER SEEN THE RAIN?** *Cowboy Music COWCDB 008*	70		1

JEFFERSON
UK, male vocalist (Geoff Turton). See Rockin' Berries **8**

Date	Title	Peak Position	Weeks at No.1	Weeks on Chart
9 Apr 69	**COLOUR OF MY LOVE** *Pye 7N 17706*	22		8

GARLAND JEFFREYS
US, male vocalist **1**

Date	Title	Peak Position	Weeks at No.1	Weeks on Chart
8 Feb 92	**HAIL HAIL ROCK 'N' ROLL** *RCA PB 49171*	72		1

JELLYBEAN
US, male producer (John Benitez) **47**

Date	Title	Peak Position	Weeks at No.1	Weeks on Chart
1 Feb 86	**SIDEWALK TALK** *EMI America EA 210* FEATURING CATHERINE BUCHANAN	47		4
26 Sep 87	**THE REAL THING** *Chrysalis CHS 3167* FEATURING STEVEN DANTE	13		10
28 Nov 87	**WHO FOUND WHO** *Chrysalis CHS JEL 1* FEATURING ELISA FIORILLO	10		10
12 Dec 87	**JINGO** *Chrysalis JEL 2*	12		10
12 Mar 88	**JUST A MIRAGE** *Chrysalis JEL 3* FEATURING ADELE BERTEI	13		10
20 Aug 88	**COMING BACK FOR MORE** *Chrysalis JEL 4* FEATURING RICHARD DARBYSHIRE	41		3

JELLYFISH
US, male vocal/instrumental group **20**

Date	Title	Peak Position	Weeks at No.1	Weeks on Chart
26 Jan 91	**THE KING IS HALF UNDRESSED** *Charisma CUSS 1*	39		6
27 Apr 91	**BABY'S COMING BACK** *Charisma CUSS 2*	51		4
3 Aug 91	**THE SCARY-GO-ROUND EP** *Charisma CUSS 3*	49		3
26 Oct 91	**I WANNA STAY HOME** *Charisma CUSS 4*	59		2
1 May 93	**THE GHOST AT NUMBER ONE** *Charisma CUSDG 10*	43		3
17 Jul 93	**NEW MISTAKE** *Charisma CUSDG 11*	55		2

JEM
UK, female vocalist (Jem Griffiths) **26**

Date	Title	Peak Position	Weeks at No.1	Weeks on Chart
26 Mar 05	**THEY** *Ato 82876685182*	6		15
25 Jun 05	**JUST A RIDE** *Ato 82876705862*	16		8
24 Sep 05	**WISH I** *Ato 82876727732*	24		3

JEMINI
UK, male/female vocal duo **3**

Date	Title	Peak Position	Weeks at No.1	Weeks on Chart
7 Jun 03	**CRY BABY** *Integral INTEG 001CD*	15		3

Silver-selling ● Gold-selling ● Platinum-selling (x multiples) ★ US No.1 | Peak Position | Weeks at No.1 | Weeks on Chart

KATHERINE JENKINS
UK, female vocalist — 2

Date	Title	Peak	No.1	Wks
2 Dec 06	GREEN GREEN GRASS OF HOME *UCJ 1717438*	62		1
7 Nov 09	BRING ME TO LIFE *Warner Brothers GBAHT0900424*	74		1

VANESSA JENKINS & BRYN WEST FEATURING TOM JONES & ROBIN GIBB
UK, male/female charity group – actors Ruth Jones & Rob Brydon & vocalists Thomas Woodward & Robin Gibb. See Bee Gees — 4

Date	Title	Peak	No.1	Wks
21 Mar 09	ISLANDS IN THE STREAM *Mercury 1799919*	1	1	4

JENTINA
UK, female vocalist (Jentina Chapman) — 6

Date	Title	Peak	No.1	Wks
3 Jul 04	BAD ASS STRIPPA *Virgin VSCDX 1873*	22		3
9 Oct 04	FRENCH KISSES *Virgin VSCDX 1877*	20		3

JEREMIH
US, male vocalist/multi-instrumentalist/producer (Jeremih Felton) — 10

Date	Title	Peak	No.1	Wks
22 Aug 09	BIRTHDAY SEX *Mercury USUV70901767*	15		10

JERU THE DAMAJA
US, male rapper (Kendrick Davis) — 1

Date	Title	Peak	No.1	Wks
7 Dec 96	YA PLAYIN YASELF *ffrr FCD 289*	67		1

JESSICA
Sweden, female vocalist (Jessica Folker) — 1

Date	Title	Peak	No.1	Wks
20 Mar 99	HOW WILL I KNOW (WHO YOU ARE) *Jive 0522412*	47		1

JESSY
Belgium, female vocalist (Jessy de Smet) — 15

Date	Title	Peak	No.1	Wks
12 Apr 03	LOOK AT ME NOW *Data 46CDS*	29		3
19 Aug 06	DANCING IN THE DARK *All Around The World CDGLOBE510* MICKY MODELLE V JESSY	10		10
30 Dec 06	OVER YOU *All Around The World CDGLOBE609* MICKY MODELLE V JESSY	35		2

JESUS & MARY CHAIN
UK, male vocal/instrumental group – Jim Reid, Bobby Gillespie, Douglas Hart & William Reid — 59

Date	Title	Peak	No.1	Wks
2 Mar 85	NEVER UNDERSTAND *Blanco Y Negro NEG 8*	47		4
8 Jun 85	YOU TRIP ME UP *Blanco Y Negro NEG 13*	55		3
12 Oct 85	JUST LIKE HONEY *Blanco Y Negro NEG 17*	45		3
26 Jul 86	SOME CANDY TALKING *Blanco Y Negro NEG 19*	13		5
2 May 87	APRIL SKIES *Blanco Y Negro NEG 24*	8		6
15 Aug 87	HAPPY WHEN IT RAINS *Blanco Y Negro NEG 25*	25		5
7 Nov 87	DARKLANDS *Blanco Y Negro NEG 29*	33		4
9 Apr 88	SIDEWALKING *Blanco Y Negro NEG 32*	30		3
23 Sep 89	BLUES FROM A GUN *Blanco Y Negro NEG 41*	32		2
18 Nov 89	HEAD ON *Blanco Y Negro NEG 42*	57		2
8 Sep 90	ROLLERCOASTER (EP) *Blanco Y Negro NEG 45*	46		2
15 Feb 92	REVERENCE *Blanco Y Negro NEG 55*	10		4
14 Mar 92	FAR GONE AND OUT *Blanco Y Negro NEG 56*	23		3
4 Jul 92	ALMOST GOLD *Blanco Y Negro NEG 57*	41		2
10 Jul 93	SOUND OF SPEED (EP) *Blanco Y Negro NEG 66CD*	30		2
30 Jul 94	SOMETIMES ALWAYS *Blanco Y Negro NEG 70CD*	22		3
22 Oct 94	COME ON *Blanco Y Negro NEG 73CD1*	52		2
17 Jun 95	I HATE ROCK 'N' ROLL *Blanco Y Negro NEG 81CD*	61		1
18 Apr 98	CRACKING UP *Creation CRESCD 292*	35		2
30 May 98	ILOVEROCKNROLL *Creation CRESCD 296*	38		1

JESUS JONES
UK, male vocal/instrumental group – Mike Edwards, Iain Baker, Jerry de Borg, Al Doughty & Simon 'Gen' Matthews — 52

Date	Title	Peak	No.1	Wks
25 Feb 89	INFO-FREAKO *Food 18*	42		3
8 Jul 89	NEVER ENOUGH *Food 21*	42		3
23 Sep 89	BRING IT ON DOWN *Food 22*	46		3
7 Apr 90	REAL REAL REAL *Food 24*	19		8
6 Oct 90	RIGHT HERE RIGHT NOW *Food 25*	31		4
12 Jan 91	INTERNATIONAL BRIGHT YOUNG THING *Food 27*	7		7
2 Mar 91	WHO WHERE WHY *Food 28*	21		7
20 Jul 91	RIGHT HERE RIGHT NOW *Food 30*	31		4
9 Jan 93	THE DEVIL YOU KNOW *Food CDPERV 1*	10		5
10 Apr 93	THE RIGHT DECISION *Food CDPERV 2*	36		3
10 Jul 93	ZEROES AND ONES *Food CDFOODS 44*	30		3
14 Jun 97	THE NEXT BIG THING *Food CDFOOD 95*	49		1
16 Aug 97	CHEMICAL #1 *Food CDFOOD 102*	71		1

JESUS LIZARD
US, male vocal/instrumental group — 2

Date	Title	Peak	No.1	Wks
6 Mar 93	PUSS *Touch And Go TG 83CD*	12		2

JESUS LOVES YOU
UK, male vocal/instrumental group — 18

Date	Title	Peak	No.1	Wks
11 Nov 89	AFTER THE LOVE *More Protein PROT 2*	68		1
23 Feb 91	BOW DOWN MISTER *More Protein PROT 8*	27		8
8 Jun 91	GENERATIONS OF LOVE *More Protein PROT 10*	35		8
12 Dec 92	SWEET TOXIC LOVE *Virgin VS 1449*	65		1

JET
Australia, male vocal/instrumental group — 20

Date	Title	Peak	No.1	Wks
6 Sep 03	ARE YOU GONNA BE MY GIRL? *Elektra E 7456CD1*	23		2
15 Nov 03	ROLLOVER DJ *Elektra E 7486CD1*	34		2
20 Mar 04	LOOK WHAT YOU'VE DONE *Elektra E 7527CD*	28		3
5 Jun 04	ARE YOU GONNA BE MY GIRL? *Elektra E 7599CD*	16		5
18 Sep 04	COLD HARD BITCH *Elektra E7607CD*	34		2
8 Jan 05	GET ME OUTTA HERE *679 679L094CD*	37		2
30 Sep 06	PUT YOUR MONEY WHERE YOUR MOUTH IS *Elektra AT0258CD*	23		3
2 Dec 06	BRING IT ON BACK *Atlantic AT0263CD*	51		1

JETHRO TULL
UK, male vocal/instrumental group – Ian Anderson*, Martin Barre, Clive Bunker (replaced by Barriemore Barlow), Glen Cornick (replaced by Jeffrey Hammond) & John Evan — 68

Date	Title	Peak	No.1	Wks
1 Jan 69	LOVE STORY *Island WIP 6048*	29		8
14 May 69	LIVING IN THE PAST *Island WIP 6056*	3		14
1 Nov 69	SWEET DREAM *Chrysalis WIP 6070*	7		11
24 Jan 70	THE WITCH'S PROMISE/TEACHER *Chrysalis WIP 6077*	4		9
18 Sep 71	LIFE IS A LONG SONG/UP THE POOL *Chrysalis WIP 6106*	11		8
11 Dec 76	RING OUT SOLSTICE BELLS (EP) *Chrysalis CXP 2*	28		6
15 Sep 84	LAP OF LUXURY *Chrysalis TULL 1*	70		2
16 Jan 88	SAID SHE WAS A DANCER *Chrysalis TULL 4*	55		4
21 Mar 92	ROCKS ON THE ROAD *Chrysalis TULLX 7*	47		3
22 May 93	LIVING IN THE (SLIGHTLY MORE RECENT) PAST *Chrysalis CDCHSS 3970*	32		3

JETS
UK, male vocal/instrumental group — 38

Date	Title	Peak	No.1	Wks
22 Aug 81	SUGAR DOLL *EMI 5211*	55		3
31 Oct 81	YES TONIGHT JOSEPHINE *EMI 5247*	25		11
6 Feb 82	LOVE MAKES THE WORLD GO ROUND *EMI 5262*	21		9
24 Apr 82	THE HONEYDRIPPER *EMI 5289*	58		3
9 Oct 82	SOMEBODY TO LOVE *EMI 5342*	56		3
6 Aug 83	BLUE SKIES *EMI 5405*	53		3
17 Dec 83	ROCKIN' AROUND THE CHRISTMAS TREE *PRT 7P 297*	62		4
13 Oct 84	PARTY DOLL *PRT JETS 2*	72		2

JETS
US, male/female vocal/instrumental group – Eddie, Elizabeth, Eugene, Haini, Kathy, LeRoy, Moana & Rudy Wolfgramm — 19

Date	Title	Peak	No.1	Wks
31 Jan 87	CRUSH ON YOU *MCA 1048*	5		13
25 Apr 87	CURIOSITY *MCA 1119*	41		4
28 May 88	ROCKET 2 U *MCA 1226*	69		2

JOAN JETT & THE BLACKHEARTS
US, female/male vocal/instrumental group – Joan Jett (Joan Larkin), Ricky Byrd, Lee Crystal (replaced by Thommy Price) & Gary Ryan (replaced by Kasim Sulton) — 21

Date	Title	Peak	No.1	Wks
24 Apr 82	I LOVE ROCK 'N' ROLL *Epic EPC A 2152* ● ★	4		10
10 Jul 82	CRIMSON AND CLOVER *Epic EPC A 2485*	60		3
20 Aug 88	I HATE MYSELF FOR LOVING YOU *London LON 195*	46		6
31 Mar 90	DIRTY DEEDS *Chrysalis CHS 3518* JOAN JETT	69		1
19 Feb 94	I LOVE ROCK 'N' ROLL *Reprise W 0232CD*	75		1

JEWEL

US, female vocalist/guitarist (Jewel Kilcher)

Date	Title / Label	Peak	Wks No.1	9
14 Jun 97	**WHO WILL SAVE YOUR SOUL** *Atlantic A 8514CD*	52		1
9 Aug 97	**YOU WERE MEANT FOR ME** *Atlantic A 5463CD*	53		1
22 Nov 97	**YOU WERE MEANT FOR ME** *Atlantic A 5463CD*	32		2
21 Nov 98	**HANDS** *Atlantic AT 0055CD*	41		2
26 Jun 99	**DOWN SO LONG** *Atlantic AT 0069CD*	38		2
30 Aug 03	**INTUITION** *Atlantic W 619CD*	52		1

JEZ & CHOOPIE

UK/Israel, male DJ/production duo

Date	Title / Label	Peak	Wks No.1	2
21 Mar 98	**YIM** *Multiply CDMULTY 31*	36		2

JFK

UK, male producer (JF Kinch)

Date	Title / Label	Peak	Wks No.1	3
15 Sep 01	**GOOD GOD** *Y2K 025CD*	71		1
26 Jan 02	**WHIPLASH** *Y2K 027CD*	47		1
4 May 02	**THE SOUND OF BLUE** *Y2K 030CD*	55		1

JHELISA

US, female vocalist (Jhelisa Anderson)

Date	Title / Label	Peak	Wks No.1	1
1 Jul 95	**FRIENDLY PRESSURE** *Dorado DOR 040CD*	75		1

JIBBS

US, male rapper (Jovan Campbell)

Date	Title / Label	Peak	Wks No.1	1
3 Feb 07	**CHAIN HANG LOW** *Geffen 1709267*	63		1

JIGSAW

UK, male vocal/instrumental group – Des Dyer, Barrie Bernard, Tony Campbell & Clive Scott

Date	Title / Label	Peak	Wks No.1	16
1 Nov 75	**SKY HIGH** *Splash CPI 1*	9		11
6 Aug 77	**IF I HAVE TO GO AWAY** *Splash CP 11*	36		5

JILTED JOHN

UK, male vocalist (Graham Fellows)

Date	Title / Label	Peak	Wks No.1	12
12 Aug 78	**JILTED JOHN** *EMI International INT 567* ○	4		12

JIMMY EAT WORLD

US, male vocal/instrumental group

Date	Title / Label	Peak	Wks No.1	11
17 Nov 01	**SALT SWEAT SUGAR** *DreamWorks 4508782*	60		1
9 Feb 02	**THE MIDDLE** *DreamWorks 4508482*	26		3
15 Jun 02	**SWEETNESS** *DreamWorks 4508342*	38		2
16 Oct 04	**PAIN** *Interscope 9864179*	38		2
9 Apr 05	**WORK** *Interscope 9880673*	49		2
15 Mar 08	**ALWAYS BE** *Interscope 1763635*	37		1

JIMMY THE HOOVER

UK, male/female vocal/instrumental group

Date	Title / Label	Peak	Wks No.1	8
25 Jun 83	**TANTALISE (WO WO EE YEH YEH)** *Innervision A 3406*	18		8

JIN

US, male rapper (Jin Au-Yeung)

Date	Title / Label	Peak	Wks No.1	1
19 Mar 05	**LEARN CHINESE** *Virgin VUSDX300*	59		1

JINGLE BELLES

US/UK, female vocal group

Date	Title / Label	Peak	Wks No.1	4
17 Dec 83	**CHRISTMAS SPECTRE** *Passion PASH 14*	37		4

JINNY

Italy, male production group

Date	Title / Label	Peak	Wks No.1	16
29 Jun 91	**KEEP WARM** *Virgin VS 1356*	68		3
22 May 93	**FEEL THE RHYTHM** *Logic 1633001022*	74		1
15 Jul 95	**KEEP WARM (REMIX)** *Multiply CDMULTY 5*	11		8
16 Dec 95	**WANNA BE WITH YOU** *Multiply CDMULTY 8*	30		4

JIVE BUNNY & THE MASTERMIXERS

UK, male DJ/production group – Andy & John Pickles, Les Hemstock & Ian Morgan

Date	Title / Label	Peak	Wks No.1	70
15 Jul 89	**SWING THE MOOD** *Music Factory Dance MFD 001* ⊛	1	5	19
14 Oct 89	**THAT'S WHAT I LIKE** *Music Factory Dance MFD 002* ●	1	3	12
2 Dec 89	**IT TAKES TWO BABY** *Spartan CIN 101* LIZ KERSHAW, BRUNO BROOKES, JIVE BUNNY & LONDONBEAT	53		2
16 Dec 89	**LET'S PARTY** *Music Factory Dance MFD 003* ●	1	1	6
17 Mar 90	**THAT SOUNDS GOOD TO ME** *Music Factory Dance MFD 004*	4		6
25 Aug 90	**CAN CAN YOU PARTY** *Music Factory Dance MFD 007*	8		6
17 Nov 90	**LET'S SWING AGAIN** *Music Factory Dance MFD 009*	19		5
22 Dec 90	**THE CRAZY PARTY MIXES** *Music Factory Dance MFD 010*	13		5
23 Mar 91	**OVER TO YOU JOHN (HERE WE GO AGAIN)** *Music Factory Dance MFD 012*	28		5
20 Jul 91	**HOT SUMMER SALSA** *Music Factory Dance MFD 013*	43		2
23 Nov 91	**ROCK 'N' ROLL DANCE PARTY** *Music Factory Dance MFD 015*	48		2

JJ

UK, male/female vocal/instrumental duo

Date	Title / Label	Peak	Wks No.1	3
9 Feb 91	**IF THIS IS LOVE** *Columbia 6566097*	55		3

JJ72

Ireland, male/female vocal/instrumental group

Date	Title / Label	Peak	Wks No.1	14
3 Jun 00	**LONG WAY SOUTH** *Lakota LAK 0015CD*	68		1
26 Aug 00	**OXYGEN** *Lakota LAK 0016CD*	23		3
4 Nov 00	**OCTOBER SWIMMER** *Lakota LAK 0018CD*	29		3
10 Feb 01	**SNOW** *Lakota LAK 0019CD*	21		3
12 Oct 02	**FORMULAE** *Columbia 6731595*	28		2
22 Feb 03	**ALWAYS AND FOREVER** *Columbia 6734325*	43		1
10 Sep 05	**COMING HOME** *Lakota LAK0035*	52		1

JKD BAND

UK, male/female vocal/instrumental session group

Date	Title / Label	Peak	Wks No.1	4
1 Jul 78	**DRAGON POWER** *Satril SAT 132*	58		4

JLS

UK, male vocal group – Jonathan 'JB' Gill, Marvin Humes, Aston Merrygold & Oritse Williams. See Helping Haiti, *X Factor* Finalists

Date	Title / Label	Peak	Wks No.1	55
25 Jul 09	**BEAT AGAIN** *Epic 88697545842* ●	1	2	27
14 Nov 09	**EVERYBODY IN LOVE** *Epic 88697562162*	1	1	16
23 Jan 10	**ONE SHOT** *Epic 88697634512*	6		12+

JM SILK

US, male production/vocal duo

Date	Title / Label	Peak	Wks No.1	6
25 Oct 86	**I CAN'T TURN AROUND** *RCA PB 49793*	62		3
7 Mar 87	**LET THE MUSIC TAKE CONTROL** *RCA PB 49767*	47		3

JO BOXERS

UK/US, male vocal/instrumental group – Dig Wayne (Timothy Wayne Ball), Chris Bostock, Dave Collard, Sean McLusky & Rob Marche

Date	Title / Label	Peak	Wks No.1	33
19 Feb 83	**BOXER BEAT** *RCA BOXX 1*	3		15
21 May 83	**JUST GOT LUCKY** *RCA BOXX 2*	7		9
13 Aug 83	**JOHNNY FRIENDLY** *RCA BOXX 3*	31		8
12 Nov 83	**JEALOUS LOVE** *RCA BOXX 4*	72		1

JO JINGLES

UK, male/female vocal group

Date	Title / Label	Peak	Wks No.1	6
13 Nov 04	**WIND THE BOBBIN UP** *Jo Jingles JJ21CD*	21		3
12 Nov 05	**DISCO** *Jo Jingles JJ27*	44		3

JO JO GUNNE

US, male vocal/instrumental group – Jay Ferguson, Matthew & Mark Andes & Curly Smith

Date	Title / Label	Peak	Wks No.1	12
25 Mar 72	**RUN RUN RUN** *Asylum AYM 501*	6		12

JOAN COLLINS FAN CLUB

UK, male vocalist/comedian

Date	Title / Label	Peak	Wks No.1	3
18 Jun 88	**LEADER OF THE PACK** *10 TEN 227*	60		3

Silver-selling ○ Gold-selling ● Platinum-selling (x multiples) ⊛ US No.1 ★ | Peak Position | Weeks at No.1 | Weeks on Chart

JOHN PAUL JOANS
UK, male vocalist — **7**

Date	Title	Peak Position	Weeks at No.1	Weeks on Chart
19 Dec 70	**MAN FROM NAZARETH** *RAK 107*	25		7

JOCASTA
UK, male vocal/instrumental group — **2**

Date	Title	Peak Position	Weeks at No.1	Weeks on Chart
15 Feb 97	**GO** *Epic 6641415*	50		1
3 May 97	**CHANGE ME** *Epic 6643902*	60		1

JOCKO
US, male rapper/DJ (Douglas Henderson), d. 15 Jul 2000 (age 82) — **3**

Date	Title	Peak Position	Weeks at No.1	Weeks on Chart
23 Feb 80	**RHYTHM TALK** *Philadelphia International PIR 8222*	56		3

JODE FEATURING YO-HANS
UK, male/female vocal trio — **2**

Date	Title	Peak Position	Weeks at No.1	Weeks on Chart
19 Dec 98	**WALK...(THE DOG) LIKE AN EGYPTIAN** *Logic 74321640332*	48		2

JODECI
US, male vocal group — **19**

Date	Title	Peak Position	Weeks at No.1	Weeks on Chart
16 Jan 93	**CHERISH** *Uptown MCSTD 1726*	56		2
11 Dec 93	**CRY FOR YOU** *Uptown MCSTD 1951*	56		1
16 Jul 94	**FEENIN'** *MCA MCSTD 1984*	18		3
28 Jan 95	**CRY FOR YOU** *Uptown MCSTD 2039*	20		3
24 Jun 95	**FREEK 'N YOU** *Uptown MCSTD 2072*	17		5
9 Dec 95	**LOVE U 4 LIFE** *Uptown MCSTD 2105*	23		3
25 May 96	**GET ON UP** *MCA MCSTD 48010*	20		2

JODIE
Australia, female vocalist (Jodie Wilson) — **1**

Date	Title	Peak Position	Weeks at No.1	Weeks on Chart
25 Feb 95	**ANYTHING YOU WANT** *Mercury MERCD 423*	47		1

JOE
US, male vocalist (Joseph Thomas) — **52**

Date	Title	Peak Position	Weeks at No.1	Weeks on Chart
22 Jan 94	**I'M IN LUV** *Mercury JOECD 1*	22		4
25 Jun 94	**THE ONE FOR ME** *Mercury JOECD 2*	34		2
22 Oct 94	**ALL OR NOTHING** *Mercury JOECD 3*	56		1
27 Apr 96	**ALL THE THINGS (YOUR MAN WON'T DO)** *Island CID 634*	34		3
14 Jun 97	**DON'T WANNA BE A PLAYER** *Jive JIVECD 410*	16		3
27 Sep 97	**THE LOVE SCENE** *Jive JIVECD 430*	22		2
10 Jan 98	**GOOD GIRLS** *Jive JIVECD 442*	29		3
22 Aug 98	**NO ONE ELSE COMES CLOSE** *Jive 0521682*	41		2
31 Oct 98	**ALL THAT I AM** *Jive 0518532*	52		1
11 Mar 00	**THANK GOD I FOUND YOU** *Columbia 6690582* MARIAH CAREY FEATURING JOE & 98o ★	10		10
15 Jul 00	**TREAT HER LIKE A LADY** *Jive 9250772*	60		1
17 Feb 01	**STUTTER** *Jive 9251632* FEATURING MYSTIKAL ★	7		8
5 May 01	**I WANNA KNOW** *Jive 9252102*	37		2
16 Feb 02	**LET'S STAY HOME TONIGHT** *Jive 9253222*	29		2
14 Sep 02	**WHAT IF A WOMAN** *Jive 9253962*	53		1
24 Apr 04	**RIDE WIT U/MORE & MORE** *Jive 82876609392* FEATURING G-UNIT	12		7

JOE PUBLIC
US, male vocal group — **5**

Date	Title	Peak Position	Weeks at No.1	Weeks on Chart
11 Jul 92	**LIVE AND LEARN** *Columbia 6575267*	43		4
28 Nov 92	**I'VE BEEN WATCHIN'** *Columbia 6587657*	75		1

BILLY JOEL
US, male vocalist/multi-instrumentalist — **146**

Date	Title	Peak Position	Weeks at No.1	Weeks on Chart
11 Feb 78	**JUST THE WAY YOU ARE** *CBS 5872*	19		9
24 Jun 78	**MOVIN' OUT (ANTHONY'S SONG)** *CBS 6412*	35		6
2 Dec 78	**MY LIFE** *CBS 6821* ○	12		15
28 Apr 79	**UNTIL THE NIGHT** *CBS 7242*	50		3
12 Apr 80	**ALL FOR LEYNA** *CBS 8325*	40		4
9 Aug 80	**IT'S STILL ROCK AND ROLL TO ME** *CBS 8753* ★	14		11
15 Oct 83	**UPTOWN GIRL** *CBS A 3775* ●	1	5	17
10 Dec 83	**TELL HER ABOUT IT** *CBS A 3655* ○ ★	4		10
18 Feb 84	**AN INNOCENT MAN** *CBS A 4142* ○	8		10
28 Apr 84	**THE LONGEST TIME** *CBS A 4280*	25		8
23 Jun 84	**LEAVE A TENDER MOMENT ALONE/GOODNIGHT SAIGON** *CBS A 4521*	29		7
22 Feb 86	**SHE'S ALWAYS A WOMAN/JUST THE WAY YOU ARE** *CBS A 6862*	53		1
20 Sep 86	**A MATTER OF TRUST** *CBS 6500577*	52		4
30 Sep 89	**WE DIDN'T START THE FIRE** *CBS JOEL 1* ★	7		10
16 Dec 89	**LENINGRAD** *CBS JOEL 3*	53		4
10 Mar 90	**I GO TO EXTREMES** *CBS JOEL 2*	70		2
29 Aug 92	**ALL SHOOK UP** *Columbia 6583437*	27		4
31 Jul 93	**THE RIVER OF DREAMS** *Columbia 6595432*	3		14
23 Oct 93	**ALL ABOUT SOUL** *Columbia 6597362*	32		4
26 Feb 94	**NO MAN'S LAND** *Columbia 6599202*	50		3

JOHANN
Germany, male producer (Johann Bley) — **1**

Date	Title	Peak Position	Weeks at No.1	Weeks on Chart
16 Mar 96	**NEW KICKS** *Perfecto PERF 118CD*	54		1

ELTON JOHN
UK, male vocalist/pianist (Reginald Dwight). The flamboyant entertainer recorded the biggest-selling single of the rock era and is the only UK act to enter both the US singles and album charts at No.1. Sir Elton, who has sold 14.5 million singles in the UK, has shifted more albums in the UK and US than any other UK male artist — **669**

Date	Title	Peak Position	Weeks at No.1	Weeks on Chart
23 Jan 71	**YOUR SONG** *DJM DJS 233*	7		12
22 Apr 72	**ROCKET MAN** *DJM DJX 501*	2		13
9 Sep 72	**HONKY CAT** *DJM DJS 269*	31		6
4 Nov 72	**CROCODILE ROCK** *DJM DJS 271* ★	5		14
20 Jan 73	**DANIEL** *DJM DJS 275*	4		10
7 Jul 73	**SATURDAY NIGHT'S ALRIGHT FOR FIGHTING** *DJM DJX 502*	7		9
29 Sep 73	**GOODBYE YELLOW BRICK ROAD** *DJM DJS 285*	6		16
8 Dec 73	**STEP INTO CHRISTMAS** *DJM DJS 290*	24		7
2 Mar 74	**CANDLE IN THE WIND** *DJM DJS 297*	11		9
1 Jun 74	**DON'T LET THE SUN GO DOWN ON ME** *DJM DJS 302*	16		8
14 Sep 74	**THE BITCH IS BACK** *DJM DJS 322*	15		7
23 Nov 74	**LUCY IN THE SKY WITH DIAMONDS** *DJM DJS 340* ★	10		10
8 Mar 75	**PHILADELPHIA FREEDOM** *DJM DJS 354* BAND ★	12		9
28 Jun 75	**SOMEONE SAVED MY LIFE TONIGHT** *DJM DJS 385*	22		5
4 Oct 75	**ISLAND GIRL** *DJM DJS 610* ★	14		8
20 Mar 76	**PINBALL WIZARD** *DJM DJS 652*	7		7
3 Jul 76	**DON'T GO BREAKING MY HEART** *Rocket ROKN 512* & KIKI DEE ● ★	1	6	14
25 Sep 76	**BENNIE AND THE JETS** *DJM DJS 10705* ★	37		5
13 Nov 76	**SORRY SEEMS TO BE THE HARDEST WORD** *Rocket ROKN 517*	11		10
26 Feb 77	**CRAZY WATER** *Rocket ROKN 521*	27		6
11 Jun 77	**BITE YOUR LIP (GET UP AND DANCE)** *Rocket ROKN 526*	28		4
15 Apr 78	**EGO** *Rocket ROKN 538*	34		6
21 Oct 78	**PART TIME LOVE** *Rocket XPRES 1* ○	15		13
16 Dec 78	**SONG FOR GUY** *Rocket XPRES 5* ○	4		10
12 May 79	**ARE YOU READY FOR LOVE** *Rocket XPRES 13*	42		6
24 May 80	**LITTLE JEANNIE** *Rocket XPRES 32*	33		7
23 Aug 80	**SARTORIAL ELOQUENCE** *Rocket XPRES 41*	44		5
21 Mar 81	**I SAW HER STANDING THERE** *DJM DJS 10965* ELTON JOHN BAND FEATURING JOHN LENNON & THE MUSCLE SHOALS HORNS	40		4
23 May 81	**NOBODY WINS** *Rocket XPRES 54*	42		5
27 Mar 82	**BLUE EYES** *Rocket XPRES 71*	8		10
12 Jun 82	**EMPTY GARDEN** *Rocket XPRES 77*	51		4
30 Apr 83	**I GUESS THAT'S WHY THEY CALL IT THE BLUES** *Rocket XPRES 91*	5		15
30 Jul 83	**I'M STILL STANDING** *Rocket EJS 1* ○	4		11
15 Oct 83	**KISS THE BRIDE** *Rocket EJS 2*	20		7
10 Dec 83	**COLD AS CHRISTMAS** *Rocket EJS 3*	33		6
26 May 84	**SAD SONGS (SAY SO MUCH)** *Rocket PH 7*	7		12
11 Aug 84	**PASSENGERS** *Rocket EJS 5* ○	5		11
20 Oct 84	**WHO WEARS THESE SHOES** *Rocket EJS 6*	50		3
2 Mar 85	**BREAKING HEARTS (AIN'T WHAT IT USED TO BE)** *Rocket EJS 7*	59		3
15 Jun 85	**ACT OF WAR** *Rocket EJS 8* & MILLIE JACKSON	32		5
12 Oct 85	**NIKITA** *Rocket EJS 9* ○	3		13
9 Nov 85	**THAT'S WHAT FRIENDS ARE FOR** *Arista ARIST 638* DIONNE WARWICK & FRIENDS FEATURING ELTON JOHN, STEVIE WONDER & GLADYS KNIGHT ★	16		9
7 Dec 85	**WRAP HER UP** *Rocket EJS 10*	12		10
1 Mar 86	**CRY TO HEAVEN** *Rocket EJS 11*	47		4
4 Oct 86	**HEARTACHE ALL OVER THE WORLD** *Rocket EJS 12*	45		4
29 Nov 86	**SLOW RIVERS** *Rocket EJS 13* & CLIFF RICHARD	44		8
20 Jun 87	**FLAMES OF PARADISE** *Columbia 6508657* JENNIFER RUSH & ELTON JOHN	59		3
16 Jan 88	**CANDLE IN THE WIND** *Rocket EJS 15*	5		11
4 Jun 88	**I DON'T WANNA GO ON WITH YOU LIKE THAT** *Rocket EJS 16*	30		8
3 Sep 88	**TOWN OF PLENTY** *Rocket EJS 17*	74		1
6 May 89	**THROUGH THE STORM** *Arista 112185* ARETHA FRANKLIN & ELTON JOHN	41		3
26 Aug 89	**HEALING HANDS** *Rocket EJS 19*	45		5
4 Nov 89	**SACRIFICE** *Rocket EJS 20*	55		3
9 Jun 90	**SACRIFICE/HEALING HANDS** *Rocket EJS 22* ⊛	1	5	15
18 Aug 90	**CLUB AT THE END OF THE STREET/WHISPERS** *Rocket EJS 23*	47		3
20 Oct 90	**YOU GOTTA LOVE SOMEONE** *Rocket EJS 24*	33		4
15 Dec 90	**EASIER TO WALK AWAY** *Rocket EJS 25*	63		2

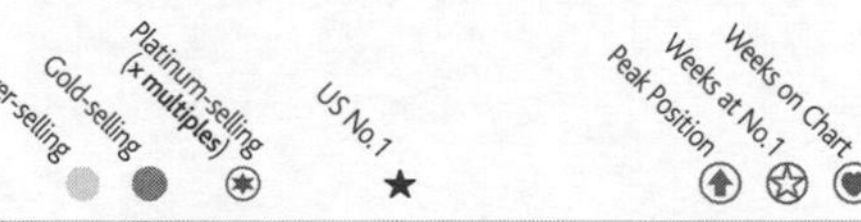

Date	Title	Peak	Wks at No.1	Wks on Chart
7 Dec 91	**DON'T LET THE SUN GO DOWN ON ME** *Epic 6576467* GEORGE MICHAEL & ELTON JOHN ● ★	1	2	10
6 Jun 92	**THE ONE** *Rocket EJS 28*	10		8
1 Aug 92	**RUNAWAY TRAIN** *Rocket EJS 29* & ERIC CLAPTON	31		4
7 Nov 92	**THE LAST SONG** *Rocket EJS 30*	21		4
22 May 93	**SIMPLE LIFE** *Rocket EJSCD 31*	44		2
20 Nov 93	**TRUE LOVE** *Rocket EJSCX 32* & KIKI DEE ●	2		10
26 Feb 94	**DON'T GO BREAKING MY HEART** *Rocket EJCD 33* WITH RuPAUL	7		7
14 May 94	**AIN'T NOTHING LIKE THE REAL THING** *London LONCD 350* MARCELLA DETROIT & ELTON JOHN	24		4
9 Jul 94	**CAN YOU FEEL THE LOVE TONIGHT** *Mercury EJCD 34*	14		9
8 Oct 94	**CIRCLE OF LIFE** *Rocket EJSCD 35*	11		12
4 Mar 95	**BELIEVE** *Rocket EJSDD 36*	15		7
20 May 95	**MADE IN ENGLAND** *Rocket EJSDD 37*	18		5
3 Feb 96	**PLEASE** *Rocket EJSCD 40*	33		3
14 Dec 96	**LIVE LIKE HORSES** *Rocket LLHDD 1* & LUCIANO PAVAROTTI	9		6
20 Sep 97	**SOMETHING ABOUT THE WAY YOU LOOK TONIGHT/ CANDLE IN THE WIND 1997** *Rocket PTCD 1* ⊛x9 ★	1	5	24
14 Feb 98	**RECOVER YOUR SOUL** *Rocket EJSCD 42*	16		3
13 Jun 98	**IF THE RIVER CAN BEND** *Rocket EJSDD 43*	32		2
6 Mar 99	**WRITTEN IN THE STARS** *Mercury EJSDD 45* & LeANN RIMES	10		8
6 Oct 01	**I WANT LOVE** *Rocket 5887072*	9		10
26 Jan 02	**THIS TRAIN DON'T STOP THERE ANYMORE** *Rocket 5888972*	24		4
13 Apr 02	**ORIGINAL SIN** *Rocket 5889992*	39		2
27 Jul 02	**YOUR SONG** *Mercury 639972* & ALESSANDRO SAFINA	4		10
21 Dec 02	**SORRY SEEMS TO BE THE HARDEST WORD** *Innocent SINCD 43* BLUE FEATURING ELTON JOHN ●	1	1	17
19 Jul 03	**ARE YOU READY FOR LOVE** *Southern Fried ECB 50LOVE*	66		1
6 Sep 03	**ARE YOU READY FOR LOVE** *Southern Fried ECB 50CDS*	1	1	13
13 Nov 04	**ALL THAT I'M ALLOWED (I'M THANKFUL)** *Rocket/Mercury 9868258*	20		5
16 Apr 05	**TURN THE LIGHTS OUT WHEN YOU LEAVE** *Rocket 9870664*	32		2
2 Jul 05	**GHETTO GOSPEL** *Interscope 9883248* 2PAC FEATURING ELTON JOHN	1	3	22
23 Jul 05	**ELECTRICITY** *Rocket 9872184*	4		4
7 Apr 07	**ROCKET MAN** *Mercury GBF080000394*	62		2
22 Dec 07	**STEP INTO CHRISTMAS** *Mercury GBAMB9500053*	53		2
9 May 09	**TINY DANCER (HOLD ME CLOSER)** *Asylum ASYLUM9CD* IRONIK FEATURING CHIPMUNK & ELTON JOHN	3		9

ROBERT JOHN
US, male vocalist (Robert John Pedrick) — 13

Date	Title	Peak	Wks at No.1	Wks on Chart
17 Jul 68	**IF YOU DON'T WANT MY LOVE** *CBS 3436*	42		5
20 Oct 79	**SAD EYES** *EMI American EA 101* ★	31		8

JOHN SILVER
Switzerland/Italy, male vocal/production duo — 2

Date	Title	Peak	Wks at No.1	Wks on Chart
25 Jan 03	**COME ON OVER** *Cream 20CD*	35		2

JOHNNA
US, female vocalist (Johnna Cummings) — 3

Date	Title	Peak	Wks at No.1	Wks on Chart
10 Feb 96	**DO WHAT YOU FEEL** *PWL International PWL 323CD*	43		2
11 May 96	**IN MY DREAMS** *PWL International PWL 325CD*	66		1

JOHNNY & CHARLEY
Spain, male vocal duo — 1

Date	Title	Peak	Wks at No.1	Wks on Chart
14 Oct 65	**LA YENKA** *Pye International 7N 25326*	49		1

JOHNNY & THE HURRICANES
US, male instrumental group – Johnny Paris (Johnny Pocisk), d. 1 May 2006, Tony Kaye, Lionel Mattice, Bo Savich, d. 4 Jan 2002, Paul Tesluk & Dave Yorko — 88

Date	Title	Peak	Wks at No.1	Wks on Chart
9 Oct 59	**RED RIVER ROCK** *London HL 8948*	3		16
25 Dec 59	**REVEILLE ROCK** *London HL 9017*	14		5
17 Mar 60	**BEATNIK FLY** *London HLI 9072*	8		19
16 Jun 60	**DOWN YONDER** *London HLX 9134*	8		11
29 Sep 60	**ROCKING GOOSE** *London HLX 9190*	3		20
2 Mar 61	**JA-DA** *London HLX 9289*	14		9
6 Jul 61	**OLD SMOKEY/HIGH VOLTAGE** *London HLX 9378*	24		8

JOHNNY BOY
UK, male/female vocal/production duo — 2

Date	Title	Peak	Wks at No.1	Wks on Chart
14 Aug 04	**YOU ARE THE GENERATION THAT BOUGHT MORE SHOES AND YOU GET WHAT YOU DESERVE** *Mercury 9866935*	50		2

JOHNNY CORPORATE
US, male production duo — 2

Date	Title	Peak	Wks at No.1	Wks on Chart
28 Oct 00	**SUNDAY SHOUTIN'** *Defected DFECT 21CDS*	45		2

JOHNNY HATES JAZZ
UK, male vocal/instrumental group – Clark Datchler, Calvin Hayes & Mike Nocito (b. Germany) — 45

Date	Title	Peak	Wks at No.1	Wks on Chart
11 Apr 87	**SHATTERED DREAMS** *Virgin VS 948*	5		14
29 Aug 87	**I DON'T WANT TO BE A HERO** *Virgin VS 1000*	11		10
21 Nov 87	**TURN BACK THE CLOCK** *Virgin VS 1017*	12		11
27 Feb 88	**HEART OF GOLD** *Virgin VS 1045*	19		7
9 Jul 88	**DON'T SAY IT'S LOVE** *Virgin VS 1081*	48		3

JOHNNY PANIC
UK, male vocal/instrumental group — 2

Date	Title	Peak	Wks at No.1	Wks on Chart
18 Sep 04	**BURN YOUR YOUTH** *Concept CDCON59*	69		1
14 May 05	**MINORITY OF ONE** *Concept CDCON63*	60		1

JOHNNY PANIC & THE BIBLE OF DREAMS
UK, male/female vocal/instrumental group. See Tears For Fears — 2

Date	Title	Peak	Wks at No.1	Wks on Chart
2 Feb 91	**JOHNNY PANIC AND THE BIBLE OF DREAMS** *Fontana PANIC 1*	70		2

JOHNSON
UK, male/female vocal/instrumental duo — 1

Date	Title	Peak	Wks at No.1	Wks on Chart
27 Mar 99	**SAY YOU LOVE ME** *Higher Ground HIGHS 18CD*	56		1

ANDREAS JOHNSON
Sweden, male vocalist (Jon Erik Andreas Johnson) — 12

Date	Title	Peak	Wks at No.1	Wks on Chart
5 Feb 00	**GLORIOUS** *WEA 254CD*	4		11
27 May 00	**THE GAMES WE PLAY** *WEA 264CD*	41		1

BRYAN JOHNSON
UK, male vocalist, d. 18 Oct 1995 (age 69) — 11

Date	Title	Peak	Wks at No.1	Wks on Chart
10 Mar 60	**LOOKING HIGH HIGH HIGH** *Decca F 11213*	20		11

CAREY JOHNSON
Australia, male vocalist (Reginald Johnson) — 8

Date	Title	Peak	Wks at No.1	Wks on Chart
25 Apr 87	**REAL FASHION REGGAE STYLE** *Oval TEN 170*	19		8

DENISE JOHNSON
UK, female vocalist — 4

Date	Title	Peak	Wks at No.1	Wks on Chart
24 Aug 91	**DON'T FIGHT IT FEEL IT** *Creation CRE 110* PRIMAL SCREAM FEATURING DENISE JOHNSON	41		2
14 May 94	**RAYS OF THE RISING SUN** *Magnet MAG 1022CD*	45		2

DON JOHNSON
US, male vocalist/actor — 12

Date	Title	Peak	Wks at No.1	Wks on Chart
18 Oct 86	**HEARTBEAT** *Epic 6500647*	46		5
5 Nov 88	**TILL I LOVED YOU (LOVE THEME FROM 'GOYA')** *CBS BARB 2* BARBRA STREISAND & DON JOHNSON	16		7

HOLLY JOHNSON
UK, male vocalist (William Johnson). See Frankie Goes To Hollywood — 38

Date	Title	Peak	Wks at No.1	Wks on Chart
14 Jan 89	**LOVE TRAIN** *MCA 1306* ●	4		11
1 Apr 89	**AMERICANOS** *MCA 1323* ●	4		11
20 May 89	**FERRY 'CROSS THE MERSEY** *PWL 41* CHRISTIANS, HOLLY JOHNSON, PAUL McCARTNEY, GERRY MARSDEN & STOCK AITKEN WATERMAN	1	3	7
24 Jun 89	**ATOMIC CITY** *MCA 1342*	18		4
30 Sep 89	**HEAVEN'S HERE** *MCA 1342*	62		2
1 Dec 90	**WHERE HAS LOVE GONE** *MCA 1460*	73		1
25 Dec 99	**THE POWER OF LOVE** *Pleasure Dome PLDCD 2005*	56		2

HOWARD JOHNSON
US, male vocalist — 6

Date	Title	Peak	Wks at No.1	Wks on Chart
4 Sep 82	**KEEPIN' LOVE NEW/SO FINE** *A&M USA 1221*	45		6

Top 100 Singles Of All Time

Based on UK Sales

* All Singles featured in the chart reached #1, except where indicated

Pos	Title Artist *Year*	Approx Sales
1	**SOMETHING ABOUT THE WAY YOU LOOK TONIGHT/ CANDLE IN THE WIND '97** ELTON JOHN *1997*	4,890,000
2	**DO THEY KNOW IT'S CHRISTMAS?** BAND AID *1984*	3,640,000
3	**BOHEMIAN RHAPSODY** QUEEN *1975*	2,290,000
4	**MULL OF KINTYRE/GIRLS' SCHOOL** WINGS *1977*	2,060,000
5	**RIVERS OF BABYLON/BROWN GIRL IN THE RING** BONEY M *1978*	2,020,000
6	**YOU'RE THE ONE THAT I WANT** JOHN TRAVOLTA & OLIVIA NEWTON-JOHN *1978*	2,015,000
7	**RELAX** FRANKIE GOES TO HOLLYWOOD *1983*	1,980,000
8	**SHE LOVES YOU** BEATLES *1963*	1,890,000
9	**UNCHAINED MELODY/(THERE'LL BE BLUEBIRDS OVER THE) WHITE CLIFFS OF DOVER** ROBSON GREEN & JEROME FLYNN *1995*	1,850,000
10	**MARY'S BOY CHILD – OH MY LORD** BONEY M *1978*	1,830,000
11	**LOVE IS ALL AROUND** WET WET WET *1994*	1,825,000
12	**I JUST CALLED TO SAY I LOVE YOU** STEVIE WONDER *1984*	1,815,000
13	**ANYTHING IS POSSIBLE / EVERGREEN** WILL YOUNG *2002*	1,790,000
14	**BARBIE GIRL** AQUA *1997*	1,770,000
15	**I WANT TO HOLD YOUR HAND** BEATLES *1963*	1,750,000
16	**BELIEVE** CHER *1998*	1,720,000
17	**(EVERYTHING I DO) I DO IT FOR YOU** BRYAN ADAMS *1991*	1,660,000
18	**LAST CHRISTMAS/EVERYTHING SHE WANTS** WHAM! *1984*	1,600,000*
19	**SUMMER NIGHTS** JOHN TRAVOLTA & OLIVIA NEWTON-JOHN *1978*	1,570,000
20	**TWO TRIBES** FRANKIE GOES TO HOLLYWOOD *1984*	1,560,000
21	**PERFECT DAY** VARIOUS ARTISTS *1997*	1,550,000
22	**IMAGINE** JOHN LENNON *1975*	1,545,000
23	**TEARS** KEN DODD *1965*	1,520,000
24	**CAN'T BUY ME LOVE** BEATLES *1964*	1,520,000
25	**DON'T YOU WANT ME** HUMAN LEAGUE *1981*	1,500,000
26	**...BABY ONE MORE TIME** BRITNEY SPEARS *1999*	1,490,000
27	**I'LL BE MISSING YOU** PUFF DADDY & FAITH EVANS (FT 112) *1997*	1,470,000
28	**I WILL ALWAYS LOVE YOU** WHITNEY HOUSTON *1992*	1,460,000
29	**KARMA CHAMELEON** CULTURE CLUB *1983*	1,450,000
30	**Y.M.C.A.** VILLAGE PEOPLE *1978*	1,430,000
31	**CARELESS WHISPER** GEORGE MICHAEL *1984*	1,420,000
32	**THREE LIONS** BADDIEL/SKINNER/ LIGHTNING SEEDS *1996*	1,415,000
33	**(WE'RE GONNA) ROCK AROUND THE CLOCK** BILL HALEY & HIS COMETS *1955*	1,410,000
34	**I FEEL FINE** BEATLES *1964*	1,410,000
35	**MY HEART WILL GO ON** CELINE DION *1998*	1,410,000
36	**THE CARNIVAL IS OVER** SEEKERS *1965*	1,405,000
37	**DAY TRIPPER/WE CAN WORK IT OUT** BEATLES *1965*	1,385,000
38	**RELEASE ME** ENGELBERT HUMPERDINCK *1967*	1,375,000
39	**THE POWER OF LOVE** JENNIFER RUSH *1985*	1,365,000
40	**GANGSTA'S PARADISE** COOLIO FT LV *1995*	1,345,000
41	**UNCHAINED MELODY** GARETH GATES *2002*	1,340,000
42	**KILLING ME SOFTLY** FUGEES *1996*	1,325,000
43	**WANNABE** SPICE GIRLS *1996*	1,300,000
44	**NEVER EVER** ALL SAINTS *1997*	1,290,000
45	**THINK TWICE** CELINE DION *1994*	1,280,000
46	**COME ON EILEEN** DEXY'S MIDNIGHT RUNNERS *1982*	1,270,000
47	**IT'S NOW OR NEVER** ELVIS PRESLEY *1960*	1,255,000
48	**EYE OF THE TIGER** SURVIVOR *1982*	1,250,000
49	**DIANA** PAUL ANKA *1957*	1,250,000
50	**HEART OF GLASS** BLONDIE *1979*	1,245,000
51	**IT WASN'T ME** SHAGGY *2001*	1,230,000
52	**TAINTED LOVE** SOFT CELL *1981*	1,230,000
53	**(IS THIS THE WAY TO) AMARILLO** TONY CHRISTIE FT PETER KAY *2005*	1,215,000
54	**GREEN GREEN GRASS OF HOME** TOM JONES *1966*	1,200,000
55	**IT'S LIKE THAT** RUN DMC VS JASON NEVINS *1998*	1,195,000
56	**BRIGHT EYES** ART GARFUNKEL *1979*	1,185,000
57	**HALLELUJAH** ALEXANDRA BURKE *2008*	1,185,000
58	**MARY'S BOY CHILD** HARRY BELAFONTE *1957*	1,180,000
59	**THE LAST WALTZ** ENGELBERT HUMPERDINCK *1967*	1,165,000
60	**HEARTBEAT/TRAGEDY** STEPS *1998*	1,150,000
61	**DON'T GIVE UP ON US** DAVID SOUL *1976*	1,150,000
62	**DO THEY KNOW IT'S CHRISTMAS?** BAND AID 20 *2004*	1,150,000

Pos	Title Artist *Year*	Approx Sales
63	**STRANGER ON THE SHORE** MR ACKER BILK *1961*	1,145,000*
64	**I LOVE YOU LOVE ME LOVE** GARY GLITTER *1973*	1,145,000
65	**EARTH SONG** MICHAEL JACKSON *1995*	1,140,000
66	**SPACEMAN** BABYLON ZOO *1996*	1,135,000
67	**MERRY XMAS EVERYBODY** SLADE *1973*	1,130,000
68	**CAN'T GET YOU OUT OF MY HEAD** KYLIE MINOGUE *2001*	1,125,000
69	**BLUE MONDAY** NEW ORDER *1983*	1,125,000*
70	**SATURDAY NIGHT** WHIGFIELD *1994*	1,120,000
71	**NO MATTER WHAT** BOYZONE *1998*	1,110,000
72	**TELETUBBIES SAY 'EH-OH!'** TELETUBBIES *1997*	1,105,000
73	**I BELIEVE/UP ON THE ROOF** ROBSON & JEROME *1995*	1,105,000
74	**I REMEMBER YOU** FRANK IFIELD *1962*	1,100,000
75	**HIT ME WITH YOUR RHYTHM STICK** IAN DURY & THE BLOCKHEADS *1978*	1,100,000
76	**2 BECOME 1** SPICE GIRLS *1996*	1,095,000
77	**THAT'S MY GOAL** SHAYNE WARD *2005*	1,090,000
78	**PURE & SIMPLE** HEAR'SAY *2001*	1,085,000
79	**GHOSTBUSTERS** RAY PARKER, JR *1984*	1,065,000*
80	**TORN** NATALIE IMBRUGLIA *1997*	1,060,000*
81	**THE YOUNG ONES** CLIFF RICHARD & THE SHADOWS *1962*	1,060,000
82	**ANOTHER BRICK IN THE WALL PART 2** PINK FLOYD *1979*	1,050,000
83	**ANGELS** ROBBIE WILLIAMS *1997*	1,045,000*
84	**BACK FOR GOOD** TAKE THAT *1995*	1,045,000
85	**BLUE (DA BA DEE)** EIFFEL 65 *1999*	1,040,000
86	**FAME** IRENE CARA *1982*	1,035,000
87	**RIDE ON TIME** BLACK BOX *1989*	1,030,000
88	**WONDERWALL** OASIS *1995*	1,025,000*
89	**DANCING QUEEN** ABBA *1976*	1,020,000
90	**STAND & DELIVER** ADAM & THE ANTS *1981*	1,015,000
91	**CAN WE FIX IT?** BOB THE BUILDER *2000*	1,010,000
92	**SAVE YOUR KISSES FOR ME** BROTHERHOOD OF MAN *1976*	1,010,000
93	**EYE LEVEL** SIMON PARK ORCHESTRA *1972*	1,005,000
94	**UPTOWN GIRL** BILLY JOEL *1983*	1,005,000
95	**I'D LIKE TO TEACH THE WORLD TO SING** NEW SEEKERS *1971*	1,005,000
96	**SUGAR SUGAR** ARCHIES *1969*	1,000,000
97	**DON'T CRY FOR ME ARGENTINA** JULIE COVINGTON *1976*	1,000,000
98	**LONG HAIRED LOVER FROM LIVERPOOL** LITTLE JIMMY OSMOND *1972*	1,000,000
99	**UNCHAINED MELODY** RIGHTEOUS BROTHERS *1965*	1,000,000
100	**SAILING** ROD STEWART *1975*	995,000

JACK JOHNSON

US, male vocalist/multi-instrumentalist/film-maker/surfer — 27

Date	Title	Peak Position	Weeks at No.1	Weeks on Chart
25 Jun 05	**GOOD PEOPLE** *Island MCSTD40417*	50		3
17 Sep 05	**BREAKDOWN** *Island MCSTD40430*	73		2
4 Mar 06	**SITTING, WAITING, WISHING** *Brushfire/Island MCSXD40407*	65		1
11 Mar 06	**BETTER TOGETHER** *Brushfire/Island 9879916*	24		5
27 May 06	**UPSIDE DOWN** *Brushfire/Island 9853873*	30		12
26 Jan 08	**IF I HAD EYES** *Brushfire/Island 1760759*	60		4

JOHNNY JOHNSON & THE BANDWAGON

US, male vocal/instrumental group – Johnny Johnson, Billy Bradley, Arthur Fullilove & Terry Lewis — 50

Date	Title	Peak Position	Weeks at No.1	Weeks on Chart
16 Oct 68	**BREAKIN' DOWN THE WALLS OF HEARTACHE** *Direction 58 3670* BANDWAGON	4		15
5 Feb 69	**YOU** *Direction 58 3923* BANDWAGON	34		4
28 May 69	**LET'S HANG ON** *Direction 58 4180* BANDWAGON	36		6
25 Jul 70	**SWEET INSPIRATION** *Bell 1111*	10		13
28 Nov 70	**(BLAME IT) ON THE PONY EXPRESS** *Bell 1128*	7		12

KEVIN JOHNSON

Australia, male vocalist — 6

Date	Title	Peak Position	Weeks at No.1	Weeks on Chart
11 Jan 75	**ROCK 'N ROLL (I GAVE YOU THE BEST YEARS OF MY LIFE)** *UK UKR 84*	23		6

LAURIE JOHNSON ORCHESTRA

UK, orchestra — 14

Date	Title	Peak Position	Weeks at No.1	Weeks on Chart
28 Sep 61	**SUCU SUCU** *Pye 7N 15383*	9		12
17 May 97	**THEME FROM 'THE PROFESSIONALS'** *Virgin VSCDT 1643* LAURIE JOHNSON'S LONDON BIG BAND	36		2

LJ JOHNSON

US, male vocalist — 6

Date	Title	Peak Position	Weeks at No.1	Weeks on Chart
7 Feb 76	**YOUR MAGIC PUT A SPELL ON ME** *Philips 6006 492*	27		6

LOU JOHNSON

US, male vocalist — 2

Date	Title	Peak Position	Weeks at No.1	Weeks on Chart
26 Nov 64	**MESSAGE TO MARTHA** *London HL 9929*	36		2

MARV JOHNSON

US, male vocalist, d. 16 May 1993 (age 54) — 40

Date	Title	Peak Position	Weeks at No.1	Weeks on Chart
12 Feb 60	**YOU GOT WHAT IT TAKES** *London HLT 9013*	7		17
5 May 60	**I LOVE THE WAY YOU LOVE** *London HLT 9109*	35		3
11 Aug 60	**AIN'T GONNA BE THAT WAY** *London HLT 9165*	50		1
22 Jan 69	**I'LL PICK A ROSE FOR MY ROSE** *Tamla Motown TMG 680*	10		11
25 Oct 69	**I MISS YOU BABY** *Tamla Motown TMG 713*	25		8

PAUL JOHNSON

UK, male vocalist. See Paradise — 7

Date	Title	Peak Position	Weeks at No.1	Weeks on Chart
21 Feb 87	**WHEN LOVE COMES CALLING** *CBS PJOHN 1*	52		5
25 Feb 89	**NO MORE TOMORROWS** *CBS PJOHN 7*	67		2

PAUL JOHNSON

US, male DJ/producer/instrumentalist — 9

Date	Title	Peak Position	Weeks at No.1	Weeks on Chart
25 Sep 99	**GET GET DOWN** *Defected DEFECT 7CDS*	5		8
27 Aug 05	**SHE GOT ME ON** *Data DATA86CDS*	70		1

PUFF JOHNSON

US, female vocalist (Ewanya Johnson) — 6

Date	Title	Peak Position	Weeks at No.1	Weeks on Chart
18 Jan 97	**OVER AND OVER** *Columbia 6640345*	20		4
12 Apr 97	**FOREVER MORE** *Work 6644075*	29		2

ROMINA JOHNSON

UK (b. Italy), female vocalist — 13

Date	Title	Peak Position	Weeks at No.1	Weeks on Chart
4 Mar 00	**MOVIN TOO FAST** *Locked On/XL Recordings LUX 117CD* ARTFUL DODGER & ROMINA JOHNSON ●	2		12
17 Jun 00	**MY FORBIDDEN LOVER** *51 Lexington CDLEX 1* FEATURING LUCI MARTIN & NORMA JEAN	59		1

Silver-selling ● Gold-selling ● Platinum-selling (× multiples) ✱ US No.1 ★ Peak Position Weeks at No.1 Weeks on Chart

SYLEENA JOHNSON
US, female vocalist

Date	Title	Peak Position	Weeks at No.1	Weeks on Chart (10)
26 Oct 02	**TONIGHT I'M GONNA LET GO** *Jive 9254252*	38		2
19 Jun 04	**ALL FALLS DOWN** *Roc-A-Fella 9862670* KANYE WEST FEATURING SYLEENA JOHNSON	10		8

ANA JOHNSSON
Sweden, female vocalist

Date	Title	Peak Position	Weeks at No.1	Weeks on Chart (6)
14 Aug 04	**WE ARE** *Epic 6751622*	8		6

JOHNSTON BROTHERS
UK, male vocal group – Johnnie Johnston (Johnny Reine), Frank Holmes, Miff King & Eddie Lester

Date	Title	Peak Position	Weeks at No.1	Weeks on Chart (33)
3 Apr 53	**OH HAPPY DAY** *Decca F 10071*	4		8
5 Nov 54	**WAIT FOR ME DARLING** *Decca F 10362* JOAN REGAN & THE JOHNSTON BROTHERS	18		1
21 Jan 55	**HAPPY DAYS AND LONELY NIGHTS** *Decca F 10389* SUZI MILLER & THE JOHNSTON BROTHERS	14		2
7 Oct 55	**HERNANDO'S HIDEAWAY** *Decca F 10608*	1	2	13
30 Dec 55	**JOIN IN AND SING AGAIN** *Decca F 10636* & THE GEORGE CHISHOLM SOUR-NOTE SIX	9		1
13 Apr 56	**NO OTHER LOVE** *Decca F 10721*	22		1
30 Nov 56	**IN THE MIDDLE OF THE HOUSE** *Decca F 10781*	27		1
7 Dec 56	**JOIN IN AND SING (NO. 3)** *Decca F 10814*	24		2
8 Feb 57	**GIVE HER MY LOVE** *Decca F 10828*	27		1
19 Apr 57	**HEART** *Decca F 10860*	23		3

BRUCE JOHNSTON
US, male keyboard player. See Beach Boys

Date	Title	Peak Position	Weeks at No.1	Weeks on Chart (4)
27 Aug 77	**PIPELINE** *CBS 5514*	33		4

JAN JOHNSTON
UK, female vocalist

Date	Title	Peak Position	Weeks at No.1	Weeks on Chart (10)
8 Feb 97	**TAKE ME BY THE HAND** *AM:PM 5821012* SUBMERGE FEATURING JAN JOHNSTON	28		2
22 Jul 00	**SKYDIVE (REMIX)** *Renaissance Recordings RENCDS 002* FREEFALL FEATURING JAN JOHNSTON	43		2
28 Nov 98	**SKYDIVE** *Stress CDSTR 89* FREEFALL FEATURING JAN JOHNSTON	75		1
21 Apr 01	**FLESH** *Perfecto PERF 05CDS*	36		2
28 Jul 01	**SILENT WORDS** *Perfecto PERF 16CDS*	57		1
8 Sep 01	**SKYDIVE (I FEEL WONDERFUL)** *Incentive CENT 22CDS* FREEFALL FEATURING JAN JOHNSTON	35		2

SABRINA JOHNSTON
US (b. Germany), female vocalist

Date	Title	Peak Position	Weeks at No.1	Weeks on Chart (19)
7 Sep 91	**PEACE** *East West YZ 616*	8		10
7 Dec 91	**FRIENDSHIP** *East West YZ 637*	58		4
11 Jul 92	**I WANNA SING** *East West YZ 661*	46		2
3 Oct 92	**PEACE** *Epic 6584377*	35		2
13 Aug 94	**SATISFY MY LOVE** *Champion CHAMPCD 311*	62		1

JIMMY JOHNSTONE, JIM KERR, SIMPLE MINDS & LAURA MCGHEE
UK, male footballer (Celtic) & male/female vocal group

Date	Title	Peak Position	Weeks at No.1	Weeks on Chart (3)
8 Apr 06	**TRIBUTE TO JINKY** *Lord Of The Wing LWSP7*	28		3

JOJO
US, female vocalist (Joanne Levesque)

Date	Title	Peak Position	Weeks at No.1	Weeks on Chart (37)
11 Sep 04	**LEAVE (GET OUT)** *Mercury 9867841*	2		8
27 Nov 04	**BABY IT'S YOU** *Mercury 9869056* FEATURING BOW WOW	8		9
13 Jan 07	**TOO LITTLE TOO LATE** *Mercury 1716751*	4		15
12 May 07	**ANYTHING** *Mercury 1734750*	21		5

JOLLY BROTHERS
Jamaica, male vocal/instrumental group

Date	Title	Peak Position	Weeks at No.1	Weeks on Chart (7)
28 Jul 79	**CONSCIOUS MAN** *United Artists UP 36415*	46		7

JOLLY ROGER
UK, male producer (Eddie Richards)

Date	Title	Peak Position	Weeks at No.1	Weeks on Chart (12)
10 Sep 88	**ACID MAN** *10 TEN 236*	23		12

JOMANDA
US, female vocal trio

Date	Title	Peak Position	Weeks at No.1	Weeks on Chart (10)
22 Apr 89	**MAKE MY BODY ROCK** *RCA PB 42749*	44		3
29 Jun 91	**GOT A LOVE FOR YOU** *Giant W 0040*	43		4
11 Sep 93	**I LIKE IT** *Big Beat A 8377CD*	67		1
13 Nov 93	**NEVER** *Big Beat A 8347CD*	40		2

JON & VANGELIS
UK, male vocalist (Jon Anderson) & Greece, male multi-instrumentalist (Evangelos Papathanassiou – Vangelis*)

Date	Title	Peak Position	Weeks at No.1	Weeks on Chart (28)
5 Jan 80	**I HEAR YOU NOW** *Polydor POSP 96*	8		11
12 Dec 81	**I'LL FIND MY WAY HOME** *Polydor JV 1* ●	6		13
30 Jul 83	**HE IS SAILING** *Polydor JV 4*	61		2
18 Aug 84	**STATE OF INDEPENDENCE** *Polydor JV 5*	67		2

JON OF THE PLEASED WIMMIN
UK, male DJ/producer (Jonathan Cooper)

Date	Title	Peak Position	Weeks at No.1	Weeks on Chart (5)
18 Feb 95	**PASSION** *Perfecto YZ 884CD*	27		3
6 Apr 96	**GIVE ME STRENGTH** *Perfecto PERF 119CD*	30		2

JON THE DENTIST VS OLLIE JAYE
UK, male DJ/production duo

Date	Title	Peak Position	Weeks at No.1	Weeks on Chart (2)
24 Jul 99	**IMAGINATION** *Tidy Trax TIDY 126CD*	72		1
10 Jun 00	**FEEL SO GOOD** *Tidy Trax TIDY 135CD*	72		1

JONAH
Holland, male production group

Date	Title	Peak Position	Weeks at No.1	Weeks on Chart (4)
22 Jul 00	**SSSST (LISTEN)** *VC Recordings VCRD 69*	25		4

JONAS BROTHERS
US, male vocal/instrumental trio

Date	Title	Peak Position	Weeks at No.1	Weeks on Chart (14)
28 Jun 08	**SOS** *Hollywood 1768733*	13		6
4 Oct 08	**BURNIN' UP/WHEN YOU LOOK ME IN THE EYES** *Polydor USHR10823884*	30		5
4 Oct 08	**PLAY MY MUSIC** *Walt Disney USWD10833809*	57		1
20 Jun 09	**PARANOID** *Hollywood USHR10924413*	56		2

ALED JONES
UK, male vocalist/TV presenter

Date	Title	Peak Position	Weeks at No.1	Weeks on Chart (27)
20 Jul 85	**MEMORY: THEME FROM THE MUSICAL 'CATS'** *BBC RESL 175*	42		4
30 Nov 85	**WALKING IN THE AIR** *HMV ALED 1* ●	5		11
14 Dec 85	**PICTURES IN THE DARK** *Virgin VS 836* MIKE OLDFIELD FEATURING ALED JONES, ANITA HEGERLAND & BARRY PALMER	50		6
20 Dec 86	**A WINTER STORY** *HMV ALED 2*	51		3
29 Dec 07	**WALKING IN THE AIR** *EMI GBAYE8500081*	72		1
19 Dec 09	**SILVER BELLS/ME AND MY TEDDY BEAR** *Bandaged CDTOG2* SIR TERRY WOGAN & ALED JONES	27		2

BARBARA JONES
Jamaica, female vocalist

Date	Title	Peak Position	Weeks at No.1	Weeks on Chart (7)
31 Jan 81	**JUST WHEN I NEEDED YOU MOST** *Sonet SON 2221*	31		7

CATHERINE ZETA JONES
UK, female vocalist/actor

Date	Title	Peak Position	Weeks at No.1	Weeks on Chart (9)
19 Sep 92	**FOR ALL TIME** *Columbia 6583547*	36		5
26 Nov 94	**TRUE LOVE WAYS** *Polygram TV TLWCD 2* DAVID ESSEX & CATHERINE ZETA JONES	38		3
1 Apr 95	**IN THE ARMS OF LOVE** *Wow! WOWCD 7101*	72		1

DEENA JONES & THE DREAMS
US, female vocal group

Date	Title	Peak Position	Weeks at No.1	Weeks on Chart (1)
12 Sep 09	**ONE NIGHT ONLY** *Columbia USLIC0602216*	67		1

DONELL JONES
US, male vocalist/producer

Date	Title	Peak Position	Weeks at No.1	Weeks on Chart (20)
15 Feb 97	**KNOCKS ME OFF MY FEET** *LaFace 74321458502*	58		1
22 Jan 00	**U KNOW WHAT'S UP** *LaFace 74321722762* ●	2		11
20 May 00	**SHORTY (GOT HER EYES ON ME)** *LaFace 74321748902*	19		3

Date	Title	Peak	Wks at No.1	Wks on Chart
2 Dec 00	**TRUE STEP TONIGHT** *NuLife 74321811312* TRUE STEPPERS FEATURING BRIAN HARVEY & DONELL JONES	25		3
24 Aug 02	**YOU KNOW THAT I LOVE YOU** *Arista 74321956962*	41		2

GEORGIA JONES
US, female vocalist — 4

Date	Title	Peak	Wks at No.1	Wks on Chart
4 May 96	**OVER & OVER** *ffrr FCD 277* PLUX FEATURING GEORGIA JONES	33		2
14 Nov 98	**ON THE TOP OF THE WORLD** *Positiva CDTIV 100* DIVA SURPRISE FEATURING GEORGIA JONES	29		2

GRACE JONES
Jamaica, female vocalist (Grace Mendoza) — 46

Date	Title	Peak	Wks at No.1	Wks on Chart
26 Jul 80	**PRIVATE LIFE** *Island WIP 6629*	17		8
20 Jun 81	**PULL UP TO THE BUMPER** *Island WIP 6696*	53		4
30 Oct 82	**THE APPLE STRETCHING/NIPPLE TO THE BOTTLE** *Island WIP 6779*	50		4
9 Apr 83	**MY JAMAICAN GUY** *Island IS 103*	56		3
12 Oct 85	**SLAVE TO THE RHYTHM** *ZTT IS 206*	12		8
18 Jan 86	**PULL UP TO THE BUMPER/LA VIE EN ROSE** *Island IS 240*	12		9
1 Mar 86	**LOVE IS THE DRUG** *Island IS 266*	35		4
15 Nov 86	**I'M NOT PERFECT (BUT I'M PERFECT FOR YOU)** *Manhattan MT 15*	56		3
7 May 94	**SLAVE TO THE RHYTHM** *Zance ZANG 50CD1*	28		2
25 Nov 00	**PULL UP TO THE BUMPER** *Club Tools 0120375 CLU* VS FUNKSTAR DE LUXE	60		1

HANNAH JONES
US, female vocalist — 9

Date	Title	Peak	Wks at No.1	Wks on Chart
14 Sep 91	**BRIDGE OVER TROUBLED WATER** *Dance Pool 6565467* PJB FEATURING HANNAH & HER SISTERS	21		8
30 Jan 93	**KEEP IT ON** *TMRC CDTMRC 7*	67		1

HOWARD JONES
UK, male vocalist/keyboard player (John Howard Jones) — 103

Date	Title	Peak	Wks at No.1	Wks on Chart
17 Sep 83	**NEW SONG** *WEA HOW 1* ●	3		15
26 Nov 83	**WHAT IS LOVE** *WEA HOW 2* ●	2		15
18 Feb 84	**HIDE AND SEEK** *WEA HOW 3*	12		9
26 May 84	**PEARL IN THE SHELL** *WEA HOW 4*	7		10
11 Aug 84	**LIKE TO GET TO KNOW YOU WELL** *WEA HOW 5* ●	4		12
9 Feb 85	**THINGS CAN ONLY GET BETTER** *WEA HOW 6* ●	6		8
20 Apr 85	**LOOK MAMA** *WEA HOW 7*	10		6
29 Jun 85	**LIFE IN ONE DAY** *WEA HOW 8*	14		7
15 Mar 86	**NO ONE IS TO BLAME** *WEA HOW 9*	16		7
4 Oct 86	**ALL I WANT** *WEA HOW 10*	35		4
29 Nov 86	**YOU KNOW I LOVE YOU...DON'T YOU** *WEA HOW 11*	43		3
21 Mar 87	**A LITTLE BIT OF SNOW** *WEA HOW 12*	70		1
4 Mar 89	**EVERLASTING LOVE** *WEA HOW 13*	62		3
11 Apr 92	**LIFT ME UP** *WEA HOW 15*	52		3

JANIE JONES
UK, female vocalist (Marion Maitchell) — 3

Date	Title	Peak	Wks at No.1	Wks on Chart
27 Jan 66	**WITCHES' BREW** *HMV POP 1495*	46		3

JIMMY JONES
US, male vocalist — 47

Date	Title	Peak	Wks at No.1	Wks on Chart
17 Mar 60	**HANDY MAN** *MGM 1051*	3		24
16 Jun 60	**GOOD TIMIN'** *MGM 1078*	1	3	15
8 Sep 60	**I JUST GO FOR YOU** *MGM 1091*	35		4
17 Nov 60	**READY FOR LOVE** *MGM 1103*	46		1
6 Apr 61	**I TOLD YOU SO** *MGM 1123*	33		3

JUGGY JONES
US, multi-instrumentalist (Henry Murray), d. 8 Feb 2005 (age 81) — 4

Date	Title	Peak	Wks at No.1	Wks on Chart
7 Feb 76	**INSIDE AMERICA** *Contempo CS 2080*	39		4

LAVINIA JONES
South Africa, female vocalist — 2

Date	Title	Peak	Wks at No.1	Wks on Chart
18 Feb 95	**SING IT TO YOU (DEE-DOOB-DEE-DOO)** *Virgin International DINDG 142*	45		2

NORAH JONES
US, female vocalist/multi-instrumentalist — 6

Date	Title	Peak	Wks at No.1	Wks on Chart
25 May 02	**DON'T KNOW WHY** *Parlophone CDCL 836*	59		1
17 Aug 02	**FEELIN' THE SAME WAY** *Parlophone CDCL 838*	72		1
13 Sep 03	**DON'T KNOW WHY/I'LL BE YOUR BABY TONIGHT** *Parlophone CDCL 848*	67		1
10 Apr 04	**SUNRISE** *Blue Note CDCL 853*	30		3

ORAN 'JUICE' JONES
US, male vocalist — 14

Date	Title	Peak	Wks at No.1	Wks on Chart
15 Nov 86	**THE RAIN** *Def Jam A 7303* ●	4		14

PAUL JONES
UK, male vocalist (Paul Pond). See Blues Band, Manfred Mann — 34

Date	Title	Peak	Wks at No.1	Wks on Chart
6 Oct 66	**HIGH TIME** *HMV POP 1554*	4		15
19 Jan 67	**I'VE BEEN A BAD BAD BOY** *HMV POP 1576*	5		9
23 Aug 67	**THINKIN' AIN'T FOR ME** *HMV POP 1602*	32		8
5 Feb 69	**AQUARIUS** *Columbia DB 8514*	45		2

QUINCY JONES
US, male producer/keyboard player — 42

Date	Title	Peak	Wks at No.1	Wks on Chart
29 Jul 78	**STUFF LIKE THAT** *A&M AMS 7367*	34		9
11 Apr 81	**AI NO CORRIDA (I-NO-KO-REE-DA)** *A&M AMS 8109* FEATURING DUNE	14		10
20 Jun 81	**RAZZAMATAZZ** *A&M 8140* FEATURING PATTI AUSTIN	11		9
5 Sep 81	**BETCHA' WOULDN'T HURT ME** *A&M AMS 8157*	52		3
13 Jan 90	**I'LL BE GOOD TO YOU** *Qwest W 2697* FEATURING RAY CHARLES & CHAKA KHAN	21		7
31 Mar 90	**SECRET GARDEN** *Qwest W 9992* FEATURING AL B SURE!, JAMES INGRAM, EL DeBARGE & BARRY WHITE	67		1
14 Sep 96	**STOMP – THE REMIXES** *Qwest W 0372CD* FEATURING MELLE MEL, COOLIO, YO-YO, SHAQUILLE O'NEAL & THE LUNIZ	28		2
1 Aug 98	**SOUL BOSSA NOVA** *Manifesto FESCD 48* COOL, THE FAB & THE GROOVY PRESENT QUINCY JONES	47		1

RICKIE LEE JONES
US, female vocalist/guitarist — 9

Date	Title	Peak	Wks at No.1	Wks on Chart
23 Jun 79	**CHUCK E.'S IN LOVE** *Warner Brothers K 17390*	18		9

SONNY JONES FEATURING TARA CHASE
Germany/Canada, male/female vocal/rap duo — 2

Date	Title	Peak	Wks at No.1	Wks on Chart
7 Oct 00	**FOLLOW YOU FOLLOW ME** *Logic 74321772892*	42		2

TAMMY JONES
UK, female vocalist — 10

Date	Title	Peak	Wks at No.1	Wks on Chart
26 Apr 75	**LET ME TRY AGAIN** *Epic EPC 3211*	5		10

TOM JONES
UK, male vocalist (Thomas Woodward). Perennially popular Welsh vocalist who has a 44-year span of UK No.1s and was the top UK solo singer of the 1960s on both sides of the Atlantic. The unmistakable Vegas veteran received the 'Outstanding Contribution to British Music' award at the 2003 BRITs — 411

Date	Title	Peak	Wks at No.1	Wks on Chart
11 Feb 65	**IT'S NOT UNUSUAL** *Decca F 12062*	1	1	14
6 May 65	**ONCE UPON A TIME** *Decca F 12121*	32		4
8 Jul 65	**WITH THESE HANDS** *Decca F 12191*	13		11
12 Aug 65	**WHAT'S NEW PUSSYCAT** *Decca F 12203*	11		10
13 Jan 66	**THUNDERBALL** *Decca F 12292*	35		4
19 May 66	**ONCE THERE WAS A TIME/NOT RESPONSIBLE** *Decca F 12390*	18		9
18 Aug 66	**THIS AND THAT** *Decca F 12461*	44		3
10 Nov 66	**GREEN GREEN GRASS OF HOME** *Decca F 22511*	1	7	22
16 Feb 67	**DETROIT CITY** *Decca F 22555*	8		10
13 Apr 67	**FUNNY FAMILIAR FORGOTTEN FEELINGS** *Decca F 12599*	7		15
26 Jul 67	**I'LL NEVER FALL IN LOVE AGAIN** *Decca F 12639*	2		25
22 Nov 67	**I'M COMING HOME** *Decca F 12693*	2		16
28 Feb 68	**DELILAH** *Decca F 12747*	2		17
17 Jul 68	**HELP YOURSELF** *Decca F 12812*	5		26
27 Nov 68	**A MINUTE OF YOUR TIME** *Decca F 12854*	14		15
14 May 69	**LOVE ME TONIGHT** *Decca F 12924*	9		12
13 Dec 69	**WITHOUT LOVE (THERE IS NOTHING)** *Decca F 12990*	10		12
18 Apr 70	**DAUGHTER OF DARKNESS** *Decca F 13013*	5		15
15 Aug 70	**I (WHO HAVE NOTHING)** *Decca F 13061*	16		11
16 Jan 71	**SHE'S A LADY** *Decca F 13113*	13		10

Silver-selling ● Gold-selling ● Platinum-selling (x multiples) ⊛ US No.1 ★ Peak Position Weeks at No.1 Weeks on Chart

Date	Title	Peak Position	Weeks at No.1	Weeks on Chart
5 Jun 71	**PUPPET MAN** *Decca F 13183*	49		2
23 Oct 71	**TILL** *Decca F 13236*	2		15
1 Apr 72	**THE YOUNG NEW MEXICAN PUPPETEER** *Decca F 13298*	6		12
14 Apr 73	**LETTER TO LUCILLE** *Decca F 13393*	31		8
7 Sep 74	**SOMETHING 'BOUT YOU BABY I LIKE** *Decca F 13550*	36		5
16 Apr 77	**SAY YOU'LL STAY UNTIL TOMORROW** *EMI 2583*	40		3
18 Apr 87	**A BOY FROM NOWHERE** *Epic OLE 1* ●	2		12
30 May 87	**IT'S NOT UNUSUAL** *Decca F 103*	17		8
2 Jan 88	**I WAS BORN TO BE ME** *Epic OLE 4*	61		1
29 Oct 88	**KISS** *China 11* ART OF NOISE FEATURING TOM JONES	5		7
29 Apr 89	**MOVE CLOSER** *Jive 203*	49		3
26 Jan 91	**COULDN'T SAY GOODBYE** *Dover ROJ 10*	51		2
16 Mar 91	**CARRYING A TORCH** *Dover ROJ 12*	57		2
4 Jul 92	**DELILAH** *The Hit Label TOM 10*	68		2
6 Feb 93	**ALL YOU NEED IS LOVE** *Childline CHILDCD 93*	19		4
5 Nov 94	**IF I ONLY KNEW** *ZTT ZANG 59CD*	11		9
25 Sep 99	**BURNING DOWN THE HOUSE** *Gut CDGUT 26* & THE CARDIGANS	7		7
18 Dec 99	**BABY, IT'S COLD OUTSIDE** *Gut CDGUT 29* & CERYS MATTHEWS	17		7
18 Mar 00	**MAMA TOLD ME NOT TO COME** *Gut CXGUT 031* & STEREOPHONICS	4		7
20 May 00	**SEX BOMB** *Gut CXGUT 33* & MOUSSE T	3		10
18 Nov 00	**YOU NEED LOVE LIKE I DO** *Gut CXGUT 36* & HEATHER SMALL	24		3
9 Nov 02	**TOM JONES INTERNATIONAL** *V2 VVR 5021083*	31		2
8 Mar 03	**BLACK BETTY/I WHO HAVE NOTHING** *V2 VVR 5021763*	50		2
29 Apr 06	**STONED IN LOVE** *Universal TV 9878360* CHICANE FEATURING TOM JONES	7		13
21 Mar 09	**ISLANDS IN THE STREAM** *Mercury 1799919* VANESSA JENKINS & BRYN WEST FEATURING TOM JONES & ROBIN GIBB	1	1	4

JONESTOWN
US, male vocal duo — 1

Date	Title	Peak	No.1	Weeks
13 Jun 98	**SWEET THANG** *Universal UMD 70376*	49		1

ALLISON JORDAN
UK, female vocalist. See Cappella — 4

Date	Title	Peak	No.1	Weeks
9 May 92	**BOY FROM NEW YORK CITY** *Arista 74321100427*	23		4

DAVID JORDAN
UK, male vocalist — 15

Date	Title	Peak	No.1	Weeks
26 Jan 08	**SUN GOES DOWN** *Mercury 1761142*	4		14
24 May 08	**MOVE ON** *Mercury 1765454*	68		1

DICK JORDAN
UK, male vocalist — 4

Date	Title	Peak	No.1	Weeks
17 Mar 60	**HALLELUJAH I LOVE HER SO** *Oriole CB 1534*	47		1
9 Jun 60	**LITTLE CHRISTINE** *Oriole CB 1548*	39		3

MONTELL JORDAN
US, male vocalist/producer — 21

Date	Title	Peak	No.1	Weeks
13 May 95	**THIS IS HOW WE DO IT** *Def Jam DEFCD 07* ★	11		8
2 Sep 95	**SOMETHIN' 4 DA HONEYZ** *Def Jam DEFCD 10*	15		4
19 Oct 96	**I LIKE** *Def Jam DEFCD 19* FEATURING SLICK RICK	24		3
23 May 98	**LET'S RIDE** *Def Jam 5686912* FEATURING MASTER P & SILKK THE SHOCKER	25		2
8 Apr 00	**GET IT ON TONITE** *Def Soul 5627222*	15		4

RONNY JORDAN
UK, male guitarist (Ronald Simpson) — 7

Date	Title	Peak	No.1	Weeks
1 Feb 92	**SO WHAT!** *Antilles ANN 14*	32		4
25 Sep 93	**UNDER YOUR SPELL** *Island CID 565*	72		1
15 Jan 94	**TINSEL TOWN** *Island CID 566*	64		1
28 May 94	**COME WITH ME** *Island CID 584*	63		1

JORIO
US, male producer (Fred Jorio) — 1

Date	Title	Peak	No.1	Weeks
24 Feb 01	**REMEMBER ME** *Wonderboy WBOYD 021*	54		1

DAVID JOSEPH
UK, male vocalist. See Hi Tension — 21

Date	Title	Peak	No.1	Weeks
26 Feb 83	**YOU CAN'T HIDE (YOUR LOVE FROM ME)** *Island IS 101*	13		9
28 May 83	**LET'S LIVE IT UP (NITE PEOPLE)** *Island IS 116*	26		5
18 Feb 84	**JOYS OF LIFE** *Island IS 153*	61		2
31 May 86	**EXPANSIONS '86 (EXPAND YOUR MIND)** *Fourth & Broadway BRW 48* CHRIS PAUL FEATURING DAVID JOSEPH	58		5

MARK JOSEPH
UK, male vocalist (Mark Joseph Muzsnyai) — 5

Date	Title	Peak	No.1	Weeks
1 Mar 03	**GET THROUGH** *Mark Joseph MJR 003*	38		1
30 Aug 03	**FLY** *14th Floor MJM01CD*	28		1
27 Mar 04	**BRINGING BACK THOSE MEMORIES** *14th Floor MJM02CD2*	34		1
26 Feb 05	**LADY LADY** *14th Floor MJM05CD2*	36		2

MARTYN JOSEPH
UK, male vocalist/guitarist — 10

Date	Title	Peak	No.1	Weeks
20 Jun 92	**DOLPHINS MAKE ME CRY** *Epic 6581347*	34		4
12 Sep 92	**WORKING MOTHER** *Epic 6582937*	65		1
9 Jan 93	**PLEASE SIR** *Epic 6588552*	45		3
3 Jun 95	**TALK ABOUT IT IN THE MORNING** *Epic 6613342*	43		2

JOURNEY
US, male vocal/instrumental group – Steve Perry*, Jonathan Cain, Neal Schon, Steve Smith & Ross Valory — 41

Date	Title	Peak	No.1	Weeks
27 Feb 82	**DON'T STOP BELIEVIN'** *CBS A 1728*	62		4
11 Sep 82	**WHO'S CRYING NOW** *CBS A 2725*	46		5
25 Apr 09	**DON'T STOP BELIEVIN'** *Columbia USSM18100116*	6		32+

RUTH JOY
UK, female vocalist (Ruth Joy Oram) — 3

Date	Title	Peak	No.1	Weeks
26 Aug 89	**DON'T PUSH IT** *MCA RJOY 1*	66		2
22 Feb 92	**FEEL** *MCA MCS 1574*	67		1

JOY DIVISION
UK, male vocal/instrumental group – Ian Curtis, d. 18 May 1980, Peter Hook, Stephen Morris & Bernard Sumner — 26

Date	Title	Peak	No.1	Weeks
28 Jun 80	**LOVE WILL TEAR US APART** *Factory FAC 23*	13		9
29 Oct 83	**LOVE WILL TEAR US APART** *Factory FAC 23*	19		7
18 Jun 88	**ATMOSPHERE** *Factory FAC 2137*	34		5
17 Jun 95	**LOVE WILL TEAR US APART** *London YOJCD 1*	19		3
6 Oct 07	**LOVE WILL TEAR US APART** *London FAC23CD*	46		2

JOY STRINGS
UK, male/female Salvation Army vocal/instrumental group — 11

Date	Title	Peak	No.1	Weeks
27 Feb 64	**IT'S AN OPEN SECRET** *Regal Zonophone RZ 501*	32		7
17 Dec 64	**A STARRY NIGHT** *Regal Zonophone RZ 504*	35		4

JOY ZIPPER
US, male/female vocal/instrumental duo — 2

Date	Title	Peak	No.1	Weeks
24 Apr 04	**BABY YOU SHOULD KNOW** *13 Amp/Vertigo 9866235*	59		1
20 Aug 05	**I** *Vertigo 9872947*	73		1

JOYRIDER
UK, male vocal/instrumental group — 4

Date	Title	Peak	No.1	Weeks
27 Jul 96	**RUSH HOUR** *Paradox PDOXD 012*	22		3
28 Sep 96	**ALL GONE AWAY** *A&M 5819552*	54		1

JT & THE BIG FAMILY
Italy, male production trio – Paul Bisiach, Mauro Ferrucci & Christian Hornbostel — 8

Date	Title	Peak	No.1	Weeks
3 Mar 90	**MOMENTS IN SOUL** *Champion CHAMP 237*	7		8

JT PLAYAZ
UK, male production trio — 4

Date	Title	Peak	No.1	Weeks
5 Apr 97	**JUST PLAYIN'** *Pukka CDJTP 1*	30		3
2 May 98	**LET'S GET DOWN** *MCA MCSTD 40161*	64		1

JTQ
UK, male vocal/instrumental group — 6

Date	Title	Peak	No.1	Weeks
3 Apr 93	**LOVE THE LIFE** *Big Life BLRD 93* WITH NOEL McKOY	34		3
3 Jul 93	**SEE A BRIGHTER DAY** *Big Life BLRDA 97* WITH NOEL McKOY	49		2
25 Feb 95	**LOVE WILL KEEP US TOGETHER** *Acid Jazz JAZID 112CD* FEATURING ALISON LIMERICK	63		1

JUANES
Colombia, male vocalist/guitarist (Juan Esteban Aristizabal Vasquez) — 2

Date	Title	Peak	Wks at No.1	Wks on Chart
29 Apr 06	**LA CAMISA NEGRA** *Interscope 9877816*	32		2

JUDAS PRIEST
UK, male vocal/instrumental group – Rob Halford, K.K. Downing, Ian Hill, Dave Holland (replaced by Scott Travis) & Glen Tipton — 51

Date	Title	Peak	Wks at No.1	Wks on Chart
20 Jan 79	**TAKE ON THE WORLD** *CBS 6915*	14		10
12 May 79	**EVENING STAR** *CBS 7312*	53		4
29 Mar 80	**LIVING AFTER MIDNIGHT** *CBS 8379*	12		7
7 Jun 80	**BREAKING THE LAW** *CBS 8644*	12		6
23 Aug 80	**UNITED** *CBS 8897*	26		8
21 Feb 81	**DON'T GO** *CBS 9520*	51		3
25 Apr 81	**HOT ROCKIN'** *CBS A 1153*	60		3
21 Aug 82	**YOU'VE GOT ANOTHER THING COMIN'** *CBS A 2611*	66		2
21 Jan 84	**FREEWHEEL BURNIN'** *CBS A 4054*	42		3
23 Apr 88	**JOHNNY B. GOODE** *Atlantic A 9114*	64		2
15 Sep 90	**PAINKILLER** *CBS 6562737*	74		1
23 Mar 91	**A TOUCH OF EVIL** *Columbia 6565897*	58		1
24 Apr 93	**NIGHT CRAWLER** *Columbia 6590972*	63		1

JUDGE DREAD
UK, male vocalist (Alex Hughes), d. 13 Mar 1998 (age 52) — 95

Date	Title	Peak	Wks at No.1	Wks on Chart
26 Aug 72	**BIG SIX** *Big Shot BI 608*	11		27
9 Dec 72	**BIG SEVEN** *Big Shot BI 613*	8		18
21 Apr 73	**BIG EIGHT** *Big Shot BI 619*	14		10
5 Jul 75	**JE T'AIME (MOI NON PLUS)** *Cactus CT 65*	9		9
27 Sep 75	**BIG TEN** *Cactus CT 77*	14		7
6 Dec 75	**CHRISTMAS IN DREADLAND/COME OUTSIDE** *Cactus CT 80*	14		7
8 May 76	**THE WINKLE MAN** *Cactus CT 90*	35		4
28 Aug 76	**Y VIVA SUSPENDERS/CONFESSIONS OF A BOUNCER** *Cactus CT 99*	27		4
2 Apr 77	**5TH ANNIVERSARY EP** *Cactus CT 98*	31		4
14 Jan 78	**UP WITH THE COCK/BIG PUNK** *Cactus CT 110*	49		1
16 Dec 78	**HOKEY COKEY/JINGLE BELLS** *EMI 2881*	64		4

JUICE
Denmark, female vocal trio — 3

Date	Title	Peak	Wks at No.1	Wks on Chart
18 Apr 98	**BEST DAYS** *Chrysalis CDCHS 5081*	28		2
22 Aug 98	**I'LL COME RUNNIN'** *Chrysalis CDCHS 5090*	48		1

JUICY
US, male/female vocal duo — 5

Date	Title	Peak	Wks at No.1	Wks on Chart
22 Feb 86	**SUGAR FREE** *Epic A 6917*	45		5

JUICY LUCY
UK, male vocal/instrumental group — 17

Date	Title	Peak	Wks at No.1	Wks on Chart
7 Mar 70	**WHO DO YOU LOVE** *Vertigo V 1*	14		12
10 Oct 70	**PRETTY WOMAN** *Vertigo 6059 015*	44		5

THOMAS JULES-STOCK
UK, male vocalist — 1

Date	Title	Peak	Wks at No.1	Wks on Chart
15 Aug 98	**DIDN'T I TELL YOU TRUE** *Mercury MERCD 501*	59		1

JULIA & COMPANY
US, female vocalist (Julia McGirt) & male instrumental group — 10

Date	Title	Peak	Wks at No.1	Wks on Chart
3 Mar 84	**BREAKIN' DOWN (SUGAR SAMBA)** *London LON 46*	15		8
23 Feb 85	**I'M SO HAPPY** *Next Plateau LON 61*	56		2

JULIET
US, female vocalist (Juliet Richardson) — 3

Date	Title	Peak	Wks at No.1	Wks on Chart
23 Apr 05	**AVALON** *Virgin VUSDX299*	24		3

JULIETTE & THE LICKS
US, female actor/vocalist & male vocal/instrumental group — 4

Date	Title	Peak	Wks at No.1	Wks on Chart
21 May 05	**YOU'RE SPEAKING MY LANGUAGE** *Hassle HOFF003CDS*	35		2
1 Oct 05	**GOT LOVE TO KILL** *Hassle HOFF005CDS*	56		1
7 Oct 06	**HOT KISS** *Hassle HOFF020CDS*	50		1

JULUKA
UK/South Africa, male/female vocal/instrumental group — 4

Date	Title	Peak	Wks at No.1	Wks on Chart
12 Feb 83	**SCATTERLINGS OF AFRICA** *Safari ZULU 1*	44		4

JUMP
UK, male instrumental group — 1

Date	Title	Peak	Wks at No.1	Wks on Chart
1 Mar 97	**FUNKATARIUM** *Heat Recordings HEATCD 005*	56		1

WALLY JUMP, JR & THE CRIMINAL ELEMENT ORCHESTRA
US, male producer (Arthur Baker) & male vocalists — 19

Date	Title	Peak	Wks at No.1	Wks on Chart
28 Feb 87	**TURN ME LOOSE** *London LON 126*	60		2
5 Sep 87	**PUT THE NEEDLE TO THE RECORD** *Cooltempo COOL 150* CRIMINAL ELEMENT ORCHESTRA	63		3
12 Dec 87	**TIGHTEN UP – I JUST CAN'T STOP DANCING** *Breakout USA 621*	24		7
19 Mar 88	**PRIVATE PARTY** *Breakout USA 624*	57		3
6 Oct 90	**EVERYBODY (RAP)** *Deconstruction PB 44701* CRIMINAL ELEMENT ORCHESTRA & WENDELL WILLIAMS	30		4

ROSEMARY JUNE
US, female vocalist — 9

Date	Title	Peak	Wks at No.1	Wks on Chart
23 Jan 59	**I'LL BE WITH YOU IN APPLE BLOSSOM TIME** *Pye International 7N 25005*	14		9

JUNGLE BOOK
UK, male production duo — 8

Date	Title	Peak	Wks at No.1	Wks on Chart
8 May 93	**THE JUNGLE BOOK GROOVE** *Hollywood HWCD 128*	14		8

JUNGLE BOYS
UK, male TV celebrities/vocal group — 6

Date	Title	Peak	Wks at No.1	Wks on Chart
20 Mar 04	**JUNGLE ROCK** *Bushtucker JUNGLE001CD*	30		5
31 Jul 04	**IN THE SUMMERTIME** *MCS JUNGLE002CD*	72		1

JUNGLE BROTHERS
US, male rap trio — 40

Date	Title	Peak	Wks at No.1	Wks on Chart
22 Oct 88	**I'LL HOUSE YOU** *Gee Street GEE 003* RICHIE RICH MEETS THE JUNGLE BROTHERS	22		5
18 Mar 89	**BLACK IS BLACK/STRAIGHT OUT OF THE JUNGLE** *Gee Street GEE 15*	72		1
31 Mar 90	**WHAT 'U' WAITIN' '4'** *Eternal W 9865*	35		5
21 Jul 90	**DOIN' OUR OWN DANG** *Eternal W 9754*	33		6
19 Jul 97	**BRAIN** *Gee Street GEE 5000388*	52		1
29 Nov 97	**JUNGLE BROTHER** *Gee Street GEE 5000493*	56		1
9 May 98	**JUNGLE BROTHER** *Gee Street GEE 5000493*	18		4
11 Jul 98	**I'LL HOUSE YOU '98 (REMIX)** *Gee Street FCD 338* RICHIE RICH MEETS THE JUNGLE BROTHERS	26		5
28 Nov 98	**BECAUSE I GOT IT LIKE THAT** *Gee Street GEE 5003593*	32		2
10 Jul 99	**VIP** *Gee Street GEE 5007958*	33		3
6 Nov 99	**GET DOWN** *Gee Street GEE 5010153*	52		1
25 Mar 00	**FREAKIN' YOU** *Gee Street GEE 5008808*	70		1
7 Feb 04	**BREATHE DON'T STOP** *Positiva/Incentive CDTIVS 201* MR ON VS THE JUNGLE BROTHERS	21		5

JUNGLE HIGH WITH BLUE PEARL
UK/Germany, male production duo & UK/US, male/female vocal/production duo — 1

Date	Title	Peak	Wks at No.1	Wks on Chart
27 Nov 93	**FIRE OF LOVE** *Logic 74321170292*	71		1

JUNIOR
UK, male vocalist (Norman Giscombe) — 57

Date	Title	Peak	Wks at No.1	Wks on Chart
24 Apr 82	**MAMA USED TO SAY** *Mercury MER 98* ●	7		13
10 Jul 82	**TOO LATE** *Mercury MER 112*	20		9
25 Sep 82	**LET ME KNOW/I CAN'T HELP IT** *Mercury MER 116*	53		3
23 Apr 83	**COMMUNICATION BREAKDOWN** *Mercury MER 134*	57		3
8 Sep 84	**SOMEBODY** *London LON 50*	64		2
9 Feb 85	**DO YOU REALLY (WANT MY LOVE)** *London LON 60*	47		4
30 Nov 85	**OH LOUISE** *London LON 75*	74		3
4 Apr 87	**ANOTHER STEP CLOSER TO YOU** *MCA KIM 5* KIM WILDE & JUNIOR	6		11
25 Aug 90	**STEP OFF** *MCA 1432* JUNIOR GISCOMBE	63		3
15 Aug 92	**THEN CAME YOU** *MCA MCS 1676* JUNIOR GISCOMBE	32		5
31 Oct 92	**ALL OVER THE WORLD** *MCA MCS 1691* JUNIOR GISCOMBE	74		1

JUNIOR JACK
Italy, male DJ/producer (Vito Lucente). See Room 5 featuring Oliver Cheatham **25**

Date	Title	Peak Position	Weeks at No.1	Weeks on Chart
16 Dec 00	**MY FEELING** *Defected DFECT 24CDS*	31		4
2 Mar 02	**THRILL ME** *VC Recordings VCRD 102*	29		3
27 Sep 03	**E SAMBA** *Defected DFTD 076CDS*	34		3
14 Feb 04	**DA HYPE** *Defected DFTD 083CDS* FEATURING ROBERT SMITH	25		4
3 Jul 04	**STUPIDISCO** *Defected DFTD 089CDS*	26		6
24 Feb 07	**DARE ME (STUPIDISCO)** *Defected DFTD150CDS* FEATURING SHENA	20		5

JUNIOR M.A.F.I.A.
US, male/female rap ensemble **2**

Date	Title	Peak Position	Weeks at No.1	Weeks on Chart
3 Feb 96	**I NEED YOU TONIGHT** *Big Beat A 8130CD* FEATURING AALIYAH	66		1
19 Oct 96	**GETTING' MONEY** *Big Beat A 5674CD*	63		1

JUNIOR SENIOR
Denmark, male vocal/instrumental duo – Jeppe Laursen & Jesper Mortensen **20**

Date	Title	Peak Position	Weeks at No.1	Weeks on Chart
8 Mar 03	**MOVE YOUR FEET** *Mercury 0198192*	3		17
9 Aug 03	**RHYTHM BANDITS** *Mercury 9810210*	22		3

JUNKIE XL
Holland, male producer (Tom Holkenborg) **19**

Date	Title	Peak Position	Weeks at No.1	Weeks on Chart
22 Jul 00	**ZEROTONINE** *Manifesto FESCD 71*	63		1
22 Jun 02	**A LITTLE LESS CONVERSATION** *RCA 74321943572* ELVIS VS JXL ⊛	1	4	12
30 Nov 02	**OBSESSION** *Nebula NEBCD 029* TIESTO & JUNKIE XL	56		1
7 Jun 03	**CATCH UP TO MY STEP** *Roadrunner RR 20209* FEATURING SOLOMON BURKE	63		1
7 May 05	**A LITTLE LESS CONVERSATION** *RCA 82876666832* ELVIS VS JXL	3		4

JUNO REACTOR
UK/Germany, male production duo **1**

Date	Title	Peak Position	Weeks at No.1	Weeks on Chart
8 Feb 97	**JUNGLE HIGH** *Perfecto PERF 133CD*	45		1

JUPITER ACE FEATURING SHEENA
UK, male/female vocal/production duo **2**

Date	Title	Peak Position	Weeks at No.1	Weeks on Chart
23 Jul 05	**1000 YEARS (JUST LEAVE ME NOW)** *Manifesto 9871706*	51		2

JURASSIC 5
US, male rap group **4**

Date	Title	Peak Position	Weeks at No.1	Weeks on Chart
25 Jul 98	**JAYOU** *Pan 018CD*	56		1
24 Oct 98	**CONCRETE SCHOOLYARD** *Pan 020CD*	35		3

CHRISTOPHER JUST
Austria, male DJ/producer **2**

Date	Title	Peak Position	Weeks at No.1	Weeks on Chart
13 Dec 97	**I'M A DISCO DANCER** *Slut Trax SLUT 001CD*	72		1
6 Feb 99	**I'M A DISCO DANCER (REMIX)** *XL Recordings XLS 105CD*	69		1

JUST 4 JOKES FEATURING MC RB
UK, male rap/production trio **1**

Date	Title	Peak Position	Weeks at No.1	Weeks on Chart
28 Sep 02	**JUMP UP** *Serious SERR 050CD*	67		1

JUST JACK
UK, male vocalist/rapper/DJ/producer (Jack Allsopp) **38**

Date	Title	Peak Position	Weeks at No.1	Weeks on Chart
20 Jan 07	**STARZ IN THEIR EYES** *Mercury 1714375*	2		20
14 Apr 07	**GLORY DAYS** *Mercury 1724905*	32		5
30 Jun 07	**WRITER'S BLOCK** *Mercury 1735872*	74		1
11 Apr 09	**EMBERS** *Mercury GBUM70818630*	17		4
29 Aug 09	**THE DAY I DIED** *Mercury GBUM70907451*	11		8

JUST LUIS
Spain, male vocalist (Luis Pizarro) **3**

Date	Title	Peak Position	Weeks at No.1	Weeks on Chart
14 Oct 95	**AMERICAN PIE** *Pro-Activ CDPTV 1*	31		2
17 Feb 96	**AMERICAN PIE** *Pro-Activ CDPTV 1*	70		1

JUSTICE
France, male production duo **11**

Date	Title	Peak Position	Weeks at No.1	Weeks on Chart
15 Jul 06	**WE ARE YOUR FRIENDS** *Ten TENCDX505* VERSUS SIMIAN	20		10
23 Jun 07	**BECAUSE** *Because/Ed Banger BEC5772072*	48		1

JIMMY JUSTICE
UK, male vocalist (James Little) **35**

Date	Title	Peak Position	Weeks at No.1	Weeks on Chart
29 Mar 62	**WHEN MY LITTLE GIRL IS SMILING** *Pye 7N 15421*	9		13
14 Jun 62	**AIN'T THAT FUNNY** *Pye 7N 15443*	8		11
23 Aug 62	**SPANISH HARLEM** *Pye 7N 15457*	20		11

JUSTIFIED ANCIENTS OF MU MU
UK, male production duo – Jimmy Cauty & Bill Drummond. See KLF, Timelords, 2K **6**

Date	Title	Peak Position	Weeks at No.1	Weeks on Chart
9 Nov 91	**IT'S GRIM UP NORTH** *KLF Communications JAMS 028*	10		6

JUSTIN
UK, male vocalist (Justin Osuji) **13**

Date	Title	Peak Position	Weeks at No.1	Weeks on Chart
22 Aug 98	**THIS BOY** *Virgin STCDT 1*	34		2
16 Jan 99	**OVER YOU** *Virgin STCDT 2*	11		4
17 Jul 99	**IT'S ALL ABOUT YOU** *Virgin STCDT 3*	34		3
22 Jan 00	**LET IT BE ME** *Innocent STCDTX 4*	15		4

BILL JUSTIS
US, male alto-saxophonist, d. 15 May 1982 (age 55) **8**

Date	Title	Peak Position	Weeks at No.1	Weeks on Chart
10 Jan 58	**RAUNCHY** *London HLS 8517*	11		8

PATRICK JUVET
Switzerland, male vocalist **19**

Date	Title	Peak Position	Weeks at No.1	Weeks on Chart
2 Sep 78	**GOT A FEELING** *Casablanca CAN 127*	34		7
4 Nov 78	**I LOVE AMERICA** *Casablanca CAN 132*	12		12

JX
UK, male producer (Jake Williams). See Planet Perfecto **36**

Date	Title	Peak Position	Weeks at No.1	Weeks on Chart
2 Apr 94	**SON OF A GUN** *Internal Dance IDC 5*	13		6
1 Apr 95	**YOU BELONG TO ME** *ffrreedom TABCD 227*	17		5
19 Aug 95	**SON OF A GUN (REMIX)** *ffrreedom TABCD 233*	6		6
18 May 96	**THERE'S NOTHING I WON'T DO** *ffrreedom TABCD 241* ●	4		13
8 Mar 97	**CLOSE TO YOUR HEART** *ffrreedom TABCD 245*	18		3
6 Mar 04	**RESTLESS** *Tidy Two TIDYTWOJX1C*	22		3

FRANK K FEATURING WISTON OFFICE
Italy, male producer (Francesco Pini) & US, male rapper **1**

Date	Title	Peak Position	Weeks at No.1	Weeks on Chart
26 Jan 91	**EVERYBODY LETS SOMEBODY LOVE** *Urban URB 66*	61		1

LEILA K
Sweden, female rapper (Laila El Khalifi) **22**

Date	Title	Peak Position	Weeks at No.1	Weeks on Chart
25 Nov 89	**GOT TO GET** *Arista 112696* ROB 'N' RAZ FEATURING LEILA K	8		14
17 Mar 90	**ROK THE NATION** *Arista 112971* ROB 'N' RAZ FEATURING LEILA K	41		3
23 Jan 93	**OPEN SESAME** *Polydor PQCD 1*	23		4
3 Jul 93	**CA PLANE POUR MOI** *Polydor PQCD 3*	69		1

K-CI & JOJO
US, male vocal duo – Cedric & Joel Hailey. See Jodeci **38**

Date	Title	Peak Position	Weeks at No.1	Weeks on Chart
27 Jul 96	**HOW DO YOU WANT IT?** *Death Row 228546532* 2PAC FEATURING K-CI & JOJO ★	17		4
30 Nov 96	**I AIN'T MAD AT CHA** *Death Row DRWCD 5* 2PAC FEATURING K-CI & JOJO	13		9
23 Aug 97	**YOU BRING ME UP** *MCA MCSTD 48057*	21		2
18 Apr 98	**ALL MY LIFE** *MCA MCSTD 48076* ★	8		11
19 Sep 98	**DON'T RUSH (TAKE LOVE SLOWLY)** *MCA MCSD 48090*	16		3
2 Oct 99	**TELL ME IT'S REAL** *MCA MCSXD 40211*	40		2
23 Sep 00	**TELL ME IT'S REAL** *AM:PM CDAMPM 135*	16		5
12 May 01	**CRAZY** *MCA MCSTD 40253*	35		2

K CREATIVE
UK, male rap/instrumental/production group **2**

Date	Title	Peak Position	Weeks at No.1	Weeks on Chart
7 Mar 92	**THREE TIMES A MAYBE** *Talkin Loud TLK 17*	58		2

ERNIE K-DOE

US, male vocalist (Ernest Kador), d. 5 Jul 2001 (age 65) **11**

Date	Title	Peak	Wks at No.1	Wks on Chart
11 May 61	**MOTHER-IN-LAW** *London HLU 9330* ★	29		7
8 Dec 07	**HERE COME THE GIRLS** *Soul Jazz SJR176CDS*	43		4

K-GEE

UK, male producer (Karl Gordon) **3**

Date	Title	Peak	Wks at No.1	Wks on Chart
4 Nov 00	**I DON'T REALLY CARE** *Instant Karma 3CD*	22		3

K-KLASS

UK, male production group – Russ Morgan, Paul Roberts, Carl Thomas & Andrew Williams **31**

Date	Title	Peak	Wks at No.1	Wks on Chart
4 May 91	**RHYTHM IS A MYSTERY** *Deconstruction CREED 1*	61		2
9 Nov 91	**RHYTHM IS A MYSTERY** *Deconstruction R 6302*	3		10
25 Apr 92	**SO RIGHT** *Deconstruction R 6309*	20		5
7 Nov 92	**DON'T STOP** *Deconstruction R 6325*	32		3
27 Nov 93	**LET ME SHOW YOU** *Deconstruction CDR 6367*	13		7
28 May 94	**WHAT YOU'RE MISSING** *Deconstruction CDRS 6380*	24		3
1 Aug 98	**BURNIN'** *Parlophone CDK 2001*	45		1

K7

US, male vocalist (Louis Sharpe) **22**

Date	Title	Peak	Wks at No.1	Wks on Chart
11 Dec 93	**COME BABY COME** *Big Life BLRD 105*	3		16
2 Apr 94	**HI DE HO** *Big Life BLRD 108* & THE SWING KIDS	17		5
25 Jun 94	**ZUNGA ZENG** *Big Life BLRD 111* & THE SWING KIDS	63		1

K3M

Italy, male production duo **1**

Date	Title	Peak	Wks at No.1	Wks on Chart
21 Mar 92	**LISTEN TO THE RHYTHM** *PWL Continental PWL 214*	71		1

K-WARREN FEATURING LEE O

UK, male vocal/production duo **2**

Date	Title	Peak	Wks at No.1	Wks on Chart
5 May 01	**COMING HOME** *Go! Beat GOBCD 41*	32		2

K2 FAMILY

UK, male rap/vocal/production group **3**

Date	Title	Peak	Wks at No.1	Wks on Chart
27 Oct 01	**BOUNCING FLOW** *Relentless RELENT 22CD*	27		3

KACI

US, female vocalist (Kaci Battaglia) **23**

Date	Title	Peak	Wks at No.1	Wks on Chart
10 Mar 01	**PARADISE** *Curb CUBC 61*	11		9
28 Jul 01	**TU AMOR** *Curb CUBX 71*	24		3
2 Feb 02	**I THINK I LOVE YOU** *Curb CUBC 076*	10		10
9 Aug 03	**I'M NOT ANYBODY'S GIRL** *Curb CUBC 091*	55		1

JOSHUA KADISON

US, male vocalist/pianist **19**

Date	Title	Peak	Wks at No.1	Wks on Chart
26 Feb 94	**JESSIE** *SBK CDSBK 43*	69		2
1 Oct 94	**JESSIE** *SBK CDSBK 43*	48		3
12 Nov 94	**BEAUTIFUL IN MY EYES** *SBK CDSBK 50*	65		1
29 Apr 95	**JESSIE** *SBK CDSBK 53*	15		10
12 Aug 95	**BEAUTIFUL IN MY EYES** *SBK CDSBKS 55*	37		3

KADOC

UK/Spain, male vocal/instrumental group **11**

Date	Title	Peak	Wks at No.1	Wks on Chart
6 Apr 96	**THE NIGHTTRAIN** *Positiva CDTIV 26*	14		8
17 Aug 96	**YOU GOT TO BE THERE** *Positiva CDTIV 58*	45		1
23 Aug 97	**ROCK THE BELLS** *Manifesto FESCD 30*	34		2

BERT KAEMPFERT

Germany, male band leader/composer/multi-instrumentalist (Berthold Kampfert), d. 21 Jun 1980 (age 56), & orchestra **10**

Date	Title	Peak	Wks at No.1	Wks on Chart
23 Dec 65	**BYE BYE BLUES** *Polydor BM 56 504*	24		10

KAISER CHIEFS

UK, male vocal/instrumental group – Ricky Wilson, Nick 'Peanut' Baines, Nick Hodgson, Simon Rix & Andrew 'Whitey' White **136**

Date	Title	Peak	Wks at No.1	Wks on Chart
29 May 04	**OH MY GOD** *Drowned In Sound DISO3*	66		1
13 Nov 04	**I PREDICT A RIOT** *B Unique BUN088CD*	22		2
5 Mar 05	**OH MY GOD** *B Unique BUN092CDX*	6		12
28 May 05	**EVERYDAY I LOVE YOU LESS AND LESS** *B Unique/Polydor BUN094CDX*	10		25
6 Aug 05	**I PREDICT A RIOT** *B Unique BUN088CD*	31		4
3 Sep 05	**I PREDICT A RIOT/SINK A SHIP** *B Unique/Polydor BUN96CD*	9		30
19 Nov 05	**MODERN WAY** *B Unique/Polydor BUN100CDX*	11		7
17 Feb 07	**RUBY** *B Unique/Polydor BUN119CD*	1	1	35
26 May 07	**EVERYTHING IS AVERAGE NOWADAYS** *B Unique/Polydor BUN125CD*	19		4
1 Sep 07	**THE ANGRY MOB** *B Unique/Polydor BUN132CD*	20		5
18 Oct 08	**NEVER MISS A BEAT** *B Unique/Polydor BUN145CD*	5		11

KAJAGOOGOO

UK, male vocal/instrumental group – Chris Hamill (Limahl*), Steve Askew, Nick Beggs, Stuart Croxford Neale & Jeremy 'Jez' Strode **50**

Date	Title	Peak	Wks at No.1	Wks on Chart
22 Jan 83	**TOO SHY** *EMI 5359* ●	1	2	13
2 Apr 83	**OOH TO BE AH** *EMI 5383*	7		8
4 Jun 83	**HANG ON NOW** *EMI 5394*	13		7
17 Sep 83	**BIG APPLE** *EMI 5423*	8		8
3 Mar 84	**THE LION'S MOUTH** *EMI 5449*	25		7
5 May 84	**TURN YOUR BACK ON ME** *EMI 5646*	47		4
21 Sep 85	**SHOULDN'T DO THAT** *Parlophone R 6106* KAJA	63		3

KALEEF

UK, male rap/vocal group **12**

Date	Title	Peak	Wks at No.1	Wks on Chart
30 Mar 96	**WALK LIKE A CHAMPION** *Payday KACD 5* KALIPHZ FEATURING PRINCE NASEEM	23		3
7 Dec 96	**GOLDEN BROWN** *Unity 010CD*	22		4
14 Jun 97	**TRIALS OF LIFE** *Unity 012CD*	75		1
11 Oct 97	**I LIKE THE WAY (THE KISSING GAME)** *Unity 015CD*	58		1
24 Jan 98	**SANDS OF TIME** *Unity 016CD*	26		3

PREEYA KALIDAS

UK, female actor/vocalist **2**

Date	Title	Peak	Wks at No.1	Wks on Chart
13 Jul 02	**SHAKALAKA BABY** *Sony Classical 6726322*	38		2

KALIN TWINS

US, male vocal duo – Hal, d. 24 Aug 2005, & Herb, d. 21 Jul 2006, Kalin **18**

Date	Title	Peak	Wks at No.1	Wks on Chart
18 Jul 58	**WHEN** *Brunswick 05751*	1	5	18

KITTY KALLEN

US, female vocalist **23**

Date	Title	Peak	Wks at No.1	Wks on Chart
2 Jul 54	**LITTLE THINGS MEAN A LOT** *Brunswick 05287* ★	1	1	23

GUNTER KALLMAN CHOIR

Germany, male/female vocal group **3**

Date	Title	Peak	Wks at No.1	Wks on Chart
24 Dec 64	**ELISABETH SERENADE** *Polydor NH 24678*	39		3

KALOMOIRA

Greece (b. US), female vocalist (Maria Kalomoira Sarantis) **1**

Date	Title	Peak	Wks at No.1	Wks on Chart
7 Jun 08	**SECRET COMBINATION** *EMI GRHV10800017*	71		1

ISRAEL KAMAKAWIWO'OLE

US, male vocalist/ukulele player, d. 26 Jun 1997 (age 38) **4**

Date	Title	Peak	Wks at No.1	Wks on Chart
21 Apr 07	**SOMEWHERE OVER THE RAINBOW** *Big Boy USMAC0100119*	68		2
4 Oct 08	**SOMEWHERE OVER THE RAINBOW** *Big Boy USMAC0100119*	46		2

KAMASUTRA FEATURING JOCELYN BROWN

Italy/US, male/female vocal/DJ/production trio **1**

Date	Title	Peak	Wks at No.1	Wks on Chart
22 Nov 97	**HAPPINESS** *Sony S3 KAMCD 2*	45		1

Silver-selling ● Gold-selling ● Platinum-selling (x multiples) ⊛ US No.1 ★ Peak Position · Weeks at No.1 · Weeks on Chart

NICK KAMEN
UK, male vocalist — 33

Date	Title	Peak	Wks No.1	Wks
8 Nov 86	EACH TIME YOU BREAK MY HEART *WEA YZ 90* ●	5		12
28 Feb 87	LOVING YOU IS SWEETER THAN EVER *WEA YZ 106*	16		9
16 May 87	NOBODY ELSE *WEA YZ 122*	47		3
28 May 88	TELL ME *WEA YZ 184*	40		5
28 Apr 90	I PROMISED MYSELF *WEA YZ 454*	50		4

INI KAMOZE
Jamaica, male vocalist (Cecil Campbell) — 15

Date	Title	Peak	Wks No.1	Wks
7 Jan 95	HERE COMES THE HOTSTEPPER *Columbia 6610472* ● ★	4		15

KANDI
US, female vocalist (Kandi Burruss) — 10

Date	Title	Peak	Wks No.1	Wks
11 Nov 00	DON'T THINK I'M NOT *Columbia 6705102*	9		10

KANDIDATE
UK, male vocal/instrumental group — 28

Date	Title	Peak	Wks No.1	Wks
19 Aug 78	DON'T WANNA SAY GOODNIGHT *RAK 280*	47		6
17 Mar 79	I DON'T WANNA LOSE YOU *RAK 289*	11		12
4 Aug 79	GIRLS GIRLS GIRLS *RAK 295*	34		7
22 Mar 80	LET ME ROCK YOU *RAK 306*	58		3

KANE
Holland, male vocal/instrumental group — 2

Date	Title	Peak	Wks No.1	Wks
4 Sep 04	RAIN DOWN ON ME *BMG 82876634262*	38		2

EDEN KANE
UK, male vocalist (Richard Sarstedt) — 73

Date	Title	Peak	Wks No.1	Wks
1 Jun 61	WELL I ASK YOU *Decca F 11353*	1	1	21
14 Sep 61	GET LOST *Decca F 11381*	10		11
18 Jan 62	FORGET ME NOT *Decca F 11418*	3		14
10 May 62	I DON'T KNOW WHY *Decca F 11460*	7		13
30 Jan 64	BOYS CRY *Fontana TF 438*	8		14

KANE GANG
UK, male vocal/instrumental group — 37

Date	Title	Peak	Wks No.1	Wks
19 May 84	SMALLTOWN CREED *Kitchenware SK 11*	60		2
7 Jul 84	CLOSEST THING TO HEAVEN *Kitchenware SK 15*	12		11
10 Nov 84	RESPECT YOURSELF *Kitchenware SK 16*	21		11
9 Mar 85	GUN LAW *Kitchenware SK 20*	53		4
27 Jun 87	MOTORTOWN *Kitchenware SK 30*	45		5
16 Apr 88	DON'T LOOK ANY FURTHER *Kitchenware SK 33*	52		4

KANO
US, male rapper (Kane Robinson) — 26

Date	Title	Peak	Wks No.1	Wks
12 Mar 05	TYPICAL ME *679 679L096CD2*	22		3
19 Mar 05	ROUTINE CHECK *WEA BEATS8* MITCHELL BROTHERS/KANO/THE STREETS	42		2
25 Jun 05	REMEMBER ME *679 679L101CD1*	71		1
24 Sep 05	NITE NITE *679 679L108CD2* FEATURING MIKE SKINNER & LEO THE LION	25		6
1 Sep 07	THIS IS THE GIRL *679 679L148CD* FEATURING CRAIG DAVID	18		11
7 Mar 09	AGAINST ALL ODDS *Ram RAMM76CD* CHASE & STATUS FEATURING KANO	45		1
7 Nov 09	ROCK N ROLLER *BPM GBWRD0900001*	44		2

KANSAS
US, male vocal/instrumental group — 7

Date	Title	Peak	Wks No.1	Wks
1 Jul 78	CARRY ON WAYWARD SON *Kirshner KIR 4932*	51		7

MORY KANTE
Guinea, male vocalist — 14

Date	Title	Peak	Wks No.1	Wks
23 Jul 88	YEKE YEKE *London LON 171*	29		9
11 Mar 95	YEKE YEKE (REMIX) *ffreedom TABCD 226*	25		3
30 Nov 96	YEKE YEKE (REMIX) *ffrr FCD 288*	28		2

KAOMA
France/Senegal/Brazil, male/female vocal/instrumental group – Michel Abihssira, Jacky Arconte, Jean-Claude Bonaventure, Loalwa Braz, Chyco Roger Dru, Fatou 'Fania' Niang & Monica Nogueira — 20

Date	Title	Peak	Wks No.1	Wks
21 Oct 89	LAMBADA *CBS 6550117* ●	4		18
27 Jan 90	DANCANDO LAMBADA *CBS 6552357*	62		2

KAOTIC CHEMISTRY
UK, male production trio — 1

Date	Title	Peak	Wks No.1	Wks
31 Oct 92	LSD (EP) *Moving Shadow SHADOW 20*	68		1

KARAJA
Germany, female vocalist (Ivana Karaja) — 1

Date	Title	Peak	Wks No.1	Wks
19 Oct 02	SHE MOVES (LALALA) *Substance SUBS 14CDS*	42		1

KARDINAL OFFISHALL
Canada, male rapper/producer (Jason D. Harrow) — 55

Date	Title	Peak	Wks No.1	Wks
18 Oct 03	CARNIVAL GIRL *Mercury 9812254* TEXAS FEATURING KARDINAL OFFISHALL	9		5
11 Oct 08	DANGEROUS *Polydor 1789479* FEATURING AKON	16		20
13 Dec 08	BEAUTIFUL *Universal 2700494* AKON FEATURING KARDINAL OFFISHALL & COLBY O'DONIS	8		30

KARIYA
US, female vocalist — 9

Date	Title	Peak	Wks No.1	Wks
8 Jul 89	LET ME LOVE YOU FOR TONIGHT *Sleeping Bag SBUK 4*	44		6
21 Oct 89	LET ME LOVE YOU FOR TONIGHT *Sleeping Bag SBUK 4*	57		3

MICK KARN
UK (b. Cyprus), male bass player (Anthony Michelides). See Dali's Car, Japan, Rain Tree Crow — 6

Date	Title	Peak	Wks No.1	Wks
9 Jul 83	AFTER A FASHION *Musicfest FEST 1* MIDGE URE & MICK KARN	39		4
17 Jan 87	BUOY *Virgin VS 910* FEATURING DAVID SYLVIAN	63		2

KARTOON KREW
US, male producer (Craig Bevan) — 6

Date	Title	Peak	Wks No.1	Wks
7 Dec 85	INSPECTOR GADGET *Champion CHAMP 6*	58		6

KASABIAN
UK, male vocal/instrumental group – Tom Meighan, Chris Edwards, Ash Hannis (replaced by Ian Matthews), Chris Karloff (replaced by Jay Mehler) & Sergio Pizzorno — 79

Date	Title	Peak	Wks No.1	Wks
22 May 04	CLUB FOOT *BMG PARADISE08*	19		3
21 Aug 04	LSF *RCA PARADISE14*	10		7
23 Oct 04	PROCESSED BEATS *RCA PARADISE21*	17		3
15 Jan 05	CUTT OFF *RCA PARADISE26*	8		7
2 Apr 05	CLUB FOOT *RCA PARADISE30*	21		5
5 Aug 06	EMPIRE *Columbia PARADISE36*	9		14
11 Nov 06	SHOOT THE RUNNER *Columbia PARADISE43*	17		7
10 Feb 07	ME PLUS ONE *Columbia PARADISE48*	22		2
13 Jun 09	FIRE *Columbia PARADISE54*	3		20
20 Jun 09	UNDERDOG *Columbia GBARL0801796*	32		9
29 Aug 09	WHERE DID ALL THE LOVE GO *Columbia PARADISE64*	30		2

KASENETZ-KATZ SINGING ORCHESTRAL CIRCUS
US, male vocal/instrumental group — 15

Date	Title	Peak	Wks No.1	Wks
20 Nov 68	QUICK JOEY SMALL (RUN JOEY RUN) *Buddah 201 022*	19		15

KATCHA
UK, male DJ/producer (Jerry Dickens) — 1

Date	Title	Peak	Wks No.1	Wks
21 Aug 99	TOUCHED BY GOD *Hooj Choons HOOJ 77CD*	57		1

KATOI
Thailand, female DJ/producer (Kat Henderson) — 1

Date	Title	Peak	Wks No.1	Wks
29 Mar 03	TOUCH YOU *Arista Dance 74321964492*	70		1

KATRINA & THE WAVES

US/UK, female/male vocal/instrumental group – Katrina Leskanich, Kimberley Rew, Alex Cooper & Vince de la Cruz

Date	Title	Peak	Wks at No.1	34
4 May 85	**WALKING ON SUNSHINE** *Capitol CL 354*	8		12
5 Jul 86	**SUN STREET** *Capitol CL 407*	22		9
8 Jun 96	**WALKING ON SUNSHINE** *EMI Premier PRESCD 2*	53		1
10 May 97	**LOVE SHINE A LIGHT** *Eternal WEA 106CD1*	3		12

KAVANA

UK, male vocalist (Anthony Kavanagh)

Date	Title	Peak	Wks at No.1	26
11 May 96	**CRAZY CHANCE** *Nemesis NMSDG 1*	35		3
24 Aug 96	**WHERE ARE YOU** *Nemesis NMSD 2*	26		2
11 Jan 97	**I CAN MAKE YOU FEEL GOOD** *Nemesis NMSDX 3*	8		5
19 Apr 97	**MFEO** *Nemesis NMSD 4*	8		4
13 Sep 97	**CRAZY CHANCE** *Nemesis NMSD 5*	16		3
29 Aug 98	**SPECIAL KIND OF SOMETHING** *Virgin VSCDT 1704*	13		4
12 Dec 98	**FUNKY LOVE** *Virgin VSCDT 1711*	32		3
20 Mar 99	**WILL YOU WAIT FOR ME** *Virgin VSCDT 1726*	29		2

NIAMH KAVANAGH

Ireland, female vocalist

Date	Title	Peak	Wks at No.1	5
12 Jun 93	**IN YOUR EYES** *Arista 74321154152*	24		5

KAWALA

UK, male vocal/instrumental/production group

Date	Title	Peak	Wks at No.1	1
26 Feb 00	**HUMANISTIC** *Pepper 9230022*	68		1

JANET KAY

UK, female vocalist (Janet Bogle)

Date	Title	Peak	Wks at No.1	24
9 Jun 79	**SILLY GAMES** *Scope SC 2* ○	2		14
11 Aug 90	**SILLY GAMES** *Arista 113452* LINDY LAYTON FEATURING JANET KAY	22		7
11 Aug 90	**SILLY GAMES (REMIX)** *Music Factory Dance MFD 006*	62		3

PETER KAY

UK, male comedian/actor/vocalist

Date	Title	Peak	Wks at No.1	56
26 Mar 05	**(IS THIS THE WAY TO) AMARILLO?** *Universal TV 9828606* TONY CHRISTIE FEATURING PETER KAY ⊛	1	7	25
31 Dec 05	**(IS THIS THE WAY TO) AMARILLO?** *Universal TV 9828606* TONY CHRISTIE FEATURING PETER KAY	58		3
24 Mar 07	**(I'M GONNA BE) 500 MILES** *EMI COMICCD01* PROCLAIMERS FEATURING BRIAN POTTER & ANDY PIPKIN	1	3	10
25 Oct 08	**THE WINNER'S SONG** *Polydor 1789241* GERALDINE	2		7
27 Dec 08	**ONCE UPON A CHRISTMAS SONG** *Polydor 1793980* GERALDINE	5		3
28 Nov 09	**THE OFFICIAL BBC CHILDREN IN NEED MEDLEY** *Epic 88697618362* PETER KAY'S ANIMATED ALL STAR BAND ●	1	2	8

DANNY KAYE

US, male vocalist (David Kaminsky), d. 3 Mar 1987 (age 74)

Date	Title	Peak	Wks at No.1	10
27 Feb 53	**WONDERFUL COPENHAGEN** *Brunswick 05023*	5		10

KAYE SISTERS

US, female vocal group – Sheila Jones, Sheila Palmer & Carole Young, d. 20 Aug 2006

Date	Title	Peak	Wks at No.1	45
25 May 56	**IVORY TOWER** *HMV POP 209* THREE KAYES	20		5
1 Nov 57	**GOTTA HAVE SOMETHING IN THE BANK FRANK** *Philips PB 751* FRANKIE VAUGHAN & THE KAYE SISTERS	8		11
3 Jan 58	**SHAKE ME I RATTLE/ALONE** *Philips PB 752*	27		1
1 May 59	**COME SOFTLY TO ME** *Philips PB 913* FRANKIE VAUGHAN & THE KAYE SISTERS	9		9
7 Jul 60	**PAPER ROSES** *Philips PB 1024*	7		19

KAYESTONE

UK, male DJ/production duo

Date	Title	Peak	Wks at No.1	1
29 Jul 00	**ATMOSPHERE** *Distinctive DISNCD 62*	55		1

KC & THE SUNSHINE BAND

US, male vocal/instrumental group – Harry 'KC' Wayne Casey, Richard Finch, Robert Johnson, Jerome Smith, d. 28 Jul 2000, & various musicians

Date	Title	Peak	Wks at No.1	104
17 Aug 74	**QUEEN OF CLUBS** *Jayboy BOY 88*	7		12
23 Nov 74	**SOUND YOUR FUNKY HORN** *Jayboy BOY 83*	17		9
29 Mar 75	**GET DOWN TONIGHT** *Jayboy BOY 93* ★	21		9
2 Aug 75	**THAT'S THE WAY (I LIKE IT)** *Jayboy BOY 99* ★	4		10
22 Nov 75	**I'M SO CRAZY ('BOUT YOU)** *Jayboy BOY 101*	34		3
17 Jul 76	**(SHAKE SHAKE SHAKE) SHAKE YOUR BOOTY** *Jayboy BOY 110* ★	22		8
11 Dec 76	**KEEP IT COMIN' LOVE** *Jayboy BOY 112*	31		8
30 Apr 77	**I'M YOUR BOOGIE MAN** *TK XB 2167* ★	41		4
6 May 78	**BOOGIE SHOES** *TK TKR 6025*	34		5
22 Jul 78	**IT'S THE SAME OLD SONG** *TK TKR 6037*	47		5
8 Dec 79	**PLEASE DON'T GO** *TK TKR 7558* ○ ★	3		12
16 Jul 83	**GIVE IT UP** *Epic EPC 3017* ●	1	3	14
24 Sep 83	**(YOU SAID) YOU'D GIMME SOME MORE** *Epic A 2760*	41		3
11 May 91	**THAT'S THE WAY (I LIKE IT) (REMIX)** *Music Factory Dance M7FAC 2*	59		2

KE

US, male vocalist (Kevin Griudis)

Date	Title	Peak	Wks at No.1	1
13 Apr 96	**STRANGE WORLD** *Venture 74321349412*	73		1

KEANE

UK, male vocal/instrumental trio – Tom Chaplin, Richard Hughes & Tim Rice-Oxley

Date	Title	Peak	Wks at No.1	79
28 Feb 04	**SOMEWHERE ONLY WE KNOW** *Island CID 849*	3		13
15 May 04	**EVERYBODY'S CHANGING** *Island CID 855*	4		9
28 Aug 04	**BEDSHAPED** *Island CID 870*	10		7
4 Dec 04	**THIS IS THE LAST TIME** *Island CID880*	18		6
3 Jun 06	**IS IT ANY WONDER** *Island CID934*	3		16
26 Aug 06	**CRYSTALL BALL** *Island/Uni-Island 1704803*	20		5
11 Nov 06	**NOTHING IN MY WAY** *Island 1712175*	19		3
27 Jan 07	**A BAD DREAM** *Island/Uni-Island 1723057*	23		4
23 Aug 08	**SPIRALING** *Island GBUM70812249*	23		15
1 Nov 08	**THE LOVERS ARE LOSING** *Island 1788773*	52		1

JOHNNY KEATING

UK, orchestra

Date	Title	Peak	Wks at No.1	14
1 Mar 62	**THEME FROM 'Z-CARS'** *Piccadilly 7N 35032*	8		14

RONAN KEATING

Ireland, male vocalist. See Boyzone

Date	Title	Peak	Wks at No.1	154
7 Aug 99	**WHEN YOU SAY NOTHING AT ALL** *Polydor 5612902* ●	1	2	17
22 Jul 00	**LIFE IS A ROLLERCOASTER** *Polydor 5619362* ●	1	1	14
2 Dec 00	**THE WAY YOU MAKE ME FEEL** *Polydor 5878862*	6		12
28 Apr 01	**LOVIN' EACH DAY** *Polydor 5876912* ○	2		14
18 May 02	**IF TOMORROW NEVER COMES** *Polydor 5707192* ●	1	1	15
21 Sep 02	**I LOVE IT WHEN WE DO** *Polydor 5709042*	5		11
7 Dec 02	**WE'VE GOT TONIGHT** *Polydor 0658612* FEATURING LULU	4		13
10 May 03	**THE LONG GOODBYE** *Polydor 0657382*	3		10
22 Nov 03	**LOST FOR WORDS** *Polydor 9813305*	9		4
21 Feb 04	**SHE BELIEVES (IN ME)** *Polydor 9816653*	2		7
15 May 04	**LAST THING ON MY MIND** *Polydor/Curb 9866595* & LeANN RIMES	5		9
9 Oct 04	**I HOPE YOU DANCE** *Polydor 9868261*	2		7
25 Dec 04	**FATHER AND SON** *Polydor 9869667* & YUSUF ISLAM	2		11
10 Jun 06	**ALL OVER AGAIN** *Polydor 9857872* & KATE RUSBY	6		6
26 Aug 06	**IRIS** *Polydor 1705359*	15		4

KEEDIE

UK, female vocalist (Keedie Babb)

Date	Title	Peak	Wks at No.1	9
23 Oct 04	**I BELIEVE MY HEART** *Innocent 8677122* DUNCAN JAMES & KEEDIE	12		7
24 Dec 05	**JERUSALEM** *Hyperactive CXSTUMP1* & THE ENGLAND CRICKET TEAM	19		2

KEVIN KEEGAN

UK, male footballer/vocalist

Date	Title	Peak	Wks at No.1	6
9 Jun 79	**HEAD OVER HEELS IN LOVE** *EMI 2965*	31		6

NELSON KEENE

UK, male vocalist (Malcolm Holland)

Date	Title	Peak	Wks at No.1	5
25 Aug 60	**IMAGE OF A GIRL** *HMV POP 771*	37		5

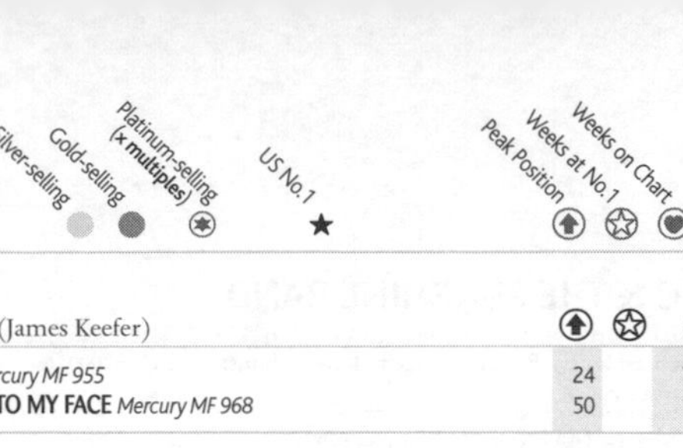

KEITH
US, male vocalist (James Keefer) — 8

Date	Title	Peak	Wks No.1	Wks
26 Jan 67	**98.6** *Mercury MF 955*	24		7
16 Mar 67	**TELL IT TO MY FACE** *Mercury MF 968*	50		1

KEITH 'N' SHANE
Ireland, male vocal duo. See Boyzone — 3

Date	Title	Peak	Wks No.1	Wks
23 Dec 00	**GIRL YOU KNOW IT'S TRUE** *Polydor 5879462*	36		3

KELIS
US, female vocalist/rapper (Kelis Rogers-Jones) — 113

Date	Title	Peak	Wks No.1	Wks
26 Feb 00	**CAUGHT OUT THERE (IMPORT)** *Virgin 8965102CD*	52		1
4 Mar 00	**CAUGHT OUT THERE** *Virgin VUSCD 158*	4		12
17 Jun 00	**GOOD STUFF** *Virgin VUSDX 164*	19		5
8 Jul 00	**GOT YOUR MONEY** *Elektra E 7077CD* OL' DIRTY BASTARD FEATURING KELIS	11		8
21 Oct 00	**GET ALONG WITH YOU** *Virgin VUSCD 174*	51		1
3 Nov 01	**YOUNG FRESH N' NEW** *Virgin VUSCD 212*	32		2
5 Oct 02	**HELP ME** *Perfecto PERF 42CDS* TIMO MAAS FEATURING KELIS	65		1
23 Aug 03	**FINEST DREAMS** *Virgin RXCD 2* RICHARD X FEATURING KELIS	8		5
23 Aug 03	**LET'S GET ILL** *Bad Boy/Island MCSTD 40331* P DIDDY FEATURING KELIS	25		3
17 Jan 04	**MILKSHAKE** *Virgin VSCDX 1863* ●	2		15
20 Mar 04	**NOT IN LOVE** *Interscope 9862023* ENRIQUE FEATURING KELIS	5		9
5 Jun 04	**TRICK ME** *Virgin VSCDX 1872*	2		14
30 Oct 04	**MILLIONAIRE** *Virgin VSCDX 1885* FEATURING ANDRE 3000	3		12
16 Apr 05	**IN PUBLIC** *Virgin VSCDT1893* FEATURING NAS	17		6
9 Sep 06	**BOSSY** *Virgin VSCDT1914* FEATURING TOO SHORT	22		5
3 Feb 07	**LIL STAR** *Virgin VSCDT1922* FEATURING CEE LO	3		14

JERRY KELLER
US, male vocalist — 14

Date	Title	Peak	Wks No.1	Wks
28 Aug 59	**HERE COMES SUMMER** *London HLR 8890*	1	1	14

FRANK KELLY
Ireland, male vocalist/actor — 5

Date	Title	Peak	Wks No.1	Wks
24 Dec 83	**CHRISTMAS COUNTDOWN** *Ritz 062*	26		4
29 Dec 84	**CHRISTMAS COUNTDOWN** *Ritz 062*	54		1

FRANKIE KELLY
US, male vocalist — 2

Date	Title	Peak	Wks No.1	Wks
2 Nov 85	**AIN'T THAT THE TRUTH** *10 TEN 87*	65		2

KEITH KELLY
UK, male vocalist (Michael Pailthorpe) — 5

Date	Title	Peak	Wks No.1	Wks
5 May 60	**TEASE ME** *Parlophone R 4640*	27		4
18 Aug 60	**LISTEN LITTLE GIRL** *Parlophone R 4676*	47		1

R KELLY
US, male vocalist/producer (Robert Kelly). R'n'B supremo whose 1998 double album R produced seven Top 20 singles, among them the inspirational 'I Believe I Can Fly', his best-selling UK single and the fourth of his six US million-sellers — 254

Date	Title	Peak	Wks No.1	Wks
9 May 92	**SHE'S GOT THAT VIBE** *Jive JIVET 292* & PUBLIC ANNOUNCEMENT	57		2
20 Nov 93	**SEX ME** *Jive JIVECD 346* & PUBLIC ANNOUNCEMENT	75		1
14 May 94	**YOUR BODY'S CALLIN'** *Jive JIVECD 353*	19		4
3 Sep 94	**SUMMER BUNNIES** *Jive JIVECD 358*	23		3
22 Oct 94	**SHE'S GOT THAT VIBE** *Jive JIVECD 364*	3		13
21 Jan 95	**BUMP N' GRIND** *Jive JIVECD 368* ★	8		9
6 May 95	**THE 4 PLAYS EPS** *Jive JIVECD 376*	23		3
11 Nov 95	**YOU REMIND ME OF SOMETHING** *Jive JIVECD 388*	24		3
2 Mar 96	**DOWN LOW (NOBODY HAS TO KNOW)** *Jive JIVERCD 392* FEATURING RONALD ISLEY	23		3
22 Jun 96	**THANK GOD IT'S FRIDAY** *Jive JIVERCD 395*	14		4
29 Mar 97	**I BELIEVE I CAN FLY** *Jive JIVECD 415* ⊛	1	3	17
19 Jul 97	**GOTHAM CITY** *Jive JIVECD 428*	9		8
18 Jul 98	**BE CAREFUL** *Jive 0521452* SPARKLE FEATURING R KELLY	7		7
26 Sep 98	**HALF ON A BABY** *Jive 0521802*	16		4
14 Nov 98	**HOME ALONE** *Jive 0522392* FEATURING KEITH MURRAY	17		5
28 Nov 98	**I'M YOUR ANGEL** *Epic 6666282* CELINE DION & R KELLY ● ★	3		13
31 Jul 99	**DID YOU EVER THINK** *Jive 0523612*	20		5
16 Oct 99	**IF I COULD TURN BACK THE HANDS OF TIME (IMPORT)** *Jive 0523182*	57		2
30 Oct 99	**IF I COULD TURN BACK THE HANDS OF TIME** *Jive 0523182* ⊛	2		19
19 Feb 00	**SATISFY YOU (IMPORT)** *Bad Boy/Arista 792832* PUFF DADDY FEATURING R KELLY	73		2
11 Mar 00	**SATISFY YOU** *Puff Daddy 74321745592* PUFF DADDY FEATURING R KELLY	8		8
22 Apr 00	**ONLY THE LOOT CAN MAKE ME HAPPY/WHEN A WOMAN'S FED UP/I CAN'T SLEEP BABY (IF I)** *Jive 9250282*	24		3
21 Oct 00	**I WISH** *Jive 9251292*	12		6
31 Mar 01	**THE STORM IS OVER** *Jive 9251852*	18		6
23 Jun 01	**FIESTA** *Jive 9252142* FEATURING JAY-Z	23		3
2 Mar 02	**THE WORLD'S GREATEST** *Jive 9253242*	4		12
25 May 02	**HONEY** *Jive 9253662* & JAY-Z	35		2
17 May 03	**IGNITION** *Jive 9254982* ●	1	4	20
23 Aug 03	**SNAKE** *Jive 82876547232* FEATURING BIG TIGGER	10		5
15 Nov 03	**STEP IN THE NAME OF LOVE/THOIA THONG** *Jive 82876573912*	14		4
29 May 04	**HOTEL** *J 82876618612* CASSIDY FEATURING R KELLY	3		14
30 Oct 04	**HAPPY PEOPLE/U SAVED ME** *Jive 82876656182*	6		11
6 Nov 04	**WONDERFUL** *Def Jam 9864606* JA RULE FEATURING R KELLY & ASHANTI	1	1	10
20 Nov 04	**SO SEXY** *Atlantic AT 0187CD* TWISTA FEATURING R KELLY	28		3
10 Sep 05	**PLAYA'S ONLY** *Jive 82876725552* FEATURING GAME	33		2
16 Dec 06	**THAT'S THAT S****** *Geffen 1717453* SNOOP DOGG FEATURING R KELLY	38		4
19 May 07	**I'M A FLIRT** *Jive 88697090232* FEATURING TI & T-PAIN	18		6
28 Jul 07	**SAME GIRL** *Nonsuch 88697126432* & USHER	26		8

ROBERTA KELLY
US, female vocalist — 3

Date	Title	Peak	Wks No.1	Wks
21 Jan 78	**ZODIACS** *Oasis/Hansa 3*	44		3

KELLY FAMILY
US/Spain/Ireland/Germany, male/female vocal/instrumental group — 1

Date	Title	Peak	Wks No.1	Wks
21 Oct 95	**AN ANGEL** *EMI CDEM 390*	69		1

JOHNNY KEMP
US (b. Bahamas), male vocalist — 1

Date	Title	Peak	Wks No.1	Wks
27 Aug 88	**JUST GOT PAID** *CBS 6514707*	68		1

TARA KEMP
US, female vocalist — 2

Date	Title	Peak	Wks No.1	Wks
20 Apr 91	**HOLD YOU TIGHT** *Giant W 0020*	69		2

GRAHAM KENDRICK
UK, male vocalist — 4

Date	Title	Peak	Wks No.1	Wks
9 Sep 89	**LET THE FLAME BURN BRIGHTER** *Power P 30*	55		4

EDDIE KENDRICKS
US, male vocalist, d. 5 Oct 1992 (age 52). See Temptations — 20

Date	Title	Peak	Wks No.1	Wks
3 Nov 73	**KEEP ON TRUCKIN'** *Tamla Motown TMG 873* ★	18		14
16 Mar 74	**BOOGIE DOWN** *Tamla Motown TMG 888*	39		4
21 Sep 85	**A NIGHT AT THE APOLLO LIVE!** *RCA PB 49935* DARYL HALL & JOHN OATES FEATURING DAVID RUFFIN & EDDIE KENDRICK	58		2

KENICKIE
UK, female/male vocal/instrumental group — 13

Date	Title	Peak	Wks No.1	Wks
14 Sep 96	**PUNKA** *Emidisc CDDISC 001*	43		2
16 Nov 96	**MILLIONAIRE SWEEPER** *Emidisc CDDISC 002*	60		1
11 Jan 97	**IN YOUR CAR** *Emidisc CDDISCX 005*	24		3
3 May 97	**NIGHTLIFE** *Emidisc CDDISCX 006*	27		2
5 Jul 97	**PUNKA** *Emidisc CDDISCS 007*	38		2
6 Jun 98	**I WOULD FIX YOU** *EMI CDEM 513*	36		2
22 Aug 98	**STAY IN THE SUN** *EMI CDEMS 520*	43		1

JANE KENNAWAY & STRANGE BEHAVIOUR
UK, female vocalist & male instrumental group — 3

Date	Title	Peak	Wks No.1	Wks
24 Jan 81	**I.O.U.** *Deram DM 436*	65		3

BRIAN KENNEDY
UK, male vocalist/guitarist — 18

Date	Title	Peak	Wks No.1	Wks
22 Jun 96	**A BETTER MAN** *RCA 74321382642*	28		3
21 Sep 96	**LIFE, LOVE AND HAPPINESS** *RCA 74321409912*	27		3
5 Apr 97	**PUT THE MESSAGE IN THE BOX** *RCA 74321462272*	37		2
31 Dec 05	**GEORGE BEST – A TRIBUTE** *Curb CUBC116* & PETER CORRY	4		10

KEVIN KENNEDY
UK, male actor/vocalist (Kevin Williams) — 1

Date	Title	Peak	Wks at No.1	Wks
24 Jun 00	**BULLDOG NATION** *D2m 74321759742*	70		1

KENNY
Ireland, male vocalist (Tony Kenny) — 16

Date	Title	Peak	Wks at No.1	Wks
3 Mar 73	**HEART OF STONE** *RAK 144*	11		13
30 Jun 73	**GIVE IT TO ME NOW** *RAK 153*	38		3

KENNY
UK, male vocal/instrumental group – Richard Driscoll, Christopher Lacklison, Chris Redburn, Yan Style & Andy Walton — 39

Date	Title	Peak	Wks at No.1	Wks
7 Dec 74	**THE BUMP** *RAK 186* ○	3		15
8 Mar 75	**FANCY PANTS** *RAK 196*	4		9
7 Jun 75	**BABY I LOVE YOU OK** *RAK 207*	12		7
16 Aug 75	**JULIE ANN** *RAK 214*	10		8

GERARD KENNY
US, male vocalist — 21

Date	Title	Peak	Wks at No.1	Wks
9 Dec 78	**NEW YORK, NEW YORK** *RCA PB 5117*	43		8
21 Jun 80	**FANTASY** *RCA PB 5256*	34		6
18 Feb 84	**THE OTHER WOMAN, THE OTHER MAN** *Impression IMS 3*	69		4
4 May 85	**NO MAN'S LAND** *WEA YZ 38*	56		3

KENT
Sweden, male vocal/instrumental group — 1

Date	Title	Peak	Wks at No.1	Wks
13 Mar 99	**747** *RCA 74321645912*	61		1

KLARK KENT
US, male vocalist/drummer (Stewart Copeland). See Police — 4

Date	Title	Peak	Wks at No.1	Wks
26 Aug 78	**DON'T CARE** *A&M AMS 7376*	48		4

KERBDOG
Ireland, male vocal/instrumental group — 5

Date	Title	Peak	Wks at No.1	Wks
12 Mar 94	**DRY RISER** *Vertigo VERCC 83*	60		1
6 Aug 94	**DUMMY CRUSHER** *Vertigo VERCD 86*	37		2
12 Oct 96	**SALLY** *Fontana KERCD 2*	69		1
29 Mar 97	**MEXICAN WAVE** *Fontana KERCD 3*	49		1

KERRI & MICK
Australia, female/male vocal duo — 3

Date	Title	Peak	Wks at No.1	Wks
28 Apr 84	**SONS AND DAUGHTERS' THEME** *A1 286*	68		3

KERRI-ANN
Ireland, female vocalist — 1

Date	Title	Peak	Wks at No.1	Wks
8 Aug 98	**DO YOU LOVE ME BOY?** *Ragtan Road 5671012*	58		1

LIZ KERSHAW & BRUNO BROOKES
UK, female/male vocal/radio DJ duo — 3

Date	Title	Peak	Wks at No.1	Wks
2 Dec 89	**IT TAKES TWO BABY** *Spartan CIN 101* LIZ KERSHAW, BRUNO BROOKES, JIVE BUNNY & LONDONBEAT	53		2
1 Dec 90	**LET'S DANCE** *Jive BRUNO 1* BRUNO & LIZ & THE RADIO 1 POSSE	54		1

NIK KERSHAW
UK, male vocalist/guitarist — 89

Date	Title	Peak	Wks at No.1	Wks
19 Nov 83	**I WON'T LET THE SUN GO DOWN ON ME** *MCA 816*	47		5
28 Jan 84	**WOULDN'T IT BE GOOD** *MCA NIK 2* ○	4		14
14 Apr 84	**DANCING GIRLS** *MCA NIK 3*	13		9
16 Jun 84	**I WON'T LET THE SUN GO DOWN ON ME** *MCA NIK 4* ○	2		13
15 Sep 84	**HUMAN RACING** *MCA NIK 5*	19		7
17 Nov 84	**THE RIDDLE** *MCA NIK 6* ○	3		11
16 Mar 85	**WIDE BOY** *MCA NIK 7*	9		8
3 Aug 85	**DON QUIXOTE** *MCA NIK 8*	10		7
30 Nov 85	**WHEN A HEART BEATS** *MCA NIK 9*	27		7
11 Oct 86	**NOBODY KNOWS** *MCA NIK 10*	44		3
13 Dec 86	**RADIO MUSICOLA** *MCA NIK 11*	43		2
4 Feb 89	**ONE STEP AHEAD** *MCA NIK 12*	55		1
27 Feb 99	**SOMEBODY LOVES YOU** *Eagle EAGXA 023*	70		1
7 Aug 99	**SOMETIMES** *Wall Of Sound WALLD 054* LES RYTHMES DIGITALES FEATURING NIK KERSHAW	56		1

KE$HA
US, female vocalist/rapper (Kesha Sebert) — 33

Date	Title	Peak	Wks at No.1	Wks
14 Nov 09	**TIK TOK** *RCA 88697619042* ★	5		23+
13 Feb 10	**BLAH BLAH BLAH** *RCA 88697659702* FEATURING 30H!3	11		9+
13 Feb 10	**YOUR LOVE IS MY DRUG** *RCA USRC10900735*	63		1

KEVIN THE GERBIL
UK, male vocalist/TV puppet (David Claridge) — 6

Date	Title	Peak	Wks at No.1	Wks
4 Aug 84	**SUMMER HOLIDAY** *Magnet RAT 3*	50		6

KEY WEST FEATURING ERIK
UK, male producer (Richard Hewson) & female vocalist — 2

Date	Title	Peak	Wks at No.1	Wks
10 Apr 93	**LOOKS LIKE I'M IN LOVE AGAIN** *PWL Sanctuary PWCD 252*	46		2

ALICIA KEYS
US, female vocalist/pianist (Alicia Cook) — 152

Date	Title	Peak	Wks at No.1	Wks
10 Nov 01	**FALLIN'** *J Records 74321903692* ★	3		10
9 Mar 02	**BROTHA PART II** *J Records 74321922142* ANGIE STONE FEATURING ALICIA KEYS & EVE	37		2
30 Mar 02	**A WOMAN'S WORTH** *J Records 74321928692*	18		8
20 Jul 02	**HOW COME YOU DON'T CALL ME** *J Records 74321943122*	26		3
5 Oct 02	**GANGSTA LOVIN'** *Interscope 4978042* EVE FEATURING ALICIA KEYS	6		8
7 Dec 02	**GIRLFRIEND** *J Records 74321974972*	24		5
20 Dec 03	**YOU DON'T KNOW MY NAME** *J Records 82876588652*	19		9
10 Apr 04	**IF I AIN'T GOT YOU** *J Records 82876608172*	18		5
10 Nov 07	**NO ONE** *J Records 88697182452* ★	6		24
8 Mar 08	**LIKE YOU'LL NEVER SEE ME AGAIN** *J Records 88697233992*	53		1
4 Oct 08	**ANOTHER WAY TO DIE** *RCA 88697413642* JACK WHITE & ALICIA KEYS	9		12
30 May 09	**NO ONE** *J Records 88697182452*	54		2
26 Sep 09	**EMPIRE STATE OF MIND** *Roc Nation USJZ10900031* JAY-Z FEATURING ALICIA KEYS ★	2		29+
3 Oct 09	**IF I AIN'T GOT YOU** *J Records 82876608172*	54		1
12 Dec 09	**DOESN'T MEAN ANYTHING** *J Records 88697621702*	8		16
12 Dec 09	**NO ONE** *J Records 88697182452*	51		1
26 Dec 09	**EMPIRE STATE OF MIND PART II** *J USJAY0900291*	4		15+
6 Feb 10	**TRY SLEEPING WITH A BROKEN HEART** *J USJAY0900254*	71		1

CHAKA KHAN
US, female vocalist (Yvette Stevens) — 97

Date	Title	Peak	Wks at No.1	Wks
2 Dec 78	**I'M EVERY WOMAN** *Warner Brothers K 17269*	11		13
31 Mar 84	**AIN'T NOBODY** *Warner Brothers RCK 1* RUFUS & CHAKA KHAN ○	8		12
20 Oct 84	**I FEEL FOR YOU** *Warner Brothers W 9209* ●	1	3	16
19 Jan 85	**THIS IS MY NIGHT** *Warner Brothers W 9097*	14		6
20 Apr 85	**EYE TO EYE** *Warner Brothers W 9009*	16		7
12 Jul 86	**LOVE OF A LIFETIME** *Warner Brothers W 8671*	52		4
21 Jan 89	**IT'S MY PARTY** *Warner Brothers W 7678*	71		2
6 May 89	**I'M EVERY WOMAN (REMIX)** *Warner Brothers W 2963*	8		8
8 Jul 89	**AIN'T NOBODY (REMIX)** *Warner Brothers W 2880* RUFUS & CHAKA KHAN	6		9
7 Oct 89	**I FEEL FOR YOU (REMIX)** *Warner Brothers W 2764*	45		2
13 Jan 90	**I'LL BE GOOD TO YOU** *Qwest W 2697* QUINCY JONES FEATURING RAY CHARLES & CHAKA KHAN	21		7
28 Mar 92	**LOVE YOU ALL MY LIFETIME** *Warner Brothers W 0087*	49		3
17 Jul 93	**DON'T LOOK AT ME THAT WAY** *Warner Brothers W 0192CD*	73		1
19 Aug 95	**WATCH WHAT YOU SAY** *Cooltempo CDCOOL 308* GURU FEATURING CHAKA KHAN	28		3
1 Mar 97	**NEVER MISS THE WATER** *Reprise W 1393CD* FEATURING ME'SHELL NDEGEOCELLO	59		1
11 Nov 00	**ALL GOOD** *Tommy Boy TBCD 2154B* DE LA SOUL FEATURING CHAKA KHAN	33		3

PRAGA KHAN
Belgium, male producer (Maurice Engelen) — 9

Date	Title	Peak	Wks at No.1	Wks
4 Apr 92	**FREE YOUR BODY/INJECTED WITH A POISON** *Profile PROFT 347* FEATURING JADE 4 U	16		6
11 Jul 92	**RAVE ALERT** *Profile PROF 369*	39		2
24 Nov 01	**INJECTED WITH POISON** *Nukleuz NUKC 0238*	52		1

KHIA
US, female vocalist (Khia Finch) — 14

Date	Title	Peak	Wks at No.1	Wks
16 Oct 04	**MY NECK MY BACK (LICK IT)** *Direction 6753802*	4		14

MARY KIANI
UK, female vocalist (Mary McKloskey). See Time Frequency — **15**

Date	Title	Peak	Wks No.1	Wks
12 Aug 95	**WHEN I CALL YOUR NAME** *Mercury MERCD 440*	18		4
23 Dec 95	**I GIVE IT ALL TO YOU/I IMAGINE** *Mercury MERCD 449*	35		4
27 Apr 96	**LET THE MUSIC PLAY** *Mercury MERCD 456*	19		3
18 Jan 97	**100%** *Mercury MERCD 469*	23		3
21 Jun 97	**WITH OR WITHOUT YOU** *Mercury MERCD 487*	46		1

KICK SQUAD
UK, male production duo — **2**

Date	Title	Peak	Wks No.1	Wks
10 Nov 90	**SOUND CLASH (CHAMPION SOUND)** *Kickin KICK 2*	59		2

KICKING BACK WITH TAXMAN
UK, male/female vocal/production duo with male rapper — **8**

Date	Title	Peak	Wks No.1	Wks
17 Mar 90	**DEVOTION** *10 TEN 297*	47		4
7 Jul 90	**EVERYTHING** *10 TEN 307*	54		4

KICKS LIKE A MULE
UK, male production duo – Nick Halkes & Richard Russell — **6**

Date	Title	Peak	Wks No.1	Wks
1 Feb 92	**THE BOUNCER** *Tribal Bass TRIBE 35*	7		6

K.I.D.
Antilles, male/female vocal/production group — **4**

Date	Title	Peak	Wks No.1	Wks
28 Feb 81	**DON'T STOP** *EMI 5143*	49		4

KID BRITISH
UK, male vocal/instrumental group — **1**

Date	Title	Peak	Wks No.1	Wks
18 Jul 09	**OUR HOUSE IS DADLESS** *Mercury GBUM70900066*	63		1

KID CREME
Belgium, male producer (Nicolas Skaravilli) — **3**

Date	Title	Peak	Wks No.1	Wks
22 Mar 03	**DOWN AND UNDER (TOGETHER)** *Ink NIBNE 13CD* FEATURING MC SHURAKANO	55		1
10 May 03	**HYPNOTISING** *Positiva CDTIV 189* FEATURING CHARLISE	31		2

KID CUDI
US/Italy, male vocal/rap/DJ/production trio – Scott Mescudi, Francesco Barbaglia & Andrea Fratangelo — **29**

Date	Title	Peak	Wks No.1	Wks
24 Jan 09	**DAY 'N' NITE** *Data DATA211CDS* VS CROOKERS	2		22
26 Sep 09	**MAKE HER SAY** *Island USUM70969614* FEATURING KANYE WEST, COMMON & LADY GAGA	67		2
13 Mar 10	**MEMORIES** *Positiva/Virgin FRZID0900950* DAVID GUETTA FEATURING KID CUDI	30		5+

KID 'N' PLAY
US, male rap duo — **7**

Date	Title	Peak	Wks No.1	Wks
18 Jul 87	**LAST NIGHT** *Cooltempo COOL 148*	71		1
26 Mar 88	**DO THIS MY WAY** *Cooltempo COOL 164*	48		3
17 Sep 88	**GITTIN' FUNKY** *Cooltempo COOL 168*	55		3

KID ROCK
US, male vocalist/rapper (Robert Ritchie) — **31**

Date	Title	Peak	Wks No.1	Wks
23 Oct 99	**COWBOY** *Atlantic AT 0076CD*	36		2
9 Sep 00	**AMERICAN BAD ASS** *Atlantic AT 0085CD*	25		4
12 May 01	**BAWITDABA** *Atlantic AT 0098CD*	41		2
12 Jul 08	**ALL SUMMER LONG** *Atlantic AT0315CD* ★	1	1	23

KID UNKNOWN
UK, male producer (Paul Fitzpatrick) — **1**

Date	Title	Peak	Wks No.1	Wks
2 May 92	**NIGHTMARE** *Warp WAP 20CD*	64		1

CAROL KIDD FEATURING TERRY WAITE
UK, female vocalist & male humanitarian — **3**

Date	Title	Peak	Wks No.1	Wks
17 Oct 92	**WHEN I DREAM** *The Hit Label HLS 1*	58		3

JOHNNY KIDD & THE PIRATES
UK, male vocalist (Frederick Heath), d. 7 Oct 1966 (age 36), & male vocal/instrumental group — **62**

Date	Title	Peak	Wks No.1	Wks
12 Jun 59	**PLEASE DON'T TOUCH** *HMV POP 615* JOHNNY KIDD	25		5
12 Feb 60	**YOU GOT WHAT IT TAKES** *HMV POP 698*	25		3
16 Jun 60	**SHAKIN' ALL OVER** *HMV POP 753*	1	1	19
6 Oct 60	**RESTLESS** *HMV POP 790*	22		7
13 Apr 61	**LINDA LU** *HMV POP 853*	47		1
10 Jan 63	**SHOT OF RHYTHM AND BLUES** *HMV POP 1088*	48		1
25 Jul 63	**I'LL NEVER GET OVER YOU** *HMV POP 1173*	4		15
28 Nov 63	**HUNGRY FOR LOVE** *HMV POP 1228*	20		10
30 Apr 64	**ALWAYS AND EVER** *HMV POP 1269*	46		1

NICOLE KIDMAN
Australia, female actor/vocalist — **17**

Date	Title	Peak	Wks No.1	Wks
6 Oct 01	**COME WHAT MAY** *Interscope 4976302* & EWAN McGREGOR	27		5
22 Dec 01	**SOMETHIN' STUPID** *Chrysalis CDCHS 5132* ROBBIE WILLIAMS & NICOLE KIDMAN ●	1	3	12

KIDS IN GLASS HOUSES
UK, male vocal/instrumental group — **3**

Date	Title	Peak	Wks No.1	Wks
31 May 08	**GIVE ME WHAT I WANT** *Roadrunner RR38522*	62		1
3 Apr 10	**MATTERS AT ALL** *Roadrunner NLA320989486*	65		2+

KIDS FROM *FAME*
US, male/female vocal/instrumental/acting/dancing group – featuring Debbie Allen, Lee Curreri, Erica Gimpel, Carlo Imperato, Valerie Landsberg, Gene Anthony Ray, d. 14 Nov 2003, & Lori Singer, backed by session musicians — **36**

Date	Title	Peak	Wks No.1	Wks
14 Aug 82	**HI-FIDELITY** *RCA 254* FEATURING VALERIE LANDSBERG ●	5		10
2 Oct 82	**STARMAKER** *RCA 280* ●	3		10
11 Dec 82	**MANNEQUIN** *RCA 299* FEATURING GENE ANTHONY RAY	50		6
9 Apr 83	**FRIDAY NIGHT (LIVE VERSION)** *RCA 320*	13		10

K.I.G.
UK, male vocal/rap group — **9**

Date	Title	Peak	Wks No.1	Wks
28 Mar 09	**HEADS SHOULDERS KNEEZ AND TOEZ** *AATW/Island 2701380*	18		9

GREG KIHN BAND
US, male vocal/instrumental group — **2**

Date	Title	Peak	Wks No.1	Wks
23 Apr 83	**JEOPARDY** *Beserkley E 9847*	63		2

KILLAH PRIEST
US, male rapper (Walter Reed) — **1**

Date	Title	Peak	Wks No.1	Wks
7 Feb 98	**ONE STEP** *Geffen GFSTD 22318*	45		1

KILLCITY
UK, female/male vocal/instrumental group — **1**

Date	Title	Peak	Wks No.1	Wks
14 Aug 04	**JUST LIKE BRUCE LEE** *Poptones MC5091SCD*	63		1

KILLER MIKE
US, male rapper (Michael Render) — **9**

Date	Title	Peak	Wks No.1	Wks
6 Apr 02	**THE WHOLE WORLD** *LaFace 74321917592* OUTKAST FEATURING KILLER MIKE	19		5
27 Jul 02	**LAND OF A MILLION DRUMS** *Atlantic AT 0134CD* OUTKAST FEATURING KILLER MIKE & SLEEPY BROWN	46		1
10 May 03	**A.D.I.D.A.S.** *Columbia 6738652* FEATURING BIG BOI	22		3

KILLERS
US, male vocal/instrumental group – Brandon Flowers, Dave Keuning, Mark Stoermer & Ronnie Vannucci, Jr — **131**

Date	Title	Peak	Wks No.1	Wks
27 Mar 04	**SOMEBODY TOLD ME** *Lizard King LIZARD009*	28		2
5 Jun 04	**MR BRIGHTSIDE** *Lizard King LIZARD 010CD2* ●	10		6
11 Sep 04	**ALL THESE THINGS THAT I'VE DONE** *Lizard King LIZARD012*	18		4
22 Jan 05	**SOMEBODY TOLD ME** *Lizard King LIZARD014CD2*	3		18
14 May 05	**SMILE LIKE YOU MEAN IT** *Lizard King LIZARD015*	11		6
23 Sep 06	**WHEN YOU WERE YOUNG** *Mercury 1707658*	2		14
2 Dec 06	**BONES** *Vertigo 1717078*	15		7
24 Feb 07	**READ MY MIND** *Vertigo 1724567*	15		14

Silver-selling ● Gold-selling ● Platinum-selling (x multiples) US No.1 ★ Peak Position Weeks at No.1 Weeks on Chart

Date	Title / Label	Peak Position	Weeks at No.1	Weeks on Chart
7 Jul 07	**FOR REASONS UNKNOWN** *Vertigo 1736030*	53		1
20 Oct 07	**TRANQUILIZE** *Mercury USUM70754276*	13		6
15 Dec 07	**DON'T SHOOT ME SANTA** *Vertigo 1750323*	34		4
15 Nov 08	**MR BRIGHTSIDE** *Mercury GBFFP0300052*	60		2
22 Nov 08	**HUMAN** *Vertigo 1789799*	3		38
14 Feb 09	**SPACEMAN** *Vertigo USUM70842814*	40		6
13 Jun 09	**MR BRIGHTSIDE** *Mercury GBFFP0300052*	59		3

KILLING JOKE
UK, male vocal/instrumental group — 51

Date	Title / Label	Peak Position	Weeks at No.1	Weeks on Chart
23 May 81	**FOLLOW THE LEADERS** *Malicious Damage EGMDS 101*	55		5
20 Mar 82	**EMPIRE SONG** *Malicious Damage EGO 4*	43		4
30 Oct 82	**BIRDS OF A FEATHER** *EG EGO 10*	64		2
25 Jun 83	**LET'S ALL (GO TO THE FIRE DANCES)** *EG EGO 11*	51		3
15 Oct 83	**ME OR YOU?** *EG EGO 14*	57		1
7 Apr 84	**EIGHTIES** *EG EGO 16*	60		5
21 Jul 84	**A NEW DAY** *EG EGO 17*	56		2
2 Feb 85	**LOVE LIKE BLOOD** *EG EGO 20*	16		9
30 Mar 85	**KINGS AND QUEENS** *EG EGO 21*	58		3
16 Aug 86	**ADORATIONS** *EG EGO 27*	42		6
18 Oct 86	**SANITY** *EG EGO 30*	70		1
7 May 94	**MILLENNIUM** *Butterfly BFLD 12*	34		2
16 Jul 94	**THE PANDEMONIUM SINGLE** *Butterfly BFLDA 17*	28		3
4 Feb 95	**JANA** *Butterfly BFLDA 21*	54		1
23 Mar 96	**DEMOCRACY** *Butterfly BFLDB 33*	39		1
26 Jul 03	**LOOSE CANNON** *Zuma Recordings ZUMAD004*	25		2
1 Apr 06	**HOSANNAS FROM THE BASEMENTS OF HELL** *Cooking Vinyl FRYCD251*	72		1

KILLS
UK, male/female vocal/instrumental duo — 5

Date	Title / Label	Peak Position	Weeks at No.1	Weeks on Chart
26 Apr 03	**FRIED MY LITTLE BRAINS** *Domino Recordings RUG 154CD*	55		1
19 Feb 05	**THE GOOD ONES** *Domino RUG190CD*	23		2
11 Jun 05	**LOVE IS A DESERTER** *Domino RUG198CD*	44		1
12 Nov 05	**NO WOW** *Domino RUG207CD*	53		1

ANDY KIM
Canada, male vocalist (Andrew Joachim) — 12

Date	Title / Label	Peak Position	Weeks at No.1	Weeks on Chart
24 Aug 74	**ROCK ME GENTLY** *Capitol CL 15787* ● ★	2		12

KINANE
Ireland, female vocalist (Bianca Kinane) — 4

Date	Title / Label	Peak Position	Weeks at No.1	Weeks on Chart
18 May 96	**ALL THE LOVER I NEED** *Coliseum TOGA 003CD*	59		1
21 Sep 96	**THE WOMAN IN ME** *Coliseum TOGA 007CD*	73		1
16 May 98	**HEAVEN** *Coalition COLA 047CD*	49		1
22 Aug 98	**SO FINE** *Coalition COLA 055CD1*	63		1

KINESIS
UK, male vocal/instrumental group — 3

Date	Title / Label	Peak Position	Weeks at No.1	Weeks on Chart
22 Mar 03	**AND THEY OBEY** *Independiente ISOM 68MS*	63		1
28 Jun 03	**FOREVER REELING** *Independiente ISOM 74MS*	65		1
27 Sep 03	**ONE WAY MIRROR** *Independiente ISOM 77MS*	71		1

KING
UK/Ireland, male vocal/instrumental group – Paul King, John Hewitt, Jim Lantsbery, Mick Roberts & Anthony Wall — 44

Date	Title / Label	Peak Position	Weeks at No.1	Weeks on Chart
12 Jan 85	**LOVE AND PRIDE** *CBS A 4988* ●	2		14
23 Mar 85	**WON'T YOU HOLD MY HAND NOW** *CBS A 6094*	24		8
17 Aug 85	**ALONE WITHOUT YOU** *CBS A 6308*	8		9
19 Oct 85	**THE TASTE OF YOUR TEARS** *CBS A 6618*	11		9
11 Jan 86	**TORTURE** *CBS A 6761*	23		4

KING ADORA
UK, male vocal/instrumental group — 6

Date	Title / Label	Peak Position	Weeks at No.1	Weeks on Chart
4 Nov 00	**SMOULDER** *Superior Quality RQSD 010CD*	62		1
3 Mar 01	**SUFFOCATE** *Superior Quality RQS 11DD*	39		2
26 May 01	**BIONIC** *Superior Quality RQS 012DD*	30		2
31 May 03	**BORN TO LOSE/KAMIKAZE** *MHR MHRCD 001*	68		1

B.B. KING
US, male vocalist/guitarist (Riley B King) — 10

Date	Title / Label	Peak Position	Weeks at No.1	Weeks on Chart
15 Apr 89	**WHEN LOVE COMES TO TOWN** *Island IS 411* U2 FEATURING B.B. KING	6		7
18 Jul 92	**SINCE I MET YOU BABY** *Virgin VS 1423* GARY MOORE & B.B. KING	59		3

BEN E KING
US, male vocalist (Benjamin Nelson). See Drifters — 35

Date	Title / Label	Peak Position	Weeks at No.1	Weeks on Chart
2 Feb 61	**FIRST TASTE OF LOVE** *London HLK 9258*	27		11
22 Jun 61	**STAND BY ME** *London HLK 9358*	27		7
5 Oct 61	**AMOR AMOR** *London HLK 9416*	38		4
14 Feb 87	**STAND BY ME** *Atlantic A 9361* ●	1	3	11
4 Jul 87	**SAVE THE LAST DANCE FOR ME** *Manhattan MT 25*	69		2

CAROLE KING
US, female vocalist/pianist (Carole Klein) — 29

Date	Title / Label	Peak Position	Weeks at No.1	Weeks on Chart
20 Sep 62	**IT MIGHT AS WELL RAIN UNTIL SEPTEMBER** *London HLU 9591*	3		13
7 Aug 71	**IT'S TOO LATE** *A&M AMS 849* ★	6		12
28 Oct 72	**IT MIGHT AS WELL RAIN UNTIL SEPTEMBER** *London HL 10391*	43		4

DAVE KING
UK, male comedian/vocalist, d. 17 Apr 2002 (age 72) — 29

Date	Title / Label	Peak Position	Weeks at No.1	Weeks on Chart
17 Feb 56	**MEMORIES ARE MADE OF THIS** *Decca F 10684* FEATURING THE KEYNOTES	5		15
13 Apr 56	**YOU CAN'T BE TRUE TO TWO** *Decca F 10720* FEATURING THE KEYNOTES	11		9
21 Dec 56	**CHRISTMAS AND YOU** *Decca F 10791*	23		2
24 Jan 58	**THE STORY OF MY LIFE** *Decca F 10973*	20		3

DIANA KING
Jamaica, female vocalist — 22

Date	Title / Label	Peak Position	Weeks at No.1	Weeks on Chart
8 Jul 95	**SHY GUY** *Columbia 6621682* ●	2		13
28 Oct 95	**AIN'T NOBODY** *Work 6625495*	13		5
1 Nov 97	**I SAY A LITTLE PRAYER** *Columbia 6651472*	17		4

EVELYN KING
US, female vocalist — 76

Date	Title / Label	Peak Position	Weeks at No.1	Weeks on Chart
13 May 78	**SHAME** *RCA PC 1122* EVELYN 'CHAMPAGNE' KING ●	39		23
3 Feb 79	**I DON'T KNOW IF IT'S RIGHT** *RCA PB 1386* EVELYN 'CHAMPAGNE' KING	67		2
27 Jun 81	**I'M IN LOVE** *RCA 95*	27		11
26 Sep 81	**IF YOU WANT MY LOVIN'** *RCA 131*	43		6
28 Aug 82	**LOVE COME DOWN** *RCA 249* ●	7		13
20 Nov 82	**BACK TO LOVE** *RCA 287*	40		4
19 Feb 83	**GET LOOSE** *RCA 315* EVELYN 'CHAMPAGNE' KING	45		5
9 Nov 85	**YOUR PERSONAL TOUCH** *RCA PB 49915*	37		5
29 Mar 86	**HIGH HORSE** *RCA PB 49891*	55		3
23 Jul 88	**HOLD ON TO WHAT YOU'VE GOT** *Manhattan MT 49*	47		3
10 Oct 92	**SHAME** *Network NWKTEN 56* ALTERN 8 VS EVELYN KING	74		1

JONATHAN KING
UK, male vocalist/producer (Kenneth King) — 128

Date	Title / Label	Peak Position	Weeks at No.1	Weeks on Chart
29 Jul 65	**EVERYONE'S GONE TO THE MOON** *Decca F 12187*	4		11
10 Jan 70	**LET IT ALL HANG OUT** *Decca F 12988*	26		7
16 Jan 71	**IT'S THE SAME OLD SONG** *B&C CB 139* WEATHERMEN	19		9
3 Apr 71	**SUGAR SUGAR** *RCA 2064* SAKKARIN	12		14
29 May 71	**LAZY BONES** *Decca F 13177*	23		8
20 Nov 71	**HOOKED ON A FEELING** *Decca F 13241*	23		10
5 Feb 72	**FLIRT** *Decca F 13276*	22		9
14 Oct 72	**LOOP DI LOVE** *UK 7* SHAG	4		13
26 Jan 74	**(I CAN'T GET NO) SATISFACTION** *UK 53* BUBBLEROCK	29		5
6 Sep 75	**UNA PALOMA BLANCA** *UK 105*	5		11
20 Sep 75	**CHICK-A-BOOM (DON'T YA JES LOVE IT)** *UK 2012 002* 53RD & A 3RD FEATURING THE SOUND OF SHAG	36		4
7 Feb 76	**IN THE MOOD** *UK 121* SOUND 9418	46		3
26 Jun 76	**IT ONLY TAKES A MINUTE** *UK 135* ONE HUNDRED TON & A FEATHER	9		9
7 Oct 78	**ONE FOR YOU ONE FOR ME** *GTO GT 237*	29		6
16 Dec 78	**LICK A SMURP FOR CHRISTMAS (ALL FALL DOWN)** *Petrol GAS 1/ Magnet MAG 139* FATHER ABRAPHART & THE SMURPS	58		4
16 Jun 79	**YOU'RE THE GREATEST LOVER** *UK International INT 586*	67		2
3 Nov 79	**GLORIA** *Ariola ARO 198*	65		3

Silver-selling ● Gold-selling ● Platinum-selling (× multiples) ✪ US No.1 ★ Peak Position · Weeks at No.1 · Weeks on Chart

PAUL KING
UK, male vocalist. See King — 3

Date	Title	Peak	No.1	Weeks
2 May 87	**I KNOW** *CBS PKING 1*	59		3

SOLOMON KING
US, male vocalist (Allen Levy), d. 20 Jan 2005 (age 74) — 28

Date	Title	Peak	No.1	Weeks
3 Jan 68	**SHE WEARS MY RING** *Columbia DB 8325*	3		18
1 May 68	**WHEN WE WERE YOUNG** *Columbia DB 8402*	21		10

KING BEE
Holland, male production/rap trio — 6

Date	Title	Peak	No.1	Weeks
26 Jan 91	**MUST BEE THE MUSIC** *Columbia 6565827* FEATURING MICHELE	44		4
23 Mar 91	**BACK BY DOPE DEMAND** *First Bass 7RUFF 6X*	61		2

KING BISCUIT TIME
UK, male vocalist/guitarist (Stephen Mason). See Beta Band — 1

Date	Title	Peak	No.1	Weeks
8 Oct 05	**C I AM 15** *No Style MC5103SCD*	67		1

KING BLUES
UK, male vocal/instrumental group — 1

Date	Title	Peak	No.1	Weeks
28 Feb 09	**SAVE THE WORLD GET THE GIRL** *Island 1798070*	68		1

KING BROTHERS
UK, male vocal/instrumental trio – Denis, Michael & Tony King — 74

Date	Title	Peak	No.1	Weeks
31 May 57	**A WHITE SPORT COAT (AND A PINK CARNATION)** *Parlophone R 4310*	6		14
9 Aug 57	**IN THE MIDDLE OF AN ISLAND** *Parlophone R 4338*	19		13
6 Dec 57	**WAKE UP LITTLE SUSIE** *Parlophone R 4367*	22		3
31 Jan 58	**PUT A LIGHT IN THE WINDOW** *Parlophone R 4389*	25		4
14 Apr 60	**STANDING ON THE CORNER** *Parlophone R 4639*	4		11
28 Jul 60	**MAIS OUI** *Parlophone R 4672*	16		10
12 Jan 61	**DOLL HOUSE** *Parlophone R 4715*	21		8
2 Mar 61	**76 TROMBONES** *Parlophone R 4737*	19		11

KING KURT
UK, male vocal/instrumental group — 16

Date	Title	Peak	No.1	Weeks
15 Oct 83	**DESTINATION ZULULAND** *Stiff BUY 189*	36		6
28 Apr 84	**MACK THE KNIFE** *Stiff BUY 199*	55		4
4 Aug 84	**BANANA BANANA** *Stiff BUY 206*	54		4
15 Nov 86	**AMERICA** *Polydor KURT 1*	73		1
2 May 87	**THE LAND OF RING DANG DO** *Polydor KURT 2*	67		1

KING SUN-D'MOET
US, male rap/DJ duo — 3

Date	Title	Peak	No.1	Weeks
11 Jul 87	**HEY LOVE** *Flame MELT 5*	66		3

KING TRIGGER
UK, male/female vocal/instrumental group — 4

Date	Title	Peak	No.1	Weeks
14 Aug 82	**THE RIVER** *Chrysalis CHS 2623*	57		4

KINGDOM COME
US, male vocal/instrumental group — 2

Date	Title	Peak	No.1	Weeks
16 Apr 88	**GET IT ON** *Polydor KCS 1*	75		1
6 May 89	**DO YOU LIKE IT** *Polydor KCS 3*	73		1

KINGMAKER
UK, male vocal/instrumental group — 22

Date	Title	Peak	No.1	Weeks
18 Jan 92	**IDIOTS AT THE WHEEL EP.** *Scorch 3*	30		3
23 May 92	**EAT YOURSELF WHOLE** *Scorch SCORCHG 5*	15		3
31 Oct 92	**ARMCHAIR ANARCHIST** *Scorch SCORCHG 6*	47		2
8 May 93	**10 YEARS ASLEEP** *Scorch CDSCORCHS 8*	15		4
19 Jun 93	**QUEEN JANE** *Scorch CDSCORS 9*	29		4
30 Oct 93	**SATURDAY'S NOT WHAT IT USED TO BE** *Scorch CDSCORCH 10*	63		1
15 Apr 95	**YOU AND I WILL NEVER SEE THINGS EYE TO EYE** *Chrysalis CDSORCHS 11*	33		3
3 Jun 95	**IN THE BEST POSSIBLE TASTE (PART 2)** *Scorch CDSCORCHS 12*	41		2

KINGS OF CONVENIENCE
Norway, male vocal/instrumental duo — 3

Date	Title	Peak	No.1	Weeks
21 Apr 01	**TOXIC GIRL** *Source SOURCDSE 1025*	44		1
14 Jul 01	**FAILURE** *Source SOURCD 036*	63		1
4 Sep 04	**I'D RATHER DANCE WITH YOU** *Source SOURCDX 102*	60		1

KINGS OF LEON
US, male vocal/instrumental group – brothers (Anthony) Caleb, (Michael) Jared & (Ivan) Nathan Followill & their cousin (Cameron) Matthew Followill — 186

Date	Title	Peak	No.1	Weeks
8 Mar 03	**HOLY ROLLER NOVACAINE** *Hand Me Down HMD21*	53		1
14 Jun 03	**WHAT I SAW** *Hand Me Down HMD23*	22		3
23 Aug 03	**MOLLY'S CHAMBERS** *Hand Me Down HMD30*	23		3
1 Nov 03	**WASTED TIME** *Hand Me Down HMD32*	51		2
28 Feb 04	**CALIFORNIA WAITING** *Hand Me Down HMD37*	61		1
6 Nov 04	**THE BUCKET** *Hand Me Down HMD41*	16		3
22 Jan 05	**FOUR KICKS** *Hand Me Down HMD45*	24		3
23 Apr 05	**KING OF THE RODEO** *Hand Me Down HMD49*	41		2
24 Mar 07	**ON CALL** *Hand Me Down 88697073602*	18		8
14 Jul 07	**FANS** *Hand Me Down 88697114112*	13		7
12 Jul 08	**FANS** *Hand Me Down 88697114112*	44		5
20 Sep 08	**SEX ON FIRE** *Hand Me Down 88697352002*	1	3	79
4 Oct 08	**USE SOMEBODY** *Hand Me Down 88697412182*	2		62
7 Mar 09	**REVELRY** *Hand Me Down 88697464632*	29		7

KINGS OF SWING ORCHESTRA
Australia, orchestra — 5

Date	Title	Peak	No.1	Weeks
1 May 82	**SWITCHED ON SWING** *Philips Swing 1*	48		5

KINGS OF TOMORROW
US, male production/instrumental duo. See Layo & Bushwacka! — 9

Date	Title	Peak	No.1	Weeks
14 Apr 01	**FINALLY** *Distance DI 2029* FEATURING JULIE McKNIGHT	54		1
29 Sep 01	**FINALLY (REMIX)** *Defected DEFECT 37CDX* FEATURING JULIE McKNIGHT	24		3
13 Apr 02	**YOUNG HEARTS** *Defected DFECT 46CDS*	45		2
25 Oct 03	**DREAMS/THROUGH** *Defected DFTD 079*	74		1
31 Jul 04	**DREAMS** *Defected DFTD 090CDS* FEATURING HAZE	69		1
26 Feb 05	**THRU** *Defected DFTD099CDS* FEATURING HAZE	55		1

KINGSMEN
US, male vocal/instrumental group — 7

Date	Title	Peak	No.1	Weeks
30 Jan 64	**LOUIE LOUIE** *Pye International 7N 25231*	26		7

SEAN KINGSTON
Jamaica (b. US), male vocalist/rapper (Kisean Anderson) — 55

Date	Title	Peak	No.1	Weeks
1 Sep 07	**BEAUTIFUL GIRLS** *RCA 88697168302* ★	1	4	17
3 Nov 07	**ME LOVE** *RCA 88697204762*	32		7
1 Mar 08	**TAKE YOU THERE** *Epic USSM10702415*	47		6
29 Mar 08	**LOVE LIKE THIS** *Phonogenic 88697287252* NATASHA BEDINGFIELD FEATURING SEAN KINGSTON	20		7
1 Aug 09	**FIRE BURNING** *Beluga Heights/Epic 88697529742*	12		15
7 Nov 09	**FACE DROP** *Beluga Heights/Epic USSM10903702*	56		3

KINGSTON TRIO
US, male vocal/instrumental trio – Dave Guard, d. 22 Mar 1991, Nick Reynolds, d. 1 Oct 2008, & Bob Shane — 15

Date	Title	Peak	No.1	Weeks
21 Nov 58	**TOM DOOLEY** *Capitol CL 14951* ★	5		14
4 Dec 59	**SAN MIGUEL** *Capitol CL 15073*	29		1

KINKS
UK, male vocal/instrumental group – Ray Davies*, Mick Avory, Dave Davies* & Pete Quaife (replaced by John Dalton), d. 23 Jun 2010. Innovative and influential 1960s band whose leader is one of the most well-respected songwriters of the rock era. Ray is still a regular visitor to the album chart 45 years after making his debut — 217

Date	Title	Peak	No.1	Weeks
13 Aug 64	**YOU REALLY GOT ME** *Pye 7N 15673*	1	2	12
29 Oct 64	**ALL DAY AND ALL OF THE NIGHT** *Pye 7N 15714*	2		14
21 Jan 65	**TIRED OF WAITING FOR YOU** *Pye 7N 15759*	1	1	10
25 Mar 65	**EVERYBODY'S GONNA BE HAPPY** *Pye 7N 15813*	17		8
27 May 65	**SET ME FREE** *Pye 7N 15854*	9		11
5 Aug 65	**SEE MY FRIEND** *Pye 7N 15919*	10		9
2 Dec 65	**TILL THE END OF THE DAY** *Pye 7N 15981*	8		12
3 Mar 66	**DEDICATED FOLLOWER OF FASHION** *Pye 7N 17064*	4		11
9 Jun 66	**SUNNY AFTERNOON** *Pye 7N 17125*	1	2	13

Silver-selling | Gold-selling | Platinum-selling (x multiples) | US No.1 | Peak Position | Weeks at No.1 | Weeks on Chart

Date	Title	Peak	No.1	Wks
24 Nov 66	**DEAD END STREET** *Pye 7N 17222*	5		11
11 May 67	**WATERLOO SUNSET** *Pye 7N 17321*	2		11
18 Oct 67	**AUTUMN ALMANAC** *Pye 7N 17400*	3		11
17 Apr 68	**WONDERBOY** *Pye 7N 17468*	36		5
17 Jul 68	**DAYS** *Pye 7N 17573*	12		10
16 Apr 69	**PLASTIC MAN** *Pye 7N 17724*	31		4
10 Jan 70	**VICTORIA** *Pye 7N 17865*	33		4
4 Jul 70	**LOLA** *Pye 7N 17961*	2		14
12 Dec 70	**APEMAN** *Pye 7N 45016*	5		14
27 May 72	**SUPERSONIC ROCKET SHIP** *RCA 2211*	16		8
27 Jun 81	**BETTER THINGS** *Arista ARIST 415*	46		5
6 Aug 83	**COME DANCING** *Arista ARIST 502*	12		9
15 Oct 83	**DON'T FORGET TO DANCE** *Arista ARIST 524*	58		3
15 Oct 83	**YOU REALLY GOT ME** *PRT KD1*	47		4
18 Jan 97	**THE DAYS EP** *When! WENX 1016*	35		2
18 Sep 04	**YOU REALLY GOT ME** *Sanctuary SANXD317*	42		2

Top 3 Best-Selling Singles

		Approximate Sales
1	YOU REALLY GOT ME	400,000
2	SUNNY AFTERNOON	370,000
3	TIRED OF WAITING FOR YOU	350,000

KINKY
UK, female rapper (Caron Geary). See Erasure — 1

Date	Title	Peak	No.1	Wks
24 Aug 96	**EVERYBODY** *Feverpitch CDFVR 1009*	71		1

KINKY MACHINE
UK, male vocal/instrumental group — 4

Date	Title	Peak	No.1	Wks
6 Mar 93	**SUPERNATURAL GIVER** *Lemon 006CD*	70		1
29 May 93	**SHOCKAHOLIC** *Oxygen GASPD 5*	70		1
14 Aug 93	**GOING OUT WITH GOD** *Oxygen GASPD 9*	74		1
2 Jul 94	**10 SECOND BIONIC MAN** *Oxygen GASPD 14*	66		1

FERN KINNEY
US, female vocalist — 11

Date	Title	Peak	No.1	Wks
16 Feb 80	**TOGETHER WE ARE BEAUTIFUL** *WEA K 79111* (Gold)	1	1	11

KIOKI
Holland/Japan, male vocal/production trio — 1

Date	Title	Peak	No.1	Wks
17 Aug 02	**DO AND DON'T FOR LOVE** *V2 VVR 5020803*	66		1

KIRA
Belgium, female vocalist (Natasja De Witte) — 5

Date	Title	Peak	No.1	Wks
1 Mar 03	**I'LL BE YOUR ANGEL** *NuLife 74321970362*	9		5

KATHY KIRBY
UK, female vocalist (Kathleen O'Rourke) — 54

Date	Title	Peak	No.1	Wks
15 Aug 63	**DANCE ON** *Decca F 11682*	11		13
7 Nov 63	**SECRET LOVE** *Decca F 11759*	4		18
20 Feb 64	**LET ME GO LOVER** *Decca F 11832*	10		11
7 May 64	**YOU'RE THE ONE** *Decca F 11892*	17		9
4 Mar 65	**I BELONG** *Decca F 12087*	36		3

BO KIRKLAND & RUTH DAVIS
US, male/female vocal duo — 9

Date	Title	Peak	No.1	Wks
4 Jun 77	**YOU'RE GONNA GET NEXT TO ME** *EMI International INT 532*	12		9

KISS
US/Israel, male vocal/instrumental group – Gene Simmons*, Paul Stanley, Peter Criss (replaced by Eric Carr) & Ace Frehley (Frehley's Comet*) (replaced by Vinnie Vincent*) — 57

Date	Title	Peak	No.1	Wks
30 Jun 79	**I WAS MADE FOR LOVIN' YOU** *Casablanca CAN 152*	50		7
20 Feb 82	**A WORLD WITHOUT HEROES** *Casablanca KISS 002*	55		3
30 Apr 83	**CREATURES OF THE NIGHT** *Casablanca KISS 4*	34		4
29 Oct 83	**LICK IT UP** *Vertigo KISS 5*	31		5
8 Sep 84	**HEAVEN'S ON FIRE** *Vertigo VER 12*	43		3
9 Nov 85	**TEARS ARE FALLING** *Vertigo KISS 6*	57		2
3 Oct 87	**CRAZY CRAZY NIGHTS** *Vertigo KISS 7*	4		9
5 Dec 87	**REASON TO LIVE** *Vertigo KISS 8*	33		7
10 Sep 88	**TURN ON THE NIGHT** *Vertigo KISS 9*	41		3
18 Nov 89	**HIDE YOUR HEART** *Vertigo KISS 10*	59		2
31 Mar 90	**FOREVER** *Vertigo KISS 11*	65		2
11 Jan 92	**GOD GAVE ROCK AND ROLL TO YOU II** *Interscope A 8696*	4		8
9 May 92	**UNHOLY** *Vertigo KISS 12*	26		2

KISS AMC
UK, female rap duo — 5

Date	Title	Peak	No.1	Wks
1 Jul 89	**A BIT OF...** *Syncopate SY 29*	58		2
19 Aug 89	**A BIT OF U2** *Syncopate SY 29*	58		2
3 Feb 90	**MY DOCS** *Syncopate XAMC 1*	66		1

KISSING THE PINK
UK, male/female vocal/instrumental group — 14

Date	Title	Peak	No.1	Wks
5 Mar 83	**LAST FILM** *Magnet KTP 3*	19		14

MAC & KATIE KISSOON
Trinidad/UK, male/female vocal duo — 33

Date	Title	Peak	No.1	Wks
19 Jun 71	**CHIRPY CHIRPY CHEEP CHEEP** *Young Blood YB 1026*	41		1
18 Jan 75	**SUGAR CANDY KISSES** *Polydor 2058 531* (Silver)	3		10
3 May 75	**DON'T DO IT BABY** *State STAT 4*	9		8
30 Aug 75	**LIKE A BUTTERFLY** *State STAT 9*	18		9
15 May 76	**THE TWO OF US** *State STAT 21*	46		5

KEVIN KITCHEN
UK, male vocalist/guitarist — 3

Date	Title	Peak	No.1	Wks
20 Apr 85	**PUT MY ARMS AROUND YOU** *China WOK 1*	64		3

JOY KITIKONTI
Italy, male producer (Massimo Chiticonti) — 2

Date	Title	Peak	No.1	Wks
17 Nov 01	**JOYENERGIZER** *BXR BXRC 0347*	57		2

EARTHA KITT
US, female vocalist, d. 25 Dec 2008 (age 81) — 34

Date	Title	Peak	No.1	Wks
1 Apr 55	**UNDER THE BRIDGES OF PARIS** *HMV B 10647*	7		10
3 Dec 83	**WHERE IS MY MAN** *Record Shack SOHO 11*	36		11
7 Jul 84	**I LOVE MEN** *Record Shack SOHO 21*	50		3
12 Apr 86	**THIS IS MY LIFE** *Record Shack SOHO 61*	73		1
1 Jul 89	**CHA CHA HEELS** *Arista 112331* & BRONSKI BEAT	32		7
5 Mar 94	**IF I LOVE YA THEN I NEED YA IF I NEED YA THEN I WANT YOU AROUND** *RCA 74321190342*	43		2

KITTIE
Canada, female vocal/instrumental group — 2

Date	Title	Peak	No.1	Wks
25 Mar 00	**BRACKISH** *Epic 6691292*	46		1
22 Jul 00	**CHARLOTTE** *Epic 6696222*	60		1

KLAXONS
Belgium, male instrumental group — 6

Date	Title	Peak	No.1	Wks
10 Dec 83	**THE CLAP CLAP SOUND** *PRT 7P 290*	45		6

KLAXONS
UK, male vocal/instrumental group – Jamie Reynolds, Steffan Halperin, James Righton & Simon Taylor-Davis — 31

Date	Title	Peak	No.1	Wks
11 Nov 06	**MAGICK** *Polydor RINSE1CD*	29		2
20 Jan 07	**GOLDEN SKANS** *Polydor RINSE002CD*	7		17
21 Apr 07	**GRAVITY'S RAINBOW** *Rinse RINSE003CD*	35		2
16 Jun 07	**IT'S NOT OVER YET** *Rinse RINSE004CD*	13		10

KLEA
UK, male/female vocal/rap/production trio — 1

Date	Title	Peak	No.1	Wks
7 Sep 02	**TIC TOC** *Incentive CENT 41CDS*	61		1

KLEEER
US, male vocal/instrumental group — 10

Date	Title	Peak	No.1	Wks
17 Mar 79	**KEEEP YOUR BODY WORKING** *Atlantic LV 21*	51		6
14 Mar 81	**GET TOUGH** *Atlantic 11560*	49		4

KLESHAY
UK, female vocal trio — 5

Date	Title	Peak	Wks at No.1	Wks on Chart
19 Sep 98	**REASONS** *Epic KLE 1CD*	33		2
20 Feb 99	**RUSH** *Epic KLE 2CD*	19		3

KLF
UK, male production duo – Jimmy Cauty & Bill Drummond. See Justified Ancients Of Mu Mu, Timelords, 2K — 51

Date	Title	Peak	Wks at No.1	Wks on Chart
11 Aug 90	**WHAT TIME IS LOVE (LIVE AT TRANCENTRAL)** *KLF Communications KLF 004* FEATURING THE CHILDREN OF THE REVOLUTION	5		12
19 Jan 91	**3AM ETERNAL** *KLF Communications KLF 005* FEATURING THE CHILDREN OF THE REVOLUTION	1	2	11
4 May 91	**LAST TRAIN TO TRANCENTRAL** *KLF Communications KLF 008* FEATURING THE CHILDREN OF THE REVOLUTION	2		9
7 Dec 91	**JUSTIFIED AND ANCIENT** *KLF Communications KLF099* GUEST VOCALS TAMMY WYNETTE	2		12
7 Mar 92	**AMERICA: WHAT TIME IS LOVE** *KLF Communications KLFUSA 004*	4		7

KLUBBHEADS
Holland, male instrumental/production group. See Da Techno Bohemian, Drunkenmunky, Hi_Tack, Itty Bitty Boozy Woozy — 10

Date	Title	Peak	Wks at No.1	Wks on Chart
11 May 96	**KLUBHOPPING** *AM:PM 5815572*	10		6
16 Aug 97	**DISCOHOPPING** *AM:PM 5823032*	35		2
15 Aug 98	**KICKIN' HARD** *Wonderboy WBOYD 011*	36		2

KLUSTER FEATURING RON CARROLL
France/US, male vocal/DJ/production trio — 1

Date	Title	Peak	Wks at No.1	Wks on Chart
28 Apr 01	**MY LOVE** *Scorpio Music 1928112*	73		1

KMC FEATURING DAHNY
Italy, male/female vocal/production trio — 2

Date	Title	Peak	Wks at No.1	Wks on Chart
25 May 02	**I FEEL SO FINE** *Incentive CENT 39CDS*	33		2

KNACK
US, male vocal/instrumental group – Doug Fieger, d. 14 Feb 2010, Benton Averre, Bruce Gary, d. 22 Aug 2006, & Prescott Niles — 14

Date	Title	Peak	Wks at No.1	Wks on Chart
30 Jun 79	**MY SHARONA** *Capitol CL 16087* ★	6		10
13 Oct 79	**GOOD GIRLS DON'T** *Capitol CL 16097*	66		2
9 May 09	**MY SHARONA** *Capitol USCA20200254*	59		2

BEVERLEY KNIGHT
UK, female vocalist (Beverley Smith) — 74

Date	Title	Peak	Wks at No.1	Wks on Chart
8 Apr 95	**FLAVOUR OF THE OLD SCHOOL** *Dome CDDOME 101*	50		2
2 Sep 95	**DOWN FOR THE ONE** *Dome CDDOME 102*	55		1
21 Oct 95	**FLAVOUR OF THE OLD SCHOOL** *Dome CDDOME 105*	33		2
23 Mar 96	**MOVING ON UP (ON THE RIGHT SIDE)** *Dome CDDOME 107*	42		1
30 May 98	**MADE IT BACK** *Parlophone Rhythm CDRHYTHM 11* FEATURING REDMAN	21		3
22 Aug 98	**REWIND (FIND A WAY)** *Parlophone Rhythm CDRHYTHS 13*	40		2
10 Apr 99	**MADE IT BACK 99 (REMIX)** *Parlophone Rhythm CDRHYTHS 18* FEATURING REDMAN	19		5
17 Jul 99	**GREATEST DAY** *Parlophone Rhythm CDRHYTHS 22*	14		5
4 Dec 99	**SISTA SISTA** *Parlophone Rhythm CDRHYTHS 26*	31		2
17 Nov 01	**GET UP** *Parlophone CDRS 6564*	17		4
9 Mar 02	**SHOULDA WOULDA COULDA** *Parlophone CDRS 6570*	10		8
6 Jul 02	**GOLD** *Parlophone CDRS 6580*	27		4
3 Jul 04	**COME AS YOU ARE** *Parlophone CDRS 6636*	9		10
9 Oct 04	**NOT TOO LATE FOR LOVE** *Parlophone CDRS 6645*	31		2
22 Jan 05	**NO MORE** *V VRECSUK003CD* RONI SIZE FEATURING BEVERLEY KNIGHT	26		4
26 Mar 05	**KEEP THIS FIRE BURNING** *Parlophone CDRS6657*	16		6
25 Mar 06	**PIECE OF MY HEART** *Parlophone CDR6684*	16		11
12 May 07	**NO MAN'S LAND** *Parlophone CDR6737*	43		2

FREDERICK KNIGHT
US, male vocalist — 10

Date	Title	Peak	Wks at No.1	Wks on Chart
10 Jun 72	**I'VE BEEN LONELY FOR SO LONG** *Stax 2025 098*	22		10

GLADYS KNIGHT & THE PIPS
US, female/male vocal/instrumental group – Gladys Knight, William Guest, Merald 'Bubba' Knight & Edward Patten, d. 25 Feb 2005 — 187

Date	Title	Peak	Wks at No.1	Wks on Chart
8 Jun 67	**TAKE ME IN YOUR ARMS AND LOVE ME** *Tamla Motown TMG 604*	13		15
27 Dec 67	**I HEARD IT THROUGH THE GRAPEVINE** *Tamla Motown TMG 629*	47		1
17 Jun 72	**JUST WALK IN MY SHOES** *Tamla Motown TMG 813*	35		8
25 Nov 72	**HELP ME MAKE IT THROUGH THE NIGHT** *Tamla Motown TMG 830*	11		17
3 Mar 73	**LOOK OF LOVE** *Tamla Motown TMG 844*	21		9
26 May 73	**NEITHER ONE OF US** *Tamla Motown TMG 855*	31		7
5 Apr 75	**THE WAY WE WERE – TRY TO REMEMBER** *Buddah BDS 428*	4		15
2 Aug 75	**BEST THING THAT EVER HAPPENED TO ME** *Buddah BDS 432*	7		10
15 Nov 75	**PART TIME LOVE** *Buddah BDS 438*	30		5
8 May 76	**MIDNIGHT TRAIN TO GEORGIA** *Buddah BDS 444* ★	10		9
21 Aug 76	**MAKE YOURS A HAPPY HOME** *Buddah BDS 447*	35		4
6 Nov 76	**SO SAD THE SONG** *Buddah BDS 448*	20		9
15 Jan 77	**NOBODY BUT YOU** *Buddah BDS 451*	34		2
28 May 77	**BABY DON'T CHANGE YOUR MIND** *Buddah BDS 458*	4		12
24 Sep 77	**HOME IS WHERE THE HEART IS** *Buddah BDS 460*	35		4
8 Apr 78	**THE ONE AND ONLY** *Buddah BDS 470*	32		5
24 Jun 78	**COME BACK AND FINISH WHAT YOU STARTED** *Buddah BDS 473*	15		13
30 Sep 78	**IT'S A BETTER THAN GOOD TIME** *Buddah BDS 478*	59		4
30 Aug 80	**TASTE OF BITTER LOVE** *CBS 8890*	35		6
8 Nov 80	**BOURGIE BOURGIE** *CBS 9081*	32		6
26 Dec 81	**WHEN A CHILD IS BORN** *CBS S 1758* JOHNNY MATHIS & GLADYS KNIGHT	74		2
9 Nov 85	**THAT'S WHAT FRIENDS ARE FOR** *Arista ARIST 638* DIONNE WARWICK & FRIENDS FEATURING ELTON JOHN, STEVIE WONDER & GLADYS KNIGHT ★	16		9
16 Jan 88	**LOVE OVERBOARD** *MCA 1223*	42		4
10 Jun 89	**LICENCE TO KILL** *MCA 1339* GLADYS KNIGHT	6		11

JORDAN KNIGHT
US, male vocalist. See New Kids On The Block — 9

Date	Title	Peak	Wks at No.1	Wks on Chart
16 Oct 99	**GIVE IT TO YOU** *Interscope 4971672*	5		9

ROBERT KNIGHT
US, male vocalist — 26

Date	Title	Peak	Wks at No.1	Wks on Chart
17 Jan 68	**EVERLASTING LOVE** *Monument MON 1008*	40		2
24 Nov 73	**LOVE ON A MOUNTAIN TOP** *Monument MNT 1875*	10		16
9 Mar 74	**EVERLASTING LOVE** *Monument MNT 2106*	19		8

MARK KNOPFLER
UK, male vocalist/guitarist. See Dire Straits, Dunblane, Notting Hillbillies — 9

Date	Title	Peak	Wks at No.1	Wks on Chart
12 Mar 83	**GOING HOME (THEME OF 'LOCAL HERO')** *Vertigo DSTR 4*	56		3
16 Mar 96	**DARLING PRETTY** *Vertigo VERCD 88*	33		2
25 May 96	**CANNIBALS** *Vertigo VERCD 89*	42		2
2 Oct 04	**BOOM LIKE THAT** *Mercury 9867839*	34		2

KNOWLEDGE
Italy, male production duo — 1

Date	Title	Peak	Wks at No.1	Wks on Chart
8 Nov 97	**AS (UNTIL THE DAY)** *ffrr FCD 312*	70		1

BUDDY KNOX
US, male vocalist, d. 14 Feb 1999 (age 65) — 5

Date	Title	Peak	Wks at No.1	Wks on Chart
10 May 57	**PARTY DOLL** *Columbia DB 3914* ★	29		3
16 Aug 62	**SHE'S GONE** *Liberty LIB 55473*	45		2

FRANKIE KNUCKLES
US, male producer — 19

Date	Title	Peak	Wks at No.1	Wks on Chart
17 Jun 89	**TEARS** *ffrr F 108* PRESENTS SATOSHI TOMIIE	50		3
21 Oct 89	**YOUR LOVE** *Trax TRAXT 3*	59		4
27 Jul 91	**THE WHISTLE SONG** *Virgin America VUS 47*	17		5
23 Nov 91	**IT'S HARD SOMETIMES** *Virgin America VUS 52*	67		1
6 Jun 92	**RAIN FALLS** *Virgin America VUST 60* FEATURING LISA MICHAELIS	48		2
27 May 95	**TOO MANY FISH** *Virgin VUSCD 89* FEATURING ADEVA	34		2
18 Nov 95	**WHADDA U WANT (FROM ME)** *Virgin VUSCD 98* FEATURING ADEVA	36		2

MOE KOFFMAN QUARTETTE
Canada, male instrumental group – leader d. 28 Mar 2001 — 2

Date	Title	Peak	Wks at No.1	Wks on Chart
28 Mar 58	**SWINGIN' SHEPHERD BLUES** *London HLJ 8549*	23		2

MIKE KOGLIN

Germany, male producer — 4

Date	Title / Label	Peak	Wks at No.1	Wks on Chart
28 Nov 98	**THE SILENCE** *Multiply CDMULTY 44*	20		2
29 May 99	**ON MY WAY** *Multiply CDMULTY 51* FEATURING BEATRICE	28		2

KOKOMO

US, male pianist/producer (Jimmy Wisner) — 7

Date	Title / Label	Peak	Wks at No.1	Wks on Chart
13 Apr 61	**ASIA MINOR** *London HLU 9305*	35		7

KOKOMO

UK, male/female vocal/instrumental group — 3

Date	Title / Label	Peak	Wks at No.1	Wks on Chart
29 May 82	**A LITTLE BIT FURTHER AWAY** *CBS A 2064*	45		3

KON KAN

Canada, male vocal/production duo – Barry Harris & Kevin Wynne — 13

Date	Title / Label	Peak	Wks at No.1	Wks on Chart
4 Mar 89	**I BEG YOUR PARDON** *Atlantic A 8969*	5		13

JOHN KONGOS

South Africa, male vocalist/multi-instrumentalist — 25

Date	Title / Label	Peak	Wks at No.1	Wks on Chart
22 May 71	**HE'S GONNA STEP ON YOU AGAIN** *Fly BUG 8*	4		14
20 Nov 71	**TOKOLOSHE MAN** *Fly BUG 14*	4		11

KONKRETE

UK, female production duo — 1

Date	Title / Label	Peak	Wks at No.1	Wks on Chart
22 Sep 01	**LAW UNTO MYSELF** *Perfecto PERF 23CDS*	60		1

KONTAKT

UK, male production duo. See Vinylgroover & The Red Hed — 4

Date	Title / Label	Peak	Wks at No.1	Wks on Chart
20 Sep 03	**SHOW ME A SIGN** *NuLife 82876557432*	19		4

KOOKS

UK, male vocal/instrumental group – Luke Pritchard, Paul Garred, Hugh Harris & Max Rafferty (replaced by Dan Logan) — 100

Date	Title / Label	Peak	Wks at No.1	Wks on Chart
23 Jul 05	**EDDIE'S GUN** *Virgin VSCDT2000*	35		1
29 Oct 05	**SOFA SONG** *Virgin VSCDT1904*	28		2
21 Jan 06	**YOU DON'T LOVE ME** *Virgin VSCDX1910*	12		5
1 Apr 06	**NAÏVE** *Virgin VSCDT1911*	5		32
1 Jul 06	**SHE MOVES IN HER OWN WAY** *Virgin VSCDT1913*	7		32
28 Oct 06	**OOH LA** *Virgin VSCDT1918*	20		7
5 Apr 08	**ALWAYS WHERE I NEED TO BE** *Virgin VSCDX1967*	3		10
5 Jul 08	**SHINE ON** *Virgin VSCDT1972*	25		9
25 Oct 08	**SWAY** *Virgin VSCDT1978*	41		2

KOOL & THE GANG

US, male vocal/instrumental group – James 'JT' Taylor, Robert 'Kool' Bell, Ronald Bell (Khalis Bayyan), George Brown, Robert Mickens, Claydes Charles Smith, d. 20 Jun 2006, Dennis Thomas & Ricky Westfield, d. 1985. The most successful US R&B band in the UK and the only American act on the record-breaking first Band Aid single — 218

Date	Title / Label	Peak	Wks at No.1	Wks on Chart
27 Oct 79	**LADIES NIGHT** *Mercury KOOL 7*	9		12
19 Jan 80	**TOO HOT** *Mercury KOOL 8*	23		8
12 Jul 80	**HANGIN' OUT** *Mercury KOOL 9*	52		4
1 Nov 80	**CELEBRATION** *De-Lite KOOL 10* ★	7		13
21 Feb 81	**JONES VS JONES/SUMMER MADNESS** *De-Lite KOOL 11*	17		11
30 May 81	**TAKE IT TO THE TOP** *De-Lite DE 2*	15		9
31 Oct 81	**STEPPIN' OUT** *De-Lite DE 4*	12		13
19 Dec 81	**GET DOWN ON IT** *De-Lite DE 5*	3		12
6 Mar 82	**TAKE MY HEART (YOU CAN HAVE IT IF YOU WANT IT)** *De-Lite DE 6*	29		7
7 Aug 82	**BIG FUN** *De-Lite DE 7*	14		8
16 Oct 82	**OOH LA LA LA (LET'S GO DANCIN')** *De-Lite DE 9*	6		9
4 Dec 82	**HI DE HI, HI DE HO** *De-Lite DE 14*	29		8
10 Dec 83	**STRAIGHT AHEAD** *De-Lite DE 15*	15		10
11 Feb 84	**JOANNA/TONIGHT** *De-Lite DE 16*	2		11
14 Apr 84	**(WHEN YOU SAY YOU LOVE SOMEBODY) IN THE HEART** *De-Lite DE 17*	7		8
24 Nov 84	**FRESH** *De-Lite DE 18*	11		12
9 Feb 85	**MISLED** *De-Lite DE 19*	28		5
11 May 85	**CHERISH** *De-Lite DE 20*	4		22
2 Nov 85	**EMERGENCY** *De-Lite DE 21*	50		3
22 Nov 86	**VICTORY** *Club JAB 44*	30		12
21 Mar 87	**STONE LOVE** *Club JAB 47*	45		4
31 Dec 88	**CELEBRATION (REMIX)** *Club JAB 78*	56		5
6 Jul 91	**GET DOWN ON IT (REMIX)** *Mercury MER 346*	69		1
27 Dec 03	**LADIES NIGHT** *Innocent SINDX53* ATOMIC KITTEN FEATURING KOOL & THE GANG	8		11

KOOPA

UK, male vocal/instrumental trio — 4

Date	Title / Label	Peak	Wks at No.1	Wks on Chart
3 Dec 05	**NO TREND** *Mad Cow MCR741*	71		1
20 Jan 07	**BLAG STEAL & BORROW** *Juxtaposition GBLFP0675801*	31		1
23 Jun 07	**THE ONE-OFF SONG FOR THE SUMMER** *Juxtaposition GBDNW0905013*	21		1
10 Nov 07	**THE CRASH** *Juxtaposition JXCD904*	16		1

KORGIS

UK, male vocal/instrumental group – James Warren, Andy Davis, Stuart Gordon & Phil Harrison — 27

Date	Title / Label	Peak	Wks at No.1	Wks on Chart
23 Jun 79	**IF I HAD YOU** *Rialto TREB 103*	13		12
24 May 80	**EVERYBODY'S GOT TO LEARN SOMETIME** *Rialto TREB 115*	5		12
30 Aug 80	**IF IT'S ALRIGHT WITH YOU BABY** *Rialto TREB 118*	56		3

KORN

US, male vocal/instrumental group — 28

Date	Title / Label	Peak	Wks at No.1	Wks on Chart
19 Oct 96	**NO PLACE TO HIDE** *Epic 6638452*	26		2
15 Feb 97	**A.D.I.D.A.S.** *Epic 6642042*	22		2
7 Jun 97	**GOOD GOD** *Epic 6646585*	25		2
22 Aug 98	**GOT THE LIFE** *Epic 6663912*	23		2
8 May 99	**FREAK ON A LEASH** *Epic 6672525*	24		2
12 Feb 00	**FALLING AWAY FROM ME** *Epic 6688692*	24		2
3 Jun 00	**MAKE ME BAD** *Epic 6694332*	25		2
1 Jun 02	**HERE TO STAY** *Epic 6727422*	12		5
21 Sep 02	**THOUGHTLESS** *Epic 6731572*	37		2
23 Aug 03	**DID MY TIME** *Epic 6741422*	15		4
3 Dec 05	**TWISTED TRANSISTOR** *Virgin VUSCD316*	27		2
24 Jun 06	**COMING UNDONE** *Virgin VUSCD323*	63		1

KOSHEEN

UK, female/male vocal/production trio – Sian Evans, Darren Decoder (Darren Beale) & Markee Substance (Mark Davies) — 31

Date	Title / Label	Peak	Wks at No.1	Wks on Chart
17 Jun 00	**EMPTY SKIES/HIDE U** *Moksha Recordings MOKSHA 05CD*	73		1
14 Apr 01	**(SLIP & SLIDE) SUICIDE** *Moksha Recordings MOKSHA 07CD*	50		2
1 Sep 01	**HIDE U (REMIX)** *Moksha/Arista 74321879412*	6		7
22 Dec 01	**CATCH** *Moksha/Arista 74321913732*	15		8
4 May 02	**HUNGRY** *Moksha/Arista 74321934392*	13		4
31 Aug 02	**HARDER** *Moksha/Arista 74321954462*	53		1
9 Aug 03	**ALL IN MY HEAD** *Moksha/Arista 82876527252*	7		7
1 Nov 03	**WASTING MY TIME** *Moksha/Arista 82876570032*	49		1

KP & ENVYI

US, female vocal/rap duo — 4

Date	Title / Label	Peak	Wks at No.1	Wks on Chart
13 Jun 98	**SWING MY WAY** *East West E 3849CD*	14		4

KRAFTWERK

Germany, male vocal/instrumental/production group – Ralf Hutter, Karl Bartos, Wolfgang Flur & Florian Schneider — 79

Date	Title / Label	Peak	Wks at No.1	Wks on Chart
10 May 75	**AUTOBAHN** *Vertigo 6147 012*	11		9
28 Oct 78	**NEON LIGHTS** *Capitol CL 15998*	53		3
9 May 81	**POCKET CALCULATOR** *EMI 5175*	39		6
11 Jul 81	**THE MODEL/COMPUTER LOVE** *EMI 5207*	36		8
26 Dec 81	**THE MODEL/COMPUTER LOVE** *EMI 5207*	1	1	13
20 Feb 82	**SHOWROOM DUMMIES** *EMI 5272*	25		5
6 Aug 83	**TOUR DE FRANCE** *EMI 5413*	22		8
25 Aug 84	**TOUR DE FRANCE** *EMI 5413*	24		11
1 Jun 91	**THE ROBOTS** *EMI EM 192*	20		4
2 Nov 91	**RADIOACTIVITY** *EMI EM 201*	43		2
23 Oct 99	**TOUR DE FRANCE** *EMI 8874210*	61		1
18 Mar 00	**EXPO 2000** *EMI CDEM 562*	27		2
19 Jul 03	**TOUR DE FRANCE 2003** *EMI CDEM 626*	20		4
27 Mar 04	**AERODYNAMIK** *EMI CDEM 637*	33		3

BILLY J KRAMER & THE DAKOTAS

UK, male vocal/instrumental group – Billy J Kramer (William Ashton), Robin MacDonald, Tony Mansfield & Michael Maxfield — 71

Date	Title / Label	Peak	Wks at No.1	Wks on Chart
2 May 63	**DO YOU WANT TO KNOW A SECRET?** *Parlophone R 5023*	2		15
1 Aug 63	**BAD TO ME** *Parlophone R 5049*	1	3	14

Date	Title	Peak	Wks at No.1	Wks on Chart
7 Nov 63	**I'LL KEEP YOU SATISFIED** *Parlophone R 5073*	4		13
27 Feb 64	**LITTLE CHILDREN** *Parlophone R 5105*	1	2	13
23 Jul 64	**FROM A WINDOW** *Parlophone R 5156*	10		8
20 May 65	**TRAINS AND BOATS AND PLANES** *Parlophone R 5285*	12		8

KRANKIES
UK, male/female vocal/comedy duo – Janette & Ian Tough — 6

Date	Title	Peak	Wks at No.1	Wks on Chart
7 Feb 81	**FAN'DABI'DOZI** *Monarch MON 21*	46		6

LENNY KRAVITZ
US, male vocalist/guitarist — 72

Date	Title	Peak	Wks at No.1	Wks on Chart
2 Jun 90	**MR CABDRIVER** *Virgin America VUS 20*	58		2
4 Aug 90	**LET LOVE RULE** *Virgin America VUS 26*	39		4
30 Mar 91	**ALWAYS ON THE RUN** *Virgin America VUS 34*	41		3
15 Jun 91	**IT AIN'T OVER TIL IT'S OVER** *Virgin America VUS 43*	11		8
14 Sep 91	**STAND BY MY WOMAN** *Virgin America VUS 45*	55		3
20 Feb 93	**ARE YOU GONNA GO MY WAY** *Virgin America VUSDG 65* ●	4		11
22 May 93	**BELIEVE** *Virgin America VUSCD 72*	30		5
28 Aug 93	**HEAVEN HELP** *Virgin America VUSDG 73*	20		7
4 Dec 93	**BUDDHA OF SUBURBIA** *Arista 74321177052* DAVID BOWIE FEATURING LENNY KRAVITZ	35		3
4 Dec 93	**IS THERE ANY LOVE IN YOUR HEART** *Virgin America VUSDG 76*	52		2
9 Sep 95	**ROCK AND ROLL IS DEAD** *Virgin America VUSCD 93*	22		3
23 Dec 95	**CIRCUS** *Virgin America VUSCD 96*	54		2
2 Mar 96	**CAN'T GET YOU OFF MY MIND** *Virgin America VUSCD 100*	54		2
16 May 98	**IF YOU CAN'T SAY NO** *Virgin VUSCD 130*	48		2
10 Oct 98	**I BELONG TO YOU** *Virgin VUSCD 138*	75		1
20 Feb 99	**FLY AWAY** *Virgin VUSCD 141* ●	1	1	10
6 Apr 02	**STILLNESS OF HEART** *Virgin VUSCD 236*	44		1
7 Feb 04	**SHOW ME YOUR SOUL** *Puff Daddy MCSTD 40350* P DIDDY, LENNY KRAVITZ, PHARRELL WILLIAMS & LOON	35		2
24 Jul 04	**CALIFORNIA** *Virgin VUSCD 294*	62		1

KRAY TWINZ FEATURING TWISTA & LETHAL B
UK/US, male rap/production group. See Lethal Bizzle — 3

Date	Title	Peak	Wks at No.1	Wks on Chart
12 Nov 05	**WHAT WE DO** *Gana/W10 GANA01CDS*	23		3

KRAZE
US, male/female production/vocal group — 6

Date	Title	Peak	Wks at No.1	Wks on Chart
22 Oct 88	**THE PARTY** *MCA 1288*	29		5
17 Jun 89	**LET'S PLAY HOUSE** *MCA 1337*	71		1

KREUZ
UK, male vocal group — 1

Date	Title	Peak	Wks at No.1	Wks on Chart
8 Jul 95	**PARTY ALL NIGHT** *Diesel DES 004C*	75		1

CHANTAL KREVIAZUK
Canada, female vocalist/pianist/guitarist — 1

Date	Title	Peak	Wks at No.1	Wks on Chart
6 Mar 99	**LEAVING ON A JET PLANE** *Epic 6666272*	59		1

KREW-KATS
UK, male vocal/instrumental group — 10

Date	Title	Peak	Wks at No.1	Wks on Chart
9 Mar 61	**TRAMBONE** *HMV POP 840*	33		10

CHAD KROEGER FEATURING JOSEY SCOTT
Canada/US, male vocal/instrumental duo – Chad Kroeger & Joseph Scott Sappington. See Nickelback, Saliva — 14

Date	Title	Peak	Wks at No.1	Wks on Chart
22 Jun 02	**HERO** *Roadrunner RR 20463* ●	4		14

KRIS KROSS
US, male rap duo – Chris Kelly & Chris Smith — 22

Date	Title	Peak	Wks at No.1	Wks on Chart
30 May 92	**JUMP** *Ruffhouse 6578547* ★	2		8
25 Jul 92	**WARM IT UP** *Ruffhouse 6582187*	16		6
17 Oct 92	**I MISSED THE BUS** *Ruffhouse 6583927*	57		1
19 Dec 92	**IT'S A SHAME** *Ruffhouse 6588587*	31		5
11 Sep 93	**ALRIGHT** *Ruffhouse 6595652*	47		2

KRISTIN
US, female actor/vocalist (Kristin Chenoweth) — 1

Date	Title	Peak	Wks at No.1	Wks on Chart
31 May 08	**DEFYING GRAVITY** *UMC USUMC0300219*	60		1

KROKUS
Switzerland/Malta, male vocal/instrumental group — 2

Date	Title	Peak	Wks at No.1	Wks on Chart
16 May 81	**INDUSTRIAL STRENGTH (EP)** *Ariola ARO 258*	62		2

KRS ONE
US, male rapper (Lawrence Parker) — 8

Date	Title	Peak	Wks at No.1	Wks on Chart
18 May 96	**RAPPAZ R N DAINJA** *Jive JIVECD 396*	47		1
8 Feb 97	**WORD PERFECT** *Jive JIVECD 418*	70		1
26 Apr 97	**STEP INTO A WORLD (RAPTURE'S DELIGHT)** *Jive JIVECD 411*	24		2
20 Sep 97	**HEARTBEAT/A FRIEND** *Jive JIVECD 431*	66		1
1 Nov 97	**DIGITAL** *ffrr FCD 316* GOLDIE FEATURING KRS ONE	13		3

KRUSH
UK, male instrumental/production duo – Cassius Campbell & Mark Gamble — 16

Date	Title	Peak	Wks at No.1	Wks on Chart
5 Dec 87	**HOUSE ARREST** *Club JAB 63* ●	3		15
14 Nov 92	**WALKING ON SUNSHINE** *Network NWK 55*	71		1

KRUSH PERSPECTIVE
US, female vocal/rap trio — 2

Date	Title	Peak	Wks at No.1	Wks on Chart
16 Jan 93	**LET'S GET TOGETHER (SO GROOVY NOW)** *Perspective PERD 7416*	61		2

KRUST
UK, male producer/instrumentalist (Keith Thompson) — 2

Date	Title	Peak	Wks at No.1	Wks on Chart
23 Oct 99	**CODED LANGUAGE** *Talkin Loud TLCD 51* FEATURING SAUL WILLIAMS	66		1
26 Jan 02	**SNAPPED IT** *Full Cycle FCY 034*	58		1

KUBB
UK, male vocal/instrumental group — 7

Date	Title	Peak	Wks at No.1	Wks on Chart
3 Sep 05	**REMAIN** *Mercury 9873116*	45		1
19 Nov 05	**WICKED SOUL** *Mercury 9874772*	25		3
18 Feb 06	**GROW** *Mercury 9876852*	18		3

KUJAY DADA
UK, male production group — 3

Date	Title	Peak	Wks at No.1	Wks on Chart
17 Jan 04	**YOUNG HEARTS** *Nebula NEBCD 057*	41		3

KULA SHAKER
UK, male vocal/instrumental group – Crispian Mills, Alonza Bevan, Jay Darlington & Paul Winterhart — 48

Date	Title	Peak	Wks at No.1	Wks on Chart
4 May 96	**GRATEFUL WHEN YOU'RE DEAD – JERRY WAS THERE** *Columbia KULACD 2*	35		3
6 Jul 96	**TATTVA** *Columbia KULACD 3K*	4		8
7 Sep 96	**HEY DUDE** *Columbia KULACD 4*	2		7
23 Nov 96	**GOVINDA** *Columbia KULACD 5*	7		8
8 Mar 97	**HUSH** *Columbia KULACD 6* ●	2		9
2 May 98	**SOUND OF DRUMS** *Columbia KULA 21CD*	3		6
6 Mar 99	**MYSTICAL MACHINE GUN** *Columbia KULA 22CD*	14		3
15 May 99	**SHOWER YOUR LOVE** *Columbia KULA 23CD*	14		4

KULAY
Philippines, male/female vocal group — 1

Date	Title	Peak	Wks at No.1	Wks on Chart
12 Sep 98	**DELICIOUS** *INCredible INCRL 4CD*	73		1

KUMARA
Holland, male production duo — 1

Date	Title	Peak	Wks at No.1	Wks on Chart
7 Oct 00	**SNAP YOUR FINGAZ** *Y2K 018CD*	70		1

CHARLIE KUNZ
US, male pianist, d. 16 Mar 1958 (age 61) — 4

Date	Title	Peak	Wks at No.1	Wks on Chart
17 Dec 54	**PIANO MEDLEY NO. 114** *Decca F 10419*	16		4

KURSAAL FLYERS
UK, male vocal/instrumental group — 10

Date	Title	Peak	Wks at No.1	Wks
20 Nov 76	**LITTLE DOES SHE KNOW** *CBS 4689*	14		10

KURUPT
US, male rapper (Ricardo Brown). See Tha Dogg Pound — 10

Date	Title	Peak	Wks at No.1	Wks
25 Aug 01	**WHERE I WANNA BE** *London LONCD 461* SHADE SHEIST FEATURING NATE DOGG & KURUPT	14		7
13 Oct 01	**IT'S OVER** *PIAS Recordings PIASB 024CDX*	21		3

KUT KLOSE
US, female vocal group — 1

Date	Title	Peak	Wks at No.1	Wks
29 Apr 95	**I LIKE** *Elektra EKR 200CD*	72		1

KYLA
UK, female vocalist (Kyla Smith) — 3

Date	Title	Peak	Wks at No.1	Wks
7 Feb 09	**DO YOU MIND** *Cadiz GBY710900011*	48		3

LI KWAN
UK, male producer (Matt Darey) — 2

Date	Title	Peak	Wks at No.1	Wks
17 Dec 94	**I NEED A MAN** *Deconstruction 74321252192*	51		2

TALIB KWELI FEATURING MARY J BLIGE
US, male/female rap/vocal duo — 1

Date	Title	Peak	Wks at No.1	Wks
18 Dec 04	**I TRY** *Island MCSTD40390*	59		1

KWS
UK, production duo – Chris King & Winston Williams — 36

Date	Title	Peak	Wks at No.1	Wks
25 Apr 92	**PLEASE DON'T GO/GAME BOY** *Network NWK 46* ●	1	5	16
22 Aug 92	**ROCK YOUR BABY** *Network NWK 54*	8		7
12 Dec 92	**HOLD BACK THE NIGHT** *Network NWK 65* FEATURES GUEST VOCAL FROM THE TRAMMPS	30		5
5 Jun 93	**CAN'T GET ENOUGH OF YOUR LOVE** *Network NWKCD 72*	71		1
9 Apr 94	**IT SEEMS TO HANG ON** *X-clusive SCLU 006CD*	58		1
2 Jul 94	**AIN'T NOBODY (LOVES ME BETTER)** *X-clusive XCLU 010CD* & GWEN DICKEY	21		4
19 Nov 94	**THE MORE I GET THE MORE I WANT** *X-clusive XCLU 011CD* FEATURING TEDDY PENDERGRASS	35		2

AIRI L
UK, female vocalist — 1

Date	Title	Peak	Wks at No.1	Wks
20 Jun 09	**WHEN LOVE TAKES OVER** *Power Music USCBK0910710*	22		1

JONNY L
UK, male producer (John Lisners). See True Steppers — 2

Date	Title	Peak	Wks at No.1	Wks
28 Aug 93	**OOH I LIKE IT** *XL Recordings XLS 44CD*	73		1
31 Oct 98	**20 DEGREES** *XL Recordings XLS 103CD*	66		1

LA BELLE EPOQUE
France, female vocal trio – Marcia Briscue, Jusy Fortes & Evelyne Lenton — 14

Date	Title	Peak	Wks at No.1	Wks
27 Aug 77	**BLACK IS BLACK** *Harvest HAR 5133* ●	2		14

LA BIONDA
Italy, vocal/instrumental group — 4

Date	Title	Peak	Wks at No.1	Wks
7 Oct 78	**ONE FOR YOU ONE FOR ME** *Philips 6198 227*	54		4

LA BOUCHE
US, female/male vocal/rap duo — 12

Date	Title	Peak	Wks at No.1	Wks
24 Sep 94	**SWEET DREAMS** *Bell 74321223912*	63		1
15 Jul 95	**BE MY LOVER** *Arista 74321265402*	27		4
30 Sep 95	**FALLING IN LOVE** *Arista 74321305102*	43		2
2 Mar 96	**BE MY LOVER (REMIX)** *Arista 74321339822*	25		4
7 Sep 96	**SWEET DREAMS** *Arista 74321398542*	44		1

LA FLEUR
Holland, male/female vocal/production group — 4

Date	Title	Peak	Wks at No.1	Wks
30 Jul 83	**BOOGIE NIGHTS** *Proto ENA 111*	51		4

LA GANZ
US, male rap/vocal/instrumental group — 1

Date	Title	Peak	Wks at No.1	Wks
9 Nov 96	**LIKE A PLAYA** *Jive JIVECD 405*	75		1

L.A. GUNS
US, male/female vocal/instrumental group — 4

Date	Title	Peak	Wks at No.1	Wks
30 Nov 91	**SOME LIE 4 LOVE** *Mercury MER 358*	61		1
21 Dec 91	**THE BALLAD OF JAYNE** *Mercury MER 361*	53		3

L.A. MIX
UK, male/female production trio – Les Adams, Emma Freilich & Mike Stevens — 25

Date	Title	Peak	Wks at No.1	Wks
10 Oct 87	**DON'T STOP (JAMMIN')** *Breakout USA 615*	47		4
21 May 88	**CHECK THIS OUT** *Breakout USA 629*	6		7
8 Jul 89	**GET LOOSE** *Breakout USA 659* PERFORMED BY JAZZI P	25		6
16 Sep 89	**LOVE TOGETHER** *Breakout USA 662* FEATURING KEVIN HENRY	66		2
15 Sep 90	**COMING BACK FOR MORE** *A&M AM 579*	50		3
19 Jan 91	**MYSTERIES OF LOVE** *A&M AM 707*	46		2
23 Mar 91	**WE SHOULDN'T HOLD HANDS IN THE DARK** *A&M AM 755*	69		1

SAM LA MORE
Australia, male producer (Sam Littlemore) — 1

Date	Title	Peak	Wks at No.1	Wks
5 Apr 03	**TAKIN' HOLD** *Underwater H20 023X*	70		1

LA ROUX
UK, female/male vocal/instrumental/production duo – Eleanor (Elly) Jackson & Ben Langmaid — 60

Date	Title	Peak	Wks at No.1	Wks
28 Mar 09	**IN FOR THE KILL** *Kitsune 2700304* ⊛	2		36
4 Jul 09	**BULLETPROOF** *Polydor 2705727* ●	1	1	20
3 Oct 09	**I'M NOT YOUR TOY** *Polydor 2719959*	27		4

DANNY LA RUE
Ireland, male vocalist (Daniel Carroll), d. 31 May 2009 (age 81) — 9

Date	Title	Peak	Wks at No.1	Wks
18 Dec 68	**ON MOTHER KELLY'S DOORSTEP** *Page One POF 108*	33		9

DENISE LA SALLE
US, female vocalist (Denise Allen) — 13

Date	Title	Peak	Wks at No.1	Wks
15 Jun 85	**MY TOOT TOOT** *Epic A 6334*	6		13

LABELLE
US, female vocal group — 9

Date	Title	Peak	Wks at No.1	Wks
22 Mar 75	**LADY MARMALADE (VOULEZ-VOUS COUCHER AVEC MOI CE SOIR)** *Epic EPC 2852* ★	17		9

PATTI LABELLE
US, female vocalist (Patricia Holt). See LaBelle — 21

Date	Title	Peak	Wks at No.1	Wks
3 May 86	**ON MY OWN** *MCA 1045* & MICHAEL McDONALD ● ★	2		13
2 Aug 86	**OH, PEOPLE** *MCA 1075*	26		6
3 Sep 94	**THE RIGHT KINDA LOVER** *MCA MCSTD 1995*	50		2

NICK LACHEY
US, male vocalist/actor/TV personality. See 98o — 1

Date	Title	Peak	Wks at No.1	Wks
10 Feb 07	**WHAT'S LEFT OF ME** *Jive 82876848622*	47		1

LACUNA COIL
Italy, male/female vocal/instrumental group — 2

Date	Title	Peak	Wks at No.1	Wks
1 Apr 06	**OUR TRUTH** *Century Media 776598*	40		1
8 Jul 06	**ENJOY THE SILENCE** *Century Media 776618*	41		1

LADIES CHOICE
UK, male vocal/instrumental group

Date	Title	Peak	Wks at No.1	Wks on Chart: 4
25 Jan 86	**FUNKY SENSATION** *Sure Delight SD 01*	41		4

LADIES FIRST
UK, female vocal trio

Date	Title	Peak	Wks at No.1	Wks on Chart: 8
24 Nov 01	**MESSIN'** *Polydor 5873422*	30		2
13 Apr 02	**I CAN'T WAIT** *Polydor 5706912*	19		6

LADY GAGA
US, female vocalist/pianist (Stefani Germanotta)

Date	Title	Peak	Wks at No.1	Wks on Chart: 208
10 Jan 09	**JUST DANCE** *Interscope 1796062* ⊛ ★	1	3	40
24 Jan 09	**POKER FACE** *Interscope 2703459* ⊛ ★	1	3	63+
9 May 09	**PAPARAZZI** *Interscope 2712117* ●	4		36
22 Aug 09	**LOVEGAME** *Interscope 2720317*	19		14
12 Sep 09	**CHILLIN'** *Interscope 2717517* WALE FEATURING LADY GAGA	12		5
26 Sep 09	**MAKE HER SAY** *Island USUM70969614* KID CUDI FEATURING KANYE WEST, COMMON & LADY GAGA	67		2
7 Nov 09	**BAD ROMANCE** *Interscope 2726752* ●	1	2	23+
5 Dec 09	**TELEPHONE** *Interscope 2734706* & BEYONCE	1	2	18+
5 Dec 09	**MONSTER** *Interscope USUM70905528*	68		1
5 Dec 09	**ALEJANDRO** *Interscope USUM70905526*	75		1
2 Jan 10	**VIDEO PHONE** *Columbia USSM10804757* BEYONCE FEATURING LADY GAGA	58		3
27 Feb 10	**JUST DANCE** *Interscope USUM70807646* FEATURING COLBY O'DONIS & AKON	62		2

LADY OF RAGE
US, female rapper (Robin Allen)

Date	Title	Peak	Wks at No.1	Wks on Chart: 1
8 Oct 94	**AFRO PUFFS** *Interscope A 8288CD*	72		1

LADY SAW
Jamaica, female vocalist (Marion Hall)

Date	Title	Peak	Wks at No.1	Wks on Chart: 3
16 Dec 00	**BUMP N GRIND (I AM FEELING HOT TONIGHT)** *Telstar CDSTAS 3129* M DUBS FEATURING LADY SAW	59		1
20 Oct 01	**SINCE I MET YOU LADY/SPARKLE OF MY EYES** *DEP International DEPD 55* UB40 FEATURING LADY SAW	40		2

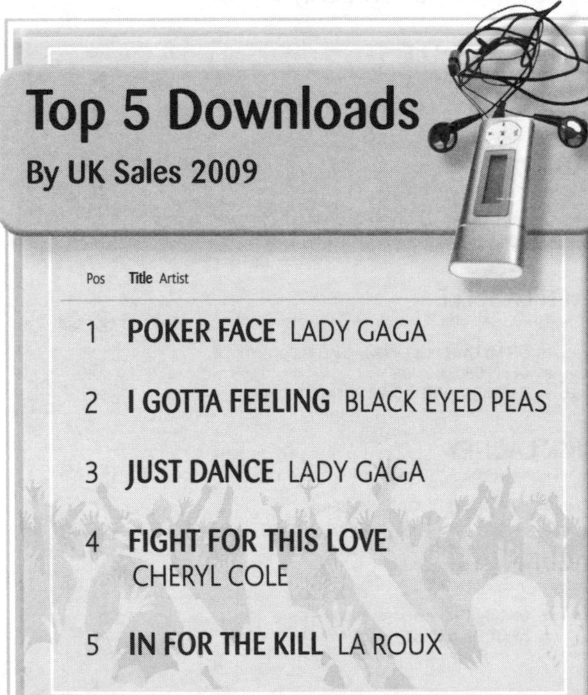

Top 5 Downloads
By UK Sales 2009

Pos	Title Artist
1	**POKER FACE** LADY GAGA
2	**I GOTTA FEELING** BLACK EYED PEAS
3	**JUST DANCE** LADY GAGA
4	**FIGHT FOR THIS LOVE** CHERYL COLE
5	**IN FOR THE KILL** LA ROUX

LADY SOVEREIGN
UK, female rapper (Louise Harman)

Date	Title	Peak	Wks at No.1	Wks on Chart: 23
26 Mar 05	**RANDOM** *Casual CDLOUPE15*	73		1
20 Aug 05	**9 TO 5** *Island CIDX898*	33		2
3 Dec 05	**HOODIE** *Island/Uni-Island CIDX914*	44		2
27 May 06	**NINE 2FIVE** *Polydor BUN105CD* ORDINARY BOYS FEATURING LADY SOVEREIGN	6		8
27 Jan 07	**LOVE ME OR HATE ME** *Island/Uni-Island 1722848*	26		6
11 Apr 09	**SO HUMAN** *Midget MID03CD*	38		4

LADYFUZZ
UK/Australia, male/female vocal group

Date	Title	Peak	Wks at No.1	Wks on Chart: 1
1 Apr 06	**BOUNCY BALL** *Transgressive TRANS024CD*	52		1

LADYHAWKE
New Zealand, female vocalist/multi-instrumentalist (Phillipa Brown)

Date	Title	Peak	Wks at No.1	Wks on Chart: 12
12 Jul 08	**PARIS IS BURNING** *Modular MODCDS058*	61		1
6 Dec 08	**MY DELIRIUM** *Modular MODCDS64*	33		5
14 Mar 09	**PARIS IS BURNING** *Modular MODCDS058*	47		3
2 May 09	**MY DELIRIUM** *Modular MODCDS64*	71		3

LADYSMITH BLACK MAMBAZO
South Africa, male vocal group

Date	Title	Peak	Wks at No.1	Wks on Chart: 26
3 Jun 95	**SWING LOW SWEET CHARIOT** *Polygram TV SWLDW 2* FEATURING CHINA BLACK	15		6
3 Jun 95	**WORLD IN UNION '95** *Polygram TV RUGBY 2* FEATURING PJ POWERS	47		5
15 Nov 97	**INKANYEZI NEZAZI (THE STAR AND THE WISEMAN)** *A&M 5823892*	33		3
11 Jul 98	**THE STAR AND THE WISEMAN** *AM:PM 5825692*	63		1
16 Oct 99	**AIN'T NO SUNSHINE** *Universal Music TV 1564332* FEATURING DES'REE	42		2
18 Dec 99	**I SHALL BE THERE** *Glow Worm 6683332* B*WITCHED FEATURING LADYSMITH BLACK MAMBAZO	13		9

LADYTRON
UK/Bulgaria, male/female vocal/production group

Date	Title	Peak	Wks at No.1	Wks on Chart: 5
7 Dec 02	**SEVENTEEN** *Invicta Hi-Fi/Telstar CDSTAS 3284*	68		1
22 Mar 03	**BLUE JEANS** *Invicta Hi-Fi/Telstar CDSTAS 3311*	43		1
12 Jul 03	**EVIL** *Invicta Hi-Fi/Telstar CXSTAS 3331*	44		1
2 Jul 05	**SUGAR** *Island CID896*	45		1
1 Oct 05	**DESTROY EVERYTHING YOU TOUCH** *Island CIDX905*	42		1

LAGUNA
Italy, male DJ/production duo. See Spiller

Date	Title	Peak	Wks at No.1	Wks on Chart: 2
1 Nov 97	**SPILLER FROM RIO (DO IT EASY)** *Positiva CDTIV 83*	40		2

LAHAYNA
UK, male vocal/instrumental group

Date	Title	Peak	Wks at No.1	Wks on Chart: 1
24 Nov 07	**IN THE CITY** *Lahayna GBTFD0700004*	33		1

LAID BACK
Denmark, male vocal/production duo

Date	Title	Peak	Wks at No.1	Wks on Chart: 4
5 May 90	**BAKERMAN** *Arista 112356*	44		4

CLEO LAINE
UK, female vocalist (Clementina Campbell)

Date	Title	Peak	Wks at No.1	Wks on Chart: 14
29 Dec 60	**LET'S SLIP AWAY** *Fontana H 269*	42		1
14 Sep 61	**YOU'LL ANSWER TO ME** *Fontana H 326*	5		13

FRANKIE LAINE
US, male vocalist (Frank Lovecchio), d. 6 Feb 2007 (age 93). Early 1950s heartthrob who spent a record 27 weeks at No.1 in 1953, 18 weeks at the top with 'I Believe' and at times had three tracks in the Top 5

Date	Title	Peak	Wks at No.1	Wks on Chart: 282
14 Nov 52	**HIGH NOON (DO NOT FORSAKE ME)** *Columbia DB 3113*	7		7
14 Nov 52	**SUGARBUSH** *Columbia DB 3123* DORIS DAY & FRANKIE LAINE	8		8
20 Mar 53	**GIRL IN THE WOOD** *Columbia DB 2907*	11		1
3 Apr 53	**I BELIEVE** *Philips PB 117*	1	18	36
8 May 53	**TELL ME A STORY** *Philips PB 126* & JIMMY BOYD	5		16
4 Sep 53	**WHERE THE WINDS BLOW** *Philips PB 167*	2		12
16 Oct 53	**HEY JOE** *Philips PB 172*	1	2	8
30 Oct 53	**ANSWER ME** *Philips PB 196*	1	8	17

		Peak	Wks at No.1	Wks on Chart
8 Jan 54	**BLOWING WILD** *Philips PB 207*	2		12
26 Mar 54	**GRANADA** *Philips PB 242*	9		2
16 Apr 54	**THE KID'S LAST FIGHT** *Philips PB 258*	3		10
13 Aug 54	**MY FRIEND** *Philips PB 316*	3		15
8 Oct 54	**THERE MUST BE A REASON** *Philips PB 306*	9		9
22 Oct 54	**RAIN RAIN RAIN** *Philips PB 311* & THE FOUR LADS	8		16
11 Mar 55	**IN THE BEGINNING** *Philips PB 404*	20		1
24 Jun 55	**COOL WATER** *Philips PB 465* WITH THE MELLOMEN	2		22
15 Jul 55	**STRANGE LADY IN TOWN** *Philips PB 478*	6		13
11 Nov 55	**HUMMING BIRD** *Philips PB 498*	16		1
25 Nov 55	**HAWKEYE** *Philips PB 519*	7		8
20 Jan 56	**SIXTEEN TONS** *Philips PB 539* WITH THE MELLOMEN	10		3
4 May 56	**HELL HATH NO FURY** *Philips PB 585*	28		1
7 Sep 56	**A WOMAN IN LOVE** *Philips PB 617*	1	4	21

Singles That Have Spent The Most Weeks At No.1

Pos	Title Artist	Weeks at No.1
1	**I BELIEVE** FRANKIE LAINE	18*
2	**(EVERYTHING I DO) I DO IT FOR YOU** BRYAN ADAMS	16
3	**LOVE IS ALL AROUND** WET WET WET	15
4	**BOHEMIAN RHAPSODY** QUEEN	14†
5	**ROSE MARIE** SLIM WHITMAN	11
6	**UMBRELLA** RIHANNA FEATURING JAY-Z	10
=	**I WILL ALWAYS LOVE YOU** WHITNEY HOUSTON	10
=	**CARA MIA** DAVID WHITFIELD, WITH CHORUS AND MANTOVANI & HIS ORCHESTRA	10
9	**YOU'RE THE ONE THAT I WANT** JOHN TRAVOLTA & OLIVIA NEWTON-JOHN	9
=	**TWO TRIBES** FRANKIE GOES TO HOLLYWOOD	9
=	**SECRET LOVE** DORIS DAY	9†
=	**OH MEIN PAPA** EDDIE CALVERT	9
=	**MULL OF KINTYRE/GIRLS' SCHOOL** WINGS	9
=	**HERE IN MY HEART** AL MARTINO	9
=	**DIANA** PAUL ANKA	9
=	**CRAZY** GNARLS BARKLEY	9
17	**WONDERFUL LAND** SHADOWS	8
=	**SUGAR SUGAR** ARCHIES	8
=	**STAY** SHAKESPEAR'S SISTER	8
=	**MAGIC MOMENTS** PERRY COMO	8
=	**IT'S NOW OR NEVER** ELVIS PRESLEY WITH THE JORDANAIRES	8
=	**ANSWER ME** FRANKIE LAINE	8
23	**YOUNG LOVE** TAB HUNTER	7
=	**WANNABE** SPICE GIRLS	7
=	**UNCHAINED MELODY/(THERE'LL BE BLUEBIRDS OVER) WHITE CLIFFS OF DOVER** ROBSON GREEN & JEROME FLYNN	7
=	**SUMMER NIGHTS** JOHN TRAVOLTA & OLIVIA NEWTON-JOHN	7
=	**MARY'S BOY CHILD** HARRY BELAFONTE	7
=	**JUST WALKIN' IN THE RAIN** JOHNNIE RAY	7
=	**IN THE SUMMERTIME** MUNGO JERRY	7
=	**I'D DO ANYTHING FOR LOVE (BUT I WON'T DO THAT)** MEAT LOAF	7
=	**I REMEMBER YOU** FRANK IFIELD	7
=	**HELLO GOODBYE** BEATLES	7
=	**GREEN GREEN GRASS OF HOME** TOM JONES	7
=	**GIVE ME YOUR WORD** TENNESSEE ERNIE FORD	7
=	**FROM ME TO YOU** BEATLES	7
=	**CATHY'S CLOWN** EVERLY BROTHERS	7
=	**BLEEDING LOVE** LEONA LEWIS	7
=	**BELIEVE** CHER	7
=	**ALL SHOOK UP** ELVIS PRESLEY WITH THE JORDANAIRES	7
=	**ALL I HAVE TO DO IS DREAM/ CLAUDETTE** EVERLY BROTHERS	7
=	**(IS THIS THE WAY TO) AMARILLO?** TONY CHRISTIE FEATURING PETER KAY	7
=	**THINK TWICE** CELINE DION	7

*based on three separate runs at number one

†based on two separate runs at number one

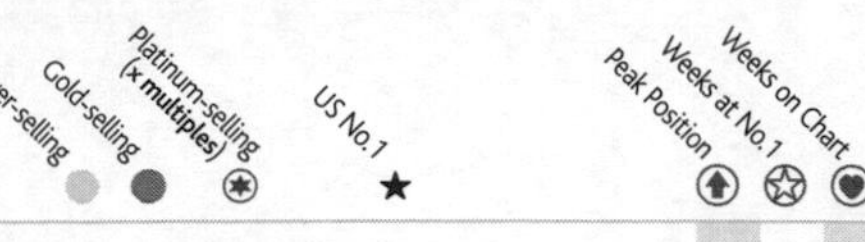

Date	Title	Peak Position	Weeks at No.1	Weeks on Chart
28 Dec 56	**MOONLIGHT GAMBLER** *Philips PB 638*	13		13
26 Apr 57	**LOVE IS A GOLDEN RING** *Philips PB 676*	19		5
4 Oct 57	**GOOD EVENING FRIENDS/UP ABOVE MY HEAD I HEAR MUSIC IN THE AIR** *Philips PB 708* & JOHNNIE RAY	25		4
13 Nov 59	**RAWHIDE** *Philips PB 965*	6		20
11 May 61	**GUNSLINGER** *Philips PB 1135*	50		1

CHRIS LAKE FEATURING LAURA V

UK, male/female vocal/production duo — 5

Date	Title	Peak Position	Weeks at No.1	Weeks on Chart
30 Sep 06	**CHANGES** *Apollo APOLLO107CDX*	27		5

GREG LAKE

UK, male vocalist/guitarist. See Emerson, Lake & Palmer, King Crimson — 12

Date	Title	Peak Position	Weeks at No.1	Weeks on Chart
6 Dec 75	**I BELIEVE IN FATHER CHRISTMAS** *Manticore K 13511*	2		7
25 Dec 82	**I BELIEVE IN FATHER CHRISTMAS** *Manticore K 13511*	72		3
24 Dec 83	**I BELIEVE IN FATHER CHRISTMAS** *Manticore K 13511*	65		2

SETH LAKEMAN

UK, male vocalist/multi-instrumentalist — 2

Date	Title	Peak Position	Weeks at No.1	Weeks on Chart
19 Aug 06	**LADY OF THE SEA (HEAR HER CALLING)** *Relentless RELCD28*	52		1
4 Nov 06	**THE WHITE HARE** *Relentless RELCD29*	47		1

LAMB

UK, male/female vocal/production duo — 4

Date	Title	Peak Position	Weeks at No.1	Weeks on Chart
29 Mar 97	**GORECKI** *Fontana LAMCD 4*	30		2
3 Apr 99	**B LINE** *Fontana LAMCD 5*	52		1
22 May 99	**ALL IN YOUR HANDS** *Fontana LAMCD 6*	71		1

ANNABEL LAMB

UK, female vocalist — 7

Date	Title	Peak Position	Weeks at No.1	Weeks on Chart
27 Aug 83	**RIDERS ON THE STORM** *A&M AM 131*	27		7

LAMBCHOP

US, male/female vocal/instrumental group — 1

Date	Title	Peak Position	Weeks at No.1	Weeks on Chart
20 May 00	**UP WITH THE PEOPLE** *City Slang 201592*	66		1

LAMBRETTAS

UK, male vocal/instrumental group – Jez Bird, d. 27 Aug 2008, Mark Ellis, Doug Sanders & Paul Wincer — 24

Date	Title	Peak Position	Weeks at No.1	Weeks on Chart
1 Mar 80	**POISON IVY** *Rocket XPRESS 25* ●	7		12
24 May 80	**D-A-A-ANCE** *Rocket XPRESS 33*	12		8
23 Aug 80	**ANOTHER DAY (ANOTHER GIRL)** *Rocket XPRESS 36*	49		4

RAY LAMONTAGNE

US, male vocalist/guitarist — 9

Date	Title	Peak Position	Weeks at No.1	Weeks on Chart
29 Jul 06	**TROUBLE** *14th Floor 14FLR15CD*	25		9

LAMPIES

US, male/female vocal cartoon group — 3

Date	Title	Peak Position	Weeks at No.1	Weeks on Chart
22 Dec 01	**LIGHT UP THE WORLD FOR CHRISTMAS** *Bluecrest LAMPCD 001*	48		3

LANCASTRIANS

UK, male vocal/instrumental group — 2

Date	Title	Peak Position	Weeks at No.1	Weeks on Chart
24 Dec 64	**WE'LL SING IN THE SUNSHINE** *Pye 7N 15732*	44		2

MAJOR LANCE

US, male vocalist, d. 3 Sep 1994 (age 55) — 2

Date	Title	Peak Position	Weeks at No.1	Weeks on Chart
13 Feb 64	**UM UM UM UM UM UM** *Columbia DB 7205*	40		2

LANDSCAPE

UK, male vocal/instrumental group – Richard James Burgess, Christopher Heaton, Andy Pask, Peter Thoms & John L Walters — 20

Date	Title	Peak Position	Weeks at No.1	Weeks on Chart
28 Feb 81	**EINSTEIN A GO-GO** *RCA 22* ●	5		13
23 May 81	**NORMAN BATES** *RCA 60*	40		7

RONNIE LANE & SLIM CHANCE

UK, male vocal/instrumental group – Ronnie Lane, d. 4 Jun 1997 (age 51). See Small Faces — 12

Date	Title	Peak Position	Weeks at No.1	Weeks on Chart
12 Jan 74	**HOW COME?** *GM GMS 011*	11		8
15 Jun 74	**THE POACHER** *GM GMS 024*	36		4

DON LANG

UK, male trombonist/vocalist (Gordon Langhorn), d. 3 Aug 1992 (age 67) — 18

Date	Title	Peak Position	Weeks at No.1	Weeks on Chart
4 Nov 55	**CLOUDBURST** *HMV POP 115* & THE MAIRANTS-LANGHORN BIG SIX	16		4
5 Jul 57	**SCHOOL DAY (RING! RING! GOES THE BELL)** *HMV POP 350* & HIS FRANTIC FIVE	26		2
23 May 58	**WITCH DOCTOR** *HMV POP 488* & HIS FRANTIC FIVE	5		11
10 Mar 60	**SINK THE BISMARK** *HMV POP 714*	43		1

k.d. lang

Canada, female vocalist (Katherine Dawn Lang) — 25

Date	Title	Peak Position	Weeks at No.1	Weeks on Chart
16 May 92	**CONSTANT CRAVING** *Sire W0100*	52		4
22 Aug 92	**CRYING** *Virgin America VUS 63* ROY ORBISON (DUET WITH k d lang)	13		6
27 Feb 93	**CONSTANT CRAVING** *Sire W0157CD*	15		8
1 May 93	**THE MIND OF LOVE** *Sire W0170CD1*	72		1
26 Jun 93	**MISS CHATELAINE** *Sire W0181CDX*	68		2
11 Dec 93	**JUST KEEP ME MOVING** *Sire W0227CD*	59		1
30 Sep 95	**IF I WERE YOU** *Sire W0319CD*	53		1
18 May 96	**YOU'RE OK** *Warner Brothers W0332CD*	44		2

THOMAS LANG

UK, male vocalist — 3

Date	Title	Peak Position	Weeks at No.1	Weeks on Chart
30 Jan 88	**THE HAPPY MAN** *Epic VOW 4*	67		3

LANGE

UK, male producer (Stuart Langelaan) — 8

Date	Title	Peak Position	Weeks at No.1	Weeks on Chart
19 Jun 99	**I BELIEVE** *Addictive 12ADD039* FEATURING SARAH DWYER	68		1
19 Jan 02	**DRIFTING AWAY** *VC Recordings VCRD 101* FEATURING SKYE	9		6
22 Feb 03	**DON'T THINK IT (FEEL IT)** *Nebula NEBCD 037* FEATURING LEAH	59		1

LANTERNS

UK, male/female vocal/instrumental trio — 1

Date	Title	Peak Position	Weeks at No.1	Weeks on Chart
6 Feb 99	**HIGHRISE TOWN** *Columbia 6665712*	50		1

MARIO LANZA

US, male vocalist (Alfredo Cocozza), d. 7 Oct 1959 (age 38) — 32

Date	Title	Peak Position	Weeks at No.1	Weeks on Chart
14 Nov 52	**BECAUSE YOU'RE MINE** *HMV DA 2017*	3		24
4 Feb 55	**DRINKING SONG** *HMV DA 2065*	13		1
18 Feb 55	**I'LL WALK WITH GOD** *HMV DA 2062*	18		2
22 Apr 55	**SERENADE** *HMV DA 2065*	15		3
14 Sep 56	**SERENADE** *HMV DA 2085*	25		2

LAPTOP

US, male vocalist/instrumentalist (Jesse Hartman) — 1

Date	Title	Peak Position	Weeks at No.1	Weeks on Chart
12 Jun 99	**NOTHING TO DECLARE** *Island CID 744*	74		1

YVES LAROCK

Switzerland, male DJ/producer (Yves 'Larock' Cheminade) — 8

Date	Title	Peak Position	Weeks at No.1	Weeks on Chart
4 Aug 07	**RISE UP** *Data DATA159CDS*	13		8

JULIUS LAROSA

US, male vocalist — 9

Date	Title	Peak Position	Weeks at No.1	Weeks on Chart
4 Jul 58	**TORERO** *RCA 1063*	15		9

LARRIKIN LOVE

UK, male vocal/instrumental group — 5

Date	Title	Peak Position	Weeks at No.1	Weeks on Chart
15 Apr 06	**EDWOULD** *Infectious WEA403CD*	49		1
8 Jul 06	**DOWNING STREET KINDLING** *Infectious WEA409CD*	35		1
23 Sep 06	**HAPPY AS ANNIE** *Infectious WEA412CD*	32		2
3 Feb 07	**A DAY IN THE LIFE** *Infectious WEA415CD*	31		1

LA'S
UK, male vocal/instrumental group

		⬆	✪	20
14 Jan 89	**THERE SHE GOES** *Go! Discs GOLAS 2*	59		4
15 Sep 90	**TIMELESS MELODY** *Go! Discs GOLAS 4*	57		2
3 Nov 90	**THERE SHE GOES** *Go! Discs GOLAS 5*	13		9
16 Feb 91	**FEELIN'** *Go! Discs GOLAS 6*	43		3
10 May 97	**FEVER PITCH THE EP** *Blanco Y Negro NEG 104CD* PRETENDERS, LA'S, ORLANDO, NICK HORNBY	65		1
2 Oct 99	**THERE SHE GOES** *Polydor 5614032*	65		1

LAS KETCHUP
Spain, female vocal trio – sisters Lola, Lucia & Pilar Munoz

		⬆	✪	26
21 Sep 02	**KETCHUP SONG (ASEREJE) (IMPORT)** *Columbia 9729602CD*	49		4
19 Oct 02	**THE KETCHUP SONG (ASEREJE)** *Columbia 6731932* ⊛	1	1	22

LASGO
Belgium, female/male vocal/production/instrumental trio – Evi Goffin, Peter Luts & Jeff Martens

		⬆	✪	34
9 Mar 02	**SOMETHING** *Positiva CDTIV 169* ●	4		15
24 Aug 02	**ALONE** *Positiva CDTIV 176*	7		8
30 Nov 02	**PRAY** *Positiva CDTIVS 182*	17		7
1 May 04	**SURRENDER** *Positiva CDTIVS 205*	24		4

LISA LASHES
UK, female DJ/producer (Lisa Rose-Wyatt)

		⬆	✪	3
8 Jul 00	**UNBELIEVABLE** *Tidy Trax TIDY 138CD*	63		1
25 Oct 03	**WHAT CAN YOU DO 4 ME?** *Tidy Trax TIDY 194C*	52		2

JAMES LAST BAND
Germany, male conductor/producer (Hans Last)

		⬆	✪	4
3 May 80	**THE SEDUCTION (LOVE THEME)** *Polydor PD 2071*	48		4

LAST RHYTHM
Italy, male instrumental/production group

		⬆	✪	1
14 Sep 96	**LAST RHYTHM** *Stress CDSTR 76*	62		1

LAST SHADOW PUPPETS
UK, male vocal/instrumental trio – Alex Turner, James Ford & Miles Kane

		⬆	✪	7
19 Apr 08	**THE AGE OF THE UNDERSTATEMENT** *Domino RUG288CD*	9		5
19 Jul 08	**STANDING NEXT TO ME** *Domino RUG301CD*	30		2

LATE SHOW
UK, male vocal/instrumental group

		⬆	✪	6
3 Mar 79	**BRISTOL STOMP** *Decca F 13822*	40		6

LATIN QUARTER
UK, male/female vocal/instrumental group

		⬆	✪	10
18 Jan 86	**RADIO AFRICA** *Rockin' Horse RH 102*	19		9
18 Apr 87	**NOMZAMO (ONE PEOPLE ONE CAUSE)** *Rockin' Horse RH 113*	73		1

LATIN THING
Canada/Spain, male/female vocal/instrumental group

		⬆	✪	1
13 Jul 96	**LATIN THING** *Faze 2 CDFAZE 33*	41		1

GINO LATINO
Italy, male rapper (Lorenzo Cherubini aka Jovanotti)

		⬆	✪	7
20 Jan 90	**WELCOME** *ffrr F 126*	17		7

LaTOUR
US, male vocalist/producer (William LaTour)

		⬆	✪	7
8 Jun 91	**PEOPLE ARE STILL HAVING SEX** *Polydor PO 147*	15		7

STACY LATTISAW
US, female vocalist

		⬆	✪	14
14 Jun 80	**JUMP TO THE BEAT** *Cotillion K 11496*	3		11
30 Aug 80	**DYNAMITE** *Atlantic K 11554*	51		3

CYNDI LAUPER
US, female vocalist

		⬆	✪	103
14 Jan 84	**GIRLS JUST WANT TO HAVE FUN** *Portrait A 3943* ●	2		12
24 Mar 84	**TIME AFTER TIME** *Portrait A 4290* ★	54		4
16 Jun 84	**TIME AFTER TIME** *Portrait A 4290* ●	3		13
1 Sep 84	**SHE BOP** *Portrait A 4620*	46		5
17 Nov 84	**ALL THROUGH THE NIGHT** *Portrait A 4849*	64		2
20 Sep 86	**TRUE COLORS** *Portrait 65000267* ★	12		11
27 Dec 86	**CHANGE OF HEART** *Portrait CYNDI 1*	67		2
28 Mar 87	**WHAT'S GOING ON** *Portrait CYN 1*	57		3
20 May 89	**I DROVE ALL NIGHT** *Epic CYN 4*	7		12
5 Aug 89	**MY FIRST NIGHT WITHOUT YOU** *Epic CYN 5*	53		4
30 Dec 89	**HEADING WEST** *Epic CYN 6*	68		1
6 Jun 92	**THE WORLD IS STONE** *Epic 6579707*	15		7
13 Nov 93	**THAT'S WHAT I THINK** *Epic 6598782*	31		4
8 Jan 94	**WHO LET IN THE RAIN** *Epic 6590392*	32		4
17 Sep 94	**HEY NOW (GIRLS JUST WANT TO HAVE FUN)** *Epic 6608072* ●	4		13
11 Feb 95	**I'M GONNA BE STRONG** *Epic 6611962*	37		2
26 Aug 95	**COME ON HOME** *Epic 6614255*	39		2
1 Feb 97	**YOU DON'T KNOW** *Epic 6641845*	27		2

LAURA
Sweden, female/male vocal/instrumental group

		⬆	✪	3
5 May 07	**RELEASE ME** *Cosmos SEWTA0700101*	47		3

LAUREL & HARDY
UK, male vocal/instrumental duo

		⬆	✪	10
22 Nov 75	**THE TRAIL OF THE LONESOME PINE** *United Artists UP 36026* WITH THE AVALON BOYS FEATURING CHILL WILLS ●	2		10

LAUREL & HARDY
UK/US, male comedy/vocal duo – Stan Laurel, d. 23 Feb 1965, & Oliver Hardy, d. 7 Aug 1957

		⬆	✪	2
2 Apr 83	**CLUNK CLICK** *CBS A 3213*	65		2

LAURNEA
US, female vocalist (Laurnea Wilkinson)

		⬆	✪	2
12 Jul 97	**DAYS OF YOUTH** *Epic 6646932*	36		2

AVRIL LAVIGNE
Canada, female vocalist/multi-instrumentalist/actor/fashion designer

		⬆	✪	112
7 Sep 02	**COMPLICATED (IMPORT)** *RCA 74321955782*	64		2
5 Oct 02	**COMPLICATED** *RCA 74321965962*	3		9
28 Dec 02	**SK8ER BOI** *RCA 74321979782*	8		9
12 Apr 03	**I'M WITH YOU** *Arista 82876506712*	7		10
19 Jul 03	**LOSING GRIP** *Arista 82876534542*	22		6
22 May 04	**DON'T TELL ME** *Arista 82876617322*	5		9
14 Aug 04	**MY HAPPY ENDING** *Arista 82876636492*	5		9
27 Nov 04	**NOBODY'S HOME** *Arista 82876663652*	24		4
9 Apr 05	**HE WASN'T** *Arista 82876683052*	23		3
10 Mar 07	**GIRLFRIEND** *Arista 88697073522* ★	2		24
23 Jun 07	**WHEN YOU'RE GONE** *RCA 88697119262*	3		19
27 Oct 07	**HOT** *RCA 88697170362*	30		6
13 Mar 10	**ALICE** *RCA USWD11037762*	59		2

JOANNA LAW
UK, female vocalist

		⬆	✪	6
7 Jul 90	**FIRST TIME EVER** *Citybeat CBE 752*	67		3
14 Sep 96	**THE GIFT** *Deconstruction 74321401912* WAY OUT WEST/MISS JOANNA LAW	15		3

STEVE LAWLER
UK, male DJ/producer

		⬆	✪	1
11 Nov 00	**RISE 'IN** *Bedrock BEDRCDS 008*	50		1

BELLE LAWRENCE
UK, female vocalist — 1

Date	Title	Peak Position	Weeks at No.1	Weeks on Chart
30 Mar 02	**EVERGREEN** *Euphoric CDUPH 024*	73		1

JOEY LAWRENCE
US, male vocalist — 15

Date	Title	Peak Position	Weeks at No.1	Weeks on Chart
26 Jun 93	**NOTHIN' MY LOVE CAN'T FIX** *EMI CDEM 271*	13		7
28 Aug 93	**I CAN'T HELP MYSELF** *EMI CDEM 277*	27		4
30 Oct 93	**STAY FOREVER** *EMI CDEM 289*	41		3
19 Sep 98	**NEVER GONNA CHANGE MY MIND** *Curb CUBC 34*	49		1

LEE LAWRENCE WITH RAY MARTIN & HIS ORCHESTRA
UK, male vocalist (Leon Siroto), d. Feb 1961 (age 40) — 10

Date	Title	Peak Position	Weeks at No.1	Weeks on Chart
20 Nov 53	**CRYING IN THE CHAPEL** *Decca F 10177*	7		6
2 Dec 55	**SUDDENLY THERE'S A VALLEY** *Columbia DB 3681*	14		4

SOPHIE LAWRENCE
UK, female vocalist/actor — 7

Date	Title	Peak Position	Weeks at No.1	Weeks on Chart
3 Aug 91	**LOVE'S UNKIND** *IQ ZB 44821*	21		7

STEVE LAWRENCE
US, male vocalist (Sidney Leibowitz) — 27

Date	Title	Peak Position	Weeks at No.1	Weeks on Chart
21 Apr 60	**FOOTSTEPS** *HMV POP 726*	4		13
18 Aug 60	**GIRLS GIRLS GIRLS** *London HLT 9166*	49		1
22 Aug 63	**I WANT TO STAY HERE** *CBS AAG 163* STEVE & EYDIE	3		13

MARIA LAWSON
UK, female vocalist — 3

Date	Title	Peak Position	Weeks at No.1	Weeks on Chart
26 Aug 06	**SLEEPWALKING** *Phonogenic 82876885032*	20		3

LAYO & BUSHWACKA!
UK, male DJ/production duo – Layo Paskin & Matthew Benjamin — 12

Date	Title	Peak Position	Weeks at No.1	Weeks on Chart
22 Jun 02	**LOVE STORY** *XL Recordings XLS 144CD*	30		2
25 Jan 03	**LOVE STORY (VS FINALLY)** *XL Recordings XLS 154CD*	8		7
16 Aug 03	**IT'S UP TO YOU (SHINING THROUGH)** *XL Recordings XLS 163CD*	25		3

LINDY LAYTON
UK, female vocalist (Belinda Layton) — 28

Date	Title	Peak Position	Weeks at No.1	Weeks on Chart
10 Feb 90	**DUB BE GOOD TO ME** *Go! Beat GOD 39* BEATS INTERNATIONAL FEATURING LINDY LAYTON ●	1	4	13
11 Aug 90	**SILLY GAMES** *Arista 113452* FEATURING JANET KAY	22		7
26 Jan 91	**ECHO MY HEART** *Arista 113845*	42		2
31 Aug 91	**WITHOUT YOU (ONE AND ONE)** *Arista 114636*	71		2
24 Apr 93	**WE GOT THE LOVE** *PWL International PWCD 250*	38		3
30 Oct 93	**SHOW ME** *PWL International PWCD 275*	47		1

LAZEE FEATURING NEVERSTORE
Sweden, male DJ/vocal/instrumental group — 1

Date	Title	Peak Position	Weeks at No.1	Weeks on Chart
4 Jul 09	**HOLD ON** *Hard2beat H2B31CDX*	46		1

PETER LAZONBY
UK, male DJ/producer — 1

Date	Title	Peak Position	Weeks at No.1	Weeks on Chart
10 Jun 00	**SACRED CYCLES** *Hooj Choons HOOJ 93CD*	49		1

DOUG LAZY
US, male rapper/producer (Gene Douglas Finley) — 9

Date	Title	Peak Position	Weeks at No.1	Weeks on Chart
15 Jul 89	**LET IT ROLL** *Atlantic A 8866* RAZE PRESENTS DOUG LAZY	27		5
4 Nov 89	**LET THE RHYTHM PUMP** *Atlantic A 8784*	45		3
26 May 90	**LET THE RHYTHM PUMP (REMIX)** *East West A 7919*	63		1

LAZY B
Denmark, male vocalist/keyboard player/guitarist/producer (Soren Nystrom Rasted). See Aqua — 4

Date	Title	Peak Position	Weeks at No.1	Weeks on Chart
26 Aug 06	**UNDERWEAR GOES INSIDE THE PANTS** *Universal TV 9878961*	30		4

LAZY TOWN
Iceland, female/male children's TV vocal group — 5

Date	Title	Peak Position	Weeks at No.1	Weeks on Chart
16 Dec 06	**BING BANG (TIME TO DANCE)** *GTV CDGTV01*	4		5

LCD
UK, male production group — 9

Date	Title	Peak Position	Weeks at No.1	Weeks on Chart
27 Jun 98	**ZORBA'S DANCE** *Virgin VSCDT 1693*	20		5
9 Oct 99	**ZORBA'S DANCE** *Virgin VSCDT 1757*	22		4

LCD SOUNDSYSTEM
US, male vocalist/instrumentalist/producer (James Murphy) & various musicians — 9

Date	Title	Peak Position	Weeks at No.1	Weeks on Chart
20 Nov 04	**MOVEMENT** *EMI DFAEMI2141CD*	52		1
12 Mar 05	**DAFT PUNK IS PLAYING AT MY HOUSE** *DFA/EMI DFAEMI2143CD*	29		3
18 Jun 05	**DISCO INFILTRATOR** *DFA/EMI DFAEMI2145CD*	49		1
8 Oct 05	**TRIBULATIONS** *DFA/EMI DFAEMI2151CD*	59		1
17 Mar 07	**NORTH AMERICAN SCUM** *DFA/EMI DFAEMI2165CD*	40		2
9 Jun 07	**ALL MY FRIENDS** *DFA/EMI DFAEMI2169CD*	41		1

LE CLICK
Sweden/US, male/female vocal duo — 2

Date	Title	Peak Position	Weeks at No.1	Weeks on Chart
30 Aug 97	**CALL ME** *Logic 74321509672*	38		2

FEDDE LE GRAND
Holland, male DJ/producer — 54

Date	Title	Peak Position	Weeks at No.1	Weeks on Chart
9 Sep 06	**PUT YOUR HANDS UP FOR DETROIT** *Data DATA140CDX*	53		2
4 Nov 06	**PUT YOUR HANDS UP FOR DETROIT** *Data DATA140CDS*	1	1	20
10 Mar 07	**THE CREEPS** *Data DATA155CDS* CAMILLE JONES & FEDDE LE GRAND	7		12
29 Sep 07	**LET ME THINK ABOUT IT** *Data DATA170CDS* IDA CORR & FEDDE LE GRAND	2		20

KELE LE ROC
UK, female vocalist (Kelly Biggs) — 17

Date	Title	Peak Position	Weeks at No.1	Weeks on Chart
31 Oct 98	**LITTLE BIT OF LOVIN'** *1st Avenue 5672812*	8		7
27 Mar 99	**MY LOVE** *1st Avenue 5636112*	8		7
30 Sep 00	**THINKING OF YOU** *Telstar CDSTAS 3136* CURTIS LYNCH JR FEATURING KELE LE ROC & RED RAT	70		1
7 Jun 03	**FEELIN' U** *London FCD 409* SHY FX & T-POWER FEATURING KELE LE ROC	34		2

DAN LE SAC VS SCROOBIUS PIP
UK, male vocal/DJ/production duo — 5

Date	Title	Peak Position	Weeks at No.1	Weeks on Chart
14 Apr 07	**THOU SHALT ALWAYS KILL** *Lex GBMYF0700001*	34		4
10 May 08	**LOOK FOR THE WOMAN** *Sunday Best SBESTC58*	72		1

LE TIGRE
US, female vocal group — 3

Date	Title	Peak Position	Weeks at No.1	Weeks on Chart
15 Jan 05	**TKO** *Universal MCSTD40398*	50		2
7 May 05	**AFTER DARK** *Universal MCSTD40411*	63		1

JOE LEAN & THE JING JANG JONG
UK, male vocal/instrumental group — 1

Date	Title	Peak Position	Weeks at No.1	Weeks on Chart
22 Mar 08	**LONELY BUOY** *Vertigo 1758362*	43		1

VICKY LEANDROS
Greece, female vocalist (Vassiliki Papathanassiou) — 29

Date	Title	Peak Position	Weeks at No.1	Weeks on Chart
8 Apr 72	**COME WHAT MAY** *Philips 6000 049*	2		16
23 Dec 72	**THE LOVE IN YOUR EYES** *Philips 6000 081*	40		8
7 Jul 73	**WHEN BOUZOUKIS PLAYED** *Philips 6000 111*	44		5

DENIS LEARY
US, male comedian/vocalist — 2

Date	Title	Peak Position	Weeks at No.1	Weeks on Chart
13 Jan 96	**ASSHOLE** *A&M 5813352*	58		2

LEAVES
Iceland, male vocal/instrumental group — 1

Date	Title	Peak Position	Weeks at No.1	Weeks on Chart
18 May 02	**RACE** *B Unique BUN 020CDS*	66		1

LED ZEPPELIN

UK, male vocal/instrumental group – Robert Plant*, John Bonham, d. 25 Sep 1980, John Paul Jones & Jimmy Page*. See Coverdale Page **7**

Date	Title	Peak Position	Weeks at No.1	Weeks on Chart
13 Sep 97	**WHOLE LOTTA LOVE** *Atlantic AT 0013CD*	21		2
24 Nov 07	**STAIRWAY TO HEAVEN** *Atlantic USSS10000007*	37		4
24 Nov 07	**WHOLE LOTTA LOVE** *Atlantic USSS10000009*	64		1

ANGEL LEE

UK, female vocalist (Angelique Beckford) **1**

Date	Title	Peak Position	Weeks at No.1	Weeks on Chart
3 Jun 00	**WHAT'S YOUR NAME?** *WEA 258CD1*	39		1

ANN LEE

UK, female vocalist (Annerley Gordon) **21**

Date	Title	Peak Position	Weeks at No.1	Weeks on Chart
11 Sep 99	**2 TIMES (IMPORT)** *ZYX 90188*	57		2
16 Oct 99	**2 TIMES** *Systematic SYSX 31* ●	2		16
4 Mar 00	**VOICES** *Systematic SYSCD 32*	27		3

BRENDA LEE

US, female vocalist (Brenda Tarpley). No other teenage singer sold more records in the early rock years than this petite vocalist, who released her first single aged 11. She is one of only a few acts in both the Rock & Roll and Country Music Halls of Fame **211**

Date	Title	Peak Position	Weeks at No.1	Weeks on Chart
17 Mar 60	**SWEET NOTHIN'S** *Brunswick 05819*	4		19
30 Jun 60	**I'M SORRY** *Brunswick 05833* ★	12		16
20 Oct 60	**I WANT TO BE WANTED** *Brunswick 05839* ★	31		6
19 Jan 61	**LET'S JUMP THE BROOMSTICK** *Brunswick 05823*	12		15
6 Apr 61	**EMOTIONS** *Brunswick 05847*	45		1
20 Jul 61	**DUM DUM** *Brunswick 05854*	22		8
16 Nov 61	**FOOL NUMBER ONE** *Brunswick 05860*	38		3
8 Feb 62	**BREAK IT TO ME GENTLY** *Brunswick 05864*	46		2
5 Apr 62	**SPEAK TO ME PRETTY** *Brunswick 05867*	3		12
21 Jun 62	**HERE COMES THAT FEELING** *Brunswick 05871*	5		12
13 Sep 62	**IT STARTED ALL OVER AGAIN** *Brunswick 05876*	15		11
29 Nov 62	**ROCKIN' AROUND THE CHRISTMAS TREE** *Brunswick 05880*	6		7
17 Jan 63	**ALL ALONE AM I** *Brunswick 05882*	7		17
28 Mar 63	**LOSING YOU** *Brunswick 05886*	10		16
18 Jul 63	**I WONDER** *Brunswick 05891*	14		9
31 Oct 63	**SWEET IMPOSSIBLE YOU** *Brunswick 05896*	28		6
9 Jan 64	**AS USUAL** *Brunswick 05899*	5		15
9 Apr 64	**THINK** *Brunswick 05903*	26		8
10 Sep 64	**IS IT TRUE** *Brunswick 05915*	17		8
10 Dec 64	**CHRISTMAS WILL BE JUST ANOTHER LONELY DAY** *Brunswick 05921*	25		5
4 Feb 65	**THANKS A LOT** *Brunswick 05927*	41		2
29 Jul 65	**TOO MANY RIVERS** *Brunswick 05936*	22		12
2 Jan 10	**ROCKIN' AROUND THE CHRISTMAS TREE** *MCA MCSTD1595*	70		1

CURTIS LEE

US, male vocalist **2**

Date	Title	Peak Position	Weeks at No.1	Weeks on Chart
31 Aug 61	**PRETTY LITTLE ANGEL EYES** *London HLX 9397*	47		2

DEE C LEE

UK, female vocalist (Diane Sealey). See Style Council **20**

Date	Title	Peak Position	Weeks at No.1	Weeks on Chart
9 Nov 85	**SEE THE DAY** *CBS A 6570* ●	3		12
8 Mar 86	**COME HELL OR WATERS HIGH** *CBS A 6869*	46		5
13 Nov 93	**NO TIME TO PLAY** *Cooltempo CDCOOL 282* GURU FEATURING DEE C LEE	25		3

GARRY LEE & SHOWDOWN

Canada, male vocal/instrumental group **3**

Date	Title	Peak Position	Weeks at No.1	Weeks on Chart
31 Jul 93	**THE RODEO SONG** *Party Dish VCD 101*	44		3

JACKIE LEE

Ireland, female vocalist (Jackie Flood) **31**

Date	Title	Peak Position	Weeks at No.1	Weeks on Chart
10 Apr 68	**WHITE HORSES** *Philips BF 1674* JACKY	10		14
2 Jan 71	**RUPERT** *Pye 7N 45003*	14		17

LEAPY LEE

UK, male vocalist (Lee Graham) **28**

Date	Title	Peak Position	Weeks at No.1	Weeks on Chart
21 Aug 68	**LITTLE ARROWS** *MCA MU 1028*	2		21
20 Dec 69	**GOOD MORNING** *MCA MK 5021*	29		7

PEGGY LEE

US, female vocalist (Norma Jean Egstrom), d. 22 Jan 2002 (age 81) **29**

Date	Title	Peak Position	Weeks at No.1	Weeks on Chart
24 May 57	**MR WONDERFUL** *Brunswick 05671*	5		13
15 Aug 58	**FEVER** *Capitol CL 14902*	5		11
23 Mar 61	**TILL THERE WAS YOU** *Capitol CL 15184*	30		4
22 Aug 92	**FEVER** *Capitol PEG 1*	75		1

TONEY LEE

US, male vocalist **4**

Date	Title	Peak Position	Weeks at No.1	Weeks on Chart
29 Jan 83	**REACH UP** *TMT 2*	64		4

TRACEY LEE

US, male rapper **1**

Date	Title	Peak Position	Weeks at No.1	Weeks on Chart
19 Jul 97	**THE THEME** *Universal UND 56133*	51		1

LEE-CABRERA

US, male production duo **10**

Date	Title	Peak Position	Weeks at No.1	Weeks on Chart
12 Apr 03	**SHAKE IT (NO TE MUEVAS TANTO)** *Credence 12CRED 035*	58		1
6 Sep 03	**SHAKE IT (MOVE A LITTLE CLOSER)** *Credence CDCRED 039* FEATURING ALEX CARTANA	16		6
15 Nov 03	**SPECIAL 2003** *Credence CDCRED 040*	45		2
10 Jul 04	**VOODOO LOVE** *C2 CDC2001*	58		1

LEEDS UNITED FC

UK, football fans/vocal group **13**

Date	Title	Peak Position	Weeks at No.1	Weeks on Chart
29 Apr 72	**LEEDS UNITED** *Chapter One SCH 168*	10		10
25 Apr 92	**LEEDS LEEDS LEEDS** *Q Music LUFC 2*	54		3

RAYMOND LEFEVRE

France, male orchestra leader, d. 27 Jun 2008 (age 78) **2**

Date	Title	Peak Position	Weeks at No.1	Weeks on Chart
15 May 68	**SOUL COAXING** *Major Minor MM 559*	46		2

LEFTFIELD

UK, male instrumental/production duo – Neil Barnes & Paul Daley **23**

Date	Title	Peak Position	Weeks at No.1	Weeks on Chart
12 Dec 92	**SONG OF LIFE** *Hard Hands HAND 002T*	59		1
13 Nov 93	**OPEN UP** *Hard Hands HAND 009CD* LYDON	13		5
25 Mar 95	**ORIGINAL** *Hard Hands HAND 18CD* FEATURING TONI HALLIDAY	18		3
5 Aug 95	**THE AFRO-LEFT EP** *Hard Hands HAND 23CD* FEATURING DJUM DJUM	22		3
20 Jan 96	**RELEASE THE PRESSURE** *Hard Hands HAND 29CD*	13		3
18 Sep 99	**AFRIKA SHOX** *Hard Hands HAND 057CD1* LEFTFIELD/BAMBAATAA	7		5
11 Dec 99	**DUSTED** *Hard Hands HAND 058CD1* LEFTFIELD/ROOTS MANUVA	28		3

JOHN LEGEND

US, male vocalist/pianist (John Stephens) **18**

Date	Title	Peak Position	Weeks at No.1	Weeks on Chart
26 Mar 05	**USED TO LOVE U** *Columbia 6758022*	29		4
18 Jun 05	**ORDINARY PEOPLE** *Columbia 6759642*	27		8
3 Sep 05	**NUMBER ONE** *Columbia 82876724532*	62		1
11 Oct 08	**GREEN LIGHT** *Columbia 88697378522* FEATURING ANDRE 3000	35		5

LEGEND B

Germany, male production duo **1**

Date	Title	Peak Position	Weeks at No.1	Weeks on Chart
22 Feb 97	**LOST IN LOVE** *Perfecto PERF 132CD*	45		1

JODY LEI

South Africa, female vocalist **2**

Date	Title	Peak Position	Weeks at No.1	Weeks on Chart
22 Feb 03	**SHOWDOWN** *Independiente ISOM 66SMS*	34		2

LEILANI

UK, female model/vocalist (Leilani Dowding) **7**

Date	Title	Peak Position	Weeks at No.1	Weeks on Chart
6 Feb 99	**MADNESS THING** *ZTT 124CD*	19		4
12 Jun 99	**DO YOU WANT ME?** *ZTT 134CD*	40		2
3 Jun 00	**FLYING ELVIS** *ZTT 145CD*	73		1

PAUL LEKAKIS

US, male vocalist **4**

Date	Title	Peak Position	Weeks at No.1	Weeks on Chart
30 May 87	**BOOM BOOM (LET'S GO BACK TO MY ROOM)** *Champion CHAMP 43*	60		4

Silver-selling ○ Gold-selling ● Platinum-selling (x multiples) ⊛ US No.1 ★ Peak Position Weeks at No.1 Weeks on Chart

LEMAR

UK, male vocalist (Lemar Obika) — 96

Date	Title	Peak	Wks No.1	Wks
30 Aug 03	**DANCE (WITH U)** *Sony Music 6741322*	2		11
29 Nov 03	**50:50/LULLABY** *Sony Music 6744185*	5		11
6 Mar 04	**ANOTHER DAY** *Sony Music 6746595*	9		6
27 Nov 04	**IF THERE'S ANY JUSTICE** *Sony Music 6756072*	3		16
9 Apr 05	**TIME TO GROW** *Sony Music 6758122*	9		10
13 Aug 05	**DON'T GIVE IT UP** *Sony Music 6760452*	21		4
9 Sep 06	**IT'S NOT THAT EASY** *White Rabbit 82876894632*	7		11
25 Nov 06	**SOMEONE SHOULD TELL YOU** *White Rabbit 88697008982*	21		6
31 Mar 07	**TICK TOCK** *White Rabbit 88697076622*	45		2
27 Aug 08	**SATURDAY NIGHT HUSTLE** *Dcypha Productions DCY010CD* SWAY FEATURING LEMAR	67		1
15 Nov 08	**IF SHE KNEW** *Epic 88697395652*	14		7
7 Mar 09	**WEIGHT OF THE WORLD** *Epic 88697460932*	31		4
27 Feb 10	**THE WAY LOVE GOES** *Epic 88697634342*	8		7+

LEMON JELLY

UK, male production duo — 11

Date	Title	Peak	Wks No.1	Wks
19 Oct 02	**SPACE WALK** *Impotent Fury/XL Recordings IFXLS 150CD*	36		2
1 Feb 03	**NICE WEATHER FOR DUCKS** *Impotent Fury/XL Recordings IFXL 156CD*	16		3
4 Dec 04	**STAY WITH YOU** *XL Recordings IFXLS201CD*	31		3
5 Feb 05	**THE SHOUTY TRACK** *XL Recordings IFXLS205CD1*	21		2
23 Jul 05	**MAKE THINGS RIGHT** *XL Recordings IFXLS211CD*	33		1

LEMON PIPERS

US, male vocal/instrumental group – Ivan Browne, Bill Albaugh, d. 20 Jan 1999, Bill Bartlett, Reg Nave & Steve Walmsley — 16

Date	Title	Peak	Wks No.1	Wks
7 Feb 68	**GREEN TAMBOURINE** *Pye International 7N 25444* ★	7		11
1 May 68	**RICE IS NICE** *Pye International 7N 25454*	41		5

LEMON TREES

UK, male vocal/instrumental group — 9

Date	Title	Peak	Wks No.1	Wks
26 Sep 92	**LOVE IS IN YOUR EYES** *Oxygen GASP 1*	75		1
7 Nov 92	**THE WAY I FEEL** *Oxygen GASP 2*	62		2
13 Feb 93	**LET IT LOOSE** *Oxygen GASPD 3*	55		2
17 Apr 93	**CHILD OF LOVE** *Oxygen GASPD 4*	55		3
3 Jul 93	**I CAN'T FACE THE WORLD** *Oxygen GASPD 6*	52		1

LEMONHEADS

US/Australia, male vocal/instrumental group — 26

Date	Title	Peak	Wks No.1	Wks
17 Oct 92	**IT'S A SHAME ABOUT RAY** *Atlantic A 7423*	70		1
5 Dec 92	**MRS ROBINSON/BEIN' AROUND** *Atlantic A 7401*	19		9
6 Feb 93	**CONFETTI/MY DRUG BUDDY** *Atlantic A 7430CD*	44		2
10 Apr 93	**IT'S A SHAME ABOUT RAY** *Atlantic A 5764CD*	31		3
16 Oct 93	**INTO YOUR ARMS** *Atlantic A 7302CD*	14		4
27 Nov 93	**IT'S ABOUT TIME** *Atlantic A 7296CD*	57		2
14 May 94	**BIG GAY HEART** *Atlantic A 7259CD*	55		2
28 Sep 96	**IF I COULD TALK I'D TELL YOU** *Atlantic A 5661CD1*	39		2
14 Dec 96	**IT'S ALL TRUE** *Atlantic A 5635CD*	61		1

LEMONESCENT

UK, female vocal group — 5

Date	Title	Peak	Wks No.1	Wks
29 Jun 02	**BEAUTIFUL** *Supertone SUPTCD 1*	70		1
9 Nov 02	**SWING MY HIPS (SEX DANCE)** *Supertone SUPTCD 2*	48		1
5 Apr 03	**HELP ME MAMA** *Supertone SUPTCD 4*	36		1
21 Jun 03	**CINDERELLA** *Supertone SUPTCD 8*	31		1
3 Jul 04	**ALL RIGHT NOW** *Supertone SUPTCD 12*	37		1

LEN

Canada, male/female vocal/DJ group – Marc & Sharon Costanzo, D Rock, DJ Moves & Planet Pea (Philip Rae) — 15

Date	Title	Peak	Wks No.1	Wks
18 Dec 99	**STEAL MY SUNSHINE** *Columbia 6685062*	8		13
10 Jun 00	**CRYPTIK SOULS CREW** *Columbia 6693832*	28		2

LENKA

Australia, female vocalist (Lenka Kripac) — 6

Date	Title	Peak	Wks No.1	Wks
23 May 09	**THE SHOW** *Epic USSM10802201*	22		6

JOHN LENNON

UK, male vocalist/multi-instrumentalist/producer/peace activist, d. 8 Dec 1980 (age 40) — 205

Date	Title	Peak	Wks No.1	Wks
9 Jul 69	**GIVE PEACE A CHANCE** *Apple 13* PLASTIC ONO BAND	2		13
1 Nov 69	**COLD TURKEY** *Apple APPLES 1001* PLASTIC ONO BAND	14		8
21 Feb 70	**INSTANT KARMA** *Apple APPLES 1003* LENNON, ONO & THE PLASTIC ONO BAND	5		9
20 Mar 71	**POWER TO THE PEOPLE** *Apple R 5892* & THE PLASTIC ONO BAND	7		9
9 Dec 72	**HAPPY XMAS (WAR IS OVER)** *Apple R 5970* JOHN & YOKO & THE PLASTIC ONO BAND WITH THE HARLEM COMMUNITY CHOIR	4		8
24 Nov 73	**MIND GAMES** *Apple R 5994*	26		9
19 Oct 74	**WHATEVER GETS YOU THROUGH THE NIGHT** *Apple R 5998* WITH THE PLASTIC ONO NUCLEAR BAND ★	36		4
4 Jan 75	**HAPPY XMAS (WAR IS OVER)** *Apple R 5970* JOHN & YOKO & THE PLASTIC ONO BAND WITH THE HARLEM COMMUNITY CHOIR	48		1
8 Feb 75	**#9 DREAM** *Apple R 6003*	23		8
3 May 75	**STAND BY ME** *Apple R 6005*	30		7
1 Nov 75	**IMAGINE** *Apple R 6009* ○	6		11
8 Nov 80	**(JUST LIKE) STARTING OVER** *Geffen K 79186* ● ★	1	1	15
20 Dec 80	**HAPPY XMAS (WAR IS OVER)** *Apple R 5970* JOHN & YOKO & THE PLASTIC ONO BAND WITH THE HARLEM COMMUNITY CHOIR	2		9
27 Dec 80	**IMAGINE** *Apple R 6009* ○	1	4	13
24 Jan 81	**WOMAN** *Geffen K 79195* ○	1	2	11
24 Jan 81	**GIVE PEACE A CHANCE** *Apple 13* PLASTIC ONO BAND	33		5
21 Mar 81	**I SAW HER STANDING THERE** *DJM DJS 10965* ELTON JOHN BAND FEATURING JOHN LENNON & THE MUSCLE SHOALS HORNS	40		4
4 Apr 81	**WATCHING THE WHEELS** *Geffen K 79207*	30		6
19 Dec 81	**HAPPY XMAS (WAR IS OVER)** *Apple R 5970* JOHN & YOKO & THE PLASTIC ONO BAND WITH THE HARLEM COMMUNITY CHOIR	28		5
20 Nov 82	**LOVE** *Parlophone R 6059*	41		7
25 Dec 82	**HAPPY XMAS (WAR IS OVER)** *Apple R 5970* JOHN & YOKO & THE PLASTIC ONO BAND WITH THE HARLEM COMMUNITY CHOIR	56		3
21 Jan 84	**NOBODY TOLD ME** *Ono Music/Polydor POSP 700*	6		6
17 Mar 84	**BORROWED TIME** *Polydor POSP 701*	32		6
30 Nov 85	**JEALOUS GUY** *Parlophone R 6117*	65		2
10 Dec 88	**IMAGINE/JEALOUS GUY/HAPPY XMAS (WAR IS OVER)** *Parlophone R 6199*	45		5
25 Dec 99	**IMAGINE** *Parlophone CDR 6534* ●	3		14
20 Dec 03	**HAPPY XMAS (WAR IS OVER)** *Parlophone CDR 6627* JOHN & YOKO & THE PLASTIC ONO BAND	33		3
15 Dec 07	**HAPPY XMAS (WAR IS OVER)** *Capitol USCA29800675* JOHN & YOKO & THE PLASTIC ONO BAND	40		3
20 Dec 08	**HAPPY XMAS (WAR IS OVER)** *Capitol USCA29800675* JOHN & YOKO & THE PLASTIC ONO BAND	67		1

JULIAN LENNON

UK, male vocalist (John Charles Julian Lennon) — 47

Date	Title	Peak	Wks No.1	Wks
6 Oct 84	**TOO LATE FOR GOODBYES** *Charisma JL 1*	6		11
15 Dec 84	**VALOTTE** *Charisma JL 2*	55		6
9 Mar 85	**SAY YOU'RE WRONG** *Charisma JL 3*	75		1
7 Dec 85	**BECAUSE** *EMI 5538*	40		7
11 Mar 89	**NOW YOU'RE IN HEAVEN** *Virgin VS 1154*	59		3
24 Aug 91	**SALTWATER** *Virgin VS 1361*	6		13
30 Nov 91	**HELP YOURSELF** *Virgin VS 1379*	53		2
25 Apr 92	**GET A LIFE** *Virgin VS 1398*	56		3
23 May 98	**DAY AFTER DAY** *Music From Another JULIAN 4CD*	66		1

ANNIE LENNOX

UK, female vocalist. See Eurythmics, Tourists — 72

Date	Title	Peak	Wks No.1	Wks
3 Dec 88	**PUT A LITTLE LOVE IN YOUR HEART** *A&M AM 484* & AL GREEN	28		8
28 Mar 92	**WHY** *RCA PB 45317*	5		8
6 Jun 92	**PRECIOUS** *RCA 74321100257*	23		5
22 Aug 92	**WALKING ON BROKEN GLASS** *RCA 74321107227*	8		8
31 Oct 92	**COLD** *RCA 74321116902*	26		4
13 Feb 93	**LITTLE BIRD/LOVE SONG FOR A VAMPIRE** *RCA 74321133832* ○	3		12
18 Feb 95	**NO MORE 'I LOVE YOUS'** *RCA 74321257162* ○	2		12
10 Jun 95	**A WHITER SHADE OF PALE** *RCA 74321284822*	16		6
30 Sep 95	**WAITING IN VAIN** *RCA 74321316132*	31		3
9 Dec 95	**SOMETHING SO RIGHT** *RCA 74321332392* FEATURING PAUL SIMON	44		2
6 Oct 07	**DARK ROAD** *RCA 88697157432*	58		1
14 Mar 09	**SHINING LIGHT** *RCA GBARL0801003*	39		3

DINO LENNY

Italy, male producer — 2

Date	Title	Peak	Wks No.1	Wks
4 May 02	**I FEEL STEREO** *Incentive CENT 40CDS*	60		1
10 May 03	**CHANGE THE WORLD** *Free 2 Air 0146685 F2A* VS THE HOUSEMARTINS	51		1

PHILLIP LEO
UK, male vocalist (Phillip Pottinger) — 3

Date	Title / Label	Peak Position	Weeks at No.1	Weeks on Chart
23 Jul 94	**SECOND CHANCE** *EMI CDEM 327*	57		2
25 Mar 95	**THINKING ABOUT YOUR LOVE** *EMI CDEM 358*	64		1

KRISTIAN LEONTIOU
UK, male vocalist — 14

Date	Title / Label	Peak Position	Weeks at No.1	Weeks on Chart
5 Jun 04	**THE STORY OF MY LIFE** *Polydor 9866632*	9		7
28 Aug 04	**SHINING** *Polydor 9867640*	13		6
4 Dec 04	**SOME SAY** *Polydor 9868904*	54		1

LES RYTHMES DIGITALES
UK, male DJ/producer (Stuart Price) — 9

Date	Title / Label	Peak Position	Weeks at No.1	Weeks on Chart
25 Apr 98	**MUSIC MAKES YOU LOSE CONTROL** *Wall Of Sound WALLD 037*	69		1
7 Aug 99	**SOMETIMES** *Wall Of Sound WALLD 054* FEATURING NIK KERHSAW	56		1
30 Oct 99	**JACQUES YOUR BODY (MAKE ME SWEAT)** *Wall Of Sound WALLD 060*	60		1
10 Sep 05	**JACQUES YOUR BODY (MAKE ME SWEAT)** *Data DATA93CDS*	9		6

LESS THAN JAKE
UK, male vocal/instrumental group — 4

Date	Title / Label	Peak Position	Weeks at No.1	Weeks on Chart
5 Aug 00	**ALL MY BEST FRIENDS ARE METALHEADS** *Golf CDSHOLE 027*	51		1
8 Sep 01	**GAINESVILLE ROCK CITY** *Golf CDSHOLE 48*	57		1
24 May 03	**SHE'S GONNA BREAK SOON** *Sire W 606CD*	39		1
27 May 06	**OVERRATED (EVERYTHING IS)/A STILL LIFE** *Sire W713CD2*	61		1

KETTY LESTER
US, female vocalist (Revoyda Frierson) — 16

Date	Title / Label	Peak Position	Weeks at No.1	Weeks on Chart
19 Apr 62	**LOVE LETTERS** *London HLN 9527*	4		12
19 Jul 62	**BUT NOT FOR ME** *London HLN 9574*	45		4

LET LOOSE
UK, male vocal/instrumental group – Richie Wermerling, Rob Jeffrey & Lee J Murray. See Childliners — 62

Date	Title / Label	Peak Position	Weeks at No.1	Weeks on Chart
24 Apr 93	**CRAZY FOR YOU** *Vertigo VERCD 74*	44		3
9 Apr 94	**SEVENTEEN** *Mercury MERCD 400*	44		2
25 Jun 94	**CRAZY FOR YOU** *Mercury MERCD 402* ●	2		24
22 Oct 94	**SEVENTEEN (REMIX)** *Mercury MERCD 406*	11		9
28 Jan 95	**ONE NIGHT STAND** *Mercury MERCD 419*	12		6
29 Apr 95	**BEST IN ME** *Mercury MERDD 428*	8		5
4 Nov 95	**EVERYBODY SAY EVERYBODY DO** *Mercury MERDD 446*	29		4
22 Jun 96	**MAKE IT WITH YOU** *Mercury MERDD 464*	7		6
7 Sep 96	**TAKE IT EASY** *Mercury MERCD 472*	25		2
16 Nov 96	**DARLING BE HOME SOON** *Mercury MERCD 475*	65		1

LETHAL BIZZLE
UK, male rapper (Maxwell Ansah). See More Fire Crew — 18

Date	Title / Label	Peak Position	Weeks at No.1	Weeks on Chart
1 Jan 05	**POW (FORWARD)** *Relentless RELDX15*	11		7
6 Aug 05	**UH OH (I'M BACK)** *V2/J-Did JAD5033613*	47		2
29 Oct 05	**FIRE** *V2/J-Did JAD5035653*	34		3
12 Nov 05	**WHAT WE DO** *Gana/W10 GANA01CDS* KRAY TWINZ FEATURING TWISTA & LETHAL B	23		3
13 Oct 07	**POLICE ON MY BACK** *V2 VVR5044933*	37		3

LeTOYA
US, female vocalist/actor (LeToya Luckett). See Destiny's Child — 3

Date	Title / Label	Peak Position	Weeks at No.1	Weeks on Chart
7 Oct 06	**TORN** *EMI CDEM705*	35		3

LETTERMEN
US, male vocal trio – Tony Butala, Bob Engemann & Jim Pike — 3

Date	Title / Label	Peak Position	Weeks at No.1	Weeks on Chart
23 Nov 61	**THE WAY YOU LOOK TONIGHT** *Capitol CL 15222*	36		3

LEVEL 42
UK, male vocal/instrumental group – Mark King*, Mike Lindup, Rowland 'Boon' Gould (replaced by Alan Murphy, d. 19 Oct 1989) & Phil Gould (replaced by Gary Husband) — 177

Date	Title / Label	Peak Position	Weeks at No.1	Weeks on Chart
30 Aug 80	**LOVE MEETING LOVE** *Polydor POSP 170*	61		4
18 Apr 81	**LOVE GAMES** *Polydor POSP 234*	38		6
8 Aug 81	**TURN IT ON** *Polydor POSP 286*	57		6
14 Nov 81	**STARCHILD** *Polydor POSP 343*	47		4
8 May 82	**ARE YOU HEARING (WHAT I HEAR)?** *Polydor POSP 396*	49		5
2 Oct 82	**WEAVE YOUR SPELL** *Polydor POSP 500*	43		4
15 Jan 83	**THE CHINESE WAY** *Polydor POSP 538*	24		8
16 Apr 83	**OUT OF SIGHT, OUT OF MIND** *Polydor POSP 570*	41		4
30 Jul 83	**THE SUN GOES DOWN (LIVING IT UP)** *Polydor POSP 622*	10		12
22 Oct 83	**MICRO KID** *Polydor POSP 643*	37		5
1 Sep 84	**HOT WATER** *Polydor POSP 697*	18		9
3 Nov 84	**THE CHANT HAS BEGUN** *Polydor POSP 710*	41		5
21 Sep 85	**SOMETHING ABOUT YOU** *Polydor POSP 759* ○	6		17
7 Dec 85	**LEAVING ME NOW** *Polydor POSP 776*	15		11
26 Apr 86	**LESSONS IN LOVE** *Polydor POSP 790* ○	3		13
14 Feb 87	**RUNNING IN THE FAMILY** *Polydor POSP 842*	6		10
25 Apr 87	**TO BE WITH YOU AGAIN** *Polydor POSP 855*	10		7
12 Sep 87	**IT'S OVER** *Polydor POSP 900*	10		8
12 Dec 87	**CHILDREN SAY** *Polydor POSP 911*	22		6
3 Sep 88	**HEAVEN IN MY HANDS** *Polydor PO 14*	12		5
29 Oct 88	**TAKE A LOOK** *Polydor PO 24*	32		4
21 Jan 89	**TRACIE** *Polydor PO 34*	25		5
28 Oct 89	**TAKE CARE OF YOURSELF** *Polydor PO 58*	39		3
17 Aug 91	**GUARANTEED** *RCA PB 44745*	17		4
19 Oct 91	**OVERTIME** *RCA PB 44997*	62		2
18 Apr 92	**MY FATHER'S SHOES** *RCA PB 45271*	55		1
26 Feb 94	**FOREVER NOW** *RCA 74321190272*	19		4
30 Apr 94	**ALL OVER YOU** *RCA 74321205662*	26		2
6 Aug 94	**LOVE IN A PEACEFUL WORLD** *RCA 74321220332*	31		3

LEVELLERS
UK, male vocal/instrumental group — 60

Date	Title / Label	Peak Position	Weeks at No.1	Weeks on Chart
21 Sep 91	**ONE WAY** *China WOK 2008*	51		2
7 Dec 91	**FAR FROM HOME** *China WOK 2010*	71		1
23 May 92	**15 YEARS (EP)** *China WOKX 2020*	11		5
10 Jul 93	**BELARUSE** *China WOKCD 2034*	12		5
30 Oct 93	**THIS GARDEN** *China WOKCD 2039*	12		4
14 May 94	**JULIE (EP)** *China WOKCD 2042*	17		3
12 Aug 95	**HOPE ST** *China WOKCD 2059*	12		5
14 Oct 95	**FANTASY** *China WOKCD 2067*	16		3
23 Dec 95	**JUST THE ONE** *China WOKCD 2076* SPECIAL GUEST JOE STRUMMER	12		8
20 Jul 96	**EXODUS – LIVE** *China WOKCD 2082*	24		2
9 Aug 97	**WHAT A BEAUTIFUL DAY** *China WOKCD 2088*	13		5
18 Oct 97	**CELEBRATE** *China WOKCD 2089*	28		2
20 Dec 97	**DOG TRAIN** *China WOKCD 2090*	24		5
14 Mar 98	**TOO REAL** *China WOKCD 2091*	46		1
24 Oct 98	**BOZOS** *China WOKCD 2096*	44		2
6 Feb 99	**ONE WAY** *China WOKCD 2102*	33		2
9 Sep 00	**HAPPY BIRTHDAY REVOLUTION** *China EW 218CD*	57		1
21 Sep 02	**COME ON** *Eagle EHAGXS 001*	44		1
18 Jan 03	**WILD AS ANGELS EP** *Eagle EHAGXS 003*	34		2
30 Apr 05	**MAKE YOU HAPPY** *Eagle EOTFXS303*	38		1

LEVERT
US, male vocal/instrumental trio — 10

Date	Title / Label	Peak Position	Weeks at No.1	Weeks on Chart
22 Aug 87	**CASANOVA** *Atlantic A 9217*	9		10

LEVERT SWEAT GILL
US, male vocal group. See Johnny Gill, Keith Sweat — 7

Date	Title / Label	Peak Position	Weeks at No.1	Weeks on Chart
14 Mar 98	**MY BODY** *East West E 3857CD*	21		3
6 Jun 98	**CURIOUS** *East West E 3842CD*	23		2
12 Sep 98	**DOOR #1** *East West E 3817CD*	45		2

HANK LEVINE
US, male orchestra leader — 4

Date	Title / Label	Peak Position	Weeks at No.1	Weeks on Chart
21 Dec 61	**IMAGE** *HMV POP 947*	45		4

LEVITICUS
UK, male producer (JJ Frost) — 1

Date	Title / Label	Peak Position	Weeks at No.1	Weeks on Chart
25 Mar 95	**BURIAL** *ffrr FCD 255*	66		1

BARRINGTON LEVY
Jamaica, male vocalist — 13

Date	Title / Label	Peak Position	Weeks at No.1	Weeks on Chart
2 Feb 85	**HERE I COME** *London LON 62*	41		4
15 Jun 91	**TRIBAL BASE** *Desire WANT 44* REBEL MC FEATURING TENOR FLY & BARRINGTON LEVY	20		6
24 Sep 94	**WORK** *MCA MCSTD 2003*	65		1
13 Oct 01	**HERE I COME (SING DJ)** *NuLife 74321895622* TALISMAN P MEETS BARRINGTON LEVY	37		2

Silver-selling ● Gold-selling ● Platinum-selling (x multiples) ⊛ US No.1 ★ Peak Position Weeks at No.1 Weeks on Chart

JONA LEWIE

UK, male vocalist (John Lewis). See Terry Dactyl & The Dinosaurs — 22

Date	Title	Peak	Wks No.1	Wks
10 May 80	YOU'LL ALWAYS FIND ME IN THE KITCHEN AT PARTIES *Stiff BUY 73*	16		9
29 Nov 80	STOP THE CAVALRY *Stiff BUY 104* ●	3		11
22 Dec 07	STOP THE CAVALRY *Stiff GB1758500190*	48		2

ANDY LEWIS & PAUL WELLER

UK, male vocal/instrumental/production duo — 1

Date	Title	Peak	Wks No.1	Wks
22 Sep 07	ARE YOU TRYING TO BE LONELY *Acid Jazz AJX193CD*	31		1

CJ LEWIS

UK, male vocalist (Steven Lewis). See Childliners — 32

Date	Title	Peak	Wks No.1	Wks
23 Apr 94	SWEETS FOR MY SWEET *Black Market BMITD 017*	3		13
23 Jul 94	EVERYTHING IS ALRIGHT (UPTIGHT) *Black Market BMITD 019*	10		7
8 Oct 94	BEST OF MY LOVE *Black Market BMITD 021*	13		6
17 Dec 94	DOLLARS *Black Market BMITD 023*	34		4
9 Sep 95	R TO THE A *Black Market BMITD 030*	34		2

DANNY J LEWIS

UK, male producer — 2

Date	Title	Peak	Wks No.1	Wks
20 Jun 98	SPEND THE NIGHT *Locked On LOX 98CD*	29		2

DARLENE LEWIS

US, female vocalist — 4

Date	Title	Peak	Wks No.1	Wks
16 Apr 94	LET THE MUSIC (LIFT YOU UP) *KMS/Eastern Bloc KMSCD 10* LOVELAND FEATURING RACHEL McFARLANE Vs DARLENE LEWIS	16		4

DEE LEWIS

UK, female vocalist — 5

Date	Title	Peak	Wks No.1	Wks
18 Jun 88	BEST OF MY LOVE *Mercury DEE 3*	47		5

DONNA LEWIS

UK, female vocalist — 16

Date	Title	Peak	Wks No.1	Wks
7 Sep 96	I LOVE YOU ALWAYS FOREVER *Atlantic A 5495CD* ●	5		14
8 Feb 97	WITHOUT LOVE *Atlantic A 5468CD*	39		2

GARY LEWIS & THE PLAYBOYS

US, male vocal/instrumental group — 7

Date	Title	Peak	Wks No.1	Wks
8 Feb 75	MY HEART'S SYMPHONY *United Artists UP 35780*	36		7

HUEY LEWIS & THE NEWS

US, male vocal/instrumental group – Huey Lewis (Hugh Cregg), Mario Cipollina, Johnny Colla, Bill Gibson, Chris Hayes & Sean Hopper — 66

Date	Title	Peak	Wks No.1	Wks
27 Oct 84	IF THIS IS IT *Chrysalis CHS 2803*	39		6
31 Aug 85	THE POWER OF LOVE *Chrysalis HUEY 1* ★	11		10
23 Nov 85	HEART AND SOUL (EP) *Chrysalis HUEY 2*	61		4
8 Feb 86	THE POWER OF LOVE/DO YOU BELIEVE IN LOVE *Chrysalis HUEY 3* ●	9		12
10 May 86	THE HEART OF ROCK AND ROLL *Chrysalis HUEY 4*	49		3
23 Aug 86	STUCK WITH YOU *Chrysalis HUEY 5* ★	12		12
6 Dec 86	HIP TO BE SQUARE *Chrysalis HUEY 6*	41		8
21 Mar 87	SIMPLE AS THAT *Chrysalis HUEY 7*	47		5
16 Jul 88	PERFECT WORLD *Chrysalis HUEY 10*	48		6

JERRY LEWIS

US, male comedian/vocalist (Joseph Levitch) — 8

Date	Title	Peak	Wks No.1	Wks
8 Feb 57	ROCK-A-BYE YOUR BABY (WITH A DIXIE MELODY) *Brunswick 05636*	12		8

JERRY LEE LEWIS

US, male vocalist/pianist — 68

Date	Title	Peak	Wks No.1	Wks
27 Sep 57	WHOLE LOTTA SHAKIN' GOIN' ON *London HLS 8457*	8		11
20 Dec 57	GREAT BALLS OF FIRE *London HLS 8529*	1	2	12
11 Apr 58	BREATHLESS *London HLS 8592*	8		7
23 Jan 59	HIGH SCHOOL CONFIDENTIAL *London HLS 8780*	12		6
1 May 59	LOVIN' UP A STORM *London HLS 8840*	28		1
9 Jun 60	BABY BABY BYE BYE *London HLS 9131*	47		1
4 May 61	WHAT'D I SAY *London HLS 9335*	10		14
6 Sep 62	SWEET LITTLE SIXTEEN *London HLS 9584*	38		5
14 Mar 63	GOOD GOLLY MISS MOLLY *London HLS 9688*	31		6
6 May 72	CHANTILLY LACE *Mercury 6052 141*	33		5

LEONA LEWIS

UK, female vocalist. See Helping Haiti — 133

Date	Title	Peak	Wks No.1	Wks
30 Dec 06	A MOMENT LIKE THIS *Syco Music 88697050872* ⊛	1	4	14
3 Nov 07	BLEEDING LOVE *Syco Music 88697175622* ⊛ ★	1	7	28
3 Nov 07	FORGIVENESS *Syco Music GBHMU0700061*	46		2
24 Nov 07	WHATEVER IT TAKES *Syco Music GBHMU0700066*	61		1
24 Nov 07	FOOTPRINTS IN THE SAND *Syco Music GBHMU0700062*	25		8
24 Nov 07	THE FIRST TIME EVER I SAW YOUR FACE *Syco Music GBHMU0700076*	73		1
1 Mar 08	BETTER IN TIME/FOOTPRINTS IN THE SAND *Syco Music 88697272002*	2		22
8 Mar 08	BETTER IN TIME *Syco Music GBHMU0700069*	23		2
15 Nov 08	FORGIVE ME *Syco Music 88697337602*	5		9
13 Dec 08	RUN *Syco Music GBHMU0800023* ●	1	2	24
21 Nov 09	HAPPY *Syco Music 88697574692* ●	2		9
21 Nov 09	RUN *Syco Music GBHMU0800023*	67		1
28 Nov 09	STOP CRYING YOUR HEART OUT *Syco Music GBHMU0900080*	29		4
20 Feb 10	I GOT YOU *Syco Music 88697653042*	14		8+

Top 3 Best-Selling Singles

		Approximate Sales
1	BLEEDING LOVE	990,000
2	A MOMENT LIKE THIS	870,000
3	RUN	630,000

LINDA LEWIS

UK, female vocalist — 31

Date	Title	Peak	Wks No.1	Wks
2 Jun 73	ROCK-A-DOODLE-DOO *Raft RA 18502*	15		11
12 Jul 75	IT'S IN HIS KISS *Arista 17*	6		8
17 Apr 76	BABY I'M YOURS *Arista 43*	33		6
2 Jun 79	I'D BE SURPRISINGLY GOOD FOR YOU *Ariola ARO 166*	40		5
19 Aug 00	REACH OUT *Skint 54CD* MIDFIELD GENERAL FEATURING LINDA LEWIS	61		1

RAMSEY LEWIS

US, male instrumental trio — 8

Date	Title	Peak	Wks No.1	Wks
15 Apr 72	WADE IN THE WATER *Chess 6145 004*	31		8

SHAZNAY LEWIS

UK, female vocalist (Tricia Lewis). See All Saints — 14

Date	Title	Peak	Wks No.1	Wks
17 Jul 04	NEVER FELT LIKE THIS BEFORE *London LONCD484*	8		10
30 Oct 04	YOU *London LONCD486*	56		1
10 May 08	DADDY O *All Around The World CDGLOBE863* WIDEBOYS FEATURING SHAZNAY LEWIS	32		3

JOHN LEYTON

UK, male actor/vocalist — 70

Date	Title	Peak	Wks No.1	Wks
3 Aug 61	JOHNNY REMEMBER ME *Top Rank JAR 577*	1	3	15
5 Oct 61	WILD WIND *Top Rank JAR 585*	2		10
28 Dec 61	SON THIS IS SHE *HMV POP 956*	15		10
15 Mar 62	LONE RIDER *HMV POP 992*	40		5
3 May 62	LONELY CITY *HMV POP 1014*	14		11
23 Aug 62	DOWN THE RIVER NILE *HMV POP 1054*	42		3
21 Feb 63	CUPBOARD LOVE *HMV POP 1122*	22		12
18 Jul 63	I'LL CUT YOUR TAIL OFF *HMV POP 1175*	36		3
20 Feb 64	MAKE LOVE TO ME *HMV POP 1264* & THE LeROYS	49		1

LEYTON BUZZARDS

UK, male vocal/instrumental group — 5

Date	Title	Peak	Wks No.1	Wks
3 Mar 79	SATURDAY NIGHT (BENEATH THE PLASTIC PALM TREES) *Chrysalis CHS 2288*	53		5

LFO

UK, male production duo — 15

Date	Title	Peak	Wks No.1	Wks
14 Jul 90	LFO *Warp WAP 5*	12		10
6 Jul 91	WE ARE BACK/NURTURE *Warp 7WAP 14*	47		3
1 Feb 92	WHAT IS HOUSE (EP) *Warp WAP 17*	62		2

LIARS
US, male vocal/instrumental group — Weeks on Chart: 1

Date	Title / Label	Peak Position	Weeks at No.1	Weeks on Chart
21 Feb 04	**THERE'S ALWAYS ROOM ON THE BROOM** *Mute CDMUTE 317*	74		1

LIBERACE
US, male pianist/vocalist (Wladziu Valentino Liberace), d. 4 Feb 1987 (age 67) — Weeks on Chart: 2

Date	Title / Label	Peak Position	Weeks at No.1	Weeks on Chart
17 Jun 55	**UNCHAINED MELODY** *Philips PB 430*	20		1
19 Oct 56	**I DON'T CARE (AS LONG AS YOU CARE FOR ME)** *Columbia DB 3834*	28		1

LIBERATION
UK, male production duo — Weeks on Chart: 3

Date	Title / Label	Peak Position	Weeks at No.1	Weeks on Chart
24 Oct 92	**LIBERATION** *ZYX 68657*	28		3

LIBERTINES
UK, male vocal/instrumental group – Pete Doherty*, Carl Barat, John Hassall & Gary Powell. See Babyshambles, Dirty Pretty Things, Littl'ans featuring Peter Doherty, Wolfman — Weeks on Chart: 20

Date	Title / Label	Peak Position	Weeks at No.1	Weeks on Chart
15 Jun 02	**WHAT A WASTER** *Rough Trade RTRADESCD 054*	37		2
12 Oct 02	**UP THE BRACKET** *Rough Trade RTRADESCD 064*	29		2
25 Jan 03	**TIME FOR HEROES** *Rough Trade RTRADESCD 074*	20		2
30 Aug 03	**DON'T LOOK BACK INTO THE SUN** *Rough Trade RTRADESCD 120*	11		4
21 Aug 04	**CAN'T STAND ME NOW** *Rough Trade RTRADSCDX 163*	2		6
6 Nov 04	**WHAT BECAME OF THE LIKELY LADS** *Rough Trade RTRADSCD 215*	9		4

LIBERTY X
UK/Ireland, female/male vocal group – Michelle Heaton, Tony Lundon, Jessica Taylor & Kelli Young. See Girls Of *FHM* — Weeks on Chart: 92

Date	Title / Label	Peak Position	Weeks at No.1	Weeks on Chart
6 Oct 01	**THINKING IT OVER** *V2 VVR 5017773* LIBERTY	5		8
15 Dec 01	**DOIN' IT** *V2 VVR 5017798* LIBERTY	14		6
25 May 02	**JUST A LITTLE** *V2 VVR 5018968* ●	1	1	16
21 Sep 02	**GOT TO HAVE YOUR LOVE** *V2 VVR 5020508*	2		12
14 Dec 02	**HOLDING ON FOR YOU** *V2 VVR 5020768*	5		11
29 Mar 03	**BEING NOBODY** *Virgin RXCD1* RICHARD X VS LIBERTY X	3		11
1 Nov 03	**JUMPIN'** *V2 VVR 5023549*	6		7
24 Jan 04	**EVERYBODY CRIES** *V2 VVR5023558*	13		5
8 Oct 05	**SONG 4 LOVERS** *Virgin/EMI VTSCDX8*	5		9
26 Nov 05	**A NIGHT TO REMEMBER** *EMI Virgin/Unique VTSCDX9*	6		6
1 Jul 06	**X** *EMI Virgin/Unique VTSCD10*	47		1

LIBIDO
Norway, male vocal/instrumental group — Weeks on Chart: 1

Date	Title / Label	Peak Position	Weeks at No.1	Weeks on Chart
31 Jan 98	**OVERTHROWN** *Fire BLAZE 119CD*	53		1

LIBRA PRESENTS TAYLOR
US, male/female vocal/production trio. See BT — Weeks on Chart: 3

Date	Title / Label	Peak Position	Weeks at No.1	Weeks on Chart
26 Oct 96	**ANOMALY – CALLING YOUR NAME** *Platipus PLATCD 24*	71		1
18 Mar 00	**ANOMALY – CALLING YOUR NAME (REMIX)** *Platipus PLATCD 56*	43		2

LICK THE TINS
UK, male/female vocal/instrumental group — Weeks on Chart: 8

Date	Title / Label	Peak Position	Weeks at No.1	Weeks on Chart
29 Mar 86	**CAN'T HELP FALLING IN LOVE** *Sedition EDIT 3308*	42		8

OLIVER LIEB PRESENTS SMOKED
Germany, male DJ/producer. See LSG — Weeks on Chart: 1

Date	Title / Label	Peak Position	Weeks at No.1	Weeks on Chart
30 Sep 00	**METROPOLIS** *Duty Free DF 019CD*	72		1

BEN LIEBRAND
Holland, male DJ/producer. See La Fleur — Weeks on Chart: 2

Date	Title / Label	Peak Position	Weeks at No.1	Weeks on Chart
9 Jun 90	**PULS(T)AR** *Epic LIEB 1*	68		2

LIEUTENANT PIGEON
UK, male vocal/instrumental group – Robert Woodward, Nigel Fletcher, Steve Johnson & Hilda Woodward, d. 22 Feb 1999 — Weeks on Chart: 29

Date	Title / Label	Peak Position	Weeks at No.1	Weeks on Chart
16 Sep 72	**MOULDY OLD DOUGH** *Decca F 13278*	1	4	19
16 Dec 72	**DESPERATE DAN** *Decca F 13365*	17		10

LIFEHOUSE
US, male vocal/instrumental group — Weeks on Chart: 4

Date	Title / Label	Peak Position	Weeks at No.1	Weeks on Chart
8 Sep 01	**HANGING BY A MOMENT** *DreamWorks 4508942*	25		4

LIGHT OF THE WORLD
UK, male vocal/instrumental group — Weeks on Chart: 25

Date	Title / Label	Peak Position	Weeks at No.1	Weeks on Chart
14 Apr 79	**SWINGIN'** *Ensign ENY 22*	45		5
14 Jul 79	**MIDNIGHT GROOVIN'** *Ensign ENY 29*	72		1
18 Oct 80	**LONDON TOWN** *Ensign ENY 43*	41		5
17 Jan 81	**I SHOT THE SHERIFF** *Ensign ENY 46*	40		5
28 Mar 81	**I'M SO HAPPY/TIME** *Ensign ENY 64*	35		6
21 Nov 81	**RIDE THE LOVE TRAIN** *EMI 5242*	49		3

LIGHTER SHADE OF BROWN
US, male rap duo — Weeks on Chart: 3

Date	Title / Label	Peak Position	Weeks at No.1	Weeks on Chart
9 Jul 94	**HEY DJ** *Mercury MERCD 401*	33		3

GORDON LIGHTFOOT
Canada, male vocalist/guitarist — Weeks on Chart: 26

Date	Title / Label	Peak Position	Weeks at No.1	Weeks on Chart
19 Jun 71	**IF YOU COULD READ MY MIND** *Reprise K 20974*	30		9
3 Aug 74	**SUNDOWN** *Reprise K 14327* ★	33		7
15 Jan 77	**THE WRECK OF THE EDMUND FITZGERALD** *Reprise K 14451*	40		4
16 Sep 78	**DAYLIGHT KATY** *Warner Brothers K 17214*	41		6

TERRY LIGHTFOOT & HIS NEW ORLEANS JAZZMEN
UK, male vocal/instrumental group — Weeks on Chart: 17

Date	Title / Label	Peak Position	Weeks at No.1	Weeks on Chart
7 Sep 61	**TRUE LOVE** *Columbia DB 4696*	33		4
23 Nov 61	**KING KONG** *Columbia SCD 2165*	29		12
3 May 62	**TAVERN IN THE TOWN** *Columbia DB 4822*	49		1

LIGHTFORCE
Germany, male production duo — Weeks on Chart: 1

Date	Title / Label	Peak Position	Weeks at No.1	Weeks on Chart
28 Oct 00	**JOIN ME** *Slinky Music SLINKY 004CD*	53		1

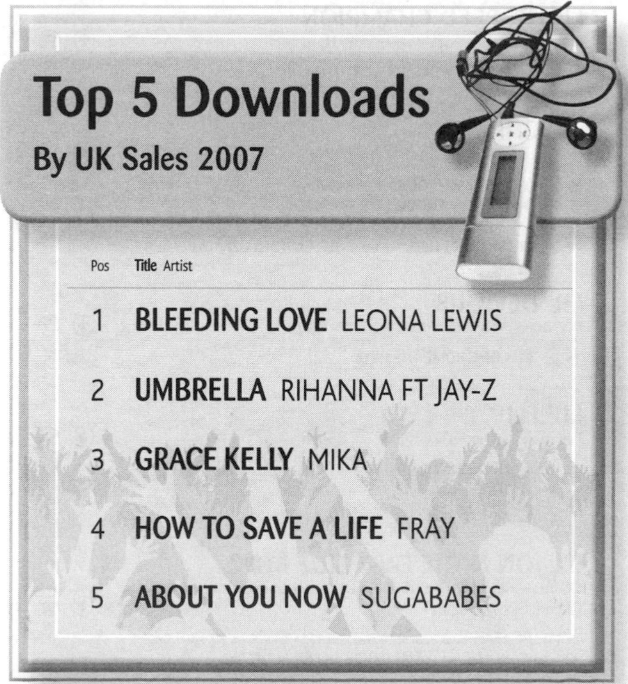

Top 5 Downloads
By UK Sales 2007

Pos	Title Artist
1	**BLEEDING LOVE** LEONA LEWIS
2	**UMBRELLA** RIHANNA FT JAY-Z
3	**GRACE KELLY** MIKA
4	**HOW TO SAVE A LIFE** FRAY
5	**ABOUT YOU NOW** SUGABABES

Silver-selling ○ Gold-selling ● Platinum-selling (x multiples) ⊛ US No.1 ★ Peak Position · Weeks at No.1 · Weeks on Chart

LIGHTHOUSE FAMILY

UK/Nigeria, male vocal/instrumental duo – Tunde Baiyewu (Tunde*) & Paul Tucker

Date	Title	Peak	Wks at No.1	Wks on Chart
				89
27 May 95	**LIFTED** *Wild Card CARDW 17*	61		2
14 Oct 95	**OCEAN DRIVE** *Wild Card 5797072*	34		3
10 Feb 96	**LIFTED** *Wild Card 5779432* ○	4		10
1 Jun 96	**OCEAN DRIVE** *Wild Card 5766192*	11		8
21 Sep 96	**GOODBYE HEARTBREAK** *Wild Card 5753492*	14		6
21 Dec 96	**LOVING EVERY MINUTE** *Wild Card 5731012*	20		7
11 Oct 97	**RAINCLOUD** *Wild Card 5717932*	6		7
10 Jan 98	**HIGH** *Wild Card 5691492* ○	4		14
27 Jun 98	**LOST IN SPACE** *Polydor 5670592*	6		8
10 Oct 98	**QUESTION OF FAITH** *Wild Card 5673932*	21		5
9 Jan 99	**POSTCARD FROM HEAVEN** *Wild Card 5633952*	24		6
24 Nov 01	**(I WISH I KNEW HOW IT WOULD FEEL TO BE) FREE/ONE** *Wild Card 5873812*	6		9
9 Mar 02	**RUN** *Wild Card 5705702*	30		3
6 Jul 02	**HAPPY** *Wild Card 5707912*	51		1

LIGHTNING SEEDS

UK, male vocal/instrumental group – Ian Broudie, Martin Campbell, Paul Hemmings & Chris Sharrock

Date	Title	Peak	Wks at No.1	Wks on Chart
				110
22 Jul 89	**PURE** *Ghetto GTG 4*	16		8
14 Mar 92	**THE LIFE OF RILEY** *Virgin VS 1402*	28		6
30 May 92	**SENSE** *Virgin VS 1414*	31		5
20 Aug 94	**LUCKY YOU** *Epic 6606282*	43		2
14 Jan 95	**CHANGE** *Epic 6609865*	13		6
15 Apr 95	**MARVELLOUS** *Epic 6614265*	24		5
22 Jul 95	**PERFECT** *Epic 6621792*	18		5
21 Oct 95	**LUCKY YOU** *Epic 6625182*	15		6
9 Mar 96	**READY OR NOT** *Epic 6629672*	20		4
1 Jun 96	**THREE LIONS (THE OFFICIAL SONG OF THE ENGLAND FOOTBALL TEAM)** *Epic 6632732* BADDIEL & SKINNER & LIGHTNING SEEDS ⊛	1	2	15
2 Nov 96	**WHAT IF...** *Epic 6638635*	14		4
18 Jan 97	**SUGAR COATED ICEBERG** *Epic 6640435*	12		4
26 Apr 97	**YOU SHOWED ME** *Epic 6643282*	8		5
13 Dec 97	**WHAT YOU SAY** *Epic 6653572*	41		5
20 Jun 98	**THREE LIONS '98** *Epic 6660982* BADDIEL & SKINNER & LIGHTNING SEEDS ⊛	1	3	13
27 Nov 99	**LIFE'S TOO SHORT** *Epic 6681502*	27		4
18 Mar 00	**SWEET SOUL SENSATIONS** *Epic 6689422*	67		1
15 Jun 02	**THREE LIONS** *Epic 6728152* BADDIEL & SKINNER & LIGHTNING SEEDS	16		6
10 Jun 06	**THREE LIONS** *Epic 82876856672* BADDIEL & SKINNER & LIGHTNING SEEDS	9		6

LIGHTSPEED CHAMPION

UK (b. US), male vocalist (Devonte Hynes)

Date	Title	Peak	Wks at No.1	Wks on Chart
				1
26 Jan 08	**TELL ME WHAT IT'S WORTH** *Domino RUG273CD*	72		1

LIL' CHRIS

UK, male vocalist (Chris Hardman)

Date	Title	Peak	Wks at No.1	Wks on Chart
				24
30 Sep 06	**CHECKIN' IT OUT** *RCA 88697002812*	3		14
16 Dec 06	**GETTING' ENOUGH** *RCA 88697035232*	17		6
10 Mar 07	**FIGURE IT OUT** *RCA 88697061382*	57		1
29 Sep 07	**WE DON'T HAVE TO TAKE OUR CLOTHES OFF** *RCA GBARL0701022*	63		3

LIL' DEVIOUS

UK, male production duo. See Percy Faith

Date	Title	Peak	Wks at No.1	Wks on Chart
				1
15 Sep 01	**COME HOME** *Rulin 16CDS*	55		1

LIL' FLIP

US, male rapper (Wesley 'Eric' Weston, Jr)

Date	Title	Peak	Wks at No.1	Wks on Chart
				6
11 Sep 04	**NEVER REALLY WAS** *Bad Boy MCSTD40372* MARIO WINANS FEATURING LIL' FLIP	44		2
30 Oct 04	**SUNSHINE** *Columbia 6751842*	14		4

LIL JON & THE EAST SIDE BOYZ

US, male rap trio – Jonathan Smith, Big Sam (Sam Norris) & Lil' Bo (Wendell Neal)

Date	Title	Peak	Wks at No.1	Wks on Chart
				40
27 Mar 04	**YEAH** *Arista 82876606012* USHER FEATURING LIL' JON & LUDACRIS ★	1	2	14
12 Feb 05	**ROLL CALL/WHAT U GON' DO** *TVT TVTUKCDX2*	38		3
26 Feb 05	**LET'S GO** *Atlantic AT0193CD* TRICK DADDY FEATURING TWISTA & LIL' JON	26		2
14 May 05	**GET LOW/LOVERS & FRIENDS** *TVT TVTUKCD9*	10		7
16 Jul 05	**GIRLFIGHT** *Virgin VUSDX301* BROOKE VALENTINE FEATURING BIG BOI & LIL' JON	35		2
23 Jan 10	**DO YOU REMEMBER** *Island 2733342* JAY SEAN FEATURING SEAN PAUL & LIL JON	13		12+

LIL' KIM

US, female rapper (Kimberly Jones)

Date	Title	Peak	Wks at No.1	Wks on Chart
				68
26 Apr 97	**NO TIME** *Atlantic A 5594CD* FEATURING PUFF DADDY	45		1
5 Jul 97	**CRUSH ON YOU** *Atlantic AT 0002CD*	36		2
16 Aug 97	**NOT TONIGHT** *Atlantic AT 0007CD*	11		5
25 Oct 97	**CRUSH ON YOU** *Atlantic AT 0002CD*	23		3
22 Aug 98	**HIT 'EM WIT DA HEE** *East West E 3824CD1* MISSY 'MISDEMEANOR' ELLIOTT FEATURING LIL' KIM	25		3
5 Feb 00	**NOTORIOUS B.I.G.** *Puff Daddy 74321737312* NOTORIOUS B.I.G. FEATURING PUFF DADDY AND LIL' KIM	16		5
2 Sep 00	**NO MATTER WHAT THEY SAY** *Atlantic 7567846972*	35		2
30 Jun 01	**LADY MARMALADE** *Interscope 4975612* CHRISTINA AGUILERA/LIL' KIM/MYA/P!NK ● ★	1	1	16
11 Aug 01	**WAIT A MINUTE** *Atlantic AT 0106CD* RAY J FEATURING LIL' KIM	54		1
22 Sep 01	**IN THE AIR TONITE** *WEA 331CD* FEATURING PHIL COLLINS	26		2
10 May 03	**THE JUMP OFF** *Atlantic AT 0151CD* FEATURING MR CHEEKS	16		7
20 Sep 03	**CAN'T HOLD US DOWN** *RCA 82876556332* CHRISTINA AGUILERA FEATURING LIL' KIM	6		9
19 Nov 05	**LIGHTERS UP** *Atlantic AT0226CD*	12		9
27 May 06	**WHOA** *Atlantic AT0241CDX*	43		3

LIL' LOUIS

US, male producer (Marvin Louis Burns)

Date	Title	Peak	Wks at No.1	Wks on Chart
				21
29 Jul 89	**FRENCH KISS** *ffrr FX 115* ○	2		11
13 Jan 90	**I CALLED U** *ffrr F 123*	16		6
26 Sep 92	**SAVED MY LIFE** *ffrr FX 197* & THE WORLD	74		1
12 Aug 00	**HOW'S YOUR EVENING SO FAR** *ffrr FCD 384* JOSH WINK & LIL' LOUIS	23		3

LIL' LOVE

Italy, male/female vocal/production trio

Date	Title	Peak	Wks at No.1	Wks on Chart
				2
27 Aug 05	**LITTLE LOVE** *Positiva CDTIVS222*	34		2

LIL' MAMA FEATURING CHRIS BROWN & T-PAIN

US, female/male rap/vocal trio

Date	Title	Peak	Wks at No.1	Wks on Chart
				3
17 May 08	**SHAWTY GET LOOSE** *Jive JIV7270821*	57		3

LIL' MO

US, female vocalist (Cynthia Long)

Date	Title	Peak	Wks at No.1	Wks on Chart
				12
21 Nov 98	**5 MINUTES** *Elektra E 3803CD* FEATURING MISSY 'MISDEMEANOR' ELLIOTT	72		1
23 Sep 00	**WHATEVER** *Virgin VUSCD 172* IDEAL US FEATURING LIL' MO	31		3
6 Apr 02	**WHERE'S MY** *EMI CDEMS 598* ADAM F FEATURING LIL' MO	37		2
15 Feb 03	**IF I COULD GO** *Elektra E 7331CD* ANGIE MARTINEZ FEATURING LIL MO	61		1
16 Aug 03	**CAN'T LET YOU GO** *Elektra E 7408CD* FABOLOUS FEATURING MIKE SHOREY & LIL' MO	14		5

LIL MO' YIN YANG

US, male instrumental/production duo. See Pianoheadz, Reel To Real featuring the Mad Stuntman

Date	Title	Peak	Wks at No.1	Wks on Chart
				2
9 Mar 96	**REACH** *Multiply CDMULTY 9*	28		2

LIL' ROMEO

US, male rapper (Percy Miller)

Date	Title	Peak	Wks at No.1	Wks on Chart
				1
22 Sep 01	**MY BABY** *Priority PTYCD 136*	67		1

LIL' WAYNE

US, male rapper (Dwayne Carter, Jr). See Young Money featuring Lloyd

Date	Title	Peak	Wks at No.1	Wks on Chart
				108
19 Feb 05	**SOLDIER** *Columbia 6757622* DESTINY'S CHILD FEATURING TI & LIL' WAYNE	4		7
22 Jul 06	**GIMME THAT REMIX** *Jive 82876880762* CHRIS BROWN FEATURING LIL' WAYNE	23		6
1 Dec 07	**SWEETEST GIRL (DOLLAR BILL)** *Columbia USSM10703185* WYCLEF JEAN FEATURING AKON, LIL WAYNE & NIIA	66		1
26 Apr 08	**LOLLIPOP** *Island 1771898* ★	26		15
27 Sep 08	**SWAGGA LIKE US** *Mercury USUM70835786* JAY-Z FEATURING KANYE WEST & LIL WAYNE	33		2

Date	Title	Peak Position	Weeks at No.1	Weeks on Chart
27 Sep 08	**MY LIFE** *Geffen 1788570* GAME FEATURING LIL WAYNE	34		7
1 Nov 08	**I'M SO PAID** *Island USUM70842012* AKON FEATURING LIL WAYNE	59		3
6 Dec 08	**MRS OFFICER** *Island 1787327* LIL WAYNE, BOBBY VALENTINO, KIDD KIDD	57		3
13 Dec 08	**LET IT ROCK** *Island 1796243* KEVIN RUDOLF FEATURING LIL' WAYNE	5		19
7 Nov 09	**DOWN** *Island 2724316* JAY SEAN FEATURING LIL WAYNE ★	3		16
14 Nov 09	**I CAN TRANSFORM YA** *JiveUSJI10900612* CHRIS BROWN FEATURING LIL' WAYNE	26		13
19 Dec 09	**FOREVER** *Interscope USUM70985104* DRAKE FEATURING KANYE WEST, LIL WAYNE & EMINEM	42		12
23 Jan 10	**DROP THE WORLD** *Cash Money USCM50901210* FEATURING EMINEM	51		4+

LILYS
US, male vocal/instrumental group — 4

Date	Title	Peak Position	Weeks at No.1	Weeks on Chart
21 Feb 98	**A NANNY IN MANHATTAN** *Che 77CD*	16		4

LIMAHL
UK, male vocalist (Chris Hamill). See Kajagoogoo — 25

Date	Title	Peak Position	Weeks at No.1	Weeks on Chart
5 Nov 83	**ONLY FOR LOVE** *EMI LML 1*	16		8
2 Jun 84	**TOO MUCH TROUBLE** *EMI LML 2*	64		3
13 Oct 84	**NEVER ENDING STORY** *EMI LML 3* ●	4		14

ALISON LIMERICK
UK, female vocalist — 41

Date	Title	Peak Position	Weeks at No.1	Weeks on Chart
30 Mar 91	**WHERE LOVE LIVES** *Arista 114208*	27		8
12 Oct 91	**COME BACK (FOR REAL LOVE)** *Arista 114530*	53		2
21 Dec 91	**MAGIC'S BACK (THEME FROM 'THE GHOSTS OF OXFORD STREET')** *RCA PB 45223* MALCOLM McLAREN FEATURING ALISON LIMERICK	42		4
29 Feb 92	**MAKE IT ON MY OWN** *Arista 114996*	16		6
18 Jul 92	**GETTING' IT RIGHT** *Arista 74321102867*	57		2
28 Nov 92	**HEAR MY CALL** *Arista 115337*	73		1
8 Jan 94	**TIME OF OUR LIVES** *Arista 74321180332*	36		4
19 Mar 94	**LOVE COME DOWN** *Arista 74321191952*	36		2
25 Feb 95	**LOVE WILL KEEP US TOGETHER** *Acid Jazz JAZID 112CD* JTQ FEATURING ALISON LIMERICK	63		1
6 Jul 96	**WHERE LOVE LIVES (REMIX)** *Arista 74321381592*	9		6
14 Sep 96	**MAKE IT ON MY OWN (REMIX)** *Arista 74321407812*	30		2
23 Aug 97	**PUT YOUR FAITH IN ME** *MBA XES 9001*	42		1
15 Mar 03	**WHERE LOVE LIVES** *Arista Dance 74321981442*	44		2

LIMIT
Holland, male vocal/production duo — 8

Date	Title	Peak Position	Weeks at No.1	Weeks on Chart
5 Jan 85	**SAY YEAH** *Portrait A 4808*	17		8

LIMMIE & THE FAMILY COOKIN'
US, male/female vocal group — Limmie, Martha & Jimmy Snell — 28

Date	Title	Peak Position	Weeks at No.1	Weeks on Chart
21 Jul 73	**YOU CAN DO MAGIC** *Avco 6105 019*	3		13
20 Oct 73	**DREAMBOAT** *Avco 6105 025*	31		5
6 Apr 74	**A WALKIN' MIRACLE** *Avco 6105 027*	6		10

LIMP BIZKIT
US, male vocal/instrumental group — Fred Durst, Wes Borland, John Otto & Sam Rivers — 62

Date	Title	Peak Position	Weeks at No.1	Weeks on Chart
15 Jul 00	**TAKE A LOOK AROUND** *Interscope 4973692* ●	3		13
11 Nov 00	**MY GENERATION** *Interscope IND 97448*	15		8
27 Jan 01	**ROLLIN'** *Interscope IND 97474* ●	1	2	13
23 Jun 01	**MY WAY** *Interscope 4975732*	6		10
10 Nov 01	**BOILER** *Interscope 4976362*	18		5
27 Sep 03	**EAT YOU ALIVE** *Interscope 9811757*	10		7
6 Dec 03	**BEHIND BLUE EYES** *Interscope 9814744*	18		6

LINA
US, female vocalist (Shelina Wade) — 1

Date	Title	Peak Position	Weeks at No.1	Weeks on Chart
3 Mar 01	**PLAYA NO MO'** *Atlantic AT 0094CD*	46		1

LINCOLN CITY FC FEATURING MICHAEL COURTNEY
UK, male football team vocalists & vocalist/actor — 1

Date	Title	Peak Position	Weeks at No.1	Weeks on Chart
4 May 02	**CHIRPY CHIRPY CHEEP CHEEP/JAGGED END** *Nap Music SLCPCD 001*	64		1

BOB LIND
US, male vocalist — 10

Date	Title	Peak Position	Weeks at No.1	Weeks on Chart
10 Mar 66	**ELUSIVE BUTTERFLY** *Fontana TF 670*	5		9
26 May 66	**REMEMBER THE RAIN** *Fontana TF 702*	46		1

LINDISFARNE
UK, male vocal/instrumental group — Alan Hull*, d. 17 Nov 1995, Rod Clements, Simon Cowe, Jesmond Dene, Ray Jackson & Ray Laidlaw — 55

Date	Title	Peak Position	Weeks at No.1	Weeks on Chart
26 Feb 72	**MEET ME ON THE CORNER** *Charisma CB 173*	5		11
13 May 72	**LADY ELEANOR** *Charisma CB 153*	3		11
23 Sep 72	**ALL FALL DOWN** *Charisma CB 191*	34		5
3 Jun 78	**RUN FOR HOME** *Mercury 6007 177* ●	10		15
7 Oct 78	**JUKE BOX GYPSY** *Mercury 6007 187*	56		4
10 Nov 90	**FOG ON THE TYNE (REVISITED)** *Best ZB 44083* GAZZA & LINDISFARNE	2		9

LINDSAY
UK, female vocalist (Lindsay Dracas) — 4

Date	Title	Peak Position	Weeks at No.1	Weeks on Chart
12 May 01	**NO DREAM IMPOSSIBLE** *Universal TV 1589562*	32		4

LINER
UK, male vocal/instrumental group — 6

Date	Title	Peak Position	Weeks at No.1	Weeks on Chart
10 Mar 79	**KEEP REACHING OUT FOR LOVE** *Atlantic K 11235*	49		3
26 May 79	**YOU AND ME** *Atlantic K 11285*	44		3

ANDY LING
UK, male producer — 1

Date	Title	Peak Position	Weeks at No.1	Weeks on Chart
13 May 00	**FIXATION** *Hooj Choons HOOJ 094CD*	55		1

LAURIE LINGO & THE DIPSTICKS
UK, male radio DJ/vocal duo — Dave Lee Travis & Paul Burnett — 7

Date	Title	Peak Position	Weeks at No.1	Weeks on Chart
17 Apr 76	**CONVOY G.B.** *State STAT 23* ●	4		7

LINK
US, male rapper (Lincoln Browder) — 1

Date	Title	Peak Position	Weeks at No.1	Weeks on Chart
7 Nov 98	**WHATCHA GONE DO?** *Relativity 6666055*	48		1

LINKIN PARK
US, male vocal/instrumental/production group — Chester Bennington, Rob Bourdon, Brad Delson, David Farrell, Joseph Hahn & Mike Shinoda — 153

Date	Title	Peak Position	Weeks at No.1	Weeks on Chart
27 Jan 01	**ONE STEP CLOSER** *Warner Brothers W 550CD*	24		4
21 Apr 01	**CRAWLING** *Warner Brothers W 556CD*	16		8
30 Jun 01	**PAPERCUT** *Warner Brothers W 562CD*	14		6
20 Oct 01	**IN THE END** *Warner Brothers W 569CD*	8		9
3 Aug 02	**HIGH VOLTAGE/POINTS OF AUTHORITY** *Warner Brothers W 588CD*	9		6
29 Mar 03	**SOMEWHERE I BELONG** *Warner Brothers W 602CD*	10		8
21 Jun 03	**FAINT** *Warner Brothers W 610CD*	15		8
20 Sep 03	**NUMB** *Warner Brothers W 622CD*	14		6
19 Jun 04	**BREAKING THE HABIT** *Warner Brothers W 645CD*	39		2
4 Dec 04	**NUMB/ENCORE** *WEA W660CD* JAY-Z VS LINKIN PARK	14		43
14 Apr 07	**WHAT I'VE DONE** *Warner Brothers W762CD1*	6		20
25 Aug 07	**BLEED IT** *Warner Brothers W772CD*	29		6
24 Nov 07	**SHADOW OF THE DAY** *Warner Brothers W790CD*	46		2
28 Jun 08	**WE MADE IT** *Warner Brothers W810CD* BUSTA RHYMES FEATURING LINKIN PARK	10		13
20 Jun 09	**NEW DIVIDE** *Warner Brothers USWB10901893*	19		12

LINOLEUM
UK, male/female vocal/instrumental group — 1

Date	Title	Peak Position	Weeks at No.1	Weeks on Chart
12 Jul 97	**MARQUIS** *Lino Vinyl LINO 004CD1*	73		1

LINX
UK, male vocal/instrumental duo — David Grant* & Peter 'Sketch' Martin — 45

Date	Title	Peak Position	Weeks at No.1	Weeks on Chart
20 Sep 80	**YOU'RE LYING** *Chrysalis CHS 2461*	15		10
7 Mar 81	**INTUITION** *Chrysalis CHS 2500* ●	7		11
13 Jun 81	**THROW AWAY THE KEY** *Chrysalis CHS 2519*	21		9
5 Sep 81	**SO THIS IS ROMANCE** *Chrysalis CHS 2546*	15		9

Silver-selling ● Gold-selling ● Platinum-selling (x multiples) ⊛ US No.1 ★ | Peak Position | Weeks at No.1 | Weeks on Chart

Date	Title	Peak Position	Weeks at No.1	Weeks on Chart
21 Nov 81	**CAN'T HELP MYSELF** *Chrysalis CHS 2565*	55		3
10 Jul 82	**PLAYTHING** *Chrysalis CHS 2621*	48		3

LIONROCK

UK, male producer (Justin Robertson) — 14

Date	Title	Peak Position	Weeks at No.1	Weeks on Chart
5 Dec 92	**LIONROCK** *Deconstruction 74321124381*	63		1
8 May 93	**PACKET OF PEACE** *Deconstruction 74321144372*	32		3
23 Oct 93	**CARNIVAL** *Deconstruction 74321164862*	34		2
27 Aug 94	**TRIPWIRE** *Deconstruction 74321204702*	44		1
6 Apr 96	**STRAIGHT AT YER HEAD** *Deconstruction 74321342972*	33		2
27 Jul 96	**FIRE UP THE SHOESAW** *Deconstruction 74321382652*	43		1
14 Mar 98	**RUDE BOY ROCK** *Concrete HARD 31CD*	20		3
30 May 98	**SCATTER & SWING** *Concrete HARD 35CD*	54		1

LIPPS INC

US, male producer (Steven Greenberg) with female vocalist (Cynthia Johnson) & session musicians — 13

Date	Title	Peak Position	Weeks at No.1	Weeks on Chart
17 May 80	**FUNKY TOWN** *Casablanca CAN 194* ● ★	2		13

LIQUID

UK, male producer (Eamon 'Ame' Downes) — 21

Date	Title	Peak Position	Weeks at No.1	Weeks on Chart
21 Mar 92	**SWEET HARMONY** *XL Recordings XLS 28*	15		6
5 Sep 92	**THE FUTURE MUSIC (EP)** *XL Recordings XLT 33*	59		2
20 Mar 93	**TIME TO GET UP** *XL Recordings XLS 40CD*	46		2
8 Jul 95	**SWEET HARMONY/ONE LOVE FAMILY** *XL Recordings XLS 65CD*	14		6
21 Oct 95	**CLOSER** *XL Recordings XLS 66CD*	47		2
25 Jul 98	**STRONG** *Higher Ground HIGHS 7CD*	59		1
21 Oct 00	**ORLANDO DAWN** *Xtravaganza XTRAV 16CDS*	53		1
13 Feb 10	**SWEET HARMONY** *Hospital NHS160* DANNY BYRD FEATURING LIQUID	64		1

LIQUID CHILD

Germany, male production duo — 2

Date	Title	Peak Position	Weeks at No.1	Weeks on Chart
23 Oct 99	**DIVING FACES** *Essential Recordings ESCD 9*	25		2

LIQUID GOLD

US, male/female vocal/instrumental group – Ellie Hope, Ray Knott, Tom Marshall, Wally 'Eddie' Rothe & Syd Twynham — 46

Date	Title	Peak Position	Weeks at No.1	Weeks on Chart
2 Dec 78	**ANYWAY YOU DO IT** *Creole CR 159*	41		7
23 Feb 80	**DANCE YOURSELF DIZZY** *Polo 1* ●	2		14
31 May 80	**SUBSTITUTE** *Polo 4*	8		9
1 Nov 80	**THE NIGHT THE WINE THE ROSES** *Polo 6*	32		7
28 Mar 81	**DON'T PANIC** *Polo 8*	42		5
21 Aug 82	**WHERE DID WE GO WRONG** *Polo 23*	56		4

LIQUID OXYGEN

US, male DJ/producer (Frankie Bones) — 2

Date	Title	Peak Position	Weeks at No.1	Weeks on Chart
28 Apr 90	**THE PLANET DANCE (MOVE YA BODY)** *Champion CHAMP 242*	56		2

LIQUID PEOPLE

UK, male vocal/instrumental/production group — 2

Date	Title	Peak Position	Weeks at No.1	Weeks on Chart
20 Jul 02	**MONSTER** *Defected DFECT 49R* VS SIMPLE MINDS	67		1
21 Jun 03	**IT'S MY LIFE** *Nebula NEBCD 045* VS TALK TALK	64		1

LIQUID STATE FEATURING MARCELLA WOODS

UK, male/female vocal/production trio. See Solar Stone, Z2 — 1

Date	Title	Peak Position	Weeks at No.1	Weeks on Chart
30 Mar 02	**FALLING** *Perfecto PERF 29CDS*	60		1

LISA LISA & CULT JAM

US, female vocalist (Lisa Velez) — 32

Date	Title	Peak Position	Weeks at No.1	Weeks on Chart
4 May 85	**I WONDER IF I TAKE YOU HOME** *CBS A 6057* WITH FULL FORCE	12		17
31 Oct 87	**LOST IN EMOTION** *CBS 6510367* ★	58		4
13 Jul 91	**LET THE BEAT HIT 'EM** *Columbia 6572867*	17		6
24 Aug 91	**LET THE BEAT HIT 'EM PART 2** *Columbia 6573747*	49		2
26 Mar 94	**SKIP TO MY LU** *Chrysalis CDCHS 5006* LISA LISA	34		3

LISA MARIE EXPERIENCE

UK, male instrumental/production duo – Neil Hynde & Dean Marriot — 17

Date	Title	Peak Position	Weeks at No.1	Weeks on Chart
27 Apr 96	**KEEP ON JUMPIN'** *ffrr FCD 271*	7		13
10 Aug 96	**DO THAT TO ME** *Positiva CDTIV 57*	33		2
16 Jun 07	**KEEP ON JUMPIN'** *Gusto CDGUS46* CORENELL & LISA MARIE EXPERIENCE	37		2

LISBON LIONS FEATURING MARTIN O'NEILL

UK, male footballers & manager (Celtic) & vocal group — 4

Date	Title	Peak Position	Weeks at No.1	Weeks on Chart
11 May 02	**THE BEST DAYS OF OUR LIVES** *Concept CDCON 32*	17		4

LIT

US, male vocal/instrumental group — 7

Date	Title	Peak Position	Weeks at No.1	Weeks on Chart
26 Jun 99	**MY OWN WORST ENEMY** *RCA 74321669992*	16		4
25 Sep 99	**ZIP – LOCK** *RCA 74321701852*	60		1
19 Aug 00	**OVER MY HEAD** *Capitol 8889532*	37		2

LITHIUM & SONYA MADAN

US/UK, male/female vocal/production duo. See Alcatraz, Echobelly, Submerge featuring Jan Johnston — 2

Date	Title	Peak Position	Weeks at No.1	Weeks on Chart
1 Mar 97	**RIDE A ROCKET** *ffrr FCD 293*	40		2

LITTL'ANS FEATURING PETER DOHERTY

UK, male vocal/instrumental group. See Babyshambles, Libertines, Wolfman — 2

Date	Title	Peak Position	Weeks at No.1	Weeks on Chart
29 Oct 05	**THEIR WAY** *Rough Trade RTRADSCD267*	22		2

DE ETTA LITTLE & NELSON PIGFORD

US, female/male vocal duo — 5

Date	Title	Peak Position	Weeks at No.1	Weeks on Chart
13 Aug 77	**YOU TAKE MY HEART AWAY** *United Artists UP 36257*	35		5

LITTLE ANGELS

UK, male vocal/instrumental group — 41

Date	Title	Peak Position	Weeks at No.1	Weeks on Chart
4 Mar 89	**BIG BAD EP** *Polydor LTLEP 2*	74		1
24 Feb 90	**KICKING UP DUST** *Polydor LTL 5*	46		4
12 May 90	**RADICAL YOUR LOVER** *Polydor LTL 6* FEATURING THE BIG BAD HORNS	34		4
4 Aug 90	**SHE'S A LITTLE ANGEL** *Polydor LTL 7*	21		3
2 Feb 91	**BONEYARD** *Polydor LTL 8*	33		4
30 Mar 91	**PRODUCT OF THE WORKING CLASS** *Polydor LTL 9*	40		2
1 Jun 91	**YOUNG GODS** *Polydor LTL 10*	34		2
20 Jul 91	**I AIN'T GONNA CRY** *Polydor LTL 11*	26		3
7 Nov 92	**TOO MUCH TOO YOUNG** *Polydor LTL 12*	22		3
9 Jan 93	**WOMANKIND** *Polydor LTLCD 13*	12		5
24 Apr 93	**SOAPBOX** *Polydor LTLCD 14*	33		4
25 Sep 93	**SAIL AWAY** *Polydor LTLCD 15*	45		3
9 Apr 94	**TEN MILES HIGH** *Polydor LTLCD 16*	18		3

LITTLE ANTHONY & THE IMPERIALS

US, male vocal group — 4

Date	Title	Peak Position	Weeks at No.1	Weeks on Chart
31 Jul 76	**BETTER USE YOUR HEAD** *United Artists UP 36141*	42		4

LITTLE BARRIE

UK, male vocal/instrumental trio — 1

Date	Title	Peak Position	Weeks at No.1	Weeks on Chart
5 Feb 05	**FREE SALUTE** *Genuine GEN032CD*	73		1

LITTLE BENNY & THE MASTERS

US, male trumpeter/vocalist (Anthony Harley), d. 30 May 2010 (age 46), & instrumental group — 7

Date	Title	Peak Position	Weeks at No.1	Weeks on Chart
2 Feb 85	**WHO COMES TO BOOGIE** *Bluebird/10 BR 13*	33		7

LITTLE BOOTS

UK, female vocalist/multi-instrumentalist (Victoria Hesketh) — 21

Date	Title	Peak Position	Weeks at No.1	Weeks on Chart
6 Jun 09	**NEW IN TOWN** *679 679L166CD*	13		6
8 Aug 09	**REMEDY** *679 679L167CD*	6		15

LITTLE CAESAR
UK, male vocal/production group

Date	Title	Peak	Wks at No.1	Wks (3)
9 Jun 90	**THE WHOLE OF THE MOON** *A1 EAU 1*	68		3

LITTLE EVA
US, female vocalist (Eva Boyd), d. 10 Apr 2003 (age 57)

Date	Title	Peak	Wks at No.1	Wks (45)
6 Sep 62	**THE LOCO-MOTION** *London HL 9581* ★	2		17
3 Jan 63	**KEEP YOUR HANDS OFF MY BABY** *London HLU 9633*	30		5
7 Mar 63	**LET'S TURKEY TROT** *London HLU 9687*	13		12
29 Jul 72	**THE LOCO-MOTION** *London HL 9581*	11		11

LITTLE JACKIE
US, female/male vocal/production duo. See Baha Men, Imani Coppola

Date	Title	Peak	Wks at No.1	Wks (6)
23 Aug 08	**THE WORLD SHOULD REVOLVE AROUND ME** *Parlophone LJ002*	14		6

LITTLE MAN TATE
UK, male vocal/instrumental group

Date	Title	Peak	Wks at No.1	Wks (7)
3 Jun 06	**WHAT? WHAT YOU GOT?** *V2 VVR5040553*	40		1
9 Sep 06	**HOUSE PARTY AT BOOTHY'S** *V2 VVR5041733*	29		1
25 Nov 06	**MAN I HATE YOUR BAND** *V2 VVR5042293*	26		1
3 Feb 07	**SEXY IN LATIN** *V2 VVR5042913*	20		2
14 Apr 07	**THIS MUST BE LOVE** *V2 VVR5044713*	33		1
21 Jun 08	**WHAT YOUR BOYFRIEND SAID** *Yellow Van YVAN01SCD*	60		1

LITTLE RICHARD
US, male vocalist/pianist (Richard Penniman)

Date	Title	Peak	Wks at No.1	Wks (116)
14 Dec 56	**RIP IT UP** *London HLO 8336*	30		1
8 Feb 57	**LONG TALL SALLY** *London HLO 8366*	3		16
22 Feb 57	**TUTTI FRUTTI** *London HLO 8366*	29		1
8 Mar 57	**SHE'S GOT IT** *London HLO 8382*	15		9
15 Mar 57	**THE GIRL CAN'T HELP IT** *London HLO 8382*	9		11
28 Jun 57	**LUCILLE** *London HLO 8446*	10		9
13 Sep 57	**JENNY JENNY** *London HLO 8470*	11		5
29 Nov 57	**KEEP A KNOCKIN'** *London HLO 8509*	21		7
28 Feb 58	**GOOD GOLLY MISS MOLLY** *London HLU 8560*	8		9
11 Jul 58	**OOH MY SOUL** *London HLO 8647*	22		4
2 Jan 59	**BABY FACE** *London HLU 8770*	2		15
3 Apr 59	**BY THE LIGHT OF THE SILVERY MOON** *London HLU 8831*	17		5
5 Jun 59	**KANSAS CITY** *London HLU 8868*	26		5
11 Oct 62	**HE GOT WHAT HE WANTED (BUT HE LOST WHAT HE HAD)** *Mercury AMT 1189*	38		4
4 Jun 64	**BAMA LAMA BAMA LOO** *London HL 9896*	20		7
2 Jul 77	**GOOD GOLLY MISS MOLLY/RIP IT UP** *Creole CR 140*	37		4
14 Jun 86	**GREAT GOSH A'MIGHTY (IT'S A MATTER OF TIME)** *MCA 1049*	62		2
25 Oct 86	**OPERATOR** *WEA YZ 89*	67		2

LITTLE STEVEN
US, male vocalist/guitarist (Steven Van Zandt)

Date	Title	Peak	Wks at No.1	Wks (3)
23 May 87	**BITTER FRUIT** *Manhattan MT 21*	66		3

LITTLE TONY
Italy, male vocalist (Anthony Ciacci)

Date	Title	Peak	Wks at No.1	Wks (3)
15 Jan 60	**TOO GOOD** *Decca F 11190*	19		3

LITTLE TREES
Denmark, female vocal group

Date	Title	Peak	Wks at No.1	Wks (7)
1 Sep 01	**HELP! I'M A FISH** *RCA 74321874652*	11		7

LIVE
US, male vocal/instrumental group

Date	Title	Peak	Wks at No.1	Wks (13)
18 Feb 95	**I ALONE** *Radioactive RAXTD 13*	48		4
1 Jul 95	**SELLING THE DRAMA** *Radioactive RAXXD 17*	30		2
7 Oct 95	**ALL OVER YOU** *Radioactive RAXTD 20*	48		1
13 Jan 96	**LIGHTNING CRASHES** *Radioactive RAXXD 23*	33		2
15 Mar 97	**LAKINI'S JUICE** *Radioactive RAD 49023*	29		2
12 Jul 97	**FREAKS** *Radioactive RAXTD 29*	60		1
5 Feb 00	**THE DOLPHINS CRY** *Radioactive RAXTD 39*	62		1

LIVE ELEMENT
US, male production duo

Date	Title	Peak	Wks at No.1	Wks (2)
26 Jan 02	**BE FREE** *Strictly Rhythm SRUKCD 11*	26		2

LIVE REPORT
UK, male/female vocal/instrumental group

Date	Title	Peak	Wks at No.1	Wks (1)
20 May 89	**WHY DO I ALWAYS GET IT WRONG** *Brouhaha CUE 7*	73		1

LIVERPOOL COLLECTIVE/KOP CHOIR
UK, football fans (Liverpool)/vocal group & choir

Date	Title	Peak	Wks at No.1	Wks (4)
18 Apr 09	**FIELDS OF ANFIELD ROAD** *Robot 012*	14		4

LIVERPOOL EXPRESS
UK, male vocal/instrumental group

Date	Title	Peak	Wks at No.1	Wks (26)
26 Jun 76	**YOU ARE MY LOVE** *Warner Brothers K 16743*	11		9
16 Oct 76	**HOLD TIGHT** *Warner Brothers K 16799*	46		2
18 Dec 76	**EVERY MAN MUST HAVE A DREAM** *Warner Brothers K 16854*	17		11
4 Jun 77	**DREAMIN'** *Warner Brothers K 16933*	40		4

LIVERPOOL FC
UK, male football team/vocalists

Date	Title	Peak	Wks at No.1	Wks (21)
28 May 77	**WE CAN DO IT (EP)** *State STAT 50*	15		4
23 Apr 83	**LIVERPOOL (WE'RE NEVER GONNA...)/LIVERPOOL (ANTHEM)** *Mean 102*	54		4
17 May 86	**SITTING ON TOP OF THE WORLD** *Columbia DB 9116*	50		2
14 May 88	**ANFIELD RAP (RED MACHINE IN FULL EFFECT)** *Virgin LFC 1*	3		6
18 May 96	**PASS & MOVE (IT'S THE LIVERPOOL GROOVE)** *Telstar LFCCD 96* & THE BOOT ROOM BOYS	4		5

LIVIN' JOY
Italy, male producers – Gianni & Paolo Visnadi – with US, female vocalist Janice Robinson (replaced by Tameka Starr)

Date	Title	Peak	Wks at No.1	Wks (44)
3 Sep 94	**DREAMER** *Undiscovered MCSTD 1993*	18		6
13 May 95	**DREAMER** *Undiscovered MCSTD 2056*	1	1	11
15 Jun 96	**DON'T STOP MOVIN'** *Undiscovered MCSTD 40041* ●	5		14
2 Nov 96	**FOLLOW THE RULES** *Undiscovered MCSTD 40081*	9		5
5 Apr 97	**WHERE CAN I FIND LOVE** *Undiscovered MCSTD 40108*	12		4
23 Aug 97	**DEEP IN YOU** *Undiscovered MCSTD 40136*	17		4

LIVING COLOUR
US, male vocal/instrumental group

Date	Title	Peak	Wks at No.1	Wks (22)
27 Oct 90	**TYPE** *Epic LCL 7*	75		1
2 Feb 91	**LOVE REARS ITS UGLY HEAD** *Epic 6565937*	12		11
1 Jun 91	**SOLACE OF YOU** *Epic 6569087*	33		5
26 Oct 91	**CULT OF PERSONALITY** *Epic 6575357*	67		2
20 Feb 93	**LEAVE IT ALONE** *Epic 6589762*	34		2
17 Apr 93	**AUSLANDER** *Epic 6591732*	53		1

LIVING IN A BOX
UK, male vocal/instrumental trio – Richard Darbyshire*, Marcus Vere & Anthony 'Tich' Critchlow

Date	Title	Peak	Wks at No.1	Wks (62)
4 Apr 87	**LIVING IN A BOX** *Chrysalis LIB 1*	5		13
13 Jun 87	**SCALES OF JUSTICE** *Chrysalis LIB 2*	30		6
26 Sep 87	**SO THE STORY GOES** *Chrysalis LIB 3* FEATURING BOBBY WOMACK	34		8
30 Jan 88	**LOVE IS THE ART** *Chrysalis LIB 4*	45		4
18 Feb 89	**BLOW THE HOUSE DOWN** *Chrysalis LIB 5*	10		9
10 Jun 89	**GATECRASHING** *Chrysalis LIB 6*	36		6
23 Sep 89	**ROOM IN YOUR HEART** *Chrysalis LIB 7* ●	5		13
30 Dec 89	**DIFFERENT AIR** *Chrysalis LIB 8*	57		3

DANDY LIVINGSTONE
Jamaica, male vocalist (Robert Livingstone)

Date	Title	Peak	Wks at No.1	Wks (19)
2 Sep 72	**SUZANNE BEWARE OF THE DEVIL** *Horse HOSS 16*	14		11
13 Jan 73	**BIG CITY/THINK ABOUT THAT** *Horse HOSS 26*	26		8

Silver-selling ● Gold-selling ● Platinum-selling (x multiples) ⊛ US No.1 ★ Peak Position · Weeks at No.1 · Weeks on Chart

LL COOL J

US, male rapper/actor (James Todd Smith) — 130

Date	Title	Peak Position	Weeks at No.1	Weeks on Chart
4 Jul 87	**I'M BAD** *Def Jam 6508567*	71		1
12 Sep 87	**I NEED LOVE** *Def Jam 6511017*	8		10
21 Nov 87	**GO CUT CREATOR GO** *Def Jam LLCJ 1*	66		2
13 Feb 88	**GOING BACK TO CALI/JACK THE RIPPER** *Def Jam LLCJ 2*	37		4
10 Jun 89	**I'M THAT TYPE OF GUY** *Def Jam LLCJ 3*	43		5
1 Dec 90	**AROUND THE WAY GIRL/MAMA SAID KNOCK YOU OUT** *Def Jam 6564470*	41		4
9 Mar 91	**AROUND THE WAY GIRL (REMIX)** *Columbia 6564470*	36		4
10 Apr 93	**HOW I'M COMIN'** *Def Jam 6591692*	37		2
20 Jan 96	**HEY LOVER** *Def Jam DEFCD 14* FEATURING BOYZ II MEN	17		4
1 Jun 96	**DOIN' IT** *Def Jam DEFCD 15*	15		3
5 Oct 96	**LOUNGIN** *Def Jam DEFCD 30*	7		8
8 Feb 97	**AIN'T NOBODY** *Geffen GFSTD 22195*	1	1	9
5 Apr 97	**HIT 'EM HIGH (THE MONSTARS' ANTHEM)** *Atlantic A 5449CD* B REAL/BUSTA RHYMES/COOLIO/LL COOL J/METHOD MAN	8		6
1 Nov 97	**PHENOMENON** *Def Jam 5681172*	9		5
28 Mar 98	**FATHER** *Def Jam 5685292*	10		5
11 Jul 98	**ZOOM** *Interscope IND 95594* DR DRE & LL COOL J	15		3
5 Dec 98	**INCREDIBLE** *Jive 0522102* KEITH MURRAY FEATURING LL COOL J	52		1
26 Oct 02	**LUV U BETTER** *Def Jam 0638722*	7		7
22 Feb 03	**PARADISE** *Def Jam 0637242* FEATURING AMERIE	18		5
22 Mar 03	**ALL I HAVE** *Epic 6736782* JENNIFER LOPEZ FEATURING LL COOL J ★	2		13
28 Aug 04	**HEADSPRUNG** *Def Jam 9863759*	25		4
26 Feb 05	**HUSH** *Def Jam 2103774* FEATURING MARCUS VEST	3		10
13 May 06	**CONTROL MYSELF** *Def Jam 9856569* FEATURING JENNIFER LOPEZ	2		13
30 Aug 08	**BABY** *Mercury USUV70801875*	56		2

LLAMA FARMERS

UK, male/female vocal/instrumental group — 2

Date	Title	Peak Position	Weeks at No.1	Weeks on Chart
6 Feb 99	**BIG WHEELS** *Beggars Banquet BBQ 333CD*	67		1
15 May 99	**GET THE KEYS AND GO** *Beggars Banquet BBQ 335CD*	74		1

KELLY LLORENNA

UK, female vocalist — 51

Date	Title	Peak Position	Weeks at No.1	Weeks on Chart
7 May 94	**SET YOU FREE** *All Around The World CDGLOBE 124* N-TRANCE FEATURING KELLY LLORENNA	39		4
24 Feb 96	**BRIGHTER DAY** *Pukka CDPUKKA 5*	43		2
14 Jan 95	**SET YOU FREE** *All Around The World CXGLOBE 126* N-TRANCE FEATURING KELLY LLORENNA ●	2		15
25 Jul 98	**HEART OF GOLD** *Diverse VERSE 2CD* FORCE & STYLES FEATURING KELLY LLORENNA	55		1
24 Mar 01	**TRUE LOVE NEVER DIES** *All Around The World CDGLOBE 240* FLIP & FILL FEATURING KELLY LLORENNA	34		3
2 Feb 02	**TRUE LOVE NEVER DIES (REMIX)** *All Around The World CDGLOBE 248* FLIP & FILL FEATURING KELLY LLORENNA	7		10
6 Jul 02	**TELL IT TO MY HEART** *All Around The World CDGLOBE 256*	9		8
30 Nov 02	**HEART OF GOLD** *All Around The World CXGLOBE 271*	19		4
6 Mar 04	**THIS TIME I KNOW IT'S FOR REAL** *All Around The World CXGLOBE 295*	14		4

LLOYD

US, male rapper/vocalist (Lloyd Polite, Jr) — 20

Date	Title	Peak Position	Weeks at No.1	Weeks on Chart
30 Apr 05	**CAUGHT UP** *The Inc 9881232* JA RULE FEATURING LLOYD	20		4
2 Jun 07	**YOU** *The Inc 1734409* FEATURING LIL WAYNE	45		3
18 Aug 07	**GET IT SHAWTY** *Universal 1743495*	72		1
9 Aug 08	**HOW WE DO IT (ROUND OUR WAY)** *Def Jam 1780769* FEATURING LUDACRIS	75		1
30 Jan 10	**BEDROCK** *Cash Money USCM50901178* YOUNG MONEY FEATURING LLOYD	9		11+

LMC

UK, male production trio – Matt Cadman, Lee Monteverde & Cris Nuttall — 14

Date	Title	Peak Position	Weeks at No.1	Weeks on Chart
7 Feb 04	**TAKE ME TO THE CLOUDS ABOVE** *All Around The World CXGLOBE 313* VS U2	1	2	12
4 Feb 06	**YOU GET WHAT YOU GIVE** *All Around The World CDGLOBE423* FEATURING RACHEL McFARLANE	30		2

LNM PROJEKT FEATURING BONNIE BAILEY

UK, male/female vocal/production group — 2

Date	Title	Peak Position	Weeks at No.1	Weeks on Chart
19 Mar 05	**EVERYWHERE** *Hed Kandi HEDKCDS012*	38		2

LNR

US, male production duo — 2

Date	Title	Peak Position	Weeks at No.1	Weeks on Chart
3 Jun 89	**WORK IT TO THE BONE** *Kool Kat KOOL 501*	64		2

LO FIDELITY ALLSTARS

UK, male vocal/instrumental group — 5

Date	Title	Peak Position	Weeks at No.1	Weeks on Chart
11 Oct 97	**DISCO MACHINE GUN** *Skint 30CD*	50		1
2 May 98	**VISION INCISION** *Skint 33CD*	30		2
28 Nov 98	**BATTLEFLAG** *Skint 38CD* FEATURING PIGEONHED	36		2

LO-RIDER FEATURING CUMBERBATCH

UK, male vocal/production duo — 2

Date	Title	Peak Position	Weeks at No.1	Weeks on Chart
2 Dec 06	**SKINNY** *Absolution CDABSOL8*	44		2

LOBO

US, male vocalist (Roland Kent LaVoie) — 25

Date	Title	Peak Position	Weeks at No.1	Weeks on Chart
19 Jun 71	**ME AND YOU AND A DOG NAMED BOO** *Philips 6073 801*	4		14
8 Jun 74	**I'D LOVE YOU TO WANT ME** *UK 68*	5		11

LOBO

Holland, male vocalist (Imrich Lobo) — 11

Date	Title	Peak Position	Weeks at No.1	Weeks on Chart
25 Jul 81	**THE CARIBBEAN DISCO SHOW** *Polydor POSP 302*	8		11

LOC

Jamaica/UK, male vocal/rap/production group — 1

Date	Title	Peak Position	Weeks at No.1	Weeks on Chart
9 Jul 05	**RING DING DING** *Street Tuff STRCDS3539*	58		1

TONE LOC

US, male rapper (Anthony Smith) — 19

Date	Title	Peak Position	Weeks at No.1	Weeks on Chart
11 Feb 89	**WILD THING/LOC'ED AFTER DARK** *Fourth & Broadway BRW 121*	21		8
20 May 89	**FUNKY COLD MEDINA/ON FIRE** *Fourth & Broadway BRW 129*	13		9
5 Aug 89	**I GOT IT GOIN' ON** *Fourth & Broadway BRW 140*	55		2

LOCK 'N' LOAD

Holland, male DJ/production duo – Nilz Pijpers & Francis Rooijen — 13

Date	Title	Peak Position	Weeks at No.1	Weeks on Chart
15 Apr 00	**BLOW YA MIND** *Pepper 9230162* ●	6		11
3 Mar 01	**HOUSE SOME MORE** *Pepper 9230422*	45		2

KIMBERLEY LOCKE

US, female vocalist/model — 2

Date	Title	Peak Position	Weeks at No.1	Weeks on Chart
31 Jul 04	**8TH WORLD WONDER** *Curb CUBC097*	49		2

HANK LOCKLIN

US, male vocalist (Lawrence Hankins Locklin), d. 8 Mar 2009 (age 91) — 41

Date	Title	Peak Position	Weeks at No.1	Weeks on Chart
11 Aug 60	**PLEASE HELP ME I'M FALLING** *RCA 1188*	9		19
15 Feb 62	**FROM HERE TO THERE TO YOU** *RCA 1273*	44		3
15 Nov 62	**WE'RE GONNA GO FISHIN'** *RCA 1305*	18		11
5 May 66	**I FEEL A CRY COMING ON** *RCA 1510*	29		8

LOCKSMITH

US, male instrumental/vocal group — 6

Date	Title	Peak Position	Weeks at No.1	Weeks on Chart
23 Aug 80	**UNLOCK THE FUNK** *Arista ARIST 364*	42		6

LOCOMOTIVE

UK, male vocal/instrumental group — 8

Date	Title	Peak Position	Weeks at No.1	Weeks on Chart
16 Oct 68	**RUDI'S IN LOVE** *Parlophone R 5718*	25		8

LODGER

UK, male/female vocal/instrumental group — 2

Date	Title	Peak Position	Weeks at No.1	Weeks on Chart
2 May 98	**I'M LEAVING** *Island CID 693*	40		2

LISA LOEB & NINE STORIES

US, female/male vocal/instrumental group — **17**

Date	Title	Peak Position	Weeks at No.1	Weeks on Chart
3 Sep 94	**STAY (I MISSED YOU)** *RCA 74321212522* ★	6		15
16 Sep 95	**DO YOU SLEEP?** *Geffen GFSTD 96*	45		2

NILS LOFGREN

US, male vocalist/guitarist — **3**

Date	Title	Peak Position	Weeks at No.1	Weeks on Chart
8 Jun 85	**SECRETS IN THE STREET** *Towerbell TOW 68*	53		3

JOHNNY LOGAN

Ireland (b. Australia), male vocalist (Sean Sherrard) — **24**

Date	Title	Peak Position	Weeks at No.1	Weeks on Chart
3 May 80	**WHAT'S ANOTHER YEAR** *Epic EPC 8572* ●	1	2	8
23 May 87	**HOLD ME NOW** *Epic LOG 1* ●	2		11
22 Aug 87	**I'M NOT IN LOVE** *Epic LOG 2*	51		5

KENNY LOGGINS

US, male vocalist/guitarist — **21**

Date	Title	Peak Position	Weeks at No.1	Weeks on Chart
28 Apr 84	**FOOTLOOSE** *CBS A 4101* ★	6		10
1 Nov 86	**DANGER ZONE** *CBS A 7188*	45		11

LOGO FEATURING DAWN JOSEPH

UK, male/female vocal/production trio — **1**

Date	Title	Peak Position	Weeks at No.1	Weeks on Chart
8 Dec 01	**DON'T PANIC** *Manifesto FESCD 89*	42		1

LINDSAY LOHAN

US, female actor/model/vocalist — **3**

Date	Title	Peak Position	Weeks at No.1	Weeks on Chart
7 May 05	**OVER** *Universal MCSTD40412*	27		3

LOLA

US, female vocalist (Lola Blank) — **1**

Date	Title	Peak Position	Weeks at No.1	Weeks on Chart
28 Mar 87	**WAX THE VAN** *Syncopate SY 1*	65		1

LOLLY

UK, female vocalist (Anna Kumble) — **44**

Date	Title	Peak Position	Weeks at No.1	Weeks on Chart
10 Jul 99	**VIVA LA RADIO** *Polydor 5639512*	6		9
18 Sep 99	**MICKEY** *Polydor 5613692* ●	4		10
4 Dec 99	**BIG BOYS DON'T CRY/ROCKIN' ROBIN** *Polydor 5615552*	10		9
6 May 00	**PER SEMPRE AMORE (FOREVER IN LOVE)** *Polydor 5617882*	11		10
9 Sep 00	**GIRLS JUST WANNA HAVE FUN** *Polydor 5619762*	14		6

LONDON BOYS

UK, male vocal duo – Edem Ephraim & Dennis Fuller, both d. 21 Sep 1996 — **46**

Date	Title	Peak Position	Weeks at No.1	Weeks on Chart
10 Dec 88	**REQUIEM** *WEA YZ 345*	59		6
1 Apr 89	**REQUIEM** *WEA YZ 345* ●	4		15
1 Jul 89	**LONDON NIGHTS** *WEA YZ 393* ●	2		9
16 Sep 89	**HARLEM DESIRE** *WEA YZ 415*	17		7
2 Dec 89	**MY LOVE** *WEA YZ 433*	46		6
16 Jun 90	**CHAPEL OF LOVE** *East West YZ 458*	75		1
19 Jan 91	**FREEDOM** *East West YZ 554*	54		2

JULIE LONDON

US, female vocalist (Julie Peck), d. 18 Oct 2000 (age 74) — **3**

Date	Title	Peak Position	Weeks at No.1	Weeks on Chart
5 Apr 57	**CRY ME A RIVER** *London HLU 8240*	22		3

LAURIE LONDON

UK, male vocalist — **12**

Date	Title	Peak Position	Weeks at No.1	Weeks on Chart
8 Nov 57	**HE'S GOT THE WHOLE WORLD IN HIS HANDS** *Parlophone R 4359* ★	12		12

LONDON STRING CHORALE

UK, orchestra & choir — **13**

Date	Title	Peak Position	Weeks at No.1	Weeks on Chart
15 Dec 73	**GALLOPING HOME** *Polydor 2058 280*	31		13

LONDON SYMPHONY ORCHESTRA

UK, orchestra — **5**

Date	Title	Peak Position	Weeks at No.1	Weeks on Chart
6 Jan 79	**THEME FROM 'SUPERMAN' (MAIN TITLE)** *Warner Brothers K 17292*	32		5

LONDONBEAT

UK/US/Trinidad, male vocal/instrumental group – Jimmy Chambers, Jimmy Helms*, George Chandler & William 'Willy M' Henshall — **47**

Date	Title	Peak Position	Weeks at No.1	Weeks on Chart
26 Nov 88	**9 A.M. (THE COMFORT ZONE)** *AnXious ANX 008*	19		10
18 Feb 89	**FALLING IN LOVE AGAIN** *AnXious ANX 007*	60		2
2 Dec 89	**IT TAKES TWO BABY** *Spartan CIN 101* LIZ KERSHAW, BRUNO BROOKES, JIVE BUNNY & LONDONBEAT	53		2
1 Sep 90	**I'VE BEEN THINKING ABOUT YOU** *AnXious ANX 14* ● ★	2		13
24 Nov 90	**A BETTER LOVE** *AnXious ANX 21*	52		5
2 Mar 91	**NO WOMAN NO CRY** *AnXious ANX 25*	64		2
20 Jul 91	**A BETTER LOVE** *AnXious ANX 32*	23		6
27 Jun 92	**YOU BRING ON THE SUN** *AnXious ANX 37*	32		4
24 Oct 92	**THAT'S HOW I FEEL ABOUT YOU** *AnXious ANX 40*	69		1
8 Apr 95	**I'M JUST YOUR PUPPET ON A ... (STRING)** *AnXious 74321270982*	55		1
20 May 95	**COME BACK** *AnXious 74321226682*	69		1

LONE JUSTICE

US, female/male vocal/instrumental group — **4**

Date	Title	Peak Position	Weeks at No.1	Weeks on Chart
7 Mar 87	**I FOUND LOVE** *Geffen GEF 18*	45		4

LONESTAR

US, male vocal/instrumental group — **24**

Date	Title	Peak Position	Weeks at No.1	Weeks on Chart
15 Apr 00	**AMAZED** *Grapevine 74321742582* ★	21		22
7 Oct 00	**SMILE** *Grapevine 74321786132*	55		2

SHORTY LONG

US, male vocalist (Frederick Long), d. 29 Jun 1969 (age 29) — **7**

Date	Title	Peak Position	Weeks at No.1	Weeks on Chart
17 Jul 68	**HERE COMES THE JUDGE** *Tamla Motown TMG 663*	30		7

LONG & THE SHORT

UK, male vocal/instrumental group — **8**

Date	Title	Peak Position	Weeks at No.1	Weeks on Chart
10 Sep 64	**THE LETTER** *Decca F 11964*	35		5
24 Dec 64	**CHOC ICE** *Decca F 12043*	40		3

LONG BLONDES

UK, female/male vocal/instrumental group — **5**

Date	Title	Peak Position	Weeks at No.1	Weeks on Chart
8 Jul 06	**WEEKEND WITHOUT MAKEUP** *Rough Trade RTRADSCD351*	28		2
4 Nov 06	**ONCE AND NEVER AGAIN** *Rough Trade RTRADSCD373*	30		2
17 Feb 07	**GIDDY STRATOSPHERES** *Rough Trade RTRADSCD387*	37		1

LONG RYDERS

US, male vocal/instrumental group — **4**

Date	Title	Peak Position	Weeks at No.1	Weeks on Chart
5 Oct 85	**LOOKING FOR LEWIS AND CLARK** *Island IS 237*	59		4

LONGPIGS

UK, male vocal/instrumental group. See Richard Hawley — **17**

Date	Title	Peak Position	Weeks at No.1	Weeks on Chart
22 Jul 95	**SHE SAID** *Mother MUMCD 66*	67		1
28 Oct 95	**JESUS CHRIST** *Mother MUMCD 68*	61		1
17 Feb 96	**FAR** *Mother MUMCD 71*	37		2
13 Apr 96	**ON AND ON** *Mother MUMCD 74*	16		3
22 Jun 96	**SHE SAID** *Mother MUMXD 77*	16		4
5 Oct 96	**LOST MYSELF** *Mother MUMCD 82*	22		3
9 Oct 99	**BLUE SKIES** *Mother MUMCD 113*	21		2
18 Dec 99	**THE FRANK SONATA** *Mother MUMCD 114*	57		1

JOE LONGTHORNE

UK, male vocalist — **6**

Date	Title	Peak Position	Weeks at No.1	Weeks on Chart
30 Apr 94	**YOUNG GIRL** *EMI CDEM 310*	61		2
10 Dec 94	**PASSING STRANGERS** *EMI CDEM 362* & LIZ DAWN	34		4

Silver-selling ○ Gold-selling ● Platinum-selling (x multiples) US No.1 ★ Peak Position Weeks at No.1 Weeks on Chart

LONGVIEW

UK, male vocal/instrumental group

				11
26 Oct 02	WHEN YOU SLEEP *4.45 Recordings LVIEW02CD*	74		1
8 Feb 03	NOWHERE *4.45 Recordings LVIEW03CD*	72		1
19 Jul 03	FURTHER *14th Floor 14FLR01CD*	27		2
11 Oct 03	CAN'T EXPLAIN *14th Floor 14FLR02CD*	51		1
10 Jul 04	IN A DREAM *14th Floor 14FLR06CD*	38		1
22 Jan 05	COMING DOWN/WHEN YOU SLEEP *14th Floor 14FLR09CD*	32		2
20 Aug 05	FURTHER *14th Floor 14FLR12CD*	24		3

LONYO

UK, male vocalist/producer (Lonyo Engele). See Bon Garcon

				9
8 Jul 00	SUMMER OF LOVE *Riverhorse RIVH CD3X* LONYO - COMME CI COMME CA	8		7
7 Apr 01	GARAGE GIRLS *Riverhorse RIVHCD 12* FEATURING MC ONYX STONE	39		2

LOOK

UK, male vocal/instrumental group – Jonny Whetstone, Mick Bass, Gus Goad & Trevor Walter

				15
20 Dec 80	I AM THE BEAT *MCA 647* ○	6		12
29 Aug 81	FEEDING TIME *MCA 736*	50		3

LOON

US, male rapper (Amir Muhadith, b. Chauncey Hawkins)

				16
10 Aug 02	I NEED A GIRL (PART ONE) *Puff Daddy 74321947242* P DIDDY FEATURING USHER & LOON	4		11
8 Mar 03	HIT THE FREEWAY *Arista 82876506372* TONI BRAXTON FEATURING LOON	29		3
7 Feb 04	SHOW ME YOUR SOUL *Puff Daddy MCSTD 40350* P DIDDY, LENNY KRAVITZ, PHARRELL WILLIAMS & LOON	35		2

LOOP DA LOOP

UK, male producer (Nick Dresti)

				4
7 Jun 97	GO WITH THE FLOW *Manifesto FESCD 24*	47		1
20 Feb 99	HAZEL *Manifesto FESCD 53*	20		3

LOOSE ENDS

UK, male/female vocal/instrumental trio

				76
23 Feb 84	TELL ME WHAT YOU WANT *Virgin VS 658*	74		1
28 Apr 84	EMERGENCY (DIAL 999) *Virgin VS 677*	41		6
21 Jul 84	CHOOSE ME (RESCUE ME) *Virgin VS 697*	59		3
23 Feb 85	HANGIN' ON A STRING (CONTEMPLATING) *Virgin VS 748*	13		13
11 May 85	MAGIC TOUCH *Virgin VS 761*	16		7
27 Jul 85	GOLDEN YEARS *Virgin VS 795*	59		4
14 Jun 86	STAY A LITTLE WHILE, CHILD *Virgin VS 819*	52		5
20 Sep 86	SLOW DOWN *Virgin VS 884*	27		7
29 Nov 86	NIGHTS OF PLEASURE *Virgin VS 919*	42		7
4 Jun 88	MR BACHELOR *Virgin VS 1080*	50		4
25 Aug 90	DON'T BE A FOOL *10 TEN 312*	13		9
17 Nov 90	LOVE'S GOT ME *10 TEN 330*	40		4
20 Jun 92	HANGIN' ON A STRING (CONTEMPLATING) (REMIX) *10 TEN 406*	25		5
5 Sep 92	MAGIC TOUCH (REMIX) *10 TEN 409*	75		1

LISA 'LEFT EYE' LOPES

US, female rapper/vocalist, d. 25 Apr 2002 (age 30)

				20
1 Apr 00	NEVER BE THE SAME AGAIN *Virgin VSCDT 1786* MELANIE C & LISA 'LEFT EYE' LOPES ●	1	1	16
27 Oct 01	THE BLOCK PARTY *LaFace 74321895912*	16		4

JENNIFER LOPEZ

US, female vocalist/producer/actor/dancer/fashion designer

				190
3 Jul 99	IF YOU HAD MY LOVE *Columbia 6675772* ★	4		13
13 Nov 99	WAITING FOR TONIGHT *Columbia 6683072*	5		12
1 Apr 00	FEELIN' SO GOOD *Columbia 6691972* FEATURING BIG PUN & FAT JOE	15		6
20 Jan 01	LOVE DON'T COST A THING *Epic 6707282* ○	1	1	11
12 May 01	PLAY *Epic 6712272*	3		12
18 Aug 01	AIN'T IT FUNNY *Epic 6717592* FEATURING JA RULE & CADILLAC TAH ★	3		9
10 Nov 01	I'M REAL *Epic 6720322* FEATURING JA RULE ★	4		15
23 Mar 02	AIN'T IT FUNNY *Epic 6724922* ★	4		13
13 Jul 02	I'M GONNA BE ALRIGHT *Epic 6728442* FEATURING NAS	3		10
30 Nov 02	JENNY FROM THE BLOCK *Epic 6733572*	3		13
22 Mar 03	ALL I HAVE *Epic 6736782* FEATURING LL COOL J ★	2		13
21 Jun 03	I'M GLAD *Epic 6740152*	11		9
20 Mar 04	BABY I LOVE U *Epic 6747902*	3		10
26 Feb 05	GET RIGHT *Epic 6757562*	1	1	14
28 May 05	HOLD YOU DOWN *Epic 6759342* FEATURING FAT JOE	6		9
13 May 06	CONTROL MYSELF *Def Jam 9856569* LL COOL J FEATURING JENNIFER LOPEZ	2		13
6 Oct 07	DO IT WELL *RCA 88697176452*	11		7
2 Feb 08	HOLD IT, DON'T DROP IT *Epic USSM10703184*	72		1

TRINI LOPEZ

US, male vocalist (Trinidad Lopez)

				37
12 Sep 63	IF I HAD A HAMMER *Reprise R 20198*	4		17
12 Dec 63	KANSAS CITY *Reprise R 20236*	35		5
12 May 66	I'M COMING HOME CINDY *Reprise R 20455*	28		5
6 Apr 67	GONNA GET ALONG WITHOUT YA NOW *Reprise R 20547*	41		5
19 Dec 81	TRINI TRAX *RCA 154*	59		5

LORD ROCKINGHAM'S XI

UK, male instrumental ensemble fronted by Harry Robinson, d. 17 Jan 1996

				21
24 Oct 58	HOOTS MON *Decca F 11059*	1	3	17
6 Feb 59	WEE TOM *Decca F 11104*	16		3
25 Sep 93	HOOTS MON *Decca 8820982*	60		1

LORD TANAMO

Jamaica, male vocalist (Joseph Gordon)

				2
1 Dec 90	I'M IN THE MOOD FOR LOVE *Mooncrest MOON 1009*	58		2

LORD TARIQ & PETER GUNZ

US, male vocal/rap duo

				3
2 May 98	DEJA VU (UPTOWN BABY) *Columbia 6658722*	21		3

JERRY LORDAN

UK, male vocalist, d. 24 Jul 1995 (age 61)

				16
8 Jan 60	I'LL STAY SINGLE *Parlophone R 4588*	26		3
26 Feb 60	WHO COULD BE BLUER *Parlophone R 4627*	16		11
2 Jun 60	SING LIKE AN ANGEL *Parlophone R 4653*	36		2

LORDI

Finland, male vocal/instrumental group

				5
10 Jun 06	HARD ROCK HALLELUJAH *Sony BMG 82876806762*	25		5

TRACI LORDS

US, female vocalist (Nora Kuzma)

				1
7 Oct 95	FALLEN ANGEL *Radioactive RAXTD 18*	72		1

LORENZ

Italy, male vocalist/model

				1
16 Sep 06	SET ME FREE *Superstar Music LORENZ17CD*	35		1

TREY LORENZ

US, male vocalist (Lloyd Lorenz Smith). See Mariah Carey

				5
21 Nov 92	SOMEONE TO HOLD *Epic 6587857*	65		2
30 Jan 93	PHOTOGRAPH OF MARY *Epic 6589542*	38		3

LORI & THE CHAMELEONS

UK, female/male vocal/instrumental group

				1
8 Dec 79	TOUCH *Sire SIR 4025*	70		1

LORRAINE

Norway, male vocal/instrumental trio

				2
22 Apr 06	I FEEL IT *Waterfall/Columbia 82876822702*	29		2

LOS BRAVOS
Spain/Germany, male vocal/instrumental group – Mike Kogel, Miguel Danus, Manuel Fernandez, d. 20 May 1967, Pablo Gomez & Tony Martinez, d. 1990 — 24

Date	Title	Peak	Wks No.1	Wks
30 Jun 66	**BLACK IS BLACK** *Decca F 22419*	2		13
8 Sep 66	**I DON'T CARE** *Decca F 22484*	16		11

LOS DEL MAR FEATURING WIL VELOZ
Canada/Cuba, male vocal/instrumental group — 7

Date	Title	Peak	Wks No.1	Wks
8 Jun 96	**MACARENA** *Pulse 8 CDLOSE 101*	43		7

LOS DEL RIO
Spain, male vocal/instrumental duo – Antonio Monge & Rafael Perdigones — 19

Date	Title	Peak	Wks No.1	Wks
1 Jun 96	**MACARENA** *RCA 74321345372* ● ★	2		19

LOS INDIOS TABAJARAS
Brazil, male guitar duo – Natalicio, d. 15 Nov 2009, & Antenor Lima — 17

Date	Title	Peak	Wks No.1	Wks
31 Oct 63	**MARIA ELENA** *RCA 1365*	5		17

LOS LOBOS
US, male vocal/instrumental group – David Hildago, Steve Berlin, Conrad Lozano, Louie Perez & Cesar Rosas — 24

Date	Title	Peak	Wks No.1	Wks
6 Apr 85	**DON'T WORRY BABY/WILL THE WOLF SURVIVE** *London LASH 4*	57		4
18 Jul 87	**LA BAMBA** *Slash LASH 13* ★	1	2	11
26 Sep 87	**COME ON LET'S GO** *Slash LASH 14*	18		9

LOS POP TOPS
Spain, male vocal/instrumental group — 6

Date	Title	Peak	Wks No.1	Wks
9 Oct 71	**MAMY BLUE** *A&M AMS 859*	35		6

LOS UMBRELLOS
Denmark, male/female vocal trio — 2

Date	Title	Peak	Wks No.1	Wks
3 Oct 98	**NO TENGO DINERO** *Virgin VUSCD 139*	33		2

JOE LOSS ORCHESTRA
UK, male orchestra leader, d. 6 Jun 1990 (age 80) — 53

Date	Title	Peak	Wks No.1	Wks
29 Jun 61	**WHEELS CHA CHA** *HMV POP 880*	21		21
19 Oct 61	**SUCU SUCU** *HMV POP 937*	48		1
29 Mar 62	**THE MAIGRET THEME** *HMV POP 995*	20		10
1 Nov 62	**MUST BE MADISON** *HMV POP 1075*	20		13
5 Nov 64	**MARCH OF THE MODS** *HMV POP 1351*	31		8

LOST
UK, male production duo — 1

Date	Title	Peak	Wks No.1	Wks
22 Jun 91	**TECHNO FUNK** *Perfecto PT 44560*	75		1

LOST BOYZ
US, male rap group — 2

Date	Title	Peak	Wks No.1	Wks
2 Nov 96	**MUSIC MAKES ME HIGH** *Universal MCSTD 48015*	42		1
12 Jul 97	**LOVE, PEACE & NAPPINESS** *Universal UND 56131*	57		1

LOST BROTHERS FEATURING G TOM MAC
UK, male vocal/production group — 9

Date	Title	Peak	Wks No.1	Wks
20 Dec 03	**CRY LITTLE SISTER (I NEED U NOW)** *Incentive CENT 60CDS*	21		9

LOST IT.COM
UK, male vocal/production duo — 1

Date	Title	Peak	Wks No.1	Wks
7 Apr 01	**ANIMAL** *Perfecto PERF 13CDS*	70		1

LOST TRIBE
UK, male production duo. See MDM, Melt featuring Little Ms Marcie, Sunburst — 4

Date	Title	Peak	Wks No.1	Wks
11 Sep 99	**GAMEMASTER** *Hooj Choons HOOJ 81CD*	24		3
6 Dec 03	**GAMEMASTER** *Liquid Asset ASSETCD 12015*	61		1

LOST WITNESS
UK, male/female vocal/production trio — 13

Date	Title	Peak	Wks No.1	Wks
29 May 99	**HAPPINESS HAPPENING** *Ministry Of Sound MOSCDS 129*	18		4
18 Sep 99	**RED SUN RISING** *Sound Of Ministry MOSCDS 133*	22		3
16 Dec 00	**7 COLOURS** *Data 15CDS*	28		3
18 May 02	**DID I DREAM (SONG TO THE SIREN)** *Data 28CDS*	28		3

LOSTPROPHETS
UK, male vocal/instrumental group – Ian Watkins, Mike Chiplin, Lee Gaze, Mike Lewis, Jamie Oliver & Stuart Richardson — 53

Date	Title	Peak	Wks No.1	Wks
8 Dec 01	**SHINOBI VS DRAGON NINJA** *Visible Noise TORMENT 17*	41		2
23 Mar 02	**THE FAKE SOUND OF PROGRESS** *Visible Noise TORMENT 20*	21		3
15 Nov 03	**BURN BURN** *Visible Noise TORMENT 30CD*	17		3
7 Feb 04	**LAST TRAIN HOME** *Visible Noise TORMENT 37CD*	8		7
15 May 04	**WAKE UP** *Visible Noise TORMENT 40CD*	18		4
4 Sep 04	**LAST SUMMER** *Visible Noise TORMENT 43CD*	13		5
4 Dec 04	**GOODBYE TONIGHT** *Visible Noise TORMENT47CD*	42		2
24 Jun 06	**ROOFTOPS (A LIBERATION BROADCAST)** *Visible Noise TORMENT73CD*	8		10
16 Sep 06	**A TOWN CALLED HYPOCRISY** *Visible Noise TORMENT86CD*	23		6
9 Dec 06	**CAN'T CATCH TOMORROW** *Visible Noise TORMENT96CD*	35		2
5 May 07	**4 AM FOREVER** *Visible Noise TORMENT105*	34		1
24 Oct 09	**IT'S NOT THE END OF THE WORLD** *Visible Noise TORMENT145*	16		3
16 Jan 10	**WHERE WE BELONG** *Visible Noise TORMENT149*	32		5

PIXIE LOTT
UK, female vocalist/pianist (Victoria Lott). See Young Soul Rebels — 69

Date	Title	Peak	Wks No.1	Wks
20 Jun 09	**MAMA DO** *Mercury 2701461* ●	1	1	18
20 Jun 09	**USE SOMEBODY** *Mercury GBUM70906591*	52		2
12 Sep 09	**BOYS AND GIRLS** *Mercury 2714871*	1	1	19
14 Nov 09	**CRY ME OUT** *Mercury GBUM70901214* ●	12		22+
20 Feb 10	**GRAVITY** *Mercury GBUM70901217*	20		8+

LOTUS EATERS
UK, male vocal/instrumental duo — 16

Date	Title	Peak	Wks No.1	Wks
2 Jul 83	**THE FIRST PICTURE OF YOU** *Sylvan SYL 1*	15		12
8 Oct 83	**YOU DON'T NEED SOMEONE NEW** *Sylvan SYL 2*	53		4

BONNIE LOU
US, male vocalist (Mary Jo Kath) — 10

Date	Title	Peak	Wks No.1	Wks
5 Feb 54	**TENNESSEE WIG WALK** *Parlophone R 3730*	4		10

LIPPY LOU
UK, female rapper/vocalist (Louise Neale) — 2

Date	Title	Peak	Wks No.1	Wks
22 Apr 95	**LIBERATION** *More Protein PROCD 105*	57		2

LOUCHIE LOU & MICHIE ONE
UK, female rap/vocal duo – Louise Gold & Michelle Charles — 37

Date	Title	Peak	Wks No.1	Wks
29 May 93	**SHOUT (IT OUT)** *ffrr FCD 211*	7		8
14 Aug 93	**SOMEBODY ELSE'S GUY** *ffrr FCD 216*	54		2
26 Aug 95	**GET DOWN ON IT** *China WOKCD 2054*	58		1
13 Apr 96	**CECILIA** *WEA 042CD1* SUGGS FEATURING LOUCHIE LOU & MICHIE ONE ●	4		19
15 Jun 96	**GOOD SWEET LOVIN'** *Indochina ID 050CD*	34		2
21 Sep 96	**NO MORE ALCOHOL** *WEA 065CD1* SUGGS FEATURING LOUCHIE LOU & MICHIE ONE	24		4
29 Oct 05	**WATERMAN** *Positiva CDTIVS224* OLAV BASOSKI FEATURING MICHIE ONE	45		1

LOUD
UK, male vocal/instrumental duo — 2

Date	Title	Peak	Wks No.1	Wks
28 Mar 92	**EASY** *China WOK 2016*	67		2

JOHN D LOUDERMILK
US, male vocalist — 10

Date	Title	Peak	Wks No.1	Wks
4 Jan 62	**THE LANGUAGE OF LOVE** *RCA 1269*	13		10

LOUIE LOUIE
US, male vocalist (Louie Cordero) — 5

Date	Title	Peak	Wks No.1	Wks
19 Dec 92	**THE THOUGHT OF IT** *Hardback YZ 724*	34		5

Silver-selling · Gold-selling · Platinum-selling (x multiples) · US No.1 · Peak Position · Weeks at No.1 · Weeks on Chart

LOUIS XIV
US, male vocal/instrumental group — **2**

Date	Title	Label	Peak Position	Weeks at No.1	Weeks on Chart
30 Jul 05	**GOD KILLED THE QUEEN**	*Atlantic AT0211CD*	68		1
22 Oct 05	**FINDING OUT TRUE LOVE IS BLIND**	*Atlantic AT0214CD*	57		1

LOUISE
UK, female vocalist/TV presenter (Louise Nurding). See Eternal — **83**

Date	Title	Label	Peak Position	Weeks at No.1	Weeks on Chart
7 Oct 95	**LIGHT OF MY LIFE**	*EMI CDEMS 397*	8		8
16 Mar 96	**IN WALKED LOVE**	*EMI CDEMS 413*	17		6
8 Jun 96	**NAKED**	*EMI CDEM 431*	5		8
31 Aug 96	**UNDIVIDED LOVE**	*EMI CDEM 441*	5		6
30 Nov 96	**ONE KISS FROM HEAVEN**	*EMI CDEM 454*	9		7
4 Oct 97	**ARMS AROUND THE WORLD**	*EMI CDEM 490*	4		7
29 Nov 97	**LET'S GO ROUND AGAIN**	*EMI CDEM 500*	10		9
4 Apr 98	**ALL THAT MATTERS**	*1st Avenue CDEM 506*	11		6
29 Jul 00	**2 FACED**	*1st Avenue CDEMS 570*	3		8
11 Nov 00	**BEAUTIFUL INSIDE**	*1st Avenue CDEMS 575*	13		4
8 Sep 01	**STUCK IN THE MIDDLE WITH YOU**	*1st Avenue CDEM 600*	4		9
27 Sep 03	**PANDORA'S KISS**	*Positive POSCDS002*	5		5

DEMI LOVATO
US, female actor/vocalist (Demetria Lovato) — **8**

Date	Title	Label	Peak Position	Weeks at No.1	Weeks on Chart
4 Oct 08	**THIS IS ME**	*Walt Disney USWD10833742* & JOE JONAS	33		2
2 May 09	**LA LA LAND**	*Walt Disney USHR10824099*	35		6

ALI LOVE
UK, male vocalist — **1**

Date	Title	Label	Peak Position	Weeks at No.1	Weeks on Chart
28 Jul 07	**SECRET SUNDAY LOVER**	*Columbia ALCD003*	45		1

COURTNEY LOVE
US, female vocalist/guitarist (Love Michelle Harrison). See Hole — **2**

Date	Title	Label	Peak Position	Weeks at No.1	Weeks on Chart
27 Mar 04	**MONO**	*Virgin VUSDX 283*	41		2

DARLENE LOVE
US, female vocalist — **5**

Date	Title	Label	Peak Position	Weeks at No.1	Weeks on Chart
19 Dec 92	**ALL ALONE ON CHRISTMAS**	*Arista 74321124767*	31		4
1 Jan 94	**ALL ALONE ON CHRISTMAS**	*Arista 74321124767*	72		1

HELEN LOVE
UK, male/female vocal/instrumental group — **2**

Date	Title	Label	Peak Position	Weeks at No.1	Weeks on Chart
20 Sep 97	**DOES YOUR HEART GO BOOM**	*Che 72CD*	71		1
19 Sep 98	**LONG LIVE THE UK MUSIC SCENE**	*Che 82CD*	65		1

MONIE LOVE
UK, female rapper (Simone Johnson) — **51**

Date	Title	Label	Peak Position	Weeks at No.1	Weeks on Chart
4 Feb 89	**I CAN DO THIS**	*Cooltempo COOL 177*	37		4
24 Jun 89	**GRANDPA'S PARTY**	*Cooltempo COOL 184*	16		9
14 Jul 90	**MONIE IN THE MIDDLE**	*Cooltempo COOL 210*	46		3
22 Sep 90	**IT'S A SHAME (MY SISTER)**	*Cooltempo COOL 219* FEATURING TRUE IMAGE	12		8
1 Dec 90	**DOWN TO EARTH**	*Cooltempo COOL 222*	31		6
6 Apr 91	**RING MY BELL**	*Cooltempo COOL 224* VS ADEVA	20		5
25 Jul 92	**FULL TERM LOVE**	*Cooltempo COOL 258*	34		4
13 Mar 93	**BORN 2 B.R.E.E.D.**	*Cooltempo CDCOOL 269*	18		5
12 Jun 93	**IN A WORD OR 2/THE POWER**	*Cooltempo CDCOOL 273*	33		3
21 Aug 93	**NEVER GIVE UP**	*Cooltempo CDCOOL 276*	41		2
22 Apr 00	**SLICE OF DA PIE**	*Relentless RELENT 2CDS*	29		2

LOVE AFFAIR
UK, male vocal/instrumental group – Steve Ellis, Maurice Bacon, Rex Brayley, Morgan Fisher, Lynton Guest & Mick Jackson — **56**

Date	Title	Label	Peak Position	Weeks at No.1	Weeks on Chart
3 Jan 68	**EVERLASTING LOVE**	*CBS 3125*	1	2	12
17 Apr 68	**RAINBOW VALLEY**	*CBS 3366*	5		13
11 Sep 68	**A DAY WITHOUT LOVE**	*CBS 3674*	6		12
19 Feb 69	**ONE ROAD**	*CBS 3994*	16		9
16 Jul 69	**BRINGING ON BACK THE GOOD TIMES**	*CBS 4300*	9		10

LOVE & MONEY
UK, male vocal/instrumental group — **23**

Date	Title	Label	Peak Position	Weeks at No.1	Weeks on Chart
24 May 86	**CANDYBAR EXPRESS**	*Mercury MONEY 1*	56		4
25 Apr 87	**LOVE AND MONEY**	*Mercury MONEY 4*	68		4
17 Sep 88	**HALLELUIAH MAN**	*Mercury MONEY 5*	63		4
14 Jan 89	**STRANGE KIND OF LOVE**	*Mercury MONEY 6*	45		5
25 Mar 89	**JOCELYN SQUARE**	*Mercury MONEY 7*	51		4
16 Nov 91	**WINTER**	*Mercury MONEY 9*	52		2

LOVE BITE
Italy, male/female vocal/production group — **1**

Date	Title	Label	Peak Position	Weeks at No.1	Weeks on Chart
7 Oct 00	**TAKE YOUR TIME**	*AM:PM CDAMPM 134*	56		1

LOVE CITY GROOVE
UK, male/female vocal/rap/instrumental group – Stephen 'Beanz' Rudden, Yinka 'Reason' Charles, Paul Hardy & Jay Williams — **11**

Date	Title	Label	Peak Position	Weeks at No.1	Weeks on Chart
8 Apr 95	**LOVE CITY GROOVE**	*Planet 3 GXY 2003CD*	7		11

LOVE CONNECTION
Italy/Germany, male/female vocal/production group — **1**

Date	Title	Label	Peak Position	Weeks at No.1	Weeks on Chart
2 Dec 00	**THE BOMB**	*Multiply CDMULTY 63*	53		1

LOVE DECADE
UK, male production group — **14**

Date	Title	Label	Peak Position	Weeks at No.1	Weeks on Chart
6 Jul 91	**DREAM ON (IS THIS A DREAM)**	*All Around The World GLOBE 100*	52		2
23 Nov 91	**SO REAL**	*All Around The World GLOBE 106*	14		7
11 Apr 92	**I FEEL YOU**	*All Around The World GLOBE 107*	34		3
6 Feb 93	**WHEN THE MORNING COMES**	*All Around The World CDGLOBE 114*	69		1
17 Feb 96	**IS THIS A DREAM?**	*All Around The World CDGLOBE 132*	39		1

LOVE DECREE
UK, male vocal/instrumental group — **4**

Date	Title	Label	Peak Position	Weeks at No.1	Weeks on Chart
16 Sep 89	**SOMETHING SO REAL (CHINHEADS THEME)**	*Ariola 112642*	61		4

LOVE/HATE
US, male vocal/instrumental group — **4**

Date	Title	Label	Peak Position	Weeks at No.1	Weeks on Chart
30 Nov 91	**EVIL TWIN**	*Columbia 6575967*	59		1
4 Apr 92	**WASTED IN AMERICA**	*Columbia 6578897*	38		3

LOVE INC
Jamaica/Canada, male/female vocal/production duo – Simone Denny & Chris Sheppard — **22**

Date	Title	Label	Peak Position	Weeks at No.1	Weeks on Chart
28 Dec 02	**YOU'RE A SUPERSTAR**	*NuLife 74321978042*	7		13
31 May 03	**BROKEN BONES**	*NuLife 8286523172*	8		7
6 Mar 04	**INTO THE NIGHT**	*NuLife 82876585782*	39		2

LOVE INC FEATURING MC NOISE
UK, male production duo & rapper — **3**

Date	Title	Label	Peak Position	Weeks at No.1	Weeks on Chart
9 Feb 91	**LOVE IS THE MESSAGE**	*Love EVOL 1*	59		3

LOVE SCULPTURE
UK, male vocal/instrumental trio – Dave Edmunds*, Tommy Riley & John Williams (replaced by Bob Jones) — **14**

Date	Title	Label	Peak Position	Weeks at No.1	Weeks on Chart
27 Nov 68	**SABRE DANCE**	*Parlophone R 5744*	5		14

A LOVE SUPREME
UK, male vocal/instrumental group — **2**

Date	Title	Label	Peak Position	Weeks at No.1	Weeks on Chart
17 Apr 99	**NIALL QUINN'S DISCO PANTS**	*A Love Supreme/Cherry Red CDVINNIE 3*	59		2

(LOVE) TATTOO
Australia, male producer (Stephen Allkins) — **1**

Date	Title	Label	Peak Position	Weeks at No.1	Weeks on Chart
6 Oct 01	**DROP SOME DRUMS**	*Positiva CDTIV 162*	58		1

LOVE TO INFINITY
UK, male/female vocal/production trio. See Soda Club — **4**

Date	Title	Label	Peak Position	Weeks at No.1	Weeks on Chart
24 Jun 95	**KEEP LOVE TOGETHER**	*Mushroom D 00467*	38		2
18 Nov 95	**SOMEDAY**	*Mushroom D 1143*	75		1
3 Aug 96	**PRAY FOR LOVE**	*Mushroom D 1213*	69		1

Silver-selling · Gold-selling · Platinum-selling (× multiples) · US No.1 ★ · Peak Position · Weeks at No.1 · Weeks on Chart

LOVE TRIBE
UK, male/female vocal/instrumental duo — 3

Date	Title	Peak Position	Weeks at No.1	Weeks on Chart
29 Jun 96	**STAND UP** *AM:PM 5816272*	23		3

LOVE UNLIMITED
US, female vocal group — 19

Date	Title	Peak Position	Weeks at No.1	Weeks on Chart
17 Jun 72	**WALKIN' IN THE RAIN WITH THE ONE I LOVE** *Uni UN 539*	14		10
25 Jan 75	**IT MAY BE WINTER OUTSIDE (BUT IN MY HEART IT'S SPRING)** *20th Century BTC 2149*	11		9

LOVE UNLIMITED ORCHESTRA
US, orchestra led by Barry White*, d. 4 Jul 2003 — 10

Date	Title	Peak Position	Weeks at No.1	Weeks on Chart
2 Feb 74	**LOVE'S THEME** *Pye International 7N 25635* ★	10		10

LOVE BITES
UK, female vocal/instrumental group — 4

Date	Title	Peak Position	Weeks at No.1	Weeks on Chart
29 Oct 05	**YOU BROKE MY HEART** *Island MCSXD40427*	13		3
11 Mar 06	**HE'S FIT** *Island MCSXD40446*	48		1

LOVEBUG
UK, male/female vocal/production trio — 2

Date	Title	Peak Position	Weeks at No.1	Weeks on Chart
18 Oct 03	**WHO'S THE DADDY** *Sony Music 6742705*	35		2

LOVEBUG STARSKI
US, male rapper (Kevin Smith) — 9

Date	Title	Peak Position	Weeks at No.1	Weeks on Chart
31 May 86	**AMITYVILLE (THE HOUSE ON THE HILL)** *Epic A 7182*	12		9

LOVEFREEKZ
UK, male producer (Mark Hadfield). See Loveland featuring the voice of Rachel McFarlane, Lucid — 6

Date	Title	Peak Position	Weeks at No.1	Weeks on Chart
5 Feb 05	**SHINE** *Positiva CDTIVS214*	6		6

LOVEHAPPY
US/UK, male/female vocal/instrumental group — 3

Date	Title	Peak Position	Weeks at No.1	Weeks on Chart
18 Feb 95	**MESSAGE OF LOVE** *MCA MCSTD 2040*	37		2
20 Jul 96	**MESSAGE OF LOVE (REMIX)** *MCA MCSTD 40052*	70		1

BILL LOVELADY
UK, male vocalist — 10

Date	Title	Peak Position	Weeks at No.1	Weeks on Chart
18 Aug 79	**REGGAE FOR IT NOW** *Charisma CB 337*	12		10

LOVELAND FEATURING RACHEL McFARLANE
UK, male/female vocal/production group — 15

Date	Title	Peak Position	Weeks at No.1	Weeks on Chart
16 Apr 94	**LET THE MUSIC (LIFT YOU UP)** *KMS/Eastern Bloc KMSCD 10* VS DARLENE LEWIS	16		4
5 Nov 94	**(KEEP ON) SHINING/HOPE (NEVER GIVE UP)** *Eastern Bloc BLOCCD 016*	37		2
14 Jan 95	**I NEED SOMEBODY** *Eastern Bloc BLOCCDX 019*	21		3
10 Jun 95	**DON'T MAKE ME WAIT** *Eastern Bloc BLOC 20CD*	22		3
2 Sep 95	**THE WONDER OF LOVE** *Eastern Bloc BLOC 22CD*	53		1
11 Nov 95	**I NEED SOMEBODY** *Eastern Bloc BLOC 23CD*	38		2

LOVER SPEAKS
UK, male vocal/instrumental duo — 5

Date	Title	Peak Position	Weeks at No.1	Weeks on Chart
16 Aug 86	**NO MORE 'I LOVE YOU'S** *A&M AM 326*	58		5

LINUS LOVES FEATURING SAM OBERNIK
UK, male/female vocal/production duo — 3

Date	Title	Peak Position	Weeks at No.1	Weeks on Chart
22 Nov 03	**STAND BACK** *Data 62CDS*	31		3

MICHAEL LOVESMITH
US, male vocalist — 1

Date	Title	Peak Position	Weeks at No.1	Weeks on Chart
5 Oct 85	**AIN'T NOTHIN' LIKE IT** *Motown ZB 40369*	75		1

LOVESTATION
UK, male/female production/vocal group — 21

Date	Title	Peak Position	Weeks at No.1	Weeks on Chart
13 Mar 93	**SHINE ON ME** *RCA 74321137912* FEATURING LISA HUNT	71		1
13 Nov 93	**BEST OF MY LOVE** *Fresh FRSHD 1*	73		1
18 Mar 95	**LOVE COME RESCUE ME** *Fresh FRSHD 22*	42		2
1 Aug 98	**TEARDROPS** *Fresh FRSHD 65*	14		6
5 Dec 98	**SENSUALITY** *Fresh FRSHD 71*	16		7
5 Feb 00	**TEARDROPS (REMIX)** *Fresh FRSHD 79*	24		4

LENE LOVICH
US, female vocalist (Lili-Marlene Premilovich) — 38

Date	Title	Peak Position	Weeks at No.1	Weeks on Chart
17 Feb 79	**LUCKY NUMBER** *Stiff BUY 42* ●	3		11
12 May 79	**SAY WHEN** *Stiff BUY 46*	19		10
20 Oct 79	**BIRD SONG** *Stiff BUY 53*	39		7
29 Mar 80	**WHAT WILL I DO WITHOUT YOU** *Stiff BUY 69*	58		3
14 Mar 81	**NEW TOY** *Stiff BUY 97*	53		5
27 Nov 82	**IT'S ONLY YOU (MEIN SCHMERZ)** *Stiff BUY 164*	68		2

LOVIN' SPOONFUL
US, male vocal/instrumental group – John Sebastian, Steve Boone, Joe Butler & Zal Yanovsky, d. 13 Dec 2002 — 33

Date	Title	Peak Position	Weeks at No.1	Weeks on Chart
14 Apr 66	**DAYDREAM** *Pye International 7N 25361*	2		13
14 Jul 66	**SUMMER IN THE CITY** *Kama Sutra KAS 200* ★	8		11
5 Jan 67	**NASHVILLE CATS** *Kama Sutra KAS 204*	26		7
9 Mar 67	**DARLING BE HOME SOON** *Kama Sutra KAS 207*	44		2

LOVINDEER
Jamaica, male vocalist (Lloyd Lovindeer) — 3

Date	Title	Peak Position	Weeks at No.1	Weeks on Chart
27 Sep 86	**MAN SHORTAGE** *TSOJ TS 1*	69		3

LOW
US, male/female vocal/instrumental group — 1

Date	Title	Peak Position	Weeks at No.1	Weeks on Chart
5 Mar 05	**CALIFORNIA** *Rough Trade RTRADSCD221*	57		1

GARY LOW
Italy (b. Spain), male vocalist (Luis Belmonte) — 3

Date	Title	Peak Position	Weeks at No.1	Weeks on Chart
8 Oct 83	**I WANT YOU** *Savoir Faire FAIS 004*	52		3

JIM LOWE & THE HIGH FIVES
US, male vocalist — 9

Date	Title	Peak Position	Weeks at No.1	Weeks on Chart
26 Oct 56	**THE GREEN DOOR** *London HLD 8317* ★	8		9

NICK LOWE
UK, male vocalist — 27

Date	Title	Peak Position	Weeks at No.1	Weeks on Chart
11 Mar 78	**I LOVE THE SOUND OF BREAKING GLASS** *Radar ADA 1*	7		8
9 Jun 79	**CRACKIN' UP** *Radar ADA 34*	34		5
25 Aug 79	**CRUEL TO BE KIND** *Radar ADA 43*	12		11
26 May 84	**HALF A BOY HALF A MAN** *F. Beat XX 34*	53		3

LOWGOLD
UK, male vocal/instrumental group — 4

Date	Title	Peak Position	Weeks at No.1	Weeks on Chart
30 Sep 00	**BEAUTY DIES YOUNG** *Nude NUD 52CD*	67		1
10 Feb 01	**MERCURY** *Nude NUD 53CD*	48		1
12 May 01	**COUNTERFEIT** *Nude NUD 55CD*	52		1
8 Sep 01	**BEAUTY DIES YOUNG (REMIX)** *Nude NUD 59CD1*	40		1

LOWRELL
US, male vocalist (Lowrell Simon) — 9

Date	Title	Peak Position	Weeks at No.1	Weeks on Chart
24 Nov 79	**MELLOW MELLOW RIGHT ON** *AVI AVIS 108*	37		9

L7
US, female vocal/instrumental group — 18

Date	Title	Peak Position	Weeks at No.1	Weeks on Chart
4 Apr 92	**PRETEND WE'RE DEAD** *Slash LASH 34*	21		7
30 May 92	**EVERGLADE** *Slash LASH 36*	27		3
12 Sep 92	**MONSTER** *Slash LASH 38*	33		3
28 Nov 92	**PRETEND WE'RE DEAD** *Slash LASH 42*	50		3
9 Jul 94	**ANDRES** *Slash LASCD 48*	34		2

Silver-selling ● Gold-selling ● Platinum-selling (x multiples) ⊛ US No.1 ★ Peak Position · Weeks at No.1 · Weeks on Chart

LSG
Germany, male DJ/producer (Oliver Lieb) — 1

Date	Title	Peak Position	Weeks at No.1	Weeks on Chart
10 May 97	**NETHERWORLD** *Hooj Choons HOOJCD 52*	63		1

L.T.D.
US, male vocal/instrumental group — 3

Date	Title	Peak Position	Weeks at No.1	Weeks on Chart
9 Sep 78	**HOLDING ON (WHEN LOVE IS GONE)** *A&M AMS 7378*	70		3

LUCAS
US (b. Denmark), male vocalist (Lucas Secon) — 4

Date	Title	Peak Position	Weeks at No.1	Weeks on Chart
6 Aug 94	**LUCAS WITH THE LID OFF** *WEA YZ 832CD*	37		4

CARRIE LUCAS
US, female vocalist — 6

Date	Title	Peak Position	Weeks at No.1	Weeks on Chart
16 Jun 79	**DANCE WITH YOU** *Solar FB 1482*	40		6

LUCIANA
UK, female vocalist (Luciana Caporaso) — 45

Date	Title	Peak Position	Weeks at No.1	Weeks on Chart
23 Apr 94	**GET IT UP FOR LOVE** *Chrysalis CDCHS 5008*	55		2
6 Aug 94	**IF YOU WANT** *Chrysalis CDCHS 5009*	47		2
5 Nov 94	**WHAT GOES AROUND/ONE MORE RIVER** *Chrysalis CDCHS 5015*	67		1
4 Nov 06	**YEAH YEAH** *Eye Industries/UMTV 1712693* BODYROX FEATURING LUCIANA	2		17
21 Jul 07	**BIGGER THAN BIG** *Eye Industries/UMTV 1740243* SUPER MAL FEATURING LUCIANA	19		4
19 Jan 08	**WHAT PLANET YOU ON** *Phonetic 1754549* BODYROX FEATURING LUCIANA	54		2
23 Feb 08	**COME ON GIRL** *Fourth & Broadway 1764408* TAIO CRUZ FEATURING LUCIANA	5		17

LUCID
UK, male/female vocal/instrumental trio – Clare Canty, Adam Carter-Ryan & Mark Hadfield. See Lovefreekz — 15

Date	Title	Peak Position	Weeks at No.1	Weeks on Chart
8 Aug 98	**I CAN'T HELP MYSELF** *ffrr FCD 339*	7		8
27 Feb 99	**CRAZY** *ffrr FCDP 355*	14		5
16 Oct 99	**STAY WITH ME TILL DAWN** *ffrr FCD 368*	25		2

LUCKY MONKEYS
UK, male instrumental/production group. See Fluke — 1

Date	Title	Peak Position	Weeks at No.1	Weeks on Chart
9 Nov 96	**BJANGO** *Hi-Life 5757132*	50		1

LUCY PEARL
US, male/female vocal/rap/instrumental/production trio — 7

Date	Title	Peak Position	Weeks at No.1	Weeks on Chart
29 Jul 00	**DANCE TONIGHT** *Virgin VSCDT 1775*	36		2
25 Nov 00	**DON'T MESS WITH MY MAN** *Virgin VSCDT 1778*	20		4
28 Jul 01	**WITHOUT YOU** *Virgin VSCDT 1805*	51		1

LUDACRIS
US, male rapper/actor (Christopher Bridges) — 113

Date	Title	Peak Position	Weeks at No.1	Weeks on Chart
9 Jun 01	**WHAT'S YOUR FANTASY** *Def Jam 5729842*	19		5
18 Aug 01	**ONE MINUTE MAN** *The Gold Mind/Elektra E 7245CD* MISSY ELLIOTT FEATURING LUDACRIS	10		8
29 Sep 01	**AREA CODES** *Def Jam 5887722* FEATURING NATE DOGG	25		3
22 Jun 02	**ROLLOUT (MY BUSINESS)** *Def Jam 5829632*	20		7
5 Oct 02	**SATURDAY (OOOH OOOH)** *Def Jam 639142*	31		2
9 Nov 02	**WHY DON'T WE FALL IN LOVE** *Columbia 6732212* AMERIE FEATURING LUDACRIS	40		2
22 Mar 03	**GOSSIP FOLKS** *Elektra E 7380CD* MISSY ELLIOTT FEATURING LUDACRIS	9		9
22 Nov 03	**STAND UP** *Def Jam South 9814001* ★	14		7
27 Mar 04	**YEAH** *Arista 82876606012* USHER FEATURING LIL' JON & LUDACRIS ★	1	2	14
21 May 05	**NUMBER ONE SPOT** *Def Jam 9881720*	30		2
13 Aug 05	**OH** *LaFace 82876711372* CIARA FEATURING LUDACRIS	4		9
22 Apr 06	**UNPREDICTABLE** *J 82876804772* JAMIE FOXX FEATURING LUDACRIS	16		6
27 Jan 07	**RUNAWAY LOVE** *Def Jam 1723705* FEATURING MARY J BLIGE	52		6
24 Feb 07	**GLAMOROUS** *A&M 1730081* FERGIE FEATURING LUDACRIS ★	6		26
9 Aug 08	**HOW WE DO IT (ROUND OUR WAY)** *Def Jam 1780769* LLOYD FEATURING LUDACRIS	75		1
20 Mar 10	**BABY** *Mercury USUM70919263* JUSTIN BIEBER FEATURING LUDACRIS	3		4+
27 Mar 10	**HOW LOW** *Mercury USUM70913041*	67		2

LUDES
Canada, male vocal/instrumental group — 1

Date	Title	Peak Position	Weeks at No.1	Weeks on Chart
18 Dec 04	**RADIO** *Double Dragon DD2018CD*	68		1

BAZ LUHRMANN
Australia, male film producer/director (Bazmark Luhrmann) — 17

Date	Title	Peak Position	Weeks at No.1	Weeks on Chart
12 Jun 99	**EVERYBODY'S FREE (TO WEAR SUNSCREEN)** *EMI CDBAZ 001* ●	1	1	16
16 Aug 08	**EVERYBODY'S FREE (TO WEAR SUNSCREEN)** *EMI AUEMO9900003*	72		1

ROBIN LUKE
US, male vocalist — 6

Date	Title	Peak Position	Weeks at No.1	Weeks on Chart
17 Oct 58	**SUSIE DARLIN'** *London HLD 8676*	23		6

LUKK FEATURING FELICIA COLLINS
US, male production duo & female vocalist — 1

Date	Title	Peak Position	Weeks at No.1	Weeks on Chart
28 Sep 85	**ON THE ONE** *Important TAN 6*	72		1

LULU
UK, female vocalist (Marie Lawrie) — 188

Date	Title	Peak Position	Weeks at No.1	Weeks on Chart
14 May 64	**SHOUT** *Decca F 11884* & THE LUVVERS	7		13
12 Nov 64	**HERE COMES THE NIGHT** *Decca F 12017*	50		1
17 Jun 65	**LEAVE A LITTLE LOVE** *Decca F 12169*	8		11
2 Sep 65	**TRY TO UNDERSTAND** *Decca F 12214*	25		8
13 Apr 67	**THE BOAT THAT I ROW** *Columbia DB 8169*	6		11
29 Jun 67	**LET'S PRETEND** *Columbia DB 8221*	11		11
8 Nov 67	**LOVE LOVES TO LOVE LOVE** *Columbia DB 8295*	32		6
28 Feb 68	**ME THE PEACEFUL HEART** *Columbia DB 8358*	9		9
5 Jun 68	**BOY** *Columbia DB 8425*	15		7
6 Nov 68	**I'M A TIGER** *Columbia DB 8500*	9		13
12 Mar 69	**BOOM BANG-A-BANG** *Columbia DB 8550*	2		13
22 Nov 69	**OH ME OH MY (I'M A FOOL FOR YOU BABY)** *Atco 226 008*	47		2
26 Jan 74	**THE MAN WHO SOLD THE WORLD** *Polydor 2001 490* ●	3		9
19 Apr 75	**TAKE YOUR MAMA FOR A RIDE** *Chelsea 2005 022*	37		4
12 Dec 81	**I COULD NEVER MISS YOU (MORE THAN I DO)** *Alfa 1700*	62		5
19 Jul 86	**SHOUT** *Jive LULU 1/Decca SHOUT 1* & THE LUVVERS	8		11
30 Jan 93	**INDEPENDENCE** *Dome CDDOME 1001*	11		5
3 Apr 93	**I'M BACK FOR MORE** *Dome CDDOME 1002* & BOBBY WOMACK	27		5
4 Sep 93	**LET ME WAKE UP IN YOUR ARMS** *Dome CDDOME 1005*	51		2
9 Oct 93	**RELIGHT MY FIRE** *RCA 74321167722* TAKE THAT FEATURING LULU ●	1	2	14
27 Nov 93	**HOW 'BOUT US** *Dome CDDOME 1007*	46		3
27 Aug 94	**GOODBYE BABY AND AMEN** *Dome CDDOME 1011*	40		2
26 Nov 94	**EVERY WOMAN KNOWS** *Dome CDDOME 1013*	44		2
29 May 99	**HURT ME SO BAD** *Rocket/Mercury 5726132*	42		2
8 Jan 00	**BETTER GET READY** *Mercury 5625852*	59		1
18 Mar 00	**WHERE THE POOR BOYS DANCE** *Mercury 1568452*	24		5
7 Dec 02	**WE'VE GOT TONIGHT** *Polydor 0658612* RONAN KEATING FEATURING LULU	4		13

BOB LUMAN
US, male vocalist, d. 27 Dec 1978 (age 41) — 21

Date	Title	Peak Position	Weeks at No.1	Weeks on Chart
8 Sep 60	**LET'S THINK ABOUT LIVING** *Warner Brothers WB 18*	6		18
15 Dec 60	**WHY WHY BYE BYE** *Warner Brothers WB 28*	46		1
4 May 61	**THE GREAT SNOWMAN** *Warner Brothers WB 37*	49		2

LUMIDEE
US, female vocalist/rapper (Lumidee Cedeno) — 15

Date	Title	Peak Position	Weeks at No.1	Weeks on Chart
9 Aug 03	**NEVER LEAVE YOU (UH OOOH UH OOOH)** *Universal MCSTD 40328*	2		13
29 Nov 03	**CRASHIN' A PARTY** *Universal MCSTD 40341* FEATURING NORE	55		1
11 Aug 07	**CRAZY** *TVT TVTUKCD24*	74		1

LUNIZ
US, male rap duo – Jerrold 'Yukmouth' Ellis, Jr. & Garrick 'Knumbskull' Husbands — 18

Date	Title	Peak Position	Weeks at No.1	Weeks on Chart
17 Feb 96	**I GOT 5 ON IT** *Noo Trybe VUSCD 101* ●	3		13
11 May 96	**PLAYA HATA** *Virgin VUSCDX 103*	20		3
31 Oct 98	**I GOT 5 ON IT (REMIX)** *Virgin VCRD 41*	28		2

LUPINE HOWL
UK, male vocal/instrumental group — 1

Date	Title	Peak Position	Weeks at No.1	Weeks on Chart
22 Jan 00	**VAPORIZER** *Vinyl Hiss VHISSCD 001*	68		1

PATTI LUPONE
US, female actor/vocalist — 2

Date	Title	Peak	No.1	Wks
25 Apr 09	**I DREAMED A DREAM** *First Night GBBKB8520105*	45		2

LURKERS
UK, male vocal/instrumental group — 11

Date	Title	Peak	No.1	Wks
3 Jun 78	**AIN'T GOT A CLUE** *Beggars Banquet BEG 6*	45		3
5 Aug 78	**I DON'T NEED TO TELL HER** *Beggars Banquet BEG 9*	49		4
3 Feb 79	**JUST THIRTEEN** *Beggars Banquet BEG 14*	66		2
9 Jun 79	**OUT IN THE DARK/CYANIDE** *Beggars Banquet BEG 19*	72		1
17 Nov 79	**NEW GUITAR IN TOWN** *Beggars Banquet BEG 28*	72		1

LUSCIOUS JACKSON
US, female vocal/instrumental group — 5

Date	Title	Peak	No.1	Wks
18 Mar 95	**DEEP SHAG/CITYSONG** *Capitol CDCL 739*	69		1
21 Oct 95	**HERE** *Capitol CDCL 758*	59		1
12 Apr 97	**NAKED EYE** *Capitol CDCL 786*	25		2
3 Jul 99	**LADYFINGERS** *Grand Royal CDCL 813*	43		1

LUSH
UK, female/male vocal/instrumental group — 19

Date	Title	Peak	No.1	Wks
10 Mar 90	**MAD LOVE (EP)** *4AD BAD 003*	55		1
27 Oct 90	**SWEETNESS AND LIGHT** *4AD BAD 0013*	47		2
19 Oct 91	**NOTHING NATURAL** *4AD AD 1016*	43		2
11 Jan 92	**FOR LOVE (EP)** *4AD BAD 2001*	35		2
11 Jun 94	**DESIRE LINES** *4AD BAD 4010CD*	60		1
11 Jun 94	**HYPOCRITE** *4AD BAD 4008CD*	52		2
20 Jan 96	**SINGLE GIRL** *4AD BAD 6001CD*	21		3
9 Mar 96	**LADYKILLERS** *4AD BAD 6002CD*	22		3
27 Jul 96	**500 (SHAKE BABY SHAKE)** *4AD BADD 6009CD*	21		3

LUSTRAL
UK, male DJ/production duo. See Ascension, Chakra, Oxygen featuring Andrea Britton, Space Brothers — 3

Date	Title	Peak	No.1	Wks
18 Oct 97	**EVERYTIME** *Hooj Choons HOOJCD 55*	60		1
4 Dec 99	**EVERYTIME (REMIX)** *Hooj Choons HOOJ 83CD*	30		2

LUZON
US, male producer (Stacy Burket) — 1

Date	Title	Peak	No.1	Wks
14 Jul 01	**THE BAGUIO TRACK** *Renaissance RENCDS 006*	67		1

LV
US, male vocalist (Larry Sanders) — 28

Date	Title	Peak	No.1	Wks
28 Oct 95	**GANGSTA'S PARADISE** *Tommy Boy MCSTD 2104* COOLIO FEATURING LV ⊛ ★	1	2	20
23 Dec 95	**THROW YOUR HANDS UP/GANGSTA'S PARADISE** *Tommy Boy TBCD 699*	24		4
4 May 96	**I AM LV** *Tommy Boy TBCD 7724*	64		1
17 Jan 09	**GANGSTA'S PARADISE** *Tommy Boy 8122747781* COOLIO FEATURING LV	31		3

ANNABELLA LWIN
Myanmar, female vocalist (Myant Myant Aye). See Bow Wow Wow — 1

Date	Title	Peak	No.1	Wks
28 Jan 95	**DO WHAT YOU DO** *Sony S2 6611235*	61		1

LWS
Italy, male production trio — 1

Date	Title	Peak	No.1	Wks
29 Oct 94	**GOSP** *Transworld TRANNY 4CD*	65		1

JOHN LYDON
UK, male vocalist. See Public Image Ltd, Sex Pistols — 6

Date	Title	Peak	No.1	Wks
13 Nov 93	**OPEN UP** *Hard Hands HAND 009CD* LEFTFIELD LYDON	13		5
2 Aug 97	**SUN** *Virgin VUSCD 122*	42		1

FRANKIE LYMON & THE TEENAGERS
US, male vocal group – Frankie Lymon, d. 28 Feb 1968, Sherman Garnes, d. 26 Feb 1977, Jimmy Merchant, Joe Negroni, d. 5 Sep 1978, & Herman Santiago — 36

Date	Title	Peak	No.1	Wks
29 Jun 56	**WHY DO FOOLS FALL IN LOVE** *Columbia DB 3772* TEENAGERS FEATURING FRANKIE LYMON	1	3	16
29 Mar 57	**I'M NOT A TEENAGE DELINQUENT** *Columbia DB 3878*	12		7
12 Apr 57	**BABY BABY** *Columbia DB 3878*	4		12
20 Sep 57	**GOODY GOODY** *Columbia DB 3983*	24		1

DES LYNAM FEATURING WIMBLEDON CHORAL SOCIETY
UK, male TV presenter/vocalist & choir — 3

Date	Title	Peak	No.1	Wks
12 Dec 98	**IF – READ TO FAURE'S 'PAVANE'** *BBC Worldwide WMSS 60062*	45		3

CURTIS LYNCH, JR FEATURING KELE LE ROC & RED RAT
UK/Jamaica, male/female vocal/production trio — 1

Date	Title	Peak	No.1	Wks
30 Sep 00	**THINKING OF YOU** *Telstar CDSTAS 3136*	70		1

KENNY LYNCH
UK, male vocalist — 59

Date	Title	Peak	No.1	Wks
30 Jun 60	**MOUNTAIN OF LOVE** *HMV POP 751*	33		3
13 Sep 62	**PUFF (UP IN SMOKE)** *HMV POP 1057*	33		6
6 Dec 62	**UP ON THE ROOF** *HMV POP 1090*	10		12
20 Jun 63	**YOU CAN NEVER STOP ME LOVING YOU** *HMV POP 1165*	10		14
16 Apr 64	**STAND BY ME** *HMV POP 1280*	39		7
27 Aug 64	**WHAT AM I TO YOU** *HMV POP 1321*	37		6
17 Jun 65	**I'LL STAY BY YOU** *HMV POP 1430*	29		7
20 Aug 83	**HALF THE DAY'S GONE AND WE HAVEN'T EARNT A PENNY** *Satril SAT 510*	50		4

LIAM LYNCH
US, male vocalist/guitarist/TV director/producer — 9

Date	Title	Peak	No.1	Wks
7 Dec 02	**UNITED STATES OF WHATEVER** *Global Warming WARMCD 17*	10		9

CHERYL LYNN
US, female vocalist (Lynda Cheryl Smith) — 2

Date	Title	Peak	No.1	Wks
8 Sep 84	**ENCORE** *Streetwave KHAN 23*	68		2

PATTI LYNN
UK, female vocalist — 5

Date	Title	Peak	No.1	Wks
10 May 62	**JOHNNY ANGEL** *Fontana H 391*	37		5

TAMI LYNN
US, female vocalist — 20

Date	Title	Peak	No.1	Wks
22 May 71	**I'M GONNA RUN AWAY FROM YOU** *Mojo 2092 001*	4		14
3 May 75	**I'M GONNA RUN AWAY FROM YOU** *Contempo Raries CS 9026*	36		6

VERA LYNN
UK, female vocalist (Vera Welch) — 46

Date	Title	Peak	No.1	Wks
14 Nov 52	**AUF WIEDERSEHEN SWEETHEART** *Decca F 9927* ★	10		1
14 Nov 52	**FORGET-ME-NOT** *Decca F 9985*	5		6
14 Nov 52	**HOMING WALTZ** *Decca F 9959*	9		3
5 Jun 53	**THE WINDSOR WALTZ** *Decca F 10092*	11		1
15 Oct 54	**MY SON MY SON** *Decca F 10372* WITH FRANK WEIR, HIS SAXOPHONE, HIS ORCHESTRA & CHORUS	1	2	14
8 Jun 56	**WHO ARE WE** *Decca F 10715*	30		1
26 Oct 56	**A HOUSE WITH LOVE IN IT** *Decca F 10799*	17		13
15 Mar 57	**THE FAITHFUL HUSSAR (DON'T CRY MY LOVE)** *Decca F 10846*	29		2
21 Jun 57	**TRAVELLIN' HOME** *Decca F 10903*	20		5

JEFF LYNNE
UK, male vocalist/guitarist/producer. See Electric Light Orchestra, Traveling Wilburys — 4

Date	Title	Peak	No.1	Wks
30 Jun 90	**EVERY LITTLE THING** *Reprise W 9799*	59		4

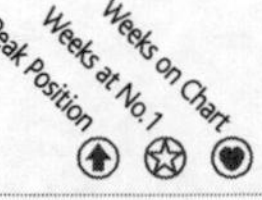

SHELBY LYNNE

US, female vocalist/guitarist (Shelby Moorer) — Total weeks on chart: 1

Date	Title	Label	Peak Position	Weeks at No.1	Weeks on Chart
29 Apr 00	**LEAVIN'**	*Mercury 5627372*	73		1

PHIL LYNOTT

Ireland, male vocalist/guitarist, d. 4 Jan 1986 (age 36). See Gary Moore, Thin Lizzy, Midge Ure — Total weeks on chart: 36

Date	Title	Label	Peak Position	Weeks at No.1	Weeks on Chart
5 Apr 80	**DEAR MISS LONELY HEARTS**	*Vertigo SOLO 1* PHILIP LYNOTT	32		6
21 Jun 80	**KING'S CALL**	*Vertigo SOLO 2*	35		6
21 Mar 81	**YELLOW PEARL**	*Vertigo SOLO 3* PHILIP LYNOTT	56		3
26 Dec 81	**YELLOW PEARL**	*Vertigo SOLO 3* PHILIP LYNOTT	14		9
18 May 85	**OUT IN THE FIELDS**	*10 TEN 49* GARY MOORE & PHIL LYNOTT	5		10
24 Jan 87	**KING'S CALL (REMIX)**	*Vertigo LYN 1* PHILIP LYNOTT	68		2

LYNYRD SKYNYRD

US, male vocal/instrumental group — Total weeks on chart: 35

Date	Title	Label	Peak Position	Weeks at No.1	Weeks on Chart
11 Sep 76	**FREE BIRD EP**	*MCA 251*	31		4
22 Dec 79	**FREE BIRD EP**	*MCA 251*	43		8
19 Jun 82	**FREE BIRD EP**	*MCA 251* ●	21		9
20 Jan 07	**SWEET HOME ALABAMA**	*MCA USMC17446153*	61		1
28 Jun 08	**SWEET HOME ALABAMA**	*MCA USMC17446153*	44		13

BARBARA LYON

US, female vocalist, d. 10 Jul 1985 (age 53) — Total weeks on chart: 12

Date	Title	Label	Peak Position	Weeks at No.1	Weeks on Chart
24 Jun 55	**STOWAWAY**	*Columbia DB 3619*	12		8
21 Dec 56	**LETTER TO A SOLDIER**	*Columbia DB 3865*	27		4

LYTE FUNKIE ONES

US, male vocal/rap trio – Rich Cronin, Brad Fischetti & Devin Lima (Harold Lima) (replaced Brian Gillis) — Total weeks on chart: 20

Date	Title	Label	Peak Position	Weeks at No.1	Weeks on Chart
22 May 99	**CAN'T HAVE YOU**	*Logic 74321649152*	54		1
18 Sep 99	**SUMMER GIRLS**	*Logic 74321701162*	16		7
5 Feb 00	**GIRL ON TV**	*Logic 74321717582*	6		9
27 Apr 02	**EVERY OTHER TIME**	*Logic 74321925502*	24		3

HUMPHREY LYTTELTON BAND

UK, male band leader, d. 25 Apr 2008 (age 86) — Total weeks on chart: 6

Date	Title	Label	Peak Position	Weeks at No.1	Weeks on Chart
13 Jul 56	**BAD PENNY BLUES**	*Parlophone R 4184*	19		6

KEVIN LYTTLE

St. Vincent, male vocalist (Lescott Coombs) — Total weeks on chart: 23

Date	Title	Label	Peak Position	Weeks at No.1	Weeks on Chart
25 Oct 03	**TURN ME ON**	*Atlantic AT 0167CD* ●	2		19
29 May 04	**LAST DROP**	*Atlantic AT 0176CD*	22		4

BIOGRAPHIES

Biographies include the nationality and category for every chart entrant.

Each entrant has at least a mini biography. The acts with the most weeks on the chart (see page 372 for the chart) each have extended biographies.

Real names are included for all solo artists and, where applicable, dates of death and age of the artist at the time. "See..." links are included for soloists who also had singles chart entries in other acts.

The best known line-up is listed for every group that had a Top 10 single, with the vocalist/leader mentioned first and the others following in alphabetical order. In cases where later replacements had similar success both people are named and, where applicable, the dates of death are also shown for every group/duo member listed.

Certified Awards are given by the BPI to mark unit sales to retailers. They were introduced in April 1973. In January 1989 the levels of unit sales to the trade required to achieve each of the awards was amended to the following amounts:

Silver symbol	●	=	200,000 units
Gold symbol	●	=	400,000 units
Platinum symbol	⊛	=	600,000 units

As from February 2005, download sales also count towards certified awards.

M–P

KEY TO ARTIST ENTRIES

Artist/Group Name — Artist/Group Biography — Silver-selling — Gold-selling — Platinum-selling — US No.1 — Peak Position — Weeks at No.1 — Weeks on Chart

Asterisks (*) indicate group members with hits in their own right that are listed elsewhere in this book

TAKE THAT

UK, male vocal group – Gary Barlow*, Howard Donald, Jason Orange, Mark Owen* & Robbie Williams* (left 1995, rejoined 2010). Comeback kings who have sold 7.4 million singles in the UK. The boys, who came back for good – as a quartet – in 2006, were the first act to score four successive No.1s since The Beatles – a feat they've achieved twice. See Helping Haiti

Artist's Total Weeks On Chart: 356

Date	Title / Label	Peak	Wks at No.1	Wks
23 Nov 91	**PROMISES** *RCA PB 45085*	38		2
8 Feb 92	**ONCE YOU'VE TASTED LOVE** *RCA PB 45257*	47		3
6 Jun 92	**IT ONLY TAKES A MINUTE** *RCA 74321101007*	7		8
15 Aug 92	**I FOUND HEAVEN** *RCA 74321108137*	15		6
10 Oct 92	**A MILLION LOVE SONGS** *RCA 74321116307*	7		9
12 Dec 92	**COULD IT BE MAGIC** *RCA 74321123137* ●	3		12
20 Feb 93	**WHY CAN'T I WAKE UP WITH YOU** *RCA 74321133102* ●	2		10
17 Jul 93	**PRAY** *RCA 74321154502* ●	1	4	11
9 Oct 93	**RELIGHT MY FIRE** *RCA 74321167722* FEATURING LULU ●	1	2	14
18 Dec 93	**BABE** *RCA 74321182122* ⊛	1	1	10
9 Apr 94	**EVERYTHING CHANGES** *RCA 74321167732* ●	1	2	10
9 Jul 94	**LOVE AIN'T HERE ANYMORE** *RCA 74321214832* ●	3		12
15 Oct 94	**SURE** *RCA 74321236622* ●	1	2	15
8 Apr 95	**BACK FOR GOOD** *RCA 74321271462* ⊛	1	4	13
5 Aug 95	**NEVER FORGET** *RCA 74321299572* ●	1	3	9
9 Mar 96	**HOW DEEP IS YOUR LOVE** *RCA 74321355592* ⊛	1	3	14
25 Nov 06	**PATIENCE** *Polydor 1714832* ●	1	4	39
10 Feb 07	**SHINE** *Polydor 1724294* ●	1	2	42
30 Jun 07	**I'D WAIT FOR LIFE** *Polydor 1736401*	17		2
27 Oct 07	**RULE THE WORLD** *Polydor 1746285* ●	2		66
6 Dec 08	**GREATEST DAY** *Polydor 1787445*	1	1	20
6 Dec 08	**PATIENCE** *Polydor 1714832*	59		1
6 Dec 08	**NEVER FORGET** *RCA GBARL9500200*	64		1
14 Feb 09	**UP ALL NIGHT** *Polydor 1796964*	14		11
13 Jun 09	**SAID IT ALL** *Polydor 2708717*	9		10
20 Jun 09	**RULE THE WORLD** *Polydor 1746285*	57		6
27 Jun 09	**GREATEST DAY** *Polydor 1787445*	73		1+

Date of entry into chart

Artist collaboration or variation on artist's name

Title of Single

Label and Catalogue Number

BPI Certified Award

A cross (+) indicates that the single was still on chart in the final week of March 2010

M
UK, male vocalist/multi-instrumentalist (Robin Scott) — 39

Date	Title	Peak	Wks at No.1	Wks on Chart
7 Apr 79	**POP MUZIK** *MCA 413* ● ★	2		14
8 Dec 79	**MOONLIGHT AND MUZAK** *MCA 541*	33		9
15 Mar 80	**THAT'S THE WAY THE MONEY GOES** *MCA 570*	45		5
22 Nov 80	**OFFICIAL SECRETS** *MCA 650*	64		2
10 Jun 89	**POP MUZIK** *Freestyle FRS 1*	15		9

BOBBY M FEATURING JEAN CARN
US, male saxophonist (Robert Militello) & female vocalist (Sarah Jean Perkins) — 3

Date	Title	Peak	Wks at No.1	Wks on Chart
29 Jan 83	**LET'S STAY TOGETHER** *Gordy TMG 1288*	53		3

M & O BAND
UK, male vocal/instrumental duo — 6

Date	Title	Peak	Wks at No.1	Wks on Chart
28 Feb 76	**LET'S DO THE LATIN HUSTLE** *Creole CR 120*	16		6

M&S PRESENTS GIRL NEXT DOOR
UK, male/female vocal/production trio – Natasha Bryce, Ricky Morrison & Fran Sidoli — 13

Date	Title	Peak	Wks at No.1	Wks on Chart
7 Apr 01	**SALSOUL NUGGET (IF U WANNA)** *ffrr FCD 393*	6		13

M-BEAT
UK, male producer (Marlon Hart) — 24

Date	Title	Peak	Wks at No.1	Wks on Chart
18 Jun 94	**INCREDIBLE** *Renk 42CD* FEATURING GENERAL LEVY	39		3
10 Sep 94	**INCREDIBLE (REMIX)** *Renk CDRENK 44* FEATURING GENERAL LEVY	8		9
17 Dec 94	**SWEET LOVE** *Renk CDRENK 49* FEATURING NAZLYN	18		7
1 Jun 96	**DO U KNOW WHERE YOU'RE COMING FROM** *Renk CDRENK 63* FEATURING JAMIROQUAI	12		5

M DUBS FEATURING LADY SAW
UK/Jamaica, male/female vocal/production duo — 1

Date	Title	Peak	Wks at No.1	Wks on Chart
16 Dec 00	**BUMP N GRIND (I AM FEELING HOT TONIGHT)** *Telstar CDSTAS 3129*	59		1

M FACTOR
UK, male DJ/production duo. See Nu-Birth, Nush, 187 Lockdown — 5

Date	Title	Peak	Wks at No.1	Wks on Chart
6 Jul 02	**MOTHER** *Serious SERR 042CD*	18		4
26 Jul 03	**COME TOGETHER** *Credence CDCRED 037*	46		1

M1
UK, male producer (Michael Woods) — 1

Date	Title	Peak	Wks at No.1	Wks on Chart
22 Feb 03	**HEAVEN SENT** *Inferno CDFERN 51*	72		1

M PEOPLE
UK, female/male vocal/instrumental/production group – Heather Small*, Paul Heard, Mike Pickering & Andrew 'Shovell' Lovell — 137

Date	Title	Peak	Wks at No.1	Wks on Chart
26 Oct 91	**HOW CAN I LOVE YOU MORE** *Deconstruction PB 44855*	29		9
7 Mar 92	**COLOUR MY LIFE** *Deconstruction PB 45241*	35		4
18 Apr 92	**SOMEDAY** *Deconstruction PB 45369* WITH HEATHER SMALL	38		3
10 Oct 92	**EXCITED** *Deconstruction 74321116337*	29		5
6 Feb 93	**HOW CAN I LOVE YOU MORE (REMIX)** *Deconstruction 74321130232*	8		8
26 Jun 93	**ONE NIGHT IN HEAVEN** *Deconstruction 74321151852*	6		11
25 Sep 93	**MOVING ON UP** *Deconstruction 74321166162*	2		11
4 Dec 93	**DON'T LOOK ANY FURTHER** *Deconstruction 74321177112*	9		10
12 Mar 94	**RENAISSANCE** *Deconstruction 74321194132*	5		7
17 Sep 94	**ELEGANTLY AMERICAN: ONE NIGHT IN HEAVEN/MOVING ON UP** *Deconstruction 74321231882*	31		2
19 Nov 94	**SIGHT FOR SORE EYES** *Deconstruction 74321245472*	6		9
4 Feb 95	**OPEN YOUR HEART** *Deconstruction 74321261532*	9		7
24 Jun 95	**SEARCH FOR THE HERO** *Deconstruction 74321287962*	9		7
14 Oct 95	**LOVE RENDEZVOUS** *Deconstruction 74321319282*	32		4
25 Nov 95	**ITCHYCOO PARK** *Deconstruction 74321330732*	11		8
4 Oct 97	**JUST FOR YOU** *M People 74321523002*	8		7
6 Dec 97	**FANTASY ISLAND** *M People 74321542932*	33		9
28 Mar 98	**ANGEL STREET** *M People 74321564182*	8		6
7 Nov 98	**TESTIFY** *M People 74321621742*	12		6
13 Feb 99	**DREAMING** *M People 74321645362*	13		4

M + M
Canada, male/female vocal/instrumental duo. See Martha & The Muffins — 4

Date	Title	Peak	Wks at No.1	Wks on Chart
28 Jul 84	**BLACK STATIONS WHITE STATIONS** *RCA 426*	46		4

M3
UK, male/female vocal/production trio — 2

Date	Title	Peak	Wks at No.1	Wks on Chart
30 Oct 99	**BAILAMOS** *Inferno CDFERN 21*	40		2

M2M
Norway, female vocal/instrumental duo — 6

Date	Title	Peak	Wks at No.1	Wks on Chart
1 Apr 00	**DON'T SAY YOU LOVE ME** *Atlantic AT 0081CD1*	16		6

TIMO MAAS
Germany, male DJ/producer — 10

Date	Title	Peak	Wks at No.1	Wks on Chart
1 Apr 00	**DER SCHIEBER** *48k/Perfecto SPECT 07CDS*	50		1
30 Sep 00	**UBIK** *Perfecto PERF10CDS2* FEATURING MARTIN BETTINGHAUS	33		2
23 Feb 02	**TO GET DOWN (ROCK THING)** *Perfecto PERF 30CDS*	14		4
11 May 02	**SHIFTER** *Perfecto PERF 31CDS* FEATURING MC CHICKABOO	38		2
5 Oct 02	**HELP ME** *Perfecto PERF 42CDS* FEATURING KELIS	65		1

PETE MAC, JR
US, male vocalist — 4

Date	Title	Peak	Wks at No.1	Wks on Chart
15 Oct 77	**THE WATER MARGIN** *BBC RESL 50*	37		4

STEVE MAC
UK, male DJ/producer (Stephen McGuinness) — 7

Date	Title	Peak	Wks at No.1	Wks on Chart
22 Oct 05	**LOVIN' YOU MORE** *Ministry Of Sound C2MOS1CDS* VS MOSQUITO FEATURING STEVE SMITH	73		1
13 Sep 08	**PADDY'S REVENGE** *All Around The World CDGLOBE987*	17		6

MAC BAND FEATURING THE McCAMPBELL BROTHERS
US, male vocal/instrumental group – Charles, Derrick, Kelvin & Ray McCampbell, Ray Flippin, Rodney Frazier, Slye Fuller & Mark Harper — 17

Date	Title	Peak	Wks at No.1	Wks on Chart
18 Jun 88	**ROSES ARE RED** *MCA 1264*	8		13
10 Sep 88	**STALEMATE** *MCA 1271*	40		4

KEITH MAC PROJECT
UK, male producer (Keith McDonald) & vocal/production collaborators — 1

Date	Title	Peak	Wks at No.1	Wks on Chart
25 Jun 94	**DE DAH DAH (SPICE OF LIFE)** *Public Demand PPDCD 3*	66		1

DAVID McALMONT
UK, male vocal/instrumental duo – David McAlmont* & Bernard Butler*. See Suede, Tears — 22

Date	Title	Peak	Wks at No.1	Wks on Chart
27 May 95	**YES** *Hut HUTCD 53* McALMONT & BUTLER	8		8
4 Nov 95	**YOU DO** *Hut HUTDG 57* McALMONT & BUTLER	17		4
27 Apr 96	**HYMN** *Blanco Y Negro NEG 87CD* ULTRAMARINE FEATURING DAVID McALMONT	65		1
9 Aug 97	**LOOK AT YOURSELF** *Hut HUTCD 87*	40		2
22 Nov 97	**DIAMONDS ARE FOREVER** *East West EW 141CD* & DAVID ARNOLD	39		2
10 Aug 02	**FALLING** *Chrysalis CDCHS 5141* McALMONT & BUTLER	23		3
9 Nov 02	**BRING IT BACK** *Chrysalis CDCHSS 5145* McALMONT & BUTLER	36		2

NEIL MacARTHUR
UK, male vocalist (Colin Blunstone). See Zombies — 5

Date	Title	Peak	Wks at No.1	Wks on Chart
5 Feb 69	**SHE'S NOT THERE** *Deram DM 225*	34		5

DAVID MACBETH
UK, male vocalist — 4

Date	Title	Peak	Wks at No.1	Wks on Chart
30 Oct 59	**MR BLUE** *Pye 7N 15231*	18		4

Silver-selling ○ Gold-selling ● Platinum-selling (x multiples) ⊛ US No.1 ★ Peak Position ⬆ Weeks at No.1 ✪ Weeks on Chart

NICKO McBRAIN

UK, male drummer (Michael McBrain). See Iron Maiden, John McEnroe & Pat Cash with the Full Metal Rackets

⬆ ✪ 1

Date	Title	Peak	Wks at No.1	Wks
13 Jul 91	**RHYTHM OF THE BEAST** *EMI NICK 1*	72		1

FRANKIE McBRIDE

Ireland, male vocalist

⬆ ✪ 15

Date	Title	Peak	Wks at No.1	Wks
9 Aug 67	**FIVE LITTLE FINGERS** *Emerald MD 1081*	19		15

MACCABEES

UK, male vocal/instrumental group

⬆ ✪ 7

Date	Title	Peak	Wks at No.1	Wks
25 Nov 06	**FIRST LOVE** *Fiction 1707085*	40		1
10 Mar 07	**ABOUT YOUR DRESS** *Fiction/Polydor 1724475*	33		2
19 May 07	**PRECIOUS TIME** *Fiction/Polydor 1732766*	49		1
19 Jan 08	**TOOTHPASTE KISSES** *Fiction/Polydor 1746533*	70		1
9 May 09	**LOVE YOU BETTER** *Fiction 2701348*	36		2

DAN McCAFFERTY

UK, male vocalist. See Nazareth

⬆ ✪ 3

Date	Title	Peak	Wks at No.1	Wks
13 Sep 75	**OUT OF TIME** *Mountain TOP 1*	41		3

CW McCALL

US, male vocalist (William Fries)

⬆ ✪ 10

Date	Title	Peak	Wks at No.1	Wks
14 Feb 76	**CONVOY** *MGM 2006 560* ○ ★	2		10

DAVID McCALLUM

UK, male actor/vocalist

⬆ ✪ 4

Date	Title	Peak	Wks at No.1	Wks
14 Apr 66	**COMMUNICATION** *Capitol CL 15439*	32		4

JESSE McCARTNEY

US, male vocalist/actor

⬆ ✪ 12

Date	Title	Peak	Wks at No.1	Wks
11 Feb 06	**BEAUTIFUL SOUL** *Angel ANGEDX7*	16		7
7 Oct 06	**RIGHT WHERE YOU WANT ME** *Angel ANGECD20*	54		1
7 Jun 08	**LEAVIN'** *Angel CASD33*	48		4

LINDA McCARTNEY

US, female vocalist (Linda Eastman), d. 17 Apr 1998 (age 55)

⬆ ✪ 7

Date	Title	Peak	Wks at No.1	Wks
28 Aug 71	**BACK SEAT OF MY CAR** *Apple R 5914* PAUL & LINDA McCARTNEY	39		5
21 Nov 98	**WIDE PRAIRIE** *Parlophone CDR 6510*	74		1
6 Feb 99	**THE LIGHT COMES FROM WITHIN** *Parlophone CDR 6513*	56		1

PAUL McCARTNEY

UK, male vocalist (James McCartney). The most successful pop music composer of the rock era is also one of the world's most popular live acts and the biggest-earning UK artist of all time. The multi-award-winning ex-Beatle's composition 'Yesterday' is the most recorded song ever

⬆ ✪ 423

Date	Title	Peak	Wks at No.1	Wks
27 Feb 71	**ANOTHER DAY** *Apple R 5889*	2		12
28 Aug 71	**BACK SEAT OF MY CAR** *Apple R 5914* PAUL & LINDA McCARTNEY	39		5
26 Feb 72	**GIVE IRELAND BACK TO THE IRISH** *Apple R 5936* WINGS	16		8
27 May 72	**MARY HAD A LITTLE LAMB** *Apple R 5949* WINGS	9		11
9 Dec 72	**HI HI HI/C MOON** *Apple R 5973* WINGS	5		13
7 Apr 73	**MY LOVE** *Apple R 5985* & WINGS ★	9		11
9 Jun 73	**LIVE AND LET DIE** *Apple R 5987* WINGS	9		14
3 Nov 73	**HELEN WHEELS** *Apple R 5993* & WINGS	12		12
2 Mar 74	**JET** *Apple R 5996* & WINGS ●	7		9
6 Jul 74	**BAND ON THE RUN** *Apple R 5997* & WINGS ○ ★	3		11
9 Nov 74	**JUNIOR'S FARM** *Apple R 5999* & WINGS	16		10
31 May 75	**LISTEN TO WHAT THE MAN SAID** *Capitol R 6006* WINGS ★	6		8
18 Oct 75	**LETTING GO** *Capitol R 6008* WINGS	41		3
15 May 76	**SILLY LOVE SONGS** *Parlophone R 6014* WINGS ○ ★	2		11
7 Aug 76	**LET 'EM IN** *Parlophone R 6015* WINGS ○	2		10
19 Feb 77	**MAYBE I'M AMAZED** *Parlophone R 6017* WINGS	28		5
19 Nov 77	**MULL OF KINTYRE/GIRLS' SCHOOL** *Parlophone R 6018* WINGS ⊛ x2	1	9	17
8 Apr 78	**WITH A LITTLE LUCK** *Parlophone R 6019* WINGS ○ ★	5		9
1 Jul 78	**I'VE HAD ENOUGH** *Parlophone R 6020* WINGS	42		7
9 Sep 78	**LONDON TOWN** *Parlophone R 6021* WINGS	60		4
7 Apr 79	**GOODNIGHT TONIGHT** *Parlophone R 6023* WINGS ○	5		10
16 Jun 79	**OLD SIAM SIR** *MPL R 6026* WINGS	35		6
1 Sep 79	**GETTING CLOSER/BABY'S REQUEST** *R 6027* WINGS	60		3
1 Dec 79	**WONDERFUL CHRISTMAS TIME** *Parlophone R 6029* ○	6		8
19 Apr 80	**COMING UP** *Parlophone R 6035* ○ ★	2		9
21 Jun 80	**WATERFALLS** *Parlophone R 6037*	9		8
10 Apr 82	**EBONY AND IVORY** *Parlophone R 6054* & STEVIE WONDER ● ★	1	3	10
3 Jul 82	**TAKE IT AWAY** *Parlophone R 6056*	15		10
9 Oct 82	**TUG OF WAR** *Parlophone R 6057*	53		3
6 Nov 82	**THE GIRL IS MINE** *Epic A 2729* MICHAEL JACKSON & PAUL McCARTNEY	8		10
15 Oct 83	**SAY SAY SAY** *Parlophone R 6062* & MICHAEL JACKSON ○ ★	2		15
17 Dec 83	**PIPES OF PEACE** *Parlophone R 6064* ○	1	2	12
6 Oct 84	**NO MORE LONELY NIGHTS (BALLAD)** *Parlophone R 6080* ○	2		15
24 Nov 84	**WE ALL STAND TOGETHER** *Parlophone R 6086* & THE FROG CHORUS ●	3		13
30 Nov 85	**SPIES LIKE US** *Parlophone R 6118*	13		10
21 Dec 85	**WE ALL STAND TOGETHER** *Parlophone R 6086* & THE FROG CHORUS	32		5
26 Jul 86	**PRESS** *Parlophone R 6133*	25		8
13 Dec 86	**ONLY LOVE REMAINS** *Parlophone R 6148*	34		5
28 Nov 87	**ONCE UPON A LONG AGO** *Parlophone R 6170*	10		7
20 May 89	**FERRY 'CROSS THE MERSEY** *PWL 41* CHRISTIANS, HOLLY JOHNSON, PAUL McCARTNEY, GERRY MARSDEN & STOCK AITKEN WATERMAN	1	3	7
20 May 89	**MY BRAVE FACE** *Parlophone R 6213*	18		5
29 Jul 89	**THIS ONE** *Parlophone R 6223*	18		6
25 Nov 89	**FIGURE OF EIGHT** *Parlophone R 6235*	42		3
17 Feb 90	**PUT IT THERE** *Parlophone R 6246*	32		2
20 Oct 90	**BIRTHDAY** *Parlophone R 6271*	29		3
8 Dec 90	**ALL MY TRIALS** *Parlophone R 6278*	35		5
9 Jan 93	**HOPE OF DELIVERANCE** *Parlophone CDR 6330*	18		6
6 Mar 93	**C'MON PEOPLE** *Parlophone CDRS 6338*	41		3
10 May 97	**YOUNG BOY** *Parlophone CDRS 6462*	19		3
19 Jul 97	**THE WORLD TONIGHT** *Parlophone CDR 6472*	23		2
27 Dec 97	**BEAUTIFUL NIGHT** *Parlophone CDR 6489*	25		4
6 Nov 99	**NO OTHER BABY/BROWN EYED HANDSOME MAN** *Parlophone CDR 6527*	42		2
10 Nov 01	**FROM A LOVER TO A FRIEND** *Parlophone CDR 6567*	45		2
2 Oct 04	**TROPIC ISLAND HUM/WE ALL STAND TOGETHER** *Parlophone CDR 6649*	21		3
10 Sep 05	**FINE LINE** *Parlophone CDR6673*	20		2
3 Dec 05	**JENNY WREN** *Parlophone CDRS6678*	22		2
30 Jun 07	**DANCE TONIGHT** *Hear Music GBCCS0700646*	26		4
22 Dec 07	**WONDERFUL CHRISTMAS TIME** *Parlophone GBCCS8401051*	44		2

LIZ McCLARNON

UK, female vocalist. See Atomic Kitten, Girls Of FHM

⬆ ✪ 5

Date	Title	Peak	Wks at No.1	Wks
25 Feb 06	**WOMAN IN LOVE/I GET THE SWEETEST FEELING** *All Around The World CXGLOBE476*	5		5

KIRSTY MacCOLL

UK, female vocalist, d. 18 Dec 2000 (age 41)

⬆ ✪ 91

Date	Title	Peak	Wks at No.1	Wks
13 Jun 81	**THERE'S A GUY WORKS DOWN THE CHIPSHOP SWEARS HE'S ELVIS** *Polydor POSP 250*	14		9
19 Jan 85	**A NEW ENGLAND** *Stiff BUY 216*	7		10
15 Nov 86	**GREETINGS TO THE NEW BRUNETTE** *Go! Discs GOD 15* BILLY BRAGG WITH JOHNNY MARR & KIRSTY MacCOLL	58		2
5 Dec 87	**FAIRYTALE OF NEW YORK** *Pogue Mahone NY 7* POGUES FEATURING KIRSTY MacCOLL ○	2		9
8 Apr 89	**FREE WORLD** *Virgin KMA 1*	43		6
1 Jul 89	**DAYS** *Virgin KMA 2*	12		9
25 May 91	**WALKING DOWN MADISON** *Virgin VS 1348*	23		7
17 Aug 91	**MY AFFAIR** *Virgin VS 1354*	56		2
14 Dec 91	**FAIRYTALE OF NEW YORK** *PM YZ 628* POGUES FEATURING KIRSTY MacCOLL	36		5
4 Mar 95	**CAROLINE** *Virgin VSCDX 1517*	58		2
24 Jun 95	**PERFECT DAY** *Virgin VSCDT 1552* & EVAN DANDO	75		1
29 Jul 95	**DAYS** *Virgin VSCDT 1558*	42		3
31 Dec 05	**FAIRYTALE OF NEW YORK** *Warner Brothers WEA400CD* POGUES FEATURING KIRSTY MacCOLL	3		5
9 Dec 06	**FAIRYTALE OF NEW YORK** *Warner Brothers WEA400CD* POGUES FEATURING KIRSTY MacCOLL	6		5
8 Dec 07	**FAIRYTALE OF NEW YORK** *Warner Brothers WEA400CD* POGUES FEATURING KIRSTY MacCOLL	4		5
29 Nov 08	**FAIRYTALE OF NEW YORK** *Warner Brothers WEA400CD* POGUES FEATURING KIRSTY MacCOLL	12		6
5 Dec 09	**FAIRYTALE OF NEW YORK** *Warner Brothers WEA400CD* POGUES FEATURING KIRSTY MacCOLL	12		5

MARILYN McCOO & BILLY DAVIS, JR

US, male/female vocal duo. See 5th Dimension

⬆ ✪ 9

Date	Title	Peak	Wks at No.1	Wks
19 Mar 77	**YOU DON'T HAVE TO BE A STAR (TO BE IN MY SHOW)** *ABC 4147* ★	7		9

VAN McCOY

US, male producer/band leader, d. 6 Jul 1979 (age 39), & orchestra — 36

Date	Title	Peak Position	Weeks at No.1	Weeks on Chart
31 May 75	**THE HUSTLE** *Avco 6105 038* WITH THE SOUL CITY SYMPHONY ●	3		12
1 Nov 75	**CHANGE WITH THE TIMES** *H&L 6105 042*	36		4
12 Feb 77	**SOUL CHA CHA** *H&L 6105 065*	34		6
9 Apr 77	**THE SHUFFLE** *H&L 6105 076* ● ★	4		14

McCOYS

US, male vocal/instrumental group – Rick Derringer (Zehringer), Ronnie Brandon, Randy Hobbs & Randy Zehringer — 18

Date	Title	Peak Position	Weeks at No.1	Weeks on Chart
2 Sep 65	**HANG ON SLOOPY** *Immediate IM 001* ★	5		14
16 Dec 65	**FEVER** *Immediate IM 021*	44		4

GEORGE McCRAE

US, male vocalist — 62

Date	Title	Peak Position	Weeks at No.1	Weeks on Chart
29 Jun 74	**ROCK YOUR BABY** *Jayboy BOY 85* ● ★	1	3	14
5 Oct 74	**I CAN'T LEAVE YOU ALONE** *Jayboy BOY 90*	9		9
14 Dec 74	**YOU CAN HAVE IT ALL** *Jayboy BOY 92*	23		9
22 Mar 75	**SING A HAPPY SONG** *Jayboy BOY 95*	38		4
19 Jul 75	**IT'S BEEN SO LONG** *Jayboy BOY 100* ●	4		11
18 Oct 75	**I AIN'T LYIN'** *Jayboy BOY 105*	12		7
24 Jan 76	**HONEY I** *Jayboy BOY 107*	33		4
25 Feb 84	**ONE STEP CLOSER (TO LOVE)** *President PT 522*	57		4

GWEN McCRAE

US, female vocalist (Gwen Mosley) — 5

Date	Title	Peak Position	Weeks at No.1	Weeks on Chart
30 Apr 88	**ALL THIS LOVE I'M GIVING** *Flame MELT 7*	63		2
13 Feb 93	**ALL THIS LOVE I'M GIVING** *KTDA CDKTDA 2* MUSIC & MYSTERY FEATURING GWEN McCRAE	36		3

McCRARYS

US, male/female vocal group — 4

Date	Title	Peak Position	Weeks at No.1	Weeks on Chart
31 Jul 82	**LOVE ON A SUMMER NIGHT** *Capitol CL 251*	52		4

MINDY McCREADY

US, female vocalist (Malinda McCready) — 3

Date	Title	Peak Position	Weeks at No.1	Weeks on Chart
1 Aug 98	**OH ROMEO** *BNA 74321597242*	41		3

DAVE McCULLEN

Belgium, male DJ/producer (David Veervoort). See Lasgo — 2

Date	Title	Peak Position	Weeks at No.1	Weeks on Chart
24 Dec 05	**B*TCH** *Nebula NEBCD078*	54		2

IAN McCULLOCH

UK, male vocalist. See Echo & The Bunnymen — 15

Date	Title	Peak Position	Weeks at No.1	Weeks on Chart
15 Dec 84	**SEPTEMBER SONG** *Korova KOW 40*	51		5
2 Sep 89	**PROUD TO FALL** *WEA YZ 417*	51		4
12 May 90	**CANDLELAND (THE SECOND COMING)** *East West YZ 452* FEATURING ELIZABETH FRASER	75		1
22 Feb 92	**LOVER LOVER LOVER** *East West YZ 643*	47		4
26 Apr 03	**SLIDLING** *Cooking Vinyl FRYCD 146X*	61		1

MARTINE McCUTCHEON

UK, female actor/vocalist (Martine Ponting) — 65

Date	Title	Peak Position	Weeks at No.1	Weeks on Chart
18 Nov 95	**ARE YOU MAN ENOUGH** *Avex UK AVEXCD 14* UNO CLIO FEATURING MARTINE McCUTCHEON	62		1
17 Apr 99	**PERFECT MOMENT** *Innocent SINCD 7* ⊛	1	2	20
11 Sep 99	**I'VE GOT YOU** *Innocent SINCD 12*	6		10
4 Dec 99	**TALKING IN YOUR SLEEP/LOVE ME** *Innocent SINCD 14* ●	6		16
4 Nov 00	**I'M OVER YOU** *Innocent SINCD 20*	2		10
3 Feb 01	**ON THE RADIO** *Innocent SINCD 21*	7		8

GENE McDANIELS

US, male vocalist — 2

Date	Title	Peak Position	Weeks at No.1	Weeks on Chart
16 Nov 61	**TOWER OF STRENGTH** *London HLG 9448*	49		2

JULIE McDERMOTT

UK, female vocalist — 4

Date	Title	Peak Position	Weeks at No.1	Weeks on Chart
26 Oct 96	**DON'T GO (2ND REMIX)** *XL Recordings XLS 78CD* AWESOME 3 FEATURING JULIE McDERMOTT	27		2
12 Oct 96	**DON'T GO** *Soundprooof MCSTD 40082* THIRD DIMENSION FEATURING JULIE McDERMOTT	34		2

CHARLES McDEVITT SKIFFLE GROUP FEATURING NANCY WHISKEY

UK, male vocal/instrumental group featuring McDevitt & Nancy Whiskey, d. 1 Feb 2003, & Marc Sharratt, d. 16 May 1991 — 20

Date	Title	Peak Position	Weeks at No.1	Weeks on Chart
12 Apr 57	**FREIGHT TRAIN** *Oriole CB 1352*	5		18
14 Jun 57	**GREENBACK DOLLAR** *Oriole CB 1371*	28		2

AMY MacDONALD

UK, female vocalist/guitarist — 29

Date	Title	Peak Position	Weeks at No.1	Weeks on Chart
28 Jul 07	**MR ROCK & ROLL** *Vertigo 1736026*	12		9
27 Oct 07	**LA** *Vertigo 1749279*	48		1
8 Dec 07	**THIS IS THE LIFE** *Vertigo 1755264*	28		17
15 Mar 08	**RUN** *Vertigo 1762441*	75		1
20 Mar 10	**DON'T TELL ME THAT IT'S OVER** *Vertigo GBUM70916512*	48		1

JANE McDONALD

UK, female vocalist/TV personality — 7

Date	Title	Peak Position	Weeks at No.1	Weeks on Chart
26 Dec 98	**CRUISE INTO CHRISTMAS MEDLEY** *Focus Music Int CDFM 2*	10		7

MICHAEL McDONALD

US, male vocalist. See Doobie Brothers — 49

Date	Title	Peak Position	Weeks at No.1	Weeks on Chart
18 Feb 84	**YAH MO B THERE** *Qwest W 9394* JAMES INGRAM WITH MICHAEL McDONALD	44		8
12 Jan 85	**YAH MO B THERE** *Qwest W 9394* JAMES INGRAM WITH MICHAEL McDONALD	12		8
3 May 86	**ON MY OWN** *MCA 1045* PATTI LABELLE & MICHAEL McDONALD ● ★	2		13
26 Jul 86	**I KEEP FORGETTIN'** *Warner Brothers K 17992*	43		6
6 Sep 86	**SWEET FREEDOM** *MCA 1073*	12		10
24 Jan 87	**WHAT A FOOL BELIEVES** *Warner Brothers W 8451* DOOBIE BROTHERS FEATURING MICHAEL McDONALD	57		3
5 Oct 02	**SWEET FREEDOM** *Serious SERR 55CD* SAFRI DUO FEATURING MICHAEL McDONALD	54		1

CARRIE McDOWELL

US, female vocalist — 3

Date	Title	Peak Position	Weeks at No.1	Weeks on Chart
26 Sep 87	**UH UH NO NO CASUAL SEX** *Motown ZV 41501*	68		3

JOE McELDERRY

UK, male vocalist. See Helping Haiti, X Factor Finalists — 8

Date	Title	Peak Position	Weeks at No.1	Weeks on Chart
26 Dec 09	**THE CLIMB** *Syco Music 88697632942* ⊛	1	1	8

JOHN McENROE & PAT CASH WITH THE FULL METAL RACKETS

US/Australia, male guitar/tennis playing duo & UK, vocal/instrumental charity ensemble — 1

Date	Title	Peak Position	Weeks at No.1	Weeks on Chart
13 Jul 91	**ROCK 'N' ROLL** *Music For Nations KUT 141*	66		1

REBA McENTIRE

US, female vocalist/actor — 1

Date	Title	Peak Position	Weeks at No.1	Weeks on Chart
19 Jun 99	**DOES HE LOVE YOU** *MCA Nashville MCSTD 55569*	62		1

MACEO & THE MACKS

US, male saxophonist (Maceo Parker) & vocal/instrumental group — 5

Date	Title	Peak Position	Weeks at No.1	Weeks on Chart
16 May 87	**CROSS THE TRACK (WE BETTER GO BACK)** *Urban IRBX 1*	54		5

BRIAN McFADDEN

Ireland, male vocalist. See Westlife — 36

Date	Title	Peak Position	Weeks at No.1	Weeks on Chart
18 Sep 04	**REAL TO ME** *Modest/Sony Music 6753032*	1	1	12
4 Dec 04	**IRISH SON** *Modest/Sony Music 6754872*	6		11
12 Feb 05	**ALMOST HERE** *Sony Music 6757352* & DELTA GOODREM	3		10
4 Jun 05	**DEMONS** *Modest/Sony Music 6759102*	28		2

Silver-selling ● Gold-selling ● Platinum-selling (x multiples) ⊛ US No.1 ★ Peak Position Weeks at No.1 Weeks on Chart

Date	Title	Peak Position	Weeks at No.1	Weeks on Chart
7 Oct 06	**EVERYBODY'S SOMEONE** *Curb/London CUBC128* LeANN RIMES & BRIAN McFADDEN	48		1

McFADDEN & WHITEHEAD

US, male vocal duo – Gene McFadden, d. 17 Jan 2006, & John Whitehead, d. 11 May 2004 — **10**

Date	Title	Peak Position	Weeks at No.1	Weeks on Chart
19 May 79	**AIN'T NO STOPPIN' US NOW** *Philadelphia International PIR 7365* ●	5		10

RACHEL McFARLANE

UK, female vocalist. — **21**

Date	Title	Peak Position	Weeks at No.1	Weeks on Chart
16 Apr 94	**LET THE MUSIC (LIFT YOU UP)** *KMS/Eastern Bloc KMSCD 10* LOVELAND FEATURING RACHEL McFARLANE Vs DARLENE LEWIS	16		4
5 Nov 94	**(KEEP ON) SHINING/HOPE (NEVER GIVE UP)** *Eastern Bloc BLOCCD 016* LOVELAND FEATURING RACHEL McFARLANE	37		2
14 Jan 95	**I NEED SOMEBODY** *Eastern Bloc BLOCCDX 019* LOVELAND FEATURING RACHEL McFARLANE	21		3
10 Jun 95	**DON'T MAKE ME WAIT** *Eastern Bloc BLOC 20CD* LOVELAND FEATURING RACHEL McFARLANE	22		3
2 Sep 95	**THE WONDER OF LOVE** *Eastern Bloc BLOC 22CD* LOVELAND FEATURING RACHEL McFARLANE	53		1
11 Nov 95	**I NEED SOMEBODY** *Eastern Bloc BLOC 23CD* LOVELAND FEATURING RACHEL McFARLANE	38		2
1 Aug 98	**LOVER** *Multiply CDMULTY 37*	38		2
29 Jan 05	**LOVER (REMIX)** *All Around The World CDGLOBE250*	36		2
4 Feb 06	**YOU GET WHAT YOU GIVE** *All Around The World CDGLOBE423* LMC FEATURING RACHEL McFARLANE	30		2

BOBBY McFERRIN

US, male vocalist — **15**

Date	Title	Peak Position	Weeks at No.1	Weeks on Chart
24 Sep 88	**DON'T WORRY BE HAPPY** *Manhattan MT 56* ★	2		11
17 Dec 88	**THINKIN' ABOUT YOUR BODY** *Manhattan BLUE 6*	46		4

McFLY

UK, male vocal/instrumental group – Tom Fletcher, Danny Jones, Harry Judd & Dougie Poynter — **112**

Date	Title	Peak Position	Weeks at No.1	Weeks on Chart
10 Apr 04	**5 COLOURS IN HER HAIR** *Universal MCSXD 40357*	1	2	12
3 Jul 04	**OBVIOUSLY** *Universal MCSXD 40364*	1	1	13
18 Sep 04	**THAT GIRL** *Universal MCSXD 40378*	3		9
27 Nov 04	**ROOM ON THE 3RD FLOOR** *Island MCSXD40389*	5		9
19 Mar 05	**ALL ABOUT YOU/YOU'VE GOT A FRIEND** *Island MCSTD40409* ●	1	1	13
27 Aug 05	**I'LL BE OK** *Island MCSXD40428*	1	1	9
29 Oct 05	**I WANNA HOLD YOU** *Island MCSXD40436*	3		4
24 Dec 05	**ULTRAVIOLET/THE BALLAD OF PAUL K** *Island MCSXD40442*	9		4
29 Jul 06	**DON'T STOP ME NOW/PLEASE, PLEASE** *Universal 1703585*	1	1	7
4 Nov 06	**STAR GIRL** *Island 1709444*	1	1	6
30 Dec 06	**SORRY'S NOT GOOD ENOUGH/FRIDAY NIGHT** *Island 1718992*	3		4
19 May 07	**BABY'S COMING BACK/TRANSYLVANIA** *Island/Uni-Island 1733933*	1	1	4
3 Nov 07	**THE HEART NEVER LIES** *Island 1749617*	3		5
26 Jul 08	**ONE FOR THE RADIO** *Super CDSUPR1*	2		4
20 Sep 08	**LIES** *Super CXSUPR2*	4		7
6 Dec 08	**DO YA/STAY WITH ME** *Super CDSUP3*	18		2

McGANNS

UK, male actors/vocal trio — **4**

Date	Title	Peak Position	Weeks at No.1	Weeks on Chart
14 Nov 98	**JUST MY IMAGINATION** *Coalition COLA 062CD*	59		1
6 Feb 99	**A HEARTBEAT AWAY** *Coalition COLA 069CD*	42		3

MIKE McGEAR

UK, male vocalist (Peter McCartney). See Scaffold — **4**

Date	Title	Peak Position	Weeks at No.1	Weeks on Chart
5 Oct 74	**LEAVE IT** *Warner Brothers K 16446*	36		4

MAUREEN McGOVERN

US, female vocalist — **8**

Date	Title	Peak Position	Weeks at No.1	Weeks on Chart
5 Jun 76	**THE CONTINENTAL** *20th Century BTC 2222*	16		8

SHANE MacGOWAN

UK, male vocalist. See Pogues — **9**

Date	Title	Peak Position	Weeks at No.1	Weeks on Chart
12 Dec 92	**WHAT A WONDERFUL WORLD** *Mute 151* NICK CAVE & SHANE MacGOWAN	72		1
3 Sep 94	**THE CHURCH OF THE HOLY SPOOK** *ZTT ZANG 57CD* & THE POPES	74		1
15 Oct 94	**THAT WOMAN'S GOT ME DRINKING** *ZTT ZANG 57CD* & THE POPES	34		3
29 Apr 95	**HAUNTED** *ZTT BANG 65CD* & SINEAD O'CONNOR	30		2
20 Apr 96	**MY WAY** *ZTT ZANG 79CD*	29		2

EWAN McGREGOR

UK, male actor/vocalist — **16**

Date	Title	Peak Position	Weeks at No.1	Weeks on Chart
15 Nov 97	**CHOOSE LIFE** *Positiva CDTIV 84* PF PROJECT FEATURING EWAN McGREGOR	6		11
6 Oct 01	**COME WHAT MAY** *Interscope 4976302* NICOLE KIDMAN & EWAN McGREGOR	27		5

FREDDIE McGREGOR

Jamaica, male vocalist — **16**

Date	Title	Peak Position	Weeks at No.1	Weeks on Chart
27 Jun 87	**JUST DON'T WANT TO BE LONELY** *Germain DG 24*	9		11
19 Sep 87	**THAT GIRL (GROOVY SITUATION)** *Polydor POSP 884*	47		5

MARY MacGREGOR

US, female vocalist — **10**

Date	Title	Peak Position	Weeks at No.1	Weeks on Chart
19 Feb 77	**TORN BETWEEN TWO LOVERS** *Ariola America AA 111* ● ★	4		10

McGUINNESS FLINT

UK, male vocal/instrumental group – Tom McGuinness, Dennis Coulson, Hughie Flint, Benny Gallagher & Graham Lyle. See Gallagher & Lyle, Manfred Mann — **26**

Date	Title	Peak Position	Weeks at No.1	Weeks on Chart
21 Nov 70	**WHEN I'M DEAD AND GONE** *Capitol CL 15662*	2		14
1 May 71	**MALT AND BARLEY BLUES** *Capitol CL 15682*	5		12

BARRY McGUIRE

US, male vocalist — **13**

Date	Title	Peak Position	Weeks at No.1	Weeks on Chart
9 Sep 65	**EVE OF DESTRUCTION** *RCA 1469* ★	3		13

McGUIRE SISTERS

US, female vocal group — **24**

Date	Title	Peak Position	Weeks at No.1	Weeks on Chart
1 Apr 55	**NO MORE** *Vogue Coral Q 72050*	20		1
15 Jul 55	**SINCERELY** *Vogue Coral Q 72050* ★	14		4
1 Jun 56	**DELILAH JONES** *Vogue Coral Q 72161*	24		2
14 Feb 58	**SUGARTIME** *Coral Q 72305* ★	14		6
1 May 59	**MAY YOU ALWAYS** *Coral Q 72356*	15		11

MACHEL

Trinidad & Tobago, male vocalist (Machel Montano) — **2**

Date	Title	Peak Position	Weeks at No.1	Weeks on Chart
14 Sep 96	**COME DIG IT** *London LONCD 386*	56		2

MACHINE HEAD

US, male vocal/instrumental group — **4**

Date	Title	Peak Position	Weeks at No.1	Weeks on Chart
27 May 95	**OLD** *Roadrunner RR 23403*	43		2
6 Dec 97	**TAKE MY SCARS** *Roadrunner RR 22573*	73		1
18 Dec 99	**FROM THIS DAY** *Roadrunner RR 21383*	74		1

STEPHANIE McINTOSH

Australia, female actor/vocalist — **1**

Date	Title	Peak Position	Weeks at No.1	Weeks on Chart
7 Jul 07	**MISTAKE** *Universal TV 1739005*	47		1

BILLY MACK

UK, male actor/vocalist (Bill Nighy) — **3**

Date	Title	Peak Position	Weeks at No.1	Weeks on Chart
27 Dec 03	**CHRISTMAS IS ALL AROUND** *Island CID 841*	26		3

CRAIG MACK

US, male rapper — **5**

Date	Title	Peak Position	Weeks at No.1	Weeks on Chart
12 Nov 94	**FLAVA IN YOUR EAR** *Bad Boy 74321242582*	57		2
1 Apr 95	**GET DOWN** *Puff Daddy 74321263402*	54		1
7 Jun 97	**SPIRIT** *Perspective 5822312* SOUNDS OF BLACKNESS FEATURING CRAIG MACK	35		2

LIZZY MACK
UK, female vocalist — 3

Date	Title	Peak	Wks No.1	Wks
5 Nov 94	**THE POWER OF LOVE** *Media MCSTD 2016* FITS OF GLOOM FEATURING LIZZY MACK	49		2
4 Nov 95	**DON'T GO** *Power Station MCSTD 40004*	52		1

LONNIE MACK
US, male guitarist/vocalist (Lonnie McIntosh) — 3

Date	Title	Peak	Wks No.1	Wks
14 Apr 79	**MEMPHIS** *Lightning LIG 9011*	47		3

MACK VIBE FEATURING JACQUELINE
US, male/female vocal/instrumental duo — 1

Date	Title	Peak	Wks No.1	Wks
4 Feb 95	**I CAN'T LET YOU GO** *MCA MCSTD 2020*	53		1

McKAY
US, female vocalist (Stephanie McKay) — 1

Date	Title	Peak	Wks No.1	Wks
23 Aug 03	**TAKE ME OVER** *Go! Beat GOBCD 57*	65		1

MARIA McKEE
US, female vocalist. See Lone Justice — 23

Date	Title	Peak	Wks No.1	Wks
15 Sep 90	**SHOW ME HEAVEN** *Epic 6563037*	1	4	14
26 Jan 91	**BREATHE** *Geffen GFS 1*	59		1
1 Aug 92	**SWEETEST CHILD** *Geffen GFS 23*	45		4
22 May 93	**I'M GONNA SOOTHE YOU** *Geffen GFSTD 39*	35		3
18 Sep 93	**I CAN'T MAKE IT ALONE** *Geffen GFSTD 53*	74		1

KENNETH McKELLAR
UK, male vocalist, d. 9 Apr 2010 (age 82) — 4

Date	Title	Peak	Wks No.1	Wks
10 Mar 66	**A MAN WITHOUT LOVE** *Decca F 12341*	30		4

GISELE MacKENZIE
Canada, female vocalist (Gisele LaFleche), d. 5 Sep 2003 (age 76) — 6

Date	Title	Peak	Wks No.1	Wks
17 Jul 53	**SEVEN LONELY DAYS** *Capitol CL 13920*	6		6

SCOTT McKENZIE
US, male vocalist (Philip Blondheim) — 18

Date	Title	Peak	Wks No.1	Wks
12 Jul 67	**SAN FRANCISCO (BE SURE TO WEAR SOME FLOWERS IN YOUR HAIR)** *CBS 2816*	1	4	17
1 Nov 67	**LIKE AN OLD TIME MOVIE** *CBS 3009* VOICE OF SCOTT McKENZIE	50		1

KEN MACKINTOSH
UK, male orchestra leader, d. 22 Nov 2005 (age 86) — 9

Date	Title	Peak	Wks No.1	Wks
15 Jan 54	**THE CREEP** *HMV BD 1295*	10		2
7 Feb 58	**RAUNCHY** *HMV POP 426*	19		6
10 Mar 60	**NO HIDING PLACE** *HMV POP 713*	45		1

BEN MACKLIN FEATURING TIGER LILY
UK/Denmark, male/female vocal/production duo — 1

Date	Title	Peak	Wks No.1	Wks
20 Jan 07	**FEEL TOGETHER** *Free2Air F2A25CDX*	71		1

BRIAN McKNIGHT
US, male vocalist/multi-instrumentalist/producer — 4

Date	Title	Peak	Wks No.1	Wks
6 Jun 98	**ANYTIME** *Motown 8607752*	48		2
3 Oct 98	**YOU SHOULD BE MINE** *Motown 8608412* FEATURING MA$E	36		2

JULIE McKNIGHT
US, female vocalist. See Layo & Bushwacka! — 6

Date	Title	Peak	Wks No.1	Wks
14 Apr 01	**FINALLY** *Distance DI 2029* KINGS OF TOMORROW FEATURING JULIE McKNIGHT	54		1
29 Sep 01	**FINALLY (REMIX)** *Defected DEFECT 37CDX* KINGS OF TOMORROW FEATURING JULIE McKNIGHT	24		3
15 Jun 02	**HOME** *Defected DFECT 51CDS*	61		1
23 Nov 02	**DIAMOND LIFE** *Distance D12409* LOUIE VEGA & JAY 'SINISTER' SEALEE STARRING JULIE McKNIGHT	52		1

VIVIENNE McKONE
UK, female vocalist — 5

Date	Title	Peak	Wks No.1	Wks
25 Jul 92	**SING (OOH-EE-OOH)** *ffrr F 183*	47		4
31 Oct 92	**BEWARE** *ffrr F 202*	69		1

McKOY
UK, male/female vocal group — 2

Date	Title	Peak	Wks No.1	Wks
6 Mar 93	**FIGHT** *Rightrack CDTUM 1*	54		2

CRAIG McLACHLAN
Australia, male vocalist/actor — 40

Date	Title	Peak	Wks No.1	Wks
16 Jun 90	**MONA** *Epic 6557847* & CHECK 1-2	2		11
4 Aug 90	**AMANDA** *Epic 6561707* & CHECK 1-2	19		6
10 Nov 90	**I ALMOST FELT LIKE CRYING** *Epic 6563107* & CHECK 1-2	50		3
23 May 92	**ONE REASON WHY** *Epic 6580677*	29		6
14 Nov 92	**ON MY OWN** *Epic 6584677*	59		2
24 Jul 93	**YOU'RE THE ONE THAT I WANT** *Epic 6595222* & DEBBIE GIBSON	13		6
25 Dec 93	**GREASE** *Epic 6600242*	44		4
8 Jul 95	**EVERYDAY** *MDMC DEVCS 6* & THE CULPRITS	65		2

SARAH McLACHLAN
Canada, female vocalist/guitarist — 34

Date	Title	Peak	Wks No.1	Wks
3 Oct 98	**ADIA** *Arista 74321613902*	18		5
14 Oct 00	**SILENCE (REMIXES)** *Nettwerk 331082* DELERIUM FEATURING SARAH McLACHLAN ●	3		16
2 Feb 02	**ANGEL** *Nettwerk 331492*	36		3
20 Mar 04	**FALLEN** *Arista 82876599282*	50		1
26 Jun 04	**WORLD ON FIRE** *Arista 82876628632*	72		1
27 Nov 04	**SILENCE 2004** *Nettwerk 332422* DELERIUM FEATURING SARAH McLACHLAN	38		8

TOMMY McLAIN
US, male vocalist — 1

Date	Title	Peak	Wks No.1	Wks
8 Sep 66	**SWEET DREAMS** *London HL 10065*	49		1

MALCOLM McLAREN
UK, male producer/vocalist, d. 8 April 2010 (age 64) — 65

Date	Title	Peak	Wks No.1	Wks
4 Dec 82	**BUFFALO GIRLS** *Charisma MALC 1* & THE WORLD'S FAMOUS SUPREME TEAM ●	9		12
26 Feb 83	**SOWETO** *Charisma MALC 2* & THE McLARENETTES	32		5
2 Jul 83	**DOUBLE DUTCH** *Charisma MALC 3* ●	3		13
17 Dec 83	**DUCK FOR THE OYSTER** *Charisma MALC 4*	54		5
1 Sep 84	**MADAM BUTTERFLY (UN BEL DI VEDREMO)** *Charisma MALC 5*	13		9
27 May 89	**WALTZ DARLING** *Epic WALTZ 2* & THE BOOTZILLA ORCHESTRA	31		8
19 Aug 89	**SOMETHING'S JUMPIN' IN YOUR SHIRT** *Epic WALTZ 3* & THE BOOTZILLA ORCHESTRA FEATURING LISA MARIE	29		7
25 Nov 89	**HOUSE OF THE BLUE DANUBE** *Epic WALTZ 4* & THE BOOTZILLA ORCHESTRA	73		1
21 Dec 91	**MAGIC'S BACK (THEME FROM 'THE GHOSTS OF OXFORD STREET')** *RCA PB 45223* FEATURING ALISON LIMERICK	42		4
3 Oct 98	**BUFFALO GALS STAMPEDE** *Virgin VSCDT 1717* & THE WORLD'S FAMOUS SUPREME TEAM PLUS RAKIM & ROGER SANCHEZ	65		1

McLEAN
UK, male vocalist (Anthony McLean). See Young Soul Rebels — 4

Date	Title	Peak	Wks No.1	Wks
20 Mar 10	**MY NAME** *Asylum 14CD*	10		4+

BITTY McLEAN
UK, male vocalist — 50

Date	Title	Peak	Wks No.1	Wks
31 Jul 93	**IT KEEP'S RAININ' (TEARS FROM MY EYES)** *Brilliant CDBRIL 1* ●	2		15
30 Oct 93	**PASS IT ON** *Brilliant CDBRIL 2*	35		3
15 Jan 94	**HERE I STAND** *Brilliant CDBRIL 3*	10		6
9 Apr 94	**DEDICATED TO THE ONE I LOVE** *Brilliant CDBRIL 4*	6		10
6 Aug 94	**WHAT GOES AROUND** *Brilliant CDBRIL 5*	36		3
8 Apr 95	**OVER THE RIVER** *Brilliant CDBRIL 9*	27		4
17 Jun 95	**WE'VE ONLY JUST BEGUN** *Brilliant CDBRIL 10*	23		5
30 Sep 95	**NOTHING CAN CHANGE THIS LOVE** *Brilliant CDBRIL 11*	55		2
27 Jan 96	**NATURAL HIGH** *Brilliant CDBRIL 12*	63		1
5 Oct 96	**SHE'S ALRIGHT** *Kuff KUFFD 9*	53		1

Silver-selling ● Gold-selling ● Platinum-selling (x multiples) ⊛ US No.1 ★ Peak Position Weeks at No.1 Weeks on Chart

DON McLEAN
US, male vocalist/guitarist — 68

Date	Title / Label	Peak	Wks at No.1	Wks on Chart
22 Jan 72	**AMERICAN PIE** *United Artists UP 35325* ★	2		16
13 May 72	**VINCENT** *United Artists UP 35359*	1	2	15
14 Apr 73	**EVERYDAY** *United Artists UP 35519*	38		5
10 May 80	**CRYING** *EMI 5051* ●	1	3	14
17 Apr 82	**CASTLES IN THE AIR** *EMI 5258*	47		8
5 Oct 91	**AMERICAN PIE** *Liberty EMCT 3*	12		10

JACKIE McLEAN
US, male saxophonist, d. 31 Mar 2006 (age 74) — 4

Date	Title / Label	Peak	Wks at No.1	Wks on Chart
7 Jul 79	**DR JACKYLL AND MISTER FUNK** *RCA PB 1575*	53		4

PHIL McLEAN
US, male radio DJ/vocalist — 4

Date	Title / Label	Peak	Wks at No.1	Wks on Chart
18 Jan 62	**SMALL SAD SAM** *Top Rank JAR 597*	34		4

McLUSKY
UK, male vocal/instrumental group — 1

Date	Title / Label	Peak	Wks at No.1	Wks on Chart
8 May 04	**THAT MAN WILL NOT HANG** *Too Pure PURE153CDS*	71		1

JACK McMANUS
UK, male vocalist/keyboard player — 2

Date	Title / Label	Peak	Wks at No.1	Wks on Chart
10 May 08	**BANG ON THE PIANO** *UMRL/Polydor 1765467*	45		2

IAN McNABB
UK, male vocalist. See Icicle Works — 7

Date	Title / Label	Peak	Wks at No.1	Wks on Chart
23 Jan 93	**IF LOVE WAS LIKE GUITARS** *This Way Up WAY 233*	67		1
2 Jul 94	**YOU MUST BE PREPARED TO DREAM** *This Way Up WAY 3199*	54		1
17 Sep 94	**GO INTO THE LIGHT** *This Way Up WAY 3699*	66		2
27 Apr 96	**DON'T PUT YOUR SPELL ON ME** *This Way Up WAY 5033*	72		1
6 Jul 96	**MERSEYBEAT** *This Way Up WAY 5266*	74		1
28 May 05	**LET THE YOUNG GIRL DO WHAT SHE WANTS TO** *Fairfield FAIRCD5*	38		1

LUTRICIA McNEAL
US, female vocalist — 43

Date	Title / Label	Peak	Wks at No.1	Wks on Chart
29 Nov 97	**AIN'T THAT JUST THE WAY** *Wildstar CDSTAS 2907* ●	6		18
23 May 98	**STRANDED** *Wildstar CXSTAS 2973* ●	3		12
26 Sep 98	**SOMEONE LOVES YOU HONEY** *Wildstar CDWILD 9*	9		7
19 Dec 98	**THE GREATEST LOVE YOU'LL NEVER KNOW** *Wildstar CDWILD 11*	17		6

PATRICK MACNEE & HONOR BLACKMAN
UK, male/female vocal/acting duo — 7

Date	Title / Label	Peak	Wks at No.1	Wks on Chart
1 Dec 90	**KINKY BOOTS** *Deram KINKY 1*	5		7

RITA MacNEIL
Canada, female vocalist — 10

Date	Title / Label	Peak	Wks at No.1	Wks on Chart
6 Oct 90	**WORKING MAN** *Polydor PO 98*	11		10

CLYDE McPHATTER
US, female vocalist, d. 13 Jun 1972 (age 39) — 1

Date	Title / Label	Peak	Wks at No.1	Wks on Chart
24 Aug 56	**TREASURE OF LOVE** *London HLE 8293*	27		1

TOM McRAE
UK, male vocalist/guitarist — 1

Date	Title / Label	Peak	Wks at No.1	Wks on Chart
24 May 03	**KARAOKE SOUL** *DB DB016CDE7JC2*	48		1

RALPH McTELL
UK, male vocalist/guitarist (Ralph May) — 18

Date	Title / Label	Peak	Wks at No.1	Wks on Chart
7 Dec 74	**STREETS OF LONDON** *Reprise K 14380* ●	2		12
20 Dec 75	**DREAMS OF YOU** *Warner Brothers K 16648*	36		6

MAD COBRA FEATURING RICHIE STEPHENS
Jamaica, male producer (Ewart Brown) & vocalist (Richard Stephenson) — 2

Date	Title / Label	Peak	Wks at No.1	Wks on Chart
15 May 93	**LEGACY** *Columbia 6592852*	64		2

MAD DONNA
US, male/female vocal/production group — 4

Date	Title / Label	Peak	Wks at No.1	Wks on Chart
4 May 02	**THE WHEELS ON THE BUS** *Star Harbour/All Around The World DISCO 0202CR*	17		4

MAD JOCKS FEATURING JOCKMASTER B.A.
UK, male vocal/instrumental parody group — 9

Date	Title / Label	Peak	Wks at No.1	Wks on Chart
19 Dec 87	**JOCK MIX 1** *Debut DEBT 3037*	46		5
18 Dec 93	**PARTY FOUR (EP)** *SMP CDSSKM 24*	57		4

MAD MOSES
US, male DJ/producer ('Mad' Mitch Moses) — 1

Date	Title / Label	Peak	Wks at No.1	Wks on Chart
16 Aug 97	**PANTHER PARTY** *Hi-Life 5744932*	50		1

MADASUN
UK, female vocal group — 13

Date	Title / Label	Peak	Wks at No.1	Wks on Chart
11 Mar 00	**DON'T YOU WORRY** *V2 VVR 5011523*	14		6
27 May 00	**WALKING ON WATER** *V2 VVR 5012418*	14		4
2 Sep 00	**FEEL GOOD** *V2 VVR 5012983*	29		3

MADCON
Norway, male vocal/rap duo – Tshawe Baqwa & Yosef Wolde-Mariam — 33

Date	Title / Label	Peak	Wks at No.1	Wks on Chart
23 Aug 08	**BEGGIN** *RCA 88697332512*	5		33

DANNY MADDEN
US, male vocalist — 2

Date	Title / Label	Peak	Wks at No.1	Wks on Chart
14 Jul 90	**THE FACTS OF LIFE** *Eternal YZ 473*	72		2

MADDER ROSE
US, male/female vocal/instrumental group — 2

Date	Title / Label	Peak	Wks at No.1	Wks on Chart
26 Mar 94	**PANIC ON** *Atlantic A 8301CD*	65		1
16 Jul 94	**CAR SONG** *Seed A 7256CD*	68		1

MADE IN LONDON
UK/Norway, female vocal group — 6

Date	Title / Label	Peak	Wks at No.1	Wks on Chart
13 May 00	**DIRTY WATER** *RCA 74321746192*	15		5
9 Sep 00	**SHUT YOUR MOUTH** *RCA 74321772602*	74		1

MADELYNE
Holland, male producer (Carlo Resoort). See 4 Strings — 1

Date	Title / Label	Peak	Wks at No.1	Wks on Chart
7 Sep 02	**BEAUTIFUL CHILD (A DEEPER LOVE)** *Xtravaganza XTRAV 36CDS*	63		1

MADEMOISELLE
France, male production/instrumental duo — 1

Date	Title / Label	Peak	Wks at No.1	Wks on Chart
8 Sep 01	**DO YOU LOVE ME** *RCA 74321878952*	56		1

MAD'HOUSE
France/Holland, male/female vocal/production trio – Mukendi Adolphe, Stephane Durand & Buse Unlu — 14

Date	Title / Label	Peak	Wks at No.1	Wks on Chart
17 Aug 02	**LIKE A PRAYER** *Serious SERR 046CD*	3		11
9 Nov 02	**HOLIDAY** *Serious SER 058CD MADHOUSE*	24		3

MADISON AVENUE
Australia, male/female vocal/production duo – Cheyne Coates & Andy Van Dorsselaer — 25

Date	Title / Label	Peak	Wks at No.1	Wks on Chart
13 Nov 99	**DON'T CALL ME BABY** *VC Recordings VCRD 56*	30		6
20 May 00	**DON'T CALL ME BABY** *VC Recordings VCRD 64* ●	1	1	12
21 Oct 00	**WHO THE HELL ARE YOU** *VC Recordings VCRD 70*	10		5
27 Jan 01	**EVERYTHING YOU NEED** *VC Recordings VCRD 82*	33		2

Silver-selling · Gold-selling · Platinum-selling (× multiples) · US No.1 ★ · Peak Position · Weeks at No.1 · Weeks on Chart

MADNESS

UK, male vocal/instrumental group – Suggs* (Graham McPherson), Mike Barson, Mark Bedford, Chris Foreman, Carl Smythe, Lee Thompson & Dan Woodgate. The 'Nutty Boys' helped kick-start the 2 Tone/ska music craze of the early 1980s and no group spent longer on the charts in the 1980s. They have sold nearly six million singles in the UK

Weeks on Chart: 274

Date	Title / Label	Peak Position	Weeks at No.1	Weeks on Chart
1 Sep 79	**THE PRINCE** *2 Tone TT 3*	16		11
10 Nov 79	**ONE STEP BEYOND** *Stiff BUY 56*	7		14
5 Jan 80	**MY GIRL** *Stiff BUY 62*	3		10
5 Apr 80	**WORK REST AND PLAY (EP)** *Stiff BUY 71*	6		8
13 Sep 80	**BAGGY TROUSERS** *Stiff BUY 84*	3		20
22 Nov 80	**EMBARRASSMENT** *Stiff BUY 102*	4		12
24 Jan 81	**RETURN OF THE LOS PALMAS SEVEN** *Stiff BUY 108*	7		11
25 Apr 81	**GREY DAY** *Stiff BUY 112*	4		10
26 Sep 81	**SHUT UP** *Stiff BUY 126*	7		9
5 Dec 81	**IT MUST BE LOVE** *Stiff BUY 134*	4		12
20 Feb 82	**CARDIAC ARREST** *Stiff BUY 140*	14		10
22 May 82	**HOUSE OF FUN** *Stiff BUY 146*	1	2	9
24 Jul 82	**DRIVING IN MY CAR** *Stiff BUY 153*	4		8
27 Nov 82	**OUR HOUSE** *Stiff BUY 163*	5		13
19 Feb 83	**TOMORROW'S (JUST ANOTHER DAY)/MADNESS (IS ALL IN THE MIND)** *Stiff BUY 169*	8		9
20 Aug 83	**WINGS OF A DOVE** *Stiff BUY 181*	2		10
5 Nov 83	**THE SUN AND THE RAIN** *Stiff BUY 192*	5		10
11 Feb 84	**MICHAEL CAINE** *Stiff BUY 196*	11		8
2 Jun 84	**ONE BETTER DAY** *Stiff BUY 201*	17		7
31 Aug 85	**YESTERDAY'S MEN** *Zarjazz JAZZ 5*	18		7
26 Oct 85	**UNCLE SAM** *Zarjazz JAZZ 7*	21		11
1 Feb 86	**SWEETEST GIRL** *Zarjazz JAZZ 8*	35		6
8 Nov 86	**(WAITING FOR) THE GHOST TRAIN** *Zarjazz JAZZ 9*	18		8
19 Mar 88	**I PRONOUNCE YOU** *Virgin VS 1054*	44		4
15 Feb 92	**IT MUST BE LOVE** *Virgin VS 1405*	6		9
25 Apr 92	**HOUSE OF FUN** *Virgin VS 1413*	40		3
8 Aug 92	**MY GIRL** *Virgin VS 1425*	27		4
28 Nov 92	**THE HARDER THEY COME** *Go! Discs GOD 93*	44		3
27 Feb 93	**NIGHT BOAT TO CAIRO** *Virgin VSCDT 1447*	56		2
31 Jul 99	**LOVESTRUCK** *Virgin VSCDT 1737*	10		7
6 Nov 99	**JOHNNY THE HORSE** *Virgin VSCDT 1740*	44		2
11 Mar 00	**DRIP FED FRED** *Virgin VSCDT 1768* FEATURING IAN DURY	55		1
6 Aug 05	**SHAME & SCANDAL** *V2 VVR5033243*	38		2
17 Mar 07	**SORRY** *Lucky Seven Records LUCKY701CDS*	23		1
26 Jan 08	**NW5** *Lucky Seven Records LUCKY70021CDS*	24		2
23 May 09	**DUST DEVIL** *Lucky Seven Records LUCKY7004CDS*	64		1

MADONNA

US, female vocalist/producer/actor (Madonna Ciccone). The most successful female artist in UK and US chart history amassed an unprecedented, decade-long 35 consecutive Top 10 singles and has an unequalled female tally of UK No.1 singles and albums. The 'Queen of Pop' has sold an incredible 17.1 million singles during her UK chart career

Weeks on Chart: 731

Date	Title / Label	Peak Position	Weeks at No.1	Weeks on Chart
14 Jan 84	**HOLIDAY** *Sire W9405*	6		11
17 Mar 84	**LUCKY STAR** *Sire W9522*	14		9
2 Jun 84	**BORDERLINE** *Sire W9260*	56		4
17 Nov 84	**LIKE A VIRGIN** *Sire W9210* ★	3		18
2 Mar 85	**MATERIAL GIRL** *Sire W9083*	3		10
8 Jun 85	**CRAZY FOR YOU** *Geffen A 6323* ★	2		15
27 Jul 85	**INTO THE GROOVE** *Sire W8934*	1	4	14
3 Aug 85	**HOLIDAY** *Sire W9405*	2		10
21 Sep 85	**ANGEL** *Sire W8881*	5		9
12 Oct 85	**GAMBLER** *Geffen A 6585*	4		12
7 Dec 85	**DRESS YOU UP** *Sire W8848*	5		11
25 Jan 86	**BORDERLINE** *Sire W9260*	2		9
26 Apr 86	**LIVE TO TELL** *Sire W8717* ★	2		12
28 Jun 86	**PAPA DON'T PREACH** *Sire W8636* ★	1	3	14
4 Oct 86	**TRUE BLUE** *Sire W8550*	1	1	15
13 Dec 86	**OPEN YOUR HEART** *Sire W8480* ★	4		9
4 Apr 87	**LA ISLA BONITA** *Sire W8378*	1	2	11
18 Jul 87	**WHO'S THAT GIRL** *Sire W8341* ★	1	1	10
19 Sep 87	**CAUSING A COMMOTION** *Sire W8224*	4		9
12 Dec 87	**THE LOOK OF LOVE** *Sire W8115*	9		7
18 Mar 89	**LIKE A PRAYER** *Sire W7539* ★	1	3	12
3 Jun 89	**EXPRESS YOURSELF** *Sire W2948*	5		10
16 Sep 89	**CHERISH** *Sire W2883*	3		8
16 Dec 89	**DEAR JESSIE** *Sire W2668*	5		9
7 Apr 90	**VOGUE** *Sire W9851* ★	1	4	14
21 Jul 90	**HANKY PANKY** *Sire W9789*	2		9
8 Dec 90	**JUSTIFY MY LOVE** *Sire W9000* ★	2		10
2 Mar 91	**CRAZY FOR YOU** *Sire W0008*	2		8
13 Apr 91	**RESCUE ME** *Sire W0024*	3		8
8 Jun 91	**HOLIDAY** *Sire W0037*	5		7

Acts With The Most Top 10 Hits

Pos	Artist	No. Top 10 Hits
1	ELVIS PRESLEY	77
2	CLIFF RICHARD	68
3	MADONNA	63
4	MICHAEL JACKSON	42
5	SHADOWS	41
6	U2	33
7	ELTON JOHN	32
=	KYLIE MINOGUE	32
9	BEATLES	28
=	ROBBIE WILLIAMS	28
11	ROD STEWART	27
12	QUEEN	26
13	MARIAH CAREY	25
14	DAVID BOWIE	24
=	PAUL McCARTNEY/WINGS	24
16	WESTLIFE	24
17	GEORGE MICHAEL	23
=	OASIS	23
19	STATUS QUO	22
=	PET SHOP BOYS	22
21	ROLLING STONES	21
=	DIANA ROSS	21
23	GIRLS ALOUD	20
=	TOM JONES	20
=	BRITNEY SPEARS	20
26	ABBA	19
=	BEE GEES	19
=	EMINEM	19
=	FRANKIE LAINE	19
=	STEVIE WONDER	19
31	BON JOVI	18
=	BOYZONE	18
=	HOLLIES	18
=	SUGABABES	18
=	TAKE THAT	18
36	LONNIE DONEGAN	17
=	ERASURE	17
=	WHITNEY HOUSTON	17
=	IRON MAIDEN	17
=	JANET JACKSON	17
=	MADNESS	17
=	UB40	17
43	BACKSTREET BOYS	16
=	MANFRED MANN	16
=	PRINCE	16
=	SLADE	16

Key: ○ Silver-selling · ● Gold-selling · ⊛ Platinum-selling (x multiples) · ★ US No.1 · Peak Position · Weeks at No.1 · Weeks on Chart

Date	Title / Label	Peak Position	Weeks at No.1	Weeks on Chart
25 Jul 92	**THIS USED TO BE MY PLAYGROUND** *Sire W0122* ○ ★	3		9
17 Oct 92	**EROTICA** *Maverick W0138*	3		9
12 Dec 92	**DEEPER AND DEEPER** *Maverick W0146*	6		9
6 Mar 93	**BAD GIRL** *Maverick W0145CD*	10		7
3 Apr 93	**FEVER** *Maverick W0168CD*	6		6
31 Jul 93	**RAIN** *Maverick W0190CD*	7		8
2 Apr 94	**I'LL REMEMBER** *Maverick W0240CD*	7		8
8 Oct 94	**SECRET** *Maverick W0268CD*	5		9
17 Dec 94	**TAKE A BOW** *Maverick W0278CD* ★	16		9
25 Feb 95	**BEDTIME STORY** *Maverick W0285CD*	4		9
26 Aug 95	**HUMAN NATURE** *Maverick W0300CD*	8		5
4 Nov 95	**YOU'LL SEE** *Maverick W0324CDX*	5		13
6 Jan 96	**OH FATHER** *Maverick W0326CDX*	16		6
23 Mar 96	**ONE MORE CHANCE** *Maverick W0337CD*	11		4
2 Nov 96	**YOU MUST LOVE ME** *Warner Brothers W0378CD*	10		6
28 Dec 96	**DON'T CRY FOR ME ARGENTINA** *Warner Brothers W0384CD* ○	3		12
29 Mar 97	**ANOTHER SUITCASE IN ANOTHER HALL** *Warner Brothers W0388CD*	7		5
7 Mar 98	**FROZEN** *Maverick W0433CD* ●	1	1	13
9 May 98	**RAY OF LIGHT** *Maverick W0444CD* ○	2		10
5 Sep 98	**DROWNED WORLD (SUBSTITUTE FOR LOVE)** *Maverick W0453CD1*	10		5
5 Dec 98	**THE POWER OF GOODBYE/LITTLE STAR** *Maverick W459CD*	6		9
13 Mar 99	**NOTHING REALLY MATTERS** *Maverick W471CD1* ○	7		9
19 Jun 99	**BEAUTIFUL STRANGER** *Maverick W495CD* ●	2		16
11 Mar 00	**AMERICAN PIE** *Maverick W519CD* ●	1	1	14
2 Sep 00	**MUSIC** *Maverick W537CD1* ● ★	1	1	23
9 Dec 00	**DON'T TELL ME** *Maverick W547CD1*	4		10
28 Apr 01	**WHAT IT FEELS LIKE FOR A GIRL** *Maverick W533CD1*	7		11
9 Nov 02	**DIE ANOTHER DAY** *Warner Brothers W595CD*	3		16
19 Apr 03	**AMERICAN LIFE (IMPORT)** *Maverick 166582*	57		1
26 Apr 03	**AMERICAN LIFE** *Maverick W603CD*	2		11
19 Jul 03	**HOLLYWOOD** *Maverick W614CD*	2		7
22 Nov 03	**ME AGAINST THE MUSIC** *Jive 82876576432* BRITNEY SPEARS FEATURING MADONNA	2		12
20 Dec 03	**NOTHING FAILS/LOVE PROFUSION** *Maverick W634CD1*	11		6
19 Nov 05	**HUNG UP** *Warner Brothers W695CD2*	1	3	29
4 Mar 06	**SORRY** *Warner Brothers W703CD1*	1	1	15
29 Jul 06	**GET TOGETHER** *Warner Brothers W725CD*	7		6
11 Nov 06	**JUMP** *Warner Brothers W744CD1*	9		6
29 Mar 08	**4 MINUTES** *Maverick W803CD1* FEATURING JUSTIN TIMBERLAKE	1	4	27
10 May 08	**GIVE IT 2 ME** *Warner Brothers W809CD2*	7		19
6 Dec 08	**MILES AWAY** *Warner Brothers W814CD*	39		2
26 Sep 09	**CELEBRATION** *Warner Brothers W819CD*	3		6

Top 3 Best-Selling Singles

		Approximate Sales
1	INTO THE GROOVE	860,000
2	LIKE A VIRGIN	780,000
3	HOLIDAY	770,000

LISA MAFFIA

UK, female vocalist. See So Solid Crew — Weeks on Chart: **27**

Date	Title / Label	Peak Position	Weeks at No.1	Weeks on Chart
30 Dec 00	**NO GOOD 4 ME** *East West OXIDE 02CD* OXIDE & NEUTRINO FEATURING MEGAMAN, ROMEO & LISA MAFFIA	6		8
3 May 03	**ALL OVER** *Independiente ISOM 69SMS*	2		11
9 Aug 03	**IN LOVE** *Independiente ISOM 75SMS*	13		4
8 Sep 07	**BAD GIRL (AT NIGHT)** *Toolroom/Apollo APOLLO114CDX* DAVE SPOON FEATURING LISA MAFFIA	36		4

MAGAZINE

UK, male vocal/instrumental group — Weeks on Chart: **7**

Date	Title / Label	Peak Position	Weeks at No.1	Weeks on Chart
11 Feb 78	**SHOT BY BOTH SIDES** *Virgin VS 200*	41		4
26 Jul 80	**SWEET HEART CONTRACT** *Virgin VS 368*	54		3

MAGIC AFFAIR

Germany/US, male/female production/vocal/rap group — Weeks on Chart: **8**

Date	Title / Label	Peak Position	Weeks at No.1	Weeks on Chart
4 Jun 94	**OMEN III** *EMI CDEM 317*	17		4
27 Aug 94	**GIVE ME ALL YOUR LOVE** *EMI CDEM 340*	30		2
5 Nov 94	**IN THE MIDDLE OF THE NIGHT** *EMI CDEM 349*	38		2

MAGIC LADY

US, female vocal duo — Weeks on Chart: **3**

Date	Title / Label	Peak Position	Weeks at No.1	Weeks on Chart
14 May 88	**BETCHA CAN'T LOSE (WITH MY LOVE)** *Motown ZB 42003*	58		3

MAGIC LANTERNS

UK, male vocal/instrumental group — Weeks on Chart: **3**

Date	Title / Label	Peak Position	Weeks at No.1	Weeks on Chart
7 Jul 66	**EXCUSE ME BABY** *CBS 202094*	44		3

MAGIC NUMBERS

Trinidad & Tobago/UK, male/female vocal/instrumental group — Weeks on Chart: **24**

Date	Title / Label	Peak Position	Weeks at No.1	Weeks on Chart
4 Jun 05	**FOREVER LOST** *Heavenly HVN151CD*	15		6
20 Aug 05	**LOVE ME LIKE YOU** *Heavenly HVN153CDS*	12		7
5 Nov 05	**LOVE'S A GAME** *Heavenly HVN154CD*	24		3
25 Feb 06	**I SEE YOU YOU SEE ME** *Heavenly HVN156CD*	20		2
28 Oct 06	**TAKE A CHANCE** *Heavenly HVN163CD*	16		5
3 Mar 07	**THIS IS A SONG** *Heavenly HVN165CD*	36		1

MAGNOLIA

Italy, male/female vocal/production duo — Weeks on Chart: **1**

Date	Title / Label	Peak Position	Weeks at No.1	Weeks on Chart
24 Jul 04	**IT'S ALL VAIN** *Data 69CDS*	55		1

MAGNUM

UK, male vocal/instrumental group — Weeks on Chart: **26**

Date	Title / Label	Peak Position	Weeks at No.1	Weeks on Chart
22 Mar 80	**MAGNUM (DOUBLE SINGLE)** *Jet 175*	47		6
12 Jul 86	**LONELY NIGHT** *Polydor POSP 798*	70		2
19 Mar 88	**DAYS OF NO TRUST** *Polydor POSP 910*	32		4
7 May 88	**START TALKING LOVE** *Polydor POSP 920*	22		4
2 Jul 88	**IT MUST HAVE BEEN LOVE** *Polydor POSP 930*	33		4
23 Jun 90	**ROCKIN' CHAIR** *Polydor PO 88*	27		4
25 Aug 90	**HEARTBROKE AND BUSTED** *Polydor PO 94*	49		2

MAGOO

US, male rapper (Melvin Barcliff) — Weeks on Chart: **4**

Date	Title / Label	Peak Position	Weeks at No.1	Weeks on Chart
13 Mar 99	**HERE WE COME** *Virgin DINSD 179* TIMBALAND/MISSY ELLIOTT & MAGOO	43		1
13 Mar 04	**COP THAT SHIT** *Unique Corp TIMBACD001* TIMBALAND/MAGOO/MISSY ELLIOTT	22		3

MAGOO:MOGWAI

UK, male vocal/instrumental group — Weeks on Chart: **1**

Date	Title / Label	Peak Position	Weeks at No.1	Weeks on Chart
4 Apr 98	**BLACK SABBATH/SWEET LEAF** *Fierce Panda NING 47CD*	60		1

SEAN MAGUIRE

UK, male actor/vocalist. See Childliners — Weeks on Chart: **34**

Date	Title / Label	Peak Position	Weeks at No.1	Weeks on Chart
20 Aug 94	**SOMEONE TO LOVE** *Parlophone CDRS 6390*	14		7
5 Nov 94	**TAKE THIS TIME** *Parlophone CDRS 6395*	27		5
25 Mar 95	**SUDDENLY** *Parlophone CDRS 6403*	18		5
24 Jun 95	**NOW I'VE FOUND YOU** *Parlophone CDLEEPYS 1*	22		3
18 Nov 95	**YOU TO ME ARE EVERYTHING** *Parlophone CDR 6420*	16		3
25 May 96	**GOOD DAY** *Parlophone CDR 6432*	12		4
3 Aug 96	**DON'T PULL YOUR LOVE** *Parlophone CDRS 6440*	14		4
29 Mar 97	**TODAY'S THE DAY** *Parlophone CDR 6459*	27		3

MAI TAI

Suriname/Holland, female vocal trio – Jetty Weels, Mildred Douglas & Carolien de Windt — Weeks on Chart: **30**

Date	Title / Label	Peak Position	Weeks at No.1	Weeks on Chart
25 May 85	**HISTORY** *Virgin VS 773* ○	8		13
3 Aug 85	**BODY AND SOUL** *Virgin VS 801*	9		13
15 Feb 86	**FEMALE INTUITION** *Virgin VS 844*	54		4

MAIN INGREDIENT

US, male vocal group — Weeks on Chart: **7**

Date	Title / Label	Peak Position	Weeks at No.1	Weeks on Chart
29 Jun 74	**JUST DON'T WANT TO BE LONELY** *RCA APBO 0205*	27		7

MAISONETTES

UK, male/female vocal/instrumental group – Laurence 'Lol' Mason, Mark Tibenham, Nick Parry, Denise Ward & Elaine Williams — Weeks on Chart: **12**

Date	Title / Label	Peak Position	Weeks at No.1	Weeks on Chart
11 Dec 82	**HEARTACHE AVENUE** *Ready Steady Go! RSG 1* ○	7		12

J MAJIK
UK, male producer (Jamie Spratling) — Weeks on Chart: 7

Date	Title	Peak Position	Weeks at No.1	Weeks on Chart
5 May 01	**LOVE IS NOT A GAME** *Defected DFECT 31CDS* FEATURING KATHY BROWN	34		2
27 Apr 02	**METROSOUND** *Kaos 001P* ADAM F & J MAJIK	54		1
22 May 04	**SCOOBY DOO/SPYCATCHER** *Infared INFRA28* & WICKAMAN	67		1
30 Aug 08	**CRAZY WORLD** *Data DATA197T* & WICKAMAN	37		3

MAKADOPOULOS & HIS GREEK SERENADERS
Greece, male/vocal instrumental group — Weeks on Chart: 14

Date	Title	Peak Position	Weeks at No.1	Weeks on Chart
20 Oct 60	**NEVER ON SUNDAY** *Palette PG 9005*	36		14

MAKAVELI
US, male rapper/actor (Tupac Shakur), d. 13 Sep 1996 (age 25). See 2Pac — Weeks on Chart: 8

Date	Title	Peak Position	Weeks at No.1	Weeks on Chart
12 Apr 97	**TO LIVE AND DIE IN LA** *Interscope IND 95529*	10		4
9 Aug 97	**TOSS IT UP** *Interscope IND 95521*	15		3
14 Feb 98	**HAIL MARY** *Interscope IND 95575*	43		1

JACK E MAKOSSA
US, male producer (Arthur Baker). See Wally Jump, Jr & The Criminal Element Orchestra — Weeks on Chart: 5

Date	Title	Peak Position	Weeks at No.1	Weeks on Chart
12 Sep 87	**THE OPERA HOUSE** *Champion CHAMP 50*	48		5

MALACHI
UK, male vocalist (Malachi Cush) — Weeks on Chart: 1

Date	Title	Peak Position	Weeks at No.1	Weeks on Chart
19 Apr 03	**JUST SAY YOU LOVE ME** *Mercury 0779072*	49		1

MALAIKA
US, female vocalist — Weeks on Chart: 1

Date	Title	Peak Position	Weeks at No.1	Weeks on Chart
31 Jul 93	**GOTTA KNOW (YOUR NAME)** *A&M 5802732*	68		1

CARL MALCOLM
Jamaica, male vocalist — Weeks on Chart: 8

Date	Title	Peak Position	Weeks at No.1	Weeks on Chart
13 Sep 75	**FATTIE BUM BUM** *UK 108*	8		8

STEPHEN MALKMUS
US, male vocalist/guitarist. See Pavement — Weeks on Chart: 1

Date	Title	Peak Position	Weeks at No.1	Weeks on Chart
28 Apr 01	**DISCRETION GROVE** *Domino RUG 123CD*	60		1

RAUL MALO
US, male vocalist/guitarist (Raul Martinez-Malo, Jr). See Mavericks — Weeks on Chart: 1

Date	Title	Peak Position	Weeks at No.1	Weeks on Chart
18 May 02	**I SAID I LOVE YOU** *Gravity 74321923082*	57		1

MAMA CASS
US, female vocalist (Ellen Cohen), d. 29 Jul 1974 (age 32). See Mamas & The Papas — Weeks on Chart: 27

Date	Title	Peak Position	Weeks at No.1	Weeks on Chart
14 Aug 68	**DREAM A LITTLE DREAM OF ME** *RCA 1726*	11		12
16 Aug 69	**IT'S GETTING BETTER** *Stateside SS 8021*	8		15

MAMAS & THE PAPAS
US, male/female vocal/instrumental group – John, d. 18 Mar 2001, & Michelle Phillips, Mama Cass Elliott (Mama Cass*), d. 29 Jul 1974, & Denny Doherty, d. 19 Jan 2007 — Weeks on Chart: 71

Date	Title	Peak Position	Weeks at No.1	Weeks on Chart
28 Apr 66	**CALIFORNIA DREAMIN'** *RCA 1503*	23		9
12 May 66	**MONDAY MONDAY** *RCA 1516* ★	3		13
28 Jul 66	**I SAW HER AGAIN** *RCA 1533*	11		11
9 Feb 67	**WORDS OF LOVE** *RCA 1564*	47		3
6 Apr 67	**DEDICATED TO THE ONE I LOVE** *RCA 1576*	2		17
26 Jul 67	**CREEQUE ALLEY** *RCA 1613*	9		11
2 Aug 97	**CALIFORNIA DREAMIN'** *MCA MCSTD 48058*	9		7

A MAN CALLED ADAM
UK, male/female production/vocal duo — Weeks on Chart: 4

Date	Title	Peak Position	Weeks at No.1	Weeks on Chart
29 Sep 90	**BAREFOOT IN THE HEAD** *Big Life BLR 28*	60		4

MAN 2 MAN MEET MAN PARRISH
US, production/vocal duo – Paul (Paul Cilione) & Miki Zone (Bruno Cilione), d. 31 Dec 1986 — Weeks on Chart: 19

Date	Title	Peak Position	Weeks at No.1	Weeks on Chart
13 Sep 86	**MALE STRIPPER** *Bolts 4*	64		3
3 Jan 87	**MALE STRIPPER** *Bolts 4* ●	4		13
4 Jul 87	**I NEED A MAN/ENERGY IS EUROBEAT** *Bolts 5* MAN TO MAN	43		3

MAN WITH NO NAME
UK, male producer (Martin Freeland) — Weeks on Chart: 6

Date	Title	Peak Position	Weeks at No.1	Weeks on Chart
30 Sep 95	**FLOOR-ESSENCE** *Perfecto PERF 108CD*	68		1
20 Jan 96	**PAINT A PICTURE** *Perfecto PERF 114CD* FEATURING HANNAH	42		2
12 Oct 96	**TELEPORT/SUGAR RUSH** *Perfecto PERF 126CD*	55		1
2 May 98	**VAVOOM!** *Perfecto PERF 159CD1*	43		1
18 Jul 98	**THE FIRST DAY (HORIZON)** *Perfecto PERF 164CD*	72		1

MANCHESTER UNITED FC
UK, male football team/vocalists — Weeks on Chart: 56

Date	Title	Peak Position	Weeks at No.1	Weeks on Chart
8 May 76	**MANCHESTER UNITED** *Decca F 13633*	50		1
21 May 83	**GLORY GLORY MAN. UNITED** *EMI 5390*	13		5
18 May 85	**WE ALL FOLLOW MAN. UNITED** *Columbia DB 9107*	10		5
19 Jun 93	**UNITED (WE LOVE YOU)** *Living Beat LBECD 026* MANCHESTER UNITED & THE CHAMPIONS	37		2
30 Apr 94	**COME ON YOU REDS** *Polygram TV MANU 2* ●	1	2	15
13 May 95	**WE'RE GONNA DO IT AGAIN** *Polygram TV MANU 952* MANCHESTER UNITED FEATURING STRYKER	6		6
4 May 96	**MOVE MOVE MOVE (THE RED TRIBE)** *Music Collection MANUCD 1* ●	6		15
29 May 99	**LIFT IT HIGH (ALL ABOUT BELIEF)** *Music Collection MANUCD 4* 1999 MANCHESTER UNITED SQUAD	11		7

MANCHILD
UK, male production duo. See Stereophonics — Weeks on Chart: 2

Date	Title	Peak Position	Weeks at No.1	Weeks on Chart
16 Sep 00	**THE CLICHES ARE TRUE** *One Little Indian 176 TP7CD* FEATURING KELLY JONES	60		1
25 Aug 01	**NOTHING WITHOUT ME** *One Little Indian 183 TP7CD*	40		1

HENRY MANCINI
US, male composer/conductor, d. 14 Jun 1994 (age 70) — Weeks on Chart: 23

Date	Title	Peak Position	Weeks at No.1	Weeks on Chart
7 Dec 61	**MOON RIVER** *RCA 1256*	44		3
24 Sep 64	**HOW SOON** *RCA 1414*	10		12
25 Mar 72	**THEME FROM 'CADE'S COUNTY'** *RCA 2182*	42		1
11 Feb 84	**MAIN THEME FROM 'THE THORNBIRDS'** *Warner Brothers 9677*	23		7

MANDO DIAO
Sweden, male vocal/instrumental group — Weeks on Chart: 2

Date	Title	Peak Position	Weeks at No.1	Weeks on Chart
5 Mar 05	**YOU CAN'T STEAL MY LOVE** *Majesty 8708962*	73		1
18 Jun 05	**GOD KNOWS** *Majesty 8726022*	64		1

GUCCI MANE FEATURING USHER
US, male rap/vocal duo — Weeks on Chart: 1

Date	Title	Peak Position	Weeks at No.1	Weeks on Chart
20 Feb 10	**SPOTLIGHT** *Warner Brothers USWB10904424*	46		1

MANFRED MANN
UK/South Africa, male vocal/instrumental group – Manfred Mann, Paul Jones* (replaced by Mike D'Abo), Mike Hugg, Tom McGuinness, Dave Richmond & Mike Vickers. One of the top acts of the 1960s and the first group from the south of England to top the US chart during the first 'British Invasion'. With a change of personnel, and a slight name change, Mann also had several big 1970s hits — Weeks on Chart: 217

Date	Title	Peak Position	Weeks at No.1	Weeks on Chart
23 Jan 64	**5-4-3-2-1** *HMV POP 1252*	5		13
16 Apr 64	**HUBBLE BUBBLE TOIL AND TROUBLE** *HMV POP 1282*	11		8
16 Jul 64	**DO WAH DIDDY DIDDY** *HMV POP 1320* ★	1	2	14
15 Oct 64	**SHA LA LA** *HMV POP 1346*	3		12
14 Jan 65	**COME TOMORROW** *HMV POP 1381*	4		9
15 Apr 65	**OH NO NOT MY BABY** *HMV POP 1413*	11		10
16 Sep 65	**IF YOU GOTTA GO GO NOW** *HMV POP 1466*	2		12
21 Apr 66	**PRETTY FLAMINGO** *HMV POP 1523*	1	3	12
7 Jul 66	**YOU GAVE ME SOMEBODY TO LOVE** *HMV POP 1541*	36		4
4 Aug 66	**JUST LIKE A WOMAN** *Fontana TF 730*	10		10
27 Oct 66	**SEMI-DETACHED SUBURBAN MR. JAMES** *Fontana TF 757*	2		12
30 Mar 67	**HA HA SAID THE CLOWN** *Fontana TF 812*	4		11
25 May 67	**SWEET PEA** *Fontana TF 828*	36		4
24 Jan 68	**MIGHTY QUINN** *Fontana TF 897*	1	2	11
12 Jun 68	**MY NAME IS JACK** *Fontana TF 943*	8		11

Silver-selling ○ Gold-selling ● Platinum-selling (x multiples) ⊛ US No.1 ★ Peak Position ⊕ Weeks at No.1 ✪ Weeks on Chart ♥

Date	Title	Peak Position	Weeks at No.1	Weeks on Chart
18 Dec 68	**FOX ON THE RUN** *Fontana TF 985*	5		12
30 Apr 69	**RAGAMUFFIN MAN** *Fontana TF 1013*	8		11
8 Sep 73	**JOYBRINGER** *Vertigo 6059 083* MANFRED MANN'S EARTH BAND	9		10
28 Aug 76	**BLINDED BY THE LIGHT** *Bronze BRO 29* MANFRED MANN'S EARTH BAND ★	6		10
20 May 78	**DAVY'S ON THE ROAD AGAIN** *Bronze BRO 52* MANFRED MANN'S EARTH BAND ○	6		12
17 Mar 79	**YOU ANGEL YOU** *Bronze BRO 68* MANFRED MANN'S EARTH BAND	54		5
7 Jul 79	**DON'T KILL IT CAROL** *Bronze BRO 77* MANFRED MANN'S EARTH BAND	45		4

MANHATTAN TRANSFER

US, male/female vocal group – Tim Hauser, Laurel Masse (replaced by Cheryl Bentyne), Alan Paul & Janis Siegel

		⊕	✪	72
7 Feb 76	**TUXEDO JUNCTION** *Atlantic K 10670*	24		6
5 Feb 77	**CHANSON D'AMOUR** *Atlantic K 10886* ●	1	3	13
28 May 77	**DON'T LET GO** *Atlantic K 10930*	32		6
18 Feb 78	**WALK IN LOVE** *Atlantic K 11075*	12		12
20 May 78	**ON A LITTLE STREET IN SINGAPORE** *Atlantic K 11136*	20		9
16 Sep 78	**WHERE DID OUR LOVE GO/JE VOULAIS TE DIRE (QUE JE T'ATTENDS)** *Atlantic K 11182*	40		4
23 Dec 78	**WHO WHAT WHEN WHERE WHY** *Atlantic K 11233*	49		6
17 May 80	**TWILIGHT ZONE – TWILIGHT TONE (MEDLEY)** *Atlantic K 11476*	25		8
21 Jan 84	**SPICE OF LIFE** *Atlantic A 9728*	19		8

MANHATTANS

US, male vocal group – George Smith, d. 16 Dec 1970 (replaced by Gerald Alston*), Edward Bivens, Kenneth Kelly, Winfred Lovett & Richard Taylor, d. 7 Dec 1987

		⊕	✪	31
19 Jun 76	**KISS AND SAY GOODBYE** *CBS 4317* ○ ★	4		11
2 Oct 76	**HURT** *CBS 4562* ○	4		11
23 Apr 77	**IT'S YOU** *CBS 5093*	43		3
26 Jul 80	**SHINING STAR** *CBS 8624*	45		4
6 Aug 83	**CRAZY** *CBS A 3578*	63		2

MANIA

UK, female vocal duo

		⊕	✪	2
7 Aug 04	**LOOKING FOR A PLACE** *RCA 82876617862*	29		2

M.A.N.I.C.

UK, male production duo

		⊕	✪	1
18 Apr 92	**I'M COMIN' HARDCORE** *Union City UCRT 2*	60		1

MANIC MC's FEATURING SARA CARLSON

UK, male production duo & female vocalist

		⊕	✪	5
12 Aug 89	**MENTAL** *RCA PB 43037*	30		5

MANIC STREET PREACHERS

UK, male vocal/instrumental group – James Dean Bradfield, Richey Edwards (presumed d. Feb 1995), Sean Moore & Nicky Wire (Nicholas Jones)

		⊕	✪	174
25 May 91	**YOU LOVE US** *Heavenly HVN 10*	62		2
10 Aug 91	**STAY BEAUTIFUL** *Columbia 6573377*	40		3
9 Nov 91	**LOVE'S SWEET EXILE/REPEAT** *Columbia 6575827*	26		3
1 Feb 92	**YOU LOVE US** *Columbia 6577247*	16		4
28 Mar 92	**SLASH 'N' BURN** *Columbia 6578737*	20		4
13 Jun 92	**MOTORCYCLE EMPTINESS** *Columbia 6580837*	17		6
19 Sep 92	**THEME FROM M.A.S.H. (SUICIDE IS PAINLESS)** *Columbia 6583827*	7		6
21 Nov 92	**LITTLE BABY NOTHING** *Columbia 6587967*	29		3
12 Jun 93	**FROM DESPAIR TO WHERE** *Columbia 6593372*	25		4
31 Jul 93	**LA TRISTESSE DURERA (SCREAM TO A SIGH)** *Columbia 6594772*	22		5
2 Oct 93	**ROSES IN THE HOSPITAL** *Columbia 6597272*	15		3
12 Feb 94	**LIFE BECOMING A LANDSLIDE** *Columbia 6600702*	36		2
11 Jun 94	**FASTER/PCP** *Epic 6604472*	16		3
13 Aug 94	**REVOL** *Epic 6606862*	22		3
15 Oct 94	**SHE IS SUFFERING** *Epic 6608952*	25		3
27 Apr 96	**A DESIGN FOR LIFE** *Epic 6630705* ○	2		11
3 Aug 96	**EVERYTHING MUST GO** *Epic 6634685*	5		6
12 Oct 96	**KEVIN CARTER** *Epic 6637752*	9		4
14 Dec 96	**AUSTRALIA** *Epic 6640445*	7		7
13 Sep 97	**STAY BEAUTIFUL** *Epic MANIC 1CD*	52		1
13 Sep 97	**LOVE'S SWEET EXILE** *Epic MANIC 2CD*	55		1
13 Sep 97	**YOU LOVE US** *Epic MANIC 3CD*	49		1
13 Sep 97	**SLASH 'N' BURN** *Epic MANIC 4CD*	54		1
13 Sep 97	**MOTORCYCLE EMPTINESS** *Epic MANIC 5CD*	41		2
13 Sep 97	**LITTLE BABY NOTHING** *Epic MANIC 6CD*	50		1
5 Sep 98	**IF YOU TOLERATE THIS YOUR CHILDREN WILL BE NEXT** *Epic 6663452* ○	1	1	11
12 Dec 98	**THE EVERLASTING** *Epic 6666862*	11		8
20 Mar 99	**YOU STOLE THE SUN FROM MY HEART** *Epic 6669532*	5		8
17 Jul 99	**TSUNAMI** *Epic 6674112*	11		5
22 Jan 00	**THE MASSES AGAINST THE CLASSES** *Epic 6685302*	1	1	7
10 Mar 01	**SO WHY SO SAD** *Epic 6708322*	8		7
10 Mar 01	**FOUND THAT SOUL** *Epic 6708332*	9		4
16 Jun 01	**OCEAN SPRAY** *Epic 6712532*	15		4
22 Sep 01	**LET ROBESON SING** *Epic 6717732*	19		2
26 Oct 02	**THERE BY THE GRACE OF GOD** *Epic 6731662*	6		5
30 Oct 04	**THE LOVE OF RICHARD NIXON** *Sony Music 6753422*	2		4
22 Jan 05	**EMPTY SOULS** *Columbia 6756102*	2		4
5 May 07	**YOUR LOVE ALONE IS NOT ENOUGH** *Columbia 88697075602*	2		10
4 Aug 07	**AUTUMNSONG** *Columbia 88697118302*	10		2
13 Oct 07	**INDIAN SUMMER** *Columbia 88697159322*	22		1
22 Mar 08	**UMBRELLA** *RCA GBARL0800128*	47		3

MANIJAMA FEATURING MUKUPA & LIL' T

Denmark/Iran, male/female vocal/production group

		⊕	✪	1
8 Feb 03	**NO NO NO** *Defected DFTD 058CDS*	66		1

BARRY MANILOW

US, male vocalist/pianist/producer (Barry Pincus)

		⊕	✪	136
22 Feb 75	**MANDY** *Arista 1* ★	11		9
6 May 78	**CAN'T SMILE WITHOUT YOU** *Arista 176*	43		7
29 Jul 78	**SOMEWHERE IN THE NIGHT/COPACABANA (AT THE COPA)** *Arista 196*	42		10
23 Dec 78	**COULD IT BE MAGIC** *Arista ARIST 229*	25		10
8 Nov 80	**LONELY TOGETHER** *Arista ARIST 373*	21		13
7 Feb 81	**I MADE IT THROUGH THE RAIN** *Arista ARIST 384*	37		6
11 Apr 81	**BERMUDA TRIANGLE** *Arista ARIST 406*	15		9
26 Sep 81	**LET'S HANG ON** *Arista ARIST 429* ○	12		11
12 Dec 81	**THE OLD SONGS** *Arista ARIST 443*	48		8
20 Feb 82	**IF I SHOULD LOVE AGAIN** *Arista ARIST 453*	66		2
17 Apr 82	**STAY** *Arista ARIST 464* FEATURING KEVIN DISIMONE & JAMES JOLIS	23		8
16 Oct 82	**I WANNA DO IT WITH YOU** *Arista ARIST 495*	8		8
4 Dec 82	**I'M GONNA SIT DOWN AND WRITE MYSELF A LETTER** *Arista ARIST 503*	36		7
25 Jun 83	**SOME KIND OF FRIEND** *Arista ARIST 516*	48		2
27 Aug 83	**YOU'RE LOOKING HOT TONIGHT** *Arista ARIST 542*	47		6
10 Dec 83	**READ 'EM AND WEEP** *Arista ARIST 551*	17		7
8 Apr 89	**PLEASE DON'T BE SCARED** *Arista 112186*	35		5
10 Apr 93	**COPACABANA (AT THE COPA) (REMIX)** *Arista 74321136912*	22		4
20 Nov 93	**COULD IT BE MAGIC** *Arista 74321174882*	36		3
6 Aug 94	**LET ME BE YOUR WINGS** *EMI CDEM 336* & DEBRA BYRD	73		1

MANIX

UK, male producer (Mark Clair). See 4 Hero

		⊕	✪	6
23 Nov 91	**MANIC MINDS** *Reinforced RIVET 1209*	63		2
7 Mar 92	**OBLIVION (HEAD IN THE CLOUDS) (EP)** *Reinforced RIVET 1212*	43		3
8 Aug 92	**RAINBOW PEOPLE** *Reinforced RIVET 1221*	57		1

MANKEY

UK, male producer (Andy Manston)

		⊕	✪	1
16 Nov 96	**BELIEVE IN ME** *Frisky DISKY 3*	74		1

MANKIND

UK, male instrumental session group

		⊕	✪	12
25 Nov 78	**DR WHO** *Pinnacle PIN 71*	25		12

AIMEE MANN

US, female vocalist/guitarist

		⊕	✪	9
31 Oct 87	**TIME STAND STILL** *Vertigo RUSH 13* RUSH WITH AIMEE MANN	42		3
28 Aug 93	**I SHOULD'VE KNOWN** *Imago 72787250437*	55		2
20 Nov 93	**STUPID THING** *Imago 74321174227*	47		2
5 Mar 94	**I SHOULD'VE KNOWN** *Imago 72787250602*	45		2

JOHNNY MANN SINGERS

US, male/female vocal group

		⊕	✪	13
12 Jul 67	**UP, UP AND AWAY** *Liberty LIB 55972*	6		13

MANSUN

UK, male vocal/instrumental group – Paul Draper, Dominic Chad, Stove King & Andie Rathbone 45

Date	Title	Peak Position	Weeks at No.1	Weeks on Chart
6 Apr 96	**ONE EP** *Parlophone CDR 6430*	37		2
15 Jun 96	**TWO EP** *Parlophone CDR 6437*	32		2
21 Sep 96	**THREE EP** *Parlophone CDR 6447*	19		3
7 Dec 96	**WIDE OPEN SPACE** *Parlophone CDR 6453*	15		4
15 Feb 97	**SHE MAKES MY NOSE BLEED** *Parlophone CDR 6458*	9		5
10 May 97	**TAXLOSS** *Parlophone CDRS 6465*	15		3
18 Oct 97	**CLOSED FOR BUSINESS** *Parlophone CDR 6482*	10		3
11 Jul 98	**LEGACY EP** *Parlophone CDR 6497*	7		4
5 Sep 98	**BEING A GIRL (PART ONE) EP** *Parlophone CDR 6503*	13		3
7 Nov 98	**NEGATIVE** *Parlophone CDR 6508*	27		2
13 Feb 99	**SIX** *Parlophone CDRS 6511*	16		3
12 Aug 00	**I CAN ONLY DISAPPOINT U** *Parlophone CDRS 6544*	8		6
18 Nov 00	**ELECTRIC MAN** *Parlophone CDRS 6550*	23		2
10 Feb 01	**FOOL** *Parlophone CDRS 6553*	28		2
2 Oct 04	**SLIPPING AWAY** *Parlophone R6650*	55		1

MANTOVANI

UK, male band leader (Annunzio Mantovani), d. 29 Mar 1980 (age 74), & orchestra 91

Date	Title	Peak Position	Weeks at No.1	Weeks on Chart
19 Dec 52	**WHITE CHRISTMAS** *Decca F 10017*	6		3
29 May 53	**THE SONG FROM MOULIN ROUGE** *Decca F 10094*	1	1	23
23 Oct 53	**SWEDISH RHAPSODY** *Decca F 10168*	2		18
18 Jun 54	**CARA MIA** *Decca F 10327* DAVID WHITFIELD, WITH CHORUS & MANTOVANI & HIS ORCHESTRA	1	10	25
11 Feb 55	**LONELY BALLERINA** *Decca F 10395*	16		4
25 Nov 55	**WHEN YOU LOSE THE ONE YOU LOVE** *Decca F 10627* DAVID WHITFIELD WITH CHORUS & MANTOVANI & HIS ORCHESTRA	7		11
31 May 57	**AROUND THE WORLD** *Decca F 10888*	20		4
14 Feb 58	**CRY MY HEART** *Decca F 10978* DAVID WHITFIELD WITH CHORUS & MANTOVANI & HIS ORCHESTRA	22		3

KURTIS MANTRONIK VS EPMD

US, male vocalist/instrumentalist/producer (Kurtis Kahleel) 1

Date	Title	Peak Position	Weeks at No.1	Weeks on Chart
15 Aug 98	**STRICTLY BUSINESS** *Parlophone CDR 6502*	43		1

MANTRONIX

US, male DJ/production/rap duo – Kurtis 'Mantronik' el Kahleel & Touré 'MC Tee' Embden (replaced by Bryce 'Luvah' Wilson) 53

Date	Title	Peak Position	Weeks at No.1	Weeks on Chart
22 Feb 86	**LADIES** *10 TEN 116*	55		4
17 May 86	**BASSLINE** *10 TEN 118*	34		6
7 Feb 87	**WHO IS IT** *10 TEN 137*	40		6
4 Jul 87	**SCREAM (PRIMAL SCREAM)** *10 TEN 169*	46		4
30 Jan 88	**SING A SONG (BREAK IT DOWN)** *10 TEN 206*	61		2
12 Mar 88	**SIMPLE SIMON (YOU GOTTA REGARD)** *10 TEN 217*	72		2
6 Jan 90	**GOT TO HAVE YOUR LOVE** *Capitol CL 559* FEATURING WONDRESS ●	4		11
12 May 90	**TAKE YOUR TIME** *Capitol CL 573* FEATURING WONDRESS	10		7
2 Mar 91	**DON'T GO MESSIN' WITH MY HEART** *Capitol CL 608*	22		5
22 Jun 91	**STEP TO ME (DO ME)** *Capitol CL 613*	59		1
9 Nov 02	**77 STRINGS** *Southern Fried ECB 35* KURTIS MANTRONIK PRESENTS CHAMONIX	71		1
28 Jun 03	**HOW DID YOU KNOW** *Southern Fried ECB 43CDS* KURTIS MANTRONIK PRESENTS CHAMONIX	16		4

MANUEL & HIS MUSIC OF THE MOUNTAINS

UK, male orchestra – leader Geoff Love*, d. 8 Jul 1991 (age 73) 31

Date	Title	Peak Position	Weeks at No.1	Weeks on Chart
28 Aug 59	**THE HONEYMOON SONG** *Columbia DB 4323*	22		9
13 Oct 60	**NEVER ON SUNDAY** *Columbia DB 4515*	29		10
13 Oct 66	**SOMEWHERE MY LOVE** *Columbia DB 7969*	42		2
31 Jan 76	**RODRIGO'S GUITAR CONCERTO DE ARANJUEZ (THEME FROM 2ND MOVEMENT)** *EMI 2383* ●	3		10

ROOTS MANUVA

UK, male rapper (Rodney Hylton Smith) 13

Date	Title	Peak Position	Weeks at No.1	Weeks on Chart
11 Dec 99	**DUSTED** *Hard Hands HAND 058CD1* LEFTFIELD/ROOTS MANUVA	28		3
4 Aug 01	**WITNESS (1 HOPE)** *Big Dada BDCDS 022*	45		2
20 Oct 01	**DREAMY DAYS** *Big Dada BDCDS 033*	53		1
8 May 04	**OH YOU WANT MORE** *Big Dada BDCDS 066* TY FEATURING ROOTS MANUVA	65		1
29 Jan 05	**COLOSSAL INSIGHT** *Big Dada BDCDS073*	33		2
2 Apr 05	**TOO COLD** *Big Dada BDCDS078*	39		3
29 Apr 06	**TRUE SKOOL** *Ninja Tune ZENCDS178* COLDCUT FEATURING ROOTS MANUVA	61		1

MARATHON

Germany/UK, male production duo 3

Date	Title	Peak Position	Weeks at No.1	Weeks on Chart
25 Jan 92	**MOVIN'** *10 TEN 395*	36		3

MARAUDERS

UK, male vocal/instrumental group 4

Date	Title	Peak Position	Weeks at No.1	Weeks on Chart
8 Aug 63	**THAT'S WHAT I WANT** *Decca F 11695*	43		4

MARBLES

UK, male vocal duo – Graham Bonnett* & Trevor Gordon 18

Date	Title	Peak Position	Weeks at No.1	Weeks on Chart
25 Sep 68	**ONLY ONE WOMAN** *Polydor 56 272*	5		12
26 Mar 69	**THE WALLS FELL DOWN** *Polydor 56 310*	28		6

MARC ET CLAUDE

Germany, male DJ/production duo 15

Date	Title	Peak Position	Weeks at No.1	Weeks on Chart
21 Nov 98	**LA** *Positiva CDTIV 104*	28		3
22 Jul 00	**I NEED YOUR LOVIN' (LIKE THE SUNSHINE)** *Positiva CDTIV 136*	12		7
6 Apr 02	**TREMBLE** *Positiva CDTIV 170*	29		3
19 Apr 03	**LOVING YOU '03** *Positiva CDTIV 190*	37		2

MARCELS

US, male vocal group – Cornelius Harp, Gene Bricker, d. 10 Dec 1983, Fred Johnson, Richard Knauss & Ronald Mundy 17

Date	Title	Peak Position	Weeks at No.1	Weeks on Chart
13 Apr 61	**BLUE MOON** *Pye International 7N 25073* ★	1	2	13
8 Jun 61	**SUMMERTIME** *Pye International 7N 25083*	46		4

LITTLE PEGGY MARCH

US, female vocalist (Margaret Battavio) 7

Date	Title	Peak Position	Weeks at No.1	Weeks on Chart
12 Sep 63	**HELLO HEARTACHE GOODBYE LOVE** *RCA 1362*	29		7

MARCO POLO

Italy, male instrumental/production duo 1

Date	Title	Peak Position	Weeks at No.1	Weeks on Chart
8 Apr 95	**A PRAYER TO THE MUSIC** *Hi-Life HICD 7*	65		1

MARCY PLAYGROUND

US, male vocal/instrumental trio 3

Date	Title	Peak Position	Weeks at No.1	Weeks on Chart
18 Apr 98	**SEX AND CANDY** *EMI CDEM 508*	29		3

MARDI GRAS

UK, male vocal/instrumental group 9

Date	Title	Peak Position	Weeks at No.1	Weeks on Chart
5 Aug 72	**TOO BUSY THINKING 'BOUT MY BABY** *Bell 1226*	19		9

MARDOUS

UK, male vocal/instrumental trio 1

Date	Title	Peak Position	Weeks at No.1	Weeks on Chart
20 Aug 05	**REVOLUTION OVER THE PHONE** *Poptones MC5102SCD*	74		1

IDA MARIA

Norway, female vocalist/guitarist (Ida Maria Borli Sivertsen) 8

Date	Title	Peak Position	Weeks at No.1	Weeks on Chart
2 Aug 08	**I LIKE YOU SO MUCH BETTER WHEN YOU'RE NAKED** *RCA 88697343092*	13		8

KELLY MARIE

UK, female vocalist (Jacqueline McKinnon) 36

Date	Title	Peak Position	Weeks at No.1	Weeks on Chart
2 Aug 80	**FEELS LIKE I'M IN LOVE** *Calibre Plus 1* ●	1	2	16
18 Oct 80	**LOVING JUST FOR FUN** *Calibre Plus 4*	21		7
7 Feb 81	**HOT LOVE** *Calibre Plus 5*	22		10
30 May 81	**LOVE TRIAL** *Calibre Plus 7*	51		3

ROSE MARIE

Ireland, female vocalist 5

Date	Title	Peak Position	Weeks at No.1	Weeks on Chart
19 Nov 83	**WHEN I LEAVE THE WORLD BEHIND** *A1 284*	63		5

Silver-selling ● Gold-selling ● Platinum-selling (x multiples) ⊛ US No.1 ★ Peak Position Weeks at No.1 Weeks on Chart

TEENA MARIE

US, female vocalist (Mary Brockert) — 28

Date	Title / Label	Peak	Wks at No.1	Wks on Chart
7 Jul 79	**I'M A SUCKER FOR YOUR LOVE** *Motown TMG 1146* CO-LEAD VOCALS RICK JAMES	43		8
31 May 80	**BEHIND THE GROOVE** *Motown TMG 1185*	6		10
11 Oct 80	**I NEED YOUR LOVIN'** *Motown TMG 1203*	28		6
26 Mar 88	**OOO LA LA LA** *Epic 6514237*	74		2
10 Nov 90	**SINCE DAY ONE** *Epic 6564297*	69		2

MARILLION

UK, male vocal/instrumental group – Derek Dick (aka Fish*, replaced by Steve Hogarth), Brian Jelliman, Diz Minnitt, Mick Pointer & Steve Rothary — 110

Date	Title / Label	Peak	Wks at No.1	Wks on Chart
20 Nov 82	**MARKET SQUARE HEROES** *EMI 5351*	60		2
12 Feb 83	**HE KNOWS YOU KNOW** *EMI 5362*	35		4
16 Apr 83	**MARKET SQUARE HEROES** *EMI 5351*	53		6
18 Jun 83	**GARDEN PARTY** *EMI 5393*	16		5
11 Feb 84	**PUNCH AND JUDY** *EMI MARIL 1*	29		4
12 May 84	**ASSASSING** *EMI MARIL 2*	22		5
18 May 85	**KAYLEIGH** *EMI MARIL 3* ●	2		14
7 Sep 85	**LAVENDER** *EMI MARIL 4*	5		9
30 Nov 85	**HEART OF LOTHIAN** *EMI MARIL 5*	29		6
23 May 87	**INCOMMUNICADO** *EMI MARIL 6*	6		5
25 Jul 87	**SUGAR MICE** *EMI MARIL 7*	22		5
7 Nov 87	**WARM WET CIRCLES** *EMI MARIL 8*	22		4
26 Nov 88	**FREAKS (LIVE)** *EMI MARIL 9*	24		3
9 Sep 89	**HOOKS IN YOU** *Capitol MARIL 10*	30		3
9 Dec 89	**UNINVITED GUEST** *EMI MARIL 11*	53		2
14 Apr 90	**EASTER** *EMI MARIL 12*	34		2
8 Jun 91	**COVER MY EYES (PAIN AND HEAVEN)** *EMI MARIL 13*	34		4
3 Aug 91	**NO ONE CAN** *EMI MARIL 14*	33		4
5 Oct 91	**DRY LAND** *EMI MARIL 15*	34		2
23 May 92	**SYMPATHY** *EMI MARIL 16*	17		3
1 Aug 92	**NO ONE CAN** *EMI MARIL 17*	26		4
26 Mar 94	**THE HOLLOW MAN** *EMI CDEMS 307*	30		2
7 May 94	**ALONE AGAIN IN THE LAP OF LUXURY** *EMI CDEMS 318*	53		3
10 Jun 95	**BEAUTIFUL** *EMI CDMARILS 18*	29		2
1 May 04	**YOU'RE GONE** *Intact CXINTACT1*	7		3
24 Jul 04	**DON'T HURT YOURSELF** *Intact CXINTACT2*	16		2
7 Apr 07	**SEE IT LIKE A BABY** *Intact GBGST0700007*	45		1
23 Jun 07	**THANKYOU WHOEVER YOU ARE** *Intact CXINTACT4*	15		1

MARILYN

UK (b. Jamaica), male vocalist (Peter Robinson) — 26

Date	Title / Label	Peak	Wks at No.1	Wks on Chart
5 Nov 83	**CALLING YOUR NAME** *Mercury MAZ 1* ●	4		12
11 Feb 84	**CRY AND BE FREE** *Mercury MAZ 2*	31		6
21 Apr 84	**YOU DON'T LOVE ME** *Mercury MAZ 3*	40		7
13 Apr 85	**BABY U LEFT ME (IN THE COLD)** *Mercury MAZ 4*	70		1

MARILYN MANSON

US, male vocal/instrumental group – Brian Warner (Marilyn Manson), Steve Bier, Scott Putesky, Jeordi White & Ken Wilson — 44

Date	Title / Label	Peak	Wks at No.1	Wks on Chart
7 Jun 97	**THE BEAUTIFUL PEOPLE** *Interscope IND 95541*	18		3
20 Sep 97	**TOURNIQUET** *Interscope IND 95552*	28		2
21 Nov 98	**THE DOPE SHOW** *Interscope IND 95610*	12		3
26 Jun 99	**ROCK IS DEAD** *Maverick W 486CD*	23		2
18 Nov 00	**DISPOSABLE TEENS** *Nothing 4974372*	12		3
3 Mar 01	**THE FIGHT SONG** *Interscope 4974912*	24		3
15 Sep 01	**THE NOBODIES** *Interscope IND 97604*	34		2
30 Mar 02	**TAINTED LOVE** *Maverick W 579CD1*	5		11
14 Jun 03	**MOBSCENE** *Interscope 9807726*	13		6
13 Sep 03	**THIS IS THE NEW SHIT** *Interscope 9810793*	29		2
16 Oct 04	**PERSONAL JESUS** *Interscope 9864166*	13		5
9 Jun 07	**HEART-SHAPED GLASSES** *Interscope 1736138*	19		2

MARINA & THE DIAMONDS

UK, female vocalist/multi-instrumentalist (Marina Diamandis) & various musicians — 9

Date	Title / Label	Peak	Wks at No.1	Wks on Chart
13 Feb 10	**HOLLYWOOD** *679/Atlantic 679L170CD*	12		9+

MARINO MARINI & HIS QUARTET

Italy, male vocal/instrumental group – Marino Marini, d. 20 Mar 1997, Sergio & Ruggiero Cori & Tony Savio — 23

Date	Title / Label	Peak	Wks at No.1	Wks on Chart
3 Oct 58	**VOLARE** *Durium DC 16632*	13		7
10 Oct 58	**COME PRIMA** *Durium DC 16632*	2		14
20 Mar 59	**CIAO CIAO BAMBINA** *Durium DC 16636*	24		2

MARIO

US, male vocalist (Mario Barrett) — 35

Date	Title / Label	Peak	Wks at No.1	Wks on Chart
12 Apr 03	**JUST A FRIEND** *J Records 82876508082*	18		4
12 Jul 03	**C'MON** *J Records 82876528282*	28		2
19 Mar 05	**LET ME LOVE YOU (IMPORT)** *J Records 82876679752*	53		1
2 Apr 05	**LET ME LOVE YOU** *J Records 82876682562* ★	2		15
9 Jul 05	**HERE I GO AGAIN** *J Records 82876705592*	11		8
18 Aug 07	**HOW DO I BREATHE** *J Records 88697121652*	21		5

MARION

UK, male vocal/instrumental group — 9

Date	Title / Label	Peak	Wks at No.1	Wks on Chart
25 Feb 95	**SLEEP** *London LONCD 360*	53		1
13 May 95	**TOYS FOR BOYS** *London LONCD 366*	57		1
21 Oct 95	**LET'S ALL GO TOGETHER** *London LONCD 371*	37		2
3 Feb 96	**TIME** *London LONCD 377*	29		2
30 Mar 96	**SLEEP (REMIX)** *London LONCD 381*	17		2
7 Mar 98	**MIYAKO HIEAWAY** *London LONCD 403*	45		1

MARK' OH

Germany, male producer (Marko Albrecht) — 3

Date	Title / Label	Peak	Wks at No.1	Wks on Chart
6 May 95	**TEARS DON'T LIE** *Systematic SYSCD 9*	24		3

PIGMEAT MARKHAM

US, male comedian/vocalist (Dewey Markham), d. 13 Dec 1981 (age 77) — 8

Date	Title / Label	Peak	Wks at No.1	Wks on Chart
17 Jul 68	**HERE COMES THE JUDGE** *Chess CRS 8077*	19		8

BIZ MARKIE

US, male rapper (Theo Hall) — 2

Date	Title / Label	Peak	Wks at No.1	Wks on Chart
26 May 90	**JUST A FRIEND** *Cold Chillin' W 9823*	55		2

YANNIS MARKOPOULOS

Greece, orchestra — 8

Date	Title / Label	Peak	Wks at No.1	Wks on Chart
17 Dec 77	**WHO PAYS THE FERRYMAN** *BBC RESL 51*	11		8

GUY MARKS

US, male vocalist (Mario Scarpo), d. 29 Nov 1987 (age 64) — 8

Date	Title / Label	Peak	Wks at No.1	Wks on Chart
13 May 78	**LOVING YOU HAS MADE ME BANANAS** *ABC 4211*	25		8

MARKY MARK & THE FUNKY BUNCH

US, male rapper/actor (Mark Wahlberg) & male/female rap/vocal/DJ/dance group — 14

Date	Title / Label	Peak	Wks at No.1	Wks on Chart
31 Aug 91	**GOOD VIBRATIONS** *Interscope A 8764* FEATURING LOLEATTA HOLLOWAY ★	14		7
2 Nov 91	**WILDSIDE** *Interscope A 8674*	42		3
12 Dec 92	**YOU GOTTA BELIEVE** *Interscope A 8680*	54		4

DAMIAN 'JR GONG' MARLEY

Jamaica, male vocalist — 11

Date	Title / Label	Peak	Wks at No.1	Wks on Chart
1 Oct 05	**WELCOME TO JAMROCK** *Island MCSD40432*	13		6
24 Dec 05	**THE MASTER HAS COME BACK** *Island MCSTD40443*	74		1
29 Apr 06	**BEAUTIFUL** *Tuff Gong MCSTD40452*	39		4

ZIGGY MARLEY & THE MELODY MAKERS

Jamaica, male vocalist/guitarist (David Marley) & male/female vocal/instrumental group — 11

Date	Title / Label	Peak	Wks at No.1	Wks on Chart
11 Jun 88	**TOMORROW PEOPLE** *Virgin VS 1049*	22		10
23 Sep 89	**LOOK WHO'S DANCING** *Virgin America VUS 5*	65		1

BOB MARLEY & THE WAILERS

Jamaica, male vocal/instrumental group – Bob Marley, Junior Braithwaite, Beverley Kelso, Bunny Livingston (aka Bunny Wailer), Cherry Smith & Peter Tosh — 173

Date	Title / Label	Peak	Wks at No.1	Wks on Chart
27 Sep 75	**NO WOMAN NO CRY** *Island WIP 6244*	22		7
25 Jun 77	**EXODUS** *Island WIP 6390*	14		9
10 Sep 77	**WAITING IN VAIN** *Island WIP 6402*	27		6
10 Dec 77	**JAMMING/PUNKY REGGAE PARTY** *Island WIP 6410* ●	9		12
25 Feb 78	**IS THIS LOVE** *Island WIP 6420*	9		9
10 Jun 78	**SATISFY MY SOUL** *Island WIP 6440*	21		10

Date	Title	Peak Position	Weeks at No.1	Weeks on Chart
20 Oct 79	**SO MUCH TROUBLE IN THE WORLD** *Island WIP 6510*	56		4
21 Jun 80	**COULD YOU BE LOVED** *Island WIP 6610*	5		12
13 Sep 80	**THREE LITTLE BIRDS** *Island WIP 6641*	17		9
13 Jun 81	**NO WOMAN NO CRY** *Island WIP 6244*	8		11
7 May 83	**BUFFALO SOLDIER** *Island/Tuff Gong IS 180*	4		12
21 Apr 84	**ONE LOVE – PEOPLE GET READY** *Island IS 169*	5		11
23 Jun 84	**WAITING IN VAIN** *Island IS 180*	31		7
8 Dec 84	**COULD YOU BE LOVED** *Island IS 210*	71		2
18 May 91	**ONE LOVE – PEOPLE GET READY** *Tuff Gong TGX 1*	42		3
19 Sep 92	**IRON LION ZION** *Tuff Gong TGX 2*	5		9
28 Nov 92	**WHY SHOULD I/EXODUS** *Tuff Gong TFX 3*	42		4
20 May 95	**KEEP ON MOVING** *Tuff Gong TGXCD 4*	17		4
8 Jun 96	**WHAT GOES AROUND COMES AROUND** *Anansi ANACS 002*	42		1
25 Sep 99	**SUN IS SHINING** *Club Tools 0066895 CLU* BOB MARLEY VERSUS FUNKSTAR DE LUXE	3		10
11 Dec 99	**TURN YOUR LIGHTS DOWN LOW** *Columbia 6684362* BOB MARLEY FEATURING LAURYN HILL	15		7
22 Jan 00	**RAINBOW COUNTRY** *Club Tools 0067225 CLU* BOB MARLEY VERSUS FUNKSTAR DELUXE	11		6
24 Jun 00	**JAMMIN'** *Tuff Gong TFXCD 9* BOB MARLEY FEATURING MC LYTE	42		2
12 Nov 05	**NO WOMAN NO CRY** *Tuff Gong TGXCD13*	58		1
19 Nov 05	**I SHOT THE SHERIFF** *Tuff Gong TGXCD14*	67		1
26 Nov 05	**SUN IS SHINING** *Tuff Gong TGXCD15*	54		1
3 Dec 05	**SLOGANS** *Tuff Gong TGXCDS11*	45		1
10 Dec 05	**AFRICA UNITE** *Tuff Gong TGXCD16*	49		1
17 Dec 05	**STAND UP JAMROCK** *Tuff Gong TGXCD17*	56		1

LENE MARLIN
Norway, female vocalist (Lene Marlin Pederson) — 20

Date	Title	Peak Position	Weeks at No.1	Weeks on Chart
11 Mar 00	**SITTING DOWN HERE** *Virgin DINSD 183*	5		11
16 Sep 00	**UNFORGIVABLE SINNER** *Virgin DINSCX 202*	13		6
13 Jan 01	**WHERE I'M HEADED** *Virgin DINSD 196*	31		2
4 Oct 03	**YOU WEREN'T THERE** *Virgin DINSD 262*	59		1

MARLO
UK, male vocal/instrumental group — 1

Date	Title	Peak Position	Weeks at No.1	Weeks on Chart
24 Jul 99	**HOW DO I KNOW?** *Polydor 5611362*	56		1

MARLY
Denmark, female vocalist (Ditte-Marie Lyfeldt) — 2

Date	Title	Peak Position	Weeks at No.1	Weeks on Chart
28 Aug 04	**YOU NEVER KNOW** *All Around The World CDGLOBE 363*	23		2

MARMADUKE DUKE
UK, male vocal/instrumental duo — 9

Date	Title	Peak Position	Weeks at No.1	Weeks on Chart
2 May 09	**RUBBER LOVER** *14th Floor GBFTG0900022*	12		9

MARMALADE
UK, male vocal/instrumental group – William 'Junior' Campbell*, Raymond Duffy (replaced by Alan Whitehead), Dean Ford, Patrick Fairley & Graham Knight — 130

Date	Title	Peak Position	Weeks at No.1	Weeks on Chart
22 May 68	**LOVIN' THINGS** *CBS 3412*	6		13
23 Oct 68	**WAIT FOR ME MARIANNE** *CBS 3708*	30		5
4 Dec 68	**OB-LA-DI OB-LA-DA** *CBS 3892*	1	3	20
11 Jun 69	**BABY MAKE IT SOON** *CBS 4287*	9		13
20 Dec 69	**REFLECTIONS OF MY LIFE** *Decca F 12982*	3		12
18 Jul 70	**RAINBOW** *Decca F 13035*	3		14
27 Mar 71	**MY LITTLE ONE** *Decca F 13135*	15		11
4 Sep 71	**COUSIN NORMAN** *Decca F 13214*	6		11
27 Nov 71	**BACK ON THE ROAD** *Decca F 13251*	35		8
1 Apr 72	**RADANCER** *Decca F 13297*	6		12
21 Feb 76	**FALLING APART AT THE SEAMS** *Target TGT 105*	9		11

MARMION
Spain/Holland, male instrumental/production duo — 2

Date	Title	Peak Position	Weeks at No.1	Weeks on Chart
18 May 96	**SCHONEBERG** *Hooj Choons HOOJCD 43*	53		1
14 Feb 98	**SCHONEBERG (REMIX)** *ffrr FCD 324*	56		1

MAROON 5
US, male vocal/instrumental group – Adam Levine, Jesse Carmichael, Matt Flynn, Mickey Madden & James Valentine. See Kanye West featuring Adam Levine — 79

Date	Title	Peak Position	Weeks at No.1	Weeks on Chart
31 Jan 04	**HARDER TO BREATHE** *J Records 82876566922*	13		7
1 May 04	**THIS LOVE** *J Records 82876608452*	3		14
4 Sep 04	**SHE WILL BE LOVED** *J Records 82876643632*	4		10
18 Dec 04	**SUNDAY MORNING** *J Records 82876668042*	27		7
23 Apr 05	**MUST GET OUT** *J Records 82876689062*	39		2
19 May 07	**MAKES ME WONDER** *A&M/Polydor 1734956*	2		15
25 Aug 07	**WAKE UP CALL** *A&M 1744501*	33		7
24 Nov 07	**WON'T GO HOME WITHOUT YOU** *Polydor USUM70731562*	44		6
14 Jun 08	**IF I NEVER SEE YOUR FACE AGAIN** *A&M/Octone USUM70731559* FEATURING RIHANNA	28		11

MARRADONA
UK, male production duo — 5

Date	Title	Peak Position	Weeks at No.1	Weeks on Chart
26 Feb 94	**OUT OF MY HEAD** *Peach PWCD 282*	38		3
26 Jul 97	**OUT OF MY HEAD (REMIX)** *Soopa SPCD 1*	39		2

M/A/R/R/S
UK, male production/instrumental group – Alex Ayuli, Rudi Tambala & Martyn & Steve Young – with DJs Dave Dorrell & Chris 'CJ' Mackintosh — 14

Date	Title	Peak Position	Weeks at No.1	Weeks on Chart
5 Sep 87	**PUMP UP THE VOLUME/ANITINA (THE FIRST TIME I SEE SHE DANCE)** *4AD AD 70*	1	2	14

MARS VOLTA
US, male vocal/instrumental group — 8

Date	Title	Peak Position	Weeks at No.1	Weeks on Chart
11 Oct 03	**INERTIATIC ESP** *Universal MCSTD 40332*	42		2
13 Mar 04	**TELEVATORS** *Universal MCSTD 40352*	41		1
26 Mar 05	**THE WIDOW** *Universal MCSTD40408*	20		4
23 Jul 05	**L'VIA L'VIAQUEZ** *Universal MCSTD40420*	53		1

MATTHEW MARSDEN
UK, male actor/vocalist — 10

Date	Title	Peak Position	Weeks at No.1	Weeks on Chart
11 Jul 98	**THE HEART'S LONE DESIRE** *Columbia 6661152*	13		7
7 Nov 98	**SHE'S GONE** *Columbia 6664915* FEATURING DESTINY'S CHILD	24		3

KYM MARSH
UK, female vocalist/actor. See Hear'Say — 21

Date	Title	Peak Position	Weeks at No.1	Weeks on Chart
19 Apr 03	**CRY** *Island MCSXD 40314*	2		12
19 Jul 03	**COME ON OVER** *Universal MCSXD 40323*	10		7
8 Nov 03	**SENTIMENTAL** *Universal MCSTD 40340*	35		2

STEVIE MARSH
UK, female vocalist — 4

Date	Title	Peak Position	Weeks at No.1	Weeks on Chart
4 Dec 59	**IF YOU WERE THE ONLY BOY IN THE WORLD** *Decca F 11181*	24		4

JOY MARSHALL
UK, female vocalist — 2

Date	Title	Peak Position	Weeks at No.1	Weeks on Chart
23 Jun 66	**THE MORE I SEE YOU** *Decca F 12422*	34		2

KEITH MARSHALL
UK, male vocalist. See Hello — 10

Date	Title	Peak Position	Weeks at No.1	Weeks on Chart
4 Apr 81	**ONLY CRYING** *Arrival PIK 2*	12		10

WAYNE MARSHALL
UK, male vocalist — 7

Date	Title	Peak Position	Weeks at No.1	Weeks on Chart
1 Oct 94	**OOH AAH (G-SPOT)** *Soultown SOULCDS 322*	29		3
3 Jun 95	**SPIRIT** *Soultown SOULCDS 00352*	58		1
24 Feb 96	**NEVER KNEW LOVE LIKE THIS** *Sony S2 6629382* PAULINE HENRY FEATURING WAYNE MARSHALL	40		2
7 Dec 96	**G SPOT (REMIX)** *MBA INTER 9006*	50		1

MARSHALL HAIN
UK, male/female vocal/instrumetnal duo – Julian Marshall & Kit Hain — 19

Date	Title	Peak Position	Weeks at No.1	Weeks on Chart
3 Jun 78	**DANCING IN THE CITY** *Harvest HAR 5157*	3		15
14 Oct 78	**COMING HOME** *Harvest HAR 5168*	39		4

MARTAY FEATURING ZZ TOP
UK/US, female/male rap/vocal/instrumental group — 2

Date	Title	Peak Position	Weeks at No.1	Weeks on Chart
16 Oct 99	**GIMME ALL YOUR LOVIN' 2000** *Riverhorse RIVHCD 2*	28		2

Silver-selling ○ Gold-selling ● Platinum-selling (x multiples) ⊛ US No.1 ★ Peak Position Weeks at No.1 Weeks on Chart

LENA MARTELL
UK, female vocalist (Helen Thomson) — 18

Date	Title	Peak Position	Weeks at No.1	Weeks on Chart
29 Sep 79	**ONE DAY AT A TIME** *Pye 7N 46021* ●	1	3	18

MARTHA & THE MUFFINS
Canada, female/male vocal/instrumental group – Martha Johnson, Carl Finkle, Mark & Tim Gane, Andy Haas & Martha Ladly — 10

Date	Title	Peak Position	Weeks at No.1	Weeks on Chart
1 Mar 80	**ECHO BEACH** *Dindisc DIN 9*	10		10

MARTIKA
US, female vocalist (Marta Marrero) — 57

Date	Title	Peak Position	Weeks at No.1	Weeks on Chart
29 Jul 89	**TOY SOLDIERS** *CBS 6550497* ○ ★	5		11
14 Oct 89	**I FEEL THE EARTH MOVE** *CBS 6552947*	7		14
13 Jan 90	**MORE THAN YOU KNOW** *CBS 6555267*	15		7
17 Mar 90	**WATER** *CBS 6557317*	59		3
17 Aug 91	**LOVE...THY WILL BE DONE** *Columbia 6573137*	9		9
30 Nov 91	**MARTIKA'S KITCHEN** *Columbia 6575687*	17		10
22 Feb 92	**COLOURED KISSES** *Columbia 6577097*	41		3

BILLIE RAY MARTIN
Germany, female vocalist (Birgit Dieckmann). See Electribe 101 — 20

Date	Title	Peak Position	Weeks at No.1	Weeks on Chart
19 Nov 94	**YOUR LOVING ARMS** *Magnet MAG 1028CD*	38		3
20 May 95	**YOUR LOVING ARMS (REMIX)** *Magnet MAG 1031CD*	6		10
2 Sep 95	**RUNNING AROUND TOWN** *Magnet MAG 1035CD*	29		2
6 Jan 96	**IMITATION OF LIFE** *Magnet MAG 1040CD*	29		3
6 Apr 96	**SPACE OASIS** *Magnet MAG 1042CD*	66		1
21 Aug 99	**HONEY** *React CDREACT 129*	54		1

DEAN MARTIN
US, male vocalist (Dino Crocetti), d. 25 Dec 1995 (age 78) — 163

Date	Title	Peak Position	Weeks at No.1	Weeks on Chart
18 Sep 53	**KISS** *Capitol CL 13893*	5		8
22 Jan 54	**THAT'S AMORE** *Capitol CL 14008*	2		11
1 Oct 54	**SWAY** *Capitol CL 14138*	6		7
22 Oct 54	**HOW DO YOU SPEAK TO AN ANGEL** *Capitol CL 14150*	15		6
28 Jan 55	**NAUGHTY LADY OF SHADY LANE** *Capitol CL 14226*	5		10
4 Feb 55	**MAMBO ITALIANO** *Capitol CL 14227*	14		2
25 Feb 55	**LET ME GO LOVER** *Capitol CL 14226*	3		9
1 Apr 55	**UNDER THE BRIDGES OF PARIS** *Capitol CL 14255*	6		8
10 Feb 56	**MEMORIES ARE MADE OF THIS** *Capitol CL 14523* ★	1	4	16
2 Mar 56	**YOUNG AND FOOLISH** *Capitol CL 14519*	20		1
27 Apr 56	**INNAMORATA** *Capitol CL 14507*	21		3
22 Mar 57	**THE MAN WHO PLAYS THE MANDOLINO** *Capitol CL 14690*	21		2
13 Jun 58	**RETURN TO ME** *Capitol CL 14844*	2		22
29 Aug 58	**VOLARE** *Capitol CL 14910*	2		14
27 Aug 64	**EVERYBODY LOVES SOMEBODY** *Reprise R 20281* ★	11		13
12 Nov 64	**THE DOOR IS STILL OPEN TO MY HEART** *Reprise R 20307*	42		4
5 Feb 69	**GENTLE ON MY MIND** *Reprise R 23343*	2		24
22 Jun 96	**THAT'S AMORE** *EMI Premier PRESCD 3*	43		2
21 Aug 99	**SWAY** *Capitol CDSWAY 001*	66		1

JUAN MARTIN
Spain, male guitarist — 7

Date	Title	Peak Position	Weeks at No.1	Weeks on Chart
28 Jan 84	**LOVE THEME FROM 'THE THORN BIRDS'** *WEA X 9518*	10		7

LINDA MARTIN
Ireland (b. UK), female vocalist — 2

Date	Title	Peak Position	Weeks at No.1	Weeks on Chart
30 May 92	**WHY ME** *Columbia 6581317*	59		2

RAY MARTIN
UK, male orchestra leader, d. 7 Feb 1988 (age 69). See Lee Lawrence — 21

Date	Title	Peak Position	Weeks at No.1	Weeks on Chart
14 Nov 52	**BLUE TANGO** *Columbia DB 3051*	8		4
20 Nov 53	**CRYING IN THE CHAPEL** *Decca F 10177* LEE LAWRENCE WITH RAY MARTIN & HIS ORCHESTRA	7		6
4 Dec 53	**SWEDISH RHAPSODY** *Columbia DB 3346*	4		4
2 Dec 55	**SUDDENLY THERE'S A VALLEY** *Columbia DB 3681* LEE LAWRENCE WITH RAY MARTIN & HIS ORCHESTRA	14		4
15 Jun 56	**CAROUSEL WALTZ** *Columbia DB 3771*	24		3

RICKY MARTIN
Puerto Rico, male vocalist/actor (Enrique Martin Morales) — 80

Date	Title	Peak Position	Weeks at No.1	Weeks on Chart
20 Sep 97	**(UN, DOS, TRES) MARIA** *Columbia 6649595*	6		6
11 Jul 98	**THE CUP OF LIFE** *Columbia 6661502*	29		3
17 Jul 99	**LIVIN' LA VIDA LOCA** *Columbia 6676405* ⊛ ★	1	3	17
20 Nov 99	**SHAKE YOUR BON-BON** *Columbia 6683412*	12		9
29 Apr 00	**PRIVATE EMOTION** *Columbia 6692692* FEATURING MEJA	9		9
4 Nov 00	**SHE BANGS** *Columbia 6705422* ○	3		15
10 Mar 01	**NOBODY WANTS TO BE LONELY** *Columbia 6709462* WITH CHRISTINA AGUILERA	4		12
28 Jul 01	**LOADED** *Columbia 6714642*	19		4
15 Oct 05	**DON'T CARE** *Sony BMG 6760667*	11		5

TONY MARTIN
US, male vocalist (Alvin Morris, Jr) — 28

Date	Title	Peak Position	Weeks at No.1	Weeks on Chart
22 Apr 55	**STRANGER IN PARADISE** *HMV B 10849*	6		13
13 Jul 56	**WALK HAND IN HAND** *HMV POP 222*	2		15

WINK MARTINDALE
US, male vocalist (Winston Martindale) — 41

Date	Title	Peak Position	Weeks at No.1	Weeks on Chart
4 Dec 59	**DECK OF CARDS** *London HLD 8962*	18		8
18 Apr 63	**DECK OF CARDS** *London HLD 8962*	5		21
20 Oct 73	**DECK OF CARDS** *Dot 109*	22		12

ALICE MARTINEAU
UK, female vocalist, d. 6 Mar 2003 (age 30) — 1

Date	Title	Peak Position	Weeks at No.1	Weeks on Chart
23 Nov 02	**IF I FALL** *Epic 6732332*	45		1

ANGIE MARTINEZ FEATURING LIL' MO & SACARIO
US, female vocal/rap trio — 1

Date	Title	Peak Position	Weeks at No.1	Weeks on Chart
15 Feb 03	**IF I COULD GO** *Elektra E 7331CD*	61		1

AL MARTINO
US, male vocalist (Alfred Cini), d. 13 Oct 2009 (age 82) — 87

Date	Title	Peak Position	Weeks at No.1	Weeks on Chart
14 Nov 52	**HERE IN MY HEART** *Capitol CL 13779* ★	1	9	18
21 Nov 52	**TAKE MY HEART** *Capitol CL 13769*	9		1
30 Jan 53	**NOW** *Capitol CL 13835*	3		12
10 Jul 53	**RACHEL** *Capitol CL 13879*	10		5
4 Jun 54	**WANTED** *Capitol CL 14128*	4		16
1 Oct 54	**THE STORY OF TINA** *Capitol CL 14163*	10		8
23 Sep 55	**THE MAN FROM LARAMIE** *Capitol CL 14343*	19		3
31 Mar 60	**SUMMERTIME** *Top Rank JAR 312*	49		1
29 Aug 63	**I LOVE YOU BECAUSE** *Capitol CL 15300*	48		1
22 Aug 70	**SPANISH EYES** *Capitol CL 15430*	49		1
14 Jul 73	**SPANISH EYES** *Capitol CL 15430*	5		21

MARVELETTES
US, female vocal group — 10

Date	Title	Peak Position	Weeks at No.1	Weeks on Chart
15 Jun 67	**WHEN YOU'RE YOUNG AND IN LOVE** *Tamla Motown TMG 609*	13		10

MARVIN & TAMARA
UK, male/female vocal duo — 9

Date	Title	Peak Position	Weeks at No.1	Weeks on Chart
7 Aug 99	**GROOVE MACHINE** *Epic 6675582*	11		5
25 Dec 99	**NORTH, SOUTH, EAST, WEST** *Epic 6684902*	38		4

HANK MARVIN
UK, male vocalist/guitarist (Brian Rankin). See Shadows — 36

Date	Title	Peak Position	Weeks at No.1	Weeks on Chart
13 Sep 69	**THROW DOWN A LINE** *Columbia DB 8615* CLIFF RICHARD & HANK MARVIN	7		9
21 Feb 70	**JOY OF LIVING** *Columbia DB 8657* CLIFF & HANK	25		8
6 Mar 82	**DON'T TALK** *Polydor POSP 420*	49		4
22 Mar 86	**LIVING DOLL** *WEA YZ 65* CLIFF RICHARD & THE YOUNG ONES FEATURING HANK B MARVIN ●	1	3	11
7 Jan 89	**LONDON KID** *Polydor 32* JEAN-MICHEL JARRE FEATURING HANK MARVIN	52		3
17 Oct 92	**WE ARE THE CHAMPIONS** *PolyGram TV PO 229* FEATURING BRIAN MAY	66		1

LEE MARVIN
US, male actor/vocalist, d. 28 Aug 1987 (age 63) — 23

Date	Title / Label	Peak Position	Weeks at No.1	Weeks on Chart
7 Feb 70	**WAND'RIN' STAR** *Paramount PARA 3004*	1	3	23

MARVIN THE PARANOID ANDROID
UK, male robot (Stephen Moore) — 4

Date	Title / Label	Peak Position	Weeks at No.1	Weeks on Chart
16 May 81	**MARVIN** *Polydor POSP 261*	53		4

RICHARD MARX
US, male vocalist — 75

Date	Title / Label	Peak Position	Weeks at No.1	Weeks on Chart
27 Feb 88	**SHOULD'VE KNOWN BETTER** *Manhattan MT 32*	50		5
14 May 88	**ENDLESS SUMMER NIGHTS** *Manhattan MT 39*	50		3
17 Jun 89	**SATISFIED** *EMI-USA MT 64* ★	52		4
2 Sep 89	**RIGHT HERE WAITING** *EMI-USA MT 72* ● ★	2		10
11 Nov 89	**ANGELIA** *EMI-USA MT 74*	45		4
24 Mar 90	**TOO LATE TO SAY GOODBYE** *EMI-USA MT 80*	38		3
7 Jul 90	**CHILDREN OF THE NIGHT** *EMI-USA MT 84*	54		2
1 Sep 90	**ENDLESS SUMMER NIGHTS/HOLD ON TO THE NIGHTS** *EMI-USA MT 89* ★	60		2
19 Oct 91	**KEEP COMING BACK** *Capitol CL 634*	55		2
9 May 92	**HAZARD** *Capitol CL 654* ●	3		15
29 Aug 92	**TAKE THIS HEART** *Capitol CL 667*	13		6
28 Nov 92	**CHAINS AROUND MY HEART** *Capitol CL 676*	29		6
29 Jan 94	**NOW AND FOREVER** *Capitol CDCLS 703*	13		6
30 Apr 94	**SILENT SCREAM** *Capitol CDCLS 714*	32		4
13 Aug 94	**THE WAY SHE LOVES ME** *Capitol CDCL 721*	38		3

MARXMAN
UK/Ireland, male rap/production group — 5

Date	Title / Label	Peak Position	Weeks at No.1	Weeks on Chart
6 Mar 93	**ALL ABOUT EVE** *Talkin Loud TLKCD 35*	28		4
1 May 93	**SHIP AHOY** *Talkin Loud TLKCD 39*	64		1

MARY JANE GIRLS
US, female vocal group — 15

Date	Title / Label	Peak Position	Weeks at No.1	Weeks on Chart
21 May 83	**CANDY MAN** *Motown TMG 1301*	60		4
25 Jun 83	**ALL NIGHT LONG** *Gordy TMG 1309*	13		9
8 Oct 83	**BOYS** *Gordy TMG 1315*	74		1
18 Feb 95	**ALL NIGHT LONG (REMIX)** *Motown TMGCD 1436*	51		1

MARY MARY
US, female vocal duo – Erica & Tina Atkins — 14

Date	Title / Label	Peak Position	Weeks at No.1	Weeks on Chart
10 Jun 00	**SHACKLES (PRAISE YOU)** *Columbia 6694202*	5		12
18 Nov 00	**I SINGS** *Columbia 6699742*	32		2

CAROLYNE MAS
US, female vocalist/guitarist — 2

Date	Title / Label	Peak Position	Weeks at No.1	Weeks on Chart
2 Feb 80	**QUOTE GOODBYE QUOTE** *Mercury 6167 873*	71		2

MASAI
UK, female vocal duo — 1

Date	Title / Label	Peak Position	Weeks at No.1	Weeks on Chart
1 Mar 03	**DO THAT THANG** *Concept CDCON 36X*	42		1

MA$E
US, male rapper (Mason Betha) — 57

Date	Title / Label	Peak Position	Weeks at No.1	Weeks on Chart
29 Mar 97	**CAN'T NOBODY HOLD ME DOWN** *Puff Daddy 74321464552* PUFF DADDY FEATURING MA$E ★	19		4
9 Aug 97	**MO MONEY MO PROBLEMS** *Puff Daddy 74321492492* NOTORIOUS B.I.G. FEATURING PUFF DADDY & MA$E ★	6		10
27 Dec 97	**FEEL SO GOOD** *Puff Daddy 74321526442*	10		8
18 Apr 98	**WHAT YOU WANT** *Puff Daddy 74321578772* FEATURING TOTAL	15		5
19 Sep 98	**HORSE AND CARRIAGE** *Epic 6662612* CAM'RON FEATURING MA$E	12		4
3 Oct 98	**YOU SHOULD BE MINE** *Motown 8608412* BRIAN McKNIGHT FEATURING MA$E	36		2
10 Oct 98	**TOP OF THE WORLD** *Atlantic AT 0046CD* BRANDY FEATURING MA$E ●	2		9
12 Dec 98	**TAKE ME THERE** *Interscope IND 95620* BLACKstreet & MYA FEATURING MA$E & BLINKY BLINK	7		9
10 Jul 99	**GET READY** *Puff Daddy 74321682612* FEATURING BLACKstreet	32		4
20 Nov 04	**WELCOME BACK/BREATHE STRETCH SHAKE** *Bad Boy MCSTD40392*	29		2

MASH
US, male conductor/arranger (Johnny Mandel) & (uncredited) male vocalists – John & Tom Bahler, Ian Freebairn-Smith & Ron Hicklin — 12

Date	Title / Label	Peak Position	Weeks at No.1	Weeks on Chart
10 May 80	**THEME FROM 'M*A*S*H' (SUICIDE IS PAINLESS)** *CBS 8536* ●	1	3	12

MASH!
UK/US, female/male vocal/rap trio — 3

Date	Title / Label	Peak Position	Weeks at No.1	Weeks on Chart
21 May 94	**U DON'T HAVE TO SAY U LOVE ME** *React CDREACT 37*	37		2
4 Feb 95	**LET'S SPEND THE NIGHT TOGETHER** *Playa CDXPLAYA 2*	66		1

MASON VS PRINCESS SUPERSTAR
Holland/US, male/female vocal/production trio – Coen Berrier, Iason Chronis & Concetta Kirschner — 16

Date	Title / Label	Peak Position	Weeks at No.1	Weeks on Chart
27 Jan 07	**EXCEEDER** *Boss DATA150CDS*	3		16

BARBARA MASON
US, female vocalist — 5

Date	Title / Label	Peak Position	Weeks at No.1	Weeks on Chart
21 Jan 84	**ANOTHER MAN** *Streetwave KHAN 3*	45		5

GLEN MASON
UK, male vocalist (Tommy Lennon) — 7

Date	Title / Label	Peak Position	Weeks at No.1	Weeks on Chart
28 Sep 56	**GLENDORA** *Parlophone R 4203*	28		2
16 Nov 56	**GREEN DOOR** *Parlophone R 4244*	24		5

MARY MASON
UK, female vocalist — 6

Date	Title / Label	Peak Position	Weeks at No.1	Weeks on Chart
8 Oct 77	**ANGEL OF THE MORNING – ANY WAY THAT YOU WANT ME (MEDLEY)** *Epic EPC 5552*	27		6

WILLY MASON
UK, male vocalist/guitarist — 7

Date	Title / Label	Peak Position	Weeks at No.1	Weeks on Chart
26 Feb 05	**OXYGEN** *Virgin VSCDX1892*	23		3
14 May 05	**SO LONG** *Virgin VSCDX1898*	45		2
3 Mar 07	**SAVE MYSELF** *Virgin VSCDT1928*	42		1
26 May 07	**WE CAN BE STRONG** *Radiate VSCDT1939*	52		1

MASQUERADE
UK, male/female vocal/rap group — 10

Date	Title / Label	Peak Position	Weeks at No.1	Weeks on Chart
11 Jan 86	**ONE NATION** *Streetwave KHAN 59*	54		6
5 Jul 86	**(SOLUTION TO) THE PROBLEM** *Streetwave KHAN 67*	64		4

MASS ORDER
US, male vocal duo — 5

Date	Title / Label	Peak Position	Weeks at No.1	Weeks on Chart
14 Mar 92	**LIFT EVERY VOICE (TAKE ME AWAY)** *Columbia 6577487*	35		3
23 May 92	**LET'S GET HAPPY** *Columbia 6580737*	45		2

MASS PRODUCTION
US, male vocal/instrumental group — 7

Date	Title / Label	Peak Position	Weeks at No.1	Weeks on Chart
12 Mar 77	**WELCOME TO OUR WORLD (OF MERRY MUSIC)** *Atlantic K 10898*	44		3
17 May 80	**SHANTE** *Atlantic K 11475*	59		4

MASS SYNDICATE FEATURING SU SU BOBIEN
US, male/female vocal/production duo — 1

Date	Title / Label	Peak Position	Weeks at No.1	Weeks on Chart
24 Oct 98	**YOU DON'T KNOW** *ffrr FCD 347*	71		1

ZEITIA MASSIAH
UK (b. Barbados), female vocalist — 2

Date	Title / Label	Peak Position	Weeks at No.1	Weeks on Chart
12 Mar 94	**I SPECIALIZE IN LOVE** *Union City UCRCD 27* ARIZONA FEATURING ZEITIA	74		1
24 Sep 94	**THIS IS THE PLACE** *Virgin VSCDT 1511*	62		1

MASSIEL
Spain, female vocalist (Maria Espinosa) — 4

Date	Title / Label	Peak Position	Weeks at No.1	Weeks on Chart
24 Apr 68	**LA LA LA** *Philips BF 1667*	35		4

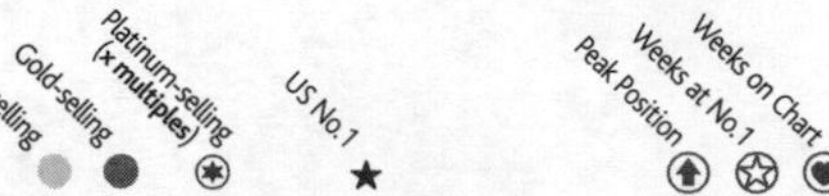

Peak Position · Weeks at No.1 · Weeks on Chart

MASSIVE ATTACK

UK, male production/vocal/instrumental trio – Grantley 'Daddy G' Marshall, Robert '3D' del Naja & Andrew 'Mushroom' Vowles (left 1998) — 40

Date	Title	Peak	Wks at No.1	Wks
23 Feb 91	**UNFINISHED SYMPATHY** *Wild Bunch WBRS 2* MASSIVE	13		9
8 Jun 91	**SAFE FROM HARM** *Wild Bunch WBRS 3*	25		6
22 Feb 92	**MASSIVE ATTACK EP** *Wild Bunch WBRS 4*	27		4
29 Oct 94	**SLY** *Wild Bunch WBRDX 5*	24		4
21 Jan 95	**PROTECTION** *Virgin WBRX 6* FEATURING TRACEY THORN	14		4
1 Apr 95	**KARMACOMA** *Virgin WBRX 7*	28		4
19 Jul 97	**RISINGSON** *Circa WBRX 8*	11		3
9 May 98	**TEARDROP** *Virgin WBRX 9*	10		6
25 Jul 98	**ANGEL** *Virgin WBRX 10*	30		2
8 Mar 03	**SPECIAL CASES** *Virgin VSCDT 1839*	15		2
25 Mar 06	**LIVE WITH ME** *Virgin VSCDX1912*	17		4
17 Oct 09	**SPLITTING THE ATOM** *Virgin GBAAA0900841*	64		1

MASSIVO FEATURING TRACY

UK, male production trio & female vocalist (Tracy Ackerman) — 11

Date	Title	Peak	Wks at No.1	Wks
26 May 90	**LOVING YOU** *Debut DEBT 3097*	25		11

MASTER BLASTER

Germany, male production trio — 1

Date	Title	Peak	Wks at No.1	Wks
7 Aug 04	**HYPNOTIC TANGO** *Mondo Pop 9867100*	64		1

MASTER SINGERS

UK, vocal ensemble — 8

Date	Title	Peak	Wks at No.1	Wks
14 Apr 66	**HIGHWAY CODE** *Parlophone R 5428*	25		6
17 Nov 66	**WEATHER FORECAST** *Parlophone R 5523*	45		2

MASTERS AT WORK PRESENT INDIA

US, male/female vocal/instrumental/production trio. See Nuyorican Soul — 6

Date	Title	Peak	Wks at No.1	Wks
5 Aug 95	**I CAN'T GET NO SLEEP** *A&M 5811412*	44		2
31 Jul 99	**TO BE IN LOVE** *Defected DEFECT 5CD* MAW PRESENTS INDIA	23		3
6 Jul 02	**BACKFIRED** *Susu CDSUSU 4* MASTERS AT WORK FEATURING INDIA	62		1

SAMMY MASTERS

US, male vocalist — 5

Date	Title	Peak	Wks at No.1	Wks
9 Jun 60	**ROCKIN' RED WING** *Warner Brothers WB 10*	36		5

PAUL MASTERSON PRESENTS SUSHI

UK, male/female vocal/production duo. See Candy Girls, Clergy, Dorothy, Hi-Gate, Sleazesisters, Yomanda — 2

Date	Title	Peak	Wks at No.1	Wks
2 Nov 02	**THE EARTHSHAKER** *NuLife 74321970372*	35		2

MATCH

UK, male vocal/instrumental group — 3

Date	Title	Peak	Wks at No.1	Wks
16 Jun 79	**BOOGIE MAN** *Flamingo FM 2*	48		3

MATCHBOX

UK, male vocal/instrumental group – Graham Fenton, Bob Burgos, Steve Bloomfield, Rusty Lipton, Fred Poke, Jimmy Redhead & Wiffle Smith — 5

Date	Title	Peak	Wks at No.1	Wks
3 Nov 79	**ROCKABILLY REBEL** *Magnet MAG 155*	18		12
19 Jan 80	**BUZZ BUZZ A DIDDLE IT** *Magnet MAG 157*	22		8
10 May 80	**MIDNITE DYNAMOS** *Magnet MAG 169*	14		12
27 Sep 80	**WHEN YOU ASK ABOUT LOVE** *Magnet MAG 191* ○	4		12
29 Nov 80	**OVER THE RAINBOW – YOU BELONG TO ME (MEDLEY)** *Magnet MAG 192*	15		11
4 Apr 81	**BABES IN THE WOOD** *Magnet MAG 193*	46		6
1 Aug 81	**LOVE'S MADE A FOOL OF YOU** *Magnet MAG 194*	63		3
29 May 82	**ONE MORE SATURDAY NIGHT** *Magnet MAG 223*	63		2
11 Apr 98	**PUSH** *Atlantic AT 0021CD 20*	38		2
4 Jul 98	**3AM** *Atlantic AT 0034CD 20*	64		1
17 Feb 01	**IF YOU'RE GONE** *Atlantic AT 0090CD 20*	50		1
22 Feb 03	**DISEASE** *Atlantic AT 0145CD 20*	50		1

MIREILLE MATHIEU

France, female vocalist — 7

Date	Title	Peak	Wks at No.1	Wks
13 Dec 67	**LA DERNIERE VALSE** *Columbia DB 8323*	26		7

JOHNNY MATHIS

US, male vocalist — 138

Date	Title	Peak	Wks at No.1	Wks
23 May 58	**TEACHER TEACHER** *Fontana H 130*	27		5
26 Sep 58	**A CERTAIN SMILE** *Fontana H 142*	4		16
19 Dec 58	**WINTER WONDERLAND** *Fontana H 165*	17		3
7 Aug 59	**SOMEONE** *Fontana H 199*	6		15
27 Nov 59	**THE BEST OF EVERYTHING** *Fontana H 218*	30		1
29 Jan 60	**MISTY** *Fontana H 219*	12		12
24 Mar 60	**YOU ARE BEAUTIFUL** *Fontana H 234*	38		9
28 Jul 60	**STARBRIGHT** *Fontana H 254*	47		2
6 Oct 60	**MY LOVE FOR YOU** *Fontana H 267*	9		18
4 Apr 63	**WHAT WILL MARY SAY** *CBS AAG 135*	49		1
25 Jan 75	**I'M STONE IN LOVE WITH YOU** *CBS 2653*	10		12
13 Nov 76	**WHEN A CHILD IS BORN (SOLEADO)** *CBS 4599* ●	1	3	12
25 Mar 78	**TOO MUCH TOO LITTLE TOO LATE** *CBS 6164* & DENIECE WILLIAMS ★	3		14
29 Jul 78	**YOU'RE ALL I NEED TO GET BY** *CBS 6483* & DENIECE WILLIAMS	45		6
11 Aug 79	**GONE GONE GONE** *CBS 7730*	15		10
26 Dec 81	**WHEN A CHILD IS BORN** *CBS S 1758* & GLADYS KNIGHT	74		2

IVAN MATIAS

US, male vocalist — 1

Date	Title	Peak	Wks at No.1	Wks
6 Apr 96	**SO GOOD (TO COME HOME TO)/I'VE HAD ENOUGH** *Arista 74321345072*	69		1

MATT BIANCO

UK, male vocal/instrumental duo — 65

Date	Title	Peak	Wks at No.1	Wks
11 Feb 84	**GET OUT YOUR LAZY BED** *WEA BIANCO 1*	15		8
14 Apr 84	**SNEAKING OUT THE BACK DOOR/MATT'S MOOD** *WEA YZ 3*	44		7
10 Nov 84	**HALF A MINUTE** *WEA YZ 26*	23		10
2 Mar 85	**MORE THAN I CAN BEAR** *WEA YZ 34*	50		7
5 Oct 85	**YEH YEH** *WEA YZ 46*	13		10
1 Mar 86	**JUST CAN'T STAND IT** *WEA YZ 62*	66		2
14 Jun 86	**DANCING IN THE STREET** *WEA YZ 72*	64		3
4 Jun 88	**DON'T BLAME IT ON THAT GIRL/WAP-BAM-BOOGIE** *WEA YZ 188*	11		13
27 Aug 88	**GOOD TIMES** *WEA YZ 302*	55		3
4 Feb 89	**NERVOUS/WAP-BAM-BOOGIE (REMIX)** *WEA YZ 328*	59		2

MATTAFIX

UK/St. Vincent, male vocal/instrumental/production duo — 7

Date	Title	Peak	Wks at No.1	Wks
20 Aug 05	**BIG CITY LIFE** *Buddhist Punk ANGEDX1*	15		7

AL MATTHEWS

US, male vocalist — 8

Date	Title	Peak	Wks at No.1	Wks
23 Aug 75	**FOOL** *CBS 3429*	16		8

CERYS MATTHEWS

UK, female vocalist. See Catatonia — 17

Date	Title	Peak	Wks at No.1	Wks
7 Mar 98	**THE BALLAD OF TOM JONES** *Gut CDGUT 18* SPACE WITH CERYS OF CATATONIA ○	4		8
18 Dec 99	**BABY, IT'S COLD OUTSIDE** *Gut CDGUT 29* TOM JONES & CERYS MATTHEWS	17		7
2 Aug 03	**CAUGHT IN THE MIDDLE** *Blanco Y Negro NEG 147CD*	47		1
19 Aug 06	**OPEN ROADS** *Rough Trade RTRADSCD357*	53		1

DAVE MATTHEWS BAND

US, male vocal/instrumental group — 2

Date	Title	Peak	Wks at No.1	Wks
1 Dec 01	**THE SPACE BETWEEN** *RCA 74321883192*	35		2

SCOTT MATTHEWS

UK, male vocalist/guitarist — 2

Date	Title	Peak	Wks at No.1	Wks
30 Sep 06	**ELUSIVE** *Island REMOCDS001*	56		2

SUMMER MATTHEWS

UK, female actor/vocalist (Holly Wilkinson) — 2

Date	Title	Peak	Wks at No.1	Wks
28 Feb 04	**LITTLE MISS PERFECT** *Sony Music 6744732*	32		2

MATTHEWS' SOUTHERN COMFORT

UK, male vocal/instrumental group – Ian Matthew McDonald, Carl Barnwell, Ramon Duffy, Mark Griffiths, Gordon Huntley & Andy Leigh — 18

Date	Title	Peak	Wks at No.1	Wks on Chart
26 Sep 70	**WOODSTOCK** *Uni UNS 526*	1	3	18

MATUMBI

UK, male vocal/instrumental group — 7

Date	Title	Peak	Wks at No.1	Wks on Chart
29 Sep 79	**POINT OF VIEW** *Matumbi RIC 101*	35		7

SUSAN MAUGHAN

UK, female vocalist — 25

Date	Title	Peak	Wks at No.1	Wks on Chart
11 Oct 62	**BOBBY'S GIRL** *Philips 326544 BF*	3		19
14 Feb 63	**HAND A HANDKERCHIEF TO HELEN** *Philips 326562 BF*	41		3
9 May 63	**SHE'S NEW TO YOU** *Philips 326586 BF*	45		3

MAUREEN

UK, female vocalist (Maureen Walsh) — 22

Date	Title	Peak	Wks at No.1	Wks on Chart
26 Nov 88	**SAY A LITTLE PRAYER** *Rhythm King DOOD 3* BOMB THE BASS FEATURING MAUREEN	10		10
16 Jun 90	**THINKING OF YOU** *Urban URB 55*	11		9
12 Jan 91	**WHERE HAS ALL THE LOVE GONE** *Urban URB 65*	51		3

PAUL MAURIAT

France, male orchestra leader, d. 3 Nov 2006 (age 81) — 14

Date	Title	Peak	Wks at No.1	Wks on Chart
21 Feb 68	**LOVE IS BLUE (L'AMOUR EST BLEU)** *Philips BF 1637* ★	12		14

MAVERICKS

US, male vocal/instrumental group – Raul Malo*, Paul Deakin, Nick Kane & Robert Reynolds — 23

Date	Title	Peak	Wks at No.1	Wks on Chart
2 May 98	**DANCE THE NIGHT AWAY** *MCA Nashville MCSTD 48081* ●	4		18
26 Sep 98	**I'VE GOT THIS FEELING** *MCA Nashville MCSTD 48095*	27		4
5 Jun 99	**SOMEONE SHOULD TELL HER** *MCA Nashville MCSTD 55567*	45		1

MAX LINEN

UK, male production duo — 1

Date	Title	Peak	Wks at No.1	Wks on Chart
17 Nov 01	**THE SOULSHAKER** *Global Cuts GC 73CD*	55		1

MAX Q

Australia, male vocal/instrumental duo — 3

Date	Title	Peak	Wks at No.1	Wks on Chart
17 Feb 90	**SOMETIMES** *Mercury MXQ 2*	53		3

MAX WEBSTER

Canada, male vocal/instrumental group — 3

Date	Title	Peak	Wks at No.1	Wks on Chart
19 May 79	**PARADISE SKIES** *Capitol CL 16079*	43		3

MAXEE

US, female vocalist (Charmayne Maxwell). See Brownstone — 1

Date	Title	Peak	Wks at No.1	Wks on Chart
17 Mar 01	**WHEN I LOOK INTO YOUR EYES** *Mercury 5628702*	55		1

MAXIM

UK, male vocalist/producer (Keith Palmer). See Prodigy — 3

Date	Title	Peak	Wks at No.1	Wks on Chart
10 Jun 00	**CARMEN QUEASY** *XL Recordings XLS 119CD*	33		2
23 Sep 00	**SCHEMING** *XL Recordings XLS 121CD*	53		1

MAXIMA FEATURING LILY

UK/Spain, male/female vocal/production duo — 2

Date	Title	Peak	Wks at No.1	Wks on Chart
14 Aug 93	**IBIZA** *Yo! Yo! CDLILY 1*	55		2

MAXIMO PARK

UK, male vocal/instrumental group – Paul Smith, Tom English, Duncan Lloyd, Archis Tiku & Lukas Wooller — 26

Date	Title	Peak	Wks at No.1	Wks on Chart
5 Mar 05	**APPLY SOME PRESSURE** *Warp WAP185CD*	20		2
14 May 05	**GRAFFITI** *Warp WAP187CDR*	15		3
30 Jul 05	**GOING MISSING** *Warp WAP190CDR*	20		3
5 Nov 05	**APPLY SOME PRESSURE** *Warp WAP198CD*	17		3
4 Mar 06	**I WANT YOU TO STAY** *Warp WAP201CD*	21		2
24 Mar 07	**OUR VELOCITY** *Warp WAP220CD*	9		9
23 Jun 07	**BOOKS FROM BOXES** *Warp WAP223CD*	16		2
1 Sep 07	**GIRLS WHO PLAY GUITARS** *Warp WAP227CD*	31		1
16 May 09	**THE KIDS ARE SICK AGAIN** *Warp WAP277CD*	50		1

MAXTREME

Holland, male production group — 1

Date	Title	Peak	Wks at No.1	Wks on Chart
9 Mar 02	**MY HOUSE IS YOUR HOUSE** *Y2K 028CD*	66		1

MAXWELL

US, male vocalist (Maxwell Menard) — 10

Date	Title	Peak	Wks at No.1	Wks on Chart
11 May 96	**...TIL THE COPS COME KNOCKIN'** *Columbia 6631792*	63		1
24 Aug 96	**ASCENSION NO ONE'S GONNA LOVE YOU, SO DON'T EVER WONDER** *Columbia 6636265*	39		3
1 Mar 97	**SUMTHIN' SUMTHIN' THE MANTRA** *Columbia 6638642*	27		3
24 May 97	**ASCENSION NO ONE'S GONNA LOVE YOU, SO DON'T EVER WONDER** *Columbia 6645952*	28		3

MAXX

Germany/Sweden/UK, male/female vocal/rap/production group – David 'Hitman' Brunner, Samira Besic (replaced by Linda Meek), Gary Bokoe (Boris Kohler), Olaf 'O Jay/Dawhite' Jeglitza, Dakota O'Neill (Frank Hassas) & George Topley (Jurgen Wind) — 24

Date	Title	Peak	Wks at No.1	Wks on Chart
21 May 94	**GET-A-WAY** *Pulse 8 CDLOSE 59* ●	4		12
6 Aug 94	**NO MORE (I CAN'T STAND IT)** *Pulse 8 CDLOSE 66*	8		8
29 Oct 94	**YOU CAN GET IT** *Pulse 8 CDLOSE 75*	21		3
22 Jul 95	**I CAN MAKE YOU FEEL LIKE** *Pulse 8 CDLOSE 88*	56		1

BILLY MAY

US, male band leader, d. 22 Jan 2004 (age 87) — 10

Date	Title	Peak	Wks at No.1	Wks on Chart
27 Apr 56	**MAIN TITLE THEME FROM 'MAN WITH THE GOLDEN ARM'** *Capitol 14551*	9		10

BRIAN MAY

UK, male vocalist/guitarist. See Queen — 33

Date	Title	Peak	Wks at No.1	Wks on Chart
5 Nov 83	**STAR FLEET** *EMI 5436* & FRIENDS	65		3
7 Dec 91	**DRIVEN BY YOU** *Parlophone R 6304*	6		9
5 Sep 92	**TOO MUCH LOVE WILL KILL YOU** *Parlophone R 6320* ●	5		9
17 Oct 92	**WE ARE THE CHAMPIONS** *PolyGram TV PO 229* HANK MARVIN FEATURING BRIAN MAY	66		1
21 Nov 92	**BACK TO THE LIGHT** *Parlophone R 6329*	19		4
19 Jun 93	**RESURRECTION** *Parlophone CDRS 6351* WITH COZY POWELL	23		3
18 Dec 93	**LAST HORIZON** *Parlophone CDR 6371*	51		2
6 Jun 98	**THE BUSINESS** *Parlophone CDR 6498*	51		1
12 Sep 98	**WHY DON'T WE TRY AGAIN** *Parlophone CDR 6504*	44		1

LISA MAY

UK, female vocalist — 2

Date	Title	Peak	Wks at No.1	Wks on Chart
15 Jul 95	**WISHING ON A STAR** *Urban Gorilla UG 3CD* 88.3 FEATURING LISA MAY	61		1
14 Sep 96	**THE CURSE OF VOODOO RAY** *Fontana VOOCD 1*	64		1

MARY MAY

UK, female vocalist — 1

Date	Title	Peak	Wks at No.1	Wks on Chart
27 Feb 64	**ANYONE WHO HAD A HEART** *Fontana TF 440*	49		1

SHERNETTE MAY

UK, female vocalist — 1

Date	Title	Peak	Wks at No.1	Wks on Chart
6 Jun 98	**ALL THE MAN THAT I NEED** *Virgin VSCDT 1691*	50		1

SIMON MAY

UK, male orchestra leader — 42

Date	Title	Peak	Wks at No.1	Wks on Chart
9 Oct 76	**SUMMER OF MY LIFE** *Pye 7N 45627* ●	7		8
21 May 77	**WE'LL GATHER LILACS – ALL MY LOVING (MEDLEY)** *Pye 7N 45688*	49		2
26 Oct 85	**HOWARD'S WAY** *BBC RESL 174* SIMON MAY ORCHESTRA	21		11
9 Aug 86	**ANYONE CAN FALL IN LOVE** *BBC RESL 191* ANITA DOBSON FEATURING THE SIMON MAY ORCHESTRA ●	4		9
20 Sep 86	**ALWAYS THERE** *BBC RESL 190* MARTI WEBB & THE SIMON MAY ORCHESTRA	13		12

JOHN MAYER

US, male vocalist/multi-instrumentalist — Weeks on Chart: 20

Date	Title	Peak	Wks at No.1	Wks
23 Aug 03	**NO SUCH THING** *Columbia 6732322*	42		1
28 Feb 04	**BIGGER THAN MY BODY** *Columbia 6744392*	72		1
26 Apr 08	**BEAT IT** *Mercury USUM70808144* FALL OUT BOY FEATURING JOHN MAYER	21		18

CURTIS MAYFIELD

US, male vocalist/guitarist, d. 26 Dec 1999 (age 57) — Weeks on Chart: 20

Date	Title	Peak	Wks at No.1	Wks
31 Jul 71	**MOVE ON UP** *Buddah 2011 080*	12		10
2 Dec 78	**NO GOODBYES** *Atlantic LV 1*	65		3
30 May 87	**(CELEBRATE) THE DAY AFTER YOU** *RCA MONK 6* BLOW MONKEYS WITH CURTIS MAYFIELD	52		2
29 Sep 90	**SUPERFLY 1990** *Capitol CL 586* & ICE-T	48		3
16 Jun 01	**ASTOUNDED** *Virgin VUSCD 194* BRAN VAN 3000 FEATURING CURTIS MAYFIELD	40		2

MAYTALS

Jamaica, male vocal/instrumental group — Weeks on Chart: 4

Date	Title	Peak	Wks at No.1	Wks
25 Apr 70	**MONKEY MAN** *Trojan TR 7711*	47		4

MAYTE

US, female vocalist/dancer (Mayte Garcia) — Weeks on Chart: 1

Date	Title	Peak	Wks at No.1	Wks
18 Nov 95	**IF EYE LOVE U 2 NIGHT** *NPG 0061635*	67		1

MAZE

US, male vocal/instrumental group — Weeks on Chart: 14

Date	Title	Peak	Wks at No.1	Wks
20 Jul 85	**TOO MANY GAMES** *Capitol CL 363* FEATURING FRANKIE BEVERLY	36		7
23 Aug 86	**I WANNA BE WITH YOU** *Capitol CL 421* FEATURING FRANKIE BEVERLY	55		3
27 May 89	**JOY AND PAIN** *Capitol CL 531*	57		4

KYM MAZELLE

US, female vocalist (Kimberley Grigsby) — Weeks on Chart: 66

Date	Title	Peak	Wks at No.1	Wks
12 Nov 88	**USELESS (I DON'T NEED YOU NOW)** *Syncopate SY 18*	53		3
14 Jan 89	**WAIT** *RCA PB 42595* ROBERT HOWARD & KYM MAZELLE	7		10
25 Mar 89	**GOT TO GET YOU BACK** *Syncopate SY 25*	29		4
7 Oct 89	**LOVE STRAIN** *Syncopate SY 30*	52		3
20 Jan 90	**WAS THAT ALL IT WAS** *Syncopate SY 32*	33		6
26 May 90	**USELESS (I DON'T NEED YOU NOW) (REMIX)** *Syncopate SY 36*	48		2
24 Nov 90	**MISSING YOU** *10 TEN 345* SOUL II SOUL FEATURING KYM MAZELLE	22		7
25 May 91	**NO ONE CAN LOVE YOU MORE THAN ME** *Parlophone R 6287*	62		2
26 Dec 92	**LOVE ME THE RIGHT WAY** *Logic 74321128097* RAPINATION & KYM MAZELLE	22		10
11 Jun 94	**NO MORE TEARS (ENOUGH IS ENOUGH)** *Ding Dong 74321209032* & JOCELYN BROWN	13		7
8 Oct 94	**GIMME ALL YOUR LOVIN'** *Ding Dong 74321231322* & JOCELYN BROWN	22		3
23 Dec 95	**SEARCHING FOR THE GOLDEN EYE** *Eternal 027CD* MOTIV 8 & KYM MAZELLE	40		3
28 Sep 96	**LOVE ME THE RIGHT WAY (REMIX)** *Logic 74321404442* RAPINATION & KYM MAZELLE	55		1
16 Aug 97	**YOUNG HEARTS RUN FREE** *EMI CDEM 488*	20		4
19 Feb 00	**TRULY** *Island Blue PFACD 4* PESHAY FEATURING KYM MAZELLE	55		1

MAZZY STAR

US, male/female vocal/instrumental duo — Weeks on Chart: 4

Date	Title	Peak	Wks at No.1	Wks
27 Aug 94	**FADE INTO YOU** *Capitol CDCL 720*	48		1
2 Nov 96	**FLOWERS IN DECEMBER** *Capitol CDCL 781*	40		2
18 Jul 09	**INTO DUST** *Capitol USCA29300475*	71		1

MC DUKE

UK, male rapper (Anthony Hilaire) — Weeks on Chart: 1

Date	Title	Peak	Wks at No.1	Wks
11 Mar 89	**I'M RIFFIN (ENGLISH RASTA)** *Music Of Life 7NOTE 25*	75		1

MC JIG

Germany, male rapper/DJ/producer — Weeks on Chart: 7

Date	Title	Peak	Wks at No.1	Wks
21 Feb 04	**CHA CHA SLIDE (IMPORT)** *ZYX 95838*	37		3
13 Mar 04	**CHA CHA SLIDE** *NM Music SLIDE001*	33		4

MC LETHAL

UK, male producer (Lee Frederick Whitney) — Weeks on Chart: 1

Date	Title	Peak	Wks at No.1	Wks
14 Nov 92	**THE RAVE DIGGER** *Network NWKT 60*	66		1

MC LYTE

US, female rapper (Lana Moorer) — Weeks on Chart: 19

Date	Title	Peak	Wks at No.1	Wks
15 Jan 94	**RUFFNECK** *Atlantic A 8336CD*	67		1
29 Jun 96	**KEEP ON, KEEPIN' ON** *East West A 4287CD* FEATURING XSCAPE	39		2
18 Jan 97	**COLD ROCK A PARTY** *East West A 3975CD*	15		4
19 Apr 97	**KEEP ON, KEEPIN' ON** *East West A 3950CD1* FEATURING XSCAPE	27		2
5 Sep 98	**I CAN'T MAKE A MISTAKE** *Elektra E 3813CD*	46		1
19 Dec 98	**IT'S ALL YOURS** *East West E 3789CD* FEATURING GINA THOMPSON	36		4
24 Jun 00	**JAMMIN'** *Tuff Gong TGXCD 9* BOB MARLEY FEATURING MC LYTE	42		2
8 May 04	**GIRLFRIEND'S STORY** *Polydor 9866362* GEMMA FOX FEATURING MC LYTE	38		3

MC MIKER 'G' & DEEJAY SVEN

Holland, male rap/vocal duo – Lucien Witteveen & Sven van Veen — Weeks on Chart: 7

Date	Title	Peak	Wks at No.1	Wks
6 Sep 86	**HOLIDAY RAP** *Debut DEBT 3008*	6		7

MC ONYX STONE

UK, male rapper (Andrew Martin) — Weeks on Chart: 3

Date	Title	Peak	Wks at No.1	Wks
7 Apr 01	**GARAGE GIRLS** *Riverhorse RIVHCD 12* LONYO FEATURING MC ONYX STONE	39		2
16 Mar 02	**WHADDA WE LIKE?** *Cooltempo CDCOOL 358* ROUND SOUND PRESENTS ONYX STONE & MC MALIBU	69		1

MC SKAT KAT & THE STRAY MOB

US, male cartoon cat (Derrick 'Delite' Stevens) & male/female animated feline rap/vocal group — Weeks on Chart: 2

Date	Title	Peak	Wks at No.1	Wks
9 Nov 91	**SKAT STRUT** *Virgin America VUS 51*	64		2

MC SOLAAR

France (b. Senegal), male rapper (Claude M'Barali) — Weeks on Chart: 6

Date	Title	Peak	Wks at No.1	Wks
20 Aug 94	**LISTEN** *Talkin Loud TLKCD 50* URBAN SPECIES FEATURING MC SOLAAR	47		2
25 Sep 99	**ALL N MY GRILL** *Elektra E 3742CD* MISSY 'MISDEMEANOR' ELLIOTT FEATURING MC SOLAAR	20		4

MC SPY-D + FRIENDS

UK, male/female rap/vocal/instrumental group — Weeks on Chart: 2

Date	Title	Peak	Wks at No.1	Wks
11 Mar 95	**THE AMAZING SPIDER MAN** *Parlophone CDR 6404*	37		2

MC TUNES

UK, male rapper (Nicholas "Lockett" Hodgson) — Weeks on Chart: 19

Date	Title	Peak	Wks at No.1	Wks
2 Jun 90	**THE ONLY RHYME THAT BITES** *ZTT ZANG 3* VERSUS 808 STATE	10		10
15 Sep 90	**TUNES SPLITS THE ATOM** *ZTT ZANG 6* VERSUS 808 STATE	18		7
1 Dec 90	**PRIMARY RHYMING** *ZTT ZANG 10*	67		1
6 Mar 99	**THE ONLY RHYME THAT BITES 99** *ZTT 125CD* VERSUS 808 STATE	53		1

MC WILDSKI

UK, male rapper (Simon Anniki) — Weeks on Chart: 10

Date	Title	Peak	Wks at No.1	Wks
8 Jul 89	**WON'T TALK ABOUT IT/BLAME IT ON THE BASSLINE** *Go! Beat GOD 33* NORMAN COOK FEATURING BILLY BRAGG/NORMAN COOK FEATURING MC WILDSKI	29		6
3 Mar 90	**WARRIOR** *Arista 112956*	49		4

M.C.R.B.

UK, male rapper (Ricky Benjamin) — Weeks on Chart: 2

Date	Title	Peak	Wks at No.1	Wks
1 Apr 00	**CHEQUE ONE-TWO** *Filter FILT 044* SUNSHIP FEATURING M.C.R.B.	75		1
28 Sep 02	**JUMP UP** *Serious SERR 050CD* JUST 4 JOKES FEATURING M.C.R.B.	67		1

M-D-EMM

UK, male producer (Mark Ryder) — Weeks on Chart: 3

Date	Title	Peak	Wks at No.1	Wks
22 Feb 92	**GET DOWN** *Strictly Underground 7STUR 13*	55		2
30 May 92	**MOVE YOUR FEET** *Strictly Underground 7STUR 15*	67		1

MDM
UK, male producer (Matt Darey). See Lost Tribe, Melt featuring Little Ms Marcie, Sunburst — 1

Date	Title	Peak	Wks No.1	Wks
27 Oct 01	MASH IT UP *NuLife 74321870472*	66		1

ME & YOU FEATURING WE THE PEOPLE BAND
Jamaica/UK, male/female vocal/instrumental group — 9

Date	Title	Peak	Wks No.1	Wks
28 Jul 79	YOU NEVER KNOW WHAT YOU'VE GOT *Laser LAS 8*	31		9

ME ME ME
UK, male vocal/instrumental group. See Fat Les — 4

Date	Title	Peak	Wks No.1	Wks
17 Aug 96	HANGING AROUND *Indolent DUFF 005CD*	19		4

ABIGAIL MEAD & NIGEL GOULDING
UK, female (Vivian Kubrick)/male instrumental/production duo — 10

Date	Title	Peak	Wks No.1	Wks
26 Sep 87	FULL METAL JACKET (I WANNA BE YOUR DRILL INSTRUCTOR) *Warner Brothers W 8187* ●	2		10

LEE MEAD
UK, male actor/vocalist — 7

Date	Title	Peak	Wks No.1	Wks
23 Jun 07	ANY DREAM WILL DO *Polydor 1739785*	2		7

MEAT BEAT MANIFESTO
UK, male production duo — 1

Date	Title	Peak	Wks No.1	Wks
20 Feb 93	MINDSTREAM *Play It Again Sam BIAS 232CD*	55		1

MEAT LOAF
US, male vocalist/multi-instrumentalist/actor (Marvin Lee Aday) — 161

Date	Title	Peak	Wks No.1	Wks
20 May 78	YOU TOOK THE WORDS RIGHT OUT OF MY MOUTH *Epic EPC 5980*	33		8
19 Aug 78	TWO OUT OF THREE AIN'T BAD *Epic EPC 6281*	32		8
10 Feb 79	BAT OUT OF HELL *Epic EPC 7018*	15		7
26 Sep 81	I'M GONNA LOVE HER FOR BOTH OF US *Epic EPC A 1580*	62		3
28 Nov 81	DEAD RINGER FOR LOVE *Epic EPC A 1697* ●	5		17
28 May 83	IF YOU REALLY WANT TO *Epic A 3357*	59		2
24 Sep 83	MIDNIGHT AT THE LOST AND FOUND *Epic A 3748*	17		8
14 Jan 84	RAZOR'S EDGE *Epic A 4080*	41		3
6 Oct 84	MODERN GIRL *Arista ARIST 585*	17		9
22 Dec 84	NOWHERE FAST *Arista ARIST 600*	67		4
23 Mar 85	PIECE OF THE ACTION *Arista ARIST 603*	47		5
30 Aug 86	ROCK 'N' ROLL MERCENARIES *Arista ARIST 666* FEATURING JOHN PARR	31		6
22 Jun 91	DEAD RINGER FOR LOVE *Epic 6569827*	53		2
27 Jun 92	TWO OUT OF THREE AIN'T BAD *Epic 6574917*	69		1
9 Oct 93	I'D DO ANYTHING FOR LOVE (BUT I WON'T DO THAT) *Virgin VSCDT 1443* ⊛ ★	1	7	19
18 Dec 93	BAT OUT OF HELL *Epic 6600062*	8		9
19 Feb 94	ROCK AND ROLL DREAMS COME THROUGH *Virgin VSCDT 1479*	11		7
7 May 94	OBJECTS IN THE REAR VIEW MIRROR MAY APPEAR CLOSER THAN THEY ARE *Virgin VSCDT 1492*	26		4
28 Oct 95	I'D LIE FOR YOU (AND THAT'S THE TRUTH) *Virgin VSCDT 1563* ●	2		11
27 Jan 96	NOT A DRY EYE IN THE HOUSE *Virgin VSCDT 1567*	7		6
27 Apr 96	RUNNIN' FOR THE RED LIGHT (I GOTTA LIFE) *Virgin VSCDX 1582*	21		3
17 Apr 99	IS NOTHING SACRED *Virgin VSCDT 1734* FEATURING PATTI RUSSO	15		4
26 Apr 03	COULDN'T HAVE SAID IT BETTER *Mercury 0656842*	31		2
6 Dec 03	MAN OF STEEL *Mercury 9815114*	21		4
21 Oct 06	IT'S ALL COMING BACK TO ME NOW *Mercury 1707714* FEATURING MARION RAVEN	6		8
19 May 07	CRY OVER ME *Mercury 1733477*	47		1

MECK
Holland, male DJ/producer (Craig Dimech) — 20

Date	Title	Peak	Wks No.1	Wks
18 Feb 06	THUNDER IN MY HEART AGAIN *Apollo/Free 2 Air APOLLO101CDX* FEATURING LEO SAYER	1	2	16
21 Apr 07	FEELS LIKE HOME *Free2Air F2A27CDS* FEATURING DINO	39		4

MECO
US, male orchestra leader (Meco Monardo) — 9

Date	Title	Peak	Wks No.1	Wks
1 Oct 77	STAR WARS THEME – CANTINA BAND *RCA XB 102* ★	7		9

GLENN MEDEIROS
US, male vocalist — 26

Date	Title	Peak	Wks No.1	Wks
18 Jun 88	NOTHING'S GONNA CHANGE MY LOVE FOR YOU *London LON 184* ●	1	4	13
3 Sep 88	LONG AND LASTING LOVE (ONCE IN A LIFETIME) *London LON 202*	42		4
30 Jun 90	SHE AIN'T WORTH IT *London LON 265* FEATURING BOBBY BROWN ★	12		9

MEDICINE HEAD
UK, male vocal/instrumental duo – John Fiddler & Peter Hope-Evans — 37

Date	Title	Peak	Wks No.1	Wks
26 Jun 71	(AND THE) PICTURES IN THE SKY *Dandelion DAN 7003*	22		8
5 May 73	ONE AND ONE IS ONE *Polydor 2001 432*	3		13
4 Aug 73	RISING SUN *Polydor 2058 389*	11		9
9 Feb 74	SLIP AND SLIDE *Polydor 2058 436*	22		7

MEDINA
Denmark, female vocalist (Andrea Valbak) — 3

Date	Title	Peak	Wks No.1	Wks
17 Oct 09	YOU AND I *EMI DKGL50900212*	39		3

BILL MEDLEY
US, male vocalist. See Righteous Brothers — 29

Date	Title	Peak	Wks No.1	Wks
31 Oct 87	(I'VE HAD) THE TIME OF MY LIFE *RCA PB 49625* & JENNIFER WARNES ★	6		12
27 Aug 88	HE AIN'T HEAVY, HE'S MY BROTHER *Scotti Brothers PO 10*	25		6
15 Dec 90	(I'VE HAD) THE TIME OF MY LIFE *RCA PB 49625* & JENNIFER WARNES ●	8		11

MEDWAY
US, male producer (Jesse Skeens) — 2

Date	Title	Peak	Wks No.1	Wks
29 Apr 00	FAT BASTARD (EP) *Hooj Choons HOOJ 92CD*	69		1
10 Mar 01	RELEASE *Hooj Choons HOOJ 105CD*	67		1

MICHAEL MEDWIN, BERNARD BRESSLAW, ALFIE BASS & LESLIE FYSON
UK, male actor/vocalists – Bresslaw*, d. 11 Jun 1893, & Bass, d. 15 Jul 1987 — 9

Date	Title	Peak	Wks No.1	Wks
30 May 58	THE SIGNATURE TUNE OF 'THE ARMY GAME' *HMV POP 490*	5		9

MEECHIE
US, female vocalist — 1

Date	Title	Peak	Wks No.1	Wks
2 Sep 95	YOU BRING ME JOY *Vibe MCSTD 2069*	74		1

TONY MEEHAN COMBO
UK, male instrumental group. See Shadows, Jet Harris & Tony Meehan — 4

Date	Title	Peak	Wks No.1	Wks
16 Jan 64	SONG OF MEXICO *Decca F 11801*	39		4

MEEKER
UK, female vocal/production duo — 1

Date	Title	Peak	Wks No.1	Wks
26 Feb 00	SAVE ME *Underwater H2O 009 CD*	60		1

MEGA CITY FOUR
UK, male vocal/instrumental group — 7

Date	Title	Peak	Wks No.1	Wks
19 Oct 91	WORDS THAT SAY *Big Life MEGA 2*	66		1
8 Feb 92	STOP (EP) *Big Life MEGA 3*	36		2
16 May 92	SHIVERING SAND *Big Life MEGA 4*	35		2
1 May 93	IRON *Big Life MEGAD 5*	48		1
17 Jul 93	WALLFLOWER *Big Life MEGAD 6*	69		1

MEGADETH
US, male vocal/instrumental group – Dave Mustaine, Dave Ellefson, Marty Friedman & Nick Menza — 32

Date	Title	Peak	Wks No.1	Wks
19 Dec 87	WAKE UP DEAD *Capitol CL 476*	65		2
27 Feb 88	ANARCHY IN THE UK *Capitol CL 480*	45		3
21 May 88	MARY JANE *Capitol CL 489*	46		2
13 Jan 90	NO MORE MR. NICE GUY *SBK 4*	13		6
29 Sep 90	HOLY WARS...THE PUNISHMENT DUE *Capitol CLP 588*	24		3
16 Mar 91	HANGAR 18 *Capitol CLS 604*	26		4
27 Jun 92	SYMPHONY OF DESTRUCTION *Capitol CLS 662*	15		3
24 Oct 92	SKIN O' MY TEETH *Capitol CLP 669*	13		3

Silver-selling ● Gold-selling ● Platinum-selling (x multiples) ⊛ US No.1 ★ Peak Position · Weeks at No.1 · Weeks on Chart

Date	Title	Peak Position	Weeks at No.1	Weeks on Chart
29 May 93	**SWEATING BULLETS** *Capitol CDCL 682*	26		3
7 Jan 95	**TRAIN OF CONSEQUENCES** *Capitol CDCL 730*	22		3

MEJA
Sweden, female vocalist (Meja Beckman) — **14**

Date	Title	Peak Position	Weeks at No.1	Weeks on Chart
24 Oct 98	**ALL 'BOUT THE MONEY** *Columbia 6665662*	12		5
29 Apr 00	**PRIVATE EMOTION** *Columbia 6692692* RICKY MARTIN FEATURING MEJA	9		9

MEKKA
UK, male producer (Jake Williams). See JX, Planet Perfecto — **1**

Date	Title	Peak Position	Weeks at No.1	Weeks on Chart
24 Mar 01	**DIAMOND BACK** *Perfecto PERF 12CDS*	67		1

MEKON
UK, male producer (John Gosling) — **2**

Date	Title	Peak Position	Weeks at No.1	Weeks on Chart
23 Sep 00	**WHAT'S GOING ON** *Wall Of Sound WALD 064* FEATURING ROXANNE SHANTE	43		1
13 Mar 04	**D-FUNKTIONAL** *Wall Of Sound WALLD092* FEATURING AFRIKA BAMBAATAA	72		1

MEL & KIM
UK, female vocal duo – Melanie, d. 18 Jan 1990, & Kim Appleby* — **51**

Date	Title	Peak Position	Weeks at No.1	Weeks on Chart
20 Sep 86	**SHOWING OUT (GET FRESH AT THE WEEKEND)** *Supreme SUPE 107* ●	3		19
7 Mar 87	**RESPECTABLE** *Supreme SUPE 111* ●	1	1	15
11 Jul 87	**F.L.M.** *Supreme SUPE 113*	7		10
27 Feb 88	**THAT'S THE WAY IT IS** *Supreme SUPE 117*	10		7

GEORGE MELACHRINO ORCHESTRA
UK, male orchestra leader, d. 18 Jun 1965 (age 56) — **9**

Date	Title	Peak Position	Weeks at No.1	Weeks on Chart
12 Oct 56	**AUTUMN CONCERTO** *HMV B 10958*	18		9

MELANIE
US, female vocalist/guitarist (Melanie Safka) — **35**

Date	Title	Peak Position	Weeks at No.1	Weeks on Chart
26 Sep 70	**RUBY TUESDAY** *Buddah 2011 038*	9		15
16 Jan 71	**WHAT HAVE THEY DONE TO MY SONG MA** *Buddah 2011 038*	39		1
1 Jan 72	**BRAND NEW KEY** *Buddah 2011 105* ★	4		12
16 Feb 74	**WILL YOU LOVE ME TOMORROW** *Neighbourhood NBH 9*	37		5
24 Sep 83	**EVERY BREATH OF THE WAY** *Neighbourhood HOOD NB1*	70		2

MELEE
US, male vocal/instrumental group — **2**

Date	Title	Peak Position	Weeks at No.1	Weeks on Chart
2 Aug 08	**BUILT TO LAST** *Warner Brothers W802CD*	58		2

MELKY SEDECK
US, male/female vocal/instrumental duo – Melky & Sedeck Jean — **9**

Date	Title	Peak Position	Weeks at No.1	Weeks on Chart
8 May 99	**RAW** *MCA MCSTD 48107*	50		1
16 Sep 00	**IT DOESN'T MATTER** *Columbia 6697782* WYCLEF JEAN FEATURING THE ROCK & MELKY SEDECK	3		8

JOHN COUGAR MELLENCAMP
US, male vocalist/guitarist — **18**

Date	Title	Peak Position	Weeks at No.1	Weeks on Chart
23 Oct 82	**JACK AND DIANE** *Riva 37* ★ JOHN COUGAR	25		8
1 Feb 86	**SMALL TOWN** *Riva JCM 5*	53		4
10 May 86	**R.O.C.K. IN THE USA** *Riva JCM 6*	67		3
3 Sep 94	**WILD NIGHT** *Mercury MERCD 409* JOHN MELLENCAMP FEATURING ME'SHELL NDEGEOCELLO	34		3

MELLOMEN
US, male session vocal group formed by Thurl Ravenscroft, d. 22 May 2005 (age 91) — **74**

Date	Title	Peak Position	Weeks at No.1	Weeks on Chart
1 Oct 54	**IF I GIVE MY HEART TO YOU** *Philips PB 325* DORIS DAY WITH THE MELLOMEN	4		11
17 Dec 54	**MAMBO ITALIANO** *Philips PB 382* ROSEMARY CLOONEY WITH THE MELLOMEN	1	3	16
20 May 55	**WHERE WILL THE DIMPLE BE** *Philips PB 428* ROSEMARY CLOONEY WITH THE MELLOMEN	6		13
24 Jun 55	**COOL WATER** *Philips PB 465* FRANKIE LAINE WITH THE MELLOMEN	2		22
20 Jan 56	**SIXTEEN TONS** *Philips PB 539* FRANKIE LAINE WITH THE MELLOMEN	10		3
28 Feb 63	**ONE BROKEN HEART FOR SALE** *RCA 1337* ELVIS PRESLEY WITH THE MELLOMEN	12		9

WILL MELLOR
UK, male actor/vocalist — **9**

Date	Title	Peak Position	Weeks at No.1	Weeks on Chart
28 Feb 98	**WHEN I NEED YOU** *Unity 017RCD*	5		6
27 Jun 98	**NO MATTER WHAT I DO** *Jive 0540012*	23		3

MELLOW TRAX
Germany, male producer (Christian Schwarnweber) — **2**

Date	Title	Peak Position	Weeks at No.1	Weeks on Chart
14 Oct 00	**OUTTA SPACE** *Substance SUBS 3CDS*	41		2

MELODIANS
Jamaica, male vocal/instrumental group — **1**

Date	Title	Peak Position	Weeks at No.1	Weeks on Chart
10 Jan 70	**SWEET SENSATION** *Trojan TR 695*	41		1

MELT FEATURING LITTLE MS MARCIE
UK, male/female vocal/production duo. See Lost Tribe, MDM, Sunburst — **1**

Date	Title	Peak Position	Weeks at No.1	Weeks on Chart
8 Apr 00	**HARD HOUSE MUSIC** *WEA 257CD*	59		1

MELTDOWN
UK/US, male instrumental/production duo — **1**

Date	Title	Peak Position	Weeks at No.1	Weeks on Chart
27 Apr 96	**MY LIFE IS IN YOUR HANDS** *Sony S3 DANU 7CD*	44		1

KATIE MELUA
UK (b. Georgia), female vocalist/guitarist (Ketevan Melua) — **55**

Date	Title	Peak Position	Weeks at No.1	Weeks on Chart
13 Dec 03	**THE CLOSEST THING TO CRAZY** *Dramatico DRAMCDS 0003*	10		20
27 Mar 04	**CALL OFF THE SEARCH** *Dramatico DRAMCDS0005*	19		4
31 Jul 04	**CRAWLING UP A HILL** *Dramatico DRAMCDS0007*	46		2
1 Oct 05	**NINE MILLION BICYCLES** *Dramatico DRAMCDS0012*	5		16
17 Dec 05	**I CRIED FOR YOU/JUST LIKE HEAVEN** *Dramatico DRAMCDS0013*	35		3
29 Apr 06	**SPIDER'S WEB** *Dramatico DRAMCDS0017*	52		1
23 Sep 06	**IT'S ONLY PAIN** *Dramatico DRAMCDS0020*	41		1
6 Oct 07	**IF YOU WERE A SAILBOAT** *Dramatico DRAMCDS0029*	23		4
22 Dec 07	**WHAT A WONDERFUL WORLD** *Dramatico TD001* EVA CASSIDY & KATIE MELUA	1	1	4

HAROLD MELVIN & THE BLUENOTES
US, male vocal group featuring Teddy Pendergrass*, d. 13 Jan 2010, & Harold Melvin, d. 24 Mar 1997 — **52**

Date	Title	Peak Position	Weeks at No.1	Weeks on Chart
13 Jan 73	**IF YOU DON'T KNOW ME BY NOW** *CBS 8496*	9		9
12 Jan 74	**THE LOVE I LOST** *Philadelphia International PIR 1879*	21		8
13 Apr 74	**SATISFACTION GUARANTEED (OR TAKE YOUR LOVE BACK)** *Philadelphia International PIR 2187*	32		6
31 May 75	**GET OUT (AND LET ME CRY)** *Route RT 06*	35		5
28 Feb 76	**WAKE UP EVERYBODY** *Philadelphia International PIR 3866*	23		7
22 Jan 77	**DON'T LEAVE ME THIS WAY** *Philadelphia International PIR 4909* FEATURING THEODORE PENDERGRASS ●	5		10
2 Apr 77	**REACHING FOR THE WORLD** *ABC 4161*	48		1
28 Apr 84	**DON'T GIVE ME UP** *London LON 47*	59		4
4 Aug 84	**TODAY'S YOUR LUCKY DAY** *London LON 52* FEATURING NIKKO	66		2

MEMBERS
UK, male vocal/instrumental group — **14**

Date	Title	Peak Position	Weeks at No.1	Weeks on Chart
3 Feb 79	**THE SOUND OF THE SUBURBS** *Virgin VS 242*	12		9
7 Apr 79	**OFFSHORE BANKING BUSINESS** *Virgin VS 248*	31		5

MEMBERS OF MAYDAY
Germany, male production duo — **4**

Date	Title	Peak Position	Weeks at No.1	Weeks on Chart
23 Jun 01	**10 IN 01** *Deviant DVNT 42CDS*	31		3
13 Apr 02	**SONIC EMPIRE** *Deviant DVNT 49CDS*	59		1

MEMPHIS BLEEK FEATURING JAY-Z
US, male rap duo — **1**

Date	Title	Peak Position	Weeks at No.1	Weeks on Chart
4 Dec 99	**WHAT YOU THINK OF THAT** *Def Jam 8708292*	58		1

MEN AT WORK
Australia, male vocal/instrumental group – Colin James Hay, Greg Ham, John Rees & Jerry Speiser — **39**

Date	Title	Peak Position	Weeks at No.1	Weeks on Chart
30 Oct 82	**WHO CAN IT BE NOW?** *Epic A 2392* ★	45		5
8 Jan 83	**DOWN UNDER** *Epic EPC A 1980* ● ★	1	3	12

Date	Title	Peak Position	Weeks at No.1	Weeks on Chart
9 Apr 83	**OVERKILL** *Epic EPC A 3220*	21		10
2 Jul 83	**IT'S A MISTAKE** *Epic EPC A 3475*	33		6
10 Sep 83	**DR HECKYLL AND MR. JIVE** *Epic EPC A 3668*	31		6

MEN OF VIZION
US, male vocal group — **2**

Date	Title	Peak Position	Weeks at No.1	Weeks on Chart
27 Mar 99	**DO YOU FEEL ME? (...FREAK YOU)** *MJJ 6670912*	36		2

MEN THEY COULDN'T HANG
UK, male vocal/instrumental group — **4**

Date	Title	Peak Position	Weeks at No.1	Weeks on Chart
2 Apr 88	**THE COLOURS** *Magnet SELL 6*	61		4

MEN WITHOUT HATS
Canada, male vocal/instrumental group – Ivan & Stefan Doroschuk & Allan McCarthy, d. 11 Aug 1995 — **11**

Date	Title	Peak Position	Weeks at No.1	Weeks on Chart
8 Oct 83	**THE SAFETY DANCE** *Statik TAK 1* ○	6		11

SERGIO MENDES
Brazil, male band leader/pianist — **15**

Date	Title	Peak Position	Weeks at No.1	Weeks on Chart
9 Jul 83	**NEVER GONNA LET YOU GO** *A&M AM 118*	45		5
24 Jun 06	**MAS QUE NADA** *Concord/UCJ 9859631* & THE BLACK EYED PEAS	6		10

ANDREA MENDEZ
UK, female vocalist — **1**

Date	Title	Peak Position	Weeks at No.1	Weeks on Chart
3 Aug 96	**BRING ME LOVE** *AM:PM 5817872*	44		1

MENSWEAR
UK, male vocal/instrumental group – Johnny Dean, Stuart Black, Matt Everitt, Chris Gentry & Simon White — **18**

Date	Title	Peak Position	Weeks at No.1	Weeks on Chart
15 Apr 95	**I'LL MANAGE SOMEHOW** *Laurel LAUCD 4*	49		1
1 Jul 95	**DAYDREAMER** *Laurel LAUCD 5*	14		4
30 Sep 95	**STARDUST** *Laurel LAUCD 6*	16		3
16 Dec 95	**SLEEPING IN** *Laurel LAUCD 7*	24		3
23 Mar 96	**BEING BRAVE** *Laurel LAUCD 8*	10		4
7 Sep 96	**WE LOVE YOU** *Laurel LAUCD 11*	22		3

MENTAL AS ANYTHING
Australia/New Zealand, male vocal/instrumental group – Martin Murphy, Chris & Peter O'Doherty, Andrew 'Greedy' Smith & David Twohill — **13**

Date	Title	Peak Position	Weeks at No.1	Weeks on Chart
7 Feb 87	**LIVE IT UP** *Epic ANY 1* ○	3		13

FREDDIE MERCURY
UK (b. Zanzibar), male vocalist, d. 24 Nov 1991 (age 45). See Queen — **79**

Date	Title	Peak Position	Weeks at No.1	Weeks on Chart
22 Sep 84	**LOVE KILLS** *CBS A 4735*	10		8
20 Apr 85	**I WAS BORN TO LOVE YOU** *CBS A 6019*	11		10
13 Jul 85	**MADE IN HEAVEN** *CBS A 6413*	57		4
21 Sep 85	**LIVING ON MY OWN** *CBS A 6555*	50		3
24 May 86	**TIME** *EMI 5559*	32		5
7 Mar 87	**THE GREAT PRETENDER** *Parlophone R 6151*	4		9
7 Nov 87	**BARCELONA** *Polydor POSP 887* & MONTSERRAT CABALLE	8		9
8 Aug 92	**BARCELONA** *Polydor PO 221* & MONTSERRAT CABALLE	2		8
12 Dec 92	**IN MY DEFENCE** *Parlophone R 6331*	8		7
6 Feb 93	**THE GREAT PRETENDER** *Parlophone CDR 6336*	29		3
31 Jul 93	**LIVING ON MY OWN** *Parlophone CDR 6355* ●	1	2	13

MERCURY REV
US, male vocal/instrumental group — **15**

Date	Title	Peak Position	Weeks at No.1	Weeks on Chart
14 Nov 98	**GODDESS ON A HIWAY** *V2 VVR 5003323*	51		1
6 Feb 99	**DELTA SUN BOTTLENECK STOMP** *V2 VVR 5005413*	26		2
22 May 99	**OPUS 40** *V2 VVR 5006963*	31		2
28 Aug 99	**GODDESS ON A HIWAY** *V2 VVR 5008498*	26		2
6 Oct 01	**NITE AND FOG** *V2 VVR 5017728*	47		1
26 Jan 02	**THE DARK IS RISING** *V2 VVR 5018713*	16		3
27 Jul 02	**LITTLE RHYMES** *V2 VVR 5019788*	51		1
29 Jan 05	**IN A FUNNY WAY** *V2 VVR 5029223*	28		2
2 Apr 05	**ACROSS YER OCEAN** *V2 VVR5031033*	54		1

MERCY MERCY
UK, male vocal/instrumental duo — **2**

Date	Title	Peak Position	Weeks at No.1	Weeks on Chart
21 Sep 85	**WHAT ARE WE GONNA DO ABOUT IT?** *Ensign ENY 522*	59		2

MERLIN
UK, male rapper (Justin Boreland) — **18**

Date	Title	Peak Position	Weeks at No.1	Weeks on Chart
27 Aug 88	**MEGABLAST/DON'T MAKE ME WAIT** *Mister-ron DOOD 2* BOMB THE BASS FEATURING MERLIN & ANTONIA/BOMB THE BASS FEATURING LORRAINE	6		9
22 Apr 89	**WHO'S IN THE HOUSE** *Rhythm King LEFT 31* BEATMASTERS FEATURING MERLIN	8		9

MERO
UK, male vocal duo — **2**

Date	Title	Peak Position	Weeks at No.1	Weeks on Chart
25 Mar 00	**IT MUST BE LOVE** *RCA 74321664772*	33		2

TONY MERRICK
UK, male vocalist — **1**

Date	Title	Peak Position	Weeks at No.1	Weeks on Chart
2 Jun 66	**LADY JANE** *Columbia DB 7913*	49		1

AVID MERRION/DAVINA McCALL/PATSY KENSIT
UK, male/female vocal trio – comedian/actor Leigh Francis, TV presenter Davina McCall & actor/TV personality Patricia (Patsy) Kensit — **5**

Date	Title	Peak Position	Weeks at No.1	Weeks on Chart
25 Dec 04	**I GOT YOU BABE/SODA POP** *BMG 82876669872*	5		5

DANIEL MERRIWEATHER
Australia, male vocalist — **57**

Date	Title	Peak Position	Weeks at No.1	Weeks on Chart
14 Apr 07	**STOP ME** *Columbia 88697078762* MARK RONSON FEATURING DANIEL MERRIWEATHER	2		17
13 Dec 08	**CASH IN MY POCKET** *Asylum ASYLUM7CD* WILEY FEATURING DANIEL MERRIWEATHER	18		9
14 Feb 09	**CHANGE** *Allido 88697432662*	8		4
30 May 09	**RED** *J Records 88697499282*	5		26
29 Aug 09	**IMPOSSIBLE** *J USJAY0800285*	67		1

MERSEYBEATS
UK, male vocal/instrumental group – John Banks, d. 20 Apr 1988, Tony Crane, Johnny Gustafson, Billy Kinsley & Aaron Williams. See Merseys — **64**

Date	Title	Peak Position	Weeks at No.1	Weeks on Chart
12 Sep 63	**IT'S LOVE THAT REALLY COUNTS** *Fontana TF 412*	24		12
16 Jan 64	**I THINK OF YOU** *Fontana TF 431*	5		17
16 Apr 64	**DON'T TURN AROUND** *Fontana TF 459*	13		11
9 Jul 64	**WISHIN' AND HOPIN'** *Fontana TF 482*	13		10
5 Nov 64	**LAST NIGHT** *Fontana TF 504*	40		3
14 Oct 65	**I LOVE YOU, YES I DO** *Fontana TF 607*	22		8
20 Jan 66	**I STAND ACCUSED** *Fontana TF 645*	38		3

MERSEYS
UK, male vocal duo – Tony Crane & Billy Kinsley. See Merseybeats — **13**

Date	Title	Peak Position	Weeks at No.1	Weeks on Chart
28 Apr 66	**SORROW** *Fontana TF 694*	4		13

MERTON PARKAS
UK, male vocal/instrumental group — **6**

Date	Title	Peak Position	Weeks at No.1	Weeks on Chart
4 Aug 79	**YOU NEED WHEELS** *Beggars Banquet BEG 22*	40		6

MERZ
UK, male vocalist/multi-instrumentalist (Conrad Lambert) — **2**

Date	Title	Peak Position	Weeks at No.1	Weeks on Chart
17 Jul 99	**MANY WEATHERS APART** *Epic 6674972*	48		1
16 Oct 99	**LOVELY DAUGHTER** *Epic 6679132*	60		1

MESH-29
UK, male vocal/instrumental trio — **1**

Date	Title	Peak Position	Weeks at No.1	Weeks on Chart
14 Jul 07	**OVER THE BARRICADE** *Media Addiction GBSAC0700001*	35		1

Peak Position / Weeks at No.1 / Weeks on Chart

MADY MESPLE & DANIELLE MILLET WITH THE PARIS OPERACOMIQUE ORCHESTRA CONDUCTED BY ALAIN LOMBARD

France, female vocal duo, male conductor & orchestra — 4

Date	Title	Peak	Wks at No.1	Wks on Chart
6 Apr 85	**FLOWER DUET (FROM LAKME)** *EMI 5481*	47		4

MESSIAH

UK, male production duo — 13

Date	Title	Peak	Wks at No.1	Wks on Chart
20 Jun 92	**TEMPLE OF DREAMS** *Kickin KICK 125*	20		5
26 Sep 92	**I FEEL LOVE** *Kickin KICK 225* FEATURING PRECIOUS WILSON	19		5
27 Nov 93	**THUNDERDOME** *WEA YZ 790CD1*	29		3

METAL GURUS

UK, male vocal/instrumental group. See Mission — 2

Date	Title	Peak	Wks at No.1	Wks on Chart
8 Dec 90	**MERRY XMAS EVERYBODY** *Mercury GURU 1*	55		2

METALLICA

US, male vocal/instrumental group – James Hetfield, Cliff Burton, d. 27 Sep 1986 (replaced by Jason Newsted, then Robert Trujillo), Kirk Hammett & Lars Ulrich — 87

Date	Title	Peak	Wks at No.1	Wks on Chart
22 Aug 87	**THE $5.98 EP – GARAGE DAYS REVISITED** *Vertigo METAL 112*	27		4
3 Sep 88	**HARVESTER OF SORROW** *Vertigo METAL 212*	20		3
22 Apr 89	**ONE** *Vertigo METAL 5*	13		7
10 Aug 91	**ENTER SANDMAN** *Vertigo METAL 7*	5		4
9 Nov 91	**THE UNFORGIVEN** *Vertigo METAL 8*	15		4
2 May 92	**NOTHING ELSE MATTERS** *Vertigo METAL 10*	6		6
31 Oct 92	**WHEREVER I MAY ROAM** *Vertigo METAL 9*	25		4
20 Feb 93	**SAD BUT TRUE** *Vertigo METCD 11*	20		3
1 Jun 96	**UNTIL IT SLEEPS** *Vertigo UKMETCX 12*	5		4
28 Sep 96	**HERO OF THE DAY** *Vertigo METCD 13*	17		4
7 Dec 96	**MAMA SAID** *Vertigo METCD 14*	19		2
22 Nov 97	**THE MEMORY REMAINS** *Vertigo METCD 15*	13		3
7 Mar 98	**THE UNFORGIVEN II** *Vertigo METDD 17*	15		4
4 Jul 98	**FUEL** *Vertigo METCD 16*	31		2
27 Feb 99	**WHISKEY IN THE JAR** *Vertigo METCD 19*	29		2
12 Aug 00	**I DISAPPEAR** *Hollywood 0113875 HWR*	35		3
5 Jul 03	**ST ANGER** *Vertigo 9865413*	9		8
4 Oct 03	**FRANTIC** *Vertigo 9811514*	16		3
24 Jan 04	**THE UNNAMED FEELING** *Vertigo 9815881*	42		2
30 Aug 08	**THE DAY THAT NEVER COMES** *Mercury GBUM70812419*	19		5
30 Aug 08	**NOTHING ELSE MATTERS** *Vertigo GBAMC9900015*	47		3
30 Aug 08	**ENTER SANDMAN** *Vertigo GBAMC9900023*	52		4
6 Sep 08	**MY APOCALYPSE** *Mercury GBUM70812435*	51		2
13 Sep 08	**CYANIDE** *Mercury GBUM70812434*	48		1

METEOR SEVEN

Germany, male producer (Jans Ebert) — 1

Date	Title	Peak	Wks at No.1	Wks on Chart
18 May 02	**UNIVERSAL MUSIC** *Bulletproof PROOF 16CD*	71		1

METEORS

UK, male vocal/instrumental group — 2

Date	Title	Peak	Wks at No.1	Wks on Chart
26 Feb 83	**JOHNNY REMEMBER ME** *ID EYE 1*	66		2

METHOD MAN

US, male rapper (Clifford Smith). See Wu-Tang Clan — 24

Date	Title	Peak	Wks at No.1	Wks on Chart
29 Apr 95	**RELEASE YO' SELF** *Def Jam DEFCD 6*	46		1
29 Jul 95	**I'LL BE THERE FOR YOU-YOU'RE ALL I NEED TO GET BY** *Def Jam DEFDX11* FEATURING MARY J BLIGE	10		5
5 Apr 97	**HIT 'EM HIGH (THE MONSTARS' ANTHEM)** *Atlantic A 5449CD* B REAL/BUSTA RHYMES/COOLIO/LL COOL J/METHOD MAN	8		6
22 May 99	**BREAK UPS 2 MAKE UPS** *Def Jam 8709272* FEATURING D'ANGELO	33		2
27 Sep 03	**LOVE @ 1ST SIGHT** *MCA MCSTD 40338* MARY J BLIGE FEATURING METHOD MAN	18		5
22 May 04	**WHAT'S HAPPENIN'** *Def Jam 9862518* FEATURING BUSTA RHYMES	17		5

METRIC

Canada, female/male vocal/instrumental group — 1

Date	Title	Peak	Wks at No.1	Wks on Chart
19 Aug 06	**MONSTER HOSPITAL** *Drowned In Sound DISOO21CD*	55		1

METRO STATION

US, male vocal/instrumental group – Trace Cyrus, Mason Musso, Blake Healy & Anthony Improgo — 18

Date	Title	Peak	Wks at No.1	Wks on Chart
14 Mar 09	**SHAKE IT** *Columbia 88697481072*	6		18

MEW

Denmark, male vocal/instrumental group — 6

Date	Title	Peak	Wks at No.1	Wks on Chart
5 Apr 03	**COMFORTING SOUNDS** *Epic 6736432*	48		1
28 Jun 03	**AM I WRY NO** *Epic 6739395*	47		1
27 Dec 03	**SHE CAME HOME FOR CHRISTMAS** *Epic 6744942*	55		1
30 Jul 05	**APOCALYPSO** *Evil Office EVIL02*	75		1
1 Oct 05	**SPECIAL** *Evil Office 6760621*	46		1
18 Feb 06	**WHY ARE YOU LOOKING GRAVE?** *Evil Office 82876755712*	53		1

MEZZOFORTE

Iceland, male instrumental group — 10

Date	Title	Peak	Wks at No.1	Wks on Chart
5 Mar 83	**GARDEN PARTY** *Steinar STE 705*	17		9
11 Jun 83	**ROCKALL** *Steinar STE 710*	75		1

MFSB

US, male instrumental session group — 18

Date	Title	Peak	Wks at No.1	Wks on Chart
27 Apr 74	**TSOP (THE SOUND OF PHILADELPHIA)** *Philadelphia International PIR 2289* FEATURING THE THREE DEGREES ★	22		9
26 Jul 75	**SEXY** *Philadelphia International PIR 3381*	37		5
31 Jan 81	**MYSTERIES OF THE WORLD** *Sound Of Philadelphia PIR 9501*	41		4

MGMT

US, male vocal/instrumental duo — 66

Date	Title	Peak	Wks at No.1	Wks on Chart
15 Mar 08	**TIME TO PRETEND** *Columbia 88697235412*	35		10
28 Jun 08	**ELECTRIC FEEL** *Columbia 88697326492*	22		6
4 Oct 08	**KIDS** *Columbia 88697387482*	16		37
17 Jan 09	**ELECTRIC FEEL** *Columbia 88697326492*	42		3
17 Jan 09	**TIME TO PRETEND** *Columbia 88697235412*	36		10

MIA

UK, female vocalist/producer (Mathangi 'Maya' Arulpragasam) — 29

Date	Title	Peak	Wks at No.1	Wks on Chart
13 Oct 07	**JIMMY** *XL Recordings XLS287CD*	66		1
13 Sep 08	**PAPER PLANES** *XL Recordings XLT396CD*	19		27
23 Jan 10	**PAPER PLANES** *XL Recordings XLT396CD*	61		1

MIAMI SOUND MACHINE

US, female/male vocal/instrumental group – Gloria Estefan*, Emilio Estefan, Juan Marcos Avila (replaced by Jorge Casas) & Enrique Garcia — 95

Date	Title	Peak	Wks at No.1	Wks on Chart
11 Aug 84	**DR BEAT** *Epic A 4614* ●	6		14
17 May 86	**BAD BOY** *Epic A 6537*	16		11
16 Jul 88	**ANYTHING FOR YOU** *Epic 6516737* GLORIA ESTEFAN & MIAMI SOUND MACHINE ★	10		16
22 Oct 88	**1-2-3-** *Epic 6529587* GLORIA ESTEFAN & MIAMI SOUND MACHINE	9		10
17 Dec 88	**RHYTHM IS GONNA GET YOU** *Epic 6545147* GLORIA ESTEFAN & MIAMI SOUND MACHINE	16		9
11 Feb 89	**CAN'T STAY AWAY FROM YOU** *Epic 6514447* GLORIA ESTEFAN & MIAMI SOUND MACHINE	7		12
17 Sep 05	**DOCTOR PRESSURE** *Breastfed BFD017CD2* MYLO VS MIAMI SOUND MACHINE	3		23

GEORGE MICHAEL

UK, male vocalist/multi-instrumentalist/producer (Georgios Panayiotou). Award-winning songwriter who became the first artist in UK chart history to release six Top 3 singles from one album (Older). His solo debut was a transatlantic million-seller. See Wham! — 299

Date	Title	Peak	Wks at No.1	Wks on Chart
4 Aug 84	**CARELESS WHISPER** *Epic A 4603* ◉ ★	1	3	17
5 Apr 86	**A DIFFERENT CORNER** *Epic A 7033* ●	1	3	10
31 Jan 87	**I KNEW YOU WERE WAITING (FOR ME)** *Epic DUET 2* ARETHA FRANKLIN & GEORGE MICHAEL ● ★	1	2	9
13 Jun 87	**I WANT YOUR SEX** *Epic LUST 1*	3		10
24 Oct 87	**FAITH** *Epic EMU 3* ★	2		12
9 Jan 88	**FATHER FIGURE** *Epic EMU 4* ★	11		6
23 Apr 88	**ONE MORE TRY** *Epic EMU 5* ★	8		7
16 Jul 88	**MONKEY** *Epic EMU 6* ★	13		6
3 Dec 88	**KISSING A FOOL** *Epic EMU 7*	18		6
25 Aug 90	**PRAYING FOR TIME** *Epic GEO 1* ★	6		7
27 Oct 90	**WAITING FOR THAT DAY** *Epic GEO 2*	23		5
15 Dec 90	**FREEDOM 90** *Epic GEO 3*	28		6

Date	Title	Peak Position	Weeks at No.1	Weeks on Chart
16 Feb 91	**HEAL THE PAIN** *Epic 6566477*	31		4
30 Mar 91	**COWBOYS AND ANGELS** *Epic 6567747*	45		3
7 Dec 91	**DON'T LET THE SUN GO DOWN ON ME** *Epic 6576467* & ELTON JOHN ○ ★	1	2	10
13 Jun 92	**TOOFUNKY** *Epic 6580587*	4		9
1 May 93	**FIVE LIVE EP** *Parlophone CDRS 6340* & QUEEN WITH LISA STANSFIELD ●	1	3	12
20 Jan 96	**JESUS TO A CHILD** *Virgin VSCDG 1571* ○	1	1	13
4 May 96	**FASTLOVE** *Virgin VSCDG 1579* ●	1	3	14
31 Aug 96	**SPINNING THE WHEEL** *Virgin VSCDG 1595* ○	2		12
1 Feb 97	**OLDER/I CAN'T MAKE YOU LOVE ME** *Virgin VSCDG 1626*	3		9
10 May 97	**STAR PEOPLE '97** *Virgin VSCDG 1641*	2		13
7 Jun 97	**WALTZ AWAY DREAMING** *Aegean AECD 01* TOBY BOURKE/GEORGE MICHAEL	10		4
20 Sep 97	**YOU HAVE BEEN LOVED/THE STRANGEST THING '97** *Virgin VSCD 1663*	2		8
31 Oct 98	**OUTSIDE** *Epic 6665625* ○	2		16
13 Mar 99	**AS** *Epic 6670122* & MARY J BLIGE ○	4		10
17 Jun 00	**IF I TOLD YOU THAT** *Arista 74321766282* WHITNEY HOUSTON & GEORGE MICHAEL	9		11
30 Mar 02	**FREEEK!** *Polydor 5706822*	7		10
10 Aug 02	**SHOOT THE DOG** *Polydor 5709242*	12		5
13 Mar 04	**AMAZING** *Aegean 6747265*	4		11
10 Jul 04	**FLAWLESS (GO TO THE CITY)** *Aegean 6750682*	8		10
13 Nov 04	**ROUND HERE** *Aegean/Sony 6754702*	32		2
8 Jul 06	**AN EASIER AFFAIR** *Epic 82876869462*	13		6
18 Nov 06	**THIS IS NOT REAL LOVE** *Aegean/Sony 88697019792* & MUTYA	15		4
26 Dec 09	**DECEMBER SONG (I DREAMED OF CHRISTMAS)** *Island 2729330*	14		2

MICHAELA

UK, female vocalist/TV presenter (Michaela Strachan) 6

Date	Title	Peak Position	Weeks at No.1	Weeks on Chart
2 Sep 89	**H-A-P-P-Y RADIO** *London H 1*	62		4
28 Apr 90	**TAKE GOOD CARE OF MY HEART** *London WAC 90*	66		2

PRAS MICHEL

US, male rapper/producer (Prakazrel Michael). See Fugees 36

Date	Title	Peak Position	Weeks at No.1	Weeks on Chart
27 Jun 98	**GHETTO SUPERSTAR (THAT IS WHAT YOU ARE)** *Interscope IND 95593* FEATURING OL' DIRTY BASTARD INTRODUCING MYA ⊛	2		17
7 Nov 98	**BLUE ANGELS** *Ruffhouse 6666215* PRAS	6		10
14 Nov 98	**ANOTHER ONE BITES THE DUST** *DreamWorks DRMCD 22364* QUEEN WITH WYCLEF JEAN FEATURING PRAS MICHEL/FREE	5		6
1 Sep 01	**MISS CALIFORNIA** *Elektra E 7192CD* DANTE THOMAS FEATURING PRAS	25		3

KEITH MICHELL

Australia, male actor/vocalist 25

Date	Title	Peak Position	Weeks at No.1	Weeks on Chart
27 Mar 71	**I'LL GIVE YOU THE EARTH (TOUS LES BATEAUX, TOUS LES OISEAUX)** *Spark SRL 1046*	30		11
26 Jan 80	**CAPTAIN BEAKY/WILFRED THE WEASEL** *Polydor POSP 106* ○	5		10
29 Mar 80	**THE TRIAL OF HISSING SID** *Polydor HISS 1* KEITH MITCHELL, CAPTAIN BEAKY & HIS BAND	53		4

MICHELLE

Canada, female vocalist (Michelle Narine). See Big Bass 1

Date	Title	Peak Position	Weeks at No.1	Weeks on Chart
8 Jun 96	**STANDING HERE ALL ALONE** *Positiva CDTIV 54*	69		1

MICHELLE

UK, female vocalist (Michelle McManus). See Idols 15

Date	Title	Peak Position	Weeks at No.1	Weeks on Chart
17 Jan 04	**ALL THIS TIME** *S 82876590652*	1	3	11
17 Apr 04	**THE MEANING OF LOVE** *S 82876604032*	16		4

YVETTE MICHELLE

US, female vocalist (Michele Bryant) 3

Date	Title	Peak Position	Weeks at No.1	Weeks on Chart
5 Apr 97	**I'M NOT FEELING YOU** *Loud 74321465222*	36		3

MICROBE

UK, male vocalist (Ian Doody) 7

Date	Title	Peak Position	Weeks at No.1	Weeks on Chart
14 May 69	**GROOVY BABY** *CBS 4158*	29		7

MICRODISNEY

Ireland, male vocal/instrumental group 3

Date	Title	Peak Position	Weeks at No.1	Weeks on Chart
21 Feb 87	**TOWN TO TOWN** *Virgin VS 927*	55		3

MIDAS

UK, male vocal/instrumental group 1

Date	Title	Peak Position	Weeks at No.1	Weeks on Chart
31 Mar 07	**DON'T DANCE** *Midas MID001*	59		1

MIDDLE OF THE ROAD

UK, male/female vocal/instrumental group – Sally Carr, Ken Andrew, Eric, d. 6 Oct 2007, & Ian McCredie 76

Date	Title	Peak Position	Weeks at No.1	Weeks on Chart
5 Jun 71	**CHIRPY CHIRPY CHEEP CHEEP** *RCA 2047*	1	5	34
4 Sep 71	**TWEEDLE DEE TWEEDLE DUM** *RCA 2110*	2		17
11 Dec 71	**SOLEY SOLEY** *RCA 2151*	5		12
25 Mar 72	**SACRAMENTO (A WONDERFUL TOWN)** *RCA 2184*	23		7
29 Jul 72	**SAMSON AND DELILAH** *RCA 2237*	26		6

MIDDLESBROUGH FC FEATURING BOB MORTIMER & CHRIS REA

UK, male footballers/vocal/instrumental group 1

Date	Title	Peak Position	Weeks at No.1	Weeks on Chart
24 May 97	**LET'S DANCE** *Magnet EW 112CD*	44		1

MALCOLM MIDDLETON

UK, male vocalist/multi-instrumentalist. See Arab Strab 1

Date	Title	Peak Position	Weeks at No.1	Weeks on Chart
29 Dec 07	**WE'RE ALL GOING TO DIE** *Full Time Hobby FTH045S*	31		1

MIDFIELD GENERAL FEATURING LINDA LEWIS

UK, male/female vocal/production duo 1

Date	Title	Peak Position	Weeks at No.1	Weeks on Chart
19 Aug 00	**REACH OUT** *Skint 54CD*	61		1

MIDGET

UK, male vocal/instrumental group 2

Date	Title	Peak Position	Weeks at No.1	Weeks on Chart
31 Jan 98	**ALL FALL DOWN** *Radarscope TINYCDS 6X*	57		1
18 Apr 98	**INVISIBLE BALLOON** *Radarscope TINYCDS 7*	66		1

MIDI XPRESS

UK, male vocal/instrumental duo 1

Date	Title	Peak Position	Weeks at No.1	Weeks on Chart
11 May 96	**CHASE** *Labello Dance LAD 26CD*	73		1

BETTE MIDLER

US, female vocalist 28

Date	Title	Peak Position	Weeks at No.1	Weeks on Chart
17 Jun 89	**WIND BENEATH MY WINGS** *Atlantic A 8972* ★	5		12
13 Oct 90	**FROM A DISTANCE** *Atlantic A 7820*	45		5
15 Jun 91	**FROM A DISTANCE** *Atlantic A 7820*	6		9
5 Dec 98	**MY ONE TRUE FRIEND** *Warner Brothers W 460CD*	58		1
4 Oct 08	**WIND BENEATH MY WINGS** *Atlantic USAT29900553*	70		1

MIDNIGHT COWBOY SOUNDTRACK

UK, male conductor (John Barry) & US, orchestra. See John Barry 4

Date	Title	Peak Position	Weeks at No.1	Weeks on Chart
8 Nov 80	**MIDNIGHT COWBOY** *United Artists UP 634*	47		4

MIDNIGHT OIL

Australia, male vocal/instrumental group – Peter Garrett, Peter Gifford (replaced by Bones Hillman), Rob Hirst, Jim Moginie & Martin Rotsey 32

Date	Title	Peak Position	Weeks at No.1	Weeks on Chart
23 Apr 88	**BEDS ARE BURNING** *Sprint OIL 1*	48		5
2 Jul 88	**THE DEAD HEART** *Sprint OIL 2*	68		2
25 Mar 89	**BEDS ARE BURNING** *Sprint OIL 3*	6		13
1 Jul 89	**THE DEAD HEART** *Sprint OIL 4*	62		4
10 Feb 90	**BLUE SKY MINE** *CBS OIL 5*	66		2
17 Apr 93	**TRUGANINI** *Columbia 6590492*	29		4
3 Jul 93	**MY COUNTRY** *Columbia 6593702*	66		1
6 Nov 93	**IN THE VALLEY** *Columbia 6598492*	60		1

MIDNIGHT STAR

US, male/female vocal/instrumental group – Belinda Lipscomb, Reggie & Vincent Calloway, Jeff Cooper, Kenneth Gant, Melvin Gentry, Bobby Lovelace, Bill Simmons & Boaz Watson 26

Date	Title	Peak Position	Weeks at No.1	Weeks on Chart
23 Feb 85	**OPERATOR** *Solar MCA 942*	66		2
28 Jun 86	**HEADLINES** *Solar MCA 1065*	16		8
4 Oct 86	**MIDAS TOUCH** *Solar MCA 1096*	8		10
7 Feb 87	**ENGINE NO. 9** *Solar MCA 1117*	64		3

Silver-selling ○ Gold-selling ● Platinum-selling (x multiples) ⊛ US No.1 ★ Peak Position Weeks at No.1 Weeks on Chart

Date	Title	Peak Position	Weeks at No.1	Weeks on Chart
2 May 87	WET MY WHISTLE *Solar MCA 1127*	60		3

MIGHTY AVENGERS
UK, male vocal/instrumental group — 2

Date	Title	Peak Position	Weeks at No.1	Weeks on Chart
26 Nov 64	SO MUCH IN LOVE *Decca F 11962*	46		2

MIGHTY DUB KATZ
UK, male producer (Norman Cook). See Beats International, Fatboy Slim, Freakpower, Housemartins, Pizzaman, Urban All Stars — 6

Date	Title	Peak Position	Weeks at No.1	Weeks on Chart
7 Dec 96	JUST ANOTHER GROOVE *ffrr FCD 287*	43		1
2 Aug 97	MAGIC CARPET RIDE *ffrr FCD 306*	24		4
7 Dec 02	LET THE DRUMS SPEAK *Southern Fried ECB 31X*	73		1

MIGHTY LEMON DROPS
UK, male vocal/instrumental group — 6

Date	Title	Peak Position	Weeks at No.1	Weeks on Chart
13 Sep 86	THE OTHER SIDE OF YOU *Blue Guitar AZUR 1*	67		1
18 Apr 87	OUT OF HAND *Blue Guitar AZUR 4*	66		3
23 Jan 88	INSIDE OUT *Blue Guitar AZUR 6*	74		2

MIGHTY MIGHTY BOSSTONES
US, male vocal/instrumental group — 6

Date	Title	Peak Position	Weeks at No.1	Weeks on Chart
25 Apr 98	THE IMPRESSION THAT I GET *Mercury 5748432*	12		5
27 Jun 98	THE RASCAL KING *Mercury 5661092*	63		1

MIGHTY MORPH'N POWER RANGERS
US, male/female teenage earth defenders – male vocalist/instrumentalist Ron Wasserman (aka Aaron Waters & The Mighty Raw) — 13

Date	Title	Peak Position	Weeks at No.1	Weeks on Chart
17 Dec 94	POWER RANGERS *RCA 74321253022* ○	3		13

MIGIL FIVE
UK, male vocal/instrumental group – Mike Felix, Lenny Blanche, Red Lambert, Gilbert Lucas (deceased) & Alan Watson — 20

Date	Title	Peak Position	Weeks at No.1	Weeks on Chart
19 Mar 64	MOCKIN' BIRD HILL *Pye 7N 15597*	10		13
4 Jun 64	NEAR YOU *Pye 7N 15645*	31		7

MIG29
Italy, male production group — 2

Date	Title	Peak Position	Weeks at No.1	Weeks on Chart
22 Feb 92	MIG29 *Champion CHAMP 292*	62		2

MIIKE SNOW
Sweden, male vocal/instrumental/production trio — 1

Date	Title	Peak Position	Weeks at No.1	Weeks on Chart
31 Oct 09	BLACK AND BLUE *Columbia 88697605811*	64		1

MIKA
UK (b. Lebanon), male vocalist/keyboard player (Michael Penniman). See Helping Haiti — 132

Date	Title	Peak Position	Weeks at No.1	Weeks on Chart
20 Jan 07	GRACE KELLY *Island 1721083* ○	1	4	40
17 Feb 07	LOLLIPOP *Casablanca/Island USC7R0600045*	59		10
7 Apr 07	LOVE TODAY *Casablanca/Island 1732069*	6		20
14 Jul 07	BIG GIRL (YOU ARE BEAUTIFUL) *Casablanca/Island 1741590*	9		19
13 Oct 07	HAPPY ENDING *Casablanca/Island 1749143*	7		19
29 Dec 07	RELAX TAKE IT EASY *Casablanca/Island 1706314*	18		16
19 Sep 09	WE ARE GOLDEN *Casablanca/Island 2716934*	4		6
5 Dec 09	RAIN *Casablanca 2726500*	72		1
27 Feb 10	BLAME IT ON THE GIRLS *Casablanca/Island USC7R0900171*	72		1

MIKE
UK, male producer (Mike Hill) — 2

Date	Title	Peak Position	Weeks at No.1	Weeks on Chart
19 Nov 94	TWANGLING THREE FINGERS IN A BOX *Pukka CDMIKE 100*	40		2

MIKE + THE MECHANICS
UK, male vocal/instrumental group – Mike Rutherford*, Paul Carrack*, Adrian Lee, Peter van Hooke & Paul Young, d. 15 Jul 2000 — 67

Date	Title	Peak Position	Weeks at No.1	Weeks on Chart
15 Feb 86	SILENT RUNNING (ON DANGEROUS GROUND) *WEA U 8908*	21		9
31 May 86	ALL I NEED IS A MIRACLE *WEA U 8765*	53		4
14 Jan 89	THE LIVING YEARS *WEA U 7717* ● ★	2		11
16 Mar 91	WORD OF MOUTH *Virgin VS 1345*	13		10
15 Jun 91	A TIME AND PLACE *Virgin VS 1351*	58		3
8 Feb 92	EVERYBODY GETS A SECOND CHANCE *Virgin VS 1396*	56		4
25 Feb 95	OVER MY SHOULDER *Virgin VSCDX 1526*	12		9
17 Jun 95	A BEGGAR ON A BEACH OF GOLD *Virgin VSCD 1535*	33		5
2 Sep 95	ANOTHER CUP OF COFFEE *Virgin VSCDT 1554*	51		4
17 Feb 96	ALL I NEED IS A MIRACLE '96 *Virgin VSCDG 1576*	27		4
1 Jun 96	SILENT RUNNING *Virgin VSCDT 1585*	61		1
5 Jun 99	NOW THAT YOU'VE GONE *Virgin VSCD 1732*	35		2
28 Aug 99	WHENEVER I STOP *Virgin VSCDT 1743*	73		1

MIKI & GRIFF
UK, male/female vocal duo – Barbara Sailsbury, d. 20 Apr 1989, & Emyr Griffith, d. 24 Sep 1995 — 25

Date	Title	Peak Position	Weeks at No.1	Weeks on Chart
2 Oct 59	HOLD BACK TOMORROW *Pye 7N 15213*	26		2
13 Oct 60	ROCKIN' ALONE (IN AN OLD ROCKIN' CHAIR) *Pye 7N 15296*	44		3
1 Feb 62	LITTLE BITTY TEAR *Pye 7N 15412*	16		13
22 Aug 63	I WANNA STAY HERE *Pye 7N 15555*	23		7

MILBURN
UK, male vocal/instrumental group — 5

Date	Title	Peak Position	Weeks at No.1	Weeks on Chart
8 Apr 06	SEND IN THE BOYS *Mercury 9853112*	22		2
22 Jul 06	CHESHIRE CAT SMILE *Mercury 9858662*	32		1
11 Nov 06	WHAT YOU COULD'VE WON *Mercury 1708383*	66		1
29 Sep 07	WHAT WILL YOU DO (WHEN THE MONEY GOES) *Mercury 1744520*	44		1

JOHN MILES
UK, male vocalist/multi-instrumentalist — 30

Date	Title	Peak Position	Weeks at No.1	Weeks on Chart
18 Oct 75	HIGH FLY *Decca F 13595*	17		6
20 Mar 76	MUSIC *Decca F 13627* ○	3		9
16 Oct 76	REMEMBER YESTERDAY *Decca F 13667*	32		5
18 Jun 77	SLOW DOWN *Decca F 13709*	10		10

ROBERT MILES
Italy, male DJ/producer/composer (Robert Concina) — 49

Date	Title	Peak Position	Weeks at No.1	Weeks on Chart
24 Feb 96	CHILDREN *Deconstruction 74321348322* ⊛	2		18
8 Jun 96	FABLE *Deconstruction 74321382622*	7		9
16 Nov 96	ONE & ONE *Deconstruction 74321427692* FEATURING MARIA NAYLER ●	3		17
29 Nov 97	FREEDOM *Deconstruction 74321536952* FEATURING KATHY SLEDGE	15		4
28 Jul 01	PATHS *Salt 002CDX* FEATURING NINA MIRANDA	74		1

CHRISTINA MILIAN
US, female vocalist/actor (Christine Flores) — 61

Date	Title	Peak Position	Weeks at No.1	Weeks on Chart
3 Mar 01	BETWEEN YOU AND ME *Def Jam 5727402* JA RULE FEATURING CHRISTINA MILIAN	26		3
26 Jan 02	AM TO PM *Def Soul 5889332*	3		11
29 Jun 02	WHEN YOU LOOK AT ME *Def Soul 5829802*	3		10
9 Nov 02	IT'S ALL GRAVY *Relentless RELENT 32CD* ROMEO FEATURING CHRISTINA MILIAN	9		6
15 May 04	DIP IT LOW *Def Jam UK 9862395*	2		13
16 Oct 04	WHATEVER U WANT *Def Jam 9864266* FEATURING JOE BUDDEN	9		7
20 May 06	SAY I *Def Jam 9857779* FEATURING YOUNG JEEZY	4		11

MILK & HONEY FEATURING GALI ATARI
Israel, male/female vocal/instrumental group — 8

Date	Title	Peak Position	Weeks at No.1	Weeks on Chart
14 Apr 79	HALLELUJAH *Polydor 2001 870* ○	5		8

MILK & SUGAR
Germany, male production duo — 7

Date	Title	Peak Position	Weeks at No.1	Weeks on Chart
12 Jan 02	LOVE IS IN THE AIR *Positiva CDTIV 166* MILK & SUGAR/JOHN PAUL YOUNG	25		3
11 Oct 03	LET THE SUNSHINE IN *Data 64CDS* FEATURING LIZZY PATTINSON	18		4

MILK INC
Belgium, male/female vocal/production duo – Regi Penxten & An Vervoort — 21

Date	Title	Peak Position	Weeks at No.1	Weeks on Chart
28 Feb 98	GOOD ENOUGH (LA VACHE) *Malarky MLKD 5* MILK INCORPORATED	23		3
25 May 02	IN MY EYES *All Around The World CDGLOBE 252*	9		8
21 Sep 02	WALK ON WATER *Positiva CDTIV 179*	10		6
11 Jan 03	LAND OF THE LIVING *Positiva CDTIV 184*	18		4

MILKY

Italy/Egypt, male/female vocal/production trio – Sabrina Elahl, Giuliano Sanchetto & Giordano Trivellato — 7

Date	Title	Peak Position	Weeks at No.1	Weeks on Chart
31 Aug 02	**JUST THE WAY YOU ARE** *Multiply CDMULTY 87*	8		6
7 Dec 02	**IN MY MIND** *Multiply CDMULTY 92*	48		1

MILLA

US (b. Ukraine), female vocalist/model/actor (Milla Jovovich) — 1

Date	Title	Peak Position	Weeks at No.1	Weeks on Chart
18 Jun 94	**GENTLEMAN WHO FELL** *SBK CDSBK 49*	65		1

FRANKIE MILLER

UK, male vocalist — 32

Date	Title	Peak Position	Weeks at No.1	Weeks on Chart
4 Jun 77	**BE GOOD TO YOURSELF** *Chrysalis CHS 2147*	27		6
14 Oct 78	**DARLIN'** *Chrysalis CHS 2255* ●	6		15
20 Jan 79	**WHEN I'M AWAY FROM YOU** *Chrysalis CHS 2276*	42		5
21 Mar 92	**CALEDONIA** *MCS 2001*	45		6

GARY MILLER

UK, male vocalist (Neville Williams), d. 15 Jun 1968 (age 46) — 35

Date	Title	Peak Position	Weeks at No.1	Weeks on Chart
21 Oct 55	**YELLOW ROSE OF TEXAS** *Pye Nixa N 15004*	13		5
13 Jan 56	**ROBIN HOOD** *Pye Nixa N 15020*	10		6
11 Jan 57	**GARDEN OF EDEN** *Pye Nixa N 15070*	14		7
19 Jul 57	**WONDERFUL WONDERFUL** *Pye Nixa N 15094*	29		1
17 Jan 58	**STORY OF MY LIFE** *Pye Nixa N 15120*	14		6
21 Dec 61	**THERE GOES THAT SONG AGAIN/THE NIGHT IS YOUNG** *Pye Nixa N 15404*	29		10

GLENN MILLER

US, male composer/band leader (Alton Glenn Miller), d. 15 Dec 1944 (age 40), & orchestra — 9

Date	Title	Peak Position	Weeks at No.1	Weeks on Chart
12 Mar 54	**MOONLIGHT SERENADE** *HMV BD 5942*	12		1
24 Jan 76	**MOONLIGHT SERENADE/LITTLE BROWN JUG/IN THE MOOD** *RCA 2644*	13		8

JODY MILLER

US, female vocalist (Myrna Brooks) — 1

Date	Title	Peak Position	Weeks at No.1	Weeks on Chart
21 Oct 65	**HOME OF THE BRAVE** *Capitol CL 15415*	49		1

MITCH MILLER

US, male, orchestra leader/instrumentalist/producer, d. 31 Jul 2010 (age 99) — 13

Date	Title	Peak Position	Weeks at No.1	Weeks on Chart
7 Oct 55	**YELLOW ROSE OF TEXAS** *Philips PB 505* ★	2		13

NED MILLER

US, male vocalist — 22

Date	Title	Peak Position	Weeks at No.1	Weeks on Chart
14 Feb 63	**FROM A JACK TO A KING** *London HL 9658*	2		21
18 Feb 65	**DO WHAT YOU DO WELL** *London HL 9937*	48		1

ROGER MILLER

US, male vocalist, d. 25 Oct 1992 (age 56) — 42

Date	Title	Peak Position	Weeks at No.1	Weeks on Chart
18 Mar 65	**KING OF THE ROAD** *Philips BF 1397*	1	1	15
3 Jun 65	**ENGINE ENGINE NO. 9** *Philips BF 1416*	33		5
21 Oct 65	**KANSAS CITY STAR** *Philips BF 1437*	48		1
16 Dec 65	**ENGLAND SWINGS** *Philips BF 1456*	13		8
27 Mar 68	**LITTLE GREEN APPLES** *Mercury MF 1021*	19		10
2 Apr 69	**LITTLE GREEN APPLES** *Mercury MF 1021*	39		3

STEVE MILLER BAND

US, male vocal/instrumental group – Steve Miller, James Cook, Tim Davis, Gary Mallaber & Lonnie Turner — 36

Date	Title	Peak Position	Weeks at No.1	Weeks on Chart
23 Oct 76	**ROCK 'N ME** *Mercury 6078 804* ★	11		9
19 Jun 82	**ABRACADABRA** *Mercury STEVE 3* ● ★	2		11
4 Sep 82	**KEEPS ME IN WONDERLAND** *Mercury STEVE 4*	52		3
11 Aug 90	**THE JOKER** *Capitol CL 583* ● ★	1	2	13

SUZI MILLER & THE JOHNSTON BROTHERS

UK, female vocalist (Renee Lester) & male vocal group. See Johnston Brothers — 2

Date	Title	Peak Position	Weeks at No.1	Weeks on Chart
21 Jan 55	**HAPPY DAYS AND LONELY NIGHTS** *Decca F 10389*	14		2

LISA MILLETT

UK, female vocalist — 8

Date	Title	Peak Position	Weeks at No.1	Weeks on Chart
3 Sep 94	**WALKIN' ON** *Go! Beat GODCD 115* SHEER BRONZE FEATURING LISA MILLETT	63		1
16 Sep 00	**BAD HABIT** *Defected DEFECT 8CDS* A.T.F.C. PRESENTS ONEPHATDEEVA FEATURING LISA MILLETT	17		3
21 Jul 01	**SOUL HEAVEN** *Direction 6713852* GOODFELLAS FEATURING LISA MILLETT	27		2
9 Feb 02	**SLEEP TALK** *Defected DFECT 43CDS* A.T.F.C. FEATURING LISA MILLETT	33		2

MILLI VANILLI

Germany/France, male 'vocal' duo – Fabrice Morvan & Rob Pilatus, d. 2 Apr 1998 (voiced by US/Germany, vocal/rap trio – John Davis, Brad Howell & Charles Shaw) — 50

Date	Title	Peak Position	Weeks at No.1	Weeks on Chart
1 Oct 88	**GIRL YOU KNOW IT'S TRUE** *Cooltempo COOL 170* ●	3		13
17 Dec 88	**BABY DON'T FORGET MY NUMBER** *Cooltempo COOL 178* ★	16		11
22 Jul 89	**BLAME IT ON THE RAIN** *Cooltempo COOL 180* ★	53		5
30 Sep 89	**GIRL I'M GONNA MISS YOU** *Cooltempo COOL 191* ● ★	2		15
2 Dec 89	**BLAME IT ON THE RAIN** *Cooltempo COOL 180*	52		5
10 Mar 90	**ALL OR NOTHING** *Cooltempo COOL 199*	74		1

MILLICAN & NESBITT

UK, male vocal duo – Alan Millican & Tim Nesbitt — 14

Date	Title	Peak Position	Weeks at No.1	Weeks on Chart
1 Dec 73	**VAYA CON DOS** *Pye 7N 45310*	20		11
18 May 74	**FOR OLD TIME'S SAKE** *Pye 7N 45357*	38		3

MILLIE

Jamaica, female vocalist (Millie Small) — 33

Date	Title	Peak Position	Weeks at No.1	Weeks on Chart
12 Mar 64	**MY BOY LOLLIPOP** *Fontana TF 449*	2		18
25 Jun 64	**SWEET WILLIAM** *Fontana TF 479*	30		9
11 Nov 65	**BLOODSHOT EYES** *Fontana TF 617*	48		1
25 Jul 87	**MY BOY LOLLIPOP** *Island WIP 6574*	46		5

MILLION DAN

UK, male rapper (Michael Dunn) — 2

Date	Title	Peak Position	Weeks at No.1	Weeks on Chart
27 Sep 03	**DOGZ N SLEDGEZ** *Gut CDGUT 52*	66		1
12 Feb 05	**BOOM BLAST** *Against The Grain ATG010R* FREESTYLERS FEATURING MILLION DAN	75		1

MILLION DEAD

UK/Australia, male vocal/instrumental group — 2

Date	Title	Peak Position	Weeks at No.1	Weeks on Chart
29 May 04	**I GAVE MY EYES TO STEVIE WONDER** *Xtra Mile XMR101*	72		1
2 Apr 05	**LIVING THE DREAM** *Xtra Mile XMR105*	60		1

MILLIONAIRE HIPPIES

UK, male producer/DJ (Danny Rampling) — 4

Date	Title	Peak Position	Weeks at No.1	Weeks on Chart
18 Dec 93	**I AM THE MUSIC HEAR ME!** *Deconstruction 74321175432*	52		3
10 Sep 94	**C'MON** *Deconstruction 74321229372*	59		1

GARRY MILLS

UK, male vocalist — 31

Date	Title	Peak Position	Weeks at No.1	Weeks on Chart
7 Jul 60	**LOOK FOR A STAR** *Top Rank JAR 336*	7		14
20 Oct 60	**TOP TEEN BABY** *Top Rank JAR 500*	24		12
22 Jun 61	**I'LL STEP DOWN** *Decca F 11358*	39		5

HAYLEY MILLS

UK, female actor/vocalist — 11

Date	Title	Peak Position	Weeks at No.1	Weeks on Chart
19 Oct 61	**LET'S GET TOGETHER** *Decca F 21396*	17		11

STEPHANIE MILLS

US, female vocalist — 33

Date	Title	Peak Position	Weeks at No.1	Weeks on Chart
18 Oct 80	**NEVER KNEW LOVE LIKE THIS BEFORE** *20th Century TC 2460* ●	4		14
23 May 81	**TWO HEARTS** *20th Century TC 2492* FEATURING TEDDY PENDERGRASS	49		5

Silver-selling ● Gold-selling ● Platinum-selling (× multiples) ✪ US No.1 ★ Peak Position · Weeks at No.1 · Weeks on Chart

Date	Title	Peak Position	Weeks at No.1	Weeks on Chart
15 Sep 84	**THE MEDICINE SONG** *Club JAB 8*	29		9
5 Sep 87	**(YOU'RE PUTTIN') A RUSH ON ME** *MCA 1187*	62		2
1 May 93	**NEVER DO YOU WRONG** *MCA MCSTD 1767*	57		2
10 Jul 93	**ALL DAY ALL NIGHT** *MCA MCSTD 1778*	68		1

WARREN MILLS
Zambia, male vocalist — **1**

Date	Title	Peak Position	Weeks at No.1	Weeks on Chart
28 Sep 85	**SUNSHINE** *Jive 99*	74		1

MILLS BROTHERS
US, male vocal group – Donald, d. 13 Nov 1999, Harry, d. 28 Jun 1982, Herbert, d. 12 Apr 1989, & John, d. 8 Dec 1967, Mills — **1**

Date	Title	Peak Position	Weeks at No.1	Weeks on Chart
30 Jan 53	**GLOW WORM** *Brunswick 05007* ★	10		1

MILLTOWN BROTHERS
UK, male vocal/instrumental group — **16**

Date	Title	Peak Position	Weeks at No.1	Weeks on Chart
2 Feb 91	**WHICH WAY SHOULD I JUMP** *A&M AM 711*	38		5
13 Apr 91	**HERE I STAND** *A&M AM 758*	41		4
6 Jul 91	**APPLE GREEN** *A&M AM 787*	43		4
22 May 93	**TURN OFF** *A&M 5802692*	55		1
17 Jul 93	**IT'S ALL OVER NOW BABY BLUE** *A&M 5803332*	48		2

MILLWALL FC
UK, football fans/vocal group — **1**

Date	Title	Peak Position	Weeks at No.1	Weeks on Chart
29 May 04	**OH MILLWALL** *Absolute CDAME4*	41		1

CB MILTON
Holland (b. Suriname), male vocalist (Clarence Becker Milton) — **5**

Date	Title	Peak Position	Weeks at No.1	Weeks on Chart
21 May 94	**IT'S A LOVING THING** *Logic 74321208062*	49		2
25 Mar 95	**IT'S A LOVING THING (REMIX)** *Logic 74321267212*	34		2
19 Aug 95	**HOLD ON** *Logic 74321292112*	62		1

GARNET MIMMS & TRUCKIN' CO
US, male vocalist & male instrumental group — **1**

Date	Title	Peak Position	Weeks at No.1	Weeks on Chart
25 Jun 77	**WHAT IT IS** *Arista 109*	44		1

MIMS
US, male rapper (Shawn Mims) — **8**

Date	Title	Peak Position	Weeks at No.1	Weeks on Chart
12 May 07	**THIS IS WHY I'M HOT** *Capitol ANGECD43* ★	18		8

MIND OF KANE
UK, male production duo — **1**

Date	Title	Peak Position	Weeks at No.1	Weeks on Chart
27 Jul 91	**STABBED IN THE BACK** *Déjà Vu DJV 007*	64		1

WAYNE FONTANA & THE MINDBENDERS
UK, male vocal/instrumental group – Wayne Fontana* (Glyn Ellis), Bob Lang, Ric Rothwell & Eric Stewart — **79**

Date	Title	Peak Position	Weeks at No.1	Weeks on Chart
11 Jul 63	**HELLO JOSEPHINE** *Fontana TF 404*	46		2
28 May 64	**STOP LOOK AND LISTEN** *Fontana TF 451*	37		4
8 Oct 64	**UM UM UM UM UM UM** *Fontana TF 497*	5		15
4 Feb 65	**GAME OF LOVE** *Fontana TF 535* ★	2		11
17 Jun 65	**JUST A LITTLE BIT TOO LATE** *Fontana TF 579*	20		7
30 Sep 65	**SHE NEEDS LOVE** *Fontana TF 611*	32		6
13 Jan 66	**A GROOVY KIND OF LOVE** *Fontana TF 644* MINDBENDERS	2		14
5 May 66	**CAN'T LIVE WITH YOU (CAN'T LIVE WITHOUT YOU)** *Fontana TF 697* MINDBENDERS	28		7
25 Aug 66	**ASHES TO ASHES** *Fontana TF 731* MINDBENDERS	14		9
20 Sep 67	**THE LETTER** *Fontana TF 869* MINDBENDERS	42		4

MINDS OF MEN
UK, male/female vocal/instrumental group — **1**

Date	Title	Peak Position	Weeks at No.1	Weeks on Chart
22 Jun 96	**BRAND NEW DAY** *Perfecto PERF 121CD*	41		1

SAL MINEO
US, male actor/vocalist, d. 12 Feb 1976 (age 37) — **11**

Date	Title	Peak Position	Weeks at No.1	Weeks on Chart
12 Jul 57	**START MOVIN' (IN MY DIRECTION)** *Philips PB 707*	16		11

MARCELLO MINERBI
Italy, orchestra — **16**

Date	Title	Peak Position	Weeks at No.1	Weeks on Chart
22 Jul 65	**ZORBA'S DANCE** *Durium DRS 54001*	6		16

MINI POPS
UK, male/female children's TV vocal group — **2**

Date	Title	Peak Position	Weeks at No.1	Weeks on Chart
26 Dec 87	**SONGS FOR CHRISTMAS '87 EP** *Bright BULB 9*	39		2

MINI VIVA
UK, female vocal duo – Frankee Connolly & Britt Love — **9**

Date	Title	Peak Position	Weeks at No.1	Weeks on Chart
19 Sep 09	**LEFT MY HEART IN TOKYO** *Xenomania/Geffen 2715592*	7		8
26 Dec 09	**I WISH** *Xenomania/Geffen 2723993*	73		1

MINIMAL CHIC FEATURING MATT GOSS
Italy/UK, male vocal/production trio. See Bros — **1**

Date	Title	Peak Position	Weeks at No.1	Weeks on Chart
2 Oct 04	**I NEED THE KEY** *Inferno CDFERN63*	54		1

MINIMAL FUNK 2
Italy, male production duo — **2**

Date	Title	Peak Position	Weeks at No.1	Weeks on Chart
18 Jul 98	**THE GROOVY THANG** *Cleveland City CLECD 13046*	65		1
18 May 02	**DEFINITION OF HOUSE** *Junior BRG 033* MINIMAL FUNK	63		1

MINIMALISTIX
Belgium, male production duo — **7**

Date	Title	Peak Position	Weeks at No.1	Weeks on Chart
16 Mar 02	**CLOSE COVER** *Data 32CDS*	12		5
19 Jul 03	**MAGIC FLY** *Data 48CDS*	36		2

MINISTERS DE LA FUNK FEATURING JOCELYN BROWN
US, male/female vocal/production group — **4**

Date	Title	Peak Position	Weeks at No.1	Weeks on Chart
11 Mar 00	**BELIEVE** *Defected DFECT 14CDS*	45		2
27 Jan 01	**BELIEVE (REMIX)** *Defected DFECT 26CDS*	42		2

MINISTRY
US, male vocal/instrumental group — **3**

Date	Title	Peak Position	Weeks at No.1	Weeks on Chart
8 Aug 92	**N.W.O.** *Sire W 0125TE*	49		1
6 Jan 96	**THE FALL** *Warner Brothers W 0328CD*	53		2

MINK DE VILLE
US, male vocal/instrumental group — **9**

Date	Title	Peak Position	Weeks at No.1	Weeks on Chart
6 Aug 77	**SPANISH STROLL** *Capitol CLX 103*	20		9

MINKY
UK, male producer (Gary Dedman) — **1**

Date	Title	Peak Position	Weeks at No.1	Weeks on Chart
30 Oct 99	**THE WEEKEND HAS LANDED** *Offbeat OFFCD 1001*	70		1

LIZA MINNELLI
US, female vocalist — **15**

Date	Title	Peak Position	Weeks at No.1	Weeks on Chart
12 Aug 89	**LOSING MY MIND** *Epic ZEE 1*	6		7
7 Oct 89	**DON'T DROP BOMBS** *Epic ZEE 2*	46		3
25 Nov 89	**SO SORRY I SAID** *Epic ZEE 3*	62		2
3 Mar 90	**LOVE PAINS** *Epic ZEE 4*	41		3

DANNII MINOGUE
Australia, female vocalist. See Childliners — **124**

Date	Title	Peak Position	Weeks at No.1	Weeks on Chart
30 Mar 91	**LOVE AND KISSES** *MCA MCS 1529*	8		8
18 May 91	**SUCCESS** *MCA MCS 1538*	11		7
27 Jul 91	**JUMP TO THE BEAT** *MCA MCS 1556*	8		6
19 Oct 91	**BABY LOVE** *MCA MCS 1580*	14		6
14 Dec 91	**I DON'T WANNA TAKE THIS PAIN** *MCA MCS 1600*	40		5
1 Aug 92	**SHOW YOU THE WAY TO GO** *MCA MCS 1671*	30		3
12 Dec 92	**LOVE'S ON EVERY CORNER** *MCA MCSR 1723*	44		4
17 Jul 93	**THIS IS IT** *MCA MCSTD 1790*	10		8
2 Oct 93	**THIS IS THE WAY** *MCA MCSTD 1935*	27		3
11 Jun 94	**GET INTO YOU** *Mushroom D 11751*	36		2
23 Aug 97	**ALL I WANNA DO** *Eternal WEA 119CD* DANNII	4		8

Key: ○ Silver-selling · ● Gold-selling · ⊛ Platinum-selling (x multiples) · ★ US No.1 · Peak Position · Weeks at No.1 · Weeks on Chart

Date	Title / Label	Peak	Wks at No.1	Wks on Chart
1 Nov 97	**EVERYTHING I WANTED** *Eternal WEA 137CD* DANNII	15		4
28 Mar 98	**DISREMEMBRANCE** *Eternal WEA 153CD* DANNII	21		3
1 Dec 01	**WHO DO YOU LOVE NOW (STRINGER)** *ffrr DFCD 002* RIVA FEATURING DANNII MINOGUE	3		15
16 Nov 02	**PUT THE NEEDLE ON IT** *London LONCD 470*	7		11
15 Mar 03	**I BEGIN TO WONDER** *London LONCD 473*	2		11
21 Jun 03	**DON'T WANNA LOSE THIS FEELING** *London LONCD 478*	5		9
6 Nov 04	**YOU WON'T FORGET ABOUT ME** *All Around The World CXGLOBE379* VS FLOWER POWER	7		5
29 Oct 05	**PERFECTION** *All Around The World CDGLOBE483* & SOUL SEEKERZ	11		3
24 Jun 06	**SO UNDER PRESSURE** *All Around The World CXGLOBE541*	20		2
15 Dec 07	**TOUCH ME LIKE THAT** *All Around The World CDGLOBE795* VS JASON NEVINS	48		1

KYLIE MINOGUE

Australia, female vocalist/actor. Chameleon-like soap star turned pop/dance diva who holds a female record 13 consecutive career-starting Top 10 singles. The million-selling 'Can't Get You Out Of My Head' topped charts in 30 countries and helped boost her total UK singles sales to 9.3 million. See Helping Haiti — 414

Date	Title / Label	Peak	Wks at No.1	Wks on Chart
23 Jan 88	**I SHOULD BE SO LUCKY** *PWL 8* ●	1	5	16
14 May 88	**GOT TO BE CERTAIN** *PWL 12* ○	2		12
6 Aug 88	**THE LOCO-MOTION** *PWL 14*	2		11
22 Oct 88	**JE NE SAIS PAS POURQUOI** *PWL 21* ○	2		13
10 Dec 88	**ESPECIALLY FOR YOU** *PWL 24* & JASON DONOVAN ●	1	3	14
6 May 89	**HAND ON YOUR HEART** *PWL 35* ●	1	1	11
5 Aug 89	**WOULDN'T CHANGE A THING** *PWL 42*	2		9
4 Nov 89	**NEVER TOO LATE** *PWL 45* ○	4		10
20 Jan 90	**TEARS ON MY PILLOW** *PWL 47* ○	1	1	8
12 May 90	**BETTER THE DEVIL YOU KNOW** *PWL 56* ○	2		10
3 Nov 90	**STEP BACK IN TIME** *PWL 64*	4		8
2 Feb 91	**WHAT DO I HAVE TO DO** *PWL 72*	6		8
1 Jun 91	**SHOCKED** *PWL 81*	6		7
7 Sep 91	**WORD IS OUT** *PWL 204*	16		5
2 Nov 91	**IF YOU WERE WITH ME NOW** *PWL 208* & KEITH WASHINGTON	4		7
30 Nov 91	**KEEP ON PUMPIN' IT** *PWL 207* VISIONMASTERS WITH TONY KING & KYLIE MINOGUE	49		1
25 Jan 92	**GIVE ME JUST A LITTLE MORE TIME** *PWL 212*	2		8
25 Apr 92	**FINER FEELINGS** *PWL International PWL 227*	11		6
22 Aug 92	**WHAT KIND OF FOOL (HEARD IT ALL BEFORE)** *PWL International PWL 241*	14		5
28 Nov 92	**CELEBRATION** *PWL International PWL 257*	20		7
10 Sep 94	**CONFIDE IN ME** *Deconstruction 74321227482* ○	2		9
26 Nov 94	**PUT YOURSELF IN MY PLACE** *Deconstruction 74321246572*	11		9
22 Jul 95	**WHERE IS THE FEELING?** *Deconstruction 74321293612*	16		3
14 Oct 95	**WHERE THE WILD ROSES GROW** *Mute CDMUTE 185* NICK CAVE + KYLIE MINOGUE	11		4
20 Sep 97	**SOME KIND OF BLISS** *Deconstruction 74321517252*	22		5
6 Dec 97	**DID IT AGAIN** *Deconstruction 74321535702*	14		6
21 Mar 98	**BREATHE** *Deconstruction 74321570132*	14		4
31 Oct 98	**GBI** *Athrob ART 021CD* TOWA TEI FEATURING KYLIE MINOGUE	63		1
1 Jul 00	**SPINNING AROUND** *Parlophone CDRS 6542* ○	1	1	11
23 Sep 00	**ON A NIGHT LIKE THIS** *Parlophone CDRS 6546*	2		8
21 Oct 00	**KIDS** *Chrysalis CDCHSS 5119* ROBBIE WILLIAMS & KYLIE MINOGUE ○	2		19
23 Dec 00	**PLEASE STAY** *Parlophone CDRS 6551*	10		7
29 Sep 01	**CAN'T GET YOU OUT OF MY HEAD** *Parlophone CDRS 6562* ⊛	1	4	25
2 Mar 02	**IN YOUR EYES** *Parlophone CDRS 6569* ○	1		17
22 Jun 02	**LOVE AT FIRST SIGHT** *Parlophone CDRS 6577*	2		12
23 Nov 02	**COME INTO MY WORLD** *Parlophone CDR 6590*	8		10
15 Nov 03	**SLOW** *Parlophone CDRS 6625*	1	1	10
13 Mar 04	**RED BLOODED WOMAN** *Parlophone CDRS 6633*	5		9
10 Jul 04	**CHOCOLATE** *Parlophone CDRS 6639*	6		7
18 Dec 04	**I BELIEVE IN YOU** *Parlophone CDRS 6656*	2		12
9 Apr 05	**GIVING YOU UP** *Parlophone CDRS6661*	6		8
17 Nov 07	**2 HEARTS** *Parlophone CDRS6751*	4		13
29 Dec 07	**WOW** *Parlophone CDRS6754*	5		19
26 Apr 08	**IN MY ARMS** *Parlophone CDR6756*	10		9
9 Aug 08	**THE ONE** *Parlophone GBAYE0703013*	36		1

MORRIS MINOR & THE MAJORS

UK, male rap/vocal/comedy trio – Tony Hawks, Paul Boross & Phil Judge — 11

Date	Title / Label	Peak	Wks at No.1	Wks on Chart
19 Dec 87	**STUTTER RAP (NO SLEEP 'TIL BEDTIME)** *10 TEN 203*	4		11

SUGAR MINOTT

Jamaica, male vocalist (Lincoln Minott), d. 10 Jul 2010 (age 54) — 16

Date	Title / Label	Peak	Wks at No.1	Wks on Chart
28 Mar 81	**GOOD THING GOING (WE'VE GOT A GOOD THING GOING)** *RCA 58* ○	4		12
17 Oct 81	**NEVER MY LOVE** *RCA 138*	52		4

MINT CONDITION

US, male vocal group — 3

Date	Title / Label	Peak	Wks at No.1	Wks on Chart
21 Jun 97	**WHAT KIND OF MAN WOULD I BE** *Wild Card 5710492*	38		2
4 Oct 97	**LET ME BE THE ONE** *Wild Card 5717132*	63		1

MINT JULEPS

UK, female vocal group — 7

Date	Title / Label	Peak	Wks at No.1	Wks on Chart
22 Mar 86	**ONLY LOVE CAN BREAK YOUR HEART** *Stiff BUY 241*	62		2
30 May 87	**EVERY KINDA PEOPLE** *Stiff BUY 257*	58		5

MINT ROYALE

UK, male production duo – Chris Baker & Neil Claxton — 25

Date	Title / Label	Peak	Wks at No.1	Wks on Chart
5 Feb 00	**DON'T FALTER** *Faith & Hope FHCD 014* FEATURING LAUREN LAVERNE	15		4
6 May 00	**TAKE IT EASY** *Faith & Hope FHCD 016* FEATURING LAUREN LAVERNE	66		1
7 Sep 02	**SEXIEST MAN IN JAMAICA** *Faith & Hope FHCD 025*	20		3
8 Feb 03	**BLUE SONG** *Illustrious/Epic FHCD 030*	35		2
3 Sep 05	**SINGIN' IN THE RAIN** *Direction 82876720492*	20		4
7 Jun 08	**SINGIN' IN THE RAIN** *Direction 82876720492*	1	2	11

MINTY

Australia, female vocalist (Angela Kelly) — 1

Date	Title / Label	Peak	Wks at No.1	Wks on Chart
23 Jan 99	**I WANNA BE FREE** *Virgin VSCDT 1728*	67		1

MINUTEMAN

UK, male vocal/instrumental group — 3

Date	Title / Label	Peak	Wks at No.1	Wks on Chart
20 Jul 02	**BIGBOY** *Ignition IGNSCD 225*	69		1
21 Sep 02	**5000 MINUTES OF PAIN** *Ignition IGNSCD 27*	75		1
15 Feb 03	**BIGBOY/MOTHER FIXATION** *Ignition IGNSCD 28X*	45		1

MIRACLES

US, male vocal group – William 'Smokey' Robinson*, Warren Moore, Bobby Rogers & Ronnie White, d. 26 Aug 1995 — 81

Date	Title / Label	Peak	Wks at No.1	Wks on Chart
24 Feb 66	**GOING TO A GO-GO** *Tamla Motown TMG 547*	44		5
22 Dec 66	**(COME 'ROUND HERE) I'M THE ONE YOU NEED** *Tamla Motown TMG 584*	37		2
27 Dec 67	**I SECOND THAT EMOTION** *Tamla Motown TMG 631* SMOKEY ROBINSON & THE MIRACLES	27		11
3 Apr 68	**IF YOU CAN WANT** *Tamla Motown TMG 648* SMOKEY ROBINSON & THE MIRACLES	50		1
7 May 69	**TRACKS OF MY TEARS** *Tamla Motown TMG 696* SMOKEY ROBINSON & THE MIRACLES	9		13
1 Aug 70	**TEARS OF A CLOWN** *Tamla Motown TMG 745* SMOKEY ROBINSON & THE MIRACLES ★	1	1	14
30 Jan 71	**(COME 'ROUND HERE) I'M THE ONE YOU NEED** *Tamla Motown TMG 761* SMOKEY ROBINSON & THE MIRACLES	13		9
5 Jun 71	**I DON'T BLAME YOU AT ALL** *Tamla Motown TMG 774* SMOKEY ROBINSON & THE MIRACLES	11		10
10 Jan 76	**LOVE MACHINE (PART 1)** *Tamla Motown TMG 1015* ○ ★	3		10
2 Oct 76	**TEARS OF A CLOWN** *Tamla Motown TMG 1048* SMOKEY ROBINSON & THE MIRACLES	34		6

MIRAGE

UK, male/female production/vocal group – Nigel Wright, Tracy Ackerman, John Davies, Robin Sellars & Nigel Stock – fronted by male/female vocalists/dancers – Kiki Billy, Debbie Fagan & Carlos & Nicos Griffiths — 31

Date	Title / Label	Peak	Wks at No.1	Wks on Chart
14 Jan 84	**GIVE ME THE NIGHT** *Passion PASH 15* FEATURING ROY GAYLE	49		4
9 May 87	**JACK MIX II/JACK MIX III** *Debut DEBT 3022*	4		11
25 Jul 87	**SERIOUS MIX** *Debut DEBT 3028*	42		4
7 Nov 87	**JACK MIX IV** *Debut DEBT 3035*	8		10
27 Feb 88	**JACK MIX VII** *Debut DEBT 3042*	50		3
2 Jul 88	**PUSH THE BEAT** *Debut DEBT 3050*	67		2
11 Nov 89	**LATINO HOUSE** *Debut DEBT 3085*	70		1

DANNY MIRROR

Holland, male vocalist (Eddy Ouwens) — 9

Date	Title / Label	Peak	Wks at No.1	Wks on Chart
17 Sep 77	**I REMEMBER ELVIS PRESLEY (THE KING IS DEAD)** *Stone SON 2121* ○	4		9

Silver-selling ● Gold-selling ● Platinum-selling (x multiples) ✪ US No.1 ★ Peak Position · Weeks at No.1 · Weeks on Chart

MIRRORBALL
UK, male/female vocal/production trio. See PF Project featuring Ewan McGregor, Tzant — **5**

Date	Title / Label	Peak Position	Weeks at No.1	Weeks on Chart
13 Feb 99	**GIVEN UP** *Multiply CDMULTY 46*	12		4
24 Jun 00	**BURNIN'** *Multiply CDMULTY 56*	47		1

MIRWAIS
France, male producer (Mirwais Ahmadzai) — **3**

Date	Title / Label	Peak Position	Weeks at No.1	Weeks on Chart
20 May 00	**DISCO SCIENCE** *Epic 6693102*	68		1
23 Dec 00	**NAÏVE SONG** *Epic 6706922*	50		2

MIS-TEEQ
UK, female vocal group – Alesha Dixon*, Su-Elise Nash, Zena Playford & Sabrena Washington — **69**

Date	Title / Label	Peak Position	Weeks at No.1	Weeks on Chart
20 Jan 01	**WHY** *Inferno CDFERN 35*	8		7
23 Jun 01	**ALL I WANT** *Telstar CDSTAS 3184*	2		11
27 Oct 01	**ONE NIGHT STAND** *Inferno/Telstar CDTAS 3208*	5		12
2 Mar 02	**B WITH ME** *Inferno/Telstar CDSTAS 3243*	5		8
29 Jun 02	**ROLL ON/THIS IS HOW WE DO IT** *Inferno/Telstar CDSTAS 3255*	7		6
29 Mar 03	**SCANDALOUS** *Telstar CDSTAS 3319*	2		11
12 Jul 03	**CAN'T GET IT BACK** *Telstar CXSTAS 3337*	8		9
29 Nov 03	**STYLE** *Telstar CDSTAS 3369*	13		5

MISH MASH
UK, male/female vocal/DJ/production trio — **4**

Date	Title / Label	Peak Position	Weeks at No.1	Weeks on Chart
15 Apr 06	**SPEECHLESS** *Data DATA100CDS*	16		4

MISHKA
Bermuda, male vocalist (Alexander Mishka Frith) — **2**

Date	Title / Label	Peak Position	Weeks at No.1	Weeks on Chart
15 May 99	**GIVE YOU ALL THE LOVE** *Creation CRESCD 311*	34		2

MISS BEHAVIN'
UK, female DJ/producer (Nichola Potterton) — **1**

Date	Title / Label	Peak Position	Weeks at No.1	Weeks on Chart
18 Jan 03	**SUCH A GOOD FEELIN'** *Tidy Two 115C*	62		1

MISS JANE
Italy/UK, male/female vocal/production trio — **1**

Date	Title / Label	Peak Position	Weeks at No.1	Weeks on Chart
30 Oct 99	**IT'S A FINE DAY** *G1 Recordings G 1001CD*	62		1

MISS SHIVA
Germany, female DJ/producer (Khadra Bungardt) — **3**

Date	Title / Label	Peak Position	Weeks at No.1	Weeks on Chart
10 Nov 01	**DREAMS** *VC Recordings VCRCD 99*	30		3

MISS X
UK, female vocalist (Joyce Blair), d. 19 Aug 2006 (age 73) — **6**

Date	Title / Label	Peak Position	Weeks at No.1	Weeks on Chart
1 Aug 63	**CHRISTINE** *Ember S 175*	37		6

MISSION
UK, male vocal/instrumental group – Wayne Hussey, Craig Adams, Mick Brown & Simon Hinkler — **58**

Date	Title / Label	Peak Position	Weeks at No.1	Weeks on Chart
14 Jun 86	**SERPENTS KISS** *Chapter 22 CHAP 6*	70		3
26 Jul 86	**GARDEN OF DELIGHT/LIKE A HURRICANE** *Chapter 22 CHAP 7*	49		4
18 Oct 86	**STAY WITH ME** *Mercury MYTH 1*	30		4
17 Jan 87	**WASTELAND** *Mercury MYTH 2*	11		6
14 Mar 87	**SEVERINA** *Mercury MYTH 3*	25		5
13 Feb 88	**TOWER OF STRENGTH** *Mercury MYTH 4*	12		7
23 Apr 88	**BEYOND THE PALE** *Mercury MYTH 6*	32		4
13 Jan 90	**BUTTERFLY ON A WHEEL** *Mercury MYTH 8*	12		4
10 Mar 90	**DELIVERANCE** *Mercury MYTH 9*	27		4
2 Jun 90	**INTO THE BLUE** *Mercury MYTH 10*	32		3
17 Nov 90	**HANDS ACROSS THE OCEAN** *Mercury MYTH 11*	28		2
25 Apr 92	**NEVER AGAIN** *Mercury MYTH 12*	34		3
20 Jun 92	**LIKE A CHILD AGAIN** *Mercury MYTH 13*	30		2
17 Oct 92	**SHADES OF GREEN** *Vertigo MYTH 14*	49		2
8 Jan 94	**TOWER OF STRENGTH (REMIX)** *Vertigo MYTCD 15*	33		3
26 Mar 94	**AFTERGLOW** *Vertigo MYTCD 16*	53		1
4 Feb 95	**SWOON** *Neverland HOOKCD 002*	73		1

MISSJONES
US, female vocalist (Tarsha Jones) — **1**

Date	Title / Label	Peak Position	Weeks at No.1	Weeks on Chart
10 Oct 98	**2 WAY STREET** *Motown 8608572*	49		1

MRS MILLS
UK, female pianist (Gladys Mills), d. 25 Feb 1978 (age 56) — **6**

Date	Title / Label	Peak Position	Weeks at No.1	Weeks on Chart
14 Dec 61	**MRS MILLS MEDLEY** *Parlophone R 4856*	18		5
31 Dec 64	**MRS MILLS PARTY MEDLEY** *Parlophone R 5214*	50		1

MRS WOOD
UK, female producer (Jane Rolink) — **6**

Date	Title / Label	Peak Position	Weeks at No.1	Weeks on Chart
16 Sep 95	**JOANNA** *React CDREACT 066*	40		2
6 Jul 96	**HEARTBREAK** *React CDREACT 78* FEATURING EVE GALLAGHER	44		1
4 Oct 97	**JOANNA** *React CDXREACT 107*	34		2
15 Aug 98	**1234** *React CDREACT 121*	54		1

MISTA E
UK, male production trio — **5**

Date	Title / Label	Peak Position	Weeks at No.1	Weeks on Chart
10 Dec 88	**DON'T BELIEVE THE HYPE** *Urban URB 28*	41		5

MR & MRS SMITH
UK, male/female instrumental/production group — **1**

Date	Title / Label	Peak Position	Weeks at No.1	Weeks on Chart
12 Oct 96	**GOTTA GET LOOSE** *Hooj Choons HOOJCD 46*	70		1

MR BEAN & SMEAR CAMPAIGN FEATURING BRUCE DICKINSON
UK, male TV comedy character/vocalist (Rowan Atkinson) & male vocal/instrumental group — **5**

Date	Title / Label	Peak Position	Weeks at No.1	Weeks on Chart
4 Apr 92	**(I WANT TO BE) ELECTED** *London LON 319*	9		5

MR BIG
UK, male vocal/instrumental group – Jeff Dicken, Edward Carter, Vince Chaulk, Peter Crowther & John Marter — **14**

Date	Title / Label	Peak Position	Weeks at No.1	Weeks on Chart
12 Feb 77	**ROMEO** *EMI 2567* ●	4		10
21 May 77	**FEEL LIKE CALLING HOME** *EMI 2610*	35		4

MR BIG
US, male vocal/instrumental group – Eric Martin, Paul Gilbert, Billy Sheehan & Pat Torpey — **17**

Date	Title / Label	Peak Position	Weeks at No.1	Weeks on Chart
7 Mar 92	**TO BE WITH YOU** *Atlantic A 7514* ★	3		11
23 May 92	**JUST TAKE MY HEART** *Atlantic A 7490*	26		4
8 Aug 92	**GREEN TINTED SIXTIES MIND** *Atlantic A 7468*	72		1
20 Nov 93	**WILD WORLD** *Atlantic A 7310CD*	59		1

MR BLOBBY
Blobbyland, male pink with yellow spots TV character/vocalist (Barry Killerby) — **16**

Date	Title / Label	Peak Position	Weeks at No.1	Weeks on Chart
4 Dec 93	**MR BLOBBY** *Destiny Music CDDMUS 104* ✪	1	3	12
16 Dec 95	**CHRISTMAS IN BLOBBYLAND** *Destiny DMUSCD 108*	36		4

MR BLOE
UK, male instrumental session band formed by Zack Lawrence — **18**

Date	Title / Label	Peak Position	Weeks at No.1	Weeks on Chart
9 May 70	**GROOVIN' WITH MR. BLOE** *DJM DJS 216*	2		18

MR FINGERS
US, male producer (Larry Heard) — **5**

Date	Title / Label	Peak Position	Weeks at No.1	Weeks on Chart
17 Mar 90	**WHAT ABOUT THIS LOVE** *ffrr F 131*	74		1
7 Mar 92	**CLOSER** *MCA MCS 1601*	50		3
23 May 92	**ON MY WAY** *MCA MCS 1630*	71		1

MR FOOD
UK, male vocalist/greedy radio character (David Sanderson) — **3**

Date	Title / Label	Peak Position	Weeks at No.1	Weeks on Chart
9 Jun 90	**...AND THAT'S BEFORE ME TEA!** *Tangible TGB 005*	62		3

MR HANKEY

US, male cartoon excrement vocalist **6**

Date	Title / Label	Peak	No.1	Wks
25 Dec 99	**MR HANKEY THE CHRISTMAS POO** *Columbia 6685582*	4		6

MR HUDSON

UK, male vocal/instrumental group – Benjamin Hudson Kasnorten McIldowie, Rob Barron, Joy Joseph, Raphael Mann & Andrew 'Wilkie' Wilkinson **62**

Date	Title / Label	Peak	No.1	Wks
3 Mar 07	**TOO LATE TOO LATE** *Mercury 1721391* & THE LIBRARY	53		1
1 Aug 09	**SUPERNOVA** *Good Music GBUM70902596* & KANYE WEST ●	2		15
26 Sep 09	**YOUNG FOREVER** *Roc Nation USJZ10900041* JAY-Z FEATURING MR HUDSON	10		23+
24 Oct 09	**WHITE LIES** *Mercury GBUM70909003*	20		3
28 Nov 09	**PLAYING WITH FIRE** *AATW/UMTV CDGLOBE1304* N-DUBZ FEATURING MR HUDSON	14		20+

MR JACK

Belgium, male producer (Lucente Vito) **2**

Date	Title / Label	Peak	No.1	Wks
25 Jan 97	**WIGGLY WORLD** *Xtravaganza 0090965*	32		2

MR LEE

US, male producer (Leroy Haggard) **6**

Date	Title / Label	Peak	No.1	Wks
6 Aug 88	**PUMP UP LONDON** *Breakout USA 639*	64		2
11 Nov 89	**GET BUSY** *Jive 231*	71		1
24 Feb 90	**GET BUSY** *Jive 231*	41		3

MR MISTER

US, male vocal/instrumental group – Richard Page, Steve Farris, Steve George & Pat Mastelotto **22**

Date	Title / Label	Peak	No.1	Wks
21 Dec 85	**BROKEN WINGS** *RCA PB 49945* ★	4		13
1 Mar 86	**KYRIE** *RCA PB 49927* ★	11		9

MR OIZO

France, male producer (Quentin Dupieux) **15**

Date	Title / Label	Peak	No.1	Wks
3 Apr 99	**FLAT BEAT** *F Communications/PIAS Recordings F 104CDUK* ⊛	1	2	15

MR ON VS THE JUNGLE BROTHERS

UK/US, male rap/production trio **5**

Date	Title / Label	Peak	No.1	Wks
7 Feb 04	**BREATHE DON'T STOP** *Positiva/Incentive CDTIVS 201*	21		5

MR PINK PRESENTS THE PROGRAM

UK, male producer (Leiam Sullivan) **4**

Date	Title / Label	Peak	No.1	Wks
19 Jan 02	**LOVE AND AFFECTION** *Manifesto FESCD 90*	22		4

MR PRESIDENT

Germany, female/male vocal trio – Lady Danii (Daniela Haak), Lazy Dee (Delroy Rennalls) & T-Seven (Judith Hildebrandt) **13**

Date	Title / Label	Peak	No.1	Wks
14 Jun 97	**COCO JAMBOO** *WEA 110CD* ●	8		11
20 Sep 97	**I GIVE YOU MY HEART** *WEA 126CD*	52		1
25 Apr 98	**JOJO ACTION** *WEA 156CD*	73		1

MR REDZ VS DJ SKRIBBLE

UK, male producers **6**

Date	Title / Label	Peak	No.1	Wks
24 May 03	**EVERYBODY COME ON (CAN U FEEL IT)** *ffrr FCD 410*	13		6

MR ROY

UK, male production trio **6**

Date	Title / Label	Peak	No.1	Wks
7 May 94	**SOMETHING ABOUT YOU** *Fresh FRSHD 11*	74		1
21 Jan 95	**SAVED** *Fresh FRSHD 21*	24		4
16 Dec 95	**SOMETHING ABOUT YOU (CAN'T BE BEAT) (REMIX)** *Fresh FRSHD 33*	49		1

MR SCRUFF

UK, male DJ/producer (Andy Carthy) **1**

Date	Title / Label	Peak	No.1	Wks
14 Dec 02	**SWEETSMOKE** *Ninja Tune ZEN 12124*	75		1

MR SMASH & FRIENDS FEATURING THE ENGLAND SUPPORTERS' BAND

UK, male producer & football fans/vocal group **1**

Date	Title / Label	Peak	No.1	Wks
8 Jun 02	**WE'RE COMING OVER** *RGR RGRCD 2*	67		1

MR V

UK, male producer (Rob Villiers) **2**

Date	Title / Label	Peak	No.1	Wks
6 Aug 94	**GIVE ME LIFE** *Cheeky CHEKCD 005*	40		2

MR VEGAS

Jamaica, male vocalist (Clifford Smith) **7**

Date	Title / Label	Peak	No.1	Wks
22 Aug 98	**HEADS HIGH** *Greensleeves GRECD 650*	71		1
13 Nov 99	**HEADS HIGH** *Greensleeves GRECD 785*	16		6

MISTURA FEATURING LLOYD MICHELS

US, male vocal/instrumental group **10**

Date	Title / Label	Peak	No.1	Wks
15 May 76	**THE FLASHER** *Route RT 30*	23		10

MITCHELL BROTHERS

UK, male rap duo **5**

Date	Title / Label	Peak	No.1	Wks
19 Mar 05	**ROUTINE CHECK** *WEA BEATS8* MITCHELL BROTHERS/KANO/THE STREETS	42		2
4 Jun 05	**HARVEY NICKS** *WEA BEATS15* FEATURING SWAY	62		1
20 Aug 05	**EXCUSE MY BROTHER** *The Beats BEATS19*	58		1
17 Nov 07	**MICHAEL JACKSON** *Beat Recordings BEATS58*	65		1

DES MITCHELL

UK, male DJ/producer **5**

Date	Title / Label	Peak	No.1	Wks
29 Jan 00	**(WELCOME) TO THE DANCE** *Code Blue BLU 008CD1*	5		5

GUY MITCHELL

US, male vocalist (Al Cernick), d. 1 Jul 1999 (age 72) **165**

Date	Title / Label	Peak	No.1	Wks
14 Nov 52	**FEET UP** *Columbia DB 3151*	2		10
13 Feb 53	**SHE WEARS RED FEATHERS** *Columbia DB 3238*	1	4	16
24 Apr 53	**PRETTY LITTLE BLACK EYED SUSIE** *Columbia DB 3255*	2		11
28 Aug 53	**LOOK AT THAT GIRL** *Philips PB 162*	1	6	14
6 Nov 53	**CHICKA BOOM** *Philips PB 178*	4		15
18 Dec 53	**CLOUD LUCKY SEVEN** *Philips PB 210*	2		16
19 Feb 54	**CUFF OF MY SHIRT** *Philips PB 225*	9		3
26 Feb 54	**SIPPIN' SODA** *Philips PB 210*	11		1
30 Apr 54	**DIME AND A DOLLAR** *Philips PB 248*	8		5
7 Dec 56	**SINGING THE BLUES** *Philips PB 650* ★	1	3	22
15 Feb 57	**KNEE DEEP IN THE BLUES** *Philips PB 669*	3		12
26 Apr 57	**ROCK-A-BILLY** *Philips PB 685*	1	1	14
26 Jul 57	**IN THE MIDDLE OF A DARK DARK NIGHT/SWEET STUFF** *Philips PB 712*	25		4
11 Oct 57	**CALL ROSIE ON THE PHONE** *Philips PB 743*	17		6
27 Nov 59	**HEARTACHES BY THE NUMBER** *Philips PB 964* ★	5		16

JONI MITCHELL

Canada, female vocalist/guitarist (Roberta Anderson) **24**

Date	Title / Label	Peak	No.1	Wks
13 Jun 70	**BIG YELLOW TAXI** *Reprise RS 20906*	11		15
4 Oct 97	**GOT 'TIL IT'S GONE** *Virgin VSCDG 1666* JANET FEATURING Q-TIP & JONI ●	6		9

WILLIE MITCHELL

US, male guitarist/producer, d. 5 Jan 2010 (age 81) **3**

Date	Title / Label	Peak	No.1	Wks
24 Apr 68	**SOUL SERENADE** *London HLU 10186*	43		1
11 Dec 76	**THE CHAMPION** *London HL 10545*	47		2

MIX FACTORY

UK, male production duo **2**

Date	Title / Label	Peak	No.1	Wks
30 Jan 93	**TAKE ME AWAY (PARADISE)** *All Around The World CDGLOBE 120*	51		2

MIXMASTER

Italy, male producer (Daniele Davoli). See Black Box, Starlight **10**

Date	Title / Label	Peak	No.1	Wks
4 Nov 89	**GRAND PIANO** *BCM 344*	9		10

Silver-selling ○ · Gold-selling ● · Platinum-selling (x multiples) · US No.1 ★ · Peak Position · Weeks at No.1 · Weeks on Chart

MIXTURES

Australia, male vocal/instrumental group – Peter Williams, Don Lebler, Chris Spooner & Fred Wieland **21**

Date	Title	Peak	Wks No.1	Wks
16 Jan 71	**THE PUSHBIKE SONG** *Polydor 2058 083*	2		21

HANK MIZELL

US, male vocalist, d. 23 Dec 1992 (age 79) **13**

Date	Title	Peak	Wks No.1	Wks
20 Mar 76	**JUNGLE ROCK** *Charly CS 1005* ○	3		13

MK

US, male producer (Mark Kinchen) **3**

Date	Title	Peak	Wks No.1	Wks
4 Feb 95	**ALWAYS** *Activ CDTV 3* FEATURING ALANA	69		1
27 May 95	**BURNING** *Activ CDTVR 6*	44		2

MN8

UK/Trinidad & Tobago, male vocal group – Gary 'G-Man' Douglas, Kingsley 'KG' Goldsmith, Tony 'Kule T' Michaels & David 'Dee Tails' Rayside. See Childliners **38**

Date	Title	Peak	Wks No.1	Wks
4 Feb 95	**I'VE GOT A LITTLE SOMETHING FOR YOU** *Columbia 6608802* ○	2		13
29 Apr 95	**IF YOU ONLY LET ME IN** *Columbia 6613252*	6		7
15 Jul 95	**HAPPY** *Columbia 6622192*	8		7
4 Nov 95	**BABY IT'S YOU** *Columbia 6624522*	22		3
24 Feb 96	**PATHWAY TO THE MOON** *Columbia 6629212*	25		2
31 Aug 96	**TUFF ACT TO FOLLOW** *Columbia 6635345*	15		3
26 Oct 96	**DREAMING** *Columbia 6638302*	21		3

MNO

Belgium, male/female production trio **2**

Date	Title	Peak	Wks No.1	Wks
28 Sep 91	**GOD OF ABRAHAM** *A&M AM 820*	66		2

MOBB DEEP

US, male rap group **12**

Date	Title	Peak	Wks No.1	Wks
24 Sep 05	**OUTTA CONTROL** *Interscope 9885436* 50 CENT FEATURING MOBB DEEP	7		11
15 Jul 06	**PUT EM' IN THEIR PLACE** *Interscope 9877787*	75		1

MOBILES

UK, female/male vocal/instrumental group – Anna Maria, David Blundell, Chris Downton, Russell Madge & Eddie & Jhon Smithson **14**

Date	Title	Peak	Wks No.1	Wks
9 Jan 82	**DROWNING IN BERLIN** *Rialto RIA 3*	9		10
27 Mar 82	**AMOUR AMOUR** *Rialto RIA 5*	45		4

MOBO ALLSTARS

UK/US, male/female vocal/instrumental collective **3**

Date	Title	Peak	Wks No.1	Wks
26 Dec 98	**AIN'T NO STOPPING US NOW** *PolyGram TV 5632302*	47		3

MOBY

US, male producer/vocalist (Richard Hall). See UHF **82**

Date	Title	Peak	Wks No.1	Wks
27 Jul 91	**GO** *Outer Rhythm FOOT 15*	46		3
19 Oct 91	**GO** *Outer Rhythm FOOT 15*	10		7
3 Jul 93	**I FEEL IT** *Equator AXISCD 001*	38		3
11 Sep 93	**MOVE** *Mute CDMUTE 158*	21		5
28 May 94	**HYMN** *Mute CDMUTE 161*	31		2
29 Oct 94	**FEELING SO REAL** *Mute CDMUTE 173*	30		2
25 Feb 95	**EVERY TIME YOU TOUCH ME** *Mute CDMUTE 176*	28		3
1 Jul 95	**INTO THE BLUE** *Mute CDMUTE 179A*	34		2
7 Sep 96	**THAT'S WHEN I REACH FOR MY REVOLVER** *Mute CDMUTE 184*	50		1
15 Nov 97	**JAMES BOND THEME** *Mute CDMUTE 210*	8		8
5 Sep 98	**HONEY** *Mute CDMUTE 218*	33		2
8 May 99	**RUN ON** *Mute LCDMUTE 221*	33		2
24 Jul 99	**BODYROCK** *Mute LCDMUTE 225*	38		2
23 Oct 99	**WHY DOES MY HEART FEEL SO BAD** *Mute CDMUTE 230*	16		4
18 Mar 00	**NATURAL BLUES** *Mute CDMUTE 251*	11		6
24 Jun 00	**PORCELAIN** *Mute LCDMUTE 252*	5		6
28 Oct 00	**WHY DOES MY HEART FEEL SO BAD** *Mute LCDMUTE 255*	17		5
11 May 02	**WE ARE ALL MADE OF STARS** *Mute LCDMUTE 268*	11		4
31 Aug 02	**EXTREME WAYS** *Mute LCDMUTE 270*	39		1
16 Nov 02	**IN THIS WORLD** *Mute LCDMUTE 276*	35		2
12 Mar 05	**LIFT ME UP** *Mute LCDMUTE340*	18		4
11 Jun 05	**SPIDERS** *Mute LCDMUTE350*	50		1
4 Feb 06	**SLIPPING AWAY** *Mute LCDMUTE365*	53		1
11 Nov 06	**NEW YORK NEW YORK** *Mute CDMUTE371* FEATURING DEBBIE HARRY	43		1
1 Sep 07	**EXTREME WAYS** *Mute CDMUTE270*	45		5

MOCK TURTLES

UK, male/female vocal/instrumental group **18**

Date	Title	Peak	Wks No.1	Wks
9 Mar 91	**CAN YOU DIG IT** *Siren SRN 136*	18		11
29 Jun 91	**AND THEN SHE SMILES** *Siren SRN 139*	44		4
15 Mar 03	**CAN YOU DIG IT** *Virgin CDMOCK 001*	19		3

MICKY MODELLE V JESSY

UK/Holland, male/female vocal/DJ/production duo – Micky Modelle & Jessy de Smet **12**

Date	Title	Peak	Wks No.1	Wks
19 Aug 06	**DANCING IN THE DARK** *All Around The World CDGLOBE510*	10		10
30 Dec 06	**OVER YOU** *All Around The World CDGLOBE609*	35		2

MODERN

UK, male/female vocal/instrumental group **1**

Date	Title	Peak	Wks No.1	Wks
26 Nov 05	**JANE FALLS DOWN** *Mercury 9874798*	35		1

MODERN ROMANCE

UK, male vocal/instrumental group – Geoff Deane (replaced by Michael J Mullins), Tony Gainsborough (replaced by Andy Kyriacou), Paul Gendler, David & Robbie Jaymes & John du Prez **77**

Date	Title	Peak	Wks No.1	Wks
15 Aug 81	**EVERYBODY SALSA** *WEA K 18815*	12		10
7 Nov 81	**AY AY AY AY MOOSEY** *WEA K 18883*	10		12
30 Jan 82	**QUEEN OF THE RAPPING SCENE (NOTHING EVER GOES THE WAY YOU PLAN)** *WEA K 18928*	37		8
14 Aug 82	**CHERRY PINK AND APPLE BLOSSOM WHITE** *WEA K 19245* FEATURING JOHN DU PREZ	15		8
13 Nov 82	**BEST YEARS OF OUR LIVES** *WEA ROM 1* ○	4		13
26 Feb 83	**HIGH LIFE** *WEA ROM 2*	8		8
7 May 83	**DON'T STOP THAT CRAZY RHYTHM** *WEA ROM 3*	14		6
6 Aug 83	**WALKING IN THE RAIN** *WEA X 9733* ○	7		12

MODERN TALKING

Germany, male vocal/production duo – Thomas Anders (Bernd Weidung) & Dieter Bohlen **22**

Date	Title	Peak	Wks No.1	Wks
15 Jun 85	**YOU'RE MY HEART, YOU'RE MY SOUL** *Magnet MAG 277*	56		7
12 Oct 85	**YOU CAN WIN IF YOU WANT** *Magnet MAG 282*	70		2
16 Aug 86	**BROTHER LOUIE** *RCA PB 40875* ○	4		10
4 Oct 86	**ATLANTIS IS CALLING (S.O.S. FOR LOVE)** *RCA PB 40969*	55		3

MODEST MOUSE

US, male vocal/instrumental group **1**

Date	Title	Peak	Wks No.1	Wks
24 Jul 04	**FLOAT ON** *Epic 6750692*	46		1

MODETTES

UK, female vocal/instrumental group **6**

Date	Title	Peak	Wks No.1	Wks
12 Jul 80	**PAINT IT BLACK** *Deram DET-R 1*	42		5
18 Jul 81	**TONIGHT** *Deram DET 3*	68		1

MODJO

France, male vocal/production duo – Yann Destangol & Romain Tranchart **29**

Date	Title	Peak	Wks No.1	Wks
16 Sep 00	**LADY (HEAR ME TONIGHT)** *Sound Of Barclay 5877582* ●	1	2	20
14 Apr 01	**CHILLIN'** *Polydor 5870092*	12		8
6 Oct 01	**WHAT I MEAN** *Polydor 5873462*	59		1

DOMENICO MODUGNO

Italy, male vocalist, d. 6 Aug 1994 (age 66) **13**

Date	Title	Peak	Wks No.1	Wks
5 Sep 58	**VOLARE** *Oriole ICB 5000* ★	10		12
27 Mar 59	**CIAO CIAO BAMBINA (PIOVE)** *Oriole ICB 1489*	29		1

MODEY LEMON

US, male vocal/instrumental group **2**

Date	Title	Peak	Wks No.1	Wks
22 May 04	**CROWS** *Mute CDMUTE 328*	75		1
28 May 05	**SLEEPWALKERS** *Mute CDMUTE331*	71		1

MOFFATTS
Canada, male vocal/instrumental group — 6

Date	Title	Peak	Wks at No.1	Wks
20 Feb 99	**CRAZY** *Chrysalis CDEM 533*	16		3
26 Jun 99	**UNTIL YOU LOVED ME** *Chrysalis CDEMS 541*	36		2
23 Oct 99	**MISERY** *EMI CDEM 551*	47		1

MOGUAI
Germany, male producer (Andre Tegeler) — 1

Date	Title	Peak	Wks at No.1	Wks
8 Feb 03	**U KNOW Y** *Hope Recordings HOPECDS 038*	62		1

MOGWAI
UK, male vocal/instrumental group — 4

Date	Title	Peak	Wks at No.1	Wks
4 Apr 98	**SWEET LEAF/BLACK SABBATH** *Fierce Panda NING 47CD* MAGOO:MOGWAI	60		1
11 Apr 98	**FEAR SATAN** *Eye-Q EYEUK 032CD*	57		1
11 Jul 98	**NO EDUCATION NO FUTURE (F**K THE CURFEW)** *Chemikal Underground CHEM 026CD*	68		1
11 Feb 06	**FRIEND OF THE NIGHT** *PIAS PIASX064CD*	38		1

MOHAIR
UK, male vocal/instrumental group — 1

Date	Title	Peak	Wks at No.1	Wks
17 Dec 05	**END OF THE LINE** *Pebble Beach ECYCD025*	52		1

MOHAWKS
UK, male instrumental group — 2

Date	Title	Peak	Wks at No.1	Wks
24 Jan 87	**THE CHAMP** *Pama PM 1*	58		2

FRANK'O MOIRAGHI FEATURING AMNESIA
Italy, male/female vocal/DJ/production duo — 4

Date	Title	Peak	Wks at No.1	Wks
1 Jun 96	**FEEL MY BODY** *Multiply CDMULTY 10*	39		2
26 Oct 96	**FEEL MY BODY (REMIX)** *Multiply CDMULTY 15*	40		2

MOIST
Canada, male vocal/instrumental group — 10

Date	Title	Peak	Wks at No.1	Wks
12 Nov 94	**PUSH** *Chrysalis CDCHS 5016*	35		3
25 Feb 95	**SILVER** *Chrysalis CDCHS 5019*	50		2
29 Apr 95	**FREAKY BE BEAUTIFUL** *Chrysalis CDCHS 5022*	47		2
19 Aug 95	**PUSH** *Chrysalis CDCHS 5024*	20		3

MOJO
UK, male instrumental/production group — 3

Date	Title	Peak	Wks at No.1	Wks
22 Aug 81	**DANCE ON** *Creole CR 17*	70		3

MOJOLATORS FEATURING CAMILLA
US, male/female vocal/production trio — 1

Date	Title	Peak	Wks at No.1	Wks
6 Oct 01	**DRIFTING** *Multiply CDMULTY 81*	52		1

MOJOS
UK, male vocal/instrumental group – Stewart James, Nicky Crouch, Keith Karlson (replaced by Lewis Collins), John Konrad & Terry O'Toole — 26

Date	Title	Peak	Wks at No.1	Wks
26 Mar 64	**EVERYTHING'S ALRIGHT** *Decca F 11853*	9		11
11 Jun 64	**WHY NOT TONIGHT** *Decca F 11918*	25		10
10 Sep 64	**SEVEN DAFFODILS** *Decca F 11959*	30		5

MOKENSTEF
US, female vocal group — 1

Date	Title	Peak	Wks at No.1	Wks
23 Sep 95	**HE'S MINE** *Def Jam DEFCD 13*	70		1

MOLELLA FEATURING THE OUTHERE BROTHERS
Italy, male producer (Maurizio Molella) & US, male rap/vocal duo – Lamar 'Hula' Mahone & Keith 'Malik' Mayberry — 10

Date	Title	Peak	Wks at No.1	Wks
16 Dec 95	**IF YOU WANNA PARTY** *Stip 030CD*	9		10

MOLLY HALF HEAD
UK, male vocal/instrumental group — 1

Date	Title	Peak	Wks at No.1	Wks
3 Jun 95	**SHINE** *Columbia 6620732*	73		1

MOLOKO
Ireland/UK, female/male vocal/instrumental/production duo – Roisin Murphy* & Mark Brydon. See Psychedelic Waltons — 39

Date	Title	Peak	Wks at No.1	Wks
24 Feb 96	**DOMINOID** *Echo ECSCD 016*	65		1
25 May 96	**FUN FOR ME** *Echo ECSCD 20*	36		2
20 Jun 98	**THE FLIPSIDE** *Echo ECSCD 54*	53		1
27 Mar 99	**SING IT BACK** *Echo ECSCD 71*	45		2
4 Sep 99	**SING IT BACK (REMIX)** *Echo ECSCD 82* ●	4		9
1 Apr 00	**THE TIME IS NOW** *Echo ECSCD 88* ●	2		10
5 Aug 00	**PURE PLEASURE SEEKER** *Echo ECSCD 99*	21		5
25 Nov 00	**INDIGO** *Echo ECSCD 104*	51		1
1 Mar 03	**FAMILIAR FEELING** *Echo ECSCD 131*	10		4
5 Jul 03	**FOREVER MORE** *Echo ECSCD 136*	17		4

MOMBASSA
UK, male production duo — 1

Date	Title	Peak	Wks at No.1	Wks
8 Mar 97	**CRY FREEDOM** *Soundproof SPCD 021*	63		1

MOMENTS
US, male vocal group – William Brown, Al Goodman & Harry Ray, d. 1 Oct 1992 — 32

Date	Title	Peak	Wks at No.1	Wks
8 Mar 75	**GIRLS** *All Platinum 6146 302* & WHATNAUTS ●	3		10
19 Jul 75	**DOLLY MY LOVE** *All Platinum 6146 306*	10		9
25 Oct 75	**LOOK AT ME (I'M IN LOVE)** *All Platinum 6146 309*	42		4
22 Jan 77	**JACK IN THE BOX** *All Platinum 6146 318* ●	7		9

TONY MOMRELLE
UK, male vocalist — 1

Date	Title	Peak	Wks at No.1	Wks
15 Aug 98	**LET ME SHOW YOU** *Art & Soul ART 1CDS*	67		1

MONACO
UK, male vocal/instrumental group. See Joy Division, New Order — 11

Date	Title	Peak	Wks at No.1	Wks
15 Mar 97	**WHAT DO YOU WANT FROM ME?** *Polydor 5731912*	11		6
31 May 97	**SWEET LIPS** *Polydor 5710552*	18		4
20 Sep 97	**SHINE (SOMEONE WHO NEEDS ME)** *Polydor 5714182*	55		1

PHAROAHE MONCH
US, male rapper (Troy Jamerson) — 11

Date	Title	Peak	Wks at No.1	Wks
19 Feb 00	**SIMON SAYS** *Rawkus RWK 205CD*	24		2
19 Aug 00	**LIGHT** *Rawkus RWK 259CD*	72		1
3 Feb 01	**OH NO** *Rawkus RWK 302* MOS DEF & NATE DOGG FEATURING PHAROAHE MONCH	24		4
1 Dec 01	**GOT YOU** *Priority PTYCD 145*	27		3
14 Sep 02	**THE LIFE** *MCA MCSTD 40292* STYLES & PHAROAHE MONCH	50		1

JAY MONDI & THE LIVING BASS
UK, female vocalist (Julie Morrison) & male producer (Chris Paul*) — 3

Date	Title	Peak	Wks at No.1	Wks
24 Mar 90	**ALL NIGHT LONG** *10 TEN 304*	63		3

MONDO KANE
UK, male production trio. See Stock Aitken Waterman — 3

Date	Title	Peak	Wks at No.1	Wks
16 Aug 86	**NEW YORK AFTERNOON** *Lisson DOLE 2*	70		3

MONE
US, male DJ/production duo — 2

Date	Title	Peak	Wks at No.1	Wks
12 Aug 95	**WE CAN MAKE IT** *A&M 5811592*	64		1
16 Mar 96	**MOVIN'** *AM:PM 5814392*	48		1

ZOOT MONEY & THE BIG ROLL BAND
UK, male vocal/instrumental group — 8

Date	Title	Peak	Wks at No.1	Wks
18 Aug 66	**BIG TIME OPERATOR** *Columbia DB 7975*	25		8

MONEY MARK
US, male vocalist/keyboard player/producer (Mark Ramos-Nishita) — 3

Date	Title / Label	Peak	Wks at No.1	Wks on Chart
28 Feb 98	**HAND IN YOUR HEAD** *Mo Wax MW066CD*	40		2
6 Jun 98	**MAYBE I'M DEAD** *Mo Wax MW089CD1*	45		1

MONICA
US, female vocalist (Monica Arnold) — 37

Date	Title / Label	Peak	Wks at No.1	Wks on Chart
29 Jul 95	**DON'T TAKE IT PERSONAL (JUST ONE OF DEM DAYS)** *Arista 74321301452*	32		3
17 Feb 96	**LIKE THIS AND LIKE THAT** *Rowdy 74321344222*	33		2
8 Jun 96	**BEFORE YOU WALK OUT OF MY LIFE** *Rowdy 74321374042*	22		3
24 May 97	**FOR YOU I WILL** *Atlantic A 5437CD*	27		2
6 Jun 98	**THE BOY IS MINE** *Atlantic AT 0036CD* BRANDY & MONICA ● ★	2		20
17 Oct 98	**THE FIRST NIGHT** *Rowdy 74321619342* ★	6		6
4 Sep 99	**ANGEL OF MINE** *Arista 74321692892* ★	55		1

MONIFAH
US, female vocalist (Monifah Carter) — 2

Date	Title / Label	Peak	Wks at No.1	Wks on Chart
30 Jan 99	**TOUCH IT** *Universal UMD 56218*	29		2

TS MONK
US, male/female vocal/instrumental group — 6

Date	Title / Label	Peak	Wks at No.1	Wks on Chart
7 Mar 81	**BON BON VIE** *Mirage K 11653*	63		2
25 Apr 81	**CANDIDATE FOR LOVE** *Mirage K 11648*	58		4

MONKEES
US, male vocal/instrumental group – Micky Dolenz, Davy Jones, Michael Nesmith & Peter Tork — 101

Date	Title / Label	Peak	Wks at No.1	Wks on Chart
5 Jan 67	**I'M A BELIEVER** *RCA 1560* ★	1	4	17
26 Jan 67	**LAST TRAIN TO CLARKSVILLE** *RCA 1547* ★	23		7
6 Apr 67	**A LITTLE BIT ME A LITTLE BIT YOU** *RCA 1580*	3		12
22 Jun 67	**ALTERNATE TITLE** *RCA 1604*	2		12
16 Aug 67	**PLEASANT VALLEY SUNDAY** *RCA 1620*	11		8
15 Nov 67	**DAYDREAM BELIEVER** *RCA 1645* ★	5		17
27 Mar 68	**VALLERI** *RCA 1673*	12		8
26 Jun 68	**D. W. WASHBURN** *RCA 1706*	17		6
26 Mar 69	**TEARDROP CITY** *RCA 1802*	44		1
25 Jun 69	**SOMEDAY MAN** *RCA 1824*	47		1
15 Mar 80	**THE MONKEES EP** *Arista ARIST 326*	33		9
18 Oct 86	**THAT WAS THEN, THIS IS NOW** *Arista ARIST 673*	68		1
1 Apr 89	**THE MONKEES EP** *Arista 112157*	62		2

MONKEY BARS/GABRIELLE WIDMAN
UK, male/female vocal/production/instrumental trio — 1

Date	Title / Label	Peak	Wks at No.1	Wks on Chart
8 May 04	**SHUGGIE LOVE** *Subliminal SUB117CD*	61		1

MONKEY HANGERZ
UK, football fans (Hartlepool United)/vocal group — 1

Date	Title / Label	Peak	Wks at No.1	Wks on Chart
19 Nov 05	**2 LITTLE BOYS/NEVER SAY DIE 2005** *Poolie Pride 1908*	24		1

MONKEY MAFIA
UK, male vocal/instrumental/production group — 3

Date	Title / Label	Peak	Wks at No.1	Wks on Chart
10 Aug 96	**WORK MI BODY** *Heavenly HVN 53CD* FEATURING PATRA	75		1
7 Jun 97	**15 STEPS (EP)** *Heavenly HVN 67CD*	67		1
2 May 98	**LONG AS I CAN SEE THE LIGHT** *Heavenly HVN 84CD*	51		1

MONKS
UK, male vocal/instrumental duo – Richard Hudson & John Ford. See Hudson-Ford, Strawbs — 9

Date	Title / Label	Peak	Wks at No.1	Wks on Chart
21 Apr 79	**NICE LEGS SHAME ABOUT HER FACE** *Carrere CAR 104*	19		9

MONO
UK, male/female vocal/instrumental duo — 1

Date	Title / Label	Peak	Wks at No.1	Wks on Chart
2 May 98	**LIFE IN MONO** *Echo ECSCD 64*	60		1

MONOBOY FEATURING DELORES
Ireland, male/female vocal/production duo — 1

Date	Title / Label	Peak	Wks at No.1	Wks on Chart
7 Jul 01	**THE MUSIC IN YOU** *Perfecto PERF 18CDS*	50		1

MATT MONRO
UK, male vocalist (Terence Parsons), d. 7 Feb 1985 (age 52) — 127

Date	Title / Label	Peak	Wks at No.1	Wks on Chart
15 Dec 60	**PORTRAIT OF MY LOVE** *Parlophone R 4714*	3		16
9 Mar 61	**MY KIND OF GIRL** *Parlophone R 4755*	5		12
18 May 61	**WHY NOT NOW/CAN THIS BE LOVE** *Parlophone R 4775*	24		9
28 Sep 61	**GONNA BUILD A MOUNTAIN** *Parlophone R 4819*	44		3
8 Feb 62	**SOFTLY AS I LEAVE YOU** *Parlophone R 4868*	10		18
14 Jun 62	**WHEN LOVE COMES ALONG** *Parlophone R 4911*	46		3
8 Nov 62	**MY LOVE AND DEVOTION** *Parlophone R 4954*	29		5
14 Nov 63	**FROM RUSSIA WITH LOVE** *Parlophone R 5068*	20		13
17 Sep 64	**WALK AWAY** *Parlophone R 5171*	4		20
24 Dec 64	**FOR MAMA** *Parlophone R 5215*	23		4
25 Mar 65	**WITHOUT YOU** *Parlophone R 5251*	37		4
21 Oct 65	**YESTERDAY** *Parlophone R 5348*	8		12
24 Nov 73	**AND YOU SMILED** *EMI 2091*	28		8

MONROE
International, female vocal group — 1

Date	Title / Label	Peak	Wks at No.1	Wks on Chart
31 Jul 04	**SMILE** *Zu ZUDB001*	60		1

GERRY MONROE
UK, male vocalist, d. 1987 (age 54) — 57

Date	Title / Label	Peak	Wks at No.1	Wks on Chart
23 May 70	**SALLY** *Chapter One CH 122*	4		20
19 Sep 70	**CRY** *Chapter One CH 128*	38		5
14 Nov 70	**MY PRAYER** *Chapter One CH 132*	9		12
17 Apr 71	**IT'S A SIN TO TELL A LIE** *Chapter One CH 144*	13		12
21 Aug 71	**LITTLE DROPS OF SILVER** *Chapter One CH 152*	37		6
12 Feb 72	**GIRL OF MY DREAMS** *Chapter One CH 159*	43		2

HOLLIS P MONROE
Canada, male DJ/producer — 1

Date	Title / Label	Peak	Wks at No.1	Wks on Chart
24 Apr 99	**I'M LONELY** *City Beat CBE 778CD*	51		1

MONSOON
UK, female/male vocal/instrumental trio — 12

Date	Title / Label	Peak	Wks at No.1	Wks on Chart
3 Apr 82	**EVER SO LONELY** *Mobile Suit Corporation CORP 2*	12		9
5 Jun 82	**SHAKTI (THE MEANING OF WITHIN)** *Mobile Suit Corporation CORP 4*	41		3

MONSTA BOY FEATURING DENZIE
UK, male vocal/production/instrumental duo — 3

Date	Title / Label	Peak	Wks at No.1	Wks on Chart
7 Oct 00	**SORRY (I DIDN'T KNOW)** *Locked On LOX 125C*	25		3

MONSTER MAGNET
US, male vocal/instrumental group — 6

Date	Title / Label	Peak	Wks at No.1	Wks on Chart
29 May 93	**TWIN EARTH** *A&M 5802812*	67		1
18 Mar 95	**NEGASONIC TEENAGE WARHEAD** *A&M 5809812*	49		1
6 May 95	**DOPES TO INFINITY** *A&M 5810332*	58		1
23 Jan 99	**POWERTRIP** *A&M 5828232*	39		2
6 Mar 99	**SPACE LORD** *A&M 5632752*	45		1

MONTAGE
UK, female vocal trio — 1

Date	Title / Label	Peak	Wks at No.1	Wks on Chart
15 Feb 97	**THERE AIN'T NOTHIN' LIKE THE LOVE** *Wild Card 5733172*	64		1

MONTANA SEXTET
US, male instrumental group — 1

Date	Title / Label	Peak	Wks at No.1	Wks on Chart
15 Jan 83	**HEAVY VIBES** *Virgin VS 560*	59		1

MONTANO VS THE TRUMPET MAN
UK, male production/instrumental duo — 1

Date	Title / Label	Peak	Wks at No.1	Wks on Chart
18 Sep 99	**ITZA TRUMPET THING** *Serious SERR 010CD*	46		1

HUGO MONTENEGRO
US, male orchestra leader, d. 6 Feb 1981 (age 56) — 26

Date	Title / Label	Peak	Wks at No.1	Wks on Chart
11 Sep 68	**THE GOOD THE BAD THE UGLY** *RCA 1727* & HIS ORCHESTRA & CHORUS	1	4	25
8 Jan 69	**HANG 'EM HIGH** *RCA 1771*	50		1

CHRIS MONTEZ
UK, male vocalist (Ezekiel Montanez) **61**

Date	Title / Label	Peak Position	Weeks at No.1	Weeks on Chart
4 Oct 62	**LET'S DANCE** *London HLU 9596*	2		18
17 Jan 63	**SOME KINDA FUN** *London HLU 9650*	10		9
30 Jun 66	**THE MORE I SEE YOU** *Pye International 7N 25369*	3		13
22 Sep 66	**THERE WILL NEVER BE ANOTHER YOU** *Pye International 7N 25381*	37		4
14 Oct 72	**LET'S DANCE** *London HL 10205*	9		14
14 Apr 79	**LET'S DANCE** *Lightning LIG 9011*	47		3

MONTROSE
US, male vocal/instrumental group **2**

Date	Title / Label	Peak Position	Weeks at No.1	Weeks on Chart
28 Jun 80	**SPACE STATION NO. 5/GOOD ROCKIN' TONIGHT** *WB HM 9*	71		2

MONTROSE AVENUE
UK, male vocal/instrumental group **4**

Date	Title / Label	Peak Position	Weeks at No.1	Weeks on Chart
28 Mar 98	**WHERE DO I STAND?** *Columbia 6656072*	38		2
20 Jun 98	**SHINE** *Columbia 6660012*	58		1
17 Oct 98	**START AGAIN** *Columbia 6664255*	59		1

MONTY PYTHON
UK, male vocal/comedy group – Eric Idle*, Graham Chapman, d. 4 Oct 1989, John Cleese, Terry Gilliam, Terry Jones & Michael Palin **9**

Date	Title / Label	Peak Position	Weeks at No.1	Weeks on Chart
5 Oct 91	**ALWAYS LOOK ON THE BRIGHT SIDE OF LIFE** *Virgin PYTH 1*	3		9

MONYAKA
US/Jamaica, male vocal/instrumental group **8**

Date	Title / Label	Peak Position	Weeks at No.1	Weeks on Chart
10 Sep 83	**GO DEH YAKA (GO TO THE TOP)** *Polydor POSP 641*	14		8

MOOD
UK, male vocal/instrumental trio **10**

Date	Title / Label	Peak Position	Weeks at No.1	Weeks on Chart
6 Feb 82	**DON'T STOP** *RCA 171*	59		4
22 May 82	**PARIS IS ONE DAY AWAY** *RCA 211*	42		5
30 Oct 82	**PASSION IN DARK ROOMS** *RCA 276*	74		1

MOOD II SWING
US, male vocal/production duo **2**

Date	Title / Label	Peak Position	Weeks at No.1	Weeks on Chart
31 Jan 04	**CAN'T GET AWAY** *Defected DFTD 078CDS*	45		2

MOODSWINGS FEATURING CHRISSIE HYNDE
UK, male production duo & US, female vocalist **4**

Date	Title / Label	Peak Position	Weeks at No.1	Weeks on Chart
12 Oct 91	**SPIRITUAL HIGH (STATE OF INDEPENDENCE)** *Arista 114528*	66		2
23 Jan 93	**SPIRITUAL HIGH (STATE OF INDEPENDENCE) (REMIX)** *Arista 74321127712*	47		2

MOODY BLUES
UK, male vocal/instrumental group – Graham Edge, Justin Hayward*, Denny Laine, John Lodge, Michael Pinder, Ray Thomas & Clint Warwick, d. 15 May 2004 **114**

Date	Title / Label	Peak Position	Weeks at No.1	Weeks on Chart
10 Dec 64	**GO NOW** *Decca F 12022*	1	1	14
4 Mar 65	**I DON'T WANT TO GO ON WITHOUT YOU** *Decca F 12095*	33		9
10 Jun 65	**FROM THE BOTTOM OF MY HEART** *Decca F 12166*	22		9
18 Nov 65	**EVERYDAY** *Decca F 12266*	44		2
27 Dec 67	**NIGHTS IN WHITE SATIN** *Deram DM 161*	19		11
7 Aug 68	**VOICES IN THE SKY** *Deram DM 196*	27		10
4 Dec 68	**RIDE MY SEE-SAW** *Deram DM 213*	42		1
2 May 70	**QUESTION** *Threshold TH 4*	2		12
6 May 72	**ISN'T LIFE STRANGE** *Threshold TH 9*	13		10
2 Dec 72	**NIGHTS IN WHITE SATIN** *Deram DM 161*	9		11
10 Feb 73	**I'M JUST A SINGER (IN A ROCK 'N' ROLL BAND)** *Threshold TH 13*	36		4
10 Nov 79	**NIGHTS IN WHITE SATIN** *Deram DM 161*	14		12
20 Aug 83	**BLUE WORLD** *Threshold TH 30*	35		5
25 Jun 88	**I KNOW YOU'RE OUT THERE SOMEWHERE** *Polydor POSP 921*	52		4

MICHAEL MOOG
US, male producer (Shivaun Gaines) **3**

Date	Title / Label	Peak Position	Weeks at No.1	Weeks on Chart
11 Dec 99	**THAT SOUND** *ffrr FCD 374*	32		2
25 Aug 01	**YOU BELONG TO ME** *Strictly Rhythm SRUKECD 04*	62		1

MOOGWAI
Switzerland, male producer (Francois Chabloz) **2**

Date	Title / Label	Peak Position	Weeks at No.1	Weeks on Chart
6 May 00	**VIOLA** *Platipus PLATCD 71*	55		1
26 May 01	**THE LABYRINTH** *Platipus PLATCD 83*	68		1

MOONEY SUZUKI
US, male vocal/instrumental group **2**

Date	Title / Label	Peak Position	Weeks at No.1	Weeks on Chart
29 Jan 05	**ALIVE AND AMPLIFIED** *Columbia SAMMY006*	38		2

MOONMAN
Holland, male DJ/producer (Ferry Corsten). See Albion, Gouryella, Starparty, System F, Veracocha **4**

Date	Title / Label	Peak Position	Weeks at No.1	Weeks on Chart
9 Aug 97	**DON'T BE AFRAID** *Heat Recordings HEATCD 009*	60		1
27 Nov 99	**DON'T BE AFRAID '99 (REMIX)** *Heat Recordings HEATCD 022*	41		2
7 Oct 00	**GALAXIA** *Heat Recordings HEATCD 025* FEATURING CHANTAL	50		1

MOONTREKKERS
UK, male instrumental group **1**

Date	Title / Label	Peak Position	Weeks at No.1	Weeks on Chart
2 Nov 61	**NIGHT OF THE VAMPIRE** *Parlophone R 4814*	50		1

MOONY
Italy, female vocalist (Monica Bragato). See DB Boulevard **9**

Date	Title / Label	Peak Position	Weeks at No.1	Weeks on Chart
15 Jun 02	**DOVE (I'LL BE LOVING YOU)** *Positiva/Cream CDMNY1*	9		8
1 Mar 03	**ACROBATS (LOOKING FOR BALANCE)** *WEA 363CD*	64		1

CHANTE MOORE
US, female vocalist **11**

Date	Title / Label	Peak Position	Weeks at No.1	Weeks on Chart
20 Mar 93	**LOVE'S TAKEN OVER** *MCA MCSTD 1744*	54		3
4 Mar 95	**FREE/SAIL ON** *MCA MCSTD 2042*	69		1
7 Apr 01	**STRAIGHT UP** *MCA MCSTD 40250*	11		7

DOROTHY MOORE
US, female vocalist **24**

Date	Title / Label	Peak Position	Weeks at No.1	Weeks on Chart
19 Jun 76	**MISTY BLUE** *Contempo CS 2087* ●	5		12
16 Oct 76	**FUNNY HOW TIME SLIPS AWAY** *Contempo CS 2092*	38		3
15 Oct 77	**I BELIEVE YOU** *Epic EPC 5573*	20		9

GARY MOORE
UK, male vocalist/guitarist. See One World Project, Thin Lizzy **103**

Date	Title / Label	Peak Position	Weeks at No.1	Weeks on Chart
21 Apr 79	**PARISIENNE WALKWAYS** *MCA 419* ●	8		11
21 Jan 84	**HOLD ON TO LOVE** *10 TEN 13*	65		3
11 Aug 84	**EMPTY ROOMS** *10 TEN 25*	51		5
18 May 85	**OUT IN THE FIELDS** *10 TEN 49* & PHIL LYNOTT	5		10
27 Jul 85	**EMPTY ROOMS** *10 TEN 58*	23		8
20 Dec 86	**OVER THE HILLS AND FAR AWAY** *10 TEN 134*	20		8
28 Feb 87	**WILD FRONTIER** *10 TEN 159*	35		5
9 May 87	**FRIDAY ON MY MIND** *10 TEN 164*	26		6
29 Aug 87	**THE LONER** *10 TEN 178*	53		5
5 Dec 87	**TAKE A LITTLE TIME (DOUBLE SINGLE)** *10 TEN 190*	75		1
14 Jan 89	**AFTER THE WAR** *Virgin GMS 1*	37		4
18 Mar 89	**READY FOR LOVE** *Virgin GMS 2*	56		2
24 Mar 90	**OH PRETTY WOMAN** *Virgin VS 1233* FEATURING ALBERT KING	48		3
12 May 90	**STILL GOT THE BLUES (FOR YOU)** *Virgin VS 1267*	31		7
18 Aug 90	**WALKING BY MYSELF** *Virgin VS 1281*	48		5
15 Dec 90	**TOO TIRED** *Virgin VS 1306*	71		1
22 Feb 92	**COLD DAY IN HELL** *Virgin VS 1393*	24		5
9 May 92	**STORY OF THE BLUES** *Virgin VS 1412*	40		4
18 Jul 92	**SINCE I MET YOU BABY** *Virgin VS 1423* & B.B. KING	59		3
24 Oct 92	**SEPARATE WAYS** *Virgin VS 1437*	59		1
8 May 93	**PARISIENNE WALKWAYS** *Virgin VSCDX 1456*	32		4
17 Jun 95	**NEED YOUR LOVE SO BAD** *Virgin VSCDG 1546*	48		2

JACKIE MOORE
US, female vocalist **5**

Date	Title / Label	Peak Position	Weeks at No.1	Weeks on Chart
15 Sep 79	**THIS TIME BABY** *CBS 7722*	49		5

MANDY MOORE
US, female vocalist/actor/fashion designer (Amanda Moore) **18**

Date	Title / Label	Peak Position	Weeks at No.1	Weeks on Chart
6 May 00	**CANDY** *Epic 6693452*	6		13
19 Aug 00	**I WANNA BE WITH YOU** *Epic 6695922*	21		5

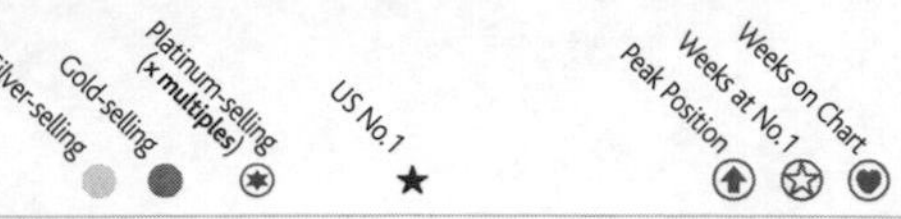

MELBA MOORE
US, female vocalist (Melba Hill) — 29

Date	Title / Label	Peak	Wks at No.1	Wks on Chart
15 May 76	**THIS IS IT** *Buddah BDS 443*	9		8
26 May 79	**PICK ME UP I'LL DANCE** *Epic EPC 7234*	48		5
9 Oct 82	**LOVE'S COMIN' AT YA** *EMI America EA 146*	15		8
15 Jan 83	**MIND UP TONIGHT** *Capitol CL 272*	22		6
5 Mar 83	**UNDERLOVE** *Capitol CL 281*	60		2

RAY MOORE
UK, male vocalist/radio presenter, d. 11 Jan 1989 (age 47) — 9

Date	Title / Label	Peak	Wks at No.1	Wks on Chart
29 Nov 86	**O' MY FATHER HAD A RABBIT** *Play 213*	24		7
5 Dec 87	**BOG EYED JOG** *Play 224*	61		2

SAM MOORE & LOU REED
US, male vocal duo. See Lou Reed, Sam & Dave — 10

Date	Title / Label	Peak	Wks at No.1	Wks on Chart
17 Jan 87	**SOUL MAN** *A&M AM 364*	30		10

TINA MOORE
US, female vocalist — 18

Date	Title / Label	Peak	Wks at No.1	Wks on Chart
30 Aug 97	**NEVER GONNA LET YOU GO** *Delirious 74321511052* ●	7		15
25 Apr 98	**NOBODY BETTER** *Delirious 74321571612*	20		3

LISA MOORISH
UK, female vocalist (Lisa Morrish). See Fat Les, Kill City — 11

Date	Title / Label	Peak	Wks at No.1	Wks on Chart
7 Jan 95	**JUST THE WAY IT IS** *Go! Beat GODCD 123*	42		3
19 Aug 95	**I'M YOUR MAN** *Go! Beat GODCD 128*	24		3
3 Feb 96	**MR FRIDAY NIGHT** *Go! Beat GODCD 137*	24		3
18 May 96	**LOVE FOR LIFE** *Go! Beat GODCD 145*	37		2

M.O.P.
US, male rap duo – Jamal Grinnage & Eric Murry — 20

Date	Title / Label	Peak	Wks at No.1	Wks on Chart
12 May 01	**COLD AS ICE** *Epic 6711762*	4		10
18 Aug 01	**ANTE UP** *Epic 6717882* FEATURING BUSTA RHYMES	7		8
1 Dec 01	**STAND CLEAR** *Chrysalis CDEM 597* ADAM F FEATURING M.O.P.	43		1
8 Jun 02	**STAND CLEAR** *Kaos KAOSCD 002* ADAM F FEATURING M.O.P.	50		1

ANGEL MORAES
US, male DJ/producer — 2

Date	Title / Label	Peak	Wks at No.1	Wks on Chart
16 Nov 96	**HEAVEN KNOWS – DEEP DEEP DOWN** *ffrr FCD 282*	72		1
17 May 97	**I LIKE IT** *AM:PM 5871792*	70		1

DAVID MORALES
US, male DJ/producer — 22

Date	Title / Label	Peak	Wks at No.1	Wks on Chart
10 Jul 93	**GIMME LUV (EENIE MEENIE MINY MO)** *Mercury MERCD 390* & THE BAD YARD CLUB	37		3
20 Nov 93	**THE PROGRAM** *Mercury MERCD 396*	66		1
24 Aug 96	**IN DE GHETTO** *Manifesto FESCD 12* & THE BAD YARD CLUB FEATURING CRYSTAL WATERS & DELTA	35		2
15 Aug 98	**NEEDIN' YOU** *Manifesto FESCD 46* PRESENTS THE FACE	8		8
24 Jun 00	**HIGHER** *Azuli AZNYCDX 120* & ALBERT CABRERA PRESENT MOCA FEATURING DEANNA	41		2
20 Jan 01	**NEEDIN' U II (REMIX)** *Manifesto FESCD 78* PRESENTS THE FACE FEATURING JULIET ROBERTS	11		5
2 Oct 04	**HOW WOULD U FEEL** *DMI DM102* FEATURING LEA LORIEN	71		1

MORCHEEBA
UK, female/male vocal/instrumental group — 14

Date	Title / Label	Peak	Wks at No.1	Wks on Chart
13 Jul 96	**TAPE LOOP** *Indochina ID 045CD*	42		1
5 Oct 96	**TRIGGER HIPPIE** *Indochina ID 052CDR*	40		2
15 Feb 97	**THE MUSIC THAT WE HEAR (MOOG ISLAND)** *Indochina ID 054CD*	47		1
11 Oct 97	**SHOULDER HOLSTER** *Indochina ID 064CD*	53		1
11 Apr 98	**BLINDFOLD** *Indochina ID 070CD*	56		1
20 Jun 98	**LET ME SEE** *Indochina ID 076CD*	46		1
29 Aug 98	**PART OF THE PROCESS** *China WOKCD 2097*	38		2
5 Aug 00	**ROME WASN'T BUILT IN A DAY** *East West EW 214CD*	34		3
31 Mar 01	**WORLD LOOKING IN** *East West EW 225CD*	48		1
6 Jul 02	**OTHERWISE** *East West EW 247CD*	64		1

MORE
UK, male vocal/instrumental group — 2

Date	Title / Label	Peak	Wks at No.1	Wks on Chart
14 Mar 81	**WE ARE THE BAND** *Atlantic K 11561*	59		2

MORE FIRE CREW
UK, male vocal/rap/production trio. See Lethal Bizzle — 10

Date	Title / Label	Peak	Wks at No.1	Wks on Chart
16 Mar 02	**OI** *Go! Beat GOBCD 48* PLATINUM 45 FEATURING MORE FIRE CREW	8		8
25 Jan 03	**BACK THEN** *Go! Beat GOBCD 54*	45		2

MOREL
US, male vocalist/producer (Richard Morel) — 1

Date	Title / Label	Peak	Wks at No.1	Wks on Chart
12 Aug 00	**TRUE (THE FAGGOT IS YOU)** *Hooj Choons HOOJ 097CD*	64		1

GEORGE MOREL FEATURING HEATHER WILDMAN
US, male/female vocal/instrumental duo — 2

Date	Title / Label	Peak	Wks at No.1	Wks on Chart
26 Oct 96	**LET'S GROOVE** *Positiva CDTIV 62*	42		2

MORGAN
UK, male vocal/instrumental duo — 1

Date	Title / Label	Peak	Wks at No.1	Wks on Chart
27 Nov 99	**MISS PARKER** *Source CDSOUR 002*	74		1

DEBELAH MORGAN
US, female vocalist — 9

Date	Title / Label	Peak	Wks at No.1	Wks on Chart
24 Feb 01	**DANCE WITH ME** *Atlantic AT 0087CD*	10		9

DERRICK MORGAN
Jamaica, male vocalist — 1

Date	Title / Label	Peak	Wks at No.1	Wks on Chart
17 Jan 70	**MOON HOP** *Crab 32*	49		1

JAMIE J MORGAN
US, male vocalist — 6

Date	Title / Label	Peak	Wks at No.1	Wks on Chart
10 Feb 90	**WALK ON THE WILD SIDE** *Tabu 6555967*	27		6

JANE MORGAN
US, female vocalist (Florence Currier) — 22

Date	Title / Label	Peak	Wks at No.1	Wks on Chart
5 Dec 58	**THE DAY THE RAINS CAME** *London HLR 8751*	1	1	16
22 May 59	**IF ONLY I COULD LIVE MY LIFE AGAIN** *London HLR 8810*	27		1
21 Jul 60	**ROMANTICA** *London HLR 9120*	39		5

MELI'SA MORGAN
US, female vocalist — 7

Date	Title / Label	Peak	Wks at No.1	Wks on Chart
9 Aug 86	**FOOL'S PARADISE** *Capitol CL 415*	41		5
25 Jun 88	**GOOD LOVE** *Capitol CL 483*	59		2

RAY MORGAN
UK, male vocalist — 6

Date	Title / Label	Peak	Wks at No.1	Wks on Chart
25 Jul 70	**THE LONG AND WINDING ROAD** *B&C CB 128*	32		6

ERICK MORILLO
US, male DJ/producer/instrumentalist. See Lil Mo' Yin Yang, Pianoheadz, Real To Reel — 4

Date	Title / Label	Peak	Wks at No.1	Wks on Chart
4 Feb 95	**HIGHER (FEEL IT)** *A&M 5809412* ERICK 'MORE' MORILLO PRESENTS RAW	74		1
26 Jun 04	**BREAK DOWN THE DOORS** *Subliminal SUB124CD* MORILLO FEATURING THE AUDIOBULLYS	44		2
12 Feb 05	**WHAT DO YOU WANT?** *Subliminal SUB138CD* MORILLO FEATURING TERRA DEVA	61		1

ALANIS MORISSETTE
Canada, female vocalist/multi-instrumentalist/producer — 58

Date	Title / Label	Peak	Wks at No.1	Wks on Chart
5 Aug 95	**YOU OUGHTA KNOW** *Maverick W 0307CD*	22		7
28 Oct 95	**HAND IN MY POCKET** *Maverick W 0312CD1*	26		3
24 Feb 96	**YOU LEARN** *Maverick W 0334CD*	24		4
20 Apr 96	**IRONIC** *Maverick W 0343CD*	11		9
3 Aug 96	**HEAD OVER FEET** *Maverick W 0355CD*	7		7

Date	Title	Peak Position	Weeks at No.1	Weeks on Chart
7 Dec 96	**ALL I REALLY WANT** *Maverick W 0382CD*	59		1
31 Oct 98	**THANK U** *Maverick W 0458CD*	5		10
13 Mar 99	**JOINING YOU** *Maverick W 472CD*	28		2
31 Jul 99	**SO PURE** *Maverick W 492CD1*	38		2
2 Mar 02	**HANDS CLEAN** *Maverick W 574CD*	12		7
17 Aug 02	**PRECIOUS ILLUSIONS** *Maverick W 582CD*	53		1
22 May 04	**EVERYTHING** *Maverick W 641CD*	22		3
31 Jul 04	**OUT IS THROUGH** *Maverick W 647CD*	56		1
12 Nov 05	**CRAZY** *Maverick W694CD1*	65		1

MORJAC FEATURING RAZ CONWAY

Denmark, male vocal/production trio — **2**

Date	Title	Peak Position	Weeks at No.1	Weeks on Chart
11 Oct 03	**STARS** *Credence CDCRED 036*	38		2

MORNING RUNNER

UK, male vocal/instrumental group — **8**

Date	Title	Peak Position	Weeks at No.1	Weeks on Chart
4 Jun 05	**DRAWING SHAPES EP** *Parlophone CDR6666*	70		1
13 Aug 05	**GONE UP IN FLAMES** *Parlophone CDRS6669*	39		2
5 Nov 05	**BE ALL YOU WANT ME TO BE** *Parlophone CDR6674*	44		1
4 Mar 06	**BURNING BENCHES** *Parlophone CDRS6683*	19		3
27 May 06	**THE GREAT ESCAPE** *Parlophone CDRS6696*	56		1

GIORGIO MORODER

Italy, male producer/synthesiser player — **36**

Date	Title	Peak Position	Weeks at No.1	Weeks on Chart
24 Sep 77	**FROM HERE TO ETERNITY** *Oasis 1* GIORGIO	16		10
17 Mar 79	**CHASE** *Casablanca CAN 144*	48		6
22 Sep 84	**TOGETHER IN ELECTRIC DREAMS** *Virgin VS 713* & PHIL OAKEY ●	3		13
29 Jun 85	**GOODYBYE BAD TIMES** *Virgin VS 772* & PHIL OAKEY	44		5
11 Jul 98	**CARRY ON** *Almighty CDALMY 120* DONNA SUMMER & GIORGIO MORODER	65		1
12 Feb 00	**THE CHASE** *Logic 74321732112* DJ EMPIRE PRESENTS GIORGIO MORODER	46		1

ENNIO MORRICONE

Italy, male conductor/composer — **12**

Date	Title	Peak Position	Weeks at No.1	Weeks on Chart
11 Apr 81	**CHI MAI (THEME FROM THE TV SERIES THE LIFE AND TIMES OF DAVID LLOYD GEORGE)** *BBC RESL 92* ●	2		12

JAMES MORRISON

UK, male vocalist/guitarist. See Helping Haiti — **93**

Date	Title	Peak Position	Weeks at No.1	Weeks on Chart
22 Jul 06	**YOU GIVE ME SOMETHING** *Polydor 9858670*	5		17
21 Oct 06	**WONDERFUL WORLD** *Polydor 1709432*	8		19
23 Dec 06	**THE PIECES DON'T FIT ANYMORE** *Polydor 1717533*	30		7
24 Mar 07	**UNDISCOVERED** *Polydor GBUM70600846*	63		3
4 Oct 08	**YOU MAKE IT REAL** *Polydor 1783983*	7		7
29 Nov 08	**BROKEN STRINGS** *Polydor 1792152* FEATURING NELLY FURTADO ●	2		31
4 Apr 09	**PLEASE DON'T STOP THE RAIN** *Polydor GBUM70810072*	33		9

MARK MORRISON

UK, male vocalist (Abdul Rahman) — **70**

Date	Title	Peak Position	Weeks at No.1	Weeks on Chart
22 Apr 95	**CRAZY** *WEA YZ 907CD*	19		4
16 Sep 95	**LET'S GET DOWN** *WEA 001CD*	39		2
16 Mar 96	**RETURN OF THE MACK** *WEA 040CD* ⊛	1	2	24
27 Jul 96	**CRAZY (REMIX)** *WEA 054CD1*	6		9
19 Oct 96	**TRIPPIN'** *WEA 079CD1*	8		6
21 Dec 96	**HORNY** *WEA 090CD1*	5		9
15 Mar 97	**MOAN AND GROAN** *WEA 096CD1*	7		6
20 Sep 97	**WHO'S THE MACK** *WEA 128CD1*	13		5
4 Sep 99	**BEST FRIEND** *WEA 221CD1* & CONNOR REEVES	23		3
14 Aug 04	**JUST A MAN/BACKSTABBERS** *2 Wikid WKDCD007*	48		1
22 Apr 06	**INNOCENT MAN** *Mona MONASP5CDS* FEATURING DMX	46		1

VAN MORRISON

Ireland, male vocalist/guitarist. See Them — **21**

Date	Title	Peak Position	Weeks at No.1	Weeks on Chart
20 Oct 79	**BRIGHT SIDE OF THE ROAD** *Mercury 6001 121*	63		3
1 Jul 89	**HAVE I TOLD YOU LATELY** *Polydor VANS 1*	74		1
9 Dec 89	**WHENEVER GOD SHINES HIS LIGHT** *Polydor VANS 2* WITH CLIFF RICHARD	20		6
15 May 93	**GLORIA** *Exile VANCD 11* & JOHN LEE HOOKER	31		3
18 Mar 95	**HAVE I TOLD YOU LATELY THAT I LOVE YOU** *RCA 74321271702* CHIEFTAINS WITH VAN MORRISON	71		1
10 Jun 95	**DAYS LIKE THIS** *Exile VANCD 12*	65		1
2 Dec 95	**NO RELIGION** *Exile 5775792*	54		1
1 Mar 97	**THE HEALING GAME** *Exile 5733912*	46		1
6 Mar 99	**PRECIOUS TIME** *Pointblank POBDX 14*	36		2
22 May 99	**BACK ON TOP** *Exile/Pointblank/Virgin POBD 15*	69		1
18 May 02	**HEY MR DJ** *Exile 5705962*	58		1

MORRISSEY

UK, male vocalist (Steven Morrissey). See Smiths — **114**

Date	Title	Peak Position	Weeks at No.1	Weeks on Chart
27 Feb 88	**SUEDEHEAD** *HMV POP 1618*	5		6
11 Jun 88	**EVERYDAY IS LIKE SUNDAY** *HMV POP 1619*	9		6
11 Feb 89	**LAST OF THE FAMOUS INTERNATIONAL PLAYBOYS** *HMV POP 1620*	6		5
29 Apr 89	**INTERESTING DRUG** *HMV POP 1621*	9		4
25 Nov 89	**OUIJA BOARD OUIJA BOARD** *HMV POP 1622*	18		4
5 May 90	**NOVEMBER SPAWNED A MONSTER** *HMV POP 1623*	12		4
20 Oct 90	**PICCADILLY PALARE** *HMV POP 1624*	18		2
23 Feb 91	**OUR FRANK** *HMV POP 1625*	26		3
13 Apr 91	**SING YOUR LIFE** *HMV POP 1626*	33		2
27 Jul 91	**PREGNANT FOR THE LAST TIME** *HMV POP 1627*	25		4
12 Oct 91	**MY LOVE LIFE** *HMV POP 1628*	29		2
9 May 92	**WE HATE IT WHEN OUR FRIENDS BECOME SUCCESSFUL** *HMV POP 1629*	17		3
18 Jul 92	**YOU'RE THE ONE FOR ME, FATTY** *HMV POP 1630*	19		3
19 Dec 92	**CERTAIN PEOPLE I KNOW** *HMV POP 1631*	35		4
12 Mar 94	**THE MORE YOU IGNORE ME THE CLOSER I GET** *Parlophone CDR 6372*	8		3
11 Jun 94	**HOLD ON TO YOUR FRIENDS** *Parlophone CDR 6383*	47		2
20 Aug 94	**INTERLUDE** *Parlophone CDR 6365* & SIOUXSIE	25		2
28 Jan 95	**BOXERS** *Parlophone CDR 6400*	23		3
2 Sep 95	**DAGENHAM DAVE** *RCA Victor 74321299802*	26		2
9 Dec 95	**THE BOY RACER** *RCA Victor 74321332952*	36		2
23 Dec 95	**SUNNY** *Parlophone CDR 6243*	42		2
2 Aug 97	**ALMA MATTERS** *Island CID 667*	16		3
18 Oct 97	**ROY'S KEEN** *Island CID 671*	42		1
10 Jan 98	**SATAN REJECTED MY SOUL** *Island CID 686*	39		2
22 May 04	**IRISH BLOOD ENGLISH HEART** *Attack ATKXS002*	3		5
24 Jul 04	**FIRST OF THE GANG TO DIE** *Attack ATKXS003*	6		7
23 Oct 04	**LET ME KISS YOU** *Attack ATKXS008*	8		3
25 Dec 04	**I HAVE FORGIVEN JESUS** *Attack ATKXS011*	10		5
9 Apr 05	**REDONDO BEACH/THERE IS A LIGHT THAT NEVER GOES OUT** *Attack ATKXD015*	11		4
8 Apr 06	**YOU HAVE KILLED ME** *Attack ATKXS017*	3		4
17 Jun 06	**THE YOUNGEST WAS THE MOST LOVED** *Attack ATKXS018*	14		2
2 Sep 06	**IN THE FUTURE WHEN ALL'S WELL** *Attack ATKXS021*	17		2
16 Dec 06	**I JUST WANT TO SEE THE BOY HAPPY** *Attack ATKXD023*	16		2
16 Feb 08	**THAT'S HOW PEOPLE GROW UP** *Decca 4780362*	14		2
14 Jun 08	**ALL YOU NEED IS ME** *Decca 4780963*	24		1
21 Feb 09	**I'M THROWING MY ARMS AROUND PARIS** *Decca F20008*	21		2
9 May 09	**SOMETHING IS SQUEEZING MY SKULL** *Polydor 4781875*	46		1

BUDDY MORROW

US, male orchestra leader (Muni Zudecoff) — **1**

Date	Title	Peak Position	Weeks at No.1	Weeks on Chart
20 Mar 53	**NIGHT TRAIN** *HMV B 10347*	12		1

BOB MORTIMER

UK, male comedian/vocalist — **9**

Date	Title	Peak Position	Weeks at No.1	Weeks on Chart
8 Jul 95	**I'M A BELIEVER** *Parlophone CDR 6412* EMF/REEVES & MORTIMER	3		8
24 May 97	**LET'S DANCE** *Magnet EW 112CD* MIDDLESBROUGH FC FEATURING BOB MORTIMER & CHRIS REA	44		1

MORTIIS

Norway, male vocal/instrumental group — **2**

Date	Title	Peak Position	Weeks at No.1	Weeks on Chart
28 Aug 04	**THE GRUDGE** *Earache MOSH284CD*	51		1
7 May 05	**DECADENT & DESPERATE** *Earache MOSH306CD*	49		1

MOS DEF

US, male rapper (Dante Smith) — **6**

Date	Title	Peak Position	Weeks at No.1	Weeks on Chart
24 Jun 00	**UMI SAYS** *Rawkus RWK 232CD*	60		1
4 Nov 00	**MISS FAT BOOTY – PART II** *Rawkus RWK 282CD* FEATURING GHOSTFACE KILLAH	64		1
3 Feb 01	**OH NO** *Rawkus RWK 302* & NATE DOGG FEATURING PHAROAHE MONCH	24		4

MICKIE MOST

UK, male vocalist/producer (Michael Haye), d. 30 May 2003 (age 64) — **1**

Date	Title	Peak Position	Weeks at No.1	Weeks on Chart
25 Jul 63	**MISTER PORTER** *Decca F 11664*	45		1

Silver-selling ○ Gold-selling ● Platinum-selling (x multiples) US No.1 ★ Peak Position · Weeks at No.1 · Weeks on Chart

MOTELS
US, female/male vocal/instrumental group — 7

Date	Title	Peak	Wks No.1	Wks
11 Oct 80	**WHOSE PROBLEM?** *Capitol CL 16162*	42		4
10 Jan 81	**DAYS ARE O.K.** *Capitol CL 16149*	41		3

WENDY MOTEN
US, female vocalist — 13

Date	Title	Peak	Wks No.1	Wks
5 Feb 94	**COME IN OUT OF THE RAIN** *EMI-USA CDMT 105*	8		9
14 May 94	**SO CLOSE TO LOVE** *EMI-USA CDMTS 106*	35		4

MOTHER
UK, male production duo — 4

Date	Title	Peak	Wks No.1	Wks
12 Jun 93	**ALL FUNKED UP** *Bosting BYSNCD 101*	34		2
1 Oct 94	**GET BACK** *Six6 SIXT 119*	73		1
31 Aug 96	**ALL FUNKED UP (REMIX)** *Six6 SIXXCD 1*	66		1

MOTHER'S PRIDE
UK, male DJ/production duo — 2

Date	Title	Peak	Wks No.1	Wks
21 Mar 98	**FLORIBUNDA** *Heat Recordings HEATCD 013*	42		1
6 Nov 99	**LEARNING TO FLY** *Devolution DEVR 001CDS*	54		1

MOTIV 8
UK, male producer (Steve Rodway) — 11

Date	Title	Peak	Wks No.1	Wks
17 Jul 93	**ROCKIN' FOR MYSELF** *Nuff Respect NUFF 002CD* FEATURING ANGIE BROWN	67		1
7 May 94	**ROCKIN' FOR MYSELF** *WEA YZ 814CD*	18		4
21 Oct 95	**BREAK THE CHAIN** *Eternal 010CD*	31		2
23 Dec 95	**SEARCHING FOR THE GOLDEN EYE** *Eternal 027CD* & KYM MAZELLE	40		3
19 Feb 05	**RIDING ON THE WINGS** *Concept CDCON52X*	44		1

MOTIVATION
Holland, male producer (Francis Louwers) — 1

Date	Title	Peak	Wks No.1	Wks
17 Nov 01	**PARA MI** *Definitive CDDEF 1*	71		1

MOTLEY CRUE
US, male vocal/instrumental group — 29

Date	Title	Peak	Wks No.1	Wks
24 Aug 85	**SMOKIN' IN THE BOYS ROOM** *Elektra EKR 16*	71		2
8 Feb 86	**HOME SWEET HOME/SMOKIN' IN THE BOYS' ROOM** *Elektra EKR 33*	51		3
1 Aug 87	**GIRLS GIRLS GIRLS** *Elektra EKR 59*	26		6
16 Jan 88	**YOU'RE ALL I NEED/WILD SIDE** *Elektra EKR 65*	23		4
4 Nov 89	**DR FEELGOOD** *Elektra EKR 97*	50		3
12 May 90	**WITHOUT YOU** *Elektra EKR 109*	39		3
7 Sep 91	**PRIMAL SCREAM** *Elektra EKR 133*	32		2
11 Jan 92	**HOME SWEET HOME** *Elektra EKR 136*	37		2
5 Mar 94	**HOOLIGAN'S HOLIDAY** *Elektra EKR 180CDX*	36		2
19 Jul 97	**AFRAID** *Elektra E 3936 CD1*	58		1
4 Jun 05	**IF I DIE TOMORROW** *Mercury 9871754*	63		1

MOTORCYCLE
US, male/female vocal/production trio — 9

Date	Title	Peak	Wks No.1	Wks
17 Jan 04	**AS THE RUSH COMES** *Positiva CDTIVS 203*	11		9

MOTORHEAD
UK, male vocal/instrumental group – Ian 'Lemmy' Kilmister, Eddie Clarke, Phil Taylor & Larry Wallis — 81

Date	Title	Peak	Wks No.1	Wks
16 Sep 78	**LOUIE LOUIE** *Bronze BRO 60*	68		2
10 Mar 79	**OVERKILL** *Bronze BRO 67*	39		7
30 Jun 79	**NO CLASS** *Bronze BRO 78*	61		4
1 Dec 79	**BOMBER** *Bronze BRO 85*	34		7
3 May 80	**THE GOLDEN YEARS EP** *Bronze BRO 92*	8		7
1 Nov 80	**ACE OF SPADES** *Bronze BRO 106*	15		12
22 Nov 80	**BEER DRINKERS AND HELL RAISERS** *Big Beat SWT 61*	43		4
21 Feb 81	**ST VALENTINE'S DAY MASSACRE EP** *Bronze BRO 116* & GIRLSCHOOL ○	5		8
11 Jul 81	**MOTORHEAD LIVE** *Bronze BRO 124*	6		7
3 Apr 82	**IRON FIST** *Bronze BRO 146*	29		5
21 May 83	**I GOT MINE** *Bronze BRO 165*	46		2
30 Jul 83	**SHINE** *Bronze BRO 167*	59		2
1 Sep 84	**KILLED BY DEATH** *Bronze BRO 185*	51		2
5 Jul 86	**DEAF FOREVER** *GWR 2*	67		1
5 Jan 91	**THE ONE TO SING THE BLUES** *Epic 6565787*	45		3
14 Nov 92	**92 TOUR (EP)** *Epic 6588096*	63		1
11 Sep 93	**ACE OF SPADES** *WGAF CDWGAF 101*	23		5
10 Dec 94	**BORN TO RAISE HELL** *Fox 74321230152* MOTORHEAD/ICE-T/WHITFIELD CRANE	47		2

MOTORS
UK, male vocal/instrumental group – Nick Garvey, Rob Hendry (replaced by Peter Bramall), Andy McMaster & Ricky Wenham — 29

Date	Title	Peak	Wks No.1	Wks
24 Sep 77	**DANCING THE NIGHT AWAY** *Virgin VS 186*	42		4
10 Jun 78	**AIRPORT** *Virgin VS 219* ○	4		13
19 Aug 78	**FORGET ABOUT YOU** *Virgin VS 222*	13		9
12 Apr 80	**LOVE AND LONELINESS** *Virgin VS 263*	58		3

MOTT THE HOOPLE
UK, male vocal/instrumental group – Ian Hunter*, Dale Griffin, Mick Ralphs & Pete Watts — 55

Date	Title	Peak	Wks No.1	Wks
12 Aug 72	**ALL THE YOUNG DUDES** *CBS 8271*	3		11
16 Jun 73	**HONALOOCHIE BOOGIE** *CBS 1530*	12		9
8 Sep 73	**ALL THE WAY FROM MEMPHIS** *CBS 1764*	10		8
24 Nov 73	**ROLL AWAY THE STONE** *CBS 1895*	8		12
30 Mar 74	**GOLDEN AGE OF ROCK AND ROLL** *CBS 2177*	16		7
22 Jun 74	**FOXY FOXY** *CBS 2439*	33		5
2 Nov 74	**SATURDAY GIGS** *CBS 2754*	41		3

MOUNT RUSHMORE PRESENTS THE KNACK
UK, male/female vocal/production trio — 1

Date	Title	Peak	Wks No.1	Wks
3 Apr 99	**YOU BETTER** *Universal MCSTD 40192*	53		1

NANA MOUSKOURI
Greece, female vocalist (Ioanna Mouschouri) — 11

Date	Title	Peak	Wks No.1	Wks
11 Jan 86	**ONLY LOVE** *Philips PH 38*	2		11

MOUSSE T
Germany, male DJ/producer (Mustafa Gundogdu) — 49

Date	Title	Peak	Wks No.1	Wks
6 Jun 98	**HORNY** *AM:PM 5826712* VERSUS HOT 'N' JUICY ●	2		17
20 May 00	**SEX BOMB** *Gut CXGUT 33* TOM JONES & MOUSSE T	3		10
10 Aug 02	**FIRE** *Serious SERR 44CDX* FEATURING EMMA LANFORD	58		1
4 Sep 04	**IS IT COS I'M COOL?** *Free 2 Air F2A1CDX* FEATURING EMMA LANFORD	9		11
18 Dec 04	**RIGHT ABOUT NOW** *Free2Air F2A2CDX* FEATURING EMMA LANFORD	28		5
12 Aug 06	**HORNY AS A DANDY** *Feverpitch/Free2air CDFEV14* VS DANDY WARHOLS	17		5

MOUTH & MACNEAL
Holland, male/female vocal duo – Willem Duyn, d. 3 Dec 2004, & Sjourkje Van't Spijker — 10

Date	Title	Peak	Wks No.1	Wks
4 May 74	**I SEE A STAR** *Decca F 13504*	8		10

MOVE
UK, male vocal/instrumental group – Roy Wood*, Bev Bevan, Trevor Burton (replaced by Rick Price), Christopher Kefford & Carl Wayne, d. 31 Aug 2004 (replaced by Jeff Lynne*) — 110

Date	Title	Peak	Wks No.1	Wks
5 Jan 67	**NIGHT OF FEAR** *Deram DM 109*	2		10
6 Apr 67	**I CAN HEAR THE GRASS GROW** *Deram DM 117*	5		10
6 Sep 67	**FLOWERS IN THE RAIN** *Regal Zonophone RZ 3001*	2		13
7 Feb 68	**FIRE BRIGADE** *Regal Zonophone RZ 3005*	3		11
25 Dec 68	**BLACKBERRY WAY** *Regal Zonophone RZ 3015*	1	1	12
23 Jul 69	**CURLY** *Regal Zonophone RZ 3021*	12		12
25 Apr 70	**BRONTOSAURUS** *Regal Zonophone RZ 3026*	7		10
3 Jul 71	**TONIGHT** *Harvest HAR 5038*	11		10
23 Oct 71	**CHINATOWN** *Harvest HAR 5043*	23		8
13 May 72	**CALIFORNIA MAN** *Harvest HAR 5050*	7		14

MOVEMENT
US, male production/rap trio — 2

Date	Title	Peak	Wks No.1	Wks
24 Oct 92	**JUMP!** *Arista 74321116677*	57		2

MOVEMENT 98 FEATURING CARROLL THOMPSON
UK, male production trio & female vocalist — 8

Date	Title	Peak	Wks No.1	Wks
19 May 90	**JOY AND HEARTBREAK** *Circa YR 45*	27		5
15 Sep 90	**SUNRISE** *Circa YR 51*	58		3

MOVIN' MELODIES PRODUCTION
Holland, male producer (Patrick Prins). See Artemesia, Ethics, Subliminal Cuts — Weeks on Chart: 3

Date	Title / Label	Peak Position	Weeks at No.1	Weeks on Chart
22 Oct 94	**LA LUNA** *Effective EFFS 017CD*	64		1
29 Jun 96	**INDICA** *Hooj Choons HOOJCD 44* MOVIN' MELODIES	62		1
26 Jul 97	**ROLLERBLADE** *Movin' Melodies 5822352* MOVIN' MELODIES	71		1

ALISON MOYET
UK, female vocalist (Geneviève Alison Moyet). See Yazoo — Weeks on Chart: 107

Date	Title / Label	Peak Position	Weeks at No.1	Weeks on Chart
23 Jun 84	**LOVE RESURRECTION** *CBS A 4497*	10		11
13 Oct 84	**ALL CRIED OUT** *CBS A 4757* ○	8		11
1 Dec 84	**INVISIBLE** *CBS A 4930*	21		10
16 Mar 85	**THAT OLE DEVIL CALLED LOVE** *CBS A 6044* ○	2		10
29 Nov 86	**IS THIS LOVE?** *CBS MOYET 1* ○	3		16
7 Mar 87	**WEAK IN THE PRESENCE OF BEAUTY** *CBS MOYET 2*	6		10
30 May 87	**ORDINARY GIRL** *CBS MOYET 3*	43		4
28 Nov 87	**LOVE LETTERS** *CBS MOYET 5* ○	4		10
6 Apr 91	**IT WON'T BE LONG** *Columbia 6567577*	50		4
1 Jun 91	**WISHING YOU WERE HERE** *Columbia 6569397*	72		1
12 Oct 91	**THIS HOUSE** *Columbia 6575157*	40		5
16 Oct 93	**FALLING** *Columbia 6595962*	42		3
12 Mar 94	**WHISPERING YOUR NAME** *Columbia 6601622*	18		7
28 May 94	**GETTING INTO SOMETHING** *Columbia 6603565*	51		2
22 Oct 94	**ODE TO BOY** *Columbia 6607952*	59		1
26 Aug 95	**SOLID WOOD** *Columbia 6623265*	44		2

MOZAIC
UK, female vocal group — Weeks on Chart: 7

Date	Title / Label	Peak Position	Weeks at No.1	Weeks on Chart
5 Aug 95	**SING IT (THE HALLELUJAH SONG)** *Perfecto PERF 106CD*	14		4
10 Aug 96	**RAYS OF THE RISING SUN** *Perfecto PERF 123CD*	32		2
30 Nov 96	**MOVING UP MOVING ON** *Perfecto PERF 131CD*	62		1

MPHO
South Africa, female vocalist (Mpho Skeef). See Young Soul Rebels — Weeks on Chart: 1

Date	Title / Label	Peak Position	Weeks at No.1	Weeks on Chart
1 Aug 09	**BOX N LOCKS** *Parlophone CDR6774*	49		1

JASON MRAZ
US, male vocalist/multi-instrumentalist — Weeks on Chart: 55

Date	Title / Label	Peak Position	Weeks at No.1	Weeks on Chart
13 Dec 08	**I'M YOURS** *Atlantic AT0308CD*	11		55

MS DYNAMITE
UK, female rapper/vocalist (Niomi McLean-Daley) — Weeks on Chart: 38

Date	Title / Label	Peak Position	Weeks at No.1	Weeks on Chart
23 Jun 01	**BOOO!** *ffrr FCD 399* STICKY FEATURING MS DYNAMITE	12		6
1 Jun 02	**IT TAKES MORE** *Polydor 5707982*	7		10
7 Sep 02	**DY-NA-MI-TEE** *Polydor 5709782*	5		10
14 Dec 02	**PUT HIM OUT** *Polydor 0658942*	19		6
8 Oct 05	**JUDGEMENT DAY** *Polydor 9873970*	25		3
20 Feb 10	**WILE OUT** *Zinc/Essential EAST001* ZINC FEATURING MS DYNAMITE	38		3

MSTRKRFT
Canada, male vocal/instrumental duo — Weeks on Chart: 2

Date	Title / Label	Peak Position	Weeks at No.1	Weeks on Chart
8 Aug 09	**HEARTBREAKER** *Geffen 2707368*	50		2

MTUME
US, male/female vocal/instrumental group — Weeks on Chart: 12

Date	Title / Label	Peak Position	Weeks at No.1	Weeks on Chart
14 May 83	**JUICY FRUIT** *Epic A 3424*	34		9
22 Sep 84	**PRIME TIME** *Epic A 4720*	57		3

MUD
UK, male vocal/instrumental group – Les Gray, d. 21 Feb 2004, Rob Davis, Dave Mount, d. 2 Dec 2006, & Ray Stiles — Weeks on Chart: 139

Date	Title / Label	Peak Position	Weeks at No.1	Weeks on Chart
10 Mar 73	**CRAZY** *RAK 146*	12		12
23 Jun 73	**HYPNOSIS** *RAK 152*	16		13
27 Oct 73	**DYNA-MITE** *RAK 159* ○	4		12
19 Jan 74	**TIGER FEET** *RAK 166* ●	1	4	11
13 Apr 74	**THE CAT CREPT IN** *RAK 170* ○	2		9
27 Jul 74	**ROCKET** *RAK 178*	6		9
30 Nov 74	**LONELY THIS CHRISTMAS** *RAK 187* ●	1	4	10
15 Feb 75	**THE SECRETS THAT YOU KEEP** *RAK 194* ○	3		9
26 Apr 75	**OH BOY** *RAK 201* ○	1	2	9
21 Jun 75	**MOONSHINE SALLY** *RAK 208*	10		7
2 Aug 75	**ONE NIGHT** *RAK 213*	32		4
4 Oct 75	**L-L-LUCY** *Private Stock PVT 41*	10		6
29 Nov 75	**SHOW ME YOU'RE A WOMAN** *Private Stock PVT 45*	8		8
15 May 76	**SHAKE IT DOWN** *Private Stock PVT 65*	12		8
27 Nov 76	**LEAN ON ME** *Private Stock PVT 85* ○	7		9
21 Dec 85	**LONELY THIS CHRISTMAS** *RAK 187*	61		3

MUDHONEY
US, male vocal/instrumental group — Weeks on Chart: 2

Date	Title / Label	Peak Position	Weeks at No.1	Weeks on Chart
17 Aug 91	**LET IT SLIDE** *Subpop SP 15154*	60		1
24 Oct 92	**SUCK YOU DRY** *Reprise W 0137*	65		1

MUDLARKS
UK, male/female vocal trio – Mary, Fred, d. 2007, & Jeff Mudd — Weeks on Chart: 19

Date	Title / Label	Peak Position	Weeks at No.1	Weeks on Chart
2 May 58	**LOLLIPOP** *Columbia DB 4099*	2		9
6 Jun 58	**BOOK OF LOVE** *Columbia DB 4133*	8		9
27 Feb 59	**THE LOVE GAME** *Columbia DB 4250*	30		1

IDRIS MUHAMMAD
US, male drummer (Leo Morris) — Weeks on Chart: 3

Date	Title / Label	Peak Position	Weeks at No.1	Weeks on Chart
17 Sep 77	**COULD HEAVEN EVER BE LIKE THIS** *Kudu 935*	42		3

MUKKAA
UK, male production duo. See Eye To Eye featuring Taka Boom, Umboza — Weeks on Chart: 1

Date	Title / Label	Peak Position	Weeks at No.1	Weeks on Chart
27 Feb 93	**BURUCHACCA** *Limbo 008*	74		1

MARIA MULDAUR
US, female vocalist (Maria D'Amato) — Weeks on Chart: 8

Date	Title / Label	Peak Position	Weeks at No.1	Weeks on Chart
29 Jun 74	**MIDNIGHT AT THE OASIS** *Reprise K 14331*	21		8

MULL HISTORICAL SOCIETY
UK, male vocal/instrumental group — Weeks on Chart: 7

Date	Title / Label	Peak Position	Weeks at No.1	Weeks on Chart
21 Jul 01	**ANIMAL CANNABUS** *Rough Trade RTRADESCD 021*	53		1
9 Feb 02	**WATCHING XANADU** *Blanco Y Negro NEG 138CD*	36		2
1 Mar 03	**THE FINAL ARREARS** *Blanco Y Negro NEG 144CD*	32		2
14 Jun 03	**AM I WRONG** *Blanco Y Negro NEG 146CD*	51		1
24 Jul 04	**HOW 'BOUT I LOVE YOU MORE** *B Unique BUN080CDS*	37		1

SHAWN MULLINS
US, male vocalist/guitarist — Weeks on Chart: 11

Date	Title / Label	Peak Position	Weeks at No.1	Weeks on Chart
6 Mar 99	**LULLABY** *Columbia 6669595*	9		10
2 Oct 99	**WHAT IS LIFE** *Columbia 6678212*	62		1

MULU
UK, male/female vocal/instrumental duo — Weeks on Chart: 1

Date	Title / Label	Peak Position	Weeks at No.1	Weeks on Chart
2 Aug 97	**PUSSYCAT** *Dedicated MULU 003CD1*	50		1

OMERO MUMBA
Ireland, male vocalist — Weeks on Chart: 2

Date	Title / Label	Peak Position	Weeks at No.1	Weeks on Chart
20 Jul 02	**LIL' BIG MAN** *Polydor 5708862*	42		2

SAMANTHA MUMBA
Ireland, female vocalist — Weeks on Chart: 69

Date	Title / Label	Peak Position	Weeks at No.1	Weeks on Chart
8 Jul 00	**GOTTA TELL YOU** *Wild Card 5618832*	2		12
28 Oct 00	**BODY II BODY** *Wild Card 5877752*	5		12
3 Mar 01	**ALWAYS COME BACK TO YOUR LOVE** *Wild Card 5879252* ○	3		15
22 Sep 01	**BABY COME ON OVER** *Wild Card 5872352*	5		10
22 Dec 01	**LATELY** *Wild Card 5705232*	6		12
26 Oct 02	**I'M RIGHT HERE** *Wild Card 0659372*	5		8

MUMFORD & SONS
UK, male vocal/instrumental group — Weeks on Chart: 26

Date	Title / Label	Peak Position	Weeks at No.1	Weeks on Chart
26 Sep 09	**LITTLE LION MAN** *Island GBUM70910618*	24		12
12 Dec 09	**WINTER WINDS** *Island GBUM70909076*	44		6
20 Feb 10	**THE CAVE** *Island 2733942*	32		8+

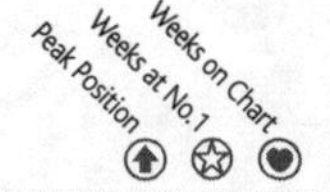

MUMM RA
UK, male vocal/instrumental group — 3

Date	Title	Peak Position	Weeks at No.1	Weeks on Chart
4 Nov 06	**OUT OF THE QUESTION** *Columbia BEXHILL06*	45		1
3 Mar 07	**WHAT WOULD STEVE DO** *Columbia BEXHILL10*	40		1
26 May 07	**SHE'S GOT YOU HIGH** *Columbia BEXHILL14*	41		1

MUNDY
Ireland, male vocalist (Edmund Enright) — 2

Date	Title	Peak Position	Weeks at No.1	Weeks on Chart
3 Aug 96	**TO YOU I BESTOW** *Epic MUNDY 1CD*	60		1
5 Oct 96	**LIFE'S A CINCH** *Epic MUNDY 2CD*	75		1

MUNGO JERRY
UK, male vocal/instrumental group – Ray Dorset, Mike Cole, Colin Earl & Paul King — 88

Date	Title	Peak Position	Weeks at No.1	Weeks on Chart
6 Jun 70	**IN THE SUMMERTIME** *Dawn DNX 2502*	1	7	20
6 Feb 71	**BABY JUMP** *Dawn DNX 2505*	1	2	13
29 May 71	**LADY ROSE** *Dawn DNX 2510*	5		12
18 Sep 71	**YOU DON'T HAVE TO BE IN THE ARMY TO FIGHT IN THE WAR** *Dawn DNX 2513*	13		8
22 Apr 72	**OPEN UP** *Dawn DNX 2514*	21		8
7 Jul 73	**ALRIGHT ALRIGHT ALRIGHT** *Dawn DNS 1037* ●	3		12
10 Nov 73	**WILD LOVE** *Dawn DNS 1051*	32		5
6 Apr 74	**LONG LEGGED WOMAN DRESSED IN BLACK** *Dawn DNS 1061*	13		9
29 May 99	**SUPPORT THE TOON – IT'S YOUR DUTY (EP)** *Saraja TOONCD 001* & TOON TRAVELLERS	57		1

MUNICH MACHINE
Germany, male instrumental session group — 8

Date	Title	Peak Position	Weeks at No.1	Weeks on Chart
10 Dec 77	**GET ON THE FUNK TRAIN** *Oasis 2*	41		4
4 Nov 78	**A WHITER SHADE OF PALE** *Oasis 5* INTRODUCING CHRIS BENNETT	42		4

MUPPETS
US, puppets fronted by Kermit The Frog — 17

Date	Title	Peak Position	Weeks at No.1	Weeks on Chart
28 May 77	**HALFWAY DOWN THE STAIRS** *Pye 7N 45698*	7		8
17 Dec 77	**THE MUPPET SHOW MUSIC HALL EP** *Pye 7NX 8004*	19		7
26 Dec 09	**BOHEMIAN RHAPSODY** *Walt Disney USWD10937466* QUEEN & THE MUPPETS	32		2

MURDERDOLLS
US, male vocal/instrumental group — 4

Date	Title	Peak Position	Weeks at No.1	Weeks on Chart
16 Nov 02	**DEAD IN HOLLYWOOD** *Roadrunner RR 20223*	54		1
26 Jul 03	**WHITE WEDDING** *Roadrunner RR 20155*	24		3

LYDIA MURDOCK
US, female vocalist — 9

Date	Title	Peak Position	Weeks at No.1	Weeks on Chart
24 Sep 83	**SUPERSTAR** *Korova KOW 30*	14		9

SHIRLEY MURDOCK
US, female vocalist — 2

Date	Title	Peak Position	Weeks at No.1	Weeks on Chart
12 Apr 86	**TRUTH OR DARE** *Elektra EKR 36*	60		2

NOEL MURPHY
Ireland, male vocalist — 4

Date	Title	Peak Position	Weeks at No.1	Weeks on Chart
27 Jun 87	**MURPHY AND THE BRICKS** *Murphy's STACK 1*	57		4

ROISIN MURPHY
Ireland, female vocalist/producer. See Moloko — 11

Date	Title	Peak Position	Weeks at No.1	Weeks on Chart
16 Jun 01	**NEVER ENOUGH** *Positiva CDTIV 156* BORIS DLUGOSCH FEATURING ROISIN MURPHY	16		4
19 Jan 02	**WONDERLAND** *Echo ECSCD 120* PSYCHEDELIC WALTONS FEATURING ROISIN MURPHY	37		2
20 Oct 07	**LET ME KNOW** *EMI CDEMS728*	28		4
12 Apr 08	**YOU KNOW ME BETTER** *EMI CDEMS741*	47		1

WALTER MURPHY & THE BIG APPLE BAND
US, male orchestra leader & band — 9

Date	Title	Peak Position	Weeks at No.1	Weeks on Chart
10 Jul 76	**A FIFTH OF BEETHOVEN** *Private Stock PVT 59* ★	28		9

ANNE MURRAY
Canada, female vocalist — 40

Date	Title	Peak Position	Weeks at No.1	Weeks on Chart
24 Oct 70	**SNOWBIRD** *Capitol CL 15654*	23		17
21 Oct 72	**DESTINY** *Capitol CL 15734*	41		4
9 Dec 78	**YOU NEEDED ME** *Capitol CL 16011* ★	22		14
21 Apr 79	**I JUST FALL IN LOVE AGAIN** *Capitol CL 16069*	58		2
19 Apr 80	**DAYDREAM BELIEVER** *Capitol CL 16123*	61		3

KEITH MURRAY
US, male rapper/vocalist — 10

Date	Title	Peak Position	Weeks at No.1	Weeks on Chart
2 Nov 96	**THE RHYME** *Jive JIVECD 407*	59		1
27 Jun 98	**SHORTY (YOU KEEP PLAYIN' WITH MY MIND)** *Jive 0521212* IMAJIN FEATURING KEITH MURRAY	22		3
14 Nov 98	**HOME ALONE** *Jive 0522392* R KELLY FEATURING KEITH MURRAY	17		5
5 Dec 98	**INCREDIBLE** *Jive 0522102* FEATURING LL COOL J	52		1

PAULINE MURRAY & THE INVISIBLE GIRLS
UK, female vocalist & male instrumental group — 2

Date	Title	Peak Position	Weeks at No.1	Weeks on Chart
2 Aug 80	**DREAM SEQUENCE (ONE)** *Illusive IVE 1*	67		2

RUBY MURRAY
UK, female vocalist, d. 17 Dec 1996 (age 61) — 114

Date	Title	Peak Position	Weeks at No.1	Weeks on Chart
3 Dec 54	**HEARTBEAT** *Columbia DB 3542*	3		16
28 Jan 55	**SOFTLY SOFTLY** *Columbia DB 3558*	1	3	23
4 Feb 55	**HAPPY DAYS AND LONELY NIGHTS** *Columbia DB 3577*	6		8
4 Mar 55	**LET ME GO LOVER** *Columbia DB 3577*	5		7
18 Mar 55	**IF ANYONE FINDS THIS I LOVE YOU** *Columbia DB 3580* WITH ANNE WARREN	4		11
1 Jul 55	**EVERMORE** *Columbia DB 3617*	3		17
14 Oct 55	**I'LL COME WHEN YOU CALL** *Columbia DB 3643*	6		7
31 Aug 56	**YOU ARE MY FIRST LOVE** *Columbia DB 3770*	16		5
12 Dec 58	**REAL LOVE** *Columbia DB 4192*	18		6
5 Jun 59	**GOODBYE JIMMY GOODBYE** *Columbia DB 4305*	10		14

JUNIOR MURVIN
Jamaica, male vocalist (Murvin Junior Smith) — 9

Date	Title	Peak Position	Weeks at No.1	Weeks on Chart
3 May 80	**POLICE AND THIEVES** *Island WIP 6539*	23		9

MUSE
UK, male vocal/instrumental trio – Matt Bellamy, Dominic Howard & Chris Wolstenholme — 103

Date	Title	Peak Position	Weeks at No.1	Weeks on Chart
26 Jun 99	**UNO** *Mushroom MUSH 50CDS*	73		1
18 Sep 99	**CAVE** *Mushroom MUSH 58CDS*	52		1
4 Dec 99	**MUSCLE MUSEUM** *Mushroom MUSH 66CDS*	43		2
4 Mar 00	**SUNBURN** *Mushroom MUSH 68CDS*	22		2
17 Jun 00	**UNINTENDED** *Mushroom MUSH 72CDSX*	20		4
21 Oct 00	**MUSCLE MUSEUM** *Mushroom MUSH 84CDSX*	25		3
24 Mar 01	**PLUG IN BABY** *Mushroom MUSH 89CDSX*	11		5
16 Jun 01	**NEW BORN** *Mushroom MUSH 92CDSX*	12		4
1 Sep 01	**BLISS** *Mushroom MUSH 96CDSX*	22		2
1 Dec 01	**HYPER MUSIC/FEELING GOOD** *Mushroom MUSH 97CDS*	24		3
29 Jun 02	**DEAD STAR/IN YOUR WORLD** *Mushroom MUSH 104CDS*	13		3
20 Sep 03	**TIME IS RUNNING OUT** *East West EW 272CD*	8		8
13 Dec 03	**HYSTERIA** *Taste Media/EastWest EW 278CD*	17		6
29 May 04	**SING FOR ABSOLUTION** *Taste Media/East West EW 285CD*	16		4
2 Oct 04	**BUTTERFLIES AND HURRICANES** *Atlantic ATUK003CD*	14		3
24 Jun 06	**SUPER MASSIVE BLACK HOLE** *Warner Brothers HEL3001CD*	4		15
9 Sep 06	**STARLIGHT** *Helium 3/Warner Bros HEL3003CD*	13		15
9 Dec 06	**KNIGHTS OF CYDONIA** *Helium 3/Warner Bros HEL3004CD*	10		4
21 Apr 07	**INVINCIBLE** *Helium 3/Warner Bros HEL3005CD*	21		2
30 Jun 07	**MAP OF THE PROBLEMATIQUE** *Warner Brothers GBAHT0500594*	18		1
19 Sep 09	**UPRISING** *Helium 3/Warner WEA458CD*	9		9
28 Nov 09	**UNDISCLOSED DESIRES** *Warner Brothers GBAHT0900322*	49		4
6 Mar 10	**RESISTANCE** *Helium 3/Warner WEA460CD*	38		2

MUSIC
UK, male vocal/instrumental group — 16

Date	Title	Peak Position	Weeks at No.1	Weeks on Chart
31 Aug 02	**TAKE THE LONG ROAD AND WALK IT** *Hut HUTDX 158*	14		3
30 Nov 02	**GETAWAY** *Hut HUTCD 162*	26		2
1 Mar 03	**THE TRUTH IS NO WORDS** *Hut HUTCD 164*	18		2
18 Sep 04	**FREEDOM FIGHTERS** *Virgin VSCDX 1883*	15		4
22 Jan 05	**BREAKIN'** *Virgin VSCDX1894*	20		3
21 Jun 08	**STRENGTH IN NUMBERS** *Polydor 1767695*	38		2

MUSIC & MYSTERY
UK, male production group & US, female vocalist

		Peak Position	Weeks at No.1	Weeks on Chart 3
13 Feb 93	**ALL THIS LOVE I'M GIVING** *KTDA CDKTDA 2* FEATURING GWEN McCRAE	36		3

MUSIC RELIEF '94
International, male/female vocal/instrumental charity ensemble

		Peak Position	Weeks at No.1	Weeks on Chart 1
5 Nov 94	**WHAT'S GOING ON** *Jive RWANDACD 1*	70		1

MUSICAL YOUTH
UK, male vocal/instrumental group – Dennis Seaton, Kelvin & Michael Grant & Freddie 'Junior' & Patrick, d. 18 Feb 1993, Waite

		Peak Position	Weeks at No.1	Weeks on Chart 55
25 Sep 82	**PASS THE DUTCHIE** *MCA YOU 1* ●	1	3	13
20 Nov 82	**YOUTH OF TODAY** *MCA YOU 2*	13		9
12 Feb 83	**NEVER GONNA GIVE YOU UP** *MCA YOU 3*	6		10
16 Apr 83	**HEARTBREAKER** *MCA YOU 4*	44		3
9 Jul 83	**TELL ME WHY** *MCA YOU 5*	33		6
22 Oct 83	**007** *MCA YOU 6*	26		6
14 Jan 84	**SIXTEEN** *MCA YOU 7*	23		8

MUSIQUE
US, female vocal group

		Peak Position	Weeks at No.1	Weeks on Chart 12
18 Nov 78	**IN THE BUSH** *CBS 6791*	16		12

MUSIQUE VS U2
UK/Ireland, male vocal/instrumental/production group. See PF Project featuring Ewan McGregor

		Peak Position	Weeks at No.1	Weeks on Chart 5
2 Jun 01	**NEW YEARS DUB** *Serious SERRO 030CD*	15		5

MUTINY UK
UK, male production duo. See Helicopter

		Peak Position	Weeks at No.1	Weeks on Chart 3
19 May 01	**SECRETS** *Sunflower VCRD 86*	47		1
25 Aug 01	**VIRUS** *VC Recordings VCRD 91*	42		2

MVP
US, male vocal/rap/production group – Rob Dinero/Rich Kid (Robert Clivilles), MC Stagga Lee (Eric Newman) & Vice Verse (Victor Matos). See C & C Music Factory

		Peak Position	Weeks at No.1	Weeks on Chart 18
2 Jul 05	**ROC YA BODY (MIC CHECK 1 2)** *Positiva CDTIVS219*	5		14
1 Apr 06	**BOUNCE SHAKE MOVE STOP** *Positiva CDTIVS227*	22		4

MXM
Italy, male production trio

		Peak Position	Weeks at No.1	Weeks on Chart 1
2 Jun 90	**NOTHING COMPARES 2 U** *London LON 267*	68		1

MY BLOODY VALENTINE
UK, male/female vocal/instrumental group

		Peak Position	Weeks at No.1	Weeks on Chart 5
5 May 90	**SOON** *Creation CRE 073*	41		3
16 Feb 91	**TO HERE KNOWS WHEN** *Creation CRE 085*	29		2

MY CHEMICAL ROMANCE
US, male vocal/instrumental group – Gerard Way, Frank Iero, Matt Pelissier, Ray Toto & Mikey Way

		Peak Position	Weeks at No.1	Weeks on Chart 65
25 Dec 04	**THANK YOU FOR THE VENOM** *Reprise W661*	71		1
19 Mar 05	**I'M NOT OKAY (I PROMISE)** *Reprise W666CD1*	19		3
4 Jun 05	**HELENA** *Reprise W671CD*	20		4
10 Sep 05	**THE GHOST OF YOU** *Reprise W683CD1*	27		2
19 Nov 05	**I'M NOT OKAY (I PROMISE)** *Reprise W666CD1*	28		4
14 Oct 06	**WELCOME TO THE BLACK PARADE** *Reprise W740CD*	1	2	21
20 Jan 07	**FAMOUS LAST WORDS** *Reprise W754CD*	8		7
31 Mar 07	**I DON'T LOVE YOU** *Reprise W758CD*	13		8
23 Jun 07	**TEENAGERS** *Reprise W771CD*	9		14
21 Feb 09	**DESOLATION ROW** *Reprise W815T*	52		1

MY LIFE STORY
UK, male/female vocal/instrumental group

		Peak Position	Weeks at No.1	Weeks on Chart 12
17 Aug 96	**12 REASONS WHY I LOVE HER** *Parlophone CDR 6442*	32		2
9 Nov 96	**SPARKLE** *Parlophone CDR 6450*	34		2
1 Mar 97	**THE KING OF KISSINGDOM** *Parlophone CDRS 6457*	35		1
17 May 97	**STRUMPET** *Parlophone CDR 6464*	27		2
23 Aug 97	**DUCHESS** *Parlophone CDR 6474*	39		1
19 Jun 99	**IT'S A GIRL THING** *IT ITR 001*	37		2
30 Oct 99	**EMPIRE LINE** *IT ITR 003*	58		1
19 Feb 00	**WALK/DON'T WALK** *IT ITR 007*	48		1

MY RED CELL
UK, male vocal/instrumental group

		Peak Position	Weeks at No.1	Weeks on Chart 1
12 Jun 04	**IN A CAGE (ON PROZAC)** *V2 VVR 5027133*	61		1

MY VITRIOL
UK, male/female vocal/instrumental group

		Peak Position	Weeks at No.1	Weeks on Chart 7
22 Jul 00	**CEMENTED SHOES** *Infectious INFECT 89CDS*	65		1
11 Nov 00	**PIECES** *Infectious INFECT 94CDS*	56		1
24 Feb 01	**ALWAYS YOUR WAY** *Infectious INFECT 95CDSX*	31		2
19 May 01	**GROUNDED** *Infectious INFECT 97CD*	29		2
27 Jul 02	**MOODSWINGS/THE GENTLE ART OF CHOKING** *Infectious INFEC 107CDSX*	39		1

MYA
US, female vocalist (Mya Harrison)

		Peak Position	Weeks at No.1	Weeks on Chart 66
27 Jun 98	**GHETTO SUPERSTAR (THAT IS WHAT YOU ARE)** *Interscope IND 95593* PRAS MICHEL FEATURING OL' DIRTY BASTARD INTRODUCING MYA ⊛	2		17
12 Dec 98	**TAKE ME THERE** *Interscope IND 95620* BLACKstreet & MYA FEATURING MASE & BLINKY BLINK	7		9
10 Feb 01	**CASE OF THE EX (WHATCHA GONNA DO)** *Interscope 4974772*	3		11
24 Mar 01	**GIRLS DEM SUGAR** *Virgin VUSCD 173* BEENIE MAN FEATURING MYA	13		5
9 Jun 01	**FREE** *Interscope 4975002*	11		6
30 Jun 01	**LADY MARMALADE** *Interscope 4975612* CHRISTINA AGUILERA/LIL' KIM/MYA/P!NK ● ★	1	1	16
20 Sep 03	**MY LOVE IS LIKE...WO!** *Interscope 9810302*	33		2

ALICIA MYERS
US, female vocalist. See Al Hudson & The Partners, One Way

		Peak Position	Weeks at No.1	Weeks on Chart 3
1 Sep 84	**YOU GET THE BEST FROM ME (SAY SAY SAY)** *MCA 914*	58		3

BILLIE MYERS
UK, female vocalist

		Peak Position	Weeks at No.1	Weeks on Chart 12
11 Apr 98	**KISS THE RAIN** *Universal UND 56182*	4		9
25 Jul 98	**TELL ME** *Universal UND 56201*	28		3

RICHARD MYHILL
UK, male vocalist

		Peak Position	Weeks at No.1	Weeks on Chart 9
1 Apr 78	**IT TAKES TWO TO TANGO** *Mercury 6007 167*	17		9

ALANNAH MYLES
Canada, female vocalist

		Peak Position	Weeks at No.1	Weeks on Chart 17
17 Mar 90	**BLACK VELVET** *East West A 8742* ● ★	2		15
16 Jun 90	**LOVE IS** *East West A 8918*	61		2

MYLO
UK, male vocalist/producer (Myles MacInnes)

		Peak Position	Weeks at No.1	Weeks on Chart 43
30 Oct 04	**DROP THE PRESSURE** *Breastfed BFD009CD*	19		7
5 Feb 05	**DESTROY ROCK AND ROLL** *Breastfed BFD014CD*	15		4
28 May 05	**IN MY ARMS** *Breastfed BFD016CD*	13		7
17 Sep 05	**DOCTOR PRESSURE** *Breastfed BFD017CD2* VS MIAMI SOUND MACHINE	3		23
21 Jan 06	**MUSCLE CAR** *Breastfed BFD019CD* FEATURING FREEFORM FIVE	38		2

MYNC PROJECT FEATURING ABIGAIL BAILEY
UK, male/female vocal/production trio

		Peak Position	Weeks at No.1	Weeks on Chart 1
22 Jul 06	**SOMETHING ON YOUR MIND** *Island APOLLO103CD*	71		1

MARIE MYRIAM
France (b. Portugal), female vocalist

		Peak Position	Weeks at No.1	Weeks on Chart 4
28 May 77	**L'OISEAU ET L'ENFANT** *Polydor 2056 634*	42		4

Silver-selling ● Gold-selling ● Platinum-selling (x multiples) ✪ US No.1 ★ Peak Position · Weeks at No.1 · Weeks on Chart

MYRON

US, male vocalist (Myron Davis) — **1**

Date	Title / Label	Peak	Wks at No.1	Wks on Chart
22 Nov 97	**WE CAN GET DOWN** *Island Black Music CID 677*	74		1

MYSTERY

Holland, male production duo. See Ron Van Den Beuken — **2**

Date	Title / Label	Peak	Wks at No.1	Wks on Chart
6 Oct 01	**MYSTERY** *Inferno CDFERN 42*	56		1
10 Aug 02	**ALL I EVER WANTED (DEVOTION)** *Xtravaganza XTRAV 33CDS*	57		1

MYSTERY JETS

UK, male vocal/instrumental group — **17**

Date	Title / Label	Peak	Wks at No.1	Wks on Chart
24 Sep 05	**YOU CAN'T FOOL ME DENNIS** *679 679L109CD*	44		2
17 Dec 05	**ALAS AGNES** *679 679L115CD*	34		1
11 Mar 06	**THE BOY WHO RAN AWAY** *679 679L122CD*	23		2
3 Jun 06	**YOU CAN'T FOOL ME DENNIS** *679 679L129CD*	41		1
16 Sep 06	**DIAMONDS IN THE DARK EP** *679 679L138CD*	47		1
15 Mar 08	**YOUNG LOVE** *679 679L152CD*	34		4
7 Jun 08	**TWO DOORS DOWN** *679 679L156CD*	24		6

MYSTIC MERLIN

US, male vocal/instrumental group — **9**

Date	Title / Label	Peak	Wks at No.1	Wks on Chart
26 Apr 80	**JUST CAN'T GIVE YOU UP** *Capitol CL 16133*	20		9

MYSTIC 3

UK, male DJ/producer (Brandon Block). See Blockster — **1**

Date	Title / Label	Peak	Wks at No.1	Wks on Chart
24 Jun 00	**SOMETHING'S GOIN' ON** *Rulin 2CDS*	63		1

MYSTICA

Israel, male production trio — **2**

Date	Title / Label	Peak	Wks at No.1	Wks on Chart
24 Jan 98	**EVER REST** *Perfecto PERF 152CD*	62		1
9 May 98	**AFRICAN HORIZON** *Perfecto PERF 161CD*	59		1

MYSTIKAL

US, male rapper (Michael Tyler) — **21**

Date	Title / Label	Peak	Wks at No.1	Wks on Chart
9 Dec 00	**SHAKE YA ASS** *Jive 9251552*	30		5
17 Feb 01	**STUTTER** *Jive 9251632* JOE FEATURING MYSTIKAL ★	7		8
3 Mar 01	**DANGER (BEEN SO LONG)** *Jive 9251722* FEATURING NIVEA	28		3
29 Dec 01	**DON'T STOP (FUNKIN' 4 JAMAICA)** *Virgin VUSCD 228* MARIAH CAREY FEATURING MYSTIKAL	32		4
23 Feb 02	**BOUNCIN' BACK** *Jive 9253272*	45		1

MYTOWN

Ireland, male vocal group — **2**

Date	Title / Label	Peak	Wks at No.1	Wks on Chart
13 Mar 99	**PARTY ALL NIGHT** *Universal UND 56231*	22		2

N-DUBZ

UK, male/female vocal/rap trio – Dino 'Dappy' & Tula 'Tulisa' Contostavlos & Richard 'Fazer' Rawson. See Young Soul Rebels — **111**

Date	Title / Label	Peak	Wks at No.1	Wks on Chart
26 May 07	**FEVA LAS VEGAS** *LRC LRC0010*	57		2
3 Nov 07	**YOU BETTER NOT WASTE MY TIME** *LRC 1744153*	26		3
11 Oct 08	**OUCH** *All Around The World CDGLOBE991*	22		9
29 Nov 08	**PAPA CAN YOU HEAR ME** *All Around The World CDGLOBE992*	19		11
3 Jan 09	**STRONG AGAIN** *AATW/UMTV GBUM70818241*	24		21
2 May 09	**NUMBER 1** *Fourth & Broadway 2701362* TINCHY STRYDER FEATURING N-DUBZ	1	3	28
23 May 09	**WOULDN'T YOU** *AATW/UMTV GBUM70818239*	64		4
21 Nov 09	**I NEED YOU** *All Around The World CDGLOBE1281*	5		11
28 Nov 09	**PLAYING WITH FIRE** *AATW/UMTV CDGLOBE1304* FEATURING MR HUDSON	14		20+
3 Apr 10	**SAY IT'S OVER** *AATW/UMTV GBCFZ0900638*	40		2+

N-JOI

UK, male production duo – Nigel Champion & Mark Franklin — **28**

Date	Title / Label	Peak	Wks at No.1	Wks on Chart
27 Oct 90	**ANTHEM** *Deconstruction PB 44041*	45		5
2 Mar 91	**ADRENALIN (EP)** *Deconstruction PT 44344*	23		5
6 Apr 91	**ANTHEM** *Deconstruction PB 44445*	8		8
22 Feb 92	**LIVE IN MANCHESTER (PARTS 1 + 2)** *Deconstruction PT 45252*	12		5
24 Jul 93	**THE DRUMSTRUCK (EP)** *Deconstruction 74321154832*	33		3
17 Dec 94	**PAPILLON** *Deconstruction 74321252132*	70		1
8 Jul 95	**BAD THINGS** *Deconstruction 74321277292*	57		1

N 'N' G FEATURING KALLAGHAN

UK, male/female vocal/production group — **6**

Date	Title / Label	Peak	Wks at No.1	Wks on Chart
1 Apr 00	**RIGHT BEFORE MY EYES** *Urban Heat UHTCD003*	12		6

*NSYNC

US, male vocal group – Lance Bass, JC Chasez*, Joey Fatone, Chris Kirkpatrick & Justin Timberlake* — **79**

Date	Title / Label	Peak	Wks at No.1	Wks on Chart
13 Sep 97	**TEARIN' UP MY HEART** *Arista 74321505152*	40		2
22 Nov 97	**I WANT YOU BACK** *Arista 74321541122*	62		1
27 Feb 99	**I WANT YOU BACK** *Transcontinental 74321646982*	5		10
26 Jun 99	**TEARIN' UP MY HEART** *Northwestside 74321675832*	9		10
8 Jan 00	**MUSIC OF MY HEART** *Epic 6678052* & GLORIA ESTEFAN	34		3
11 Mar 00	**BYE BYE BYE** *Jive 9250202* ●	3		8
22 Jul 00	**I'LL NEVER STOP** *Jive 9250762*	13		6
16 Sep 00	**IT'S GONNA BE ME** *Jive 9251082* ★	9		8
2 Dec 00	**THIS I PROMISE YOU** *Jive 9251302*	21		7
21 Jul 01	**POP** *Jive 9252422*	9		8
8 Dec 01	**GONE** *Jive 9252772*	24		4
27 Apr 02	**GIRLFRIEND** *Jive 9253312* FEATURING NELLY	2		12

N-TRANCE

UK, male production duo – Dale Longworth & Kevin O'Toole & male/female vocalists. See Freeloaders — **86**

Date	Title / Label	Peak	Wks at No.1	Wks on Chart
7 May 94	**SET YOU FREE** *All Around The World CDGLOBE 124* FEATURING KELLY LLORENNA	39		4
22 Oct 94	**TURN UP THE POWER** *All Around The World CDGLOBE 125*	23		3
14 Jan 95	**SET YOU FREE** *All Around The World CXGLOBE 126* FEATURING KELLY LLORENNA ●	2		15
16 Sep 95	**STAYIN' ALIVE** *All Around The World CDGLOBE 131* FEATURING RICARDO DA FORCE ●	2		11
24 Feb 96	**ELECTRONIC PLEASURE** *All Around The World CDGLOBE 135*	11		4
5 Apr 97	**D.I.S.C.O.** *All Around The World CDGLOBE 153*	11		6
23 Aug 97	**THE MIND OF THE MACHINE** *All Around The World CDGLOBE 159*	15		4
1 Nov 97	**DA YA THINK I'M SEXY?** *All Around The World CDGLOBE 150* FEATURING ROD STEWART	7		10
12 Sep 98	**PARADISE CITY** *All Around The World CDGLOBE 140*	28		3
19 Dec 98	**TEARS IN THE RAIN** *All Around The World CDGLOBE 185*	53		1
20 May 00	**SHAKE YA BODY** *All Around The World CDGLOBE 204*	37		1
22 Sep 01	**SET YOU FREE** *All Around The World CXGLOBE 242*	4		11
14 Sep 02	**FOREVER** *All Around The World CXGLOBE 257*	6		8
19 Jul 03	**DESTINY** *All Around The World CDGLOBE 282*	37		2
4 Dec 04	**I'M IN HEAVEN** *All Around The World CDGLOBE343*	46		2
8 Jan 05	**SET YOU FREE** *All Around The World CXGLOBE 242*	64		1

N-TYCE

UK, female vocal group — **15**

Date	Title / Label	Peak	Wks at No.1	Wks on Chart
5 Jul 97	**HEY DJ! (PLAY THAT SONG)** *Telstar CDSTAS 2885*	20		2
13 Sep 97	**WE COME TO PARTY** *Telstar CDSTAS 2915*	12		4
28 Feb 98	**TELEFUNKIN'** *Telstar CXSTAS 2944*	16		5
6 Jun 98	**BOOM BOOM** *Telstar CDSTAS 2971*	18		4

NADA SURF

US, male vocal/instrumental group — **1**

Date	Title / Label	Peak	Wks at No.1	Wks on Chart
24 May 03	**INSIDE OF LOVE** *Heavenly HVN 133CD*	73		1

NADIA

Portugal, female vocalist (Nadia Almada) — **5**

Date	Title / Label	Peak	Wks at No.1	Wks on Chart
11 Dec 04	**A LITTLE BIT OF ACTION** *Virgin/EMI VTSCDX6*	27		5

JIMMY NAIL

UK, male actor/vocalist (James Bradford) — **73**

Date	Title / Label	Peak	Wks at No.1	Wks on Chart
27 Apr 85	**LOVE DON'T LIVE HERE ANYMORE** *Virgin VS 764* ●	3		11
11 Jul 92	**AIN'T NO DOUBT** *East West YZ 686* ●	1	3	12
3 Oct 92	**LAURA** *East West YZ 702*	58		2
26 Nov 94	**CROCODILE SHOES** *East West YZ 867CD* ●	4		20
11 Feb 95	**COWBOY DREAMS** *East West YZ 878CD*	13		7
6 May 95	**CALLING OUT YOUR NAME** *East West YZ 935CD*	65		1
28 Oct 95	**BIG RIVER** *East West EW 008CD*	18		5
23 Dec 95	**LOVE** *East West EW 018CD1*	33		4
3 Feb 96	**BIG RIVER (REMIX)** *East West EW 024CD*	72		2
16 Nov 96	**COUNTRY BOY** *East West EW 070CD*	25		8
21 Nov 98	**THE FLAME STILL BURNS** *London LONCD 420* WITH STRANGE FRUIT	47		1

YAEL NAIM

France, female vocalist/multi-instrumentalist — 9

Date	Title / Label	Peak Position	Weeks at No.1	Weeks on Chart
16 Feb 08	**NEW SOUL** *Tôt Ou Tard FR79W0700370*	30		9

NAKATOMI

UK, male/female production group — 4

Date	Title / Label	Peak Position	Weeks at No.1	Weeks on Chart
7 Feb 98	**CHILDREN OF THE NIGHT** *Peach PCHCD 006*	47		2
26 Oct 02	**CHILDREN OF THE NIGHT** *Jive 9254212*	31		2

NAKED EYES

UK, male vocal/instrumental duo — 3

Date	Title / Label	Peak Position	Weeks at No.1	Weeks on Chart
23 Jul 83	**ALWAYS SOMETHING THERE TO REMIND ME** *EMI 5334*	59		3

NALIN & KANE

Germany, male DJ/production duo — 7

Date	Title / Label	Peak Position	Weeks at No.1	Weeks on Chart
1 Nov 97	**BEACHBALL** *ffrr FCD 318*	48		1
28 Mar 98	**PLANET VIOLET** *Logic 74321565702* NALIN I.N.C.	51		1
3 Oct 98	**BEACHBALL (REMIX)** *London FCD 349*	17		5

NAPOLEON XIV

US, male vocalist (Jerry Samuels) — 10

Date	Title / Label	Peak Position	Weeks at No.1	Weeks on Chart
4 Aug 66	**THEY'RE COMING TO TAKE ME AWAY HA-HAAA!** *Warner Brothers WB 5831*	4		10

NARCOTIC THRUST

UK, male DJ/production duo – Stuart Crichton & Andy Morris — 11

Date	Title / Label	Peak Position	Weeks at No.1	Weeks on Chart
10 Aug 02	**SAFE FROM HARM** *ffrr FCD 406*	24		3
17 Apr 04	**I LIKE IT** *Free 2 Air 0153656F2A*	9		6
22 Jan 05	**WHEN THE DAWN BREAKS** *Free2Air F2A3CDX*	28		2

NAS

US, male rapper (Nasir Jones) — 69

Date	Title / Label	Peak Position	Weeks at No.1	Weeks on Chart
28 May 94	**IT AIN'T HARD TO TELL** *Columbia 6604702*	64		1
17 Aug 96	**IF I RULED THE WORLD** *Columbia 6634022*	12		7
25 Jan 97	**STREET DREAMS** *Columbia 6641302*	12		4
14 Jun 97	**HEAD OVER HEELS** *Epic 6645942* ALLURE FEATURING NAS	18		3
29 May 99	**HATE ME NOW** *Columbia 6672565* FEATURING PUFF DADDY	14		6
15 Jan 00	**NASTRADAMUS** *Columbia 6685572*	24		3
22 Jan 00	**HOT BOYZ** *Elektra E 7002CD* MISSY 'MISDEMEANOR' ELLIOTT FEATURING NAS, EVE & Q-TIP	18		3
21 Apr 01	**OOCHIE WALLY** *Columbia 6710852* QB FINEST FEATURING NAS & BRAVEHEARTS	30		1
2 Feb 02	**GOT UR SELF A** *Columbia 6723022*	30		5
13 Jul 02	**I'M GONNA BE ALRIGHT** *Epic 6728442* JENNIFER LOPEZ FEATURING NAS	3		10
25 Jan 03	**MADE YOU LOOK** *Columbia 6734792*	27		3
5 Apr 03	**I CAN** *Columbia 6737385*	19		7
20 Nov 04	**BRIDGING THE GAP** *Columbia 6754682*	18		4
16 Apr 05	**IN PUBLIC** *Virgin VSCDT1893* KELIS FEATURING NAS	17		6
3 Feb 07	**HIP HOP IS DEAD** *Def Jam 1721323* FEATURING WILL.I.AM	35		4
23 Aug 08	**HERO** *Mercury USUM70821210* FEATURING KERI HILSON	70		2

JOHNNY NASH

US, male vocalist — 106

Date	Title / Label	Peak Position	Weeks at No.1	Weeks on Chart
7 Aug 68	**HOLD ME TIGHT** *Regal Zonophone RZ 3010*	5		16
8 Jan 69	**YOU GOT SOUL** *Major Minor MM 586*	6		12
2 Apr 69	**CUPID** *Major Minor MM 603*	6		12
1 Apr 72	**STIR IT UP** *CBS 7800*	13		12
24 Jun 72	**I CAN SEE CLEARLY NOW** *CBS 8113* ★	5		15
7 Oct 72	**THERE ARE MORE QUESTIONS THAN ANSWERS** *CBS 8351*	9		9
14 Jun 75	**TEARS ON MY PILLOW** *CBS 3220* ●	1	1	11
11 Oct 75	**LET'S BE FRIENDS** *CBS 3597*	42		3
12 Jun 76	**(WHAT A) WONDERFUL WORLD** *Epic EPC 4294*	25		7
9 Nov 85	**ROCK ME BABY** *2000 AD FED 19*	47		4
15 Apr 89	**I CAN SEE CLEARLY NOW (REMIX)** *Epic JN 1*	54		5

KATE NASH

UK, female vocalist/multi-instrumentalist — 49

Date	Title / Label	Peak Position	Weeks at No.1	Weeks on Chart
7 Jul 07	**FOUNDATIONS** *Fiction/Polydor 1735509*	2		31
22 Sep 07	**MOUTHWASH** *Fiction/Polydor 1744949*	23		8
15 Dec 07	**PUMPKIN SOUP** *Fiction/Polydor 1754566*	23		10

NASHVILLE TEENS

UK, male vocal/instrumental group – Arthur Sharp, Ray Phillips, John Allen, John Hawken, Barry Jenkins & Pete Shannon — 37

Date	Title / Label	Peak Position	Weeks at No.1	Weeks on Chart
9 Jul 64	**TOBACCO ROAD** *Decca F 11930*	6		13
22 Oct 64	**GOOGLE EYE** *Decca F 12000*	10		11
4 Mar 65	**FIND MY WAY BACK HOME** *Decca F 12089*	34		6
20 May 65	**THIS LITTLE BIRD** *Decca F 12143*	38		4
3 Feb 66	**THE HARD WAY** *Decca F 12316*	45		3

NATASHA

UK, female vocalist (Natasha England) — 16

Date	Title / Label	Peak Position	Weeks at No.1	Weeks on Chart
5 Jun 82	**IKO IKO** *Towerbell TOW 22*	10		11
4 Sep 82	**THE BOOM BOOM ROOM** *Towerbell TOW 25*	44		5

ULTRA NATE

US, female vocalist (Ultra Nate Wyche) — 41

Date	Title / Label	Peak Position	Weeks at No.1	Weeks on Chart
9 Dec 89	**IT'S OVER NOW** *Eternal YZ 440*	62		3
23 Feb 91	**IS IT LOVE** *Eternal YZ 509* BASEMENT BOYS PRESENT ULTRA NATE	71		1
29 Jan 94	**SHOW ME** *Warner Brothers W 0219CD*	62		1
14 Jun 97	**FREE** *AM:PM 5822432* ●	4		17
24 Jan 98	**FREE (REMIX)** *AM:PM 5825012*	33		2
18 Apr 98	**FOUND A CURE** *AM:PM 5826452*	6		7
25 Jul 98	**NEW KIND OF MEDICINE** *AM:PM 5827492*	14		5
22 Jul 00	**DESIRE** *AM:PM CDAMPM 133*	40		2
9 Jun 01	**GET IT UP (THE FEELING)** *AM:PM CDAMPM 140*	51		1
28 May 05	**FREAK ON** *Hed Kandi HEDKCDX010* STONEBRIDGE VS ULTRA NATE	37		2

NATHAN

UK, male vocalist (Nathan Fagan-Gayle) — 5

Date	Title / Label	Peak Position	Weeks at No.1	Weeks on Chart
12 Mar 05	**COME INTO MY ROOM** *V2 JAD5029593*	37		2
24 Mar 07	**DO WITHOUT MY LOVE** *Mona MONA7NATCDS*	44		3

NATIVE

UK, male production duo. See Beat Renegades, Dream Frequency, Quake featuring Marcia Rae, Red — 2

Date	Title / Label	Peak Position	Weeks at No.1	Weeks on Chart
10 Feb 01	**FEEL THE DRUMS** *Slinky Music SLINKY 009CD*	46		2

NATTY

UK (b. US), male vocalist (Alexander Modiano) — 2

Date	Title / Label	Peak Position	Weeks at No.1	Weeks on Chart
2 Aug 08	**JULY** *Atlantic VAP003CD*	53		2

NATURAL

US, male vocal group — 2

Date	Title / Label	Peak Position	Weeks at No.1	Weeks on Chart
10 Aug 02	**PUT YOUR ARMS AROUND ME** *Ariola 74321947892*	32		2

NATURAL BORN CHILLERS

UK, male production duo — 3

Date	Title / Label	Peak Position	Weeks at No.1	Weeks on Chart
1 Nov 97	**ROCK THE FUNKY BEAT** *East West EW 138CD1*	30		3

NATURAL BORN GROOVES

Belgium, male DJ/production duo — 3

Date	Title / Label	Peak Position	Weeks at No.1	Weeks on Chart
2 Nov 96	**FORERUNNER** *XL Recordings XLS 76CD*	64		1
19 Apr 97	**GROOVEBIRD** *Positiva CDTIV 75*	21		2

NATURAL LIFE

UK, male vocal/instrumental group — 3

Date	Title / Label	Peak Position	Weeks at No.1	Weeks on Chart
7 Mar 92	**NATURAL LIFE** *Tribe NLIFE 3*	47		3

NATURAL SELECTION

US, male vocal/instrumental duo — 2

Date	Title / Label	Peak Position	Weeks at No.1	Weeks on Chart
9 Nov 91	**DO ANYTHING** *East West A 8724*	69		2

NATURALS

UK, male vocal/instrumental group — 9

Date	Title / Label	Peak Position	Weeks at No.1	Weeks on Chart
20 Aug 64	**I SHOULD HAVE KNOWN BETTER** *Parlophone R 5165*	24		9

DAVID NAUGHTON
US, male actor/vocalist — 6

Date	Title	Peak	Wks No.1	Wks
25 Aug 79	**MAKIN' IT** *RSO 32*	44		6

NATURI NAUGHTON
US, female vocalist/actor. See 3LW — 4

Date	Title	Peak	Wks No.1	Wks
26 Sep 09	**FAME** *Universal USLS50909502*	33		4

NAUGHTY BOY
UK, male production duo – Marcus Lee & Will Paton — 8

Date	Title	Peak	Wks No.1	Wks
14 Jan 06	**PHAT BEACH (I'LL BE READY)** *Ministry Of Sound PHAT01CDS*	36		3
13 Mar 10	**NEVER BE YOUR WOMAN** *Relentless/Virgin RELCD65* PRESENTS WILEY FEATURING EMELI SANDE	8		5+

NAUGHTY BY NATURE
US, male rap trio — 19

Date	Title	Peak	Wks No.1	Wks
9 Nov 91	**O.P.P.** *Big Life BLR 62*	73		1
20 Jun 92	**O.P.P.** *Big Life BLR 74*	35		3
30 Jan 93	**HIP HOP HOORAY** *Big Life BLRD 89*	22		3
19 Jun 93	**IT'S ON** *Big Life BLRD 99*	48		2
27 Nov 93	**HIP HOP HOORAY (REMIX)** *Big Life BLRDA 104*	20		4
29 Apr 95	**FEEL ME FLOW** *Big Life BLRD 115*	23		3
11 Sep 99	**JAMBOREE** *Arista 74321692882* FEATURING ZHANE	51		1
19 Oct 02	**FEELS GOOD (DON'T WORRY BOUT A THING)** *Island CID 806* FEATURING 3LW	44		1
8 Jan 05	**O.P.P.** *Tommy Boy 5046759840*	71		1

MARIA NAYLER
UK, female vocalist — 26

Date	Title	Peak	Wks No.1	Wks
9 Mar 96	**BE AS ONE** *7pm 74321342962* SASHA & MARIA	17		4
16 Nov 96	**ONE & ONE** *Deconstruction 74321427692* ROBERT MILES FEATURING MARIA NAYLER ●	3		17
7 Mar 98	**NAKED AND SACRED** *Deconstruction 74321534242*	32		3
5 Sep 98	**WILL YOU BE WITH ME/LOVE IS THE GOD** *Deconstruction 74321591772*	65		1
27 May 00	**ANGRY SKIES** *Deconstruction 74321759492*	42		1

NAZARETH
UK, male vocal/instrumental group – Dan McCafferty, Pete Agnew, Manny Charlton, John Locke, Billy Rankin & Darrell Sweet, d. 30 Apr 1999 — 75

Date	Title	Peak	Wks No.1	Wks
5 May 73	**BROKEN DOWN ANGEL** *Mooncrest MOON 1*	9		11
21 Jul 73	**BAD BAD BOY** *Mooncrest MOON 9*	10		9
13 Oct 73	**THIS FLIGHT TONIGHT** *Mooncrest MOON 14*	11		13
23 Mar 74	**SHANGHAI'D IN SHANGHAI** *Mooncrest MOON 22*	41		4
14 Jun 75	**MY WHITE BICYCLE** *Mooncrest MOON 47*	14		8
15 Nov 75	**HOLY ROLLER** *Mountain TOP 3*	36		4
24 Sep 77	**HOT TRACKS EP** *Mountain NAZ 1*	15		11
18 Feb 78	**GONE DEAD TRAIN** *Mountain NAZ 002*	49		2
13 May 78	**PLACE IN YOUR HEART** *Mountain TOP 37*	70		2
27 Jan 79	**MAY THE SUN SHINE** *Mountain NAZ 003*	22		8
28 Jul 79	**STAR** *Mountain TOP 45*	54		3

ME'SHELL NDEGEOCELLO
US (b. Germany), female vocalist/bass guitarist (Michelle Johnson) — 5

Date	Title	Peak	Wks No.1	Wks
12 Feb 94	**IF THAT'S YOUR BOYFIEND (HE WASN'T LAST NIGHT)** *Maverick W 0223CD1*	74		1
3 Sep 94	**WILD NIGHT** *Mercury MERCD 409* JOHN MELLENCAMP FEATURING ME'SHELL NDEGEOCELLO	34		3
1 Mar 97	**NEVER MISS THE WATER** *Reprise W 1393CD* CHAKA KHAN FEATURING ME'SHELL NDEGEOCELLO	59		1

YOUSSOU N'DOUR
Senegal, male vocalist — 35

Date	Title	Peak	Wks No.1	Wks
3 Jun 89	**SHAKING THE TREE** *Virgin VS 1167* & PETER GABRIEL	61		3
22 Dec 90	**SHAKING THE TREE** *Virgin VS 1322* & PETER GABRIEL	57		4
25 Jun 94	**7 SECONDS** *Columbia 6605082* (FEATURING NENEH CHERRY) ●	3		25
14 Jan 95	**UNDECIDED** *Columbia 6609712*	53		2
10 Oct 98	**HOW COME** *Interscope IND 95598* & CANIBUS	52		1

NE-YO
US, male vocalist/producer/actor (Shaffer Smith) — 165

Date	Title	Peak	Wks No.1	Wks
25 Mar 06	**SO SICK** *Def Jam 9854185* ★	1	1	15
1 Jul 06	**SEXY LOVE** *Def Jam 1701192*	5		13
26 Aug 06	**BACK LIKE THAT** *Def Jam 1705586* GHOSTFACE KILLAH FEATURING NE-YO & KANYE WEST	46		2
14 Apr 07	**BECAUSE OF YOU** *Def Jam 1732579*	4		16
13 Oct 07	**CAN WE CHILL** *Def Jam 1747442*	62		1
20 Oct 07	**HATE THAT I LOVE YOU** *Def Jam 1751369* RIHANNA FEATURING NE-YO	15		19
17 May 08	**CLOSER** *Def Jam 1776445* ●	1	1	31
6 Sep 08	**MISS INDEPENDENT** *Mercury USUM70826981*	6		22
20 Dec 08	**MAD** *Mercury USUM70833542*	19		13
24 Jan 09	**CAMERA PHONE** *Geffen 1795606* GAME FEATURING NE-YO	48		3
23 May 09	**KNOCK YOU DOWN** *Interscope 2711463* KERI HILSON FEATURING KANYE WEST & NE-YO	5		21
28 Nov 09	**BABY BY ME** *Interscope 2727064* 50 CENT FEATURING NE-YO	17		9

NEARLY GOD
UK, male/female vocal/instrumental group. See Starving Souls, Tricky — 2

Date	Title	Peak	Wks No.1	Wks
20 Apr 96	**POEMS** *Durban Poison DPCD 3*	28		2

TERRY NEASON
UK, female vocalist/comedian — 1

Date	Title	Peak	Wks No.1	Wks
25 Jun 94	**LIFEBOAT** *WEA YZ 830*	72		1

NEBULA II
UK, male production duo — 3

Date	Title	Peak	Wks No.1	Wks
1 Feb 92	**SÉANCE/ATHEAMA** *Reinforced RIVET 1211*	55		2
16 May 92	**FLATLINERS** *J4M 12NEBULA 2*	54		1

NED'S ATOMIC DUSTBIN
UK, male vocal/instrumental group — 24

Date	Title	Peak	Wks No.1	Wks
14 Jul 90	**KILL YOUR TELEVISION** *Chapter 22 CHAP 48*	53		2
27 Oct 90	**UNTIL YOU FIND OUT** *Chapter 22 CHAP 52*	51		2
9 Mar 91	**HAPPY** *Columbia 6566807*	16		4
21 Sep 91	**TRUST** *Furtive 6574627*	21		4
10 Oct 92	**NOT SLEEPING AROUND** *Furtive 6583866*	19		3
5 Dec 92	**INTACT** *Furtive 6588166*	36		6
25 Mar 95	**ALL I ASK OF MYSELF IS THAT I HOLD TOGETHER** *Furtive 6613565*	33		2
15 Jul 95	**STUCK** *Furtive 6620562*	64		1

RAJA NEE
US, female vocalist (Alicia Knott) — 2

Date	Title	Peak	Wks No.1	Wks
4 Mar 95	**TURN IT UP** *Perspective 5874872*	42		2

JOEY NEGRO
UK, male producer (Dave Lee) — 27

Date	Title	Peak	Wks No.1	Wks
16 Nov 91	**DO WHAT YOU FEEL** *10 TEN 391*	36		3
21 Dec 91	**REACHIN'** *Republic LIC 160* PRESENTS PHASE II	70		1
18 Jul 92	**ENTER YOUR FANTASY EP** *10 TEN 397*	35		3
25 Sep 93	**WHAT HAPPENED TO THE MUSIC** *Virgin VSCD 1466*	51		2
19 Feb 00	**MUST BE THE MUSIC** *Incentive CENT 4CDS* FEATURING TAKA BOOM	8		5
16 Sep 00	**SATURDAY** *Yola CDX03* FEATURING TAKA BOOM	41		1
18 Mar 06	**MAKE A MOVE ON ME** *Data DATA82CDS*	11		12

NEIL
UK, male hippy/TV comedy character (Nigel Planer) — 10

Date	Title	Peak	Wks No.1	Wks
14 Jul 84	**HOLE IN MY SHOE** *WEA YZ 10* ●	2		10

VINCE NEIL
US, male vocalist (Vince Wharton). See Motley Crue — 1

Date	Title	Peak	Wks No.1	Wks
3 Oct 92	**YOU'RE INVITED (BUT YOUR FRIEND CAN'T COME)** *Hollywood HWD 123*	63		1

NEIL'S CHILDREN
UK, male vocal/instrumental trio — 1

Date	Title	Peak	Wks No.1	Wks
18 Jun 05	**ALWAYS THE SAME** *Poptones MC5100SCD*	56		1

NEJA

Italy, female vocalist (Agnese Cacciola) — 1

Date	Title	Peak Position	Weeks at No.1	Weeks on Chart
26 Sep 98	**RESTLESS (I KNOW YOU KNOW)** *Panorama CDPAN 1*	47		1

NEK

Italy, male vocalist (Filippo Neviani) — 1

Date	Title	Peak Position	Weeks at No.1	Weeks on Chart
29 Aug 98	**LAURA** *Coalition COLA 054CD*	59		1

NELLY

US, male rapper/vocalist/actor (Cornell Haynes, Jr) — 197

Date	Title	Peak Position	Weeks at No.1	Weeks on Chart
11 Nov 00	**(HOT S**T) COUNTRY GRAMMAR** *Universal MCSTD 40242*	7		9
24 Feb 01	**EI** *Universal MCSTD 40249*	11		5
19 May 01	**RIDE WIT ME** *Universal MCSTD 40252* FEATURING CITY SPUD ●	3		12
15 Sep 01	**BATTER UP** *Universal MCSTD 40261* & ST LUNATICS	28		2
27 Oct 01	**WHERE'S THE PARTY AT** *Columbia 6719012* JAGGED EDGE FEATURING NELLY	25		3
27 Apr 02	**GIRLFRIEND** *Jive 9253312* N SYNC FEATURING NELLY	2		12
29 Jun 02	**HOT IN HERRE** *Universal MCSTD 40289* ● ★	4		15
26 Oct 02	**DILEMMA** *Universal MCSTD 40299* FEATURING KELLY ROWLAND ⊛ ★	1	2	21
15 Mar 03	**WORK IT** *Universal MCSXD 40312* FEATURING JUSTIN TIMBERLAKE	7		11
20 Sep 03	**SHAKE YA TAILFEATHER** *Bad Boy MCSTD 40337* ,NELLY, P DIDDY & MURPHY LEE ★	10		7
13 Dec 03	**IZ U** *Universal MCSTD 40346*	36		4
11 Sep 04	**MY PLACE/FLAP YOUR WINGS** *Universal MCSTD 40379*	1	1	11
4 Dec 04	**TILT YA HEAD BACK** *Universal MCSTD40396* & CHRISTINA AGUILERA	5		12
5 Mar 05	**OVER AND OVER** *Curb/Derrty/Island MCSTD40402* FEATURING TIM McGRAW	1	1	12
25 Jun 05	**N DEY SAY** *Universal MCSXD40414*	6		7
16 Jul 05	**GET IT POPPIN'** *Atlantic AT0210CD* FAT JOE FEATURING NELLY	34		3
28 Jan 06	**NASTY GIRL** *Bad Boy AT0229CDX* NOTORIOUS B.I.G. FEATURING DIDDY, NELLY, JAGGED EDGE AND AVERY STORM	1	2	19
25 Mar 06	**GRILLZ** *Universal MCSTD40453* FEATURING PAUL WALL, ALI & GIPP ★	24		7
30 Sep 06	**CALL ON ME** *Virgin VUSCD330* JANET & NELLY	18		5
26 Apr 08	**PARTY PEOPLE** *Island 1771901* & FERGIE	14		11
9 Aug 08	**BODY ON ME** *Island 1781914* FEATURING AKON & ASHANTI	17		9

Top 3 Best-Selling Singles

	Title	Approximate Sales
1	DILEMMA	770,000
2	HOT IN HERRE	290,000
3	NASTY GIRL	280,000

NELSON

US, male vocal/instrumental duo — 3

Date	Title	Peak Position	Weeks at No.1	Weeks on Chart
27 Oct 90	**(CAN'T LIVE WITHOUT YOUR) LOVE AND AFFECTION** *DGC GEF 82* ★	54		3

BILL NELSON

UK, male vocalist/multi-instrumentalist. See Be Bop Deluxe — 12

Date	Title	Peak Position	Weeks at No.1	Weeks on Chart
24 Feb 79	**FURNITURE MUSIC** *Harvest HAR 5176* BILL NELSON'S RED NOISE	59		3
5 May 79	**REVOLT INTO STYLE** *Harvest HAR 5183* BILL NELSON'S RED NOISE	69		2
5 Jul 80	**DO YOU DREAM IN COLOUR?** *Cocteau COQ 1*	52		4
13 Jun 81	**YOUTH OF NATION ON FIRE** *Mercury WILL 2*	73		3

PHYLLIS NELSON

US, female vocalist, d. 12 Jan 1998 (age 47) — 24

Date	Title	Peak Position	Weeks at No.1	Weeks on Chart
23 Feb 85	**MOVE CLOSER** *Carrere CAR 337* ●	1	1	21
21 May 94	**MOVE CLOSER** *EMI CDEMCT 9*	34		3

RICKY NELSON

US, female vocalist, d. 31 Dec 1985 (age 45) — 150

Date	Title	Peak Position	Weeks at No.1	Weeks on Chart
21 Feb 58	**STOOD UP** *London HLP 8542*	27		2
22 Aug 58	**POOR LITTLE FOOL** *London HLP 8670* ★	4		14
7 Nov 58	**SOMEDAY** *London HLP 8732*	9		13
21 Nov 58	**I GOT A FEELING** *London HLP 8732*	27		1
17 Apr 59	**IT'S LATE** *London HLP 8817*	3		20
15 May 59	**NEVER BE ANYONE ELSE BUT YOU** *London HLP 8817*	14		10
4 Sep 59	**SWEETER THAN YOU** *London HLP 8927*	19		3
11 Sep 59	**JUST A LITTLE TOO MUCH** *London HLP 8927*	11		8
15 Jan 60	**I WANNA BE LOVED** *London HLP 9021*	30		1
7 Jul 60	**YOUNG EMOTIONS** *London HLP 9121*	48		1
1 Jun 61	**HELLO MARY LOU/TRAVELLIN' MAN** *London HLP 9347* ★	2		18
16 Nov 61	**EVERLOVIN'** *London HLP 9440* RICK NELSON	23		5
29 Mar 62	**YOUNG WORLD** *London HLP 9524*	19		13
30 Aug 62	**TEENAGE IDOL** *London HLP 9583* RICK NELSON	39		4
17 Jan 63	**IT'S UP TO YOU** *London HLP 9648* RICK NELSON	22		9
17 Oct 63	**FOOLS RUSH IN** *Brunswick 05895* RICK NELSON	12		9
30 Jan 64	**FOR YOU** *Brunswick 05900* RICK NELSON	14		10
21 Oct 72	**GARDEN PARTY** *MCA MU 1165* RICK NELSON	41		4
24 Aug 91	**HELLO MARY LOU (GOODBYE HEART)** *Liberty EMCT 2*	45		5

SANDY NELSON

US, male drummer (Sander Nelson) — 42

Date	Title	Peak Position	Weeks at No.1	Weeks on Chart
6 Nov 59	**TEEN BEAT** *Top Rank JAR 197*	9		12
14 Dec 61	**LET THERE BE DRUMS** *London HLP 9466*	3		16
22 Mar 62	**DRUMS ARE MY BEAT** *London HLP 9521*	30		6
7 Jun 62	**DRUMMIN' UP A STORM** *London HLP 9558*	39		8

SHARA NELSON

UK, female vocalist. See Massive Attack — 23

Date	Title	Peak Position	Weeks at No.1	Weeks on Chart
24 Jul 93	**DOWN THAT ROAD** *Cooltempo CDCOOL 275*	19		6
18 Sep 93	**ONE GOODBYE IN TEN** *Cooltempo CDCOOL 279*	21		5
12 Feb 94	**UPTIGHT** *Cooltempo CDCOOL 286*	19		5
4 Jun 94	**NOBODY** *Cooltempo CDCOOL 290*	49		1
10 Sep 94	**INSIDE OUT/DOWN THAT ROAD (REMIX)** *Cooltempo CDCOOLX 295*	34		3
16 Sep 95	**ROUGH WITH THE SMOOTH** *Cooltempo CDCOOL 311*	30		2
5 Dec 98	**SENSE OF DANGER** *Pagan 024CDS* PRESENCE FEATURING SHARA NELSON	61		1

WILLIE NELSON

US, male vocalistguitarist — 13

Date	Title	Peak Position	Weeks at No.1	Weeks on Chart
31 Jul 82	**ALWAYS ON MY MIND** *CBS A 2511*	49		3
7 Apr 84	**TO ALL THE GIRLS I'VE LOVED BEFORE** *CBS A 4252* JULIO IGLESIAS & WILLIE NELSON	17		10

NENA

Germany, female/male vocal/instrumental group – Gabriele 'Nena' Kerner, Rolf Brendel, Jürgen Dehmel, Carlo Karges, d. 30 Jan 2002, & JOrn-Uwe Fahrenkrog-Petersen — 14

Date	Title	Peak Position	Weeks at No.1	Weeks on Chart
4 Feb 84	**99 RED BALLOONS** *Epic A 4074* ●	1	3	12
5 May 84	**JUST A DREAM** *Epic A 3249*	70		2

NEO CORTEX

Italy, male production trio — 1

Date	Title	Peak Position	Weeks at No.1	Weeks on Chart
23 Oct 04	**ELEMENTS** *All Around The World CDGLOBE332*	67		1

N*E*R*D

US, male vocal/production trio – Pharrell Williams (Pharrell*), Shae Haley & Chad Hugo — 37

Date	Title	Peak Position	Weeks at No.1	Weeks on Chart
9 Jun 01	**LAPDANCE** *Virgin VUSCD 196* FEATURING LEE HARVEY & VITA	33		2
26 Jan 02	**DIDDY** *Puff Daddy 74321911652* P DIDDY FEATURING THE NEPTUNES	19		4
10 Aug 02	**ROCK STAR** *Virgin VUSCD 253*	15		4
29 Mar 03	**PROVIDER/LAPDANCE** *Virgin VUSCD 262*	20		4
27 Mar 04	**SHE WANTS TO MOVE** *Virgin VUSDX 284*	5		12
26 Jun 04	**MAYBE** *Virgin VUSDX 291*	25		5
21 Jun 08	**EVERYONE NOSE (ALL THE GIRLS STANDING IN THE LINE FOR THE BATHROOM)** *Interscope 1778235*	41		6

FRANCES NERO

US, female vocalist — 9

Date	Title	Peak Position	Weeks at No.1	Weeks on Chart
13 Apr 91	**FOOTSTEPS FOLLOWING ME** *Debut DEBT 3109*	17		9

NERO & THE GLADIATORS

UK, male instrumental group — 6

Date	Title	Peak Position	Weeks at No.1	Weeks on Chart
23 Mar 61	**ENTRY OF THE GLADIATORS** *Decca F 11329*	37		5
27 Jul 61	**IN THE HALL OF THE MOUNTAIN KING** *Decca F 11367*	48		1

ANN NESBY

US, female vocalist — 3

Date	Title	Peak Position	Weeks at No.1	Weeks on Chart
21 Dec 96	**WITNESS (EP)** *AM:PM 5875612*	42		2
17 May 97	**HOLD ON (EP)** *AM:PM 5822332*	75		1

MICHAEL NESMITH
US, male vocalist (Robert Nesmith). See Monkees

Date	Title	Peak	Wks No.1	Wks 6
26 Mar 77	**RIO** *Island WIP 6373*	28		6

NETWORK
UK, male producer (Tim Laws)

Date	Title	Peak	Wks No.1	Wks 4
12 Dec 92	**BROKEN WINGS** *Chrysalis CHS 3923*	46		4

NEVADA
UK, male/female vocal/instrumental group

Date	Title	Peak	Wks No.1	Wks 1
8 Jan 83	**IN THE BLEAK MID WINTER** *Polydor POSP 203*	71		1

ROBBIE NEVIL
US, male vocalist

Date	Title	Peak	Wks No.1	Wks 24
20 Dec 86	**C'EST LA VIE** *Manhattan MT 14*	3		11
2 May 87	**DOMINOES** *Manhattan MT 19*	26		6
11 Jul 87	**WOT'S IT TO YA** *Manhattan MT 24*	43		7

TOM NEVILLE
UK, male DJ/producer

Date	Title	Peak	Wks No.1	Wks 1
6 Mar 04	**JUST FUCK** *Nukleuz 0555PNUK*	60		1

NEVILLE BROTHERS
US, male vocal/instrumental group

Date	Title	Peak	Wks No.1	Wks 7
25 Nov 89	**WITH GOD ON OUR SIDE** *A&M AM 545*	47		6
7 Jul 90	**BIRD ON A WIRE** *A&M AM 568*	72		1

JASON NEVINS
US, male DJ/producer

Date	Title	Peak	Wks No.1	Wks 30
21 Feb 98	**IT'S LIKE THAT (GERMAN IMPORT)** *Columbia 6652932* RUN DMC VS JASON NEVINS	63		3
14 Mar 98	**IT'S LIKE THAT (AMERICAN IMPORT)** *Columbia 6652932* RUN DMC VS JASON NEVINS	65		1
21 Mar 98	**IT'S LIKE THAT** *Sm:)e Communications SM 90652* RUN DMC VS JASON NEVINS ⊛	1	6	16
18 Apr 98	**IT'S TRICKY (IMPORT)** *Epidrome EPD 6656982* RUN DMC VS JASON NEVINS	74		1
26 Jun 99	**INSANE IN THE BRAIN** *INCredible INCRL 17CD* VS CYPRESS HILL	19		3
16 Aug 03	**I'M IN HEAVEN** *Free 2 Air/Incentive 0148665 F2A* PRESENTS UKNY FEATURING HOLLY JAMES	9		5
15 Dec 07	**TOUCH ME LIKE THAT** *All Around The World CDGLOBE795* DANNII MINOGUE VS JASON NEVINS	48		1

NEW ATLANTIC
UK, male production duo

Date	Title	Peak	Wks No.1	Wks 15
29 Feb 92	**I KNOW** *3 Beat 3BT 1*	12		7
3 Oct 92	**INTO THE FUTURE** *3 Beat 3BT 2* FEATURING LINDA WRIGHT	70		1
13 Feb 93	**TAKE OFF SOME TIME** *3 Beat 3BTCD 14*	64		1
26 Nov 94	**THE SUNSHINE AFTER THE RAIN** *3 Beat TABCD 223* NEW ATLANTIC/U4EA FEATURING BERRI	26		6

NEW EDITION
US, male vocal group – Ricky Bell, Michael Bivins, Bobby Brown* (replaced by Johnny Gill*), Ronnie DeVoe & Ralph Tresvant*

Date	Title	Peak	Wks No.1	Wks 36
16 Apr 83	**CANDY GIRL** *London LON 21* ●	1	1	13
13 Aug 83	**POPCORN LOVE** *London LON 31*	43		5
23 Feb 85	**MR TELEPHONE MAN** *MCA 938*	19		9
15 Apr 89	**CRUCIAL** *MCA 23934*	70		1
10 Aug 96	**HIT ME OFF** *MCA MCSTD 48014*	20		4
7 Jun 97	**SOMETHING ABOUT YOU** *MCA MCSTD 48032*	16		4

NEW FOUND GLORY
US, male vocal/instrumental group

Date	Title	Peak	Wks No.1	Wks 8
16 Jun 01	**HIT OR MISS (WAITED TOO LONG)** *MCA 1558232*	58		1
3 Aug 02	**MY FRIENDS OVER YOU** *MCA MCSXD 40286*	30		3
19 Oct 02	**HEAD ON COLLISION** *MCA MCSXD 40298*	64		1
12 Jun 04	**ALL DOWNHILL FROM HERE** *Geffen 9862523*	58		1
11 Sep 04	**FAILURE'S NOT FLATTERING** *Geffen MCSTD40380*	67		1
26 Feb 05	**I DON'T WANNA KNOW** *Geffen 2103972*	48		1

A NEW GENERATION
UK, male vocal/instrumental group

Date	Title	Peak	Wks No.1	Wks 5
26 Jun 68	**SMOKEY BLUES AWAY** *Spark SRL 1007*	38		5

NEW KIDS ON THE BLOCK
US, male vocal group – Jon & Jordan Knight, Joey McIntyre, Donnie Wahlberg & Danny Wood. See Upper Street

Date	Title	Peak	Wks No.1	Wks 92
16 Sep 89	**HANGIN' TOUGH** *CBS BLOCK 1* ★	52		4
11 Nov 89	**YOU GOT IT (THE RIGHT STUFF)** *CBS BLOCK 2* ●	1	3	13
6 Jan 90	**HANGIN' TOUGH** *CBS BLOCK 3*	1	2	9
17 Mar 90	**I'LL BE LOVING YOU (FOREVER)** *CBS BLOCK 4* ★	5		8
12 May 90	**COVER GIRL** *CBS BLOCK 5*	4		8
16 Jun 90	**STEP BY STEP** *CBS BLOCK 6* ● ★	2		7
4 Aug 90	**TONIGHT** *CBS BLOCK 7*	3		10
13 Oct 90	**LET'S TRY AGAIN/DIDN'T I BLOW YOUR MIND** *CBS BLOCK 8*	8		5
8 Dec 90	**THIS ONE'S FOR THE CHILDREN** *CBS BLOCK 9*	9		7
9 Feb 91	**GAMES** *CBS 6566267*	14		4
18 May 91	**CALL IT WHAT YOU WANT** *Columbia 6567857*	12		5
14 Dec 91	**IF YOU GO AWAY** *Columbia 6576667*	9		5
19 Feb 94	**DIRTY DAWG** *Columbia 6600362* NKOTB	27		3
26 Mar 94	**NEVER LET YOU GO** *Columbia 6602072* NKOTB	42		2
13 Sep 08	**SUMMERTIME** *Interscope 1781712*	34		2

NEW MODEL ARMY
UK, male vocal/instrumental group

Date	Title	Peak	Wks No.1	Wks 33
27 Apr 85	**NO REST** *EMI NMA 1*	28		5
3 Aug 85	**THE ACOUSTICS (EP)** *EMI NMA 2*	49		2
30 Nov 85	**BRAVE NEW WORLD** *EMI NMA 3*	57		1
8 Nov 86	**51ST STATE** *EMI NMA 4*	71		2
28 Feb 87	**POISON STREET** *EMI NMA 5*	64		1
26 Sep 87	**WHITE COATS (EP)** *EMI NMA 6*	50		3
21 Jan 89	**STUPID QUESTION** *EMI NMA 7*	31		3
11 Mar 89	**VAGABONDS** *EMI NMA 8*	37		3
10 Jun 89	**GREEN AND GREY** *EMI NMA 9*	37		3
8 Sep 90	**GET ME OUT** *EMI NMA 10*	34		3
3 Nov 90	**PURITY** *EMI NMA 11*	61		2
8 Jun 91	**SPACE** *EMI NMA 12*	39		2
20 Feb 93	**HERE COMES THE WAR** *Epic 6589352*	25		2
24 Jul 93	**LIVING IN THE ROSE (THE BALLADS EP)** *Epic 6592492*	51		1

NEW MUSIK
UK, male vocal/instrumental group

Date	Title	Peak	Wks No.1	Wks 27
6 Oct 79	**STRAIGHT LINES** *GTO GT 255*	53		5
19 Jan 80	**LIVING BY NUMBERS** *GTO GT 261*	13		8
26 Apr 80	**THIS WORLD OF WATER** *GTO GT 268*	31		7
12 Jul 80	**SANCTUARY** *GTO GT 275*	31		7

NEW ORDER
UK, male/female vocal/instrumental group – Bernard Sumner, Gillian Gilbert, Peter Hook & Stephen Morris

Date	Title	Peak	Wks No.1	Wks 200
14 Mar 81	**CEREMONY** *Factory FAC 33*	34		5
3 Oct 81	**PROCESSION/EVERYTHING'S GONE GREEN** *Factory FAC 53*	38		5
22 May 82	**TEMPTATION** *Factory FAC 63*	29		7
19 Mar 83	**BLUE MONDAY** *Factory FAC 73*	12		17
13 Aug 83	**BLUE MONDAY** *Factory FAC 73*	9		21
3 Sep 83	**CONFUSION** *Factory FAC 93*	12		7
28 Apr 84	**THIEVES LIKE US** *Factory FAC 103*	18		5
25 May 85	**THE PERFECT KISS** *Factory FAC 123*	46		4
9 Nov 85	**SUB-CULTURE** *Factory FAC 133*	63		4
29 Mar 86	**SHELLSHOCK** *Factory FAC 143*	28		5
27 Sep 86	**STATE OF THE NATION** *Factory FAC 153*	30		3
27 Sep 86	**THE PEEL SESSIONS (1ST JUNE 1982)** *Strange Fruit SFPS 001*	54		1
15 Nov 86	**BIZARRE LOVE TRIANGLE** *Factory FAC 163*	56		2
1 Aug 87	**TRUE FAITH** *Factory FAC 183/7*	4		10
19 Dec 87	**TOUCHED BY THE HAND OF GOD** *Factory FAC 1937*	20		7
7 May 88	**BLUE MONDAY (REMIX)** *Factory FAC 737*	3		11
10 Dec 88	**FINE TIME** *Factory FAC 2237*	11		8
11 Mar 89	**ROUND AND ROUND** *Factory FAC 2637*	21		7
9 Sep 89	**RUN 2** *Factory FAC 273*	49		2
2 Jun 90	**WORLD IN MOTION...** *Factory/MCA FAC 2937* ENGLANDNEWORDER ●	1	2	12
17 Apr 93	**REGRET** *Centredate Co NUOCD 1*	4		7
3 Jul 93	**RUINED IN A DAY** *Centredate Co NUOCD 2*	22		4
4 Sep 93	**WORLD (THE PRICE OF LOVE)** *Centredate Co NUOCD 3*	13		5
18 Dec 93	**SPOOKY** *Centredate Co NUOCD 4*	22		4
19 Nov 94	**TRUE FAITH (REMIX)** *Centredate Co NUOCD 5*	9		8
21 Jan 95	**NINETEEN63** *London NUOCD 6*	21		4
5 Aug 95	**BLUE MONDAY (2ND REMIX)** *London NUOCD 7*	17		4

Date	Title	Peak Position	Weeks at No.1	Weeks on Chart
25 Aug 01	**CRYSTAL** *London NUOCD 8*	8		4
1 Dec 01	**60 MILES AN HOUR** *London NOUCD 9*	29		2
27 Apr 02	**HERE TO STAY** *London NUOCD 11*	15		3
15 Jun 02	**WORLD IN MOTION...** *London NUOCD 12* ENGLANDNEWORDER	43		2
30 Nov 02	**CONFUSION** *Whacked WACKT 002CD* ARTHUR BAKER VS NEW ORDER	64		1
19 Mar 05	**KRAFTY** *London NUOCD13*	8		4
28 May 05	**JETSTREAM** *London NUOCD14* FEATURING ANA MANTRONIC	20		2
8 Oct 05	**WAITING FOR THE SIRENS' CALL** *London NUOCD15*	21		2
11 Mar 06	**BLUE MONDAY** *New State NSER017*	73		1

NEW POWER GENERATION

US, male/female vocal/instrumental group – members included Prince*, Tommy Barbarella, Michael Bland, Rosie Gaines*, Kirk Johnson, Marva King, Mayte* Garcia, Anthony 'Tony M' Mosley, Levi Seacer, Jr, Rhonda Smith & Sonny Thompson — 64

Date	Title	Peak Position	Weeks at No.1	Weeks on Chart
31 Aug 91	**GETT OFF** *Paisley Park W 0056* PRINCE & THE NEW POWER GENERATION	4		8
21 Sep 91	**CREAM** *Paisley Park W 0061* PRINCE & THE NEW POWER GENERATION ★	15		7
7 Dec 91	**DIAMONDS AND PEARLS** *Paisley Park W 0075* PRINCE & THE NEW POWER GENERATION	25		6
28 Mar 92	**MONEY DON'T MATTER 2 NIGHT** *Paisley Park W 0091* PRINCE & THE NEW POWER GENERATION	19		5
27 Jun 92	**THUNDER** *Paisley Park W 01132P* PRINCE & THE NEW POWER GENERATION	28		3
18 Jul 92	**SEXY MF/STROLLIN'** *Paisley Park W 0123* PRINCE & THE NEW POWER GENERATION	4		7
10 Oct 92	**MY NAME IS PRINCE** *Paisley Park W 0132* PRINCE & THE NEW POWER GENERATION	7		5
14 Nov 92	**MY NAME IS PRINCE (REMIX)** *Paisley Park W 0142T* PRINCE & THE NEW POWER GENERATION	51		1
5 Dec 92	**7** *Paisley Park W 0147* PRINCE & THE NEW POWER GENERATION	27		6
13 Mar 93	**THE MORNING PAPERS** *Paisley Park W 0162CD* PRINCE & THE NEW POWER GENERATION	52		3
1 Apr 95	**GET WILD** *NPG 0061045*	19		4
19 Aug 95	**THE GOOD LIFE** *NPG 0061515*	29		3
5 Jul 97	**THE GOOD LIFE** *NPG 0061515*	15		5
21 Nov 98	**COME ON** *RCA 74321634722*	65		1

NEW RADICALS

US, male/female vocal/instrumental group – Gregg Alexander, Danielle Brisebois* & session musicians — 18

Date	Title	Peak Position	Weeks at No.1	Weeks on Chart
3 Apr 99	**YOU GET WHAT YOU GIVE** *MCA MCSTD 48111* ●	5		17
25 Sep 99	**SOMEDAY WE'LL KNOW** *MCA MCSTD 40217*	48		1

NEW RHODES

UK, male vocal/instrumental group — 3

Date	Title	Peak Position	Weeks at No.1	Weeks on Chart
7 Aug 04	**I WISH I WAS YOU** *Moshi Moshi MOSHI11CD*	63		1
26 Feb 05	**YOU'VE GIVEN ME SOMETHING THAT I CAN'T GIVE BACK** *Moshi Moshi MOSHI15CD*	38		1
27 Aug 05	**FROM THE BEGINNING** *Moshi Moshi MOSHI24CD*	64		1

NEW SEEKERS

UK/Australia/Germany, female/male vocal group – Peter Doyle, d. 22 Oct 2001, Eve Graham, Marty Kristian, Paul Layton & Lyn Paul* — 143

Date	Title	Peak Position	Weeks at No.1	Weeks on Chart
17 Oct 70	**WHAT HAVE THEY DONE TO MY SONG MA** *Philips 6006 027*	44		2
10 Jul 71	**NEVER ENDING SONG OF LOVE** *Philips 6006 125*	2		19
18 Dec 71	**I'D LIKE TO TEACH THE WORLD TO SING (IN PERFECT HARMONY)** *Polydor 2058 184*	1	4	21
4 Mar 72	**BEG, STEAL OR BORROW** *Polydor 2058 201*	2		13
10 Jun 72	**CIRCLES** *Polydor 2058 242*	4		16
2 Dec 72	**COME SOFTLY TO ME** *Polydor 2058 315* FEATURING MARTY KRISTIAN	20		11
24 Feb 73	**PINBALL WIZARD – SEE ME FEEL ME (MEDLEY)** *Polydor 2058 338*	16		8
7 Apr 73	**NEVERTHELESS** *Polydor 2058 340* EVE GRAHAM & THE NEW SEEKERS	34		5
16 Jun 73	**GOODBYE IS JUST ANOTHER WORD** *Polydor 2058 368*	36		5
24 Nov 73	**YOU WON'T FIND ANOTHER FOOL LIKE ME** *Polydor 2058 421* ●	1	1	16
9 Mar 74	**I GET A LITTLE SENTIMENTAL OVER YOU** *Polydor 2058 439* ●	5		9
14 Aug 76	**IT'S SO NICE (TO HAVE YOU HOME)** *CBS 4391*	44		4
29 Jan 77	**I WANNA GO BACK** *CBS 4786*	25		4
15 Jul 78	**ANTHEM (ONE DAY IN EVERY WEEK)** *CBS 6413*	21		10

NEW VAUDEVILLE BAND

UK, male vocal/instrumental studio group formed by Geoff Stephens & fronted by Allen Klein — 43

Date	Title	Peak Position	Weeks at No.1	Weeks on Chart
8 Sep 66	**WINCHESTER CATHEDRAL** *Fontana TF 741* ★	4		19
26 Jan 67	**PEEK-A-BOO** *Fontana TF 784* FEATURING TRISTRAM	7		11
11 May 67	**FINCHLEY CENTRAL** *Fontana TF 824*	11		9
2 Aug 67	**GREEN STREET GREEN** *Fontana TF 853*	37		4

NEW VISION

US, male vocal/instrumental duo. See Lee-Cabrera, David Morales — 2

Date	Title	Peak Position	Weeks at No.1	Weeks on Chart
29 Jan 00	**(JUST) ME AND YOU** *AM:PM CDAMPM 128*	23		2

NEW WORLD

Australia/UK, male vocal/instrumental group – John Kane, John Lee & Mel Noonan — 53

Date	Title	Peak Position	Weeks at No.1	Weeks on Chart
27 Feb 71	**ROSE GARDEN** *RAK 111*	15		11
3 Jul 71	**TOM-TOM TURNAROUND** *RAK 117*	6		15
4 Dec 71	**KARA KARA** *RAK 123*	17		13
13 May 72	**SISTER JANE** *RAK 130*	9		13
12 May 73	**ROOF TOP SINGING** *RAK 148*	50		1

NEW YORK CITY

US, male vocal group — 11

Date	Title	Peak Position	Weeks at No.1	Weeks on Chart
21 Jul 73	**I'M DOING FINE NOW** *RCA 2351*	20		11

NEW YORK SKYY

US, male/female vocal/instrumental group — 2

Date	Title	Peak Position	Weeks at No.1	Weeks on Chart
16 Jan 82	**LET'S CELEBRATE** *Epic EPC A 1898*	67		2

NEW YOUNG PONY CLUB

UK, female/male vocal/instrumental group — 3

Date	Title	Peak Position	Weeks at No.1	Weeks on Chart
31 Mar 07	**THE BOMB** *Island/Modular NYPCCD002*	47		1
14 Jul 07	**ICE CREAM** *Island/Modular MODCDS40*	40		2

NEWBEATS

US, male vocal group – Larry Henley, Dean & Marc Mathis — 22

Date	Title	Peak Position	Weeks at No.1	Weeks on Chart
10 Sep 64	**BREAD AND BUTTER** *Hickory 1269*	15		9
23 Oct 71	**RUN BABY RUN** *London HL 10341*	10		13

BOOKER NEWBURY III

US, male vocalist — 11

Date	Title	Peak Position	Weeks at No.1	Weeks on Chart
28 May 83	**LOVE TOWN** *Polydor POSP 613*	6		8
8 Oct 83	**TEDDY BEAR** *Polydor POSP 637*	44		3

MICKEY NEWBURY

US, male vocalist (Milton Newbury), d. 29 Sep 2002 (age 62) — 5

Date	Title	Peak Position	Weeks at No.1	Weeks on Chart
1 Jul 72	**AMERICAN TRILOGY** *Elektra K 12047*	42		5

NEWCLEUS

US, male/female rap/instrumental group — 6

Date	Title	Peak Position	Weeks at No.1	Weeks on Chart
3 Sep 83	**JAM ON REVENGE (THE WIKKI WIKKI SONG)** *Beckett BKS 8*	44		6

ANTHONY NEWLEY

UK, male actor/vocalist, d. 14 Apr 1999 (age 67) — 130

Date	Title	Peak Position	Weeks at No.1	Weeks on Chart
1 May 59	**I'VE WAITED SO LONG** *Decca F 11127*	3		15
8 May 59	**IDLE ON PARADE EP** *Decca DFE 6566*	13		4
12 Jun 59	**PERSONALITY** *Decca F 11142*	6		12
15 Jan 60	**WHY** *Decca F 11194*	1	4	18
24 Mar 60	**DO YOU MIND** *Decca F 11220*	1	1	15
14 Jul 60	**IF SHE SHOULD COME TO YOU** *Decca F 11254*	4		15
24 Nov 60	**STRAWBERRY FAIR** *Decca F 11295*	3		11
16 Mar 61	**AND THE HEAVENS CRIED** *Decca F 11331*	6		12
15 Jun 61	**POP GOES THE WEASEL/BEE BOM** *Decca F 11362*	12		9
3 Aug 61	**WHAT KIND OF FOOL AM I?** *Decca F 11376*	36		8
25 Jan 62	**D-DARLING** *Decca F 11419*	25		6
26 Jul 62	**THAT NOISE** *Decca F 11486*	34		5

BRAD NEWMAN

UK, male vocalist (Charles Thomas), d. 18 Jan 1999 (age 50) — 1

Date	Title	Peak Position	Weeks at No.1	Weeks on Chart
22 Feb 62	**SOMEBODY TO LOVE** *Fontana H 357*	47		1

DAVE NEWMAN

UK, male vocalist — 6

Date	Title	Peak Position	Weeks at No.1	Weeks on Chart
15 Apr 72	**THE LION SLEEPS TONIGHT** *Pye 7N 45134*	34		6

Silver-selling ○ · Gold-selling ● · Platinum-selling (x multiples) ⊛ · US No.1 ★ · Peak Position · Weeks at No.1 · Weeks on Chart

NEWS
UK, male vocal/instrumental group — 3

Date	Title / Label	Peak Position	Weeks at No.1	Weeks on Chart
29 Aug 81	**AUDIO VIDEO** *George 1*	52		3

NEWTON
UK, male vocalist (William Myers) — 6

Date	Title / Label	Peak Position	Weeks at No.1	Weeks on Chart
15 Jul 95	**SKY HIGH** *Bags Of Fun BAGSCD 6*	56		2
15 Feb 97	**SOMETIMES WHEN WE TOUCH** *Dominion CDDMIN 202*	32		3
16 Aug 97	**DON'T WORRY** *Dominion CDDMIN 206*	61		1

JUICE NEWTON
US, female vocalist (Judith Newton) — 6

Date	Title / Label	Peak Position	Weeks at No.1	Weeks on Chart
2 May 81	**ANGEL OF THE MORNING** *Capitol CL 16189*	43		6

OLIVIA NEWTON-JOHN
Australia (b. UK), female vocalist/actor. Cambridge-born pop/country superstar who dominated the airwaves in the summer of 1978 with back-to-back transatlantic *Grease* million-sellers. This much-loved breast-cancer survivor, who has sold 6.6 million UK singles, has long been hopelessly devoted to health, environmental and animal-rights issues — 234

Date	Title / Label	Peak Position	Weeks at No.1	Weeks on Chart
20 Mar 71	**IF NOT FOR YOU** *Pye International 7N 25543*	7		11
23 Oct 71	**BANKS OF THE OHIO** *Pye International 7N 25568*	6		17
11 Mar 72	**WHAT IS LIFE** *Pye International 7N 25575*	16		8
13 Jan 73	**TAKE ME HOME COUNTRY ROADS** *Pye International 7N 25599*	15		13
16 Mar 74	**LONG LIVE LOVE** *Pye International 7N 25638*	11		8
12 Oct 74	**I HONESTLY LOVE YOU** *EMI 2216* ★	22		6
11 Jun 77	**SAM** *EMI 2616*	6		11
20 May 78	**YOU'RE THE ONE THAT I WANT** *RSO 006* JOHN TRAVOLTA & OLIVIA NEWTON-JOHN ⊛ ★	1	9	26
16 Sep 78	**SUMMER NIGHTS** *RSO 18* JOHN TRAVOLTA & OLIVIA NEWTON-JOHN ⊛	1	7	19
4 Nov 78	**HOPELESSLY DEVOTED TO YOU** *RSO 17* ●	2		11
16 Dec 78	**A LITTLE MORE LOVE** *EMI 2879* ○	4		12
30 Jun 79	**DEEPER THAN THE NIGHT** *EMI 2954*	64		3
21 Jun 80	**XANADU** *Jet 185* & ELECTRIC LIGHT ORCHESTRA ○	1	2	11
23 Aug 80	**MAGIC** *Jet 196* ★	32		7
25 Oct 80	**SUDDENLY** *Jet 7002* & CLIFF RICHARD	15		7
10 Oct 81	**PHYSICAL** *EMI 5234* ○ ★	7		16
16 Jan 82	**LANDSLIDE** *EMI 5257*	18		9
17 Apr 82	**MAKE A MOVE ON ME** *EMI 5291*	43		3
23 Oct 82	**HEART ATTACK** *EMI 5347*	46		4
15 Jan 83	**I HONESTLY LOVE YOU** *EMI 5360*	52		4
12 Nov 83	**TWIST OF FATE** *EMI 5438*	57		2
22 Dec 90	**GREASE MEGAMIX** *Polydor PO 114* JOHN TRAVOLTA & OLIVIA NEWTON-JOHN	3		10
23 Mar 91	**GREASE – THE DREAM MIX** *PWL/Polydor PO 136* FRANKIE VALLI, JOHN TRAVOLTA & OLIVIA NEWTON-JOHN	47		2
4 Jul 92	**I NEED LOVE** *Mercury MER 370*	75		1
9 Dec 95	**HAD TO BE** *EMI CDEMS 410* CLIFF RICHARD & OLIVIA NEWTON-JOHN	22		4
25 Jul 98	**YOU'RE THE ONE THAT I WANT** *Polydor 0441332* JOHN TRAVOLTA & OLIVIA NEWTON-JOHN	4		9

NEXT
US, male vocal trio — 8

Date	Title / Label	Peak Position	Weeks at No.1	Weeks on Chart
6 Jun 98	**TOO CLOSE** *Arista 74321580672* ★	24		3
16 Sep 00	**WIFEY** *Arista 74321790912*	19		5

NEXT OF KIN
UK, male vocal/instrumental group — 6

Date	Title / Label	Peak Position	Weeks at No.1	Weeks on Chart
20 Feb 99	**24 HOURS FROM YOU** *Universal MCSTD 40201*	13		4
19 Jun 99	**MORE LOVE** *Universal MCSTD 40207*	33		2

NIAGRA
UK, male/female vocal/DJ/production duo — 1

Date	Title / Label	Peak Position	Weeks at No.1	Weeks on Chart
27 Sep 97	**CLOUDBURST** *Freeflow FLOW CD2*	65		1

NICE
UK, male vocal/instrumental group — 15

Date	Title / Label	Peak Position	Weeks at No.1	Weeks on Chart
10 Jul 68	**AMERICA** *Immediate IM 068*	21		15

PAUL NICHOLAS
UK, male actor/vocalist, d. 14 Apr 1999 (age 67) — 31

Date	Title / Label	Peak Position	Weeks at No.1	Weeks on Chart
17 Apr 76	**REGGAE LIKE IT USED TO BE** *RSO 2090 185*	17		8
9 Oct 76	**DANCING WITH THE CAPTAIN** *RSO 2090 206*	8		9
4 Dec 76	**GRANDMA'S PARTY** *RSO 2090 216* ○	9		11
9 Jul 77	**HEAVEN ON THE 7TH FLOOR** *RSO 2090 249*	40		3

SUE NICHOLLS
UK, female actor/vocalist — 8

Date	Title / Label	Peak Position	Weeks at No.1	Weeks on Chart
3 Jul 68	**WHERE WILL YOU BE** *Pye 7N 17565*	17		8

NICKELBACK
Canada, male vocal/instrumental group – Chad Kroeger*, Mike Kroeger, Ryan Peake & Ryan Vikedal — 136

Date	Title / Label	Peak Position	Weeks at No.1	Weeks on Chart
23 Feb 02	**HOW YOU REMIND ME (IMPORT)** *Roadrunner 23203323CD*	65		2
9 Mar 02	**HOW YOU REMIND ME** *Roadrunner 23203325* ● ★	4		21
7 Sep 02	**TOO BAD** *Roadrunner RR 20375*	9		9
7 Dec 02	**NEVER AGAIN** *Roadrunner RR 20255*	30		2
27 Sep 03	**SOMEDAY** *Roadrunner RR 20088*	6		9
27 Mar 04	**FEELIN' WAY TOO DAMN GOOD** *Roadrunner RR39983*	39		2
8 Oct 05	**PHOTOGRAPH** *Roadrunner RR39553*	29		3
25 Feb 06	**FAR AWAY** *Roadrunner RR39483*	40		2
27 Oct 07	**ROCKSTAR** *Roadrunner RR39323* ●	2		50
2 Feb 08	**HOW YOU REMIND ME** *Roadrunner NLA320119533*	55		4
14 Jun 08	**PHOTOGRAPH** *Roadrunner RR39553*	18		14
20 Sep 08	**FAR AWAY** *Roadrunner RR39483*	41		5
22 Nov 08	**GOTTA BE SOMEBODY** *Roadrunner RR38332*	20		5
4 Apr 09	**I'D COME FOR YOU** *Roadrunner NLA320888016*	67		2
20 Jun 09	**IF TODAY WAS YOUR LAST DAY** *Roadrunner NLA320887846*	64		6

STEVIE NICKS
US, female vocalist/guitarist. See Fleetwood Mac — 34

Date	Title / Label	Peak Position	Weeks at No.1	Weeks on Chart
15 Aug 81	**STOP DRAGGIN' MY HEART AROUND** *WEA K 79231* WITH TOM PETTY & THE HEARTBREAKERS	50		4
25 Jan 86	**I CAN'T WAIT** *Parlophone R 6110*	54		4
29 Mar 86	**TALK TO ME** *Parlophone R 6124*	68		2
6 May 89	**ROOMS ON FIRE** *EMI EM 90*	16		7
12 Aug 89	**LONG WAY TO GO** *EMI EM 97*	60		2
11 Nov 89	**WHOLE LOTTA TROUBLE** *EMI EM 114*	62		2
24 Aug 91	**SOMETIMES IT'S A BITCH** *EMI EM 203*	40		4
9 Nov 91	**I CAN'T WAIT** *EMI EM 214*	47		2
2 Jul 94	**MAYBE LOVE** *EMI CDEMS 328*	42		3
29 Apr 06	**DREAMS** *Positiva CDTIV232* DEEP DISH FEATURING STEVIE NICKS	14		4

NICOLE
Germany, female vocalist (Nicole Hohloch) — 10

Date	Title / Label	Peak Position	Weeks at No.1	Weeks on Chart
8 May 82	**A LITTLE PEACE** *CBS A 2365* ○	1	2	9
21 Aug 82	**GIVE ME MORE TIME** *CBS A 2467*	75		1

NICOLE
US, female vocalist (Nicole McCloud) — 9

Date	Title / Label	Peak Position	Weeks at No.1	Weeks on Chart
28 Dec 85	**NEW YORK EYES** *Portrait A 6805* WITH TIMMY THOMAS	41		7
26 Dec 92	**ROCK THE HOUSE** *React 12REACT 12* SOURCE FEATURING NICOLE	63		1
6 Jul 96	**RUNNIN' AWAY** *Ore AG 18CD*	69		1

REMI NICOLE
UK, female actor/vocalist — 1

Date	Title / Label	Peak Position	Weeks at No.1	Weeks on Chart
1 Sep 07	**GO MR SUNSHINE** *Island 1744537*	57		1

NICOLETTE
UK, female vocalist (Nicolette Suwoton) — 1

Date	Title / Label	Peak Position	Weeks at No.1	Weeks on Chart
23 Dec 95	**NO GOVERNMENT** *Talkin Loud TLCD 1*	67		1

NIGEL & MARVIN
Trinidad & Tobago, male vocal duo – Nigel & Marvin Lewis — 10

Date	Title / Label	Peak Position	Weeks at No.1	Weeks on Chart
18 May 02	**FOLLOW DA LEADER** *Relentless RELENT 19CD*	5		10

NIGHTBREED
Holland, male production duo. See Angel City — 1

Date	Title / Label	Peak Position	Weeks at No.1	Weeks on Chart
9 Oct 04	**PACK OF WOLVES** *Ram RAMM52CD*	45		1

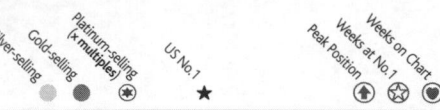

NIGHTCRAWLERS

UK, male vocalist (John Reid) & various instrumental/production/vocal collaborators. See Childliners

Date	Title	Peak Position	Weeks at No.1	Weeks on Chart
				36
15 Oct 94	**PUSH THE FEELING ON** *ffrr FCD 245*	22		5
4 Mar 95	**PUSH THE FEELING ON** *ffrr FCD 257*	3		11
27 May 95	**SURRENDER YOUR LOVE** *Final Vinyl 74321283982*	7		7
9 Sep 95	**DON'T LET THE FEELING GO** *Final Vinyl 74321298822*	13		4
20 Jan 96	**LET'S PUSH IT** *Final Vinyl 74321328142* FEATURING JOHN REID	23		4
20 Apr 96	**SHOULD I EVER (FALL IN LOVE)** *Arista 74321358072*	34		2
27 Jul 96	**KEEP ON PUSHING OUR LOVE** *Arista 74321390422* FEATURING JOHN REID & ALYSHA WARREN	30		2
3 Jul 99	**NEVER KNEW LOVE** *Riverhorse RIVHCD 1*	59		1

MAXINE NIGHTINGALE

UK, female vocalist

Date	Title	Peak Position	Weeks at No.1	Weeks on Chart
				16
1 Nov 75	**RIGHT BACK WHERE WE STARTED FROM** *United Artists UP 36015*	8		8
12 Mar 77	**LOVE HIT ME** *United Artists UP 36215*	11		8

NIGHTMARES ON WAX

UK, male producer (George Evelyn) & various rap/vocal/instrumental collaborators

Date	Title	Peak Position	Weeks at No.1	Weeks on Chart
				6
27 Oct 90	**AFTERMATH/I'M FOR REAL** *Warp WAP 6*	38		5
26 Jun 99	**FINER** *Warp WAP 123CD*	63		1

NIGHTWISH

Finland, male/female vocal/instrumental group

Date	Title	Peak Position	Weeks at No.1	Weeks on Chart
				1
9 Oct 04	**WISH I HAD AN ANGEL** *Nuclear Blast NB1336CD*	60		1

NIGHTWRITERS

US, male producer (Frankie Knuckles)

Date	Title	Peak Position	Weeks at No.1	Weeks on Chart
				2
23 May 92	**LET THE MUSIC USE YOU** *ffreedom TABX 112*	51		2

NIKKE? NICOLE!

US, female rapper (Nicole Miller)

Date	Title	Peak Position	Weeks at No.1	Weeks on Chart
				1
1 Jun 91	**NIKKE DOES IT BETTER** *Love EVOL 5*	73		1

MARKUS NIKOLAI

Germany, male producer

Date	Title	Peak Position	Weeks at No.1	Weeks on Chart
				1
6 Oct 01	**BUSHES** *Southern Fried ECB 24CD*	74		1

KURT NILSEN

Norway, male vocalist/guitarist

Date	Title	Peak Position	Weeks at No.1	Weeks on Chart
				3
29 May 04	**SHE'S SO HIGH** *RCA 82876610882*	25		3

NILSSON

US, male vocalist (Harry Nilsson), d. 15 Jan 1994 (age 52)

Date	Title	Peak Position	Weeks at No.1	Weeks on Chart
				55
27 Sep 69	**EVERYBODY'S TALKIN'** *RCA 1876*	23		15
5 Feb 72	**WITHOUT YOU** *RCA 2165* ★	1	5	20
3 Jun 72	**COCONUT** *RCA 2214*	42		5
16 Oct 76	**WITHOUT YOU** *RCA 2733*	22		8
20 Aug 77	**ALL I THINK ABOUT IS YOU** *RCA PB 9104*	43		3
19 Feb 94	**WITHOUT YOU** *RCA 74321193092*	47		4

CHARLOTTE NILSSON

Sweden, female vocalist

Date	Title	Peak Position	Weeks at No.1	Weeks on Chart
				4
3 Jul 99	**TAKE ME TO YOUR HEAVEN** *Arista 74321686952*	20		4

NINA & FREDERIK

Denmark, female/male vocal duo – Baroness Nina & Baron Frederik von Pallandt, d. 15 May 1994

Date	Title	Peak Position	Weeks at No.1	Weeks on Chart
				29
18 Dec 59	**MARY'S BOY CHILD** *Columbia DB 4375*	26		1
10 Mar 60	**LISTEN TO THE OCEAN** *Columbia DB 4332*	46		2
17 Nov 60	**LITTLE DONKEY** *Columbia DB 4536*	3		10
28 Sep 61	**LONGTIME BOY** *Columbia DB 4703*	43		3
5 Oct 61	**SUCU SUCU** *Columbia DB 4632*	23		13

NINA SKY

US, female vocal duo – Natalie & Nicole Albino

Date	Title	Peak Position	Weeks at No.1	Weeks on Chart
				11
17 Jul 04	**MOVE YA BODY** *Universal MCSTD40373*	6		11

NINE BLACK ALPS

UK, male vocal/instrumental group

Date	Title	Peak Position	Weeks at No.1	Weeks on Chart
				8
19 Mar 05	**SHOT DOWN** *Island CID885*	25		2
4 Jun 05	**NOT EVERYONE** *Island CID892*	31		2
20 Aug 05	**UNSATISFIED** *Island CID899*	30		2
12 Nov 05	**JUST FRIENDS** *Island CID915*	52		1
4 Aug 07	**BURN FASTER** *Island/Uni-Island 1741825*	42		1

NINE INCH NAILS

US, male vocalist/multi-instrumentalist (Trent Reznor) & various male instrumental collaborators

Date	Title	Peak Position	Weeks at No.1	Weeks on Chart
				23
14 Sep 91	**HEAD LIKE A HOLE** *TVT IS 484*	45		4
16 Nov 91	**SIN** *TVT IS 508*	35		2
9 Apr 94	**MARCH OF THE PIGS** *TVT CID 592*	45		3
18 Jun 94	**CLOSER** *TVT CID 596*	25		3
13 Sep 97	**THE PERFECT DRUG** *Interscope IND 95542*	43		1
18 Dec 99	**WE'RE IN THIS TOGETHER** *Island 4971832*	39		2
30 Apr 05	**THE HAND THAT FEEDS** *Island CID888*	7		3
6 Aug 05	**ONLY** *Island CID903*	20		3
21 Apr 07	**SURVIVALISM** *Interscope 1730194*	29		2

999

UK, male vocal/instrumental group

Date	Title	Peak Position	Weeks at No.1	Weeks on Chart
				13
25 Nov 78	**HOMICIDE** *United Artists UP 36467*	40		3
27 Oct 79	**FOUND OUT TOO LATE** *Radar ADA 46*	69		2
16 May 81	**OBSESSED** *Albion ION 1011*	71		1
18 Jul 81	**LIL RED RIDING HOOD** *Albion ION 1017*	59		3
14 Nov 81	**INDIAN RESERVATION** *Albion ION 1023*	51		4

911

UK, male vocal trio – Lee Brennan, Jimmy Constable & Simon Dawbarn. See Upper Street

Date	Title	Peak Position	Weeks at No.1	Weeks on Chart
				94
11 May 96	**NIGHT TO REMEMBER** *Ginga CDGINGA 1*	38		2
10 Aug 96	**LOVE SENSATION** *Ginga CDGINGA 2*	21		4
9 Nov 96	**DON'T MAKE ME WAIT** *Ginga VSCDT 1618*	10		8
22 Feb 97	**THE DAY WE FIND LOVE** *Virgin VSCDG 1619*	4		8
3 May 97	**BODYSHAKIN'** *Virgin VSCDT 1634*	3		7
12 Jul 97	**THE JOURNEY** *Virgin VSCDT 1645*	3		7
1 Nov 97	**PARTY PEOPLE...FRIDAY NIGHT** *Ginga VSCDT 1658*	5		10
4 Apr 98	**ALL I WANT IS YOU** *Virgin VSCDT 1681*	4		7
4 Jul 98	**HOW DO YOU WANT ME TO LOVE YOU?** *Ginga VSCDT 1686*	10		9
24 Oct 98	**MORE THAN A WOMAN** *Virgin VSCDT 1707*	2		13
23 Jan 99	**A LITTLE BIT MORE** *Virgin VSCDT 1719* ●	1	1	9
15 May 99	**PRIVATE NUMBER** *Virgin VSCDT 1730*	3		7
23 Oct 99	**WONDERLAND** *Virgin VSCDT 1755*	13		3

9.9

US, female vocal trio

Date	Title	Peak Position	Weeks at No.1	Weeks on Chart
				3
6 Jul 85	**ALL OF ME FOR ALL OF YOU** *RCA PB 49951*	53		3

NINE YARDS

UK, male vocal group

Date	Title	Peak Position	Weeks at No.1	Weeks on Chart
				3
21 Nov 98	**LONELINESS IS GONE** *Virgin VSCDT 1696*	70		1
10 Apr 99	**MATTER OF TIME** *Virgin VSCDT 1723*	59		1
28 Aug 99	**ALWAYS FIND A WAY** *Virgin VSCDT 1746*	50		1

1910 FRUITGUM CO

US, male vocal/instrumental group – Joey Levine, Mark Gutkowski, Frank Jeckell, Pat Karwan, Floyd Marcus & Steve Mortkowitz

Date	Title	Peak Position	Weeks at No.1	Weeks on Chart
				16
20 Mar 68	**SIMON SAYS** *Pye International 7N 25447*	2		16

1927

Australia, male vocal/instrumental group

Date	Title	Peak Position	Weeks at No.1	Weeks on Chart
				6
22 Apr 89	**THAT'S WHEN I THINK OF YOU** *WEA YZ 351*	46		6

Silver-selling ● Gold-selling ● Platinum-selling (x multiples) ⊛ US No.1 ★ Peak Position Weeks at No.1 Weeks on Chart

98o
US, male vocal group – Justin Jeffre, Drew & Nick Lachey* & Jeff Timmons 17

Date	Title	Peak Position	Weeks at No.1	Weeks on Chart
29 Nov 97	**INVISIBLE MAN** *Motown 8607092*	66		1
31 Oct 98	**TRUE TO YOUR HEART** *Motown 8608832* FEATURING STEVIE WONDER	51		1
13 Mar 99	**BECAUSE OF YOU** *Motown 8609012*	36		2
11 Mar 00	**THANK GOD I FOUND YOU** *Columbia 6690582* MARIAH CAREY FEATURING JOE & 98o ★	10		10
11 Mar 00	**THE HARDEST THING** *Universal MCSTD 40228*	29		2
2 Dec 00	**GIVE ME JUST ONE MORE NIGHT (UNA NOCHE)** *Universal MCSTD 40243*	61		1

99TH FLOOR ELEVATORS
UK, male DJ/production duo 5

Date	Title	Peak Position	Weeks at No.1	Weeks on Chart
12 Aug 95	**HOOKED** *Labello Dance LAD 18CD* FEATURING TONY DE VIT	28		2
30 Mar 96	**I'LL BE THERE** *Labello Dance LAD 25CD2* FEATURING TONY DE VIT	37		2
8 Apr 00	**HOOKED (REMIX)** *Tripoli Trax TTRAX 061CD*	66		1

NIO
UK, male vocalist/rapper/producer (Robert Medcalf) 1

Date	Title	Peak Position	Weeks at No.1	Weeks on Chart
23 Aug 03	**DO YOU THINK YOU'RE SPECIAL?** *Echo ECSCX 132*	52		1

NIRVANA
UK/Ireland, male vocal/instrumental duo 6

Date	Title	Peak Position	Weeks at No.1	Weeks on Chart
15 May 68	**RAINBOW CHASER** *Island WIP 6029*	34		6

NIRVANA
US, male vocal/instrumental trio – Kurt Cobain, d. 5 Apr 1994, Dave Grohl & Krist Novoselic. See Foo Fighters 36

Date	Title	Peak Position	Weeks at No.1	Weeks on Chart
30 Nov 91	**SMELLS LIKE TEEN SPIRIT** *DGC DGCS 5*	7		6
14 Mar 92	**COME AS YOU ARE** *DGC DGCS 7*	9		5
25 Jul 92	**LITHIUM** *DGC DGCS 9*	11		6
12 Dec 92	**IN BLOOM** *Geffen GFS 34*	28		7
6 Mar 93	**OH THE GUILT** *Touch And Go TG 83CD*	12		2
11 Sep 93	**HEART-SHAPED BOX** *Geffen GFSTD 54*	5		5
18 Dec 93	**ALL APOLOGIES/RAPE ME** *Geffen GFSTD 66*	32		5

NITRO DELUXE
US, male vocalist/producer (Manny Scretching) 16

Date	Title	Peak Position	Weeks at No.1	Weeks on Chart
14 Feb 87	**THIS BRUTAL HOUSE** *Cooltempo COOL 142*	47		7
13 Jun 87	**THIS BRUTAL HOUSE** *Cooltempo COOL 142*	62		4
6 Feb 88	**LET'S GET BRUTAL** *Cooltempo COOL 142*	24		5

NITZER EBB
UK, male vocal/production duo 3

Date	Title	Peak Position	Weeks at No.1	Weeks on Chart
11 Jan 92	**GODHEAD** *Mute 1MUTE 135T*	56		1
11 Apr 92	**ASCEND** *Mute CDMUTE 145*	52		1
4 Mar 95	**KICK IT** *Mute LCDMUTE 155*	75		1

NIVEA
US, female vocalist (Nivea Hamilton) 8

Date	Title	Peak Position	Weeks at No.1	Weeks on Chart
3 Mar 01	**DANGER (BEEN SO LONG)** *Jive 9251722* MYSTIKAL FEATURING NIVEA	28		3
4 May 02	**RUN AWAY (I WANNA BE WITH U)/DON'T MESS WITH THE RADIO** *Jive 9253362*	48		1
21 Sep 02	**DON'T MESS WITH MY MAN** *Jive 9254082* FEATURING BRIAN & BRANDON CASEY	41		2
10 May 03	**LAUNDROMAT/DON'T MESS WITH MY MAN** *Jive 9254822*	33		2

NIZLOPI
UK, male vocal/instrumental duo – Luke Concannon & John Parker 15

Date	Title	Peak Position	Weeks at No.1	Weeks on Chart
24 Dec 05	**JCB SONG** *FDM FDMNIZ004* ●	1	1	15

NNEKA
Nigeria, female vocalist/guitarist (Nneka Egbuna) 6

Date	Title	Peak Position	Weeks at No.1	Weeks on Chart
5 Sep 09	**HEARTBEAT** *Yo Mama DEK560800002*	20		6

NO AUTHORITY
US, male vocal group 1

Date	Title	Peak Position	Weeks at No.1	Weeks on Chart
14 Mar 98	**DON'T STOP** *Epic 6655592*	54		1

NO DICE
UK, male vocal/instrumental group 2

Date	Title	Peak Position	Weeks at No.1	Weeks on Chart
5 May 79	**COME DANCING** *EMI 2927*	65		2

NO DOUBT
US, female/male vocal/instrumental group – Gwen Stefani*, Tom Dumont, Tony Kanai & Adrian Young 74

Date	Title	Peak Position	Weeks at No.1	Weeks on Chart
26 Oct 96	**JUST A GIRL** *Interscope IND 80034*	38		2
22 Feb 97	**DON'T SPEAK** *Interscope IND 95515* ●	1	3	18
5 Jul 97	**JUST A GIRL** *Interscope IND 95539*	3		7
4 Oct 97	**SPIDERWEBS** *Interscope IND 95551*	16		3
20 Dec 97	**SUNDAY MORNING** *Interscope IND 95566*	50		3
12 Jun 99	**NEW** *Higher Ground HIGHS 22CD*	30		2
25 Mar 00	**EX-GIRLFRIEND** *Interscope 4972992*	23		3
7 Oct 00	**SIMPLE KIND OF LIFE** *Interscope 4974162*	69		1
16 Feb 02	**HEY BABY** *Interscope 4976682*	2		9
15 Jun 02	**HELLA GOOD** *Interscope 4977362*	12		7
12 Oct 02	**UNDERNEATH IT ALL** *Interscope 4977792*	18		5
6 Dec 03	**IT'S MY LIFE** *Interscope 9813724*	20		7
13 Mar 04	**IT'S MY LIFE/BATHWATER** *Interscope 9861993*	17		7

NO MERCY
US, male vocal trio – Marty Cintron III & Ariel & Gabriel Hernandez 26

Date	Title	Peak Position	Weeks at No.1	Weeks on Chart
18 Jan 97	**WHERE DO YOU GO** *Arista 74321401502* ●	2		15
24 May 97	**PLEASE DON'T GO** *Arista 74321481372*	4		7
6 Sep 97	**KISS YOU ALL OVER** *Arista 74321514452*	16		4

NO REASON
UK, male vocal group 1

Date	Title	Peak Position	Weeks at No.1	Weeks on Chart
11 Sep 04	**MAN LIKE ME** *Mad As Toast TOAST001*	53		1

NO SWEAT
Ireland, male vocal/instrumental group 5

Date	Title	Peak Position	Weeks at No.1	Weeks on Chart
13 Oct 90	**HEART AND SOUL** *London LON 274*	64		4
2 Feb 91	**TEAR DOWN THE WALLS** *London LON 257*	61		1

NO WAY JOSE
UK, male production/vocal/instrumental group 6

Date	Title	Peak Position	Weeks at No.1	Weeks on Chart
3 Aug 85	**TEQUILA** *Fourth & Broadway BRW 28*	47		6

NO WAY SIS
UK, male vocal/instrumental group 4

Date	Title	Peak Position	Weeks at No.1	Weeks on Chart
21 Dec 96	**I'D LIKE TO TEACH THE WORLD TO SING** *EMI CDEM 461*	27		4

NOAH & THE WHALE
UK, male vocal/instrumental group – Charlie & Doug Fink, Tom Hobden & Matt Owens 14

Date	Title	Peak Position	Weeks at No.1	Weeks on Chart
26 Jul 08	**5 YEAR'S TIME** *Vertigo 1774960*	7		14

NODDY
UK, male cartoon vocalist & female vocal trio 4

Date	Title	Peak Position	Weeks at No.1	Weeks on Chart
20 Dec 03	**MAKE WAY FOR NODDY** *BMG 82876582142*	29		4

NODESHA
US, female vocalist (Nodesha Felix) 8

Date	Title	Peak Position	Weeks at No.1	Weeks on Chart
6 Sep 03	**MISS PERFECT** *BMG 82876556742* ABS FEATURING NODESHA	5		7
1 Nov 03	**GET IT WHILE IT'S HOT** *Arista 82876559592*	55		1

JIM NOIR
UK, male vocalist/multi-instrumentalist (Alan Roberts) 2

Date	Title	Peak Position	Weeks at No.1	Weeks on Chart
13 May 06	**MY PATCH** *My Dad Recordings MY013CD*	65		1
22 Jul 06	**EANIE MEANY** *My Dad Recordings MY011CDX*	67		1

Silver-selling ○ · Gold-selling ● · Platinum-selling (x multiples) · US No.1 ★ · Peak Position · Weeks at No.1 · Weeks on Chart

NOISE NEXT DOOR

UK, male vocal/instrumental trio — Weeks on chart: 10

Date	Title	Peak Position	Weeks at No.1	Weeks on Chart
6 Nov 04	**LOCK UP YA DAUGHTERS/MINISTRY OF MAYHEM** *Us & Them USTHEMS10*	12		4
19 Feb 05	**CALENDAR GIRL** *Us & Them USTHEMS12*	11		4
11 Jun 05	**SHE MIGHT** *Us & Them WEA386CD1*	27		2

NOISETTES

UK, female/male vocal/instrumental trio – Shingai Shoniwa, Jamie Morrison & Dan Smith — Weeks on chart: 40

Date	Title	Peak Position	Weeks at No.1	Weeks on Chart
2 Dec 06	**DON'T GIVE UP** *Vertigo 9844295*	73		1
10 Feb 07	**SISTER ROSETTA (CAPTURE THE SPIRIT)** *Vertigo 1723267*	63		1
4 Apr 09	**DON'T UPSET THE RHYTHM** *Vertigo 1798000*	2		20
20 Jun 09	**NEVER FORGET YOU** *Mercury GBUM70817778*	20		18

BERNIE NOLAN

Ireland, female actor/vocalist. See Nolans — Weeks on chart: 3

Date	Title	Peak Position	Weeks at No.1	Weeks on Chart
6 Mar 04	**MACUSHLA** *Laurel Bank 4KATECD1*	38		3

NOLANS

Ireland, female vocal group – Anne, Bernadette (Bernie Nolan*), Coleen, Denise, Linda & Maureen Nolan — Weeks on chart: 90

Date	Title	Peak Position	Weeks at No.1	Weeks on Chart
6 Oct 79	**SPIRIT BODY AND SOUL** *Epic EPC 7796* NOLAN SISTERS	34		6
22 Dec 79	**I'M IN THE MOOD FOR DANCING** *Epic EPC 8068* ●	3		15
12 Apr 80	**DON'T MAKE WAVES** *Epic EPC 8349*	12		11
13 Sep 80	**GOTTA PULL MYSELF TOGETHER** *Epic EPC 8878* ○	9		13
6 Dec 80	**WHO'S GONNA ROCK YOU** *Epic EPC 9325*	12		11
14 Mar 81	**ATTENTION TO ME** *Epic EPC 9571* ○	9		13
15 Aug 81	**CHEMISTRY** *Epic EPC A 1485*	15		8
20 Feb 82	**DON'T LOVE ME TOO HARD** *Epic EPC A 1927*	14		12
1 Apr 95	**I'M IN THE MOOD FOR DANCING** *Living Beat LBECD 31*	51		1

NOMAD

UK, male/female production/vocal duo – Damon Rochefort & Sharon Dee Clarke – with various production/rap/vocal collaborators — Weeks on chart: 22

Date	Title	Peak Position	Weeks at No.1	Weeks on Chart
2 Feb 91	**(I WANNA GIVE YOU) DEVOTION** *Rumour RUMA 25* FEATURING MC MIKEE FREEDOM ○	2		10
4 May 91	**JUST A GROOVE** *Rumour RUMA 33*	16		6
28 Sep 91	**SOMETHING SPECIAL** *Rumour RUMA 35*	73		1
25 Apr 92	**YOUR LOVE IS LIFTING ME** *Rumour RUMA 48*	60		2
7 Nov 92	**24 HOURS A DAY** *Rumour RUMA 60*	61		1
25 Nov 95	**(I WANNA GIVE YOU) DEVOTION (REMIX)** *Rumour RUMACD 75*	42		2

NONCHALANT

US, female vocalist (Tanya Pointer) — Weeks on chart: 1

Date	Title	Peak Position	Weeks at No.1	Weeks on Chart
29 Jun 96	**5 O'CLOCK** *MCA MCSTD 48011*	44		1

PETER NOONE

UK, male vocalist. See Herman's Hermits — Weeks on chart: 9

Date	Title	Peak Position	Weeks at No.1	Weeks on Chart
22 May 71	**OH YOU PRETTY THING** *RAK 114*	12		9

NOOTROPIC

UK, male instrumental/production duo — Weeks on chart: 1

Date	Title	Peak Position	Weeks at No.1	Weeks on Chart
16 Mar 96	**I SEE ONLY YOU** *Hi-Life 5779832*	42		1

NORE

US, male rapper (Victor Santiago, Jr) — Weeks on chart: 9

Date	Title	Peak Position	Weeks at No.1	Weeks on Chart
21 Sep 02	**NOTHIN'** *Def Jam 639262*	11		7
29 Nov 03	**CRASHIN' A PARTY** *Universal MCSTD 40341* LUMIDEE FEATURING NORE	55		1
22 May 04	**NOTHIN'** *Def Jam 639262*	72		1

NORTH & SOUTH

UK, male vocal/instrumental group – Lee Otter, Sam Chapman, James Hurst & Tom Lowe — Weeks on chart: 16

Date	Title	Peak Position	Weeks at No.1	Weeks on Chart
17 May 97	**I'M A MAN NOT A BOY** *RCA 74321461142*	7		5
9 Aug 97	**TARANTINO'S NEW STAR** *RCA 74321501242*	18		5
8 Nov 97	**BREATHING** *RCA 74321528422*	27		2
4 Apr 98	**NO SWEAT '98** *RCA 74321562212*	29		4

NORTHERN HEIGHTZ

UK, male/female vocal/DJ/production group — Weeks on chart: 3

Date	Title	Peak Position	Weeks at No.1	Weeks on Chart
20 Mar 04	**LOOK AT US** *Iconic CDXIC002*	29		3

NORTHERN LINE

UK/South Africa, male vocal group — Weeks on chart: 12

Date	Title	Peak Position	Weeks at No.1	Weeks on Chart
9 Oct 99	**RUN FOR YOUR LIFE** *Global Talent GTR 002CDS1*	18		4
11 Mar 00	**LOVE ON THE NORTHERN LINE** *Global Talent GTR 003CDS1*	15		5
17 Jun 00	**ALL AROUND THE WORLD** *Global Talent GTR 004CDS1*	27		3

NORTHERN UPROAR

UK, male vocal/instrumental group — Weeks on chart: 11

Date	Title	Peak Position	Weeks at No.1	Weeks on Chart
21 Oct 95	**ROLLERCOASTER/ROUGH BOYS** *Heavenly HVN 047CD*	41		2
3 Feb 96	**FROM A WINDOW/THIS MORNING** *Heavenly HVN 051CD*	17		3
20 Apr 96	**LIVIN' IT UP** *Heavenly HVN 52CD*	24		2
22 Jun 96	**TOWN** *Heavenly HVN 54CD*	48		1
7 Jun 97	**ANY WAY YOU LOOK** *Heavenly HVN 70CD*	36		2
23 Aug 97	**A GIRL I ONCE KNEW** *Heavenly HVN 73CD*	63		1

NORTHSIDE

UK, male vocal/instrumental group — Weeks on chart: 12

Date	Title	Peak Position	Weeks at No.1	Weeks on Chart
9 Jun 90	**SHALL WE TAKE A TRIP/MOODY PLACES** *Factory FAC 268*	50		5
3 Nov 90	**MY RISING STAR** *Factory FAC 2987*	32		3
1 Jun 91	**TAKE 5** *Factory FAC 3087*	40		4

FREDDIE NOTE & THE RUDIES

Jamaica, male vocal/instrumental group — Weeks on chart: 2

Date	Title	Peak Position	Weeks at No.1	Weeks on Chart
10 Oct 70	**MONTEGO BAY** *Trojan TR 7791*	45		2

NOTORIOUS B.I.G.

US, male rapper (Christopher Wallace), d. 9 Mar 1997 (age 24) — Weeks on chart: 56

Date	Title	Peak Position	Weeks at No.1	Weeks on Chart
29 Oct 94	**JUICY** *Bad Boy 74321240102*	72		1
1 Apr 95	**BIG POPPA** *Puff Daddy 74321263412*	63		1
15 Jul 95	**CAN'T YOU SEE** *Tommy Boy TBCD 700* TOTAL FEATURING THE NOTORIOUS B.I.G.	43		2
19 Aug 95	**ONE MORE CHANCE/STAY WITH ME** *Puff Daddy 74321300782*	34		2
3 May 97	**HYPNOTIZE** *Puff Daddy 74321466412* ★	10		4
9 Aug 97	**MO MONEY MO PROBLEMS** *Puff Daddy 74321492492* FEATURING PUFF DADDY & MA$E ★	6		10
14 Feb 98	**SKY'S THE LIMIT** *Puff Daddy 74321587992* FEATURING 112	35		2
18 Jul 98	**RUNNIN'** *Black Jam BJAM 9005* 2PAC & THE NOTORIOUS B.I.G.	15		3
5 Feb 00	**NOTORIOUS B.I.G.** *Puff Daddy 74321737312* FEATURING PUFF DADDY & LIL' KIM	16		5
31 Jan 04	**RUNNIN' (DYIN' TO LIVE)** *Interscope 9815329* 2PAC & THE NOTORIOUS B.I.G.	17		6
28 Jan 06	**NASTY GIRL** *Bad Boy AT0229CDX* FEATURING DIDDY, NELLY, JAGGED EDGE AND AVERY STORM	1	2	19
6 May 06	**SPIT YOUR GAME** *Bad Boy AT0240CDX*	64		1

NOTTINGHAM FOREST FC & PAPER LACE

UK, male football team/vocalists — Weeks on chart: 6

Date	Title	Peak Position	Weeks at No.1	Weeks on Chart
4 Mar 78	**WE'VE GOT THE WHOLE WORLD IN OUR HANDS** *Warner Brothers K 17110*	24		6

HEATHER NOVA

Bermuda, female vocalist/guitarist (Heather Frith) — Weeks on chart: 1

Date	Title	Peak Position	Weeks at No.1	Weeks on Chart
25 Feb 95	**WALK THIS WORLD** *Butterfly BFLD 19*	69		1

NANCY NOVA

UK, female vocalist (Carol Holness) — Weeks on chart: 2

Date	Title	Peak Position	Weeks at No.1	Weeks on Chart
4 Sep 82	**NO NO NO** *EMI 5328*	63		2

NOVACANE VS NO ONE DRIVING

UK, male production duo — Weeks on chart: 1

Date	Title	Peak Position	Weeks at No.1	Weeks on Chart
15 Jun 02	**LOVE BE MY LOVER (PLAYA SOL)** *Direction 6727792*	69		1

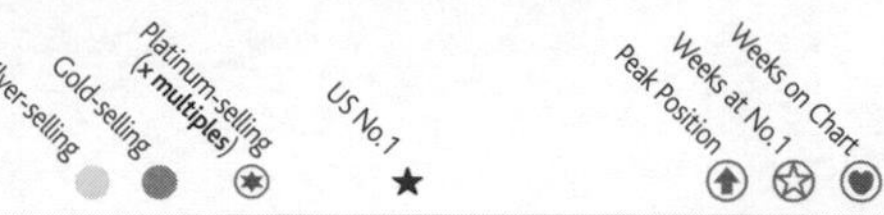

NOVASPACE
Germany, male/female vocal/production duo — 3

Date	Title / Label	Peak Position	Weeks at No.1	Weeks on Chart
22 Feb 03	**TIME AFTER TIME** *Substance SUBS 15CDS*	29		3

TOM NOVY
Germany, male DJ/producer (Thomas Reichold) — 26

Date	Title / Label	Peak Position	Weeks at No.1	Weeks on Chart
2 May 98	**SUPERSTAR** *D:disco 74321569352* NOVY VERSUS ENIAC	32		3
3 Jun 00	**PUMPIN'** *Positiva CDTIVS 132* NOVY VERSUS ENIAC	19		3
2 Sep 00	**I ROCK** *Rulin 3CDS*	55		1
4 Aug 01	**NOW OR NEVER** *Rulin 14CDS* FEATURING LIMA	64		1
3 Dec 05	**YOUR BODY** *Data DATA102CDS* FEATURING MICHAEL MARSHALL	10		14
12 Aug 06	**TAKE IT (CLOSING TIME)** *Data DATA132CDS* & LIMA	31		4

NRG
UK, male DJ/producer (Neil Rumney). See DJ Flavours, Smokin Beats featuring Lyn Eden — 3

Date	Title / Label	Peak Position	Weeks at No.1	Weeks on Chart
29 Mar 97	**NEVER LOST HIS HARDCORE** *Top Banana TOPCD 04*	71		1
12 Dec 98	**NEVER LOST HIS HARDCORE (REMIX)** *Top Banana TOPCD 010*	61		1
20 Mar 04	**NEVER LOST HIS HARDCORE** *Tidy Trax TIDY200T2*	59		1

NT GANG
Germany, male production trio. See B-Tribe, Sacred Spirit — 1

Date	Title / Label	Peak Position	Weeks at No.1	Weeks on Chart
2 Apr 88	**WAM BAM** *Cooltempo COOL 163*	71		1

NU-BIRTH
UK, male production duo. See M Factor, Nush, 187 Lockdown — 2

Date	Title / Label	Peak Position	Weeks at No.1	Weeks on Chart
6 Sep 97	**ANYTIME** *XL Recordings XLS 85CD*	48		1
6 Jun 98	**ANYTIME** *Locked On LOX 97CD*	41		1

NU CIRCLES FEATURING EMMA B
UK, male/female vocal/production trio — 1

Date	Title / Label	Peak Position	Weeks at No.1	Weeks on Chart
8 Feb 03	**WHAT YOU NEED (TONIGHT)** *East West EW 258CD*	46		1

NU COLOURS
UK, male/female vocal group — 11

Date	Title / Label	Peak Position	Weeks at No.1	Weeks on Chart
6 Jun 92	**TEARS** *Wild Card CARD 1*	55		2
10 Oct 92	**POWER** *Wild Card CARD 3*	64		1
5 Jun 93	**WHAT IN THE WORLD** *Wild Card CARDD 4*	57		2
27 Nov 93	**POWER (REMIX)** *Wild Card CARDD 5*	40		2
25 May 96	**DESIRE** *Wild Card 5763652*	31		2
24 Aug 96	**SPECIAL KIND OF LOVER** *Wild Card 5752012*	38		2

NU GENERATION
UK, male producer (Aston Harvey) — 9

Date	Title / Label	Peak Position	Weeks at No.1	Weeks on Chart
29 Jan 00	**IN YOUR ARMS (RESCUE ME)** *Concept CDCON 7*	8		8
21 Oct 00	**NOWHERE TO RUN 2000** *Concept CDCON 16*	66		1

NU MATIC
UK, male production duo — 1

Date	Title / Label	Peak Position	Weeks at No.1	Weeks on Chart
8 Aug 92	**SPRING IN MY STEP** *XL Recordings XLS 31*	58		1

NU SHOOZ
US, female/male vocal/instrumental duo – Valerie Day & John Smith — 17

Date	Title / Label	Peak Position	Weeks at No.1	Weeks on Chart
24 May 86	**I CAN'T WAIT** *Atlantic A 9446* (silver)	2		14
26 Jul 86	**POINT OF NO RETURN** *Atlantic A 9392*	48		3

NU SOUL FEATURING KELLI RICH
US, male/female vocal/instrumental trio — 2

Date	Title / Label	Peak Position	Weeks at No.1	Weeks on Chart
13 Jan 96	**HIDE-A-WAY** *ffrr FCD 269*	27		2

NUANCE FEATURING VIKKI LOVE
US, male producer (Ron Dean Miller) & female vocalist — 3

Date	Title / Label	Peak Position	Weeks at No.1	Weeks on Chart
19 Jan 85	**LOVERIDE** *Fourth & Broadway BRW 20*	59		3

NUKLEUZ DJs
UK, male DJs/producers — 14

Date	Title / Label	Peak Position	Weeks at No.1	Weeks on Chart
24 Aug 02	**DJ NATION** *Nukleuz NUKFB 0440*	40		2
8 Feb 03	**DJ NATION (BOOTLEG EDITION)** *Nukleuz 0468 FNUK*	33		2
9 Aug 03	**SUMMER EDITION** *Nukleuz 0542 FNUK* DJ NATION	59		2
15 Nov 03	**DJ NATION – HARDER EDITION** *Nukleuz 0572 FBNUK*	48		3
17 Jan 04	**DJ NATION (BOOTLEG EDITION)** *Nukleuz 0468 FNUK*	63		2
27 Mar 04	**X-RATED** *Amato 0501FBNUK* DJ NATION	52		3

GARY NUMAN
UK, male vocalist/synthesizer player (Gary Webb) — 171

Date	Title / Label	Peak Position	Weeks at No.1	Weeks on Chart
19 May 79	**ARE 'FRIENDS' ELECTRIC?** *Beggars Banquet BEG 18* TUBEWAY ARMY (gold)	1	4	16
1 Sep 79	**CARS** *Beggars Banquet BEG 23* (gold)	1	1	11
24 Nov 79	**COMPLEX** *Beggars Banquet BEG 29* (silver)	6		9
24 May 80	**WE ARE GLASS** *Beggars Banquet BEG 35*	5		7
30 Aug 80	**I DIE: YOU DIE** *Beggars Banquet BEG 46*	6		7
20 Dec 80	**THIS WRECKAGE** *Beggars Banquet BEG 50*	20		7
29 Aug 81	**SHE'S GOT CLAWS** *Beggars Banquet BEG 62*	6		6
5 Dec 81	**LOVE NEEDS NO DISGUISE** *Beggars Banquet BEG 33* & DRAMATIS	33		7
6 Mar 82	**MUSIC FOR CHAMELEONS** *Beggars Banquet BEG 70*	19		7
19 Jun 82	**WE TAKE MYSTERY (TO BED)** *Beggars Banquet BEG 77*	9		4
28 Aug 82	**WHITE BOYS AND HEROES** *Beggars Banquet BEG 81*	20		4
3 Sep 83	**WARRIORS** *Beggars Banquet BEG 95*	20		5
22 Oct 83	**SISTER SURPRISE** *Beggars Banquet BEG 101*	32		3
3 Nov 84	**BERSERKER** *Numa NU 4*	32		5
22 Dec 84	**MY DYING MACHINE** *Numa NU 6*	66		1
9 Feb 85	**CHANGE YOUR MIND** *Polydor POSP 722* SHARPE & NUMAN	17		8
25 May 85	**THE LIVE EP** *Numa NUM 7*	27		4
10 Aug 85	**YOUR FASCINATION** *Numa NU 9*	46		5
21 Sep 85	**CALL OUT THE DOGS** *Numa NU 11*	49		2
16 Nov 85	**MIRACLES** *Numa NU 13*	49		3
19 Apr 86	**THIS IS LOVE** *Numa NU 16*	28		3
28 Jun 86	**I CAN'T STOP** *Numa NU 17*	27		4
4 Oct 86	**NEW THING FROM LONDON TOWN** *Numa NU 19* SHARPE & NUMAN	52		3
6 Dec 86	**I STILL REMEMBER** *Numa NU 21*	74		1
28 Mar 87	**RADIO HEART** *GFM 109* RADIO HEART FEATURING GARY NUMAN	35		6
13 Jun 87	**LONDON TIMES** *GFM 112* RADIO HEART FEATURING GARY NUMAN	48		2
19 Sep 87	**CARS (E REG MODEL)/ARE 'FRIENDS' ELECTRIC? (REMIX)** *Beggars Banquet BEG 199*	16		7
30 Jan 88	**NO MORE LIES** *Polydor POSP 894* SHARPE & NUMAN	34		3
1 Oct 88	**NEW ANGER** *Illegal ILS 1003*	46		2
3 Dec 88	**AMERICA** *Illegal ILS 1004*	49		1
3 Jun 89	**I'M ON AUTOMATIC** *Polydor PO 43* SHARPE & NUMAN	44		2
16 Mar 91	**HEART** *IRS NUMAN 1*	43		2
21 Mar 92	**THE SKIN GAME** *Numa NU 23*	68		1
1 Aug 92	**MACHINE + SOUL** *Numa NUM 124*	72		1
4 Sep 93	**CARS (2ND REMIX)** *Beggars Banquet BEG 264CD*	53		1
16 Mar 96	**CARS (2ND REMIX)** *Polygram TV PRMCD 1*	17		4
13 Jul 02	**RIP** *Jagged Halo JHCD5*	29		2
5 Jul 03	**CRAZIER** *Jagged Halo JHCDX6* VS RICO	13		3
29 Jul 06	**IN A DARK PLACE** *Cooking Vinyl MORTALCDS001*	63		1
11 Aug 07	**THE LEATHER SEA** *Submission Ltd SUB03CD2* VS ADE FENTON	72		1

NUMBER ONE CUP
US, male vocal/instrumental group — 1

Date	Title / Label	Peak Position	Weeks at No.1	Weeks on Chart
2 Mar 96	**DIVEBOMB** *Blue Rose BRRC 10032*	61		1

JOSE NUNEZ FEATURING OCTAHVIA
US, male/female vocal/DJ/production duo. See Choo Choo Project — 2

Date	Title / Label	Peak Position	Weeks at No.1	Weeks on Chart
5 Sep 98	**IN MY LIFE** *Ministry Of Sound MOSCDS 126*	56		1
5 Jun 99	**HOLD ON** *Ministry Of Sound MOSCDS 130*	44		1

BOBBY NUNN
US, male vocalist — 3

Date	Title / Label	Peak Position	Weeks at No.1	Weeks on Chart
4 Feb 84	**DON'T KNOCK IT (UNTIL YOU TRY IT)** *Motown TMG 1323*	65		3

NUSH
UK, male production duo. See M Factor, Nu-Birth, 187 Lockdown — 7

Date	Title / Label	Peak Position	Weeks at No.1	Weeks on Chart
23 Jul 94	**U GIRLS** *Blunted Vinyl BLNCDX 006*	58		1
22 Apr 95	**MOVE THAT BODY** *Blunted Vinyl BLNCD 012*	46		2
16 Sep 95	**U GIRLS (LOOK SO SEXY) (REMIX)** *Blunted Vinyl BLNCD 13*	15		4

NUT
UK, female vocalist (Cat Goscovitch) — 4

Date	Title	Peak	Wks at No.1	Wks on Chart
8 Jun 96	**BRAINS** *Epic NUTCD 2*	64		1
21 Sep 96	**CRAZY** *Epic NUTCD 5*	56		1
11 Jan 97	**SCREAM** *Epic NUTCD 6*	43		2

PAOLO NUTINI
UK, male vocalist/guitarist — 100

Date	Title	Peak	Wks at No.1	Wks on Chart
8 Jul 06	**LAST REQUEST** *Atlantic ATUK034CD*	5		25
30 Sep 06	**JENNY DON'T BE HASTY** *Atlantic ATUK043CD*	20		11
9 Dec 06	**REWIND** *Atlantic ATUK050CD*	27		9
10 Mar 07	**NEW SHOES** *Atlantic ATUK057CD*	21		13
30 May 09	**CANDY** *Atlantic ATUK087CDX*	19		11
22 Aug 09	**COMING UP EASY** *Atlantic ATUK089CD*	62		1
10 Oct 09	**LAST REQUEST** *Atlantic ATUK034CD*	41		3
24 Oct 09	**PENCIL FULL OF LEAD** *Atlantic ATUK091CD*	17		21
30 Jan 10	**TEN TEN** *Atlantic GBAHS0900105*	51		6

NUTTIN' NYCE
US, female vocal group — 2

Date	Title	Peak	Wks at No.1	Wks on Chart
10 Jun 95	**DOWN 4 WHATEVA** *Jive JIVECD 365*	62		1
12 Aug 95	**FROGGY STYLE** *Jive JIVECD 381*	68		1

NUYORICAN SOUL
US, male/female vocal/DJ/production group. See Masters At Work — 10

Date	Title	Peak	Wks at No.1	Wks on Chart
8 Feb 97	**RUNAWAY** *Talkin Loud TLCD 20* FEATURING INDIA	24		6
10 May 97	**IT'S ALRIGHT, I FEEL IT!** *Talkin Loud TLCD 22* FEATURING JOCELYN BROWN	26		2
25 Oct 97	**I AM THE BLACK GOLD OF THE SUN** *Talkin Loud TLCD 26* FEATURING JOCELYN BROWN	31		2

N.W.A.
US, male rap/DJ/production group – Dr Dre* (Andre Young), Easy-E* (Eric Wright), d. 26 Mar 1995, Ice Cube* (O'Shea Jackson), MC Ren (Lorenzo Patterson) & Yella (Antoine Carraby) — 15

Date	Title	Peak	Wks at No.1	Wks on Chart
9 Sep 89	**EXPRESS YOURSELF** *Fourth & Broadway BRW 144*	50		4
26 May 90	**EXPRESS YOURSELF** *Fourth & Broadway BRW 144*	26		5
1 Sep 90	**GANGSTA, GANGSTA** *Fourth & Broadway BRW 191*	70		1
10 Nov 90	**100 MILES AND RUNNIN'** *Fourth & Broadway BRW 200*	38		3
23 Nov 91	**ALWAYZ INTO SOMETHIN'** *Fourth & Broadway BRW 238*	60		2

NYCC
Germany, male rap trio — 6

Date	Title	Peak	Wks at No.1	Wks on Chart
30 May 98	**FIGHT FOR YOUR RIGHT (TO PARTY)** *Control 0042645 CON*	14		5
19 Sep 98	**CAN YOU FEEL IT (ROCK DA HOUSE)** *Control 0042785 CON*	68		1

NYLON
Iceland, female vocal group — 3

Date	Title	Peak	Wks at No.1	Wks on Chart
22 Jul 06	**LOSING A FRIEND** *Believer Music BELIEVECDS1*	29		2
4 Nov 06	**CLOSER** *Believer Music BELIEVECDS2*	64		1

NYLON MOON
Italy, male instrumental duo — 2

Date	Title	Peak	Wks at No.1	Wks on Chart
13 Apr 96	**SKY PLUS** *Positiva CDTIV 50*	43		2

MICHAEL NYMAN
UK, male conductor/composer/pianist — 2

Date	Title	Peak	Wks at No.1	Wks on Chart
19 Mar 94	**THE HEART ASKS PLEASURE FIRST/THE PROMISE** *Virgin VEND 3*	60		2

O-TOWN
US, male vocal group – Ashley Parker Angel, Erik-Michael Estrada, Dan Miller, Trevor Penick & Jacob Underwood — 27

Date	Title	Peak	Wks at No.1	Wks on Chart
28 Apr 01	**LIQUID DREAMS** *J Records 74321853212*	3		10
4 Aug 01	**ALL OR NOTHING** *J Records 74321877952*	4		10
3 Nov 01	**WE FIT TOGETHER** *J Records 74321893692*	20		4
23 Feb 02	**LOVE SHOULD BE A CRIME** *J Records 74321920232*	38		2
15 Feb 03	**THESE ARE THE DAYS** *J Records 82876503052*	36		1

O-ZONE
Moldova, male vocal trio – Dan Balan, Radu Sirbu & Arsenie Todiras — 17

Date	Title	Peak	Wks at No.1	Wks on Chart
19 Jun 04	**DRAGOSTEA DIN TEI** *Jive 82876618412*	3		17

PAUL OAKENFOLD
UK, male DJ/producer. See Elementfour, Perfecto Allstarz, Virus — 30

Date	Title	Peak	Wks at No.1	Wks on Chart
25 Aug 01	**PLANET ROCK** *Tommy Boy TBCD 2266* PRESENTS AFRIKA BAMBAATAA	47		1
22 Jun 02	**SOUTHERN SUN/READY STEADY GO** *Perfecto PERF 17CDS*	16		4
31 Aug 02	**STARRY EYED SURPRISE** *Perfecto PERF 27CDS*	6		8
22 Feb 03	**THE HARDER THEY COME** *Perfecto PERF 49CDSX*	38		2
27 Sep 03	**HYPNOTISED** *Perfecto EW 271CD*	57		1
3 Jun 06	**FASTER KILL PUSSYCAT** *Perfecto CDPER008* FEATURING BRITTANY MURPHY	7		14

PHIL OAKEY
UK, male vocalist. See Human League — 19

Date	Title	Peak	Wks at No.1	Wks on Chart
22 Sep 84	**TOGETHER IN ELECTRIC DREAMS** *Virgin VS 713* GIORGIO MORODER & PHIL OAKEY	3		13
29 Jun 85	**GOODYBYE BAD TIMES** *Virgin VS 772* GIORGIO MORODER & PHIL OAKEY	44		5
26 Apr 03	**LA TODAY** *Xtravaganza XTRAV 37CDS* ALEX GOLD FEATURING PHILIP OAKEY	68		1

OASIS
UK, male vocal/instrumental group – Noel & Liam Gallagher*, Paul Arthurs, Tony McCarroll (replaced by Tony White) & Paul McGuigan. Outspoken, Beatles-influenced rockers who put the swagger into Britpop and imploded in 2009 after shifting 8.1 million UK singles. They racked up 16 successive Top 10 entries and a record 134 cumulative weeks on the singles chart in 1996 — 404

Date	Title	Peak	Wks at No.1	Wks on Chart
23 Apr 94	**SUPERSONIC** *Creation CRESCD 176*	31		14
2 Jul 94	**SHAKERMAKER** *Creation CRESCD 182*	11		15
20 Aug 94	**LIVE FOREVER** *Creation CRESCD 185*	10		18
22 Oct 94	**CIGARETTES AND ALCOHOL** *Creation CRESCD 190*	7		35
31 Dec 94	**WHATEVER** *Creation CRESCD 195*	3		50
6 May 95	**SOME MIGHT SAY** *Creation CRESCD 204*	1	1	27
13 May 95	**SOME MIGHT SAY** *Creation CRE 204T*	71		1
26 Aug 95	**ROLL WITH IT** *Creation CRESCD 212*	2		18
11 Nov 95	**WONDERWALL** *Creation CRESCD 215*	2		34
25 Nov 95	**WIBBLING RIVALRY (INTERVIEWS WITH NOEL AND LIAM GALLAGHER)** *Fierce Panda NING 12CD* OAS*S	52		2
2 Mar 96	**DON'T LOOK BACK IN ANGER** *Creation CRESCD 221*	1	1	24
19 Jul 97	**D'YOU KNOW WHAT I MEAN?** *Creation CRESCD 256*	1	1	18
4 Oct 97	**STAND BY ME** *Creation CRESCD 273*	2		18
24 Jan 98	**ALL AROUND THE WORLD** *Creation CRESCD 282*	1	1	9
19 Feb 00	**GO LET IT OUT** *Big Brother RKIDSCD 001*	1	1	12
29 Apr 00	**WHO FEELS LOVE?** *Big Brother RKIDSCD 003*	4		8
15 Jul 00	**SUNDAY MORNING CALL** *Big Brother RKIDSCD 004*	4		6
27 Apr 02	**THE HINDU TIMES** *Big Brother RKIDSCD 23*	1	1	11
29 Jun 02	**STOP CRYING YOUR HEART OUT** *Big Brother RKIDSCD 24*	2		10
5 Oct 02	**LITTLE BY LITTLE/SHE IS LOVE** *Big Brother RKIDSCD 26*	2		8
15 Feb 03	**SONGBIRD** *Big Brother RKIDSCD 27*	3		10
28 May 05	**LYLA** *Big Brother RKIDSCD29*	1	1	13
3 Sep 05	**THE IMPORTANCE OF BEING IDLE** *Big Brother RKIDSCD31*	1	1	19
10 Dec 05	**LET THERE BE LOVE** *Big Brother RKIDSCD32*	2		10
3 Nov 07	**LORD DON'T SLOW ME DOWN** *Big Brother GBUM70709751*	10		3
11 Oct 08	**THE SHOCK OF THE LIGHTNING** *Big Brother RKIDSCD52*	3		5
13 Dec 08	**I'M OUTTA TIME** *Big Brother RKIDSCD55*	12		2
21 Mar 09	**FALLING DOWN** *Big Brother RKIDSCD56*	10		3
14 Nov 09	**STOP CRYING YOUR HEART OUT** *Big Brother RKIDSCD 24*	71		1

Top 3 Best-Selling Singles

		Approximate Sales
1	WONDERWALL	1,025,000
2	D'YOU KNOW WHAT I MEAN?	720,000
3	DON'T LOOK BACK IN ANGER	660,000

SAM OBERNIK
Ireland, female vocalist — 14

Date	Title	Peak	Wks at No.1	Wks on Chart
20 Jul 02	**IT JUST WON'T DO** *Underwater H2O 016CD* TIM DELUXE FEATURING SAM OBERNIK	14		7
22 Nov 03	**STAND BACK** *Data 62CDS* LINUS LOVES FEATURING SAM OBERNIK	31		3
16 Aug 08	**BADITUDE** *Toolroom CDTOOLABS1* SPOON, HARRIS & OBERNIK	29		4

OBERNKIRCHEN CHILDREN'S CHOIR
Germany, male/female choir — Weeks on Chart: 26

Date	Title / Label	Peak Position	Weeks at No.1	Weeks on Chart
22 Jan 54	**HAPPY WANDERER** *Parlophone R 3799*	2		26

OBI PROJECT FEATURING HARRY, ASHER D & DJ WHAT?
UK, male vocal/rap/DJ/production group. See Studio B — Weeks on Chart: 1

Date	Title / Label	Peak Position	Weeks at No.1	Weeks on Chart
4 Aug 01	**BABY, CAN I GET YOUR NUMBER** *East West EW 235CD*	75		1

DERMOT O'BRIEN
Ireland, male vocalist/accordion player, d. 22 May 2007 (age 74) — Weeks on Chart: 2

Date	Title / Label	Peak Position	Weeks at No.1	Weeks on Chart
20 Oct 66	**THE MERRY PLOUGHBOY** *Envoy ENV 016*	46		2

BILLY OCEAN
Trinidad & Tobago, male vocalist (Leslie Charles) — Weeks on Chart: 153

Date	Title / Label	Peak Position	Weeks at No.1	Weeks on Chart
21 Feb 76	**LOVE REALLY HURTS WITHOUT YOU** *GTO GT 52* ●	2		10
10 Jul 76	**L.O.D. (LOVE ON DELIVERY)** *GTO GT 62*	19		8
13 Nov 76	**STOP ME (IF YOU'VE HEARD IT ALL BEFORE)** *GTO GT 72*	12		11
19 Mar 77	**RED LIGHT SPELLS DANGER** *GTO GT 85* ●	2		10
1 Sep 79	**AMERICAN HEARTS** *GTO GT 244*	54		5
19 Jan 80	**ARE YOU READY** *GTO GT 259*	42		7
13 Oct 84	**CARIBBEAN QUEEN (NO MORE LOVE ON THE RUN)** *Jive 77* ● ★	6		14
19 Jan 85	**LOVERBOY** *Jive 80*	15		10
11 May 85	**SUDDENLY** *Jive 90* ●	4		14
17 Aug 85	**MYSTERY LADY** *Jive 98*	49		4
25 Jan 86	**WHEN THE GOING GETS TOUGH, THE TOUGH GET GOING** *Jive 114* ●	1	4	13
12 Apr 86	**THERE'LL BE SAD SONGS (TO MAKE YOU CRY)** *Jive 117* ★	12		13
9 Aug 86	**LOVE ZONE** *Jive 124*	49		3
11 Oct 86	**BITTERSWEET** *Jive 133*	44		4
10 Jan 87	**LOVE IS FOREVER** *Jive 134*	34		7
6 Feb 88	**GET OUTTA MY DREAMS GET INTO MY CAR** *Jive BOS 1* ● ★	3		11
7 May 88	**CALYPSO CRAZY** *Jive BOS 2*	35		4
6 Aug 88	**THE COLOUR OF LOVE** *Jive BOS 3*	65		3
6 Feb 93	**PRESSURE** *Jive BOSCD 6*	55		2

OCEAN COLOUR SCENE
UK, male vocal/instrumental group – Simon Fowler, Steve Cradock, Oscar Harrison & Damon Minchella (replaced by Dan Sealey). See England United — Weeks on Chart: 74

Date	Title / Label	Peak Position	Weeks at No.1	Weeks on Chart
23 Mar 91	**YESTERDAY TODAY** *!Phfft FIT 2*	49		1
17 Feb 96	**THE RIVERBOAT SONG** *MCA MCSTD 40021*	15		5
6 Apr 96	**YOU'VE GOT IT BAD** *MCA MCSTD 40036*	7		4
15 Jun 96	**THE DAY WE CAUGHT THE TRAIN** *MCA MCSTD 40046*	4		11
28 Sep 96	**THE CIRCLE** *MCA MCSTD 40077*	6		6
28 Jun 97	**HUNDRED MILE HIGH CITY** *MCA MCSTD 40133*	4		7
6 Sep 97	**TRAVELLERS TUNE** *MCA MCSTD 40144*	5		5
22 Nov 97	**BETTER DAY** *MCA MCSTD 40151*	9		5
28 Feb 98	**IT'S A BEAUTIFUL THING** *MCA MCSTD 40157*	12		4
4 Sep 99	**PROFIT IN PEACE** *Island CID 757*	13		5
27 Nov 99	**SO LOW** *Island CID 759*	34		2
8 Jul 00	**JULY/I AM THE NEWS** *Island CID 763*	31		2
7 Apr 01	**UP ON THE DOWN SIDE** *Island CID 774*	19		3
14 Jul 01	**MECHANICAL WONDER** *Island CID 779*	49		1
22 Dec 01	**CRAZY LOWDOWN WAYS** *Island CID 787*	64		1
12 Jul 03	**I JUST NEED MYSELF** *Sanctuary SANXD 159X*	13		3
6 Sep 03	**MAKE THE DEAL** *Sanctuary SANXD 219*	35		2
10 Jan 04	**GOLDEN GATE BRIDGE** *Sanctuary SANXD 244*	40		3
19 Mar 05	**FREE MY NAME** *Sanctuary SANXS344*	23		2
2 Jul 05	**THIS DAY SHOULD LAST FOREVER** *Sanctuary SANXS380*	53		1
28 Apr 07	**I TOLD YOU SO** *Moseley Shoals CXOCS1*	34		1

OCEANIC
UK, male/female production/vocal trio – David Harry, Frank Crofts & Jorinde Williams — Weeks on Chart: 26

Date	Title / Label	Peak Position	Weeks at No.1	Weeks on Chart
24 Aug 91	**INSANITY** *Dead Dead Good GOOD 4* ●	3		15
30 Nov 91	**WICKED LOVE** *Dead Dead Good GOOD 5*	25		5
13 Jun 92	**CONTROLLING ME** *Dead Dead Good GOOD 14*	14		5
14 Nov 92	**IGNORANCE** *Dead Dead Good GOOD 22* FEATURING SIOBHAN MAHER	72		1

OCEANLAB
UK/Finland, male production trio. See Dirt Devils — Weeks on Chart: 5

Date	Title / Label	Peak Position	Weeks at No.1	Weeks on Chart
27 Apr 02	**CLEAR BLUE WATER** *Code Blue BLU 024CD1* FEATURING JUSTINE SUISSA	48		1
1 May 04	**SATELLITE** *NuLife 82876614002*	19		4

OCEANSIZE
UK, male vocal/instrumental group — Weeks on Chart: 1

Date	Title / Label	Peak Position	Weeks at No.1	Weeks on Chart
14 Feb 04	**CATALYST** *Beggars Banquet BBQ 375CD*	73		1

DES O'CONNOR
UK, male comedian/vocalist — Weeks on Chart: 117

Date	Title / Label	Peak Position	Weeks at No.1	Weeks on Chart
1 Nov 67	**CARELESS HANDS** *Columbia DB 8275* WITH THE MICHAEL SAMMES SINGERS	6		17
8 May 68	**I PRETEND** *Columbia DB 8397*	1	1	36
20 Nov 68	**1-2-3 O'LEARY** *Columbia DB 8492*	4		11
7 May 69	**DICK-A-DUM-DUM (KING'S ROAD)** *Columbia DB 8566*	14		10
29 Nov 69	**LONELINESS** *Columbia DB 8632*	18		11
14 Mar 70	**I'LL GO ON HOPING** *Columbia DB 8661*	30		7
26 Sep 70	**THE TIPS OF MY FINGERS** *Columbia DB 8713*	15		15
8 Nov 86	**THE SKYE BOAT SONG** *Tembo TML 119* ROGER WHITTAKER & DES O'CONNOR	10		10

HAZEL O'CONNOR
UK, female vocalist — Weeks on Chart: 46

Date	Title / Label	Peak Position	Weeks at No.1	Weeks on Chart
16 Aug 80	**EIGHTH DAY** *A&M AMS 7553* ●	5		11
25 Oct 80	**GIVE ME AN INCH** *A&M AMS 7569*	41		4
21 Mar 81	**D-DAYS** *Albion ION 1009* ●	10		9
23 May 81	**WILL YOU** *A&M AMS 8131* ●	8		10
1 Aug 81	**(COVER PLUS) WE'RE ALL GROWN UP** *Albion ION 1018*	41		6
3 Oct 81	**HANGING AROUND** *Albion ION 1022*	45		3
23 Jan 82	**CALLS THE TUNE** *A&M AMS 8203*	60		3

SINEAD O'CONNOR
Ireland, female vocalist. See Massive Attack — Weeks on Chart: 67

Date	Title / Label	Peak Position	Weeks at No.1	Weeks on Chart
16 Jan 88	**MANDINKA** *Ensign ENY 611*	17		9
20 Jan 90	**NOTHING COMPARES 2 U** *Ensign ENY 630* ⊛ ★	1	4	14
21 Jul 90	**THE EMPEROR'S NEW CLOTHES** *Ensign ENY 633*	31		5
20 Oct 90	**THREE BABIES** *Ensign ENY 635*	42		4
8 Jun 91	**MY SPECIAL CHILD** *Ensign ENY 646*	42		3
14 Dec 91	**SILENT NIGHT** *Ensign ENY 652*	60		4
12 Sep 92	**SUCCESS HAS MADE A FAILURE OF OUR HOME** *Ensign ENY 656*	18		4
12 Dec 92	**DON'T CRY FOR ME ARGENTINA** *Ensign ENY 657*	53		4
19 Feb 94	**YOU MADE ME THE THIEF OF YOUR HEART** *Island CID 588*	42		3
26 Nov 94	**THANK YOU FOR HEARING ME** *Ensign CDENYS 662*	13		7
29 Apr 95	**HAUNTED** *ZTT BANG 65CD* SHANE MacGOWAN & SINEAD O'CONNOR	30		2
26 Aug 95	**FAMINE** *Ensign CDENY 663*	51		1
17 May 97	**GOSPEL OAK EP** *Chrysalis CDCHS 5051*	28		3
6 Dec 97	**THIS IS A REBEL SONG** *Columbia 6652992*	60		1
24 Aug 02	**TROY (THE PHOENIX FROM THE FLAME)** *Devolution DEVR 003CDS*	48		1
29 Sep 07	**ILLEGAL ATTACKS** *Fiction 1724668* IAN BROWN FEATURING SINEAD O'CONNOR	16		2

OCTOPUS
UK/France, male vocal/instrumental group — Weeks on Chart: 5

Date	Title / Label	Peak Position	Weeks at No.1	Weeks on Chart
22 Jun 96	**YOUR SMILE** *Food CDFOODS 78*	42		2
14 Sep 96	**SAVED** *Food CDFOODS 84*	40		2
23 Nov 96	**JEALOUSY** *Food CDFOODS 87*	59		1

OCTAVE ONE FEATURING ANN SAUNDERSON
US, male/female vocal/production group — Weeks on Chart: 2

Date	Title / Label	Peak Position	Weeks at No.1	Weeks on Chart
16 Feb 02	**BLACKWATER** *Concept/430 West CDCON 26*	47		1
28 Sep 02	**BLACKWATER** *Concept/430 West CDCON 34*	69		1

ALAN O'DAY
US, male vocalist — Weeks on Chart: 3

Date	Title / Label	Peak Position	Weeks at No.1	Weeks on Chart
2 Jul 77	**UNDERCOVER ANGEL** *Atlantic K 10926* ★	43		3

COLBY O'DONIS

US, male vocalist/guitarist/producer/actor (Colby O'Donis Colon). See Evanescence — **32**

Date	Title	Peak	Wks No.1	Wks
13 Dec 08	**BEAUTIFUL** *Universal 2700494* AKON FEATURING KARDINAL OFFISHALL & COLBY O'DONIS	8		30
27 Feb 10	**JUST DANCE** *Interscope USUM70807646* LADY GAGA FEATURING COLBY O'DONIS & AKON	62		2

DANIEL O'DONNELL

Ireland, male vocalist — **71**

Date	Title	Peak	Wks No.1	Wks
12 Sep 92	**I JUST WANT TO DANCE WITH YOU** *Ritz 250P*	20		7
2 Jan 93	**THE THREE BELLS** *Ritz RITZCD 239*	71		1
8 May 93	**THE LOVE IN YOUR EYES** *Ritz RITZCD 257*	47		3
7 Aug 93	**WHAT EVER HAPPENED TO OLD FASHIONED LOVE** *Ritz RITZCD 262*	21		5
16 Apr 94	**SINGING THE BLUES** *Ritz RITZCD 270*	23		3
26 Nov 94	**THE GIFT** *Ritz RITZCD 275*	46		3
10 Jun 95	**SECRET LOVE** *Ritz RITZCD 285* & MARY DUFF	28		3
9 Mar 96	**TIMELESS** *Ritz RITZCD 293* & MARY DUFF	32		3
28 Sep 96	**FOOTSTEPS** *Ritz RITZCD 300*	25		5
7 Jun 97	**THE LOVE SONGS EP** *Ritz RITZCD 306*	27		4
11 Apr 98	**GIVE A LITTLE LOVE** *Ritz RITZCD 315*	7		5
17 Oct 98	**THE MAGIC IS THERE** *Ritz RZCD 320*	16		4
20 Mar 99	**THE WAY DREAMS ARE** *Ritz RZCD 325*	18		3
24 Jul 99	**UNO MAS** *Ritz RZCD 326*	25		3
18 Dec 99	**A CHRISTMAS KISS** *Ritz RZCD 330*	20		4
15 Apr 00	**LIGHT A CANDLE** *Ritz RZCD 335*	23		4
16 Dec 00	**MORNING HAS BROKEN** *Ritz RZCD 341*	32		4
13 Dec 03	**YOU RAISE ME UP** *Rosette ROSCD 310*	22		4
23 Sep 06	**CRUSH ON YOU** *Rosette ROSCD325*	21		3

ODYSSEY

US/Virgin Islands, male/female vocal trio – Tony Reynolds, Lillian & Louise Lopez — **82**

Date	Title	Peak	Wks No.1	Wks
24 Dec 77	**NATIVE NEW YORKER** *RCA PC 1129* ○	5		11
21 Jun 80	**USE IT UP AND WEAR IT OUT** *RCA PB 1962* ○	1	2	12
13 Sep 80	**IF YOU'RE LOOKING FOR A WAY OUT** *RCA 5* ○	6		15
17 Jan 81	**HANG TOGETHER** *RCA 23*	36		7
30 May 81	**GOING BACK TO MY ROOTS** *RCA 85* ○	4		12
19 Sep 81	**IT WILL BE ALRIGHT** *RCA 128*	43		5
12 Jun 82	**INSIDE OUT** *RCA 226* ○	3		11
11 Sep 82	**MAGIC TOUCH** *RCA 275*	41		5
17 Aug 85	**(JOY) I KNOW IT** *Mirror BUTCH 12*	51		4

ESTHER & ABI OFARIM

Israel, female/male vocal duo – Esther Zaled & Abraham Reichstadt — **22**

Date	Title	Peak	Wks No.1	Wks
14 Feb 68	**CINDERELLA ROCKEFELLA** *Philips BF 1640*	1	3	13
19 Jun 68	**ONE MORE DANCE** *Philips BF 1678*	13		9

OFF-SHORE

Germany, male production duo – Peter Harder & Jens Lissat — **12**

Date	Title	Peak	Wks No.1	Wks
22 Dec 90	**I CAN'T TAKE THE POWER** *CBS 6565707*	7		11
17 Aug 91	**I GOT A LITTLE SONG** *Dance Pool 6568257*	64		1

OFFSPRING

US, male vocal/instrumental group – Brian 'Dexter' Holland, Greg Kriesel, Kevin 'Noodles' Wasserman & Ron Welty — **64**

Date	Title	Peak	Wks No.1	Wks
25 Feb 95	**SELF ESTEEM** *Epitaph CDSHOLE 001*	37		3
19 Aug 95	**GOTTA GET AWAY** *Out Of Step WOOS 2CDS*	43		2
1 Feb 97	**ALL I WANT** *Epitaph 64912*	31		2
26 Apr 97	**GONE AWAY** *Epitaph 64982*	42		1
30 Jan 99	**PRETTY FLY (FOR A WHITE GUY)** *Columbia 6668802* ●	1	1	11
8 May 99	**WHY DON'T YOU GET A JOB** *Columbia 6673545*	2		8
11 Sep 99	**THE KIDS AREN'T ALRIGHT** *Columbia 6677632*	11		6
4 Dec 99	**SHE'S GOT ISSUES** *Columbia 6683772*	41		2
18 Nov 00	**ORIGINAL PRANKSTER** *Columbia 6699972*	6		8
31 Mar 01	**WANT YOU BAD** *Columbia 6709292*	15		9
7 Jul 01	**MILLION MILES AWAY** *Columbia 6714082*	21		4
31 Jan 04	**HIT THAT** *Columbia 6745475*	11		7
5 Jun 04	**(CAN'T GET MY) HEAD AROUND YOU** *Columbia 6748262*	48		1

OH WELL

Germany, male production group — **7**

Date	Title	Peak	Wks No.1	Wks
14 Oct 89	**OH WELL** *Parlophone R 6236*	28		6
3 Mar 90	**RADAR LOVE** *Parlophone R 6244*	65		1

OHIO EXPRESS

US, male vocal/instrumental group – Joey Levine, Tim Corwin, Doug Grassel, Dean Krastan, Jim Pflayer & Dale Powers — **15**

Date	Title	Peak	Wks No.1	Wks
5 Jun 68	**YUMMY YUMMY YUMMY** *Pye International 7N 25459*	5		15

OHIO PLAYERS

US, male vocal/instrumental group — **4**

Date	Title	Peak	Wks No.1	Wks
10 Jul 76	**WHO'D SHE COO** *Mercury PLAY 001*	43		4

O'JAYS

US, male vocal group – Eddie Levert, Bill Isles, Bobby Massey, William Powell, d. 26 May 1977, & Walter Williams — **72**

Date	Title	Peak	Wks No.1	Wks
23 Sep 72	**BACK STABBERS** *CBS 8270*	14		9
3 Mar 73	**LOVE TRAIN** *CBS 1181* ★	9		13
31 Jan 76	**I LOVE MUSIC** *Philadelphia International PIR 3879*	13		9
12 Feb 77	**DARLIN' DARLIN' BABY (SWEET, TENDER, LOVE)** *Philadelphia International PIR 4834*	24		6
8 Apr 78	**I LOVE MUSIC** *Philadelphia International PIR 6093*	36		3
17 Jun 78	**USED TA BE MY GIRL** *Philadelphia International PIR 6332*	12		12
30 Sep 78	**BRANDY** *Philadelphia International PIR 6658*	21		9
29 Sep 79	**SING A HAPPY SONG** *Philadelphia International PIR 7825*	39		6
30 Jul 83	**PUT OUR HEADS TOGETHER** *Philadelphia International A 3642*	45		5

OK GO

US, male vocal/instrumental group — **9**

Date	Title	Peak	Wks No.1	Wks
22 Mar 03	**GET OVER IT** *Capitol CDR 6603*	21		3
25 Feb 06	**A MILLION WAYS** *Angel ANGECD9*	43		1
30 Sep 06	**HERE IT GOES AGAIN** *Angel ANGECD22*	36		5

JOHN O'KANE

UK, male vocalist — **4**

Date	Title	Peak	Wks No.1	Wks
9 May 92	**STAY WITH ME** *Circa YR 88*	41		4

OL' DIRTY BASTARD

US, male rapper (Russell Jones), d. 13 Nov 2004 (age 35). See Wu-Tang Clan — **25**

Date	Title	Peak	Wks No.1	Wks
27 Jun 98	**GHETTO SUPERSTAR (THAT IS WHAT YOU ARE)** *Interscope IND 95593* PRAS MICHEL FEATURING OL' DIRTY BASTARD INTRODUCING MYA ⊛	2		17
8 Jul 00	**GOT YOUR MONEY** *Elektra E 7077CD* FEATURING KELIS	11		8

OLD SKOOL ORCHESTRA

UK, male DJ/production duo. See Stretch 'N' Vern present Maddog — **1**

Date	Title	Peak	Wks No.1	Wks
23 Jan 99	**B-BOY HUMP** *East West EW 186CD1*	55		1

MIKE OLDFIELD

UK, male producer/multi-instrumentalist — **113**

Date	Title	Peak	Wks No.1	Wks
13 Jul 74	**MIKE OLDFIELD'S SINGLE (THEME FROM TUBULAR BELLS)** *Virgin VS 101*	31		6
20 Dec 75	**IN DULCE JUBILO/ON HORSEBACK** *Virgin VS 131*	4		10
27 Nov 76	**PORTSMOUTH** *Virgin VS 163* ○	3		12
23 Dec 78	**TAKE 4 (EP)** *Virgin VS 238*	72		3
21 Apr 79	**GUILTY** *Virgin VS 245*	22		8
8 Dec 79	**BLUE PETER** *Virgin VS 317*	19		9
20 Mar 82	**FIVE MILES OUT** *Virgin VS 464* FEATURING MAGGIE REILLY	43		5
12 Jun 82	**FAMILY MAN** *Virgin VS 489* FEATURING MAGGIE REILLY	45		6
28 May 83	**MOONLIGHT SHADOW** *Virgin VS 586* WITH VOCALS BY MAGGIE REILLY ○	4		17
14 Jan 84	**CRIME OF PASSION** *Virgin VS 648* FEATURING MAGGIE REILLY	61		3
30 Jun 84	**TO FRANCE** *Virgin VS 686* FEATURING MAGGIE REILLY	48		7
14 Dec 85	**PICTURES IN THE DARK** *Virgin VS 836* FEATURING ALED JONES, ANITA HEGERLAND & BARRY PALMER	50		6
3 Oct 92	**SENTINEL** *WEA YZ 698*	10		6
19 Dec 92	**TATTOO** *WEA YZ 708*	33		5
17 Apr 93	**THE BELL** *WEA YZ 737CD*	50		2
9 Oct 93	**MOONLIGHT SHADOW** *Virgin VSCDT 1477*	52		2
17 Dec 94	**HIBERNACULUM** *WEA YZ 871CD*	47		3
2 Sep 95	**LET THERE BE LIGHT** *WEA YZ 880CD*	51		1
22 Nov 97	**WOMEN OF IRELAND** *WEA YZ 093CD*	70		1
24 Apr 99	**FAR ABOVE THE CLOUDS** *WEA 206CD1*	53		1

SALLY OLDFIELD
UK, female vocalist — 13

Date	Title / Label	Peak	Wks at No.1	Wks on Chart
9 Dec 78	**MIRRORS** *Bronze BRO 66*	19		13

MISTY OLDLAND
UK, female vocalist (Michele Oldland) — 7

Date	Title / Label	Peak	Wks at No.1	Wks on Chart
16 Oct 93	**GOT ME A FEELING** *Columbia 6597872*	59		2
12 Mar 94	**A FAIR AFFAIR (JE T'AIME)** *Columbia 6601612*	49		4
9 Jul 94	**I WROTE YOU A SONG** *Columbia 6603732*	73		1

OLGA
Italy, male production group — 1

Date	Title / Label	Peak	Wks at No.1	Wks on Chart
1 Oct 94	**I'M A BITCH** *UMM 144UKCD*	68		1

OLIVE
UK, female/male vocal/instrumental/production trio – Ruth-Ann Boyle, Tim Kellett & Robin Taylor-Firth — 24

Date	Title / Label	Peak	Wks at No.1	Wks on Chart
7 Sep 96	**YOU'RE NOT ALONE** *RCA 74321406272*	42		4
15 Mar 97	**MIRACLE** *RCA 74321461242*	41		2
17 May 97	**YOU'RE NOT ALONE** *RCA 74321473232*	1	2	13
16 Aug 97	**OUTLAW** *RCA 74321508372*	14		4
8 Nov 97	**MIRACLE (REMIX)** *RCA 74321530842*	41		1

OLIVER
US, male vocalist (William Swafford), d. 12 Feb 2000 (age 54) — 18

Date	Title / Label	Peak	Wks at No.1	Wks on Chart
9 Aug 69	**GOOD MORNING STARSHINE** *CBS 4435*	6		18

FRANKIE OLIVER
UK, male vocalist — 1

Date	Title / Label	Peak	Wks at No.1	Wks on Chart
7 Jun 97	**GIVE HER WHAT SHE WANTS** *Island Jamaica IJCD 2011*	58		1

OLLIE & JERRY
US, male vocal/instrumental duo – Ollie E Brown & Jerry Knight — 14

Date	Title / Label	Peak	Wks at No.1	Wks on Chart
23 Jun 84	**BREAKIN'...THERE'S NO STOPPING US** *Polydor POSP 690*	5		11
9 Mar 85	**ELECTRIC BOOGALOO** *Polydor POSP 730*	57		3

OLYMPIC ORCHESTRA
UK, orchestra — 15

Date	Title / Label	Peak	Wks at No.1	Wks on Chart
1 Oct 83	**REILLY** *Red Bus RBUS 82*	26		15

OLYMPIC RUNNERS
UK, male vocal/instrumental group — 21

Date	Title / Label	Peak	Wks at No.1	Wks on Chart
13 May 78	**WHATEVER IT TAKES** *RCA PC 5078*	61		2
14 Oct 78	**GET IT WHILE YOU CAN** *Polydor RUN 7*	35		6
20 Jan 79	**SIR DANCEALOT** *Polydor POSP 17*	35		6
28 Jul 79	**THE BITCH** *Polydor POSP 63*	37		7

OLYMPICS
US, male vocal group — 9

Date	Title / Label	Peak	Wks at No.1	Wks on Chart
3 Oct 58	**WESTERN MOVIES** *HMV POP 528*	12		8
19 Jan 61	**I WISH I COULD SHIMMY LIKE MY SISTER KATE** *Vogue V 9174*	40		1

OMAR
UK, male vocalist (Omar Lye-Fook aka Hammer) — 18

Date	Title / Label	Peak	Wks at No.1	Wks on Chart
22 Jun 91	**THERE'S NOTHING LIKE THIS** *Talkin Loud TLK 9*	14		7
23 May 92	**YOUR LOSS MY GAIN** *Talkin Loud TLK 22*	47		2
26 Sep 92	**MUSIC** *Talkin Loud TLK 28*	53		2
23 Jul 94	**OUTSIDE/SATURDAY** *RCA 74321213982*	43		2
15 Oct 94	**KEEP STEPPIN'** *RCA 74321233682*	57		1
2 Aug 97	**SAY NOTHIN'** *RCA 74321502872*	29		2
18 Oct 97	**GOLDEN BROWN** *RCA 74321525122*	37		2

OMARION
US, male vocalist/actor (Omari Grandberry). See B2K — 24

Date	Title / Label	Peak	Wks at No.1	Wks on Chart
23 Jul 05	**O** *Epic 6759862*	47		2
8 Oct 05	**LET ME HOLD YOU (IMPORT)** *Sony BMG 6760602* BOW WOW FEATURING OMARION	64		2
22 Oct 05	**LET ME HOLD YOU** *Columbia 6760605* BOW WOW FEATURING OMARION	27		6
17 Feb 07	**ICE BOX** *Epic 88697079682*	14		12
9 Jun 07	**ENTOURAGE** *Columbia/Sony Urban 88697098442*	58		2

OMC
New Zealand, male vocal/production duo – Paul Fuemana, d. 31 Jan 2010, & Alan Jansson — 17

Date	Title / Label	Peak	Wks at No.1	Wks on Chart
20 Jul 96	**HOW BIZARRE** *Polydor 5776202*	5		16
18 Jan 97	**ON THE RUN** *Polydor 5732452*	56		1

JO O'MEARA
UK, female vocalist/actor. See S Club 7 — 5

Date	Title / Label	Peak	Wks at No.1	Wks on Chart
8 Oct 05	**WHAT HURTS THE MOST** *Sanctuary SANXS403*	13		5

OMNI TRIO
UK, male producer (Rob Haigh) — 4

Date	Title / Label	Peak	Wks at No.1	Wks on Chart
7 Jul 01	**THE ANGELS & SHADOWS PROJECT** *Moving Shadow SHADOW 150CD*	44		3
26 Jul 03	**RENEGADE SNARES** *Moving Shadow SHADOW 166*	61		1

ONE
UK, male vocal group — 2

Date	Title / Label	Peak	Wks at No.1	Wks on Chart
11 Jan 97	**ONE MORE CHANCE** *Mercury MERDD 478*	31		2

PHOEBE ONE
UK, female rapper (Phoebe Espirit) — 3

Date	Title / Label	Peak	Wks at No.1	Wks on Chart
12 Dec 98	**DOIN' OUR THING/ONE MAN'S BITCH** *Mecca Recordings MECX 1020*	59		1
15 May 99	**GET ON IT** *Mecca Recordings MECX 1026*	38		2

ONE DOVE
UK, male/female vocal/production trio — 9

Date	Title / Label	Peak	Wks at No.1	Wks on Chart
7 Aug 93	**WHITE LOVE** *Boy's Own BOICD 14*	43		3
16 Oct 93	**BREAKDOWN** *Boy's Own BOICD 15*	24		3
15 Jan 94	**WHY DON'T YOU TAKE ME** *Boy's Own BOICD 16*	30		3

187 LOCKDOWN
UK, male production duo – Danny Harrison & Julian Jonah. See M Factor, Nu-Birth, Nush, Reflex featuring MC Viper — 16

Date	Title / Label	Peak	Wks at No.1	Wks on Chart
15 Nov 97	**GUNMAN** *East West EW 140CD*	16		4
25 Apr 98	**KUNG-FU** *East West EW 155CD*	9		5
25 Jul 98	**GUNMAN** *East West EW 176CD*	17		4
3 Oct 98	**THE DON** *East West EW 180CD*	29		2
13 Feb 99	**ALL 'N' ALL** *East West EW 194CD* (FEATURING D'EMPRESS)	43		1

1 GIANT LEAP FEATURING MAXI JAZZ & ROBBIE WILLIAMS
UK, male production duo – Duncan Bridgeman & Jamie Catto, rapper (Maxwell Frazer) & vocalist. See Faithless, Take That — 6

Date	Title / Label	Peak	Wks at No.1	Wks on Chart
20 Apr 02	**MY CULTURE** *Palm Pictures PPCD 70732*	9		6

ONE HUNDRED TON & A FEATHER
UK, male vocalist (Jonathan King) — 9

Date	Title / Label	Peak	Wks at No.1	Wks on Chart
26 Jun 76	**IT ONLY TAKES A MINUTE** *UK 135*	9		9

100% FEATURING JENNIFER JOHN
UK, male/female vocal/production trio — 6

Date	Title / Label	Peak	Wks at No.1	Wks on Chart
25 Dec 04	**JUST CAN'T WAIT (SATURDAY)** *CR2 CDC2X005*	28		6

ONE MINUTE SILENCE
UK, male vocal/rap/instrumental group — 2

Date	Title / Label	Peak	Wks at No.1	Wks on Chart
20 Jan 01	**FISH OUT OF WATER** *V2 VVR 5013213*	56		1
5 Jul 03	**I WEAR MY SKIN** *Taste Media TMCDSX 5005*	44		1

ONE NIGHT ONLY

UK, male vocal/instrumental group – George Craig, Sam Ford, Mark Hayton, Daniel Parkin & Jack Sails — 19

Date	Title	Peak Position	Weeks at No.1	Weeks on Chart
10 Nov 07	**YOU AND ME** *Vertigo 1747365*	46		1
2 Feb 08	**JUST FOR TONIGHT** *Vertigo 1753471*	9		16
10 May 08	**IT'S ABOUT TIME** *Vertigo 1765451*	37		1
26 Jul 08	**YOU AND ME** *Vertigo 1747365*	55		1

112

US, male vocal/instrumental/production group – Daron Jones, Michael Keith, Quinnes 'Q' Parker & Marvin 'Slim' Scandrick — 34

Date	Title	Peak Position	Weeks at No.1	Weeks on Chart
28 Jun 97	**I'LL BE MISSING YOU** *Puff Daddy 74321499102* PUFF DADDY & FAITH EVANS FEATURING 112 ⊛x2 ★	1	6	21
10 Jan 98	**ALL CRIED OUT** *Epic 6652715* ALLURE FEATURING 112	12		5
14 Feb 98	**SKY'S THE LIMIT** *Puff Daddy 74321587992* NOTORIOUS B.I.G. FEATURING 112	35		2
30 Jun 01	**IT'S OVER NOW** *Puff Daddy 74321849912*	22		3
8 Sep 01	**PEACHES AND CREAM** *Arista 74321882632*	32		3

ONE THE JUGGLER

UK, male vocal/instrumental group — 1

Date	Title	Peak Position	Weeks at No.1	Weeks on Chart
19 Feb 83	**PASSION KILLER** *Regard RG 107*	71		1

1000 CLOWNS

US, male/female vocal/rap group — 4

Date	Title	Peak Position	Weeks at No.1	Weeks on Chart
22 May 99	**(NOT THE) GREATEST RAPPER** *Elektra E 3759CD*	23		4

ONEREPUBLIC

US, male vocal/instrumental group – Ryan Tedder, Drew Brown, Zach Filkins, Eddie Fisher & Brent Kutzle — 74

Date	Title	Peak Position	Weeks at No.1	Weeks on Chart
13 Oct 07	**APOLOGIZE** *Interscope 1750152* TIMBALAND PRESENTS ONEREPUBLIC	3		42
23 Feb 08	**STOP AND STARE** *Interscope 1763784*	4		23
7 Jun 08	**SAY (ALL I NEED)** *Interscope 1772305*	51		3
16 Jan 10	**ALL THE RIGHT MOVES** *Universal USUM70984099*	26		6

ONE TRUE VOICE

UK, male vocal group – Anton Gordon, Matt Johnson, Daniel Pearce, Keith Semple & Jamie Shaw — 14

Date	Title	Peak Position	Weeks at No.1	Weeks on Chart
28 Dec 02	**SACRED TRUST/AFTER YOU'RE GONE** *Ebul/Jive 9201532* ●	2		9
14 Jun 03	**SHAKESPEARE'S WAY WITH WORDS** *Ebul/Jive 9201582*	10		5

ONE 2 MANY

Norway, male/female vocal/instrumental trio — 11

Date	Title	Peak Position	Weeks at No.1	Weeks on Chart
12 Nov 88	**DOWNTOWN** *A&M AM 476*	65		4
3 Jun 89	**DOWNTOWN** *A&M AM 456*	43		7

ONE WAY

US, male/female vocal/instrumental group — 8

Date	Title	Peak Position	Weeks at No.1	Weeks on Chart
8 Dec 79	**MUSIC** *MCA 542* FEATURING AL HUDSON	56		6
29 Jun 85	**LET'S TALK ABOUT SHHH** *MCA 972*	64		2

ONE WORLD PROJECT

UK/US, male vocal/instrumental charity ensemble – Jon Anderson, Gerry Beckley & Dewey Bunnell (America*), Boy George*, Celena Cherry (Honeyz*), Barry & Robin Gibb* (Bee Gees*), Kenney Jones (Faces*, Small Faces*, Who*), Hank Linderman, Gary Moore*, Mike Read, Cliff Richard*, Rick Wakeman, Russell Watson*, Brian Wilson*, Steve Winwood* & Bill Wyman* — 4

Date	Title	Peak Position	Weeks at No.1	Weeks on Chart
5 Feb 05	**GRIEF NEVER GROWS OLD** *One World OWR1*	4		4

ALEXANDER O'NEAL

US, male vocalist — 110

Date	Title	Peak Position	Weeks at No.1	Weeks on Chart
28 Dec 85	**SATURDAY LOVE** *Tabu A 6829* CHERRELLE WITH ALEXANDER O'NEAL	6		11
15 Feb 86	**IF YOU WERE HERE TONIGHT** *Tabu A 6391*	13		10
5 Apr 86	**A BROKEN HEART CAN MEND** *Tabu A 6244*	53		4
6 Jun 87	**FAKE** *Tabu 6508917*	33		6
31 Oct 87	**CRITICIZE** *Tabu 6512117*	4		14
6 Feb 88	**NEVER KNEW LOVE LIKE THIS** *Tabu 6513827* FEATURING CHERRELLE	26		7
28 May 88	**THE LOVERS** *Tabu 6515957*	28		4
23 Jul 88	**(WHAT CAN I SAY) TO MAKE YOU LOVE ME** *Tabu 6528527*	27		5
24 Sep 88	**FAKE '88** *Tabu 6529497*	16		7
10 Dec 88	**CHRISTMAS SONG (CHESTNUTS ROASTING ON AN OPEN FIRE)/ THANK YOU FOR A GOOD YEAR** *Tabu 6531827*	30		5
25 Feb 89	**HEARSAY '89** *Tabu 6544667*	56		2
2 Sep 89	**SUNSHINE** *Tabu 6551917*	72		1
9 Dec 89	**HITMIX (OFFICIAL BOOTLEG MEGA-MIX)** *Tabu 6555047*	19		7
24 Mar 90	**SATURDAY LOVE (REMIX)** *Tabu 6558007* CHERRELLE WITH ALEXANDER O'NEAL	55		2
12 Jan 91	**ALL TRUE MAN** *Tabu 6565717*	18		6
23 Mar 91	**WHAT IS THIS THING CALLED LOVE** *Tabu 6567317*	53		2
11 May 91	**SHAME ON ME** *Tabu 6568737*	71		1
9 May 92	**SENTIMENTAL** *Tabu 6580147*	53		2
30 Jan 93	**LOVE MAKES NO SENSE** *Tabu AMCD 7708*	26		6
3 Jul 93	**IN THE MIDDLE** *Tabu 5877152*	32		3
25 Sep 93	**ALL THAT MATTERS TO ME** *Tabu 6577232*	67		1
2 Nov 96	**LET'S GET TOGETHER** *EMI Premier PRESCD 11*	38		2
2 Aug 97	**BABY COME TO ME** *One World Entertainment OWECD 1* FEATURING CHERRELLE	56		1
12 Dec 98	**CRITICIZE '98 MIX** *One World Entertainment OWECD 3*	51		1

SHAQUILLE O'NEAL

US, male rapper/basketball player — 6

Date	Title	Peak Position	Weeks at No.1	Weeks on Chart
26 Mar 94	**I'M OUTSTANDING** *Jive JIVECD 349*	70		1
14 Sep 96	**STOMP – THE REMIXES** *Qwest W 0372CD* QUINCY JONES FEATURING MELLE MEL, COOLIO, YO-YO, SHAQUILLE O'NEAL & THE LUNIZ	28		2
1 Feb 97	**YOU CAN'T STOP THE REIGN** *Interscope IND 95522*	40		2
17 Oct 98	**THE WAY IT'S GOIN' DOWN (T.W.I.S.M. FOR LIFE)** *A&M 5827932*	62		1

ONES

US, male DJ/production trio – Paul Alexander, JoJo Americo & Nashom Wooden — 14

Date	Title	Peak Position	Weeks at No.1	Weeks on Chart
20 Oct 01	**FLAWLESS** *Positiva CDTIV 164*	7		13
1 Mar 03	**SUPERSTAR** *Positiva CDTIVS 186*	45		1

ONLY ONES

UK, male vocal/instrumental group — 2

Date	Title	Peak Position	Weeks at No.1	Weeks on Chart
1 Feb 92	**ANOTHER GIRL – ANOTHER PLANET** *Columbia 6577507*	57		2

YOKO ONO

Japan, female vocalist. See John Lennon — 7

Date	Title	Peak Position	Weeks at No.1	Weeks on Chart
28 Feb 81	**WALKING ON THIN ICE** *Geffen K 79202*	35		5
14 Jun 03	**WALKING ON THIN ICE (REMIX)** *Parlophone CDMINDS 002*	35		2

BEN ONONO

UK, male vocalist — 4

Date	Title	Peak Position	Weeks at No.1	Weeks on Chart
15 Mar 03	**ON MY MIND** *Junior/Parlophone CDR 6595* FUTURESHOCK FEATURING BEN ONONO	51		1
17 May 03	**MY LOVE IS ALWAYS** *Illustrious CDILL 016* SAFFRON HILL FEATURING BEN ONONO	28		3

ONSLAUGHT

UK, male vocal/instrumental group — 3

Date	Title	Peak Position	Weeks at No.1	Weeks on Chart
6 May 89	**LET THERE BE ROCK** *London LON 224*	50		3

ONYX

US, male rap group — 8

Date	Title	Peak Position	Weeks at No.1	Weeks on Chart
28 Aug 93	**SLAM** *Columbia 6596302*	31		4
27 Nov 93	**THROW YA GUNZ** *Columbia 6598312*	34		3
20 Feb 99	**ROC-IN-IT** *Independiente ISOM 21MS* DEEJAY PUNK-ROC VS ONYX	59		1

ONYX FEATURING GEMMA J

UK, male/female vocal/production trio — 1

Date	Title	Peak Position	Weeks at No.1	Weeks on Chart
11 Dec 04	**EVERY LITTLE TIME** *Data DATA78CDS*	66		1

OO LA LA

UK, male vocal/instrumental group — 2

Date	Title	Peak Position	Weeks at No.1	Weeks on Chart
5 Sep 92	**OO...AH...CANTONA** *North Speed OOAH 1*	64		2

OOBERMAN

UK, male/female vocal/instrumental group — 5

Date	Title / Label	Peak Position	Weeks at No.1	Weeks on Chart
8 May 99	**BLOSSOMS FALLING** *Independiente ISOM 26MS*	39		2
17 Jul 99	**MILLION SUNS** *Independiente ISOM 30MS*	43		1
23 Oct 99	**TEARS FROM A WILLOW** *Independiente ISOM 37MS*	63		1
8 Apr 00	**SHORLEY WALL** *Independiente ISOM 41MS*	47		1

OPEN

UK, male vocal/instrumental group — 4

Date	Title / Label	Peak Position	Weeks at No.1	Weeks on Chart
13 Mar 04	**CLOSE MY EYES** *Polydor 9817294*	46		1
3 Jul 04	**JUST WANT TO LIVE** *Loog 9866489*	52		1
11 Sep 04	**ELEVATION** *Loog 9867495*	54		1
13 Nov 04	**NEVER ENOUGH** *Loog 9868779*	53		1

OPEN ARMS FEATURING ROWETTA

UK, male/female vocal/instrumental group. See Flip & Fill — 1

Date	Title / Label	Peak Position	Weeks at No.1	Weeks on Chart
15 Jun 96	**HEY MR DJ** *All Around The World CDGLOBE 136*	62		1

OPERABABES

UK, female vocal duo — 1

Date	Title / Label	Peak Position	Weeks at No.1	Weeks on Chart
6 Jul 02	**ONE FINE DAY** *Sony Classical 6727062*	54		1

OPM

US, male vocal/rap/instrumental group – Big B (Bryan Mahoney), John E. Necro, Casper (Jeff Turney), Gary P Dean (replaced by Shane Mayo), Etienne Franc (replaced by Matt Rowe) & Jonathan Williams — 18

Date	Title / Label	Peak Position	Weeks at No.1	Weeks on Chart
14 Jul 01	**HEAVEN IS A HALFPIPE** *Atlantic AT 0107CD* ●	4		14
12 Jan 02	**EL CAPITAN** *East West AT 0118CD*	20		4

OPTIMYSTIC

UK, male/female vocal group — 6

Date	Title / Label	Peak Position	Weeks at No.1	Weeks on Chart
17 Sep 94	**CAUGHT UP IN MY HEART** *WEA YZ 841CD*	49		3
10 Dec 94	**NOTHING BUT LOVE** *WEA YZ 864CD1*	37		2
13 May 95	**BEST THING IN THE WORLD** *WEA YZ 920CD*	70		1

OPUS

Austria, male vocal/instrumental group – Herwig Rüdisser, Günter Grasmuck, Niki Gruber, Kurt Rene Plisnier & Ewald Pfleger — 15

Date	Title / Label	Peak Position	Weeks at No.1	Weeks on Chart
15 Jun 85	**LIVE IS LIFE** *Polydor POSP 743* ●	6		15

OPUS III

UK, male/female vocal/production group – Kirsty Hawkshaw, Kevin Dodds, Ian Munro & Nigel Walton — 10

Date	Title / Label	Peak Position	Weeks at No.1	Weeks on Chart
22 Feb 92	**IT'S A FINE DAY** *PWL International PWL 215*	5		8
27 Jun 92	**I TALK TO THE WIND** *PWL International PWL 235*	52		1
11 Jun 94	**WHEN YOU MADE THE MOUNTAIN** *PWL International PWL 302*	71		1

ORANGE

UK, male vocal/instrumental group — 1

Date	Title / Label	Peak Position	Weeks at No.1	Weeks on Chart
8 Oct 94	**JUDY OVER THE RAINBOW** *Chrysalis CDCHS 5012*	73		1

ORANGE JUICE

UK, male vocal/instrumental group – Edwyn Collins*, Steven Daly (replaced by Zeke Manyika), James Kirk (replaced by Malcolm Ross) & David McClymont — 34

Date	Title / Label	Peak Position	Weeks at No.1	Weeks on Chart
7 Nov 81	**L.O.V.E...LOVE** *Polydor POSP 357*	65		2
30 Jan 82	**FELICITY** *Polydor POSP 386*	63		3
21 Aug 82	**TWO HEARTS TOGETHER/HOKOYO** *Polydor POSP 470*	60		2
23 Oct 82	**I CAN'T HELP MYSELF** *Polydor POSP 522*	42		3
19 Feb 83	**RIP IT UP** *Polydor POSP 547*	8		11
4 Jun 83	**FLESH OF MY FLESH** *Polydor OJ 4*	41		6
25 Feb 84	**BRIDGE** *Polydor OJ 5*	67		2
12 May 84	**WHAT PRESENCE?** *Polydor OJ 6*	47		4
27 Oct 84	**LEAN PERIOD** *Polydor OJ 7*	74		1

ORB

UK, male production/instrumental duo – Alex Patterson (Duncan Alex Patterson) & Kris 'Thrash' Weston (replaced by Thomas Fehlmann & Andy Hughes, d. 12 Jun 1999, then Simon Phillips) — 32

Date	Title / Label	Peak Position	Weeks at No.1	Weeks on Chart
15 Jun 91	**PERPETUAL DAWN** *Big Life BLRD 46*	61		1
20 Jun 92	**BLUE ROOM** *Big Life BLRT 75*	8		6
17 Oct 92	**ASSASSIN** *Big Life BLRT 81*	12		5
13 Nov 93	**LITTLE FLUFFY CLOUDS** *Big Life BLRD 98*	10		5
5 Feb 94	**PERPETUAL DAWN** *Big Life BLRD 46*	18		5
27 May 95	**OXBOW LAKES** *Island CID 609*	38		2
8 Feb 97	**TOXYGENE** *Island CID 652*	4		4
24 May 97	**ASYLUM** *Island CID 657*	20		2
24 Feb 01	**ONCE MORE** *Island CIDX 767*	38		2

ROY ORBISON

US, male vocalist, d. 6 Dec 1988 (age 52). The 'Big O' was the most popular US singer in Britain during the 'Beat Boom' era. The distinctive vocalist, who had a hit span of 44 years, was enjoying a successful comeback when he died. See Traveling Wilburys — 345

Date	Title / Label	Peak Position	Weeks at No.1	Weeks on Chart
28 Jul 60	**ONLY THE LONELY** *London HLU 9149*	1	2	24
27 Oct 60	**BLUE ANGEL** *London HLU 9207*	11		16
25 May 61	**RUNNING SCARED** *London HLU 9342* ★	9		15
28 Sep 61	**CRYIN'** *London HLU 9405*	25		9
8 Mar 62	**DREAM BABY** *London HLU 9511*	2		14
28 Jun 62	**THE CROWD** *London HLU 9561*	40		4
8 Nov 62	**WORKIN' FOR THE MAN** *London HLU 9607*	50		1
28 Feb 63	**IN DREAMS** *London HLU 9676*	6		23
30 May 63	**FALLING** *London HLU 9727*	9		11
19 Sep 63	**BLUE BAYOU/MEAN WOMAN BLUES** *London HLU 9777*	3		19
20 Feb 64	**BORNE ON THE WIND** *London HLU 9845*	15		10
30 Apr 64	**IT'S OVER** *London HLU 9882*	1	2	18
10 Sep 64	**OH PRETTY WOMAN** *London HLU 9919* ★	1	3	18
19 Nov 64	**PRETTY PAPER** *London HLU 9930*	6		11
11 Feb 65	**GOODNIGHT** *London HLU 9951*	14		9
22 Jul 65	**(SAY) YOU'RE MY GIRL** *London HLU 9978*	23		8
9 Sep 65	**RIDE AWAY** *London HLU 9986*	34		6
4 Nov 65	**CRAWLIN' BACK** *London HLU 10000*	19		9
27 Jan 66	**BREAKIN' UP IS BREAKIN' MY HEART** *London HLU 10015*	22		6
7 Apr 66	**TWINKLE TOES** *London HLU 10034*	29		5
16 Jun 66	**LANA** *London HLU 10051*	15		9
18 Aug 66	**TOO SOON TO KNOW** *London HLU 10067*	3		17
1 Dec 66	**THERE WON'T BE MANY COMING HOME** *London HLU 10096*	12		9
23 Feb 67	**SO GOOD** *London HLU 10113*	32		6
24 Jul 68	**WALK ON** *London HLU 10206*	39		10
25 Sep 68	**HEARTACHE** *London HLU 10222*	44		4
30 Apr 69	**MY FRIEND** *London HLU 10261*	35		4
13 Sep 69	**PENNY ARCADE** *London HLU 10285*	27		14
14 Jan 89	**YOU GOT IT** *Virgin VS 1166* ●	3		10
1 Apr 89	**SHE'S A MYSTERY TO ME** *Virgin VS 1173*	27		5
4 Jul 92	**I DROVE ALL NIGHT** *MCA MCS 1652*	7		10
22 Aug 92	**CRYING** *Virgin America VUS 63* (DUET WITH k.d. lang)	13		6
7 Nov 92	**HEARTBREAK RADIO** *Virgin America VUS 68*	36		3
13 Nov 93	**I DROVE ALL NIGHT** *Virgin America VUSCD 79*	47		2

WILLIAM ORBIT

UK, male producer (William Wainwright) — 29

Date	Title / Label	Peak Position	Weeks at No.1	Weeks on Chart
26 Jun 93	**WATER FROM A VINE LEAF** *Guerilla VSCDT 1465*	59		1
18 Dec 99	**BARBER'S ADAGIO FOR STRINGS** *WEA 247CD* ●	4		15
6 May 00	**RAVEL'S PAVANE POUR UNE INFANTE DEFUNTE** *WEA 269CD*	31		2
19 Jul 03	**FEEL GOOD TIME** *Columbia 6741062* P!NK FEATURING WILLIAM ORBIT	3		11

ORBITAL

UK, male instrumental duo – Paul & Phil Hartnoll — 58

Date	Title / Label	Peak Position	Weeks at No.1	Weeks on Chart
24 Mar 90	**CHIME** *ffrr F 85*	17		7
22 Sep 90	**OMEN** *ffrr 145*	46		3
19 Jan 91	**SATAN** *ffrr FX 149*	31		4
15 Feb 92	**MUTATIONS EP** *ffrr FX 181*	24		3
26 Sep 92	**RADICCIO EP** *Internal LIARX 1*	37		2
21 Aug 93	**LUSH** *Internal LIECD 7*	43		2
24 Sep 94	**ARE WE HERE** *Internal LIECD 15*	33		2
27 May 95	**BELFAST** *Volume VOLCD 1*	53		1
27 Apr 96	**THE BOX** *Internal LIECD 30*	11		4
11 Jan 97	**SATAN** *Internal LIECD 37*	3		6
19 Apr 97	**THE SAINT** *ffrr FCD 296*	3		7
20 Mar 99	**STYLE** *ffrr FCD 358*	13		4
17 Jul 99	**NOTHING LEFT** *ffrr FCDP 365*	32		2
11 Mar 00	**BEACHED** *ffrr FCD 377* & ANGELO BADALAMENTI	36		3
28 Apr 01	**FUNNY BREAK (ONE IS ENOUGH)** *ffrr FCDP 395*	21		3

Date	Title	Peak Position	Weeks at No.1	Weeks on Chart
8 Jun 02	**REST AND PLAY EP** *ffrr FCD 407*	33		3
17 Jul 04	**ONE PERFECT SUNRISE** *Orbital Music ORBITALCD03X*	29		2

ORCHESTRA ON THE HALF SHELL

US, male production duo **6**

Date	Title	Peak Position	Weeks at No.1	Weeks on Chart
15 Dec 90	**TURTLE RHAPSODY** *SBK 17*	36		6

ORCHESTRAL MANOEUVRES IN THE DARK

UK, male vocal/instrumental group – Andy McCluskey (George Andrew McCluskey), Paul Humphreys, Martin Cooper & Malcolm Holmes **201**

Date	Title	Peak Position	Weeks at No.1	Weeks on Chart
9 Feb 80	**RED FRAME WHITE LIGHT** *Dindisc DIN 6*	67		2
10 May 80	**MESSAGES** *Dindisc DIN 15*	13		11
4 Oct 80	**ENOLA GAY** *Dindisc DIN 22* ●	8		15
29 Aug 81	**SOUVENIR** *Dindisc DIN 24* ●	3		12
24 Oct 81	**JOAN OF ARC** *Dindisc DIN 36* ●	5		14
23 Jan 82	**MAID OF ORLEANS (THE WALTZ JOAN OF ARC)** *Dindisc DIN 40* ●	4		10
19 Feb 83	**GENETIC ENGINEERING** *Virgin VS 527*	20		8
9 Apr 83	**TELEGRAPH** *Virgin VS 580*	42		4
14 Apr 84	**LOCOMOTION** *Virgin VS 660*	5		11
16 Jun 84	**TALKING LOUD AND CLEAR** *Virgin VS 685*	11		10
8 Sep 84	**TESLA GIRLS** *Virgin VS 705*	21		8
10 Nov 84	**NEVER TURN AWAY** *Virgin VS 727*	70		2
25 May 85	**SO IN LOVE** *Virgin VS 766*	27		7
20 Jul 85	**SECRET** *Virgin VS 796*	34		7
26 Oct 85	**LA FEMME ACCIDENT** *Virgin VS 811*	42		4
3 May 86	**IF YOU LEAVE** *Virgin VS 843*	48		4
6 Sep 86	**(FOREVER) LIVE AND DIE** *Virgin VS 888*	11		10
15 Nov 86	**WE LOVE YOU** *Virgin VS 911*	54		5
2 May 87	**SHAME** *Virgin VS 938*	52		3
6 Feb 88	**DREAMING** *Virgin VS 987*	50		3
2 Jul 88	**DREAMING** *Virgin VS 987*	60		3
30 Mar 91	**SAILING ON THE SEVEN SEAS** *Virgin VS 1310*	3		13
6 Jul 91	**PANDORA'S BOX** *Virgin VS 1331*	7		10
14 Sep 91	**THEN YOU TURN AWAY** *Virgin VS 1368*	50		4
7 Dec 91	**CALL MY NAME** *Virgin VS 1380*	50		2
15 May 93	**STAND ABOVE ME** *Virgin VSCDG 1444*	21		4
17 Jul 93	**DREAM OF ME (BASED ON LOVE'S THEME)** *Virgin VSCDT 1461*	24		5
18 Sep 93	**EVERYDAY** *Virgin VSCDT 1471*	59		2
17 Aug 96	**WALKING ON THE MILKY WAY** *Virgin VSCDT 1599*	17		5
2 Nov 96	**UNIVERSAL** *Virgin VSCDT 1606*	55		1
26 Sep 98	**THE OMD REMIXES** *Virgin VSCDT 1694*	35		2

ORDINARY BOYS

UK, male vocal/instrumental group – Samuel Preston, William J Brown, Simon Goldring, James Gregory & Charles 'Chuck' Stanley **49**

Date	Title	Peak Position	Weeks at No.1	Weeks on Chart
17 Apr 04	**WEEK IN WEEK OUT** *B Unique WEA372CD*	36		3
10 Jul 04	**TALK TALK TALK** *B Unique WEA377CD*	17		3
2 Oct 04	**SEASIDE** *B Unique WEA379CD*	27		2
18 Jun 05	**BOYS WILL BE BOYS** *B Unique WEA389CD2*	16		3
10 Sep 05	**LIFE WILL BE THE DEATH OF ME** *B Unique WEA394CD1*	50		1
21 Jan 06	**BOYS WILL BE BOYS** *B Unique WEA389CD2*	3		15
27 May 06	**NINE 2FIVE** *Polydor BUN105CD* FEATURING LADY SOVEREIGN	6		8
21 Oct 06	**LONELY AT THE TOP** *B Unique/Polydor BUN112CD*	10		4
13 Jan 07	**I LUV U** *B Unique/Polydor BUN118CD*	7		10

RAUL ORELLANA

Spain, male producer **8**

Date	Title	Peak Position	Weeks at No.1	Weeks on Chart
30 Sep 89	**THE REAL WILD HOUSE** *RCA BCM 322*	29		8

O.R.G.A.N.

Spain, male DJ/producer (Vidana Crespo) **2**

Date	Title	Peak Position	Weeks at No.1	Weeks on Chart
16 May 98	**TO THE WORLD** *Multiply CDMULTY 34*	33		2

ORIGIN

UK, male production duo **1**

Date	Title	Peak Position	Weeks at No.1	Weeks on Chart
12 Aug 00	**WIDE EYED ANGEL** *Lost Language LOST 001CD*	73		1

ORIGIN UNKNOWN

UK, male instrumental/production duo **3**

Date	Title	Peak Position	Weeks at No.1	Weeks on Chart
13 Jul 96	**VALLEY OF THE SHADOWS** *Ram RAMM 16CD*	60		1
11 May 02	**TRULY ONE** *Ram RAMM 38CD*	53		1
20 Sep 03	**HOTNESS** *Ram RAMM 45* DYNAMITE MC & ORIGIN UNKNOWN	66		1

ORIGINAL

US, male vocal/instrumental duo – Everett Bradley & Walter Taieb. See Diva Surprise featuring Georgia Jones **14**

Date	Title	Peak Position	Weeks at No.1	Weeks on Chart
14 Jan 95	**I LUV U BABY** *Ore AG 8CD*	31		3
19 Aug 95	**I LUV U BABY (REMIX)** *Ore/XL Recordings AGR 8CD* ●	2		9
11 Nov 95	**B 2 GETHER** *Ore/XL Recordings AG 12CD*	29		2

ORIGINAL CAST RECORDING

International, male/female vocal group **4**

Date	Title	Peak Position	Weeks at No.1	Weeks on Chart
26 Jul 08	**HONEY HONEY** *Polydor GBUM70809210*	69		4

ORION

UK, male/female vocal/instrumental/production duo. See Angelic, Citizen Caned, DT8 Project, Jurgen Vries **2**

Date	Title	Peak Position	Weeks at No.1	Weeks on Chart
7 Oct 00	**ETERNITY** *Incentive CENT 11CDS*	38		2

ORION TOO

Belgium, male/female vocal/production duo **1**

Date	Title	Peak Position	Weeks at No.1	Weeks on Chart
9 Nov 02	**HOPE AND WAIT** *Data 4CDS*	46		1

TONY ORLANDO

US, male vocalist (Michael Anthony Orlando Cassavitis). See Dawn **11**

Date	Title	Peak Position	Weeks at No.1	Weeks on Chart
5 Oct 61	**BLESS YOU** *Fontana H 330*	5		11

ORLONS

US, female/male vocal group **3**

Date	Title	Peak Position	Weeks at No.1	Weeks on Chart
27 Dec 62	**DON'T HANG UP** *Cameo Parkway C 231*	39		3

ORN

UK, male DJ/producer (Omio Nourizadeh) **1**

Date	Title	Peak Position	Weeks at No.1	Weeks on Chart
1 Mar 97	**SNOW** *Deconstruction 74321447612*	61		1

STACIE ORRICO

US, female vocalist **26**

Date	Title	Peak Position	Weeks at No.1	Weeks on Chart
23 Aug 03	**STUCK** *Virgin VUSCD 269*	9		8
1 Nov 03	**THERE'S GOTTA BE MORE TO LIFE** *Virgin VUSCD 275*	12		8
24 Jan 04	**I PROMISE** *Virgin VUSDX 280*	22		4
12 Jun 04	**I COULD BE THE ONE** *Virgin VUSDX 289*	34		2
2 Sep 06	**I'M NOT MISSING YOU** *Virgin VUSCD329*	22		4

ORSON

US, male vocal/instrumental group – Jason Pebworth, George Astasio, Chris Cano, Johnny Lonely & Kevin Roentgen **44**

Date	Title	Peak Position	Weeks at No.1	Weeks on Chart
11 Mar 06	**NO TOMORROW** *Mercury 9876828*	1	1	18
20 May 06	**BRIGHT IDEA** *Mercury 9856127*	11		16
12 Aug 06	**HAPPINESS** *Mercury 1703849*	27		5
20 Oct 07	**AIN'T NO PARTY** *Mercury 1746453*	21		5

BETH ORTON

UK, female vocalist/guitarist **15**

Date	Title	Peak Position	Weeks at No.1	Weeks on Chart
1 Feb 97	**TOUCH ME WITH YOUR LOVE** *Heavenly HVN 64CD*	60		1
5 Apr 97	**SOMEONE'S DAUGHTER** *Heavenly HVN 65CD*	49		1
14 Jun 97	**SHE CRIES YOUR NAME** *Heavenly HVN 68CD*	40		2
13 Dec 97	**BEST BIT EP** *Heavenly HVN 72CD* FEATURING TERRY CALLIER	36		3
13 Mar 99	**STOLEN CAR** *Heavenly HVN 89CD*	34		2
25 Sep 99	**CENTRAL RESERVATION** *Heavenly HVN 92CD1*	37		2
16 Nov 02	**ANYWHERE** *Heavenly HVN 125CDS*	55		1
12 Apr 03	**THINKING ABOUT TOMORROW** *Heavenly HVN 129CD*	57		1
11 Feb 06	**CONCEIVED** *EMI CDEM681*	44		2

JEFFREY OSBORNE

US, male vocalist. See LTD **38**

Date	Title	Peak Position	Weeks at No.1	Weeks on Chart
17 Sep 83	**DON'T YOU GET SO MAD** *A&M AM 140*	54		2
14 Apr 84	**STAY WITH ME TONIGHT** *A&M AM 188*	18		11
23 Jun 84	**ON THE WINGS OF LOVE** *A&M AM 198*	11		14
20 Oct 84	**DON'T STOP** *A&M AM 222*	61		2
26 Jul 86	**SOWETO** *A&M AM 334*	44		6
15 Aug 87	**LOVE POWER** *Arista RIS 27* DIONNE WARWICK & JEFFREY OSBORNE	63		3

Silver-selling ● Gold-selling ● Platinum-selling (x multiples) ⊛ US No.1 ★ — Peak Position · Weeks at No.1 · Weeks on Chart

JOAN OSBORNE
US, female vocalist/guitarist — 13

Date	Title	Peak Position	Weeks at No.1	Weeks on Chart
10 Feb 96	ONE OF US *Blue Gorilla JOACD 1*	6		10
8 Jun 96	ST TERESA *Blue Gorilla JOACD 3*	33		3

TONY OSBORNE SOUND
UK, orchestra leader, d. 1 Mar 2009 (age 86) — 3

Date	Title	Peak Position	Weeks at No.1	Weeks on Chart
23 Feb 61	MAN FROM MADRID *HMV POP 827* FEATURING JOANNE BROWN	50		1
3 Feb 73	THE SHEPHERD'S SONG *Philips 6006 266*	46		2

KELLY OSBOURNE
UK, female vocalist/actor/TV personality/fashion designer — 41

Date	Title	Peak Position	Weeks at No.1	Weeks on Chart
24 Aug 02	PAPA DON'T PREACH (IMPORT) *Epic 6729152CD*	65		3
21 Sep 02	PAPA DON'T PREACH *Epic 6731602*	3		10
8 Feb 03	SHUT UP *Epic 6735552*	12		6
20 Dec 03	CHANGES *Sanctuary SANXD 34* OZZY & KELLY OSBOURNE ●	1	1	16
21 May 05	ONE WORD *Sanctuary SANXS349*	9		6

OZZY OSBOURNE
UK, male vocalist (John Osbourne). See Black Sabbath — 65

Date	Title	Peak Position	Weeks at No.1	Weeks on Chart
13 Sep 80	CRAZY TRAIN *Jet 197* OZZY OSBOURNE'S BLIZZARD OF OZ	49		4
15 Nov 80	MR CROWLEY *Jet 7003* OZZY OSBOURNE'S BLIZZARD OF OZ	46		3
26 Nov 83	BARK AT THE MOON *Epic A 3915*	21		8
2 Jun 84	SO TIRED *Epic A 4452*	20		9
1 Feb 86	SHOT IN THE DARK *Epic A 6859*	20		6
9 Aug 86	THE ULTIMATE SIN/LIGHTNING STRIKES *Epic A 7311*	72		1
20 May 89	CLOSE MY EYES FOREVER *Dreamland PB 49409* LITA FORD DUET WITH OZZY OSBOURNE	47		3
28 Sep 91	NO MORE TEARS *Epic 6574407*	32		3
30 Nov 91	MAMA I'M COMING HOME *Epic 6576177*	46		2
25 Nov 95	PERRY MASON *Epic 6626395*	23		2
31 Aug 96	I JUST WANT YOU *Epic 6635702*	43		1
8 Jun 02	DREAMER/GETS ME THROUGH *Epic 6724122*	18		6
20 Dec 03	CHANGES *Sanctuary SANXD 34* OZZY & KELLY OSBOURNE ●	1	1	16
24 Dec 05	IN MY LIFE *Epic 82876743122*	63		1

OSIBISA
Ghana/Nigeria, male vocal/instrumental group — 12

Date	Title	Peak Position	Weeks at No.1	Weeks on Chart
17 Jan 76	SUNSHINE DAY *Bronze BRO 20*	17		6
5 Jun 76	DANCE THE BODY MUSIC *Bronze BRO 26*	31		6

DONNY OSMOND
US, male vocalist. See Osmonds — 123

Date	Title	Peak Position	Weeks at No.1	Weeks on Chart
17 Jun 72	PUPPY LOVE *MGM 2006 104*	1	5	23
16 Sep 72	TOO YOUNG *MGM 2006 113*	5		15
11 Nov 72	WHY *MGM 2006 119*	3		20
10 Mar 73	THE TWELFTH OF NEVER *MGM 2006 199*	1	1	14
18 Aug 73	YOUNG LOVE *MGM 2006 300* ●	1	4	10
10 Nov 73	WHEN I FALL IN LOVE *MGM 2006 365* ●	4		13
9 Nov 74	WHERE DID ALL THE GOOD TIMES GO *MGM 2006 468*	18		10
26 Sep 87	I'M IN IT FOR LOVE *Virgin VS 994*	70		1
6 Aug 88	SOLDIER OF LOVE *Virgin VS 1094*	29		8
12 Nov 88	IF IT'S LOVE THAT YOU WANT *Virgin VS 1140*	70		2
9 Feb 91	MY LOVE IS A FIRE *Capitol CL 600*	64		2
2 Oct 04	BREEZE ON BY *Decca 9863140*	8		5

DONNY & MARIE OSMOND
US, male/female vocal duo — 37

Date	Title	Peak Position	Weeks at No.1	Weeks on Chart
3 Aug 74	I'M LEAVING IT (ALL) UP TO YOU *MGM 2006 446* ●	2		12
14 Dec 74	MORNING SIDE OF THE MOUNTAIN *MGM 2006 274* ●	5		12
21 Jun 75	MAKE THE WORLD GO AWAY *MGM 2006 523*	18		6
17 Jan 76	DEEP PURPLE *MGM 2006 561*	25		7

LITTLE JIMMY OSMOND
US, male vocalist — 50

Date	Title	Peak Position	Weeks at No.1	Weeks on Chart
25 Nov 72	LONG HAIRED LOVER FROM LIVERPOOL *MGM 2006 109*	1	5	27
31 Mar 73	TWEEDLE DEE *MGM 2006 175*	4		13
23 Mar 74	I'M GONNA KNOCK ON YOUR DOOR *MGM 2006 389*	11		10

MARIE OSMOND
US, female vocalist (Olive Marie Osmond) — 15

Date	Title	Peak Position	Weeks at No.1	Weeks on Chart
17 Nov 73	PAPER ROSES *MGM 2006 315*	2		15

OSMOND BOYS
US, male vocal group — 6

Date	Title	Peak Position	Weeks at No.1	Weeks on Chart
9 Nov 91	BOYS WILL BE BOYS *Curb 6573847*	65		2
11 Jan 92	SHOW ME THE WAY *Curb 6577227*	60		4

OSMONDS
US, male vocal group – Donny Osmond*, Alan, Jay, Merrill & Wayne Osmond — 94

Date	Title	Peak Position	Weeks at No.1	Weeks on Chart
25 Mar 72	DOWN BY THE LAZY RIVER *MGM 2006 096*	40		5
11 Nov 72	CRAZY HORSES *MGM 2006 142*	2		18
14 Jul 73	GOING HOME *MGM 2006 288*	4		10
27 Oct 73	LET ME IN *MGM 2006 321* ●	2		14
20 Apr 74	I CAN'T STOP *MCA 129*	12		10
24 Aug 74	LOVE ME FOR A REASON *MGM 2006 458* ●	1	3	9
1 Mar 75	HAVING A PARTY *MGM 2006 492*	28		8
24 May 75	THE PROUD ONE *MGM 2006 520* ●	5		8
15 Nov 75	I'M STILL GONNA NEED YOU *MGM 2006 551*	32		4
30 Oct 76	I CAN'T LIVE A DREAM *Polydor 2066 726*	37		5
23 Sep 95	CRAZY HORSES (REMIX) *Polydor 5793212*	50		1
12 Jun 99	CRAZY HORSES (REMIX) *Polydor 5611372*	34		2

GILBERT O'SULLIVAN
Ireland, male vocalist/pianist (Raymond O'Sullivan) — 145

Date	Title	Peak Position	Weeks at No.1	Weeks on Chart
28 Nov 70	NOTHING RHYMED *MAM 3*	8		11
3 Apr 71	UNDERNEATH THE BLANKET GO *MAM 13*	40		4
24 Jul 71	WE WILL *MAM 30*	16		11
27 Nov 71	NO MATTER HOW I TRY *MAM 53*	5		15
4 Mar 72	ALONE AGAIN (NATURALLY) *MAM 66* ★	3		12
17 Jun 72	OOH-WAKKA-DOO-WAKKA-DAY *MAM 78*	8		11
21 Oct 72	CLAIR *MAM 84*	1	2	14
17 Mar 73	GET DOWN *MAM 96*	1	2	13
15 Sep 73	OOH BABY *MAM 107*	18		7
10 Nov 73	WHY OH WHY OH WHY *MAM 111* ●	6		14
9 Feb 74	HAPPINESS IS ME AND YOU *MAM 114*	19		7
24 Aug 74	A WOMAN'S PLACE *MAM 122*	42		3
14 Dec 74	CHRISTMAS SONG *MAM 124*	12		6
14 Jun 75	I DON'T LOVE YOU BUT I THINK I LIKE YOU *MAM 130*	14		6
27 Sep 80	WHAT'S IN A KISS? *CBS 8929*	19		9
24 Feb 90	SO WHAT *Dover ROJ 3*	70		2

OTHER TWO
UK, female/male vocal/instrumental duo – Gillian Gilbert & Stephen Morris. See New Order — 5

Date	Title	Peak Position	Weeks at No.1	Weeks on Chart
9 Nov 91	TASTY FISH *Factory FAC 3297*	41		3
6 Nov 93	SELFISH *London TWOCD 1*	46		2

OTHERS
UK, male vocal/instrumental group — 7

Date	Title	Peak Position	Weeks at No.1	Weeks on Chart
29 May 04	THIS IS FOR THE POOR *Poptones MC5090SCD*	42		1
6 Nov 04	STAN BOWLES *Vertigo 9868521*	36		2
29 Jan 05	LACKEY *Vertigo 9869350*	21		3
16 Apr 05	WILLIAM *Poptones 9870861*	29		1

JOHNNY OTIS
US, male vocalist/band leader (John Veliotis) — 22

Date	Title	Peak Position	Weeks at No.1	Weeks on Chart
22 Nov 57	MA HE'S MAKING EYES AT ME *Capitol CL 14794* & HIS ORCHESTRA WITH MARIE ADAMS & THE THREE TONS OF JOY	2		15
10 Jan 58	BYE BYE BABY *Capitol CL 14817* JOHNNY OTIS SHOW, VOCALS BY MARIE ADAMS & JOHNNY OTIS	20		7

OTT
Ireland, male vocal group — 18

Date	Title	Peak Position	Weeks at No.1	Weeks on Chart
15 Feb 97	LET ME IN *Epic 6642052*	12		5
17 May 97	FOREVER GIRL *Epic 6645082*	24		3
23 Aug 97	ALL OUT OF LOVE *Epic 6649152*	11		4
24 Jan 98	THE STORY OF LOVE *Epic OTT 1CD*	11		6

OTTAWAN

France/Belgium, male production duo – Daniel Vangarde (Daniel Bangalter) & Jean Kluger – with Martinique/France, male/female vocal duo – Jean Patrick & Annette — **45**

Date	Title	Peak Position	Weeks at No.1	Weeks on Chart
13 Sep 80	**D.I.S.C.O.** *Carrere CAR 161* ●	2		18
13 Dec 80	**YOU'RE OK** *Carrere CAR 168*	56		6
29 Aug 81	**HANDS UP (GIVE ME YOUR HEART)** *Carrere CAR 183* ○	3		15
5 Dec 81	**HELP, GET ME SOME HELP!** *Carrere CAR 215*	49		6

JOHN OTWAY

UK, male vocal/instrumental duo — **15**

Date	Title	Peak Position	Weeks at No.1	Weeks on Chart
3 Dec 77	**REALLY FREE** *Polydor 2058 951* & WILD WILLY BARRETT	27		8
5 Jul 80	**DK 50-80** *Polydor 2059 250* OTWAY & BARRETT	45		4
12 Oct 02	**BUNSEN BURNER** *U-vibe OTWAY 02Z*	9		3

OUI 3

UK/US/Switzerland, male/female rap/vocal/production trio — **21**

Date	Title	Peak Position	Weeks at No.1	Weeks on Chart
20 Feb 93	**FOR WHAT IT'S WORTH** *MCA MCSTD 1736*	28		6
24 Apr 93	**ARMS OF SOLITUDE** *MCA MCSTD 1759*	54		2
17 Jul 93	**BREAK FROM THE OLD ROUTINE** *MCA MCSTD 1793*	17		6
23 Oct 93	**FOR WHAT IT'S WORTH** *MCA MCSTD 1941*	26		3
29 Jan 94	**FACT OF LIFE** *MCA MCSTD 1939*	38		2
27 May 95	**JOY OF LIVING** *MCA MCSTD 2057*	55		2

OUR DAUGHTER'S WEDDING

US, male vocal/instrumental trio — **6**

Date	Title	Peak Position	Weeks at No.1	Weeks on Chart
1 Aug 81	**LAWNCHAIRS** *EMI America EA 124*	49		6

OUR HOUSE

Australia, male instrumental/production duo — **1**

Date	Title	Peak Position	Weeks at No.1	Weeks on Chart
31 Aug 96	**FLOOR SPACE** *Perfecto PERF 125CD*	52		1

OUR KID

UK, male vocal/instrumental group – Kevin Rown, Terry Baccino, Brian Farrell & Terry McCreith — **11**

Date	Title	Peak Position	Weeks at No.1	Weeks on Chart
29 May 76	**YOU JUST MIGHT SEE ME CRY** *Polydor 2058 729* ○	2		11

OUR LADY PEACE

Canada, male vocal/instrumental group — **1**

Date	Title	Peak Position	Weeks at No.1	Weeks on Chart
15 Jan 00	**ONE MAN ARMY** *Epic 6688662*	70		1

OUR TRIBE/ONE TRIBE

UK/US, male/female vocal/instrumental group. See Dusted, Faithless, Rollo, Sphinx — **13**

Date	Title	Peak Position	Weeks at No.1	Weeks on Chart
20 Jun 92	**WHAT HAVE YOU DONE (IS THIS ALL)** *Inner Rhythm HEART 03* ONE TRIBE FEATURING GEM	52		2
27 Mar 93	**I BELIEVE IN YOU** *ffreedom TABCD 117* OUR TRIBE	42		2
30 Apr 94	**HOLD THAT SUCKER DOWN** *Cheeky CHEKCD 004* OT QUARTET	24		3
21 May 94	**LOVE COME HOME** *Triangle BLUESCD 001* OUR TRIBE WITH FRANKE PHAROAH & KRISTINE W	73		1
13 May 95	**HIGH AS A KITE** *ffrr FCD 259* ONE TRIBE FEATURING ROGER	55		1
30 Sep 95	**HOLD THAT SUCKER DOWN (REMIX)** *Cheeky CHEKCD 009* OT QUARTET	26		3
9 Dec 00	**HOLD THAT SUCKER DOWN** *Champion CHAMPCD 786* OT QUARTET	45		1

OUT OF MY HAIR

UK, male vocal/instrumental group — **1**

Date	Title	Peak Position	Weeks at No.1	Weeks on Chart
1 Jul 95	**MISTER JONES** *RCA 74321267812*	73		1

OUT OF OFFICE

UK, male/female vocal/production duo — **5**

Date	Title	Peak Position	Weeks at No.1	Weeks on Chart
22 Sep 07	**HANDS UP** *Frenetic FRE1CDX*	52		2
23 Feb 08	**BREAK OF DAWN 2008** *Frenetic FRE7CDX*	41		3

OUTHERE BROTHERS

US, male rap/vocal duo – Lamar 'Hula' Mahone & Keith 'Malik' Mayberry — **50**

Date	Title	Peak Position	Weeks at No.1	Weeks on Chart
18 Mar 95	**DON'T STOP (WIGGLE WIGGLE)** *Stip YZ 917CD* ●	1	1	15
17 Jun 95	**BOOM BOOM BOOM** *Stip YZ 938CD* ●	1	4	15
23 Sep 95	**LA LA LA HEY HEY** *Stip YZ 974CD*	7		7
16 Dec 95	**IF YOU WANNA PARTY** *Stip 030CD* MOLELLA FEATURING THE OUTHERE BROTHERS	9		10
25 Jan 97	**LET ME HEAR YOU SAY 'OLE OLE'** *Stip 089CD*	18		3

OUTKAST

US, male rap/vocal duo – 'Andre 3000' Benjamin & Antwan 'Big Boi' Patton — **71**

Date	Title	Peak Position	Weeks at No.1	Weeks on Chart
23 Dec 00	**B.O.B. (BOMBS OVER BAGHDAD)** *LaFace 74321822942*	61		1
3 Feb 01	**MS JACKSON (IMPORT)** *LaFace 73008245252*	48		4
3 Mar 01	**MS JACKSON** *LaFace 74321836822* ○ ★	2		10
9 Jun 01	**SO FRESH SO CLEAN** *LaFace 74321863402*	16		8
6 Apr 02	**THE WHOLE WORLD** *LaFace 74321917592* FEATURING KILLER MIKE	19		5
27 Jul 02	**LAND OF A MILLION DRUMS** *Atlantic AT 0134CD* FEATURING KILLER MIKE & SLEEPY BROWN	46		1
4 Oct 03	**GHETTO MUSICK** *Arista 82876567232*	55		1
22 Nov 03	**HEY YA!** *Arista 82876580102* ★	3		21
3 Apr 04	**THE WAY YOU MOVE** *Arista 82876605672* FEATURING SLEEPY BROWN ★	7		10
3 Jul 04	**ROSES** *Arista 82876624392*	4		7
9 Sep 06	**MORRIS BROWN** *LaFace 82876808422*	43		3

OUTLANDER

Belgium, male producer (Marcus Salon) — **3**

Date	Title	Peak Position	Weeks at No.1	Weeks on Chart
31 Aug 91	**VAMP** *R&S RSUK 1*	51		2
7 Feb 98	**THE VAMP (REVISITED)** *R&S RS 97113CDX*	62		1

OUTLANDISH

Morocco/Pakistan/Honduras, male rap/production trio — **2**

Date	Title	Peak Position	Weeks at No.1	Weeks on Chart
31 May 03	**GUANTANAMO** *RCA 82876517702*	31		2

OUTLAWS

UK, male instrumental group — **4**

Date	Title	Peak Position	Weeks at No.1	Weeks on Chart
13 Apr 61	**SWINGIN' LOW** *HMV POP 844*	46		2
8 Jun 61	**AMBUSH** *HMV POP 877*	43		2

OUTRAGE

US, male vocal/production duo — **2**

Date	Title	Peak Position	Weeks at No.1	Weeks on Chart
11 Mar 95	**TALL 'N' HANDSOME** *Effective ECFL 001CD*	57		1
23 Nov 96	**TALL 'N' HANDSOME (REMIX)** *Positiva CDTIV 64*	51		1

OUTSIDAZ FEATURING RAH DIGGA & MELANIE BLATT

US/UK, male/female rap/vocal group. See All Saints, Artful Dodger featuring Melanie Blatt — **2**

Date	Title	Peak Position	Weeks at No.1	Weeks on Chart
2 Mar 02	**I'M LEAVIN'** *Rufflife RLCDM 03*	41		2

OUTWORK FEATURING MR GEE

Italy, male vocal/production duo — **2**

Date	Title	Peak Position	Weeks at No.1	Weeks on Chart
16 Dec 06	**ELEKTRO** *Defected DFTD137CDS*	49		2

OVACAST & BECKY MEASURES

UK, male/female vocal/instrumental group — **1**

Date	Title	Peak Position	Weeks at No.1	Weeks on Chart
10 Mar 07	**NO BIG DEAL** *Logik BECKY1*	67		1

OVERLANDERS

UK, male/female vocal/instrumental group – Laurie Mason, Paul Arnold, Pete Bartholomew, David Walsh & Terry Widlake — **10**

Date	Title	Peak Position	Weeks at No.1	Weeks on Chart
13 Jan 66	**MICHELLE** *Pye 7N 17034*	1	3	10

OVERWEIGHT POOCH FEATURING CE CE PENISTON

US, female rapper (Tonya Davis) & female vocalist — **2**

Date	Title	Peak Position	Weeks at No.1	Weeks on Chart
18 Jan 92	**I LIKE IT** *A&M AM 847*	58		2

MARK OWEN

UK, male vocalist. See Take That — 37

Date	Title	Peak	Wks No.1	Wks
30 Nov 96	**CHILD** *RCA 74321424422* ●	3		15
15 Feb 97	**CLEMENTINE** *RCA 74321454992*	3		6
23 Aug 97	**I AM WHAT I AM** *RCA 74321501222*	29		3
16 Aug 03	**FOUR MINUTE WARNING** *Universal MCSTD 40329*	4		9
8 Nov 03	**ALONE WITHOUT YOU** *Universal MCSXD 40342*	26		2
19 Jun 04	**MAKIN' OUT** *Sedna CXSEDNA1*	30		1
3 Sep 05	**BELIEVE IN THE BOOGIE** *Sedna SEDNACS1*	57		1

REG OWEN

UK, male orchestra leader, d. 23 May 1978 (age 57) — 10

Date	Title	Peak	Wks No.1	Wks
27 Feb 59	**MANHATTAN SPIRITUAL** *Pye International 7N 25009*	20		8
27 Oct 60	**OBSESSION** *Palette PG 9004*	43		2

SID OWEN

UK, male actor/vocalist (David Sutton) — 6

Date	Title	Peak	Wks No.1	Wks
16 Dec 95	**BETTER BELIEVE IT (CHILDREN IN NEED)** *Trinity TDM 001CD* SID OWEN & PATSY PALMER	60		1
8 Jul 00	**GOOD THING GOING** *Mushroom MUSH 74CDS*	14		5

ROBERT OWENS

US, male vocalist — 6

Date	Title	Peak	Wks No.1	Wks
7 Dec 91	**I'LL BE YOUR FRIEND** *Perfecto PB 45161*	75		2
26 Apr 97	**I'LL BE YOUR FRIEND (REMIX)** *Perfecto PERF 137CD1*	25		2
24 Feb 01	**MINE TO GIVE** *Science QEDCD 10* PHOTEK FEATURING ROBERT OWENS	44		1
15 Feb 03	**LAST NIGHT A DJ BLEW MY MIND** *Illustrious CDILL 013* FAB FOR FEATURING ROBERT OWENS	34		1

OWL CITY

US, male vocalist/keyboard player (Adam Young) — 13

Date	Title	Peak	Wks No.1	Wks
16 Jan 10	**FIREFLIES** *Island USUM70972068* ● ★	1	3	13+

OXIDE & NEUTRINO

UK, male rap/production duo – Mark Oseitutu & Alex Rivers. See So Solid Crew — 45

Date	Title	Peak	Wks No.1	Wks
6 May 00	**BOUND 4 DA RELOAD (CASUALTY)** *East West OXIDE01CD1* ●	1	1	11
30 Dec 00	**NO GOOD 4 ME** *East West OXIDE 02CD* FEATURING MEGAMAN, ROMEO & LISA MAFFIA	6		8
26 May 01	**UP MIDDLE FINGER** *East West OXIDE 03CD*	7		7
28 Jul 01	**DEVIL'S NIGHTMARE** *East West OXIDE 07CD1*	16		5
8 Dec 01	**RAP DIS/ONLY WANNA KNOW U COS URE FAMOUS** *East West OXIDE 08CD*	12		8
28 Sep 02	**DEM GIRLZ (I DON'T KNOW WHY)** *East West OXIDE 09CD* FEATURING KOWDEAN	10		6

OXYGEN FEATURING ANDREA BRITTON

UK, male/female vocal/production trio. See Ascension, Chakra, Essence, Lustral, Space Brothers — 3

Date	Title	Peak	Wks No.1	Wks
11 Jan 03	**AM I ON YOUR MIND** *Innocent SINCD 40*	30		3

OYSTAR

UK, male vocal/instrumental group — 1

Date	Title	Peak	Wks No.1	Wks
19 Jan 08	**I FOUGHT THE LLOYDS** *Tone Def GBQAJ0700001*	25		1

OZOMATLI

US, male vocal/instrumental group — 2

Date	Title	Peak	Wks No.1	Wks
20 Mar 99	**CUT CHEMIST SUITE** *Almo Sounds CDALM 62*	58		1
22 May 99	**SUPER BOWL SUNDAE** *Almo Sounds CDALM 63*	68		1

JAMESY P

St. Vincent, male vocalist (James Morgan) — 5

Date	Title	Peak	Wks No.1	Wks
24 Sep 05	**NOOKIE** *Smoove SMOOVE04CDS*	14		5

JAZZI P

UK, female rapper (Pauline Bennett) — 13

Date	Title	Peak	Wks No.1	Wks
8 Jul 89	**GET LOOSE** *Breakout USA 659* L.A. MIX PERFORMED BY JAZZI P	25		6
9 Jun 90	**FEEL THE RHYTHM** *A&M USA 691*	51		3
3 Aug 91	**REBEL WOMAN** *DNA 7DNA 001* DNA FEATURING JAZZI P	42		4

P DIDDY

US, male rapper/producer/fashion designer (Sean Combs). Native New Yorker and serial collaborator whose poignant tribute to the Notorious B.I.G., his slain rapper friend, shifted more than 1.4 million copies to become rap's top-selling single ever — 224

Date	Title	Peak	Wks No.1	Wks
29 Mar 97	**CAN'T NOBODY HOLD ME DOWN** *Puff Daddy 74321464552* PUFF DADDY FEATURING MASE ★	19		4
26 Apr 97	**NO TIME** *Atlantic A 5594CD* LIL' KIM FEATURING PUFF DADDY	45		1
28 Jun 97	**I'LL BE MISSING YOU** *Puff Daddy 74321499102* PUFF DADDY & FAITH EVANS FEATURING 112 ⊛x2 ★	1	6	21
9 Aug 97	**MO MONEY MO PROBLEMS** *Puff Daddy 74321492492* NOTORIOUS B.I.G. FEATURING PUFF DADDY & MASE ★	6		10
13 Sep 97	**SOMEONE** *RCA 74321513942* SWV FEATURING PUFF DADDY	34		2
1 Nov 97	**BEEN AROUND THE WORLD** *Puff Daddy 74321539442* PUFF DADDY & THE FAMILY	20		6
7 Feb 98	**IT'S ALL ABOUT THE BENJAMINS** *Puff Daddy 74321561972* PUFF DADDY & THE FAMILY	18		3
1 Aug 98	**COME WITH ME (IMPORT)** *Epic 34K78954* PUFF DADDY FEATURING JIMMY PAGE	75		1
8 Aug 98	**COME WITH ME** *Epic 6662842* PUFF DADDY FEATURING JIMMY PAGE	2		10
1 May 99	**ALL NIGHT LONG** *Puff Daddy 74321625592* FAITH EVANS FEATURING PUFF DADDY	23		3
29 May 99	**HATE ME NOW** *Columbia 6672565* NAS FEATURING PUFF DADDY	14		6
21 Aug 99	**PE 2000** *Puff Daddy 74321694982* PUFF DADDY FEATURING HURRICANE G	13		4
20 Nov 99	**BEST FRIEND** *Puff Daddy 74321712312* PUFF DADDY FEATURING MARIO WINANS	24		4
5 Feb 00	**NOTORIOUS B.I.G.** *Puff Daddy 74321737312* NOTORIOUS B.I.G. FEATURING PUFF DADDY AND LIL' KIM	16		5
19 Feb 00	**SATISFY YOU (IMPORT)** *Bad Boy/Arista 792832* PUFF DADDY FEATURING R KELLY	73		2
11 Mar 00	**SATISFY YOU** *Puff Daddy 74321745592* PUFF DADDY FEATURING R KELLY	8		8
6 Oct 01	**BAD BOY FOR LIFE** *Arista 74321889982* FEATURING BLACK ROB & MARK CURRY	13		6
26 Jan 02	**DIDDY** *Puff Daddy 74321911652* FEATURING THE NEPTUNES	19		4
8 Jun 02	**PASS THE COURVOISIER – PART II** *J Records 74321937902* BUSTA RHYMES, P DIDDY & PHARRELL	16		7
10 Aug 02	**I NEED A GIRL (PART ONE)** *Puff Daddy 74321947242* FEATURING USHER & LOON	4		11
29 Mar 03	**BUMP BUMP BUMP** *Epic 6736452* B2K FEATURING P DIDDY ★	11		8
23 Aug 03	**LET'S GET ILL** *Bad Boy MCSTD 40331* FEATURING KELIS	25		3
20 Sep 03	**SHAKE YA TAILFEATHER** *Bad Boy MCSTD 40337* NELLY, P DIDDY & MURPHY LEE ★	10		7
7 Feb 04	**SHOW ME YOUR SOUL** *Puff Daddy MCSTD 40350* P DIDDY, LENNY KRAVITZ, PHARRELL WILLIAMS & LOON	35		2
15 May 04	**PASS THE COURVOISIER – PART II** *J Records 74321937902* BUSTA RHYMES, P DIDDY & PHARRELL	71		1
5 Jun 04	**I DON'T WANNA KNOW (IMPORT)** *Universal 9862372PMI* MARIO WINANS FEATURING ENYA & P DIDDY	71		1
12 Jun 04	**I DON'T WANNA KNOW** *Bad Boy MCSTD40369* MARIO WINANS FEATURING ENYA & P DIDDY ●	1	1	14
28 Jan 06	**NASTY GIRL** *Bad Boy AT0229CDX* NOTORIOUS B.I.G. FEATURING DIDDY, NELLY, JAGGED EDGE AND AVERY STORM	1	2	19
7 Oct 06	**COME TO ME** *Atlantic AT0260CD* FEATURING NICOLE SCHERZINGER	4		12
16 Dec 06	**TELL ME** *Atlantic AT0268CD* FEATURING CHRISTINA AGUILERA	8		17
3 Mar 07	**LAST NIGHT** *Atlantic AT0273CD* FEATURING KEYSHIA COLE	14		16
14 Jul 07	**I'LL BE MISSING YOU** *Bad Boy USBB40300019* PUFF DADDY FEATURING FAITH EVANS	32		2
8 Sep 07	**THROUGH THE PAIN (SHE TOLD ME)** *Bad Boy AT0283CD* FEATURING MARIO WINANS	50		2
14 Feb 09	**I'LL BE MISSING YOU** *Bad Boy USBB40300019* PUFF DADDY FEATURING FAITH EVANS	68		2

TALISMAN P MEETS BARRINGTON LEVY

UK/Jamaica, male vocal duo — 2

Date	Title	Peak	Wks No.1	Wks
13 Oct 01	**HERE I COME (SING DJ)** *NuLife 74321895622*	37		2

PJB FEATURING HANNAH & HER SISTERS

UK, male producer (Pete Bellotte) & US, female vocalist (Hannah Jones*) & backing group — 8

Date	Title	Peak	Wks No.1	Wks
14 Sep 91	**BRIDGE OVER TROUBLED WATER** *Dance Pool 6565467*	21		8

PETEY PABLO
US, male rapper (Moses Barrett) — Weeks on Chart: 11

Date	Title	Peak	Wks at No.1	Wks on Chart
9 Feb 02	**I** *Jive 9253092*	51		1
15 Jan 05	**GOODIES (IMPORT)** *Jive 82876648252* CIARA FEATURING PETEY PABLO	68		1
29 Jan 05	**GOODIES** *LaFace 82876673132* CIARA FEATURING PETEY PABLO ★	1	1	9

THOM PACE
US, male vocalist — Weeks on Chart: 15

Date	Title	Peak	Wks at No.1	Wks on Chart
19 May 79	**MAYBE** *RSO 34*	14		15

PACIFICA
UK, male production duo — Weeks on Chart: 1

Date	Title	Peak	Wks at No.1	Wks on Chart
31 Jul 99	**LOST IN THE TRANSLATION** *Wildstar CDWILD 25*	54		1

PACK FEATURING NIGEL BENN
UK, male/female production/vocal group with male rapper/boxer — Weeks on Chart: 2

Date	Title	Peak	Wks at No.1	Wks on Chart
8 Dec 90	**STAND AND FIGHT** *IQ ZB 44237*	61		2

PACKABEATS
UK, male instrumental group — Weeks on Chart: 1

Date	Title	Peak	Wks at No.1	Wks on Chart
23 Feb 61	**GYPSY BEAT** *Parlophone R 4729*	49		1

PADDINGTONS
UK, male vocal/instrumental group — Weeks on Chart: 6

Date	Title	Peak	Wks at No.1	Wks on Chart
23 Oct 04	**21/SOME OLD GIRL** *Poptones MC5093SCD*	47		1
7 May 05	**PANIC ATTACK** *Poptones 9870603*	25		2
23 Jul 05	**50 TO A POUND** *Poptones 9872739*	32		2
29 Oct 05	**SORRY** *Poptones 9873961*	41		1

JOSE PADILLA FEATURING ANGELA JOHN
Spain/UK, male/female vocal/DJ duo — Weeks on Chart: 1

Date	Title	Peak	Wks at No.1	Wks on Chart
8 Aug 98	**WHO DO YOU LOVE** *Manifesto FESCD 45*	59		1

PAFFENDORF
Germany, male production duo – Gottfried Engels & Ramon Zenker. See Bellini, E-Trax, Fragma, Hardfloor, Interactive — Weeks on Chart: 8

Date	Title	Peak	Wks at No.1	Wks on Chart
15 Jun 02	**BE COOL** *Data 29CDS*	7		7
26 Apr 03	**CRAZY SEXY MARVELLOUS** *Data 51CDS*	52		1

PAGANINI TRAXX
Italy, male DJ/producer (Sam Paganini) — Weeks on Chart: 1

Date	Title	Peak	Wks at No.1	Wks on Chart
1 Feb 97	**ZOE** *Sony S3 DANCUCD 18X*	47		1

JIMMY PAGE
UK, male guitarist. See Coverdale Page, Led Zeppelin, Yardbirds — Weeks on Chart: 16

Date	Title	Peak	Wks at No.1	Wks on Chart
17 Dec 94	**GALLOWS POLE** *Fontana PPCD 2* & ROBERT PLANT	35		3
11 Apr 98	**MOST HIGH** *Mercury 5687512* PAGE & PLANT	26		2
1 Aug 98	**COME WITH ME (IMPORT)** *Epic 34K78954* PUFF DADDY FEATURING JIMMY PAGE	75		1
8 Aug 98	**COME WITH ME** *Epic 6662842* PUFF DADDY FEATURING JIMMY PAGE	2		10

PATTI PAGE
US, female vocalist (Clara Ann Fowler) — Weeks on Chart: 5

Date	Title	Peak	Wks at No.1	Wks on Chart
27 Mar 53	**(HOW MUCH IS) THAT DOGGIE IN THE WINDOW** *Oriole CB 1156* ★	9		5

TOMMY PAGE
US, male vocalist — Weeks on Chart: 3

Date	Title	Peak	Wks at No.1	Wks on Chart
26 May 90	**I'LL BE YOUR EVERYTHING** *Sire W 9959* ★	53		3

PAGLIARO
Canada, male vocalist (Michel Pagliaro) — Weeks on Chart: 6

Date	Title	Peak	Wks at No.1	Wks on Chart
19 Feb 72	**LOVING YOU AIN'T EASY** *Pye 7N 45111*	31		6

PAID + LIVE FEATURING LAURYN HILL
US, male/female vocal/rap/production trio. See Fugees — Weeks on Chart: 1

Date	Title	Peak	Wks at No.1	Wks on Chart
27 Dec 97	**ALL MY TIME** *One World Entertainment OWECD 2*	57		1

ELAINE PAIGE
UK, female vocalist/actor (Elaine Bickerstaff) — Weeks on Chart: 41

Date	Title	Peak	Wks at No.1	Wks on Chart
21 Oct 78	**DON'T WALK AWAY TILL I TOUCH YOU** *EMI 2862*	46		5
6 Jun 81	**MEMORY** *Polydor POSP 279* ●	6		12
30 Jan 82	**MEMORY** *Polydor POSP 279*	67		3
14 Apr 84	**SOMETIMES (THEME FROM 'CHAMPIONS')** *Island IS 174*	72		1
5 Jan 85	**I KNOW HIM SO WELL** *RCA CHESS 3* & BARBARA DICKSON ●	1	4	16
21 Nov 87	**THE SECOND TIME (THEME FROM 'BILITIS')** *WEA YZ 163*	69		1
21 Jan 95	**HYMNE A L'AMOUR** *WEA YZ 899CD*	68		1
24 Oct 98	**MEMORY** *WEA 197CD*	36		2

HAL PAIGE & THE WHALERS
US, male vocal/instrumental group — Weeks on Chart: 1

Date	Title	Peak	Wks at No.1	Wks on Chart
25 Aug 60	**GOING BACK TO MY HOME TOWN** *Melodisc MEL 1553*	50		1

JENNIFER PAIGE
US, female vocalist (Jennifer Scoggins) — Weeks on Chart: 13

Date	Title	Peak	Wks at No.1	Wks on Chart
12 Sep 98	**CRUSH** *EAR 0039425 ERE* ●	4		12
20 Mar 99	**SOBER** *EAR 0044185 ERE*	68		1

ORCHESTRE DE CHAMBRE JEAN-FRANCOIS PAILLARD
France, male conductor & orchestra — Weeks on Chart: 3

Date	Title	Peak	Wks at No.1	Wks on Chart
20 Aug 88	**THEME FROM 'VIETNAM' (CANON IN D)** *Debut DEBT 3053*	61		3

PALE
Ireland, male vocal/instrumental trio — Weeks on Chart: 2

Date	Title	Peak	Wks at No.1	Wks on Chart
13 Jun 92	**DOGS WITH NO TAILS** *A&M AM 866*	51		2

PALE FOUNTAINS
UK, male vocal/instrumental group — Weeks on Chart: 6

Date	Title	Peak	Wks at No.1	Wks on Chart
27 Nov 82	**THANK YOU** *Virgin VS 557*	48		6

PALE SAINTS
UK, male/female vocal/instrumental group — Weeks on Chart: 1

Date	Title	Peak	Wks at No.1	Wks on Chart
6 Jul 91	**KINKY LOVE** *4AD AD 1009*	72		1

PALE X
Holland, male producer (Michael Pollen) — Weeks on Chart: 1

Date	Title	Peak	Wks at No.1	Wks on Chart
3 Feb 01	**NITRO** *Nukleuz NUKP 0280*	74		1

PALLADIUM
UK, male vocal/instrumental group — Weeks on Chart: 1

Date	Title	Peak	Wks at No.1	Wks on Chart
17 Nov 07	**HIGH 5** *Virgin VSCDT1957*	44		1

NERINA PALLOT
UK, female vocalist/guitarist — Weeks on Chart: 14

Date	Title	Peak	Wks at No.1	Wks on Chart
18 Aug 01	**PATIENCE** *Polydor 5872122*	61		1
27 May 06	**EVERYBODY'S GONE TO WAR** *14th Floor 14FLR13CD*	14		9
14 Oct 06	**SOPHIA** *14th Floor 14FLR16CD*	32		3
20 Jan 07	**LEARNING TO BREATHE** *14th Floor 14FLR18CD*	70		1

JHAY PALMER FEATURING MC IMAGE
UK, male vocal/rap duo — Weeks on Chart: 1

Date	Title	Peak	Wks at No.1	Wks on Chart
27 Apr 02	**HELLO** *Bagatrix CDBTX 002*	69		1

Silver-selling ○ Gold-selling ● Platinum-selling (x multiples) US No.1 ★ Peak Position Weeks at No.1 Weeks on Chart

ROBERT PALMER

UK, male vocalist (Alan Palmer), d. 20 Sep 2003 (age 54). See Power Station — 129

Date	Title	Peak Position	Weeks at No.1	Weeks on Chart
20 May 78	**EVERY KINDA PEOPLE** *Island WIP 6425*	53		4
7 Jul 79	**BAD CASE OF LOVIN' YOU (DOCTOR DOCTOR)** *Island WIP 6481*	61		2
6 Sep 80	**JOHNNY AND MARY** *Island WIP 6638*	44		8
22 Nov 80	**LOOKING FOR CLUES** *Island WIP 6651*	33		9
13 Feb 82	**SOME GUYS HAVE ALL THE LUCK** *Island WIP 6754*	16		8
2 Apr 83	**YOU ARE IN MY SYSTEM** *Island IS 104*	53		4
18 Jun 83	**YOU CAN HAVE IT (TAKE MY HEART)** *Island IS 121*	66		2
10 May 86	**ADDICTED TO LOVE** *Island IS 270* ○ ★	5		15
19 Jul 86	**I DIDN'T MEAN TO TURN YOU ON** *Island IS 283*	9		9
1 Nov 86	**DISCIPLINE OF LOVE** *Island IS 242*	68		1
26 Mar 88	**SWEET LIES** *Island IS 352*	58		3
11 Jun 88	**SIMPLY IRRESISTABLE** *EMI EM 61*	44		4
15 Oct 88	**SHE MAKES MY DAY** *EMI EM 65*	6		12
13 May 89	**CHANGE HIS WAYS** *EMI EM 85*	28		7
26 Aug 89	**IT COULD HAPPEN TO YOU** *EMI EM 99*	71		1
3 Nov 90	**I'LL BE YOUR BABY TONIGHT** *EMI EM 167* & UB40	6		10
5 Jan 91	**MERCY MERCY ME – I WANT YOU** *EMI EM 173*	9		9
15 Jun 91	**DREAMS TO REMEMBER** *EMI 193*	68		1
7 Mar 92	**EVERY KINDA PEOPLE (REMIX)** *Island IS 498*	43		3
17 Oct 92	**WITCHCRAFT** *EMI EM 251*	50		3
9 Jul 94	**GIRL U WANT** *EMI CDEMS 331*	57		2
3 Sep 94	**KNOW BY NOW** *EMI CDEMS 343*	25		5
24 Dec 94	**YOU BLOW ME AWAY** *EMI CDEMS 350*	38		4
14 Oct 95	**RESPECT YOURSELF** *EMI CDEMS 399*	45		2
18 Jan 03	**ADDICTED TO LOVE** *Serious SER 606CD* SHAKE B4 USE VS ROBERT PALMER	42		1

SUZANNE PALMER

UK, female vocalist — 5

Date	Title	Peak Position	Weeks at No.1	Weeks on Chart
18 Jan 97	**I BELIEVE** *AM:PM 5820752* ABSOLUTE FEATURING SUZANNE PALMER	38		2
14 Nov 98	**ALRIGHT** *Twisted UK TWCD 10039* CLUB 69 FEATURING SUZANNE PALMER	70		1
29 Jun 02	**643 (LOVE'S ON FIRE)** *Nebula VCRD 106* DJ TIESTO FEATURING SUZANNE PALMER	36		2

PAN POSITION

Italy/Venezuela, male production trio — 1

Date	Title	Peak Position	Weeks at No.1	Weeks on Chart
18 Jun 94	**ELEPHANT PAW (GET DOWN TO THE FUNK)** *Positiva CDTIV 13*	55		1

PANDORA'S BOX

US, female/male vocal/instrumental group — 3

Date	Title	Peak Position	Weeks at No.1	Weeks on Chart
21 Oct 89	**IT'S ALL COMING BACK TO ME NOW** *Virgin VS 1216*	51		3

DARRYL PANDY

US, male vocalist — 5

Date	Title	Peak Position	Weeks at No.1	Weeks on Chart
14 Dec 96	**LOVE CAN'T TURN AROUND** *4 Liberty LIBTCD 27R* FARLEY 'JACKMASTER' FUNK FEATURING DARRYL PANDY	40		2
20 Feb 99	**RAISE YOUR HANDS** *VC Recordings VCRD 44* BIG ROOM GIRL FEATURING DARRYL PANDY	40		2
2 Oct 99	**SUNSHINE & HAPPINESS** *Azuli AZNYCD 103* DARRYL PANDY/NERIO'S DUBWORK	68		1

PANIC! AT THE DISCO

US, male vocal/instrumental group — 27

Date	Title	Peak Position	Weeks at No.1	Weeks on Chart
13 May 06	**BUT IT'S BETTER IF YOU DO** *Decaydance/Fueled By Ramen AT0242CD*	23		5
19 Aug 06	**LYING IS THE MOST FUN A GIRL CAN HAVE** *Decaydance/Fueled By Ramen AT0247CD*	39		2
4 Nov 06	**I WRITE SINS NOT TRAGEDIES** *Decaydance/Fueled By Ramen AT0259CD*	25		10
22 Mar 08	**NINE IN THE AFTERNOON** *Decaydance/Fueled By Ramen AT0303CD* PANIC AT THE DISCO	13		10

PANJABI MC

UK, male DJ/producer (Rajinder Singh) — 19

Date	Title	Peak Position	Weeks at No.1	Weeks on Chart
4 Jan 03	**MUNDIAN TO BACH KE (IMPORT)** *Big Star Big CDM 076CD*	59		3
25 Jan 03	**MUNDIAN TO BACH KE** *Showbiz/Instant Karma KARMA 28CD*	5		13
5 Jul 03	**JOGI/BEWARE OF THE BOYS** *Showbiz/Dharma DHARMA 1CDS* FEATURING JAY-Z	25		3

PANTERA

US, male vocal/instrumental group — 8

Date	Title	Peak Position	Weeks at No.1	Weeks on Chart
10 Oct 92	**MOUTH FOR WAR** *Atco A 5845T*	73		1
27 Feb 93	**WALK** *Atco B 6076CD*	35		2
19 Mar 94	**I'M BROKEN** *Atco B 5832CD1*	19		2
22 Oct 94	**PLANET CARAVAN** *East West A 5836CD1*	26		3

PAPA ROACH

US, male vocal/instrumental group – Jacoby Shaddix, Dave Buckner, Tobin Esperance & Jerry Horton — 27

Date	Title	Peak Position	Weeks at No.1	Weeks on Chart
17 Feb 01	**LAST RESORT** *DreamWorks 4509212*	3		10
5 May 01	**BETWEEN ANGELS AND INSECTS** *DreamWorks 4509092*	17		6
22 Jun 02	**SHE LOVES ME NOT** *DreamWorks 4508182*	14		8
2 Nov 02	**TIME AND TIME AGAIN** *DreamWorks 4508052*	54		1
18 Sep 04	**GETTING AWAY WITH MURDER** *Geffen 9863647*	45		2

PAPER DOLLS

UK, female vocal group — 13

Date	Title	Peak Position	Weeks at No.1	Weeks on Chart
13 Mar 68	**SOMETHING HERE IN MY HEART (KEEPS A-TELLIN' ME NO)** *Pye 7N 17456*	11		13

PAPER LACE

UK, male vocal/instrumental group – Phil Wright, Cliff Fish, Chris Morris & Michael Vaughan — 41

Date	Title	Peak Position	Weeks at No.1	Weeks on Chart
23 Feb 74	**BILLY, DON'T BE A HERO** *Bus Stop BUS 1014* ●	1	3	14
4 May 74	**THE NIGHT CHICAGO DIED** *Bus Stop BUS 1016* ○ ★	3		11
24 Aug 74	**THE BLACK EYED BOYS** *Bus Stop BUS 1019*	11		10
4 Mar 78	**WE'VE GOT THE WHOLE WORLD IN OUR HANDS** *Warner Brothers K 17110* NOTTINGHAM FOREST FC & PAPER LACE	24		6

PAPERDOLLS

UK, female vocal group — 1

Date	Title	Peak Position	Weeks at No.1	Weeks on Chart
12 Sep 98	**GONNA MAKE YOU BLUSH** *MCA MCSTD 40175*	65		1

PAPPA BEAR FEATURING VAN DER TOORN

Antilles/Holland, male rap/vocal duo — 1

Date	Title	Peak Position	Weeks at No.1	Weeks on Chart
16 May 98	**CHERISH** *Universal UMD 70316*	47		1

PAR-T-ONE VS INXS

Italy/Australia, male vocal/instrumental/production group — 6

Date	Title	Peak Position	Weeks at No.1	Weeks on Chart
3 Nov 01	**I'M SO CRAZY** *Credence CDCRED 016*	19		6

PARA BEATS FEATURING CARMEN REECE

UK, male/female vocal/production duo — 1

Date	Title	Peak Position	Weeks at No.1	Weeks on Chart
27 Aug 05	**U GOT ME** *Onetwo ONETCDS003*	59		1

VANESSA PARADIS

France, female vocalist — 30

Date	Title	Peak Position	Weeks at No.1	Weeks on Chart
13 Feb 88	**JOE LE TAXI** *FA Productions POSP 902*	3		10
10 Oct 92	**BE MY BABY** *Remark PO 235*	6		15
27 Feb 93	**SUNDAY MORNINGS** *Remark PZCD 251*	49		4
24 Jul 93	**JUST AS LONG AS YOU ARE THERE** *Remark PZCD 272*	57		1

PARADISE

UK, male vocal/instrumental group — 4

Date	Title	Peak Position	Weeks at No.1	Weeks on Chart
10 Sep 83	**ONE MIND, TWO HEARTS** *Priority P 1*	42		4

PARADISE

UK, male/female vocal/production group — 1

Date	Title	Peak Position	Weeks at No.1	Weeks on Chart
9 Jul 05	**SEE THE LIGHT** *Turbulence CDTURB1*	73		1

PARADISE LOST

UK, male vocal/instrumental group — 3

Date	Title	Peak Position	Weeks at No.1	Weeks on Chart
20 May 95	**THE LAST TIME** *Music For Nations CDKUT 165*	60		1
7 Oct 95	**FOREVER FAILURE** *Music For Nations CDKUT 169*	66		1
28 Jun 97	**SAY JUST WORDS** *Music For Nations CDKUT 174*	53		1

PARADISE ORGANISATION
UK, male production duo — 1

Date	Title	Peak	Wks at No.1	Wks
23 Jan 93	**PRAYER TOWER** *Cowboy RODEO 13*	70		1

PARADOX
UK, male production/rap duo — 2

Date	Title	Peak	Wks at No.1	Wks
24 Feb 90	**JAILBREAK** *Ronin 7R2*	66		2

NORRIE PARAMOR
UK, male orchestra leader/producer, d. 9 Sep 1979 (age 65) — 8

Date	Title	Peak	Wks at No.1	Wks
17 Mar 60	**THEME FROM 'A SUMMER PLACE'** *Columbia DB 4419*	36		2
22 Mar 62	**THEME FROM 'Z CARS'** *Columbia DB 4789*	33		6

PARAMORE
US, female/male vocal/instrumental group — 25

Date	Title	Peak	Wks at No.1	Wks
30 Jun 07	**MISERY BUSINESS (AUSTRALIA RELEASE)** *Atlantic AT0279CD*	17		8
8 Dec 07	**CRUSH CRUSH CRUSH** *Fueled By Ramen AT0295CD*	61		1
17 May 08	**THAT'S WHAT YOU GET** *Fueled By Ramen AT0312CD*	55		3
27 Dec 08	**DECODE** *Fueled By Ramen USAT20804057*	52		6
26 Sep 09	**IGNORANCE** *Fueled By Ramen AT0347CD*	14		6
10 Apr 10	**THE ONLY EXCEPTION** *Fueled By Ramen USAT20902323*	57		1+

PARAMOUNTS
UK, male vocal/instrumental group — 7

Date	Title	Peak	Wks at No.1	Wks
16 Jan 64	**POISON IVY** *Parlophone R 5093*	35		7

PARCHMENT
UK, male/female vocal/instrumental group — 5

Date	Title	Peak	Wks at No.1	Wks
16 Sep 72	**LIGHT UP THE FIRE** *Pye 7N 45178*	31		5

PARIS
UK, male/female vocal instrumental trio — 4

Date	Title	Peak	Wks at No.1	Wks
19 Jun 82	**NO GETTING OVER YOU** *RCA 222*	49		4

PARIS
UK, male rapper/vocalist (Oscar Jackson) — 2

Date	Title	Peak	Wks at No.1	Wks
21 Jan 95	**GUERRILLA FUNK** *Virgin PTYCD 100*	38		2

PARIS & SHARP
UK, male production duo — 1

Date	Title	Peak	Wks at No.1	Wks
1 Dec 01	**APHRODITE** *Cream 16CD*	61		1

PARIS ANGELS
UK, male/female vocal/instrumental group — 5

Date	Title	Peak	Wks at No.1	Wks
3 Nov 90	**SCOPE** *Sheer Joy SHEER 0047*	75		1
20 Jul 91	**PERFUME** *Virgin VS 1360*	55		3
21 Sep 91	**FADE** *Virgin VS 1365*	70		1

MICA PARIS
UK, female vocalist (Michelle Wallen) — 63

Date	Title	Peak	Wks at No.1	Wks
7 May 88	**MY ONE TEMPTATION** *Fourth & Broadway BRW 85*	7		11
30 Jul 88	**LIKE DREAMERS DO** *Fourth & Broadway BRW 108* FEATURING COURTNEY PINE	26		5
22 Oct 88	**BREATHE LIFE INTO ME** *Fourth & Broadway BRW 115*	26		10
21 Jan 89	**WHERE IS THE LOVE** *Fourth & Broadway BRW 122* & WILL DOWNING	19		7
6 Oct 90	**CONTRIBUTION** *Fourth & Broadway BRW 188*	33		4
1 Dec 90	**SOUTH OF THE RIVER** *Fourth & Broadway BRW 199*	50		2
23 Feb 91	**IF I LOVE U 2 NITE** *Fourth & Broadway BRW 207*	43		3
31 Aug 91	**YOUNG SOUL REBELS** *Big Life BLR 57*	61		3
3 Apr 93	**I NEVER FELT LIKE THIS BEFORE** *Fourth & Broadway BRCD 263*	15		5
5 Jun 93	**I WANNA HOLD ON TO YOU** *Fourth & Broadway BRCD 275*	27		3
7 Aug 93	**TWO IN A MILLION** *Fourth & Broadway BRCD 285*	51		2
4 Dec 93	**WHISPER A PRAYER** *Fourth & Broadway BRCD 287*	65		1
8 Apr 95	**ONE** *Cooltempo CDCOOL 304*	29		4
16 May 98	**STAY** *Cooltempo CDCOOL 334*	40		2
14 Nov 98	**BLACK ANGEL** *Cooltempo CDCOOL 341*	72		1

PARIS RED
US, female vocalist — 2

Date	Title	Peak	Wks at No.1	Wks
29 Feb 92	**GOOD FRIEND** *Columbia 6569417*	61		1
15 May 93	**PROMISES** *Columbia 6592342*	59		1

RYAN PARIS
Italy, male vocalist (Fabio Roscioli) — 10

Date	Title	Peak	Wks at No.1	Wks
3 Sep 83	**DOLCE VITA** *Carrere CAR 289*	5		10

JOHN PARISH & POLLY JEAN HARVEY
US, male/female vocal/instrumental/production duo — 1

Date	Title	Peak	Wks at No.1	Wks
23 Nov 96	**THAT WAS MY VEIL** *Island CID 648*	75		1

SIMON PARK ORCHESTRA
UK, male orchestra leader — 24

Date	Title	Peak	Wks at No.1	Wks
25 Nov 72	**EYE LEVEL** *Columbia DB 8946*	41		2
15 Sep 73	**EYE LEVEL** *Columbia DB 8946* ◉	1	4	22

GRAHAM PARKER & THE RUMOUR
UK, male vocal/instrumental group — 16

Date	Title	Peak	Wks at No.1	Wks
19 Mar 77	**THE PINK PARKER EP** *Vertigo PARK 001*	24		5
22 Apr 78	**HEY LORD DON'T ASK ME QUESTIONS** *Vertigo PARK 002* GRAHAM PARKER	32		7
20 Mar 82	**TEMPORARY BEAUTY** *RCA PARK 100*	50		4

RAY PARKER, JR
US, male vocalist/guitarist. See Raydio — 50

Date	Title	Peak	Wks at No.1	Wks
25 Aug 84	**GHOSTBUSTERS** *Arista ARIST 580* ● ★	2		31
18 Jan 86	**GIRLS ARE MORE FUN** *Arista ARIST 641*	46		4
3 Oct 87	**I DON'T THINK THAT MAN SHOULD SLEEP ALONE** *Geffen GEF 27*	13		10
30 Jan 88	**OVER YOU** *Geffen GEF 33*	65		2
10 Nov 07	**GHOSTBUSTERS** *Arista USAR18400008*	70		1
8 Nov 08	**GHOSTBUSTERS** *Arista USAR18400008*	49		1
7 Nov 09	**GHOSTBUSTERS** *Arista USAR18400008*	57		1

ROBERT PARKER
US, male vocalist — 8

Date	Title	Peak	Wks at No.1	Wks
4 Aug 66	**BAREFOOTIN'** *Island WI 286*	24		8

SARA PARKER
US, female vocalist — 2

Date	Title	Peak	Wks at No.1	Wks
12 Apr 97	**MY LOVE IS DEEP** *Manifesto FESCD 22*	22		2

JIMMY PARKINSON
Australia, male vocalist — 19

Date	Title	Peak	Wks at No.1	Wks
2 Mar 56	**THE GREAT PRETENDER** *Columbia DB 3729*	9		13
17 Aug 56	**WALK HAND IN HAND** *Columbia DB 3775*	26		2
9 Nov 56	**IN THE MIDDLE OF THE HOUSE** *Columbia DB 3833*	26		4

ALEX PARKS
UK, female vocalist — 14

Date	Title	Peak	Wks at No.1	Wks
29 Nov 03	**MAYBE THAT'S WHAT IT TAKES** *Polydor 9814581*	3		9
28 Feb 04	**CRY** *Polydor 9816986*	13		4
4 Feb 06	**HONESTY** *Polydor 9876837*	56		1

PARKS & WILSON
UK, male production duo — 1

Date	Title	Peak	Wks at No.1	Wks
9 Sep 00	**FEEL THE DRUM (EP)** *Hooj Choons HOOJ 099CD*	71		1

JOHN PARR
UK, male vocalist — 24

Date	Title	Peak	Wks at No.1	Wks
14 Sep 85	**ST ELMO'S FIRE (MAN IN MOTION)** *London LON 73* ○ ★	6		13
18 Jan 86	**NAUGHTY NAUGHTY** *London 80*	58		3
30 Aug 86	**ROCK 'N' ROLL MERCENARIES** *Arista ARIST 666* MEAT LOAF FEATURING JOHN PARR	31		6
24 Jun 06	**NEW HORIZON** *Gusto CDGUS35* VERSUS TOMMYKNOCKERS	43		2

Silver-selling ● Gold-selling ● Platinum-selling (x multiples) ㊉ US No.1 ★ Peak Position · Weeks at No.1 · Weeks on Chart

DEAN PARRISH

US, male vocalist (Phil Anastasi) — 5

Date	Title	Peak	Wks No.1	Wks
8 Feb 75	**I'M ON MY WAY** *UK USA 2*	38		5

MAN PARRISH

US, male producer/DJ (Manuel Parrish) — 26

Date	Title	Peak	Wks No.1	Wks
26 Mar 83	**HIP HOP, BE BOP (DON'T STOP)** *Polydor POSP 575*	41		6
23 Mar 85	**BOOGIE DOWN (BRONX)** *Boiling Point POSP 731*	56		4
13 Sep 86	**MALE STRIPPER** *Bolts 4* MAN 2 MAN MEET MAN PARRISH	64		3
3 Jan 87	**MALE STRIPPER** *Bolts 4* MAN 2 MAN MEET MAN PARRISH ●	4		13

KAREN PARRY

UK, female vocalist — 12

Date	Title	Peak	Wks No.1	Wks
28 Dec 02	**I THINK WE'RE ALONE NOW** *All Around The World CDGLOBE267* PASCAL FEATURING KAREN PARRY	23		5
24 Jul 04	**DISCOLAND** *All Around The World CDGLOBE 346* FLIP & FILL FEATURING KAREN PARRY	11		7

BILL PARSONS

US, male vocalist — 2

Date	Title	Peak	Wks No.1	Wks
10 Apr 59	**ALL AMERICAN BOY** *London HL 8798*	22		2

ALAN PARSONS PROJECT

UK, male vocal/instrumental group — 4

Date	Title	Peak	Wks No.1	Wks
15 Jan 83	**OLD AND WISE** *Arista ARIST 494*	74		1
10 Mar 84	**DON'T ANSWER ME** *Arista ARIST 553*	58		3

PARTIZAN

UK, male DJ/production duo. See Camisra, Escrima, Grifters, Tall Paul — 3

Date	Title	Peak	Wks No.1	Wks
8 Feb 97	**DRIVE ME CRAZY** *Multiply CDMULTY 17*	36		2
6 Dec 97	**KEEP YOUR LOVE** *Multiply CDMULTY 29* FEATURING NATALIE ROBB	53		1

PARTNERS IN KRYME

US, male rap/production duo – James Alpern & Richard Usher — 10

Date	Title	Peak	Wks No.1	Wks
21 Jul 90	**TURTLE POWER** *SBK TURTLE 1* ●	1	4	10

DAVID PARTON

UK, male vocalist — 9

Date	Title	Peak	Wks No.1	Wks
15 Jan 77	**ISN'T SHE LOVELY** *Pye 7N 45663* ●	4		9

DOLLY PARTON

US, female vocalist/guitarist — 34

Date	Title	Peak	Wks No.1	Wks
15 May 76	**JOLENE** *RCA 2675*	7		10
21 Feb 81	**9 TO 5** *RCA 325* ★	47		5
12 Nov 83	**ISLANDS IN THE STREAM** *RCA 378* KENNY ROGERS & DOLLY PARTON ● ★	7		15
7 Apr 84	**HERE YOU COME AGAIN** *RCA 395*	75		1
16 Apr 94	**THE DAY I FALL IN LOVE** *Columbia 6600282* & JAMES INGRAM	64		2
19 Oct 02	**IF** *Sanctuary SANX 139X*	73		1

STELLA PARTON

US, female vocalist — 4

Date	Title	Peak	Wks No.1	Wks
22 Oct 77	**THE DANGER OF A STRANGER** *Elektra K 12272*	35		4

DON PARTRIDGE

UK, male vocalist/one-man band — 32

Date	Title	Peak	Wks No.1	Wks
7 Feb 68	**ROSIE** *Columbia DB 8330*	4		12
29 May 68	**BLUE EYES** *Columbia DB 8416*	3		13
19 Feb 69	**BREAKFAST ON PLUTO** *Columbia DB 8538*	26		7

PARTRIDGE FAMILY

US, male/female actors/vocal/instrumental group featuring David Cassidy* & Shirley Jones — 53

Date	Title	Peak	Wks No.1	Wks
13 Feb 71	**I THINK I LOVE YOU** *Bell 1130* STARRING SHIRLEY JONES FEATURING DAVID CASSIDY ★	18		9
26 Feb 72	**IT'S ONE OF THOSE NIGHTS (YES LOVE)** *Bell 1203* STARRING SHIRLEY JONES FEATURING DAVID CASSIDY	11		11
8 Jul 72	**BREAKING UP IS HARD TO DO** *Bell MABEL 1* STARRING SHIRLEY JONES FEATURING DAVID CASSIDY	3		13
3 Feb 73	**LOOKING THROUGH THE EYES OF LOVE** *Bell 1278* STARRING DAVID CASSIDY	9		9
19 May 73	**WALKING IN THE RAIN** *Bell 1293* STARRING DAVID CASSIDY	10		11

PARTY ANIMALS

Holland, male rap/instrumental/production group — 3

Date	Title	Peak	Wks No.1	Wks
1 Jun 96	**HAVE YOU EVER BEEN MELLOW** *Mokum DB 17553*	56		1
19 Oct 96	**HAVE YOU EVER BEEN MELLOW (EP)** *Mokum DB 17413*	43		2

PARTY BOYS

UK, male vocal trio — 2

Date	Title	Peak	Wks No.1	Wks
10 Jan 04	**BUILD ME UP BUTTERCUP 2003** *Liberty CDUP 001*	44		2

PARTY FAITHFUL

UK, male/female vocal/instrumental group — 1

Date	Title	Peak	Wks No.1	Wks
22 Jul 95	**BRASS, LET THERE BE HOUSE** *Ore AG 10CD*	54		1

PASADENAS

UK, male vocal/instrumental group – John Andrew Banfield, Jeff Aaron Brown, David & Michael Milliner & Hamish Seelochan — 57

Date	Title	Peak	Wks No.1	Wks
28 May 88	**TRIBUTE (RIGHT ON)** *CBS PASA 1*	5		14
17 Sep 88	**RIDING ON A TRAIN** *CBS PASA 2*	13		9
26 Nov 88	**ENCHANTED LADY** *CBS PASA 3*	31		6
12 May 90	**LOVE THING** *CBS PASA 4*	22		5
14 Jul 90	**REELING** *CBS PASA 5*	75		1
1 Feb 92	**I'M DOING FINE NOW** *Columbia 6577187* ●	4		10
4 Apr 92	**MAKE IT WITH YOU** *Columbia 6579257*	20		4
6 Jun 92	**I BELIEVE IN MIRACLES** *Columbia 6580567*	34		3
29 Aug 92	**MOVING IN THE RIGHT DIRECTION** *Columbia 6583417*	49		2
21 Nov 92	**LET'S STAY TOGETHER** *Columbia 6587747*	22		3

PASCAL FEATURING KAREN PARRY

UK, male/female vocal/production duo. See Flip & Fill — 5

Date	Title	Peak	Wks No.1	Wks
28 Dec 02	**I THINK WE'RE ALONE NOW** *All Around The World CDGLOBE267*	23		5

PASSENGERS

UK/Ireland, male vocal/instrumental/production charity group – Brian Eno & U2. See Roxy Music — 9

Date	Title	Peak	Wks No.1	Wks
2 Dec 95	**MISS SARAJEVO** *Island CID 625* ●	6		9

PASSION

UK, male vocal/rap group — 1

Date	Title	Peak	Wks No.1	Wks
25 Jan 97	**SHARE YOUR LOVE (NO DIGGITY)** *Charm CRTCDS 269*	62		1

PASSIONS

UK, male/female vocal/instrumental group — 8

Date	Title	Peak	Wks No.1	Wks
31 Jan 81	**I'M IN LOVE WITH A GERMAN FILM STAR** *Polydor POSP 222*	25		8

PAT & MICK

UK, male vocal/radio DJ duo – Pat Sharp (Patrick Sharpin) & Mick Brown — 27

Date	Title	Peak	Wks No.1	Wks
9 Apr 88	**LET'S ALL CHANT/ON THE NIGHT** *PWL 10*	11		9
25 Mar 89	**I HAVEN'T STOPPED DANCING YET** *PWL 33*	9		8
14 Apr 90	**USE IT UP AND WEAR IT OUT** *PWL 55*	22		6
23 Mar 91	**GIMME SOME** *PWL 75*	53		2
15 May 93	**HOT HOT HOT** *PWL International PARKCD 1*	47		2

PATIENCE & PRUDENCE

US, female vocal duo — 8

Date	Title	Peak	Wks No.1	Wks
2 Nov 56	**TONIGHT YOU BELONG TO ME** *London HLU 8321*	28		3
1 Mar 57	**GONNA GET ALONG WITHOUT YA NOW** *London HLU 8369*	22		5

PATRA
Jamaica, female vocalist (Dorothy Smith) — 11

Date	Title	Peak	Wks No.1	Wks on Chart
25 Dec 93	**FAMILY AFFAIR** *Polydor PZCD 304* SHABBA RANKS FEATURING PATRA & TERRY & MONICA	18		8
30 Sep 95	**PULL UP TO THE BUMPER** *Epic 6623942*	50		2
10 Aug 96	**WORK MI BODY** *Heavenly HVN 53CD* MONKEY MAFIA FEATURING PATRA	75		1

PATRIC
UK, male vocalist (Marcus Patrick). See Worlds Apart — 2

Date	Title	Peak	Wks No.1	Wks on Chart
9 Jul 94	**LOVE ME** *Bell 74321215352*	54		2

DEE PATTEN
UK, male DJ/producer — 1

Date	Title	Peak	Wks No.1	Wks on Chart
30 Jan 99	**WHO'S THE BAD MAN** *Higher Ground HIGHS 15CD*	42		1

KELLEE PATTERSON
US, female vocalist — 7

Date	Title	Peak	Wks No.1	Wks on Chart
18 Feb 78	**IF IT DON'T FIT DON'T FORCE IT** *EMI International INT 544*	44		7

RAHSAAN PATTERSON
US, male vocalist — 2

Date	Title	Peak	Wks No.1	Wks on Chart
26 Jul 97	**STOP BY** *MCA MCSTD 48055*	50		1
21 Mar 98	**WHERE YOU ARE** *MCA MCSTD 48073*	55		1

BILLY PAUL
US, male vocalist (Paul Williams) — 44

Date	Title	Peak	Wks No.1	Wks on Chart
13 Jan 73	**ME AND MRS JONES** *Epic EPC 1055* ★	12		9
12 Jan 74	**THANKS FOR SAVING MY LIFE** *Philadelphia International PIR 1928*	33		6
22 May 76	**LET'S MAKE A BABY** *Philadelphia International PIR 4144*	30		5
30 Apr 77	**LET 'EM IN** *Philadelphia International PIR 5143*	26		5
16 Jul 77	**YOUR SONG** *Philadelphia International PIR 5391*	37		7
19 Nov 77	**ONLY THE STRONG SURVIVE** *Philadelphia International PIR 5699*	33		7
14 Jul 79	**BRING THE FAMILY BACK** *Philadelphia International PIR 7456*	51		5

CHRIS PAUL
UK, male producer. See Isotonik — 8

Date	Title	Peak	Wks No.1	Wks on Chart
31 May 86	**EXPANSIONS '86 (EXPAND YOUR MIND)** *Fourth & Broadway BRW 48* FEATURING DAVID JOSEPH	58		5
21 Nov 87	**BACK IN MY ARMS** *Syncopate SY 5*	74		2
13 Aug 88	**TURN THE MUSIC UP** *Syncopate SY 13*	73		1

LES PAUL & MARY FORD
US, male guitarist (Les Poisfuss), d. 12 Aug 2009, & female vocalist (Colleen Summers), d. 30 Sep 1977 — 4

Date	Title	Peak	Wks No.1	Wks on Chart
20 Nov 53	**VAYA CON DIOS** *Capitol CL 13943* ★	7		4

LYN PAUL
UK, female vocalist (Lynda Belcher). See New Seekers — 6

Date	Title	Peak	Wks No.1	Wks on Chart
28 Jun 75	**IT OUGHTA SELL A MILLION** *Polydor 2058 602*	37		6

OWEN PAUL
UK, male vocalist (Owen Paul McGee) — 14

Date	Title	Peak	Wks No.1	Wks on Chart
31 May 86	**MY FAVOURITE WASTE OF TIME** *Epic A 7125*	3		14

SEAN PAUL
Jamaica, male vocalist (Sean Paul Henriques) — 150

Date	Title	Peak	Wks No.1	Wks on Chart
21 Sep 02	**GIMME THE LIGHT** *VP VPCD 6400*	32		7
15 Feb 03	**GIMME THE LIGHT** *VP/Atlantic AT 0146CD*	5		10
24 May 03	**GET BUSY** *VP/Atlantic AT 0155CD* ★	4		7
19 Jul 03	**BREATHE (IMPORT)** *Arista 82876534002* BLU CANTRELL FEATURING SEAN PAUL	59		3
9 Aug 03	**BREATHE** *Arista 82876545722* BLU CANTRELL FEATURING SEAN PAUL	1	4	18
6 Sep 03	**LIKE GLUE** *VP/Atlantic AT 0162CD*	3		10
18 Oct 03	**BABY BOY** *Columbia 6744082* BEYONCE FEATURING SEAN PAUL ★	2		11
17 Jan 04	**I'M STILL IN LOVE WITH YOU** *VP/Atlantic AT 0170CDX* FEATURING SASHA	6		14
24 Sep 05	**WE BE BURNIN'** *VP/Atlantic AT0218CDX*	2		19
10 Dec 05	**EVER BLAZIN'** *VP/Atlantic AT0227CD*	12		8
25 Mar 06	**TEMPERATURE** *VP/Atlantic AT0235CD* ★	11		12
20 May 06	**CRY BABY CRY** *Arista 82876804672* SANTANA FEATURING SEAN PAUL & JOSS STONE	71		1
22 Jul 06	**NEVER GONNA BE THE SAME** *VP/Atlantic AT0248CD*	22		5
23 Sep 06	**DO IT TO IT** *Capitol CDCL878* CHERISH FEATURING SEAN PAUL	30		4
4 Nov 06	**(WHEN YOU GONNA) GIVE IT UP TO ME** *VP/Atlantic AT0265CD* FEATURING KEYSHIA COLE	31		6
29 Aug 09	**SO FINE** *Atlantic AT0343CD*	25		3
23 Jan 10	**DO YOU REMEMBER** *Island 2733342* JAY SEAN FEATURING SEAN PAUL & LIL JON	13		12+

PAUL & PAULA
UK, male/female vocal duo – Ray Hilderbrand & Jill Jackson — 31

Date	Title	Peak	Wks No.1	Wks on Chart
14 Feb 63	**HEY PAULA** *Philips 304012 BF* ★	8		17
18 Apr 63	**YOUNG LOVERS** *Philips 304016 BF*	9		14

LUCIANO PAVAROTTI
Italy, male vocalist, d. 6 Sep 2007 (age 71) — 33

Date	Title	Peak	Wks No.1	Wks on Chart
16 Jun 90	**NESSUN DORMA** *Decca PAV 03*	2		11
24 Oct 92	**MISERERE** *London LON 329* ZUCCHERO WITH LUCIANO PAVAROTTI	15		5
30 Jul 94	**LIBIAMO/LA DONNA E MOBILE** *Teldec YZ 843CD* JOSE CARRERAS, PLACIDO DOMINGO & LUCIANO PAVAROTTI	21		4
14 Dec 96	**LIVE LIKE HORSES** *Rocket LLHDD 1* ELTON JOHN & LUCIANO PAVAROTTI	9		6
25 Jul 98	**YOU'LL NEVER WALK ALONE** *Decca 4607982* CARRERAS/DOMINGO/PAVAROTTI WITH MEHTA	35		4
15 Sep 07	**NESSUN DORMA** *Decca PAVOX3*	24		3

PAVEMENT
US, male vocal/instrumental group — 6

Date	Title	Peak	Wks No.1	Wks on Chart
28 Nov 92	**WATERY, DOMESTIC (EP)** *Big Cat ABB 38T*	58		1
12 Feb 94	**CUT YOUR HAIR** *Big Cat ABB 55SCD*	52		1
8 Feb 97	**STEREO** *Domino RUG 51CD*	48		1
3 May 97	**SHADY LANE** *Domino RUG 53CD*	40		1
22 May 99	**CARROT ROPE** *Domino RUG 90CD1*	27		2

RITA PAVONE
Italy, female vocalist — 19

Date	Title	Peak	Wks No.1	Wks on Chart
1 Dec 66	**HEART** *RCA 1553*	27		12
19 Jan 67	**YOU ONLY YOU** *RCA 1561*	21		7

PAY AS U GO
UK, male rap/production group — 4

Date	Title	Peak	Wks No.1	Wks on Chart
27 Apr 02	**CHAMPAGNE DANCE** *So Urban 6721362*	13		4

FREDA PAYNE
US, female vocalist — 30

Date	Title	Peak	Wks No.1	Wks on Chart
5 Sep 70	**BAND OF GOLD** *Invictus INV 502*	1	6	19
21 Nov 70	**DEEPER AND DEEPER** *Invictus INV 505*	33		9
27 Mar 71	**CHERISH WHAT IS DEAR TO YOU** *Invictus INV 509*	46		2

TAMMY PAYNE
UK, female vocalist — 2

Date	Title	Peak	Wks No.1	Wks on Chart
20 Jul 91	**TAKE ME NOW** *Talkin Loud TLK 12*	55		2

HEATHER PEACE
UK, female actor/vocalist — 1

Date	Title	Peak	Wks No.1	Wks on Chart
13 May 00	**THE ROSE** *RCA 74321742892*	56		1

PEACE BY PIECE
UK, male vocal group — 2

Date	Title	Peak	Wks No.1	Wks on Chart
21 Sep 96	**SWEET SISTER** *Blanco Y Negro NEG94CD*	46		1
25 Apr 98	**NOBODY'S BUSINESS** *Blanco Y Negro NEG110CD1*	50		1

Silver-selling ● Gold-selling ● Platinum-selling (x multiples) ⊛ US No.1 ★ | Peak Position | Weeks at No.1 | Weeks on Chart

PEACH
UK/Belgium, female/male vocal/production group — Weeks on Chart: 1

Date	Title	Peak Position	Weeks at No.1	Weeks on Chart
17 Jan 98	**ON MY OWN** *Mute CDMUTE 215*	69		1

PEACHES
Canada, female vocalist/producer (Merrill Nisker) — Weeks on Chart: 6

Date	Title	Peak Position	Weeks at No.1	Weeks on Chart
15 Jun 02	**SET IT OFF** *Epic 6726862*	36		2
17 Jan 04	**KICK IT** *XL Recordings XLS176CD* FEATURING IGGY POP	39		3
15 Jul 06	**DOWNTOWN** *XL Recordings XLS235CD*	50		1

PEACHES & HERB
US, female/male vocal duo – Linda Green & Herbert Feemster — Weeks on Chart: 23

Date	Title	Peak Position	Weeks at No.1	Weeks on Chart
20 Jan 79	**SHAKE YOUR GROOVE THING** *Polydor 2066 992*	26		10
21 Apr 79	**REUNITED** *Polydor POSP 43* ● ★	4		13

PEARL JAM
US, male vocal/instrumental group – Eddie Vedder, Jeff Ament, Stone Gossard, Dave Krusen (replaced by Dave Abbruzzese, followed by Jack Irons, then Matt Cameron) & Mike McCready — Weeks on Chart: 43

Date	Title	Peak Position	Weeks at No.1	Weeks on Chart
15 Feb 92	**ALIVE** *Epic 6575727*	16		6
18 Apr 92	**EVEN FLOW** *Epic 6578577*	27		3
26 Sep 92	**JEREMY** *Epic 6582587*	15		4
1 Jan 94	**DAUGHTER** *Epic 6600202*	18		5
28 May 94	**DISSIDENT** *Epic 6604415*	14		4
26 Nov 94	**SPIN THE BLACK CIRCLE** *Epic 6610362*	10		3
25 Feb 95	**NOT FOR YOU** *Epic 6612032*	34		2
16 Dec 95	**MERKINBALL EP** *Epic 6627162*	25		3
17 Aug 96	**WHO YOU ARE** *Epic 6635392*	18		2
31 Jan 98	**GIVEN TO FLY** *Epic 6653942*	12		3
23 May 98	**WISHLIST** *Epic 6657902*	30		2
14 Aug 99	**LAST KISS** *Epic 6674792*	42		1
13 May 00	**NOTHING AS IT SEEMS** *Epic 6693742*	22		2
22 Jul 00	**LIGHT YEARS** *Epic 6696282*	52		1
9 Nov 02	**I AM MINE** *Epic 6733082*	26		2

PEARLS
UK, female vocal duo – Lynn Cornell* & Ann Simmons — Weeks on Chart: 24

Date	Title	Peak Position	Weeks at No.1	Weeks on Chart
27 May 72	**THIRD FINGER, LEFT HAND** *Bell 1217*	31		6
23 Sep 72	**YOU CAME YOU SAW YOU CONQUERED** *Bell 1254*	32		5
24 Mar 73	**YOU ARE EVERYTHING** *Bell 1284*	41		3
1 Jun 74	**GUILTY** *Bell 1352*	10		10

JOHNNY PEARSON
UK, male orchestra leader/pianist — Weeks on Chart: 15

Date	Title	Peak Position	Weeks at No.1	Weeks on Chart
18 Dec 71	**SLEEPY SHORES** *Penny Farthing PEN 778*	8		15

PEBBLES
US, female vocalist (Perri McKissack) — Weeks on Chart: 17

Date	Title	Peak Position	Weeks at No.1	Weeks on Chart
19 Mar 88	**GIRLFRIEND** *MCA 1233*	8		11
28 May 88	**MERCEDES BOY** *MCA 1248*	42		4
27 Oct 90	**GIVING YOU THE BENEFIT** *MCA 1448*	73		2

PEDDLERS
UK, male/female vocal/instrumental group — Weeks on Chart: 14

Date	Title	Peak Position	Weeks at No.1	Weeks on Chart
7 Jan 65	**LET THE SUNSHINE IN** *Philips BF 1375*	50		1
23 Aug 69	**BIRTH** *CBS 4449*	17		9
31 Jan 70	**GIRLIE** *CBS 4720*	34		4

PEE BEE SQUAD
UK, male vocalist/radio presenter (Paul Burnett). See Laurie Lingo & The Dipsticks — Weeks on Chart: 3

Date	Title	Peak Position	Weeks at No.1	Weeks on Chart
5 Oct 85	**RUGGED AND MEAN, BUTCH AND ON SCREEN** *Project PRO 3*	52		3

ANN PEEBLES
US, female vocalist — Weeks on Chart: 3

Date	Title	Peak Position	Weeks at No.1	Weeks on Chart
20 Apr 74	**I CAN'T STAND THE RAIN** *London HL 10428*	41		3

PEECH BOYS
US, male vocal/instrumental group — Weeks on Chart: 3

Date	Title	Peak Position	Weeks at No.1	Weeks on Chart
30 Oct 82	**DON'T MAKE ME WAIT** *TMT 7001*	49		3

DONALD PEERS
UK, male vocalist, d. 9 Aug 1973 (age 65) — Weeks on Chart: 28

Date	Title	Peak Position	Weeks at No.1	Weeks on Chart
29 Dec 66	**GAMES THAT LOVERS PLAY** *Columbia DB 8079*	46		1
18 Dec 68	**PLEASE DON'T GO** *Columbia DB 8502*	3		21
24 Jun 72	**GIVE ME ONE MORE CHANCE** *Decca F 13302*	36		6

PELE
UK, male/female vocal/instrumental group — Weeks on Chart: 3

Date	Title	Peak Position	Weeks at No.1	Weeks on Chart
15 Feb 92	**MEGALOMANIA** *M&G MAGS 20*	73		1
13 Jun 92	**FAIR BLOWS THE WIND FOR FRANCE** *M&G MAGS 24*	62		1
31 Jul 93	**FAT BLACK HEART** *M&G MAGCD 43*	75		1

MARTI PELLOW
UK, male vocalist. See Wet Wet Wet — Weeks on Chart: 9

Date	Title	Peak Position	Weeks at No.1	Weeks on Chart
16 Jun 01	**CLOSE TO YOU** *Mercury MERDD 532*	9		6
1 Dec 01	**I'VE BEEN AROUND THE WORLD** *Mercury 5887772*	28		2
22 Nov 03	**A LOT OF LOVE** *Universal TV 9813763*	59		1

JACK PENATE
UK, male vocalist/guitarist — Weeks on Chart: 22

Date	Title	Peak Position	Weeks at No.1	Weeks on Chart
30 Jun 07	**TORN ON THE PLATFORM** *XL Recordings XLS276CD*	7		10
29 Sep 07	**SECOND, MINUTE OR HOUR** *XL Recordings XLS290CD*	17		7
22 Dec 07	**HAVE I BEEN A FOOL** *XL Recordings XLS391CD*	73		1
11 Apr 09	**TONIGHT'S TODAY** *XL Recordings XLS420CD*	23		2
27 Jun 09	**BE THE ONE** *XL Recordings XLS442CD*	35		2

DEBBIE PENDER
US, female vocalist — Weeks on Chart: 1

Date	Title	Peak Position	Weeks at No.1	Weeks on Chart
30 May 98	**MOVIN' ON** *AM:PM 5826492*	41		1

TEDDY PENDERGRASS
US, male vocalist (Theodore Pendergrass), d. 13 Jan 2010 (age 59). See Harold Melvin & The Bluenotes — Weeks on Chart: 24

Date	Title	Peak Position	Weeks at No.1	Weeks on Chart
21 May 77	**THE WHOLE TOWN'S LAUGHING AT ME** *Philadelphia International PIR 5116*	44		3
28 Oct 78	**ONLY YOU/CLOSE THE DOOR** *Philadelphia International PIR 6713*	41		6
23 May 81	**TWO HEARTS** *20th Century TC 2492*	49		5
25 Jan 86	**HOLD ME** *Asylum EKR 32* & WHITNEY HOUSTON	44		5
28 May 88	**JOY** *Elektra EKR 75*	58		3
19 Nov 94	**THE MORE I GET THE MORE I WANT** *X-clusive XCLU 011CD* KWS FEATURING TEDDY PENDERGRASS	35		2

PENDULUM
Australia, male vocal/DJ/production group – Rob Swire, Peredur ap Gwynedd, Paul Harding, Paul Kodish, Gareth McGrillen & Ben Mount — Weeks on Chart: 38

Date	Title	Peak Position	Weeks at No.1	Weeks on Chart
6 Mar 04	**ANOTHER PLANET/VOYAGER** *Breakbeat Kaos BBK003*	46		2
30 Apr 05	**GUNS AT DAWN** *Breakbeat Kaos BBK008* DJ BARON FEATURING PENDULUM	71		1
9 Jul 05	**TARANTULA/FASTEN YOUR SEATBELT** *Breakbeat Kaos BBK009SCD* & FRESH FEATURING SPYDA	60		1
1 Oct 05	**SLAM/OUT HERE** *Breakbeat Kaos BBK011SCD*	34		2
9 Jun 07	**BLOOD SUGAR/AXLE GRINDER** *Breakbeat Kaos GBKBH0720001*	62		3
17 Nov 07	**GRANITE** *Warner Brothers WEA436CD*	29		6
3 May 08	**PROPANE NIGHTMARES** *Warner Brothers WEA455CD*	9		20
24 May 08	**BLOOD SUGAR/AXLE GRINDER** *Breakbeat Kaos BBK020*	74		1
9 Aug 08	**THE OTHER SIDE** *Warner Brothers WEA450CD*	54		2

CE CE PENISTON
US, female vocalist (Cecilia Peniston) — Weeks on Chart: 53

Date	Title	Peak Position	Weeks at No.1	Weeks on Chart
12 Oct 91	**FINALLY** *A&M AM 822*	29		7
11 Jan 92	**WE GOT A LOVE THANG** *A&M AM 846*	6		8
18 Jan 92	**I LIKE IT** *A&M AM 847* OVERWEIGHT POOCH FEATURING CE CE PENISTON	58		2
21 Mar 92	**FINALLY** *A&M AM 858* ●	2		8
23 May 92	**KEEP ON WALKIN'** *A&M AM 878*	10		6
5 Sep 92	**CRAZY LOVE** *A&M AM 0060*	44		3
12 Dec 92	**INSIDE THAT I CRIED** *A&M AM 0121*	42		2

Date	Title / Label	Peak Position	Weeks at No.1	Weeks on Chart
15 Jan 94	**I'M IN THE MOOD** *A&M 5804552*	16		4
2 Apr 94	**KEEP GIVIN' ME YOUR LOVE** *A&M 5805492*	36		2
6 Aug 94	**HIT BY LOVE** *A&M 5806932*	33		2
13 Sep 97	**FINALLY** *AM:PM 5823432*	26		5
7 Feb 98	**SOMEBODY ELSE'S GUY** *AM:PM 5825112*	13		4

DAWN PENN

Jamaica, female vocalist (Dawn Pickering) — 12

Date	Title / Label	Peak Position	Weeks at No.1	Weeks on Chart
11 Jun 94	**YOU DON'T LOVE ME (NO NO NO)** *Big Beat A 8295CD* ○	3		12

BARBARA PENNINGTON

US, female vocalist — 8

Date	Title / Label	Peak Position	Weeks at No.1	Weeks on Chart
27 Apr 85	**FAN THE FLAME** *Record Shack SOHO 37*	62		3
27 Jul 85	**ON A CROWDED STREET** *Record Shack SOHO 49*	57		5

TRICIA PENROSE

UK, female actor/vocalist — 2

Date	Title / Label	Peak Position	Weeks at No.1	Weeks on Chart
7 Dec 96	**WHERE DID OUR LOVE GO** *RCA 74321428152*	71		1
4 Mar 00	**DON'T WANNA BE ALONE** *Doop DP 2001CD*	44		1

PENTANGLE

UK, male/female vocal/instrumental group — 4

Date	Title / Label	Peak Position	Weeks at No.1	Weeks on Chart
28 May 69	**ONCE I HAD A SWEETHEART** *Big T BIG 124*	46		1
14 Feb 70	**LIGHT FLIGHT** *Big T BIG 128*	43		3

PENTHOUSE 4

UK, male vocal/production duo — 3

Date	Title / Label	Peak Position	Weeks at No.1	Weeks on Chart
23 Apr 88	**BUST THIS HOUSE DOWN** *Syncopate SY 10*	56		3

PEOPLE'S CHOICE

US, male vocal/instrumental group — 9

Date	Title / Label	Peak Position	Weeks at No.1	Weeks on Chart
20 Sep 75	**DO IT ANY WAY YOU WANNA** *Philadelphia International PIR 3500*	36		5
21 Jan 78	**JAM JAM JAM (ALL NIGHT LONG)** *Philadelphia International PIR 5891*	40		4

PEPE DELUXE

Finland, male DJ/production group — 3

Date	Title / Label	Peak Position	Weeks at No.1	Weeks on Chart
26 May 01	**BEFORE YOU LEAVE** *Catskills 6712392*	20		3

DANNY PEPPERMINT & THE JUMPING JACKS

US, male vocal/instrumental group — 8

Date	Title / Label	Peak Position	Weeks at No.1	Weeks on Chart
18 Jan 62	**PEPPERMINT TWIST** *London HLL 9478*	26		8

PEPPERS

France, male instrumental duo – Mat Camison & Pierre Dahan — 12

Date	Title / Label	Peak Position	Weeks at No.1	Weeks on Chart
26 Oct 74	**PEPPER BOX** *Spark SRL 1100*	6		12

PEPSI & SHIRLIE

UK, female vocal duo – Helen DeMacque & Shirlie Holliman — 24

Date	Title / Label	Peak Position	Weeks at No.1	Weeks on Chart
17 Jan 87	**HEARTACHE** *Polydor POSP 837* ○	2		12
30 May 87	**GOODBYE STRANGER** *Polydor POSP 865*	9		7
26 Sep 87	**CAN'T GIVE ME LOVE** *Polydor POSP 885*	58		3
12 Dec 87	**ALL RIGHT NOW** *Polydor POSP 896*	50		2

PERAN

Holland, male producer (Peran van Dijk) — 2

Date	Title / Label	Peak Position	Weeks at No.1	Weeks on Chart
23 Mar 02	**GOOD TIME** *Incentive CENT 37CDS*	37		2

PERCEPTION

UK, male/female vocal/production group — 2

Date	Title / Label	Peak Position	Weeks at No.1	Weeks on Chart
7 Mar 92	**FEED THE FEELING** *Talkin Loud TLK 17*	58		2

LANCE PERCIVAL

UK, male vocalist/comedian — 3

Date	Title / Label	Peak Position	Weeks at No.1	Weeks on Chart
28 Oct 65	**SHAME AND SCANDAL IN THE FAMILY** *Parlophone R 5335*	37		3

A PERFECT CIRCLE

UK, male vocal/instrumental group — 2

Date	Title / Label	Peak Position	Weeks at No.1	Weeks on Chart
18 Nov 00	**THE HOLLOW** *Virgin VUSCD 181*	72		1
13 Jan 01	**3 LIBRAS** *Virgin VUSCD 184*	49		1

PERFECT DAY

UK, male vocal/instrumental group — 4

Date	Title / Label	Peak Position	Weeks at No.1	Weeks on Chart
21 Jan 89	**LIBERTY TOWN** *London LON 214*	58		3
1 Apr 89	**JANE** *London LON 188*	68		1

PERFECT PHASE

Holland, male production duo — 8

Date	Title / Label	Peak Position	Weeks at No.1	Weeks on Chart
25 Dec 99	**HORNY HORNS** *Positiva CDTIV 123*	21		7
12 Jun 04	**BLOW YOUR HORNY HORNS** *Feverpitch 12FEV3*	75		1

PERFECTLY ORDINARY PEOPLE

UK, male production duo — 3

Date	Title / Label	Peak Position	Weeks at No.1	Weeks on Chart
22 Oct 88	**THEME FROM P.O.P.** *Urban URB 25*	61		3

PERFECTO ALLSTARZ

UK, male instrumental/production duo – Paul Oakenfold & Steve Osborne. See Oakenfold, Rise, Virus — 11

Date	Title / Label	Peak Position	Weeks at No.1	Weeks on Chart
4 Feb 95	**REACH UP (PAPA'S GOT A BRAND NEW PIG BAG)** *Perfecto YZ 892CD* ○	6		11

PERFUME

UK, male vocal/instrumental group — 1

Date	Title / Label	Peak Position	Weeks at No.1	Weeks on Chart
10 Feb 96	**HAVEN'T SEEN YOU** *Aromasound AROMA 005CDS*	71		1

EMILIO PERICOLI

Italy, male vocalist — 14

Date	Title / Label	Peak Position	Weeks at No.1	Weeks on Chart
28 Jun 62	**AL DI LA** *Warner Brothers WB 69*	30		14

CARL PERKINS

US, male vocalist/guitarist, d. 19 Jan 1998 (age 65) — 8

Date	Title / Label	Peak Position	Weeks at No.1	Weeks on Chart
18 May 56	**BLUE SUEDE SHOES** *London HLU 8271*	10		8

PERPETUAL MOTION

UK, male instrumental/production group — 5

Date	Title / Label	Peak Position	Weeks at No.1	Weeks on Chart
2 May 98	**KEEP ON DANCIN' (LET'S GO)** *Positiva CDTIV 90*	12		5

KATY PERRY

US, female vocalist/guitarist (Katheryn Hudson) — 119

Date	Title / Label	Peak Position	Weeks at No.1	Weeks on Chart
9 Aug 08	**I KISSED A GIRL** *Virgin VSCDT1976* ● ★	1	5	30
4 Oct 08	**HOT N COLD** *Virgin VSCDT1980* ●	4		35
31 Jan 09	**THINKING OF YOU** *Virgin VSCDT1985*	27		11
16 May 09	**WAKING UP IN VEGAS** *Virgin VSCDT1993*	19		17
26 Dec 09	**STARSTRUKK** *Asylum/Photo Finish USAT20802558* 30H!3 FEATURING KATY PERRY ●	3		16+
6 Feb 10	**IF WE EVER MEET AGAIN** *Interscope 2733439* TIMBALAND FEATURING KATY PERRY	3		10+

STEVE PERRY

UK, male vocalist — 1

Date	Title / Label	Peak Position	Weeks at No.1	Weeks on Chart
4 Aug 60	**STEP BY STEP** *HMV POP 745*	41		1

NINA PERSSON & DAVID ARNOLD

Sweden/UK, female/male vocal/instrumental/production duo. See Cardigans — 1

Date	Title / Label	Peak Position	Weeks at No.1	Weeks on Chart
29 Apr 00	**THEME FROM 'RANDALL & HOPKIRK (DECEASED)'** *Island CID 762*	49		1

JON PERTWEE

UK, male vocalist/actor, d. 20 May 1996 (age 76) — 7

Date	Title / Label	Peak Position	Weeks at No.1	Weeks on Chart
1 Mar 80	**WORZEL SONG** *Decca F 13885*	33		7

Silver-selling ● Gold-selling ● Platinum-selling (x multiples) US No.1 ★ Peak Position Weeks at No.1 Weeks on Chart

PESHAY

UK, male DJ/producer (Paul Pesce) — 6

Date	Title	Peak Position	Weeks at No.1	Weeks on Chart
9 May 98	**MILES FROM HOME** *Mo Wax MW092*	75		1
17 Jul 99	**SWITCH** *Island Blue PFACD 1*	59		1
19 Feb 00	**TRULY** *Island Blue PFACD 4* FEATURING KYM MAZELLE	55		1
4 May 02	**YOU GOT ME BURNING/FUZION** *Cubik Music CUBIKSAMPCD 001* FEATURING CO-ORDINATE	41		2
24 Aug 02	**SATISFY MY LOVE** *Cubik Music CUBIK 002CD* VERSUS FLYTRONIX	67		1

PET SHOP BOYS

UK, male vocal/instrumental duo – Neil Tennant & Chris Lowe. Critically acclaimed music video pioneers who have scored more UK hits (45 and counting) than any other duo and amassed total UK singles sales of 5.4 million. 'West End Girls' won 'Best British Single' at the 1987 BRIT Awards — 260

Date	Title	Peak Position	Weeks at No.1	Weeks on Chart
23 Nov 85	**WEST END GIRLS** *Parlophone R 6115* ● ★	1	2	15
8 Mar 86	**LOVE COMES QUICKLY** *Parlophone R 6116*	19		9
31 May 86	**OPPORTUNITIES (LET'S MAKE LOTS OF MONEY)** *Parlophone R 6129*	11		8
4 Oct 86	**SUBURBIA** *Parlophone R 6140*	8		9
27 Jun 87	**IT'S A SIN** *Parlophone R 6158* ●	1	3	11
22 Aug 87	**WHAT HAVE I DONE TO DESERVE THIS** *Parlophone R 6163* & DUSTY SPRINGFIELD ●	2		9
24 Oct 87	**RENT** *Parlophone R 6168*	8		7
12 Dec 87	**ALWAYS ON MY MIND** *Parlophone R 6171* ●	1	4	11
2 Apr 88	**HEART** *Parlophone R 6177* ●	1	3	10
24 Sep 88	**DOMINO DANCING** *Parlophone R 6190*	7		8
26 Nov 88	**LEFT TO MY OWN DEVICES** *Parlophone R 6198*	4		8
8 Jul 89	**IT'S ALRIGHT** *Parlophone R 6220*	5		8
6 Oct 90	**SO HARD** *Parlophone R 6269*	4		6
24 Nov 90	**BEING BORING** *Parlophone R 6275*	20		8
23 Mar 91	**WHERE THE STREETS HAVE NO NAME – CAN'T TAKE MY EYES OFF YOU/HOW CAN YOU EXPECT ME TO BE TAKEN SERIOUSLY** *Parlophone R 6285*	4		8
8 Jun 91	**JEALOUSY** *Parlophone R 6283*	12		5
26 Oct 91	**DJ CULTURE** *Parlophone R 6301*	13		3
23 Nov 91	**DJ CULTURE (REMIX)** *Parlophone 12RX 6301*	40		2
21 Dec 91	**WAS IT WORTH IT** *Parlophone R 6306*	24		4
12 Jun 93	**CAN YOU FORGIVE HER** *Parlophone CDR 6348*	7		7
18 Sep 93	**GO WEST** *Parlophone CDR 6356*	2		9
11 Dec 93	**I WOULDN'T NORMALLY DO THIS KIND OF THING** *Parlophone CDR 6370*	13		7
16 Apr 94	**LIBERATION** *Parlophone CDR 6377*	14		5
11 Jun 94	**ABSOLUTELY FABULOUS** *Spaghetti CDR 6382* ABSOLUTELY FABULOUS	6		7
10 Sep 94	**YESTERDAY WHEN I WAS MAD** *Parlophone CDRS 6386*	13		4
5 Aug 95	**PANINARO '95** *Parlophone CDRS 6414*	15		4
4 May 96	**BEFORE** *Parlophone CDRS 6431*	7		5
24 Aug 96	**SE A VIDA E (THAT'S THE WAY LIFE IS)** *Parlophone CDR 6443*	8		8
23 Nov 96	**SINGLE** *Parlophone CDRS 6452*	14		3
29 Mar 97	**RED LETTER DAY** *Parlophone CDR 6460*	9		3
5 Jul 97	**SOMEWHERE** *Parlophone CDR 6470*	9		5
31 Jul 99	**I DON'T KNOW WHAT YOU WANT BUT I CAN'T GIVE IT TO YOU** *Parlophone CDR 6523*	15		3
9 Oct 99	**NEW YORK CITY BOY** *Parlophone CDR 6525*	14		4
15 Jan 00	**YOU ONLY TELL ME YOU LOVE ME WHEN YOU'RE DRUNK** *Parlophone CDR 6533*	8		4
30 Mar 02	**HOME AND DRY** *Parlophone CDRS 6572*	14		6
27 Jul 02	**I GET ALONG** *Parlophone CDRS 6581*	18		3
29 Nov 03	**MIRACLES** *Parlophone CDRS 6620*	10		4
10 Apr 04	**FLAMBOYANT** *Parlophone CDRS 6629*	12		4
20 May 06	**I'M WITH STUPID** *Parlophone CDR6690*	8		3
5 Aug 06	**MINIMAL** *Parlophone CDR6708*	19		3
28 Oct 06	**NUMB** *Parlophone CDR6723*	23		2
17 Mar 07	**SHE'S MADONNA** *Chrysalis CDCHS5163* ROBBIE WILLIAMS & PET SHOP BOYS	16		3
28 Mar 09	**LOVE ETC** *Parlophone CDR6765*	14		3
13 Jun 09	**DID YOU SEE ME COMING** *Parlophone CDRS6772*	21		1
26 Dec 09	**IT DOESN'T OFTEN SNOW AT CHRISTMAS** *Parlophone CDRS6784*	40		1

PETER & GORDON

UK, male vocal/instrumental duo – Peter Asher & Gordon Waller, d. 17 Jul 2009 — 77

Date	Title	Peak Position	Weeks at No.1	Weeks on Chart
12 Mar 64	**A WORLD WITHOUT LOVE** *Columbia DB 7225* ★	1	2	14
4 Jun 64	**NOBODY I KNOW** *Columbia DB 7292*	10		11
8 Apr 65	**TRUE LOVE WAYS** *Columbia DB 7524*	2		15
24 Jun 65	**TO KNOW YOU IS TO LOVE YOU** *Columbia DB 7617*	5		10
21 Oct 65	**BABY I'M YOURS** *Columbia DB 7729*	19		9
24 Feb 66	**WOMAN** *Columbia DB 7834*	28		7
22 Sep 66	**LADY GODIVA** *Columbia DB 8003*	16		11

PETER BJORN & JOHN FEATURING BERGSMAN

Sweden, male/female vocal/instrumental/production group — 13

Date	Title	Peak Position	Weeks at No.1	Weeks on Chart
19 Aug 06	**YOUNG FOLKS** *Wichita WEBB107SCD*	35		2
8 Sep 07	**YOUNG FOLKS** *Wichita WEBB107SCD*	13		11

PETER, PAUL & MARY

US, male/female vocal trio – Mary Travers, d. 16 Sep 2009, Paul Stookey & Peter Yarrow — 38

Date	Title	Peak Position	Weeks at No.1	Weeks on Chart
10 Oct 63	**BLOWING IN THE WIND** *Warner Brothers WB 104*	13		16
16 Apr 64	**TELL IT ON THE MOUNTAIN** *Warner Brothers WB 127*	33		4
15 Oct 64	**THE TIMES THEY ARE A-CHANGIN'** *Warner Brothers WB 142*	44		2
17 Jan 70	**LEAVIN' ON A JET PLANE** *Warner Brothers WB 7340* ★	2		16

PETERS & LEE

UK, male/female vocal/instrumental duo – Lenny Peters, d. 10 Oct 1992, & Dianne Lee — 57

Date	Title	Peak Position	Weeks at No.1	Weeks on Chart
26 May 73	**WELCOME HOME** *Philips 6006 307*	1	1	24
3 Nov 73	**BY YOUR SIDE** *Philips 6006 339*	39		4
20 Apr 74	**DON'T STAY AWAY TOO LONG** *Philips 6006 388* ●	3		15
17 Aug 74	**RAINBOW** *Philips 6006 406*	17		7
6 Mar 76	**HEY MR MUSIC MAN** *Philips 6006 502*	16		7

JONATHAN PETERS PRESENTS LUMINAIRE

US, male/female vocal/DJ/production duo — 1

Date	Title	Peak Position	Weeks at No.1	Weeks on Chart
24 Jul 99	**FLOWER DUET** *Pelican PELID 001*	75		1

RAY PETERSON

US, male vocalist, d. 25 Jan 2005 (age 65) — 9

Date	Title	Peak Position	Weeks at No.1	Weeks on Chart
4 Sep 59	**THE WONDER OF YOU** *RCA 1131*	23		1
24 Mar 60	**ANSWER ME** *RCA 1175*	47		1
19 Jan 61	**CORRINE, CORRINA** *London HLX 9246*	41		7

TOM PETTY & THE HEARTBREAKERS

US, male vocal/instrumental group — 43

Date	Title	Peak Position	Weeks at No.1	Weeks on Chart
25 Jun 77	**ANYTHING THAT'S ROCK 'N' ROLL** *Shelter WIP 6396*	36		3
13 Aug 77	**AMERICAN GIRL** *Shelter WIP 6403*	40		5
15 Aug 81	**STOP DRAGGIN' MY HEART AROUND** *WEA K 79231* STEVIE NICKS WITH TOM PETTY & THE HEARTBREAKERS	50		4
13 Apr 85	**DON'T COME AROUND HERE NO MORE** *MCA 926*	50		4
13 May 89	**I WON'T BACK DOWN** *MCA 1334* TOM PETTY	28		10
12 Aug 89	**RUNNIN' DOWN A DREAM** *MCA 1359* TOM PETTY	55		4
25 Nov 89	**FREE FALLIN'** *MCA 1381* TOM PETTY	64		2
29 Jun 91	**LEARNING TO FLY** *MCA MCS 1555*	46		4
4 Apr 92	**TOO GOOD TO BE TRUE** *MCA MCS 1616*	34		3
30 Oct 93	**SOMETHING IN THE AIR** *MCA MCSTD 1945* TOM PETTY	53		2
12 Mar 94	**MARY JANE'S LAST DANCE** *MCA MCSTD 1966* TOM PETTY	52		2

PEYTON

UK, male production group — 1

Date	Title	Peak Position	Weeks at No.1	Weeks on Chart
22 May 04	**A HIGHER PLACE** *Hed Kandi HEDK12006*	68		1

PF PROJECT FEATURING EWAN McGREGOR

UK, male production duo – Moussa Clarke & Jamie White – & actor/vocalist — 11

Date	Title	Peak Position	Weeks at No.1	Weeks on Chart
15 Nov 97	**CHOOSE LIFE** *Positiva CDTIV 84*	6		11

PHANTOM PLANET

US, male vocal/instrumental group – Alex Greenwald, Jeff Conrad, Sam Farrar & Darren Robinson — 14

Date	Title	Peak Position	Weeks at No.1	Weeks on Chart
19 Mar 05	**CALIFORNIA** *Epic 6726672*	9		14

PHARAO

Germany, male/female vocal/instrumental group — 2

Date	Title	Peak Position	Weeks at No.1	Weeks on Chart
4 Mar 95	**THERE IS A STAR** *Epic 6611832*	43		2

PHARCYDE

US, male rap group — 6

Date	Title	Peak Position	Weeks at No.1	Weeks on Chart
31 Jul 93	**PASSIN' ME BY** *Atlantic A 8360CD*	55		3

Silver-selling ● · Gold-selling ● · Platinum-selling (x multiples) · US No.1 ★ · Peak Position · Weeks at No.1 · Weeks on Chart

Date	Title / Label	Peak Position	Weeks at No.1	Weeks on Chart
6 Apr 96	**RUNNIN'** *Go! Beat GODCD 142*	36		2
10 Aug 96	**SHE SAID** *Go! Beat GODCD 144*	51		1

PHARELL WILLIAMS
US, male vocalist/producer – (Pharrell Williams) see N*E*R*D — 86

Date	Title / Label	Peak Position	Weeks at No.1	Weeks on Chart
8 Jun 02	**PASS THE COURVOISIER – PART II** *J Records 74321937902* BUSTA RHYMES, P DIDDY & PHARRELL	16		7
10 Aug 02	**BOYS** *Jive 9253912* BRITNEY SPEARS FEATURING PHARRELL WILLIAMS	7		8
5 Apr 03	**BEAUTIFUL** *Capitol CDCL 842* SNOOP DOGG FEATURING PHARRELL	23		20
16 Aug 03	**FRONTIN'** *Arista 82876553332* FEATURING JAY-Z	6		10
29 Nov 03	**LIGHT YOUR ASS ON FIRE** *Arista 82876572512* BUSTA RHYMES FEATURING PHARRELL	62		1
7 Feb 04	**SHOW ME YOUR SOUL** *Puff Daddy MCSTD 40350* P DIDDY, LENNY KRAVITZ, PHARRELL WILLIAMS & LOON	35		2
15 May 04	**PASS THE COURVOISIER – PART II** *J Records 74321937902* BUSTA RHYMES, P DIDDY & PHARRELL	71		1
11Dec 04	**DROP IT LIKE IT'S HOT** *Geffen 2103461* SNOOP DOGG FEATURING PHARRELL ★	10		11
5 Mar 05	**LET'S GET BLOWN** *Geffen 9880425* SNOOP DOGG FEATURING PHARRELL	13		6
12 Nov 05	**CAN I HAVE IT LIKE THAT** *Virgin VUSCD315* PHARRELL FEATURING GWEN STEFANI	3		11
4 Feb 06	**ANGEL** *Virgin VUSCD317*	15		4
26 Aug 06	**NUMBER ONE** *Virgin VUSDX333* PHARRELL FEATURING KANYE WEST	31		5

PHASE II
US, male vocal/production group — 2

Date	Title / Label	Peak Position	Weeks at No.1	Weeks on Chart
18 Mar 89	**REACHIN'** *Republic LICT 006*	70		1
21 Dec 91	**REACHIN' (REMIX)** *Republic LICT 160* JOEY NEGRO PRESENTS PHASE II	70		1

PHAT 'N' PHUNKY
UK, male production duo — 1

Date	Title / Label	Peak Position	Weeks at No.1	Weeks on Chart
14 Jun 97	**LET'S GROOVE** *Chase CDCHASE 8*	61		1

PHATS & SMALL
UK, male DJ/production duo – Jason Hayward & Russell Small — 36

Date	Title / Label	Peak Position	Weeks at No.1	Weeks on Chart
10 Apr 99	**TURN AROUND** *Multiply CDMULTY 49* ●	2		16
14 Aug 99	**FEEL GOOD** *Multiply CDMULTY 54*	7		8
4 Dec 99	**TONITE** *Multiply CDMULTY 57*	11		6
30 Jun 01	**THIS TIME AROUND** *Multiply CDMULTY 75*	15		5
24 Nov 01	**CHANGE** *Multiply CDMULTY 80*	45		1

PHATT B
Holland, male DJ/producer (Bernsquil Verndoom) — 1

Date	Title / Label	Peak Position	Weeks at No.1	Weeks on Chart
11 Nov 00	**AND DA DRUM MACHINE** *NuLife 74321801902*	58		1

PhD
UK, male vocal/instrumental trio – Jim Diamond*, Anthony Hymas & Simon Phillips — 14

Date	Title / Label	Peak Position	Weeks at No.1	Weeks on Chart
3 Apr 82	**I WON'T LET YOU DOWN** *WEA K 79209* ●	3		14

BARRINGTON PHELOUNG
Australia, male conductor — 2

Date	Title / Label	Peak Position	Weeks at No.1	Weeks on Chart
13 Mar 93	**INSPECTOR MORSE' THEME** *Virgin VSCDT 1458*	61		2

PHILADELPHIA INTERNATIONAL ALL-STARS
US, male/female vocal ensemble — 8

Date	Title / Label	Peak Position	Weeks at No.1	Weeks on Chart
13 Aug 77	**LET'S CLEAN UP THE GHETTO** *Philadelphia International PIR 5451*	34		8

PHILHARMONIA ORCHESTRA, CONDUCTOR LORIN MAAZEL
US, orchestra & male conductor — 7

Date	Title / Label	Peak Position	Weeks at No.1	Weeks on Chart
30 Jul 69	**THUS SPAKE ZARATHUSTRA** *Columbia DB 8607*	33		7

CHYNNA PHILLIPS
US, female vocalist. See Wilson Phillips — 1

Date	Title / Label	Peak Position	Weeks at No.1	Weeks on Chart
3 Feb 96	**NAKED AND SACRED** *EMI CDEM 409*	62		1

ESTHER PHILLIPS
US, female vocalist (Esther Jones), d. 7 Aug 1984 (age 48) — 8

Date	Title / Label	Peak Position	Weeks at No.1	Weeks on Chart
4 Oct 75	**WHAT A DIFFERENCE A DAY MAKES** *Kudu 925*	6		8

SARAH PHILLIPS
UK, female vocalist — 1

Date	Title / Label	Peak Position	Weeks at No.1	Weeks on Chart
3 Apr 10	**AUTUMN – TRIBUTE TO DEBBIE PHILLIPS** *Bacon Empire GBKZT1010001*	49		1

PHIXX
UK, male vocal group – Mikey Green, Andrew Kinlochan, Nikk Mager, Chris Park & Peter Smith — 15

Date	Title / Label	Peak Position	Weeks at No.1	Weeks on Chart
8 Nov 03	**HOLD ON ME** *Concept CDCON 51X*	10		4
20 Mar 04	**LOVE REVOLUTION** *Concept CDCON 55X*	13		5
3 Jul 04	**WILD BOYS** *Concept CON 56X*	12		3
5 Feb 05	**STRANGE LOVE** *Concept CDCON60X*	19		3

PHOENIX
France, male vocal/instrumental group — 3

Date	Title / Label	Peak Position	Weeks at No.1	Weeks on Chart
3 Feb 01	**IF I EVER FEEL BETTER** *Source DINSD 210*	65		1
1 May 04	**RUN RUN RUN** *Source SOURCD094*	66		1
24 Jul 04	**EVERYTHING IS EVERYTHING** *Source SOURCDX097*	74		1

PAUL PHOENIX
UK, male vocalist — 4

Date	Title / Label	Peak Position	Weeks at No.1	Weeks on Chart
3 Nov 79	**NUNC DIMITTIS** *Different HAVE 20*	56		4

PHOTEK
UK, male producer (Rupert Parkes) — 4

Date	Title / Label	Peak Position	Weeks at No.1	Weeks on Chart
22 Mar 97	**NI-TEN-ICHI-RYU (TWO SWORDS TECHNIQUE)** *Science QEDCD 2*	37		2
28 Feb 98	**MODUS OPERANDI** *Virgin QEDCD 6*	66		1
24 Feb 01	**MINE TO GIVE** *Science QEDCD 10* FEATURING ROBERT OWENS	44		1

PHOTOS
UK, male/female vocal/instrumental group — 4

Date	Title / Label	Peak Position	Weeks at No.1	Weeks on Chart
17 May 80	**IRENE** *Epic EPC 8517*	56		4

PHUNKY PHANTOM
UK, male producer (Lawrence Nelson). See Gat Decor, Rest Assured — 3

Date	Title / Label	Peak Position	Weeks at No.1	Weeks on Chart
16 May 98	**GET UP STAND UP** *Club For Life DISNCD 44*	27		3

PHUTURE ASSASSINS
UK, male production/vocal trio — 1

Date	Title / Label	Peak Position	Weeks at No.1	Weeks on Chart
6 Jun 92	**FUTURE SOUND (EP)** *Suburban Base SUBBASE 010*	64		1

EDITH PIAF
France, female vocalist (Edith Gassion), d. 11 Oct 1963 (age 47) — 15

Date	Title / Label	Peak Position	Weeks at No.1	Weeks on Chart
12 May 60	**MILORD** *Columbia DC 754*	41		4
3 Nov 60	**MILORD** *Columbia DC 754*	24		11

PIANOHEADZ
US, male DJ/production duo. See Lil Mo' Yin Yang, Real To Reel — 2

Date	Title / Label	Peak Position	Weeks at No.1	Weeks on Chart
11 Jul 98	**IT'S OVER (DISTORTION)** *Incredible Music INCRL 3CD*	39		2

PIANOMAN
UK, male producer (James Sammon). See Bass Boyz — 8

Date	Title / Label	Peak Position	Weeks at No.1	Weeks on Chart
15 Jun 96	**BLURRED** *ffreedom TABCD 243*	6		7
26 Apr 97	**PARTY PEOPLE (LIVE YOUR LIFE BE FREE)** *3 Beat 3 BTDCD 1*	43		1

MARK PICCHIOTTI PRESENTS BASSTOY FEATURING DANA
US, male/female vocal/DJ/production duo. See Absolute, Sandstorm — 5

Date	Title / Label	Peak Position	Weeks at No.1	Weeks on Chart
19 Jan 02	**RUNNIN'** *Black & Blue NEOCD 073*	13		5

BOBBY 'BORIS' PICKETT & THE CRYPT-KICKERS

US, male vocal/instrumental group – Bobby Pickett, d. 25 Apr 2007, Leon Russell, Johnny McCrae, Ricky Page & Gary Paxton **15**

Date	Title / Label	Peak Position	Weeks at No.1	Weeks on Chart
1 Sep 73	**MONSTER MASH** *London HL 10320* ○ ★	3		13
8 Nov 08	**MONSTER MASH** *Old Gold USDEI9004341*	60		1
7 Nov 09	**MONSTER MASH** *Old Gold USDEI9004341*	61		1

WILSON PICKETT

US, male vocalist, d. 19 Jan 2006 (age 64) **61**

Date	Title / Label	Peak Position	Weeks at No.1	Weeks on Chart
23 Sep 65	**IN THE MIDNIGHT HOUR** *Atlantic AT 4036*	12		11
25 Nov 65	**DON'T FIGHT IT** *Atlantic AT 4052*	29		8
10 Mar 66	**634-5789** *Atlantic AT 4072*	36		5
1 Sep 66	**LAND OF 1000 DANCES** *Atlantic 584-039*	22		9
15 Dec 66	**MUSTANG SALLY** *Atlantic 584-066*	28		7
27 Sep 67	**FUNKY BROADWAY** *Atlantic 584 130*	43		3
11 Sep 68	**I'M A MIDNIGHT MOVER** *Atlantic 584 203*	38		6
8 Jan 69	**HEY JUDE** *Atlantic 584 236*	16		9
21 Nov 87	**IN THE MIDNIGHT HOUR** *Motown ZB 41583*	62		3

PICKETTYWITCH

UK, male/female vocal/instrumental group – Polly Brown*, Martin Bridges, Bob Brittain, Maggie Farren, Keith Hall, Mike Tomich & Chris Warren **34**

Date	Title / Label	Peak Position	Weeks at No.1	Weeks on Chart
28 Feb 70	**THAT SAME OLD FEELING** *Pye 7N 17887*	5		14
4 Jul 70	**(IT'S LIKE A) SAD OLD KINDA MOVIE** *Pye 7N 17951*	16		10
7 Nov 70	**BABY I WON'T LET YOU DOWN** *Pye 7N 45002*	27		10

MAURO PICOTTO

Italy, male producer. See CRW, R.A.F. **23**

Date	Title / Label	Peak Position	Weeks at No.1	Weeks on Chart
12 Jun 99	**LIZARD (GONNA GET YOU)** *VC Recordings VCRD 50*	27		3
20 Nov 99	**LIZARD (GONNA GET YOU) (REMIX)** *VC Recordings VCRD 57*	33		2
15 Jul 00	**IGUANA** *VC Recordings VCRD 68*	33		3
13 Jan 01	**KOMODO (SAVE A SOUL)** *VC Recordings VCRDX 85*	13		5
11 Aug 01	**LIKE THIS LIKE THAT** *VC Recordings VCRD 92*	21		4
25 Aug 01	**VERDI** *BXR BXRP 0318*	74		1
16 Mar 02	**PULSAR 2002** *BXR/Nukleuz BXRCA 0162*	35		3
3 Aug 02	**BACK TO CALI** *BXR BXRC 0433*	42		2

PIGBAG

UK, male instrumental group – Chris Hamlin (left 1982), Andrew Carpenter, Roger Freeman (replaced by Brian Nevill), James Johnstone, Chris Lee, Ollie Moore, Mark Smith, Simon Underwood & Oscar Verden **20**

Date	Title / Label	Peak Position	Weeks at No.1	Weeks on Chart
7 Nov 81	**SUNNY DAY** *Y Records Y 12*	53		3
27 Feb 82	**GETTING UP** *Y Records Y 16*	61		3
3 Apr 82	**PAPA'S GOT A BRAND NEW PIGBAG** *Y Records Y 10*	3		11
10 Jul 82	**THE BIG BEAN** *Y Records Y 24*	40		3

PIGLETS

UK, female vocal session group fronted by Barbara Kay **12**

Date	Title / Label	Peak Position	Weeks at No.1	Weeks on Chart
6 Nov 71	**JOHNNY REGGAE** *Bell 1180*	3		12

PIGEON DETECTIVES

UK, male vocal/instrumental group **35**

Date	Title / Label	Peak Position	Weeks at No.1	Weeks on Chart
18 Nov 06	**I FOUND OUT** *Dance To The Radio DTTR018CD*	39		2
10 Mar 07	**ROMANTIC TYPE** *Dance To The Radio DTTR026CD*	19		2
26 May 07	**I'M NOT SORRY** *Dance To The Radio DTTR029CD*	12		6
18 Aug 07	**TAKE HER BACK** *Dance To The Radio DTTR034CD*	20		10
24 Nov 07	**I FOUND OUT** *Dance To The Radio DTTR040CD*	42		5
17 May 08	**THIS IS AN EMERGENCY** *Dance To The Radio DTTR043CD*	14		8
9 Aug 08	**EVERYBODY WANTS ME** *Dance To The Radio DTTR045CD*	51		2

PILOT

UK, male vocal/instrumental trio – David Paton, Billy Lyall, d. 1 Dec 1989, & Stuart Tosh **29**

Date	Title / Label	Peak Position	Weeks at No.1	Weeks on Chart
2 Nov 74	**MAGIC** *EMI 2217*	11		11
18 Jan 75	**JANUARY** *EMI 2255* ○	1	3	10
19 Apr 75	**CALL ME ROUND** *EMI 2287*	34		4
27 Sep 75	**JUST A SMILE** *EMI 2338*	31		4

PILTDOWN MEN

US, male instrumental session group **36**

Date	Title / Label	Peak Position	Weeks at No.1	Weeks on Chart
8 Sep 60	**MACDONALD'S CAVE** *Capitol CL 15149*	14		18
12 Jan 61	**PILTDOWN RIDES AGAIN** *Capitol CL 15175*	14		10
9 Mar 61	**GOODNIGHT MRS. FLINTSTONE** *Capitol CL 15186*	18		8

COURTNEY PINE

UK, male saxophonist **6**

Date	Title / Label	Peak Position	Weeks at No.1	Weeks on Chart
30 Jul 88	**LIKE DREAMERS DO** *Fourth & Broadway BRW 108* MICA PARIS FEATURING COURTNEY PINE	26		5
7 Jul 90	**I'M STILL WAITING** *Mango MNG 749* FEATURING CARROLL THOMPSON	66		1

PING PING & AL VERLANE

Belgium, male vocal duo **4**

Date	Title / Label	Peak Position	Weeks at No.1	Weeks on Chart
28 Sep 61	**SUCU SUCU** *Oriole CB 1589*	41		4

P!NK

US, female vocalist/guitarist/producer (Alecia Moore). Energetic, BRIT-winning ('Best International Female', 2003) superstar who crashed into No.1 on *Billboard* magazine's list of 'Pop Songs Artists' of the 2000s ahead of the likes of Kelly Clarkson, Rihanna, Justin Timberlake and Beyonce **268**

Date	Title / Label	Peak Position	Weeks at No.1	Weeks on Chart
10 Jun 00	**THERE YOU GO** *LaFace 74321757602*	6		9
30 Sep 00	**MOST GIRLS** *LaFace 74321792012*	5		8
27 Jan 01	**YOU MAKE ME SICK** *LaFace 74321828702*	9		6
30 Jun 01	**LADY MARMALADE** *Interscope 4975612* CHRISTINA AGUILERA/LIL' KIM/MYA/P!NK ● ★	1	1	16
26 Jan 02	**GET THE PARTY STARTED** *Arista 74321913382* ○	2		15
25 May 02	**DON'T LET ME GET ME** *Arista 74321939212*	6		11
28 Sep 02	**JUST LIKE A PILL** *Arista 74321959652*	1	1	11
14 Dec 02	**FAMILY PORTRAIT (IMPORT)** *Arista 74321982102*	66		1
21 Dec 02	**FAMILY PORTRAIT** *Arista 74321982052*	11		9
19 Jul 03	**FEEL GOOD TIME** *Columbia 6741062* FEATURING WILLIAM ORBIT	3		11
8 Nov 03	**TROUBLE** *Arista 82876572172*	7		12
7 Feb 04	**GOD IS A DJ** *Arista 82876589472*	11		6
1 May 04	**LAST TO KNOW** *Arista 82876611732*	21		4
25 Mar 06	**STUPID GIRLS** *RCA 82876811902*	4		12
3 Jun 06	**WHO KNEW** *LaFace 82876847012*	5		26
2 Sep 06	**U & UR HAND** *LaFace 82876880802*	10		19
2 Dec 06	**NOBODY KNOWS** *LaFace 88697032862*	27		4
10 Mar 07	**LEAVE ME ALONE (I'M LONELY)** *LaFace USLF20600028*	34		15
4 Oct 08	**SO WHAT** *LaFace 88697372772* ★	1	3	27
10 Jan 09	**SOBER** *LaFace 88697425072*	9		20
4 Apr 09	**PLEASE DON'T LEAVE ME** *LaFace 88697471622*	12		17
25 Jul 09	**FUNHOUSE** *LaFace 88697556452*	29		8
14 Nov 09	**I DON'T BELIEVE YOU** *LaFace USLF20800180*	62		1

PINK FLOYD

UK, male vocal/instrumental group – Syd Barrett, d. 7 Jul 2006 (replaced by David Gilmour*), Nick Mason, Roger Waters* & Rick Wright, d. 15 Sep 2008 **55**

Date	Title / Label	Peak Position	Weeks at No.1	Weeks on Chart
30 Mar 67	**ARNOLD LAYNE** *Columbia DB 8156*	20		8
22 Jun 67	**SEE EMILY PLAY** *Columbia DB 8214*	6		12
1 Dec 79	**ANOTHER BRICK IN THE WALL (PART 2)** *Harvest HAR 5194* ⊛ ★	1	5	12
7 Aug 82	**WHEN THE TIGERS BROKE FREE** *Harvest HAR 5222*	39		5
7 May 83	**NOT NOW JOHN** *Harvest HAR 5224*	30		4
19 Dec 87	**ON THE TURNING AWAY** *EMI EM 34*	55		4
25 Jun 88	**ONE SLIP** *EMI EM 52*	50		3
4 Jun 94	**TAKE IT BACK** *EMI CDEMS 309*	23		4
29 Oct 94	**HIGH HOPES/KEEP TALKING** *EMI CDEMS 342*	26		3

PINK GREASE

UK, male vocal/instrumental group **5**

Date	Title / Label	Peak Position	Weeks at No.1	Weeks on Chart
26 Jun 04	**THE PINK GREASE** *Mute CDMUTE316*	75		1
22 Jan 05	**STRIP** *Mute CDMUTE325*	36		2
9 Apr 05	**PEACHES** *Mute CDMUTE343*	44		2

PINKEES

UK, male vocal/instrumental group **9**

Date	Title / Label	Peak Position	Weeks at No.1	Weeks on Chart
18 Sep 82	**DANGER GAMES** *Creole CR 39*	8		9

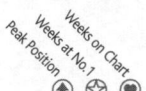

PINKERTON'S ASSORTED COLOURS
UK, male vocal/instrumental group – Samuel Kemp, Barrie Bernard (replaced by Stuart Colman), Dave Holland, Tom Long & Tony Newman — 12

Date	Title / Label	Peak	Wks No.1	Wks
13 Jan 66	**MIRROR MIRROR** *Decca F 12307*	9		11
21 Apr 66	**DON'T STOP LOVIN' ME BABY** *Decca F 12377*	50		1

PINKY & PERKY
UK, male/female vocal/porcine TV puppet duo — 3

Date	Title / Label	Peak	Wks No.1	Wks
29 May 93	**REET PETITE** *Telstar CDPIGGY 1*	47		3

LISA PIN-UP
UK, female DJ/producer (Lisa Chilcott) — 4

Date	Title / Label	Peak	Wks No.1	Wks
25 May 02	**TURN UP THE SOUND** *Nukleuz NUKC 0406*	60		1
21 Dec 02	**BLOW YOUR MIND (I AM THE WOMAN)** *Nukleuz 0450 FNUK*	60		3

PIONEERS
Jamaica, male vocal/instrumental group – Glen Adams, Sidney & Derrick Crooks, George Dekker & Jackie Robinson — 34

Date	Title / Label	Peak	Wks No.1	Wks
18 Oct 69	**LONG SHOT KICK DE BUCKET** *Trojan TR 672*	21		11
31 Jul 71	**LET YOUR YEAH BE YEAH** *Trojan TR 7825*	5		12
15 Jan 72	**GIVE AND TAKE** *Trojan TR 7846*	35		6
29 Mar 80	**LONG SHOT KICK DE BUCKET** *Trojan TRO 9063*	42		5

BILLIE PIPER
UK, female vocalist/actor — 75

Date	Title / Label	Peak	Wks No.1	Wks
11 Jul 98	**BECAUSE WE WANT TO** *Innocent SINCD 2* BILLIE	1	1	12
17 Oct 98	**GIRLFRIEND** *Innocent SINCD 3* BILLIE	1	1	12
19 Dec 98	**SHE WANTS YOU** *Innocent SINDXX 6* BILLIE	3		13
3 Apr 99	**HONEY TO THE BEE** *Innocent SINCD 8* BILLIE	3		11
27 May 00	**DAY & NIGHT** *Innocent SINDX 11*	1	1	12
30 Sep 00	**SOMETHING DEEP INSIDE** *Innocent SINDX 19*	4		9
23 Dec 00	**WALK OF LIFE** *Innocent SINDX 23*	25		5
27 Jan 07	**HONEY TO THE BEE** *Innocent SINCD 8* BILLIE	17		1

PIPETTES
UK, female vocal trio — 6

Date	Title / Label	Peak	Wks No.1	Wks
26 Nov 05	**DIRTY MIND** *Memphis Industries MI053CDS*	63		1
8 Apr 06	**YOUR KISSES ARE WASTED ON ME** *Memphis Industries MI062CDS*	35		1
15 Jul 06	**PULL SHAPES** *Memphis Industries MI071CDS*	26		3
7 Oct 06	**JUDY** *Memphis Industries MI077CDS*	46		1

PIPKINS
UK, male vocal duo – Roger Greenaway & Tony Burrows* — 10

Date	Title / Label	Peak	Wks No.1	Wks
28 Mar 70	**GIMME DAT DING** *Columbia DB 8662*	6		10

PIRANHAS
UK, male vocal/instrumental group – Bob Grover, Richard Adland, Phil Collis, John Helmer & Reginald Hornsbury — 21

Date	Title / Label	Peak	Wks No.1	Wks
2 Aug 80	**TOM HARK** *Sire SIR 4044*	6		12
16 Oct 82	**ZAMBESI** *Dakota DAK 6* FEATURING BORING BOB GROVER	17		9

PIRATES FEATURING ENYA, SHOLA AMA, NAILA BOSS & ISHANI
UK, male production duo – Man De Lev & Ryan Perara – & Ireland/UK, female vocalists – Eithne Ni Bhraonian, Mathurin Campbell, Naila Boss & Ishani — 8

Date	Title / Label	Peak	Wks No.1	Wks
11 Sep 04	**YOU SHOULD REALLY KNOW** *Relentless RELCD9*	8		8

PITBULL
US, male rapper (Armando Perez) — 48

Date	Title / Label	Peak	Wks No.1	Wks
18 Feb 06	**SHAKE** *TVT TVTUKCD0020* YING YANG TWINS FEATURING PITBULL	49		2
4 Jul 09	**I KNOW YOU WANT ME (CALLE OCHO)** *Positiva CDTIV289*	4		18
22 Aug 09	**HOTEL ROOM SERVICE** *J Records 88697608242*	9		18
19 Sep 09	**NOW I'M THAT CHICK** *Jive USJI10900435* LIVVI FRANC FEATURING PITBULL	40		3
30 Jan 10	**SHUT IT DOWN** *J USJAY0900143* FEATURING AKON	33		5
3 Apr 10	**ALL NIGHT LONG** *Syco Music GBHMU0900055* ALEXANDRA BURKE FEATURING PITBULL	59		2+

PITCHSHIFTER
UK, male vocal/instrumental group — 4

Date	Title / Label	Peak	Wks No.1	Wks
28 Feb 98	**GENIUS** *Geffen GFSTD 22324*	71		1
26 Sep 98	**MICROWAVED** *Geffen GFSTD 22348*	54		1
21 Oct 00	**DEAD BATTERY** *MCA MCSTD 40241*	71		1
29 Jun 02	**SHUTDOWN** *Mayan MYNX 008X*	66		1

GENE PITNEY
US, male vocalist, d. 5 Apr 2006 (age 66). One of the most distinctive vocal stylists of the rock era was among the few US acts who racked up hit after hit in the 'Beat Boom' era. Oddly, though, his first No.1 took 28 years to achieve — 212

Date	Title / Label	Peak	Wks No.1	Wks
23 Mar 61	**(I WANNA) LOVE MY LIFE AWAY** *London HL 9270*	26		11
8 Mar 62	**TOWN WITHOUT PITY** *HMV POP 952*	32		6
5 Dec 63	**TWENTY FOUR HOURS FROM TULSA** *United Artists UP 1035*	5		19
5 Mar 64	**THAT GIRL BELONGS TO YESTERDAY** *United Artists UP 1045*	7		12
15 Oct 64	**IT HURTS TO BE IN LOVE** *United Artists UP 1063*	36		4
12 Nov 64	**I'M GONNA BE STRONG** *Stateside SS 358*	2		14
18 Feb 65	**I MUST BE SEEING THINGS** *Stateside SS 390*	6		10
10 Jun 65	**LOOKING THROUGH THE EYES OF LOVE** *Stateside SS 420*	3		12
4 Nov 65	**PRINCESS IN RAGS** *Stateside SS 471*	9		12
17 Feb 66	**BACKSTAGE** *Stateside SS 490*	4		10
9 Jun 66	**NOBODY NEEDS YOUR LOVE** *Stateside SS 518*	2		13
10 Nov 66	**JUST ONE SMILE** *Stateside SS 558*	8		12
23 Feb 67	**(IN THE) COLD LIGHT OF DAY** *Stateside SS 597*	38		6
15 Nov 67	**SOMETHING'S GOTTEN HOLD OF MY HEART** *Stateside SS 2060*	5		13
3 Apr 68	**SOMEWHERE IN THE COUNTRY** *Stateside SS 2103*	19		9
27 Nov 68	**YOURS UNTIL TOMORROW** *Stateside SS 2131*	34		7
5 Mar 69	**MARIA ELENA** *Stateside SS 2142*	25		6
14 Mar 70	**A STREET CALLED HOPE** *Stateside SS 2164*	37		5
3 Oct 70	**SHADY LADY** *Stateside SS 2177*	29		8
28 Apr 73	**24 SYCAMORE** *Pye International 7N 25606*	34		7
2 Nov 74	**BLUE ANGEL** *Bronze BRO 11*	39		4
14 Jan 89	**SOMETHING'S GOTTEN HOLD OF MY HEART** *Parlophone R 6201* MARC ALMOND FEATURING SPECIAL GUEST STAR GENE PITNEY	1	4	12

MARIO PIU
Italy, male DJ/producer — 14

Date	Title / Label	Peak	Wks No.1	Wks
11 Dec 99	**COMMUNICATION (SOMEBODY ANSWER THE PHONE)** *Incentive CENT 2CDS*	5		9
10 Mar 01	**THE VISION** *BXR BXRC 0253* PRESENTS DJ ARABESQUE	16		5

PIXIES
US, male/female vocal/instrumental group — 13

Date	Title / Label	Peak	Wks No.1	Wks
1 Apr 89	**MONKEY GONE TO HEAVEN** *4AD AD 904*	60		3
1 Jul 89	**HERE COMES YOUR MAN** *4AD AD 909*	54		1
28 Jul 90	**VELOURIA** *4AD AD 0009*	28		3
10 Nov 90	**DIG FOR FIRE** *4AD AD 0014*	62		1
8 Jun 91	**PLANET OF SOUND** *4AD AD 1008*	27		3
4 Oct 97	**DEBASER** *4AD BADO 7010CD*	23		2

PIZZAMAN
UK, male producer (Norman Cook). See Beats International, Freakpower, Housemartins, Mighty Dub Katz, Urban All Stars — 18

Date	Title / Label	Peak	Wks No.1	Wks
27 Aug 94	**TRIPPIN' ON SUNSHINE** *Loaded CDLOAD 16*	33		2
10 Jun 95	**SEX ON THE STREETS** *Cowboy CDLOAD 24*	24		4
18 Nov 95	**HAPPINESS** *Cowboy CDLOAD 29*	19		4
6 Jan 96	**SEX ON THE STREETS** *Cowboy CDLOAD 24*	23		4
1 Jun 96	**TRIPPIN' ON SUNSHINE** *Cowboy CDLOAD 32*	18		3
14 Sep 96	**HELLO HONKY TONKS (ROCK YOUR BODY)** *Cowboy CDLOAD 39*	41		1

PIZZICATO FIVE
Japan, male/female vocal/instrumental group — 1

Date	Title / Label	Peak	Wks No.1	Wks
1 Nov 97	**MON AMOUR TOKYO** *Matador OLE 2902*	72		1

PJ
Canada, male producer (Paul Jacobs) — 2

Date	Title / Label	Peak	Wks No.1	Wks
20 Sep 97	**HAPPY DAYS** *Deconstruction 74321511822*	72		1
4 Sep 99	**HAPPY DAYS (REMIX)** *Defected DFECT 6CDS*	57		1

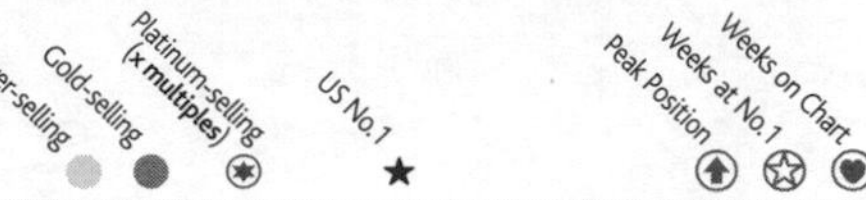

PKA
UK, male producer (Phil Kelsey) — Total weeks: 2

Date	Title / Label	Peak Position	Weeks at No.1	Weeks on Chart
20 Apr 91	**TEMPERATURE RISING** *Stress SS 4*	68		1
7 Mar 92	**POWERSIGN (ONLY YOUR LOVE)** *Stress PKA 1*	70		1

PLACEBO
Belgium/Sweden/UK, male vocal/instrumental group – Brian Molko, Stefan Olsdal & Robert Schultzberg (replaced by Steve Hewitt). See Alpinestars featuring Brian Molko — Total weeks: 58

Date	Title / Label	Peak Position	Weeks at No.1	Weeks on Chart
28 Sep 96	**TEENAGE ANGST** *Elevator Music FLOORCD 3*	30		3
1 Feb 97	**NANCY BOY** *Elevator Music FLOORCD 4*	4		6
24 May 97	**BRUISE PRISTINE** *Elevator Music FLOORCD 5*	14		3
15 Aug 98	**PURE MORNING** *Hut FLOORCD 6*	4		6
10 Oct 98	**YOU DON'T CARE ABOUT US** *Hut FLOORCD 7*	5		5
6 Feb 99	**EVERY YOU EVERY ME** *Hut FLOORDX 9*	11		5
29 Jul 00	**TASTE IN MEN** *Hut FLOORD 11*	16		6
7 Oct 00	**SLAVE TO THE WAGE** *Hut FLOORDX 12*	19		3
22 Mar 03	**BITTER END** *Hut FLOORDX 16*	12		5
28 Jun 03	**THIS PICTURE** *Hut FLOORCD 18*	23		2
27 Sep 03	**SPECIAL NEEDS** *Hut FLOORCD 19*	27		2
6 Mar 04	**ENGLISH SUMMER RAIN** *Hut FLOORDX 21*	23		2
30 Oct 04	**TWENTY YEARS** *Virgin FLOORDX24*	18		3
18 Mar 06	**BECAUSE I WANT YOU** *Virgin FLOORCD25*	13		3
1 Jul 06	**INFRA-RED** *Virgin FLOORCD29*	42		1
21 Oct 06	**MEDS** *Virgin FLOORCD30* FEATURING ALISON MOSSHART	35		1
3 Feb 07	**RUNNING UP THAT HILL** *Virgin GBAAA0300682*	66		1
16 Jan 10	**RUNNING UP THAT HILL** *Virgin GBAAA0300682*	44		1

PLAIN WHITE T'S
US, male vocal/instrumental group – Tom Higgenson, De'Mar Hamilton, Tim Lopez, Mike Retondo & Dave Tirio — Total weeks: 34

Date	Title / Label	Peak Position	Weeks at No.1	Weeks on Chart
28 Jul 07	**HEY THERE DELILAH** *Hollywood/Angel ANGECDX52* ★	2		31
19 Jan 08	**HATE (I REALLY DON'T LIKE YOU)** *Hollywood/Angel CASD9*	53		3

PLAN B
UK, male rapper/DJ (Ben Drew) — Total weeks: 27

Date	Title / Label	Peak Position	Weeks at No.1	Weeks on Chart
22 Jul 06	**MAMA (LOVES A CRACKHEAD)** *679 679L135CD*	41		1
14 Nov 09	**END CREDITS** *Vertigo 2723595* CHASE & STATUS FEATURING PLAN B	9		13
23 Jan 10	**STAY TOO LONG** *679/Atlantic 679L171CD*	9		12+
10 Apr 10	**SHE SAID** *679/Atlantic 679L172CD*	3		1+

PLANET FUNK
Italy/UK/Finland, male vocal/instrumental/production group – Marco Baroni, Domenico 'GG' Canu, Sergio Della Monica, Alex Neri, Alessandro Sommella & guest vocalists — Total weeks: 13

Date	Title / Label	Peak Position	Weeks at No.1	Weeks on Chart
10 Feb 01	**CHASE THE SUN** *Virgin VSCDT 1749*	5		9
26 Apr 03	**WHO SAID (STUCK IN THE UK)** *Illustrious/Bustin L CDILL 015*	36		2
16 Aug 03	**THE SWITCH** *Illustrious/Epic CDILL 017*	52		1
19 Mar 05	**THE SWITCH** *Direction 6757882*	66		1

PLANET PATROL
US, male vocal group — Total weeks: 3

Date	Title / Label	Peak Position	Weeks at No.1	Weeks on Chart
17 Sep 83	**CHEAP THRILLS** *Polydor POSP 639*	64		3

PLANET PERFECTO
UK, male DJ/production trio – Ian Masterson, Paul Oakenfold & Jake Williams. See Elementfour, JX, Mekka, Oakenfold, Perfecto Allstarz, Virus — Total weeks: 15

Date	Title / Label	Peak Position	Weeks at No.1	Weeks on Chart
14 Aug 99	**NOT OVER YET 99** *Code Blue BLU OO4CD* FEATURING GRACE	16		4
13 Nov 99	**BULLET IN THE GUN** *Perfecto PERF 3CDS*	15		4
16 Sep 00	**BULLET IN THE GUN 2000 (REMIX)** *Perfecto PERF 03CDSX*	7		6
29 Sep 01	**BITES DA DUST** *Perfecto PERF 19CDS*	52		1

PLANETS
UK, male vocal/instrumental group — Total weeks: 8

Date	Title / Label	Peak Position	Weeks at No.1	Weeks on Chart
18 Aug 79	**LINES** *Rialto TREB 104*	36		6
25 Oct 80	**DON'T LOOK DOWN** *Rialto TREB 116*	66		2

PLANK 15
UK, male producer (Andrew Holt) — Total weeks: 1

Date	Title / Label	Peak Position	Weeks at No.1	Weeks on Chart
2 Feb 02	**STRINGS OF LIFE** *Multiply CDMULTY 82*	60		1

ROBERT PLANT
UK, male vocalist. See Honeydrippers, Led Zeppelin — Total weeks: 35

Date	Title / Label	Peak Position	Weeks at No.1	Weeks on Chart
9 Oct 82	**BURNING DOWN ONE SIDE** *Swansong SSK 19429*	73		1
16 Jul 83	**BIG LOG** *WEA B 9848*	11		10
30 Jan 88	**HEAVEN KNOWS** *Es Paranza A 9373*	33		5
28 Apr 90	**HURTING KIND (I'VE GOT MY EYES ON YOU)** *Es Paranza A 8985*	45		3
8 May 93	**29 PALMS** *Fontana FATEX 1*	21		5
3 Jul 93	**I BELIEVE** *Fontana FATEX 2*	64		2
25 Dec 93	**IF I WERE A CARPENTER** *Fontana FATEX 4*	63		2
17 Dec 94	**GALLOWS POLE** *Fontana PPCD 2* JIMMY PAGE & ROBERT PLANT	35		3
11 Apr 98	**MOST HIGH** *Mercury 5687512* PAGE & PLANT	26		2
7 May 05	**SHINE IT ALL AROUND** *Universal MCSTD40412* & THE STRANGE SENSATION	32		2

PLASMATICS
US, female/male vocal/instrumental group — Total weeks: 4

Date	Title / Label	Peak Position	Weeks at No.1	Weeks on Chart
26 Jul 80	**BUTCHER BABY** *Stiff BUY 76*	55		4

PLASTIC BERTRAND
Belgium, male vocalist (Roger Jouret) — Total weeks: 17

Date	Title / Label	Peak Position	Weeks at No.1	Weeks on Chart
13 May 78	**CA PLANE POUR MOI** *Sire 6078 616*	8		12
5 Aug 78	**SHA LA LA LA LEE** *Vertigo 6059 209*	39		5

PLASTIC BOY FEATURING ROZALLA
Belgium/Zimbabwe, male/female vocal/production duo — Total weeks: 1

Date	Title / Label	Peak Position	Weeks at No.1	Weeks on Chart
22 Nov 03	**LIVE ANOTHER LIFE** *Inferno CDFERN 59*	55		1

PLASTIC PENNY
UK, male vocal/instrumental group – Brian Keith, Mick Graham, Tony Murray, Nigel Olsson & Paul Raymond — Total weeks: 10

Date	Title / Label	Peak Position	Weeks at No.1	Weeks on Chart
3 Jan 68	**EVERYTHING I AM** *Page One POF 051*	6		10

PLATINUM 45 FEATURING MORE FIRE CREW
UK, male vocal/rap/production group – Ozzie B (Osmond Bowes), Lethal Bizzle (Maxwell Ansah), C Matthews, Neeko (D Hector) & C Wilson — Total weeks: 8

Date	Title / Label	Peak Position	Weeks at No.1	Weeks on Chart
16 Mar 02	**OI** *Go! Beat GOBCD 48*	8		8

PLATINUM HOOK
US, male vocal/instrumental group — Total weeks: 1

Date	Title / Label	Peak Position	Weeks at No.1	Weeks on Chart
2 Sep 78	**STANDING ON THE VERGE (OF GETTING IT ON)** *Motown TMG 1115*	72		1

PLATNUM
UK, female/male vocal trio – Aaron Evers, Michelle McKenna & Mina Poli — Total weeks: 24

Date	Title / Label	Peak Position	Weeks at No.1	Weeks on Chart
23 Feb 08	**WHAT'S IT GONNA BE** *Hard2Beat H2B02CDS* H TWO O FEATURING PLATNUM (Silver)	2		16
11 Oct 08	**LOVE SHY** *Hard2beat H2B12CDS*	12		8

PLATTERS
US, male/female vocal group – Tony Williams, d. 14 Aug 1992, David Lynch, d. 2 Jan 1981, Herb Reed, Paul Robi, d. 1 Feb 1989, & Zola Taylor, d. 30 Apr 2007 — Total weeks: 92

Date	Title / Label	Peak Position	Weeks at No.1	Weeks on Chart
7 Sep 56	**THE GREAT PRETENDER/ONLY YOU** *Mercury MT 117* ★	5		16
2 Nov 56	**MY PRAYER** *Mercury MT 120* ★	4		13
25 Jan 57	**YOU'LL NEVER NEVER KNOW/IT ISN'T RIGHT** *Mercury MT 130*	23		3
17 May 57	**I'M SORRY** *Mercury MT 145*	18		8
16 May 58	**TWILIGHT TIME** *Mercury MT 214* ★	3		18
16 Jan 59	**SMOKE GETS IN YOUR EYES** *Mercury AMT 1016* ★	1	1	20
28 Aug 59	**REMEMBER WHEN** *Mercury AMT 1053*	25		2
29 Jan 60	**HARBOUR LIGHTS** *Mercury AMT 1081*	11		12

PLAYER
US/UK, male vocal/instrumental group — Total weeks: 7

Date	Title / Label	Peak Position	Weeks at No.1	Weeks on Chart
25 Feb 78	**BABY COME BACK** *RSO 2090 254* ★	32		7

PLAYERS ASSOCIATION

US, male vocal/instrumental session group formed by Chris Hills & Danny Weiss — 17

Date	Title	Peak Position	Weeks at No.1	Weeks on Chart
10 Mar 79	**TURN THE MUSIC UP** *Vanguard VS 5011*	8		9
5 May 79	**RIDE THE GROOVE** *Vanguard VS 5012*	42		5
9 Feb 80	**WE GOT THE GROOVE** *Vanguard VS 5016*	61		3

PLAYGROUP

UK, male producer (Trevor Jackson) — 1

Date	Title	Peak Position	Weeks at No.1	Weeks on Chart
24 Nov 01	**NUMBER ONE** *Source SOURCD 026*	66		1

PLAYTHING

Italy, male production duo. See Triple X — 6

Date	Title	Peak Position	Weeks at No.1	Weeks on Chart
5 May 01	**INTO SPACE** *Manifesto FESCD 81*	48		1
24 Aug 02	**DO YOU SEE THE LIGHT** *Data 33CDS* SNAP! VS PLAYTHING	14		5

PLIES FEATURING AKON

US, male rap duo — 2

Date	Title	Peak Position	Weeks at No.1	Weeks on Chart
5 Apr 08	**HYPNOTIZED** *Atlantic AT0301CD*	66		2

PLUMB

US, female vocalist (Tiffany Arbuckle-Lee) — 2

Date	Title	Peak Position	Weeks at No.1	Weeks on Chart
14 Feb 04	**REAL** *Curb CUBC 095*	41		2

PLUMMET

US, male/female vocal/production duo — 12

Date	Title	Peak Position	Weeks at No.1	Weeks on Chart
26 Apr 03	**DAMAGED** *Serious SER 68CD*	12		10
8 May 04	**CHERISH THE DAY** *Manifesto 9866389*	35		2

PLUS 44

US, male vocal/instrumental group — 2

Date	Title	Peak Position	Weeks at No.1	Weeks on Chart
24 Feb 07	**WHEN YOUR HEART STOPS BEATING** *Interscope 1724085*	47		2

PLUS ONE FEATURING SIRRON

UK, male production duo & male rapper — 4

Date	Title	Peak Position	Weeks at No.1	Weeks on Chart
19 May 90	**IT'S HAPPENIN'** *MCA 1405*	40		4

PLUX FEATURING GEORGIA JONES

US, male/female vocal/instrumental group — 2

Date	Title	Peak Position	Weeks at No.1	Weeks on Chart
4 May 96	**OVER & OVER** *ffrr FCD 277*	33		2

PM DAWN

US, male rap/production duo – Attrell & Jarrett Cordes — 39

Date	Title	Peak Position	Weeks at No.1	Weeks on Chart
8 Jun 91	**A WATCHER'S POINT OF VIEW (DON'T CHA THINK)** *Gee Street GEE 32*	36		5
17 Aug 91	**SET ADRIFT ON A MEMORY BLISS** *Gee Street GEE 33* ★	3		8
19 Oct 91	**PAPER DOLL** *Gee Street GEE 35*	49		3
22 Feb 92	**REALITY USED TO BE A GOOD FRIEND OF MINE** *Gee Street GEE 37*	29		4
7 Nov 92	**I'D DIE WITHOUT YOU** *Gee Street GEE 39*	30		5
13 Mar 93	**LOOKING THROUGH PATIENT EYES** *Gee Street GESCD 47*	11		7
12 Jun 93	**MORE THAN LIKELY** *Gee Street GESCD 49* FEATURING BOY GEORGE	40		3
30 Sep 95	**DOWNTOWN VENUS** *Gee Street GESCD 63*	58		2
6 Apr 96	**SOMETIMES I MISS YOU SO MUCH** *Gee Street GESCD 65*	58		1
31 Oct 98	**GOTTA...MOVIN' ON UP** *Gee Street GEE 5003933* FEATURING KY-MANI	68		1

POB FEATURING DJ PATRICK REID

UK, male DJ/production duo — 1

Date	Title	Peak Position	Weeks at No.1	Weeks on Chart
11 Dec 99	**BLUEBOTTLE/FLY** *Platipus PLAT 63CD*	74		1

P.O.D.

US, male vocal/instrumental group — 10

Date	Title	Peak Position	Weeks at No.1	Weeks on Chart
2 Feb 02	**ALIVE** *Atlantic AT 0119CD*	19		6
18 May 02	**YOUTH OF THE NATION** *East West AT 0127CD*	36		2
7 Jun 03	**SLEEPING AWAKE** *Maverick W 608CD*	42		1
24 Jan 04	**WILL YOU** *Atlantic AT 0169CD*	68		1

POETS

UK, male vocal/instrumental group — 5

Date	Title	Peak Position	Weeks at No.1	Weeks on Chart
29 Oct 64	**NOW WE'RE THRU** *Decca F 11995*	31		5

POGUES

Ireland/UK, male/female vocal/instrumental group – Shane MacGowan*, Philip Chevron (Philip Ryan), James Fearnley (replaced by James McNally), Jem Finer, Caitlin O'Riordan (replaced by Darryl Hunt), Andrew Ranken, Peter 'Spider' Stacy & Terry Woods (replaced by David Coulter) — 96

Date	Title	Peak Position	Weeks at No.1	Weeks on Chart
6 Apr 85	**A PAIR OF BROWN EYES** *Stiff BUY 220*	72		2
22 Jun 85	**SALLY MACLENNANE** *Stiff BUY 224*	51		4
14 Sep 85	**DIRTY OLD TOWN** *Stiff BUY 229*	62		3
8 Mar 86	**POGUETRY IN MOTION EP** *Stiff BUY 243*	29		6
30 Aug 86	**HAUNTED** *MCA 1084*	42		4
28 Mar 87	**THE IRISH ROVER** *Stiff BUY 258* & THE DUBLINERS	8		8
5 Dec 87	**FAIRYTALE OF NEW YORK** *Pogue Mahone NY 7* FEATURING KIRSTY MacCOLL ●	2		9
5 Mar 88	**IF I SHOULD FALL FROM GRACE WITH GOD** *Pogue Mahone PG 1*	58		3
16 Jul 88	**FIESTA** *Pogue Mahone PG 2*	24		5
17 Dec 88	**YEAH YEAH YEAH YEAH YEAH** *Pogue Mahone YZ 355*	43		4
8 Jul 89	**MISTY MORNING, ALBERT BRIDGE** *PM YZ 407*	41		3
16 Jun 90	**JACK'S HEROES/WHISKEY IN THE JAR** *Pogue Mahone YZ 500* & THE DUBLINERS	63		2
15 Sep 90	**SUMMER IN SIAM** *PM YZ 519*	64		2
21 Sep 91	**A RAINY NIGHT IN SOHO** *PM YZ 603*	67		1
14 Dec 91	**FAIRYTALE OF NEW YORK** *PM YZ 628* FEATURING KIRSTY MacCOLL	36		5
30 May 92	**HONKY TONK WOMEN** *PM YZ 673*	56		2
21 Aug 93	**TUESDAY MORNING** *PM YZ 758CD*	18		5
22 Jan 94	**ONCE UPON A TIME** *PM YZ 771CD*	66		2
31 Dec 05	**FAIRYTALE OF NEW YORK** *Warner Brothers WEA400CD* FEATURING KIRSTY MacCOLL	3		5
9 Dec 06	**FAIRYTALE OF NEW YORK** *Warner Brothers WEA400CD* FEATURING KIRSTY MacCOLL	6		5
8 Dec 07	**FAIRYTALE OF NEW YORK** *Warner Brothers WEA400CD* FEATURING KIRSTY MacCOLL	4		5
29 Nov 08	**FAIRYTALE OF NEW YORK** *Warner Brothers WEA400CD* FEATURING KIRSTY MacCOLL	12		6
5 Dec 09	**FAIRYTALE OF NEW YORK** *Warner Brothers WEA400CD* FEATURING KIRSTY MacCOLL	12		5

POINT BREAK

UK, male vocal trio – Brett Adams, Declan Bennett & David Oliver — 21

Date	Title	Peak Position	Weeks at No.1	Weeks on Chart
9 Oct 99	**DO WE ROCK** *Eternal WEA 216CD1*	29		2
22 Jan 00	**STAND TOUGH** *Eternal WEA 248CD2*	7		5
22 Apr 00	**FREAKYTIME** *Eternal WEA 265CD1*	13		6
5 Aug 00	**YOU** *Eternal WEA 290CD1*	14		5
2 Dec 00	**WHAT ABOUT US** *Eternal WEA 314CD1*	24		3

POINTER SISTERS

US, female vocal group – Anita, Bonnie (left 1977), June, d. 11 Apr 2006, & Ruth Pointer — 87

Date	Title	Peak Position	Weeks at No.1	Weeks on Chart
3 Feb 79	**EVERYBODY IS A STAR** *Planet K 12324*	61		3
17 Mar 79	**FIRE** *Planet K 12339*	34		8
22 Aug 81	**SLOWHAND** *Planet K 12530*	10		11
5 Dec 81	**SHOULD I DO IT?** *Reprise K 12578*	50		5
14 Apr 84	**AUTOMATIC** *Planet RPS 105* ●	2		15
23 Jun 84	**JUMP (FOR MY LOVE)** *Planet RPS 106*	6		10
11 Aug 84	**I NEED YOU** *Planet RPS 107*	25		9
27 Oct 84	**I'M SO EXCITED** *Planet RPS 108*	11		11
12 Jan 85	**NEUTRON DANCE** *Planet RPS 109*	31		7
20 Jul 85	**DARE ME** *RCA PB 49957*	17		8

POISON

US, male vocal/instrumental group — 43

Date	Title	Peak Position	Weeks at No.1	Weeks on Chart
23 May 87	**TALK DIRTY TO ME** *Music For Nations KUT 125*	67		1
7 May 88	**NOTHIN' BUT A GOOD TIME** *Capitol CL 486*	35		3
5 Nov 88	**FALLEN ANGEL** *Capitol CL 500*	59		1
11 Feb 89	**EVERY ROSE HAS ITS THORN** *Capitol CL 520* ★	13		9
29 Apr 89	**YOUR MAMA DON'T DANCE** *Capitol CL 523*	13		7
23 Sep 89	**NOTHIN' BUT A GOOD TIME** *Capitol CL 539*	48		3
30 Jun 90	**UNSKINNY BOP** *Capitol CL 582*	15		7
27 Oct 90	**SOMETHING TO BELIEVE IN** *Enigma CL 594*	35		4
23 Nov 91	**SO TELL ME WHY** *Capitol CL 640*	25		2
13 Feb 93	**STAND** *Capitol CDCL 679*	25		3
24 Apr 93	**UNTIL YOU SUFFER SOME (FIRE AND ICE)** *Capitol CDCL 685*	32		3

Peak Position / Weeks at No.1 / Weeks on Chart

POKER PETS FEATURING NATE JAMES
Sweden/UK, male vocal/production trio — 1

Date	Title	Peak	Wks at No.1	Wks on Chart
25 Jun 05	**LOVIN' YOU** *Positiva CDTIVS218*	43		1

POLECATS
UK, male vocal/instrumental group — 18

Date	Title	Peak	Wks at No.1	Wks on Chart
7 Mar 81	**JOHN I'M ONLY DANCING/BIG GREEN CAR** *Mercury POLE 1*	35		8
16 May 81	**ROCKABILLY GUY** *Mercury POLE 2*	35		6
22 Aug 81	**JEEPSTER/MARIE CELESTE** *Mercury POLE 3*	53		4

POLICE
UK/US, male vocal/instrumental trio – Sting* (Gordon Sumner), Stewart Copeland (Klark Kent*) & Andy Summers — 153

Date	Title	Peak	Wks at No.1	Wks on Chart
7 Oct 78	**CAN'T STAND LOSING YOU** *A&M AMS 7381*	42		5
28 Apr 79	**ROXANNE** *A&M AMS 7348*	12		9
7 Jul 79	**CAN'T STAND LOSING YOU** *A&M AMS 7381* ●	2		11
22 Sep 79	**MESSAGE IN A BOTTLE** *A&M AMS 7474* ●	1	3	11
17 Nov 79	**FALL OUT** *Illegal IL 001*	47		4
1 Dec 79	**WALKING ON THE MOON** *A&M AMS 7494* ●	1	1	10
16 Feb 80	**SO LONELY** *A&M AMS 7402* ●	6		10
14 Jun 80	**SIX PACK** *A&M AMPP 6001*	17		4
27 Sep 80	**DON'T STAND SO CLOSE TO ME** *A&M AMS 7564* ●	1	4	10
13 Dec 80	**DE DO DO DO, DE DA DA DA** *A&M AMS 7578* ●	5		8
26 Sep 81	**INVISIBLE SUN** *A&M AMS 8164* ●	2		8
24 Oct 81	**EVERY LITTLE THING SHE DOES IS MAGIC** *A&M AMS 8174* ●	1	1	13
12 Dec 81	**SPIRITS IN THE MATERIAL WORLD** *A&M AMS 8194* ●	12		8
28 May 83	**EVERY BREATH YOU TAKE** *A&M AM 117* ● ★	1	4	11
23 Jul 83	**WRAPPED AROUND YOUR FINGER** *A&M AM 127*	7		7
5 Nov 83	**SYNCHRONICITY II** *A&M AM 153*	17		4
14 Jan 84	**KING OF PAIN** *A&M AM 176*	17		5
11 Oct 86	**DON'T STAND SO CLOSE TO ME (REMIX)** *A&M AM 354*	24		4
13 May 95	**CAN'T STAND LOSING YOU (LIVE)** *A&M 5810372*	27		2
20 Dec 97	**ROXANNE '97** *A&M 5824552* STING & THE POLICE	17		6
5 Aug 00	**WHEN THE WORLD IS RUNNING DOWN** *Pagan 039CDS* DIFFERENT GEAR VERSUS THE POLICE	28		3

SU POLLARD
UK, female actor/vocalist — 11

Date	Title	Peak	Wks at No.1	Wks on Chart
5 Oct 85	**COME TO ME (I AM WOMAN)** *Rainbow RBR 1*	71		1
1 Feb 86	**STARTING TOGETHER** *Rainbow RBR 4* ●	2		10

JIMI POLO
US, male vocalist (James Perri) — 5

Date	Title	Peak	Wks at No.1	Wks on Chart
9 Nov 91	**NEVER GOIN' DOWN/BORN TO BE ALIVE** *MCA MCS 1578* ADAMSKI FEATURING JIMI POLO/ADAMSKI FEATURING SOHO	51		2
1 Aug 92	**EXPRESS YOURSELF** *Perfecto 74321101827*	59		2
9 Aug 97	**EXPRESS YOURSELF** *Perfecto PERF 146CD1*	62		1

POLOROID
UK, male/female vocal/production trio — 2

Date	Title	Peak	Wks at No.1	Wks on Chart
11 Oct 03	**SO DAMN BEAUTIFUL** *Decode/Telstar CXSTAS 3351*	28		2

POLTERGEIST
UK, male producer (Simon Berry). See Art Of Trance, Vicious Circles — 2

Date	Title	Peak	Wks at No.1	Wks on Chart
6 Jul 96	**VICIOUS CIRCLES** *Manifesto FESCD 8*	32		2

PETER POLYCARPOU
UK, male vocalist/actor — 4

Date	Title	Peak	Wks at No.1	Wks on Chart
20 Feb 93	**LOVE HURTS** *Soundtrack Music CDEM 259*	26		4

POLYGON WINDOW
UK, male producer (Richard James). See AFX, Aphex Twin, Powerpill — 1

Date	Title	Peak	Wks at No.1	Wks on Chart
3 Apr 93	**QUOTH** *Warp WAP 33CD*	49		1

POLYPHONIC SPREE
US, male/female vocal/instrumental ensemble — 5

Date	Title	Peak	Wks at No.1	Wks on Chart
2 Nov 02	**HANGING AROUND** *679 Recordings 679L 012CD*	39		1
22 Feb 03	**LIGHT AND DAY** *679 Recordings 679L 015CD*	40		1
26 Jul 03	**SOLDIER GIRL** *679 Recordings 679L 014CD*	26		2
7 Aug 04	**HOLD ME NOW** *Good CDPOLY1*	72		1

PONDLIFE
UK, male production group — 8

Date	Title	Peak	Wks at No.1	Wks on Chart
18 Jun 05	**RING DING DING** *Gut CDSNOG14*	11		8

PONI-TAILS
UK, female vocal group – Toni Cistone, Patti McCabe, d. 17 Jan 1989, & Laverne Novak — 14

Date	Title	Peak	Wks at No.1	Wks on Chart
19 Sep 58	**BORN TOO LATE** *HMV POP 516*	5		11
10 Apr 59	**EARLY TO BED** *HMV POP 596*	26		3

BRIAN POOLE & THE TREMELOES
UK, male vocal/instrumental group – Brian Poole, Alan Blakely, d. 10 Jun 1996, Alan Howard, Dave Munden, Brian Scott & Rick West — 91

Date	Title	Peak	Wks at No.1	Wks on Chart
4 Jul 63	**TWIST AND SHOUT** *Decca F 11694*	4		14
12 Sep 63	**DO YOU LOVE ME** *Decca F 11739*	1	3	14
28 Nov 63	**I CAN DANCE** *Decca F 11771*	31		8
30 Jan 64	**CANDY MAN** *Decca F 11823*	6		13
7 May 64	**SOMEONE SOMEONE** *Decca F 11893*	2		17
20 Aug 64	**TWELVE STEPS TO LOVE** *Decca F 11951*	32		7
31 Dec 64	**THREE BELLS** *Decca F 12037*	17		10
22 Jul 65	**I WANT CANDY** *Decca F 12197*	25		8

GLYN POOLE
UK, male vocalist — 8

Date	Title	Peak	Wks at No.1	Wks on Chart
20 Oct 73	**MILLY MOLLY MANDY** *York SYK 565*	35		8

IAN POOLEY
Germany, male DJ/producer — 3

Date	Title	Peak	Wks at No.1	Wks on Chart
10 Mar 01	**900 DEGREES** *V2 VVR 5015143*	57		1
11 Aug 01	**BALMES** *V2 VVR 5016613* FEATURING ESTHERO	65		1
23 Nov 02	**PIHA** *Honchos Music HONM019CD* & MAGIK J	53		1

POP!
UK, male/female vocal group — 8

Date	Title	Peak	Wks at No.1	Wks on Chart
12 Jun 04	**HEAVEN AND EARTH** *Jive 82876619582*	14		2
11 Sep 04	**CAN'T SAY GOODBYE** *Jive 82876639492*	26		3
22 Jan 05	**SERIOUS** *Ebul/Jive 82876668682*	16		3

IGGY POP
US, male vocalist (James Newell Osterberg) — 31

Date	Title	Peak	Wks at No.1	Wks on Chart
13 Dec 86	**REAL WILD CHILD (WILD ONE)** *A&M AM 368*	10		11
10 Feb 90	**LIVIN' ON THE EDGE OF THE NIGHT** *Virgin America VUS 18*	51		4
13 Oct 90	**CANDY** *Virgin America VUS 29*	67		1
5 Jan 91	**WELL DID YOU EVAH!** *Chrysalis CHS 3646* DEBORAH HARRY & IGGY POP	42		4
4 Sep 93	**THE WILD AMERICA (EP)** *Virgin America VUSCD 74*	63		1
21 May 94	**BESIDE YOU** *Virgin America VUSCD 77*	47		2
23 Nov 96	**LUST FOR LIFE** *Virgin VUSCD 116*	26		2
7 Mar 98	**THE PASSENGER** *Virgin VSCDT 1689*	22		3
17 Jan 04	**KICK IT** *XL Recordings XLS 176CD* PEACHES FEATURING IGGY POP	39		3

POP WILL EAT ITSELF
UK, male vocal/instrumental group – Graham Crabb, Clinton Mansell, Richard March & Adam Mole — 43

Date	Title	Peak	Wks at No.1	Wks on Chart
30 Jan 88	**THERE IS NO LOVE BETWEEN US ANYMORE** *Chapter 22 CHAP 20*	66		1
23 Jul 88	**DEF CON ONE** *Chapter 22 PWEI 001*	63		4
11 Feb 89	**CAN U DIG IT** *RCA PB 42621*	38		4
22 Apr 89	**WISE UP! SUCKER** *RCA PB 42761*	41		3
2 Sep 89	**VERY METAL NOISE POLLUTION (EP)** *RCA PB 42883*	45		3
9 Jun 90	**TOUCHED BY THE HAND OF CICCIOLINA** *RCA PB 43735*	28		4
13 Oct 90	**DANCE OF THE MAD** *RCA PB 44023*	32		2
12 Jan 91	**X Y & ZEE** *RCA PB 44243*	15		4
1 Jun 91	**92 DEGREES** *RCA PB 44555*	23		3
6 Jun 92	**KARMADROME/EAT ME DRINK ME LOVE ME** *RCA PB 45467*	17		2
29 Aug 92	**BULLETPROOF!** *RCA 74321110137*	24		3
16 Jan 93	**GET THE GIRL! KILL THE BADDIES!** *RCA 74321128802*	9		4
16 Oct 93	**RSVP/FAMILIUS HORRIBILUS** *Infectious INFECT 1CD*	27		2
12 Mar 94	**ICH BIN EIN AUSLANDER** *Infectious INFECT 4CD*	28		2
10 Sep 94	**EVERYTHING'S COOL** *Infectious INFECT 9CD*	23		2

POPPERS PRESENTS AURA
UK, male/female vocal/production group — 1

Date	Title	Peak	Wks at No.1	Wks on Chart
25 Oct 97	**EVERY LITTLE TIME** *VC Recordings VCRD 26*	44		1

POPPY FAMILY
Canada, male/female vocal duo – Susan & Terry Jacks* — 14

Date	Title	Peak Position	Weeks at No.1	Weeks on Chart
15 Aug 70	**WHICH WAY YOU GOIN' BILLY** *Decca F 22976*	7		14

POPPY FIELDS
UK, male vocal/instrumental group. See Alarm — 2

Date	Title	Peak Position	Weeks at No.1	Weeks on Chart
21 Feb 04	**45 RPM** *Snapper Music SMASCD055*	28		2

PORN KINGS
UK, male instrumental/production duo – Kenny Hayes & Davy T (Dave O'Connor) — 12

Date	Title	Peak Position	Weeks at No.1	Weeks on Chart
28 Sep 96	**UP TO NO GOOD** *All Around The World CDGLOBE 145*	28		2
21 Jun 97	**AMOUR (C'MON)** *All Around The World CDGLOBE 152*	17		3
16 Jan 99	**UP TO THE WILDSTYLE** *All Around The World CDGLOBE 170* VERSUS DJ SUPREME	10		4
10 Feb 01	**SLEDGER** *All Around The World CDGLOBE 229*	71		1
22 Mar 03	**SHAKE YA SHIMMY** *All Around The World CXGLOBE 213* VERSUS FLIP & FILL FEATURING 740 BOYZ	28		2

PORNO
Italy, male production group — 1

Date	Title	Peak Position	Weeks at No.1	Weeks on Chart
4 Feb 06	**MUSIC POWER** *Data DATA96CDS*	72		1

PORNO FOR PYROS
US, male vocal/instrumental group — 2

Date	Title	Peak Position	Weeks at No.1	Weeks on Chart
5 Jun 93	**PETS** *Warner Brothers W 0177CD*	53		2

PORTISHEAD
UK, female/male vocal/instrumental trio – Beth Gibbons*, Geoff Barrow & Adrian Utley — 22

Date	Title	Peak Position	Weeks at No.1	Weeks on Chart
13 Aug 94	**SOUR TIMES** *Go! Beat GOLCD 116*	57		1
14 Jan 95	**GLORY BOX** *Go! Beat GODCD 120*	13		7
22 Apr 95	**SOUR TIMES** *Go! Beat GOLCD 116*	13		4
20 Sep 97	**ALL MINE** *Go! Beat 5715972*	8		4
22 Nov 97	**OVER** *Go! Beat 5710932*	25		2
14 Mar 98	**ONLY YOU** *Go! Beat 5694752*	35		2
5 Apr 08	**MACHINE GUN** *Go! Discs GBUM70801442*	52		2

GARY PORTNOY
US, male vocalist — 3

Date	Title	Peak Position	Weeks at No.1	Weeks on Chart
25 Feb 84	**THEME FROM 'CHEERS'** *Starblend CHEER 1*	58		3

PORTOBELLA
UK, male/female vocal/instrumental group — 1

Date	Title	Peak Position	Weeks at No.1	Weeks on Chart
26 Jun 04	**COVERED IN PUNK** *Island CID 862*	54		1

PORTRAIT
US, male vocal group — 6

Date	Title	Peak Position	Weeks at No.1	Weeks on Chart
27 Mar 93	**HERE WE GO AGAIN** *Capitol CDCL 683*	37		3
8 Apr 95	**I CAN CALL YOU** *Capitol CDCL 740*	61		1
8 Jul 95	**HOW DEEP IS YOUR LOVE** *Capitol CDCL 751*	41		2

PORTSMOUTH SINFONIA
UK, 'orchestra' — 4

Date	Title	Peak Position	Weeks at No.1	Weeks on Chart
12 Sep 81	**CLASSICAL MUDDLEY** *Island WIP 6736*	38		4

SANDY POSEY
US, female vocalist — 32

Date	Title	Peak Position	Weeks at No.1	Weeks on Chart
15 Sep 66	**BORN A WOMAN** *MGM 1321*	24		11
5 Jan 67	**SINGLE GIRL** *MGM 1330*	15		13
13 Apr 67	**WHAT A WOMAN IN LOVE WON'T DO** *MGM 1335*	48		3
6 Sep 75	**SINGLE GIRL** *MGM 2006 533*	35		5

POSIES
US, male vocal/instrumental group — 1

Date	Title	Peak Position	Weeks at No.1	Weeks on Chart
19 Mar 94	**DEFINITE DOOR** *Geffen GFSTD 68*	67		1

POSITIVE FORCE
US, female vocal duo — 9

Date	Title	Peak Position	Weeks at No.1	Weeks on Chart
22 Dec 79	**WE GOT THE FUNK** *Sugarhill SHL 102*	18		9

POSITIVE GANG
UK, male/female vocal/instrumental/production group — 5

Date	Title	Peak Position	Weeks at No.1	Weeks on Chart
17 Apr 93	**SWEET FREEDOM** *PWL Continental PWCD 261*	34		4
31 Jul 93	**SWEET FREEDOM PART 2** *PWL Continental PWCD 264*	67		1

POSITIVE K
US, male rapper (Darryl Gibson) — 2

Date	Title	Peak Position	Weeks at No.1	Weeks on Chart
15 May 93	**I GOT A MAN** *Fourth & Broadway BRCD 280*	43		2

MIKE POST
UK, male orchestra leader — 18

Date	Title	Peak Position	Weeks at No.1	Weeks on Chart
9 Aug 75	**AFTERNOON OF THE RHINO** *Warner Brothers K 16588* MIKE POST COALITION	47		2
16 Jan 82	**THEME FROM 'HILL STREET BLUES'** *Elektron K 12576* FEATURING LARRY CARLTON	25		11
29 Sep 84	**THE A TEAM** *RCA 443*	45		5

ROBERT POST
Norway, male vocalist/guitarist (Robert Fylling) — 2

Date	Title	Peak Position	Weeks at No.1	Weeks on Chart
3 Sep 05	**GOT NONE** *Mercury 9872370*	42		2

POTBELLEEZ
Ireland/Australia, male vocal/production group — 2

Date	Title	Peak Position	Weeks at No.1	Weeks on Chart
21 Jun 08	**DON'T HOLD BACK** *Frenetic FRE10CDX*	54		2

POTTERS
UK, football fans (Stoke City)/vocal group — 2

Date	Title	Peak Position	Weeks at No.1	Weeks on Chart
1 Apr 72	**WE'LL BE WITH YOU** *Pye JT 100*	34		2

P.O.V. FEATURING JADE
US, male vocal group & female vocal trio — 3

Date	Title	Peak Position	Weeks at No.1	Weeks on Chart
5 Feb 94	**ALL THRU THE NITE** *Giant 74321187552*	32		3

POWDER
UK, male/female vocal/instrumental group — 1

Date	Title	Peak Position	Weeks at No.1	Weeks on Chart
24 Jun 95	**AFRODISIAC** *Parkway PARK 002CD*	72		1

BRYAN POWELL
UK, male vocalist — 3

Date	Title	Peak Position	Weeks at No.1	Weeks on Chart
13 Mar 93	**IT'S ALRIGHT** *Talkin Loud TLKCD 34*	73		1
15 May 93	**I THINK OF YOU** *Talkin Loud TLKCD 38*	61		1
7 Aug 93	**NATURAL** *Talkin Loud TLKCD 41*	73		1

COZY POWELL
UK, male drummer, d. 5 Apr 1998 (age 50) — 38

Date	Title	Peak Position	Weeks at No.1	Weeks on Chart
8 Dec 73	**DANCE WITH THE DEVIL** *RAK 164* ●	3		15
25 May 74	**THE MAN IN BLACK** *RAK 173*	18		8
10 Aug 74	**NA NA NA** *RAK 180*	10		10
10 Nov 79	**THEME ONE** *Ariola ARO 189*	62		2
19 Jun 93	**RESURRECTION** *Parlophone CDRS 6351* BRIAN MAY WITH COZY POWELL	23		3

POWER OF DREAMS
Ireland, male vocal/instrumental group — 2

Date	Title	Peak Position	Weeks at No.1	Weeks on Chart
19 Jan 91	**AMERICAN DREAM** *Polydor PO 117*	74		1
11 Apr 92	**THERE I GO AGAIN** *Polydor PO 200*	65		1

POWER STATION
UK/US, male vocal/instrumental group — 17

Date	Title	Peak Position	Weeks at No.1	Weeks on Chart
16 Mar 85	**SOME LIKE IT HOT** *Parlophone R 6091*	14		8
11 May 85	**GET IT ON** *Parlophone R 6096*	22		7
9 Nov 85	**COMMUNICATION** *Parlophone R 6114*	75		1
12 Oct 96	**SHE CAN ROCK IT** *Chrysalis CDCHS 5039*	63		1

POWERCUT FEATURING NUBIAN PRINZ
US, male vocal/instrumental group — 4

Date	Title	Peak Position	Weeks at No.1	Weeks on Chart
22 Jun 91	**GIRLS** *Eternal YZ 570*	50		4

POWERHOUSE
UK, male production duo — 4

Date	Title	Peak Position	Weeks at No.1	Weeks on Chart
20 Dec 97	**RHYTHM OF THE NIGHT** *Satellite 74321522592*	38		4

POWERHOUSE FEATURING DUANE HARDEN
US, male vocal/DJ/production duo — 5

Date	Title	Peak Position	Weeks at No.1	Weeks on Chart
22 May 99	**WHAT YOU NEED** *Defected DEFECT 3CDS*	13		5

POWERPILL
UK, male producer (Richard James). See AFX, Aphex Twin, Polygon Window — 3

Date	Title	Peak Position	Weeks at No.1	Weeks on Chart
6 Jun 92	**PAC-MAN** *ffrreedom TABX 110*	43		3

WILL POWERS
US, female vocalist (Lynn Goldsmith) — 9

Date	Title	Peak Position	Weeks at No.1	Weeks on Chart
1 Oct 83	**KISSING WITH CONFIDENCE** *Island IS 134*	17		9

POWERS THAT BE
UK/Sweden, male production duo — 1

Date	Title	Peak Position	Weeks at No.1	Weeks on Chart
26 Jul 03	**PLANET ROCK/FUNKY PLANET** *Defected DFTD 074*	63		1

DANIEL POWTER
Canada, male vocalist/pianist — 39

Date	Title	Peak Position	Weeks at No.1	Weeks on Chart
6 Aug 05	**BAD DAY** *Warner Brothers W682CD1* ★	2		38
20 Sep 08	**NEXT PLANE HOME** *Warner Brothers W811CD*	70		1

PPK
Russia, male production/instrumental duo – Sergey Pimenov & Alexander Polyakov — 17

Date	Title	Peak Position	Weeks at No.1	Weeks on Chart
8 Dec 01	**RESURRECTION** *Perfecto PERF 32CDS*	3		15
26 Oct 02	**RELOAD** *Perfecto PERF 41CDS*	39		2

PQM FEATURING CICA
US, male/female vocal/production duo — 1

Date	Title	Peak Position	Weeks at No.1	Weeks on Chart
9 Dec 00	**THE FLYING SONG** *Renaissance/Yoshitoshi RENCD 004*	68		1

PEREZ PRADO
Cuba, male orchestra leader (Damas Prado), d. 14 Sep 1989 (age 72) — 57

Date	Title	Peak Position	Weeks at No.1	Weeks on Chart
25 Mar 55	**CHERRY PINK AND APPLE BLOSSOM WHITE** *HMV B 10833* PEREZ 'PREZ' PRADO & HIS ORCHESTRA, THE KING OF THE MAMBO ★	1	2	17
25 Jul 58	**PATRICIA** *RCA 1067* ★	8		16
10 Dec 94	**GUAGLIONE** *RCA 74321250192* PEREZ 'PREZ' PRADO & HIS ORCHESTRA	41		6
8 Apr 95	**GUAGLIONE** *RCA 74321250192* PEREZ 'PREZ' PRADO & HIS ORCHESTRA ●	2		18

PRAISE
UK, male/female vocal/production trio – Miriam Stockley, Simon Goldenberg & Geoff MacCormack — 7

Date	Title	Peak Position	Weeks at No.1	Weeks on Chart
2 Feb 91	**ONLY YOU** *Epic 6566117*	4		7

PRAISE CATS
US, male producer (Eric 'E-Smoove' Miller). See E-Smoove featuring Latanza Waters, Thick D — 5

Date	Title	Peak Position	Weeks at No.1	Weeks on Chart
26 Oct 02	**SHINED ON ME** *PIAS Recordings PIASX 028CD*	56		1
21 May 05	**SHINED ON ME** *All Around The World CDGLOBE380* FEATURING ANDREA LOVE	24		4

PRATT & McCLAIN WITH BROTHERLOVE
US, male vocal duo — 6

Date	Title	Peak Position	Weeks at No.1	Weeks on Chart
1 Oct 77	**HAPPY DAYS** *Reprise K 14435*	31		6

PRAXIS FEATURING KATHY BROWN
UK, male/female vocal/production duo — 5

Date	Title	Peak Position	Weeks at No.1	Weeks on Chart
25 Nov 95	**TURN ME OUT (TURN TO SUGAR)** *Stress CDSTR 40*	44		2
20 Sep 97	**TURN ME OUT (TURN TO SUGAR) (REMIX)** *ffrr FCD 314*	35		3

PRAYING MANTIS
UK, male vocal/instrumental group — 2

Date	Title	Peak Position	Weeks at No.1	Weeks on Chart
31 Jan 81	**CHEATED** *Arista ARIST 378*	69		2

PRECIOUS
UK, female vocal group – Kalli Clark-Sternberg, Jenny Frost, Anya Lahiri, Sophie McDonnell & Louise Rose. See Route One featuring Jenny Frost — 20

Date	Title	Peak Position	Weeks at No.1	Weeks on Chart
29 May 99	**SAY IT AGAIN** *EMI CDEM 544* ●	6		11
1 Apr 00	**REWIND** *EMI CDEM 557*	11		5
15 Jul 00	**IT'S GONNA BE MY WAY** *EMI CDEMS 569*	27		3
25 Nov 00	**NEW BEGINNING** *EMI CDEM 573*	50		1

PRECOCIOUS BRATS FEATURING KEVIN & PERRY
UK, male/female vocal/production/comedy group. See Clergy, Harry Enfield, Hi-Gate — 4

Date	Title	Peak Position	Weeks at No.1	Weeks on Chart
6 May 00	**BIG GIRL** *Virgin VTSCD 1*	16		4

PREFAB SPROUT
UK, male vocal/instrumental group – Paddy & Martin McAloon, Mick Salmon (replaced by Graham Lant, then Neil Conti) & Wendy Smith — 60

Date	Title	Peak Position	Weeks at No.1	Weeks on Chart
28 Jan 84	**DON'T SING** *Kitchenware SK 9*	62		2
20 Jul 85	**FARON YOUNG** *Kitchenware SK 22*	74		1
9 Nov 85	**WHEN LOVE BREAKS DOWN** *Kitchenware SK 21*	25		10
8 Feb 86	**JOHNNY JOHNNY** *Kitchenware SK 24*	64		2
13 Feb 88	**CARS AND GIRLS** *Kitchenware SK 35*	44		5
30 Apr 88	**THE KING OF ROCK 'N' ROLL** *Kitchenware SK 37*	7		10
23 Jul 88	**HEY MANHATTAN** *Kitchenware SK 38*	72		2
18 Aug 90	**LOOKING FOR ATLANTIS** *Kitchenware SK 47*	51		3
20 Oct 90	**WE LET THE STARS GO** *Kitchenware SK 48*	50		3
5 Jan 91	**JORDAN: THE EP** *Kitchenware SK 49*	35		4
13 Jun 92	**THE SOUND OF CRYING** *Kitchenware SK 58*	23		5
8 Aug 92	**IF YOU DON'T LOVE ME** *Kitchenware SK 60*	33		4
3 Oct 92	**ALL THE WORLD LOVES LOVERS** *Kitchenware SK 62*	61		2
9 Jan 93	**LIFE OF SURPRISES** *Kitchenware SKCD 63*	24		4
10 May 97	**A PRISONER OF THE PAST** *Columbia SKZD 70*	30		2
2 Aug 97	**ELECTRIC GUITARS** *Columbia SKZD 71*	53		1

PRELUDE
UK, male/female vocal group — 26

Date	Title	Peak Position	Weeks at No.1	Weeks on Chart
26 Jan 74	**AFTER THE GOLDRUSH** *Dawn DNS 1052*	21		9
26 Apr 80	**PLATINUM BLONDE** *EMI 5046*	45		7
22 May 82	**AFTER THE GOLDRUSH** *After Hours AFT 02*	28		7
31 Jul 82	**ONLY THE LONELY** *After Hours AFT 06*	55		3

PRESENCE
UK, male/female vocal/production group — 2

Date	Title	Peak Position	Weeks at No.1	Weeks on Chart
5 Dec 98	**SENSE OF DANGER** *Pagan 024CDS* FEATURING SHARA NELSON	61		1
19 Jun 99	**FUTURE LOVE** *Pagan 028CDS*	66		1

PRESIDENTS OF THE UNITED STATES OF AMERICA
US, male vocal/instrumental trio – Chris Ballew, Dave Dederer & Jason Finn — 21

Date	Title	Peak Position	Weeks at No.1	Weeks on Chart
6 Jan 96	**LUMP** *Columbia 6624962*	15		7
20 Apr 96	**PEACHES** *Columbia 6631072*	8		7
20 Jul 96	**DUNE BUGGY** *Columbia 6634892*	15		4
2 Nov 96	**MACH 5** *Columbia 6638812*	29		2
1 Aug 98	**VIDEO KILLED THE RADIO STAR** *Maverick W 0450CD*	52		1

Silver-selling ● Gold-selling ● Platinum-selling (x multiples) ⊛ US No.1 ★ Peak Position Weeks at No.1 Weeks on Chart

ELVIS PRESLEY

US, male vocalist/actor. 'The King' of rock 'n' roll has sold more records, had more hits and collected more awards around the globe than any other artist. The most imitated and influential entertainer of all-time has a 48-year chart span of No.1 singles and a 46-year span of No.1 albums and has sold 21 million singles in the UK alone

Date	Title	Peak Position	Weeks at No.1	Weeks on Chart (1304)
11 May 56	**HEARTBREAK HOTEL** *HMV POP 182* ★	2		22
25 May 56	**BLUE SUEDE SHOES** *HMV POP 213*	9		10
13 Jul 56	**I WANT YOU I NEED YOU I LOVE YOU** *HMV POP 235* ★	14		11
21 Sep 56	**HOUND DOG** *HMV POP 249* ★	2		23
16 Nov 56	**BLUE MOON** *HMV POP 272*	9		11
23 Nov 56	**I DON'T CARE IF THE SUN DON'T SHINE** *HMV POP 272*	23		4
7 Dec 56	**LOVE ME TENDER** *HMV POP 253* ★	11		9
15 Feb 57	**MYSTERY TRAIN** *HMV POP 295*	25		5
8 Mar 57	**RIP IT UP** *HMV POP 305*	27		1
10 May 57	**TOO MUCH** *HMV POP 330* WITH THE JORDANAIRES ★	6		9
14 Jun 57	**ALL SHOOK UP** *HMV POP 359* WITH THE JORDANAIRES ★	1	7	21
12 Jul 57	**(LET ME BE YOUR) TEDDY BEAR** *RCA 1013* WITH THE JORDANAIRES ★	3		19
30 Aug 57	**PARALYSED** *HMV POP 378*	8		10
4 Oct 57	**PARTY** *RCA 1020* WITH THE JORDANAIRES	2		15
18 Oct 57	**GOT A LOT O' LIVIN' TO DO** *RCA 1020* WITH THE JORDANAIRES	17		4
1 Nov 57	**TRYING TO GET TO YOU** *HMV POP 408*	16		4
1 Nov 57	**LOVING YOU** *RCA 1013* WITH THE JORDANAIRES	24		2
8 Nov 57	**LAWDY MISS CLAWDY** *HMV POP 408*	15		5
15 Nov 57	**SANTA BRING MY BABY BACK TO ME** *RCA 1025*	7		8
17 Jan 58	**I'M LEFT YOU'RE RIGHT SHE'S GONE** *HMV POP 428*	21		3
24 Jan 58	**JAILHOUSE ROCK** *RCA 1028* ★	1	3	14
31 Jan 58	**JAILHOUSE ROCK EP** *RCA RCX 106* WITH THE JORDANAIRES	18		5
28 Feb 58	**DON'T** *RCA 1043* WITH THE JORDANAIRES ★	2		11
2 May 58	**WEAR MY RING AROUND YOUR NECK** *RCA 1058* WITH THE JORDANAIRES	3		10
25 Jul 58	**HARD HEADED WOMAN** *RCA 1070* WITH THE JORDANAIRES ★	2		11
3 Oct 58	**KING CREOLE** *RCA 1081* WITH THE JORDANAIRES	2		15
23 Jan 59	**ONE NIGHT/I GOT STUNG** *RCA 1100*	1	3	12
24 Apr 59	**A FOOL SUCH AS I/I NEED YOUR LOVE TONIGHT** *RCA 1113* WITH THE JORDANAIRES	1	5	15
24 Jul 59	**A BIG HUNK O' LOVE** *RCA 1136* WITH THE JORDANAIRES ★	4		9
12 Feb 60	**STRICTLY ELVIS EP** *RCA RCX 175*	26		1
7 Apr 60	**STUCK ON YOU** *RCA 1187* WITH THE JORDANAIRES ★	3		14
28 Jul 60	**A MESS OF BLUES** *RCA 1194* WITH THE JORDANAIRES	2		18
3 Nov 60	**IT'S NOW OR NEVER** *RCA 1207* WITH THE JORDANAIRES ★	1	8	19
19 Jan 61	**ARE YOU LONESOME TONIGHT** *RCA 1216* WITH THE JORDANAIRES ★	1	4	15
9 Mar 61	**WOODEN HEART** *RCA 1226*	1	6	27
25 May 61	**SURRENDER** *RCA 1227* WITH THE JORDANAIRES ★	1	4	15
7 Sep 61	**WILD IN THE COUNTRY/I FEEL SO BAD** *RCA 1244* WITH THE JORDANAIRES	4		12
2 Nov 61	**(MARIE'S THE NAME) HIS LATEST FLAME/LITTLE SISTER** *RCA 1258*	1	4	13
1 Feb 62	**ROCK A HULA BABY/CAN'T HELP FALLING IN LOVE** *RCA 1270* WITH THE JORDANAIRES	1	4	20
10 May 62	**GOOD LUCK CHARM** *RCA 1280* WITH THE JORDANAIRES ★	1	5	17
21 Jun 62	**FOLLOW THAT DREAM EP** *RCA RCX 211*	34		2
30 Aug 62	**SHE'S NOT YOU** *RCA 1303* WITH THE JORDANAIRES	1	3	14
29 Nov 62	**RETURN TO SENDER** *RCA 1320* WITH THE JORDANAIRES	1	3	14
28 Feb 63	**ONE BROKEN HEART FOR SALE** *RCA 1337* WITH THE MELLOMEN	12		9
4 Jul 63	**(YOU'RE THE) DEVIL IN DISGUISE** *RCA 1355* WITH THE JORDANAIRES	1	1	12
24 Oct 63	**BOSSA NOVA BABY** *RCA 1374* WITH THE JORDANAIRES	13		8
19 Dec 63	**KISS ME QUICK** *RCA 1375* WITH THE JORDANAIRES	14		10
12 Mar 64	**VIVA LAS VEGAS** *RCA 1390* WITH THE JORDANAIRES	17		12
25 Jun 64	**KISSIN' COUSINS** *RCA 1404* WITH THE JORDANAIRES	10		11
20 Aug 64	**SUCH A NIGHT** *RCA 1411* WITH THE JORDANAIRES	13		10
29 Oct 64	**AIN'T THAT LOVIN' YOU BABY** *RCA 1422*	15		8
3 Dec 64	**BLUE CHRISTMAS** *RCA 1430* WITH THE JORDANAIRES	11		7
11 Mar 65	**DO THE CLAM** *RCA 1443* WITH THE JORDANAIRES JUBILEE FOUR AND CAROL LOMBARD TRIO	19		8
27 May 65	**CRYING IN THE CHAPEL** *RCA 1455* WITH THE JORDANAIRES	1	2	15
11 Nov 65	**TELL ME WHY** *RCA 1489* WITH THE JORDANAIRES	15		10
24 Feb 66	**BLUE RIVER** *RCA 1504*	22		7
7 Apr 66	**FRANKIE AND JOHNNY** *RCA 1509*	21		9
7 Jul 66	**LOVE LETTERS** *RCA 1526*	6		10
13 Oct 66	**ALL THAT I AM** *RCA 1545* WITH THE JORDANAIRES	18		8
1 Dec 66	**IF EVERY DAY WAS LIKE CHRISTMAS** *RCA 1557* WITH THE JORDANIARES AND IMPERIALS QUARTET	9		7
9 Feb 67	**INDESCRIBABLY BLUE** *RCA 1565* WITH THE JORDANIARES AND IMPERIALS QUARTET	21		5
11 May 67	**YOU GOTTA STOP/LOVE MACHINE** *RCA 1593*	38		5
16 Aug 67	**LONG LEGGED GIRL (WITH THE SHORT DRESS ON)** *RCA 1616* WITH THE JORDANAIRES	49		2
21 Feb 68	**GUITAR MAN** *RCA 1663*	19		9
15 May 68	**U.S. MALE** *RCA 1688* WITH THE JORDANAIRES	15		8
17 Jul 68	**YOUR TIME HASN'T COME YET BABY** *RCA 1714* WITH THE JORDANAIRES	22		11
16 Oct 68	**YOU'LL NEVER WALK ALONE** *RCA 1747* WITH THE JORDANAIRES	44		3
26 Feb 69	**IF I CAN DREAM** *RCA 1795*	11		10
11 Jun 69	**IN THE GHETTO** *RCA 1831*	2		17
6 Sep 69	**CLEAN UP YOUR OWN BACK YARD** *RCA 1869*	21		7
29 Nov 69	**SUSPICIOUS MINDS** *RCA 1900* ★	2		14
28 Feb 70	**DON'T CRY DADDY** *RCA 1916*	8		11
16 May 70	**KENTUCKY RAIN** *RCA 1949*	21		12
11 Jul 70	**THE WONDER OF YOU** *RCA 1974*	1	6	21
14 Nov 70	**I'VE LOST YOU** *RCA 1999*	9		12
9 Jan 71	**YOU DON'T HAVE TO SAY YOU LOVE ME** *RCA 2046*	9		10
20 Mar 71	**THERE GOES MY EVERYTHING** *RCA 2060* VOCAL ACCOMPANIMENT: THE IMPERIALS QUARTET	6		11
15 May 71	**RAGS TO RICHES** *RCA 2084*	9		11
17 Jul 71	**HEARTBREAK HOTEL/HOUND DOG** *RCA Maximillion 2104*	10		12
2 Oct 71	**I'M LEAVIN'** *RCA 2125* VOCAL ACCOMPANIMENT: THE IMPERIALS QUARTET	23		9
4 Dec 71	**I JUST CAN'T HELP BELIEVING** *RCA 2158* VOCAL ACCOMPANIMENT: THE IMPERIALS QUARTET AND THE SWEET INSPIRATIONS	6		16
11 Dec 71	**JAILHOUSE ROCK** *RCA Maximillion 2153*	42		5
1 Apr 72	**UNTIL IT'S TIME FOR YOU TO GO** *RCA 2188* VOCAL ACCOMPANIMENT: THE IMPERIALS QUARTET	5		9
17 Jun 72	**AMERICAN TRILOGY** *RCA 2229*	8		11
30 Sep 72	**BURNING LOVE** *RCA 2267*	7		9
16 Dec 72	**ALWAYS ON MY MIND** *RCA 2304* VOCAL ACCOMPANIMENT: JD SUMNER AND THE STAMPS	9		13
26 May 73	**POLK SALAD ANNIE** *RCA 2359*	23		7
11 Aug 73	**FOOL** *RCA 2393*	15		10
24 Nov 73	**RAISED ON ROCK** *RCA 2435*	36		7
16 Mar 74	**I'VE GOT A THING ABOUT YOU BABY** *RCA APBO 0196* VOCAL ACCOMPANIMENT: JD SUMNER AND THE STAMPS	33		5
13 Jul 74	**IF YOU TALK IN YOUR SLEEP** *RCA APBO 0280*	40		3
16 Nov 74	**MY BOY** *RCA 2458* ●	5		13
18 Jan 75	**PROMISED LAND** *RCA PB 10074*	9		8
24 May 75	**T.R.O.U.B.L.E.** *RCA 2562*	31		4
29 Nov 75	**GREEN GREEN GRASS OF HOME** *RCA 2635*	29		7
1 May 76	**HURT** *RCA 2674*	37		5
4 Sep 76	**GIRL OF MY BEST FRIEND** *RCA 2729*	9		12
25 Dec 76	**SUSPICION** *RCA 2768*	9		12
5 Mar 77	**MOODY BLUE** *RCA PB 0857* VOCAL ACCOMPANIMENT JD SUMNER AND THE STAMPS QUARTET, KATHY WESTMORELAND, MYRNA SMITH	6		9
13 Aug 77	**WAY DOWN** *RCA PB 0998* VOCAL ACCOMPANIMENT JD SUMNER AND THE STAMPS QUARTET, K WESTMORELAND, S NEILSON AND M SMITH ●	1	5	13
3 Sep 77	**ALL SHOOK UP** *RCA PB 2694* WITH THE JORDANAIRES	41		2
3 Sep 77	**ARE YOU LONESOME TONIGHT** *RCA PB 2699* WITH THE JORDANAIRES	46		1
3 Sep 77	**CRYING IN THE CHAPEL** *RCA PB 2708* WITH THE JORDANAIRES	43		2
3 Sep 77	**IT'S NOW OR NEVER** *RCA PB 2698* WITH THE JORDANAIRES	39		2
3 Sep 77	**JAILHOUSE ROCK** *RCA PB 2695* WITH THE JORDANAIRES	44		2
3 Sep 77	**RETURN TO SENDER** *RCA PB 2706* WITH THE JORDANAIRES	42		3
3 Sep 77	**THE WONDER OF YOU** *RCA PB 2709*	48		1
3 Sep 77	**WOODEN HEART** *RCA PB 2700*	49		1
10 Dec 77	**MY WAY** *RCA PB 1165* VOCAL ACCOMPANIMENT JD SUMNER AND THE STAMPS, THE SWEET INSPIRATIONS AND KATHY WESTMORELAND	9		8
24 Jun 78	**DON'T BE CRUEL** *RCA PB 9265* ★	24		12
15 Dec 79	**IT WON'T SEEM LIKE CHRISTMAS (WITHOUT YOU)** *RCA PB 9464*	13		6
30 Aug 80	**IT'S ONLY LOVE/BEYOND THE REEF** *RCA 4* ●	3		10
6 Dec 80	**SANTA CLAUS IS BACK IN TOWN** *RCA 16*	41		6
14 Feb 81	**GUITAR MAN** *RCA 43*	43		4
18 Apr 81	**LOVING ARMS** *RCA 48*	47		6
13 Mar 82	**ARE YOU LONESOME TONIGHT** *RCA 196* VOCAL ACCOMPANIMENT JD SUMNER AND THE STAMPS, THE SWEET INSPIRATIONS AND KATHY WESTMORELAND	25		7
26 Jun 82	**THE SOUND OF YOUR CRY** *RCA 232*	59		2
5 Feb 83	**JAILHOUSE ROCK** *RCA 1028*	27		6
7 May 83	**BABY I DON'T CARE** *RCA 332*	61		3
3 Dec 83	**I CAN HELP** *RCA 369*	30		9
10 Nov 84	**THE LAST FAREWELL** *RCA 459*	48		6
19 Jan 85	**THE ELVIS MEDLEY** *RCA 476* WITH THE JORDANAIRES	51		3
10 Aug 85	**ALWAYS ON MY MIND** *RCA PB 49944*	59		4
11 Apr 87	**AIN'T THAT LOVIN' YOU BABY/BOSSA NOVA BABY** *RCA ARON 1*	47		5
22 Aug 87	**LOVE ME TENDER/IF I CAN DREAM** *RCA ARON 2*	56		3
16 Jan 88	**STUCK ON YOU** *RCA PB 49595* WITH THE JORDANAIRES	58		2
17 Aug 91	**ARE YOU LONESOME TONIGHT (LIVE)** *RCA PB 49177*	68		2
29 Aug 92	**DON'T BE CRUEL** *RCA 74321110777* WITH THE JORDANAIRES	42		2
11 Nov 95	**THE TWELFTH OF NEVER** *RCA 74321320122*, VOCAL ACCOMPANIMENT THE VOICE	21		3
18 May 96	**HEARTBREAK HOTEL/I WAS THE ONE** *RCA 74321336862*	45		1
24 May 97	**ALWAYS ON MY MIND** *RCA 74321485412*	13		6
14 Apr 01	**SUSPICIOUS MINDS** *RCA 74321855822*	15		4
10 Nov 01	**AMERICA THE BEAUTIFUL** *RCA 74321904022*	69		1
22 Jun 02	**A LITTLE LESS CONVERSATION** *RCA 74321943572* ELVIS VS JXL ⊛	1	4	12
4 Oct 03	**RUBBERNECKIN'** *RCA 82876543412*	5		8
17 Jul 04	**THAT'S ALL RIGHT** *RCA 82876619212*	3		7
15 Jan 05	**JAILHOUSE ROCK** *RCA 82876667152*	1	1	7
22 Jan 05	**ONE NIGHT/I GOT STUNG** *RCA 82876666682*	1	1	6

Top Acts By Weeks On Chart

Pos	Artist	Weeks on Chart
1	ELVIS PRESLEY	1303
2	CLIFF RICHARD	1177
3	SHADOWS	772
4	MADONNA	731
5	ELTON JOHN	669
6	MICHAEL JACKSON	662
7	DIANA ROSS	568
8	ROD STEWART	477
9	DAVID BOWIE	457
10	BEATLES	456
11	QUEEN	445
12	FRANK SINATRA	440
13	STATUS QUO	432
=	STEVIE WONDER	432
15	PAUL McCARTNEY/WINGS	423
16	KYLIE MINOGUE	414
17	TOM JONES	411
18	OASIS	404
19	ROLLING STONES	382
20	MARIAH CAREY	376
21	ROBBIE WILLIAMS	364
22	U2	359
23	TAKE THAT	357
24	BEE GEES	354
25	UB40	350
26	EVERLY BROTHERS	345
=	ROY ORBISON	345
28	RIHANNA	333
29	KANYE WEST	332
30	WHITNEY HOUSTON	331
=	BRITNEY SPEARS	331
32	SHIRLEY BASSEY	329
=	PERRY COMO	329
=	JAY-Z	329
35	JIM REEVES	322
36	LONNIE DONEGAN	321
37	FOUR TOPS	318
=	HOLLIES	318
=	BEYONCE	318
40	PRINCE	309
41	PAT BOONE	308
42	SUPREMES	306
43	JANET JACKSON	304
44	GEORGE MICHAEL	299
=	DONNA SUMMER	299
46	SLADE	296
47	AKON	294
48	SHAKIN' STEVENS	292
49	JUSTIN TIMBERLAKE	288
50	EMINEM	284
51	HOT CHOCOLATE	283
52	FRANKIE LAINE	282
53	BEACH BOYS	281
=	BILLY FURY	281
55	WESTLIFE	277
56	MADNESS	274
57	SUGABABES	273
58	P!NK	268
59	DEPECHE MODE	262
60	ABBA	260
=	PET SHOP BOYS	260
62	ELECRTRIC LIGHT ORCHESTRA	255
=	GIRLS ALOUD	255
64	CELINE DION	254
=	R KELLY	254
66	JACKSON 5	253
67	PHIL COLLINS	251
=	ADAM FAITH	251
69	NAT 'KING' COLE	250
70	BON JOVI	249
71	BRYAN ADAMS	248
72	PETULA CLARK	247
=	SIMPLY RED	247
=	WHO	247
75	ANDY WILLIAMS	245
76	CONNIE FRANCIS	244
77	FRANKIE VAUGHAN	241
78	ENGELBERT HUMPERDINCK	240
79	BLACK EYED PEAS	237
=	T REX	237
81	BOYZONE	234
=	OLIVIA NEWTON-JOHN	234
83	KEN DODD	233
84	CHRISTINA AGUILERA	231
85	DURAN DURAN	230
86	CHER	229
87	TIMBALAND	228
88	TINA TURNER	227
89	ERASURE	226
90	PUFF DADDY/P DIDDY	224
91	FLEETWOOD MAC	223
92	TREMELOES	222
93	KOOL & THE GANG	218
94	KINKS	217
=	MANFRED MANN	217
96	WET WET WET	214
97	EURYTHMICS	212
=	GENE PITNEY	212
99	HERMAN'S HERMITS	211
=	BRENDA LEE	211
=	DUSTY SPRINGFIELD	211

Date	Title	Peak Position	Weeks at No.1	Weeks on Chart
29 Jan 05	**A FOOL SUCH AS I/I NEED YOUR LOVE TONIGHT** *RCA 82876666582*	2		5
5 Feb 05	**IT'S NOW OR NEVER** *RCA 82876666592*	1	1	4
12 Feb 05	**ARE YOU LONESOME TONIGHT?** *RCA 82876666602*	2		6
19 Feb 05	**WOODEN HEART** *RCA 82876666612*	2		5
26 Feb 05	**SURRENDER** *RCA 82876666692*	2		5
5 Mar 05	**(MARIE'S THE NAME) HIS LATEST FLAME** *RCA 82876666702*	3		4
12 Mar 05	**ROCK-A-HULA BABY** *RCA 82876666732*	3		4
19 Mar 05	**GOOD LUCK CHARM** *RCA 82876666752*	2		4
26 Mar 05	**SHE'S NOT YOU** *RCA 82876666762*	3		4
2 Apr 05	**RETURN TO SENDER** *RCA 82876666772*	5		4
9 Apr 05	**(YOU'RE THE) DEVIL IN DISGUISE** *RCA 82876666782*	2		5
16 Apr 05	**CRYING IN THE CHAPEL** *RCA 82876666802*	2		4
23 Apr 05	**THE WONDER OF YOU** *RCA 82876666812*	4		4
30 Apr 05	**WAY DOWN** *RCA 82876666822*	2		4
7 May 05	**A LITTLE LESS CONVERSATION** *RCA 82876666832* ELVIS VS JXL	3		4
25 Aug 07	**SUSPICIOUS MINDS** *RCA Victor 88697147212*	11		4
1 Sep 07	**BLUE SUEDE SHOES** *RCA Victor 88697122382*	11		2
1 Sep 07	**MY BABY LEFT ME** *Memphis Recording Service MHC400451001*	18		2
8 Sep 07	**HOUND DOG** *RCA 88697122402*	14		2
15 Sep 07	**(LET ME BE YOUR) TEDDY BEAR** *RCA 88697124782*	14		1
22 Sep 07	**PARTY** *RCA 88697125142*	14		1
29 Sep 07	**DON'T** *RCA 88697125152*	14		1
6 Oct 07	**HARD HEADED WOMAN** *RCA 88697125162*	15		1
13 Oct 07	**KING CREOLE** *RCA 88697125172*	15		1
20 Oct 07	**A BIG HUNK O' LOVE** *RCA 88697125182*	12		1
27 Oct 07	**WEAR MY RING AROUND YOUR NECK** *RCA 88697125192*	16		1
3 Nov 07	**IF I CAN DREAM** *RCA 88697125202*	17		2
10 Nov 07	**VIVA LAS VEGAS** *RCA 88697125212*	15		1
17 Nov 07	**IN THE GHETTO** *RCA 88697125222*	13		1
24 Nov 07	**YOU DON'T HAVE TO SAY YOU LOVE ME** *RCA 88697125232*	16		1
1 Dec 07	**ALWAYS ON MY MIND** *RCA 88697125242*	17		1
8 Dec 07	**AN AMERICAN TRILOGY** *RCA 88697125252*	12		1
15 Dec 07	**BURNING LOVE** *RCA 88697125262*	13		1

Top 3 Best-Selling Singles

		Approximate Sales
1	IT'S NOW OR NEVER	1,225,000
2	ARE YOU LONESOME TONIGHT	880,000
3	JAILHOUSE ROCK	870,000

LISA MARIE PRESLEY
US, female vocalist — 5

Date	Title	Peak Position	Weeks at No.1	Weeks on Chart
12 Jul 03	**LIGHTS OUT** *Capitol CDCL 844*	16		5

PRESSURE DROP
UK, male vocal/instrumental duo — 2

Date	Title	Peak Position	Weeks at No.1	Weeks on Chart
21 Mar 98	**SILENTLY BAD MINDED** *Higher Ground HIGHS 6CD*	53		1
17 Mar 01	**WARRIOR SOUND** *Higher Ground 6697192*	72		1

BILLY PRESTON
US, male vocalist/keyboard player, d. 6 Jun 2006 (age 59) — 51

Date	Title	Peak Position	Weeks at No.1	Weeks on Chart
23 Apr 69	**GET BACK** *Apple R 5777* BEATLES WITH BILLY PRESTON ★	1	6	17
2 Jul 69	**THAT'S THE WAY GOD PLANNED IT** *Apple 12*	11		10
16 Sep 72	**OUTA SPACE** *A&M AMS 7007*	44		3
3 Apr 76	**GET BACK** *Apple R 5777* BEATLES WITH BILLY PRESTON	28		5
15 Dec 79	**WITH YOU I'M BORN AGAIN** *Motown TMG 1159* & SYREETA ●	2		11
8 Mar 80	**IT WILL COME IN TIME** *Motown TMG 1175* & SYREETA	47		4
22 Apr 89	**GET BACK** *Apple R 5777* BEATLES WITH BILLY PRESTON	74		1

JOHNNY PRESTON
US, male vocalist (Johnny Courville) — 46

Date	Title	Peak Position	Weeks at No.1	Weeks on Chart
12 Feb 60	**RUNNING BEAR** *Mercury AMT 1079* ★	1	2	16
21 Apr 60	**CRADLE OF LOVE** *Mercury AMT 1092*	2		16
28 Jul 60	**I'M STARTING TO GO STEADY** *Mercury AMT 1104*	49		1
11 Aug 60	**FEEL SO FINE** *Mercury AMT 1104*	18		10
8 Dec 60	**CHARMING BILLY** *Mercury AMT 1114*	34		3

MIKE PRESTON
UK, male vocalist — 33

Date	Title	Peak Position	Weeks at No.1	Weeks on Chart
30 Oct 59	**MR BLUE** *Decca F 11167*	12		8
25 Aug 60	**I'D DO ANYTHING** *Decca F 11255*	23		10
22 Dec 60	**TOGETHERNESS** *Decca F 11287*	41		5
9 Mar 61	**MARRY ME** *Decca F 11335*	14		10

PRETENDERS
US/UK, female/male vocal/instrumental group – Chrissie Hynde*, Martin Chambers, Pete Farndon, d. 14 Apr 1983 (replaced by Malcolm Foster), & James 'Honeyman' Scott, d. 16 Jun 1982 (replaced by Robbie McIntosh) — 132

Date	Title	Peak Position	Weeks at No.1	Weeks on Chart
10 Feb 79	**STOP YOUR SOBBING** *Real ARE 6*	34		9
14 Jul 79	**KID** *Real ARE 9*	33		7
17 Nov 79	**BRASS IN POCKET** *Real ARE 11* ●	1	2	17
5 Apr 80	**TALK OF THE TOWN** *Real ARE 12*	8		8
14 Feb 81	**MESSAGE OF LOVE** *Real ARE 15*	11		7
12 Sep 81	**DAY AFTER DAY** *Real ARE 17*	45		4
14 Nov 81	**I GO TO SLEEP** *Real ARE 18*	7		10
2 Oct 82	**BACK ON THE CHAIN GANG** *Real ARE 19*	17		9
26 Nov 83	**2000 MILES** *Real ARE 20*	15		9
9 Jun 84	**THIN LINE BETWEEN LOVE AND HATE** *Real ARE 22*	49		3
11 Oct 86	**DON'T GET ME WRONG** *Real YZ 85*	10		9
13 Dec 86	**HYMN TO HER** *Real YZ 93*	8		12
15 Aug 87	**IF THERE WAS A MAN** *Real YZ 149* FOR 007	49		6
23 Apr 94	**I'LL STAND BY YOU** *Real YZ 815CD*	10		10
2 Jul 94	**NIGHT IN MY VEINS** *Real YZ 825CD*	25		5
15 Oct 94	**977** *WEA YZ 848CD1*	66		2
14 Oct 95	**KID** *WEA 014CD*	73		1
10 May 97	**FEVER PITCH THE EP** *Blanco Y Negro NEG 104CD* PRETENDERS, LA'S, ORLANDO, NICK HORNBY	65		1
15 May 99	**HUMAN** *WEA 207CD*	33		3

PRETTY BOY FLOYD
US, male vocal/instrumental group — 1

Date	Title	Peak Position	Weeks at No.1	Weeks on Chart
10 Mar 90	**ROCK AND ROLL (IS GONNA SET THE NIGHT ON FIRE)** *MCA 1393*	75		1

PRETTY RICKY
US, male rap/vocal group — 8

Date	Title	Peak Position	Weeks at No.1	Weeks on Chart
24 Sep 05	**GRIND WITH ME** *Atlantic AT0212CDX*	26		6
25 Feb 06	**YOUR BODY** *Atlantic AT0231CD1*	37		2

PRETTY THINGS
UK, male vocal/instrumental group – Phil May, Brian Pendleton, d. 16 May 2001, Viv Prince (replaced by Skip Alan), John Stax & Dick Taylor — 41

Date	Title	Peak Position	Weeks at No.1	Weeks on Chart
18 Jun 64	**ROSALYN** *Fontana TF 469*	41		5
22 Oct 64	**DON'T BRING ME DOWN** *Fontana TF 503*	10		11
25 Feb 65	**HONEY I NEED** *Fontana TF 537*	13		10
15 Jul 65	**CRY TO ME** *Fontana TF 585*	28		7
20 Jan 66	**MIDNIGHT TO SIX MAN** *Fontana TF 647*	46		1
5 May 66	**COME SEE ME** *Fontana TF 688*	43		5
21 Jul 66	**A HOUSE IN THE COUNTRY** *Fontana TF 722*	50		2

ALAN PRICE SET
UK, male vocalist/pianist. See Animals — 87

Date	Title	Peak Position	Weeks at No.1	Weeks on Chart
31 Mar 66	**I PUT A SPELL ON YOU** *Decca F 12367*	9		10
14 Jul 66	**HI LILI HI LO** *Decca F 12442*	11		12
2 Mar 67	**SIMON SMITH AND HIS AMAZING DANCING BEAR** *Decca F 12570*	4		12
2 Aug 67	**THE HOUSE THAT JACK BUILT** *Decca F 12641*	4		10
15 Nov 67	**SHAME** *Decca F 12691*	45		2
31 Jan 68	**DON'T STOP THE CARNIVAL** *Decca F 12731*	13		8
10 Apr 71	**ROSETTA** *CBS 7108* FAME & PRICE TOGETHER	11		10
25 May 74	**JARROW SONG** *Warner Brothers K 16372* ALAN PRICE	6		9
29 Apr 78	**JUST FOR YOU** *Jet UP 36358* ALAN PRICE	43		7
17 Feb 79	**BABY OF MINE/JUST FOR YOU** *Jet 135* ALAN PRICE	32		3
30 Apr 88	**CHANGES** *Ariola 109911* ALAN PRICE	54		4

KELLY PRICE
US, female vocalist — 10

Date	Title	Peak Position	Weeks at No.1	Weeks on Chart
7 Nov 98	**FRIEND OF MINE** *Island Black Music CID 723*	25		3
8 May 99	**SECRET LOVE** *Island Black Music CID 739*	26		2
30 Dec 00	**HEARTBREAK HOTEL** *Arista 74321820572* WHITNEY HOUSTON FEATURING FAITH EVANS & KELLY PRICE	25		5

LLOYD PRICE
US, male vocalist — 36

Date	Title	Peak Position	Weeks at No.1	Weeks on Chart
13 Feb 59	**STAGGER LEE** *HMV POP 580* ★	7		14
15 May 59	**WHERE WERE YOU (ON OUR WEDDING DAY)?** *HMV POP 598*	15		6
12 Jun 59	**PERSONALITY** *HMV POP 626*	9		10
11 Sep 59	**I'M GONNA GET MARRIED** *HMV POP 650*	23		5
21 Apr 60	**LADY LUCK** *HMV POP 712*	45		1

Silver-selling ● Gold-selling ● Platinum-selling (x multiples) ⊛ US No.1 ★ Peak Position · Weeks at No.1 · Weeks on Chart

PRICKLY HEAT

UK, male producer (T Binns) — Weeks on Chart: 1

Date	Title	Peak Position	Weeks at No.1	Weeks on Chart
26 Dec 98	**OOOIE, OOOIE, OOOIE** *Virgin VSCDT 1727*	57		1

DICKIE PRIDE

UK, male vocalist (Richard Kneller), d. 26 Mar 1969 (age 28) — Weeks on Chart: 1

Date	Title	Peak Position	Weeks at No.1	Weeks on Chart
30 Oct 59	**PRIMROSE LANE** *Columbia DB 4340*	28		1

MAXI PRIEST

UK, male vocalist (Max Elliott) — Weeks on Chart: 106

Date	Title	Peak Position	Weeks at No.1	Weeks on Chart
29 Mar 86	**STROLLIN' ON** *10 TEN 84*	32		9
12 Jul 86	**IN THE SPRINGTIME** *10 TEN 127*	54		3
8 Nov 86	**CRAZY LOVE** *10 TEN 135*	67		5
4 Apr 87	**LET ME KNOW** *10 TEN 156*	49		4
24 Oct 87	**SOME GUYS HAVE ALL THE LUCK** *10 TEN 198*	12		12
20 Feb 88	**HOW CAN WE EASE THE PAIN** *10 TEN 207* FEATURING BERES HAMMOND	41		6
4 Jun 88	**WILD WORLD** *10 TEN 221*	5		9
27 Aug 88	**GOODBYE TO LOVE AGAIN** *10 TEN 238*	57		3
9 Jun 90	**CLOSE TO YOU** *10 TEN 294* ★	7		10
1 Sep 90	**PEACE THROUGHOUT THE WORLD** *10 TEN 317* FEATURING JAZZIE B	41		4
1 Dec 90	**HUMAN WORK OF ART** *10 TEN 328*	71		4
24 Aug 91	**HOUSECALL** *Epic 6573477* SHABBA RANKS FEATURING MAXI PRIEST	31		7
5 Oct 91	**THE MAXI PRIEST EP** *10 TEN 343*	62		3
26 Sep 92	**GROOVIN' IN THE MIDNIGHT** *10 TEN 412*	50		2
28 Nov 92	**JUST WANNA KNOW/FE' REAL** *10 TEN 416* MAXI PRIEST/MAXI PRIEST FEATURING APACHE INDIAN	33		3
20 Mar 93	**ONE MORE CHANCE** *10 TENCD 420*	40		3
8 May 93	**HOUSECALL (REMIX)** *Epic 6592842* SHABBA RANKS FEATURING MAXI PRIEST	8		8
31 Jul 93	**WAITING IN VAIN** *GRP MCSTD 1921* LEE RITENOUR & MAXI PRIEST	65		2
22 Jun 96	**THAT GIRL** *Virgin VUSDX 106* FEATURING SHAGGY	15		7
21 Sep 96	**WATCHING THE WORLD GO BY** *Virgin VUSD 108*	36		2

PRIMA DONNA

UK, male/female vocal group — Weeks on Chart: 4

Date	Title	Peak Position	Weeks at No.1	Weeks on Chart
26 Apr 80	**LOVE ENOUGH FOR TWO** *Ariola ARO 221*	48		4

LOUIS PRIMA

US, male vocalist/trumpeter/band leader, d. 24 Aug 1978 (age 66) — Weeks on Chart: 1

Date	Title	Peak Position	Weeks at No.1	Weeks on Chart
21 Feb 58	**BUONA SERA** *Capitol CL 14841*	25		1

PRIMAL SCREAM

UK, male vocal/instrumental group – Bobby Gillespie, Martin Duffy, Andrew Innes, Gary 'Mani' Mounfield, Harry Olsen, Philip Tomanov (replaced by Paul Mulraney, then Darrin Mooney) & Robert Young — Weeks on Chart: 69

Date	Title	Peak Position	Weeks at No.1	Weeks on Chart
3 Mar 90	**LOADED** *Creation CRE 070*	16		9
18 Aug 90	**COME TOGETHER** *Creation CRE 078*	26		6
22 Jun 91	**HIGHER THAN THE SUN** *Creation CRE 096*	40		2
24 Aug 91	**DON'T FIGHT IT FEEL IT** *Creation CRE 110* FEATURING DENISE JOHNSON	41		2
8 Feb 92	**DIXIE-NARCO EP** *Creation CRE 117*	11		6
12 Mar 94	**ROCKS/FUNKY JAM** *Creation CRESCD 129*	7		5
18 Jun 94	**JAILBIRD** *Creation CRESCD 145*	29		2
10 Dec 94	**(I'M GONNA) CRY MYSELF BLIND** *Creation CRESCD 183*	49		2
15 Jun 96	**THE BIG MAN AND THE SCREAM TEAM MEET THE BARMY ARMY UPTOWN** *Creation CRESCD 194* PRIMAL SCREAM, IRVINE WELSH & ON U-SOUND	17		2
17 May 97	**KOWALSKI** *Creation CRESCD 245*	8		3
28 Jun 97	**STAR** *Creation CRESCD 263*	16		3
25 Oct 97	**BURNING WHEEL** *Creation CRESCD 272*	17		2
20 Nov 99	**SWASTIKA EYES** *Creation CRESCD 326*	22		2
1 Apr 00	**KILL ALL HIPPIES** *Creation CRESCD 332*	24		2
23 Sep 00	**ACCELERATOR** *Creation CRESCD 333*	34		1
3 Aug 02	**MISS LUCIFER** *Columbia 6728252*	25		2
9 Nov 02	**AUTOBAHN 66** *Columbia 6733122*	44		1
29 Nov 03	**SOME VELVET MORING** *Columbia 6744022*	44		2
27 May 06	**COUNTRY GIRL** *Columbia 82876834272*	5		13
19 Aug 06	**DOLLS** *Columbia 82876871632*	40		1
26 Jul 08	**CAN'T GO BACK** *B Unique BUN140CD*	48		1

PRIME MOVERS

US, male vocal/instrumental group — Weeks on Chart: 1

Date	Title	Peak Position	Weeks at No.1	Weeks on Chart
8 Feb 86	**ON THE TRAIL** *Island IS 263*	74		1

PRIMITIVE RADIO GODS

US, male vocalist (Chris O'Connor) — Weeks on Chart: 1

Date	Title	Peak Position	Weeks at No.1	Weeks on Chart
30 Mar 96	**STANDING OUTSIDE A BROKEN PHONE BOOTH WITH MONEY IN MY HAND** *Columbia 6627692*	74		1

PRIMITIVES

UK/Australia, female/male vocal/instrumental group – Tracy Tracy (Tracy Cattell), Paul Court, Steve Dullaghan (replaced by Andy Hobson) & Pete Tweedie (replaced by Tig Williams) — Weeks on Chart: 27

Date	Title	Peak Position	Weeks at No.1	Weeks on Chart
27 Feb 88	**CRASH** *Lazy PB 41761*	5		10
30 Apr 88	**OUT OF REACH** *Lazy PB 42011*	25		4
3 Sep 88	**WAY BEHIND ME** *Lazy PB 42209*	36		4
29 Jul 89	**SICK OF IT** *Lazy PB 42947*	24		4
30 Sep 89	**SECRETS** *Lazy PB 43173*	49		3
3 Aug 91	**YOU ARE THE WAY** *RCA PB 44481*	58		2

PRINCE

US, male vocalist/producer/multi-instrumentalist (Prince Rogers Nelson). Multi-monikered musical maestro who waited 14 years for a solo No.1 (credited to 'Symbol') but famously penned Sinead O'Connor's 1990 chart-topper 'Nothing Compares 2 U'. The diminutive Minneapolis native is one of the most popular live acts of all time — Weeks on Chart: 309

Date	Title	Peak Position	Weeks at No.1	Weeks on Chart
19 Jan 80	**I WANNA BE YOUR LOVER** *Warner Brothers K 17537*	41		3
29 Jan 83	**1999** *Warner Brothers W 9896* & THE REVOLUTION	25		7
30 Apr 83	**LITTLE RED CORVETTE** *Warner Brothers W 9688*	54		6
26 Nov 83	**LITTLE RED CORVETTE** *Warner Brothers W 9436*	66		2
30 Jun 84	**WHEN DOVES CRY** *Warner Brothers W 9286* ● ★	4		15
22 Sep 84	**PURPLE RAIN** *Warner Brothers W 9174* & THE REVOLUTION	8		9
8 Dec 84	**I WOULD DIE 4 U** *Warner Brothers W 9121* & THE REVOLUTION	58		6
19 Jan 85	**1999/LITTLE RED CORVETTE** *Warner Brothers W 1999* & THE REVOLUTION ●	2		10
23 Feb 85	**LET'S GO CRAZY/TAKE ME WITH YOU** *Warner Brothers W 2000* & THE REVOLUTION ★	7		9
25 May 85	**PAISLEY PARK** *WEA W 9052* & THE REVOLUTION	18		10
27 Jul 85	**RASPBERRY BERET** *WEA W 8929* & THE REVOLUTION	25		8
26 Oct 85	**POP LIFE** *Paisley Park W 8858* & THE REVOLUTION	60		2
8 Mar 86	**KISS** *Paisley Park W 8751* & THE REVOLUTION ★	6		9
14 Jun 86	**MOUNTAINS** *Paisley Park W 8711* & THE REVOLUTION	45		4
16 Aug 86	**GIRLS AND BOYS** *Paisley Park W 8586* & THE REVOLUTION	11		8
1 Nov 86	**ANOTHERLOVERHOLENYOHEAD** *Paisley Park W 8521*	36		3
14 Mar 87	**SIGN O' THE TIMES** *Paisley Park W 8399*	10		9
20 Jun 87	**IF I WAS YOUR GIRLFRIEND** *Paisley Park W 8334*	20		6
15 Aug 87	**U GOT THE LOOK** *Paisley Park W 8289*	11		9
28 Nov 87	**I COULD NEVER TAKE THE PLACE OF YOUR MAN** *Paisley Park W 8288*	29		6
7 May 88	**ALPHABET STREET** *Paisley Park W 7900*	9		6
23 Jul 88	**GLAM SLAM** *Paisley Park W 7806*	29		4
5 Nov 88	**I WISH U HEAVEN** *Paisley Park W 7745*	24		5
24 Jun 89	**BATDANCE** *Warner Brothers W 2924* ● ★	2		12
9 Sep 89	**PARTYMAN** *Warner Brothers W 2814*	14		6
18 Nov 89	**THE ARMS OF ORION** *Warner Brothers W 2757* WITH SHEENA EASTON	27		5
4 Aug 90	**THIEVES IN THE TEMPLE** *Paisley Park W 9751*	7		6
10 Nov 90	**NEW POWER GENERATION** *Paisley Park W 9525*	26		4
31 Aug 91	**GETT OFF** *Paisley Park W 0056* & THE NEW POWER GENERATION	4		8
21 Sep 91	**CREAM** *Paisley Park W 0061* & THE NEW POWER GENERATION ★	15		7
7 Dec 91	**DIAMONDS AND PEARLS** *Paisley Park W 0075* & THE NEW POWER GENERATION	25		6
28 Mar 92	**MONEY DON'T MATTER 2 NIGHT** *Paisley Park W 0091* & THE NEW POWER GENERATION	19		5
27 Jun 92	**THUNDER** *Paisley Park W 01132P* & THE NEW POWER GENERATION	28		3
18 Jul 92	**SEXY MF/STROLLIN'** *Paisley Park W 0123* & THE NEW POWER GENERATION	4		7
10 Oct 92	**MY NAME IS PRINCE** *Paisley Park W 0132* & THE NEW POWER GENERATION	7		5
14 Nov 92	**MY NAME IS PRINCE (REMIX)** *Paisley Park W 0142T* & THE NEW POWER GENERATION	51		1
5 Dec 92	**7** *Paisley Park W 0147* & THE NEW POWER GENERATION	27		6
13 Mar 93	**THE MORNING PAPERS** *Paisley Park W 0162CD* & THE NEW POWER GENERATION	52		3
16 Oct 93	**PEACH** *Paisley Park W 0210CD*	14		5
11 Dec 93	**CONTROVERSY** *Paisley Park W 0215CD1*	5		5
9 Apr 94	**THE MOST BEAUTIFUL GIRL IN THE WORLD** *NPG 60155* (SYMBOL) ●	1	3	12
4 Jun 94	**THE BEAUTIFUL EXPERIENCE** *NPG 60212*	18		3
10 Sep 94	**LETITGO** *Warner Brothers W 0260CD*	30		4
18 Mar 95	**PURPLE MEDLEY** *Warner Brothers W 0289CD*	33		2
23 Sep 95	**EYE HATE U** *Warner Brothers W 0315CD* ARTIST FORMERLY KNOWN AS PRINCE (AFKAP)	20		3
9 Dec 95	**GOLD** *Warner Brothers W 0325CDX* ARTIST FORMERLY KNOWN AS PRINCE (AFKAP)	10		9

Date	Title	Peak Position	Weeks at No.1	Weeks on Chart
3 Aug 96	**DINNER WITH DELORES** *Warner Brothers 9362437422* ARTIST FORMERLY KNOWN AS PRINCE (AFKAP)	36		2
14 Dec 96	**BETCHA BY GOLLY WOW!** *NPG CDEMS 463* ARTIST	11		7
8 Mar 97	**THE HOLY RIVER** *EMI CDEM 467* ARTIST	19		3
9 Jan 99	**1999** *Warner Brothers W 467CD* & THE REVOLUTION	10		4
18 Dec 99	**1999** *Warner Brothers W 467CD* & THE REVOLUTION	40		5
26 Feb 00	**THE GREATEST ROMANCE EVER SOLD** *NPG 74321745002* ARTIST	65		1
20 Nov 04	**CINNAMON GIRL** *Columbia 6751422*	43		1
8 Apr 06	**BLACK SWEAT** *Universal MCSTD40457*	43		1
10 Jun 06	**FURY** *Universal MCSTD40462*	60		1
21 Nov 09	**PURPLE RAIN** *Warner Brothers 8122799678*	62		1

PRINCE BUSTER
Jamaica, male vocalist (Cecil Campbell) — 16

Date	Title	Peak Position	Weeks at No.1	Weeks on Chart
23 Feb 67	**AL CAPONE** *Blue Beat BB 324*	18		13
4 Apr 98	**WHINE AND GRINE** *Island CID 691*	21		3

PRINCE CHARLES & THE CITY BEAT BAND
US, male vocalist/producer (Charles Alexander) & male/female vocal/instrumental group — 2

Date	Title	Peak Position	Weeks at No.1	Weeks on Chart
22 Feb 86	**WE CAN MAKE IT HAPPEN** *PRT 7P 348*	56		2

PRINCESS
UK, female vocalist (Desiree Heslop) — 44

Date	Title	Peak Position	Weeks at No.1	Weeks on Chart
3 Aug 85	**SAY I'M YOUR NO. 1** *Supreme SUPE 101*	7		12
9 Nov 85	**AFTER THE LOVE HAS GONE** *Supreme SUPE 103*	28		13
19 Apr 86	**I'LL KEEP ON LOVING YOU** *Supreme SUPE 105*	16		8
5 Jul 86	**TELL ME TOMORROW** *Supreme SUPE 106*	34		5
25 Oct 86	**IN THE HEAT OF A PASSIONATE MOMENT** *Supreme SUPE 109*	74		1
13 Jun 87	**RED HOT** *Polydor POSP 868*	58		5

PRINCESS IVORI
US, female rapper (Taryn Gresham) — 2

Date	Title	Peak Position	Weeks at No.1	Weeks on Chart
17 Mar 90	**WANTED** *Supreme SUPE 163*	69		2

PRINCESS SUPERSTAR
US, female vocalist/DJ (Concetta Kirschner) — 23

Date	Title	Peak Position	Weeks at No.1	Weeks on Chart
2 Mar 02	**BAD BABYSITTER** *Rapster/!K7 RR 007CDM*	11		7
27 Jan 07	**EXCEEDER** *Boss DATA150CDS* MASON VS PRINCESS SUPERSTAR	3		16

PRIVATE LIVES
UK, male vocal/instrumental duo — 4

Date	Title	Peak Position	Weeks at No.1	Weeks on Chart
11 Feb 84	**LIVING IN A WORLD (TURNED UPSIDE DOWN)** *EMI PRIV 2*	53		4

PRIZNA FEATURING DEMOLITION MAN
UK, male rap/production duo — 2

Date	Title	Peak Position	Weeks at No.1	Weeks on Chart
29 Apr 95	**FIRE** *Labello Blanco NLBCDX 18*	33		2

PJ PROBY
US, male vocalist (James Marcus Smith) — 91

Date	Title	Peak Position	Weeks at No.1	Weeks on Chart
28 May 64	**HOLD ME** *Decca F 11904*	3		15
3 Sep 64	**TOGETHER** *Decca F 11967*	8		11
10 Dec 64	**SOMEWHERE** *Liberty LIB 10182*	6		12
25 Feb 65	**I APOLOGISE** *Liberty LIB 10188*	11		8
8 Jul 65	**LET THE WATER RUN DOWN** *Liberty LIB 10206*	19		8
30 Sep 65	**THAT MEANS A LOT** *Liberty LIB 10215*	30		6
25 Nov 65	**MARIA** *Liberty LIB 10218*	8		9
10 Feb 66	**YOU'VE COME BACK** *Liberty LIB 10223*	25		7
16 Jun 66	**TO MAKE A BIG MAN CRY** *Liberty LIB 10236*	34		3
27 Oct 66	**I CAN'T MAKE IT ALONE** *Liberty LIB 10250*	37		5
6 Mar 68	**IT'S YOUR DAY TODAY** *Liberty LIB 15046*	32		5
28 Dec 96	**YESTERDAY HAS GONE** *EMI Premier CDPRESX 13* & MARC ALMOND FEATURING THE MY LIFE STORY ORCHESTRA	58		2

PROCLAIMERS
UK, male vocal/instrumental duo – Charlie & Craig Reid — 69

Date	Title	Peak Position	Weeks at No.1	Weeks on Chart
14 Nov 87	**LETTER FROM AMERICA** *Chrysalis CHS 3178* ●	3		10
5 Mar 88	**MAKE MY HEART FLY** *Chrysalis CLAIM 1*	63		3
27 Aug 88	**I'M GONNA BE (500 MILES)** *Chrysalis CLAIM 2*	11		11
12 Nov 88	**SUNSHINE ON LEITH** *Chrysalis CLAIM 3*	41		5
11 Feb 89	**I'M ON MY WAY** *Chrysalis CLAIM 4*	43		4
24 Nov 90	**KING OF THE ROAD (EP)** *Chrysalis CLAIM 5*	9		8
19 Feb 94	**LET'S GET MARRIED** *Chrysalis CDCLAIMS 6*	21		4
16 Apr 94	**WHAT MAKES YOU CRY** *Chrysalis CDCLAIMS 7*	38		3
22 Oct 94	**THESE ARMS OF MINE** *Chrysalis CDCLAIM 8*	51		2
24 Mar 07	**(I'M GONNA BE) 500 MILES** *EMI COMICCD01* FEATURING BRIAN POTTER & ANDY PIPKIN	1	3	10
24 Mar 07	**I'M GONNA BE (500 MILES)** *Chrysalis GBAYK8800055*	26		7
8 Sep 07	**LIFE WITH YOU** *W14 1742097*	58		2

PROCOL HARUM
UK, male vocal/instrumental group – Gary Brooker, Matthew Fisher, Bobby Harrison, David Knights, Keith Reid & Ray Royer (replaced by Robin Trower) — 56

Date	Title	Peak Position	Weeks at No.1	Weeks on Chart
25 May 67	**A WHITER SHADE OF PALE** *Deram DM 126*	1	6	15
4 Oct 67	**HOMBURG** *Regal Zonophone RZ 3003*	6		10
24 Apr 68	**QUITE RIGHTLY SO** *Regal Zonophone RZ 3007*	50		1
18 Jun 69	**SALTY DOG** *Regal Zonophone RZ 3109*	44		3
22 Apr 72	**A WHITER SHADE OF PALE** *Magnifly ECHO 10*	13		13
5 Aug 72	**CONQUISTADOR** *Chrysalis CHS 2003*	22		7
23 Aug 75	**PANDORA'S BOX** *Chrysalis CHS 2073*	16		7

PRODIGY
UK, male vocal/instrumental group – Liam Howlett, Keith Flint, Keith "Maxim" Palmer & Leeroy Thornhill — 194

Date	Title	Peak Position	Weeks at No.1	Weeks on Chart
24 Aug 91	**CHARLY** *XL Recordings XLS 21* ●	3		10
4 Jan 92	**EVERYBODY IN THE PLACE (EP)** *XL Recordings XLS 26*	2		9
26 Sep 92	**FIRE/JERICHO** *XL Recordings XLS 30*	11		4
21 Nov 92	**OUT OF SPACE/RUFF IN THE JUNGLE BIZNESS** *XL Recordings XLS 35* ●	5		12
17 Apr 93	**WIND IT UP (REWOUND)** *XL Recordings XLS 39CD*	11		7
16 Oct 93	**ONE LOVE** *XL Recordings XLS 47CD*	8		6
28 May 94	**NO GOOD (START THE DANCE)** *XL Recordings XLS 51CD*	4		12
24 Sep 94	**VOODOO PEOPLE** *XL Recordings XLS 54CD*	13		5
18 Mar 95	**POISON** *XL Recordings XLS 58CD*	15		6
30 Mar 96	**FIRESTARTER** *XL Recordings XLS 70CD* ●	1	3	19
20 Apr 96	**CHARLY** *XL Recordings XLS 21*	66		1
20 Apr 96	**FIRE/JERICHO** *XL Recordings XLS 30*	63		1
20 Apr 96	**NO GOOD (START THE DANCE)** *XL Recordings XLS 51CD*	57		2
20 Apr 96	**OUT OF SPACE/RUFF IN THE JUNGLE BIZNESS** *XL Recordings XLS 35*	52		2
20 Apr 96	**POISON** *XL Recordings XLS 58CD*	62		1
20 Apr 96	**VOODOO PEOPLE** *XL Recordings XLS 54CD*	75		1
20 Apr 96	**WIND IT UP (REWOUND)** *XL Recordings XLS 39CD*	71		1
27 Apr 96	**EVERYBODY IN THE PLACE (EP)** *XL Recordings XLS 26*	69		1
23 Nov 96	**BREATHE** *XL Recordings XLS 80CD* ⊛	1	2	17
14 Dec 96	**FIRESTARTER** *XL Recordings XLS 70CD*	53		11
29 Nov 97	**SMACK MY BITCH UP** *XL Recordings XLS 90CD*	8		10
13 Jul 02	**BABY'S GOT A TEMPER** *XL Recordings XLS 145CD*	5		6
11 Sep 04	**GIRLS** *XL Recordings XLS 195CD*	19		4
4 Dec 04	**CHARLY** *XL Recordings XLXV1506*	73		1
15 Oct 05	**VOODOO PEOPLE/OUT OF SPACE** *XL Recordings XLS219CD*	20		4
21 Feb 09	**OMEN** *Take Me To The Hospital HOSPCDS02*	4		19
7 Mar 09	**INVADERS MUST DIE** *Take Me To The Hospital GBCEJ0800437*	49		2
25 Apr 09	**WARRIOR'S DANCE** *Take Me To The Hospital HOSPCDS04*	13		17
12 Sep 09	**TAKE ME TO THE HOSPITAL** *Take Me To The Hospital HOSPCDS05*	38		2
12 Dec 09	**INVADERS MUST DIE** *Take Me To The Hospital GBCEJ0800437*	74		1

PROFESSIONALS
UK, male vocal/instrumental group — 4

Date	Title	Peak Position	Weeks at No.1	Weeks on Chart
11 Oct 80	**1-2-3-** *Virgin VS 376*	43		4

PROGRESS FUNK
Italy, male production trio — 1

Date	Title	Peak Position	Weeks at No.1	Weeks on Chart
11 Oct 97	**AROUND MY BRAIN** *Deconstruction 74321518182*	73		1

PROGRESS PRESENTS THE BOY WUNDA
UK, male DJ/producer (Robert Webster) — 10

Date	Title	Peak Position	Weeks at No.1	Weeks on Chart
18 Dec 99	**EVERYBODY** *Manifesto FESCD 65*	7		10

PROJECT FEATURING GERIDEAU
US, male producer (Jose Burgos) & male vocalist (Theo Gerideau) — 1

Date	Title	Peak Position	Weeks at No.1	Weeks on Chart
27 Aug 94	**BRING IT BACK 2 LUV** *Fruittree FTREE 10CD*	65		1

Silver-selling ● Gold-selling ● Platinum-selling (x multiples) US No.1 ★ Peak Position Weeks at No.1 Weeks on Chart

PROJECT 1

UK, male producer (Mark Williams) — 3

Date	Title	Peak Position	Weeks at No.1	Weeks on Chart
16 May 92	**ROUGHNECK (EP)** *Rising High RSN 22*	49		2
29 Aug 92	**DON GARGON COMIN'** *Rising High RSN 35*	64		1

PRONG

US, male vocal/instrumental trio — 1

Date	Title	Peak Position	Weeks at No.1	Weeks on Chart
25 Apr 92	**WHOSE FIST IS THIS ANYWAY EP** *Epic 6580026*	58		1

PROPAGANDA

Germany, male/female vocal/instrumental group — 35

Date	Title	Peak Position	Weeks at No.1	Weeks on Chart
17 Mar 84	**DR MABUSE** *ZTT ZTAS 2*	27		9
4 May 85	**DUEL** *ZTT ZTAS 8*	21		12
10 Aug 85	**P MACHINERY** *ZTT ZTAS 12*	50		5
28 Apr 90	**HEAVEN GIVE ME WORDS** *Virgin VS 1245*	36		5
8 Sep 90	**ONLY ONE WORD** *Virgin VS 1271*	71		4

PROPELLERHEADS

UK, male production/instrumental duo – Alex Gifford & Will White — 15

Date	Title	Peak Position	Weeks at No.1	Weeks on Chart
7 Dec 96	**TAKE CALIFORNIA** *Wall Of Sound WALLD 024*	69		1
17 May 97	**SPYBREAK!** *Wall Of Sound WALLD 029X*	40		1
18 Oct 97	**ON HER MAJESTY'S SECRET SERVICE** *East West EW 136CD* & DAVID ARNOLD	7		5
20 Dec 97	**HISTORY REPEATING** *Wall Of Sound WALLD 036* & SHIRLEY BASSEY	19		7
27 Jun 98	**BANG ON!** *Wall Of Sound WALLD 039*	53		1

PROPHETS OF SOUND

UK, male/instrumental/production duo — 2

Date	Title	Peak Position	Weeks at No.1	Weeks on Chart
14 Nov 98	**HIGH** *Distinctive DISNCD 47*	73		1
23 Feb 02	**NEW DAWN** *Ink NIBNE 10CD*	51		1

PROSPECT PARK/CAROLYN HARDING

UK, male/female vocal/production duo — 1

Date	Title	Peak Position	Weeks at No.1	Weeks on Chart
8 Aug 98	**MOVIN' ON** *AM:PM 5827312*	55		1

BRIAN PROTHEROE

UK, male vocalist — 6

Date	Title	Peak Position	Weeks at No.1	Weeks on Chart
7 Sep 74	**PINBALL** *Chrysalis CHS 2043*	22		6

PROTOCOL

UK, male vocal/instrumental group — 3

Date	Title	Peak Position	Weeks at No.1	Weeks on Chart
22 Oct 05	**SHE WAITS FOR ME** *Polydor 9871400*	65		1
4 Feb 06	**WHERE'S THE PLEASURE** *Polydor 9876559*	27		2

PROUD MARY

UK, male vocal/instrumental group — 1

Date	Title	Peak Position	Weeks at No.1	Weeks on Chart
25 Aug 01	**VERY BEST FRIEND** *Sour Mash JDNCSCD 004*	75		1

DOROTHY PROVINE

US, female actor/vocalist — 15

Date	Title	Peak Position	Weeks at No.1	Weeks on Chart
7 Dec 61	**DON'T BRING LULU** *Warner Brothers WB 53*	17		12
28 Jun 62	**CRAZY WORDS CRAZY TUNE** *Warner Brothers WB 70*	45		3

ERIC PRYDZ

Sweden, male DJ/producer — 49

Date	Title	Peak Position	Weeks at No.1	Weeks on Chart
21 Aug 04	**WOZ NOT WOZ** *C2 CDC2002* & STEVE ANGELLO	55		1
25 Sep 04	**CALL ON ME** *Data 68CDS*	1	5	25
13 Jan 07	**PROPER EDUCATION** *Data/Positiva DATA144CDS* VS FLOYD	2		10
6 Sep 08	**PJANOO** *Data DATA200CDS*	2		13

PSEUDO ECHO

Australia, male vocal/instrumental group – Brian Canham, Pierre Giglotti & James & Vince Dingli — 12

Date	Title	Peak Position	Weeks at No.1	Weeks on Chart
18 Jul 87	**FUNKY TOWN** *RCA PB 49705*	8		12

PSYCHEDELIC FURS

UK, male vocal/instrumental group — 31

Date	Title	Peak Position	Weeks at No.1	Weeks on Chart
2 May 81	**DUMB WAITERS** *CBS A 1166*	59		2
27 Jun 81	**PRETTY IN PINK** *CBS A 1327*	43		5
31 Jul 82	**LOVE MY WAY** *CBS A 2549*	42		6
31 Mar 84	**HEAVEN** *CBS A 4300*	29		6
16 Jun 84	**GHOST IN YOU** *CBS A 4470*	68		2
23 Aug 86	**PRETTY IN PINK** *CBS A 7242*	18		9
9 Jul 88	**ALL THAT MONEY WANTS** *CBS FURS 4*	75		1

PSYCHEDELIC WALTONS

UK, male production duo. See Soul II Soul — 3

Date	Title	Peak Position	Weeks at No.1	Weeks on Chart
19 Jan 02	**WONDERLAND** *Echo ECSCD 120* FEATURING ROISIN MURPHY	37		2
12 Apr 03	**PAYBACK TIME** *Sony Music 6737622* DYSFUNCTIONAL PSYCHEDELIC WALTONS	48		1

PSYCHIC TV

UK, male/female vocal/instrumental group — 4

Date	Title	Peak Position	Weeks at No.1	Weeks on Chart
26 Apr 86	**GODSTAR** *Temple TOPY 009*	67		2
20 Sep 86	**GOOD VIBRATIONS/ROMAN P** *Temple TOPY 23*	65		2

PUBLIC ANNOUNCEMENT

US, male vocal group — 5

Date	Title	Peak Position	Weeks at No.1	Weeks on Chart
9 May 92	**SHE'S GOT THAT VIBE** *Jive JIVET 292* R KELLY & PUBLIC ANNOUNCEMENT	57		2
20 Nov 93	**SEX ME** *Jive JIVECD 346* R KELLY & PUBLIC ANNOUNCEMENT	75		1
4 Jul 98	**BODY BUMPIN' (YIPPIE-YI-YO)** *A&M 5826972*	38		2

PUBLIC DEMAND

UK, male vocal group — 2

Date	Title	Peak Position	Weeks at No.1	Weeks on Chart
15 Feb 97	**INVISIBLE** *ZTT ZANG 85CD*	41		2

PUBLIC DOMAIN

UK, male vocal/production trio – James Allan, Alistair MacIssac & Mark Sherry — 18

Date	Title	Peak Position	Weeks at No.1	Weeks on Chart
2 Dec 00	**OPERATION BLADE (BASS IN THE PLACE)** *Xtravaganza X2H1 CDS* FEATURING CHUCK D ●	5		13
23 Jun 01	**ROCK DA FUNKY BEATS** *Xtrahard X2H3 CDS* FEATURING CHUCK D	19		3
12 Jan 02	**TOO MANY MC'S/LET ME CLEAR MY THROAT** *Xtrahard X2H 8CDS*	34		2

PUBLIC ENEMY

US, male rap/DJ group — 53

Date	Title	Peak Position	Weeks at No.1	Weeks on Chart
21 Nov 87	**REBEL WITHOUT A PAUSE** *Def Jam 6512457*	37		7
9 Jan 88	**BRING THE NOISE** *Def Jam 6513357*	32		5
2 Jul 88	**DON'T BELIEVE THE HYPE** *Def Jam 6528337*	18		5
15 Oct 88	**NIGHT OF THE LIVING BASEHEADS** *Def Jam 6530460*	63		2
24 Jun 89	**FIGHT THE POWER** *Motown ZB 42877*	29		5
20 Jan 90	**WELCOME TO THE TERRORDOME** *Def Jam 6554760*	18		4
7 Apr 90	**911 IS A JOKE** *Def Jam 6558377*	41		3
23 Jun 90	**BROTHERS GONNA WORK IT OUT** *Def Jam 6560181*	46		2
3 Nov 90	**CAN'T DO NUTTIN' FOR YA MAN** *Def Jam 6563857*	53		2
12 Oct 91	**CAN'T TRUSS IT** *Def Jam 6575307*	22		4
25 Jan 92	**SHUT 'EM DOWN** *Def Jam 6577617*	21		3
11 Apr 92	**NIGHTTRAIN** *Def Jam 6578647*	55		2
13 Aug 94	**GIVE IT UP** *Def Jam DEFCD1*	18		3
29 Jul 95	**SO WATCHA GONNA DO NOW** *Def Jam DEFCD5*	50		1
6 Jun 98	**HE GOT GAME** *Def Jam 5689852* FEATURING STEPHEN STILLS	16		4
25 Sep 99	**DO YOU WANNA GO OUR WAY???** *PIAS Recordings PIASX 005CDX*	66		1

PUBLIC IMAGE LTD

UK, male vocal/instrumental group – leader John Lydon*. See Sex Pistols — 61

Date	Title	Peak Position	Weeks at No.1	Weeks on Chart
21 Oct 78	**PUBLIC IMAGE** *Virgin VS 228*	9		8
7 Jul 79	**DEATH DISCO (PARTS 1 & 2)** *Virgin VS 274*	20		7
20 Oct 79	**MEMORIES** *Virgin VS 299*	60		2
4 Apr 81	**FLOWERS OF ROMANCE** *Virgin VS 397*	24		7
17 Sep 83	**THIS IS NOT A LOVE SONG** *Virgin VS 529*	5		10
19 May 84	**BAD LIFE** *Virgin VS 675*	71		2
1 Feb 86	**RISE** *Virgin VS 841*	11		8
3 May 86	**HOME** *Virgin VS 855*	75		1
22 Aug 87	**SEATTLE** *Virgin VS 988*	47		4
6 May 89	**DISAPPOINTED** *Virgin VS 1181*	38		5
20 Oct 90	**DON'T ASK ME** *Virgin VS 1231*	22		5

Silver-selling ○ Gold-selling ● Platinum-selling (x multiples) ㊉ US No.1 ★ Peak Position · Weeks at No.1 · Weeks on Chart

Date	Title / Label	Peak Position	Weeks at No.1	Weeks on Chart
22 Feb 92	**CRUEL** *Virgin VS 1390*	49		2

PUDDLE OF MUDD

US, male vocal/instrumental group – Wes Scantlin, Doug Ardito, Paul Phillips & Greg Upchurch — 22

Date	Title / Label	Peak Position	Weeks at No.1	Weeks on Chart
23 Feb 02	**CONTROL** *Geffen 4976822*	15		5
15 Jun 02	**BLURRY** *Geffen 4977352*	8		9
28 Sep 02	**SHE HATES ME** *Geffen 4978052*	14		7
13 Dec 03	**AWAY FROM ME** *Geffen 9814810*	55		1

PUDSEY'S BEAUTIFUL DREAMERS WITH THE TARTAN ARMY

UK, male/female vocal charity ensemble — 2

Date	Title / Label	Peak Position	Weeks at No.1	Weeks on Chart
22 Nov 08	**WE HAVE A DREAM** *Somnium Habemus SHSP24861*	40		2

TITO PUENTE Jr & THE LATIN RHYTHM FEATURING TITO PUENTE, INDIA & CALI ALEMAN

US, male/female vocal/instrumental group — 3

Date	Title / Label	Peak Position	Weeks at No.1	Weeks on Chart
16 Mar 96	**OYE COMO VA** *Media MCSTD 40013*	36		2
19 Jul 97	**OYE COMO VA (REMIX)** *Nukleuz MCSTD 40120*	56		1

PULP

UK, male/female vocal/instrumental group – Jarvis Cocker*, Nicholas Banks, Candida Doyle, Steve Mackey & Russell Senior (replaced by Mark Webber) — 74

Date	Title / Label	Peak Position	Weeks at No.1	Weeks on Chart
27 Nov 93	**LIP GLOSS** *Island CID 567*	50		2
2 Apr 94	**DO YOU REMEMBER THE FIRST TIME** *Island CID 574*	33		4
4 Jun 94	**THE SISTERS EP** *Island CID 595*	19		4
3 Jun 95	**COMMON PEOPLE** *Island CID 613* ○	2		13
7 Oct 95	**MIS-SHAPES/SORTED FOR ES & WIZZ** *Island CIDX 620* ○	2		11
9 Dec 95	**DISCO 2000** *Island CID 623* ○	7		11
6 Apr 96	**SOMETHING CHANGED** *Island CID 632*	10		7
7 Sep 96	**DO YOU REMEMBER THE FIRST TIME** *Island CID 574*	73		1
22 Nov 97	**HELP THE AGED** *Island CID 679*	8		9
28 Mar 98	**THIS IS HARDCORE** *Island CID 695*	12		4
20 Jun 98	**A LITTLE SOUL** *Island CID 708*	22		2
19 Sep 98	**PARTY HARD** *Island CID 719*	29		2
20 Oct 01	**THE TREES/SUNRISE** *Island CID 786*	23		2
27 Apr 02	**BAD COVER VERSION** *Island CIDX 794*	27		2

PULSE FEATURING ANTOINETTE ROBERSON

US, male/female vocal/production duo. See Boss — 3

Date	Title / Label	Peak Position	Weeks at No.1	Weeks on Chart
25 May 96	**THE LOVER THAT YOU ARE** *ffrr FCD 278*	22		3

PUNK CHIC

Sweden, male producer (Johan Strandkvist) — 1

Date	Title / Label	Peak Position	Weeks at No.1	Weeks on Chart
6 Oct 01	**DJ SPINNIN'** *WEA 333CD*	69		1

PUNX

Germany, male production trio — 1

Date	Title / Label	Peak Position	Weeks at No.1	Weeks on Chart
16 Nov 02	**THE ROCK** *Data 38CDS*	59		1

PURE REASON REVOLUTION

UK, male vocal/instrumental group — 2

Date	Title / Label	Peak Position	Weeks at No.1	Weeks on Chart
1 May 04	**APPRENTICE OF THE UNIVERSE** *Poptones MC5089SCD*	74		1
23 Apr 05	**THE BRIGHT AMBASSADORS OF MORNING** *Sony Music 6758072*	68		1

PURE SUGAR

UK, male/female vocal/instrumental trio — 1

Date	Title / Label	Peak Position	Weeks at No.1	Weeks on Chart
24 Oct 98	**DELICIOUS** *Geffen GFSTD 22355*	70		1

PURESSENCE

UK, male vocal/instrumental group — 7

Date	Title / Label	Peak Position	Weeks at No.1	Weeks on Chart
23 May 98	**THIS FEELING** *Island CID 688*	33		2
8 Aug 98	**IT DOESN'T MATTER ANYMORE** *Island CID 703*	47		1
21 Nov 98	**ALL I WANT** *Island CID 722*	39		2
5 Oct 02	**WALKING DEAD** *Island CIDX 803*	40		1
22 Sep 07	**DROP DOWN TO EARTH** *Reaction REACTRR002*	56		1

PURETONE

Australia, male producer (Josh Abrahams) — 17

Date	Title / Label	Peak Position	Weeks at No.1	Weeks on Chart
12 Jan 02	**ADDICTED TO BASS** *Gut GDGUS 6*	2		15
10 May 03	**STUCK IN A GROOVE** *Illustrious CDILL 014*	26		2

JAMES & BOBBY PURIFY

US, male vocal duo — 16

Date	Title / Label	Peak Position	Weeks at No.1	Weeks on Chart
24 Apr 76	**I'M YOUR PUPPET** *Mercury 6167 324*	12		10
7 Aug 76	**MORNING GLORY** *Mercury 6167 380*	27		6

PURPLE HEARTS

UK, male vocal/instrumental group — 5

Date	Title / Label	Peak Position	Weeks at No.1	Weeks on Chart
22 Sep 79	**MILLIONS LIKE US** *Fiction FICS 003*	57		3
8 Mar 80	**JIMMY** *Fiction FICS 9*	60		2

PURPLE KINGS

UK, male production duo — 3

Date	Title / Label	Peak Position	Weeks at No.1	Weeks on Chart
15 Oct 94	**THAT'S THE WAY YOU DO IT** *Positiva CDTIV 21*	26		3

PUSH

Belgium, male producer (Dirk Dierickx) — 19

Date	Title / Label	Peak Position	Weeks at No.1	Weeks on Chart
15 May 99	**UNIVERSAL NATION** *Inferno CDFERN 16*	36		2
9 Oct 99	**UNIVERSAL NATION (REMIX)** *Inferno CDFERN 20*	35		2
23 Sep 00	**TILL WE MEET AGAIN** *Inferno CDFERN 29*	46		1
12 May 01	**STRANGE WORLD** *Inferno CDFERN 38*	21		4
20 Oct 01	**PLEASE SAVE ME** *Five AM/Inferno FAMFERN 1CD* SUNSCREEM VS PUSH	36		2
3 Nov 01	**THE LEGACY** *Inferno CDFERN 43*	22		4
4 May 02	**TRANZY STATE OF MIND** *Inferno CDFERN 45*	31		2
5 Oct 02	**STRANGE WORLD/THE LEGACY** *Inferno CDFERN 49*	55		1
15 Mar 03	**UNIVERSAL NATION** *Inferno CDFERN 53*	54		1

PUSSY 2000

UK, male production duo — 1

Date	Title / Label	Peak Position	Weeks at No.1	Weeks on Chart
3 Nov 01	**IT'S GONNA BE ALRIGHT** *Ink NIBNE 9CD*	70		1

PUSSYCAT

Holland, male/female vocal instrumental group – Tonny Betty, Marianne Kowalczyk, Theo Coumans, John Theunissen, Theo Wetzels & Lou Wille — 30

Date	Title / Label	Peak Position	Weeks at No.1	Weeks on Chart
28 Aug 76	**MISSISSIPPI** *Sonet SON 2077* ●	1	4	22
25 Dec 76	**SMILE** *Sonet SON 2096*	24		8

PUSSYCAT DOLLS

US, female vocal group – Nicole Scherzinger*, Carmit Bachar, Ashley Roberts, Jessica Sutta, Melody Thornton & Kimberly Wyatt — 179

Date	Title / Label	Peak Position	Weeks at No.1	Weeks on Chart
10 Sep 05	**DON'T CHA (IMPORT)** *Polydor AMB000468322* FEATURING BUSTA RHYMES	44		1
17 Sep 05	**DON'T CHA** *A&M/Polydor 9885052* FEATURING BUSTA RHYMES ○	1	3	37
10 Dec 05	**STICKWITU** *A&M 9888583*	1	2	17
11 Mar 06	**BEEP** *A&M 9852860* FEATURING WILL.I.AM	2		11
1 Jul 06	**BUTTONS** *A&M 1700854* FEATURING SNOOP DOGG	3		16
30 Sep 06	**I DON'T NEED A MAN** *A&M/Polydor 1709094*	7		10
13 Sep 08	**WHEN I GROW UP** *Interscope 1783453*	3		17
8 Nov 08	**I HATE THIS PART** *Interscope 1791558*	12		19
7 Feb 09	**WHATCHA THINK ABOUT THAT** *Interscope 1799050* & MISSY ELLIOTT	9		12
28 Mar 09	**JAI HO! (YOU ARE MY DESTINY)** *Polydor USUM70954362* AR RAHMAN & PUSSYCAT DOLLS FEATURING NICOLE SCHERZINGER	3		22
13 Jun 09	**HUSH HUSH** *Interscope USUM70832594*	17		15
20 Mar 10	**JAI HO! (YOU ARE MY DESTINY)** *Polydor USUM70954362* AR RAHMAN & PUSSYCAT DOLLS FEATURING NICOLE SCHERZINGER	58		2+

PYRAMIDS

Jamaica, male vocal/instrumental group. See Symarip — 4

Date	Title / Label	Peak Position	Weeks at No.1	Weeks on Chart
22 Nov 67	**TRAIN TOUR TO RAINBOW CITY** *President PT 161*	35		4

PYTHON LEE JACKSON

Australia, male vocal/instrumental session group featuring Rod Stewart* — 12

Date	Title / Label	Peak Position	Weeks at No.1	Weeks on Chart
30 Sep 72	**IN A BROKEN DREAM** *Young Blood YB 1002*	3		12

BIOGRAPHIES

Biographies include the nationality and category for every chart entrant.

Each entrant has at least a mini biography. The acts with the most weeks on the chart (see page 372 for the chart) each have extended biographies.

Real names are included for all solo artists and, where applicable, dates of death and age of the artist at the time. "See..." links are included for soloists who also had singles chart entries in other acts.

The best known line-up is listed for every group that had a Top 10 single, with the vocalist/leader mentioned first and the others following in alphabetical order. In cases where later replacements had similar success both people are named and, where applicable, the dates of death are also shown for every group/duo member listed.

Certified Awards are given by the BPI to mark unit sales to retailers. They were introduced in April 1973. In January 1989 the levels of unit sales to the trade required to achieve each of the awards was amended to the following amounts:

Silver symbol	●	=	200,000 units
Gold symbol	●	=	400,000 units
Platinum symbol	⊛	=	600,000 units

As from February 2005, download sales also count towards certified awards.

Q–T

KEY TO ARTIST ENTRIES

Artist/Group Name — Artist/Group Biography — Silver-selling — Gold-selling — Platinum-selling — US No.1 — Peak Position — Weeks at No.1 — Weeks on Chart

Asterisks (*) indicate group members with hits in their own right that are listed elsewhere in this book

TAKE THAT

UK, male vocal group – Gary Barlow*, Howard Donald, Jason Orange, Mark Owen* & Robbie Williams* (left 1995, rejoined 2010). Comeback kings who have sold 7.4 million singles in the UK. The boys, who came back for good – as a quartet – in 2006, were the first act to score four successive No.1s since The Beatles – a feat they've achieved twice. See Helping Haiti

Artist's Total Weeks On Chart: 356

Date	Title / Label	Peak	Wks at No.1	Wks
23 Nov 91	**PROMISES** *RCA PB 45085*	38		2
8 Feb 92	**ONCE YOU'VE TASTED LOVE** *RCA PB 45257*	47		3
6 Jun 92	**IT ONLY TAKES A MINUTE** *RCA 74321101007*	7		8
15 Aug 92	**I FOUND HEAVEN** *RCA 74321108137*	15		6
10 Oct 92	**A MILLION LOVE SONGS** *RCA 74321116307*	7		9
12 Dec 92	**COULD IT BE MAGIC** *RCA 74321123137* ●	3		12
20 Feb 93	**WHY CAN'T I WAKE UP WITH YOU** *RCA 74321133102* ●	2		10
17 Jul 93	**PRAY** *RCA 74321154502* ●	1	4	11
9 Oct 93	**RELIGHT MY FIRE** *RCA 74321167722* FEATURING LULU ●	1	2	14
18 Dec 93	**BABE** *RCA 74321182122* ⊛	1	1	10
9 Apr 94	**EVERYTHING CHANGES** *RCA 74321167732* ●	1	2	10
9 Jul 94	**LOVE AIN'T HERE ANYMORE** *RCA 74321214832* ●	3		12
15 Oct 94	**SURE** *RCA 74321236622* ●	1	2	15
8 Apr 95	**BACK FOR GOOD** *RCA 74321271462* ⊛	1	4	13
5 Aug 95	**NEVER FORGET** *RCA 74321299572* ●	1	3	9
9 Mar 96	**HOW DEEP IS YOUR LOVE** *RCA 74321355592* ⊛	1	3	14
25 Nov 06	**PATIENCE** *Polydor 1714832* ●	1	4	39
10 Feb 07	**SHINE** *Polydor 1724294* ●	1	2	42
30 Jun 07	**I'D WAIT FOR LIFE** *Polydor 1736401*	17		2
27 Oct 07	**RULE THE WORLD** *Polydor 1746285* ●	2		66
6 Dec 08	**GREATEST DAY** *Polydor 1787445*	1	1	20
6 Dec 08	**PATIENCE** *Polydor 1714832*	59		1
6 Dec 08	**NEVER FORGET** *RCA GBARL9500200*	64		1
14 Feb 09	**UP ALL NIGHT** *Polydor 1796964*	14		11
13 Jun 09	**SAID IT ALL** *Polydor 2708717*	9		10
20 Jun 09	**RULE THE WORLD** *Polydor 1746285*	57		6
27 Jun 09	**GREATEST DAY** *Polydor 1787445*	73		1+

Date of entry into chart

Artist collaboration or variation on artist's name

Title of Single

Label and Catalogue Number

BPI Certified Award

A cross (+) indicates that the single was still on chart in the final week of March 2010

Q

UK, male producer (Mark Taylor)

Date	Title	Peak Position	Weeks at No.1	Weeks on Chart
				6
5 Jun 93	**GET HERE** *Arista 74321145972* FEATURING TRACY ACKERMAN	37		4
12 Mar 94	**(EVERYTHING I DO) I DO IT FOR YOU** *Bell 74321193062* FEATURING TONY JACKSON	47		2

QATTARA

UK, male production duo. See Alex Whitcombe & Big C

Date	Title	Peak Position	Weeks at No.1	Weeks on Chart
				2
15 Mar 97	**COME WITH ME** *Positiva CDTIV 71*	31		2

QB FINEST FEATURING NAS & BRAVEHEARTS

US, male rap group

Date	Title	Peak Position	Weeks at No.1	Weeks on Chart
				3
21 Apr 01	**OOCHIE WALLY** *Columbia 6710852*	30		3

Q-BASS

UK, male producer (Dan Donnelly)

Date	Title	Peak Position	Weeks at No.1	Weeks on Chart
				1
8 Feb 92	**HARDCORE WILL NEVER DIE** *Suburban Base SUBBASE 007*	64		1

Q-CLUB

Italy, male/female vocal/instrumental group

Date	Title	Peak Position	Weeks at No.1	Weeks on Chart
				3
6 Jan 96	**TELL IT TO MY HEART** *Manifesto FESCD 5*	28		3

QFX

UK, male/female vocal/instrumental/production group

Date	Title	Peak Position	Weeks at No.1	Weeks on Chart
				18
6 May 95	**FREEDOM (EP)** *Epidemic EPICD 004*	41		3
3 Feb 96	**EVERYTIME YOU TOUCH ME** *Epidemic EPICD 006*	22		4
3 Aug 96	**YOU GOT THE POWER** *Epidemic EPICD 007*	33		3
18 Jan 97	**FREEDOM 2** *Epidemic EPICD 008*	21		4
20 Mar 99	**SAY YOU'LL BE MINE** *Quality Recordings QUAL 005CD*	34		2
23 Aug 03	**FREEDOM** *Data 57CDS*	36		2

Q-TEE

UK, female rapper (Tatiana Mais)

Date	Title	Peak Position	Weeks at No.1	Weeks on Chart
				7
21 Apr 90	**AFRIKA** *SBK 7008* HISTORY FEATURING Q-TEE	42		5
10 Feb 96	**GIMME THAT BODY** *Heavenly HVN 48CD*	40		2

Q-TEX

UK, male/female production/vocal group

Date	Title	Peak Position	Weeks at No.1	Weeks on Chart
				7
9 Apr 94	**THE POWER OF LOVE** *Stoatin' VSCDG 1666*	65		1
26 Nov 94	**BELIEVE** *23rd Precinct THIRD 2CD*	41		2
15 Jun 96	**LET THE LOVE** *23rd Precinct THIRD 4CD*	30		2
30 Nov 96	**DO YOU WANT ME** *23rd Precinct THIRD 5CD*	48		1
28 Jun 97	**POWER OF LOVE '97 (REMIX)** *23rd Precinct THIRD 7CD*	49		1

Q-TIP

US, male rapper (John Davis). See Deee-Lite, A Tribe Called Quest

Date	Title	Peak Position	Weeks at No.1	Weeks on Chart
				23
4 Oct 97	**GOT 'TIL IT'S GONE** *Virgin VSCDG 1666* JANET FEATURING Q-TIP & JONI ○	6		9
19 Jun 99	**GET INVOLVED** *Hollywood 0101185 HWR* RAPHAEL SAADIQ & Q-TIP	36		2
22 Jan 00	**HOT BOYZ** *Elektra E 7002CD* MISSY MISDEMEANOR ELLIOTT FEATURING NAS, EVE & Q-TIP	18		3
12 Feb 00	**BREATHE AND STOP** *Arista 74321727062*	12		7
6 May 00	**VIVRANT THING** *Arista 74321751302*	39		2

QUAD CITY DJS

US, male rap duo

Date	Title	Peak Position	Weeks at No.1	Weeks on Chart
				1
15 Nov 97	**SPACE JAM** *Atlantic EW 773*	57		1

QUADROPHONIA

Belgium/Holland, male production duo

Date	Title	Peak Position	Weeks at No.1	Weeks on Chart
				15
13 Apr 91	**QUADROPHONIA** *ARS 6567687*	14		9
6 Jul 91	**THE WAVE OF THE FUTURE** *ARS 6569937*	40		3
21 Dec 91	**FIND THE TIME (PART ONE)** *ARS 6576260*	41		3

QUADS

UK, male vocal/instrumental group

Date	Title	Peak Position	Weeks at No.1	Weeks on Chart
				2
22 Sep 79	**THERE MUST BE THOUSANDS** *Big Bear BB 23*	66		2

QUAKE FEATURING MARCIA RAE

UK, male/female vocal/production trio. See Beat Renegades, Dream Frequency, Native, Red

Date	Title	Peak Position	Weeks at No.1	Weeks on Chart
				1
29 Aug 98	**THE DAY WILL COME** *ffrr FCD 344*	53		1

QUANTUM JUMP

UK, male vocal/instrumental group – Rupert Hine, Trevor Morris, John Parry & Mark Warner

Date	Title	Peak Position	Weeks at No.1	Weeks on Chart
				10
2 Jun 79	**THE LONE RANGER** *Electric WOT 33* ○	5		10

QUARTERFLASH

US, male/female vocal/instrumental group

Date	Title	Peak Position	Weeks at No.1	Weeks on Chart
				5
27 Feb 82	**HARDEN MY HEART** *Geffen GEF A 1838*	49		5

QUARTZ

UK, male production duo – Ronnie Herel & Dave Rawlings

Date	Title	Peak Position	Weeks at No.1	Weeks on Chart
				19
17 Mar 90	**WE'RE COMIN' AT YA** *Mercury ITMR 2* FEATURING STEPZ	65		2
2 Feb 91	**IT'S TOO LATE** *Mercury ITM 3* INTRODUCING DINA CARROLL	8		14
15 Jun 91	**NAKED LOVE (JUST SAY YOU WANT ME)** *Mercury ITM 4* & DINA CARROLL	39		3

JAKIE QUARTZ

France, female vocalist (Jacqueline Cuchet)

Date	Title	Peak Position	Weeks at No.1	Weeks on Chart
				3
11 Mar 89	**A LA VIE, A L'AMOUR** *PWL 30*	55		3

QUARTZ LOCK FEATURING LONNIE GORDON

UK/US, male/female vocal/instrumental/production trio

Date	Title	Peak Position	Weeks at No.1	Weeks on Chart
				2
7 Oct 95	**LOVE EVICTION** *X-Plode BANG 2CD*	32		2

SUZI QUATRO

US, female vocalist/guitarist (Suzy Quatrocchio)

Date	Title	Peak Position	Weeks at No.1	Weeks on Chart
				122
19 May 73	**CAN THE CAN** *RAK 150* ○	1	1	14
28 Jul 73	**48 CRASH** *RAK 158*	3		9
27 Oct 73	**DAYTONA DEMON** *RAK 161*	14		13
9 Feb 74	**DEVIL GATE DRIVE** *RAK 167* ●	1	2	11
29 Jun 74	**TOO BIG** *RAK 175*	14		6
9 Nov 74	**THE WILD ONE** *RAK 185*	7		10
8 Feb 75	**YOUR MAMA WON'T LIKE ME** *RAK 191*	31		5
5 Mar 77	**TEAR ME APART** *RAK 248*	27		6
18 Mar 78	**IF YOU CAN'T GIVE ME LOVE** *RAK 271* ○	4		13
22 Jul 78	**THE RACE IS ON** *RAK 278*	43		5
11 Nov 78	**STUMBLIN' IN** *RAK 285* & CHRIS NORMAN	41		8
20 Oct 79	**SHE'S IN LOVE WITH YOU** *RAK 299*	11		9
19 Jan 80	**MAMA'S BOY** *RAK 303*	34		5
5 Apr 80	**I'VE NEVER BEEN IN LOVE** *RAK 307*	56		3
25 Oct 80	**ROCK HARD** *Dreamland DLSP 6*	68		2
13 Nov 82	**HEART OF STONE** *Polydor POSP 477*	60		3

FINLEY QUAYE

UK, male vocalist/guitarist

Date	Title	Peak Position	Weeks at No.1	Weeks on Chart
				23
21 Jun 97	**SUNDAY SHINING** *Epic 6644552*	16		6
13 Sep 97	**EVEN AFTER ALL** *Epic 6649712*	10		5
29 Nov 97	**IT'S GREAT WHEN WE'RE TOGETHER** *Epic 6653382*	29		3
7 Mar 98	**YOUR LOVE GETS SWEETER** *Epic 6656065*	16		5
15 Aug 98	**ULTRA STIMULATION** *Epic 6660792*	51		1
23 Sep 00	**SPIRITUALIZED** *Epic 6698032*	26		3

Silver-selling ○ · Gold-selling ● · Platinum-selling (x multiples) ⊛ · US No.1 ★ · Peak Position · Weeks at No.1 · Weeks on Chart

QUEEN

UK, male vocal/instrumental group – Freddie Mercury*, d. 24 Nov 1991, John Deacon, Brian May* & Roger Taylor*. Legendary rock group and music video pioneers who were the first group to have No.1s in four successive decades (1970s-2000s). The epic 'Bohemian Rhapsody' was the first single to top the chart in four calendar years (1975, 1976, 1991 & 1992). They have sold 11.9 million singles in the UK **445**

Date	Title / Label	Peak Position	Weeks at No.1	Weeks on Chart
9 Mar 74	**SEVEN SEAS OF RHYE** *EMI 2121*	10		10
26 Oct 74	**KILLER QUEEN** *EMI 2229* ○	2		12
25 Jan 75	**NOW I'M HERE** *EMI 2256*	11		7
8 Nov 75	**BOHEMIAN RHAPSODY** *EMI 2375* ⊛	1	9	17
3 Jul 76	**YOU'RE MY BEST FRIEND** *EMI 2494*	7		8
27 Nov 76	**SOMEBODY TO LOVE** *EMI 2565*	2		9
19 Mar 77	**TIE YOUR MOTHER DOWN** *EMI 2593*	31		4
4 Jun 77	**QUEEN'S FIRST EP** *EMI 2623*	17		10
22 Oct 77	**WE ARE THE CHAMPIONS** *EMI 2708* ●	2		12
25 Feb 78	**SPREAD YOUR WINGS** *EMI 2757*	34		4
28 Oct 78	**BICYCLE RACE/FAT BOTTOMED GIRLS** *EMI 2870* ○	11		12
10 Feb 79	**DON'T STOP ME NOW** *EMI 2910* ○	9		12
14 Jul 79	**LOVE OF MY LIFE** *EMI 2959*	63		2
20 Oct 79	**CRAZY LITTLE THING CALLED LOVE** *EMI 5001* ● ★	2		14
2 Feb 80	**SAVE ME** *EMI 5022*	11		6
14 Jun 80	**PLAY THE GAME** *EMI 5076*	14		8
6 Sep 80	**ANOTHER ONE BITES THE DUST** *EMI 5102* ★	7		9
6 Dec 80	**FLASH** *EMI 5126* ○	10		13
14 Nov 81	**UNDER PRESSURE** *EMI 5250* & DAVID BOWIE ○	1	2	11
1 May 82	**BODY LANGUAGE** *EMI 5293*	25		6
12 Jun 82	**LAS PALABRAS DE AMOR** *EMI 5316*	17		8
21 Aug 82	**BACKCHAT** *EMI 5325*	40		4
4 Feb 84	**RADIO GA GA** *EMI QUEEN 1* ○	2		9
14 Apr 84	**I WANT TO BREAK FREE** *EMI QUEEN 2* ○	3		15
28 Jul 84	**IT'S A HARD LIFE** *EMI QUEEN 3*	6		9
22 Sep 84	**HAMMER TO FALL** *EMI QUEEN 4*	13		7
8 Dec 84	**THANK GOD IT'S CHRISTMAS** *EMI QUEEN 5*	21		6
16 Nov 85	**ONE VISION** *EMI QUEEN 6*	7		10
29 Mar 86	**A KIND OF MAGIC** *EMI QUEEN 7*	3		11
21 Jun 86	**FRIENDS WILL BE FRIENDS** *EMI QUEEN 8*	14		8
27 Sep 86	**WHO WANTS TO LIVE FOREVER** *EMI QUEEN 9*	24		5
13 May 89	**I WANT IT ALL** *Parlophone QUEEN 10* ○	3		7
1 Jul 89	**BREAKTHRU'** *Parlophone QUEEN 11*	7		7
19 Aug 89	**THE INVISIBLE MAN** *Parlophone QUEEN 12*	12		6
21 Oct 89	**SCANDAL** *Parlophone QUEEN 14*	25		4
9 Dec 89	**THE MIRACLE** *Parlophone QUEEN 15*	21		5
26 Jan 91	**INNUENDO** *Parlophone QUEEN 16* ○	1	1	6
16 Mar 91	**I'M GOING SLIGHTLY MAD** *Parlophone QUEEN 17*	22		5
25 May 91	**HEADLONG** *Parlophone QUEEN 18*	14		4
26 Oct 91	**THE SHOW MUST GO ON** *Parlophone QUEEN 19*	16		10
21 Dec 91	**BOHEMIAN RHAPSODY/THESE ARE THE DAYS OF OUR LIVES** *Parlophone QUEEN 20* ⊛	1	5	14
1 May 93	**FIVE LIVE EP** *Parlophone CDRS 6340* GEORGE MICHAEL & QUEEN WITH LISA STANSFIELD ●	1	3	12
4 Nov 95	**HEAVEN FOR EVERYONE** *Parlophone CDQUEEN 21* ○	2		12
23 Dec 95	**A WINTER'S TALE** *Parlophone CDQUEENS 22*	6		6
9 Mar 96	**TOO MUCH LOVE WILL KILL YOU** *Parlophone CDQUEEN 23*	15		6
29 Jun 96	**LET ME LIVE** *Parlophone CDQUEENS 24*	9		4
30 Nov 96	**YOU DON'T FOOL ME – THE REMIXES** *Parlophone CDQUEEN 25*	17		4
17 Jan 98	**NO-ONE BUT YOU/TIE YOUR MOTHER DOWN** *Parlophone CD QUEEN 27*	13		4
14 Nov 98	**ANOTHER ONE BITES THE DUST** *DreamWorks DRMCD 22364* WITH WYCLEF JEAN FEATURING PRAS MICHEL/FREE	5		6
18 Dec 99	**UNDER PRESSURE (REMIX)** *Parlophone CDQUEEN 28* & DAVID BOWIE	14		7
29 Jul 00	**WE WILL ROCK YOU** *RCA 74321774022* FIVE & QUEEN	1	1	13
29 Mar 03	**FLASH** *Nebula NEBCD 041* & VANGUARD	15		4
23 Dec 06	**ANOTHER ONE BITES THE DUST** *Positiva CDTIVS250* VS THE MIAMI PROJECT	31		4
12 Apr 08	**DON'T STOP ME NOW** *Parlophone GBCEE9300011*	47		13
20 Sep 08	**C-LEBRITY** *Parlophone 2370102* & PAUL RODGERS	33		1
28 Nov 09	**WHO WANTS TO LIVE FOREVER** *EMI GBCEE8600010*	63		1
26 Dec 09	**BOHEMIAN RHAPSODY** *Walt Disney USWD10937466* & THE MUPPETS	32		2

Top 3 Best-Selling Singles

		Approximate Sales
1	BOHEMIAN RHAPSODY	2,290,000
2	WE ARE THE CHAMPIONS	760,000
3	UNDER PRESSURE	700,000

QUEEN LATIFAH

US, female rapper/vocalist/actor (Dana Owens) **17**

Date	Title / Label	Peak Position	Weeks at No.1	Weeks on Chart
24 Mar 90	**MAMA GAVE BIRTH TO THE SOUL CHILDREN** *Gee Street GEE 26* + DE LA SOUL	14		7
26 May 90	**FIND A WAY** *Ahead Of Our Time CCUT 8* COLDCUT FEATURING QUEEN LATIFAH	52		2
31 Aug 91	**FLY GIRL** *Gee Street GEE 34*	67		1
26 Jun 93	**WHAT'CHA GONNA DO** *Epic 6593072* SHABBA RANKS FEATURING QUEEN LATIFAH	21		4
26 Mar 94	**U.N.I.T.Y.** *Motown TMGCD 1422*	74		1
12 Apr 97	**MR BIG STUFF** *Motown 5736572* QUEEN LATIFAH, SHADES & FREE	31		2

QUEEN PEN

US, female rapper (Lynise Walters) **10**

Date	Title / Label	Peak Position	Weeks at No.1	Weeks on Chart
7 Mar 98	**MAN BEHIND THE MUSIC** *Interscope IND 95562*	38		2
9 May 98	**ALL MY LOVE** *Interscope IND 95584* FEATURING ERIC WILLIAMS	11		5
5 Sep 98	**IT'S TRUE** *Interscope IND 95597*	24		3

QUEENS OF THE STONE AGE

US, male vocal/instrumental group **22**

Date	Title / Label	Peak Position	Weeks at No.1	Weeks on Chart
26 Aug 00	**THE LOST ART OF KEEPING A SECRET** *Interscope 4973922*	31		2
16 Nov 02	**NO ONE KNOWS** *Interscope 4978122*	15		7
19 Apr 03	**GO WITH THE FLOW** *Interscope 4978702*	21		3
30 Aug 03	**FIRST IT GIVETH** *Interscope 9810505*	33		2
26 Mar 05	**LITTLE SISTER** *Interscope 9880670*	18		5
23 Jul 05	**IN MY HEAD** *Interscope 9883541*	44		1
16 Jun 07	**3'S & 7'S** *Interscope 1735379*	19		2

QUEENSRYCHE

US, male vocal/instrumental group **21**

Date	Title / Label	Peak Position	Weeks at No.1	Weeks on Chart
13 May 89	**EYES OF A STRANGER** *EMI USA MT 65*	59		1
10 Nov 90	**EMPIRE** *EMI USA MT 90*	61		1
20 Apr 91	**SILENT LUCIDITY** *EMI USA MT 94*	34		5
6 Jul 91	**BEST I CAN** *EMI USA MT 97*	36		3
7 Sep 91	**JET CITY WOMAN** *EMI USA MT 98*	39		2
8 Aug 92	**SILENT LUCIDITY** *EMI USA MT 104*	18		4
28 Jan 95	**I AM I** *EMI CDMT 109*	40		2
25 Mar 95	**BRIDGE** *EMI CDMTS 111*	40		3

QUENCH

Australia, male instrumental/production duo **1**

Date	Title / Label	Peak Position	Weeks at No.1	Weeks on Chart
17 Feb 96	**DREAMS** *Infectious INFECT 3CD*	75		1

QUENTIN & ASH

UK, female actors/vocal duo **3**

Date	Title / Label	Peak Position	Weeks at No.1	Weeks on Chart
6 Jul 96	**TELL HIM** *East West EW 049CD*	25		3

? (QUESTION MARK) & THE MYSTERIANS

US, male vocal/instrumental group **4**

Date	Title / Label	Peak Position	Weeks at No.1	Weeks on Chart
17 Nov 66	**96 TEARS** *Cameo Parkway C 428* ★	37		4

QUESTIONS

UK, male/female vocal/instrumental group **8**

Date	Title / Label	Peak Position	Weeks at No.1	Weeks on Chart
23 Apr 83	**PRICE YOU PAY** *Respond KOB 702*	56		3
17 Sep 83	**TEAR SOUP** *Respond KOB 705*	66		1
10 Mar 84	**TUESDAY SUNSHINE** *Respond KOB 707*	46		4

QUICK

UK, male vocal/instrumental duo **7**

Date	Title / Label	Peak Position	Weeks at No.1	Weeks on Chart
15 May 82	**RHYTHM OF THE JUNGLE** *Epic EPC A 2013*	41		7

TOMMY QUICKLY & THE REMO FOUR

UK, male vocalist (Tommy Quigley) **8**

Date	Title / Label	Peak Position	Weeks at No.1	Weeks on Chart
22 Oct 64	**WILD SIDE OF LIFE** *Pye 7N 15708*	33		8

QUIET FIVE

UK, male vocal/instrumental group **3**

Date	Title / Label	Peak Position	Weeks at No.1	Weeks on Chart
13 May 65	**WHEN THE MORNING SUN DRIES THE DEW** *Parlophone R 5273*	45		1

Silver-selling ● Gold-selling ● Platinum-selling (x multiples) ⊛ US No.1 ★ | Peak Position | Weeks at No.1 | Weeks on Chart

Date	Title	Label	Peak Position	Weeks at No.1	Weeks on Chart
21 Apr 66	**HOMEWARD BOUND**	*Parlophone R 5421*	44		2

QUIET RIOT
US, male vocal/instrumental group — **5**

Date	Title	Label	Peak Position	Weeks at No.1	Weeks on Chart
3 Dec 83	**METAL HEALTH/CUM ON FEEL THE NOIZE**	*Epic A 3968*	45		5

EIMEAR QUINN
Ireland, female vocalist — **2**

Date	Title	Label	Peak Position	Weeks at No.1	Weeks on Chart
15 Jun 96	**THE VOICE**	*Polydor 5768842*	40		2

PAUL QUINN & EDWYN COLLINS
UK, male vocal/instrumental duo — **2**

Date	Title	Label	Peak Position	Weeks at No.1	Weeks on Chart
11 Aug 84	**PALE BLUE EYES**	*Swamplands SWP 1*	72		2

SINEAD QUINN
UK, female vocalist — **15**

Date	Title	Label	Peak Position	Weeks at No.1	Weeks on Chart
22 Feb 03	**I CAN'T BREAK DOWN**	*Mercury 0637282*	2		12
12 Jul 03	**WHAT YOU NEED IS**	*Fontana 9808972*	19		3

QUIREBOYS
UK, male vocal/instrumental group — **27**

Date	Title	Label	Peak Position	Weeks at No.1	Weeks on Chart
4 Nov 89	**7 O'CLOCK**	*Parlophone R 6230*	36		4
6 Jan 90	**HEY YOU**	*Parlophone R 6241*	14		7
7 Apr 90	**I DON'T LOVE YOU ANYMORE**	*Parlophone R 6248*	24		6
8 Sep 90	**THERE SHE GOES AGAIN/MISLED**	*Parlophone R 6267*	37		4
10 Oct 92	**TRAMPS AND THIEVES**	*Parlophone R 6323*	41		3
20 Feb 93	**BROTHER LOUIE**	*Parlophone CDR 6335*	32		3

QUIVVER
UK, male producer (John Graham). See Tilt — **3**

Date	Title	Label	Peak Position	Weeks at No.1	Weeks on Chart
5 Mar 94	**SAXY LADY**	*A&M 5805152*	56		2
18 Nov 95	**BELIEVE IN ME**	*Perfecto PERF 111CD*	56		1

QUO VADIS
UK, male production trio — **1**

Date	Title	Label	Peak Position	Weeks at No.1	Weeks on Chart
16 Dec 00	**SONIC BOOM (LIFE'S TOO SHORT)**	*Serious SERR 028CD*	49		1

QWILO & FELIX DA HOUSECAT
US, male DJ/production duo — **1**

Date	Title	Label	Peak Position	Weeks at No.1	Weeks on Chart
6 Sep 97	**DIRTY MOTHA**	*Manifesto FESCD 29*	66		1

EDDIE RABBITT
US, male vocalist/guitarist, d. 7 May 1998 (age 56) — **14**

Date	Title	Label	Peak Position	Weeks at No.1	Weeks on Chart
27 Jan 79	**EVERY WHICH WAY BUT LOOSE**	*Elektra K 12331*	41		9
28 Feb 81	**I LOVE A RAINY NIGHT**	*Elektra K 12498* ★	53		5

STEVE RACE
UK, male pianist, d. 22 Jun 2009 (age 88) — **9**

Date	Title	Label	Peak Position	Weeks at No.1	Weeks on Chart
28 Feb 63	**PIED PIPER (THE BEEJE)**	*Parlophone R 4981*	29		9

RACEY
UK, male vocal/instrumental group – Phil Fursdon, Richard Gower, Peter Miller & Clive Wilson — **44**

Date	Title	Label	Peak Position	Weeks at No.1	Weeks on Chart
25 Nov 78	**LAY YOUR LOVE ON ME**	*RAK 284* ●	3		14
31 Mar 79	**SOME GIRLS**	*RAK 291* ●	2		11
18 Aug 79	**BOY OH BOY**	*RAK 297*	22		9
20 Dec 80	**RUNAROUND SUE**	*RAK 325*	13		10

RACING CARS
UK, male vocal/instrumental group — **7**

Date	Title	Label	Peak Position	Weeks at No.1	Weeks on Chart
12 Feb 77	**THEY SHOOT HORSES DON'T THEY**	*Chrysalis CHS 2129*	14		7

RACONTEURS
US, male vocal/instrumental group – Jack White* (John Gillis), Brendan Benson*, Patrick Keeler & Jack Lawrence — **20**

Date	Title	Label	Peak Position	Weeks at No.1	Weeks on Chart
6 May 06	**STEADY AS SHE GOES**	*XL Recordings XLS229CD*	4		16
12 Aug 06	**HANDS**	*XL Recordings XLS236CD*	29		2
4 Nov 06	**BROKEN BOY SOLDIER**	*XL Recordings XLS248CD*	22		2

JIMMY RADCLIFFE
US, male vocalist, d. 27 Jul 1973 (age 36) — **2**

Date	Title	Label	Peak Position	Weeks at No.1	Weeks on Chart
4 Feb 65	**LONG AFTER TONIGHT IS ALL OVER**	*Stateside SS 374*	40		2

RADHA KRISHNA TEMPLE
UK, male/female vocal/instrumental group — **17**

Date	Title	Label	Peak Position	Weeks at No.1	Weeks on Chart
13 Sep 69	**HARE KRISHNA MANTRA**	*Apple 15*	12		9
28 Mar 70	**GOVINDA**	*Apple 25*	23		8

RADICAL ROB
UK, male producer (Rob McLuhan) — **1**

Date	Title	Label	Peak Position	Weeks at No.1	Weeks on Chart
11 Jan 92	**MONKEY WAH**	*R&S RSUK 8*	67		1

RADIO 4
US, male vocal/instrumental group — **2**

Date	Title	Label	Peak Position	Weeks at No.1	Weeks on Chart
24 Jul 04	**PARTY CRASHERS**	*City Slang 5494920*	75		1
18 Sep 04	**ABSOLUTE AFFIRMATION**	*Labels 5498032*	61		1

RADIO HEART FEATURING GARY NUMAN
UK, male instrumental duo & male vocalist — **8**

Date	Title	Label	Peak Position	Weeks at No.1	Weeks on Chart
28 Mar 87	**RADIO HEART**	*GFM 109*	35		6
13 Jun 87	**LONDON TIMES**	*GFM 112*	48		2

RADIO STARS
UK, male vocal/instrumental group — **3**

Date	Title	Label	Peak Position	Weeks at No.1	Weeks on Chart
4 Feb 78	**NERVOUS WRECK**	*Chiswick NS 23*	39		3

RADIOHEAD
UK, male vocal/instrumental group – Thom Yorke, Colin & Jonny Greenwood, Ed O'Brien & Phil Selway — **72**

Date	Title	Label	Peak Position	Weeks at No.1	Weeks on Chart
13 Feb 93	**ANYONE CAN PLAY GUITAR**	*Parlophone CDR 6333*	32		2
22 May 93	**POP IS DEAD**	*Parlophone CDR 6345*	42		2
18 Sep 93	**CREEP**	*Parlophone CDR 6359*	7		6
8 Oct 94	**MY IRON LUNG**	*Parlophone CDR 6394*	24		2
11 Mar 95	**HIGH AND DRY/PLANET TELEX**	*Parlophone CDRS 6405*	17		4
27 May 95	**FAKE PLASTIC TREES**	*Parlophone CDR 6411*	20		4
2 Sep 95	**JUST**	*Parlophone CDR 6415*	19		3
3 Feb 96	**STREET SPIRIT (FADE OUT)**	*Parlophone CDRS 6419*	5		4
7 Jun 97	**PARANOID ANDROID**	*Parlophone CDODATA 01*	3		5
6 Sep 97	**KARMA POLICE**	*Parlophone CDODATAS 03*	8		4
24 Jan 98	**NO SURPRISES**	*Parlophone CDODATAS 04*	4		7
2 Jun 01	**PYRAMID SONG**	*Parlophone CDSFHEIT 45102*	5		5
18 Aug 01	**KNIVES OUT**	*Parlophone CDFEIT 45103*	13		4
7 Jun 03	**THERE THERE**	*Parlophone CDR 6608*	4		4
30 Aug 03	**GO TO SLEEP**	*Parlophone CDRS 6613*	12		4
29 Nov 03	**2 + 2 = 5**	*Parlophone CDRS 6623*	15		3
26 Jan 08	**JIGSAW FALLING INTO PLACE**	*XL Recordings XLS326CD*	30		2
12 Apr 08	**NUDE**	*XL Recordings XLS350CD*	21		2
14 Jun 08	**CREEP**	*Parlophone CDR 6359*	37		4
4 Oct 08	**RECKONER**	*Warner/Chappell GBSTK0700007*	74		1

RADISH
US, male vocal/instrumental group — **3**

Date	Title	Label	Peak Position	Weeks at No.1	Weeks on Chart
30 Aug 97	**LITTLE PINK STARS**	*Mercury MERCD 494*	32		2
15 Nov 97	**SIMPLE SINCERITY**	*Mercury MERCD 498*	50		1

CORINNE BAILEY RAE
UK, female vocalist/guitarist (Corinne Bailey) — **29**

Date	Title	Label	Peak Position	Weeks at No.1	Weeks on Chart
19 Nov 05	**LIKE A STAR**	*EMI CDEM678*	34		4
4 Mar 06	**PUT YOUR RECORDS ON**	*Good Groove/EMI CDEM683*	2		19
10 Jun 06	**TROUBLE SLEEPING**	*Good Groove/EMI CDEM692*	40		2
14 Oct 06	**LIKE A STAR**	*EMI CDEM710*	32		4

Silver-selling ● Gold-selling ● Platinum-selling (× multiples) ★ US No.1 | Peak Position · Weeks at No.1 · Weeks on Chart

FONDA RAE
US, female vocalist — 4

Date	Title / Label	Peak Position	Weeks at No.1	Weeks on Chart
6 Oct 84	**TUCH ME** *Streetwave KHAN 28*	49		4

JESSE RAE
UK, male vocalist — 2

Date	Title / Label	Peak Position	Weeks at No.1	Weeks on Chart
11 May 85	**OVER THE SEA** *Scotland Video YZ 36*	65		2

RAE & CHRISTIAN FEATURING VEBA
UK, male/female vocal/production trio — 1

Date	Title / Label	Peak Position	Weeks at No.1	Weeks on Chart
6 Mar 99	**ALL I ASK** *Grand Central GCD 120*	67		1

RAF
Italy, male producer (Mauro Picotto). See CRW — 6

Date	Title / Label	Peak Position	Weeks at No.1	Weeks on Chart
14 Mar 92	**WE'VE GOT TO LIVE TOGETHER** *PWL Continental PWL 218*	34		3
5 Mar 94	**TAKE ME HIGHER** *Media MRLCD 0012*	71		1
23 Mar 96	**TAKE ME HIGHER (REMIX)** *Media MCSTD 40026*	59		1
27 Jul 96	**ANGEL'S SYMPHONY** *Media MCSTD 40051*	73		1

GERRY RAFFERTY
UK, male vocalist/guitarist. See Stealers Wheel — 47

Date	Title / Label	Peak Position	Weeks at No.1	Weeks on Chart
18 Feb 78	**BAKER STREET** *United Artists UP 36346* ●	3		15
26 May 79	**NIGHT OWL** *United Artists UP 36512* ●	5		13
18 Aug 79	**GET IT RIGHT NEXT TIME** *United Artists BP 301*	30		9
22 Mar 80	**BRING IT ALL HOME** *United Artists BP 340*	54		4

Top 50 Catalogue Downloads

Titles that originally charted prior to the launch of the Official Download Chart in September 2004.

Pos	Title	Artist	Original Charting Year
1	**KILLING IN THE NAME**	RAGE AGAINST THE MACHINE	1993
2	**DON'T STOP BELIEVIN'**	JOURNEY	1982
3	**FAIRYTALE OF NEW YORK**	POGUES FT KIRSTY MACCOLL	1987
4	**ALL I WANT FOR CHRISTMAS IS YOU**	MARIAH CAREY	1994
5	**MAN IN THE MIRROR**	MICHAEL JACKSON	1988
6	**I DON'T WANT TO MISS A THING**	AEROSMITH	1998
7	**DON'T STOP ME NOW**	QUEEN	1979
8	**SWEET CHILD O' MINE**	GUNS N' ROSES	1988
9	**EYE OF THE TIGER**	SURVIVOR	1982
10	**LIVIN' ON A PRAYER**	BON JOVI	1986
11	**BILLIE JEAN**	MICHAEL JACKSON	1983
12	**THRILLER**	MICHAEL JACKSON	1983
13	**IRIS**	GOO GOO DOLLS	1998
14	**RUN**	SNOW PATROL	2004
15	**IN THE AIR TONIGHT**	PHIL COLLINS	1981
16	**I'M GONNA BE (500 MILES)**	PROCLAIMERS	1988
17	**SMELLS LIKE TEEN SPIRIT**	NIRVANA	1991
18	**YOU GOT THE LOVE**	SOURCE FT CANDI STATON	1991
19	**HEAVEN**	DJ SAMMY & YANOU FT DO	2002
20	**LOSE YOURSELF**	EMINEM	2002
21	**WONDERWALL**	OASIS	1995
22	**SWEET HOME ALABAMA**	LYNYRD SKYNYRD	1974*
23	**SUMMER OF '69**	BRYAN ADAMS	1985
24	**INSOMNIA**	FAITHLESS	1995
25	**BITTER SWEET SYMPHONY**	VERVE	1997
26	**ANGELS**	ROBBIE WILLIAMS	1997
27	**WITH OR WITHOUT YOU**	U2	1987
28	**SOMEBODY TOLD ME**	KILLERS	2004
29	**9 TO 5**	DOLLY PARTON	1981
30	**SMOOTH CRIMINAL**	MICHAEL JACKSON	1988
31	**BEAT IT**	MICHAEL JACKSON	1983
32	**BOHEMIAN RHAPSODY**	QUEEN	1975
33	**HERO**	ENRIQUE IGLESIAS	2002
34	**7 NATION ARMY**	WHITE STRIPES	2003
35	**LAST CHRISTMAS**	WHAM!	1984
36	**TIME OF YOUR LIFE (GOOD RIDDANCE)**	GREEN DAY	1998
37	**JUMP AROUND**	HOUSE OF PAIN	1992
38	**U CAN'T TOUCH THIS**	MC HAMMER	1990
39	**CRAZY IN LOVE**	BEYONCE	2003
40	**WHERE IS THE LOVE**	BLACK EYED PEAS	2003
41	**DANCE WITH MY FATHER**	LUTHER VANDROSS	2004
42	**(EVERYTHING I DO) I DO IT FOR YOU**	BRYAN ADAMS	1991
43	**IN DA CLUB**	50 CENT	2003
44	**FAST CAR**	TRACY CHAPMAN	1988
45	**TEARDROP**	MASSIVE ATTACK	1998
46	**YEAH**	USHER FT LIL' JON & LUDACRIS	2004
47	**YELLOW**	COLDPLAY	2000
48	**I WANT YOU BACK**	JACKSON 5	1970
49	**SUPERSTITION**	STEVIE WONDER	1973
50	**PAINT IT, BLACK**	ROLLING STONES	1966

* Never charted in the UK before 2004. However, was a US hit in 1974

Date	Title / Label	Peak	Wks at No.1	Wks on Chart
21 Jun 80	**ROYAL MILE** *United Artists BP 354*	67		2
10 Mar 90	**BAKER STREET (REMIX)** *EMI EM 132*	53		4

RAGE
UK, male production duo – Barry Leng & Duncan Hannant – with male vocalist Tony Jackson

15

Date	Title / Label	Peak	Wks at No.1	Wks on Chart
31 Oct 92	**RUN TO YOU** *Pulse 8 LOSE 33*	3		11
27 Feb 93	**WHY DON'T YOU** *Pulse 8 CDLOSE 39*	44		2
15 May 93	**HOUSE OF THE RISING SUN** *Pulse 8 CDLOSE 43*	41		2

RAGE AGAINST THE MACHINE
US, male vocal/instrumental group – Zack de la Rocha, Tim Commerford, Tom Morello & Brad Wilk

22

Date	Title / Label	Peak	Wks at No.1	Wks on Chart
27 Feb 93	**KILLING IN THE NAME** *Epic 6584922*	25		4
8 May 93	**BULLET IN THE HEAD** *Epic 6592582*	16		4
4 Sep 93	**BOMBTRACK** *Epic 6594712*	37		2
13 Apr 96	**BULLS ON PARADE** *Epic 6631522*	8		3
7 Sep 96	**PEOPLE OF THE SUN** *Epic 6636282*	26		2
6 Nov 99	**GUERRILLA RADIO** *Epic 6683142*	32		2
15 Apr 00	**SLEEP NOW IN THE FIRE** *Epic 6691362*	43		2
26 Dec 09	**KILLING IN THE NAME** *Epic 6584922*	1	1	3

RAGGA TWINS
UK, male vocal duo

10

Date	Title / Label	Peak	Wks at No.1	Wks on Chart
10 Nov 90	**ILLEGAL GUNSHOT/SPLIFFHEAD** *Shut Up And Dance SUAD 7*	51		2
6 Apr 91	**WIPE THE NEEDLE/JUGGLING** *Shut Up And Dance SUAD 12S*	71		2
6 Jul 91	**HOOLIGAN 69** *Shut Up And Dance SUAD 16S*	56		2
7 Mar 92	**MIXED TRUTH/BRING UP THE MIC SOME MORE** *Shut Up And Dance SUAD 27S*	65		2
11 Jul 92	**SHINE EYE** *Shut Up And Dance SUAD 32S* FEATURING JUNIOR REID	63		2

RAGHAV
Canada, male vocalist (Raghav Mathur)

37

Date	Title / Label	Peak	Wks at No.1	Wks on Chart
24 Jan 04	**SO CONFUSED** *2PSL 2PSLCD02* 2PLAY FEATURING RAGHAV & JUCXI	6		13
22 May 04	**IT CAN'T BE RIGHT** *2PSL/inferno 2PSLCD04* 2PLAY FEATURING RAGHAV & NAILA BOSS	8		7
28 Feb 04	**CAN'T GET ENOUGH** *A&R ANR1CDS*	10		8
4 Sep 04	**LET'S WORK IT OUT** *V2 ARV5028628* FEATURING JAHAZIEL	15		3
19 Feb 05	**ANGEL EYES** *A&R/V2 ARV5028638*	7		6

RAGING SPEEDHORN
UK, male vocal/instrumental group

2

Date	Title / Label	Peak	Wks at No.1	Wks on Chart
16 Jun 01	**THE GUSH** *ZTT GIR004CD*	47		1
6 Jul 02	**THE HATE SONG** *ZTT RSH001CD*	69		1

RAGTIMERS
UK, male instrumental session group

8

Date	Title / Label	Peak	Wks at No.1	Wks on Chart
16 Mar 74	**THE STING** *Pye 7N 45323*	31		8

RAH BAND
UK, male/female instrumental session group formed by Richard A. Hewson. See Key West featuring Erik

50

Date	Title / Label	Peak	Wks at No.1	Wks on Chart
9 Jul 77	**THE CRUNCH** *Good Earth GD 7*	6		12
1 Nov 80	**FALCON** *DJM DJS 10954*	35		7
7 Feb 81	**SLIDE** *DJM DJS 10964*	50		7
1 May 82	**PERFUMED GARDEN** *KR 5*	45		7
9 Jul 83	**MESSAGES FROM THE STARS** *TMT 5*	42		5
19 Jan 85	**ARE YOU SATISFIED? (FUNKA NOVA)** *RCA 470*	70		2
30 Mar 85	**CLOUDS ACROSS THE MOON** *RCA PB 40025*	6		10

AR RAHMAN & PUSSYCAT DOLLS FEATURING NICOLE SCHERZINGER
India/US, male/female vocal/production group

24

Date	Title / Label	Peak	Wks at No.1	Wks on Chart
28 Mar 09	**JAI HO! (YOU ARE MY DESTINY)** *Polydor USUM70954362*	3		22
20 Mar 10	**JAI HO! (YOU ARE MY DESTINY)** *Polydor USUM70954362*	58		2+

RAILWAY CHILDREN
UK, male vocal/instrumental group

13

Date	Title / Label	Peak	Wks at No.1	Wks on Chart
24 Mar 90	**EVERY BEAT OF THE HEART** *Virgin VS 1237*	68		2
2 Jun 90	**MUSIC STOP** *Virgin VS 1255*	66		2
20 Oct 90	**SO RIGHT** *Virgin VS 1289*	68		1
2 Feb 91	**EVERY BEAT OF THE HEART** *Virgin VS 1237*	24		6
20 Apr 91	**SOMETHING SO GOOD** *Virgin VS 1318*	57		2

RAIN BAND
UK, male vocal/instrumental group

2

Date	Title / Label	Peak	Wks at No.1	Wks on Chart
1 Mar 03	**EASY RIDER** *Temptation TEMPTCD 003*	63		1
19 Jul 03	**KNEE DEEP AND DOWN** *Temptation TEMPTCD 007*	56		1

RAIN TREE CROW
UK, male vocal/instrumental group

1

Date	Title / Label	Peak	Wks at No.1	Wks on Chart
30 Mar 91	**BLACKWATER** *Virgin VS 1340*	62		1

RAINBOW
UK, male vocal/instrumental group – Ritchie Blackmore; members also included Graham Bonnet*, Tony Carey, Ronnie James Dio, Roger Glover, Cozy Powell*, d. 5 Apr 1998, & Joe Lynn Turner

62

Date	Title / Label	Peak	Wks at No.1	Wks on Chart
17 Sep 77	**KILL THE KING** *Polydor 2066 845*	44		3
8 Apr 78	**LONG LIVE ROCK 'N' ROLL** *Polydor 2066 913*	33		3
30 Sep 78	**L.A. CONNECTION** *Polydor 2066 968*	40		4
15 Sep 79	**SINCE YOU'VE BEEN GONE** *Polydor POSP 70* ●	6		10
16 Feb 80	**ALL NIGHT LONG** *Polydor POSP 104* ●	5		11
31 Jan 81	**I SURRENDER** *Polydor POSP 221* ●	3		10
20 Jun 81	**CAN'T HAPPEN HERE** *Polydor POSP 251*	20		8
11 Jul 81	**KILL THE KING** *Polydor POSP 274*	41		4
3 Apr 82	**STONE COLD** *Polydor POSP 421*	34		4
27 Aug 83	**STREET OF DREAMS** *Polydor POSP 631*	52		3
5 Nov 83	**CAN'T LET YOU GO** *Polydor POSP 654*	43		2

RAINBOW COTTAGE
UK, male vocal/instrumental group

4

Date	Title / Label	Peak	Wks at No.1	Wks on Chart
6 Mar 76	**SEAGULL** *Penny Farthing PEN 906*	33		4

RAINBOW (GEORGE & ZIPPY)
UK, male puppet vocalists

6

Date	Title / Label	Peak	Wks at No.1	Wks on Chart
14 Dec 02	**IT'S A RAINBOW** *BBC Music ZIPPCD1X*	15		6

RAINMAKERS
US, male vocal/instrumental group

11

Date	Title / Label	Peak	Wks at No.1	Wks on Chart
7 Mar 87	**LET MY PEOPLE GO-GO** *Mercury MER 238*	18		11

MARVIN RAINWATER
US, male vocalist/guitarist

22

Date	Title / Label	Peak	Wks at No.1	Wks on Chart
7 Mar 58	**WHOLE LOTTA WOMAN** *MGM 974*	1	3	15
6 Jun 58	**I DIG YOU BABY** *MGM 980*	19		7

RAISSA
UK, female vocalist (Raissa Khan-Panni)

1

Date	Title / Label	Peak	Wks at No.1	Wks on Chart
12 Feb 00	**HOW LONG DO I GET** *Polydor 5616282*	47		1

BONNIE RAITT
US, female vocalist/guitarist

9

Date	Title / Label	Peak	Wks at No.1	Wks on Chart
14 Dec 91	**I CAN'T MAKE YOU LOVE ME** *Capitol CL 639*	50		4
9 Apr 94	**LOVE SNEAKIN' UP ON YOU** *Capitol CDCL 713*	69		1
18 Jun 94	**YOU** *Capitol CDCLS 718*	31		2
11 Nov 95	**ROCK STEADY** *Capitol CDCL 763* & BRYAN ADAMS	50		2

DIONNE RAKEEM
UK, female vocalist

2

Date	Title / Label	Peak	Wks at No.1	Wks on Chart
4 Aug 01	**SWEETER THAN WINE** *Virgin VSCDT 1809*	46		2

RAKES
UK, male vocal/instrumental group

9

Date	Title / Label	Peak	Wks at No.1	Wks on Chart
9 Oct 04	**STRASBOURG** *City Rockers ROCKERS28CD*	57		1
30 Apr 05	**RETREAT** *Moshi Moshi MOSHI18CD*	24		2
13 Aug 05	**WORK WORK WORK (PUB CLUB SLEEP)** *V2 VVR5032778*	28		2
12 Nov 05	**22 GRAND JOB** *V2 VVR5034618*	39		1
11 Mar 06	**ALL TOO HUMAN** *V2 VVR5036208*	22		2
24 Mar 07	**WE DANCED TOGETHER** *V2 VVR5042753*	38		1

RAKIM

US, male rapper (William Griffin, Jr). See Eric B & Rakim — 17

Date	Title / Label	Peak	Wks at No.1	Wks on Chart
27 Dec 97	**GUESS WHO'S BACK** *Universal UND 56151*	32		3
22 Aug 98	**STAY A WHILE** *Universal UND 56203*	53		1
3 Oct 98	**BUFFALO GALS STAMPEDE** *Virgin VSCDT 1717* MALCOLM McLAREN & THE WORLD'S FAMOUS SUPREME TEAM PLUS RAKIM & ROGER SANCHEZ	65		1
31 Aug 02	**ADDICTIVE** *Interscope 4977782* TRUTH HURTS FEATURING RAKIM	3		12

TONY RALLO & THE MIDNIGHT BAND

France/US, male vocal/instrumental group — 8

Date	Title / Label	Peak	Wks at No.1	Wks on Chart
23 Feb 80	**HOLDIN' ON** *Calibre CAB 150*	34		8

SHERYL LEE RALPH

US, female vocalist/actor — 2

Date	Title / Label	Peak	Wks at No.1	Wks on Chart
26 Jan 85	**IN THE EVENING** *Arista ARIST 595*	64		2

RAM JAM

US, male vocal/instrumental group – Myke Scavone, Bill Bartlett, Howie Blauvelt, d. 25 Oct 1993, & Peter Charles — 20

Date	Title / Label	Peak	Wks at No.1	Wks on Chart
10 Sep 77	**BLACK BETTY** *Epic EPC 5492* ●	7		12
17 Feb 90	**BLACK BETTY** *Epic 6554307*	13		8

RAM TRILOGY

UK, male production trio — 3

Date	Title / Label	Peak	Wks at No.1	Wks on Chart
6 Jul 02	**CHAPTER FOUR** *Ram RAMM 39*	71		1
20 Jul 02	**CHAPTER FIVE** *Ram RAMM 40*	62		1
3 Aug 02	**CHAPTER SIX** *Ram RAMM 41*	60		1

RAMBLERS (FROM THE ABBEY HEY JUNIOR SCHOOL)

UK, children's choir — 15

Date	Title / Label	Peak	Wks at No.1	Wks on Chart
13 Oct 79	**THE SPARROW** *Decca F 13860* ●	11		15

KAREN RAMIREZ

US, female vocalist (Karen Ramelize) — 15

Date	Title / Label	Peak	Wks at No.1	Wks on Chart
28 Mar 98	**TROUBLED GIRL** *Manifesto FESCD 31*	50		1
27 Jun 98	**LOOKING FOR LOVE** *Manifesto FESCD 44* ●	8		11
21 Nov 98	**IF WE TRY** *Manifesto FESCD 50*	23		3

RAMMSTEIN

Germany, male vocal/instrumental group — 12

Date	Title / Label	Peak	Wks at No.1	Wks on Chart
25 May 02	**ICH WILL** *Universal MCSXD 40280*	30		2
23 Nov 02	**FEUER FREI** *Universal MCSXD 40302*	35		2
14 Aug 04	**MEIN TEIL (IMPORT)** *Universal 9866978*	61		2
30 Oct 04	**AMERIKA** *Universal MCSTD 40394*	38		2
12 Mar 05	**KEINE LUST** *Universal MCSTD40405*	35		2
29 Oct 05	**BENZIN** *Universal 9874302*	58		1
1 Apr 06	**MANN GEGEN MANN** *Universal MCSXD40451*	59		1

RAMONES

US, male vocal/instrumental group – Joey (Jeffrey Hyman), d. 15 Apr 2001, Dee Dee (Douglas Colvin), d. 5 Jun 2002, Johnny (John Cummings), d. 15 Sep 2004, & Tommy (Tomas Erdelyi, replaced by Marky (Marc Bell)) Ramone — 32

Date	Title / Label	Peak	Wks at No.1	Wks on Chart
21 May 77	**SHEENA IS A PUNK ROCKER** *Sire RAM 001*	22		7
6 Aug 77	**SWALLOW MY PRIDE** *Sire 6078 607*	36		3
30 Sep 78	**DON'T COME CLOSE** *Sire SRE 1031*	39		5
8 Sep 79	**ROCK 'N' ROLL HIGH SCHOOL** *Sire SRE 4021*	67		2
26 Jan 80	**BABY I LOVE YOU** *Sire SIR 4031*	8		9
19 Apr 80	**DO YOU REMEMBER ROCK 'N' ROLL RADIO** *Sire SIR 4037*	54		3
10 May 86	**SOMEBODY PUT SOMETHING IN MY DRINK/SOMETHING TO BELIEVE IN** *Beggars Banquet BEG 157*	69		1
19 Dec 92	**POISON HEART** *Chrysalis CHS 3917*	69		2

RAMP

UK, male instrumental/production duo. See Slacker — 1

Date	Title / Label	Peak	Wks at No.1	Wks on Chart
8 Jun 96	**ROCK THE DISCOTEK** *Loaded LOADCD 30*	49		1

RAMPAGE

UK, male DJ/production group — 1

Date	Title / Label	Peak	Wks at No.1	Wks on Chart
25 Nov 95	**THE MONKEES** *Almo Sounds CDALMOS 017*	51		1

RAMPAGE FEATURING BILLY LAWRENCE

US, male rap/vocal duo — 1

Date	Title / Label	Peak	Wks at No.1	Wks on Chart
18 Oct 97	**TAKE IT TO THE STREETS** *Elektra E 3914CD*	58		1

RAMRODS

US, male/female instrumental group – Vinny Lee (d.), Claire & Richard Litke & Eugene Moore — 12

Date	Title / Label	Peak	Wks at No.1	Wks on Chart
23 Feb 61	**RIDERS IN THE SKY** *London HLU 9282*	8		12

RAMSEY & FEN FEATURING LYNSEY MOORE

UK, male/female vocal/production trio — 1

Date	Title / Label	Peak	Wks at No.1	Wks on Chart
10 Jun 00	**LOVE BUG** *Nebula VCNEBD 4*	75		1

RANCID

US, male vocal/instrumental group — 3

Date	Title / Label	Peak	Wks at No.1	Wks on Chart
7 Oct 95	**TIME BOMB** *Out Of Step WOOS 8CDS*	56		1
27 Sep 03	**FALL BACK DOWN** *Hellcat W 618CD*	42		2

RANGERS FC

UK, football fans/vocal group — 2

Date	Title / Label	Peak	Wks at No.1	Wks on Chart
4 Oct 97	**GLASGOW RANGERS (NINE IN A ROW)** *Gers GERSCD 1*	54		2

RANK 1

Holland, male production duo – Piet Bervoets & Benno de Goeij — 5

Date	Title / Label	Peak	Wks at No.1	Wks on Chart
15 Apr 00	**AIRWAVE** *Manifesto FESCD 69*	10		5

SHABBA RANKS

Jamaica, male vocalist (Rexton Gordon) — 67

Date	Title / Label	Peak	Wks at No.1	Wks on Chart
16 Mar 91	**SHE'S A WOMAN** *Virgin VS 1333* SCRITTI POLITTI FEATURING SHABBA RANKS	20		7
18 May 91	**TRAILER LOAD A GIRLS** *Epic 6568747*	63		2
24 Aug 91	**HOUSECALL** *Epic 6573477* FEATURING MAXI PRIEST	31		7
8 Aug 92	**MR LOVERMAN** *Epic 6582517*	23		7
28 Nov 92	**SLOW AND SEXY** *Epic 6587727* FEATURING JOHNNY GILL	17		7
6 Mar 93	**I WAS A KING** *Motown TMGCD 1414* EDDIE MURPHY FEATURING SHABBA RANKS	64		1
13 Mar 93	**MR LOVERMAN** *Epic 6590782*	3		11
8 May 93	**HOUSECALL (REMIX)** *Epic 6592842* FEATURING MAXI PRIEST	8		8
26 Jun 93	**WHAT'CHA GONNA DO** *Epic 6593072* FEATURING QUEEN LATIFAH	21		4
25 Dec 93	**FAMILY AFFAIR** *Polydor PZCD 304* FEATURING PATRA & TERRY & MONICA	18		8
29 Apr 95	**LET'S GET IT ON** *Epic 6614122*	22		3
5 Aug 95	**SHINE EYE GAL** *Epic 6622332* (FEATURING MYKAL ROSE)	46		2

RAPINATION

Italy, male instrumental/production duo — 12

Date	Title / Label	Peak	Wks at No.1	Wks on Chart
26 Dec 92	**LOVE ME THE RIGHT WAY** *Logic 74321128097* & KYM MAZELLE	22		10
10 Jul 93	**HERE'S MY A** *Logic 74321153092* FEATURING CAROL KENYON	69		1
28 Sep 96	**LOVE ME THE RIGHT WAY (REMIX)** *Logic 74321404442* & KYM MAZELLE	55		1

RAPPIN' 4-TAY

US, male rapper (Anthony Forte) — 5

Date	Title / Label	Peak	Wks at No.1	Wks on Chart
24 Jun 95	**I'LL BE AROUND** *Cooltempo CDCOOL 306* FEATURING THE SPINNERS	30		4
30 Sep 95	**PLAYAZ CLUB** *Cooltempo CDCOOL 310*	63		1

RAPTURE

US, male vocal/instrumental group — 7

Date	Title / Label	Peak	Wks at No.1	Wks on Chart
6 Sep 03	**HOUSE OF JEALOUS LOVERS** *XL Recordings XLS 167CD*	27		2
13 Dec 03	**SISTER SAVIOUR** *DFA/Output/Vertigo 9814181*	51		1
21 Feb 04	**LOVE IS ALL** *DFA/Output/Vertigo 9816876*	38		1
16 Sep 06	**GET MYSELF INTO IT** *Vertigo 1705165*	36		2
16 Dec 06	**WAYUH (PEOPLE DON'T DANCE NO MORE)** *Vertigo 1713573*	65		1

Peak Position Weeks at No.1 Weeks on Chart

RARE
UK, male/female vocal/instrumental group **1**

Date	Title	Peak	Wks at No.1	Wks on Chart
17 Feb 96	**SOMETHING WILD** *Equator AXISCD 011*	57		1

RARE BIRD
UK, male vocal/instrumental group **8**

Date	Title	Peak	Wks at No.1	Wks on Chart
14 Feb 70	**SYMPATHY** *Charisma CB 120*	27		8

RASMUS
Finland, male vocal/instrumental group – Lauri Yionen, Aki Hakala, Eero Heinonen & Pauli Rantasalmi **24**

Date	Title	Peak	Wks at No.1	Wks on Chart
17 Apr 04	**IN THE SHADOWS** *Universal MCSXD 40351*	3		16
21 Aug 04	**GUILTY** *Universal MCSTD 40376*	15		6
13 Nov 04	**FIRST DAY OF MY LIFE** *Universal MCSTD 40391*	50		1
17 Sep 05	**NO FEAR** *Universal MCSXD40429*	43		1

ROLAND RAT SUPERSTAR
UK, male rodent rapper/vocalist/TV character (voiced by David Claridge) **20**

Date	Title	Peak	Wks at No.1	Wks on Chart
19 Nov 83	**RAT RAPPING** *Rodent RAT 1*	14		12
28 Apr 84	**LOVE ME TENDER** *Rodent RAT 2*	32		7
2 Mar 85	**NO. 1 RAT FAN** *Rodent RAT 4*	72		1

RATPACK
UK, male vocal/production duo **3**

Date	Title	Peak	Wks at No.1	Wks on Chart
6 Jun 92	**SEARCHIN' FOR MY RIZLA** *Big Giant BIGT 02*	58		3

RATTLES
Germany, male vocal/instrumental group – Edna Bejarano, Herbert Bornhold, Kurt Lungen & Frank Mille **15**

Date	Title	Peak	Wks at No.1	Wks on Chart
3 Oct 70	**THE WITCH** *Decca F 23058*	8		15

RATTY
Germany, male production group **1**

Date	Title	Peak	Wks at No.1	Wks on Chart
24 Mar 01	**SUNRISE (HERE I AM)** *Neo NEOCD 051*	51		1

RAVEN MAIZE
UK, male producer (Dave Lee). **9**

Date	Title	Peak	Wks at No.1	Wks on Chart
5 Aug 89	**FOREVER TOGETHER** *Republic LIC 014*	67		1
18 Aug 01	**THE REAL LIFE** *Rulin 18CDS*	12		6
17 Aug 02	**FASCINATED** *Rulin 27CDS*	37		2

RAVEONETTES
Denmark, male/female vocal/instrumental group **7**

Date	Title	Peak	Wks at No.1	Wks on Chart
21 Dec 02	**ATTACK OF THE GHOSTRIDERS** *Columbia 6733892*	73		1
30 Aug 03	**THAT GREAT LOVE SOUND** *Columbia RAVEON005*	34		2
20 Dec 03	**HEARTBREAK STROLL** *Columbia RAVEON008*	49		1
22 May 04	**THAT GREAT LOVE SOUND** *Columbia RAVEON010*	52		1
23 Jul 05	**LOVE IN A TRASHCAN** *Columbia RAVEON017*	26		2

RAVESIGNAL III
UK, male producer (CJ Bolland). See Sonic Solution **2**

Date	Title	Peak	Wks at No.1	Wks on Chart
14 Dec 91	**HORSEPOWER** *R&S RSUK 6*	61		2

RAW SILK
US, male/female production/vocal group **12**

Date	Title	Peak	Wks at No.1	Wks on Chart
16 Oct 82	**DO IT TO THE MUSIC** *KR 14*	18		9
10 Sep 83	**JUST IN TIME** *West End WEND 2*	49		3

RAW STYLUS
UK, male/female vocal/instrumental duo **1**

Date	Title	Peak	Wks at No.1	Wks on Chart
26 Oct 96	**BELIEVE IN ME** *Wired 234*	66		1

LOU RAWLS
US, male vocalist, d. 6 Jan 2006 (age 72) **10**

Date	Title	Peak	Wks at No.1	Wks on Chart
31 Jul 76	**YOU'LL NEVER FIND ANOTHER LOVE LIKE MINE** *Philadelphia International PIR 4372*	10		10

JIMMY RAY
UK, male vocalist (James Edwards) **6**

Date	Title	Peak	Wks at No.1	Wks on Chart
25 Oct 97	**ARE YOU JIMMY RAY?** *Sony S2 6650125*	13		5
14 Feb 98	**GOIN' TO VEGAS** *Sony S2 6654652*	49		1

JOHNNIE RAY
US, male vocalist, d. 25 Feb 1990 (age 63) **168**

Date	Title	Peak	Wks at No.1	Wks on Chart
14 Nov 52	**WALKING MY BABY BACK HOME** *Columbia DB 3060*	12		1
19 Dec 52	**FAITH CAN MOVE MOUNTAINS** *Columbia DB 3154* & THE FOUR LADS	7		3
3 Apr 53	**MA SAYS PA SAYS** *Columbia DB 3242* DORIS DAY & JOHNNIE RAY	12		1
10 Apr 53	**SOMEBODY STOLE MY GAL** *Philips PB 123*	6		7
17 Apr 53	**FULL TIME JOB** *Columbia DB 3242* DORIS DAY & JOHNNIE RAY	11		1
24 Jul 53	**LET'S WALK THATA-WAY** *Philips PB 157* DORIS DAY & JOHNNIE RAY	4		14
9 Apr 54	**SUCH A NIGHT** *Philips PB 244*	1	1	18
8 Apr 55	**IF YOU BELIEVE** *Philips PB 379*	7		11
20 May 55	**PATHS OF PARADISE** *Philips PB 441*	20		1
7 Oct 55	**HERNANDO'S HIDEAWAY** *Philips PB 495*	11		5
14 Oct 55	**HEY THERE** *Philips PB 495*	5		9
28 Oct 55	**SONG OF THE DREAMER** *Philips PB 516*	10		5
17 Feb 56	**WHO'S SORRY NOW** *Philips PB 546*	17		2
20 Apr 56	**AIN'T MISBEHAVIN'** *Philips PB 580*	17		7
12 Oct 56	**JUST WALKIN' IN THE RAIN** *Philips PB 624*	1	7	19
18 Jan 57	**YOU DON'T OWE ME A THING** *Philips PB 655*	12		15
8 Feb 57	**LOOK HOMEWARD ANGEL** *Philips PB 655*	7		16
10 May 57	**YES TONIGHT JOSEPHINE** *Philips PB 686*	1	3	16
6 Sep 57	**BUILD YOUR LOVE (ON A STRONG FOUNDATION)** *Philips PB 721*	17		7
4 Oct 57	**GOOD EVENING FRIENDS/UP ABOVE MY HEAD I HEAR MUSIC IN THE AIR** *Philips PB 708* FRANKIE LAINE & JOHNNIE RAY	25		4
4 Dec 59	**I'LL NEVER FALL IN LOVE AGAIN** *Philips PB 952*	26		6

NICOLE RAY
US, female vocalist (Nicole Wray) **5**

Date	Title	Peak	Wks at No.1	Wks on Chart
22 Aug 98	**MAKE IT HOT** *East West E 3821CD* NICOLE FEATURING MISSY 'MISDEMEANOR' ELLIOTT	22		4
5 Dec 98	**I CAN'T SEE** *East West E 3801CD*	55		1

RAYDIO
US, male vocal/instrumental group **21**

Date	Title	Peak	Wks at No.1	Wks on Chart
8 Apr 78	**JACK AND JILL** *Arista 161*	11		12
8 Jul 78	**IS THIS A LOVE THING** *Arista 193*	27		9

DANA RAYNE
US, female vocalist **8**

Date	Title	Peak	Wks at No.1	Wks on Chart
15 Jan 05	**OBJECT OF MY DESIRE** *Incentive CENTMOS1CDS*	7		8

RAYVON
Barbados, male rapper/vocalist (Bruce Brewster) **26**

Date	Title	Peak	Wks at No.1	Wks on Chart
8 Jul 95	**IN THE SUMMERTIME** *Virgin VSCDT 1542* SHAGGY FEATURING RAYVON	5		9
9 Jun 01	**ANGEL** *MCA MCSTD 40257* SHAGGY FEATURING RAYVON ● ★	1	3	16
3 Aug 02	**2-WAY** *MCA MCSTD 40287*	67		1

RAZE
US, male producer (Vaughan Mason) & various male/female vocal/rap collaborators **48**

Date	Title	Peak	Wks at No.1	Wks on Chart
1 Nov 86	**JACK THE GROOVE** *Champion CHAMP 23*	20		15
28 Feb 87	**LET THE MUSIC MOVE U** *Champion CHAMP 27*	57		3
31 Dec 88	**BREAK 4 LOVE** *Champion CHAMP 67*	28		11
15 Jul 89	**LET IT ROLL** *Atlantic A 8866* PRESENTS DOUG LAZY	27		5
2 Sep 89	**BREAK 4 LOVE** *Champion CHAMP 67*	59		5
27 Jan 90	**ALL 4 LOVE (BREAK 4 LOVE 1990)** *Champion CHAMP 228* FEATURING LADY J & SECRETARY OF ENTERTAINMENT	30		5
10 Feb 90	**CAN YOU FEEL IT/CAN YOU FEEL IT** *Champion CHAMP 227* RAZE/CHAMPIONSHIP LEGEND	62		1
24 Sep 94	**BREAK 4 LOVE (REMIX)** *Champion CHAMPCD 314*	44		2
29 Mar 03	**BREAK 4 LOVE (REMIX)** *Champion CHAMPCD 784*	64		1

RAZORLIGHT

UK/Sweden, male vocal/instrumental group – Johnny Borrell, Bjorn Agren, Carl Dalemo & Christian Smith-Pancorvo (replaced by Andy Burrows) — 113

Date	Title / Label	Peak	Wks No.1	Wks
30 Aug 03	**ROCK 'N' ROLL LIES** *Vertigo 9800413*	56		1
22 Nov 03	**RIP IT UP** *Vertigo 9814046*	42		1
7 Feb 04	**STUMBLE AND FALL** *Vertigo 9816397*	27		3
26 Jun 04	**GOLDEN TOUCH** *Vertigo 9866836*	9		7
25 Sep 04	**VICE** *Vertigo 9867759*	18		4
11 Dec 04	**RIP IT UP** *Vertigo 9869077*	20		5
23 Apr 05	**SOMEWHERE ELSE** *Vertigo 9869893*	2		22
8 Jul 06	**IN THE MORNING** *Vertigo 1701088*	3		23
7 Oct 06	**AMERICA** *Vertigo 1705368*	1	1	27
23 Dec 06	**BEFORE I FALL TO PIECES** *Vertigo 1714372*	17		11
31 Mar 07	**I CAN'T STOP THIS FEELING I'VE GOT** *Vertigo 1724345*	44		2
25 Oct 08	**WIRE TO WIRE** *Vertigo 1785877*	5		7

RE-FLEX

UK, male vocal/instrumental group — 9

Date	Title / Label	Peak	Wks No.1	Wks
28 Jan 84	**THE POLITICS OF DANCING** *EMI FLEX 2*	28		9

CHRIS REA

UK, male vocalist/guitarist — 130

Date	Title / Label	Peak	Wks No.1	Wks
7 Oct 78	**FOOL (IF YOU THINK IT'S OVER)** *Magnet MAG 111*	30		7
21 Apr 79	**DIAMONDS** *Magnet MAG 144*	44		3
27 Mar 82	**LOVING YOU** *Magnet MAG 215*	65		3
1 Oct 83	**I CAN HEAR YOUR HEARTBEAT** *Magnet MAG 244*	60		2
17 Mar 84	**I DON'T KNOW WHAT IT IS BUT I LOVE IT** *Magnet MAG 255*	65		2
30 Mar 85	**STAINSBY GIRLS** *Magnet MAG 276*	26		10
29 Jun 85	**JOSEPHINE** *Magnet MAG 280*	67		2
29 Mar 86	**IT'S ALL GONE** *Magnet MAG 283*	69		1
31 May 86	**ON THE BEACH** *Magnet MAG 294*	57		8
6 Jun 87	**LET'S DANCE** *Magnet MAG 299*	12		10
29 Aug 87	**LOVING YOU AGAIN** *Magnet MAG 300*	47		4
5 Dec 87	**JOYS OF CHRISTMAS** *Magnet MAG 314*	67		1
13 Feb 88	**QUE SERA** *Magnet MAG 318*	73		2
13 Aug 88	**ON THE BEACH SUMMER '88** *WEA YZ 195*	12		6
22 Oct 88	**I CAN HEAR YOUR HEARTBEAT** *WEA YZ 320*	74		2
17 Dec 88	**DRIVING HOME FOR CHRISTMAS (EP)** *WEA YZ 325*	53		3
18 Feb 89	**WORKING ON IT** *WEA YZ 350*	53		3
14 Oct 89	**THE ROAD TO HELL (PART 2)** *WEA YZ 431*	10		9
10 Feb 90	**TELL ME THERE'S A HEAVEN** *East West YZ 455*	24		6
5 May 90	**TEXAS** *East West YZ 468*	69		1
16 Feb 91	**AUBERGE** *East West YZ 555*	16		6
6 Apr 91	**HEAVEN** *East West YZ 566*	57		2
29 Jun 91	**LOOKING FOR THE SUMMER** *East West YZ 584*	49		3
9 Nov 91	**WINTER SONG** *East West YZ 629*	27		4
24 Oct 92	**NOTHING TO FEAR** *East West YZ 699*	16		4
28 Nov 92	**GOD'S GREAT BANANA SKIN** *East West YZ 706*	31		3
30 Jan 93	**SOFT TOP HARD SHOULDER** *East West YZ 710CD*	53		2
23 Oct 93	**JULIA** *East West YZ 722CD*	18		5
12 Nov 94	**YOU CAN GO YOUR OWN WAY** *East West YZ 835CD*	28		3
24 Dec 94	**TELL ME THERE'S A HEAVEN** *East West YZ 885CD*	70		1
16 Nov 96	**DISCO' LA PASSIONE** *East West EW072CD* & SHIRLEY BASSEY	41		1
24 May 97	**LET'S DANCE** *Magnet EW 112CD* MIDDLESBROUGH FC FEATURING BOB MORTIMER & CHRIS REA	44		1
15 Dec 07	**DRIVING HOME FOR CHRISTMAS** *Warner Brothers GBAHS9904091*	33		3
13 Dec 08	**DRIVING HOME FOR CHRISTMAS** *Warner Brothers GBAHS9904091*	53		4
19 Dec 09	**DRIVING HOME FOR CHRISTMAS** *Warner Brothers GBAHS9904091*	40		3

REACT 2 RHYTHM

UK, male production group — 1

Date	Title / Label	Peak	Wks No.1	Wks
28 Jun 97	**INTOXICATION** *Jackpot WIN 014CD*	73		1

REACTOR

UK, male vocal/instrumental group — 1

Date	Title / Label	Peak	Wks No.1	Wks
10 Apr 04	**FEELING THE LOVE** *Liberty CDREACT001*	56		1

EDDI READER

UK, female vocalist (Sadenia Reader). See Fairground Attraction — 14

Date	Title / Label	Peak	Wks No.1	Wks
4 Jun 94	**PATIENCE OF ANGELS** *Blanco Y Negro NEG 68CD*	33		5
13 Aug 94	**JOKE (I'M LAUGHING)** *Blanco Y Negro NEG 72CD*	42		3
5 Nov 94	**DEAR JOHN** *Blanco Y Negro NEG 75CD1*	48		2
22 Jun 96	**TOWN WITHOUT PITY** *Blanco Y Negro NEG 90CDX*	26		3
21 Aug 99	**FRAGILE THING** *Track 0004A* BIG COUNTRY FEATURING EDDI READER	69		1

READY FOR THE WORLD

US, male vocal/instrumental group — 8

Date	Title / Label	Peak	Wks No.1	Wks
26 Oct 85	**OH SHEILA** *MCA 1005* ★	50		5
14 Mar 87	**LOVE YOU DOWN** *MCA 1110*	60		3

REAL & RICHARDSON FEATURING JOBABE

UK, male/female vocal/production trio — 1

Date	Title / Label	Peak	Wks No.1	Wks
10 May 03	**SUNSHINE ON A RAINY DAY** *Nukleuz 0489 CNUK*	69		1

REAL EMOTION

UK, male/female vocal/instrumental group — 1

Date	Title / Label	Peak	Wks No.1	Wks
1 Jul 95	**BACK FOR GOOD** *Living Beat LBECD 34*	67		1

(MC SAR &) THE REAL McCOY

Germany/US, male/female rap/vocal trio – Olaf "O-Jay" Jeglitza, Vanessa Mason & Patricia Petersen (voiced by Karin Kasar) — 36

Date	Title / Label	Peak	Wks No.1	Wks
6 Nov 93	**ANOTHER NIGHT** *Logic 74321173732*	61		1
5 Nov 94	**ANOTHER NIGHT** *Logic 74321236992* ●	2		12
28 Jan 95	**RUN AWAY** *Logic 74321258822* ●	6		10
22 Apr 95	**LOVE AND DEVOTION** *Logic 74321272702*	11		8
26 Aug 95	**COME AND GET YOUR LOVE** *Logic 74321301272* REAL McCOY	19		4
11 Nov 95	**AUTOMATIC LOVER (CALL FOR LOVE)** *Logic 74321325042* REAL McCOY	58		1

REAL PEOPLE

UK, male vocal/instrumental group — 8

Date	Title / Label	Peak	Wks No.1	Wks
16 Feb 91	**OPEN YOUR MIND (LET ME IN)** *CBS 6566127*	70		1
20 Apr 91	**THE TRUTH** *Columbia 6567877*	73		1
6 Jul 91	**WINDOW PANE (EP)** *Columbia 6569327*	60		1
11 Jan 92	**THE TRUTH** *Columbia 6576987*	41		3
23 May 92	**BELIEVER** *Columbia 6580067*	38		2

REAL ROXANNE

US, female rapper (Joanne Martinez) — 10

Date	Title / Label	Peak	Wks No.1	Wks
28 Jun 86	**BANG ZOOM (LET'S GO GO)** *Cooltempo COOL 124* WITH HITMAN HOWIE TEE	11		9
12 Nov 88	**RESPECT** *Cooltempo COOL 176*	71		1

REAL THING

UK, male vocal group – Chris & Eddie Amoo, Ray Lake & Dave Smith — 121

Date	Title / Label	Peak	Wks No.1	Wks
5 Jun 76	**YOU TO ME ARE EVERYTHING** *Pye International 7N 25709* ●	1	3	11
4 Sep 76	**CAN'T GET BY WITHOUT YOU** *Pye 7N 45618* ●	2		10
12 Feb 77	**YOU'LL NEVER KNOW WHAT YOU'RE MISSING** *Pye 7N 45662*	16		9
30 Jul 77	**LOVE'S SUCH A WONDERFUL THING** *Pye 7N 45701*	33		5
4 Mar 78	**WHENEVER YOU WANT MY LOVE** *Pye 7N 46045*	18		9
3 Jun 78	**LET'S GO DISCO** *Pye 7N 46078*	39		7
12 Aug 78	**RAININ' THROUGH MY SUNSHINE** *Pye 7N 46113*	40		8
17 Feb 79	**CAN YOU FEEL THE FORCE** *Pye 7N 46147* ●	5		11
21 Jul 79	**BOOGIE DOWN (GET FUNKY NOW)** *Pye 7P 109*	33		6
22 Nov 80	**SHE'S A GROOVY FREAK** *Calibre CAB 105*	52		4
8 Mar 86	**YOU TO ME ARE EVERYTHING (THE DECADE REMIX 78-86)** *PRT 7P 349*	5		13
24 May 86	**CAN'T GET BY WITHOUT YOU (THE SECOND DECADE REMIX)** *PRT 7P 352*	6		13
2 Aug 86	**CAN YOU FEEL THE FORCE ('86 REMIX)** *PRT 7P 358*	24		6
25 Oct 86	**STRAIGHT TO THE HEART** *Jive 129*	71		2
23 Apr 05	**SO MUCH LOVE TO GIVE** *All Around The World CDGLOBE412* FREELOADERS FEATURING THE REAL THING	9		7

REAL TO REEL

US, male vocal group — 2

Date	Title / Label	Peak	Wks No.1	Wks
21 Apr 84	**LOVE ME LIKE THIS** *Arista ARIST 565*	68		2

REBEL MC

UK, male rapper (Michael West). See Conquering Lion — 52

Date	Title / Label	Peak	Wks No.1	Wks
27 May 89	**JUST KEEP ROCKIN'** *Desire WANT 9* DOUBLE TROUBLE & THE REBEL MC	11		12
7 Oct 89	**STREET TUFF** *Desire WANT 18* DOUBLE TROUBLE & THE REBEL MC	3		14
31 Mar 90	**BETTER WORLD** *Desire WANT 25*	20		6
2 Jun 90	**REBEL MUSIC** *Desire WANT 31*	53		2
6 Apr 91	**WICKEDEST SOUND** *Desire WANT 40* FEATURING TENOR FLY	43		6

Date	Title	Peak Position	Weeks at No.1	Weeks on Chart
15 Jun 91	**TRIBAL BASE** *Desire WANT 44* FEATURING TENOR FLY & BARRINGTON LEVY	20		6
31 Aug 91	**BLACK MEANING GOOD** *Desire WANT 47*	73		1
21 Mar 92	**RICH AH GETTING RICHER** *Big Life BLR 70* INTRODUCING LITTLE T	48		4
8 Aug 92	**HUMANITY** *Big Life BLR 78* FEATURING LINCOLM THOMPSON	62		1

EZZ RECO & THE LAUNCHERS WITH BOSIE GRANT

Jamaica, male vocal/instrumental group — 4

Date	Title	Peak Position	Weeks at No.1	Weeks on Chart
5 Mar 64	**KING OF KINGS** *Columbia DB 7217*	44		4

RECOIL

UK, male vocal/instrumental group — 1

Date	Title	Peak Position	Weeks at No.1	Weeks on Chart
21 Mar 92	**FAITH HEALER** *Mute 110*	60		1

RED

UK, male production duo. See Beat Renegades, Dream Frequency, Quake featuring Marcia Rae — 1

Date	Title	Peak Position	Weeks at No.1	Weeks on Chart
20 Jan 01	**HEAVEN & EARTH** *Slinky Music SLINKY 008CD*	41		1

RED BOX

UK, male vocal/instrumental duo – Simon Toulson-Clarke & Julian Close — 28

Date	Title	Peak Position	Weeks at No.1	Weeks on Chart
24 Aug 85	**LEAN ON ME (AH-LI-AYO)** *Sire W 8926* ●	3		14
25 Oct 86	**FOR AMERICA** *Sire YZ 84*	10		12
31 Jan 87	**HEART OF THE SUN** *Sire YZ 100*	71		2

RED CAR AND THE BLUE CAR

UK, male TV advert cartoon racing cars (Bob Saker) — 4

Date	Title	Peak Position	Weeks at No.1	Weeks on Chart
14 Dec 91	**HOME FOR CHRISTMAS DAY** *Virgin VS 1394*	44		4

RED CARPET

Belgium, male/female vocal/production trio — 3

Date	Title	Peak Position	Weeks at No.1	Weeks on Chart
11 Dec 04	**ALRIGHT** *Positiva CDTIVS212*	58		2
14 Jan 06	**ALRIGHT** *Positiva CDTIVS231*	74		1

RED DRAGON WITH BRIAN & TONY GOLD

Jamaica, male vocal trio – Leroy May, Brian Thompson & Patrick Anthony Morrison — 15

Date	Title	Peak Position	Weeks at No.1	Weeks on Chart
30 Jul 94	**COMPLIMENTS ON YOUR KISS** *Mango CIDM 820* ●	2		15

RED EYE

UK, male production duo — 1

Date	Title	Peak Position	Weeks at No.1	Weeks on Chart
3 Dec 94	**KUT IT** *Champion CHAMPCD 315*	62		1

RED 5

Germany, male producer (Thomas Kukula) — 10

Date	Title	Peak Position	Weeks at No.1	Weeks on Chart
10 May 97	**I LOVE YOU...STOP!** *Multiply CDMULTY 20*	11		5
20 Dec 97	**LIFT ME UP** *Multiply CDMULTY 30*	26		5

RED HILL CHILDREN

UK, male/female choir — 2

Date	Title	Peak Position	Weeks at No.1	Weeks on Chart
30 Nov 96	**WHEN CHILDREN RULE THE WORLD** *Really Useful 5797262*	40		2

RED HOT CHILI PEPPERS

US, male vocal/instrumental group – Anthony Kiedis, Michael 'Flea' Balzary, John Frusciante*, Dave Navarro & Chad Smith — 134

Date	Title	Peak Position	Weeks at No.1	Weeks on Chart
10 Feb 90	**HIGHER GROUND** *EMI-USA MT 75*	55		3
23 Jun 90	**TASTE THE PAIN** *EMI-USA MT 85*	29		3
8 Sep 90	**HIGHER GROUND** *EMI-USA MT 88*	54		3
14 Mar 92	**UNDER THE BRIDGE** *Warner Brothers W 0084*	26		4
15 Aug 92	**BREAKING THE GIRL** *Warner Brothers W 0126*	41		3
5 Feb 94	**GIVE IT AWAY** *Warner Brothers W 0225CD1*	9		4
30 Apr 94	**UNDER THE BRIDGE** *Warner Brothers W 0237CDX*	13		6
2 Sep 95	**WARPED** *Warner Brothers W 0316CD*	31		2
21 Oct 95	**MY FRIENDS** *Warner Brothers W 0317CD*	29		2
17 Feb 96	**AEROPLANE** *Warner Brothers W 0331CD*	11		3
14 Jun 97	**LOVE ROLLERCOASTER** *Geffen GFSTD 22188*	7		8
12 Jun 99	**SCAR TISSUE** *Warner Brothers W 490CD*	15		6
4 Sep 99	**AROUND THE WORLD** *Warner Brothers W 500CD1*	35		2
12 Feb 00	**OTHERSIDE** *Warner Brothers W 510CD1*	33		2
19 Aug 00	**CALIFORNICATION** *Warner Brothers W 534CD1*	16		5
13 Jan 01	**ROAD TRIPPIN'** *Warner Brothers W 546CD1*	30		2
13 Jul 02	**BY THE WAY** *Warner Brothers W 580CD1*	2		10
2 Nov 02	**THE ZEPHYR SONG** *Warner Brothers W 592CD*	11		10
22 Feb 03	**CAN'T STOP** *Warner Brothers W 599CD*	22		6
28 Jun 03	**UNIVERSALLY SPEAKING** *Warner Brothers W 609CD*	27		2
22 Nov 03	**FORTUNE FADED** *Warner Brothers W 630CD*	11		5
6 May 06	**DANI CALIFORNIA** *Warner Brothers W715CD1*	2		17
22 Jul 06	**TELL ME BABY** *Warner Brothers W726CD1*	16		8
25 Nov 06	**SNOW (HEY HO)** *Warner Brothers W751CD1*	16		13
24 Feb 07	**DESECRATION SMILE** *Warner Brothers W756CD2*	27		2
12 May 07	**HUMP DE BUMP** *Warner Brothers W763CDX*	41		3

RED LIGHT COMPANY

UK, male vocal/instrumental group — 2

Date	Title	Peak Position	Weeks at No.1	Weeks on Chart
15 Nov 08	**SCHEME EUGENE** *Lavolta 021*	69		1
14 Mar 09	**ARTS AND CRAFTS** *Lavolta 022X*	53		1

RED 'N' WHITE MACHINES

UK, football fans (Southampton)/vocal group — 1

Date	Title	Peak Position	Weeks at No.1	Weeks on Chart
24 May 03	**SOUTHAMPTON BOYS** *Centric CEN 008*	16		1

RED RAW FEATURING 007

UK, male vocal/instrumental duo. See Clock — 1

Date	Title	Peak Position	Weeks at No.1	Weeks on Chart
28 Oct 95	**OOH LA LA LA** *Media MCSTD 2065*	59		1

RED SNAPPER

UK, male vocal/instrumental group — 1

Date	Title	Peak Position	Weeks at No.1	Weeks on Chart
21 Nov 98	**IMAGE OF YOU** *Warp WAP 111CD*	60		1

REDBONE

US, male vocal/instrumental group – Lolly & Pat Vegas, Anthony Bellamy & Peter De Poe — 12

Date	Title	Peak Position	Weeks at No.1	Weeks on Chart
25 Sep 71	**THE WITCH QUEEN OF NEW ORLEANS** *Epic EPC 7351*	2		12

REDD KROSS

US, male vocal/instrumental group — 4

Date	Title	Peak Position	Weeks at No.1	Weeks on Chart
5 Feb 94	**VISIONARY** *This Way Up WAY 2733*	75		1
10 Sep 94	**YESTERDAY ONCE MORE** *A&M 5807932*	45		2
1 Feb 97	**GET OUT OF MYSELF** *This Way Up WAY 5466*	63		1

REDD SQUARE FEATURING TIFF LACEY

UK, male/female vocal/production group — 1

Date	Title	Peak Position	Weeks at No.1	Weeks on Chart
26 Oct 02	**IN YOUR HANDS** *Inferno CDFERN 50*	64		1

SHARON REDD

US, female vocalist, d. 1 May 1992 (age 46) — 32

Date	Title	Peak Position	Weeks at No.1	Weeks on Chart
28 Feb 81	**CAN YOU HANDLE IT** *Epic EPC 9572*	31		8
2 Oct 82	**NEVER GIVE YOU UP** *Prelude PRL A 2755*	20		9
15 Jan 83	**IN THE NAME OF LOVE** *Prelude PRL A 2905*	31		5
22 Oct 83	**LOVE HOW YOU FEEL** *Prelude A 3868*	39		5
1 Feb 92	**CAN YOU HANDLE IT** *EMI EM 219* DNA FEATURING SHARON REDD	17		5

OTIS REDDING

US, male vocalist, d. 10 Dec 1967 (age 26) — 124

Date	Title	Peak Position	Weeks at No.1	Weeks on Chart
25 Nov 65	**MY GIRL** *Atlantic AT 4050*	11		16
7 Apr 66	**SATISFACTION** *Atlantic AT 4080*	33		4
14 Jul 66	**MY LOVER'S PRAYER** *Atlantic 584 019*	37		6
25 Aug 66	**I CAN'T TURN YOU LOOSE** *Atlantic 584 030*	29		8
24 Nov 66	**FA FA FA FA FA (SAD SONG)** *Atlantic 584 049*	23		9
26 Jan 67	**TRY A LITTLE TENDERNESS** *Atlantic 584 070*	46		4
23 Mar 67	**DAY TRIPPER** *Stax 601 005*	43		6
4 May 67	**LET ME COME ON HOME** *Stax 601 007*	48		1
15 Jun 67	**SHAKE** *Stax 601 011*	28		10
19 Jul 67	**TRAMP** *Stax 601 012* & CARLA THOMAS	18		11
11 Oct 67	**KNOCK ON WOOD** *Stax 601 021* & CARLA THOMAS	35		5
14 Feb 68	**MY GIRL** *Atlantic 584 092*	36		9

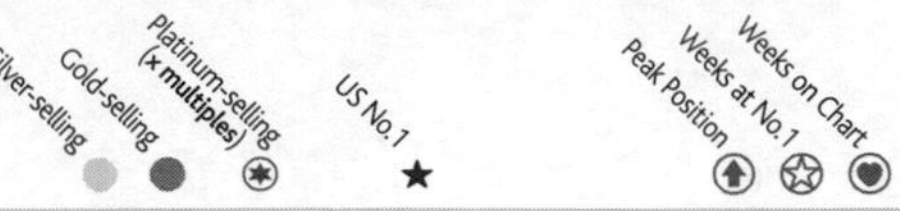

Date	Title	Peak Position	Weeks at No.1	Weeks on Chart
21 Feb 68	**(SITTIN' ON) THE DOCK OF THE BAY** *Stax 601 031* ★	3		15
29 May 68	**THE HAPPY SONG (DUM-DUM)** *Stax 601 040*	24		5
31 Jul 68	**HARD TO HANDLE** *Atlantic 584 199*	15		12
9 Jul 69	**LOVE MAN** *Atco 226 001*	43		3

HELEN REDDY

Australia, female vocalist — 18

Date	Title	Peak Position	Weeks at No.1	Weeks on Chart
18 Jan 75	**ANGIE BABY** *Capitol CL 15799* ★	5		10
28 Nov 81	**I CAN'T SAY GOODBYE TO YOU** *MCA 744*	43		8

REDHEAD KINGPIN & THE FBI

US, male rapper (David Guppy) & male vocal/rap group — 11

Date	Title	Peak Position	Weeks at No.1	Weeks on Chart
22 Jul 89	**DO THE RIGHT THING** *10 TEN 271*	13		10
2 Dec 89	**SUPERBAD SUPERSLICK** *10 TEN 286*	68		1

REDMAN

US, male rapper (Reggie Noble) — 43

Date	Title	Peak Position	Weeks at No.1	Weeks on Chart
25 Apr 98	**RAP SCHOLAR** *East West E 3853CD* DAS EFX FEATURING REDMAN	42		1
30 May 98	**MADE IT BACK** *Parlophone Rhythm CDRHYTHM 11* BEVERLEY KNIGHT FEATURING REDMAN	21		3
24 Oct 98	**HOW DEEP IS YOUR LOVE** *Island Black Music CID 725* DRU HILL FEATURING REDMAN	9		8
10 Apr 99	**MADE IT BACK 99 (REMIX)** *Parlophone Rhythm CDRHYTHS 18* BEVERLEY KNIGHT FEATURING REDMAN	19		5
12 Jun 99	**DA GOODNESS** *Def Jam 8709232*	52		1
22 Jul 00	**OOOH** *Tommy Boy TBCD 2102B* DE LA SOUL FEATURING REDMAN	29		2
15 Sep 01	**SMASH SUMTHIN'** *Def Jam 5886932* ADAM F FEATURING REDMAN	11		7
31 Aug 02	**SMASH SUMTHIN'** *Kaos KOASCD 003* ADAM F FEATURING REDMAN	47		2
23 Nov 02	**DIRRTY** *RCA 74321962722* CHRISTINA AGUILERA FEATURING REDMAN ⊛	1	2	9
11 Jan 03	**REACT** *J Records 74321988492* ERICK SERMON FEATURING REDMAN	14		5

REDNEX

Sweden, male/female vocal/instrumental group – Göran Danielsson, Annika Ljungberg, Anders Arstrand, Urban Landgren, Jonas Nilsson & Kent Olander — 23

Date	Title	Peak Position	Weeks at No.1	Weeks on Chart
17 Dec 94	**COTTON EYE JOE** *Internal Affairs KGBCD 016* ⊛	1	2	16
25 Mar 95	**OLD POP IN AN OAK** *Internal Affairs KGBCD 019*	12		6
21 Oct 95	**WILD 'N FREE** *Internal Affairs KGBCD 024*	55		1

REDS UNITED

UK, football fans (Manchester United)/vocal group — 13

Date	Title	Peak Position	Weeks at No.1	Weeks on Chart
6 Dec 97	**SING UP FOR THE CHAMPIONS** *Music Collection MANUCD 2* ● (silver)	12		9
9 May 98	**UNITED CALYPSO '98** *Music Collection MANUCD 3*	33		4

REDSKINS

UK, male vocal/instrumental trio — 12

Date	Title	Peak Position	Weeks at No.1	Weeks on Chart
10 Nov 84	**KEEP ON KEEPIN' ON** *Decca F 1*	43		5
22 Jun 85	**BRING IT DOWN (THIS INSANE THING)** *Decca F 2*	33		5
22 Feb 86	**THE POWER IS YOURS** *Decca F 3*	59		2

ALEX REECE

UK, male DJ/producer — 7

Date	Title	Peak Position	Weeks at No.1	Weeks on Chart
16 Dec 95	**FEEL THE SUNSHINE** *Blunted Vinyl BLNCD 016*	69		1
11 May 96	**FEEL THE SUNSHINE (REMIX)** *Fourth & Broadway BRCD 332*	26		3
27 Jul 96	**CANDLES** *Fourth & Broadway BRCD 333*	33		2
16 Nov 96	**ACID LAB** *Fourth & Broadway BRCD 344*	64		1

JIMMY REED

US, male vocalist/guitarist/harmonica player (Mathis Reed), d. 29 Aug 1976 (age 50) — 2

Date	Title	Peak Position	Weeks at No.1	Weeks on Chart
10 Sep 64	**SHAME SHAME SHAME** *Stateside SS 330*	45		2

LOU REED

US, male vocalist (Lou Firbank). See Velvet Underground — 26

Date	Title	Peak Position	Weeks at No.1	Weeks on Chart
12 May 73	**WALK ON THE WILD SIDE** *RCA 2303*	10		9
17 Jan 87	**SOUL MAN** *A&M AM 364* SAM MOORE & LOU REED	30		10
31 Jul 04	**SATELLITE OF LOVE 04** *NuLife 82876636472*	10		7

DAN REED NETWORK

US, male vocal/instrumental group — 16

Date	Title	Peak Position	Weeks at No.1	Weeks on Chart
20 Jan 90	**COME BACK BABY** *Mercury DRN 2*	51		3
17 Mar 90	**RAINBOW CHILD** *Mercury DRN 3*	60		3
21 Jul 90	**STARDATE 1990/RAINBOW CHILD** *Mercury DRN 4*	39		4
8 Sep 90	**LOVER/MONEY** *Mercury DRN 5*	45		3
13 Jul 91	**MIX IT UP** *Mercury MER 345*	49		2
21 Sep 91	**BABY NOW I** *Mercury MER 352*	65		1

REEF

UK, male vocal/instrumental group – Gary Stringer, Jack Bessant, Dominic Greensmith, Kenwyn House & Benmont Tench — 48

Date	Title	Peak Position	Weeks at No.1	Weeks on Chart
15 Apr 95	**GOOD FEELING** *Sony S2 6613602*	24		4
3 Jun 95	**NAKED** *Sony S2 6620622*	11		5
5 Aug 95	**WEIRD** *Sony S2 6622772*	19		3
2 Nov 96	**PLACE YOUR HANDS** *Sony S2 6635712*	6		7
25 Jan 97	**COME BACK BRIGHTER** *Sony S2 6640972*	8		5
5 Apr 97	**CONSIDERATION** *Sony S2 6643125*	13		4
2 Aug 97	**YER OLD** *Sony S2 6647032*	21		3
10 Apr 99	**I'VE GOT SOMETHING TO SAY** *Sony S2 6669545*	15		6
5 Jun 99	**SWEETY** *Sony S2 6673732*	46		1
11 Sep 99	**NEW BIRD** *Sony S2 6678512*	73		1
12 Aug 00	**SET THE RECORD STRAIGHT** *Sony S2 6695952*	19		5
16 Dec 00	**SUPERHERO** *Sony S2 6699382*	55		1
19 May 01	**ALL I WANT** *Sony S2 6708222*	51		1
25 Jan 03	**GIVE ME YOUR LOVE** *Sony S2 6731645*	44		1
28 Jun 03	**WASTER** *Reef Recordings SMASCD 051X*	56		1

REEL

Ireland, male vocal group — 3

Date	Title	Peak Position	Weeks at No.1	Weeks on Chart
24 Nov 01	**LIFT ME UP** *Universal TV 0154632*	39		1
8 Jun 02	**YOU TAKE ME AWAY** *Universal TV 0190182*	31		2

REEL BIG FISH

US, male vocal/instrumental group — 1

Date	Title	Peak Position	Weeks at No.1	Weeks on Chart
6 Apr 02	**SOLD OUT EP** *Jive 9270002*	62		1

REEL 2 REAL

US, male vocal/production duo – Erick Morillo & Mark Quashie — 53

Date	Title	Peak Position	Weeks at No.1	Weeks on Chart
12 Feb 94	**I LIKE TO MOVE IT** *Positiva CDTIV 10* FEATURING THE MAD STUNTMAN ● (silver)	5		20
2 Jul 94	**GO ON MOVE** *Positiva CDTIV 15* FEATURING THE MAD STUNTMAN	7		9
1 Oct 94	**CAN YOU FEEL IT** *Positiva CDTIV 22* FEATURING THE MAD STUNTMAN	13		5
3 Dec 94	**RAISE YOUR HANDS** *Positiva CDTIV 27* FEATURING THE MAD STUNTMAN	14		6
6 Jul 96	**JAZZ IT UP** *Positiva CDTIV 59*	7		7
1 Apr 95	**CONWAY** *Positiva CDTIVS 30* FEATURING THE MAD STUNTMAN	27		4
5 Oct 96	**ARE YOU READY FOR SOME MORE?** *Positiva CDTIV 56*	24		2

REELISTS

UK, male vocal/production duo — 6

Date	Title	Peak Position	Weeks at No.1	Weeks on Chart
25 May 02	**FREAK MODE** *Go! Beat GOBCD 45*	16		6

MAUREEN REES

UK, female TV personality/vocalist — 4

Date	Title	Peak Position	Weeks at No.1	Weeks on Chart
20 Dec 97	**DRIVING IN MY CAR** *Eagle EAGXS 014*	49		4

TONY REES & THE COTTAGERS

UK, football fans (Fulham)/vocal group — 1

Date	Title	Peak Position	Weeks at No.1	Weeks on Chart
10 May 75	**VIVA EL FULHAM** *Sonet SON 2059*	46		1

REESE PROJECT

US, male producer (Kevin Saunderson). See Inner City, Tronikhouse — 7

Date	Title	Peak Position	Weeks at No.1	Weeks on Chart
8 Aug 92	**THE COLOUR OF LOVE** *Network NWK 1*	52		2
12 Dec 92	**I BELIEVE** *Network NWKT 63*	74		1
13 Mar 93	**SO DEEP** *Network NWKCD 68*	54		2
24 Sep 94	**THE COLOUR OF LOVE (REMIX)** *Network NWKCD 81*	55		1
6 May 95	**DIRECT-ME** *Network NWKCD 87*	44		1

CONNOR REEVES

UK, male vocalist — 18

Date	Title	Peak	Wks at No.1	Wks
30 Aug 97	**MY FATHER'S SON** *Wildstar CDWILD 1*	12		5
22 Nov 97	**EARTHBOUND** *Wildstar CDWILD 2*	14		4
11 Apr 98	**READ MY MIND** *Wildstar CXWILD 4*	19		4
3 Oct 98	**SEARCHING FOR A SOUL** *Wildstar CDWILD 6*	28		2
4 Sep 99	**BEST FRIEND** *WEA 221CD1* MARK MORRISON & CONNOR REEVES	23		3

JIM REEVES

US, male vocalist, d. 31 Jul 1964 (age 39). The velvet-voiced country music balladeer who achieved most of his UK chart success after he was tragically killed in a plane crash. Shortly after his death, 'Gentleman Jim' had a record eight albums simultaneously in the Top 20 — 322

Date	Title	Peak	Wks at No.1	Wks
24 Mar 60	**HE'LL HAVE TO GO** *RCA 1168*	12		31
16 Mar 61	**WHISPERING HOPE** *RCA 1223*	50		1
23 Nov 61	**YOU'RE THE ONLY GOOD THING (THAT HAPPENED TO ME)** *RCA 1261*	17		19
28 Jun 62	**ADIOS AMIGO** *RCA 1293*	23		21
22 Nov 62	**I'M GONNA CHANGE EVERYTHING** *RCA 1317*	42		2
13 Jun 63	**WELCOME TO MY WORLD** *RCA 1342*	6		15
17 Oct 63	**GUILTY** *RCA 1364*	29		7
20 Feb 64	**I LOVE YOU BECAUSE** *RCA 1385*	5		39
18 Jun 64	**I WON'T FORGET YOU** *RCA 1400*	3		26
5 Nov 64	**THERE'S A HEARTACHE FOLLOWING ME** *RCA 1423*	6		13
4 Feb 65	**IT HURTS SO MUCH (TO SEE YOU)** *RCA 1437*	8		10
15 Apr 65	**NOT UNTIL NEXT TIME** *RCA 1446*	13		12
6 May 65	**HOW LONG HAS IT BEEN** *RCA 1445*	45		5
15 Jul 65	**THIS WORLD IS NOT MY HOME** *RCA 1412*	22		9
11 Nov 65	**IS IT REALLY OVER** *RCA 1488*	17		9
18 Aug 66	**DISTANT DRUMS** *RCA 1537*	1	5	25
2 Feb 67	**I WON'T COME IN WHILE HE'S THERE** *RCA 1563*	12		11
26 Jul 67	**TRYING TO FORGET** *RCA 1611*	33		5
22 Nov 67	**I HEARD A HEART BREAK LAST NIGHT** *RCA 1643*	38		6
27 Mar 68	**PRETTY BROWN EYES** *RCA 1672*	33		5
25 Jun 69	**WHEN TWO WORLDS COLLIDE** *RCA 1830*	17		17
6 Dec 69	**BUT YOU LOVE ME, DADDY** *RCA 1899*	15		16
21 Mar 70	**NOBODY'S FOOL** *RCA 1915*	32		5
12 Sep 70	**ANGELS DON'T LIE** *RCA 1997*	32		3
26 Jun 71	**I LOVE YOU BECAUSE/HE'LL HAVE TO GO/MOONLIGHT & ROSES** *RCA Maximillion 2092*	34		8
19 Feb 72	**YOU'RE FREE TO GO** *RCA 2174*	48		2

MARTHA REEVES & THE VANDELLAS

US, female vocal trio – Martha Reeves, Annette Beard (replaced by Betty Kelly) & Rosalind Ashford — 85

Date	Title	Peak	Wks at No.1	Wks
29 Oct 64	**DANCING IN THE STREET** *Stateside SS 345*	28		8
1 Apr 65	**NOWHERE TO RUN** *Tamla Motown TMG 502*	26		8
1 Dec 66	**I'M READY FOR LOVE** *Tamla Motown TMG 582*	22		8
30 Mar 67	**JIMMY MACK** *Tamla Motown TMG 599*	21		9
17 Jan 68	**HONEY CHILE** *Tamla Motown TMG 636*	30		9
15 Jan 69	**DANCING IN THE STREET** *Tamla Motown TMG 684*	4		12
16 Apr 69	**NOWHERE TO RUN** *Tamla Motown TMG 694*	42		3
29 Aug 70	**JIMMY MACK** *Tamla Motown TMG 599*	21		12
13 Feb 71	**FORGET ME NOT** *Tamla Motown TMG 762*	11		8
8 Jan 72	**BLESS YOU** *Tamla Motown TMG 794*	33		5
23 Jul 88	**NOWHERE TO RUN** *A&M AM 444*	52		3

VIC REEVES

UK, male comedian/vocalist (Jim Moir). See Shaun The Sheep — 29

Date	Title	Peak	Wks at No.1	Wks
27 Apr 91	**BORN FREE** *Sense SIGH 710* & THE ROMAN NUMERALS	6		6
26 Oct 91	**DIZZY** *Sense SIGH 712* & THE WONDER STUFF (silver-selling)	1	2	12
14 Dec 91	**ABIDE WITH ME** *Sense SIGH 713*	47		3
8 Jul 95	**I'M A BELIEVER** *Parlophone CDR 6412* EMF/REEVES & MORTIMER	3		8

REFLEKT FEATURING DELLINE BASS

UK, male/female vocal/production trio — 5

Date	Title	Peak	Wks at No.1	Wks
5 Mar 05	**NEED TO FEEL LOVED** *Positiva CDTIVS213*	14		5

REFLEX FEATURING MC VIPER

UK, male rap/production trio. See 187 Lockdown — 1

Date	Title	Peak	Wks at No.1	Wks
19 May 01	**PUT YOUR HANDS UP** *Gusto CDGUS 2*	72		1

REFUGEE ALLSTARS

Haiti/US, male vocal/instrumental group — 14

Date	Title	Peak	Wks at No.1	Wks
28 Jun 97	**WE TRYING TO STAY ALIVE** *Columbia 6646815* WYCLEF JEAN & THE REFUGEE ALLSTARS	13		5
6 Sep 97	**THE SWEETEST THING** *Columbia 6649785* FEATURING LAURYN HILL	18		4
27 Sep 97	**GUANTANAMERA** *Columbia 6650852* WYCLEF JEAN & THE REFUGEE ALLSTARS	25		2
27 Oct 01	**LOVING YOU (OLE OLE OLE)** *Blacklist 0133045 ERE* BRIAN HARVEY & THE REFUGEE CREW	20		3

JOAN REGAN

UK, female vocalist — 62

Date	Title	Peak	Wks at No.1	Wks
11 Dec 53	**RICOCHET** *Decca F 10193* & THE SQUADRONAIRES	8		5
14 May 54	**SOMEONE ELSE'S ROSES** *Decca F 10257*	5		8
1 Oct 54	**IF I GIVE MY HEART TO YOU** *Decca F 10373*	3		11
5 Nov 54	**WAIT FOR ME DARLING** *Decca F 10362* & THE JOHNSTON BROTHERS	18		1
25 Mar 55	**PRIZE OF GOLD** *Decca F 10432*	6		8
6 May 55	**OPEN UP YOUR HEART** *Decca F 10474* JOAN & RUSTY REGAN	19		1
1 May 59	**MAY YOU ALWAYS** *HMV POP 593*	9		16
5 Feb 60	**HAPPY ANNIVERSARY** *Pye 7N 15238*	29		2
28 Jul 60	**PAPA LOVES MAMA** *Pye 7N 15278*	29		8
24 Nov 60	**ONE OF THE LUCKY ONES** *Pye 7N 15310*	47		1
5 Jan 61	**IT MUST BE SANTA** *Pye 7N 15303*	42		1

REGENTS

UK, male/female vocal/instrumental group — 14

Date	Title	Peak	Wks at No.1	Wks
22 Dec 79	**7TEEN** *Rialto TREB 111*	11		12
7 Jun 80	**SEE YOU LATER** *Arista ARIST 350*	55		2

REGGAE BOYZ

Jamaica, male vocal/instrumental group — 1

Date	Title	Peak	Wks at No.1	Wks
27 Jun 98	**KICK IT** *Universal MCSTD 40167*	59		1

REGGAE PHILHARMONIC ORCHESTRA

UK, male/female vocal/instrumental group — 11

Date	Title	Peak	Wks at No.1	Wks
19 Nov 88	**MINNIE THE MOOCHER** *Mango IS 378*	35		9
28 Jul 90	**LOVELY THING** *Mango MNG 742*	71		2

REGINA

US, female vocalist (Regina Richards) — 3

Date	Title	Peak	Wks at No.1	Wks
1 Feb 86	**BABY LOVE** *Funkin' Marvellous MARV 01*	50		3

REID

UK, male vocal trio — 12

Date	Title	Peak	Wks at No.1	Wks
8 Oct 88	**ONE WAY OUT** *Syncopate SY 16*	66		2
11 Feb 89	**REAL EMOTION** *Syncopate SY 24*	65		2
15 Apr 89	**GOOD TIMES** *Syncopate SY 27*	55		6
21 Oct 89	**LOVIN' ON THE SIDE** *Syncopate REID 1*	71		2

JUNIOR REID

Jamaica, male vocalist (Delroy Reid). See Black Uhuru — 27

Date	Title	Peak	Wks at No.1	Wks
10 Sep 88	**STOP THIS CRAZY THING** *Ahead Of Our Time CCUT 4* COLDCUT FEATURING JUNIOR REID & THE AHEAD OF OUR TIME ORCHESTRA	21		7
14 Jul 90	**I'M FREE** *Raw TV RTV 9* SOUP DRAGONS FEATURING JUNIOR REID	5		12
11 Jul 92	**SHINE EYE** *Shut Up And Dance SUAD 32S* RAGGA TWINS FEATURING JUNIOR REID	63		2
4 Nov 06	**IT'S OKAY** *Geffen 1713921* GAME FEATURING JUNIOR REID	26		6

MIKE REID

UK, male actor/comedian/vocalist, d. 29 Jul 2007 (age 67) — 10

Date	Title	Peak	Wks at No.1	Wks
22 Mar 75	**UGLY DUCKLING** *Pye 7N 45434*	10		8
24 Apr 99	**THE MORE I SEE YOU** *Telstar TV CDSTAS 3049* BARBARA WINDSOR & MIKE REID	46		2

NEIL REID

UK, male vocalist — 26

Date	Title	Peak	Wks at No.1	Wks
1 Jan 72	**MOTHER OF MINE** *Decca F 13264*	2		20
8 Apr 72	**THAT'S WHAT I WANT TO BE** *Decca F 13300*	45		6

TOMMY REILLY
UK, male vocalist — **2**

Date	Title / Label	Peak	Wks at No.1	Wks on Chart
7 Feb 09	**GIMME A CALL** *Polydor GBUM70905402*	14		2

KEITH RELF
UK, male vocalist, d. 14 May 1976 (age 33). See Yardbirds — **1**

Date	Title / Label	Peak	Wks at No.1	Wks on Chart
26 May 66	**MR ZERO** *Columbia DB 7920*	50		1

R.E.M.
US, male vocal/instrumental group – Michael Stipe, Bill Berry, Peter Buck & Mike Mills — **187**

Date	Title / Label	Peak	Wks at No.1	Wks on Chart
28 Nov 87	**THE ONE I LOVE** *IRS IRM 46*	51		8
30 Apr 88	**FINEST WORKSONG** *IRS IRM 161*	50		2
4 Feb 89	**STAND** *Warner Brothers W 7577*	51		3
3 Jun 89	**ORANGE CRUSH** *Warner Brothers W 2960*	28		5
12 Aug 89	**STAND** *Warner Brothers W 2833*	48		2
9 Mar 91	**LOSING MY RELIGION** *Warner Brothers W 0015*	19		9
18 May 91	**SHINY HAPPY PEOPLE** *Warner Brothers W 0027*	6		11
17 Aug 91	**NEAR WILD HEAVEN** *Warner Brothers W 0055*	27		4
21 Sep 91	**THE ONE I LOVE** *IRS IRM 178*	16		6
16 Nov 91	**RADIO SONG** *Warner Brothers W 0072*	28		3
14 Dec 91	**IT'S THE END OF THE WORLD AS WE KNOW IT** *IRS IRM 180*	39		4
3 Oct 92	**DRIVE** *Warner Brothers W 0136*	11		5
28 Nov 92	**MAN ON THE MOON** *Warner Brothers W 0143*	18		8
20 Feb 93	**THE SIDEWINDER SLEEPS TONITE** *Warner Brothers W 0152CD1*	17		6
17 Apr 93	**EVERYBODY HURTS** *Warner Brothers W 0169CD1* ●	7		12
24 Jul 93	**NIGHTSWIMMING** *Warner Brothers W 0184CD*	27		5
11 Dec 93	**FIND THE RIVER** *Warner Brothers W 0211CD*	54		1
17 Sep 94	**WHAT'S THE FREQUENCY, KENNETH** *Warner Brothers W 0265CD*	9		7
12 Nov 94	**BANG AND BLAME** *Warner Brothers W 0275CD*	15		4
4 Feb 95	**CRUSH WITH EYELINER** *Warner Brothers W 0281CD*	23		3
15 Apr 95	**STRANGE CURRENCIES** *Warner Brothers W 0290CD*	9		4
29 Jul 95	**TONGUE** *Warner Brothers W 0308CD*	13		5
31 Aug 96	**E – BOW THE LETTER** *Warner Brothers W 0369CD*	4		5
2 Nov 96	**BITTERSWEET ME** *Warner Brothers W 0377CDX*	19		2
14 Dec 96	**ELECTROLITE** *Warner Brothers W 0383CDX*	29		2
24 Oct 98	**DAYSLEEPER** *Warner Brothers W 0455CD*	6		6
19 Dec 98	**LOTUS** *Warner Brothers W 466CD*	26		5
20 Mar 99	**AT MY MOST BEAUTIFUL** *Warner Brothers W 477CD*	10		4
5 Feb 00	**THE GREAT BEYOND** *Warner Brothers W 516CD*	3		10
12 May 01	**IMITATION OF LIFE** *Warner Brothers W 559CD*	6		9
4 Aug 01	**ALL THE WAY TO RENO** *Warner Brothers W 568CDX*	24		3
1 Dec 01	**I'LL TAKE THE RAIN** *Warner Brothers W 573CD*	44		1
25 Oct 03	**BAD DAY** *Warner Brothers W 624CD1*	8		7
17 Jan 04	**ANIMAL** *Warner Brothers W 633CD*	33		2
9 Oct 04	**LEAVING NEW YORK** *Warner Brothers W 654CD1*	5		5
11 Dec 04	**AFTERMATH** *Warner Brothers W658CD2*	41		2
12 Mar 05	**ELECTRON BLUE** *Warner Brothers W665CD2*	26		2
23 Jul 05	**WANDERLUST** *Warner Brothers W676CD2*	27		2
23 Feb 08	**SUPERNATURAL SUPERSERIOUS** *Warner Brothers W798CD*	54		3

REMADY
Switzerland, male producer (Benjamin Muhlethaler) — **1**

Date	Title / Label	Peak	Wks at No.1	Wks on Chart
27 Feb 10	**NO SUPERSTAR** *Maelstrom GBDLM0990669*	75		1

REMBRANDTS
US, male vocal/instrumental duo – Phil Solem & Danny Wilde — **28**

Date	Title / Label	Peak	Wks at No.1	Wks on Chart
2 Sep 95	**I'LL BE THERE FOR YOU** *Elektra A 4390CD* ●	3		12
20 Jan 96	**THIS HOUSE IS NOT A HOME** *East West A 4336CD*	58		1
24 May 97	**I'LL BE THERE FOR YOU** *East West A 4390CD* ●	5		15

REMY ZERO
US, male vocal/instrumental group — **1**

Date	Title / Label	Peak	Wks at No.1	Wks on Chart
27 Apr 02	**SAVE ME** *Elektra E 7297CD*	55		1

RENAISSANCE
UK, male/female vocal/instrumental group – Annie Haslam, John Camp, Michael Dunford, Terry Sullivan & John Trout — **11**

Date	Title / Label	Peak	Wks at No.1	Wks on Chart
15 Jul 78	**NORTHERN LIGHTS** *Warner Brothers K 17177* ●	10		11

RENE & ANGELA
US, male/female vocal duo — **15**

Date	Title / Label	Peak	Wks at No.1	Wks on Chart
15 Jun 85	**SAVE YOUR LOVE (FOR NUMBER 1)** *Club JAB 14* FEATURING KURTIS BLOW	66		2
7 Sep 85	**I'LL BE GOOD** *Club JAB 18*	22		10
2 Nov 85	**SECRET RENDEZVOUS** *Champion CHAMP 5*	54		3

RENE & YVETTE
UK, male/female vocal/TV comedy character duo — **4**

Date	Title / Label	Peak	Wks at No.1	Wks on Chart
22 Nov 86	**JE T'AIME (ALLO ALLO)/RENE DMC (DEVASTATING MACHO CHARISMA)** *Sedition EDIT 3319*	57		4

NICOLE RENEE
US, female vocalist — **1**

Date	Title / Label	Peak	Wks at No.1	Wks on Chart
12 Dec 98	**STRAWBERRY** *Atlantic AT 0050CD*	55		1

RENEE & RENATO
UK/Italy, female/male vocal duo – Hilary Lester & Renato Pagliari, d. 29 July 2009 — **22**

Date	Title / Label	Peak	Wks at No.1	Wks on Chart
30 Oct 82	**SAVE YOUR LOVE** *Hollywood HWD 003* ●	1	4	16
12 Feb 83	**JUST ONE MORE KISS** *Hollywood HWD 006*	48		6

RENEGADE SOUNDWAVE
UK, male vocal/production trio — **7**

Date	Title / Label	Peak	Wks at No.1	Wks on Chart
3 Feb 90	**PROBABLY A ROBBERY** *Mute 102*	38		6
5 Feb 94	**RENEGADE SOUNDWAVE** *Mute CDMUTE 146*	64		1

REO SPEEDWAGON
US, male vocal/instrumental group – Kevin Cronin, Neil Doughty, Alan Gratzer, Bruce Hall & Gary Richrath — **38**

Date	Title / Label	Peak	Wks at No.1	Wks on Chart
11 Apr 81	**KEEP ON LOVING YOU** *Epic EPC 9544* ★	7		14
27 Jun 81	**TAKE IT ON THE RUN** *Epic EPC A 1207*	19		14
16 Mar 85	**CAN'T FIGHT THIS FEELING** *Epic A 4880* ★	16		10

REPARATA & THE DELRONS
US, female vocal group — **12**

Date	Title / Label	Peak	Wks at No.1	Wks on Chart
20 Mar 68	**CAPTAIN OF YOUR SHIP** *Bell 1002*	13		10
18 Oct 75	**SHOES** *Dart 2066 562* REPARATA	43		2

REPUBLICA
UK/Nigeria, female/male vocal/instrumental group – Samantha 'Saffron' Sprackling, Dave Barbarossa, Tim Dorney, Johnny Male & Andy Todd — **18**

Date	Title / Label	Peak	Wks at No.1	Wks on Chart
27 Apr 96	**READY TO GO** *Deconstruction 74321326132*	43		2
1 Mar 97	**READY TO GO** *Deconstruction 74321421332*	13		6
3 May 97	**DROP DEAD GORGEOUS** *Deconstruction 74321408442*	7		7
3 Oct 98	**FROM RUSH HOUR WITH LOVE** *Deconstruction 74321610472*	20		3

RESEARCH
UK, male vocal/instrumental group — **5**

Date	Title / Label	Peak	Wks at No.1	Wks on Chart
27 Nov 04	**SHE'S NOT LEAVING** *At Large FUGCD005*	73		1
3 Sep 05	**C'MON CHAMELEON/I LOVE YOU BUT** *At Large FUGCD008*	63		1
29 Oct 05	**THE WAY YOU USED TO SMILE** *At Large FUGCD010*	66		1
25 Feb 06	**LONELY HEARTS STILL BEAT THE SAME** *At Large FUGCD013*	50		1
17 Jun 06	**THE HARD TIMES** *At Large FUGCD015*	73		1

RESONANCE FEATURING THE BURRELLS
US, male vocal/production trio — **1**

Date	Title / Label	Peak	Wks at No.1	Wks on Chart
26 May 01	**DJ** *Strictly Rhythm SRUKCD 02*	67		1

RESOURCE
Germany, male vocal/production group — **2**

Date	Title / Label	Peak	Wks at No.1	Wks on Chart
31 May 03	**I JUST DIED IN YOUR ARMS** *Substance SUBS17CDS*	42		2

REST ASSURED
UK, male production trio. See Gat Decor, Phunky Phantom — **7**

Date	Title / Label	Peak	Wks at No.1	Wks on Chart
28 Feb 98	**TREAT INFAMY** *ffrr FCD 333*	14		7

REUBEN
UK, male vocal/instrumental trio — 4

Date	Title / Label	Peak	Wks No.1	Wks
19 Jun 04	**FREDDY KRUEGER** *Xtra Mile XMR102*	53		1
28 Aug 04	**MOVING TO BLACKWATER** *Xtra Mile XMR104*	59		1
25 Jun 05	**A KICK I N THE MOUTH** *Xtra Mile XMR108*	58		1
17 Sep 05	**KEEP IT TO YOURSELF** *Xtra Mile XMR109*	62		1

REUNION
US, male session vocal group — 4

Date	Title / Label	Peak	Wks No.1	Wks
21 Sep 74	**LIFE IS A ROCK (BUT THE RADIO ROLLED ME)** *RCA PB 10056*	33		4

REVELATION
UK, male/female vocal/production group — 2

Date	Title / Label	Peak	Wks No.1	Wks
10 May 03	**JUST BE DUB TO ME** *Multiply CDMULTY 99*	36		2

REVEREND & THE MAKERS
UK, male/female vocal/instrumental group – Jon 'The Reverend' McClure, Ed Cosens, Stuart Doughty, Tom Jarvis, Laura Manuel, Joe Moskow & Richy Westley — 28

Date	Title / Label	Peak	Wks No.1	Wks
19 May 07	**HEAVYWEIGHT CHAMPION OF THE WORLD** *Wall Of Sound WOS009CD*	8		21
8 Sep 07	**HE SAID HE LOVED ME** *Wall Of Sound WOS014CD*	16		6
1 Dec 07	**OPEN YOUR WINDOW** *Wall Of Sound WOS020CD*	65		1

REVIVAL 3000
UK, male DJ/production trio — 1

Date	Title / Label	Peak	Wks No.1	Wks
1 Nov 97	**THE MIGHTY HIGH** *Hi-Life 5718092*	47		1

REVOLTING COCKS
UK, male vocal/instrumental group — 1

Date	Title / Label	Peak	Wks No.1	Wks
18 Sep 93	**DA YA THINK I'M SEXY** *Devotion CDDVN 111*	61		1

DEBBIE REYNOLDS
US, female vocalist (Mary Reynolds) — 17

Date	Title / Label	Peak	Wks No.1	Wks
30 Aug 57	**TAMMY** *Coral Q 72274* ★	2		17

JODY REYNOLDS
US, male vocalist, d. 7 Nov 2008 (age 75) — 1

Date	Title / Label	Peak	Wks No.1	Wks
14 Apr 79	**ENDLESS SLEEP** *Lightning LIG 9015*	66		1

LJ REYNOLDS
US, male vocalist — 3

Date	Title / Label	Peak	Wks No.1	Wks
30 Jun 84	**DON'T LET NOBODY HOLD YOU DOWN** *Club JAB 5*	53		3

REYNOLDS GIRLS
UK, female vocal duo – Aisling & Linda Reynolds — 12

Date	Title / Label	Peak	Wks No.1	Wks
25 Feb 89	**I'D RATHER JACK** *PWL 25*	8		12

REZILLOS
UK, male/female vocal/instrumental group — 21

Date	Title / Label	Peak	Wks No.1	Wks
12 Aug 78	**TOP OF THE POPS** *Sire SIR 4001*	17		9
25 Nov 78	**DESTINATION VENUS** *Sire SIR 4008*	43		4
18 Aug 79	**I WANNA BE YOUR MAN/I CAN'T STAND MY BABY** *Sensible SAB 1*	71		2
26 Jan 80	**MOTORBIKE BEAT** *Dindisc DIN 5* REVILLOS	45		6

REZONANCE Q
UK, male/female vocal/production duo. See Eyeopener — 2

Date	Title / Label	Peak	Wks No.1	Wks
1 Mar 03	**SOMEDAY** *All Around The World CXGLOBE 266*	29		2

RHAPSODY FEATURING WARREN G & SISSEL
US/Norway, male/female rap/vocal group — 7

Date	Title / Label	Peak	Wks No.1	Wks
10 Jan 98	**PRINCE IGOR** *Def Jam 5749652*	15		7

RHC
UK/US, male/female production/vocal duo — 1

Date	Title / Label	Peak	Wks No.1	Wks
11 Jan 92	**FEVER CALLED LOVE** *R&S RSUK 9*	65		1

RHIANNA
UK, female vocalist (Rhianna Kelly) — 6

Date	Title / Label	Peak	Wks No.1	Wks
1 Jun 02	**OH BABY** *Sony S2 6726232*	18		5
14 Sep 02	**WORD LOVE** *Sony S2 6730115*	41		1

RHODA WITH THE SPECIAL A.K.A.
UK, female vocalist & male vocal/instrumental group — 5

Date	Title / Label	Peak	Wks No.1	Wks
23 Jan 82	**THE BOILER** *2 Tone CHSTT 18*	35		5

RHYMEFEST FEATURING KANYE WEST
US, male rap/DJ/production duo — 2

Date	Title / Label	Peak	Wks No.1	Wks
25 Feb 06	**BRAND NEW** *J Records 82876778842*	32		2

BUSTA RHYMES
US, male rapper/actor (Trevor Smith) — 168

Date	Title / Label	Peak	Wks No.1	Wks
11 May 96	**WOO-HAH!! GOT YOU ALL IN CHECK** *Elektra EKR 220CD*	8		7
21 Sep 96	**IT'S A PARTY** *Elektra EKR 226CD* FEATURING ZHANE	23		2
5 Apr 97	**HIT 'EM HIGH (THE MONSTARS' ANTHEM)** *Atlantic A 5449CD* B REAL/BUSTA RHYMES/COOLIO/LL COOL J/METHOD MAN	8		6
3 May 97	**DO MY THING** *Elektra EKR 235CD*	39		1
18 Oct 97	**PUT YOUR HANDS WHERE MY EYES COULD SEE** *Elektra E 3900CD*	16		3
20 Dec 97	**DANGEROUS** *Elektra E 3877CD*	32		4
18 Apr 98	**TURN IT UP/FIRE IT UP** *Elektra E 3847CD* ●	2		10
11 Jul 98	**ONE** *Elektra E 3833CD1* FEATURING ERYKAH BADU	23		3
30 Jan 99	**GIMME SOME MORE** *Elektra E 3782CD*	5		6
1 May 99	**WHAT'S IT GONNA BE?!** *Elektra E 3762CD1* FEATURING JANET	6		7
22 Jul 00	**GET OUT** *Elektra E 7075CD*	57		1
16 Dec 00	**FIRE** *East West E 7136CD*	60		1
18 Aug 01	**ANTE UP** *Epic 6717882* M.O.P. FEATURING BUSTA RHYMES	7		8
16 Mar 02	**BREAK YA NECK** *J Records 74321922332*	11		6
8 Jun 02	**PASS THE COURVOISIER – PART II** *J Records 74321937902* BUSTA RHYMES, P DIDDY & PHARRELL	16		7
8 Feb 03	**MAKE IT CLAP** *J Records 82876502062* FEATURING SPLIFF STAR	16		4
7 Jun 03	**I KNOW WHAT YOU WANT** *J Records 82876528292* & MARIAH CAREY	3		13
29 Nov 03	**LIGHT YOUR ASS ON FIRE** *Arista 82876572512* FEATURING PHARRELL	62		1
15 May 04	**PASS THE COURVOISIER – PART II** *J Records 74321937902* BUSTA RHYMES, P DIDDY & PHARRELL	71		1
22 May 04	**WHAT'S HAPPENIN'** *Def Jam 9862518* METHOD MAN FEATURING BUSTA RHYMES	17		5
10 Sep 05	**DON'T CHA (IMPORT)** *Polydor AMB000468322* PUSSYCAT DOLLS FEATURING BUSTA RHYMES	44		1
17 Sep 05	**DON'T CHA** *A&M/Polydor 9885052* PUSSYCAT DOLLS FEATURING BUSTA RHYMES ●	1	3	37
20 May 06	**TOUCH IT** *Interscope 9855966*	6		7
15 Jul 06	**I LOVE MY CHICK** *Interscope 1702859*	8		10
7 Jun 08	**RUN THE SHOW** *Epic USSM10800485* KAT DELUNA FEATURING BUSTA RHYMES	41		3
28 Jun 08	**WE MADE IT** *Warner Brothers W810CD* FEATURING LINKIN PARK	10		13
15 Aug 09	**WORLD GO ROUND** *Island USUM70852215* FEATURING ESTELLE	66		1

DYLAN RHYMES FEATURING KATHERINE ELLIS
UK, male/female vocal/production duo — 1

Date	Title / Label	Peak	Wks No.1	Wks
29 Jan 05	**SALTY** *Kingsize KS093D1*	70		1

RHYTHIM IS RHYTHIM
US, male producer (Derrick May) — 1

Date	Title / Label	Peak	Wks No.1	Wks
11 Nov 89	**STRINGS OF LIFE** *Kool Kat KOOL 509*	74		1

RHYTHM ETERNITY
UK, male/female production/vocal group — 1

Date	Title / Label	Peak	Wks No.1	Wks
23 May 92	**PINK CHAMPAGNE** *Dead Dead Good GOOD 15T*	72		1

RHYTHM FACTOR
US, male/female vocal/instrumental group — 2

Date	Title / Label	Peak	Wks No.1	Wks
29 Apr 95	**YOU BRING ME JOY** *Multiply CDMULTY 4*	53		2

RHYTHM MASTERS

UK/Malta, male DJ/production duo. See Big Room Girl featuring Darryl Pandy, Rhythmatic Junkies — 4

Date	Title	Peak Position	Weeks at No.1	Weeks on Chart
16 Aug 97	**COME ON YALL** *Faze 2 CDFAZE 37*	49		1
6 Dec 97	**ENTER THE SCENE** *Distinctive DISNCD 40* DJ SUPREME VS THE RHYTHM MASTERS	49		1
18 Aug 01	**UNDERGROUND** *Black & Blue NEOCD 056*	50		1
30 Mar 02	**GHETTO** *Black & Blue NEOCD 074* FEATURING JOE WATSON	71		1

RHYTHM-N-BASS

UK, male vocal group — 4

Date	Title	Peak Position	Weeks at No.1	Weeks on Chart
19 Sep 92	**ROSES** *Epic 6582907*	56		2
3 Jul 93	**CAN'T STOP THIS FEELING** *Epic 6592002*	59		2

RHYTHM OF LIFE

UK, male DJ/producer (Steve Burgess) — 2

Date	Title	Peak Position	Weeks at No.1	Weeks on Chart
13 May 00	**YOU PUT ME IN HEAVEN WITH YOUR TOUCH** *Xtravaganza XTRAV 4CDS*	24		2

RHYTHM ON THE LOOSE

UK, male producer (Geoff Hibbert) — 2

Date	Title	Peak Position	Weeks at No.1	Weeks on Chart
19 Aug 95	**BREAK OF DAWN** *Six6 SIXCD 126*	36		2

RHYTHM QUEST

UK, male producer (Mark Hadfield) — 2

Date	Title	Peak Position	Weeks at No.1	Weeks on Chart
20 Jun 92	**CLOSER TO ALL YOUR DREAMS** *Network NWK 40*	45		2

RHYTHM SECTION

UK, male production group — 1

Date	Title	Peak Position	Weeks at No.1	Weeks on Chart
18 Jul 92	**MIDSUMMER MADNESS (EP)** *Rhythm Section RSEC 006*	66		1

RHYTHM SOURCE

UK, male/female vocal/instrumental group — 1

Date	Title	Peak Position	Weeks at No.1	Weeks on Chart
17 Jun 95	**LOVE SHINE** *A&M 5810672*	74		1

RHYTHMATIC

UK, male production duo — 3

Date	Title	Peak Position	Weeks at No.1	Weeks on Chart
12 May 90	**TAKE ME BACK** *Network NWK 8*	71		2
3 Nov 90	**FREQUENCY** *Network NWK 13*	62		1

RHYTHMATIC JUNKIES

UK, male vocal/production group. See Rhythm Masters — 1

Date	Title	Peak Position	Weeks at No.1	Weeks on Chart
15 May 99	**THE FEELIN (CLAP YOUR HANDS)** *Sound Of Ministry RIDE 2CDS*	67		1

RHYTHMKILLAZ

Holland, male production duo. See Chocolate Puma, Goodmen, Jark Prongo, Riva featuring Dannii Minogue, Tomba Vira — 2

Date	Title	Peak Position	Weeks at No.1	Weeks on Chart
31 Mar 01	**WACK ASS MF** *Incentive CENT 18CDS*	32		2

RIALTO

UK, male vocal/instrumental group — 8

Date	Title	Peak Position	Weeks at No.1	Weeks on Chart
8 Nov 97	**MONDAY MORNING 5:19** *East West EW 116CD*	37		2
17 Jan 98	**UNTOUCHABLE** *East West EW 107CD1*	20		3
28 Mar 98	**DREAM ANOTHER DREAM** *East West EW 156CD1*	39		2
17 Oct 98	**SUMMER'S OVER** *China WOKCDR 2099*	60		1

ROSIE RIBBONS

UK, female vocalist — 7

Date	Title	Peak Position	Weeks at No.1	Weeks on Chart
2 Nov 02	**BLINK** *T2 CDSTAS 3288*	12		4
25 Jan 03	**A LITTLE BIT** *T2 CDSTAS 3312*	19		3

DAMIEN RICE

Ireland, male vocalist/guitarist — 26

Date	Title	Peak Position	Weeks at No.1	Weeks on Chart
1 Nov 03	**CANNONBALL** *DRM/14th Floor DR03CD1*	32		2
17 Jul 04	**CANNONBALL** *DRM/14th Floor DR03CD1*	19		7
25 Dec 04	**THE BLOWER'S DAUGHTER** *14th Floor DR06CD1*	27		5
2 Apr 05	**VOLCANO** *DRM/14th Floor DR07CD1*	29		3
2 Jul 05	**UNPLAYED PIANO** *DRM/14th Floor DR08CD* & LISA HANNIGAN	24		3
2 Dec 06	**9 CRIMES** *DRM/14th Floor DR09CD*	29		5
17 Feb 07	**ROOTLESS TREE** *Heffa/14th Floor DR10CD*	50		1

REVA RICE & GREG ELLIS

US/UK, female/male vocal/acting duo — 2

Date	Title	Peak Position	Weeks at No.1	Weeks on Chart
27 Mar 93	**NEXT TIME YOU FALL IN LOVE** *Really Useful RURCD 12*	59		2

CHARLIE RICH

US, male vocalist/keyboard player, d. 25 Jul 1995 (age 62) — 29

Date	Title	Peak Position	Weeks at No.1	Weeks on Chart
16 Feb 74	**THE MOST BEAUTIFUL GIRL** *CBS 1897* ★	2		14
13 Apr 74	**BEHIND CLOSED DOORS** *Epic EPC 1539*	16		10
1 Feb 75	**WE LOVE EACH OTHER** *Epic EPC 2868*	37		5

RICHIE RICH

UK, male DJ/producer (Richard Morgan) — 16

Date	Title	Peak Position	Weeks at No.1	Weeks on Chart
16 Jul 88	**TURN IT UP** *Club JAR 68*	48		3
22 Oct 88	**I'LL HOUSE YOU** *Gee Street GEE 003* MEETS THE JUNGLE BROTHERS	22		5
10 Dec 88	**MY DJ (PUMP IT UP SOME)** *Gee Street GEE 7*	74		1
2 Sep 89	**SALSA HOUSE** *ffrr F 113*	50		3
9 Mar 91	**YOU USED TO SALSA** *ffrr F 156* FEATURING RALPHI ROSARIO	52		3
29 Mar 97	**STAY WITH ME** *Castle CATX 1001* & ESERA TUAOLO	58		1

RISHI RICH PROJECT

UK, male/female vocal/rap/production group – Rishpal Rekhi & various musicians, including Juggy D (Jagwinder Dhaliwal), Veronica Mehta, Mumzy Stranger (Muhammad Ahmed) & Jay Sean* (Kamaljit Jhooti) — 15

Date	Title	Peak Position	Weeks at No.1	Weeks on Chart
20 Sep 03	**DANCE WITH YOU (NACHNA TERE NAAL)** *Relentless RELCD1* FEATURING JAY SEAN	12		5
3 Jul 04	**EYES ON YOU** *Relentless RELDX5* JAY SEAN FEATURING RISHI RICH PROJECT	6		10

TONY RICH PROJECT

US, male vocalist (Antonio Jeffries) — 22

Date	Title	Peak Position	Weeks at No.1	Weeks on Chart
4 May 96	**NOBODY KNOWS** *LaFace 74321356422*	4		17
31 Aug 96	**LIKE A WOMAN** *LaFace 74321401612*	27		4
14 Dec 96	**LEAVIN'** *LaFace 74321438382*	52		1

RICH KIDS

UK, male vocal/instrumental group — 5

Date	Title	Peak Position	Weeks at No.1	Weeks on Chart
28 Jan 78	**RICH KIDS** *EMI 2738*	24		5

CLIFF RICHARD

UK, male vocalist (Harry Webb). The most successful British act of all time, whose UK singles sales stand at an unrivalled 21.4 million. Sir Cliff has had more hit singles than any other artist (including No.1s in five different decades) and more Top 10 albums than any other UK act — 1177

Date	Title	Peak Position	Weeks at No.1	Weeks on Chart
12 Sep 58	**MOVE IT** *Columbia DB 4178* & THE DRIFTERS	2		17
21 Nov 58	**HIGH CLASS BABY** *Columbia DB 4203* & THE DRIFTERS	7		10
30 Jan 59	**LIVIN' LOVIN' DOLL** *Columbia DB 4249* & THE DRIFTERS	20		6
8 May 59	**MEAN STREAK** *Columbia DB 4290* & THE DRIFTERS	10		9
15 May 59	**NEVER MIND** *Columbia DB 4290* & THE DRIFTERS	21		2
10 Jul 59	**LIVING DOLL** *Columbia DB 4306* & THE DRIFTERS	1	6	23
9 Oct 59	**TRAVELLIN' LIGHT** *Columbia DB 4351* & THE SHADOWS	1	5	17
9 Oct 59	**DYNAMITE** *Columbia DB 4351* & THE SHADOWS	16		4
15 Jan 60	**EXPRESSO BONGO EP** *Columbia SEG 7971* & THE SHADOWS	14		7
22 Jan 60	**A VOICE IN THE WILDERNESS** *Columbia DB 4398* & THE SHADOWS	2		16
24 Mar 60	**FALL IN LOVE WITH YOU** *Columbia DB 4431* & THE SHADOWS	2		15
30 Jun 60	**PLEASE DON'T TEASE** *Columbia DB 4479* & THE SHADOWS	1	3	18
22 Sep 60	**NINE TIMES OUT OF TEN** *Columbia DB 4506* & THE SHADOWS	3		12
1 Dec 60	**I LOVE YOU** *Columbia DB 4547* & THE SHADOWS	1	2	16
2 Mar 61	**THEME FOR A DREAM** *Columbia DB 4593* & THE SHADOWS	3		14
30 Mar 61	**GEE WHIZ IT'S YOU** *Columbia DC 756* & THE SHADOWS	4		14
22 Jun 61	**A GIRL LIKE YOU** *Columbia DB 4667* & THE SHADOWS	3		14
19 Oct 61	**WHEN THE GIRL IN YOUR ARMS IS THE GIRL IN YOUR HEART** *Columbia DB 4716*	3		15
11 Jan 62	**THE YOUNG ONES** *Columbia DB 4761* & THE SHADOWS	1	6	21
10 May 62	**I'M LOOKING OUT THE WINDOW/DO YOU WANNA DANCE** *Columbia DB 4828* & THE SHADOWS	2		17
6 Sep 62	**IT'LL BE ME** *Columbia DB 4886* & THE SHADOWS	2		12

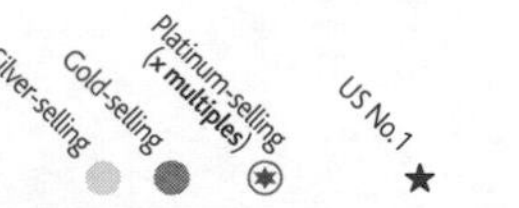

Date	Title	Peak Position	Weeks at No.1	Weeks on Chart
6 Dec 62	**THE NEXT TIME/BACHELOR BOY** *Columbia DB 4950* & THE SHADOWS	1	3	18
21 Feb 63	**SUMMER HOLIDAY** *Columbia DB 4977* & THE SHADOWS	1	3	18
9 May 63	**LUCKY LIPS** *Columbia DB 7034* & THE SHADOWS	4		15
22 Aug 63	**IT'S ALL IN THE GAME** *Columbia DB 7089*	2		13
7 Nov 63	**DON'T TALK TO HIM** *Columbia DB 7150* & THE SHADOWS	2		14
6 Feb 64	**I'M THE LONELY ONE** *Columbia DB 7203* & THE SHADOWS	8		10
30 Apr 64	**CONSTANTLY** *Columbia DB 7272*	4		13
2 Jul 64	**ON THE BEACH** *Columbia DB 7305* & THE SHADOWS	7		13
8 Oct 64	**THE TWELFTH OF NEVER** *Columbia DB 7372*	8		11
10 Dec 64	**I COULD EASILY FALL** *Columbia DB 7420* & THE SHADOWS	6		11
11 Mar 65	**THE MINUTE YOU'RE GONE** *Columbia DB 7496*	1	1	14
10 Jun 65	**ON MY WORD** *Columbia DB 7596*	12		10
19 Aug 65	**THE TIME IN BETWEEN** *Columbia DB 7660* & THE SHADOWS	22		8
4 Nov 65	**WIND ME UP (LET ME GO)** *Columbia DB 7745*	2		16
24 Mar 66	**BLUE TURNS TO GREY** *Columbia DB 7866* & THE SHADOWS	15		9
21 Jul 66	**VISIONS** *Columbia DB 7968*	7		12
13 Oct 66	**TIME DRAGS BY** *Columbia DB 8017* & THE SHADOWS	10		12
15 Dec 66	**IN THE COUNTRY** *Columbia DB 8094* & THE SHADOWS	6		10
16 Mar 67	**IT'S ALL OVER** *Columbia DB 8150*	9		10
8 Jun 67	**I'LL COME RUNNING** *Columbia DB 8210*	26		8
16 Aug 67	**THE DAY I MET MARIE** *Columbia DB 8245*	10		14
15 Nov 67	**ALL MY LOVE** *Columbia DB 8293*	6		12
20 Mar 68	**CONGRATULATIONS** *Columbia DB 8376*	1	2	13
26 Jun 68	**I'LL LOVE YOU FOREVER TODAY** *Columbia DB 8437*	27		6
25 Sep 68	**MARIANNE** *Columbia DB 8476*	22		8
27 Nov 68	**DON'T FORGET TO CATCH ME** *Columbia DB 8503* & THE SHADOWS	21		10
26 Feb 69	**GOOD TIMES (BETTER TIMES)** *Columbia DB 8548*	12		11
28 May 69	**BIG SHIP** *Columbia DB 8581*	8		10
13 Sep 69	**THROW DOWN A LINE** *Columbia DB 8615* & HANK MARVIN	7		9
6 Dec 69	**WITH THE EYES OF A CHILD** *Columbia DB 8641*	20		11
21 Feb 70	**JOY OF LIVING** *Columbia DB 8657* CLIFF (Richard) & HANK (Marvin)	25		8
6 Jun 70	**GOODBYE SAM HELLO SAMANTHA** *Columbia DB 8685*	6		15
5 Sep 70	**I AIN'T GOT TIME ANYMORE** *Columbia DB 8708*	21		7
23 Jan 71	**SUNNY HONEY GIRL** *Columbia DB 8747*	19		8
10 Apr 71	**SILVERY RAIN** *Columbia DB 8774*	27		6
17 Jul 71	**FLYING MACHINE** *Columbia DB 8797*	37		7
13 Nov 71	**SING A SONG OF FREEDOM** *Columbia DB 8836*	13		12
11 Mar 72	**JESUS** *Columbia DB 8864*	35		3
26 Aug 72	**LIVING IN HARMONY** *Columbia DB 8917*	12		10
17 Mar 73	**POWER TO ALL OUR FRIENDS** *EMI 2012*	4		12
12 May 73	**HELP IT ALONG/TOMORROW RISING** *EMI 2022*	29		6
1 Dec 73	**TAKE ME HIGH** *EMI 2088*	27		12
18 May 74	**(YOU KEEP ME) HANGIN' ON** *EMI 2150*	13		8
7 Feb 76	**MISS YOU NIGHTS** *EMI 2376*	15		10
8 May 76	**DEVIL WOMAN** *EMI 2458*	9		8
21 Aug 76	**I CAN'T ASK FOR ANY MORE THAN YOU** *EMI 2499*	17		8
4 Dec 76	**HEY MR. DREAM MAKER** *EMI 2559*	31		5
5 Mar 77	**MY KINDA LIFE** *EMI 2584*	15		8
16 Jul 77	**WHEN TWO WORLDS DRIFT APART** *EMI 2633*	46		3
31 Mar 79	**GREEN LIGHT** *EMI 2920*	57		3
21 Jul 79	**WE DON'T TALK ANYMORE** *EMI 2975*	1	4	14
3 Nov 79	**HOT SHOT** *EMI 5003*	46		5
2 Feb 80	**CARRIE** *EMI 5006*	4		10
16 Aug 80	**DREAMIN'** *EMI 5095*	8		10
25 Oct 80	**SUDDENLY** *Jet 7002* OLIVIA NEWTON-JOHN & CLIFF RICHARD	15		7
24 Jan 81	**A LITTLE IN LOVE** *EMI 5123*	15		8
29 Aug 81	**WIRED FOR SOUND** *EMI 5221*	4		9
21 Nov 81	**DADDY'S HOME** *EMI 5251*	2		12
17 Jul 82	**THE ONLY WAY OUT** *EMI 5318*	10		9
25 Sep 82	**WHERE DO WE GO FROM HERE** *EMI 5341*	60		3
4 Dec 82	**LITTLE TOWN** *EMI 5348*	11		7
19 Feb 83	**SHE MEANS NOTHING TO ME** *Capitol CL 276* PHIL EVERLY & CLIFF RICHARD	9		9
16 Apr 83	**TRUE LOVE WAYS** *EMI 5385* WITH THE LONDON PHILHARMONIC ORCHESTRA	8		8
4 Jun 83	**DRIFTING** *DJM SHEILA 1* SHEILA WALSH & CLIFF RICHARD	64		2
3 Sep 83	**NEVER SAY DIE (GIVE A LITTLE BIT MORE)** *EMI 5415*	15		7
26 Nov 83	**PLEASE DON'T FALL IN LOVE** *EMI 5437*	7		9
31 Mar 84	**BABY YOU'RE DYNAMITE/OCEAN DEEP** *EMI 5457*	27		7
3 Nov 84	**SHOOTING FROM THE HEART** *EMI RICH 1*	51		4
9 Feb 85	**HEART USER** *EMI RICH 2*	46		3
14 Sep 85	**SHE'S SO BEAUTIFUL** *EMI 5531*	17		9
7 Dec 85	**IT'S IN EVERY ONE OF US** *EMI 5537*	45		6
22 Mar 86	**LIVING DOLL** *WEA YZ 65* & THE YOUNG ONES FEATURING HANK B MARVIN	1	3	11
4 Oct 86	**ALL I ASK OF YOU** *Polydor POSP 802* & SARAH BRIGHTMAN	3		16
29 Nov 86	**SLOW RIVERS** *Rocket EJS 13* ELTON JOHN & CLIFF RICHARD	44		8
20 Jun 87	**MY PRETTY ONE** *EMI EM 4*	6		10
29 Aug 87	**SOME PEOPLE** *EMI EM 18*	3		10
31 Oct 87	**REMEMBER ME** *EMI EM 31*	35		4
13 Feb 88	**TWO HEARTS** *EMI EM 42*	34		3
3 Dec 88	**MISTLETOE AND WINE** *EMI EM 78*	1	4	8
10 Jun 89	**THE BEST OF ME** *EMI EM 78*	2		7
26 Aug 89	**I JUST DON'T HAVE THE HEART** *EMI EM 101*	3		8

Top 40 Acts By Singles Sales

Pos	Artist	Approximate Sales
1	CLIFF RICHARD	21,400,000
2	ELVIS PRESLEY	21,000,000
3	BEATLES	20,800,000
4	MADONNA	17,200,000
5	ELTON JOHN	14,800,000
6	MICHAEL JACKSON	14,300,000
7	QUEEN	11,900,000
8	ABBA	10,900,000
9	DAVID BOWIE	10,200,000
10	PAUL McCARTNEY/WINGS	10,200,000
11	ROD STEWART	9,600,000
12	ROLLING STONES	9,400,000
13	KYLIE MINOGUE	9,300,000
14	STEVIE WONDER	8,500,000
15	OASIS	8,200,000
16	WHITNEY HOUSTON	7,900,000
17	SPICE GIRLS	7,800,000
18	GEORGE MICHAEL	7,500,000
19	TAKE THAT	7,400,000
20	SHAKIN' STEVENS	7,300,000
21	BEE GEES	7,200,000
22	STATUS QUO	7,000,000
23	ROBBIE WILLIAMS	6,900,000
24	BOYZONE	6,900,000
25	BLONDIE	6,800,000
26	U2	6,800,000
27	BONEY M	6,700,000
28	SLADE	6,700,000
29	OLIVIA NEWTON-JOHN	6,600,000
30	BRITNEY SPEARS	6,600,000
31	WESTLIFE	6,600,000
32	TOM JONES	6,500,000
33	UB40	6,400,000
34	CELINE DION	6,300,000
35	EMINEM	6,100,000
36	MARIAH CAREY	6,000,000
37	POLICE	6,000,000
38	MADNESS	5,900,000
39	DIANA ROSS	5,700,000
40	WHAM!	5,700,000

Silver-selling ● Gold-selling ● Platinum-selling (x multiples) ⊛ US No.1 ★ Peak Position Weeks at No.1 Weeks on Chart

Top 40 Acts By Download Sales

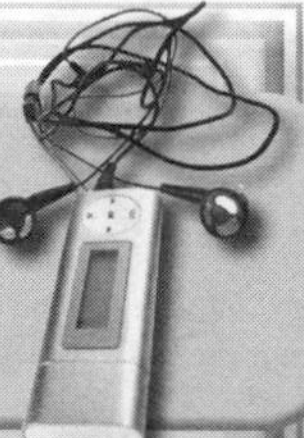

Pos	Artist	Approximate Sales
1	RIHANNA	4,400,000
2	BEYONCE	3,850,000
3	LADY GAGA	3,750,000
4	KANYE WEST	3,620,000
5	BLACK EYED PEAS	3,410,000
6	AKON	3,200,000
7	JUSTIN TIMBERLAKE	2,940,000
8	MICHAEL JACKSON	2,765,000
9	JAY-Z	2,670,000
10	TAKE THAT	2,570,000
11	TIMBALAND	2,460,000
12	LEONA LEWIS	2,450,000
13	EMINEM	2,450,000
14	KINGS OF LEON	2,430,000
15	GIRLS ALOUD	2,270,000
16	DIZZEE RASCAL	2,165,000
17	KATY PERRY	2,130,000
18	NELLY FURTADO	2,130,000
19	PUSSYCAT DOLLS	2,085,000
20	MADONNA	2,075,000
21	SUGABABES	2,055,000
22	NE-YO	2,030,000
23	BRITNEY SPEARS	2,010,000
24	KILLERS	2,000,000
25	FLO RIDA	1,995,000
26	ALICIA KEYS	1,990,000
27	P!NK	1,960,000
28	COLDPLAY	1,870,000
29	SNOW PATROL	1,805,000
30	LILY ALLEN	1,790,000
31	50 CENT	1,765,000
32	CALVIN HARRIS	1,665,000
33	CHERYL COLE	1,645,000
34	CHRIS BROWN	1,625,000
35	OASIS	1,585,000
36	N-DUBZ	1,585,000
37	ROBBIE WILLIAMS	1,540,000
38	ALEXANDRA BURKE	1,520,000
39	QUEEN	1,515,000
40	U2	1,510,000

Date	Title	Peak Position	Weeks at No.1	Weeks on Chart
14 Oct 89	**LEAN ON YOU** *EMI EM 105*	17		6
9 Dec 89	**WHENEVER GOD SHINES HIS LIGHT** *Polydor VANS 2* VAN MORRISON WITH CLIFF RICHARD	20		6
24 Feb 90	**STRONGER THAN THAT** *EMI EM 129*	14		5
25 Aug 90	**SILHOUETTES** *EMI EM 152*	10		7
13 Oct 90	**FROM A DISTANCE** *EMI EM 155*	11		6
8 Dec 90	**SAVIOUR'S DAY** *EMI XMAS 90* ●	1	1	7
14 Sep 91	**MORE TO LIFE** *EMI EM 205*	23		5
7 Dec 91	**WE SHOULD BE TOGETHER** *EMI XMAS 91*	10		6
11 Jan 92	**THIS NEW YEAR** *EMI EMS 216*	30		2
5 Dec 92	**I STILL BELIEVE IN YOU** *EMI EM 255*	7		6
27 Mar 93	**PEACE IN OUR TIME** *EMI CDEMS 265*	8		5
12 Jun 93	**HUMAN WORK OF ART** *EMI CDEMS 267*	24		4
2 Oct 93	**NEVER LET GO** *EMI CDEM 281*	32		3
18 Dec 93	**HEALING LOVE** *EMI CDEM 294*	19		5
10 Dec 94	**ALL I HAVE TO DO IS DREAM/MISS YOU NIGHTS** *EMI CDEMS 359* PHIL EVERLY & CLIFF RICHARD/CLIFF RICHARD	14		9
21 Oct 95	**MISUNDERSTOOD MAN** *EMI CDEM 394*	19		3
9 Dec 95	**HAD TO BE** *EMI CDEMS 410* & OLIVIA NEWTON-JOHN	22		4
30 Mar 96	**THE WEDDING** *EMI CDEM 422* FEATURING HELEN HOBSON	40		1
25 Jan 97	**BE WITH ME ALWAYS** *EMI CDEM 453*	52		1
24 Oct 98	**CAN'T KEEP THIS FEELING IN** *EMI CDEM 526*	10		4
7 Aug 99	**THE MIRACLE** *Blacknight CDEM 546*	23		2
27 Nov 99	**THE MILLENNIUM PRAYER** *Papillon PROMISECD 01* ⊛ x2	1	3	16
15 Dec 01	**SOMEWHERE OVER THE RAINBOW/WHAT A WONDERFUL WORLD** *Papillon CLIFFCX 1*	11		6
13 Apr 02	**LET ME BE THE ONE** *Papillon CLIFFCD 2*	29		3
20 Dec 03	**SANTA'S LIST** *EMI SANTA 02*	5		5
23 Oct 04	**SOMETHIN' IS GOIN' ON** *Decca/UCJ 4756419*	9		3
25 Dec 04	**I CANNOT GIVE YOU MY LOVE** *Decca/UCJ 4756611*	13		4
21 May 05	**WHAT CAR** *Decca/UCJ 4756943*	12		3
23 Dec 06	**21ST CENTURY CHRISTMAS/MOVE IT** *EMI 3799312*	2		3
10 Nov 07	**WHEN I NEED YOU** *EMI 5114522*	38		2
29 Dec 07	**MISTLETOE AND WINE** *EMI EUEDD03124413*	68		1
20 Sep 08	**THANK YOU FOR A LIFETIME** *EMI 2364622*	3		3
26 Sep 09	**SINGING THE BLUES** *EMI 6878852* & THE SHADOWS	40		1

CALVIN RICHARDSON

US, male vocalist — 1

Date	Title	Peak Position	Weeks at No.1	Weeks on Chart
27 Mar 04	**I'VE GOT TO MOVE** *Hollywood HOL004CD*	74		1

LIONEL RICHIE

US, male vocalist/pianist/producer. See Commodores — 197

Date	Title	Peak Position	Weeks at No.1	Weeks on Chart
12 Sep 81	**ENDLESS LOVE** *Motown TMG 1240* DIANA ROSS & LIONEL RICHIE ★	7		12
20 Nov 82	**TRULY** *Motown TMG 1284* ● ★	6		11
29 Jan 83	**YOU ARE** *Motown TMG 1290*	43		7
7 May 83	**MY LOVE** *Motown TMG 1300*	70		3
1 Oct 83	**ALL NIGHT LONG (ALL NIGHT)** *Motown TMG 1319* ★	2		16
3 Dec 83	**RUNNING WITH THE NIGHT** *Motown TMG 1324*	9		12
10 Mar 84	**HELLO** *Motown TMG 1330* ● ★	1	6	15
23 Jun 84	**STUCK ON YOU** *Motown TMG 1341*	12		12
20 Oct 84	**PENNY LOVER** *Motown TMG 1356*	18		7
16 Nov 85	**SAY YOU, SAY ME** *Motown ZB 40421* ★	8		11
26 Jul 86	**DANCING ON THE CEILING** *Motown LIO 1*	7		11
11 Oct 86	**LOVE WILL CONQUER ALL** *Motown LIO 2*	45		5
20 Dec 86	**BALLERINA GIRL/DEEP RIVER WOMAN** *Motown LIO 3*	17		8
28 Mar 87	**SELA** *Motown LIO 4*	43		6
9 May 92	**DO IT TO ME** *Motown TMG 1407*	33		6
22 Aug 92	**MY DESTINY** *Motown TMG 1408*	7		13
28 Nov 92	**LOVE OH LOVE** *Motown TMG 1413*	52		4
6 Apr 96	**DON'T WANNA LOSE YOU** *Mercury MERDD 461*	17		5
23 Nov 96	**STILL IN LOVE** *Mercury MERDD 477*	66		1
27 Jun 98	**CLOSEST THING TO HEAVEN** *Mercury 5661312*	26		2
21 Oct 00	**ANGEL** *Mercury 5726702*	18		5
23 Dec 00	**DON'T STOP THE MUSIC** *Mercury 5688992*	34		5
17 Mar 01	**TENDER HEART** *Mercury 5728462*	29		3
23 Jun 01	**I FORGOT** *Mercury 5729922*	34		2
26 Apr 03	**TO LOVE A WOMAN** *Mercury 0779082* FEATURING ENRIQUE IGLESIAS	19		4
20 Mar 04	**JUST FOR YOU** *Mercury 9862072*	20		4
30 Sep 06	**I CALL IT LOVE** *Def Jam 1707683*	45		5
28 Mar 09	**JUST GO** *Mercury USUM70852644*	52		2

SHANE RICHIE

UK, male actor/vocalist — 14

Date	Title	Peak Position	Weeks at No.1	Weeks on Chart
6 Dec 03	**I'M YOUR MAN** *BMG 82876576932* ●	2		14

JONATHAN RICHMAN & THE MODERN LOVERS

US, male vocal/instrumental group – Jonathan Richman, Greg Keranen, Leroy Radcliffe & D Sharpe

Date	Title	Peak Position	Weeks at No.1	Weeks on Chart
				27
16 Jul 77	**ROADRUNNER** *Beserkley BZZ 1*	11		9
29 Oct 77	**EGYPTIAN REGGAE** *Beserkley BZZ 2* ○	5		14
21 Jan 78	**MORNING OF OUR LIVES** *Beserkley BZZ 7* MODERN LOVERS	29		4

ADAM RICKITT

UK, male actor/vocalist

Date	Title	Peak Position	Weeks at No.1	Weeks on Chart
				19
26 Jun 99	**I BREATHE AGAIN** *Polydor 5611862* ○	5		10
16 Oct 99	**EVERYTHING MY HEART DESIRES** *Polydor 5614492*	15		6
5 Feb 00	**BEST THING** *Polydor 5616142*	25		3

RICKY

UK, male vocal/instrumental group

Date	Title	Peak Position	Weeks at No.1	Weeks on Chart
				3
18 Sep 04	**THAT EXTRA MILE** *Garcia GARCIA005CD*	50		1
5 Feb 05	**THE JOURNEY/STOP KNOCKING THE WALLS DOWN** *Beat Crazy BEAT001CD* AMSTERDAM/RICKY	32		1
1 Jul 06	**WE ARE ENGLAND** *Beat Crazy BEAT007CD*	54		1

RIDE

UK, male vocal/instrumental group – Mark Gardner, Andy Bell, Laurence Colbert & Stephen Queralt

Date	Title	Peak Position	Weeks at No.1	Weeks on Chart
				22
27 Jan 90	**RIDE (EP)** *Creation CRE 072T*	71		2
14 Apr 90	**PLAY EP** *Creation CRE 07T2*	32		3
29 Sep 90	**FALL EP** *Creation CRE 075T*	34		3
16 Mar 91	**TODAY FOREVER** *Creation CRE 100T*	14		4
15 Feb 92	**LEAVE THEM ALL BEHIND** *Creation CRE 123T*	9		3
25 Apr 92	**TWISTERELLA** *Creation CRE 150T*	36		2
30 Apr 94	**BIRDMAN** *Creation CRESCD 155*	38		2
25 Jun 94	**HOW DOES IT FEEL TO FEEL** *Creation CRESCD 184*	58		1
8 Oct 94	**I DON'T KNOW WHERE IT COMES FROM** *Creation CRESCD 189R*	46		1
24 Feb 96	**BLACK NITE CRASH** *Creation CRESCD 199*	67		1

RIDER & TERRY VENABLES

UK, male vocal/instrumental group & football pundit/vocalist

Date	Title	Peak Position	Weeks at No.1	Weeks on Chart
				2
1 Jun 02	**ENGLAND CRAZY** *East West EW 248CD*	46		2

ANDREW RIDGELEY

UK, male vocalist. See Wham!

Date	Title	Peak Position	Weeks at No.1	Weeks on Chart
				3
31 Mar 90	**SHAKE** *Epic AJR 1*	58		3

STAN RIDGWAY

US, male vocalist. See Wall Of Voodoo

Date	Title	Peak Position	Weeks at No.1	Weeks on Chart
				12
5 Jul 86	**CAMOUFLAGE** *IRS IRM 114*	4		12

RIFLES

UK, male vocal/instrumental group

Date	Title	Peak Position	Weeks at No.1	Weeks on Chart
				6
11 Jun 05	**WHEN I'M ALONE** *Xtra Mile XMR007CD*	64		1
5 Nov 05	**LOCAL BOY** *Right Hook RHK001CD*	36		2
18 Mar 06	**REPEATED OFFENDER** *Red Ink 82876786922*	26		1
15 Jul 06	**SHE'S GOT STANDARDS** *Red Ink 82876856172*	32		1
28 Oct 06	**PEACE & QUIET** *Red Ink 82876897652*	48		1

RIGHEIRA

Italy, male vocal duo

Date	Title	Peak Position	Weeks at No.1	Weeks on Chart
				3
24 Sep 83	**VAMOS A LA PLAYA** *A&M AM 137*	53		3

RIGHT SAID FRED

UK, male vocal/instrumental trio – Richard & Fred Fairbrass & Rob Manzoli

Date	Title	Peak Position	Weeks at No.1	Weeks on Chart
				67
27 Jul 91	**I'M TOO SEXY** *Tug SNOG 1* ● ★	2		16
7 Dec 91	**DON'T TALK JUST KISS** *Tug SNOG 2*. GUEST VOCALS: JOCELYN BROWN	3		11
21 Mar 92	**DEEPLY DIPPY** *Tug SNOG 3* ○	1	3	14
1 Aug 92	**THOSE SIMPLE THINGS/DAYDREAM** *Tug SNOG 4*	29		5
27 Feb 93	**STICK IT OUT** *Tug CDCOMIC 1* & FRIENDS	4		7
23 Oct 93	**BUMPED** *Tug CDSNOG 7*	32		4
18 Dec 93	**HANDS UP (4 LOVERS)** *Tug CDSNOG 8*	60		3
19 Mar 94	**WONDERMAN** *Tug CDSNOG 9*	55		1
13 Oct 01	**YOU'RE MY MATE** *Kingsize 74321895632*	18		5
12 May 07	**I'M TOO SEXY 2007** *Gut CDSNOG20*	56		1

RIGHTEOUS BROTHERS

US, male vocal duo – Bill Medley & Bobby Hatfield, d. 5 Nov 2003

Date	Title	Peak Position	Weeks at No.1	Weeks on Chart
				86
14 Jan 65	**YOU'VE LOST THAT LOVIN' FEELIN'** *London HLU 9943* ★	1	2	10
12 Aug 65	**UNCHAINED MELODY** *London HL 9975*	14		12
13 Jan 66	**EBB TIDE** *London HL 10011*	48		2
14 Apr 66	**(YOU'RE MY) SOUL AND INSPIRATION** *Verve VS 535* ★	15		10
10 Nov 66	**WHITE CLIFFS OF DOVER** *London HL 10086*	21		9
22 Dec 66	**ISLAND IN THE SUN** *Verve VS 547*	24		5
12 Feb 69	**YOU'VE LOST THAT LOVIN' FEELIN'** *London HL 10241*	10		11
19 Nov 77	**YOU'VE LOST THAT LOVIN' FEELIN'** *Phil Spector International 2010 022*	42		4
27 Oct 90	**UNCHAINED MELODY** *Verve/Polydor PO 101* ⊛	1	4	14
15 Dec 90	**YOU'VE LOST THAT LOVIN' FEELIN'/EBB TIDE** *Verve/Polydor PO 116*	3		9

RIHANNA

Barbados, female vocalist/model (Robyn Rihanna Fenty). Songwriter with more 21st century US No.1s (6) than any other female. The indefatigable 'Umbrella' was, at 10 weeks, the longest-running UK No.1 since 'Love Is All Around' in 1994

Date	Title	Peak Position	Weeks at No.1	Weeks on Chart
				333
3 Sep 05	**PON DE REPLAY** *Def Jam 9884878*	2		16
10 Dec 05	**IF IT'S LOVIN' THAT YOU WANT** *Def Jam 9888412*	11		8
22 Apr 06	**SOS** *Def Jam 9877821* ★	2		13
22 Jul 06	**UNFAITHFUL** *Def Jam 1702249*	2		16
28 Oct 06	**WE RIDE** *Def Jam 1709084*	17		5
26 May 07	**UMBRELLA** *Def Jam 1735491* FEATURING JAY-Z ○ ★	1	10	51
28 Jul 07	**SHUT UP AND DRIVE** *Def Jam 1746118*	5		21
20 Oct 07	**HATE THAT I LOVE YOU** *Def Jam 1751369* FEATURING NE-YO	15		19
15 Dec 07	**DON'T STOP THE MUSIC** *Def Jam 1762161* ○	4		34
24 May 08	**TAKE A BOW** *Def Jam 1773577* ● ★	1	2	23
14 Jun 08	**IF I NEVER SEE YOUR FACE AGAIN** *A&M/Octone USUM70731559* MAROON 5 FEATURING RIHANNA	28		11
14 Jun 08	**DISTURBIA** *Def Jam USUM70814476* ○ ★	3		32
15 Nov 08	**LIVE YOUR LIFE** *Atlantic AT0325CD* TI FEATURING RIHANNA ★	2		20
29 Nov 08	**REHAB** *Def Jam USUM70735519* FEATURING JUSTIN TIMBERLAKE	16		13
12 Sep 09	**RUN THIS TOWN** *Roc Nation USJZ10900011* JAY-Z FEATURING RIHANNA & KANYE WEST	1	1	12
5 Dec 09	**RUSSIAN ROULETTE** *Def Jam USUM70905503* ○	2		19+
5 Dec 09	**WAIT YOUR TURN** *Def Jam USUM70904699*	45		2
23 Jan 10	**HARD** *Def Jam USUM70912183* FEATURING YOUNG JEEZY	42		6
30 Jan 10	**RUDE BOY** *Def Jam USUM70912307* ★	2		11+
6 Feb 10	**STRANDED (HAITI MON AMOUR)** *MTV Networks USYP61000005* JAY-Z FEATURING BONO, THE EDGE & RIHANNA	41		1

Top 3 Best-Selling Singles

		Approximate Sales
1	UMBRELLA	690,000
2	DISTURBIA	430,000
3	DON'T STOP THE MUSIC	390,000

RIKKI & DAZ FEATURING GLEN CAMPBELL

UK/US, male vocal/instrumental/production trio. See Barndance Boys, Bus Stop, Uniting Nations

Date	Title	Peak Position	Weeks at No.1	Weeks on Chart
				8
30 Nov 02	**RHINESTONE COWBOY (GIDDY UP GIDDY UP)** *Serious SER 059CD*	12		8

CHERYL PEPSII RILEY

US, female vocalist

Date	Title	Peak Position	Weeks at No.1	Weeks on Chart
				1
28 Jan 89	**THANKS FOR MY CHILD** *CBS 6531537*	75		1

JEANNIE C RILEY

US, female vocalist (Jeannie Stephenson)

Date	Title	Peak Position	Weeks at No.1	Weeks on Chart
				15
16 Oct 68	**HARPER VALLEY P.T.A.** *Polydor 56 748* ★	12		15

TEDDY RILEY

US, male producer/vocalist. See Blackstreet, Guy

Date	Title	Peak Position	Weeks at No.1	Weeks on Chart
				5
21 Mar 92	**IS IT GOOD TO YOU** *MCA MCS 1611* FEATURING TAMMY LUCAS	53		2
19 Jun 93	**BABY BE MINE** *MCA MCSTD 1772* BLACKstreet FEATURING TEDDY RILEY	37		3

Peak Position
Weeks at No.1
Weeks on Chart

RIMES FEATURING SHAILA PROSPERE
UK, male/female rap/vocal duo — 1

Date	Title	Peak	Wks at No.1	Wks on Chart
22 May 99	**IT'S OVER** *Universal MCSTD 40199*	51		1

LeANN RIMES
US, female vocalist/actor (Margaret LeAnn Rimes) — 107

Date	Title	Peak	Wks at No.1	Wks on Chart
7 Mar 98	**HOW DO I LIVE** *Curb CUBCX 30* ⊛	7		34
12 Sep 98	**LOOKING THROUGH YOUR EYES/COMMITMENT** *Curb CUBC 32*	38		2
12 Dec 98	**BLUE** *Curb CUBC 39*	23		6
6 Mar 99	**WRITTEN IN THE STARS** *Mercury EJSDD 45* ELTON JOHN & LeANN RIMES	10		8
18 Dec 99	**CRAZY** *Curb CUBC 52*	36		3
25 Nov 00	**CAN'T FIGHT THE MOONLIGHT** *Curb CUBCX 58* ●	1	1	17
31 Mar 01	**I NEED YOU** *Curb CUBCX 60*	13		7
23 Feb 02	**BUT I DO LOVE YOU** *Curb CUBC 075*	20		4
12 Oct 02	**LIFE GOES ON** *Curb CUBCX 085*	11		8
8 Mar 03	**SUDDENLY** *Curb CUBC 088*	47		1
23 Aug 03	**WE CAN** *Curb CUBC 092*	27		2
14 Feb 04	**THIS LOVE** *Curb CUNC 096*	54		1
15 May 04	**LAST THING ON MY MIND** *Polydor/Curb 9866595* RONAN KEATING & LeANN RIMES	5		9
10 Jun 06	**AND IT FEELS LIKE** *Curb/London CUBC122*	22		2
7 Oct 06	**EVERYBODY'S SOMEONE** *Curb/London CUBC128* & BRIAN McFADDEN	48		1
6 Oct 07	**NOTHIN' BETTER TO DO** *Curb CUBC145*	48		2

RIMSHOTS
US, male vocal/instrumental group — 5

Date	Title	Peak	Wks at No.1	Wks on Chart
19 Jul 75	**7-6-5-4-3-2-1 (BLOW YOUR WHISTLE)** *All Platinum 6146 304*	26		5

RIO & MARS
France/UK, male/female vocal/instrumental duo — 3

Date	Title	Peak	Wks at No.1	Wks on Chart
28 Jan 95	**BOY I GOTTA HAVE YOU** *Dome CDDOME 1014*	43		2
13 Apr 96	**BOY I GOTTA HAVE YOU** *Feverpitch CDFVR 1007*	46		1

MIGUEL RIOS
Spain, male vocalist — 12

Date	Title	Peak	Wks at No.1	Wks on Chart
11 Jul 70	**SONG OF JOY** *A&M AMS 790*	16		12

RIOT ACT
US/Canada, male/female vocal/production trio — 1

Date	Title	Peak	Wks at No.1	Wks on Chart
4 Jun 05	**CALIFORNIA SOUL** *Nebula NEBCD070*	59		1

RIP PRODUCTIONS
UK, male production duo. See Carnival featuring RIP vs Red Rat, Cohen vs Deluxe, Tim Deluxe, Double 99, Saffron Hill featuring Ben Onono — 1

Date	Title	Peak	Wks at No.1	Wks on Chart
29 Nov 97	**THE CHANT (WE R)/RIP PRODUCTIONS** *Satellite 74321534022*	50		1

MINNIE RIPERTON
US, female vocalist, d. 12 Jul 1979 (age 31) — 10

Date	Title	Peak	Wks at No.1	Wks on Chart
12 Apr 75	**LOVING YOU** *Epic EPC 3121* ● ★	2		10

RISE
UK, male production duo. See Perfecto Allstarz, Virus — 1

Date	Title	Peak	Wks at No.1	Wks on Chart
3 Sep 94	**THE SINGLE** *East West YZ 839CD*	70		1

RITCHIE FAMILY
US, female vocal group – Cheryl Jackson, Gwen Oliver & Cassandra Wooten — 19

Date	Title	Peak	Wks at No.1	Wks on Chart
23 Aug 75	**BRAZIL** *Polydor 2058 625*	41		4
18 Sep 76	**THE BEST DISCO IN TOWN** *Polydor 2058 777*	10		9
17 Feb 79	**AMERICAN GENERATION** *Mercury 6007 199*	49		6

LEE RITENOUR & MAXI PRIEST
US, male guitarist — 2

Date	Title	Peak	Wks at No.1	Wks on Chart
31 Jul 93	**WAITING IN VAIN** *GRP MCSTD 1921*	65		2

RITMO-DYNAMIC
France, male producer (Laurent Debuire) — 1

Date	Title	Peak	Wks at No.1	Wks on Chart
15 Nov 03	**CALINDA** *Xtravaganza XTRAV42CDS*	68		1

TEX RITTER
US, male vocalist (Maurice Ritter), d. 3 Jan 1974 (age 68) — 14

Date	Title	Peak	Wks at No.1	Wks on Chart
22 Jun 56	**WAYWARD WIND** *Capitol CL 14581*	8		14

RIVAL SCHOOLS
US, male vocal/instrumental group — 2

Date	Title	Peak	Wks at No.1	Wks on Chart
30 Mar 02	**USED FOR GLUE** *Mercury 5889652*	42		1
20 Jul 02	**GOOD THINGS** *Mercury 5829662*	74		1

RIVER CITY PEOPLE
UK, male/female vocal/instrumental group — 27

Date	Title	Peak	Wks at No.1	Wks on Chart
12 Aug 89	**(WHAT'S WRONG WITH) DREAMING** *EMI EM 95*	70		3
3 Mar 90	**WALKING ON ICE** *EMI EM 130*	62		2
30 Jun 90	**CARRY THE BLAME/CALIFORNIA DREAMIN'** *EMI EM 145*	13		10
22 Sep 90	**(WHAT'S WRONG WITH) DREAMING** *EMI EM 156*	40		3
2 Mar 91	**WHEN I WAS YOUNG** *EMI EM 176*	62		2
28 Sep 91	**SPECIAL WAY** *EMI EM 207*	44		3
22 Feb 92	**STANDING IN THE NEED OF LOVE** *EMI EM 216*	36		4

RIVER DETECTIVES
UK, male vocal/instrumental duo — 4

Date	Title	Peak	Wks at No.1	Wks on Chart
29 Jul 89	**CHAINS** *WEA YZ 383*	51		4

RIVER OCEAN FEATURING INDIA
US, male producer (Louie Vega*) & female vocalist — 2

Date	Title	Peak	Wks at No.1	Wks on Chart
26 Feb 94	**LOVE AND HAPPINESS (YEMAYA Y OCHUN)** *Cooltempo CDCOOL 287*	50		2

ROBBIE RIVERA PRESENTS RHYTHM BANGERS
Puerto Rico, male DJ/producer — 8

Date	Title	Peak	Wks at No.1	Wks on Chart
2 Sep 00	**BANG** *Multiply CDMULTY 64*	13		7
12 Oct 02	**SEX** *352 Recordings 352 CD001* ROBBIE RIVERA FEATURING BILLY PAUL W	55		1

SANDY RIVERA
US, male producer. See Kings Of Tomorrow — 7

Date	Title	Peak	Wks at No.1	Wks on Chart
18 Jan 03	**CHANGES** *Defected DFTD 059R* FEATURING HAZE	48		2
5 Apr 03	**I CAN'T STOP** *Defected DFTD 063R*	58		1
5 May 07	**LOLLIPOP** *Data DATA158CDS* DADA FEATURING SANDY RIVERA & TRIX	18		4

DANNY RIVERS
UK, male vocalist — 3

Date	Title	Peak	Wks at No.1	Wks on Chart
12 Jan 61	**CAN'T YOU HEAR MY HEART** *Decca F 11294*	36		3

RM PROJECT
UK, male production group — 1

Date	Title	Peak	Wks at No.1	Wks on Chart
3 Jul 99	**GET IT UP** *Inferno CDFERN 15*	49		1

RMXCRW FEATURING EBON-E PLUS AMBUSH
Holland/Suriname, male production group — 2

Date	Title	Peak	Wks at No.1	Wks on Chart
17 Jan 04	**TURN ME ON** *Digi Dance 871486697203*	52		2

ROACH MOTEL
UK, male production duo. See Fire Island, Heller & Farley Project — 2

Date	Title	Peak	Wks at No.1	Wks on Chart
21 Aug 93	**AFRO SLEEZE/TRANSATLANTIC** *Junior Boy's Own JBO 1412*	73		1
10 Dec 94	**HAPPY BIZZNESS/WILD LUV** *Junior Boy's Own JBO 24*	75		1

ROACHFORD
UK, male vocal/instrumental group – Andrew Roachford, Hawi Gondre & Chris & Derrick Taylor — 61

Date	Title	Peak	Wks at No.1	Wks on Chart
18 Jun 88	**CUDDLY TOY** *CBS ROA 2*	61		4
14 Jan 89	**CUDDLY TOY** *CBS ROA 4*	4		9

Date	Title	Peak Position	Weeks at No.1	Weeks on Chart
18 Mar 89	**FAMILY MAN** *CBS ROA 5*	25		6
1 Jul 89	**KATHLEEN** *CBS ROA 6*	43		5
13 Apr 91	**GET READY!** *Columbia 6567057*	22		8
19 Mar 94	**ONLY TO BE WITH YOU** *Columbia 6601562*	21		7
18 Jun 94	**LAY YOUR LOVE ON ME** *Columbia 6603722*	36		5
20 Aug 94	**THIS GENERATION** *Columbia 6607452*	38		4
3 Dec 94	**CRY FOR ME** *Columbia 6610742*	46		2
1 Apr 95	**I KNOW YOU DON'T LOVE ME** *Columbia 6612525*	42		2
11 Oct 97	**THE WAY I FEEL** *Columbia 6650142*	20		4
14 Feb 98	**HOW COULD I? (INSECURITY)** *Columbia 6653462*	34		3
11 Jul 98	**NAKED WITHOUT YOU** *Columbia 6659362*	53		2

ROB 'N' RAZ FEATURING LEILA K
Sweden, male production duo – Robert Wåtz & Rasmus Lindwall – & female rapper (Leila el Khalifi) — 17

Date	Title	Peak Position	Weeks at No.1	Weeks on Chart
25 Nov 89	**GOT TO GET** *Arista 112696*	8		14
17 Mar 90	**ROK THE NATION** *Arista 112971*	41		3

KATE ROBBINS & BEYOND
UK, female vocalist/actor & male vocal group — 10

Date	Title	Peak Position	Weeks at No.1	Weeks on Chart
30 May 81	**MORE THAN IN LOVE** *RCA 69* ●	2		10

MARTY ROBBINS
US, male vocalist (Marty Robinson), d. 8 Dec 1982 (age 57) — 33

Date	Title	Peak Position	Weeks at No.1	Weeks on Chart
29 Jan 60	**EL PASO** *Fontana H 233* ★	19		9
26 May 60	**BIG IRON** *Fontana H 229*	48		1
27 Sep 62	**DEVIL WOMAN** *CBS AAG 114*	5		17
17 Jan 63	**RUBY ANN** *CBS AAG 128*	24		6

AUSTIN ROBERTS
US, male vocalist — 7

Date	Title	Peak Position	Weeks at No.1	Weeks on Chart
25 Oct 75	**ROCKY** *Private Stock PVT 33*	22		7

JOE ROBERTS
UK, male vocalist — 17

Date	Title	Peak Position	Weeks at No.1	Weeks on Chart
28 Aug 93	**BACK IN MY LIFE** *ffrr FCD 215*	59		1
29 Jan 94	**LOVER** *ffrr FCD 220*	22		5
14 May 94	**BACK IN MY LIFE** *ffrr FCD 230*	39		3
6 Aug 94	**ADORE** *ffrr FCD 240*	45		3
18 Feb 95	**YOU ARE EVERYTHING** *Columbia 6611755* MELANIE WILLIAMS & JOE ROBERTS	28		4
24 Feb 96	**HAPPY DAYS** *Grass Green GRASS 10CD* SWEET MERCY FEATURING JOE ROBERTS	63		1

JULIET ROBERTS
UK, female vocalist. See Working Week — 34

Date	Title	Peak Position	Weeks at No.1	Weeks on Chart
31 Jul 93	**CAUGHT IN THE MIDDLE** *Cooltempo CDCOOL 272*	24		6
6 Nov 93	**FREE LOVE** *Cooltempo CDCOOL 281*	25		3
19 Mar 94	**AGAIN/I WANT YOU** *Cooltempo CDCOOL 285*	33		3
2 Jul 94	**CAUGHT IN THE MIDDLE (REMIX)** *Cooltempo CDCOOL 291*	14		5
15 Oct 94	**I WANT YOU** *Cooltempo CDCOOL 297*	28		3
31 Jan 98	**SO GOOD/FREE LOVE 98 (REMIX)** *Delirious 74321554002*	15		4
23 Jan 99	**BAD GIRLS/I LIKE** *Delirious DELICD 11*	17		5
20 Jan 01	**NEEDIN' U II (REMIX)** *Manifesto FESCD 78* DAVID MORALES PRESENTS THE FACE FEATURING JULIET ROBERTS	11		5

MALCOLM ROBERTS
UK, male vocalist, d. 7 Feb 2003 (age 58) — 29

Date	Title	Peak Position	Weeks at No.1	Weeks on Chart
11 May 67	**TIME ALONE WILL TELL** *RCA 1578*	45		2
30 Oct 68	**MAY I HAVE THE NEXT DREAM WITH YOU** *Major Minor MM 581*	8		15
22 Nov 69	**LOVE IS ALL** *Major Minor MM 637*	12		12

BA ROBERTSON
UK, male vocalist (Brian Alexander Robertson) — 60

Date	Title	Peak Position	Weeks at No.1	Weeks on Chart
28 Jul 79	**BANG BANG** *Asylum K 13152* ●	2		12
27 Oct 79	**KNOCKED IT OFF** *Asylum K 12396* ●	8		12
1 Mar 80	**KOOL IN THE KAFTAN** *Asylum K 12427*	17		12
31 May 80	**TO BE OR NOT TO BE** *Asylum K 12449*	9		11
17 Oct 81	**HOLD ME** *Swansong BAM 1* & MAGGIE BELL	11		8
17 Dec 83	**TIME** *Epic A 3983* FRIDA & BA ROBERTSON	45		5

DON ROBERTSON
US (b. China), male pianist/whistler — 9

Date	Title	Peak Position	Weeks at No.1	Weeks on Chart
11 May 56	**THE HAPPY WHISTLER** *Capitol CL 14575*	8		9

ROBBIE ROBERTSON
Canada, male vocalist/guitarist. See Band — 11

Date	Title	Peak Position	Weeks at No.1	Weeks on Chart
23 Jul 88	**SOMEWHERE DOWN THE CRAZY RIVER** *Geffen GEF 40*	15		10
11 Apr 98	**TAKE YOUR PARTNER BY THE HAND** *Polydor 5693272* HOWIE B FEATURING ROBBIE ROBERTSON	74		1

IVO ROBIC
Croatia, male vocalist, d. 9 Mar 2000 (age 77) — 1

Date	Title	Peak Position	Weeks at No.1	Weeks on Chart
6 Nov 59	**MORGEN** *Polydor 23923*	23		1

FLOYD ROBINSON
US, male vocalist — 9

Date	Title	Peak Position	Weeks at No.1	Weeks on Chart
16 Oct 59	**MAKIN' LOVE** *RCA 1146*	9		9

SMOKEY ROBINSON
US, male vocalist (William Robinson). See Miracles — 64

Date	Title	Peak Position	Weeks at No.1	Weeks on Chart
23 Feb 74	**JUST MY SOUL RESPONDING** *Tamla Motown TMG 883*	35		6
24 Feb 79	**POPS WE LOVE YOU** *Motown TMG 1136* DIANA ROSS, MARVIN GAYE, SMOKEY ROBINSON & STEVIE WONDER	66		5
9 May 81	**BEING WITH YOU** *Motown TMG 1223* ●	1	2	13
13 Mar 82	**TELL ME TOMORROW** *Motown TMG 1255*	51		4
28 Mar 87	**JUST TO SEE HER** *Motown ZB 41147*	52		6
17 Sep 88	**INDESTRUCTIBLE** *Arista 111717* FOUR TOPS FEATURING SMOKEY ROBINSON	55		4
25 Feb 89	**INDESTRUCTIBLE** *Arista 112074* FOUR TOPS FEATURING SMOKEY ROBINSON	30		7
27 Dec 67	**I SECOND THAT EMOTION** *Tamla Motown TMG 631* & THE MIRACLES	27		11
3 Apr 68	**IF YOU CAN WANT** *Tamla Motown TMG 648* & THE MIRACLES	50		1
7 May 69	**TRACKS OF MY TEARS** *Tamla Motown TMG 696* & THE MIRACLES	9		13
1 Aug 70	**TEARS OF A CLOWN** *Tamla Motown TMG 745* & THE MIRACLES ★	1	1	14
30 Jan 71	**(COME 'ROUND HERE) I'M THE ONE YOU NEED** *Tamla Motown TMG 761* & THE MIRACLES	13		9
5 Jun 71	**I DON'T BLAME YOU AT ALL** *Tamla Motown TMG 774* & THE MIRACLES	11		10
2 Oct 76	**TEARS OF A CLOWN** *Tamla Motown TMG 1048* & THE MIRACLES	34		6

TOM ROBINSON BAND
UK, male vocalist — 41

Date	Title	Peak Position	Weeks at No.1	Weeks on Chart
22 Oct 77	**2-4-6-8 MOTORWAY** *EMI 2715* ●	5		9
18 Feb 78	**DON'T TAKE NO FOR AN ANSWER** *EMI 2749*	18		6
13 May 78	**UP AGAINST THE WALL** *EMI 2787*	33		6
17 Mar 79	**BULLY FOR YOU** *EMI 2916*	68		2
25 Jun 83	**WAR BABY** *Panic NIC 2* TOM ROBINSON	6		9
12 Nov 83	**LISTEN TO THE RADIO: ATMOSPHERICS** *Panic NIC 3* TOM ROBINSON	39		6
15 Sep 84	**RIKKI DON'T LOSE THAT NUMBER** *Castaway TR 2* TOM ROBINSON	58		3

VICKI SUE ROBINSON
US, female vocalist, d. 27 Apr 2000 (age 45) — 1

Date	Title	Peak Position	Weeks at No.1	Weeks on Chart
27 Sep 97	**HOUSE OF JOY** *Logic 74321511492*	48		1

ROBSON & JEROME
UK, male actors/vocal duo – Robson Green & Jerome Flynn — 45

Date	Title	Peak Position	Weeks at No.1	Weeks on Chart
20 May 95	**UNCHAINED MELODY/(THERE'LL BE BLUEBIRDS OVER) WHITE CLIFFS OF DOVER** *RCA 74321284362* ROBSON GREEN & JEROME FLYNN ⊛x2	1	7	17
11 Nov 95	**I BELIEVE/UP ON THE ROOF** *RCA 74321326882* ⊛	1	4	14
9 Nov 96	**WHAT BECOMES OF THE BROKENHEARTED/SATURDAY NIGHT AT THE MOVIES/YOU'LL NEVER WALK ALONE** *RCA 74321424732* ●	1	2	14

ROBYN
Sweden, female vocalist (Robin Carlsson) — 67

Date	Title	Peak Position	Weeks at No.1	Weeks on Chart
20 Jul 96	**YOU'VE GOT THAT SOMETHIN'** *RCA 74321393462*	54		1
16 Aug 97	**DO YOU KNOW (WHAT IT TAKES)** *RCA 74321509932*	26		3
7 Mar 98	**SHOW ME LOVE** *RCA 74321555032*	8		6
30 May 98	**DO YOU REALLY WANT ME** *RCA 74321582982*	20		4
11 Aug 07	**WITH EVERY HEARTBEAT** *Konichiwa KORMCD008* WITH KLEERUP	1	1	25

Silver-selling ● Gold-selling ● Platinum-selling (x multiples) ✪ US No.1 ★ Peak Position Weeks at No.1 Weeks on Chart

Date	Title	Peak	Wks at No.1	Wks on Chart
3 Nov 07	**HANDLE ME** *Konichiwa 1751222*	17		9
12 Jan 08	**BE MINE** *Konichiwa 1759899*	10		12
26 Apr 08	**WHO'S THAT GIRL** *Konichiwa 1768011*	26		5
29 Nov 08	**DREAM ON** *Data DATA208CDS* CHRISTIAN FALK FEATURING ROBYN	29		2

ROC PROJECT FEATURING TINA ARENA

US/Australia, male/female vocal/production duo — 1

Date	Title	Peak	Wks at No.1	Wks on Chart
12 Apr 03	**NEVER (PAST TENSE)** *Illustrious CDILL 010*	42		1

ERIN ROCHA

UK, female vocalist — 5

Date	Title	Peak	Wks at No.1	Wks on Chart
27 Dec 03	**CAN'T DO RIGHT FOR DOING WRONG** *Flying Sparks TDBCDS76*	36		5

ROCHELLE

US, female vocalist (Rochelle Darlington) — 6

Date	Title	Peak	Wks at No.1	Wks on Chart
1 Feb 86	**MY MAGIC MAN** *Warner Brothers W 8838*	27		6

CHUBB ROCK

US (b. Jamaica), male rapper (Richard Simpson) — 1

Date	Title	Peak	Wks at No.1	Wks on Chart
19 Jan 91	**TREAT 'EM RIGHT** *Champion CHAMP 272*	67		1

ROCK AID ARMENIA

International, male vocal/instrumental charity ensemble — 5

Date	Title	Peak	Wks at No.1	Wks on Chart
16 Dec 89	**SMOKE ON THE WATER** *Life Aid Armenia ARMEN 001*	39		5

ROCK CANDY

UK, male vocal/instrumental group — 6

Date	Title	Peak	Wks at No.1	Wks on Chart
11 Sep 71	**REMEMBER** *MCA MK 5069*	32		6

ROCK GODDESS

UK, female vocal/instrumental group — 5

Date	Title	Peak	Wks at No.1	Wks on Chart
5 Mar 83	**MY ANGEL** *A&M AMS 8311*	64		2
24 Mar 84	**I DIDN'T KNOW I LOVED YOU (TILL I SAW YOU ROCK 'N' ROLL)** *A&M AMS 185*	57		3

ROCKER'S REVENGE

US, male producer (Arthur Baker) & male/female vocal collaborators — 20

Date	Title	Peak	Wks at No.1	Wks on Chart
14 Aug 82	**WALKING ON SUNSHINE** *London LON 11* FEATURING DONNIE CALVIN ●	4		13
29 Jan 83	**THE HARDER THEY COME** *London LON 18*	30		7

ROCKET FROM THE CRYPT

US, male vocal/instrumental group — 7

Date	Title	Peak	Wks at No.1	Wks on Chart
27 Jan 96	**BORN IN 69** *Elemental ELM 32CD*	68		1
13 Apr 96	**YOUNG LIVERS** *Elemental ELM 33CDS*	67		1
14 Sep 96	**ON A ROPE** *Elemental ELM 38CDS1*	12		4
29 Aug 98	**LIPSTICK** *Elemental ELM 48CDS1*	64		1

ROCKFORD FILES

UK, male instrumental/production duo — 4

Date	Title	Peak	Wks at No.1	Wks on Chart
11 Mar 95	**YOU SEXY DANCER** *Escapade/Rumour CDJAPE 7*	34		3
6 Apr 96	**YOU SEXY DANCER** *Escapade CDJAPE 14*	59		1

ROCKIN' BERRIES

UK, male vocal/instrumental group – Geoff Turton (Jefferson*), Roy Austin, Terry Bond, Chuck Botfield & Chris Lea — 41

Date	Title	Peak	Wks at No.1	Wks on Chart
1 Oct 64	**I DIDN'T MEAN TO HURT YOU** *Piccadilly 7N 35197*	43		1
15 Oct 64	**HE'S IN TOWN** *Piccadilly 7N 35203*	3		13
21 Jan 65	**WHAT IN THE WORLD'S COME OVER YOU** *Piccadilly 7N 35217*	23		7
13 May 65	**POOR MAN'S SON** *Piccadilly 7N 35236*	5		11
26 Aug 65	**YOU'RE MY GIRL** *Piccadilly 7N 35254*	40		7
6 Jan 66	**THE WATER IS OVER MY HEAD** *Piccadilly 7N 35270*	43		2

ROCKSTEADY CREW

US, male/female vocal/breakdancing group – Daisy Castro, Richard Colon, Kenneth Gabbert, Jeffrey Greene, Gabriel Marcano & Lorenzo Soto — 16

Date	Title	Peak	Wks at No.1	Wks on Chart
1 Oct 83	**(HEY YOU) THE ROCKSTEADY CREW** *Charisma/Virgin RSC 1* ●	6		12
5 May 84	**UPROCK** *Charisma/Virgin RSC 2*	64		4

ROCKWELL

US, male vocalist (Kennedy Gordy) — 11

Date	Title	Peak	Wks at No.1	Wks on Chart
4 Feb 84	**SOMEBODY'S WATCHING ME** *Motown TMG 1331*	6		11

ROCOCO

UK/Italy, male/female production/vocal group — 5

Date	Title	Peak	Wks at No.1	Wks on Chart
16 Dec 89	**ITALO HOUSE MIX** *Mercury MER 314*	54		5

RODEO JONES

UK/Grenada, male/female vocal/instrumental trio — 2

Date	Title	Peak	Wks at No.1	Wks on Chart
30 Jan 93	**NATURAL WORLD** *A&M AMCD 0165*	75		1
3 Apr 93	**SHADES OF SUMMER** *A&M AMCD 212*	59		1

CLODAGH RODGERS

UK, female vocalist — 59

Date	Title	Peak	Wks at No.1	Wks on Chart
26 Mar 69	**COME BACK AND SHAKE ME** *RCA 1792*	3		14
9 Jul 69	**GOODNIGHT MIDNIGHT** *RCA 1852*	4		12
8 Nov 69	**BILJO** *RCA 1891*	22		9
4 Apr 70	**EVERYBODY GO HOME THE PARTY'S OVER** *RCA 1930*	47		2
20 Mar 71	**JACK IN THE BOX** *RCA 2066*	4		10
9 Oct 71	**LADY LOVE BUG** *RCA 2117*	28		12

JIMMIE RODGERS

US, male vocalist — 37

Date	Title	Peak	Wks at No.1	Wks on Chart
1 Nov 57	**HONEYCOMB** *Columbia DB 3986* ★	30		1
20 Dec 57	**KISSES SWEETER THAN WINE** *Columbia DB 4052*	7		11
28 Mar 58	**OH OH, I'M FALLING IN LOVE AGAIN** *Columbia DB 4078*	18		6
19 Dec 58	**WOMAN FROM LIBERIA** *Columbia DB 4206*	18		6
14 Jun 62	**ENGLISH COUNTRY GARDEN** *Columbia DB 4847*	5		13

PAUL RODGERS

UK, male vocalist. See Bad Company, Firm, Free, Law — 3

Date	Title	Peak	Wks at No.1	Wks on Chart
12 Feb 94	**MUDDY WATER BLUES** *Victory ROGCD 1*	45		2
20 Sep 08	**C-LEBRITY** *Parlophone 2370102* QUEEN & PAUL RODGERS	33		1

TOMMY ROE

US, male vocalist — 74

Date	Title	Peak	Wks at No.1	Wks on Chart
6 Sep 62	**SHEILA** *HMV POP 1060* ★	3		14
6 Dec 62	**SUSIE DARLIN'** *HMV POP 1092*	37		5
21 Mar 63	**THE FOLK SINGER** *HMV POP 1138*	4		13
26 Sep 63	**EVERYBODY** *HMV POP 1207*	9		14
16 Apr 69	**DIZZY** *Stateside SS 2143* ★	1	1	19
23 Jul 69	**HEATHER HONEY** *Stateside SS 2152*	24		9

ROFO

Belgium, male producer (Fonny de Wulf) — 3

Date	Title	Peak	Wks at No.1	Wks on Chart
1 Aug 92	**ROFO'S THEME** *PWL Continental PWLT 236*	44		3

ROGER

US, male vocalist (Roger Troutman), d. 25 Apr 1999 (age 47). See Zapp — 8

Date	Title	Peak	Wks at No.1	Wks on Chart
17 Oct 87	**I WANT TO BE YOUR MAN** *Reprise W 8229*	61		4
12 Nov 88	**BOOM! THERE SHE WAS** *Virgin VS 1143* SCRITTI POLITTI FEATURING ROGER	55		3
13 May 95	**HIGH AS A KITE** *ffrr FCD 259* ONE TRIBE FEATURING ROGER	55		1

JULIE ROGERS

UK, female vocalist (Julie Rolls) — 38

Date	Title	Peak	Wks at No.1	Wks on Chart
13 Aug 64	**THE WEDDING** *Mercury MF 820* WITH JOHNNY ARTHEY & HIS ORCHESTRA & CHORUS	3		23
10 Dec 64	**LIKE A CHILD** *Mercury MF 838*	20		9
25 Mar 65	**HAWAIIAN WEDDING SONG** *Mercury MF 849*	31		6

Silver-selling ○ | Gold-selling ● | Platinum-selling (x multiples) | US No.1 ★ | Peak Position | Weeks at No.1 | Weeks on Chart

KENNY ROGERS

US, male vocalist — 113

Date	Title / Label	Peak Position	Weeks at No.1	Weeks on Chart
18 Oct 69	**RUBY DON'T TAKE YOUR LOVE TO TOWN** *Reprise RS 20829* & THE FIRST EDITION	2		23
7 Feb 70	**SOMETHING'S BURNING** *Reprise RS 20888* & THE FIRST EDITION	8		14
30 Apr 77	**LUCILLE** *United Artists UP 36242* ○	1	1	14
17 Sep 77	**DAYTIME FRIENDS** *United Artists UP 36289*	39		4
2 Jun 79	**SHE BELIEVES IN ME** *United Artists UP 36533*	42		7
26 Jan 80	**COWARD OF THE COUNTY** *United Artists UP 614* ●	1	2	12
15 Nov 80	**LADY** *United Artists UP 635* ★	12		12
12 Feb 83	**WE'VE GOT TONIGHT** *Liberty UP 658* & SHEENA EASTON	28		7
22 Oct 83	**EYES THAT SEE IN THE DARK** *RCA 358*	61		1
12 Nov 83	**ISLANDS IN THE STREAM** *RCA 378* & DOLLY PARTON ○ ★	7		15
20 Oct 07	**THE GAMBLER** *Liberty USCN17800055*	22		4

ROGUE TRADERS

Australia/UK, female/male vocal/instrumental group – Natalie Bassingthwaighte, James Ash (Jamie Appleby), Steve Davis (replaced by Tim Henwood) & Cameron McGlinchey — 20

Date	Title / Label	Peak Position	Weeks at No.1	Weeks on Chart
15 Jul 06	**VOODOO CHILD** *RCA 82876866312*	3		18
28 Oct 06	**WATCHING YOU** *Sony BMG 88697019672*	33		2

ROKOTTO

UK, male vocal/instrumental group — 10

Date	Title / Label	Peak Position	Weeks at No.1	Weeks on Chart
22 Oct 77	**BOOGIE ON UP** *State STAT 62*	40		4
10 Jun 78	**FUNK THEORY** *State STAT 80*	49		6

ROLL DEEP

UK, male rap collective — 11

Date	Title / Label	Peak Position	Weeks at No.1	Weeks on Chart
30 Jul 05	**THE AVENUE** *Relentless RELDX19*	11		7
22 Oct 05	**SHAKE A LEG** *Relentless RELDX22*	24		4

ROLLERGIRL

Germany, female vocalist (Nicci Saft) — 3

Date	Title / Label	Peak Position	Weeks at No.1	Weeks on Chart
16 Sep 00	**DEAR JESSIE** *Neo NEOCD038*	22		3

ROLLING STONES

UK, male vocal/instrumental group – Mick Jagger*, Brian Jones, Keith Richards, Mick Taylor, Charlie Watts, Ron Wood & Bill Wyman*. No act has earned more money from touring than the world's No.1 rock group. They have a 41-year span of Top 20 singles and have amassed more Top 10 albums in the UK and US than any other group — 382

Date	Title / Label	Peak Position	Weeks at No.1	Weeks on Chart
25 Jul 63	**COME ON** *Decca F 11675*	21		14
14 Nov 63	**I WANNA BE YOUR MAN** *Decca F 11764*	12		16
27 Feb 64	**NOT FADE AWAY** *Decca F 11845*	3		15
2 Jul 64	**IT'S ALL OVER NOW** *Decca F 11934*	1	1	15
19 Nov 64	**LITTLE RED ROOSTER** *Decca F 12014*	1	1	12
4 Mar 65	**THE LAST TIME** *Decca F 12104*	1	3	13
26 Aug 65	**(I CAN'T GET NO) SATISFACTION** *Decca F 12220* ★	1	2	12
28 Oct 65	**GET OFF OF MY CLOUD** *Decca F 12263* ★	1	3	12
10 Feb 66	**NINETEENTH NERVOUS BREAKDOWN** *Decca F 12331*	2		8
19 May 66	**PAINT IT, BLACK** *Decca F 12395* ★	1	1	10
29 Sep 66	**HAVE YOU SEEN YOUR MOTHER BABY STANDING IN THE SHADOW** *Decca F 12497*	5		8
19 Jan 67	**LET'S SPEND THE NIGHT TOGETHER/RUBY TUESDAY** *Decca F 12546* ★	3		10
23 Aug 67	**WE LOVE YOU/DANDELION** *Decca F 12654*	8		8
29 May 68	**JUMPIN' JACK FLASH** *Decca F 12782*	1	2	11
9 Jul 69	**HONKY TONK WOMEN** *Decca F 12952* ★	1	5	17
24 Apr 71	**BROWN SUGAR/BITCH/LET IT ROCK** *Rolling Stones RS 19100* ★	2		13
3 Jul 71	**STREET FIGHTING MAN** *Decca F 13195*	21		8
29 Apr 72	**TUMBLING DICE** *Rolling Stones RS 19103*	5		8
1 Sep 73	**ANGIE** *Rolling Stones RS 19105* ○ ★	5		10
3 Aug 74	**IT'S ONLY ROCK AND ROLL** *Rolling Stones RS 19114*	10		7
20 Sep 75	**OUT OF TIME** *Decca F 13597*	45		2
1 May 76	**FOOL TO CRY** *Rolling Stones RS 19121*	6		10
3 Jun 78	**MISS YOU/FAR AWAY EYES** *Rolling Stones EMI 2802* ○ ★	3		13
30 Sep 78	**RESPECTABLE** *Rolling Stones EMI 2861*	23		9
5 Jul 80	**EMOTIONAL RESCUE** *Rolling Stones RSR 105*	9		8
4 Oct 80	**SHE'S SO COLD** *Rolling Stones RSR 106*	33		6
29 Aug 81	**START ME UP** *Rolling Stones RSR 108*	7		9
12 Dec 81	**WAITING ON A FRIEND** *Rolling Stones RSR 109*	50		6
12 Jun 82	**GOING TO A GO GO** *Rolling Stones RSR 110*	26		6
2 Oct 82	**TIME IS ON MY SIDE** *Rolling Stones RSR 111*	62		2
12 Nov 83	**UNDERCOVER OF THE NIGHT** *Rolling Stones RSR 113*	11		9
11 Feb 84	**SHE WAS HOT** *Rolling Stones RSR 114*	42		4
21 Jul 84	**BROWN SUGAR** *Rolling Stones SUGAR 1*	58		2
15 Mar 86	**HARLEM SHUFFLE** *Rolling Stones A 6864*	13		7
2 Sep 89	**MIXED EMOTIONS** *Rolling Stones 6551937*	36		5
2 Dec 89	**ROCK AND A HARD PLACE** *Rolling Stones 6554227*	63		1
23 Jun 90	**PAINT IT, BLACK** *London LON 264*	61		3
30 Jun 90	**ALMOST HEAR YOU SIGH** *Rolling Stones 6560657*	31		5
30 Mar 91	**HIGHWIRE** *Rolling Stones 6567567*	29		4
1 Jun 91	**RUBY TUESDAY (LIVE)** *Rolling Stones 6568927*	59		2
16 Jul 94	**LOVE IS STRONG** *Virgin VSCDT 1503*	14		5
8 Oct 94	**YOU GOT ME ROCKING** *Virgin VSCDG 1518*	23		3
10 Dec 94	**OUT OF TEARS** *Virgin VSCDT 1524*	36		4
15 Jul 95	**I GO WILD** *Virgin VSCDX 1539*	29		3
11 Nov 95	**LIKE A ROLLING STONE** *Virgin VSCDT 1562*	12		5
4 Oct 97	**ANYBODY SEEN MY BABY?** *Virgin VSCDT 1653*	22		3
7 Feb 98	**SAINT OF ME** *Virgin VSCDT 1667*	26		2
22 Aug 98	**OUT OF CONTROL** *Virgin VSCDT 1700*	51		1
28 Dec 02	**DON'T STOP** *Virgin VSCDT 1838*	36		2
13 Sep 03	**SYMPATHY FOR THE DEVIL** *Mercury 9810612*	14		6
3 Sep 05	**STREETS OF LOVE/ROUGH JUSTICE** *Virgin VSCDT1905*	15		4
17 Dec 05	**RAIN FALL DOWN** *Virgin VSCDX1907*	33		2
2 Sep 06	**BIGGEST MISTAKE** *Virgin VSCDX1916*	51		1
2 Jun 07	**PAINT IT, BLACK** *ABKCO/Decca GBAAA9100024*	70		1

ROLLINS BAND

US, male vocal/instrumental group — 4

Date	Title / Label	Peak Position	Weeks at No.1	Weeks on Chart
12 Sep 92	**TEARING** *Imago 72787250187*	54		2
10 Sep 94	**LIAR/DISCONNECTED** *Imago 74321213052*	27		2

ROLLO

UK, male producer (Rowland Armstrong). See Dusted, Faithless, Our Tribe/One Tribe, Sphinx — 8

Date	Title / Label	Peak Position	Weeks at No.1	Weeks on Chart
29 Jan 94	**GET OFF YOUR HIGH HORSE** *Cheeky CHEKCD 003* ROLLO GOES CAMPING	43		2
1 Oct 94	**GET OFF YOUR HIGH HORSE** *Cheeky CHEKCD 003* ROLLO GOES CAMPING	47		2
10 Jun 95	**LOVE, LOVE, LOVE – HERE I COME** *Cheeky CHEKCD 007* ROLLO GOES MYSTIC	32		2
8 Jun 96	**LET THIS BE A PRAYER** *Cheeky CHEKCD 013* ROLLO GOES SPIRITUAL WITH PAULINE TAYLOR	26		2

ROMAN HOLLIDAY

UK, male vocal/instrumental group — 19

Date	Title / Label	Peak Position	Weeks at No.1	Weeks on Chart
2 Apr 83	**STAND BY** *Jive 31*	61		3
2 Jul 83	**DON'T TRY TO STOP IT** *Jive 39*	14		9
24 Sep 83	**MOTORMANIA** *Jive 49*	40		7

ROMEO

UK, male rapper (Marvin Dawkins). See So Solid Crew — 24

Date	Title / Label	Peak Position	Weeks at No.1	Weeks on Chart
30 Dec 00	**NO GOOD 4 ME** *East West OXIDE 02CD* OXIDE & NEUTRINO FEATURING MEGAMAN, ROMEO & LISA MAFFIA	6		8
24 Aug 02	**ROMEO DUNN** *Relentless RELENT 29CD*	3		9
9 Nov 02	**IT'S ALL GRAVY** *Relentless RELENT 32CD* FEATURING CHRISTINA MILIAN	9		6
6 Dec 03	**I SEE GIRLS (CRAZY)** *Multiply CDMULTY 109* STUDIO B/ROMEO & HARRY BROOKS	52		1

MAX ROMEO

Jamaica, male vocalist (Maxwell Smith) — 25

Date	Title / Label	Peak Position	Weeks at No.1	Weeks on Chart
28 May 69	**WET DREAM** *Unity UN 503*	10		25

HARRY 'CHOO CHOO' ROMERO

US, male DJ/producer. See Choo Choo Project — 3

Date	Title / Label	Peak Position	Weeks at No.1	Weeks on Chart
22 May 99	**JUST CAN'T GET ENOUGH** *AM:PM CDAMPM 121* PRESENTS INAYA DAY	39		2
1 Sep 01	**I WANT OUT (I CAN'T BELIEVE)** *Perfecto PERF 22CDS*	51		1

RONALDO'S REVENGE

UK, male production duo. See Disco Tex presents Cloudburst, Full Intention, Hustlers Convention featuring Dave Laudat & Ondrea Duverney, Sex-O-Sonique, Shena — 2

Date	Title / Label	Peak Position	Weeks at No.1	Weeks on Chart
1 Aug 98	**MAS QUE MANCADA** *AM:PM 5827532*	37		2

RONDO VENEZIANO
Italy, orchestra — **3**

Date	Title	Peak	Wks at No.1	Wks on Chart
22 Oct 83	**LA SERENISSIMA (THEME FROM 'VENICE IN PERIL')** *Ferroway 7 RON 1*	58		3

RONETTES
US, female vocal group – Veronica Bennett (Ronnie Spector), Estelle Bennett, d. 11 Feb 2009, & Nedra Talley — **34**

Date	Title	Peak	Wks at No.1	Wks on Chart
17 Oct 63	**BE MY BABY** *London HLU 9793*	4		13
9 Jan 64	**BABY I LOVE YOU** *London HLU 9826*	11		14
27 Aug 64	**(THE BEST PART OF) BREAKING UP** *London HLU 9905*	43		3
8 Oct 64	**DO I LOVE YOU** *London HLU 9922*	35		4

MARK RONSON
UK, male DJ/producer — **80**

Date	Title	Peak	Wks at No.1	Wks on Chart
1 Nov 03	**OOH WEE** *Elektra E 7490CD*	15		7
25 Mar 06	**JUST** *Columbia 88697272032* FEATURING ALEX GREENWALD	48		2
14 Apr 07	**STOP ME** *Columbia 88697078762* FEATURING DANIEL MERRIWEATHER	2		17
21 Apr 07	**GOD PUT A SMILE ON YOUR FACE** *Columbia GBARL0602010* RONSON FEATURING DAPTONE HORNS	63		1
21 Apr 07	**NO ONE KNOWS** *RCA GBARL0700217*	66		1
7 Jul 07	**OH MY GOD** *Columbia 88697113172* FEATURING LILY ALLEN	8		11
29 Sep 07	**VALERIE** *Columbia 88697186332* FEATURING AMY WINEHOUSE	2		39
8 Mar 08	**JUST** *Columbia 88697272032* FEATURING PHANTOM PLANET	36		2

MICK RONSON WITH JOE ELLIOTT
UK, male vocalist/guitarist, d. 29 Apr 1993 (age 46). See Mott The Hoople — **1**

Date	Title	Peak	Wks at No.1	Wks on Chart
7 May 94	**DON'T LOOK DOWN** *Epic 6603582*	55		1

LINDA RONSTADT
US, female vocalist/guitarist — **34**

Date	Title	Peak	Wks at No.1	Wks on Chart
8 May 76	**TRACKS OF MY TEARS** *Asylum K 13034*	42		3
28 Jan 78	**BLUE BAYOU** *Asylum K 13106*	35		4
26 May 79	**ALISON** *Asylum K 13149*	66		2
11 Jul 87	**SOMEWHERE OUT THERE** *MCA 1132* & JAMES INGRAM	8		13
11 Nov 89	**DON'T KNOW MUCH** *Elektra EKR 101* & AARON NEVILLE ●	2		12

ROOFTOP SINGERS
US, male/female vocal/instrumental trio – Erik Darling, d. 2 Aug 2008, William Svanoe & Lynne Taylor — **12**

Date	Title	Peak	Wks at No.1	Wks on Chart
31 Jan 63	**WALK RIGHT IN** *Fontana TF 271700* ★	10		12

ROOM 5 FEATURING OLIVER CHEATHAM
Italy, male producer (Vito Lucente) & US, male vocalist. See Junior Jack — **17**

Date	Title	Peak	Wks at No.1	Wks on Chart
5 Apr 03	**MAKE LUV** *Positiva CDTIV 187* ●	1	4	15
6 Dec 03	**MUSIC AND YOU** *Positiva CDTIVS 197*	38		2

ROONEY
US, male vocal/instrumental group — **3**

Date	Title	Peak	Wks at No.1	Wks on Chart
26 Jun 04	**I'M SHAKIN'** *Geffen 9862557*	73		1
15 Sep 07	**WHEN DID YOUR HEART GO MISSING?** *Geffen 1745789*	45		2

ROOSTER
UK, male vocal/instrumental group – Nick Atkinson, Dave Neale, Luke Potashnick & Ben Smyth — **22**

Date	Title	Peak	Wks at No.1	Wks on Chart
23 Oct 04	**COME GET SOME** *Brightside 82876652382*	7		6
22 Jan 05	**STARING AT THE SUN** *Brightside 82876670952*	5		8
7 May 05	**YOU'RE SO RIGHT FOR ME** *Wichita WEBB078SCD*	14		4
23 Jul 05	**DEEP AND MEANINGLESS** *Brightside 82876708392*	29		2
22 Jul 06	**HOME** *Brightside 82876862852*	33		2

ROOTJOOSE
UK, male vocal/instrumental group — **3**

Date	Title	Peak	Wks at No.1	Wks on Chart
17 May 97	**CAN'T KEEP LIVING THIS WAY** *Rage RAGECD 2*	73		1
2 Aug 97	**MR FIXIT** *Rage RAGECDX 3*	54		1
4 Oct 97	**LONG WAY** *Rage RAGECD 5*	68		1

ROOTS
US, male rap/production group — **6**

Date	Title	Peak	Wks at No.1	Wks on Chart
3 May 97	**WHAT THEY DO** *Geffen GFSTD 22240*	49		1
6 Mar 99	**YOU GOT ME** *MCA MCSTD 48110* FEATURING ERYKAH BADU	31		2
12 Apr 03	**THE SEED (2.0)** *MCA MCSTD 40316* FEATURING CODY CHESTNUTT	33		2
16 Aug 03	**BREAKS YOU OFF** *MCA MCSTD 40330* FEATURING MUSIQ	59		1

ROSE OF ROMANCE ORCHESTRA
UK, orchestra — **1**

Date	Title	Peak	Wks at No.1	Wks on Chart
9 Jan 82	**TARA'S THEME FROM 'GONE WITH THE WIND'** *BBC RESL 108*	71		1

ROSE ROYCE
US, female/male vocal/instrumental group – Gwen Dickey*, Kenji Brown, Ken Copeland, Fred Dunn, Henry Garner, Lequient Jobe, Mike Moore, Victor Nix & Terrai Santiel — **113**

Date	Title	Peak	Wks at No.1	Wks on Chart
25 Dec 76	**CAR WASH** *MCA 267* ★	9		12
22 Jan 77	**PUT YOUR MONEY WHERE YOUR MOUTH IS** *MCA 259*	44		5
2 Apr 77	**I WANNA GET NEXT TO YOU** *MCA 278*	14		8
24 Sep 77	**DO YOUR DANCE** *Whitfield K 17006*	30		6
14 Jan 78	**WISHING ON A STAR** *Whitfield K 17060* ●	3		14
6 May 78	**IT MAKES YOU FEEL LIKE DANCIN'** *Whitfield K 17148*	16		10
16 Sep 78	**LOVE DON'T LIVE HERE ANYMORE** *Whitfield K 17236* ●	2		10
3 Feb 79	**I'M IN LOVE (AND I LOVE THE FEELING)** *Whitfield K 17291*	51		4
17 Nov 79	**IS IT LOVE YOU'RE AFTER** *Whitfield K 17456*	13		13
8 Mar 80	**OOH BOY** *Whitfield K 17575*	46		7
21 Nov 81	**R.R. EXPRESS** *Warner Brothers K 17875*	52		3
1 Sep 84	**MAGIC TOUCH** *Streetwave KHAN 21*	43		8
6 Apr 85	**LOVE ME RIGHT NOW** *Streetwave KHAN 39*	60		3
11 Jun 88	**CAR WASH/IS IT LOVE YOU'RE AFTER** *MCA 1253*	20		7
31 Oct 98	**CAR WASH** *MCA MCSTD 48096* FEATURING GWEN DICKEY	18		3

ROSE TATTOO
Australia, male vocal/instrumental group — **4**

Date	Title	Peak	Wks at No.1	Wks on Chart
11 Jul 81	**ROCK 'N' ROLL OUTLAW** *Carrere CAR 200*	60		4

JIMMY ROSELLI
US, male vocalist — **8**

Date	Title	Peak	Wks at No.1	Wks on Chart
5 Mar 83	**WHEN YOUR OLD WEDDING RING WAS NEW** *A1 282*	51		5
20 Jun 87	**WHEN YOUR OLD WEDDING RING WAS NEW** *First Night SCORE 9*	52		3

MARIO ROSENSTOCK
Ireland, male actor/comedian/impressionist/vocalist — **1**

Date	Title	Peak	Wks at No.1	Wks on Chart
4 Mar 06	**JOSE AND HIS AMAZING TECHNICOLOR OVERCOAT** *Angel ANGECD11*	45		1

ROSETTA LIFE FEATURING BILLY BRAGG
UK, male/female vocal/instrumental group — **5**

Date	Title	Peak	Wks at No.1	Wks on Chart
12 Nov 05	**WE LAUGHED** *Cooking Vinyl FRYCD252*	11		5

DIANA ROSS
US, female vocalist (Diane Earle). Before starting her successful solo career, this Supreme-ly talented lady was lead singer of the most popular female group of the 1960s. She sang on hit singles for 33 successive years and has amassed more chart albums in the UK than any other US female. See Supremes — **568**

Date	Title	Peak	Wks at No.1	Wks on Chart
30 Aug 67	**REFLECTIONS** *Tamla Motown TMG 616* & THE SUPREMES	5		14
29 Nov 67	**IN AND OUT OF LOVE** *Tamla Motown TMG 632* & THE SUPREMES	13		13
10 Apr 68	**FOREVER CAME TODAY** *Tamla Motown TMG 650* & THE SUPREMES	28		8
3 Jul 68	**SOME THINGS YOU NEVER GET USED TO** *Tamla Motown TMG 662* & THE SUPREMES	34		6
20 Nov 68	**LOVE CHILD** *Tamla Motown TMG 677* & THE SUPREMES ★	15		14
29 Jan 69	**I'M GONNA MAKE YOU LOVE ME** *Tamla Motown TMG 685* & THE SUPREMES & THE TEMPTATIONS	3		12
23 Apr 69	**I'M LIVING IN SHAME** *Tamla Motown TMG 695* & THE SUPREMES	14		10
16 Jul 69	**NO MATTER WHAT SIGN YOU ARE** *Tamla Motown TMG 704* & THE SUPREMES	37		7
20 Sep 69	**I SECOND THAT EMOTION** *Tamla Motown TMG 709* & THE SUPREMES & THE TEMPTATIONS	18		8
13 Dec 69	**SOMEDAY WE'LL BE TOGETHER** *Tamla Motown TMG 721* & THE SUPREMES ★	13		13
21 Mar 70	**WHY (MUST WE FALL IN LOVE)** *Tamla Motown TMG 730* & THE SUPREMES & THE TEMPTATIONS	31		7
18 Jul 70	**REACH OUT AND TOUCH** *Tamla Motown TMG 743*	33		5

Date	Title	Peak Position	Weeks at No.1	Weeks on Chart
12 Sep 70	**AIN'T NO MOUNTAIN HIGH ENOUGH** *Tamla Motown TMG 751* ★	6		12
3 Apr 71	**REMEMBER ME** *Tamla Motown TMG 768*	7		12
31 Jul 71	**I'M STILL WAITING** *Tamla Motown TMG 781*	1	4	14
30 Oct 71	**SURRENDER** *Tamla Motown TMG 792*	10		11
13 May 72	**DOOBEDOOD'NDOOBE DOOBEDOOD'NDOOBE** *Tamla Motown TMG 812*	12		9
14 Jul 73	**TOUCH ME IN THE MORNING** *Tamla Motown TMG 861* ★	9		13
5 Jan 74	**ALL OF MY LIFE** *Tamla Motown TMG 880*	9		13
23 Mar 74	**YOU ARE EVERYTHING** *Tamla Motown TMG 890* & MARVIN GAYE ○	5		12
4 May 74	**LAST TIME I SAW HIM** *Tamla Motown TMG 893*	35		4
20 Jul 74	**STOP LOOK LISTEN (TO YOUR HEART)** *Tamla Motown TMG 906* & MARVIN GAYE	25		8
24 Aug 74	**BABY LOVE** *Tamla Motown TMG 915* & THE SUPREMES	12		10
28 Sep 74	**LOVE ME** *Tamla Motown TMG 917*	38		5
29 Mar 75	**SORRY DOESN'T ALWAYS MAKE IT RIGHT** *Tamla Motown TMG 941*	23		9
3 Apr 76	**THEME FROM 'MAHOGANY' (DO YOU KNOW WHERE YOU'RE GOING TO)** *Tamla Motown TMG 1010* ★	5		8
24 Apr 76	**LOVE HANGOVER** *Tamla Motown TMG 1024* ★	10		10
10 Jul 76	**I THOUGHT IT TOOK A LITTLE TIME** *Tamla Motown TMG 1032*	32		5
16 Oct 76	**I'M STILL WAITING** *Tamla Motown TMG 1041*	41		4
19 Nov 77	**GETTIN' READY FOR LOVE** *Motown TMG 1090*	23		7
22 Jul 78	**LOVIN' LIVIN' AND GIVIN'** *Motown TMG 1112*	54		6
18 Nov 78	**EASE ON DOWN THE ROAD** *MCA 396* & MICHAEL JACKSON	45		4
24 Feb 79	**POPS WE LOVE YOU** *Motown TMG 1136* DIANA ROSS, MARVIN GAYE, SMOKEY ROBINSON & STEVIE WONDER	66		5
21 Jul 79	**THE BOSS** *Motown TMG 1150*	40		7
6 Oct 79	**NO ONE GETS THE PRIZE** *Motown TMG 1160*	59		3
24 Nov 79	**IT'S MY HOUSE** *Motown TMG 1169*	32		10
19 Jul 80	**UPSIDE DOWN** *Motown TMG 1195* ○ ★	2		12
20 Sep 80	**MY OLD PIANO** *Motown TMG 1202* ○	5		9
15 Nov 80	**I'M COMING OUT** *Motown TMG 1210*	13		10
17 Jan 81	**IT'S MY TURN** *Motown TMG 1217*	16		8
28 Mar 81	**ONE MORE CHANCE** *Motown TMG 1227*	49		5
13 Jun 81	**CRYIN' MY HEART OUT FOR YOU** *Motown TMG 1233*	58		3
12 Sep 81	**ENDLESS LOVE** *Motown TMG 1240* & LIONEL RICHIE ★	7		12
7 Nov 81	**WHY DO FOOLS FALL IN LOVE** *Capitol CL 226* ○	4		12
23 Jan 82	**TENDERNESS** *Motown TMG 1248*	73		2
30 Jan 82	**MIRROR MIRROR** *Capitol CL 234*	36		5
29 May 82	**WORK THAT BODY** *Capitol CL 241*	7		11
7 Aug 82	**IT'S NEVER TOO LATE** *Capitol CL 256*	41		4
23 Oct 82	**MUSCLES** *Capitol CL 268*	15		9
15 Jan 83	**SO CLOSE** *Capitol CL 277*	43		4
23 Jul 83	**PIECES OF ICE** *Capitol CL 298*	46		3
7 Jul 84	**ALL OF YOU** *CBS A 4522* JULIO IGLESIAS & DIANA ROSS	43		8
15 Sep 84	**TOUCH BY TOUCH** *Capitol CL 337*	47		6
28 Sep 85	**EATEN ALIVE** *Capitol CL 372*	71		1
25 Jan 86	**CHAIN REACTION** *Capitol CL 386* ●	1	3	17
3 May 86	**EXPERIENCE** *Capitol CL 400*	47		3
13 Jun 87	**DIRTY LOOKS** *EMI EM 2*	49		3
8 Oct 88	**MR LEE** *EMI EM 73*	58		2
26 Nov 88	**LOVE HANGOVER (REMIX)** *Motown ZB 42307*	75		1
18 Feb 89	**STOP! IN THE NAME OF LOVE** *Motown ZB 41963* & THE SUPREMES	62		1
6 May 89	**WORKIN' OVERTIME** *EMI EM 91*	32		5
29 Jul 89	**PARADISE** *EMI EM 94*	61		2
7 Jul 90	**I'M STILL WAITING (REMIX)** *Motown ZB 43781*	21		6
30 Nov 91	**WHEN YOU TELL ME THAT YOU LOVE ME** *EMI EM 217* ○	2		11
15 Feb 92	**THE FORCE BEHIND THE POWER** *EMI EM 221*	27		3
20 Jun 92	**ONE SHINING MOMENT** *EMI EM 239*	10		8
28 Nov 92	**IF WE HOLD ON TOGETHER** *EMI EM 257*	11		10
13 Mar 93	**HEART (DON'T CHANGE MY MIND)** *EMI CDEM 261*	31		3
9 Oct 93	**CHAIN REACTION** *EMI CDEM 290*	20		5
11 Dec 93	**YOUR LOVE** *EMI CDEM 299*	14		8
2 Apr 94	**THE BEST YEARS OF MY LIFE** *EMI CDEM 305*	28		4
9 Jul 94	**WHY DO FOOLS FALL IN LOVE/I'M COMING OUT (REMIX)** *EMI CDEM 332*	36		4
2 Sep 95	**TAKE ME HIGHER** *EMI CDEM 388*	32		4
25 Nov 95	**I'M GONE** *EMI CDEMS 402*	36		3
17 Feb 96	**I WILL SURVIVE** *EMI CDEM 415*	14		4
21 Dec 96	**IN THE ONES YOU LOVE** *EMI CDEM 457*	34		4
6 Nov 99	**NOT OVER YOU YET** *EMI CDEM 553*	9		7
24 Dec 05	**WHEN YOU TELL ME THAT YOU LOVE ME** *S 82876767382* WESTLIFE FEATURING DIANA ROSS	2		8

RICKY ROSS

UK, male vocalist/guitarist. See Deacon Blue — 3

Date	Title	Peak Position	Weeks at No.1	Weeks on Chart
18 May 96	**RADIO ON** *Epic 6631352*	35		2
10 Aug 96	**GOOD EVENING PHILADELPHIA** *Epic 6635335*	58		1

FRANCIS ROSSI

UK, male vocalist/guitarist. See Status Quo — 6

Date	Title	Peak Position	Weeks at No.1	Weeks on Chart
11 May 85	**MODERN ROMANCE (I WANT TO FALL IN LOVE AGAIN)** *Vertigo FROS 1* & BERNARD FROST	54		4
3 Aug 96	**GIVE MYSELF TO LOVE** *Virgin VSCDT 1594* OF STATUS QUO	42		2

NINI ROSSO

Italy, male trumpeter (Celeste Rosso), d. 5 Oct 1994 (age 68) — 14

Date	Title	Peak Position	Weeks at No.1	Weeks on Chart
26 Aug 65	**IL SILENZIO** *Durium DRS 54000*	8		14

ASHER ROTH

US, male rapper — 11

Date	Title	Peak Position	Weeks at No.1	Weeks on Chart
28 Mar 09	**I LOVE COLLEGE** *Island USUM70853293*	26		11

DAVID LEE ROTH

US, male vocalist. See Van Halen — 15

Date	Title	Peak Position	Weeks at No.1	Weeks on Chart
23 Feb 85	**CALIFORNIA GIRLS** *Warner Brothers W 9102*	68		2
5 Mar 88	**JUST LIKE PARADISE** *Warner Brothers W 8119*	27		7
3 Sep 88	**DAMN GOOD/STAND UP** *Warner Brothers W 7753*	72		1
12 Jan 91	**A LIL' AIN'T ENOUGH** *Warner Brothers W 0002*	32		3
19 Feb 94	**SHE'S MY MACHINE** *Reprise W 0229CD*	64		1
28 May 94	**NIGHT LIFE** *Reprise W 0249CD*	72		1

ROTTERDAM TERMINATION SOURCE

Holland, male production duo — 6

Date	Title	Peak Position	Weeks at No.1	Weeks on Chart
7 Nov 92	**POING** *SEP EDGE 74*	27		4
25 Dec 93	**MERRY X-MESS** *React CDREACT 33*	73		2

ROUND SOUND PRESENTS ONYX STONE & MC MALIBU

UK, male rap/production group — 1

Date	Title	Peak Position	Weeks at No.1	Weeks on Chart
16 Mar 02	**WHADDA WE LIKE?** *Cooltempo CDCOOL 358*	69		1

DEMIS ROUSSOS

Greece, male vocalist/multi-instrumentalist. See Aphrodite's Child — 44

Date	Title	Peak Position	Weeks at No.1	Weeks on Chart
22 Nov 75	**HAPPY TO BE ON AN ISLAND IN THE SUN** *Philips 6042 033* ○	5		10
28 Feb 76	**CAN'T SAY HOW MUCH I LOVE YOU** *Philips 6042 114*	35		5
26 Jun 76	**THE ROUSSOS PHENOMENON EP** *Philips DEMIS 001* ○	1	1	12
2 Oct 76	**WHEN FOREVER HAS GONE** *Philips 6042 186* ○	2		10
19 Mar 77	**BECAUSE** *Philips 6042 245*	39		4
18 Jun 77	**KYRILA (EP)** *Philips DEMIS 002*	33		3

ROUTE ONE FEATURING JENNY FROST

UK, male/female vocal/production group. See Atomic Kitten — 1

Date	Title	Peak Position	Weeks at No.1	Weeks on Chart
22 Oct 05	**CRASH LANDING** *All Around The World CDGLOBE446*	47		1

ROUTERS

US, male instrumental group — 7

Date	Title	Peak Position	Weeks at No.1	Weeks on Chart
27 Dec 62	**LET'S GO** *Warner Brothers WB 77*	32		7

MARIA ROWE

UK, female vocalist — 2

Date	Title	Peak Position	Weeks at No.1	Weeks on Chart
20 May 95	**SEXUAL** *ffrr FCD 248*	67		2

KELLY ROWLAND

US, female vocalist/actor (Kelendria Rowland). See Destiny's Child — 121

Date	Title	Peak Position	Weeks at No.1	Weeks on Chart
26 Oct 02	**DILEMMA** *Universal MCSTD 40299* NELLY FEATURING KELLY ROWLAND ⊛ ★	1	2	21
28 Dec 02	**STOLE (IMPORT)** *Columbia 6732122*	57		5
8 Feb 03	**STOLE** *Columbia 6735182*	2		14
10 May 03	**CAN'T NOBODY** *Columbia 6738142*	5		10
16 Aug 03	**TRAIN ON A TRACK** *Columbia 6742155*	20		4
15 Apr 06	**HERE WE GO** *Atlantic AT0238CD* TRINA FEATURING KELLY ROWLAND	15		8
16 Jun 07	**LIKE THIS** *Columbia 88697110322* FEATURING EVE	4		12
19 Jan 08	**WORK** *RCA 88697268382*	4		20
10 May 08	**DAYLIGHT** *RCA 88697288752* FEATURING TRAVIS McCOY	14		7
20 Jun 09	**WHEN LOVE TAKES OVER** *Positiva CDTIV287* DAVID GUETTA FEATURING KELLY ROWLAND ●	1	1	20

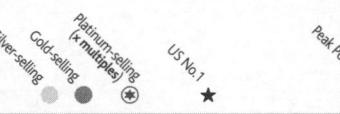

Silver-selling ○ Gold-selling ● Platinum-selling (x multiples) ⊛ US No.1 ★ Peak Position · Weeks at No.1 · Weeks on Chart

JOHN ROWLES
New Zealand, male vocalist — 28

Date	Title	Peak	Wks at No.1	Wks on Chart
13 Mar 68	**IF I ONLY HAD TIME** *MCA MU 1000*	3		18
19 Jun 68	**HUSH NOT A WORD TO MARY** *MCA MU 1023*	12		10

LISA ROXANNE
UK, female vocalist (Lisa Roxanne Naraine) — 2

Date	Title	Peak	Wks at No.1	Wks on Chart
9 Jun 01	**NO FLOW** *Palm Pictures PPCD 70542*	18		2

ROXETTE
Sweden, female/male vocal/instrumental duo – Marie Fredriksson & Per Gessle — 148

Date	Title	Peak	Wks at No.1	Wks on Chart
22 Apr 89	**THE LOOK** *EMI EM 87* ★	7		10
15 Jul 89	**DRESSED FOR SUCCESS** *EMI EM 96*	48		5
28 Oct 89	**LISTEN TO YOUR HEART** *EMI EM 108* ★	62		3
2 Jun 90	**IT MUST HAVE BEEN LOVE** *EMI EM 141* ○ ★	3		14
11 Aug 90	**LISTEN TO YOUR HEART/DANGEROUS** *EMI EM 149* ★	6		9
27 Oct 90	**DRESSED FOR SUCCESS** *EMI EM 162*	18		7
9 Mar 91	**JOYRIDE** *EMI EM 177* ★	4		10
11 May 91	**FADING LIKE A FLOWER** *EMI EM 190*	12		6
7 Sep 91	**THE BIG L** *EMI EM 204*	21		6
23 Nov 91	**SPENDING MY TIME** *EMI EM 215*	22		4
28 Mar 92	**CHURCH OF YOUR HEART** *EMI EM 227*	21		4
1 Aug 92	**HOW DO YOU DO!** *EMI EM 241*	13		7
7 Nov 92	**QUEEN OF RAIN** *EMI EM 253*	28		4
24 Jul 93	**ALMOST UNREAL** *EMI CDEM 268*	7		9
18 Sep 93	**IT MUST HAVE BEEN LOVE** *EMI CDEM 285*	10		8
26 Mar 94	**SLEEPING IN MY CAR** *EMI CDEM 314*	14		6
4 Jun 94	**CRASH! BOOM! BANG!** *EMI CDEM 324*	26		5
17 Sep 94	**FIREWORKS** *EMI CDEM 345*	30		4
3 Dec 94	**RUN TO YOU** *EMI CDEMS 360*	27		6
8 Apr 95	**VULNERABLE** *EMI CDEM 369*	44		2
25 Nov 95	**THE LOOK (REMIX)** *EMI CDEMS 406*	28		3
30 Mar 96	**YOU DON'T UNDERSTAND ME** *EMI CDEM 418*	42		2
20 Jul 96	**JUNE AFTERNOON** *EMI CDEM 437*	52		1
20 Mar 99	**WISH I COULD FLY** *EMI CDEM 537*	11		7
9 Oct 99	**STARS** *EMI CDEM 550*	56		1
6 Aug 05	**FADING LIKE A FLOWER** *All Around The World CDGLOBE426* DANCING DJS VS ROXETTE	18		5

ROXY MUSIC
UK, male vocal/instrumental group – Bryan Ferry*; members also included Brian Eno*, Eddie Jobson, Andy Mackay, Phil Manzanera*, Graham Simpson & Paul Thompson — 155

Date	Title	Peak	Wks at No.1	Wks on Chart
19 Aug 72	**VIRGINIA PLAIN** *Island WIP 6144*	4		12
10 Mar 73	**PYJAMARAMA** *Island WIP 6159*	10		12
17 Nov 73	**STREET LIFE** *Island WIP 6173*	9		12
12 Oct 74	**ALL I WANT IS YOU** *Island WIP 6208*	12		8
11 Oct 75	**LOVE IS THE DRUG** *Island WIP 6248* ○	2		10
27 Dec 75	**BOTH ENDS BURNING** *Island WIP 6262*	25		7
22 Oct 77	**VIRGINIA PLAIN** *Polydor 2001 739*	11		6
3 Mar 79	**TRASH** *Polydor POSP 32*	40		6
28 Apr 79	**DANCE AWAY** *Polydor POSP 44* ●	2		14
11 Aug 79	**ANGEL EYES** *Polydor POSP 67* ○	4		11
17 May 80	**OVER YOU** *Polydor POSP 93* ○	5		9
2 Aug 80	**OH YEAH (ON THE RADIO)** *Polydor 2001 972*	5		8
8 Nov 80	**THE SAME OLD SCENE** *Polydor ROXY 1*	12		7
21 Feb 81	**JEALOUS GUY** *EG ROXY 2* ●	1	2	11
3 Apr 82	**MORE THAN THIS** *EG ROXY 3* ○	6		8
19 Jun 82	**AVALON** *EG ROXY 4*	13		6
25 Sep 82	**TAKE A CHANCE WITH ME** *EG ROXY 5*	26		6
27 Apr 96	**LOVE IS THE DRUG (REMIX)** *EG VSCDT 1580*	33		2

BILLY JOE ROYAL
US, male vocalist — 4

Date	Title	Peak	Wks at No.1	Wks on Chart
7 Oct 65	**DOWN IN THE BOONDOCKS** *CBS 201802*	38		4

CENTRAL BAND OF THE ROYAL AIR FORCE, CONDUCTOR W/CDR A.E. SIMS O.B.E.
UK, military band — 1

Date	Title	Peak	Wks at No.1	Wks on Chart
21 Oct 55	**THE DAMBUSTERS MARCH** *HMV B 10877*	18		1

ROYAL BALLET SINFONIA & GAVIN SUTHERLAND
UK, male/female orchestra & conductor/composer/pianist — 3

Date	Title	Peak	Wks at No.1	Wks on Chart
8 Apr 06	**RADIO 4 UK THEME** *Sweetspot SSUKCDS001*	29		3

ROYAL GIGOLOS
Germany/UK, male vocal/production group — 3

Date	Title	Peak	Wks at No.1	Wks on Chart
31 Jul 04	**CALIFORNIA DREAMIN'** *Manifesto 9866931*	44		3

ROYAL GUARDSMEN
US, male vocal/instrumental group – Barry Winslow, Bill Balough, Chris Nunley, Tom Richards & Billy Taylor — 17

Date	Title	Peak	Wks at No.1	Wks on Chart
19 Jan 67	**SNOOPY VS. THE RED BARON** *Stateside SS 574*	8		13
6 Apr 67	**RETURN OF THE RED BARON** *Stateside SS 2010*	37		4

ROYAL HOUSE
US, male producer (Todd Terry). See Black Riot, Gypsymen, Swan Lake — 18

Date	Title	Peak	Wks at No.1	Wks on Chart
10 Sep 88	**CAN YOU PARTY** *Champion CHAMP 79*	14		14
7 Jan 89	**YEAH! BUDDY** *Champion CHAMP 91*	35		4

ROYAL PHILHARMONIC ORCHESTRA ARRANGED & CONDUCTED BY LOUIS CLARK
UK, orchestra — 19

Date	Title	Peak	Wks at No.1	Wks on Chart
25 Jul 81	**HOOKED ON CLASSICS** *RCA 109* ○	2		11
24 Oct 81	**HOOKED ON CAN-CAN** *RCA 151*	47		3
10 Jul 82	**BBC WORLD CUP GRANDSTAND** *BBC RESL 116* ROYAL PHILHARMONIC ORCHESTRA	61		3
7 Aug 82	**IF YOU KNEW SOUSA (AND FRIENDS)** *RCA 256*	71		2

PIPES & DRUMS & MILITARY BAND OF THE ROYAL SCOTS DRAGOON GUARDS
UK, military band — 43

Date	Title	Peak	Wks at No.1	Wks on Chart
1 Apr 72	**AMAZING GRACE** *RCA 2191*	1	5	27
19 Aug 72	**HEYKENS SERENADE/THE DAY IS ENDED** *RCA 2251*	30		7
2 Dec 72	**LITTLE DRUMMER BOY** *RCA 2301*	13		9

ROYALLE DELITE
US, female vocal group — 6

Date	Title	Peak	Wks at No.1	Wks on Chart
14 Sep 85	**(I'LL BE A) FREAK FOR YOU** *Streetwave KHAN 51*	45		6

ROYKSOPP
Norway, male vocal/instrumental/production duo — 20

Date	Title	Peak	Wks at No.1	Wks on Chart
15 Dec 01	**POOR LENO** *Wall Of Sound WALLD 073*	59		1
17 Aug 02	**REMIND ME/SO EASY** *Wall Of Sound WALLD 074X*	21		3
30 Nov 02	**POOR LENO** *Wall Of Sound WALLD 079V*	38		2
8 Mar 03	**EPLE** *Wall Of Sound WALLD 080V*	16		3
28 Jun 03	**SPARKS** *Wall Of Sound WALLD 084V*	41		1
9 Jul 05	**ONLY THIS MOMENT** *Wall Of Sound WALLD104*	33		2
8 Oct 05	**49 PERCENT** *Wall Of Sound WALLD107X*	55		1
17 Dec 05	**WHAT ELSE IS THERE?** *Wall Of Sound WALLD111*	32		5
28 Mar 09	**HAPPY UP HERE** *Wall Of Sound WALL049T*	44		2

ROYWORLD
UK, male vocal/instrumental group — 4

Date	Title	Peak	Wks at No.1	Wks on Chart
24 May 08	**DUST** *Virgin VSCDT1962*	29		4

LITA ROZA
UK, female vocalist, d. 14 Aug 2008 (age 82) — 18

Date	Title	Peak	Wks at No.1	Wks on Chart
13 Mar 53	**(HOW MUCH IS) THAT DOGGIE IN THE WINDOW** *Decca F 10070*	1	1	11
7 Oct 55	**HEY THERE** *Decca F 10611*	17		2
23 Mar 56	**JIMMY UNKNOWN** *Decca F 10679*	15		5

ROZALLA
Zimbabwe (b. Zambia), female vocalist (Rozalla Miller) — 49

Date	Title	Peak	Wks at No.1	Wks on Chart
27 Apr 91	**FAITH (IN THE POWER OF LOVE)** *Pulse 8 LOSE 7*	65		2
7 Sep 91	**EVERYBODY'S FREE (TO FEEL GOOD)** *Pulse 8 LOSE 13* ○	6		11
16 Nov 91	**FAITH (IN THE POWER OF LOVE)** *Pulse 8 LOSE 15*	11		6
22 Feb 92	**ARE YOU READY TO FLY** *Pulse 8 LOSE 21*	14		6

Date	Title	Peak Position	Weeks at No.1	Weeks on Chart
9 May 92	**LOVE BREAKDOWN** *Pulse 8 LOSE 25*	65		2
15 Aug 92	**IN 4 CHOONS LATER** *Pulse 8 LOSE 29*	50		2
30 Oct 93	**DON'T PLAY WITH ME** *Pulse 8 CDLOSE 52*	50		1
5 Feb 94	**I LOVE MUSIC** *Epic 6598932*	18		5
6 Aug 94	**THIS TIME I FOUND LOVE** *Epic 6603742*	33		3
29 Oct 94	**YOU NEVER LOVE THE SAME WAY TWICE** *Epic 6609052*	16		5
4 Mar 95	**BABY** *Epic 6611955*	26		3
31 Aug 96	**EVERYBODY'S FREE (TO FEEL GOOD) (REMIX)** *Pulse 8 CDLOSE 110*	30		2
22 Nov 03	**LIVE ANOTHER LIFE** *Inferno CDFERN 59* PLASTIC BOY FEATURING ROZALLA	55		1

RUBBADUBB
UK, male/female vocal/instrumental group — 1

Date	Title	Peak Position	Weeks at No.1	Weeks on Chart
18 Jul 98	**TRIBUTE TO OUR ANCESTORS** *Perfecto PERF 165CD*	56		1

RUBETTES
UK, male vocal/instrumental group – Paul Da Vinci* (first hit only), Alan Williams, Mick Clarke, Bill Hurd, John Richardson & Tony Thorpe — 68

Date	Title	Peak Position	Weeks at No.1	Weeks on Chart
4 May 74	**SUGAR BABY LOVE** *Polydor 2058 442*	1	4	10
13 Jul 74	**TONIGHT** *Polydor 2058 499*	12		9
16 Nov 74	**JUKE BOX JIVE** *Polydor 2058 529*	3		12
8 Mar 75	**I CAN DO IT** *State STAT 1*	7		9
21 Jun 75	**FOE-DEE-O-DEE** *State STAT 7*	15		6
22 Nov 75	**LITTLE DARLING** *State STAT 13*	30		5
1 May 76	**YOU'RE THE REASON WHY** *State STAT 20*	28		4
25 Sep 76	**UNDER ONE ROOF** *State STAT 27*	40		3
12 Feb 77	**BABY I KNOW** *State STAT 37*	10		10

MARIA RUBIA
UK, female vocalist/model. See Fragma — 13

Date	Title	Peak Position	Weeks at No.1	Weeks on Chart
13 Jan 01	**EVERYTIME YOU NEED ME** *Positiva CDTIVS 147* FRAGMA FEATURING MARIA RUBIA	3		11
19 May 01	**SAY IT** *Neo NEOCD 055*	40		2

PAULINA RUBIO
Mexico, female vocalist/actor (Paulina Rubio Dosamantes) — 1

Date	Title	Peak Position	Weeks at No.1	Weeks on Chart
28 Sep 02	**DON'T SAY GOODBYE** *Universal MCSXD 40291*	68		1

RUBY & THE ROMANTICS
US, female/male vocal group — 6

Date	Title	Peak Position	Weeks at No.1	Weeks on Chart
28 Mar 63	**OUR DAY WILL COME** *London HLR 9679* ★	38		6

RUDENKO
Russia, male DJ/producer (Leonid Rudenko) — 3

Date	Title	Peak Position	Weeks at No.1	Weeks on Chart
28 Feb 09	**EVERYBODY** *Data DATA213CDS*	24		3

KEVIN RUDOLF FEATURING LIL' WAYNE
US, male vocal/rap/instrumental/production duo – Kevin Rudolf & Dwayne Carter, Jr. — 19

Date	Title	Peak Position	Weeks at No.1	Weeks on Chart
13 Dec 08	**LET IT ROCK** *Island 1796243*	5		19

RUFF DRIVERZ
UK, male/female vocal/DJ/production duo – Chris Brown & Brad Carter — 21

Date	Title	Peak Position	Weeks at No.1	Weeks on Chart
7 Feb 98	**DON'T STOP** *Inferno CDFERN 003*	30		2
23 May 98	**DEEPER LOVE** *Inferno CDFERN 006*	19		3
24 Oct 98	**SHAME** *Inferno CXFERN 9*	51		2
28 Nov 98	**DREAMING** *Inferno CXFERN 11* PRESENTS ARROLA	10		8
24 Apr 99	**LA MUSICA** *Inferno CDFERN 14* PRESENTS ARROLA	14		4
2 Oct 99	**WAITING FOR THE SUN** *Inferno CDFERN 19*	37		2

RUFF ENDZ
US, male vocal duo — 5

Date	Title	Peak Position	Weeks at No.1	Weeks on Chart
19 Aug 00	**NO MORE** *Epic 6696202*	11		5

FRANCES RUFFELLE
UK, female actor/vocalist — 6

Date	Title	Peak Position	Weeks at No.1	Weeks on Chart
16 Apr 94	**LONELY SYMPHONY** *Virgin VSCDT 1499*	25		6

BRUCE RUFFIN
Jamaica, male vocalist (Bernado Balderamus) — 23

Date	Title	Peak Position	Weeks at No.1	Weeks on Chart
1 May 71	**RAIN** *Trojan TR 7814*	19		11
24 Jun 72	**MAD ABOUT YOU** *Rhino RNO 101*	9		12

DAVID RUFFIN
US, male vocalist, d. 1 Jun 1991 (age 50). See Temptations — 10

Date	Title	Peak Position	Weeks at No.1	Weeks on Chart
17 Jan 76	**WALK AWAY FROM LOVE** *Tamla Motown TMG 1017*	10		8
21 Sep 85	**A NIGHT AT THE APOLLO LIVE!** *RCA PB 49935* DARYL HALL & JOHN OATES FEATURING DAVID RUFFIN & EDDIE KENDRICK	58		2

JIMMY RUFFIN
US, male vocalist — 106

Date	Title	Peak Position	Weeks at No.1	Weeks on Chart
27 Oct 66	**WHAT BECOMES OF THE BROKENHEARTED** *Tamla Motown TMG 577*	10		15
9 Feb 67	**I'VE PASSED THIS WAY BEFORE** *Tamla Motown TMG 593*	29		7
20 Apr 67	**GONNA GIVE HER ALL THE LOVE I'VE GOT** *Tamla Motown TMG 603*	26		6
9 Aug 69	**I'VE PASSED THIS WAY BEFORE** *Tamla Motown TMG 703*	33		6
28 Feb 70	**FAREWELL IS A LONELY SOUND** *Tamla Motown TMG 726*	8		16
4 Jul 70	**I'LL SAY FOREVER MY LOVE** *Tamla Motown TMG 740*	7		12
17 Oct 70	**IT'S WONDERFUL (TO BE LOVED BY YOU)** *Tamla Motown TMG 753*	6		14
27 Jul 74	**WHAT BECOMES OF THE BROKENHEARTED** *Tamla Motown TMG 911*	4		12
2 Nov 74	**FAREWELL IS A LONELY SOUND** *Tamla Motown TMG 922*	30		5
16 Nov 74	**TELL ME WHAT YOU WANT** *Polydor 2058 433*	39		4
3 May 80	**HOLD ON TO MY LOVE** *RSO 57*	7		8
26 Jan 85	**THERE WILL NEVER BE ANOTHER YOU** *EMI 5541*	68		1

RUFFNECK FEATURING YAVAHN
US, male/female vocal/production group — 6

Date	Title	Peak Position	Weeks at No.1	Weeks on Chart
11 Nov 95	**EVERYBODY BE SOMEBODY** *Positiva CDTIV 46*	13		4
7 Sep 96	**MOVE YOUR BODY** *Positiva CDTIV 61*	60		1
1 Dec 01	**EVERYBODY BE SOMEBODY (REMIX)** *Strictly Rhythm SRUKCD 08*	66		1

RUFUS & CHAKA KHAN
US, male vocal/instrumental group & female vocalist — 21

Date	Title	Peak Position	Weeks at No.1	Weeks on Chart
31 Mar 84	**AIN'T NOBODY** *Warner Brothers RCK 1*	8		12
8 Jul 89	**AIN'T NOBODY (REMIX)** *Warner Brothers W 2880*	6		9

RUMBLE STRIPS
UK, male vocal/instrumental group — 3

Date	Title	Peak Position	Weeks at No.1	Weeks on Chart
31 Mar 07	**ALARM CLOCK** *Fallout 1723936*	41		1
23 Jun 07	**MOTORCYCLE** *Fallout 1727123*	46		1
15 Sep 07	**GIRLS AND BOYS IN LOVE** *Fallout 1745159*	64		1

RUMPLE-STILTS-SKIN
US, male/female vocal/instrumental group — 4

Date	Title	Peak Position	Weeks at No.1	Weeks on Chart
24 Sep 83	**I THINK I WANT TO DANCE WITH YOU** *Polydor POSP 649*	51		4

RUN TINGS
UK, male producer (Winston Meikle) — 1

Date	Title	Peak Position	Weeks at No.1	Weeks on Chart
16 May 92	**FIRES BURNING** *Suburban Base SUBBASE 009*	58		1

TODD RUNDGREN
US, male vocalist/guitarist — 8

Date	Title	Peak Position	Weeks at No.1	Weeks on Chart
30 Jun 73	**I SAW THE LIGHT** *Bearsville K 15506*	36		6
14 Dec 85	**LOVING YOU'S A DIRTY JOB BUT SOMEBODY'S GOTTA DO IT** *CBS A 6662* BONNIE TYLER, GUEST VOCALS TODD RUNDGREN	73		2

RUN DMC
US, male rap/DJ trio – Joseph 'Run' Simmons, Darryl 'DMC' McDaniels & Jason 'Jam-Master Jay' Mizell, d. 30 Oct 2002 — 62

Date	Title	Peak Position	Weeks at No.1	Weeks on Chart
19 Jul 86	**MY ADIDAS/PETER PIPER** *London LON 101*	62		2
6 Sep 86	**WALK THIS WAY** *London LON 104*	8		10
7 Feb 87	**YOU BE ILLIN'** *Profile LON 118*	42		4
30 May 87	**IT'S TRICKY** *Profile LON 130*	16		7
12 Dec 87	**CHRISTMAS IN HOLLIS** *Profile LON 163*	56		4
21 May 88	**RUN'S HOUSE** *London LON 177*	37		4
2 Sep 89	**GHOSTBUSTERS** *MCA 1360*	65		2
1 Dec 90	**WHAT'S IT ALL ABOUT** *Profile PROF 315*	48		3

Silver-selling ● Gold-selling ● Platinum-selling (x multiples) ⊛ US No.1 ★ Peak Position · Weeks at No.1 · Weeks on Chart

Date	Title	Peak Position	Weeks at No.1	Weeks on Chart
27 Mar 93	**DOWN WITH THE KING** *Profile PROFCD 39*	69		2
21 Feb 98	**IT'S LIKE THAT (GERMAN IMPORT)** *Columbia 6652932* VS JASON NEVINS	63		3
14 Mar 98	**IT'S LIKE THAT (AMERICAN IMPORT)** *Columbia 6652932* VS JASON NEVINS	65		1
21 Mar 98	**IT'S LIKE THAT** *Sm:)e Communications SM 90652* VS JASON NEVINS ⊛	1	6	16
18 Apr 98	**IT'S TRICKY (IMPORT)** *Epidrome EPD 6656982* VS JASON NEVINS	74		1
19 Apr 03	**IT'S TRICKY 2003** *Arista 82876513712* FEATURING JACKNIFE LEE	20		3

RUNRIG

UK, male vocal/instrumental group — 32

Date	Title	Peak Position	Weeks at No.1	Weeks on Chart
29 Sep 90	**CAPTURE THE HEART (EP)** *Chrysalis CHS 3594*	49		2
7 Sep 91	**HEARTHAMMER (EP)** *Chrysalis CHS 3754*	25		4
9 Nov 91	**FLOWER OF THE WEST** *Chrysalis CHS 3805*	43		2
6 Mar 93	**WONDERFUL** *Chrysalis CDCHS 3952*	29		3
15 May 93	**THE GREATEST FLAME** *Chrysalis CDCHS 3975*	36		3
7 Jan 95	**THIS TIME OF YEAR** *Chrysalis CDCHS 5018*	38		2
6 May 95	**AN UBHAL AS AIRDE (THE HIGHEST APPLE)** *Chrysalis CDCHS 5021*	18		5
4 Nov 95	**THINGS THAT ARE** *Chrysalis CDCHS 5029*	40		2
12 Oct 96	**RHYTHM OF MY HEART** *Chrysalis CDCHS 5035*	24		2
11 Jan 97	**THE GREATEST FLAME** *Chrysalis CDCHSS 5045*	30		3
24 Nov 07	**LOCH LOMOND** *Ridge RRS48* & THE TARTAN ARMY	9		4

RuPAUL

US, female vocalist/drag persona (RuPaul Charles) — 19

Date	Title	Peak Position	Weeks at No.1	Weeks on Chart
26 Jun 93	**SUPERMODEL (YOU BETTER WORK)** *Union City UCRD 21*	39		4
18 Sep 93	**HOUSE OF LOVE/BACK TO MY ROOTS** *Union City UCRD 23*	40		2
22 Jan 94	**SUPERMODEL/LITTLE DRUMMER BOY (REMIX)** *Union City UCRD 25*	61		2
26 Feb 94	**DON'T GO BREAKING MY HEART** *Rocket EJCD 33* ELTON JOHN WITH RuPAUL	7		7
25 May 94	**HOUSE OF LOVE** *Union City UCRDG 29*	68		1
28 Feb 98	**IT'S RAINING MEN...THE SEQUEL** *Logic 74321555412* MARTHA WASH FEATURING RuPAUL	21		3

RUPEE

Barbados (b. Germany), male vocalist (Rupert Clarke) — 2

Date	Title	Peak Position	Weeks at No.1	Weeks on Chart
23 Oct 04	**TEMPTED TO TOUCH** *Atlantic AT0185CD*	44		2

RUSH

Canada, male vocal/instrumental group – Geddy Lee, Alex Lifeson & Neal Peart — 47

Date	Title	Peak Position	Weeks at No.1	Weeks on Chart
11 Feb 78	**CLOSER TO THE HEART** *Mercury RUSH 7*	36		3
15 Mar 80	**SPIRIT OF RADIO** *Mercury RADIO 7*	13		7
28 Mar 81	**VITAL SIGNS/A PASSAGE TO BANGKOK** *Mercury VITAL 7*	41		4
28 Mar 81	**A PASSAGE TO BANGKOK** *Mercury VITAL 7*	41		4
31 Oct 81	**TOM SAWYER** *Mercury Exit 7*	25		6
4 Sep 82	**NEW WORLD MAN** *Mercury RUSH 8*	42		3
30 Oct 82	**SUBDIVISIONS** *Mercury RUSH 9*	53		2
7 May 83	**COUNTDOWN/NEW WORLD MAN (LIVE)** *Mercury RUSH 10*	36		5
26 May 84	**THE BODY ELECTRIC** *Mercury RUSH 11*	56		3
12 Oct 85	**THE BIG MONEY** *Vertigo RUSH 12*	46		3
31 Oct 87	**TIME STAND STILL** *Vertigo RUSH 13* WITH AIMEE MANN	42		3
23 Apr 88	**PRIME MOVER** *Vertigo RUSH 14*	43		3
7 Mar 92	**ROLL THE BONES** *Atlantic A 7524*	49		1

DONELL RUSH

US, male vocalist — 1

Date	Title	Peak Position	Weeks at No.1	Weeks on Chart
5 Dec 92	**SYMPHONY** *ID 6587977*	66		1

ED RUSH & OPTICAL

UK, male production duo — 2

Date	Title	Peak Position	Weeks at No.1	Weeks on Chart
1 Jun 02	**PACMAN/VESSEL** *Virus VRS 010* ED RUSH & OPTICAL/UNIVERSAL	61		1
20 Nov 04	**REMIXES – VOLUME 2** *Virus VRS014B*	69		1

JENNIFER RUSH

US, female vocalist (Heidi Stern) — 58

Date	Title	Peak Position	Weeks at No.1	Weeks on Chart
29 Jun 85	**THE POWER OF LOVE** *CBS A 5003* ⊛	1	5	36
14 Dec 85	**RING OF ICE** *CBS A 4745*	14		10
20 Jun 87	**FLAMES OF PARADISE** *Columbia 6508657* & ELTON JOHN	59		3
27 May 89	**TILL I LOVED YOU** *CBS 6548437* PLACIDO DOMINGO & JENNIFER RUSH	24		9

PATRICE RUSHEN

US, female vocalist/pianist — 25

Date	Title	Peak Position	Weeks at No.1	Weeks on Chart
1 Mar 80	**HAVEN'T YOU HEARD** *Elektra K 12414*	62		3
24 Jan 81	**NEVER GONNA GIVE YOU UP (WON'T LET YOU BE)** *Elektra K 12494*	66		3
24 Apr 82	**FORGET ME NOTS** *Elektra K 13173*	8		11
10 Jul 82	**I WAS TIRED OF BEING ALONE** *Elektra K 13184*	39		5
9 Jun 84	**FEELS SO REAL (WON'T LET GO)** *Elektra E 9742*	51		3

RUSLANA

Ukraine, female vocalist/multi-instrumentalist (Ruslana Lyzhychko) — 1

Date	Title	Peak Position	Weeks at No.1	Weeks on Chart
19 Jun 04	**WILD DANCES** *Liberty 5490542*	47		1

RUSSELL

US, male vocalist (Russell Taylor) — 1

Date	Title	Peak Position	Weeks at No.1	Weeks on Chart
27 May 00	**FOOL FOR LOVE** *Rulin ICDS*	52		1

BRENDA RUSSELL

US, female vocalist/keyboard player (Brenda Gordon) — 17

Date	Title	Peak Position	Weeks at No.1	Weeks on Chart
19 Apr 80	**SO GOOD SO RIGHT/IN THE THICK OF IT** *A&M AM 7515*	51		5
12 Mar 88	**PIANO IN THE DARK** *Breakout USA 623*	23		12

RUTH

UK, male vocal/instrumental group — 1

Date	Title	Peak Position	Weeks at No.1	Weeks on Chart
12 Apr 97	**I DON'T KNOW** *Arc 5737812*	66		1

PAUL RUTHERFORD

UK, male vocalist. See Frankie Goes To Hollywood — 6

Date	Title	Peak Position	Weeks at No.1	Weeks on Chart
8 Oct 88	**GET REAL** *Fourth & Broadway BRW 113*	47		3
19 Aug 89	**OH WORLD** *Fourth & Broadway BRW 136*	61		3

RUTHLESS RAP ASSASSINS

UK, male rap trio — 2

Date	Title	Peak Position	Weeks at No.1	Weeks on Chart
9 Jun 90	**JUST MELLOW** *Syncopate SY 35*	75		1
1 Sep 90	**AND IT WASN'T A DREAM** *Syncopate SY 38*	75		1

RUTLES

UK, male vocal/instrumental group — 5

Date	Title	Peak Position	Weeks at No.1	Weeks on Chart
15 Apr 78	**I MUST BE IN LOVE** *Warner Brothers K 17125*	39		4
16 Nov 96	**SHANGRI-LA** *Virgin America VUSCD 117*	68		1

RUTS

UK, male vocal/instrumental group – Malcolm Owen, d. 14 Jul 1980, Paul Fox, d. 21 Oct 2007, John Jennings & Dave Ruffy — 28

Date	Title	Peak Position	Weeks at No.1	Weeks on Chart
16 Jun 79	**BABYLON'S BURNING** *Virgin VS 271*	7		11
8 Sep 79	**SOMETHING THAT I SAID** *Virgin VS 285*	29		5
19 Apr 80	**STARING AT THE RUDE BOYS** *Virgin VS 327*	22		8
30 Aug 80	**WEST ONE (SHINE ON ME)** *Virgin VS 370*	43		4

BARRY RYAN

UK, male vocalist (Barry Sapherson). See Paul & Barry Ryan — 33

Date	Title	Peak Position	Weeks at No.1	Weeks on Chart
23 Oct 68	**ELOISE** *MGM 1442*	2		12
19 Feb 69	**LOVE IS LOVE** *MGM 1464*	25		4
4 Oct 69	**HUNT** *Polydor 56 348*	34		5
21 Feb 70	**MAGICAL SPIEL** *Polydor 56 370*	49		1
16 May 70	**KITSCH** *Polydor 2001 035*	37		6
15 Jan 72	**CAN'T LET YOU GO** *Polydor 2001 256*	32		5

JOSHUA RYAN

US, male DJ/producer/drummer (Joshua Topolsky) — 3

Date	Title	Peak Position	Weeks at No.1	Weeks on Chart
27 Jan 01	**PISTOL WHIP** *NuLife 74321825482*	29		3

LEE RYAN

UK, male vocalist. See Blue — 19

Date	Title	Peak Position	Weeks at No.1	Weeks on Chart
30 Jul 05	**ARMY OF LOVERS** *Brightside 82876713182*	3		9
22 Oct 05	**TURN YOUR CAR AROUND** *Brightside 82876743372*	12		6
11 Feb 06	**WHEN I THINK OF YOU** *Brightside 82876782892*	15		4

Key: ○ Silver-selling · ● Gold-selling · ⊛ Platinum-selling (x multiples) · ★ US No.1 · Peak Position · Weeks at No.1 · Weeks on Chart

MARION RYAN
UK, female vocalist (Marion Sapherson), d. 15 Jan 1999 (age 67) — 11

Date	Title / Label	Peak	Wks at No.1	Wks on Chart
24 Jan 58	**LOVE ME FOREVER** *Pye Nixa N 15121*	5		11

PAUL & BARRY RYAN
UK, male vocal duo – Paul, d. 28 Nov 1992, & Barry Ryan* — 43

Date	Title / Label	Peak	Wks at No.1	Wks on Chart
11 Nov 65	**DON'T BRING ME YOUR HEARTACHES** *Decca F 12260*	13		9
3 Feb 66	**HAVE PITY ON THE BOY** *Decca F 12319*	18		6
12 May 66	**I LOVE HER** *Decca F 12391*	17		8
14 Jul 66	**I LOVE HOW YOU LOVE ME** *Decca F 12445*	21		7
29 Sep 66	**HAVE YOU EVER LOVED SOMEBODY** *Decca F 12494*	49		1
8 Dec 66	**MISSY MISSY** *Decca F 12520*	43		4
2 Mar 67	**KEEP IT OUT OF SIGHT** *Decca F 12567*	30		6
29 Jun 67	**CLAIRE** *Decca F 12633*	47		2

REBEKAH RYAN
UK, female vocalist — 5

Date	Title / Label	Peak	Wks at No.1	Wks on Chart
18 May 96	**YOU LIFT ME UP** *MCA MCSTD 40022*	26		3
7 Sep 96	**JUST A LITTLE BIT OF LOVE** *MCA MCSTD 40063*	51		1
17 May 97	**WOMAN IN LOVE** *MCA MCSTD 40109*	64		1

RYANDAN
Canada, male vocal duo — 1

Date	Title / Label	Peak	Wks at No.1	Wks on Chart
29 Sep 07	**LIKE THE SUN** *UCJ 1747339*	69		1

ALEXANDER RYBAK
Belarus, male vocalist/pianist — 2

Date	Title / Label	Peak	Wks at No.1	Wks on Chart
30 May 09	**FAIRYTALE** *EMI NO23B0900001*	10		2

BOBBY RYDELL
US, male vocalist (Robert Ridarelli) — 60

Date	Title / Label	Peak	Wks at No.1	Wks on Chart
10 Mar 60	**WILD ONE** *Columbia DB 4429*	7		15
1 Sep 60	**VOLARE** *Columbia DB 4495*	22		6
30 Jun 60	**SWINGING SCHOOL** *Columbia DB 4471*	44		1
15 Dec 60	**SWAY** *Columbia DB 4545*	12		13
23 Mar 61	**GOOD TIME BABY** *Columbia DB 4600*	42		7
19 Apr 62	**TEACH ME TO TWIST** *Columbia DB 4802* CHUBBY CHECKER & BOBBY RYDELL	45		1
20 Dec 62	**JINGLE BELL ROCK** *Cameo Parkway C 205* CHUBBY CHECKER & BOBBY RYDELL	40		3
23 May 63	**FORGET HIM** *Cameo Parkway C 108*	13		14

MARK RYDER
UK, male producer (Mark Rydquist). See Fantasy UFO, M-D-Emm — 2

Date	Title / Label	Peak	Wks at No.1	Wks on Chart
31 Mar 01	**JOY** *Relentless/Public Demand RELENT9CDS*	34		2

MITCH RYDER & THE DETROIT WHEELS
US, male vocal/instrumental group — 5

Date	Title / Label	Peak	Wks at No.1	Wks on Chart
10 Feb 66	**JENNY TAKE A RIDE** *Stateside SS 481*	33		5

SHAUN RYDER
UK, male vocalist. See Happy Mondays — 2

Date	Title / Label	Peak	Wks at No.1	Wks on Chart
9 Nov 96	**DON'T TAKE MY KINDNESS FOR WEAKNESS** *Radioactive MCSTD 48024* HEADS WITH SHAUN RYDER	60		1
22 Jul 00	**BARCELONA (FRIENDS UNTIL THE END)** *Decca 46672772* RUSSELL WATSON & SHAUN RYDER	68		1

RYTHM SYNDICATE
US, male vocal/instrumental group — 5

Date	Title / Label	Peak	Wks at No.1	Wks on Chart
27 Jul 91	**P.A.S.S.I.O.N.** *Impact American EM 197*	58		5

RYZE
UK, male vocal trio — 1

Date	Title / Label	Peak	Wks at No.1	Wks on Chart
2 Nov 02	**IN MY LIFE** *Inferno Cool CDFERN 48*	46		1

ROBIN S
US, female vocalist (Robin Stone) — 49

Date	Title / Label	Peak	Wks at No.1	Wks on Chart
16 Jan 93	**SHOW ME LOVE** *Champion CHAMPCD 300*	59		4
13 Mar 93	**SHOW ME LOVE** *Champion CHAMPCD 300*	6		13
31 Jul 93	**LUV 4 LUV** *Champion CHAMPCD 301*	11		7
4 Dec 93	**WHAT I DO BEST** *Champion CHAMPCD 307*	43		2
19 Mar 94	**I WANT TO THANK YOU** *Champion CHAMPCD 310*	48		1
5 Nov 94	**BACK IT UP** *Champion CHAMPCD 312*	43		2
8 Mar 97	**SHOW ME LOVE (REMIX)** *Champion CHAMPCD 326*	9		5
12 Jul 97	**IT MUST BE LOVE** *Atlantic A 5596CD*	37		2
4 Oct 97	**YOU GOT THE LOVE** *Champion CHAMPCD 330* T2 FEATURING ROBIN S	62		1
7 Dec 02	**SHOW ME LOVE** *Champion CHAMPCD 796*	61		1
28 Mar 09	**SHOW ME LOVE** *Champion CHAMPC1204*	72		1
4 Apr 09	**SHOW ME LOVE** *Data DATA212CDS* STEVE ANGELLO & LAIDBACK LUKE FEATURING ROBIN S	11		10

S CLUB JUNIORS
UK, female/male vocal group/actors – Jay Asforis, Daisy Evans, Calvin Goldspink, Stacey McClean, Aaron Renfree, Hannah Richings, Frankie Sandford & Rochelle Wiseman. See I Dream featuring Frankie & Calvin — 52

Date	Title / Label	Peak	Wks at No.1	Wks on Chart
4 May 02	**ONE STEP CLOSER** *Polydor 5707332* ○	2		16
3 Aug 02	**AUTOMATIC HIGH** *Polydor 5708922*	2		13
19 Oct 02	**NEW DIRECTION** *Polydor 0659702*	2		13
21 Dec 02	**PUPPY LOVE/SLEIGH RIDE** *Polydor 0658442*	6		10
12 Jul 03	**FOOL NO MORE** *Polydor 9808754* S CLUB 8	4		8
11 Oct 03	**SUNDOWN** *19/Universal 9811790* S CLUB 8	4		10
10 Jan 04	**DON'T TELL ME YOU'RE SORRY** *Polydor 9815342* S CLUB 8	11		8

S CLUB 7
UK, female/male vocal group/actors – Jo O'Meara*, Tina Barrett, Paul Cattermole, John Lee, Bradley McIntosh, Hannah Spearritt & Rachel Stevens*. See Girls Of *FHM*, Upper Street — 192

Date	Title / Label	Peak	Wks at No.1	Wks on Chart
19 Jun 99	**BRING IT ALL BACK** *Polydor 5610852* ⊛	1	1	15
2 Oct 99	**S CLUB PARTY** *Polydor 5614172* ●	2		14
25 Dec 99	**TWO IN A MILLION/YOU'RE MY NUMBER ONE** *Polydor 5615962* ○	2		11
3 Jun 00	**REACH** *Polydor 5618302* ●	2		17
23 Sep 00	**NATURAL** *Polydor 5677602*	3		16
9 Dec 00	**NEVER HAD A DREAM COME TRUE** *Polydor 5879032* ●	1	1	18
5 May 01	**DON'T STOP MOVIN'** *Polydor 5870842* ⊛	1	2	19
1 Dec 01	**HAVE YOU EVER** *Polydor 5705002*	1	1	14
23 Feb 02	**YOU** *Polydor 5705822*	2		14
30 Nov 02	**ALIVE** *Polydor 0658912* S CLUB	5		16
7 Jun 03	**SAY GOODBYE/LOVE AIN'T GONNA WAIT FOR YOU** *Polydor 9807140* S CLUB	2		12

S-EXPRESS
UK, male producer (Mark Moore) with female/male vocalists – Chilo Harlo, Linda Love & Michellé Ndrika (all replaced by Sonique*) — 50

Date	Title / Label	Peak	Wks at No.1	Wks on Chart
16 Apr 88	**THEME FROM S-EXPRESS** *Rhythm King LEFT 21* ○	1	2	13
23 Jul 88	**SUPERFLY GUY** *Rhythm King LEFT 28*	5		9
18 Feb 89	**HEY MUSIC LOVER** *Rhythm King LEFT 30*	6		10
16 Sep 89	**MANTRA FOR A STATE MIND** *Rhythm King LEFT 35*	21		8
15 Sep 90	**NOTHING TO LOSE** *Rhythm King SEXY 01*	32		4
30 May 92	**FIND 'EM, FOOL 'EM, FORGET 'EM** *Rhythm King 6580137*	43		2
11 May 96	**THEME FROM S-EXPRESS (REMIX)** *Rhythm King SEXY 9CD*	14		4

S-J
UK, female vocalist (Sarah Jiminez-Heany) — 4

Date	Title / Label	Peak	Wks at No.1	Wks on Chart
11 Jan 97	**FEVER** *React CDREACT 93*	46		1
24 Jan 98	**I FEEL DIVINE** *React CDREACT 113*	30		2
7 Nov 98	**SHIVER** *React CDREACT 138*	59		1

RAPHAEL SAADIQ
US, male vocalist (Raphael Wiggins). See Lucy Pearl, Tony Toni Tone — 4

Date	Title / Label	Peak	Wks at No.1	Wks on Chart
23 Nov 96	**STRESSED OUT** *Jive JIVECD 404* A TRIBE CALLED QUEST FEATURING FAITH EVANS & RAPHAEL SAADIQ	33		2
19 Jun 99	**GET INVOLVED** *Hollywood 0101185 HWR* & Q-TIP	36		2

SABRE FEATURING PREZIDENT BROWN
Jamaica, male vocal/DJ duo — 1

Date	Title / Label	Peak	Wks at No.1	Wks on Chart
19 Aug 95	**WRONG OR RIGHT** *Greensleeves GRECD 485*	71		1

SABRES OF PARADISE
UK, male production trio — 8

Date	Title / Label	Peak Position	Weeks at No.1	Weeks on Chart
2 Oct 93	**SMOKEBELCH II** *Sabres Of Paradise PT 009CD*	55		3
9 Apr 94	**THEME** *Sabres Of Paradise PT 014CD*	56		3
17 Sep 94	**WILMOT** *Warp WAP 50CD*	36		2

SABRINA
Italy, female vocalist (Norma Sabrina Salerno) — 22

Date	Title / Label	Peak Position	Weeks at No.1	Weeks on Chart
6 Feb 88	**BOYS (SUMMERTIME LOVE)** *Ibiza IBIZ 1*	60		3
11 Jun 88	**BOYS (SUMMERTIME LOVE)** *Ibiza IBIZ 1* ● (silver)	3		11
1 Oct 88	**ALL OF ME** *PWL 19*	25		7
1 Jul 89	**LIKE A YO-YO** *Videogram DCUP 1*	72		1

SACRED SPIRIT
Germany, male instrumental/production/composition trio. See B-Tribe, NT Gang — 5

Date	Title / Label	Peak Position	Weeks at No.1	Weeks on Chart
15 Apr 95	**YEHA-NOHA (WISHES OF HAPPINESS AND PROSPERITY)** *Virgin VSCDT 1514*	71		1
18 Nov 95	**YEHA-NOHA (WISHES OF HAPPINESS AND PROSPERITY)** *Virgin VSCDT 1514*	37		2
16 Mar 96	**WINTER CEREMONY (TOR-CHENEY-NAHANA)** *Virgin VSCDT 1574*	45		2

SAD CAFE
UK, male vocal/instrumental group – Paul Young, d. 17 Jul 2000, Tony Cresswell, Vic Emerson, Mike Hehir, Lenni, Ashley Mulford, John Stimpson & Ian Wilson — 44

Date	Title / Label	Peak Position	Weeks at No.1	Weeks on Chart
22 Sep 79	**EVERY DAY HURTS** *RCA PB 5180* ● (silver)	3		12
19 Jan 80	**STRANGE LITTLE GIRL** *RCA PB 5202*	32		5
15 Mar 80	**MY OH MY** *RCA SAD 3*	14		11
21 Jun 80	**NOTHING LEFT TOULOUSE** *RCA SAD 4*	62		4
27 Sep 80	**LA-DI-DA** *RCA SAD 5*	41		6
20 Dec 80	**I'M IN LOVE AGAIN** *RCA SAD 6*	40		6

SADE
Nigeria/UK, female/male vocal/instrumental group – Helen Folasade Adu, Paul Cooke (left 1984), Paul S Denman, Andrew Hale & Stuart Matthewman — 69

Date	Title / Label	Peak Position	Weeks at No.1	Weeks on Chart
25 Feb 84	**YOUR LOVE IS KING** *Epic A 4137*	6		12
26 May 84	**WHEN AM I GONNA MAKE A LIVING** *Epic A 4437*	36		5
15 Sep 84	**SMOOTH OPERATOR** *Epic A 4655*	19		10
12 Oct 85	**THE SWEETEST TABOO** *Epic A 6609*	31		5
11 Jan 86	**IS IT A CRIME** *Epic A 6742*	49		3
2 Apr 88	**LOVE IS STRONGER THAN PRIDE** *Epic SADE 1*	44		3
4 Jun 88	**PARADISE** *Epic SADE 2*	29		7
10 Oct 92	**NO ORDINARY LOVE** *Epic 6583567*	26		3
28 Nov 92	**FEEL NO PAIN** *Epic 6588297*	56		2
8 May 93	**KISS OF LIFE** *Epic 6591162*	44		3
5 Jun 93	**NO ORDINARY LOVE** *Epic 6583562*	14		8
31 Jul 93	**CHERISH THE DAY** *Epic 6594812*	53		2
18 Nov 00	**BY YOUR SIDE** *Epic 6699992*	17		5
24 Mar 01	**KING OF SORROW** *Epic 6708672*	59		1

STAFF SERGEANT BARRY SADLER
US, male vocalist, d. 5 Nov 1989 (age 49) — 8

Date	Title / Label	Peak Position	Weeks at No.1	Weeks on Chart
24 Mar 66	**BALLAD OF THE GREEN BERETS** *RCA 1506* ★	24		8

SAFFRON
UK (b. Nigeria), female vocalist (Samantha Sprackling). See Republica — 2

Date	Title / Label	Peak Position	Weeks at No.1	Weeks on Chart
16 Jan 93	**CIRCLES** *WEA SAFF 9CD*	60		2

SAFFRON HILL FEATURING BEN ONONO
UK, male vocal/DJ/production duo. See Cohen vs Deluxe, Tim Deluxe, Double 99, RIP Productions — 3

Date	Title / Label	Peak Position	Weeks at No.1	Weeks on Chart
17 May 03	**MY LOVE IS ALWAYS** *Illustrious CDILL 016*	28		3

SAFRI DUO
Denmark, male instrumental/production duo – Morten Friis & Uffe Savery — 10

Date	Title / Label	Peak Position	Weeks at No.1	Weeks on Chart
3 Feb 01	**PLAYED A LIVE (THE BONGO SONG)** *AM:PM CDAMPM 141*	6		9
5 Oct 02	**SWEET FREEDOM** *Serious SERR 55CD* FEATURING MICHAEL McDONALD	54		1

MIKE SAGAR
UK, male vocal/instrumental group — 5

Date	Title / Label	Peak Position	Weeks at No.1	Weeks on Chart
8 Dec 60	**DEEP FEELING** *HMV POP 819*	44		5

SAGAT
US, male rapper (Faustin Lenon) — 6

Date	Title / Label	Peak Position	Weeks at No.1	Weeks on Chart
4 Dec 93	**FUNK DAT** *ffrr FCD 224*	25		5
3 Dec 94	**LUVSTUFF** *ffrr FCD 250*	71		1

CAROLE BAYER SAGER
US, female vocalist — 9

Date	Title / Label	Peak Position	Weeks at No.1	Weeks on Chart
28 May 77	**YOU'RE MOVING OUT TODAY** *Elektra K 12257*	6		9

BALLY SAGOO
UK (b. India), male producer (Baljit Singh Sagoo) — 8

Date	Title / Label	Peak Position	Weeks at No.1	Weeks on Chart
3 Sep 94	**CHURA LIYA** *Columbia 6607092*	64		1
22 Apr 95	**CHOLI KE PEECHE** *Columbia 6613352*	45		1
19 Oct 96	**DIL CHEEZ (MY HEART...)** *Higher Ground 6634882*	12		3
1 Feb 97	**TUM BIN JIYA** *Higher Ground 6641372*	21		3

SAILOR
Norway/UK/Germany, male vocal/instrumental group – Georg Kajanus, Henry Marsh, Phil Pickett & Grant Serpell — 24

Date	Title / Label	Peak Position	Weeks at No.1	Weeks on Chart
6 Dec 75	**A GLASS OF CHAMPAGNE** *Epic EPC 3770* ● (silver)	2		12
27 Mar 76	**GIRLS GIRLS GIRLS** *Epic EPC 3858*	7		8
19 Feb 77	**ONE DRINK TOO MANY** *Epic EPC 4804*	35		4

SAINT FEATURING SUZANNA DEE
UK, male/female vocal/production trio — 2

Date	Title / Label	Peak Position	Weeks at No.1	Weeks on Chart
12 Apr 03	**SHOW ME HEAVEN** *Inferno CXFERN 52*	36		2

ST ANDREWS CHORALE
UK, church choir — 5

Date	Title / Label	Peak Position	Weeks at No.1	Weeks on Chart
14 Feb 76	**CLOUD 99** *Decca F 13617*	31		5

ST CECILIA
UK, male vocal/instrumental group — 17

Date	Title / Label	Peak Position	Weeks at No.1	Weeks on Chart
19 Jun 71	**LEAP UP AND DOWN (WAVE YOUR KNICKERS IN THE AIR)** *Polydor 2058 104*	12		17

SAINT ETIENNE
UK, female/male vocal/instrumental trio – Sarah Cracknell*, Bob Stanley & Peter Wiggs — 57

Date	Title / Label	Peak Position	Weeks at No.1	Weeks on Chart
18 May 91	**NOTHING CAN STOP US/SPEEDWELL** *Heavenly HVN 009*	54		3
7 Sep 91	**ONLY LOVE CAN BREAK YOUR HEART/FILTHY** *Heavenly HVN 12*	39		4
16 May 92	**JOIN OUR CLUB/PEOPLE GET REAL** *Heavenly HVN 15*	21		3
17 Oct 92	**AVENUE** *Heavenly HVN 2312*	40		2
13 Feb 93	**YOU'RE IN A BAD WAY** *Heavenly HVN 25CD*	12		5
22 May 93	**HOBART PAVING/WHO DO YOU THINK YOU ARE** *Heavenly HVN 29CD*	23		5
18 Dec 93	**I WAS BORN ON CHRISTMAS DAY** *Heavenly HVN 36CD* CO STARRING TIM BURGESS	37		5
19 Feb 94	**PALE MOVIE** *Heavenly HVN 37CD*	28		3
28 May 94	**LIKE A MOTORWAY** *Heavenly HVN 40CD*	47		2
1 Oct 94	**HUG MY SOUL** *Heavenly HVN 42CD*	32		2
11 Nov 95	**HE'S ON THE PHONE** *Heavenly HVN 50CDR* FEATURING ETIENNE DAHO	11		5
7 Feb 98	**SYLVIE** *Creation CRESCD 279X*	12		3
2 May 98	**THE BAD PHOTOGRAPHER** *Creation CRESCD 290*	27		2
20 May 00	**TELL ME WHY (THE RIDDLE)** *Deviant DVNT 36CDS* PAUL VAN DYK FEATURING SAINT ETIENNE	7		5
24 Jun 00	**HEART FAILED (IN THE BACK OF A TAXI)** *Mantra MNT 54CD*	50		1
20 Jan 01	**BOY IS CRYING** *Mantra MNT 60CD1*	34		2
7 Sep 02	**ACTION** *Mantra MNT 73CD*	41		1
29 Mar 03	**SOFT LIKE ME** *Mantra MNT 78CD*	40		1
18 Jun 05	**SIDE STREETS** *Sanctuary SANXS378*	36		1
12 Nov 05	**A GOOD THING** *Sanctuary SANXS412*	70		1
21 Feb 09	**METHOD OF MODERN LOVE** *Heavenly HVN185CDR*	56		1

ST GERMAIN
France, male producer (Ludovic Navarre) — 3

Date	Title / Label	Peak Position	Weeks at No.1	Weeks on Chart
31 Aug 96	**ALABAMA BLUES (REVISITED)** *F Communications F 050CD*	50		1
10 Mar 01	**ROSE ROUGE** *Blue Note CDROSE 001*	54		2

BARRY ST JOHN
UK, female vocalist — 1

Date	Title / Label	Peak Position	Weeks at No.1	Weeks on Chart
9 Dec 65	**COME AWAY MELINDA** *Columbia DB 7783*	47		1

ST JOHN'S COLLEGE SCHOOL CHOIR & THE BAND OF THE GRENADIER GUARDS
UK, choir & military band — 3

Date	Title / Label	Peak Position	Weeks at No.1	Weeks on Chart
3 May 86	**THE QUEEN'S BIRTHDAY SONG** *Columbia Q1*	40		3

ST LOUIS UNION
UK, male vocal/instrumental group — 10

Date	Title / Label	Peak Position	Weeks at No.1	Weeks on Chart
13 Jan 66	**GIRL** *Decca F 12318*	11		10

CRISPIAN ST. PETERS
UK, male vocalist (Robin Smith), d. 8 Jun 2010 (age 71) — 31

Date	Title / Label	Peak Position	Weeks at No.1	Weeks on Chart
6 Jan 66	**YOU WERE ON MY MIND** *Decca F 12287*	2		14
31 Mar 66	**PIED PIPER** *Decca F 12359*	5		13
15 Sep 66	**CHANGES** *Decca F 12480*	47		4

ST PHILIPS CHOIR
UK, choir — 4

Date	Title / Label	Peak Position	Weeks at No.1	Weeks on Chart
12 Dec 87	**SING FOR EVER** *BBC RESL 222*	49		4

ST WINIFRED'S SCHOOL CHOIR
UK, female/male choir – soloist Dawn Ralph. See Brian & Michael, Bill Tarmey — 11

Date	Title / Label	Peak Position	Weeks at No.1	Weeks on Chart
22 Nov 80	**THERE'S NO ONE QUITE LIKE GRANDMA** *MFP FP 900* ●	1	2	11

BUFFY SAINTE-MARIE
Canada, female vocalist/guitarist — 29

Date	Title / Label	Peak Position	Weeks at No.1	Weeks on Chart
17 Jul 71	**SOLDIER BLUE** *RCA 2081*	7		18
18 Mar 72	**I'M GONNA BE A COUNTRY GIRL AGAIN** *Vanguard VRS 35143*	34		5
8 Feb 92	**THE BIG ONES GET AWAY** *Ensign ENY 650*	39		5
4 Jul 92	**FALLEN ANGELS** *Ensign ENY 655*	57		1

SAINTS
Australia, male vocal/instrumental group — 4

Date	Title / Label	Peak Position	Weeks at No.1	Weeks on Chart
16 Jul 77	**THIS PERFECT DAY** *Harvest HAR 5130*	34		4

KYU SAKAMOTO
Japan, male vocalist, d. 12 Aug 1985 (age 43) — 13

Date	Title / Label	Peak Position	Weeks at No.1	Weeks on Chart
27 Jun 63	**SUKIYAKI** *HMV POP 1171* ★	6		13

SYLVIAN SAKAMOTO
Japan, male keyboard player (Ryuichi Sakamoto). See Yellow Magic Orchestra — 15

Date	Title / Label	Peak Position	Weeks at No.1	Weeks on Chart
7 Aug 82	**BAMBOO HOUSES/BAMBOO MUSIC** *Virgin VS 510*	30		4
2 Jul 83	**FORBIDDEN COLOURS** *Virgin VS 601* DAVID SYLVIAN & RYUICHI SAKAMOTO	16		8
13 Jun 92	**HEARTBEAT (TAINAI KAIKI II) RETURNING TO THE WOMB** *Virgin America VUS 57* DAVID SYLVIAN/RYUICHI SAKAMOTO FEATURING INGRID CHAVEZ	58		3

SAKKARIN
UK, male vocalist (Jonathan King) — 14

Date	Title / Label	Peak Position	Weeks at No.1	Weeks on Chart
3 Apr 71	**SUGAR SUGAR** *RCA 2064*	12		14

SALAD
UK/Holland, male/female vocal/instrumental group — 5

Date	Title / Label	Peak Position	Weeks at No.1	Weeks on Chart
11 Mar 95	**DRINK THE ELIXIR** *Island Red CIRD 104*	66		1
13 May 95	**MOTORBIKE TO HEAVEN** *Island Red CIRD 106*	42		1
16 Sep 95	**GRANITE STATUE** *Island Red CIRD 108*	50		1
26 Oct 96	**I WANT YOU** *Island CID 646*	60		1
17 May 97	**CARDBOY KING** *Island CID 654*	65		1

SALFORD JETS
UK, male vocal/instrumental group — 2

Date	Title / Label	Peak Position	Weeks at No.1	Weeks on Chart
31 May 80	**WHO YOU LOOKING AT** *RCA PB 5239*	72		2

SALIVA
US, male vocal/instrumental group — 1

Date	Title / Label	Peak Position	Weeks at No.1	Weeks on Chart
15 Mar 03	**ALWAYS** *Mercury 0637082*	47		1

SALT TANK
UK, male production duo — 4

Date	Title / Label	Peak Position	Weeks at No.1	Weeks on Chart
11 May 96	**EUGINA** *Internal LIECD 29*	40		2
3 Jul 99	**DIMENSION** *Hooj Choons HOOJ 74CD*	52		1
9 Dec 00	**EUGINA (REMIX)** *Lost Language LOST 004CD*	58		1

SALT-N-PEPA
US/Jamaica, female rap/DJ trio – Cheryl 'Salt' James, Sandra 'Pepa' Denton & Deidra 'Spinderella' Roper — 123

Date	Title / Label	Peak Position	Weeks at No.1	Weeks on Chart
26 Mar 88	**PUSH IT/I AM DOWN** *ffrr FFR 2*	41		6
25 Jun 88	**PUSH IT/TRAMP** *Champion CHAMP 51/ffrr FFR 2* ○	2		13
3 Sep 88	**SHAKE YOUR THANG (IT'S YOUR THING)** *ffrr FFR 11* FEATURING E.U.	22		8
12 Nov 88	**TWIST AND SHOUT** *ffrr FFR 16*	4		9
14 Apr 90	**EXPRESSION** *ffrr F 127*	40		6
25 May 91	**DO YOU WANT ME** *ffrr F 151*	5		12
31 Aug 91	**LET'S TALK ABOUT SEX** *ffrr F 162* FEATURING PSYCHOTROPIC ○	2		13
30 Nov 91	**YOU SHOWED ME** *ffrr F 174*	15		9
28 Mar 92	**EXPRESSION (REMIX)** *ffrr F 182*	23		6
3 Oct 92	**START ME UP** *ffrr F 196*	39		3
9 Oct 93	**SHOOP** *ffrr FCD 219*	29		3
19 Mar 94	**WHATTA MAN** *ffrr FCD 222* WITH EN VOGUE	7		10
28 May 94	**SHOOP (REMIX)** *ffrr FCD 234*	13		8
12 Nov 94	**NONE OF YOUR BUSINESS** *ffrr FCD 244*	19		5
21 Dec 96	**CHAMPAGNE** *MCA MCSTD 48025*	23		6
29 Nov 97	**R U READY** *ffrr FCDP 322*	24		2
11 Dec 99	**THE BRICK TRACK VERSUS GITTY UP** *ffrr FCD 373* SALTNPEPA	22		4

SAM & DAVE
US, male vocal duo – Sam Moore & Dave Prater, d. 9 Apr 1998 — 39

Date	Title / Label	Peak Position	Weeks at No.1	Weeks on Chart
16 Mar 67	**SOOTHE ME** *Stax 601 004*	35		8
1 Nov 67	**SOUL MAN** *Stax 601 023*	24		14
13 Mar 68	**I THANK YOU** *Stax 601 030*	34		9
29 Jan 69	**SOUL SISTER BROWN SUGAR** *Atlantic 584 237*	15		8

SAM & MARK
UK, male vocal duo – Sam Nixon & Mark Rhodes. See Idols — 13

Date	Title / Label	Peak Position	Weeks at No.1	Weeks on Chart
21 Feb 04	**WITH A LITTLE HELP FROM MY FRIENDS/MEASURE OF A MAN** *19 19RECS9*	1	1	10
5 Jun 04	**THE SUN HAS COME YOUR WAY** *19/UMTV 9866906*	19		3

SAM THE SHAM & THE PHARAOHS
US, male vocal/instrumental group — 18

Date	Title / Label	Peak Position	Weeks at No.1	Weeks on Chart
24 Jun 65	**WOOLY BULLY** *MGM 1269*	11		15
4 Aug 66	**LIL' RED RIDING HOOD** *MGM 1315*	46		3

SAMANDA
UK, female vocal duo — 4

Date	Title / Label	Peak Position	Weeks at No.1	Weeks on Chart
20 Oct 07	**BARBIE GIRL** *BMG 88697186502*	26		4

RICHIE SAMBORA
US, male vocalist/guitarist. See Bon Jovi — 4

Date	Title / Label	Peak Position	Weeks at No.1	Weeks on Chart
7 Sep 91	**BALLAD OF YOUTH** *Mercury MER 350*	59		1
7 Mar 98	**HARD TIMES COME EASY** *Mercury 5686972*	37		2
1 Aug 98	**IN IT FOR LOVE** *Mercury 5660632*	58		1

Silver-selling · Gold-selling · Platinum-selling (x multiples) · US No.1 · Peak Position · Weeks at No.1 · Weeks on Chart

SAME DIFFERENCE
UK, male/female vocal duo — 3

Date	Title	Peak Position	Weeks at No.1	Weeks on Chart
6 Dec 08	**WE R ONE** *Syco Music 88697414672*	13		3

SAMIM
Germany, male DJ/producer (Samim Winiger) — 6

Date	Title	Peak Position	Weeks at No.1	Weeks on Chart
3 Nov 07	**HEATER** *Data DATA176CDS*	12		6

MICHAEL SAMMES SINGERS
UK, male/female vocal ensemble – leader d. 19 May 2001 (age 73) — 164

Date	Title	Peak Position	Weeks at No.1	Weeks on Chart
3 May 57	**ROUND AND ROUND** *Decca F 10875* JIMMY YOUNG WITH THE MICHAEL SAMMES SINGERS	30		1
21 Mar 58	**TO BE LOVED** *HMV POP 459* MALCOLM VAUGHAN WITH THE MICHAEL SAMMES SINGERS	14		12
18 Apr 58	**I MAY NEVER PASS THIS WAY AGAIN** *HMV POP 468* RONNIE HILTON WITH THE MICHAEL SAMMES SINGERS	27		3
17 Oct 58	**MORE THAN EVER (COME PRIMA)** *HMV POP 538* MALCOLM VAUGHAN WITH THE MICHAEL SAMMES SINGERS	5		14
9 Jan 59	**THE WORLD OUTSIDE** *HMV POP 559* RONNIE HILTON WITH THE MICHAEL SAMMES SINGERS	18		6
27 Feb 59	**LITTLE DRUMMER BOY** *Parlophone R 4528* MICHAEL FLANDERS WITH THE MICHAEL SAMMES SINGERS	20		3
1 Jan 60	**STARRY EYED** *Columbia DB 4378* MICHAEL HOLLIDAY WITH THE MICHAEL SAMMES SINGERS	1	1	13
15 Dec 60	**DONALD WHERE'S YOUR TROOSERS** *Top Rank JAR 427* ANDY STEWART WITH THE MICHAEL SAMMES SINGERS	37		1
12 Jan 61	**A SCOTTISH SOLDIER** *Top Rank JAR 512* ANDY STEWART WITH THE MICHAEL SAMMES SINGERS	19		40
1 Jun 61	**THE BATTLE'S O'ER** *Top Rank JAR 565* ANDY STEWART WITH THE MICHAEL SAMMES SINGERS	28		13
26 Mar 64	**UNCHAINED MELODY** *Columbia DB 7234* JIMMY YOUNG WITH THE MICHAEL SAMMES SINGERS	43		3
15 Sep 66	**SOMEWHERE MY LOVE** *HMV POP 1546* MIKE SAMMES SINGERS	22		19
12 Jul 67	**SOMEWHERE MY LOVE** *HMV POP 1546* MIKE SAMMES SINGERS	14		19
1 Nov 67	**CARELESS HANDS** *Columbia DB 8275* DES O'CONNOR WITH THE MICHAEL SAMMES SINGERS	6		17

DAVE SAMPSON
UK, male vocalist — 6

Date	Title	Peak Position	Weeks at No.1	Weeks on Chart
19 May 60	**SWEET DREAMS** *Columbia DB 4449*	29		6

DAZ SAMPSON
UK, male vocalist/producer (Darren Sampson). See Barndance Boys, Bus Stop, Rikki & Daz featuring Glen Campbell, Uniting Nations — 6

Date	Title	Peak Position	Weeks at No.1	Weeks on Chart
20 May 06	**TEENAGE LIFE** *Ebul/Jive 82876834222*	8		6

GEORGE SAMPSON
UK, male dancer/actor — 3

Date	Title	Peak Position	Weeks at No.1	Weeks on Chart
6 Dec 08	**GET UP ON THE DANCE FLOOR/HEADZ UP** *Syco Music 88697438462*	30		3

SAMSON
UK, male vocal/instrumental group — 6

Date	Title	Peak Position	Weeks at No.1	Weeks on Chart
4 Jul 81	**RIDING WITH THE ANGELS** *RCA 67*	55		3
24 Jul 82	**LOSING MY GRIP** *Polydor POSP 471*	63		2
5 Mar 83	**RED SKIES** *Polydor POSP 554*	65		1

SIDNEY SAMSON FEATURING WIZARD SLEEVE
Holland/US, male rap/DJ/instrumental/production group – Sidney Samson, Mike Beatz (Michael Barnett), Lex One (Alex Cruz) & Pusher Fm (Pedro Calcano) — 13

Date	Title	Peak Position	Weeks at No.1	Weeks on Chart
16 Jan 10	**RIVERSIDE (LET'S GO)** *Data DATA225CDX*	2		13+

SAN JOSE FEATURING RODRIGUEZ ARGENTINA
UK, male instrumental group featuring Rod Argent. See Argent, Silsoe, Zombies — 8

Date	Title	Peak Position	Weeks at No.1	Weeks on Chart
17 Jun 78	**ARGENTINE MELODY (CANCION DE ARGENTINA)** *MCA 369*	14		8

SAN REMO STRINGS
US, male instrumental session group — 8

Date	Title	Peak Position	Weeks at No.1	Weeks on Chart
18 Dec 71	**FESTIVAL TIME** *Tamla Motown TMG 795*	39		8

JUNIOR SANCHEZ FEATURING DAJAE
US, male/female vocal/DJ/production duo — 2

Date	Title	Peak Position	Weeks at No.1	Weeks on Chart
16 Oct 99	**B WITH U** *Manifesto FESCD 62*	31		2

ROGER SANCHEZ
US, male DJ/producer — 21

Date	Title	Peak Position	Weeks at No.1	Weeks on Chart
3 Oct 98	**BUFFALO GALS STAMPEDE** *Virgin VSCDT 1717* MALCOLM McLAREN & THE WORLD'S FAMOUS SUPREME TEAM PLUS RAKIM & ROGER SANCHEZ	65		1
20 Feb 99	**I WANT YOUR LOVE** *Perpetual PERPCDS 001* PRESENTS TWILIGHT	31		2
29 Jan 00	**I NEVER KNEW** *INCredible INCS 4CD*	24		2
14 Jul 01	**ANOTHER CHANCE** *Defected DFECT 35CD*	1	1	12
15 Dec 01	**YOU CAN'T CHANGE ME** *Defected DFECT 41CDS* FEATURING ARMAND VAN HELDEN AND N'DEA DAVENPORT	25		4

HAYLEY SANDERSON
UK, female vocalist/saxophonist — 1

Date	Title	Peak Position	Weeks at No.1	Weeks on Chart
19 Aug 06	**SOMETHING IN THE AIR** *Transistor Project CDTRANSP2*	61		1

CHRIS SANDFORD
UK, male actor/vocalist — 9

Date	Title	Peak Position	Weeks at No.1	Weeks on Chart
12 Dec 63	**NOT TOO LITTLE NOT TOO MUCH** *Decca F 11778*	17		9

SANDPIPERS
US, male vocal trio – Jim Brady, Michael Piano & Richard Shoff — 33

Date	Title	Peak Position	Weeks at No.1	Weeks on Chart
15 Sep 66	**GUANTANAMERA** *Pye International 7N 25380*	7		17
5 Jun 68	**QUANDO M'INNAMORO (A MAN WITHOUT LOVE)** *A&M AMS 723*	33		6
26 Mar 69	**KUMBAYA** *A&M AMS 744*	38		2
27 Nov 76	**HANG ON SLOOPY** *Satril SAT 114*	32		8

SANDRA
Germany, female vocalist (Sandra Lauer) — 8

Date	Title	Peak Position	Weeks at No.1	Weeks on Chart
17 Dec 88	**EVERLASTING LOVE** *Siren SRN 85*	45		8

JODIE SANDS
US, female vocalist — 10

Date	Title	Peak Position	Weeks at No.1	Weeks on Chart
17 Oct 58	**SOMEDAY (YOU'LL WANT ME TO WANT YOU)** *HMV POP 533*	14		10

TOMMY SANDS
US, male vocalist — 7

Date	Title	Peak Position	Weeks at No.1	Weeks on Chart
4 Aug 60	**OLD OAKEN BUCKET** *Capitol CL 15143*	25		7

SANDSTORM
US, male producer (Mark Picchiotti). See Absolute, Basstoy — 1

Date	Title	Peak Position	Weeks at No.1	Weeks on Chart
13 May 00	**THE RETURN OF NOTHING** *Renaissance Recordings RENCDS 001*	54		1

SAMANTHA SANG
Australia, female vocalist (Cheryl Gray) — 13

Date	Title	Peak Position	Weeks at No.1	Weeks on Chart
4 Feb 78	**EMOTION** *Private Stock PVT 128*	11		13

SANTA
North Pole, male vocalist (Father Christmas) — 1

Date	Title	Peak Position	Weeks at No.1	Weeks on Chart
31 Dec 05	**IS THIS THE WAY TO AMARILLO (SANTA'S GROTTO)** *Sony 82876767312*	30		1

SANTA CLAUS & THE CHRISTMAS TREES
UK, male vocal/instrumental group — 10

Date	Title	Peak Position	Weeks at No.1	Weeks on Chart
11 Dec 82	**SINGALONG-A-SANTA** *Polydor IVY 1*	19		5
10 Dec 83	**SINGALONG-A-SANTA AGAIN** *Polydor IVY 2*	39		5

SANTA ESMERALDA & LEROY GOMEZ
UK/France, male/female vocal/instrumental group — 5

Date	Title	Peak Position	Weeks at No.1	Weeks on Chart
12 Nov 77	**DON'T LET ME BE MISUNDERSTOOD** *Philips 6042 325*	41		5

SANTANA
US, male vocal/instrumental group – Carlos Santana; members also included David Brown, Alex Ligertwood, Leon Patillo, Gregg Rolie, Neal Schon, Michael Shrieve & Greg Walker — 56

Date	Title	Peak Position	Weeks at No.1	Weeks on Chart
28 Sep 74	**SAMBA PA TI** *CBS 2561*	27		7
15 Oct 77	**SHE'S NOT THERE** *CBS 5671*	11		12
25 Nov 78	**WELL ALL RIGHT** *CBS 6755*	53		3
22 Mar 80	**ALL I EVER WANTED** *CBS 8160*	57		3
23 Oct 99	**SMOOTH** *Arista 74321709492* FEATURING ROB THOMAS	75		1
1 Apr 00	**SMOOTH** *Arista 74321748762* FEATURING ROB THOMAS ★	3		10
5 Aug 00	**MARIA MARIA** *Arista 74321769372* FEATURING THE PRODUCT G&B ★	6		9
23 Nov 02	**THE GAME OF LOVE** *Arista 74321959442* FEATURING MICHELLE BRANCH	16		8
20 May 06	**CRY BABY CRY** *Arista 82876804672* FEATURING SEAN PAUL & JOSS STONE	71		1
23 Dec 06	**ILLEGAL** *Epic 88697009202* SHAKIRA FEATURING CARLOS SANTANA	34		2

JUELZ SANTANA
US, male rapper/producer/actor (LaRon James) — 33

Date	Title	Peak Position	Weeks at No.1	Weeks on Chart
25 Mar 06	**THERE IT GO (THE WHISTLE SONG)** *Def Jam 9853444*	47		2
17 Aug 02	**OH BOY** *Roc-A-Fella 0639642* CAM'RON FEATURING JUELZ SANTANA	13		7
8 Feb 03	**HEY MA** *Roc-A-Fella 0637242* CAM'RON FEATURING JUELZ SANTANA	8		10
11 Feb 06	**RUN IT!** *Jive 82876780532* CHRIS BROWN FEATURING JUELZ SANTANA ★	2		14

SANTO & JOHNNY
UK, male guitar duo — 5

Date	Title	Peak Position	Weeks at No.1	Weeks on Chart
16 Oct 59	**SLEEP WALK** *Pye International 7N 25037* ★	22		4
31 Mar 60	**TEARDROP** *Parlophone R 4619*	50		1

SANTOGOLD
US, female vocalist/producer (Santi White) — 4

Date	Title	Peak Position	Weeks at No.1	Weeks on Chart
10 May 08	**LES ARTISTES** *Atlantic ATUK078CD*	27		4

SANTOS
Italy, male DJ/producer (Sante Pucello) — 6

Date	Title	Peak Position	Weeks at No.1	Weeks on Chart
20 Jan 01	**CAMELS** *Incentive CENT 15CDS*	9		6

MIKE SARNE
UK, male vocalist (Mike Scheuer) — 43

Date	Title	Peak Position	Weeks at No.1	Weeks on Chart
10 May 62	**COME OUTSIDE** *Parlophone R 4902* WITH WENDY RICHARD	1	2	19
30 Aug 62	**WILL I WHAT** *Parlophone R 4932* WITH BILLIE DAVIS	18		10
10 Jan 63	**JUST FOR KICKS** *Parlophone R 4974*	22		7
28 Mar 63	**CODE OF LOVE** *Parlophone R 5010*	29		7

JOY SARNEY
UK, female vocalist — 6

Date	Title	Peak Position	Weeks at No.1	Weeks on Chart
7 May 77	**NAUGHTY NAUGHTY NAUGHTY** *Alaska ALA 2005*	26		6

SARR BAND
Italy/UK/France, male/female vocal/instrumental group — 1

Date	Title	Peak Position	Weeks at No.1	Weeks on Chart
16 Sep 78	**MAGIC MANDRAKE** *Calendar Day 111*	68		1

PETER SARSTEDT
UK, male vocalist — 25

Date	Title	Peak Position	Weeks at No.1	Weeks on Chart
5 Feb 69	**WHERE DO YOU GO TO MY LOVELY** *United Artists UP 2262*	1	4	16
4 Jun 69	**FROZEN ORANGE JUICE** *United Artists UP 35021*	10		9

ROBIN SARSTEDT
UK, male vocalist (Clive Sarstedt) — 9

Date	Title	Peak Position	Weeks at No.1	Weeks on Chart
8 May 76	**MY RESISTANCE IS LOW** *Decca F 13624*	3		9

SARTORELLO
Italy, male/female vocal/instrumental duo — 1

Date	Title	Peak Position	Weeks at No.1	Weeks on Chart
10 Aug 96	**MOVE BABY MOVE** *Multiply CDMULTY 12*	56		1

SASH!
Germany, male DJ/production group – Sascha Lappessen, Ralf Kappmeier, Thomas Ludke & various vocalists — 116

Date	Title	Peak Position	Weeks at No.1	Weeks on Chart
1 Mar 97	**ENCORE UNE FOIS** *Multiply CDMULTY 18* ●	2		15
5 Jul 97	**ECUADOR** *Multiply CDMULTY 23* FEATURING RODRIGUEZ ●	2		12
18 Oct 97	**STAY** *Multiply CDMULTY 26* FEATURING LA TREC ●	2		14
4 Apr 98	**LA PRIMAVERA** *Multiply CXMULTY 32* ○	3		12
15 Aug 98	**MYSTERIOUS TIMES** *Multiply CDMULTY 40* FEATURING TINA COUSINS ○	2		12
28 Nov 98	**MOVE MANIA** *Multiply CDMULTY 45* FEATURING SHANNON	8		10
3 Apr 99	**COLOUR THE WORLD** *Multiply CDMULTY 48*	15		6
12 Feb 00	**ADELANTE** *Multiply CDMULTY 60*	2		10
22 Apr 00	**JUST AROUND THE HILL** *Multiply CDMULTY 62*	8		7
23 Sep 00	**WITH MY OWN EYES** *Multiply CDMULTY 67*	10		5
25 Oct 08	**RAINDROPS (ENCORE UNE FOIS)** *Hard2Beat H2B15CDS* FEATURING STUNT	9		13

SASHA
UK, male producer (Alexander Coe) — 16

Date	Title	Peak Position	Weeks at No.1	Weeks on Chart
31 Jul 93	**TOGETHER** *ffrr FCD 212* DANNY CAMPBELL & SASHA	57		1
19 Feb 94	**HIGHER GROUND** *Deconstruction 74321189002* WITH SAM MOLLISON	19		3
27 Aug 94	**MAGIC** *Deconstruction 74321221862* WITH SAM MOLLISON	32		4
9 Mar 96	**BE AS ONE** *7pm 74321342962* & MARIA	17		4
23 Sep 00	**SCORCHIO** *Arista 74321788222* SASHA/EMERSON	23		3
31 Aug 02	**WAVY GRAVY** *Arista 74321960602*	64		1

JOE SATRIANI
US, male guitarist — 1

Date	Title	Peak Position	Weeks at No.1	Weeks on Chart
13 Feb 93	**THE SATCH EP** *Relativity 6589532*	53		1

SATURATED SOUL FEATURING MISS BUNTY
US/UK/Holland, male/female vocal/production trio — 1

Date	Title	Peak Position	Weeks at No.1	Weeks on Chart
14 Aug 04	**GOT TO RELEASE** *Defected DFTD093*	56		1

SATURDAY NIGHT BAND
US, male vocal/instrumental group — 9

Date	Title	Peak Position	Weeks at No.1	Weeks on Chart
1 Jul 78	**COME ON DANCE DANCE** *CBS 6367*	16		9

SATURDAYS
UK/Ireland, female vocal group – Una Healy, Mollie King, Frankie Sandford, Vanessa White & Rochelle Wiseman — 103

Date	Title	Peak Position	Weeks at No.1	Weeks on Chart
9 Aug 08	**IF THIS IS LOVE** *Fascination 1771961*	8		9
25 Oct 08	**UP** *Fascination 1785660*	5		30
20 Dec 08	**ISSUES** *Fascination 1794029*	4		18
14 Mar 09	**JUST CAN'T GET ENOUGH** *Fascination 1799707*	2		10
13 Jun 09	**WORK** *Fascination 2707835*	22		10
17 Oct 09	**FOREVER IS OVER** *Fascination 2720426*	2		8
12 Dec 09	**EGO** *Fascination 2727784*	9		18+

ANNE SAVAGE
UK, female DJ/producer — 1

Date	Title	Peak Position	Weeks at No.1	Weeks on Chart
19 Apr 03	**HELLRAISER** *Tidy Trax TIDY 186T*	74		1

CHANTAY SAVAGE
US, female vocalist — 9

Date	Title	Peak Position	Weeks at No.1	Weeks on Chart
4 May 96	**I WILL SURVIVE** *RCA 74321377682*	12		8
8 Nov 97	**REMINDING ME (OF SEF)** *Relativity 6560762* COMMON FEATURING CHANTAY SAVAGE	59		1

EDNA SAVAGE
UK, female vocalist, d. 31 Dec 2000 (age 64) — 1

Date	Title	Peak Position	Weeks at No.1	Weeks on Chart
13 Jan 56	**ARRIVEDERCI DARLING** *Parlophone R 4097*	19		1

SAVAGE GARDEN

Australia, male vocal/instrumental duo – Darren Hayes* & Daniel Jones

Date	Title / Label	Peak Position	Weeks at No.1	Weeks on Chart
				101
21 Jun 97	**I WANT YOU** *Columbia 6645452*	11		7
27 Sep 97	**TO THE MOON AND BACK** *Columbia 6648932*	55		1
28 Feb 98	**TRULY MADLY DEEPLY** *Columbia 6656022* ⊛ ★	4		23
22 Aug 98	**TO THE MOON AND BACK** *Columbia 6662882* ○	3		16
12 Dec 98	**I WANT YOU '98 (REMIX)** *Columbia 6667332*	12		10
10 Jul 99	**THE ANIMAL SONG** *Columbia 6675882*	16		6
13 Nov 99	**I KNEW I LOVED YOU** *Columbia 6683102* ★	10		12
1 Apr 00	**CRASH AND BURN** *Columbia 6690442*	14		6
29 Jul 00	**AFFIRMATION** *Columbia 6696882*	8		10
25 Nov 00	**HOLD ME** *Columbia 6706032*	16		7
31 Mar 01	**THE BEST THING** *Columbia 6709852*	35		3

TELLY SAVALAS

US, male actor/vocalist (Aristottle Savalas), d. 22 Jan 1994 (age 70)

Date	Title / Label	Peak Position	Weeks at No.1	Weeks on Chart
				12
22 Feb 75	**IF** *MCA 174* ○	1	2	9
31 May 75	**YOU'VE LOST THAT LOVIN' FEELIN'** *MCA 189*	47		3

SAVANA

UK (b. Jamaica), male rapper

Date	Title / Label	Peak Position	Weeks at No.1	Weeks on Chart
				1
24 Jul 04	**PRETTY LADY** *Jetstar JECDS1805*	48		1

SAVANNA

UK, male vocal/instrumental group

Date	Title / Label	Peak Position	Weeks at No.1	Weeks on Chart
				4
10 Oct 81	**I CAN'T TURN AWAY** *R&B RBS 203*	61		4

SAW DOCTORS

Ireland, male vocal/instrumental group

Date	Title / Label	Peak Position	Weeks at No.1	Weeks on Chart
				11
12 Nov 94	**SMALL BIT OF LOVE** *Shamtown SAW001CD*	24		3
27 Jan 96	**WORLD OF GOOD** *Shamtown SAW002CD*	15		3
13 Jul 96	**TO WIN JUST ONCE** *Shamtown SAW004CD*	14		2
6 Dec 97	**SIMPLE THINGS** *Shamtown SAW006CD*	56		1
1 Jun 02	**THIS IS ME** *Shamtown SAW012CD*	31		1
15 Oct 05	**STARS OVER CLOUGHANOVER** *Shamtown SAW014CD*	69		1

NITIN SAWHNEY FEATURING ESKA

UK, male/female vocal/instrumental/production duo

Date	Title / Label	Peak Position	Weeks at No.1	Weeks on Chart
				1
28 Jul 01	**SUNSET** *V2 VVR 5016768*	65		1

SAXON

UK, male vocal/instrumental group

Date	Title / Label	Peak Position	Weeks at No.1	Weeks on Chart
				61
22 Mar 80	**WHEELS OF STEEL** *Carrere CAR 143*	20		11
21 Jun 80	**747 (STRANGERS IN THE NIGHT)** *Carrere CAR 151*	13		9
28 Jun 80	**BACKS TO THE WALL** *Carrere HM 6*	64		2
28 Jun 80	**BIG TEASER/RAINBOW THEME** *Carrere HM 5*	66		2
29 Nov 80	**STRONG ARM OF THE LAW** *Carrere CAR 170*	63		3
11 Apr 81	**AND THE BANDS PLAYED ON** *Carrere CAR 180*	12		8
18 Jul 81	**NEVER SURRENDER** *Carrere CAR 204*	18		6
31 Oct 81	**PRINCESS OF THE NIGHT** *Carrere CAR 208*	57		3
23 Apr 83	**POWER AND THE GLORY** *Carrere SAXON 1*	32		5
30 Jul 83	**NIGHTMARE** *Carrere CAR 284*	50		3
31 Aug 85	**BACK ON THE STREETS** *Parlophone R 6103*	75		1
29 Mar 86	**ROCK 'N' ROLL GYPSY** *Parlophone R 6112*	72		1
30 Aug 86	**WAITING FOR THE NIGHT** *EMI 5575*	66		2
5 Mar 88	**RIDE LIKE THE WIND** *EMI EM 43*	52		4
30 Apr 88	**I CAN'T WAIT ANYMORE** *EMI EM 54*	71		1

AL SAXON

UK, male vocalist (Allan Fowler)

Date	Title / Label	Peak Position	Weeks at No.1	Weeks on Chart
				10
16 Jan 59	**YOU'RE THE TOP CHA** *Fontana H 164*	17		4
28 Aug 59	**ONLY SIXTEEN** *Fontana H 205*	24		3
22 Dec 60	**BLUE-EYED BOY** *Fontana H 278*	39		2
7 Sep 61	**THERE I'VE SAID IT AGAIN** *Piccadilly 7N 35011*	48		1

LEO SAYER

UK, male vocalist (Gerard Sayer)

Date	Title / Label	Peak Position	Weeks at No.1	Weeks on Chart
				167
15 Dec 73	**THE SHOW MUST GO ON** *Chrysalis CHS 2023* ○	2		13
15 Jun 74	**ONE MAN BAND** *Chrysalis CHS 2045*	6		9
14 Sep 74	**LONG TALL GLASSES** *Chrysalis CHS 2052*	4		9
30 Aug 75	**MOONLIGHTING** *Chrysalis CHS 2076* ○	2		8
30 Oct 76	**YOU MAKE ME FEEL LIKE DANCING** *Chrysalis CHS 2119* ○ ★	2		12
29 Jan 77	**WHEN I NEED YOU** *Chrysalis CHS 2127* ● ★	1	3	13
9 Apr 77	**HOW MUCH LOVE** *Chrysalis CHS 2140*	10		8
10 Sep 77	**THUNDER IN MY HEART** *Chrysalis CHS 2163*	22		8
16 Sep 78	**I CAN'T STOP LOVIN' YOU (THOUGH I TRY)** *Chrysalis CHS 2240* ○	6		11
25 Nov 78	**RAINING IN MY HEART** *Chrysalis CHS 2277*	21		10
5 Jul 80	**MORE THAN I CAN SAY** *Chrysalis CHS 2442* ○	2		11
13 Mar 82	**HAVE YOU EVER BEEN IN LOVE** *Chrysalis CHS 2596*	10		9
19 Jun 82	**HEART (STOP BEATING IN TIME)** *Chrysalis CHS 2616*	22		10
12 Mar 83	**ORCHARD ROAD** *Chrysalis CHS 2677*	16		8
15 Oct 83	**TILL YOU COME BACK TO ME** *Chrysalis LEO 01*	51		3
8 Feb 86	**UNCHAINED MELODY** *Chrysalis LEO 3*	54		4
13 Feb 93	**WHEN I NEED YOU** *Chrysalis CDCHS 3926*	65		2
8 Aug 98	**YOU MAKE ME FEEL LIKE DANCING** *Brothers Organisation CDBRUV 8* GROOVE GENERATION FEATURING LEO SAYER	32		3
18 Feb 06	**THUNDER IN MY HEART AGAIN** *Apollo/Free 2 Air APOLLO101CDX* MECK FEATURING LEO SAYER	1	2	16

ALEXEI SAYLE

UK, male 'rapper'/comedian

Date	Title / Label	Peak Position	Weeks at No.1	Weeks on Chart
				8
25 Feb 84	**'ULLO JOHN GOT A NEW MOTOR?** *Island IS 162*	15		8

SCAFFOLD

UK, male vocal/instrumental trio – John Gorman, Mike McGear (McCartney) & Roger McGough

Date	Title / Label	Peak Position	Weeks at No.1	Weeks on Chart
				62
22 Nov 67	**THANK U VERY MUCH** *Parlophone R 5643*	4		12
27 Mar 68	**DO YOU REMEMBER** *Parlophone R 5679*	34		5
6 Nov 68	**LILY THE PINK** *Parlophone R 5734*	1	4	24
1 Nov 69	**GIN GAN GOOLIE** *Parlophone R 5812*	38		12
1 Jun 74	**LIVERPOOL LOU** *Warner Brothers K 16400*	7		9

BOZ SCAGGS

US, male vocalist (Willam Royce Scaggs)

Date	Title / Label	Peak Position	Weeks at No.1	Weeks on Chart
				31
30 Oct 76	**LOWDOWN** *CBS 4563*	28		4
22 Jan 77	**WHAT CAN I SAY** *CBS 4869*	10		10
14 May 77	**LIDO SHUFFLE** *CBS 5136*	13		9
10 Dec 77	**HOLLYWOOD** *CBS 5836*	33		8

SCANTY SANDWICH

UK, male DJ/producer (Richard Marshall)

Date	Title / Label	Peak Position	Weeks at No.1	Weeks on Chart
				8
29 Jan 00	**BECAUSE OF YOU** *Southern Fried ECB 18CDS*	3		8

SCARFACE

US, male rapper (Brad Jordan)

Date	Title / Label	Peak Position	Weeks at No.1	Weeks on Chart
				6
11 Mar 95	**HAND OF THE DEAD BODY** *Virgin America VUSCD 88* FEATURING ICE CUBE	41		2
5 Aug 95	**I SEEN A MAN DIE** *Virgin America VUSCD 94*	55		2
5 Jul 97	**GAME OVER** *Virgin VUSCD 121*	34		2

SCARFO

UK, male vocal/instrumental group

Date	Title / Label	Peak Position	Weeks at No.1	Weeks on Chart
				2
19 Jul 97	**ALKALINE** *Deceptive BLUFF 044CD*	61		1
18 Oct 97	**COSMONAUT NO. 7** *Deceptive BLUFF 053CD*	67		1

SCARLET

UK, female vocal/instrumental duo

Date	Title / Label	Peak Position	Weeks at No.1	Weeks on Chart
				18
21 Jan 95	**INDEPENDENT LOVE SONG** *WEA YZ 820CD*	12		12
29 Apr 95	**I WANNA BE FREE (TO BE WITH HIM)** *WEA YZ 913CD*	21		4
5 Aug 95	**LOVE HANGOVER** *WEA YZ 969CD*	54		1
6 Jul 96	**BAD GIRL** *WEA 046CD*	54		1

SCARLET FANTASTIC

UK, female/male vocal/instrumental duo

Date	Title / Label	Peak Position	Weeks at No.1	Weeks on Chart
				12
3 Oct 87	**NO MEMORY** *Arista RIS 36*	24		10
23 Jan 88	**PLUG ME IN (TO THE CENTRAL LOVE LINE)** *Arista 109693*	67		2

SCARLET PARTY

UK, male vocal/instrumental group

Date	Title / Label	Peak Position	Weeks at No.1	Weeks on Chart
				5
16 Oct 82	**101 DAM-NATIONS** *Parlophone R 6058*	44		5

SCATMAN JOHN
US, male vocalist (John Larkin), d. 3 Dec 1999 (age 57) — 19

Date	Title	Peak	Wks at No.1	Wks
13 May 95	**SCATMAN (SKI-BA-BOP-BA-DOP-BOP)** *RCA 74321281712* ●	3		12
2 Sep 95	**SCATMAN'S WORLD** *RCA 74321289952*	10		7

MICHAEL SCHENKER GROUP
Germany/UK, male vocal/instrumental group — 9

Date	Title	Peak	Wks at No.1	Wks
13 Sep 80	**ARMED AND READY** *Chrysalis CHS 2455*	53		3
8 Nov 80	**CRY FOR THE NATIONS** *Chrysalis CHS 2471*	56		3
11 Sep 82	**DANCER** *Chrysalis CHS 2636*	52		3

NICOLE SCHERZINGER
US, female vocalist/dancer/model. See Pussycat Dolls — 59

Date	Title	Peak	Wks at No.1	Wks
7 Oct 06	**COME TO ME** *Atlantic AT0260CD* P DIDDY FEATURING NICOLE SCHERZINGER	4		12
20 Oct 07	**BABY LOVE** *Polydor 1753014* FEATURING WILL.I.AM	14		9
16 Feb 08	**SCREAM** *Interscope 1764136* TIMBALAND FEATURING KERI HILSON & NICOLE SCHERZINGER	12		14
28 Mar 09	**JAI HO! (YOU ARE MY DESTINY)** *Polydor USUM70954362* AR RAHMAN & PUSSYCAT DOLLS FEATURING NICOLE SCHERZINGER	3		22
20 Mar 10	**JAI HO! (YOU ARE MY DESTINY)** *Polydor USUM70954362* AR RAHMAN & PUSSYCAT DOLLS FEATURING NICOLE SCHERZINGER	58		2+

SCHNAPPI
Germany, cartoon crocodile vocalist (Joy Gruttmann) — 3

Date	Title	Peak	Wks at No.1	Wks
15 Oct 05	**SCHNAPPI** *Universal TV 9873701*	32		3

SCENT
Italy/Ireland, male/female vocal/production trio — 3

Date	Title	Peak	Wks at No.1	Wks
21 Aug 04	**UP AND DOWN** *Positiva CDTIVS209*	23		3

LALO SCHIFRIN
Argentina, male pianist/conductor — 11

Date	Title	Peak	Wks at No.1	Wks
9 Oct 76	**JAWS** *CTI CTSP 005*	14		9
25 Oct 97	**BULLITT** *warner.esp WESP 002CD*	36		2

SCHILLER
Germany, male production duo — 3

Date	Title	Peak	Wks at No.1	Wks
28 Apr 01	**DAS GLOCKENSPIEL** *Data 22CDS*	17		3

PETER SCHILLING
Germany, male vocalist — 6

Date	Title	Peak	Wks at No.1	Wks
5 May 84	**MAJOR TOM (COMING HOME)** *PSP/WEA X 9438*	42		6

PHILIP SCHOFIELD
UK, male vocalist/TV presenter — 6

Date	Title	Peak	Wks at No.1	Wks
5 Dec 92	**CLOSE EVERY DOOR** *Really Useful RUR 11*	27		6

SCHOOL OF ROCK
US, male/female actors/vocalists — 2

Date	Title	Peak	Wks at No.1	Wks
21 Feb 04	**SCHOOL OF ROCK** *Atlantic AT 0172CD*	51		2

SCIENCE DEPT FEATURING ERIRE
UK, male/female vocal/production trio. See Danny Howells & Dick Trevor featuring Erire — 1

Date	Title	Peak	Wks at No.1	Wks
10 Nov 01	**BREATHE** *Renaissance RENCDS 010*	64		1

SCIENTIST
UK, male producer (Phivos Sebastiane) — 13

Date	Title	Peak	Wks at No.1	Wks
6 Oct 90	**THE EXORCIST** *Kickin KICK 1*	62		3
1 Dec 90	**THE EXORCIST (REMIX)** *Kickin KICK 1TR*	46		3
15 Dec 90	**THE BEE** *Kickin KICK 35*	47		6
11 May 91	**SPIRAL SYMPHONY** *Kickin KICK 5*	74		1

SCISSOR SISTERS
US/Singapore, male/female vocal/instrumental group – Jake Shears (Jason Sellards), Babydaddy (Scott Hoffman), Del Marquis (Derek Gruen), Ana Matronic (Ana Lynch) & Paddy Boom (Paddy Seacor) — 84

Date	Title	Peak	Wks at No.1	Wks
8 Nov 03	**LAURA** *Polydor 9812788*	54		2
31 Jan 04	**COMFORTABLY NUMB** *Polydor 9815883*	10		7
10 Apr 04	**TAKE YOUR MAMA** *Polydor 9866277*	17		6
19 Jun 04	**LAURA** *Polydor 9866833*	12		10
23 Oct 04	**MARY** *Polydor 9868282*	14		6
8 Jan 05	**COMFORTABLY NUMB** *Polydor 9815883*	74		1
15 Jan 05	**FILTHY/GORGEOUS** *Polydor 9869799*	5		9
9 Sep 06	**I DON'T FEEL LIKE DANCIN'** *Polydor 1705491*	1	4	33
9 Dec 06	**LAND OF A THOUSAND WORDS** *Polydor 1712488*	19		4
17 Mar 07	**SHE'S MY MAN** *Polydor 1721313*	29		4
9 Jun 07	**KISS YOU OFF** *Polydor 1726298*	43		1
14 Jul 07	**I CAN'T DECIDE** *Polydor GBUM70602614*	64		1

SCOOBIE
UK, football fans (Celtic)/vocal/production group — 3

Date	Title	Peak	Wks at No.1	Wks
22 Dec 01	**THE MAGNIFICENT 7** *Big Tongue BTR 001CDS*	58		2
1 Jun 02	**THE MAGNIFICENT 7** *Big Tongue BTR 001CDSX*	71		1

SCOOCH
UK, male/female vocal group – Caroline Barnes, David Ducasse, Natalie Powers & Russ Spencer — 26

Date	Title	Peak	Wks at No.1	Wks
6 Nov 99	**WHEN MY BABY** *Accolade CDACS 002*	29		4
22 Jan 00	**MORE THAN I NEEDED TO KNOW** *Accolade CDACS 003*	5		5
6 May 00	**THE BEST IS YET TO COME** *Accolade CDAC 004*	12		5
5 Aug 00	**FOR SURE** *Accolade CDACS 005*	15		6
31 Mar 07	**FLYING THE FLAG (FOR YOU)** *Warner Brothers WEA421CD*	5		6

SCOOTER
UK/Germany, male vocal/instrumental trio – H.P. Baxxter (Hans Peter Geerdes), Ferris Bueller (Soren Buhler, replaced by Axel Coon (Axel Broszeit) then Jay Frog (Jurgen Frosch)) & Rick J Jordan (Hendrik Stedler) — 83

Date	Title	Peak	Wks at No.1	Wks
21 Oct 95	**MOVE YOUR ASS** *Club Tools 0061675 CLU*	23		4
17 Feb 96	**BACK IN THE UK** *Club Tools 0061955 CLU*	18		3
25 May 96	**REBEL YELL** *Club Tools 0062575 CLU*	30		2
19 Oct 96	**I'M RAVING** *Club Tools 0063015 CLU*	33		3
17 May 97	**FIRE** *Club Tools 0060005 CLU*	45		2
22 Jun 02	**THE LOGICAL SONG** *Sheffield Tunes 0139295 STU* ●	2		15
21 Sep 02	**NESSAJA** *Sheffield Tunes 0142165 STU*	4		9
7 Dec 02	**POSSE (I NEED YOU ON THE FLOOR)** *Sheffield Tunes 0143775 STU*	15		7
5 Apr 03	**WEEKEND** *Sheffield Tunes 0147315 STU*	12		10
5 Jul 03	**THE NIGHT** *Sheffield Tunes 0149005 STU*	16		5
18 Oct 03	**MARIA (I LIKE IT LOUD)** *Sheffield Tunes 0151135 STU* VS MARC ACARDIPANE & DICK RULES	16		4
10 Jul 04	**JIGGA JIGGA** *All Around The World CXGLOBE 348*	48		1
26 Apr 08	**THE QUESTION IS WHAT IS THE QUESTION** *All Around The World CDGLOBE769*	49		6
7 Jun 08	**JUMPING ALL OVER THE WORLD** *All Around The World CDGLOBE940*	28		11
20 Dec 08	**JUMP THAT ROCK** *All Around The World CDGLOBE1006* VS STATUS QUO	57		1

SCORPIONS
Germany, male vocal/instrumental group – Klaus Meine, Francis Buckholz, Matthias Jabs, Herman Rarebell & Rudolf Schenker — 35

Date	Title	Peak	Wks at No.1	Wks
26 May 79	**IS THERE ANYBODY THERE/ANOTHER PIECE OF MEAT** *Harvest HAR 5185*	39		4
25 Aug 79	**LOVEDRIVE** *Harvest HAR 5188*	69		2
31 May 80	**MAKE IT REAL** *Harvest HAR 5206*	72		2
20 Sep 80	**THE ZOO** *Harvest HAR 5212*	75		1
3 Apr 82	**NO ONE LIKE YOU** *Harvest HAR 5219*	64		4
17 Jul 82	**CAN'T LIVE WITHOUT YOU** *Harvest HAR 5221*	63		2
4 Jun 88	**RHYTHM OF LOVE** *Harvest HAR 5240*	59		2
18 Feb 89	**PASSION RULES THE GAME** *Harvest HAR 5242*	74		1
1 Jun 91	**WIND OF CHANGE** *Vertigo VER 54*	53		3
28 Sep 91	**WIND OF CHANGE** *Vertigo VER 58* ●	2		9
30 Nov 91	**SEND ME AN ANGEL** *Vertigo VER 60*	27		5

SCOTLAND WORLD CUP SQUAD
UK, male footballer vocalists — 27

Date	Title	Peak	Wks at No.1	Wks
22 Jun 74	**EASY EASY** *Polydor 2058 452*	20		4
27 May 78	**OLE OLA (MULHER BRASILEIRA)** *Riva 15* ROD STEWART FEATURING THE SCOTTISH WORLD CUP FOOTBALL SQUAD	4		6
1 May 82	**WE HAVE A DREAM** *WEA K 19145*	5		9

Date	Title	Peak	Wks No.1	Wks
9 Jun 90	**SAY IT WITH PRIDE** *RCA PB 43791*	45		3
15 Jun 96	**PURPLE HEATHER** *Warner Brothers W 0354CD* ROD STEWART WITH THE SCOTTISH EURO '96 SQUAD	16		5

JACK SCOTT

Canada, male vocalist (Jack Scafone, Jr) — 28

Date	Title	Peak	Wks No.1	Wks
10 Oct 58	**MY TRUE LOVE** *London HLU 8626*	9		10
25 Sep 59	**THE WAY I WALK** *London HLL 8912*	30		1
10 Mar 60	**WHAT IN THE WORLD'S COME OVER YOU** *Top Rank JAR 280*	11		15
2 Jun 60	**BURNING BRIDGES** *Top Rank JAR 375*	32		2

JAMIE SCOTT

UK, male vocalist/guitarist — 7

Date	Title	Peak	Wks No.1	Wks
4 Sep 04	**JUST** *Sony Music 6752282*	29		2
22 Jan 05	**SEARCHING** *Sony Music 6757332*	33		3
8 Sep 07	**WHEN WILL I SEE YOUR FACE AGAIN** *Polydor 1742251* & THE TOWN	41		2

JILL SCOTT

US, female vocalist/actor — 11

Date	Title	Peak	Wks No.1	Wks
4 Nov 00	**GETTIN' IN THE WAY** *Epic 6705272*	30		3
7 Apr 01	**A LONG WALK** *Epic 6710382*	54		1
6 Nov 04	**GOLDEN** *Epic 6751772*	59		1
16 Sep 06	**DAYDREAMIN'** *Atlantic AT0252CD* LUPE FIASCO FEATURING JILL SCOTT	25		6

LINDA SCOTT

US, female vocalist (Linda Sampson) — 14

Date	Title	Peak	Wks No.1	Wks
18 May 61	**I'VE TOLD EVERY LITTLE STAR** *Columbia DB 4638*	7		13
14 Sep 61	**DON'T BET MONEY HONEY** *Columbia DB 4692*	50		1

MIKE SCOTT

UK, male vocalist/guitarist. See Waterboys — 4

Date	Title	Peak	Wks No.1	Wks
16 Sep 95	**BRING 'EM ALL IN** *Chrysalis CDCHS 5025*	56		1
11 Nov 95	**BUILDING THE CITY OF LIGHT** *Chrysalis CDCHS 5026*	60		1
27 Sep 97	**LOVE ANYWAY** *Chrysalis CDCHS 5064*	50		1
14 Feb 98	**RARE, PRECIOUS AND GONE** *Chrysalis CDCHS 5073*	74		1

MILLIE SCOTT

US, female vocalist — 11

Date	Title	Peak	Wks No.1	Wks
12 Apr 86	**PRISONER OF LOVE** *Fourth & Broadway BRW 45*	52		4
23 Aug 86	**AUTOMATIC** *Fourth & Broadway BRW 51*	56		3
21 Feb 87	**EV'RY LITTLE BIT** *Fourth & Broadway BRW 58*	63		4

SIMON SCOTT

UK (b. India), male vocalist — 8

Date	Title	Peak	Wks No.1	Wks
13 Aug 64	**MOVE IT BABY** *Parlophone R 5164*	37		8

TONI SCOTT

Holland, male rapper (Peter van der Bosch) — 6

Date	Title	Peak	Wks No.1	Wks
15 Apr 89	**THAT'S HOW I'M LIVING/THE CHIEF** *Champion CHAMP 97*	48		4
10 Feb 90	**GET INTO IT/THAT'S HOW I'M LIVING** *Champion CHAMP 232* TONY SCOTT	63		2

SCOTT & LEON

UK, male production duo — 6

Date	Title	Peak	Wks No.1	Wks
30 Sep 00	**YOU USED TO HOLD ME** *AM:PM CDAMPM 137*	19		4
19 May 01	**SHINE ON** *AM:PM CDAMPM 143*	34		2

LISA SCOTT-LEE

UK, female vocalist. See Girls Of *FHM*, Steps — 17

Date	Title	Peak	Wks No.1	Wks
24 May 03	**LATELY** *Fontana 9800295*	6		8
20 Sep 03	**TOO FAR GONE** *Fontana 9811643*	11		4
4 Dec 04	**GET IT ON** *Inspired INSPMOS1CDS* INTENSO PROJECT FEATURING LISA SCOTT-LEE	23		3
22 Oct 05	**ELECTRIC** *Concept CDCON68X*	13		2

SCOTTISH RUGBY TEAM WITH RONNIE BROWNE

UK, male vocalists/rugby players & male vocalist/instrumentalist (Ronald Grant) — 1

Date	Title	Peak	Wks No.1	Wks
2 Jun 90	**FLOWER OF SCOTLAND** *Greentrax STRAX 1001*	73		1

SCOUTING FOR GIRLS

UK, male vocal/instrumental trio – Roy Stride, Greg Churchouse & Peter Ellard — 100

Date	Title	Peak	Wks No.1	Wks
30 Jun 07	**IT'S NOT ABOUT YOU** *Epic 88697102422*	31		4
8 Sep 07	**SHE'S SO LOVELY** *Epic 88697147742*	7		41
15 Dec 07	**ELVIS AIN'T DEAD** *Epic 88697191162*	8		23
29 Mar 08	**HEARTBEAT** *Epic 88697271242*	10		23
2 Aug 08	**IT'S NOT ABOUT YOU** *White Rabbit 88697343052*	38		5
8 Nov 08	**I WISH I WAS JAMES BOND** *Epic 88697395662*	40		3
10 Apr 10	**THIS AIN'T A LOVE SONG** *Epic 88697632852*	1	1	1+

SCREAMING BLUE MESSIAHS

US/UK, male vocal/instrumental trio — 6

Date	Title	Peak	Wks No.1	Wks
16 Jan 88	**I WANNA BE A FLINTSTONE** *WEA YZ 166*	28		6

SCREAMING TREES

US, male vocal/instrumental group — 2

Date	Title	Peak	Wks No.1	Wks
6 Mar 93	**NEARLY LOST YOU EP** *Epic 6582372*	50		1
1 May 93	**DOLLAR BILL** *Epic 6591792*	52		1

SCRIPT

Ireland, male vocal/instrumental trio – Danny O'Donoghue, Glen Power & Mark Sheehan — 74

Date	Title	Peak	Wks No.1	Wks
3 May 08	**WE CRY** *RCA 88697291572*	15		15
2 Aug 08	**THE MAN WHO CAN'T BE MOVED** *Phonogenic 88697350612*	2		30
25 Oct 08	**BREAK EVEN** *Phonogenic 88697418467*	21		24
28 Mar 09	**TALK YOU DOWN** *Phonogenic GBARL0800145*	47		3
5 Sep 09	**THE MAN WHO CAN'T BE MOVED** *Phonogenic 88697350612*	69		2

SCRITTI POLITTI

UK, male vocal/instrumental group – Green Gartside (Paul Strohmeyer), Nial Jinks (replaced by David Gamson) & Tom Morley (replaced by Fred Maher) — 78

Date	Title	Peak	Wks No.1	Wks
21 Nov 81	**THE SWEETEST GIRL** *Rough Trade RT 091*	64		3
22 May 82	**FAITHLESS** *Rough Trade RT 101*	56		4
7 Aug 82	**ASYLUMS IN JERUSALEM/JACQUES DERRIDA** *Rough Trade RT 111*	43		5
10 Mar 84	**WOOD BEEZ (PRAY LIKE ARETHA FRANKLIN)** *Virgin VS 657*	10		12
9 Jun 84	**ABSOLUTE** *Virgin VS 680*	17		9
17 Nov 84	**HYPNOTIZE** *Virgin VS 725*	68		2
11 May 85	**THE WORD GIRL** *Virgin VS 747* FEATURING RANKING ANN	6		12
7 Sep 85	**PERFECT WAY** *Virgin VS 780*	48		5
7 May 88	**OH PATTI (DON'T FEEL SORRY FOR LOVERBOY)** *Virgin VS 1006*	13		9
27 Aug 88	**FIRST BOY IN THIS TOWN (LOVE SICK)** *Virgin VS 1082*	63		3
12 Nov 88	**BOOM! THERE SHE WAS** *Virgin VS 1143* FEATURING ROGER	55		3
16 Mar 91	**SHE'S A WOMAN** *Virgin VS 1333* FEATURING SHABBA RANKS	20		7
3 Aug 91	**TAKE ME IN YOUR ARMS AND LOVE ME** *Virgin VS 1346* & SWEETIE IRIE	47		3
31 Jul 99	**TINSELTOWN TO THE BOOGIEDOWN** *Virgin VSCDT 1731*	46		1

SCUMFROG

Holland, male producer (Jesse Houk). See Dutch featuring Crystal Waters — 3

Date	Title	Peak	Wks No.1	Wks
11 May 02	**LOVING THE ALIEN** *Positiva CDTIV 172* VS BOWIE	41		1
31 May 03	**MUSIC REVOLUTION** *Positiva CDTIV 191*	46		2

SE:SA FEATURING SHARON PHILLIPS

Germany/UK, male/female vocal/instrumental trio — 1

Date	Title	Peak	Wks No.1	Wks
1 Dec 07	**LIKE THIS LIKE THAT** *Positiva CDTIVS263*	63		1

SEA FRUIT

UK, male vocal/instrumental group — 1

Date	Title	Peak	Wks No.1	Wks
24 Jul 99	**HELLO WORLD** *Electric Canyon ECCD 3055*	59		1

SEA LEVEL
US, male instrumental group — 4

Date	Title / Label	Peak Position	Weeks at No.1	Weeks on Chart
17 Feb 79	**FIFTY-FOUR** *Capricorn POSP 28*	63		4

SEAFOOD
UK, male/female vocal/instrumental group — 2

Date	Title / Label	Peak Position	Weeks at No.1	Weeks on Chart
28 Jul 01	**CLOAKING** *Infectious INFEC 103CDS*	71		1
1 May 04	**GOOD REASON** *Cooking Vinyl FRYCD189*	65		1

SEAGULLS SKA
UK, football fans (Brighton & Hove Albion)/vocal group — 3

Date	Title / Label	Peak Position	Weeks at No.1	Weeks on Chart
15 Jan 05	**TOM HARK (WE WANT FALMER)** *Falmer For All FALMER001*	17		3

SEAHORSES
UK, male vocal/instrumental group – Chris Helme, Stuart Fletcher, John Squire* & Andy Watts — 26

Date	Title / Label	Peak Position	Weeks at No.1	Weeks on Chart
10 May 97	**LOVE IS THE LAW** *Geffen GFSTD 22243*	3		7
26 Jul 97	**BLINDED BY THE SUN** *Geffen GFSTD 22266*	7		7
11 Oct 97	**LOVE ME AND LEAVE ME** *Geffen GFSTD 22292*	16		4
13 Dec 97	**YOU CAN TALK TO ME** *Geffen GFSTD 22297*	15		8

SEAL
UK, male vocalist (Sealhenry Samuel). See Adamski — 84

Date	Title / Label	Peak Position	Weeks at No.1	Weeks on Chart
8 Dec 90	**CRAZY** *ZTT ZANG 8* ●	2		15
4 May 91	**FUTURE LOVE EP** *ZTT ZANG 11*	12		6
20 Jul 91	**THE BEGINNING** *ZTT ZANG 21*	24		6
16 Nov 91	**KILLER (EP)** *ZTT ZANG 23*	8		8
29 Feb 92	**VIOLET** *ZTT ZANG 27*	39		2
21 May 94	**PRAYER FOR THE DYING** *ZTT ZANG 51CD*	14		5
30 Jul 94	**KISS FROM A ROSE** *ZTT ZANG 52CD1*	20		5
5 Nov 94	**NEWBORN FRIEND** *ZTT ZANG 58CD*	45		2
15 Jul 95	**KISS FROM A ROSE/I'M ALIVE** *ZTT ZANG 70CD* ● ★	4		13
9 Dec 95	**DON'T CRY/PRAYER FOR THE DYING** *ZTT ZANG 75CD*	51		2
29 Mar 97	**FLY LIKE AN EAGLE** *ZTT ZEAL 1CD*	13		5
14 Nov 98	**HUMAN BEINGS** *Warner Brothers W 464CD*	50		1
12 Oct 02	**MY VISION** *Rulin 26CDS* JAKATTA FEATURING SEAL	6		8
20 Sep 03	**GET IT TOGETHER** *Warner Brothers W 620CD*	25		3
22 Nov 03	**LOVE'S DIVINE** *Warner Brothers W 629CD*	68		1
17 Nov 07	**AMAZING** *Warner Brothers W788CD*	74		1
3 Oct 09	**KISS FROM A ROSE** *Warner Brothers USWB19900917*	57		1

JAY SEAN
UK, male vocalist/rapper/producer (Kamaljit Jhooti) — 72

Date	Title / Label	Peak Position	Weeks at No.1	Weeks on Chart
20 Sep 03	**DANCE WITH YOU (NACHNA TERE NAAL)** *Relentless RELCD1* RISHI RICH PROJECT FEATURING JAY SEAN	12		5
3 Jul 04	**EYES ON YOU** *Relentless RELDX5* FEATURING RISHI RICH PROJECT	6		10
6 Nov 04	**STOLEN** *Relentless RELDX11*	4		6
2 Feb 08	**RIDE IT** *2Point9 CXJAY2P91*	11		12
3 May 08	**MAYBE** *2 Point 9/Jayded CXJAY2P92*	19		6
19 Jul 08	**STAY** *2 Point 9/Jayded CXJAY2P93*	59		1
31 Jan 09	**TONIGHT** *2 Point 9/Jayded CXJAY2P94*	23		4
7 Nov 09	**DOWN** *Island 2724316* FEATURING LIL WAYNE ★	3		16
23 Jan 10	**DO YOU REMEMBER** *Island 2733342* FEATURING SEAN PAUL & LIL JON	13		12+

SEARCHERS
UK, male vocal/instrumental group – Tony Jackson*, d. 18 Aug 2003 (replaced by Frank Allen), Chris Curtis, d. 28 Feb 2005, John McNally & Mike Pender — 128

Date	Title / Label	Peak Position	Weeks at No.1	Weeks on Chart
27 Jun 63	**SWEETS FOR MY SWEET** *Pye 7N 15533*	1	2	16
10 Oct 63	**SWEET NOTHIN'S** *Phillips BF 1274*	48		2
24 Oct 63	**SUGAR AND SPICE** *Pye 7N 15566*	2		13
16 Jan 64	**NEEDLES AND PINS** *Pye 7N 15594*	1	3	15
16 Apr 64	**DON'T THROW YOUR LOVE AWAY** *Pye 7N 15630*	1	2	11
16 Jul 64	**SOMEDAY WE'RE GONNA LOVE AGAIN** *Pye 7N 15670*	11		8
17 Sep 64	**WHEN YOU WALK IN THE ROOM** *Pye 7N 15694*	3		12
3 Dec 64	**WHAT HAVE THEY DONE TO THE RAIN** *Pye 7N 15739*	13		11
4 Mar 65	**GOODBYE MY LOVE** *Pye 7N 15794*	4		11
8 Jul 65	**HE'S GOT NO LOVE** *Pye 7N 15878*	12		10
14 Oct 65	**WHEN I GET HOME** *Pye 7N 15950*	35		3
16 Dec 65	**TAKE ME FOR WHAT I'M WORTH** *Pye 7N 15992*	20		8
21 Apr 66	**TAKE IT OR LEAVE IT** *Pye 7N 17094*	31		6
13 Oct 66	**HAVE YOU EVER LOVED SOMEBODY** *Pye 7N 17170*	48		2

SEASHELLS
UK, female vocal group — 5

Date	Title / Label	Peak Position	Weeks at No.1	Weeks on Chart
9 Sep 72	**MAYBE I KNOW** *CBS 8218*	32		5

SEB
UK, male keyboard player (Sebastian Wronski) — 1

Date	Title / Label	Peak Position	Weeks at No.1	Weeks on Chart
18 Feb 95	**SUGAR SHACK** *React CDREACT 50*	61		1

SEBADOH
US, male vocal/instrumental group — 4

Date	Title / Label	Peak Position	Weeks at No.1	Weeks on Chart
27 Jul 96	**BEAUTY OF THE RIDE** *Domino RUG 47CD*	74		1
30 Jan 99	**FLAME** *Domino RUG 80CD1*	30		3

JON SECADA
Cuba, male vocalist (Juan Secada) — 42

Date	Title / Label	Peak Position	Weeks at No.1	Weeks on Chart
18 Jul 92	**JUST ANOTHER DAY** *SBK 35* ●	5		15
31 Oct 92	**DO YOU BELIEVE IN US** *SBK 37*	30		4
6 Feb 93	**ANGEL** *SBK CDSBK 39*	23		5
17 Jul 93	**DO YOU REALLY WANT ME** *SBK CDSBK 41*	30		4
16 Oct 93	**I'M FREE** *SBK CDSBK 44*	50		2
14 May 94	**IF YOU GO** *SBK CDSBK 51*	39		5
4 Feb 95	**MENTAL PICTURE** *SBK CDSBK 54*	44		2
16 Dec 95	**IF I NEVER KNEW YOU (LOVE THEME FROM 'POCAHONTAS')** *Walt Disney WD 7023C* & SHANICE	51		4
14 Jun 97	**TOO LATE, TOO SOON** *SBK CDSBK 57*	43		1

SECCHI FEATURING ORLANDO JOHNSON
Italy, male producer (Stefano Secchi) & US, male vocalist — 3

Date	Title / Label	Peak Position	Weeks at No.1	Weeks on Chart
4 May 91	**I SAY YEAH** *Epic 6568467*	46		3

HARRY SECOMBE
UK, male vocalist/comedian, d. 12 Apr 2001 (age 79) — 35

Date	Title / Label	Peak Position	Weeks at No.1	Weeks on Chart
9 Dec 55	**ON WITH THE MOTLEY** *Philips PB 523*	16		3
3 Oct 63	**IF I RULED THE WORLD** *Philips BF 1261*	18		17
23 Feb 67	**THIS IS MY SONG** *Philips BF 1539*	2		15

SECOND CITY SOUND
UK, male vocal/instrumental group — 8

Date	Title / Label	Peak Position	Weeks at No.1	Weeks on Chart
20 Jan 66	**TCHAIKOVSKY ONE** *Decca F 12310*	22		7
2 Apr 69	**DREAM OF OLWEN** *Major Minor MM 600*	43		1

SECOND IMAGE
UK, male vocal/instrumental group — 11

Date	Title / Label	Peak Position	Weeks at No.1	Weeks on Chart
24 Jul 82	**STAR** *Polydor POSP 457*	60		2
2 Apr 83	**BETTER TAKE TIME** *Polydor POSP 565*	67		2
26 Nov 83	**DON'T YOU** *MCA 848*	68		2
11 Aug 84	**SING AND SHOUT** *MCA 882*	53		3
2 Feb 85	**STARTING AGAIN** *MCA 936*	65		2

SECOND PHASE
US, male production duo — 2

Date	Title / Label	Peak Position	Weeks at No.1	Weeks on Chart
21 Sep 91	**MENTASM** *R&S RSUK 2*	48		2

SECOND PROTOCOL
UK, male production duo — 2

Date	Title / Label	Peak Position	Weeks at No.1	Weeks on Chart
23 Sep 00	**BASSLICK** *East West 216CD*	58		2

SECRET AFFAIR
UK, male vocal/instrumental group — 34

Date	Title / Label	Peak Position	Weeks at No.1	Weeks on Chart
1 Sep 79	**TIME FOR ACTION** *I-Spy SEE 1*	13		10
10 Nov 79	**LET YOUR HEART DANCE** *I-Spy SEE 3*	32		6
8 Mar 80	**MY WORLD** *I-Spy SEE 5*	16		9
23 Aug 80	**SOUND OF CONFUSION** *I-Spy SEE 8*	45		5
17 Oct 81	**DO YOU KNOW** *I-Spy SEE 10*	57		4

Silver-selling · Gold-selling · Platinum-selling (x multiples) · US No.1 ★ · Peak Position · Weeks at No.1 · Weeks on Chart

SECRET KNOWLEDGE
UK/US, male/female vocal/instrumental duo — Weeks on Chart: 2

Date	Title / Label	Peak Position	Weeks at No.1	Weeks on Chart
27 Apr 96	**LOVE ME NOW** *Deconstruction 74321342432*	66		1
24 Aug 96	**SUGAR DADDY** *Deconstruction 74321400242*	75		1

SECRET LIFE
UK, male vocal/production duo — Weeks on Chart: 10

Date	Title / Label	Peak Position	Weeks at No.1	Weeks on Chart
12 Dec 92	**AS ALWAYS** *Cowboy 7RODEO 9*	45		4
7 Aug 93	**LOVE SO STRONG** *Cowboy RODEO 18CD*	38		2
7 May 94	**SHE HOLDS THE KEY** *Pulse 8 CDLOSE 58*	63		1
29 Oct 94	**I WANT YOU** *Pulse 8 CDLOSE 71*	70		1
28 Jan 95	**LOVE SO STRONG (REMIX)** *Pulse 8 CDLOSE 79*	37		2

SECRET MACHINES
US, male vocal/instrumental trio — Weeks on Chart: 6

Date	Title / Label	Peak Position	Weeks at No.1	Weeks on Chart
7 Aug 04	**NOWHERE AGAIN** *Reprise W648CD*	49		1
8 Jan 05	**SAD AND LONELY** *East West E 7625*	38		3
23 Apr 05	**THE ROAD LEADS WHERE IT'S LED** *679 Recordings W669CD2*	56		1
8 Apr 06	**LIGHTNING BLUE EYES** *Warner Brothers W707CD1*	57		1

SECTION-X
France, male instrumental duo — Weeks on Chart: 1

Date	Title / Label	Peak Position	Weeks at No.1	Weeks on Chart
8 Mar 97	**ATLANTIS** *Perfecto PERF 136CD*	42		1

NEIL SEDAKA
US, male vocalist/pianist — Weeks on Chart: 190

Date	Title / Label	Peak Position	Weeks at No.1	Weeks on Chart
24 Apr 59	**I GO APE** *RCA 1115*	9		13
13 Nov 59	**OH CAROL** *RCA 1152*	3		17
14 Apr 60	**STAIRWAY TO HEAVEN** *RCA 1178*	8		15
1 Sep 60	**YOU MEAN EVERYTHING TO ME** *RCA 1198*	45		3
2 Feb 61	**CALENDAR GIRL** *RCA 1220*	8		14
18 May 61	**LITTLE DEVIL** *RCA 1236*	9		12
21 Dec 61	**HAPPY BIRTHDAY SWEET SIXTEEN** *RCA 1266*	3		18
19 Apr 62	**KING OF CLOWNS** *RCA 1282*	23		11
19 Jul 62	**BREAKING UP IS HARD TO DO** *RCA 1298* ★	7		16
22 Nov 62	**NEXT DOOR TO AN ANGEL** *RCA 1319*	29		4
30 May 63	**LET'S GO STEADY AGAIN** *RCA 1343*	42		3
7 Oct 72	**OH CAROL/BREAKING UP IS HARD TO DO/LITTLE DEVIL** *RCA Maximillion 2259*	19		14
4 Nov 72	**BEAUTIFUL YOU** *RCA 2269*	43		3
24 Feb 73	**THAT'S WHEN THE MUSIC TAKES ME** *RCA 2310*	18		10
2 Jun 73	**STANDING ON THE INSIDE** *MGM 2006 267*	26		9
25 Aug 73	**OUR LAST SONG TOGETHER** *MGM 2006 307*	31		8
9 Feb 74	**A LITTLE LOVIN'** *Polydor 2058 434*	34		6
22 Jun 74	**LAUGHTER IN THE RAIN** *Polydor 2058 494* ★	15		9
22 Mar 75	**THE QUEEN OF 1964** *Polydor 2058 546*	35		5

MAX SEDGLEY
UK, male DJ/producer/drummer/keyboard player — Weeks on Chart: 3

Date	Title / Label	Peak Position	Weeks at No.1	Weeks on Chart
17 Jul 04	**HAPPY** *Sunday Best SBESTC14*	30		3

SEDUCTION
US, female vocal trio — Weeks on Chart: 1

Date	Title / Label	Peak Position	Weeks at No.1	Weeks on Chart
21 Apr 90	**HEARTBEAT** *Breakout USA 685*	75		1

SEEKERS
Australia, female/male vocal/instrumental group – Judith Durham*, Athol Guy, Keith Potger & Bruce Woodley — Weeks on Chart: 120

Date	Title / Label	Peak Position	Weeks at No.1	Weeks on Chart
7 Jan 65	**I'LL NEVER FIND ANOTHER YOU** *Columbia DB 7431*	1	2	23
15 Apr 65	**A WORLD OF OUR OWN** *Columbia DB 7532*	3		18
28 Oct 65	**THE CARNIVAL IS OVER** *Columbia DB 7711*	1	3	17
24 Mar 66	**SOMEDAY ONE DAY** *Columbia DB 7867*	11		11
8 Sep 66	**WALK WITH ME** *Columbia DB 8000*	10		12
24 Nov 66	**MORNINGTOWN RIDE** *Columbia DB 8060*	2		15
23 Feb 67	**GEORGY GIRL** *Columbia DB 8134*	3		11
20 Sep 67	**WHEN WILL THE GOOD APPLES FALL** *Columbia DB 8273*	11		12
13 Dec 67	**EMERALD CITY** *Columbia DB 8313*	50		1

SEELENLUFT FEATURING MICHAEL SMITH
Switzerland/US, male rap/production duo — Weeks on Chart: 1

Date	Title / Label	Peak Position	Weeks at No.1	Weeks on Chart
4 Oct 03	**MANILA** *Back Yard BACK 10CSC1*	70		1

BOB SEGER & THE SILVER BULLET BAND
US, male vocal/instrumental group — Weeks on Chart: 30

Date	Title / Label	Peak Position	Weeks at No.1	Weeks on Chart
30 Sep 78	**HOLLYWOOD NIGHTS** *Capitol CL 16004*	42		6
3 Feb 79	**WE'VE GOT TONITE** *Capitol CL 16028*	41		6
24 Oct 81	**HOLLYWOOD NIGHTS** *Capitol CL 223*	49		3
6 Feb 82	**WE'VE GOT TONITE** *Capitol CL 235*	60		4
9 Apr 83	**EVEN NOW** *Capitol CL 284*	73		2
28 Jan 95	**WE'VE GOT TONIGHT** *Capitol CDCLS 734*	22		5
29 Apr 95	**NIGHT MOVES** *Capitol CDCL 741*	45		2
29 Jul 95	**HOLLYWOOD NIGHTS** *Capitol CDCL 749*	52		1
10 Feb 96	**LOCK AND LOAD** *Capitol CDCL 765*	57		1

SHEA SEGER
US, female vocalist — Weeks on Chart: 1

Date	Title / Label	Peak Position	Weeks at No.1	Weeks on Chart
5 May 01	**CLUTCH** *RCA 74321828142*	47		1

SEIKO & DONNIE WAHLBERG
Japan/US, female/male vocal duo — Weeks on Chart: 5

Date	Title / Label	Peak Position	Weeks at No.1	Weeks on Chart
18 Aug 90	**THE RIGHT COMBINATION** *Epic 6562037*	44		5

SELECTER
UK, male/female vocal/instrumental group – Pauline Black; members also included Megan Amanor, Charley Anderson, Charley Bembridge, Desmond Brown, Neol Davies & Arthur Hendrickson — Weeks on Chart: 28

Date	Title / Label	Peak Position	Weeks at No.1	Weeks on Chart
13 Oct 79	**ON MY RADIO** *2 Tone CHSTT 4*	8		9
2 Feb 80	**THREE MINUTE HERO** *2 Tone CHSTT 8*	16		6
29 Mar 80	**MISSING WORDS** *2 Tone CHSTT 10*	23		8
23 Aug 80	**THE WHISPER** *Chrysalis CHS 1*	36		5

SELENA VS X MEN
UK, female/male vocal/production trio — Weeks on Chart: 1

Date	Title / Label	Peak Position	Weeks at No.1	Weeks on Chart
14 Jul 01	**GIVE IT UP** *Go! Beat GOBCD 40*	61		1

SELFISH CUNT
UK, male vocal/instrumental group — Weeks on Chart: 1

Date	Title / Label	Peak Position	Weeks at No.1	Weeks on Chart
17 Jul 04	**AUTHORITY CONFRONTATION** *Horseglue UHU008*	66		1

PETER SELLERS
UK, male comedian/vocalist (Richard Sellers), d. 24 Jul 1980 (age 54) — Weeks on Chart: 39

Date	Title / Label	Peak Position	Weeks at No.1	Weeks on Chart
2 Aug 57	**ANY OLD IRON** *Parlophone R 4337*	17		11
10 Nov 60	**GOODNESS GRACIOUS ME** *Parlophone R 4702* & SOPHIA LOREN	4		14
12 Jan 61	**BANGERS AND MASH** *Parlophone R 4724* & SOPHIA LOREN	22		5
23 Dec 65	**A HARD DAY'S NIGHT** *Parlophone R 5393*	14		7
27 Nov 93	**A HARD DAY'S NIGHT** *EMI CDEMS 293*	52		2

MICHAEL SEMBELLO
US, male vocalist/guitarist — Weeks on Chart: 6

Date	Title / Label	Peak Position	Weeks at No.1	Weeks on Chart
20 Aug 83	**MANIAC** *Casablanca CAN 1017* ★	43		6

SEMISONIC
US, male vocal/instrumental group — Weeks on Chart: 20

Date	Title / Label	Peak Position	Weeks at No.1	Weeks on Chart
10 Jul 99	**SECRET SMILE** *MCA MCSTD 40210*	13		11
6 Nov 99	**CLOSING TIME** *MCA MCDXD 40221*	25		5
1 Apr 00	**SINGING IN MY SLEEP** *MCA MCSTD 40227*	39		2
3 Mar 01	**CHEMISTRY** *MCA MCSTD 40248*	35		2

SEMPRINI
UK, male pianist (Fernando Riccardo Alberto Semprini), d. 19 Jan 1990 (age 81) — Weeks on Chart: 8

Date	Title / Label	Peak Position	Weeks at No.1	Weeks on Chart
16 Mar 61	**THEME FROM 'EXODUS'** *HMV POP 842*	25		8

SENSELESS THINGS
UK, male vocal/instrumental group — Weeks on Chart: 19

Date	Title / Label	Peak Position	Weeks at No.1	Weeks on Chart
22 Jun 91	**EVERYBODY'S GONE** *Epic 6569807*	73		1
28 Sep 91	**GOT IT AT THE DELMAR** *Epic 6574497*	50		3
11 Jan 92	**EASY TO SMILE** *Epic 6576957*	18		4
11 Apr 92	**HOLD IT DOWN** *Epic 6579267*	19		4
5 Dec 92	**HOMOPHOBIC ASSHOLE** *Epic 6588337*	52		2

Date	Title	Peak Position	Weeks at No.1	Weeks on Chart
13 Feb 93	**PRIMARY INSTINCT** *Epic 6589402*	41		2
12 Jun 93	**TOO MUCH KISSING** *Epic 6592502*	69		1
5 Nov 94	**CHRISTINE KEELER** *Epic 6609572*	56		1
28 Jan 95	**SOMETHING TO MISS** *Epic 6611162*	57		1

SENSER

UK, male/female vocal/instrumental group — 5

Date	Title	Peak Position	Weeks at No.1	Weeks on Chart
25 Sep 93	**THE KEY** *Ultimate TOPP 019CD*	47		1
19 Mar 94	**SWITCH** *Ultimate TOPP 022CD*	39		2
23 Jul 94	**AGE OF PANIC** *Ultimate TOPP 027CD*	52		1
17 Aug 96	**CHARMING DEMONS** *Ultimate TOPP 045CD*	42		1

SEPTEMBER

Sweden, female vocalist (Petra Marklund) — 27

Date	Title	Peak Position	Weeks at No.1	Weeks on Chart
19 Apr 08	**CRY FOR YOU** *Hard2Beat H2B03CDS*	5		22
21 Mar 09	**CAN'T GET OVER** *Hard2Beat H2B23CDS*	14		5

SEPULTURA

Brazil, male vocal/instrumental group — 12

Date	Title	Peak Position	Weeks at No.1	Weeks on Chart
2 Oct 93	**TERRITORY** *Roadrunner RR 23823*	66		2
26 Feb 94	**REFUSE-RESIST** *Roadrunner RR 23773*	51		2
4 Jun 94	**SLAVE NEW WORLD** *Roadrunner RR 23745*	46		2
24 Feb 96	**ROOTS BLOODY ROOTS** *Roadrunner RR 23205*	19		2
17 Aug 96	**RATAMAHATTA** *Roadrunner RR 23145*	23		2
14 Dec 96	**ATTITUDE** *Roadrunner RR 22995*	46		2

SERAFIN

UK, male vocal/instrumental group — 2

Date	Title	Peak Position	Weeks at No.1	Weeks on Chart
17 May 03	**THINGS FALL APART** *Taste Media TMCDSX 5003*	49		1
16 Aug 03	**DAY BY DAY** *Taste Media TMCDSX 5006*	49		1

SERAPHIM SUITE

UK, male/female vocal/production trio. See Jeremy Healy & Amos, Mica Paris — 2

Date	Title	Peak Position	Weeks at No.1	Weeks on Chart
27 Mar 04	**HEART** *Inferno CDFERN61*	45		2

SERIAL DIVA

UK, male/female production group — 3

Date	Title	Peak Position	Weeks at No.1	Weeks on Chart
18 Jan 97	**KEEP HOPE ALIVE** *Sound Of Ministry SOMCD 26*	57		1
15 May 99	**PEARL RIVER** *Low Sense SENSECD 24* THREE 'N' ONE PRESENTS JOHNNY SHAKER FEATURING SERIAL DIVA	32		2

SERIOUS DANGER

UK, male producer (Richard Phillips) — 4

Date	Title	Peak Position	Weeks at No.1	Weeks on Chart
20 Dec 97	**DEEPER** *Fresh FRSHD 68*	40		3
2 May 98	**HIGH NOON** *Fresh FRSHD 69*	54		1

SERIOUS INTENTION

US, male production/vocal group — 6

Date	Title	Peak Position	Weeks at No.1	Weeks on Chart
16 Nov 85	**YOU DON'T KNOW (OH-OH-OH)** *Important TAN 8*	75		1
5 Apr 86	**SERIOUS** *Pow Wow LON 93*	51		5

SERIOUS ROPE

UK, male producer (Damon Rochefort). See Mista E, Nomad — 3

Date	Title	Peak Position	Weeks at No.1	Weeks on Chart
22 May 93	**HAPPINESS** *Rumour RUMACD 64* PRESENTS SHARON DEE CLARK	54		2
1 Oct 94	**HAPPINESS – YOU MAKE ME HAPPY (REMIX)** *Mercury MERCD 407*	70		1

ERICK SERMON

US, male rapper/producer — 8

Date	Title	Peak Position	Weeks at No.1	Weeks on Chart
6 Oct 01	**MUSIC** *Polydor 4976222* FEATURING MARVIN GAYE	36		2
11 Jan 03	**REACT** *J Records 74321988492* FEATURING REDMAN	14		5
19 Apr 03	**LOVE IZ** *J Records 82876510971*	72		1

SERTAB

Turkey, female vocalist (Sertab Erener) — 1

Date	Title	Peak Position	Weeks at No.1	Weeks on Chart
21 Jun 03	**EVERY WAY THAT I CAN** *Columbia 6739621*	72		1

SET THE TONE

UK, male/female vocal/instrumental group — 4

Date	Title	Peak Position	Weeks at No.1	Weeks on Chart
22 Jan 83	**DANCE SUCKER** *Island WIP 6836*	62		2
26 Mar 83	**RAP YOUR LOVE** *Island IS 110*	67		2

SETTLERS

UK, male/female vocal/instrumental group — 5

Date	Title	Peak Position	Weeks at No.1	Weeks on Chart
16 Oct 71	**THE LIGHTNING TREE** *York SYK 505*	36		5

BRIAN SETZER ORCHESTRA

US, male vocal/instrumental group. See Stray Cats — 3

Date	Title	Peak Position	Weeks at No.1	Weeks on Chart
3 Apr 99	**JUMP JIVE AN' WAIL** *Interscope IND 95601*	34		3

TAJA SEVELLE

US, female vocalist — 13

Date	Title	Peak Position	Weeks at No.1	Weeks on Chart
20 Feb 88	**LOVE IS CONTAGIOUS** *Paisley Park W 8257*	7		9
14 May 88	**WOULDN'T YOU LOVE TO LOVE ME** *Paisley Park W 8127*	59		4

702

US, female vocal group — 10

Date	Title	Peak Position	Weeks at No.1	Weeks on Chart
14 Dec 96	**STEELO** *Motown 8606072*	41		2
29 Nov 97	**NO DOUBT** *Motown 8607052*	59		1
7 Aug 99	**WHERE MY GIRLS AT?** *Motown TMGCD 1500*	22		4
27 Nov 99	**YOU DON'T KNOW** *Motown TMGCD 1502*	36		3

740 BOYZ

US, male vocal/instrumental duo — 3

Date	Title	Peak Position	Weeks at No.1	Weeks on Chart
4 Nov 95	**SHIMMY SHAKE** *MCA MCSTD 40002*	54		1
22 Mar 03	**SHAKE YA SHIMMY** *All Around The World CXGLOBE 213* PORN KINGS VERSUS FLIP & FILL FEATURING 740 BOYZ	28		2

SEVEN GRAND HOUSING AUTHORITY

UK, male producer (Terence Parker) — 1

Date	Title	Peak Position	Weeks at No.1	Weeks on Chart
23 Oct 93	**THE QUESTION** *Olympic ELYCD 010*	70		1

7669

US, female vocal group — 1

Date	Title	Peak Position	Weeks at No.1	Weeks on Chart
18 Jun 94	**JOY** *Motown TMGCD 1429*	60		1

7TH HEAVEN

UK, male vocal/instrumental group — 5

Date	Title	Peak Position	Weeks at No.1	Weeks on Chart
14 Sep 85	**HOT FUN** *Mercury MER 199*	47		5

SEVERINE

France, female vocalist (Josiane Grizeau) — 11

Date	Title	Peak Position	Weeks at No.1	Weeks on Chart
24 Apr 71	**UN BANC, UN ABRE, UNE RUE** *Philips 6009 135*	9		11

DAVID SEVILLE

US, male vocalist (Ross Bagdasarian), d. 16 Jan 1972 (age 52). See Alfi & Harry, Chipmunks — 6

Date	Title	Peak Position	Weeks at No.1	Weeks on Chart
23 May 58	**WITCH DOCTOR** *London HLU 8619* ★	11		6

SEX CLUB FEATURING BROWN SUGAR

US, male/female vocal/instrumental duo — 1

Date	Title	Peak Position	Weeks at No.1	Weeks on Chart
28 Jan 95	**BIG DICK MAN** *Club Tools CLU 60775*	67		1

SEX-O-SONIQUE

UK, male instrumental/production duo. See Full Intention, Hustlers Convention featuring Dave Laudat & Ondrea Duverney, Ronaldo's Revenge — 3

Date	Title	Peak Position	Weeks at No.1	Weeks on Chart
6 Dec 97	**I THOUGHT IT WAS YOU** *ffrr FCD 321*	32		3

SEX PISTOLS

UK, male vocal/instrumental group – Johnny Rotten (John Lydon), Paul Cook, Steve Jones, Glen Matlock (replaced by Sid Vicious* (John Ritchie/Beverley, d. 2 Feb 1979))

Date	Title	Peak Position	Weeks at No.1	Weeks on Chart (96)
18 Dec 76	**ANARCHY IN THE UK** *EMI 2566*	38		4
4 Jun 77	**GOD SAVE THE QUEEN** *Virgin VS 181* ●	2		9
9 Jul 77	**PRETTY VACANT** *Virgin VS 184* ●	6		8
22 Oct 77	**HOLIDAYS IN THE SUN** *Virgin VS 191*	8		6
8 Jul 78	**NO ONE IS INNOCENT/MY WAY** *Virgin VS 220* PUNK PRAYER BY RONALD BIGGS	7		10
3 Mar 79	**SOMETHING ELSE/FRIGGIN' IN THE RIGGIN'** *Virgin VS 240* ●	3		12
7 Apr 79	**SILLY THING** *Virgin VS 256* ●	6		8
30 Jun 79	**C'MON EVERYBODY** *Virgin VS 272* ●	3		9
13 Oct 79	**THE GREAT ROCK 'N' ROLL SWINDLE** *Virgin VS 290*	21		6
14 Jun 80	**(I'M NOT YOUR) STEPPING STONE** *Virgin VS 339*	21		8
3 Oct 92	**ANARCHY IN THE U.K.** *Virgin VS 1431*	33		3
5 Dec 92	**PRETTY VACANT** *Virgin VS 1448*	56		2
27 Jul 96	**PRETTY VACANT (LIVE)** *Virgin VUSCD 113*	18		3
8 Jun 02	**GOD SAVE THE QUEEN** *Virgin VSCDT 1832*	15		3
13 Oct 07	**ANARCHY IN THE U.K.** *Virgin EMI2566*	70		1
20 Oct 07	**GOD SAVE THE QUEEN** *Virgin VS181*	42		1
27 Oct 07	**PRETTY VACANT** *Virgin VS 184*	65		1
3 Nov 07	**HOLIDAYS IN THE SUN** *Virgin VS 191*	74		2

DENNY SEYTON & THE SABRES

UK, male vocal/instrumental group

Date	Title	Peak Position	Weeks at No.1	Weeks on Chart (2)
17 Sep 64	**THE WAY YOU LOOK TONIGHT** *Mercury MF 824*	48		2

SFX

UK, male production duo

Date	Title	Peak Position	Weeks at No.1	Weeks on Chart (3)
15 May 93	**LEMMINGS** *Parlophone CDR 6343*	51		3

SHABOOM

UK, male instrumental/production group

Date	Title	Peak Position	Weeks at No.1	Weeks on Chart (1)
31 Jul 99	**SWEET SENSATION** *WEA 218CD1*	64		1

SHACK

UK, male vocal/instrumental group

Date	Title	Peak Position	Weeks at No.1	Weeks on Chart (4)
26 Jun 99	**COMEDY** *London LONCD 427*	44		1
14 Aug 99	**NATALIE'S PARTY** *London LONCD 436*	63		1
11 Mar 00	**OSCAR** *London LONCD 445*	67		1
4 Oct 03	**BYRDS TURN TO STONE** *North Country NCCDB 002*	63		1

SHADES

US, female vocal group

Date	Title	Peak Position	Weeks at No.1	Weeks on Chart (3)
12 Apr 97	**MR BIG STUFF** *Motown 5736572* QUEEN LATIFAH, SHADES & FREE	31		2
20 Sep 97	**SERENADE** *Motown 8606892*	75		1

SHADES OF LOVE

US, male instrumental/production duo

Date	Title	Peak Position	Weeks at No.1	Weeks on Chart (1)
22 Apr 95	**KEEP IN TOUCH (BODY TO BODY)** *Vicious Muzik MUZCD 102*	64		1

SHADES OF RHYTHM

UK, male production/vocal trio

Date	Title	Peak Position	Weeks at No.1	Weeks on Chart (25)
2 Feb 91	**HOMICIDE/EXORCIST** *ZTT ZANG 13*	53		3
13 Apr 91	**SWEET SENSATION** *ZTT ZANG 18*	54		4
20 Jul 91	**THE SOUND OF EDEN** *ZTT ZANG 22*	35		5
30 Nov 91	**EXTACY** *ZTT ZANG 24*	16		7
20 Feb 93	**SWEET REVIVAL (KEEP IT COMIN')** *ZTT ZANG 40CD*	61		1
11 Sep 93	**THE SOUND OF EDEN** *ZTT ZANG 44CD*	37		3
5 Nov 94	**THE WANDERING DRAGON** *Public Demand PPDCD 5*	55		1
21 Jun 97	**PSYCHO BASE** *Coalition CRUM 002CD*	57		1

SHADOWS

UK, male vocal/instrumental group – Hank Marvin* & Bruce Welch; members also included Brian Bennett, John Farrar, Jet Harris*, Brian Locking, Tony Meehan* & John Rostill, d. 26 Nov 1973. The most successful instrumental act of all time started out as Cliff Richard's backing band. Britain's most influential and most imitated act before The Beatles were the first British group to top the album chart

Date	Title	Peak Position	Weeks at No.1	Weeks on Chart (772)
12 Sep 58	**MOVE IT** *Columbia DB 4178* CLIFF RICHARD & THE DRIFTERS	2		17
21 Nov 58	**HIGH CLASS BABY** *Columbia DB 4203* CLIFF RICHARD & THE DRIFTERS	7		10
30 Jan 59	**LIVIN' LOVIN' DOLL** *Columbia DB 4249* CLIFF RICHARD & THE DRIFTERS	20		6
8 May 59	**MEAN STREAK** *Columbia DB 4290* CLIFF RICHARD & THE DRIFTERS	10		9
15 May 59	**NEVER MIND** *Columbia DB 4290* CLIFF RICHARD & THE DRIFTERS	21		2
10 Jul 59	**LIVING DOLL** *Columbia DB 4306* CLIFF RICHARD & THE DRIFTERS	1	6	23
9 Oct 59	**TRAVELLIN' LIGHT** *Columbia DB 4351* CLIFF RICHARD & THE SHADOWS	1	5	17
9 Oct 59	**DYNAMITE** *Columbia DB 4351* CLIFF RICHARD & THE SHADOWS	16		4
15 Jan 60	**EXPRESSO BONGO EP** *Columbia SEG 7971* CLIFF RICHARD & THE SHADOWS	14		7
22 Jan 60	**A VOICE IN THE WILDERNESS** *Columbia DB 4398* CLIFF RICHARD & THE SHADOWS	2		16
24 Mar 60	**FALL IN LOVE WITH YOU** *Columbia DB 4431* CLIFF RICHARD & THE SHADOWS	2		15
30 Jun 60	**PLEASE DON'T TEASE** *Columbia DB 4479* CLIFF RICHARD & THE SHADOWS	1	3	18
21 Jul 60	**APACHE** *Columbia DB 4484*	1	5	21
22 Sep 60	**NINE TIMES OUT OF TEN** *Columbia DB 4506* CLIFF RICHARD & THE SHADOWS	3		12
10 Nov 60	**MAN OF MYSTERY/THE STRANGER** *Columbia DB 4530*	5		15
1 Dec 60	**I LOVE YOU** *Columbia DB 4547* CLIFF RICHARD & THE SHADOWS	1	2	16
9 Feb 61	**F.B.I.** *Columbia DB 4580*	6		19
2 Mar 61	**THEME FOR A DREAM** *Columbia DB 4593* CLIFF RICHARD & THE SHADOWS	3		14
30 Mar 61	**GEE WHIZ IT'S YOU** *Columbia DC 756* CLIFF RICHARD & THE SHADOWS	4		14
11 May 61	**FRIGHTENED CITY** *Columbia DB 4637*	3		20
22 Jun 61	**A GIRL LIKE YOU** *Columbia DB 4667* CLIFF RICHARD & THE SHADOWS	3		14
7 Sep 61	**KON-TIKI** *Columbia DB 4698*	1	1	12
16 Nov 61	**THE SAVAGE** *Columbia DB 4726*	10		8
11 Jan 62	**THE YOUNG ONES** *Columbia DB 4761* CLIFF RICHARD & THE SHADOWS	1	6	21
1 Mar 62	**WONDERFUL LAND** *Columbia DB 4790*	1	8	19
10 May 62	**I'M LOOKING OUT THE WINDOW/DO YOU WANNA DANCE** *Columbia DB 4828* CLIFF RICHARD & THE SHADOWS	2		17
2 Aug 62	**GUITAR TANGO** *Columbia DB 4870*	4		15
6 Sep 62	**IT'LL BE ME** *Columbia DB 4886* CLIFF RICHARD & THE SHADOWS	2		12
6 Dec 62	**THE NEXT TIME/BACHELOR BOY** *Columbia DB 4950* CLIFF RICHARD & THE SHADOWS	1	3	18
13 Dec 62	**DANCE ON!** *Columbia DB 4948*	1	1	15
21 Feb 63	**SUMMER HOLIDAY** *Columbia DB 4977* CLIFF RICHARD & THE SHADOWS	1	3	18
7 Mar 63	**FOOT TAPPER** *Columbia DB 4984*	1	1	16
9 May 63	**LUCKY LIPS** *Columbia DB 7034* CLIFF RICHARD & THE SHADOWS	4		15
6 Jun 63	**ATLANTIS** *Columbia DB 7047*	2		17
19 Sep 63	**SHINDIG** *Columbia DB 7106*	6		12
7 Nov 63	**DON'T TALK TO HIM** *Columbia DB 7150* CLIFF RICHARD & THE SHADOWS	2		14
5 Dec 63	**GERONIMO** *Columbia DB 7163*	11		12
6 Feb 64	**I'M THE LONELY ONE** *Columbia DB 7203* CLIFF RICHARD & THE SHADOWS	8		10
5 Mar 64	**THEME FOR YOUNG LOVERS** *Columbia DB 7231*	12		10
7 May 64	**THE RISE AND FALL OF FLINGEL BUNT** *Columbia DB 7261*	5		14
2 Jul 64	**ON THE BEACH** *Columbia DB 7305* CLIFF RICHARD & THE SHADOWS	7		13
3 Sep 64	**RHYTHM AND GREENS** *Columbia DB 7342*	22		7
3 Dec 64	**GENIE WITH THE LIGHT BROWN LAMP** *Columbia DB 7416*	17		10
10 Dec 64	**I COULD EASILY FALL** *Columbia DB 7420* CLIFF RICHARD & THE SHADOWS	6		11
11 Feb 65	**MARY ANNE** *Columbia DB 7476*	17		10
10 Jun 65	**STINGRAY** *Columbia DB 7588*	19		7
5 Aug 65	**DON'T MAKE MY BABY BLUE** *Columbia DB 7650*	10		10
19 Aug 65	**THE TIME IN BETWEEN** *Columbia DB 7660* CLIFF RICHARD & THE SHADOWS	22		8
25 Nov 65	**WAR LORD** *Columbia DB 7769*	18		9
17 Mar 66	**I MET A GIRL** *Columbia DB 7853*	22		5
24 Mar 66	**BLUE TURNS TO GREY** *Columbia DB 7866* CLIFF RICHARD & THE SHADOWS	15		9
7 Jul 66	**A PLACE IN THE SUN** *Columbia DB 7952*	24		6
13 Oct 66	**TIME DRAGS BY** *Columbia DB 8017* CLIFF RICHARD & THE SHADOWS	10		12
3 Nov 66	**THE DREAMS I DREAM** *Columbia DB 8034*	42		6
15 Dec 66	**IN THE COUNTRY** *Columbia DB 8094* CLIFF RICHARD & THE SHADOWS	6		10
13 Apr 67	**MAROC 7** *Columbia DB 8170*	24		8
27 Nov 68	**DON'T FORGET TO CATCH ME** *Columbia DB 8503* CLIFF RICHARD & THE SHADOWS	21		10
8 Mar 75	**LET ME BE THE ONE** *EMI 2269*	12		9
16 Dec 78	**DON'T CRY FOR ME ARGENTINA** *EMI 2890* ●	5		14
28 Apr 79	**THEME FROM 'THE DEER HUNTER' (CAVATINA)** *EMI 2939* ●	9		14

Date	Title / Label	Peak Position	Weeks at No.1	Weeks on Chart
26 Jan 80	**RIDERS IN THE SKY** *EMI 5027*	12		12
23 Aug 80	**EQUINOXE (PART V)** *Polydor POSP 148*	50		3
2 May 81	**THE THIRD MAN** *Polydor POSP 255*	44		4
26 Sep 09	**SINGING THE BLUES** *EMI 6878852* CLIFF RICHARD & THE SHADOWS	40		1

SHAFT

UK, male production duo – Mark Pritchard & Adrian Hughes — **9**

Date	Title / Label	Peak Position	Weeks at No.1	Weeks on Chart
21 Dec 91	**ROOBARB AND CUSTARD** *ffrreedom TAB 100*	7		8
25 Jul 92	**MONKEY** *ffrreedom TAB 114*	61		1

SHAFT

UK, male production duo – Elliot Ireland & Alex Rizzo. See Da Muttz — **19**

Date	Title / Label	Peak Position	Weeks at No.1	Weeks on Chart
4 Sep 99	**(MUCHO MAMBO) SWAY** *Wonderboy WBYD 015* ○	2		12
20 May 00	**MAMBO ITALIANO** *Wonderboy WBDD 017*	12		6
21 Jul 01	**KIKI RIRI BOOM** *Wonderboy WBOYD 026*	62		1

SHAG

UK, male vocalist (Jonathan King) — **17**

Date	Title / Label	Peak Position	Weeks at No.1	Weeks on Chart
14 Oct 72	**LOOP DI LOVE** *UK 7*	4		13
20 Sep 75	**CHICK-A-BOOM (DON'T YA JES LOVE IT)** *UK 2012 002* 53RD & A 3RD FEATURING THE SOUND OF SHAG	36		4

SHAGGY

Jamaica, male vocalist (Orville Burrell) — **145**

Date	Title / Label	Peak Position	Weeks at No.1	Weeks on Chart
6 Feb 93	**OH CAROLINA** *Greensleeves GRECD 361* ●	1	2	19
10 Jul 93	**SOON BE DONE** *Greensleeves GRECD 380*	46		3
8 Jul 95	**IN THE SUMMERTIME** *Virgin VSCDT 1542* FEATURING RAYVON	5		9
23 Sep 95	**BOOMBASTIC** *Virgin VSCDT 1536* ●	1	1	12
13 Jan 96	**WHY YOU TREAT ME SO BAD** *Virgin VSCDT 1566* FEATURING GRAND PUBA	11		5
23 Mar 96	**SOMETHING DIFFERENT/THE TRAIN IS COMING** *Virgin VSCDX 1581* FEATURING WAYNE WONDER	21		5
22 Jun 96	**THAT GIRL** *Virgin VUSDX 106* MAXI PRIEST FEATURING SHAGGY	15		7
19 Jul 97	**PIECE OF MY HEART** *Virgin VSCDT 1647* FEATURING MARSHA	7		6
17 Feb 01	**IT WASN'T ME** *MCA 1558032* FEATURING RICARDO 'RIKROK' DUCENT	31		3
10 Mar 01	**IT WASN'T ME** *MCA 1558022* FEATURING RICARDO 'RIKROK' DUCENT ⊛ ★	1	1	20
9 Jun 01	**ANGEL** *MCA MCSTD 40257* FEATURING RAYVON ● ★	1	3	16
29 Sep 01	**LUV ME LUV ME** *MCA MCSTD 40263*	5		10
1 Dec 01	**DANCE AND SHOUT/HOPE** *MCA MCSTD 40272*	19		7
23 Mar 02	**ME JULIE** *Island CID 793* ALI G & SHAGGY ○	2		14
9 Nov 02	**HEY SEXY LADY** *MCA MCSTD 40304* FEATURING BRIAN & TONY GOLD	10		7
3 Jul 04	**YOUR EYES** *VP VPCD6415* RIK ROK FEATURING SHAGGY	57		1
17 Sep 05	**WILD 2NITE** *Geffen MCSXD40431*	61		1

SHAH

UK, female vocalist (Sarah Morriss) — **1**

Date	Title / Label	Peak Position	Weeks at No.1	Weeks on Chart
6 Jun 98	**SECRET LOVE** *Evocative EVOKE 5CDS*	69		1

SHAI

US, male vocal group — **6**

Date	Title / Label	Peak Position	Weeks at No.1	Weeks on Chart
19 Dec 92	**IF I EVER FALL IN LOVE** *MCA MCS 1727*	36		6

SHAKATAK

UK, female/male vocal/instrumental group – Bill Sharpe (Sharpe & Numan*), Roger Odell, Jackie Rawe (replaced by Norma Lewis), Jill Saward, Steve Underwood (replaced by George Anderson), Keith Winter & Nigel Wright — **85**

Date	Title / Label	Peak Position	Weeks at No.1	Weeks on Chart
8 Nov 80	**FEELS LIKE THE RIGHT TIME** *Polydor POSP 188*	41		5
7 Mar 81	**LIVING IN THE UK** *Polydor POSP 230*	52		4
25 Jul 81	**BRAZILIAN DAWN** *Polydor POSP 282*	48		3
21 Nov 81	**EASIER SAID THAN DONE** *Polydor POSP 375*	12		17
3 Apr 82	**NIGHT BIRDS** *Polydor POSP 407*	9		8
19 Jun 82	**STREETWALKIN'** *Polydor POSP 452*	38		6
4 Sep 82	**INVITATIONS** *Polydor POSP 502*	24		7
6 Nov 82	**STRANGER** *Polydor POSP 530*	43		3
4 Jun 83	**DARK IS THE NIGHT** *Polydor POSP 595*	15		8
27 Aug 83	**IF YOU COULD SEE ME NOW** *Polydor POSP 635*	49		4
7 Jul 84	**DOWN ON THE STREET** *Polydor POSP 688*	9		11
15 Sep 84	**DON'T BLAME IT ON LOVE** *Polydor POSP 699*	55		3
16 Nov 85	**DAY BY DAY** *Polydor POSP 770* FEATURING AL JARREAU	53		3
24 Oct 87	**MR MANIC AND SISTER COOL** *Polydor MANIC 1*	56		3

SHAKE B4 USE VS ROBERT PALMER

UK, male vocal/instrumental/production group — **1**

Date	Title / Label	Peak Position	Weeks at No.1	Weeks on Chart
18 Jan 03	**ADDICTED TO LOVE** *Serious SER 606CD*	42		1

SHAKEDOWN

Switzerland, male DJ/production duo – Sebastien & Stephan Kohler — **10**

Date	Title / Label	Peak Position	Weeks at No.1	Weeks on Chart
11 May 02	**AT NIGHT** *Defected DFECT 50CDS*	6		8
28 Jun 03	**DROWSY WITH HOPE** *Defected DFTD 071CDS*	46		2

SHAKESPEAR'S SISTER

UK/US, female vocal/instrumental duo – Marcella Detroit* (Marcella Levy) & Siobhan Fahey — **52**

Date	Title / Label	Peak Position	Weeks at No.1	Weeks on Chart
29 Jul 89	**YOU'RE HISTORY** *ffrr F 112*	7		9
14 Oct 89	**RUN SILENT** *ffrr F 119*	54		3
10 Mar 90	**DIRTY MIND** *ffrr F 128*	71		1
12 Oct 91	**GOODBYE CRUEL WORLD** *London LON 309*	59		2
25 Jan 92	**STAY** *London LON 314* ●	1	8	16
16 May 92	**I DON'T CARE** *London LON 318*	7		7
18 Jul 92	**GOODBYE CRUEL WORLD** *London LON 322*	32		4
7 Nov 92	**HELLO (TURN YOUR RADIO ON)** *London LON 330*	14		6
27 Feb 93	**MY 16TH APOLOGY (EP)** *London LONCD 337*	61		1
22 Jun 96	**I CAN DRIVE** *London LONCD 383*	30		3

SHAKIRA

Colombia, female vocalist/multi-instrumentalist/producer (Shakira Ripoll) — **131**

Date	Title / Label	Peak Position	Weeks at No.1	Weeks on Chart
9 Mar 02	**WHENEVER WHEREVER** *Epic 6724262* ●	2		19
3 Aug 02	**UNDERNEATH YOUR CLOTHES** *Epic 6729532*	3		15
23 Nov 02	**OBJECTION (TANGO)** *Epic 6733402*	17		8
11 Mar 06	**DON'T BOTHER** *Epic 82876792812*	9		5
17 Jun 06	**HIPS DON'T LIE** *Epic 82876842702* FEATURING WYCLEF JEAN ★	1	2	38
23 Dec 06	**ILLEGAL** *Epic 88697009202* FEATURING CARLOS SANTANA	34		2
14 Apr 07	**BEAUTIFUL LIAR** *Columbia 88697091242* BEYONCE & SHAKIRA ○	1	3	21
19 Sep 09	**SHE WOLF** *Epic 88697562052* ○	4		16
28 Nov 09	**DID IT AGAIN** *Epic USSM10904793*	26		7

SHALAMAR

US, male/female vocal trio – Gerald Brown (replaced by Howard Hewitt), Jeffrey Daniel (replaced by Micki Free) & Jody Watley* (replaced by Delisa Davis) — **134**

Date	Title / Label	Peak Position	Weeks at No.1	Weeks on Chart
14 May 77	**UPTOWN FESTIVAL** *Soul Train FB 0885*	30		5
9 Dec 78	**TAKE THAT TO THE BANK** *RCA FB 1379*	20		12
24 Nov 79	**THE SECOND TIME AROUND** *Solar FB 1709*	45		9
9 Feb 80	**RIGHT IN THE SOCKET** *Solar SO 2*	44		6
30 Aug 80	**I OWE YOU ONE** *Solar SO 11*	13		10
28 Mar 81	**MAKE THAT MOVE** *Solar SO 17*	30		10
27 Mar 82	**I CAN MAKE YOU FEEL GOOD** *Solar K 12599*	7		11
12 Jun 82	**A NIGHT TO REMEMBER** *Solar K 13162*	5		12
4 Sep 82	**THERE IT IS** *Solar K 13194* ○	5		10
27 Nov 82	**FRIENDS** *Solar CHUM 1*	12		10
11 Jun 83	**DEAD GIVEAWAY** *Solar E 9819*	8		10
13 Aug 83	**DISAPPEARING ACT** *Solar E 9807*	18		8
15 Oct 83	**OVER AND OVER** *Solar E 9792*	23		6
24 Mar 84	**DANCING IN THE SHEETS** *CBS A 4171*	41		3
31 Mar 84	**DEADLINE USA** *MCA 866*	52		3
24 Nov 84	**AMNESIA** *Solar/MCA SHAL 1*	61		2
2 Feb 85	**MY GIRL LOVES ME** *MCA SHAL 2*	45		3
26 Apr 86	**A NIGHT TO REMEMBER (REMIX)** *MCA SHAL 3*	52		4

SHAM ROCK

Ireland, male/female vocal/instrumental group — **11**

Date	Title / Label	Peak Position	Weeks at No.1	Weeks on Chart
7 Nov 98	**TELL ME MA** *Jive 0522352*	13		11

SHAM 69

UK, male vocal/instrumental group – Jimmy Pursey, Mark Cain (replaced by Rick Goldstein), Albie Maskell (replaced by Dave Treganna) & Dave Parsons — **56**

Date	Title / Label	Peak Position	Weeks at No.1	Weeks on Chart
13 May 78	**ANGELS WITH DIRTY FACES** *Polydor 2059 023*	19		10
29 Jul 78	**IF THE KIDS ARE UNITED** *Polydor 2059 050*	9		9
14 Oct 78	**HURRY UP HARRY** *Polydor POSP 7*	10		8
24 Mar 79	**QUESTIONS AND ANSWERS** *Polydor POSP 27*	18		9
4 Aug 79	**HERSHAM BOYS** *Polydor PSOP 64*	6		9
27 Oct 79	**YOU'RE A BETTER MAN THAN I** *Polydor POSP 82*	49		5
12 Apr 80	**TELL THE CHILDREN** *Polydor POSP 136*	45		3
24 Jun 06	**HURRY UP ENGLAND – THE PEOPLE'S ANTHEM** *Parlophone CDR6704* & THE SPECIAL ASSEMBLY	10		3

SHAMEN

UK, male production/rap/vocal trio – Colin Angus, Will Sinnott, d. 23 May 1991, & Richard 'Mr C' West — Weeks on Chart: **77**

Date	Title / Label	Peak	Wks at No.1	Wks on Chart
7 Apr 90	**PRO-GEN** *One Little Indian 36 TP7*	55		4
22 Sep 90	**MAKE IT MINE** *One Little Indian 46 TP7*	42		5
6 Apr 91	**HYPERREAL** *One Little Indian 48 TP7*	29		5
27 Jul 91	**MOVE ANY MOUNTAIN (REMIX)/PRO-GEN '91** *One Little Indian 52 TP7*	4		10
18 Jul 92	**LSI** *One Little Indian 68 TP7*	6		8
5 Sep 92	**EBENEEZER GOODE** *One Little Indian 78 TP7* ●	1	4	10
7 Nov 92	**BOSS DRUM** *One Little Indian 88 TP7*	4		7
7 Nov 92	**BOSS DRUM (REMIX)** *One Little Indian 88 TP12*	58		1
19 Dec 92	**PHOREVER PEOPLE** *One Little Indian 98 TP7* ●	5		10
6 Mar 93	**RE:EVOLUTION** *One Little Indian 118 TP7CD* WITH TERENCE McKENNA	18		2
6 Nov 93	**THE SOS EP** *One Little Indian 108 TP7CD*	14		4
19 Aug 95	**DESTINATION ESCHATON** *One Little Indian 128 TP7CDL*	15		4
21 Oct 95	**TRANSAMAZONIA** *One Little Indian 138 TP7CD*	28		2
10 Feb 96	**HEAL (THE SEPARATION)** *One Little Indian 158 TP7CDL*	31		2
21 Dec 96	**MOVE ANY MOUNTAIN (2ND REMIX)** *One Little Indian 169 TP7CD*	35		3

SHAMPOO

UK, female vocal duo — Weeks on Chart: **28**

Date	Title / Label	Peak	Wks at No.1	Wks on Chart
30 Jul 94	**TROUBLE** *Food CDFOOD 51*	11		12
15 Oct 94	**VIVA LA MEGABABES** *Food CDFOOD 54*	27		4
18 Feb 95	**DELICIOUS** *Food CDFOOD 58*	21		4
5 Aug 95	**TROUBLE** *Food CDFOODS 66*	36		3
13 Jul 96	**GIRL POWER** *Food CDFOOD 76*	25		4
21 Sep 96	**I KNOW WHAT BOYS LIKE** *Food CDFOOD 83*	42		1

JIMMY SHAND

UK, male band leader/accordion player, d. 23 Dec 2000 (age 92) — Weeks on Chart: **2**

Date	Title / Label	Peak	Wks at No.1	Wks on Chart
23 Dec 55	**BLUEBELL POLKA** *Parlophone R 3436*	20		2

PAUL SHANE & THE YELLOWCOATS

UK, male vocalist/actor (George Speight) & male/female vocal/instrumental group — Weeks on Chart: **5**

Date	Title / Label	Peak	Wks at No.1	Wks on Chart
16 May 81	**HI DE HI (HOLIDAY ROCK)** *EMI 5180*	36		5

SHANGRI-LAS

US, female vocal group – Mary & Betty Weiss, Mary Anne, d. 14 Mar 1970, & Marge Ganser, d. 28 Jul 1996 — Weeks on Chart: **57**

Date	Title / Label	Peak	Wks at No.1	Wks on Chart
8 Oct 64	**REMEMBER (WALKIN' IN THE SAND)** *Red Bird RB 10008*	14		13
14 Jan 65	**LEADER OF THE PACK** *Red Bird RB 10014* ★	11		9
14 Oct 72	**LEADER OF THE PACK** *Kama Sutra 2013 024*	3		14
5 Jun 76	**LEADER OF THE PACK** *Charly CS 1009/Contempo CS 7032*	7		11
12 Jun 76	**LEADER OF THE PACK** *Contempo CS 9032*	7		10

SHANICE

US, female vocalist (Shanice Wilson) — Weeks on Chart: **24**

Date	Title / Label	Peak	Wks at No.1	Wks on Chart
23 Nov 91	**I LOVE YOUR SMILE** *Motown ZB 44907*	55		4
22 Feb 92	**I LOVE YOUR SMILE (REMIX)** *Motown TMG 1401*	2		10
14 Nov 92	**LOVIN' YOU** *Motown TMG 1409*	54		1
16 Jan 93	**SAVING FOREVER FOR YOU** *Giant W 0148CD*	42		3
13 Aug 94	**I LIKE** *Motown TMGCD 1427*	49		2
16 Dec 95	**IF I NEVER KNEW YOU (LOVE THEME FROM 'POCAHONTAS')** *Walt Disney WD 7023C* JON SECADA & SHANICE	51		4

SHANKS & BIGFOOT

UK, male production duo – Daniel Langsman & Stephen Meade. See Doolally — Weeks on Chart: **24**

Date	Title / Label	Peak	Wks at No.1	Wks on Chart
29 May 99	**SWEET LIKE CHOCOLATE** *Chocolate Boy 0530352* ⊛	1	2	16
29 Jul 00	**SING-A-LONG** *Pepper 9230232*	12		8

SHANNON

US, female vocalist (Brenda Shannon Greene) — Weeks on Chart: **54**

Date	Title / Label	Peak	Wks at No.1	Wks on Chart
19 Nov 83	**LET THE MUSIC PLAY** *Club LET 1*	14		15
7 Apr 84	**GIVE ME TONIGHT** *Club JAB 1*	24		7
30 Jun 84	**SWEET SOMEBODY** *Club JAB 3*	25		8
20 Jul 85	**STRONGER TOGETHER** *Club JAB 15*	46		6
6 Dec 97	**IT'S OVER LOVE** *Manifesto FESCD 37* TODD TERRY PRESENTS SHANNON	16		8
28 Nov 98	**MOVE MANIA** *Multiply CDMULTY 45* SASH! FEATURING SHANNON	8		10

DEL SHANNON

US, male vocalist (Charles Westover), d. 8 Feb 1990 (age 55) — Weeks on Chart: **147**

Date	Title / Label	Peak	Wks at No.1	Wks on Chart
27 Apr 61	**RUNAWAY** *London HLX 9317* ★	1	3	22
14 Sep 61	**HATS OFF TO LARRY** *London HLX 9402*	6		12
7 Dec 61	**SO LONG BABY** *London HLX 9462*	10		11
15 Mar 62	**HEY LITTLE GIRL** *London HLX 9515*	2		15
6 Sep 62	**CRY MYSELF TO SLEEP** *London HLX 9587*	29		6
11 Oct 62	**SWISS MAID** *London HLX 0609*	2		17
17 Jan 63	**LITTLE TOWN FLIRT** *London HLX 9653*	4		13
25 Apr 63	**TWO KINDS OF TEARDROPS** *London HLX 9710*	5		13
22 Aug 63	**TWO SILHOUETTES** *London HLX 9761*	23		8
24 Oct 63	**SUE'S GOTTA BE MINE** *London HLU 9800*	21		8
12 Mar 64	**MARY JANE** *Stateside SS 269*	35		5
30 Jul 64	**HANDY MAN** *Stateside SS 317*	36		4
14 Jan 65	**KEEP SEARCHIN' (WE'LL FOLLOW THE SUN)** *Stateside SS 368*	3		11
18 Mar 65	**STRANGER IN TOWN** *Stateside SS 395*	40		2

SHARON SHANNON & STEVE EARLE

Ireland/US, female/male vocal/instrumental duo — Weeks on Chart: **3**

Date	Title / Label	Peak	Wks at No.1	Wks on Chart
7 Jun 08	**THE GALWAY GIRL** *The Daisy Label LRLCDS020*	67		3

ROXANNE SHANTE

US, female rapper (Lolita Shante Gooden) — Weeks on Chart: **11**

Date	Title / Label	Peak	Wks at No.1	Wks on Chart
1 Aug 87	**HAVE A NICE DAY** *Breakout USA 612*	58		3
4 Jun 88	**GO ON GIRL** *Breakout USA 633*	55		3
29 Oct 88	**SHARP AS A KNIFE** *Club JAB 73* BRANDON COOKE FEATURING ROXANNE SHANTE	45		3
14 Apr 90	**GO ON GIRL (REMIX)** *Breakout USA 689*	74		1
23 Sep 00	**WHAT'S GOING ON** *Wall Of Sound WALLD 064* MEKON FEATURING ROXANNE SHANTE	43		1

SHAPESHIFTERS

UK/Sweden, male DJ/production duo – Simon Marlin & Max Reich — Weeks on Chart: **32**

Date	Title / Label	Peak	Wks at No.1	Wks on Chart
24 Jul 04	**LOLA'S THEME** *Positiva CDTIVS 207* ●	1	1	15
26 Mar 05	**BACK TO BASICS** *Positiva CDTIVS216*	10		8
18 Mar 06	**INCREDIBLE** *Positiva CDTIVS233*	12		5
5 Aug 06	**SENSITIVITY** *Positiva CDTIV238* & CHIC	40		2
14 Jul 07	**PUSHER** *Positiva CDTIVS258*	56		1
27 Oct 07	**NEW DAY** *Positiva CDTIVS262*	72		1

HELEN SHAPIRO

UK, female vocalist — Weeks on Chart: **119**

Date	Title / Label	Peak	Wks at No.1	Wks on Chart
23 Mar 61	**DON'T TREAT ME LIKE A CHILD** *Columbia DB 4589*	3		20
29 Jun 61	**YOU DON'T KNOW** *Columbia DB 4670*	1	3	23
28 Sep 61	**WALKIN' BACK TO HAPPINESS** *Columbia DB 4715*	1	3	19
15 Feb 62	**TELL ME WHAT HE SAID** *Columbia DB 4782*	2		15
3 May 62	**LET'S TALK ABOUT LOVE** *Columbia DB 4824*	23		7
12 Jul 62	**LITTLE MISS LONELY** *Columbia DB 4869*	8		11
18 Oct 62	**KEEP AWAY FROM OTHER GIRLS** *Columbia DB 4908*	40		6
7 Feb 63	**QUEEN FOR TONIGHT** *Columbia DB 4966*	33		5
25 Apr 63	**WOE IS ME** *Columbia DB 7026*	35		6
24 Oct 63	**LOOK WHO IT IS** *Columbia DB 7130*	47		3
23 Jan 64	**FEVER** *Columbia DB 7190*	38		4

SHARADA HOUSE GANG

Italy, male/female vocal/instrumental group — Weeks on Chart: **4**

Date	Title / Label	Peak	Wks at No.1	Wks on Chart
12 Aug 95	**KEEP IT UP** *Media MCSTD 2071*	36		2
11 May 96	**LET THE RHYTHM MOVE YOU** *Media MCSTD 40035*	50		1
18 Oct 97	**GYPSY BOY, GYPSY GIRL** *Gut CXGUT 12*	52		1

SHARAM

US, male DJ/producer (Sharam Tayebi). See Deep Dish — Weeks on Chart: **11**

Date	Title / Label	Peak	Wks at No.1	Wks on Chart
30 Dec 06	**PATT (PARTY ALL THE TIME)** *Data DATA138CDS*	8		11

SHARKEY

UK, male DJ/producer/keyboard player (Jonathan Kneath) — Weeks on Chart: **1**

Date	Title / Label	Peak	Wks at No.1	Wks on Chart
8 Mar 97	**REVOLUTIONS (EP)** *React CDREACT 95*	53		1

FEARGAL SHARKEY

UK, male vocalist (Sean Feargal Sharkey). See Assembly, Undertones — 58

Date	Title	Peak Position	Weeks at No.1	Weeks on Chart
13 Oct 84	**LISTEN TO YOUR FATHER** *Zarjazz JAZZ 1*	23		7
29 Jun 85	**LOVING YOU** *Virgin VS 770*	26		10
12 Oct 85	**A GOOD HEART** *Virgin VS 808* ●	1	2	16
4 Jan 86	**YOU LITTLE THIEF** *Virgin VS 840*	5		9
5 Apr 86	**SOMEONE TO SOMEBODY** *Virgin VS 828*	64		3
16 Jan 88	**MORE LOVE** *Virgin VS 992*	44		5
16 Mar 91	**I'VE GOT NEWS FOR YOU** *Virgin VS 1294*	12		8

SHARONETTES

UK, female vocal group — 8

Date	Title	Peak Position	Weeks at No.1	Weeks on Chart
26 Apr 75	**PAPA OOM MOW MOW** *Black Magic BM 102*	26		5
12 Jul 75	**GOING TO A GO-GO** *Black Magic BM 104*	46		3

DEE DEE SHARP

US, female vocalist (Dione LaRue) — 2

Date	Title	Peak Position	Weeks at No.1	Weeks on Chart
25 Apr 63	**DO THE BIRD** *Cameo Parkway C 244*	46		2

SHARPAY

US, female actor/vocalist (Ashley Tisdale) — 1

Date	Title	Peak Position	Weeks at No.1	Weeks on Chart
6 Oct 07	**FABULOUS** *Walt Disney USWD10732093*	64		1

SHARPE & NUMAN

UK, male vocal/instrumental duo — 16

Date	Title	Peak Position	Weeks at No.1	Weeks on Chart
9 Feb 85	**CHANGE YOUR MIND** *Polydor POSP 722*	17		8
4 Oct 86	**NEW THING FROM LONDON TOWN** *Numa NU 19*	52		3
30 Jan 88	**NO MORE LIES** *Polydor POSP 894*	34		3
3 Jun 89	**I'M ON AUTOMATIC** *Polydor PO 43*	44		2

ROCKY SHARPE & THE REPLAYS

UK, male/female vocal/instrumental group — 41

Date	Title	Peak Position	Weeks at No.1	Weeks on Chart
16 Dec 78	**RAMA LAMA DING DONG** *Chiswick CHIS 104*	17		10
24 Mar 79	**IMAGINATION** *Chiswick CHIS 110*	39		6
25 Aug 79	**LOVE WILL MAKE YOU FAIL IN SCHOOL** *Chiswick CHIS 114* FEATURING THE TOP LINERS	60		4
9 Feb 80	**MARTIAN HOP** *Chiswick CHIS 121*	55		4
17 Apr 82	**SHOUT SHOUT (KNOCK YOURSELF OUT)** *Chiswick DICE 3*	19		9
7 Aug 82	**CLAP YOUR HANDS** *RAK 345*	54		3
26 Feb 83	**IF YOU WANNA BE HAPPY** *Polydor POSP 560*	46		5

SHAUN THE SHEEP

UK, cartoon sheep vocalist (Vic Reeves). See Wonderstuff — 2

Date	Title	Peak Position	Weeks at No.1	Weeks on Chart
22 Dec 07	**LIFE'S A TREAT** *Tug CDSNOG24*	20		2

BEN SHAW FEATURING ADELE HOLNESS

UK, male/female vocal/production duo — 1

Date	Title	Peak Position	Weeks at No.1	Weeks on Chart
14 Jul 01	**SO STRONG** *Fire Recordings ERIF 009CDS*	72		1

MARK SHAW

UK, male vocalist (Mark Tiplady). See Then Jerico — 1

Date	Title	Peak Position	Weeks at No.1	Weeks on Chart
17 Nov 90	**LOVE SO BRIGHT** *EMI EM 161*	54		1

SANDIE SHAW

UK, female vocalist (Sandra Goodrich) — 165

Date	Title	Peak Position	Weeks at No.1	Weeks on Chart
8 Oct 64	**(THERE'S) ALWAYS SOMETHING THERE TO REMIND ME** *Pye 7N 15704*	1	3	11
10 Dec 64	**GIRL DON'T COME** *Pye 7N 15743*	3		12
18 Feb 65	**I'LL STOP AT NOTHING** *Pye 7N 15783*	4		11
13 May 65	**LONG LIVE LOVE** *Pye 7N 15841*	1	3	14
23 Sep 65	**MESSAGE UNDERSTOOD** *Pye 7N 15940*	6		10
18 Nov 65	**HOW CAN YOU TELL** *Pye 7N 15987*	21		9
27 Jan 66	**TOMORROW** *Pye 7N 17036*	9		9
19 May 66	**NOTHING COMES EASY** *Pye 7N 17086*	14		9
8 Sep 66	**RUN** *Pye 7N 17163*	32		5
24 Nov 66	**THINK SOMETIMES ABOUT ME** *Pye 7N 17212*	32		4
19 Jan 67	**I DON'T NEED ANYTHING** *Pye 7N 17239*	50		1
16 Mar 67	**PUPPET ON A STRING** *Pye 7N 17272*	1	3	18
12 Jul 67	**TONIGHT IN TOKYO** *Pye 7N 17346*	21		6
4 Oct 67	**YOU'VE NOT CHANGED** *Pye 7N 17378*	18		12
7 Feb 68	**TODAY** *Pye 7N 17441*	27		7
12 Feb 69	**MONSIEUR DUPONT** *Pye 7N 17675*	6		15
14 May 69	**THINK IT ALL OVER** *Pye 7N 17726*	42		4
21 Apr 84	**HAND IN GLOVE** *Rough Trade RT 130*	27		5
14 Jun 86	**ARE YOU READY TO BE HEARTBROKEN** *Polydor POSP 793*	68		1
12 Nov 94	**NOTHING LESS THAN BRILLIANT** *Virgin VSCDT 1521*	66		2

TRACY SHAW

UK, female actor/vocalist — 1

Date	Title	Peak Position	Weeks at No.1	Weeks on Chart
4 Jul 98	**HAPPENIN' ALL OVER AGAIN** *Recognition CDREC 2*	46		1

WINIFRED SHAW

UK, female vocalist, d. 2 May 1982 (age 83) — 4

Date	Title	Peak Position	Weeks at No.1	Weeks on Chart
14 Aug 76	**LULLABY OF BROADWAY** *United Artists UP 36131*	42		4

SHE ROCKERS

UK, female rap duo — 2

Date	Title	Peak Position	Weeks at No.1	Weeks on Chart
13 Jan 90	**JAM IT JAM** *Jive 233*	58		2

GEORGE SHEARING

US (b. UK), male pianist — 15

Date	Title	Peak Position	Weeks at No.1	Weeks on Chart
19 Jul 62	**LET THERE BE LOVE** *Capitol CL 15257* NAT 'KING' COLE WITH GEORGE SHEARING	11		14
4 Oct 62	**BAUBLES, BANGLES AND BEADS** *Capitol CL 15269*	49		1

GARY SHEARSTON

Australia, male vocalist — 8

Date	Title	Peak Position	Weeks at No.1	Weeks on Chart
5 Oct 74	**I GET A KICK OUT OF YOU** *Charisma CB 234*	7		8

SHED SEVEN

UK, male vocal/instrumental group – Rick Witter, Paul Banks, Tim Gladwin & Alan Leach — 50

Date	Title	Peak Position	Weeks at No.1	Weeks on Chart
25 Jun 94	**DOLPHIN** *Polydor YORCD 2*	28		4
27 Aug 94	**SPEAKEASY** *Polydor YORCD 3*	24		3
12 Nov 94	**OCEAN PIE** *Polydor YORCD 4*	33		2
13 May 95	**WHERE HAVE YOU BEEN TONIGHT?** *Polydor YORCD 5*	23		2
27 Jan 96	**GETTING BETTER** *Polydor 5778912*	14		3
23 Mar 96	**GOING FOR GOLD** *Polydor 5762152*	8		5
18 May 96	**BULLY BOY** *Polydor 5765972*	22		3
31 Aug 96	**ON STANDBY** *Polydor 5752732*	12		4
23 Nov 96	**CHASING RAINBOWS** *Polydor 5759292*	17		5
14 Mar 98	**SHE LEFT ME ON FRIDAY** *Polydor 5695412*	11		4
23 May 98	**THE HEROES** *Polydor 5699172*	18		3
22 Aug 98	**DEVIL IN YOUR SHOES (WALKING ALL OVER)** *Polydor 5672072*	37		2
5 Jun 99	**DISCO DOWN** *Polydor 5638752*	13		6
5 May 01	**CRY FOR HELP** *Artful CDX 35ARTFUL*	30		2
24 May 03	**WHY CAN'T I BE YOU?** *Taste Media TMCDSX 5004*	23		2

SHEEP ON DRUGS

UK, male vocal/instrumental duo — 5

Date	Title	Peak Position	Weeks at No.1	Weeks on Chart
27 Mar 93	**15 MINUTES OF FAME** *Transglobal CID 564*	44		2
30 Oct 93	**FROM A TO H AND BACK AGAIN** *Transglobal CID 575*	40		2
14 May 94	**LET THE GOOD TIMES ROLL** *Transglobal CID 576*	56		1

SHEER BRONZE FEATURING LISA MILLETT

UK, male producer (Charles Eve) & female vocalist — 1

Date	Title	Peak Position	Weeks at No.1	Weeks on Chart
3 Sep 94	**WALKIN' ON** *Go! Beat GODCD 115*	63		1

SHEER ELEGANCE

UK, male vocal group — 23

Date	Title	Peak Position	Weeks at No.1	Weeks on Chart
20 Dec 75	**MILKY WAY** *Pye International 7N 25697*	18		10
3 Apr 76	**LIFE IS TOO SHORT GIRL** *Pye International 7N 25703*	9		9
24 Jul 76	**IT'S TEMPTATION** *Pye International 7N 25717*	41		4

SHADE SHEIST FEATURING NATE DOGG & KURUPT

US, male rap trio — 7

Date	Title	Peak Position	Weeks at No.1	Weeks on Chart
25 Aug 01	**WHERE I WANNA BE** *London LONCD 461*	14		7

Silver-selling ● Gold-selling ● Platinum-selling (x multiples) ✪ US No.1 ★ Peak Position · Weeks at No.1 · Weeks on Chart

DOUG SHELDON
UK, male vocalist — 15

Date	Title / Label	Peak Position	Weeks at No.1	Weeks on Chart
9 Nov 61	**RUNAROUND SUE** *Decca F 11398*	36		3
4 Jan 62	**YOUR MA SAID YOU CRIED IN YOUR SLEEP LAST NIGHT** *Decca F 11416*	29		6
7 Feb 63	**I SAW LINDA YESTERDAY** *Decca F 11564*	36		6

PETE SHELLEY
UK, male vocalist. See Buzzcocks — 1

Date	Title / Label	Peak Position	Weeks at No.1	Weeks on Chart
12 Mar 83	**TELEPHONE OPERATOR** *Genetic XX1*	66		1

PETER SHELLEY
UK, male vocalist (Peter McNeish) — 20

Date	Title / Label	Peak Position	Weeks at No.1	Weeks on Chart
14 Sep 74	**GEE BABY** *Magnet MAG 12*	4		10
22 Mar 75	**LOVE ME LOVE MY DOG** *Magnet MAG 22* ●	3		10

ANNE SHELTON
UK, female vocalist (Patricia Sibley), d. 31 Jul 1994 (age 65) — 31

Date	Title / Label	Peak Position	Weeks at No.1	Weeks on Chart
16 Dec 55	**ARRIVEDERCI DARLING** *HMV POP 146*	17		4
13 Apr 56	**SEVEN DAYS** *Philips PB 567*	20		4
24 Aug 56	**LAY DOWN YOUR ARMS** *Philips PB 616*	1	4	14
20 Nov 59	**VILLAGE OF ST. BERNADETTE** *Philips PB 969*	27		1
26 Jan 61	**SAILOR** *Philips PB 1096*	10		8

SHENA
UK, female vocalist (Shena McSween) — 18

Date	Title / Label	Peak Position	Weeks at No.1	Weeks on Chart
2 Aug 97	**LET THE BEAT HIT 'EM** *VC Recordings VCRD 24*	28		2
1 Sep 01	**I'LL BE WAITING** *Rulin 17CDS* FULL INTENTION PRESENTS SHENA	44		1
4 Oct 03	**WILDERNESS** *Direction 6742692* JURGEN VRIES FEATURING SHENA	20		3
24 Feb 07	**DARE ME (STUPIDISCO)** *Defected DFTD150CDS* JUNIOR JACK FEATURING SHENA	20		5
14 Apr 07	**GUILTY** *Hed Kandi HK32CDS* DE SOUZA FEATURING SHENA	46		2
14 Jun 08	**WATCH OUT** *Data DATA190CDS* ALEX GAUDINO FEATURING SHENA	16		5

VONDA SHEPARD
US, female vocalist/pianist/bass player/actor — 9

Date	Title / Label	Peak Position	Weeks at No.1	Weeks on Chart
5 Dec 98	**SEARCHIN' MY SOUL** *Epic 6666332*	10		9

SHEPHERD SISTERS
US, female vocal group — 6

Date	Title / Label	Peak Position	Weeks at No.1	Weeks on Chart
15 Nov 57	**ALONE** *HMV POP 411*	14		6

SHERBET
Australia, male vocal/instrumental group — 10

Date	Title / Label	Peak Position	Weeks at No.1	Weeks on Chart
25 Sep 76	**HOWZAT** *Epic EPC 4574* ●	4		10

TONY SHERIDAN & THE BEATLES
UK, male vocalist & vocal/instrumental group — 1

Date	Title / Label	Peak Position	Weeks at No.1	Weeks on Chart
6 Jun 63	**MY BONNIE** *Polydor NH 66833*	48		1

ALLAN SHERMAN
US, male comedian (Allan Copelon), d. 27 Nov 1973 (age 48) — 10

Date	Title / Label	Peak Position	Weeks at No.1	Weeks on Chart
12 Sep 63	**HELLO MUDDAH HELLO FADDAH** *Warner Brothers WB 106*	14		10

BOBBY SHERMAN
US, male vocalist — 4

Date	Title / Label	Peak Position	Weeks at No.1	Weeks on Chart
31 Oct 70	**JULIE DO YA LOVE ME** *CBS 5144*	28		4

SHERRICK
US, male vocalist (Lamotte Smith), d. 22 Jan 1999 (age 41) — 10

Date	Title / Label	Peak Position	Weeks at No.1	Weeks on Chart
1 Aug 87	**JUST CALL** *Warner Brothers W 8380*	23		8
21 Nov 87	**LET'S BE LOVERS TONIGHT** *Warner Brothers W 8146*	63		2

PLUTO SHERVINGTON
Jamaica, male vocalist — 20

Date	Title / Label	Peak Position	Weeks at No.1	Weeks on Chart
7 Feb 76	**DAT** *Opal Pal 5*	6		8
10 Apr 76	**RAM GOAT LIVER** *Trojan TR 7978*	43		4
6 Mar 82	**YOUR HONOUR** *KR 4* PLUTO	19		8

HOLLY SHERWOOD
US, female vocalist — 7

Date	Title / Label	Peak Position	Weeks at No.1	Weeks on Chart
5 Feb 72	**DAY BY DAY** *Bell 1182*	29		7

TONY SHEVETON
UK, male vocalist — 1

Date	Title / Label	Peak Position	Weeks at No.1	Weeks on Chart
13 Feb 64	**MILLION DRUMS** *Oriole CB 1895*	49		1

SHIFTY
US, male rapper (Seth Binzer, aka Shifty Shellshock). See Crazy Town — 3

Date	Title / Label	Peak Position	Weeks at No.1	Weeks on Chart
11 Sep 04	**SLIDE ALONG SIDE** *Maverick W649CD*	29		3

SHIMMON & WOOLFSON
UK, male DJ/production duo. See Sundance — 1

Date	Title / Label	Peak Position	Weeks at No.1	Weeks on Chart
10 Jan 98	**WELCOME TO THE FUTURE** *React CDREACT 119*	69		1

SHIMON & ANDY C
UK, male DJ/production duo — 5

Date	Title / Label	Peak Position	Weeks at No.1	Weeks on Chart
15 Sep 01	**BODY ROCK** *Ram RAMM 34CD*	58		2
12 Jan 02	**BODY ROCK** *Ram RAMM 34CD*	28		3

SHINEDOWN
US, male vocal/instrumental group — 1

Date	Title / Label	Peak Position	Weeks at No.1	Weeks on Chart
4 Jul 09	**SECOND CHANCE** *Atlantic AT0340CD*	74		1

SHINEHEAD
Jamaica (b. UK), male vocalist (Edmund Aiken) — 6

Date	Title / Label	Peak Position	Weeks at No.1	Weeks on Chart
3 Apr 93	**JAMAICAN IN NEW YORK** *Elektra EKR 161CD*	30		5
26 Jun 93	**LET 'EM IN** *Elektra EKR 168CD*	70		1

SHINING
UK, male vocal/instrumental group — 2

Date	Title / Label	Peak Position	Weeks at No.1	Weeks on Chart
6 Jul 02	**I WONDER HOW** *Zuma ZUMAD 002*	58		1
14 Sep 02	**YOUNG AGAIN** *Zuma ZUMASCD 03B*	52		1

SHINS
UK, male vocal/instrumental group — 3

Date	Title / Label	Peak Position	Weeks at No.1	Weeks on Chart
13 Mar 04	**SO SAYS I** *Sub Pop SPCD621*	73		1
3 Feb 07	**PHANTOM LIMB** *Transgressive TRANS046CD*	42		1
21 Apr 07	**AUSTRALIA** *Transgressive TRANS051CD*	62		1

SHIRELLES
US, female vocal group – Shirley (Owens) Alston, Addie Harris, d. 10 Jun 1982, Doris Kenner, d. 4 Feb 2000, & Beverly Lee — 29

Date	Title / Label	Peak Position	Weeks at No.1	Weeks on Chart
9 Feb 61	**WILL YOU LOVE ME TOMORROW** *Top Rank JAR 540* ★	4		15
31 May 62	**SOLDIER BOY** *HMV POP 1019* ★	23		9
23 May 63	**FOOLISH LITTLE GIRL** *Stateside SS 181*	38		5

SHIRLEY & COMPANY
US, female vocalist & male vocal/instrumental group – Shirley Pixley Goodman, d. 5 Jul 2009 — 9

Date	Title / Label	Peak Position	Weeks at No.1	Weeks on Chart
8 Feb 75	**SHAME SHAME SHAME** *All Platinum 6146 301*	6		9

SHITDISCO
UK, male vocal/instrumental group — 1

Date	Title / Label	Peak Position	Weeks at No.1	Weeks on Chart
4 Nov 06	**REACTOR PARTY** *Fierce Panda NING191CD*	73		1

SHIVA
UK, male/female vocal/instrumental trio — Total weeks on chart: 5

Date	Title / Label	Peak Position	Weeks at No.1	Weeks on Chart
13 May 95	**WORK IT OUT** *ffrr FCD 261*	36		2
19 Aug 95	**FREEDOM** *ffrr FCD 263*	18		3

SHIVAREE
US, female/male vocal/instrumental group — Total weeks on chart: 1

Date	Title / Label	Peak Position	Weeks at No.1	Weeks on Chart
17 Feb 01	**GOODNIGHT MOON** *Capitol CDCL 825*	63		1

SHO NUFF
US, male vocal/instrumental group — Total weeks on chart: 4

Date	Title / Label	Peak Position	Weeks at No.1	Weeks on Chart
24 May 80	**IT'S ALRIGHT** *Ensign ENY 37*	53		4

MICHELLE SHOCKED
US, female vocalist/guitarist (Karen Michelle Johnston) — Total weeks on chart: 10

Date	Title / Label	Peak Position	Weeks at No.1	Weeks on Chart
8 Oct 88	**ANCHORAGE** *Cooking Vinyl LON 193*	60		4
14 Jan 89	**IF LOVE WAS A TRAIN** *Cooking Vinyl LON 212*	63		3
11 Mar 89	**WHEN I GROW UP** *Cooking Vinyl LON 219*	67		3

SHOCKING BLUE
Holland, female/male vocal/instrumental group – Mariska Veres, d. 2 Dec 2006, Cor Van Der Beek, d. 2 Apr 1998, Klaasje Van Der Wal & Robbie Van Leewen — Total weeks on chart: 14

Date	Title / Label	Peak Position	Weeks at No.1	Weeks on Chart
17 Jan 70	**VENUS** *Penny Farthing PEN 702* ★	8		11
25 Apr 70	**MIGHTY JOE** *Penny Farthing PEN 713*	43		3

SHOLAN
Israel/Germany, male/female vocal/production duo — Total weeks on chart: 1

Date	Title / Label	Peak Position	Weeks at No.1	Weeks on Chart
5 Apr 03	**CAN YOU FEEL (WHAT I'M GOING THROUGH)** *Data 39CDS*	47		1

TROY SHONDELL
US, male vocalist (Gary Schelton) — Total weeks on chart: 11

Date	Title / Label	Peak Position	Weeks at No.1	Weeks on Chart
2 Nov 61	**THIS TIME** *London HLG 9432*	22		11

SHONTELLE
Barbados, female vocalist (Shontelle Layne) — Total weeks on chart: 27

Date	Title / Label	Peak Position	Weeks at No.1	Weeks on Chart
31 Jan 09	**T-SHIRT** *Universal 1797835*	6		15
11 Apr 09	**STUCK WITH EACH OTHER** *Universal USUM70900875* FEATURING AKON	23		9
15 Aug 09	**BATTLE CRY** *Universal USHBR0810104*	61		3

SHOOTING PARTY
UK, male vocal/instrumental duo — Total weeks on chart: 2

Date	Title / Label	Peak Position	Weeks at No.1	Weeks on Chart
31 Mar 90	**LET'S HANG ON** *Lisson DOLE 15*	66		2

MIKE SHOREY
US, male vocalist — Total weeks on chart: 8

Date	Title / Label	Peak Position	Weeks at No.1	Weeks on Chart
16 Aug 03	**CAN'T LET YOU GO** *Elektra E 7408CD* FABOLOUS FEATURING MIKE SHOREY & LIL' MO	14		5
2 Apr 05	**BABY** *Atlantic AT0199CDX* FABOLOUS FEATURING MIKE SHOREY	41		3

SHORTIE VS BLACK LEGEND
Italy, male vocal/production trio — Total weeks on chart: 2

Date	Title / Label	Peak Position	Weeks at No.1	Weeks on Chart
4 Aug 01	**SOMEBODY** *WEA 328CDX*	37		2

SHOUT OUT LOUDS
Sweden, male/female vocal/instrumental group — Total weeks on chart: 2

Date	Title / Label	Peak Position	Weeks at No.1	Weeks on Chart
24 Sep 05	**THE COMEBACK** *EMI CDEM668*	63		1
4 Mar 06	**PLEASE PLEASE PLEASE** *EMI CDEM684*	53		1

SHOWADDYWADDY
UK, male vocal/instrumental group – Dave Bartram, Buddy Gask, Malcolm Allured, Romeo Challenger, Rod Deas, Russ Field, Al James & Trevor Oakes — Total weeks on chart: 209

Date	Title / Label	Peak Position	Weeks at No.1	Weeks on Chart
18 May 74	**HEY ROCK AND ROLL** *Bell 1357* ○	2		14
17 Aug 74	**ROCK 'N' ROLL LADY** *Bell 1374*	15		9
30 Nov 74	**HEY MR. CHRISTMAS** *Bell 1387*	13		8
22 Feb 75	**SWEET MUSIC** *Bell 1403*	14		9
17 May 75	**THREE STEPS TO HEAVEN** *Bell 1426* ○	2		11
6 Sep 75	**HEARTBEAT** *Bell 1450*	7		7
15 Nov 75	**HEAVENLY** *Bell 1460*	34		6
29 May 76	**TROCADERO** *Bell 1476*	32		3
6 Nov 76	**UNDER THE MOON OF LOVE** *Bell 1495* ●	1	3	15
5 Mar 77	**WHEN** *Arista 91* ○	3		11
23 Jul 77	**YOU GOT WHAT IT TAKES** *Arista 126* ○	2		10
5 Nov 77	**DANCIN' PARTY** *Arista 149* ○	4		11
25 Mar 78	**I WONDER WHY** *Arista 174* ○	2		11
24 Jun 78	**A LITTLE BIT OF SOAP** *Arista 191* ○	5		12
4 Nov 78	**PRETTY LITTLE ANGEL EYES** *Arista ARIST 222* ○	5		12
31 Mar 79	**REMEMBER THEN** *Arista 247*	17		8
28 Jul 79	**SWEET LITTLE ROCK 'N' ROLLER** *Arista 278*	15		9
10 Nov 79	**A NIGHT AT DADDY GEE'S** *Arista 314*	39		5
27 Sep 80	**WHY DO LOVERS BREAK EACH OTHER'S HEARTS** *Arista ARIST 359*	22		10
29 Nov 80	**BLUE MOON** *Arista ARIST 379*	32		9
13 Jun 81	**MULTIPLICATION** *Arista ARIST 416*	39		4
28 Nov 81	**FOOTSTEPS** *Bell 1499*	31		9
28 Aug 82	**WHO PUT THE BOMP (IN THE BOMP-A-BOMP-A-BOMP)** *RCA 236*	37		6

SHOWDOWN
US, male vocal/instrumental group — Total weeks on chart: 3

Date	Title / Label	Peak Position	Weeks at No.1	Weeks on Chart
17 Dec 77	**KEEP DOIN' IT** *State STAT 63*	41		3

SHOWSTOPPERS
US, male vocal group — Total weeks on chart: 25

Date	Title / Label	Peak Position	Weeks at No.1	Weeks on Chart
13 Mar 68	**AIN'T NOTHING BUT A HOUSEPARTY** *Beacon 3-100*	11		15
13 Nov 68	**EENY MEENY** *MGM 1436*	33		7
30 Jan 71	**AIN'T NOTHING BUT A HOUSEPARTY** *Beacon BEA 100*	33		3

SHRIEKBACK
UK, male vocal/instrumental group — Total weeks on chart: 4

Date	Title / Label	Peak Position	Weeks at No.1	Weeks on Chart
28 Jul 84	**HAND ON MY HEART** *Arista SHRK 1*	52		4

SHRINK
Holland, male DJ/production trio — Total weeks on chart: 4

Date	Title / Label	Peak Position	Weeks at No.1	Weeks on Chart
10 Oct 98	**NERVOUS BREAKDOWN** *VC Recordings VCRD 42*	42		2
19 Aug 00	**ARE YOU READY TO PARTY** *NuLife 74321783772*	39		2

SHUT UP & DANCE
UK, male production/vocal duo – Philip 'PJ' Johnson & Carlton 'Smiley' Hyman — Total weeks on chart: 14

Date	Title / Label	Peak Position	Weeks at No.1	Weeks on Chart
21 Apr 90	**£20 TO GET IN** *Shut Up And Dance SUAD 3*	56		3
28 Jul 90	**LAMBORGHINI** *Shut Up And Dance SUAD 4*	55		2
8 Feb 92	**AUTOBIOGRAPHY OF A CRACKHEAD/THE GREEN MAN** *Shut Up And Dance SUAD 21*	43		2
30 May 92	**RAVING I'M RAVING** *Shut Up And Dance SUAD 30S* FEATURING PETER BOUNCER	2		2
15 Aug 92	**THE ART OF MOVING BUTTS** *Shut Up And Dance SUAD 34S* FEATURING ERIN	69		1
1 Apr 95	**SAVE IT 'TIL THE MOURNING AFTER** *Pulse 8 PULS 84CD*	25		3
8 Jul 95	**I LUV U** *Pulse 8 PULS 90CD* FEATURING RICHIE DAVIS & PROFESSOR T	68		1

SHY
UK, male vocal/instrumental group — Total weeks on chart: 3

Date	Title / Label	Peak Position	Weeks at No.1	Weeks on Chart
19 Apr 80	**GIRL (IT'S ALL I HAVE)** *Gallery GA 1*	60		3

SHY FX
UK, male producer (Andre Williams) — Total weeks on chart: 23

Date	Title / Label	Peak Position	Weeks at No.1	Weeks on Chart
1 Oct 94	**ORIGINAL NUTTAH** *Sound Of Underground SOUR 008CD* U.K. APACHI WITH SHY FX	39		3
20 Mar 99	**BAMBAATA 2012** *Ebony EBR 020CD*	60		1
6 Apr 02	**SHAKE UR BODY** *Positiva CDTIV 171* & T-POWER FEATURING DI	7		11
23 Nov 02	**DON'T WANNA KNOW** *ffrr FCD 408* SHY FX/T POWER/DI & SKIBADEE	19		4
28 Dec 02	**WOLF** *Ebony Dubs EBD001*	60		1

Date	Title / Label	Peak	Wks at No.1	Wks on Chart
7 Jun 03	**FEELIN' U** *London FCD 409* & T-POWER FEATURING KELE LE ROC	34		2
21 Jan 06	**EVERYDAY** *Soundboy SBOY002* & T-POWER FEATURING TOP CAT	75		1

SHYHEIM
US, male rapper (Shyheim Franklin) — 1

Date	Title / Label	Peak	Wks at No.1	Wks on Chart
8 Jun 96	**THIS IZ REAL** *Noo Trybe VUSCD 105*	61		1

SHYSTIE
UK, female rapper (Chanelle Calica) — 3

Date	Title / Label	Peak	Wks at No.1	Wks on Chart
17 Jul 04	**ONE WISH** *Polydor 9866875*	40		2
2 Oct 04	**MAKE IT EASY** *Polydor 9867988*	59		1

SIA
Australia, female vocalist (Sia Furler) — 10

Date	Title / Label	Peak	Wks at No.1	Wks on Chart
3 Jun 00	**TAKEN FOR GRANTED** *Long Lost Brother S002CD1*	10		5
18 Aug 01	**DESTINY** *Ultimate Dilemma UDRCDS 043* ZERO 7 FEATURING SIA & SOPHIE	30		3
1 May 04	**BREATHE ME** *Go! Beat 9866392*	71		1
29 May 04	**SOMERSAULT** *Ultimate Dilemma EW290CD* ZERO 7 FEATURING SIA	56		1

LABI SIFFRE
UK, male vocalist/guitarist — 44

Date	Title / Label	Peak	Wks at No.1	Wks on Chart
27 Nov 71	**IT MUST BE LOVE** *Pye International 7N 25572*	14		12
25 Mar 72	**CRYING LAUGHING LOVING LYING** *Pye International 7N 25576*	11		9
29 Jul 72	**WATCH ME** *Pye International 7N 25586*	29		6
4 Apr 87	**(SOMETHING INSIDE) SO STRONG** *China WOK 12*	4		13
21 Nov 87	**NOTHIN'S GONNA CHANGE** *China WOK 16*	52		4

SIGNAL 1 & SIGNAL 2
UK, male radio DJ & vocalists — 2

Date	Title / Label	Peak	Wks at No.1	Wks on Chart
3 Jun 06	**STANDING TOGETHER – WORLD CUP 2006** *Signal 1 SIGNAL1CDS*	67		2

SIGNUM
Holland, male production duo — 6

Date	Title / Label	Peak	Wks at No.1	Wks on Chart
28 Nov 98	**WHAT YA GOT 4 ME** *Tidy Trax TIDY 118CD*	70		1
31 Jul 99	**COMING ON STRONG** *Tidy Trax TIDY 128T*	66		1
9 Feb 02	**WHAT YA GOT 4 ME** *Tidy Trax TIDY 163CD*	35		3
29 Jun 02	**COMING ON STRONG** *Tidy Two TIDYTWO 104CD* FEATURING SCOTT MAC	50		1

SIGUE SIGUE SPUTNIK
UK, male vocal/instrumental group – Martin Degville, Tony James, Chris Kavanagh, Ray Mayhew, Neil Whitmore & Yana YaYa (Jane Farrimond) — 20

Date	Title / Label	Peak	Wks at No.1	Wks on Chart
1 Mar 86	**LOVE MISSILE F1-11** *Parlophone SSS 1* ●	3		9
7 Jun 86	**TWENTY-FIRST CENTURY BOY** *Parlophone SSS 2*	20		5
19 Nov 88	**SUCCESS** *Parlophone SSS 3*	31		3
1 Apr 89	**DANCERAMA** *Parlophone SSS 5*	50		2
20 May 89	**ALBINONI VS STAR WARS** *Parlophone SSS 4*	75		1

SIGUR ROS
Iceland, male vocal/instrumental group — 12

Date	Title / Label	Peak	Wks at No.1	Wks on Chart
24 May 03	**()** *Pias Recordings CD10FAT02*	72		1
10 Dec 05	**HOPPIPOLLA** *EMI CDEM673*	24		11

SIL
Holland, male DJ/production duo — 1

Date	Title / Label	Peak	Wks at No.1	Wks on Chart
11 Apr 98	**WINDOWS '98** *Hooj Choons HOOJCD 60*	58		1

SILENCERS
UK, male vocal/instrumental group — 7

Date	Title / Label	Peak	Wks at No.1	Wks on Chart
25 Jun 88	**PAINTED MOON** *RCA HUSH 1*	57		4
27 May 89	**SCOTTISH RAIN** *RCA PB 42701*	71		2
15 May 93	**I CAN FEEL IT** *RCA 74321147112*	62		1

SILENT UNDERDOG
UK, male producer (Paul Hardcastle). See Direct Drive, First Light — 1

Date	Title / Label	Peak	Wks at No.1	Wks on Chart
16 Feb 85	**PAPA'S GOT A BRAND NEW PIGBAG** *Kaz 50*	73		1

SILICONE SOUL FEATURING LOUISE CLARE MARSHALL
UK, male/female vocal/production trio — 5

Date	Title / Label	Peak	Wks at No.1	Wks on Chart
6 Oct 01	**RIGHT ON!** *Soma/VC Recordings VCRD 96*	15		5

SILJE
Norway, female vocalist (Silje Nergaard) — 6

Date	Title / Label	Peak	Wks at No.1	Wks on Chart
15 Dec 90	**TELL ME WHERE YOU'RE GOING** *EMI EM 159*	55		6

SILK
US, male vocal group — 10

Date	Title / Label	Peak	Wks at No.1	Wks on Chart
24 Apr 93	**FREAK ME** *Elektra EKR 165CD* ★	46		5
5 Jun 93	**GIRL U FOR ME** *Elektra EKR 167CD*	67		2
9 Oct 93	**BABY IT'S YOU** *Elektra EKR 173CD*	44		2
26 Feb 94	**FREAK ME** *Elektra EKR 165CD*	72		1

SILKIE
UK, male/female vocal/instrumental group — 6

Date	Title / Label	Peak	Wks at No.1	Wks on Chart
23 Sep 65	**YOU'VE GOT TO HIDE YOUR LOVE AWAY** *Fontana TF 603*	28		6

SILSOE
UK, male instrumental/production duo — 4

Date	Title / Label	Peak	Wks at No.1	Wks on Chart
21 Jun 86	**AZTEC GOLD** *CBS A 7231*	48		4

LUCIE SILVAS
UK, female vocalist/pianist (Lucie Silverman) — 19

Date	Title / Label	Peak	Wks at No.1	Wks on Chart
17 Jun 00	**IT'S TOO LATE** *EMI CDEM 565*	62		1
16 Oct 04	**WHAT YOU'RE MADE OF** *Mercury 9867463*	7		7
29 Jan 05	**BREATHE IN** *Mercury 2103631*	6		7
14 May 05	**THE GAME IS WON** *Mercury 9870820*	38		2
6 Aug 05	**DON'T LOOK BACK** *Mercury 9872943*	34		2

SILVER BULLET
UK, male rapper (Richard Brown) — 20

Date	Title / Label	Peak	Wks at No.1	Wks on Chart
2 Sep 89	**BRING FORTH THE GUILLOTINE** *Tam Tam TTT 013*	70		1
9 Dec 89	**20 SECONDS TO COMPLY** *Tam Tam 7TTT 019*	11		10
3 Mar 90	**BRING FORTH THE GUILLOTINE** *Tam Tam TTT 013*	45		5
13 Apr 91	**UNDERCOVER ANARCHIST** *Parlophone R 6284*	33		4

SILVER CITY
UK, male producer (Greg Fenton) — 1

Date	Title / Label	Peak	Wks at No.1	Wks on Chart
30 Oct 93	**LOVE INFINITY** *Silver City GFJMCD 1*	62		1

SILVER CONVENTION
Germany/US, female vocal trio – Penny McLean, Linda Thompson & Ramona Wulf — 35

Date	Title / Label	Peak	Wks at No.1	Wks on Chart
5 Apr 75	**SAVE ME** *Magnet MAG 26*	30		7
15 Nov 75	**FLY ROBIN FLY** *Magnet MAG 43* ★	28		8
3 Apr 76	**GET UP AND BOOGIE** *Magnet MAG 55*	7		11
19 Jun 76	**TIGER BABY/NO NO JOE** *Magnet MAG 69*	41		4
29 Jan 77	**EVERYBODY'S TALKIN' 'BOUT LOVE** *Magnet MAG 81*	25		5

SILVER SUN
UK, male vocal/instrumental group — 13

Date	Title / Label	Peak	Wks at No.1	Wks on Chart
2 Nov 96	**LAVA** *Polydor 5756872*	54		1
22 Feb 97	**LAST DAY** *Polydor 5732432*	48		1
3 May 97	**GOLDEN SKIN** *Polydor 5738272*	32		2
5 Jul 97	**JULIA** *Polydor 5711752*	51		1
18 Oct 97	**LAVA** *Polydor 5714242*	35		2
20 Jun 98	**TOO MUCH, TOO LITTLE, TOO LATE** *Polydor 5699152*	20		4
26 Sep 98	**I'LL SEE YOU AROUND** *Polydor 5674532*	26		2

SILVERCHAIR
Australia, male vocal/instrumental group — 8

Date	Title / Label	Peak	Wks at No.1	Wks on Chart
29 Jul 95	**PURE MASSACRE** *Murmur 6622642*	71		1
9 Sep 95	**TOMORROW** *Murmur 6623952*	59		2
5 Apr 97	**FREAK** *Murmur 6640765*	34		2
19 Jul 97	**ABUSE ME** *Murmur 6647905*	40		2
15 May 99	**ANA'S SONG** *Columbia 6673452*	45		1

Silver-selling ● Gold-selling ● Platinum-selling (x multiples) ✪ US No.1 ★ Peak Position · Weeks at No.1 · Weeks on Chart

DOOLEY SILVERSPOON
US, male vocalist

3

Date	Title / Label	Peak Position	Weeks at No.1	Weeks on Chart
31 Jan 76	**LET ME BE THE NUMBER 1 (LOVE OF YOUR LIFE)** *Seville SEV 1020*	44		3

HARRY SIMEONE CHORALE
US, choir – leader d. 22 Feb 2005 (age 93)

14

Date	Title / Label	Peak Position	Weeks at No.1	Weeks on Chart
13 Feb 59	**LITTLE DRUMMER BOY** *Top Rank JAR 101*	13		7
22 Dec 60	**ONWARD CHRISTIAN SOLDIERS** *Ember EMBS 118*	35		2
21 Dec 61	**ONWARD CHRISTIAN SOLDIERS** *Ember EMBS 118*	36		3
20 Dec 62	**ONWARD CHRISTIAN SOLDIERS** *Ember EMBS 144*	38		2

SIMIAN
UK, male vocal/instrumental group

11

Date	Title / Label	Peak Position	Weeks at No.1	Weeks on Chart
14 Jun 03	**LA BREEZE** *Source SOURCD 069*	55		1
15 Jul 06	**WE ARE YOUR FRIENDS** *Ten TENCDX505* JUSTICE VERSUS SIMIAN	20		10

SIMIAN MOBILE DISCO
UK, male DJ/production duo

1

Date	Title / Label	Peak Position	Weeks at No.1	Weeks on Chart
15 Aug 09	**AUDACITY OF HUGE** *Wichita WEBB224S*	60		1

SIMILOU
Sweden, male vocal/instrumental duo

6

Date	Title / Label	Peak Position	Weeks at No.1	Weeks on Chart
5 Aug 06	**ALL THIS LOVE** *Direction 82876883502*	20		6

GENE SIMMONS
US (b. Israel), male vocalist/guitarist (Chaim Witz). See Kiss

4

Date	Title / Label	Peak Position	Weeks at No.1	Weeks on Chart
27 Jan 79	**RADIOACTIVE** *Casablanca CAN 134*	41		4

SIMON
UK, male producer (Simon Pearson)

2

Date	Title / Label	Peak Position	Weeks at No.1	Weeks on Chart
31 Mar 01	**FREE AT LAST** *Positiva CDTIV 152*	36		2

CARLY SIMON
US, female vocalist

85

Date	Title / Label	Peak Position	Weeks at No.1	Weeks on Chart
16 Dec 72	**YOU'RE SO VAIN** *Elektra K 12077* ★	3		15
31 Mar 73	**THE RIGHT THING TO DO** *Elektra K 12095*	17		9
16 Mar 74	**MOCKINGBIRD** *Elektra K 12134* & JAMES TAYLOR	34		5
6 Aug 77	**NOBODY DOES IT BETTER** *Elektra K 12261* ●	7		12
21 Aug 82	**WHY** *WEA K 79300*	10		13
24 Jan 87	**COMING AROUND AGAIN** *Arista ARIST 687*	10		12
10 Jun 89	**WHY** *WEA U 7501*	56		5
20 Apr 91	**YOU'RE SO VAIN** *Elektra EKR 123*	41		5
22 Dec 01	**SON OF A GUN (BETCHA THINK THIS SONG)** *Virgin VUSCDX 232* JANET JACKSON WITH CARLY SIMON FEATURING MISSY ELLIOTT	13		9

JOE SIMON
US, male vocalist

10

Date	Title / Label	Peak Position	Weeks at No.1	Weeks on Chart
16 Jun 73	**STEP BY STEP** *Mojo 2093 030*	14		10

PAUL SIMON
US, male vocalist/guitarist. See Simon & Garfunkel

90

Date	Title / Label	Peak Position	Weeks at No.1	Weeks on Chart
19 Feb 72	**MOTHER AND CHILD REUNION** *CBS 7793*	5		12
29 Apr 72	**ME AND JULIO DOWN BY THE SCHOOLYARD** *CBS 7964*	15		9
16 Jun 73	**TAKE ME TO THE MARDI GRAS** *CBS 1578*	7		11
22 Sep 73	**LOVES ME LIKE A ROCK** *CBS 1700*	39		5
10 Jan 76	**50 WAYS TO LEAVE YOUR LOVER** *CBS 3887* ★	23		6
3 Dec 77	**SLIP SLIDIN' AWAY** *CBS 5770*	36		5
6 Sep 80	**LATE IN THE EVENING** *Warner Brothers K 17666*	58		4
13 Sep 86	**YOU CAN CALL ME AL** *Warner Brothers W 8667* ●	4		13
13 Dec 86	**THE BOY IN THE BUBBLE** *Warner Brothers W 8509*	26		8
6 Oct 90	**THE OBVIOUS CHILD** *Warner Brothers W 9549*	15		10
9 Dec 95	**SOMETHING SO RIGHT** *RCA 74321332392* ANNIE LENNOX FEATURING PAUL SIMON	44		2
3 Jun 06	**FATHER AND DAUGHTER** *Warner Brothers W719CD*	31		5

RONNI SIMON
UK, male vocalist

2

Date	Title / Label	Peak Position	Weeks at No.1	Weeks on Chart
13 Aug 94	**B GOOD 2 ME** *Network NWKCD 80*	73		1
10 Jun 95	**TAKE YOU THERE** *Network NWKCD 85*	58		1

TITO SIMON
Jamaica, male vocalist (Keith Foster)

4

Date	Title / Label	Peak Position	Weeks at No.1	Weeks on Chart
8 Feb 75	**THIS MONDAY MORNING FEELING** *Horse HOSS 57*	45		4

SIMON & GARFUNKEL
US, male vocal/instrumental duo – Paul Simon* & Art Garfunkel*

87

Date	Title / Label	Peak Position	Weeks at No.1	Weeks on Chart
24 Mar 66	**HOMEWARD BOUND** *CBS 202045*	9		12
16 Jun 66	**I AM A ROCK** *CBS 202303*	17		10
10 Jul 68	**MRS. ROBINSON** *CBS 3443* ★	4		12
8 Jan 69	**MRS. ROBINSON (EP)** *CBS EP 6400*	9		5
30 Apr 69	**THE BOXER** *CBS 4162*	6		14
21 Feb 70	**BRIDGE OVER TROUBLED WATER** *CBS 4790* ★	1	3	20
7 Oct 72	**AMERICA** *CBS 8336*	25		7
7 Dec 91	**A HAZY SHADE OF WINTER/SILENT NIGHT/SEVEN O'CLOCK NEWS** *Columbia 6576537*	30		6
15 Feb 92	**THE BOXER** *Columbia 6578067*	75		1

SIMONE
US, male/female production/vocal group

1

Date	Title / Label	Peak Position	Weeks at No.1	Weeks on Chart
23 Nov 91	**MY FAMILY DEPENDS ON ME** *Strictly Rhythm A 8678*	75		1

NINA SIMONE
US, female vocalist/pianist (Eunice Waymon), d. 21 Apr 2003 (age 70)

62

Date	Title / Label	Peak Position	Weeks at No.1	Weeks on Chart
5 Aug 65	**I PUT A SPELL ON YOU** *Philips BF 1415*	49		1
16 Oct 68	**AIN'T GOT NO-I GOT LIFE/DO WHAT YOU GOTTA DO** *RCA 1743*	2		18
15 Jan 69	**TO LOVE SOMEBODY** *RCA 1779*	5		9
15 Jan 69	**I PUT A SPELL ON YOU** *Philips BF 1736*	28		4
31 Oct 87	**MY BABY JUST CARES FOR ME** *Charly CYZ 7112* ●	5		11
9 Jul 94	**FEELING GOOD** *Mercury MERCD 403*	40		3
29 Apr 06	**AIN'T GOT NO-I GOT LIFE** *Sony BMG TV 82876708212* VS GROOVEFINDER	30		16

VICTOR SIMONELLI PRESENTS SOLUTION
US, male/female vocal/production duo

1

Date	Title / Label	Peak Position	Weeks at No.1	Weeks on Chart
2 Nov 96	**FEELS SO RIGHT** *Soundproof MCSTD 40068*	63		1

SIMPLE KID
UK, male vocalist (Ciaran McFeely)

3

Date	Title / Label	Peak Position	Weeks at No.1	Weeks on Chart
13 Sep 03	**THE AVERAGE MAN** *2M 2M005CD*	72		1
14 Feb 04	**TRUCK ON** *2M 2M007CD*	38		2

SIMPLE MINDS
UK, male vocal/instrumental group – Jim Kerr, Charles Burchill, Mel Gaynor, John Giblin & Michael MacNeil

194

Date	Title / Label	Peak Position	Weeks at No.1	Weeks on Chart
12 May 79	**LIFE IN A DAY** *Zoom ZUM 10*	62		2
23 May 81	**THE AMERICAN** *Virgin VS 410*	59		3
15 Aug 81	**LOVE SONG** *Virgin VS 434*	47		4
7 Nov 81	**SWEAT IN A BULLET** *Virgin VS 451*	52		3
10 Apr 82	**PROMISED YOU A MIRACLE** *Virgin VS 488*	13		11
28 Aug 82	**GLITTERING PRIZE** *Virgin VS 511*	16		11
13 Nov 82	**SOMEONE SOMEWHERE (IN SUMMERTIME)** *Virgin VS 538*	36		5
26 Nov 83	**WATERFRONT** *Virgin VS 636*	13		10
28 Jan 84	**SPEED YOUR LOVE TO ME** *Virgin VS 649*	20		4
24 Mar 84	**UP ON THE CATWALK** *Virgin VS 661*	27		5
20 Apr 85	**DON'T YOU FORGET ABOUT ME** *Virgin VS 749* ● ★	7		24
12 Oct 85	**ALIVE AND KICKING** *Virgin VS 817*	7		11
1 Feb 86	**SANCTIFY YOURSELF** *Virgin SM 1*	10		7
12 Apr 86	**ALL THE THINGS SHE SAID** *Virgin VS 860*	9		9
15 Nov 86	**GHOSTDANCING** *Virgin VS 907*	13		8
20 Jun 87	**PROMISED YOU A MIRACLE** *Virgin SM 2*	19		7
18 Feb 89	**BELFAST CHILD** *Virgin SMX 3* ●	1	2	11
22 Apr 89	**THIS IS YOUR LAND** *Virgin SMX 4*	13		4
29 Jul 89	**KICK IT IN** *Virgin SM 5*	15		5
9 Dec 89	**THE AMSTERDAM EP** *Virgin SMX 6*	18		6
23 Mar 91	**LET THERE BE LOVE** *Virgin VS 1332*	6		7
25 May 91	**SEE THE LIGHTS** *Virgin VS 1343*	20		4
31 Aug 91	**STAND BY LOVE** *Virgin VS 1358*	13		4
26 Oct 91	**REAL LIFE** *Virgin VS 1382*	34		3
10 Oct 92	**LOVE SONG/ALIVE AND KICKING** *Virgin VS 1440*	6		6
28 Jan 95	**SHE'S A RIVER** *Virgin VSCDX 1509*	9		5
8 Apr 95	**HYPNOTISED** *Virgin VSCDX 1534*	18		5
14 Mar 98	**GLITTERBALL** *Chrysalis CDCHSS 5078*	18		2

Date	Title	Peak	Wks at No.1	Wks on Chart
30 May 98	**WAR BABIES** *Chrysalis CDCHSS 5088*	43		1
2 Feb 02	**BELFAST TRANCE** *Nebula BELFCD 001* JOHN 'OO' FLEMING VS SIMPLE MINDS	74		1
30 Mar 02	**CRY** *Eagle EAGXS 218*	47		1
20 Jul 02	**MONSTER** *Defected DFECT 49R* LIQUID PEOPLE VS SIMPLE MINDS	67		1
17 Sep 05	**HOME** *Sanctuary SANXS388*	41		1
8 Apr 06	**TRIBUTE TO JINKY** *Lord Of The Wing LWSP7* JIMMY JOHNSTONE, JIM KERR, SIMPLE MINDS & LAURA MCGHEE	28		3

SIMPLE PLAN
US, male vocal/instrumental group

Date	Title	Peak	Wks at No.1	10
5 Jul 03	**ADDICTED** *Lava/Atlantic AT 0158CD*	63		1
5 Mar 05	**SHUT UP** *Lava AT0195CD*	44		2
2 Jul 05	**WELCOME TO MY LIFE** *Lava AT0206CD1*	49		1
23 Feb 08	**WHEN I'M GONE** *Atlantic AT0297CDX*	26		4
26 Apr 08	**YOUR LOVE IS A LIE** *Atlantic AT0306CD*	63		2

SIMPLICIOUS
US, male/female vocal group

Date	Title	Peak	Wks at No.1	9
29 Sep 84	**LET HER FEEL IT** *Fourth & Broadway BRW 13*	65		3
2 Feb 85	**LET HER FEEL IT** *Fourth & Broadway BRW 18*	34		6

SIMPLY RED
UK, male vocal/instrumental group – Mick Hucknall; members also included Tony Bowers, Chris Joyce, Tim Kellett, Ian Kirkham, Fritz McIntyre & Sylvan Richardson. Stylish, internationally popular outfit who have graced the Top 10 for almost 25 years. 'Fairground' rode to the top with sales of almost 800,000

Date	Title	Peak	Wks at No.1	247
15 Jun 85	**MONEY'S TOO TIGHT TO MENTION** *Elektra EKR 9*	13		12
21 Sep 85	**COME TO MY AID** *Elektra EKR 19*	66		2
16 Nov 85	**HOLDING BACK THE YEARS** *Elektra EKR 29*	51		4
8 Mar 86	**JERICHO** *WEA YZ 63*	53		3
17 May 86	**HOLDING BACK THE YEARS** *WEA YZ 70* ● ★	2		13
9 Aug 86	**OPEN UP THE RED BOX** *WEA YZ 75*	61		4
14 Feb 87	**THE RIGHT THING** *WEA YZ 103*	11		10
23 May 87	**INFIDELITY** *Elektra YZ 114*	31		5
28 Nov 87	**EV'RY TIME WE SAY GOODBYE** *Elektra YZ 161*	11		9
12 Mar 88	**I WON'T FEEL BAD** *Elektra YZ 172*	68		3
28 Jan 89	**IT'S ONLY LOVE** *Elektra YZ 349*	13		8
8 Apr 89	**IF YOU DON'T KNOW ME BY NOW** *Elektra YZ 377* ● ★	2		10
8 Jul 89	**A NEW FLAME** *WEA YZ 404*	17		8
28 Oct 89	**YOU'VE GOT IT** *WEA YZ 424*	46		3
21 Sep 91	**SOMETHING GOT ME STARTED** *East West YZ 614*	11		8
30 Nov 91	**STARS** *East West YZ 626*	8		10
8 Feb 92	**FOR YOUR BABIES** *East West YZ 642*	9		8
2 May 92	**THRILL ME** *East West YZ 671*	33		5
25 Jul 92	**YOUR MIRROR** *East West YZ 689*	17		4
21 Nov 92	**MONTREAUX EP** *East West YZ 716*	11		10
30 Sep 95	**FAIRGROUND** *East West EW 001CD2* ⊛	1	4	14
16 Dec 95	**REMEMBERING THE FIRST TIME** *East West EW 015CD1*	22		6
24 Feb 96	**NEVER NEVER LOVE** *East West EW 029CD1*	18		4
22 Jun 96	**WE'RE IN THIS TOGETHER** *East West EW 046CDX*	11		6
9 Nov 96	**ANGEL** *East West EW 074CD1* ●	4		13
20 Sep 97	**NIGHT NURSE** *East West EW 129CD1* SLY & ROBBIE FEATURING SIMPLY RED	14		8
16 May 98	**SAY YOU LOVE ME** *East West EW 164CD*	7		7
22 Aug 98	**THE AIR I BREATHE** *East West EW 181CD1*	6		7
12 Dec 98	**GHETTO GIRL** *East West EW 191CD1*	34		2
30 Oct 99	**AIN'T THAT A LOT OF LOVE** *East West EW 208CD1*	14		6
19 Feb 00	**YOUR EYES** *East West EW 212CD1*	26		2
29 Mar 03	**SUNRISE** *Simplyred.com SRS 001CD*	7		11
19 Jul 03	**FAKE** *Simplyred.com SRS 002CD*	21		4
13 Dec 03	**YOU MAKE ME FEEL BRAND NEW** *Simplyred.com SRS 003CD*	7		9
10 Apr 04	**HOME** *Simplyred.com SRS 004CD*	40		2
22 Oct 05	**PERFECT LOVE** *Simplyred.com SRS005CD2*	30		3
7 Oct 06	**OH! WHAT A GIRL!** *Simplyred.com SRS007CD1*	57		1
17 Mar 07	**SO NOT OVER YOU** *Simplyred.com SRS009CD2*	34		2
9 Jun 07	**STAY** *Simplyred.com SRS010CD*	36		1

SIMPLY RED & WHITE
UK, football fans (Sunderland)/vocal group

Date	Title	Peak	Wks at No.1	4
6 Apr 96	**DAYDREAM BELIEVER (CHEER UP PETER REID)** *Ropery SHAYISGOD 1D*	41		4

SIMPLY SMOOTH
US, male/female vocal group

Date	Title	Peak	Wks at No.1	1
17 Oct 98	**LADY (YOU BRING ME UP)** *Big Bang CDBANG 07*	70		1

ASHLEE SIMPSON
US, female vocalist/actor

Date	Title	Peak	Wks at No.1	28
9 Oct 04	**PIECES OF ME** *Geffen 9863812*	4		10
5 Feb 05	**LALA** *Geffen 2103876*	11		6
11 Feb 06	**BOYFRIEND** *Geffen 9850111*	12		5
3 May 08	**OUTTA MY HEAD (AY YA YA)** *Geffen 1768688*	24		7

JESSICA SIMPSON
US, female vocalist/actor

Date	Title	Peak	Wks at No.1	46
22 Apr 00	**I WANNA LOVE YOU FOREVER** *Columbia 6691272*	7		11
15 Jul 00	**I THINK I'M IN LOVE WITH YOU** *Columbia 6695942*	15		7
14 Jul 01	**IRRESISTIBLE** *Columbia 6714102*	11		6
26 Jun 04	**WITH YOU** *Columbia 6748302*	7		8
10 Sep 05	**THESE BOOTS ARE MADE FOR WALKIN'** *Columbia 6760652*	4		10
10 Feb 07	**A PUBLIC AFFAIR** *Columbia 88697060712*	20		4

PAUL SIMPSON FEATURING ADEVA
US, male producer & female vocalist

Date	Title	Peak	Wks at No.1	8
25 Mar 89	**MUSICAL FREEDOM (MOVING ON UP)** *Cooltempo COOL 182*	22		8

VIDA SIMPSON
US, female vocalist

Date	Title	Peak	Wks at No.1	1
18 Feb 95	**OOHHH BABY** *Hi-Life HICD 6*	70		1

SIMPSONS
US, male/female TV cartoon vocal group – Bart, Homer, Lisa, Maggie & Marge Simpson (Dan Castellaneta, Nancy Cartwright, Yeardley Smith & Julie Kavner)

Date	Title	Peak	Wks at No.1	23
26 Jan 91	**DO THE BARTMAN** *Geffen GEF 87* ●	1	3	12
6 Apr 91	**DEEP DEEP TROUBLE** *Geffen GEF 88* FEATURING BART & HOMER	7		7
11 Aug 07	**SPIDER PIG** *Rhino US95X0700015*	23		4

JOYCE SIMS
US, female vocalist

Date	Title	Peak	Wks at No.1	36
19 Apr 86	**ALL AND ALL** *London LON 94*	16		10
13 Jun 87	**LIFETIME LOVE** *London LON 137*	34		6
9 Jan 88	**COME INTO MY LIFE** *London LON 161*	7		9
23 Apr 88	**WALK AWAY** *London LON 176*	24		6
17 Jun 89	**LOOKING FOR A LOVE** *ffrr F 109*	39		4
27 May 95	**COME INTO MY LIFE (REMIX)** *Club Tools 0060435 CLU*	72		1

KYM SIMS
US, female vocalist

Date	Title	Peak	Wks at No.1	23
7 Dec 91	**TOO BLIND TO SEE IT** *Atco B 8667* ●	5		12
28 Mar 92	**TAKE MY ADVICE** *Atco B 8591*	13		7
27 Jun 92	**A LITTLE BIT MORE** *Atco B 8528*	30		3
8 Jun 96	**WE GOTTA LOVE** *Pulse 8 CDLOSE 104*	58		1

SIN WITH SEBASTIAN
Germany, male vocalist (Sebastian Roth)

Date	Title	Peak	Wks at No.1	2
16 Sep 95	**SHUT UP (AND SLEEP WITH ME)** *Sing Sing 74321253592*	44		1
27 Jan 96	**SHUT UP (AND SLEEP WITH ME) (REMIX)** *Sing Sing 74321337972*	46		1

FRANK SINATRA
US, male vocalist/actor, d. 14 May 1998 (age 82). No single has spent longer on the chart than the legendary song stylist's 'My Way'. The first artist to top the UK album chart is regarded by many as 'the greatest singer of the 20th century'. 'Ol' Blue Eyes' has achieved UK singles sales of more than five million

Date	Title	Peak	Wks at No.1	440
9 Jul 54	**YOUNG AT HEART** *Capitol CL 14064*	12		1
16 Jul 54	**THREE COINS IN THE FOUNTAIN** *Capitol CL 14120*	1	3	19
10 Jun 55	**YOU MY LOVE** *Capitol CL 14240*	13		7
5 Aug 55	**LEARNIN' THE BLUES** *Capitol CL 14296* ★	2		13
2 Sep 55	**NOT AS A STRANGER** *Capitol CL 14326*	18		1
13 Jan 56	**LOVE AND MARRIAGE** *Capitol CL 14503*	3		8
20 Jan 56	**(LOVE IS) THE TENDER TRAP** *Capitol CL 14511*	2		9
15 Jun 56	**SONGS FOR SWINGING LOVERS (LP)** *Capitol LCT 6106*	12		8
22 Nov 57	**ALL THE WAY** *Capitol CL 14800*	3		19
29 Nov 57	**CHICAGO** *Capitol CL 14800*	21		1
7 Feb 58	**WITCHCRAFT** *Capitol CL 14819*	12		8
14 Nov 58	**MR SUCCESS** *Capitol CL 14956*	25		4

Date	Title	Peak Position	Weeks at No.1	Weeks on Chart
10 Apr 59	**FRENCH FOREIGN LEGION** *Capitol CL 14997*	18		5
15 May 59	**COME DANCE WITH ME (LP)** *Capitol LCT 6179*	30		1
28 Aug 59	**HIGH HOPES** *Capitol CL 15052*	6		15
7 Apr 60	**IT'S NICE TO GO TRAV'LING** *Capitol CL 15116*	48		2
16 Jun 60	**RIVER STAY 'WAY FROM MY DOOR** *Capitol CL 15135*	18		9
8 Sep 60	**NICE 'N' EASY** *Capitol CL 15150*	15		12
24 Nov 60	**OL' MACDONALD** *Capitol CL 15168*	11		8
20 Apr 61	**MY BLUE HEAVEN** *Capitol CL 15193*	33		7
28 Sep 61	**GRANADA** *Reprise R 20010*	15		8
23 Nov 61	**THE COFFEE SONG** *Reprise R 20035*	39		3
5 Apr 62	**EVERYBODY'S TWISTING** *Reprise R 20063*	22		12
13 Dec 62	**ME AND MY SHADOW** *Reprise R 20128* & SAMMY DAVIS, JR	20		9
7 Mar 63	**MY KIND OF GIRL** *Reprise R 20148* WITH COUNT BASIE	35		6
24 Sep 64	**HELLO DOLLY** *Reprise R 20351* WITH COUNT BASIE	47		1
12 May 66	**STRANGERS IN THE NIGHT** *Reprise R 23052* ★	1	3	20
29 Sep 66	**SUMMER WIND** *Reprise R 20509*	36		5
15 Dec 66	**THAT'S LIFE** *Reprise RS 20531*	44		5
23 Mar 67	**SOMETHIN' STUPID** *Reprise RS 23166* NANCY SINATRA & FRANK SINATRA ★	1	2	18
23 Aug 67	**THE WORLD WE KNEW** *Reprise R 20610*	33		11
2 Apr 69	**MY WAY** *Reprise RS 20817*	5		122
4 Oct 69	**LOVE'S BEEN GOOD TO ME** *Reprise R 20852*	8		18
6 Mar 71	**I WILL DRINK THE WINE** *Reprise R 23487*	16		12
20 Dec 75	**I BELIEVE I'M GONNA LOVE YOU** *Reprise K 14400*	34		7
9 Aug 80	**THEME FROM 'NEW YORK, NEW YORK'** *Reprise K 14502*	59		4
22 Feb 86	**THEME FROM NEW YORK, NEW YORK** *Reprise K 14502* ●	4		10
4 Dec 93	**I'VE GOT YOU UNDER MY SKIN** *Island CID 578* WITH BONO	4		9
16 Apr 94	**MY WAY** *Reprise W 0163CD*	45		2
30 Jan 99	**THEY ALL LAUGHED** *Reprise W 469CD*	41		1

Singles That Have Spent The Most Weeks On Chart

Pos	Title Artist	Weeks on Chart
1	**MY WAY** FRANK SINATRA	124
2	**CHASING CARS** SNOW PATROL	96
3	**SEX ON FIRE** KINGS OF LEON	79
4	**RULE THE WORLD** TAKE THAT	72
5	**AMAZING GRACE** JUDY COLLINS	67
6	**POKER FACE** LADY GAGA	63
7	**USE SOMEBODY** KINGS OF LEON	62
8	**RELAX** FRANKIE GOES TO HOLLYWOOD	59
9	**ROCK AROUND THE CLOCK** BILL HALEY & HIS COMETS	57
=	**RELEASE ME** ENGELBERT HUMPERDINCK	57
=	**REHAB** AMY WINEHOUSE	57
12	**STRANGER ON THE SHORE** MR ACKER BILK WITH THE LEON YOUNG STRING CHORALE	55
=	**I'M YOURS** JASON MRAZ	55
14	**BLUE MONDAY** NEW ORDER	54
15	**LOW** FLO RIDA FT T-PAIN	53
16	**MERRY XMAS EVERYBODY** SLADE	51
=	**UMBRELLA** RIHANNA FT JAY-Z	51
18	**WHATEVER** OASIS	50
=	**ROCKSTAR** NICKELBACK	50
20	**LET'S TWIST AGAIN** CHUBBY CHECKER	44
=	**LEADER OF THE PACK** SHANGRI-LAS	44
=	**TAINTED LOVE** SOFT CELL	44
=	**GOLD DIGGER** KANYE WEST FT JAMIE FOXX	44
=	**MERCY** DUFFY	44
25	**IMAGINE** JOHN LENNON	43
=	**WHITE LINES (DON'T DON'T DO IT)** GRANDMASTER FLASH & MELLE MEL	43
=	**NUMB/ENCORE** JAY-Z VS LINKIN PARK	43
=	**VIVA LA VIDA** COLDPLAY	43
29	**HOW TO SAVE A LIFE** FRAY	42
=	**SHINE** TAKE THAT	42
=	**APOLOGIZE** TIMBALAND PRESENTS ONEREPUBLIC	42
=	**SINGLE LADIES (PUT A RING ON IT)** BEYONCE	42
=	**JUST DANCE** LADY GAGA	42
=	**I GOTTA FEELING** BLACK EYED PEAS	42
35	**DECK OF CARDS** WINK MARTINDALE	41
=	**(IS THIS THE WAY TO) AMARILLO?** TONY CHRISTIE	41
=	**SHE'S SO LOVELY** SCOUTING FOR GIRLS	41
38	**A SCOTTISH SOLDIER** ANDY STEWART WITH THE MICHAEL SAMMES SINGERS	40
=	**TIE A YELLOW RIBBON ROUND THE OLD OAK TREE** DAWN FT TONY ORLANDO	40
=	**RIVERS OF BABYLON/BROWN GIRL IN THE RING** BONEY M	40
=	**FAIRYTALE OF NEW YORK** POGUES FT KIRSTY MacCOLL	40
=	**THREE LIONS** BADDIEL & SKINNER & LIGHTNING SEEDS	40
=	**I LIKE THE WAY** BODYROCKERS	40
=	**YOU'RE BEAUTIFUL** JAMES BLUNT	40
=	**PATIENCE** TAKE THAT	40
=	**GRACE KELLY** MIKA	40
47	**JAILHOUSE ROCK** ELVIS PRESLEY	39
=	**I LOVE YOU BECAUSE** JIM REEVES	39
=	**FEEL GOOD INC** GORILLAZ	39
=	**EVERYTIME WE TOUCH** CASCADA	39
=	**VALERIE** MARK RONSON FT AMY WINEHOUSE	39
=	**BLACK & GOLD** SAM SPARRO	39
=	**DANCE WIV ME** DIZZEE RASCAL FT CALVIN HARRIS & CHROME	39

NANCY SINATRA

US, female vocalist — 117

Date	Title / Label	Peak	Wks at No.1	Wks on Chart
27 Jan 66	**THESE BOOTS ARE MADE FOR WALKIN'** *Reprise R 20432* ★	1	4	14
28 Apr 66	**HOW DOES THAT GRAB YOU DARLIN'** *Reprise R 20461*	19		8
19 Jan 67	**SUGAR TOWN** *Reprise RS 20527*	8		10
23 Mar 67	**SOMETHIN' STUPID** *Reprise RS 23166* & FRANK SINATRA ★	1	2	18
5 Jul 67	**YOU ONLY LIVE TWICE/JACKSON** *Reprise RS 20595* NANCY SINATRA/ NANCY SINATRA & LEE HAZLEWOOD	11		19
8 Nov 67	**LADYBIRD** *Reprise RS 20629* & LEE HAZLEWOOD	47		1
29 Nov 69	**THE HIGHWAY SONG** *Reprise RS 20869*	21		10
21 Aug 71	**DID YOU EVER** *Reprise K 14093* & LEE HAZLEWOOD	2		19
23 Oct 04	**LET ME KISS YOU** *Attack ATKXS005*	46		1
4 Jun 05	**SHOT YOU DOWN** *Source SOURCDX111* AUDIO BULLYS FEATURING NANCY SINATRA	3		17

SINCLAIR

UK, male vocalist (Mike Sinclair) — 8

Date	Title / Label	Peak	Wks at No.1	Wks on Chart
21 Aug 93	**AIN'T NO CASANOVA** *Dome CDDOME 1004*	28		5
26 Feb 94	**(I WANNA KNOW) WHY** *Dome CDDOME 1009*	58		2
6 Aug 94	**DON'T LIE** *Dome CDDOME 1010*	70		1

BOB SINCLAR

France, male DJ/producer — 61

Date	Title / Label	Peak	Wks at No.1	Wks on Chart
20 Mar 99	**MY ONLY LOVE** *East West EW 196CD* FEATURING LEE A GENESIS	56		1
19 Aug 00	**I FEEL FOR YOU** *Defected DFECT 18CDS*	9		5
7 Apr 01	**DARLIN'** *Defected DFECT 30CDS* FEATURING JAMES WILLIAMS	46		1
25 Jan 03	**THE BEAT GOES ON** *Defected DFTD 062CDS*	33		2
2 Aug 03	**KISS MY EYES** *Defected DFTD 070CDX*	67		1
22 Oct 05	**LOVE GENERATION** *Defected DFTD111CDX* FEATURING GARY NESTA PINE	12		17
15 Jul 06	**WORLD, HOLD ON (CHILDREN OF THE SKY)** *Defected DFTD132CDX* FEATURING STEVE EDWARDS	9		12
7 Oct 06	**ROCK THIS PARTY (EVERYBODY DANCE NOW)** *Defected DFTD142CDX* & CUTEE B	3		15
9 Jun 07	**SOUND OF FREEDOM** *Defected DFTD157CDS* BOB SINCLAIR, CUTEE B & DOLLARMAN	14		4
9 Aug 08	**WHAT I WANT** *Hard2Beat H2B10CDX* PRESENTS FIREBALL	52		2
11 Oct 08	**WHAT A WONDERFUL WORLD** *Defected/ Positiva CDTIV275* AXWELL & BOB SINCLAR FEATURING RON CARROLL	48		1

SINDY

UK, female doll vocalist — 1

Date	Title / Label	Peak	Wks at No.1	Wks on Chart
5 Oct 96	**SATURDAY NIGHT** *Love This LUVTHISCD 13*	70		1

SINE

US, male/female vocal/instrumental group — 9

Date	Title / Label	Peak	Wks at No.1	Wks on Chart
10 Jun 78	**JUST LET ME DO MY THING** *CBS 6351*	33		9

SINGING CORNER MEETS DONOVAN

UK, male vocal/comedy duo — 1

Date	Title / Label	Peak	Wks at No.1	Wks on Chart
1 Dec 90	**JENNIFER JUNIPER** *Fontana SYP 1*	68		1

DON CHARLES PRESENTS THE SINGING DOGS

Denmark, dog vocalists — 4

Date	Title / Label	Peak	Wks at No.1	Wks on Chart
25 Nov 55	**THE SINGING DOGS (MEDLEY)/OH SUSANNA** *Nixa N 15009*	13		4

SINGING NUN

Belgium, female vocalist/guitarist (Jeanine Deckers), d. 31 Mar 1985 (age 51) — 14

Date	Title / Label	Peak	Wks at No.1	Wks on Chart
5 Dec 63	**DOMINIQUE** *Philips BF 1293* ★	7		14

SINGING SHEEP

UK, synthesized sheep 'vocalists' (produced by Jeff Mutton aka Richard Branson) — 5

Date	Title / Label	Peak	Wks at No.1	Wks on Chart
18 Dec 82	**BAA BAA BLACK SHEEP** *Sheep BAA 1*	42		5

MAXINE SINGLETON

US, female vocalist — 3

Date	Title / Label	Peak	Wks at No.1	Wks on Chart
2 Apr 83	**YOU CAN'T RUN FROM LOVE** *Creole CR 50*	57		3

SINITTA

UK (b. US), female vocalist (Sinitta Malone) — 104

Date	Title / Label	Peak	Wks at No.1	Wks on Chart
8 Mar 86	**SO MACHO/CRUISING** *Fanfare FAN 7* ●	2		28
11 Oct 86	**FEELS LIKE THE FIRST TIME** *Fanfare FAN 8*	45		5
25 Jul 87	**TOY BOY** *Fanfare FAN 12* ○	4		14
12 Dec 87	**G.T.O.** *Fanfare FAN 14*	15		9
19 Mar 88	**CROSS MY BROKEN HEART** *Fanfare FAN 15* ○	6		9
24 Sep 88	**I DON'T BELIEVE IN MIRACLES** *Fanfare FAN 16*	22		8
3 Jun 89	**RIGHT BACK WHERE WE STARTED FROM** *Fanfare FAN 18* ○	4		10
7 Oct 89	**LOVE ON A MOUNTAIN TOP** *Fanfare FAN 21*	20		6
21 Apr 90	**HITCHIN' A RIDE** *Fanfare FAN 24*	24		6
22 Sep 90	**LOVE AND AFFECTION** *Fanfare FAN 31*	62		3
4 Jul 92	**SHAME SHAME SHAME** *Arista 74321100327*	28		4
17 Apr 93	**THE SUPREME EP** *Arista 74321139592*	49		2

SINNAMON

US, male vocal/instrumental group — 1

Date	Title / Label	Peak	Wks at No.1	Wks on Chart
28 Sep 96	**I NEED YOU NOW** *Worx WORXCD 003*	70		1

SIOUXSIE & THE BANSHEES

UK, male/female vocal/instrumental group – Susan 'Siouxsie' Ballion, Peter 'Budgie' Clark, Steve Severin & various musicians — 151

Date	Title / Label	Peak	Wks at No.1	Wks on Chart
26 Aug 78	**HONG KONG GARDEN** *Polydor 2059 052* ○	7		10
31 Mar 79	**THE STAIRCASE (MYSTERY)** *Polydor POSP 9*	24		8
7 Jul 79	**PLAYGROUND TWIST** *Polydor POSP 59*	28		6
29 Sep 79	**MITTAGEISEN (METAL POSTCARD)** *Polydor 2059 151*	47		3
15 Mar 80	**HAPPY HOUSE** *Polydor POSP 117*	17		8
7 Jun 80	**CHRISTINE** *Polydor 2059 249*	22		8
6 Dec 80	**ISRAEL** *Polydor POSP 205*	41		8
30 May 81	**SPELLBOUND** *Polydor POSP 273*	22		8
1 Aug 81	**ARABIAN KNIGHTS** *Polydor PSOP 309*	32		7
29 May 82	**FIRE WORKS** *Polydor POSPG 450*	22		6
9 Oct 82	**SLOWDIVE** *Polydor POSP 510*	41		4
4 Dec 82	**MELT/IL EST NE LE DIVIN ENFANT** *Polydor POSP 539*	49		5
1 Oct 83	**DEAR PRUDENCE** *Wonderland SHE 4* ○	3		8
24 Mar 84	**SWIMMING HORSES** *Wonderland SHE 6*	28		4
2 Jun 84	**DAZZLE** *Wonderland SHE 7*	33		3
27 Oct 84	**THE THORN EP** *Wonderland SHE 8*	47		3
26 Oct 85	**CITIES IN DUST** *Wonderland SHE 9*	21		6
8 Mar 86	**CANDYMAN** *Wonderland SHE 10*	34		5
17 Jan 87	**THIS WHEEL'S ON FIRE** *Wonderland SHE 11*	14		6
28 Mar 87	**THE PASSENGER** *Wonderland SHE 12*	41		6
25 Jul 87	**SONG FROM THE EDGE OF THE WORLD** *Wonderland SHE 13*	59		3
30 Jul 88	**PEEK-A-BOO** *Wonderland SHE 14*	16		6
8 Oct 88	**THE KILLING JAR** *Wonderland SHE 15*	41		3
3 Dec 88	**THE LAST BEAT OF MY HEART** *Wonderland SHE 16*	44		1
25 May 91	**KISS THEM FOR ME** *Wonderland SHE 19*	32		4
13 Jul 91	**SHADOWTIME** *Wonderland SHE 20*	57		1
25 Jul 92	**FACE TO FACE** *Wonderland SHE 21*	21		4
20 Aug 94	**INTERLUDE** *Parlophone CDR 6365* MORRISSEY & SIOUXSIE	25		2
7 Jan 95	**O BABY** *Wonderland SHECD 22*	34		3
18 Feb 95	**STARGAZER** *Wonderland SHECD 23*	64		1
15 Sep 07	**INTO A SWAN** *W14 1742056* SIOUXSIE	59		1

SIR DOUGLAS QUINTET

US, male vocal/instrumental group — 10

Date	Title / Label	Peak	Wks at No.1	Wks on Chart
17 Jun 65	**SHE'S ABOUT A MOVER** *London HLU 9964*	15		10

SIR KILLALOT VS ROBO BABE

UK, male robot rapper & female vocalist — 3

Date	Title / Label	Peak	Wks at No.1	Wks on Chart
30 Dec 00	**ROBOT WARS (ANDROID LOVE)** *Polydor 5879362*	51		3

SIR MIX-A-LOT

US, male rapper (Anthony Ray) — 2

Date	Title / Label	Peak	Wks at No.1	Wks on Chart
8 Aug 92	**BABY GOT BACK** *Def American DEFA 20* ★	56		2

SIRENS

UK, female vocal group — 1

Date	Title / Label	Peak	Wks at No.1	Wks on Chart
28 Aug 04	**BABY (OFF THE WALL)** *Kitchenware SKCD742*	49		1

SISQO

US, male vocalist/producer/actor (Mark Andrews). See Dru Hill — 43

Date	Title / Label	Peak	Wks at No.1	Wks on Chart
12 Feb 00	**GOT TO GET IT** *Def Soul 5626442*	14		4

Date	Title	Peak Position	Weeks at No.1	Weeks on Chart
22 Apr 00	**THONG SONG** *Def Soul 5688902* ○	3		14
30 Sep 00	**UNLEASH THE DRAGON** *Def Soul 5726432*	6		7
16 Dec 00	**INCOMPLETE** *Def Soul 5727542* ★	13		8
28 Jul 01	**DANCE FOR ME** *Def Soul 5887002*	6		10

SISTER BLISS

UK, female producer (Ayalah Bentovim). See Faithless — 11

Date	Title	Peak Position	Weeks at No.1	Weeks on Chart
15 Oct 94	**CANTGETAMAN CANTGETAJOB (LIFE'S A BITCH)** *Go! Beat GODCD 124* WITH COLETTE	31		4
15 Jul 95	**OH! WHAT A WORLD** *Go! Beat GODCD 126* WITH COLETTE	40		2
29 Jun 96	**BADMAN** *Junk Dog JDOGCD 1*	51		1
7 Oct 00	**SISTER SISTER** *Multiply CDMULTY 68*	34		2
24 Mar 01	**DELIVER ME** *Multiply CXMULTY 72* FEATURING JOHN MARTYN	31		2

SISTER SLEDGE

US, female vocal group – Debbie, Joni, Kathy* & Kim Sledge — 111

Date	Title	Peak Position	Weeks at No.1	Weeks on Chart
21 Jun 75	**MAMA NEVER TOLD ME** *Atlantic K 10619*	20		6
17 Mar 79	**HE'S THE GREATEST DANCER** *Cotillion K 11257*	6		11
26 May 79	**WE ARE FAMILY** *Cotillion K 11293*	8		10
11 Aug 79	**LOST IN MUSIC** *Cotillion K 11337*	17		10
19 Jan 80	**GOT TO LOVE SOMEBODY** *Cotillion K 11404*	34		4
28 Feb 81	**ALL AMERICAN GIRLS** *Atlantic K 11656*	41		5
26 May 84	**THINKING OF YOU** *Cotillion B 9744*	11		13
8 Sep 84	**LOST IN MUSIC (REMIX)** *Cotillion B 9718* ○	4		12
17 Nov 84	**WE ARE FAMILY (REMIX)** *Cotillion B 9692*	33		4
1 Jun 85	**FRANKIE** *Atlantic A 9547* ●	1	4	16
31 Aug 85	**DANCING ON THE JAGGED EDGE** *Atlantic A 9520*	50		3
23 Jan 93	**WE ARE FAMILY (2ND REMIX)** *Atlantic A 4508CD*	5		8
13 Mar 93	**LOST IN MUSIC (2ND REMIX)** *Atlantic A 4509CD*	14		5
12 Jun 93	**THINKING OF YOU (REMIX)** *Atlantic A 4515CD*	17		4

SISTER 2 SISTER

Australia, female vocal duo — 5

Date	Title	Peak Position	Weeks at No.1	Weeks on Chart
22 Apr 00	**SISTER** *Mushroom MUSH 70CDS*	18		4
28 Oct 00	**WHAT'S A GIRL TO DO** *Mushroom MUSH 76CDS*	61		1

SISTERS OF MERCY

UK/US, male/female vocal/instrumental group – Andrew Eldritch; varying line-ups included Craig Adams, Tim Bricheno, Andreas Bruhn, Wayne Hussey, Tony James, Gary Marx & Patricia Morrison — 40

Date	Title	Peak Position	Weeks at No.1	Weeks on Chart
16 Jun 84	**BODY AND SOUL/TRAIN** *Merciful Release MR 029*	46		3
20 Oct 84	**WALK AWAY** *Merciful Release MR 033*	45		3
9 Mar 85	**NO TIME TO CRY** *Merciful Release MR 035*	63		2
3 Oct 87	**THIS CORROSION** *Merciful Release MR 39*	7		6
27 Feb 88	**DOMINION** *Merciful Release MR 43*	13		6
18 Jun 88	**LUCRETIA MY REFLECTION** *Merciful Release MR 45*	20		4
13 Oct 90	**MORE** *Merciful Release MR 47*	14		4
22 Dec 90	**DOCTOR JEEP** *Merciful Release MR 51*	37		4
2 May 92	**TEMPLE OF LOVE** *Merciful Release MR 53*	3		5
28 Aug 93	**UNDER THE GUN** *Merciful Release MR 59CDX*	19		3

SIVUCA

Brazil, male guitarist/keyboard player (Severino Dias de Oliveira), d. 14 Dec 2006 (age 76) — 3

Date	Title	Peak Position	Weeks at No.1	Weeks on Chart
28 Jul 84	**AIN'T NO SUNSHINE** *London LON 51*	56		3

SIX BY SEVEN

UK, male vocal/instrumental group — 2

Date	Title	Peak Position	Weeks at No.1	Weeks on Chart
9 May 98	**CANDLELIGHT** *Mantra MNT 34CD*	70		1
2 Mar 02	**IOU LOVE** *Mantra MNT 68CD1*	48		1

6 BY SIX

UK, male instrumental/production duo — 1

Date	Title	Peak Position	Weeks at No.1	Weeks on Chart
4 May 96	**INTO YOUR HEART** *Six6 SIXCD 130*	51		1

SIX CHIX

UK, female vocal group — 1

Date	Title	Peak Position	Weeks at No.1	Weeks on Chart
26 Feb 00	**ONLY THE WOMEN KNOW** *EMI CDCHIX 001*	72		1

666

Germany, male production duo — 5

Date	Title	Peak Position	Weeks at No.1	Weeks on Chart
3 Oct 98	**ALARMA** *Danceteria CDDAN 001*	58		1
25 Nov 00	**DEVIL** *Echo ECSCD 102*	18		4

SIXPENCE NONE THE RICHER

US, female/male vocal/instrumental group – Leigh Nash, Dale Baker, Justin Cary, Sean Kelly & Matt Slocum — 17

Date	Title	Peak Position	Weeks at No.1	Weeks on Chart
29 May 99	**KISS ME** *Elektra E 3750CD* ○	4		12
18 Sep 99	**THERE SHE GOES** *Elektra E 3728CD*	14		5

60FT DOLLS

UK, male vocal/instrumental group — 4

Date	Title	Peak Position	Weeks at No.1	Weeks on Chart
3 Feb 96	**STAY** *Indolent DOLLS 002CD*	48		1
11 May 96	**TALK TO ME** *Indolent DOLLS 003CD*	37		1
20 Jul 96	**HAPPY SHOPPER** *Indolent DOLLS 005CD*	38		1
9 May 98	**ALISON'S ROOM** *Indolent DOLLS 007CD1*	61		1

SIZE 9

UK, male producer (Josh Wink) — 4

Date	Title	Peak Position	Weeks at No.1	Weeks on Chart
17 Jun 95	**I'M READY** *Virgin America VUSCD 92*	52		1
11 Nov 95	**I'M READY** *VC Recordings VCRD 2* JOSH WINK'S SIZE 9	30		3

RONI SIZE/REPRAZENT

UK, male male/female vocal/instrumental/production group — 32

Date	Title	Peak Position	Weeks at No.1	Weeks on Chart
14 Jun 97	**SHARE THE FALL** *Talkin Loud TLCD 21*	37		2
13 Sep 97	**HEROES** *Talkin Loud TLCD 25*	31		2
15 Nov 97	**BROWN PAPER BAG** *Talkin Loud TLCD 28*	20		3
14 Mar 98	**WATCHING WINDOWS** *Talkin Loud TLCD 31*	28		2
7 Oct 00	**WHO TOLD YOU** *Talkin Loud TLCD 61*	17		3
24 Mar 01	**DIRTY BEATS** *Talkin Loud TLCDD 63*	32		3
23 Jun 01	**LUCKY PRESSURE** *Talkin Loud TLCD 64*	58		1
19 Oct 02	**SOUND ADVICE** *Full Cycle FCY 044* RONI SIZE	69		1
9 Nov 02	**PLAYTIME** *Full Cycle FCY 045* RONI SIZE	53		2
7 Dec 02	**SCRAMBLED EGGS/SWINGS & ROUNDABOUTS** *Full Cycle FCY 046* RONI SIZE	57		1
18 Jan 03	**FEEL THE HEAT** *Full Cycle FCY 048* RONI SIZE	55		1
22 Feb 03	**SNAPSHOT 3/SORRY FOR YOU** *Full Cycle FCY 033* RONI SIZE	61		1
12 Jul 03	**SIREN SOUNDS/AT THE MOVIES** *Full Cycle FCY 054* RONI SIZE	67		1
6 Sep 03	**SOUND ADVICE/FORGET ME KNOTS** *Full Cycle FCY 056* RONI SIZE	61		1
17 Apr 04	**STRICTLY SOCIAL/AUTUMN** *Liquid V LQD001* RONI SIZE	70		1
24 Apr 04	**BAMBAKITA/FASSY HOLE** *V Recordings V045* RONI SIZE	60		1
9 Oct 04	**OUT OF BREATH** *V VRECUK002X* RONI SIZE FEATURING RAHZEL	44		2
22 Jan 05	**NO MORE** *V VRECSUK003CD* RONI SIZE FEATURING BEVERLEY KNIGHT	26		4

SIZZLA

Jamaica, male rapper (Miguel Collins) — 2

Date	Title	Peak Position	Weeks at No.1	Weeks on Chart
17 Apr 99	**RAIN SHOWERS** *Xterminator EXTCDS 76*	51		2

SKANDAL

UK, male vocal group — 1

Date	Title	Peak Position	Weeks at No.1	Weeks on Chart
14 Oct 00	**CHAMPAGNE HIGHWAY** *Prestige Management CDGING 1*	53		1

SKANDI GIRLS

Sweden/Norway/Finland, female vocal group — 3

Date	Title	Peak Position	Weeks at No.1	Weeks on Chart
25 Dec 04	**DO THE CAN CAN** *Intelligent IR001CDX*	38		3

SKATALITES

Jamaica, male vocal instrumental group — 6

Date	Title	Peak Position	Weeks at No.1	Weeks on Chart
20 Apr 67	**GUNS OF NAVARONE** *Island WI 168*	36		6

SKEE-LO

US, male rapper (Antoine Roundtree) — 10

Date	Title	Peak Position	Weeks at No.1	Weeks on Chart
9 Dec 95	**I WISH** *Wild Card 5777752*	15		8
27 Apr 96	**TOP OF THE STAIRS** *Wild Card 5763352*	38		2

Silver-selling ● Gold-selling ● Platinum-selling (x multiples) ⊛ US No.1 ★ Peak Position · Weeks at No.1 · Weeks on Chart

PETER SKELLERN
UK, male vocalist/keyboard player — 24

Date	Title	Peak Position	Weeks at No.1	Weeks on Chart
23 Sep 72	**YOU'RE A LADY** *Decca F 13333*	3		11
29 Mar 75	**HOLD ON TO LOVE** *Decca F 13568*	14		9
28 Oct 78	**LOVE IS THE SWEETEST THING** *Mercury 6008 603* FEATURING GRIMETHORPE COLLIERY BAND	60		4

SKEPTA
UK, male vocalist/DJ/producer (Joseph Adenuga) — 4

Date	Title	Peak Position	Weeks at No.1	Weeks on Chart
28 Mar 09	**SUNGLASSES AT NIGHT** *GBSYA0900003*	64		1
27 Mar 10	**BAD BOY** *Boy Betta Know JMECD033*	35		3+

SKID ROW
US, male vocal/instrumental group — 27

Date	Title	Peak Position	Weeks at No.1	Weeks on Chart
18 Nov 89	**YOUTH GONE WILD** *Atlantic A 8935*	42		3
3 Feb 90	**18 AND LIFE** *Atlantic A 8883*	12		6
31 Mar 90	**I REMEMBER YOU** *East West A 8836*	36		4
15 Jun 91	**MONKEY BUSINESS** *Atlantic A 7673*	19		3
14 Sep 91	**SLAVE TO THE GRIND** *Atlantic A 7603*	43		2
23 Nov 91	**WASTED TIME** *Atlantic A 7570*	20		3
29 Aug 92	**YOUTH GONE WILD/DELIVERING THE GOODS** *Atlantic A 7444*	22		4
18 Nov 95	**BREAKIN' DOWN** *Atlantic A 7135CD1*	48		2

SKIDS
UK, male vocal/instrumental group – Richard Jobson, Stuart Adamson, d. 16 Dec 2001, Mike Baillie, Tom Kellichan & Bill Simpson (replaced by Russell Webb) — 60

Date	Title	Peak Position	Weeks at No.1	Weeks on Chart
23 Sep 78	**SWEET SUBURBIA** *Virgin VS 227*	70		3
4 Nov 78	**THE SAINTS ARE COMING** *Virgin VS 232*	48		3
17 Feb 79	**INTO THE VALLEY** *Virgin VS 241*	10		11
26 May 79	**MASQUERADE** *Virgin VS 262*	14		9
29 Sep 79	**CHARADE** *Virgin VS 288*	31		6
24 Nov 79	**WORKING FOR THE YANKEE DOLLAR** *Virgin VS 306*	20		11
1 Mar 80	**ANIMATION** *Virgin VS 323*	56		3
16 Aug 80	**CIRCUS GAMES** *Virgin VS 359*	32		7
18 Oct 80	**GOODBYE CIVILIAN** *Virgin VS 373*	52		4
6 Dec 80	**WOMAN IN WINTER** *Virgin VSK 101*	49		3

SKIN
UK/Germany, male vocal/instrumental group — 19

Date	Title	Peak Position	Weeks at No.1	Weeks on Chart
25 Dec 93	**THE SKIN UP (EP)** *Parlophone CDR 6363*	67		2
12 Mar 94	**HOUSE OF LOVE** *Parlophone CDR 6374*	45		2
30 Apr 94	**MONEY/UNBELIEVABLE** *Parlophone CDRS 6381*	18		3
23 Jul 94	**TOWER OF STRENGTH** *Parlophone CDRS 6387*	19		3
15 Oct 94	**LOOK BUT DON'T TOUCH (EP)** *Parlophone CDRS 6391*	33		3
20 May 95	**TAKE ME DOWN TO THE RIVER** *Parlophone CDRS 6409*	26		2
23 Mar 96	**HOW LUCKY YOU ARE** *Parlophone CDR 6425*	32		2
18 May 96	**PERFECT DAY** *Parlophone CDR 6433*	33		2

SKIN
UK, female vocalist (Deborah Dyer). See Skunk Anansie — 4

Date	Title	Peak Position	Weeks at No.1	Weeks on Chart
20 Jul 02	**GOOD TIMES** *Columbia 6727672* ED CASE & SKIN	49		1
7 Jun 03	**TRASHED** *EMI CDEM 622*	30		2
20 Sep 03	**FAITHFULNESS** *EMI CDEM 624*	64		1

SKIN UP
UK, male producer (Jason Cohen) — 8

Date	Title	Peak Position	Weeks at No.1	Weeks on Chart
7 Sep 91	**IVORY** *Love EVOL 4*	48		2
14 Mar 92	**A JUICY RED APPLE** *Love EVOL 11*	32		4
18 Jul 92	**ACCELERATE** *Love EVOL 17*	45		2

SKINNY
UK, male vocal/instrumental/production duo — 2

Date	Title	Peak Position	Weeks at No.1	Weeks on Chart
11 Apr 98	**FAILURE** *Cheeky CHEKCD 023*	31		2

SKIP RAIDERS FEATURING JADA
UK, male/female vocal/DJ/production trio — 1

Date	Title	Peak Position	Weeks at No.1	Weeks on Chart
15 Jul 00	**ANOTHER DAY** *Perfecto PERF 4CDS*	46		1

SKIPWORTH & TURNER
US, male vocal/instrumental duo — 12

Date	Title	Peak Position	Weeks at No.1	Weeks on Chart
27 Apr 85	**THINKING ABOUT YOUR LOVE** *Fourth & Broadway BRW 23*	24		10
21 Jan 89	**MAKE IT LAST** *Fourth & Broadway BRW 118*	60		2

SKUNK ANANSIE
UK, female/male vocal/instrumental group — 41

Date	Title	Peak Position	Weeks at No.1	Weeks on Chart
25 Mar 95	**SELLING JESUS** *One Little Indian 101 TP7CD*	46		1
17 Jun 95	**I CAN DREAM** *One Little Indian 121 TP7CD*	41		2
2 Sep 95	**CHARITY** *One Little Indian 131 TP7CD*	40		2
27 Jan 96	**WEAK** *One Little Indian 141 TP7CD*	20		5
27 Apr 96	**CHARITY** *One Little Indian 151 TP7CD*	20		3
28 Sep 96	**ALL I WANT** *One Little Indian 161 TP7CD*	14		4
30 Nov 96	**TWISTED (EVERYDAY HURTS)** *One Little Indian 171 TP7CDL*	26		4
1 Feb 97	**HEDONISM (JUST BECAUSE YOU FEEL GOOD)** *One Little Indian 181 TP7CD*	13		6
14 Jun 97	**BRAZEN 'WEEP'** *One Little Indian 191 TP7CD1*	11		5
13 Mar 99	**CHARLIE BIG POTATO** *Virgin VSCDT 1725*	17		3
22 May 99	**SECRETLY** *Virgin VSCDT 1733*	16		4
7 Aug 99	**LATELY** *Virgin VSCDT 1738*	33		2

SKY
UK/Australia, male instrumental group – John Williams*, Herbie Flowers, Tristan Fry, Francis Monkman & Kevin Peek — 11

Date	Title	Peak Position	Weeks at No.1	Weeks on Chart
5 Apr 80	**TOCCATA** *Ariola ARO 300*	5		11

SKYHOOKS
Australia, male vocal/instrumental group — 1

Date	Title	Peak Position	Weeks at No.1	Weeks on Chart
9 Jun 79	**WOMEN IN UNIFORM** *United Artists UP 36508*	73		1

SKYLARK
UK/France, male DJ/production group — 1

Date	Title	Peak Position	Weeks at No.1	Weeks on Chart
27 Mar 04	**THAT'S MORE LIKE IT** *Credence CDCRED042*	62		1

SLACKER
UK, male production duo. See Ramp — 4

Date	Title	Peak Position	Weeks at No.1	Weeks on Chart
26 Apr 97	**SCARED** *XL Recordings XLS 84CD*	36		2
30 Aug 97	**YOUR FACE** *XL Recordings XLS 87CD*	33		2

SLADE
UK, male vocal/instrumental group – Noddy Holder, Dave Hill, Jimmy Lea & Don Powell. Flamboyant 1970s superstars who were the first act to have three singles debut at No.1. They have had a record 12 separate entries for their million-selling Christmas classic, which was recorded on a hot summer's day in New York — 296

Date	Title	Peak Position	Weeks at No.1	Weeks on Chart
19 Jun 71	**GET DOWN AND GET WITH IT** *Polydor 2058 112*	16		14
30 Oct 71	**COZ I LUV YOU** *Polydor 2058 155*	1	4	15
5 Feb 72	**LOOK WOT YOU DUN** *Polydor 2058 195*	4		10
3 Jun 72	**TAKE ME BAK 'OME** *Polydor 2058 231*	1	1	13
2 Sep 72	**MAMA WEER ALL CRAZEE NOW** *Polydor 2058 274*	1	3	10
25 Nov 72	**GUDBUY T' JANE** *Polydor 2058 312*	2		13
3 Mar 73	**CUM ON FEEL THE NOIZE** *Polydor 2058 339*	1	4	12
30 Jun 73	**SKWEEZE ME PLEEZE ME** *Polydor 2058 377* ●	1	3	10
6 Oct 73	**MY FREND STAN** *Polydor 2058 407* ●	2		8
15 Dec 73	**MERRY XMAS EVERYBODY** *Polydor 2058 422* ⊛	1	5	9
6 Apr 74	**EVERYDAY** *Polydor 2058 453* ●	3		7
6 Jul 74	**THE BANGIN' MAN** *Polydor 2058 492*	3		7
19 Oct 74	**FAR FAR AWAY** *Polydor 2058 522* ●	2		6
15 Feb 75	**HOW DOES IT FEEL** *Polydor 2058 547*	15		7
17 May 75	**THANKS FOR THE MEMORY (WHAM BAM THANK YOU MAM)** *Polydor 2058 585*	7		7
22 Nov 75	**IN FOR A PENNY** *Polydor 2058 663*	11		8
7 Feb 76	**LET'S CALL IT QUITS** *Polydor 2058 690*	11		7
5 Feb 77	**GYPSY ROAD HOG** *Barn 2014 105*	48		2
29 Oct 77	**MY BABY LEFT ME – THAT'S ALL RIGHT (MEDLEY)** *Barn 2014 114*	32		4
18 Oct 80	**SLADE LIVE AT READING '80 (EP)** *Cheapskate CHEAP 5*	44		5
27 Dec 80	**MERRY XMAS EVERYBODY** *Cheapskate CHEAP 11* & THE READING CHOIR	70		2
31 Jan 81	**WE'LL BRING THE HOUSE DOWN** *Cheapskate CHEAPO 16*	10		9
4 Apr 81	**WHEELS AIN'T COMING DOWN** *Cheapskate CHEAPO 21*	60		3
19 Sep 81	**LOCK UP YOUR DAUGHTERS** *RCA 124*	29		8
19 Dec 81	**MERRY XMAS EVERYBODY** *Polydor 2058 422*	32		4
27 Mar 82	**RUBY RED** *RCA 191*	51		3
27 Nov 82	**(AND NOW – THE WALTZ) C'EST LA VIE** *RCA 291*	50		6
25 Dec 82	**MERRY XMAS EVERYBODY** *Polydor 2058 422*	67		3

○ Silver-selling ● Gold-selling ✪ Platinum-selling (x multiples) ★ US No.1 — Peak Position | Weeks at No.1 | Weeks on Chart

Date	Title / Label	Peak Position	Weeks at No.1	Weeks on Chart
19 Nov 83	**MY OH MY** *RCA 373* ●	2		11
10 Dec 83	**MERRY XMAS EVERYBODY** *Polydor 2058 422*	20		5
4 Feb 84	**RUN RUN AWAY** *RCA 385*	7		10
17 Nov 84	**ALL JOIN HANDS** *RCA 455*	15		9
15 Dec 84	**MERRY XMAS EVERYBODY** *Polydor 2058 422*	47		4
26 Jan 85	**7 YEAR BITCH** *RCA 475*	60		3
23 Mar 85	**MYZSTERIOUS MIZSTER JONES** *RCA PB 40027*	50		5
30 Nov 85	**DO YOU BELIEVE IN MIRACLES** *RCA PB 40449*	54		6
21 Dec 85	**MERRY XMAS EVERYBODY** *Polydor POSP 780*	48		3
27 Dec 86	**MERRY XMAS EVERYBODY** *Polydor POSP 780*	71		1
21 Feb 87	**STILL THE SAME** *RCA PB 41137*	73		2
19 Oct 91	**RADIO WALL OF SOUND** *Polydor PO 180*	21		5
26 Dec 98	**MERRY XMAS EVERYBODY '98 REMIX** *Polydor 5633532* VS FLUSH	30		3
9 Dec 06	**MERRY XMAS EVERYBODY** *Universal TV 1713754*	21		5
15 Dec 07	**MERRY XMAS EVERYBODY** *Universal TV 1713754*	20		4
13 Dec 08	**MERRY XMAS EVERYBODY** *Universal TV 1713754*	32		4
12 Dec 09	**MERRY XMAS EVERYBODY** *Universal TV 1713754*	35		4

SLAM
UK, male production duo — 4

Date	Title / Label	Peak Position	Weeks at No.1	Weeks on Chart
17 Feb 01	**POSITIVE EDUCATION** *VC Recordings VCRD 84*	44		2
17 Mar 01	**NARCO TOURISTS** *Soma 100CD* VS UNKLE	66		1
7 Jul 01	**LIFETIMES** *Soma 107CDS* FEATURING TYRONE PALMER	61		1

SLAMM
UK, male vocal/instrumental group — 6

Date	Title / Label	Peak Position	Weeks at No.1	Weeks on Chart
17 Jul 93	**ENERGIZE** *PWL International PWCD 266*	57		2
23 Oct 93	**VIRGINIA PLAIN** *PWL International PWCD 274*	60		1
22 Oct 94	**THAT'S WHERE MY MIND GOES** *PWL International PWCD 310*	68		1
4 Feb 95	**CAN'T GET BY** *PWL International PWCD 316*	47		2

LUKE SLATER
UK, male DJ/producer — 2

Date	Title / Label	Peak Position	Weeks at No.1	Weeks on Chart
16 Sep 00	**ALL EXHALE** *Novamute CDNOMU 79*	74		1
6 Apr 02	**NOTHING AT ALL** *Mute CDMUTE 261*	70		1

SLAUGHTER
US, male vocal/instrumental group — 2

Date	Title / Label	Peak Position	Weeks at No.1	Weeks on Chart
29 Sep 90	**UP ALL NIGHT** *Chrysalis CHS 3556*	62		1
2 Feb 91	**FLY TO THE ANGELS** *Chrysalis CHS 3634*	55		1

SLAVE
US, male/female vocal/instrumental group — 3

Date	Title / Label	Peak Position	Weeks at No.1	Weeks on Chart
8 Mar 80	**JUST A TOUCH OF LOVE** *Atlantic/Cotillion K 11442*	64		3

SLAYER
US, male vocal/instrumental group — 3

Date	Title / Label	Peak Position	Weeks at No.1	Weeks on Chart
13 Jun 87	**CRIMINALLY INSANE** *Def Jam LON 133*	64		1
26 Oct 91	**SEASONS IN THE ABYSS** *Def American DEFA 9*	51		1
9 Sep 95	**SERENITY IN MURDER** *American Recordings 74321312482*	50		1

SLEAZESISTERS
UK, male producer (Paul Masterson). See Candy Girls, Clergy, Dorothy, Hi-Gate, Paul Masterson presents Sushi, Yomanda — 3

Date	Title / Label	Peak Position	Weeks at No.1	Weeks on Chart
29 Jul 95	**SEX** *Pulse 8 CDLOSE 92* WITH VIKKI SHEPARD	53		1
30 Mar 96	**LET'S WHIP IT UP (YOU GO GIRL)** *Pulse 8 CDLOSE 102* WITH VIKKI SHEPARD	46		1
26 Sep 98	**WORK IT UP** *Logic 74321616622* SLEAZE SISTERS	74		1

KATHY SLEDGE
US, female vocalist. See Sister Sledge — 7

Date	Title / Label	Peak Position	Weeks at No.1	Weeks on Chart
16 May 92	**TAKE ME BACK TO LOVE AGAIN** *Epic 6579837*	62		2
18 Feb 95	**ANOTHER STAR** *NRC DEACD*	54		1
29 Nov 97	**FREEDOM** *Deconstruction 74321536952* ROBERT MILES FEATURING KATHY SLEDGE	15		4

PERCY SLEDGE
US, male vocalist — 34

Date	Title / Label	Peak Position	Weeks at No.1	Weeks on Chart
12 May 66	**WHEN A MAN LOVES A WOMAN** *Atlantic 584 001* ★	4		17
4 Aug 66	**WARM AND TENDER LOVE** *Atlantic 584 034*	34		7
14 Feb 87	**WHEN A MAN LOVES A WOMAN** *Atlantic YZ 96* ○	2		10

SLEEPER
UK, female/male vocal/instrumental group – Louise Wener, Andy Maclure, Kenadiid Osman & Jonathan Stewart — 29

Date	Title / Label	Peak Position	Weeks at No.1	Weeks on Chart
21 May 94	**DELICIOUS** *Indolent SLEEP 003CD*	75		1
21 Jan 95	**INBETWEENER** *Indolent SLEEP 006CD*	16		4
8 Apr 95	**VEGAS** *Indolent SLEEP 008CD*	33		3
7 Oct 95	**WHAT DO I DO NOW?** *Indolent SLEEP 009CD*	14		4
4 May 96	**SALE OF THE CENTURY** *Indolent SLEEP 011CD*	10		5
13 Jul 96	**NICE GUY EDDIE** *Indolent SLEEP 013CD*	10		5
5 Oct 96	**STATUESQUE** *Indolent SLEEP 014CD1*	17		3
4 Oct 97	**SHE'S A GOOD GIRL** *Indolent SLEEP 015CD*	28		2
6 Dec 97	**ROMEO ME** *Indolent SLEEP 17CD1*	39		2

SLEEPY JACKSON
Australia, male vocal/instrumental trio — 3

Date	Title / Label	Peak Position	Weeks at No.1	Weeks on Chart
19 Jul 03	**VAMPIRE RACECOURSE** *Virgin DINSD 261*	50		1
25 Oct 03	**GOOD DANCERS** *Virgin DINSD 265*	71		1
29 Jul 06	**GOD LEAD YOUR SOUL** *Virgin DINSDX278*	69		1

SLICK
US, male/female vocal/instrumental group — 15

Date	Title / Label	Peak Position	Weeks at No.1	Weeks on Chart
16 Jun 79	**SPACE BASS** *Fantasy FTC 176*	16		10
15 Sep 79	**SEXY CREAM** *Fantasy FTC 182*	47		5

GRACE SLICK
US, female vocalist (Grace Wing). See Jefferson Airplane — 4

Date	Title / Label	Peak Position	Weeks at No.1	Weeks on Chart
24 May 80	**DREAMS** *RCA PB 9534*	50		4

SLICK RICK
US (b. UK), male rapper (Richard Walters). See Doug E Fresh & The Get Fresh Crew — 12

Date	Title / Label	Peak Position	Weeks at No.1	Weeks on Chart
10 Jun 89	**IF I'M NOT YOUR LOVER** *Uptown W 2908* AL B SURE! FEATURING SLICK RICK	54		3
19 Oct 96	**I LIKE** *Def Jam DEFCD 19* MONTELL JORDAN FEATURING SLICK RICK	24		3
6 Oct 07	**HIP HOP POLICE** *Universal 1751125* CHAMILLIONAIRE FEATURING SLICK RICK	50		6

SLIK
UK, male vocal/instrumental group – Midge Ure*, Kenny Hyslop, Jim McGinlay & Billy McIsaac — 18

Date	Title / Label	Peak Position	Weeks at No.1	Weeks on Chart
17 Jan 76	**FOREVER AND EVER** *Bell 1464* ●	1	1	9
8 May 76	**REQUIEM** *Bell 1478*	24		9

SLIPKNOT
US, male vocal/instrumental group — 25

Date	Title / Label	Peak Position	Weeks at No.1	Weeks on Chart
11 Mar 00	**WAIT AND BLEED** *Roadrunner RR21125*	27		3
16 Sep 00	**SPIT IT OUT** *Roadrunner RR20903*	28		2
10 Nov 01	**LEFT BEHIND** *Roadrunner 23203352*	24		4
20 Jul 02	**MY PLAGUE** *Roadrunner RR 20453*	43		2
26 Jun 04	**DUALITY** *Roadrunner RR 39880*	15		6
30 Oct 04	**VERMILION** *Roadrunner RR 39770*	31		2
25 Jun 05	**BEFORE I FORGET** *Roadrunner RR39688*	35		1
2 Aug 08	**PSYCHOSOCIAL** *Roadrunner NLA320886994*	67		5

SLIPMATT
UK, male producer (Matt Nelson). See SL2 — 2

Date	Title / Label	Peak Position	Weeks at No.1	Weeks on Chart
19 Apr 03	**SPACE** *Concept CDCON 37*	41		2

SLIPSTREEM
UK, male production duo — 7

Date	Title / Label	Peak Position	Weeks at No.1	Weeks on Chart
19 Dec 92	**WE ARE RAVING – THE ANTHEM** *Boogie Food 7BF 1*	18		7

SLITS
UK, female vocal/instrumental group — 3

Date	Title / Label	Peak Position	Weeks at No.1	Weeks on Chart
13 Oct 79	**TYPICAL GIRLS/I HEARD IT THROUGH THE GRAPEVINE** *Island WIP 6505*	60		3

Silver-selling ● Gold-selling ● Platinum-selling (x multiples) ✪ US No.1 ★ Peak Position Weeks at No.1 Weeks on Chart

SLK
UK, male/female rap group — 3

Date	Title / Label	Peak Position	Weeks at No.1	Weeks on Chart
19 Mar 05	**HYPE! HYPE!** *Smoove SMOOVE01CDS*	22		3

PF SLOAN
US, male vocalist (Philip Gary Schlein) — 3

Date	Title / Label	Peak Position	Weeks at No.1	Weeks on Chart
4 Nov 65	**SINS OF THE FAMILY** *RCA 1482*	38		3

SLO-MOSHUN
UK, male production duo — 4

Date	Title / Label	Peak Position	Weeks at No.1	Weeks on Chart
5 Feb 94	**BELLS OF NY** *Six6 SIXCD 108*	29		3
30 Jul 94	**HELP MY FRIEND** *Six6 SIXCD 117*	52		1

SLOWDIVE
UK, male/female vocal/instrumental group — 2

Date	Title / Label	Peak Position	Weeks at No.1	Weeks on Chart
15 Jun 91	**CATCH THE BREEZE/SHINE** *Creation CRE 112*	52		1
29 May 93	**OUTSIDE YOUR ROOM (EP)** *Creation CRESCD 119*	69		1

SL2
UK, male production duo – John 'Lime' Fernandez & Matt 'Slipmatt' Nelson — 25

Date	Title / Label	Peak Position	Weeks at No.1	Weeks on Chart
2 Nov 91	**DJS TAKE CONTROL/WAY IN MY BRAIN** *XL Recordings XLS 24*	11		6
18 Apr 92	**ON A RAGGA TIP** *XL Recordings XLS 29* ●	2		11
19 Dec 92	**WAY IN MY BRAIN (REMIX)/DRUMBEATS** *XL Recordings XLS 36*	26		6
15 Feb 97	**ON A RAGGA TIP '97 (REMIX)** *XL Recordings XLSR 29CD*	31		2

SLUSNIK LUNA
Finland, male DJ/production duo — 2

Date	Title / Label	Peak Position	Weeks at No.1	Weeks on Chart
1 Sep 01	**SUN** *Incentive CENT 29CDS*	40		2

SLY & THE FAMILY STONE
US, male/female vocal/instrumental group – Sylvester Stewart, Greg Errico, Larry Graham, Jerry Martini, Cynthia Robinson, Freddie & Rosie Stewart — 42

Date	Title / Label	Peak Position	Weeks at No.1	Weeks on Chart
10 Jul 68	**DANCE TO THE MUSIC** *Direction 58 3568*	7		14
2 Oct 68	**M'LADY** *Direction 58 3707*	32		7
19 Mar 69	**EVERYDAY PEOPLE** *Direction 58 3938* ★	36		5
8 Jan 72	**FAMILY AFFAIR** *Epic EPC 7632* ★	15		8
15 Apr 72	**RUNNIN' AWAY** *Epic EPC 7810*	17		8

SLY FOX
US, male vocal duo – Michael Camacho & Gary Cooper — 16

Date	Title / Label	Peak Position	Weeks at No.1	Weeks on Chart
31 May 86	**LET'S GO ALL THE WAY** *Capitol CL 403*	3		16

SLY & ROBBIE
Jamaica, male vocal/instrumental duo — 23

Date	Title / Label	Peak Position	Weeks at No.1	Weeks on Chart
4 Apr 87	**BOOPS (HERE TO GO)** *Fourth & Broadway BRW 61*	12		11
25 Jul 87	**FIRE** *Fourth & Broadway BRW 71*	60		4
20 Sep 97	**NIGHT NURSE** *East West EW 129CD1* FEATURING SIMPLY RED	14		8

SMALL ADS
UK, male vocal/instrumental group — 3

Date	Title / Label	Peak Position	Weeks at No.1	Weeks on Chart
18 Apr 81	**SMALL ADS** *Bronze BRO 115*	63		3

SMALL FACES
UK, male vocal/instrumental group – Steve Marriott, d. 20 Apr 1991, Kenney Jones, Ronnie Lane*, d. 4 Jun 1997, & Ian McLagan — 137

Date	Title / Label	Peak Position	Weeks at No.1	Weeks on Chart
2 Sep 65	**WHATCHA GONNA DO ABOUT IT** *Decca F 12208*	14		12
10 Feb 66	**SHA LA LA LA LEE** *Decca F 12317*	3		11
12 May 66	**HEY GIRL** *Decca F 12393*	10		9
11 Aug 66	**ALL OR NOTHING** *Decca F 12470*	1	1	12
17 Nov 66	**MY MIND'S EYE** *Decca F 12500*	4		11
9 Mar 67	**I CAN'T MAKE IT** *Decca F 12565*	26		7
8 Jun 67	**HERE COME THE NICE** *Immediate IM 050*	12		10
9 Aug 67	**ITCHYCOO PARK** *Immediate IM 057*	3		14
6 Dec 67	**TIN SOLDIER** *Immediate IM 062*	9		12
17 Apr 68	**LAZY SUNDAY** *Immediate IM 064*	2		11
10 Jul 68	**UNIVERSAL** *Immediate IM 069*	16		11
19 Mar 69	**AFTERGLOW OF YOUR LOVE** *Immediate IM 077*	36		1
13 Dec 75	**ITCHYCOO PARK** *Immediate IMS 102*	9		11
20 Mar 76	**LAZY SUNDAY** *Immediate IMS 106*	39		5

HEATHER SMALL
UK, female vocalist. See M People — 12

Date	Title / Label	Peak Position	Weeks at No.1	Weeks on Chart
20 May 00	**PROUD** *Arista 74321757112*	16		5
19 Aug 00	**HOLDING ON** *Arista 74321781332*	58		1
30 Jul 05	**PROUD** *Arista 82876669182*	33		3
18 Nov 00	**YOU NEED LOVE LIKE I DO** *Gut CXGUT 36* TOM JONES & HEATHER SMALL	24		3

SMALLER
UK, male vocal/instrumental group — 2

Date	Title / Label	Peak Position	Weeks at No.1	Weeks on Chart
28 Sep 96	**WASTED** *Better BETSCD 006*	72		1
29 Mar 97	**IS** *Better BETSCD 008*	55		1

SMART E'S
UK, male production trio – Nick Arnold, Chris Howell & Tom Orton — 9

Date	Title / Label	Peak Position	Weeks at No.1	Weeks on Chart
11 Jul 92	**SESAME'S TREET** *Suburban Base SUBBASE 125*	2		9

S*M*A*S*H
UK, male vocal/instrumental group — 1

Date	Title / Label	Peak Position	Weeks at No.1	Weeks on Chart
6 Aug 94	**(I WANT TO) KILL SOMEBODY** *Hi-Rise FLATSCD 5*	26		1

SMASH MOUTH
US, male vocal/instrumental group — 9

Date	Title / Label	Peak Position	Weeks at No.1	Weeks on Chart
25 Oct 97	**WALKIN' ON THE SUN** *Interscope IND 95555*	19		4
31 Jul 99	**ALL STAR** *Interscope IND 4971182*	24		5

SMASHING PUMPKINS
US, male/female vocal/instrumental group – Billy Corgan, Jimmy Chamberlain, James Iha & D'Arcy Wretzky — 37

Date	Title / Label	Peak Position	Weeks at No.1	Weeks on Chart
5 Sep 92	**I AM ONE** *Hut HUTT 18*	73		1
3 Jul 93	**CHERUB ROCK** *Hut HUTCD 31*	31		2
25 Sep 93	**TODAY** *Hut HUTCD 37*	44		2
5 Mar 94	**DISARM** *Hut HUTCD 43*	11		3
28 Oct 95	**BULLET WITH BUTTERFLY WINGS** *Virgin HUTCD 63*	20		3
10 Feb 96	**1979** *Virgin HUTCD 67*	16		3
18 May 96	**TONIGHT TONIGHT** *Virgin HUTDX 69*	7		6
23 Nov 96	**THIRTY THREE** *Virgin HUTCD 78*	21		2
14 Jun 97	**THE END IS THE BEGINNING IS THE END** *Warner Brothers W0404CD*	10		4
23 Aug 97	**THE END IS THE BEGINNING IS THE END (REMIX)** *Warner Brothers W0410CD*	72		1
30 May 98	**AVA ADORE** *Hut HUTCD 101*	11		4
19 Sep 98	**PERFECT** *Hut HUTCD 106*	24		2
4 Mar 00	**STAND INSIDE YOUR LOVE** *Hut HUTCD 127*	23		2
23 Sep 00	**TRY TRY TRY** *Hut HUTCD 140*	73		1
14 Jul 07	**TARANTULA** *Warner Brothers W769CD*	59		1

SMELLS LIKE HEAVEN
UK, male producer (Fabio Paras). See Outrage — 1

Date	Title / Label	Peak Position	Weeks at No.1	Weeks on Chart
10 Jul 93	**LONDRES STRUTT** *Deconstruction 74321154312*	57		1

AARON SMITH FEATURING LUVLI
US, male/female vocal/production duo — 5

Date	Title / Label	Peak Position	Weeks at No.1	Weeks on Chart
14 Jan 06	**DANCIN'** *Boss BOSSMOS02CDS*	20		5

ANN-MARIE SMITH
UK, female vocalist — 5

Date	Title / Label	Peak Position	Weeks at No.1	Weeks on Chart
23 Jan 93	**MUSIC** *Synthetic CDR 6334* FARGETTA & ANNE-MARIE SMITH	34		2
18 Mar 95	**ROCKIN' MY BODY** *Media MCSTD 2021* 49ERS FEATURING ANN-MARIE SMITH	31		2
15 Jul 95	**(YOU'RE MY ONE AND ONLY) TRUE LOVE** *Media MCSTD 2060*	46		1

Silver-selling ● Gold-selling ● Platinum-selling (× multiples) ⊛ US No.1 ★ Peak Position · Weeks at No.1 · Weeks on Chart

ELLIOTT SMITH

US, male vocalist/guitarist (Steven Smith), d. 21 Oct 2003 (age 34) — 3

Date	Title	Peak Position	Weeks at No.1	Weeks on Chart
19 Dec 98	**WALTZ #2 (XO)** *DreamWorks DRMCD 22347*	52		1
1 May 99	**BABY BRITAIN** *DreamWorks DRMDM 50950*	55		1
8 Jul 00	**SON OF SAM** *DreamWorks DRMCD 4509492*	55		1

HURRICANE SMITH

UK, male vocalist (Norman Smith), d. 3 Mar 2008 (age 85) — 35

Date	Title	Peak Position	Weeks at No.1	Weeks on Chart
12 Jun 71	**DON'T LET IT DIE** *Columbia DB 8785*	2		12
29 Apr 72	**OH BABE WHAT WOULD YOU SAY?** *Columbia DB 8878*	4		16
2 Sep 72	**WHO WAS IT** *Columbia DB 8916*	23		7

JIMMY SMITH

US, male organist, d. 8 Feb 2005 (age 79) — 3

Date	Title	Peak Position	Weeks at No.1	Weeks on Chart
28 Apr 66	**GOT MY MOJO WORKING** *Verve VS 536*	48		3

KEELY SMITH

US, female vocalist (Dorothy Keely) — 10

Date	Title	Peak Position	Weeks at No.1	Weeks on Chart
18 Mar 65	**YOU'RE BREAKIN' MY HEART** *Reprise R 20346*	14		10

MANDY SMITH

UK, female vocalist/model — 2

Date	Title	Peak Position	Weeks at No.1	Weeks on Chart
20 May 89	**DON'T YOU WANT ME BABY** *PWL 37*	59		2

MEL SMITH

UK, male vocalist/comedian — 10

Date	Title	Peak Position	Weeks at No.1	Weeks on Chart
5 Dec 87	**ROCKIN' AROUND THE CHRISTMAS TREE** *10 TEN 2* MEL & KIM ●	3		7
21 Dec 91	**ANOTHER BLOOMING CHRISTMAS** *Epic 6576877*	59		3

MURIEL SMITH

US, female vocalist, d. 13 Sep 1985 (age 62) — 17

Date	Title	Peak Position	Weeks at No.1	Weeks on Chart
15 May 53	**HOLD ME THRILL ME KISS ME** *Philips PB 122*	3		17

OC SMITH

US, male vocalist (Ocie Smith), d. 23 Nov 2001 (age 65) — 23

Date	Title	Peak Position	Weeks at No.1	Weeks on Chart
29 May 68	**SON OF HICKORY HOLLER'S TRAMP** *CBS 3343*	2		15
26 Mar 77	**TOGETHER** *Caribou CRB 4910*	25		8

PATTI SMITH GROUP

US, female/male vocal/instrumental group – Patti Smith, JD Daugherty, Lenny Kaye, Ivan Kral & Richard Sohl, d. 3 Jun 1990 — 16

Date	Title	Peak Position	Weeks at No.1	Weeks on Chart
29 Apr 78	**BECAUSE THE NIGHT** *Arista 181* ●	5		12
19 Aug 78	**PRIVILEGE (SET ME FREE)** *Arista 197*	72		1
2 Jun 79	**FREDERICK** *Arista 264*	63		3

REX SMITH & RACHEL SWEET

US, male/female vocal duo — 7

Date	Title	Peak Position	Weeks at No.1	Weeks on Chart
22 Aug 81	**EVERLASTING LOVE** *CBS A 1405*	35		7

RICHARD JON SMITH

South Africa, male vocalist — 2

Date	Title	Peak Position	Weeks at No.1	Weeks on Chart
16 Jul 83	**SHE'S THE MASTER OF THE GAME** *Jive 38*	63		2

WHISTLING JACK SMITH

UK, male whistler (Billy Moeller) — 12

Date	Title	Peak Position	Weeks at No.1	Weeks on Chart
2 Mar 67	**I WAS KAISER BILL'S BATMAN** *Deram DM 112*	5		12

WILL SMITH

US, male actor/rapper. See Jazzy Jeff & The Fresh Prince — 135

Date	Title	Peak Position	Weeks at No.1	Weeks on Chart
16 Aug 97	**MEN IN BLACK** *Columbia 6648682* ⊛ ★	1	4	16
13 Dec 97	**JUST CRUISIN'** *Columbia 6653482*	23		6
7 Feb 98	**GETTIN' JIGGY WIT IT** *Columbia 6655605* ● ★	3		10
1 Aug 98	**JUST THE TWO OF US** *Columbia 6662092*	2		10
5 Dec 98	**MIAMI** *Columbia 6666782*	3		14
13 Feb 99	**BOY YOU KNOCK ME OUT** *MJJ 6674742* TATYANA ALI FEATURING WILL SMITH ●	3		9
10 Jul 99	**WILD WILD WEST** *Columbia 6675962* FEATURING DRU HILL ● ★	2		16
20 Nov 99	**WILL 2K** *Columbia 6684452*	2		11
25 Mar 00	**FREAKIN' IT** *Columbia 6691052*	15		8
10 Aug 02	**BLACK SUITS COMIN' (NOD YA HEAD)** *Columbia 6730135* FEATURING TRA-KNOX	3		10
2 Apr 05	**SWITCH** *Interscope 9881083*	4		22
5 Nov 05	**PARTY STARTER** *Interscope 9886574*	19		3

SMITHS

UK, male vocal/instrumental group – Morrissey* (Steven Morrissey), Mike Joyce, Johnny Marr (John Maher) & Andy Rourke — 105

Date	Title	Peak Position	Weeks at No.1	Weeks on Chart
12 Nov 83	**THIS CHARMING MAN** *Rough Trade RT 136*	25		12
28 Jan 84	**WHAT DIFFERENCE DOES IT MAKE** *Rough Trade RT 146*	12		9
2 Jun 84	**HEAVEN KNOWS I'M MISERABLE NOW** *Rough Trade RT 156*	10		8
1 Sep 84	**WILLIAM, IT WAS REALLY NOTHING** *Rough Trade RT 166*	17		6
9 Feb 85	**HOW SOON IS NOW** *Rough Trade RT 176*	24		6
30 Mar 85	**SHAKESPEARE'S SISTER** *Rough Trade RT 181*	26		4
13 Jul 85	**THE JOKE ISN'T FUNNY ANYMORE** *Rough Trade RT 186*	49		3
5 Oct 85	**THE BOY WITH THE THORN IN HIS SIDE** *Rough Trade RT 191*	23		5
31 May 86	**BIG MOUTH STRIKES AGAIN** *Rough Trade RT 192*	26		4
2 Aug 86	**PANIC** *Rough Trade RT 193*	11		8
1 Nov 86	**ASK** *Rough Trade RT 194*	14		5
7 Feb 87	**SHOPLIFTERS OF THE WORLD UNITE** *Rough Trade RT 195*	12		4
25 Apr 87	**SHEILA TAKE A BOW** *Rough Trade RT 196*	10		5
22 Aug 87	**GIRLFRIEND IN A COMA** *Rough Trade RT 197*	13		5
14 Nov 87	**I STARTED SOMETHING I COULDN'T FINISH** *Rough Trade RT 198*	23		4
19 Dec 87	**LAST NIGHT I DREAMT THAT SOMEBODY LOVED ME** *Rough Trade RT 200*	30		4
15 Aug 92	**THIS CHARMING MAN** *WEA YZ 0001*	8		5
12 Sep 92	**HOW SOON IS NOW** *WEA YX 0002*	16		4
24 Oct 92	**THERE IS A LIGHT THAT NEVER GOES OUT** *WEA YZ 0003*	25		3
18 Feb 95	**ASK** *WEA YZ 0004CDX*	62		1

SMOKE

UK, male vocal/instrumental group — 3

Date	Title	Peak Position	Weeks at No.1	Weeks on Chart
9 Mar 67	**MY FRIEND JACK** *Columbia DB 8115*	45		3

SMOKE CITY

Brazil/UK/Germany, female/male vocal/instrumental trio – Nina Miranda, Mark Brown & Chris Franck — 5

Date	Title	Peak Position	Weeks at No.1	Weeks on Chart
12 Apr 97	**UNDERWATER LOVE** *Jive JIVECD 422*	4		5

SMOKE 2 SEVEN

UK, female vocal trio — 2

Date	Title	Peak Position	Weeks at No.1	Weeks on Chart
16 Mar 02	**BEEN THERE DONE THAT** *Curb CUBCX 077*	26		2

SMOKIE

UK, male vocal/instrumental group – Chris Norman, Alan Silson, Pete Spencer & Terry Utley. See Suzi Quatro — 125

Date	Title	Peak Position	Weeks at No.1	Weeks on Chart
19 Jul 75	**IF YOU THINK YOU KNOW HOW TO LOVE ME** *RAK 206* SMOKEY	3		9
4 Oct 75	**DON'T PLAY YOUR ROCK 'N' ROLL TO ME** *RAK 217* SMOKEY	8		7
31 Jan 76	**SOMETHING'S BEEN MAKING ME BLUE** *RAK 227*	17		8
25 Sep 76	**I'LL MEET YOU AT MIDNIGHT** *RAK 241*	11		9
4 Dec 76	**LIVING NEXT DOOR TO ALICE** *RAK 244* ●	5		11
19 Mar 77	**LAY BACK IN THE ARMS OF SOMEONE** *RAK 251*	12		9
16 Jul 77	**IT'S YOUR LIFE** *RAK 260*	5		9
15 Oct 77	**NEEDLES AND PINS** *RAK 263* ●	10		9
28 Jan 78	**FOR A FEW DOLLARS MORE** *RAK 267*	17		6
20 May 78	**OH CAROL** *RAK 276* ●	5		13
23 Sep 78	**MEXICAN GIRL** *RAK 283*	19		9
19 Apr 80	**TAKE GOOD CARE OF MY BABY** *RAK 309*	34		7
13 May 95	**LIVING NEXT DOOR TO ALICE (WHO THE F**K IS ALICE)** *NOW CDWAG 245* FEATURING ROY CHUBBY BROWN	64		2
26 Aug 95	**LIVING NEXT DOOR TO ALICE (WHO THE F**K IS ALICE)** *NOW CDWAG 245* FEATURING ROY CHUBBY BROWN ●	3		17

SMOKIN' BEATS FEATURING LYN EDEN

UK, male/female vocal/DJ/production trio. See DJ Flavours, NRG — 3

Date	Title	Peak Position	Weeks at No.1	Weeks on Chart
17 Jan 98	**DREAMS** *AM:PM 5624711*	23		3

Silver-selling ● Gold-selling ● Platinum-selling (× multiples) ⊛ US No.1 ★ Peak Position · Weeks at No.1 · Weeks on Chart

SMOKIN' MOJO FILTERS
UK/US, male/female vocal/instrumental charity group — 5

Date	Title	Peak	Wks at No.1	Wks on Chart
23 Dec 95	**COME TOGETHER (WAR CHILD)** *Go! Discs GODCD 136*	19		5

SMOOTH
US, female vocalist (Juanita Stokes) — 7

Date	Title	Peak	Wks at No.1	Wks on Chart
22 Jul 95	**MIND BLOWIN'** *Jive JIVECD 379*	36		2
7 Oct 95	**IT'S SUMMERTIME (LET IT GET INTO YOU)** *Jive JIVECD 383*	46		1
16 Mar 96	**LOVE GROOVE (GROOVE WITH YOU)** *Jive JIVECD 390*	46		1
16 Mar 96	**WE GOT IT** *MCA MCSTD 48009* IMMATURE FEATURING SMOOTH	26		2
6 Jul 96	**UNDERCOVER LOVER** *Jive JIVECD 397*	41		1

JOE SMOOTH
US, male producer (Joseph Welbon) — 4

Date	Title	Peak	Wks at No.1	Wks on Chart
4 Feb 89	**PROMISED LAND** *DJ International DJIN 6*	56		4

SMOOTH TOUCH
US, male production duo — 1

Date	Title	Peak	Wks at No.1	Wks on Chart
2 Apr 94	**HOUSE OF LOVE (IN MY HOUSE)** *Six6 SIXCD 112*	58		1

JEAN JACQUES SMOOTHIE
UK, male DJ/producer (Steve Robson) — 7

Date	Title	Peak	Wks at No.1	Wks on Chart
13 Oct 01	**2 PEOPLE** *Echo ECSCD 112*	12		7

SMUJJI
Jamaica, male vocalist (Sean McLeod) — 9

Date	Title	Peak	Wks at No.1	Wks on Chart
13 Mar 04	**MUST BE LOVE** *Def Jam UK 9817508* FYA FEATURING SMUJJI	13		7
31 Jul 04	**KO** *Def Jam 9867077*	43		2

SMURFS
Smurfland/Holland, cartoon characters vocal group — 52

Date	Title	Peak	Wks at No.1	Wks on Chart
3 Jun 78	**THE SMURF SONG** *Decca F 13759* FATHER ABRAHAM & THE SMURFS ●	2		17
30 Sep 78	**DIPPETY DAY** *Decca F 13798* FATHER ABRAHAM & THE SMURFS ●	13		12
2 Dec 78	**CHRISTMAS IN SMURFLAND** *Decca F 13819* FATHER ABRAHAM & THE SMURFS	19		7
7 Sep 96	**I'VE GOT A LITTLE PUPPY** *EMI TV CDSMURF 100*	4		10
21 Dec 96	**YOUR CHRISTMAS WISH** *EMI TV CDSMURF 102*	8		6

PATTY SMYTH WITH DON HENLEY
US, female/male vocal duo — 6

Date	Title	Peak	Wks at No.1	Wks on Chart
3 Oct 92	**SOMETIMES LOVE JUST AIN'T ENOUGH** *MCA MCS 1692*	22		6

SNAKEBITE
Italy, male production trio — 2

Date	Title	Peak	Wks at No.1	Wks on Chart
9 Aug 97	**THE BIT GOES ON** *Multiply CDMULTY 22*	25		2

SNAP!
Germany, male production duo – Benito Benites (Michael Munzing) & John 'Virgo' Garrett III (Luca Anzilotti) – & various US, male/female vocalist/rappers – Thea Austin, Turbo B (Durron Butler), Penny Ford*, Niki Haris & Summer (Paula Brown) — 136

Date	Title	Peak	Wks at No.1	Wks on Chart
24 Mar 90	**THE POWER** *Arista 113133* ●	1	2	15
16 Jun 90	**OOOPS UP** *Arista 113296* ●	5		12
22 Sep 90	**CULT OF SNAP** *Arista 113596*	8		7
8 Dec 90	**MARY HAD A LITTLE BOY** *Arista 113831*	8		10
30 Mar 91	**SNAP MEGAMIX** *Arista 114169*	10		6
21 Dec 91	**THE COLOUR OF LOVE** *Arista 114678*	54		3
4 Jul 92	**RHYTHM IS A DANCER** *Arista 115309* ●	1	6	19
9 Jan 93	**EXTERMINATE!** *Arista 74321106962* FEATURING NIKI HARIS	2		11
12 Jun 93	**DO YOU SEE THE LIGHT (LOOKING FOR)** *Arista 74321147622* FEATURING NIKI HARIS	10		8
17 Sep 94	**WELCOME TO TOMORROW** *Arista 74321223852* FEATURING SUMMER ●	6		14
1 Apr 95	**THE FIRST THE LAST THE ETERNITY (TIL THE END)** *Arista 74321254672* FEATURING SUMMER	15		7
28 Oct 95	**THE WORLD IN MY HANDS** *Arista 74321314792* FEATURING SUMMER	44		1
13 Apr 96	**RAME** *Arista 74321368902* FEATURING RUKMANI	50		1
24 Aug 96	**THE POWER 96** *Arista 74321398672* FEATURING EINSTEIN	42		1
24 Aug 02	**DO YOU SEE THE LIGHT** *Data 33CDS* VS PLAYTHING	14		5
17 May 03	**RHYTHM IS A DANCER** *Data 47CDS*	17		4
6 Sep 03	**THE POWER (OF BHANGRA)** *Data 60CDS* VS MOTIVO	34		2
24 May 08	**RHYTHM IS A DANCER** *Logic 74321102572*	23		5
28 Jun 08	**RHYTHM IS A DANCER 08** *Luma Music LUMA0099*	43		5

SNEAKER PIMPS
UK, female/male vocal/instrumental group – Kelli Dayton (aka Kelli Ali), Chris Corner, Liam Howe & Joe Wilson — 19

Date	Title	Peak	Wks at No.1	Wks on Chart
19 Oct 96	**6 UNDERGROUND** *Clean Up CUP 023CDD*	15		4
15 Mar 97	**SPIN SPIN SUGAR** *Clean Up CUP 033CDS*	21		3
7 Jun 97	**6 UNDERGROUND** *Clean Up CUP 036CDS*	9		4
30 Aug 97	**POST MODERN SLEAZE** *Clean Up CUP 038CDM*	22		3
7 Feb 98	**SPIN SPIN SUGAR (REMIX)** *Clean Up CUP 037X*	46		2
21 Aug 99	**LOW FIVE** *Clean Up CUP 052CDS*	39		2
30 Oct 99	**TEN TO TWENTY** *Clean Up CUP 054CDS*	56		1

SNEAKY SOUND SYSTEM
Australia, male vocal/instrumental group — 3

Date	Title	Peak	Wks at No.1	Wks on Chart
29 Nov 08	**UFO** *14th Floor SNEAK2CD2*	52		1
10 Oct 09	**I WILL BE HERE** *14th Floor 14FLR39CD* TIESTO & SNEAKY SOUNDSYSTEM	44		2

DAVID SNEDDON
UK, male vocalist — 33

Date	Title	Peak	Wks at No.1	Wks on Chart
25 Jan 03	**STOP LIVING THE LIE** *Mercury 0637292*	1	2	18
3 May 03	**DON'T LET GO** *Mercury 9800069*	3		10
23 Aug 03	**BEST OF ORDER** *Fontana 9810277*	19		3
8 Nov 03	**BABY GET HIGHER** *Fontana 9813422*	38		2

SNIFF 'N' THE TEARS
UK, male vocal/instrumental group — 5

Date	Title	Peak	Wks at No.1	Wks on Chart
23 Jun 79	**DRIVER'S SEAT** *Chiswick CHIS 105*	42		5

SNOOP DOGG
US, male rapper (Calvin Broadus) — 177

Date	Title	Peak	Wks at No.1	Wks on Chart
4 Dec 93	**WHAT'S MY NAME?** *Death Row A 8337CD* SNOOP DOGGY DOGG	20		8
12 Feb 94	**GIN AND JUICE** *Death Row A 8316CD* SNOOP DOGGY DOGG	39		3
20 Aug 94	**DOGGY DOGG WORLD** *Death Row A 8289CD* SNOOP DOGGY DOGG	32		3
14 Dec 96	**SNOOP'S UPSIDE YA HEAD** *Interscope IND 95520* SNOOP DOGGY DOGG FEATURING CHARLIE WILSON	12		7
26 Apr 97	**WANTED DEAD OR ALIVE** *Def Jam 5744052* 2PAC & SNOOP DOGGY DOGG	16		3
3 May 97	**VAPORS** *Interscope IND 95530* SNOOP DOGGY DOGG	18		2
20 Sep 97	**WE JUST WANNA PARTY WITH YOU** *Columbia 6649902* SNOOP DOGGY DOGG FEATURING JD	21		2
24 Jan 98	**THA DOGGFATHER** *Interscope IND 95550* SNOOP DOGGY DOGG	36		2
12 Dec 98	**COME AND GET WITH ME** *Elektra E 3787CD* KEITH SWEAT FEATURING SNOOP DOGG	58		1
25 Mar 00	**STILL DRE** *Interscope 4972862* DR DRE FEATURING SNOOP DOGGY DOGG	6		10
3 Feb 01	**THE NEXT EPISODE** *Interscope 4974762* DR DRE FEATURING SNOOP DOGGY DOGG	3		10
17 Mar 01	**X** *Epic 6709072* XZIBIT FEATURING SNOOP DOOG	14		7
28 Apr 01	**SNOOP DOGG** *Priority PTYCD 134*	13		5
30 Nov 02	**FROM THA CHUUUCH TO DA PALACE** *Priority 5516102*	27		6
1 Mar 03	**THE STREETS** *Def Jam 0779852* WC FEATURING SNOOP DOGG & NATE DOGG	48		2
5 Apr 03	**BEAUTIFUL** *Capitol CDCL 842* FEATURING PHARRELL	23		20
14 Feb 04	**THE NEXT EPISODE** *Interscope 4974762* DR DRE FEATURING SNOOP DOGGY DOGG	58		2
14 Aug 04	**I WANNA THANK YOU** *J Records 82876624782* ANGIE STONE FEATURING SNOOP DOGG	31		3
11 Dec 04	**DROP IT LIKE IT'S HOT** *Geffen 2103461* FEATURING PHARRELL ★	10		11
5 Mar 05	**LET'S GET BLOWN** *Geffen 9880425* FEATURING PHARRELL	13		6
7 May 05	**SIGNS** *Geffen 9881782* FEATURING CHARLIE WILSON & JUSTIN TIMBERLAKE	2		16
27 Aug 05	**UPS AND DOWN** *Geffen 9883732*	36		2
1 Jul 06	**BUTTONS** *A&M 1700854* PUSSYCAT DOLLS FEATURING SNOOP DOGG	3		16
28 Oct 06	**GANGSTA WALK** *All Around The World CDGLOBE565* COOLIO FEATURING SNOOP DOGG	67		1
16 Dec 06	**THAT'S THAT S****** *Geffen 1717453* FEATURING R KELLY	38		4
13 Jan 07	**I WANNA LOVE YOU** *Universal 1722994* AKON FEATURING SNOOP DOGGY DOGG ★	3		20
5 Apr 08	**SENSUAL SEDUCTION** *Geffen 1766332*	24		5

SNOW
Canada, male vocalist (Darrin O'Brien) 18

Date	Title	Peak	Wks No.1	Wks
13 Mar 93	**INFORMER** *East West America A 8436CD* ○ ★	2		15
5 Jun 93	**GIRL I'VE BEEN HURT** *East West America A 8417CD*	48		2
4 Sep 93	**UHH IN YOU** *Atlantic A 8378CD*	67		1

MARK SNOW
US, male keyboard player/composer (Martin Fulterman) 15

Date	Title	Peak	Wks No.1	Wks
30 Mar 96	**THE X FILES** *Warner Brothers W 0341CD* ○	2		15

PHOEBE SNOW
US, female vocalist/guitarist (Phoebe Laub) 7

Date	Title	Peak	Wks No.1	Wks
6 Jan 79	**EVERY NIGHT** *CBS 6842*	37		7

SNOW PATROL
UK, male vocal/instrumental group – Gary Lightbody, Nathan Connelly, Jonny Quinn, Tom Simpson & Paul Wilson 206

Date	Title	Peak	Wks No.1	Wks
27 Sep 03	**SPITTING GAMES** *Polydor 9809350*	54		1
7 Feb 04	**RUN** *Fiction/Polydor 9816353*	5		11
24 Apr 04	**CHOCOLATE** *Fiction/Polydor 9866355*	24		6
24 Jul 04	**SPITTING GAMES** *Fiction/Polydor 9867126*	23		5
6 Nov 04	**HOW TO BE DEAD** *Polydor 9868777*	39		2
29 Apr 06	**YOU'RE ALL I HAVE** *Fiction 9853867*	7		28
29 Jul 06	**CHASING CARS** *Fiction 1704397*	6		17
18 Nov 06	**SET THE FIRE TO THE THIRD BAR** *Fiction 1714673* FEATURING MARTHA WAINWRIGHT	18		10
13 Jan 07	**CHASING CARS** *Fiction 1704397*	9		74
10 Feb 07	**OPEN YOUR EYES** *Fiction/Polydor 1723992*	26		8
12 May 07	**SIGNAL FIRE** *Fiction/Polydor 1734375*	4		9
18 Oct 08	**TAKE BACK THE CITY** *Fiction 1784828*	6		8
29 Nov 08	**RUN** *Fiction 9816353*	28		6
20 Dec 08	**CRACK THE SHUTTERS** *Fiction 1794020*	43		8
14 Nov 09	**JUST SAY YES** *Fiction 2724796*	15		6
21 Nov 09	**CHASING CARS** *Fiction 1704397*	39		5
28 Nov 09	**SET THE FIRE TO THE THIRD BAR** *Fiction 1714673* FEATURING MARTHA WAINWRIGHT	56		2

SNOWMEN
UK, male vocal/instrumental group 12

Date	Title	Peak	Wks No.1	Wks
12 Dec 81	**HOKEY COKEY** *Stiff ODB 1*	18		8
18 Dec 82	**XMAS PARTY** *Solid STOP 006*	44		4

SNUG
UK, male vocal/instrumental group 1

Date	Title	Peak	Wks No.1	Wks
18 Apr 98	**BEATNIK GIRL** *WEA 151CDX*	55		1

SO
UK, male vocal/instrumental group 3

Date	Title	Peak	Wks No.1	Wks
13 Feb 88	**ARE YOU SURE** *Parlophone R 6173*	62		3

SO SOLID CREW
UK, male/female rap/production collective – members included Asher D* (Ashley Walters), Lisa Maffia*, Harvey* (Michael Harvey, Jr), Oxide & Neutrino* (Mark Oseitutu & Alex Rivers) & Romeo* (Marvin Dawkins) 43

Date	Title	Peak	Wks No.1	Wks
18 Aug 01	**21 SECONDS** *Relentless RELENT 16CD* ○	1	1	15
17 Nov 01	**THEY DON'T KNOW** *Relentless RELENT 26CD*	3		9
19 Jan 02	**HATERS** *Relentless/Independiente RELENT 23CD* PRESENTS MR SHABZ	8		7
20 Apr 02	**RIDE WID US** *Relentless ISOM 55SMS*	19		6
27 Sep 03	**BROKEN SILENCE** *Independiente ISOM 71MS*	9		5
3 Apr 04	**SO GRIMEY** *Independiente ISOM 82MS*	62		1

S.O.A.P.
Denmark, female vocal duo 2

Date	Title	Peak	Wks No.1	Wks
25 Jul 98	**THIS IS HOW WE PARTY** *Columbia 6661295*	36		2

SOAPY
UK, male instrumental/production duo 2

Date	Title	Peak	Wks No.1	Wks
14 Sep 96	**HORNY AS FUNK** *WEA 074CD*	35		2

GINO SOCCIO
Canada, male keyboard player 5

Date	Title	Peak	Wks No.1	Wks
28 Apr 79	**DANCER** *Warner Brothers K 17357*	46		5

SODA CLUB
UK, male production duo. See Love To Infinity 12

Date	Title	Peak	Wks No.1	Wks
9 Nov 02	**TAKE MY BREATH AWAY** *Concept CDCON 33* FEATURING HANNAH ALETHA	16		4
8 Mar 03	**HEAVEN IS A PLACE ON EARTH** *Concept CDCON 39* FEATURING HANNAH ALETHA	13		4
23 Aug 03	**KEEP LOVE TOGETHER** *Concept CDCON 44X* FEATURING ANDREA ANATOLA	31		2
28 Aug 04	**AIN'T NO LOVE (AIN'T NO USE)** *Concept CDCON58X* FEATURING ASHLEY JADE	40		2

SOFT CELL
UK, male vocal/instrumental duo – Marc Almond* & David Ball 110

Date	Title	Peak	Wks No.1	Wks
1 Aug 81	**TAINTED LOVE** *Some Bizzare BZS 2* ●	1	2	30
14 Nov 81	**BED SITTER** *Some Bizzare BZS 6* ○	4		12
6 Feb 82	**SAY HELLO WAVE GOODBYE** *Some Bizzare BZS 7* ○	3		9
29 May 82	**TORCH** *Some Bizzare BZS 9* ○	2		9
21 Aug 82	**WHAT** *Some Bizzare BZS 11* ○	3		8
4 Dec 82	**WHERE THE HEART IS** *Some Bizzare BZS 16*	21		7
5 Mar 83	**NUMBERS/BARRIERS** *Some Bizzare BZS 17*	25		4
24 Sep 83	**SOUL INSIDE** *Some Bizzare BZS 20*	16		5
25 Feb 84	**DOWN IN THE SUBWAY** *Some Bizzare BZS 22*	24		6
9 Feb 85	**TAINTED LOVE** *Some Bizzare BZS 2*	43		6
23 Mar 91	**SAY HELLO WAVE GOODBYE '91** *Mercury SOFT 1* SOFT CELL/MARC ALMOND	38		3
18 May 91	**TAINTED LOVE** *Mercury SOFT 2* SOFT CELL/MARC ALMOND	5		8
28 Sep 02	**MONOCULTURE** *Cooking Vinyl FRYCD 132X*	52		1
8 Feb 03	**THE NIGHT** *Cooking Vinyl FRYCD 135X*	39		2

SOHO
UK, female/male vocal/instrumental trio – Jacqueline & Pauline Cuff & Timothy London 11

Date	Title	Peak	Wks No.1	Wks
5 May 90	**HIPPY CHICK** *Savage 7SAV 106*	67		1
19 Jan 91	**HIPPY CHICK** *Savage 7SAV 106*	8		8
9 Nov 91	**BORN TO BE ALIVE** *MCA MCS 1578* ADAMSKI FEATURING SOHO	51		2

SOHO DOLLS
UK, female/male vocal/instrumental group 1

Date	Title	Peak	Wks No.1	Wks
27 Nov 04	**PRINCE HARRY** *Poptones MC5096SCD*	57		1

SOIL
US, male vocal/instrumental group 2

Date	Title	Peak	Wks No.1	Wks
9 Nov 02	**HALO** *J Records 74321970132*	74		1
5 Jun 04	**REDEFINE** *J Records 82876618512*	68		1

SOLANGE
US, female vocalist/actor (Solange Knowles) 3

Date	Title	Peak	Wks No.1	Wks
23 Aug 08	**I DECIDED** *Geffen 1781082*	27		3

SOLAR STONE
UK, male DJ/production duo. See Liquid State featuring Marcella Woods, Z2 5

Date	Title	Peak	Wks No.1	Wks
21 Feb 98	**THE IMPRESSIONS EP** *Hooj Choons HOOJCD 57*	75		1
6 Nov 99	**SEVEN CITIES** *Hooj Choons HOOJ 85CD*	39		2
28 Sep 02	**SEVEN CITIES** *Lost Language LOST 018CD*	44		2

SOLDIERS
UK, male soldiers/vocal trio 1

Date	Title	Peak	Wks No.1	Wks
19 Dec 09	**A SOLDIER'S CHRISTMAS LETTER** *Rhino 5186570592*	65		1

SOLID GOLD CHARTBUSTERS
UK, male/female vocal/production group 1

Date	Title	Peak	Wks No.1	Wks
25 Dec 99	**I WANNA 1-2-1 WITH YOU** *Virgin VSCDT 1765*	62		1

SOLID HARMONIE
UK/US, female vocal group — 11

Date	Title / Label	Peak Position	Weeks at No.1	Weeks on Chart
31 Jan 98	**I'LL BE THERE FOR YOU** *Jive JIVECD 437*	18		3
18 Apr 98	**I WANT YOU TO WANT ME** *Jive JIVECD 452*	16		3
15 Aug 98	**I WANNA LOVE YOU** *Jive 0521742*	20		4
21 Nov 98	**TO LOVE ONCE AGAIN** *Jive 0522472*	55		1

SOLID SESSIONS
Holland, male production duo — 1

Date	Title / Label	Peak Position	Weeks at No.1	Weeks on Chart
14 Sep 02	**JANEIRO** *Positiva CDTIV 175*	47		1

SOLITAIRE
UK, male production duo — 3

Date	Title / Label	Peak Position	Weeks at No.1	Weeks on Chart
29 Nov 03	**I LIKE LOVE (I LOVE LOVE)** *Susu CDSUSU21*	57		2
26 Mar 05	**YOU GOT THE LOVE** *Susu CDSUSU30*	63		1

SOLO
UK, male/female producer/vocal duo — 4

Date	Title / Label	Peak Position	Weeks at No.1	Weeks on Chart
20 Jul 91	**RAINBOW (SAMPLE FREE)** *Reverb RVBT 003*	59		2
18 Jan 92	**COME ON!** *Reverb RVBT 008*	75		1
11 Sep 93	**COME ON! (REMIX)** *Stoatin' STOAT 003CD*	63		1

SAL SOLO
UK, male vocalist (Christopher Stevens). See Classix Nouveau — 13

Date	Title / Label	Peak Position	Weeks at No.1	Weeks on Chart
15 Dec 84	**SAN DAMIANO (HEART AND SOUL)** *MCA 930*	15		10
6 Apr 85	**MUSIC AND YOU** *MCA 946* WITH THE LONDON COMMUNITY GOSPEL CHOIR	52		3

SOLO (US)
US, male vocal group — 3

Date	Title / Label	Peak Position	Weeks at No.1	Weeks on Chart
3 Feb 96	**HEAVEN** *Perspective 5875212*	35		2
30 Mar 96	**WHERE DO U WANT ME TO PUT IT** *Perspective 5875312*	45		1

SOLU MUSIC FEATURING KIMBLEE
US, male/female vocal/production trio — 9

Date	Title / Label	Peak Position	Weeks at No.1	Weeks on Chart
17 Jun 06	**FADE** *Ministry Of Sound HK19CDS*	18		9

MARTIN SOLVEIG
France, male DJ/producer — 10

Date	Title / Label	Peak Position	Weeks at No.1	Weeks on Chart
24 Apr 04	**ROCKING MUSIC** *Defected DFTD082CDS*	35		4
26 Jun 04	**I'M A GOOD MAN** *Defected DFTD091CDS*	57		1
6 Aug 05	**EVERYBODY** *Defected DFTD107CDS*	22		4
11 Feb 06	**JEALOUSY** *Defected DFTD121CDX*	62		1

BELOUIS SOME
UK, male vocalist (Neville Keighley) — 26

Date	Title / Label	Peak Position	Weeks at No.1	Weeks on Chart
27 Apr 85	**IMAGINATION** *Parlophone R 6097*	50		7
18 Jan 86	**IMAGINATION** *Parlophone R 1986*	17		10
12 Apr 86	**SOME PEOPLE** *Parlophone R 6130*	33		7
16 May 87	**LET IT BE WITH YOU** *Parlophone R 6154*	53		2

JIMMY SOMERVILLE
UK, male vocalist. See Bronski Beat, Communards — 53

Date	Title / Label	Peak Position	Weeks at No.1	Weeks on Chart
11 Nov 89	**COMMENT TE DIRE ADIEU** *London LON 241* FEATURING JUNE MILES-KINGSTON	14		9
13 Jan 90	**YOU MAKE ME FEEL (MIGHTY REAL)** *London LON 249*	5		8
17 Mar 90	**READ MY LIPS (ENOUGH IS ENOUGH)** *London LON 254*	26		6
3 Nov 90	**TO LOVE SOMEBODY** *London LON 281*	8		11
2 Feb 91	**SMALLTOWN BOY (REMIX)** *London LON 287* WITH BRONSKI BEAT	32		4
10 Aug 91	**RUN FROM LOVE** *London LON 301*	52		2
28 Jan 95	**HEARTBEAT** *London LONCD 358*	24		4
27 May 95	**HURT SO GOOD** *London LONCD 364*	15		6
28 Oct 95	**BY YOUR SIDE** *London LONCD 372*	41		2
13 Sep 97	**DARK SKY** *Gut CXGUT 11*	66		1

SOMETHIN' FOR THE PEOPLE FEATURING TRINA & TAMARA
US, male/female vocal/instrumental group — 1

Date	Title / Label	Peak Position	Weeks at No.1	Weeks on Chart
7 Feb 98	**MY LOVE IS THE SHHH!** *Warner Brothers W 0427CD*	64		1

SOMETHING CORPORATE
US, male vocal/instrumental group — 3

Date	Title / Label	Peak Position	Weeks at No.1	Weeks on Chart
29 Mar 03	**PUNK ROCK PRINCESS** *MCA MCSTD 40315*	33		2
12 Jul 03	**IF YOU C JORDAN** *MCA MCSTD 40324*	68		1

SOMORE FEATURING DAMON TRUEITT
US, male/vocal/production group — 2

Date	Title / Label	Peak Position	Weeks at No.1	Weeks on Chart
24 Jan 98	**I REFUSE (WHAT YOU WANT)** *XL Recordings XLS 93CD*	21		2

SON OF DORK
UK, male vocal/instrumental group – James Bourne, Danny Hall, Chris Leonard, Steven Rushton & David Williams. See Busted, Stamford Amp — 10

Date	Title / Label	Peak Position	Weeks at No.1	Weeks on Chart
19 Nov 05	**TICKET OUTTA LOSERVILLE** *Mercury 9875191*	3		6
28 Jan 06	**EDDIE'S SONG** *Mercury 9876652*	10		4

SONGSTRESS
US, male vocal/production duo — 1

Date	Title / Label	Peak Position	Weeks at No.1	Weeks on Chart
27 Feb 99	**SEE LINE WOMAN '99** *Locked On LOX 106CD*	64		1

SONIA
UK, female vocalist (Sonia Evans) — 78

Date	Title / Label	Peak Position	Weeks at No.1	Weeks on Chart
24 Jun 89	**YOU'LL NEVER STOP ME LOVING YOU** *Chrysalis CHS 3385*	1	2	13
7 Oct 89	**CAN'T FORGET YOU** *Chrysalis CHS 3419*	17		6
9 Dec 89	**LISTEN TO YOUR HEART** *Chrysalis CHS 3465*	10		10
7 Apr 90	**COUNTING EVERY MINUTE** *Chrysalis CHS 3492*	16		7
23 Jun 90	**YOU'VE GOT A FRIEND** *Jive CHILD 90* BIG FUN & SONIA FEATURING GARY BARNACLE	14		6
25 Aug 90	**END OF THE WORLD** *Chrysalis CHS 3557*	18		7
1 Jun 91	**ONLY FOOLS (NEVER FALL IN LOVE)** *IQ ZB 44613*	10		8
31 Aug 91	**BE YOUNG BE FOOLISH BE HAPPY** *IQ ZB 44935*	22		5
16 Nov 91	**YOU TO ME ARE EVERYTHING** *IQ ZB 45121*	13		5
12 Sep 92	**BOOGIE NIGHTS** *Arista 74321113467*	30		3
1 May 93	**BETTER THE DEVIL YOU KNOW** *Arista 74321146872*	15		7
30 Jul 94	**HOPELESSLY DEVOTED TO YOU** *Cockney COCCD 2*	61		1

SONIC SOLUTION
UK/Belgium, male production duo — 1

Date	Title / Label	Peak Position	Weeks at No.1	Weeks on Chart
4 Apr 92	**BEATSTIME** *R&S RSUK 11*	59		1

SONIC SURFERS
Holland, male production duo — 2

Date	Title / Label	Peak Position	Weeks at No.1	Weeks on Chart
20 Mar 93	**TAKE ME UP** *A&M AMCD 210*	61		1
30 Jul 94	**DON'T GIVE IT UP** *Brilliant CDBRIL 6* SONIC SURFERS FEATURING JOCELYN BROWN	54		1

SONIC YOUTH
US, male/female vocal/instrumental group — 14

Date	Title / Label	Peak Position	Weeks at No.1	Weeks on Chart
11 Jul 92	**100%** *DGC DGCS 11*	28		4
7 Nov 92	**YOUTH AGAINST FASCISM** *Geffen GFS 26*	52		2
3 Apr 93	**SUGAR KANE** *Geffen GFSTD 37*	26		3
7 May 94	**BULL IN THE HEATHER** *Geffen GFSTD 72*	24		2
10 Sep 94	**SUPERSTAR** *A&M 5807932*	45		2
11 Jul 98	**SUNDAY** *Geffen GFSTD 22332*	72		1

SONIQUE
UK, female vocalist/DJ (Sonia Clarke). See S-Express — 47

Date	Title / Label	Peak Position	Weeks at No.1	Weeks on Chart
13 Jun 98	**I PUT A SPELL ON YOU** *Serious SERR 001CD*	36		2
5 Dec 98	**IT FEELS SO GOOD** *Serious SERR 004CD1*	24		3
3 Jun 00	**IT FEELS SO GOOD** *Universal MCSTD 40233* ⊛	1	3	17
16 Sep 00	**SKY** *Universal MCSTD 40240*	2		10
9 Dec 00	**I PUT A SPELL ON YOU** *Universal MCSTD 40245*	8		10
31 May 03	**CAN'T MAKE MY MIND UP** *Serious 9807217*	17		4
13 Sep 03	**ALIVE** *Serious 9811500*	70		1

SONNY

US, male vocalist (Salvatore Bono), d. 5 Jan 1998 (age 62). See Sonny & Cher — 11

Date	Title / Label	Peak Position	Weeks at No.1	Weeks on Chart
19 Aug 65	**LAUGH AT ME** *Atlantic AT 4038*	9		11

SONNY & CHER

US, male/female vocal duo – Sonny* Bono, d. 5 Jan 1998, & Cher* (Cherilyn LaPierre) — 78

Date	Title / Label	Peak Position	Weeks at No.1	Weeks on Chart
12 Aug 65	**I GOT YOU BABE** *Atlantic AT 4035* ★	1	2	12
16 Sep 65	**BABY DON'T GO** *Reprise R 20309*	11		9
21 Oct 65	**BUT YOU'RE MINE** *Atlantic AT 4047*	17		8
17 Feb 66	**WHAT NOW MY LOVE** *Atlantic AT 4069*	13		11
30 Jun 66	**HAVE I STAYED TOO LONG** *Atlantic 584 018*	42		3
8 Sep 66	**LITTLE MAN** *Atlantic 584 040*	4		10
17 Nov 66	**LIVING FOR YOU** *Atlantic 584 057*	44		4
2 Feb 67	**THE BEAT GOES ON** *Atlantic 584 078*	29		8
15 Jan 72	**ALL I EVER NEED IS YOU** *MCA MU 1145*	8		12
22 May 93	**I GOT YOU BABE** *Epic 6592402*	66		1

SONO

Germany, male production duo — 1

Date	Title / Label	Peak Position	Weeks at No.1	Weeks on Chart
16 Jun 01	**KEEP CONTROL** *Code Blue BLU 020CD1*	66		1

SON'Z OF A LOOP DA LOOP ERA

UK, male producer (Daniel Whidett) — 4

Date	Title / Label	Peak Position	Weeks at No.1	Weeks on Chart
15 Feb 92	**FAR OUT** *Suburban Base SUBBASE 008*	36		3
17 Oct 92	**PEACE + LOVEISM** *Suburban Base SUBBASE 14*	60		1

SONS & DAUGHTERS

UK, male/female vocal/instrumental group — 3

Date	Title / Label	Peak Position	Weeks at No.1	Weeks on Chart
16 Oct 04	**JOHNNY CASH** *Domino RUG186CD*	68		1
4 Jun 05	**DANCE ME IN** *Domino RUG196CD*	40		1
27 Aug 05	**TASTE THE LAST GIRL** *Domino RUG206CD*	75		1

SOOPA HOOPZ FEATURING QPR MASSIVE

UK, male football fans (Queens Park Rangers)/vocal group — 1

Date	Title / Label	Peak Position	Weeks at No.1	Weeks on Chart
16 Oct 04	**SOOPA HOOPZ** *Sniper Alley SNIPER001*	54		1

SORROWS

UK, male vocal/instrumental group — 8

Date	Title / Label	Peak Position	Weeks at No.1	Weeks on Chart
16 Sep 65	**TAKE A HEART** *Piccadilly 7N 35260*	21		8

S.O.S. BAND

US, male/female vocal/instrumental group — 46

Date	Title / Label	Peak Position	Weeks at No.1	Weeks on Chart
19 Jul 80	**TAKE YOUR TIME (DO IT RIGHT) PART 1** *Tabu TBU 8564*	51		4
26 Feb 83	**GROOVIN' (THAT'S WHAT WE'RE DOIN')** *Tabu TBU A 3120*	72		1
7 Apr 84	**JUST BE GOOD TO ME** *Tabu A 3626*	13		11
4 Aug 84	**JUST THE WAY YOU LIKE IT** *Tabu A 4621*	32		7
13 Oct 84	**WEEKEND GIRL** *Tabu A 4785*	51		5
29 Mar 86	**THE FINEST** *Tabu A 6997*	17		10
5 Jul 86	**BORROWED LOVE** *Tabu A 7241*	50		5
2 May 87	**NO LIES** *Tabu 6504447*	64		3

AARON SOUL

UK, male vocalist (Aaron Anyia) — 4

Date	Title / Label	Peak Position	Weeks at No.1	Weeks on Chart
2 Jun 01	**RING RING RING** *Def Soul 5689042*	14		4

DAVID SOUL

US, male actor/vocalist (David Solberg) — 56

Date	Title / Label	Peak Position	Weeks at No.1	Weeks on Chart
18 Dec 76	**DON'T GIVE UP ON US** *Private Stock PVT 84* ⊛ ★	1	4	16
26 Mar 77	**GOING IN WITH MY EYES OPEN** *Private Stock PVT 99* ○	2		8
27 Aug 77	**SILVER LADY** *Private Stock PVT 115* ●	1	3	14
17 Dec 77	**LET'S HAVE A QUIET NIGHT IN** *Private Stock PVT 130*	8		9
27 May 78	**IT SURE BRINGS OUT THE LOVE IN YOUR EYES** *Private Stock PVT 137*	12		9

JIMMY SOUL

US, male vocalist (James McCleese), d. 25 Jun 1988 (age 45) — 5

Date	Title / Label	Peak Position	Weeks at No.1	Weeks on Chart
11 Jul 63	**IF YOU WANNA BE HAPPY** *Stateside SS 178* ★	39		2
15 Jun 91	**IF YOU WANNA BE HAPPY** *Epic 6569647*	68		3

SOUL ASYLUM

US, male vocal/instrumental group – David Pirner, Karl Mueller, d. 17 Jun 2005, Dan Murphy & Grant Young (replaced by Sterling Campbell) — 33

Date	Title / Label	Peak Position	Weeks at No.1	Weeks on Chart
19 Jun 93	**RUNAWAY TRAIN** *Columbia 6593902*	37		8
4 Sep 93	**SOMEBODY TO SHOVE** *Columbia 6596492*	34		3
13 Nov 93	**RUNAWAY TRAIN** *Columbia 6593902*	7		11
22 Jan 94	**BLACK GOLD** *Columbia 6598442*	26		4
26 Mar 94	**SOMEBODY TO SHOVE** *Columbia 6602245*	32		3
15 Jul 95	**MISERY** *Columbia 6621092*	30		3
2 Dec 95	**JUST LIKE ANYONE** *Columbia 6624785*	52		1

SOUL AVENGERZ FEATURING JAVINE

UK, male/female vocal/production trio — 1

Date	Title / Label	Peak Position	Weeks at No.1	Weeks on Chart
14 Oct 06	**DON'T LET THE MORNING COME** *Positiva CDTIVS244*	49		1

SOUL BROTHERS

UK, male vocal/instrumental group — 3

Date	Title / Label	Peak Position	Weeks at No.1	Weeks on Chart
22 Apr 65	**I KEEP RINGING MY BABY** *Decca F 12116*	43		3

SOUL CENTRAL FEATURING KATHY BROWN

UK, male production duo – Paul Timothy & Andy Ward – & US, female vocalist — 7

Date	Title / Label	Peak Position	Weeks at No.1	Weeks on Chart
22 Jan 05	**STRINGS OF LIFE (STRONGER ON MY OWN)** *Defected DFTD094CDS*	6		7

SOUL CITY ORCHESTRA

UK, male production duo — 1

Date	Title / Label	Peak Position	Weeks at No.1	Weeks on Chart
11 Dec 93	**IT'S JURASSIC** *London JURCD 1*	70		1

SOUL CONTROL

Germany, male vocal/rap duo — 2

Date	Title / Label	Peak Position	Weeks at No.1	Weeks on Chart
18 Sep 04	**CHOCOLATE (CHOCO CHOCO)** *Tug CDSNOG12*	25		2

SOUL FAMILY SENSATION

UK/US, male/female vocal/production trio — 4

Date	Title / Label	Peak Position	Weeks at No.1	Weeks on Chart
11 May 91	**I DON'T EVEN KNOW IF I SHOULD CALL YOU BABY** *One Little Indian 47 TP7*	49		4

SOUL FOR REAL

US, male vocal group — 4

Date	Title / Label	Peak Position	Weeks at No.1	Weeks on Chart
8 Jul 95	**CANDY RAIN** *Uptown MCSTD 2052*	23		2
23 Mar 96	**EVERY LITTLE THING I DO** *Uptown MCSTD 48005*	31		2

SOUL II SOUL

UK, male/female vocal/instrumental/production group – Jazzie B (Beresford Romeo) & Nellee Hooper; members also included Phillip 'Daddae' Harvey, Simon Law, Doreen Waddell, d. 1 Mar 2002, Caron Wheeler & Rose Windross — 89

Date	Title / Label	Peak Position	Weeks at No.1	Weeks on Chart
21 May 88	**FAIRPLAY** *10 TEN 228* FEATURING ROSE WINDROSS	63		3
17 Sep 88	**FEEL FREE** *10 TEN 239* FEATURING DO'REEN	64		2
18 Mar 89	**KEEP ON MOVING** *10 TEN 263* FEATURING CARON WHEELER	5		12
10 Jun 89	**BACK TO LIFE (HOWEVER DO YOU WANT ME)** *10 TEN 265* FEATURING CARON WHEELER ○	1	4	14
9 Dec 89	**GET A LIFE** *10 TEN 284* ○	3		13
5 May 90	**A DREAM'S A DREAM** *10 TEN 300*	6		6
24 Nov 90	**MISSING YOU** *10 TEN 345* FEATURING KYM MAZELLE	22		7
4 Apr 92	**JOY** *10 TEN 350*	4		7
13 Jun 92	**MOVE ME NO MOUNTAIN** *10 TEN 400* LEAD VOCALS KOFI	31		4
26 Sep 92	**JUST RIGHT** *10 TEN 410*	38		2
6 Nov 93	**WISH** *Virgin VSCDG 1480*	24		4
22 Jul 95	**LOVE ENUFF** *Virgin VSCDT 1527*	12		6
21 Oct 95	**I CARE** *Virgin VSCDT 1560*	17		4
19 Oct 96	**KEEP ON MOVING** *Virgin VSCDT 1612* FEATURING CARON WHEELER	31		2
30 Aug 97	**REPRESENT** *Island CID 668*	39		2
8 Nov 97	**PLEASURE DOME** *Island CID 669*	51		1

Silver-selling ● Gold-selling ● Platinum-selling (x multiples) ★ US No.1 | Peak Position | Weeks at No.1 | Weeks on Chart

SOUL PROVIDERS FEATURING MICHELLE SHELLERS
UK/US, male/female vocal/production trio — 1

Date	Title / Label	Peak	Wks at No.1	Wks
14 Jul 01	**RISE** *AM:PM CDAMPM 147*	59		1

S.O.U.L. S.Y.S.T.E.M. INTRODUCING MICHELLE VISAGE
US, male/female production/vocal group — 5

Date	Title / Label	Peak	Wks at No.1	Wks
16 Jan 93	**IT'S GONNA BE A LOVELY DAY** *Arista 74321125692*	17		5

SOUL U*NIQUE
UK, male/female vocal group — 2

Date	Title / Label	Peak	Wks at No.1	Wks
19 Feb 00	**BE MY FRIEND** *M&J MAJCD 2*	53		1
29 Jul 00	**3IL (THRILL)** *M&J MAJCD 3*	66		1

SOULED OUT
Italy/US/UK, male/female production/vocal group — 1

Date	Title / Label	Peak	Wks at No.1	Wks
9 May 92	**IN MY LIFE** *Columbia 6578367*	75		1

SOULJA BOY TELL'EM
US, male rapper/producer (DeAndre Way) — 45

Date	Title / Label	Peak	Wks at No.1	Wks
24 Nov 07	**CRANK THAT (SOULJA BOY)** *Interscope 1755233* ★	2		26
19 Apr 08	**YAHHH!** *Interscope 1766763* FEATURING ARAB	49		2
9 May 09	**KISS ME THRU THE PHONE** *Interscope 2709754* FEATURING SAMMIE	6		17

SOULSEARCHER
US, male/female vocal/production duo – Thea Austin & Marc Pomeroy. See Snap! — 9

Date	Title / Label	Peak	Wks at No.1	Wks
13 Feb 99	**CAN'T GET ENOUGH** *Defected DEFECT 1CDS*	8		7
8 Apr 00	**DO IT TO ME AGAIN** *Defected DEFECT 15CDS*	32		2

SOULWAX
Belgium, male vocal/instrumental duo — 11

Date	Title / Label	Peak	Wks at No.1	Wks
25 Mar 00	**CONVERSATION INTERCOM** *Pias Recordings PIASB 018CD*	65		1
24 Jun 00	**MUCH AGAINST EVERYONE'S ADVICE** *Pias Recordings PIASB 026CD*	56		1
30 Sep 00	**TOO MANY DJ'S** *Pias Recordings PIASB 036CD*	40		2
3 Mar 01	**CONVERSATION INTERCOM (REMIX)** *Pias Recordings PIASB 046CD*	50		1
21 Aug 04	**ANY MINUTE NOW** *Pias Recordings PIASB 126CDM*	34		2
29 Jan 05	**E TALKING** *PIAS PIASB136CD*	27		2
9 Jul 05	**EXCUSE** *PIAS PIASB156CD*	35		2

SOUND BLUNTZ
Germany, male vocal/production group — 2

Date	Title / Label	Peak	Wks at No.1	Wks
30 Nov 02	**BILLIE JEAN** *Incentive CENT 51CDS*	32		2

SOUND DE-ZIGN
Holland, male DJ/production duo — 5

Date	Title / Label	Peak	Wks at No.1	Wks
14 Apr 01	**HAPPINESS** *NuLife 74321844002*	19		5

SOUND FACTORY
Sweden, male production/vocal duo — 1

Date	Title / Label	Peak	Wks at No.1	Wks
5 Jun 93	**2 THE RHYTHM** *Logic 74321149422*	72		1

SOUND 5
UK, male vocal/instrumental group — 1

Date	Title / Label	Peak	Wks at No.1	Wks
24 Apr 99	**ALA KABOO** *Gut CDGUT 23*	69		1

SOUND 9418
UK, male vocalist (Jonathan King) — 3

Date	Title / Label	Peak	Wks at No.1	Wks
7 Feb 76	**IN THE MOOD** *UK 121*	46		3

SOUND OF ONE FEATURING GLADEZZ
US, male production group & female vocalist — 1

Date	Title / Label	Peak	Wks at No.1	Wks
20 Nov 93	**AS I AM** *Cooltempo CDCOOL 280*	65		1

SOUNDBWOY ENT
UK, male/female vocal/instrumental group — 5

Date	Title / Label	Peak	Wks at No.1	Wks
29 Apr 06	**NEVER WANNA SAY** *Smoove SMOOVE05CDS*	18		5

SOUNDGARDEN
US, male vocal/instrumental group — 24

Date	Title / Label	Peak	Wks at No.1	Wks
11 Apr 92	**JESUS CHRIST POSE** *A&M AM 862*	30		3
20 Jun 92	**RUSTY CAGE** *A&M AM 874*	41		1
21 Nov 92	**OUTSHINED** *A&M AM 0102*	50		1
26 Feb 94	**SPOONMAN** *A&M 5805392*	20		3
30 Apr 94	**THE DAY I TRIED TO LIVE** *A&M 5805952*	42		2
20 Aug 94	**BLACK HOLE SUN** *A&M 5807532*	12		5
28 Jan 95	**FELL ON BLACK DAYS** *A&M 5809472*	24		2
18 May 96	**PRETTY NOOSE** *A&M 5816202*	14		3
28 Sep 96	**BURDEN IN MY HAND** *A&M 5818552*	33		2
28 Dec 96	**BLOW UP THE OUTSIDE WORLD** *A&M 5819862*	40		2

SOUNDMAN & DON LLOYDIE WITH ELISABETH TROY
UK, male/female vocal/production group — 2

Date	Title / Label	Peak	Wks at No.1	Wks
25 Feb 95	**GREATER LOVE** *Sound Of Underground SOJURCD 016*	49		2

SOUNDS INCORPORATED
UK, male instrumental group — 11

Date	Title / Label	Peak	Wks at No.1	Wks
23 Apr 64	**THE SPARTANS** *Columbia DB 7239*	30		6
30 Jul 64	**SPANISH HARLEM** *Columbia DB 7321*	35		5

SOUNDS NICE
UK, male vocal/instrumental group — 11

Date	Title / Label	Peak	Wks at No.1	Wks
6 Sep 69	**LOVE AT FIRST SIGHT (JE T'AIME...MOI NON PLUS)** *Parlophone R 5797*	18		11

SOUNDS OF BLACKNESS
US, male/female vocal group — 32

Date	Title / Label	Peak	Wks at No.1	Wks
22 Jun 91	**OPTIMISTIC** *Perspective PERSS 786*	45		4
28 Sep 91	**THE PRESSURE PART 1** *Perspective PERSS 816*	71		1
15 Feb 92	**OPTIMISTIC** *Perspective PERSS 849*	28		4
25 Apr 92	**THE PRESSURE PART 1 (REMIX)** *Perspective PERSS 867*	49		2
8 May 93	**I'M GOING ALL THE WAY** *Perspective 5874252*	27		3
26 Mar 94	**I BELIEVE** *A&M 5874512*	17		4
2 Jul 94	**GLORYLAND** *Mercury MERCD 404* DARYL HALL & THE SOUNDS OF BLACKNESS	36		4
20 Aug 94	**EVERYTHING IS GONNA BE ALRIGHT** *A&M 5874672*	29		3
14 Jan 95	**I'M GOING ALL THE WAY** *A&M 5874832*	14		4
7 Jun 97	**SPIRIT** *Perspective 5822312* FEATURING CRAIG MACK	35		2
14 Feb 98	**THE PRESSURE (2ND REMIX)** *AM:PM 5824872*	46		1

SOUNDS ORCHESTRAL
UK, orchestra fronted by Johnny Pearson — 18

Date	Title / Label	Peak	Wks at No.1	Wks
3 Dec 64	**CAST YOUR FATE TO THE WIND** *Piccadilly 7N 35206*	5		16
8 Jul 65	**MOONGLOW** *Piccadilly 7N 35248*	43		2

SOUNDSATION
UK, male production trio — 1

Date	Title / Label	Peak	Wks at No.1	Wks
14 Jan 95	**PEACE AND JOY** *ffrreedom TABCD 224*	48		1

SOUNDSCAPE
UK, male DJ/production group — 1

Date	Title / Label	Peak	Wks at No.1	Wks
14 Feb 98	**DUBPLATE CULTURE** *Satellite 74321552002*	61		1

SOUNDSOURCE
UK, male production duo — 1

Date	Title / Label	Peak	Wks at No.1	Wks
11 Jan 92	**TAKE ME UP** *ffrr FX 177*	62		1

SOUNDTRACK OF OUR LIVES
Sweden, male vocal/instrumental group — 1

Date	Title / Label	Peak	Wks at No.1	Wks
12 Mar 05	**HEADING FOR A BREAKDOWN** *WEA WEA383CD*	70		1

SOUP DRAGONS

UK, male vocal/instrumental group – Sean Dickinson, Sushil K Dade, Jim McCulloch & Ross Sinclair (replaced by Paul Quinn) — **23**

Date	Title	Peak Position	Weeks at No.1	Weeks on Chart
20 Jun 87	**CAN'T TAKE NO FOR AN ANSWER** *Raw TV RTV 3*	65		1
5 Sep 87	**SOFT AS YOUR FACE** *Raw TV RTV 4*	66		2
14 Jul 90	**I'M FREE** *Raw TV RTV 9* FEATURING JUNIOR REID	5		12
20 Oct 90	**MOTHER UNIVERSE** *Big Life BLR 30*	26		5
11 Apr 92	**DIVINE THING** *Big Life BLR 68*	53		3

SOURCE

UK, male producer (John Truelove) — **41**

Date	Title	Peak Position	Weeks at No.1	Weeks on Chart
2 Feb 91	**YOU GOT THE LOVE** *Truelove TLOVE 7001* FEATURING CANDI STATON ●	4		11
26 Dec 92	**ROCK THE HOUSE** *React 12REACT 12* FEATURING NICOLE	63		1
1 Mar 97	**YOU GOT THE LOVE (REMIX)** *React CDREACT 89* FEATURING CANDI STATON	3		8
23 Aug 97	**CLOUDS** *XL Recordings XLS 83CD*	38		2
1 Jan 05	**YOU GOT THE LOVE (IMPORT)** *ZYX GDC22218* FEATURING CANDI STATON	60		3
18 Feb 06	**YOU GOT THE LOVE (2ND REMIX)** *Positiva CDTIVS230* FEATURING CANDI STATON	7		16

SOURMASH

UK, male production trio — **1**

Date	Title	Peak Position	Weeks at No.1	Weeks on Chart
23 Dec 00	**PILGRIMAGE/MESCALITO** *Hooj Choons HOOJ 102CD*	73		1

SOUTH

UK, male vocal/instrumental group — **4**

Date	Title	Peak Position	Weeks at No.1	Weeks on Chart
17 Mar 01	**PAINT THE SILENCE** *Mo Wax MWR 134CD*	69		1
23 Aug 03	**LOOSEN YOUR HOLD** *Double Dragon DD 2010CD*	73		1
3 Apr 04	**COLOURS IN WAVES** *Sanctuary SANXD249*	60		1
14 Aug 04	**MOTIVELESS CRIME** *Sanctuary SANXD286*	72		1

JOE SOUTH

US, male vocalist (Joe Souter) — **11**

Date	Title	Peak Position	Weeks at No.1	Weeks on Chart
5 Mar 69	**GAMES PEOPLE PLAY** *Capitol CL 15579*	6		11

SOUTH ST. PLAYER

US, male vocalist/producer (Roland Clark) — **1**

Date	Title	Peak Position	Weeks at No.1	Weeks on Chart
2 Sep 00	**WHO KEEPS CHANGING YOUR MIND** *Cream 4CD*	49		1

JERI SOUTHERN

US, female vocalist (Genevieve Hering), d. 4 Aug 1991 (age 64) — **3**

Date	Title	Peak Position	Weeks at No.1	Weeks on Chart
21 Jun 57	**FIRE DOWN BELOW** *Brunswick 05665*	22		3

SOUTHLANDERS

Jamaica/UK, male vocal group — **10**

Date	Title	Peak Position	Weeks at No.1	Weeks on Chart
22 Nov 57	**ALONE** *Decca F 10946*	17		10

SOUTHSIDE SPINNERS

Holland, male production duo – Benjamin Kuyten & Marco Verkuylen — **7**

Date	Title	Peak Position	Weeks at No.1	Weeks on Chart
27 May 00	**LUVSTRUCK** *AM:PM CDAMPM 132*	9		7

SOUVERNANCE

Holland, male production duo — **1**

Date	Title	Peak Position	Weeks at No.1	Weeks on Chart
31 Aug 02	**HAVIN' A GOOD TIME** *Positiva CDTIV 174*	63		1

SOUVLAKI

UK, male producer (Mark Summers) — **4**

Date	Title	Peak Position	Weeks at No.1	Weeks on Chart
15 Feb 97	**INFERNO** *Wonderboy WBOYD 003*	24		3
8 Aug 98	**MY TIME** *Wonderboy WBOYD 009*	63		1

SOVEREIGN COLLECTION

UK, orchestra — **6**

Date	Title	Peak Position	Weeks at No.1	Weeks on Chart
3 Apr 71	**MOZART 40** *Capitol CL 15676*	27		6

RED SOVINE

US, male vocalist (Woodrow Wilson Sovine), d. 4 Apr 1980 (age 61) — **8**

Date	Title	Peak Position	Weeks at No.1	Weeks on Chart
13 Jun 81	**TEDDY BEAR** *Starday SD 142* ●	4		8

SOX

UK, female vocal/instrumental group — **1**

Date	Title	Peak Position	Weeks at No.1	Weeks on Chart
15 Apr 95	**GO FOR THE HEART** *Living Beat LBECD 33*	47		1

BOB B SOXX & THE BLUE JEANS

US, male/female vocal group — **2**

Date	Title	Peak Position	Weeks at No.1	Weeks on Chart
31 Jan 63	**ZIP-A-DEE-DOO-DAH** *London HLU 9646*	45		2

KIM SOZZI

US, female vocalist — **3**

Date	Title	Peak Position	Weeks at No.1	Weeks on Chart
9 Jun 07	**BREAK UP** *Substance SUBS25CDS*	23		3

SPACE

France, male instrumental trio – Didier Marouani, Roland Romanelli & Jannick Top — **12**

Date	Title	Peak Position	Weeks at No.1	Weeks on Chart
13 Aug 77	**MAGIC FLY** *Pye International 7N 25746* ●	2		12

SPACE

UK, male vocal/instrumental group – Tommy Scott, Francis Griffiths, James Murphy & Andrew Parle. See England United — **52**

Date	Title	Peak Position	Weeks at No.1	Weeks on Chart
6 Apr 96	**NEIGHBOURHOOD** *Gut CDGUT 1*	56		1
8 Jun 96	**FEMALE OF THE SPECIES** *Gut CDGUT 2*	14		10
7 Sep 96	**ME AND YOU VERSUS THE WORLD** *Gut CXGUT 4*	9		6
2 Nov 96	**NEIGHBOURHOOD** *Gut GXGUT 5*	11		6
22 Feb 97	**DARK CLOUDS** *Gut CDGUT 6*	14		4
10 Jan 98	**AVENGING ANGELS** *Gut CDGUT 16*	6		8
7 Mar 98	**THE BALLAD OF TOM JONES** *Gut CDGUT 18* WITH CERYS OF CATATONIA ●	4		8
4 Jul 98	**BEGIN AGAIN** *Gut CDGUT 019*	21		4
5 Dec 98	**THE BAD DAYS EP** *Gut CDGUT 22*	20		3
8 Jul 00	**DIARY OF A WIMP** *Gut CDGUT 34*	49		1
6 Mar 04	**SUBURBAN ROCK 'N' ROLL** *R&M Entertainment RAMCDS001*	67		1

SPACE BABY

UK, male producer (Matt Darey). See Lost Tribe, MDM, Melt featuring Little Ms Marcie, Sunburst — **1**

Date	Title	Peak Position	Weeks at No.1	Weeks on Chart
8 Jul 95	**FREE YOUR MIND** *Hooj Choons HOOJ 34CD*	55		1

SPACE BROTHERS

UK, male production duo. See Ascension, Chakra, Essence, Lustral, Oxygen featuring Andrea Britton — **19**

Date	Title	Peak Position	Weeks at No.1	Weeks on Chart
17 May 97	**SHINE** *Manifesto FESCD 23*	23		3
13 Dec 97	**FORGIVEN (I FEEL YOUR LOVE)** *Manifesto FESCD 36*	27		7
10 Jul 99	**LEGACY (SHOW ME LOVE)** *Manifesto FESCD 55*	31		3
9 Oct 99	**HEAVEN WILL COME** *Manifesto FESCD 61*	25		2
5 Feb 00	**SHINE 2000 (REMIX)** *Manifesto FESCD 67*	18		4

SPACE COWBOY

UK (b. France), male DJ/producer (Nick Dresti) — **4**

Date	Title	Peak Position	Weeks at No.1	Weeks on Chart
6 Jul 02	**I WOULD DIE 4 U** *Southern Fried ECB 29*	55		2
2 Aug 03	**JUST PUT YOUR HAND IN MINE** *Southern Fried ECB 37CD*	71		1
3 Feb 07	**MY EGYPTIAN LOVER** *Tiger Trax TIGDRE25CD* FEATURING NADIA OH	45		1

SPACE FROG

Germany, male production duo — **1**

Date	Title	Peak Position	Weeks at No.1	Weeks on Chart
16 Mar 02	**X RAY FOLLOW ME** *Tripoli Trax TTRAX 082CD*	70		1

SPACE KITTENS

UK, male instrumental/production group — **1**

Date	Title	Peak Position	Weeks at No.1	Weeks on Chart
13 Apr 96	**STORM** *Hooj Choons HOOJCD 41*	58		1

Silver-selling ● Gold-selling ● Platinum-selling (x multiples) US No.1 ★ Peak Position Weeks at No.1 Weeks on Chart

SPACE MANOEUVRES
UK, male producer (John Graham) — 2

Date	Title	Peak Position	Weeks at No.1	Weeks on Chart
29 Jan 00	**STAGE ONE** *Hooj Choons HOOJ 79CD*	25		2

SPACE MONKEY
UK, male producer (Paul Goodchild) — 4

Date	Title	Peak Position	Weeks at No.1	Weeks on Chart
8 Oct 83	**CAN'T STOP RUNNING** *Innervision A 3742*	53		4

SPACE MONKEYZ VS GORILLAZ
UK, male instrumental/production duo & UK/US/Japan, male/female virtual cartoon group — 1

Date	Title	Peak Position	Weeks at No.1	Weeks on Chart
3 Aug 02	**LIL' DUB CHEFIN'** *Parlophone CDR 6584*	73		1

SPACE RAIDERS
UK, male production trio — 1

Date	Title	Peak Position	Weeks at No.1	Weeks on Chart
28 Mar 98	**GLAM RAID** *Skint 32CD*	68		1

SPACE 2000
UK, male vocal/instrumental duo — 1

Date	Title	Peak Position	Weeks at No.1	Weeks on Chart
12 Aug 95	**DO U WANNA FUNK** *Wired 218*	50		1

SPACECORN
Sweden, male DJ/producer (Daniel Ellenson) — 1

Date	Title	Peak Position	Weeks at No.1	Weeks on Chart
28 Apr 01	**AXEL F** *69 SN 069CD*	74		1

SPACEDUST
UK, male production duo – Paul Glancey & Duncan Glasson — 12

Date	Title	Peak Position	Weeks at No.1	Weeks on Chart
24 Oct 98	**GYM AND TONIC** *East West EW 188CD* ●	1	1	10
27 Mar 99	**LET'S GET DOWN** *East West EW 195CD*	20		2

SPACEHOG
UK, male vocal/instrumental group — 8

Date	Title	Peak Position	Weeks at No.1	Weeks on Chart
11 May 96	**IN THE MEANTIME** *Sire 7559643162*	70		1
28 Dec 96	**IN THE MEANTIME** *Sire 7559643162*	29		6
7 Feb 98	**CARRY ON** *Sire W 0428CD*	43		1

SPACEMAID
UK, male vocal/instrumental group — 1

Date	Title	Peak Position	Weeks at No.1	Weeks on Chart
5 Apr 97	**BABY COME ON** *Big Star STARC 105*	70		1

SPAGHETTI SURFERS
UK, male instrumental/production duo — 1

Date	Title	Peak Position	Weeks at No.1	Weeks on Chart
22 Jul 95	**MISIRLOU (THE THEME TO THE MOTION PICTURE 'PULP FICTION')** *Tempo Toons CDTOON 4*	55		1

SPAGNA
Italy, female vocalist (Ivana Spagna) — 23

Date	Title	Peak Position	Weeks at No.1	Weeks on Chart
25 Jul 87	**CALL ME** *CBS 6502797*	2		12
17 Oct 87	**EASY LADY** *CBS 6511697*	62		3
20 Aug 88	**EVERY GIRL AND BOY** *CBS SPAG 1*	23		8

SPAN
Norway, male vocal/instrumental group — 1

Date	Title	Peak Position	Weeks at No.1	Weeks on Chart
21 Feb 04	**DON'T THINK THE WAY THEY DO** *Island CID 846*	52		1

SPANDAU BALLET
UK, male vocal/instrumental group – Tony Hadley*, John Keeble, Gary and Martin Kemp & Steve Norman — 159

Date	Title	Peak Position	Weeks at No.1	Weeks on Chart
15 Nov 80	**TO CUT A LONG STORY SHORT** *Reformation CHS 2473* ●	5		11
24 Jan 81	**THE FREEZE** *Reformation CHS 2486*	17		8
4 Apr 81	**MUSCLEBOUND/GLOW** *Reformation CHS 2509*	10		10
18 Jul 81	**CHANT NO. 1 (I DON'T NEED THIS PRESSURE ON)** *Reformation CHS 2528* ●	3		10
14 Nov 81	**PAINT ME DOWN** *Reformation CHS 2560*	30		5
30 Jan 82	**SHE LOVED LIKE DIAMOND** *Reformation CHS 2585*	49		4
17 Apr 82	**INSTINCTION** *Reformation CHS 2602*	10		11
2 Oct 82	**LIFELINE** *Reformation CHS 2642*	7		9
12 Feb 83	**COMMUNICATION** *Reformation CHS 2662*	12		10
23 Apr 83	**TRUE** *Reformation SPAN 1* ●	1	4	12
13 Aug 83	**GOLD** *Reformation SPAN 2* ●	2		9
9 Jun 84	**ONLY WHEN YOU LEAVE** *Reformation SPAN 3*	3		10
25 Aug 84	**I'LL FLY FOR YOU** *Reformation SPAN 4*	9		9
20 Oct 84	**HIGHLY STRUNG** *Reformation SPAN 5*	15		5
8 Dec 84	**ROUND AND ROUND** *Reformation SPAN 6*	18		8
26 Jul 86	**FIGHT FOR OURSELVES** *Reformation A 7264*	15		7
8 Nov 86	**THROUGH THE BARRICADES** *Reformation SPANS 1*	6		10
14 Feb 87	**HOW MANY LIES** *Reformation SPANS 2*	34		4
3 Sep 88	**RAW** *CBS SPANS 3*	47		3
26 Aug 89	**BE FREE WITH YOUR LOVE** *CBS SPANS 4*	42		4

SPANKOX
Italy, male producer (Agostino Carollo). See Motivo — 1

Date	Title	Peak Position	Weeks at No.1	Weeks on Chart
9 Oct 04	**TO THE CLUB** *Inferno CDFERN62*	69		1

SPARKLE
US, female vocalist (Stephanie Edwards) — 10

Date	Title	Peak Position	Weeks at No.1	Weeks on Chart
18 Jul 98	**BE CAREFUL** *Jive 0521452* FEATURING R KELLY	7		7
7 Nov 98	**TIME TO MOVE ON** *Jive 0522032*	40		2
28 Aug 99	**LOVIN' YOU YOU** *Jive 0523452*	65		1

SPARKLEHORSE
US, male vocal/instrumental group — 2

Date	Title	Peak Position	Weeks at No.1	Weeks on Chart
31 Aug 96	**RAINMAKER** *Capitol CDCL 777*	61		1
17 Oct 98	**SICK OF GOODBYES** *Parlophone CDCLS 808*	57		1

SPARKS
US/UK, male vocal/instrumental group – Ron & Russell Mael, Norman Diamond, d. 10 Sep 2004, Adrian Fisher, d. 31 Mar 2000, & Martin Gordon — 81

Date	Title	Peak Position	Weeks at No.1	Weeks on Chart
4 May 74	**THIS TOWN AIN'T BIG ENOUGH FOR THE BOTH OF US** *Island WIP 6193* ●	2		10
20 Jul 74	**AMATEUR HOUR** *Island WIP 6203*	7		9
19 Oct 74	**NEVER TURN YOUR BACK ON MOTHER EARTH** *Island WIP 6211*	13		7
18 Jan 75	**SOMETHING FOR THE GIRL WITH EVERYTHING** *Island WIP 6221*	17		7
19 Jul 75	**GET IN THE SWING** *Island WIP 6236*	27		7
4 Oct 75	**LOOKS LOOKS LOOKS** *Island WIP 6249*	26		4
21 Apr 79	**THE NUMBER ONE SONG IN HEAVEN** *Virgin VS 244*	14		12
21 Jul 79	**BEAT THE CLOCK** *Virgin VS 270*	10		9
27 Oct 79	**TRYOUTS FOR THE HUMAN RACE** *Virgin VS 289*	45		5
29 Oct 94	**WHEN DO I GET TO SING 'MY WAY'** *Logic 74321234472*	38		3
11 Mar 95	**WHEN I KISS YOU (I HEAR CHARLIE PARKER)** *Logic 74321264272*	36		2
20 May 95	**WHEN DO I GET TO SING 'MY WAY'** *Logic 74321274002*	32		2
9 Mar 96	**NOW THAT I OWN THE BBC** *Logic 74321348672*	60		1
25 Oct 97	**THE NUMBER ONE SONG IN HEAVEN** *Roadrunner RR 22692*	70		1
13 Dec 97	**THIS TOWN AIN'T BIG ENOUGH FOR THE BOTH OF US** *Roadrunner RR 22513* VS FAITH NO MORE	40		2

JORDIN SPARKS
US, female vocalist — 73

Date	Title	Peak Position	Weeks at No.1	Weeks on Chart
12 Apr 08	**TATTOO** *Jive GBCTA0700266*	24		15
26 Apr 08	**NO AIR** *Jive 88697296612* FEATURING CHRIS BROWN ●	3		27
17 Jan 09	**ONE STEP AT A TIME** *Jive GBCTA0700276*	16		8
20 Jun 09	**BATTLEFIELD** *Jive 88697553682*	11		15
3 Oct 09	**SOS (LET THE MUSIC PLAY)** *Jive GBCTA0900220*	13		8

TOMMY SPARKS
Sweden, male vocalist — 3

Date	Title	Peak Position	Weeks at No.1	Weeks on Chart
16 May 09	**SHE'S GOT ME DANCING** *Island 2705868*	22		3

SAM SPARRO
Australia, male vocalist/keyboard player/producer (Sam Falson) — 41

Date	Title	Peak Position	Weeks at No.1	Weeks on Chart
29 Mar 08	**BLACK & GOLD** *Island 1766841*	2		39
9 Aug 08	**21ST CENTURY LIFE** *Island 1780494*	44		2

BUBBA SPARXXX
US, male rapper (Warren Mathis) — 13

Date	Title	Peak Position	Weeks at No.1	Weeks on Chart
24 Nov 01	**UGLY** *Interscope 4976542*	7		10
9 Mar 02	**LOVELY** *Interscope 4976752*	24		2
20 Mar 04	**DELIVERANCE** *Interscope 9862013*	55		1

SPEAR OF DESTINY
UK, male vocal/instrumental group — 43

Date	Title	Peak Position	Weeks at No.1	Weeks on Chart
21 May 83	**THE WHEEL** *Epic A 3372*	59		5
21 Jan 84	**PRISONER OF LOVE** *Epic A 4068*	59		3
14 Apr 84	**LIBERATOR** *Epic A 4310*	67		2
15 Jun 85	**ALL MY LOVE (ASK NOTHING)** *Epic A 6333*	61		3
10 Aug 85	**COME BACK** *Epic A 6445*	55		3
7 Feb 87	**STRANGERS IN OUR TOWN** *10 TEN 148*	49		4
4 Apr 87	**NEVER TAKE ME ALIVE** *10 TEN 162*	14		11
25 Jul 87	**WAS THAT YOU** *10 TEN 173*	55		4
3 Oct 87	**THE TRAVELLER** *10 TEN 189*	44		3
24 Sep 88	**SO IN LOVE WITH YOU** *Virgin VS 1123*	36		5

SPEARHEAD
US, male/female vocal/instrumental group — 5

Date	Title	Peak Position	Weeks at No.1	Weeks on Chart
17 Dec 94	**OF COURSE YOU CAN** *Capitol CDCL 733*	74		1
22 Apr 95	**HOLE IN THE BUCKET** *Capitol CDCL 742*	55		1
15 Jul 95	**PEOPLE IN THA MIDDLE** *Capitol CDCLS 752*	49		2
15 Mar 97	**WHY OH WHY** *Capitol CDCL 785*	45		1

BILLIE JO SPEARS
US, female vocalist — 40

Date	Title	Peak Position	Weeks at No.1	Weeks on Chart
12 Jul 75	**BLANKET ON THE GROUND** *United Artists UP 35805*	6		13
17 Jul 76	**WHAT I'VE GOT IN MIND** *United Artists UP 36118*	4		13
11 Dec 76	**SING ME AN OLD FASHIONED SONG** *United Artists UP 36179*	34		9
21 Jul 79	**I WILL SURVIVE** *United Artists UP 601*	47		5

BRITNEY SPEARS
US, female vocalist/actor. The youngest million-selling female in UK chart history smashed the first-week sales record for a debut act when the raunchy, back-to-school ditty '...Baby One More Time' sold 464,000 copies to land at No.1. Her UK singles sales stand at 6.6 million — 331

Date	Title	Peak Position	Weeks at No.1	Weeks on Chart
27 Feb 99	**BABY ONE MORE TIME** *Jive 0521692* ⊛x2 ★	1	2	22
26 Jun 99	**SOMETIMES** *Jive 0523202* ●	3		16
2 Oct 99	**(YOU DRIVE ME) CRAZY** *Jive 0550582* ○	5		11
29 Jan 00	**BORN TO MAKE YOU HAPPY** *Jive 9250022* ○	1	1	12
13 May 00	**OOPS!...I DID IT AGAIN** *Jive 9250542* ●	1	1	14
26 Aug 00	**LUCKY** *Jive 9251022* ○	5		11
16 Dec 00	**STRONGER** *Jive 9251502*	7		10
7 Apr 01	**DON'T LET ME BE THE LAST TO KNOW** *Jive 9252032*	12		8
27 Oct 01	**I'M A SLAVE 4 U** *Jive 9252892*	4		14
2 Feb 02	**OVERPROTECTED** *Jive 9253072*	4		12
13 Apr 02	**I'M NOT A GIRL NOT YET A WOMAN** *Jive 9253472*	2		10
10 Aug 02	**BOYS** *Jive 9253912* FEATURING PHARRELL WILLIAMS	7		8
16 Nov 02	**I LOVE ROCK 'N' ROLL** *Jive 9254222*	13		8
22 Nov 03	**ME AGAINST THE MUSIC** *Jive 82876576432* FEATURING MADONNA	2		12
13 Mar 04	**TOXIC** *Jive 82876602092* ○	1	1	14
26 Jun 04	**EVERYTIME** *Jive 82876626202*	1	1	14
13 Nov 04	**MY PREROGATIVE** *Jive 82876652582*	3		12
12 Mar 05	**DO SOMETHIN'** *Jive 82876682132*	6		9
27 Oct 07	**GIMME MORE** *Jive 88697186762*	3		18
29 Dec 07	**PIECE OF ME** *Jive 88697221762*	2		23
5 Apr 08	**BREAK THE ICE** *Jive 88697290262*	15		11
15 Nov 08	**WOMANIZER** *Jive 88697409422* ○ ★	3		20
13 Dec 08	**CIRCUS** *Jive 88697455282*	13		18
11 Apr 09	**IF YOU SEEK AMY** *Jive 88697487822*	20		11
1 Aug 09	**RADAR** *Jive USJI10700730*	46		3
21 Nov 09	**3** *Jive USJI10900602* ★	7		10

SPECIAL D
Germany, male producer (Dennis Horstmann) & female vocalist (Laura Nori) — 11

Date	Title	Peak Position	Weeks at No.1	Weeks on Chart
17 Apr 04	**COME WITH ME** *All Around The World CDGLOBE 340*	6		11

SPECIAL NEEDS
UK, male vocal/instrumental group — 2

Date	Title	Peak Position	Weeks at No.1	Weeks on Chart
16 Oct 04	**FRANCESCA – THE MADDENING GLARE/WINTER** *Poptones MC5092SCD*	69		1
25 Jun 05	**BLUES SKIES** *Mercury 9872234*	56		1

SPECIALS
UK, male vocal/instrumental group – Jerry Dammers, John Bradbury, Horace Gentleman (Stephen Panter), Lynval Golding (b. Jamaica), Terry Hall*, Roddy Radiation (Roderick Byers) & Neville Staple (b. Jamaica) — 101

Date	Title	Peak Position	Weeks at No.1	Weeks on Chart
28 Jul 79	**GANGSTERS** *2 Tone CHSTT 1* SPECIAL A.K.A. ○	6		12
27 Oct 79	**A MESSAGE TO YOU RUDY/NITE CLUB** *2 Tone CHSTT 5* (FEATURING RICO) ○	10		14
26 Jan 80	**THE SPECIAL A.K.A. LIVE! EP** *2 Tone CHSTT 7* SPECIAL A.K.A. ○	1	2	10
24 May 80	**RAT RACE/RUDE BUOYS OUTA JAIL** *2 Tone CHSTT 11*	5		9
20 Sep 80	**STEREOTYPE/INTERNATIONAL JET SET** *2 Tone CHSTT 13*	6		8
13 Dec 80	**DO NOTHING/MAGGIE'S FARM** *2 Tone CHSTT 16* ○	4		11
20 Jun 81	**GHOST TOWN** *2 Tone CHSTT 17* ●	1	3	14
23 Jan 82	**THE BOILER** *2 Tone CHSTT 18* RHODA WITH THE SPECIAL A.K.A.	35		5
3 Sep 83	**RACIST FRIENDS/BRIGHT LIGHTS** *2 Tone CHSTT 25* SPECIAL A.K.A.	60		3
17 Mar 84	**NELSON MANDELA** *2 Tone CHSTT 26* SPECIAL A.K.A.	9		10
8 Sep 84	**WHAT I LIKE MOST ABOUT YOU IS YOUR GIRLFRIEND** *2 Tone CHSTT 27* SPECIAL A.K.A.	51		4
10 Feb 96	**HYPROCRITE** *Kuff KUFFD 3*	66		1

SPECTRUM
UK, male production/instrumental trio — 1

Date	Title	Peak Position	Weeks at No.1	Weeks on Chart
26 Sep 92	**TRUE LOVE WILL FIND YOU IN THE END** *Silvertone ORE 44*	70		1

CHRIS SPEDDING
UK, male vocalist/guitarist — 8

Date	Title	Peak Position	Weeks at No.1	Weeks on Chart
23 Aug 75	**MOTOR BIKING** *RAK 210*	14		8

SPEECH
US, male vocalist (Todd Thomas) — 2

Date	Title	Peak Position	Weeks at No.1	Weeks on Chart
17 Feb 96	**LIKE MARVIN GAYE SAID (WHAT'S GOING ON)** *Cooltempo CDCOOL 314*	35		2

SPEEDWAY
UK, male/female vocal/instrumental duo – Jim Duguid & Jill Jackson — 10

Date	Title	Peak Position	Weeks at No.1	Weeks on Chart
6 Sep 03	**GENIE IN A BOTTLE/SAVE YOURSELF** *Innocent SINCD 47*	10		4
21 Feb 04	**CAN'T TURN BACK** *Innocent SINDX 55*	12		4
19 Jun 04	**IN AND OUT** *Innocent SINDX 61*	31		2

SPEEDY
UK, male/female vocal/instrumental group — 1

Date	Title	Peak Position	Weeks at No.1	Weeks on Chart
9 Nov 96	**BOY WONDER** *Boiler House! BOIL 2CD*	56		1

REGINA SPEKTOR
US (b. Russia), female vocalist/pianist — 4

Date	Title	Peak Position	Weeks at No.1	Weeks on Chart
15 Jul 06	**ON THE RADIO** *Sire W718CD*	60		1
3 Mar 07	**FIDELITY** *Sire W737CD1*	45		3

SPEKTRUM
UK, male/female vocal/instrumental group — 1

Date	Title	Peak Position	Weeks at No.1	Weeks on Chart
18 Sep 04	**KINDA NEW** *Non Stop SPEKD004*	70		1

SPELLBOUND
India, female vocal duo — 1

Date	Title	Peak Position	Weeks at No.1	Weeks on Chart
31 May 97	**HEAVEN ON EARTH** *East West EW 098CD*	73		1

JOHNNIE SPENCE
UK, male orchestra leader — 15

Date	Title	Peak Position	Weeks at No.1	Weeks on Chart
1 Mar 62	**THEME FROM 'DR KILDARE'** *Parlophone R 4872*	15		15

Silver-selling ○ Gold-selling ● Platinum-selling (x multiples) ⊛ US No.1 ★ Peak Position Weeks at No.1 Weeks on Chart

DON SPENCER
Australia, male vocalist — 12

Date	Title	Peak Position	Weeks at No.1	Weeks on Chart
21 Mar 63	**FIREBALL** *HMV POP 1087*	32		12

TRACIE SPENCER
US, female vocalist — 3

Date	Title	Peak Position	Weeks at No.1	Weeks on Chart
4 May 91	**THIS HOUSE** *Capitol CL 612*	65		2
6 Nov 99	**IT'S ALL ABOUT YOU (NOT ABOUT ME)** *Parlophone Rhythm Series CDCL 815*	65		1

JON SPENCER BLUES EXPLOSION
US, male vocal/instrumental group — 3

Date	Title	Peak Position	Weeks at No.1	Weeks on Chart
10 May 97	**WAIL** *Mute CDMUTE 204*	66		1
6 Apr 02	**SHE SAID** *Mute LCDMUTE 263*	58		1
6 Jul 02	**SWEET N SOUR** *Mute LCDMUTE 271*	66		1

SPHINX
UK/US, male vocal/instrumental group. See Dusted, Faithless, Our Tribe/One Tribe, Rollo — 2

Date	Title	Peak Position	Weeks at No.1	Weeks on Chart
25 Mar 95	**WHAT HOPE HAVE I** *Champion CHAMPCD 318*	43		2

SPICE GIRLS
UK, female vocal group – Victoria Beckham* (nee Adams), Melanie B* (Melanie Brown), Emma Bunton*, Melanie C* (Melanie Chisholm) & Geri Halliwell*. See England United — 184

Date	Title	Peak Position	Weeks at No.1	Weeks on Chart
20 Jul 96	**WANNABE** *Virgin VSCDX 1588* ⊛ ★	1	7	26
26 Oct 96	**SAY YOU'LL BE THERE** *Virgin VSCDT 1601* ⊛	1	2	17
28 Dec 96	**2 BECOME 1** *Virgin VSCDT 1607* ⊛	1	3	23
15 Mar 97	**MAMA/WHO DO YOU THINK YOU ARE** *Virgin VSCDT 1623* ⊛	1	3	15
25 Oct 97	**SPICE UP YOUR LIFE** *Virgin VSCDT 1660* ⊛	1	1	15
27 Dec 97	**TOO MUCH** *Virgin VSCDR 1669* ⊛	1	2	15
21 Mar 98	**STOP** *Virgin VSCDT 1679* ○	2		17
1 Aug 98	**VIVA FOREVER** *Virgin VSCDT 1692* ⊛	1	2	13
26 Dec 98	**GOODBYE** *Virgin VSCDT 1721* ⊛	1	1	21
4 Nov 00	**HOLLER/LET LOVE LEAD THE WAY** *Virgin VSCDT 1788* ○	1	1	17
17 Nov 07	**HEADLINES (FRIENDSHIP NEVER ENDS)** *Virgin HEADCD100*	11		5

Top 3 Best-Selling Singles

		Approximate Sales
1	WANNABE	1,300,000
2	2 BECOME 1	1,095,000
3	SAY YOU'LL BE THERE	940,000

SPIDER
UK, male vocal/instrumental group — 5

Date	Title	Peak Position	Weeks at No.1	Weeks on Chart
5 Mar 83	**WHY D'YA LIE TO ME** *RCA 313*	65		2
10 Mar 84	**HERE WE GO ROCK 'N' ROLL** *A&M AM 180*	57		3

SPILLER
Italy, male producer (Cristiano Spiller). See Sophie Ellis-Bextor, Laguna, Theaudience — 26

Date	Title	Peak Position	Weeks at No.1	Weeks on Chart
26 Aug 00	**GROOVEJET (IF THIS AIN'T LOVE)** *Positiva CDTIV 137* ●	1	1	24
2 Feb 02	**CRY BABY** *Positiva CDTIVS 167*	40		2

SPIN CITY
UK/Ireland, male vocal group — 3

Date	Title	Peak Position	Weeks at No.1	Weeks on Chart
26 Aug 00	**LANDSLIDE** *Epic 6696132*	30		3

SPIN DOCTORS
US, male vocal/instrumental group – Christopher Barron, Aaron Comess, Eric Schenkman (replaced by Anthony Krizan) & Mark White — 28

Date	Title	Peak Position	Weeks at No.1	Weeks on Chart
15 May 93	**TWO PRINCES** *Epic 6591452* ○	3		15
14 Aug 93	**LITTLE MISS CAN'T BE WRONG** *Epic 6584892*	23		5
9 Oct 93	**JIMMY OLSEN'S BLUES** *Epic 6597582*	40		2
4 Dec 93	**WHAT TIME IS IT** *Epic 6599552*	56		1
25 Jun 94	**CLEOPATRA'S CAT** *Epic 6604192*	29		2
30 Jul 94	**YOU LET YOUR HEART GO TOO FAST** *Epic 6606612*	66		1
29 Oct 94	**MARY JANE** *Epic 6609772*	55		1

Date	Title	Peak Position	Weeks at No.1	Weeks on Chart
8 Jun 96	**SHE USED TO BE MINE** *Epic 6632682*	55		1

SPINAL TAP
UK/US, male vocal/instrumental group — 3

Date	Title	Peak Position	Weeks at No.1	Weeks on Chart
28 Mar 92	**BITCH SCHOOL** *MCA 1624*	35		2
2 May 92	**THE MAJESTY OF ROCK** *MCA MCS 1629*	61		1

SPINTO BAND
US, male vocal/instrumental group — 2

Date	Title	Peak Position	Weeks at No.1	Weeks on Chart
3 Jun 06	**DID I TELL YOU** *Radiate RDTCDX17*	55		1
26 Aug 06	**OH MANDY** *Radiate RDTCDX18*	54		1

SPIRAL TRIBE
UK, male/female vocal/rap/DJ/production collective — 2

Date	Title	Peak Position	Weeks at No.1	Weeks on Chart
29 Aug 92	**BREACH THE PEACE (EP)** *Butterfly BLRT 79*	66		1
21 Nov 92	**FORWARD THE REVOLUTION** *Butterfly BLRT 85*	70		1

SPIRITS
UK, male/female vocal duo — 5

Date	Title	Peak Position	Weeks at No.1	Weeks on Chart
19 Nov 94	**DON'T BRING ME DOWN** *MCA MCSTD 2018*	31		3
8 Apr 95	**SPIRIT INSIDE** *MCA MCSTD 2045*	39		2

SPIRITUALIZED
UK, male/female vocal/instrumental group — 19

Date	Title	Peak Position	Weeks at No.1	Weeks on Chart
30 Jun 90	**ANYWAY THAT YOU WANT ME/STEP INTO THE BREEZE** *Dedicated ZB 43783*	75		1
17 Aug 91	**RUN** *Dedicated SPIRT 002*	59		1
25 Jul 92	**MEDICATION** *Dedicated SPIRT 005T*	55		1
23 Oct 93	**ELECTRIC MAINLINE** *Dedicated SPIRT 007CD*	49		1
4 Feb 95	**LET IT FLOW** *Dedicated SPIRT 009CD SPIRITUALIZED ELECTRIC MAINLINE*	30		2
9 Aug 97	**ELECTRICITY** *Dedicated SPIRIT 012CD1*	32		2
14 Feb 98	**I THINK I'M IN LOVE** *Dedicated SPIRIT 014CD*	27		2
6 Jun 98	**THE ABBEY ROAD EP** *Dedicated SPIRT 015CD*	39		2
15 Sep 01	**STOP YOUR CRYING** *Spaceman OPM 002*	18		3
8 Dec 01	**OUT OF SIGHT** *Spaceman OPM 005*	65		1
23 Feb 02	**DO IT ALL OVER AGAIN** *Spaceman OPM 007*	31		2
13 Sep 03	**SHE KISSED ME (IT FELT LIKE A HIT)** *Sanctuary SANXD 222*	38		1

SPIRO & WIX
UK, male instrumental/production duo — 2

Date	Title	Peak Position	Weeks at No.1	Weeks on Chart
10 Aug 96	**TARA'S THEME** *EMI Premier PRESCD 4*	29		2

SHARLEEN SPITERI
UK, female vocalist/guitarist. See Texas — 9

Date	Title	Peak Position	Weeks at No.1	Weeks on Chart
12 Jul 08	**ALL THE TIMES I CRIED** *Mercury 1769267*	26		8
13 Mar 10	**XANADU** *Mercury GBUM70912805*	71		1

SPITTING IMAGE
UK, male/female TV comedy puppets — 18

Date	Title	Peak Position	Weeks at No.1	Weeks on Chart
10 May 86	**THE CHICKEN SONG** *Virgin SPIT 1* ○	1	3	11
6 Dec 86	**SANTA CLAUS IS ON THE DOLE/FIRST ATHEIST TABERNACLE CHOIR** *Virgin VS 921*	22		7

SPLINTER
UK, male vocal/instrumental duo — 10

Date	Title	Peak Position	Weeks at No.1	Weeks on Chart
2 Nov 74	**COSTAFINE TOWN** *Dark Horse AMS 7135*	17		10

SPLIT ENZ
New Zealand, male/female vocal/instrumental group — 15

Date	Title	Peak Position	Weeks at No.1	Weeks on Chart
16 Aug 80	**I GOT YOU** *A&M AMS 7546*	12		11
23 May 81	**HISTORY NEVER REPEATS** *A&M AMS 8128*	63		4

A SPLIT SECOND
Belgium, male production duo — 1

Date	Title	Peak Position	Weeks at No.1	Weeks on Chart
14 Dec 91	**FLESH** *ffrr FX 178*	68		1

SPLODGENESSABOUNDS

UK, male/female vocal/instrumental group – Max Splodge (Martyn Everest), Ray 'Wiffy' Archer, Pat (Delroy Washington) Thetic Von Dale Chiptooth, Miles Flat, Winston Forbe, Baby Greensleeves, Roger Rodent & Desert Island Joe Lurche Slythe — 17

Date	Title	Peak	Wks at No.1	Wks
14 Jun 80	**SIMON TEMPLAR/TWO PINTS OF LAGER AND A PACKET OF CRISPS PLEASE** *Deram BUM 1*	7		8
6 Sep 80	**TWO LITTLE BOYS/HORSE** *Deram ROLF 1*	26		7
13 Jun 81	**COWPUNK MEDLUM** *Deram BUM 3*	69		2

SPOILED & ZIGO

Israel, male DJ/production duo — 3

Date	Title	Peak	Wks at No.1	Wks
12 Aug 00	**MORE & MORE** *Manifesto FESCD 72*	31		3

SPONGE

US, male vocal/instrumental group — 1

Date	Title	Peak	Wks at No.1	Wks
19 Aug 95	**PLOWED** *Work 6623162*	74		1

SPOOKS

US, male/female vocal/rap group – Ming Xia (Irina Perez), Booka-T (Booker Tucker), Joe Davis, Hypno (Chenjerai Kumanyika) & Water Water (Jerel Spruill), d. 21 Sep 2003 — 17

Date	Title	Peak	Wks at No.1	Wks
27 Jan 01	**THINGS I'VE SEEN** *Artemis ANTCD 6706722*	6		10
5 May 01	**KARMA HOTEL** *Artemis ANTCD 6709012*	15		6
15 Sep 01	**SWEET REVENGE** *Artemis 6718072*	67		1

SPOOKY

UK, male production duo — 1

Date	Title	Peak	Wks at No.1	Wks
13 Mar 93	**SCHMOO** *Guerilla GRRR 45CD*	72		1

DAVE SPOON

UK, male radio DJ/producer (Simon Neale) — 8

Date	Title	Peak	Wks at No.1	Wks
8 Sep 07	**BAD GIRL (AT NIGHT)** *Toolroom/Apollo APOLLO114CDX* FEATURING LISA MAFFIA	36		4
16 Aug 08	**BADITUDE** *Toolroom CDTOOLABS1* SPOON, HARRIS & OBERNIK	29		4

SPORTY THIEVZ

US, male rap/vocal group — 6

Date	Title	Peak	Wks at No.1	Wks
10 Jul 99	**NO PIGEONS** *Columbia 6676022*	21		6

SPOTNICKS

Sweden, male instrumental group — 37

Date	Title	Peak	Wks at No.1	Wks
14 Jun 62	**ORANGE BLOSSOM SPECIAL** *Oriole CB 1724*	29		10
6 Sep 62	**ROCKET MAN** *Oriole CB 1755*	38		9
31 Jan 63	**HAVA NAGILA** *Oriole CB 1790*	13		12
25 Apr 63	**JUST LISTEN TO MY HEART** *Oriole CB 1818*	36		6

DUSTY SPRINGFIELD

UK, female vocalist (Mary O'Brien), d. 2 Mar 1999 (age 59). One of the most successful UK females of the 1960s, who had a string of successes after the Springfields split. The distinctive vocalist, who was often voted the UK's 'Top Female Singer', influenced many 21st-century artists — 211

Date	Title	Peak	Wks at No.1	Wks
21 Nov 63	**I ONLY WANT TO BE WITH YOU** *Philips BF 1292*	4		18
20 Feb 64	**STAY AWHILE** *Philips BF 1313*	13		10
2 Jul 64	**I JUST DON'T KNOW WHAT TO DO WITH MYSELF** *Philips BF 1348*	3		12
22 Oct 64	**LOSING YOU** *Philips BF 1369*	9		13
18 Feb 65	**YOUR HURTIN' KIND OF LOVE** *Philips BF 1396*	37		4
1 Jul 65	**IN THE MIDDLE OF NOWHERE** *Philips BF 1418*	8		10
16 Sep 65	**SOME OF YOUR LOVIN'** *Philips BF 1430*	8		12
27 Jan 66	**LITTLE BY LITTLE** *Philips BF 1466*	17		9
31 Mar 66	**YOU DON'T HAVE TO SAY YOU LOVE ME** *Philips BF 1482*	1	1	13
7 Jul 66	**GOING BACK** *Philips BF 1502*	10		10
15 Sep 66	**ALL I SEE IS YOU** *Philips BF 1510*	9		12
23 Feb 67	**I'LL TRY ANYTHING** *Philips BF 1553*	13		9
25 May 67	**GIVE ME TIME** *Philips BF 1577*	24		6
10 Jul 68	**I CLOSE MY EYES AND COUNT TO TEN** *Philips BF 1682*	4		12
4 Dec 68	**SON OF A PREACHER MAN** *Philips BF 1730*	9		9
20 Sep 69	**AM I THE SAME GIRL** *Philips BF 1811*	43		4
19 Sep 70	**HOW CAN I BE SURE** *Philips 6006 045*	36		4
20 Oct 79	**BABY BLUE** *Mercury DUSTY 4*	61		5
22 Aug 87	**WHAT HAVE I DONE TO DESERVE THIS** *Parlophone R 6163* PET SHOP BOYS & DUSTY SPRINGFIELD ●	2		9
25 Feb 89	**NOTHING HAS BEEN PROVED** *Parlophone R 6207*	16		7
2 Dec 89	**IN PRIVATE** *Parlophone R 6234*	14		10
26 May 90	**REPUTATION** *Parlophone R 6253*	38		6
24 Nov 90	**ARRESTED BY YOU** *Parlophone R 6266*	70		2
30 Oct 93	**HEART AND SOUL** *Columbia 6598562* CILLA BLACK WITH DUSTY SPRINGFIELD	75		1
10 Jun 95	**WHEREVER WOULD I BE** *Columbia 6620592* & DARYL HALL	44		3
4 Nov 95	**ROLL AWAY** *Columbia 6623682*	68		1

RICK SPRINGFIELD

Australia, male vocalist/guitarist/actor (Richard Springthorpe) — 13

Date	Title	Peak	Wks at No.1	Wks
14 Jan 84	**HUMAN TOUCH/SOULS** *RCA RICK 1*	23		7
24 Mar 84	**JESSIE'S GIRL** *RCA RICK 2* ★	43		6

SPRINGFIELDS

UK, female/male vocal/instrumental trio – Dusty Springfield*, d. 2 Mar 1999, Tim Field (replaced by Mike Hurst) & Tom Springfield — 66

Date	Title	Peak	Wks at No.1	Wks
31 Aug 61	**BREAKAWAY** *Philips BF 1168*	31		8
16 Nov 61	**BAMBINO** *Philips BF 1178*	16		11
13 Dec 62	**ISLAND OF DREAMS** *Philips 326557 BF*	5		26
28 Mar 63	**SAY I WON'T BE THERE** *Philips 326577 BF*	5		15
25 Jul 63	**COME ON HOME** *Philips BF 1253*	31		6

BRUCE SPRINGSTEEN

US, male vocalist/guitarist/harmonica player — 147

Date	Title	Peak	Wks at No.1	Wks
22 Nov 80	**HUNGRY HEART** *CBS 9309*	44		4
13 Jun 81	**THE RIVER** *CBS A 1179*	35		6
26 May 84	**DANCING IN THE DARK** *CBS A 4436*	28		7
6 Oct 84	**COVER ME** *CBS A 4662*	38		5
12 Jan 85	**DANCING IN THE DARK** *CBS A 4436* ●	4		16
23 Mar 85	**COVER ME** *CBS A 4662*	16		8
15 Jun 85	**I'M ON FIRE/BORN IN THE USA** *CBS A 6342* ●	5		12
3 Aug 85	**GLORY DAYS** *CBS A 6375*	17		6
14 Dec 85	**SANTA CLAUS IS COMIN' TO TOWN/MY HOMETOWN** *CBS A 6773* ●	9		5
29 Nov 86	**WAR** *CBS 6501937*	18		7
7 Feb 87	**FIRE** *CBS 6503817*	54		2
23 May 87	**BORN TO RUN** *CBS BRUCE 2*	16		4
3 Oct 87	**BRILLIANT DISGUISE** *CBS 6511417*	20		5
12 Dec 87	**TUNNEL OF LOVE** *CBS 6512957*	45		4
18 Jun 88	**TOUGHER THAN THE REST** *CBS BRUCE 3*	13		8
24 Sep 88	**SPARE PARTS** *CBS BRUCE 4*	32		3
21 Mar 92	**HUMAN TOUCH** *Columbia 6578727*	11		5
23 May 92	**BETTER DAYS** *Columbia 6578907*	34		3
25 Jul 92	**57 CHANNELS (AND NOTHIN' ON)** *Columbia 6581387*	32		4
24 Oct 92	**LEAP OF FAITH** *Columbia 6583697*	46		3
10 Apr 93	**LUCKY TOWN (LIVE)** *Columbia 6592282*	48		3
19 Mar 94	**STREETS OF PHILADELPHIA** *Columbia 6600652* ●	2		12
22 Apr 95	**SECRET GARDEN** *Columbia 6612955*	44		3
11 Nov 95	**HUNGRY HEART** *Columbia 6626252*	28		3
4 May 96	**THE GHOST OF TOM JOAD** *Columbia 6630315*	26		2
19 Apr 97	**SECRET GARDEN** *Columbia 6643245*	17		4
14 Dec 02	**LONESOME DAY** *Columbia 6734082*	39		2
29 Dec 07	**SANTA CLAUS IS COMIN' TO TOWN/MY HOMETOWN** *Sony Music USSM17500461*	60		1

SPRINGWATER

UK, male multi-instrumentalist (Phil Cordell) — 12

Date	Title	Peak	Wks at No.1	Wks
23 Oct 71	**I WILL RETURN** *Polydor 2058 141*	5		12

SPRINKLER

UK/US, male/female vocal/rap group — 2

Date	Title	Peak	Wks at No.1	Wks
11 Jul 98	**LEAVE 'EM SOMETHING TO DESIRE** *Island CID 706*	45		2

SPUNGE

UK, male vocal/instrumental group — 3

Date	Title	Peak	Wks at No.1	Wks
15 Jun 02	**JUMP ON DEMAND** *B Unique BUN 022CDX*	39		2
24 Aug 02	**ROOTS** *B Unique BUN 030CDX*	52		1

SPYRO GYRA

US, male instrumental group — 10

Date	Title	Peak	Wks at No.1	Wks
21 Jul 79	**MORNING DANCE** *Infinity INF 111*	17		10

Silver-selling ● Gold-selling ● Platinum-selling (x multiples) ✪ US No.1 ★ Peak Position · Weeks at No.1 · Weeks on Chart

SQUEEZE

UK, male vocal/instrumental group – Chris Difford & Glenn Tilbrook (Difford & Tilbrook*); members also included Paul Gunn (replaced by Gilson Lavis), Jools Holland* (replaced by Paul Carrack*) & Henry Kakoulli (replaced by John Bentley)

Date	Title	Peak Position	Weeks at No.1	Weeks on Chart: 123
8 Apr 78	**TAKE ME I'M YOURS** *A&M AMS 7335*	19		9
10 Jun 78	**BANG BANG** *A&M AMS 7360*	49		5
18 Nov 78	**GOODBYE GIRL** *A&M AMS 7398*	63		2
24 Mar 79	**COOL FOR CATS** *A&M AMS 7426* ●	2		11
2 Jun 79	**UP THE JUNCTION** *A&M AMS 7444* ●	2		11
8 Sep 79	**SLAP AND TICKLE** *A&M AMS 7466*	24		8
1 Mar 80	**ANOTHER NAIL IN MY HEART** *A&M AMS 7507*	17		9
10 May 80	**PULLING MUSSELS (FROM THE SHELL)** *A&M AMS 7523*	44		6
16 May 81	**IS THAT LOVE** *A&M AMS 8129*	35		8
25 Jul 81	**TEMPTED** *A&M AMS 8147*	41		5
10 Oct 81	**LABELLED WITH LOVE** *A&M AMS 8166* ●	4		10
24 Apr 82	**BLACK COFFEE IN BED** *A&M AMS 8219*	51		4
23 Oct 82	**ANNIE GET YOUR GUN** *A&M AMS 8259*	43		4
15 Jun 85	**LAST TIME FOREVER** *A&M AM 255*	45		5
8 Aug 87	**HOURGLASS** *A&M AM 4000*	16		10
17 Oct 87	**TRUST ME TO OPEN MY MOUTH** *A&M AM 412*	72		1
25 Apr 92	**COOL FOR CATS** *A&M AM 860*	62		2
24 Jul 93	**THIRD RAIL** *A&M 5803372*	39		3
11 Sep 93	**SOME FANTASTIC PLACE** *A&M 5803792*	73		1
9 Sep 95	**THIS SUMMER** *A&M 5811912*	36		3
18 Nov 95	**ELECTRIC TRAINS** *A&M 5812692*	44		2
15 Jun 96	**HEAVEN KNOWS** *A&M 5816052*	27		2
24 Aug 96	**THIS SUMMER** *A&M 5818412*	32		2

BILLY SQUIER

US, male vocalist/guitarist

Date	Title	Peak Position	Weeks at No.1	Weeks on Chart: 3
3 Oct 81	**THE STROKE** *Capitol CL 214*	52		3

JOHN SQUIRE

UK, male vocalist/guitarist. See Seahorses, Stone Roses

Date	Title	Peak Position	Weeks at No.1	Weeks on Chart: 2
2 Nov 02	**JOE LOUIS** *North Country NCCDB 001*	43		1
14 Feb 04	**ROOM IN BROOKLYN** *North Country NCCDA 003*	44		1

DOROTHY SQUIRES

UK, female vocalist (Edna Squires), d. 14 Apr 1998 (age 83)

Date	Title	Peak Position	Weeks at No.1	Weeks on Chart: 56
5 Jun 53	**I'M WALKING BEHIND YOU** *Polygon P 1068*	12		1
24 Aug 61	**SAY IT WITH FLOWERS** *Columbia DB 4665* & RUSS CONWAY	23		10
20 Sep 69	**FOR ONCE IN MY LIFE** *President PT 267*	24		11
21 Feb 70	**TILL** *President PT 281*	25		11
8 Aug 70	**MY WAY** *President PT 305*	25		23

STABBS

Finland/US/Cameroon, male/female production/vocal group

Date	Title	Peak Position	Weeks at No.1	Weeks on Chart: 1
24 Dec 94	**JOY AND HAPPINESS** *Hi-Life HICD 3*	65		1

STACCATO

UK/Holland, male/female vocal/instrumental duo

Date	Title	Peak Position	Weeks at No.1	Weeks on Chart: 1
20 Jul 96	**I WANNA KNOW** *Multiply CDMULTY 11*	65		1

WARREN STACEY

UK, male vocalist

Date	Title	Peak Position	Weeks at No.1	Weeks on Chart: 3
23 Mar 02	**MY GIRL MY GIRL** *Def Soul 5889932*	26		3

JIM STAFFORD

US, male vocalist

Date	Title	Peak Position	Weeks at No.1	Weeks on Chart: 16
27 Apr 74	**SPIDERS AND SNAKES** *MGM 2006 374*	14		8
6 Jul 74	**MY GIRL BILL** *MGM 2006 423*	20		8

JO STAFFORD

US, female vocalist, d. 16 Jul 2008 (age 91)

Date	Title	Peak Position	Weeks at No.1	Weeks on Chart: 28
14 Nov 52	**YOU BELONG TO ME** *Columbia DB 3152* ★	1	1	19
19 Dec 52	**JAMBALAYA** *Columbia DB 3169*	11		2
7 May 54	**MAKE LOVE TO ME** *Philips PB 233* ★	8		1
9 Dec 55	**SUDDENLY THERE'S A VALLEY** *Philips PB 509*	12		6

TERRY STAFFORD

US, male vocalist, d. 17 Mar 1996 (age 54)

Date	Title	Peak Position	Weeks at No.1	Weeks on Chart: 9
7 May 64	**SUSPICION** *London HLU 9871*	31		9

STAGECOACH FEATURING PENNY FOSTER

UK, male/female vocal charity ensemble

Date	Title	Peak Position	Weeks at No.1	Weeks on Chart: 1
18 Oct 03	**ANGEL LOOKING THROUGH** *Stagecoach Theatre SCR00001*	59		1

STAIFFI & HIS MUSTAFAS

France, male vocal/instrumental group

Date	Title	Peak Position	Weeks at No.1	Weeks on Chart: 1
28 Jul 60	**MUSTAFA CHA CHA CHA** *Pye International 7N 25057*	43		1

STAIND

US, male vocal/instrumental group

Date	Title	Peak Position	Weeks at No.1	Weeks on Chart: 11
15 Sep 01	**IT'S BEEN A WHILE** *Elektra E 7252CD1*	15		6
1 Dec 01	**OUTSIDE** *Elektra E 7277CD*	33		2
23 Feb 02	**FOR YOU** *Elektra E 7281CD*	55		1
24 May 03	**PRICE TO PAY** *Elektra E 7417CD*	36		2

STAKKA BO

Sweden, male vocalist/rapper (Johan Renck)

Date	Title	Peak Position	Weeks at No.1	Weeks on Chart: 12
25 Sep 93	**HERE WE GO** *Polydor PZCD 280*	13		8
18 Dec 93	**DOWN THE DRAIN** *Polydor PZCD 301*	64		4

FRANK STALLONE

US, male vocalist

Date	Title	Peak Position	Weeks at No.1	Weeks on Chart: 2
22 Oct 83	**FAR FROM OVER** *RSO 95*	68		2

STAMFORD AMP

UK, male vocal/instrumental group

Date	Title	Peak Position	Weeks at No.1	Weeks on Chart: 2
12 Oct 02	**ANYTHING FOR YOU** *Mercury 638982*	33		2

STAMFORD BRIDGE

UK, football fans (Chelsea)/vocal group

Date	Title	Peak Position	Weeks at No.1	Weeks on Chart: 1
16 May 70	**CHELSEA** *Penny Farthing PEN 715*	47		1

STAN

UK, male vocal/production duo – Simon Andrew & Kevin Stagg

Date	Title	Peak Position	Weeks at No.1	Weeks on Chart: 3
31 Jul 93	**SUNTAN** *Hug CDBUM 1*	40		3

STANDS

UK, male vocal/instrumental group

Date	Title	Peak Position	Weeks at No.1	Weeks on Chart: 8
16 Aug 03	**WHEN THIS RIVER ROLLS OVER YOU** *Echo ECSCD 142*	32		1
25 Oct 03	**I NEED YOU** *Echo ECSCX 146*	39		2
21 Feb 04	**HERE SHE COMES AGAIN** *Echo ECSCX 148*	25		2
5 Jun 04	**OUTSIDE YOUR DOOR** *Echo ECSCX 151*	49		1
21 May 05	**DO IT LIKE YOU LIKE** *Echo ECSCX165*	28		2

LISA STANSFIELD

UK, female vocalist

Date	Title	Peak Position	Weeks at No.1	Weeks on Chart: 127
25 Mar 89	**PEOPLE HOLD ON** *Ahead Of Our Time CCUT 5* COLDCUT FEATURING LISA STANSFIELD	11		9
12 Aug 89	**THIS IS THE RIGHT TIME** *Arista 112512*	13		8
28 Oct 89	**ALL AROUND THE WORLD** *Arista 112693* ●	1	2	14
10 Feb 90	**LIVE TOGETHER** *Arista 112914*	10		6
12 May 90	**WHAT DID I DO TO YOU (EP)** *Arista 113168*	25		4
19 Oct 91	**CHANGE** *Arista 114820*	10		7
21 Dec 91	**ALL WOMAN** *Arista 115000*	20		8
14 Mar 92	**TIME TO MAKE YOU MINE** *Arista 115113*	14		8
6 Jun 92	**SET YOUR LOVING FREE** *Arista 74321100587*	28		4
19 Dec 92	**SOMEDAY (I'M COMING BACK)** *Arista 74321123567*	10		9
1 May 93	**FIVE LIVE EP** *Parlophone CDRS 6340* GEORGE MICHAEL & QUEEN WITH LISA STANSFIELD ●	1	3	12
5 Jun 93	**IN ALL THE RIGHT PLACES** *MCA MCSTD 1780*	8		11
23 Oct 93	**SO NATURAL** *Arista 74321169132*	15		5
11 Dec 93	**LITTLE BIT OF HEAVEN** *Arista 74321178202*	32		4
18 Jan 97	**PEOPLE HOLD ON** *Arista 74321452012* VS THE DIRTY ROTTEN SCOUNDRELS	4		6

Date	Title	Peak Position	Weeks at No.1	Weeks on Chart
22 Mar 97	**THE REAL THING** *Arista 74321463222*	9		7
21 Jun 97	**NEVER NEVER GONNA GIVE YOU UP** *Arista 74321490392*	25		3
4 Oct 97	**THE LINE** *RCA 74321511372*	64		1
23 Jun 01	**LET'S CALL IT LOVE** *Arista 74321863422*	48		1

STANTON WARRIORS
UK, male production duo — Weeks on Chart: **1**

Date	Title	Peak Position	Weeks at No.1	Weeks on Chart
22 Sep 01	**DA ANTIDOTE** *Mob MOBCD 006*	69		1

STAPLE SINGERS
US, male/female vocal/instrumental group — Weeks on Chart: **14**

Date	Title	Peak Position	Weeks at No.1	Weeks on Chart
10 Jun 72	**I'LL TAKE YOU THERE** *Stax 2025 110* ★	30		8
8 Jun 74	**IF YOU'RE READY (COME GO WITH ME)** *Stax 2025 224*	34		6

CYRIL STAPLETON
UK, male orchestra leader, d. 25 Feb 1974 (age 59) — Weeks on Chart: **41**

Date	Title	Peak Position	Weeks at No.1	Weeks on Chart
27 May 55	**ELEPHANT TANGO** *Decca F 10488*	19		4
23 Sep 55	**BLUE STAR (THE MEDIC THEME)** *Decca F 10599* CYRIL STAPLETON ORCHESTRA FEATURING JULIE DAWN	2		12
6 Apr 56	**THE ITALIAN THEME** *Decca F 10703*	18		2
1 Jun 56	**THE HAPPY WHISTLER** *Decca F 10735* CYRIL STAPLETON ORCHESTRA FEATURING DESMOND LANE, PENNY WHISTLE	22		4
19 Jul 57	**FORGOTTEN DREAMS** *Decca F 10912*	27		5
16 May 58	**ON THE STREET WHERE YOU LIVE** *Decca F 11018* DAVID WHITFIELD WITH CYRIL STAPLETON & HIS ORCHESTRA	16		14

STAR PILOTS
Sweden, male vocal group — Weeks on Chart: **4**

Date	Title	Peak Position	Weeks at No.1	Weeks on Chart
30 May 09	**IN THE HEAT OF THE NIGHT** *Hard2beat H2B18CDS*	21		4

STAR SPANGLES
UK, male vocal/instrumental group — Weeks on Chart: **2**

Date	Title	Peak Position	Weeks at No.1	Weeks on Chart
19 Apr 03	**STAY AWAY FROM ME** *Parlophone CDR 6604*	52		1
12 Jul 03	**I LIVE FOR SPEED** *Capitol CDR 6609*	60		1

STARCHASER
Italy, male DJ/production trio — Weeks on Chart: **4**

Date	Title	Peak Position	Weeks at No.1	Weeks on Chart
22 Jun 02	**LOVE WILL SET YOU FREE (JAMBE MYTH)** *Rulin 23CDS*	24		4

STARDUST
France, male/female vocal/instrumental group — Weeks on Chart: **29**

Date	Title	Peak Position	Weeks at No.1	Weeks on Chart
8 Oct 77	**ARIANA** *Satril SAT 120*	42		3
1 Aug 98	**MUSIC SOUNDS BETTER WITH YOU (IMPORT)** *Roule 305*	55		3
22 Aug 98	**MUSIC SOUNDS BETTER WITH YOU** *Virgin DINSD 175* ⊛	2		23

ALVIN STARDUST
UK, male vocalist (Bernard Jewry) — Weeks on Chart: **119**

Date	Title	Peak Position	Weeks at No.1	Weeks on Chart
3 Nov 73	**MY COO-CA-CHOO** *Magnet MAG 1* ●	2		21
16 Feb 74	**JEALOUS MIND** *Magnet MAG 5*	1	1	11
4 May 74	**RED DRESS** *Magnet MAG 8*	7		8
31 Aug 74	**YOU YOU YOU** *Magnet MAG 13* ○	6		10
30 Nov 74	**TELL ME WHY** *Magnet MAG 19*	16		8
1 Feb 75	**GOOD LOVE CAN NEVER DIE** *Magnet MAG 21*	11		9
12 Jul 75	**SWEET CHEATIN' RITA** *Magnet MAG 32*	37		4
5 Sep 81	**PRETEND** *Stiff BUY 124* ○	4		10
21 Nov 81	**A WONDERFUL TIME UP THERE** *Stiff BUY 132*	56		8
5 May 84	**I FEEL LIKE BUDDY HOLLY** *Chrysalis CHS 2784*	7		11
27 Oct 84	**I WON'T RUN AWAY** *Chrysalis CHS 2829*	7		13
15 Dec 84	**SO NEAR TO CHRISTMAS** *Chrysalis CHS 2835*	29		4
23 Mar 85	**GOT A LITTLE HEARTACHE** *Chrysalis CHS 2856*	55		2

STARFIGHTER
Belgium, male producer (Philip Dirix) — Weeks on Chart: **3**

Date	Title	Peak Position	Weeks at No.1	Weeks on Chart
5 Feb 00	**APACHE** *Sound Of Ministry MOSCDS 136*	31		3

STARGARD
US, female vocal group — Weeks on Chart: **14**

Date	Title	Peak Position	Weeks at No.1	Weeks on Chart
28 Jan 78	**THEME FROM 'WHICH WAY IS UP'** *MCA 346*	19		7
15 Apr 78	**LOVE IS SO EASY** *MCA 354*	45		1
9 Sep 78	**WHAT YOU WAITING FOR** *MCA 382*	39		6

STARGATE
Norway/US, male/female vocal/rap/production group — Weeks on Chart: **1**

Date	Title	Peak Position	Weeks at No.1	Weeks on Chart
7 Sep 02	**EASIER SAID THAN DONE** *Telstar CDSTAS 3269*	55		1

STARGAZERS
UK, male/female vocal group – Marie Benson (replaced by Eula Parker), Cliff Adams*, d. 22 Oct 2001, Fred Datchler & Ronnie Milne (replaced by Dave Carey) — Weeks on Chart: **68**

Date	Title	Peak Position	Weeks at No.1	Weeks on Chart
13 Feb 53	**BROKEN WINGS** *Decca F 10047*	1	1	12
19 Feb 54	**I SEE THE MOON** *Decca F 10213*	1	6	15
9 Apr 54	**HAPPY WANDERER** *Decca F 10259*	12		1
17 Dec 54	**FINGER OF SUSPICION** *Decca F 10394* DICKIE VALENTINE WITH THE STARGAZERS	1	3	15
4 Mar 55	**SOMEBODY** *Decca F 10437*	20		1
3 Jun 55	**CRAZY OTTO RAG** *Decca F 10523*	18		3
9 Sep 55	**CLOSE THE DOOR** *Decca F 10594*	6		9
11 Nov 55	**TWENTY TINY FINGERS** *Decca F 10626*	4		11
22 Jun 56	**HOT DIGGITY (DOG ZIGGITY BOOM)** *Decca F 10731*	28		1

STARGAZERS
UK, male vocal/instrumental group — Weeks on Chart: **3**

Date	Title	Peak Position	Weeks at No.1	Weeks on Chart
6 Feb 82	**GROOVE BABY GROOVE (EP)** *Epic EPC A 1924*	56		3

STARJETS
UK, male vocal/instrumental group — Weeks on Chart: **5**

Date	Title	Peak Position	Weeks at No.1	Weeks on Chart
8 Sep 79	**WAR STORIES** *Epic EPC 7770*	51		5

STARLAND VOCAL BAND
US, male/female vocal group — Weeks on Chart: **10**

Date	Title	Peak Position	Weeks at No.1	Weeks on Chart
7 Aug 76	**AFTERNOON DELIGHT** *RCA 2716* ★	18		10

STARLIGHT
Italy, male production trio – Daniele Davoli, Mirko Limono & Valerio Semplici. See Black Box — Weeks on Chart: **11**

Date	Title	Peak Position	Weeks at No.1	Weeks on Chart
19 Aug 89	**NUMERO UNO** *Citybeat CBE 742*	9		11

STARPARTY
Holland, male production duo. See Albion, Generator, Gouryella, Moonman, System F, Veracocha — Weeks on Chart: **2**

Date	Title	Peak Position	Weeks at No.1	Weeks on Chart
26 Feb 00	**I'M IN LOVE** *Incentive CENT 5CDS*	26		2

EDWIN STARR
US, male vocalist (Charles Hatcher), d. 2 Apr 2003 (age 61) — Weeks on Chart: **70**

Date	Title	Peak Position	Weeks at No.1	Weeks on Chart
12 May 66	**STOP HER ON SIGHT (SOS)** *Polydor BM 56 702*	35		8
18 Aug 66	**HEADLINE NEWS** *Polydor 56 717*	39		3
11 Dec 68	**STOP HER ON SIGHT (SOS)/HEADLINE NEWS** *Polydor 56 753*	11		11
13 Sep 69	**25 MILES** *Tamla Motown TMG 672*	36		6
24 Oct 70	**WAR** *Tamla Motown TMG 754* ★	3		12
20 Feb 71	**STOP THE WAR NOW** *Tamla Motown TMG 764*	33		1
27 Jan 79	**CONTACT** *20th Century BTC 2396* ○	6		12
26 May 79	**H.A.P.P.Y. RADIO** *20th Century TC 2408*	9		11
1 Jun 85	**IT AIN'T FAIR** *Hippodrome HIP 101*	56		4
30 Oct 93	**WAR** *Weekend CDWEEK 103* & SHADOW	69		2

FREDDIE STARR
UK, male comedian/vocalist (Fred Smith) — Weeks on Chart: **14**

Date	Title	Peak Position	Weeks at No.1	Weeks on Chart
23 Feb 74	**IT'S YOU** *Tiffany 6121 501*	9		10
20 Dec 75	**WHITE CHRISTMAS** *Thunderbird THE 102*	41		4

KAY STARR
US, female vocalist (Katherine Starks) — Weeks on Chart: **58**

Date	Title	Peak Position	Weeks at No.1	Weeks on Chart
5 Dec 52	**COMES A-LONG A-LOVE** *Capitol CL 13808*	1	1	16
24 Apr 53	**SIDE BY SIDE** *Capitol CL 13871*	7		4
19 Mar 54	**CHANGING PARTNERS** *Capitol CL 14050*	4		14
15 Oct 54	**AM I A TOY OR A TREASURE** *Capitol CL 14151*	17		4
17 Feb 56	**ROCK AND ROLL WALTZ** *HMV POP 168* ★	1	1	20

Silver-selling ○ | Gold-selling ● | Platinum-selling (x multiples) | US No.1 ★ | Peak Position | Weeks at No.1 | Weeks on Chart

RINGO STARR
UK, male drummer/vocalist (Richard Starkey). See Beatles — **56**

Date	Title	Peak Position	Weeks at No.1	Weeks on Chart
17 Apr 71	IT DON'T COME EASY *Apple R 5898*	4		11
1 Apr 72	BACK OFF BOOGALOO *Apple R 5944*	2		10
27 Oct 73	PHOTOGRAPH *Apple R 5992* ★	8		13
23 Feb 74	YOU'RE SIXTEEN *Apple R 5995* ○ ★	4		10
30 Nov 74	ONLY YOU *Apple R 6000*	28		11
6 Jun 92	WEIGHT OF THE WORLD *Private Music 115392*	74		1

STARS ON 54
US, female vocal trio — **3**

Date	Title	Peak Position	Weeks at No.1	Weeks on Chart
28 Nov 98	IF YOU COULD READ MY MIND *Tommy Boy TBCD 7497*	23		3

STARSAILOR
UK, male vocal/instrumental group – James Walsh, Ben Byrne, James Stelfox & Barry Westhead — **44**

Date	Title	Peak Position	Weeks at No.1	Weeks on Chart
17 Feb 01	FEVER *Chrysalis 555123*	18		3
5 May 01	GOOD SOULS *Chrysalis CDCHS 5125*	12		6
29 Sep 01	ALCOHOLIC *Chrysalis CDCHSS 5130*	10		6
22 Dec 01	LULLABY *Chrysalis CDCHS 5131*	36		4
30 Mar 02	POOR MISGUIDED FOOL *Chrysalis CDCHS 5136*	23		3
13 Sep 03	SILENCE IS EASY *EMI CDEM 625*	9		8
29 Nov 03	BORN AGAIN *EMI CDEMS 632*	40		2
13 Mar 04	FOUR TO THE FLOOR *EMI CDEM634*	24		4
15 Oct 05	THE CROSSFIRE *EMI CDEM671*	22		3
4 Feb 06	THIS TIME *EMI CDEM679*	24		3
20 May 06	KEEP US TOGETHER *EMI CDEM691*	47		1
14 Mar 09	TELL ME IT'S NOT OVER *Virgin VSCDT1984*	73		1

STARSHIP
US/UK, male/female vocal/instrumental group – Mickey Thomas, Grace Slick, Craig Chaquico, Aynsley Dunbar (replaced by Donny Baldwin), David Freiberg, Paul Kantner (left 1984) & Pete Sears — **41**

Date	Title	Peak Position	Weeks at No.1	Weeks on Chart
26 Jan 80	JANE *Grunt FB 1750* JEFFERSON STARSHIP	21		9
16 Nov 85	WE BUILT THIS CITY *RCA PB 49929* ★	12		12
8 Feb 86	SARA *RCA PB 49893* ★	66		3
11 Apr 87	NOTHING'S GONNA STOP US NOW *Grunt FB 49757* ● ★	1	4	17

STARSOUND
Holland, male producer (Jaap Eggermont) & various male/female vocal/instrumental 'soundalikes' including Claudia Hoogendoorn, Okkie Huysdens, Bas Muys, Jody Pijper, Tony Sherman & Hans Vermeulen — **37**

Date	Title	Peak Position	Weeks at No.1	Weeks on Chart
18 Apr 81	STARS ON 45 *CBS A 1102* ● ★	2		14
4 Jul 81	STARS ON 45 VOLUME 2 *CBS A 1407* ○	2		10
19 Sep 81	STARS ON 45 VOLUME 3 *CBS A 1521*	17		6
27 Feb 82	STARS ON STEVIE *CBS A 2041*	14		7

STARTRAX
UK, male/female vocal group — **8**

Date	Title	Peak Position	Weeks at No.1	Weeks on Chart
1 Aug 81	STARTRAX CLUB DISCO *Picksy KSY 1001*	18		8

STARTURN ON 45 (PINTS)
UK, male vocal/production trio — **9**

Date	Title	Peak Position	Weeks at No.1	Weeks on Chart
24 Oct 81	STARTURN ON 45 (PINTS) *V Tone 003*	45		4
30 Apr 88	PUMP UP THE BITTER *Pacific DRINK 1*	12		5

STARVATION
International, male/female vocal/instrumental charity assembly — **6**

Date	Title	Peak Position	Weeks at No.1	Weeks on Chart
9 Mar 85	STARVATION/TAM-TAM POUR L'ETHIOPE *Zarjazz JAZZ 3*	33		6

STARVING SOULS
UK, male vocal/instrumental group. See Nearly God — **1**

Date	Title	Peak Position	Weeks at No.1	Weeks on Chart
21 Oct 95	I BE THE PROPHET *Durban Poison DPCD 1*	66		1

STATE OF MIND
UK, male/female vocal/production group — **3**

Date	Title	Peak Position	Weeks at No.1	Weeks on Chart
18 Apr 98	THIS IS IT *Ministry Of Sound MOSCDS 123*	30		2
25 Jul 98	TAKE CONTROL *Ministry Of Sound MOSCDS 124*	46		1

STATE ONE
UK/Germany, male production group — **1**

Date	Title	Peak Position	Weeks at No.1	Weeks on Chart
27 Sep 03	FOREVER AND A DAY *Incentive CENT 54CDS*	62		1

STATIC REVENGER
US, male DJ/producer (Dennis White) — **3**

Date	Title	Peak Position	Weeks at No.1	Weeks on Chart
7 Jul 01	HAPPY PEOPLE *Incentive/Rulin CENRUL 1CDS*	23		3

STATIC-X
US, male vocal/instrumental group — **1**

Date	Title	Peak Position	Weeks at No.1	Weeks on Chart
6 Oct 01	BLACK AND WHITE *Warner Brothers W 560CD*	65		1

STATLER BROTHERS
US, male vocal group — **4**

Date	Title	Peak Position	Weeks at No.1	Weeks on Chart
24 Feb 66	FLOWERS ON THE WALL *CBS 201976*	38		4

CANDI STATON
US, female vocalist (Canzata Staton) — **90**

Date	Title	Peak Position	Weeks at No.1	Weeks on Chart
29 May 76	YOUNG HEARTS RUN FREE *Warner Brothers K 16730* ○	2		13
18 Sep 76	DESTINY *Warner Brothers K 16806*	41		3
23 Jul 77	NIGHTS ON BROADWAY *Warner Brothers K 16972* ○	6		12
3 Jun 78	HONEST I DO LOVE YOU *Warner Brothers K 17164*	48		5
24 Apr 82	SUSPICIOUS MINDS *Sugarhill SH 112*	31		9
31 May 86	YOUNG HEARTS RUN FREE (REMIX) *Warner Brothers W 8680*	47		5
2 Feb 91	YOU GOT THE LOVE *Truelove TLOVE 7001* SOURCE FEATURING CANDI STATON ○	4		11
1 Mar 97	YOU GOT THE LOVE (REMIX) *React CDREACT 89* SOURCE FEATURING CANDI STATON	3		8
17 Apr 99	LOVE ON LOVE *React CDREACT 143*	27		3
7 Aug 99	YOUNG HEARTS RUN FREE *React CDREACT 158*	29		2
1 Jan 05	YOU GOT THE LOVE (IMPORT) *ZYX GDC22218* SOURCE FEATURING CANDI STATON	60		3
18 Feb 06	YOU GOT THE LOVE (2ND REMIX) *Positiva CDTIVS230* SOURCE FEATURING CANDI STATON	7		16

STATUS IV
US, male vocal group — **3**

Date	Title	Peak Position	Weeks at No.1	Weeks on Chart
9 Jul 83	YOU AIN'T REALLY DOWN *TMT 4*	56		3

STATUS QUO
UK, male vocal/instrumental group – Francis Rossi, Andy Bown, John Coghlan (replaced by Jeff Rich), Alan Lancaster (replaced by John Edwards) & Rick Parfitt. No group has had more chart singles than this three-chord boogie band, who have remained at the top for over 40 years, with only the Beatles and the Stones amassing more Top 20 albums — **432**

Date	Title	Peak Position	Weeks at No.1	Weeks on Chart
24 Jan 68	PICTURES OF MATCHSTICK MEN *Pye 7N 17449*	7		12
21 Aug 68	ICE IN THE SUN *Pye 7N 17581*	8		12
28 May 69	ARE YOU GROWING TIRED OF MY LOVE *Pye 7N 17728*	46		3
2 May 70	DOWN THE DUSTPIPE *Pye 7N 17907*	12		17
7 Nov 70	IN MY CHAIR *Pye 7N 17998*	21		14
13 Jan 73	PAPER PLANE *Vertigo 6059 071*	8		11
14 Apr 73	MEAN GIRL *Pye 7N 45229*	20		11
8 Sep 73	CAROLINE *Vertigo 6059 085* ○	5		13
4 May 74	BREAK THE RULES *Vertigo 6059 101*	8		8
7 Dec 74	DOWN DOWN *Vertigo 6059 114* ○	1	1	11
17 May 75	ROLL OVER LAY DOWN *Vertigo QUO 13*	9		8
14 Feb 76	RAIN *Vertigo 6059 133*	7		7
10 Jul 76	MYSTERY SONG *Vertigo 6059 146*	11		9
11 Dec 76	WILD SIDE OF LIFE *Vertigo 6059 153* ○	9		12
8 Oct 77	ROCKIN' ALL OVER THE WORLD *Vertigo 6059 184* ●	3		16
2 Sep 78	AGAIN AND AGAIN *Vertigo QUO 1*	13		9
25 Nov 78	ACCIDENT PRONE *Vertigo QUO 2*	36		8
22 Sep 79	WHATEVER YOU WANT *Vertigo 6059 242* ○	4		9
24 Nov 79	LIVING ON AN ISLAND *Vertigo 6059 248*	16		10
11 Oct 80	WHAT YOU'RE PROPOSING *Vertigo QUO 3* ○	2		11
6 Dec 80	LIES/DON'T DRIVE MY CAR *Vertigo QUO 4* ○	11		10
28 Feb 81	SOMETHING 'BOUT YOU BABY I LIKE *Vertigo QUO 5*	9		7
28 Nov 81	ROCK 'N' ROLL *Vertigo QUO 6* ○	8		11
27 Mar 82	DEAR JOHN *Vertigo QUO 7*	10		8
12 Jun 82	SHE DON'T FOOL ME *Vertigo QUO 8*	36		5
30 Oct 82	CAROLINE (LIVE AT THE NEC) *Vertigo QUO 10*	13		7
10 Sep 83	OL' RAG BLUES *Vertigo QUO 11*	9		8
5 Nov 83	A MESS OF THE BLUES *Vertigo QUO 12*	15		6
10 Dec 83	MARGUERITA TIME *Vertigo QUO 14* ○	3		11

Date	Title / Label	Peak Position	Weeks at No.1	Weeks on Chart
19 May 84	**GOING DOWN TOWN TONIGHT** *Vertigo QUO 15*	20		6
27 Oct 84	**THE WANDERER** *Vertigo QUO 16*	7		11
17 May 86	**ROLLIN' HOME** *Vertigo QUO 18*	9		6
26 Jul 86	**RED SKY** *Vertigo QUO 19*	19		8
4 Oct 86	**IN THE ARMY NOW** *Vertigo QUO 20* ●	2		14
6 Dec 86	**DREAMIN'** *Vertigo QUO 21*	15		8
26 Mar 88	**AIN'T COMPLAINING** *Vertigo QUO 22*	19		6
21 May 88	**WHO GETS THE LOVE** *Vertigo QUO 23*	34		4
20 Aug 88	**RUNNING ALL OVER THE WORLD** *Vertigo QUAID 1*	17		6
3 Dec 88	**BURNING BRIDGES (ON AND OFF AND ON AGAIN)** *Vertigo QUO 25* ●	5		10
28 Oct 89	**NOT AT ALL** *Vertigo QUO 26*	50		2
29 Sep 90	**ANNIVERSARY WALTZ – PART 1** *Vertigo QUO 28* ●	2		9
15 Dec 90	**ANNIVERSARY WALTZ – PART 2** *Vertigo QUO 29*	16		7
7 Sep 91	**CAN'T GIVE YOU MORE** *Vertigo QUO 30*	37		3
18 Jan 92	**ROCK 'TIL YOU DROP** *Vertigo QUO 32*	38		3
10 Oct 92	**ROADHOUSE MEDLEY (ANNIVERSARY WALTZ PART 25)** *Vertigo QUO 33*	21		4
6 Aug 94	**I DIDN'T MEAN IT** *Vertigo QUOCD 34*	21		4
22 Oct 94	**SHERRI DON'T FAIL ME NOW** *Vertigo QUOCD 35*	38		2
3 Dec 94	**RESTLESS** *Polydor QUOCD 36*	39		2
4 Nov 95	**WHEN YOU WALK IN THE ROOM** *Polygram TV 5775122*	34		2
2 Mar 96	**FUN FUN FUN** *Polygram TV 5762972* WITH THE BEACH BOYS	24		4
13 Apr 96	**DON'T STOP** *Polygram TV 5766352*	35		2
9 Nov 96	**ALL AROUND MY HAT** *Polygram TV 5759452*	47		1
20 Mar 99	**THE WAY IT GOES** *Eagle EAGXS 075*	39		2
12 Jun 99	**LITTLE WHITE LIES** *Eagle EAGXS 101*	47		1
2 Oct 99	**TWENTY WILD HORSES** *Eagle EAGXS 105*	53		1
13 May 00	**MONY MONY** *Universal TV 1580132*	48		1
17 Aug 02	**JAM SIDE DOWN** *Universal TV 0192352*	17		3
9 Nov 02	**ALL STAND UP (NEVER SAY NEVER)** *Universal TV 0194872*	51		1
25 Sep 04	**YOU'LL COME 'ROUND** *Universal TV 9868038*	14		3
4 Dec 04	**THINKING OF YOU** *Universal TV 9825824*	21		3
24 Sep 05	**THE PARTY AIN'T OVER YET** *Sanctuary SANXS400*	11		3
12 Nov 05	**ALL THAT COUNTS IS LOVE** *Sanctuary SANXS413*	29		2
22 Sep 07	**BEGINNING OF THE END** *Fourth Cord QUOSP002*	48		1
20 Dec 08	**IT'S CHRISTMAS TIME** *Fourth Cord 1793139*	40		2
20 Dec 08	**JUMP THAT ROCK** *All Around The World CDGLOBE1006* SCOOTER VS STATUS QUO	57		1

STAXX FEATURING CAROL LEEMING

UK, male production duo — 11

Date	Title / Label	Peak Position	Weeks at No.1	Weeks on Chart
2 Oct 93	**JOY** *Champion CHAMPCD 303*	25		6
20 May 95	**YOU** *Champion CHAMPCD 316*	50		1
13 Sep 97	**JOY (REMIX)** *Champion CHAMPCD 328*	14		4

STEALERS WHEEL

UK, male vocal/instrumental group – Gerry Rafferty*, Rod Coombes, Joe Egan, Paul Pilnick & Tony Williams — 22

Date	Title / Label	Peak Position	Weeks at No.1	Weeks on Chart
26 May 73	**STUCK IN THE MIDDLE WITH YOU** *A&M AMS 7036*	8		10
1 Sep 73	**EVERYTHING'L TURN OUT FINE** *A&M AMS 7079*	33		6
26 Jan 74	**STAR** *A&M AMS 7094*	25		6

STEAM

US, male vocal/instrumental trio – Paul Leka, Gary DeCarlo & Dale Frashuer — 14

Date	Title / Label	Peak Position	Weeks at No.1	Weeks on Chart
31 Jan 70	**NA NA HEY HEY KISS HIM GOODBYE** *Fontana TF 1058* ★	9		14

ANTHONY STEEL & THE RADIO REVELLERS

UK, male actor/vocalist, d. 21 Mar 2001 (age 81), & UK, male vocal group — 6

Date	Title / Label	Peak Position	Weeks at No.1	Weeks on Chart
10 Sep 54	**WEST OF ZANZIBAR** *Polygon P 1114*	11		6

STEEL PULSE

UK, male vocal/instrumental group — 12

Date	Title / Label	Peak Position	Weeks at No.1	Weeks on Chart
1 Apr 78	**KU KLUX KHAN** *Island WIP 6428*	41		4
8 Jul 78	**PRODIGAL SON** *Island WIP 6449*	35		6
23 Jun 79	**SOUND SYSTEM** *Island WIP 6490*	71		2

TOMMY STEELE

UK, male vocalist (Tommy Hicks) — 147

Date	Title / Label	Peak Position	Weeks at No.1	Weeks on Chart
26 Oct 56	**ROCK WITH THE CAVEMAN** *Decca F 10795* & THE STEELMEN	13		5
14 Dec 56	**SINGING THE BLUES** *Decca F 10819* & THE STEELMEN	1	1	15
15 Feb 57	**KNEE DEEP IN THE BLUES** *Decca F 10849* & THE STEELMEN	15		9
3 May 57	**BUTTERFINGERS** *Decca F 10877* & THE STEELMEN	8		18
16 Aug 57	**WATER WATER/HANDFUL OF SONGS** *Decca F 10923* & THE STEELMEN	5		17
30 Aug 57	**SHIRALEE** *Decca F 10896*	11		4
22 Nov 57	**HEY YOU** *Decca F 10941*	28		1
7 Mar 58	**NAIROBI** *Decca F 10991*	3		11
25 Apr 58	**HAPPY GUITAR** *Decca F 10976*	20		5
18 Jul 58	**THE ONLY MAN ON THE ISLAND** *Decca F 11041*	16		8
14 Nov 58	**COME ON, LET'S GO** *Decca F 11072*	10		13
14 Aug 59	**TALLAHASSEE LASSIE** *Decca F 11152*	16		5
28 Aug 59	**GIVE GIVE GIVE** *Decca F 11152*	28		2
4 Dec 59	**LITTLE WHITE BULL** *Decca F 11177*	6		17
23 Jun 60	**WHAT A MOUTH** *Decca F 11245*	5		11
29 Dec 60	**MUST BE SANTA** *Decca F 11299*	40		1
17 Aug 61	**WRITING ON THE WALL** *Decca F 11372*	30		5

STEELEYE SPAN

UK, male/female vocal/instrumental group – Maddy Prior, Tim Hart, d. 24 Dec 2009, Bob Johnson, Rick Kemp, Peter Knight & Nigel Pegrum — 18

Date	Title / Label	Peak Position	Weeks at No.1	Weeks on Chart
8 Dec 73	**GAUDETE** *Chrysalis CHS 2007*	14		9
15 Nov 75	**ALL AROUND MY HAT** *Chrysalis CHS 2078* ●	5		9

STEELY DAN

US, male vocal/instrumental group — 21

Date	Title / Label	Peak Position	Weeks at No.1	Weeks on Chart
30 Aug 75	**DO IT AGAIN** *ABC 4075*	39		4
11 Dec 76	**HAITIAN DIVORCE** *ABC 4152*	17		9
29 Jul 78	**FM (NO STATIC AT ALL)** *MCA 374*	49		5
10 Mar 79	**RIKKI DON'T LOSE THAT NUMBER** *ABC 4241*	58		3

GWEN STEFANI

US, female vocalist/actor/fashion designer. See No Doubt — 123

Date	Title / Label	Peak Position	Weeks at No.1	Weeks on Chart
25 Aug 01	**LET ME BLOW YA MIND** *Interscope 4976052* EVE FEATURING GWEN STEFANI	4		12
27 Nov 04	**WHAT YOU WAITING FOR** *Interscope 9864986*	4		14
26 Mar 05	**RICH GIRL** *Interscope 9880219* FEATURING EVE	4		12
4 Jun 05	**HOLLABACK GIRL** *Interscope 9882326* ★	8		14
10 Sep 05	**COOL** *Interscope 9884356*	11		10
12 Nov 05	**CAN I HAVE IT LIKE THAT** *Virgin VUSCD315* PHARRELL FEATURING GWEN STEFANI	3		11
17 Dec 05	**LUXURIOUS** *Interscope 9888344*	44		2
16 Dec 06	**WIND IT UP** *Interscope 1717388*	3		10
3 Feb 07	**THE SWEET ESCAPE** *Interscope 1724450* FEATURING AKON	2		28
16 Jun 07	**4 IN THE MORNING** *Interscope 1735560*	22		8
20 Oct 07	**NOW THAT YOU GOT IT** *Interscope 1747456*	59		2

JIM STEINMAN

US, male producer — 9

Date	Title / Label	Peak Position	Weeks at No.1	Weeks on Chart
4 Jul 81	**ROCK 'N' ROLL DREAMS COME THROUGH** *Epic EPC A 1236* VOCALS BY RORY DODD	52		7
23 Jun 84	**TONIGHT IS WHAT IT MEANS TO BE YOUNG** *MCA 889* & FIRE INC	67		2

STEINSKI & MASS MEDIA

US, male producer/DJ (Steve Stein) — 2

Date	Title / Label	Peak Position	Weeks at No.1	Weeks on Chart
31 Jan 87	**WE'LL BE RIGHT BACK** *Fourth & Broadway BRW 59*	63		2

STELLA BROWNE

UK, male production duo — 3

Date	Title / Label	Peak Position	Weeks at No.1	Weeks on Chart
20 May 00	**EVERY WOMAN NEEDS LOVE** *Perfecto PERF 06*	55		1
9 Feb 02	**NEVER KNEW LOVE** *Perfecto PERF 26CDS*	42		2

STELLASTARR*

US, male/female vocal/instrumental group — 3

Date	Title / Label	Peak Position	Weeks at No.1	Weeks on Chart
31 May 03	**SOMEWHERE ACROSS FOREVER** *Twenty-20 TWENTYCDS001*	73		1
27 Sep 03	**JENNY** *Twenty-20 TWENTYCDS002*	61		1
20 Mar 04	**MY COCO** *RCA 82876599082*	46		1

STELLAR PROJECT FEATURING BRANDI EMMA

Italy/US, male/female vocal/production group — 4

Date	Title / Label	Peak Position	Weeks at No.1	Weeks on Chart
14 Aug 04	**GET UP STAND UP** *Data 74CDS*	14		4

Silver-selling ○ Gold-selling ● Platinum-selling (x multiples) ⊛ US No.1 ★ Peak Position · Weeks at No.1 · Weeks on Chart

RICHIE STEPHENS

Jamaica, male vocalist (Richard Stephenson) — Weeks on Chart: 3

Date	Title	Peak	Wks No.1	Wks
15 May 93	**LEGACY** *Columbia 6592852* MAD COBRA FEATURING RICHIE STEPHENS	64		2
9 Aug 97	**COME GIVE ME YOUR LOVE** *Delirious 74321450442*	62		1

MARTIN STEPHENSON & THE DAINTEES

UK, male vocal/instrumental group — Weeks on Chart: 7

Date	Title	Peak	Wks No.1	Wks
8 Nov 86	**BOAT TO BOLIVIA** *Kitchenware SL 27*	70		2
17 Jan 87	**TROUBLE TOWN** *Kitchenware SK 13*	58		3
27 Jun 92	**BIG SKY NEW LIGHT** *Kitchenware SK 57*	71		2

STEPPENWOLF

US/Canada, male vocal/instrumental group — Weeks on Chart: 14

Date	Title	Peak	Wks No.1	Wks
11 Jun 69	**BORN TO BE WILD** *Stateside SS 8017*	30		9
27 Feb 99	**BORN TO BE WILD** *MCA MCSTD 48104*	18		5

STEPS

UK, female/male vocal group – Lee Latchford-Evans, Claire Richards (H & Claire*), Lisa Scott-Lee*, Faye Tozer & Ian 'H' Watkins (H & Claire*). See Girls Of *FHM*, Russell Watson & Faye Tozer — Weeks on Chart: 204

Date	Title	Peak	Wks No.1	Wks
22 Nov 97	**5, 6, 7, 8** *Jive JIVECD 438* ○	14		17
2 May 98	**LAST THING ON MY MIND** *Jive 0518492* ○	6		14
5 Sep 98	**ONE FOR SORROW** *Jive 0519092* ○	2		11
21 Nov 98	**HEARTBEAT/TRAGEDY** *Ebul/Jive 0519142* ⊛	1	1	30
20 Mar 99	**BETTER BEST FORGOTTEN** *Ebul/Jive 0519242* ●	2		17
24 Jul 99	**LOVE'S GOT A HOLD ON MY HEART** *Ebul/Jive 0519372* ○	2		12
23 Oct 99	**AFTER THE LOVE HAS GONE** *Ebul/Jive 0519462* ○	5		11
25 Dec 99	**SAY YOU'LL BE MINE/BETTER THE DEVIL YOU KNOW** *Ebul/Jive 9201008* ●	4		17
15 Apr 00	**DEEPER SHADE OF BLUE** *Ebul/Jive 9201022*	4		9
15 Jul 00	**WHEN I SAID GOODBYE/SUMMER OF LOVE** *Ebul/Jive 9201162*	5		11
28 Oct 00	**STOMP** *Ebul/Jive 9201212*	1	1	11
6 Jan 01	**IT'S THE WAY YOU MAKE ME FEEL/TOO BUSY THINKING ABOUT MY BABY** *Ebul/Jive 9201232*	2		11
16 Jun 01	**HERE AND NOW/YOU'LL BE SORRY** *Ebul/Jive 9201372*	4		10
6 Oct 01	**CHAIN REACTION/ONE FOR SORROW** *Ebul/Jive 9201442* ○	2		12
15 Dec 01	**WORDS ARE NOT ENOUGH/I KNOW HIM SO WELL** *Ebul/Jive 9201452*	5		11

STEREO MC'S

UK/Kenya, male/female vocal/rap/production group — Weeks on Chart: 37

Date	Title	Peak	Wks No.1	Wks
29 Sep 90	**ELEVATE MY MIND** *Fourth & Broadway BRW 186*	74		1
9 Mar 91	**LOST IN MUSIC** *Fourth & Broadway BRW 198*	46		3
26 Sep 92	**CONNECTED** *Fourth & Broadway BRW 262*	18		6
5 Dec 92	**STEP IT UP** *Fourth & Broadway BRW 266*	12		12
20 Feb 93	**GROUND LEVEL** *Fourth & Broadway BRCD 268*	19		5
29 May 93	**CREATION** *Fourth & Broadway BRCD 276*	19		4
26 May 01	**DEEP DOWN AND DIRTY** *Island CID 777*	17		5
1 Sep 01	**WE BELONG IN THIS WORLD TOGETHER** *Island CID 782*	59		1

STEREO NATION

UK, male vocal duo — Weeks on Chart: 3

Date	Title	Peak	Wks No.1	Wks
17 Aug 96	**I'VE BEEN WAITING** *EMI Premier PRESCD 5*	53		1
27 Oct 01	**LAILA** *Wizard WIZ 015* TAZ & STEREO NATION	44		2

STEREO STAR FEATURING MIA J

UK, male/female vocal/production group — Weeks on Chart: 1

Date	Title	Peak	Wks No.1	Wks
23 Apr 05	**UTOPIA (WHERE I WANT TO BE)** *Free2Air F2A5CDX*	66		1

STEREOLAB

UK/France/Australia, male/female vocal/instrumental group — Weeks on Chart: 6

Date	Title	Peak	Wks No.1	Wks
8 Jan 94	**JENNY ONDIOLINE/FRENCH DISCO** *Duophonic UHF DUHFCD 01*	75		1
30 Jul 94	**PING PONG** *Duophonic UHF DUHFCD 04*	45		2
12 Nov 94	**WOW AND FLUTTER** *Duophonic UHF DUHFCD 07*	70		1
2 Mar 96	**CYBELE'S REVERIE** *Duophonic UHF DUHFCD 10*	62		1
13 Sep 97	**MISS MODULAR** *Duophonic UHF DUHFCD 16*	60		1

STEREOPHONICS

UK, male vocal/instrumental group – Kelly Jones, Stuart Cable (left 2004), d. 7 Jun 2010, Richard Jones & Javier Weyler. Distinctive Welsh band who arrived on the scene with a 'Best Newcomer' BRIT in 1998. They had 10 Top 5 hits before breaking their chart-topping duck with 'Dakota'. Drummer Cable died shortly after his new project, Killing For Company, released their debut LP — Weeks on Chart: 165

Date	Title	Peak	Wks No.1	Wks
29 Mar 97	**LOCAL BOY IN THE PHOTOGRAPH** *V2 SPHD 2*	51		1
31 May 97	**MORE LIFE IN A TRAMP'S VEST** *V2 SPHD 4*	33		2
23 Aug 97	**A THOUSAND TREES** *V2 VVR 5000443*	22		3
8 Nov 97	**TRAFFIC** *V2 VVR 5000948*	20		3
21 Feb 98	**LOCAL BOY IN THE PHOTOGRAPH** *V2 VVR 5001283*	14		4
21 Nov 98	**THE BARTENDER AND THE THIEF** *V2 VVR 5004653*	3		12
6 Mar 99	**JUST LOOKING** *V2 VVR 5005310*	4		9
15 May 99	**PICK A PART THAT'S NEW** *V2 VVR 5006778*	4		9
4 Sep 99	**I WOULDN'T BELIEVE YOUR RADIO** *V2 VVR 5008823*	11		7
20 Nov 99	**HURRY UP AND WAIT** *V2 VVR 5009323*	11		8
18 Mar 00	**MAMA TOLD ME NOT TO COME** *Gut CXGUT 031* TOM JONES & STEREOPHONICS	4		7
31 Mar 01	**MR WRITER** *V2 VVR 5015938*	5		12
23 Jun 01	**HAVE A NICE DAY** *V2 VVR 5016248*	5		9
6 Oct 01	**STEP ON MY OLD SIZE NINES** *V2 VVR 5016253*	16		5
15 Dec 01	**HANDBAGS AND GLADRAGS** *V2 VVR 5017752* ○	4		15
13 Apr 02	**VEGAS TWO TIMES** *V2 VVR 5019173*	23		2
31 May 03	**MADAME HELGA** *V2 VVR 5021743*	4		4
2 Aug 03	**MAYBE TOMORROW** *V2 VVR 5021898*	3		8
22 Nov 03	**SINCE I TOLD YOU IT'S OVER** *V2 VVR 5022628*	16		4
21 Feb 04	**MOVIESTAR** *V2 VVR 5024658*	5		5
12 Mar 05	**DAKOTA** *V2 VVR5031048*	1	1	20
2 Jul 05	**SUPERMAN** *V2 VVR5031068*	13		4
1 Oct 05	**DEVIL** *V2 VVR5034058*	11		2
3 Dec 05	**REWIND** *V2 VVR5035048*	17		2
6 Oct 07	**IT MEANS NOTHING** *V2 VVR5048643*	12		6
22 Dec 07	**MY FRIENDS** *V2 1754688*	32		1
28 Nov 09	**INNOCENT** *Mercury GBUV70903592*	54		1

STEREOPOL FEATURING NEVADA

Sweden/UK, male vocal/production group — Weeks on Chart: 2

Date	Title	Peak	Wks No.1	Wks
29 Mar 03	**DANCIN' TONIGHT** *Rulin 28CDS*	36		2

STERIOGRAM

New Zealand, male vocal/instrumental group — Weeks on Chart: 4

Date	Title	Peak	Wks No.1	Wks
20 Nov 04	**WALKIE TALKIE MAN** *EMI CDEMS652*	19		4

STETSASONIC

US, male rap/DJ group — Weeks on Chart: 3

Date	Title	Peak	Wks No.1	Wks
24 Sep 88	**TALKIN' ALL THAT JAZZ** *Breakout USA 640*	73		2
7 Nov 98	**TALKIN' ALL THAT JAZZ (REMIX)** *Tommy Boy TBCD 7310A*	54		1

CAT STEVENS

UK, male vocalist/guitarist (Steven Georgiou/Yusuf Islam) — Weeks on Chart: 108

Date	Title	Peak	Wks No.1	Wks
20 Oct 66	**I LOVE MY DOG** *Deram DM 102*	28		7
12 Jan 67	**MATTHEW AND SON** *Deram DM 110*	2		10
30 Mar 67	**I'M GONNA GET ME A GUN** *Deram DM 118*	6		10
2 Aug 67	**A BAD NIGHT** *Deram DM 140*	20		8
20 Dec 67	**KITTY** *Deram DM 156*	47		1
27 Jun 70	**LADY D'ARBANVILLE** *Island WIP 6086*	8		13
28 Aug 71	**MOON SHADOW** *Island WIP 6092*	22		11
1 Jan 72	**MORNING HAS BROKEN** *Island WIP 6121*	9		13
9 Dec 72	**CAN'T KEEP IT IN** *Island WIP 6152*	13		12
24 Aug 74	**ANOTHER SATURDAY NIGHT** *Island WIP 6206*	19		8
2 Jul 77	**(REMEMBER THE DAYS OF THE) OLD SCHOOL YARD** *Island WIP 6387*	44		3
25 Dec 04	**FATHER AND SON** *Polydor 9869667* RONAN KEATING & YUSUF ISLAM	2		11
7 Apr 07	**WILD WORLD** *Island GBAAN7000041*	52		1

CONNIE STEVENS

US, female vocalist (Concetta Ingolia) — Weeks on Chart: 20

Date	Title	Peak	Wks No.1	Wks
5 May 60	**KOOKIE KOOKIE (LEND ME YOUR COMB)** *Warner Brothers WB 5* EDWARD BYRNES & CONNIE STEVENS	27		8
5 May 60	**SIXTEEN REASONS** *Warner Brothers WB 3*	9		12

RACHEL STEVENS

UK, female vocalist/actor. See S Club 7 — Weeks on Chart: 51

Date	Title	Peak	Wks at No.1	Wks
27 Sep 03	**SWEET DREAMS MY LA EX** *Polydor 9811874*	2		10
20 Dec 03	**FUNKY DORY** *Polydor 9814984*	26		4
24 Jul 04	**SOME GIRLS** *Polydor 9867433*	2		12
16 Oct 04	**MORE MORE MORE** *Polydor 9868325*	3		8
9 Apr 05	**NEGOTIATE WITH LOVE** *Polydor 9870784*	10		6
16 Jul 05	**SO GOOD** *Polydor 9872237*	10		6
15 Oct 05	**I SAID NEVER AGAIN (BUT HERE WE ARE)** *Polydor 9874240*	12		5

RAY STEVENS

US, male vocalist/comedian (Ray Ragsdale) — Weeks on Chart: 64

Date	Title	Peak	Wks at No.1	Wks
16 May 70	**EVERYTHING IS BEAUTIFUL** *CBS 4953* ★	6		16
13 Mar 71	**BRIDGET THE MIDGET (THE QUEEN OF THE BLUES)** *CBS 7070*	2		14
25 Mar 72	**TURN YOUR RADIO ON** *CBS 7634*	33		4
25 May 74	**THE STREAK** *Janus 6146 201* ★	1	1	12
21 Jun 75	**MISTY** *Janus 6146 204*	2		10
27 Sep 75	**INDIAN LOVE CALL** *Janus 6146 205*	34		4
5 Mar 77	**IN THE MOOD** *Warner Brothers K 16875*	31		4

RICKY STEVENS

UK, male vocalist — Weeks on Chart: 7

Date	Title	Peak	Wks at No.1	Wks
14 Dec 61	**I CRIED FOR YOU** *Columbia DB 4739*	34		7

SHAKIN' STEVENS

UK, male vocalist (Michael Barratt). Hip-swivelling Welsh entertainer who added his distinctive 1950s rock 'n' roll feel to both new songs and old favourites. 'Shaky' was the most successful UK singles chart artist of the 1980s and has sold 7.3 million singles in the UK alone — Weeks on Chart: 292

Date	Title	Peak	Wks at No.1	Wks
16 Feb 80	**HOT DOG** *Epic EPC 8090*	24		9
16 Aug 80	**MARIE MARIE** *Epic EPC 8725*	19		10
28 Feb 81	**THIS OLE HOUSE** *Epic EPC 9555*	1	3	17
2 May 81	**YOU DRIVE ME CRAZY** *Epic A 1165*	2		12
25 Jul 81	**GREEN DOOR** *Epic A 1354*	1	4	12
10 Oct 81	**IT'S RAINING** *Epic A 1643*	10		9
16 Jan 82	**OH JULIE** *Epic EPC A 1742*	1	1	10
24 Apr 82	**SHIRLEY** *Epic EPC A 2087*	6		6
21 Aug 82	**GIVE ME YOUR HEART TONIGHT** *Epic EPC A 2656*	11		10
16 Oct 82	**I'LL BE SATISFIED** *Epic EPC A 2846*	10		8
11 Dec 82	**THE SHAKIN' STEVENS EP** *Epic SHAKY 1*	2		7
23 Jul 83	**IT'S LATE** *Epic A 3565*	11		7
5 Nov 83	**CRY JUST A LITTLE BIT** *Epic A 3774*	3		12
7 Jan 84	**A ROCKIN' GOOD WAY** *Epic A 4071* SHAKY & BONNIE	5		9
24 Mar 84	**A LOVE WORTH WAITING FOR** *Epic A 4291*	2		10
15 Sep 84	**A LETTER TO YOU** *Epic A 4677*	10		8
24 Nov 84	**TEARDROPS** *Epic A 4882*	5		9
2 Mar 85	**BREAKING UP MY HEART** *Epic A 6072*	14		7
12 Oct 85	**LIPSTICK POWDER AND PAINT** *Epic A 6610*	11		9
7 Dec 85	**MERRY CHRISTMAS EVERYONE** *Epic A 6769*	1	2	8
8 Feb 86	**TURNING AWAY** *Epic A 6819*	15		7
1 Nov 86	**BECAUSE I LOVE YOU** *Epic SHAKY 2*	14		10
20 Dec 86	**MERRY CHRISTMAS EVERYONE** *Epic A 6769*	58		3
27 Jun 87	**A LITTLE BOOGIE WOOGIE (IN THE BACK OF MY MIND)** *Epic SHAKY 3*	12		10
19 Sep 87	**COME SEE ABOUT ME** *Epic SHAKY 4*	24		6
28 Nov 87	**WHAT DO YOU WANT TO MAKE THOSE EYES AT ME FOR** *Epic SHAKY 5*	5		8
23 Jul 88	**FEEL THE NEED IN ME** *Epic SHAKY 6*	26		5
15 Oct 88	**HOW MANY TEARS CAN YOU HIDE** *Epic SHAKY 7*	47		4
10 Dec 88	**TRUE LOVE** *Epic SHAKY 8*	23		6
18 Feb 89	**JEZEBEL** *Epic SHAKY 9*	58		2
13 May 89	**LOVE ATTACK** *Epic SHAKY 10*	28		4
24 Feb 90	**I MIGHT** *Epic SHAKY 11*	18		6
12 May 90	**YES I DO** *Epic SHAKY 12*	60		2
18 Aug 90	**PINK CHAMPAGNE** *Epic SHAKY 13*	59		2
13 Oct 90	**MY CUTIE CUTIE** *Epic SHAKY 14*	75		1
15 Dec 90	**THE BEST CHRISTMAS OF THEM ALL** *Epic SHAKY 15*	19		4
7 Dec 91	**I'LL BE HOME THIS CHRISTMAS** *Epic 6576507*	34		5
10 Oct 92	**RADIO** *Epic 6584367* SHAKY FEATURING ROGER TAYLOR	37		3
25 Jun 05	**TROUBLE/THIS OLE HOUSE** *Virgin/EMI VTSCD7*	20		3
15 Dec 07	**MERRY CHRISTMAS EVERYONE** *RCA GBBBM8500013*	22		4
13 Dec 08	**MERRY CHRISTMAS EVERYONE** *RCA GBBBM8500013*	36		4
12 Dec 09	**MERRY CHRISTMAS EVERYONE** *RCA GBBBM8500013*	47		4

STEVENSON'S ROCKET

UK, male vocal/instrumental group — Weeks on Chart: 5

Date	Title	Peak	Wks at No.1	Wks
29 Nov 75	**ALRIGHT BABY** *Magnet MAG 47*	37		5

AL STEWART

UK, male vocalist/guitarist — Weeks on Chart: 6

Date	Title	Peak	Wks at No.1	Wks
29 Jan 77	**YEAR OF THE CAT** *RCA 2771*	31		6

AMII STEWART

US, female vocalist — Weeks on Chart: 61

Date	Title	Peak	Wks at No.1	Wks
7 Apr 79	**KNOCK ON WOOD** *Atlantic/Hansa K 11214* ★	6		12
16 Jun 79	**LIGHT MY FIRE/137 DISCO HEAVEN (MEDLEY)** *Atlantic/Hansa K 11278*	5		11
3 Nov 79	**JEALOUSY** *Atlantic/Hansa K 11386*	58		3
19 Jan 80	**THE LETTER/PARADISE BIRD** *Atlantic/Hansa K 11424*	39		4
19 Jul 80	**MY GUY – MY GIRL (MEDLEY)** *Atlantic/Hansa K 11550* & JOHNNY BRISTOL	39		5
29 Dec 84	**FRIENDS** *RCA 471*	12		11
17 Aug 85	**KNOCK ON WOOD/LIGHT MY FIRE (REMIX)** *Sedition EDIT 3303*	7		12
25 Jan 86	**MY GUY – MY GIRL (MEDLEY)** *Sedition EDIT 3310* & DEON ESTUS	63		3

ANDY STEWART

UK, male vocalist, d. 11 Oct 1993 (age 59) — Weeks on Chart: 67

Date	Title	Peak	Wks at No.1	Wks
15 Dec 60	**DONALD WHERE'S YOUR TROOSERS** *Top Rank JAR 427* WITH THE MICHAEL SAMMES SINGERS	37		1
12 Jan 61	**A SCOTTISH SOLDIER** *Top Rank JAR 512* WITH THE MICHAEL SAMMES SINGERS	19		40
1 Jun 61	**THE BATTLE'S O'ER** *Top Rank JAR 565* WITH THE MICHAEL SAMMES SINGERS	28		13
12 Aug 65	**DR FINLAY** *HMV POP 1454*	43		5
9 Dec 89	**DONALD WHERE'S YOUR TROOSERS** *Stone SON 2353*	4		8

BILLY STEWART

US, male vocalist, d. 17 Jan 1970 (age 32) — Weeks on Chart: 2

Date	Title	Peak	Wks at No.1	Wks
8 Sep 66	**SUMMERTIME** *Chess CRS 8040*	39		2

DAVE STEWART

UK, male keyboard player/producer — Weeks on Chart: 30

Date	Title	Peak	Wks at No.1	Wks
14 Mar 81	**WHAT BECOMES OF THE BROKENHEARTED** *Stiff BROKEN 1* GUEST VOCALS: COLIN BLUNSTONE	13		10
19 Sep 81	**IT'S MY PARTY** *Stiff BROKEN 2* WITH BARBARA GASKIN	1	4	13
13 Aug 83	**BUSY DOING NOTHING** *Broken 5* WITH BARBARA GASKIN	49		4
14 Jun 86	**THE LOCOMOTION** *Broken 8* WITH BARBARA GASKIN	70		3

DAVE STEWART

UK, male guitarist/producer. See Eurythmics, Tourists, Vegas — Weeks on Chart: 21

Date	Title	Peak	Wks at No.1	Wks
24 Feb 90	**LILY WAS HERE** *RCA ZB 43045* DAVID A STEWART FEATURING CANDY DULFER	6		12
18 Aug 90	**JACK TALKING** *RCA PB 43907* & THE SPIRITUAL COWBOYS	69		2
3 Sep 94	**HEART OF STONE** *East West YZ 845CD*	36		5
6 Nov 04	**OLD HABITS DIE HARD** *Virgin VSCDX1887* MICK JAGGER & DAVE STEWART	45		2

JERMAINE STEWART

US, male vocalist, d. 17 Mar 1997 (age 39) — Weeks on Chart: 42

Date	Title	Peak	Wks at No.1	Wks
9 Aug 86	**WE DON'T HAVE TO...** *10 TEN 96*	2		14
1 Nov 86	**JODY** *10 TEN 143*	50		4
16 Jan 88	**SAY IT AGAIN** *10 TEN 188*	7		12
2 Apr 88	**GET LUCKY** *Siren SRN 82*	13		9
24 Sep 88	**DON'T TALK DIRTY TO ME** *Siren SRN 86*	61		3

JOHN STEWART

US, male vocalist — Weeks on Chart: 6

Date	Title	Peak	Wks at No.1	Wks
30 Jun 79	**GOLD** *RSO 35*	43		6

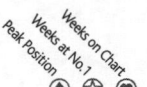

Peak Position | Weeks at No.1 | Weeks on Chart

In the entries below, ○ marks silver-selling, ● gold-selling and ★ US No.1. The tables take their column headings from these printed labels: Peak = Peak Position, Wks No.1 = Weeks at No.1, Wks = Weeks on Chart.

ROD STEWART

UK, male vocalist. The perennially popular, gravel-voiced rock superstar is one of the biggest-selling UK acts ever in the US, with 16 Top 10 singles and 10 Top 5 LPs, and has a 33-year span of chart-topping US albums. See Faces, Helping Haiti

Total weeks on chart: 477

Date	Title	Peak	Wks No.1	Wks
4 Sep 71	**REASON TO BELIEVE/MAGGIE MAY** *Mercury 6052 097* ★	1	5	21
12 Aug 72	**YOU WEAR IT WELL** *Mercury 6052 171*	1	1	12
18 Nov 72	**ANGEL/WHAT MADE MILWAUKEE FAMOUS (HAS MADE A LOSER OUT OF ME)** *Mercury 6052 198*	4		11
5 May 73	**I'VE BEEN DRINKING** *RAK RR4* JEFF BECK & ROD STEWART	27		6
8 Sep 73	**OH NO NOT MY BABY** *Mercury 6052 371*	6		9
5 Oct 74	**FAREWELL – BRING IT ON HOME TO ME/YOU SEND ME** *Mercury 6167 033*	7		7
7 Dec 74	**YOU CAN MAKE ME DANCE SING OR ANYTHING (EVEN TAKE THE DOG FOR A WALK, MEND A FUSE, FOLD AWAY THE IRONING BOARD, OR ANY OTHER DOMESTIC SHORTCOMINGS)** *Warner Brothers K 16494* & THE FACES	12		9
16 Aug 75	**SAILING** *Warner Brothers K 16600* ●	1	4	11
15 Nov 75	**THIS OLD HEART OF MINE** *Riva 1*	4		9
5 Jun 76	**TONIGHT'S THE NIGHT** *Riva 3* ★	5		9
21 Aug 76	**THE KILLING OF GEORGIE** *Riva 4*	2		10
4 Sep 76	**SAILING** *Warner Brothers K 16600* ○	3		20
20 Nov 76	**GET BACK** *Riva 6*	11		9
4 Dec 76	**MAGGIE MAY** *Mercury 6160 006*	31		7
23 Apr 77	**I DON'T WANT TO TALK ABOUT IT/FIRST CUT IS THE DEEPEST** *Riva 7* ○	1	4	13
15 Oct 77	**YOU'RE IN MY HEART** *Riva 11* ○	3		10
28 Jan 78	**HOTLEGS/I WAS ONLY JOKING** *Riva 10* ○	5		8
27 May 78	**OLE OLA (MULHER BRASILEIRA)** *Riva 15* FEATURING THE SCOTTISH WORLD CUP FOOTBALL SQUAD	4		6
18 Nov 78	**DA 'YA THINK I'M SEXY** *Riva 17* ● ★	1	1	13
3 Feb 79	**AIN'T LOVE A BITCH** *Riva 18* ○	11		8
5 May 79	**BLONDES (HAVE MORE FUN)** *Riva 19*	63		3
31 May 80	**IF LOVING YOU IS WRONG (I DON'T WANT TO BE RIGHT)** *Riva 23*	23		9
8 Nov 80	**PASSION** *Riva 26*	17		10
20 Dec 80	**MY GIRL** *Riva 28*	32		7
17 Oct 81	**TONIGHT I'M YOURS (DON'T HURT ME)** *Riva 33*	8		13
12 Dec 81	**YOUNG TURKS** *Riva 34*	11		9
27 Feb 82	**HOW LONG** *Riva 35*	41		4
4 Jun 83	**BABY JANE** *Warner Brothers W 9608* ○	1	3	14
27 Aug 83	**WHAT AM I GONNA DO** *Warner Brothers W 9564*	3		8
10 Dec 83	**SWEET SURRENDER** *Warner Brothers W 9440*	23		9
26 May 84	**INFATUATION** *Warner Brothers W 9256*	27		7
28 Jul 84	**SOME GUYS HAVE ALL THE LUCK** *Warner Brothers W 9204*	15		10
24 May 86	**LOVE TOUCH** *Warner Brothers W 8668*	27		8
12 Jul 86	**EVERY BEAT OF MY HEART** *Warner Brothers W 8625* ○	2		9
20 Sep 86	**ANOTHER HEARTACHE** *Warner Brothers W 8631*	54		2
28 Mar 87	**SAILING** *Warner Brothers K 16600*	41		3
28 May 88	**LOST IN YOU** *Warner Brothers W 7927*	21		6
13 Aug 88	**FOREVER YOUNG** *Warner Brothers W 7796*	57		3
6 May 89	**MY HEART CAN'T TELL YOU NO** *Warner Brothers W 7729*	49		4
11 Nov 89	**THIS OLD HEART OF MINE** *Warner Brothers W 2686*	51		3
13 Jan 90	**DOWNTOWN TRAIN** *Warner Brothers W 2647*	10		12
24 Nov 90	**IT TAKES TWO** *Warner Brothers ROD 1* & TINA TURNER	5		8
16 Mar 91	**RHYTHM OF MY HEART** *Warner Brothers W 0017* ○	3		11
15 Jun 91	**THE MOTOWN SONG** *Warner Brothers W 0030*	10		8
7 Sep 91	**BROKEN ARROW** *Warner Brothers W 0059*	54		3
7 Mar 92	**PEOPLE GET READY** *Epic 6577567* JEFF BECK & ROD STEWART	49		3
18 Apr 92	**YOUR SONG/BROKEN ARROW** *Warner Brothers W 0104*	41		4
5 Dec 92	**TOM TRAUBERT'S BLUES (WALTZING MATILDA)** *Warner Brothers W 0144* ○	6		9
20 Feb 93	**RUBY TUESDAY** *Warner Brothers W 0158CD*	11		6
17 Apr 93	**SHOTGUN WEDDING** *Warner Brothers W 0171CD*	21		4
26 Jun 93	**HAVE I TOLD YOU LATELY** *Warner Brothers W 0185CD*	5		9
21 Aug 93	**REASON TO BELIEVE** *Warner Brothers W 0198CD1*	51		3
18 Dec 93	**PEOPLE GET READY** *Warner Brothers W 0226CD1*	45		4
15 Jan 94	**ALL FOR LOVE** *A&M 5804772* BRYAN ADAMS, ROD STEWART & STING ○ ★	2		13
20 May 95	**YOU'RE THE STAR** *Warner Brothers W 0296CD*	19		5
19 Aug 95	**LADY LUCK** *Warner Brothers W 0310CD1*	56		1
15 Jun 96	**PURPLE HEATHER** *Warner Brothers W 0354CD* WITH THE SCOTTISH EURO '96 SQUAD	16		5
14 Dec 96	**IF WE FALL IN LOVE TONIGHT** *Warner Brothers W 0380CD*	58		1
1 Nov 97	**DA YA THINK I'M SEXY?** *All Around The World CDGLOBE 150* N-TRANCE FEATURING ROD STEWART	7		10
30 May 98	**OOH LA LA** *Warner Brothers W 0446CD*	16		5
5 Sep 98	**ROCKS** *Warner Brothers W 0452CD1*	55		1
17 Apr 99	**FAITH OF THE HEART** *Universal UND 56235*	60		1
24 Mar 01	**I CAN'T DENY IT** *Atlantic AT 0096CD*	26		2

STEX

UK, male vocalist (Andrew Enamejewa)

Total weeks on chart: 2

Date	Title	Peak	Wks No.1	Wks
19 Jan 91	**STILL FEEL THE RAIN** *Some Bizzare SBZ 7002*	63		2

STICKY FEATURING MS DYNAMITE

UK, male/female rap/vocal/production duo

Total weeks on chart: 6

Date	Title	Peak	Wks No.1	Wks
23 Jun 01	**BOOO!** *ffrr FCD 399*	12		6

STIFF DYLANS

UK, male vocal/instrumental group

Total weeks on chart: 3

Date	Title	Peak	Wks No.1	Wks
9 Aug 08	**ULTRAVIOLET** *Columbia 88697341552*	41		3

STIFF LITTLE FINGERS

UK, male vocal/instrumental group

Total weeks on chart: 39

Date	Title	Peak	Wks No.1	Wks
29 Sep 79	**STRAW DOGS** *Chrysalis CHS 2368*	44		4
16 Feb 80	**AT THE EDGE** *Chrysalis CHS 2406*	15		9
24 May 80	**NOBODY'S HERO/TIN SOLDIERS** *Chrysalis CHS 2424*	36		5
2 Aug 80	**BACK TO FRONT** *Chrysalis CHS 2447*	49		4
28 Mar 81	**JUST FADE AWAY** *Chrysalis CHS 2510*	47		6
30 May 81	**SILVER LINING** *Chrysalis CHS 2517*	68		3
23 Jan 82	**LISTEN EP** *Chrysalis CHS 2580*	33		6
18 Sep 82	**BITS OF KIDS** *Chrysalis CHS 2637*	73		2

CURTIS STIGERS

US, male vocalist/saxophonist

Total weeks on chart: 34

Date	Title	Peak	Wks No.1	Wks
18 Jan 92	**I WONDER WHY** *Arista 114716*	5		10
28 Mar 92	**YOU'RE ALL THAT MATTERS TO ME** *Arista 115273*	6		12
11 Jul 92	**SLEEPING WITH THE LIGHTS ON** *Arista 74321102307*	53		4
17 Oct 92	**NEVER SAW A MIRACLE** *Arista 74321117257*	34		4
3 Jun 95	**THIS TIME** *Arista 74321286962*	28		3
2 Dec 95	**KEEP ME FROM THE COLD** *Arista 74321319162*	57		1

STILLS

Canada, male vocal/instrumental group

Total weeks on chart: 5

Date	Title	Peak	Wks No.1	Wks
6 Sep 03	**REMEMBERESE** *679 Recordings 679L 026CD*	75		1
28 Feb 04	**LOLA STARS AND STRIPES** *679 Recordings 679L 036CD1*	39		2
8 May 04	**CHANGES ARE NO GOOD** *679 Recordings 679L 072CD2*	51		1
28 Aug 04	**STILL IN LOVE SONG** *679 Recordings 679L079CD2*	45		1

STEPHEN STILLS

US, male vocalist/guitarist. See Crosby, Stills, Nash & Young

Total weeks on chart: 8

Date	Title	Peak	Wks No.1	Wks
13 Mar 71	**LOVE THE ONE YOU'RE WITH** *Atlantic 2091 046*	37		4
6 Jun 98	**HE GOT GAME** *Def Jam 5689852* PUBLIC ENEMY FEATURING STEPHEN STILLS	16		4

STILTSKIN

UK, male vocal/instrumental group – Ray Wilson, Peter Lawlor, Ross McFarlane & Craig Simister

Total weeks on chart: 15

Date	Title	Peak	Wks No.1	Wks
7 May 94	**INSIDE** *White Water LEV 1CD* ○	1	1	13
24 Sep 94	**FOOTSTEPS** *White Water WWRD 2*	34		2

STING

UK, male vocalist/multi-instrumentalist (Gordon Sumner). See Police

Total weeks on chart: 166

Date	Title	Peak	Wks No.1	Wks
14 Aug 82	**SPREAD A LITTLE HAPPINESS** *A&M AMS 8242*	16		8
8 Jun 85	**IF YOU LOVE SOMEBODY SET THEM FREE** *A&M AM 258*	26		7
24 Aug 85	**LOVE IS THE SEVENTH WAVE** *A&M AM 272*	41		5
19 Oct 85	**FORTRESS AROUND YOUR HEART** *A&M AM 286*	49		3
7 Dec 85	**RUSSIANS** *A&M AM 292*	12		12
15 Feb 86	**MOON OVER BOURBON STREET** *A&M AM 305*	44		4
7 Nov 87	**WE'LL BE TOGETHER** *A&M AM 410*	41		4
20 Feb 88	**ENGLISHMAN IN NEW YORK** *A&M AM 431*	51		3
9 Apr 88	**FRAGILE** *A&M AM 439*	70		2
11 Aug 90	**ENGLISHMAN IN NEW YORK (REMIX)** *A&M AM 580*	15		7
12 Jan 91	**ALL THIS TIME** *A&M AM 713*	22		4
9 Mar 91	**MAD ABOUT YOU** *A&M AM 721*	56		2
4 May 91	**THE SOUL CAGES** *A&M AM 759*	57		1
29 Aug 92	**IT'S PROBABLY ME** *A&M AM 883* WITH ERIC CLAPTON	30		5
13 Feb 93	**IF I EVER LOSE MY FAITH IN YOU** *A&M AMCD 0172*	14		6
24 Apr 93	**SEVEN DAYS** *A&M 5802232*	25		4
19 Jun 93	**FIELDS OF GOLD** *A&M 5803012*	16		6
4 Sep 93	**SHAPE OF MY HEART** *A&M 5803532*	57		1

Date	Title	Peak	Wks at No.1	Wks on Chart
20 Nov 93	**DEMOLITION MAN** *A&M 5804512*	21		4
15 Jan 94	**ALL FOR LOVE** *A&M 5804772* BRYAN ADAMS, ROD STEWART & STING ● ★	2		13
26 Feb 94	**NOTHING 'BOUT ME** *A&M 5805292*	32		3
29 Oct 94	**WHEN WE DANCE** *A&M 5808612*	9		7
11 Feb 95	**THIS COWBOY SONG** *A&M 5809652* FEATURING PATO BANTON	15		6
20 Jan 96	**SPIRITS IN THE MATERIAL WORLD** *MCA MCSTD 2113* PATO BANTON WITH STING	36		2
2 Mar 96	**LET YOUR SOUL BE YOUR PILOT** *A&M 5813312*	15		4
11 May 96	**YOU STILL TOUCH ME** *A&M 5815472*	27		3
22 Jun 96	**LIVE AT TFI FRIDAY EP** *A&M 5817652*	53		2
14 Sep 96	**I WAS BROUGHT TO MY SENSES** *A&M 5818912*	31		2
30 Nov 96	**I'M SO HAPPY I CAN'T STOP CRYING** *A&M 5820312*	54		1
20 Dec 97	**ROXANNE '97** *A&M 5824552* & THE POLICE	17		6
25 Sep 99	**BRAND NEW DAY** *A&M 4971522*	13		5
29 Jan 00	**DESERT SONG** *A&M 4972412* FEATURING CHEB MAMI	15		6
22 Apr 00	**AFTER THE RAIN HAS GONE** *A&M 4973262*	31		4
10 May 03	**RISE & FALL** *Wildstar CDWILD 45* CRAIG DAVID & STING	2		10
27 Sep 03	**SEND YOUR LOVE** *A&M 9810103*	30		2
20 Dec 03	**WHENEVER I SAY YOUR NAME** *A&M 9815304* & MARY J BLIGE	60		1
29 May 04	**STOLEN CAR (TAKE ME DANCING)** *A&M 9862266*	60		1

BYRON STINGILY

US, male vocalist. See Ten City — 14

Date	Title	Peak	Wks at No.1	Wks on Chart
25 Jan 97	**GET UP (EVERYBODY)** *Manifesto FESCD 19*	14		5
1 Nov 97	**SING A SONG** *Manifesto FESCD 35*	38		2
31 Jan 98	**YOU MAKE ME FEEL (MIGHTY REAL)** *Manifesto FESCD 38*	13		4
13 Jun 98	**TESTIFY** *Manifesto FESCD 42*	48		1
12 Feb 00	**THAT'S THE WAY LOVE IS** *Manifesto FESCD 66*	32		2

STINX

UK, female vocal duo — 3

Date	Title	Peak	Wks at No.1	Wks on Chart
24 Mar 01	**WHY DO YOU KEEP ON RUNNING BOY** *HEBS 1*	49		3

STIX 'N' STONED

UK, male instrumental/production duo. See Clergy, Hi-Gate — 2

Date	Title	Peak	Wks at No.1	Wks on Chart
20 Jul 96	**OUTRAGEOUS** *Positiva CDTIV 52*	39		2

CATHERINE STOCK

UK, female vocalist — 6

Date	Title	Peak	Wks at No.1	Wks on Chart
18 Oct 86	**TO HAVE AND TO HOLD** *Sierra FED 29*	17		6

STOCK AITKEN WATERMAN

UK, male production trio – Michael Stock, Matthew Aitken & Peter Waterman — 36

Date	Title	Peak	Wks at No.1	Wks on Chart
25 Jul 87	**ROADBLOCK** *Breakout USA 611*	13		9
24 Oct 87	**MR SLEAZE** *London NANA 14* ●	3		10
12 Dec 87	**PACKJAMMED (WITH THE PARTY POSSE)** *Breakout USA 620*	41		6
21 May 88	**ALL THE WAY** *MCA GOAL 1* ENGLAND FOOTBALL TEAM & THE SOUND OF STOCK AITKEN & WATERMAN	64		2
3 Dec 88	**SS PAPARAZZI** *PWL 22*	68		2
20 May 89	**FERRY 'CROSS THE MERSEY** *PWL 41* CHRISTIANS, HOLLY JOHNSON, PAUL McCARTNEY, GERRY MARSDEN & STOCK AITKEN WATERMAN	1	3	7

RHET STOLLER

UK, male guitarist — 8

Date	Title	Peak	Wks at No.1	Wks on Chart
12 Jan 61	**CHARIOT** *Decca F 11302*	26		8

MORRIS STOLOFF

US, male orchestra leader, d. 16 Apr 1980 (age 81) — 11

Date	Title	Peak	Wks at No.1	Wks on Chart
1 Jun 56	**MOONGLOW/THEME FROM 'PICNIC'** *Brunswick 05553* ★	7		11

ANGIE STONE

US, female vocalist/keyboard player/producer (Angela Brown) — 24

Date	Title	Peak	Wks at No.1	Wks on Chart
15 Apr 00	**LIFE STORY** *Arista 74321748492*	22		3
16 Dec 00	**KEEP YOUR WORRIES** *Virgin VUSCD 177* GURU'S JAZZAMATAZZ FEATURING ANGIE STONE	57		1
9 Mar 02	**BROTHA PART II** *J Records 74321922142* FEATURING ALICIA KEYS & EVE	37		2
27 Jul 02	**WISH I DIDN'T MISS YOU** *J Records 74321939182*	30		5
27 Dec 03	**SIGNED SEALED DELIVERED I'M YOURS** *Innocent SINCD 54* BLUE FEATURING STEVIE WONDER & ANGIE STONE	11		10
14 Aug 04	**I WANNA THANK YOU** *J Records 82876624782* FEATURING SNOOP DOGG	31		3

JOSS STONE

UK, female vocalist/actor (Joscelyn Stoker) — 33

Date	Title	Peak	Wks at No.1	Wks on Chart
7 Feb 04	**FELL IN LOVE WITH A BOY** *Relentless RELCD3*	18		5
22 May 04	**SUPER DUPER LOVE (ARE YOU DIGGIN ON ME)** *Relentless RELCD4*	18		4
25 Sep 04	**YOU HAD ME** *Relentless RELDX10*	9		8
11 Dec 04	**RIGHT TO BE WRONG** *Relentless RELDX13*	29		6
26 Mar 05	**SPOILED** *Relentless RELCD16*	32		2
16 Jul 05	**DON'T CHA WANNA RIDE** *Relentless RELCD20*	20		4
20 May 06	**CRY BABY CRY** *Arista 82876804672* SANTANA FEATURING SEAN PAUL & JOSS STONE	71		1
17 Mar 07	**TELL ME 'BOUT IT** *Relentless/Virgin RELCD35*	28		3

R & J STONE

UK, male/female vocal duo. Russell & Joanne Stone, d. 1979 — 9

Date	Title	Peak	Wks at No.1	Wks on Chart
10 Jan 76	**WE DO IT** *RCA 2616* ●	5		9

STONE ROSES

UK, male vocal/instrumental group – Ian Brown*, Gary 'Mani' Mounfield, John Squire* & Alan "Reni" Wren (replaced by Robbie Maddix) — 77

Date	Title	Peak	Wks at No.1	Wks on Chart
29 Jul 89	**SHE BANGS THE DRUMS** *Silvertone ORE 6*	36		3
25 Nov 89	**WHAT THE WORLD IS WAITING FOR/FOOL'S GOLD** *Silvertone ORE 13* ●	8		14
6 Jan 90	**SALLY CINNAMON** *Revolver REV 36*	46		5
3 Mar 90	**ELEPHANT STONE** *Silvertone ORE 1*	8		6
17 Mar 90	**MADE OF STONE** *Silvertone ORE 2*	20		4
31 Mar 90	**SHE BANGS THE DRUMS** *Silvertone ORE 6*	34		3
14 Jul 90	**ONE LOVE** *Silvertone ORE 17*	4		7
15 Sep 90	**WHAT THE WORLD IS WAITING FOR/FOOL'S GOLD** *Silvertone ORE 13*	22		5
14 Sep 91	**I WANNA BE ADORED** *Silvertone ORE 31*	20		3
11 Jan 92	**WATERFALL** *Silvertone ORE 35*	27		4
11 Apr 92	**I AM THE RESURRECTION** *Silvertone ORE 40*	33		2
30 May 92	**FOOL'S GOLD** *Silvertone ORET 13*	73		1
3 Dec 94	**LOVE SPREADS** *Geffen GFSTD 84*	2		8
11 Mar 95	**TEN STOREY LOVE SONG** *Geffen GFSTD 87*	11		3
29 Apr 95	**FOOL'S GOLD** *Silvertone ORECD 71*	25		3
11 Nov 95	**BEGGING YOU** *Geffen GFSTD 22060*	15		3
6 Mar 99	**FOOL'S GOLD (REMIX)** *Jive Electro 0523092*	25		3

STONE SOUR

US, male vocal/instrumental group — 3

Date	Title	Peak	Wks at No.1	Wks on Chart
15 Mar 03	**BOTHER** *Roadrunner RR 20243*	28		2
19 Jul 03	**INHALE** *Roadrunner RR 20093*	63		1

STONE TEMPLE PILOTS

US, male vocal/instrumental group — 11

Date	Title	Peak	Wks at No.1	Wks on Chart
27 Mar 93	**SEX TYPE THING** *Atlantic A 5769CD*	60		2
4 Sep 93	**PLUSH** *Atlantic A 7349CD*	23		4
27 Nov 93	**SEX TYPE THING** *Atlantic A 7293CD*	55		2
20 Aug 94	**VASOLINE** *Atlantic A 5650CD*	48		2
10 Dec 94	**INTERSTATE LOVE SONG** *Atlantic A 7192CD*	53		1

STONEBRIDGE

Sweden, male DJ/producer (Sten Hollstrom) — 22

Date	Title	Peak	Wks at No.1	Wks on Chart
13 Mar 04	**PUT EM HIGH** *Hed Kandi HEDK12004*	59		2
28 Aug 04	**PUT EM HIGH** *Hed Kandi HEDKCDS008* FEATURING THERESE	6		13
29 Jan 05	**TAKE ME AWAY** *Hed Kandi HEDKCDS009* FEATURING THERESE	9		5
28 May 05	**FREAK ON** *Hed Kandi HEDKCDX010* VS ULTRA NATE	37		2

STONEBRIDGE McGUINNESS

UK, male vocal/instrumental duo — 2

Date	Title	Peak	Wks at No.1	Wks on Chart
14 Jul 79	**OO-EEH BABY** *RCA PB 5163*	54		2

STONEFREE

UK, male vocalist (Tony Stone) — 1

Date	Title	Peak	Wks at No.1	Wks on Chart
23 May 87	**CAN'T SAY 'BYE** *Ensign ENY 607*	73		1

Silver-selling ○ Gold-selling ● Platinum-selling (x multiples) ⊛ US No.1 ★ Peak Position · Weeks at No.1 · Weeks on Chart

STONEPROOF
UK, male producer (John Graham) — Weeks on Chart: **1**

Date	Title / Label	Peak	Wks at No.1	Wks on Chart
15 May 99	**EVERYTHING'S NOT YOU** *VC Recordings VCRD 47*	68		1

STOP THE VIOLENCE
US, male/female rap charity assembly — Weeks on Chart: **1**

Date	Title / Label	Peak	Wks at No.1	Wks on Chart
18 Feb 89	**SELF DESTRUCTION** *Jive BDPST 1*	75		1

STORM
UK, male/female vocal/instrumental group — Weeks on Chart: **10**

Date	Title / Label	Peak	Wks at No.1	Wks on Chart
17 Nov 79	**IT'S MY HOUSE** *Scope SC 10*	36		10

STORM
Germany, male production duo – Rolf Ellmer & Markus Loeffel, d. 11 Jan 2006 (age 39) — Weeks on Chart: **19**

Date	Title / Label	Peak	Wks at No.1	Wks on Chart
29 Aug 98	**STORM** *Positiva CDTIV 94*	32		2
12 Aug 00	**TIME TO BURN** *Data 16CDS* ○	3		10
23 Dec 00	**STORM ANIMAL** *Data 20CDS*	21		5
26 May 01	**STORM (REMIX)** *Positiva CDTIV 154*	32		2

DANNY STORM
UK, male vocalist — Weeks on Chart: **4**

Date	Title / Label	Peak	Wks at No.1	Wks on Chart
12 Apr 62	**HONEST I DO** *Piccadilly 7N 35025*	42		4

REBECCA STORM
UK, female vocalist/actor — Weeks on Chart: **13**

Date	Title / Label	Peak	Wks at No.1	Wks on Chart
13 Jul 85	**THE SHOW (THEME FROM 'CONNIE')** *Towerbell TVP 3*	22		13

STORY OF THE YEAR
US, male vocal/instrumental group — Weeks on Chart: **1**

Date	Title / Label	Peak	Wks at No.1	Wks on Chart
12 Jun 04	**UNTIL THE DAY I DIE** *Maverick W 643CD*	62		1

IZZY STRADLIN'
US, male vocalist/guitarist (Jeffrey Isbell). See Guns N' Roses — Weeks on Chart: **2**

Date	Title / Label	Peak	Wks at No.1	Wks on Chart
26 Sep 92	**PRESSURE DROP** *Geffen GFS 25*	45		2

NICK STRAKER BAND
UK, male vocal/instrumental group — Weeks on Chart: **15**

Date	Title / Label	Peak	Wks at No.1	Wks on Chart
2 Aug 80	**A WALK IN THE PARK** *CBS 8525*	20		12
15 Nov 80	**LEAVING ON THE MIDNIGHT TRAIN** *CBS 9088*	61		3

PETER STRAKER & THE HANDS OF DR TELENY
UK, male vocal/instrumental group — Weeks on Chart: **4**

Date	Title / Label	Peak	Wks at No.1	Wks on Chart
19 Feb 72	**THE SPIRIT IS WILLING** *RCA 2163*	40		4

STRANGELOVE
UK, male vocal/instrumental group — Weeks on Chart: **8**

Date	Title / Label	Peak	Wks at No.1	Wks on Chart
20 Apr 96	**LIVING WITH THE HUMAN MACHINES** *Food CDFOOD 70*	53		1
15 Jun 96	**BEAUTIFUL ALONE** *Food CDFOOD 81*	35		2
19 Oct 96	**SWAY** *Food CDFOOD 82*	47		1
26 Jul 97	**THE GREATEST SHOW ON EARTH** *Food CDFOOD 97*	36		2
11 Oct 97	**FREAK** *Food CDFOOD 105*	43		1
21 Feb 98	**ANOTHER NIGHT IN** *Food CDFOOD 110*	46		1

STRANGLERS
UK, male vocal/instrumental group – Hugh Cornwell; members also included Jet Black, Jean-Jacques Burnel, John Ellis, Dave Greenfield, Paul Roberts & Baz Warne — Weeks on Chart: **198**

Date	Title / Label	Peak	Wks at No.1	Wks on Chart
19 Feb 77	**(GET A) GRIP (ON YOURSELF)** *United Artists UP 36211*	44		4
21 May 77	**PEACHES/GO BUDDY GO** *United Artists UP 36248* ○	8		14
30 Jul 77	**SOMETHING BETTER CHANGE/STRAIGHTEN OUT** *United Artists UP 36277*	9		8
24 Sep 77	**NO MORE HEROES** *United Artists UP 36300*	8		9
4 Feb 78	**FIVE MINUTES** *United Artists UP 36350*	11		9
6 May 78	**NICE 'N' SLEAZY** *United Artists UP 36379*	18		8
12 Aug 78	**WALK ON BY** *United Artists UP 36429*	21		8
18 Aug 79	**DUCHESS** *United Artists BP 308*	14		9
20 Oct 79	**NUCLEAR DEVICE (THE WIZARD OF AUS)** *United Artists BP 318*	36		4
1 Dec 79	**DON'T BRING HARRY (EP)** *United Artists STR 1*	41		3
22 Mar 80	**BEAR CAGE** *United Artists BP 344*	36		5
7 Jun 80	**WHO WANTS THE WORLD** *United Artists BPX 355*	39		4
31 Jan 81	**THROWN AWAY** *Liberty BP 383*	42		4
14 Nov 81	**LET ME INTRODUCE YOU TO THE FAMILY** *Liberty BP 405*	42		3
9 Jan 82	**GOLDEN BROWN** *Liberty BP 407* ●	2		12
24 Apr 82	**LA FOLIE** *Liberty BP 410*	47		3
24 Jul 82	**STRANGE LITTLE GIRL** *Liberty BP 412*	7		9
8 Jan 83	**EUROPEAN FEMALE** *Epic EPC A 2893*	9		6
26 Feb 83	**MIDNIGHT SUMMER DREAM** *Epic EPC A 3167*	35		4
6 Aug 83	**PARADISE** *Epic A 3387*	48		3
6 Oct 84	**SKIN DEEP** *Epic A 4738*	15		7
1 Dec 84	**NO MERCY** *Epic A 4921*	37		7
16 Feb 85	**LET ME DOWN EASY** *Epic A 6045*	48		4
23 Aug 86	**NICE IN NICE** *Epic 6500557*	30		5
18 Oct 86	**ALWAYS THE SUN** *Epic SOLAR 1*	30		5
13 Dec 86	**BIG IN AMERICA** *Epic HUGE 1*	48		6
7 Mar 87	**SHAKIN' LIKE A LEAF** *Epic SHEIK 1*	58		4
9 Jan 88	**ALL DAY AND ALL OF THE NIGHT** *Epic VICE 1*	7		7
28 Jan 89	**GRIP '89 (GET A) GRIP (ON YOURSELF) (REMIX)** *EMI EM 84*	33		3
17 Feb 90	**96 TEARS** *Epic TEARS 1*	17		6
21 Apr 90	**SWEET SMELL OF SUCCESS** *Epic TEARS 2*	65		2
5 Jan 91	**ALWAYS THE SUN (REMIX)** *Epic 6564307*	29		5
30 Mar 91	**GOLDEN BROWN (REMIX)** *Epic 6567617*	68		2
22 Aug 92	**HEAVEN OR HELL** *Psycho WOK 2025*	46		2
14 Feb 04	**BIG THING COMING** *Liberty 5480692*	31		2
24 Apr 04	**LONG BLACK VEIL** *EMI 05489062*	51		1
23 Sep 06	**THE SPECTRE OF LOVE** *Liberty 3750342*	57		1

STRAW
UK, male vocal/instrumental group — Weeks on Chart: **4**

Date	Title / Label	Peak	Wks at No.1	Wks on Chart
6 Feb 99	**THE AEROPLANE SONG** *WEA 196CD*	37		2
24 Apr 99	**MOVING TO CALIFORNIA** *WEA 205CD*	50		1
3 Mar 01	**SAILING OFF THE EDGE OF THE WORLD** *Columbia 6708452*	52		1

STRAWBERRY SWITCHBLADE
UK, female vocal/instrumental duo – Jill Bryson & Rose McDowall — Weeks on Chart: **26**

Date	Title / Label	Peak	Wks at No.1	Wks on Chart
17 Nov 84	**SINCE YESTERDAY** *Korova KOW 38*	5		17
23 Mar 85	**LET HER GO** *Korova KOW 39*	59		5
21 Sep 85	**JOLENE** *Korova KOW 42*	53		4

STRAWBS
UK, male vocal/instrumental group – Dave Cousins; members also included Sandy Denny, John Ford, Richard Hudson (Hudson Ford*),Tony Hooper, Sonja Kristina, Dave Lambert, Rick Wakeman & Blue Weaver (Derek Weaver) — Weeks on Chart: **27**

Date	Title / Label	Peak	Wks at No.1	Wks on Chart
28 Oct 72	**LAY DOWN** *A&M AMS 7035*	12		13
27 Jan 73	**PART OF THE UNION** *A&M AMS 7047*	2		11
6 Oct 73	**SHINE ON SILVER SUN** *A&M AMS 7082*	34		3

STRAY CATS
US, male vocal/instrumental trio – Brian Setzer, Lee Rocker (Leon Drucher) & Slim Jim Phantom (James McDonnell) — Weeks on Chart: **49**

Date	Title / Label	Peak	Wks at No.1	Wks on Chart
29 Nov 80	**RUNAWAY BOYS** *Arista SCAT 1* ○	9		10
7 Feb 81	**ROCK THIS TOWN** *Arista SCAT 2*	9		8
25 Apr 81	**STRAY CAT STRUT** *Arista SCAT 3*	11		10
20 Jun 81	**THE RACE IS ON** *Swansong SSK 19425* DAVE EDMUNDS & THE STRAY CATS	34		6
7 Nov 81	**YOU DON'T BELIEVE ME** *Arista SCAT 4*	57		3
6 Aug 83	**(SHE'S) SEXY AND 17** *Arista SCAT 6*	29		9
4 Mar 89	**BRING IT BACK AGAIN** *EMI USA MT 62*	64		3

STREETBAND
UK, male vocal/instrumental group — Weeks on Chart: **6**

Date	Title / Label	Peak	Wks at No.1	Wks on Chart
4 Nov 78	**TOAST/HOLD ON** *Logo GO 325*	18		6

STREETS
UK, male rapper/producer (Mike Skinner) — Weeks on Chart: **75**

Date	Title / Label	Peak	Wks at No.1	Wks on Chart
20 Oct 01	**HAS IT COME TO THIS** *679 Recordings 679L 001CD1*	18		5
27 Apr 02	**LET'S PUSH THINGS FORWARD** *Locked On/679 679005CD1*	30		3
3 Aug 02	**WEAK BECOME HEROES** *Locked On/679 Recordings 679007CD*	27		3
2 Nov 02	**DON'T MUG YOURSELF** *Locked On/679 Recordings 008CDX*	21		3
8 May 04	**FIT BUT YOU KNOW IT** *Locked On/679 Recordings 679L071CD2*	4		10
31 Jul 04	**DRY YOUR EYES** *Locked On/679 Recordings 679L077CD1*	1	1	13

Date	Title	Peak Position	Weeks at No.1	Weeks on Chart
9 Oct 04	**BLINDED BY THE LIGHTS** *Locked On/679 Recordings 679L085CD*	10		7
11 Dec 04	**COULD WELL BE IN** *Locked On/679 Recordings 679L092CD*	30		5
19 Mar 05	**ROUTINE CHECK** *WEA BEATS8* MITCHELL BROTHERS/KANO/THE STREETS	42		2
24 Sep 05	**NITE NITE** *679 679L108CD2* KANO FEATURING MIKE SKINNER & LEO THE LION	25		6
8 Apr 06	**WHEN YOU WASN'T FAMOUS** *679 679L125CD1*	8		7
10 Jun 06	**NEVER WENT TO CHURCH** *679 679L132CD1*	20		5
30 Sep 06	**PRANGIN' OUT** *Locked On/679 679L141CD1* FEATURING PETE DOHERTY	25		4
27 Sep 08	**EVERYTHING IS BORROWED** *679 GBFFS0800087*	37		2

BARBRA STREISAND

US, female vocalist/actor/film producer/director — 155

Date	Title	Peak Position	Weeks at No.1	Weeks on Chart
20 Jan 66	**SECOND HAND ROSE** *CBS 202025*	14		13
30 Jan 71	**STONEY END** *CBS 5321*	27		11
30 Mar 74	**THE WAY WE WERE** *CBS 1915* ★	31		6
9 Apr 77	**LOVE THEME FROM 'A STAR IS BORN' (EVERGREEN)** *CBS 4855* ● ★	3		19
25 Nov 78	**YOU DON'T BRING ME FLOWERS** *CBS 6803* BARBRA & NEIL ● ★	5		12
3 Nov 79	**NO MORE TEARS (ENOUGH IS ENOUGH)** *Casablanca CAN 174/CBS 8000* DONNA SUMMER & BARBRA STREISAND ● ★	3		13
4 Oct 80	**WOMAN IN LOVE** *CBS 8966* ● ★	1	3	16
6 Dec 80	**GUILTY** *CBS 9315* & BARRY GIBB	34		10
30 Jan 82	**COMIN' IN AND OUT OF YOUR LIFE** *CBS A 1789*	66		3
20 Mar 82	**MEMORY** *CBS A 1903*	34		6
5 Nov 88	**TILL I LOVED YOU (LOVE THEME FROM 'GOYA')** *CBS BARB 2* & DON JOHNSON	16		7
7 Mar 92	**PLACES THAT BELONG TO YOU** *Columbia 6577947*	17		5
5 Jun 93	**WITH ONE LOOK** *Columbia 6593422*	30		3
15 Jan 94	**THE MUSIC OF THE NIGHT** *Columbia 6597382* (DUET WITH MICHAEL CRAWFORD)	54		3
30 Apr 94	**AS IF WE NEVER SAID GOODBYE (FROM SUNSET BOULEVARD)** *Columbia 6603572*	20		3
8 Feb 97	**I FINALLY FOUND SOMEONE** *A&M 5820832* & BRYAN ADAMS	10		7
15 Nov 97	**TELL HIM** *Epic 6653052* & CELINE DION ●	3		15
30 Oct 99	**IF YOU EVER LEAVE ME** *Columbia 6681242* BARBARA STREISAND/VINCE GILL	26		3

STRESS

UK, male vocal/instrumental trio — 1

Date	Title	Peak Position	Weeks at No.1	Weeks on Chart
13 Oct 90	**BEAUTIFUL PEOPLE** *Eternal YZ 495*	74		1

STRETCH

UK, male vocal/instrumental group — 9

Date	Title	Peak Position	Weeks at No.1	Weeks on Chart
8 Nov 75	**WHY DID YOU DO IT** *Anchor ANC 1021*	16		9

STRETCH 'N' VERN PRESENT MADDOG

UK, male instrumental/production duo – Stuart Collins & Julian Peake — 14

Date	Title	Peak Position	Weeks at No.1	Weeks on Chart
14 Sep 96	**I'M ALIVE** *ffrr FCD 284*	6		9
9 Aug 97	**GET UP! GO INSANE!** *ffrr FCD 304*	17		5

STRICT INSTRUCTOR

Russia, female vocalist (Lana Cox) — 1

Date	Title	Peak Position	Weeks at No.1	Weeks on Chart
24 Oct 98	**STEP-TWO-THREE-FOUR** *All Around The World CDGLOBE 155*	49		1

STRIKE

UK/Australia, male/female production/vocal trio – Matt Cantor, Andy Gardner & Victoria Newton — 24

Date	Title	Peak Position	Weeks at No.1	Weeks on Chart
24 Dec 94	**U SURE DO** *Fresh FRSHD 19*	31		5
1 Apr 95	**U SURE DO** *Fresh FRSHD 19*	4		9
23 Sep 95	**THE MORNING AFTER (FREE AT LAST)** *Fresh FRSHD 37*	38		1
29 Jun 96	**INSPIRATION** *Fresh FRSHD 45*	27		2
16 Nov 96	**MY LOVE IS FOR REAL** *Fresh FRSHD 46*	35		2
31 May 97	**I HAVE PEACE** *Fresh FRSHD 58*	17		4
25 Sep 99	**U SURE DO (REMIX)** *Fresh FRSHD 78*	53		1

STRIKERS

US, male vocal/instrumental group — 5

Date	Title	Peak Position	Weeks at No.1	Weeks on Chart
6 Jun 81	**BODY MUSIC** *Epic A 1290*	45		5

STRING-A-LONGS

US, male instrumental group – Jimmy Torres, Don Allen, Aubrey Lee De Cordova, Keith McCormack & Richard Stephens — 16

Date	Title	Peak Position	Weeks at No.1	Weeks on Chart
23 Feb 61	**WHEELS** *London HLU 9278*	8		16

STRINGS OF LOVE

Italy, male/female production/vocal group — 2

Date	Title	Peak Position	Weeks at No.1	Weeks on Chart
3 Mar 90	**NOTHING HAS BEEN PROVED** *Breakout USA 688*	59		2

STROKES

US, male vocal/instrumental group – Julian Casablancas, Nikolai Fraiture, Albert Hammond Jr, Fab Moretti, & Nick Valensi — 36

Date	Title	Peak Position	Weeks at No.1	Weeks on Chart
7 Jul 01	**HARD TO EXPLAIN/NEW YORK CITY COPS** *Rough Trade RTRADESCD 023*	16		5
7 Jul 01	**MODERN AGE** *Rough Trade RTRADESCD 010*	68		3
17 Nov 01	**LAST NIGHT** *Rough Trade RTRADESCD 041*	14		5
5 Oct 02	**SOMEDAY** *Rough Trade RTRADESCD 063*	27		2
18 Oct 03	**12:51** *Rough Trade RTRADESCD 140*	7		4
21 Feb 04	**REPTILLA** *Rough Trade RTRADESCD 155*	17		5
13 Nov 04	**THE END HAS NO END** *Rough Trade RTRADSCD 205*	27		2
17 Dec 05	**JUICEBOX** *Rough Trade RTRADSCDX282*	5		8
1 Apr 06	**HEART IN A CAGE** *Rough Trade RTRADSCDX305*	25		2

JOE STRUMMER

UK (b. Turkey), male vocalist/guitarist (John Mellor), d. 23 Dec 2002 (age 50). See Clash — 17

Date	Title	Peak Position	Weeks at No.1	Weeks on Chart
2 Aug 86	**LOVE KILLS** *CBS A 7244*	69		1
23 Dec 95	**JUST THE ONE** *China WOKCD 2076* LEVELLERS, SPECIAL GUEST JOE STRUMMER	12		8
29 Jun 96	**ENGLAND'S IRIE** *Radioactive RAXTD 25* BLACK GRAPE FEATURING JOE STRUMMER & KEITH ALLEN	6		4
18 Oct 03	**COMA GIRL** *Hellcat 11362* & THE MESCALEROS	33		2
27 Dec 03	**REDEMPTION SONG/ARMS ALOFT** *Hellcat 11482* & THE MESCALEROS	46		2

TINCHY STRYDER

UK, male vocalist/rapper (Kwasi Danquah). See Young Soul Rebels — 72

Date	Title	Peak Position	Weeks at No.1	Weeks on Chart
9 Aug 08	**STRYDERMAN** *Island 1781881*	73		2
22 Nov 08	**WHERE'S YOUR LOVE** *Warner Brothers GBAHT0800447* CRAIG DAVID FEATURNG TINCHY STRYDER	58		1
17 Jan 09	**TAKE ME BACK** *Fourth & Broadway 1797027* FEATURING TAIO CRUZ	3		19
2 May 09	**NUMBER 1** *Fourth & Broadway 2701362* FEATURING N-DUBZ	1	3	28
15 Aug 09	**NEVER LEAVE YOU** *Fourth & Broadway 2713078* FEATURING AMELLE BERRABAH	1	1	13
29 Aug 09	**YOU'RE NOT ALONE** *Fourth & Broadway GBUM70908594*	14		9

STUART

Holland, male DJ/producer (Sjoerd Wijdoogen) — 2

Date	Title	Peak Position	Weeks at No.1	Weeks on Chart
5 Apr 03	**FREE (LET IT BE)** *Product/Incentive PFT 07CDS*	41		2

CHAD STUART & JEREMY CLYDE

UK, male vocal/instrumental duo — 7

Date	Title	Peak Position	Weeks at No.1	Weeks on Chart
28 Nov 63	**YESTERDAY'S GONE** *Ember EMBS 180*	37		7

STUDIO B

UK, male vocalist/producer (Harry Brooks, Jr.). See OBI Project featuring Harry, Asher D & DJ What?, So Solid Crew — 23

Date	Title	Peak Position	Weeks at No.1	Weeks on Chart
6 Dec 03	**I SEE GIRLS (CRAZY)** *Multiply CDMULTY 109* STUDIO B/ROMEO & HARRY BROOKS	52		1
9 Apr 05	**I SEE GIRLS** *Data BOSSMOS1CDS*	12		19
22 Apr 06	**C'MON GET IT ON** *Loaded LOAD110CD*	28		3

STUDIO 45

Germany, male DJ/production duo — 2

Date	Title	Peak Position	Weeks at No.1	Weeks on Chart
20 Feb 99	**FREAK IT!** *Azuli AZNYCD 090*	36		2

STUDIO 2

Jamaica, male vocalist (Errol Jones) — 1

Date	Title	Peak Position	Weeks at No.1	Weeks on Chart
27 Jun 98	**TRAVELLING MAN** *Multiply CDMULTY 35*	40		1

AMY STUDT
UK, female vocalist/pianist — 26

Date	Title / Label	Peak	Wks No.1	Wks
13 Jul 02	**JUST A LITTLE GIRL** *Polydor 5708802*	14		6
21 Jun 03	**MISFIT** *Polydor 9800107*	6		10
11 Oct 03	**UNDER THE THUMB** *Polydor 9811793*	10		6
24 Jan 04	**ALL I WANNA DO** *19/Polydor 9815012*	21		4

STUMP
UK/Ireland, male vocal/instrumental group — 1

Date	Title / Label	Peak	Wks No.1	Wks
13 Aug 88	**CHARLTON HESTON** *Ensign ENY 614*	72		1

STUNT
UK, male DJ/production group — 14

Date	Title / Label	Peak	Wks No.1	Wks
21 Jan 06	**RAINDROPS** *Data DATA108CDS*	51		1
25 Oct 08	**RAINDROPS (ENCORE UNE FOIS)** *Hard2Beat H2B15CDS* SASH! FEATURING STUNT	9		13

STUNTMASTERZ
UK, male production duo – Pete Cook & Steve Harris — 9

Date	Title / Label	Peak	Wks No.1	Wks
3 Mar 01	**THE LADYBOY IS MINE** *East West EW 226CD*	10		9

STUTZ BEARCATS & THE DENIS KING ORCHESTRA
UK, male/female vocal group & orchestra — 6

Date	Title / Label	Peak	Wks No.1	Wks
24 Apr 82	**THE SONG THAT I SING (THEME FROM 'WE'LL MEET AGAIN')** *Multi-Media Tapes MMT 6*	36		6

STYLE COUNCIL
UK, male/female vocal/instrumental group – Paul Weller*, Dee C Lee*, Mick Talbot & Steve White. See Council Collective — 103

Date	Title / Label	Peak	Wks No.1	Wks
19 Mar 83	**SPEAK LIKE A CHILD** *Polydor TSC 1* ○	4		8
28 May 83	**MONEY GO ROUND (PART 1)** *Polydor TSC 2*	11		7
13 Aug 83	**LONG HOT SUMMER/PARIS MATCH** *Polydor TSC 3* ○	3		9
19 Nov 83	**SOLID BOND IN YOUR HEART** *Polydor TSC 4*	11		8
18 Feb 84	**MY EVER CHANGING MOODS** *Polydor TSC 5*	5		7
26 May 84	**GROOVIN' (YOU'RE THE BEST THING)/BIG BOSS GROOVE** *Polydor TSC 6*	5		8
13 Oct 84	**SHOUT TO THE TOP** *Polydor TSC 7*	7		8
11 May 85	**WALLS COME TUMBLING DOWN!** *Polydor TSC 8*	6		7
6 Jul 85	**COME TO MILTON KEYNES** *Polydor TSC 9*	23		5
28 Sep 85	**THE LODGERS** *Polydor TSC 10*	13		6
5 Apr 86	**HAVE YOU EVER HAD IT BLUE** *Polydor CINE 1*	14		6
17 Jan 87	**IT DIDN'T MATTER** *Polydor TSC 12*	9		5
14 Mar 87	**WAITING** *Polydor TSC 13*	52		3
31 Oct 87	**WANTED** *Polydor TSC 14*	20		4
28 May 88	**LIFE AT A TOP PEOPLE'S HEALTH FARM** *Polydor TSC 15*	28		3
23 Jul 88	**HOW SHE THREW IT ALL AWAY (EP)** *Polydor TSC 16*	41		2
18 Feb 89	**PROMISED LAND** *Polydor TSC 17*	27		5
27 May 89	**LONG HOT SUMMER 89 (REMIX)** *Polydor LHS 1*	48		2

STYLES P
US, male rapper/producer (David Styles) — 4

Date	Title / Label	Peak	Wks No.1	Wks
14 Sep 02	**THE LIFE** *MCA MCSTD 40292* STYLES & PHAROAHE MONCH	50		1
25 Dec 04	**LOCKED UP** *Universal E9864569* AKON FEATURING STYLES P	61		3

DARREN STYLES
UK, male producer — 20

Date	Title / Label	Peak	Wks No.1	Wks
5 Apr 03	**LET ME FLY** *Nukleuz 0432 CNUK* DARREN STYLES/MARK BREEZE	59		1
31 Jul 04	**YOU'RE SHINING** *All Around The World CDGLOBE346* STYLES & BREEZE	19		4
12 Mar 05	**HEARTBEATZ** *All Around The World CDGLOBE342* STYLES & BREEZE FEATURING KAREN DANZIG	16		4
7 Apr 07	**SAVE ME** *All Around The World CXGLOBE566*	70		1
8 Sep 07	**SURE FEELS GOOD** *All Around The World CDGLOBE696* ULTRABEAT VS DARREN STYLES	52		1
19 Jul 08	**DISCOLIGHTS** *All Around The World CDGLOBE937* ULTRABEAT VS DARREN STYLES	23		9

STYLISTICS
US, male vocal group – Russell Thompkins, Jr, James Dunn, Airrion Love, Herbie Murrell & James Smith — 143

Date	Title / Label	Peak	Wks No.1	Wks
24 Jun 72	**BETCHA BY GOLLY WOW** *Avco 6105 011*	13		12
4 Nov 72	**I'M STONE IN LOVE WITH YOU** *Avco 6105 015*	9		10
17 Mar 73	**BREAK UP TO MAKE UP** *Avco 6105 020*	34		5
30 Jun 73	**PEEK-A-BOO** *Avco 6105 023*	35		6
19 Jan 74	**ROCKIN' ROLL BABY** *Avco 6105 026*	6		9
13 Jul 74	**YOU MAKE ME FEEL BRAND NEW** *Avco 6105 028* ○	2		14
19 Oct 74	**LET'S PUT IT ALL TOGETHER** *Avco 6105 032*	9		9
25 Jan 75	**STAR ON A TV SHOW** *Avco 6105 035*	12		8
10 May 75	**SING BABY SING** *Avco 6105 036* ○	3		10
26 Jul 75	**CAN'T GIVE YOU ANYTHING (BUT MY LOVE)** *Avco 6105 039* ●	1	3	11
15 Nov 75	**NA NA IS THE SADDEST WORD** *Avco 6105 041* ○	5		10
14 Feb 76	**FUNKY WEEKEND** *Avco 6105 044*	10		7
24 Apr 76	**CAN'T HELP FALLING IN LOVE** *Avco 6105 050*	4		7
7 Aug 76	**16 BARS** *H&L 6105 059*	7		9
27 Nov 76	**YOU'LL NEVER GET TO HEAVEN EP** *H&L STYL 001*	24		9
26 Mar 77	**7000 DOLLARS AND YOU** *H&L 6105 073*	24		7

STYLUS TROUBLE
UK, male producer (Pete Heller). See Fire Island, Heller & Farley Project — 1

Date	Title / Label	Peak	Wks No.1	Wks
23 Jun 01	**SPUTNIK** *Junior London BRG 014*	63		1

STYX
US, male vocal/instrumental group – Dennis DeYoung, Chuck & John, d. 16 Jul 1996, Panozzo, Tommy Shaw & James Young — 18

Date	Title / Label	Peak	Wks No.1	Wks
5 Jan 80	**BABE** *A&M AMS 7489* ○ ★	6		10
24 Jan 81	**THE BEST OF TIMES** *A&M AMS 8102*	42		5
18 Jun 83	**DON'T LET IT END** *A&M AM 120*	56		3

SUB FOCUS
UK, male producer (Nick Douwma) — 6

Date	Title / Label	Peak	Wks No.1	Wks
19 Mar 05	**X RAY/SCARECROW** *Ramm Records RAMM 054*	60		1
8 Aug 09	**ROCK IT/FOLLOW THE LIGHT** *Ramm Records RAMM78CD*	38		3
30 Jan 10	**COULD THIS BE REAL** *Ramm Records RAMM82CD*	41		2

SUB SUB
UK, male instrumental/production trio – Jimi Goodwin & Andy & Jez Williams. See Doves — 12

Date	Title / Label	Peak	Wks No.1	Wks
10 Apr 93	**AIN'T NO LOVE (AIN'T NO USE)** *Rob's CDROB 9* FEATURING MELANIE WILLIAMS ○	3		11
19 Feb 94	**RESPECT** *Rob's CDROB 19*	49		1

SUBCIRCUS
Denmark/UK, male vocal/instrumental group — 2

Date	Title / Label	Peak	Wks No.1	Wks
26 Apr 97	**YOU LOVE YOU** *Echo ECSCD 34*	61		1
12 Jul 97	**86'D** *Echo ECSCX 43*	56		1

SUBLIME
US, male vocal/instrumental group — 1

Date	Title / Label	Peak	Wks No.1	Wks
5 Jul 97	**WHAT I GOT** *Gasoline Alley MCSTD 48045*	71		1

SUBLIMINAL CUTS
Holland, male producer (Patrick Prins). See Artemesia, Ethics, Movin' Melodies — 3

Date	Title / Label	Peak	Wks No.1	Wks
15 Oct 94	**LE VOIE LE SOLEIL** *XL Recordings XLS 53CD*	69		1
20 Jul 96	**LE VOIE LE SOLEIL (REMIX)** *XL Recordings XLSR 53CD*	23		2

SUBMERGE FEATURING JAN JOHNSTON
US/UK, male/female vocal/instrumental/production duo — 2

Date	Title / Label	Peak	Wks No.1	Wks
8 Feb 97	**TAKE ME BY THE HAND** *AM:PM 5821012*	28		2

SUBSONIC 2
UK, male rap/DJ duo — 3

Date	Title / Label	Peak	Wks No.1	Wks
13 Jul 91	**THE UNSUNG HEROES OF HIP HOP** *Unity 6577947*	63		3

SUBTERRANIA FEATURING ANN CONSUELO

Sweden, male producer (Niklas Windahl) & (b. Ecuador), female vocalist — **1**

Date	Title	Peak	Wks at No.1	Wks on Chart
5 Jun 93	**DO IT FOR LOVE** *Champion CHAMPCD 297*	68		1

SUBWAYS

UK, male/female vocal/instrumental group — **10**

Date	Title	Peak	Wks at No.1	Wks on Chart
2 Apr 05	**OH YEAH** *WEA WEA384CD1*	25		3
2 Jul 05	**ROCK & ROLL QUEEN** *Infectious WEA390CD1*	22		2
24 Sep 05	**WITH YOU** *Infectious WEA392CD*	29		2
24 Dec 05	**NO GOODBYES** *Infectious WEA398CD*	27		2
28 Jun 08	**ALRIGHT** *Infectious WEA447X*	44		1

SUEDE

UK, male vocal/instrumental group – Brett Anderson*, Bernard Butler* (replaced by Richard Oakes), Neil Codling (replaced by Alex Lee), Simon Gilbert & Mat Osman — **75**

Date	Title	Peak	Wks at No.1	Wks on Chart
23 May 92	**THE DROWNERS/TO THE BIRDS** *Nude NUD 1CD*	49		2
26 Sep 92	**METAL MICKEY** *Nude NUD 3CD*	17		3
6 Mar 93	**ANIMAL NITRATE** *Nude NUD 4CD*	7		7
29 May 93	**SO YOUNG** *Nude NUD 5CD*	22		3
26 Feb 94	**STAY TOGETHER** *Nude NUD 9CD*	3		6
24 Sep 94	**WE ARE THE PIGS** *Nude NUD 10CD*	18		3
19 Nov 94	**THE WILD ONES** *Nude NUD 11CD1*	18		4
11 Feb 95	**NEW GENERATION** *Nude NUD 12CD2*	21		4
10 Aug 96	**TRASH** *Nude NUD 21CD1*	3		6
26 Oct 96	**BEAUTIFUL ONES** *Nude NUD 23CD1*	8		5
25 Jan 97	**SATURDAY NIGHT** *Nude NUD 24CD1*	6		4
19 Apr 97	**LAZY** *Nude NUD 27CD*	9		3
23 Aug 97	**FILMSTAR** *Nude NUD 30CD1*	9		4
24 Apr 99	**ELECTRICITY** *Nude NUD 43CD1*	5		5
3 Jul 99	**SHE'S IN FASHION** *Nude NUD 44CD1*	13		5
18 Sep 99	**EVERYTHING WILL FLOW** *Nude NUD 45CD1*	24		2
20 Nov 99	**CAN'T GET ENOUGH** *Nude NUD 47CD1*	23		2
28 Sep 02	**POSITIVITY** *Epic 6729495*	16		2
30 Nov 02	**OBSESSIONS** *Epic 6732942*	29		2
18 Oct 03	**ATTITUDE/GOLDEN GUN** *Sony Music 6743585*	14		3

SUENO LATINO

Italy, male production duo — **6**

Date	Title	Peak	Wks at No.1	Wks on Chart
23 Sep 89	**SUENO LATINO** *BCM 323* FEATURING CAROLINA DAMAS	47		5
11 Nov 00	**SUENO LATINO (REMIX)** *Distinctive DISNCD 64*	68		1

SUGABABES

UK, female vocal group – Keisha Buchanan (replaced by Jade Ewen*), Mutya Buena* (replaced by Amelle Berrabah) & Siobhan Donaghy* (replaced by Heidi Range). Line-up change queens who are arguably the most successful girl group of the 21st century. At 18, Buchanan, Buena and Range were the youngest all-girl group to reach No.1 (with 'Freak Like Me'). See Tinchy Stryder — **273**

Date	Title	Peak	Wks at No.1	Wks on Chart
23 Sep 00	**OVERLOAD** *London LONCD 449*	6		8
30 Dec 00	**NEW YEAR** *London LONCD 455*	12		9
21 Apr 01	**RUN FOR COVER** *London LONCD 459*	13		7
28 Jul 01	**SOUL SOUND** *London LONCD 460*	30		2
4 May 02	**FREAK LIKE ME** *Island CID 798* ●	1	1	14
24 Aug 02	**ROUND ROUND** *Island CIDX 804* ●	1	1	13
23 Nov 02	**STRONGER/ANGELS WITH DIRTY FACES** *Island CIDX 813*	7		13
22 Mar 03	**SHAPE** *Island CIDX 817*	11		9
25 Oct 03	**HOLE IN THE HEAD** *Island CIDX 836*	1	1	13
27 Dec 03	**TOO LOST IN YOU** *Island CID 844*	10		13
3 Apr 04	**IN THE MIDDLE** *Island MCSXD 40360*	8		8
4 Sep 04	**CAUGHT IN A MOMENT** *Universal MCSXD 40371*	8		7
8 Oct 05	**PUSH THE BUTTON** *Island CID911* ●	1	3	23
17 Dec 05	**UGLY** *Island CIDX918*	3		15
18 Mar 06	**RED DRESS** *Island CID922*	4		10
17 Jun 06	**FOLLOW ME HOME** *Island CID936*	32		3
11 Nov 06	**EASY** *Island 1712313*	8		6
24 Mar 07	**WALK THIS WAY** *Fascination/Island 1724331* VS GIRLS ALOUD	1	1	6
29 Sep 07	**ABOUT YOU NOW** *Island 1748657*	1	4	32
8 Dec 07	**CHANGE** *Island 1755606*	13		11
8 Mar 08	**DENIAL** *Island GBUM70708340*	15		10
4 Oct 08	**GIRLS** *Island 1787323*	3		15
10 Jan 09	**NO CAN DO** *Island 1795155*	23		4
12 Sep 09	**GET SEXY** *Island 2717468*	2		8
21 Nov 09	**ABOUT A GIRL** *Island 2725741*	8		8
6 Mar 10	**WEAR MY KISS** *Island 2732016*	7		6+

SUGARCOMA

UK, male/female vocal/instrumental group — **1**

Date	Title	Peak	Wks at No.1	Wks on Chart
13 Apr 02	**YOU DRIVE ME CRAZY/WINGDINGS** *Music For Nations CDKUT 190*	57		1

SUGAR

US, male vocal/instrumental trio — **7**

Date	Title	Peak	Wks at No.1	Wks on Chart
31 Oct 92	**A GOOD IDEA** *Creation CRE 143*	65		1
30 Jan 93	**IF I CAN'T CHANGE YOUR MIND** *Creation CRESCD 149*	30		2
21 Aug 93	**TILTED** *Creation CRECD 156*	48		1
3 Sep 94	**YOUR FAVOURITE THING** *Creation CRESCD 186*	40		2
29 Oct 94	**BELIEVE WHAT YOU'RE SAYING** *Creation CRESCD 193*	73		1

SUGAR CANE

US, male/female vocal group — **5**

Date	Title	Peak	Wks at No.1	Wks on Chart
30 Sep 78	**MONTEGO BAY** *Ariola Hansa AHA 524*	54		5

SUGAR RAY

US, male vocal/instrumental group – Mark McGrath, Craig 'DJ Homicide' Bullock, Stan Frazier, Murphy Karges & Rodney Sheppard — **12**

Date	Title	Peak	Wks at No.1	Wks on Chart
31 Jan 98	**FLY** *Atlantic AT 0008CD*	58		1
29 May 99	**EVERY MORNING** *Lava AT 0065CD*	10		9
20 Oct 01	**WHEN IT'S OVER** *Atlantic 020114CD*	32		2

SUGARCUBES

Iceland, male/female vocal/instrumental group — **22**

Date	Title	Peak	Wks at No.1	Wks on Chart
14 Nov 87	**BIRTHDAY** *One Little Indian 7TP 7*	65		3
30 Jan 88	**COLD SWEAT** *One Little Indian 7TP 9*	56		4
16 Apr 88	**DEUS** *One Little Indian 7TP 10*	51		3
3 Sep 88	**BIRTHDAY** *One Little Indian 7TP 11*	65		3
16 Sep 89	**REGINA** *One Little Indian 26 TP7*	55		2
11 Jan 92	**HIT** *One Little Indian 62 TP7*	17		6
3 Oct 92	**BIRTHDAY (REMIX)** *One Little Indian 104 TP12*	64		1

SUGARHILL GANG

US, male rap trio – Henry Jackson (Big Bank Hank), Guy (Master Gee) O'Brien & Michael (Wonder Mike) Wright — **16**

Date	Title	Peak	Wks at No.1	Wks on Chart
1 Dec 79	**RAPPER'S DELIGHT** *Sugarhill SHL 101* ●	3		11
11 Sep 82	**THE LOVER IN YOU** *Sugarhill SH 116*	54		3
25 Nov 89	**RAPPER'S DELIGHT (REMIX)** *Sugarhill SHRD 0007*	58		2

SUGGS

UK, male vocalist (Graham McPherson). See Fink Brothers, Madness — **46**

Date	Title	Peak	Wks at No.1	Wks on Chart
12 Aug 95	**I'M ONLY SLEEPING/OFF ON HOLIDAY** *WEA YZ 975CD*	7		6
14 Oct 95	**CAMDEN TOWN** *WEA 019CD*	14		6
16 Dec 95	**THE TUNE** *WEA 031CD*	33		3
13 Apr 96	**CECILIA** *WEA 042CD1* FEATURING LOUCHIE LOU & MICHIE ONE ●	4		19
21 Sep 96	**NO MORE ALCOHOL** *WEA 065CD1* FEATURING LOUCHIE LOU & MICHIE ONE	24		4
17 May 97	**BLUE DAY** *WEA 112CD* & CO FEATURING CHELSEA TEAM	22		5
5 Sep 98	**I AM** *WEA 174CD*	38		3

JUSTINE SUISSA

Holland, female vocalist — **3**

Date	Title	Peak	Wks at No.1	Wks on Chart
27 Apr 02	**CLEAR BLUE WATER** *Code Blue BLU 024CD1* OCEANLAB FEATURING JUSTINE SUISSA	48		1
20 Mar 04	**BURNED WITH DESIRE** *Nebula NEBCDX 055* ARMIN VAN BUUREN FEATURING JUSTINE SUISSA	45		2

SULTANA

Italy, male instrumental/production trio — **1**

Date	Title	Peak	Wks at No.1	Wks on Chart
26 Mar 94	**TE AMO** *Union City UCRD 28*	57		1

SULTANS OF PING FC

Ireland, male vocal/instrumental group — **12**

Date	Title	Peak	Wks at No.1	Wks on Chart
8 Feb 92	**WHERE'S ME JUMPER** *Divine ATHY 01*	67		2
9 May 92	**STUPID KID** *Divine ATHY 02*	67		1
10 Oct 92	**VERONICA** *Divine ATHY 03*	69		1
9 Jan 93	**YOU TALK TOO MUCH** *Rhythm King 6588872*	26		3
11 Sep 93	**TEENAGE PUNKS** *Epic 6595792* SULTANS OF PING	49		2

Date	Title / Label	Peak	Wks at No.1	Wks on Chart
30 Oct 93	**MICHIKO** *Epic 6598222* SULTANS OF PING	43		2
19 Feb 94	**WAKE UP AND SCRATCH ME** *Epic 6601122* SULTANS OF PING	50		1

SUM 41

Canada, male vocal/instrumental group – Deryck Whibley, Dave Baksh, Steve Jocz & Jason McCaslin — **40**

Date	Title / Label	Peak	Wks at No.1	Wks on Chart
13 Oct 01	**FAT LIP** *Def Jam 5888012*	8		9
15 Dec 01	**IN TOO DEEP** *Mercury 5888982*	13		11
6 Apr 02	**MOTIVATION** *Mercury 5889452*	21		7
29 Jun 02	**IT'S WHAT WE'RE ALL ABOUT** *Columbia 6728642*	32		3
30 Nov 02	**STILL WAITING** *Mercury 0638342*	16		7
22 Feb 03	**THE HELL SONG** *Mercury 0637202*	35		3

DONNA SUMMER

US, female vocalist (LaDonna Gaines). Disco queen from Massachusetts with no less than 11 million-selling US singles to her credit. Her controversial debut single, recorded in Germany, was banned by some radio stations for its 'explicit' content — **299**

Date	Title / Label	Peak	Wks at No.1	Wks on Chart
17 Jan 76	**LOVE TO LOVE YOU BABY** *GTO GT 17*	4		9
29 May 76	**COULD IT BE MAGIC** *GTO GT 60*	40		7
25 Dec 76	**WINTER MELODY** *GTO GT 76*	27		6
9 Jul 77	**I FEEL LOVE** *GTO GT 100* ●	1	4	11
20 Aug 77	**DOWN DEEP INSIDE (THEME FROM 'THE DEEP')** *Casablanca CAN 111* ●	5		10
24 Sep 77	**I REMEMBER YESTERDAY** *GTO GT 107*	14		7
3 Dec 77	**LOVE'S UNKIND** *GTO GT 113* ●	3		13
10 Dec 77	**I LOVE YOU** *Casablanca CAN 114*	10		9
25 Feb 78	**RUMOUR HAS IT** *Casablanca CAN 122*	19		8
22 Apr 78	**BACK IN LOVE AGAIN** *GTO GT 117*	29		7
10 Jun 78	**LAST DANCE** *Casablanca TGIF 2*	51		9
14 Oct 78	**MACARTHUR PARK** *Casablanca CAN 131* ● ★	5		10
17 Feb 79	**HEAVEN KNOWS** *Casablanca CAN 141*	34		8
12 May 79	**HOT STUFF** *Casablanca CAN 151* ★	11		10
7 Jul 79	**BAD GIRLS** *Casablanca CAN 155* ● ★	14		10
1 Sep 79	**DIM ALL THE LIGHTS** *Casablanca CAN 162*	29		9
3 Nov 79	**NO MORE TEARS (ENOUGH IS ENOUGH)** *Casablanca CAN 174/CBS 8000* & BARBRA STREISAND ● ★	3		13
16 Feb 80	**ON THE RADIO** *Casablanca NB 2236*	32		6
21 Jun 80	**SUNSET PEOPLE** *Casablanca CAN 198*	46		5
27 Sep 80	**THE WANDERER** *Geffen K 79180*	48		6
17 Jan 81	**COLD LOVE** *Geffen K 79193*	44		3
10 Jul 82	**LOVE IS IN CONTROL (FINGER ON THE TRIGGER)** *Warner Brothers K 79302*	18		11
6 Nov 82	**STATE OF INDEPENDENCE** *Warner Brothers K 79344*	14		11
4 Dec 82	**I FEEL LOVE (REMIX)** *Casablanca FEEL 7*	21		10
5 Mar 83	**THE WOMAN IN ME** *Warner Brothers U 9983*	62		2
18 Jun 83	**SHE WORKS HARD FOR THE MONEY** *Mercury DONNA 1*	25		8
24 Sep 83	**UNCONDITIONAL LOVE** *Mercury DONNA 2*	14		12
21 Jan 84	**STOP LOOK AND LISTEN** *Mercury DONNA 3*	57		2
24 Oct 87	**DINNER WITH GERSHWIN** *Warner Brothers U 8237*	13		11
23 Jan 88	**ALL SYSTEMS GO** *WEA U 8122*	54		3
25 Feb 89	**THIS TIME I KNOW IT'S FOR REAL** *Warner Brothers U 7780* ●	3		14
27 May 89	**I DON'T WANNA GET HURT** *Warner Brothers U 7567*	7		9
26 Aug 89	**LOVE'S ABOUT TO CHANGE MY HEART** *Warner Brothers U 7494*	20		6
25 Nov 89	**WHEN LOVE TAKES OVER YOU** *WEA U 7361*	72		1
17 Nov 90	**STATE OF INDEPENDENCE** *Warner Brothers U 2857*	45		3
12 Jan 91	**BREAKAWAY** *Warner Brothers U 3308*	49		4
30 Nov 91	**WORK THAT MAGIC** *Warner Brothers U 5937*	74		1
12 Nov 94	**MELODY OF LOVE (WANNA BE LOVED)** *Mercury MERCD 418*	21		3
9 Sep 95	**I FEEL LOVE** *Manifesto FESCD 1*	8		5
6 Apr 96	**STATE OF INDEPENDENCE (REMIX)** *Manifesto FESCD 7* FEATURING THE ALL STAR CHOIR	13		5
11 Jul 98	**CARRY ON** *Almighty CDALMY 120* & GIORGIO MORODER	65		1
30 Oct 99	**I WILL GO WITH YOU (CON TE PARTIRO)** *Epic 6682092*	44		1

SUMMER DAZE

UK, male instrumental/production duo — **1**

Date	Title / Label	Peak	Wks at No.1	Wks on Chart
26 Oct 96	**SAMBA MAGIC** *VC Recordings VCRD 14*	61		1

MARK SUMMERS

UK, male producer — **6**

Date	Title / Label	Peak	Wks at No.1	Wks on Chart
26 Jan 91	**SUMMER'S MAGIC** *Fourth & Broadway BRW 205*	27		6

SUNBLOCK

Holland, male production duo – Magnus Nordin & Martin Pihl – & female vocalists — **26**

Date	Title / Label	Peak	Wks at No.1	Wks on Chart
21 Jan 06	**I'LL BE READY** *Manifesto 9876550*	4		11
20 May 06	**FIRST TIME** *Manifesto 9878335*	9		9
28 Apr 07	**BABY BABY** *Universal TV 1727061* FEATURING SANDY	16		6

SUNBURST

UK, male producer (Matt Darey). See Lost Tribe, MDM, Melt featuring Little Ms Marcie — **1**

Date	Title / Label	Peak	Wks at No.1	Wks on Chart
8 Jul 00	**EYEBALL (EYEBALL PAUL'S THEME)** *Virgin/EMI VTSCD 4*	48		1

SUNDANCE

UK, male production duo. See Shimmon & Woolfson — **7**

Date	Title / Label	Peak	Wks at No.1	Wks on Chart
8 Nov 97	**SUNDANCE** *React CDREACT 109*	33		2
3 Oct 98	**SUNDANCE '98 (REMIX)** *React CDREACTX 136*	37		2
27 Feb 99	**THE LIVING DREAM** *React CDREACT 134*	56		1
5 Feb 00	**WON'T LET THIS FEELING GO** *Inferno CDFERN 23*	40		2

SUNDAYS

UK, female/male vocal/instrumental group — **12**

Date	Title / Label	Peak	Wks at No.1	Wks on Chart
11 Feb 89	**CAN'T BE SURE** *Rough Trade RT 218*	45		5
3 Oct 92	**GOODBYE** *Parlophone R 6319*	27		2
20 Sep 97	**SUMMERTIME** *Parlophone CDRS 6475*	15		4
22 Nov 97	**CRY** *Parlophone CDR 6487*	43		1

SUNDRAGON

UK, male vocal/instrumental duo — **1**

Date	Title / Label	Peak	Wks at No.1	Wks on Chart
21 Feb 68	**GREEN TAMBOURINE** *MGM 1380*	50		1

SUNFIRE

US, male vocal trio — **11**

Date	Title / Label	Peak	Wks at No.1	Wks on Chart
12 Mar 83	**YOUNG, FREE AND SINGLE** *Warner Brothers W 9897*	20		11

SUNFREAKZ FEATURING ANDREA BRITTON

Belgium/UK, male/female vocal/DJ/production duo — **3**

Date	Title / Label	Peak	Wks at No.1	Wks on Chart
28 Jul 07	**COUNTING DOWN THE DAYS** *Positiva CDTIVS245*	37		3

SUNKIDS FEATURING CHANCE

US, male/female vocal/production trio — **2**

Date	Title / Label	Peak	Wks at No.1	Wks on Chart
13 Nov 99	**RESCUE ME** *AM:PM CDAMPM 126*	50		2

SUNNY

UK (b. India), female vocalist (Heather Wheatman) — **10**

Date	Title / Label	Peak	Wks at No.1	Wks on Chart
30 Mar 74	**DOCTOR'S ORDERS** *CBS 2068*	7		10

SUNSCREEM

UK, male/female vocal/instrumental group — **36**

Date	Title / Label	Peak	Wks at No.1	Wks on Chart
29 Feb 92	**PRESSURE** *Sony S2 6578017*	60		2
18 Jul 92	**LOVE U MORE** *Sony S2 6581727*	23		6
17 Oct 92	**PERFECT MOTION** *Sony S2 6584057*	18		5
9 Jan 93	**BROKEN ENGLISH** *Sony S2 6589032*	13		5
27 Mar 93	**PRESSURE US** *Sony S2 6591102*	19		5
2 Sep 95	**WHEN** *Sony S2 6623222*	47		2
18 Nov 95	**EXODUS** *Sony S2 6625342*	40		2
20 Jan 96	**WHITE SKIES** *Sony S2 6627425*	25		3
23 Mar 96	**SECRETS** *Sony S2 6629342*	36		2
6 Sep 97	**CATCH** *Pulse 8 CDLOSE 117*	55		1
20 Oct 01	**PLEASE SAVE ME** *Five AM/Inferno FAMFERN 1CD* VS PUSH	36		2
16 Nov 02	**PERFECT MOTION** *Five AM FAM 15CD*	71		1

SUNSET STRIPPERS

UK, male production trio – Harry Diamond, Sergei Hall & Kieron McTernan — **13**

Date	Title / Label	Peak	Wks at No.1	Wks on Chart
19 Mar 05	**FALLING STARS** *Direction 6758312*	3		13

SUNSHINE UNDERGROUND
UK, male vocal/instrumental group — 5

Date	Title	Peak Position	Weeks at No.1	Weeks on Chart
28 Jan 06	**COMMERCIAL BREAKDOWN** *City Rockers ROCKERS32CD*	48		1
27 May 06	**I AIN'T LOSING ANY SLEEP** *City Rockers ROCKERS33CD*	47		1
26 Aug 06	**PUT YOU IN YOUR PLACE** *City Rockers ROCKERS35CD*	39		1
11 Nov 06	**COMMERCIAL BREAKDOWN** *City Rockers ROCKERS37CD*	46		1
17 Mar 07	**BORDERS** *City Rockers ROCKERS38CD*	56		1

SUNSHIP FEATURING M.C.R.B.
UK, male rap/production duo — 1

Date	Title	Peak Position	Weeks at No.1	Weeks on Chart
1 Apr 00	**CHEQUE ONE-TWO** *Filter FILT 044*	75		1

SUPAFLY INC
UK, male vocal/production trio — 10

Date	Title	Peak Position	Weeks at No.1	Weeks on Chart
17 Sep 05	**LET'S GET DOWN** *Eye Industries/UMTV 9873464* SUPAFLY VS FISHBOWL	22		3
9 Sep 06	**MOVING TOO FAST** *Data DATA133CDS*	23		7

SUPATONIC
UK, male vocal/instrumental duo — 1

Date	Title	Peak Position	Weeks at No.1	Weeks on Chart
6 Nov 04	**I WISH IT WASN'T TRUE** *Fluff Alley FLUFFA0001*	69		1

SUPER FURRY ANIMALS
UK, male vocal/instrumental group — 48

Date	Title	Peak Position	Weeks at No.1	Weeks on Chart
9 Mar 96	**HOMETOWN UNICORN** *Creation CRESCD 222*	47		1
11 May 96	**GOD! SHOW ME MAGIC** *Creation CRESCD 231*	33		2
13 Jul 96	**SOMETHING 4 THE WEEKEND** *Creation CRESCD 235*	18		3
12 Oct 96	**IF YOU DON'T WANT ME TO DESTROY YOU** *Creation CRESCD 243*	18		2
14 Dec 96	**THE MAN DON'T GIVE A FUCK** *Creation CRESCD 247*	22		2
24 May 97	**HERMANN LOVES PAULINE** *Creation CRESCD 252*	26		2
26 Jul 97	**THE INTERNATIONAL LANGUAGE OF SCREAMING** *Creation CRESCD 269*	24		2
4 Oct 97	**PLAY IT COOL** *Creation CRESCD 275*	27		2
6 Dec 97	**DEMONS** *Creation CRESCD 283*	27		2
6 Jun 98	**ICE HOCKEY HAIR** *Creation CRESCD 288*	12		3
22 May 99	**NORTHERN LITES** *Creation CRESCD 314*	11		4
21 Aug 99	**FIRE IN MY HEART** *Creation CRESCD 323*	25		3
29 Jan 00	**DO OR DIE** *Creation CRESCD 329*	20		2
21 Jul 01	**JUXTAPOZED WITH U** *Epic 6712242*	14		4
20 Oct 01	**(DRAWING) RINGS AROUND THE WORLD** *Epic 6719082*	28		2
26 Jan 02	**IT'S NOT THE END OF THE WORLD?** *Epic 6721752*	30		2
26 Jul 03	**GOLDEN RETRIEVER** *Epic 6739062*	13		3
1 Nov 03	**HELLO SUNSHINE** *Epic 6743602*	31		2
9 Oct 04	**THE MAN DON'T GIVE A FUCK** *Epic 6753041*	16		2
27 Aug 05	**LAZER BEAM** *Epic 6760111*	28		2
25 Aug 07	**SHOW YOUR HAND** *Rough Trade RTRADSCD402*	46		1

SUPER MAL FEATURING LUCIANA
UK, male/female vocal/production group — 4

Date	Title	Peak Position	Weeks at No.1	Weeks on Chart
21 Jul 07	**BIGGER THAN BIG** *Eye Industries/UMTV 1740243*	19		4

SUPERCAR
Italy, male DJ/production duo — 6

Date	Title	Peak Position	Weeks at No.1	Weeks on Chart
13 Feb 99	**TONITE** *Pepper 0530202*	15		5
21 Aug 99	**COMPUTER LOVE** *Pepper 0530392* FEATURING MIKAELA	67		1

SUPERCAT
Jamaica, male vocalist (William Maragh) — 5

Date	Title	Peak Position	Weeks at No.1	Weeks on Chart
1 Aug 92	**IT FE DONE** *Columbia 6582737*	66		1
6 May 95	**MY GIRL JOSEPHINE** *Columbia 6614702* FEATURING JACK RADICS	22		4

SUPERFUNK
France, male production trio — 2

Date	Title	Peak Position	Weeks at No.1	Weeks on Chart
4 Mar 00	**LUCKY STAR** *Virgin DINSD 198* FEATURING RON CARROLL	42		1
10 Jun 00	**THE YOUNG MC** *Virgin DINSD 206*	62		1

SUPERGRASS
UK, male vocal/instrumental trio – Gaz Coombes, Danny Goffey & Mick Quinn (with Rob Coombes) — 70

Date	Title	Peak Position	Weeks at No.1	Weeks on Chart
29 Oct 94	**CAUGHT BY THE FUZZ** *Parlophone CDR 6396*	43		2
18 Feb 95	**MANSIZE ROOSTER** *Parlophone CDR 6402*	20		3
25 Mar 95	**LOSE IT** *Sub Pop SP 281*	75		1
13 May 95	**LENNY** *Parlophone CDR 6410*	10		3
15 Jul 95	**ALRIGHT/TIME** *Parlophone CDR 6413* ●	2		10
9 Mar 96	**GOING OUT** *Parlophone CDR 6428*	5		6
12 Apr 97	**RICHARD III** *Parlophone CDR 6461*	2		5
21 Jun 97	**SUN HITS THE SKY** *Parlophone CDR 6469*	10		4
18 Oct 97	**LATE IN THE DAY** *Parlophone CDRS 6484*	18		4
5 Jun 99	**PUMPING ON YOUR STEREO** *Parlophone CDR 6518*	11		7
18 Sep 99	**MOVING** *Parlophone CDR 6524*	9		5
4 Dec 99	**MARY** *Parlophone CDR 6531*	36		4
13 Jul 02	**NEVER DONE NOTHING LIKE THAT BEFORE** *Parlophone R 6583*	75		1
28 Sep 02	**GRACE** *Parlophone CDRS 6586*	13		4
8 Feb 03	**SEEN THE LIGHT** *Parlophone CDR 6592*	22		3
5 Jun 04	**KISS OF LIFE** *Parlophone CDR 6638*	23		3
20 Aug 05	**ST PETERSBURG** *Parlophone CDR6670*	22		3
5 Nov 05	**LOW C** *Parlophone CDR6675*	52		1
29 Mar 08	**BAD BLOOD** *Parlophone CDR6755*	73		1

SUPERMEN LOVERS FEATURING MANI HOFFMAN
France, male vocal/production duo – Guillaume Atlan & Mani Hoffman — 17

Date	Title	Peak Position	Weeks at No.1	Weeks on Chart
15 Sep 01	**STARLIGHT** *Independiente ISOM 53MS* ●	2		17

SUPERMODE
Sweden, male DJ/production duo. See Steve Angello, Axwell — 9

Date	Title	Peak Position	Weeks at No.1	Weeks on Chart
29 Jul 06	**TELL ME WHY** *Data DATA121CDS*	13		9

SUPERNATURALS
UK, male vocal/instrumental group — 15

Date	Title	Peak Position	Weeks at No.1	Weeks on Chart
26 Oct 96	**LAZY LOVER** *Food CDFOOD 85*	34		2
8 Feb 97	**THE DAY BEFORE YESTERDAY'S MAN** *Food CDFOODS 88*	25		3
26 Apr 97	**SMILE** *Food CDFOOD 92*	23		2
12 Jul 97	**LOVE HAS PASSED AWAY** *Food CDFOOD 99*	38		2
25 Oct 97	**PREPARE TO LAND** *Food CDFOODS 106*	48		1
1 Aug 98	**I WASN'T BUILT TO GET UP** *Food CDFOOD 112*	25		3
24 Oct 98	**SHEFFIELD SONG** *Food CDFOODS 115*	45		1
13 Mar 99	**EVEREST** *Food CDFOOD 119*	52		1

SUPERNOVA
UK, male/female vocal/instrumental duo — 1

Date	Title	Peak Position	Weeks at No.1	Weeks on Chart
11 May 96	**SOME MIGHT SAY** *Sing Sing 74321369442*	55		1

SUPERSISTER
UK, female vocal group — 8

Date	Title	Peak Position	Weeks at No.1	Weeks on Chart
14 Oct 00	**COFFEE** *Gut CXGUT 35*	16		5
25 Aug 01	**SHOPPING** *Gut CXGUT 37*	36		2
17 Nov 01	**SUMMER GONNA COME AGAIN** *Gut CDGUT 38*	51		1

SUPERSTAR
UK, male vocal/instrumental group — 2

Date	Title	Peak Position	Weeks at No.1	Weeks on Chart
7 Feb 98	**EVERY DAY I FALL APART** *Camp Fabulous CFAB 003CD*	66		1
25 Apr 98	**SUPERSTAR** *Camp Fabulous CFAB 007CD*	49		1

SUPERTRAMP
US/UK, male vocal/instrumental group – Roger Hodgson, Rick Davies, John Helliwell, Bob Siebenberg & Dougie Thomson — 52

Date	Title	Peak Position	Weeks at No.1	Weeks on Chart
15 Feb 75	**DREAMER** *A&M AMS 7132*	13		10
25 Jun 77	**GIVE A LITTLE BIT** *A&M AMS 7293*	29		7
31 Mar 79	**THE LOGICAL SONG** *A&M AMS 7427*	7		11
30 Jun 79	**BREAKFAST IN AMERICA** *A&M AMS 7451*	9		10
27 Oct 79	**GOODBYE STRANGER** *A&M AMS 7481*	57		3
30 Oct 82	**IT'S RAINING AGAIN** *A&M AMS 8255* FEATURING VOCALS BY ROGER HODGSON	26		11

Silver-selling ● Gold-selling ● Platinum-selling (x multiples) ⊛ US No.1 ★ Peak Position · Weeks at No.1 · Weeks on Chart

SUPREMES

US, female vocal trio – Diana Ross*, Florence Ballard, d. 22 Feb 1976, & Mary Wilson. The first female trio to top the UK chart had a record-shattering 12 US No.1s before Ross left in 1969. They are, arguably, the most successful girl group of all time **306**

Date	Title	Peak Position	Weeks at No.1	Weeks on Chart
3 Sep 64	**WHERE DID OUR LOVE GO** *Stateside SS 327* ★	3		14
22 Oct 64	**BABY LOVE** *Stateside SS 350* ★	1	2	15
21 Jan 65	**COME SEE ABOUT ME** *Stateside SS 376* ★	27		6
25 Mar 65	**STOP IN THE NAME OF LOVE** *Tamla Motown TMG 501* ★	7		12
10 Jun 65	**BACK IN MY ARMS AGAIN** *Tamla Motown TMG 516* ★	40		5
9 Dec 65	**I HEAR A SYMPHONY** *Tamla Motown TMG 543* ★	39		5
8 Sep 66	**YOU CAN'T HURRY LOVE** *Tamla Motown TMG 575* ★	3		12
1 Dec 66	**YOU KEEP ME HANGIN' ON** *Tamla Motown TMG 585* ★	8		10
2 Mar 67	**LOVE IS HERE AND NOW YOU'RE GONE** *Tamla Motown TMG 597* ★	17		10
11 May 67	**THE HAPPENING** *Tamla Motown TMG 607* ★	6		12
30 Aug 67	**REFLECTIONS** *Tamla Motown TMG 616* DIANA ROSS & THE SUPREMES	5		14
29 Nov 67	**IN AND OUT OF LOVE** *Tamla Motown TMG 632* DIANA ROSS & THE SUPREMES	13		13
10 Apr 68	**FOREVER CAME TODAY** *Tamla Motown TMG 650* DIANA ROSS & THE SUPREMES	28		8
3 Jul 68	**SOME THINGS YOU NEVER GET USED TO** *Tamla Motown TMG 662* DIANA ROSS & THE SUPREMES	34		6
20 Nov 68	**LOVE CHILD** *Tamla Motown TMG 677* DIANA ROSS & THE SUPREMES ★	15		14
29 Jan 69	**I'M GONNA MAKE YOU LOVE ME** *Tamla Motown TMG 685* DIANA ROSS & THE SUPREMES & THE TEMPTATIONS	3		12
23 Apr 69	**I'M LIVING IN SHAME** *Tamla Motown TMG 695* DIANA ROSS & THE SUPREMES	14		10
16 Jul 69	**NO MATTER WHAT SIGN YOU ARE** *Tamla Motown TMG 704* DIANA ROSS & THE SUPREMES	37		7
20 Sep 69	**I SECOND THAT EMOTION** *Tamla Motown TMG 709* DIANA ROSS & THE SUPREMES & THE TEMPTATIONS	18		8
13 Dec 69	**SOMEDAY WE'LL BE TOGETHER** *Tamla Motown TMG 721* DIANA ROSS & THE SUPREMES ★	13		13
21 Mar 70	**WHY (MUST WE FALL IN LOVE)** *Tamla Motown TMG 730* DIANA ROSS & THE SUPREMES & THE TEMPTATIONS	31		7
2 May 70	**UP THE LADDER TO THE ROOF** *Tamla Motown TMG 735*	6		15
16 Jan 71	**STONED LOVE** *Tamla Motown TMG 760*	3		13
26 Jun 71	**RIVER DEEP MOUNTAIN HIGH** *Tamla Motown TMG 777* & THE FOUR TOPS	11		10
21 Aug 71	**NATHAN JONES** *Tamla Motown TMG 782*	5		11
20 Nov 71	**YOU GOTTA HAVE LOVE IN YOUR HEART** *Tamla Motown TMG 793* & THE FOUR TOPS	25		10
4 Mar 72	**FLOY JOY** *Tamla Motown TMG 804*	9		10
15 Jul 72	**AUTOMATICALLY SUNSHINE** *Tamla Motown TMG 821*	10		9
21 Apr 73	**BAD WEATHER** *Tamla Motown TMG 847*	37		4
24 Aug 74	**BABY LOVE** *Tamla Motown TMG 915* DIANA ROSS & THE SUPREMES	12		10
18 Feb 89	**STOP! IN THE NAME OF LOVE** *Motown ZB 41963* DIANA ROSS & THE SUPREMES	62		1

AL B SURE!

US, male vocalist (Albert Brown) **13**

Date	Title	Peak Position	Weeks at No.1	Weeks on Chart
16 Apr 88	**NITE AND DAY** *Uptown W 8192*	44		5
30 Jul 88	**OFF ON YOUR OWN (GIRL)** *Uptown W 7870*	70		2
10 Jun 89	**IF I'M NOT YOUR LOVER** *Uptown W 2908* FEATURING SLICK RICK	54		3
31 Mar 90	**SECRET GARDEN** *Qwest W 9992* QUINCY JONES FEATURING AL B SURE!, JAMES INGRAM, EL DeBARGE & BARRY WHITE	67		1
12 Jun 93	**BLACK TIE WHITE NOISE** *Arista 74321148682* DAVID BOWIE FEATURING AL B. SURE!	36		2

SUREAL

UK, male/female vocal/production group **4**

Date	Title	Peak Position	Weeks at No.1	Weeks on Chart
7 Oct 00	**YOU TAKE MY BREATH AWAY** *Cream 7CD*	15		4

SURFACE

US, male vocal/instrumental trio **14**

Date	Title	Peak Position	Weeks at No.1	Weeks on Chart
23 Jul 83	**FALLING IN LOVE** *Salsoul SAL 104*	67		3
23 Jun 84	**WHEN YOUR 'EX' WANTS YOU BACK** *Salsoul SAL 106*	52		4
28 Feb 87	**HAPPY** *CBS 6503937*	56		5
12 Jan 91	**THE FIRST TIME** *Columbia 6564767* ★	60		2

SURFACE NOISE

UK, male producer (Chris Palmer) **11**

Date	Title	Peak Position	Weeks at No.1	Weeks on Chart
31 May 80	**THE SCRATCH** *WEA K 18291*	26		8
30 Aug 80	**DANCIN' ON A WIRE** *Groove Productions GP 102*	59		3

SURFARIS

US, male vocal/instrumental group – Ron Wilson, d. 19 May 1989, Bob Berryhill, Pat Connolly, Jim Fuller & Jim Pash **14**

Date	Title	Peak Position	Weeks at No.1	Weeks on Chart
25 Jul 63	**WIPE OUT** *London HLD 9751*	5		14

SURPRISE SISTERS

UK, female vocal group **3**

Date	Title	Peak Position	Weeks at No.1	Weeks on Chart
13 Mar 76	**LA BOOGA ROOGA** *Good Earth GD 1*	38		3

SURVIVOR

US, male vocal/instrumental group – Dave Bickler (replaced by Jimi Jamison), Marc Droubay, Stephan Ellis, Jim Peterik & Frankie Sullivan **30**

Date	Title	Peak Position	Weeks at No.1	Weeks on Chart
31 Jul 82	**EYE OF THE TIGER** *Scotti Brothers SCT A 2411* ● ★	1	4	15
1 Feb 86	**BURNING HEART** *Scotti Brothers A 6708*	5		11
27 Jan 07	**EYE OF THE TIGER** *Arista USVR10400292*	47		4

SUTHERLAND BROTHERS

UK, male vocal/instrumental duo – Iain & Gavin Sutherland **20**

Date	Title	Peak Position	Weeks at No.1	Weeks on Chart
3 Apr 76	**ARMS OF MARY** *CBS 4001* & QUIVER	5		12
20 Nov 76	**SECRETS** *CBS 4668* & QUIVER	35		4
2 Jun 79	**EASY COME EASY GO** *CBS 7121*	50		4

PAT SUZUKI

US, female vocalist (Chiyoko Suzuki) **1**

Date	Title	Peak Position	Weeks at No.1	Weeks on Chart
14 Apr 60	**I ENJOY BEING A GIRL** *RCA 1171*	49		1

SVENSON & GIELEN

Belgium, male production duo. See Airscape, Blue Bamboo, Cubic 22, Johan Gielen presents Abnea, Transformer 2 **2**

Date	Title	Peak Position	Weeks at No.1	Weeks on Chart
22 Sep 01	**THE BEAUTY OF SILENCE** *Xtrahard/Xtravaganza X2H 5CDS*	41		2

BILLY SWAN

US, male vocalist **13**

Date	Title	Peak Position	Weeks at No.1	Weeks on Chart
14 Dec 74	**I CAN HELP** *Monument MNT 2752* ● ★	6		9
24 May 75	**DON'T BE CRUEL** *Monument MNT 3244*	42		4

SWAN LAKE

US, male producer (Todd Terry). See Black Riot, Gypsymen, Royal House **4**

Date	Title	Peak Position	Weeks at No.1	Weeks on Chart
17 Sep 88	**IN THE NAME OF LOVE** *Champion CHAMP 86*	53		4

SWANS WAY

UK, male/female vocal/instrumental trio **12**

Date	Title	Peak Position	Weeks at No.1	Weeks on Chart
4 Feb 84	**SOUL TRAIN** *Exit EXT 3*	20		7
26 May 84	**ILLUMINATIONS** *Balgier PH 5*	57		5

SWAY

UK, male rapper/vocalist/producer (Derek Safo) **6**

Date	Title	Peak Position	Weeks at No.1	Weeks on Chart
4 Jun 05	**HARVEY NICKS** *WEA BEATS15* MITCHELL BROTHERS FEATURING SWAY	62		1
28 Jan 06	**LITTLE DEREK** *All City ACM0017CDS*	38		2
27 Aug 08	**SATURDAY NIGHT HUSTLE** *Dcypha Productions DCY010CD* FEATURING LEMAR	67		1
28 Feb 09	**SILVER & GOLD** *Dcypha GBPVV0800081* FEATURING AKON	61		1
7 Nov 09	**MERCEDES BENZ** *Dcypha GBJVA0900002*	53		1

PATRICK SWAYZE FEATURING WENDY FRASER

US, male vocalist/actor, d. 14 Sep 2009 (age 57), & female vocalist **11**

Date	Title	Peak Position	Weeks at No.1	Weeks on Chart
26 Mar 88	**SHE'S LIKE THE WIND** *RCA PB 49565*	17		11

KEITH SWEAT

US, male vocalist **23**

Date	Title	Peak Position	Weeks at No.1	Weeks on Chart
20 Feb 88	**I WANT HER** *Vintertainment EKR 68*	26		10
14 May 88	**SOMETHING JUST AIN'T RIGHT** *Vintertainment EKR 72*	55		3
14 May 94	**HOW DO YOU LIKE IT** *Elektra EKR 185CD*	71		1
22 Jun 96	**TWISTED** *Elektra EKR 223CD*	39		2
23 Nov 96	**JUST A TOUCH** *Elektra EKR 227CD*	35		2
3 May 97	**NOBODY** *Elektra EKR 233CD* FEATURING ATHENA CAGE	30		2

Date	Title	Peak Position	Weeks at No.1	Weeks on Chart
6 Dec 97	**I WANT HER (REMIX)** *Elektra E 3887CD*	44		1
12 Dec 98	**COME AND GET WITH ME** *Elektra E 3787CD* FEATURING SNOOP DOGG	58		1
27 Mar 99	**I'M NOT READY** *Elektra E 3767CD*	53		1

MICHELLE SWEENEY
US, female vocalist — **1**

Date	Title	Peak Position	Weeks at No.1	Weeks on Chart
29 Oct 94	**THIS TIME** *Big Beat A 8229CD*	57		1

SWEET
UK, male vocal/instrumental group – Brian Connolly, d. 9 Feb 1997, Steve Priest, Andy Scott & Mick Tucker, d. 14 Feb 2002 — **159**

Date	Title	Peak Position	Weeks at No.1	Weeks on Chart
13 Mar 71	**FUNNY FUNNY** *RCA 2051*	13		14
12 Jun 71	**CO-CO** *RCA 2087*	2		15
16 Oct 71	**ALEXANDER GRAHAM BELL** *RCA 2121*	33		5
5 Feb 72	**POPPA JOE** *RCA 2164*	11		12
10 Jun 72	**LITTLE WILLY** *RCA 2225*	4		14
9 Sep 72	**WIG-WAM BAM** *RCA 2260*	4		13
13 Jan 73	**BLOCKBUSTER** *RCA 2305*	1	5	15
5 May 73	**HELL RAISER** *RCA 2357*	2		11
22 Sep 73	**THE BALLROOM BLITZ** *RCA 2403* ●	2		9
19 Jan 74	**TEENAGE RAMPAGE** *RCA LPBO 5004* ●	2		8
13 Jul 74	**THE SIX TEENS** *RCA LPBO 5037*	9		7
9 Nov 74	**TURN IT DOWN** *RCA 2480*	41		2
15 Mar 75	**FOX ON THE RUN** *RCA 2524* ●	2		10
12 Jul 75	**ACTION** *RCA 2578*	15		6
24 Jan 76	**LIES IN YOUR EYES** *RCA 2641*	35		4
28 Jan 78	**LOVE IS LIKE OXYGEN** *Polydor POSP 1* ●	9		9
26 Jan 85	**IT'S...IT'S...THE SWEET MIX** *Anagram ANA 28*	45		5

RACHEL SWEET
US, female vocalist — **15**

Date	Title	Peak Position	Weeks at No.1	Weeks on Chart
9 Dec 78	**B-A-B-Y** *Stiff BUY 39*	35		8
22 Aug 81	**EVERLASTING LOVE** *CBS A 1405* REX SMITH & RACHEL SWEET	35		7

SWEET DREAMS
UK, male/female vocal duo – Polly Brown* & Tony Jackson, d. 18 Aug 2003 — **12**

Date	Title	Peak Position	Weeks at No.1	Weeks on Chart
20 Jul 74	**HONEY HONEY** *Bradley's BRAD 7408*	10		12

SWEET DREAMS
UK, male/female vocal trio — **7**

Date	Title	Peak Position	Weeks at No.1	Weeks on Chart
9 Apr 83	**I'M NEVER GIVING UP** *Ariola ARO 333*	21		7

SWEET FEMALE ATTITUDE
UK, female vocal duo – Leanne Brown & Catherine Cassidy — **17**

Date	Title	Peak Position	Weeks at No.1	Weeks on Chart
15 Apr 00	**FLOWERS** *Milkk 267CD* ●	2		12
7 Oct 00	**8 DAYS A WEEK** *WEA 296CD*	43		4
19 Apr 08	**FLOWERS** *WEA DEA620000108*	62		1

SWEET MERCY FEATURING JOE ROBERTS
UK, male vocal/instrumental/production trio — **1**

Date	Title	Peak Position	Weeks at No.1	Weeks on Chart
24 Feb 96	**HAPPY DAYS** *Grass Green GRASS 10CD*	63		1

SWEET PEOPLE
Switzerland, male/female instrumental group — **10**

Date	Title	Peak Position	Weeks at No.1	Weeks on Chart
4 Oct 80	**ET LES OISEAUX CHANTAIENT (AND THE BIRDS WERE SINGING)** *Polydor POSP 179*	4		8
29 Aug 87	**ET LES OISEAUX CHANTAIENT (AND THE BIRDS WERE SINGING)** *Polydor POSP 179*	73		2

SWEET SENSATION
Jamaica/UK, male vocal group – Marcel King, Junior Daye, Roy Flowers, Vincent James, Barry Johnson, St Clair L Palmer, Gary Shaugnessy & Leroy Smith — **17**

Date	Title	Peak Position	Weeks at No.1	Weeks on Chart
14 Sep 74	**SAD SWEET DREAMER** *Pye 7N 45385* ●	1	1	10
18 Jan 75	**PURELY BY COINCIDENCE** *Pye 7N 45421*	11		7

SWEET TEE
US, female rapper (Toi Jackson) — **8**

Date	Title	Peak Position	Weeks at No.1	Weeks on Chart
16 Jan 88	**IT'S LIKE THAT Y'ALL/I GOT DA FEELIN'** *Cooltempo COOL 160*	31		6
13 Aug 94	**THE FEELING** *Deep Distraxion OILYCD 029* TIN TIN OUT FEATURING SWEET TEE	32		2

SWEETBACK
UK, male vocal/instrumental group — **1**

Date	Title	Peak Position	Weeks at No.1	Weeks on Chart
29 Mar 97	**YOU WILL RISE** *Epic 6643155*	64		1

SWEETBOX
US/Germany, female/male vocal/production duo – Tina Harris & Rosan Roberto — **12**

Date	Title	Peak Position	Weeks at No.1	Weeks on Chart
22 Aug 98	**EVERYTHING'S GONNA BE ALRIGHT** *RCA 74321606842*	5		12

SWERVEDRIVER
UK, male vocal/instrumental group — **3**

Date	Title	Peak Position	Weeks at No.1	Weeks on Chart
10 Aug 91	**SANDBLASTED (EP)** *Creation CRE 102*	67		1
30 May 92	**NEVER LOST THAT FEELING** *Creation CRE 120*	62		1
14 Aug 93	**DUEL** *Creation CRESCD 136*	60		1

TAYLOR SWIFT
US, female vocalist/guitarist/pianist/actor — **40**

Date	Title	Peak Position	Weeks at No.1	Weeks on Chart
28 Feb 09	**LOVE STORY** *Mercury USCJY0803450* ●	2		18
21 Mar 09	**WHITE HORSE** *Mercury USCJY0803264*	60		1
9 May 09	**TEARDROPS ON MY GUITAR** *Mercury USCJY0603137*	51		7
8 Aug 09	**YOU BELONG WITH ME** *Mercury USCJY0803328*	30		12
23 Jan 10	**LOVE STORY** *Mercury USCJY0803450*	70		1
27 Feb 10	**TODAY WAS A FAIRYTALE** *Mercury GBUM71000028*	57		1

MAMPI SWIFT
UK, male DJ/producer (Philip Anim) — **1**

Date	Title	Peak Position	Weeks at No.1	Weeks on Chart
5 Jun 04	**HI-TEK/DRUNKEN STARS** *Charge Recordings CHRG024*	72		1

SWIMMING WITH SHARKS
Germany, female vocal duo — **3**

Date	Title	Peak Position	Weeks at No.1	Weeks on Chart
7 May 88	**CARELESS LOVE** *WEA YZ 173*	63		3

SWING FEATURING DR ALBAN
US/Nigeria, male rap/vocal duo — **1**

Date	Title	Peak Position	Weeks at No.1	Weeks on Chart
29 Apr 95	**SWEET DREAMS** *Logic 74321251552*	59		1

SWING 52
US, male vocal/instrumental group — **1**

Date	Title	Peak Position	Weeks at No.1	Weeks on Chart
25 Feb 95	**COLOR OF MY SKIN** *ffrr FCD 256*	60		1

SWING OUT SISTER
UK, female/male vocal/instrumental trio – Corinne Drewery, Andy Connell & Martin Jackson (left 1988) — **55**

Date	Title	Peak Position	Weeks at No.1	Weeks on Chart
25 Oct 86	**BREAKOUT** *Mercury SWING 2* ●	4		14
10 Jan 87	**SURRENDER** *Mercury SWING 3*	7		8
18 Apr 87	**TWILIGHT WORLD** *Mercury SWING 4*	32		6
11 Jul 87	**FOOLED BY A SMILE** *Mercury SWING 5*	43		4
8 Apr 89	**YOU ON MY MIND** *Fontana SWING 6*	28		9
8 Jul 89	**WHERE IN THE WORLD** *Fontana SWING 7*	47		4
11 Apr 92	**AM I THE SAME GIRL** *Fontana SWING 9*	21		6
20 Jun 92	**NOTGONNACHANGE** *Fontana SWING 10*	49		2
27 Aug 94	**LA LA (MEANS I LOVE YOU)** *Fontana SWIDD 11*	37		2

SWINGING BLUE JEANS
UK, male vocal/instrumental group – Ray Ennis, Les Braid, d. 31 Jul 2005, Ralph Ellis & Norman Kuhike — **57**

Date	Title	Peak Position	Weeks at No.1	Weeks on Chart
20 Jun 63	**IT'S TOO LATE NOW** *HMV POP 1170*	30		9
12 Dec 63	**HIPPY HIPPY SHAKE** *HMV POP 1242*	2		17
19 Mar 64	**GOOD GOLLY MISS MOLLY** *HMV POP 1273*	11		10
4 Jun 64	**YOU'RE NO GOOD** *HMV POP 1304*	3		13
20 Jan 66	**DON'T MAKE ME OVER** *HMV POP 1501*	31		8

Silver-selling ● Gold-selling ● Platinum-selling (x multiples) ⊛ US No.1 ★ Peak Position · Weeks at No.1 · Weeks on Chart

SWIRL 360
US, male vocal duo — Total weeks on chart: 1

Date	Title / Label	Peak Position	Weeks at No.1	Weeks on Chart
14 Nov 98	**HEY NOW NOW** *Mercury 5665352*	61		1

SWITCH
US, male vocal/instrumental group — Total weeks on chart: 3

Date	Title / Label	Peak Position	Weeks at No.1	Weeks on Chart
10 Nov 84	**KEEPING SECRETS** *Total Experience RCA XE 502*	61		3

SWITCHES
UK, male vocal/instrumental group — Total weeks on chart: 2

Date	Title / Label	Peak Position	Weeks at No.1	Weeks on Chart
10 Feb 07	**DRAMA QUEEN** *Atlantic ATUK052CD*	61		1
28 Apr 07	**LAY DOWN THE LAW** *Atlantic ATUK059CD*	51		1

SWITCHFOOT
US, male vocal/instrumental group — Total weeks on chart: 2

Date	Title / Label	Peak Position	Weeks at No.1	Weeks on Chart
14 Aug 04	**MEANT TO LIVE** *Columbia 6750812*	29		2

SWV
US, female vocal trio – Cheryl 'Koko' Gamble, Tamara 'Taj' Johnson & Leanne 'Lelee' Lyons — Total weeks on chart: 43

Date	Title / Label	Peak Position	Weeks at No.1	Weeks on Chart
1 May 93	**I'M SO INTO YOU** *RCA 74321144972*	17		6
26 Jun 93	**WEAK** *RCA 74321153352* ★	33		3
28 Aug 93	**RIGHT HERE** *RCA 74321160482*	3		12
26 Feb 94	**DOWNTOWN** *RCA 74321189012*	19		5
11 Jun 94	**ANYTHING** *RCA 74321212212*	24		3
25 May 96	**YOU'RE THE ONE** *RCA 74321383312*	13		3
21 Dec 96	**IT'S ALL ABOUT U** *RCA 74321442152*	36		5
12 Apr 97	**CAN WE** *Jive JIVECD 423*	18		4
13 Sep 97	**SOMEONE** *RCA 74321513942* FEATURING PUFF DADDY	34		2

SYBIL
US, female vocalist (Sybil Lynch) — Total weeks on chart: 69

Date	Title / Label	Peak Position	Weeks at No.1	Weeks on Chart
1 Nov 86	**FALLING IN LOVE** *Champion CHAMP 22*	68		3
25 Apr 87	**LET YOURSELF GO** *Champion CHAMP 42*	32		6
29 Aug 87	**MY LOVE IS GUARANTEED** *Champion CHAMPX 55*	42		5
22 Jul 89	**DON'T MAKE ME OVER** *Champion CHAMP 213*	59		5
14 Oct 89	**DON'T MAKE ME OVER** *Champion CHAMP 213*	19		6
27 Jan 90	**WALK ON BY** *PWL 48*	6		9
21 Apr 90	**CRAZY FOR YOU** *PWL 53*	71		1
16 Jan 93	**THE LOVE I LOST** *PWL Sanctuary PWCD 253* WEST END FEATURING SYBIL	3		13
20 Mar 93	**WHEN I'M GOOD AND READY** *PWL International PWCD 260*	5		13
26 Jun 93	**BEYOND YOUR WILDEST DREAMS** *PWL International PWCD 265*	41		2
11 Sep 93	**STRONGER TOGETHER** *PWL International PWCD 269*	41		2
11 Dec 93	**MY LOVE IS GUARANTEED (REMIX)** *PWL International PWCD 277*	48		1
9 Mar 96	**SO TIRED OF BEING ALONE** *PWL International PWL 324CD*	53		1
8 Mar 97	**WHEN I'M GOOD AND READY (REMIX)** *Next Plateau NP 14183*	66		1
26 Jul 97	**STILL A THRILL** *Coalition COLA 007CD*	55		1

SYLK 130
US, male production duo — Total weeks on chart: 2

Date	Title / Label	Peak Position	Weeks at No.1	Weeks on Chart
25 Apr 98	**LAST NIGHT A DJ SAVED MY LIFE** *Sony S2 SYLK 1CD*	33		2

SYLVER
Belgium, male/female vocal/DJ/production duo — Total weeks on chart: 1

Date	Title / Label	Peak Position	Weeks at No.1	Weeks on Chart
1 Jun 02	**TURN THE TIDE** *Pepper 9230562*	56		1

SYLVESTER
US, male vocalist (Sylvester James), d. 16 Dec 1988 (age 41) — Total weeks on chart: 45

Date	Title / Label	Peak Position	Weeks at No.1	Weeks on Chart
19 Aug 78	**YOU MAKE ME FEEL (MIGHTY REAL)** *Fantasy FTC 160* ●	8		15
18 Nov 78	**DANCE (DISCO HEAT)** *Fantasy FTC 163*	29		12
31 Mar 79	**I (WHO HAVE NOTHING)** *Fantasy FTC 171*	46		5
7 Jul 79	**STARS** *Fantasy FTC 177*	47		3
11 Sep 82	**DO YOU WANNA FUNK** *London LON 13* WITH PATRICK COWLEY	32		8
3 Sep 83	**BAND OF GOLD** *London LON 33*	67		2

SYLVIA
US, female vocalist (Sylvia Vanderpool) — Total weeks on chart: 11

Date	Title / Label	Peak Position	Weeks at No.1	Weeks on Chart
23 Jun 73	**PILLOW TALK** *London HL 10415*	14		11

SYLVIA
Sweden, female vocalist (Sylvia Vrethammar) — Total weeks on chart: 33

Date	Title / Label	Peak Position	Weeks at No.1	Weeks on Chart
10 Aug 74	**Y VIVA ESPANA** *Sonet SON 2037* ●	4		28
26 Apr 75	**HASTA LA VISTA** *Sonet SON 2055*	38		5

DAVID SYLVIAN
UK, male vocalist (David Batt). See Japan, Rain Tree Crow — Total weeks on chart: 36

Date	Title / Label	Peak Position	Weeks at No.1	Weeks on Chart
7 Aug 82	**BAMBOO HOUSES/BAMBOO MUSIC** *Virgin VS 510* SYLVIAN SAKAMOTO	30		4
2 Jul 83	**FORBIDDEN COLOURS** *Virgin VS 601* & RYUICHI SAKAMOTO	16		8
2 Jun 84	**RED GUITAR** *Virgin VS 633*	17		5
18 Aug 84	**THE INK IN THE WELL** *Virgin VS 700*	36		3
3 Nov 84	**PULLING PUNCHES** *Virgin VS 717*	56		2
14 Dec 85	**WORDS WITH THE SHAMEN** *Virgin VS 835*	72		1
9 Aug 86	**TAKING THE VEIL** *Virgin VS 815*	53		3
17 Jan 87	**BUOY** *Virgin VS 910* MICK KARN FEATURING DAVID SYLVIAN	63		2
10 Oct 87	**LET THE HAPPINESS IN** *Virgin VS 1001*	66		1
13 Jun 92	**HEARTBEAT (TAINAI KAIKI II) RETURNING TO THE WOMB** *Virgin America VUS 57* DAVID SYLVIAN/RYUICHI SAKAMOTO FEATURING INGRID CHAVEZ	58		3
28 Aug 93	**JEAN THE BIRDMAN** *Virgin VSCDG 1462* & ROBERT FRIPP	68		2
27 Mar 99	**I SURRENDER** *Virgin VSCDT 1722*	40		2

SYMARIP
UK, male vocal/instrumental group. See Pyramids — Total weeks on chart: 3

Date	Title / Label	Peak Position	Weeks at No.1	Weeks on Chart
2 Feb 80	**SKINHEAD MOONSTOMP** *Trojan TRO 9062*	54		3

SYMBOLS
UK, male vocal/instrumental group — Total weeks on chart: 15

Date	Title / Label	Peak Position	Weeks at No.1	Weeks on Chart
2 Aug 67	**BYE BYE BABY** *President PT 144*	44		3
3 Jan 68	**BEST PART OF BREAKING UP** *President PT 173*	25		12

TERRI SYMON
UK, female vocalist — Total weeks on chart: 1

Date	Title / Label	Peak Position	Weeks at No.1	Weeks on Chart
10 Jun 95	**I WANT TO KNOW WHAT LOVE IS** *A&M 5810592*	54		1

SYMPOSIUM
UK, male vocal/instrumental group — Total weeks on chart: 10

Date	Title / Label	Peak Position	Weeks at No.1	Weeks on Chart
22 Mar 97	**FAREWELL TO TWILIGHT** *Infectious INFECT 34CD*	25		2
31 May 97	**THE ANSWER TO WHY I HATE YOU** *Infectious INFECT 37CD*	32		2
30 Aug 97	**FAIRWEATHER FRIEND** *Infectious INFECT 44CD*	25		3
14 Mar 98	**AVERAGE MAN** *Infectious INFECT 52CD*	45		1
16 May 98	**BURY YOU** *Infectious INFECT 55CDS*	41		1
18 Jul 98	**BLUE** *Infectious INFECT 57CD*	48		1

SYNTAX
UK, male production duo — Total weeks on chart: 4

Date	Title / Label	Peak Position	Weeks at No.1	Weeks on Chart
8 Feb 03	**PRAY** *Illustrious/Epic CDILL 012*	28		3
28 Feb 04	**BLISS** *Illustrious/Epic CDILLX 020*	69		1

SYREETA
US, female vocalist (Rita Wright), d. 6 Jul 2004 (age 57) — Total weeks on chart: 30

Date	Title / Label	Peak Position	Weeks at No.1	Weeks on Chart
21 Sep 74	**SPINNIN' AND SPINNIN'** *Tamla Motown TMG 912*	49		3
1 Feb 75	**YOUR KISS IS SWEET** *Tamla Motown TMG 933*	12		8
12 Jul 75	**HARMOUR LOVE** *Tamla Motown TMG 954*	32		4
15 Dec 79	**WITH YOU I'M BORN AGAIN** *Motown TMG 1159* BILLY PRESTON & SYREETA ●	2		11
8 Mar 80	**IT WILL COME IN TIME** *Motown TMG 1175* BILLY PRESTON & SYREETA	47		4

SYSTEM
US, male vocal/production duo — Total weeks on chart: 2

Date	Title / Label	Peak Position	Weeks at No.1	Weeks on Chart
9 Jun 84	**I WANNA MAKE YOU FEEL GOOD** *Polydor POSP 685*	73		2

SYSTEM F
Holland, male DJ/producer (Ferry Corsten). See Albion, Gouryella, Moonman, Starparty, Veracocha — Total weeks on chart: 10

Date	Title / Label	Peak Position	Weeks at No.1	Weeks on Chart
3 Apr 99	**OUT OF THE BLUE** *Essential Recordings 5704052*	14		6
6 May 00	**CRY** *Essential Recordings ESCD 14*	19		4

SYSTEM OF A DOWN
US/Lebanon, male vocal/instrumental group **12**

Date	Title / Label	Peak	Wks at No.1	Wks on Chart
3 Nov 01	**CHOP SUEY** *Columbia 6720342*	17		4
23 Mar 02	**TOXICITY** *Columbia 6725022*	25		3
27 Jul 02	**ARIALS** *Columbia 6728692*	34		2
10 Sep 05	**QUESTION** *American/Columbia 6760562*	41		1
26 Nov 05	**HPNOTIZE** *American/Columbia 82876741302*	48		2

SYSTEM OF LIFE
UK, male production duo **1**

Date	Title / Label	Peak	Wks at No.1	Wks on Chart
29 May 04	**LUV IS COOL** *Freedream CDFDREAM1*	63		1

SYSTEM PRESENTS KERRI B
UK, male/female vocal/production group **1**

Date	Title / Label	Peak	Wks at No.1	Wks on Chart
8 Nov 03	**IF YOU LEAVE ME NOW** *All Around The World CDGLOBE 288*	55		1

SYSTEM 7
UK/France, male/female instrumental/production duo **2**

Date	Title / Label	Peak	Wks at No.1	Wks on Chart
13 Feb 93	**7:7 EXPANSION** *Butterfly BFLD 2*	39		1
17 Jul 93	**SINBAD QUEST** *Butterfly BFLD 8*	74		1

JAMIE T
UK, male vocalist/guitarist (Jamie Treays) **34**

Date	Title / Label	Peak	Wks at No.1	Wks on Chart
15 Jul 06	**SHEILA** *Virgin VSCDT1917*	15		13
21 Oct 06	**IF YOU GOT THE MONEY** *Virgin VSCDT1921*	13		5
20 Jan 07	**CALM DOWN DEAREST** *Virgin VSCDT1923*	9		5
11 Jul 09	**STICKS N STONES** *Virgin VSCDT1991*	15		8
12 Sep 09	**CHAKA DEMUS** *Virgin VSCDT1995*	23		3

T-BOZ
US, female vocalist (Tionne 'T-Boz' Watkins). See TLC **2**

Date	Title / Label	Peak	Wks at No.1	Wks on Chart
23 Nov 96	**TOUCH MYSELF** *LaFace 74321422882*	48		1
14 Apr 01	**MY GETAWAY** *Maverick W549CD* TIONNE 'T-BOZ' WATKINS	44		1

T-CONNECTION
US, male vocal/instrumental group **27**

Date	Title / Label	Peak	Wks at No.1	Wks on Chart
18 Jun 77	**DO WHAT YOU WANNA DO** *TK XC 9109*	11		8
14 Jan 78	**ON FIRE** *TK TKR 6006*	16		5
10 Jun 78	**LET YOURSELF GO** *TK TKR 6024*	52		3
24 Feb 79	**AT MIDNIGHT** *TK TKR 7517*	53		5
5 May 79	**SATURDAY NIGHT** *TK TKR 7536*	41		6

T-EMPO
UK, male production duo **4**

Date	Title / Label	Peak	Wks at No.1	Wks on Chart
7 May 94	**SATURDAY NIGHT SUNDAY MORNING** *ffrr FCD 232*	19		3
9 Nov 96	**THE LOOK OF LOVE/THE BLUE ROOM** *ffrr FCD 281*	71		1

T FACTORY
Italy, male production group **2**

Date	Title / Label	Peak	Wks at No.1	Wks on Chart
13 Apr 02	**MESSAGE IN A BOTTLE** *Inferno CDFERN 44*	51		2

T-PAIN
US, male rapper/producer (Faheem Najm) **104**

Date	Title / Label	Peak	Wks at No.1	Wks on Chart
13 May 06	**I'M SPRUNG** *Jive 82876734862*	30		6
19 May 07	**I'M A FLIRT** *Jive 88697090232* R KELLY FEATURING TI & T-PAIN	18		6
29 Sep 07	**GOOD LIFE** *Def Jam 1752306* KANYE WEST FEATURING T-PAIN	23		16
3 Nov 07	**KISS KISS** *Jive 88697385242* CHRIS BROWN FEATURING T-PAIN ★	38		5
16 Feb 08	**LOW** *Atlantic AT0302CD* FLO-RIDA FEATURING T-PAIN ★	2		48
8 Mar 08	**CHURCH** *Jive 88697280942* FEATURING TEDDY VERSETI	35		11
17 May 08	**SHAWTY GET LOOSE** *Jive JIV7270821* LIL' MAMA FEATURING CHRIS BROWN & T-PAIN	57		3
27 Sep 08	**KISS KISS** *Jive 88697385242* CHRIS BROWN FEATURING T-PAIN	39		2
1 Nov 08	**FREEZE** *Jive USJI10801038* FEATURING CHRIS BROWN	62		2
30 May 09	**LOW** *Atlantic AT0302CD* FLO RIDA FEATURING T-PAIN	44		5

T-POWER
UK, male DJ/producer (Mark Royal). See Ebony Dusters **14**

Date	Title / Label	Peak	Wks at No.1	Wks on Chart
13 Apr 96	**POLICE STATE** *Sound Of Underground TPOWCD 001*	63		1
6 Apr 02	**SHAKE UR BODY** *Positiva CDTIV 171* SHY FX & T-POWER FEATURING DI	7		11
7 Jun 03	**FEELIN' U** *London FCD 409* SHY FX & T-POWER FEATURING KELE LE ROC	34		2

T REX
UK, male vocal/instrumental group – Marc Bolan*, d. 16 Sep 1977, Steve Currie, d. 28 Apr 1981, Mickey Finn, d. 11 Jan 2003, Bill Legend & Steve Peregrine Took, d. 27 Oct 1980. Ill-fated glam rockers who enjoyed 11 consecutive Top 10 hits between 1970 and 1973 before becoming extinct following the death of Bolan (who died a calendar month after Elvis) **237**

Date	Title / Label	Peak	Wks at No.1	Wks on Chart
8 May 68	**DEBORA** *Regal Zonophone RZ 3008* TYRANNOSAURUS REX	34		7
4 Sep 68	**ONE INCH ROCK** *Regal Zonophone RZ 3011* TYRANNOSAURUS REX	28		7
9 Aug 69	**KING OF THE RUMBLING SPIRES** *Regal Zonophone RZ 3022* TYRANNOSAURUS REX	44		1
24 Oct 70	**RIDE A WHITE SWAN** *Fly BUG 1*	2		20
27 Feb 71	**HOT LOVE** *Fly BUG 6*	1	6	17
10 Jul 71	**GET IT ON** *Fly BUG 10*	1	4	13
13 Nov 71	**JEEPSTER** *Fly BUG 16*	2		15
29 Jan 72	**TELEGRAM SAM** *T Rex 101*	1	2	12
1 Apr 72	**DEBORA/ONE INCH ROCK** *Magnifly ECHO 102* TYRANNOSAURUS REX	7		10
13 May 72	**METAL GURU** *EMI MARC 1*	1	4	14
16 Sep 72	**CHILDREN OF THE REVOLUTION** *EMI MARC 2*	2		10
9 Dec 72	**SOLID GOLD EASY ACTION** *EMI MARC 3*	2		11
10 Mar 73	**20TH CENTURY BOY** *EMI MARC 4*	3		9
16 Jun 73	**THE GROOVER** *EMI MARC 5*	4		9
24 Nov 73	**TRUCK ON (TYKE)** *EMI MARC 6*	12		11
9 Feb 74	**TEENAGE DREAM** *EMI MARC 7* MARC BOLAN & T REX	13		5
13 Jul 74	**LIGHT OF LOVE** *EMI MARC 8*	22		5
16 Nov 74	**ZIP GUN BOOGIE** *EMI MARC 9*	41		3
12 Jul 75	**NEW YORK CITY** *EMI MARC 10*	15		8
11 Oct 75	**DREAMY LADY** *EMI MARC 11* DISCO PARTY	30		5
6 Mar 76	**LONDON BOYS** *EMI MARC 13*	40		3
19 Jun 76	**I LOVE TO BOOGIE** *EMI MARC 14*	13		9
2 Oct 76	**LASER LOVE** *EMI MARC 15*	41		4
2 Apr 77	**THE SOUL OF MY SUIT** *EMI MARC 16*	42		3
9 May 81	**RETURN OF THE ELECTRIC WARRIOR (EP)** *Rarn MBSF 001* MARC BOLAN & T REX	50		4
19 Sep 81	**YOU SCARE ME TO DEATH** *Cherry Red CHERRY 29* MARC BOLAN & T REX	51		4
27 Mar 82	**TELEGRAM SAM** *T Rex 101*	69		2
18 May 85	**MEGAREX** *Marc On Wax TANX 1* MARC BOLAN & T REX	72		2
9 May 87	**GET IT ON (REMIX)** *Marc On Wax MARC 10* MARC BOLAN & T REX	54		4
24 Aug 91	**20TH CENTURY BOY** *Marc On Wax MARC 501*	13		8
7 Oct 00	**GET IT ON** *All Around The World CDGLOBE 225* BUS STOP FEATURING T REX	59		1
22 Sep 07	**GET IT ON** *Universal TV 1744374*	71		1

T-SHIRT
UK, female vocal duo **1**

Date	Title / Label	Peak	Wks at No.1	Wks on Chart
13 Sep 97	**YOU SEXY THING** *Eternal WEA 122CD*	63		1

T-SPOON
Holland, male/female vocal/rap/instrumental group – Anatevka Bos, Linda Estelle, Prince Peration (Remy de Groot) & Shamrock (Shalamon Baskin) **15**

Date	Title / Label	Peak	Wks at No.1	Wks on Chart
19 Sep 98	**SEX ON THE BEACH** *Control 0042395 CON* ●	2		13
23 Jan 99	**TOM'S PARTY** *Control 0043505 CON*	27		2

T2 FEATURING ROBIN S
US, male producer (Tony Stewart) **1**

Date	Title / Label	Peak	Wks at No.1	Wks on Chart
4 Oct 97	**YOU GOT THE LOVE** *Champion CHAMPCD 330*	62		1

T2
UK, male DJ/producer (Tafazwa Tawonezvi) **23**

Date	Title / Label	Peak	Wks at No.1	Wks on Chart
24 Nov 07	**HEARTBROKEN** *All Around The World CDGLOBE760* FEATURING JODIE ●	2		20
22 Mar 08	**GONNA BE MINE** *Gusto/2NV CDGUST59* ADDICTIVE FEATURING T2	47		3

TABERNACLE
UK, male instrumental/production group **2**

Date	Title / Label	Peak	Wks at No.1	Wks on Chart
4 Mar 95	**I KNOW THE LORD** *Good Groove CDGG 1*	62		1
3 Feb 96	**I KNOW THE LORD (REMIX)** *Good Groove CDGGX 1*	55		1

TACK HEAD
US/UK, male instrumental/production group

Date	Title	Peak	Wks No.1	3
30 Jun 90	**DANGEROUS SEX** *SBK 7014*	48		3

TAFFY
UK (b. US), female vocalist (Katherine Quaye)

Date	Title	Peak	Wks No.1	14
10 Jan 87	**I LOVE MY RADIO (MY DEE JAY'S RADIO)** *Transglobal TYPE 1*	6		10
18 Jul 87	**STEP BY STEP** *Transglobal TYPE 5*	59		4

TAG TEAM
US, male rap duo

Date	Title	Peak	Wks No.1	8
8 Jan 94	**WHOOMP! (THERE IT IS)** *Club Tools SHXCD 1*	34		5
29 Jan 94	**ADDAMS FAMILY (WHOOMP!)** *Atlas PZCD 305*	53		1
10 Sep 94	**WHOOMP! (THERE IT IS) (REMIX)** *Club Tools SHXR 1*	48		2

TAIKO
Germany, male DJ/production duo

Date	Title	Peak	Wks No.1	1
29 Jun 02	**SILENCE** *Nukleuz NUKC 0330*	72		1

TAK TIX
US, male/female vocal/production group

Date	Title	Peak	Wks No.1	2
20 Jan 96	**FEEL LIKE SINGING** *Dub Dub 5813212*	33		2

TAKE 5
US, male vocal group

Date	Title	Peak	Wks No.1	4
7 Nov 98	**I GIVE** *Edel 0039635 ERE*	70		1
27 Mar 99	**NEVER HAD IT SO GOOD** *Edel 0043975 ERE*	34		3

TAKE THAT
UK, male vocal group – Gary Barlow*, Howard Donald, Jason Orange, Mark Owen* & Robbie Williams* (left 1995, rejoined 2010). Comeback kings who have sold 7.4 million singles in the UK. The boys, who came back for good – as a quartet – in 2006, were the first act to score four successive No.1s since The Beatles – a feat they've achieved twice. See Helping Haiti

Date	Title	Peak	Wks No.1	357
23 Nov 91	**PROMISES** *RCA PB 45085*	38		2
8 Feb 92	**ONCE YOU'VE TASTED LOVE** *RCA PB 45257*	47		3
6 Jun 92	**IT ONLY TAKES A MINUTE** *RCA 74321101007*	7		8
15 Aug 92	**I FOUND HEAVEN** *RCA 74321108137*	15		6
10 Oct 92	**A MILLION LOVE SONGS** *RCA 74321116307*	7		9
12 Dec 92	**COULD IT BE MAGIC** *RCA 74321123137* ○	3		12
20 Feb 93	**WHY CAN'T I WAKE UP WITH YOU** *RCA 74321133102* ○	2		10
17 Jul 93	**PRAY** *RCA 74321154502* ●	1	4	11
9 Oct 93	**RELIGHT MY FIRE** *RCA 74321167722* FEATURING LULU ○	1	2	14
18 Dec 93	**BABE** *RCA 74321182122* ⊛	1	1	10
9 Apr 94	**EVERYTHING CHANGES** *RCA 74321167732* ○	1	2	10
9 Jul 94	**LOVE AIN'T HERE ANYMORE** *RCA 74321214832* ○	3		12
15 Oct 94	**SURE** *RCA 74321236622* ○	1	2	15
8 Apr 95	**BACK FOR GOOD** *RCA 74321271462* ⊛	1	4	13
5 Aug 95	**NEVER FORGET** *RCA 74321299572* ●	1	3	9
9 Mar 96	**HOW DEEP IS YOUR LOVE** *RCA 74321355592* ⊛	1	3	14
25 Nov 06	**PATIENCE** *Polydor 1714832* ●	1	4	39
10 Feb 07	**SHINE** *Polydor 1724294* ●	1	2	42
30 Jun 07	**I'D WAIT FOR LIFE** *Polydor 1736401*	17		2
27 Oct 07	**RULE THE WORLD** *Polydor 1746285* ●	2		66
6 Dec 08	**GREATEST DAY** *Polydor 1787445*	1	1	20
6 Dec 08	**PATIENCE** *Polydor 1714832*	59		1
6 Dec 08	**NEVER FORGET** *RCA GBARL9500200*	64		1
14 Feb 09	**UP ALL NIGHT** *Polydor 1796964*	14		11
13 Jun 09	**SAID IT ALL** *Polydor 2708717*	9		10
20 Jun 09	**RULE THE WORLD** *Polydor 1746285*	57		6
27 Jun 09	**GREATEST DAY** *Polydor 1787445*	73		1

Top 3 Best-Selling Singles

		Approximate Sales
1	BACK FOR GOOD	1,045,000
2	RULE THE WORLD	730,000
3	HOW DEEP IS YOUR LOVE	590,000

TAKEN BY TREES
Sweden, female vocalist (Victoria Bergsman). See Concretes, Peter Bjorn & John featuring Bergsman

Date	Title	Peak	Wks No.1	6
28 Nov 09	**SWEET CHILD O' MINE** *Rough Trade GBCVZ0702111*	23		6

TAKING BACK SUNDAY
US, male vocal/instrumental group

Date	Title	Peak	Wks No.1	4
2 Oct 04	**A DECADE UNDER THE INFLUENCE** *Victory VR236CD*	70		1
3 Jun 06	**MAKEDAMN SURE** *Warner Brothers W716CD1*	36		2
2 Sep 06	**TWENTY-TWENTY SURGERY** *Warner Brothers W728CD2*	60		1

TALI
New Zealand, female rapper/DJ/producer (Natalia Scott)

Date	Title	Peak	Wks No.1	5
10 Aug 02	**LYRIC ON MY LIP** *Full Cycle FCY 042*	75		1
7 Feb 04	**BLAZIN'** *Full Cycle FCYCDS 059*	42		2
15 May 04	**LYRIC ON MY LIP** *Full Cycle FCYCDS 065*	39		2

TALK TALK
UK, male vocal/instrumental group

Date	Title	Peak	Wks No.1	74
24 Apr 82	**TALK TALK** *EMI 5284*	52		4
24 Jul 82	**TODAY** *EMI 5314*	14		13
13 Nov 82	**TALK TALK (REMIX)** *EMI 5352*	23		10
19 Mar 83	**MY FOOLISH FRIEND** *EMI 5373*	57		3
14 Jan 84	**IT'S MY LIFE** *EMI 5443*	46		5
7 Apr 84	**SUCH A SHAME** *EMI 5433*	49		6
11 Aug 84	**DUM DUM GIRL** *EMI 5480*	74		1
18 Jan 86	**LIFE'S WHAT YOU MAKE IT** *EMI 5540*	16		9
15 Mar 86	**LIVING IN ANOTHER WORLD** *EMI 5551*	48		4
17 May 86	**GIVE IT UP** *Parlophone R 6131*	59		3
19 May 90	**IT'S MY LIFE** *Parlophone R 6254*	13		9
1 Sep 90	**LIFE'S WHAT YOU MAKE IT** *Parlophone R 6264*	23		6
21 Jun 03	**IT'S MY LIFE** *Nebula NEBCD 045* LIQUID PEOPLE VS TALK TALK	64		1

TALKING HEADS
US/UK, male/female vocal/instrumental group – David Byrne, Chris Frantz, Jerry Harrison & Tina Weymouth

Date	Title	Peak	Wks No.1	54
7 Feb 81	**ONCE IN A LIFETIME** *Sire SIR 4048*	14		10
9 May 81	**HOUSES IN MOTION** *Sire SIR 4050*	50		3
21 Jan 84	**THIS MUST BE THE PLACE** *sire W 9451*	51		3
3 Nov 84	**SLIPPERY PEOPLE** *EMI 5504*	68		2
12 Oct 85	**ROAD TO NOWHERE** *EMI 5530*	6		16
8 Feb 86	**AND SHE WAS** *EMI 5543*	17		8
6 Sep 86	**WILD WILD LIFE** *EMI 5567*	43		4
16 May 87	**RADIO HEAD** *EMI EM 1*	52		2
13 Aug 88	**BLIND** *EMI EM 68*	59		3
10 Oct 92	**LIFETIME PILING UP** *EMI EM 250*	50		3

TALKSPORT ALLSTARS
UK, male radio DJs/vocal group

Date	Title	Peak	Wks No.1	2
17 Jun 06	**WE'RE ENGLAND (TOM HARK)** *Nonsuch 82876857452*	37		2

TALL PAUL
UK, male DJ/producer (Paul Newman). See Camisra, Escrima, Grifters, Partizan

Date	Title	Peak	Wks No.1	15
29 Mar 97	**ROCK DA HOUSE** *VC Recordings VCRD 18*	12		4
29 May 99	**BE THERE** *Duty Free DF 009CD*	45		1
8 Apr 00	**FREEBASE** *Duty Free DF 015CD*	43		2
2 Jun 01	**ROCK DA HOUSE (REMIX)** *VC Recordings VCRD 89*	29		2
18 Aug 01	**PRECIOUS HEART** *Duty Freee/Decode DFTELCD 001* VS INXS	14		5
13 Apr 02	**EVERYBODY'S A ROCK STAR** *Duty Free DFTELCD 003*	60		1

TAMBA TRIO
Argentina, male vocal/instrumental group

Date	Title	Peak	Wks No.1	2
18 Jul 98	**MAS QUE NADA** *Talkin Loud TLCD 34*	34		2

TAMPERER FEATURING MAYA
Italy, male/female vocal/production trio – Maya Days, Mario Fargetta & Alex Farolfi. See Fargetta

Date	Title	Peak	Wks No.1	38
25 Apr 98	**FEEL IT** *Pepper 0530032* ○	1	1	17
14 Nov 98	**IF YOU BUY THIS RECORD YOUR LIFE WILL BE BETTER** *Pepper 0530082* ○	3		14
12 Feb 00	**HAMMER TO THE HEART** *Pepper 9230038*	6		7

TAMS

US, male vocal group – Joseph Pope, d. 16 Mar 1996, Albert Cottle, Horace Key, Charles Pope & Robert Smith — 31

Date	Title / Label	Peak	Wks at No.1	Wks on Chart
14 Feb 70	**BE YOUNG BE FOOLISH BE HAPPY** *Stateside SS 2123*	32		7
31 Jul 71	**HEY GIRL DON'T BOTHER ME** *Probe PRO 532*	1	3	17
21 Nov 87	**THERE AIN'T NOTHING LIKE SHAGGIN'** *Virgin VS 1029*	21		7

NORMA TANEGA

US, female vocalist/guitarist — 8

Date	Title / Label	Peak	Wks at No.1	Wks on Chart
7 Apr 66	**WALKING MY CAT NAMED DOG** *Stateside SS 496*	22		8

CHILDREN OF TANSLEY SCHOOL

UK, male/female school choir — 4

Date	Title / Label	Peak	Wks at No.1	Wks on Chart
28 Mar 81	**MY MUM IS ONE IN A MILLION** *EMI 5151*	27		4

JIMMY TARBUCK

UK, male vocalist/comedian — 2

Date	Title / Label	Peak	Wks at No.1	Wks on Chart
16 Nov 85	**AGAIN** *Safari SAFE 68*	68		2

BILL TARMEY

UK, male vocalist/actor (William Cleworth-Piddington) — 9

Date	Title / Label	Peak	Wks at No.1	Wks on Chart
3 Apr 93	**ONE VOICE** *Arista 74321140852*	16		4
19 Feb 94	**WIND BENEATH MY WINGS** *EMI CDEM 304*	40		3
19 Nov 94	**IOU** *EMI CDEM 361*	55		2

VINCE MARTIN & THE TARRIERS

US, male vocal/instrumental trio — 6

Date	Title / Label	Peak	Wks at No.1	Wks on Chart
14 Dec 56	**CINDY OH CINDY** *London HLN 8340*	26		1
1 Mar 57	**BANANA BOAT SONG** *Columbia DB 3891* TARRIERS	15		5

TARTAN ARMY

UK, football fans (Scotland)/vocal group — 10

Date	Title / Label	Peak	Wks at No.1	Wks on Chart
6 Jun 98	**SCOTLAND BE GOOD** *Precious Organisation JWLCD 33*	54		4
24 Nov 07	**LOCH LOMOND** *Ridge RRS48* RUNRIG & THE TARTAN ARMY	9		4
22 Nov 08	**WE HAVE A DREAM** *Somnium Habemus SHSP24861* PUDSEY'S BEAUTIFUL DREAMERS WITH THE TARTAN ARMY	40		2

A TASTE OF HONEY

UK, female vocal group – Janice Johnson, Donald Johnson, Perry Kibble, d. Feb 1999, & Hazel Payne — 19

Date	Title / Label	Peak	Wks at No.1	Wks on Chart
17 Jun 78	**BOOGIE OOGIE OOGIE** *Capitol CL 15988* ● ★	3		16
18 May 85	**BOOGIE OOGIE OOGIE (REMIX)** *Capitol CL 357*	59		3

TASTE XPERIENCE FEATURING NATASHA PEARL

UK, male/female vocal/instrumental/production group — 1

Date	Title / Label	Peak	Wks at No.1	Wks on Chart
6 Nov 99	**SUMMERSAULT** *Manifesto FESCD 64*	66		1

TATA BOX INHIBITORS

Holland, male production duo. See Trancesetters — 1

Date	Title / Label	Peak	Wks at No.1	Wks on Chart
3 Feb 01	**FREET** *Hooj Choons HOOJ 103CD*	67		1

TATJANA

Croatia, female vocalist (Tatjana Simic) — 2

Date	Title / Label	Peak	Wks at No.1	Wks on Chart
21 Sep 96	**SANTA MARIA** *Love This LUVTHISCDX 4*	40		2

T.A.T.U.

Russia, female vocal duo – Lena Katina & Julia Volkova — 32

Date	Title / Label	Peak	Wks at No.1	Wks on Chart
25 Jan 03	**ALL THE THINGS SHE SAID (IMPORT)** *Interscope 0193332*	44		2
8 Feb 03	**ALL THE THINGS SHE SAID** *Interscope 0196972* ●	1	4	15
31 May 03	**NOT GONNA GET US** *Interscope 9806961*	7		8
8 Oct 05	**ALL ABOUT US** *Interscope 9885764*	8		6
18 Feb 06	**FRIEND OR FOE** *Interscope 9850070*	48		1

TAVARES

US, male vocal/instrumental group – Antone, Arthur, Feliciano & Perry Lee & Ralph Tavares — 77

Date	Title / Label	Peak	Wks at No.1	Wks on Chart
10 Jul 76	**HEAVEN MUST BE MISSING AN ANGEL** *Capitol CL 15876* ●	4		11
9 Oct 76	**DON'T TAKE AWAY THE MUSIC** *Capitol CL 15886* ●	4		10
5 Feb 77	**MIGHTY POWER OF LOVE** *Capitol CL 15905*	25		6
9 Apr 77	**WHODUNNIT** *Capitol CL 15914*	5		10
2 Jul 77	**ONE STEP AWAY** *Capitol CL 15930*	16		7
18 Mar 78	**THE GHOST OF LOVE** *Capitol CL 15968*	29		6
6 May 78	**MORE THAN A WOMAN** *Capitol CL 15977*	7		11
12 Aug 78	**SLOW TRAIN TO PARADISE** *Capitol CL 15996*	62		3
22 Feb 86	**HEAVEN MUST BE MISSING AN ANGEL** *Capitol TAV 1*	12		9
3 May 86	**IT ONLY TAKES A MINUTE** *Capitol TAV 2*	46		4

ANDY TAYLOR

UK, male vocalist/guitarist. See Duran Duran, Power Station — 2

Date	Title / Label	Peak	Wks at No.1	Wks on Chart
20 Oct 90	**LOLA** *A&M AM 596*	60		2

BECKY TAYLOR

UK, female vocalist — 1

Date	Title / Label	Peak	Wks at No.1	Wks on Chart
16 Jun 01	**SONG OF DREAMS** *EMI Classics 8794880*	60		1

FELICE TAYLOR

US, female vocalist — 13

Date	Title / Label	Peak	Wks at No.1	Wks on Chart
25 Oct 67	**I FEEL LOVE COMIN' ON** *President PT 155*	11		13

JAMES TAYLOR

US, male vocalist/guitarist — 23

Date	Title / Label	Peak	Wks at No.1	Wks on Chart
21 Nov 70	**FIRE AND RAIN** *Warner Brothers WB 6104*	42		3
28 Aug 71	**YOU'VE GOT A FRIEND** *Warner Brothers K 16085* ★	4		15
16 Mar 74	**MOCKINGBIRD** *Elektra K 12134* CARLY SIMON & JAMES TAYLOR	34		5

JOHN TAYLOR

UK, male vocalist/bass guitarist (Nigel John Taylor). See Duran Duran, Power Station — 4

Date	Title / Label	Peak	Wks at No.1	Wks on Chart
15 Mar 86	**I DO WHAT I DO...THEME FOR '9 1/2 WEEKS'** *Parlophone R 6125*	42		4

JOHNNIE TAYLOR

US, male vocalist, d. 31 May 2000 (age 62) — 7

Date	Title / Label	Peak	Wks at No.1	Wks on Chart
24 Apr 76	**DISCO LADY** *CBS 4044* ★	25		7

JT TAYLOR

US, male vocalist (James Taylor). See Kool & The Gang — 5

Date	Title / Label	Peak	Wks at No.1	Wks on Chart
24 Aug 91	**LONG HOT SUMMER NIGHT** *MCA MCS 1567*	63		2
30 Nov 91	**FEEL THE NEED** *MCA MCS 1592*	57		1
18 Apr 92	**FOLLOW ME** *MCA MCS 1617*	59		2

PAULINE TAYLOR

UK, female vocalist — 3

Date	Title / Label	Peak	Wks at No.1	Wks on Chart
8 Jun 96	**LET THIS BE A PRAYER** *Cheeky CHEKCD 013* ROLLO GOES SPIRITUAL WITH PAULINE TAYLOR	26		2
9 Nov 96	**CONSTANTLY WAITING** *Cheeky CHEKCD 015*	51		1

R DEAN TAYLOR

Canada, male vocalist (Richard Dean Taylor) — 48

Date	Title / Label	Peak	Wks at No.1	Wks on Chart
19 Jun 68	**GOTTA SEE JANE** *Tamla Motown TMG 656*	17		12
3 Apr 71	**INDIANA WANTS ME** *Tamla Motown TMG 763*	2		15
11 May 74	**THERE'S A GHOST IN MY HOUSE** *Tamla Motown TMG 896* ●	3		12
31 Aug 74	**WINDOW SHOPPING** *Polydor 2058 502*	36		5
21 Sep 74	**GOTTA SEE JANE** *Tamla Motown TMG 918*	41		4

ROGER TAYLOR

UK, male vocalist/drummer/guitarist (Roger Meddows-Taylor). See Cross, Queen — 18

Date	Title / Label	Peak	Wks at No.1	Wks on Chart
18 Apr 81	**FUTURE MANAGEMENT** *EMI 5157*	49		4
16 Jun 84	**MAN ON FIRE** *EMI 5478*	66		2
10 Oct 92	**RADIO** *Epic 6584367* SHAKY FEATURING ROGER TAYLOR	37		3
14 May 94	**NAZIS** *Parlophone CDR 6379*	22		2

Silver-selling ○ · Gold-selling ● · Platinum-selling (x multiples) ⊛ · US No.1 ★ · Peak Position · Weeks at No.1 · Weeks on Chart

Date	Title / Label	Peak Position	Weeks at No.1	Weeks on Chart
1 Oct 94	**FOREIGN SAND** *Parlophone CDR 6389* & YOSHIKI	26		2
26 Nov 94	**HAPPINESS** *Parlophone CDRS 6399*	32		2
10 Oct 98	**PRESSURE ON** *Parlophone CDR 6507*	45		1
10 Apr 99	**SURRENDER** *Parlophone CDRS 6517*	38		2

TAZ

UK (b. Jamaica), male rapper (Tesmond Rowe) — **4**

Date	Title / Label	Peak Position	Weeks at No.1	Weeks on Chart
27 Oct 01	**LAILA** *Wizard WIZ 015* & STEREO NATION	44		2
26 Jun 04	**CAN'T CONTAIN ME** *Def Jam UK/Mercury 9866825*	46		2

TC

Italy, male production group — **5**

Date	Title / Label	Peak Position	Weeks at No.1	Weeks on Chart
14 Mar 92	**BERRY** *Union City UCRT 13* 1991	73		1
21 Nov 92	**FUNKY GUITAR** *Union City UCRT 13* 1992	40		2
10 Jul 93	**HARMONY** *Union City UCRD 20* 1993	51		2

KIRI TE KANAWA

New Zealand, female vocalist — **11**

Date	Title / Label	Peak Position	Weeks at No.1	Weeks on Chart
28 Sep 91	**WORLD IN UNION** *Columbia 6574817*	4		11

TEACH-IN

Holland, male/female vocal/instrumental group — **7**

Date	Title / Label	Peak Position	Weeks at No.1	Weeks on Chart
12 Apr 75	**DING-A-DONG** *Polydor 2058 570*	13		7

TEAM

UK, male vocal/instrumental group — **5**

Date	Title / Label	Peak Position	Weeks at No.1	Weeks on Chart
1 Jun 85	**WICKY WACKY HOUSE PARTY** *EMI 5519*	55		5

TEAM DEC

UK, male/female vocal charity group led by Declan Donnelly. See Ant & Dec — **1**

Date	Title / Label	Peak Position	Weeks at No.1	Weeks on Chart
28 Feb 09	**WAKE ME UP BEFORE YOU GO GO** *ITV Music GBZWE0900002*	64		1

TEAM DEEP

Belgium, male production duo — **1**

Date	Title / Label	Peak Position	Weeks at No.1	Weeks on Chart
17 May 97	**MORNINGLIGHT** *Multiply CDMULTY 19*	42		1

TEARDROP EXPLODES

UK, male vocal/instrumental group – Julian Cope, David Balfe, Gary Dwyer & Alan Gill (replaced by Troy Tate) — **50**

Date	Title / Label	Peak Position	Weeks at No.1	Weeks on Chart
27 Sep 80	**WHEN I DREAM** *Mercury TEAR 1*	47		6
31 Jan 81	**REWARD** *Vertigo TEAR 2* ○	6		13
2 May 81	**TREASON (IT'S JUST A STORY)** *Mercury TEAR 3*	18		8
29 Aug 81	**PASSIONATE FRIEND** *Mercury TEAR 5*	25		10
21 Nov 81	**COLOURS FLY AWAY** *Mercury TEAR 6*	54		3
19 Jun 82	**TINY CHILDREN** *Mercury TEAR 7*	44		7
19 Mar 83	**YOU DISAPPEAR FROM VIEW** *Mercury TEAR 8*	41		3

TEARS

UK, male vocal/instrumental duo – Brett Anderson* & Bernard Butler*. See McAlmont & Butler, Suede — **6**

Date	Title / Label	Peak Position	Weeks at No.1	Weeks on Chart
7 May 05	**REFUGEES** *Independiente ISOM92MS*	9		4
9 Jul 05	**LOVERS** *Independiente ISOM95MS*	24		2

TEARS FOR FEARS

UK, male vocal/instrumental duo – Roland Orzabal & Curt Smith. See Johnny Panic & The Bible Of Dreams — **145**

Date	Title / Label	Peak Position	Weeks at No.1	Weeks on Chart
2 Oct 82	**MAD WORLD** *Mercury IDEA 3* ○	3		16
5 Feb 83	**CHANGE** *Mercury IDEA 4* ○	4		9
30 Apr 83	**PALE SHELTER** *Mercury IDEA 5*	5		8
3 Dec 83	**THE WAY YOU ARE** *Mercury IDEA 6*	24		8
18 Aug 84	**MOTHER'S TALK** *Mercury IDEA 7*	14		8
1 Dec 84	**SHOUT** *Mercury IDEA 8* ○ ★	4		16
30 Mar 85	**EVERYBODY WANTS TO RULE THE WORLD** *Mercury IDEA 9* ○ ★	2		14
22 Jun 85	**HEAD OVER HEELS** *Mercury IDEA 10*	12		9
31 Aug 85	**SUFFER THE CHILDREN** *Mercury IDEA 1*	52		4
7 Sep 85	**PALE SHELTER** *Mercury IDEA 2*	73		2
12 Oct 85	**I BELIEVE (A SOULFUL RECORDING)** *Mercury IDEA 11*	23		4
22 Feb 86	**EVERYBODY WANTS TO RULE THE WORLD** *Mercury IDEA 9*	73		1
31 May 86	**EVERYBODY WANTS TO RUN THE WORLD** *Mercury RACE 1*	5		7
2 Sep 89	**SOWING THE SEEDS OF LOVE** *Fontana IDEA 12*	5		9
18 Nov 89	**WOMAN IN CHAINS** *Fontana IDEA 13*	26		8
3 Mar 90	**ADVICE FOR THE YOUNG AT HEART** *Fontana IDEA 14*	36		4
22 Feb 92	**LAID SO LOW (TEARS ROLL DOWN)** *Fontana IDEA 17*	17		5
25 Apr 92	**WOMAN IN CHAINS** *Fontana IDEA 16* FEATURING OLETA ADAMS	57		1
29 May 93	**BREAK IT DOWN AGAIN** *Mercury IDECD 18*	20		5
31 Jul 93	**COLD** *Mercury IDECD 19*	72		1
7 Oct 95	**RAOUL AND THE KINGS OF SPAIN** *Epic 6624765*	31		3
29 Jun 96	**GOD'S MISTAKE** *Epic 6634185*	61		1
5 Mar 05	**CLOSEST THING TO HEAVEN** *Gut CDGUT66*	40		2

TECHNATION

UK, male production duo — **1**

Date	Title / Label	Peak Position	Weeks at No.1	Weeks on Chart
7 Apr 01	**SEA OF BLUE** *Slinky Music SLINK 012CD*	56		1

TECHNICIAN 2

UK, male production group — **1**

Date	Title / Label	Peak Position	Weeks at No.1	Weeks on Chart
14 Nov 92	**PLAYING WITH THE BOY** *MCA MCS 1710*	70		1

TECHNIQUE

UK, female vocal/instrumental duo — **2**

Date	Title / Label	Peak Position	Weeks at No.1	Weeks on Chart
10 Apr 99	**SUN IS SHINING** *Creation CRESCD 306*	64		1
28 Aug 99	**YOU + ME** *Creation CRESCD 315*	56		1

TECHNO TWINS

UK, male/female vocal/instrumental duo — **2**

Date	Title / Label	Peak Position	Weeks at No.1	Weeks on Chart
16 Jan 82	**FALLING IN LOVE AGAIN** *PRT 7P 224*	70		2

TECHNOHEAD

UK, female/male production/instrumental duo – Lee Newman, d. 4 Aug 1995, & Michael Wells. See GTO, Tricky Disco — **20**

Date	Title / Label	Peak Position	Weeks at No.1	Weeks on Chart
3 Feb 96	**I WANNA BE A HIPPY** *Mokum DB 17703* ○	6		14
27 Apr 96	**HAPPY BIRTHDAY** *Mokum DB 17593*	18		5
12 Oct 96	**BANANA-NA-NA (DUMB DI DUMB)** *Mokum DB 17473*	64		1

TECHNOTRONIC

Belgium, male producer (Jo Bogaert aka Thomas De Quincey) & various Belgium/UK rappers/vocalists including Felly Kilingi (Ya Kid K), MC Eric (Eric Martin) & Ya Kid K (Manuela Kamosi Moaso Djogi) — **69**

Date	Title / Label	Peak Position	Weeks at No.1	Weeks on Chart
2 Sep 89	**PUMP UP THE JAM** *Swanyard SYR 4* FEATURING FELLY ●	2		15
3 Feb 90	**GET UP (BEFORE THE NIGHT IS OVER)** *Swanyard SYR 8* FEATURING YA KID K ○	2		10
7 Apr 90	**THIS BEAT IS TECHNOTRONIC** *Swanyard SYR 9* FEATURING MC ERIC	14		7
14 Jul 90	**ROCKIN' OVER THE BEAT** *Swanyard SYR 14* FEATURING YA KID K	9		9
6 Oct 90	**MEGAMIX** *Swanyard SYR 19*	6		8
15 Dec 90	**TURN IT UP** *Swanyard SYD 9* FEATURING MELISSA & EINSTEIN	42		4
25 May 91	**MOVE THAT BODY** *ARS 6568377* FEATURING REGGIE	12		7
3 Aug 91	**WORK** *ARS 6573317* FEATURING REGGIE	40		4
14 Dec 96	**PUMP UP THE JAM** *Worx WORXCD 004* FEATURING FELLY	36		2
5 Nov 05	**PUMP UP THE JAM** *Data DATA94CDS* DONS FEATURING TECHNOTRONIC	22		3

TEDDY BEARS

US, female/male vocal trio – Annette Kleinbard (Carol Connors), Marshall Leib, d. 15 Mar 2002, & Phil Spector* — **17**

Date	Title / Label	Peak Position	Weeks at No.1	Weeks on Chart
19 Dec 58	**TO KNOW HIM IS TO LOVE HIM** *London HLN 8733* ★	2		16
14 Apr 79	**TO KNOW HIM IS TO LOVE HIM** *Lightning LIG 9015*	66		1

TEEBONE FEATURING MC KIE & MC SPARKS

UK, male rap/production trio — **2**

Date	Title / Label	Peak Position	Weeks at No.1	Weeks on Chart
5 Aug 00	**FLY BI** *East West EW 217CD*	43		2

TEENAGE FANCLUB

UK, male vocal/instrumental group — **23**

Date	Title / Label	Peak Position	Weeks at No.1	Weeks on Chart
24 Aug 91	**STAR SIGN** *Creation CRE 105*	44		2
2 Nov 91	**THE CONCEPT** *Creation CRE 111*	51		1
8 Feb 92	**WHAT YOU DO TO ME (EP)** *Creation CRE 115*	31		2
26 Jun 93	**RADIO** *Creation CRESCD 130*	31		2
2 Oct 93	**NORMAN 3** *Creation CRESCD 142*	50		1

Silver-selling ● Gold-selling ● Platinum-selling (x multiples) ⊛ US No.1 ★ Peak Position · Weeks at No.1 · Weeks on Chart

Date	Title	Peak Position	Weeks at No.1	Weeks on Chart
2 Apr 94	**FALLIN'** *Epic 6602622* & DE LA SOUL	59		1
8 Apr 95	**MELLOW DOUBT** *Creation CRESCD 175*	34		2
27 May 95	**SPARKY'S DREAM** *Creation CRESCD 201*	40		2
2 Sep 95	**NEIL JUNG** *Creation CRESCD 210*	62		1
16 Dec 95	**HAVE LOST IT (EP)** *Creation CRESCD 216*	53		1
12 Jul 97	**AIN'T THAT ENOUGH** *Creation CRESCD 228*	17		3
30 Aug 97	**I DON'T WANT CONTROL OF YOU** *Creation CRESCD 238*	43		1
29 Nov 97	**START AGAIN** *Creation CRESCD 280*	54		1
28 Oct 00	**I NEED DIRECTION** *Columbia 6699512*	48		1
2 Mar 02	**NEAR TO ME** *Geographic GEOG 013CD* & JAD FAIR	68		1
4 Sep 04	**ASSOCIATION** *Geographic GEOG 29CD* INTERNATIONAL AIRPORT/ TEENAGE FANCLUB	75		1

TOWA TEI FEATURING KYLIE MINOGUE

Japan/Australia, male/female vocal/DJ/production duo. See Deee-Lite — 1

Date	Title	Peak Position	Weeks at No.1	Weeks on Chart
31 Oct 98	**GBI** *Athrob ART 021CD*	63		1

TEKNO TOO

UK, male producer (André Jacobs) — 2

Date	Title	Peak Position	Weeks at No.1	Weeks on Chart
13 Jul 91	**JET-STAR** *D-Zone DANCE 012*	56		2

TELEPOPMUSIK

France/UK, male/female vocal/instrumental/production group — 1

Date	Title	Peak Position	Weeks at No.1	Weeks on Chart
2 Mar 02	**BREATHE** *Chrysalis CDCHS 5133*	42		1

TELETUBBIES

UK, male/female children's TV vocal group – Dipsy, Laa-Laa, Po & Tinky Winky — 32

Date	Title	Peak Position	Weeks at No.1	Weeks on Chart
13 Dec 97	**TELETUBBIES SAY EH-OH!** *BBC Worldwide Music WMXS 00092* ⊛x2	1	2	32

TELEVISION

US, male vocal/instrumental group — 10

Date	Title	Peak Position	Weeks at No.1	Weeks on Chart
16 Apr 77	**MARQUEE MOON** *Elektra K 12252*	30		4
30 Jul 77	**PROVE IT** *Elektra K 12262*	25		4
22 Apr 78	**FOXHOLE** *Elektra K 12287*	36		2

TELEX

Belgium, male vocal/instrumental trio — 7

Date	Title	Peak Position	Weeks at No.1	Weeks on Chart
21 Jul 79	**ROCK AROUND THE CLOCK** *Sire SIR 4020*	34		7

SEBASTIEN TELLIER

France, male producer/multi-instrumentalist — 1

Date	Title	Peak Position	Weeks at No.1	Weeks on Chart
8 Oct 05	**LA RITOURNELLE** *Lucky Number LUCKY004CD*	66		1

TINIE TEMPAH

UK, male rapper (Patrick Okogwu, Jr.) — 5

Date	Title	Peak Position	Weeks at No.1	Weeks on Chart
13 Mar 10	**PASS OUT** *EMI GB7TP0900005*	1	2	5+

TEMPER TRAP

Australia, male vocal/instrumental group – Dougy Mandagi, Jonathon Aherne, Toby Dundas & Lorenzo Sillitto — 26

Date	Title	Peak Position	Weeks at No.1	Weeks on Chart
15 Aug 09	**SWEET DISPOSITION** *Infectious INFECT103S* ●	6		26

TEMPERANCE SEVEN

UK, male vocal/instrumental group – Paul McDowell, Colin Bowles, John R.T. Davies, Martin Fry, John Gieves-Watson, Phillip Harrison, Cephas Howard, Brian Innes & Alan Swainston Cooper — 45

Date	Title	Peak Position	Weeks at No.1	Weeks on Chart
30 Mar 61	**YOU'RE DRIVING ME CRAZY** *Parlophone R 4757*	1	1	16
15 Jun 61	**PASADENA** *Parlophone R 4781*	4		17
28 Sep 61	**HARD HEARTED HANNAH/CHILI BOM BOM** *Parlophone R 4823*	28		4
7 Dec 61	**CHARLESTON** *Parlophone R 4851*	22		8

TEMPLE OF THE DOG

US, male vocal/instrumental group — 2

Date	Title	Peak Position	Weeks at No.1	Weeks on Chart
24 Oct 92	**HUNGER STRIKE** *A&M AM 0091*	51		2

NINO TEMPO & APRIL STEVENS

US, male/female vocal duo — 19

Date	Title	Peak Position	Weeks at No.1	Weeks on Chart
7 Nov 63	**DEEP PURPLE** *London HLK 9782* ★	17		11
16 Jan 64	**WHISPERING** *London HLK 9829*	20		8

TEMPTATIONS

US, male vocal/instrumental group – members included Dennis Edwards*, Melvin Franklin, d. 23 Feb 1995, Eddie Kendricks*, d. 5 Oct 1992, David Ruffin*, d. 1 Jun 1991, Richard Street, Otis Williams & Paul Williams, d. 17 Aug 1973 — 203

Date	Title	Peak Position	Weeks at No.1	Weeks on Chart
18 Mar 65	**MY GIRL** *Stateside SS 378* ★	43		1
1 Apr 65	**IT'S GROWING** *Tamla Motown TMG 504*	45		2
14 Jul 66	**AIN'T TOO PROUD TO BEG** *Tamla Motown TMG 565*	21		11
6 Oct 66	**BEAUTY IS ONLY SKIN DEEP** *Tamla Motown TMG 578*	18		10
15 Dec 66	**(I KNOW) I'M LOSING YOU** *Tamla Motown TMG 587*	19		9
6 Sep 67	**YOU'RE MY EVERYTHING** *Tamla Motown TMG 620*	26		15
6 Mar 68	**I WISH IT WOULD RAIN** *Tamla Motown TMG 641*	45		1
12 Jun 68	**I COULD NEVER LOVE ANOTHER** *Tamla Motown TMG 658*	47		1
29 Jan 69	**I'M GONNA MAKE YOU LOVE ME** *Tamla Motown TMG 685* DIANA ROSS & THE SUPREMES & THE TEMPTATIONS	3		12
5 Mar 69	**GET READY** *Tamla Motown TMG 688*	10		9
23 Aug 69	**CLOUD NINE** *Tamla Motown TMG 707*	15		10
20 Sep 69	**I SECOND THAT EMOTION** *Tamla Motown TMG 709* DIANA ROSS & THE SUPREMES & THE TEMPTATIONS	18		8
17 Jan 70	**I CAN'T GET NEXT TO YOU** *Tamla Motown TMG 722* ★	13		9
21 Mar 70	**WHY (MUST WE FALL IN LOVE)** *Tamla Motown TMG 730* DIANA ROSS & THE SUPREMES & THE TEMPTATIONS	31		7
13 Jun 70	**PSYCHEDELIC SHACK** *Tamla Motown TMG 741*	33		7
19 Sep 70	**BALL OF CONFUSION** *Tamla Motown TMG 749*	7		15
22 May 71	**JUST MY IMAGINATION (RUNNING AWAY WITH ME)** *Tamla Motown TMG 773* ★	8		16
5 Feb 72	**SUPERSTAR (REMEMBER HOW YOU GOT WHERE YOU ARE)** *Tamla Motown TMG 800*	32		5
15 Apr 72	**TAKE A LOOK AROUND** *Tamla Motown TMG 808*	13		10
13 Jan 73	**PAPA WAS A ROLLIN' STONE** *Tamla Motown TMG 839* ★	14		8
29 Sep 73	**LAW OF THE LAND** *Tamla Motown TMG 866*	41		4
12 Jun 82	**STANDING ON THE TOP (PART 1)** *Motown TMG 1263* FEATURING RICK JAMES	53		3
17 Nov 84	**TREAT HER LIKE A LADY** *Motown TMG 1365*	12		10
15 Aug 87	**PAPA WAS A ROLLIN' STONE (REMIX)** *Motown ZB 41431*	31		6
6 Feb 88	**LOOK WHAT YOU STARTED** *Motown ZB 41733*	63		2
21 Oct 89	**ALL I WANT FROM YOU** *Motown ZB 43233*	71		1
15 Feb 92	**MY GIRL** *Epic 6576767*	2		10
22 Feb 92	**THE JONES'** *Motown TMG 1403*	69		1

10 C.C.

UK, male vocal/instrumental group – Lol Creme, Kevin Godley (Godley & Creme*), Graham Gouldman* & Eric Stewart — 133

Date	Title	Peak Position	Weeks at No.1	Weeks on Chart
23 Sep 72	**DONNA** *UK 6*	2		13
19 May 73	**RUBBER BULLETS** *UK 36*	1	1	15
25 Aug 73	**THE DEAN AND I** *UK 48*	10		8
15 Jun 74	**WALL STREET SHUFFLE** *UK 69*	10		10
14 Sep 74	**SILLY LOVE** *UK 77*	24		7
5 Apr 75	**LIFE IS A MINESTRONE** *Mercury 6008 010*	7		8
31 May 75	**I'M NOT IN LOVE** *Mercury 6008 014* ●	1	2	11
29 Nov 75	**ART FOR ART'S SAKE** *Mercury 6008 017*	5		10
20 Mar 76	**I'M MANDY FLY ME** *Mercury 6008 019*	6		9
11 Dec 76	**THINGS WE DO FOR LOVE** *Mercury 6008 022* ●	6		11
16 Apr 77	**GOOD MORNING JUDGE** *Mercury 6008 025* ●	5		12
12 Aug 78	**DREADLOCK HOLIDAY** *Mercury 6008 035* ●	1	1	13
7 Aug 82	**RUN AWAY** *Mercury MER 113*	50		4
18 Mar 95	**I'M NOT IN LOVE** *Avex UK AVEXCD 2*	29		2

TEN CITY

US, male vocal/instrumental trio – Byron Stingily*, Byron Burke & Herb Lawson — 21

Date	Title	Peak Position	Weeks at No.1	Weeks on Chart
21 Jan 89	**THAT'S THE WAY LOVE IS** *Atlantic A 8963*	8		10
8 Apr 89	**DEVOTION** *Atlantic A 8916*	29		4
22 Jul 89	**WHERE DO WE GO** *Atlantic A 8864*	60		1
27 Oct 90	**WHATEVER MAKES YOU HAPPY** *Atlantic A 7819*	60		2
15 Aug 92	**ONLY TIME WILL TELL/MY PEACE OF HEAVEN** *East West America A 8516*	63		2
11 Sep 93	**FANTASY** *Columbia 6595042*	45		2

10 REVOLUTIONS

UK, male production group — 1

Date	Title	Peak Position	Weeks at No.1	Weeks on Chart
30 Aug 03	**TIME FOR THE REVOLUTION** *Incentive CENT 53CDS*	59		1

TEN SHARP

Holland, male vocal/instrumental duo – Marcel Kapteijn & Niels Hermes — 15

Date	Title	Peak Position	Weeks at No.1	Weeks on Chart
21 Mar 92	**YOU** *Columbia 6566647*	10		13
20 Jun 92	**AIN'T MY BEATING HEART** *Columbia 6580947*	63		2

10,000 MANIACS

US, female/male vocal/instrumental group — 7

Date	Title	Peak Position	Weeks at No.1	Weeks on Chart
12 Sep 92	**THESE ARE DAYS** *Elektra EKR 156*	58		3
10 Apr 93	**CANDY EVERYBODY WANTS** *Elektra EKR 160CD1*	47		3
23 Oct 93	**BECAUSE THE NIGHT** *Elektra EKR 175CD*	65		1

TEN YEARS AFTER

UK, male vocal/instrumental group – Alvin Lee, Chick Churchill, Ric Lee & Leo Lyons — 18

Date	Title	Peak Position	Weeks at No.1	Weeks on Chart
6 Jun 70	**LOVE LIKE A MAN** *Deram DM 299*	10		18

TENACIOUS D

US, male vocal/instrumental duo — 6

Date	Title	Peak Position	Weeks at No.1	Weeks on Chart
23 Nov 02	**WONDERBOY** *Epic 6733512*	34		2
11 Nov 06	**POD** *Columbia 88697029612*	24		4

DANNY TENAGLIA

US, male DJ/producer — 5

Date	Title	Peak Position	Weeks at No.1	Weeks on Chart
5 Sep 98	**MUSIC IS THE ANSWER (DANCING' & PRANCIN')** *Twisted UK TWCD 10038* & CELEDA	36		3
10 Apr 99	**TURN ME ON** *Twisted UK TWCD 10045* FEATURING LIZ TORRES	53		1
23 Oct 99	**MUSIC IS THE ANSWER (REMIX)** *Twisted UK TWCD 10052* & CELEDA	50		1

TENOR FLY

UK, male vocalist (Jonathan Sutter) — 17

Date	Title	Peak Position	Weeks at No.1	Weeks on Chart
6 Apr 91	**WICKEDEST SOUND** *Desire WANT 40* REBEL MC FEATURING TENOR FLY	43		6
15 Jun 91	**TRIBAL BASE** *Desire WANT 44* REBEL MC FEATURING TENOR FLY & BARRINGTON LEVY	20		6
7 Jan 95	**BRIGHT SIDE OF LIFE** *Mango CIDM 825*	51		2
7 Feb 98	**B-BOY STANCE** *Freskanova FND 7* FREESTYLERS FEATURING TENOR FLY	23		3

TENPOLE TUDOR

UK, male vocal/instrumental group – Eddie Tudor-Pole, Dave Crippen, Bob Kingston & Garry Long — 40

Date	Title	Peak Position	Weeks at No.1	Weeks on Chart
7 Apr 79	**WHO KILLED BAMBI** *Virgin VS 256* ●	6		8
13 Oct 79	**ROCK AROUND THE CLOCK** *Virgin VS 290*	21		6
25 Apr 81	**SWORDS OF A THOUSAND MEN** *Stiff BUY 109* ●	6		12
1 Aug 81	**WUNDERBAR** *Stiff BUY 120*	16		9
14 Nov 81	**THROWING MY BABY OUT WITH THE BATHWATER** *Stiff BUY 129*	49		5

TENTH PLANET

UK, male/female vocal/production group — 1

Date	Title	Peak Position	Weeks at No.1	Weeks on Chart
14 Apr 01	**GHOSTS** *Nebula NEBCD 015*	59		1

TERRA FIRMA

Italy, male producer (Claudio Giussani) — 1

Date	Title	Peak Position	Weeks at No.1	Weeks on Chart
18 May 96	**FLOATING** *Platipus PLAT 21CD*	64		1

TERRIS

UK, male vocal/instrumental group — 1

Date	Title	Peak Position	Weeks at No.1	Weeks on Chart
17 Mar 01	**FABRICATED LUNACY** *Blanco Y Negro NEG 130CD*	62		1

TERROR SQUAD FEATURING FAT JOE & REMY

US, male/female rap group — 5

Date	Title	Peak Position	Weeks at No.1	Weeks on Chart
16 Oct 04	**LEAN BACK** *Universal MCSTD 40385* ★	24		5

TERRORIZE

UK, male producer (Shaun Imrei) — 6

Date	Title	Peak Position	Weeks at No.1	Weeks on Chart
2 May 92	**IT'S JUST A FEELING** *Hamster STER 1*	52		3
22 Aug 92	**FEEL THE RHYTHM** *Hamster 12STER2*	69		1
14 Nov 92	**IT'S JUST A FEELING** *Hamster STER 8*	47		2

TERRORVISION

UK, male vocal/instrumental group – Tony Wright, Leigh Marklew, David Shuttleworth & Mark Yates — 55

Date	Title	Peak Position	Weeks at No.1	Weeks on Chart
19 Jun 93	**AMERICAN TV** *Total Vegas CDVEGAS 3*	63		1
30 Oct 93	**NEW POLICY ONE** *Total Vegas CDVEGAS 4*	42		2
8 Jan 94	**MY HOUSE** *Total Vegas CDVEGAS 5*	29		4
9 Apr 94	**OBLIVION** *Total Vegas CDVEGAS 6*	21		5
25 Jun 94	**MIDDLEMAN** *Total Vegas CDVEGAS 7*	25		4
3 Sep 94	**PRETEND BEST FRIEND** *Total Vegas CDVEGASS 8*	25		3
29 Oct 94	**ALICE WHAT'S THE MATTER** *Total Vegas CDVEGAS 9*	24		4
18 Mar 95	**SOME PEOPLE SAY** *Total Vegas CDVEGAS 10*	22		3
2 Mar 96	**PERSEVERANCE** *Total Vegas CDVEGAS 11*	5		4
4 May 96	**CELEBRITY HIT LIST** *Total Vegas CDVEGAS 12*	20		3
20 Jul 96	**BAD ACTRESS** *Total Vegas CDVEGAS 13*	10		3
11 Jan 97	**EASY** *Total Vegas CDVEGAS 14*	12		4
3 Oct 98	**JOSEPHINE** *Total Vegas CDVEGAS 15*	23		2
30 Jan 99	**TEQUILA** *Total Vegas CDVEGAS 16*	2		10
15 May 99	**III WISHES** *Total Vegas CDVEGAS 17*	42		1
27 Jan 01	**D'YA WANNA GO FASTER** *Papillon BTFLYX0007*	28		2

HELEN TERRY

UK, female vocalist — 6

Date	Title	Peak Position	Weeks at No.1	Weeks on Chart
12 May 84	**LOVE LIES LOST** *Virgin VS 678*	34		6

TONY TERRY

US, male vocalist — 6

Date	Title	Peak Position	Weeks at No.1	Weeks on Chart
27 Feb 88	**LOVEY DOVEY** *Epic TONY 2*	44		6

TODD TERRY PROJECT

US, male producer. See Black Riot, Gypsymen, Royal House, Swan Lake — 33

Date	Title	Peak Position	Weeks at No.1	Weeks on Chart
12 Nov 88	**WEEKEND** *Sleeping Bag SBUK 1T*	56		3
14 Oct 95	**WEEKEND (REMIX)** *Ore AG 13CD*	28		3
13 Jul 96	**KEEP ON JUMPIN'** *Manifesto FESCD 11* TODD TERRY FEATURING MARTHA WASH & JOCELYN BROWN	8		6
12 Jul 97	**SOMETHING GOIN' ON** *Manifesto FESCD 25* TODD TERRY FEATURING MARTHA WASH & JOCELYN BROWN	5		10
6 Dec 97	**IT'S OVER LOVE** *Manifesto FESCD 37* TODD TERRY PRESENTS SHANNON	16		8
11 Apr 98	**READY FOR A NEW DAY** *Manifesto FESCD 40* TODD TERRY FEATURING MARTHA WASH	20		2
3 Jul 99	**LET IT RIDE** *Innocent RESTCD 1*	58		1

TESLA

US, male vocal/instrumental group — 1

Date	Title	Peak Position	Weeks at No.1	Weeks on Chart
27 Apr 91	**SIGNS** *Geffen GFS 3*	70		1

TEST ICICLES

UK, male vocal/instrumental group — 5

Date	Title	Peak Position	Weeks at No.1	Weeks on Chart
13 Aug 05	**BOA VS PYTHON** *Domino RUG205CD*	46		1
5 Nov 05	**CIRCLE SQUARE TRIANGLE** *Domino RUG210CD*	25		2
28 Jan 06	**WHAT'S YOUR DAMAGE?** *Domino RUG217CD*	31		2

JOE TEX

US, female vocalist (Joe Arlington), d. 13 Aug 1982 (age 49) — 11

Date	Title	Peak Position	Weeks at No.1	Weeks on Chart
23 Apr 77	**AIN'T GONNA BUMP NO MORE (WITH NO BIG FAT WOMAN)** *Epic EPC 5035* ●	2		11

TEXAS

UK, female/male vocal/instrumental group – Sharleen Spiteri*, Michael Bannister, Eddie Campbell, Stuart Kerr (replaced by Richard Hynd, then Neil Payne), Johnny McElhone, Ally McErlaine & Tony McGovern — Weeks on Chart: 150

Date	Title	Peak Position	Weeks at No.1	Weeks on Chart
4 Feb 89	**I DON'T WANT A LOVER** *Mercury TEX 1*	8		11
6 May 89	**THRILL HAS GONE** *Mercury TEX 2*	60		3
5 Aug 89	**EVERYDAY NOW** *Mercury TEX 3*	44		5
2 Dec 89	**PRAYER FOR YOU** *Mercury TEX 4*	73		1
7 Sep 91	**WHY BELIEVE IN YOU** *Mercury TEX 5*	66		1
26 Oct 91	**IN MY HEART** *Mercury TEX 6*	74		1
8 Feb 92	**ALONE WITH YOU** *Mercury TEX 7*	32		4
25 Apr 92	**TIRED OF BEING ALONE** *Mercury TEX 8*	19		6
11 Sep 93	**SO CALLED FRIEND** *Mercury TEXCD 9*	30		3
30 Oct 93	**YOU OWE IT ALL TO ME** *Vertigo TEXCD 10*	39		3
12 Feb 94	**SO IN LOVE WITH YOU** *Vertigo TEXCD 11*	28		2
18 Jan 97	**SAY WHAT YOU WANT** *Mercury MERDD 480* ●	3		10
19 Apr 97	**HALO** *Mercury MERCD 482*	10		7
9 Aug 97	**BLACK EYED BOY** *Mercury MERCD 490*	5		6
15 Nov 97	**PUT YOUR ARMS AROUND ME** *Mercury MERCD 497*	10		8
21 Mar 98	**SAY WHAT YOU WANT/INSANE** *Mercury MERCD 499* FEATURING THE WU-TANG CLAN	4		7
1 May 99	**IN OUR LIFETIME** *Mercury MERCD 517* ●	4		9
28 Aug 99	**SUMMER SON** *Mercury MERDD 520*	5		9
27 Nov 99	**WHEN WE ARE TOGETHER** *Mercury MERDD 525*	12		9
14 Oct 00	**IN DEMAND** *Mercury MERDD 528*	6		10
20 Jan 01	**INNER SMILE** *Mercury MERDD 531*	6		8
21 Jul 01	**I DON'T WANT A LOVER (REMIX)** *Mercury MERCD 533*	16		4
18 Oct 03	**CARNIVAL GIRL** *Mercury 9812254* FEATURING KARDINAL OFFISHALL	9		5
20 Dec 03	**I'LL SEE IT THROUGH** *Mercury 9815221*	40		3
13 Aug 05	**GETAWAY** *Mercury 9872946*	6		5
12 Nov 05	**CAN'T RESIST** *Mercury 9874784*	13		3
21 Jan 06	**SLEEP** *Mercury 9876292*	6		7

THAT KID CHRIS

US, male DJ/producer (Chris Staropoli) — Weeks on Chart: 1

Date	Title	Peak Position	Weeks at No.1	Weeks on Chart
22 Feb 97	**FEEL THA VIBE** *Manifesto FESCD 16*	52		1

THAT PETROL EMOTION

UK/US, male vocal/instrumental group — Weeks on Chart: 24

Date	Title	Peak Position	Weeks at No.1	Weeks on Chart
11 Apr 87	**BIG DECISION** *Polydor TPE 1*	43		7
11 Jul 87	**DANCE** *Polydor TPE 2*	64		2
17 Oct 87	**GENIUS MOVE** *Virgin VS 1002*	65		2
31 Mar 90	**ABANDON** *Virgin VS 1242*	73		1
1 Sep 90	**HEY VENUS** *Virgin VS 1290*	49		4
9 Feb 91	**TINGLE** *Virgin VS 1312*	49		4
27 Apr 91	**SENSITIZE** *Virgin VS 1261*	55		4

THE THE

UK, male vocalist/multi-instrumentalist (Matt Johnson) & various male instrumental collaborators — Weeks on Chart: 52

Date	Title	Peak Position	Weeks at No.1	Weeks on Chart
4 Dec 82	**UNCERTAIN SMILE** *Epic EPC A 2787*	68		3
17 Sep 83	**THIS IS THE DAY** *Epic A 3710*	71		3
9 Aug 86	**HEARTLAND** *Some Bizzare TRUTH 2*	29		10
25 Oct 86	**INFECTED** *Some Bizzare TRUTH 3*	48		5
24 Jan 87	**SLOW TRAIN TO DAWN** *Some Bizzare TENSE 1*	64		2
23 May 87	**SWEET BIRD OF TRUTH** *Epic TENSE 2*	55		2
1 Apr 89	**THE BEAT(EN) GENERATION** *Epic EMU 8*	18		5
22 Jul 89	**GRAVITATE TO ME** *Epic EMU 9*	63		3
7 Oct 89	**ARMAGEDDON DAYS ARE HERE (AGAIN)** *Epic EMU 10*	70		2
2 Mar 91	**SHADES OF BLUE (EP)** *Epic 6557968*	54		1
16 Jan 93	**DOGS OF LUST** *Epic 6584572*	25		4
17 Apr 93	**SLOW EMOTION REPLAY** *Epic 6590772*	35		3
19 Jun 93	**LOVE IS STRONGER THAN DEATH** *Epic 6593712*	39		3
15 Jan 94	**DIS-INFECTED EP** *Epic 6598112*	17		4
4 Feb 95	**I SAW THE LIGHT** *Epic 6610912*	31		2

THEATRE OF HATE

UK, male vocal/instrumental group — Weeks on Chart: 9

Date	Title	Peak Position	Weeks at No.1	Weeks on Chart
23 Jan 82	**DO YOU BELIEVE IN THE WESTWORLD** *Burning Rome BRR 2*	40		7
29 May 82	**THE HOP** *Burning Rome BRR 3*	70		2

THEAUDIENCE

UK, male/female vocal/instrumental group. See Sophie Ellis-Bextor, Spiller — Weeks on Chart: 5

Date	Title	Peak Position	Weeks at No.1	Weeks on Chart
7 Mar 98	**IF YOU CAN'T DO IT WHEN YOU'RE YOUNG, WHEN CAN YOU DO IT?** *Mercury AUDCD 2*	48		1
23 May 98	**A PESSIMIST IS NEVER DISAPPOINTED** *Mercury AUDCD 3*	27		2
8 Aug 98	**I KNOW ENOUGH (I DON'T GET ENOUGH)** *Elleffe AUCD 4*	25		2

THEE UNSTRUNG

UK, male vocal/instrumental group — Weeks on Chart: 2

Date	Title	Peak Position	Weeks at No.1	Weeks on Chart
13 Nov 04	**CONTRARY MARY/YOU** *Poptones MC5094SCD*	59		1
7 May 05	**PSYCHO** *Vertigo 9870969*	41		1

THEM

UK, male vocal/instrumental group – Van Morrison*, Pete Bardens, Billy Harrison, Alan Henderson & Jackie & Pat McAuley — Weeks on Chart: 23

Date	Title	Peak Position	Weeks at No.1	Weeks on Chart
7 Jan 65	**BABY PLEASE DON'T GO** *Decca F 12018*	10		9
25 Mar 65	**HERE COMES THE NIGHT** *Decca 12094*	2		12
9 Feb 91	**BABY PLEASE DON'T GO** *London LON 292*	65		2

THEN JERICO

UK, male vocal/instrumental group — Weeks on Chart: 36

Date	Title	Peak Position	Weeks at No.1	Weeks on Chart
31 Jan 87	**LET HER FALL** *London LON 97*	65		3
25 Jul 87	**THE MOTIVE (LIVING WITHOUT YOU)** *London LON 145*	18		12
24 Oct 87	**MUSCLE DEEP** *London LON 156*	48		4
28 Jan 89	**BIG AREA** *London LON 204*	13		7
8 Apr 89	**WHAT DOES IT TAKE** *London LON 223*	33		4
12 Aug 89	**SUGAR BOX** *London LON 235*	22		6

THERAPY?

UK/Ireland, male vocal/instrumental group – Andy Cairns, Fyfe Ewing (replaced by Graham Hopkins), Martin McCarrick (left 2003) & Michael McKeegan — Weeks on Chart: 33

Date	Title	Peak Position	Weeks at No.1	Weeks on Chart
31 Oct 92	**TEETHGRINDER** *A&M AM 0097*	30		2
20 Mar 93	**SHORTSHARPSHOCK EP** *A&M AMCD 208*	9		4
12 Jun 93	**FACE THE STRANGE EP** *A&M 5803052*	18		3
28 Aug 93	**OPAL MANTRA** *A&M 5803612*	13		3
29 Jan 94	**NOWHERE** *A&M 5805052*	18		4
12 Mar 94	**TRIGGER INSIDE** *A&M 5805352*	22		3
11 Jun 94	**DIE LAUGHING** *A&M 5805892*	29		2
27 May 95	**INNOCENT X** *Volume VOLCD 1*	53		1
3 Jun 95	**STORIES** *A&M 5811052*	14		3
29 Jul 95	**LOOSE** *A&M 5811652*	25		3
18 Nov 95	**DIANE** *A&M 5812912*	26		2
14 Mar 98	**CHURCH OF NOISE** *A&M 5825392*	29		2
30 May 98	**LONELY, CRYIN', ONLY** *A&M 0441212*	32		1

THERESE

Sweden, female vocalist (Therese Grankvist) — Weeks on Chart: 19

Date	Title	Peak Position	Weeks at No.1	Weeks on Chart
28 Aug 04	**PUT EM HIGH** *Hed Kandi HEDKCDS008* STONEBRIDGE FEATURING THERESE	6		13
29 Jan 05	**TAKE ME AWAY** *Hed Kandi HEDKCDS009* STONEBRIDGE FEATURING THERESE	9		5
19 May 07	**FEELIN' ME** *Positiva CDTIVS255*	61		1

THESE ANIMAL MEN

UK, male vocal/instrumental group — Weeks on Chart: 3

Date	Title	Peak Position	Weeks at No.1	Weeks on Chart
24 Sep 94	**THIS IS THE SOUND OF YOUTH** *Hi-Rise FLATSCD 7*	72		1
8 Feb 97	**LIFE SUPPORTING MACHINE** *Hut HUTCD 76*	62		1
12 Apr 97	**LIGHT EMITTING ELECTRICAL WAVE** *Hut HUTCD 81*	72		1

THEY MIGHT BE GIANTS

US, male vocal/instrumental duo – John Flansburgh & John Linnell — Weeks on Chart: 18

Date	Title	Peak Position	Weeks at No.1	Weeks on Chart
3 Mar 90	**BIRDHOUSE IN YOUR SOUL** *Elektra EKR 104*	6		11
2 Jun 90	**ISTANBUL (NOT CONSTANTINOPLE)** *Elektra EKR 110*	61		2
28 Jul 01	**BOSS OF ME** *PIAS PIASREST 001CD*	21		5

THICK D

US, male producer (Eric 'E-Smoove' Miller). See E-Smoove featuring Latanza Waters, Praise Cats — Weeks on Chart: 3

Date	Title	Peak Position	Weeks at No.1	Weeks on Chart
12 Oct 02	**INSATIABLE** *Multiply CDMULTY 88*	35		3

ROBIN THICKE
US, male vocalist/producer — 7

Date	Title	Peak Position	Weeks at No.1	Weeks on Chart
30 Jun 07	**LOST WITHOUT U** *Interscope 1736885*	11		7

THIN LIZZY
Ireland/UK, male vocal/instrumental group – Phil Lynott*, d. 4 Jan 1986; members also included Brian Downey, Scott Gorham, Gary Moore*, Brian Robertson, Midge Ure* & Snowy White* — 128

Date	Title	Peak Position	Weeks at No.1	Weeks on Chart
20 Jan 73	**WHISKEY IN THE JAR** *Decca F 13355*	6		12
29 May 76	**THE BOYS ARE BACK IN TOWN** *Vertigo 6059 139*	8		10
14 Aug 76	**JAILBREAK** *Vertigo 6059 150*	31		4
15 Jan 77	**DON'T BELIEVE A WORD** *Vertigo LIZZY 001*	12		7
13 Aug 77	**DANCIN' IN THE MOONLIGHT (IT'S CAUGHT ME IN THE SPOTLIGHT)** *Vertigo 6059 177*	14		8
13 May 78	**ROSALIE – COWGIRLS' SONG (MEDLEY)** *Vertigo LIZZY 2*	20		13
3 Mar 79	**WAITING FOR AN ALIBI** *Vertigo LIZZY 003*	9		8
16 Jun 79	**DO ANYTHING YOU WANT TO** *Vertigo LIZZY 004*	14		9
20 Oct 79	**SARAH** *Vertigo LIZZY 5*	24		13
24 May 80	**CHINATOWN** *Vertigo LIZZY 6*	21		9
27 Sep 80	**KILLER ON THE LOOSE** *Vertigo LIZZY 7*	10		7
2 May 81	**KILLERS LIVE EP** *Vertigo LIZZY 8*	19		7
8 Aug 81	**TROUBLE BOYS** *Vertigo LIZZY 9*	53		4
6 Mar 82	**HOLLYWOOD (DOWN ON YOUR LUCK)** *Vertigo LIZZY 10*	53		3
12 Feb 83	**COLD SWEAT** *Vertigo LIZZY 11*	27		5
7 May 83	**THUNDER AND LIGHTNING** *Vertigo LIZZY 12*	39		2
6 Aug 83	**THE SUN GOES DOWN** *Vertigo LIZZY 13*	52		3
26 Jan 91	**DEDICATION** *Vertigo LIZZY 14*	35		3
23 Mar 91	**THE BOYS ARE BACK IN TOWN** *Vertigo LIZZY 15*	63		1

3RD BASS
US, male rap/DJ trio — 5

Date	Title	Peak Position	Weeks at No.1	Weeks on Chart
10 Feb 90	**THE GAS FACE** *Def Jam 6556270*	71		1
7 Apr 90	**BROOKLYN-QUEENS** *Def Jam 6558307*	61		2
22 Jun 91	**POP GOES THE WEASEL** *Def Jam 6569547*	64		2

THIRD DIMENSION FEATURING JULIE McDERMOTT
UK, male/female vocal/instrumental group — 2

Date	Title	Peak Position	Weeks at No.1	Weeks on Chart
12 Oct 96	**DON'T GO** *Soundprooof MCSTD 40082*	34		2

3RD EDGE
UK, male vocal/production group — 9

Date	Title	Peak Position	Weeks at No.1	Weeks on Chart
31 Aug 02	**IN AND OUT** *Q Zone/Parlophone CDR 6568*	15		5
8 Feb 03	**KNOW YOU WANNA** *Parlophone CDRS 6596*	17		4

THIRD EYE BLIND
US, male vocal/instrumental group — 6

Date	Title	Peak Position	Weeks at No.1	Weeks on Chart
27 Sep 97	**SEMI-CHARMED LIFE** *Elektra E 3907CD*	33		5
21 Mar 98	**HOW'S IT GOING TO BE** *Elektra E 3863CD*	51		1

3RD STOREE
US, male vocal group — 1

Date	Title	Peak Position	Weeks at No.1	Weeks on Chart
5 Jun 99	**IF EVER** *Yab Yum E 3752CD*	53		1

3RD WISH
US, male vocal trio — 6

Date	Title	Peak Position	Weeks at No.1	Weeks on Chart
18 Dec 04	**OBSESSION (SI ES AMOR)** *Three8 CXTHREE8004*	15		6

THIRD WORLD
Jamaica, male vocal/instrumental group – William Clarke, Stephen Coore, Michael Cooper, Richard Daley, Irvin Jarrett & Willie Stewart — 53

Date	Title	Peak Position	Weeks at No.1	Weeks on Chart
23 Sep 78	**NOW THAT WE'VE FOUND LOVE** *Island WIP 6457*	10		9
6 Jan 79	**COOL MEDITATION** *Island WIP 6469*	17		10
16 Jun 79	**TALK TO ME** *Island WIP 6496*	56		5
6 Jun 81	**DANCING ON THE FLOOR (HOOKED ON LOVE)** *CBS A 1214*	10		15
17 Apr 82	**TRY JAH LOVE** *CBS A 2063*	47		6
9 Mar 85	**NOW THAT WE'VE FOUND LOVE** *Island IS 219*	22		8

THIRST
UK, male rap/vocal/production group — 2

Date	Title	Peak Position	Weeks at No.1	Weeks on Chart
6 Jul 91	**THE ENEMY WITHIN** *10 TEN 379*	61		2

THIRTEEN SENSES
UK, male vocal/instrumental group — 8

Date	Title	Peak Position	Weeks at No.1	Weeks on Chart
12 Jun 04	**DO NO WRONG** *Vertigo 9866746*	38		2
25 Sep 04	**INTO THE FIRE** *Vertigo 9867851*	35		2
22 Jan 05	**THRU THE GLASS** *Vertigo 9869347*	18		3
9 Apr 05	**THE SALT WOUND ROUTINE** *Vertigo 9870781*	45		1

1300 DRUMS FEATURING THE UNJUSTIFIED ANCIENTS OF MU
UK, male vocal/instrumental/production group. See KLF — 4

Date	Title	Peak Position	Weeks at No.1	Weeks on Chart
18 May 96	**OOH! AAH! CANTONA** *Dynamo DYND 5*	11		4

THIRTY SECONDS TO MARS
US, male vocal/instrumental group — 23

Date	Title	Peak Position	Weeks at No.1	Weeks on Chart
12 May 07	**THE KILL** *Virgin 3933652*	64		1
22 Sep 07	**THE KILL (REBIRTH)** *Virgin 3933652*	28		9
16 Feb 08	**FROM YESTERDAY** *Virgin VUSCD340*	37		2
12 Dec 09	**KINGS AND QUEENS** *Virgin VUSCD346*	28		10
10 Apr 10	**THIS IS WAR** *Virgin USVI20900430*	59		1+

THIS ISLAND EARTH
UK, male/female vocal/instrumental group — 5

Date	Title	Peak Position	Weeks at No.1	Weeks on Chart
5 Jan 85	**SEE THAT GLOW** *Magnet MAG 266*	47		5

THIS MORTAL COIL
UK, male/female vocal/instrumental group — 3

Date	Title	Peak Position	Weeks at No.1	Weeks on Chart
22 Oct 83	**SONG TO THE SIREN** *4AD AD 310*	66		3

THIS WAY UP
UK, male vocal/instrumental duo — 2

Date	Title	Peak Position	Weeks at No.1	Weeks on Chart
22 Aug 87	**TELL ME WHY** *Virgin VS 954*	72		2

THIS YEAR'S BLONDE
UK, male/female vocal/production duo — 8

Date	Title	Peak Position	Weeks at No.1	Weeks on Chart
10 Oct 81	**PLATINUM POP** *Creole CR 19*	46		5
14 Nov 87	**WHO'S THAT MIX** *Debut DEBT 3034*	62		3

SANDI THOM
UK, female vocalist/guitarist (Alexandria Thom) — 33

Date	Title	Peak Position	Weeks at No.1	Weeks on Chart
15 Oct 05	**I WISH I WAS A PUNK ROCKER** *Viking Legacy VIKINGS04*	55		1
27 May 06	**I WISH I WAS A PUNK ROCKER (WITH FLOWERS IN MY HAIR)** *RCA 82876843422* ●	1		22
2 Sep 06	**WHAT IF I'M RIGHT** *RCA 82876891252*	22		8
24 May 08	**THE DEVIL'S BEAT** *RCA 88697280362*	58		2

BJ THOMAS
US, male vocalist (Billy Joe Thomas) — 4

Date	Title	Peak Position	Weeks at No.1	Weeks on Chart
21 Feb 70	**RAINDROPS KEEP FALLING ON MY HEAD** *Wand WN 1* ★	38		4

DANTE THOMAS FEATURING PRAS
US, male vocal/rap/production duo. See Fugees — 3

Date	Title	Peak Position	Weeks at No.1	Weeks on Chart
1 Sep 01	**MISS CALIFORNIA** *Elektra E 7192CD*	25		3

EVELYN THOMAS
US, female vocalist — 29

Date	Title	Peak Position	Weeks at No.1	Weeks on Chart
24 Jan 76	**WEAK SPOT** *20th Century BTC 1014*	26		7
17 Apr 76	**DOOMSDAY** *20th Century BTC 1017*	41		2
21 Apr 84	**HIGH ENERGY** *Record Shack SOHO 18*	5		17
25 Aug 84	**MASQUERADE** *Record Shack SOHO 25*	60		3

JAMO THOMAS
US, male vocalist — 2

Date	Title	Peak Position	Weeks at No.1	Weeks on Chart
26 Feb 69	**I SPY FOR THE FBI** *Polydor 56 755*	44		2

KENNY THOMAS

UK, male vocalist — 54

Date	Title	Peak	Wks at No.1	Wks
26 Jan 91	**OUTSTANDING** *Cooltempo COOL 227*	12		10
1 Jun 91	**THINKING ABOUT YOUR LOVE** *Cooltempo COOL 235*	4		13
5 Oct 91	**BEST OF YOU** *Cooltempo COOL 243*	11		7
30 Nov 91	**TENDER LOVE** *Cooltempo COOL 247*	26		6
10 Jul 93	**STAY** *Cooltempo CDCOOL 271*	22		6
4 Sep 93	**TRIPPIN' ON YOUR LOVE** *Cooltempo CDCOOL 277*	17		5
6 Nov 93	**PIECE BY PIECE** *Cooltempo CDCOOL 283*	36		3
14 May 94	**DESTINY** *Cooltempo CDCOOL 289*	59		1
2 Sep 95	**WHEN I THINK OF YOU** *Cooltempo CDCOOL 309*	27		3

LILLO THOMAS

US, male vocalist — 10

Date	Title	Peak	Wks at No.1	Wks
27 Apr 85	**SETTLE DOWN** *Capitol CL 356*	66		2
21 Mar 87	**SEXY GIRL** *Capitol CL 445*	23		5
30 May 87	**I'M IN LOVE** *Capitol CL 450*	54		3

NATASHA THOMAS

Denmark, female vocalist — 1

Date	Title	Peak	Wks at No.1	Wks
22 Apr 06	**SKIN DEEP** *Simply Vinyl SIMPCD003*	54		1

NICKY THOMAS

Jamaica, male vocalist (Cecil Thomas) — 14

Date	Title	Peak	Wks at No.1	Wks
13 Jun 70	**LOVE OF THE COMMON PEOPLE** *Trojan TR 7750*	9		14

ROB THOMAS

US, male vocalist/multi-instrumentalist. See Matchbox 20 — 22

Date	Title	Peak	Wks at No.1	Wks
23 Oct 99	**SMOOTH** *Arista 74321709492* SANTANA FEATURING ROB THOMAS	75		1
1 Apr 00	**SMOOTH** *Arista 74321748762* SANTANA FEATURING ROB THOMAS ★	3		10
28 May 05	**LONELY NO MORE** *Atlantic AT0203CD*	11		10
1 Oct 05	**THIS IS HOW A HEART BREAKS** *Atlantic AT0219CD*	67		1

RUFUS THOMAS

US, male vocalist, d. 15 Dec 2001 (age 84) — 12

Date	Title	Peak	Wks at No.1	Wks
11 Apr 70	**DO THE FUNKY CHICKEN** *Stax 144*	18		12

TASHA THOMAS

US, female vocalist, d. 8 Nov 1984 (age 34) — 3

Date	Title	Peak	Wks at No.1	Wks
20 Jan 79	**SHOOT ME (WITH YOUR LOVE)** *Atlantic LV 4*	59		3

TIMMY THOMAS

US, male vocalist/keyboard player — 20

Date	Title	Peak	Wks at No.1	Wks
24 Feb 73	**WHY CAN'T WE LIVE TOGETHER** *Mojo 2027 012*	12		11
28 Dec 85	**NEW YORK EYES** *Portrait A 6805* NICOLE WITH TIMMY THOMAS	41		7
14 Jul 90	**WHY CAN'T WE LIVE TOGETHER (REMIX)** *TK TKR 1*	54		2

THOMAS & TAYLOR

US, male/female vocal duo — 5

Date	Title	Peak	Wks at No.1	Wks
17 May 86	**YOU CAN'T BLAME LOVE** *Cooltempo COOL 123*	53		5

CAROL THOMPSON

UK, female vocalist — 9

Date	Title	Peak	Wks at No.1	Wks
19 May 90	**JOY AND HEARTBREAK** *Circa YR 45* MOVEMENT 98 FEATURING CARROLL THOMPSON	27		5
7 Jul 90	**I'M STILL WAITING** *Mango MNG 749* COURTNEY PINE FEATURING CARROLL THOMPSON	66		1
15 Sep 90	**SUNRISE** *Circa YR 51* MOVEMENT 98 FEATURING CARROLL THOMPSON	58		3

CHRIS THOMPSON

US, male vocalist — 5

Date	Title	Peak	Wks at No.1	Wks
27 Oct 79	**IF YOU REMEMBER ME** *Planet K 12389*	42		5

SUE THOMPSON

US, female vocalist (Eva Sue McKee) — 9

Date	Title	Peak	Wks at No.1	Wks
2 Nov 61	**SAD MOVIES (MAKE ME CRY)** *Polydor NH 66967*	46		2
21 Jan 65	**PAPER TIGER** *Hickory 1284*	30		7

THOMPSON TWINS

UK/New Zealand, male/female vocal/instrumental trio – Tom Bailey, Alannah Currie & Joe Leeway (left 1986) — 110

Date	Title	Peak	Wks at No.1	Wks
6 Nov 82	**LIES** *Arista ARIST 486*	67		3
29 Jan 83	**LOVE ON YOUR SIDE** *Arista ARIST 504*	9		12
16 Apr 83	**WE ARE DETECTIVE** *Arista ARIST 526*	7		9
16 Jul 83	**WATCHING** *Arista TWINS 1*	33		6
19 Nov 83	**HOLD ME NOW** *Arista TWINS 2* ●	4		15
4 Feb 84	**DOCTOR DOCTOR** *Arista TWINS 3* ○	3		10
31 Mar 84	**YOU TAKE ME UP** *Arista TWINS 4* ○	2		9
7 Jul 84	**SISTER OF MERCY** *Arista TWINS 5*	11		9
8 Dec 84	**LAY YOUR HANDS ON ME** *Arista TWINS 6* ○	13		9
31 Aug 85	**DON'T MESS WITH DOCTOR DREAM** *Arista TWINS 9*	15		6
19 Oct 85	**KING FOR A DAY** *Arista TWINS 7*	22		6
7 Dec 85	**REVOLUTION** *Arista TWINS 10*	56		4
21 Mar 87	**GET THAT LOVE** *Arista TWINS 12*	66		3
15 Oct 88	**IN THE NAME OF LOVE '88** *Arista 111808*	46		3
28 Sep 91	**COME INSIDE** *Warner Brothers W 0058*	56		4
25 Jan 92	**THE SAINT** *Warner Brothers W 0080*	53		2

EDDIE THONEICK & KURD MAVERICK

Germany, male DJ/production duo — 2

Date	Title	Peak	Wks at No.1	Wks
27 May 06	**LOVE SENSATION 2006** *All Around The World CDGLOBE531*	39		2

TRACEY THORN

UK, female vocalist. See Everything But The Girl — 5

Date	Title	Peak	Wks at No.1	Wks
21 Jan 95	**PROTECTION** *Virgin WBRX 6* MASSIVE ATTACK FEATURING TRACEY THORN	14		4
10 Mar 07	**IT'S ALL TRUE** *Virgin VSCDX1932*	75		1

DAVID THORNE

US, male vocalist — 8

Date	Title	Peak	Wks at No.1	Wks
24 Jan 63	**ALLEY CAT SONG** *Stateside SS 141*	21		8

KEN THORNE

UK, male pianist & orchestra leader — 15

Date	Title	Peak	Wks at No.1	Wks
18 Jul 63	**THEME FROM THE FILM 'THE LEGION'S LAST PATROL'** *HMV POP 1176*	4		15

THOSE 2 GIRLS

UK, female vocal duo — 4

Date	Title	Peak	Wks at No.1	Wks
5 Nov 94	**WANNA MAKE YOU GO...UUH!** *Final Vinyl 74321233782*	74		1
4 Mar 95	**ALL I WANT** *Final Vinyl 74321254202*	36		3

THOUSAND YARD STARE

UK, male vocal/instrumental group — 5

Date	Title	Peak	Wks at No.1	Wks
26 Oct 91	**SEASONSTREAM (EP)** *Stifled Aardvark AARD 5T*	65		1
8 Feb 92	**COMEUPPANCE** *Stifled Aardvark AARD 007*	37		2
11 Jul 92	**SPINDRIFT (EP)** *Stifled Aardvark AARDT 010*	58		1
8 May 93	**VERSION OF ME** *Polydor AARDC 012*	57		1

THRASHING DOVES

UK, male vocal/instrumental group — 3

Date	Title	Peak	Wks at No.1	Wks
24 Jan 87	**BEAUTIFUL IMBALANCE** *A&M TDOVE 1*	50		3

THREE AMIGOS

UK, male production trio — 8

Date	Title	Peak	Wks at No.1	Wks
3 Jul 99	**LOUIE LOUIE** *Inferno CDFERN 17*	15		6
24 Mar 01	**25 MILES 2001** *Wonderboy WBOYD 25*	30		2

3 COLOURS RED

UK, male vocal/instrumental group — 17

Date	Title	Peak	Wks at No.1	Wks
18 Jan 97	**NUCLEAR HOLIDAY** *Creation CRESCD 250*	22		2
15 Mar 97	**SIXTY MILE SMILE** *Creation CRESCD 254*	20		3
10 May 97	**PURE** *Creation CRESCD 265*	28		1
12 Jul 97	**COPPER GIRL** *Creation CRESCD 270*	30		2
8 Nov 97	**THIS IS MY HOLLYWOOD** *Creation CRESCD 277*	48		1
23 Jan 99	**BEAUTIFUL DAY** *Creation CRESCD 308*	11		6
29 May 99	**THIS IS MY TIME** *Creation CRESCD 313*	36		2

THREE DEGREES
US, female vocal trio – Sheila Ferguson*, Valerie Holiday & Fayette Pinkney, d. 27 Jun 2009 — Total weeks: 113

Date	Title	Peak	Wks No.1	Wks
13 Apr 74	**YEAR OF DECISION** *Philadelphia International PIR 2073*	13		10
27 Apr 74	**TSOP (THE SOUND OF PHILADELPHIA)** *Philadelphia International PIR 2289* MFSB FEATURING THE THREE DEGREES ★	22		9
13 Jul 74	**WHEN WILL I SEE YOU AGAIN** *Philadelphia International PIR 2155* ●	1	2	16
2 Nov 74	**GET YOUR LOVE BACK** *Philadelphia International PIR 2737*	34		4
12 Apr 75	**TAKE GOOD CARE OF YOURSELF** *Philadelphia International PIR 3177* ●	9		9
5 Jul 75	**LONG LOST LOVER** *Philadelphia International PIR 3352*	40		4
1 May 76	**TOAST OF LOVE** *Epic EPC 4215*	36		4
7 Oct 78	**GIVIN' UP GIVIN' IN** *Ariola ARO 130*	12		10
13 Jan 79	**WOMAN IN LOVE** *Ariola ARO 141* ●	3		11
24 Mar 79	**THE RUNNER** *Ariola ARO 154* ●	10		10
23 Jun 79	**THE GOLDEN LADY** *Ariola ARO 170*	56		3
29 Sep 79	**JUMP THE GUN** *Ariola ARO 183*	48		5
24 Nov 79	**MY SIMPLE HEART** *Ariola ARO 202* ●	9		11
5 Oct 85	**THE HEAVEN I NEED** *Supreme SUPE 102*	42		5
26 Dec 98	**LAST CHRISTMAS** *Wildstar CDWILD 15* ALIEN VOICES FEATURING THE THREE DEGREES	54		2

THREE DOG NIGHT
US, male vocal/instrumental trio – Danny Hutton, Chuck Negron & Cory Wells — Total weeks: 23

Date	Title	Peak	Wks No.1	Wks
8 Aug 70	**MAMA TOLD ME NOT TO COME** *Stateside SS 8052* ★	3		14
29 May 71	**JOY TO THE WORLD** *Probe PRO 523* ★	24		9

THREE DRIVES
Holland, male vocal/instrumental duo — Total weeks: 9

Date	Title	Peak	Wks No.1	Wks
27 Jun 98	**GREECE 2000** *Hooj Choons HOOJCD 63*	44		1
30 Jan 99	**GREECE 2000 (REMIX)** *Hooj Choons HOOJ 70CD*	12		4
17 Nov 01	**SUNSET ON IBIZA** *Xtravaganza XTRAV 27CDS* THREE DRIVES ON A VINYL	44		2
7 Jun 03	**CARRERA 2** *Nebula NEBCD 043*	57		1
14 Aug 04	**AIR TRAFFIC** *Nebula NEBCD 056*	75		1

THREE GOOD REASONS
UK, male vocal/instrumental group — Total weeks: 3

Date	Title	Peak	Wks No.1	Wks
10 Mar 66	**NOWHERE MAN** *Mercury MF 899*	47		3

3 JAYS
UK, male vocal/production trio — Total weeks: 5

Date	Title	Peak	Wks No.1	Wks
31 Jul 99	**FEELING IT TOO** *Multiply CDMULTY 53*	17		5

3LW
US, female vocal trio – Adrienne Bailon, Naturi Naughton* (replaced by Jessica Benson) & Kiely Williams — Total weeks: 13

Date	Title	Peak	Wks No.1	Wks
2 Jun 01	**NO MORE (BABY I'MA DO RIGHT)** *Epic 6712722*	6		9
8 Sep 01	**PLAYAS GON' PLAY** *Epic 6717932*	21		3
19 Oct 02	**FEELS GOOD (DON'T WORRY BOUT A THING)** *Island CID 806* NAUGHTY BY NATURE FEATURING 3LW	44		1

THREE 'N' ONE
Germany, male production duo — Total weeks: 3

Date	Title	Peak	Wks No.1	Wks
7 Jun 97	**REFLECT** *ffrr FCD 301*	66		1
15 May 99	**PEARL RIVER** *Low Sense SENSECD 24* PRESENTS JOHNNY SHAKER FEATURING SERIAL DIVA	32		2

30H!3
US, male vocal duo – Sean Foreman & Nathaniel Motte — Total weeks: 34

Date	Title	Peak	Wks No.1	Wks
25 Jul 09	**DON'T TRUST ME** *Photo Finish/Atlantic PF001CD*	21		9
26 Dec 09	**STARSTRUKK** *Asylum/Photo Finish USAT20802558* FEATURING KATY PERRY ●	3		16+
13 Feb 10	**BLAH BLAH BLAH** *RCA 88697659702* KE$HA FEATURING 30H!3	11		9+

365
UK, male vocal group — Total weeks: 1

Date	Title	Peak	Wks No.1	Wks
25 Nov 06	**ONE TOUCH** *Innocent ANGEDX24*	60		1

THREE 6 MAFIA
US, male rap group — Total weeks: 2

Date	Title	Peak	Wks No.1	Wks
18 Feb 06	**STAY FLY** *Sony Urban 82876783062*	33		2

3SL
UK, male vocal trio. See Idols — Total weeks: 10

Date	Title	Peak	Wks No.1	Wks
20 Apr 02	**TAKE IT EASY** *Epic 6724042*	11		6
7 Sep 02	**TOUCH ME TEASE ME** *Epic 6727875*	16		4

3 OF A KIND
UK, female/male vocal/rap trio – Liana Caruana (Miz Tipzta), Nicholas Gallante (Devine MC) & Marc Portelli (Marky P) — Total weeks: 14

Date	Title	Peak	Wks No.1	Wks
21 Aug 04	**BABYCAKES** *Relentless RELDX6* ●	1	1	14

3T
US, male vocal group – brothers Tariano (Taj), Taryll & Tito (TJ) Jackson — Total weeks: 45

Date	Title	Peak	Wks No.1	Wks
27 Jan 96	**ANYTHING** *MJJ 6627152* ●	2		14
4 May 96	**24-Jul** *MJJ 6631995*	11		7
24 Aug 96	**WHY** *Epic 6636482* FEATURING MICHAEL JACKSON	2		9
7 Dec 96	**I NEED YOU** *Epic 6639912* ●	3		10
5 Apr 97	**GOTTA BE YOU** *Epic 6643645* 3T: RAP BY HERBIE	10		5

THRICE
US, male vocal/instrumental group — Total weeks: 1

Date	Title	Peak	Wks No.1	Wks
18 Oct 03	**ALL THAT'S LEFT** *Island US 9811957*	69		1

THRILLS
Ireland, male vocal/instrumental group — Total weeks: 18

Date	Title	Peak	Wks No.1	Wks
22 Mar 03	**ONE HORSE TOWN** *Virgin VSCDT 1845*	18		3
21 Jun 03	**BIG SUR** *Virgin VSCDT 1852*	17		4
6 Sep 03	**SANTA CRUZ (YOU'RE NOT THAT FAR)** *Virgin VSCDT 1862*	33		2
6 Dec 03	**DON'T STEAL OUR SUN** *Virgin VSCD 1864*	45		1
11 Sep 04	**WHATEVER HAPPENED TO COREY HAIM?** *Virgin VSCDX 1876*	22		4
27 Nov 04	**NOT FOR ALL THE LOVE IN THE WORLD** *Virgin VSCDX1890*	39		2
2 Apr 05	**THE IRISH KEEP GATE-CRASHING** *Virgin VSCDT1895*	48		1
28 Jul 07	**NOTHING CHANGES AROUND HERE** *Virgin VSCDT1947*	40		1

THRILLSEEKERS
UK, male producer/keyboard player (Steve Helstrip) — Total weeks: 3

Date	Title	Peak	Wks No.1	Wks
17 Feb 01	**SYNAESTHESIA (FLY AWAY)** *Neo NEOCD1 050* FEATURING SHERYL DEANE	28		2
7 Sep 02	**DREAMING OF YOU** *Data 36CDS*	48		1

THROWING MUSES
US, female/male vocal/instrumental group — Total weeks: 6

Date	Title	Peak	Wks No.1	Wks
9 Feb 91	**COUNTING BACKWARDS** *4AD AD 1001*	70		2
1 Aug 92	**FIREPILE (EP)** *4AD BAD 2012*	46		1
24 Dec 94	**BRIGHT YELLOW GUN** *4AD BAD 4018CD*	51		2
10 Aug 96	**SHARK** *4AD BAD 6016CD*	53		1

THS – THE HORN SECTION
US, male vocal/instrumental duo — Total weeks: 3

Date	Title	Peak	Wks No.1	Wks
18 Aug 84	**LADY SHINE (SHINE ON)** *Fourth & Broadway BRW 10*	54		3

HARRY THUMANN
Germany, male producer (Harald Thumann), d. Aug 2001. See Wonder Dog — Total weeks: 6

Date	Title	Peak	Wks No.1	Wks
21 Feb 81	**UNDERWATER** *Decca F 13901*	41		6

THUNDER
UK, male vocal/instrumental group — Total weeks: 56

Date	Title	Peak	Wks No.1	Wks
17 Feb 90	**DIRTY LOVE** *EMI EM 126*	32		4
12 May 90	**BACKSTREET SYMPHONY** *EMI EM 137*	25		4
14 Jul 90	**GIMME SOME LOVIN'** *EMI EM 148*	36		3
29 Sep 90	**SHE'S SO FINE** *EMI EM 158*	34		3
23 Feb 91	**LOVE WALKED IN** *EMI EM 175*	21		4
15 Aug 92	**LOW LIFE IN HIGH PLACES** *EMI EM 242*	22		5

Date	Title	Peak Position	Weeks at No.1	Weeks on Chart
10 Oct 92	**EVERYBODY WANTS HER** *EMI EM 249*	36		4
13 Feb 93	**A BETTER MAN** *EMI CDBETTER 1*	18		4
19 Jun 93	**LIKE A SATELLITE (EP)** *EMI CDEM 272*	28		2
7 Jan 95	**STAND UP** *EMI CDEM 365*	23		4
25 Feb 95	**RIVER OF PAIN** *EMI CDEM 367*	31		2
6 May 95	**CASTLES IN THE SAND** *EMI CDEMS 372*	30		3
23 Sep 95	**IN A BROKEN DREAM** *EMI CDEMS 384*	26		2
25 Jan 97	**DON'T WAIT UP** *Raw Power RAWX 1020*	27		2
5 Apr 97	**LOVE WORTH DYING FOR** *Raw Power RAWX 1043*	60		1
7 Feb 98	**THE ONLY ONE** *Eagle EAGXA 016*	31		2
27 Jun 98	**PLAY THAT FUNKY MUSIC** *Eagle EAGXS 030*	39		2
20 Mar 99	**YOU WANNA KNOW** *Eagle EAGXA 037*	49		1
31 May 03	**LOSER** *STC Recordings STC20032*	48		1
4 Dec 04	**I LOVE YOU MORE THAN ROCK N ROLL** *STC STC20044*	27		2
16 Dec 06	**THE DEVIL MADE ME DO IT** *STC STC20066*	40		1

THUNDERBUGS

UK/Germany/France, female vocal/instrumental group – Jane Vaughan, Brigitta Jansen, Stef Maillard & Nicky Shaw

Date	Title	Peak Position	Weeks at No.1	Weeks on Chart
				15
18 Sep 99	**FRIENDS FOREVER** *1st Avenue 6676932*	5		10
18 Dec 99	**IT'S ABOUT TIME YOU WERE MINE** *1st Avenue 6683972*	43		5

THUNDERCLAP NEWMAN

UK, male vocal/instrumental group – Andy Newman, John Keene, d. 21 Mar 2002, & Jimmy McCulloch, d. 27 Sep 1979

Date	Title	Peak Position	Weeks at No.1	Weeks on Chart
				13
11 Jun 69	**SOMETHING IN THE AIR** *Track 604 031*	1	3	12
27 Jun 70	**ACCIDENTS** *Track 2094 001*	46		1

THUNDERTHIGHS

US, female vocal group

Date	Title	Peak Position	Weeks at No.1	Weeks on Chart
				5
22 Jun 74	**CENTRAL PARK ARREST** *Philips 6006 386*	30		5

THURSDAY

US, male vocal/instrumental group

Date	Title	Peak Position	Weeks at No.1	Weeks on Chart
				1
25 Oct 03	**SIGNALS OVER THE AIR** *Island US 9812292*	62		1

BOBBY THURSTON

US, male vocalist/percussionist

Date	Title	Peak Position	Weeks at No.1	Weeks on Chart
				10
29 Mar 80	**CHECK OUT THE GROOVE** *Epic EPC 8348*	10		10

TI

US, male rapper/producer/actor (Clifford Harris, Jr)

Date	Title	Peak Position	Weeks at No.1	Weeks on Chart
				98
19 Feb 05	**SOLDIER** *Columbia 6757622* DESTINY'S CHILD FEATURING TI & LIL'WAYNE	4		7
26 Mar 05	**BRING EM OUT** *Atlantic AT0196CD*	59		1
17 Jun 06	**WHY YOU WANNA** *Atlantic AT0244CD*	22		7
18 Nov 06	**MY LOVE** *Jive 88697020502* JUSTIN TIMBERLAKE FEATURING TI ★	2		19
27 Jan 07	**PAC'S LIFE** *Interscope 1723503* 2PAC FEATURING TI & ASHANTI	21		6
19 May 07	**I'M A FLIRT** *Jive 88697090232* R KELLY FEATURING TI & T-PAIN	18		6
27 Sep 08	**WHATEVER YOU LIKE** *Atlantic USAT20803177* ★	47		10
15 Nov 08	**LIVE YOUR LIFE** *Atlantic AT0325CD* FEATURING RIHANNA ★	2		20
7 Feb 09	**DEAD AND GONE** *Atlantic AT0333CD* FEATURING JUSTIN TIMBERLAKE	4		18
6 Jun 09	**WHATEVER YOU LIKE** *Atlantic USAT20803177*	53		2
5 Sep 09	**REMEMBER ME** *Atlantic USAT20901697* FEATURING MARY J BLIGE	34		2

TIFFANY

US, female vocalist (Tiffany Darwish)

Date	Title	Peak Position	Weeks at No.1	Weeks on Chart
				45
16 Jan 88	**I THINK WE'RE ALONE NOW** *MCA 1211* ● ★	1	3	13
19 Mar 88	**COULD'VE BEEN** *MCA TIFF 2* ★	4		9
4 Jun 88	**I SAW HIM STANDING THERE** *MCA TIFF 3*	8		7
6 Aug 88	**FEELINGS OF FOREVER** *MCA TIFF 4*	52		2
12 Nov 88	**RADIO ROMANCE** *MCA TIFF 5*	13		11
11 Feb 89	**ALL THIS TIME** *MCA TIFF 6*	47		3

TIGA

Canada, male DJ/producer (Tiga Sontag)

Date	Title	Peak Position	Weeks at No.1	Weeks on Chart
				8
11 May 02	**SUNGLASSES AT NIGHT** *City Rockers ROCKERS 15CD* & ZYNTHERIUS	25		3
6 Sep 03	**HOT IN HERRE** *Skint 90CD*	46		2
19 Jun 04	**PLEASURE FROM THE BASS** *Different DIFB1028CDM*	57		1
29 Oct 05	**YOU GONNA WANT ME** *Different DIFB1043CDM*	64		1
6 May 06	**(FAR FROM) HOME** *Different DIFB1048CDM*	65		1

TIGER

UK/Ireland, male/female vocal/instrumental group

Date	Title	Peak Position	Weeks at No.1	Weeks on Chart
				5
31 Aug 96	**RACE** *Trade 2 TRDCD 004*	37		2
16 Nov 96	**MY PUPPET PAL** *Trade 2 TRDCD 005*	62		1
22 Feb 97	**ON THE ROSE** *Trade 2 TRDCD 008*	57		1
22 Aug 98	**FRIENDS** *Trade 2 TRDCD 013*	72		1

TIGERSTYLE

UK, male vocal/instrumental group

Date	Title	Peak Position	Weeks at No.1	Weeks on Chart
				1
14 Jun 08	**NACHNA ONDA NEI** *Kismet USA560638295*	62		1

TIGERTAILZ

US, male vocal/instrumental group

Date	Title	Peak Position	Weeks at No.1	Weeks on Chart
				2
24 Jun 89	**LOVE BOMB BABY** *Music For Nations KUT 132*	75		1
16 Feb 91	**HEAVEN** *Music For Nations KUT 137*	71		1

TIGHT FIT

UK, male producer (Ken Gold) & uncredited male/female vocal group; then UK, male/female vocal trio – Steve Grant (initially voiced by Roy Ward), Denise Gyngell & Julie Harris

Date	Title	Peak Position	Weeks at No.1	Weeks on Chart
				49
18 Jul 81	**BACK TO THE SIXTIES** *Jive 002*	4		11
26 Sep 81	**BACK TO THE SIXTIES PART 2** *Jive 005*	33		5
23 Jan 82	**THE LION SLEEPS TONIGHT** *Jive 9* ●	1	3	15
1 May 82	**FANTASY ISLAND** *Jive 13* ●	5		12
31 Jul 82	**SECRET HEART** *Jive 20*	41		6

TIK & TOK

UK, male vocal duo

Date	Title	Peak Position	Weeks at No.1	Weeks on Chart
				2
8 Oct 83	**COOL RUNNING** *Survival SUR 0116*	69		2

TANITA TIKARAM

UK (b. Germany), female vocalist/guitarist

Date	Title	Peak Position	Weeks at No.1	Weeks on Chart
				31
30 Jul 88	**GOOD TRADITION** *WEA YZ 196*	10		10
22 Oct 88	**TWIST IN MY SOBRIETY** *WEA YZ 321*	22		8
14 Jan 89	**CATHEDRAL SONG** *WEA YZ 331*	48		3
18 Mar 89	**WORLD OUTSIDE YOUR WINDOW** *WEA YZ 363*	58		2
13 Jan 90	**WE ALMOST GOT IT TOGETHER** *WEA YZ 443*	52		3
9 Feb 91	**ONLY THE ONES WE LOVE** *East West YZ 558*	69		1
4 Feb 95	**I MIGHT BE CRYING** *East West YZ 879CD*	64		2
6 Jun 98	**STOP LISTENING** *Mother MUMCD 102*	67		1
29 Aug 98	**I DON'T WANNA LOSE AT LOVE** *Mother MUMCD 105*	73		1

JOHNNY TILLOTSON

US, male vocalist

Date	Title	Peak Position	Weeks at No.1	Weeks on Chart
				50
1 Dec 60	**POETRY IN MOTION** *London HLA 9231*	1	2	15
2 Feb 61	**JIMMY'S GIRL** *London HLA 9275*	43		2
12 Jul 62	**IT KEEPS RIGHT ON A HURTIN'** *London HLA 9550*	31		10
4 Oct 62	**SEND ME THE PILLOW YOU DREAM ON** *London HLA 9598*	21		10
27 Dec 62	**I CAN'T HELP IT** *London HLA 9642*	41		6
9 May 63	**OUT OF MY MIND** *London HLA 9695*	34		5
14 Apr 79	**POETRY IN MOTION** *Lightning LIG 9016*	67		2

TILT

UK, male instrumental/production group

Date	Title	Peak Position	Weeks at No.1	Weeks on Chart
				8
2 Dec 95	**I DREAM** *Perfecto PERF 112CD*	69		1
10 May 97	**MY SPIRIT** *Perfecto PERF 139CD*	61		1
13 Sep 97	**PLACES** *Perfecto PERF 149CD*	64		1
7 Feb 98	**BUTTERFLY** *Perfecto PERF 154CD1* FEATURING ZEE	41		1
27 Mar 99	**CHILDREN** *Deconstruction 74321648172*	51		1
8 May 99	**INVISIBLE** *Hooj Choons HOOJ 73CD*	20		2
12 Feb 00	**DARK SCIENCE (EP)** *Hooj Choons HOOJ 87CD*	55		1

TIMBALAND

US, male rapper/multi-instrumentalist/producer (Tim Mosley). Grammy-winner who has successfully bridged the gap between rap and pop, including production credits on Russia's 2008 Eurovision Song Contest-winning 'Believe'. The video for his grammatically-incorrect No.1 'The Way I Are' was shot in Salford, Greater Manchester

Date	Title	Peak Position	Weeks at No.1	Weeks on Chart: 228
23 Jan 99	**GET ON THE BUS** *East West E 3780CD* DESTINY'S CHILD FEATURING TIMBALAND	15		5
13 Mar 99	**HERE WE COME** *Virgin DINSD 179* TIMBALAND/MISSY ELLIOTT & MAGOO	43		1
19 Jun 99	**LOBSTER & SCRIMP** *Virgin DINSD 186* FEATURING JAY-Z	48		1
21 Jul 01	**WE NEED A RESOLUTION** *Blackground VUSCD 206* AALIYAH FEATURING TIMBALAND	20		6
13 Mar 04	**COP THAT SHIT** *Unique Corp TIMBACD001* TIMBALAND/MAGOO/MISSY ELLIOTT	22		3
9 Sep 06	**PROMISCUOUS** *Geffen 1706030* NELLY FURTADO FEATURING TIMBALAND ★	3		14
14 Apr 07	**GIVE IT TO ME** *Interscope 1732199* FEATURING NELLY FURTADO & JUSTIN TIMBERLAKE ★	1	1	26
30 Jun 07	**ANONYMOUS** *Def Jam 1736310* BOBBY VALENTINO FEATURING TIMBALAND	25		6
7 Jul 07	**THE WAY I ARE** *Interscope 1742316* FEATURING DOE & KERI HILSON	1	2	36
25 Aug 07	**AYO TECHNOLOGY** *Interscope 1746158* 50 CENT FEATURING JUSTIN TIMBERLAKE & TIMBALAND	2		27
13 Oct 07	**APOLOGIZE** *Interscope 1750152* PRESENTS ONEREPUBLIC	3		42
16 Feb 08	**SCREAM** *Interscope 1764136* FEATURING KERI HILSON & NICOLE SCHERZINGER	12		14
12 Apr 08	**ELEVATOR** *Atlantic AT0317CD* FLO RIDA FEATURING TIMBALAND	20		14
2 May 09	**RETURN THE FAVOUR** *Polydor USUM70804618* KERI HILSON FEATURING TIMBALAND	19		7
12 Dec 09	**MORNING AFTER DARK** *Interscope 2728036* FEATURING SO SHY & NELLY FURTADO	6		14
6 Feb 10	**IF WE EVER MEET AGAIN** *Interscope 2733439* FEATURING KATY PERRY	3		10+
3 Apr 10	**CARRY OUT** *Interscope USUM70915229* FEATURING JUSTIN TIMBERLAKE	16		2+

JUSTIN TIMBERLAKE

US, male vocalist/producer/actor. Photogenic, world-conquering superstar who 'justified' his split from record-breaking boy band *NSync by amassing 13 Top 5 entries from two hit-heavy, multi-million-selling albums: Justified and Futuresex/Lovesounds

Date	Title	Peak Position	Weeks at No.1	Weeks on Chart: 291
2 Nov 02	**LIKE I LOVE YOU** *Jive 9254342* ●	2		16
15 Feb 03	**CRY ME A RIVER** *Jive 9254632*	2		12
15 Mar 03	**WORK IT** *Universal MCSXD 40312* NELLY FEATURING JUSTIN TIMBERLAKE	7		11
24 May 03	**ROCK YOUR BODY (IMPORT)** *Jive 9254962*	46		1
31 May 03	**ROCK YOUR BODY** *Jive 9254952*	2		13
27 Sep 03	**SENORITA** *Jive 82876563442*	13		8
7 May 05	**SIGNS** *Geffen 9881782* SNOOP DOGG FEATURING CHARLIE WILSON & JUSTIN TIMBERLAKE	2		16
2 Sep 06	**SEXYBACK** *Jive 82876870882* ★	1	1	31
18 Nov 06	**MY LOVE** *Jive 88697020502* FEATURING TI ★	2		19
3 Feb 07	**WHAT GOES AROUND COMES AROUND** *Jive 88697058012* ★	4		22
14 Apr 07	**GIVE IT TO ME** *Interscope 1732199* TIMBALAND FEATURING NELLY FURTADO & JUSTIN TIMBERLAKE ★	1	1	26
23 Jun 07	**LOVESTONED I THINK SHE KNOWS** *Jive USJI10600495*	11		15
25 Aug 07	**AYO TECHNOLOGY** *Interscope 1746158* 50 CENT FEATURING JUSTIN TIMBERLAKE & TIMBALAND	2		27
29 Mar 08	**4 MINUTES** *Maverick W803CD1* MADONNA FEATURING JUSTIN TIMBERLAKE	1	4	27
7 Feb 09	**DEAD AND GONE** *Atlantic AT0333CD* TI FEATURING JUSTIN TIMBERLAKE	4		18
18 Apr 09	**LOVE SEX MAGIC** *RCA 88697520672* CIARA FEATURING JUSTIN TIMBERLAKE	5		14
29 Nov 08	**REHAB** *Def Jam USUM70735519* RIHANNA FEATURING JUSTIN TIMBERLAKE	16		13
3 Apr 10	**CARRY OUT** *Interscope USUM70915229* TIMBALAND FEATURING JUSTIN TIMBERLAKE	16		2+

TIMBUK 3

US, male/female vocal/instrumental duo

Date	Title	Peak Position	Weeks at No.1	Weeks on Chart: 7
31 Jan 87	**THE FUTURE'S SO BRIGHT I GOTTA WEAR SHADES** *IRS IRM 126*	21		7

TIME FREQUENCY

UK, male instrumental/production group – Jon Campbell, Paul Inglis, Colin McNeil & Kyle Ramsey – with various female vocalists

Date	Title	Peak Position	Weeks at No.1	Weeks on Chart: 34
6 Jun 92	**REAL LOVE** *Jive JIVET 307*	60		1
9 Jan 93	**NEW EMOTION** *Internal Affairs KGBCD 009*	36		6
12 Jun 93	**THE ULTIMATE HIGH/THE POWER ZONE** *Internal Affairs KGBCD 010*	17		11
6 Nov 93	**REAL LOVE (REMIX)** *Internal Affairs KGBCD 011*	8		8
28 May 94	**SUCH A PHANTASY** *Internal Affairs KGBCD 013*	25		4
8 Oct 94	**DREAMSCAPE '94** *Internal Affairs KGBCD 015*	32		3
31 Aug 02	**REAL LOVE 2002** *Jive 9253782*	43		1

TIME OF THE MUMPH

UK, male producer (Mark Mumford)

Date	Title	Peak Position	Weeks at No.1	Weeks on Chart: 1
11 Feb 95	**CONTROL** *Fresh FRSHD 24*	69		1

TIME UK

UK, male vocal/instrumental group

Date	Title	Peak Position	Weeks at No.1	Weeks on Chart: 3
8 Oct 83	**THE CABARET** *Red Bus/Aroadia TIM 123*	63		3

TIME ZONE

US/UK, male vocal/instrumental/production group

Date	Title	Peak Position	Weeks at No.1	Weeks on Chart: 9
19 Jan 85	**WORLD DESTRUCTION** *Virgin VS 743*	44		9

TIMEBOX

UK, male vocal/instrumental group

Date	Title	Peak Position	Weeks at No.1	Weeks on Chart: 4
24 Jul 68	**BEGGIN'** *Deram DM 194*	38		4

TIMELORDS

UK, male production duo – Jimmy Cauty & Bill Drummond. See KLF, Justified Ancients Of Mu Mu, 2K

Date	Title	Peak Position	Weeks at No.1	Weeks on Chart: 9
4 Jun 88	**DOCTORIN' THE TARDIS** *KLF Communications KLF 003*	1	1	9

TIMEX SOCIAL CLUB

US, male vocal group

Date	Title	Peak Position	Weeks at No.1	Weeks on Chart: 9
13 Sep 86	**RUMORS** *Cooltempo COOL 133*	13		9

TIN MACHINE

UK/US, male vocal/instrumental group

Date	Title	Peak Position	Weeks at No.1	Weeks on Chart: 10
1 Jul 89	**UNDER THE GOD** *EMI-USA MT 68*	51		2
9 Sep 89	**TIN MACHINE/MAGGIE'S FARM (LIVE)** *EMI-USA MT 73*	48		2
24 Aug 91	**YOU BELONG IN ROCK 'N' ROLL** *London LON 305*	33		3
2 Nov 91	**BABY UNIVERSAL** *London LON 310*	48		3

TIN TIN OUT

UK, male instrumental/production duo – Lindsay Edwards & Darren Stokes

Date	Title	Peak Position	Weeks at No.1	Weeks on Chart: 42
13 Aug 94	**THE FEELING** *Deep Distraxion OILYCD 029* FEATURING SWEET TEE	32		2
25 Mar 95	**ALWAYS SOMETHING THERE TO REMIND ME** *WEA YZ 911CD* FEATURING ESPIRITU	14		5
8 Feb 97	**ALL I WANNA DO** *VC Recordings VCRD 15*	31		2
10 May 97	**DANCE WITH ME** *VC Recordings VCRD 17* FEATURING TONY HADLEY	35		2
20 Sep 97	**STRINGS FOR YASMIN** *VC Recordings VCRD 20*	31		3
28 Mar 98	**HERE'S WHERE THE STORY ENDS** *VC Recordings VCRD 30* FEATURING SHELLEY NELSON	7		10
12 Sep 98	**SOMETIMES** *VC Recordings VCRD 34* FEATURING SHELLEY NELSON	20		4
11 Sep 99	**ELEVEN TO FLY** *VC Recordings VCRDX 52* FEATURING WENDY PAGE	26		2
13 Nov 99	**WHAT I AM** *VC Recordings VCRD 53* FEATURING EMMA BUNTON ●	2		12

TINDERSTICKS

UK, male vocal/instrumental group

Date	Title	Peak Position	Weeks at No.1	Weeks on Chart: 7
5 Feb 94	**KATHLEEN (EP)** *This Way Up WAY 2833CD*	61		1
18 Mar 95	**NO MORE AFFAIRS** *This Way Up WAY 3833*	58		1
12 Aug 95	**TRAVELLING LIGHT** *This Way Up WAY 4533*	51		1
7 Jun 97	**BATHTIME** *This Way Up WAY 6166*	38		1
1 Nov 97	**RENTED ROOMS** *This Way Up WAY 6566*	56		1
4 Sep 99	**CAN WE START AGAIN?** *Island CID 756*	54		1
2 Aug 03	**SOMETIMES IT HURTS** *Beggars Banquet BBQ369CD*	60		1

TING TINGS
UK, female/male vocal/instrumental duo – Katie White & Jules de Martino — 66

Date	Title / Label	Peak Position	Weeks at No.1	Weeks on Chart
24 May 08	**THAT'S NOT MY NAME** *Columbia 88697293792* ●	1	1	31
31 May 08	**GREAT DJ** *Columbia GBARL0701283*	33		8
31 May 08	**SHUT UP AND LET ME GO** *Columbia 88697328482*	6		23
18 Oct 08	**BE THE ONE** *Columbia 88697385012*	28		3
7 Mar 09	**WE WALK** *Columbia 88697455201*	58		1

TINGO TANGO
Italy, male producer (Marco Bongiovanni) — 2

Date	Title / Label	Peak Position	Weeks at No.1	Weeks on Chart
21 Jul 90	**IT IS JAZZ** *Champion CHAMP 250*	68		2

TINMAN
UK, male producer (Paul Dakeyne) — 9

Date	Title / Label	Peak Position	Weeks at No.1	Weeks on Chart
20 Aug 94	**EIGHTEEN STRINGS** *ffrr FCD 242*	9		8
3 Jun 95	**GUDVIBE** *ffrr FCD 262*	49		1

TINY DANCERS
UK, male vocal/instrumental group — 4

Date	Title / Label	Peak Position	Weeks at No.1	Weeks on Chart
31 Mar 07	**I WILL WAIT FOR YOU** *Parlophone CDR6733*	36		2
9 Jun 07	**HANNAH WE KNOW** *Parlophone CDR6740*	33		2

TINY TIM
US, male vocalist (Herbert Khaury), d. 30 Nov 1996 (age 66) — 1

Date	Title / Label	Peak Position	Weeks at No.1	Weeks on Chart
5 Feb 69	**GREAT BALLS OF FIRE** *Reprise RS 20802*	45		1

ROB TISSERA, VINYLGROOVER & THE RED HED
UK, male production trio — 1

Date	Title / Label	Peak Position	Weeks at No.1	Weeks on Chart
10 Jul 04	**STAY** *Tidy Trax TIDYTWO133C*	61		1

TITANIC
Norway/UK, male vocal/instrumental group – Roy Robinson, Kenny Aas, Kjell Aasperud, John Lorck & Janny Loseth — 12

Date	Title / Label	Peak Position	Weeks at No.1	Weeks on Chart
25 Sep 71	**SULTANA** *CBS 5365*	5		12

TITIYO
Sweden, female vocalist (Titiyo Jah) — 6

Date	Title / Label	Peak Position	Weeks at No.1	Weeks on Chart
3 Mar 90	**AFTER THE RAIN** *Arista 112722*	60		3
6 Oct 90	**FLOWERS** *Arista 113212*	71		1
5 Feb 94	**TELL ME I'M NOT DREAMING** *Arista 74321185622*	45		2

TJR FEATURING XAVIER
UK, male instrumental/DJ/production trio — 2

Date	Title / Label	Peak Position	Weeks at No.1	Weeks on Chart
27 Sep 97	**JUST GETS BETTER** *Multiply CDMULTY 25*	28		2

TLC
US, female vocal/rap trio – Lisa 'Left Eye' Lopes*, d. 25 Apr 2002, Rozonda 'Chilli' Thomas & Tionne 'T-Boz'* Watkins — 85

Date	Title / Label	Peak Position	Weeks at No.1	Weeks on Chart
20 Jun 92	**AIN'T 2 PROUD 2 BEG** *Arista 115265*	13		5
22 Aug 92	**BABY-BABY-BABY** *LaFace 74321111297*	55		3
24 Oct 92	**WHAT ABOUT YOUR FRIENDS** *LaFace 74321118177*	59		2
21 Jan 95	**CREEP** *LaFace 74321254212* ★	22		4
22 Apr 95	**RED LIGHT SPECIAL** *LaFace 74321273662*	18		4
5 Aug 95	**WATERFALLS** *LaFace 74321298812* ● ★	4		14
4 Nov 95	**DIGGIN' ON YOU** *LaFace 74321319252*	18		5
13 Jan 96	**CREEP** *LaFace 74321340942*	6		7
3 Apr 99	**NO SCRUBS** *LaFace 74321660952* ⊛ ★	3		19
28 Aug 99	**UNPRETTY** *LaFace 74321695842* ★	6		11
18 Dec 99	**DEAR LIE** *LaFace 74321724012*	31		9
14 Dec 02	**GIRL TALK** *Arista 74321983502*	30		2

T99
Belgium, male production duo — 10

Date	Title / Label	Peak Position	Weeks at No.1	Weeks on Chart
11 May 91	**ANASTHASIA** *XL Recordings XLS 19*	14		6
19 Oct 91	**NOCTURNE** *Emphasis 6574097*	33		4

ART & DOTTY TODD
US, male/female vocal duo – Art Todd, d. 10 Oct 2007, & Dorothy Todd, d. 12 Dec 2000 — 7

Date	Title / Label	Peak Position	Weeks at No.1	Weeks on Chart
13 Feb 53	**BROKEN WINGS** *HMV B 10399*	6		7

TOGETHER
UK, male production group — 8

Date	Title / Label	Peak Position	Weeks at No.1	Weeks on Chart
4 Aug 90	**HARDCORE UPROAR** *ffrr F 143*	12		8

TOKENS
US, male vocal group — 12

Date	Title / Label	Peak Position	Weeks at No.1	Weeks on Chart
21 Dec 61	**THE LION SLEEPS TONIGHT (WIMOWEH)** *RCA 1263* ★	11		12

TOKYO DRAGONS
UK, male vocal/instrumental group — 3

Date	Title / Label	Peak Position	Weeks at No.1	Weeks on Chart
26 Jun 04	**TEENAGE SCREAMERS** *Island CID 864*	61		1
23 Oct 04	**GET 'EM OFF** *Island CID 876*	75		1
5 Mar 05	**WHAT THE HELL** *Island/Uni-Island CID883*	59		1

TOKYO GHETTO PUSSY
Germany, male instrumental/production duo. See Jam & Spoon featuring Plavka, Storm — 4

Date	Title / Label	Peak Position	Weeks at No.1	Weeks on Chart
16 Sep 95	**EVERYBODY ON THE FLOOR (PUMP IT)** *Epic 6611132*	26		2
16 Mar 96	**I KISS YOUR LIPS** *Epic 6623212*	55		2

TOL & TOL
Holland, male instrumental duo — 2

Date	Title / Label	Peak Position	Weeks at No.1	Weeks on Chart
14 Apr 90	**ELENI** *Dover ROJ 5*	73		2

TOM TOM CLUB
US/Jamaica, male/female vocal/instrumental group – Chris Frantz, Tina Weymouth, Adrian Belew, Monte Browne, Tyrone Downie, Uziah 'Sticky' Thompson & Lani, Laura & Loric Weymouth — 20

Date	Title / Label	Peak Position	Weeks at No.1	Weeks on Chart
20 Jun 81	**WORDY RAPPINGHOOD** *Island WIP 6694*	7		9
10 Oct 81	**GENIUS OF LOVER** *Island WIP 6735*	65		2
7 Aug 82	**UNDER THE BOARDWALK** *Island WIP 6762*	22		9

TOMBA VIRA
Holland, male production duo. See Chocolate Puma, Goodmen, Jark Prongo, Rhythmkillaz, Riva featuring Dannii Minogue — 1

Date	Title / Label	Peak Position	Weeks at No.1	Weeks on Chart
16 Jun 01	**THE SOUND OF OH YEAH** *VC Recordings VCRD 88*	51		1

TOMCAT
UK, male vocal/instrumental group — 1

Date	Title / Label	Peak Position	Weeks at No.1	Weeks on Chart
14 Oct 00	**CRAZY** *Virgin VSCSDT 1785*	48		1

TOMCRAFT
Germany, male DJ/producer (Thomas Bruckner) — 15

Date	Title / Label	Peak Position	Weeks at No.1	Weeks on Chart
10 May 03	**LONELINESS** *Data 52CDS*	1	1	13
25 Oct 03	**BRAINWASHED (CALL YOU)** *Data 63CDS*	43		2

RICKY TOMLINSON
UK, male actor/vocalist (Eric Tomlinson) — 5

Date	Title / Label	Peak Position	Weeks at No.1	Weeks on Chart
10 Nov 01	**ARE YOU LOOKIN' AT ME** *All Around The World CDRICKY 1*	28		3
23 Dec 06	**CHRISTMAS MY A*SE** *Liberty 3837292*	25		2

TOMMI
UK, female vocal group — 8

Date	Title / Label	Peak Position	Weeks at No.1	Weeks on Chart
5 Jul 03	**LIKE WHAT** *Sony Music 6739095*	12		8

TOMSKI
UK, male producer (Tom Jankiewicz) — 3

Date	Title / Label	Peak Position	Weeks at No.1	Weeks on Chart
18 Apr 98	**14 HOURS TO SAVE THE EARTH** *Xtravaganza 0091515 EXT*	42		1
12 Feb 00	**LOVE WILL COME** *Xtravaganza XTRAV 6CDS* FEATURING JAN JOHNSTON	31		2

TONEDEF ALLSTARS
UK, male footballers/boxer/actor vocal group — 4

Date	Title	Peak	Wks No.1	Wks
17 Jun 06	WHO DO YOU THINK YOU ARE KIDDING JURGEN KLINSMANN *Tone Def CDTONE1*	13		4

TONGUE 'N' CHEEK
UK, male/female vocal/instrumental trio — 28

Date	Title	Peak	Wks No.1	Wks
27 Feb 88	NOBODY (CAN LOVE ME) *Criminal BUS 6* TONGUE IN CHEEK	59		6
25 Nov 89	ENCORE *Syncopate SY 33*	41		4
14 Apr 90	TOMORROW *Syncopate SY 34*	20		7
4 Aug 90	FORGET ME NOTS *Syncopate SY 37*	37		5
19 Jan 91	NOBODY *Syncopate SY 39*	26		6

TONIGHT
UK, male vocal/instrumental group — 10

Date	Title	Peak	Wks No.1	Wks
28 Jan 78	DRUMMER MAN *Target TDS 1*	14		8
20 May 78	MONEY THAT'S YOUR PROBLEM *Target TDS 2*	66		2

TONY! TONI! TONE!
US, male vocal trio — 12

Date	Title	Peak	Wks No.1	Wks
30 Jun 90	OAKLAND STROKE *Wing 7*	50		5
9 Mar 91	IT NEVER RAINS (IN SOUTHERN CALIFORNIA) *Wing 10*	69		2
4 Sep 93	IF I HAD NO LOOT *Polydor PZCD 292* TONY TONI TONE	44		3
3 May 97	LET'S GET DOWN *Mercury MERCD 485* TONY TONI TONE FEATURING DJ QUIK	33		2

TOP
UK, male vocal/instrumental trio — 2

Date	Title	Peak	Wks No.1	Wks
20 Jul 91	NUMBER ONE DOMINATOR *Island IS 496*	67		2

TOPLOADER
UK, male vocal/instrumental group – Joseph Washbourn, Julian Deane, Rob Green, Dan Hipgrave & Matt Knight — 56

Date	Title	Peak	Wks No.1	Wks
22 May 99	ACHILLES HEEL *Sony S2 6671612*	64		1
7 Aug 99	LET THE PEOPLE KNOW *Sony S2 6677132*	52		1
4 Mar 00	DANCING IN THE MOONLIGHT *Sony S2 6689412*	19		7
13 May 00	ACHILLES HEEL *Sony S2 6691872*	8		7
2 Sep 00	JUST HOLD ON *Sony S2 6696242*	20		4
25 Nov 00	DANCING IN THE MOONLIGHT *Sony S2 6699852* (silver)	7		25
21 Apr 01	ONLY FOR A WHILE *Sony S2 6708612*	19		4
17 Aug 02	TIME OF MY LIFE *Sony S2 6728862*	18		7

TOPOL
Israel, male vocalist (Chaim Topol) — 20

Date	Title	Peak	Wks No.1	Wks
20 Apr 67	IF I WERE A RICH MAN *CBS 202651*	9		20

MEL TORME
US, female vocalist, d. 5 Jun 1999 (age 73) — 32

Date	Title	Peak	Wks No.1	Wks
27 Apr 56	MOUNTAIN GREENERY *Vogue Coral Q 72150*	4		24
3 Jan 63	COMING HOME BABY *London HLK 9643*	13		8

TORNADOS
UK, male instrumental group – George Bellamy, Heinz* Burt, d. 7 Apr 2000, Alan Caddy, d. 16 Aug 2000, Clem Cattini & Roger Jackson — 59

Date	Title	Peak	Wks No.1	Wks
30 Aug 62	TELSTAR *Decca F 11494* ★	1	5	25
10 Jan 63	GLOBETROTTER *Decca F 11562*	5		11
21 Mar 63	ROBOT *Decca F 11606*	17		12
6 Jun 63	THE ICE CREAM MAN *Decca F 11662*	18		9
10 Oct 63	DRAGONFLY *Decca F 11745*	41		2

MITCHELL TOROK
US, male vocalist — 19

Date	Title	Peak	Wks No.1	Wks
28 Sep 56	WHEN MEXICO GAVE UP THE RHUMBA *Brunswick 05586*	6		18
11 Jan 57	RED LIGHT GREEN LIGHT *Brunswick 05626*	29		1

EMILIANA TORRINI
Iceland, female vocalist — 3

Date	Title	Peak	Wks No.1	Wks
10 Jun 00	EASY *One Little Indian 274 TP7CD*	63		1
9 Sep 00	UNEMPLOYED IN SUMMERTIME *One Little Indian 275 TP7CD*	63		1
3 Feb 01	TO BE FREE *One Little Indian 276TP 7CDL*	44		1

PETE TOSH
Jamaica, male vocalist (Winston McIntosh), d. 11 Sep 1987 (age 42) — 12

Date	Title	Peak	Wks No.1	Wks
21 Oct 78	(YOU GOTTA WALK) DON'T LOOK BACK *Rolling Stones 2859*	43		7
2 Apr 83	JOHNNY B GOODE *EMI RIC 115*	48		5

TOTAL
US, female vocal group — 11

Date	Title	Peak	Wks No.1	Wks
15 Jul 95	CAN'T YOU SEE *Tommy Boy TBCD 700* FEATURING THE NOTORIOUS B.I.G.	43		2
14 Sep 96	KISSIN' YOU *Arista 74321404172*	29		2
15 Feb 97	DO YOU THINK ABOUT US *Puff Daddy 74321458492*	49		1
18 Apr 98	WHAT YOU WANT *Puff Daddy 74321578772* MA$E FEATURING TOTAL	15		5
30 Sep 00	I WONDER WHY HE'S THE GREATEST DJ *Tommy Boy TBCD 2100* TONY TOUCH FEATURING TOTAL	68		1

TOTAL CONTRAST
UK, male vocal/instrumental duo — 22

Date	Title	Peak	Wks No.1	Wks
3 Aug 85	TAKES A LITTLE TIME *London LON 71*	17		10
19 Oct 85	HIT AND RUN *London LON 76*	41		5
1 Mar 86	THE RIVER *London LON 83*	44		3
10 May 86	WHAT YOU GONNA DO ABOUT IT *London LON 95*	63		4

TOTO
US, male vocal/instrumental group – Bobby Kimball; members also included David Hungate, Steve Lukather, David Paich, Jeff Porcaro, d. 5 Aug 1992, Mike Porcaro & Steve Porcaro — 35

Date	Title	Peak	Wks No.1	Wks
10 Feb 79	HOLD THE LINE *CBS 6784*	14		11
5 Feb 83	AFRICA *CBS A 2510* (silver) ★	3		10
9 Apr 83	ROSANNA *CBS A 2079*	12		8
18 Jun 83	I WON'T HOLD YOU BACK *CBS A 3392*	37		5
18 Nov 95	I WILL REMEMBER *Columbia 6626552*	64		1

TOTO COELO
UK, female vocal group – Lacey Bond, Lindsey Danvers, Sheen Doran, Ros Holness & Anita Mahadervan — 14

Date	Title	Peak	Wks No.1	Wks
7 Aug 82	I EAT CANNIBALS PART 1 *Radialchoice TIC 10*	8		10
13 Nov 82	DRACULA'S TANGO/MUCHO MACHO *Radialchoice TIC 11*	54		4

TOTTENHAM HOTSPUR FA CUP FINAL SQUAD
UK, male vocalists/footballers — 23

Date	Title	Peak	Wks No.1	Wks
9 May 81	OSSIE'S DREAM (SPURS ARE ON THEIR WAY TO WEMBLEY) *Rockney SHELF 1*	5		8
1 May 82	TOTTENHAM TOTTENHAM *Rockney SHELF 2*	19		7
9 May 87	HOT SHOT TOTTENHAM *Rainbow RBR 16*	18		5
11 May 91	WHEN THE YEAR ENDS IN 1 *A1 A 1324*	44		3

TONY TOUCH FEATURING TOTAL
US, male/female vocal/production group — 1

Date	Title	Peak	Wks No.1	Wks
30 Sep 00	I WONDER WHY HE'S THE GREATEST DJ *Tommy Boy TBCD 2100*	68		1

TOUCH & GO
UK, female/male vocal/instrumental/production group – Vanessa Lancaster, Charlie Gillett, David Lowe, James Lynch & Gordon Nelki — 12

Date	Title	Peak	Wks No.1	Wks
7 Nov 98	WOULD YOU...? *V2 VVR 5003083* (silver)	3		12

TOUCH OF SOUL
Italy, male production trio — 3

Date	Title	Peak	Wks No.1	Wks
19 May 90	WE GOT THE LOVE *Cooltempo COOL 204*	46		3

TOUR DE FORCE
UK, male production trio — 1

Date	Title	Peak	Wks No.1	Wks
16 May 98	CATALAN *East West EW 161CD*	71		1

TOURISTS

UK, male/female vocal/instrumental group – Annie Lennox*, David A Stewart*, Eddy Chinn, Peet Combes & Jim Toomey. See Eurythmics

Date	Title	Peak	No.1	40
9 Jun 79	**BLIND AMONG THE FLOWERS** *Logo GO 350*	52		5
8 Sep 79	**THE LONELIEST MAN IN THE WORLD** *Logo GO 360*	32		7
10 Nov 79	**I ONLY WANT TO BE WITH YOU** *Logo GO 370* ●	4		14
9 Feb 80	**SO GOOD TO BE BACK HOME AGAIN** *Logo TOUR 1*	8		9
18 Oct 80	**DON'T SAY I TOLD YOU SO** *RCA TOUR 2*	40		5

TOUTES LES FILLES

UK, female vocal group

Date	Title	Peak	No.1	1
4 Sep 99	**THAT'S WHAT LOVE CAN DO** *London LONCD 434*	44		1

TOWERS OF LONDON

UK, male vocal/instrumental group

Date	Title	Peak	No.1	5
19 Mar 05	**ON A NOOSE** *TVT TOLCD01*	32		1
9 Jul 05	**FUCK IT UP** *TVT TOLCD2*	46		1
26 Nov 05	**HOW RUDE SHE WAS** *TVT TOLCD3*	30		1
27 May 06	**AIR GUITAR** *TVT TOLCD4*	32		1
24 Feb 07	**I'M A RAT** *TVT TOLCD5*	46		1

CAROL LYNN TOWNES

US, female vocalist

Date	Title	Peak	No.1	7
4 Aug 84	**99.5** *Polydor POSP 693*	47		4
19 Jan 85	**BELIEVE IN THE BEAT** *Polydor POSP 720*	56		3

FUZZ TOWNSHEND

UK, male drummer/producer (Richard Townshend)

Date	Title	Peak	No.1	1
6 Sep 97	**HELLO DARLIN'** *Echo ECSCD 46*	51		1

PETE TOWNSHEND

UK, male vocalist/guitarist. See High Numbers, Who

Date	Title	Peak	No.1	17
5 Apr 80	**ROUGH BOYS** *Atco K 11460*	39		6
21 Jun 80	**LET MY LOVE OPEN YOUR DOOR** *Atco k 11486*	46		6
21 Aug 82	**UNIFORMS (CORPS D'ESPRIT)** *Atco K 11751*	48		5

TOXIC TWO

US, male production duo

Date	Title	Peak	No.1	6
7 Mar 92	**RAVE GENERATOR** *PWL International PWL 223*	13		6

TOY-BOX

Denmark, male/female vocal duo

Date	Title	Peak	No.1	2
18 Sep 99	**BEST FRIENDS** *Edel 0058245 ERE*	41		2

TOY DOLLS

UK, male vocal/instrumental trio – Michael 'Olga' Algar, Pete 'Zulu' Robson & 'Little' Paul Smith

Date	Title	Peak	No.1	12
1 Dec 84	**NELLIE THE ELEPHANT** *Volume VOL 11*	4		12

TOYAH

UK, female vocalist (Toyah Willcox)

Date	Title	Peak	No.1	87
14 Feb 81	**FOUR FROM TOYAH EP** *Safari TOY 1* ●	4		14
16 May 81	**I WANT TO BE FREE** *Safari SAFE 34* ●	8		11
3 Oct 81	**THUNDER IN THE MOUNTAINS** *Safari SAFE 38* ●	4		9
28 Nov 81	**FOUR MORE FROM TOYAH EP** *Safari TOY 2*	14		9
22 May 82	**BRAVE NEW WORLD** *Safari SAFE 45*	21		8
17 Jul 82	**IEYA** *Safari SAFE 28*	48		5
9 Oct 82	**BE LOUD BE PROUD (BE HEARD)** *Safari SAFE 52*	30		7
24 Sep 83	**REBEL RUN** *Safari SAFE 56*	24		5
19 Nov 83	**THE VOW** *Safari SAFE 58*	50		5
27 Apr 85	**DON'T FALL IN LOVE (I SAID)** *Portrait A 6160*	22		6
29 Jun 85	**SOUL PASSING THROUGH SOUL** *Portrait A 6359*	57		3
25 Apr 87	**ECHO BEACH** *EG EGO 31*	54		5

TOYS

US, female vocal trio – Barbara Harris, June Montiero & Barbara Parritt

Date	Title	Peak	No.1	17
4 Nov 65	**A LOVER'S CONCERTO** *Stateside SS 460*	5		13
27 Jan 66	**ATTACK** *Stateside SS 483*	36		4

T'PAU

UK, female/male vocal/instrumental group – Carol Decker, Tim Burgess, Michael Chetwood, Paul Jackson, Ronnie Rogers & Taj Wyzgowski (replaced by Dean Howard)

Date	Title	Peak	No.1	77
8 Aug 87	**HEART AND SOUL** *Siren SRN 41*	4		13
24 Oct 87	**CHINA IN YOUR HAND** *Siren SRN 64* ●	1	5	15
30 Jan 88	**VALENTINE** *Siren SRN 69*	9		8
2 Apr 88	**SEX TALK (LIVE)** *Siren SRN 80*	23		7
25 Jun 88	**I WILL BE WITH YOU** *Siren SRN 87*	14		6
1 Oct 88	**SECRET GARDEN** *Siren SRN 93*	18		7
3 Dec 88	**ROAD TO OUR DREAM** *Siren SRN 100*	42		6
25 Mar 89	**ONLY THE LONELY** *Siren SRN 107*	28		6
18 May 91	**WHENEVER YOU NEED ME** *Siren SRN 140*	16		6
27 Jul 91	**WALK ON AIR** *Siren SRN 142*	62		2
20 Feb 93	**VALENTINE** *Virgin VALEG 1*	53		1

TQ

US, male rapper (Terrance Quaites)

Date	Title	Peak	No.1	35
30 Jan 99	**WESTSIDE** *Epic 6668105*	4		9
1 May 99	**BYE BYE BABY** *Epic 6672372*	7		7
21 Aug 99	**BETTER DAYS** *Epic 6677535*	32		2
4 Sep 99	**SUMMERTIME** *Northwestside 74321694672* ANOTHER LEVEL FEATURING TQ	7		7
29 Apr 00	**DAILY** *Epic 6692752*	14		5
13 Oct 01	**LET'S GET BACK TO BED...BOY** *Epic 6718662* SARAH CONNOR FEATURING TQ	16		5

TRACIE

UK, female vocalist (Tracie Young)

Date	Title	Peak	No.1	24
26 Mar 83	**THE HOUSE THAT JACK BUILT** *Respond KOB 701*	9		8
16 Jul 83	**GIVE IT SOME EMOTION** *Respond KOB 704*	24		9
14 Apr 84	**SOUL'S ON FIRE** *Respond KOB 708*	73		2
9 Jun 84	**(I LOVE YOU) WHEN YOU SLEEP** *Respond KOB 710*	59		3
17 Aug 85	**I CAN'T LEAVE YOU ALONE** *Respond SBS 1* TRACIE YOUNG	60		2

JEANIE TRACY

US, female vocalist

Date	Title	Peak	No.1	3
11 Jun 94	**IF THIS IS LOVE** *Pulse 8 CDLOSE 63*	73		1
5 Nov 94	**DO YOU BELIEVE IN THE WONDER** *Pulse 8 CDLOSE 74*	57		1
13 May 95	**IT'S A MAN'S MAN'S MAN'S WORLD** *Pulse 8 CDLOSE 89* & BOBBY WOMACK	73		1

TRAFFIC

UK, male vocal/instrumental group – Steve Winwood*, Jim Capaldi*, d. 26 Jan 2005, Dave Mason & Chris Wood, d. 12 Jul 1983

Date	Title	Peak	No.1	40
1 Jun 67	**PAPER SUN** *Island WIP 6002*	5		10
6 Sep 67	**HOLE IN MY SHOE** *Island WIP 6017*	2		14
29 Nov 67	**HERE WE GO ROUND THE MULBERRY BUSH** *Island WIP 6025*	8		12
6 Mar 68	**NO FACE, NO NAME, NO NUMBER** *Island WIP 6030*	40		4

TRAIN

US, male vocal/instrumental group – Patrick Monahan, Charlie Colin, Rob Hotchkiss, Jimmy Stafford & Scott Underwood

Date	Title	Peak	No.1	10
11 Aug 01	**DROPS OF JUPITER (TELL ME)** *Columbia 6714472*	10		8
2 Mar 02	**SHE'S ON FIRE** *Columbia 6722812*	49		2

TRAMAINE

US, female vocalist (Tramaine Hawkins)

Date	Title	Peak	No.1	2
5 Oct 85	**FALL DOWN (SPIRIT OF LOVE)** *A&M AM 281*	60		2

TRAMMPS

US, male vocal group – Ronnie Baker, Ed Cermanski, Norman Harris & Earl Young

Date	Title	Peak	No.1	55
23 Nov 74	**ZING WENT THE STRINGS OF MY HEART** *Buddah BDS 405*	29		10
1 Feb 75	**SIXTY MINUTE MAN** *Buddah BDS 415*	40		4

Silver-selling ● Gold-selling ● Platinum-selling (x multiples) ⊛ US No.1 ★ | Peak Position | Weeks at No.1 | Weeks on Chart

Date	Title	Peak Position	Weeks at No.1	Weeks on Chart
11 Oct 75	**HOLD BACK THE NIGHT** *Buddah BDS 437*	5		8
13 Mar 76	**THAT'S WHERE THE HAPPY PEOPLE GO** *Atlantic K 10703*	35		8
24 Jul 76	**SOUL SEARCHIN' TIME** *Atlantic K 10797*	42		3
14 May 77	**DISCO INFERNO** *Atlantic K 10914*	16		7
24 Jun 78	**DISCO INFERNO** *Atlantic K 11135*	47		10
12 Dec 92	**HOLD BACK THE NIGHT** *Network NWK 65* KWS FEATURES GUEST VOCAL FROM THE TRAMMPS	30		5

TRANCESETTERS

Holland, male production duo. See Tata Box Inhibitors — 2

Date	Title	Peak Position	Weeks at No.1	Weeks on Chart
4 Mar 00	**ROACHES** *Hooj Choons HOOJ 89CD*	55		1
9 Jun 01	**SYNERGY** *Hooj Choons HOOJ 107CD*	72		1

TRANS-X

Canada, male/female vocal/instrumental duo – Pascal Languirand & Laurie Gill — 9

Date	Title	Peak Position	Weeks at No.1	Weeks on Chart
13 Jul 85	**LIVING ON VIDEO** *Boiling Point POSP 650*	9		9

TRANSA

UK, male DJ/production duo — 2

Date	Title	Peak Position	Weeks at No.1	Weeks on Chart
30 Aug 97	**PROPHASE** *Perfecto PERF 147CD*	65		1
21 Feb 98	**ENERVATE** *Perfecto PERF 155CD*	42		1

TRANSATLANTIC SOUL

US, male DJ/producer (Roger Sanchez). See El Mariachi, Funk Junkeez — 1

Date	Title	Peak Position	Weeks at No.1	Weeks on Chart
22 Mar 97	**RELEASE YO SELF** *Deconstruction 74321459102*	43		1

TRANSFER

UK, male/female vocal/production trio — 1

Date	Title	Peak Position	Weeks at No.1	Weeks on Chart
3 Nov 01	**POSSESSION** *Multiply CDMULTY 76*	54		1

TRANSFORMER 2

Belgium/Holland, male/female vocal/instrumental group — 1

Date	Title	Peak Position	Weeks at No.1	Weeks on Chart
24 Feb 96	**JUST CAN'T GET ENOUGH** *Positiva CDTIV 49*	45		1

TRANSISTER

UK/US, male/female vocal/instrumental group — 1

Date	Title	Peak Position	Weeks at No.1	Weeks on Chart
28 Mar 98	**LOOK WHO'S PERFECT NOW** *Virgin VSCDT 1678*	56		1

TRANSPLANTS

US, male vocal/instrumental group — 4

Date	Title	Peak Position	Weeks at No.1	Weeks on Chart
19 Apr 03	**DIAMONDS AND GUNS** *Hellcat 11082*	27		2
19 Jul 03	**DJ DJ** *Hellcat 11122*	49		1
17 Sep 05	**GANGSTERS AND THUGS** *Atlantic AT0213CD*	35		1

TRANSVISION VAMP

UK, female/male vocal/instrumental group – Wendy James*, Tex Axile (Anthony Doughty), Pol Burton (left 1989), Dave Parsons & Nick Christian Sayer — 59

Date	Title	Peak Position	Weeks at No.1	Weeks on Chart
16 Apr 88	**TELL THAT GIRL TO SHUT UP** *MCA TVV 2*	45		3
25 Jun 88	**I WANT YOUR LOVE** *MCA TVV 3*	5		13
17 Sep 88	**REVOLUTION BABY** *MCA TVV 4*	30		5
19 Nov 88	**SISTER MOON** *MCA TVV 5*	41		5
1 Apr 89	**BABY I DON'T CARE** *MCA TVV 6*	3		11
10 Jun 89	**THE ONLY ONE** *MCA TVV 7*	15		6
5 Aug 89	**LANDSLIDE OF LOVE** *MCA TVV 8*	14		5
4 Nov 89	**BORN TO BE SOLD** *MCA TVV 9*	22		4
13 Apr 91	**(I JUST WANNA) B WITH U** *MCA TVV 10*	30		4
22 Jun 91	**IF LOOKS COULD KILL** *MCA TVV 11*	41		3

TRASH

UK, male vocal/instrumental group — 3

Date	Title	Peak Position	Weeks at No.1	Weeks on Chart
25 Oct 69	**GOLDEN SLUMBERS/CARRY THAT WEIGHT** *Apple 17*	35		3

TRASHMEN

US, male vocal/instrumental group — 1

Date	Title	Peak Position	Weeks at No.1	Weeks on Chart
2 May 09	**SURFIN BIRD** *Charly GBAJC9902168*	50		1

TRASH CAN SINATRAS

UK, male vocal/instrumental group — 1

Date	Title	Peak Position	Weeks at No.1	Weeks on Chart
24 Apr 93	**HAYFEVER** *Go! Discs GODCD 98*	61		1

TRAVEL

France, male producer (Laurent Gutbier) — 2

Date	Title	Peak Position	Weeks at No.1	Weeks on Chart
24 Apr 99	**BULGARIAN** *Tidy Trax TIDY 121CD*	67		2

TRAVELING WILBURYS

US/UK, male vocal/instrumental group – Bob Dylan*, George Harrison*, d. 29 Nov 2001, Jeff Lynne*, Roy Orbison*, d. 6 Dec 1988, & Tom Petty* — 19

Date	Title	Peak Position	Weeks at No.1	Weeks on Chart
29 Oct 88	**HANDLE WITH CARE** *Wilbury W 7732*	21		13
11 Mar 89	**END OF THE LINE** *Wilbury W 7637*	52		4
30 Jun 90	**NOBODY'S CHILD** *Wilbury W 9773*	44		2

TRAVIS

UK, male vocal/instrumental group – Fran Healy, Andrew Dunlop, Douglas Payne & Neil Primrose — 101

Date	Title	Peak Position	Weeks at No.1	Weeks on Chart
12 Apr 97	**U16 GIRLS** *Independiente ISOM 1MS*	40		2
28 Jun 97	**ALL I WANT TO DO IS ROCK** *Independiente ISOM 3MS*	39		2
23 Aug 97	**TIED TO THE 90'S** *Independiente ISOM 5MS*	30		2
25 Oct 97	**HAPPY** *Independiente ISOM 6SMS*	38		2
11 Apr 98	**MORE THAN US EP** *Independiente ISOM 11MS*	16		3
20 Mar 99	**WRITING TO REACH YOU** *Independiente ISOM 22MS*	14		5
29 May 99	**DRIFTWOOD** *Independiente ISOM 27SMS*	13		5
14 Aug 99	**WHY DOES IT ALWAYS RAIN ON ME** *Independiente ISOM 33MS*	10		8
20 Nov 99	**TURN** *Independiente ISOM 39SMS*	8		11
17 Jun 00	**COMING AROUND** *Independiente ISOM 45SMS*	5		10
9 Jun 01	**SING** *Independiente ISOM 49SMS*	3		14
29 Sep 01	**SIDE** *Independiente ISOM 54SMS*	14		8
6 Apr 02	**FLOWERS IN THE WINDOW** *Independiente ISOM 56SMS*	18		7
11 Oct 03	**RE-OFFENDER** *Independiente ISOM 78SMS*	7		4
27 Dec 03	**THE BEAUTIFUL OCCUPATION** *Independiente ISOM 81SMS*	48		3
3 Apr 04	**LOVE WILL COME THROUGH** *Independiente ISOM 84MS*	28		3
30 Oct 04	**WALKING IN THE SUN** *Independiente ISOM 88SMS*	20		3
28 Apr 07	**CLOSER** *Independiente ISOM118MS*	10		6
21 Jul 07	**SELFISH JEAN** *Independiente ISOM123MS*	30		2
29 Sep 07	**MY EYES** *Independiente ISOM124MS*	60		1

RANDY TRAVIS

US, male vocalist/guitarist (Randy Traywick) — 6

Date	Title	Peak Position	Weeks at No.1	Weeks on Chart
21 May 88	**FOREVER AND EVER, AMEN** *Warner Brothers W 8384*	55		6

JOHN TRAVOLTA

US, male actor/vocalist — 90

Date	Title	Peak Position	Weeks at No.1	Weeks on Chart
20 May 78	**YOU'RE THE ONE THAT I WANT** *RSO 006* & OLIVIA NEWTON-JOHN ⊛ ★	1	9	26
16 Sep 78	**SUMMER NIGHTS** *RSO 18* & OLIVIA NEWTON-JOHN ⊛	1	7	19
7 Oct 78	**SANDY** *Polydor POSP 6* ●	2		15
2 Dec 78	**GREASED LIGHTNIN'** *Polydor POSP 14* ●	11		9
22 Dec 90	**GREASE MEGAMIX** *Polydor PO 114* & OLIVIA NEWTON-JOHN	3		10
23 Mar 91	**GREASE – THE DREAM MIX** *PWL/Polydor PO 136* FRANKIE VALLI, JOHN TRAVOLTA & OLIVIA NEWTON-JOHN	47		2
25 Jul 98	**YOU'RE THE ONE THAT I WANT** *Polydor 0441332* & OLIVIA NEWTON-JOHN	4		9

TREMELOES

UK, male vocal/instrumental group – Brian Poole (left 1966), Len Hawkes, Alan Blakely, d. 10 Jun 1996, Dave Munden & Ricky West. The band who were famously signed by Decca on the day the label rejected the Beatles. After a string of hits backing Poole, they amassed an even longer chart tally in their own right — 222

Date	Title	Peak Position	Weeks at No.1	Weeks on Chart
4 Jul 63	**TWIST AND SHOUT** *Decca F 11694* BRIAN POOLE & THE TREMELOES	4		14
12 Sep 63	**DO YOU LOVE ME** *Decca F 11739* BRIAN POOLE & THE TREMELOES	1	3	14
28 Nov 63	**I CAN DANCE** *Decca F 11771* BRIAN POOLE & THE TREMELOES	31		8
30 Jan 64	**CANDY MAN** *Decca F 11823* BRIAN POOLE & THE TREMELOES	6		13
7 May 64	**SOMEONE SOMEONE** *Decca F 11893* BRIAN POOLE & THE TREMELOES	2		17
20 Aug 64	**TWELVE STEPS TO LOVE** *Decca F 11951* BRIAN POOLE & THE TREMELOES	32		7
31 Dec 64	**THREE BELLS** *Decca F 12037* BRIAN POOLE & THE TREMELOES	17		10
22 Jul 65	**I WANT CANDY** *Decca F 12197* BRIAN POOLE & THE TREMELOES	25		8
2 Feb 67	**HERE COMES MY BABY** *CBS 202519*	4		11
27 Apr 67	**SILENCE IS GOLDEN** *CBS 2723*	1	3	15

Date	Title	Peak Position	Weeks at No.1	Weeks on Chart
2 Aug 67	**EVEN THE BAD TIMES ARE GOOD** *CBS 2930*	4		13
8 Nov 67	**BE MINE** *CBS 3043*	39		2
17 Jan 68	**SUDDENLY YOU LOVE ME** *CBS 3234*	6		11
8 May 68	**HELULE HELULE** *CBS 2889*	14		9
18 Sep 68	**MY LITTLE LADY** *CBS 3680*	6		12
11 Dec 68	**I SHALL BE RELEASED** *CBS 3873*	29		5
19 Mar 69	**HELLO WORLD** *CBS 4065*	14		8
1 Nov 69	**(CALL ME) NUMBER ONE** *CBS 4582*	2		14
21 Mar 70	**BY THE WAY** *CBS 4815*	35		6
12 Sep 70	**ME AND MY LIFE** *CBS 5139*	4		18
10 Jul 71	**HELLO BUDDY** *CBS 7294*	32		7

JACKIE TRENT

UK, female vocalist (Yvonne Burgess) — 17

Date	Title	Peak Position	Weeks at No.1	Weeks on Chart
22 Apr 65	**WHERE ARE YOU NOW (MY LOVE)** *Pye 7N 15776*	1	1	11
1 Jul 65	**WHEN THE SUMMERTIME IS OVER** *Pye 7N 15865*	39		2
2 Apr 69	**I'LL BE THERE** *Pye 7N 17693*	38		4

RALPH TRESVANT

US, male vocalist. See New Edition — 28

Date	Title	Peak Position	Weeks at No.1	Weeks on Chart
12 Jan 91	**SENSITIVITY** *MCA MCS 1462*	18		8
15 Aug 92	**THE BEST THINGS IN LIFE ARE FREE** *Perspective PERSS 7400* LUTHER VANDROSS & JANET JACKSON WITH SPECIAL GUESTS BBD & RALPH TRESVANT ●	2		13
16 Dec 95	**THE BEST THINGS IN LIFE ARE FREE (REMIX)** *A&M 5813092* LUTHER VANDROSS & JANET JACKSON WITH SPECIAL GUESTS BBD & RALPH TRESVANT	7		7

TREVOR & SIMON

UK, male production duo — 5

Date	Title	Peak Position	Weeks at No.1	Weeks on Chart
10 Jun 00	**HANDS UP** *Substance SUBS 1CDS*	12		5

TRI

UK, male vocal/instrumental group — 1

Date	Title	Peak Position	Weeks at No.1	Weeks on Chart
2 Sep 95	**WE GOT THE LOVE** *Epic 6623642*	61		1

TRIBAL HOUSE

US, male producer (Winston Jones) — 2

Date	Title	Peak Position	Weeks at No.1	Weeks on Chart
3 Feb 90	**MOTHERLAND-A-FRI-CA** *Cooltempo COOL 198*	57		2

TONY TRIBE

Jamaica, male vocalist — 2

Date	Title	Peak Position	Weeks at No.1	Weeks on Chart
16 Jul 69	**RED RED WINE** *Downtown DT 419*	46		2

A TRIBE CALLED QUEST

US, male rap/DJ trio — 18

Date	Title	Peak Position	Weeks at No.1	Weeks on Chart
18 Aug 90	**BONITA APPLEBUM** *Jive 256*	47		3
19 Jan 91	**CAN I KICK IT** *Jive 265*	15		7
11 Jun 94	**OH MY GOD** *Jive JIVECD 355*	68		1
13 Jul 96	**1NCE AGAIN** *Jive JIVECD 399*	34		2
23 Nov 96	**STRESSED OUT** *Jive JIVECD 404* FEATURING FAITH EVANS & RAPHAEL SAADIQ	33		2
23 Aug 97	**THE JAM EP** *Jive JIVECD 427*	61		1
29 Aug 98	**FIND A WAY** *Jive 0518982*	41		2

A TRIBE OF TOFFS

UK, male vocal/instrumental group — 5

Date	Title	Peak Position	Weeks at No.1	Weeks on Chart
24 Dec 88	**JOHN KETLEY (IS A WEATHERMAN)** *Completely Different DAFT 1*	21		5

OBIE TRICE

US, male rapper — 16

Date	Title	Peak Position	Weeks at No.1	Weeks on Chart
1 Nov 03	**GOT SOME TEETH** *Interscope 9813061*	8		11
14 Feb 04	**THE SET UP (YOU DON'T KNOW)** *Interscope 9815333* FEATURING NATE DOGG	32		3
16 Sep 06	**SNITCH** *Interscope 1705438* FEATURING AKON	44		2

TRICK DADDY

US, male rapper (Maurice Young) — 3

Date	Title	Peak Position	Weeks at No.1	Weeks on Chart
26 Feb 05	**LET'S GO** *Atlantic AT0193CD* FEATURING TWISTA & LIL' JON	26		2
28 May 05	**SUGAR (GIMME SOME)** *Atlantic AT0202CDX*	61		1

TRICKBABY

UK, female vocal/instrumental group — 2

Date	Title	Peak Position	Weeks at No.1	Weeks on Chart
12 Oct 96	**INDIE-YARN** *Logic 74321423152*	47		2

TRICKSTER

UK, male producer (Liam Sullivan) — 3

Date	Title	Peak Position	Weeks at No.1	Weeks on Chart
4 Apr 98	**MOVE ON UP** *AM:PM 5825812*	19		3

TRICKY

UK, male vocalist/rapper/producer (Adrian Thaws). See Nearly God, Starving Souls — 29

Date	Title	Peak Position	Weeks at No.1	Weeks on Chart
5 Feb 94	**AFTERMATH** *Fourth & Broadway BRCD 288*	69		1
28 Jan 95	**OVERCOME** *Fourth & Broadway BRCD 304*	34		3
15 Apr 95	**BLACK STEEL** *Fourth & Broadway BRCDX 320*	28		3
5 Aug 95	**THE HELL EP** *Fourth & Broadway BRCD 326* VS THE GRAVEDIGGAZ	12		3
11 Nov 95	**PUMPKIN** *Fourth & Broadway BRCD 330*	26		2
9 Nov 96	**CHRISTIANSANDS** *Fourth & Broadway BRCD 340*	36		2
23 Nov 96	**MILK** *Mushroom D 1494* GARBAGE FEATURING TRICKY	10		8
11 Jan 97	**TRICKY KID** *Fourth & Broadway BRCD 341*	28		2
3 May 97	**MAKES ME WANNA DIE** *Fourth & Broadway BRCD 348*	29		2
30 May 98	**MONEY GREED/BROKEN HOMES** *Island CID 701*	25		2
21 Aug 99	**FOR REAL** *Island CID 753*	45		1

TRICKY DISCO

UK, male/female production duo — 10

Date	Title	Peak Position	Weeks at No.1	Weeks on Chart
28 Jul 90	**TRICKY DISCO** *Warp WAP 7*	14		8
20 Apr 91	**HOUSE FLY** *Warp 7WAP 11*	55		2

TRIFFIDS

Australia, male vocal/instrumental group — 1

Date	Title	Peak Position	Weeks at No.1	Weeks on Chart
6 Feb 88	**A TRICK OF THE LIGHT** *Island IS 350*	73		1

TRINA & TAMARA

US, female vocal duo — 3

Date	Title	Peak Position	Weeks at No.1	Weeks on Chart
7 Feb 98	**MY LOVE IS THE SHHH!** *Warner Brothers W 0427CD* SOMETHIN' FOR THE PEOPLE FEATURING TRINA & TAMARA	64		1
12 Jun 99	**WHAT'D YOU COME HERE FOR?** *Columbia 6673382*	46		2

TRINA

US, female vocalist (Katrina Taylor) — 9

Date	Title	Peak Position	Weeks at No.1	Weeks on Chart
19 Oct 02	**NO PANTIES** *Atlantic AT 0141CD*	45		1
15 Apr 06	**HERE WE GO** *Atlantic AT0238CD* FEATURING KELLY ROWLAND	15		8

TRINIDAD & TOBAGO TARTAN ARMY

Trinidad & Tobago, football fans/vocal/instrumental group — 2

Date	Title	Peak Position	Weeks at No.1	Weeks on Chart
17 Jun 06	**SCOTLAND SCOTLAND JASON SCOTLAND** *1745 Trading QUEST001*	30		2

TRINIDAD OIL COMPANY

Trinidad & Tobago, male vocal/instrumental group — 5

Date	Title	Peak Position	Weeks at No.1	Weeks on Chart
21 May 77	**THE CALENDAR SONG (JANUARY, FEBRUARY, MARCH, APRIL, MAY)** *Harvest HAR 5122*	34		5

TRINITY-X

UK, male/female vocal/production trio — 3

Date	Title	Peak Position	Weeks at No.1	Weeks on Chart
19 Oct 02	**FOREVER** *All Around The World CXGLOBE 255*	19		3

TRIO

Germany, male vocal/instrumental trio – Stephan Remmler, Peter Behrens & Gert 'Kralle' Krawinkel — 10

Date	Title	Peak Position	Weeks at No.1	Weeks on Chart
3 Jul 82	**DA DA DA** *Mobile Suit Corporation CORP 5* ●	2		10

TRIPLE EIGHT

UK, male vocal group – Josh Barnett, Jamie Bell, Ian 'Sparx' Farquharson (left 2004), Stewart Macintosh (joined 2005), Justin 'Mysterio' Scott & David Wilcox (left 2004) **10**

Date	Title	Peak Position	Weeks at No.1	Weeks on Chart
3 May 03	**KNOCK OUT** *Polydor 9800048*	8		4
2 Aug 03	**GIVE ME A REASON** *Polydor 9809137*	9		5
11 Jun 05	**GOOD 2 GO** *Osmosis OSMU88802*	42		1

TRIPLE X

Italy, male production duo. See Plaything **2**

Date	Title	Peak Position	Weeks at No.1	Weeks on Chart
30 Oct 99	**FEEL THE SAME** *Ministry Of Sound MOSCDS 135*	32		2

TRIPPING DAISY

US, male vocal/instrumental group **1**

Date	Title	Peak Position	Weeks at No.1	Weeks on Chart
30 Mar 96	**PIRANHA** *Island CID 638*	72		1

TRISCO

UK, male production duo **2**

Date	Title	Peak Position	Weeks at No.1	Weeks on Chart
30 Jun 01	**MUSAK** *Positiva CDTIV 155*	28		2

TRIUMPH

Canada, male vocal/instrumental trio **2**

Date	Title	Peak Position	Weeks at No.1	Weeks on Chart
22 Nov 80	**I LIVE FOR THE WEEKEND** *RCA 13*	59		2

TRIVIUM

US, male vocal/instrumental group **2**

Date	Title	Peak Position	Weeks at No.1	Weeks on Chart
14 Oct 06	**ANTHEM (WE ARE THE FIRE)** *Roadrunner RR39293*	40		2

TROGGS

UK, male vocal/instrumental group – Reg Presley, Ronnie Bond, d. 13 Nov 1992, Chris Britton & Pete Staples **87**

Date	Title	Peak Position	Weeks at No.1	Weeks on Chart
5 May 66	**WILD THING** *Fontana TF 689* ★	2		12
14 Jul 66	**WITH A GIRL LIKE YOU** *Fontana TF 717*	1	2	12
29 Sep 66	**I CAN'T CONTROL MYSELF** *Page One POF 001*	2		14
15 Dec 66	**ANY WAY YOU WANT ME** *Page One POF 010*	8		10
16 Feb 67	**GIVE IT TO ME** *Page One POF 015*	12		10
1 Jun 67	**NIGHT OF THE LONG GRASS** *Page One POF 022*	17		6
26 Jul 67	**HI HI HAZEL** *Page One POF 030*	42		3
18 Oct 67	**LOVE IS ALL AROUND** *Page One POF 040*	5		14
28 Feb 68	**LITTLE GIRL** *Page One POF 056*	37		4
30 Oct 93	**WILD THING** *Weekend CDWEEK 103* & WOLF	69		2

TRONIKHOUSE

US, male producer (Kevin Saunderson). See Inner City, Reese Project **1**

Date	Title	Peak Position	Weeks at No.1	Weeks on Chart
14 Mar 92	**UP TEMPO** *KMS UK KMSUK 1*	68		1

TROPHY BOYZ

UK, male vocal group **1**

Date	Title	Peak Position	Weeks at No.1	Weeks on Chart
6 Aug 05	**DU THE DUDEK** *Diablo DIACD010*	49		1

TROUBADOURS DU ROI BAUDOUIN

Zaire, male/female vocal group **11**

Date	Title	Peak Position	Weeks at No.1	Weeks on Chart
19 Mar 69	**SANCTUS (MISSA LUBA)** *Philips BF 1732*	28		11

TROUBLE FUNK

US, male vocal/instrumental group **3**

Date	Title	Peak Position	Weeks at No.1	Weeks on Chart
27 Jun 87	**WOMAN OF PRINCIPLE** *Fourth & Broadway BRW 70*	65		3

TROY

US, male actor/vocalist (Zac Efron) **3**

Date	Title	Peak Position	Weeks at No.1	Weeks on Chart
6 Oct 07	**GOTTA GO MY OWN WAY** *Walt Disney USWD10732098* GABRIELLA & TROY	40		2
6 Oct 07	**BET ON IT** *Walt Disney USWD10732099*	65		1

DORIS TROY

US, female vocalist (Dorris Higginson), d. 16 Feb 2004 (age 67) **12**

Date	Title	Peak Position	Weeks at No.1	Weeks on Chart
19 Nov 64	**WHATCHA GONNA DO ABOUT IT** *Atlantic AT 4011*	37		12

TRU FAITH & DUB CONSPIRACY

UK, male production group **5**

Date	Title	Peak Position	Weeks at No.1	Weeks on Chart
9 Sep 00	**FREAK LIKE ME** *Public Demand CDTIV 138*	12		5

TRUBBLE

UK, male/female vocal/production trio **5**

Date	Title	Peak Position	Weeks at No.1	Weeks on Chart
26 Dec 98	**DANCING BABY (OOGA-CHAKA)** *Island YYCD 1*	21		5

TRUCE

UK, female vocal group **6**

Date	Title	Peak Position	Weeks at No.1	Weeks on Chart
2 Sep 95	**THE FINEST** *Big Life BLRD 118*	54		1
30 Mar 96	**CELEBRATION OF LIFE** *Big Life BLRD 126*	51		1
29 Nov 97	**NOTHIN' BUT A PARTY** *Big Life BLRD 138*	71		1
5 Sep 98	**EYES DON'T LIE** *Big Life BLRD 146*	20		3

TRUCKS

UK/Norway, male vocal/instrumental group **2**

Date	Title	Peak Position	Weeks at No.1	Weeks on Chart
5 Oct 02	**IT'S JUST PORN MUM** *Gut CDGUT 43*	35		2

ANDREA TRUE CONNECTION

US, female vocalist & male instrumental session group **16**

Date	Title	Peak Position	Weeks at No.1	Weeks on Chart
17 Apr 76	**MORE MORE MORE** *Buddah BDS 442*	5		10
4 Mar 78	**WHAT'S YOUR NAME WHAT'S YOUR NUMBER** *Buddah BDS 467*	34		6

TRUE FAITH & BRIDGETTE GRACE WITH FINAL CUT

US, male/female production/vocal group **4**

Date	Title	Peak Position	Weeks at No.1	Weeks on Chart
2 Mar 91	**TAKE ME AWAY** *Network NWK 20*	51		4

TRUE PARTY

UK, male vocal/production group **6**

Date	Title	Peak Position	Weeks at No.1	Weeks on Chart
2 Dec 00	**WHAZZUP** *Positiva CDBUD 001*	13		6

TRUE STEPPERS

UK, male production/instrumental duo – Jonny Linders & Andy Lysandrou. See Jonny L **31**

Date	Title	Peak Position	Weeks at No.1	Weeks on Chart
29 Apr 00	**BUGGIN'** *NuLife 74321753342* FEATURING DANE BOWERS	6		8
26 Aug 00	**OUT OF YOUR MIND** *NuLife 74321782942* & DANE BOWERS FEATURING VICTORIA BECKHAM ●	2		20
2 Dec 00	**TRUE STEP TONIGHT** *NuLife 74321811312* FEATURING BRIAN HARVEY & DONELL JONES	25		3

TRUMAN & WOLFF FEATURING STEEL HORSES

UK, male rap/production group **1**

Date	Title	Peak Position	Weeks at No.1	Weeks on Chart
22 Aug 98	**COME AGAIN** *Multiply CDMULTY 38*	57		1

JONNY TRUNK & WISBEY

US, male record label owner & actor/impressionist **3**

Date	Title	Peak Position	Weeks at No.1	Weeks on Chart
1 Sep 07	**THE LADIES' BRAS** *Trunk GBKTV0700001*	27		3

TRUSSEL

US, male vocal/instrumental group **4**

Date	Title	Peak Position	Weeks at No.1	Weeks on Chart
8 Mar 80	**LOVE INJECTION** *Elektra K 12412*	43		4

TRUTH

UK, male vocal/instrumental duo **6**

Date	Title	Peak Position	Weeks at No.1	Weeks on Chart
3 Feb 66	**GIRL** *Pye 7N 17035*	27		6

TRUTH
UK, male vocal/instrumental group — Weeks on chart: 16

Date	Title / Label	Peak Position	Weeks at No.1	Weeks on Chart
11 Jun 83	**CONFUSION (HITS US EVERY TIME)** *Formation TRUTH 1*	22		7
27 Aug 83	**A STEP IN THE RIGHT DIRECTION** *Formation TRUTH 2*	32		7
4 Feb 84	**NO STONE UNTURNED** *Formation TRUTH 3*	66		2

TRUTH HURTS FEATURING RAKIM
US, female vocal/rap duo – Shari Watson & William Griffin, Jr — Weeks on chart: 12

Date	Title / Label	Peak Position	Weeks at No.1	Weeks on Chart
31 Aug 02	**ADDICTIVE** *Interscope 4977782*	3		12

TSD
UK, female vocal group — Weeks on chart: 2

Date	Title / Label	Peak Position	Weeks at No.1	Weeks on Chart
17 Feb 96	**HEART AND SOUL** *Avex UK AVEXCD 21*	69		1
30 Mar 96	**BABY I LOVE YOU** *Avex UK AVEXCD 34*	64		1

TUBBY T
UK, male vocalist (Anthony Robinson) — Weeks on chart: 3

Date	Title / Label	Peak Position	Weeks at No.1	Weeks on Chart
21 Sep 02	**TALES OF THE HOOD** *Go! Beat GOBCD 51*	47		1
24 May 03	**BIG N BASHY** *Virgin VSCDT 1847* FALLACY FEATURING TUBBY T	45		2

TUBE & BERGER FEATURING CHRISSIE HYNDE
Germany/US, male/female vocal/instrumental/production trio. See Pretenders — Weeks on chart: 3

Date	Title / Label	Peak Position	Weeks at No.1	Weeks on Chart
7 Feb 04	**STRAIGHT AHEAD** *Direction 6746222*	29		3

TUBES
US, male vocal/instrumental group — Weeks on chart: 18

Date	Title / Label	Peak Position	Weeks at No.1	Weeks on Chart
19 Nov 77	**WHITE PUNKS ON DOPE** *A&M AMS 7323*	28		4
28 Apr 79	**PRIME TIME** *A&M AMS 7423*	34		10
12 Sep 81	**DON'T WANT TO WAIT ANYMORE** *Capitol CL 208*	60		4

BARBARA TUCKER
US, female vocalist — Weeks on chart: 19

Date	Title / Label	Peak Position	Weeks at No.1	Weeks on Chart
5 Mar 94	**BEAUTIFUL PEOPLE** *Positiva CDTIV 11*	23		3
26 Nov 94	**I GET LIFTED** *Positiva CDTIV 23*	33		2
23 Sep 95	**STAY TOGETHER** *Positiva CDTIV 39*	46		1
8 Aug 98	**EVERYBODY DANCE (THE HORN SONG)** *Positiva CDTIV 96*	28		2
18 Mar 00	**STOP PLAYING WITH MY MIND** *Positiva CDTIV 127* FEATURING DARYL D'BONNEAU	17		4
14 May 05	**MOST PRECIOUS LOVE** *Defected DFTD100CDS* BLAZE PRESENTS UDA FEATURING BARBARA TUCKER	44		3
29 Apr 06	**MOST PRECIOUS LOVE** *Defected DFTD125CDX* BLAZE FEATURING BARBARA TUCKER	17		4

JUNIOR TUCKER
Jamaica, male vocalist — Weeks on chart: 2

Date	Title / Label	Peak Position	Weeks at No.1	Weeks on Chart
2 Jun 90	**DON'T TEST** *10 TEN 299*	54		2

LOUISE TUCKER
UK, female vocalist — Weeks on chart: 5

Date	Title / Label	Peak Position	Weeks at No.1	Weeks on Chart
9 Apr 83	**MIDNIGHT BLUE** *Ariola ARO 289*	59		5

TOMMY TUCKER
US, male vocalist (Robert Higginbotham), d. 22 Jan 1982 (age 42) — Weeks on chart: 10

Date	Title / Label	Peak Position	Weeks at No.1	Weeks on Chart
26 Mar 64	**HI-HEEL SNEAKERS** *Pye 7N 25238*	23		10

TUFF JAM
UK, male production duo — Weeks on chart: 1

Date	Title / Label	Peak Position	Weeks at No.1	Weeks on Chart
10 Oct 98	**NEED GOOD LOVE** *Locked On LOX 99CD*	44		1

TUKAN
Denmark, male production duo — Weeks on chart: 3

Date	Title / Label	Peak Position	Weeks at No.1	Weeks on Chart
15 Dec 01	**LIGHT A RAINBOW** *Incentive CENT 33CDS*	38		3

KT TUNSTALL
UK, female vocalist/guitarist (Kate Tunstall) — Weeks on chart: 63

Date	Title / Label	Peak Position	Weeks at No.1	Weeks on Chart
5 Mar 05	**BLACK HORSE AND THE CHERRY TREE** *Relentless RELCD14*	28		3
21 May 05	**OTHER SIDE OF THE WORLD** *Relentless RELCD18*	13		19
10 Sep 05	**SUDDENLY I SEE** *Relentless RELCD21*	12		25
17 Dec 05	**UNDER THE WEATHER** *Relentless RELCD23*	39		2
25 Mar 06	**ANOTHER PLACE TO FALL** *Relentless RELCD24*	52		2
25 Aug 07	**HOLD ON** *Relentless RELCD40*	21		8
1 Dec 07	**SAVING MY FACE** *Relentless RELCD46*	50		2
15 Mar 08	**IF ONLY** *Relentless RELCD48*	45		2

TURIN BRAKES
UK, male vocal/instrumental duo – Olly Knights & Gale 'Magpie' Paridjanian — Weeks on chart: 18

Date	Title / Label	Peak Position	Weeks at No.1	Weeks on Chart
3 Mar 01	**THE DOOR** *Source SOURCDS 024*	67		1
12 May 01	**UNDERDOG (SAVE ME)** *Source SOURCDSE 1015*	39		2
11 Aug 01	**MIND OVER MONEY** *Source SOURCD 038*	31		2
27 Oct 01	**EMERGENCY 72** *Source SOURCD 041*	41		1
2 Nov 02	**LONG DISTANCE** *Source SOURCDX 064*	22		2
1 Mar 03	**PAIN KILLER** *Source SOURCD 068*	5		3
7 Jun 03	**AVERAGE MAN** *Source SOURCD 085*	35		2
11 Oct 03	**5 MILE (THESE ARE THE DAYS)** *Source SOURCD 089*	31		2
28 May 05	**FISHING FOR A DREAM** *Source SOURCDX109*	32		2
13 Aug 05	**OVER AND OVER** *Source SOURCDX114*	62		1

FRANK TURNER
UK, male vocalist/guitarist — Weeks on chart: 2

Date	Title / Label	Peak Position	Weeks at No.1	Weeks on Chart
1 Nov 08	**LONG LIVE THE QUEEN** *Xtra Mile GBHAH0800024*	65		1
12 Sep 09	**THE ROAD** *Xtra Mile GBM830900030*	62		1

IKE & TINA TURNER
US, male/female vocal/instrumental duo – Ike Turner, d. 12 Dec 2007 — Weeks on chart: 44

Date	Title / Label	Peak Position	Weeks at No.1	Weeks on Chart
9 Jun 66	**RIVER DEEP MOUNTAIN HIGH** *London HL 10046*	3		13
28 Jul 66	**TELL HER I'M NOT HOME** *Warner Brothers WB 5753*	48		1
27 Oct 66	**A LOVE LIKE YOURS** *London HL 10083*	16		10
12 Feb 69	**RIVER DEEP MOUNTAIN HIGH** *London HLU 10242*	33		7
8 Sep 73	**NUTBUSH CITY LIMITS** *United Artists UP 35582*	4		13

RUBY TURNER
UK (b. Jamaica), female vocalist — Weeks on chart: 31

Date	Title / Label	Peak Position	Weeks at No.1	Weeks on Chart
25 Jan 86	**IF YOU'RE READY (COME GO WITH ME)** *Jive 109* FEATURING JONATHAN BUTLER	30		7
29 Mar 86	**I'M IN LOVE** *Jive 118*	61		4
13 Sep 86	**BYE BABY** *Jive 126*	52		3
14 Mar 87	**I'D RATHER GO BLIND** *Jive RTS 1*	24		8
16 May 87	**I'M IN LOVE** *Jive RTS 2*	57		2
13 Jan 90	**IT'S GONNA BE ALRIGHT** *Jive RTS 7*	57		3
5 Feb 94	**STAY WITH ME BABY** *M&G MAGCD 53*	39		3
9 Dec 95	**SHAKABOOM!** *Telstar HUNTCD 1* HUNTER FEATURING RUBY TURNER	64		1

SAMMY TURNER
US, male vocalist (Samuel Black) — Weeks on chart: 2

Date	Title / Label	Peak Position	Weeks at No.1	Weeks on Chart
13 Nov 59	**ALWAYS** *London HLX 8963*	26		2

TINA TURNER
US, female vocalist (Anna Mae Bullock). The veteran Nutbush native went from soul superstar to rock royalty. She has a US/UK chart span of 49 years and her *Private Dancer* album sold over 15 million copies worldwide. The perennially popular live performer took home four Grammys in 1985. See Ike & Tina Turner — Weeks on chart: 227

Date	Title / Label	Peak Position	Weeks at No.1	Weeks on Chart
19 Nov 83	**LET'S STAY TOGETHER** *Capitol CL 316* ●	6		13
25 Feb 84	**HELP** *Capitol CL 325*	40		6
16 Jun 84	**WHAT'S LOVE GOT TO DO WITH IT** *Capitol CL 334* ● ★	3		16
15 Sep 84	**BETTER BE GOOD TO ME** *Capitol CL 338*	45		5
17 Nov 84	**PRIVATE DANCER** *Capitol CL 343*	26		9
2 Mar 85	**I CAN'T STAND THE RAIN** *Capitol CL 352*	57		3
20 Jul 85	**WE DON'T NEED ANOTHER HERO (THUNDERDOME)** *Capitol CL 364* ●	3		12
12 Oct 85	**ONE OF THE LIVING** *Capitol CL 376*	55		2
2 Nov 85	**IT'S ONLY LOVE** *A&M AM 285* BRYAN ADAMS & TINA TURNER	29		6
23 Aug 86	**TYPICAL MALE** *Capitol CL 419*	33		6
8 Nov 86	**TWO PEOPLE** *Capitol CL 430*	43		4
14 Mar 87	**WHAT YOU GET IS WHAT YOU SEE** *Capitol CL 439*	30		7
13 Jun 87	**BREAK EVERY RULE** *Capitol CL 452*	43		3
20 Jun 87	**TEARING US APART** *Duck W 8299* ERIC CLAPTON & TINA TURNER	56		3

Key: Silver-selling ○ · Gold-selling ● · Platinum-selling (x multiples) ⊛ · US No.1 ★ · Peak Position · Weeks at No.1 · Weeks on Chart

Date	Title / Label	Peak Position	Weeks at No.1	Weeks on Chart
19 Mar 88	**ADDICTED TO LOVE (LIVE)** *Capitol CL 484*	71		2
2 Sep 89	**THE BEST** *Capitol CL 543* ○	5		12
18 Nov 89	**I DON'T WANNA LOSE YOU** *Capitol CL 553*	8		11
17 Feb 90	**STEAMY WINDOWS** *Capitol CL 560*	13		6
11 Aug 90	**LOOK ME IN THE HEART** *Capitol CL 584*	31		6
13 Oct 90	**BE TENDER WITH ME BABY** *Capitol CL 593*	28		4
24 Nov 90	**IT TAKES TWO** *Warner Brothers ROD 1* ROD STEWART & TINA TURNER	5		8
21 Sep 91	**NUTBUSH CITY LIMITS** *Capitol CL 630*	23		5
23 Nov 91	**WAY OF THE WORLD** *Capitol CL 637*	13		7
15 Feb 92	**LOVE THING** *Capitol CL 644*	29		4
6 Jun 92	**I WANT YOU NEAR ME** *Capitol CL 659*	22		4
22 May 93	**I DON'T WANNA FIGHT** *Parlophone CDRS 6346*	7		9
28 Aug 93	**DISCO INFERNO** *Parlophone CDR 6357*	12		6
30 Oct 93	**WHY MUST WE WAIT UNTIL TONIGHT** *Parlophone CDR 6366*	16		4
18 Nov 95	**GOLDENEYE** *Parlophone CDR 007 1001*	10		9
23 Mar 96	**WHATEVER YOU WANT** *Parlophone CDRS 6429*	23		6
8 Jun 96	**ON SILENT WINGS** *Parlophone CDR 6434*	13		6
27 Jul 96	**MISSING YOU** *Parlophone CDRS 6441*	12		5
19 Oct 96	**SOMETHING BEAUTIFUL REMAINS** *Parlophone CDR 6448*	27		2
21 Dec 96	**IN YOUR WILDEST DREAMS** *Parlophone CDR 6451* FEATURING BARRY WHITE	32		3
30 Oct 99	**WHEN THE HEARTACHE IS OVER** *Parlophone CDR 6529*	10		7
12 Feb 00	**WHATEVER YOU NEED** *Parlophone CDRS 6532*	27		3
6 Nov 04	**OPEN ARMS** *Parlophone CDCLS862*	25		3

TURNTABLE ORCHESTRA

US, male producer (Hipolito Torrales) — **4**

Date	Title / Label	Peak Position	Weeks at No.1	Weeks on Chart
21 Jan 89	**YOU'RE GONNA MISS ME** *Republic LIC 012*	52		4

TURTLES

US, male vocal/instrumental group – Mark Volman, Howard Kaylan, Don Murray, Al Nichol, Chuck Portz & Jim Tucker — **39**

Date	Title / Label	Peak Position	Weeks at No.1	Weeks on Chart
23 Mar 67	**HAPPY TOGETHER** *London HL 10115* ★	12		12
15 Jun 67	**SHE'D RATHER BE WITH ME** *London HLU 10135*	4		15
30 Oct 68	**ELENORE** *London HL 10223*	7		12

T.W.A.

UK, male instrumental/production group — **1**

Date	Title / Label	Peak Position	Weeks at No.1	Weeks on Chart
16 Sep 95	**NASTY GIRLS** *Mercury MERCD 441*	51		1

SHANIA TWAIN

Canada, female vocalist (Eileen Edwards) — **128**

Date	Title / Label	Peak Position	Weeks at No.1	Weeks on Chart
28 Feb 98	**YOU'RE STILL THE ONE** *Mercury 5684932*	10		10
13 Jun 98	**WHEN** *Mercury 5661192*	18		4
28 Nov 98	**FROM THIS MOMENT ON** *Mercury 5665632*	9		8
22 May 99	**THAT DON'T IMPRESS ME MUCH** *Mercury 8708032* ⊛	3		21
2 Oct 99	**MAN! I FEEL LIKE A WOMAN** *Mercury 5623242* ○	3		18
26 Feb 00	**DON'T BE STUPID (YOU KNOW I LOVE YOU)** *Mercury 1721492*	5		11
16 Nov 02	**I'M GONNA GETCHA GOOD!** *Mercury 1722732*	4		15
22 Mar 03	**KA-CHING** *Mercury 1722872*	8		8
14 Jun 03	**FOREVER AND FOR ALWAYS** *Mercury 9807734*	6		10
6 Sep 03	**THANK YOU BABY!** *Mercury 9810628*	11		7
29 Nov 03	**WHEN YOU KISS ME/UP!** *Mercury 9814004*	21		5
4 Dec 04	**PARTY FOR TWO** *Mercury 2103240* & MARK McGRATH	10		9
12 Mar 05	**DON'T** *Mercury 9880435*	30		2

TWANG

UK, male vocal/instrumental group – Phil Etheridge, Matty Clinton, Stuart Hartland, Martin Saunders & Jon Watkin — **17**

Date	Title / Label	Peak Position	Weeks at No.1	Weeks on Chart
24 Mar 07	**WIDE AWAKE** *B Unique/Polydor BUN121CD*	15		7
2 Jun 07	**EITHER WAY** *B Unique/Polydor BUN126CD*	8		6
8 Sep 07	**TWO LOVERS** *B Unique/Polydor BUN134CDS*	34		2
8 Dec 07	**PUSH THE GHOST** *B Unique/Polydor BUN137CDS*	63		1
8 Aug 09	**BARNEY RUBBLE** *B Unique BUN152CD*	59		1

TWEENIES

UK, male/female/canine children's TV vocal group – Bella, Fizz, Jake & Milo (Tweenies), Judy & Max (adults) & Doodles & Izzles (dogs) — **54**

Date	Title / Label	Peak Position	Weeks at No.1	Weeks on Chart
11 Nov 00	**NUMBER 1** *BBC Music WMSS 60332* ○	5		23
31 Mar 01	**BEST FRIENDS FOREVER** *BBC Music WMSS 60382*	12		10
4 Aug 01	**DO THE LOLLIPOP** *BBC Music WMSS 60452*	17		8
15 Dec 01	**I BELIEVE IN CHRISTMAS** *BBC Music WMSS 60502*	9		6
14 Sep 02	**HAVE FUN GO MAD** *BBC Music WMSS 60572*	20		7

TWEET

US, female vocalist/guitarist (Charlene Keys) — **13**

Date	Title / Label	Peak Position	Weeks at No.1	Weeks on Chart
11 May 02	**OOPS (OH MY)** *Elektra E 7306CD*	5		8
7 Sep 02	**CALL ME** *Elektra E 7326CD*	35		2
19 Mar 05	**TURN DA LIGHTS OFF** *Atlantic AT0200CD* FEATURING MISSY ELLIOTT	29		3

TWEETS

UK, male producer (Henry Hadaway) & uncredited feathered instrumentalists — **34**

Date	Title / Label	Peak Position	Weeks at No.1	Weeks on Chart
12 Sep 81	**THE BIRDIE SONG (BIRDIE DANCE)** *PRT 7P 219* ●	2		23
5 Dec 81	**LET'S ALL SING LIKE THE BIRDIES SING** *PRT 7P 226*	44		6
18 Dec 82	**THE BIRDIE SONG (BIRDIE DANCE)** *PRT 7P 219*	46		5

20 FINGERS

US, male production duo — **14**

Date	Title / Label	Peak Position	Weeks at No.1	Weeks on Chart
26 Nov 94	**SHORT DICK MAN** *Multiply CDMULT 12* FEATURING GILLETTE	21		4
30 Sep 95	**LICK IT** *ZYX 75908* FEATURING ROULA	48		3
30 Sep 95	**SHORT SHORT MAN** *Multiply CXMULTY 7* FEATURING GILLETTE	11		7

21ST CENTURY GIRLS

UK, female vocal/instrumental group — **4**

Date	Title / Label	Peak Position	Weeks at No.1	Weeks on Chart
12 Jun 99	**21ST CENTURY GIRLS** *EMI NTNCDS 001*	16		4

24

US, male producer/musical director (Sean Callery) — **1**

Date	Title / Label	Peak Position	Weeks at No.1	Weeks on Chart
12 Feb 05	**THE LONGEST DAY** *Nebula NEBCD064*	56		1

TWENTY 4 SEVEN

UK, male vocal group — **1**

Date	Title / Label	Peak Position	Weeks at No.1	Weeks on Chart
12 Jun 04	**HIDE** *Diablo Music MND2*	42		1

TWENTY 4 SEVEN FEATURING CAPTAIN HOLLYWOOD

Holland/Germany, female/male vocal/dance trio – Nancy Coolen, Giovanni 'Hanks' Falco & Wolfgang 'Jacks' Reiss & US, male rapper (Tony Dawson-Harrison) — **20**

Date	Title / Label	Peak Position	Weeks at No.1	Weeks on Chart
22 Sep 90	**I CAN'T STAND IT** *BCM BCMR 395*	7		10
24 Nov 90	**ARE YOU DREAMING** *BCM 07504*	17		10

29 PALMS

UK, male producer (Pete Lorimar) — **1**

Date	Title / Label	Peak Position	Weeks at No.1	Weeks on Chart
25 May 02	**TOUCH THE SKY** *Mushroom PERF 35CDS*	51		1

22-20'S

UK, male vocal/instrumental group — **8**

Date	Title / Label	Peak Position	Weeks at No.1	Weeks on Chart
17 Apr 04	**WHY DON'T YOU DO IT FOR ME** *Heavenly HVN 138CD*	41		2
10 Jul 04	**SHOOT YOUR GUN** *Heavenly HVN 141CD*	30		2
25 Sep 04	**22 DAYS** *Heavenly HVN 144CDS*	34		2
12 Feb 05	**SUCH A FOOL** *Heavenly HVN148CDS*	29		2

TWICE AS MUCH

UK, male vocal/instrumental duo — **9**

Date	Title / Label	Peak Position	Weeks at No.1	Weeks on Chart
16 Jun 66	**SITTIN' ON A FENCE** *Immediate IM 033*	25		9

TWIGGY

UK, female model/vocalist (Lesley Hornby) — **10**

Date	Title / Label	Peak Position	Weeks at No.1	Weeks on Chart
14 Aug 76	**HERE I GO AGAIN** *Mercury 6007 100*	17		10

TWIN HYPE

US, male rap duo — **2**

Date	Title / Label	Peak Position	Weeks at No.1	Weeks on Chart
15 Jul 89	**DO IT TO THE CROWD** *Profile PROF 255*	65		2

Silver-selling ● Gold-selling ● Platinum-selling (× multiples) ⊛ US No.1 ★ Peak Position · Weeks at No.1 · Weeks on Chart

TWINKLE

UK, female vocalist (Lynn Ripley) — 20

Date	Title / Label	Peak Position	Weeks at No.1	Weeks on Chart
26 Nov 64	**TERRY** *Decca F 12013*	4		15
25 Feb 65	**GOLDEN LIGHTS** *Decca F 12076*	21		5

TWISTA

US, male rapper/producer (Carl Mitchell) — 45

Date	Title / Label	Peak Position	Weeks at No.1	Weeks on Chart
10 Apr 04	**SLOW JAMZ** *Atlantic AT 0174CD* ★	3		10
3 Jul 04	**OVERNIGHT CELEBRITY** *Atlantic AT 0180CD*	16		7
14 Aug 04	**SUNSHINE (IMPORT)** *Atlantic 7567932652CD*	60		3
11 Sep 04	**SUNSHINE** *Atlantic AT 0181CD*	3		10
20 Nov 04	**SO SEXY** *Atlantic AT 0187CD* FEATURING R KELLY	28		3
9 Apr 05	**HOPE** *Capitol 8694660* FEATURING FAITH EVANS	25		5
26 Feb 05	**LET'S GO** *Atlantic AT0193CD* TRICK DADDY FEATURING TWISTA & LIL' JON	26		2
12 Nov 05	**WHAT WE DO** *Gana/W10 GANA01CDS* KRAY TWINZ FEATURING TWISTA & LETHAL B	23		3
26 Nov 05	**GIRL TONITE** *Atlantic AT0225CDX* FEATURING TREY SONGZ	47		2

TWISTED INDIVIDUAL

UK, male DJ/producer (Lee Greenaway) — 1

Date	Title / Label	Peak Position	Weeks at No.1	Weeks on Chart
9 Aug 03	**BANDWAGON BLUES** *Formation FORM 12102*	51		1

TWISTED SISTER

US, male vocal/instrumental group — 28

Date	Title / Label	Peak Position	Weeks at No.1	Weeks on Chart
26 Mar 83	**I AM (I'M ME)** *Atlantic A 9854*	18		9
28 May 83	**THE KIDS ARE BACK** *Atlantic A 9827*	32		6
20 Aug 83	**YOU CAN'T STOP ROCK 'N' ROLL** *Atlantic A 9792*	43		4
2 Jun 84	**WE'RE NOT GONNA TAKE IT** *Atlantic A 9657*	58		6
18 Jan 86	**LEADER OF THE PACK** *Atlantic A 9478*	47		3

TWISTED X

UK, football fans (England)/vocal group — 3

Date	Title / Label	Peak Position	Weeks at No.1	Weeks on Chart
19 Jun 04	**BORN IN ENGLAND** *Universal TV 9867021*	9		3

CONWAY TWITTY

US, male vocalist (Harold Jenkins), d. 5 Jun 1993 (age 59) — 36

Date	Title / Label	Peak Position	Weeks at No.1	Weeks on Chart
14 Nov 58	**IT'S ONLY MAKE BELIEVE** *MGM 992* ★	1	5	15
27 Mar 59	**STORY OF MY LOVE** *MGM 1003*	30		1
21 Aug 59	**MONA LISA** *MGM 1029*	5		14
21 Jul 60	**IS A BLUE BIRD BLUE** *MGM 1082*	43		3
23 Feb 61	**C'EST SI BON** *MGM 1118*	40		3

2 BAD MICE

UK, male production duo — 4

Date	Title / Label	Peak Position	Weeks at No.1	Weeks on Chart
15 Feb 92	**HOLD IT DOWN** *Moving Shadow SHADOW 14*	70		1
8 Aug 92	**HOLD IT DOWN** *Moving Shadow SHADOW 14*	48		2
7 Sep 96	**BOMBSCARE** *Arista 74321397662*	46		1

TWO COWBOYS

Italy, male production duo – Maurizio Braccagni & Roberto Gallo Salsotto — 11

Date	Title / Label	Peak Position	Weeks at No.1	Weeks on Chart
9 Jul 94	**EVERYBODY GONFI-GON** *3 Beat TABCD 221*	7		11

2 EIVISSA

Germany, female vocal duo — 6

Date	Title / Label	Peak Position	Weeks at No.1	Weeks on Chart
4 Oct 97	**OH LA LA LA** *Club Tools 0063475 CLU*	13		6

2 FOR JOY

UK, male production duo — 3

Date	Title / Label	Peak Position	Weeks at No.1	Weeks on Chart
1 Dec 90	**IN A STATE** *Mercury MER 333*	61		1
9 Nov 91	**LET THE BASS KICK** *All Around The World GLOBE 102*	67		2

2 FUNKY 2 FEATURING KATHRYN DION

UK, male production duo & female vocalist — 4

Date	Title / Label	Peak Position	Weeks at No.1	Weeks on Chart
6 Nov 93	**BROTHERS AND SISTERS** *Logic 74321170772*	56		2
30 Nov 96	**BROTHERS AND SISTERS (REMIX)** *All Around The World CDGLOBE 138*	36		2

2 HOUSE

US, male rap duo — 1

Date	Title / Label	Peak Position	Weeks at No.1	Weeks on Chart
21 Mar 92	**GO TECHNO** *Atlantic A 7519*	65		1

2 IN A ROOM

US, male rap/vocal/production duo – Rafael Vargas & Roger Pauletta (replaced by Edwin Ovalles) — 15

Date	Title / Label	Peak Position	Weeks at No.1	Weeks on Chart
18 Nov 89	**SOMEBODY IN THE HOUSE SAY YEAH!** *Big Life BLR 12*	66		1
26 Jan 91	**WIGGLE IT** *Positiva CDTIV 18* ●	3		8
6 Apr 91	**SHE'S GOT ME GOING CRAZY** *SBK 23*	54		2
22 Oct 94	**EL TRAGO (THE DRINK)** *SBK 19*	34		2
8 Apr 95	**AHORA ES (NOW IS THE TIME)** *Positiva CDTIV 32*	43		1
17 Aug 96	**GIDDY-UP** *Encore CDCOR 008*	74		1

2 IN A TENT

UK, male production duo. See Stock Aitken Waterman — 7

Date	Title / Label	Peak Position	Weeks at No.1	Weeks on Chart
17 Dec 94	**WHEN I'M CLEANING WINDOWS (TURNED OUT NICE AGAIN)** *Love This SPONCD 1*	25		5
13 May 95	**BOOGIE WOOGIE BUGLE BOY (DON'T STOP)** *Bald Cat BALCD 1* 2 IN A TANK	48		1
6 Jan 96	**WHEN I'M CLEANING WINDOWS (TURNED OUT NICE AGAIN)** *Love This SPONCD 1*	62		1

2 MAD

UK, male production duo — 4

Date	Title / Label	Peak Position	Weeks at No.1	Weeks on Chart
9 Feb 91	**THINKING ABOUT YOUR BODY** *Big Life BLR 37*	43		4

TWO MAN SOUND

Belgium, male vocal/instrumental group — 7

Date	Title / Label	Peak Position	Weeks at No.1	Weeks on Chart
20 Jan 79	**QUE TAL AMERICA** *Miracle M 1*	46		7

TWO MEN, A DRUM MACHINE & A TRUMPET

UK, male instrumental/production duo. See Fine Young Cannibals — 17

Date	Title / Label	Peak Position	Weeks at No.1	Weeks on Chart
9 Jan 88	**I'M TIRED OF GETTING PUSHED AROUND** *London LON 141*	18		8
25 Jun 88	**HEAT IT UP** *Jive 174* WEE PAPA GIRL RAPPERS FEATURING TWO MEN & A DRUM MACHINE	21		9

TWO NATIONS

UK, male vocal/instrumental group — 1

Date	Title / Label	Peak Position	Weeks at No.1	Weeks on Chart
20 Jun 87	**THAT'S THE WAY IT FEELS** *10 TEN 168*	74		1

TWO PEOPLE

UK, male vocal/instrumental duo — 2

Date	Title / Label	Peak Position	Weeks at No.1	Weeks on Chart
31 Jan 87	**HEAVEN** *Polydor POSP 844*	63		2

2WO THIRD3

UK, male vocal trio — 15

Date	Title / Label	Peak Position	Weeks at No.1	Weeks on Chart
19 Feb 94	**HEAR ME CALLING** *Epic 6600642*	48		3
11 Jun 94	**EASE THE PRESSURE** *Epic 6604782*	45		2
8 Oct 94	**I WANT THE WORLD** *Epic 6608542*	20		5
17 Dec 94	**I WANT TO BE ALONE** *Epic 6610852*	29		5

2-4 FAMILY

UK/US/Korea, male/female vocal/rap group — 1

Date	Title / Label	Peak Position	Weeks at No.1	Weeks on Chart
29 May 99	**LEAN ON ME (WITH THE FAMILY)** *Epic 6670132*	69		1

2 UNLIMITED

Belgium, male producers – Jean-Paul de Coster & Phil Wilde – & Holland, male/female vocal/rap duo – Ray Slijngaard & Anita Doth — 112

Date	Title / Label	Peak Position	Weeks at No.1	Weeks on Chart
5 Oct 91	**GET READY FOR THIS** *PWL Continental PWL 206*	2		15
25 Jan 92	**TWILIGHT ZONE** *PWL Continental PWL 211*	2		10
2 May 92	**WORKAHOLIC** *PWL Continental PWL 228*	4		7
15 Aug 92	**THE MAGIC FRIEND** *PWL Continental PWL 240*	11		7
30 Jan 93	**NO LIMIT** *PWL Continental PWCD 256*	1	5	16
8 May 93	**TRIBAL DANCE** *PWL Continental PWCD 262*	4		11
4 Sep 93	**FACES** *PWL Continental PWCD 268*	8		7
20 Nov 93	**MAXIMUM OVERDRIVE** *PWL Continental PWCD 276*	15		8
19 Feb 94	**LET THE BEAT CONTROL YOUR BODY** *PWL Continental PWCD 280*	6		9

Silver-selling ● Gold-selling ● Platinum-selling (x multiples) US No.1 ★ Peak Position Weeks at No.1 Weeks on Chart

Date	Title	Peak Position	Weeks at No.1	Weeks on Chart
21 May 94	**THE REAL THING** *PWL Continental PWCD 306*	6		7
1 Oct 94	**NO ONE** *PWL Continental PWCD 314*	17		6
25 Mar 95	**HERE I GO** *PWL Continental PWCD 317*	22		3
21 Oct 95	**DO WHAT'S GOOD FOR ME** *PWL 322CD*	16		4
11 Jul 98	**WANNA GET UP** *Big Life BLRD 143*	38		2

2K

UK, male production duo. See Justified Ancients Of Mu Mu, KLF, Timelords — **2**

Date	Title	Peak Position	Weeks at No.1	Weeks on Chart
25 Oct 97	*****K THE MILLENNIUM** *Blast First BFFP 146CDK*	28		2

2PAC

US, male rapper/actor (Tupac Shakur), d. 13 Sep 1996 (age 25). See Makaveli — **107**

Date	Title	Peak Position	Weeks at No.1	Weeks on Chart
13 Apr 96	**CALIFORNIA LOVE** *Death Row DRWCD 3* FEATURING DR DRE	6		8
27 Jul 96	**HOW DO YOU WANT IT?** *Death Row 228546532* FEATURING K-CI & JOJO ★	17		4
30 Nov 96	**I AIN'T MAD AT CHA** *Death Row DRWCD 5* FEATURING K-CI & JOJO	13		9
26 Apr 97	**WANTED DEAD OR ALIVE** *Def Jam 5744052* & SNOOP DOGGY DOGG	16		3
10 Jan 98	**I WONDER IF HEAVEN GOT A GHETTO** *Jive JIVECD 446*	21		4
13 Jun 98	**DO FOR LOVE** *Jive 0518512* FEATURING ERIC WILLIAMS	12		4
18 Jul 98	**RUNNIN'** *Black Jam BJAM 9005* & THE NOTORIOUS B.I.G.	15		3
28 Nov 98	**HAPPY HOME** *Eagle EAGXS 058*	17		2
20 Feb 99	**CHANGES** *Jive 0522832* ●	3		12
3 Jul 99	**DEAR MAMA** *Jive 0523702*	27		3
23 Jun 01	**UNTIL THE END OF TIME** *Interscope 4975812*	4		11
10 Nov 01	**LETTER 2 MY UNBORN** *Interscope 4976142*	21		5
22 Feb 03	**THUGZ MANSION** *Interscope 4978542*	24		5
31 Jan 04	**RUNNIN' (DYIN' TO LIVE)** *Interscope 9815329* & THE NOTORIOUS B.I.G.	17		6
2 Jul 05	**GHETTO GOSPEL** *Interscope 9883248* FEATURING ELTON JOHN	1	3	22
27 Jan 07	**PAC'S LIFE** *Interscope 1723503* FEATURING TI & ASHANTI	21		6

2PLAY

UK, male vocalist/rapper/producer (Wesley Johnson) — **16**

Date	Title	Peak Position	Weeks at No.1	Weeks on Chart
24 Jan 04	**SO CONFUSED** *2PSL 2PSLCD02* FEATURING RAGHAV & JUCXI	6		13
4 Dec 04	**CARELESS WHISPER** *Inferno 2PSLCD06* FEATURING THOMAS JULES/ JUCXI D	29		3

TY FEATURING ROOTS MANUVA

UK, male rap duo — **1**

Date	Title	Peak Position	Weeks at No.1	Weeks on Chart
8 May 04	**OH YOU WANT MORE** *Big Dada BDCDS 066*	65		1

TYGERS OF PAN TANG

UK, male vocal/instrumental group — **15**

Date	Title	Peak Position	Weeks at No.1	Weeks on Chart
14 Feb 81	**HELLBOUND** *MCA 672*	48		3
27 Mar 82	**LOVE POTION NO. 9** *MCA 769*	45		6
10 Jul 82	**RENDEZVOUS** *MCA 777*	49		4
11 Sep 82	**PARIS BY AIR** *MCA 790*	63		2

BONNIE TYLER

UK, female vocalist (Gaynor Hopkins) — **83**

Date	Title	Peak Position	Weeks at No.1	Weeks on Chart
30 Oct 76	**LOST IN FRANCE** *RCA 2734*	9		10
19 Mar 77	**MORE THAN A LOVER** *RCA PB 5008*	27		6
3 Dec 77	**IT'S A HEARTACHE** *RCA PB 5057* ●	4		12
30 Jun 79	**MARRIED MEN** *RCA PB 5164*	35		6
19 Feb 83	**TOTAL ECLIPSE OF THE HEART** *CBS TYLER 1* ● ★	1	2	12
7 May 83	**FASTER THAN THE SPEED OF NIGHT** *CBS A 3338*	43		4
25 Jun 83	**HAVE YOU EVER SEEN THE RAIN** *CBS A 3517*	47		3
7 Jan 84	**A ROCKIN' GOOD WAY** *Epic A 4071* SHAKY & BONNIE	5		9
31 Aug 85	**HOLDING OUT FOR A HERO** *CBS A 4251* ●	2		13
14 Dec 85	**LOVING YOU'S A DIRTY JOB BUT SOMEBODY'S GOTTA DO IT** *CBS A 6662*, GUEST VOCALS TODD RUNDGREN	73		2
28 Dec 91	**HOLDING OUT FOR A HERO** *Total TYLER 10*	69		2
27 Jan 96	**MAKING LOVE (OUT OF NOTHING AT ALL)** *East West EW 010CD*	45		2
20 Sep 08	**TOTAL ECLIPSE OF THE HEART** *RCA GBBBN8300002*	57		2

TYMES

US, male/female vocal group – George Williams, Donald Banks, Norman Burnett, Terri Gonzales &Melanie Moore — **41**

Date	Title	Peak Position	Weeks at No.1	Weeks on Chart
25 Jul 63	**SO MUCH IN LOVE** *Cameo Parkway P 871* ★	21		8
15 Jan 69	**PEOPLE** *Direction 58 3903*	16		10
21 Sep 74	**YOU LITTLE TRUSTMAKER** *RCA 2456*	18		9
21 Dec 74	**MS GRACE** *RCA 2493* ●	1	1	11
17 Jan 76	**GOD'S GONNA PUNISH YOU** *RCA 2626*	41		3

TYMES 4

UK, female vocal group — **5**

Date	Title	Peak Position	Weeks at No.1	Weeks on Chart
25 Aug 01	**BODYROCK** *Edel 0118635 ERE*	23		3
15 Dec 01	**SHE GOT GAME** *Blacklist 0133135 EREP*	40		2

TYPICALLY TROPICAL

UK, male vocal/instrumental/production duo – Jeff Calvert & Max West — **11**

Date	Title	Peak Position	Weeks at No.1	Weeks on Chart
5 Jul 75	**BARBADOS** *Gull GULS 14* ●	1	1	11

TYREE

US, male producer (Tyree Cooper) — **10**

Date	Title	Peak Position	Weeks at No.1	Weeks on Chart
25 Feb 89	**TURN UP THE BASS** *ffrr FFR 24* FEATURING KOOL ROCK STEADY	12		7
6 May 89	**HARDCORE HIP HOUSE** *DJ International DJIN 11*	70		2
2 Dec 89	**MOVE YOUR BODY** *CBS 6554707* FEATURING JMD	72		1

TYRESE

US, male vocalist (Tyrese Gibson) — **8**

Date	Title	Peak Position	Weeks at No.1	Weeks on Chart
31 Jul 99	**NOBODY ELSE** *RCA 74321688282*	59		1
25 Sep 99	**SWEET LADY** *RCA 74321700842*	55		1
26 Jul 03	**HOW YOU GONNA ACT LIKE THAT** *J Records 82876544892*	30		4
23 Sep 06	**PULLIN' ME BACK** *Capitol CDR6710* CHINGY FEATURING TYRESE	44		2

TYRREL CORPORATION

UK, male vocal/production duo — **9**

Date	Title	Peak Position	Weeks at No.1	Weeks on Chart
14 Mar 92	**THE BOTTLE** *Volante TYR 1*	71		1
15 Aug 92	**GOING HOME** *Volante TYR 2*	58		2
10 Oct 92	**WAKING WITH A STRANGER/ONE DAY** *Volante TYRS 3*	59		1
24 Sep 94	**YOU'RE NOT HERE** *Cooltempo CDCOOL 292*	42		2
14 Jan 95	**BETTER DAYS AHEAD** *Cooltempo CDCOOLS 303*	29		3

TZANT

UK, male rap/instrumental duo. See Mirrorball, PF Project featuring Ewan McGregor — **10**

Date	Title	Peak Position	Weeks at No.1	Weeks on Chart
7 Sep 96	**HOT AND WET (BELIEVE IT)** *Logic 74321376832*	36		2
25 Apr 98	**SOUNDS OF WICKEDNESS** *Logic 74321568842*	11		6
22 Aug 98	**BOUNCE WITH THE MASSIVE** *Logic 74321602102*	39		2

JUDIE TZUKE

UK, female vocalist — **10**

Date	Title	Peak Position	Weeks at No.1	Weeks on Chart
14 Jul 79	**STAY WITH ME TILL DAWN** *Rocket XPRES 17*	16		10

BIOGRAPHIES

Biographies include the nationality and category for every chart entrant.

Each entrant has at least a mini biography. The acts with the most weeks on the chart (see page 372 for the chart) each have extended biographies.

Real names are included for all solo artists and, where applicable, dates of death and age of the artist at the time. "See..." links are included for soloists who also had singles chart entries in other acts.

The best known line-up is listed for every group that had a Top 10 single, with the vocalist/leader mentioned first and the others following in alphabetical order. In cases where later replacements had similar success both people are named and, where applicable, the dates of death are also shown for every group/duo member listed.

Certified Awards are given by the BPI to mark unit sales to retailers. They were introduced in April 1973. In January 1989 the levels of unit sales to the trade required to achieve each of the awards was amended to the following amounts:

Silver symbol	●	=	200,000 units
Gold symbol	●	=	400,000 units
Platinum symbol	⊛	=	600,000 units

As from February 2005, download sales also count towards certified awards.

U–X

KEY TO ARTIST ENTRIES

Artist/Group Name — Artist/Group Biography — Silver-selling — Gold-selling — Platinum-selling — US No.1 ★ — Peak Position — Weeks at No.1 — Weeks on Chart

Asterisks (*) indicate group members with hits in their own right that are listed elsewhere in this book

TAKE THAT

UK, male vocal group – Gary Barlow*, Howard Donald, Jason Orange, Mark Owen* & Robbie Williams* (left 1995, rejoined 2010). Comeback kings who have sold 7.4 million singles in the UK. The boys, who came back for good – as a quartet – in 2006, were the first act to score four successive No.1s since The Beatles – a feat they've achieved twice. See Helping Haiti

Artist's Total Weeks On Chart: 356

Date	Title / Label	Peak	Wks at No.1	Wks
23 Nov 91	**PROMISES** *RCA PB 45085*	38		2
8 Feb 92	**ONCE YOU'VE TASTED LOVE** *RCA PB 45257*	47		3
6 Jun 92	**IT ONLY TAKES A MINUTE** *RCA 74321101007*	7		8
15 Aug 92	**I FOUND HEAVEN** *RCA 74321108137*	15		6
10 Oct 92	**A MILLION LOVE SONGS** *RCA 74321116307*	7		9
12 Dec 92	**COULD IT BE MAGIC** *RCA 74321123137* ●	3		12
20 Feb 93	**WHY CAN'T I WAKE UP WITH YOU** *RCA 74321133102* ●	2		10
17 Jul 93	**PRAY** *RCA 74321154502* ●	1	4	11
9 Oct 93	**RELIGHT MY FIRE** *RCA 74321167722* FEATURING LULU ●	1	2	14
18 Dec 93	**BABE** *RCA 74321182122* ⊛	1	1	10
9 Apr 94	**EVERYTHING CHANGES** *RCA 74321167732* ●	1	2	10
9 Jul 94	**LOVE AIN'T HERE ANYMORE** *RCA 74321214832* ●	3		12
15 Oct 94	**SURE** *RCA 74321236622* ●	1	2	15
8 Apr 95	**BACK FOR GOOD** *RCA 74321271462* ⊛	1	4	13
5 Aug 95	**NEVER FORGET** *RCA 74321299572* ●	1	3	9
9 Mar 96	**HOW DEEP IS YOUR LOVE** *RCA 74321355592* ⊛	1	3	14
25 Nov 06	**PATIENCE** *Polydor 1714832* ●	1	4	39
10 Feb 07	**SHINE** *Polydor 1724294* ●	1	2	42
30 Jun 07	**I'D WAIT FOR LIFE** *Polydor 1736401*	17		2
27 Oct 07	**RULE THE WORLD** *Polydor 1746285* ●	2		66
6 Dec 08	**GREATEST DAY** *Polydor 1787445*	1	1	20
6 Dec 08	**PATIENCE** *Polydor 1714832*	59		1
6 Dec 08	**NEVER FORGET** *RCA GBARL9500200*	64		1
14 Feb 09	**UP ALL NIGHT** *Polydor 1796964*	14		11
13 Jun 09	**SAID IT ALL** *Polydor 2708717*	9		10
20 Jun 09	**RULE THE WORLD** *Polydor 1746285*	57		6
27 Jun 09	**GREATEST DAY** *Polydor 1787445*	73		1+

Date of entry into chart

Artist collaboration or variation on artist's name

Title of Single — Label and Catalogue Number — BPI Certified Award

A cross (+) indicates that the single was still on chart in the final week of March 2010

UB40

UK, male vocal/instrumental group – Ali Campbell*, James Brown, Robin Campbell, Earl Falconer, Norman Hassan, Brian Travers, Mickey Virtue & Terence Wilson. Reggae-infused Birmingham collective who brought the genre to a new, transatlantic audience. Named after the UK unemployment benefit form, they have sold 6.4 million UK singles during a career that has spawned 40 Top 40 hits — 350

Date	Title	Peak	Wks at No.1	Wks on Chart
8 Mar 80	**KING/FOOD FOR THOUGHT** *Graduate GRAD 6* ○	4		13
14 Jun 80	**MY WAY OF THINKING/I THINK IT'S GOING TO RAIN** *Graduate GRAD 8*	6		10
1 Nov 80	**THE EARTH DIES SCREAMING/DREAM A LIE** *Graduate GRAD 10*	10		12
23 May 81	**DON'T LET IT PASS YOU BY/DON'T SLOW DOWN** *DEP International DEP 1*	16		9
8 Aug 81	**ONE IN TEN** *DEP International DEP 2*	7		10
13 Feb 82	**I WON'T CLOSE MY EYES** *DEP International DEP 3*	32		6
15 May 82	**LOVE IS ALL IS ALRIGHT** *DEP International DEP 4*	29		7
28 Aug 82	**SO HERE I AM** *DEP International DEP 5*	25		9
5 Feb 83	**I'VE GOT MINE** *DEP International DEP 6*	45		4
20 Aug 83	**RED RED WINE** *DEP International DEP 7* ● ★	1	3	14
15 Oct 83	**PLEASE DON'T MAKE ME CRY** *DEP International DEP 8*	10		8
10 Dec 83	**MANY RIVERS TO CROSS** *DEP International DEP 9*	16		8
17 Mar 84	**CHERRY OH BABY** *DEP International DEP 10*	12		8
22 Sep 84	**IF IT HAPPENS AGAIN** *DEP International DEP 11*	9		8
1 Dec 84	**RIDDLE ME** *DEP International DEP 15*	59		2
3 Aug 85	**I GOT YOU BABE** *DEP International DEP 20* FEATURING CHRISSIE HYNDE ●	1	1	13
26 Oct 85	**DON'T BREAK MY HEART** *DEP International DEP 22* ○	3		13
12 Jul 86	**SING OUR OWN SONG** *DEP International DEP 23*	5		9
27 Sep 86	**ALL I WANT TO DO** *DEP International DEP 24*	41		4
17 Jan 87	**RAT IN MI KITCHEN** *DEP International DEP 25*	12		7
9 May 87	**WATCHDOGS** *DEP International DEP 26*	39		4
10 Oct 87	**MAYBE TOMORROW** *DEP International DEP 27*	14		8
27 Feb 88	**RECKLESS** *EMI EM 41* AFRIKA BAMBAATAA FEATURING UB40 & FAMILY	17		8
18 Jun 88	**BREAKFAST IN BED** *DEP International DEP 29* FEATURING CHRISSIE HYNDE	6		11
20 Aug 88	**WHERE DID I GO WRONG** *DEP International DEP 30*	26		6
17 Jun 89	**I WOULD DO FOR YOU** *DEP International DEP 32*	45		4
18 Nov 89	**HOMELY GIRL** *DEP International DEP 33*	6		10
27 Jan 90	**HERE I AM (COME AND TAKE ME)** *DEP International DEP 34*	46		3
31 Mar 90	**KINGSTON TOWN** *DEP International DEP 35* ○	4		12
28 Jul 90	**WEAR YOU TO THE BALL** *DEP International DEP 36*	35		6
3 Nov 90	**I'LL BE YOUR BABY TONIGHT** *EMI EM 167* ROBERT PALMER & UB40	6		10
1 Dec 90	**IMPOSSIBLE LOVE** *DEP International DEP 37*	47		2
2 Feb 91	**THE WAY YOU DO THE THINGS YOU DO** *DEP International DEP 38*	49		3
12 Dec 92	**ONE IN TEN** *ZTT ZANG 39* 808 STATE Vs UB40	17		8
22 May 93	**(I CAN'T HELP) FALLING IN LOVE WITH YOU** *DEP International DEPDG 40* ⊛ ★	1	2	16
21 Aug 93	**HIGHER GROUND** *DEP International DEPD 41*	8		9
11 Dec 93	**BRING ME YOUR CUP** *DEP International DEPD 42*	24		6
2 Apr 94	**C'EST LA VIE** *DEP International DEPD 43*	37		3
27 Aug 94	**REGGAE MUSIC** *DEP International DEPDG 44*	28		2
4 Nov 95	**UNTIL MY DYING DAY** *DEP International DEPD 45*	15		6
30 Aug 97	**TELL ME IS IT TRUE** *DEP International DEPD 48*	14		4
15 Nov 97	**ALWAYS THERE** *DEP International DEPD 49*	53		1
10 Oct 98	**COME BACK DARLING** *DEP International DEPD 50*	10		6
19 Dec 98	**HOLLY HOLY** *DEP International DEPD 51*	31		3
1 May 99	**THE TRAIN IS COMING** *DEP International DEPD 52*	30		2
9 Dec 00	**LIGHT MY FIRE** *DEP International DEPD 53*	63		1
20 Oct 01	**SINCE I MET YOU LADY/SPARKLE OF MY EYES** *DEP International DEPD 55* FEATURING LADY SAW	40		2
2 Mar 02	**COVER UP** *DEP International DEPD 56*	54		1
8 Nov 03	**SWING LOW** *DEP International DEPX 58* FEATURING UNITED COLOURS OF SOUND	15		14
18 Jun 05	**KISS AND SAY GOODBYE** *DEP International DEPDX59*	19		4
10 Sep 05	**REASONS** *DEP International DEPDX60* UB40/HUNTERZ/DHOL BLASTERS	75		1

UBM

Germany, male/female vocal/instrumental group — 1

Date	Title	Peak	Wks at No.1	Wks on Chart
23 May 98	**LOVIN' YOU** *Logic 74321571692*	46		1

UD PROJECT

Canada/Germany, male vocal/production group — 10

Date	Title	Peak	Wks at No.1	Wks on Chart
4 Oct 03	**SUMMER JAM** *Free 2 Air/Kontor 0150795KON*	14		6
21 Feb 04	**SATURDAY NIGHT** *Free 2 Air/Kontor 0152955KON*	19		4

UFO

UK/Germany, male vocal/instrumental group — 31

Date	Title	Peak	Wks at No.1	Wks on Chart
5 Aug 78	**ONLY YOU CAN ROCK ME** *Chrysalis CHS 2241*	50		4
27 Jan 79	**DOCTOR DOCTOR** *Chrysalis CHS 2287*	35		6
31 Mar 79	**SHOOT SHOOT** *Chrysalis CHS 2318*	48		5
12 Jan 80	**YOUNG BLOOD** *Chrysalis CHS 2399*	36		5
17 Jan 81	**LONELY HEART** *Chrysalis CHS 2482*	41		5
30 Jan 82	**LET IT RAIN** *Chrysalis CHS 2576*	62		3
19 Mar 83	**WHEN IT'S TIME TO ROCK** *Chrysalis CHS 2672*	70		3

UGLY DUCKLING

US, male rap/production trio — 1

Date	Title	Peak	Wks at No.1	Wks on Chart
13 Oct 01	**A LITTLE SAMBA** *XL Recordings XLS 135CD*	70		1

UGLY KID JOE

US, male vocal/instrumental group – Whitfield Crane, Cordell Crockett, Mark Davis (replaced by Shannon Larkin), Klaus Eichstadt & Dave Fortman — 28

Date	Title	Peak	Wks at No.1	Wks on Chart
16 May 92	**EVERYTHING ABOUT YOU** *Mercury MER 367*	3		9
22 Aug 92	**NEIGHBOUR** *Mercury MER 374*	28		4
31 Oct 92	**SO DAMN COOL** *Mercury MER 383*	44		2
13 Mar 93	**CAT'S IN THE CRADLE** *Mercury MERCD 385*	7		9
19 Jun 93	**BUSY BEE** *Mercury MERCD 389*	39		2
8 Jul 95	**MILKMAN'S SON** *Mercury MERDD 435*	39		2

UGLY RUMOURS

UK, male vocal/instrumental group — 1

Date	Title	Peak	Wks at No.1	Wks on Chart
10 Mar 07	**WAR** *Tone Def GBQAJ0600001*	21		1

UHF

US, male producer (Richard Hall). See Moby — 4

Date	Title	Peak	Wks at No.1	Wks on Chart
14 Dec 91	**UHF/EVERYTHING** *XL Recordings XLS 25*	46		4

TILLMANN UHRMACHER

Germany, male DJ/producer — 4

Date	Title	Peak	Wks at No.1	Wks on Chart
16 Sep 00	**BASSFLY** *Liquid Asset ASSETCD 004* TILLMANN + REIS	70		1
23 Mar 02	**ON THE RUN** *Direction 6721352*	16		3

UK

UK, male vocal/instrumental group — 1

Date	Title	Peak	Wks at No.1	Wks on Chart
30 Jun 79	**NOTHING TO LOSE** *Polydor POSP 55*	67		2
3 Aug 96	**SMALL TOWN BOY** *Media MCSTD 40049*	74		1

UK APACHE

UK, male vocalist/rapper (Abdul Wahab Lafta) — 4

Date	Title	Peak	Wks at No.1	Wks on Chart
1 Oct 94	**ORIGINAL NUTTAH** *Sound Of Underground SOUR 008CD* U.K. APACHI WITH SHY FX	39		3
28 Jul 01	**SIGNS** *Outcaste OUT 38CD1* DJ BADMARSH & SHRI FEATURING UK APACHE	63		1

UK MIXMASTERS

UK, male producer (Nigel Wright). See Doctor Spin, Shakatak — 15

Date	Title	Peak	Wks at No.1	Wks on Chart
2 Feb 91	**THE NIGHT FEVER MEGAMIX** *IQ ZB 44339*	23		5
27 Jul 91	**LUCKY 7 MEGAMIX** *IQ ZB 44731*	43		3
7 Dec 91	**BARE NECESSITIES MEGAMIX** *Connect ZB 35135*	14		7

UK PLAYERS

UK, male vocal/instrumental group — 3

Date	Title	Peak	Wks at No.1	Wks on Chart
14 May 83	**LOVE'S GONNA GET YOU** *RCA 326*	52		3

UK SUBS

UK, male vocal/instrumental group — 39

Date	Title	Peak	Wks at No.1	Wks on Chart
23 Jun 79	**STRANGLEHOLD** *Gem GEMS 5*	26		8
8 Sep 79	**TOMORROW'S GIRLS** *Gem GEMS 10*	28		6
1 Dec 79	**SHE'S NOT THERE/KICKS (EP)** *Gem GEMS 14*	36		7
8 Mar 80	**WARHEAD** *Gem GEMS 23*	30		4
17 May 80	**TEENAGE** *Gem GEMS 30*	32		5
25 Oct 80	**PARTY IN PARIS** *Gem GEMS 42*	37		4
18 Apr 81	**KEEP ON RUNNIN' (TILL YOU BURN)** *Gem GEMS 45*	41		5

TRACEY ULLMAN

US (b. UK), female vocalist/comedian — 49

Date	Title	Peak	Wks at No.1	Wks
19 Mar 83	**BREAKAWAY** *Stiff BUY 168*	4		11
24 Sep 83	**THEY DON'T KNOW** *Stiff BUY 180*	2		11
3 Dec 83	**MOVE OVER DARLING** *Stiff BUY 195*	8		9
3 Mar 84	**MY GUY** *Stiff BUY 197*	23		6
28 Jul 84	**SUNGLASSES** *Stiff BUY 205*	18		9
27 Oct 84	**HELPLESS** *Stiff BUY 211*	61		3

ULTIMATE KAOS

UK, male vocal group – Haydon Eshun, Jomo Baxter, Jayde Delpratt, Ryan Elliott & Nick Grant. See Childliners — 28

Date	Title	Peak	Wks at No.1	Wks
22 Oct 94	**SOME GIRLS** *Wild Card CARDD 12*	9		9
21 Jan 95	**HOOCHIE BOOTY** *Wild Card CARDW 14*	17		4
1 Apr 95	**SHOW A LITTLE LOVE** *Wild Card CARDW 18*	23		5
1 Jul 95	**RIGHT HERE** *Wild Card 5795832*	18		4
8 Mar 97	**CASANOVA** *Polydor 5759312*	24		3
18 Jul 98	**CASANOVA** *Mercury MERCD 505*	29		2
5 Jun 99	**ANYTHING YOU WANT (I'VE GOT IT)** *Mercury MERCD 510*	52		1

ULTRA

UK, male vocal/instrumental group — 22

Date	Title	Peak	Wks at No.1	Wks
18 Apr 98	**SAY YOU DO** *East West EW 124CD*	11		7
4 Jul 98	**SAY IT ONCE** *East West EW 171CD*	16		6
10 Oct 98	**THE RIGHT TIME** *East West EW 182CD*	28		3
16 Jan 99	**RESCUE ME** *East West EW 193CD1*	8		6

ULTRA HIGH

UK, male vocalist (Michael McCloud) — 3

Date	Title	Peak	Wks at No.1	Wks
2 Dec 95	**STAY WITH ME** *MCA MCSTD 40007*	36		2
20 Jul 96	**ARE YOU READY FOR LOVE** *MCA MCSTD 40039*	45		1

ULTRABEAT

UK, male/female vocal/DJ/production group – Mike Di Scala, Chris Henry, Ian Redman & Rebecca Rudd (since 2006) — 47

Date	Title	Peak	Wks at No.1	Wks
16 Aug 03	**PRETTY GREEN EYES** *All Around The World CXGLOBE 281*	2		14
27 Dec 03	**FEELIN' FINE** *All Around The World CXGLOBE 320*	12		12
11 Sep 04	**BETTER THAN LIFE** *All Around The World CDGLOBE 360*	23		5
8 Jan 05	**PRETTY GREEN EYES** *All Around The World CXGLOBE 281*	68		1
1 Oct 05	**FEEL IT WITH ME** *All Around The World CDGLOBE410*	57		1
6 May 06	**ELYSIUM (I GO CRAZY)** *All Around The World CDGLOBE488* VS SCOTT BROWN	35		4
8 Sep 07	**SURE FEELS GOOD** *All Around The World CDGLOBE696* VS DARREN STYLES	52		1
19 Jul 08	**DISCOLIGHTS** *All Around The World CDGLOBE937* VS DARREN STYLES	23		9

ULTRACYNIC

UK, male/female production/vocal group — 3

Date	Title	Peak	Wks at No.1	Wks
29 Aug 92	**NOTHING IS FOREVER** *380 PEW 2*	50		2
19 Apr 97	**NOTHING IS FOREVER (REMIX)** *All Around The World CDGLOBE 139*	47		1

ULTRAMARINE

UK, male production duo — 4

Date	Title	Peak	Wks at No.1	Wks
24 Jul 93	**KINGDOM** *Blanco Y Negro NEG 65CD*	46		2
29 Jan 94	**BAREFOOT (EP)** *Blanco Y Negro NEG 67CD*	61		1
27 Apr 96	**HYMN** *Blanco Y Negro NEG 87CD* FEATURING DAVID McALMONT	65		1

ULTRA-SONIC

UK, male production duo — 2

Date	Title	Peak	Wks at No.1	Wks
3 Sep 94	**OBSESSION** *Clubscene DCSRT 027*	75		1
21 Sep 96	**DO YOU BELIEVE IN LOVE** *Clubscene DCSRT 070*	47		1

ULTRASOUND

UK, male/female vocal/instrumental group — 5

Date	Title	Peak	Wks at No.1	Wks
7 Mar 98	**BEST WISHES** *Nude NUD 33CD*	68		1
13 Jun 98	**STAY YOUNG** *Nude NUD 35CD1*	30		2
10 Apr 99	**FLOODLIT WORLD** *Nude NUD 41CD1*	39		2

ULTRAVOX

UK, male vocal/instrumental group – Midge Ure*, Warren Cann (replaced by Mark Brzezicki), Chris Cross (Chris Allen) & Billy Currie — 142

Date	Title	Peak	Wks at No.1	Wks
5 Jul 80	**SLEEPWALK** *Chrysalis CHS 2441*	29		11
18 Oct 80	**PASSING STRANGERS** *Chrysalis CHS 2457*	57		4
17 Jan 81	**VIENNA** *Chrysalis CHS 2481*	2		14
28 Mar 81	**SLOW MOTION** *Island WIP 6691*	33		4
6 Jun 81	**ALL STOOD STILL** *Chrysalis CHS 2522*	8		10
22 Aug 81	**THE THIN WALL** *Chrysalis CHS 2540*	14		8
7 Nov 81	**THE VOICE** *Chrysalis CHS 2559*	16		12
25 Sep 82	**REAP THE WILD WIND** *Chrysalis CHS 2639*	12		9
27 Nov 82	**HYMN** *Chrysalis CHS 2657*	11		11
19 Mar 83	**VISIONS IN BLUE** *Chrysalis CHS 2676*	15		6
4 Jun 83	**WE CAME TO DANCE** *Chrysalis VOX 1*	18		7
11 Feb 84	**ONE SMALL DAY** *Chrysalis VOX 2*	27		6
19 May 84	**DANCING WITH TEARS IN MY EYES** *Chrysalis UV 1*	3		11
7 Jul 84	**LAMENT** *Chrysalis UV 2*	22		7
20 Oct 84	**LOVE'S GREAT ADVENTURE** *Chrysalis UV 3*	12		9
27 Sep 86	**SAME OLD STORY** *Chrysalis UV 4*	31		4
22 Nov 86	**ALL FALL DOWN** *Chrysalis UV 5*	30		5
6 Feb 93	**VIENNA** *Chrysalis CDCHSS 3936*	13		4

UMBOZA

UK, male instrumental/production duo. See Eye To Eye featuring Taka Boom, Mukkaa — 9

Date	Title	Peak	Wks at No.1	Wks
23 Sep 95	**CRY INDIA** *Positiva CDTIV 43*	19		4
20 Jul 96	**SUNSHINE** *Positiva CDTIV 47*	14		5

PIERO UMILIANI

Italy, male orchestra leader, d. 14 Feb 2001 (age 74) — 8

Date	Title	Peak	Wks at No.1	Wks
30 Apr 77	**MAH NA MAH NA** *EMI International INT 530*	8		8

UN-CUT

UK, male/female vocal/production trio — 4

Date	Title	Peak	Wks at No.1	Wks
29 Mar 03	**MIDNIGHT** *WEA 364CD2*	26		3
28 Jun 03	**FALLIN'** *WEA 368CD*	63		1

UNA MAS

UK, male production duo — 1

Date	Title	Peak	Wks at No.1	Wks
6 Apr 02	**I WILL FOLLOW** *Defected DFECT 47CDS*	55		1

UNATION

UK, male/female vocal/instrumental trio — 3

Date	Title	Peak	Wks at No.1	Wks
5 Jun 93	**HIGHER AND HIGHER** *MCA MCSTD 1773*	42		2
7 Aug 93	**DO YOU BELIEVE IN LOVE** *MCA MCSTD 1796*	75		1

UNBELIEVABLE TRUTH

UK, male vocal/instrumental group — 5

Date	Title	Peak	Wks at No.1	Wks
14 Feb 98	**HIGHER THAN REASON** *Virgin VSCDT 1676*	38		2
9 May 98	**SOLVED** *Virgin VSCDT 1684*	39		2
18 Jul 98	**SETTLE DOWN/DUNE SEA** *Virgin VSCDT 1697*	46		1

UNCANNY ALLIANCE

US, female/male vocal/production duo — 5

Date	Title	Peak	Wks at No.1	Wks
19 Dec 92	**I GOT MY EDUCATION** *A&M AM 0128*	39		5

UNCLE KRACKER

US, male vocalist/rapper/DJ (Matt Shafer) — 18

Date	Title	Peak	Wks at No.1	Wks
8 Sep 01	**FOLLOW ME** *Atlantic AT 0108CD*	3		18

UNCLE SAM

US, male vocalist (Sam Turner) — 2

Date	Title	Peak	Wks at No.1	Wks
16 May 98	**I DON'T EVER WANT TO SEE YOU AGAIN** *Epic 6656382*	30		2

UNDERCOVER
UK, male vocal/instrumental/production trio – John Matthews, Jon Jules & Steve Mac (Steve McCutcheon)

Date	Title	Peak Position	Weeks at No.1	Weeks on Chart (30)
15 Aug 92	**BAKER STREET** *PWL International PWL 239*	2		14
14 Nov 92	**NEVER LET HER SLIP AWAY** *PWL International PWL 255*	5		11
6 Feb 93	**I WANNA STAY WITH YOU** *PWL International PWL 258*	28		3
14 Aug 93	**LOVESICK** *PWL International PWCD 271* FEATURING JOHN MATTHEWS	62		1
3 Jul 04	**VIVA ENGLAND** *MCS MCSRECS1*	49		1

UNDERTAKERS
UK, male vocal/instrumental group

Date	Title	Peak Position	Weeks at No.1	Weeks on Chart (1)
9 Apr 64	**JUST A LITTLE BIT** *Pye 7N 15607*	49		1

UNDERTONES
UK, male vocal/instrumental group – Feargal Sharkey*, Michael Bradley, Billy Doherty, Damien & John O'Neill

Date	Title	Peak Position	Weeks at No.1	Weeks on Chart (67)
21 Oct 78	**TEENAGE KICKS** *Sire SIR 4007*	31		6
3 Feb 79	**GET OVER YOU** *Sire SIR 4010*	57		4
28 Apr 79	**JIMMY JIMMY** *Sire SIR 4015*	16		10
21 Jul 79	**HERE COMES THE SUMMER** *Sire SIR 4022*	34		6
20 Oct 79	**YOU'VE GOT MY NUMBER (WHY DON'T YOU USE IT)** *Sire SIR 4024*	32		6
5 Apr 80	**MY PERFECT COUSIN** *Sire SIR 4038*	9		10
5 Jul 80	**WEDNESDAY WEEK** *Sire SIR 4042*	11		9
2 May 81	**IT'S GOING TO HAPPEN!** *Ardeck ARDS 8*	18		9
25 Jul 81	**JULIE OCEAN** *Ardeck ARDS 9*	41		5
9 Jul 83	**TEENAGE KICKS** *Ardeck ARDS 1*	60		2

UNDERWORLD
UK, male vocal/instrumental trio – Karl Hyde, Rick Smith & Darren Emerson (left 2000)

Date	Title	Peak Position	Weeks at No.1	Weeks on Chart (48)
18 Dec 93	**SPIKEE/DOGMAN GO WOOF** *Junior Boy's Own JBO 17CD* UNDERWORLD	63		1
25 Jun 94	**DARK AND LONG** *Junior Boy's Own JBO 19CDS*	57		1
13 May 95	**BORN SLIPPY** *Junior Boy's Own JBO 29CDS*	52		2
18 May 96	**PEARL'S GIRL** *Junior Boy's Own JBO 38CDS1*	24		1
13 Jul 96	**BORN SLIPPY (REMIX)** *Junior Boy's Own JBO 44CDS1* ●	2		21
9 Nov 96	**PEARL'S GIRL** *Junior Boy's Own JBO 45CDS1*	22		3
27 Mar 99	**PUSH UPSTAIRS** *Junior Boy's Own JBO 5006173*	12		4
5 Jun 99	**JUMBO** *JBO 5007193*	21		2
28 Aug 99	**KING OF SNAKE** *JBO 5008798*	17		3
2 Sep 00	**COWGIRL** *JBO 5012518*	24		2
14 Sep 02	**TWO MONTHS OFF** *JBO 5020098*	12		4
1 Feb 03	**DINOSAUR ADVENTURE 3D** *JBO 05020528*	34		1
8 Nov 03	**BORN SLIPPY NUXX** *JBO 5024703*	27		3

UNDISPUTED TRUTH
US, male/female vocal group

Date	Title	Peak Position	Weeks at No.1	Weeks on Chart (4)
22 Jan 77	**YOU + ME = LOVE** *Warner Brothers K 16804*	43		4

U96
Germany, male production/vocal group

Date	Title	Peak Position	Weeks at No.1	Weeks on Chart (7)
29 Aug 92	**DAS BOOT** *M&G MAGS 28*	18		5
4 Jun 94	**INSIDE YOUR DREAMS** *Logic 74321209722*	44		1
29 Jun 96	**CLUB BIZARRE** *Urban 5750152*	70		1

UNION FEATURING THE ENGLAND WORLD CUP SQUAD
UK/Holland, male instrumental group & UK, male vocalists/rugby players

Date	Title	Peak Position	Weeks at No.1	Weeks on Chart (7)
12 Oct 91	**SWING LOW (RUN WITH THE BALL)** *Columbia 6575317*	16		7

UNION GAP FEATURING GARY PUCKETT
US, male vocal/instrumental group – Gary Puckett, Dwight Bement, Kerry Chater, Paul Wheatbread & Gary Withem

Date	Title	Peak Position	Weeks at No.1	Weeks on Chart (47)
17 Apr 68	**YOUNG GIRL** *CBS 3365*	1	4	17
7 Aug 68	**LADY WILLPOWER** *CBS 3551*	5		16
28 Aug 68	**WOMAN WOMAN** *CBS 3110* GARY PUCKETT & THE UNION GAP	48		1
15 Jun 74	**YOUNG GIRL** *CBS 8202* GARY PUCKETT & THE UNION GAP ●	6		13

UNIQUE
US, male/female vocal/production group

Date	Title	Peak Position	Weeks at No.1	Weeks on Chart (7)
10 Sep 83	**WHAT I GOT IS WHAT YOU NEED** *Prelude A 3707*	27		7

UNIQUE 3
UK, male production group

Date	Title	Peak Position	Weeks at No.1	Weeks on Chart (12)
4 Nov 89	**THE THEME** *10 TEN 285*	61		3
14 Apr 90	**MUSICAL MELODY/WEIGHT FOR THE BASS** *10 TEN 298*	29		5
10 Nov 90	**RHYTHM TAKES CONTROL** *10 TEN 327* FEATURING KARIN	41		3
16 Nov 91	**NO MORE** *10 TEN 387*	74		1

UNIT FOUR PLUS TWO
UK, male vocal/instrumental group – Peter Moules, Hugh Halliday, Ron Garwood, Howard Lubin, David Meikle, Thomas Moeller & Brian Parker, d. 2002

Date	Title	Peak Position	Weeks at No.1	Weeks on Chart (29)
13 Feb 64	**GREEN FIELDS** *Decca F 11821*	48		2
25 Feb 65	**CONCRETE AND CLAY** *Decca F 12071*	1	1	15
13 May 65	**YOU'VE NEVER BEEN IN LOVE LIKE THIS BEFORE** *Decca F 12144*	14		11
17 Mar 66	**BABY NEVER SAY GOODBYE** *Decca F 12333*	49		1

UNITED CITIZEN FEDERATION FEATURING SARAH BRIGHTMAN
UK, male/female vocal/production trio

Date	Title	Peak Position	Weeks at No.1	Weeks on Chart (1)
14 Feb 98	**STARSHIP TROOPERS** *Coalition COLA 040CD*	58		1

UNITED KINGDOM SYMPHONY
UK, orchestra

Date	Title	Peak Position	Weeks at No.1	Weeks on Chart (4)
27 Jul 85	**SHADES (THEME FROM THE CROWN PAINT TELEVISION COMMERCIAL)** *Food For Thought YUM 108*	68		4

UNITING NATIONS
UK, male vocal/production trio – Paul Keenan (b. Portugal), Craig Powell & Daz (Darren) Sampson. See Barndance Boys, Bus Stop, Rikki & Daz featuring Glen Campbell

Date	Title	Peak Position	Weeks at No.1	Weeks on Chart (33)
4 Dec 04	**OUT OF TOUCH** *Gusto CDGUS13*	7		21
6 Aug 05	**YOU AND ME** *Gusto CDGUS18*	15		7
19 Nov 05	**AI NO CORRIDA** *Gusto CDGUS25* FEATURING LAURA MORE	18		4
8 Dec 07	**DO IT YOURSELF (GO OUT AND GET IT)** *Gusto CDGUS55*	64		1

UNITONE ROCKERS FEATURING STEEL
UK, male instrumental/production duo & male vocalist (Errol Nicholson)

Date	Title	Peak Position	Weeks at No.1	Weeks on Chart (1)
26 Jun 93	**CHILDREN OF THE REVOLUTION** *The Hit Label HLC 4*	60		1

UNITY
UK, male/female production/vocal group

Date	Title	Peak Position	Weeks at No.1	Weeks on Chart (2)
31 Aug 91	**UNITY** *Cardiac CNY6*	64		2

UNIVERSAL
Australia, male vocal group

Date	Title	Peak Position	Weeks at No.1	Weeks on Chart (6)
2 Aug 97	**ROCK ME GOOD** *London LONCD 397*	19		4
18 Oct 97	**MAKE IT WITH YOU** *London LONCD 404*	33		2

UNKLE
US/UK, male DJ/production duo – Josh Davis & James Lavelle

Date	Title	Peak Position	Weeks at No.1	Weeks on Chart (13)
20 Feb 99	**BE THERE** *Mo Wax MW 108CD1* FEATURING IAN BROWN	8		6
17 Mar 01	**NARCO TOURISTS** *Soma 100CD* SLAM VS UNKLE	66		1
6 Sep 03	**EYE FOR AN EYE** *Mo Wax/Island CIDX 826*	31		2
15 Nov 03	**IN A STATE** *Mo Wax/Island CID 839*	44		2
27 Nov 04	**REIGN** *Mo Wax GUSIN007CDS* FEATURING IAN BROWN	40		2

UNKLEJAM
UK, male vocal/instrumental trio

Date	Title	Peak Position	Weeks at No.1	Weeks on Chart (4)
10 Mar 07	**LOVE YA** *Virgin VSCDX1925*	54		1
16 Jun 07	**WHAT AM I FIGHTING FOR** *Virgin VSCDX1937*	16		3

Silver-selling ● Gold-selling ● Platinum-selling (x multiples) ⊛ US No.1 ★ Peak Position Weeks at No.1 Weeks on Chart

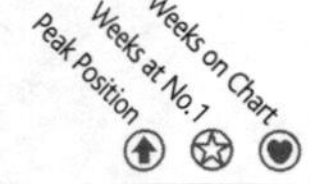

UNO CLIO FEATURING MARTINE McCUTCHEON
UK, male/female vocal/instrumental/production group — 1

Date	Title	Peak	Wks No.1	Wks
18 Nov 95	**ARE YOU MAN ENOUGH** *Avex UK AVEXCD 14*	62		1

UNTOUCHABLES
US, male vocal/instrumental group — 16

Date	Title	Peak	Wks No.1	Wks
6 Apr 85	**FREE YOURSELF** *Stiff BUY 221*	26		11
27 Jul 85	**I SPY FOR THE FBI** *Stiff BUY 227*	59		5

UP YER RONSON FEATURING MARY PEARCE
UK, male/female vocal/instrumental group — 7

Date	Title	Peak	Wks No.1	Wks
5 Aug 95	**LOST IN LOVE** *Hi-Life 5795572*	27		3
30 Mar 96	**ARE YOU GONNA BE THERE?** *Hi-Life 5763272*	27		2
19 Apr 97	**I WILL BE RELEASED** *Hi-Life 5737352*	32		2

PHIL UPCHURCH COMBO
US, male instrumental group — 2

Date	Title	Peak	Wks No.1	Wks
5 May 66	**YOU CAN'T SIT DOWN** *Sue WI 4005*	39		2

UPPER ROOM
UK, male vocal/instrumental group — 5

Date	Title	Peak	Wks No.1	Wks
11 Mar 06	**ALL OVER THIS TOWN** *Columbia 82876728002*	38		2
20 May 06	**BLACK AND WHITE** *Columbia 82876836562*	22		3

UPPER STREET
UK/US, male vocal group – Dane Bowers* (Another Level), Jimmy Constable (911), Bradley McIntosh (S Club 7) & Danny Wood (New Kids On The Block) — 1

Date	Title	Peak	Wks No.1	Wks
4 Nov 06	**THE ONE** *Concept CDCON70*	35		1

UPSETTERS
Jamaica, male instrumental group — 15

Date	Title	Peak	Wks No.1	Wks
4 Oct 69	**RETURN OF DJANGO/DOLLAR IN THE TEETH** *Upsetter US 301*	5		15

UPSIDE DOWN
UK, male vocal group — 16

Date	Title	Peak	Wks No.1	Wks
20 Jan 96	**CHANGE YOUR MIND** *World CDWORLD 1A*	11		7
13 Apr 96	**EVERY TIME I FALL IN LOVE** *World CDWORLD 2A*	18		4
29 Jun 96	**NEVER FOUND A LOVE LIKE THIS BEFORE** *World CDWORLD 3A*	19		3
23 Nov 96	**IF YOU LEAVE ME NOW** *World CDWORLD 4A*	27		2

URBAN ALL STARS
UK, male producer (Norman Cook). See Beats International, Norman Cook, Fatboy Slim, Freakpower, Housemartins, Mighty Dub Katz, Pizzaman — 2

Date	Title	Peak	Wks No.1	Wks
27 Aug 88	**IT BEGAN IN AFRICA** *Urban URB 23*	64		2

URBAN BLUES PROJECT PRESENTS MICHAEL PROCTER
US, male vocal/instrumental group — 1

Date	Title	Peak	Wks No.1	Wks
10 Aug 96	**LOVE DON'T LIVE** *AM:PM 5817932*	55		1

URBAN COOKIE COLLECTIVE
UK, male/female production/vocal group – Rohan Heath, Diane Charlemagne, Simon Bentall & Peter Samson — 40

Date	Title	Peak	Wks No.1	Wks
10 Jul 93	**THE KEY THE SECRET** *Pulse 8 CDLOSE 48* ●	2		16
13 Nov 93	**FEELS LIKE HEAVEN** *Pulse 8 CDLOSE 55*	5		9
19 Feb 94	**SAIL AWAY** *Pulse 8 CDLOSE 56*	18		4
23 Apr 94	**HIGH ON A HAPPY VIBE** *Pulse 8 CDLOSE 60*	31		3
15 Oct 94	**BRING IT ON HOME** *Pulse 8 CDLOSE 73*	56		1
27 May 95	**SPEND THE DAY** *Pulse 8 CDLOSE 85*	59		1
9 Sep 95	**REST OF MY LOVE** *Pulse 8 CDLOSE 93*	67		1
16 Dec 95	**SO BEAUTIFUL** *Pulse 8 CDLOSE 100*	68		1
24 Aug 96	**THE KEY THE SECRET (REMIX)** *Pulse 8 CDLOSE 109* UCC	52		1
15 Jan 05	**THE KEY THE SECRET 2005** *Feverpitch CDFEVS4*	31		3

URBAN DISCHARGE FEATURING SHE
US, male/female vocal/instrumental group — 1

Date	Title	Peak	Wks No.1	Wks
27 Jan 96	**WANNA DROP A HOUSE (ON THAT BITCH)** *MCA MCSTD 40020*	51		1

URBAN HYPE
UK, male production duo – Mark Chitty & Robert Dibden — 12

Date	Title	Peak	Wks No.1	Wks
11 Jul 92	**A TRIP TO TRUMPTON** *Faze 2 FAZE 5*	6		8
17 Oct 92	**THE FEELING** *Faze 2 FAZE 10*	67		1
9 Jan 93	**LIVING IN A FANTASY** *Faze 2 CDFAZE 13*	57		3

URBAN SHAKEDOWN
UK, male production duo — 8

Date	Title	Peak	Wks No.1	Wks
27 Jun 92	**SOME JUSTICE** *Urban Shakedown URBST 1*	23		5
12 Sep 92	**BASS SHAKE** *Urban Shakedown URBST 2* FEATURING MICKY FINN	59		2
10 Jun 95	**SOME JUSTICE** *Urban Shakedown URBCD 3* FEATURING DBO	49		1

URBAN SOUL
US, male producer (Roland Clark) — 11

Date	Title	Peak	Wks No.1	Wks
30 Mar 91	**ALRIGHT** *Cooltempo COOL 231*	60		4
21 Sep 91	**ALRIGHT (REMIX)** *Cooltempo COOL 244*	43		3
28 Mar 92	**ALWAYS** *Cooltempo COOL 251*	41		3
13 Jun 98	**LOVE IS SO NICE** *VC Recordings VCRD 33*	75		1

URBAN SPECIES
UK, male rap/vocal/production trio — 10

Date	Title	Peak	Wks No.1	Wks
12 Feb 94	**SPIRITUAL LOVE** *Talkin Loud TLKCD 45*	35		4
16 Apr 94	**BROTHER** *Talkin Loud TLKCD 47*	40		3
20 Aug 94	**LISTEN** *Talkin Loud TLKCD 50* FEATURING MC SOLAAR	47		2
6 Mar 99	**BLANKET** *Talkin Loud TLDD 39* FEATURING IMOGEN HEAP	56		1

URBNRI
UK, male vocal/instrumental group — 2

Date	Title	Peak	Wks No.1	Wks
9 Feb 08	**YOUNG FREE AND SINGLE** *Fortress XPH001*	34		1
28 Jun 08	**BACK ME UP** *Fortress FORT002*	42		1

MIDGE URE
UK, male vocalist. See Rich Kids, Slik, Ultravox, Visage — 56

Date	Title	Peak	Wks No.1	Wks
12 Jun 82	**NO REGRETS** *Chrysalis CHS 2618*	9		10
9 Jul 83	**AFTER A FASHION** *Musicfest FEST 1* & MICK KARN	39		4
14 Sep 85	**IF I WAS** *Chrysalis URE 1* ●	1	1	11
16 Nov 85	**THAT CERTAIN SMILE** *Chrysalis URE 2*	28		4
8 Feb 86	**WASTELANDS** *Chrysalis URE 3*	46		3
7 Jun 86	**CALL OF THE WILD** *Chrysalis URE 4*	27		8
20 Aug 88	**ANSWERS TO NOTHING** *Chrysalis URE 5*	49		4
19 Nov 88	**DEAR GOD** *Chrysalis URE 6*	55		4
17 Aug 91	**COLD COLD HEART** *Arista 114555*	17		7
25 May 96	**BREATHE** *Arista 74321371172*	70		1

URGE OVERKILL
US, male vocal/instrumental trio — 6

Date	Title	Peak	Wks No.1	Wks
21 Aug 93	**SISTER HAVANA** *Geffen GFSTD 51*	67		1
16 Oct 93	**POSITIVE BLEEDING** *Geffen GFSTD 57*	61		1
19 Nov 94	**GIRL, YOU'LL BE A WOMAN SOON** *MCA MCSTD 2024*	37		4

URUSEI YATSURA
UK, male/female vocal/instrumental group — 4

Date	Title	Peak	Wks No.1	Wks
22 Feb 97	**STRATEGIC HAMLETS** *Che 67CD*	64		1
28 Jun 97	**FAKE FUR** *Che 70CD*	58		1
21 Feb 98	**HELLO TIGER** *Che 75CD1*	40		1
6 Jun 98	**SLAIN BY ELF** *Che 80CD1*	63		1

US5
Germany, male vocal group — 2

Date	Title	Peak	Wks No.1	Wks
7 Oct 06	**MARIA** *Triple-M Trans Con 2401001*	38		2

US3

UK, male production duo — Weeks on Chart: 14

Date	Title	Peak Position	Weeks at No.1	Weeks on Chart
10 Jul 93	**RIDDIM** *Blue Note CDCL 686* FEATURING TUKKA YOOT	34		6
25 Sep 93	**CANTALOOP** *Blue Note CDCL 696* FEATURING RAHSAAN	23		5
28 May 94	**I GOT IT GOIN' ON** *Blue Note CDCL 708* FEATURING KOBIE POWELL & RAHSAAN	52		2
1 Mar 97	**COME ON EVERYBODY (GET DOWN)** *Blue Note CDCL 784*	38		1

USA FOR AFRICA

International, male/female vocal/instrumental charity assembly — Weeks on Chart: 9

Date	Title	Peak Position	Weeks at No.1	Weeks on Chart
13 Apr 85	**WE ARE THE WORLD** *CBS USAID 1* ○ ★	1	2	9

USED

US, male vocal/instrumental group — Weeks on Chart: 2

Date	Title	Peak Position	Weeks at No.1	Weeks on Chart
22 Mar 03	**THE TASTE OF INK** *Reprise W601CD*	52		1
5 Feb 05	**TAKE IT AWAY** *Reprise W662CD2*	44		1

USHER

US, male vocalist/producer/actor (Usher Raymond IV) — Weeks on Chart: 155

Date	Title	Peak Position	Weeks at No.1	Weeks on Chart
18 Mar 95	**THINK OF YOU** *LaFace 74321269252*	70		1
31 Jan 98	**YOU MAKE ME WANNA...** *LaFace 74321560652* ○	1	1	13
2 May 98	**NICE AND SLOW** *LaFace 74321579102* ★	24		5
3 Feb 01	**POP YA COLLAR** *LaFace 74321828692*	2		9
7 Jul 01	**U REMIND ME** *LaFace 74321863382* ★	3		9
20 Oct 01	**U GOT IT BAD** *LaFace 74321898552* ★	5		8
20 Apr 02	**U TURN** *LaFace 74321934092*	16		6
10 Aug 02	**I NEED A GIRL (PART ONE)** *Puff Daddy 74321947242* P DIDDY FEATURING USHER & LOON	4		11
27 Mar 04	**YEAH** *Arista 82876606012* FEATURING LIL' JON & LUDACRIS ★	1	2	14
10 Jul 04	**BURN** *LaFace 82876624362* ★	1	2	12
13 Nov 04	**CONFESSIONS PART II/MY BOO** *LaFace 82876655292* ★	5		13
5 Mar 05	**CAUGHT UP** *LaFace 82876679142*	9		9
28 Jul 07	**SAME GIRL** *Nonsuch 88697126432* R KELLY & USHER	26		8
5 Apr 08	**LOVE IN THIS CLUB** *LaFace 88697305772* FEATURING YOUNG JEEZY ★	4		22
5 Jul 08	**MOVING MOUNTAINS** *LaFace 88697337242*	25		12
20 Feb 10	**SPOTLIGHT** *Warner Brothers USWB10904424* GUCCI MANE FEATURING USHER	46		1
3 Apr 10	**OMG** *LaFace USLF20900103* FEATURING WILL.I.AM	8		2+

USURA

Italy, male producer (Walter Cremonini) & various male/female production/vocal collaborators including Alessandro Gilardi, Claudio Varola, Michele Comis & Elisa Spreafichi — Weeks on Chart: 15

Date	Title	Peak Position	Weeks at No.1	Weeks on Chart
23 Jan 93	**OPEN YOUR MIND** *Deconstruction 74321128042*	7		9
10 Jul 93	**SWEAT** *Deconstruction 74321154602*	29		3
6 Dec 97	**OPEN YOUR MIND** *Malarky MLKD 4*	21		3

UTAH SAINTS

UK, male instrumental/production duo – Tim Garbutt & Jez Willis — Weeks on Chart: 61

Date	Title	Peak Position	Weeks at No.1	Weeks on Chart
24 Aug 91	**WHAT CAN YOU DO FOR ME** *ffrr F 164*	10		11
6 Jun 92	**SOMETHING GOOD** *ffrr F 187*	4		9
8 May 93	**BELIEVE IN ME** *ffrr FCD 209*	8		6
17 Jul 93	**I WANT YOU** *ffrr FCD 213*	25		5
25 Jun 94	**I STILL THINK OF YOU** *ffrr FCD 225*	32		2
2 Sep 95	**OHIO** *ffrr FCD 264*	42		2
5 Feb 00	**LOVE SONG** *Echo ECSCD 83*	37		2
20 May 00	**FUNKY MUSIC** *Echo ECSCX 96*	23		2
23 Feb 08	**SOMETHING GOOD 08** *Data DATA183CDS*	8		22

U2

Ireland/UK, male vocal/instrumental group – Paul 'Bono'* Hewson, Adam Clayton*, David 'The Edge' Evans & Larry Mullen, Jr Stadium-packing rock heavyweights who have won 6 BRITs for 'Best International Group' and 22 Grammys, more than any other band. They have sold 6.7 million UK singles and 150 million records worldwide. See Passengers — Weeks on Chart: 359

Date	Title	Peak Position	Weeks at No.1	Weeks on Chart
8 Aug 81	**FIRE** *Island WIP 6679*	35		6
17 Oct 81	**GLORIA** *Island WIP 6733*	55		4
3 Apr 82	**A CELEBRATION** *Island WIP 6770*	47		4
22 Jan 83	**NEW YEARS DAY** *Island WIP 6848*	10		8
2 Apr 83	**TWO HEARTS BEAT AS ONE** *Island IS 109*	18		5
15 Sep 84	**PRIDE (IN THE NAME OF LOVE)** *Island IS 202*	3		11
4 May 85	**THE UNFORGETTABLE FIRE** *Island IS 220*	6		6
28 Mar 87	**WITH OR WITHOUT YOU** *Island IS 319* ★	4		11
6 Jun 87	**I STILL HAVEN'T FOUND WHAT I'M LOOKING FOR** *Island IS 328* ★	6		11
12 Sep 87	**WHERE THE STREETS HAVE NO NAME** *Island IS 340*	4		6
26 Dec 87	**IN GOD'S COUNTRY (IMPORT)** *Island 7-99385*	48		4
1 Oct 88	**DESIRE** *Island IS 400* ○	1	1	8
17 Dec 88	**ANGEL OF HARLEM** *Island IS 402*	9		6
15 Apr 89	**WHEN LOVE COMES TO TOWN** *Island IS 411* FEATURING B.B. KING	6		7
24 Jun 89	**ALL I WANT IS YOU** *Island IS 422*	4		6
2 Nov 91	**THE FLY** *Island IS 500* ○	1	1	6
14 Dec 91	**MYSTERIOUS WAYS** *Island IS 509*	13		7
7 Mar 92	**ONE** *Island IS 515*	7		6
20 Jun 92	**EVEN BETTER THAN THE REAL THING** *Island IS 525*	12		7
11 Jul 92	**EVEN BETTER THAN THE REAL THING (REMIX)** *Island REAL U2*	8		7
5 Dec 92	**WHO'S GONNA RIDE YOUR WILD HORSES** *Island IS 550*	14		8
4 Dec 93	**STAY (FARAWAY, SO CLOSE)** *Island CID 578* ○	4		9
17 Jun 95	**HOLD ME, THRILL ME, KISS ME, KILL ME** *Atlantic A 7131CD* ●	2		14
15 Feb 97	**DISCOTHEQUE** *Island CID 649* ○	1	1	11
26 Apr 97	**STARING AT THE SUN** *Island CID 658*	3		6
2 Aug 97	**LAST NIGHT ON EARTH** *Island CID 664*	10		5
4 Oct 97	**PLEASE** *Island CIDX 673*	7		4
20 Dec 97	**IF GOD WILL SEND HIS ANGELS** *Island CID 684*	12		6
31 Oct 98	**SWEETEST THING** *Island CID 727* ○	3		13
21 Oct 00	**BEAUTIFUL DAY** *Island CIDX 766* ○	1	1	16
10 Feb 01	**STUCK IN A MOMENT YOU CAN'T GET OUT OF** *Island CIDX 770*	2		8
2 Jun 01	**NEW YEARS DUB** *Serious SERRO 030CD* MUSIQUE VS U2	15		5
28 Jul 01	**ELEVATION** *Island CIDX 780*	3		8
1 Dec 01	**WALK ON** *Island CIDX 788*	5		8
2 Nov 02	**ELECTRICAL STORM** *Island CIDX 808*	5		13
7 Feb 04	**TAKE ME TO THE CLOUDS ABOVE** *All Around The World CXGLOBE 313* LMC VS U2	1	2	12
20 Nov 04	**VERTIGO** *Island CIDX 878*	1	1	13
19 Feb 05	**SOMETIMES YOU CAN'T MAKE IT ON YOUR OWN** *Island CIDX886*	1	1	9
19 Feb 05	**ALL BECAUSE OF YOU (IMPORT)** *Island 0249870322CD*	51		1
18 Jun 05	**CITY OF BLINDING LIGHTS** *Island CIDX890*	2		9
22 Oct 05	**ALL BECAUSE OF YOU** *Island CIDX906*	4		4
8 Apr 06	**ONE** *Geffen MCSTD40458* MARY J BLIGE & U2	2		19
11 Nov 06	**THE SAINTS ARE COMING** *Mercury 1713137* & GREEN DAY	2		6
13 Jan 07	**WINDOW IN THE SKIES** *Mercury 1718124*	4		4
25 Oct 08	**WITH OR WITHOUT YOU** *Mercury GBAAN8790003*	66		1
28 Feb 09	**GET ON YOUR BOOTS** *Vertigo 1798676*	12		5
16 May 09	**MAGNIFICENT** *Vertigo 2701248*	42		1
6 Jun 09	**WITH OR WITHOUT YOU** *Mercury GBAAN8790003*	43		2
19 Sep 09	**I'LL GO CRAZY IF I DON'T GO CRAZY TONIGHT** *Vertigo 2716225*	32		1
10 Oct 09	**WITH OR WITHOUT YOU** *Mercury GBAAN8790003*	63		2

Top 3 Best-Selling Singles

		Approximate Sales
1	WITH OR WITHOUT YOU	460,000
2	PRIDE (IN THE NAME OF LOVE)	420,000
3	HOLD ME THRILL ME KISS ME KILL ME	380,000

V

UK, male vocal group – Antony Brant, Aaron Buckingham, Mark Harle, Kevin McDaid & Leon Pisani — Weeks on Chart: 15

Date	Title	Peak Position	Weeks at No.1	Weeks on Chart
5 Jun 04	**BLOOD SWEAT & TEARS** *Universal MCSXD 40362*	6		5
21 Aug 04	**HIP TO HIP/CAN YOU FEEL IT** *Universal MCSXD 40374*	5		6
20 Nov 04	**YOU STOOD UP** *Universal MCSXD 40388*	12		4

VAGABOND

UK, male vocal/instrumental group — Weeks on Chart: 1

Date	Title	Peak Position	Weeks at No.1	Weeks on Chart
15 Aug 09	**DON'T WANNA RUN NO MORE** *Geffen 2711585*	41		1

HOLLY VALANCE

Australia, female vocalist/actor (Holly Vukadinovic) — Weeks on Chart: 49

Date	Title	Peak Position	Weeks at No.1	Weeks on Chart
11 May 02	**KISS KISS** *London LONCD 464* ○	1	1	16
12 Oct 02	**DOWN BOY** *London LONCD 469*	2		14
21 Dec 02	**NAUGHTY GIRL** *London LONCD 472*	16		9
8 Nov 03	**STATE OF MIND** *London LONCD 482*	8		10

Silver-selling ● Gold-selling ● Platinum-selling (x multiples) ⊛ US No.1 ★ Peak Position Weeks at No.1 Weeks on Chart

RICKY VALANCE
UK, male vocalist (David Spencer) — 16

Date	Title / Label	Peak Position	Weeks at No.1	Weeks on Chart
25 Aug 60	**TELL LAURA I LOVE HER** *Columbia DB 4493*	1	3	16

RITCHIE VALENS
UK, male vocalist (Ritchie Valenzuela), d. 3 Feb 1959 (age 17) — 5

Date	Title / Label	Peak Position	Weeks at No.1	Weeks on Chart
6 Mar 59	**DONNA** *London HL 8803*	29		1
1 Aug 87	**LA BAMBA** *RCA PB 41435*	49		4

CATERINA VALENTE WITH WERNER MULLER & THE RIAS DANCE ORCHESTRA
France, female vocalist, d. 28 Dec 1998 (age 78) — 14

Date	Title / Label	Peak Position	Weeks at No.1	Weeks on Chart
19 Aug 55	**THE BREEZE AND I** *Polydor BM 6002*	5		14

VALENTINE BROTHERS
US, male vocal duo — 1

Date	Title / Label	Peak Position	Weeks at No.1	Weeks on Chart
23 Apr 83	**MONEY'S TOO TIGHT TO MENTION** *Energy NRG 1*	73		1

BROOKE VALENTINE FEATURING BIG BOI & LIL' JON
US, female/male vocal/rap trio — 2

Date	Title / Label	Peak Position	Weeks at No.1	Weeks on Chart
16 Jul 05	**GIRLFIGHT** *Virgin VUSDX301*	35		2

DICKIE VALENTINE
UK, male vocalist (Richard Brice), d. 6 May 1971 (age 41) — 92

Date	Title / Label	Peak Position	Weeks at No.1	Weeks on Chart
20 Feb 53	**BROKEN WINGS** *Decca F 9954*	12		1
13 Mar 53	**ALL THE TIME AND EVERYWHERE** *Decca F 10038*	9		3
5 Jun 53	**IN A GOLDEN COACH** *Decca F 10098*	7		1
5 Nov 54	**ENDLESS** *Decca F 10346*	19		1
17 Dec 54	**MR SANDMAN** *Decca F 10415*	5		12
17 Dec 54	**FINGER OF SUSPICION** *Decca F 10394* WITH THE STARGAZERS	1	3	15
18 Feb 55	**A BLOSSOM FELL** *Decca F 10430*	9		10
3 Jun 55	**I WONDER** *Decca F 10493*	4		15
25 Nov 55	**CHRISTMAS ALPHABET** *Decca F 10628*	1	3	7
16 Dec 55	**OLD PIANO RAG** *Decca F 10645*	15		5
7 Dec 56	**CHRISTMAS ISLAND** *Decca F 10798*	8		5
27 Dec 57	**SNOWBOUND FOR CHRISTMAS** *Decca F 10950*	28		1
13 Mar 59	**VENUS** *Pye Nixa 7N 15192*	20		8
23 Oct 59	**ONE MORE SUNRISE (MORGEN)** *Pye 7N 15221*	14		8

BOBBY VALENTINO
US, male vocalist (Bobby Wilson) — 22

Date	Title / Label	Peak Position	Weeks at No.1	Weeks on Chart
2 Jul 05	**SLOW DOWN** *Def Jam 9883239*	4		10
8 Oct 05	**TELL ME** *Def Jam 9885686*	38		3
30 Jun 07	**ANONYMOUS** *Def Jam 1736310* FEATURING TIMBALAND	25		6
6 Dec 08	**MRS OFFICER** *Island 1787327* LIL WAYNE, BOBBY VALENTINO, KIDD KIDD	57		3

JOE VALINO
US, male vocalist (Joseph Paolino), d. 26 Dec 1996 (age 67) — 2

Date	Title / Label	Peak Position	Weeks at No.1	Weeks on Chart
18 Jan 57	**THE GARDEN OF EDEN** *HMV POP 283*	23		2

FRANKIE VALLI
US, male vocalist (Francis Castellucio). See Four Seasons — 52

Date	Title / Label	Peak Position	Weeks at No.1	Weeks on Chart
12 Dec 70	**YOU'RE READY NOW** *Philips 320226*	11		13
1 Feb 75	**MY EYES ADORED YOU** *Private Stock PVT 1* ● ★	5		11
21 Jun 75	**SWEARIN' TO GOD** *Private Stock PVT 21*	31		5
17 Apr 76	**FALLEN ANGEL** *Private Stock PVT 51*	11		7
26 Aug 78	**GREASE** *RSO 012* ● ★	3		14
23 Mar 91	**GREASE – THE DREAM MIX** *PWL/Polydor PO 136* FRANKIE VALLI, JOHN TRAVOLTA & OLIVIA NEWTON-JOHN	47		2

VAMPIRE WEEKEND
US, male vocal/instrumental group — 22

Date	Title / Label	Peak Position	Weeks at No.1	Weeks on Chart
9 Feb 08	**A PUNK** *XL Recordings GBBKS0700527*	55		5
24 May 08	**OXFORD COMMA** *Abeano GBBKS0700526*	38		8
8 Nov 08	**A PUNK** *Abeano GB1410700081*	63		6
23 Jan 10	**COUSINS** *XL Recordings XLS473*	39		3

ARMIN VAN BUUREN
Holland, male DJ/producer — 10

Date	Title / Label	Peak Position	Weeks at No.1	Weeks on Chart
14 Feb 98	**BLUE FEAR** *Xtravaganza 0091485 EXT ARMIN*	45		1
12 Feb 00	**COMMUNICATION** *AM:PM CDAMPM 129 ARMIN*	18		3
10 May 03	**YET ANOTHER DAY** *Nebula NEBCD 042* FEATURING RAY WILSON	70		1
20 Mar 04	**BURNED WITH DESIRE** *Nebula NEBCDX 055* FEATURING JUSTINE SUISSA	45		2
28 Aug 04	**BLUE FEAR 2004** *Nebula NEBCD061*	52		2
2 Jul 05	**SHIVERS/SERENITY** *Nebula NEBCD069*	72		1

MARK VAN DALE WITH ENRICO
Belgium, male DJ/production duo — 1

Date	Title / Label	Peak Position	Weeks at No.1	Weeks on Chart
3 Oct 98	**WATER WAVE** *Club Tools 0065815 CLU*	71		1

DAVID VAN DAY
UK, male vocalist (David Day). See Dollar, Guys 'N' Dolls — 3

Date	Title / Label	Peak Position	Weeks at No.1	Weeks on Chart
14 May 83	**YOUNG AMERICANS TALKING** *WEA DAY 1*	43		3

RON VAN DEN BEUKEN
Holland, male DJ/producer. See Mystery — 1

Date	Title / Label	Peak Position	Weeks at No.1	Weeks on Chart
19 Jun 04	**TIMELESS (KEEP ON MOVIN')** *Manifesto 9866717*	65		1

GEORGE VAN DUSEN
UK, male vocalist (Albert Thomas Harrington), d. 1992 — 4

Date	Title / Label	Peak Position	Weeks at No.1	Weeks on Chart
17 Dec 88	**IT'S PARTY TIME AGAIN** *Bri-Tone 7BT 001*	43		4

PAUL VAN DYK
Germany, male DJ/producer — 37

Date	Title / Label	Peak Position	Weeks at No.1	Weeks on Chart
17 May 97	**FORBIDDEN FRUIT** *Deviant DVNT 18CDR*	69		1
15 Nov 97	**WORDS** *Deviant DVNT 26CDS* FEATURING TONI HALLIDAY	54		1
5 Sep 98	**FOR AN ANGEL** *Deviant DVNT 24CDS*	28		4
20 Nov 99	**ANOTHER WAY/AVENUE** *Deviant DVNT 35CDS*	13		7
20 May 00	**TELL ME WHY (THE RIDDLE)** *Deviant DVNT 36CDS* FEATURING SAINT ETIENNE	7		5
2 Dec 00	**WE ARE ALIVE** *Deviant DVNT 38CDS*	15		6
12 Jul 03	**NOTHING BUT YOU** *Positiva CDTIVS 192* FEATURING HEMSTOCK	14		5
18 Oct 03	**TIMES OF OUR LIVES/CONNECTED** *Positiva CDTIVS 196* FEATURING VEGA 4	28		2
17 Apr 04	**CRUSH** *Positiva CDTIVS 204* FEATURING SECOND SUN	42		3
17 Sep 05	**THE OTHER SIDE** *Positiva CDTIVS221* FEATURING WAYNE JACKSON	58		1
13 Jun 09	**FOR AN ANGEL 2009** *New State DEW760900011*	68		2

LEROY VAN DYKE
US, male vocalist — 20

Date	Title / Label	Peak Position	Weeks at No.1	Weeks on Chart
4 Jan 62	**WALK ON BY** *Mercury AMT 1166*	5		17
26 Apr 62	**BIG MAN IN A BIG HOUSE** *Mercury AMT 1173*	34		3

NIELS VAN GOGH
Germany, male DJ/producer — 1

Date	Title / Label	Peak Position	Weeks at No.1	Weeks on Chart
10 Apr 99	**PULVERTURM** *Logic 74321649192*	75		1

VAN HALEN
US/Holland, male vocal/instrumental group – David Lee Roth* (replaced by Sammy Hagar*), Michael Anthony (Michael Sobolewski), Alex & Eddie Van Halen — 51

Date	Title / Label	Peak Position	Weeks at No.1	Weeks on Chart
28 Jun 80	**RUNNIN' WITH THE DEVIL** *Warner Brothers HM 10*	52		3
4 Feb 84	**JUMP** *Warner Brothers W 9384* ★	7		13
19 May 84	**PANAMA** *Warner Brothers W 9273*	61		2
5 Apr 86	**WHY CAN'T THIS BE LOVE** *Warner Brothers W 8740*	8		14
12 Jul 86	**DREAMS** *Warner Brothers W 8642*	62		2
6 Aug 88	**WHEN IT'S LOVE** *Warner Brothers W 7816*	28		7
1 Apr 89	**FEELS SO GOOD** *Warner Brothers W 7565*	63		1
22 Jun 91	**POUNDCAKE** *Warner Brothers W 0045*	74		1
19 Oct 91	**TOP OF THE WORLD** *Warner Brothers W 0066*	63		1
27 Mar 93	**JUMP (LIVE)** *Warner Brothers W 0155CD*	26		3
21 Jan 95	**DON'T TELL ME** *Warner Brothers W 0280CD*	27		2
1 Apr 95	**CAN'T STOP LOVING YOU** *Warner Brothers W 0288CD*	33		2

ARMAND VAN HELDEN

US, male DJ/producer. See Duck Sauce — 118

Date	Title	Peak Position	Weeks at No.1	Weeks on Chart
8 Mar 97	**THE FUNK PHENOMENA** *ZYX 8523U8*	38		2
8 Nov 97	**ULTRAFUNKULA** *ffrr FCD 317*	46		1
6 Feb 99	**YOU DON'T KNOW ME** *ffrr FCD 357* FEATURING DUANE HARDEN ●	1	1	11
1 May 99	**FLOWERZ** *ffrr FCD 361* FEATURING ROLAND CLARK	18		6
20 May 00	**KOOCHY** *ffrr FCDP 379*	4		7
3 Nov 01	**WHY CAN'T YOU FREE SOME TIME** *ffrr FCD 402*	34		2
15 Dec 01	**YOU CAN'T CHANGE ME** *Defected DFECT 41CDS* ROGER SANCHEZ FEATURING ARMAND VAN HELDEN & N'DEA DAVENPORT	25		4
1 May 04	**HEAR MY NAME** *Southern Fried ECB64CDS*	34		2
11 Sep 04	**MY MY MY** *Southern Fried ECB67CDS*	15		15
2 Jul 05	**INTO YOUR EYES** *Southern Fried ECB78CDS*	48		2
1 Oct 05	**WHEN THE LIGHTS GO DOWN** *Southern Fried ECB85CDS*	70		1
17 Jun 06	**MYMYMY** *Southern Fried ECB97CDS* FEATURING TARA	12		16
12 May 07	**NYC BEAT** *Southern Fried ECB113CDS*	22		15
1 Sep 07	**I WANT YOUR SOUL** *Southern Fried ECD125CDS*	19		11
30 May 09	**BONKERS** *Dirtee Stank STANK005CDS* DIZZEE RASCAL FEATURING ARMAND VAN HELDEN ●	1	1	23

DENISE VAN OUTEN

UK, female actor/TV personality/vocalist — 16

Date	Title	Peak Position	Weeks at No.1	Weeks on Chart
26 Dec 98	**ESPECIALLY FOR YOU** *RCA 74321644722* DENISE & JOHNNY	3		12
29 Jun 02	**CAN'T TAKE MY EYES OFF YOU** *Columbia 6721052* ANDY WILLIAMS & DENISE VAN OUTEN	23		4

VAN TWIST

Belgium, male instrumental/production duo — 2

Date	Title	Peak Position	Weeks at No.1	Weeks on Chart
16 Feb 85	**SHAFT** *Polydor POSP 729*	57		2

DESPINA VANDI

Greece, female vocalist — 1

Date	Title	Peak Position	Weeks at No.1	Weeks on Chart
20 Mar 04	**GIA** *Positiva CDTIVS 199*	63		1

LUTHER VANDROSS

US, male vocalist/producer, d. 1 July 2005 (age 54). See Change — 157

Date	Title	Peak Position	Weeks at No.1	Weeks on Chart
19 Feb 83	**NEVER TOO MUCH** *Epic EPC A 3101*	44		6
26 Jul 86	**GIVE ME THE REASON** *Epic A 7288*	60		3
21 Feb 87	**GIVE ME THE REASON** *Epic 6502167*	71		2
28 Mar 87	**SEE ME** *Epic LUTH 1*	60		4
11 Jul 87	**I REALLY DIDN'T MEAN IT** *Epic LUTH 3*	16		10
5 Sep 87	**STOP TO LOVE** *Epic LUTH 2*	24		7
7 Nov 87	**SO AMAZING** *Epic LUTH 4*	33		6
23 Jan 88	**GIVE ME THE REASON** *Epic LUTH 5*	26		6
16 Apr 88	**I GAVE IT UP (WHEN I FELL IN LOVE)** *Epic LUTH 6*	28		5
9 Jul 88	**THERE'S NOTHING BETTER THAN LOVE** *Epic LUTH 7* DUET WITH GREGORY HINES	72		1
8 Oct 88	**ANY LOVE** *Epic LUTH 8*	31		4
4 Feb 89	**SHE WON'T TALK TO ME** *Epic LUTH 9*	34		4
22 Apr 89	**COME BACK** *Epic LUTH 10*	53		3
28 Oct 89	**NEVER TOO MUCH (REMIX)** *Epic LUTH 12*	13		7
6 Jan 90	**HERE AND NOW** *Epic LUTH 13*	43		3
27 Apr 91	**POWER OF LOVE – LOVE POWER** *Epic 6568227*	46		5
18 Jan 92	**THE RUSH** *Epic 6577237*	53		3
15 Aug 92	**THE BEST THINGS IN LIFE ARE FREE** *Perspective PERSS 7400* & JANET JACKSON WITH SPECIAL GUESTS BBD & RALPH TRESVANT ●	2		13
22 May 93	**LITTLE MIRACLES (HAPPEN EVERY DAY)** *Epic 6590442*	28		3
18 Sep 93	**HEAVEN KNOWS** *Epic 6596522*	34		3
4 Dec 93	**LOVE IS ON THE WAY** *Epic 6599592*	38		2
17 Sep 94	**ENDLESS LOVE** *Epic 6608062* & MARIAH CAREY	3		16
26 Nov 94	**LOVE THE ONE YOU'RE WITH** *Epic 6610612*	31		4
4 Feb 95	**ALWAYS AND FOREVER** *Epic 6611942*	20		5
15 Apr 95	**AIN'T NO STOPPING US NOW** *Epic 6614242*	22		3
11 Nov 95	**POWER OF LOVE – LOVE POWER (REMIX)** *Epic 6625902*	31		3
16 Dec 95	**THE BEST THINGS IN LIFE ARE FREE (REMIX)** *A&M 5813092* & JANET JACKSON WITH SPECIAL GUESTS BBD & RALPH TRESVANT	7		7
23 Dec 95	**EVERY YEAR EVERY CHRISTMAS** *Epic 6627762*	43		2
12 Oct 96	**YOUR SECRET LOVE** *Epic 6638385*	14		5
28 Dec 96	**I CAN MAKE IT BETTER** *Epic 6640632*	44		2
20 Oct 01	**TAKE YOU OUT** *J Records 74321899442*	59		1
28 Feb 04	**DANCE WITH MY FATHER** *J Records 82876569982*	21		4
21 Oct 06	**SHINE** *J Records 88697025032*	50		2
5 Sep 09	**DANCE WITH MY FATHER** *J Records 82876569982*	38		2
26 Dec 09	**DANCE WITH MY FATHER** *J Records 82876569982*	48		1

VANESSA-MAE

Singapore, female vocalist/violinist (Vanessa-Mae Vanakorn Nicholson) — 21

Date	Title	Peak Position	Weeks at No.1	Weeks on Chart
28 Jan 95	**TOCCATA AND FUGUE** *EMI Classics MAE 886812*	16		10
20 May 95	**RED HOT** *EMI CDMAE 2*	37		2
18 Nov 95	**CLASSICAL GAS** *EMI CDEM 404*	41		2
26 Oct 96	**I'M A DOUN FOR LACK O' JOHNNIE (A LITTLE SCOTTISH FANTASY)** *EMI CDMAE 3*	28		2
25 Oct 97	**STORM** *EMI CDEM 497*	54		1
20 Dec 97	**I FEEL LOVE** *EMI CDEM 503*	41		2
5 Dec 98	**DEVIL'S THRILL/REFLECTION** *EMI CDEM 530*	53		1
28 Jul 01	**WHITE BIRD** *EMI CDVAN 002*	66		1

VANGELIS

Greece, male keyboard/synthesizer player (Evangelos Papathanassiou). See Aphrodite's Child, Jon & Vangelis — 25

Date	Title	Peak Position	Weeks at No.1	Weeks on Chart
9 May 81	**CHARIOTS OF FIRE – TITLES** *Polydor POSP 246* ★	12		10
11 Jul 81	**HEAVEN AND HELL, THIRD MOVEMENT (THEME FROM THE BBC-TV SERIES 'THE COSMOS)** *BBC 1*	48		6
24 Apr 82	**CHARIOTS OF FIRE – TITLES** *Polydor POSP 246*	41		7
31 Oct 92	**CONQUEST OF PARADISE** *East West YZ 704*	60		2

VANILLA

UK, female vocal group — 10

Date	Title	Peak Position	Weeks at No.1	Weeks on Chart
22 Nov 97	**NO WAY NO WAY** *EMI CDEM 487*	14		8
23 May 98	**TRUE TO US** *EMI CDEM 509*	36		2

VANILLA FUDGE

US, male vocal/instrumental group — 11

Date	Title	Peak Position	Weeks at No.1	Weeks on Chart
9 Aug 67	**YOU KEEP ME HANGIN' ON** *Atlantic 584 123*	18		11

VANILLA ICE

US, male rapper (Robert van Winkle) — 39

Date	Title	Peak Position	Weeks at No.1	Weeks on Chart
24 Nov 90	**ICE ICE BABY** *SBK 18* ⊛ ★	1	4	13
2 Feb 91	**PLAY THAT FUNKY MUSIC** *SBK 20*	10		6
30 Mar 91	**I LOVE YOU** *SBK 22*	45		5
29 Jun 91	**ROLLIN' IN MY 5.0** *SBK 27*	27		4
10 Aug 91	**SATISFACTION** *SBK 29*	22		4
13 Feb 10	**UNDER PRESSURE (ICE ICE BABY)** *Sony BMG 88697658992* JEDWARD FEATURING VANILLA ICE	2		7

VANITY FARE

UK, male vocal/instrumental group – Terry Brice, Dick Allix, Tony Goulden, Tony Jarrett & Barry Landerman — 34

Date	Title	Peak Position	Weeks at No.1	Weeks on Chart
28 Aug 68	**I LIVE FOR THE SUN** *Page One POF 075*	20		9
23 Jul 69	**EARLY IN THE MORNING** *Page One POF 142*	8		12
27 Dec 69	**HITCHIN' A RIDE** *Page One POF 158*	16		13

JOE T VANNELLI PROJECT

Italy, male DJ/producer — 2

Date	Title	Peak Position	Weeks at No.1	Weeks on Chart
17 Jun 95	**SWEETEST DAY OF MAY** *Positiva CDTIV 36*	45		2

RANDY VANWARMER

US, male vocalist (Randall Van Wormer), d. 12 Jan 2004 (age 48) — 11

Date	Title	Peak Position	Weeks at No.1	Weeks on Chart
4 Aug 79	**JUST WHEN I NEEDED YOU MOST** *Bearsville WIP 6516* ●	8		11

VAPORS

UK, male vocal/instrumental group – David Fenton, Edward Bazalgette & Howard & Steve Smith — 23

Date	Title	Peak Position	Weeks at No.1	Weeks on Chart
9 Feb 80	**TURNING JAPANESE** *United Artists BP 334* ●	3		13
5 Jul 80	**NEWS AT TEN** *United Artists BP 345*	44		4
11 Jul 81	**JIMMIE JONES** *Liberty BP 401*	44		6

VARDIS

UK, male vocal/instrumental trio — 4

Date	Title	Peak Position	Weeks at No.1	Weeks on Chart
27 Sep 80	**LET'S GO** *Logo VAR 1*	59		4

Silver-selling ● Gold-selling ● Platinum-selling (x multiples) ★ US No.1 — Peak Position / Weeks at No.1 / Weeks on Chart

HALO VARGA

US, male producer (Brian Varga) — 1

Date	Title	Peak Position	Weeks at No.1	Weeks on Chart
9 Dec 00	**FUTURE** *Hooj Choons HOOJ 101CD*	67		1

VARIOUS ARTISTS (EPs & LPs)

121

Date	Title	Peak Position	Weeks at No.1	Weeks on Chart
15 Jun 56	**CAROUSEL – ORIGINAL SOUNDTRACK (LP)** *Capitol LCT 6105*	26		2
29 Jun 56	**ALL STAR HIT PARADE** *Decca F 10752*	2		9
26 Jul 57	**ALL STAR HIT PARADE NO. 2** *Decca 10915*	15		7
9 Dec 89	**THE FOOD CHRISTMAS EP** *Food 23*	63		1
20 Jan 90	**THE FURTHER ADVENTURES OF THE NORTH** *Deconstruction PT 43372*	64		2
2 Nov 91	**THE APPLE EP** *Apple APP 1*	60		1
11 Jul 92	**FOURPLAY (EP)** *XL Recordings XLFP 1*	45		2
7 Nov 92	**THE FRED EP** *Heavenly HVN 19*	26		3
24 Apr 93	**GIMME SHELTER (EP)** *Food CDORDERA 1*	23		4
5 Jun 93	**SUBPLATES VOLUME 1 (EP)** *Suburban Base SUBBASE 24CD*	69		1
9 Oct 93	**THE TWO TONE EP** *2 Tone CHSTT 31*	30		3
4 Nov 95	**HELP (EP)** *Go! Discs GODCD 135*	51		2
16 Mar 96	**NEW YORK UNDERCOVER 4-TRACK EP** *Uptown MCSTD 48002*	39		1
30 Mar 96	**DANGEROUS MINDS EP** *MCA MCSTD 48007*	35		1
29 Nov 97	**PERFECT DAY** *Chrysalis CDNEED 01* ⊛x2	1	3	21
12 Sep 98	**THE FULL MONTY-MONSTER MIX** *RCA Victor 74321602582*	62		1
26 Sep 98	**TRADE (EP) (DISC 2)** *Tidy Trax TREP 2*	75		1
10 Apr 99	**THANK ABBA FOR THE MUSIC** *Epic ABCD 1* ●	4		13
25 Dec 99	**IT'S ONLY ROCK 'N' ROLL** *Universal TV 1566012*	19		10
17 Jun 00	**PERFECT DAY (RE-RECORDING)** *Chrysalis 8887840*	69		1
10 Nov 01	**HARD BEAT EP 19** *Nukleuz NUKPA 0369*	71		1
19 Nov 05	**UNITED NATIONS OF HOUSE – VOLUME 1** *CR2 CDC2014*	71		1
3 Dec 05	**EVER FALLEN IN LOVE (WITH SOMEONE YOU SHOULDN'T'VE)** *EMI PEELCD1*	28		2
17 May 80	**CALIBRE CUTS** *Calibre CAB 502* VARIOUS ARTISTS (MONTAGES)	75		2
25 Nov 89	**DEEP HEAT '89** *Deep Heat DEEP 10* VARIOUS ARTISTS (MONTAGES)	12		11
3 Mar 90	**THE BRITS 1990** *RCA PB 43565* VARIOUS ARTISTS (MONTAGES)	2		7
28 Apr 90	**THE SIXTH SENSE** *Deep Heat DEEP 12* VARIOUS ARTISTS (MONTAGES)	49		2
10 Nov 90	**TIME TO MAKE THE FLOOR BURN** *Megabass MEGAX 1* VARIOUS ARTISTS (MONTAGES)	16		9

JUNIOR VASQUEZ

US, male DJ/producer (Donald Mattern) — 5

Date	Title	Peak Position	Weeks at No.1	Weeks on Chart
15 Jul 95	**GET YOUR HANDS OFF MY MAN!** *Tribal UK/Positiva CDTIV 37*	22		3
31 Aug 96	**IF MADONNA CALLS** *Multiply CDMULTY 13*	24		2

VAST

Australia, male vocal/instrumental group — 1

Date	Title	Peak Position	Weeks at No.1	Weeks on Chart
16 Sep 00	**FREE** *Mushroom MUSH 79CDS*	55		1

SVEN VATH

Germany, male producer/DJ — 5

Date	Title	Peak Position	Weeks at No.1	Weeks on Chart
24 Jul 93	**L'ESPERANZA** *Eye Q YZ 757*	63		2
6 Nov 93	**AN ACCIDENT IN PARADISE** *Eye Q YZ 778CD*	57		2
22 Oct 94	**HARLEQUIN – THE BEAUTY AND THE BEAST** *Eye Q YZ 857*	72		1

FRANKIE VAUGHAN

UK, male vocalist (Frank Abelson), d. 17 Sep 1999 (age 71). Liverpool's first major chart artist was one of the UK's top heartthrobs/entertainers in the 1950s. His movie appearance alongside Marilyn Monroe in 1960 was the inspiration for the group name Frankie Goes To Hollywood — 241

Date	Title	Peak Position	Weeks at No.1	Weeks on Chart
29 Jan 54	**ISTANBUL (NOT CONSTANTINOPLE)** *HMV B 10599* WITH THE PETER KNIGHT SINGERS	11		1
28 Jan 55	**HAPPY DAYS AND LONELY NIGHTS** *HMV B 10783*	12		3
22 Apr 55	**TWEEDLE DEE** *Philips PB 423*	17		1
2 Dec 55	**SEVENTEEN** *Philips PB 511*	18		3
3 Feb 56	**MY BOY FLAT TOP** *Philips PB 544*	20		2
9 Nov 56	**THE GREEN DOOR** *Philips PB 640*	2		15
11 Jan 57	**THE GARDEN OF EDEN** *Philips PB 660*	1	4	13
4 Oct 57	**MAN ON FIRE/WANDERIN' EYES** *Philips PB 729*	6		12
1 Nov 57	**GOTTA HAVE SOMETHING IN THE BANK FRANK** *Philips PB 751* & THE KAYE SISTERS	8		11
20 Dec 57	**KISSES SWEETER THAN WINE** *Philips PB 775*	8		11
7 Mar 58	**CAN'T GET ALONG WITHOUT YOU/WE ARE NOT ALONE** *Philips PB 793*	11		6
9 May 58	**KEWPIE DOLL** *Philips PB 825*	10		12
1 Aug 58	**WONDERFUL THINGS** *Philips PB 834*	22		6
10 Oct 58	**AM I WASTING MY TIME ON YOU** *Philips PB 865*	25		4
30 Jan 59	**THAT'S MY DOLL** *Philips PB 895*	28		2
1 May 59	**COME SOFTLY TO ME** *Philips PB 913* & THE KAYE SISTERS	9		9
24 Jul 59	**THE HEART OF A MAN** *Philips PB 930*	5		14
18 Sep 59	**WALKIN' TALL** *Philips PB 931*	28		2
29 Jan 60	**WHAT MORE DO YOU WANT** *Philips PB 985*	25		2
22 Sep 60	**KOOKIE LITTLE PARADISE** *Philips PB 1054*	31		5
27 Oct 60	**MILORD** *Philips PB 1066*	34		6
9 Nov 61	**TOWER OF STRENGTH** *Philips PB 1195*	1	3	13
1 Feb 62	**DON'T STOP TWIST** *Philips PB 1219*	22		7
27 Sep 62	**HERCULES** *Philips 326542 BF*	42		4
24 Jan 63	**LOOP-DE-LOOP** *Philips 326566 BF*	5		21
20 Jun 63	**HEY MAMA** *Philips BF 1254*	21		9
4 Jun 64	**HELLO DOLLY** *Philips BF 1339*	18		11
11 Mar 65	**SOMEONE MUST HAVE HURT YOU A LOT** *Philips BF 1394*	46		1
23 Aug 67	**THERE MUST BE A WAY** *Columbia DB 8248*	7		21
15 Nov 67	**SO TIRED** *Columbia DB 8298*	21		9
28 Feb 68	**NEVERTHELESS** *Columbia DB 8354*	29		5

MALCOLM VAUGHAN

UK, male vocalist (Malcolm Thomas), d. 9 Feb 2010 (age 80) — 105

Date	Title	Peak Position	Weeks at No.1	Weeks on Chart
1 Jul 55	**EVERY DAY OF MY LIFE** *HMV B 10874*	5		16
27 Jan 56	**WITH YOUR LOVE** *HMV POP 130* WITH THE PETER KNIGHT SINGERS	18		3
26 Oct 56	**ST. THERESE OF THE ROSES** *HMV POP 250*	3		20
12 Apr 57	**THE WORLD IS MINE** *HMV POP 303*	29		3
10 May 57	**CHAPEL OF THE ROSES** *HMV POP 325*	13		8
29 Nov 57	**MY SPECIAL ANGEL** *HMV POP 419*	3		14
21 Mar 58	**TO BE LOVED** *HMV POP 459* WITH THE MICHAEL SAMMES SINGERS	14		12
17 Oct 58	**MORE THAN EVER (COME PRIMA)** *HMV POP 538* WITH THE MICHAEL SAMMES SINGERS	5		14
27 Feb 59	**WAIT FOR ME/WILLINGLY** *HMV POP 590*	13		15

NORMAN VAUGHAN

UK, male comedian/vocalist, d. 17 May 2002 (age 75) — 5

Date	Title	Peak Position	Weeks at No.1	Weeks on Chart
17 May 62	**SWINGING IN THE RAIN** *Pye 7N 15438*	34		5

SARAH VAUGHAN

US, female vocalist, d. 3 Apr 1990 (age 66) — 34

Date	Title	Peak Position	Weeks at No.1	Weeks on Chart
27 Sep 57	**PASSING STRANGERS** *Mercury MT 164* BILLY ECKSTINE & SARAH VAUGHAN	22		2
11 Sep 59	**BROKEN HEARTED MELODY** *Mercury AMT 1057*	7		13
29 Dec 60	**LET'S/SERENATA** *Columbia DB 4542*	37		4
12 Mar 69	**PASSING STRANGERS** *Mercury MF 1082* BILLY ECKSTINE & SARAH VAUGHAN	20		15

BILLY VAUGHN

US, male orchestra leader, d. 26 Sep 1991 (age 72) — 8

Date	Title	Peak Position	Weeks at No.1	Weeks on Chart
27 Jan 56	**SHIFTING WHISPERING SANDS** *London HLD 8205* BILLY VAUGHN ORCHESTRA & CHORUS, NARRATION BY KEN NORDINE	20		1
23 Mar 56	**THEME FROM THE 'THREEPENNY OPERA'** *London HLD 8238*	12		7

VAULTS

UK, male vocal/instrumental group — 1

Date	Title	Peak Position	Weeks at No.1	Weeks on Chart
20 Mar 04	**NO SLEEP NO NEED EP** *Red Flag RFO9CDS*	70		1

VBIRDS

UK, female cartoon vocal group — 3

Date	Title	Peak Position	Weeks at No.1	Weeks on Chart
3 May 03	**VIRTUALITY** *Liberty CDVIRT001*	21		3

BOBBY VEE

US, male vocalist (Robert Velline) — 134

Date	Title	Peak Position	Weeks at No.1	Weeks on Chart
19 Jan 61	**RUBBER BALL** *London HLG 9255*	4		11
13 Apr 61	**MORE THAN I CAN SAY/STAYING IN** *London HLG 9316*	4		16
3 Aug 61	**HOW MANY TEARS** *London HLG 9389*	10		13
26 Oct 61	**TAKE GOOD CARE OF MY BABY** *London HLG 9438* ★	3		16
21 Dec 61	**RUN TO HIM** *London HLG 9470*	6		15
8 Mar 62	**PLEASE DON'T ASK ABOUT BARBARA** *Liberty LIB 55419*	29		9
7 Jun 62	**SHARING YOU** *Liberty LIB 55451*	10		13
27 Sep 62	**A FOREVER KIND OF LOVE** *Liberty LIB 10046*	13		19
7 Feb 63	**THE NIGHT HAS A THOUSAND EYES** *Liberty LIB 10069*	3		12
20 Jun 63	**BOBBY TOMORROW** *Liberty LIB 55530*	21		10

LOUIE VEGA

US, male producer (Luis Vager). See Lil Mo' Yin Yang, Nuyorican Soul, Masters At Work — **5**

Date	Title / Label	Peak	Wks at No.1	Wks on Chart
5 Oct 91	**RIDE ON THE RHYTHM** *Atlantic A 7602* LITTLE LOUIE VEGA & MARC ANTHONY	71		1
23 May 92	**RIDE ON THE RHYTHM** *Atlantic A 7486* & MARK ANTHONY	70		1
31 Jan 98	**RIDE ON THE RHYTHM (REMIX)** *Perfecto PERF 151CD1* LITTLE LOUIE & MARC ANTHONY	36		2
23 Nov 02	**DIAMOND LIFE** *Distance D12409* & JAY 'SINISTER' SEALEE STARRING JULIE McKNIGHT	52		1

SUZANNE VEGA

US, female vocalist/guitarist — **52**

Date	Title / Label	Peak	Wks at No.1	Wks on Chart
18 Jan 86	**SMALL BLUE THING** *A&M AM 294*	65		3
22 Mar 86	**MARLENE ON THE WALL** *A&M AM 309*	21		9
7 Jun 86	**LEFT OF CENTER** *A&M AM 320* FEATURING JOE JACKSON	32		9
23 May 87	**LUKA** *A&M VEGA 1*	23		8
18 Jul 87	**TOM'S DINER** *A&M VEGA 2*	58		3
19 May 90	**BOOK OF DREAMS** *A&M AM 559*	66		1
28 Jul 90	**TOM'S DINER** *A&M AM 592* DNA FEATURING SUZANNE VEGA ○	2		10
22 Aug 92	**IN LIVERPOOL** *A&M AM 0029*	52		2
24 Oct 92	**99.9o F** *A&M AM 0085*	46		2
19 Dec 92	**BLOOD MAKES NOISE** *A&M AM 0112*	60		3
6 Mar 93	**WHEN HEROES GO DOWN** *A&M AMCD 0158*	58		1
22 Feb 97	**NO CHEAP THRILL** *A&M 5818692*	40		1

TATA VEGA

US, female vocalist (Carmen Rosa Vega) — **4**

Date	Title / Label	Peak	Wks at No.1	Wks on Chart
26 May 79	**GET IT UP FOR LOVE/I JUST KEEP THINKING ABOUT YOU BABY** *Motown TMG 1140*	52		4

VEGAS

UK, male vocal/instrumental duo — **10**

Date	Title / Label	Peak	Wks at No.1	Wks on Chart
19 Sep 92	**POSSESSED** *RCA 74321110437*	32		4
28 Nov 92	**SHE** *RCA 74321124657*	43		4
3 Apr 93	**WALK INTO THE WIND** *RCA 74321122462*	65		2

VEILS

UK, male vocal/instrumental group — **2**

Date	Title / Label	Peak	Wks at No.1	Wks on Chart
7 Feb 04	**THE WILD SON** *Rough Trade RTRADESCD 154*	74		1
19 Jun 04	**THE TIDE THAT LEFT AND NEVER CAME BACK** *Rough Trade RTRADSCD 164*	63		1

TOM VEK

UK, male vocalist/guitarist — **3**

Date	Title / Label	Peak	Wks at No.1	Wks on Chart
2 Apr 05	**I AIN'T SAYING MY GOODBYES** *Go Beat/Polydor 9870674*	45		1
2 Jul 05	**C-C (YOU SET THE FIRE IN ME)** *Go Beat/Polydor 9871846*	60		1
5 Nov 05	**NOTHING BUT GREEN LIGHTS** *Go Beat 9874748*	59		1

ROSIE VELA

US, female vocalist (Roseanne Vela) — **7**

Date	Title / Label	Peak	Wks at No.1	Wks on Chart
17 Jan 87	**MAGIC SMILE** *A&M AM 369*	27		7

VELVELETTES

US, female vocal group — **7**

Date	Title / Label	Peak	Wks at No.1	Wks on Chart
31 Jul 71	**THESE THINGS WILL KEEP ME LOVING YOU** *Tamla Motown TMG 780*	34		7

VELVET REVOLVER

US, male vocal/instrumental group — **5**

Date	Title / Label	Peak	Wks at No.1	Wks on Chart
24 Jul 04	**SLITHER** *RCA 82876633312*	35		3
23 Oct 04	**FALL TO PIECES** *RCA 82876647692*	32		2

VELVET UNDERGROUND

US, male/female vocal/instrumental group — **1**

Date	Title / Label	Peak	Wks at No.1	Wks on Chart
12 Mar 94	**VENUS IN FURS (LIVE)** *Sire W 0224CD*	71		1

VELVETS

US, male vocal group — **2**

Date	Title / Label	Peak	Wks at No.1	Wks on Chart
11 May 61	**THAT LUCKY OLD SUN** *London HLU 9328*	46		1
17 Aug 61	**TONIGHT (COULD BE THE NIGHT)** *London HLU 9372*	50		1

VENGABOYS

Holland, male DJ/production duo – Dennis Van Den Driesschen & Wessel Van Diepen – & Holland/Trinidad/Brazil, male/female vocal/dance group – Yorick Bakker, Roy Den Burger, Robin Pors, Denise Post-Van Rijswijk & Kim Sassabone — **99**

Date	Title / Label	Peak	Wks at No.1	Wks on Chart
28 Nov 98	**UP AND DOWN** *Positiva CDTIV 105* ●	4		15
13 Mar 99	**WE LIKE TO PARTY (THE VENGABUS)** *Positiva CDTIV 108* ●	3		14
26 Jun 99	**BOOM BOOM BOOM BOOM!!** *Positiva CDTIV 114* ●	1	1	15
11 Sep 99	**WE'RE GOING TO IBIZA! (IMPORT)** *Jive 550422*	69		1
18 Sep 99	**WE'RE GOING TO IBIZA!** *Positiva CDTIVS 119* ●	1	1	12
18 Dec 99	**KISS (WHEN THE SUN DON'T SHINE)** *Positiva CDTIV 122* ○	3		18
11 Mar 00	**SHALALA LALA** *Positiva CDTIV 126* ○	5		10
8 Jul 00	**UNCLE JOHN FROM JAMAICA** *Positiva CDTIV 135*	6		7
14 Oct 00	**CHEEKAH BOW WOW (THAT COMPUTER SONG)** *Positiva CDTIV 142*	19		5
24 Feb 01	**FOREVER AS ONE** *Positiva CDTIV 148*	28		2

VENT 414

UK, male vocal/instrumental group — **1**

Date	Title / Label	Peak	Wks at No.1	Wks on Chart
28 Sep 96	**FIXER** *Polydor 5753292*	71		1

VENTURES

US, male instrumental group – Bob Bogle, d. 14 Jun 2009, Nokie Edwards, Mel Taylor, d. 11 Aug 1996, & Don Wilson — **31**

Date	Title / Label	Peak	Wks at No.1	Wks on Chart
8 Sep 60	**WALK DON'T RUN** *Top Rank JAR 417*	8		13
1 Dec 60	**PERFIDIA** *London HLG 9232*	4		13
9 Mar 61	**RAM-BUNK-SHUSH** *London HLG 9292*	45		1
11 May 61	**LULLABY OF THE LEAVES** *London HLG 9344*	43		4

VERACOCHA

Holland, male production duo. See Gouryella, Moonman, Starparty, System F — **4**

Date	Title / Label	Peak	Wks at No.1	Wks on Chart
15 May 99	**CARTE BLANCHE** *Positiva CDTIV 110*	22		4

VERBALICIOUS

UK, female rapper (Natalia Cappuccini, b. Natalie Keery-Fisher) — **5**

Date	Title / Label	Peak	Wks at No.1	Wks on Chart
5 Mar 05	**DON'T PLAY NICE** *All Around The World/Adventure VERCD1*	11		5

VERKA SERDUCHKA

Ukraine, male comedian/vocalist (Andriy Danylko) — **1**

Date	Title / Label	Peak	Wks at No.1	Wks on Chart
26 May 07	**DANCING LASHA TUMBAI (UKRAINE)** *Danilko DKBV70705142*	28		1

VERNONS GIRLS

UK, female vocal group — **31**

Date	Title / Label	Peak	Wks at No.1	Wks on Chart
17 May 62	**LOVER PLEASE** *Decca F 11450*	16		9
23 Aug 62	**LOVER PLEASE/YOU KNOW WHAT I MEAN** *Decca F 11450*	39		11
6 Sep 62	**LOCO-MOTION** *Decca F 11495*	47		1
3 Jan 63	**FUNNY ALL OVER** *Decca F 11549*	31		8
18 Apr 63	**DO THE BIRD** *Decca F 11629*	44		2

VERNON'S WONDERLAND

Germany, male producer (Matthias Hoffmann). See Brainchild, Cygnus X — **1**

Date	Title / Label	Peak	Wks at No.1	Wks on Chart
25 May 96	**VERNON'S WONDERLAND** *Eye Q Classics EYECL 004CD*	59		1

VERONICAS

Australia, female vocal duo – Jessica & Lisa Origliasso – & male/female instrumental group — **23**

Date	Title / Label	Peak	Wks at No.1	Wks on Chart
6 Jun 09	**UNTOUCHED** *Warner Brothers USWB10704602*	8		19
10 Oct 09	**4 EVER** *Sire W820CD2*	17		4

VERTICAL HORIZON

US, male vocal/instrumental group — **2**

Date	Title / Label	Peak	Wks at No.1	Wks on Chart
26 Aug 00	**EVERYTHING YOU WANT** *RCA 74321748692* ★	42		2

Silver-selling ● Gold-selling ● Platinum-selling (x multiples) ⊛ US No.1 ★ Peak Position Weeks at No.1 Weeks on Chart

VERUCA SALT

Date	Title / Label	Peak Position	Weeks at No.1	Weeks on Chart
	US, female/male vocal/instrumental group			5
2 Jul 94	**SEETHER** *Scared Hitless FRET 003CD*	61		1
3 Dec 94	**SEETHER** *Hi-Rise FLATSDG 12*	73		1
4 Feb 95	**NUMBER ONE BLIND** *Hi-Rise FLATSDG 16*	68		1
22 Feb 97	**VOLCANO GIRLS** *Outpost OPRCD 22197*	56		1
30 Aug 97	**BENJAMIN** *Outpost OPRCD 22261*	75		1

VERVE

Date	Title / Label	Peak Position	Weeks at No.1	Weeks on Chart
	UK, male vocal/instrumental group – Richard Ashcroft*, Simon Jones, Nick McCabe, Peter Salisbury & Simon Tong			67
4 Jul 92	**SHE'S A SUPERSTAR** *Hut 16*	66		1
22 May 93	**BLUE** *Hut HUTCD 29*	69		1
13 May 95	**THIS IS MUSIC** *Hut HUTCD 54*	35		3
24 Jun 95	**ON YOUR OWN** *Hut HUTCD 55*	28		2
30 Sep 95	**HISTORY** *Hut HUTDX 59*	24		3
28 Jun 97	**BITTER SWEET SYMPHONY** *Hut HUTDG 82* ●	2		13
13 Sep 97	**THE DRUGS DON'T WORK** *Hut HUTDG 88* ●	1	1	13
6 Dec 97	**LUCKY MAN** *Hut HUTDG 92*	7		13
30 May 98	**SONNET (IMPORT)** *Hut 8950752*	74		1
12 Jul 08	**BITTER SWEET SYMPHONY** *Hut HUTDG 82*	58		5
16 Aug 08	**LOVE IS NOISE** *Parlophone VERVE004*	4		11
29 Nov 08	**RATHER BE** *Parlophone CDR6762*	56		1

Top 3 Best-Selling Singles

		Approximate Sales
1	BITTER SWEET SYMPHONY	530,000
2	THE DRUGS DON'T WORK	460,000
3	LUCKY MAN	250,000

A VERY GOOD FRIEND OF MINE

Date	Title / Label	Peak Position	Weeks at No.1	Weeks on Chart
	Italy, male/female vocal/instrumental/production group			1
3 Jul 99	**JUST ROUND** *Positiva CDTIV 109*	55		1

VEX RED

Date	Title / Label	Peak Position	Weeks at No.1	Weeks on Chart
	UK, male vocal/instrumental group			1
2 Mar 02	**CAN'T SMILE** *Virgin VUSCD 237*	45		1

VHS OR BETA

Date	Title / Label	Peak Position	Weeks at No.1	Weeks on Chart
	US, male vocal/instrumental group			2
16 Apr 05	**THE MELTING MOON** *Astralwerks ASW68320*	63		1
6 Aug 05	**NIGHT ON FIRE** *Astralwerks ASWCD12624*	69		1

VIBRATORS

Date	Title / Label	Peak Position	Weeks at No.1	Weeks on Chart
	UK, male vocal/instrumental group			8
18 Mar 78	**AUTOMATIC LOVER** *Epic EPC 6137*	35		5
17 Jun 78	**JUDY SAYS (KNOCK YOU IN THE HEAD)** *Epic EPC 6393*	70		3

VICE SQUAD

Date	Title / Label	Peak Position	Weeks at No.1	Weeks on Chart
	UK, male/female vocal/instrumental group			1
13 Feb 82	**OUT OF REACH** *Zonophone Z 26*	68		1

VICIOUS CIRCLES

Date	Title / Label	Peak Position	Weeks at No.1	Weeks on Chart
	UK, male producer (Simon Berry). See Art Of Trance, Poltergeist			1
16 Dec 00	**VICIOUS CIRCLES** *Platipus PLATCD 82*	68		1

VICIOUS PINK

Date	Title / Label	Peak Position	Weeks at No.1	Weeks on Chart
	UK, male/female vocal/instrumental duo			4
15 Sep 84	**CCCAN'T YOU SEE** *Parlophone R 6074*	67		4

MARIA VIDAL

Date	Title / Label	Peak Position	Weeks at No.1	Weeks on Chart
	US, female vocalist (Maria Fernandez-Vidal)			13
24 Aug 85	**BODY ROCK** *EMI America EA 189*	11		13

VIDEO KIDS

Date	Title / Label	Peak Position	Weeks at No.1	Weeks on Chart
	Holland, male/female vocal/production duo			1
5 Oct 85	**WOODPECKERS FROM SPACE** *Epic A 6504*	72		1

VIDEO SYMPHONIC

Date	Title / Label	Peak Position	Weeks at No.1	Weeks on Chart
	UK, orchestra			3
24 Oct 81	**THE FLAME TREES OF THIKA** *EMI 5222*	42		3

VIENNA PHILHARMONIC ORCHESTRA

Date	Title / Label	Peak Position	Weeks at No.1	Weeks on Chart
	Austria, orchestra			14
18 Dec 71	**THEME FROM 'THE ONEDIN LINE'** *Decca F 13259*	15		14

VIEW

Date	Title / Label	Peak Position	Weeks at No.1	Weeks on Chart
	UK, male vocal/instrumental group – Kyle Falconer, Steven Morrison, Pete Reilly & Kieren Webster			30
12 Aug 06	**WASTED LITTLE DJS** *1965 OLIVECD007*	15		7
28 Oct 06	**SUPERSTAR TRADESMAN** *1965 OLIVECD006*	15		4
20 Jan 07	**SAME JEANS** *1965 OLIVECD015*	3		14
5 May 07	**THE DON** *1965 OLIVECD021*	33		2
7 Jul 07	**FACE FOR THE RADIO** *1965 OLIVECD024*	69		1
8 Nov 08	**5 REBECCAS** *1965 OLIVECD060*	57		1
14 Feb 09	**SHOCK HORROR** *1965 OLIVECD056*	64		1

VIEW FROM THE HILL

Date	Title / Label	Peak Position	Weeks at No.1	Weeks on Chart
	UK, male/female vocal/instrumental trio			6
19 Jul 86	**NO CONVERSATION** *EMI 5565*	58		3
21 Feb 87	**I'M NO REBEL** *EMI 5580*	59		3

VIKKI

Date	Title / Label	Peak Position	Weeks at No.1	Weeks on Chart
	UK, female vocalist (Aeone Victoria Watson)			3
4 May 85	**LOVE IS…** *PRT 7P 326*	49		3

VILLAGE PEOPLE

Date	Title / Label	Peak Position	Weeks at No.1	Weeks on Chart
	US, male vocal group – Alexander Briley, David Hodo, Glenn Hughes, d. 4 Mar 2001, Randy Jones, Felipe Rose & Victor Willis (replaced by Ray Simpson)			66
3 Dec 77	**SAN FRANCISCO (YOU'VE GOT ME)** *DJM DJS 10817*	45		5
25 Nov 78	**Y.M.C.A.** *Mercury 6007 192* ⊛	1	3	16
17 Mar 79	**IN THE NAVY** *Mercury 6007 209* ●	2		9
16 Jun 79	**GO WEST** *Mercury 6007 221*	15		8
9 Aug 80	**CAN'T STOP THE MUSIC** *Mercury MER 16*	11		11
9 Feb 85	**SEX OVER THE PHONE** *Record Shack SOHO 34*	59		5
4 Dec 93	**Y.M.C.A. (REMIX)** *Bell 74321177182*	12		7
28 May 94	**IN THE NAVY (REMIX)** *Bell 74321198192*	36		2
27 Nov 99	**Y.M.C.A. (2ND REMIX)** *Wrasse WRASX 002*	35		3

V.I.M.

Date	Title / Label	Peak Position	Weeks at No.1	Weeks on Chart
	UK, male production group			1
26 Jan 91	**MAGGIE'S LAST PARTY** *F2 BOZ 1*	68		1

GENE VINCENT

Date	Title / Label	Peak Position	Weeks at No.1	Weeks on Chart
	US, male vocalist (Eugene Craddock), d. 12 Oct 1971 (age 36)			51
13 Jul 56	**BE BOP A LULA** *Capitol CL 14599*	16		7
12 Oct 56	**RACE WITH THE DEVIL** *Capitol CL 14628*	28		1
19 Oct 56	**BLUE JEAN BOP** *Capitol CL 14637*	16		5
8 Jan 60	**WILD CAT** *Capitol CL 15099*	21		6
10 Mar 60	**MY HEART** *Capitol CL 15115*	16		8
16 Jun 60	**PISTOL PACKIN' MAMA** *Capitol CL 15136*	15		9
1 Jun 61	**SHE SHE LITTLE SHEILA** *Capitol CL 15202*	22		11
31 Aug 61	**I'M GOING HOME (TO SEE MY BABY)** *Capitol CL 15215*	36		4

VINDALOO SUMMER SPECIAL

Date	Title / Label	Peak Position	Weeks at No.1	Weeks on Chart
	UK, male/female vocal/instrumental group			3
19 Jul 86	**ROCKIN' WITH RITA (HEAD TO TOE)** *Vindaloo UGH 13*	56		3

VINES
Australia, male vocal/instrumental group — 14

Date	Title	Peak Position	Weeks at No.1	Weeks on Chart
20 Apr 02	**HIGHLY EVOLVED** *Heavenly HVN 112CD*	32		2
29 Jun 02	**GET FREE** *Heavenly HVN 113CD*	24		3
19 Oct 02	**OUTTATHAWAY** *Heavenly HVN 120CDS*	20		2
20 Mar 04	**RIDE** *Heavenly HVN 137CD*	25		3
5 Jun 04	**WINNING DAYS** *Heavenly HVN 139CDS*	42		2
17 Jun 06	**ANYSOUND** *Heavenly HVN160CD*	63		1
14 Oct 06	**DON'T LISTEN TO THE RADIO** *Heavenly HVN162CD*	66		1

BOBBY VINTON
US, male vocalist (Stanley Vinton) — 29

Date	Title	Peak Position	Weeks at No.1	Weeks on Chart
2 Aug 62	**ROSES ARE RED (MY LOVE)** *Columbia DB 4878* ★	15		8
19 Dec 63	**THERE I'VE SAID IT AGAIN** *Columbia DB 7179* ★	34		10
29 Sep 90	**BLUE VELVET** *Epic 6505240* ★	2		10
17 Nov 90	**ROSES ARE RED (MY LOVE)** *Epic 6564677*	71		1

VINYLGROOVER & THE RED HED
UK, male production duo. See Kontakt — 1

Date	Title	Peak Position	Weeks at No.1	Weeks on Chart
27 Jan 01	**ROK DA HOUSE** *Nukleuz NUKP 0285*	72		1
10 Jul 04	**STAY** *Tidy Trax TIDYTWO133C* ROB TISSERA & VINYLGROOVER	61		1

VIOLENT DELIGHT
UK, male vocal/instrumental group — 5

Date	Title	Peak Position	Weeks at No.1	Weeks on Chart
1 Mar 03	**I WISH I WAS A GIRL** *WEA 362CD*	25		3
21 Jun 03	**ALL YOU EVER DO** *WEA 367CD*	38		1
13 Sep 03	**TRANSMISSION** *WEA 370CD*	64		1

VIOLINSKI
UK, male instrumental group — 9

Date	Title	Peak Position	Weeks at No.1	Weeks on Chart
17 Feb 79	**CLOG DANCE** *Jet 136*	17		9

VIPER
Belgium, male production group — 1

Date	Title	Peak Position	Weeks at No.1	Weeks on Chart
7 Feb 98	**THE TWISTER** *Hooj Choons HOOJCD 59*	55		1

REFLEX FEATURING MC VIPER
UK, male rapper (Jamie Thomas) — 2

Date	Title	Peak Position	Weeks at No.1	Weeks on Chart
19 May 01	**PUT YOUR HANDS UP** *Gusto CDGUS 2*	72		1
14 Sep 02	**SELECTA (URBAN HEROES)** *Soundproof SPR 1CD* JAMESON & VIPER	51		1

VIPERS SKIFFLE GROUP
UK, male vocal/instrumental group – Wally Whyton, d. 22 Jan 1997, Johnny Booker, d. 19 Mar 2007, John Pilgrim, Tony Tolhurst & Jean Van Der Bosch — 18

Date	Title	Peak Position	Weeks at No.1	Weeks on Chart
25 Jan 57	**DON'T YOU ROCK ME DADDY-O** *Parlophone R 4261*	10		9
22 Mar 57	**CUMBERLAND GAP** *Parlophone R 4289*	10		6
31 May 57	**STREAMLINE TRAIN** *Parlophone R 4308*	23		3

V.I.P.'S
UK, male vocal/instrumental group — 4

Date	Title	Peak Position	Weeks at No.1	Weeks on Chart
6 Sep 80	**THE QUARTER MOON** *Gem GEMS 39*	55		4

VIRUS
UK, male instrumental/production duo. See Elementfour, Oakenfold, Perfecto Allstarz — 3

Date	Title	Peak Position	Weeks at No.1	Weeks on Chart
26 Aug 95	**SUN** *Perfecto PERF 107CD*	62		1
25 Jan 97	**MOON** *Perfecto PERF 134CD*	36		2

VISAGE
UK, male vocal/instrumental group – Steve Strange, Billy Currie, Rusty Egan, Dave Formula, John McGeoch & Midge Ure* — 56

Date	Title	Peak Position	Weeks at No.1	Weeks on Chart
20 Dec 80	**FADE TO GREY** *Polydor POSP 194* ●	8		15
14 Mar 81	**MIND OF A TOY** *Polydor POSP 236*	13		8
11 Jul 81	**VISAGE** *Polydor POSP 293*	21		7
13 Mar 82	**DAMNED DON'T CRY** *Polydor POSP 390*	11		8
26 Jun 82	**NIGHT TRAIN** *Polydor POSP 441*	12		10
13 Nov 82	**PLEASURE BOYS** *Polydor POSP 523*	44		3
1 Sep 84	**LOVE GLOVE** *Polydor POSP 691*	54		3
28 Aug 93	**FADE TO GREY (REMIX)** *Polydor PZCD 282*	39		2

VISCOUNTS
UK, male vocal group — 18

Date	Title	Peak Position	Weeks at No.1	Weeks on Chart
13 Oct 60	**SHORT'NIN' BREAD** *Pye 7N 15287*	16		8
14 Sep 61	**WHO PUT THE BOMP** *Pye 7N 15379*	21		10

VISION
UK, male vocal/instrumental group — 1

Date	Title	Peak Position	Weeks at No.1	Weeks on Chart
9 Jul 83	**LOVE DANCE** *MVM 2886*	74		1

VISIONMASTERS AND TONY KING FEATURING KYLIE MINOGUE
UK, male production duo, male instrumentalist & Australia, female vocalist — 1

Date	Title	Peak Position	Weeks at No.1	Weeks on Chart
30 Nov 91	**KEEP ON PUMPIN' IT** *PWL 207*	49		1

VITA
US, female vocalist (LaVita Raynor) — 12

Date	Title	Peak Position	Weeks at No.1	Weeks on Chart
9 Jun 01	**LAPDANCE** *Virgin VUSCD 196* N*E*R*D FEATURING LEE HARVEY & VITA	33		2
12 Oct 02	**DOWN 4 U** *Murder Inc 0639002* IRV GOTTI PRESENTS JA RULE, ASHANTI, CHARLI BALTIMORE & VITA	4		10

VITAMIN C
US, female vocalist (Colleen Fitzpatrick) — 1

Date	Title	Peak Position	Weeks at No.1	Weeks on Chart
19 Jul 03	**LAST NITE** *V2 VVR 5023283*	70		1

SORAYA VIVIAN
UK, female vocalist — 1

Date	Title	Peak Position	Weeks at No.1	Weeks on Chart
16 Mar 02	**WHEN YOU'RE GONE** *Activ 8 ACT 501*	59		1

VIXEN
US, female vocal/instrumental group — 21

Date	Title	Peak Position	Weeks at No.1	Weeks on Chart
3 Sep 88	**EDGE OF A BROKEN HEART** *Manhattan MT 48*	51		4
4 Mar 89	**CRYIN'** *EMI Manhattan MT 60*	27		4
3 Jun 89	**LOVE MADE ME** *EMI-USA MT 66*	36		4
2 Sep 89	**EDGE OF A BROKEN HEART** *EMI-USA MT 48*	59		2
28 Jul 90	**HOW MUCH LOVE** *EMI-USA MT 87*	35		3
20 Oct 90	**LOVE IS A KILLER** *EMI-USA MT 91*	41		2
16 Mar 91	**NOT A MINUTE TOO SOON** *EMI America MT 93*	37		2

KATE VOEGELE
US, female vocalist/multi-instrumentalist — 2

Date	Title	Peak Position	Weeks at No.1	Weeks on Chart
11 Oct 08	**HALLELUJAH** *Polydor USUM70812275*	53		2

VOGGUE
Canada, female vocal duo — 6

Date	Title	Peak Position	Weeks at No.1	Weeks on Chart
18 Jul 81	**DANCIN' THE NIGHT AWAY** *Mercury MER 76*	39		6

VOICE OF THE BEEHIVE
US/UK, male/female vocal/instrumental group — 51

Date	Title	Peak Position	Weeks at No.1	Weeks on Chart
14 Nov 87	**I SAY NOTHING** *London LON 151*	45		5
5 Mar 88	**I WALK THE EARTH** *London LON 169*	42		4
14 May 88	**DON'T CALL ME BABY** *London LON 175*	15		10
23 Jul 88	**I SAY NOTHING** *London LON 190*	22		6
22 Oct 88	**I WALK THE EARTH** *London LON 206*	46		4
13 Jul 91	**MONSTERS AND ANGELS** *London LON 302*	17		10
28 Sep 91	**I THINK I LOVE YOU** *London LON 308*	25		6
11 Jan 92	**PERFECT PLACE** *London LON 312*	37		6

VOICES OF LIFE
US, male/female vocal/production duo. See JM Silk — 2

Date	Title	Peak Position	Weeks at No.1	Weeks on Chart
21 Mar 98	**THE WORD IS LOVE (SAY THE WORD)** *AM:PM 5825272*	26		2

STERLING VOID
US, male producer (Duane Pelt) — 3

Date	Title / Label	Peak	Wks at No.1	Wks
4 Feb 89	**RUNAWAY GIRL/IT'S ALL RIGHT** *ffrr FFR 21*	53		3

VOLATILE AGENTS FEATURING SIMONE BENN
UK, male/female vocal/production trio — 3

Date	Title / Label	Peak	Wks at No.1	Wks
15 Dec 01	**HOOKED ON YOU** *Melting Pot MPRCD 10*	54		3

VOLCANO
Norway, male production group — 4

Date	Title / Label	Peak	Wks at No.1	Wks
23 Jul 94	**MORE TO LOVE** *Deconstruction 74321221832*	32		3
18 Nov 95	**THAT'S THE WAY LOVE IS** *EXP EXPCD 002* WITH SAM CARTWRIGHT	72		1

VON BONDIES
US, male vocal/instrumental group — 3

Date	Title / Label	Peak	Wks at No.1	Wks
14 Feb 04	**C'MON C'MON** *Sire W635CD*	21		2
15 May 04	**TELL ME WHAT YOU SEE** *Sire W639CD*	43		1

VOODOO & SERANO
Germany, male production duo — 6

Date	Title / Label	Peak	Wks at No.1	Wks
3 Feb 01	**BLOOD IS PUMPIN'** *Xtrahard X2H2 CDS*	19		4
16 Aug 03	**OVERLOAD** *All Around The World CDGLOBE 284*	30		2

VOYAGE
UK/France, male vocal/instrumental group — 27

Date	Title / Label	Peak	Wks at No.1	Wks
17 Jun 78	**FROM EAST TO WEST/SCOTS MACHINE** *GTO GT 224*	13		13
25 Nov 78	**SOUVENIRS** *GTO GT 241*	56		7
24 Mar 79	**LET'S FLY AWAY** *GTO GT 245*	38		7

VOYAGER
UK, male vocal/instrumental group — 8

Date	Title / Label	Peak	Wks at No.1	Wks
26 May 79	**HALFWAY HOTEL** *Mountain VOY 001*	33		8

JURGEN VRIES
UK, male DJ/producer (Darren Tate). See Angelic, Citizen Caned, DT8 Project, Orion — 20

Date	Title / Label	Peak	Wks at No.1	Wks
14 Sep 02	**THE THEME** *Direction 6730952*	13		4
1 Feb 03	**THE OPERA SONG (BRAVE NEW WORLD)** *Direction 6734642* FEATURING CMC	3		10
4 Oct 03	**WILDERNESS** *Direction 6742692* FEATURING SHENA	20		3
19 Jun 04	**TAKE MY HAND** *Direction 6749932* FEATURING ANDREA BRITTON	23		3

VS
UK, male/female vocal/rap group – Marvin Humes, Blimi, Chinyere McKenzie, Jaime Summaz (Jaime Douglas) & Ryan Taylor — 15

Date	Title / Label	Peak	Wks at No.1	Wks
6 Mar 04	**LOVE YOU LIKE MAD** *Innocent SINCD 59*	7		7
19 Jun 04	**CALL U SEXY** *Innocent SINDX 62*	11		6
23 Oct 04	**MAKE IT HOT** *Innocent SINDX 66*	29		2

VYBE
US, female vocal group — 1

Date	Title / Label	Peak	Wks at No.1	Wks
7 Oct 95	**WARM SUMMER DAZE** *Fourth & Broadway BRCD 315*	60		1

KRISTINE W
US, female vocalist (Kristine Weitz) — 8

Date	Title / Label	Peak	Wks at No.1	Wks
21 May 94	**LOVE COME HOME** *Triangle BLUESCD 001* OUR TRIBE WITH FRANKE PHAROAH & KRISTINE W	73		1
25 Jun 94	**FEEL WHAT YOU WANT** *Champion CHAMPCD 304*	33		3
25 May 96	**ONE MORE TRY** *Champion CHAMPCD 317*	41		1
21 Dec 96	**LAND OF THE LIVING** *Champion CHAMPCD 324*	57		1
5 Jul 97	**FEEL WHAT YOU WANT** *Champion CHAMPCD 329*	40		2

ADAM WADE
US, male vocalist — 6

Date	Title / Label	Peak	Wks at No.1	Wks
8 Jun 61	**TAKE GOOD CARE OF HER** *HMV POP 843*	38		6

WAG YA TAIL
UK, male production group — 1

Date	Title / Label	Peak	Wks at No.1	Wks
3 Oct 92	**XPAND YA MIND (EXPANSIONS)** *PWL International PWL 238*	49		1

WAH!
UK, male vocalist/guitarist (Pete Wylie) & various male/female vocal/instrumental collaborators — 26

Date	Title / Label	Peak	Wks at No.1	Wks
25 Dec 82	**THE STORY OF THE BLUES** *Eternal JF 1*	3		12
19 Mar 83	**HOPE (I WISH YOU'D BELIEVE ME)** *WEA X 9880*	37		5
30 Jun 84	**COME BACK** *Beggars Banquet BEG 111* MIGHTY WAH	20		9

WAIKIKIS
Belgium, male instrumental group — 2

Date	Title / Label	Peak	Wks at No.1	Wks
11 Mar 65	**HAWAII TATTOO** *Pye International 7N 25286*	41		2

RUFUS WAINWRIGHT
Canada, male vocalist/guitarist/pianist — 3

Date	Title / Label	Peak	Wks at No.1	Wks
7 Aug 04	**I DON'T KNOW WHAT IT IS** *DreamWorks 9863229*	74		1
19 May 07	**GOING TO A TOWN** *Polydor USUM70725561*	54		2

JOHN WAITE
UK, male vocalist. See Babys, Bad English — 13

Date	Title / Label	Peak	Wks at No.1	Wks
29 Sep 84	**MISSING YOU** *EMI America EA 182* ★	9		11
13 Feb 93	**MISSING YOU** *Chrysalis CDCHS 3938*	56		2

WAITRESSES
US, male/female vocal/instrumental group — 4

Date	Title / Label	Peak	Wks at No.1	Wks
18 Dec 82	**CHRISTMAS WRAPPING** *Ze/Island WIP 6821*	45		4

JOHNNY WAKELIN
UK, male vocalist — 20

Date	Title / Label	Peak	Wks at No.1	Wks
18 Jan 75	**BLACK SUPERMAN (MUHAMMAD ALI)** *Pye 7N 45420* & THE KINSHASA BAND	7		10
24 Jul 76	**IN ZAIRE** *Pye 7N 45595*	4		10

NARADA MICHAEL WALDEN
US, male vocalist/drummer/producer (Michael Walden) — 28

Date	Title / Label	Peak	Wks at No.1	Wks
23 Feb 80	**TONIGHT I'M ALL RIGHT** *Atlantic K 11437*	34		9
26 Apr 80	**I SHOULDA LOVED YA** *Atlantic K 11413*	8		9
23 Apr 88	**DIVINE EMOTIONS** *Reprise W 7967* NARADA	8		10

WALE FEATURING LADY GAGA
US, male/female rap/vocal duo — 5

Date	Title / Label	Peak	Wks at No.1	Wks
12 Sep 09	**CHILLIN'** *Interscope 2717517*	12		5

DOUG WALKER
UK, male vocalist/pianist — 1

Date	Title / Label	Peak	Wks at No.1	Wks
15 Mar 08	**THE MYSTERY** *Warner Brothers GBAHT0800042*	36		1

GARY WALKER
US, male vocalist/drummer (Gary Leeds). See Walker Brothers — 12

Date	Title / Label	Peak	Wks at No.1	Wks
24 Feb 66	**YOU DON'T LOVE ME** *CBS 202036*	26		6
26 May 66	**TWINKIE LEE** *CBS 202081*	26		6

JOHN WALKER
US, male vocalist /guitarist (John Maus). See Walker Brothers — 6

Date	Title / Label	Peak	Wks at No.1	Wks
5 Jul 67	**ANNABELLA** *Philips BF 1593*	24		6

SCOTT WALKER
US, male vocalist (Scott Engel). See Walker Brothers — 30

Date	Title / Label	Peak	Wks at No.1	Wks
6 Dec 67	**JACKIE** *Philips BF 1628*	22		9
1 May 68	**JOANNA** *Philips BF 1662*	7		11
11 Jun 69	**LIGHTS OF CINCINNATI** *Philips BF 1793*	13		10

JUNIOR WALKER & THE ALL-STARS
US, male vocal/instrumental group — 59

Date	Title / Label	Peak	Wks at No.1	Wks
18 Aug 66	**HOW SWEET IT IS** *Tamla Motown TMG 571*	22		10
2 Apr 69	**(I'M A) ROAD RUNNER** *Tamla Motown TMG 691*	12		12
18 Oct 69	**WHAT DOES IT TAKE (TO WIN YOUR LOVE)** *Tamla Motown TMG 712*	13		12
26 Aug 72	**WALK IN THE NIGHT** *Tamla Motown TMG 824*	16		11
27 Jan 73	**TAKE ME GIRL I'M READY** *Tamla Motown TMG 840*	16		9
30 Jun 73	**WAY BACK HOME** *Tamla Motown TMG 857*	35		5

TERRI WALKER
UK, female vocalist — 4

Date	Title / Label	Peak	Wks at No.1	Wks
1 Mar 03	**GUESS YOU DIDN'T LOVE ME** *Def Soul 779962*	60		1
17 May 03	**CHING CHING (LOVIN' YOU STILL)** *Def Soul 9800075*	38		2
26 Mar 05	**WHOOPSIE DAISY** *Mercury 9870690*	41		1

WALKER BROTHERS
US, male vocal/instrumental trio – Scott Walker* (Scott Engel), Gary Walker* (Gary Leeds) & John Walker* (John Maus) — 93

Date	Title / Label	Peak	Wks at No.1	Wks
29 Apr 65	**LOVE HER** *Philips BF 1409*	20		13
19 Aug 65	**MAKE IT EASY ON YOURSELF** *Philips BF 1428*	1	1	14
2 Dec 65	**MY SHIP IS COMING IN** *Philips BF 1454*	3		12
3 Mar 66	**THE SUN AIN'T GONNA SHINE ANYMORE** *Philips BF 1473*	1	4	11
14 Jul 66	**(BABY) YOU DON'T HAVE TO TELL ME** *Philips BF 1497*	13		8
22 Sep 66	**ANOTHER TEAR FALLS** *Philips BF 1514*	12		8
15 Dec 66	**DEADLIER THAN THE MALE** *Philips BF 1537*	32		6
9 Feb 67	**STAY WITH ME BABY** *Philips BF 1548*	26		6
18 May 67	**WALKING IN THE RAIN** *Philips BF 1576*	26		6
17 Jan 76	**NO REGRETS** *GTO GT 42*	7		9

WALKMEN
US, male vocal/instrumental group — 2

Date	Title / Label	Peak	Wks at No.1	Wks
1 May 04	**THE RAT** *WEA W640CD*	45		1
10 Jul 04	**LITTLE HOUSE OF SAVAGES** *Record Collection W646CD*	72		1

WALL OF SOUND FEATURING GERALD LETHAN
US, male production duo & male vocalist — 1

Date	Title / Label	Peak	Wks at No.1	Wks
31 Jul 93	**CRITICAL (IF ONLY YOU KNEW)** *Positiva CDTIV 4*	73		1

WALL OF VOODOO
US, male vocal/instrumental group — 3

Date	Title / Label	Peak	Wks at No.1	Wks
19 Mar 83	**MEXICAN RADIO** *Illegal ILS 36*	64		3

JERRY WALLACE
US, male vocalist, d. 5 May 2008 (age 79) — 1

Date	Title / Label	Peak	Wks at No.1	Wks
23 Jun 60	**YOU'RE SINGING OUR LOVE SONG TO SOMEBODY ELSE** *London HLH 9110*	46		1

RIK WALLER
UK, male vocalist — 12

Date	Title / Label	Peak	Wks at No.1	Wks
16 Mar 02	**I WILL ALWAYS LOVE YOU** *Liberty CDRIK 001*	6		8
6 Jul 02	**SOMETHING INSIDE (SO STRONG)** *Liberty CDRIK 002*	25		4

WALLFLOWERS
US, male vocal/instrumental group — 1

Date	Title / Label	Peak	Wks at No.1	Wks
12 Jul 97	**ONE HEADLIGHT** *Interscope IND 95532*	54		1

BOB WALLIS & HIS STORYVILLE JAZZ BAND
UK, male vocal/instrumental group – leader d. 10 Jan 1991 (age 56) — 7

Date	Title / Label	Peak	Wks at No.1	Wks
6 Jul 61	**I'M SHY MARY ELLEN (I'M SHY)** *Pye Jazz 7NJ 2043*	44		2
4 Jan 62	**COME ALONG PLEASE** *Pye Jazz 7NJ 2048*	33		5

JOE WALSH
US, male vocalist/guitarist. See Eagles — 15

Date	Title / Label	Peak	Wks at No.1	Wks
16 Jul 77	**ROCKY MOUNTAIN EP** *ABC ABE 12002*	39		4
8 Jul 78	**LIFE'S BEEN GOOD** *Asylum K 13129*	14		11

SHEILA WALSH & CLIFF RICHARD
UK, female vocalist — 2

Date	Title / Label	Peak	Wks at No.1	Wks
4 Jun 83	**DRIFTING** *DJM SHEILA 1*	64		2

STEVE WALSH
UK, male vocalist/DJ, d. 4 Jul 1988 (age 29) — 18

Date	Title / Label	Peak	Wks at No.1	Wks
18 Jul 87	**I FOUND LOVIN'** *A1 299*	9		13
12 Dec 87	**LET'S GET TOGETHER (TONITE)** *A1 303*	74		1
30 Jul 88	**AIN'T NO STOPPING US NOW (PARTY FOR THE WORLD)** *A1 304*	44		4

TREVOR WALTERS
UK, male vocalist — 22

Date	Title / Label	Peak	Wks at No.1	Wks
24 Oct 81	**LOVE ME TONIGHT** *Magnet MAG 198*	27		8
21 Jul 84	**STUCK ON YOU** *Sanity IS 002*	9		12
1 Dec 84	**NEVER LET HER SLIP AWAY** *Polydor POSP 716*	73		2

WAMDUE PROJECT
US, male DJ/producer (Chris Brann) — 19

Date	Title / Label	Peak	Wks at No.1	Wks
20 Nov 99	**KING OF MY CASTLE (IMPORT)** *Orange ORCDM 53584CD*	61		1
27 Nov 99	**KING OF MY CASTLE** *AM:PM CDAMPM 127* ●	1	1	16
15 Apr 00	**YOU'RE THE REASON** *AM:PM CDAMPM 130*	39		2

WANG CHUNG
UK, male vocal/instrumental trio — 12

Date	Title / Label	Peak	Wks at No.1	Wks
28 Jan 84	**DANCE HALL DAYS** *Geffen A 3837*	21		12

WANNADIES
Sweden, male/female vocal/instrumental group — 12

Date	Title / Label	Peak	Wks at No.1	Wks
18 Nov 95	**MIGHT BE STARS** *Indolent DIE 003CD1*	51		2
24 Feb 96	**HOW DOES IT FEEL** *Indolent DIE 004CD1*	53		1
20 Apr 96	**YOU & ME SONG** *Indolent DIE 005CD*	18		3
7 Sep 96	**SOMEONE SOMEWHERE** *Indolent DIE 006CD*	38		1
26 Apr 97	**HIT** *Indolent DIE 009CD1*	20		2
5 Jul 97	**SHORTY** *Indolent DIE 010CD1*	41		2
4 Mar 00	**YEAH** *RCA 74321745552*	56		1

DEXTER WANSELL
US, male keyboard player — 3

Date	Title / Label	Peak	Wks at No.1	Wks
20 May 78	**ALL NIGHT LONG** *Philadelphia International PIR 6255*	59		3

WAR
US, male vocal/instrumental group — 32

Date	Title / Label	Peak	Wks at No.1	Wks
24 Jan 76	**LOW RIDER** *Island WIP 6267*	12		7
26 Jun 76	**ME AND BABY BROTHER** *Island WIP 6303*	21		7
14 Jan 78	**GALAXY** *MCA 339*	14		7
15 Apr 78	**HEY SENORITA** *MCA 359*	40		2
10 Apr 82	**YOU GOT THE POWER** *RCA 201*	58		4
6 Apr 85	**GROOVIN'** *Bluebird BR 16*	43		5

ANITA WARD
US, female vocalist — 11

Date	Title / Label	Peak	Wks at No.1	Wks
2 Jun 79	**RING MY BELL** *TK TKR 7543* ● ★	1	2	11

BILLY WARD
US, male vocal group — 13

Date	Title / Label	Peak	Wks at No.1	Wks
13 Sep 57	**STARDUST** *London HLU 8465*	13		12
29 Nov 57	**DEEP PURPLE** *London HLU 8502*	30		1

CHRISSY WARD
US, female vocalist — 2

Date	Title / Label	Peak	Wks at No.1	Wks
24 Jun 95	**RIGHT AND EXACT** *Ore AG 6CD*	62		1
8 Feb 97	**RIGHT AND EXACT (REMIX)** *Ore AG 21CD*	59		1

CLIFFORD T WARD
UK, male vocalist/keyboard player, d. 18 Dec 2001 (age 57) — 16

Date	Title / Label	Peak	Wks at No.1	Wks
30 Jun 73	**GAYE** *Charisma CB 205*	8		11
26 Jan 74	**SCULLERY** *Charisma CB 221*	37		5

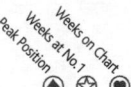

Silver-selling ○ Gold-selling ● Platinum-selling (x multiples) ⊛ US No.1 ★ — Peak Position | Weeks at No.1 | Weeks on Chart

MICHAEL WARD
UK, male vocalist — 13

Date	Title	Peak	Wks at No.1	Wks on Chart
29 Sep 73	**LET THERE BE PEACE ON EARTH (LET IT BEGIN WITH ME)** *Philips 6006 340*	15		13

SHAYNE WARD
UK, male vocalist — 63

Date	Title	Peak	Wks at No.1	Wks on Chart
31 Dec 05	**THAT'S MY GOAL** *Syco Music 82876779272* ⊛	1	4	21
22 Apr 06	**NO PROMISES** *Syco Music 82876825902*	2		16
22 Jul 06	**STAND BY ME** *Syco Music 82876869132*	14		4
6 Oct 07	**NO U HANG UP/IF THAT'S OKAY WITH YOU** *Syco Music 88697131702*	2		11
1 Dec 07	**BREATHLESS** *Syco Music 88697188422*	6		10
8 Dec 07	**IF THAT'S OK WITH YOU** *Syco Music GBHMU0700027*	72		1

WARD BROTHERS
UK, male vocal/instrumental trio — 8

Date	Title	Peak	Wks at No.1	Wks on Chart
10 Jan 87	**CROSS THAT BRIDGE** *Siren 37*	32		8

MATHIAS WARE FEATURING ROB TAYLOR
Germany, male vocal/production duo — 1

Date	Title	Peak	Wks at No.1	Wks on Chart
9 Mar 02	**HEY LITTLE GIRL** *Manifesto FESCD 91*	42		1

WARM JETS
UK/Canada, male vocal/instrumental group — 4

Date	Title	Peak	Wks at No.1	Wks on Chart
14 Feb 98	**NEVER NEVER** *Island WAY 6766*	37		2
25 Apr 98	**HURRICANE** *Island CID 697*	34		2

WARM SOUNDS
UK, male vocal duo — 6

Date	Title	Peak	Wks at No.1	Wks on Chart
4 May 67	**BIRDS AND BEES** *Deram DM 120*	27		6

TONI WARNE
UK, female vocalist — 4

Date	Title	Peak	Wks at No.1	Wks on Chart
25 Apr 87	**BEN** *Mint CHEW 110*	50		4

JENNIFER WARNES
US, female vocalist — 37

Date	Title	Peak	Wks at No.1	Wks on Chart
15 Jan 83	**UP WHERE WE BELONG** *Island WIP 6830* JOE COCKER & JENNIFER WARNES ○ ★	7		13
25 Jul 87	**FIRST WE TAKE MANHATTAN** *Cypress PB 49709*	74		1
31 Oct 87	**(I'VE HAD) THE TIME OF MY LIFE** *RCA PB 49625* BILL MEDLEY & JENNIFER WARNES ★	6		12
15 Dec 90	**(I'VE HAD) THE TIME OF MY LIFE** *RCA PB 49625* BILL MEDLEY & JENNIFER WARNES ○	8		11

WARP BROTHERS
Germany, male DJ/production duo – Jurgen Dohrgroup & Oliver Goedicke — 18

Date	Title	Peak	Wks at No.1	Wks on Chart
11 Nov 00	**PHATT BASS (IMPORT)** *Dos Or Die BMSCDM 40009*	58		3
9 Dec 00	**PHATT BASS** *NuLife 74321817102* VERSUS AQUAGEN	9		8
17 Feb 01	**WE WILL SURVIVE** *NuLife 74321832722*	19		4
29 Dec 01	**BLAST THE SPEAKERS** *NuLife 74321899162*	40		3

WARRANT
US, male vocal/instrumental group — 7

Date	Title	Peak	Wks at No.1	Wks on Chart
17 Nov 90	**CHERRY PIE** *CBS 6562587*	59		2
9 Mar 91	**CHERRY PIE** *Columbia 6566867*	35		5

ALYSHA WARREN
UK, female vocalist (Alison Wallen) — 4

Date	Title	Peak	Wks at No.1	Wks on Chart
24 Sep 94	**I'M SO IN LOVE** *Wild Card CARDD 10*	61		1
25 Mar 95	**I THOUGHT I MEANT THE WORLD TO YOU** *Wild Card CARDD 16*	40		1
27 Jul 96	**KEEP ON PUSHING OUR LOVE** *Arista 74321390422* NIGHTCRAWLERS FEATURING JOHN REID & ALYSHA WARREN	30		2

NIKITA WARREN
Italy, female vocalist — 1

Date	Title	Peak	Wks at No.1	Wks on Chart
13 Jul 96	**I NEED YOU** *VC Recordings VCRD 12*	48		1

WARRIOR
UK, male/female vocal/production duo — 7

Date	Title	Peak	Wks at No.1	Wks on Chart
21 Oct 00	**WARRIOR** *Incentive CENT 12CDS*	19		4
30 Jun 01	**VOODOO** *Incentive CENT 26CDS*	37		2
4 Oct 03	**X** *Incentive CENT 56CDS*	64		1

DIONNE WARWICK
US, female vocalist — 101

Date	Title	Peak	Wks at No.1	Wks on Chart
13 Feb 64	**ANYONE WHO HAD A HEART** *Pye International 7N 25234*	42		3
16 Apr 64	**WALK ON BY** *Pye International 7N 25241*	9		14
30 Jul 64	**YOU'LL NEVER GET TO HEAVEN** *Pye International 7N 25256*	20		8
8 Oct 64	**REACH OUT FOR ME** *Pye International 7N 25265*	23		7
1 Apr 65	**YOU CAN HAVE HIM** *Pye International 7N 25290*	37		5
13 Mar 68	**VALLEY OF THE DOLLS** *Pye International 7N 25445*	28		8
15 May 68	**DO YOU KNOW THE WAY TO SAN JOSE** *Pye International 7N 25457*	8		10
19 Oct 74	**THEN CAME YOU** *Atlantic K 10495* DIONNE WARWICKE & THE DETROIT SPINNERS ★	29		6
23 Oct 82	**HEARTBREAKER** *Arista ARIST 496* ○	2		13
11 Dec 82	**ALL THE LOVE IN THE WORLD** *Arista ARIST 507* ○	10		10
26 Feb 83	**YOURS** *Arista ARIST 518*	66		2
28 May 83	**I'LL NEVER LOVE THIS WAY AGAIN** *Arista ARIST 530*	62		3
9 Nov 85	**THAT'S WHAT FRIENDS ARE FOR** *Arista ARIST 638* & FRIENDS FEATURING ELTON JOHN, STEVIE WONDER & GLADYS KNIGHT ★	16		9
15 Aug 87	**LOVE POWER** *Arista RIS 27* & JEFFREY OSBORNE	63		3

WAS (NOT WAS)
US, male instrumental/production duo – David (David Weiss) & Don (Don Fagenson) Was – with male vocalists – 'Sweet Pea' Atkinson & 'Sir' Harry Bowens – & various instrumental collaborators — 58

Date	Title	Peak	Wks at No.1	Wks on Chart
3 Mar 84	**OUT COME THE FREAKS** *Ze/Geffen A 4178*	41		5
18 Jul 87	**SPY IN THE HOUSE OF LOVE** *Fontana WAS 2*	51		7
3 Oct 87	**WALK THE DINOSAUR** *Fontana WAS 3*	10		10
6 Feb 88	**SPY IN THE HOUSE OF LOVE** *Fontana WAS 2*	21		8
7 May 88	**OUT COME THE FREAKS (AGAIN)** *Fontana WAS 4*	44		3
16 Jul 88	**ANYTHING CAN HAPPEN** *Fontana WAS 5*	67		3
26 May 90	**PAPA WAS A ROLLING STONE** *Fontana WAS 7*	12		7
11 Aug 90	**HOW THE HEART BEHAVES** *Fontana WAS 8*	53		3
23 May 92	**LISTEN LIKE THIEVES** *Fontana WAS 10*	58		2
11 Jul 92	**SHAKE YOUR HEAD** *Fontana WAS 11*	4		9
26 Sep 92	**SOMEWHERE IN AMERICA (THERE'S A STREET NAMED AFTER MY DAD)** *Fontana WAS 12*	57		1

MARTHA WASH
US, female vocalist. See Weather Girls — 34

Date	Title	Peak	Wks at No.1	Wks on Chart
28 Nov 92	**CARRY ON** *RCA 74321125457*	74		1
6 Mar 93	**GIVE IT TO YOU** *RCA 74321136562*	37		4
10 Jul 93	**RUNAROUND/CARRY ON (REMIX)** *RCA 74321153702*	49		2
18 Feb 95	**I FOUND LOVE/TAKE A TOKE** *Columbia 6612112* C & C MUSIC FACTORY/C & C MUSIC FACTORY FEATURING MARTHA WASH	26		2
13 Jul 96	**KEEP ON JUMPIN'** *Manifesto FESCD 11* TODD TERRY FEATURING MARTHA WASH & JOCELYN BROWN	8		6
12 Jul 97	**SOMETHING GOIN' ON** *Manifesto FESCD 25* TODD TERRY FEATURING MARTHA WASH & JOCELYN BROWN	5		10
25 Oct 97	**CARRY ON (2ND REMIX)** *Delirious DELICD 6*	49		1
28 Feb 98	**IT'S RAINING MEN...THE SEQUEL** *Logic 74321555412* FEATURING RuPAUL	21		3
11 Apr 98	**READY FOR A NEW DAY** *Manifesto FESCD 40* TODD TERRY FEATURING MARTHA WASH	20		2
15 Aug 98	**CATCH THE LIGHT** *Logic 74321587912*	45		1
3 Jul 99	**COME** *Logic 74321653942*	64		1
5 Feb 00	**IT'S RAINING MEN** *Logic 74321726282*	56		1

DINAH WASHINGTON
US, female vocalist (Ruth Jones), d. 14 Dec 1963 (age 39) — 8

Date	Title	Peak	Wks at No.1	Wks on Chart
30 Nov 61	**SEPTEMBER IN THE RAIN** *Mercury AMT 1162*	35		4
4 Apr 92	**MAD ABOUT THE BOY** *Mercury DINAH 1*	41		4

GROVER WASHINGTON, JR
US, male saxophonist, d. 17 Dec 1999 (age 56) — 7

Date	Title	Peak	Wks at No.1	Wks on Chart
16 May 81	**JUST THE TWO OF US** *Elektra K 12514*	34		7

SARAH WASHINGTON
UK, female vocalist — 13

Date	Title / Label	Peak Position	Weeks at No.1	Weeks on Chart
14 Aug 93	**I WILL ALWAYS LOVE YOU** *Almighty CDALMY 33*	12		7
27 Nov 93	**CARELESS WHISPER** *Almighty CDALMY 43*	45		2
25 May 96	**HEAVEN** *AM:PM 5815332*	28		2
12 Oct 96	**EVERYTHING** *AM:PM 5818872*	30		2

GENO WASHINGTON & THE RAM JAM BAND
US, male vocalist — 20

Date	Title / Label	Peak Position	Weeks at No.1	Weeks on Chart
19 May 66	**WATER** *Piccadilly 7N 35312*	39		8
21 Jul 66	**HI HI HAZEL** *Piccadilly 7N 35329*	45		4
6 Oct 66	**QUE SERA SERA** *Piccadilly 7N 35346*	43		3
2 Feb 67	**MICHAEL** *Piccadilly 7N 35359*	39		5

W.A.S.P.
US, male vocal/instrumental group — 38

Date	Title / Label	Peak Position	Weeks at No.1	Weeks on Chart
31 May 86	**WILD CHILD** *Capitol CL 388*	71		2
11 Oct 86	**95 – NASTY** *Capitol CL 432*	70		1
29 Aug 87	**SCREAM UNTIL YOU LIKE IT** *Capitol CL 458*	32		5
31 Oct 87	**I DON'T NEED NO DOCTOR (LIVE)** *Capitol CL 469*	31		5
20 Feb 88	**LIVE ANMIMAL (F**K LIKE A BEAST)** *Music For Nations KUT 109*	61		3
4 Mar 89	**MEAN MAN** *Capitol CL 521*	21		5
27 May 89	**THE REAL ME** *Capitol CL 534*	23		5
9 Sep 89	**FOREVER FREE** *Capitol CL 546*	25		5
4 Apr 92	**CHAINSAW CHARLIE (MURDERS IN THE NEW MORGUE)** *Parlophone RS 6308*	17		2
6 Jun 92	**THE IDOL** *Parlophone RPD 6314*	41		2
31 Oct 92	**I AM ONE** *Parlophone 10RG 6324*	56		1
23 Oct 93	**SUNSET AND BABYLON** *Capitol CDCL 698*	38		2

WATER BABIES
UK, male/female vocal/instrumental group — 3

Date	Title / Label	Peak Position	Weeks at No.1	Weeks on Chart
24 Dec 05	**UNDER THE TREE** *Angel ANGECD8*	27		3

WATERBOYS
UK, male vocal/instrumental group – Mike Scott*, Anthony Thistlethwaite, Karl Wallinger, Steve Wickham & Kevin Wilkinson — 33

Date	Title / Label	Peak Position	Weeks at No.1	Weeks on Chart
2 Nov 85	**THE WHOLE OF THE MOON** *Ensign ENY 520*	26		7
14 Jan 89	**FISHERMAN'S BLUES** *Ensign ENY 621*	32		6
1 Jul 89	**AND A BANG ON THE EAR** *Ensign ENY 624*	51		4
6 Apr 91	**THE WHOLE OF THE MOON** *Ensign ENY 642*	3		9
8 Jun 91	**FISHERMAN'S BLUES** *Ensign ENY 645*	75		1
15 May 93	**THE RETURN OF PAN** *Geffen GFSTD 42*	24		3
24 Jul 93	**GLASTONBURY SONG** *Geffen GFSTD 49*	29		3

WATERFRONT
UK, male vocal/instrumental duo — 19

Date	Title / Label	Peak Position	Weeks at No.1	Weeks on Chart
15 Apr 89	**BROKEN ARROW** *Polydor WON 3*	63		2
27 May 89	**CRY** *Polydor WON 1*	17		13
9 Sep 89	**NATURE OF LOVE** *Polydor WON 2*	63		4

WATERGATE
Turkey, male DJ/producer (Orhan Terzi). See DJ Quicksilver — 10

Date	Title / Label	Peak Position	Weeks at No.1	Weeks on Chart
13 May 00	**HEART OF ASIA** *Positiva CDTIV 129*	3		10

DENNIS WATERMAN
UK, male vocalist/actor — 17

Date	Title / Label	Peak Position	Weeks at No.1	Weeks on Chart
25 Oct 80	**I COULD BE SO GOOD FOR YOU** *EMI 5009* & GEORGE COLE ●	3		12
17 Dec 83	**WHAT ARE WE GONNA GET 'ER INDOORS** *EMI MIN 101* WITH THE DENNIS WATERMAN BAND	21		5

CRYSTAL WATERS
US, female vocalist — 59

Date	Title / Label	Peak Position	Weeks at No.1	Weeks on Chart
18 May 91	**GYPSY WOMAN (LA DA DEE)** *A&M AM 772* ●	2		10
7 Sep 91	**MAKIN' HAPPY** *A&M AM 790*	18		6
11 Jan 92	**MEGAMIX** *A&M AM 843*	39		3
3 Oct 92	**GYPSY WOMAN (LA DA DEE) (REMIX)** *Epic 6584377*	35		2
23 Apr 94	**100% PURE LOVE** *A&M 8586692*	15		7
2 Jul 94	**GHETTO DAY** *A&M 8589592*	40		2
25 Nov 95	**RELAX** *Manifesto FESCD 4*	37		2
24 Aug 96	**IN DE GHETTO** *Manifesto FESCD 12* DAVID MORALES & THE BAD YARD CLUB FEATURING CRYSTAL WATERS & DELTA	35		2
19 Apr 97	**SAY…IF YOU FEEL ALRIGHT** *Mercury 5742912*	45		1
20 Sep 03	**MY TIME** *Illustrious/Epic CDILL 018* DUTCH FEATURING CRYSTAL WATERS	22		4
24 Mar 07	**DESTINATION CALABRIA** *Data DATA153CDS* ALEX GAUDINO FEATURING CRYSTAL WATERS	4		20

MUDDY WATERS
US, male vocalist/guitarist (McKinley Morganfield), d. 30 Apr 1983 (age 68) — 6

Date	Title / Label	Peak Position	Weeks at No.1	Weeks on Chart
16 Jul 88	**MANNISH BOY** *Epic MUD 1*	51		6

ROGER WATERS
UK, male vocalist/bass guitarist (George Roger Waters). See Pink Floyd — 8

Date	Title / Label	Peak Position	Weeks at No.1	Weeks on Chart
30 May 87	**RADIO WAVES** *Harvest EM 6*	74		1
26 Dec 87	**THE TIDE IS TURNING (AFTER LIVE AID)** *Harvest EM 37*	54		4
5 Sep 92	**WHAT GOD WANTS PART 1** *Columbia 6581395*	35		3

LAUREN WATERWORTH
UK, female vocalist — 3

Date	Title / Label	Peak Position	Weeks at No.1	Weeks on Chart
1 Jun 02	**BABY NOW THAT I'VE FOUND YOU** *Jive 9253622*	24		3

MICHAEL WATFORD
US, male vocalist — 2

Date	Title / Label	Peak Position	Weeks at No.1	Weeks on Chart
26 Feb 94	**SO INTO YOU** *East West A 8309CD*	53		2

JODY WATLEY
US, female vocalist. See Shalamar — 35

Date	Title / Label	Peak Position	Weeks at No.1	Weeks on Chart
9 May 87	**LOOKING FOR A NEW LOVE** *MCA 1107*	13		11
17 Oct 87	**DON'T YOU WANT ME** *MCA 1198*	55		3
8 Apr 89	**REAL LOVE** *MCA 1324*	31		7
12 Aug 89	**FRIENDS** *MCA 1352* WITH ERIC B & RAKIM	21		6
10 Feb 90	**EVERYTHING** *MCA 1395*	74		2
11 Apr 92	**I'M THE ONE YOU NEED** *MCA MCS 1608*	50		3
21 May 94	**WHEN A MAN LOVES A WOMAN** *MCA MCSTD 1964*	33		2
25 Apr 98	**OFF THE HOOK** *Atlantic AT 0024CD1*	51		1

JOHNNY 'GUITAR' WATSON
US, male vocalist/guitarist, d. 17 May 1996 (age 61) — 8

Date	Title / Label	Peak Position	Weeks at No.1	Weeks on Chart
28 Aug 76	**I NEED IT** *DJM DJS 10694*	35		5
23 Apr 77	**A REAL MOTHER FOR YA** *DJM DJS 10762*	44		3

RUSSELL WATSON
UK, male vocalist. See One World Project — 13

Date	Title / Label	Peak Position	Weeks at No.1	Weeks on Chart
30 Oct 99	**SWING LOW '99** *Universal TV 4669502*	38		2
22 Jul 00	**BARCELONA (FRIENDS UNTIL THE END)** *Decca 46672772* & SHAUN RYDER	68		1
18 May 02	**SOMEONE LIKE YOU** *Decca 4730002* & FAYE TOZER	10		4
21 Dec 02	**NOTHING SACRED – A SONG FOR KIRSTY** *Decca 4737402*	17		5
29 Apr 06	**CAN'T HELP FALLING IN LOVE** *Decca 4757841*	69		1

BEN WATT FEATURING ESTELLE
UK, male/female vocal/instrumental/production duo — 1

Date	Title / Label	Peak Position	Weeks at No.1	Weeks on Chart
12 Feb 05	**OUTSPOKEN – PART 1** *Buzzin Fly 010BUZZCD*	74		1

BARRATT WAUGH
UK, male vocalist — 1

Date	Title / Label	Peak Position	Weeks at No.1	Weeks on Chart
26 Jul 03	**SKIP A BEAT** *BNW BNWCD02*	56		1

WAVELENGTH
UK, male vocal group — 12

Date	Title / Label	Peak Position	Weeks at No.1	Weeks on Chart
10 Jul 82	**HURRY HOME** *Ariola ARO 281*	17		12

WAX
US/UK, male vocal/instrumental duo — 16

Date	Title / Label	Peak Position	Weeks at No.1	Weeks on Chart
12 Apr 86	**RIGHT BETWEEN THE EYES** *RCA PB 40509*	60		5
1 Aug 87	**BRIDGE TO YOUR HEART** *RCA PB 41405*	12		11

Silver-selling ● Gold-selling ● Platinum-selling (x multiples) ★ US No.1 · Peak Position · Weeks at No.1 · Weeks on Chart

ANTHONY WAY
UK, male vocalist — 2

Date	Title	Peak	Wks at No.1	Wks
15 Apr 95	**PANIS ANGELICUS** *Decca 4481642*	55		2

A WAY OF LIFE
US, male vocal/instrumental/production group — 3

Date	Title	Peak	Wks at No.1	Wks
21 Apr 90	**TRIPPIN' ON YOUR LOVE** *Eternal YZ 4664*	55		3

WAY OF THE WEST
UK, male vocal/instrumental group — 5

Date	Title	Peak	Wks at No.1	Wks
25 Apr 81	**DON'T SAY THAT'S JUST FOR WHITE BOYS** *Mercury MER 66*	54		5

WAY OUT WEST
UK, male production duo — 17

Date	Title	Peak	Wks at No.1	Wks
3 Dec 94	**AJARE** *Deconstruction 74321243802*	52		1
2 Mar 96	**DOMINATION** *Deconstruction 74321342822*	38		2
14 Sep 96	**THE GIFT** *Deconstruction 74321401912* WAY OUT WEST/ MISS JOANNA LAW	15		5
30 Aug 97	**BLUE** *Deconstruction 74321477512*	41		2
29 Nov 97	**AJARE (REMIX)** *Deconstruction 74321521352*	36		2
9 Dec 00	**THE FALL** *Wow 005CD*	61		1
18 Aug 01	**INTENSIFY** *Distinctive Breaks DISNCD 74*	46		1
30 Mar 02	**MINDCIRCUS** *Distinctive Breaks DISNCD 80* FEATURING TRICIA LEE KELSHALL	39		2
21 Sep 02	**STEALTH** *Distinctive Breaks DISNCD 90* FEATURING KIRSTY HAWKSHAW	67		1

BRUCE WAYNE
Germany, male DJ/producer — 2

Date	Title	Peak	Wks at No.1	Wks
13 Dec 97	**READY** *Logic 74321527012*	44		1
4 Jul 98	**NO GOOD FOR ME** *Logic 74321587052*	70		1

JAN WAYNE
Germany, male DJ/producer (Jan Christiansen) — 8

Date	Title	Peak	Wks at No.1	Wks
9 Nov 02	**BECAUSE THE NIGHT** *Product PDT 02CDS*	14		5
29 Mar 03	**TOTAL ECLIPSE OF THE HEART** *Product PDT 10CDS*	28		3

JEFF WAYNE
US, male producer/keyboard player — 21

Date	Title	Peak	Wks at No.1	Wks
9 Sep 78	**THE EVE OF THE WAR** *CBS 6496* JEFF WAYNE'S WAR OF THE WORLDS	36		8
10 Jul 82	**MATADOR** *CBS A 2493*	57		3
25 Nov 89	**THE EVE OF THE WAR** *CBS 6551267* JEFF WAYNE'S WAR OF THE WORLDS	3		10

WE ARE SCIENTISTS
UK, male vocal/instrumental trio — 13

Date	Title	Peak	Wks at No.1	Wks
9 Jul 05	**NOBODY MOVE NOBODY GET HURT** *Virgin VUSCD303*	56		1
15 Oct 05	**THE GREAT ESCAPE** *Virgin VUSDX308*	37		2
4 Mar 06	**IT'S A HIT** *Virgin VUSCD319*	29		2
13 May 06	**NOBODY MOVE NOBODY GET HURT** *Virgin VUSCD325*	21		4
15 Mar 08	**AFTER HOURS** *Virgin VSCDT1970*	15		3
21 Jun 08	**CHICK LIT** *Virgin VSCDT1971*	37		1

WEATHER GIRLS
US, female vocal duo – Izora Rhodes Armstead, d. 16 Sep 2004, & Martha Wash — 14

Date	Title	Peak	Wks at No.1	Wks
27 Aug 83	**IT'S RAINING MEN** *CBS A 2924*	73		3
3 Mar 84	**IT'S RAINING MEN** *CBS A 2924* ●	2		11

WEATHER PROPHETS
UK, male vocal/instrumental group — 2

Date	Title	Peak	Wks at No.1	Wks
28 Mar 87	**SHE COMES FROM THE RAIN** *Elevation ACID 1*	62		2

WEATHERMEN
UK, male vocalist (Jonathan King) — 9

Date	Title	Peak	Wks at No.1	Wks
16 Jan 71	**IT'S THE SAME OLD SONG** *B&C CB 139*	19		9

MARTI WEBB
UK, female vocalist — 42

Date	Title	Peak	Wks at No.1	Wks
9 Feb 80	**TAKE THAT LOOK OFF YOUR FACE** *Polydor POSP 100* ●	3		12
19 Apr 80	**TELL ME ON A SUNDAY** *Polydor POSP 111*	67		2
20 Sep 80	**YOUR EARS SHOULD BE BURNING NOW** *Polydor POSP 166*	61		4
8 Jun 85	**BEN** *Starblend STAR 6*	5		11
20 Sep 86	**ALWAYS THERE** *BBC RESL 190* & THE SIMON MAY ORCHESTRA	13		12
6 Jun 87	**I CAN'T LET GO** *Rainbow RBR 12*	65		1

WEBB BROTHERS
US, male vocal/instrumental duo — 1

Date	Title	Peak	Wks at No.1	Wks
17 Feb 01	**I CAN'T BELIEVE YOU'RE GONE** *WEA 320CD*	69		1

SIMON WEBBE
UK, male vocalist. See Blue — 49

Date	Title	Peak	Wks at No.1	Wks
3 Sep 05	**LAY YOUR HANDS** *Innocent SINCD76*	4		16
19 Nov 05	**NO WORRIES** *Innocent SINDX77*	4		16
4 Mar 06	**AFTER ALL THIS TIME** *Innocent SINDX79*	16		6
4 Nov 06	**COMING AROUND AGAIN** *Angel ANGECD25*	12		7
17 Feb 07	**MY SOUL PLEADS FOR YOU** *Innocent ANGECD28*	45		3
30 Jun 07	**GRACE/RIDE THE STORM** *Angel ANGECD46*	36		1

JOAN WEBER
US, female vocalist, d. 13 May 1981 (age 45) — 1

Date	Title	Peak	Wks at No.1	Wks
18 Feb 55	**LET ME GO LOVER** *Philips PB 389* ★	16		1

NIKKI WEBSTER
Australia, female vocalist — 1

Date	Title	Peak	Wks at No.1	Wks
8 Jun 02	**STRAWBERRY KISSES** *Gotham 74321943642*	64		1

WEDDING PRESENT
UK, male vocal/instrumental group – David Gedge, Keith Gregory (replaced by Darren Belk, Jayne Lockey, then Terry de Castro), Peter Solowka (replaced by Paul Dorrington, then Simon Cleave) & Simon Smith (replaced by Kari Paavola) — 42

Date	Title	Peak	Wks at No.1	Wks
5 Mar 88	**NOBODY'S TWISTING YOUR ARM** *Reception REC 009*	46		2
1 Oct 88	**WHY ARE YOU BEING SO REASONABLE NOW** *Reception REC 011*	42		2
7 Oct 89	**KENNEDY** *RCA PB 43117*	33		3
17 Feb 90	**BRASSNECK** *RCA PB 43403*	24		3
29 Sep 90	**3 SONGS EP** *RCA PB 44021*	25		4
11 May 91	**DALLIANCE** *RCA PB 44495*	29		3
27 Jul 91	**LOVENEST** *RCA PT 44750*	58		1
18 Jan 92	**BLUE EYES** *RCA PB 45185*	26		2
15 Feb 92	**GO-GO DANCER** *RCA PB 45183*	20		1
14 Mar 92	**THREE** *RCA PB 45181*	14		2
18 Apr 92	**SILVER SHORTS** *RCA PB 45311*	14		1
16 May 92	**COME PLAY WITH ME** *RCA PB 45313*	10		2
13 Jun 92	**CALIFORNIA** *RCA PB 43515*	16		1
18 Jul 92	**FLYING SAUCER** *RCA 74321101157*	22		1
15 Aug 92	**BOING!** *RCA 74321101177*	19		1
19 Sep 92	**LOVE SLAVE** *RCA 74321101167*	17		1
17 Oct 92	**STICKY** *RCA 74321116917*	17		1
14 Nov 92	**THE QUEEN OF OUTER SPACE** *RCA 74321116927*	23		1
19 Dec 92	**NO CHRISTMAS** *RCA 74321116937*	25		1
10 Sep 94	**YEAH YEAH YEAH YEAH YEAH** *Island CID 585*	51		2
26 Nov 94	**IT'S A GAS** *Island CID 591*	71		1
31 Aug 96	**2, 3, GO** *Cooking Vinyl FRYCD 048*	67		1
25 Jan 97	**MONTREAL** *Cooking Vinyl FRYCD 053*	40		1
27 Nov 04	**INTERSTATE 5** *Scopitones TONECD018*	62		1
12 Feb 05	**I'M FROM FURTHER NORTH THAN YOU** *Scopitones TONECD019*	34		3

FRED WEDLOCK
UK, male vocalist (Peter Frederick Wedlock), d. 4 Mar 2010 (age 67) — 10

Date	Title	Peak	Wks at No.1	Wks
31 Jan 81	**OLDEST SWINGER IN TOWN** *Rocket XPRES 46* ●	6		10

WEE PAPA GIRL RAPPERS
UK, female rap duo – Samantha & Sandra Lawrence — 27

Date	Title	Peak	Wks at No.1	Wks
12 Mar 88	**FAITH** *Jive 164*	60		4
25 Jun 88	**HEAT IT UP** *Jive 174* FEATURING TWO MEN & A DRUM MACHINE	21		9
1 Oct 88	**WEE RULE** *Jive 185*	6		9
24 Dec 88	**SOULMATE** *Jive 193*	45		4
25 Mar 89	**BLOW THE HOUSE DOWN** *Jive 197*	65		1

BERT WEEDON
UK, male guitarist — 38

Date	Title / Label	Peak	Wks No.1	Wks
15 May 59	**GUITAR BOOGIE SHUFFLE** *Top Rank JAR 117*	10		9
20 Nov 59	**NASHVILLE BOOGIE** *Top Rank JAR 221*	29		2
10 Mar 60	**BIG BEAT BOOGIE** *Top Rank JAR 300*	37		4
9 Jun 60	**TWELFTH STREET RAG** *Top Rank JAR 360*	47		2
28 Jul 60	**APACHE** *Top Rank JAR 415*	24		4
27 Oct 60	**SORRY ROBBIE** *Top Rank JAR 517*	28		11
2 Feb 61	**GINCHY** *Top Rank JAR 537*	35		5
4 May 61	**MR GUITAR** *Top Rank JAR 559*	47		1

WEEKEND
International, male/female vocal/instrumental group — 5

Date	Title / Label	Peak	Wks No.1	Wks
14 Dec 85	**CHRISTMAS MEDLEY/AULD LANG SYNE** *Lifestyle XY 1*	47		5

WEEKEND PLAYERS
UK, male/female vocal/production duo. See Groove Armada — 5

Date	Title / Label	Peak	Wks No.1	Wks
8 Sep 01	**21ST CENTURY** *Multiply CXMULTY 78*	22		4
16 Mar 02	**INTO THE SUN** *Multiply CXMULTY 84*	42		1

MICHELLE WEEKS
US, female vocalist — 7

Date	Title / Label	Peak	Wks No.1	Wks
2 Aug 97	**MOMENT OF MY LIFE** *Ministry Of Sound MOSCDS 1* BOBBY D'AMBROSIO FEATURING MICHELLE WEEKS	23		3
8 Nov 97	**DON'T GIVE UP** *Ministry Of Sound MOSCDS 2*	28		2
11 Jul 98	**GIVE ME LOVE** *VC Recordings VCRD 37* DJ DADO VS MICHELLE WEEKS	59		1
3 May 03	**THE LIGHT** *Defected DFTD 064X*	69		1

WEEN
US, male vocal/instrumental group — 3

Date	Title / Label	Peak	Wks No.1	Wks
29 Aug 98	**BEACON LIGHT** *Elektra E 4100CD*	20		3

WEEZER
US, male vocal/instrumental group – Rivers Cuomo, Brian Bell, Matt Sharp (replaced by Mikey Welsh, then Scott Shriner) & Pat Wilson — 31

Date	Title / Label	Peak	Wks No.1	Wks
11 Feb 95	**UNDONE – THE SWEATER SONG** *Geffen GFSTD 85*	35		2
6 May 95	**BUDDY HOLLY** *Geffen GFSTD 88*	12		7
22 Jul 95	**SAY IT AIN'T SO** *Geffen GFSTD 95*	37		2
5 Oct 96	**EL SCORCHO** *Geffen GFSTD 22167*	50		1
14 Jul 01	**HASH PIPE** *Geffen 4975642*	21		2
3 Nov 01	**ISLAND IN THE SUN** *Geffen 4976162*	31		2
14 Sep 02	**KEEP FISHIN'** *Geffen 04977922*	29		2
14 May 05	**BEVERLY HILLS** *Geffen 9881791*	9		6
27 Aug 05	**WE ARE ALL ON DRUGS** *Geffen 9883495*	47		1
28 Jun 08	**PORK AND BEANS** *Geffen 1774361*	33		4
31 Jan 09	**BEVERLY HILLS** *Geffen 9881791*	59		2

FRANK WEIR
UK, male saxophonist/orchestra leader, d. 12 May 1981 (age 70) — 4

Date	Title / Label	Peak	Wks No.1	Wks
15 Sep 60	**CARIBBEAN HONEYMOON** *Oriole CB 1559*	42		4

WEIRD SCIENCE
UK, male DJ/production duo — 1

Date	Title / Label	Peak	Wks No.1	Wks
1 Jul 00	**FEEL THE NEED** *NuLife 74321751982*	62		1

DENISE WELCH
UK, female actor/TV personality/vocalist (Jacqueline Denise Welch) — 3

Date	Title / Label	Peak	Wks No.1	Wks
4 Nov 95	**YOU DON'T HAVE TO SAY YOU LOVE ME/CRY ME A RIVER** *Virgin VSCDT 1569*	23		3

PAUL WELLER
UK, male vocalist (John Weller). See Council Collective, Jam, Style Council — 96

Date	Title / Label	Peak	Wks No.1	Wks
18 May 91	**INTO TOMORROW** *Freedom High FHP 1* PAUL WELLER MOVEMENT	36		3
15 Aug 92	**UH HUH OH YEH** *Go! Discs GOD 86*	18		5
10 Oct 92	**ABOVE THE CLOUDS** *Go! Discs GOD 91*	47		2
17 Jul 93	**SUNFLOWER** *Go! Discs GODCD 102*	16		5
4 Sep 93	**WILD WOOD** *Go! Discs GODCD 104*	14		3
13 Nov 93	**THE WEAVER (EP)** *Go! Discs GODCD 107*	18		3
9 Apr 94	**HUNG UP** *Go! Discs GODCD 111*	11		3
5 Nov 94	**OUT OF THE SINKING** *Go! Discs GODCD 121*	20		3
6 May 95	**THE CHANGINGMAN** *Go! Discs GODCD 127*	7		4
22 Jul 95	**YOU DO SOMETHING TO ME** *Go! Discs GODCD 130*	9		6
30 Sep 95	**BROKEN STONES** *Go! Discs GODCD 132*	20		4
9 Mar 96	**OUT OF THE SINKING** *Go! Discs GODCD 143*	16		2
17 Aug 96	**PEACOCK SUIT** *Go! Discs GODCD 149*	5		5
9 Aug 97	**BRUSHED** *Island CID 666*	14		3
11 Oct 97	**FRIDAY STREET** *Island CID 676*	21		2
6 Dec 97	**MERMAIDS** *Island CID 683*	30		2
14 Nov 98	**BRAND NEW START** *Island CID 711*	16		3
9 Jan 99	**WILD WOOD** *Island CID 734*	22		3
2 Sep 00	**SWEET PEA, MY SWEET PEA** *Island CID 764*	44		1
14 Sep 02	**IT'S WRITTEN IN THE STARS** *Independiente ISOM 63SMS*	7		3
30 Nov 02	**LEAFY MYSTERIES** *Independiente ISOM 65SMS*	23		2
26 Jun 04	**THE BOTTLE** *V2 VVR 5026913*	13		3
11 Sep 04	**WISHING ON A STAR** *V2 VVR 5026928*	11		5
27 Nov 04	**THINKING OF YOU** *V2 VVR5028463*	18		3
26 Mar 05	**EARLY MORNING RAIN** *V2 VVR5030597*	40		1
30 Jul 05	**FROM THE FLOORBOARDS UP** *V2 VVR5033413*	6		4
8 Oct 05	**COME ON/LET'S GO** *V2 VVR5033223*	15		2
17 Dec 05	**HERE'S THE GOOD NEWS** *V2 VVR5034603*	21		2
18 Nov 06	**WILD BLUE YONDER** *V2 VVR5043983*	22		2
21 Jul 07	**THIS OLD TOWN** *Regal Recordings GB01A0700935* & GRAHAM COXON	39		2
22 Sep 07	**ARE YOU TRYING TO BE LONELY** *Acid Jazz AJX193CD* ANDY LEWIS & PAUL WELLER	31		1
7 Jun 08	**HAVE YOU MADE UP YOUR MIND/ECHOES AROUND THE SUN** *Island 1772838*	19		2
6 Sep 08	**ALL I WANNA DO/PUSH IT ALONG** *Island 1781131*	28		1
15 Nov 08	**SEA SPRAY/22 DREAMS** *Island 1790117*	59		1

BRANDI WELLS
US, female vocalist (Marguerite Pinder Bannister), d. 25 Mar 2003 (age 47) — 1

Date	Title / Label	Peak	Wks No.1	Wks
20 Feb 82	**WATCH OUT** *Virgin VS 479*	74		1

HOUSTON WELLS
UK, male vocalist (Andrew Smith), d. — 10

Date	Title / Label	Peak	Wks No.1	Wks
1 Aug 63	**ONLY THE HEARTACHES** *Parlophone R 5031*	22		10

MARY WELLS
US, female vocalist, d. 26 Jul 1992 (age 49) — 25

Date	Title / Label	Peak	Wks No.1	Wks
21 May 64	**MY GUY** *Stateside SS 288* ★	5		14
30 Jul 64	**ONCE UPON A TIME** *Stateside SS 316* MARVIN GAYE & MARY WELLS	50		1
8 Jul 72	**MY GUY** *Tamla Motown TMG 820*	14		10

TERRI WELLS
US, female vocalist — 9

Date	Title / Label	Peak	Wks No.1	Wks
2 Jul 83	**YOU MAKE IT HEAVEN** *Phillyworld PWS 111*	53		2
5 May 84	**I'LL BE AROUND** *Phillyworld LON 48*	17		7

ALEX WELSH
UK, male vocal/instrumental group – leader d. 25 Jun 1982 (age 52) — 4

Date	Title / Label	Peak	Wks No.1	Wks
10 Aug 61	**TANSY** *Columbia DB 4686*	45		4

WENDY & LISA
US, female vocal/instrumental duo — 31

Date	Title / Label	Peak	Wks No.1	Wks
5 Sep 87	**WATERFALL** *Virgin VS 999*	66		4
16 Jan 88	**SIDE SHOW** *Virgin VS 1012*	49		5
18 Feb 89	**ARE YOU MY BABY** *Virgin VS 1156*	70		3
29 Apr 89	**LOLLY LOLLY** *Virgin VS 1175*	64		3
8 Jul 89	**SATISFACTION** *Virgin VS 1194*	27		8
18 Nov 89	**WATERFALL (REMIX)** *Virgin VS 1223*	69		2
30 Jun 90	**STRUNG OUT** *Virgin VS 1272*	44		5
10 Nov 90	**RAINBOW LAKE** *Virgin VS 1280*	70		1

WES
Cameroon, male vocalist (Wes Alane) — 7

Date	Title / Label	Peak	Wks No.1	Wks
14 Feb 98	**ALANE** *Epic 6654682*	11		6
27 Jun 98	**I LOVE FOOTBALL** *Epic 6660772*	75		1

Silver-selling ◦ | Gold-selling ● | Platinum-selling (x multiples) ⊛ | US No.1 ★ | Peak Position | Weeks at No.1 | Weeks on Chart

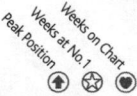

DODIE WEST
UK, female vocalist

		Peak	No.1	4
14 Jan 65	**GOING OUT OF MY HEAD** *Decca F 12046*	39		4

KANYE WEST
US, male rapper/producer/record label owner. Outspoken Jay-Z protege who has successfully teamed up with some of the biggest names in pop and rock. With his help, Jay-Z achieved his first UK No.1 as a lead artist ('Run This Town') and Ray Charles bagged his first US No.1 as a songwriter (for an 'I Got A Woman' sample on 'Gold Digger')

		Peak	No.1	332
3 Apr 04	**THROUGH THE WIRE** *Roc-A-Fella 9862270*	9		9
19 Jun 04	**ALL FALLS DOWN** *Roc-A-Fella 9862670* FEATURING SYLEENA JOHNSON	10		8
26 Jun 04	**TALK ABOUT OUR LOVE** *Atlantic AT 0177CD* BRANDY FEATURING KANYE WEST	6		10
11 Sep 04	**JESUS WALKS** *Roc-A-Fella 9863964*	16		6
16 Jul 05	**DIAMONDS FROM SIERRA LEONE** *Roc-A-Fella 9883229*	8		12
1 Oct 05	**GOLD DIGGER** *Roc-A-Fella 9885699* FEATURING JAMIE FOXX ◦ ★	2		44
17 Dec 05	**HEARD 'EM SAY** *Roc-A-Fella 9888416* FEATURING ADAM LEVINE	22		11
25 Feb 06	**BRAND NEW** *J Records 82876778842* RHYMEFEST FEATURING KANYE WEST	32		2
18 Mar 06	**TOUCH THE SKY** *Roc-A-Fella 9852115* FEATURING LUPE FIASCO	6		12
1 Jul 06	**EXTRAVAGANZA** *J Records 8287689422* JAMIE FOXX FEATURING KANYE WEST	43		2
26 Aug 06	**NUMBER ONE** *Virgin VUSDX333* PHARRELL FEATURING KANYE WEST	31		5
26 Aug 06	**BACK LIKE THAT** *Def Jam 1705586* FEATURING NE-YO & GHOSTFACED KILLAH	46		2
18 Aug 07	**STRONGER** *Def Jam 1744463* ★	1	2	30
29 Sep 07	**GOOD LIFE** *Def Jam 1752306* FEATURING T-PAIN	23		16
5 Jan 08	**HOMECOMING** *Def Jam 1761789* FEATURING CHRIS MARTIN	9		16
15 Mar 08	**AMERICAN BOY** *Atlantic AT0304CD* ESTELLE FEATURING KANYE WEST	1	4	32
12 Apr 08	**FLASHING LIGHTS** *Def Jam 1768251* FEATURING DWELE	29		10
27 Sep 08	**SWAGGA LIKE US** *Mercury USUM70835786* JAY-Z FEATURING KANYE WEST & LIL WAYNE	33		2
4 Oct 08	**LOVE LOCKDOWN** *Def Jam 1791479*	8		23
6 Dec 08	**HEARTLESS** *Roc-A-Fella USUM70840511*	10		18
23 May 09	**KNOCK YOU DOWN** *Interscope 2711463* KERI HILSON FEATURING KANYE WEST & NE-YO	5		21
1 Aug 09	**SUPERNOVA** *Good Music GBUM70902596* MR HUDSON & KANYE WEST ◦	2		15
12 Sep 09	**RUN THIS TOWN** *Roc Nation USJZ10900011* JAY-Z FEATURING RIHANNA & KANYE WEST	1	1	12
26 Sep 09	**MAKE HER SAY** *Island USUM70969614* KID CUDI FEATURING KANYE WEST, COMMON & LADY GAGA	67		2
19 Dec 09	**FOREVER** *Interscope USUM70985104* DRAKE FEATURING KANYE WEST, LIL WAYNE & EMINEM	42		12

KEITH WEST
UK, male vocalist (Keith Hopkins)

		Peak	No.1	18
9 Aug 67	**EXCERPT FROM A TEENAGE OPERA** *Parlophone R 5623*	2		15
22 Nov 67	**SAM** *Parlophone R 5651*	38		3

TILL WEST & DJ DELICIOUS
Germany, male production duo

		Peak	No.1	3
15 Jul 06	**SAME MAN** *Data DATA119CDS*	36		3

WEST END
UK, female vocal group

		Peak	No.1	2
19 Aug 95	**LOVE RULES** *RCA 74321292702*	44		2

WEST END FEATURING SYBIL
UK, male production trio – Eddie Gordon, Mike Stock & Pete Waterman – & US, female vocalist (Sybil Lynch). See Childliners

		Peak	No.1	13
16 Jan 93	**THE LOVE I LOST** *PWL Sanctuary PWCD 253*	3		13

WEST HAM UNITED CUP SQUAD
UK, male football team vocalists

		Peak	No.1	2
10 May 75	**I'M FOREVER BLOWING BUBBLES** *Pye 7N 45470*	31		2

WEST STREET MOB
US, male/female DJ/vocal trio

		Peak	No.1	3
8 Oct 83	**BREAK DANCIN' – ELECTRIC BOOGIE** *Sugarhill SH 128*	64		3

WESTBAM
Germany, male producer (Maximilian Lenz)

		Peak	No.1	9
9 Jul 94	**CELEBRATION GENERATION** *Low Spirit PQCD 5*	48		2
19 Nov 94	**BAM BAM BAM** *Low Spirit PZCD 329*	57		1
3 Jun 95	**WIZARDS OF THE SONIC** *Urban PZCD 344*	32		2
23 Mar 96	**ALWAYS MUSIC** *Low Spirit 5779152* WESTBAM/KOON + STEPHENSON	51		1
13 Jun 98	**WIZARDS OF THE SONIC (REMIX)** *Wonderboy WBOYD 010* VS RED JERRY	43		2
28 Nov 98	**ROOF IS ON FIRE** *Logic 74321633162*	58		1

WESTLIFE
Ireland, male vocal group – Nicky Byrne, Kian Egan, Mark Feehily, Shane Filan & Bryan McFadden* (left 2004). Photogenic balladeers whose career-starting record run of seven successive No.1s and 22 consecutive Top 5 hits could prove to be unbreakable. They were the top-selling group of the 2000s, with singles sales approaching six million, and only Robbie Williams sold more records in that decade. See Helping Haiti

		Peak	No.1	277
1 May 99	**SWEAR IT AGAIN** *RCA 74321662062* ●	1	2	13
21 Aug 99	**IF I LET YOU GO** *RCA 74321692352* ◦	1	1	11
30 Oct 99	**FLYING WITHOUT WINGS** *RCA 74321709162* ◦	1	1	13
25 Dec 99	**I HAVE A DREAM/SEASONS IN THE SUN** *RCA 74321726012* ⊛	1	4	17
8 Apr 00	**FOOL AGAIN** *RCA 74321751562*	1	1	12
30 Sep 00	**AGAINST ALL ODDS (TAKE A LOOK AT ME NOW)** *Columbia 6698872* MARIAH CAREY FEATURING WESTLIFE ◦	1	2	12
11 Nov 00	**MY LOVE** *RCA 74321802802*	1	1	10
30 Dec 00	**WHAT MAKES A MAN** *RCA 74321826252* ●	2		13
17 Mar 01	**UPTOWN GIRL** *RCA 74321841692* ◦	1	1	16
17 Nov 01	**QUEEN OF MY HEART** *RCA 74321899142* ◦	1	1	15
2 Mar 02	**WORLD OF OUR OWN** *RCA 74321919242* ◦	1	1	13
1 Jun 02	**BOP BOP BABY** *S 74321940452*	5		10
16 Nov 02	**UNBREAKABLE** *S 74321975222* ◦	1	1	16
5 Apr 03	**TONIGHT/MISS YOU NIGHTS** *S 74321986802*	3		10
27 Sep 03	**HEY WHATEVER** *S 82876560862*	4		7
29 Nov 03	**MANDY** *S 82876570742*	1	1	9
6 Mar 04	**OBVIOUS** *S 82876596322*	3		8
5 Nov 05	**YOU RAISE ME UP** *S 82876739522*	1	2	17
24 Dec 05	**WHEN YOU TELL ME THAT YOU LOVE ME** *S 82876767382* FEATURING DIANA ROSS	2		8
4 Mar 06	**AMAZING** *S 82876806252*	4		6
18 Nov 06	**THE ROSE** *S 88697032652*	1	1	7
10 Nov 07	**HOME** *S 88697189872*	3		12
8 Dec 07	**I'M ALREADY THERE** *S GBARL0701126*	62		1
1 Mar 08	**US AGAINST THE WORLD** *S 88697253142*	8		8
27 Dec 08	**I'M ALREADY THERE** *S GBARL0701126*	63		1
7 Nov 09	**WHAT ABOUT NOW** *Syco Music 88697611282* ◦	2		12

WESTWORLD
UK/US, male/female vocal/instrumental trio

		Peak	No.1	23
21 Feb 87	**SONIC BOOM BOY** *RCA BOOM 1*	11		7
2 May 87	**BA-NA-NA-BAM-BOO** *RCA BOOM 2*	37		5
25 Jul 87	**WHERE THE ACTION IS** *RCA BOOM 3*	54		4
17 Oct 87	**SILVERMAC** *RCA BOOM 4*	42		5
15 Oct 88	**EVERYTHING GOOD IS BAD** *RCA PB 42243*	72		2

WET WET WET
UK, male vocal/instrumental group – Marti Pellow* (Mark McLoughlin), Graeme Clark, Tom Cunningham & Neil Mitchell. Glasgow band who will forever be remembered for their 1.8-million-selling Four Weddings & A Funeral ... ballad 'Love Is All Around', which locked down the No.1 spot for a group record 15 consecutive weeks and accounts for more than a third of their total UK singles sales of 5 million

		Peak	No.1	214
11 Apr 87	**WISHING I WAS LUCKY** *Precious Organisation JEWEL 3*	6		14
25 Jul 87	**SWEET LITTLE MYSTERY** *Precious Organisation JEWEL 4*	5		12
5 Dec 87	**ANGEL EYES (HOME AND AWAY)** *Precious Organisation JEWEL 6*	5		12
19 Mar 88	**TEMPTATION** *Precious Organisation JEWEL 7*	12		8
14 May 88	**WITH A LITTLE HELP FROM MY FRIENDS** *Childline CHILD 1* ◦	1	4	11
30 Sep 89	**SWEET SURRENDER** *Precious Organisation JEWEL 9*	6		8
9 Dec 89	**BROKE AWAY** *Precious Organisation JEWEL 10*	19		7
10 Mar 90	**HOLD BACK THE RIVER** *Precious Organisation JEWEL 11*	31		4
11 Aug 90	**STAY WITH ME HEARTACHE/I FEEL FINE** *Precious Organisation JEWEL 13*	30		4
14 Sep 91	**MAKE IT TONIGHT** *Precious Organisation JEWEL 15*	37		3
2 Nov 91	**PUT THE LIGHT ON** *Precious Organisation JEWEL 16*	56		2
4 Jan 92	**GOODNIGHT GIRL** *Precious Organisation JEWEL 17*	1	4	11
21 Mar 92	**MORE THAN LOVE** *Precious Organisation JEWEL 18*	19		5
11 Jul 92	**LIP SERVICE (EP)** *Precious Organisation JEWEL 19*	15		5
8 May 93	**BLUE FOR YOU/THIS TIME (LIVE)** *Precious Organisation JWLCD 20*	38		2

Date	Title / Label	Peak Position	Weeks at No.1	Weeks on Chart
6 Nov 93	**SHED A TEAR** *Precious Organisation JWLCD 21*	22		5
8 Jan 94	**COLD COLD HEART** *Precious Organisation JWLCD 22*	20		4
21 May 94	**LOVE IS ALL AROUND** *Precious Organisation JWLCD 23* ⊛ **x2**	1	15	37
25 Mar 95	**JULIA SAYS** *Precious Organisation JWLDD 24* ○	3		9
17 Jun 95	**DON'T WANT TO FORGIVE ME NOW** *Precious Organisation JWLDD 25*	7		8
30 Sep 95	**SOMEWHERE SOMEHOW** *Precious Organisation JWLDD 26*	7		7
2 Dec 95	**SHE'S ALL ON MY MIND** *Precious Organisation JWLDD 27*	17		7
30 Mar 96	**MORNING** *Precious Organisation JWLDD 28*	16		4
22 Mar 97	**IF I NEVER SEE YOU AGAIN** *Precious Organisation JWLCD 29*	3		9
14 Jun 97	**STRANGE** *Precious Organisation JWLCD 30*	13		5
16 Aug 97	**YESTERDAY** *Precious Organisation JWLCD 31*	4		6
13 Nov 04	**ALL I WANT** *Mercury 9868448*	14		3
17 Nov 07	**TOO MANY PEOPLE** *Dry DRY2SCX*	46		1
16 Feb 08	**WEIGHTLESS** *Dry DRY3SCX*	10		1

WE'VE GOT A FUZZBOX & WE'RE GONNA USE IT

UK, female vocal/instrumental group — 39

Date	Title / Label	Peak Position	Weeks at No.1	Weeks on Chart
26 Apr 86	**XX SEX/RULES AND REGULATIONS** *Vindaloo UGH 11*	41		7
15 Nov 86	**LOVE IS THE SLUG** *Vindaloo UGH 14*	31		4
7 Feb 87	**WHAT'S THE POINT** *Vindaloo YZ 101*	51		2
25 Feb 89	**INTERNATIONAL RESCUE** *WEA YZ 347* FUZZBOX	11		10
20 May 89	**PINK SUNSHINE** *WEA YZ 401* FUZZBOX	14		10
5 Aug 89	**SELF!** *WEA YZ 408* FUZZBOX	24		6

WHALE

Sweden, male/female vocal/instrumental group — 8

Date	Title / Label	Peak Position	Weeks at No.1	Weeks on Chart
19 Mar 94	**HOBO HUMPIN' SLOBO BABE** *East West YZ 798CD*	46		2
15 Jul 95	**I'LL DO YA** *Hut HUTDG 51*	53		1
25 Nov 95	**HOBO HUMPIN' SLOBO BABE** *Hut HUTCD 64*	15		4
4 Jul 98	**FOUR BIG SPEAKERS** *Hut HUTCD 96* FEATURING BUS 75	69		1

WHAM!

UK, male vocal duo – George Michael* & Andrew Ridgeley* — 151

Date	Title / Label	Peak Position	Weeks at No.1	Weeks on Chart
16 Oct 82	**YOUNG GUNS (GO FOR IT)** *Innervision IVL A 2766* ○	3		17
15 Jan 83	**WHAM RAP** *Innervision IVL A 2442*	8		11
14 May 83	**BAD BOYS** *Innervision A 3143* ○	2		14
30 Jul 83	**CLUB TROPICANA** *Innervision A 3613*	4		11
3 Dec 83	**CLUB FANTASTIC MEGAMIX** *Innervision A 3586*	15		8
26 May 84	**WAKE ME UP BEFORE YOU GO GO** *Epic A 4440* ● ★	1	2	16
13 Oct 84	**FREEDOM** *Epic A 4743* ●	1	3	14
15 Dec 84	**LAST CHRISTMAS/EVERYTHING SHE WANTS** *Epic A 4949* ⊛ ★	2		13
23 Nov 85	**I'M YOUR MAN** *Epic A 6716* ●	1	2	12
14 Dec 85	**LAST CHRISTMAS** *Epic WHAM 1*	6		7
21 Jun 86	**THE EDGE OF HEAVEN/WHERE DID YOUR HEART GO** *Epic FIN 1* ○	1	2	10
20 Dec 86	**LAST CHRISTMAS** *Epic 6502697*	45		4
8 Dec 07	**LAST CHRISTMAS** *RCA GBBBM8400019*	14		5
6 Dec 08	**LAST CHRISTMAS** *RCA GBBBM8400019*	26		5
12 Dec 09	**LAST CHRISTMAS** *RCA GBBBM8400019*	34		4

SARAH WHATMORE

UK, female vocalist — 17

Date	Title / Label	Peak Position	Weeks at No.1	Weeks on Chart
21 Sep 02	**WHEN I LOST YOU** *RCA 74321965952*	6		9
22 Feb 03	**AUTOMATIC** *RCA 82876504612*	11		8

REBECCA WHEATLEY

UK, female actor/vocalist — 8

Date	Title / Label	Peak Position	Weeks at No.1	Weeks on Chart
26 Feb 00	**STAY WITH ME (BABY)** *BBC Music WMSS 60222*	10		8

WHEATUS

US, male vocal/instrumental group – Brendan & Peter Brown, Phil A. Jimenez & Rich Liegey — 38

Date	Title / Label	Peak Position	Weeks at No.1	Weeks on Chart
17 Feb 01	**TEENAGE DIRTBAG** *Columbia 6707962* ●	2		20
14 Jul 01	**A LITTLE RESPECT** *Columbia 6714282*	3		12
26 Jan 02	**WANNABE GANGSTER/LEROY** *Columbia 6721272*	22		5
6 Sep 03	**AMERICAN IN AMSTERDAM** *Columbia 6741072*	59		1

CARON WHEELER

UK, female vocalist — 42

Date	Title / Label	Peak Position	Weeks at No.1	Weeks on Chart
18 Mar 89	**KEEP ON MOVING** *10 TEN 263* SOUL II SOUL FEATURING CARON WHEELER	5		12
10 Jun 89	**BACK TO LIFE (HOWEVER DO YOU WANT ME)** *10 TEN 265* SOUL II SOUL FEATURING CARON WHEELER ○	1	4	14
8 Sep 90	**LIVIN' IN THE LIGHT** *RCA PB 43939*	14		6
10 Nov 90	**UK BLAK** *RCA PB 43719*	40		4

Date	Title / Label	Peak Position	Weeks at No.1	Weeks on Chart
9 Feb 91	**DON'T QUIT** *RCA PB 44259*	53		3
7 Nov 92	**I ADORE YOU** *Perspective PERSS 7407*	59		2
11 Sep 93	**BEACH OF THE WAR GODDESS** *EMI CDEM 282*	75		1

BILL WHELAN

Ireland, male conductor/composer — 16

Date	Title / Label	Peak Position	Weeks at No.1	Weeks on Chart
17 Dec 94	**RIVERDANCE** *Son RTEBUACD 1* FEATURING ANUNA & THE RTE CONCERT ORCHESTRA ○	9		16

WHEN IN ROME

UK, male vocal/instrumental group — 3

Date	Title / Label	Peak Position	Weeks at No.1	Weeks on Chart
28 Jan 89	**THE PROMISE** *10 TEN 244*	58		3

Acts With The Most No.1s

Pos	Artist	No.1 singles
1	ELVIS PRESLEY	21
2	BEATLES	17
3	CLIFF RICHARD	14
=	WESTLIFE	14
5	MADONNA	13
6	SHADOWS	12
7	TAKE THAT	11
8	ABBA	9
=	SPICE GIRLS	9
10	ROLLING STONES	8
=	OASIS	8
12	ELTON JOHN	7
=	GEORGE MICHAEL	7
=	MICHAEL JACKSON	7
=	KYLIE MINOGUE	7
=	U2	7
=	McFLY	7
=	EMINEM	7
19	QUEEN	6
=	SLADE	6
=	ROD STEWART	6
=	BLONDIE	6
=	SUGABABES	6
=	ROBBIE WILLIAMS	6
=	BOYZONE	6

Silver-selling ● Gold-selling ● Platinum-selling (x multiples) ⊛ US No.1 ★ Peak Position Weeks at No.1 Weeks on Chart

WHIGFIELD

Denmark, female vocalist (Sannie Carlson) — 52

Date	Title / Label	Peak Position	Weeks at No.1	Weeks on Chart
17 Sep 94	**SATURDAY NIGHT** *Systematic SYSCD 3* ⊛	1	4	18
10 Dec 94	**ANOTHER DAY** *Systematic SYSCD 6* ●	7		10
10 Jun 95	**THINK OF YOU** *Systematic SYCDP 10*	7		11
9 Sep 95	**CLOSE TO YOU** *Systematic SYCDP 18*	13		7
16 Dec 95	**LAST CHRISTMAS/BIG TIME** *Systematic SYSCD 24*	21		5
10 Oct 98	**SEXY EYES – REMIXES** *ZYX 8085R8*	68		1

WHIPPING BOY

Ireland, male vocal/instrumental group — 4

Date	Title / Label	Peak Position	Weeks at No.1	Weeks on Chart
14 Oct 95	**WE DON'T NEED NOBODY ELSE** *Columbia 6622205*	51		1
3 Feb 96	**WHEN WE WERE YOUNG** *Columbia 6628062*	46		2
25 May 96	**TWINKLE** *Columbia 6632272*	55		1

WHISPERS

US, male vocal group – Nicholas Caldwell, Leaveil Degree, Marcus Hutson & Wallace & Walter Scott — 52

Date	Title / Label	Peak Position	Weeks at No.1	Weeks on Chart
2 Feb 80	**AND THE BEAT GOES ON** *Solar SO 1* ●	2		12
10 May 80	**LADY** *Solar SO 4*	55		3
12 Jul 80	**MY GIRL** *Solar SO 8*	26		6
14 Mar 81	**IT'S A LOVE THING** *Solar SO 16*	9		11
13 Jun 81	**I CAN MAKE IT BETTER** *Solar SO 19*	44		5
19 Jan 85	**CONTAGIOUS** *MCA 937*	56		3
28 Mar 87	**AND THE BEAT GOES ON** *Solar MCA 1126*	45		4
23 May 87	**ROCK STEADY** *Solar MCA 1152*	38		6
15 Aug 87	**SPECIAL F/X** *Solar MCA 1178*	69		2

WHISTLE

US, male rap/DJ trio – Rickford Bennett, Garvin Dublin & Brian Faust — 8

Date	Title / Label	Peak Position	Weeks at No.1	Weeks on Chart
1 Mar 86	**(NOTHIN' SERIOUS) JUST BUGGIN'** *Champion CHAMP 12*	7		8

ALEX WHITCOMBE & BIG C

UK, male DJ/production duo. See Qattara — 1

Date	Title / Label	Peak Position	Weeks at No.1	Weeks on Chart
23 May 98	**ICE RAIN** *Xtravaganza 0091075 EXT*	44		1

BARRY WHITE

US, male vocalist/producer, d. 4 July 2003 (age 58). See Love Unlimited Orchestra — 138

Date	Title / Label	Peak Position	Weeks at No.1	Weeks on Chart
9 Jun 73	**I'M GONNA LOVE YOU JUST A LITTLE BIT MORE BABY** *Pye International 7N 25610*	23		7
26 Jan 74	**NEVER NEVER GONNA GIVE YA UP** *Pye International 7N 25633*	14		11
17 Aug 74	**CAN'T GET ENOUGH OF YOUR LOVE BABE** *Pye International 7N 25661* ★	8		12
2 Nov 74	**YOU'RE THE FIRST THE LAST MY EVERYTHING** *20th Century BTC 2133* ●	1	2	14
8 Mar 75	**WHAT AM I GONNA DO WITH YOU** *20th Century BTC 2177*	5		8
24 May 75	**I'LL DO ANYTHING YOU WANT ME TO** *20th Century BTC 2208*	20		6
27 Dec 75	**LET THE MUSIC PLAY** *20th Century BTC 2265*	9		8
6 Mar 76	**YOU SEE THE TROUBLE WITH ME** *20th Century BTC 2277* ●	2		10
21 Aug 76	**BABY, WE BETTER TRY TO GET IT TOGETHER** *20th Century BTC 2298*	15		7
13 Nov 76	**DON'T MAKE ME WAIT TOO LONG** *20th Century BTC 2309*	17		8
5 Mar 77	**I'M QUALIFIED TO SATISFY** *20th Century BTC 2328*	37		5
15 Oct 77	**IT'S ECSTASY WHEN YOU LAY DOWN NEXT TO ME** *20th Century BTC 2350*	40		3
16 Dec 78	**JUST THE WAY YOU ARE** *20th Century BTC 2380* ●	12		12
24 Mar 79	**SHA LA LA MEANS I LOVE YOU** *20th Century BTC 1041*	55		6
7 Nov 87	**SHO' YOU RIGHT** *Breakout USA 614*	14		7
16 Jan 88	**NEVER NEVER GONNA GIVE YA UP (REMIX)** *Club JAB 59*	63		2
31 Mar 90	**SECRET GARDEN** *Qwest W 9992* QUINCY JONES FEATURING AL B SURE!, JAMES INGRAM, EL DeBARGE & BARRY WHITE	67		1
21 Jan 95	**PRACTICE WHAT YOU PREACH/LOVE IS THE ICON** *A&M 5808992*	20		4
8 Apr 95	**I ONLY WANT TO BE WITH YOU** *A&M 5810252*	36		2
21 Dec 96	**IN YOUR WILDEST DREAMS** *Parlophone CDR 6451* TINA TURNER FEATURING BARRY WHITE	32		3
4 Nov 00	**LET THE MUSIC PLAY (REMIX)** *Wonderboy WBOYD 020*	45		2

CHRIS WHITE

UK, male vocalist — 4

Date	Title / Label	Peak Position	Weeks at No.1	Weeks on Chart
20 Mar 76	**SPANISH WINE** *Charisma CB 272*	37		4

JACK WHITE & ALICIA KEYS

US, male/female vocal/instrumental duo – John Gillis & Alicia Cook. See Raconteurs, White Stripes — 12

Date	Title / Label	Peak Position	Weeks at No.1	Weeks on Chart
4 Oct 08	**ANOTHER WAY TO DIE** *RCA 88697413642*	9		12

KARYN WHITE

US, female vocalist — 38

Date	Title / Label	Peak Position	Weeks at No.1	Weeks on Chart
5 Nov 88	**THE WAY YOU LOVE ME** *Warner Brothers W 7773*	42		5
18 Feb 89	**SECRET RENDEZVOUS** *Warner Brothers W 7562*	52		3
10 Jun 89	**SUPERWOMAN** *Warner Brothers W 2920*	11		13
9 Sep 89	**SECRET RENDEZVOUS** *Warner Brothers W 2855*	22		9
17 Aug 91	**ROMANTIC** *Warner Brothers W 0028* ★	23		5
18 Jan 92	**THE WAY I FEEL ABOUT YOU** *Warner Brothers W 0073*	65		2
24 Sep 94	**HUNGAH** *Warner Brothers W 0264CD*	69		1

KEISHA WHITE

UK, female vocalist. See Oakenfold — 11

Date	Title / Label	Peak Position	Weeks at No.1	Weeks on Chart
27 Mar 04	**WATCHA GONNA DO** *Radar RAD005CD*	53		1
5 Mar 05	**DON'T CARE WHO KNOWS** *Warner Brothers WEA382CD2*	29		2
11 Mar 06	**THE WEAKNESS IN ME** *Korova KOW1001CD1*	17		5
1 Jul 06	**DON'T MISTAKE ME** *Korova KOW1007CD1*	48		2
30 Sep 06	**I CHOOSE LIFE** *Korova KOW1012CD1*	63		1

LAURA WHITE

UK, female vocalist. See X Factor Finalists — 2

Date	Title / Label	Peak Position	Weeks at No.1	Weeks on Chart
14 Nov 09	**YOU SHOULD HAVE KNOWN** *DCW GB5VW0900001*	32		2

SNOWY WHITE

UK, male vocalist/guitarist (Terence White). See Thin Lizzy — 12

Date	Title / Label	Peak Position	Weeks at No.1	Weeks on Chart
24 Dec 83	**BIRD OF PARADISE** *Towerbell TOW 42* ●	6		10
28 Dec 85	**FOR YOU** *R4 FOR 3*	65		2

TAM WHITE

UK, male vocalist, d. 21 Jun 2010 (age 67) — 4

Date	Title / Label	Peak Position	Weeks at No.1	Weeks on Chart
15 Mar 75	**WHAT IN THE WORLD'S COME OVER YOU** *RAK 193*	36		4

TONY JOE WHITE

US, male vocalist/guitarist — 10

Date	Title / Label	Peak Position	Weeks at No.1	Weeks on Chart
6 Jun 70	**GROUPIE GIRL** *Monument MON 1043*	22		10

WHITE & TORCH

UK, male vocal/instrumental duo — 4

Date	Title / Label	Peak Position	Weeks at No.1	Weeks on Chart
2 Oct 82	**PARADE** *Chrysalis CHS 2641*	54		4

WHITE LIES

UK, male vocal/instrumental group — 10

Date	Title / Label	Peak Position	Weeks at No.1	Weeks on Chart
4 Oct 08	**DEATH** *Fiction 1782724*	52		1
4 Apr 09	**FAREWELL TO THE FAIRGROUND** *Fiction 2700376*	33		5
24 Jan 09	**TO LOSE MY LIFE** *Fiction 1793327*	34		4

WHITE PLAINS

UK, male vocal session group featuring Tony Burrows* — 56

Date	Title / Label	Peak Position	Weeks at No.1	Weeks on Chart
7 Feb 70	**MY BABY LOVES LOVIN'** *Deram DM 280*	9		11
18 Apr 70	**I'VE GOT YOU ON MY MIND** *Deram DM 291*	17		11
24 Oct 70	**JULIE DO YA LOVE ME** *Deram DM 315*	8		14
12 Jun 71	**WHEN YOU ARE A KING** *Deram DM 333*	13		11
17 Feb 73	**STEP INTO A DREAM** *Deram DM 371*	21		9

WHITE ROSE MOVEMENT

UK, male/female vocal/instrumental group — 1

Date	Title / Label	Peak Position	Weeks at No.1	Weeks on Chart
12 Nov 05	**ALSATIAN** *Independiente ISOM99MS*	54		1

WHITE STRIPES

US, male/female vocal/instrumental duo – Jack White* (John Gillis) & Meg White — 55

Date	Title / Label	Peak Position	Weeks at No.1	Weeks on Chart
24 Nov 01	**HOTEL YORBA** *XL Recordings XLS 139CD*	26		2
9 Mar 02	**FELL IN LOVE WITH A GIRL** *XL Recordings XLS 142CD*	21		2

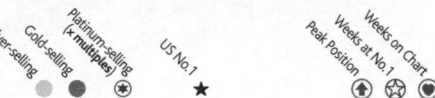

Date	Title	Peak Position	Weeks at No.1	Weeks on Chart
14 Sep 02	**DEAD LEAVES AND THE DIRTY GROUND** *XL Recordings 148CD*	25		2
3 May 03	**7 NATION ARMY** *XL Recordings XLS 162CD*	7		5
13 Sep 03	**I JUST DON'T KNOW WHAT TO DO WITH MYSELF** *XL Recordings XLS 166CD*	13		5
29 Nov 03	**THE HARDEST BUTTON TO BUTTON** *XL Recordings XLS 173CD*	23		3
27 Nov 04	**JOLENE – LIVE UNDER BLACKPOOL LIGHTS** *XL Recordings XLS207CD*	16		4
11 Jun 05	**BLUE ORCHID** *XL Recordings XLS216CD1*	9		7
3 Sep 05	**MY DOORBELL** *XL Recordings XLS218CD*	10		9
26 Nov 05	**THE DENIAL TWIST** *XL Recordings XLS223CD*	10		4
16 Jun 07	**ICKY THUMP** *XL Recordings XLS277CD*	2		7
22 Sep 07	**YOU DON'T KNOW WHAT LOVE IS** *XL Recordings XLS293CD*	18		3
12 Jan 08	**CONQUEST** *XL Recordings XLS320A*	30		2

WHITE TOWN

UK (b. India), male vocalist/producer (Jyoti Mishra) — Total weeks on chart: 10

Date	Title	Peak Position	Weeks at No.1	Weeks on Chart
25 Jan 97	**YOUR WOMAN** *Chrysalis CDCHS 5052* ●	1	1	9
24 May 97	**UNDRESSED** *Chrysalis CDCHS 5058*	57		1

WHITE ZOMBIE

US, male vocal/instrumental group — Total weeks on chart: 4

Date	Title	Peak Position	Weeks at No.1	Weeks on Chart
20 May 95	**MORE HUMAN THAN HUMAN** *Geffen GFSTD 92*	51		2
18 May 96	**ELECTRIC HEAD PART 2 (THE ECSTASY)** *Geffen GFSXD 22140*	31		2

WHITEHEAD BROTHERS

US, male vocal duo — Total weeks on chart: 5

Date	Title	Peak Position	Weeks at No.1	Weeks on Chart
14 Jan 95	**YOUR LOVE IS A 187** *Motown TMGCD 1434*	32		3
13 May 95	**FORGET I WAS A G** *Motown TMGCD 1441*	40		2

WHITEHOUSE

US/UK, male vocal/instrumental/production duo — Total weeks on chart: 1

Date	Title	Peak Position	Weeks at No.1	Weeks on Chart
15 Aug 98	**AIN'T NO MOUNTAIN HIGH ENOUGH** *Beautiful Noise BNOISE 2CD*	60		1

WHITEOUT

UK, male vocal/instrumental group — Total weeks on chart: 2

Date	Title	Peak Position	Weeks at No.1	Weeks on Chart
24 Sep 94	**DETROIT** *Silvertone ORECD 66*	73		1
18 Feb 95	**JACKIE'S RACING** *Silvertone ORECD 68*	72		1

WHITESNAKE

UK/US, male vocal/instrumental group – David Coverdale*; members also included Warren di Martini, Aynsley Dunbar, Jon Lord, Ian Paice, Cozy Powell*, Rudy Sarzo, Steve Vai* & Adrian Vandenberg — Total weeks on chart: 112

Date	Title	Peak Position	Weeks at No.1	Weeks on Chart
24 Jun 78	**SNAKEBITE (EP)** *EMI International INEP 751* DAVID COVERDALE'S WHITESNAKE	61		3
10 Nov 79	**LONG WAY FROM HOME** *United Artists BP 324*	55		2
26 Apr 80	**FOOL FOR YOUR LOVING** *United Artists BP 352*	13		9
12 Jul 80	**READY AN' WILLING (SWEET SATISFACTION)** *United Artists BP 363*	43		4
22 Nov 80	**AIN'T NO LOVE IN THE HEART OF THE CITY** *Sunburst/Liberty BP 381*	51		4
11 Apr 81	**DON'T BREAK MY HEART AGAIN** *Liberty BP 395*	17		9
6 Jun 81	**WOULD I LIE TO YOU** *Liberty BP 399*	37		6
6 Nov 82	**HERE I GO AGAIN/BLOODY LUXURY** *Liberty BP 416*	*34*		*10*
13 Aug 83	**GUILTY OF LOVE** *Liberty BP 420*	31		5
14 Jan 84	**GIVE ME MORE TIME** *Liberty BP 422*	29		4
28 Apr 84	**STANDING IN THE SHADOW** *Liberty BP 423*	62		2
9 Feb 85	**LOVE AIN'T NO STRANGER** *Liberty BP 424*	44		4
28 Mar 87	**STILL OF THE NIGHT** *EMI 5606*	16		8
6 Jun 87	**IS THIS LOVE** *EMI EM 3*	9		11
31 Oct 87	**HERE I GO AGAIN (REMIX)** *EMI EM 35*	9		11
6 Feb 88	**GIVE ME ALL YOUR LOVE** *EMI EM 23*	18		6
2 Dec 89	**FOOL FOR YOUR LOVING** *EMI EM 123*	43		2
10 Mar 90	**THE DEEPER THE LOVE** *EMI EM 128*	35		3
25 Aug 90	**NOW YOU'RE GONE** *EMI EM 150*	31		4
6 Aug 94	**IS THIS LOVE/SWEET LADY LUCK** *EMI CDEM 329*	25		4
7 Jun 97	**TOO MANY TEARS** *EMI CDEM 471* DAVID COVERDALE & WHITESNAKE	46		1

WHITEY

UK, male DJ/producer (Nathan Whitey) — Total weeks on chart: 1

Date	Title	Peak Position	Weeks at No.1	Weeks on Chart
5 Mar 05	**NON STOP/A WALK IN THE DARK** *1234 1234CDS06*	67		1

DAVID WHITFIELD

UK, male vocalist, d. 16 Jan 1980 (age 54) — Total weeks on chart: 190

Date	Title	Peak Position	Weeks at No.1	Weeks on Chart
2 Oct 53	**BRIDGE OF SIGHS** *Decca F 10129*	9		1
16 Oct 53	**ANSWER ME** *Decca F 10192*	1	2	14
11 Dec 53	**RAGS TO RICHES** *Decca F 10207* WITH STANLEY BLACK & HIS ORCHESTRA	3		11
19 Feb 54	**THE BOOK** *Decca F 10242*	5		15
18 Jun 54	**CARA MIA** *Decca F 10327* WITH CHORUS AND MANTOVANI & HIS ORCHESTRA	1	10	25
12 Nov 54	**SANTO NATALE (MERRY CHRISTMAS)** *Decca F 10399*	2		10
11 Feb 55	**BEYOND THE STARS** *Decca F 10458*	8		9
27 May 55	**MAMA** *Decca F 10515*	12		11
8 Jul 55	**EV'RYWHERE** *Decca F 10515* WITH THE ROLAND SHAW ORCHESTRA	3		20
25 Nov 55	**WHEN YOU LOSE THE ONE YOU LOVE** *Decca F 10627* WITH CHORUS & MANTOVANI & HIS ORCHESTRA	7		11
2 Mar 56	**MY SEPTEMBER LOVE** *Decca F 10690*	3		24
24 Aug 56	**MY SON JOHN** *Decca F 10769*	22		4
31 Aug 56	**MY UNFINISHED SYMPHONY** *Decca F 10769*	29		1
25 Jan 57	**ADORATION WALTZ** *Decca F 10833* WITH THE ROLAND SHAW ORCHESTRA	9		11
5 Apr 57	**I'LL FIND YOU** *Decca F 10864*	27		4
14 Feb 58	**CRY MY HEART** *Decca F 10978* WITH CHORUS & MANTOVANI & HIS ORCHESTRA	22		3
16 May 58	**ON THE STREET WHERE YOU LIVE** *Decca F 11018* WITH CYRIL STAPLETON & HIS ORCHESTRA	16		14
8 Aug 58	**THE RIGHT TO LOVE** *Decca F 11039*	30		1
24 Nov 60	**I BELIEVE** *Decca F 11289*	49		1

SLIM WHITMAN

US, male vocalist/guitarist (Otis Whitman, Jr) — Total weeks on chart: 77

Date	Title	Peak Position	Weeks at No.1	Weeks on Chart
15 Jul 55	**ROSE MARIE** *London HL 8061*	1	11	19
29 Jul 55	**INDIAN LOVE CALL** *London L 1149*	7		12
23 Sep 55	**CHINA DOLL** *London L 1149*	15		2
9 Mar 56	**TUMBLING TUMBLEWEEDS** *London HLU 8230*	19		2
13 Apr 56	**I'M A FOOL** *London HLU 8252*	16		4
22 Jun 56	**SERENADE** *London HLU 8287*	8		15
12 Apr 57	**I'LL TAKE YOU HOME AGAIN KATHLEEN** *London HLP 8403*	7		13
5 Oct 74	**HAPPY ANNIVERSARY** *United Artists UP 35728*	14		10

ROGER WHITTAKER

Kenya, male vocalist/whistler/guitarist — Total weeks on chart: 85

Date	Title	Peak Position	Weeks at No.1	Weeks on Chart
8 Nov 69	**DURHAM TOWN (THE LEAVIN')** *Columbia DB 8613*	12		18
11 Apr 70	**I DON'T BELIEVE IN 'IF' ANYMORE** *Columbia DB 8664*	8		18
10 Oct 70	**NEW WORLD IN THE MORNING** *Columbia DB 8718*	17		14
3 Apr 71	**WHY** *Columbia DB 8752*	47		1
2 Oct 71	**MAMMY BLUE** *Columbia DB 8822*	31		10
26 Jul 75	**THE LAST FAREWELL** *EMI 2294* ●	2		14
8 Nov 86	**THE SKYE BOAT SONG** *Tembo TML 119* & DES O'CONNOR	10		10

WHO

UK, male vocal/instrumental group – Roger Daltrey*, John Entwistle, d. 27 Jun 2002, Keith Moon, d. 7 Sep 1978 (replaced by Kenney Jones), & Pete Townshend*. Mid-1960s Mod R&B band who became rock legends, thanks in no small part to their revolutionary live performances and their groundbreaking rock opera *Tommy* — Total weeks on chart: 247

Date	Title	Peak Position	Weeks at No.1	Weeks on Chart
18 Feb 65	**I CAN'T EXPLAIN** *Brunswick 05926*	8		13
27 May 65	**ANYWAY ANYHOW ANYWHERE** *Brunswick 05935*	10		12
4 Nov 65	**MY GENERATION** *Brunswick 05944*	2		13
10 Mar 66	**SUBSTITUTE** *Reaction 591 001*	5		13
24 Mar 66	**A LEGAL MATTER** *Brunswick 05956*	32		6
1 Sep 66	**I'M A BOY** *Reaction 591 004*	2		13
1 Sep 66	**THE KIDS ARE ALRIGHT** *Brunswick 05965*	41		3
15 Dec 66	**HAPPY JACK** *Reaction 591 010*	3		11
27 Apr 67	**PICTURES OF LILY** *Track 604 002*	4		10
26 Jul 67	**THE LAST TIME/UNDER MY THUMB** *Track 604 006*	44		3
18 Oct 67	**I CAN SEE FOR MILES** *Track 604 011*	10		12
19 Jun 68	**DOGS** *Track 604 023*	25		5
23 Oct 68	**MAGIC BUS** *Track 604 024*	26		6
19 Mar 69	**PINBALL WIZARD** *Track 604 027*	4		13
4 Apr 70	**THE SEEKER** *Track 604 036*	19		11
8 Aug 70	**SUMMERTIME BLUES** *Track 2094 002*	38		4
10 Jul 71	**WON'T GET FOOLED AGAIN** *Track 2094 009*	9		12
23 Oct 71	**LET'S SEE ACTION** *Track 2094 012*	16		12
24 Jun 72	**JOIN TOGETHER** *Track 2094 102*	9		9
13 Jan 73	**RELAY** *Track 2094 106*	21		5
13 Oct 73	**5.15** *Track 2094 115*	20		6
24 Jan 76	**SQUEEZE BOX** *Polydor 2121 275*	10		9
30 Oct 76	**SUBSTITUTE** *Polydor 2058 803*	7		7
22 Jul 78	**WHO ARE YOU** *Polydor WHO 1*	18		12

Silver-selling ○ | Gold-selling ● | Platinum-selling (x multiples) | US No.1 ★ | Peak Position | Weeks at No.1 | Weeks on Chart

Date	Title	Peak Position	Weeks at No.1	Weeks on Chart
28 Apr 79	**LONG LIVE ROCK** *Polydor WHO 2*	48		5
7 Mar 81	**YOU BETTER YOU BET** *Polydor WHO 004*	9		8
9 May 81	**DON'T LET GO THE COAT** *Polydor WHO 005*	47		4
2 Oct 82	**ATHENA** *Polydor WHO 6*	40		4
26 Nov 83	**READY STEADY WHO (EP)** *Polydor WHO 7*	58		2
20 Feb 88	**MY GENERATION** *Polydor POSP 907*	68		2
27 Jul 96	**MY GENERATION** *Polydor 8546372*	31		2

WHO DA FUNK
US, male production duo — 8

Date	Title	Peak Position	Weeks at No.1	Weeks on Chart
26 Oct 02	**SHINY DISCO BALLS (IMPORT)** *Subusa 5000007432304* FEATURING JESSICA EVE	69		1
2 Nov 02	**SHINY DISCO BALLS** *Cream 22CD* FEATURING JESSICA EVE	15		5
15 Feb 03	**STING ME RED (YOU THINK YOU'RE SO)** *Cream 19CDS* FEATURING TERRA DEVA	32		2

WHODINI
US, male rap duo — 10

Date	Title	Peak Position	Weeks at No.1	Weeks on Chart
25 Dec 82	**MAGIC'S WAND** *Jive 28*	47		6
17 Mar 84	**MAGIC'S WAND (THE WHODINI ELECTRIC EP)** *Jive 61*	63		4

WHOOLIGANZ
US, male rap duo — 2

Date	Title	Peak Position	Weeks at No.1	Weeks on Chart
13 Aug 94	**PUT YOUR HANDZ UP** *Positiva CDTIV 17*	53		2

WHOOSH
UK, male production trio — 1

Date	Title	Peak Position	Weeks at No.1	Weeks on Chart
13 Sep 97	**WHOOSH** *Wonderboy WBOYD 006*	72		1

WHYCLIFFE
UK, male vocalist/instrumentalist (Donovan Whycliffe Bramwell) — 2

Date	Title	Peak Position	Weeks at No.1	Weeks on Chart
20 Nov 93	**HEAVEN** *MCA MCSTD 1944*	56		1
2 Apr 94	**ONE MORE TIME** *MCA MCSTD 1955*	72		1

WIDEBOYS
UK, male vocal/production trio — 9

Date	Title	Peak Position	Weeks at No.1	Weeks on Chart
27 Oct 01	**SAMBUCA** *Locked On/679 Recordings 679L 002CD* FEATURING DENNIS G	15		6
10 May 08	**DADDY O** *All Around The World CDGLOBE863* FEATURING SHAZNAY LEWIS	32		3

JANE WIEDLIN
US, female vocalist. See Go-Go's — 14

Date	Title	Peak Position	Weeks at No.1	Weeks on Chart
6 Aug 88	**RUSH HOUR** *Manhattan MT 36*	12		11
29 Oct 88	**INSIDE A DREAM** *Manhattan MT 55*	64		3

WIFI FEATURING MELANIE M
UK, male/female vocal group — 2

Date	Title	Peak Position	Weeks at No.1	Weeks on Chart
17 Mar 07	**BE WITHOUT YOU** *All Around The World CDGLOBE625*	42		2

WIGAN'S CHOSEN FEW
Canada, male vocal/instrumental group — 11

Date	Title	Peak Position	Weeks at No.1	Weeks on Chart
18 Jan 75	**FOOTSEE** *Pye Disco Demand DDS 111*	9		11

WIGAN'S OVATION
UK, male vocal/instrumental group — 19

Date	Title	Peak Position	Weeks at No.1	Weeks on Chart
15 Mar 75	**SKIING IN THE SNOW** *Spark SRL 1122*	12		10
28 Jun 75	**PER-SO-NAL-LY** *Spark SRL 1129*	38		6
29 Nov 75	**SUPER LOVE** *Spark SRL 1133*	41		3

WIGWAM
UK, male vocal/instrumental duo. See Blur, Betty Boo, Fat Les — 1

Date	Title	Peak Position	Weeks at No.1	Weeks on Chart
15 Apr 06	**WIGWAM** *Instant Karma DHARMA9CD2*	60		1

WILCO
US, male vocal/instrumental group — 1

Date	Title	Peak Position	Weeks at No.1	Weeks on Chart
17 Apr 99	**CAN'T STAND IT** *Reprise W 475CD1*	67		1

JACK WILD
UK, male actor/vocalist, d. 1 Mar 2006 (age 53) — 2

Date	Title	Peak Position	Weeks at No.1	Weeks on Chart
2 May 70	**SOME BEAUTIFUL** *Capitol CL 15635*	46		2

WILD CHERRY
US, male vocal/instrumental group – Robert Parissi, Mark Avsec, Bryan Bassett, Ron Beitle & Allen Wentz — 11

Date	Title	Peak Position	Weeks at No.1	Weeks on Chart
9 Oct 76	**PLAY THAT FUNKY MUSIC** *Epic EPC 4593* ★	7		11

WILD COLOUR
UK, male/female vocal/instrumental group — 2

Date	Title	Peak Position	Weeks at No.1	Weeks on Chart
14 Oct 95	**DREAMS** *Perfecto PERF 105CD*	25		2

WILD WEEKEND
UK, male vocal/instrumental group — 2

Date	Title	Peak Position	Weeks at No.1	Weeks on Chart
29 Apr 89	**BREAKIN' UP** *Parlophone R 6204*	74		1
5 May 90	**WHO'S AFRAID OF THE BIG BAD LOVE** *Parlophone R 6249*	70		1

WILDCHILD
UK, male DJ/producer (Roger McKenzie), d. 25 Nov 1995 (age 24) — 20

Date	Title	Peak Position	Weeks at No.1	Weeks on Chart
22 Apr 95	**LEGENDS OF THE DARK BLACK – PART 2** *Hi-Life HICD 9*	34		3
21 Oct 95	**RENEGADE MASTER** *Hi-Life 5771312*	11		4
23 Nov 96	**JUMP TO MY BEAT** *Hi-Life 5757372*	30		2
17 Jan 98	**RENEGADE MASTER** *Hi-Life 5692792* ○	3		10
25 Apr 98	**BAD BOY** *Polydor 5716072* FEATURING JOMALSKI	38		1

EUGENE WILDE
US, male vocalist (Ron Broomfield). See Simplicious — 15

Date	Title	Peak Position	Weeks at No.1	Weeks on Chart
13 Oct 84	**GOTTA GET YOU HOME TONIGHT** *Fourth & Broadway BRW 15*	18		9
2 Feb 85	**PERSONALITY** *Fourth & Broadway BRW 18*	34		6

KIM WILDE
UK, female vocalist (Kim Smith) — 194

Date	Title	Peak Position	Weeks at No.1	Weeks on Chart
21 Feb 81	**KIDS IN AMERICA** *RAK 327* ●	2		13
9 May 81	**CHEQUERED LOVE** *RAK 330* ○	4		9
1 Aug 81	**WATER ON GLASS/BOYS** *RAK 334*	11		8
14 Nov 81	**CAMBODIA** *RAK 336*	12		12
17 Apr 82	**VIEW FROM A BRIDGE** *RAK 342*	16		7
16 Oct 82	**CHILD COME AWAY** *RAK 352*	43		4
30 Jul 83	**LOVE BLONDE** *RAK 360*	23		8
12 Nov 83	**DANCING IN THE DARK** *RAK 365*	67		2
13 Oct 84	**THE SECOND TIME** *MCA KIM 1*	29		6
8 Dec 84	**THE TOUCH** *MCA KIM 2*	56		3
27 Apr 85	**RAGE TO LOVE** *MCA KIM 3*	19		8
25 Oct 86	**YOU KEEP ME HANGIN' ON** *MCA KIM 4* ○ ★	2		14
4 Apr 87	**ANOTHER STEP CLOSER TO YOU** *MCA KIM 5* & JUNIOR	6		11
8 Aug 87	**SAY YOU REALLY WANT ME** *MCA KIM 6*	29		5
5 Dec 87	**ROCKIN' AROUND THE CHRISTMAS TREE** *10 TEN 2* MEL & KIM ○	3		7
14 May 88	**HEY MISTER HEARTACHE** *MCA KIM 7*	31		5
16 Jul 88	**YOU CAME** *MCA KIM 8* ○	3		11
1 Oct 88	**NEVER TRUST A STRANGER** *MCA KIM 9*	7		9
3 Dec 88	**FOUR LETTER WORD** *MCA KIM 10*	6		12
4 Mar 89	**LOVE IN THE NATURAL WAY** *MCA KIM 11*	32		6
14 Apr 90	**IT'S HERE** *MCA KIM 12*	42		4
16 Jun 90	**TIME** *MCA KIM 13*	71		3
15 Dec 90	**I CAN'T SAY GOODBYE** *MCA KIM 14*	51		3
2 May 92	**LOVE IS HOLY** *MCA KIM 15*	16		6
27 Jun 92	**HEART OVER MIND** *MCA KIM 16*	34		3
12 Sep 92	**WHO DO YOU THINK YOU ARE** *MCA KIM 17*	49		3
10 Jul 93	**IF I CAN'T HAVE YOU** *MCA KIMTD 18*	12		8
13 Nov 93	**IN MY LIFE** *MCA KIMTD 19*	54		1
14 Oct 95	**BREAKIN' AWAY** *MCA KIMTD 21*	43		2
10 Feb 96	**THIS I SWEAR** *MCA KIMTD 22*	46		1

MARTY WILDE

UK, male vocalist (Reg Smith) — 117

Date	Title	Peak Position	Weeks at No.1	Weeks on Chart
11 Jul 58	**ENDLESS SLEEP** *Philips PB 835*	4		14
6 Mar 59	**DONNA** *Philips PB 902*	3		18
5 Jun 59	**A TEENAGER IN LOVE** *Philips PB 926*	2		17
25 Sep 59	**SEA OF LOVE** *Philips PB 959*	3		12
11 Dec 59	**BAD BOY** *Philips PB 972*	7		8
10 Mar 60	**JOHNNY ROCCO** *Philips PB 1002*	30		4
19 May 60	**THE FIGHT** *Philips PB 1022*	47		1
22 Dec 60	**LITTLE GIRL** *Philips PB 1078*	16		9
26 Jan 61	**RUBBER BALL** *Philips PB 1101*	9		9
27 Jul 61	**HIDE AND SEEK** *Philips PB 1240*	47		2
9 Nov 61	**TOMORROW'S CLOWN** *Philips PB 1191*	33		5
24 May 62	**JEZEBEL** *Philips PB 1240*	19		11
25 Oct 62	**EVER SINCE YOU SAID GOODBYE** *Philips 326546 BF*	31		7

MATTHEW WILDER

US, male vocalist (Matthew Weiner) — 11

Date	Title	Peak Position	Weeks at No.1	Weeks on Chart
21 Jan 84	**BREAK MY STRIDE** *Epic A 3908* ●	4		11

WILDHEARTS

UK, male vocal/instrumental group — 32

Date	Title	Peak Position	Weeks at No.1	Weeks on Chart
20 Nov 93	**TV TAN** *Bronze YZ 784CD*	53		2
19 Feb 94	**CAFFEINE BOMB** *Bronze YZ 794CD*	31		3
9 Jul 94	**SUCKERPUNCH** *Bronze YZ 828CD*	38		2
28 Jan 95	**IF LIFE IS LIKE A LOVE BANK I WANT AN OVERDRAFT/GEORDIE IN WONDERLAND** *Bronze YZ 874CD*	31		3
6 May 95	**I WANNA GO WHERE THE PEOPLE GO** *East West YZ 923CD*	16		3
29 Jul 95	**JUST IN LUST** *East West YZ 967CD*	28		2
20 Apr 96	**SICK OF DRUGS** *Round WILD 1CDX*	14		3
29 Jun 96	**RED LIGHT GREEN LIGHT EP** *Round WILD 2CD*	30		2
16 Aug 97	**ANTHEM** *Mushroom MUSH 6CD*	21		2
18 Oct 97	**URGE** *Mushroom MUSH 14CD*	26		2
12 Oct 02	**VANILLA RADIO** *Round/Snapper SMASCD 048X*	26		2
1 Feb 03	**STORMY IN THE NORTH KARMA IN THE SOUTH** *Snapper Music SMASCD 049X*	17		2
24 May 03	**SO INTO YOU** *Gut CXGUT 49*	22		2
15 Nov 03	**TOP OF THE WORLD** *Gut CXGUT 54*	26		2

WILEY

UK, male rapper/producer (Richard Cowie) — 47

Date	Title	Peak Position	Weeks at No.1	Weeks on Chart
17 Apr 04	**WOT DO U CALL IT?** *XL Recordings XLS179CD*	31		4
21 Aug 04	**PIES** *XL Recordings XLS188CD*	45		2
3 May 08	**WEARING MY ROLEX** *Asylum ASYLUM1CD2*	2		20
25 Oct 08	**SUMMERTIME** *Asylum ASYLUM5CDX*	45		1
13 Dec 08	**CASH IN MY POCKET** *Asylum ASYLUM7CD* FEATURING DANIEL MERRIWEATHER	18		9
9 Jan 10	**TAKE THAT** *Universal 2728893* & CHEW FU	20		6
13 Mar 10	**NEVER BE YOUR WOMAN** *Relentless/Virgin RELCD65* NAUGHTY BOY PRESENTS WILEY FEATURING EMELI SANDE	8		5+

JONATHAN WILKES

UK, male vocalist — 2

Date	Title	Peak Position	Weeks at No.1	Weeks on Chart
17 Mar 01	**JUST ANOTHER DAY** *Innocent SINCD 25*	24		2

SUE WILKINSON

UK, female vocalist/model, d. Mar 2005 (age 61) — 8

Date	Title	Peak Position	Weeks at No.1	Weeks on Chart
2 Aug 80	**YOU GOTTA BE A HUSTLER IF YOU WANNA GET ON** *Cheapskate CHEAP 2*	25		8

WILL.I.AM

US, male vocalist/rapper/multi-instrumentalist/producer (William Adams, Jr.). See Steve Aoki featuring Zuper Blahq — 87

Date	Title	Peak Position	Weeks at No.1	Weeks on Chart
11 Mar 06	**BEEP** *A&M 9852860* PUSSYCAT DOLLS FEATURING WILL.I.AM	2		11
3 Feb 07	**HIP HOP IS DEAD** *Def Jam 1721323* NAS FEATURING WILL.I.AM	35		4
22 Sep 07	**I GOT IT FROM MY MAMA** *Interscope 1747759*	38		5
20 Oct 07	**BABY LOVE** *Polydor 1753014* NICOLE SCHERZINGER FEATURING WILL.I.AM	14		9
2 Feb 08	**THE GIRL IS MINE** *Epic 88697226202* MICHAEL JACKSON FEATURING WILL.I.AM	32		5
29 Mar 08	**HEARTBREAKER** *A&M 1771789* FEATURING CHERYL COLE	4		24
23 Aug 08	**IN THE AYER** *Atlantic AT0322CD1* FLO RIDA FEATURING WILL.I.AM	29		9
7 Nov 09	**3 WORDS** *Fascination 2729724* CHERYL COLE FEATURING WILL.I.AM	4		18
3 Apr 10	**OMG** *LaFace USLF20900103* USHER FEATURING WILL.I.AM	8		2+

WILL TO POWER

US, male/female vocal/instrumental trio – Bob Rosenberg, Maria Mendez (replaced by Elin Michaels) & Dr J — 18

Date	Title	Peak Position	Weeks at No.1	Weeks on Chart
7 Jan 89	**BABY I LOVE YOUR WAY – FREEBIRD** *Epic 6530947* ★	6		9
22 Dec 90	**I'M NOT IN LOVE** *Epic 6565377*	29		9

ALYSON WILLIAMS

US, female vocalist — 28

Date	Title	Peak Position	Weeks at No.1	Weeks on Chart
4 Mar 89	**SLEEP TALK** *Def Jam 6546567*	17		9
6 May 89	**MY LOVE IS SO RAW** *Def Jam 6548987* FEATURING NIKKI D	34		5
19 Aug 89	**I NEED YOUR LOVIN'** *Def Jam 6551437*	8		11
18 Nov 89	**I SECOND THAT EMOTION** *Def Jam 6554567* WITH CHUCK STANLEY	44		3

ANDY WILLIAMS

US, male vocalist. Easy-on-the-ear balladeer and top-rated 1960s TV show host who first tasted success in his family group the Williams Brothers in the mid-1940s. Andy has a 42-year span of Top 10 singles and has earned 17 gold albums in the US — 245

Date	Title	Peak Position	Weeks at No.1	Weeks on Chart
19 Apr 57	**BUTTERFLY** *London HLA 8399* ★	1	2	16
21 Jun 57	**I LIKE YOUR KIND OF LOVE** *London HLA 8437*	16		10
14 Jun 62	**STRANGER ON THE SHORE** *CBS AAG 103*	30		10
21 Mar 63	**CAN'T GET USED TO LOSING YOU** *CBS AAG 138*	2		18
27 Feb 64	**A FOOL NEVER LEARNS** *CBS AAG 182*	40		4
16 Sep 65	**ALMOST THERE** *CBS 201813*	2		17
24 Feb 66	**MAY EACH DAY** *CBS 202042*	19		8
22 Sep 66	**IN THE ARMS OF LOVE** *CBS 202300*	33		7
4 May 67	**MUSIC TO WATCH GIRLS BY** *CBS 2675*	33		6
2 Aug 67	**MORE AND MORE** *CBS 2886*	45		1
13 Mar 68	**CAN'T TAKE MY EYES OFF YOU** *CBS 3298*	5		18
7 May 69	**HAPPY HEART** *CBS 4062*	19		10
14 Mar 70	**CAN'T HELP FALLING IN LOVE** *CBS 4818*	3		17
1 Aug 70	**IT'S SO EASY** *CBS 5113*	13		14
21 Nov 70	**HOME LOVIN' MAN** *CBS 5267*	7		12
20 Mar 71	**(WHERE DO I BEGIN) LOVE STORY** *CBS 7020*	4		18
5 Aug 72	**LOVE THEME FROM THE GODFATHER** *CBS 8166*	42		9
8 Dec 73	**SOLITAIRE** *CBS 1824*	4		18
18 May 74	**GETTING OVER YOU** *CBS 2181*	35		5
31 May 75	**YOU LAY SO EASY ON MY MIND** *CBS 3167*	32		7
6 Mar 76	**THE OTHER SIDE OF ME** *CBS 3903*	42		3
27 Mar 99	**MUSIC TO WATCH GIRLS BY** *Columbia 6671322*	9		6
29 Jun 02	**CAN'T TAKE MY EYES OFF YOU** *Columbia 6721052* & DENISE VAN OUTEN	23		4
8 Dec 07	**IT'S THE MOST WONDERFUL TIME OF THE YEAR** *Sony BMG 88697207452*	21		5
20 Dec 08	**IT'S THE MOST WONDERFUL TIME OF THE YEAR** *Sony BMG 88697207452*	63		2

ANDY & DAVID WILLIAMS

US, male vocal duo — 5

Date	Title	Peak Position	Weeks at No.1	Weeks on Chart
24 Mar 73	**I DON'T KNOW WHY** *MCA MUS 1183*	37		5

BILLY WILLIAMS

US, male vocalist, d. 17 Oct 1972 (age 61) — 9

Date	Title	Peak Position	Weeks at No.1	Weeks on Chart
2 Aug 57	**I'M GONNA SIT RIGHT DOWN AND WRITE MYSELF A LETTER** *Vogue Coral Q 72266*	22		9

DANNY WILLIAMS

South Africa, male vocalist, d. 6 Dec 2005 (age 63) — 74

Date	Title	Peak Position	Weeks at No.1	Weeks on Chart
25 May 61	**WE WILL NEVER BE THIS YOUNG AGAIN** *HMV POP 839*	44		3
6 Jul 61	**THE MIRACLE OF YOU** *HMV POP 885*	41		8
2 Nov 61	**MOON RIVER** *HMV POP 932*	1	2	19
18 Jan 62	**JEANNIE** *HMV POP 968*	14		14
12 Apr 62	**WONDERFUL WORLD OF THE YOUNG** *HMV POP 1002*	8		13
5 Jul 62	**TEARS** *HMV POP 1035*	22		7
28 Feb 63	**MY OWN TRUE LOVE** *HMV POP 1112*	45		3
30 Jul 77	**DANCIN' EASY** *Ensign ENY 3*	30		7

DENIECE WILLIAMS

US, female vocalist (Deniece Chandler) — 59

Date	Title	Peak Position	Weeks at No.1	Weeks on Chart
2 Apr 77	**FREE** *CBS 4978* ●	1	2	10
30 Jul 77	**THAT'S WHAT FRIENDS ARE FOR** *CBS 5432* ●	8		11
12 Nov 77	**BABY BABY MY LOVE'S ALL FOR YOU** *CBS 5779*	32		5
25 Mar 78	**TOO MUCH TOO LITTLE TOO LATE** *CBS 6164* JOHNNY MATHIS & DENIECE WILLIAMS ★	3		14

Silver-selling ● Gold-selling ● Platinum-selling (x multiples) ⊛ US No.1 ★ | Peak Position | Weeks at No.1 | Weeks on Chart

Date	Title	Peak	Wks at No.1	Wks on Chart
29 Jul 78	**YOU'RE ALL I NEED TO GET BY** *CBS 6483* JOHNNY MATHIS & DENIECE WILLIAMS	45		6
5 May 84	**LET'S HEAR IT FOR THE BOY** *CBS A 4319* ● ★	2		13

DIANA WILLIAMS
US, female vocalist — 3

Date	Title	Peak	Wks at No.1	Wks on Chart
25 Jul 81	**TEDDY BEAR'S LAST RIDE** *Capitol CL 207*	54		3

DON WILLIAMS
US, male vocalist/guitarist — 16

Date	Title	Peak	Wks at No.1	Wks on Chart
19 Jun 76	**I RECALL A GYPSY WOMAN** *ABC 4098*	13		10
23 Oct 76	**YOU'RE MY BEST FRIEND** *ABC 4144*	35		6

ERIC WILLIAMS
US, male vocalist. See Blackstreet — 9

Date	Title	Peak	Wks at No.1	Wks on Chart
9 May 98	**ALL MY LOVE** *Interscope IND 95584* QUEEN PEN FEATURING ERIC WILLIAMS	11		5
13 Jun 98	**DO FOR LOVE** *Jive 0518512* 2PAC FEATURING ERIC WILLIAMS	12		4

FREEDOM WILLIAMS
US, male rapper (Frederick Williams) — 31

Date	Title	Peak	Wks at No.1	Wks on Chart
15 Dec 90	**GONNA MAKE YOU SWEAT (EVERYBODY DANCE NOW)** *CBS 6564540* C & C MUSIC FACTORY (FEATURING FREEDOM WILLIAMS) ★	3		12
30 Mar 91	**HERE WE GO** *Columbia 6567557* C & C MUSIC FACTORY (FEATURING FREEDOM WILLIAMS)	20		7
6 Jul 91	**THINGS THAT MAKE YOU GO HMMM** *Columbia 6566907* C & C MUSIC FACTORY (FEATURING FREEDOM WILLIAMS)	4		11
5 Jun 93	**VOICE OF FREEDOM** *Columbia 6593342*	62		1

GEOFFREY WILLIAMS
UK, male vocalist — 8

Date	Title	Peak	Wks at No.1	Wks on Chart
11 Apr 92	**IT'S NOT A LOVE THING** *EMI EM 228*	63		2
22 Aug 92	**SUMMER BREEZE** *EMI EM 245*	56		3
18 Jan 97	**DRIVE** *Hands On CDHOR 11*	52		2
19 Apr 97	**SEX LIFE** *Hands On CDHOR 12*	71		1

IRIS WILLIAMS
UK, female vocalist — 8

Date	Title	Peak	Wks at No.1	Wks on Chart
27 Oct 79	**HE WAS BEAUTIFUL (CAVATINA) (THE THEME FROM 'THE DEER HUNTER')** *Columbia DB 9070*	18		8

JOHN WILLIAMS
Australia, male guitarist. See Sky — 11

Date	Title	Peak	Wks at No.1	Wks on Chart
19 May 79	**CAVATINA** *Cube BUG 80*	13		11

JOHN WILLIAMS
US, male conductor/composer — 15

Date	Title	Peak	Wks at No.1	Wks on Chart
18 Dec 82	**THEME FROM 'E.T. (THE EXTRA-TERRESTRIAL)'** *MCA 800*	17		10
14 Aug 93	**THEME FROM 'JURASSIC PARK'** *MCA MCSTD 1927*	45		2
4 Jun 05	**BATTLE OF THE HEROES – STAR WARS** *Sony Classical 6759562* & THE LSO	25		3

KENNY WILLIAMS
US, male vocalist — 7

Date	Title	Peak	Wks at No.1	Wks on Chart
19 Nov 77	**(YOU'RE) FABULOUS BABE** *Decca FR 13731*	35		7

LARRY WILLIAMS
US, male vocalist/pianist, d. 7 Jan 1980 (age 44) — 18

Date	Title	Peak	Wks at No.1	Wks on Chart
20 Sep 57	**SHORT FAT FANNIE** *London HLN 8472*	21		8
17 Jan 58	**BONY MORONIE** *London HLU 8532*	11		10

LENNY WILLIAMS
US, male vocalist — 7

Date	Title	Peak	Wks at No.1	Wks on Chart
5 Nov 77	**SHOO DOO FU FU OOH** *ABC 4194*	38		4
16 Sep 78	**YOU GOT ME RUNNING** *ABC 4228*	67		3

MASON WILLIAMS
US, male guitarist/composer/writer/poet — 13

Date	Title	Peak	Wks at No.1	Wks on Chart
28 Aug 68	**CLASSICAL GAS** *Warner Brothers WB 7190*	9		13

MAURICE WILLIAMS & THE ZODIACS
US, male vocal group — 9

Date	Title	Peak	Wks at No.1	Wks on Chart
5 Jan 61	**STAY** *Top Rank JAR 526* ★	14		9

MELANIE WILLIAMS
UK, female vocalist — 21

Date	Title	Peak	Wks at No.1	Wks on Chart
10 Apr 93	**AIN'T NO LOVE (AIN'T NO USE)** *Rob's CDROB 9* SUB SUB FEATURING MELANIE WILLIAMS ●	3		11
9 Apr 94	**ALL CRIED OUT** *Columbia 6601872*	60		2
11 Jun 94	**EVERYDAY THANG** *Columbia 6604712*	38		3
17 Sep 94	**NOT ENOUGH** *Columbia 6607752*	65		1
18 Feb 95	**YOU ARE EVERYTHING** *Columbia 6611755* & JOE ROBERTS	28		4

MICHELLE WILLIAMS
US, female vocalist/producer/actor (Tenitra Michelle Williams). See Destiny's Child — 1

Date	Title	Peak	Wks at No.1	Wks on Chart
4 Oct 08	**WE BREAK THE DAWN** *Columbia USSM10800922*	47		1

ROBBIE WILLIAMS
UK, male vocalist. Ever-popular showman whose 40 Top 10 hits and 13 No.1s (solo and with Take That) made him rich beyond his wildest dreams. In 2005, the self-penned 'Angels' won a BRIT award for 'Best Single' from 25 years of the BRITs – his record 16th BRIT statue. See Helping Haiti, 1 Giant Leap featuring Maxi Jazz & Robbie Williams — 364

Date	Title	Peak	Wks at No.1	Wks on Chart
10 Aug 96	**FREEDOM** *Chrysalis CDFREE 1* ●	2		14
26 Apr 97	**OLD BEFORE I DIE** *Chrysalis CDCHS 5055*	2		11
26 Jul 97	**LAZY DAYS** *Chrysalis CDCHS 5063*	8		5
27 Sep 97	**SOUTH OF THE BORDER** *Chrysalis CDCHS 5068*	14		4
13 Dec 97	**ANGELS** *Chrysalis CDCHS 5072* ⊛ x2	4		27
28 Mar 98	**LET ME ENTERTAIN YOU** *Chrysalis CDCHSS 5080* ●	3		12
19 Sep 98	**MILLENNIUM** *Chrysalis CDCHS 5099* ●	1	1	21
12 Dec 98	**NO REGRETS** *Chrysalis CDCHS 5100*	4		13
27 Mar 99	**STRONG** *Chrysalis CDCHS 5107*	4		9
20 Nov 99	**SHE'S THE ONE/IT'S ONLY US** *Chrysalis CDCHS 5112* ●	1	1	20
12 Aug 00	**ROCK DJ** *Chrysalis CDCHS 5118* ⊛	1	1	20
21 Oct 00	**KIDS** *Chrysalis CDCHSS 5119* & KYLIE MINOGUE ●	2		19
23 Dec 00	**SUPREME** *Chrysalis CDCHSS 5120*	4		10
21 Apr 01	**LET LOVE BE YOUR ENERGY** *Chrysalis CDCHS 5124*	10		11
21 Jul 01	**ETERNITY/THE ROAD TO MANDALAY** *Chrysalis CDCHS 5126*	1	2	16
22 Dec 01	**SOMETHIN' STUPID** *Chrysalis CDCHS 5132* & NICOLE KIDMAN ●	1	3	12
20 Apr 02	**MY CULTURE** *Palm Pictures PPCD 70732* 1 GIANT LEAP FEATURING MAXI JAZZ & ROBBIE WILLIAMS	9		6
14 Dec 02	**FEEL** *Chrysalis CDCHS 5150*	4		15
26 Apr 03	**COME UNDONE** *Chrysalis CDCHS 5151*	4		11
9 Aug 03	**SOMETHING BEAUTIFUL** *Chrysalis CDCHS 5152*	3		8
15 Nov 03	**SEXED UP** *Chrysalis CDCHS 5153*	10		9
16 Oct 04	**RADIO** *Chrysalis CDCHSS 5156*	1	1	8
18 Dec 04	**MISUNDERSTOOD** *Chrysalis CDCHSS 5157*	8		8
15 Oct 05	**TRIPPING** *Chrysalis CDCHSS5158*	2		15
24 Dec 05	**ADVERTISING SPACE** *Chrysalis CDCHSS5159*	8		11
3 Jun 06	**SIN SIN SIN** *Chrysalis CDCHS5160*	22		3
9 Sep 06	**RUDEBOX** *Chrysalis CDCHS5161*	4		9
18 Nov 06	**LOVELIGHT** *Chrysalis CDCHS5162*	8		7
17 Mar 07	**SHE'S MADONNA** *Chrysalis CDCHS5163* & PET SHOP BOYS	16		3
24 Oct 09	**BODIES** *Virgin VSCDT1998* ●	2		8
21 Nov 09	**YOU KNOW ME** *Virgin VSCDT2002* ●	6		16
20 Mar 10	**MORNING SUN** *Chrysalis GBFFG0900001*	45		3

Top 3 Best-Selling Singles

	Title	Approximate Sales
1	ANGELS	1,045,000
2	ROCK DJ	630,000
3	MILLENNIUM	480,000

VANESSA WILLIAMS
US, female vocalist/actor — 24

Date	Title	Peak	Wks at No.1	Wks on Chart
20 Aug 88	**THE RIGHT STUFF** *Wing 3*	71		1
25 Mar 89	**DREAMIN'** *Wing 4*	74		2
19 Aug 89	**THE RIGHT STUFF (REMIX)** *Wing WINR 3*	62		2
21 Mar 92	**SAVE THE BEST FOR LAST** *Polydor PO 192* ★	3		11
8 Apr 95	**THE SWEETEST DAYS** *Mercury MERCD 422*	41		2
8 Jul 95	**THE WAY THAT YOU LOVE ME** *Mercury MERCD 439*	52		1
16 Sep 95	**COLOURS OF THE WIND** *Walt Disney WD 7677CD*	21		5

VESTA WILLIAMS
US, female vocalist — 13

Date	Title	Peak	Wks at No.1	Wks on Chart
20 Dec 86	**ONCE BITTEN TWICE SHY** *A&M AM 362*	14		13

WENDELL WILLIAMS
US, male rapper — 6

Date	Title	Peak	Wks at No.1	Wks on Chart
6 Oct 90	**EVERYBODY (RAP)** *Deconstruction PB 44701* CRIMINAL ELEMENT ORCHESTRA & WENDELL WILLIAMS	30		4
18 May 91	**SO GROOVY** *Deconstruction PB 44567*	74		2

BRUCE WILLIS
US, male vocalist/actor (Walter Bruce Willis) — 30

Date	Title	Peak	Wks at No.1	Wks on Chart
7 Mar 87	**RESPECT YOURSELF** *Motown ZB 41117*	7		10
30 May 87	**UNDER THE BOARDWALK** *Motown ZB 41349* ○	2		15
12 Sep 87	**SECRET AGENT MAN – JAMES BOND IS BACK** *Motown ZB 41437*	43		4
23 Jan 88	**COMIN' RIGHT UP** *Motown ZB 41453*	73		1

MATT WILLIS
UK, male vocalist/multi-instrumentalist. See Busted — 15

Date	Title	Peak	Wks at No.1	Wks on Chart
27 May 06	**UP ALL NIGHT** *Mercury 9858520*	7		4
26 Aug 06	**HEY KID** *Mercury 1705075*	11		5
16 Dec 06	**DON'T LET IT GO TO WASTE** *Mercury 1713567*	19		4
28 Apr 07	**CRASH** *Mercury 1729795*	31		2

VIOLA WILLS
US, female vocalist, d. 6 May 2009 (age 69) — 16

Date	Title	Peak	Wks at No.1	Wks on Chart
6 Oct 79	**GONNA GET ALONG WITHOUT YOU NOW** *Ariola/Hansa AHA 546* ○	8		10
15 Mar 86	**BOTH SIDES NOW/DARE TO DREAM** *Streetwave KHAN 66*	35		6

MARIA WILLSON
UK, female vocalist — 3

Date	Title	Peak	Wks at No.1	Wks on Chart
9 Aug 03	**CHOOZA LOOZA** *Telstar CDSTAS 3343*	29		2
1 Nov 03	**MR ALIBI** *Telstar CDSTAS 3355*	43		1

AL WILSON
US, male vocalist, d. 21 Apr 2008 (age 68) — 5

Date	Title	Peak	Wks at No.1	Wks on Chart
23 Aug 75	**THE SNAKE** *Bell 1436*	41		5

BRIAN WILSON
US, male vocalist/multi-instrumentalist. See Beach Boys, One World Project — 5

Date	Title	Peak	Wks at No.1	Wks on Chart
2 Oct 04	**WONDERFUL** *Must Destroy MDA001X*	29		2
18 Dec 04	**GOOD VIBRATIONS** *Nonesuch NS001CD*	30		2
17 Dec 05	**WHAT I REALLY WANT FOR CHRISTMAS** *Arista 82876764802*	66		1

CHARLIE WILSON
US, male vocalist/multi-instrumentalist. See Gap Band — 23

Date	Title	Peak	Wks at No.1	Wks on Chart
14 Dec 96	**SNOOP'S UPSIDE YA HEAD** *Interscope IND 95520* SNOOP DOGGY DOGG FEATURING CHARLIE WILSON	12		7
7 May 05	**SIGNS** *Geffen 9881782* SNOOP DOGG FEATURING CHARLIE WILSON & JUSTIN TIMBERLAKE	2		16

DOOLEY WILSON
US, male actor/vocalist (Arthur Wilson), d. 30 May 1953 (age 59) — 9

Date	Title	Peak	Wks at No.1	Wks on Chart
3 Dec 77	**AS TIME GOES BY** *United Artists UP 36331*	15		9

GRETCHEN WILSON
US, female vocalist/guitarist — 2

Date	Title	Peak	Wks at No.1	Wks on Chart
4 Sep 04	**REDNECK WOMAN** *Epic 6751732*	42		2

JACKIE WILSON
US, male vocalist, d. 21 Jan 1984 (age 49) — 97

Date	Title	Peak	Wks at No.1	Wks on Chart
15 Nov 57	**REET PETITE (THE SWEETEST GIRL IN TOWN)** *Coral Q 72290*	6		14
14 Mar 58	**TO BE LOVED** *Coral Q 72306*	23		8
15 Sep 60	**(YOU WERE MADE FOR) ALL MY LOVE** *Coral Q 72407*	33		7
22 Dec 60	**ALONE AT LAST** *Coral Q 72412*	50		1
14 May 69	**(YOUR LOVE KEEPS LIFTING ME) HIGHER AND HIGHER** *MCA BAG 2*	11		11
29 Jul 72	**I GET THE SWEETEST FEELING** *MCA MU 1160*	9		13
3 May 75	**I GET THE SWEETEST FEELING/(YOUR LOVE KEEPS LIFTING ME) HIGHER AND HIGHER** *Brunswick BR 18*	25		8
29 Nov 86	**REET PETITE (THE SWEETEST GIRL IN TOWN)** *SMP SKM 3* ●	1	4	17
28 Feb 87	**I GET THE SWEETEST FEELING** *SMP SKM 1* ○	3		11
4 Jul 87	**(YOUR LOVE KEEPS LIFTING ME) HIGHER AND HIGHER** *SMP SKM 10*	15		7

MARI WILSON
UK, female vocalist — 34

Date	Title	Peak	Wks at No.1	Wks on Chart
6 Mar 82	**BEAT THE BEAT** *Compact PINK 2*	59		3
8 May 82	**BABY IT'S TRUE** *Compact PINK 3*	42		6
11 Sep 82	**JUST WHAT I ALWAYS WANTED** *Compact PINK 4*	8		10
13 Nov 82	**(BEWARE) BOYFRIEND** *Compact PINK 5*	51		4
19 Mar 83	**CRY ME A RIVER** *Compact PINK 6*	27		7
11 Jun 83	**WONDERFUL** *Compact PINK 7*	47		4

MERI WILSON
US, female vocalist, d. 28 Dec 2002 (age 53) — 10

Date	Title	Peak	Wks at No.1	Wks on Chart
27 Aug 77	**TELEPHONE MAN** *Pye International 7N 25747* ○	6		10

MIKE 'HITMAN' WILSON
US, male producer — 1

Date	Title	Peak	Wks at No.1	Wks on Chart
22 Sep 90	**ANOTHER SLEEPLESS NIGHT** *Arista 113506*	74		1

TOM WILSON
UK, male radio DJ/producer, d. 25 Mar 2004 (age 52) — 4

Date	Title	Peak	Wks at No.1	Wks on Chart
2 Dec 95	**TECHNOCAT** *Pukka CDPUKKA 4* TECHNOCAT FEATURING TOM WILSON	33		3
16 Mar 96	**LET YOUR BODY GO** *Clubscene DCSRT 050*	60		1

VICTORIA WILSON JAMES
US, female vocalist — 1

Date	Title	Peak	Wks at No.1	Wks on Chart
9 Aug 97	**REACH 4 THE MELODY** *Sony S3 VWJCD1*	72		1

WILSON PHILLIPS
US, female vocal trio – Chynna Phillips & Carnie & Wendy Wilson — 33

Date	Title	Peak	Wks at No.1	Wks on Chart
26 May 90	**HOLD ON** *SBK 6* ★	6		12
18 Aug 90	**RELEASE ME** *SBK 11* ★	36		5
10 Nov 90	**IMPULSIVE** *SBK 16*	42		3
11 May 91	**YOU'RE IN LOVE** *SBK 25* ★	29		5
23 May 92	**YOU WON'T SEE ME CRY** *SBK 34*	18		5
22 Aug 92	**GIVE IT UP** *SBK 36*	36		3

WILT
Ireland, male vocal/instrumental group — 3

Date	Title	Peak	Wks at No.1	Wks on Chart
8 Apr 00	**RADIO DISCO** *Mushroom MUSH 71CDS*	56		1
8 Jul 00	**OPEN ARMS** *Mushroom MUSH 75CDS*	59		1
13 Jul 02	**DISTORTION** *Mushroom MUSH 103CDS*	66		1

W.I.P. FEATURING EMMIE
UK, male/female vocal/production trio — 1

Date	Title	Peak	Wks at No.1	Wks on Chart
16 Feb 02	**I WON'T LET YOU DOWN** *Decode/Telstar CDSTAS 3210*	53		1

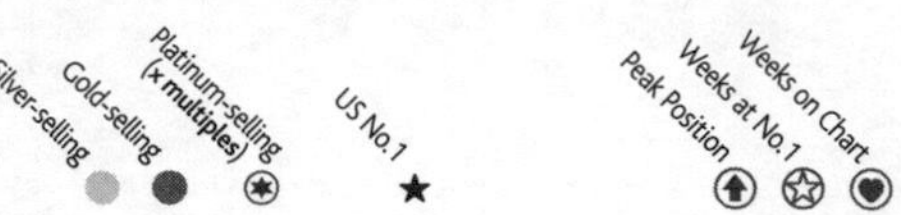

WIMBLEDON CHORAL SOCIETY
UK, male/female choral group **8**

Date	Title	Peak Position	Weeks at No.1	Weeks on Chart
4 Jul 98	**WORLD CUP '98 – PAVANE** *Telstar CDSTAS 2979*	26		5
12 Dec 98	**IF – READ TO FAURE'S 'PAVANNE'** *BBC Worldwide WMSS 60062* DES LYNAM FEATURING WIMBLEDON CHORAL SOCIETY	45		3

WIN
UK, male vocal/instrumental group **3**

Date	Title	Peak Position	Weeks at No.1	Weeks on Chart
4 Apr 87	**SUPER POPOID GROOVE** *Swamplands LON 128*	63		3

WINANS
US, male vocal group **1**

Date	Title	Peak Position	Weeks at No.1	Weeks on Chart
30 Nov 85	**LET MY PEOPLE GO (PART 1)** *Qwest W 8874*	71		1

MARIO WINANS
US, male vocalist/producer **23**

Date	Title	Peak Position	Weeks at No.1	Weeks on Chart
20 Nov 99	**BEST FRIEND** *Puff Daddy 74321712312* PUFF DADDY FEATURING MARIO WINANS	24		4
5 Jun 04	**I DON'T WANNA KNOW (IMPORT)** *Universal 9862372PMI* FEATURING ENYA & P DIDDY	71		1
12 Jun 04	**I DON'T WANNA KNOW** *Bad Boy MCSTD40369* FEATURING ENYA & P DIDDY ●	1	1	14
11 Sep 04	**NEVER REALLY WAS** *Bad Boy MCSTD40372* FEATURING LIL' FLIP	44		2
8 Sep 07	**THROUGH THE PAIN (SHE TOLD ME)** *Bad Boy AT0283CD* P DIDDY FEATURING MARIO WINANS	50		2

WINDJAMMER
US, male vocal/instrumental group **12**

Date	Title	Peak Position	Weeks at No.1	Weeks on Chart
30 Jun 84	**TOSSING AND TURNING** *MCA 897*	18		12

BARBARA WINDSOR & MIKE REID
UK, female/male actors/vocal duo **2**

Date	Title	Peak Position	Weeks at No.1	Weeks on Chart
24 Apr 99	**THE MORE I SEE YOU** *Telstar CDSTAS 3049*	46		2

AMY WINEHOUSE
UK, female vocalist **179**

Date	Title	Peak Position	Weeks at No.1	Weeks on Chart
18 Oct 03	**STRONGER THAN ME** *Island CID 830*	71		1
24 Jan 04	**TAKE THE BOX** *Island CID 840*	57		1
17 Apr 04	**IN MY BED/YOU SENT ME FLYING** *Island CID 852*	60		1
4 Sep 04	**PUMPS/HELP YOURSELF** *Island CID 865*	69		1
28 Oct 06	**REHAB** *Island 1709534*	7		57
13 Jan 07	**YOU KNOW I'M NO GOOD** *Island 1720848*	18		11
14 Apr 07	**BACK TO BLACK** *Island/Uni-Island 1732325*	25		34
4 Aug 07	**TEARS DRY ON THEIR OWN** *Island 1744544*	16		19
29 Sep 07	**VALERIE** *Columbia 88697186332* MARK RONSON FEATURING AMY WINEHOUSE	2		39
13 Oct 07	**VALERIE** *Island GBUM70702678*	37		13
22 Dec 07	**LOVE IS A LOSING GAME** *Island 1755398*	46		2

WING & A PRAYER FIFE & DRUM CORPS
US, male/female vocal/instrumental session group **7**

Date	Title	Peak Position	Weeks at No.1	Weeks on Chart
24 Jan 76	**BABY FACE** *Atlantic K 10705*	12		7

WINGER
US, male vocal/instrumental group **3**

Date	Title	Peak Position	Weeks at No.1	Weeks on Chart
19 Jan 91	**MILES AWAY** *Atlantic A 7802*	56		3

PETE WINGFIELD
UK, male vocalist/keyboard player **7**

Date	Title	Peak Position	Weeks at No.1	Weeks on Chart
28 Jun 75	**EIGHTEEN WITH A BULLET** *Island WIP 6231*	7		7

JOSH WINK
US, male DJ/producer (Joshua Winkelman). See Size 9 **30**

Date	Title	Peak Position	Weeks at No.1	Weeks on Chart
6 May 95	**DON'T LAUGH** *XL Recordings XLS 62CD* WINX	38		2
21 Oct 95	**HIGHER STATE OF CONSCIOUSNESS** *Manifesto FESCD 3*	8		12
2 Mar 96	**HYPNOTIZIN'** *XL Recordings XLS 71CD* WINX	35		2
27 Jul 96	**HIGHER STATE OF CONSCIOUSNESS '96 REMIXES** *Manifesto FESCD 9* WINK	7		10
12 Aug 00	**HOW'S YOUR EVENING SO FAR** *ffrr FCD 384* & LIL' LOUIS	23		3
11 Aug 07	**HIGHER STATE OF CONSCIOUSNESS** *Strictly Rhythm SR12640CDX* WINK	70		1

KATE WINSLET
UK, female actor/vocalist **14**

Date	Title	Peak Position	Weeks at No.1	Weeks on Chart
8 Dec 01	**WHAT IF** *EMI/Liberty CDKATE 001* ●	6		14

EDGAR WINTER GROUP
US, male vocal/instrumental group **9**

Date	Title	Peak Position	Weeks at No.1	Weeks on Chart
26 May 73	**FRANKENSTEIN** *Epic EPC 1440* ★	18		9

RUBY WINTERS
US, female vocalist **35**

Date	Title	Peak Position	Weeks at No.1	Weeks on Chart
5 Nov 77	**I WILL** *Creole CR 141*	4		13
29 Apr 78	**COME TO ME** *Creole CR 153*	11		12
26 Aug 78	**I WON'T MENTION IT AGAIN** *Creole CR 160*	45		5
16 Jun 79	**BABY LAY DOWN** *Creole CR 171*	43		5

STEVE WINWOOD
UK, male vocalist/guitarist/keyboard player. See Blind Faith, One World Project, Spencer Davis Group, Traffic **33**

Date	Title	Peak Position	Weeks at No.1	Weeks on Chart
17 Jan 81	**WHILE YOU SEE A CHANCE** *Island WIP 6655*	45		5
9 Oct 82	**VALERIE** *Island WIP 6818*	51		4
28 Jun 86	**HIGHER LOVE** *Island IS 288* ★	13		9
13 Sep 86	**FREEDOM OVERSPILL** *Island IS 294*	69		1
24 Jan 87	**BACK IN THE HIGH LIFE AGAIN** *Island IS 303*	53		2
19 Sep 87	**VALERIE (REMIX)** *Island IS 336*	19		8
11 Jun 88	**ROLL WITH IT** *Virgin VS 1085* ★	53		4

WIRE
UK, male vocal/instrumental group **4**

Date	Title	Peak Position	Weeks at No.1	Weeks on Chart
27 Jan 79	**OUTDOOR MINER** *Harvest HAR 5172*	51		3
13 May 89	**EARDRUM BUZZ** *Mute 87*	68		1

NICKY WIRE
UK, male vocalist/bass player. See Manic Street Preachers **1**

Date	Title	Peak Position	Weeks at No.1	Weeks on Chart
30 Sep 06	**BREAK MY HEART SLOWLY** *Red Ink ENOLAD001*	74		1

WIRED
Holland/Finland, male instrumental/production duo **1**

Date	Title	Peak Position	Weeks at No.1	Weeks on Chart
20 Feb 99	**TRANSONIC** *Future Groove CDFGR 001*	73		1

WIRELESS
UK, male vocal/instrumental group **2**

Date	Title	Peak Position	Weeks at No.1	Weeks on Chart
28 Jun 97	**I NEED YOU** *Chrysalis CHCHS 5059*	68		1
7 Feb 98	**IN LOVE WITH THE FAMILIAR** *Chrysalis CDCHS 5075*	69		1

NORMAN WISDOM
UK, male actor/comedian/vocalist **20**

Date	Title	Peak Position	Weeks at No.1	Weeks on Chart
19 Feb 54	**DON'T LAUGH AT ME** *Columbia DB 3133*	3		15
15 Mar 57	**WISDOM OF A FOOL** *Columbia DB 3903*	13		5

WISD'ME
Italy, male/female vocal/production group **2**

Date	Title	Peak Position	Weeks at No.1	Weeks on Chart
11 Mar 00	**OFF THE WALL** *Positiva CDTIV 125*	33		2

WISEGUYS
UK, male DJ/producer (Theo Keating). See DJ Touche **13**

Date	Title	Peak Position	Weeks at No.1	Weeks on Chart
6 Jun 98	**OOH LA LA** *Wall Of Sound WALLD 038*	55		1
12 Sep 98	**START THE COMMOTION** *Wall Of Sound WALLD 044*	66		1
5 Jun 99	**OOH LA LA** *Wall Of Sound WALLD 038X* ●	2		10
11 Sep 99	**START THE COMMOTION** *Wall Of Sound WALLD 059*	47		1

BILL WITHERS
US, male vocalist/guitarist — 34

Date	Title	Peak	Wks at No.1	Wks on Chart
12 Aug 72	**LEAN ON ME** *A&M AMS 7004* ★	18		9
14 Jan 78	**LOVELY DAY** *CBS 5773*	7		8
25 May 85	**OH YEAH!** *CBS A 6154*	60		3
10 Sep 88	**LOVELY DAY (REMIX)** *CBS 6530017*	4		9
23 May 09	**AIN'T NO SUNSHINE** *Columbia USSM17100268*	40		5

WITNESS
UK, male vocal/instrumental group — 2

Date	Title	Peak	Wks at No.1	Wks on Chart
13 Mar 99	**SCARS** *Island CID 740*	71		1
19 Jun 99	**AUDITION** *Island CID 749*	71		1

WIZZARD
UK, male vocal/instrumental group – Roy Wood*, Mike Burney, Charley Grima, Bill Hunt, Hugh McDowell, Nick Pentelow, Rick Price & Keith Smart — 90

Date	Title	Peak	Wks at No.1	Wks on Chart
9 Dec 72	**BALL PARK INCIDENT** *Harvest HAR 5062*	6		12
21 Apr 73	**SEE MY BABY JIVE** *Harvest HAR 5070* ●	1	4	17
1 Sep 73	**ANGEL FINGERS** *Harvest HAR 5076* ○	1	1	10
8 Dec 73	**I WISH IT COULD BE CHRISTMAS EVERY DAY** *Harvest HAR 5079* FEATURING VOCAL BACKING BY THE SUEDETTES PLUS THE STOCKLAND GREEN BILATERAL SCHOOL FIRST YEAR CHOIR WITH ADDITIONAL NOISES BY MISS SNOB AND CLASS 3C ○	4		9
27 Apr 74	**ROCK 'N' ROLL WINTER** *Warner Brothers K 16357*	6		7
10 Aug 74	**THIS IS THE STORY OF MY LIFE (BABY)** *Warner Brothers K 16434*	34		4
21 Dec 74	**ARE YOU READY TO ROCK** *Warner Brothers K 16497*	8		10
19 Dec 81	**I WISH IT COULD BE CHRISTMAS EVERY DAY** *Harvest HAR 5173* FEATURING VOCAL BACKING BY THE SUEDETTES PLUS THE STOCKLAND GREEN BILATERAL SCHOOL FIRST YEAR CHOIR WITH ADDITIONAL NOISES BY MISS SNOB AND CLASS 3C	41		4
15 Dec 84	**I WISH IT COULD BE CHRISTMAS EVERY DAY** *Harvest HAR 5173* FEATURING VOCAL BACKING BY THE SUEDETTES PLUS THE STOCKLAND GREEN BILATERAL SCHOOL FIRST YEAR CHOIR WITH ADDITIONAL NOISES BY MISS SNOB AND CLASS 3C	23		4
8 Dec 07	**I WISH IT COULD BE CHRISTMAS EVERY DAY** *EMI GBAYE7300088*	16		5
13 Dec 08	**I WISH IT COULD BE CHRISTMAS EVERY DAY** *EMI GBAYE7300088*	31		4
12 Dec 09	**I WISH IT COULD BE CHRISTMAS EVERY DAY** *EMI GBAYE7300088*	45		4

ANDREW WK
US, male vocalist/multi-instrumentalist (Andrew Wilkes-Krier) — 5

Date	Title	Peak	Wks at No.1	Wks on Chart
10 Nov 01	**PARTY HARD** *Mercury 5888132*	19		4
9 Mar 02	**SHE IS BEAUTIFUL** *Mercury 5889522*	55		1

JAH WOBBLE'S INVADERS OF THE HEART
UK, male vocalist/bass player/producer (John Wardle) — 10

Date	Title	Peak	Wks at No.1	Wks on Chart
1 Feb 92	**VISIONS OF YOU** *Oval 103*	35		5
30 Apr 94	**BECOMING MORE LIKE GOD** *Island CID 571*	36		2
25 Jun 94	**THE SUN DOES RISE** *Island CIDX 587*	41		3

TERRY WOGAN
UK, male TV & radio presenter/vocalist — 7

Date	Title	Peak	Wks at No.1	Wks on Chart
7 Jan 78	**FLORAL DANCE** *Philips 6006 592*	21		5
19 Dec 09	**SILVER BELLS/ME AND MY TEDDY BEAR** *Bandaged CDTOG2* SIR TERRY WOGAN & ALED JONES	27		2

PATRICK WOLF
Ireland, male vocalist/multi-instrumentalist (Patrick Apps) — 2

Date	Title	Peak	Wks at No.1	Wks on Chart
12 Feb 05	**THE LIBERTINE** *Tomlab TOM46*	67		1
21 Apr 07	**THE MAGIC POSITION** *A&M/Polydor 1726001*	69		1

WOLFMAN
UK, male vocalist/guitarist (Peter Wolfe) — 8

Date	Title	Peak	Wks at No.1	Wks on Chart
24 Apr 04	**FOR LOVERS** *Rough Trade RTRADSCD177* FEATURING PETE DOHERTY	7		6
11 Dec 04	**NAPOLEON** *Beyond Bedlam BEBAD001CDS*	44		1
4 Jun 05	**ICE CREAM GUERILLA** *Beyond Bedlam BEBAD002CDS*	60		1

WOLFMOTHER
Australia, male vocal/instrumental trio — 7

Date	Title	Peak	Wks at No.1	Wks on Chart
29 Apr 06	**DIMENSION** *Modular CID928*	49		2
29 Jul 06	**WOMAN** *Modular CID933*	31		3
30 Sep 06	**LOVE TRAIN** *Modular 1707877*	62		1
2 Dec 06	**JOKER & THE THIEF** *Island/Modular 1715494*	64		1

WOLFSBANE
UK, male vocal/instrumental group — 1

Date	Title	Peak	Wks at No.1	Wks on Chart
5 Oct 91	**EZY** *Def American DEFA 11*	68		1

BOBBY WOMACK
US, male vocalist/guitarist — 24

Date	Title	Peak	Wks at No.1	Wks on Chart
16 Jun 84	**TELL ME WHY** *Motown TMG 1339*	60		3
16 Feb 85	**(NO MATTER HOW HIGH I GET) I'LL STILL BE LOOKIN' UP TO YOU** *MCA 919* WILTON FELDER FEATURING BOBBY WOMACK & INTRODUCING ALLTRINA GRAYSON	63		2
5 Oct 85	**I WISH HE DIDN'T TRUST ME SO MUCH** *MCA 994*	64		2
26 Sep 87	**SO THE STORY GOES** *Chrysalis LIB 3* LIVING IN A BOX FEATURING BOBBY WOMACK	34		8
7 Nov 87	**LIVING IN A BOX** *MCA 1210*	70		2
3 Apr 93	**I'M BACK FOR MORE** *Dome CDDOME 1002* LULU & BOBBY WOMACK	27		5
13 May 95	**IT'S A MAN'S MAN'S MAN'S WORLD** *Pulse 8 CDLOSE 89* JEANIE TRACY & BOBBY WOMACK	73		1
19 Jun 04	**CALIFORNIA DREAMIN'** *EMI WOMACK001*	59		1

LEE ANN WOMACK
US, female vocalist/guitarist — 2

Date	Title	Peak	Wks at No.1	Wks on Chart
9 Jun 01	**I HOPE YOU DANCE** *MCA Nashville MCSTD 40254*	40		2

WOMACK & WOMACK
US, male/female vocal/instrumental duo – Cecil & Linda Womack (Linda Cooke) — 51

Date	Title	Peak	Wks at No.1	Wks on Chart
28 Apr 84	**LOVE WARS** *Elektra E 9799*	14		10
30 Jun 84	**BABY I'M SCARED OF YOU** *Elektra E 9733*	72		2
6 Dec 86	**SOUL LOVE – SOUL MAN** *Manhattan MT 16*	58		6
6 Aug 88	**TEARDROPS** *Fourth & Broadway BRW 101* ○	3		17
12 Nov 88	**LIFE'S JUST A BALLGAME** *Fourth & Broadway BRW 116*	32		5
25 Feb 89	**CELEBRATE THE WORLD** *Fourth & Broadway BRW 125*	19		8
5 Feb 94	**SECRET STAR** *Warner Brothers W 0222CD* HOUSE OF ZEKKARIYAS AKA WOMACK & WOMACK	46		3

WOMBATS
UK/Norway, male vocal/instrumental group — 31

Date	Title	Peak	Wks at No.1	Wks on Chart
28 Apr 07	**BACKFIRE AT THE DISCO** *Kids KIDS012CD*	67		1
7 Jul 07	**KILL THE DIRECTOR** *14th Floor 14FLR22CD*	35		2
20 Oct 07	**LET'S DANCE TO JOY DIVISION** *14th Floor 14FLR26CD*	15		10
19 Jan 08	**MOVING TO NEW YORK** *14th Floor 14FLR28CD*	13		11
3 May 08	**BACKFIRE AT THE DISCO** *14th Floor 14FLR30CD*	40		3
19 Jul 08	**KILL THE DIRECTOR** *14th Floor 14FLR22CD*	48		2
27 Dec 08	**IS THIS CHRISTMAS?** *14th Floor 14FLR33CD*	49		1
14 Mar 09	**MY CIRCUITBOARD CITY** *14th Floor 14FLR34CD*	69		1

WOMBLES
Wimbledon Common (UK), male/female puppet vocalists — 98

Date	Title	Peak	Wks at No.1	Wks on Chart
26 Jan 74	**THE WOMBLING SONG** *CBS 1794*	4		23
6 Apr 74	**REMEMBER YOU'RE A WOMBLE** *CBS 2241*	3		16
22 Jun 74	**BANANA ROCK** *CBS 2465*	9		13
12 Oct 74	**MINUETTO ALLEGRETTO** *CBS 2710*	16		9
7 Dec 74	**WOMBLING MERRY CHRISTMAS** *CBS 2842* ○	2		8
10 May 75	**WOMBLING WHITE TIE AND TAILS** *CBS 3266*	22		7
9 Aug 75	**SUPER WOMBLE** *CBS 3480*	20		6
13 Dec 75	**LET'S WOMBLE TO THE PARTY TONIGHT** *CBS 3794*	34		5
21 Mar 98	**REMEMBER YOU'RE A WOMBLE** *Columbia 6656202*	13		5
13 Jun 98	**WOMBLING SONG (UNDERGROUND OVERGROUND)** *Columbia 6660412*	27		3
30 Dec 00	**I WISH IT COULD BE A WOMBLING CHRISTMAS** *Dramatico DRAMCDS 0001X* FEATURING ROY WOOD	22		3

STEVIE WONDER

US, male vocalist/pianist (Steveland Judkins). Legendary blind songwriter and live favourite responsible for the top-selling Motown single of all time, 'I Just Called To Say I Love You', which sold an incredible 1.8 million copies in the UK alone. He has sold 8.5 million singles in the UK since 1966

Date	Title / Label	Peak Position	Weeks at No.1	Weeks on Chart (432)
3 Feb 66	**UPTIGHT** *Tamla Motown TMG 545*	14		10
18 Aug 66	**BLOWIN' IN THE WIND** *Tamla Motown TMG 570*	36		5
5 Jan 67	**A PLACE IN THE SUN** *Tamla Motown TMG 588*	20		5
26 Jul 67	**I WAS MADE TO LOVE HER** *Tamla Motown TMG 613*	5		15
25 Oct 67	**I'M WONDERING** *Tamla Motown TMG 626*	22		8
8 May 68	**SHOO BE DOO BE DOO DA DAY** *Tamla Motown TMG 653*	46		4
18 Dec 68	**FOR ONCE IN MY LIFE** *Tamla Motown TMG 679*	3		13
19 Mar 69	**DON'T KNOW WHY I LOVE YOU** *Tamla Motown TMG 690*	14		11
16 Jul 69	**MY CHERIE AMOUR** *Tamla Motown TMG 690*	4		15
15 Nov 69	**YESTER-ME YESTER-YOU YESTERDAY** *Tamla Motown TMG 717*	2		13
28 Mar 70	**NEVER HAD A DREAM COME TRUE** *Tamla Motown TMG 731*	6		12
18 Jul 70	**SIGNED SEALED DELIVERED I'M YOURS** *Tamla Motown TMG 744*	15		10
21 Nov 70	**HEAVEN HELP US ALL** *Tamla Motown TMG 757*	29		11
15 May 71	**WE CAN WORK IT OUT** *Tamla Motown TMG 772*	27		7
22 Jan 72	**IF YOU REALLY LOVE ME** *Tamla Motown TMG 798*	20		7
3 Feb 73	**SUPERSTITION** *Tamla Motown TMG 841* ★	11		9
19 May 73	**YOU ARE THE SUNSHINE OF MY LIFE** *Tamla Motown TMG 852* ★	7		11
13 Oct 73	**HIGHER GROUND** *Tamla Motown TMG 869*	29		5
12 Jan 74	**LIVING FOR THE CITY** *Tamla Motown TMG 881*	15		9
13 Apr 74	**HE'S MISSTRA KNOW IT ALL** *Tamla Motown TMG 892*	10		9
19 Oct 74	**YOU HAVEN'T DONE NOTHIN'** *Tamla Motown TMG 921* ★	30		5
11 Jan 75	**BOOGIE ON REGGAE WOMAN** *Tamla Motown TMG 928*	12		8
18 Dec 76	**I WISH** *Tamla Motown TMG 1054* ● ★	5		10
9 Apr 77	**SIR DUKE** *Motown TMG 1068* ● ★	2		9
10 Sep 77	**ANOTHER STAR** *Motown TMG 1083*	29		5
24 Feb 79	**POPS WE LOVE YOU** *Motown TMG 1136* DIANA ROSS, MARVIN GAYE, SMOKEY ROBINSON & STEVIE WONDER	66		5
24 Nov 79	**SEND ONE YOUR LOVE** *Motown TMG 1149*	52		3
26 Jan 80	**BLACK ORCHID** *Motown TMG 1173*	63		3
29 Mar 80	**OUTSIDE MY WINDOW** *Motown TMG 1179*	52		4
13 Sep 80	**MASTERBLASTER (JAMMIN')** *Motown TMG 1204* ●	2		10
27 Dec 80	**I AIN'T GONNA STAND FOR IT** *Motown TMG 1215*	10		10
7 Mar 81	**LATELY** *Motown TMG 1226* ●	3		13
25 Jul 81	**HAPPY BIRTHDAY** *Motown TMG 1235* ●	2		11
23 Jan 82	**THAT GIRL** *Motown TMG 1254*	39		6
10 Apr 82	**EBONY AND IVORY** *Parlophone R 6054* PAUL McCARTNEY & STEVIE WONDER ● ★	1	3	10
5 Jun 82	**DO I DO** *Motown TMG 1269*	10		7
25 Sep 82	**RIBBON IN THE SKY** *Motown TMG 1280*	45		4
25 Aug 84	**I JUST CALLED TO SAY I LOVE YOU** *Motown TMG 1349* ⊛ ★	1	6	26
1 Dec 84	**LOVE LIGHT IN FLIGHT** *Motown TMG 1364*	44		5
29 Dec 84	**DON'T DRIVE DRUNK** *Motown TMG 1372*	62		3
7 Sep 85	**PART-TIME LOVER** *Motown ZB 40351* ● ★	3		12
9 Nov 85	**THAT'S WHAT FRIENDS ARE FOR** *Arista ARIST 638* DIONNE WARWICK & FRIENDS FEATURING ELTON JOHN, STEVIE WONDER & GLADYS KNIGHT ★	16		9
23 Nov 85	**GO HOME** *Motown ZB 40501*	67		2
8 Mar 86	**OVERJOYED** *Motown ZB 40567*	17		8
17 Jan 87	**STRANGER ON THE SHORE OF LOVE** *Motown WOND 2*	55		3
31 Oct 87	**SKELETONS** *Motown ZB 41439*	59		3
28 May 88	**GET IT** *Motown ZB 41883* & MICHAEL JACKSON	37		4
6 Aug 88	**MY LOVE** *CBS JULIO 2* JULIO IGLESIAS FEATURING STEVIE WONDER	5		11
20 May 89	**FREE** *Motown ZB 42855*	49		5
12 Oct 91	**FUN DAY** *Motown ZB 44957*	63		1
25 Feb 95	**FOR YOUR LOVE** *Motown TMGCD 1437*	23		4
22 Jul 95	**TOMORROW ROBINS WILL SING** *Motown 8603732*	71		1
19 Jul 97	**HOW COME, HOW LONG** *Epic 6646202* BABYFACE FEATURING STEVIE WONDER	10		5
31 Oct 98	**TRUE TO YOUR HEART** *Motown 8608832* 98o FEATURING STEVIE WONDER	51		1
27 Dec 03	**SIGNED SEALED DELIVERED I'M YOURS** *Innocent SINCD 54* BLUE FEATURING STEVIE WONDER & ANGIE STONE	11		10
28 May 05	**SO WHAT THE FUSS** *Motown TMGCDX1510*	19		4
10 Dec 05	**POSITIVITY** *Motown TMGCD1512* FEATURING AISHA MORRIS	54		1
27 Sep 08	**SUPERSTITION** *Simply 12 S12DJ055*	65		1
26 Sep 09	**SUPERSTITION** *Simply 12 S12DJ055*	69		1

WAYNE WONDER

Jamaica, male vocalist (VonWayne Charles)

Date	Title / Label	Peak Position	Weeks at No.1	Weeks on Chart (19)
23 Mar 96	**SOMETHING DIFFERENT/THE TRAIN IS COMING** *Virgin VSCDX 1581* SHAGGY FEATURING WAYNE WONDER	21		5
28 Jun 03	**NO LETTING GO** *VP/Atlantic AT 0154CD*	3		8
8 Nov 03	**BOUNCE ALONG** *Atlantic AT 0165CD*	19		6

WONDER DOG

Germany, male canine superhero. See Harry Thumann

Date	Title / Label	Peak Position	Weeks at No.1	Weeks on Chart (7)
21 Aug 82	**RUFF MIX** *Flip 001*	31		7

WONDER STUFF

UK, male vocal/instrumental group – Miles Hunt, Martin Bell, Paul Clifford, Martin Gilks, d. 3 Apr 2006, Rob Jones, d. 30 Jul 1993 (replaced by Paul Clifford), & Malcolm Treece

Date	Title / Label	Peak Position	Weeks at No.1	Weeks on Chart (66)
7 May 88	**GIVE GIVE GIVE ME MORE MORE MORE** *Polydor GONE 3*	72		1
16 Jul 88	**A WISH AWAY** *Polydor GONE 4*	43		5
24 Sep 88	**IT'S YER MONEY I'M AFTER BABY** *Polydor GONE 5*	40		3
11 Mar 89	**WHO WANTS TO BE THE DISCO KING** *Polydor GONE 6*	28		3
23 Sep 89	**DON'T LET ME DOWN GENTLY** *Polydor GONE 7*	19		4
11 Nov 89	**GOLDEN GREEN/GET TOGETHER** *Polydor GONE 8*	33		3
12 May 90	**CIRCLESQUARE** *Polydor GONE 10*	20		4
13 Apr 91	**THE SIZE OF A COW** *Polydor GONE 11*	5		7
25 May 91	**CAUGHT IN MY SHADOW** *Polydor GONE 12*	18		3
7 Sep 91	**SLEEP ALONE** *Polydor GONE 13*	43		2
26 Oct 91	**DIZZY** *Sense SIGH 712* VIC REEVES & THE WONDER STUFF ●	1	2	12
25 Jan 92	**WELCOME TO THE CHEAP SEATS (EP)** *Polydor GONE 14*	8		5
25 Sep 93	**ON THE ROPES (EP)** *Polydor GONCD 15*	10		4
27 Nov 93	**FULL OF LIFE (HAPPY NOW)** *Polydor GONCD 16*	28		3
26 Mar 94	**HOT LOVE NOW** *Polydor GONCD 17*	19		3
10 Sep 94	**UNBEARABLE** *Polydor GONCD 18*	16		3

WONDERS

US, male vocal/instrumental group

Date	Title / Label	Peak Position	Weeks at No.1	Weeks on Chart (3)
22 Feb 97	**THAT THING YOU DO!** *Play-Tone 6640552*	22		3

BRENTON WOOD

US, male vocalist (Alfred Smith)

Date	Title / Label	Peak Position	Weeks at No.1	Weeks on Chart (14)
27 Dec 67	**GIMME LITTLE SIGN** *Liberty LBF 15021*	8		14

ROY WOOD

UK, male vocalist/multi-instrumentalist (Ulysses Adrian Wood). See Electric Light Orchestra, Move, Wizzard

Date	Title / Label	Peak Position	Weeks at No.1	Weeks on Chart (44)
11 Aug 73	**DEAR ELAINE** *Harvest HAR 5074*	18		8
1 Dec 73	**FOREVER** *Harvest HAR 5078*	8		13
15 Jun 74	**GOING DOWN THE ROAD** *Harvest HAR 5083*	13		7
31 May 75	**OH WHAT A SHAME** *Jet 754*	13		7
22 Nov 86	**WATERLOO** *IRS IRM 125* DOCTOR & THE MEDICS FEATURING ROY WOOD	45		4
23 Dec 95	**I WISH IT COULD BE CHRISTMAS EVERYDAY** *Woody 001CD* ROY WOOD BIG BAND	59		2
30 Dec 00	**I WISH IT COULD BE A WOMBLING CHRISTMAS** *Dramatico DRAMCDS 0001X* WOMBLES FEATURING ROY WOOD	22		3

WOODENTOPS

UK, male/female vocal/instrumental group

Date	Title / Label	Peak Position	Weeks at No.1	Weeks on Chart (1)
11 Oct 86	**EVERYDAY LIVING** *Rough Trade RT 178*	72		1

MARCELLA WOODS

UK, female vocalist. See Out Of Office

Date	Title / Label	Peak Position	Weeks at No.1	Weeks on Chart (13)
15 Jul 00	**BEAUTIFUL** *Incentive CENT 7CDS* MATT DAREY'S MASH UP PRESENTS MARCELLA WOODS	21		4
30 Mar 02	**FALLING** *Perfecto PERF 29CDS* LIQUID STATE FEATURING MARCELLA WOODS	60		1
20 Apr 02	**BEAUTIFUL** *Incentive CENT 38CDS* MATT DAREY FEATURING MARCELLA WOODS	10		6
14 Dec 02	**U SHINE ON** *Incentive CENT 50CDS* MATT DAREY & MARCELLA WOODS	34		2

MICHAEL WOODS

UK, male DJ/producer. See M1, M3, Out Of Office, Warrior

Date	Title / Label	Peak Position	Weeks at No.1	Weeks on Chart (2)
21 Jun 03	**IF U WANT ME** *Incentive CENT 48CDS* FEATURING IMOGEN BAILEY	46		1
29 Nov 03	**SOLEX (CLOSE TO THE EDGE)** *Free 2 Air 0151865F2A*	52		1

EDWARD WOODWARD

UK, male actor/vocalist, d. 16 Nov 2009 (age 79)

Date	Title / Label	Peak Position	Weeks at No.1	Weeks on Chart (2)
16 Jan 71	**THE WAY YOU LOOK TONIGHT** *DJM DJS 232*	42		2

WOOKIE
UK, male vocalist/producer (Jason Chue) — 11

Date	Title	Peak Position	Weeks at No.1	Weeks on Chart
3 Jun 00	**WHAT'S GOING ON** *Soul II Soul S2CD 001*	45		1
12 Aug 00	**BATTLE** *Soul II Soul S2SPCD 001* FEATURING LAIN	10		7
12 May 01	**BACK UP (TO ME)** *Soul II Soul S2SPCD 003* FEATURING LAIN	38		3

SHEB WOOLEY
US, male actor/vocalist, d. 16 Sep 2003 (age 82) — 8

Date	Title	Peak Position	Weeks at No.1	Weeks on Chart
20 Jun 58	**PURPLE PEOPLE EATER** *MGM 981* ★	12		8

WOOLPACKERS
UK, male/female actors/vocal group – Terry Dyddgen-Jones, Steve Halliwell, Billy Hartman, Alun Lewis & Lisa Riley — 24

Date	Title	Peak Position	Weeks at No.1	Weeks on Chart
16 Nov 96	**HILLBILLY ROCK HILLBILLY ROLL** *RCA 74321425412* ●	5		14
29 Nov 97	**LINE DANCE PARTY** *RCA 74321512262*	25		10

WORKING WEEK
UK, male/female vocal/instrumental trio — 2

Date	Title	Peak Position	Weeks at No.1	Weeks on Chart
9 Jun 84	**VENCEREMOS – WE WILL WIN** *Virgin VS 684*	64		2

WORLD OF TWIST
UK, male/female vocal/instrumental group — 12

Date	Title	Peak Position	Weeks at No.1	Weeks on Chart
24 Nov 90	**THE STORM** *Circa YR 55*	42		5
23 Mar 91	**SONS OF THE STAGE** *Circa YR 62*	47		3
12 Oct 91	**SWEETS** *Circa YR 72*	58		2
22 Feb 92	**SHE'S A RAINBOW** *Circa YR 82*	62		2

WORLD PARTY
UK, male vocalist/keyboard player (Karl Wallinger) & various male/female vocal/instrumental collaborators. See Waterboys — 29

Date	Title	Peak Position	Weeks at No.1	Weeks on Chart
14 Feb 87	**SHIP OF FOOLS** *Ensign ENY 606*	42		6
16 Jun 90	**MESSAGE IN THE BOX** *Ensign ENY 631*	39		6
15 Sep 90	**WAY DOWN NOW** *Ensign ENY 634*	66		2
18 May 91	**THANK YOU WORLD** *Ensign ENY 643*	68		1
10 Apr 93	**IS IT LIKE TODAY** *Ensign CDENY 658*	19		6
10 Jul 93	**GIVE IT ALL AWAY** *Ensign CDENY 659*	43		3
2 Oct 93	**ALL I GAVE** *Ensign CDENY 658*	37		3
7 Jun 97	**BEAUTIFUL DREAM** *Chrysalis CDCHS 5053*	31		2

WORLD PREMIERE
US, male vocal/instrumental group — 1

Date	Title	Peak Position	Weeks at No.1	Weeks on Chart
28 Jan 84	**SHARE THE NIGHT** *Epic A 4133*	64		1

WORLD WARRIOR
UK, male producer (Simon Harris*). See Ambassadors Of Funk featuring MC Mario — 1

Date	Title	Peak Position	Weeks at No.1	Weeks on Chart
16 Apr 94	**STREET FIGHTER II** *Living Beat LBECD 27*	70		1

WORLDS APART
UK, male vocal group — 17

Date	Title	Peak Position	Weeks at No.1	Weeks on Chart
27 Mar 93	**HEAVEN MUST BE MISSING AN ANGEL** *Arista 74321139362*	29		3
3 Jul 93	**WONDERFUL WORLD** *Arista 74321153402*	51		1
25 Sep 93	**EVERLASTING LOVE** *Bell 74321164802*	20		4
26 Mar 94	**COULD IT BE I'M FALLING IN LOVE** *Bell 74321189952*	15		6
4 Jun 94	**BEGGIN' TO BE WRITTEN** *Bell 74321211982*	29		3

WORLD'S FAMOUS SUPREME TEAM
US, male rap/DJ duo – Ronald Larkins & Larry Price – with various male/female rap/vocal collaborators — 19

Date	Title	Peak Position	Weeks at No.1	Weeks on Chart
4 Dec 82	**BUFFALO GIRLS** *Charisma MALC 1* MALCOLM McLAREN & THE WORLD'S FAMOUS SUPREME TEAM ●	9		12
25 Feb 84	**HEY DJ** *Charisma TEAM 1*	52		5
8 Dec 90	**OPERAA HOUSE** *Virgin VS 1273* WORLD'S FAMOUS SUPREME TEAM SHOW	75		1
3 Oct 98	**BUFFALO GALS STAMPEDE** *Virgin VSCDT 1717* MALCOLM McLAREN & THE WORLD'S FAMOUS SUPREME TEAM PLUS RAKIM & ROGER SANCHEZ	65		1

W.O.S.P.
UK, male/female vocal/production duo — 1

Date	Title	Peak Position	Weeks at No.1	Weeks on Chart
17 Nov 01	**GETTING' INTO U** *Data 26CDS*	48		1

WRECKX-N-EFFECT
US, male rap/vocal duo — 18

Date	Title	Peak Position	Weeks at No.1	Weeks on Chart
13 Jan 90	**JUICY** *Motown ZB 43295* WRECKS-N-EFFECT	29		7
5 Dec 92	**RUMP SHAKER** *MCA MCS 1725*	24		7
7 May 94	**WRECKX SHOP** *MCA MCSTD 1969* FEATURING APACHE INDIAN	26		2
13 Aug 94	**RUMP SHAKER** *MCA MCSTD 1989*	40		2

BETTY WRIGHT
US, female vocalist — 23

Date	Title	Peak Position	Weeks at No.1	Weeks on Chart
25 Jan 75	**SHOORAH SHOORAH** *RCA 2491*	27		7
19 Apr 75	**WHERE IS THE LOVE** *RCA 2548*	25		7
8 Feb 86	**PAIN** *Cooltempo COOL 117*	42		6
9 Sep 89	**KEEP LOVE NEW** *Sure Delight SD 11*	71		3

IAN WRIGHT
UK, male footballer/vocalist — 2

Date	Title	Peak Position	Weeks at No.1	Weeks on Chart
28 Aug 93	**DO THE RIGHT THING** *M&G MAGCD 45*	43		2

RUBY WRIGHT
US, female vocalist, d. 9 Mar 2004 (age 90) — 23

Date	Title	Peak Position	Weeks at No.1	Weeks on Chart
16 Apr 54	**BIMBO** *Parlophone R 3816*	7		5
22 May 59	**THREE STARS** *Parlophone R 4556*	19		10

STEVE WRIGHT
UK, male vocalist/radio presenter — 10

Date	Title	Peak Position	Weeks at No.1	Weeks on Chart
27 Nov 82	**I'M ALRIGHT** *RCA 296* YOUNG STEVE & THE AFTERNOON BOYS	40		6
15 Oct 83	**GET SOME THERAPY** *RCA 362* & THE SISTERS OF SOUL	75		1
1 Dec 84	**THE GAY CAVALIEROS (THE STORY SO FAR)** *MCA 925*	61		3

WUBBLE-U
UK, male production group — 1

Date	Title	Peak Position	Weeks at No.1	Weeks on Chart
7 Mar 98	**PETAL** *Indolent DGOL 003CD1*	55		1

WURZELS
UK, male vocal/instrumental group – Alan John 'Adge' Cutler, d. 5 May 1974, Tommy Banner, Tony Baylis & Pete Budd — 33

Date	Title	Peak Position	Weeks at No.1	Weeks on Chart
2 Feb 67	**DRINK UP THY ZIDER** *Columbia DB 8081* ADGE CUTLER & THE WURZELS	45		1
15 May 76	**COMBINE HARVESTER (BRAND NEW KEY)** *EMI 2450* ●	1	2	13
11 Sep 76	**I AM A CIDER DRINKER (PALOMA BLANCA)** *EMI 2520*	3		9
25 Jun 77	**FARMER BILL'S COWMAN (I WAS KAISER BILL'S BATMAN)** *EMI 2637*	32		5
11 Aug 01	**COMBINE HARVESTER 2001 (REMIX)** *EMI Gold CDWURZ 001*	39		2
12 Oct 02	**DON'T LOOK BACK IN ANGER** *EMI Gold 5515082*	59		1
5 May 07	**I AM A CIDER DRINKER 2007** *EMI Gold 3926532* FEATURING TONY BLACKBURN	57		1
6 Oct 07	**ONE FOR THE BRISTOL CITY** *CIA CIA004* BRISTOL CITY & THE WURZELS	66		1

WU-TANG CLAN
US, male rap/instrumental group – Genius/GZA* (Gary Crice), Ghostface Killah* (Dennis Coles), Inspectah Deck (Jason Hunter), Masta Killa (Elgin Turner), Method Man* (Clifford Smith), Ol' Dirty Bastard* (Russell Jones), d. 13 Nov 2004, Raekwon (Corey Woods) & U-God (Lamont Hawkins) — 21

Date	Title	Peak Position	Weeks at No.1	Weeks on Chart
16 Aug 97	**TRIUMPH** *Loud 74321510212* FEATURING CAPPADONNA	46		1
21 Mar 98	**SAY WHAT YOU WANT/INSANE** *Mercury MERCD 499* TEXAS FEATURING THE WU-TANG CLAN	4		7
25 Nov 00	**GRAVEL PIT** *Loud 6705182*	6		13

WWF SUPERSTARS

US/UK, male wrestlers/vocalists – Big Boss Man (Raymond Traylor), d. 22 Sep 2004, British Bulldog (David Smith), 'Hacksaw' Jim Duggan, Bret 'The Hitman' Hart, Nasty Boys (Brian Yandrisovitz & Jerome Saganovitch), Randy Savage (Randall Poffo), Tatanka (Christopher Chavis) & Undertaker (Mark Calaway)

Date	Title	Peak Position	Weeks at No.1	Weeks on Chart
				15
12 Dec 92	**SLAM JAM** *Arista 74321124887* ●	4		9
3 Apr 93	**WRESTLEMANIA** *Arista 74321136832*	14		5
10 Jul 93	**USA** *Arista 74321153092* FEATURING HACKSAW JIM DUGGAN	71		1

ROBERT WYATT

UK, male vocalist (Robert Wyatt-Ellidge)

Date	Title	Peak Position	Weeks at No.1	Weeks on Chart
				11
28 Sep 74	**I'M A BELIEVER** *Virgin VS 114*	29		5
7 May 83	**SHIPBUILDING** *Rough Trade RT 115*	35		6

MICHAEL WYCOFF

US, male vocalist

Date	Title	Peak Position	Weeks at No.1	Weeks on Chart
				2
23 Jul 83	**(DO YOU REALLY LOVE ME) TELL ME LOVE** *RCA 348*	60		2

PETE WYLIE

UK, male vocalist/guitarist. See Wah!

Date	Title	Peak Position	Weeks at No.1	Weeks on Chart
				18
3 May 86	**SINFUL** *Eternal MDM 7*	13		10
13 Sep 86	**DIAMOND GIRL** *Eternal MDM 12*	57		3
13 Apr 91	**SINFUL! (SCARY JIGGIN' WITH DOCTOR LOVE)** *Siren SRN 138* WITH THE FARM	28		5

BILL WYMAN

UK, male vocalist/bass guitarist (William Perks). See One World Project, Rolling Stones

Date	Title	Peak Position	Weeks at No.1	Weeks on Chart
				13
25 Jul 81	**(SI SI) JE SUIS UN ROCK STAR** *A&M AMS 8144*	14		9
20 Mar 82	**A NEW FASHION** *A&M AMS 8209*	37		4

TAMMY WYNETTE

US, female vocalist (Virginia Wynette Pugh), d. 6 Apr 1998 (age 55)

Date	Title	Peak Position	Weeks at No.1	Weeks on Chart
				35
26 Apr 75	**STAND BY YOUR MAN** *Epic EPC 7137* ●	1	3	12
28 Jun 75	**D.I.V.O.R.C.E.** *Epic EPC 3361*	12		7
12 Jun 76	**I DON'T WANNA PLAY HOUSE** *Epic EPC 4091*	37		4
7 Dec 91	**JUSTIFIED AND ANCIENT** *KLF Communications KLF099* KLF, GUEST VOCALS TAMMY WYNETTE ●	2		12

MARK WYNTER

UK, male vocalist/actor (Terence Lewis)

Date	Title	Peak Position	Weeks at No.1	Weeks on Chart
				80
25 Aug 60	**IMAGE OF A GIRL** *Decca F 11263*	11		10
10 Nov 60	**KICKING UP THE LEAVES** *Decca F 11279*	24		10
9 Mar 61	**DREAM GIRL** *Decca F 11323*	27		5
8 Jun 61	**EXCLUSIVELY YOURS** *Decca F 11354*	32		7
4 Oct 62	**VENUS IN BLUE JEANS** *Pye 7N 15466*	4		15
13 Dec 62	**GO AWAY LITTLE GIRL** *Pye 7N 15492*	6		11
6 Jun 63	**SHY GIRL** *Pye 7N 15525*	28		6
14 Nov 63	**IT'S ALMOST TOMORROW** *Pye 7N 15577*	12		12
9 Apr 64	**ONLY YOU (AND YOU ALONE)** *Pye 7N 15626*	38		4

MALCOLM X

US, male vocalist/political orator (Malcolm Little), d. 21 Feb 1965 (age 39)

Date	Title	Peak Position	Weeks at No.1	Weeks on Chart
				4
7 Apr 84	**NO SELL OUT** *Tommy Boy IS 165*	60		4

RICHARD X

UK, male DJ/producer (Richard Phillips)

Date	Title	Peak Position	Weeks at No.1	Weeks on Chart
				16
29 Mar 03	**BEING NOBODY** *Virgin RXCD1* VS LIBERTY X	3		11
23 Aug 03	**FINEST DREAMS** *Virgin RXCD 2* FEATURING KELIS	8		5

X FACTOR FINALISTS

UK, male/female charity vocalists – *X Factor* finalists from series 5 & 6, including Alexandra Burke*, JLS*, Eoghan Quigg, Diana Vickers & Laura White* ('Hero') & John & Edward (Jedward*), Joe McElderry*, Olly Murs & Stacey Solomon ('You Are Not Alone')

Date	Title	Peak Position	Weeks at No.1	Weeks on Chart
				19
8 Nov 08	**HERO** *Syco Music 88697407362* ⊛	1	3	12
28 Nov 09	**YOU ARE NOT ALONE** *Syco Music 88697622212*	1	1	7

XAVIER

US, male/female vocal/instrumental group

Date	Title	Peak Position	Weeks at No.1	Weeks on Chart
				3
20 Mar 82	**WORK THAT SUCKER TO DEATH/LOVE IS ON THE ONE** *Liberty UP 651*	53		3

XAVIER

US, male vocalist (Xavier Smith)

Date	Title	Peak Position	Weeks at No.1	Weeks on Chart
				3
27 Sep 97	**JUST GETS BETTER** *Multiply CDMULTY 25* TJR FEATURING XAVIER	28		2
27 Aug 05	**GIVE ME THE NIGHT** *Virgin TENCDX501*	65		1

X-ECUTIONERS FEATURING MIKE SHINODA AND MR HAHN OF LINKIN PARK

US, male rap/vocal/DJ/production group

Date	Title	Peak Position	Weeks at No.1	Weeks on Chart
				9
13 Apr 02	**IT'S GOIN' DOWN** *Epic 6725642*	7		9

XPANSIONS

UK, male producer (Richie Malone aka Richard Goldman)

Date	Title	Peak Position	Weeks at No.1	Weeks on Chart
				21
6 Oct 90	**ELEVATION** *Optimism 113683*	49		5
23 Feb 91	**MOVE YOUR BODY** *Arista 113683*	7		9
15 Jun 91	**WHAT YOU WANT** *Arista 114246* FEATURING DALE JOYNER	55		2
26 Aug 95	**MOVE YOUR BODY** *Arista 74321294982* 95	14		4
30 Nov 02	**ELEVATION (MOVE YOUR BODY) 2002** *RM RMRCD 10*	70		1

X-PRESS 2

UK, male production trio – Ashley Beedle, Darren House & Darren Rock

Date	Title	Peak Position	Weeks at No.1	Weeks on Chart
				27
5 Jun 93	**LONDON X-PRESS** *Junior Boy's Own JBO 12*	59		1
16 Oct 93	**SAY WHAT!** *Junior Boy's Own JBO 16CD*	32		2
30 Jul 94	**ROCK 2 HOUSE/ HIP HOUSIN'** *Junior Boy's Own JBO 21CD* FEATURING LO-PRO	55		2
9 Mar 96	**THE SOUND** *Junior Boy's Own JBO 36CD*	38		1
12 Oct 96	**TRANZ EURO XPRESS** *Junior Boy's Own JBO 42CD*	45		1
30 Sep 00	**AC/DC** *Skint 57*	60		1
28 Apr 01	**MUZIKIZUM** *Skint 65*	52		1
20 Oct 01	**SMOKE MACHINE** *Skint 69*	43		1
20 Apr 02	**LAZY** *Skint 74CD*	2		13
21 Sep 02	**I WANT YOU BACK** *Skint 81CD*	50		1
8 Oct 05	**GIVE IT** *Skint SKINT111CD* FEATURING KURT WAGNER	33		2
30 Sep 06	**KILL 100** *Skint SKINT124CD*	59		1

X-RAY SPEX

UK, male/female vocal/instrumental group

Date	Title	Peak Position	Weeks at No.1	Weeks on Chart
				33
29 Apr 78	**THE DAY THE WORLD TURNED DAY-GLO** *EMI International INT 553*	23		8
22 Jul 78	**IDENTITY** *EMI International INT 563*	24		10
4 Nov 78	**GERM FREE ADOLESCENCE** *EMI International INT 573*	19		11
21 Apr 79	**HIGHLY INFLAMMABLE** *EMI International INT 583*	45		4

XSCAPE

US, female vocal group

Date	Title	Peak Position	Weeks at No.1	Weeks on Chart
				15
20 Nov 93	**JUST KICKIN' IT** *Columbia 6598622*	49		2
5 Nov 94	**JUST KICKIN' IT** *Columbia 6608642*	54		2
7 Oct 95	**FEELS SO GOOD** *Columbia 6625022*	34		2
27 Jan 96	**WHO CAN I RUN TO** *Columbia 6628112*	31		3
29 Jun 96	**KEEP ON, KEEPIN' ON** *East West A 4287CD* MC LYTE FEATURING XSCAPE	39		2
19 Apr 97	**KEEP ON, KEEPIN' ON** *East West A 3950CD1* MC LYTE FEATURING XSCAPE	27		2
22 Aug 98	**THE ARMS OF THE ONE WHO LOVES YOU** *Columbia 6662522*	46		2

XSTASIA

UK, male/female vocal/production duo

Date	Title	Peak Position	Weeks at No.1	Weeks on Chart
				1
17 Mar 01	**SWEETNESS** *Liquid Asset ASSETCD 005*	65		1

X-STATIC

Italy, male/female vocal/instrumental group

Date	Title	Peak Position	Weeks at No.1	Weeks on Chart
				2
4 Feb 95	**I'M STANDING (HIGHER)** *Positiva CDTIV 25*	41		2

XTC

UK/Malta, male vocal/instrumental group – Andy Partridge, Terry Chambers, Dave Gregory & Colin Moulding — 70

Date	Title	Peak Position	Weeks at No.1	Weeks on Chart
12 May 79	**LIFE BEGINS AT THE HOP** *Virgin VS 259*	54		4
22 Sep 79	**MAKING PLANS FOR NIGEL** *Virgin VS 282*	17		11
6 Sep 80	**GENERALS AND MAJORS/DON'T LOSE YOUR TEMPER** *Virgin VS 365*	32		8
18 Oct 80	**TOWERS OF LONDON** *Virgin VS 372*	31		5
24 Jan 81	**SGT ROCK (IS GOING TO HELP ME)** *Virgin VS 384*	16		9
23 Jan 82	**SENSES WORKING OVERTIME** *Virgin VS 462*	10		9
27 Mar 82	**BALL AND CHAIN** *Virgin VS 482*	58		4
15 Oct 83	**LOVE ON A FARMBOY'S WAGES** *Virgin VS 613*	50		4
29 Sep 84	**ALL YOU PRETTY GIRLS** *Virgin VS 709*	55		5
28 Jan 89	**MAYOR OF SIMPLETON** *Virgin VS 1158*	46		5
4 Apr 92	**THE DISAPPOINTED** *Virgin VS 1404*	33		5
13 Jun 92	**THE BALLAD OF PETER PUMPKINHEAD** *Virgin VS 1415*	71		1

XTM & DJ CHUCKY PRESENTS ANNIA

Spain, male/female vocal/DJ/production group – Eva Marti & Toni & Xasqui Ten Martinez — 22

Date	Title	Peak Position	Weeks at No.1	Weeks on Chart
7 Jun 03	**FLY ON THE WINGS OF LOVE** *Serious SER 62CD*	8		19
2 Apr 05	**GIVE ME YOUR LOVE** *Wonderboy 9870368*	28		3

XZIBIT

US, male rapper/actor (Alvin Joiner IV) — 16

Date	Title	Peak Position	Weeks at No.1	Weeks on Chart
17 Mar 01	**X** *Epic 6709072* FEATURING SNOOP DOOG	14		7
16 Nov 02	**MULTIPLY** *Epic 6731552*	39		2
5 Feb 05	**HEY NOW (MEAN MUGGIN')** *Columbia 6756482*	9		7

BIOGRAPHIES

Biographies include the nationality and category for every chart entrant.

Each entrant has at least a mini biography. The acts with the most weeks on the chart (see page 372 for the chart) each have extended biographies.

Real names are included for all solo artists and, where applicable, dates of death and age of the artist at the time. "See..." links are included for soloists who also had singles chart entries in other acts.

The best known line-up is listed for every group that had a Top 10 single, with the vocalist/leader mentioned first and the others following in alphabetical order. In cases where later replacements had similar success both people are named and, where applicable, the dates of death are also shown for every group/duo member listed.

Certified Awards are given by the BPI to mark unit sales to retailers. They were introduced in April 1973. In January 1989 the levels of unit sales to the trade required to achieve each of the awards was amended to the following amounts:

Silver symbol	●	=	200,000 units
Gold symbol	●	=	400,000 units
Platinum symbol	⊛	=	600,000 units

As from February 2005, download sales also count towards certified awards.

Y–Z

KEY TO ARTIST ENTRIES

Artist/Group Name · Artist/Group Biography · Silver-selling ○ · Gold-selling ● · Platinum-selling ⊛ · US No.1 ★ · Peak Position · Weeks at No.1 · Weeks on Chart

Asterisks (*) indicate group members with hits in their own right that are listed elsewhere in this book

TAKE THAT

UK, male vocal group – Gary Barlow*, Howard Donald, Jason Orange, Mark Owen* & Robbie Williams* (left 1995, rejoined 2010). Comeback kings who have sold 7.4 million singles in the UK. The boys, who came back for good – as a quartet – in 2006, were the first act to score four successive No.1s since The Beatles – a feat they've achieved twice. See Helping Haiti

Artist's Total Weeks On Chart: 356

Date	Title	Label and Catalogue Number	Award	Peak Position	Weeks at No.1	Weeks on Chart
23 Nov 91	**PROMISES**	*RCA PB 45085*		38		2
8 Feb 92	**ONCE YOU'VE TASTED LOVE**	*RCA PB 45257*		47		3
6 Jun 92	**IT ONLY TAKES A MINUTE**	*RCA 74321101007*		7		8
15 Aug 92	**I FOUND HEAVEN**	*RCA 74321108137*		15		6
10 Oct 92	**A MILLION LOVE SONGS**	*RCA 74321116307*		7		9
12 Dec 92	**COULD IT BE MAGIC**	*RCA 74321123137*	○	3		12
20 Feb 93	**WHY CAN'T I WAKE UP WITH YOU**	*RCA 74321133102*	○	2		10
17 Jul 93	**PRAY**	*RCA 74321154502*	●	1	4	11
9 Oct 93	**RELIGHT MY FIRE** FEATURING LULU	*RCA 74321167722*	○	1	2	14
18 Dec 93	**BABE**	*RCA 74321182122*	⊛	1	1	10
9 Apr 94	**EVERYTHING CHANGES**	*RCA 74321167732*	○	1	2	10
9 Jul 94	**LOVE AIN'T HERE ANYMORE**	*RCA 74321214832*	○	3		12
15 Oct 94	**SURE**	*RCA 74321236622*	○	1	2	15
8 Apr 95	**BACK FOR GOOD**	*RCA 74321271462*	⊛	1	4	13
5 Aug 95	**NEVER FORGET**	*RCA 74321299572*	●	1	3	9
9 Mar 96	**HOW DEEP IS YOUR LOVE**	*RCA 74321355592*	⊛	1	3	14
25 Nov 06	**PATIENCE**	*Polydor 1714832*	●	1	4	39
10 Feb 07	**SHINE**	*Polydor 1724294*	●	1	2	42
30 Jun 07	**I'D WAIT FOR LIFE**	*Polydor 1736401*		17		2
27 Oct 07	**RULE THE WORLD**	*Polydor 1746285*	●	2		66
6 Dec 08	**GREATEST DAY**	*Polydor 1787445*		1	1	20
6 Dec 08	**PATIENCE**	*Polydor 1714832*		59		1
6 Dec 08	**NEVER FORGET**	*RCA GBARL9500200*		64		1
14 Feb 09	**UP ALL NIGHT**	*Polydor 1796964*		14		11
13 Jun 09	**SAID IT ALL**	*Polydor 2708717*		9		10
20 Jun 09	**RULE THE WORLD**	*Polydor 1746285*		57		6
27 Jun 09	**GREATEST DAY**	*Polydor 1787445*		73		1+

Date of entry into chart

Artist collaboration or variation on artist's name

Title of Single

Label and Catalogue Number

BPI Certified Award

A cross (+) indicates that the single was still on chart in the final week of March 2010

Silver-selling ○ Gold-selling ● Platinum-selling (x multiples) ⊛ US No.1 ★ — Peak Position / Weeks at No.1 / Weeks on Chart

Y?N-VEE
US, female vocal group — Weeks on Chart: 1

Date	Title / Label	Peak Position	Weeks at No.1	Weeks on Chart
17 Dec 94	**CHOCOLATE** *RAL RALCD 2*	65		1

Y&T
US, male vocal/instrumental group — Weeks on Chart: 4

Date	Title / Label	Peak Position	Weeks at No.1	Weeks on Chart
13 Aug 83	**MEAN STREAK** *A&M AM 135*	41		4

Y-TRAXX
Belgium, male producer (Frederique de Backer) — Weeks on Chart: 2

Date	Title / Label	Peak Position	Weeks at No.1	Weeks on Chart
24 May 97	**MYSTERY LAND (EP)** *ffrr FCD 292*	63		1
20 Sep 03	**MYSTERY LAND** *Nebula NEBT 047* FEATURING NEVE	70		1

Y-TRIBE FEATURING ELISABETH TROY
UK, male/female vocal/instrumental/production trio — Weeks on Chart: 3

Date	Title / Label	Peak Position	Weeks at No.1	Weeks on Chart
18 Dec 99	**ENOUGH IS ENOUGH** *Northwest 10 NORTHCD 002*	49		3

WEIRD AL YANKOVIC
US, male vocalist/comedian — Weeks on Chart: 8

Date	Title / Label	Peak Position	Weeks at No.1	Weeks on Chart
7 Apr 84	**EAT IT** *Scotti Brothers A 4257*	36		7
4 Jul 92	**SMELLS LIKE NIRVANA** *Scotti Brothers PO 219*	58		1

YARBROUGH & PEOPLES
US, male/female vocal/instrumental duo – Calvin Yarbrough & Alisa Peoples — Weeks on Chart: 20

Date	Title / Label	Peak Position	Weeks at No.1	Weeks on Chart
27 Dec 80	**DON'T STOP THE MUSIC** *Mercury MER 53* ○	7		12
5 May 84	**DON'T WASTE YOUR TIME** *Total Experience XE 501*	60		3
11 Jan 86	**GUILTY** *Total Experience FB 49905*	53		3
5 Jul 86	**I WOULDN'T LIE** *Total Experience FB 49841*	61		2

YARDBIRDS
UK, male vocal/instrumental group – Keith Relf*, d. 14 May 1976, Chris Dreja, Jim McCarty, Paul Samwell-Smith (replaced by Jimmy Page*), Anthony Topham (replaced by Eric Clapton*, then Jeff Beck*) — Weeks on Chart: 62

Date	Title / Label	Peak Position	Weeks at No.1	Weeks on Chart
12 Nov 64	**GOOD MORNING LITTLE SCHOOLGIRL** *Columbia DB 7391*	44		4
18 Mar 65	**FOR YOUR LOVE** *Columbia DB 7499*	3		12
17 Jun 65	**HEART FULL OF SOUL** *Columbia DB 7594*	2		13
14 Oct 65	**EVIL HEARTED YOU/STILL I'M SAD** *Columbia DB 7706*	3		10
3 Mar 66	**SHAPES OF THINGS** *Columbia DB 7848*	3		9
2 Jun 66	**OVER UNDER SIDEWAYS DOWN** *Columbia DB 7928*	10		9
27 Oct 66	**HAPPENINGS TEN YEARS TIME AGO** *Columbia DB 8024*	43		5

TONY YAYO FEATURING 50 CENT
US, male rap duo. See G-Unit — Weeks on Chart: 3

Date	Title / Label	Peak Position	Weeks at No.1	Weeks on Chart
24 Sep 05	**SO SEDUCTIVE** *Interscope 9884360*	28		3

YAZOO
UK, female/male vocal/instrumental duo – Alison Moyet* & Vince Clarke — Weeks on Chart: 55

Date	Title / Label	Peak Position	Weeks at No.1	Weeks on Chart
17 Apr 82	**ONLY YOU** *Mute 020* ○	2		14
17 Jul 82	**DON'T GO** *Mute YAZ 001* ○	3		11
20 Nov 82	**THE OTHER SIDE OF LOVE** *Mute YAZ 002*	13		9
21 May 83	**NOBODY'S DIARY** *Mute YAZ 003* ○	3		11
8 Dec 90	**SITUATION** *Mute YAZ 4*	14		8
4 Sep 99	**ONLY YOU** *Mute CDYAZ 5*	38		2

YAZZ
UK, female vocalist (Yasmin Evans) — Weeks on Chart: 69

Date	Title / Label	Peak Position	Weeks at No.1	Weeks on Chart
20 Feb 88	**DOCTORIN' THE HOUSE** *Ahead Of Our Time CCUT 2* COLDCUT FEATURING YAZZ & THE PLASTIC POPULATION	6		9
23 Jul 88	**THE ONLY WAY IS UP** *Big Life BLR 4* & THE PLASTIC POPULATION ●	1	5	15
29 Oct 88	**STAND UP FOR YOUR LOVE RIGHTS** *Big Life BLR 5* ○	2		12
4 Feb 89	**FINE TIME** *Big Life BLR 6*	9		8
29 Apr 89	**WHERE HAS ALL THE LOVE GONE** *Big Life BLR 8*	16		6
23 Jun 90	**TREAT ME GOOD** *Big Life BLR 24*	20		5
28 Mar 92	**ONE TRUE WOMAN** *Polydor PO 198*	60		2
31 Jul 93	**HOW LONG** *Polydor PZCD 252* & ASWAD	31		5
2 Apr 94	**HAVE MERCY** *Polydor PZCD 309*	42		3
9 Jul 94	**EVERYBODY'S GOT TO LEARN SOMETIME** *Polydor PZCD 316*	56		2
28 Sep 96	**GOOD THING GOING** *East West EW 062CD*	53		1
22 Mar 97	**NEVER CAN SAY GOODBYE** *East West EW 081CD*	61		1

YEAH YEAH YEAHS
US, male/female vocal/instrumental trio — Weeks on Chart: 16

Date	Title / Label	Peak Position	Weeks at No.1	Weeks on Chart
16 Nov 02	**MACHINE** *Wichita Recordings WEBB 036SCD*	37		2
26 Apr 03	**DATE WITH THE NIGHT** *Dress Up 0657442*	16		2
5 Jul 03	**PIN** *Dress Up 9808085*	29		2
4 Oct 03	**MAPS** *Dress Up 9811413*	26		2
13 Nov 04	**Y CONTROL** *Dress Up 9868816*	54		1
1 Apr 06	**GOLD LION** *Fiction 9877351*	18		3
1 Jul 06	**TURN INTO** *Fiction 1700277*	53		1
18 Apr 09	**ZERO** *Polydor 2702826*	49		3

YEAH YOU'S
UK, male vocal/instrumental group — Weeks on Chart: 2

Date	Title / Label	Peak Position	Weeks at No.1	Weeks on Chart
27 Jun 09	**15 MINUTES** *Island 2709161*	36		2

TRISHA YEARWOOD
US, female vocalist/actor (Patricia Yearwood) — Weeks on Chart: 1

Date	Title / Label	Peak Position	Weeks at No.1	Weeks on Chart
9 Aug 97	**HOW DO I LIVE** *MCA MCSTD 48064*	66		1

YELL!
UK, male vocal duo – Daniel James (Colin Heywood) & Paul Varney — Weeks on Chart: 8

Date	Title / Label	Peak Position	Weeks at No.1	Weeks on Chart
20 Jan 90	**INSTANT REPLAY** *Fanfare FAN 22*	10		8

YELLO
Switzerland, male vocal/production duo – Dieter Meier & Boris Blank (Hans Strickler) — Weeks on Chart: 42

Date	Title / Label	Peak Position	Weeks at No.1	Weeks on Chart
25 Jun 83	**I LOVE YOU** *Stiff BUY 176*	41		4
26 Nov 83	**LOST AGAIN** *Stiff BUY 191*	73		1
9 Aug 86	**GOLDRUSH** *Mercury MER 218*	54		3
22 Aug 87	**THE RHYTHM DIVINE** *Mercury MER 253* FEATURING SHIRLEY BASSEY	54		2
27 Aug 88	**THE RACE** *Mercury YELLO 1*	7		11
17 Dec 88	**TIED UP** *Mercury YELLO 2*	60		5
25 Mar 89	**OF COURSE I'M LYING** *Mercury YELLO 3*	23		8
22 Jul 89	**BLAZING SADDLES** *Mercury YELLO 4*	47		2
8 Jun 91	**RUBBERBANDMAN** *Mercury YELLO 5*	58		2
5 Sep 92	**JUNGLE BILL** *Mercury MER 376*	61		2
7 Nov 92	**THE RACE/BOSTICH** *Mercury MER 382*	55		1
15 Oct 94	**HOW HOW** *Mercury MERCD 414*	59		1

YELLOW DOG
US/UK, male vocal/instrumental group – Kenny Young, Herbie Armstrong, Gerry Conway, Jim Gannon, Gary Roberts & Gary Taylor — Weeks on Chart: 13

Date	Title / Label	Peak Position	Weeks at No.1	Weeks on Chart
4 Feb 78	**JUST ONE MORE NIGHT** *Virgin VS 195* ○	8		9
22 Jul 78	**WAIT UNTIL MIDNIGHT** *Virgin VS 217*	54		4

YELLOW MAGIC ORCHESTRA
Japan, male instrumental/production trio — Weeks on Chart: 11

Date	Title / Label	Peak Position	Weeks at No.1	Weeks on Chart
14 Jun 80	**COMPUTER GAME (THEME FROM 'THE INVADERS')** *A&M AMS 7502*	17		11

YELLOWCARD
US, male vocal/instrumental group — Weeks on Chart: 3

Date	Title / Label	Peak Position	Weeks at No.1	Weeks on Chart
12 Jun 04	**WAY AWAY** *Capitol CDCLS 855*	63		1
18 Sep 04	**OCEAN AVENUE** *Capitol CDCLS 860*	65		1
18 Mar 06	**LIGHTS AND SOUNDS** *Parlophone CDCLS875*	59		1

YEOVIL TOWN FC
UK, football fans/vocal group — Weeks on Chart: 1

Date	Title / Label	Peak Position	Weeks at No.1	Weeks on Chart
28 Feb 04	**YEOVIL TRUE** *Yeovil Town FC YEOVILTOWN188*	36		1

Silver-selling ● Gold-selling ● Platinum-selling (x multiples) US No.1 ★ Peak Position · Weeks at No.1 · Weeks on Chart

YES

UK, male vocal/instrumental group – Jon Anderson; members also included Peter Banks, Bill Bruford*, Geoff Downes, Trevor Horn, Steve Howe*, Tony Kaye, Patrick Moraz*, Chris Squire*, Rick Wakeman & Alan White

Date	Title	Peak Position	Weeks at No.1	Weeks on Chart (39)
17 Sep 77	**WONDEROUS STORIES** *Atlantic K 10999*	7		9
26 Nov 77	**GOING FOR THE ONE** *Atlantic K 11047*	24		4
9 Sep 78	**DON'T KILL THE WHALE** *Atlantic K 11184*	36		4
12 Nov 83	**OWNER OF A LONELY HEART** *Atco B 9817* ★	28		9
31 Mar 84	**LEAVE IT** *Atco B 9787*	56		4
3 Oct 87	**LOVE WILL FIND A WAY** *Atco B 9449*	73		1
28 May 05	**OWNER OF A LONELY HEART** *Data DATA92CDS* MAX GRAHAM VS YES	9		8

YETI

UK, male vocal/instrumental group

Date	Title	Peak Position	Weeks at No.1	Weeks on Chart (3)
9 Apr 05	**NEVER LOSE YOUR SENSE OF WONDER** *Moshi Moshi MOSHI17CD*	36		2
10 Sep 05	**KEEP PUSHIN' ON** *Moshi Moshi MOSHI23CD*	57		1

YIN & YAN

UK, male vocal duo

Date	Title	Peak Position	Weeks at No.1	Weeks on Chart (5)
29 Mar 75	**IF** *EMI 2282*	25		5

YING YANG TWINS

US, male rap duo

Date	Title	Peak Position	Weeks at No.1	Weeks on Chart (4)
17 Sep 05	**WAIT (THE WHISPER SONG)** *TVT TVTUKCD16*	47		2
18 Feb 06	**SHAKE** *TVT TVTUKCD0020* FEATURING PITBULL	49		2

DWIGHT YOAKAM

US, male vocalist/guitarist

Date	Title	Peak Position	Weeks at No.1	Weeks on Chart (2)
10 Jul 99	**CRAZY LITTLE THING CALLED LOVE** *Reprise W 497CD*	43		2

YOHANNA

Iceland (b. Denmark), female vocalist (Johanna Jonsdottir)

Date	Title	Peak Position	Weeks at No.1	Weeks on Chart (1)
30 May 09	**IS IT TRUE** *EMI ISV440900601*	49		1

YOMANDA

UK, male DJ/producer (Paul Masterson). See Candy Girls, Clergy, Dorothy, Hi-Gate, Sleazesisters

Date	Title	Peak Position	Weeks at No.1	Weeks on Chart (21)
24 Jul 99	**SYNTH & STRINGS** *1st Avenue FESCD 59*	8		10
11 Mar 00	**SUNSHINE** *1st Avenue FESCD 68*	16		6
2 Sep 00	**ON THE LEVEL** *Manifesto FESCD 73*	28		2
26 Jul 03	**YOU'RE FREE** *Incentive CENT 55CDS*	22		3

YORK

Germany, male instrumental/production duo – Jorg & Torsten Stenzel

Date	Title	Peak Position	Weeks at No.1	Weeks on Chart (21)
9 Oct 99	**THE AWAKENING** *Manifesto FESCD 60*	11		5
10 Jun 00	**ON THE BEACH** *Manifesto FESCD 70*	4		10
18 Nov 00	**FAREWELL TO THE MOON** *Manifesto FESCD 76*	37		2
27 Jan 01	**THE FIELDS OF LOVE** *Club Tools 0124095 CLU* ATB FEATURING YORK	16		4

THOM YORKE

UK, male vocalist/guitarist. See Radiohead

Date	Title	Peak Position	Weeks at No.1	Weeks on Chart (2)
2 Sep 06	**HARROWDOWN HILL** *XL Recordings XLS238CD*	23		2

YOSH PRESENTS LOVEDEEJAY AKEMI

Holland, male producer (Yoshida Rosenboom)

Date	Title	Peak Position	Weeks at No.1	Weeks on Chart (5)
29 Jul 95	**IT'S WHAT'S UPFRONT THAT COUNTS** *Limbo LIMB 46CD*	69		1
2 Dec 95	**IT'S WHAT'S UPFRONT THAT COUNTS (REMIX)** *Limbo LIMB 50CD*	31		2
20 Apr 96	**THE SCREAMER** *Limbo LIMB 54CD*	38		2

YOTHU YINDI

Australia, male/female vocal/instrumental group

Date	Title	Peak Position	Weeks at No.1	Weeks on Chart (1)
15 Feb 92	**TREATY** *Hollywood HWD 116*	72		1

YOU ME AT SIX

UK, male vocal/instrumental group

Date	Title	Peak Position	Weeks at No.1	Weeks on Chart (4)
6 Jun 09	**FINDERS KEEPERS** *Slam Dunk SLAMD007*	33		2
19 Sep 09	**KISS AND TELL** *Virgin VSCDT1996*	42		1
20 Feb 10	**UNDERDOG** *Virgin GBAAA0900856*	49		1

FARON YOUNG

US, male vocalist, d. 10 Dec 1996 (age 64)

Date	Title	Peak Position	Weeks at No.1	Weeks on Chart (23)
15 Jul 72	**IT'S FOUR IN THE MORNING** *Mercury 6052 140*	3		23

JIMMY YOUNG

UK, male vocalist/radio DJ

Date	Title	Peak Position	Weeks at No.1	Weeks on Chart (88)
9 Jan 53	**FAITH CAN MOVE MOUNTAINS** *Decca F 9986*	11		1
21 Aug 53	**ETERNALLY** *Decca F 10130*	8		9
6 May 55	**UNCHAINED MELODY** *Decca F 10502*	1	3	19
16 Sep 55	**THE MAN FROM LARAMIE** *Decca F 10597*	1	4	12
23 Dec 55	**SOMEONE ON YOUR MIND** *Decca F 10640*	13		5
16 Mar 56	**CHAIN GANG** *Decca F 10694*	9		6
8 Jun 56	**WAYWARD WIND** *Decca F 10736*	27		1
22 Jun 56	**RICH MAN POOR MAN** *Decca F 10736*	25		1
28 Sep 56	**MORE** *Decca F 10774*	4		17
3 May 57	**ROUND AND ROUND** *Decca F 10875* WITH THE MICHAEL SAMMES SINGERS	30		1
10 Oct 63	**MISS YOU** *Columbia DB 7119*	15		13
26 Mar 64	**UNCHAINED MELODY** *Columbia DB 7234* WITH THE MICHAEL SAMMES SINGERS	43		3

JOHN PAUL YOUNG

Australia, male vocalist

Date	Title	Peak Position	Weeks at No.1	Weeks on Chart (19)
29 Apr 78	**LOVE IS IN THE AIR** *Ariola ARO 117* ●	5		13
14 Nov 92	**LOVE IS IN THE AIR (REMIX)** *Columbia 6587697*	49		3
12 Jan 02	**LOVE IS IN THE AIR** *Positiva CDTIV 166* MILK & SUGAR/JOHN PAUL YOUNG	25		3

KAREN YOUNG

UK, female vocalist

Date	Title	Peak Position	Weeks at No.1	Weeks on Chart (21)
6 Sep 69	**NOBODY'S CHILD** *Major Minor MM 625*	6		21

KAREN YOUNG

US, female vocalist, d. 26 Jan 1991 (age 39)

Date	Title	Peak Position	Weeks at No.1	Weeks on Chart (9)
19 Aug 78	**HOT SHOT** *Atlantic K 11180*	34		7
24 Feb 79	**HOT SHOT** *Atlantic LV 8*	75		1
15 Nov 97	**HOT SHOT '97** *Distinctive DISNCD 37*	68		1

NEIL YOUNG

Canada, male vocalist/guitarist. See Crosby, Stills, Nash & Young

Date	Title	Peak Position	Weeks at No.1	Weeks on Chart (22)
11 Mar 72	**HEART OF GOLD** *Reprise K 14140* ★	10		11
6 Jan 79	**FOUR STRONG WINDS** *Reprise K 14493*	57		4
27 Feb 93	**HARVEST MOON** *Reprise W 0139CD*	36		3
17 Jul 93	**THE NEEDLE AND THE DAMAGE DONE** *Reprise W 0191CD*	75		1
30 Oct 93	**LONG MAY YOU RUN (LIVE)** *Reprise W 0207CD*	71		1
9 Apr 94	**PHILADELPHIA** *Reprise W 0242CD*	62		2

PAUL YOUNG

UK, male vocalist. See Q-Tips, Streetband

Date	Title	Peak Position	Weeks at No.1	Weeks on Chart (134)
18 Jun 83	**WHEREVER I LAY MY HAT (THAT'S MY HOME)** *CBS A 3371* ●	1	3	15
10 Sep 83	**COME BACK AND STAY** *CBS A 3636* ●	4		9
19 Nov 83	**LOVE OF THE COMMON PEOPLE** *CBS A 3585* ●	2		13
13 Oct 84	**I'M GONNA TEAR YOUR PLAYHOUSE DOWN** *CBS A 4786*	9		7
8 Dec 84	**EVERYTHING MUST CHANGE** *CBS A 4972* ● ★	9		11
9 Mar 85	**EVERY TIME YOU GO AWAY** *CBS A 6300* ●	4		11
22 Jun 85	**TOMB OF MEMORIES** *CBS A 6321*	16		8
4 Oct 86	**WONDERLAND** *CBS YOUNG 1*	24		5
29 Nov 86	**SOME PEOPLE** *CBS YOUNG 2*	56		3
7 Feb 87	**WHY DOES A MAN HAVE TO BE STRONG** *CBS YOUNG 3*	63		2
12 May 90	**SOFTLY WHISPERING I LOVE YOU** *CBS YOUNG 4*	21		6
7 Jul 90	**OH GIRL** *CBS YOUNG 5*	25		6
6 Oct 90	**HEAVEN CAN WAIT** *CBS YOUNG 6*	71		2
12 Jan 91	**CALLING YOU** *CBS YOUNG 7*	57		2
30 Mar 91	**SENZA UNA DONNA (WITHOUT A WOMAN)** *London LON 294* ZUCCHERO & PAUL YOUNG	4		12
10 Aug 91	**BOTH SIDES NOW** *MCA MCS 1546* CLANNAD & PAUL YOUNG	74		1
26 Oct 91	**DON'T DREAM IT'S OVER** *Columbia 6574117*	20		5

Silver-selling ● Gold-selling ● Platinum-selling (x multiples) ⊛ US No.1 ★ | Peak Position | Weeks at No.1 | Weeks on Chart

Date	Title / Label	Peak	Wks at No.1	Wks on Chart
25 Sep 93	**NOW I KNOW WHAT MADE OTIS BLUE** *Columbia 6596412*	14		7
27 Nov 93	**HOPE IN A HOPELESS WORLD** *Columbia 6598652*	42		3
23 Apr 94	**IT WILL BE YOU** *Columbia 6602812*	34		4
17 May 97	**I WISH YOU LOVE** *East West EW 100CD1*	33		2

RETTA YOUNG
US, female vocalist — 7

Date	Title / Label	Peak	Wks at No.1	Wks on Chart
24 May 75	**SENDING OUT AN S.O.S.** *All Platinum 6146 305*	28		7

WILL YOUNG
UK, male vocalist — 157

Date	Title / Label	Peak	Wks at No.1	Wks on Chart
9 Mar 02	**ANYTHING IS POSSIBLE/EVERGREEN** *S 74321926142* ⊛x3	1	3	16
8 Jun 02	**LIGHT MY FIRE** *S 74321943002* ●	1	2	20
5 Oct 02	**THE LONG AND WINDING ROAD/SUSPICIOUS MINDS** *S 74321965972* & GARETH GATES/GARETH GATES ●	1	2	18
30 Nov 02	**DON'T LET ME DOWN/YOU AND I** *S 74321981272* ●	2		13
6 Dec 03	**LEAVE RIGHT NOW** *S 82876578562* ●	1	2	18
27 Mar 04	**YOUR GAME** *S 82876603622*	3		9
17 Jul 04	**FRIDAY'S CHILD** *S 82876634152*	4		6
26 Nov 05	**SWITCH IT ON** *S 82876752292*	5		6
28 Jan 06	**ALL TIME LOVE** *Sony BMG 82876779602*	3		16
29 Apr 06	**WHO AM I** *Sony BMG 82876821792*	11		17
27 Sep 08	**CHANGES** *19/RCA 88697344452*	10		9
15 Nov 08	**GRACE** *RCA 88697419892*	33		7
14 Mar 09	**LET IT GO** *19/RCA 88697468662*	58		1
21 Nov 09	**HOPES & FEARS** *RCA GBCTA0900313*	65		1

Top 3 Best-Selling Singles

		Approximate Sales
1	ANYTHING IS POSSIBLE/EVERGREEN	1,790,000
2	LEAVE RIGHT NOW	550,000
3	LIGHT MY FIRE	370,000

YOUNG & COMPANY
US, male/female vocal/instrumental group — 12

Date	Title / Label	Peak	Wks at No.1	Wks on Chart
1 Nov 80	**I LIKE (WHAT YOU'RE DOING TO ME)** *Excalibur EXC 501*	20		12

YOUNG & MOODY BAND
UK, male vocal/instrumental duo — 4

Date	Title / Label	Peak	Wks at No.1	Wks on Chart
10 Oct 81	**DON'T DO THAT** *Bronze BRO 130*	63		4

YOUNG BLACK TEENAGERS
US, male rap group — 3

Date	Title / Label	Peak	Wks at No.1	Wks on Chart
9 Apr 94	**TAP THE BOTTLE** *MCA MCSTD 1967*	39		3

YOUNG BUCK
US, male rapper (David Brown). See G-Unit — 1

Date	Title / Label	Peak	Wks at No.1	Wks on Chart
23 Oct 04	**LET ME IN** *Interscope 9864517*	62		1

YOUNG DISCIPLES
UK/US, male/female vocal/instrumental trio — 17

Date	Title / Label	Peak	Wks at No.1	Wks on Chart
13 Oct 90	**GET YOURSELF TOGETHER** *Talkin Loud TLK 2*	68		1
23 Feb 91	**APPARENTLY NOTHIN'** *Talkin Loud TLK 5*	46		4
3 Aug 91	**APPARENTLY NOTHIN'** *Talkin Loud TLK 5*	13		7
5 Oct 91	**GET YOURSELF TOGETHER** *Talkin Loud TLK 15*	65		2
5 Sep 92	**YOUNG DISCIPLES (EP)** *Talkin Loud TLKX 18*	48		3

YOUNG HEART ATTACK
US, male/female vocal/instrumental group — 2

Date	Title / Label	Peak	Wks at No.1	Wks on Chart
10 Apr 04	**TOMMY SHOTS** *XL RecordingsXLS183CD*	54		1
17 Jul 04	**STARLITE** *XL Recordings XLS191CD*	69		1

YOUNG IDEA
UK, male vocal duo – Tony Cox & Douglas McRae-Brown — 6

Date	Title / Label	Peak	Wks at No.1	Wks on Chart
29 Jun 67	**WITH A LITTLE HELP FROM MY FRIENDS** *Columbia DB 8205*	10		6

YOUNG JEEZY
US, male rapper (Jay Jenkins) — 43

Date	Title / Label	Peak	Wks at No.1	Wks on Chart
4 Feb 06	**SOUL SURVIVOR** *Def Jam 9889047* FEATURING AKON	16		4
20 May 06	**SAY I** *Def Jam 9857779* CHRISTINA MILIAN FEATURING YOUNG JEEZY	4		11
5 Apr 08	**LOVE IN THIS CLUB** *LaFace 88697305772* USHER FEATURING YOUNG JEEZY ★	4		22
23 Jan 10	**HARD** *Def Jam USUM70912183* RIHANNA FEATURING JEEZY	42		6

YOUNG KNIVES
UK, male vocal/instrumental trio — 7

Date	Title / Label	Peak	Wks at No.1	Wks on Chart
11 Mar 06	**HERE COMES THE RUMOUR MILL** *Transgressive TRANS020CD*	36		1
1 Jul 06	**SHE'S ATTRACTED TO** *Transgressive TRANS031CD*	38		1
26 Aug 06	**WEEKENDS AND BLEAK DAYS (HOT SUMMER)** *Transgressive TRANS035CD*	35		2
11 Nov 06	**THE DECISION** *Transgressive TRANS042CD*	60		1
10 Nov 07	**TERRA FIRMA** *Transgressive TRANS056CD*	43		1
8 Mar 08	**UP ALL NIGHT** *Transgressive TRANS068CD*	45		1

YOUNG MC
US (b. UK), male rapper (Marvin Young) — 7

Date	Title / Label	Peak	Wks at No.1	Wks on Chart
15 Jul 89	**BUST A MOVE** *Delicious Vinyl BRW 137*	73		2
17 Feb 90	**PRINCIPAL'S OFFICE** *Delicious Vinyl BRW 161*	54		3
17 Aug 91	**THAT'S THE WAY LOVE GOES** *Capitol CL 623*	65		2

YOUNG MONEY FEATURING LLOYD
US, male rap/vocal group – Lil Wayne* (Dwayne Carter, Jr), Drake* (Aubrey Graham), Gudda Gudda (Carl Lilly), Jae Millz (Jarvis Mills), Nicki Minaj (Onika Maraj), Tyga (Michael Stevenson) & Lloyd* (Lloyd Polite, Jr) — 11

Date	Title / Label	Peak	Wks at No.1	Wks on Chart
30 Jan 10	**BEDROCK** *Cash Money USCM50901178*	9		11+

YOUNG OFFENDERS
Ireland, male vocal/instrumental group — 1

Date	Title / Label	Peak	Wks at No.1	Wks on Chart
7 Mar 98	**THAT'S WHY WE LOSE CONTROL** *Columbia 6651942*	60		1

YOUNG RASCALS
US, male vocal/instrumental group – Felix Cavaliere, Eddie Brigati, Gene Cornish & Dino Danelli — 17

Date	Title / Label	Peak	Wks at No.1	Wks on Chart
25 May 67	**GROOVIN'** *Atlantic 584 111* ★	8		13
16 Aug 67	**A GIRL LIKE YOU** *Atlantic 584 128*	37		4

YOUNG SOUL REBELS
UK/South Africa, male/female vocal group – Bashy (Ashley Thomas), V.V. Brown* (Vanessa Brown), Chipmunk* (Jahmaal Fyffe), Domino Go, Egypt, Frankmusik* (Vincent Frank, b. Vincent Turner), Matt Hazell, Ironik* (James Charters), Kid British, Pixie Lott* (Victoria Lott), McLean* (Anthony McLean), MPHO* (Mpho Skeef), N-Dubz*, Tinchy Stryder* (Kwasi Danquah), Ayak Thiik (b. Sudan) & London Community Gospel Choir. See Sal Solo — 5

Date	Title / Label	Peak	Wks at No.1	Wks on Chart
31 Oct 09	**I GOT SOUL** *Island GBUM70911405*	10		5

YOUNG STANLEY
UK, male builders/football fans/vocal/instrumental group — 1

Date	Title / Label	Peak	Wks at No.1	Wks on Chart
10 Jun 06	**SING IT FOR ENGLAND** *Young Stanley YSCD442*	58		1

SYDNEY YOUNGBLOOD
Germany (b. US), male vocalist (Sydney Ford) — 30

Date	Title / Label	Peak	Wks at No.1	Wks on Chart
26 Aug 89	**IF ONLY I COULD** *Circa YR 34* ●	3		13
9 Dec 89	**SIT AND WAIT** *Circa YR 40*	16		8
31 Mar 90	**I'D RATHER GO BLIND** *Circa YR 43*	44		5
29 Jun 91	**HOOKED ON YOU** *Circa YR 65*	72		2
20 Mar 93	**ANYTHING** *RCA 74321138672*	48		2

YOUNGER YOUNGER 28'S
UK, male/female vocal/instrumental group — 1

Date	Title / Label	Peak	Wks at No.1	Wks on Chart
5 Jun 99	**WE'RE GOING OUT** *V2 VVR 5006943*	61		1

Silver-selling ● Gold-selling ● Platinum-selling (x multiples) ⊛ US No.1 ★ Peak Position Weeks at No.1 Weeks on Chart

YOURCODENAMEIS:MILO
UK, male vocal/instrumental group

Date	Title	Peak Position	Weeks at No.1	Weeks on Chart
				2
16 Oct 04	**SCHTEEVE** *Fiction 9868526*	58		1
23 Apr 05	**17** *Fiction 9871093*	65		1

Z FACTOR
UK, male DJ/producer (Dave Lee). See Akabu featuring Linda Clifford, Hed Boys, Il Padrinos featuring Jocelyn Brown, Jakatta, Li Kwan, Joey Negro, Phase II

Date	Title	Peak Position	Weeks at No.1	Weeks on Chart
				2
21 Feb 98	**GOTTA KEEP PUSHIN'** *ffrr FCD 329*	47		1
17 Nov 01	**RIDE THE RHYTHM** *Direction 6718482*	52		1

Z2 VOCAL BY ALISON RIVERS
UK, male production duo. See Liquid State featuring Marcella Woods, Solar Stone

Date	Title	Peak Position	Weeks at No.1	Weeks on Chart
				1
26 Feb 00	**I WANT YOU** *Platipus PLATCD 67*	61		1

HELMUT ZACHARIAS
Germany, male violinist/orchestra leader, d. 28 Feb 2002 (age 82)

Date	Title	Peak Position	Weeks at No.1	Weeks on Chart
				11
29 Oct 64	**TOKYO MELODY** *Polydor YNH 52341*	9		11

PIA ZADORA
US, female vocalist/actor (Pia Schipani)

Date	Title	Peak Position	Weeks at No.1	Weeks on Chart
				6
27 Oct 84	**WHEN THE RAIN BEGINS TO FALL** *Arista ARIST 584* JERMAINE JACKSON & PIA ZADORA	68		2
12 Nov 88	**DANCE OUT OF MY HEAD** *Epic 6528867* PIA	65		4

ZAGER & EVANS
US, male vocalist/guitarists – Denny Zager & Rick Evans

Date	Title	Peak Position	Weeks at No.1	Weeks on Chart
				13
9 Aug 69	**IN THE YEAR 2525 (EXORDIUM AND TERMINUS)** *RCA 1860* ★	1	3	13

MICHAEL ZAGER BAND
US, male/female vocal/instrumental session group

Date	Title	Peak Position	Weeks at No.1	Weeks on Chart
				12
1 Apr 78	**LET'S ALL CHANT** *Private Stock PVT 143*	8		12

GHEORGHE ZAMFIR
Romania, male pan piper player

Date	Title	Peak Position	Weeks at No.1	Weeks on Chart
				9
21 Aug 76	**(LIGHT OF EXPERIENCE) DOINA DE JALE** *Epic EPC 4310*	4		9

TOMMY ZANG
US, male vocalist

Date	Title	Peak Position	Weeks at No.1	Weeks on Chart
				1
16 Feb 61	**HEY GOOD LOOKING** *Polydor NH 66957*	45		1

ZAPP
US, male vocal/instrumental group

Date	Title	Peak Position	Weeks at No.1	Weeks on Chart
				6
25 Jan 86	**IT DOESN'T REALLY MATTER** *Warner Brothers W 8879*	57		3
24 May 86	**COMPUTER LOVE (PART 1)** *Warner Brothers W 8805*	64		3

FRANCESCO ZAPPALA
Italy, male producer

Date	Title	Peak Position	Weeks at No.1	Weeks on Chart
				3
10 Aug 91	**WE GOTTA DO IT** *Fourth & Broadway BRW 225* DJ PROFESSOR FEATURING FRANCESCO ZAPPALA	57		2
2 May 92	**NO WAY OUT** *PWL Continental PWL 230*	69		1

LENA ZAVARONI
UK, female vocalist, d. 1 Oct 1999 (age 35)

Date	Title	Peak Position	Weeks at No.1	Weeks on Chart
				14
9 Feb 74	**MA HE'S MAKING EYES AT ME** *Philips 6006 367* ●	10		11
1 Jun 74	**PERSONALITY** *Philips 6006 391*	33		3

ZED BIAS
UK, male producer (Dave Jones)

Date	Title	Peak Position	Weeks at No.1	Weeks on Chart
				4
15 Jul 00	**NEIGHBOURHOOD** *Locked On LOX 122CD*	25		4

ZEE
UK, female vocalist (Lesley Cowling)

Date	Title	Peak Position	Weeks at No.1	Weeks on Chart
				4
6 Jul 96	**DREAMTIME** *Perfecto PERF 122CD*	31		2
22 Mar 97	**SAY MY NAME** *Perfecto PERF 135CD*	36		1
7 Feb 98	**BUTTERFLY** *Perfecto PERF 154CD1* TILT FEATURING ZEE	41		1

ZENA
UK, female vocalist (Zena McNally). See Honeyz

Date	Title	Peak Position	Weeks at No.1	Weeks on Chart
				2
19 Jul 03	**LET'S GET THIS PARTY STARTED** *Serious SER 69CD*	69		1
14 Aug 04	**BEEN AROUND THE WORLD** *Mercury 9867014* FEATURING VYBZ KARTEL	44		1

ZEPHYRS
UK, male vocal/instrumental group

Date	Title	Peak Position	Weeks at No.1	Weeks on Chart
				1
18 Mar 65	**SHE'S LOST YOU** *Columbia DB 7481*	48		1

ZERO B
UK, male producer (Peter Ryding)

Date	Title	Peak Position	Weeks at No.1	Weeks on Chart
				6
22 Feb 92	**THE EP** *ffrreedom TAB 102*	32		4
24 Jul 93	**RECONNECTION (EP)** *Internal LIECD 6*	54		2

ZERO VU FEATURING LORNA B
UK, male/female vocal/production group

Date	Title	Peak Position	Weeks at No.1	Weeks on Chart
				1
15 Mar 97	**FEELS SO GOOD** *Avex UK AVEXCD 53*	69		1

ZERO ZERO
UK, male production duo

Date	Title	Peak Position	Weeks at No.1	Weeks on Chart
				1
10 Aug 91	**ZEROXED** *Kickin KICK 9*	71		1

ZERO 7
UK, male production duo – Henry Binns & Sam Hardaker

Date	Title	Peak Position	Weeks at No.1	Weeks on Chart
				6
18 Aug 01	**DESTINY** *Ultimate Dilemma UDRCDS 043* FEATURING SIA & SOPHIE	30		3
17 Nov 01	**IN THE WAITING LINE** *Ultimate Dilemma UDRCDS 045*	47		1
30 Mar 02	**DISTRACTIONS** *Ultimate Dilemma UDRCDS 046*	45		1
29 May 04	**SOMERSAULT** *Ultimate Dilemma EW290CD* FEATURING SIA	56		1

ZHANE
US, female vocal duo

Date	Title	Peak Position	Weeks at No.1	Weeks on Chart
				18
11 Sep 93	**HEY MR DJ** *Epic 6596102*	26		5
19 Mar 94	**GROOVE THANG** *Motown TMGCD 1423*	34		3
20 Aug 94	**VIBE** *Motown TMGCD 1430*	67		1
25 Feb 95	**SHAME** *Jive JIVECD 372*	66		1
21 Sep 96	**IT'S A PARTY** *Elektra EKR 226CD* BUSTA RHYMES FEATURING ZHANE	23		2
8 Mar 97	**4 MORE** *Tommy Boy TBCD 7779A* DE LA SOUL FEATURING ZHANE	52		1
26 Apr 97	**REQUEST LINE** *Motown 8606452*	22		3
30 Aug 97	**CRUSH** *Motown 5716712*	44		1
11 Sep 99	**JAMBOREE** *Arista 74321692882* NAUGHTY BY NATURE FEATURING ZHANE	51		1

ZIG & ZAG
Planet Zog, male vocal/alien TV puppet duo – Zigmund & Zagnatius Zogly (Ciaran Morrison & Mick O'Hara b. Ireland)

Date	Title	Peak Position	Weeks at No.1	Weeks on Chart
				12
24 Dec 94	**THEM GIRLS THEM GIRLS** *RCA 74321251042*	5		9
1 Jul 95	**HANDS UP! HANDS UP!** *RCA 74321284392*	21		3

ZIMMERS
UK, male/female pensioners/vocal group

Date	Title	Peak Position	Weeks at No.1	Weeks on Chart
				2
9 Jun 07	**MY GENERATION** *Xphonics XPH006*	26		2

ZION TRAIN
UK, male/female vocal/instrumental group

Date	Title	Peak Position	Weeks at No.1	Weeks on Chart
				1
27 Jul 96	**RISE** *China WOKCD 2085*	61		1

ZODIAC MINDWARP & THE LOVE REACTION

UK, male vocal/instrumental group — Weeks on Chart: 11

Date	Title / Label	Peak Position	Weeks at No.1	Weeks on Chart
9 May 87	**PRIME MOVER** *Mercury ZOD 1*	18		6
14 Nov 87	**BACKSEAT EDUCATION** *Mercury ZOD 2*	49		3
2 Apr 88	**PLANET GIRL** *Mercury ZOD 3*	63		2

ZOE

UK, female vocalist (Zoe Pollock) — Weeks on Chart: 22

Date	Title / Label	Peak Position	Weeks at No.1	Weeks on Chart
10 Nov 90	**SUNSHINE ON A RAINY DAY** *M&G MAGS 6*	53		5
24 Aug 91	**SUNSHINE ON A RAINY DAY (REMIX)** *M&G MAGS 14* ●	4		11
2 Nov 91	**LIGHTNING** *M&G MAGS 18*	37		4
29 Feb 92	**HOLY DAYS** *M&G MAGS 21*	72		2

ZOMBIE NATION

Germany, male production duo – Emanuel 'Mooner' Gunther & Florian 'Splank' Senfter — Weeks on Chart: 16

Date	Title / Label	Peak Position	Weeks at No.1	Weeks on Chart
2 Sep 00	**KERNKRAFT 400 (IMPORT)** *TRANSK 002*	61		1
30 Sep 00	**KERNKRAFT 400** *Data 11CDS* ●	2		15

ROB ZOMBIE

US, male vocalist (Robert Cummings). See White Zombie — Weeks on Chart: 2

Date	Title / Label	Peak Position	Weeks at No.1	Weeks on Chart
26 Dec 98	**DRAGULA** *Geffen GFSTD 22367*	44		2

ZOMBIES

UK, male vocal/instrumental group — Weeks on Chart: 16

Date	Title / Label	Peak Position	Weeks at No.1	Weeks on Chart
13 Aug 64	**SHE'S NOT THERE** *Decca F 11940*	12		11
11 Feb 65	**TELL HER NO** *Decca F 12072*	42		5

ZOO EXPERIENCE FEATURING DESTRY

UK, male production/DJ duo & male vocalist (Destry Spigner) — Weeks on Chart: 1

Date	Title / Label	Peak Position	Weeks at No.1	Weeks on Chart
22 Aug 92	**LOVE'S GOTTA HOLD ON ME** *Cooltempo COOL 261*	66		1

ZUCCHERO

Italy, male vocalist/guitarist (Adelmo Fornaciari) — Weeks on Chart: 24

Date	Title / Label	Peak Position	Weeks at No.1	Weeks on Chart
30 Mar 91	**SENZA UNA DONNA (WITHOUT A WOMAN)** *London LON 294* & PAUL YOUNG	4		12
18 Jan 92	**DIAMANTE** *London LON 313* WITH RANDY CRAWFORD	44		7
24 Oct 92	**MISERERE** *London LON 329* WITH LUCIANO PAVAROTTI	15		5

ZUTONS

UK, male/female vocal/instrumental group – David McCabe, Boyan Chowdhury, Abi Harding, Paul Molloy, Sean Payne & Russell Pritchard — Weeks on Chart: 48

Date	Title / Label	Peak Position	Weeks at No.1	Weeks on Chart
31 Jan 04	**PRESSURE POINT** *Deltasonic DLTCDV016*	19		3
17 Apr 04	**YOU WILL YOU WON'T** *Must Destroy DARK03CD*	22		3
3 Jul 04	**REMEMBER ME** *Deltasonic DLTCD 2024*	39		2
30 Oct 04	**DON'T EVER THINK (TOO MUCH)** *Deltasonic DLTCD 2026*	15		3
25 Dec 04	**CONFUSION** *Deltasonic DLTCD 030*	37		2
15 Apr 06	**WHY WON'T YOU GIVE ME YOUR LOVE** *Deltasonic DLTCD2046*	9		8
24 Jun 06	**VALERIE** *Deltasonic DLTCD047*	9		19
30 Sep 06	**OH STACEY (LOOK WHAT YOU'VE DONE!)** *Deltasonic DLTCD053*	24		3
9 Dec 06	**IT'S THE LITTLE THINGS WE DO** *Deltasonic DLTCD2058*	47		1
31 May 08	**ALWAYS RIGHT BEHIND YOU** *Deltasonic DLTCD076*	26		4

Top 3 Best-Selling Singles

		Approximate Sales
1	VALERIE	160,000
2	WHY WON'T YOU GIVE ME YOUR LOVE	45,000
3	ALWAYS RIGHT BEHIND YOU	30,000

ZWAN

US, male vocal/instrumental group — Weeks on Chart: 3

Date	Title / Label	Peak Position	Weeks at No.1	Weeks on Chart
8 Mar 03	**HONESTLY** *Reprise W 600CD*	28		2
14 Jun 03	**LYRIC** *Reprise W 607CD*	44		1

ZZ TOP

US, male vocal/instrumental trio – Billy Gibbons, Frank Beard & Dusty Hill — Weeks on Chart: 94

Date	Title / Label	Peak Position	Weeks at No.1	Weeks on Chart
3 Sep 83	**GIMME ALL YOUR LOVIN'** *Warner Brothers W 9693*	61		3
26 Nov 83	**SHARP DRESSED MAN** *Warner Brothers W 9576*	53		3
31 Mar 84	**TV DINNERS** *Warner Brothers W 9334*	67		3
6 Oct 84	**GIMME ALL YOUR LOVIN'** *Warner Brothers W 9693*	10		15
15 Dec 84	**SHARP DRESSED MAN** *Warner Brothers W 9576*	22		10
23 Feb 85	**LEGS** *Warner Brothers W 9272*	16		7
13 Jul 85	**SUMMER HOLIDAY (EP)** *Warner Brothers W 8946*	51		5
19 Oct 85	**SLEEPING BAG** *Warner Brothers W 2001*	27		5
15 Feb 86	**STAGES** *Warner Brothers W 2002*	43		3
19 Apr 86	**ROUGH BOY** *Warner Brothers W 2003*	23		9
4 Oct 86	**VELCRO FLY** *Warner Brothers W 8650*	54		3
21 Jul 90	**DOUBLEBACK** *Warner Brothers W 9812*	29		6
13 Apr 91	**MY HEAD'S IN MISSISSIPPI** *Warner Brothers W 0009*	37		5
11 Apr 92	**VIVA LAS VEGAS** *Warner Brothers W 0098*	10		7
20 Jun 92	**ROUGH BOY** *Warner Brothers W 0111*	49		3
29 Jan 94	**PINCUSHION** *RCA 74321184732*	15		3
7 May 94	**BREAKAWAY** *RCA 74321192282*	60		1
29 Jun 96	**WHAT'S UP WITH THAT** *RCA 74321394822*	58		1
16 Oct 99	**GIMME ALL YOUR LOVIN' 2000** *Riverhorse RIVHCD 2* MARTAY FEATURING ZZ TOP	28		2

A BRIEF TIMELINE OF THE EP CHART

1954 – British EPs (or 'extended play') are released for the first time. In the US, EPs had not proven particularly successful. In the UK the format was popular amongst music buyers, falling as it did between the 45rpm single and the LP. The standard EP would include four tracks. Prior to the launch of the separate chart, EPs from artists such as Louis Armstrong, Lonnie Donegan, Elvis Presley, Anthony Newley and Cliff Richard sold in sufficient numbers to reach the Singles Chart.

1960 – A Top 10 EP Chart is launched in the trade paper Record Retailer on 12th March 1960. The film soundtrack 'Expresso Bongo' by Cliff Richard is the first No.1. The chart is extended to a Top 15 the following week and a Top 20 a week after that.

1966 – The popularity of EPs dwindles due to the growing success of albums in general and the success of budget albums, often reissues, in particular. The chart is reduced to a Top 10 in April.

1967 – The chart is discontinued in December, with 'The Beach Boys Hits' by the Beach Boys the final No.1.

1968 – 2001 – EPs continue to be released, but they now appear in either the Official Singles Chart or Album Chart depending on the chart rules. Over the years, the rules governing eligibility for the Official Charts have changed on various occasions. The number of tracks, playing time and dealer price (the price the retailer pays for the EP as opposed to the amount charged to the record buyer) are all factors that determine whether the EP qualifies for the Official Singles Chart or the Official Album Chart.

EP s

KEY TO EP ENTRIES

Weeks on Chart
Weeks at No.1
Peak Position

Artist's Total Weeks On Chart

BEATLES

Date	Title / Label and Catalogue Number	Peak	Wks at No.1	Wks on Chart (392)
20 Jul 63	**TWIST AND SHOUT** *Parlophone GEP 8882*	1	21	64
21 Sep 63	**THE BEATLES' HITS** *Parlophone GEP 8880*	1	3	43
9 Nov 63	**THE BEATLES (NO. 1)** *Parlophone GEP 8883*	2		29
8 Feb 64	**ALL MY LOVING** *Parlophone GEP 8891*	1	8	44
4 Jul 64	**LONG TALL SALLY** *Parlophone GEP 8913*	1	7	37
14 Nov 64	**EXTRACTS FROM THE FILM 'A HARD DAY'S NIGHT'** *Parlophone GEP 8920*	1	6	30
9 Jan 65	**EXTRACTS FROM THE ALBUM 'A HARD DAY'S NIGHT'** *Parlophone GEP 8924*	8		17
10 Apr 65	**BEATLES FOR SALE** *Parlophone GEP 8931*	1	6	47
12 Jun 65	**BEATLES FOR SALE (NO. 2)** *Parlophone GEP 8938*	5		24
11 Dec 65	**THE BEATLES' MILLION SELLERS** *Parlophone GEP 8946*	1	4	26
12 Mar 66	**YESTERDAY** *Parlophone GEP 8948*	1	8	13
16 Jul 66	**NOWHERE MAN** *Parlophone GEP 8952*	4		18

Date of entry into chart — Title of EP — Label and Catalogue Number

ALEXANDER BROTHERS

1

Date	Title	Peak Position	Weeks at No.1	Weeks on Chart
5 Mar 66	NOBODY'S CHILD *Pye NEP 24231*	20		1

ANIMALS

55

Date	Title	Peak Position	Weeks at No.1	Weeks on Chart
9 Jan 65	THE ANIMALS IS HERE *Columbia SEG 8374*	3		37
23 Oct 65	THE ANIMALS ARE BACK *Columbia SEG 8452*	8		14
17 Sep 66	ANIMAL TRACKS *Columbia SEG 8499*	7		4

RICHARD ANTHONY

11

Date	Title	Peak Position	Weeks at No.1	Weeks on Chart
2 May 64	RICHARD ANTHONY *Columbia SEG 8298*	18		1
11 Jul 64	WALKIN' ALONE *Columbia SEG 8319*	6		10

CHET ATKINS

1

Date	Title	Peak Position	Weeks at No.1	Weeks on Chart
21 Dec 63	GUITAR GENIUS *RCA Victor RCX 7118*	19		1

BACHELORS

98

Date	Title	Peak Position	Weeks at No.1	Weeks on Chart
14 Mar 64	BACHELORS VOLUME 2 *Decca DFE 8564*	7		30
21 Mar 64	BACHELORS *Decca DFE 8529*	5		22
9 May 64	BACHELORS' HITS *Decca DFE 8595*	1	2	32
8 Jan 66	BACHELORS' HITS VOLUME 2 *Decca DFE 8637*	9		14

JOAN BAEZ

97

Date	Title	Peak Position	Weeks at No.1	Weeks on Chart
17 Apr 65	DON'T THINK TWICE, IT'S ALRIGHT *Fontana TFE 18007*	10		23
17 Apr 65	SILVER DAGGER AND OTHER THINGS *Fontana TFE 18005*	3		33
26 Mar 66	WITH GOD ON OUR SIDE *Fontana TFE 18012*	1	1	36
2 Jul 66	A HARD RAIN'S GONNA FALL *Fontana TFE 18013*	7		5

KENNY BALL & HIS JAZZMEN

67

Date	Title	Peak Position	Weeks at No.1	Weeks on Chart
2 Dec 61	KENNY'S BIG FOUR *Pye NJE1080*	3		24
3 Mar 62	KENNY BALL'S HIT PARADE *Pye NJE1082*	5		43

CHRIS BARBER'S JAZZ BAND

1

Date	Title	Peak Position	Weeks at No.1	Weeks on Chart
25 Jun 60	BARBER'S BEST VOLUME 1 *Decca DFE 6382*	11		1

BAROCK AND ROLL ENSEMBLE

12

Date	Title	Peak Position	Weeks at No.1	Weeks on Chart
29 May 65	EINE KLEINE BEATLE MUSIC *HMV 7EG8887*	4		12

JOHN BARRY 7 + 4

25

Date	Title	Peak Position	Weeks at No.1	Weeks on Chart
25 Feb 61	THE JOHN BARRY SOUND *Columbia SEG 8069*	4		25

LIONEL BART

1

Date	Title	Peak Position	Weeks at No.1	Weeks on Chart
26 Mar 60	BART FOR BART'S SAKE *Decca DFE 6619*	20		1

SHIRLEY BASSEY

78

Date	Title	Peak Position	Weeks at No.1	Weeks on Chart
22 Oct 60	FABULOUS MISS BASSEY *Columbia SEG 8027*	5		15
21 Jan 61	AS LONG AS HE NEEDS ME *Columbia SEG 8063*	3		57
18 Feb 61	FABULOUS MISS BASSEY NO 2 *Columbia SEG 8068*	15		2
2 Dec 61	SHIRLEY NO 2 *Columbia SEG 8116*	15		3
28 Nov 64	DYNAMIC SHIRLEY BASSEY *Columbia SEG 8369*	15		1

BBC SYMPHONY ORCHESTRA

1

Date	Title	Peak Position	Weeks at No.1	Weeks on Chart
23 Mar 60	PLANET SUITE – MARS AND JUPITER *HMV 7ER 5122*	14		1

BEACH BOYS

108

Date	Title	Peak Position	Weeks at No.1	Weeks on Chart
29 Aug 64	FUN, FUN, FUN *Capitol EAP1 20603*	19		1
14 Nov 64	FOUR BY THE BEACH BOYS *Capitol EAP1 5267*	11		8
14 May 66	THE BEACH BOYS HITS *Capitol EAP1 20781*	1	32	82
12 Nov 66	GOD ONLY KNOWS *Capitol EAP6 2458*	3		17

BEATLES

392

Date	Title	Peak Position	Weeks at No.1	Weeks on Chart
20 Jul 63	TWIST AND SHOUT *Parlophone GEP 8882*	1	21	64
21 Sep 63	THE BEATLES' HITS *Parlophone GEP 8880*	1	3	43
9 Nov 63	THE BEATLES (NO. 1) *Parlophone GEP 8883*	2		29
8 Feb 64	ALL MY LOVING *Parlophone GEP 8891*	1	8	44
4 Jul 64	LONG TALL SALLY *Parlophone GEP 8913*	1	7	37
14 Nov 64	EXTRACTS FROM THE FILM 'A HARD DAY'S NIGHT' *Parlophone GEP 8920*	1	6	30
9 Jan 65	EXTRACTS FROM THE ALBUM 'A HARD DAY'S NIGHT' *Parlophone GEP 8924*	8		17
10 Apr 65	BEATLES FOR SALE *Parlophone GEP 8931*	1	6	47
12 Jun 65	BEATLES FOR SALE (NO. 2) *Parlophone GEP 8938*	5		24
11 Dec 65	THE BEATLES' MILLION SELLERS *Parlophone GEP 8946*	1	4	26
12 Mar 66	YESTERDAY *Parlophone GEP 8948*	1	8	13
16 Jul 66	NOWHERE MAN *Parlophone GEP 8952*	4		18

HARRY BELAFONTE

2

Date	Title	Peak Position	Weeks at No.1	Weeks on Chart
16 Apr 60	SCARLET RIBBONS *RCA RCX 1049*	18		1
9 Dec 61	BELAFONTE AT CHRISTMAS TIME *RCA RCX 163*	18		1

TONY BENNETT

72

Date	Title	Peak Position	Weeks at No.1	Weeks on Chart
4 Dec 65	WHEN JOANNA LOVED ME *CBS EP 6066*	5		19
21 May 66	TILL *CBS EP 6071*	7		6
7 Jan 67	THE BEST OF BENNETT *CBS EP 6151*	2		47

ELMER BERNSTEIN

1

Date	Title	Peak Position	Weeks at No.1	Weeks on Chart
12 Mar 60	STACCATO *Capitol EAP1 1287*	6		1

CHUCK BERRY

68

Date	Title	Peak Position	Weeks at No.1	Weeks on Chart
5 Oct 63	CHUCK BERRY *Pye International NEP 44011*	7		14
5 Oct 63	CHUCK AND BO *Pye International NEP 44009* & BO DIDDLEY	6		22
30 Nov 63	CHUCK AND BO VOLUME 2 *Pye International NEP 44012* & BO DIDDLEY	15		2
8 Feb 64	THE BEST OF CHUCK BERRY *Pye International NEP 44018*	5		25
15 Feb 64	CHUCK AND BO VOLUME 3 *Pye International NEP 44017* & BO DIDDLEY	12		5

DAVE BERRY

6

Date	Title	Peak Position	Weeks at No.1	Weeks on Chart
10 Jul 65	CAN I GET IT FROM YOU *Decca DFE 8625*	12		6

MIKE BERRY

4

Date	Title	Peak Position	Weeks at No.1	Weeks on Chart
31 Aug 63	A TRIBUTE TO BUDDY HOLLY *HMV 7EG8808*	17		4

BEVERLEY SISTERS

2

Date	Title	Peak Position	Weeks at No.1	Weeks on Chart
24 Dec 60	THE BEVS FOR CHRISTMAS *Decca DFE 6611*	11		2

BIG THREE

17

Date	Title	Peak Position	Weeks at No.1	Weeks on Chart
14 Dec 63	AT THE CAVERN *Decca DFE 8552*	6		17

MR ACKER BILK

134

Date	Title	Peak Position	Weeks at No.1	Weeks on Chart
12 Mar 60	ACKER'S AWAY *Columbia SEG 7940*	16		2
2 Apr 60	MR ACKER BILK REQUESTS VOLUME 2 *Pye NJE1072*	11		8
7 May 60	MR ACKER BILK MARCHES ON *Pye NJE1061*	12		2
11 Jun 60	MR ACKER BILK SINGS *Pye NJE1067*	15		1
5 Nov 60	SEVEN AGES OF ACKER *Columbia SEG 8029*	6		23
4 Mar 61	CLARINET JAMBOREE *Columbia SEG 8053* & TERRY LIGHTFOOT	19		1
18 Mar 61	SEVEN AGES OF ACKER VOLUME 2 *Columbia SEG 8076*	9		12
26 Aug 61	ACKER NO. 1 *Columbia SEG 8089*	6		5
13 Jan 62	ACKER NO. 2 *Columbia SEG 8102*	11		7
14 Apr 62	FOUR HITS AND A MISTER *Columbia SEG 8156*	2		56
29 Sep 62	BAND OF THIEVES *Columbia SEG 8178*	6		17

CILLA BLACK

	Peak Position	Weeks at No.1	Weeks on Chart
			29
25 Apr 64 ANYONE WHO HAD A HEART *Parlophone GEP 8901*	5		17
17 Oct 64 IT'S FOR YOU *Parlophone GEP 8916*	12		8
17 Sep 66 CILLA'S HITS *Parlophone GEP 8954*	6		4

BOOKER T & THE MG'S

	Peak Position	Weeks at No.1	Weeks on Chart
			1
27 Feb 65 R&B WITH BOOKER T VOL. 2 *Atlantic AET 6002*	19		1

PAT BOONE

	Peak Position	Weeks at No.1	Weeks on Chart
			5
12 Mar 60 JOURNEY TO THE CENTRE OF THE EARTH *London RED 1244*	8		5

VICTOR BORGE

	Peak Position	Weeks at No.1	Weeks on Chart
			2
7 Jan 61 PHONETIC PUNCTUATION *Philips BBE 12154*	15		2

WILFRED BRAMBELL AND HARRY H CORBETT

	Peak Position	Weeks at No.1	Weeks on Chart
			33
8 Jun 63 THE FACTS OF LIFE FROM STEPTOE AND SON *Pye NEP 24169*	4		28
21 Dec 63 THE WAGES OF SIN *Pye NEP 24180*	10		5

JOE BROWN

	Peak Position	Weeks at No.1	Weeks on Chart
			1
28 Sep 63 JOE BROWN HIT PARADE *Piccadilly NEP 34025*	20		1

DAVE BRUBECK

	Peak Position	Weeks at No.1	Weeks on Chart
			41
26 Mar 60 BRUBECK IN EUROPE *Fontana TFE 17196*	15		1
30 Sep 61 TAKE FIVE *Fontana TFE 17307*	4		40

BYRDS

	Peak Position	Weeks at No.1	Weeks on Chart
			5
19 Feb 66 THE TIMES THEY ARE A-CHANGIN' *CBS EP 6069*	15		4
15 Oct 66 EIGHT MILES HIGH *CBS EP 6077*	8		1

ED BYRNES

	Peak Position	Weeks at No.1	Weeks on Chart
			1
25 Mar 61 KOOKIE *Warner Brothers WEP 6010*	20		1

IAN CARMICHAEL

	Peak Position	Weeks at No.1	Weeks on Chart
			3
23 Dec 61 HOUSE AT POOH CORNER *HMV 7EG 117*	10		3

JOHNNY CASH

	Peak Position	Weeks at No.1	Weeks on Chart
			2
4 Jun 66 MEAN AS HELL – BALLADS FROM THE TRUE WEST *CBS EP 6073*	8		2

RAY CHARLES

	Peak Position	Weeks at No.1	Weeks on Chart
			41
12 Jan 63 I CAN'T STOP LOVING YOU *HMV 7EG 8781*	10		36
21 Sep 63 TAKE THESE CHAINS FROM MY HEART *HMV 7EG 8812*	16		5

CHUBBY CHECKER

	Peak Position	Weeks at No.1	Weeks on Chart
			46
17 Mar 62 KING OF THE TWIST *Columbia SEG 8155*	3		43
2 Feb 63 DANCING PARTY *Cameo Parkway CPE 550*	17		3

CHER

	Peak Position	Weeks at No.1	Weeks on Chart
			1
22 Oct 66 THE HITS OF CHER *Liberty LEP 4047*	10		1

MAURICE CHEVALIER & HAYLEY MILLS

	Peak Position	Weeks at No.1	Weeks on Chart
			1
9 Feb 63 IN SEARCH OF THE CASTAWAYS (OST) *Decca DFE 8512*	18		1

PETULA CLARK

	Peak Position	Weeks at No.1	Weeks on Chart
			31
15 Jul 61 THE SOUND OF MUSIC *Pye NEP 24138*	4		19
20 Feb 65 DOWNTOWN *Pye NEP 24206*	12		6
29 Apr 67 THIS IS MY SONG *Pye NEP 24279*	6		6

DAVE CLARK FIVE

	Peak Position	Weeks at No.1	Weeks on Chart
			35
18 Jan 64 THE DAVE CLARK FIVE *Columbia SEG 8289*	3		24
23 Jan 65 THE HITS OF THE DAVE CLARK FIVE *Columbia SEG 8381*	20		1
25 Sep 65 WILD WEEKEND *Columbia SEG 8447*	10		10

EDDIE COCHRAN

	Peak Position	Weeks at No.1	Weeks on Chart
			51
7 May 60 SOMETHIN' ELSE *London REV 1239*	6		11
18 Jun 60 C'MON EVERYBODY *London REV 1214*	2		38
16 Feb 63 NEVER TO BE FORGOTTEN *Liberty LEP 2052*	18		2

NAT 'KING' COLE

	Peak Position	Weeks at No.1	Weeks on Chart
			94
28 May 60 LOVE IS THE THING *Capitol EAP1 824*	2		23
15 Oct 60 UNFORGETTABLE *Capitol EAP 20053*	2		62
22 Apr 61 TENDERLY *Capitol EAP1 20108*	9		9

PERRY COMO

	Peak Position	Weeks at No.1	Weeks on Chart
			1
18 Jun 60 YOU'LL NEVER WALK ALONE *RCA RCX 1018*	20		1

RUSS CONWAY

	Peak Position	Weeks at No.1	Weeks on Chart
			25
9 Apr 60 TIME TO CELEBRATE NO 2 *Columbia SEG 7995*	17		3
13 Aug 60 ANOTHER SIX *Columbia SEG 7905*	12		5
29 Oct 60 ROCKING HORSE COWBOY *Columbia SEG 8028*	12		3
24 Dec 60 MORE PARTY POPS *Columbia SEG 7957*	7		8
29 Apr 61 MY CONCERTO FOR YOU NO. 2 *Columbia SEG 8079*	11		6

PETER COOK & DUDLEY MOORE

	Peak Position	Weeks at No.1	Weeks on Chart
			3
29 Jan 66 BY APPOINTMENT *Decca DFE 8644*	18		3

CRICKETS

	Peak Position	Weeks at No.1	Weeks on Chart
			6
18 Jun 60 FOUR MORE *Coral FEP 2000*	7		5
20 Jan 62 IT'S SO EASY *Coral FEP 2014*	18		1

BOBBY VEE & THE CRICKETS

	Peak Position	Weeks at No.1	Weeks on Chart
			16
20 Apr 63 JUST FOR FUN *Liberty LEP 2084*	1	1	16

BING CROSBY

	Peak Position	Weeks at No.1	Weeks on Chart
			6
3 Dec 60 MERRY CHRISTMAS PART 1 *Columbia OE 9069*	9		6

CRYSTALS

	Peak Position	Weeks at No.1	Weeks on Chart
			1
1 Feb 64 DA DOO RON RON *London REU 1381*	18		1

DAKOTAS

	Peak Position	Weeks at No.1	Weeks on Chart
			1
14 Dec 63 MEET THE DAKOTAS *Parlophone GEP 8888*	19		1

BOBBY DARIN

	Peak Position	Weeks at No.1	Weeks on Chart
			9
19 Mar 60 THAT'S ALL *London REK 1243*	6		9

SAMMY DAVIS, JR

	Peak Position	Weeks at No.1	Weeks on Chart
			3
30 Jul 60 STARRING SAMMY DAVIS, VOLUME 1 *Brunswick OE 9146*	20		1
31 Aug 63 SAMMY DAVIS, JR IMPERSONATING *Reprise R 30004*	18		2

SPENCER DAVIS GROUP
34

Date	Title	Peak Position	Weeks at No.1	Weeks on Chart
23 Oct 65	**YOU PUT THE HURT ON ME** *Fontana TE 17444*	4		27
21 May 66	**SITTIN' AND THINKIN'** *Fontana TE 17463*	3		7

DORIS DAY
6

Date	Title	Peak Position	Weeks at No.1	Weeks on Chart
19 Mar 60	**PILLOW TALK** *Philips BBE 429684*	11		6

DAVE DEE, DOZY, BEAKY, MICK & TICH
3

Date	Title	Peak Position	Weeks at No.1	Weeks on Chart
4 Mar 67	**LOOS OF ENGLAND** *Fontana TE 17488*	8		3

KARL DENVER
29

Date	Title	Peak Position	Weeks at No.1	Weeks on Chart
15 Sep 62	**BY A SLEEPY LAGOON** *Decca DFE 8501*	2		20
24 Nov 62	**KARL DENVER HITS** *Decca DFE 8504*	7		9

KEN DODD
19

Date	Title	Peak Position	Weeks at No.1	Weeks on Chart
22 Feb 64	**STILL** *Columbia SEG 8297*	18		1
25 Dec 65	**DODDY AND THE DIDDY MEN** *Columbia SEG 8466*	4		17
7 Jan 67	**DIDDYNESS** *Columbia SEG 8524*	8		1

LONNIE DONEGAN
8

Date	Title	Peak Position	Weeks at No.1	Weeks on Chart
1 Oct 60	**YANKEE DOODLE DONEGAN** *Pye Nixa NEP 24127*	8		8

DONOVAN
36

Date	Title	Peak Position	Weeks at No.1	Weeks on Chart
21 Aug 65	**THE UNIVERSAL SOLDIER** *Pye NEP24219*	1	8	30
5 Mar 66	**DONOVAN, VOLUME ONE** *Pye NEP24239*	12		6

VAL DOONICAN
44

Date	Title	Peak Position	Weeks at No.1	Weeks on Chart
20 Feb 65	**GREEN SHADES OF VAL DOONICAN** *Decca DFE 8608*	1	4	39
28 May 66	**DOONICAN'S IRISH STEW** *Decca DFE 8656*	4		5

LEE DORSEY
4

Date	Title	Peak Position	Weeks at No.1	Weeks on Chart
3 Sep 66	**YOU'RE BREAKIN' ME UP** *Stateside SE 1043*	7		4

BOB DYLAN
57

Date	Title	Peak Position	Weeks at No.1	Weeks on Chart
3 Jul 65	**BOB DYLAN** *CBS EP 6051*	3		41
19 Feb 66	**ONE TOO MANY MORNINGS** *CBS EP 6070*	8		8
15 Oct 66	**MR. TAMBOURINE MAN** *CBS EP 6078*	4		8

DUANE EDDY
37

Date	Title	Peak Position	Weeks at No.1	Weeks on Chart
30 Jul 60	**YEP!** *London REW 1217*	16		2
10 Dec 60	**TWANGY** *London REW 1257*	4		30
18 Feb 61	**BECAUSE THEY'RE YOUNG** *London REW 1252*	17		1
20 May 61	**THE LONELY ONE** *London REW 1216*	16		1
1 Jul 61	**PEPE** *London REW 1287*	10		3

TOMMY EDWARDS
1

Date	Title	Peak Position	Weeks at No.1	Weeks on Chart
16 Apr 60	**THE WAYS OF LOVE** *MGM EP 712*	15		1

BERN ELLIOTT & THE FENMEN
5

Date	Title	Peak Position	Weeks at No.1	Weeks on Chart
18 Jan 64	**BERN ELLIOTT AND THE FENMEN** *Decca DFE 8561*	10		5

IVOR EMMANUEL
5

Date	Title	Peak Position	Weeks at No.1	Weeks on Chart
21 Jan 61	**LAND OF SONG** *Delyse EDP 210*	13		5

EVERLY BROTHERS
13

Date	Title	Peak Position	Weeks at No.1	Weeks on Chart
7 May 60	**THE EVERLY BROTHERS – NO. 5** *London RE 1229*	7		6
23 Jul 60	**THE EVERLY BROTHERS** *London RE 1113*	15		1
23 Jul 60	**THE EVERLY BROTHERS – NO. 4** *London RE 1174*	8		5
9 Jun 62	**THE EVERLY BROTHERS – NO. 6** *London RE 16065*	20		1

ADAM FAITH
97

Date	Title	Peak Position	Weeks at No.1	Weeks on Chart
17 Sep 60	**ADAM'S HIT PARADE** *Parlophone GEP8811*	1	3	77
11 Mar 61	**ADAM NO. 1** *Parlophone GEP8824*	4		13
10 Jun 61	**ADAM NO. 3** *Parlophone GEP8831*	19		1
17 Mar 62	**ADAM FAITH NO. 1** *Parlophone GEP8851*	12		4
23 Mar 63	**ADAM'S LATEST HITS** *Parlophone GEP8877*	20		1
13 Mar 65	**A MESSAGE TO MARTHA – FROM ADAM** *Parlophone GEP8929*	17		1

MARIANNE FAITHFULL
19

Date	Title	Peak Position	Weeks at No.1	Weeks on Chart
19 Jun 65	**GO AWAY FROM MY WORLD** *Decca DFE 8624*	4		19

GEORGIE FAME
48

Date	Title	Peak Position	Weeks at No.1	Weeks on Chart
16 Jan 65	**RHYTHM AND BLUES AT THE FLAMINGO** *Columbia SEG 8382*	8		13
5 Jun 65	**FATS FOR FAME** *Columbia SEG 8406*	15		2
17 Dec 66	**GETAWAY** *Columbia SEG 8518*	7		7
10 Jun 67	**GEORGIE FAME** *CBS EP 6363*	2		26

CHRIS FARLOWE
13

Date	Title	Peak Position	Weeks at No.1	Weeks on Chart
15 Jan 66	**FARLOWE IN THE MIDNIGHT HOUR** *Immediate IMEP001*	6		13

JULIE FELIX
6

Date	Title	Peak Position	Weeks at No.1	Weeks on Chart
13 Aug 66	**SONGS FROM THE FROST REPORT** *Fontana TE 17494*	5		6

GRACIE FIELDS
1

Date	Title	Peak Position	Weeks at No.1	Weeks on Chart
26 Nov 60	**OUR GRACIE SINGS COMEDY SONGS** *HMV 7EG 8299*	16		1

ELLA FITZGERALD
7

Date	Title	Peak Position	Weeks at No.1	Weeks on Chart
11 Jun 60	**WITH A SONG IN MY HEART** *HMV 7EG 8503*	10		3
13 Aug 60	**MOODS OF ELLA** *HMV 7EG 8392*	17		1
27 Aug 60	**ELLA SINGS IRVING BERLIN** *HMV 7EG 8563*	17		3

WAYNE FONTANA & THE MINDBENDERS
20

Date	Title	Peak Position	Weeks at No.1	Weeks on Chart
12 Dec 64	**UM, UM, UM, UM, UM, UM** *Fontana TE17435*	7		19
15 May 65	**THE GAME OF LOVE** *Fontana TE147449*	19		1

EMILE FORD & THE CHECKMATES
23

Date	Title	Peak Position	Weeks at No.1	Weeks on Chart
9 Apr 60	**EMILE** *Pye NEP 24119*	1	3	23

FOUR PENNIES
15

Date	Title	Peak Position	Weeks at No.1	Weeks on Chart
1 Aug 64	**SPIN WITH THE PENNIES** *Philips BE 12562*	6		15

FOUR TOPS
97

Date	Title	Peak Position	Weeks at No.1	Weeks on Chart
29 Oct 66	**THE FOUR TOPS** *Tamla Motown TME 2012*	2		58
11 Mar 67	**FOUR TOPS HITS** *Tamla Motown TME 2018*	1	22	39

FOURMOST
5

Date	Title	Peak Position	Weeks at No.1	Weeks on Chart
29 Feb 64	**FOURMOST SOUND** *Parlophone GEP 8917*	15		5

CONNIE FRANCIS
17

Date	Title	Peak Position	Weeks at No.1	Weeks on Chart
7 Jan 61	**HEARTACHES** *MGM EP 677*	14		2
21 Jan 61	**FIRST LADY OF RECORD** *MGM EP 742*	7		15

FREDDIE & THE DREAMERS — 14

Date	Title	Peak Position	Weeks at No.1	Weeks on Chart
19 Oct 63	**IF YOU GOTTA MAKE A FOOL OF SOMEBODY** *Columbia SEG 8275*	8		11
8 Feb 64	**SONGS FROM THE FILM 'WHAT A CRAZY WORLD'** *Columbia SEG 8287*	15		2
4 Jul 64	**OVER YOU** *Columbia SEG 8323*	17		1

BILLY FURY — 75

Date	Title	Peak Position	Weeks at No.1	Weeks on Chart
9 Jun 62	**PLAY IT COOL** *Decca DFE 6708*	2		45
10 Nov 62	**BILLY FURY HITS** *Decca DFE 8505*	8		30

BILLY FURY & THE TORNADOS — 16

Date	Title	Peak Position	Weeks at No.1	Weeks on Chart
25 May 63	**BILLY FURY AND THE TORNADOS** *Decca DFE 8525*	2		16

JUDY GARLAND — 3

Date	Title	Peak Position	Weeks at No.1	Weeks on Chart
5 Dec 64	**MAGGIE MAY** *Capitol EAP 1 20630*	18		3

MARVIN GAYE — 8

Date	Title	Peak Position	Weeks at No.1	Weeks on Chart
15 Apr 67	**ORIGINALS FROM MARVIN GAYE** *Tamla Motown TME 2019*	3		8

GERRY & THE PACEMAKERS — 49

Date	Title	Peak Position	Weeks at No.1	Weeks on Chart
13 Jul 63	**HOW DO YOU LIKE IT?** *Columbia SEG 8257*	2		35
22 Feb 64	**YOU'LL NEVER WALK ALONE** *Columbia SEG 8295*	8		8
18 Apr 64	**I'M THE ONE** *Columbia SEG 8311*	11		5
10 Oct 64	**DON'T LET THE SUN CATCH YOU CRYING** *Columbia SEG 8346*	15		1

RON GRAINER ORCHESTRA — 1

Date	Title	Peak Position	Weeks at No.1	Weeks on Chart
20 Jan 62	**THEME MUSIC FROM 'INSPECTOR MAIGRET'** *Warner Brothers WEP 6012*	13		1

TONY HANCOCK — 39

Date	Title	Peak Position	Weeks at No.1	Weeks on Chart
12 May 62	**LITTLE PIECES OF HANCOCK** *Pye NEP 24146*	6		39

FRANCOISE HARDY — 23

Date	Title	Peak Position	Weeks at No.1	Weeks on Chart
4 Jul 64	**C'EST FAB** *Pye NEP 24188*	5		21
10 Oct 64	**C'EST FRANCOISE** *Pye NEP 24193*	18		2

JET HARRIS & TONY MEEHAN — 21

Date	Title	Peak Position	Weeks at No.1	Weeks on Chart
29 Jun 63	**JET AND TONY** *Decca DFE 8528*	3		21

ROLF HARRIS — 2

Date	Title	Peak Position	Weeks at No.1	Weeks on Chart
22 Oct 66	**ROLF HARRIS AND SHAMUS O'SHEAN THE LEPRACHAUN** *Columbia SEG 8508*	9		2

HEINZ — 9

Date	Title	Peak Position	Weeks at No.1	Weeks on Chart
1 Feb 64	**LIVE IT UP** *Decca DRE 8559*	12		9

HERMAN'S HERMITS — 42

Date	Title	Peak Position	Weeks at No.1	Weeks on Chart
30 Jan 65	**HERMANIA** *Columbia SEG 8380*	19		1
12 Jun 65	**MRS. BROWN YOU'VE GOT A LOVELY DAUGHTER** *Columbia SEG 8440*	3		21
25 Sep 65	**HERMAN'S HERMITS HITS** *Columbia SEG 8442*	10		10
27 Aug 66	**MUSIC FROM THE SOUNDTRACK 'HOLD ON'** *Columbia SEG 8503*	4		10

EDMUND HOCKRIDGE — 6

Date	Title	Peak Position	Weeks at No.1	Weeks on Chart
21 May 60	**MOST HAPPY FELLA** *Pye NEP 24122*	8		4
8 Apr 61	**THE MUSIC MAN** *Pye NEP 24135*	20		2

HOLLIES — 33

Date	Title	Peak Position	Weeks at No.1	Weeks on Chart
6 Jun 64	**THE HOLLIES** *Parlophone GEP 8909*	6		8
27 Jun 64	**JUST ONE LOOK** *Parlophone GEP 8911*	10		8
25 Sep 65	**I'M ALIVE** *Parlophone GEP 8142*	5		15
9 Jul 66	**I CAN'T LET GO** *Parlophone GEP 8951*	9		2

BUDDY HOLLY — 90

Date	Title	Peak Position	Weeks at No.1	Weeks on Chart
19 Mar 60	**THE LATE, GREAT BUDDY HOLLY** *Coral FEP 2044*	4		43
22 Jul 61	**RAVE ON** *Coral FE 2005*	9		22
26 Aug 61	**BUDDY HOLLY NO. 1** *Brunswick OE 9456*	18		2
2 Sep 61	**HEARTBEAT** *Coral FEP 2015*	13		6
17 Mar 62	**LISTEN TO ME** *Coral FEP 2002*	12		17

ROBERT HORTON — 8

Date	Title	Peak Position	Weeks at No.1	Weeks on Chart
12 Mar 60	**SUNDAY NIGHT AT THE LONDON PALLADIUM** *Pye NEP 24118*	7		8

HOWLIN' WOLF — 4

Date	Title	Peak Position	Weeks at No.1	Weeks on Chart
10 Oct 64	**TELL ME** *Pye International NEP 44032*	16		4

FRANK IFIELD — 103

Date	Title	Peak Position	Weeks at No.1	Weeks on Chart
8 Dec 62	**FRANK IFIELD'S HITS** *Columbia SEG 8211*	1	12	59
22 Jun 63	**MORE OF FRANK IFIELD'S HITS** *Columbia SEG 8254*	4		15
21 Sep 63	**JUST ONE MORE CHANCE** *Columbia SEG 8262*	5		13
12 Oct 63	**VIVA IFIELD** *Columbia SEG 8270*	11		11
25 Jan 64	**PLEASE** *Columbia SEG 8288*	18		3
18 Apr 64	**DON'T BLAME ME** *Columbia SEG 8300*	19		2

JAY & THE AMERICANS — 1

Date	Title	Peak Position	Weeks at No.1	Weeks on Chart
1 Oct 66	**LIVING WITH JAY AND THE AMERICANS** *United Artists UEP 1017*	10		1

PAUL JONES — 31

Date	Title	Peak Position	Weeks at No.1	Weeks on Chart
6 May 67	**PRIVILEGE** *HMV 7EG 8975*	1	3	31

TOM JONES — 28

Date	Title	Peak Position	Weeks at No.1	Weeks on Chart
10 Apr 65	**ON STAGE** *Decca DFE 8617*	3		28

EDEN KANE — 8

Date	Title	Peak Position	Weeks at No.1	Weeks on Chart
29 Sep 62	**HITS** *Decca DFE 8503*	12		8

JOHNNY KIDD & THE PIRATES — 7

Date	Title	Peak Position	Weeks at No.1	Weeks on Chart
14 Jan 61	**SHAKIN' ALL OVER** *HMV 7EG 8628*	11		7

KINKS — 79

Date	Title	Peak Position	Weeks at No.1	Weeks on Chart
12 Dec 64	**KINKSIZE SESSION** *Pye NEP2400*	1	1	22
30 Jan 65	**KINKSIZE HITS** *Pye NEP24203*	3		21
25 Sep 65	**KWYET KINKS** *Pye NEP24221*	1	7	32
23 Jul 66	**DEDICATED KINKS** *Pye NEP24258*	7		4

KATHY KIRBY — 10

Date	Title	Peak Position	Weeks at No.1	Weeks on Chart
28 Nov 64	**KATHY KIRBY VOLUME 2** *Decca DFE 8596*	20		1
6 Mar 65	**BBC TV'S SONG FOR EUROPE** *Decca DFE 8611*	9		9

EARTHA KITT — 1

Date	Title	Peak Position	Weeks at No.1	Weeks on Chart
1 Dec 62	**REVISITED** *London RER 1266*	18		1

BILLY J. KRAMER WITH THE DAKOTAS — 11

Date	Title	Peak Position	Weeks at No.1	Weeks on Chart
26 Oct 63	**THE BILLY J. KRAMER HITS** *Parlophone GEP8885*	8		11

FRANKIE LAINE — 12

Date	Title	Peak Position	Weeks at No.1	Weeks on Chart
22 Jul 61	**WESTERN FAVOURITES** *Philips BBE 12447*	7		12

MARIO LANZA — 30

Date	Title	Peak Position	Weeks at No.1	Weeks on Chart
16 Apr 60	**THE GREAT CARUSO** *RCA RCX 1046*	16		1
23 Apr 60	**THE STUDENT PRINCE** *Camden RCX 133*	8		27
24 Dec 60	**SINGS CHRISTMAS CAROLS** *RCA RCX 162*	10		2

BRENDA LEE — 11

Date	Title	Peak Position	Weeks at No.1	Weeks on Chart
10 Nov 62	**SPEAK TO ME GENTLY** *Brunswick OE 9488*	18		3
3 Aug 63	**ALL ALONE AM I** *Brunswick OE 9492*	8		8

JERRY LEE LEWIS — 11

Date	Title	Peak Position	Weeks at No.1	Weeks on Chart
6 Oct 62	**JERRY LEE LEWIS – NO. 4** *London RES 1296*	13		5
27 Oct 62	**JERRY LEE LEWIS – NO. 5** *London RES 1336*	14		6

JOHN LEYTON — 13

Date	Title	Peak Position	Weeks at No.1	Weeks on Chart
10 Mar 62	**JOHN LEYTON** *Top Rank JKP3016*	11		13

TERRY LIGHTFOOT'S NEW ORLEANS JAZZMEN — 1

Date	Title	Peak Position	Weeks at No.1	Weeks on Chart
4 Mar 61	**CLARINET JAMBOREE** *Columbia SEG 8053*	19		1

LONDON PHILHARMONIC ORCHESTRA — 15

Date	Title	Peak Position	Weeks at No.1	Weeks on Chart
9 May 64	**LAWRENCE OF ARABIA VOLUME 1** *Colpix PXE 300*	13		14
13 Mar 65	**LAWRENCE OF ARABIA VOLUME 2** *Colpix PXE 302*	18		1

TRINI LOPEZ — 11

Date	Title	Peak Position	Weeks at No.1	Weeks on Chart
7 Dec 63	**TRINI LOPEZ AT P.J.'S** *Reprise R 30013*	11		7
19 Sep 64	**AMERICA** *Reprise R 30014*	16		4

JOE LOSS & HIS ORCHESTRA — 4

Date	Title	Peak Position	Weeks at No.1	Weeks on Chart
16 Dec 61	**DANCING TIME FOR LATINS** *HMV 7EG 8587*	17		3
27 Jan 62	**LATIN STYLE** *HMV 7EG 8725*	19		1

LOVIN' SPOONFUL — 13

Date	Title	Peak Position	Weeks at No.1	Weeks on Chart
25 Jun 66	**DID YOU EVER HAVE TO MAKE UP YOUR MIND** *Kama Sutra KEP 300*	3		11
27 Aug 66	**JUG BAND MUSIC** *Kama Sutra KEP 301*	8		2

JEANETTE MacDONALD & NELSON EDDY — 1

Date	Title	Peak Position	Weeks at No.1	Weeks on Chart
23 Apr 60	**INDIAN LOVE CALL** *RCA RCX 1020*	12		1

KENNETH McKELLAR — 7

Date	Title	Peak Position	Weeks at No.1	Weeks on Chart
26 Mar 60	**KENNETH McKELLAR SINGS HANDEL** *Decca DFE 6663*	12		3
3 Sep 60	**HANDEL'S ARIAS** *Decca DFE 6623*	9		1
24 Sep 60	**KENNETH McKELLAR NO. 2** *Decca DFE 6394*	13		1
17 Dec 60	**ROAD TO THE ISLES** *Decca DFE 6575*	8		2

HENRY MANCINI — 10

Date	Title	Peak Position	Weeks at No.1	Weeks on Chart
18 Apr 64	**THE PINK PANTHER** *RCA Victor RCX 7136*	14		10

MANFRED MANN — 111

Date	Title	Peak Position	Weeks at No.1	Weeks on Chart
21 Nov 64	**GROOVIN' WITH MANFRED MANN** *HMV 7EG 8876*	3		18
12 Jun 65	**THE ONE IN THE MIDDLE** *HMV 7EG8908*	1	7	38
27 Nov 65	**NO LIVING WITHOUT LOVING** *HMV 7EG 8922*	1	7	24
16 Apr 66	**MACHINES** *HMV 7EG 8942*	1	1	13
11 Jun 66	**INSTRUMENTAL ASYLUM** *HMV 7EG 8949*	3		9
15 Oct 66	**AS WAS** *HMV 7EG 8962*	4		9

MANTOVANI & HIS ORCHESTRA — 70

Date	Title	Peak Position	Weeks at No.1	Weeks on Chart
12 Mar 60	**MANTOVANI'S BIG FOUR** *Decca DFE 6148*	6		31
2 Apr 60	**DREAMS OF OLWEN** *Decca DFE 6618*	17		4
1 Apr 61	**EXODUS AND OTHER THEMES** *Decca DFE 6671*	3		35

MARY MARTIN — 2

Date	Title	Peak Position	Weeks at No.1	Weeks on Chart
9 Apr 60	**SOUTH PACIFIC** *Philips BBE 12261*	20		2

WINK MARTINDALE — 12

Date	Title	Peak Position	Weeks at No.1	Weeks on Chart
13 Jul 63	**DECK OF CARDS** *London RED 1370*	11		12

MIREILLE MATHIEU — 6

Date	Title	Peak Position	Weeks at No.1	Weeks on Chart
12 Aug 67	**MIREILLE MATHIEU** *Fontana TE 17492*	9		6

JOHNNY MATHIS — 4

Date	Title	Peak Position	Weeks at No.1	Weeks on Chart
7 May 60	**MEET MISTER MATHIS** *Fontana TFE 17177*	18		1
15 Apr 61	**IT'S LOVE** *Fontana TFE 17319*	20		1
26 Aug 61	**FOUR HITS** *Fontana TFE 17275*	17		1
7 Oct 61	**FOUR SHOW HITS** *Fontana TFE 17317*	17		1

MERSEYBEATS — 37

Date	Title	Peak Position	Weeks at No.1	Weeks on Chart
21 Mar 64	**I THINK OF YOU** *Fontana TE17423*	8		12
11 Apr 64	**ON STAGE** *Fontana TE117422*	2		25

MIKI & GRIFF — 22

Date	Title	Peak Position	Weeks at No.1	Weeks on Chart
3 Sep 60	**THIS IS MIKI AND GRIFF** *Pye NEP 24116*	2		22

GEORGE MITCHELL MINSTRELS — 66

Date	Title	Peak Position	Weeks at No.1	Weeks on Chart
9 Dec 61	**CHRISTMAS WITH THE MINSTRELS** *HMV 7EG 8714*	4		10
23 Jun 62	**THE BLACK AND WHITE MINSTREL SHOW** *HMV 7EG 8724*	1	1	56

MOJOS — 3

Date	Title	Peak Position	Weeks at No.1	Weeks on Chart
17 Oct 64	**THE MOJOS** *Decca DFE 8591*	12		3

MATT MONRO — 7

Date	Title	Peak Position	Weeks at No.1	Weeks on Chart
29 Feb 64	**SONG FOR EUROPE** *Parlophone GEP 8898*	16		6
22 May 65	**SOMEWHERE** *Parlophone GEP 8932*	19		1

MOODY BLUES — 14

Date	Title	Peak Position	Weeks at No.1	Weeks on Chart
12 Jun 65	**THE MOODY BLUES** *Decca DFE 8622*	12		14

NEW CHRISTY MINSTRELS — 10

Date	Title	Peak Position	Weeks at No.1	Weeks on Chart
19 Mar 66	**THREE WHEELS ON MY WAGON** *CBS EP 6057*	5		10

BOB NEWHART — 65

Date	Title	Peak Position	Weeks at No.1	Weeks on Chart
10 Jun 61	**THE BUTTON-DOWN MIND OF BOB NEWHART VOLUME 1** *Warner Brothers WEP 6031*	2		64
20 Oct 62	**THE BUTTON-DOWN MIND STRIKES BACK** *Warner Brothers WEP 6042*	20		1

ANTHONY NEWLEY — 9

Date	Title	Peak Position	Weeks at No.1	Weeks on Chart
16 Apr 60	**TONY'S HITS** *Decca DFE 6629*	6		9

NINA & FREDERIK — 169

Date	Title	Peak Position	Weeks at No.1	Weeks on Chart
12 Mar 60	**NINA AND FREDERIK VOLUME 1** *Columbia SEG 7926*	2		115
2 Apr 60	**NINA AND FREDERIK NO. 1** *Pye Nixa NEP 44002*	13		2
23 Apr 60	**NINA AND FREDERIK NO. 2** *Pye Nixa NEP 44003*	8		7
11 Jun 60	**NINA AND FREDERIK VOLUME 2** *Columbia SEG 7997*	3		26

Date	Title	Peak Position	Weeks at No.1	Weeks on Chart
26 Nov 60	**NINA AND FREDERIK NO. 3** *Columbia SEG 8049*	8		7
18 Nov 61	**CHRISTMAS AT HOME WITH NINA AND FREDERIK** *Columbia SEG 8111*	2		9
15 Dec 62	**WHITE CHRISTMAS** *Columbia SEG 8215*	11		3

ROY ORBISON 101

Date	Title	Peak Position	Weeks at No.1	Weeks on Chart
1 Jun 63	**ONLY THE LONELY** *London REU 1274*	15		11
10 Aug 63	**IN DREAMS** *London REU 1373*	6		44
29 Aug 64	**IT'S OVER** *London REU 1435*	3		23
9 Jan 65	**OH PRETTY WOMAN** *London REU 1437*	9		15
27 Mar 65	**ROY ORBISON'S STAGE SHOW HITS** *London REU 1439*	10		8

PETER & GORDON 1

Date	Title	Peak Position	Weeks at No.1	Weeks on Chart
22 Aug 64	**JUST FOR YOU** *Columbia SEG 8337*	20		1

PETER, PAUL & MARY 99

Date	Title	Peak Position	Weeks at No.1	Weeks on Chart
30 Nov 63	**PETER, PAUL AND MARY** *Warner Brothers WEP 6114*	3		79
18 Apr 64	**MOVING** *Warner Brothers WEP 6119*	16		2
28 Nov 64	**BLOWIN' IN THE WIND** *Warner Brothers EP 55*	13		12
8 May 65	**IN THE WIND VOLUME 1** *Warner Brothers WEP 6135*	12		6

PINKY & PERKY 4

Date	Title	Peak Position	Weeks at No.1	Weeks on Chart
23 Dec 61	**CHRISTMAS WITH PINKY AND PERKY** *Columbia SEG 8122*	16		4

GENE PITNEY 26

Date	Title	Peak Position	Weeks at No.1	Weeks on Chart
29 Feb 64	**TWENTY FOUR HOURS FROM TULSA** *United Artists UEP 1001*	7		16
27 Feb 65	**THAT GIRL BELONGS TO YESTERDAY** *Stateside SE 1028*	13		7
9 Jul 66	**BACKSTAGE** *Stateside SE 1040*	6		3

ELVIS PRESLEY 366

Date	Title	Peak Position	Weeks at No.1	Weeks on Chart
12 Mar 60	**STRICTLY ELVIS** *RCA RCX 175*	1	5	64
19 Mar 60	**TOUCH OF GOLD** *RCA RCX 1045*	8		11
2 Apr 60	**TOUCH OF GOLD VOLUME 2** *RCA RCX 1048*	10		13
5 Nov 60	**SUCH A NIGHT** *RCA RCX 190*	4		62
26 Nov 60	**ELVIS SINGS CHRISTMAS SONGS** *RCA RCX 121*	16		5
26 Aug 61	**JAILHOUSE ROCK (OST)** *RCA RCX 106*	14		7
16 Sep 61	**PEACE IN THE VALLEY** *RCA RCX 101*	12		10
9 Jun 62	**FOLLOW THAT DREAM (OST)** *RCA RCX 211*	1	20	51
3 Nov 62	**KID GALAHAD (OST)** *RCA Victor RCX 7106*	1	18	44
18 Apr 64	**LOVE IN LAS VEGAS (OST)** *RCA Victor RCX 7141*	3		25
14 May 64	**ELVIS FOR YOU VOLUME 1** *RCA Victor RCX 7142*	11		6
20 Jun 64	**ELVIS FOR YOU VOLUME 2** *RCA Victor RCX 7143*	18		1
10 Jul 65	**TICKLE ME (OST)** *RCA Victor RCX 7173*	3		26
4 Sep 65	**TICKLE ME VOLUME 2 (OST)** *RCA Victor RCX 7174*	8		18
1 Jul 67	**EASY COME EASY GO (OST)** *RCA Victor RCX 7187*	1	3	23

PRETTY THINGS 37

Date	Title	Peak Position	Weeks at No.1	Weeks on Chart
12 Dec 64	**THE PRETTY THINGS** *Fontana TE 17434*	6		28
23 Oct 65	**RAININ' IN MY HEART** *Fontana TE 17442*	12		9

LOUIS PRIMA 2

Date	Title	Peak Position	Weeks at No.1	Weeks on Chart
25 Jun 60	**STRICTLY PRIMA** *Capitol EAP 1 1132*	12		2

PJ PROBY 11

Date	Title	Peak Position	Weeks at No.1	Weeks on Chart
9 Jan 65	**P.J. PROBY** *Liberty LEP 2192*	13		6
9 Oct 65	**SOMEWHERE** *Liberty LEP 2229*	19		5

JIM REEVES 79

Date	Title	Peak Position	Weeks at No.1	Weeks on Chart
1 Dec 62	**SONGS TO WARM THE HEART** *RCA RCX 173*	12		12
4 Apr 64	**WELCOME TO MY WORLD** *RCA Victor RCX 7119*	6		25
15 Aug 64	**FROM THE HEART VOLUME 1** *RCA Victor RCX 7131*	4		26
12 Sep 64	**SONGS TO WARM THE HEART VOLUME 2** *RCA Victor RCX 215*	9		10
26 Sep 64	**FROM THE HEART VOLUME 2** *RCA Victor RCX 7145*	14		1
3 Dec 66	**CHRISTMAS CARD FROM JIM REEVES** *RCA Victor RCX 7185*	3		5

CLIFF RICHARD 432

Date	Title	Peak Position	Weeks at No.1	Weeks on Chart
12 Mar 60	**CLIFF SINGS NO. 1** *Columbia SEG 7979* & THE SHADOWS	4		18
12 Mar 60	**EXPRESSO BONGO (OST)** *Columbia SEG 7971* & THE SHADOWS	1	2	28
19 Mar 60	**CLIFF SINGS NO. 2** *Columbia SEG 7987* & THE SHADOWS	3		36
4 Jun 60	**CLIFF SINGS NO. 3** *Columbia SEG 8005*	2		15
10 Dec 60	**CLIFF'S SILVER DISCS** *Columbia SEG 8050* & THE SHADOWS	1	3	57
11 Feb 61	**ME AND MY SHADOWS NO. 1** *Columbia SEG 8065* & THE SHADOWS	5		23
29 Apr 61	**ME AND MY SHADOWS NO. 2** *Columbia SEG 8071* & THE SHADOWS	8		4
29 Apr 61	**ME AND MY SHADOWS NO. 3** *Columbia SEG 8078* & THE SHADOWS	6		11
4 Nov 61	**LISTEN TO CLIFF NO. 1** *Columbia SEG 8105* & THE SHADOWS	17		2
18 Nov 61	**DREAM** *Columbia SEG 8119* & THE SHADOWS	3		51
10 Feb 62	**CLIFF'S HIT PARADE** *Columbia SEG 8133* & THE SHADOWS	4		42
14 Apr 62	**HITS FROM 'THE YOUNG ONES'** *Columbia SEG 8159* & THE SHADOWS	1	2	40
23 Jun 62	**CLIFF RICHARD NO. 2** *Columbia SEG 8203* & THE SHADOWS	19		2
18 May 63	**HOLIDAY CARNIVAL** *Columbia SEG 8246* & THE SHADOWS	1	3	22
15 Jun 63	**HITS FROM 'SUMMER HOLIDAY'** *Columbia SEG 8250* & THE SHADOWS	4		21
19 Oct 63	**CLIFF'S LUCKY LIPS** *Columbia SEG 8269* & THE SHADOWS	17		5
16 Nov 63	**LOVE SONGS** *Columbia SEG 8272*	4		15
30 May 64	**CLIFF SINGS 'DON'T TALK TO HIM'** *Columbia SEG 8299* & THE SHADOWS	15		1
15 Aug 64	**WONDERFUL LIFE** *Columbia SEG 8338* & THE SHADOWS	3		21
22 May 65	**CLIFF'S HITS FROM 'ALADDIN AND HIS WONDERFUL LAMP'** *Columbia SEG 8395* & THE SHADOWS	20		1
24 Jul 65	**LOOK INTO MY EYES, MARIA** *Columbia SEG 8405*	15		1
30 Oct 65	**TAKE FOUR** *Columbia SEG 8450* & THE SHADOWS	4		16

TEX RITTER 1

Date	Title	Peak Position	Weeks at No.1	Weeks on Chart
8 Dec 62	**DECK OF CARDS** *Capitol EAP 1323*	19		1

PADDY ROBERTS 90

Date	Title	Peak Position	Weeks at No.1	Weeks on Chart
12 Mar 60	**STRICTLY FOR GROWN UPS** *Decca DFE 6584*	1	19	66
30 Jul 60	**PADDY ROBERTS STRIKES AGAIN** *Decca DFE 6641*	1	2	24

ROLLING STONES 154

Date	Title	Peak Position	Weeks at No.1	Weeks on Chart
18 Jan 64	**THE ROLLING STONES** *Decca DFE 8560*	1	14	58
22 Aug 64	**FIVE BY FIVE** *Decca DFE 8590*	1	21	54
19 Jun 65	**GOT LIVE IF YOU WANT IT** *Decca DFE 8620*	1	2	42

SEARCHERS 106

Date	Title	Peak Position	Weeks at No.1	Weeks on Chart
21 Sep 63	**AIN'T GONNA KISS YOU** *Pye NEP24177*	1	4	24
14 Dec 63	**SWEETS FOR MY SWEET** *Pye NEP24183*	5		18
29 Feb 64	**HUNGRY FOR LOVE** *Pye NEP24184*	4		19
12 Dec 64	**SEARCHERS PLAY THE SYSTEM** *Pye NEP24201*	4		18
27 Mar 65	**WHEN YOU WALK IN THE ROOM** *Pye NEP24204*	12		2
8 May 65	**BUMBLE BEE** *Pye NEP24218*	1	2	17
25 Sep 65	**SEARCHERS '65** *Pye NEP24222*	15		8

HARRY SECOMBE 68

Date	Title	Peak Position	Weeks at No.1	Weeks on Chart
2 Apr 60	**SACRED SONGS** *Philips BBE 12300*	9		38
14 May 60	**LAND OF MY FATHERS** *Philips BBE 12207*	8		22
30 Jul 60	**AT YOUR REQUEST VOLUME 2** *Philips BBE 12237*	17		1
24 Dec 60	**SACRED SONGS VOLUME 2** *Philips BBE 12393*	15		4
5 May 62	**TAUBER FAVOURITES** *Philips BBE 12131*	18		1
28 Jul 62	**SHOW SOUVENIRS** *Philips BBE 12513*	18		2

PETE SEEGER 1

Date	Title	Peak Position	Weeks at No.1	Weeks on Chart
3 Oct 64	**IN CONCERT** *CBS AGG 32055*	18		1

SEEKERS 166

Date	Title	Peak Position	Weeks at No.1	Weeks on Chart
24 Jul 65	**THE SEEKERS** *Columbia SEG 8425*	1	3	50
16 Jul 66	**HITS FROM THE SEEKERS** *Columbia SEG 8496*	1	?	73
11 Feb 67	**MORNINGTOWN RIDE** *Columbia SEG 822*	1	1	43

PETER SELLERS 4

Date	Title	Peak Position	Weeks at No.1	Weeks on Chart
28 May 60	**THE BEST OF SELLERS** *Parlophone GEP 8770*	15		2
27 Aug 60	**THE BEST OF SELLERS NO. 2** *Parlophone GEP 8784*	8		2

SHADOWS — 462

Date	Title	Peak Position	Weeks at No.1	Weeks on Chart
21 Jan 61	**THE SHADOWS** *Columbia SEG 8061*	1	20	86
10 Jun 61	**THE SHADOWS TO THE FORE** *Columbia SEG 8094*	1	28	116
10 Feb 62	**SPOTLIGHT ON THE SHADOWS** *Columbia SEG 8135*	1	8	59
9 Jun 62	**THE SHADOWS NO. 2** *Columbia SEG 8148*	12		16
11 Aug 62	**THE SHADOWS NO. 3** *Columbia SEG 8166*	13		4
22 Sep 62	**THE WONDERFUL LAND OF THE SHADOWS** *Columbia SEG 8171*	6		34
13 Oct 62	**THE BOYS** *Columbia SEG 8193*	1	3	46
23 Feb 63	**OUT OF THE SHADOWS** *Columbia SEG 8218*	3		21
9 Mar 63	**DANCE ON WITH THE SHADOWS** *Columbia SEG 8233*	16		5
22 Jun 63	**OUT OF THE SHADOWS NO. 2** *Columbia SEG 8249*	20		1
21 Sep 63	**LOS SHADOWS** *Columbia SEG 8278*	4		18
12 Oct 63	**FOOT TAPPING WITH THE SHADOWS** *Columbia SEG 8268*	7		10
14 Dec 63	**SHINDIG WITH THE SHADOWS** *Columbia SEG 8286*	9		4
20 Jun 64	**THOSE BRILLIANT SHADOWS** *Columbia SEG 8321*	6		14
3 Oct 64	**DANCE WITH THE SHADOWS** *Columbia SEG8342*	20		1
24 Oct 64	**RHYTHM AND GREENS (OST)** *Columbia SEG 8362*	8		14
27 Mar 65	**THEMES FROM 'ALADDIN AND HIS WONDERFUL LAMP'** *Columbia SEG 8396*	14		2
5 Jun 65	**DANCE WITH THE SHADOWS NO. 3** *Columbia SEG 8408*	16		2
1 Oct 66	**THOSE TALENTED SHADOWS** *Columbia SEG 8500*	9		2
19 Nov 66	**THUNDERBIRDS ARE GO (OST)** *Columbia SEG 8510*	6		7

JIMMY SHAND & HIS BAND — 3

Date	Title	Peak Position	Weeks at No.1	Weeks on Chart
6 Jan 62	**DANCE WITH JIMMY SHAND NO. 2** *Parlophone GEP 8823*	15		3

DEL SHANNON — 22

Date	Title	Peak Position	Weeks at No.1	Weeks on Chart
27 Jan 62	**DEL SHANNON** *London RCX 1332*	14		2
30 Mar 63	**DEL SHANNON NO. 2** *London RCX 1346*	9		20

HELEN SHAPIRO — 97

Date	Title	Peak Position	Weeks at No.1	Weeks on Chart
25 Nov 61	**HELEN** *Columbia SEG 8128*	1	9	43
10 Feb 62	**HELEN'S HIT PARADSE** *Columbia SEG 8136*	1	4	41
13 Oct 62	**A TEENAGER SINGS THE BLUES** *Columbia SEG 8170*	15		5
6 Oct 62	**MORE HITS FROM HELEN** *Columbia SEG 8174*	12		8

SANDIE SHAW — 26

Date	Title	Peak Position	Weeks at No.1	Weeks on Chart
30 Jan 65	**(THERE'S) ALWAYS SOMETHING THERE TO REMIND ME** *Pye NEP24208*	9		12
22 Apr 67	**TELL THE BOYS** *Pye NEP24281*	4		14

SHIRLEY & LEE — 5

Date	Title	Peak Position	Weeks at No.1	Weeks on Chart
25 Jun 60	**SHIRLEY AND LEE** *Vogue VE 170145*	16		5

HARRY SIMEONE CHORALE — 7

Date	Title	Peak Position	Weeks at No.1	Weeks on Chart
9 Dec 61	**GOLDEN HITS OF THE HARRY SIMEONE CHORALE** *Ember EP 4504*	8		7

SIMON & GARFUNKEL — 11

Date	Title	Peak Position	Weeks at No.1	Weeks on Chart
18 Jun 66	**I AM A ROCK** *CBS EP 6074*	4		11

FRANK SINATRA — 53

Date	Title	Peak Position	Weeks at No.1	Weeks on Chart
26 Mar 60	**COME DANCE WITH ME NO. 1** *Capitol EAP 1 1609*	11		2
2 Apr 60	**THE SONG IS YOU** *Fontana TFE 17253*	19		1
16 Apr 60	**SONGS FOR SWINGIN' LOVERS NO. 1** *Capitol EAP 1 653*	20		1
23 Apr 60	**THE LADY IS A TRAMP** *Capitol EAP 1013*	7		19
9 Jul 60	**I'VE GOT A CRUSH ON YOU** *Fontana TFE 17254*	14		1
29 Oct 60	**COME FLY WITH ME (PART 4)** *Capitol EAP 4920*	10		4
26 Nov 60	**COME DANCE WITH ME NO. 2** *Capitol EAP 21069*	13		10
14 Jan 61	**ALL THE WAY** *Capitol EAP 21069*	6		15

ALLAN SMETHURST — 12

Date	Title	Peak Position	Weeks at No.1	Weeks on Chart
5 Jun 65	**THE SINGING POSTMAN** *Ralph Tuck BEV 152*	20		2
10 Dec 66	**FIRST DELIVERY** *Parlophone GEP 8956*	7		10

JIMMY SMITH — 1

Date	Title	Peak Position	Weeks at No.1	Weeks on Chart
23 Jul 66	**SWINGING WITH THE INCREDIBLE JIMMY SMITH** *Verve VEP 5022*	10		1

SPOTNICKS — 29

Date	Title	Peak Position	Weeks at No.1	Weeks on Chart
30 Mar 63	**ON THE AIR** *Oriole EP 7075*	2		27
19 Oct 63	**THE SPOTNICKS IN PARIS** *Oriole EP 7078*	17		2

DUSTY SPRINGFIELD — 51

Date	Title	Peak Position	Weeks at No.1	Weeks on Chart
28 Mar 64	**I ONLY WANT TO BE WITH YOU** *Philips BE 12560*	8		19
19 Sep 64	**DUSTY** *Philips BE 12564*	3		20
8 May 65	**DUSTY IN NEW YORK** *Philips BE 12572*	13		9
7 Aug 65	**MADEMOISELLE DUSTY** *Philips BE 12579*	17		3

TOMMY STEELE — 14

Date	Title	Peak Position	Weeks at No.1	Weeks on Chart
12 Mar 60	**TOMMY THE TOREADOR (OST)** *Decca DFE 6607*	4		14

ANDY STEWART — 54

Date	Title	Peak Position	Weeks at No.1	Weeks on Chart
17 Jun 61	**ANDY SINGS** *Top Rank JKP 3009*	3		48
27 Jan 62	**ANDY STEWART SINGS** *Top Rank JKP 3004*	12		6

BARBRA STREISAND — 14

Date	Title	Peak Position	Weeks at No.1	Weeks on Chart
15 Jan 66	**MY MAN** *CBS NEP 24221*	8		13
11 Jun 66	**EN FRANCAIS** *CBS EP 6048*	10		1

SUPREMES — 12

Date	Title	Peak Position	Weeks at No.1	Weeks on Chart
1 May 65	**THE SUPREMES HITS** *Tamla Motown TME 2008*	6		12

SWINGING BLUE JEANS — 8

Date	Title	Peak Position	Weeks at No.1	Weeks on Chart
18 Apr 64	**SHAKE WITH THE SWINGING BLUE JEANS** *HMV 7EG 8850*	13		8

SWINGLE SINGERS — 15

Date	Title	Peak Position	Weeks at No.1	Weeks on Chart
16 May 64	**JAZZ SEBASTIAN BACH** *Philips BE 12557*	11		14
1 May 65	**JAZZ SEBASTIAN BACH VOLUME 2** *Philips BE12558*	18		1

TEMPERANCE SEVEN — 57

Date	Title	Peak Position	Weeks at No.1	Weeks on Chart
13 May 61	**THE MUSICK** *Argo EAF 14*	2		21
23 Sep 61	**TEMPERANCE SEVEN** *Parlophone GEP 8840*	3		36

TEMPTATIONS — 3

Date	Title	Peak Position	Weeks at No.1	Weeks on Chart
3 Apr 65	**THE TEMPTATIONS** *Tamla Motown TME 2004*	18		1
18 Feb 67	**IT'S THE TEMPTATIONS** *Tamla Motown TME 2010*	8		2

THEM — 18

Date	Title	Peak Position	Weeks at No.1	Weeks on Chart
20 Mar 65	**THEM** *Decca DFE 8612*	5		18

TORNADOS — 88

Date	Title	Peak Position	Weeks at No.1	Weeks on Chart
15 Dec 62	**THE SOUND OF THE TORNADOS** *Decca DFE 8510*	2		26
2 Feb 63	**TELSTAR** *Decca DFE 8511*	4		22
13 Apr 63	**MORE SOUNDS FROM THE TORNADOS** *Decca DFE 8521*	8		11
25 May 63	**BILLY FURY AND THE TORNADOS** *Decca DFE 8525* BILLY FURY & THE TORNADOS	2		16
17 Aug 63	**TORNADO ROCK** *Decca DFE 8533*	7		13

TOTTENHAM HOTSPUR FA CUP SQUAD — 3

Date	Title	Peak Position	Weeks at No.1	Weeks on Chart
10 Jun 67	**SPURS GO MARCHING ON** *Columbia SEG 8532*	6		3

Peak Position | Weeks at No.1 | Weeks on Chart

TROGGS — 4

Date	Title	Peak Position	Weeks at No.1	Weeks on Chart
25 Mar 67	**TROGGS TOPS** *Page One POE001*	8		4

UNIT FOUR PLUS TWO — 5

Date	Title	Peak Position	Weeks at No.1	Weeks on Chart
5 Jun 65	**UNIT FOUR PLUS TWO** *Decca DFE 8619*	11		5

PAUL VAN KEMPEN — 20

Date	Title	Peak Position	Weeks at No.1	Weeks on Chart
19 Mar 60	**1812 OVERTURE** *Philips ABE 10054*	11		20

SARAH VAUGHAN — 2

Date	Title	Peak Position	Weeks at No.1	Weeks on Chart
26 Mar 60	**SMOOTH SARAH** *Mercury ZEP 10054*	11		2

BOBBY VEE — 47

Date	Title	Peak Position	Weeks at No.1	Weeks on Chart
26 Aug 61	**BOBBY VEE NO. 1** *London REG 1278*	19		1
22 Dec 62	**SINCERELY** *Liberty LEP 2053*	8		24
20 Apr 63	**JUST FOR FUN** *Liberty LEP 2084* & THE CRICKETS	1	1	16
29 Jun 63	**A FOREVER KIND OF LOVE** *Liberty LEP 2089*	14		4
5 Oct 63	**BOBBY VEE'S BIGGEST HITS** *Stateside LEP 2102*	16		2

VENTURES — 1

Date	Title	Peak Position	Weeks at No.1	Weeks on Chart
13 May 61	**THE VENTURES** *London REG 1279*	20		1

GENE VINCENT — 1

Date	Title	Peak Position	Weeks at No.1	Weeks on Chart
6 Oct 62	**RACE WITH THE DEVIL** *Capitol EAP 1 20354*	19		1

WALKER BROTHERS — 32

Date	Title	Peak Position	Weeks at No.1	Weeks on Chart
18 Jun 66	**I NEED YOU** *Philips BE 12596*	1	13	25
10 Dec 66	**SOLO JOHN – SOLO SCOTT** *Philips BE 12597*	4		7

FATS WALLER — 2

Date	Title	Peak Position	Weeks at No.1	Weeks on Chart
3 Sep 60	**FATS WALLER** *RCA RCX 1053*	14		2

DIONNE WARWICK — 10

Date	Title	Peak Position	Weeks at No.1	Weeks on Chart
15 Aug 64	**IT'S LOVE THAT REALLY COUNTS** *Pye International NEP 44024X*	18		1
3 Oct 64	**DON'T MAKE ME OVER** *Pye International NEP 44026*	13		9

GENO WASHINGTON & THE RAM JAM BAND — 3

Date	Title	Peak Position	Weeks at No.1	Weeks on Chart
4 Feb 67	**HI!** *Pye NEP 34054*	7		3

DAVID WHITFIELD — 3

Date	Title	Peak Position	Weeks at No.1	Weeks on Chart
24 Jun 61	**ROSE MARIE (SELECTION)** *Decca DFE 6669*	15		2
28 Apr 62	**EXCERPTS FROM THE DESERT SONG** *Decca DFE 6707*	16		1

WHO — 20

Date	Title	Peak Position	Weeks at No.1	Weeks on Chart
26 Nov 66	**READY STEADY WHO** *Reaction 592001*	1	5	20

ARTHUR WILKINSON ORCHESTRA — 14

Date	Title	Peak Position	Weeks at No.1	Weeks on Chart
8 Jan 66	**BEATLE CRACKER MUSIC** *HMV 7EG 8919*	7		14

ANDY WILLIAMS — 55

Date	Title	Peak Position	Weeks at No.1	Weeks on Chart
7 Aug 65	**ANDY WILLIAMS FAVOURITES** *CBS EP 6054*	3		38
4 Dec 65	**ANDY WILLIAMS FAVOURITES VOLUME 2** *CBS EP 6055*	17		2
14 Jan 67	**ANDY'S NEWEST HITS** *CBS EP 6172*	6		15

YARDBIRDS — 33

Date	Title	Peak Position	Weeks at No.1	Weeks on Chart
28 Aug 65	**FIVE YARDBIRDS** *Columbia SEG 8421*	5		33

ANONYMOUS COVER VERSIONS — 22

Date	Title	Peak Position	Weeks at No.1	Weeks on Chart
27 Apr 63	**TOP TEN RECORD NO 3** *Aral TPS 503*	15		6
23 Nov 63	**TOP TEN RECORD NO 7** *Aral TPS 507*	16		3
15 Feb 64	**TOP TEN RECORD NO 9** *Aral TPS 509*	17		2
21 Mar 64	**TOP TEN RECORD CLUB** *Aral TPS 510*	17		1
22 Feb 64	**TOP SIX** *Top Six SIX 1*	10		4
21 Mar 64	**TOP SIX VOLUME 2** *Top Six SIX 2*	10		4
11 Apr 64	**TOP SIX VOLUME 3** *Top Six SIX 3*	16		2

ORIGINAL FILM SOUNDTRACKS — 150

Date	Title	Peak Position	Weeks at No.1	Weeks on Chart
14 May 60	**CAROUSEL NO. 1** *Capitol EAP 1 694*	12		11
6 Aug 60	**SOUTH PACIFIC NO. 1** *RCA RCX 181*	1	10	86
6 Aug 60	**SEVEN BRIDES FOR SEVEN BROTHERS** *MGM EP 513*	9		15
1 Oct 60	**THE KING AND I** *Capitol EAP 3 740*	12		5
17 Jun 61	**NEVER ON SUNDAY** *London RET 1280*	8		11
1 Jul 61	**SEVEN BRIDES FOR SEVEN BROTHERS VOLUME 2** *MGM EP 514*	18		1
25 Aug 62	**SOME PEOPLE** *Pye NEP 24158*	2		21

ORIGINAL BROADWAY STAGE CAST SOUNDTRACKS — 37

Date	Title	Peak Position	Weeks at No.1	Weeks on Chart
10 Sep 60	**MY FAIR LADY NO. 4** *Philips BBE 12254*	20		2
14 Oct 61	**THE SOUND OF MUSIC** *Philips BBE 12463*	13		4
19 May 62	**WEST SIDE STORY** *Philips BBE 12243*	5		26
26 Jan 63	**WEST SIDE STORY** *CBS EP 5604*	15		5

ORIGINAL LONDON STAGE CAST SOUNDTRACKS — 24

Date	Title	Peak Position	Weeks at No.1	Weeks on Chart
21 May 60	**SALAD DAYS** *Oriole MG 20004*	19		1
4 Jun 60	**FOLLOW THAT GIRL** *Oriole EP 7030*	19		1
18 Nov 61	**OLIVER** *Decca DFE 6680*	5		21
21 Apr 62	**THE SOUND OF MUSIC** *HMV 7EG 8733*	19		1

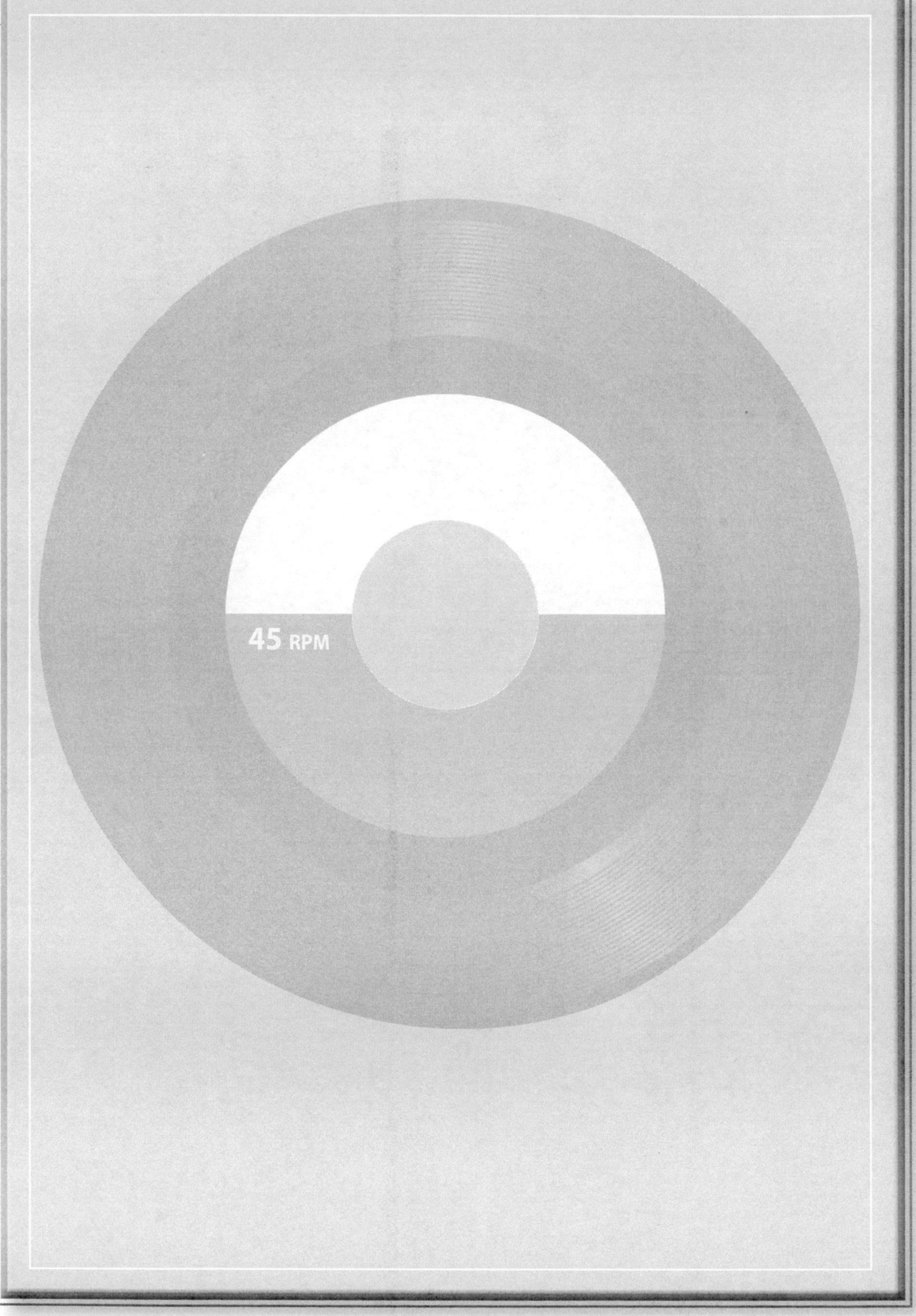
45 RPM

Singles Index

45 RPM

KEY TO INDEX ENTRIES

Album Title | Artist/Group | Peak Position | Year of Release

	Peak Position	Year of Release
A BA NI BI IZHAR COHEN & ALPHABETA	20	1978
'A' BOMB IN WARDOUR STREET JAM	1	1978
A9 ARIEL	28	2000
THE A TEAM MIKE POST	45	1984
A&E GOLDFRAPP	10	2008
AAAH D YAAA GOATS	53	1993
AARON'S PARTY (COME GET IT) AARON CARTER	51	2000
ABACAB GENESIS	9	1981
ABACUS (WHEN I FALL IN LOVE) AXUS	62	1998
ABANDON [A] DARE	71	1989
ABANDON [B] THAT PETROL EMOTION	73	1990
ABANDON SHIP BLAGGERS I.T.A.	48	1994
ABBA-ESQUE EP ERASURE	1	1992
THE ABBEY ROAD EP SPIRITUALIZED	39	1998
ABC JACKSON 5	8	1970

Title	Artist	Peak Position	Year of Release
()	SIGUR ROS	72	2003
21 GUNS	GREEN DAY	36	2009

A

Title	Artist	Peak Position	Year of Release
A BA NI BI	IZHAR COHEN & ALPHABETA	20	1978
'A' BOMB IN WARDOUR STREET	JAM	1	1978
A9	ARIEL	28	2000
THE A TEAM	MIKE POST	45	1984
A&E	GOLDFRAPP	10	2008
AAAH D YAAA	GOATS	53	1993
AARON'S PARTY (COME GET IT)	AARON CARTER	51	2000
ABACAB	GENESIS	9	1981
ABACUS (WHEN I FALL IN LOVE)	AXUS	62	1998
ABANDON [A]	DARE	71	1989
ABANDON [B]	THAT PETROL EMOTION	73	1990
ABANDON SHIP	BLAGGERS I.T.A.	48	1994
ABBA-ESQUE EP	ERASURE	1	1992
THE ABBEY ROAD EP	SPIRITUALIZED	39	1998
ABC	JACKSON 5	8	1970
ABC AND D...	BLUE BAMBOO	23	1994
A.B.C. (FALLING IN LOVE'S NOT EASY)	DIRECT DRIVE	75	1985
ABIDE WITH ME	INSPIRATIONAL CHOIR	36	1984
ABIDE WITH ME	VIC REEVES	47	1991
ABOUT A GIRL	SUGABABES	8	2009
ABOUT LOVE	ROY DAVIS, JR	70	2004
ABOUT 3AM	DARK STAR	50	1999
ABOUT YOU NOW	SUGABABES	1	2007
ABOUT YOUR DRESS	MACCABEES	33	2007
ABOVE THE CLOUDS	PAUL WELLER	47	1992
ABRACADABRA	STEVE MILLER BAND	2	1982
ABRAHAM MARTIN AND JOHN	MARVIN GAYE	9	1970
ABSENT FRIENDS	DIVINE COMEDY	38	2004
ABSOLUTE	SCRITTI POLITTI	17	1984
ABSOLUT(E)	CLAUDIA BRUCKEN	71	1990
ABSOLUTE AFFIRMATION	RADIO 4	61	2004
ABSOLUTE BEGINNERS [A]	JAM	4	1981
ABSOLUTE BEGINNERS [B]	DAVID BOWIE	2	1986
ABSOLUTE E-SENSUAL	JAKI GRAHAM	69	1995
ABSOLUTE REALITY	ALARM	35	1985
ABSOLUTELY EVERYBODY	VANESSA AMOROSI	7	2000
ABSOLUTELY FABULOUS	ABSOLUTELY FABULOUS	6	1994
ABSTAIN	FIVE THIRTY	75	1990
ABSURD	FLUKE	25	1997
ABUSE ME	SILVERCHAIR	40	1997
AC/DC	X-PRESS 2	60	2000
ACAPULCO 1922	KENNY BALL & HIS JAZZMEN	27	1963
ACCELERATE	SKIN UP	45	1992
ACCELERATOR	PRIMAL SCREAM	34	2000
ACCEPTABLE IN THE 80S	CALVIN HARRIS	10	2007
ACCESS	DJ MISJAH & DJ TIM	16	1996
ACCIDENT OF BIRTH	BRUCE DICKINSON	54	1997
ACCIDENT PRONE	STATUS QUO	36	1978
ACCIDENT WAITING TO HAPPEN (EP)	BILLY BRAGG	33	1992
ACCIDENTLY IN LOVE	COUNTING CROWS	28	2004
ACCIDENTS	THUNDERCLAP NEWMAN	46	1970
ACCIDENTS WILL HAPPEN	ELVIS COSTELLO	28	1979
ACE OF SPADES	MOTORHEAD	15	1980
ACES HIGH	IRON MAIDEN	20	1984
ACHILLES HEEL	TOPLOADER	8	2000
ACHY BREAKY HEART	BILLY RAY CYRUS	3	1992
ACHY BREAKY HEART	ALVIN & THE CHIPMUNKS FEATURING BILLY RAY CYRUS	53	1992
ACID LAB	ALEX REECE	64	1996
ACID MAN	JOLLY ROGER	23	1988
ACID TRAK	DILLINJA	71	2004
ACKEE 1-2-3	BEAT	54	1983
THE ACOUSTICS (EP)	NEW MODEL ARMY	49	1985
ACPERIENCE	HARDFLOOR	60	1997
ACROBATS (LOOKING FOR BALANCE)	MOONY	64	2003
ACROSS YER OCEAN	MERCURY REV	54	2005
ACRYLIC	COURTEENERS	44	2007
ACT OF WAR	ELTON JOHN & MILLIE JACKSON	32	1985
ACTION [A]	SWEET	15	1975
ACTION [A]	DEF LEPPARD	14	1994
ACTION [B]	SAINT ETIENNE	41	2002
ACTION AND DRAMA	BIS	50	1999
ACTIV 8 (COME WITH ME)	ALTERN 8	3	1991
ACTIVATED	GERALD ALSTON	73	1989
ACTUALLY IT'S DARKNESS	IDLEWILD	23	2000
ADAGIO FOR STRINGS	TIESTO	37	2005
ADDAMS FAMILY (WHOOMP!)	TAG TEAM	53	1994
ADDAMS GROOVE	HAMMER	4	1991
ADDICTED [A]	SIMPLE PLAN	63	2003
ADDICTED [B]	ENRIQUE IGLESIAS	11	2003
ADDICTED TO BASS	PURETONE	2	2002
ADDICTED TO LOVE	ROBERT PALMER	5	1986
ADDICTED TO LOVE	SHAKE B4 USE VS ROBERT PALMER	42	2002
ADDICTED TO LOVE (LIVE)	TINA TURNER	71	1988
ADDICTED TO YOU	ALEC EMPIRE	64	2002
ADDICTION	ALMIGHTY	38	1993
ADDICTIVE	TRUTH HURTS	3	2002
ADELANTE	SASH!	2	2000
ADIA	SARAH McLACHLAN	18	1998
A.D.I.D.A.S. [A]	KORN	22	1997
A.D.I.D.A.S. [B]	KILLER MIKE FEATURING BIG BOI	22	2003
ADIDAS WORLD	EDWYN COLLINS	71	1997
ADIEMUS	ADIEMUS	48	1995
ADIOS AMIGO	JIM REEVES	23	1962
ADMIT IT	ESMEE DENTERS	56	2010
ADORATION WALTZ	DAVID WHITFIELD	9	1957
ADORATIONS	KILLING JOKE	42	1986
ADORE	JOE ROBERTS	45	1994
ADORED AND EXPLORED	MARC ALMOND	25	1995
ADRENALIN (EP)	N-JOI	23	1991
ADRIENNE	CALLING	18	2002
ADRIFT (CAST YOUR MIND)	ANTARCTICA	72	2000
ADULT EDUCATION	DARYL HALL & JOHN OATES	63	1984
ADVENTURE [A]	BE YOUR OWN PET	36	2006
THE ADVENTURE [B]	ANGELS & AIRWAVES	20	2006
THE ADVENTURES OF THE LOVE CRUSADER	SARAH BRIGHTMAN & THE STARSHIP TROOPERS	53	1979
ADVERTISING SPACE	ROBBIE WILLIAMS	8	2005
ADVICE FOR THE YOUNG AT HEART	TEARS FOR FEARS	36	1990
AERODYNAMIK	KRAFTWERK	33	2004
AEROPLANE	RED HOT CHILI PEPPERS	11	1996
THE AEROPLANE SONG	STRAW	37	1999
AFFAIR	CHERRELLE	67	1989
AFFIRMATION	SAVAGE GARDEN	8	2000
AFRAID	MOTLEY CRUE	58	1997
AFRICA	TOTO	3	1983
AFRICA UNITE	BOB MARLEY & THE WAILERS	49	2005
AFRICAN AND WHITE	CHINA CRISIS	45	1982
AFRICAN DREAM	WASIS DIOP FEATURING LENA FIAGBE	44	1996
AFRICAN HORIZON	MYSTICA	59	1998
AFRICAN REIGN	DEEP C	75	1991
AFRICAN WALTZ	JOHNNY DANKWORTH	9	1961
AFRIKA	HISTORY FEATURING Q-TEE	42	1990
AFRIKA SHOX	LEFTFIELD/BAMBAATAA	7	1999
AFRO DIZZI ACT	CRY SISCO!	42	1989
AFRO KING	EMF	51	1995
AFRO PUFFS	LADY OF RAGE	72	1994
AFRO SLEEZE	ROACH MOTEL	73	1993
AFRODISIAC [A]	POWDER	72	1995
AFRODISIAC [B]	BRANDY	11	2004
THE AFRO-LEFT EP	LEFTFIELD FEATURING DJUM DJUM	22	1995
AFTER A FASHION	MIDGE URE & MICK KARN	39	1983
AFTER ALL [A]	FRANK & WALTERS	11	1993
AFTER ALL [B]	DELERIUM FEATURING JAEL	46	2003
AFTER ALL THESE YEARS	FOSTER & ALLEN	43	1986
AFTER ALL THIS TIME	SIMON WEBBE	16	2006
AFTER DARK	LE TIGRE	63	2005
AFTER HOURS [A]	BLUETONES	26	2002
AFTER HOURS [B]	WE ARE SCIENTISTS	15	2008
AFTER LOVE	BLANK & JONES	57	2000
AFTER THE FIRE	ROGER DALTREY	50	1985
AFTER THE GOLDRUSH	PRELUDE	21	1974
AFTER THE LOVE	JESUS LOVES YOU	68	1989
AFTER THE LOVE HAS GONE [A]	EARTH, WIND & FIRE	4	1979
AFTER THE LOVE HAS GONE [A]	DAMAGE	42	2001
AFTER THE LOVE HAS GONE [B]	PRINCESS	28	1985
AFTER THE LOVE HAS GONE [C]	STEPS	5	1999
AFTER THE RAIN	TITIYO	60	1990
AFTER THE RAIN HAS FALLEN	STING	31	2000
AFTER THE WAR	GARY MOORE	37	1989
AFTER THE WATERSHED	CARTER – THE UNSTOPPABLE SEX MACHINE	11	1991
AFTER YOU'RE GONE	ONE TRUE VOICE	2	2002
AFTER YOU'VE GONE	ALICE BABS	43	1963
AFTERGLOW	MISSION	53	1994
AFTERGLOW OF YOUR LOVE	SMALL FACES	36	1969
AFTERMATH [A]	NIGHTMARES ON WAX	38	1990
AFTERMATH [B]	TRICKY	69	1994
AFTERMATH [C]	R.E.M.	41	2004
AFTERNOON DELIGHT	STARLAND VOCAL BAND	18	1976
AFTERNOON OF THE RHINO	MIKE POST COALITION	47	1975
(AFTERNOON) SOAPS	ARAB STRAP	74	1998
AFTERNOONS & COFFEESPOONS	CRASH TEST DUMMIES	23	1994
AGADOO	BLACK LACE	2	1984
AGAIN [A]	JIMMY TARBUCK	68	1985
AGAIN [B]	JANET JACKSON	6	1993
AGAIN [C]	JULIET ROBERTS	33	1994
AGAIN [D]	FAITH EVANS	12	2005
AGAIN AND AGAIN	STATUS QUO	13	1978
AGAINST ALL ODDS [A]	STEVE BROOKSTEIN	1	2005
AGAINST ALL ODDS [B]	CHASE & STATUS FEATURING KANO	45	2009
AGAINST ALL ODDS (TAKE A LOOK AT ME NOW)	PHIL COLLINS	2	1984
AGAINST ALL ODDS (TAKE A LOOK AT ME NOW)	MARIAH CAREY FEATURING WESTLIFE	1	2000
AGAINST THE WIND	MAIRE BRENNAN	64	1992
AGE AIN'T NOTHING BUT A NUMBER	AALIYAH	32	1995
AGE OF LONELINESS	ENIGMA	21	1994
AGE OF LOVE	AGE OF LOVE	38	1997
AGE OF PANIC	SENSER	52	1994
THE AGE OF THE UNDERSTATEMENT	LAST SHADOW PUPPETS	9	2008
AGENT DAN	AGENT PROVOCATEUR	49	1997
AGNES QUEEN OF SORROW	BONNIE 'PRINCE' BILLY	69	2004
AHORA ES (NOW IS THE TIME)	2 IN A ROOM	43	1995
AI NO CORRIDA	UNITING NATIONS FEATURING LAURA MORE	18	2005

Title / Artist	Peak Position	Year of Release
AI NO CORRIDA (I-NO-KO-REE-DA) QUINCY JONES FEATURING DUNE	14	1981
AIKEA-GUINEA COCTEAU TWINS	41	1985
AIN'T COMPLAINING STATUS QUO	19	1988
AIN'T DOIN' NOTHIN' JET BRONX & THE FORBIDDEN	49	1977
AIN'T GOIN' TO GOA ALABAMA 3	40	1998
AIN'T GOING DOWN (TILL THE SUN COMES UP) GARTH BROOKS	13	1994
AIN'T GONNA BE THAT WAY MARV JOHNSON	50	1960
AIN'T GONNA BUMP NO MORE (WITH NO BIG FAT WOMAN) JOE TEX	2	1977
AIN'T GONNA CRY AGAIN PETER COX	37	1997
AIN'T GONNA WASH FOR A WEEK BROOK BROTHERS	13	1961
AIN'T GOT A CLUE LURKERS	45	1978
AIN'T GOT NO-I GOT LIFE NINA SIMONE	2	1968
AIN'T IT FUN GUNS N' ROSES	9	1993
AIN'T IT FUNNY JENNIFER LOPEZ	2	2001
AIN'T LOVE A BITCH ROD STEWART	11	1979
AIN'T MISBEHAVIN' JOHNNIE RAY	17	1956
AIN'T MISBEHAVIN' TOMMY BRUCE & THE BRUISERS	3	1960
AIN'T MY BEATING HEART TEN SHARP	1	1992
AIN'T NO CASANOVA SINCLAIR	28	1993
AIN'T NO DOUBT JIMMY NAIL	1	1992
AIN'T NO EASY WAY BLACK REBEL MOTORCYCLE CLUB	21	2005
AIN'T NO LOVE (AIN'T NO USE) SUB SUB FEATURING MELANIE WILLIAMS	3	1993
AIN'T NO LOVE (AIN'T NO USE) SODA CLUB FEATURING ASHLEY JADE	40	2004
AIN'T NO LOVE IN THE HEART OF THE CITY WHITESNAKE	51	1980
AIN'T NO MAN DINA CARROLL	16	1992
AIN'T NO MOUNTAIN HIGH ENOUGH DIANA ROSS	6	1970
AIN'T NO MOUNTAIN HIGH ENOUGH JOCELYN BROWN	35	1998
AIN'T NO MOUNTAIN HIGH ENOUGH WHITEHOUSE	60	1998
AIN'T NO MOUNTAIN HIGH ENOUGH – REMEMBER ME (MEDLEY) BOYSTOWN GANG	46	1981
AIN'T NO NEED TO HIDE SANDY B	60	1997
AIN'T NO OTHER MAN CHRISTINA AGUILERA	2	2006
AIN'T NO PARTY ORSON	21	2007
AIN'T NO PLAYA JAY-Z FEATURING FOXY BROWN	31	1997
AIN'T NO PLEASING YOU CHAS & DAVE	2	1982
AIN'T NO REST FOR THE WICKED CAGE THE ELEPHANT	32	2008
AIN'T NO STOPPIN US DJ LUCK & MC NEAT FEATURING JJ	8	2000
AIN'T NO STOPPIN' US NOW McFADDEN & WHITEHEAD	5	1979
AIN'T NO STOPPIN' US NOW BIG DADDY KANE	44	1990
AIN'T NO STOPPING ENIGMA	11	1981
AIN'T NO STOPPING US NOW LUTHER VANDROSS	22	1995
AIN'T NO STOPPING US NOW MOBO ALLSTARS	47	1998
AIN'T NO STOPPING US NOW (PARTY FOR THE WORLD) STEVE WALSH	44	1988
AIN'T NO SUNSHINE MICHAEL JACKSON	8	1972
AIN'T NO SUNSHINE SIVUCA	56	1984
AIN'T NO SUNSHINE LADYSMITH BLACK MAMBAZO FEATURING DES'REE	42	1999
AIN'T NOBODY RUFUS & CHAKA KHAN	6	1984
AIN'T NOBODY JAKI GRAHAM	44	1994
AIN'T NOBODY DIANA KING	13	1995
AIN'T NOBODY LL COOL J	1	1997
AIN'T NOBODY COURSE	8	1997
AIN'T NOBODY BETTER INNER CITY	10	1989
AIN'T NOBODY (LOVES ME BETTER) KWS & GWEN DICKEY	21	1994
AIN'T NOTHIN' LIKE IT MICHAEL LOVESMITH	75	1985
AIN'T NOTHING BUT A HOUSEPARTY SHOWSTOPPERS	11	1968
AIN'T NOTHING BUT A HOUSEPARTY PHIL FEARON	60	1986
AIN'T NOTHING GOIN' ON BUT THE RENT GWEN GUTHRIE	5	1986
AIN'T NOTHING GONNA KEEP ME FROM YOU TERI DE SARIO	52	1978
AIN'T NOTHING LIKE THE REAL THING MARVIN GAYE & TAMMI TERRELL	34	1968
AIN'T NOTHING LIKE THE REAL THING MARCELLA DETROIT & ELTON JOHN	24	1994
AIN'T NOTHING WRONG HOUSTON	33	2005
AIN'T SHE SWEET BEATLES	29	1964
AIN'T TALKIN' 'BOUT DUB APOLLO 440	7	1997
AIN'T THAT A LOT OF LOVE SIMPLY RED	14	1999
AIN'T THAT A SHAME PAT BOONE	7	1955
AIN'T THAT A SHAME FATS DOMINO	23	1957
AIN'T THAT A SHAME FOUR SEASONS	38	1963
AIN'T THAT ENOUGH TEENAGE FANCLUB	17	1997
AIN'T THAT ENOUGH FOR YOU JOHN DAVIS & THE MONSTER ORCHESTRA	70	1979
AIN'T THAT FUNNY JIMMY JUSTICE	8	1962
(AIN'T THAT) JUST LIKE ME HOLLIES	25	1963
AIN'T THAT JUST THE WAY LUTRICIA McNEAL	6	1997
AIN'T THAT LOVIN' YOU BABY ELVIS PRESLEY	15	1964
AIN'T THAT THE TRUTH FRANKIE KELLY	65	1985
AIN'T TOO PROUD TO BEG TEMPTATIONS	21	1966
AIN'T 2 PROUD 2 BEG TLC	13	1992
AIN'T WE FUNKIN' NOW BROTHERS JOHNSON	43	1978
AIN'T WHAT YOU DO BIG BROVAZ	15	2003
AIR GUITAR TOWERS OF LONDON	32	2006
AIR HOSTESS BUSTED	2	2004
THE AIR I BREATHE SIMPLY RED	6	1998
THE AIR THAT I BREATHE HOLLIES	2	1974
AIR TRAFFIC THREE DRIVES	75	2004
AIR 2000 ALBION	59	2000
AIR WE BREATHE ALISHA'S ATTIC	12	1997
THE AIR YOU BREATHE BOMB THE BASS	52	1991
AIRHEAD [A] THOMAS DOLBY	53	1988
AIRHEAD [B] GIRLS@PLAY	18	2001
AIRPLANE GARDENS FAMILY CAT	69	1993
AIRPORT MOTORS	4	1978
AIRWAVE RANK 1	10	2000
AISHA DEATH IN VEGAS	9	2000
AISY WAISY CARTOONS	16	1999
AJARE WAY OUT WEST	36	1994
AL CAPONE PRINCE BUSTER	18	1967
AL DI LA EMILIO PERICOLI	30	1962
ALA KABOO SOUND 5	69	1999
ALABAMA BLUES (REVISITED) ST GERMAIN	50	1996
ALABAMA JUBILEE FERKO STRING BAND	20	1955
ALABAMA SONG DAVID BOWIE	23	1980
ALAN BEAN HEFNER	58	2001
ALANE WES	11	1998
ALARM CALL BJORK	33	1998
ALARM CLOCK RUMBLE STRIPS	41	2007
ALARMA 666	58	1998
ALAS AGNES MYSTERY JETS	34	2005
ALBATROSS FLEETWOOD MAC	1	1968
ALBINONI VS STAR WARS SIGUE SIGUE SPUTNIK	75	1989
ALBION BABYSHAMBLES	8	2005
ALCOHOLIC STARSAILOR	10	2001
ALEJANDRO LADY GAGA	75	2009
ALEXANDER GRAHAM BELL SWEET	33	1971
ALFIE [A] CILLA BLACK	9	1966
ALFIE [B] LILY ALLEN	15	2007
ALIBI DAVID GRAY	71	2006
ALICE AVRIL LAVIGNE	59	2010
ALICE I WANT YOU JUST FOR ME FULL FORCE	9	1985
ALICE WHAT'S THE MATTER TERRORVISION	24	1994
ALICE (WHO THE X IS ALICE?) (LIVING NEXT DOOR TO ALICE) GOMPIE	17	1995
ALISHA RULES THE WORLD ALISHA'S ATTIC	12	1996
ALISON LINDA RONSTADT	66	1979
ALISON'S ROOM 60FT DOLLS	61	1998
ALIVE [A] PEARL JAM	16	1992
ALIVE [B] HELIOTROPIC FEATURING VERNA V	33	1999
ALIVE [C] BEASTIE BOYS	28	1999
ALIVE [D] P.O.D.	19	2002
ALIVE [E] ALIVE FEATURING D D KLEIN	49	2002
ALIVE [F] S CLUB	5	2002
ALIVE [G] SONIQUE	70	2003
ALIVE AND AMPLIFIED MOONEY SUZUKI	38	2005
ALIVE AND KICKING SIMPLE MINDS	6	1985
ALIVE AND KICKING EAST SIDE BEAT	26	1992
ALKALINE SCARFO	61	1997
ALL ABLAZE IAN BROWN	20	2005
ALL ABOUT EVE MARXMAN	28	1993
ALL ABOUT LOVIN' YOU BON JOVI	9	2003
ALL ABOUT SOUL BILLY JOEL	32	1993
ALL ABOUT US [A] PETER ANDRE	3	1997
ALL ABOUT US [B] T.A.T.U.	8	2005
ALL ABOUT YOU McFLY	1	2005
ALL ALONE AM I BRENDA LEE	7	1963
ALL ALONE ON CHRISTMAS DARLENE LOVE	31	1992
ALL ALONG THE WATCHTOWER JIMI HENDRIX EXPERIENCE	5	1968
ALL ALONG THE WATCHTOWER (EP) JIMI HENDRIX	52	1990
ALL AMERICAN BOY BILL PARSONS	22	1959
ALL AMERICAN GIRLS SISTER SLEDGE	41	1981
ALL AND ALL JOYCE SIMS	16	1986
ALL APOLOGIES NIRVANA	32	1993
ALL AROUND MY HAT STEELEYE SPAN	5	1975
ALL AROUND MY HAT STATUS QUO	47	1996
ALL AROUND THE WORLD [A] JAM	13	1977
ALL AROUND THE WORLD [B] LISA STANSFIELD	1	1989
ALL AROUND THE WORLD [C] JASON DONOVAN	41	1993
ALL AROUND THE WORLD [D] OASIS	1	1998
ALL AROUND THE WORLD [E] NORTHERN LINE	27	2000
ALL BECAUSE OF YOU [A] GEORDIE	6	1973
ALL BECAUSE OF YOU {B] U2	4	2005
ALL 'BOUT THE MONEY MEJA	12	1998
ALL BY MYSELF ERIC CARMEN	12	1976
ALL BY MYSELF CELINE DION	6	1996
ALL CRIED OUT [A] ALISON MOYET	8	1984
ALL CRIED OUT [B] MELANIE WILLIAMS	60	1994
ALL CRIED OUT [C] ALLURE FEATURING 112	12	1998
ALL DAY ALL NIGHT STEPHANIE MILLS	68	1993
ALL DAY AND ALL OF THE NIGHT KINKS	2	1964
ALL DAY AND ALL OF THE NIGHT STRANGLERS	7	1988
ALL DOWNHILL FROM HERE NEW FOUND GLORY	58	2004
ALL DRESSED IN LOVE JENNIFER HUDSON	72	2008
ALL EXHALE LUKE SLATER	74	2000
ALL EYES CHIKINKI	74	2004
ALL FALL DOWN [A] LINDISFARNE	34	1972
ALL FALL DOWN [B] FIVE STAR	15	1985
ALL FALL DOWN [C] ULTRAVOX	30	1986
ALL FALL DOWN [D] MIDGET	57	1998
ALL FALLS DOWN KANYE WEST FEATURING SYLEENA JOHNSON	10	2004
ALL FIRED UP PAT BENATAR	19	1988

Title / Artist	Peak Position	Year of Release
ALL FOR LEYNA BILLY JOEL	40	1980
ALL FOR LOVE BRYAN ADAMS, ROD STEWART & STING	2	1994
ALL FOR YOU JANET JACKSON	3	2001
ALL 4 LOVE COLOR ME BADD	5	1991
ALL 4 LOVE (BREAK 4 LOVE 1990) RAZE FEATURING LADY J & SECRETARY OF ENTERTAINMENT	30	1990
ALL FUNKED UP MOTHER	34	1993
ALL GOD'S CHILDREN BELINDA CARLISLE	66	1999
ALL GONE AWAY JOYRIDER	54	1996
ALL GOOD DE LA SOUL FEATURING CHAKA KHAN	33	2000
ALL GOOD THINGS (COME TO AN END) NELLY FURTADO	4	2006
ALL HOOKED UP ALL SAINTS	7	2001
ALL I AM (IS LOVING YOU) BLUEBELLS	58	1985
ALL I ASK RAE & CHRISTIAN FEATURING VEBA	67	1999
ALL I ASK OF MYSELF IS THAT I HOLD TOGETHER NED'S ATOMIC DUSTBIN	33	1995
ALL I ASK OF YOU CLIFF RICHARD & SARAH BRIGHTMAN	3	1986
ALL I DO CLEPTOMANIACS FEATURING BRYAN CHAMBERS	23	2001
ALL I EVER NEED IS YOU SONNY & CHER	8	1972
ALL I EVER WANTED [A] SANTANA	57	1980
ALL I EVER WANTED [B] HUMAN LEAGUE	47	2001
ALL I EVER WANTED [C] BASSHUNTER	2	2008
ALL I EVER WANTED (DEVOTION) MYSTERY	57	2002
ALL I GAVE WORLD PARTY	37	1993
ALL I GOT NEWTON FAULKNER	59	2007
ALL I HAVE JENNIFER LOPEZ FEATURING LL COOL J	2	2003
ALL I HAVE TO DO IS DREAM EVERLY BROTHERS	1	1958
ALL I HAVE TO DO IS DREAM BOBBIE GENTRY & GLEN CAMPBELL	3	1969
ALL I HAVE TO DO IS DREAM PHIL EVERLY & CLIFF RICHARD	14	1994
ALL I HAVE TO GIVE BACKSTREET BOYS	2	1998
(ALL I KNOW) FEELS LIKE FOREVER JOE COCKER	25	1992
ALL I NEED AIR	29	1998
ALL I NEED IS A MIRACLE MIKE + THE MECHANICS	27	1986
ALL I NEED IS EVERYTHING AZTEC CAMERA	34	1984
ALL I NEED IS YOUR SWEET LOVIN' GLORIA GAYNOR	44	1975
ALL I NEED TO KNOW EMMA BUNTON	60	2007
ALL I REALLY WANT ALANIS MORISSETTE	59	1996
ALL I REALLY WANT TO DO BYRDS	4	1965
ALL I REALLY WANT TO DO CHER	9	1965
ALL I SEE IS YOU DUSTY SPRINGFIELD	9	1966
ALL I THINK ABOUT IS YOU NILSSON	43	1977
ALL I WANNA DO [A] SHERYL CROW	4	1994
ALL I WANNA DO [A] JOANNE FARRELL	40	1995
ALL I WANNA DO [A] AMY STUDT	21	2004
ALL I WANNA DO [B] TIN TIN OUT	31	1997
ALL I WANNA DO [C] DANNII	4	1997
ALL I WANNA DO [D] PAUL WELLER	28	2008
ALL I WANNA DO IS MAKE LOVE TO YOU HEART	8	1990
ALL I WANT [A] HOWARD JONES	35	1986
ALL I WANT [B] THOSE 2 GIRLS	36	1995
ALL I WANT [C] SKUNK ANANSIE	14	1996
ALL I WANT [D] SUSANNA HOFFS	32	1996
ALL I WANT [E] OFFSPRING	31	1997
ALL I WANT [F] PURESSENCE	39	1998
ALL I WANT [G] REEF	51	2001
ALL I WANT [H] MIS-TEEQ	2	2001
ALL I WANT [I] WET WET WET	14	2004
ALL I WANT FOR CHRISTMAS IS A BEATLE DORA BRYAN	20	1963
ALL I WANT FOR CHRISTMAS IS YOU MARIAH CAREY	2	1994
ALL I WANT FROM YOU TEMPTATIONS	71	1989
ALL I WANT IS EVERYTHING DEF LEPPARD	38	1996
ALL I WANT IS YOU [A] ROXY MUSIC	12	1974
ALL I WANT IS YOU [B] U2	4	1989
ALL I WANT IS YOU [B] BELLEFIRE	18	2002
ALL I WANT IS YOU [C] BRYAN ADAMS	22	1992
ALL I WANT IS YOU [D] 911	4	1998
ALL I WANT TO DO UB40	41	1986
ALL I WANT TO DO IS ROCK TRAVIS	39	1997
ALL I WANTED IN TUA NUA	69	1988
ALL IN MY HEAD KOSHEEN	7	2003
ALL IN YOUR HANDS LAMB	71	1999
ALL IS FULL OF LOVE BJORK	24	1999
ALL JOIN HANDS SLADE	15	1984
ALL KINDS OF EVERYTHING DANA	1	1970
ALL MAPPED OUT DEPARTURE	30	2004
ALL MINE PORTISHEAD	8	1997
ALL MY BEST FRIENDS ARE METALHEADS LESS THAN JAKE	51	2000
ALL MY FRIENDS LCD SOUNDSYSTEM	41	2007
ALL MY LIFE [A] MAJOR HARRIS	61	1983
ALL MY LIFE [B] K-CI & JOJO	8	1998
ALL MY LIFE [C] FOO FIGHTERS	5	2002
ALL MY LOVE [A] CLIFF RICHARD	6	1967
ALL MY LOVE [B] HERNANDEZ	58	1989
ALL MY LOVE [C] QUEEN PEN FEATURING ERIC WILLIAMS	11	1998
ALL MY LOVE (ASK NOTHING) SPEAR OF DESTINY	61	1985
ALL MY LOVING DOWLANDS	33	1964
ALL MY TIME PAID + LIVE FEATURING LAURYN HILL	57	1997
ALL MY TRIALS PAUL McCARTNEY	35	1990
ALL 'N' ALL 187 LOCKDOWN (FEATURING D'EMPRESS)	43	1999
ALL N MY GRILL MISSY 'MISDEMEANOR' ELLIOTT FEATURING MC SOLAAR	20	1999
ALL NIGHT ALL RIGHT PETER ANDRE FEATURING WARREN G	16	1998
ALL NIGHT DISCO PARTY BRAKES	67	2005
ALL NIGHT HOLIDAY RUSS ABBOT	20	1985
ALL NIGHT LONG [A] DEXTER WANSELL	59	1978
ALL NIGHT LONG [B] RAINBOW	5	1980
ALL NIGHT LONG [C] CLOUD	72	1981
ALL NIGHT LONG [D] MARY JANE GIRLS	13	1983
ALL NIGHT LONG [D] JAY MONDI & THE LIVING BASS	63	1990
ALL NIGHT LONG [E] GANT	67	1997
ALL NIGHT LONG [F] FAITH EVANS FEATURING PUFF DADDY	23	1999
ALL NIGHT LONG [G] BLAZIN' SQUAD	54	2006
ALL NIGHT LONG [H] ALEXANDRA BURKE FEATURING PITBULL	59	2010
ALL NIGHT LONG (ALL NIGHT) LIONEL RICHIE	2	1983
ALL NITE (DON'T STOP) JANET JACKSON	19	2004
(ALL OF A SUDDEN) MY HEART SINGS PAUL ANKA	10	1959
ALL OF ME SABRINA	25	1988
ALL OF ME FOR ALL OF YOU 9.9	53	1985
ALL OF ME LOVES ALL OF YOU BAY CITY ROLLERS	4	1974
ALL OF MY HEART ABC	5	1982
ALL OF MY LIFE DIANA ROSS	9	1974
ALL OF THE GIRLS (ALL AI-DI-GIRL DEM) CARNIVAL FEATURING RIP VS RED RAT	51	1998
ALL OF YOU SAMMY DAVIS, JR	28	1956
ALL OF YOU JULIO IGLESIAS & DIANA ROSS	43	1984
ALL OF YOUR DAYS WILL BE BLESSED ED HARCOURT	35	2003
ALL ON BLACK ALKALINE TRIO	60	2003
ALL OR NOTHING [A] SMALL FACES	1	1966
ALL OR NOTHING [A] DOGS D'AMOUR	53	1993
ALL OR NOTHING [B] MILLI VANILLI	74	1990
ALL OR NOTHING [C] JOE	56	1994
ALL OR NOTHING [D] CHER	12	1999
ALL OR NOTHING [E] O-TOWN	4	2001
ALL OUT OF LOVE [A] AIR SUPPLY	11	1980
ALL OUT OF LOVE [A] OTT	11	1997
ALL OUT OF LOVE [A] FOUNDATION FEATURING NATALIE ROSSI	40	2003
ALL OUT OF LOVE [B] H & CLAIRE	10	2002
ALL OUT TO GET YOU BEAT	22	1981
ALL OVER LISA MAFFIA	2	2003
ALL OVER AGAIN RONAN KEATING & KATE RUSBY	6	2006
ALL OVER ME [A] SUZI CARR	45	1994
ALL OVER ME [B] GRAHAM COXON	19	2004
ALL OVER THE WORLD [A] FRANCOISE HARDY	16	1965
ALL OVER THE WORLD [B] ELECTRIC LIGHT ORCHESTRA	11	1980
ALL OVER THE WORLD [C] JUNIOR GISCOMBE	74	1992
ALL OVER THIS TOWN UPPER ROOM	38	2006
ALL OVER YOU [A] LEVEL 42	26	1994
ALL OVER YOU [B] LIVE	48	1995
ALL POSSIBILITIES BADLY DRAWN BOY	24	2003
ALL RIGHT CHRISTOPHER CROSS	51	1983
ALL RIGHT NOW FREE	2	1970
ALL RIGHT NOW PEPSI & SHIRLIE	50	1987
ALL RIGHT NOW LEMONESCENT	37	2004
ALL RISE BLUE	4	2001
ALL SHE WANTS IS DURAN DURAN	9	1989
ALL SHE WROTE ROSS COPPERMAN	39	2007
ALL SHOOK UP ELVIS PRESLEY	1	1957
ALL SHOOK UP BILLY JOEL	27	1992
ALL SPARKS EDITORS	21	2006
ALL STAND UP (NEVER SAY NEVER) STATUS QUO	51	2002
ALL STAR SMASH MOUTH	24	1999
ALL STAR HIT PARADE VARIOUS ARTISTS	2	1956
ALL STAR HIT PARADE NO. 2 VARIOUS ARTISTS	15	1957
ALL STOOD STILL ULTRAVOX	8	1981
ALL SUMMER LONG KID ROCK	1	2008
ALL SUSSED OUT ALMIGHTY	28	1996
ALL SYSTEMS GO DONNA SUMMER	54	1988
ALL THAT COUNTS IS LOVE STATUS QUO	29	2005
ALL THAT GLITTERS GARY GLITTER	48	1981
ALL THAT I AM [A] ELVIS PRESLEY	18	1966
ALL THAT I AM [B] JOE	52	1998
ALL THAT I CAN SAY MARY J BLIGE	29	1999
ALL THAT I GOT IS YOU GHOSTFACE KILLAH	11	1997
ALL THAT I NEED BOYZONE	1	1998
ALL THAT I'M ALLOWED (I'M THANKFUL) ELTON JOHN	20	2004
ALL THAT MATTERED (LOVE YOU DOWN) DE NUIT	38	2002
ALL THAT MATTERS LOUISE	11	1998
ALL THAT MATTERS TO ME ALEXANDER O'NEAL	67	1993
ALL THAT MONEY WANTS PSYCHEDELIC FURS	75	1988
ALL THAT SHE WANTS ACE OF BASE	1	1993
ALL THAT'S LEFT THRICE	69	2003
ALL THE LOVE IN THE WORLD [A] CONSORTIUM	22	1969
ALL THE LOVE IN THE WORLD [B] DIONNE WARWICK	10	1982
ALL THE LOVER I NEED KINANE	59	1996
ALL THE MAN THAT I NEED [A] WHITNEY HOUSTON	13	1990

Title / Artist	Peak Position	Year of Release
ALL THE MAN THAT I NEED [B] SHERNETTE MAY	50	1998
ALL THE MONEY'S GONE BABYLON ZOO	46	1999
ALL THE MYTHS ON SUNDAY DIESEL PARK WEST	66	1989
ALL THE RIGHT MOVES ONEREPUBLIC	26	2010
ALL THE SMALL THINGS BLINK-182	2	2000
ALL THE THINGS DILLINJA	71	2004
ALL THE THINGS SHE SAID [A] SIMPLE MINDS	9	1986
ALL THE THINGS SHE SAID [B] T.A.T.U.	1	2003
ALL THE THINGS (YOUR MAN WON'T DO) JOE	34	1996
ALL THE TIME AND EVERYWHERE DICKIE VALENTINE	9	1953
ALL THE TIMES I CRIED SHARLEEN SPITERI	26	2008
ALL THE WAY [A] FRANK SINATRA	3	1957
ALL THE WAY [B] ENGLAND FOOTBALL TEAM & THE SOUND OF STOCK, AITKEN & WATERMAN	64	1988
ALL THE WAY [C] CRAIG DAVID	3	2005
ALL THE WAY FROM AMERICA JOAN ARMATRADING	54	1980
ALL THE WAY FROM MEMPHIS MOTT THE HOOPLE	10	1973
ALL THE WAY FROM MEMPHIS CONTRABAND	65	1991
ALL THE WAY TO RENO R.E.M.	24	2001
ALL THE WORLD LOVES LOVERS PREFAB SPROUT	61	1992
ALL THE YOUNG DUDES MOTT THE HOOPLE	3	1972
ALL THE YOUNG DUDES BRUCE DICKINSON	23	1990
ALL THESE THINGS I HATE BULLET FOR MY VALENTINE	29	2006
ALL THESE THINGS THAT I'VE DONE KILLERS	18	2004
ALL THIS LOVE SIMILOU	20	2006
ALL THIS LOVE I'M GIVING GWEN McCRAE	63	1988
ALL THIS LOVE I'M GIVING MUSIC & MYSTERY FEATURING GWEN McCRAE	36	1993
ALL THIS TIME [A] TIFFANY	47	1989
ALL THIS TIME [B] STING	22	1991
ALL THIS TIME [C] MICHELLE	1	2003
ALL THOSE YEARS AGO GEORGE HARRISON	13	1981
ALL THROUGH THE NIGHT CYNDI LAUPER	64	1984
ALL THRU THE NITE P.O.V. FEATURING JADE	32	1994
ALL TIME HIGH RITA COOLIDGE	75	1983
ALL TIME LOVE WILL YOUNG	3	2006
ALL TOGETHER NOW FARM	4	1990
ALL TOGETHER NOW EVERTON FC	24	1995
ALL TOMORROW'S PARTIES JAPAN	38	1983
ALL TOO HUMAN RAKES	22	2006
ALL TRUE MAN ALEXANDER O'NEAL	18	1991
ALL WOMAN LISA STANSFIELD	20	1991
ALL YOU EVER DO VIOLENT DELIGHT	38	2003
ALL YOU GOOD GOOD PEOPLE EP EMBRACE	8	1997
ALL YOU NEED IS HATE DELGADOS	72	2003
ALL YOU NEED IS LOVE BEATLES	1	1967
ALL YOU NEED IS LOVE TOM JONES	19	1993
ALL YOU NEED IS ME MORRISSEY	24	2008
ALL YOU PRETTY GIRLS XTC	55	1984
ALL YOU WANTED MICHELLE BRANCH	33	2002
ALLEY CAT SONG DAVID THORNE	21	1963
ALLEY OOP HOLLYWOOD ARGYLES	24	1960
ALLY'S TARTAN ARMY ANDY CAMERON	6	1978
ALMA MATTERS MORRISSEY	16	1997
ALMAZ RANDY CRAWFORD	4	1987
ALMOST DOESN'T COUNT BRANDY	15	1999
ALMOST EASY AVENGED SEVENFOLD	67	2007
ALMOST GOLD JESUS & MARY CHAIN	41	1992
ALMOST HEAR YOU SIGH ROLLING STONES	31	1990
ALMOST HERE BRIAN McFADDEN & DELTA GOODREM	3	2005
ALMOST SATURDAY NIGHT DAVE EDMUNDS	58	1981
ALMOST SEE YOU (SOMEWHERE) CHINA BLACK	31	1995
ALMOST THERE ANDY WILLIAMS	2	1965
ALMOST UNREAL ROXETTE	7	1993
ALONE [A] PETULA CLARK	8	1957
ALONE [A] SHEPHERD SISTERS	14	1957
ALONE [A] SOUTHLANDERS	17	1957
ALONE [A] KAYE SISTERS	27	1958
ALONE [B] HEART	3	1987
ALONE [B] GLEE CAST	47	2010
ALONE [C] BIG COUNTRY	24	1993
ALONE [D] BEE GEES	5	1997
ALONE [E] LASGO	7	2002
ALONE AGAIN IN THE LAP OF LUXURY MARILLION	53	1994
ALONE AGAIN (NATURALLY) GILBERT O'SULLIVAN	3	1972
ALONE AGAIN OR DAMNED	27	1987
ALONE AT LAST JACKIE WILSON	50	1960
ALONE WITH YOU TEXAS	32	1992
ALONE WITHOUT YOU [A] KING	8	1985
ALONE WITHOUT YOU [B] MARK OWEN	26	2003
ALONG CAME CAROLINE MICHAEL COX	41	1960
ALPHA BETA GAGA AIR	44	2004
ALPHABET STREET PRINCE	9	1988
ALREADY GONE KELLY CLARKSON	66	2009
ALRIGHT [A] JANET JACKSON	20	1990
ALRIGHT [B] URBAN SOUL	43	1991
ALRIGHT [C] KRIS KROSS	47	1993
ALRIGHT [D] CAST	13	1995
ALRIGHT [E] SUPERGRASS	2	1995
ALRIGHT [F] JAMIROQUAI	6	1997
ALRIGHT [G] CLUB 69 FEATURING SUZANNE PALMER	70	1998
ALRIGHT [H] RED CARPET	58	2004
ALRIGHT [I] BEAT UP	58	2005
ALRIGHT [J] SUBWAYS	44	2008
ALRIGHT [K] JAMES DOMAN	50	2008
ALRIGHT ALRIGHT ALRIGHT MUNGO JERRY	3	1973
ALRIGHT BABY STEVENSON'S ROCKET	37	1975
ALSATIAN WHITE ROSE MOVEMENT	54	2005
ALSO SPRACH ZARATHUSTRA (2001) DEODATO	7	1973
ALTERNATE TITLE MONKEES	2	1967
ALWAYS [A] SAMMY TURNER	26	1959
ALWAYS [B] ATLANTIC STARR	3	1987
ALWAYS [C] URBAN SOUL	41	1992
ALWAYS [D] ERASURE	4	1994
ALWAYS [E] BON JOVI	2	1994
ALWAYS [F] MK FEATURING ALANA	69	1995
ALWAYS [G] SALIVA	47	2003
ALWAYS [H] BLINK-182	36	2005
ALWAYS A PERMANENT STATE DAVID JAMES	60	2001
ALWAYS AND EVER JOHNNY KIDD & THE PIRATES	46	1964
ALWAYS AND FOREVER [A] HEATWAVE	9	1978
ALWAYS AND FOREVER [A] LUTHER VANDROSS	20	1995
ALWAYS AND FOREVER [B] JJ72	43	2003
ALWAYS AND FOREVER [C] CHOCOLATE PUMA	43	2006
ALWAYS BE JIMMY EAT WORLD	37	2008
ALWAYS BE MY BABY MARIAH CAREY	3	1996
ALWAYS BREAKING MY HEART BELINDA CARLISLE	8	1996
ALWAYS COME BACK TO YOUR LOVE SAMANTHA MUMBA	3	2001
ALWAYS FIND A WAY NINE YARDS	50	1999
ALWAYS HAVE, ALWAYS WILL ACE OF BASE	12	1998
ALWAYS LOOK ON THE BRIGHT SIDE OF LIFE MONTY PYTHON	3	1991
ALWAYS LOOK ON THE BRIGHT SIDE OF LIFE CORONATION STREET CAST FEATURING BILL WADDINGTON	35	1995
ALWAYS MUSIC WESTBAM/KOON + STEPHENSON	51	1996
ALWAYS ON MY MIND ELVIS PRESLEY	9	1972
ALWAYS ON MY MIND WILLIE NELSON	49	1982
ALWAYS ON MY MIND PET SHOP BOYS	1	1987
ALWAYS ON THE RUN LENNY KRAVITZ	41	1991
ALWAYS ON TIME JA RULE FEATURING ASHANTI	6	2002
ALWAYS REMEMBER TO RESPECT AND HONOUR YOUR MOTHER DUSTED	31	2001
ALWAYS RIGHT BEHIND YOU ZUTONS	26	2008
ALWAYS SOMETHING THERE TO REMIND ME NAKED EYES	59	1983
ALWAYS SOMETHING THERE TO REMIND ME TIN TIN OUT FEATURING ESPIRITU	14	1995
ALWAYS THE LAST TO KNOW DEL AMITRI	13	1992
ALWAYS THE LONELY ONE ALAN DREW	48	1963
ALWAYS THE SAME NEIL'S CHILDREN	56	2005
ALWAYS THE SUN STRANGLERS	29	1986
ALWAYS THERE [A] MARTI WEBB & THE SIMON MAY ORCHESTRA	13	1986
ALWAYS THERE [B] INCOGNITO FEATURING JOCELYN BROWN	6	1991
ALWAYS THERE [C] UB40	53	1997
ALWAYS TOMORROW GLORIA ESTEFAN	24	1992
ALWAYS WHERE I NEED TO BE KOOKS	3	2008
ALWAYS YOU AND ME RUSS CONWAY	33	1962
ALWAYS YOUR WAY MY VITRIOL	31	2001
ALWAYS YOURS GARY GLITTER	1	1974
ALWAYZ INTO SOMETHIN' N.W.A.	60	1991
AM I A TOY OR A TREASURE KAY STARR	17	1954
AM I ON YOUR MIND OXYGEN FEATURING ANDREA BRITTON	30	2002
AM I RIGHT (EP) ERASURE	15	1991
AM I THAT EASY TO FORGET ENGELBERT HUMPERDINCK	3	1968
AM I THE SAME GIRL DUSTY SPRINGFIELD	43	1969
AM I THE SAME GIRL SWING OUT SISTER	21	1992
AM I WASTING MY TIME ON YOU FRANKIE VAUGHAN	25	1958
AM I WRONG [A] ETIENNE DE CRECY	44	2001
AM I WRONG [B] MULL HISTORICAL SOCIETY	51	2003
AM I WRY NO MEW	47	2003
AM TO PM CHRISTINA MILIAN	3	2002
AMANDA [A] STUART GILLIES	13	1973
AMANDA [B] CRAIG McLACHLAN & CHECK 1-2	19	1990
AMARANTINE ENYA	53	2005
AMATEUR HOUR SPARKS	7	1974
AMAZED LONESTAR	21	2000
AMAZING [A] AEROSMITH	57	1993
AMAZING [B] GEORGE MICHAEL	4	2004
AMAZING [C] WESTLIFE	4	2006
AMAZING [D] SEAL	74	2007
AMAZING GRACE JUDY COLLINS	5	1970
AMAZING GRACE PIPES & DRUMS & MILITARY BAND OF THE ROYAL SCOTS DRAGOON GUARDS	1	1972
THE AMAZING SPIDER MAN MC SPY-D + FRIENDS	37	1995
AMAZON CHANT AIRSCAPE	46	1998
AMBUSH OUTLAWS	43	1961
AMEN (DON'T BE AFRAID) FLASH BROTHERS	75	2004
AMERICA [A] NICE	21	1968
AMERICA [A] KING KURT	73	1986
AMERICA [B] SIMON & GARFUNKEL	25	1972
AMERICA [C] DAVID ESSEX	32	1974
AMERICA [D] GARY NUMAN	49	1988
AMERICA [E] RAZORLIGHT	1	2006

Title / Artist	Peak Position	Year of Release
AMERICA (I LOVE AMERICA) FULL INTENTION	32	1996
AMERICA THE BEAUTIFUL ELVIS PRESLEY	69	2001
AMERICA: WHAT TIME IS LOVE KLF	4	1992
AMERICA – WORLD CUP THEME 1994 LEONARD BERNSTEIN, ORCHESTRA & CHORUS	44	1994
THE AMERICAN SIMPLE MINDS	59	1981
AMERICAN BAD ASS KID ROCK	25	2000
AMERICAN BOY ESTELLE FEATURING KANYE WEST	1	2008
AMERICAN DREAM [A] CROSBY, STILLS, NASH & YOUNG	55	1989
AMERICAN DREAM [B] POWER OF DREAMS	74	1991
AMERICAN DREAM [C] JAKATTA	3	2001
AMERICAN ENGLISH IDLEWILD	15	2002
AMERICAN GENERATION RITCHIE FAMILY	49	1979
AMERICAN GIRL TOM PETTY & THE HEARTBREAKERS	40	1977
AMERICAN GIRLS COUNTING CROWS	33	2002
AMERICAN HEARTS BILLY OCEAN	54	1977
AMERICAN IDIOT GREEN DAY	3	2004
AMERICAN IN AMSTERDAM WHEATUS	59	2003
AMERICAN LIFE MADONNA	2	2003
AMERICAN PIE DON McLEAN	2	1972
AMERICAN PIE JUST LUIS	31	1995
AMERICAN PIE CHUPITO	54	1995
AMERICAN PIE MADONNA	1	2000
AMERICAN TRILOGY [A] ELVIS PRESLEY	8	1972
AMERICAN TRILOGY [A] MICKEY NEWBURY	42	1972
AMERICAN TRILOGY [B] DELGADOS	61	2000
AMERICAN TV TERRORVISION	63	1993
AMERICAN WOMAN GUESS WHO	19	1970
AMERICANOS HOLLY JOHNSON	4	1989
AMERIKA RAMMSTEIN	38	2004
AMIGO BLACK SLATE	9	1980
AMIGOS PARA SIEMPRE (FRIENDS FOR LIFE) JOSE CARRERAS & SARAH BRIGHTMAN	11	1992
AMITYVILLE (THE HOUSE ON THE HILL) LOVEBUG STARSKI	12	1986
AMNESIA [A] SHALAMAR	61	1984
AMNESIA [B] CHUMBAWAMBA	10	1998
AMONG MY SOUVENIRS CONNIE FRANCIS	11	1959
AMOR JULIO IGLESIAS	32	1982
AMOR AMOR BEN E. KING	38	1961
AMOUR AMOUR MOBILES	45	1982
AMOUR (C'MON) PORN KINGS	17	1997
AMOUREUSE KIKI DEE	13	1973
THE AMSTERDAM EP SIMPLE MINDS	18	1989
AN ACCIDENT IN PARADISE SVEN VATH	57	1993
AN AFFAIR TO REMEMBER VIC DAMONE	29	1957
AN ANGEL KELLY FAMILY	69	1995
AN EASIER AFFAIR GEORGE MICHAEL	13	2006
AN ENGLISH GENTLEMAN JAMES DEAN BRADFIELD	31	2006
AN EVERLASTING LOVE ANDY GIBB	10	1978
AN HONEST MISTAKE BRAVERY	7	2005
AN INNOCENT MAN BILLY JOEL	8	1984
AN OLYMPIC RECORD BARRON KNIGHTS	35	1968
AN OPEN LETTER TO NYC BEASTIE BOYS	38	2004
AN UBHAL AS AIRDE (THE HIGHEST APPLE) RUNRIG	18	1995
ANALOGUE (ALL IWANT) A-HA	10	2006
ANARCHY IN THE UK SEX PISTOLS	33	1976
ANARCHY IN THE UK MEGADETH	45	1988
ANARCHY IN THE UK GREEN JELLY	27	1993
ANA'S SONG SILVERCHAIR	45	1999
ANASTHASIA T99	14	1991
ANCHOR CAVE IN	53	2003
ANCHORAGE MICHELLE SHOCKED	60	1988
AND A BANG ON THE EAR WATERBOYS	51	1989
AND DA DRUM MACHINE PHATT B	58	2000
AND I LOVE YOU SO PERRY COMO	3	1973
AND I WISH DOOLEYS	52	1981
AND I'M TELLING YOU I'M NOT GOING JENNIFER HOLLIDAY	32	1982
AND I'M TELLING YOU I'M NOT GOING DONNA GILES	27	1994
AND I'M TELLING YOU I'M NOT GOING JENNIFER HUDSON	32	2009
AND IT FEELS LIKE LeANN RIMES	22	2006
AND IT HURTS DAYEENE	63	1999
AND IT WASN'T A DREAM RUTHLESS RAP ASSASSINS	75	1990
(AND NOW – THE WALTZ) C'EST LA VIE SLADE	50	1982
AND SHE WAS TALKING HEADS	17	1986
AND SO I WILL WAIT FOR YOU DEE FREDRIX	56	1993
AND SO IS LOVE KATE BUSH	26	1994
...AND STONES BLUE AEROPLANES	63	1990
...AND THAT'S BEFORE ME TEA! MR FOOD	62	1990
...(AND THAT'S NO LIE) HEAVEN 17	52	1985
AND THE BAND PLAYED ON (DOWN AMONG THE DEAD MEN) FLASH & THE PAN	54	1978
AND THE BANDS PLAYED ON SAXON	12	1981
AND THE BEAT GOES ON WHISPERS	2	1980
AND THE HEAVENS CRIED ANTHONY NEWLEY	6	1961
AND THE LEADER ROCKS ON GARY GLITTER	58	1992
(AND THE) PICTURES IN THE SKY MEDICINE HEAD	22	1971
AND THE SUN WILL SHINE JOSE FELICIANO	25	1969
AND THEN SHE KISSED ME GARY GLITTER	39	1981
AND THEN SHE SMILES MOCK TURTLES	44	1991
AND THEN THE RAIN FALLS BLUE AMAZON	53	1997
AND THEY OBEY KINESIS	63	2003
AND YOU SMILED MATT MONRO	28	1973
ANDRES L7	34	1994
ANDROGYNY GARBAGE	24	2001
ANFIELD RAP (RED MACHINE IN FULL EFFECT) LIVERPOOL FC	3	1988
ANGEL [A] ROD STEWART	4	1972
ANGEL [B] ARETHA FRANKLIN	37	1973
ANGEL [B] SIMPLY RED	4	1996
ANGEL [C] MADONNA	5	1985
ANGEL [D] AEROSMITH	69	1988
ANGEL [E] EURYTHMICS	23	1990
ANGEL [F] JON SECADA	23	1993
ANGEL [G] A-HA	41	1993
ANGEL [H] GOLDIE	41	1995
ANGEL [I] MASSIVE ATTACK	30	1998
ANGEL [J] TINA COUSINS	46	1999
ANGEL [K] RALPH FRIDGE	20	2000
ANGEL [L] LIONEL RICHIE	18	2000
ANGEL [M] SHAGGY FEATURING RAYVON	1	2001
ANGEL [N] SARAH McLACHLAN	36	2002
ANGEL [O] CORRS	16	2004
ANGEL [P] PHARRELL WILLIAMS	15	2006
THE ANGEL AND THE GAMBLER IRON MAIDEN	18	1998
ANGEL EYES [A] ROXY MUSIC	4	1979
ANGEL EYES [B] RAGHAV	7	2005
ANGEL EYES (HOME AND AWAY) WET WET WET	5	1987
ANGEL FACE GLITTER BAND	4	1974
ANGEL FINGERS WIZZARD	1	1973
ANGEL IN BLUE J GEILS BAND	55	1982
ANGEL IN THE NIGHT BASSHUNTER	14	2008
ANGEL INTERCEPTOR ASH	14	1995
ANGEL (LADADI O-HEYO) JAM & SPOON	26	1995
ANGEL LOOKING THROUGH STAGECOACH FEATURING PENNY FOSTER	59	2003
ANGEL OF HARLEM U2	9	1988
ANGEL OF MINE ETERNAL	4	1997
ANGEL OF MINE MONICA	55	1999
ANGEL OF THE MORNING PP ARNOLD	29	1968
ANGEL OF THE MORNING JUICE NEWTON	43	1981
ANGEL OF THE MORNING – ANY WAY THAT YOU WANT ME (MEDLEY) MARY MASON	27	1977
ANGEL ON MY SHOULDER GARETH GATES	22	2007
ANGEL STREET M PEOPLE	8	1998
ANGELA JONES MICHAEL COX	7	1960
ANGELEYES ABBA	3	1979
ANGELIA RICHARD MARX	45	1989
ANGELO BROTHERHOOD OF MAN	1	1977
ANGELS ROBBIE WILLIAMS	4	1997
ANGELS ALL ANGELS	48	2006
THE ANGELS & SHADOWS PROJECT OMNI TRIO	44	2001
ANGELS DON'T LIE JIM REEVES	32	1970
ANGELS GO BALD: TOO HOWIE B	36	1997
ANGEL'S HEAP FINN	41	1995
ANGELS OF THE SILENCES COUNTING CROWS	41	1996
ANGEL'S SYMPHONY R.A.F.	73	1996
ANGELS WITH DIRTY FACES [A] SHAM 69	19	1978
ANGELS WITH DIRTY FACES [B] SUGABABES	7	2002
ANGIE ROLLING STONES	5	1973
ANGIE BABY HELEN REDDY	5	1975
ANGRY AT THE BIG OAK TREE FRANK IFIELD	25	1964
ANGRY CHAIR ALICE IN CHAINS	33	1993
THE ANGRY MOB KAISER CHIEFS	20	2007
ANGRY SKIES MARIA NAYLER	42	2000
ANIMAL [A] DEF LEPPARD	6	1987
ANIMAL [B] LOST IT.COM	70	2001
ANIMAL [C] R.E.M.	33	2003
ANIMAL [D] DUELS	47	2006
ANIMAL ARMY BABYLON ZOO	17	1996
ANIMAL CANNABUS MULL HISTORICAL SOCIETY	53	2001
ANIMAL INSTINCT [A] COMMODORES	74	1985
ANIMAL INSTINCT [B] CRANBERRIES	54	1999
ANIMAL NITRATE SUEDE	7	1993
THE ANIMAL SONG SAVAGE GARDEN	16	1999
ANIMATION SKIDS	56	1980
ANITINA (THE FIRST TIME I SEE SHE DANCE) M/A/R/R/S	1	1987
ANNABELLA JOHN WALKER	24	1967
ANNIE GET YOUR GUN SQUEEZE	43	1982
ANNIE I'M NOT YOUR DADDY KID CREOLE & THE COCONUTS	2	1982
ANNIE LET'S NOT WAIT GUILLEMOTS	27	2007
ANNIE'S SONG JAMES GALWAY	3	1974
ANNIE'S SONG JOHN DENVER	1	1978
ANNIVERSARY WALTZ ANITA HARRIS	21	1968
ANNIVERSARY WALTZ – PART 1 STATUS QUO	2	1990
ANNIVERSARY WALTZ – PART 2 STATUS QUO	16	1990
ANOMALY – CALLING YOUR NAME LIBRA PRESENTS TAYLOR	43	1996
ANONYMOUS BOBBY VALENTINO FEATURING TIMBALAND	25	2007
ANOTHER BLOOMING CHRISTMAS MEL SMITH	59	1991
ANOTHER BODY MURDERED FAITH NO MORE & BOO-YAA T.R.I.B.E.	26	1993
ANOTHER BRICK IN THE WALL (PART 2) PINK FLOYD	1	1979
ANOTHER CHANCE ROGER SANCHEZ	1	2001
ANOTHER CUP OF COFFEE MIKE + THE MECHANICS	51	1995
ANOTHER DAY [A] PAUL McCARTNEY	2	1971
ANOTHER DAY [B] WHIGFIELD	7	1994
ANOTHER DAY [C] BUCKSHOT LEFONQUE	65	1997
ANOTHER DAY [D] SKIP RAIDERS FEATURING JADA	46	2000
ANOTHER DAY [D] LEMAR	9	2004

Title	Artist	Peak Position	Year of Release
ANOTHER DAY (ANOTHER GIRL)	LAMBRETTAS	49	1980
ANOTHER DAY IN PARADISE	PHIL COLLINS	2	1989
ANOTHER DAY IN PARADISE	JAM TRONIK	19	1990
ANOTHER DAY IN PARADISE	BRANDY & RAY J	5	2001
ANOTHER FINE MESS	CHESNEY HAWKES	48	2005
ANOTHER FUNNY HONEYMOON	DAVID DUNDAS	29	1977
ANOTHER GIRL – ANOTHER PLANET	ONLY ONES	57	1992
ANOTHER HEARTACHE	ROD STEWART	54	1986
ANOTHER KIND OF LOVE	HUGH CORNWELL	71	1988
ANOTHER LONELY NIGHT IN NEW YORK	ROBIN GIBB	71	1984
ANOTHER LOVER	DANE	9	2001
ANOTHER MAN	BARBARA MASON	45	1984
ANOTHER MONSTERJAM	SIMON HARRIS FEATURING EINSTEIN	65	1989
ANOTHER MORNING STONER	...AND YOU WILL KNOW US BY THE TRAIL OF THE DEAD	54	2002
ANOTHER NAIL IN MY HEART	SQUEEZE	17	1980
ANOTHER NIGHT [A]	ARETHA FRANKLIN	54	1986
ANOTHER NIGHT [B]	JASON DONOVAN	18	1990
ANOTHER NIGHT [C]	(MC SAR &) THE REAL McCOY	2	1993
ANOTHER NIGHT IN	STRANGELOVE	46	1998
ANOTHER ONE BITES THE DUST	QUEEN	7	1980
ANOTHER ONE BITES THE DUST	QUEEN WITH WYCLEF JEAN FEATURING PRAS MICHEL/FREE	5	1998
ANOTHER ONE BITES THE DUST	QUEEN VS THE MIAMI PROJECT	31	2006
ANOTHER PART OF ME	MICHAEL JACKSON	15	1988
ANOTHER PEARL	BADLY DRAWN BOY	41	2000
ANOTHER PIECE OF MEAT	SCORPIONS	39	1979
ANOTHER PLACE TO FALL	KT TUNSTALL	52	2006
ANOTHER PLANET	PENDULUM	46	2004
ANOTHER ROCK AND ROLL CHRISTMAS	GARY GLITTER	7	1984
ANOTHER SAD LOVE SONG	TONI BRAXTON	15	1993
ANOTHER SATURDAY NIGHT	SAM COOKE	23	1963
ANOTHER SATURDAY NIGHT	CAT STEVENS	19	1974
ANOTHER SILENT DAY	ADVENTURES	71	1984
ANOTHER SLEEPLESS NIGHT [A]	JIMMY CLANTON	50	1960
ANOTHER SLEEPLESS NIGHT [B]	MIKE 'HITMAN' WILSON	74	1990
ANOTHER SLEEPLESS NIGHT [B]	SHAWN CHRISTOPHER	50	1991
ANOTHER STAR	STEVIE WONDER	29	1977
ANOTHER STAR	KATHY SLEDGE	54	1995
ANOTHER STEP CLOSER TO YOU	KIM WILDE & JUNIOR	6	1987
ANOTHER SUITCASE IN ANOTHER HALL	BARBARA DICKSON	18	1977
ANOTHER SUITCASE IN ANOTHER HALL	MADONNA	7	1997
ANOTHER TEAR FALLS	WALKER BROTHERS	12	1966
ANOTHER TIME ANOTHER PLACE	ENGELBERT HUMPERDINCK	13	1971
ANOTHER WAY	PAUL VAN DYK	13	1999
ANOTHER WAY TO DIE	JACK WHITE & ALICIA KEYS	9	2008
ANOTHER WEEKEND	FIVE STAR	18	1988
ANOTHERLOVERHOLENYOHEAD	PRINCE	36	1986
ANSWER ME	DAVID WHITFIELD	1	1953
ANSWER ME	FRANKIE LAINE	1	1953
ANSWER ME	RAY PETERSON	47	1960
ANSWER ME	BARBARA DICKSON	9	1976
THE ANSWER TO WHY I HATE YOU	SYMPOSIUM	32	1997
ANSWERING BELL	RYAN ADAMS	39	2002
ANSWERS TO NOTHING	MIDGE URE	49	1988
ANT RAP	ADAM & THE ANTS	3	1981
ANTE UP	M.O.P. FEATURING BUSTA RHYMES	7	2001
ANTHEM [A]	N-JOI	8	1990
ANTHEM [B]	WILDHEARTS	21	1997
THE ANTHEM [C]	GOOD CHARLOTTE	10	2003
ANTHEM [D]	FILO & PERI FEATURING ERIC LUMIERE	39	2007
ANTHEM (ONE DAY IN EVERY WEEK)	NEW SEEKERS	21	1978
ANTHEM (WE ARE THE FIRE)	TRIVIUM	40	2006
ANTI-SOCIAL	ANTHRAX	44	1989
ANTMUSIC	ADAM & THE ANTS	2	1980
THE ANTMUSIC EP (THE B-SIDES)	ADAM & THE ANTS	46	1982
ANY DREAM WILL DO	JASON DONOVAN	1	1991
ANY DREAM WILL DO	LEE MEAD	2	2007
ANY LOVE	LUTHER VANDROSS	31	1988
ANY MINUTE NOW	SOULWAX	34	2004
ANY OLD IRON	PETER SELLERS	17	1957
ANY OLD TIME	FOUNDATIONS	48	1968
ANY ROAD	GEORGE HARRISON	37	2003
ANY TIME ANY PLACE	JANET JACKSON	13	1994
ANY WAY YOU LOOK	NORTHERN UPROAR	36	1997
ANY WAY YOU WANT ME	TROGGS	8	1966
ANYBODY SEEN MY BABY?	ROLLING STONES	22	1997
ANYMORE	SARAH CRACKNELL	39	1996
ANYONE CAN FALL IN LOVE	ANITA DOBSON FEATURING THE SIMON MAY ORCHESTRA	4	1986
ANYONE CAN PLAY GUITAR	RADIOHEAD	32	1993
ANYONE FOR TENNIS (THE SAVAGE SEVEN THEME)	CREAM	40	1968
ANYONE OF US (STUPID MISTAKE)	GARETH GATES	1	2002
ANYONE WHO HAD A HEART	CILLA BLACK	1	1964
ANYONE WHO HAD A HEART	DIONNE WARWICK	42	1964
ANYONE WHO HAD A HEART	MARY MAY	49	1964
ANYSOUND	VINES	63	2006
ANYTHING [A]	DIRECT DRIVE	67	1985
ANYTHING [B]	DAMNED	32	1986
ANYTHING [C]	SYDNEY YOUNGBLOOD	48	1993
ANYTHING [D]	CULTURE BEAT	5	1994
ANYTHING [E]	SWV	24	1994
ANYTHING [F]	3T	2	1996
ANYTHING [G]	DAMAGE	68	1996
ANYTHING [H]	JAY-Z	18	2000
ANYTHING [I]	JOJO	21	2007
ANYTHING BUT DOWN	SHERYL CROW	19	1999
ANYTHING CAN HAPPEN	WAS (NOT WAS)	67	1988
ANYTHING CAN HAPPEN IN THE NEXT HALF HOUR	ENTER SHIKARI	27	2007
ANYTHING FOR YOU [A]	GLORIA ESTEFAN & MIAMI SOUND MACHINE	10	1988
ANYTHING FOR YOU [B]	STAMFORD AMP	33	2002
ANYTHING GOES	HARPERS BIZARRE	33	1967
ANYTHING IS POSSIBLE [A]	DEBBIE GIBSON	51	1991
ANYTHING IS POSSIBLE [B]	WILL YOUNG	1	2002
ANYTHING THAT'S ROCK 'N' ROLL	TOM PETTY & THE HEARTBREAKERS	36	1977
ANYTHING YOU WANT	JODIE	47	1995
ANYTHING YOU WANT (I'VE GOT IT)	ULTIMATE KAOS	52	1999
ANYTIME [A]	NU-BIRTH	41	1997
ANYTIME [B]	BRIAN McKNIGHT	48	1998
ANYTIME YOU NEED A FRIEND	MARIAH CAREY	8	1994
ANYWAY [A]	HONEYCRACK	67	1996
ANYWAY [B]	DUCK SAUCE	22	2009
ANYWAY ANYHOW ANYWHERE	WHO	10	1965
ANYWAY THAT YOU WANT ME	SPIRITUALIZED	75	1990
ANYWAY YOU DO IT	LIQUID GOLD	41	1978
ANYWAY YOU WANT IT	DAVE CLARK FIVE	25	1964
ANYWHERE [A]	DUBSTAR	37	1995
ANYWHERE [B]	BETH ORTON	55	2002
ANYWHERE FOR YOU	BACKSTREET BOYS	4	1997
ANYWHERE IS	ENYA	7	1995
APACHE [A]	SHADOWS	1	1960
APACHE [A]	BERT WEEDON	24	1960
APACHE [B]	STARFIGHTER	31	2000
APACHE DROPOUT	EDGAR BROUGHTON BAND	33	1971
APEMAN	KINKS	5	1970
APHRODITE	PARIS & SHARP	61	2001
APOCALYPSO	MEW	75	2005
APOLLO 9	ADAM ANT	13	1984
APOLOGIES TO INSECT LIFE	BRITISH SEA POWER	36	2003
APOLOGIZE	TIMBALAND PRESENTS ONEREPUBLIC	3	2007
APPARENTLY NOTHIN'	YOUNG DISCIPLES	13	1991
APPARENTLY NOTHING	BRAND NEW HEAVIES	32	2000
THE APPLE EP	VARIOUS ARTISTS (EP'S & LP'S)	60	1991
APPLE GREEN	MILLTOWN BROTHERS	43	1991
APPLE OF MY EYE	ED HARCOURT	61	2002
THE APPLE STRETCHING	GRACE JONES	50	1982
APPLE TREE	ERYKAH BADU	47	1997
APPLEJACK	JET HARRIS & TONY MEEHAN	4	1963
APPLY SOME PRESSURE	MAXIMO PARK	17	2005
APPRENTICE OF THE UNIVERSE	PURE REASON REVOLUTION	74	2004
APRIL LOVE	PAT BOONE	7	1957
APRIL SKIES	JESUS & MARY CHAIN	8	1987
AQUARIUS	PAUL JONES	45	1969
AQUARIUS/LET THE SUNSHINE IN (MEDLEY)	FIFTH DIMENSION	11	1969
ARABIAN KNIGHTS	SIOUXSIE & THE BANSHEES	32	1981
ARE EVERYTHING	BUZZCOCKS	61	1980
ARE 'FRIENDS' ELECTRIC?	TUBEWAY ARMY	1	1979
ARE WE HERE	ORBITAL	33	1994
ARE YOU BEING SERVED	GRACE BROTHERS	51	1996
ARE YOU BEING SERVED SIR	JOHN INMAN	39	1975
ARE YOU BLUE OR ARE YOU BLIND?	BLUETONES	31	1995
ARE YOU DREAMING	TWENTY 4 SEVEN FEATURING CAPTAIN HOLLYWOOD	17	1990
ARE YOU GETTING ENOUGH OF WHAT MAKES YOU HAPPY	HOT CHOCOLATE	17	1980
ARE YOU GONNA BE MY GIRL?	JET	16	2003
ARE YOU GONNA BE THERE?	UP YER RONSON FEATURING MARY PEARCE	27	1996
ARE YOU GONNA GO MY WAY	LENNY KRAVITZ	4	1993
ARE YOU GROWING TIRED OF MY LOVE	STATUS QUO	46	1969
ARE YOU HAPPY NOW?	MICHELLE BRANCH	31	2003
ARE YOU HEARING (WHAT I HEAR)?	LEVEL 42	49	1982
ARE YOU IN	INCUBUS	34	2002
ARE YOU JIMMY RAY?	JIMMY RAY	13	1997
ARE YOU LONESOME TONIGHT	ELVIS PRESLEY	1	1961
ARE YOU LOOKIN' AT ME	RICKY TOMLINSON	28	2001
ARE YOU MAN ENOUGH	UNO CLIO FEATURING MARTINE McCUTCHEON	62	1995
ARE YOU MINE	BROS	12	1991
ARE YOU MY BABY	WENDY & LISA	70	1989
ARE YOU OUT THERE	CRESCENDO	20	1995
ARE YOU READY [A]	BILLY OCEAN	42	1980
ARE YOU READY? [B]	BREAK MACHINE	27	1984
ARE YOU READY [C]	AC/DC	34	1991
ARE YOU READY [D]	GYRES	71	1996
(ARE YOU READY) DO THE BUS STOP	FATBACK BAND	18	1975
ARE YOU READY FOR LOVE [A]	ELTON JOHN	1	1979

Title / Artist	Peak Position	Year of Release
ARE YOU READY FOR LOVE [B] ULTRA HIGH	45	1996
ARE YOU READY FOR SOME MORE? REEL 2 REAL	24	1996
ARE YOU READY TO BE HEARTBROKEN SANDIE SHAW	68	1986
ARE YOU READY TO FLY ROZALLA	14	1992
ARE YOU READY TO PARTY SHRINK	39	2000
ARE YOU READY TO ROCK WIZZARD	8	1975
ARE YOU SATISFIED? (FUNKA NOVA) RAH BAND	70	1985
ARE YOU STILL HAVING FUN? EAGLE-EYE CHERRY	21	2000
ARE YOU SURE [A] ALLISONS	2	1961
ARE YOU SURE [B] SO	62	1988
ARE YOU THAT SOMEBODY? AALIYAH	11	1998
(ARE YOU) THE ONE THAT I'VE BEEN... NICK CAVE & THE BAD SEEDS	67	1997
ARE YOU TRYING TO BE LONELY ANDY LEWIS & PAUL WELLER	31	2007
AREA FUTUREHEADS	18	2005
AREA CODES LUDACRIS FEATURING NATE DOGG	25	2001
ARGENTINA JEREMY HEALY & AMOS	30	1997
ARGENTINE MELODY (CANCION DE ARGENTINA) SAN JOSE FEATURING RODRIGUEZ ARGENTINA	14	1978
ARIA ACKER BILK, HIS CLARINET & STRINGS	5	1976
ARIALS SYSTEM OF A DOWN	34	2002
ARIANA STARDUST	42	1977
ARIENNE TASMIN ARCHER	30	1993
ARIZONA SKY CHINA CRISIS	47	1986
ARMAGEDDON DAYS ARE HERE (AGAIN) THE THE	70	1989
ARMAGEDDON IT DEF LEPPARD	20	1988
ARMCHAIR ANARCHIST KINGMAKER	47	1992
ARMED AND EXTREMELY DANGEROUS FIRST CHOICE	16	1973
ARMED AND READY MICHAEL SCHENKER GROUP	53	1980
ARMS ALOFT JOE STRUMMER & THE MESCALEROS	46	2003
ARMS AROUND THE WORLD LOUISE	4	1997
ARMS OF LOREN E'VOKE	25	1996
ARMS OF MARY SUTHERLAND BROTHERS & QUIVER	5	1976
THE ARMS OF THE ONE WHO LOVES YOU XSCAPE	46	1998
THE ARMS OF ORION PRINCE WITH SHEENA EASTON	27	1989
ARMS OF SOLITUDE OUI 3	54	1993
ARMY BEN FOLDS FIVE	28	1999
ARMY DREAMERS KATE BUSH	16	1980
ARMY OF LOVERS LEE RYAN	3	2005
ARMY OF ME BJORK	10	1995
ARMY OF TWO DUM DUMS	27	2001
ARNOLD LAYNE PINK FLOYD	20	1967
ARNOLD LAYNE DAVID GILMOUR	19	2007
AROUND MY BRAIN PROGRESS FUNK	73	1997
AROUND THE WAY GIRL LL COOL J	36	1990
AROUND THE WORLD [A] RONNIE HILTON	4	1957
AROUND THE WORLD [A] BING CROSBY	5	1957
AROUND THE WORLD [A] GRACIE FIELDS	8	1957
AROUND THE WORLD [A] MANTOVANI	20	1957
AROUND THE WORLD [B] EAST 17	3	1994
AROUND THE WORLD [C] DAFT PUNK	5	1997
AROUND THE WORLD [D] RED HOT CHILI PEPPERS	35	1999
AROUND THE WORLD [E] AQUA	26	2000
AROUND THE WORLD [F] ATC	15	2002
ARRANGED MARRIAGE APACHE INDIAN	16	1993
ARRESTED BY YOU DUSTY SPRINGFIELD	70	1990
ARRIVEDERCI DARLING ANNE SHELTON	17	1955
ARRIVEDERCI DARLING EDNA SAVAGE	19	1956

Title / Artist	Peak Position	Year of Release
ARSENAL NUMBER ONE ARSENAL FC	46	2000
ART FOR ART'S SAKE 10 C.C.	5	1975
THE ART OF DRIVING BLACK BOX RECORDER	53	2000
THE ART OF LOSING AMERICAN HI-FI	75	2003
ART OF LOVE ART OF NOISE	67	1990
THE ART OF MOVING BUTTS SHUT UP & DANCE FEATURING ERIN	69	1992
THE ART OF PARTIES JAPAN	48	1981
ARTHUR DALEY ('E'S ALRIGHT) FIRM	14	1982
ARTHUR'S THEME (BEST THAT YOU CAN DO) CHRISTOPHER CROSS	7	1981
ARTS AND CRAFTS RED LIGHT COMPANY	53	2009
AS GEORGE MICHAEL & MARY J BLIGE	4	1999
AS ALWAYS FARLEY 'JACKMASTER' FUNK FEATURING RICKY DILLARD	49	1989
AS ALWAYS SECRET LIFE	45	1992
AS GOOD AS IT GETS GENE	23	1999
AS I AM SOUND OF ONE FEATURING GLADEZZ	65	1993
AS I LAY ME DOWN SOPHIE B HAWKINS	24	1995
AS I LOVE YOU SHIRLEY BASSEY	1	1958
AS I SAT SADLY BY HER SIDE NICK CAVE & THE BAD SEEDS	42	2001
AS IF WE NEVER SAID GOODBYE (FROM SUNSET BOULEVARD) BARBRA STREISAND	20	1994
AS LONG AS HE NEEDS ME SHIRLEY BASSEY	2	1960
AS LONG AS THE PRICE IS RIGHT DR FEELGOOD	40	1979
AS LONG AS YOU FOLLOW FLEETWOOD MAC	66	1988
AS LONG AS YOU LOVE ME BACKSTREET BOYS	3	1997
AS LONG AS YOU'RE GOOD TO ME JUDY CHEEKS	30	1995
AS TEARS GO BY MARIANNE FAITHFULL	9	1964
AS THE RUSH COMES MOTORCYCLE	11	2003
AS THE TIME GOES BY FUNKAPOLITAN	41	1981
AS TIME GOES BY RICHARD ALLAN	43	1960
AS TIME GOES BY DOOLEY WILSON	15	1977
AS TIME GOES BY JASON DONOVAN	26	1992
AS (UNTIL THE DAY) KNOWLEDGE	70	1997
AS USUAL BRENDA LEE	5	1964
AS WE DO DJ ZINC	72	2002
AS YOU LIKE IT ADAM FAITH	5	1962
ASCEND NITZER EBB	62	1992
ASCENSION NO ONE'S GONNA LOVE YOU, SO DON'T EVER WONDER MAXWELL	28	1996
ASHES EMBRACE	11	2004
ASHES AND DIAMONDS ZAINE GRIFF	68	1980
ASHES TO ASHES [A] MINDBENDERS	14	1966
ASHES TO ASHES [B] DAVID BOWIE	1	1980
ASHES TO ASHES [C] FAITH NO MORE	15	1997
ASIA MINOR KOKOMO	35	1961
ASK SMITHS	14	1986
ASK THE LORD HIPSWAY	50	1985
ASLEEP IN THE BACK ELBOW	19	2002
ASS LIKE THAT EMINEM	4	2005
ASSASSIN ORB	12	1992
ASSASSINATOR 13 CHIKINKI	72	2003
ASSASSING MARILLION	22	1984
ASSESSMENT BETA BAND	31	2004
ASSHOLE DENIS LEARY	58	1996
ASSOCIATION INTERNATIONAL AIRPORT/ TEENAGE FANCLUB	75	2004
ASTOUNDED BRAN VAN 3000 FEATURING CURTIS MAYFIELD	40	2001
ASTRAL AMERICA APOLLO 440	36	1994
ASYLUM ORB	20	1997
ASYLUMS IN JERUSALEM SCRITTI POLITTI	43	1982
AT HOME HE'S A TOURIST GANG OF FOUR	58	1979
AT MIDNIGHT T-CONNECTION	53	1979
AT MY MOST BEAUTIFUL R.E.M.	10	1999
AT NIGHT SHAKEDOWN	6	2002

Title / Artist	Peak Position	Year of Release
AT THE CLUB DRIFTERS	3	1965
AT THE EDGE STIFF LITTLE FINGERS	15	1980
AT THE END IIO	20	2003
AT THE HOP DANNY & THE JUNIORS	3	1958
AT THE MOVIES RONI SIZE	67	2003
AT THE PALACE (PARTS 1 & 2) WILFRID BRAMBELL & HARRY H CORBETT	25	1963
AT THE RIVER GROOVE ARMADA	19	1999
AT THE TOP OF THE STAIRS FORMATIONS	28	1971
AT THIS TIME OF YEAR CRAIG	14	2000
(AT YOUR BEST) YOU ARE LOVE AALIYAH	27	1994
ATHEAMA NEBULA II	55	1992
ATHENA WHO	40	1982
ATLANTIS [A] SHADOWS	2	1963
ATLANTIS [B] DONOVAN	23	1968
ATLANTIS [C] SECTION-X	42	1997
ATLANTIS IS CALLING (S.O.S. FOR LOVE) MODERN TALKING	55	1986
ATMOSPHERE [A] RUSS ABBOT	7	1984
ATMOSPHERE [B] JOY DIVISION	34	1988
ATMOSPHERE [C] KAYESTONE	55	2000
ATMOSPHERIC ROAD FAMILY CAT	69	1993
ATOM BOMB FLUKE	20	1996
ATOM POWERED ACTION (EP) BIS	54	1996
ATOMIC BLONDIE	1	1980
ATOMIC CITY HOLLY JOHNSON	18	1989
ATTACK [A] TOYS	36	1966
ATTACK [B] EXPLOITED	50	1982
ATTACK ME WITH YOUR LOVE CAMEO	65	1985
ATTACK OF THE GHOSTRIDERS RAVEONETTES	73	2002
ATTENTION! COMMANDER TOM	23	2005
ATTENTION TO ME NOLANS	9	1981
ATTITUDE [A] SEPULTURA	46	1996
ATTITUDE [B] ALIEN ANT FARM	66	2002
ATTITUDE [C] SUEDE	14	2003
AUBERGE CHRIS REA	16	1991
AUDACITY OF HUGE SIMIAN MOBILE DISCO	60	2009
AUDIO VIDEO NEWS	52	1981
AUDITION WITNESS	71	1999
AUF WIEDERSEHEN SWEETHEART VERA LYNN	10	1952
AUGUST OCTOBER ROBIN GIBB	45	1970
AULD LANG SYNE WEEKEND	47	1985
AUSLANDER LIVING COLOUR	53	1993
AUSTRALIA [A] MANIC STREET PREACHERS	7	1996
AUSTRALIA [B] SHINS	62	2007
AUTHORITY CONFRONTATION SELFISH CUNT	66	2004
AUTO DRIVE HERBIE HANCOCK	33	1983
AUTOBAHN KRAFTWERK	11	1975
AUTOBAHN 66 PRIMAL SCREAM	44	2002
AUTOBIOGRAPHY OF A CRACKHEAD SHUT UP & DANCE	43	1992
AUTOMATIC [A] POINTER SISTERS	2	1984
AUTOMATIC [B] MILLIE SCOTT	56	1986
AUTOMATIC [C] FLOORPLAY	50	1996
AUTOMATIC [D] SARAH WHATMORE	11	2003
AUTOMATIC HIGH S CLUB JUNIORS	2	2002
AUTOMATIC LOVER [A] DEE D JACKSON	4	1978
AUTOMATIC LOVER [B] VIBRATORS	35	1978
AUTOMATIC LOVER (CALL FOR LOVE) REAL McCOY	58	1995
AUTOMATICALLY SUNSHINE SUPREMES	10	1972
AUTOMATIK BEAT RENEGADES	73	2001
AUTOPHILIA BLUETONES	18	2000
AUTUMN [A] RONI SIZE	70	2004
AUTUMN [B] SARAH PHILLIPS	49	2010
AUTUMN ALMANAC KINKS	3	1967
AUTUMN CONCERTO GEORGE MELACHRINO ORCHESTRA	18	1956
AUTUMN LEAVES COLDCUT	50	1994
AUTUMN LOVE ELECTRA	51	1989

Title / Artist	Peak Position	Year of Release
AUTUMN TACTICS CHICANE	44	2000
AUTUMNSONG MANIC STREET PREACHERS	10	2007
AVA ADORE SMASHING PUMPKINS	11	1998
AVALON [A] ROXY MUSIC	13	1982
AVALON [B] JULIET	24	2005
AVE MARIA SHIRLEY BASSEY	31	1962
AVE MARIA LESLEY GARRETT & AMANDA THOMPSON	16	1993
AVE MARIA ANDREA BOCELLI	65	1999
AVENGING ANGELS SPACE	6	1998
AVENUE [A] SAINT ETIENNE	40	1992
AVENUE [B] PAUL VAN DYK	13	1999
THE AVENUE [C] ROLL DEEP	11	2005
AVENUES AND ALLEYWAYS TONY CHRISTIE	26	1973
AVERAGE MAN [A] SYMPOSIUM	45	1998
AVERAGE MAN [B] TURIN BRAKES	35	2003
THE AVERAGE MAN [C] SIMPLE KID	72	2003
THE AWAKENING YORK	11	1999
AWAY FROM HERE ENEMY	8	2007
AWAY FROM HOME DR ALBAN	42	1994
AWAY FROM ME PUDDLE OF MUDD	55	2003
AWFUL HOLE	42	1999
AXEL F HAROLD FALTERMEYER	2	1985
AXEL F CLOCK	7	1995
AXEL F SPACECORN	74	2001
AXEL F CRAZY FROG	1	2005
AXLE GRINDER PENDULUM	62	2007
AY AY AY AY MOOSEY MODERN ROMANCE	10	1981
AYLA AYLA	22	1999
AYO TECHNOLOGY 50 CENT & JUSTIN TIMBERLAKE	2	2007
AZTEC GOLD SILSOE	48	1986
AZTEC LIGHTNING (THEME FROM BBC WORLD CUP GRANDSTAND) HEADS	45	1986

B

Title / Artist	Peak Position	Year of Release
B 2 GETHER ORIGINAL	29	1995
B BOY BABY MUTYA BUENA	73	2008
B GOOD 2 ME RONNI SIMON	73	1994
B LINE LAMB	52	1999
B WITH ME MIS-TEEQ	5	2002
B WITH U JUNIOR SANCHEZ FEATURING DAJAE	31	1999
BAA BAA BLACK SHEEP SINGING SHEEP	42	1982
BAAL'S HYMN (EP) DAVID BOWIE	29	1982
BA-BA-BANKROBBERY (ENGLISH VERSION) EAV	63	1986
BABARABATIRI GYPSYMEN	32	2001
BABE [A] STYX	6	1980
BABE [B] TAKE THAT	1	1993
BABES IN THE WOOD MATCHBOX	46	1981
BABETTE TOMMY BRUCE	50	1962
BABIES ASHFORD & SIMPSON	56	1985
BABOOSHKA KATE BUSH	5	1980
B-A-B-Y RACHEL SWEET	35	1978
THE BABY [A] HOLLIES	26	1972
BABY [B] HALO JAMES	43	1990
BABY [C] ROZALLA	26	1995
BABY [D] FABOLOUS FEATURING MIKE SHOREY	41	2005
BABY [E] LL COOL J	56	2008
BABY [F] JUSTIN BIEBER FEATURING LUDACRIS	3	2010
BABY BABY [A] FRANKIE LYMON & THE TEENAGERS	4	1957
BABY BABY [B] EIGHTH WONDER	65	1988
BABY BABY [C] AMY GRANT	2	1991
BABY BABY [D] CORONA	5	1995
BABY BABY [D] SUNBLOCK FEATURING SANDY	16	2007
BABY-BABY-BABY TLC	55	1992
BABY BABY BYE BYE JERRY LEE LEWIS	47	1960
BABY BABY MY LOVE'S ALL FOR YOU DENIECE WILLIAMS	32	1977
BABY BE MINE BLACKSTREET FEATURING TEDDY RILEY	37	1993
BABY BLUE DUSTY SPRINGFIELD	61	1979
BABY BOY [A] BIG BROVAZ	4	2003
BABY BOY [B] BEYONCE FEATURING SEAN PAUL	2	2003
BABY BRITAIN ELLIOTT SMITH	55	1999
BABY BY ME 50 CENT FEATURING NE-YO	17	2009
BABY, CAN I GET YOUR NUMBER OBI PROJECT FEATURING HARRY, ASHER D & DJ WHAT?	75	2001
BABY CAN I HOLD YOU BOYZONE	2	1997
BABY COME BACK [A] EQUALS	1	1968
BABY COME BACK [A] PATO BANTON	1	1994
BABY COME BACK [B] PLAYER	32	1978
BABY COME ON SPACEMAID	70	1997
BABY COME ON OVER SAMANTHA MUMBA	5	2001
BABY COME TO ME PATTI AUSTIN & JAMES INGRAM	11	1983
BABY COME TO ME ALEXANDER O'NEAL FEATURING CHERRELLE	56	1997
BABY DID A BAD BAD THING CHRIS ISAAK	44	1999
BABY DON'T CHANGE YOUR MIND GLADYS KNIGHT & THE PIPS	4	1977
BABY DON'T CRY [A] LALAH HATHAWAY	54	1991
BABY DON'T CRY [B] INXS	20	1992
BABY DON'T FORGET MY NUMBER MILLI VANILLI	16	1989
BABY DON'T GET HOOKED ON ME MAC DAVIS	29	1972
BABY DON'T GO [A] SONNY & CHER	11	1965
BABY DON'T GO [B] 4MANDU	47	1996
BABY FACE LITTLE RICHARD	2	1959
BABY FACE BOBBY DARIN	40	1962
BABY FACE WING & A PRAYER FIFE & DRUM CORPS	12	1976
BABY FRATELLI FRATELLIS	24	2007
BABY GET HIGHER DAVID SNEDDON	38	2003
BABY GOODBYE FRIDAY HILL	5	2005
BABY GOT BACK SIR MIX-A-LOT	56	1992
BABY I DON'T CARE [A] BUDDY HOLLY	12	1961
BABY I DON'T CARE [A] ELVIS PRESLEY	61	1983
BABY I DON'T CARE [B] TRANSVISION VAMP	3	1989
BABY I DON'T CARE [B] JENNIFER ELLISON	6	2003
BABY I KNOW RUBETTES	10	1977
BABY I LOVE YOU [A] RONETTES	11	1964
BABY I LOVE YOU [A] DAVE EDMUNDS	8	1973
BABY I LOVE YOU [A] RAMONES	8	1980
BABY I LOVE YOU [A] TSD	64	1996
BABY I LOVE YOU [B] ARETHA FRANKLIN	39	1967
BABY I LOVE U [C] JENNIFER LOPEZ	3	2004
BABY I LOVE YOU OK KENNY	12	1975
BABY I LOVE YOUR WAY PETER FRAMPTON	43	1976
BABY I LOVE YOUR WAY BIG MOUNTAIN	2	1994
BABY I LOVE YOUR WAY – FREEBIRD WILL TO POWER	6	1989
BABY I NEED YOUR LOVIN' FOURMOST	24	1964
BABY I WON'T LET YOU DOWN PICKETTYWITCH	27	1970
BABY I'M A-WANT YOU BREAD	14	1972
BABY I'M SCARED OF YOU WOMACK & WOMACK	72	1984
BABY I'M YOURS PETER & GORDON	19	1965
BABY I'M YOURS LINDA LEWIS	33	1976
BABY, IT'S COLD OUTSIDE TOM JONES & CERYS MATTHEWS	17	1999
BABY IT'S TRUE MARI WILSON	42	1982
BABY IT'S YOU [A] DAVE BERRY	24	1964
BABY IT'S YOU [A] BEATLES	7	1995
BABY IT'S YOU [B] SILK	44	1993
BABY IT'S YOU [C] MN8	22	1995
BABY IT'S YOU [D] JOJO FEATURING BOW WOW	8	2004
BABY JANE ROD STEWART	1	1983
BABY JUMP MUNGO JERRY	1	1971
BABY LAY DOWN RUBY WINTERS	43	1979
BABY LEE JOHN LEE HOOKER WITH ROBERT CRAY	65	1996
BABY LET ME TAKE YOU HOME ANIMALS	21	1964
BABY LOVE [A] SUPREMES	1	1964
BABY LOVE [A] HONEY BANE	58	1981
BABY LOVE [B] REGINA	50	1986
BABY LOVE [B] DANNII MINOGUE	14	1991
BABY LOVE [C] NICOLE SCHERZINGER FEATURING WILL.I.AM	14	2007
BABY LOVER PETULA CLARK	12	1958
BABY MAKE IT SOON MARMALADE	9	1969
BABY MY HEART CRICKETS	33	1960
BABY NEVER SAY GOODBYE UNIT FOUR PLUS TWO	49	1966
BABY NOW I DAN REED NETWORK	65	1991
BABY NOW THAT I'VE FOUND YOU FOUNDATIONS	1	1967
BABY NOW THAT I'VE FOUND YOU LAUREN WATERWORTH	24	2002
BABY OF MINE ALAN PRICE	32	1979
BABY (OFF THE WALL) SIRENS	49	2004
BABY ONE MORE TIME BRITNEY SPEARS	1	1999
BABY PHAT DE LA SOUL	55	2002
BABY PLAYS AROUND (EP) ELVIS COSTELLO	65	1989
BABY PLEASE DON'T GO THEM	10	1965
BABY ROO CONNIE FRANCIS	5	1961
BABY SITTIN' BOBBY ANGELO & THE TUXEDOS	30	1961
BABY SITTIN' BOOGIE BUZZ CLIFFORD	17	1961
BABY STOP CRYING BOB DYLAN	13	1978
BABY TAKE A BOW ADAM FAITH	22	1962
BABY TALK ALISHA	67	1986
BABY U LEFT ME (IN THE COLD) MARILYN	70	1985
BABY UNIVERSAL TIN MACHINE	48	1991
BABY WANTS TO RIDE HANI	70	2000
BABY, WE BETTER TRY TO GET IT TOGETHER BARRY WHITE	15	1976
BABY WE CAN'T GO WRONG CILLA BLACK	36	1974
BABY WHAT A BIG SURPRISE CHICAGO	41	1977
BABY WHAT I MEAN DRIFTERS	49	1965
BABY WHEN THE LIGHT DAVID GUETTA FEATURING COZI	50	2007
(BABY) YOU DON'T HAVE TO TELL ME WALKER BROTHERS	13	1966
BABY YOU SHOULD KNOW JOY ZIPPER	59	2004
BABY YOU'RE DYNAMITE CLIFF RICHARD	27	1984
BABYCAKES 3 OF A KIND	1	2004
BABYLON [A] BLACK DOG FEATURING OFRA HAZA	65	1999
BABYLON [B] DAVID GRAY	5	2000
BABYLON A.D. (SO GLAD FOR THE MADNESS) CRADLE OF FILTH	35	2003
BABYLON'S BURNING RUTS	7	1979
BABY'S COMING BACK JELLYFISH	51	1991
BABY'S COMING BACK McFLY	1	2007
BABY'S FIRST CHRISTMAS CONNIE FRANCIS	30	1961
BABY'S GOT A TEMPER PRODIGY	5	2002
BABY'S REQUEST WINGS	60	1979
BABYSHAMBLES PETE DOHERTY	32	2004
BACHELOR BOY CLIFF RICHARD & THE SHADOWS	1	1962
BACHELORETTE BJORK	21	1997
BACK AGAIN BOY KILL BOY	26	2006
BACK AND FORTH [A] CAMEO	11	1987

Title / Artist	Peak Position	Year of Release
BACK AND FORTH [B] AALIYAH	16	1994
BACK AROUND ELEVATOR SUITE	71	2000
BACK BY DOPE DEMAND KING BEE	61	1991
BACK FOR GOOD TAKE THAT	1	1995
BACK FOR GOOD REAL EMOTION	67	1995
BACK FOR ME CANDEE JAY	23	2004
BACK FROM THE EDGE BRUCE DICKINSON	68	1996
BACK HERE BBMAK	5	1999
BACK HOME ENGLAND WORLD CUP SQUAD	1	1970
BACK IN LOVE AGAIN DONNA SUMMER	29	1978
BACK IN MY ARMS CHRIS PAUL	74	1987
BACK IN MY ARMS AGAIN SUPREMES	40	1965
BACK IN MY ARMS (ONCE AGAIN) HAZELL DEAN	41	1984
BACK IN MY LIFE [A] JOE ROBERTS	39	1993
BACK IN MY LIFE [B] ALICE DEEJAY	4	1999
BACK IN POWER GLITTERATI	62	2005
BACK IN THE DAY [A] AHMAD	64	1994
BACK IN THE DAY [B] ASHER D	43	2002
BACK IN THE HIGH LIFE AGAIN STEVE WINWOOD	53	1987
BACK IN THE UK SCOOTER	18	1996
BACK IN THE U.S.S.R. BEATLES	19	1976
BACK IT UP ROBIN S	43	1994
BACK LIKE THAT GHOSTFACE KILLAH FEATURING NE-YO & KANYE WEST	46	2006
BACK ME UP URBNRI	42	2008
THE BACK OF LOVE ECHO & THE BUNNYMEN	19	1982
BACK OF MY HAND JAGS	17	1979
BACK OFF BOOGALOO RINGO STARR	2	1972
BACK ON MY FEET AGAIN FOUNDATIONS	18	1968
BACK ON THE CHAIN GANG PRETENDERS	17	1982
BACK ON THE RADIO HISS	65	2003
BACK ON THE ROAD [A] MARMALADE	35	1971
BACK ON THE ROAD [B] EARTH, WIND & FIRE		1980
BACK ON THE STREETS SAXON	75	1985
BACK ON TOP VAN MORRISON	69	1999
BACK SEAT OF MY CAR PAUL & LINDA McCARTNEY	39	1971
BACK STABBERS O'JAYS	14	1972
BACK STREET LUV CURVED AIR	4	1971
BACK THEN MORE FIRE CREW	45	2003
BACK TO BASICS SHAPESHIFTERS	10	2005
BACK TO BLACK AMY WINEHOUSE	25	2007
BACK TO CALI MAURO PICOTTO	42	2002
BACK TO EARTH YVES DERUYTER	56	2001
BACK TO FRONT [A] STIFF LITTLE FINGERS	49	1980
BACK TO FRONT [B] ADAMSKI	63	1992
BACK TO LIFE (HOWEVER DO YOU WANT ME) SOUL II SOUL FEATURING CARON WHEELER	1	1989
BACK TO LOVE [A] EVELYN KING	40	1982
BACK TO LOVE [B] BRAND NEW HEAVIES FEATURING N'DEA DAVENPORT	23	1994
BACK TO LOVE [C] E-Z ROLLERS	61	2003
BACK TO MY ROOTS RuPAUL	40	1993
BACK TO REALITY INTELLIGENT HOODLUM	55	1990
BACK TO SCHOOL AGAIN FOUR TOPS	62	1982
BACK TO THE LIGHT BRIAN MAY	19	1992
BACK TO THE OLD SCHOOL BASSHEADS	12	1992
BACK TO THE SIXTIES TIGHT FIT	4	1981
BACK TO THE SIXTIES PART 2 TIGHT FIT	33	1981
BACK TO YOU BRYAN ADAMS	18	1997
BACK TOGETHER [A] BABYBIRD	22	1999
BACK TOGETHER [B] HARDSOUL FEATURING RON CARROLL	60	2004
BACK TOGETHER AGAIN ROBERTA FLACK & DONNY HATHAWAY	3	1980
BACK TOGETHER AGAIN INNER CITY	49	1993
BACK UP (TO ME) WOOKIE FEATURING LAIN	38	2001
BACK WHEN ALLSTARS	19	2002
BACK WITH THE BOYS AGAIN JOE FAGIN	53	1986
BACK WITH THE KILLER AGAIN AUTEURS	45	1996
BACKCHAT QUEEN	40	1982
BACKFIELD IN MOTION JB'S ALL STARS	48	1984
BACKFIRE AT THE DISCO WOMBATS	40	2007
BACKFIRED [A] DEBBIE HARRY	32	1981
BACKFIRED [B] MASTERS AT WORK FEATURING INDIA	62	2002
BACKS TO THE WALL SAXON	64	1980
BACKSEAT EDUCATION ZODIAC MINDWARP & THE LOVE REACTION	49	1987
BACKSTABBERS MARK MORRISON	48	2004
BACKSTAGE GENE PITNEY	4	1966
BACKSTREET SYMPHONY THUNDER	25	1990
BACKSTROKIN' FATBACK	41	1980
BAD MICHAEL JACKSON	3	1987
BAD ACTRESS TERRORVISION	10	1996
BAD AMBASSADOR DIVINE COMEDY	34	2001
BAD ASS STRIPPA JENTINA	22	2004
BAD BABYSITTER PRINCESS SUPERSTAR	11	2002
BAD BAD BOY NAZARETH	10	1973
BAD BLOOD SUPERGRASS	73	2008
BAD BOY [A] MARTY WILDE	7	1959
BAD BOY [B] ADICTS	75	1983
BAD BOY [C] MIAMI SOUND MACHINE	16	1986
BAD BOY [D] WILDCHILD FEATURING JOMALSKI	38	1998
BAD BOY [E] SKEPTA	35	2010
BAD BOY FOR LIFE P DIDDY FEATURING BLACK ROB & MARK CURRY	13	2001
BAD BOYS [A] WHAM!	2	1983
BAD BOYS [B] INNER CIRCLE	52	1993
BAD BOYS [C] ALEXANDRA BURKE FEATURING FLO RIDA	1	2009
BAD BOYS HOLLER BOO 5050	73	2002
BAD CASE OF LOVIN' YOU (DOCTOR DOCTOR) ROBERT PALMER	61	1979
BAD COVER VERSION PULP	27	2002
BAD DAY [A] CARMEL	15	1983
BAD DAY [B] R.E.M.	8	2003
BAD DAY [C] DANIEL POWTER	2	2005
THE BAD DAYS EP SPACE	20	1998
A BAD DREAM KEANE	23	2007
BAD FEELINGS BEATINGS	68	2002
BAD GIRL [A] MADONNA	10	1993
BAD GIRL [B] SCARLET	54	1996
BAD GIRL [C] DJ RAP	32	1998
BAD GIRL (AT NIGHT) DAVE SPOON FEATURING LISA MAFFIA	36	2007
BAD GIRLS DONNA SUMMER	14	1979
BAD GIRLS JULIET ROBERTS	17	1999
BAD HABIT A.T.F.C. PRESENTS ONEPHATDEEVA FEATURING LISA MILLETT	17	2000
BAD HABITS JENNY BURTON	68	1985
BAD INTENTIONS DR DRE FEATURING KNOC-TURN'AL	4	2002
BAD LIFE PUBLIC IMAGE LTD	71	1984
BAD LOVE ERIC CLAPTON	25	1990
BAD LUCK FM	54	1989
BAD MAN COCKNEY REJECTS	65	1980
BAD MEDICINE BON JOVI	17	1988
BAD MOON RISING CREEDENCE CLEARWATER REVIVAL	1	1969
A BAD NIGHT CAT STEVENS	20	1967
BAD OLD DAYS CO-CO	13	1978
BAD OLD MAN BABYBIRD	31	1998
BAD PENNY BLUES HUMPHREY LYTTELTON BAND	19	1956
THE BAD PHOTOGRAPHER SAINT ETIENNE	27	1998
BAD ROMANCE LADY GAGA	1	2009
BAD THING CRY OF LOVE	60	1994
BAD THINGS [A] N-JOI	57	1995
BAD THINGS [B] JACE EVERETT	49	2009
BAD TIME JAYHAWKS	70	1995
BAD TO ME BILLY J KRAMER & THE DAKOTAS	1	1963
THE BAD TOUCH BLOODHOUND GANG	4	2000
A BAD TOWN BIG SOUND AUTHORITY	54	1985
BAD WEATHER SUPREMES	37	1973
BAD YOUNG BROTHER DEREK B	16	1988
BADABOOM B2K FEATURING FABOLOUS	26	2004
BADDER BADDER SCHWING FREDDY FRESH FEATURING FATBOY SLIM	34	1999
BADDEST RUFFEST BACKYARD DOG	15	2001
BADGE CREAM	18	1969
BADITUDE SPOON, HARRIS & OBERNIK	29	2008
BADMAN SISTER BLISS	51	1996
THE BADMAN IS ROBBIN' HIJACK	56	1990
BAG IT UP GERI HALLIWELL	1	2000
BAGGY TROUSERS MADNESS	3	1980
THE BAGUIO TRACK LUZON	67	2001
BAILAMOS [A] ENRIQUE IGLESIAS	4	1999
BAILAMOS [B] M3	40	1999
BAILANDO CON LOBOS CABANA	65	1995
BAKER STREET GERRY RAFFERTY	3	1978
BAKER STREET UNDERCOVER	2	1992
BAKERMAN LAID BACK	44	1990
BALL AND CHAIN XTC	58	1982
BALL OF CONFUSION TEMPTATIONS	7	1970
BALL PARK INCIDENT WIZZARD	6	1972
BALLA BABY CHINGY	34	2004
BALLAD OF A LANDLORD TERRY HALL	50	1997
THE BALLAD OF BONNIE AND CLYDE GEORGIE FAME	1	1967
THE BALLAD OF CHASEY LAIN BLOODHOUND GANG	15	2000
BALLAD OF DAVY CROCKETT BILL HAYES	2	1956
THE BALLAD OF DAVY CROCKETT TENNESSEE ERNIE FORD	6	1956
BALLAD OF DAVY CROCKETT DICK JAMES	18	1956
BALLAD OF DAVY CROCKETT MAX BYGRAVES	20	1956
THE BALLAD OF JAYNE L.A. GUNS	53	1991
THE BALLAD OF JOHN AND YOKO BEATLES	1	1969
THE BALLAD OF LUCY JORDAN MARIANNE FAITHFULL	48	1979
BALLAD OF PALADIN DUANE EDDY	10	1962
THE BALLAD OF PAUL K McFLY	9	2005
THE BALLAD OF PETER PUMPKINHEAD XTC	71	1992
THE BALLAD OF PETER PUMPKINHEAD CRASH TEST DUMMIES	30	1995
THE BALLAD OF SPOTTY MULDOON PETER COOK	34	1965
BALLAD OF THE GREEN BERETS STAFF SERGEANT BARRY SADLER	24	1966
THE BALLAD OF TOM JONES SPACE WITH CERYS OF CATATONIA	4	1998
BALLAD OF YOUTH RICHIE SAMBORA	59	1991
BALLERINA GIRL LIONEL RICHIE	17	1986
BALLERINA (PRIMA DONNA) STEVE HARLEY	51	1983
BALLOON CATHERINE WHEEL	59	1992
BALLOONS FOALS	39	2007
THE BALLROOM BLITZ SWEET	2	1973
BALLROOM BLITZ TIA CARRERE	26	1992
THE BALLROOM OF ROMANCE CHRIS DE BURGH	40	1986
BALMES IAN POOLEY FEATURING ESTHERO	65	2001
BAM BAM BAM WESTBAM	57	1994
BAMA BOOGIE WOOGIE CLEVELAND EATON	35	1978
BAMA LAMA BAMA LOO LITTLE RICHARD	20	1964
BAMBAATA 2012 SHY FX	60	1999
BAMBAKITA RONI SIZE	60	2004
BAMBINO SPRINGFIELDS	16	1961
BAMBOO HOUSES SYLVIAN SAKAMOTO	30	1982
BAMBOOGIE BAMBOO	2	1998
BANANA BANANA KING KURT	54	1984
BANANA BOAT SONG HARRY BELAFONTE	2	1957
BANANA BOAT SONG SHIRLEY BASSEY	8	1957
BANANA BOAT SONG TARRIERS	15	1957

Title / Artist	Peak Position	Year of Release
BANANA REPUBLIC BOOMTOWN RATS	3	1980
BANANA ROCK WOMBLES	9	1974
THE BANANA SONG GSP	38	1992
BANANA SPLITS (TRA LA LA SONG) DICKIES	7	1979
BA-NA-NA-BAM-BOO WESTWORLD	37	1987
BANANA-NA-NA (DUMB DI DUMB) TECHNOHEAD	64	1996
BAND OF GOLD [A] DON CHERRY	6	1956
BAND OF GOLD [B] FREDA PAYNE	1	1970
BAND OF GOLD [B] SYLVESTER	67	1983
BAND ON THE RUN PAUL McCARTNEY & WINGS	3	1974
THE BAND PLAYED THE BOOGIE C.C.S.	36	1973
BANDAGES HOT HOT HEAT	25	2003
BANDWAGON BLUES TWISTED INDIVIDUAL	51	2003
BANG [A] BLUR	24	1991
BANG [B] ROBBIE RIVERA PRESENTS RHYTHM BANGERS	13	2000
BANG AND BLAME R.E.M.	15	1994
BANG BANG [A] SQUEEZE	49	1978
BANG BANG [B] BA ROBERTSON	2	1979
BANG BANG (MY BABY SHOT ME DOWN) CHER	3	1966
BANG BANG YOU'RE DEAD DIRTY PRETTY THINGS	5	2006
BANG ON! PROPELLERHEADS	53	1998
BANG ON THE PIANO JACK McMANUS	45	2008
BANG ZOOM (LET'S GO GO) REAL ROXANNE WITH HITMAN HOWIE TEE	11	1986
BANGERS AND MASH PETER SELLERS & SOPHIA LOREN	22	1961
BANGIN' BASS DA TECHNO BOHEMIAN	63	1997
THE BANGIN' MAN SLADE	3	1974
BANGLA DESH GEORGE HARRISON	10	1971
BANJO BOY JAN & KJELD	36	1960
BANJO BOY GEORGE FORMBY	40	1960
BANJO'S BACK IN TOWN ALMA COGAN	17	1955
BANKROBBER CLASH	12	1980
BANKROBBER AUDIOWEB	19	1997
BANKS OF THE OHIO OLIVIA NEWTON-JOHN	6	1971
THE BANNER MAN BLUE MINK	3	1971
BANQUET BLOC PARTY	13	2004
BARBADOS TYPICALLY TROPICAL	1	1975
BARBARA ANN BEACH BOYS	3	1966
BARBARELLA ALISHA'S ATTIC	34	1999
BARBER'S ADAGIO FOR STRINGS WILLIAM ORBIT	4	1999
BARBIE GIRL AQUA	1	1997
BARBIE GIRL SAMANDA	26	2007
BARCELONA [A] FREDDIE MERCURY & MONTSERRAT CABALLE	2	1987
BARCELONA [B] D KAY & EPSILON FEATURING STAMINA MC	14	2003
BARCELONA (FRIENDS UNTIL THE END) RUSSELL WATSON & SHAUN RYDER	68	2000
BARE NECESSITIES MEGAMIX UK MIXMASTERS	14	1991
BAREFOOT (EP) ULTRAMARINE	61	1994
BAREFOOT IN THE HEAD A MAN CALLED ADAM	60	1990
BAREFOOTIN' ROBERT PARKER	24	1966
BARK AT THE MOON OZZY OSBOURNE	21	1983
BARMY LONDON ARMY CHARLIE HARPER	68	1980
BARNEY (...& ME) BOO RADLEYS	48	1994
BARNEY RUBBLE TWANG	59	2009
BARREL OF A GUN DEPECHE MODE	4	1997
BARRIERS SOFT CELL	25	1983
THE BARTENDER AND THE THIEF STEREOPHONICS	3	1998
BASEMENT TRACK HIGH CONTRAST	65	2003
BASKET CASE GREEN DAY	7	1995
BASKET CASE FREEFALLER	36	2005
THE BASS EP FERGIE	47	2002
BASS (HOW LOW CAN YOU GO) SIMON HARRIS	12	1988
BASS SHAKE URBAN SHAKEDOWN FEATURING MICKY FINN	59	1992
BASSCAD AUTECHRE	56	1994
BASSFLY TILLMAN + REIS	70	2000
BASSLICK SECOND PROTOCOL	58	2000
BASSLINE MANTRONIX	34	1986
BASTARDO CHARLOTTE HATHERLEY	31	2005
BAT OUT OF HELL MEAT LOAF	8	1979
BATDANCE PRINCE	2	1989
BATHTIME TINDERSTICKS	38	1997
BATHWATER NO DOUBT	17	2004
BATMAN THEME NEAL HEFTI	55	1988
BATTER UP NELLY & ST LUNATICS	28	2001
BATTLE WOOKIE FEATURING LAIN	10	2000
BATTLE CRY SHONTELLE	61	2009
THE BATTLE OF NEW ORLEANS LONNIE DONEGAN	2	1959
THE BATTLE OF NEW ORLEANS JOHNNY HORTON	16	1959
BATTLE OF THE HEROES – STAR WARS JOHN WILLIAMS & THE LSO	25	2005
BATTLE OF THE SEXES FAITH, HOPE & CHARITY	53	1990
BATTLE OF WHO COULD CARE LESS BEN FOLDS FIVE	26	1997
BATTLEFIELD JORDIN SPARKS	11	2009
BATTLEFLAG LO FIDELITY ALLSTARS FEATURING PIGEONHED	36	1999
THE BATTLE'S O'ER ANDY STEWART	28	1961
BATTLESHIP CHAINS GEORGIA SATELLITES	44	1987
BAUBLES, BANGLES AND BEADS GEORGE SHEARING	49	1962
BAWITDABA KID ROCK	41	2001
BBC WORLD CUP GRANDSTAND ROYAL PHILHARMONIC ORCHESTRA	61	1982
B-BOY HUMP OLD SKOOL ORCHESTRA	55	1999
B-BOY STANCE FREESTYLERS FEATURING TENOR FLY	23	1998
BE AGGRESSIVE FAITH NO MORE	3	1993
BE ALL YOU WANT ME TO BE MORNING RUNNER	44	2005
BE ALONE NO MORE ANOTHER LEVEL FEATURING JAY-Z	6	1998
BE ANGLED JAM & SPOON FEATURING REA	31	2002
BE AS ONE SASHA & MARIA	17	1996
BE BOP A LULA GENE VINCENT	16	1956
BE CAREFUL SPARKLE FEATURING R KELLY	7	1998
BE COOL PAFFENDORF	7	2002
BE FAITHFUL FATMAN SCOOP FEATURING THE CROOKLYN CLAN	1	2003
BE FREE LIVE ELEMENT	26	2002
BE FREE WITH YOUR LOVE SPANDAU BALLET	42	1989
BE GENTLE WITH ME BOY LEAST LIKELY TO	62	2006
BE GOOD TO YOURSELF FRANKIE MILLER	27	1977
BE HAPPY MARY J BLIGE	30	1994
BE LOUD BE PROUD (BE HEARD) TOYAH	30	1982
BE MINE [A] LANCE FORTUNE	4	1960
BE MINE [B] TREMELOES	39	1967
BE MINE [C] CHARLOTTE	59	1998
BE MINE [D] DAVID GRAY	23	2003
BE MINE [E] ROBYN	10	2008
BE MINE TONIGHT JAMMERS	65	1983
BE MY BABY [A] RONETTES	4	1963
BE MY BABY [B] VANESSA PARADIS	6	1992
BE MY BABY [C] CAPPELLA	53	1997
BE MY DOWNFALL DEL AMITRI	30	1992
BE MY ENEMY DEPARTURE	41	2004
BE MY FRIEND SOUL U*NIQUE	53	2000
BE MY GIRL [A] JIM DALE	2	1957
BE MY GIRL [B] DENNISONS	46	1963
BE MY GUEST FATS DOMINO	11	1959
BE MY LIGHT BE MY GUIDE GENE	54	1994
BE MY LOVER LA BOUCHE	25	1995
BE MY NUMBER TWO JOE JACKSON	70	1984
BE MY TWIN BROTHER BEYOND	14	1989
BE NEAR ME ABC	26	1985
BE ON YOU FLO RIDA	51	2009
BE QUICK OR BE DEAD IRON MAIDEN	2	1992
BE QUIET AND DRIVE (FAR AWAY) DEFTONES	50	1998
BE STIFF DEVO	71	1978
BE TENDER WITH ME BABY TINA TURNER	28	1990
BE THANKFUL FOR WHAT YOU'VE GOT WILLIAM DE VAUGHN	31	1974
BE THE FIRST TO BELIEVE A1	6	1999
BE THE ONE [A] TING TINGS	28	2008
BE THE ONE [B] JACK PENATE	35	2009
BE THERE [A] TALL PAUL	45	1999
BE THERE [B] UNKLE FEATURING IAN BROWN	8	1999
BE WITH ME ALWAYS CLIFF RICHARD	52	1997
BE WITH YOU [A] BANGLES	23	1989
BE WITH YOU [B] ATOMIC KITTEN	2	2002
BE WITHOUT YOU [A] MARY J BLIGE	32	2006
BE WITHOUT YOU [B] WIFI FEATURING MELANIE M	42	2007
BE YOUNG BE FOOLISH BE HAPPY TAMS	32	1970
BE YOUNG BE FOOLISH BE HAPPY SONIA	22	1991
BE YOURSELF [A] CELEDA	61	1999
BE YOURSELF [B] AUDIOSLAVE	40	2005
BEACH BABY FIRST CLASS	13	1974
BEACH BOYS MEDLEY BEACH BOYS	47	1981
BEACH BUMP BABY FORD	68	1990
BEACH OF THE WAR GODDESS CARON WHEELER	75	1993
BEACHBALL NALIN & KANE	17	1997
BEACHBOY GOLD GIDEA PARK	11	1981
BEACHED ORBITAL & ANGELO BADALAMENTI	36	2000
BEACON LIGHT WEEN	20	1998
BEAR CAGE STRANGLERS	36	1980
BEAST AND THE HARLOT AVENGED SEVENFOLD	47	2006
BEAT AGAIN JLS	1	2009
A BEAT CALLED LOVE GRID	64	1990
BEAT DIS BOMB THE BASS	2	1988
BEAT FOR BEATNIKS JOHN BARRY ORCHESTRA	40	1960
THE BEAT GOES ON [A] SONNY & CHER	29	1967
BEAT GOES ON [B] ALL SEEING I	11	1998
THE BEAT GOES ON [C] BOB SINCLAR	33	2003
THE BEAT IS ROCKIN' ERICK E	25	2007
BEAT IT MICHAEL JACKSON	3	1983
BEAT IT FALL OUT BOY FEATURING JOHN MAYER	21	2008
BEAT MAMA CAST	9	1999
BEAT STREET BREAKDOWN GRANDMASTER MELLE MEL & THE FURIOUS FIVE	42	1984
BEAT SURRENDER JAM	1	1982
BEAT THE BEAT MARI WILSON	59	1982
BEAT THE CLOCK SPARKS	10	1979
BEAT YOUR HEART OUT DISTILLERS	74	2004
THE BEAT(EN) GENERATION THE THE	18	1989
BEATIN' THE HEAT JACK 'N' CHILL	42	1988
BEATING HEART BABY HEAD AUTOMATICA	44	2005
BEATLES AND THE STONES HOUSE OF LOVE	36	1990
BEATLES MOVIE MEDLEY BEATLES	10	1982
BEATNIK FLY JOHNNY & THE HURRICANES	8	1960
BEATNIK GIRL SNUG	55	1998
BEATSTIME SONIC SOLUTION	59	1992
BEAUTIFUL [A] MARILLION	29	1995
BEAUTIFUL [B] MATT DAREY'S MASH UP PRESENTS MARCELLA WOODS	10	2000
BEAUTIFUL [C] BIGFELLA FEATURING NOEL McCALLA	52	2002
BEAUTIFUL [D] LEMONESCENT	70	2002

Title	Artist	Peak Position	Year of Release
BEAUTIFUL [E]	ATHLETE	41	2002
BEAUTIFUL [F]	CHRISTINA AGUILERA	1	2003
BEAUTIFUL [G]	SNOOP DOGG	23	2003
BEAUTIFUL [H]	DAMIAN 'JR GONG' MARLEY	39	2006
BEAUTIFUL [I]	AKON FEATURING KARDINAL OFFISHALL & COLBY O'DONIS	8	2008
BEAUTIFUL [J]	EMINEM	12	2009
BEAUTIFUL ALONE	STRANGELOVE	35	1996
BEAUTIFUL CHILD (A DEEPER LOVE)	MADELYNE	63	2002
BEAUTIFUL DAY [A]	3 COLOURS RED	11	1999
BEAUTIFUL DAY [B]	U2	1	2000
BEAUTIFUL DREAM	WORLD PARTY	31	1997
THE BEAUTIFUL EXPERIENCE	PRINCE	18	1994
BEAUTIFUL GIRL [A]	INXS	23	1993
BEAUTIFUL GIRL [B]	SEAN KINGSTON	1	2007
BEAUTIFUL IMBALANCE	THRASHING DOVES	50	1987
BEAUTIFUL IN MY EYES	JOSHUA KADISON	37	1994
BEAUTIFUL INSIDE	LOUISE	13	2000
BEAUTIFUL LIAR	BEYONCE & SHAKIRA	1	2007
BEAUTIFUL LIFE	ACE OF BASE	15	1996
BEAUTIFUL LOVE [A]	ADEVA	57	1989
BEAUTIFUL LOVE [B]	JULIAN COPE	32	1991
BEAUTIFUL LOVER	BROTHERHOOD OF MAN	15	1978
BEAUTIFUL NIGHT	PAUL McCARTNEY	25	1997
BEAUTIFUL NOISE	NEIL DIAMOND	13	1976
THE BEAUTIFUL OCCUPATION	TRAVIS	48	2003
BEAUTIFUL ONES [A]	SUEDE	8	1996
BEAUTIFUL ONES [B]	BILLIAM	32	2007
BEAUTIFUL PEOPLE [A]	STRESS	74	1990
BEAUTIFUL PEOPLE [B]	BIG COUNTRY	72	1991
BEAUTIFUL PEOPLE [C]	BARBARA TUCKER	23	1994
THE BEAUTIFUL PEOPLE [D]	MARILYN MANSON	18	1997
BEAUTIFUL SON	HOLE	54	1993
BEAUTIFUL SOUL	JESSE McCARTNEY	16	2006
BEAUTIFUL STRANGER	MADONNA	2	1999
BEAUTIFUL SUNDAY	DANIEL BOONE	21	1972
BEAUTIFUL YOU	NEIL SEDAKA	43	1972
BEAUTY AND THE BEAST [A]	DAVID BOWIE	39	1978
BEAUTY AND THE BEAST [B]	CELINE DION & PEABO BRYSON	9	1992
BEAUTY DIES YOUNG	LOWGOLD	40	2000
BEAUTY IS ONLY SKIN DEEP	TEMPTATIONS	18	1966
THE BEAUTY OF SILENCE	SVENSON & GIELEN	41	2001
BEAUTY OF THE RIDE	SEBADOH	74	1996
BEAUTY ON THE FIRE	NATALIE IMBRUGLIA	26	2002
BEAUTY'S ONLY SKIN DEEP	ASWAD	31	1989
BECAUSE [A]	DEMIS ROUSSOS	39	1977
BECAUSE [B]	JULIAN LENNON	40	1985
BECAUSE [C]	JUSTICE	48	2007
BECAUSE I GOT HIGH	AFROMAN	1	2001
BECAUSE I GOT IT LIKE THAT	JUNGLE BROTHERS	32	1998
BECAUSE I LOVE YOU [A]	GEORGIE FAME	15	1967
BECAUSE I LOVE YOU [B]	SHAKIN' STEVENS	14	1986
BECAUSE I LOVE YOU (THE POSTMAN SONG)	STEVIE B	6	1991
BECAUSE I WANT YOU	PLACEBO	13	2006
BECAUSE OF LOVE [A]	BILLY FURY	18	1962
BECAUSE OF LOVE [B]	JANET JACKSON	19	1994
BECAUSE OF YOU [A]	DEXY'S MIDNIGHT RUNNERS	13	1986
BECAUSE OF YOU [B]	GABRIELLE	24	1994
BECAUSE OF YOU [C]	980	36	1999
BECAUSE OF YOU [D]	SCANTY SANDWICH	3	2000
BECAUSE OF YOU [E]	MARQUES HOUSTON	51	2004
BECAUSE OF YOU [F]	KELLY CLARKSON	7	2005
BECAUSE OF YOU [G]	NE-YO	4	2007
BECAUSE THE NIGHT	PATTI SMITH GROUP	5	1978
BECAUSE THE NIGHT	CO-RO FEATURING TARLISA	61	1992
BECAUSE THE NIGHT	10,000 MANIACS	65	1993
BECAUSE THE NIGHT	JAN WAYNE	14	2002
BECAUSE THE NIGHT	CASCADA	28	2008
BECAUSE THEY'RE YOUNG	DUANE EDDY & THE REBELS	2	1960
BECAUSE THEY'RE YOUNG	JAMES DARREN	29	1960
BECAUSE WE WANT TO	BILLIE	1	1998
BECAUSE YOU	COSMIC ROUGH RIDERS	34	2003
BECAUSE YOU LOVED ME (THEME FROM UP CLOSE AND PERSONAL)	CELINE DION	5	1996
BECAUSE YOU'RE MINE	MARIO LANZA	3	1952
BECAUSE YOU'RE MINE	NAT 'KING' COLE	6	1952
BECAUSE YOU'RE YOUNG	CLASSIX NOUVEAUX	43	1982
BECOMING MORE LIKE ALFIE	DIVINE COMEDY	27	1996
BECOMING MORE LIKE GOD	JAH WOBBLE'S INVADERS OF THE HEART	36	1994
BED	J HOLIDAY	32	2007
BED OF NAILS	ALICE COOPER	38	1989
BED OF ROSES	BON JOVI	13	1993
BED SITTER	SOFT CELL	4	1981
BEDROCK	YOUNG MONEY FEATURING LLOYD	9	2010
BEDS ARE BURNING	MIDNIGHT OIL	6	1988
THE BED'S TOO BIG WITHOUT YOU	SHEILA HYLTON	35	1981
BEDSHAPED	KEANE	10	2004
BEDTIME STORY	MADONNA	4	1995
THE BEE	SCIENTIST	47	1990
BEE BOM	ANTHONY NEWLEY	12	1961
BEE STING	CAMOUFLAGE FEATURING MYSTI	48	1977
BEEF	GARY CLAIL	64	1990
BEEN A LONG TIME	FOG	27	1994
BEEN AROUND THE WORLD [A]	PUFF DADDY & THE FAMILY	20	1997
BEEN AROUND THE WORLD [B]	ZENA FEATURING VYBZ KARTEL	44	2004
BEEN CAUGHT STEALING	JANE'S ADDICTION	34	1991
BEEN IT	CARDIGANS	56	1996
BEEN THERE DONE THAT	SMOKE 2 SEVEN	26	2002
BEEN THINKING ABOUT YOU	MARTINE GIRAULT	63	1995
BEEN TRAINING DOGS	COOPER TEMPLE CLAUSE	20	2002
BEEP	PUSSYCAT DOLLS FEATURING WILL.I.AM	2	2006
BEEP ME 911	MISSY 'MISDEMEANOR' ELLIOTT	14	1998
BEEPER	COUNT & SINDEN FEATURING KID SISTER	69	2008
BEER DRINKERS AND HELL RAISERS	MOTORHEAD	43	1980
BEETHOVEN (I LOVE TO LISTEN TO)	EURYTHMICS	25	1987
BEETLEBUM	BLUR	1	1997
BEFORE	PET SHOP BOYS	7	1996
BEFORE I FALL TO PIECES	RAZORLIGHT	17	2006
BEFORE I FORGET	SLIPKNOT	35	2005
BEFORE TODAY	EVERYTHING BUT THE GIRL	25	1997
BEFORE YOU LEAVE	PEPE DELUXE	20	2001
BEFORE YOU LOVE ME	ALSOU	27	2001
BEFORE YOU WALK OUT OF MY LIFE	MONICA	22	1996
BEG, STEAL OR BORROW	NEW SEEKERS	2	1972
A BEGGAR ON A BEACH OF GOLD	MIKE + THE MECHANICS	33	1995
BEGGIN'	TIMEBOX	38	1968
BEGGIN'	FRANKIE VALLI & THE FOUR SEASONS	32	2007
BEGGIN'	MADCON	5	2008
BEGGIN' TO BE WRITTEN	WORLDS APART	29	1994
BEGGING YOU	STONE ROSES	15	1995
BEGIN AGAIN	SPACE	21	1998
BEGIN THE BEGUINE (VOLVER A EMPEZAR)	JULIO IGLESIAS	1	1981
THE BEGINNING	SEAL	24	1991
BEGINNING OF THE END	STATUS QUO	48	2007
THE BEGINNING OF THE TWIST	FUTUREHEADS	20	2008
BEHIND A PAINTED SMILE	ISLEY BROTHERS	5	1969
BEHIND BLUE EYES	LIMP BIZKIT	18	2003
BEHIND CLOSED DOORS [A]	CHARLIE RICH	16	1974
BEHIND CLOSED DOORS [B]	PETER ANDRE	4	2009
BEHIND THE COUNTER	FALL	75	1993
BEHIND THE GROOVE	TEENA MARIE	6	1980
BEHIND THE MASK	ERIC CLAPTON	15	1987
BEHIND THE WHEEL	DEPECHE MODE	21	1988
BEHIND THESE HAZEL EYES	KELLY CLARKSON	9	2005
BEIN' AROUND	LEMONHEADS	19	1992
BEING A GIRL (PART ONE) EP	MANSUN	13	1998
BEING BOILED	HUMAN LEAGUE	6	1982
BEING BORING	PET SHOP BOYS	20	1990
BEING BRAVE	MENSWEAR	10	1996
BEING NOBODY	RICHARD X VS LIBERTY X	3	2003
BEING WITH YOU	SMOKEY ROBINSON	1	1981
BEL AMOUR	BEL AMOUR	23	2001
BELARUSE	LEVELLERS	12	1993
BELFAST [A]	BONEY M	8	1977
BELFAST [B]	BARNBRACK	45	1985
BELFAST [C]	ENERGY ORCHARD	52	1990
BELFAST [D]	ORBITAL	53	1995
BELFAST BOY	DON FARDON	32	1970
BELFAST CHILD	SIMPLE MINDS	1	1989
BELFAST TRANCE	JOHN 'OO' FLEMING & SIMPLE MINDS	74	2002
BELIEVE [A]	LENNY KRAVITZ	30	1993
BELIEVE [B]	Q-TEX	41	1994
BELIEVE [C]	ELTON JOHN	15	1995
BELIEVE [D]	GOLDIE	36	1998
BELIEVE [E]	CHER	1	1998
BELIEVE [F]	MINISTERS DE LA FUNK FEATURING JOCELYN BROWN	42	2000
BELIEVE [G]	IAN VAN DAHL	27	2004
BELIEVE [H]	CHEMICAL BROTHERS	18	2005
BELIEVE IN ME [A]	UTAH SAINTS	8	1993
BELIEVE IN ME [B]	QUIVVER	56	1995
BELIEVE IN ME [C]	MANKEY	74	1996
BELIEVE IN ME [D]	RAW STYLUS	66	1996
BELIEVE IN THE BEAT	CAROL LYNN TOWNES	56	1985
BELIEVE IN THE BOOGIE	MARK OWEN	57	2005
BELIEVE WHAT YOU'RE SAYING	SUGAR	73	1994
BELIEVER	REAL PEOPLE	38	1992
BELIEVERS	BAZ	36	2001
THE BELL	MIKE OLDFIELD	50	1993
BELL BOTTOM BLUES	ALMA COGAN	4	1954
BELL BOTTOMED TEAR	BEAUTIFUL SOUTH	16	1992
THE BELLE OF ST MARK	SHEILA E	18	1985
BELLISSIMA	DJ QUICKSILVER	4	1997
BELLS OF AVIGNON	MAX BYGRAVES	36	1961
BELLS OF NY	SLO-MOSHUN	29	1994
BELLY DANCER (BANANZA)	AKON	5	2005
BELO HORIZONTI	HEARTISTS	40	1997
BEN	MICHAEL JACKSON	7	1972
BEN	MARTI WEBB	5	1985
BEN	TONI WARNE	50	1987
BEND IT	DAVE DEE, DOZY, BEAKY, MICK & TICH	2	1966
BEND ME SHAPE ME	AMEN CORNER	3	1968
BEND ME SHAPE ME	AMERICAN BREED	24	1968
BENEDICTUS	BRAINBUG	24	1997
BENJAMIN	VERUCA SALT	75	1997
BENNIE AND THE JETS	ELTON JOHN	37	1976
BENNY'S THEME	PAUL HENRY & MAYSON GLEN ORCHESTRA	39	1978

Title / Artist	Peak Position	Year of Release
BENTLEY'S GONNA SORT YOU OUT! BENTLEY RHYTHM ACE	17	1997
BENZIN RAMMSTEIN	58	2005
BERMUDA TRIANGLE BARRY MANILOW	15	1981
BERNADETTE FOUR TOPS	8	1967
BERRY TC 1991	73	1992
BERSERKER GARY NUMAN	32	1984
BESAME MUCHO JET HARRIS	22	1962
BESIDE YOU IGGY POP	47	1994
THE BEST TINA TURNER	5	1989
BEST BIT EP BETH ORTON FEATURING TERRY CALLIER	36	1997
THE BEST CHRISTMAS OF THEM ALL SHAKIN' STEVENS	19	1990
BEST DAYS JUICE	28	1998
THE BEST DAYS OF OUR LIVES LISBON LIONS FEATURING MARTIN O'NEILL	17	2002
THE BEST DISCO IN TOWN RITCHIE FAMILY	10	1976
BEST FRIEND [A] BEAT	22	1980
BEST FRIEND [B] MARK MORRISON & CONNOR REEVES	23	1999
BEST FRIEND [C] PUFF DADDY FEATURING MARIO WINANS	24	1999
BEST FRIENDS [A] TOY-BOX	41	1999
BEST FRIENDS [B] ALLSTARS	20	2001
BEST FRIENDS FOREVER TWEENIES	12	2001
BEST FRIEND'S GIRL ELECTRASY	41	1998
BEST I CAN QUEENSRYCHE	36	1991
BEST IN ME LET LOOSE	8	1995
THE BEST IS YET TO COME SCOOCH	12	2000
BEST KEPT SECRET CHINA CRISIS	36	1987
BEST LOVE COURSE	51	1997
THE BEST OF BOTH WORLDS HANNAH MONTANA	43	2007
THE BEST OF EVERYTHING JOHNNY MATHIS	30	1959
THE BEST OF LOVE MICHAEL BOLTON	14	1997
THE BEST OF ME [A] CLIFF RICHARD	2	1989
THE BEST OF ME [B] BRYAN ADAMS	47	1999
BEST OF MY LOVE [A] EMOTIONS	4	1977
BEST OF MY LOVE [A] DEE LEWIS	47	1988
BEST OF MY LOVE [A] LOVESTATION	73	1993
BEST OF MY LOVE [A] CJ LEWIS	13	1994
BEST OF MY LOVE [B] JAVINE	18	2004
BEST OF ORDER DAVID SNEDDON	19	2003
THE BEST OF TIMES STYX	42	1981
BEST OF YOU [A] KENNY THOMAS	11	1991
BEST OF YOU [B] FOO FIGHTERS	4	2005
(THE BEST PART OF) BREAKING UP RONETTES	43	1964
BEST PART OF BREAKING UP SYMBOLS	25	1968
(THE BEST PART OF) BREAKING UP RONI GRIFFITH	63	1984
BEST REGRETS GENEVA	38	1997
BEST THING [A] ADAM RICKITT	25	2000
THE BEST THING [B] SAVAGE GARDEN	35	2001
BEST THING IN THE WORLD OPTIMYSTIC	70	1995
BEST THING THAT EVER HAPPENED TO ME GLADYS KNIGHT & THE PIPS	7	1975
THE BEST THINGS IN LIFE ARE FREE LUTHER VANDROSS & JANET JACKSON WITH SPECIAL GUESTS BBD & RALPH TRESVANT	2	1992
BEST WISHES ULTRASOUND	68	1998
THE BEST YEARS OF MY LIFE DIANA ROSS	28	1994
BEST YEARS OF OUR LIVES MODERN ROMANCE	4	1982
BET ON IT TROY	65	2007
BET YER LIFE I DO HERMAN'S HERMITS	22	1970
BETA EMPIRION	75	1997
BETCHA BY GOLLY WOW STYLISTICS	13	1972
BETCHA BY GOLLY WOW! ARTIST	11	1996
BETCHA CAN'T LOSE (WITH MY LOVE) MAGIC LADY	58	1988
BETCHA CAN'T WAIT E-17	12	1999

Title / Artist	Peak Position	Year of Release
BETCHA' WOULDN'T HURT ME QUINCY JONES	52	1981
BETTE DAVIS' EYES KIM CARNES	10	1981
BETTER TOM BAXTER	67	2007
BETTER BOYZONE	22	2008
BETTER BE GOOD TO ME TINA TURNER	45	1984
BETTER BELIEVE IT (CHILDREN IN NEED) SID OWEN & PATSY PALMER	60	1995
BETTER BEST FORGOTTEN STEPS	2	1999
BETTER DAY OCEAN COLOUR SCENE	9	1997
BETTER DAYS [A] GUN	33	1989
BETTER DAYS [B] BRUCE SPRINGSTEEN	34	1992
BETTER DAYS [C] TQ	32	1999
BETTER DAYS AHEAD TYRREL CORPORATION	29	1995
BETTER DO BETTER HARD-FI	14	2006
BETTER DO IT SALSA GIBSON BROTHERS	12	1980
BETTER GET READY LULU	59	2000
BETTER IN TIME LEONA LEWIS	2	2008
A BETTER LOVE LONDONBEAT	23	1990
BETTER LOVE NEXT TIME DR HOOK	8	1980
BETTER MADE HEADSWIM	42	1998
A BETTER MAN [A] THUNDER	18	1993
A BETTER MAN [B] BRIAN KENNEDY	28	1996
BETTER OFF ALONE DJ JURGEN PRESENTS ALICE DEEJAY	2	1999
BETTER OFF AS TWO FRANKMUSIC	26	2009
BETTER OFF WITH HIM A	52	2005
BETTER OFF WITHOUT YOU HAZELL DEAN	72	1991
BETTER TAKE TIME SECOND IMAGE	67	1983
BETTER THAN LIFE ULTRABEAT	23	2004
BETTER THE DEVIL YOU KNOW [A] KYLIE MINOGUE	2	1990
BETTER THE DEVIL YOU KNOW [A] SONIA	15	1993
BETTER THE DEVIL YOU KNOW [B] STEPS	4	1999
BETTER THINGS KINKS	46	1981
BETTER TOGETHER JACK JOHNSON	24	2006
BETTER USE YOUR HEAD LITTLE ANTHONY & THE IMPERIALS	42	1976
BETTER WATCH OUT ANT & DEC	10	1996
BETTER WORLD REBEL MC	20	1990
BETTY BETTY BETTY LONNIE DONEGAN	11	1958
(BETWEEN A) ROCK AND A HARD PLACE CUTTING CREW	66	1989
BETWEEN ANGELS AND INSECTS PAPA ROACH	17	2001
BETWEEN ME AND YOU JA RULE FEATURING CHRISTINA MILIAN	26	2001
BETWEEN THE SHEETS ISLEY BROTHERS	52	1983
BETWEEN THE WARS (EP) BILLY BRAGG	15	1985
BEVERLY HILLS WEEZER	9	2005
BEWARE VIVIENNE McKONE	69	1992
(BEWARE) BOYFRIEND MARI WILSON	51	1982
BEWARE OF THE BOYS PANJABI MC FEATURING JAY-Z	25	2003
BEWARE OF THE DOG JAMELIA	10	2006
BEYOND THE INVISIBLE ENIGMA	26	1997
BEYOND THE PALE MISSION	32	1988
BEYOND THE REEF ELVIS PRESLEY	3	1980
BEYOND THE SEA (LA MER) GEORGE BENSON	60	1985
BEYOND THE STARS DAVID WHITFIELD	8	1955
BEYOND TIME BLANK & JONES	53	2001
BEYOND YOUR WILDEST DREAMS LONNIE GORDON	48	1990
BEYOND YOUR WILDEST DREAMS SYBIL	41	1993
THE BHOYS ARE BACK IN TOWN DANCE TO TIPPERARY	44	2003
BICYCLE RACE QUEEN	11	1978
BIG APPLE KAJAGOOGOO	8	1983
BIG AREA THEN JERICO	13	1989
BIG BAD EP LITTLE ANGELS	74	1989
BIG BAD JOHN JIMMY DEAN	2	1961

Title / Artist	Peak Position	Year of Release
BIG BAD MAMMA FOXY BROWN FEATURING DRU HILL	12	1997
THE BIG BEAN PIGBAG	40	1982
THE BIG BEAT [A] FATS DOMINO	20	1958
BIG BEAT [B] CAPPELLA	16	1994
BIG BEAT BOOGIE BERT WEEDON	37	1960
BIG BIG WORLD EMILIA	5	1998
BIG BOSS GROOVE STYLE COUNCIL	5	1984
BIG BOYS DON'T CRY LOLLY	10	1999
BIG BROTHER UK TV THEME ELEMENTFOUR	4	2000
BIG BUBBLES, NO TROUBLES ELLIS, BEGGS & HOWARD	41	1988
BIG CITY DANDY LIVINGSTONE	26	1973
BIG CITY LIFE MATTAFIX	15	2005
BIG DEAL BOBBY G	46	1984
BIG DECISION THAT PETROL EMOTION	43	1987
BIG DICK MAN SEX CLUB FEATURING BROWN SUGAR	67	1995
BIG EIGHT JUDGE DREAD	14	1973
BIG FUN [A] KOOL & THE GANG	14	1982
BIG FUN [B] GAP BAND	4	1986
BIG FUN [C] INNER CITY FEATURING KEVIN SAUNDERSON	8	1988
BIG GAY HEART LEMONHEADS	55	1994
BIG GIRL PRECOCIOUS BRATS/KEVIN & PERRY	16	2000
BIG GIRL (YOU ARE BEAUTIFUL) MIKA	9	2007
BIG GIRLS DON'T CRY FOUR SEASONS	13	1963
BIG GIRLS DON'T CRY (PERSONAL) FERGIE	2	2007
BIG GREEN CAR POLECATS	35	1981
BIG GUN AC/DC	23	1993
A BIG HUNK O' LOVE ELVIS PRESLEY	4	1959
THE BIG HURT MAUREEN EVANS	26	1960
THE BIG HURT TONI FISHER	30	1960
BIG IN AMERICA STRANGLERS	48	1986
BIG IN JAPAN ALPHAVILLE	8	1984
BIG IRON MARTY ROBBINS	48	1960
THE BIG L ROXETTE	21	1991
BIG LOG ROBERT PLANT	11	1983
BIG LOVE [A] FLEETWOOD MAC	9	1987
BIG LOVE [B] PETE HELLER	12	1999
BIG LOVE [C] FRESH	58	2003
BIG MAN FOUR PREPS	2	1958
THE BIG MAN AND THE SCREAM TEAM MEET THE BARMY ARMY UPTOWN PRIMAL SCREAM, IRVINE WELSH & ON U-SOUND	17	1996
BIG MAN IN A BIG HOUSE LEROY VAN DYKE	34	1962
BIG ME FOO FIGHTERS	19	1996
BIG MISTAKE NATALIE IMBRUGLIA	2	1998
THE BIG MONEY RUSH	46	1985
BIG MOUTH STRIKES AGAIN SMITHS	26	1986
BIG N BASHY FALLACY FEATURING TUBBY T	45	2003
BIG NEW PRINZ FALL	59	1988
BIG NIGHT OUT FUN LOVIN' CRIMINALS	29	1998
THE BIG ONE BLACK	54	1988
THE BIG ONES GET AWAY BUFFY SAINTE-MARIE	39	1992
BIG PANTY WOMAN BAREFOOT MAN	21	1998
BIG PIMPIN' JAY-Z	29	2000
BIG POPPA NOTORIOUS B.I.G.	63	1995
BIG PUNK JUDGE DREAD	49	1978
BIG RIVER JIMMY NAIL	18	1995
BIG SCARY ANIMAL BELINDA CARLISLE	12	1972
BIG SEVEN JUDGE DREAD	8	1993
BIG SHIP CLIFF RICHARD	8	1972
BIG SIX JUDGE DREAD	11	1969
THE BIG SKY KATE BUSH	37	1986
BIG SKY NEW LIGHT MARTIN STEPHENSON & THE DAINTEES	71	1992
BIG SPENDER SHIRLEY BASSEY	21	1967
BIG SUR THRILLS	17	2003
BIG TEASER SAXON	66	1980
BIG TEN JUDGE DREAD	14	1975

Title / Artist	Peak Position	Year of Release
BIG THING COMING STRANGLERS	31	2004
BIG TIME [A] RICK JAMES	41	1980
BIG TIME [B] PETER GABRIEL	13	1987
BIG TIME [C] WHIGFIELD	21	1995
BIG TIME OPERATOR ZOOT MONEY & THE BIG ROLL BAND	25	1966
BIG TIME SENSUALITY BJORK	17	1993
BIG WEDGE FISH	25	1990
BIG WHEELS LLAMA FARMERS	67	1999
BIG YELLOW TAXI JONI MITCHELL	11	1970
BIG YELLOW TAXI AMY GRANT	20	1995
BIG YELLOW TAXI COUNTING CROWS FEATURING VANESSA CARLTON	16	2003
BIGAMY AT CHRISTMAS TONY FERRINO	42	1996
BIGBOY MINUTEMAN	45	2002
BIGGER BETTER DEAL DESERT EAGLE DISCS FEATURING KEISHA	67	2003
BIGGER THAN BIG SUPER MAL FEATURING LUCIANA	19	2007
BIGGER THAN MY BODY JOHN MAYER	72	2004
BIGGEST HORIZON CLINT BOON EXPERIENCE	70	2000
BIGGEST MISTAKE ROLLING STONES	51	2006
BIKINI GIRLS WITH MACHINE GUNS CRAMPS	35	1990
BIKO PETER GABRIEL	38	1980
BILJO CLODAGH RODGERS	22	1969
BILL BAILEY BOBBY DARIN	34	1960
BILL MCCAI CORAL	23	2003
BILLIE JEAN MICHAEL JACKSON	1	1983
BILLIE JEAN BATES	67	1996
BILLIE JEAN SOUND BLUNTZ	32	2002
BILLS, BILLS, BILLS DESTINY'S CHILD	6	1999
BILLS 2 PAY GLAMMA KID	17	2000
BILLY BOY DICK CHARLESWORTH & HIS CITY GENTS	43	1961
BILLY, DON'T BE A HERO PAPER LACE	1	1974
BIMBO RUBY WRIGHT	7	1954
BING BANG (TIME TO DANCE) LAZY TOWN	4	2006
BINGO CATCH	23	1997
BINGO BANGO BASEMENT JAXX	13	2000
BIOLOGY GIRLS ALOUD	4	2005
BIONIC KING ADORA	30	2001
BIONIC SANTA CHRIS HILL	10	1976
BIRD DOG EVERLY BROTHERS	2	1958
BIRD OF PARADISE SNOWY WHITE	6	1984
BIRD ON A WIRE NEVILLE BROTHERS	72	1990
BIRD SONG LENE LOVICH	39	1979
BIRDHOUSE IN YOUR SOUL THEY MIGHT BE GIANTS	6	1990
THE BIRDIE SONG (BIRDIE DANCE) TWEETS	2	1981
BIRDMAN RIDE	38	1994
THE BIRDS AND THE BEES ALMA COGAN	25	1956
THE BIRDS AND THE BEES JEWEL AKENS	29	1965
BIRDS AND BEES WARM SOUNDS	27	1967
BIRDS FLY (WHISPER TO A SCREAM) ICICLE WORKS	53	1984
BIRDS OF A FEATHER KILLING JOKE	64	1982
BIRTH PEDDLERS	17	1969
BIRTHDAY [A] SUGARCUBES	64	1987
BIRTHDAY [B] PAUL McCARTNEY	29	1990
BIRTHDAY SEX JEREMIH	15	2009
BIS VS THE DIY CORPS (EP) BIS	45	1996
THE BIT GOES ON SNAKEBITE	25	1997
A BIT OF U2 KISS AMC	58	1989
BITCH [A] ROLLING STONES	2	1971
THE BITCH [B] OLYMPIC RUNNERS	37	1979
BITCH [C] MEREDITH BROOKS	6	1997
B*TCH [D] DAVE McCULLEN	54	2005
THE BITCH IS BACK ELTON JOHN	15	1974
BITCH SCHOOL SPINAL TAP	35	1992
BITCH WITH A PERM TIM DOG	49	1994
BITCHES BREW INSPIRAL CARPETS	36	1992
BITE YOUR LIP (GET UP AND DANCE) ELTON JOHN	28	1977
BITES DA DUST PLANET PERFECTO	52	2001
BITS AND PIECES [A] DAVE CLARK FIVE	2	1964
BITS + PIECES [B] ARTEMESIA	46	1995
BITS OF KIDS STIFF LITTLE FINGERS	73	1982
BITTER END PLACEBO	12	2003
BITTER FRUIT LITTLE STEVEN	66	1987
BITTER SWEET MARC ALMOND	40	1988
BITTER SWEET SYMPHONY VERVE	2	1997
BITTER TEARS INXS	30	1991
THE BITTEREST PILL (I EVER HAD TO SWALLOW) JAM	2	1982
BITTERSWEET BILLY OCEAN	44	1986
BITTERSWEET BUNDLE OF MAN GRAHAM COXON	22	2004
BITTERSWEET ME R.E.M.	19	1996
BIZARRE LOVE TRIANGLE NEW ORDER	56	1986
BIZZI'S PARTY BIZZI	62	1997
BJANGO LUCKY MONKEYS	50	1996
BLACK AND BLUE MIIKE SNOW	64	2009
BLACK & GOLD SAM SPARRO	2	2008
BLACK AND WHITE [A] GREYHOUND	6	1971
BLACK AND WHITE [B] STATIC-X	65	2001
BLACK AND WHITE [C] UPPER ROOM	22	2006
BLACK & WHITE ARMY BLACK & WHITE ARMY	26	1998
BLACK AND WHITE TOWN DOVES	6	2005
BLACK ANGEL MICA PARIS	72	1998
BLACK BEAR FRANK CORDELL	44	1961
BLACK BETTY RAM JAM	7	1977
BLACK BETTY TOM JONES	50	2003
BLACK BOOK E.Y.C.	13	1994
BLACK CAT JANET JACKSON	15	1990
BLACK CHERRY GOLDFRAPP	28	2004
BLACK COFFEE ALL SAINTS	1	2000
BLACK COFFEE IN BED SQUEEZE	51	1982
BLACK EYED BOY TEXAS	5	1997
THE BLACK EYED BOYS PAPER LACE	11	1974
BLACK GIRL FOUR PENNIES	20	1964
BLACK GOLD SOUL ASYLUM	26	1994
BLACK HEART MARC & THE MAMBAS	49	1983
BLACK HILLS OF DAKOTA DORIS DAY	7	1954
BLACK HISTORY MONTH DEATH FROM ABOVE 1979	48	2005
BLACK HOLE SUN SOUNDGARDEN	12	1994
BLACK HORSE AND THE CHERRY TREE KT TUNSTALL	28	2005
BLACK IS BLACK [A] LOS BRAVOS	2	1966
BLACK IS BLACK [A] LA BELLE EPOQUE	2	1977
BLACK IS BLACK [B] JUNGLE BROTHERS	72	1989
BLACK JESUS EVERLAST	37	2001
BLACK LODGE ANTHRAX	53	1993
BLACK MAGIC WOMAN FLEETWOOD MAC	37	1968
BLACK MAN RAY CHINA CRISIS	14	1985
BLACK MEANING GOOD REBEL MC	73	1991
BLACK METALLIC (EP) CATHERINE WHEEL	68	1991
BLACK NIGHT DEEP PURPLE	2	1970
BLACK NITE CRASH RIDE	67	1996
BLACK OR WHITE MICHAEL JACKSON	1	1991
BLACK ORCHID STEVIE WONDER	63	1980
BLACK PEARL HORACE FAITH	13	1970
BLACK PUDDING BERTHA (THE QUEEN OF NORTHERN SOUL) GOODIES	19	1975
BLACK SABBATH MAGOO:MOGWAI	60	1998
BLACK SKIN BLUE EYED BOYS EQUALS	9	1971
BLACK STATIONS WHITE STATIONS M + M	46	1984
BLACK STEEL TRICKY	28	1995
BLACK STOCKINGS JOHN BARRY SEVEN	27	1960
BLACK SUITS COMIN' (NOD YA HEAD) WILL SMITH FEATURING TRA-KNOX	3	2002
BLACK SUPERMAN (MUHAMMAD ALI) JOHNNY WAKELIN & THE KINSHASA BAND	7	1975
BLACK SWEAT PRINCE	43	2006
BLACK TIE WHITE NOISE DAVID BOWIE FEATURING AL B. SURE!	36	1993
BLACK VELVET ALANNAH MYLES	2	1990
BLACK VELVET BAND DUBLINERS	15	1967
BLACK WHITE ASIAN DUB FOUNDATION	52	1998
BLACKBERRY WAY MOVE	1	1969
BLACKBIRD ON THE WIRE BEAUTIFUL SOUTH	23	1997
BLACKBOARD JUMBLE BARRON KNIGHTS	52	1981
BLACKEN MY THUMB DATSUNS	48	2004
BLACKENED BLUE EYES CHARLATANS	28	2006
BLACKER THAN BLACK GOODBYE MR MACKENZIE	61	1990
BLACKERTHREETRACKER EP CURVE	39	1993
BLACKWATER [A] RAIN TREE CROW	62	1991
BLACKWATER [B] OCTAVE ONE FEATURING ANN SAUNDERSON	47	2002
BLAG STEAL & BORROW KOOPA	31	2007
BLAH HELTAH SKELTAH & ORIGINOO GUNN CLAPPAZ AS THE FABULOUS FIVE	60	1996
BLAH BLAH BLAH KE$SHA FEATURING 3OH!3	11	2010
BLAME IT ON ME D:REAM	25	1994
BLAME IT ON THE BASSLINE NORMAN COOK FEATURING MC WILDSKI	1	1989
BLAME IT ON THE BOOGIE JACKSONS	8	1978
BLAME IT ON THE BOOGIE MICK JACKSON	15	1978
BLAME IT ON THE BOOGIE BIG FUN	4	1989
BLAME IT ON THE BOOGIE CLOCK	16	1998
BLAME IT ON THE BOSSA NOVA EYDIE GORME	32	1963
BLAME IT ON THE GIRLS MIKA	72	2010
(BLAME IT) ON THE PONY EXPRESS JOHNNY JOHNSON & THE BANDWAGON	7	1970
BLAME IT ON THE RAIN MILLI VANILLI	52	1989
BLAME IT ON THE WEATHERMAN B*WITCHED	1	1999
BLANKET URBAN SPECIES FEATURING IMOGEN HEAP	56	1999
BLANKET ON THE GROUND BILLIE JO SPEARS	6	1975
BLASPHEMOUS RUMOURS DEPECHE MODE	16	1984
BLAST THE SPEAKERS WARP BROTHERS	40	2002
BLAZE OF GLORY JON BON JOVI	13	1990
BLAZIN' TALI	42	2004
BLAZING SADDLES YELLO	47	1989
BLEACH EASYWORLD	67	2002
BLEED CATATONIA	46	1996
BLEED IT LINKIN PARK	29	2007
BLEED ME WHITE EAT	73	1993
BLEEDING LOVE LEONA LEWIS	1	2007
BLESS YOU [A] TONY ORLANDO	5	1961
BLESS YOU [B] MARTHA REEVES & THE VANDELLAS	33	1972
BLIND [A] TALKING HEADS	59	1988
BLIND [B] BAD COMPANY	59	2002
BLIND [C] HERCULES & LOVE AFFAIR	40	2008
BLIND AMONG THE FLOWERS TOURISTS	52	1979
BLIND MAN AEROSMITH	23	1994
BLIND PILOTS COOPER TEMPLE CLAUSE	37	2003
BLIND VISION BLANCMANGE	10	1983
BLINDED BY THE LIGHT MANFRED MANN'S EARTH BAND	6	1976
BLINDED BY THE LIGHTS STREETS	10	2004
BLINDED BY THE SUN SEAHORSES	7	1997
BLINDFOLD MORCHEEBA	56	1998
THE BLINDFOLD (EP) CURVE	68	1991
BLINK ROSIE RIBBONS	12	2002
BLISS [A] MUSE	22	2001
BLISS [B] SYNTAX	69	2004
THE BLOCK PARTY LISA 'LEFT EYE' LOPES	16	2001
BLOCK ROCKIN' BEATS CHEMICAL BROTHERS	1	1997
BLOCKBUSTER SWEET	1	1973

Title / Artist	Peak Position	Year of Release
BLONDE HAIR BLUE JEANS CHRIS DE BURGH	51	1994
BLONDES (HAVE MORE FUN) ROD STEWART	63	1979
BLOOD EDITORS	18	2005
BLOOD BANK BON IVER	37	2009
BLOOD IS PUMPIN' VOODOO & SERANO	19	2001
BLOOD MAKES NOISE SUZANNE VEGA	60	1992
BLOOD MUSIC (EP) EARTHLING	69	1996
BLOOD OF EDEN PETER GABRIEL	43	1993
BLOOD ON OUR HANDS DEATH FROM ABOVE 1979	33	2005
BLOOD ON THE DANCE FLOOR MICHAEL JACKSON	1	1997
BLOOD SUGAR PENDULUM	62	2007
BLOOD SWEAT & TEARS V	6	2004
THE BLOOD THAT MOVES THE BODY A-HA	25	1988
BLOODNOK'S ROCK 'N' ROLL CALL GOONS	3	1956
BLOODSHOT EYES MILLIE	48	1965
BLOODSPORTS FOR ALL CARTER-THE UNSTOPPABLE SEX MACHINE	48	1991
BLOODY LUXURY WHITESNAKE	34	1982
A BLOSSOM FELL NAT 'KING' COLE	3	1955
A BLOSSOM FELL DICKIE VALENTINE	9	1955
A BLOSSOM FELL RONNIE HILTON	10	1955
BLOSSOMS FALLING OOBERMAN	39	1999
BLOW AWAY GEORGE HARRISON	51	1979
BLOW THE HOUSE DOWN [A] LIVING IN A BOX	10	1989
BLOW THE HOUSE DOWN [B] WEE PAPA GIRL RAPPERS	65	1989
BLOW UP THE OUTSIDE WORLD SOUNDGARDEN	40	1996
BLOW YA MIND LOCK 'N' LOAD	6	2000
BLOW YOUR HORNY HORNS PERFECT PHASE	75	2004
BLOW YOUR MIND JAMIROQUAI	12	1993
BLOW YOUR MIND (I AM THE WOMAN) LISA PIN-UP	60	2002
BLOW YOUR WHISTLE DJ DUKE	15	1994
THE BLOWER'S DAUGHTER DAMIEN RICE	27	2005
BLOWIN' IN THE WIND STEVIE WONDER	36	1966
BLOWIN' ME UP JC CHASEZ	13	2004
BLOWING IN THE WIND PETER, PAUL & MARY	13	1963
BLOWING WILD FRANKIE LAINE	2	1954
BLUE [A] FINE YOUNG CANNIBALS	41	1985
BLUE [B] VERVE	69	1993
BLUE [C] WAY OUT WEST	41	1997
BLUE [D] SYMPOSIUM	48	1998
BLUE [E] LeANN RIMES	23	1998
BLUE ANGEL [A] ROY ORBISON	11	1960
BLUE ANGEL [B] GENE PITNEY	39	1974
BLUE ANGELS PRAS	6	1998
BLUE BAYOU ROY ORBISON	3	1963
BLUE BAYOU LINDA RONSTADT	35	1978
BLUE BLUE HEARTACHES JOHNNY DUNCAN & THE BLUE GRASS BOYS	27	1957
BLUE CHRISTMAS ELVIS PRESLEY	11	1964
BLUE (DA BA DEE) EIFFEL 65	1	1999
BLUE DAY SUGGS & CO FEATURING CHELSEA TEAM	22	1997
BLUE EMOTION FIAT LUX	59	1984
BLUE-EYED BOY AL SAXON	39	1960
BLUE EYES [A] DON PARTRIDGE	3	1968
BLUE EYES [B] ELTON JOHN	8	1982
BLUE EYES [C] WEDDING PRESENT	26	1992
BLUE FEAR ARMIN	45	1998
BLUE FLOWERS DR OCTAGON	66	1996
BLUE FOR YOU WET WET WET	38	1993
BLUE GIRL BRUISERS	31	1963
BLUE GUITAR JUSTIN HAYWARD & JOHN LODGE	8	1975
BLUE HAT FOR A BLUE DAY NICK HEYWARD	14	1983
BLUE HOTEL CHRIS ISAAK	17	1991
BLUE IS THE COLOUR CHELSEA FC	5	1972
BLUE JEAN DAVID BOWIE	6	1984
BLUE JEAN BOP GENE VINCENT	16	1956
BLUE JEANS LADYTRON	43	2003
BLUE LIGHT RED LIGHT (SOMEONE'S THERE) HARRY CONNICK, JR	54	1991
BLUE LOVE (CALL MY NAME) DNA FEATURING JOE NYE	66	1992
BLUE MONDAY [A] FATS DOMINO	23	1957
BLUE MONDAY [B] NEW ORDER	3	1983
BLUE MOON ELVIS PRESLEY	9	1956
BLUE MOON MARCELS	1	1961
BLUE MOON SHOWADDYWADDY	32	1980
BLUE MOON JOHN ALFORD	9	1996
BLUE MORNING BLUE DAY FOREIGNER	45	1979
BLUE NOTE HARRISONS	69	2006
BLUE ORCHID WHITE STRIPES	9	2005
BLUE PETER MIKE OLDFIELD	19	1979
BLUE RIVER ELVIS PRESLEY	22	1966
BLUE ROOM ORB	8	1992
THE BLUE ROOM T-EMPO	71	1996
BLUE SAVANNAH ERASURE	3	1990
BLUE SKIES [A] JOHN DUMMER & HELEN APRIL	54	1982
BLUE SKIES [B] JETS	53	1983
BLUE SKIES [C] BT FEATURING TORI AMOS	26	1996
BLUE SKIES [D] LONGPIGS	21	1999
BLUE SKY MINE MIDNIGHT OIL	66	1990
BLUE SONG MINT ROYALE	35	2003
BLUE STAR (THE MEDIC THEME) CYRIL STAPLETON ORCHESTRA FEATURING JULIE DAWN	2	1955
BLUE STAR (THE MEDIC THEME) CHARLIE APPLEWHITE	20	1955
BLUE STAR (THE MEDIC THEME) RON GOODWIN	20	1955
BLUE SUEDE SHOES ELVIS PRESLEY	9	1956
BLUE SUEDE SHOES CARL PERKINS	10	1956
BLUE TANGO RAY MARTIN	8	1952
BLUE TOMORROW CHELSEA FC	22	2000
BLUE TURNS TO GREY CLIFF RICHARD & THE SHADOWS	15	1966
BLUE VELVET BOBBY VINTON	2	1990
BLUE WATER [A] FIELDS OF THE NEPHILIM	75	1987
BLUE WATER [B] BLACK ROCK FEATURING DEBRA ANDREW	36	2005
BLUE WEEKEND KARL DENVER	33	1962
BLUE WORLD MOODY BLUES	35	1983
BLUEBEARD COCTEAU TWINS	33	1994
BLUEBELL POLKA JIMMY SHAND	20	1955
BLUEBERRY HILL FATS DOMINO	6	1956
BLUEBERRY HILL JOHN BARRY ORCHESTRA	34	1960
BLUEBIRDS FLYING HIGH JAMES FOX	15	2008
BLUEBIRDS OVER THE MOUNTAIN BEACH BOYS	33	1969
BLUEBOTTLE POB FEATURING DJ PATRICK REID	74	1999
BLUEBOTTLE BLUES GOONS	4	1956
BLUER THAN BLUE ROLF HARRIS	30	1969
THE BLUES ARE STILL BLUE BELLE & SEBASTIAN	25	2006
BLUES BAND (EP) BLUES BAND	68	1980
BLUES FROM A GUN JESUS & MARY CHAIN	32	1989
BLUES SKIES SPECIAL NEEDS	56	2005
BLUETONIC BLUETONES	19	1995
BLURRED PIANOMAN	6	1996
BLURRY PUDDLE OF MUDD	8	2002
BO DIDDLEY BUDDY HOLLY	4	1963
BOA VS PYTHON TEST ICICLES	46	2005
THE BOAT THAT I ROW LULU	6	1967
BOAT TO BOLIVIA MARTIN STEPHENSON & THE DAINTEES	70	1986
B.O.B. (BOMBS OVER BAGHDAD) OUTKAST	61	2000
BOBBY TOMORROW BOBBY VEE	21	1963
BOBBY'S GIRL SUSAN MAUGHAN	3	1962
BODIES [A] DROWNING POOL	34	2002
BODIES [B] ROBBIE WILLIAMS	2	2009
BODY FUNKY GREEN DOGS	46	1999
BODY AND SOUL [A] SISTERS OF MERCY	46	1984
BODY AND SOUL [B] MAI TAI	9	1985
BODY AND SOUL [C] ANITA BAKER	48	1994
BODY BUMPIN' (YIPPIE-YI-YO) PUBLIC ANNOUNCEMENT	38	1998
THE BODY ELECTRIC RUSH	56	1984
BODY GROOVE ARCHITECHS FEATURING NANA	3	2000
BODY HEAT JAMES BROWN	36	1977
BODY IN MOTION ATLANTIC OCEAN	15	1994
BODY LANGUAGE [A] DETROIT SPINNERS	40	1980
BODY LANGUAGE [B] DOOLEYS	46	1980
BODY LANGUAGE [C] QUEEN	25	1982
BODY LANGUAGE [D] ADVENTURES OF STEVIE V	29	1990
BODY MOVIN' [A] BEASTIE BOYS	15	1998
BODY MOVIN [D] DRUMSOUND/SIMON BASSLINE SMITH	66	2004
BODY MUSIC STRIKERS	45	1981
BODY ON ME NELLY FEATURING AKON & ASHANTI	17	2008
BODY ROCK [A] MARIA VIDAL	11	1985
BODY ROCK [B] SHIMON & ANDY C	28	2001
BODY ROCKIN' ERROL BROWN	51	1987
THE BODY SHINE (EP) BILLY HENDRIX	55	1998
BODY TALK IMAGINATION	4	1981
BODY II BODY SAMANTHA MUMBA	5	2000
BODY WORK HOT STREAK	19	1983
BODYCRASH BUY NOW!	55	2008
BODYROCK [A] MOBY	38	1999
BODYROCK [B] TYMES 4	23	2001
BODYSHAKIN' 911	3	1997
BOG EYED JOG RAY MOORE	61	1987
BOHEMIAN LIKE YOU DANDY WARHOLS	5	2000
BOHEMIAN RHAPSODY QUEEN	1	1975
BOHEMIAN RHAPSODY BAD NEWS	44	1987
BOHEMIAN RHAPSODY BRAIDS	21	1996
BOHEMIAN RHAPSODY ROLF HARRIS	50	1996
BOHEMIAN RHAPSODY G4	9	2005
BOHEMIAN RHAPSODY QUEEN & THE MUPPETS	32	2009
THE BOILER [A] RHODA WITH THE SPECIAL A.K.A.	35	1982
BOILER [B] LIMP BIZKIT	18	2001
BOING! WEDDING PRESENT	19	1992
BOLL WEEVIL SONG BROOK BENTON	30	1961
BOM DIGI BOM (THINK ABOUT THE WAY) ICE MC	38	1996
THE BOMB [A] LOVE CONNECTION	53	2000
THE BOMB [B] NEW YOUNG PONY CLUB	47	2007
BOMB DIGGY ANOTHER LEVEL	6	1999
THE BOMB! (THESE SOUNDS FALL INTO MY MIND) BUCKETHEADS	5	1995
BOMBADIN 808 STATE	67	1994
BOMBER MOTORHEAD	34	1979
BOMBS FAITHLESS FEATURING HARRY COLLIER	26	2006
BOMBSCARE 2 BAD MICE	46	1996
BOMBTRACK RAGE AGAINST THE MACHINE	37	1993
BON BON VIE TS MONK	63	1981
BOND 808 STATE	57	1996
BONE DRIVEN BUSH	49	1997
BONES KILLERS	15	2006
BONEY M MEGAMIX BONEY M	7	1988
BONEYARD LITTLE ANGELS	33	1991
BONITA APPLEBUM A TRIBE CALLED QUEST	47	1990
BONITA MANANA ESPIRITU	50	1994
BONKERS DIZZEE RASCAL FEATURING ARMAND VAN HELDEN	1	2009

Title	Artist	Peak Position	Year of Release
BONNIE CAME BACK	DUANE EDDY & THE REBELS	12	1960
BONY MORONIE	LARRY WILLIAMS	11	1958
BOO! FOREVER	BOO RADLEYS	67	1992
BOOGALOO PARTY	FLAMINGOS	26	1969
BOOGIE [A]	DIVE	35	1998
BOOGIE [B]	BRAND NEW HEAVIES FEATURING NICOLE	66	2004
BOOGIE AT RUSSIAN HILL	JOHN LEE HOOKER	53	1993
BOOGIE DOWN [A]	EDDIE KENDRICKS	39	1974
BOOGIE DOWN [B]	AL JARREAU	63	1983
BOOGIE DOWN (BRONX)	MAN PARRISH	56	1985
BOOGIE DOWN (GET FUNKY NOW)	REAL THING	33	1979
BOOGIE MAN	MATCH	48	1979
BOOGIE NIGHTS	HEATWAVE	2	1977
BOOGIE NIGHTS	LA FLEUR	51	1983
BOOGIE NIGHTS	SONIA	30	1992
BOOGIE ON REGGAE WOMAN	STEVIE WONDER	12	1975
BOOGIE ON UP	ROKOTTO	40	1977
BOOGIE OOGIE OOGIE	A TASTE OF HONEY	3	1978
BOOGIE SHOES	KC & THE SUNSHINE BAND	34	1978
BOOGIE 2NITE	BOOTY LUV	3	2006
BOOGIE TOWN	F.L.B.	46	1979
BOOGIE WONDERLAND	EARTH, WIND & FIRE WITH THE EMOTIONS	4	1979
BOOGIE WOOGIE BUGLE BOY (DON'T STOP)	2 IN A TANK	48	1995
THE BOOK	DAVID WHITFIELD	5	1954
BOOK OF DAYS	ENYA	10	1992
BOOK OF DREAMS	SUZANNE VEGA	66	1990
BOOK OF LOVE	MUDLARKS	8	1958
BOOKS	BELLE & SEBASTIAN	20	2004
BOOKS FROM BOXES	MAXIMO PARK	16	2007
BOOM BANG-A-BANG	LULU	2	1969
BOOM BLAST	FREESTYLERS FEATURING MILLION DAN	75	2005
BOOM BOOM [A]	BLACK SLATE	51	1980
BOOM BOOM [B]	JOHN LEE HOOKER	16	1992
BOOM BOOM [C]	DEFINITION OF SOUND	59	1995
BOOM BOOM [D]	N-TYCE	18	1998
BOOM BOOM [E]	BASIL BRUSH FEATURING INDIA BEAU	44	2003
BOOM BOOM BOOM	OUTHERE BROTHERS	1	1995
BOOM BOOM BOOM BOOM!!	VENGABOYS	1	1999
BOOM BOOM (LET'S GO BACK TO MY ROOM)	PAUL LEKAKIS	60	1987
BOOM BOOM POW	BLACK EYED PEAS	1	2009
THE BOOM BOOM ROOM	NATASHA	44	1982
BOOM LIKE THAT	MARK KNOPFLER	34	2004
BOOM ROCK SOUL	BENZ	62	1995
BOOM SELECTION	GENIUS CRU	12	2001
BOOM! SHAKE THE ROOM	JAZZY JEFF & THE FRESH PRINCE	1	1993
BOOM! THERE SHE WAS	SCRITTI POLITTI FEATURING ROGER	55	1988
BOOMBASTIC	SHAGGY	1	1995
BOOO	STICKY FEATURING MS DYNAMITE	12	2001
BOOPS (HERE TO GO)	SLY & ROBBIE	12	1987
BOOTI CALL	BLACKSTREET	56	1994
BOOTIE CALL	ALL SAINTS	1	1998
BOOTY LA LA	BUGZ IN THE ATTIC	44	2005
BOOTYLICIOUS	DESTINY'S CHILD	2	2001
BOOTZILLA	BOOTSY'S RUBBER BAND	43	1978
BOP BOP BABY	WESTLIFE	5	2002
BOP GUN (ONE NATION)	ICE CUBE FEATURING GEORGE CLINTON	22	1994
BORA BORA	DA HOOL	35	1998
BORDERLINE	MADONNA	2	1984
BORDERLINE	MICHAEL GRAY FEATURING SHELLEY POOLE	12	2006
BORDERS	SUNSHINE UNDERGROUND	56	2007
BORN A WOMAN	SANDY POSEY	24	1966
BORN AGAIN [A]	CHRISTIANS	25	1988
BORN AGAIN [B]	BADLY DRAWN BOY	16	2002
BORN AGAIN [C]	STARSAILOR	40	2003
BORN DEAD	BODY COUNT	28	1994
BORN FREE	VIC REEVES & THE ROMAN NUMERALS	6	1991
BORN IN ENGLAND	TWISTED X	9	2004
BORN IN 69	ROCKET FROM THE CRYPT	68	1996
BORN IN THE GHETTO	FUNKY POETS	72	1994
BORN IN THE 70'S	ED HARCOURT	61	2004
BORN IN THE USA	BRUCE SPRINGSTEEN	5	1985
BORN OF FRUSTRATION	JAMES	13	1992
BORN ON THE 5TH OF NOVEMBER	CARTER-THE UNSTOPPABLE SEX MACHINE	35	1995
BORN SLIPPY	UNDERWORLD	2	1995
BORN SLIPPY NUXX	UNDERWORLD	27	2003
BORN THIS WAY (LET'S DANCE)	COOKIE CREW	23	1989
BORN TO BE ALIVE [A]	PATRICK HERNANDEZ	10	1979
BORN TO BE ALIVE [B]	ADAMSKI FEATURING SOHO	51	1991
BORN TO BE MY BABY	BON JOVI	22	1988
BORN TO BE SOLD	TRANSVISION VAMP	22	1989
BORN TO BE WILD	STEPPENWOLF	18	1969
BORN TO BE WITH YOU	CHORDETTES	8	1956
BORN TO BE WITH YOU	DAVE EDMUNDS	5	1973
BORN TO LIVE AND BORN TO DIE	FOUNDATIONS	46	1969
BORN TO LOSE	KING ADORA	68	2003
BORN TO MAKE YOU HAPPY	BRITNEY SPEARS	1	2000
BORN TO RAISE HELL	MOTORHEAD/ICE-T/WHITFIELD CRANE	47	1994
BORN TO RUN	BRUCE SPRINGSTEEN	16	1987
BORN TO TRY	DELTA GOODREM	3	2003
BORN TOO LATE	PONI-TAILS	5	1958
BORN 2 B.R.E.E.D.	MONIE LOVE	18	1993
BORN WITH A SMILE ON MY FACE	STEPHANIE DE SYKES WITH RAIN	2	1974
BORNE ON THE WIND	ROY ORBISON	15	1964
BORROWED LOVE	S.O.S. BAND	50	1986
BORROWED TIME	JOHN LENNON	32	1984
BORSALINO	BOBBY CRUSH	37	1972
THE BOSS	DIANA ROSS	40	1979
THE BOSS	BRAXTONS	31	1997
BOSS DRUM	SHAMEN	4	1992
BOSS GUITAR	DUANE EDDY & THE REBELETTES	27	1963
BOSS OF ME	THEY MIGHT BE GIANTS	21	2001
BOSSA NOVA BABY	ELVIS PRESLEY	13	1963
BOSSY	KELIS FEATURING TOO SHORT	22	2006
BOSTICH	YELLO	55	1992
THE BOSTON TEA PARTY	SENSATIONAL ALEX HARVEY BAND	13	1976
BOTH ENDS BURNING	ROXY MUSIC	25	1975
BOTH SIDES NOW	JUDY COLLINS	14	1970
BOTH SIDES NOW	VIOLA WILLS	35	1986
BOTH SIDES NOW	CLANNAD & PAUL YOUNG	74	1991
BOTH SIDES OF THE STORY	PHIL COLLINS	7	1993
BOTHER	STONE SOUR	28	2003
THE BOTTLE [A]	TYRREL CORPORATION	71	1992
THE BOTTLE [B]	CHRISTIANS	39	1993
THE BOTTLE [B]	PAUL WELLER	13	2004
BOTTLE LIVING	DAVE GAHAN	36	2003
BOTTLE ROCKET	GO! TEAM	64	2005
BOULEVARD OF BROKEN DREAMS [A]	BEATMASTERS	62	1991
BOULEVARD OF BROKEN DREAMS [B]	GREEN DAY	5	2004
BOUNCE	SARAH CONNOR	14	2004
BOUNCE ALONG	WAYNE WONDER	19	2003
BOUNCE, ROCK, SKATE, ROLL	BABY DC FEATURING IMAJIN	45	1999
BOUNCE SHAKE MOVE STOP	MVP	22	2006
BOUNCE WITH THE MASSIVE	TZANT	39	1998
THE BOUNCER	KICKS LIKE A MULE	7	1992
BOUNCIN' BACK	MYSTIKAL	45	2002
BOUNCING FLOW	K2 FAMILY	27	2001
BOUNCY BALL	LADYFUZZ	52	2006
BOUND 4 DA RELOAD (CASUALTY)	OXIDE & NEUTRINO	1	2000
BOUNDARIES	LEENA CONQUEST & HIP HOP FINGER	67	1994
BOURGIE BOURGIE	GLADYS KNIGHT & THE PIPS	32	1980
BOUT	JAMELIA FEATURING RAH DIGGA	37	2003
BOW DOWN MISTER	JESUS LOVES YOU	27	1991
BOW WOW (THAT'S MY NAME)	LIL BOW WOW	6	2001
BOW WOW WOW	FUNKDOOBIEST	34	1994
THE BOX	ORBITAL	11	1996
BOX N LOCKS	MPHO	49	2009
BOX SET GO	HIGH	28	1991
THE BOXER [A]	SIMON & GARFUNKEL	6	1969
THE BOXER [B]	CHEMICAL BROTHERS	41	2005
BOXER BEAT	JO BOXERS	3	1983
BOXERS	MORRISSEY	23	1995
BOY	LULU	15	1968
THE BOY DOES NOTHING	ALESHA	5	2008
THE BOY DONE GOOD	BILLY BRAGG	55	1997
BOY FROM NEW YORK CITY	DARTS	2	1978
BOY FROM NEW YORK CITY	ALLISON JORDAN	23	1992
A BOY FROM NOWHERE	TOM JONES	2	1987
BOY FROM SCHOOL	HOT CHIP	40	2006
BOY I GOTTA HAVE YOU	RIO & MARS	43	1995
BOY (I NEED YOU)	MARIAH CAREY FEATURING CAM'RON	17	2003
THE BOY IN THE BUBBLE	PAUL SIMON	26	1986
BOY IS CRYING	SAINT ETIENNE	34	2001
THE BOY IS MINE	BRANDY & MONICA	2	1998
A BOY NAMED SUE	JOHNNY CASH	4	1969
BOY NEXT DOOR	JAMELIA	42	2000
BOY OH BOY	RACEY	22	1979
BOY ON TOP OF THE NEWS	DIESEL PARK WEST	58	1992
BOY OR A GIRL	IMPERIAL DRAG	54	1996
THE BOY RACER	MORRISSEY	36	1995
THE BOY WHO CAME BACK	MARC ALMOND	52	1984
THE BOY WHO RAN AWAY	MYSTERY JETS	23	2006
THE BOY WITH THE THORN IN HIS SIDE	SMITHS	23	1985
THE BOY WITH X-RAY EYES	BABYLON ZOO	32	1996
BOY WONDER	SPEEDY	56	1996
BOY YOU KNOCK ME OUT	TATYANA ALI FEATURING WILL SMITH	3	1999
BOYFRIEND [A]	ASHLEE SIMPSON	12	2006
BOYFRIEND [B]	ALPHABEAT	15	2008
BOYS [A]	KIM WILDE	11	1981
BOYS [B]	MARY JANE GIRLS	74	1983
BOYS [C]	B.O.N.	15	2001
BOYS [D]	BRITNEY SPEARS FEAUTRING PHARRELL WILLIAMS	7	2002
BOYS AND GIRLS [A]	HUMAN LEAGUE	48	1981
BOYS AND GIRLS [B]	CHEEKY GIRLS	50	2004
BOYS AND GIRLS [C]	PIXIE LOTT	1	2009
THE BOYS ARE BACK IN TOWN	THIN LIZZY	8	1976
THE BOYS ARE BACK IN TOWN	GLADIATORS	70	1996
THE BOYS ARE BACK IN TOWN	HAPPY MONDAYS	24	1999
BOYS BETTER	DANDY WARHOLS	36	1998
BOYS CRY	EDEN KANE	8	1964
BOYS DON'T CRY	CURE	22	1986

Title / Artist	Peak Position	Year of Release
THE BOYS IN THE OLD BRIGHTON BLUE BRIGHTON & HOVE ALBION FC	65	1983
BOYS KEEP SWINGIN' DAVID BOWIE	7	1979
THE BOYS OF SUMMER DON HENLEY	12	1985
THE BOYS OF SUMMER DJ SAMMY	2	2003
THE BOYS OF SUMMER ATARIS	49	2003
BOYS (SUMMERTIME LOVE) SABRINA	3	1988
BOYS WILL BE BOYS [A] OSMOND BOYS	65	1991
BOYS WILL BE BOYS [B] ORDINARY BOYS	3	2005
BOZOS LEVELLERS	44	1998
BRACKISH KITTIE	46	2000
BRAIN JUNGLE BROTHERS	52	1997
BRAIN STEW GREEN DAY	28	1996
BRAINS NUT	64	1996
BRAINSTORM ARCTIC MONKEYS	2	2007
BRAINWASHED (CALL YOU) TOMCRAFT	43	2003
BRAND NEW [A] FINITRIBE	69	1994
BRAND NEW [B] RHYMEFEST FEATURING KANYE WEST	32	2006
BRAND NEW DAY [A] DARKMAN	74	1995
BRAND NEW DAY [B] MINDS OF MEN	41	1996
BRAND NEW DAY [C] STING	13	1999
BRAND NEW FRIEND LLOYD COLE & THE COMMOTIONS	19	1985
BRAND NEW KEY MELANIE	4	1972
BRAND NEW LOVER DEAD OR ALIVE	31	1986
BRAND NEW START PAUL WELLER	16	1998
BRANDY [A] SCOTT ENGLISH	12	1971
BRANDY [B] O'JAYS	21	1978
BRAS ON 45 (FAMILY VERSION) IVOR BIGGUN & THE D CUPS	50	1981
BRASS IN POCKET PRETENDERS	1	1979
BRASS, LET THERE BE HOUSE PARTY FAITHFUL	54	1995
BRASSNECK WEDDING PRESENT	24	1990
BRAVE NEW WORLD DAVID ESSEX	55	1978
BRAVE NEW WORLD TOYAH	21	1982
BRAVE NEW WORLD NEW MODEL ARMY	57	1985
BRAZEN 'WEEP' SKUNK ANANSIE	11	1997
BRAZIL CRISPY & COMPANY	26	1975
BRAZIL RITCHIE FAMILY	41	1975
BRAZILIAN DAWN SHAKATAK	48	1981
BRAZILIAN LOVE AFFAIR GEORGE DUKE	36	1980
BRAZILIAN LOVE SONG NAT 'KING' COLE	34	1962
BREACH THE PEACE (EP) SPIRAL TRIBE	66	1992
BREAD AND BUTTER NEWBEATS	15	1964
BREAK AWAY BEACH BOYS	6	1969
BREAK DANCIN' – ELECTRIC BOOGIE WEST STREET MOB	64	1983
BREAK DOWN THE DOORS MORILLO FEATURING THE AUDIOBULLYS	44	2004
BREAK EVEN SCRIPT	21	2008
BREAK EVERY RULE TINA TURNER	43	1987
BREAK 4 LOVE RAZE	28	1989
BREAK FROM THE OLD ROUTINE OUI 3	17	1993
BREAK IT DOWN AGAIN TEARS FOR FEARS	20	1993
BREAK IT TO ME GENTLY BRENDA LEE	46	1962
BREAK MY HEART SLOWLY NICKY WIRE	74	2006
BREAK MY STRIDE MATTHEW WILDER	4	1984
BREAK MY WORLD DARK GLOBE FEATURING AMANDA GHOST	52	2004
BREAK OF DAWN RHYTHM ON THE LOOSE	36	1995
BREAK OF DAWN 2008 OUT OF OFFICE	41	2008
BREAK ON THROUGH DOORS	64	1991
BREAK THE CHAIN [A] MOTIV 8	31	1995
BREAK THE CHAIN [B] ELKIE BROOKS	55	1987
BREAK THE ICE BRITNEY SPEARS	15	2008
BREAK THE NIGHT WITH COLOUR RICHARD ASHCROFT	3	2006
BREAK THE RULES STATUS QUO	8	1974
BREAK UP KIM SOZZI	23	2007
BREAK UP TO MAKE UP STYLISTICS	34	1973
BREAK UPS 2 MAKE UPS METHOD MAN FEATURING D'ANGELO	33	1999
BREAK YA NECK BUSTA RHYMES	11	2002
BREAK YOUR HEART TAIO CRUZ	1	2009
BREAKADAWN DE LA SOUL	39	1993
BREAKAWAY [A] SPRINGFIELDS	31	1961
BREAKAWAY [B] GALLAGHER & LYLE	35	1976
BREAKAWAY [C] TRACEY ULLMAN	4	1983
BREAKAWAY [D] DONNA SUMMER	49	1991
BREAKAWAY [E] KIM APPLEBY	56	1993
BREAKAWAY [F] ZZ TOP	60	1994
BREAKAWAY [G] KELLY CLARKSON	22	2006
BREAKBEAT ERA BREAKBEAT ERA	38	1998
BREAKDANCE PARTY BREAK MACHINE	9	1984
BREAKDOWN [A] ONE DOVE	24	1993
BREAKDOWN [B] DOUBLE SIX	59	1999
BREAKDOWN [C] JACK JOHNSON	73	2005
BREAKFAST ASSOCIATES	49	1985
BREAKFAST AT TIFFANY'S DEEP BLUE SOMETHING	1	1996
BREAKFAST IN AMERICA SUPERTRAMP	9	1979
BREAKFAST IN BED SHEILA HYLTON	57	1979
BREAKFAST IN BED UB40 FEATURING CHRISSIE HYNDE	6	1988
BREAKFAST ON PLUTO DON PARTRIDGE	26	1969
BREAKIN' MUSIC	20	2005
BREAKIN' AWAY KIM WILDE	43	1995
BREAKIN' DOWN SKID ROW	48	1995
BREAKIN' DOWN (SUGAR SAMBA) JULIA & COMPANY	15	1984
BREAKIN' DOWN THE WALLS OF HEARTACHE BANDWAGON	4	1968
BREAKIN' IN A BRAND NEW BROKEN HEART CONNIE FRANCIS	12	1961
BREAKIN'...THERE'S NO STOPPING US OLLIE & JERRY	5	1984
BREAKIN' UP WILD WEEKEND	74	1989
BREAKIN' UP IS BREAKIN' MY HEART ROY ORBISON	22	1966
BREAKING AWAY JAKI GRAHAM	16	1986
BREAKING FREE CAST OF HIGH SCHOOL MUSICAL	9	2006
BREAKING GLASS (EP) DAVID BOWIE	54	1978
BREAKING HEARTS (AIN'T WHAT IT USED TO BE) ELTON JOHN	59	1985
BREAKING POINT BOURGIE BOURGIE	48	1984
BREAKING THE GIRL RED HOT CHILI PEPPERS	41	1992
BREAKING THE HABIT LINKIN PARK	39	2004
BREAKING THE LAW JUDAS PRIEST	12	1980
BREAKING UP IS HARD TO DO NEIL SEDAKA	7	1962
BREAKING UP IS HARD TO DO PARTRIDGE FAMILY STARRING SHIRLEY JONES FEATURING DAVID CASSIDY	3	1972
BREAKING UP MY HEART SHAKIN' STEVENS	14	1985
BREAKING UP THE GIRL GARBAGE	27	2002
BREAKING US IN TWO JOE JACKSON	59	1983
BREAKOUT [A] SWING OUT SISTER	4	1986
BREAKOUT [B] FOO FIGHTERS	29	2000
THE BREAKS KURTIS BLOW	47	1980
BREAKS YOU OFF ROOTS FEATURING MUSIQ	59	2003
BREAKTHRU' QUEEN	7	1989
BREATH OF LIFE ERASURE	8	1992
BREATHE [A] MARIA McKEE	59	1991
BREATHE [B] MIDGE URE	70	1996
BREATHE [C] PRODIGY	1	1996
BREATHE [D] KYLIE MINOGUE	14	1998
BREATHE [E] BLUE AMAZON	73	2000
BREATHE [F] FAITH HILL	33	2000
BREATHE [G] SCIENCE DEPT FEATURING ERIRE	64	2001
BREATHE [H] TELEPOPMUSIK	42	2002
BREATHE [I] BLU CANTRELL FEATURING SEAN PAUL	1	2003
BREATHE [J] FABOLOUS	28	2004
BREATHE [K] ERASURE	4	2005
BREATHE (A LITTLE DEEPER) BLAMELESS	27	1996
BREATHE A SIGH DEF LEPPARD	43	1996
BREATHE AGAIN TONI BRAXTON	2	1994
BREATHE AND STOP Q-TIP	12	2000
BREATHE DON'T STOP MR ON VS THE JUNGLE BROTHERS	21	2004
BREATHE EASY BLUE	4	2004
BREATHE IN [A] FROU FROU	44	2002
BREATHE IN [B] LUCIE SILVAS	6	2005
BREATHE LIFE INTO ME MICA PARIS	26	1988
BREATHE ME SIA	71	2004
BREATHE SLOW ALESHA DIXON	3	2009
BREATHE STRETCH SHAKE MA$E	29	2004
BREATHING [A] KATE BUSH	16	1980
BREATHING [B] NORTH & SOUTH	27	1997
BREATHING IS E-ZEE E-ZEE POSSEE FEATURING TARA NEWLEY	72	1991
BREATHLESS [A] JERRY LEE LEWIS	8	1958
BREATHLESS [B] CORRS	1	2000
BREATHLESS [C] NICK CAVE & THE BAD SEEDS	45	2004
BREATHLESS [D] SHAYNE WARD	6	2007
THE BREEZE AND I CATERINA VALENTE	5	1955
THE BREEZE AND I FENTONES	48	1962
BREEZE ON BY DONNY OSMOND	8	2004
BRIAN WILSON BARENAKED LADIES	73	1999
BRICK BEN FOLDS FIVE	26	1998
BRICK HOUSE COMMODORES	32	1977
THE BRICK TRACK VERSUS GITTY UP SALTNPEPA	22	1999
BRIDESHEAD THEME GEOFFREY BURGON	48	1981
BRIDGE [A] ORANGE JUICE	67	1984
THE BRIDGE [B] CACTUS WORLD NEWS	74	1986
BRIDGE [C] QUEENSRYCHE	40	1995
BRIDGE OF SIGHS DAVID WHITFIELD	9	1953
BRIDGE OVER TROUBLED WATER SIMON & GARFUNKEL	1	1970
BRIDGE OVER TROUBLED WATER LINDA CLIFFORD	28	1979
BRIDGE OVER TROUBLED WATER PJB FEATURING HANNAH & HER SISTERS	21	1991
BRIDGE TO YOUR HEART WAX	12	1987
BRIDGET THE MIDGET (THE QUEEN OF THE BLUES) RAY STEVENS	2	1971
BRIDGING THE GAP NAS	18	2004
THE BRIGHT AMBASSADORS OF MORNING PURE REASON REVOLUTION	68	2005
BRIGHT EYES ART GARFUNKEL	1	1979
BRIGHT EYES STEPHEN GATELY	3	2000
BRIGHT IDEA ORSON	11	2006
THE BRIGHT LIGHT TANYA DONELLY	64	1997
BRIGHT LIGHTS SPECIAL A.K.A.	60	1983
BRIGHT SIDE OF LIFE TENOR FLY	16	1995
BRIGHT SIDE OF THE ROAD VAN MORRISON	63	1979
BRIGHT YELLOW GUN THROWING MUSES	51	1994
BRIGHTER DAY KELLY LLORENNA	43	1996
BRIGHTER THAN SUNSHINE AQUALUNG	37	2003
BRIGHTEST STAR DRIZABONE	45	1994
BRILLIANT DISGUISE BRUCE SPRINGSTEEN	20	1987
BRILLIANT FEELING FULL MONTY ALLSTARS FEATURING TJ DAVIS	72	1996
BRILLIANT MIND FURNITURE	21	1986
BRIMFUL OF ASHA CORNERSHOP	1	1997
BRING A LITTLE WATER SYLVIE LONNIE DONEGAN	7	1956
BRING 'EM ALL IN MIKE SCOTT	56	1995
BRING EM OUT TI	59	2005
BRING FORTH THE GUILLOTINE SILVER BULLET	45	1989
BRING IT ALL BACK S CLUB 7	1	1999
BRING IT ALL HOME GERRY RAFFERTY	54	1980
BRING IT BACK McALMONT & BUTLER	36	2002

Title / Artist	Peak Position	Year of Release
BRING IT BACK AGAIN [A] STRAY CATS	64	1989
BRING IT BACK AGAIN [B] EARLIES	61	2005
BRING IT BACK 2 LUV PROJECT FEATURING GERIDEAU	65	1994
BRING IT DOWN (THIS INSANE THING) REDSKINS	33	1985
BRING IT ON [A] N'DEA DAVENPORT	52	1998
BRING IT ON [B] GOMEZ	21	1999
BRING IT ON [C] NICK CAVE & THE BAD SEEDS	58	2003
BRING IT ON [D] ALISTAIR GRIFFIN	5	2004
BRING IT ON BACK JET	51	2006
BRING IT ON...BRING IT ON JAMES BROWN	45	1983
BRING IT ON DOWN JESUS JONES	46	1989
BRING IT ON HOME URBAN COOKIE COLLECTIVE	56	1994
BRING IT ON HOME TO ME ANIMALS	7	1965
BRING IT ON TO MY LOVE DE NADA	24	2002
BRING ME CLOSER ALTERED IMAGES	29	1983
BRING ME EDELWEISS EDELWEISS	5	1989
BRING ME LOVE ANDREA MENDEZ	44	1996
BRING ME TO LIFE EVANESCENCE	1	2003
BRING ME TO LIFE KATHERINE JENKINS	74	2009
BRING ME YOUR CUP UB40	24	1993
BRING MY FAMILY BACK FAITHLESS	14	1999
BRING ON THE DANCING HORSES ECHO & THE BUNNYMEN	21	1985
BRING THE FAMILY BACK BILLY PAUL	51	1979
BRING THE NOISE PUBLIC ENEMY	32	1988
BRING THE NOISE ANTHRAX FEATURING CHUCK D	14	1991
BRING UP THE MIC SOME MORE RAGGA TWINS	65	1992
BRING YOUR DAUGHTER...TO THE SLAUGHTER IRON MAIDEN	1	1991
BRINGING BACK THOSE MEMORIES MARK JOSEPH	34	2004
BRINGING ON BACK THE GOOD TIMES LOVE AFFAIR	9	1969
BRISTOL STOMP LATE SHOW	40	1979
BRITANNIA RAG WINIFRED ATWELL	5	1952
BRITE SIDE DEBORAH HARRY	59	1989
BRITISH HUSTLE HI TENSION	8	1978
THE BRITISH WAY OF LIFE CHORDS	54	1980
THE BRITS 1990 VARIOUS ARTISTS (MONTAGES)	2	1990
BROKE [A] BETA BAND	30	2001
BROKE [B] CASSIUS HENRY	31	2002
BROKE [C] CAPTAIN	34	2006
BROKE AWAY WET WET WET	19	1989
BROKEN ARROW [A] WATERFRONT	63	1989
BROKEN ARROW [B] ROD STEWART	41	1991
BROKEN BONES LOVE INC	8	2003
BROKEN BOY SOLDIER RACONTEURS	22	2006
BROKEN DOLL TOMMY BRUCE & THE BRUISERS	36	1960
BROKEN DOWN ANGEL NAZARETH	9	1973
BROKEN ENGLISH SUNSCREEM	13	1993
A BROKEN HEART CAN MEND ALEXANDER O'NEAL	53	1986
BROKEN HEART (THIRTEEN VALLEYS) BIG COUNTRY	47	1988
BROKEN HEARTED KEN DODD	15	1970
BROKEN HEARTED GIRL BEYONCE	27	2009
BROKEN HEARTED MELODY SARAH VAUGHAN	7	1959
BROKEN HEELS ALEXANDRA BURKE	8	2009
BROKEN HOMES TRICKY	25	1998
BROKEN LAND ADVENTURES	20	1988
BROKEN NOSE CATHERINE WHEEL	48	1998
BROKEN SILENCE SO SOLID CREW	9	2003
BROKEN STONES PAUL WELLER	20	1995
BROKEN STRINGS JAMES MORRISON FEATURING NELLY FURTADO	2	2008
BROKEN WINGS [A] STARGAZERS	1	1953
BROKEN WINGS [A] ART & DOTTY TODD	6	1953
BROKEN WINGS [A] DICKIE VALENTINE	12	1953
BROKEN WINGS [B] MR MISTER	4	1986
BROKEN WINGS [B] NETWORK	46	1992
THE BROKEN YEARS HIPSWAY	72	1985
BRONTOSAURUS MOVE	7	1970
BROOKLYN BEATS SCOTTI DEEP	67	1997
BROOKLYN-QUEENS 3RD BASS	61	1990
BROTHA PART II ANGIE STONE FEATURING ALICIA KEYS & EVE	37	2002
BROTHER [A] C.C.S.	25	1972
BROTHER [B] URBAN SPECIES	40	1994
BROTHER BRIGHT CA VA CA VA	65	1983
BROTHER LOUIE [A] HOT CHOCOLATE	7	1973
BROTHER LOUIE [A] QUIREBOYS	32	1993
BROTHER LOUIE [B] MODERN TALKING	4	1986
BROTHER OF MINE ANDERSON BRUFORD WAKEMAN HOWE	63	1989
BROTHERS AND SISTERS 2 FUNKY 2 FEATURING KATHRYN DION	36	1993
BROTHERS GONNA WORK IT OUT PUBLIC ENEMY	46	1990
BROTHERS IN ARMS DIRE STRAITS	16	1985
BROWN-EYED HANDSOME MAN BUDDY HOLLY	3	1963
BROWN EYED HANDSOME MAN PAUL McCARTNEY	42	1999
BROWN GIRL IN THE RING BONEY M	1	1978
BROWN PAPER BAG RONI SIZE/REPRAZENT	20	1997
BROWN SKIN INDIA.ARIE	29	2001
BROWN SUGAR [A] ROLLING STONES	2	1971
BROWN SUGAR [B] D'ANGELO	24	1995
BRUISE PRISTINE PLACEBO	14	1997
BRUISED WATER CHICANE VERSUS NATASHA BEDINGFIELD	42	2008
BRUISES CHAIRLIFT	50	2008
BRUSHED PAUL WELLER	14	1997
BRUTAL-8-E ALTERN 8	43	1992
BUBBLE FLUKE	37	1994
BUBBLIN' BLUE	9	2004
BUBBLING HOT PATO BANTON WITH RANKING ROGER	15	1995
BUBBLY COLBIE CAILLAT	58	2007
BUCCI BAG ANDREA DORIA	57	2003
BUCK ROGERS FEEDER	5	2001
THE BUCKET KINGS OF LEON	16	2004
THE BUCKET OF WATER SONG FOUR BUCKETEERS	26	1980
BUDDHA OF SUBURBIA DAVID BOWIE FEATURING LENNY KRAVITZ	35	1993
BUDDY DE LA SOUL	7	1989
BUDDY HOLLY WEEZER	12	1995
BUDDY X NENEH CHERRY	35	1993
BUDDY X 99 DREEM TEEM Vs NENEH CHERRY	15	1999
BUFFALO BILL'S LAST SCRATCH BARRON KNIGHTS	49	1983
BUFFALO GALS STAMPEDE MALCOLM McLAREN & THE WORLD'S FAMOUS SUPREME TEAM PLUS RAKIM & ROGER SANCHEZ	65	1998
BUFFALO GIRLS MALCOLM McLAREN & THE WORLD'S FAMOUS SUPREME TEAM	9	1982
BUFFALO SOLDIER BOB MARLEY & THE WAILERS	4	1983
BUFFALO STANCE NENEH CHERRY	3	1988
THE BUG DIRE STRAITS	67	1992
BUG A BOO DESTINY'S CHILD	9	1999
BUG IN THE BASSBIN INNERZONE ORCHESTRA	68	1996
BUG POWDER DUST BOMB THE BASS FEATURING JUSTIN WARFIELD	24	1994
BUGGIN' TRUE STEPPERS FEATURING DANE BOWERS	6	2000
BUGS HEPBURN	14	1999
BUILD [A] HOUSEMARTINS	15	1987
BUILD [B] INNOCENCE	72	1992
BUILD ME UP BUTTERCUP FOUNDATIONS	2	1968
BUILD ME UP BUTTERCUP 2003 PARTY BOYS	44	2004
BUILD YOUR LOVE (ON A STRONG FOUNDATION) JOHNNIE RAY	17	1957
BUILDING THE CITY OF LIGHT MIKE SCOTT	60	1995
BUILT TO LAST MELEE	58	2008
BULGARIAN TRAVEL	67	1999
BULL IN THE HEATHER SONIC YOUTH	24	1994
BULLDOG NATION KEVIN KENNEDY	70	2000
BULLET FLUKE	23	1995
BULLET COMES CHARLATANS	32	1995
BULLET IN THE GUN PLANET PERFECTO	7	1999
BULLET IN THE HEAD RAGE AGAINST THE MACHINE	16	1993
BULLET WITH BUTTERFLY WINGS SMASHING PUMPKINS	20	1995
BULLETPROOF! [A] POP WILL EAT ITSELF	24	1992
BULLETPROOF [B] LA ROUX	1	2009
BULLETS EDITORS	27	2005
BULLFROG GTO	72	1991
BULLITPROOF BREAKBEAT ERA	65	2000
BULLITT LALO SCHIFRIN	36	1997
BULLS ON PARADE RAGE AGAINST THE MACHINE	8	1996
BULLY BOY SHED SEVEN	22	1996
BULLY FOR YOU TOM ROBINSON BAND	68	1979
THE BUMP KENNY	3	1974
BUMP BUMP BUMP B2K FEATURING P DIDDY	11	2003
BUMP N' GRIND R KELLY	8	1995
BUMP N GRIND (I AM FEELING HOT TONIGHT) M DUBS FEATURING LADY SAW	59	2000
BUMP/RUN DADDY RUN FUN LOVIN' CRIMINALS	50	2001
BUMPED RIGHT SAID FRED	32	1993
A BUNCH OF THYME FOSTER & ALLEN	18	1982
BUNSEN BURNER JOHN OTWAY	9	2002
BUONA SERA LOUIS PRIMA	25	1958
BUONA SERA MR ACKER BILK & HIS PARAMOUNT JAZZ BAND	7	1960
BUONA SERA BAD MANNERS	34	1981
BUOY MICK KARN FEATURING DAVID SYLVIAN	63	1987
BURDEN IN MY HAND SOUNDGARDEN	33	1996
BURIAL LEVITICUS	66	1995
BURIED ALIVE BY LOVE H.I.M.	30	2003
BURLESQUE FAMILY	13	1972
BURN [A] DOCTOR & THE MEDICS	29	1986
BURN [B] TINA ARENA	47	1999
BURN [C] USHER	1	2004
BURN [D] ALKALINE TRIO	34	2006
BURN BABY BURN [A] HUDSON- FORD	15	1974
BURN BABY BURN [B] ASH	13	2001
BURN BURN LOSTPROPHETS	17	2003
BURN FASTER NINE BLACK ALPS	42	2007
BURN IT UP BEATMASTERS WITH PP ARNOLD	14	1988
BURN RUBBER ON ME (WHY YOU WANNA HURT ME) GAP BAND	22	1981
BURN YOUR YOUTH JOHNNY PANIC	69	2004
BURNED WITH DESIRE ARMIN VAN BUUREN FEATURING JUSTINE SUISSA	45	2004
BURNIN' [A] DAFT PUNK	30	1997
BURNIN' [B] K-KLASS	45	1998
BURNIN' [C] MIRRORBALL	47	2000
BURNIN' HOT JERMAINE JACKSON	32	1980
BURNIN' LOVE CON FUNK SHUN	68	1986
BURNIN' UP JONAS BROTHERS	30	2008

Title / Artist	Peak Position	Year of Release
BURNING [A] MK	44	1995
BURNING [B] BABY BUMPS	17	1998
BURNING BENCHES MORNING RUNNER	19	2006
BURNING BRIDGES JACK SCOTT	32	1960
BURNING BRIDGES (ON AND OFF AND ON AGAIN) STATUS QUO	5	1988
BURNING CAR JOHN FOXX	35	1980
BURNING DOWN ONE SIDE ROBERT PLANT	73	1982
BURNING DOWN THE HOUSE TOM JONES & THE CARDIGANS	7	1999
BURNING HEART SURVIVOR	5	1986
BURNING LOVE ELVIS PRESLEY	7	1972
BURNING OF THE MIDNIGHT LAMP JIMI HENDRIX EXPERIENCE	18	1967
BURNING THE GROUND DURAN DURAN	31	1989
BURNING UP [A] TONY DE VIT	25	1995
BURNING UP [B] BINI & MARTINI	65	2001
BURNING WHEEL PRIMAL SCREAM	17	1997
BURST DARLING BUDS	50	1988
BURUCHACCA MUKKAA	74	1993
BURUNDI BLACK BURUNDI STEIPHENSON BLACK	31	1971
BURUNDI BLUES BEATS INTERNATIONAL	51	1990
BURY YOU SYMPOSIUM	41	1998
BUS STOP HOLLIES	5	1966
BUSHEL AND A PECK VIVIAN BLAINE	12	1953
BUSHES MARKUS NIKOLAI	74	2001
THE BUSINESS [A] BRIAN MAY	51	1998
BUSINESS [B] EMINEM	6	2003
BUST A MOVE YOUNG MC	73	1989
BUST THIS HOUSE DOWN PENTHOUSE 4	56	1988
BUST YOUR WINDOWS GLEE CAST	57	2010
BUSTED RAY CHARLES	21	1963
BUSY BEE UGLY KID JOE	39	1993
BUSY DOING NOTHING DAVE STEWART WITH BARBARA GASKIN	49	1983
BUT I DO LOVE YOU LeANN RIMES	20	2002
BUT I FEEL GOOD GROOVE ARMADA	50	2003
BUT IT'S BETTER IF YOU DO PANIC! AT THE DISCO	23	2006
BUT NOT FOR ME ELLA FITZGERALD	25	1959
BUT NOT FOR ME KETTY LESTER	45	1962
BUT YOU LOVE ME DADDY JIM REEVES	15	1969
BUT YOU'RE MINE SONNY & CHER	17	1965
BUTCHER BABY PLASMATICS	55	1980
BUTTERCUP CARL ANDERSON	49	1985
BUTTERFINGERS TOMMY STEELE & THE STEELMEN	8	1957
BUTTERFLIES AND HURRICANES MUSE	14	2004
BUTTERFLY [A] ANDY WILLIAMS	1	1957
BUTTERFLY [A] CHARLIE GRACIE	12	1957
BUTTERFLY [B] DANYEL GERARD	11	1971
BUTTERFLY [C] MARIAH CAREY	22	1997
BUTTERFLY [D] TILT FEATURING ZEE	41	1998
BUTTERFLY [E] CRAZY TOWN	3	2001
BUTTERFLY KISSES BOB CARLISLE	56	1997
BUTTERFLY ON A WHEEL MISSION	12	1990
BUTTONS PUSSYCAT DOLLS FEATURING SNOOP DOGG	3	2006
BUY IT IN BOTTLES RICHARD ASHCROFT	26	2003
BUZZ BUZZ A DIDDLE IT MATCHBOX	22	1980
BUZZIN' ASIAN DUB FOUNDATION	31	1998
BY MY SIDE INXS	42	1991
BY THE DEVIL (I WAS TEMPTED) BLUE MINK	26	1973
BY THE FOUNTAINS OF ROME EDMUND HOCKRIDGE	17	1956
BY THE FOUNTAINS OF ROME DAVID HUGHES	27	1956
BY THE LIGHT OF THE SILVERY MOON LITTLE RICHARD	17	1959
BY THE TIME THIS NIGHT IS OVER KENNY G WITH PEABO BRYSON	56	1993
BY THE WAY [A] BIG THREE	22	1963
BY THE WAY [B] TREMELOES	35	1970
BY THE WAY [C] RED HOT CHILI PEPPERS	2	2002
BY YOUR SIDE [A] PETERS & LEE	39	1973
BY YOUR SIDE [B] JIMMY SOMERVILLE	41	1995
BY YOUR SIDE [C] SADE	17	2000
BYE BABY RUBY TURNER	52	1986
BYE BYE MARIAH CAREY	30	2008
BYE BYE BABY [A] JOHNNY OTIS SHOW, VOCALS BY MARIE ADAMS & JOHNNY OTIS	20	1958
BYE BYE BABY [B] SYMBOLS	44	1967
BYE BYE BABY [B] BAY CITY ROLLERS	1	1975
BYE BYE BABY [C] TONY JACKSON & THE VIBRATIONS	38	1964
BYE BYE BABY [D] TQ	7	1999
BYE BYE BLUES BERT KAEMPFERT	24	1966
BYE BYE BOY JENNIFER ELLISON	13	2004
BYE BYE BYE *NSYNC	3	2000
BYE BYE LOVE EVERLY BROTHERS	6	1957
B.Y.O.F. (BRING YOUR OWN FUNK) FANTASTIC FOUR	62	1979
BYRDS TURN TO STONE SHACK	63	2003

C

Title / Artist	Peak Position	Year of Release
C-C (YOU SET THE FIRE IN ME) TOM VEK	60	2005
C I AM 15 KING BISCUIT TIME	67	2005
C-LEBRITY QUEEN & PAUL RODGERS	33	2008
C MOON WINGS	5	1972
C U WHEN U GET THERE COOLIO FEATURING 40 THEVZ	3	1997
C30, C60, C90, GO BOW WOW WOW	34	1980
CA PLANE POUR MOI PLASTIC BERTRAND	8	1978
CA PLANE POUR MOI LEILA K	69	1993
CABARET [A] LOUIS ARMSTRONG	1	1968
THE CABARET [B] TIME UK	63	1983
CACHARPAYA (ANDES PUMPSA DAESI) INCANTATION	12	1982
CAFÉ DEL MAR ENERGY 52	12	1997
CAFFEINE BOMB WILDHEARTS	31	1994
CALEDONIA FRANKIE MILLER	45	1992
CALENDAR GIRL [A] NEIL SEDAKA	8	1961
CALENDAR GIRL [B] NOISE NEXT DOOR	11	2005
THE CALENDAR SONG (JANUARY, FEBRUARY, MARCH, APRIL, MAY) TRINIDAD OIL COMPANY	34	1977
CALIBRE CUTS VARIOUS ARTISTS (MONTAGES)	75	1980
CALIFORNIA [A] WEDDING PRESENT	16	1992
CALIFORNIA [B] BELINDA CARLISLE	31	1997
CALIFORNIA [C] LENNY KRAVITZ	62	2004
CALIFORNIA [D] LOW	57	2005
CALIFORNIA [E] PHANTOM PLANET	9	2005
CALIFORNIA DREAMIN' MAMAS & THE PAPAS	9	1966
CALIFORNIA DREAMIN' COLORADO	45	1978
CALIFORNIA DREAMIN' RIVER CITY PEOPLE	13	1990
CALIFORNIA DREAMIN' ROYAL GIGOLOS	44	2004
CALIFORNIA DREAMIN' BOBBY WOMACK	59	2004
CALIFORNIA GIRLS BEACH BOYS	26	1965
CALIFORNIA GIRLS DAVID LEE ROTH	68	1985
CALIFORNIA HERE I COME [A] FREDDY CANNON	25	1960
CALIFORNIA HERE I COME [B] SOPHIE B HAWKINS	53	1992
CALIFORNIA LOVE 2PAC FEATURING DR DRE	6	1996
CALIFORNIA MAN MOVE	7	1972
CALIFORNIA SAGA-CALIFORNIA BEACH BOYS	37	1973
CALIFORNIA SCREAMIN' CARRIE	55	1998
CALIFORNIA SOUL RIOT ACT	59	2005
CALIFORNIA WAITING KINGS OF LEON	61	2004
CALIFORNIA'S BLEEDING AMEN	52	2004
CALIFORNICATION RED HOT CHILI PEPPERS	16	2000
CALINDA RITMO-DYNAMIC	68	2003
THE CALL BACKSTREET BOYS	8	2001
CALL AND ANSWER BARENAKED LADIES	52	1999
CALL HER YOUR SWEETHEART FRANK IFIELD	24	1967
CALL IT FATE RICHIE DAN	34	2000
CALL IT LOVE DEUCE	11	1995
CALL IT ROCK 'N' ROLL GREAT WHITE	67	1991
CALL IT WHAT YOU WANT [A] NEW KIDS ON THE BLOCK	12	1991
CALL IT WHAT YOU WANT [B] CREDIT TO THE NATION	57	1993
CALL ME [A] BLONDIE	1	1980
CALL ME [B] GO WEST	12	1985
CALL ME [C] SPAGNA	2	1987
CALL ME [D] LE CLICK	38	1997
CALL ME [E] JAMELIA	11	2000
CALL ME [F] TWEET	35	2002
(CALL ME) NUMBER ONE TREMELOES	2	1969
CALL ME ROUND PILOT	34	1975
CALL ME WHEN YOU'RE SOBER EVANESCENCE	4	2006
CALL MY NAME [A] ORCHESTRAL MANOEUVRES IN THE DARK	50	1991
CALL MY NAME [B] CHARLOTTE CHURCH	10	2005
CALL OF THE WILD [A] MIDGE URE	27	1986
CALL OF THE WILD [B] GUSGUS	75	2003
CALL OFF THE SEARCH KATIE MELUA	19	2004
CALL ON ME [A] ERIC PRYDZ	1	2004
CALL ON ME [B] JANET & NELLY	18	2006
CALL OUT THE DOGS GARY NUMAN	49	1985
CALL ROSIE ON THE PHONE GUY MITCHELL	17	1957
CALL THE MAN CELINE DION	11	1997
CALL THE SHOTS GIRLS ALOUD	3	2007
CALL U SEXY VS	11	2004
THE CALL UP CLASH	40	1980
CALL UP THE GROUPS BARRON KNIGHTS WITH DUKE D'MOND	3	1964
CALLING GERI HALLIWELL	7	2001
CALLING ALL GIRLS ATL	12	2004
CALLING ALL THE HEROES IT BITES	6	1986
CALLING AMERICA ELECTRIC LIGHT ORCHESTRA	28	1986
CALLING ELVIS DIRE STRAITS	21	1991
CALLING OCCUPANTS OF INTERPLANETARY CRAFT (THE RECOGNISED ANTHEM OF WORLD CONTACT DAY) CARPENTERS	9	1977
CALLING OUT YOUR NAME JIMMY NAIL	65	1995
CALLING YOU PAUL YOUNG	57	1991
CALLING YOUR NAME MARILYN	4	1983
CALLS THE TUNE HAZEL O'CONNOR	60	1982
CALM DOWN (BASS KEEPS PUMPIN') CHRIS & JAMES	74	1994
CALM DOWN DEAREST JAMIE T	9	2007
CALYPSO CRAZY BILLY OCEAN	35	1988
CAMBODIA KIM WILDE	12	1981
CAMDEN TOWN SUGGS	14	1995
CAMEL BOBSLED RACE DJ SHADOW	62	1997
CAMELS SANTOS	9	2001
CAMERA PHONE GAME FEATURING NE-YO	48	2009
CAMOUFLAGE STAN RIDGWAY	4	1986
CAMPIONE 2000 E-TYPE	58	2000
CAN CAN BAD MANNERS	3	1981
CAN CAN 62 PETER JAY & THE JAYWALKERS	31	1962
CAN CAN YOU PARTY JIVE BUNNY & THE MASTERMIXERS	8	1990
CAN I CASHMERE	29	1985
CAN I GET A... JAY-Z FEATURING AMIL & JA RULE	24	1999
CAN I GET A WITNESS SAM BROWN	15	1989
CAN I GET OVER DEFINITION OF SOUND	61	1992

Title	Artist	Peak Position	Year of Release
CAN I HAVE IT LIKE THAT	PHARRELL FEATURING GWEN STEFANI	3	2005
CAN I KICK IT	A TRIBE CALLED QUEST	15	1991
CAN I PLAY WITH MADNESS	IRON MAIDEN	3	1988
CAN I TAKE YOU HOME LITTLE GIRL	DRIFTERS	10	1975
CAN I TOUCH YOU...THERE?	MICHAEL BOLTON	6	1995
CAN I TRUST YOU	BACHELORS	26	1966
CAN THE CAN	SUZI QUATRO	1	1973
CAN THIS BE LOVE	MATT MONRO	24	1961
CAN U DANCE	KENNY 'JAMMIN' JASON & DJ 'FAST' EDDIE SMITH	71	1987
CAN U DIG IT [A]	POP WILL EAT ITSELF	38	1989
CAN U DIG IT [B]	JAMX & DELEON	40	2002
CAN U FEEL IT	DEEP CREED '94	59	1994
CAN WE	SWV	18	1997
CAN WE CHILL	NE-YO	62	2007
CAN WE FIX IT	BOB THE BUILDER	1	2000
CAN WE START AGAIN?	TINDERSTICKS	54	1999
CAN WE TALK...	CODE RED	29	1997
CAN YOU DIG IT	MOCK TURTLES	19	1991
CAN YOU DO IT	GEORDIE	13	1973
CAN YOU FEEL IT [A]	JACKSONS	6	1981
CAN YOU FEEL IT [A]	V	5	2004
CAN YOU FEEL IT [B]	ELEVATION	62	1992
CAN YOU FEEL IT [C]	REEL 2 REAL FEATURING THE MAD STUNTMAN	13	1994
CAN YOU FEEL IT [D]	CLS	46	1998
CAN YOU FEEL IT (ROCK DA HOUSE)	NYCC	68	1998
CAN YOU FEEL IT/CAN YOU FEEL IT	RAZE/CHAMPIONSHIP LEGEND	62	1990
CAN YOU FEEL THE FORCE	REAL THING	5	1979
CAN YOU FEEL THE LOVE TONIGHT	ELTON JOHN	14	1994
(CAN YOU) FEEL THE PASSION	BLUE PEARL	14	1992
CAN YOU FEEL (WHAT I'M GOING THROUGH)	SHOLAN	47	2003
CAN YOU FORGIVE HER	PET SHOP BOYS	7	1993
CAN YOU FORGIVE ME	KARL DENVER	32	1963
CAN YOU HANDLE IT	SHARON REDD	31	1981
CAN YOU HANDLE IT	DNA FEATURING SHARON REDD	17	1992
CAN YOU KEEP A SECRET	BROTHER BEYOND	22	1988
CAN YOU PARTY	ROYAL HOUSE	14	1988
CAN YOU PLEASE CRAWL OUT YOUR WINDOW	BOB DYLAN	17	1966
CAN YOUR PUSSY DO THE DOG?	CRAMPS	68	1985
CANCER FOR THE CURE	EELS	60	2000
CANDIDA	DAWN	9	1971
CANDIDATE FOR LOVE	TS MONK	58	1981
CANDLE IN THE WIND	ELTON JOHN	1	1974
CANDLEFIRE	DAWN OF THE REPLICANTS	52	1998
CANDLELAND (THE SECOND COMING)	IAN McCULLOCH FEATURING ELIZABETH FRASER	75	1990
CANDLELIGHT	SIX BY SEVEN	70	1998
CANDLES	ALEX REECE	33	1996
CANDY [A]	CAMEO	27	1986
CANDY [B]	IGGY POP	67	1990
CANDY [C]	MANDY MOORE	6	2000
CANDY [D]	ASH	20	2001
CANDY [E]	PAOLO NUTINI	19	2009
CANDY EVERYBODY WANTS	10,000 MANIACS	47	1993
CANDY GIRL [A]	NEW EDITION	1	1983
CANDY GIRL [B]	BABYBIRD	14	1997
CANDY MAN [A]	BRIAN POOLE & THE TREMELOES	6	1964
CANDY MAN [B]	MARY JANE GIRLS	60	1983
CANDY RAIN	SOUL FOR REAL	23	1995
CANDY SHOP	50 CENT	4	2005
CANDYBAR EXPRESS	LOVE & MONEY	56	1986
CANDYMAN [A]	SIOUXSIE & THE BANSHEES	34	1986
CANDYMAN [B]	CHRISTINA AGUILERA	17	2007
CANNED HEAT	JAMIROQUAI	4	1999
CANNIBALS	MARK KNOPFLER	42	1996
CANNONBALL [A]	DUANE EDDY & THE REBELS	22	1959
CANNONBALL [B]	DAMIEN RICE	19	2003
CANNONBALL (EP)	BREEDERS	40	1993
CAN'T BE SURE	SUNDAYS	45	1989
CAN'T BE WITH YOU TONIGHT	JUDY BOUCHER	2	1987
CAN'T BUY ME LOVE	BEATLES	1	1964
CAN'T BUY ME LOVE	ELLA FITZGERALD	34	1964
CAN'T CATCH TOMORROW	LOSTPROPHETS	35	2006
CAN'T CHANGE ME	CHRIS CORNELL	62	1999
CAN'T CONTAIN ME	TAZ	46	2004
CAN'T CRY ANYMORE	SHERYL CROW	33	1995
CAN'T DO A THING (TO STOP ME)	CHRIS ISAAK	36	1993
CAN'T DO NUTTIN' FOR YA MAN	PUBLIC ENEMY	53	1990
CAN'T DO RIGHT FOR DOING WRONG	ERIN ROCHA	36	2003
CAN'T EXPLAIN	LONGVIEW	51	2003
CAN'T FAKE THE FEELING	GERALDINE HUNT	44	1980
CAN'T FIGHT THE MOONLIGHT	LeANN RIMES	1	2000
CAN'T FIGHT THIS FEELING	REO SPEEDWAGON	16	1985
CAN'T FORGET YOU	SONIA	17	1989
CAN'T GET ALONG WITHOUT YOU [A]	FRANKIE VAUGHAN	11	1958
CAN'T GET ALONG (WITHOUT YOU) [B]	HARD-FI	45	2007
CAN'T GET ANY HARDER	JAMES BROWN	59	1993
CAN'T GET AWAY	MOOD II SWING	45	2004
CAN'T GET BY	SLAMM	47	1995
CAN'T GET BY WITHOUT YOU	REAL THING	2	1976
CAN'T GET ENOUGH [A]	BAD COMPANY	15	1974
CAN'T GET ENOUGH [B]	SOULSEARCHER	8	1999
CAN'T GET ENOUGH [C]	SUEDE	23	1999
CAN'T GET ENOUGH [D]	RAGHAV	10	2004
CAN'T GET ENOUGH [E]	INFADELS	43	2006
CAN'T GET ENOUGH OF YOU	EDDY GRANT	13	1981
CAN'T GET ENOUGH OF YOUR LOVE [A]	DARTS	43	1979
CAN'T GET ENOUGH OF YOUR LOVE [B]	TAYLOR DAYNE	14	1993
CAN'T GET ENOUGH OF YOUR LOVE [B]	KWS	71	1993
CAN'T GET ENOUGH OF YOUR LOVE BABE	BARRY WHITE	8	1974
CAN'T GET IT BACK	MIS-TEEQ	8	2003
(CAN'T GET MY) HEAD AROUND YOU	OFFSPRING	48	2004
CAN'T GET OUT OF BED	CHARLATANS	24	1994
CAN'T GET OVER	SEPTEMBER	14	2009
CAN'T GET THE BEST OF ME	CYPRESS HILL	35	2000
CAN'T GET USED TO LOSING YOU	ANDY WILLIAMS	2	1963
CAN'T GET USED TO LOSING YOU	BEAT	3	1983
CAN'T GET USED TO LOSING YOU	COLOUR GIRL	31	2000
CAN'T GET YOU OFF MY MIND	LENNY KRAVITZ	54	1996
CAN'T GET YOU OUT OF MY HEAD	KYLIE MINOGUE	1	2001
CAN'T GET YOU OUT OF MY THOUGHTS	DUM DUMS	18	2000
CAN'T GIVE ME LOVE	PEPSI & SHIRLIE	58	1987
CAN'T GIVE YOU ANYTHING (BUT MY LOVE)	STYLISTICS	1	1975
CAN'T GIVE YOU MORE	STATUS QUO	37	1991
CAN'T GO BACK	PRIMAL SCREAM	48	2008
CAN'T HAPPEN HERE	RAINBOW	20	1981
CAN'T HAVE YOU	LYTE FUNKIE ONES	54	1999
CAN'T HELP FALLING IN LOVE	ELVIS PRESLEY	1	1962
CAN'T HELP FALLING IN LOVE	ANDY WILLIAMS	3	1970
CAN'T HELP FALLING IN LOVE	STYLISTICS	4	1976
CAN'T HELP FALLING IN LOVE	LICK THE TINS	42	1986
CAN'T HELP FALLING IN LOVE	RUSSELL WATSON	69	2006
CAN'T HELP IT	HAPPY CLAPPERS	18	1996
CAN'T HELP MYSELF	LINX	55	1981
CAN'T HOLD US DOWN	CHRISTINA AGUILERA FEATURING LIL' KIM	6	2003
CAN'T I?	NAT 'KING' COLE	6	1953
CAN'T KEEP IT IN	CAT STEVENS	13	1972
CAN'T KEEP LIVING THIS WAY	ROOTJOOSE	73	1997
CAN'T KEEP ME SILENT	ANGELIC	12	2001
CAN'T KEEP THIS FEELING IN	CLIFF RICHARD	10	1998
CAN'T KNOCK THE HUSTLE	JAY-Z FEATURING MARY J BLIGE	30	1997
CAN'T LET GO	EARTH, WIND & FIRE	46	1979
CAN'T LET GO	MARIAH CAREY	20	1992
CAN'T LET HER GO	BOYZ II MEN	23	1998
CAN'T LET YOU GO [A]	BARRY RYAN	32	1972
CAN'T LET YOU GO [B]	RAINBOW	43	1983
CAN'T LET YOU GO [C]	FABOLOUS	14	2003
CAN'T LIVE WITH YOU (CAN'T LIVE WITHOUT YOU)	MINDBENDERS	28	1966
CAN'T LIVE WITHOUT YOU	SCORPIONS	63	1982
(CAN'T LIVE WITHOUT YOUR) LOVE AND AFFECTION	NELSON	54	1990
CAN'T MAKE MY MIND UP	SONIQUE	17	2003
CAN'T NOBODY	KELLY ROWLAND	5	2003
CAN'T NOBODY HOLD ME DOWN	PUFF DADDY FEATURING MA$E	19	1997
CAN'T RESIST	TEXAS	13	2005
CAN'T SAY 'BYE	STONEFREE	73	1987
CAN'T SAY GOODBYE	POP!	26	2004
CAN'T SAY HOW MUCH I LOVE YOU	DEMIS ROUSSOS	35	1976
CAN'T SEE ME	IAN BROWN	21	1998
CAN'T SET THE RULES ABOUT LOVE	ADAM ANT	47	1990
CAN'T SHAKE LOOSE	AGNETHA FALTSKOG	63	1983
CAN'T SHAKE THE FEELING	BIG FUN	8	1989
CAN'T SMILE	VEX RED	45	2002
CAN'T SMILE WITHOUT YOU	BARRY MANILOW	43	1978
CAN'T SMILE WITHOUT YOU	JAMES BULLER	51	1999
CAN'T SPEAK FRENCH	GIRLS ALOUD	9	2008
CAN'T STAND IT	WILCO	67	1999
CAN'T STAND LOSING YOU	POLICE	2	1978
CAN'T STAND ME NOW	LIBERTINES	2	2004
CAN'T STAY AWAY FROM YOU	GLORIA ESTEFAN & MIAMI SOUND MACHINE	7	1989
CAN'T STOP [A]	AFTER 7	54	1990
CAN'T STOP [B]	RED HOT CHILI PEPPERS	22	2003
CAN'T STOP A RIVER	DUNCAN JAMES	59	2006
CAN'T STOP LOVING YOU [A]	VAN HALEN	33	1995
CAN'T STOP LOVING YOU [B]	PHIL COLLINS	28	2002
CAN'T STOP MOVING	SONNY J	40	2008
CAN'T STOP RUNNING	SPACE MONKEY	53	1983
CAN'T STOP THE MUSIC	VILLAGE PEOPLE	11	1980
CAN'T STOP THESE THINGS	CHINA DRUM	65	1996
CAN'T STOP THIS FEELING	RHYTHM-N-BASS	59	1993
CAN'T STOP THIS THING WE STARTED	BRYAN ADAMS	12	1991
CAN'T TAKE MY EYES OFF YOU	ANDY WILLIAMS	5	1968
CAN'T TAKE MY EYES OFF YOU	BOYSTOWN GANG	4	1982
CAN'T TAKE MY EYES OFF YOU	ANDY WILLIAMS & DENISE VAN OUTEN	23	2002

Title / Artist	Peak Position	Year of Release
CAN'T TAKE NO FOR AN ANSWER SOUP DRAGONS	65	1987
CAN'T TAKE YOUR LOVE PAULINE HENRY	30	1994
CAN'T TRUSS IT PUBLIC ENEMY	22	1991
CAN'T TURN BACK SPEEDWAY	12	2004
CAN'T WAIT ANOTHER MINUTE FIVE STAR	7	1986
CAN'T WAIT TO BE WITH YOU JAZZY JEFF & THE FRESH PRINCE	29	1994
CAN'T YOU HEAR MY HEART DANNY RIVERS	36	1961
CAN'T YOU HEAR MY HEART BEAT? GOLDIE & THE GINGERBREADS	25	1965
CAN'T YOU HEAR THE BEAT OF A BROKEN HEART IAIN GREGORY	39	1962
CAN'T YOU SEE TOTAL FEATURING THE NOTORIOUS B.I.G.	43	1995
CAN'T YOU SEE THAT SHE'S MINE DAVE CLARK FIVE	10	1964
(CAN'T YOU) TRIP LIKE I DO FILTER & THE CRYSTAL METHOD	39	1997
CANTALOOP US3 FEATURING KOBIE POWELL & RAHSAAN	23	1993
CANTGETAMAN CANTGETAJOB (LIFE'S A BITCH) SISTER BLISS WITH COLETTE	31	1994
CANTO DELLA TERRA ANDREA BOCELLI	24	1999
CANTON (LIVE) JAPAN	42	1983
CANTONESE BOY JAPAN	24	1982
CAPOIERA INFARED VS GIL FELIX	67	2003
CAPSTICK COMES HOME TONY CAPSTICK & THE CARLTON MAIN/FRICKLEY COLLIERY BAND	3	1981
THE CAPTAIN BIFFY CLYRO	17	2009
CAPTAIN BEAKY KEITH MICHELL	5	1980
CAPTAIN DREAD DREADZONE	49	1995
CAPTAIN KREMMEN (RETRIBUTION) KENNY EVERETT & MIKE VICKERS	32	1977
THE CAPTAIN OF HER HEART DOUBLE	8	1986
CAPTAIN OF YOUR SHIP REPARATA & THE DELRONS	13	1968
CAPTAIN SCARLET THEME BARRY GRAY ORCHESTRA WITH PETER BECKETT – KEYBOARDS	53	1986
CAPTURE THE FLAG FRESH	70	2005
CAPTURE THE HEART (EP) RUNRIG	49	1990
CAR 67 DRIVER 67	7	1979
CAR BOOT SALE BILL	73	1993
CAR SONG MADDER ROSE	68	1994
CAR WASH ROSE ROYCE	9	1977
CAR WASH GWEN DICKEY	72	1990
CAR WASH CHRISTINA AGUILERA & MISSY ELLIOTT	4	2004
CARA MIA DAVID WHITFIELD WITH CHORUS & MANTOVANI & HIS ORCHESTRA	1	1954
CARAMEL CITY HIGH FEATURING EVE	9	2002
CARAVAN [A] DUANE EDDY	42	1961
CARAVAN [B] INSPIRAL CARPETS	30	1991
CARAVAN GIRL GOLDFRAPP	54	2008
CARAVAN OF LOVE ISLEY JASPER ISLEY	52	1985
CARAVAN OF LOVE HOUSEMARTINS	1	1986
CARAVAN SONG BARBARA DICKSON	41	1980
CARBON KID ALPINESTARS FEATURING BRIAN MOLKO	63	2002
CARDBOY KING SALAD	65	1997
CARDIAC ARREST MADNESS	14	1982
CAREFUL (STRESS) HORSE	44	1990
CARELESS HANDS DES O'CONNOR	6	1967
CARELESS LOVE SWIMMING WITH SHARKS	63	1988
CARELESS MEMORIES DURAN DURAN	37	1981
CARELESS WHISPER GEORGE MICHAEL	1	1984
CARELESS WHISPER SARAH WASHINGTON	45	1993
CARELESS WHISPER 2PLAY FEATURING THOMAS JULES & JUCXI D	29	2004
CARIBBEAN BLUE ENYA	13	1991
THE CARIBBEAN DISCO SHOW LOBO	8	1981
CARIBBEAN HONEYMOON FRANK WEIR	42	1960
CARIBBEAN QUEEN (NO MORE LOVE ON THE RUN) BILLY OCEAN	6	1984
CARMEN QUEASY MAXIM	33	2000
CARNATION LIAM GALLAGHER & STEVE CRADDOCK	6	1999
CARNAVAL DE PARIS DARIO G	5	1998
CARNIVAL [A] LIONROCK	34	1993
CARNIVAL [B] CARDIGANS	35	1995
CARNIVAL GIRL TEXAS FEATURING KARDINAL OFFISHALL	9	2003
CARNIVAL IN HEAVEN MALANDRA BURROWS	49	1997
THE CARNIVAL IS OVER SEEKERS	1	1965
CAROLINA MOON CONNIE FRANCIS	1	1958
CAROLINE [A] STATUS QUO	5	1973
CAROLINE [B] KIRSTY MacCOLL	58	1995
CAROLYNA MELANIE C	49	2007
CAROUSEL- ORIGINAL SOUNDTRACK (LP) VARIOUS ARTISTS (EP'S & LP'S)	26	1956
CAROUSEL WALTZ RAY MARTIN	24	1956
CARRERA 2 THREE DRIVES	57	2003
CARRIE [A] CLIFF RICHARD	4	1980
CARRIE [B] EUROPE	22	1987
CARRIE-ANNE HOLLIES	3	1967
CARRION BRITISH SEA POWER	36	2003
CARROT ROPE PAVEMENT	27	1999
CARRY ME HOME GLOWORM	9	1994
CARRY ON [A] MARTHA WASH	49	1992
CARRY ON [B] SPACEHOG	43	1998
CARRY ON [C] DONNA SUMMER & GIORGIO MORODER	65	1998
CARRY ON WAYWARD SON KANSAS	51	1978
CARRY OUT TIMBALAND FEATURING JUSTIN TIMBERLAKE	16	2010
CARRY THAT WEIGHT TRASH	35	1969
CARRY THE BLAME RIVER CITY PEOPLE	13	1990
CARRY YOU HOME JAMES BLUNT	20	2008
CARRYING A TORCH TOM JONES	57	1991
CARS [A] GARY NUMAN	1	1979
CARS [B] FEAR FACTORY	57	1999
CARS AND GIRLS PREFAB SPROUT	44	1986
CARTE BLANCHE VERACOCHA	22	1999
CARTOON HEROES AQUA	7	2000
CARTROUBLE ADAM & THE ANTS	33	1981
CASABLANCA KENNY BALL & HIS JAZZMEN	21	1963
CASANOVA [A] PETULA CLARK	39	1963
CASANOVA [B] COFFEE	13	1980
CASANOVA [B] BABY D	67	1994
CASANOVA [C] LEVERT	9	1987
CASANOVA [C] ULTIMATE KAOS	24	1997
CASCADE FUTURE SOUND OF LONDON	27	1993
CASE OF THE EX (WHATCHA GONNA DO) MYA	3	2001
CASH IN MY POCKET WILEY FEATURING DANIEL MERRIWEATHER	18	2008
CASH MACHINE HARD-FI	14	2006
CASINO ROYALE [A] HERB ALPERT & THE TIJUANA BRASS	27	1967
CASINO ROYALE [A] DJ ZINC	58	2001
CASSIUS FOALS	26	2008
CASSIUS 1999 CASSIUS	7	1999
CAST YOUR FATE TO THE WIND SOUNDS ORCHESTRAL	5	1964
CASTLE ROCK BLUETONES	7	1996
CASTLES IN SPAIN ARMOURY SHOW	69	1984
CASTLES IN THE AIR [A] DON McLEAN	47	1982
CASTLES IN THE AIR [B] COLOUR FIELD	51	1985
CASTLES IN THE SAND THUNDER	30	1995
CASTLES IN THE SKY IAN VAN DAHL	3	2001
CASUAL SUB (BURNING SPEAR) ETA	28	1997
CAT AMONG THE PIGEONS BROS	2	1988
THE CAT CAME BACK SONNY JAMES	30	1956
THE CAT CREPT IN MUD	2	1974
CAT PEOPLE (PUTTING OUT THE FIRE) DAVID BOWIE	26	1982
CATALAN TOUR DE FORCE	71	1998
CATALYST OCEANSIZE	73	2004
CATCH [A] CURE	27	1987
CATCH [B] SUNSCREEM	55	1997
CATCH [C] KOSHEEN	15	2001
CATCH A FALLING STAR PERRY COMO	9	1958
CATCH A FIRE HADDAWAY	39	1995
CATCH ME ABSOLUTE	69	1998
CATCH ME UP GOMEZ	36	2004
CATCH MY FALL BILLY IDOL	63	1988
CATCH THE BREEZE SLOWDIVE	52	1991
CATCH THE FIRE DRIZABONE	54	1991
CATCH THE LIGHT MARTHA WASH	45	1998
CATCH THE SUN DOVES	32	2000
CATCH THE WIND DONOVAN	4	1965
CATCH UP TO MY STEP JUNKIE XL FEATURING SOLOMON BURKE	63	2003
CATCH US IF YOU CAN DAVE CLARK FIVE	5	1965
CATCH YOU SOPHIE ELLIS-BEXTOR	8	2007
CATERINA PERRY COMO	37	1962
THE CATERPILLAR CURE	14	1984
CATH BLUEBELLS	38	1983
CATHEDRAL PARK DUBSTAR	41	1997
CATHEDRAL SONG TANITA TIKARAM	48	1989
CATHY'S CLOWN EVERLY BROTHERS	1	1960
CAT'S IN THE CRADLE UGLY KID JOE	7	1993
CAT'S IN THE CRADLE JASON DOWNS FEATURING MILK	65	2001
CAUGHT A LITE SNEEZE TORI AMOS	20	1996
CAUGHT BY THE FUZZ SUPERGRASS	43	1994
CAUGHT BY THE RIVER DOVES	29	2002
CAUGHT IN A MOMENT SUGABABES	8	2004
CAUGHT IN MY SHADOW WONDER STUFF	18	1991
CAUGHT IN THE MIDDLE [A] JULIET ROBERTS	14	1993
CAUGHT IN THE MIDDLE [B] A1	2	2002
CAUGHT IN THE MIDDLE [C] CERYS MATTHEWS	47	2003
CAUGHT OUT THERE KELIS	4	2000
CAUGHT UP [A] USHER	9	2005
CAUGHT UP [B] JA RULE FEATURING LLOYD	20	2005
CAUGHT UP IN MY HEART OPTIMYSTIC	49	1994
CAUGHT UP IN THE RAPTURE ANITA BAKER	51	1987
CAUSING A COMMOTION MADONNA	4	1987
CAVATINA JOHN WILLIAMS	13	1979
CAVE [A] MUSE	52	1999
THE CAVE [B] MUMFORD & SONS	32	2010
CCCAN'T YOU SEE VICIOUS PINK	67	1984
CECILIA SUGGS FEATURING LOUCHIE LOU & MICHIE ONE	4	1996
THE CEDAR ROOM DOVES	33	2000
CELEBRATE [A] AN EMOTIONAL FISH	46	1990
CELEBRATE [B] HORSE	49	1994
CELEBRATE [C] LEVELLERS	28	1997
CELEBRATE OUR LOVE ALICE DEEJAY	17	2001
(CELEBRATE) THE DAY AFTER YOU BLOW MONKEYS WITH CURTIS MAYFIELD	52	1987
CELEBRATE THE WORLD WOMACK & WOMACK	19	1989
CELEBRATE YOUR MOTHER EIGHTIES MATCHBOX B-LINE DISASTER	66	2002
CELEBRATION [A] KOOL & THE GANG	7	1980
CELEBRATION [A] KYLIE MINOGUE	20	1992
A CELEBRATION U2	47	1982
CELEBRATION [B] MADONNA	3	2009
CELEBRATION GENERATION WESTBAM	48	1994
CELEBRATION OF LIFE TRUCE	51	1996
CELEBRITY HIT LIST TERRORVISION	20	1996
CELEBRITY SKIN HOLE	19	1998
CELL 151 STEVE HACKETT	66	1983
THE CELTIC SOUL BROTHERS KEVIN ROWLAND & DEXY'S MIDNIGHT RUNNERS	20	1982

Title / Artist	Peak Position	Year of Release
THE CELTS ENYA	29	1992
CEMENT FEEDER	53	1997
CEMENTED SHOES MY VITRIOL	65	2000
CENTER CITY FAT LARRY'S BAND	31	1977
CENTERFOLD J GEILS BAND	3	1982
CENTERFOLD ADAM AUSTIN	41	1999
CENTRAL PARK ARREST THUNDERTHIGHS	30	1974
CENTRAL RESERVATION BETH ORTON	37	1999
CENTURY INTASTELLA	70	1991
CEREMONY NEW ORDER	34	1981
CERTAIN PEOPLE I KNOW MORRISSEY	35	1992
A CERTAIN SMILE JOHNNY MATHIS	4	1958
THE CERTAINTY OF CHANCE DIVINE COMEDY	49	1998
C'EST LA VIE [A] ROBBIE NEVIL	3	1987
C'EST LA VIE [B] UB40	37	1994
C'EST LA VIE [C] B*WITCHED	1	1998
C'EST LA VIE [D] JEAN-MICHEL JARRE FEATURING NATACHA	40	2000
C'EST SI BON CONWAY TWITTY	40	1961
CH-CHECK IT OUT BEASTIE BOYS	8	2004
CHA CHA CHA FLIPMODE SQUAD	54	1998
CHA CHA HEELS EARTHA KITT & BRONSKI BEAT	32	1989
CHA CHA SLIDE DJ CASPER	1	2004
CHA CHA SLIDE MC JIG	33	2004
CHA CHA TWIST DETROIT COBRAS	59	2004
CHACARRON EL CHOMBO	20	2006
CHAIN GANG [A] JIMMY YOUNG	9	1956
CHAIN GANG [B] SAM COOKE	9	1960
CHAIN HANG LOW JIBBS	63	2007
CHAIN OF FOOLS ARETHA FRANKLIN	43	1967
CHAIN REACTION [A] DIANA ROSS	1	1986
CHAIN REACTION [A] STEPS	2	2001
CHAIN REACTION [B] HURRICANE #1	30	1997
CHAIN-GANG SMILE BROTHER BEYOND	57	1987
CHAINS [A] COOKIES	50	1963
CHAINS [B] RIVER DETECTIVES	51	1989
CHAINS [C] TINA ARENA	6	1995
CHAINS AROUND MY HEART RICHARD MARX	29	1992
CHAINS OF LOVE ERASURE	11	1988
CHAINSAW CHARLIE (MURDERS IN THE NEW MORGUE) W.A.S.P.	17	1992
CHAIRMAN OF THE BOARD CHAIRMEN OF THE BOARD	48	1971
CHAKA DEMUS JAMIE T	23	2009
CHALK DUST-THE UMPIRE STRIKES BACK BRAT	19	1982
THE CHAMP MOHAWKS	58	1987
CHAMPAGNE SALT-N-PEPA	23	1996
CHAMPAGNE DANCE PAY AS U GO	13	2002
CHAMPAGNE HIGHWAY SKANDAL	53	2000
THE CHAMPION WILLIE MITCHELL	47	1976
CHANCE BIG COUNTRY	9	1983
CHANCES HOT CHOCOLATE	32	1982
CHANGE [A] TEARS FOR FEARS	4	1983
CHANGE [B] DAVID GRANT	55	1987
CHANGE [C] LISA STANSFIELD	10	1991
CHANGE [D] INCOGNITO	52	1992
CHANGE [E] BLIND MELON	35	1994
CHANGE [F] LIGHTNING SEEDS	13	1995
CHANGE [G] DAPHNE	71	1995
CHANGE [H] PHATS & SMALL	45	2001
CHANGE [I] SUGABABES	13	2007
CHANGE [J] DANIEL MERRIWEATHER	8	2009
CHANGE CLOTHES JAY-Z	32	2003
CHANGE HIS WAYS ROBERT PALMER	28	1989
CHANGE (IN THE HOUSE OF FLIES) DEFTONES	53	2000
CHANGE ME JOCASTA	60	1997
CHANGE MY MIND BLUESKINS	56	2004
CHANGE OF HEART [A] CHANGE	17	1984
CHANGE OF HEART [B] CYNDI LAUPER	67	1986
A CHANGE OF HEART [C] BERNARD BUTLER	45	1998
CHANGE THE WORLD [A] ERIC CLAPTON	18	1996
CHANGE THE WORLD [B] DINO LENNY VS THE HOUSEMARTINS	51	2003
CHANGE WITH THE TIMES VAN McCOY	36	1975
A CHANGE WOULD DO YOU GOOD SHERYL CROW	8	1997
CHANGE YOUR MIND [A] SHARPE & NUMAN	17	1985
CHANGE YOUR MIND [B] UPSIDE DOWN	11	1996
CHANGES [A] CRISPIAN ST PETERS	47	1966
CHANGES [B] IMAGINATION	31	1983
CHANGES [C] ALAN PRICE	54	1988
CHANGES [D] 2PAC	3	1999
CHANGES [E] SANDY RIVERA FEATURING HAZE	48	2002
CHANGES [F] OZZY & KELLY OSBOURNE	1	2003
CHANGES [G] CHRIS LAKE FEATURING LAURA V	27	2006
CHANGES [H] GARETH GATES	14	2007
CHANGES [I] WILL YOUNG	10	2008
CHANGES ARE NO GOOD STILLS	51	2004
CHANGING FOR YOU CHI-LITES	61	1983
CHANGING PARTNERS KAY STARR	4	1954
CHANGING PARTNERS BING CROSBY	9	1954
THE CHANGINGMAN PAUL WELLER	7	1995
CHANNEL Z B-52's	61	1990
CHANSON D'AMOUR MANHATTAN TRANSFER	1	1977
THE CHANT HAS BEGUN LEVEL 42	41	1984
THE CHANT HAS JUST BEGUN ALARM	48	1984
CHANT NO. 1 (I DON'T NEED THIS PRESSURE ON) SPANDAU BALLET	3	1981
THE CHANT (WE R)/RIP PRODUCTIONS RIP PRODUCTIONS	50	1997
CHANTILLY LACE BIG BOPPER	12	1958
CHANTILLY LACE JERRY LEE LEWIS	33	1972
CHAPEL OF LOVE [A] DIXIE CUPS	22	1964
CHAPEL OF LOVE [B] LONDON BOYS	75	1990
CHAPEL OF THE ROSES MALCOLM VAUGHAN	13	1957
CHAPTER FIVE RAM TRILOGY	62	2002
CHAPTER FOUR RAM TRILOGY	71	2002
CHAPTER SIX RAM TRILOGY	60	2002
CHARADE SKIDS	31	1979
CHARIOT [A] RHET STOLLER	26	1961
CHARIOT [B] PETULA CLARK	39	1963
CHARIOTS OF FIRE – TITLES VANGELIS	12	1981
CHARITY SKUNK ANANSIE	20	1995
CHARLESTON TEMPERANCE SEVEN	22	1961
CHARLIE BIG POTATO SKUNK ANANSIE	17	1999
CHARLIE BROWN COASTERS	6	1959
CHARLIE'S ANGELS 2000 APOLLO FOUR FORTY	29	2000
CHARLOTTE [A] KITTIE	60	2000
CHARLOTTE [B] AIR TRAFFIC	33	2007
CHARLOTTE ANNE JULIAN COPE	35	1988
CHARLOTTE SOMETIMES CURE	44	1981
CHARLTON HESTON STUMP	72	1988
CHARLY PRODIGY	3	1991
CHARMAINE BACHELORS	6	1963
CHARMING BILLY JOHNNY PRESTON	34	1960
CHARMING DEMONS SENSER	42	1996
CHARMLESS MAN BLUR	5	1996
CHASE GIORGIO MORODER	48	1979
CHASE MIDI XPRESS	73	1996
THE CHASE DJ EMPIRE PRESENTS GIORGIO MORODER	46	2000
CHASE THE SUN PLANET FUNK	5	2001
CHASING CARS SNOW PATROL	6	2006
CHASING FOR THE BREEZE ASWAD	51	1984
CHASING PAVEMENTS ADELE	2	2008
CHASING RAINBOWS SHED SEVEN	17	1996
CHEAP THRILLS PLANET PATROL	64	1983
CHEATED PRAYING MANTIS	69	1981
CHECK IT OUT (EVERYBODY) BMR FEATURING FELICIA	29	1999
CHECK ON IT BEYONCE FEATURING SLIM THUG	3	2006
CHECK OUT THE GROOVE BOBBY THURSTON	10	1980
CHECK THE MEANING RICHARD ASHCROFT	11	2002
CHECK THIS OUT L.A. MIX	6	1988
CHECK YO SELF ICE CUBE FEATURING DAS EFX	36	1993
CHECKIN' IT OUT LIL' CHRIS	3	2006
CHEEKAH BOW WOW (THAT COMPUTER SONG) VENGABOYS	19	2000
CHEEKY BONIFACE	25	2002
CHEEKY ARMADA ILLICIT FEATURING GRAM'MA FUNK	72	2000
CHEEKY FLAMENCO CHEEKY GIRLS	29	2004
CHEEKY SONG (TOUCH MY BUM) CHEEKY GIRLS	2	2002
CHEERS THEN BANANARAMA	45	1982
CHELSEA STAMFORD BRIDGE	47	1970
CHELSEA DAGGER FRATELLIS	5	2006
CHEMICAL #1 JESUS JONES	71	1997
CHEMICAL WORLD BLUR	28	1993
THE CHEMICALS BETWEEN US BUSH	46	1999
CHEMISTRY [A] NOLANS	15	1981
CHEMISTRY [B] SEMISONIC	35	2001
CHEQUE ONE-TWO SUNSHIP FEATURING M.C.R.B.	75	2000
CHEQUERED LOVE KIM WILDE	4	1981
CHERI BABE HOT CHOCOLATE	31	1974
CHERISH [A] DAVID CASSIDY	2	1972
CHERISH [A] JODECI	56	1993
CHERISH [B] KOOL & THE GANG	4	1985
CHERISH [B] PAPPA BEAR FEATURING VAN DER TOORN	47	1998
CHERISH [C] MADONNA	3	1989
CHERISH THE DAY SADE	53	1993
CHERISH THE DAY PLUMMET	35	2004
CHERISH WHAT IS DEAR TO YOU FREDA PAYNE	46	1971
CHERRY LIPS (DER ERDBEERMUND) CULTURE BEAT	55	1990
CHERRY LIPS (GO BABY GO) GARBAGE	22	2002
CHERRY OH BABY UB40	12	1984
CHERRY PIE [A] JESS CONRAD	39	1960
CHERRY PIE [B] WARRANT	35	1990
CHERRY PINK AND APPLE BLOSSOM WHITE EDDIE CALVERT	1	1955
CHERRY PINK AND APPLE BLOSSOM WHITE PEREZ 'PREZ' PRADO & HIS ORCHESTRA, THE KING OF THE MAMBO	1	1955
CHERRY PINK AND APPLE BLOSSOM WHITE MODERN ROMANCE FEATURING JOHN DU PREZ	15	1982
CHERUB ROCK SMASHING PUMPKINS	31	1993
CHERYL'S GOIN' HOME ADAM FAITH	46	1966
CHESHIRE CAT SMILE MILBURN	32	2006
CHESTNUT MARE BYRDS	19	1971
CHEWING GUM ANNIE	25	2004
CHI MAI (THEME FROM THE TV SERIES THE LIFE AND TIMES OF DAVID LLOYD GEORGE) ENNIO MORRICONE	2	1981
CHIC MYSTIQUE CHIC	48	1992
CHICAGO [A] FRANK SINATRA	21	1957
CHICAGO [B] KIKI DEE	28	1977
CHICK-A-BOOM (DON'T YA JES LOVE IT) 53RD & A 3RD FEATURING THE SOUND OF SHAG	36	1975
CHICK CHICK CHICKEN NATALIE CASEY	72	1984
CHICK LIT WE ARE SCIENTISTS	37	2008

	Peak Position	Year of Release
CHICKA BOOM GUY MITCHELL	4	1953
CHICKEN EIGHTIES MATCHBOX B-LINE DISASTER	30	2003
CHICKEN PAYBACK BEES	28	2005
THE CHICKEN SONG SPITTING IMAGE	1	1986
THE CHIEF TONI SCOTT	48	1989
CHIEF INSPECTOR WALLY BADAROU	46	1985
CHIHUAHUA [A] BOW WOW WOW	51	1981
CHIHUAHUA [B] DJ BOBO	36	2003
CHIHUAHUA [B] DARE	45	2003
CHIKKI CHIKKI AHH AHH BABY FORD	54	1988
CHILD [A] DEFINITION OF SOUND	48	1996
CHILD [B] MARK OWEN	3	1996
CHILD COME AWAY KIM WILDE	43	1982
CHILD OF LOVE LEMON TREES	55	1993
CHILD OF THE UNIVERSE DJ TAUCHER	74	1999
CHILD STAR MARC ALMOND	41	1995
CHILDREN [A] EMF	19	1991
CHILDREN [B] ROBERT MILES	2	1996
CHILDREN [B] TILT	51	1999
CHILDREN [B] 4CLUBBERS	45	2002
CHILDREN [C] BATTLE	60	2006
CHILDREN OF PARADISE BONEY M	66	1981
CHILDREN OF THE NIGHT [A] RICHARD MARX	54	1990
CHILDREN OF THE NIGHT [B] NAKATOMI	31	1998
CHILDREN OF THE REVOLUTION T REX	2	1972
CHILDREN OF THE REVOLUTION BABY FORD	53	1989
CHILDREN OF THE REVOLUTION UNITONE ROCKERS FEATURING STEEL	60	1993
CHILDREN OF THE WORLD ANA ANN & THE LONDON COMMUNITY CHOIR	44	2004
CHILDREN SAY LEVEL 42	22	1987
CHILDREN'S CHILDREN AGENT BLUE	62	2005
A CHILD'S PRAYER HOT CHOCOLATE	7	1975
CHILI BOM BOM TEMPERANCE SEVEN	28	1961
CHILL OUT (THINGS GONNA CHANGE) JOHN LEE HOOKER	45	1995
CHILL TO THE PANIC DEEP C	73	1991
CHILLIN' [A] MODJO	12	2001
CHILLIN' [B] WALE FEATURING LADY GAGA	12	2009
CHILLIN' OUT CURTIS HAIRSTON	57	1986
CHIME ORBITAL	17	1990
CHINA TORI AMOS	51	1992
CHINA DOLL [A] SLIM WHITMAN	15	1955
CHINA DOLL [B] JULIAN COPE	53	1989
CHINA GIRL DAVID BOWIE	2	1983
CHINA IN YOUR HAND T'PAU	1	1987
CHINA TEA RUSS CONWAY	5	1959
CHINATOWN [A] MOVE	23	1971
CHINATOWN [B] THIN LIZZY	21	1980
CHINESE BAKERY AUTEURS	42	1994
CHINESE BURN HEAVY STEREO	45	1996
CHINESE DEMOCRACY GUNS N' ROSES	27	2008
THE CHINESE WAY LEVEL 42	24	1983
CHING CHING (LOVIN' YOU STILL) TERRI WALKER	38	2003
CHIP DIDDY CHIP CHIPMUNK	21	2009
CHIQUITITA ABBA	2	1979
CHIRPY CHIRPY CHEEP CHEEP MIDDLE OF THE ROAD	1	1971
CHIRPY CHIRPY CHEEP CHEEP MAC & KATIE KISSOON	41	1971
CHIRPY CHIRPY CHEEP CHEEP LINCOLN CITY FC FEATURING MICHAEL COURTNEY	64	2002
THE CHISELERS FALL	60	1996
CHOC ICE LONG & THE SHORT	40	1964
CHOCOLATE [A] Y?N-VEE	65	1994
CHOCOLATE [B] SNOW PATROL	24	2004
CHOCOLATE [C] KYLIE MINOGUE	6	2004
CHOCOLATE BOX BROS	9	1989
CHOCOLATE CAKE CROWDED HOUSE	69	1991
CHOCOLATE (CHOCO CHOCO) SOUL CONTROL	25	2004
CHOCOLATE GIRL DEACON BLUE	43	1988
CHOCOLATE SALTY BALLS (PS I LOVE YOU) CHEF	1	1998
CHOCOLATE SENSATION LENNY FONTANA & DJ SHORTY	39	2000
CHOICE? BLOW MONKEYS FEATURING SYLVIA TELLA	22	1989
CHOK THERE APACHE INDIAN	30	1993
CHOLI KE PEECHE BALLY SAGOO	45	1995
CHOOSE COLOR ME BADD	65	1994
CHOOSE LIFE PF PROJECT FEATURING EWAN McGREGOR	6	1997
CHOOSE ME (RESCUE ME) LOOSE ENDS	59	1984
CHOOZA LOOZA MARIA WILLSON	29	2003
CHOP SUEY SYSTEM OF A DOWN	17	2001
CHORUS ERASURE	3	1991
THE CHOSEN FEW DOOLEYS	7	1979
CHOSEN ONE CONCRETES	54	2006
CHRISTIAN CHINA CRISIS	12	1983
CHRISTIANSANDS TRICKY	36	1996
CHRISTINE [A] MISS X	37	1963
CHRISTINE [B] SIOUXSIE & THE BANSHEES	22	1980
CHRISTINE KEELER SENSELESS THINGS	56	1994
CHRISTMAS ALPHABET DICKIE VALENTINE	1	1955
CHRISTMAS AND YOU DAVE KING	23	1956
CHRISTMAS COUNTDOWN FRANK KELLY	26	1983
CHRISTMAS IN BLOBBYLAND MR BLOBBY	36	1995
CHRISTMAS IN DREADLAND JUDGE DREAD	14	1975
CHRISTMAS IN HOLLIS RUN DMC	56	1987
CHRISTMAS IN SMURFLAND FATHER ABRAHAM & THE SMURFS	19	1978
CHRISTMAS IS ALL AROUND BILLY MACK	26	2003
CHRISTMAS ISLAND DICKIE VALENTINE	8	1956
A CHRISTMAS KISS DANIEL O'DONNELL	20	1999
CHRISTMAS MEDLEY WEEKEND	47	1985
CHRISTMAS MY A*SE RICKY TOMLINSON	25	2006
CHRISTMAS ON 45 HOLLY & THE IVYS	40	1981
CHRISTMAS RAPPIN' KURTIS BLOW	30	1979
CHRISTMAS RAPPING DIZZY HEIGHTS	49	1982
CHRISTMAS SLIDE BASIL BRUSH FEATURING INDIA BEAU	44	2003
CHRISTMAS SONG (CHESTNUTS ROASTING ON AN OPEN FIRE) [A] ALEXANDER O'NEAL	30	1988
THE CHRISTMAS SONG [A] NAT 'KING' COLE	51	1991
CHRISTMAS SONG [B] GILBERT O'SULLIVAN	12	1974
CHRISTMAS SPECTRE JINGLE BELLES	37	1983
CHRISTMAS THROUGH YOUR EYES GLORIA ESTEFAN	8	1992
CHRISTMAS TIME BRYAN ADAMS	55	1985
CHRISTMAS TIME (DON'T LET THE BELLS END) DARKNESS	2	2003
CHRISTMAS WILL BE JUST ANOTHER LONELY DAY BRENDA LEE	25	1964
CHRISTMAS WRAPPING WAITRESSES	45	1982
THE CHRONICLES OF A BOHEMIAN TEENAGER GET CAPE. WEAR CAPE. FLY.	38	2006
THE CHRONICLES OF LIFE AND DEATH GOOD CHARLOTTE	30	2005
CHRONOLOGIE PART 4 JEAN-MICHEL JARRE	55	1993
CHUCK E.'S IN LOVE RICKIE LEE JONES	18	1979
CHUNG KUO (REVISITED) ADDAMS & GEE	72	1991
CHURA LIYA BALLY SAGOO	64	1994
CHURCH T-PAIN FEATURING TEDDY VERSETI	35	2008
CHURCH OF FREEDOM AMOS	54	1995
THE CHURCH OF THE HOLY SPOOK SHANE MacGOWAN & THE POPES	74	1994
CHURCH OF NOISE THERAPY?	29	1998
CHURCH OF THE POISON MIND CULTURE CLUB	20	1983
CHURCH OF YOUR HEART ROXETTE	21	1992
CIAO CIAO BAMBINA MARINO MARINI & HIS QUARTET	24	1959
CIAO CIAO BAMBINA DOMENICO MODUGNO	29	1959
CIGARETTES AND ALCOHOL OASIS	7	1994
CINDERELLA LEMONESCENT	31	2003
CINDERELLA ROCKEFELLA ESTHER & ABI OFARIM	1	1968
CINDY INCIDENTALLY FACES	2	1973
CINDY OH CINDY EDDIE FISHER	5	1956
CINDY OH CINDY TONY BRENT	16	1956
CINDY OH CINDY VINCE MARTIN & THE TARRIERS	26	1956
CINDY'S BIRTHDAY SHANE FENTON & THE FENTONES	19	1962
CINNAMON GIRL PRINCE	43	2004
CIRCLE [A] EDIE BRICKELL & THE NEW BOHEMIANS	74	1989
THE CIRCLE [B] OCEAN COLOUR SCENE	6	1996
CIRCLE IN THE SAND BELINDA CARLISLE	4	1988
CIRCLE OF LIFE ELTON JOHN	11	1994
CIRCLE OF ONE OLETA ADAMS	73	1991
CIRCLE SQUARE TRIANGLE TEST ICICLES	25	2005
CIRCLES [A] NEW SEEKERS	4	1972
CIRCLES [B] SAFFRON	60	1993
CIRCLES [C] ADAM F	20	1997
CIRCLESQUARE WONDER STUFF	20	1990
CIRCUS [A] LENNY KRAVITZ	54	1995
CIRCUS [B] ERIC CLAPTON	39	1998
THE CIRCUS [C] ERASURE	6	1987
CIRCUS [D] BRITNEY SPEARS	13	2008
CIRCUS GAMES SKIDS	32	1980
CITIES IN DUST SIOUXSIE & THE BANSHEES	21	1985
THE CITY IS AT STANDSTILL LIAM FROST & SLOWDOWN FAMILY	74	2006
THE CITY IS MINE JAY-Z FEATURING BLACKSTREET	38	1998
CITY LIGHTS DAVID ESSEX	24	1976
CITY OF BLINDING LIGHTS U2	2	2005
CITYSONG LUSCIOUS JACKSON	69	1995
CIVIL SIN BOY KILL BOY	44	2006
THE CIVIL WAR EP GUNS N' ROSES	11	1993
CLAIR GILBERT O'SULLIVAN	1	1972
CLAIRE PAUL & BARRY RYAN	47	1967
THE CLAIRVOYANT IRON MAIDEN	6	1988
CLAP BACK JA RULE	9	2003
THE CLAP CLAP SOUND KLAXONS	45	1983
CLAP YOUR HANDS [A] ROCKY SHARPE & THE REPLAYS	54	1982
CLAP YOUR HANDS [B] CAMISRA	34	1999
THE CLAPPING SONG SHIRLEY ELLIS	6	1965
THE CLAPPING SONG BELLE STARS	11	1982
CLARE FAIRGROUND ATTRACTION	49	1989
CLASH CITY ROCKERS CLASH	35	1978
CLASSIC ADRIAN GURVITZ	8	1982
CLASSIC GIRL JANE'S ADDICTION	60	1991
CLASSICAL GAS MASON WILLIAMS	9	1968
CLASSICAL GAS VANESSA-MAE	41	1995
CLASSICAL MUDDLEY PORTSMOUTH SINFONIA	38	1981
CLAUDETTE EVERLY BROTHERS	1	1958
CLEAN CLEAN BUGGLES	38	1980
CLEAN UP YOUR EYES DYKEENIES	53	2007
CLEAN UP YOUR OWN BACK YARD ELVIS PRESLEY	21	1969
CLEANIN' OUT MY CLOSET EMINEM	4	2002
CLEAR BLUE WATER OCEANLAB FEATURING JUSTINE SUISSA	48	2002
CLEMENTINE [A] BOBBY DARIN	8	1960
CLEMENTINE [B] MARK OWEN	3	1997
CLEOPATRA'S CAT SPIN DOCTORS	29	1994
CLEOPATRA'S THEME CLEOPATRA	3	1998
CLEVER KICKS HISS	49	2003

	Peak Position	Year of Release
THE CLICHES ARE TRUE MANCHILD FEATURING KELLY JONES	60	2000
THE CLIMB MILEY CYRUS	11	2009
THE CLIMB JOE McELDERRY	1	2009
CLIMB EV'RY MOUNTAIN SHIRLEY BASSEY	1	1961
CLINT EASTWOOD GORILLAZ	4	2001
CLIPPED CURVE	36	1991
CLOAKING SEAFOOD	71	2001
CLOCKS COLDPLAY	9	2003
CLOG DANCE VIOLINSKI	17	1979
CLOSE...BUT ECHOBELLY	59	1994
CLOSE BUT NO CIGAR THOMAS DOLBY	22	1992
CLOSE COVER MINIMALISTIX	12	2002
CLOSE EVERY DOOR PHILIP SCOFIELD	27	1992
CLOSE MY EYES OPEN	46	2004
CLOSE MY EYES FOREVER LITA FORD DUET WITH OZZY OSBOURNE	47	1989
CLOSE THE DOOR [A] STARGAZERS	6	1955
CLOSE THE DOOR [B] TEDDY PENDERGRASS	41	1978
CLOSE TO ME CURE	13	1985
CLOSE TO PERFECTION MIQUEL BROWN	63	1985
CLOSE (TO THE EDIT) ART OF NOISE	8	1985
CLOSE TO YOU [A] MAXI PRIEST	7	1990
CLOSE TO YOU [B] BRAND NEW HEAVIES FEATURING N'DEA DAVENPORT	38	1995
CLOSE TO YOU [C] WHIGFIELD	13	1995
CLOSE TO YOU [D] MARTI PELLOW	9	2001
CLOSE TO YOUR HEART JX	18	1997
CLOSE YOUR EYES TONY BENNETT	18	1955
CLOSED FOR BUSINESS MANSUN	10	1997
CLOSER [A] MR FINGERS	50	1992
CLOSER [B] NINE INCH NAILS	25	1994
CLOSER [C] LIQUID	47	1995
CLOSER [D] NYLON	64	2006
CLOSER [E] TRAVIS	10	2007
CLOSER [F] NE-YO	1	2008
THE CLOSER I GET TO YOU ROBERTA FLACK & DONNY HATHAWAY	42	1978
CLOSER THAN CLOSE ROSIE GAINES	4	1997
CLOSER THAN MOST BEAUTIFUL SOUTH	22	2000
CLOSER TO ALL YOUR DREAMS RHYTHM QUEST	45	1992
CLOSER TO ME FIVE	4	2001
CLOSER TO THE HEART RUSH	36	1978
THE CLOSEST THING TO CRAZY KATIE MELUA	10	2003
CLOSEST THING TO HEAVEN [A] KANE GANG	12	1984
CLOSEST THING TO HEAVEN [B] LIONEL RICHIE	26	1998
CLOSEST THING TO HEAVEN [C] TEARS FOR FEARS	40	2005
CLOSING TIME [A] DEACON BLUE	42	1991
CLOSING TIME [B] SEMISONIC	25	1999
CLOTHES OFF GYM CLASS HEROES	5	2007
CLOUD 8 FRAZIER CHORUS	52	1990
CLOUD 99 ST ANDREWS CHORALE	31	1976
CLOUD LUCKY SEVEN GUY MITCHELL	2	1953
CLOUD NINE TEMPTATIONS	15	1969
CLOUD NUMBER 9 BRYAN ADAMS	6	1999
CLOUDBURST [A] DON LANG & THE MAIRANTS-LANGHORN BIG SIX	16	1955
CLOUDBURST [B] NIAGRA	65	1997
CLOUDBURSTING KATE BUSH	20	1985
CLOUDS SOURCE	38	1997
CLOUDS ACROSS THE MOON RAH BAND	6	1985
THE CLOUDS WILL SOON ROLL BY TONY BRENT	20	1958
CLOWN SHOES JOHNNY BURNETTE	35	1962
CLUB AT THE END OF THE STREET ELTON JOHN	47	1990
CLUB BIZARRE U96	70	1996
CLUB COUNTRY ASSOCIATES	13	1982
CLUB FANTASTIC MEGAMIX WHAM!	15	1983
CLUB FOOT KASABIAN	19	2004
CLUB FOR LIFE '98 CHRIS & JAMES	66	1998
CLUB LONELY GROOVE CONNEKTION 2	54	1998
CLUB TROPICANA WHAM!	4	1983
CLUBBED TO DEATH ROB DOUGAN	24	2002
CLUBBIN' MARQUES HOUSTON	15	2004
CLUBLAND ELVIS COSTELLO & THE ATTRACTIONS	60	1980
CLUMSY FERGIE	62	2007
CLUNK CLICK LAUREL & HARDY	65	1983
CLUTCH SHEA SEGER	47	2001
C'MERE INTERPOL	19	2005
C'MON [A] MILLIONAIRE HIPPIES	59	1994
C'MON [B] MARIO	28	2003
C'MON AND GET MY LOVE D MOB WITH CATHY DENNIS	15	1989
C'MON BILLY PJ HARVEY	29	1995
C'MON CHAMELEON RESEARCH	63	2005
C'MON CINCINNATI DELAKOTA FEATURING ROSE SMITH	55	1998
C'MON C'MON VON BONDIES	21	2004
C'MON EVERY BEATBOX BIG AUDIO DYNAMITE	51	1986
C'MON EVERYBODY EDDIE COCHRAN	6	1959
C'MON EVERYBODY SEX PISTOLS	3	1979
C'MON GET IT ON STUDIO B	28	2006
C'MON KIDS BOO RADLEYS	18	1996
C'MON LET'S GO GIRLSCHOOL	42	1981
C'MON MARIANNE GRAPEFRUIT	31	1968
C'MON PEOPLE PAUL McCARTNEY	41	1993
C'MON PEOPLE (WE'RE MAKING IT NOW) RICHARD ASHCROFT	21	2000
COAST IS CLEAR CURVE	34	1991
COCHISE AUDIOSLAVE	24	2003
COCK A DOODLE DO IT EGGS ON LEGS	42	1995
COCKNEY TRANSLATION SMILEY CULTURE	71	1985
CO-CO SWEET	2	1971
COCO JAMBOO MR PRESIDENT	8	1997
COCOA CLIPZ	71	2004
COCOMOTION EL COCO	31	1978
COCONUT NILSSON	42	1972
COCOON BJORK	35	2002
CODE OF LOVE MIKE SARNE	29	1963
CODE RED [A] CONQUERING LION	53	1994
CODE RED [B] BOXER REBELLION	61	2004
CODED LANGUAGE KRUST FEATURING SAUL WILLIAMS	66	1999
COFFEE SUPERSISTER	16	2000
COFFEE + TEA BLUR	11	1999
THE COFFEE SONG FRANK SINATRA	39	1961
COGNOSCENTI VERSUS THE INTELLIGENTSIA CUBAN BOYS	4	1999
COLD [A] ANNIE LENNOX	26	1992
COLD [B] TEARS FOR FEARS	72	1993
COLD AS CHRISTMAS ELTON JOHN	33	1983
COLD AS ICE FOREIGNER	24	1978
COLD AS ICE M.O.P.	4	2001
COLD COLD HEART [A] MIDGE URE	17	1991
COLD COLD HEART [B] WET WET WET	20	1994
COLD DAY IN HELL GARY MOORE	24	1992
COLD DAY IN THE SUN FOO FIGHTERS	64	2006
COLD HARD BITCH JET	34	2004
COLD HEARTED PAULA ABDUL	46	1990
COLD LIGHT OF DAY HALO	49	2002
COLD LOVE DONNA SUMMER	44	1981
COLD ROCK A PARTY MC LYTE	15	1997
COLD SHOULDER [A] CULTURE CLUB	2	1999
COLD SHOULDER [B] ADELE	18	2008
COLD SWEAT [A] THIN LIZZY	27	1983
COLD SWEAT [B] SUGARCUBES	56	1988
COLD TURKEY PLASTIC ONO BAND	14	1969
COLD WIND ARCADE FIRE	52	2005
COLD WORLD GENIUS/GZA FEATURING D'ANGELO	40	1996
COLDCUT'S CHRISTMAS BREAK COLDCUT	67	1989
COLETTE BILLY FURY	9	1960
COLOR OF MY SKIN SWING 52	60	1995
COLOSSAL INSIGHT ROOTS MANUVA	33	2005
COLOSSUS FRESH BC	74	2004
THE COLOUR FIELD COLOUR FIELD	43	1984
COLOUR MY LIFE M PEOPLE	35	1992
THE COLOUR OF LOVE [A] BILLY OCEAN	65	1988
THE COLOUR OF LOVE [B] SNAP!	54	1991
THE COLOUR OF LOVE [C] REESE PROJECT	52	1992
COLOUR OF MY LOVE JEFFERSON	22	1969
COLOUR THE WORLD SASH!	15	1999
COLOURBLIND DARIUS	1	2002
COLOURED KISSES MARTIKA	41	1992
COLOURS [A] DONOVAN	4	1965
THE COLOURS [B] MEN THEY COULDN'T HANG	61	1988
COLOURS FADED FRANCESCA BERLIN	60	2006
COLOURS FLY AWAY TEARDROP EXPLODES	54	1981
COLOURS IN WAVES SOUTH	60	2004
COLOURS OF THE WIND VANESSA WILLIAMS	21	1995
COMA AROMA INAURA	57	1996
COMA GIRL JOE STRUMMER & THE MESCALEROS	33	2003
THE COMANCHEROS LONNIE DONEGAN	14	1962
COMBINE HARVESTER (BRAND NEW KEY) WURZELS	1	1976
COME MARTHA WASH	64	1999
COME AGAIN TRUMAN & WOLFF FEATURING STEEL HORSES	57	1998
COME ALONG PLEASE BOB WALLIS & HIS STORYVILLE JAZZ BAND	33	1962
COME AND GET IT BADFINGER	4	1970
COME AND GET ME CLEOPATRA	29	2000
COME AND GET SOME COOKIE CREW	42	1989
COME AND GET WITH ME KEITH SWEAT FEATURING SNOOP DOGG	58	1998
COME AND GET YOUR LOVE REAL McCOY	19	1995
COME AND STAY WITH ME MARIANNE FAITHFULL	4	1965
COME AS YOU ARE [A] NIRVANA	9	1992
COME AS YOU ARE [B] BEVERLEY KNIGHT	9	2004
COME AWAY MELINDA BARRY ST JOHN	47	1965
COME BABY COME K7	3	1993
COME BACK [A] MIGHTY WAH	20	1984
COME BACK [B] SPEAR OF DESTINY	55	1985
COME BACK [C] LUTHER VANDROSS	53	1989
COME BACK [D] LONDONBEAT	69	1995
COME BACK [E] JESSICA GARLICK	13	2002
COME BACK AND FINISH WHAT YOU STARTED GLADYS KNIGHT & THE PIPS	15	1978
COME BACK AND SHAKE ME CLODAGH RODGERS	3	1969
COME BACK AND STAY PAUL YOUNG	4	1983
COME BACK AROUND FEEDER	14	2002
COME BACK BABY DAN REED NETWORK	51	1990
COME BACK BRIGHTER REEF	8	1997
COME BACK DARLING UB40	10	1998
COME BACK (FOR REAL LOVE) ALISON LIMERICK	53	1991
COME BACK JONEE DEVO	60	1978
COME BACK MY LOVE DARTS	2	1978
COME BACK TO ME [A] JANET JACKSON	20	1990
COME BACK TO ME [B] ANGELHEART FEATURING ROCHELLE HARRIS	68	1996
COME BACK TO WHAT YOU KNOW EMBRACE	6	1998
COME BACK TOMORROW INSPIRAL CARPETS	43	2003
COME CLEAN HILARY DUFF	18	2004
COME DANCE WITH ME (LP) FRANK SINATRA	30	1959
COME DANCING [A] NO DICE	65	1979
COME DANCING [B] KINKS	12	1983

	Peak Position	Year of Release
COME DIG IT MACHEL	56	1996
COME GET MY LOVIN' DIONNE	69	1989
COME GET SOME ROOSTER	7	2004
COME GIVE ME YOUR LOVE RICHIE STEPHENS	62	1997
COME HELL OR WATERS HIGH DEE C LEE	46	1986
COME HOME [A] DAVE CLARK FIVE	16	1965
COME HOME [B] JAMES	32	1990
COME HOME [C] LIL' DEVIOUS	55	2001
COME HOME BILLY BIRD DIVINE COMEDY	25	2004
COME HOME WITH ME BABY DEAD OR ALIVE	62	1989
COME IN OUT OF THE RAIN WENDY MOTEN	8	1994
COME INSIDE THOMPSON TWINS	56	1991
COME INTO MY LIFE [A] JOYCE SIMS	7	1988
COME INTO MY LIFE [B] GALA	38	1998
COME INTO MY ROOM NATHAN	37	2005
COME INTO MY WORLD KYLIE MINOGUE	8	2002
COME LIVE WITH ME HEAVEN 17	5	1983
COME NEXT SPRING TONY BENNETT	29	1956
COME ON [A] ROLLING STONES	21	1963
COME ON! [B] SOLO	63	1992
COME ON [C] DJ SEDUCTION	37	1992
COME ON [D] JESUS & MARY CHAIN	52	1994
COME ON [E] NEW POWER GENERATION	65	1998
COME ON [F] LEVELLERS	44	2002
COME ON [G] D4	50	2002
COME ON (AND DO IT) FPI PROJECT	59	1993
COME ON, COME ON BRONSKI BEAT	20	1986
COME ON DANCE DANCE SATURDAY NIGHT BAND	16	1978
COME ON EILEEN DEXY'S MIDNIGHT RUNNERS WITH THE EMERALD EXPRESS	1	1982
COME ON ENGLAND! [A] ENGLAND'S BARMY ARMY	45	1999
COME ON ENGLAND [B] 4-4-2	2	2004
COME ON EVERYBODY (GET DOWN) URGE OVERKILL	37	1997
COME ON GIRL TAIO CRUZ FEATURING LUCIANA	5	2008
COME ON HOME [A] SPRINGFIELDS	31	1963
COME ON HOME [B] WAYNE FONTANA	16	1966
COME ON HOME [C] EVERYTHING BUT THE GIRL	44	1986
COME ON HOME [D] CYNDI LAUPER	39	1995
COME ON, LET'S GO [A] TOMMY STEELE	10	1958
COME ON, LET'S GO [A] LOS LOBOS	18	1987
COME ON/LET'S GO [B] PAUL WELLER	15	2005
COME ON OVER [A] JOHN SILVER	35	2003
COME ON OVER [B] KYM MARSH	10	2003
COME ON OVER BABY (ALL I WANT IS YOU) CHRISTINA AGUILERA	8	2000
COME ON OVER TO MY PLACE DRIFTERS	9	1965
COME ON YALL RHYTHM MASTERS	49	1997
COME ON YOU REDS MANCHESTER UNITED FOOTBALL CLUB	1	1994
COME OUTSIDE MIKE SARNE WITH WENDY RICHARD	1	1962
COME OUTSIDE JUDGE DREAD	14	1975
COME PLAY WITH ME WEDDING PRESENT	10	1992
COME PRIMA MARINO MARINI & HIS QUARTET	2	1958
(COME 'ROUND HERE) I'M THE ONE YOU NEED SMOKEY ROBINSON & THE MIRACLES	13	1966
COME SEE ABOUT ME SUPREMES	27	1965
COME SEE ABOUT ME SHAKIN' STEVENS	24	1987
COME SEE ME PRETTY THINGS	43	1966
COME SOFTLY TO ME FLEETWOODS	6	1959
COME SOFTLY TO ME FRANKIE VAUGHAN & THE KAYE SISTERS	9	1959
COME SOFTLY TO ME NEW SEEKERS FEATURING MARTY KRISTIAN	20	1972
COME TO DADDY APHEX TWIN	36	1997
COME TO ME [A] JULIE GRANT	31	1964
COME TO ME [B] RUBY WINTERS	11	1978
COME TO ME [C] ATEED	56	2003
COME TO ME [D] P DIDDY FEATURING NICOLE SCHERZINGER	4	2006
COME TO ME (I AM WOMAN) SU POLLARD	71	1985
COME TO MILTON KEYNES STYLE COUNCIL	23	1985
COME TO MY AID SIMPLY RED	66	1985
COME TO MY PARTY KEITH HARRIS & ORVILLE WITH DIPPY	44	1983
COME TO THE DANCE BARRON KNIGHTS WITH DUKE D'MOND	42	1964
COME TOGETHER [A] BEATLES	4	1969
COME TOGETHER [A] MICHAEL JACKSON	3	1992
COME TOGETHER (WAR CHILD) [A] SMOKIN' MOJO FILTERS	19	1995
COME TOGETHER [B] PRIMAL SCREAM	26	1990
COME TOGETHER [C] M FACTOR	46	2003
COME TOGETHER AS ONE WILL DOWNING	48	1990
COME TOMORROW MANFRED MANN	4	1965
COME UNDONE [A] DURAN DURAN	13	1993
COME UNDONE [B] ROBBIE WILLIAMS	4	2003
COME WHAT MAY [A] VICKY LEANDROS	2	1972
COME WHAT MAY [B] NICOLE KIDMAN & EWAN McGREGOR	27	2001
COME WITH ME [A] JESSE GREEN	29	1977
COME WITH ME [B] RONNY JORDAN	63	1994
COME WITH ME [C] QATTARA	31	1997
COME WITH ME [D] PUFF DADDY FEATURING JIMMY PAGE	2	1998
COME WITH ME [E] SPECIAL D	6	2004
COME WITH US CHEMICAL BROTHERS	14	2002
THE COMEBACK SHOUT OUT LOUDS	63	2005
COMEDY SHACK	44	1999
COMES A-LONG A-LOVE KAY STARR	1	1952
COMEUPPANCE THOUSAND YARD STARE	37	1992
COMFORTABLY NUMB SCISSOR SISTERS	10	2004
COMFORTING SOUNDS MEW	48	2003
COMIN' BACK CRYSTAL METHOD	73	1998
COMIN' HOME [A] DELANEY & BONNIE & FRIENDS FEATURING ERIC CLAPTON	16	1969
COMIN' HOME [B] DANGER DANGER	75	1992
COMIN' IN AND OUT OF YOUR LIFE BARBRA STREISAND	66	1982
COMIN' ON STRONG [A] BROKEN ENGLISH	18	1987
COMIN' ON STRONG [B] DESIYA FEATURING MELISSA YIANNAKOU	74	1992
COMIN' RIGHT UP BRUCE WILLIS	73	1988
COMING AROUND TRAVIS	5	2000
COMING AROUND AGAIN [A] CARLY SIMON	10	1987
COMING AROUND AGAIN [B] SIMON WEBBE	12	2006
COMING BACK DJ DADO	63	1998
COMING BACK FOR MORE [A] L.A. MIX	50	1990
COMING BACK FOR MORE [B] JELLYBEAN FEATURING RICHARD DARBYSHIRE	41	1988
COMING DOWN [A] CULT	50	1994
COMING DOWN [B] LONGVIEW	32	2005
COMING HOME [A] DAVID ESSEX	24	1976
COMING HOME [B] MARSHALL HAIN	39	1978
COMING HOME [C] K WARREN FEATURING LEE O	32	2001
COMING HOME [D] JJ72	52	2005
COMING HOME BABY MEL TORME	13	1963
COMING HOME NOW BOYZONE	4	1996
COMING ON STRONG SIGNUM FEATURING SCOTT MAC	66	1999
COMING OUT OF THE DARK GLORIA ESTEFAN	25	1991
COMING UNDONE KORN	63	2006
COMING UP PAUL McCARTNEY	2	1980
COMING UP EASY PAOLO NUTINI	62	2009
COMING UP ROSES CURVE	51	1998
COMMENT TE DIRE ADIEU JIMMY SOMERVILLE FEATURING JUNE MILES~KINGSTON	14	1989
COMMERCIAL BREAKDOWN SUNSHINE UNDERGROUND	46	2006
COMMITMENT LeANN RIMES	38	1998
COMMON PEOPLE PULP	2	1995
COMMUNICATION [A] DAVID McCALLUM	32	1966
COMMUNICATION [B] SPANDAU BALLET	12	1983
COMMUNICATION [C] POWER STATION	75	1985
COMMUNICATION [D] ARMIN	18	2000
COMMUNICATION BREAKDOWN JUNIOR	57	1983
COMMUNICATION (SOMEBODY ANSWER THE PHONE) MARIO PIU	5	1999
THE COMPASS DAVE CLARKE	46	2001
COMPLETE JAIMESON	4	2003
COMPLETE CONTROL CLASH	28	1977
THE COMPLETE DOMINATOR HUMAN RESOURCE	18	1991
THE COMPLETE STELLA (REMIX) JAM & SPOON	66	1992
COMPLEX GARY NUMAN	6	1979
COMPLICATED AVRIL LAVIGNE	3	2002
COMPLIMENTS ON YOUR KISS RED DRAGON WITH BRIAN & TONY GOLD	2	1994
COMPUTER GAME (THEME FROM 'THE INVADERS') YELLOW MAGIC ORCHESTRA	17	1980
COMPUTER LOVE [A] KRAFTWERK	1	1981
COMPUTER LOVE (PART 1) [B] ZAPP	64	1986
COMPUTER LOVE [C] SUPERCAR FEATURING MIKAELA	67	1999
CON LOS ANOS QUE ME QUEDIN GLORIA ESTEFAN	40	1993
CON TE PARTIRO ANDREA BOCELLI	69	2007
CONCEIVED BETH ORTON	44	2006
THE CONCEPT TEENAGE FANCLUB	51	1991
CONCRETE AND CLAY UNIT FOUR PLUS TWO	1	1965
CONCRETE AND CLAY RANDY EDELMAN	11	1976
CONCRETE SCHOOLYARD JURASSIC 5	35	1998
CONDEMNATION DEPECHE MODE	9	1993
CONFESSIN' (THAT I LOVE YOU) FRANK IFIELD	1	1963
CONFESSIONS OF A BOUNCER JUDGE DREAD	27	1976
CONFESSIONS PART II USHER	5	2004
CONFESSIONS PART II GLEE CAST	14	2010
CONFETTI LEMONHEADS	44	1993
CONFIDE IN ME KYLIE MINOGUE	2	1994
CONFUSION [A] LEE DORSEY	38	1966
CONFUSION [B] ELECTRIC LIGHT ORCHESTRA	8	1979
CONFUSION [C] NEW ORDER	12	1983
CONFUSION [C] ARTHUR BAKER VS NEW ORDER	64	2002
CONFUSION [D] ZUTONS	37	2005
CONFUSION GIRL (SHAME SHAME SHAME) FRANKMUSIK	27	2009
CONFUSION (HITS US EVERY TIME) TRUTH	22	1983
CONGO [A] BOSS	54	1994
CONGO [B] GENESIS	29	1997
CONGO SQUARE GREAT WHITE	62	1991
CONGRATULATIONS CLIFF RICHARD	1	1968
CONNECTED [A] STEREO MC'S	18	1992
CONNECTED [B] PAUL VAN DYK FEATURING VEGA 4	28	2003
CONNECTION ELASTICA	17	1994
CONQUEST WHITE STRIPES	30	2008
CONQUEST OF PARADISE VANGELIS	60	1992
CONQUISTADOR [A] PROCOL HARUM	22	1972
CONQUISTADOR [B] ESPIRITU	47	1993
CONSCIENCE JAMES DARREN	30	1962
CONSCIOUS MAN JOLLY BROTHERS	46	1979
CONSIDER YOURSELF MAX BYGRAVES	50	1960
CONSIDERATION REEF	13	1997

Title	Artist	Peak Position	Year of Release
A CONSPIRACY	BLACK CROWES	45	1995
CONSTANT CRAVING	k.d. lang	15	1992
CONSTANTLY	CLIFF RICHARD	4	1964
CONSTANTLY WAITING	PAULINE TAYLOR	51	1996
CONTACT [A]	EDWIN STARR	6	1979
CONTACT… [B]	EAT STATIC	67	1998
CONTAGIOUS	WHISPERS	56	1985
THE CONTINENTAL	MAUREEN McGOVERN	16	1976
CONTRARY MARY	THEE UNSTRUNG	59	2004
CONTRIBUTION	MICA PARIS	33	1990
CONTROL [A]	JANET JACKSON	42	1986
CONTROL [B]	TIME OF THE MUMPH	69	1995
CONTROL [C]	PUDDLE OF MUDD	15	2002
CONTROL MYSELF	LL COOL J FEATURING JENNIFER LOPEZ	2	2006
CONTROLLING ME	OCEANIC	14	1992
CONTROVERSY	PRINCE	5	1993
CONVERSATION INTERCOM	SOULWAX	50	2000
CONVERSATIONS	CILLA BLACK	7	1969
CONVOY	CW McCALL	2	1976
CONVOY GB	LAURIE LINGO & THE DIPSTICKS	4	1976
CONWAY	REEL 2 REAL FEATURING THE MAD STUNTMAN	27	1995
COOCHY COO	EN-CORE FEATURING STEPHEN EMMANUEL & ESKA	32	2000
COOKIE JAR	GYM CLASS HEROES	6	2008
COOKIN' UP YAH BRAIN	4 HERO	59	1992
COOL	GWEN STEFANI	11	2005
COOL BABY	CHARLIE GRACIE	26	1958
COOL FOR CATS	SQUEEZE	2	1979
COOL JERK	GO-GOS	60	1991
COOL MEDITATION	THIRD WORLD	17	1979
COOL OUT TONIGHT	DAVID ESSEX	23	1977
COOL RUNNING	TIK & TOK	69	1983
COOL WATER	FRANKIE LAINE	2	1955
COP THAT SHIT	TIMBALAND/MAGOO/MISSY ELLIOTT	22	2004
COPACABANA (AT THE COPA)	BARRY MANILOW	22	1978
COPPER GIRL	3 COLOURS RED	30	1997
COPPERHEAD ROAD	STEVE EARLE	45	1988
COPS AND ROBBERS	HOOSIERS	24	2008
CORNER OF THE EARTH	JAMIROQUAI	31	2002
CORNERSHOP	BABYBIRD	37	1997
CORNFLAKE GIRL	TORI AMOS	4	1994
CORONATION RAG	WINIFRED ATWELL	5	1953
CORPSES	IAN BROWN	14	1998
CORRINE, CORRINA	RAY PETERSON	41	1961
COSMIC GIRL	JAMIROQUAI	6	1996
COSMONAUT NO. 7	SCARFO	67	1997
THE COST OF LIVING EP	CLASH	22	1979
COSTAFINE TOWN	SPLINTER	17	1974
COSY PRISONS	A-HA	39	2006
COTTON EYE JOE	REDNEX	1	1994
COTTONFIELDS	BEACH BOYS	5	1970
COULD HAVE TOLD YOU SO	HALO JAMES	6	1990
COULD HEAVEN EVER BE LIKE THIS	IDRIS MUHAMMAD	42	1977
COULD I HAVE THIS KISS FOREVER	WHITNEY HOUSTON & ENRIQUE IGLESIAS	7	2000
COULD IT BE	JAHEIM	33	2001
COULD IT BE FOREVER	DAVID CASSIDY	2	1972
COULD IT BE FOREVER	GEMINI	38	1996
COULD IT BE I'M FALLING IN LOVE	DETROIT SPINNERS	11	1973
COULD IT BE I'M FALLING IN LOVE	DAVID GRANT & JAKI GRAHAM	5	1985
COULD IT BE I'M FALLING IN LOVE	WORLDS APART	15	1994
COULD IT BE I'M FALLING IN LOVE EP	DETROIT SPINNERS	32	1977
COULD IT BE MAGIC	DONNA SUMMER	40	1976
COULD IT BE MAGIC	BARRY MANILOW	25	1979
COULD IT BE MAGIC	TAKE THAT	3	1992
COULD THIS BE REAL	SUB FOCUS	41	2010
COULD WELL BE IN	STREETS	30	2004
COULD YOU BE LOVED	BOB MARLEY & THE WAILERS	5	1980
COULDN'T GET IT RIGHT	CLIMAX BLUES BAND	10	1976
COULDN'T HAVE SAID IT BETTER	MEAT LOAF	31	2003
COULDN'T SAY GOODBYE	TOM JONES	51	1991
COULD'VE BEEN	TIFFANY	4	1988
COULD'VE BEEN ME	BILLY RAY CYRUS	24	1992
COULD'VE BEEN YOU	CHER	31	1992
COUNT ON ME [A]	JULIE GRANT	24	1963
COUNT ON ME [B]	WHITNEY HOUSTON	12	1996
COUNT YOUR BLESSINGS	BING CROSBY	11	1955
COUNTDOWN	RUSH	36	1983
COUNTERFEIT	LOWGOLD	52	2001
COUNTING BACKWARDS	THROWING MUSES	70	1991
COUNTING DOWN THE DAYS [A]	NATALIE IMBRUGLIA	23	2005
COUNTING DOWN THE DAYS [B]	SUNFREAKZ FEATURING ANDREA BRITTON	37	2007
COUNTING EVERY MINUTE	SONIA	16	1990
COUNTING SHEEP	AIRHEAD	35	1991
COUNTING TEARDROPS	EMILE FORD & THE CHECKMATES	4	1960
COUNTING THE DAYS	ABI	44	1998
COUNTRY BOY [A]	FATS DOMINO	19	1960
COUNTRY BOY [B]	HEINZ	26	1963
COUNTRY BOY [C]	JIMMY NAIL	25	1996
COUNTRY GIRL	PRIMAL SCREAM	5	2006
COUNTRY HOUSE	BLUR	1	1995
THE COUNTRY OF THE BLIND	FAITH BROTHERS	63	1985
COUNTRY ROADS	HERMES HOUSE BAND	7	2001
COURSE BRUV	GENIUS CRU	39	2001
COUSIN NORMAN	MARMALADE	6	1971
COUSINS	VAMPIRE WEEKEND	39	2010
COVER FROM THE SKY	DEACON BLUE	31	1991
COVER GIRL	NEW KIDS ON THE BLOCK	4	1990
COVER ME	BRUCE SPRINGSTEEN	16	1984
COVER MY EYES (PAIN AND HEAVEN)	MARILLION	34	1991
(COVER PLUS) WE'RE ALL GROWN UP	HAZEL O'CONNOR	41	1981
COVER UP	UB40	54	2002
COVERED IN PUNK	PORTOBELLA	54	2004
COVERS EP	EVERYTHING BUT THE GIRL	13	1992
COWARD OF THE COUNTY	KENNY ROGERS	1	1980
COWBOY [A]	KID ROCK	36	1999
COWBOY [B]	CHIPZ	44	2007
COWBOY DREAMS	JIMMY NAIL	13	1995
COWBOY JIMMY JOE	ALMA COGAN	37	1961
COWBOYS AND ANGELS	GEORGE MICHAEL	45	1991
COWBOYS AND INDIANS	CROSS	74	1987
COWBOYS & KISSES	ANASTACIA	28	2001
COWGIRL	UNDERWORLD	24	2000
COWPUNCHER'S CANTATA	MAX BYGRAVES	6	1952
COWPUNK MEDLUM	SPLODGENESSABOUNDS	69	1981
COZ I LUV YOU	SLADE	1	1971
CRACK A BOTTLE	EMINEM	3	2009
CRACK THE SHUTTERS	SNOW PATROL	43	2008
CRACKERS INTERNATIONAL EP	ERASURE	2	1988
CRACKIN' UP [A]	TOMMY HUNT	39	1975
CRACKIN' UP [B]	NICK LOWE	34	1979
CRACKING UP [C]	JESUS & MARY CHAIN	35	1998
CRACKLIN' ROSIE	NEIL DIAMOND	3	1970
CRADLE	ATOMIC KITTEN	10	2005
CRADLE OF LOVE [A]	JOHNNY PRESTON	2	1960
CRADLE OF LOVE [B]	BILLY IDOL	34	1990
CRANK	CATHERINE WHEEL	66	1993
CRANK THAT (SOULJA BOY)	SOULJA BOY TELL'EM	2	2007
CRASH [A]	PRIMITIVES	5	1988
CRASH [B]	FEEDER	48	1997
CRASH [C]	MATT WILLIS	31	2007
THE CRASH [D]	KOOPA	16	2007
CRASH AND BURN	SAVAGE GARDEN	14	2000
CRASH! BOOM! BANG!	ROXETTE	26	1994
CRASH LANDING	ROUTE ONE FEATURING JENNY FROST	47	2005
CRASHED THE WEDDING	BUSTED	1	2003
CRASHIN' A PARTY	LUMIDEE FEATURING NORE	55	2003
CRASHIN' IN	CHARLATANS	31	1995
CRAWL [A]	HEADSWIM	64	1995
CRAWL [B]	CHRIS BROWN	35	2010
CRAWL HOME	DESERT SESSIONS	41	2003
CRAWLIN' BACK	ROY ORBISON	19	1965
CRAWLING	LINKIN PARK	16	2001
CRAWLING FROM THE WRECKAGE	DAVE EDMUNDS	59	1979
CRAWLING IN THE DARK	HOOBASTANK	47	2002
CRAWLING UP A HILL	KATIE MELUA	46	2004
CRAYZY MAN	BLAST FEATURING VDC	22	1994
CRAZIER	GARY NUMAN VS RICO	13	2003
CRAZY [A]	MUD	12	1973
CRAZY [B]	MANHATTANS	63	1983
CRAZY [C]	ICEHOUSE	38	1987
CRAZY [D]	BOYS	57	1990
CRAZY [E]	PATSY CLINE	14	1990
CRAZY [E]	JULIO IGLESIAS	43	1994
CRAZY [E]	LeANN RIMES	36	1999
CRAZY [F]	SEAL	2	1990
CRAZY [F]	ALANIS MORISSETTE	65	2005
CRAZY [G]	BOB GELDOF	65	1994
CRAZY [H]	AEROSMITH	23	1994
CRAZY [I]	ETERNAL	15	1994
CRAZY [J]	MARK MORRISON	6	1995
CRAZY [K]	NUT	56	1996
CRAZY [L]	AWESOME	63	1998
CRAZY [M]	MOFFATTS	16	1999
CRAZY [N]	LUCID	14	1999
CRAZY [O]	TOMCAT	48	2000
CRAZY [P]	K-CI & JOJO	35	2001
CRAZY [Q]	ANDY BELL	35	2005
CRAZY [R]	GNARLS BARKLEY	1	2006
CRAZY [S]	LUMIDEE	74	2007
CRAZY BEAT	BLUR	18	2003
CRAZY CHANCE	KAVANA	16	1996
CRAZY CHICK	CHARLOTTE CHURCH	2	2005
CRAZY CRAZY NIGHTS	KISS	4	1987
CRAZY CUTS	GRANDMIXER DST	71	1983
CRAZY DREAM	JIM DALE	24	1958
CRAZY (FOR ME)	FREDDIE JACKSON	41	1988
CRAZY FOR YOU [A]	MADONNA	2	1985
CRAZY FOR YOU [B]	SYBIL	71	1990
CRAZY FOR YOU [C]	INCOGNITO FEATURING CHYNA	59	1991
CRAZY FOR YOU [D]	LET LOOSE	2	1993
CRAZY HORSES	OSMONDS	2	1972
CRAZY IN LOVE	BEYONCE	1	2003
CRAZY LITTLE PARTY GIRL	AARON CARTER	7	1998
CRAZY LITTLE THING CALLED LOVE	QUEEN	2	1979
CRAZY LITTLE THING CALLED LOVE	DWIGHT YOAKAM	43	1999
CRAZY LOVE [A]	PAUL ANKA	26	1958
CRAZY LOVE [B]	MAXI PRIEST	67	1986
CRAZY LOVE [C]	CE CE PENISTON	44	1992
CRAZY LOVE [D]	MJ COLE	10	2000
CRAZY LOWDOWN WAYS	OCEAN COLOUR SCENE	64	2001
CRAZY OTTO RAG	STARGAZERS	18	1955

Title	Artist	Peak Position	Year of Release
THE CRAZY PARTY MIXES	JIVE BUNNY & THE MASTERMIXERS	13	1990
CRAZY RAP	AFROMAN	10	2002
CRAZY SEXY MARVELLOUS	PAFFENDORF	52	2003
CRAZY TRAIN	OZZY OSBOURNE'S BLIZZARD OF OZ	49	1980
CRAZY WATER	ELTON JOHN	27	1977
CRAZY WORDS CRAZY TUNE	DOROTHY PROVINE	45	1962
CRAZY WORLD	J MAJIK & WICKAMAN	37	2008
CRAZY YOU	GUN	21	1997
CREAM [A]	PRINCE & THE NEW POWER GENERATION	15	1991
CREAM [B]	BLANK & JONES	24	1999
CREAM (ALWAYS RISES TO THE TOP)	GREGG DIAMOND BIONIC BOOGIE	61	1979
CREATION	STEREO MC'S	19	1993
CREATURES OF THE NIGHT	KISS	34	1983
CREDO	FISH	38	1992
THE CREEP [A]	KEN MACKINTOSH	10	1954
CREEP [B]	RADIOHEAD	7	1993
CREEP [C]	TLC	6	1995
THE CREEPS	CAMILLE JONES & FEDDE LE GRAND	7	2007
THE CREEPS (YOU'RE GIVING ME)	FREAKS	9	2007
CREEQUE ALLEY	MAMAS & THE PAPAS	9	1967
CREOLE JAZZ	MR ACKER BILK & HIS PARAMOUNT JAZZ BAND	22	1961
CRESCENT MOON	LYNDEN DAVID HALL	45	1998
CRICKETS SING FOR ANAMARIA	EMMA	15	2004
CRIME OF PASSION	MIKE OLDFIELD FEATURING MAGGIE REILLY	61	1984
CRIMINALLY INSANE	SLAYER	64	1987
CRIMSON AND CLOVER	JOAN JETT & THE BLACKHEARTS	60	1982
CRISPY BACON	LAURENT GARNIER	60	1997
CRITICAL (IF ONLY YOU KNEW)	WALL OF SOUND FEATURING GERALD LETHAN	73	1993
CRITICIZE	ALEXANDER O'NEAL	4	1987
CROCKETT'S THEME	JAN HAMMER	2	1987
CROCODILE ROCK	ELTON JOHN	5	1972
CROCODILE SHOES	JIMMY NAIL	4	1994
CROOKED TEETH	DEATH CAB FOR CUTIE	69	2006
CROSS MY BROKEN HEART	SINITTA	6	1988
CROSS MY HEART	EIGHTH WONDER	13	1988
CROSS THAT BRIDGE	WARD BROTHERS	32	1987
CROSS THE TRACK (WE BETTER GO BACK)	MACEO & THE MACKS	54	1987
THE CROSSFIRE	STARSAILOR	22	2005
CROSSROADS [A]	TRACY CHAPMAN	61	1989
CROSSROADS [B]	BLAZIN' SQUAD	1	2002
CROSSTOWN TRAFFIC	JIMI HENDRIX EXPERIENCE	37	1969
THE CROWD	ROY ORBISON	40	1962
THE CROWN	GARY BYRD & THE GB EXPERIENCE	6	1983
CROWS	MODEY LEMON	75	2004
CRUCIAL	NEW EDITION	70	1989
CRUCIFIED	ARMY OF LOVERS	31	1991
CRUCIFY	TORI AMOS	15	1992
CRUEL	PUBLIC IMAGE LTD	49	1992
THE CRUEL SEA	DAKOTAS	18	1963
CRUEL SUMMER	BANANARAMA	8	1983
CRUEL SUMMER	ACE OF BASE	8	1998
CRUEL TO BE KIND	NICK LOWE	12	1979
CRUISE INTO CHRISTMAS MEDLEY	JANE McDONALD	10	1998
CRUISIN'	D'ANGELO	31	1996
CRUISING	SINITTA	2	1986
THE CRUNCH	RAH BAND	6	1977
CRUSH [A]	ZHANE	44	1997
CRUSH [B]	JENNIFER PAIGE	4	1998
CRUSH [C]	DARREN HAYES	19	2003
CRUSH [D]	PAUL VAN DYK FEATURING SECOND SUN	42	2004
CRUSH CRUSH CRUSH	PARAMORE	61	2007
CRUSH ME	HOUSE OF LOVE	67	1992
CRUSH ON YOU [A]	JETS	5	1987
CRUSH ON YOU [A]	AARON CARTER	9	1997
CRUSH ON YOU [A]	DANIEL O'DONNELL	21	2006
CRUSH ON YOU [B]	LIL' KIM	23	1997
CRUSH TONIGHT	FAT JOE FEATURING GINUWINE	42	2002
CRUSH WITH EYELINER	R.E.M.	23	1995
CRUSHED BY THE WHEELS OF INDUSTRY	HEAVEN 17	17	1983
CRUSHED LIKE FRUIT	INME	25	2002
CRY [A]	GERRY MONROE	38	1970
CRY [B]	GODLEY & CREME	19	1985
CRY [C]	WATERFRONT	17	1989
CRY [D]	SUNDAYS	43	1997
CRY [E]	SYSTEM F	19	2000
CRY [F]	MICHAEL JACKSON	25	2001
CRY [G]	SIMPLE MINDS	47	2002
CRY [H]	FAITH HILL	25	2002
CRY [I]	KYM MARSH	2	2003
CRY [J]	ALEX PARKS	13	2004
CRY AND BE FREE	MARILYN	31	1984
CRY BABY [A]	SPILLER	40	2002
CRY BABY [B]	JEMINI	15	2003
CRY BABY CRY	SANTANA FEATURING SEAN PAUL & JOSS STONE	71	2006
CRY BOY CRY	BLUE ZOO	13	1982
CRY DIGNITY	DUB WAR	59	1996
CRY FOR HELP [A]	RICK ASTLEY	7	1991
CRY FOR HELP [B]	SHED SEVEN	30	2001
CRY FOR ME	ROACHFORD	46	1994
CRY FOR THE NATIONS	MICHAEL SCHENKER GROUP	56	1980
CRY FOR YOU [A]	JODECI	20	1993
CRY FOR YOU [B]	SEPTEMBER	5	2008
CRY FREEDOM [A]	GEORGE FENTON & JONAS GWANGWA	75	1988
CRY FREEDOM [B]	MOMBASSA	63	1997
CRY INDIA	UMBOZA	19	1995
CRY JUST A LITTLE BIT	SHAKIN' STEVENS	3	1983
CRY LIKE A BABY	BOX TOPS	15	1968
CRY LITTLE SISTER (I NEED U NOW)	LOST BROTHERS FEATURING G TOM MAC	21	2003
CRY ME A RIVER [A]	JULIE LONDON	22	1957
CRY ME A RIVER [A]	MARI WILSON	27	1983
CRY ME A RIVER [A]	DENISE WELCH	23	1995
CRY ME A RIVER [A]	MICHAEL BUBLE	34	2009
CRY ME A RIVER [B]	JUSTIN TIMBERLAKE	2	2003
CRY ME OUT	PIXIE LOTT	12	2009
CRY MY HEART	DAVID WHITFIELD	22	1958
CRY MYSELF TO SLEEP	DEL SHANNON	29	1962
CRY OVER ME	MEAT LOAF	47	2007
CRY TO BE FOUND	DEL AMITRI	40	1998
CRY TO HEAVEN	ELTON JOHN	47	1986
CRY TO ME	PRETTY THINGS	28	1965
CRY WOLF	A-HA	5	1986
CRYIN' [A]	ROY ORBISON	25	1961
CRYIN' [B]	VIXEN	27	1989
CRYIN' [C]	AEROSMITH	17	1993
CRYIN' MY HEART OUT FOR YOU	DIANA ROSS	58	1981
CRYIN' TIME	RAY CHARLES	50	1966
CRYING	DON McLEAN	1	1980
CRYING	ROY ORBISON (DUET WITH k.d. lang)	13	1992
CRYING AT THE DISCOTEQUE	ALCAZAR	13	2001
THE CRYING GAME	DAVE BERRY	5	1964
THE CRYING GAME	BOY GEORGE	22	1992
CRYING IN THE CHAPEL	LEE LAWRENCE WITH RAY MARTIN & HIS ORCHESTRA	7	1953
CRYING IN THE CHAPEL	ELVIS PRESLEY	1	1965
CRYIN' IN THE RAIN [A]	EVERLY BROTHERS	6	1962
CRYING IN THE RAIN [A]	A-HA	13	1990
CRYING IN THE RAIN [B]	CULTURE BEAT	29	1996
CRYING LAUGHING LOVING LYING	LABI SIFFRE	11	1972
CRYING LIGHTNING	ARCTIC MONKEYS	12	2009
CRYING OVER YOU	KEN BOOTHE	11	1975
THE CRYING SCENE	AZTEC CAMERA	70	1990
CRYPTIK SOULS CREW	LEN	28	2000
CRYSTAL	NEW ORDER	8	2001
CRYSTAL CLEAR	GRID	27	1993
THE CRYSTAL LAKE	GRANDADDY	38	2001
CRYSTALL BALL	KEANE	20	2006
CUBA	GIBSON BROTHERS	41	1979
CUBA	EL MARIACHI	38	1996
CUBAN PETE	JIM CARREY	31	1995
CUBIK	808 STATE	10	1990
CUDDLY TOY	ROACHFORD	4	1988
CUFF OF MY SHIRT	GUY MITCHELL	9	1954
CULT OF PERSONALITY	LIVING COLOUR	67	1991
CULT OF SNAP	SNAP!	8	1990
CULT OF SNAP	HI POWER	73	1990
CUM ON FEEL THE NOIZE	SLADE	1	1973
CUM ON FEEL THE NOIZE	QUIET RIOT	45	1983
CUMBERLAND GAP	LONNIE DONEGAN	1	1957
CUMBERLAND GAP	VIPERS SKIFFLE GROUP	10	1957
THE CUP OF LIFE	RICKY MARTIN	29	1998
CUPBOARD LOVE	JOHN LEYTON	22	1963
CUPID [A]	SAM COOKE	7	1961
CUPID [A]	JOHNNY NASH	6	1969
CUPID [B]	JC 001	56	1993
CUPID-I'VE LOVED YOU FOR A LONG TIME (MEDLEY)	DETROIT SPINNERS	4	1980
CUPID'S CHOKEHOLD/BREAKFAST IN AMERICA	GYM CLASS HEROES	3	2007
THE CURE & THE CAUSE	FISH GO DEEP FEATURING TRACEY K	23	2006
CURIOSITY	JETS	41	1987
CURIOUS	LEVERT SWEAT GILL	23	1998
CURLY	MOVE	12	1969
THE CURSE OF VOODOO RAY	LISA MAY	64	1996
CURTAIN FALLS	BLUE	4	2004
CURVY COLA BOTTLE BODY	CHICO	45	2007
CUT CHEMIST SUITE	OZOMATLI	58	1999
CUT HERE	CURE	54	2001
CUT ME DOWN	LLOYD COLE & THE COMMOTIONS	38	1986
CUT SOME RUG	BLUETONES	7	1996
CUT THE CAKE	AVERAGE WHITE BAND	31	1975
CUT YOUR HAIR	PAVEMENT	52	1994
A CUTE SWEET LOVE ADDICTION	JOHNNY GILL	46	1994
CUTS ACROSS THE LAND	DUKE SPIRIT	45	2004
CUTS BOTH WAYS	GLORIA ESTEFAN	49	1990
CUTT OFF	KASABIAN	8	2005
THE CUTTER	ECHO & THE BUNNYMEN	8	1983
CUTTY SARK	JOHN BARRY SEVEN	35	1962
CYANIDE [A]	LURKERS	72	1979
CYANIDE [B]	METALLICA	48	2008
CYBELE'S REVERIE	STEREOLAB	62	1996
CYCLONE	DUB PISTOLS	63	1998
THE CYPHER: PART 3	FRANKIE CUTLASS	59	1997

D

Title	Artist	Peak Position	Year of Release
D-DARLING	ANTHONY NEWLEY	25	1962
D-DAYS	HAZEL O'CONNOR	10	1981
D-FUNKTIONAL	MEKON FEATURING AFRIKA BAMBAATAA	72	2004
DA ANTIDOTE	STANTON WARRIORS	69	2001

Title / Artist	Peak Position	Year of Release
DA DA DA TRIO	2	1982
DA DOO RON RON CRYSTALS	5	1963
DA-FORCE BEDLAM	68	1999
DA FUNK DAFT PUNK	7	1997
DA GOODNESS REDMAN	52	1999
DA HYPE JUNIOR JACK FEATURING ROBERT SMITH	25	2004
DA LICKS DJ FRESH	60	2003
DA 'YA THINK I'M SEXY ROD STEWART	1	1978
DA YA THINK I'M SEXY REVOLTING COCKS	61	1993
DA YA THINK I'M SEXY? N-TRANCE FEATURING ROD STEWART	7	1997
DA YA THINK I'M SEXY? GIRLS OF *FHM*	10	2004
D-A-A-ANCE LAMBRETTAS	12	1980
DADDY COOL [A] BONEY M	6	1976
DADDY COOL [B] DARTS	6	1977
DADDY DON'T YOU WALK SO FAST DANIEL BOONE	17	1971
DADDY O WIDEBOYS FEATURING SHAZNAY LEWIS	32	2008
DADDY'S GONE GLASVEGAS	12	2008
DADDY'S HOME CLIFF RICHARD	2	1981
DADDY'S LITTLE GIRL NIKKI D	75	1991
DAFT PUNK IS PLAYING AT MY HOUSE LCD SOUNDSYSTEM	29	2005
DAGENHAM DAVE MORRISSEY	26	1995
DAILY TQ	14	2000
DAKOTA STEREOPHONICS	1	2005
DALLIANCE WEDDING PRESENT	29	1991
DAMAGED PLUMMET	12	2003
THE DAMBUSTERS MARCH CENTRAL BAND OF THE ROYAL AIR FORCE, CONDUCTOR W/ CDR A.E. SIMS O.B.E.	18	1955
DAMN DAMN LEASH BE YOUR OWN PET	68	2005
DAMN GOOD DAVID LEE ROTH	72	1988
DAMN I WISH I WAS YOUR LOVER SOPHIE B HAWKINS	14	1992
DAMNED DON'T CRY VISAGE	11	1982
DAMNED ON 45 CAPTAIN SENSIBLE	6	1984
DANCANDO LAMBADA KAOMA	62	1990
DANCE [A] THAT PETROL EMOTION	64	1987
THE DANCE [B] GARTH BROOKS	36	1995
DANCE A LITTLE BIT CLOSER CHARO & THE SALSOUL ORCHESTRA	44	1978
DANCE AND SHOUT SHAGGY	19	2001
DANCE AWAY ROXY MUSIC	2	1979
DANCE COMMANDER ELECTRIC SIX	40	2003
DANCE DANCE [A] DESKEE	74	1990
DANCE DANCE [B] FALL OUT BOY	8	2006
DANCE DANCE DANCE BEACH BOYS	24	1965
DANCE DANCE DANCE (YOWSAH YOWSAH YOWSAH) CHIC	6	1977
DANCE (DISCO HEAT) SYLVESTER	29	1978
DANCE FOR ME [A] SISQO	6	2001
DANCE FOR ME [B] MARY J BLIGE FEATURING COMMON	13	2002
DANCE, GET DOWN (FEEL THE GROOVE) AL HUDSON	57	1978
DANCE HALL DAYS WANG CHUNG	21	1984
DANCE INTO THE LIGHT PHIL COLLINS	9	1996
DANCE LADY DANCE CROWN HEIGHTS AFFAIR	44	1979
DANCE LITTLE LADY DANCE TINA CHARLES	6	1976
DANCE LITTLE SISTER (PART ONE) TERENCE TRENT D'ARBY	20	1987
DANCE ME IN SONS & DAUGHTERS	40	2005
DANCE ME UP GARY GLITTER	25	1984
DANCE NO MORE E-LUSTRIOUS FEATURING DEBORAH FRENCH	58	1992
DANCE OF THE CUCKOOS (THE LAUREL AND HARDY THEME) BAND OF THE BLACK WATCH	37	1975
DANCE OF THE MAD POP WILL EAT ITSELF	32	1990
DANCE ON! [A] SHADOWS	1	1962
DANCE ON [A] KATHY KIRBY	11	1963
DANCE ON [B] MOJO	70	1981
DANCE OUT OF MY HEAD PIA	65	1988
DANCE STANCE DEXY'S MIDNIGHT RUNNERS	40	1980
DANCE SUCKER SET THE TONE	62	1983
DANCE THE BODY MUSIC OSIBISA	31	1976
DANCE THE KUNG FU CARL DOUGLAS	35	1974
DANCE THE NIGHT AWAY MAVERICKS	4	1998
DANCE TO THE MUSIC SLY & THE FAMILY STONE	7	1968
DANCE TO THE MUSIC HUSTLERS CONVENTION FEATURING DAVE LAUDAT & ONDREA DUVERNEY	71	1995
DANCE TO THE RHYTHM BULLETPROOF	62	2001
DANCE TONIGHT [A] LUCY PEARL	36	2000
DANCE TONIGHT [B] PAUL McCARTNEY	26	2007
DANCE WIT ME RICK JAMES	53	1982
DANCE WITH ME [A] DRIFTERS	17	1960
DANCE WITH ME [B] PETER BROWN	57	1978
DANCE WITH ME [C] CONTROL	17	1991
DANCE WITH ME [D] TIN TIN OUT FEATURING TONY HADLEY	35	1997
DANCE WITH ME [E] DEBELAH MORGAN	10	2001
DANCE WITH MY FATHER LUTHER VANDROSS	21	2004
DANCE WITH THE DEVIL COZY POWELL	3	1973
DANCE WITH THE GUITAR MAN DUANE EDDY & THE REBELETTES	4	1962
DANCE (WITH U) LEMAR	2	2003
DANCE WITH YOU CARRIE LUCAS	40	1979
DANCE WITH YOU (NACHNA TERE NAAL) RISHI RICH PROJECT FEATURING JAY SEAN	12	2003
DANCE WIV ME DIZZEE RASCAL FEATURING CALVIN HARRIS & CHROME	1	2008
DANCE YOURSELF DIZZY LIQUID GOLD	2	1980
DANCE4LIFE TIESTO FEATURING MAXI JAZZ	67	2006
DANCEFLOOR HOLLOWAYS	41	2007
DANCEHALL MOOD ASWAD	48	1993
DANCEHALL QUEEN CHEVELLE FRANKLYN/ BEENIE MAN	70	1997
DANCER [A] GINO SOCCIO	46	1979
DANCER [B] MICHAEL SCHENKER GROUP	52	1982
DANCERAMA SIGUE SIGUE SPUTNIK	50	1989
DANCIN' AARON SMITH FEATURING LUVLI	20	2005
DANCIN' EASY DANNY WILLIAMS	30	1977
DANCIN' IN THE KEY OF LIFE STEVE ARRINGTON	21	1985
DANCIN' IN THE MOONLIGHT (IT'S CAUGHT ME IN THE SPOTLIGHT) THIN LIZZY	14	1977
DANCIN' ON A WIRE SURFACE NOISE	59	1980
DANCIN' PARTY CHUBBY CHECKER	19	1962
DANCIN' PARTY SHOWADDYWADDY	4	1977
DANCIN' THE NIGHT AWAY VOGGUE	39	1981
DANCIN' TONIGHT STEREOPOL FEATURING NEVADA	36	2003
DANCING BABY (OOGA-CHAKA) TRUBBLE	21	1998
DANCING GIRLS NIK KERSHAW	13	1984
DANCING IN OUTER SPACE ATMOSFEAR	46	1979
DANCING IN THE CITY MARSHALL HAIN	3	1978
DANCING IN THE DARK [A] KIM WILDE	67	1983
DANCING IN THE DARK [B] BRUCE SPRINGSTEEN	4	1984
DANCING IN THE DARK [C] 4TUNE 500	75	2003
DANCING IN THE DARK [D] MICKY MODELLE V JESSY	10	2006
DANCING IN THE DARK EP BIG DADDY	21	1985
DANCING IN THE MOONLIGHT TOPLOADER	7	2000
DANCING IN THE SHEETS SHALAMAR	41	1984
DANCING IN THE STREET [A] MARTHA REEVES & THE VANDELLAS	4	1964
DANCING IN THE STREET [A] DAVID BOWIE & MICK JAGGER	1	1985
DANCING IN THE STREET [B] MATT BIANCO	64	1986
DANCING LASHA TUMBAI (UKRAINE) VERKA SERDUCHKA	28	2007
(DANCING) ON A SATURDAY NIGHT BARRY BLUE	2	1973
DANCING ON THE CEILING LIONEL RICHIE	7	1986
DANCING ON THE FLOOR (HOOKED ON LOVE) THIRD WORLD	10	1981
DANCING ON THE JAGGED EDGE SISTER SLEDGE	50	1985
DANCING QUEEN ABBA	1	1976
DANCING QUEEN ABBACADABRA	57	1992
DANCING THE NIGHT AWAY MOTORS	42	1977
DANCING TIGHT GALAXY FEATURING PHIL FEARON	4	1983
DANCING WITH MYSELF GEN X	62	1980
DANCING WITH MYSELF (EP) GENERATION X	60	1981
DANCING WITH TEARS IN MY EYES ULTRAVOX	3	1984
DANCING WITH THE CAPTAIN PAUL NICHOLAS	8	1976
DANDELION ROLLING STONES	8	1967
DANGER [A] AC/DC	48	1985
DANGER [B] BLAHZAY BLAHZAY	56	1996
DANGER (BEEN SO LONG) MYSTIKAL FEATURING NIVEA	28	2001
DANGER GAMES PINKEES	8	1982
DANGER HIGH VOLTAGE ELECTRIC SIX	2	2002
THE DANGER OF A STRANGER STELLA PARTON	35	1977
DANGER ZONE KENNY LOGGINS	45	1986
DANGEROUS [A] PENNYE FORD	43	1985
DANGEROUS [B] ROXETTE	6	1990
DANGEROUS [C] BUSTA RHYMES	32	1997
DANGEROUS [D] KARDINAL OFFISHALL FEATURING AKON	16	2008
DANGEROUS [E] CASCADA	67	2009
DANGEROUS MINDS EP AARON HALL:DE VANTE:SISTA FEATURING CRAIG MACK	35	1996
DANGEROUS SEX TACK HEAD	48	1990
DANI CALIFORNIA RED HOT CHILI PEPPERS	2	2006
DANIEL [A] ELTON JOHN	4	1973
DANIEL [B] BAT FOR LASHES	36	2009
DARE GORILLAZ	1	2005
DARE ME POINTER SISTERS	17	1985
DARE ME (STUPIDISCO) JUNIOR JACK FEATURING SHENA	20	2007
DARE TO DREAM VIOLA WILLS	35	1986
DARK ALAN (AILEIN DUNN) CAPERCAILLIE	65	1995
DARK AND LONG UNDERWORLD	57	1994
DARK CLOUDS SPACE	14	1997
DARK IS LIGHT ENOUGH DUKE SPIRIT	55	2004
THE DARK IS RISING MERCURY REV	16	2002
DARK IS THE NIGHT [A] SHAKATAK	15	1983
DARK IS THE NIGHT [B] A-HA	19	1993
DARK LADY CHER	36	1974
DARK MOON TONY BRENT	17	1957
DARK NIGHT GORKY'S ZYGOTIC MYNCI	49	1997
DARK ROAD ANNIE LENNOX	58	2007
DARK SCIENCE (EP) TILT	55	2000
DARK SIDE OF THE MOON ERNESTO VS BASTIAN	48	2005
DARK SKY JIMMY SOMERVILLE	66	1997
DARK THERAPY ECHOBELLY	20	1996
DARKHEART BOMB THE BASS FEATURING SPIKEY TEE	35	1994
DARKLANDS JESUS & MARY CHAIN	33	1987
DARKTOWN STRUTTERS BALL JOE BROWN & THE BRUVVERS	34	1960
DARLIN' [A] BEACH BOYS	11	1968
DARLIN' [A] DAVID CASSIDY	16	1975
DARLIN' [B] FRANKIE MILLER	6	1978

Title / Artist	Peak Position	Year of Release
DARLIN' [C] BOB SINCLAR FEATURING JAMES WILLIAMS	46	2001
DARLIN' DARLIN' BABY (SWEET, TENDER, LOVE) O'JAYS	24	1977
DARLING BE HOME SOON LOVIN' SPOONFUL	44	1967
DARLING BE HOME SOON LET LOOSE	65	1996
DARLING PRETTY MARK KNOPFLER	33	1996
DARTS OF PLEASURE FRANZ FERDINAND	44	2003
DAS BOOT U96	18	1992
DAS GLOCKENSPIEL SCHILLER	17	2001
DAT PLUTO SHERVINGTON	6	1976
DATE WITH THE NIGHT YEAH YEAH YEAH	16	2003
DAUGHTER PEARL JAM	18	1994
DAUGHTER OF DARKNESS TOM JONES	5	1970
DAVID GUSGUS	52	2003
DAVID WATTS JAM	25	1978
DAVID'S SONG (MAIN THEME FROM 'KIDNAPPED') VLADIMIR COSMA	64	1979
DAVY'S ON THE ROAD AGAIN MANFRED MANN'S EARTH BAND	6	1978
DAWN [A] FLINTLOCK	30	1976
DAWN [B] TONY DE VIT	56	2000
DAWN OF THE DEAD DOES IT OFFEND YOU, YEAH?	41	2008
DAY AFTER DAY [A] BADFINGER	10	1972
DAY AFTER DAY [B] PRETENDERS	45	1981
DAY AFTER DAY [C] JULIAN LENNON	66	1998
DAY & NIGHT BILLIE PIPER	1	2000
THE DAY BEFORE YESTERDAY'S MAN SUPERNATURALS	25	1997
THE DAY BEFORE YOU CAME ABBA	32	1982
THE DAY BEFORE YOU CAME BLANCMANGE	22	1984
DAY BY DAY [A] HOLLY SHERWOOD	29	1972
DAY BY DAY [B] SHAKATAK FEATURING AL JARREAU	53	1985
DAY BY DAY [C] SERAFIN	49	2003
THE DAY THE EARTH CAUGHT FIRE CITY BOY	67	1979
THE DAY I DIED JUST JACK	11	2009
THE DAY I FALL IN LOVE DOLLY PARTON & JAMES INGRAM	64	1994
THE DAY I MET MARIE CLIFF RICHARD	10	1967
THE DAY I TRIED TO LIVE SOUNDGARDEN	42	1994
DAY-IN DAY-OUT [A] DAVID BOWIE	17	1987
DAY IN DAY OUT [B] FEEDER	31	1999
A DAY IN THE LIFE [A] BLACK RIOT	68	1988
A DAY IN THE LIFE [B] LARRIKIN LOVE	31	2007
A DAY IN THE LIFE OF VINCE PRINCE RUSS ABBOT	61	1982
THE DAY IS ENDED PIPES & DRUMS & MILITARY BAND OF THE ROYAL SCOTS DRAGOON GUARDS	30	1972
THE DAY IT RAINED FOREVER AURORA	29	2002
DAY 'N' NITE KID CUDI VS CROOKERS	2	2009
THE DAY THE RAINS CAME JANE MORGAN	1	1958
THE DAY THAT CURLY BILLY SHOT DOWN CRAZY SAM MCGHEE HOLLIES	24	1973
THE DAY THAT NEVER COMES METALLICA	19	2008
DAY TIME 4 STRINGS	48	2000
DAY TRIP TO BANGOR (DIDN'T WE HAVE A LOVELY TIME) FIDDLER'S DRAM	3	1979
DAY TRIPPER BEATLES	1	1965
DAY TRIPPER OTIS REDDING	43	1967
THE DAY WE CAUGHT THE TRAIN OCEAN COLOUR SCENE	4	1996
THE DAY WE FIND LOVE 911	4	1997
THE DAY WILL COME QUAKE FEATURING MARCIA RAE	53	1998
A DAY WITHOUT LOVE LOVE AFFAIR	6	1968
THE DAY THE WORLD TURNED DAY-GLO X-RAY SPEX	23	1978
DAYDREAM [A] LOVIN' SPOONFUL	2	1966
DAYDREAM [A] RIGHT SAID FRED	29	1992
DAYDREAM [B] BACK TO THE PLANET	52	1993
DAYDREAM BELIEVER MONKEES	5	1967
DAYDREAM BELIEVER ANNE MURRAY	61	1980
DAYDREAM BELIEVER (CHEER UP PETER REID) SIMPLY RED & WHITE	41	1996
DAYDREAM IN BLUE I MONSTER	20	2001
DAYDREAMER [A] DAVID CASSIDY	1	1973
DAYDREAMER [B] MENSWEAR	14	1995
DAYDREAMIN' [A] TATYANA ALI	6	1998
DAYDREAMIN' [B] LUPE FIASCO FEATURING JILL SCOTT	25	2006
DAYDREAMING PENNY FORD	43	1993
DAYLIGHT KELLY ROWLAND FEATURING TRAVIS McCOY	14	2008
DAYLIGHT FADING COUNTING CROWS	54	1997
DAYLIGHT KATY GORDON LIGHTFOOT	41	1978
DAYS KINKS	12	1968
DAYS KIRSTY MacCOLL	12	1989
DAYS ARE O.K. MOTELS	41	1981
THE DAYS EP KINKS	35	1997
DAYS GO BY DIRTY VEGAS	16	2001
DAYS LIKE THESE BILLY BRAGG	43	1985
DAYS LIKE THIS [A] SHEENA EASTON	43	1989
DAYS LIKE THIS [B] VAN MORRISON	65	1995
DAYS LIKE THIS [C] SHAUN ESCOFFERY	53	2002
DAYS OF NO TRUST MAGNUM	32	1988
DAYS OF OUR LIVEZ BONE THUGS-N-HARMONY	37	1997
THE DAYS OF PEARLY SPENCER MARC ALMOND	4	1992
DAYS OF YOUTH LAURNEA	36	1997
DAYSLEEPER R.E.M.	6	1998
DAYTIME FRIENDS KENNY ROGERS	39	1977
DAYTONA DEMON SUZI QUATRO	14	1973
DAYZ LIKE THAT FIERCE	11	1999
DAZZ BRICK	36	1977
DAZZLE SIOUXSIE & THE BANSHEES	33	1984
DE DAH DAH (SPICE OF LIFE) KEITH MAC PROJECT	66	1994
DE DO DO DO, DE DA DA DA POLICE	5	1980
DE NIRO DISCO EVANGELISTS	59	1993
DEAD AND GONE TI FEATURING JUSTIN TIMBERLAKE	4	2009
DEAD A'S DJ HYPE	58	2001
DEAD BATTERY PITCHSHIFTER	71	2000
DEAD CITIES EXPLOITED	31	1981
DEAD END STREET KINKS	5	1966
DEAD FROM THE WAIST DOWN CATATONIA	7	1999
DEAD GIVEAWAY SHALAMAR	8	1983
THE DEAD HEART MIDNIGHT OIL	62	1988
DEAD HUSBAND DEEJAY PUNK-ROC	71	1998
DEAD IN HOLLYWOOD MURDERDOLLS	54	2002
DEAD LEAVES AND THE DIRTY GROUND WHITE STRIPES	25	2002
DEAD MAN WALKING DAVID BOWIE	32	1997
DEAD OR ALIVE LONNIE DONEGAN	7	1956
DEAD POP STARS ALTERED IMAGES	67	1981
DEAD RINGER FOR LOVE MEAT LOAF	5	1981
DEAD STAR MUSE	13	2002
DEADLIER THAN THE MALE WALKER BROTHERS	32	1966
DEADLINE DUTCH FORCE	35	2000
DEADLINE USA SHALAMAR	52	1984
DEADWEIGHT BECK	23	1997
DEADWOOD DIRTY PRETTY THINGS	20	2006
DEAF FOREVER MOTORHEAD	67	1986
THE DEAL PAT CAMPBELL	31	1969
THE DEAN AND I 10 C.C.	10	1973
DEAR ADDY KID CREOLE & THE COCONUTS	29	1982
DEAR BOOPSIE PAM HALL	54	1986
DEAR DELILAH GRAPEFRUIT	21	1968
DEAR ELAINE ROY WOOD	18	1973
DEAR GOD MIDGE URE	55	1988
DEAR JESSIE MADONNA	5	1989
DEAR JESSIE ROLLERGIRL	22	2000
DEAR JOHN [A] STATUS QUO	10	1982
DEAR JOHN [B] EDDI READER	48	1994
DEAR LIE TLC	31	1999
DEAR LONELY HEARTS NAT 'KING' COLE	37	1962
DEAR MAMA 2PAC	27	1999
DEAR MISS LONELY HEARTS PHILIP LYNOTT	32	1980
DEAR MRS. APPLEBEE DAVID GARRICK	22	1966
DEAR PRUDENCE SIOUXSIE & THE BANSHEES	3	1983
DEATH WHITE LIES	52	2008
DEATH DISCO (PARTS 1 & 2) PUBLIC IMAGE LTD	20	1979
DEATH OF A CLOWN DAVE DAVIES	3	1967
DEBASER PIXIES	23	1997
DEBORA TYRANNOSAURUS REX	7	1968
A DECADE UNDER THE INFLUENCE TAKING BACK SUNDAY	70	2004
DECADENCE DANCE EXTREME	36	1991
DECADENT & DESPERATE MORTIIS	49	2005
THE DECEIVER ALARM	51	1984
DECEMBER ALL ABOUT EVE	34	1989
DECEMBER BRINGS ME BACK TO YOU ANDY ABRAHAM & MICHAEL UNDERWOOD	18	2006
DECEMBER '63 (OH WHAT A NIGHT) FOUR SEASONS	1	1976
DECEMBER SONG (I DREAMED OF CHRISTMAS) GEORGE MICHAEL	14	2009
DECEMBER WILL BE MAGIC AGAIN KATE BUSH	29	1980
DECENT DAYS AND NIGHTS FUTUREHEADS	26	2004
DECEPTION FERGIE	47	2000
THE DECISION YOUNG KNIVES	60	2006
DECK OF CARDS WINK MARTINDALE	5	1959
DECK OF CARDS MAX BYGRAVES	13	1973
DECLARATION OF WAR HADOUKEN	66	2008
DECODE PARAMORE	52	2008
DEDICATED FOLLOWER OF FASHION KINKS	4	1966
DEDICATED TO THE ONE I LOVE MAMAS & THE PAPAS	2	1967
DEDICATED TO THE ONE I LOVE BITTY McLEAN	6	1994
DEDICATION THIN LIZZY	35	1991
DEEE-LITE THEME DEEE-LITE	25	1990
DEEP EAST 17	5	1993
THE DEEP GLOBAL COMMUNICATION	51	1997
DEEP AND MEANINGLESS ROOSTER	29	2005
DEEP AND WIDE AND TALL AZTEC CAMERA	55	1988
DEEP DEEP DOWN HEPBURN	16	2000
DEEP DEEP TROUBLE SIMPSONS FEATURING BART & HOMER	7	1991
DEEP DOWN AND DIRTY STEREO MC'S	17	2001
DEEP FEELING MIKE SAGAR	44	1960
DEEP FOREST DEEP FOREST	20	1994
DEEP HEAT '89 VARIOUS ARTISTS (MONTAGES)	12	1989
DEEP (I'M FALLING DEEPER) ARIEL	47	1997
DEEP IN MY HEART CLUBHOUSE	55	1991
DEEP IN THE HEART OF TEXAS DUANE EDDY	19	1962
DEEP IN YOU LIVIN' JOY	17	1997
DEEP INSIDE MARY J BLIGE	42	1999
DEEP MENACE (SPANK) D'MENACE	20	1998
DEEP PURPLE BILLY WARD	30	1957
DEEP PURPLE NINO TEMPO & APRIL STEVENS	17	1963
DEEP PURPLE DONNY & MARIE OSMOND	25	1976
DEEP RIVER WOMAN LIONEL RICHIE	17	1986
DEEP SEA AQUANUTS	75	2002
DEEP SHAG LUSCIOUS JACKSON	69	1995
DEEPER [A] ESCRIMA	27	1995
DEEPER [B] DELIRIOUS?	20	1997
DEEPER [C] SERIOUS DANGER	40	1997
DEEPER AND DEEPER [A] FREDA PAYNE	33	1970
DEEPER AND DEEPER [B] MADONNA	6	1992

Title / Artist	Peak Position	Year of Release
A DEEPER LOVE [A] CLIVILLES & COLE	15	1992
A DEEPER LOVE [A] ARETHA FRANKLIN	5	1994
DEEPER LOVE [A] RUFF DRIVERZ	19	1998
DEEPER LOVE (SYMPHONIC PARADISE) [B] BBE	19	1998
DEEPER SHADE OF BLUE STEPS	4	2000
DEEPER THAN THE NIGHT OLIVIA NEWTON-JOHN	64	1979
THE DEEPER THE LOVE WHITESNAKE	35	1990
DEEPER UNDERGROUND JAMIROQUAI	1	1998
DEEPEST BLUE DEEPEST BLUE	7	2003
DEEPLY DIPPY RIGHT SAID FRED	1	1992
DEF CON ONE POP WILL EAT ITSELF	63	1988
DEFINITE DOOR POSIES	67	1994
DEFINITION OF HOUSE MINIMAL FUNK	63	2002
DEFYING GRAVITY KRISTIN	60	2008
DEFYING GRAVITY GLEE CAST	38	2010
DÉJÀ VU [A] E-SMOOVE FEATURING LATANZA WATERS	63	1998
DÉJÀ VU [B] BEYONCE FEATURING JAY-Z	1	2006
DEJA VU (UPTOWN BABY) LORD TARIQ & PETER GUNZ	21	1998
DELAWARE PERRY COMO	3	1960
DELICATE TERENCE TRENT D'ARBY FEATURING DES'REE	14	1993
DELICIOUS [A] SLEEPER	75	1994
DELICIOUS [B] SHAMPOO	21	1995
DELICIOUS [C] CATHERINE WHEEL	53	1997
DELICIOUS [D] DENI HINES FEATURING DON-E	52	1998
DELICIOUS [E] KULAY	73	1998
DELICIOUS [F] PURE SUGAR	70	1998
DELILAH TOM JONES	2	1968
DELILAH SENSATIONAL ALEX HARVEY BAND	7	1975
DELILAH JONES McGUIRE SISTERS	24	1956
DELIVER ME SISTER BLISS FEATURING JOHN MARTYN	31	2001
DELIVERANCE [A] MISSION	27	1990
DELIVERANCE [B] BUBBA SPARXXX	55	2004
DELIVERING THE GOODS SKID ROW	22	1992
DELIVERY BABYSHAMBLES	6	2007
DELLA AND THE DEALER HOYT AXTON	48	1980
DELTA LADY JOE COCKER	10	1969
DELTA SUN BOTTLENECK STOMP MERCURY REV	26	1999
DEM GIRLZ (I DON'T KNOW WHY) OXIDE & NEUTRINO FEATURING KOWDEAN	10	2002
DEMOCRACY KILLING JOKE	39	1996
DEMOLITION MAN STING	21	1993
DEMONS [A] SUPER FURRY ANIMALS	27	1997
DEMONS [B] FATBOY SLIM FEATURING MACY GRAY	16	2001
DEMONS [C] BRIAN McFADDEN	28	2005
DENIAL SUGABABES	15	2008
THE DENIAL TWIST WHITE STRIPES	10	2005
DENIS BLONDIE	2	1978
DENISE FOUNTAINS OF WAYNE	57	1999
DER KOMMISSAR AFTER THE FIRE	47	1983
DER SCHIEBER TIMO MAAS	50	2000
DESAFINADO STAN GETZ & CHARLIE BYRD	11	1962
DESAFINADO ELLA FITZGERALD	38	1962
DESECRATION SMILE RED HOT CHILI PEPPERS	27	2007
DESERT DROUGHT CAST	45	2001
DESERT SONG STING FEATURING CHEB MAMI	15	2000
DESIDERATA LES CRANE	7	1972
A DESIGN FOR LIFE MANIC STREET PREACHERS	2	1996
DESIRE [A] U2	1	1988
DESIRE [B] NU COLOURS	31	1996
DESIRE [C] BBE	19	1998
DESIRE [D] DJ ERIC	67	2000
DESIRE [E] ULTRA NATE	40	2000
DESIRE [F] GERI HALLIWELL	22	2005
DESIRE LINES LUSH	60	1994
DESIRE ME DOLL	28	1979
DESIREE NEIL DIAMOND	39	1977
DESOLATION ROW MY CHEMICAL ROMANCE	52	2009
DESPERATE BUT NOT SERIOUS ADAM ANT	33	1982
DESPERATE DAN LIEUTENANT PIGEON	17	1972
THE DESPERATE HOURS MARC ALMOND	45	1990
DESTINATION DT8 FEATURING ROXANNE WILDE	23	2003
DESTINATION CALABRIA ALEX GAUDINO FEATURING CRYSTAL WATERS	4	2007
DESTINATION ESCHATON SHAMEN	15	1995
DESTINATION SUNSHINE BALEARIC BILL	36	1999
DESTINATION VENUS REZILLOS	43	1978
DESTINATION ZULULAND KING KURT	36	1983
DESTINY [A] ANNE MURRAY	41	1972
DESTINY [B] CANDI STATON	41	1976
DESTINY [C] JACKSONS	39	1979
DESTINY [C] N-TRANCE	37	2003
DESTINY [D] BABY D	69	1993
DESTINY [E] KENNY THOMAS	59	1994
DESTINY [F] DEM 2	58	1998
DESTINY [G] ZERO 7 FEATURING SIA & SOPHIE	30	2001
DESTINY CALLING JAMES	17	1998
DESTROY EVERYTHING YOU TOUCH LADYTRON	42	2005
DESTROY ROCK AND ROLL MYLO	15	2005
DETROIT WHITEOUT	73	1994
DETROIT CITY TOM JONES	8	1967
DEUS SUGARCUBES	51	1988
DEUTSCHER GIRLS ADAM & THE ANTS	13	1982
DEVIL [A] 666	18	2000
DEVIL [B] STEREOPHONICS	11	2005
DEVIL GATE DRIVE SUZI QUATRO	1	1974
DEVIL IN A MIDNIGHT MASS BILLY TALENT	66	2006
DEVIL IN YOUR SHOES (WALKING ALL OVER) SHED SEVEN	37	1998
DEVIL INSIDE INXS	47	1988
THE DEVIL MADE ME DO IT THUNDER	40	2006
DEVIL OR ANGEL BILLY FURY	58	1982
THE DEVIL WENT DOWN TO GEORGIA CHARLIE DANIELS BAND	14	1979
DEVIL WOMAN [A] MARTY ROBBINS	5	1962
DEVIL WOMAN [B] CLIFF RICHARD	9	1976
THE DEVIL YOU KNOW JESUS JONES	10	1993
THE DEVIL'S ANSWER ATOMIC ROOSTER	4	1971
DEVIL'S BALL DOUBLE	71	1987
THE DEVIL'S BEAT SANDI THOM	58	2008
DEVIL'S GUN CJ & CO	43	1977
DEVILS HAIRCUT BECK	22	1996
DEVIL'S NIGHTMARE OXIDE & NEUTRINO	16	2001
DEVIL'S THRILL VANESSA-MAE	53	1998
DEVIL'S TOY ALMIGHTY	36	1991
DEVOTED TO YOU CACIQUE	69	1985
DEVOTION [A] TEN CITY	29	1989
DEVOTION [B] KICKING BACK WITH TAXMAN	47	1990
DEVOTION [C] DAVE HOLMES	66	2001
DIABLA FUNK D'VOID	70	2001
DIABLO GRID	32	1995
DIAL MY HEART BOYS	61	1988
DIAMANTE ZUCCHERO WITH RANDY CRAWFORD	44	1992
DIAMOND BACK MEKKA	67	2001
DIAMOND DEW GORKY'S ZYGOTIC MYNCI	42	1997
DIAMOND DOGS DAVID BOWIE	21	1974
DIAMOND GIRL PETE WYLIE	57	1986
DIAMOND LIFE LOUIE VEGA & JAY 'SINISTER' SEALEE STARRING JULIE McKNIGHT	52	2002
DIAMOND LIGHTS GLENN & CHRIS	12	1987
DIAMOND RINGS CHIPMUNK FEATURING EMELI SANDE	6	2009
DIAMOND SMILES BOOMTOWN RATS	13	1979
DIAMONDS [A] JET HARRIS & TONY MEEHAN	1	1963
DIAMONDS [B] CHRIS REA	44	1979
DIAMONDS [C] HERB ALPERT	27	1987
DIAMONDS AND GUNS TRANSPLANTS	27	2003
DIAMONDS AND PEARLS PRINCE & THE NEW POWER GENERATION	25	1991
DIAMONDS ARE FOREVER SHIRLEY BASSEY	38	1972
DIAMONDS ARE FOREVER DAVID McALMONT & DAVID ARNOLD	39	1997
DIAMONDS FROM SIERRA LEONE KANYE WEST	8	2005
DIAMONDS IN THE DARK EP MYSTERY JETS	47	2006
DIANA PAUL ANKA	1	1957
DIANE [A] BACHELORS	1	1964
DIANE [B] THERAPY?	26	1995
DIARY OF A WIMP SPACE	49	2000
THE DIARY OF HORACE WIMP ELECTRIC LIGHT ORCHESTRA	8	1979
DICK-A-DUM-DUM (KING'S ROAD) DES O'CONNOR	14	1969
DID I DREAM (SONG TO THE SIREN) LOST WITNESS	28	2002
DID I TELL YOU SPINTO BAND	55	2006
DID IT AGAIN [A] KYLIE MINOGUE	14	1997
DID IT AGAIN [B] SHAKIRA	26	2009
DID MY TIME KORN	15	2003
DID YOU EVER NANCY SINATRA & LEE HAZLEWOOD	2	1971
DID YOU EVER REALLY LOVE ME NICKI FRENCH	55	1995
DID YOU EVER THINK R KELLY	20	1999
DID YOU HAVE TO LOVE ME LIKE YOU DID COCONUTS	60	1983
DID YOU SEE ME COMING PET SHOP BOYS	21	2009
DIDDY P DIDDY FEATURING THE NEPTUNES	19	2002
DIDN'T I BLOW YOUR MIND NEW KIDS ON THE BLOCK	8	1990
DIDN'T I (BLOW YOUR MIND THIS TIME) DELFONICS	22	1971
DIDN'T I TELL YOU TRUE THOMAS JULES-STOCK	59	1998
DIDN'T WE ALMOST HAVE IT ALL WHITNEY HOUSTON	14	1987
DIE ANOTHER DAY MADONNA	3	2002
DIE LAUGHING THERAPY?	29	1994
DIE YOUNG BLACK SABBATH	41	1980
DIFFERENCES GUYVER	72	2003
DIFFERENT AIR LIVING IN A BOX	57	1989
A DIFFERENT BEAT BOYZONE	1	1996
A DIFFERENT CORNER GEORGE MICHAEL	1	1986
DIFFERENT STORY BOWA FEATURING MALA	64	1991
DIFFERENT STROKES ISOTONIK	12	1992
DIFFERENT TIME DIFFERENT PLACE JULIA FORDHAM	41	1994
DIFFERENT WORLD IRON MAIDEN	3	2007
DIG FOR FIRE PIXIES	62	1990
DIG, LAZARUS, DIG NICK CAVE & THE BAD SEEDS	66	2008
DIGERIDOO APHEX TWIN	55	1992
DIGGI LOO-DIGGI LEY HERREYS	46	1984
DIGGIN' MY POTATOES HEINZ & THE WILD BOYS	49	1965
DIGGIN' ON YOU TLC	18	1995
DIGGING THE DIRT PETER GABRIEL	24	1992
DIGGING THE GRAVE FAITH NO MORE	16	1995
DIGGING YOUR SCENE BLOW MONKEYS	12	1986
DIGITAL GOLDIE FEATURING KRS ONE	13	1997
DIGITAL LOVE DAFT PUNK	14	2001
DIGNITY [A] DEACON BLUE	20	1988
DIGNITY [B] BOB DYLAN	33	1995

	Peak Position	Year of Release
DIL CHEEZ (MY HEART...) BALLY SAGOO	12	1996
DILEMMA NELLY FEATURING KELLY ROWLAND	1	2002
DIM ALL THE LIGHTS DONNA SUMMER	29	1979
DIME AND A DOLLAR GUY MITCHELL	8	1954
DIMENSION [A] SALT TANK	52	1999
DIMENSION [B] WOLFMOTHER	49	2006
DIMPLES JOHN LEE HOOKER	23	1964
DIN DA DA KEVIN AVIANCE	65	1998
DINAH BLACKNUSS	56	1997
DING DONG GEORGE HARRISON	38	1975
DING DONG SONG GUNTHER & THE SUNSHINE GIRLS	14	2004
DING-A-DONG TEACH-IN	13	1975
DINNER WITH DELORES ARTIST FORMERLY KNOWN AS PRINCE (AFKAP)	36	1996
DINNER WITH GERSHWIN DONNA SUMMER	13	1987
DINOSAUR ADVENTURE 3D UNDERWORLD	34	2003
DIP IT LOW CHRISTINA MILIAN	2	2004
DIPPETY DAY FATHER ABRAHAM & THE SMURFS	13	1978
DIRECT-ME REESE PROJECT	44	1995
DIRGE DEATH IN VEGAS	24	2000
DIRRTY CHRISTINA AGUILERA FEATURING REDMAN	1	2002
DIRT DEATH IN VEGAS	61	1997
DIRT OFF YOUR SHOULDER JAY-Z	12	2004
DIRTEE CASH DIZZEE RASCAL	10	2009
DIRTY BEATS RONI SIZE/REPRAZENT	32	2001
DIRTY CASH ADVENTURES OF STEVIE V	2	1990
DIRTY DAWG NKOTB	27	1994
DIRTY DEEDS JOAN JETT	69	1990
DIRTY DEEDS DONE DIRT CHEAP AC/DC	47	1993
DIRTY DIANA MICHAEL JACKSON	4	1988
DIRTY FUNK STEVE APPLETON	67	2009
DIRTY HARRY GORILLAZ	6	2005
DIRTY HARRY'S REVENGE ADAM F FEATURING BEENIE MAN	50	2002
DIRTY LAUNDRY DON HENLEY	59	1983
DIRTY LITTLE SECRET ALL-AMERICAN REJECTS	18	2006
DIRTY LOOKS DIANA ROSS	49	1987
DIRTY LOVE THUNDER	32	1990
DIRTY MIND [A] SHAKESPEAR'S SISTER	71	1990
DIRTY MIND [B] PIPETTES	63	2005
DIRTY MONEY DEE FREDRIX	74	1993
DIRTY MOTHA QWILO & FELIX DA HOUSECAT	66	1997
DIRTY OLD TOWN POGUES	62	1985
DIRTY OLD TOWN BHOYS FROM PARADISE	46	2004
DIRTY STICKY FLOORS DAVE GAHAN	18	2003
DIRTY WATER MADE IN LONDON	15	2000
DISAPPEAR INXS	21	1990
DISAPPEARING ACT SHALAMAR	18	1983
DISAPPOINTED [A] PUBLIC IMAGE LTD	38	1989
DISAPPOINTED [B] ELECTRONIC	6	1992
THE DISAPPOINTED [C] XTC	33	1992
DISARM SMASHING PUMPKINS	11	1994
DISCIPLINE OF LOVE ROBERT PALMER	68	1986
D.I.S.C.O. OTTAWAN	2	1980
D.I.S.C.O. N-TRANCE	11	1997
DISCO JO JINGLES	44	2005
DISCO CHICO	24	2006
DISCO 2000 PULP	7	1995
DISCO BABES FROM OUTER SPACE BABE INSTINCT	21	1999
DISCO BEATLEMANIA DBM	45	1977
DISCO CONNECTION ISAAC HAYES MOVEMENT	10	1976
DISCO COP BLUE ADONIS FEATURING LIL' MISS MAX	27	1998
DISCO DOWN [A] SHED SEVEN	13	1999
DISCO DOWN [B] HOUSE OF GLASS	72	2001
DISCO DUCK (PART ONE) RICK DEES & HIS CAST OF IDIOTS	6	1976
DISCO INFERNO TRAMMPS	16	1977
DISCO INFERNO TINA TURNER	12	1993
DISCO INFILTRATOR LCD SOUNDSYSTEM	49	2005
DISCO' LA PASSIONE CHRIS REA & SHIRLEY BASSEY	41	1996
DISCO LADY JOHNNIE TAYLOR	25	1976
DISCO MACHINE GUN LO FIDELITY ALLSTARS	50	1997
DISCO MUSIC (I LIKE IT) J.A.L.N. BAND	21	1976
DISCO NIGHTS (ROCK FREAK) GQ	42	1979
DISCO QUEEN HOT CHOCOLATE	11	1975
DISCO SCIENCE MIRWAIS	68	2000
DISCO STOMP HAMILTON BOHANNON	6	1975
DISCOBUG '97 FREAKYMAN	68	1997
DISCOHOPPING KLUBBHEADS	35	1997
DISCOLAND FLIP & FILL FEATURING KAREN PARRY	11	2004
DISCOLIGHTS ULTRABEAT VERSUS DARREN STYLES	23	2008
DISCONNECTED ROLLINS BAND	27	1994
DISCO'S REVENGE GUSTO	9	1996
DISCOTHEQUE U2	1	1997
DISCRETION GROVE STEPHEN MALKMUS	60	2001
DISEASE MATCHBOX 20	50	2003
DISENCHANTED COMMUNARDS	29	1986
DISILLUSION BADLY DRAWN BOY	26	2000
DIS-INFECTED EP THE THE	17	1994
DISPOSABLE TEENS MARILYN MANSON	12	2000
DISREMEMBRANCE DANNII	21	1998
DISSIDENT PEARL JAM	14	1994
THE DISTANCE CAKE	22	1997
DISTANT DRUMS JIM REEVES	1	1966
DISTANT STAR ANTHONY HOPKINS	75	1986
DISTANT SUN CROWDED HOUSE	19	1993
DISTORTION WILT	66	2002
DISTRACTIONS ZERO 7	45	2002
DISTURBIA RIHANNA	3	2008
DIVA [A] DANA INTERNATIONAL	11	1998
DIVA [B] BEYONCE	72	2009
DIVA LADY DIVINE COMEDY	52	2006
DIVE! DIVE! DIVE! BRUCE DICKINSON	45	1990
DIVE IN CATCH	44	1998
DIVE TO PARADISE EUROGROOVE	31	1995
DIVEBOMB NUMBER ONE CUP	61	1996
DIVINE EMOTIONS NARADA	8	1988
DIVINE HAMMER BREEDERS	59	1993
DIVINE THING SOUP DRAGONS	53	1992
DIVING 4 STRINGS	38	2002
DIVING FACES LIQUID CHILD	25	1999
D.I.V.O.R.C.E. BILLY CONNOLLY	1	1975
D.I.V.O.R.C.E. TAMMY WYNETTE	12	1975
DIXIE-NARCO EP PRIMAL SCREAM	11	1992
DIZZY TOMMY ROE	1	1969
DIZZY VIC REEVES & THE WONDER STUFF	1	1991
D.J. [A] DAVID BOWIE	29	1979
DJ [B] RESONANCE FEATURING THE BURRELLS	67	2001
DJ [C] H & CLAIRE	3	2002
DJ [D] JAMELIA	9	2004
DJ CULTURE PET SHOP BOYS	13	1991
DJ DJ TRANSPLANTS	49	2003
DJ NATION NUKLEUZ DJ'S	40	2002
DJ NATION – HARDER EDITION NUKLEUZ DJs	48	2003
DJ SPINNIN' PUNK CHIC	69	2001
DJS FANS AND FREAKS BLANK & JONES	45	2002
DJS TAKE CONTROL SL2	11	1991
DK 50-80 OTWAY & BARRETT	45	1980
DO AND DON'T FOR LOVE KIOKI	66	2002
DO ANYTHING NATURAL SELECTION	69	1991
DO ANYTHING YOU WANT TO THIN LIZZY	14	1979
DO ANYTHING YOU WANT TO DO RODS	9	1977
DO EVERYTHING I TAUGHT YOU ALTERKICKS	71	2005
DO FOR LOVE 2PAC FEATURING ERIC WILLIAMS	12	1998
DO FRIES GO WITH THAT SHAKE GEORGE CLINTON	57	1986
DO I GIFTED	60	1997
DO I DO STEVIE WONDER	10	1982
DO I HAVE TO SAY THE WORDS BRYAN ADAMS	30	1992
DO I LOVE YOU RONETTES	35	1964
DO I QUALIFY? LYNDEN DAVID HALL	26	1998
DO IT [A] TONY DI BART	21	1994
DO IT [B] NELLY FURTADO	75	2007
DO IT AGAIN CHEMICAL BROTHERS	12	2007
DO IT AGAIN [A] BEACH BOYS	1	1968
DO IT AGAIN [B] STEELY DAN	39	1975
DO IT AGAIN [C] COOKIE	52	2005
DO IT AGAIN-BILLIE JEAN (MEDLEY) CLUBHOUSE	11	1983
DO IT ALL OVER AGAIN SPIRITUALIZED	31	2002
DO IT ANY WAY YOU WANNA PEOPLE'S CHOICE	36	1975
DO IT DO IT AGAIN RAFFAELLA CARRA	9	1978
DO IT FOR LOVE [A] DANNI'ELLE GAHA	52	1993
DO IT FOR LOVE [B] SUBTERRANIA FEATURING ANN CONSUELO	68	1993
DO IT FOR LOVE [C] 4MANDU	45	1996
DO IT LIKE YOU LIKE STANDS	28	2005
DO IT NOW BRAINBASHERS	64	2000
DO IT PROPERLY ('NO WAY BACK')/NO WAY BACK ADONIS FEATURING 2 PUERTO RICANS, A BLACK MAN & A DOMINICAN	47	1987
DO IT TO IT CHERISH FEATURING SEAN PAUL	30	2006
DO IT TO ME LIONEL RICHIE	33	1992
DO IT TO ME AGAIN SOULSEARCHER	32	2000
DO IT TO THE CROWD TWIN HYPE	65	1989
DO IT TO THE MUSIC RAW SILK	18	1982
DO IT 2 ME CUSHH	31	2007
DO IT WELL JENNIFER LOPEZ	11	2007
DO IT WITH MADONNA ANDROIDS	15	2003
DO IT YOURSELF (GO OUT AND GET IT) UNITING NATIONS	64	2007
DO ME BELL BIV DEVOE	56	1990
DO ME RIGHT INNER CITY	47	1996
DO ME WRONG MEL BLATT	18	2003
DO MY THING BUSTA RHYMES	39	1997
DO NO WRONG THIRTEEN SENSES	38	2004
DO NOT DISTURB BANANARAMA	31	1985
DO NOT PASS ME BY HAMMER	14	1992
DO NOTHING SPECIALS	4	1980
DO OR DIE SUPER FURRY ANIMALS	20	2000
DO RE ME SO FAR SO GOOD CARTER-THE UNSTOPPABLE SEX MACHINE	22	1992
DO SOMETHING [A] MACY GRAY	51	1999
DO SOMETHIN' [B] BRITNEY SPEARS	6	2005
DO THAT THANG MASAI	42	2003
DO THAT TO ME LISA MARIE EXPERIENCE	33	1996
DO THAT TO ME ONE MORE TIME CAPTAIN & TENNILLE	7	1980
DO THE BARTMAN SIMPSONS	1	1991
DO THE BIRD VERNONS GIRLS	44	1963
DO THE BIRD DEE DEE SHARP	46	1963
DO THE CAN CAN SKANDI GIRLS	38	2005
DO THE CLAM ELVIS PRESLEY	19	1965
DO THE CONGA BLACK LACE	10	1984
DO THE FUNKY CHICKEN RUFUS THOMAS	18	1970
(DO) THE HUCKLEBUCK COAST TO COAST	5	1981
DO THE LOLLIPOP TWEENIES	17	2001
DO THE RIGHT THING [A] REDHEAD KINGPIN & THE FBI	13	1989
DO THE RIGHT THING [B] IAN WRIGHT	43	1993
(DO THE) SPANISH HUSTLE FATBACK BAND	10	1976
DO THEY KNOW IT'S CHRISTMAS? BAND AID	1	1984

Title / Artist	Peak Position	Year of Release
DO THEY KNOW IT'S CHRISTMAS? BAND AID II	1	1989
DO THEY KNOW IT'S CHRISTMAS? BAND AID 20	1	2004
DO THIS! DO THAT! FREEFALLER	8	2005
DO THIS MY WAY KID 'N' PLAY	48	1988
DO U FEEL 4 ME EDEN	51	1993
DO U KNOW WHERE YOU'RE COMING FROM M-BEAT FEATURING JAMIROQUAI	12	1996
DO U STILL? EAST 17	7	1996
DO U WANNA FUNK SPACE 2000	50	1995
DO WAH DIDDY DJ OTZI	9	2001
DO WAH DIDDY DIDDY MANFRED MANN	1	1964
DO WAH DIDDY DIDDY BLUE MELONS	70	1996
DO WATCHA DO HYPER GO GO & ADEVA	54	1996
DO WE ROCK POINT BREAK	29	1999
DO WHAT WE WOULD ACZESS	65	2001
DO WHAT YOU DO [A] JERMAINE JACKSON	6	1985
DO WHAT YOU DO [B] ANNABELLA LWIN	61	1995
DO WHAT YOU DO (EARWORM SONG) CLINT BOON EXPERIENCE	63	2000
DO WHAT YOU DO WELL NED MILLER	48	1965
DO WHAT YOU FEEL [A] JOEY NEGRO	36	1991
DO WHAT YOU FEEL [B] JOHNNA	43	1996
DO WHAT YOU GOTTA DO NINA SIMONE	2	1968
DO WHAT YOU GOTTA DO FOUR TOPS	11	1969
DO WHAT YOU WANNA DO T-CONNECTION	11	1977
DO WHAT'S GOOD FOR ME 2 UNLIMITED	16	1995
DO WITHOUT MY LOVE NATHAN	44	2007
DO YA [A] INNER CITY	44	1994
DO YA [B] McFLY	18	2008
DO YA DO YA (WANNA PLEASE ME) SAMANTHA FOX	10	1986
DO YA WANNA GET FUNKY WITH ME PETER BROWN	43	1978
DO YOU BELIEVE IN LOVE [A] HUEY LEWIS & THE NEWS	9	1986
DO YOU BELIEVE IN LOVE [B] UNATION	75	1993
DO YOU BELIEVE IN LOVE [C] ULTRA-SONIC	47	1996
DO YOU BELIEVE IN MIRACLES SLADE	54	1985
DO YOU BELIEVE IN SHAME DURAN DURAN	30	1989
DO YOU BELIEVE IN THE WESTWORLD THEATRE OF HATE	40	1982
DO YOU BELIEVE IN THE WONDER JEANIE TRACY	57	1994
DO YOU BELIEVE IN US JON SECADA	30	1992
DO YOU DREAM IN COLOUR? BILL NELSON	52	1980
DO YOU EVER THINK OF ME? ANTONY COSTA	19	2006
DO YOU FEEL LIKE I FEEL BELINDA CARLISLE	29	1991
DO YOU FEEL LIKE WE DO PETER FRAMPTON	39	1976
DO YOU FEEL ME? (...FREAK YOU) MEN OF VIZION	36	1999
DO YOU FEEL MY LOVE EDDY GRANT	8	1980
DO YOU KNOW [A] SECRET AFFAIR	57	1981
DO YOU KNOW [B] MICHELLE GAYLE	6	1997
DO YOU KNOW (I GO CRAZY) ANGEL CITY	8	2004
DO YOU KNOW (THE PING PONG SONG) ENRIQUE IGLESIAS	3	2007
DO YOU KNOW THE WAY TO SAN JOSE DIONNE WARWICK	8	1968
DO YOU KNOW (WHAT IT TAKES) ROBYN	26	1997
DO YOU LIKE IT KINGDOM COME	73	1989
DO YOU LOVE ME [A] BRIAN POOLE & THE TREMELOES	1	1963
DO YOU LOVE ME [A] DAVE CLARK FIVE	30	1963
DO YOU LOVE ME [A] DEEP FEELING	34	1970
DO YOU LOVE ME [A] DUKE BAYSEE	46	1995
DO YOU LOVE ME [A] MADEMOISELLE	56	2001
DO YOU LOVE ME [B] NICK CAVE & THE BAD SEEDS	68	1994
DO YOU LOVE ME BOY? KERRI-ANN	58	1998
DO YOU LOVE ME LIKE YOU SAY TERENCE TRENT D'ARBY	14	1993
DO YOU LOVE WHAT YOU FEEL INNER CITY	16	1989
DO YOU MIND [A] ANTHONY NEWLEY	1	1960
DO YOU MIND [B] KYLA	48	2009
DO YOU REALISE FLAMING LIPS	32	2002
DO YOU REALLY LIKE IT DJ PIED PIPER & THE MASTERS OF CEREMONIES	1	2001
(DO YOU REALLY LOVE ME) TELL ME LOVE MICHAEL WYCOFF	60	1983
DO YOU REALLY LOVE ME TOO BILLY FURY	13	1964
DO YOU REALLY WANT ME [A] JON SECADA	30	1993
DO YOU REALLY WANT ME [B] ROBYN	20	1998
DO YOU REALLY (WANT MY LOVE) JUNIOR	47	1985
DO YOU REALLY WANT TO HURT ME CULTURE CLUB	43	1982
DO YOU REMEMBER [A] SCAFFOLD	34	1968
DO YOU REMEMBER [B] JAY SEAN FEATURING SEAN PAUL & LIL JON	13	2010
DO YOU REMEMBER HOUSE BLAZE FEATURING PALMER BROWN	55	2002
DO YOU REMEMBER (LIVE) PHIL COLLINS	57	1990
DO YOU REMEMBER ROCK 'N' ROLL RADIO RAMONES	54	1980
DO YOU REMEMBER THE FIRST TIME PULP	33	1994
DO YOU SEE WARREN G	29	1995
DO YOU SEE THE LIGHT SNAP! VS PLAYTHING	14	2002
DO YOU SEE THE LIGHT (LOOKING FOR) SNAP! FEATURING NIKI HARIS	10	1993
DO YOU SLEEP? LISA LOEB & NINE STORIES	45	1995
DO YOU THINK ABOUT US TOTAL	49	1997
DO YOU THINK YOU'RE SPECIAL? NIO	52	2003
DO YOU UNDERSTAND ALMIGHTY	38	1996
DO YOU WANNA DANCE [A] CLIFF RICHARD & THE SHADOWS	2	1962
DO YOU WANNA DANCE [B] BARRY BLUE	7	1973
DO YOU WANNA FUNK SYLVESTER WITH PATRICK COWLEY	32	1982
DO YOU WANNA GET FUNKY C & C MUSIC FACTORY	27	1994
DO YOU WANNA GO OUR WAY??? PUBLIC ENEMY	66	1999
DO YOU WANNA HOLD ME? BOW WOW WOW	47	1983
DO YOU WANNA PARTY DJ SCOTT FEATURING LORNA B	36	1995
DO YOU WANNA TOUCH ME (OH YEAH!) GARY GLITTER	2	1973
DO YOU WANT IT RIGHT NOW DEGREES OF MOTION FEATURING BITI	26	1992
DO YOU WANT ME [A] SALT-N-PEPA	5	1991
DO YOU WANT ME [B] Q-TEX	48	1996
DO YOU WANT ME? [C] LEILANI	40	1999
DO YOU WANT ME TO FOUR PENNIES	47	1964
DO YOU WANT THE TRUTH OR SOMETHING BEAUTIFUL PALOMA FAITH	64	2010
DO YOU WANT TO FRANZ FERDINAND	4	2005
DO YOU WANT TO KNOW A SECRET? BILLY J KRAMER & THE DAKOTAS	2	1963
DO YOUR DANCE ROSE ROYCE	30	1977
DO YOUR THING BASEMENT JAXX	32	2005
DOA FOO FIGHTERS	25	2005
THE DOCTOR DOOBIE BROTHERS	73	1989
DR BEAT MIAMI SOUND MACHINE	6	1984
DOCTOR DOCTOR [A] UFO	35	1979
DOCTOR DOCTOR [B] THOMPSON TWINS	3	1984
DR FEELGOOD MOTLEY CRUE	50	1989
DR FINLAY ANDY STEWART	43	1965
DR GREENTHUMB CYPRESS HILL	34	1999
DR HECKYLL AND MR JIVE MEN AT WORK	31	1983
DR JACKYLL AND MISTER FUNK JACKIE McLEAN	53	1979
DOCTOR JEEP SISTERS OF MERCY	37	1990
DOCTOR JONES AQUA	1	1998
DR KISS KISS 5000 VOLTS	8	1976
DR LOVE TINA CHARLES	4	1976
DR MABUSE PROPAGANDA	27	1984
DOCTOR MY EYES JACKSON 5	9	1973
DOCTOR PRESSURE MYLO VS MIAMI SOUND MACHINE	3	2005
DR STEIN HELLOWEEN	57	1988
DR WHO MANKIND	25	1978
DOCTORIN' THE HOUSE COLDCUT FEATURING YAZZ & THE PLASTIC POPULATION	6	1988
DOCTORIN' THE TARDIS TIMELORDS	1	1988
DOCTOR'S ORDERS SUNNY	7	1974
DOES HE LOVE YOU REBA McENTIRE	62	1999
DOES IT FEEL GOOD B.T. EXPRESS	52	1980
DOES IT FEEL GOOD TO YOU DJ CARL COX	35	1992
DOES SHE HAVE A FRIEND GENE CHANDLER	28	1980
DOES THAT RING A BELL DYNASTY	53	1983
DOES THIS HURT BOO RADLEYS	67	1992
DOES THIS TRAIN STOP ON MERSEYSIDE AMSTERDAM	53	2005
DOES YOUR CHEWING GUM LOSE IT'S FLAVOUR LONNIE DONEGAN	3	1959
DOES YOUR HEART GO BOOM HELEN LOVE	71	1997
DOES YOUR MOTHER KNOW ABBA	4	1979
DOESN'T ANYBODY KNOW MY NAME? VINCE HILL	50	1969
DOESN'T MEAN ANYTHING ALICIA KEYS	8	2009
DOESN'T REALLY MATTER JANET JACKSON	5	2000
DOG DADA	71	1993
DOG DAYS ARE OVER FLORENCE + THE MACHINE	23	2010
DOG EAT DOG ADAM & THE ANTS	4	1980
DOG ON WHEELS BELLE & SEBASTIAN	59	1997
DOG TRAIN LEVELLERS	24	1997
DOGGY DOGG WORLD SNOOP DOGGY DOGG	32	1994
DOGMAN GO WOOF UNDERWORLD	63	1993
DOGMONAUT 2000 (IS THERE ANYONE OUT THERE) FRIGID VINEGAR	53	1999
DOGS WHO	25	1968
DOGS OF LUST THE THE	25	1993
DOGS OF WAR EXPLOITED	63	1981
DOGS WITH NO TAILS PALE	51	1992
DOGZ N SLEDGEZ MILLION DAN	66	2003
DOIN' IT [A] LL COOL J	15	1996
DOIN' IT [B] LIBERTY	14	2001
DOIN' IT IN A HAUNTED HOUSE YVONNE GAGE	45	1984
DOIN' OUR OWN DANG JUNGLE BROTHERS	33	1990
DOIN' OUR THING PHOEBE ONE	59	1998
DOIN' THE DO BETTY BOO	7	1990
DOING ALRIGHT WITH THE BOYS GARY GLITTER	6	1975
DOING IT RIGHT GO! TEAM	55	2007
DOLCE VITA RYAN PARIS	5	1983
DOLL HOUSE KING BROTHERS	21	1961
DOLL PARTS HOLE	16	1995
DOLLAR BILL SCREAMING TREES	52	1993
DOLLAR IN THE TEETH UPSETTERS	5	1969
DOLLARS CJ LEWIS	34	1994
DOLLARS IN THE HEAVENS GENEVA	59	1999
DOLLS PRIMAL SCREAM	40	2006
DOLLY MY LOVE MOMENTS	10	1975
DOLPHIN SHED SEVEN	28	1994
THE DOLPHINS CRY LIVE	62	2000
DOLPHINS MAKE ME CRY MARTYN JOSEPH	34	1992
DOLPHINS WERE MONKEYS IAN BROWN	5	2000
DOMINATION WAY OUT WEST	38	1996
DOMINATOR HUMAN RESOURCE	36	1991
DOMINION SISTERS OF MERCY	13	1988

	Peak Position	Year of Release
DOMINIQUE SINGING NUN	7	1963
DOMINO DANCING PET SHOP BOYS	7	1988
DOMINOES ROBBIE NEVIL	26	1987
DOMINOID MOLOKO	65	1996
DOMINOS BIG PINK	27	2009
THE DON 187 LOCKDOWN	29	1998
THE DON VIEW	33	2007
DON GARGON COMIN' PROJECT 1	64	1992
DON JUAN DAVE DEE, DOZY, BEAKY, MICK & TICH	23	1969
DON QUIXOTE NIK KERSHAW	10	1985
DONALD WHERE'S YOUR TROOSERS ANDY STEWART	4	1960
DONKEY CART FRANK CHACKSFIELD	26	1956
DONNA [A] MARTY WILDE	3	1959
DONNA [A] RITCHIE VALENS	29	1959
DONNA [B] 10 C.C.	2	1972
DON'T [A] ELVIS PRESLEY	2	1958
DON'T [B] SHANIA TWAIN	30	2005
DON'T ANSWER ME [A] CILLA BLACK	6	1966
DON'T ANSWER ME [B] ALAN PARSONS PROJECT	58	1984
DON'T ARGUE CABARET VOLTAIRE	69	1987
DON'T ASK ME PUBLIC IMAGE LTD	22	1990
DON'T ASK ME WHY EURYTHMICS	25	1989
DON'T BE A DUMMY JOHN DU CANN	33	1979
DON'T BE A FOOL LOOSE ENDS	13	1990
DON'T BE A STRANGER DINA CARROLL	3	1993
DON'T BE AFRAID AARON HALL	56	1992
DON'T BE AFRAID MOONMAN	41	1997
DON'T BE CRUEL [A] BILL BLACK'S COMBO	32	1960
DON'T BE CRUEL [A] BILLY SWAN	42	1975
DON'T BE CRUEL [A] ELVIS PRESLEY	24	1978
DON'T BE CRUEL [B] BOBBY BROWN	13	1988
DON'T BE STUPID (YOU KNOW I LOVE YOU) SHANIA TWAIN	5	2000
DON'T BELIEVE A WORD THIN LIZZY	12	1977
DON'T BELIEVE IN LOVE DIDO	54	2008
DON'T BELIEVE THE HYPE PUBLIC ENEMY	18	1988
DON'T BELIEVE THE HYPE MISTA E	41	1988
DON'T BET MONEY HONEY LINDA SCOTT	50	1961
DON'T BLAME IT ON LOVE SHAKATAK	55	1984
DON'T BLAME IT ON THAT GIRL MATT BIANCO	11	1988
DON'T BLAME ME EVERLY BROTHERS	20	1961
DON'T BLAME ME FRANK IFIELD	8	1964
DON'T BOTHER SHAKIRA	9	2006
DON'T BREAK MY HEART UB40	3	1985
DON'T BREAK MY HEART AGAIN WHITESNAKE	17	1981
DON'T BREAK THE HEART THAT LOVES YOU CONNIE FRANCIS	39	1962
DON'T BRING HARRY (EP) STRANGLERS	41	1979
DON'T BRING LULU DOROTHY PROVINE	17	1961
DON'T BRING ME DOWN [A] PRETTY THINGS	10	1964
DON'T BRING ME DOWN [B] ANIMALS	6	1966
DON'T BRING ME DOWN [C] ELECTRIC LIGHT ORCHESTRA	3	1979
DON'T BRING ME DOWN [D] SPIRITS	31	1994
DON'T BRING ME YOUR HEARTACHES PAUL & BARRY RYAN	13	1965
DON'T CALL ME BABY [A] VOICE OF THE BEEHIVE	15	1988
DON'T CALL ME BABY [B] MADISON AVENUE	1	1999
DON'T CALL THIS LOVE LEON JACKSON	3	2008
DON'T CARE [A] KLARK KENT	48	1978
DON'T CARE [B] ANGELS REVERSE	71	2002
DON'T CARE [C] RICKY MARTIN	11	2005
DON'T CARE WHO KNOWS KEISHA WHITE	29	2005
DON'T CHA PUSSYCAT DOLLS FEATURING BUSTA RHYMES	1	2005
DON'T CHA WANNA RIDE JOSS STONE	20	2005
DON'T COME AROUND HERE NO MORE TOM PETTY & THE HEARTBREAKERS	50	1985
DON'T COME CLOSE RAMONES	39	1978
DON'T COME HOME TOO SOON DEL AMITRI	15	1998
DON'T COME TO STAY HOT HOUSE	70	1987
DON'T CRY [A] ASIA	33	1983
DON'T CRY [B] BOY GEORGE	60	1988
DON'T CRY [C] GUNS N' ROSES	8	1991
DON'T CRY [D] SEAL	51	1995
DON'T CRY DADDY ELVIS PRESLEY	8	1970
DON'T CRY FOR ME ARGENTINA JULIE COVINGTON	1	1976
DON'T CRY FOR ME ARGENTINA SHADOWS	5	1979
DON'T CRY FOR ME ARGENTINA SINEAD O'CONNOR	53	1992
DON'T CRY FOR ME ARGENTINA MADONNA	3	1996
DON'T CRY FOR ME ARGENTINA MIKE FLOWERS POPS	30	1996
DON'T CRY OUT LOUD ELKIE BROOKS	12	1978
DON'T DANCE MIDAS	59	2007
DON'T DIE JUST YET DAVID HOLMES	33	1998
DON'T DO IT BABY MAC & KATIE KISSOON	9	1975
DON'T DO THAT [A] GEORDIE	32	1972
DON'T DO THAT [B] YOUNG & MOODY BAND	63	1981
DON'T DON'T TELL ME NO SOPHIE B HAWKINS	36	1994
DON'T DREAM DOVE	37	1999
DON'T DREAM IT'S OVER CROWDED HOUSE	25	1987
DON'T DREAM IT'S OVER PAUL YOUNG	20	1991
DON'T DRIVE DRUNK STEVIE WONDER	62	1984
DON'T DRIVE MY CAR STATUS QUO	11	1980
DON'T DROP BOMBS LIZA MINNELLI	46	1989
DON'T EVER CHANGE CRICKETS	5	1962
DON'T EVER THINK (TOO MUCH) ZUTONS	15	2004
DON'T FALL IN LOVE (I SAID) TOYAH	22	1985
DON'T FALTER MINT ROYALE FEATURING LAUREN LAVERNE	15	2000
(DON'T FEAR) THE REAPER BLUE OYSTER CULT	16	1978
(DON'T FEAR) THE REAPER APOLLO 440	35	1995
DON'T FIGHT IT WILSON PICKETT	29	1965
DON'T FIGHT IT FEEL IT PRIMAL SCREAM FEATURING DENISE JOHNSON	41	1991
DON'T FORBID ME PAT BOONE	2	1957
DON'T FORGET ABOUT US MARIAH CAREY	11	2005
DON'T FORGET ME (WHEN I'M GONE) GLASS TIGER	29	1986
DON'T FORGET TO CATCH ME CLIFF RICHARD	21	1968
DON'T FORGET TO DANCE KINKS	58	1983
DON'T FORGET TO REMEMBER BEE GEES	2	1968
DON'T GET ME WRONG PRETENDERS	10	1986
(DON'T) GIVE HATE A CHANCE JAMIROQUAI	27	2005
DON'T GIVE IT UP [A] SONIC SURFERS	54	1994
DON'T GIVE IT UP [B] LEMAR	21	2005
DON'T GIVE IT UP [C] SIOBHAN DONAGHY	45	2007
DON'T GIVE ME UP HAROLD MELVIN & THE BLUENOTES	59	1984
DON'T GIVE ME YOUR LIFE ALEX PARTY	2	1995
DON'T GIVE UP [A] PETER GABRIEL & KATE BUSH	9	1986
DON'T GIVE UP [B] MICHELLE WEEKS	28	1997
DON'T GIVE UP [C] CHICANE FEATURING BRYAN ADAMS	1	2000
DON'T GIVE UP [D] NOISETTES	73	2006
DON'T GIVE UP ON US DAVID SOUL	1	1976
DON'T GO [A] JUDAS PRIEST	51	1981
DON'T GO [B] YAZOO	3	1982
DON'T GO [B] LIZZY MACK	52	1995
DON'T GO [C] HOTHOUSE FLOWERS	11	1988
DON'T GO [D] AWESOME 3 FEATURING JULIE McDERMOTT	27	1992
DON'T GO [D] THIRD DIMENSION FEATURING JULIE McDERMOTT	34	1996
DON'T GO [E] DUALERS	61	2006
DON'T GO BREAKING MY HEART ELTON JOHN & KIKI DEE	1	1976
DON'T GO BREAKING MY HEART ELTON JOHN WITH RuPAUL	7	1994
DON'T GO MESSIN' WITH MY HEART MANTRONIX	22	1991
DON'T GO THERE GIGGS FEATURING B.o.B.	60	2010
DON'T HANG UP ORLONS	39	1963
DON'T HOLD BACK [A] CHANSON	33	1979
DON'T HOLD BACK [B] POTBELLEEZ	54	2008
DON'T HURT YOURSELF MARILLION	16	2004
DON'T IT MAKE MY BROWN EYES BLUE CRYSTAL GAYLE	5	1977
DON'T IT MAKE YOU FEEL GOOD STEFAN DENNIS	16	1989
DON'T JUMP OFF THE ROOF DAD TOMMY COOPER	40	1961
DON'T KILL IT CAROL MANFRED MANN'S EARTH BAND	45	1979
DON'T KILL THE WHALE YES	36	1978
DON'T KNOCK IT (UNTIL YOU TRY IT) BOBBY NUNN	65	1984
DON'T KNOCK THE ROCK BILL HALEY & HIS COMETS	7	1957
DON'T KNOW MUCH LINDA RONSTADT & AARON NEVILLE	2	1989
DON'T KNOW WHAT TO TELL YA AALIYAH	22	2003
DON'T KNOW WHAT YOU GOT (TILL IT'S GONE) CINDERELLA	54	1989
DON'T KNOW WHY NORAH JONES	59	2002
DON'T KNOW WHY I LOVE YOU STEVIE WONDER	14	1969
DON'T LAUGH WINX	38	1995
DON'T LAUGH AT ME NORMAN WISDOM	3	1954
DON'T LEAVE FAITHLESS	21	1996
DON'T LEAVE HOME DIDO	25	2004
DON'T LEAVE ME [A] BLACKSTREET	6	1997
DON'T LEAVE ME [B] MALANDRA BURROWS	54	1998
DON'T LEAVE ME BEHIND EVERYTHING BUT THE GIRL	72	1986
DON'T LEAVE ME THIS WAY HAROLD MELVIN & THE BLUENOTES	5	1977
DON'T LEAVE ME THIS WAY THELMA HOUSTON	13	1977
DON'T LEAVE ME THIS WAY COMMUNARDS WITH SARAH-JANE MORRIS	1	1986
DON'T LET 'EM GRIND YOU DOWN EXPLOITED & ANTI-PASTI	70	1981
DON'T LET GO [A] MANHATTAN TRANSFER	32	1977
DON'T LET GO [B] DAVID SNEDDON	3	2003
DON'T LET GO (LOVE) EN VOGUE	5	1997
DON'T LET GO THE COAT WHO	47	1981
DON'T LET HIM STEAL YOUR HEART AWAY PHIL COLLINS	45	1983
DON'T LET HIM TOUCH YOU ANGELETTES	35	1972
DON'T LET HIM WASTE YOUR TIME JARVIS COCKER	36	2007
DON'T LET IT DIE HURRICANE SMITH	2	1971
DON'T LET IT END STYX	56	1983
DON'T LET IT FADE AWAY DARTS	18	1978
DON'T LET IT GET YOU DOWN ECHO & THE BUNNYMEN	50	1997
DON'T LET IT GO TO WASTE MATT WILLIS	19	2006
DON'T LET IT GO TO YOUR HEAD BRAND NEW HEAVIES FEATURING N'DEA DAVENPORT	24	1992
DON'T LET IT PASS YOU BY UB40	16	1981
DON'T LET IT SHOW ON YOUR FACE ADEVA	34	1992
DON'T LET LOVE GET YOU DOWN ARCHIE BELL & THE DRELLS	49	1986

Title	Artist	Peak Position	Year of Release
DON'T LET ME BE MISUNDERSTOOD	ANIMALS	3	1965
DON'T LET ME BE MISUNDERSTOOD	SANTA ESMERALDA & LEROY GOMEZ	41	1977
DON'T LET ME BE MISUNDERSTOOD	COSTELLO SHOW FEATURING THE CONFEDERATES	33	1986
DON'T LET ME BE MISUNDERSTOOD	JOE COCKER	53	1996
DON'T LET ME BE THE LAST TO KNOW	BRITNEY SPEARS	12	2001
DON'T LET ME DOWN [A]	FARM	36	1991
DON'T LET ME DOWN [B]	WILL YOUNG	2	2002
DON'T LET ME DOWN GENTLY	WONDER STUFF	19	1989
DON'T LET ME GET ME	P!NK	6	2002
DON'T LET NOBODY HOLD YOU DOWN	LJ REYNOLDS	53	1984
DON'T LET THE FEELING GO	NIGHTCRAWLERS	13	1995
DON'T LET THE MORNING COME	SOUL AVENGERZ FEATURING JAVINE	49	2006
DON'T LET THE RAIN COME DOWN	RONNIE HILTON	21	1964
DON'T LET THE STARS GET IN YOUR EYES	PERRY COMO WITH THE RAMBLERS	1	1953
DON'T LET THE SUN CATCH YOU CRYING	GERRY & THE PACEMAKERS	6	1964
DON'T LET THE SUN GO DOWN ON ME	ELTON JOHN	16	1974
DON'T LET THE SUN GO DOWN ON ME	GEORGE MICHAEL & ELTON JOHN	1	1991
DON'T LET THE SUN GO DOWN ON ME	OLETA ADAMS	33	1991
DON'T LET THEM	ASHANTI	38	2005
DON'T LET THIS MOMENT END	GLORIA ESTEFAN	28	1999
DON'T LIE [A]	SINCLAIR	70	1994
DON'T LIE [B]	BLACK EYED PEAS	6	2005
DON'T LISTEN TO THE RADIO	VINES	66	2006
DON'T LOOK ANY FURTHER	DENNIS EDWARDS FEATURING SIEDAH GARRETT	45	1984
DON'T LOOK ANY FURTHER	KANE GANG	52	1988
DON'T LOOK ANY FURTHER	M PEOPLE	9	1993
DON'T LOOK AT ME THAT WAY	CHAKA KHAN	73	1993
DON'T LOOK BACK [A]	BOSTON	43	1978
DON'T LOOK BACK [B]	FINE YOUNG CANNIBALS	34	1989
DON'T LOOK BACK [C]	LLOYD COLE	59	1990
DON'T LOOK BACK [D]	LUCIE SILVAS	34	2005
DON'T LOOK BACK IN ANGER	OASIS	1	1996
DON'T LOOK BACK IN ANGER	WURZELS	59	2002
DON'T LOOK BACK INTO THE SUN	LIBERTINES	11	2003
DON'T LOOK DOWN [A]	PLANETS	16	1980
DON'T LOOK DOWN [B]	MICK RONSON WITH JOE ELLIOTT	55	1994
DON'T LOOK DOWN – THE SEQUEL	GO WEST	13	1985
DON'T LOSE THE MAGIC	SHAWN CHRISTOPHER	30	1992
DON'T LOSE YOUR TEMPER	XTC	32	1980
DON'T LOVE ME TOO HARD	NOLANS	14	1982
DON'T LOVE YOU NO MORE	CRAIG DAVID	4	2005
DON'T MAKE ME (FALL IN LOVE WITH YOU)	BABBITY BLUE	48	1965
DON'T MAKE ME OVER [A]	SWINGING BLUE JEANS	31	1966
DON'T MAKE ME OVER [B]	SYBIL	19	1989
DON'T MAKE ME WAIT [A]	PEECH BOYS	49	1982
DON'T MAKE ME WAIT [B]	BOMB THE BASS FEATURING LORRAINE	6	1988
DON'T MAKE ME WAIT [C]	LOVELAND FEATURING RACHEL McFARLANE	22	1995
DON'T MAKE ME WAIT [D]	911	10	1996
DON'T MAKE ME WAIT TOO LONG [A]	BARRY WHITE	17	1976
DON'T MAKE ME WAIT TOO LONG [B]	ROBERTA FLACK	44	1980
DON'T MAKE MY BABY BLUE	SHADOWS	10	1965
DON'T MAKE WAVES	NOLANS	12	1980
DON'T MARRY HER	BEAUTIFUL SOUTH	8	1996
DON'T MATTER	AKON	3	2007
DON'T MESS WITH DOCTOR DREAM	THOMPSON TWINS	15	1985
DON'T MESS WITH MY MAN [A]	LUCY PEARL	20	2000
DON'T MESS WITH MY MAN [B]	NIVEA FEATURING BRIAN & BRANDON CASEY	41	2002
DON'T MESS WITH MY MAN [C]	BOOTY LUV	11	2007
DON'T MESS WITH THE RADIO	NIVEA	75	2002
DON'T MISS THE PARTY LINE	BIZZ NIZZ	7	1990
DON'T MISTAKE ME	KEISHA WHITE	48	2006
DON'T MUG YOURSELF	STREETS	21	2002
DON'T NEED A GUN	BILLY IDOL	26	1987
DON'T NEED THE SUN TO SHINE (TO MAKE ME SMILE)	GABRIELLE	9	2001
DON'T PANIC	LIQUID GOLD	42	1981
DON'T PANIC	LOGO FEATURING DAWN JOSEPH	42	2001
DON'T PAY THE FERRYMAN	CHRIS DE BURGH	48	1982
DON'T PHUNK WITH MY HEART	BLACK EYED PEAS	3	2005
DON'T PLAY NICE	VERBALICIOUS	11	2005
DON'T PLAY THAT SONG	ARETHA FRANKLIN	13	1970
DON'T PLAY THAT SONG AGAIN	NICKI FRENCH	34	2000
DON'T PLAY WITH ME	ROZALLA	50	1993
DON'T PLAY YOUR ROCK 'N' ROLL TO ME	SMOKEY	8	1975
DON'T PULL YOUR LOVE	SEAN MAGUIRE	14	1996
DON'T PUSH IT	RUTH JOY	66	1989
DON'T PUSH IT, DON'T FORCE IT	LEON HAYWOOD	12	1980
DON'T PUT YOUR SPELL ON ME	IAN McNABB	72	1996
DON'T QUIT	CARON WHEELER	53	1991
DON'T RUSH (TAKE LOVE SLOWLY)	K-CI & JOJO	16	1998
DON'T SAY GOODBYE	PAULINA RUBIO	68	2002
DON'T SAY I TOLD YOU SO	TOURISTS	40	1980
DON'T SAY IT'S LOVE	JOHNNY HATES JAZZ	48	1988
DON'T SAY IT'S OVER	GUN	19	1994
DON'T SAY THAT'S JUST FOR WHITE BOYS	WAY OF THE WEST	54	1981
DON'T SAY YOU LOVE ME [A]	M2M	16	2000
DON'T SAY YOU LOVE ME [B]	ERASURE	15	2005
DON'T SAY YOUR LOVE IS KILLING ME	ERASURE	23	1997
DON'T SET ME FREE	RAY CHARLES	37	1963
DON'T SHED A TEAR	PAUL CARRACK	60	1989
DON'T SHOOT ME SANTA	KILLERS	34	2007
DON'T SING	PREFAB SPROUT	62	1984
DON'T SLEEP IN THE SUBWAY	PETULA CLARK	12	1967
DON'T SLOW DOWN	UB40	16	1981
DON'T SPEAK	NO DOUBT	1	1997
DON'T SPEAK	CLUELESS	61	1997
DON'T STAND SO CLOSE TO ME	POLICE	1	1980
DON'T STAND SO CLOSE TO ME	GLEE CAST	62	2010
DON'T STAY AWAY TOO LONG	PETERS & LEE	3	1974
DON'T STEAL OUR SUN	THRILLS	45	2003
DON'T STOP [A]	FLEETWOOD MAC	32	1977
DON'T STOP [A]	STATUS QUO	35	1996
DON'T STOP [B]	K.I.D.	49	1981
DON'T STOP [C]	MOOD	59	1982
DON'T STOP [D]	JEFFREY OSBORNE	61	1984
DON'T STOP [E]	K-KLASS	32	1992
DON'T STOP [F]	HAMMER	72	1994
DON'T STOP [G]	RUFF DRIVERZ	30	1998
DON'T STOP [H]	NO AUTHORITY	54	1998
DON'T STOP [I]	ATB	3	1999
DON'T STOP [J]	ROLLING STONES	36	2002
DON'T STOP BELIEVIN'	JOURNEY	6	1982
DON'T STOP BELIEVIN'	GLEE CAST	2	2009
DON'T STOP FUNKIN' 4 JAMAICA	MARIAH CAREY	32	2002
DON'T STOP IT NOW	HOT CHOCOLATE	11	1976
DON'T STOP (JAMMIN')	L.A. MIX	47	1987
DON'T STOP LOVIN' ME BABY	PINKERTON'S ASSORTED COLOURS	50	1966
DON'T STOP ME NOW [A]	QUEEN	9	1979
DON'T STOP ME NOW [B]	McFLY	1	2006
DON'T STOP MOVIN' [A]	LIVIN' JOY	5	1996
DON'T STOP MOVIN' [B]	S CLUB 7	1	2001
DON'T STOP NOW [A]	GENE FARROW & GF BAND	71	1978
DON'T STOP NOW [B]	CROWDED HOUSE	41	2007
DON'T STOP THAT CRAZY RHYTHM	MODERN ROMANCE	14	1983
DON'T STOP THE CARNIVAL	ALAN PRICE SET	13	1968
DON'T STOP THE DANCE	BRYAN FERRY	21	1985
DON'T STOP THE FEELING	ROY AYERS	56	1980
DON'T STOP THE MUSIC [A]	YARBOROUGH & PEOPLES	7	1981
DON'T STOP THE MUSIC [B]	LIONEL RICHIE	34	2000
DON'T STOP THE MUSIC [C]	RIHANNA	4	2007
DON'T STOP THE ROCK	FREESTYLE	73	2009
DON'T STOP 'TIL YOU GET ENOUGH	MICHAEL JACKSON	3	1979
DON'T STOP TWIST	FRANKIE VAUGHAN	22	1962
DON'T STOP (WIGGLE WIGGLE)	OUTHERE BROTHERS	1	1995
DON'T TAKE AWAY THE MUSIC	TAVARES	4	1976
DON'T TAKE IT LYIN' DOWN	DOOLEYS	60	1978
DON'T TAKE IT PERSONAL	JERMAINE JACKSON	69	1989
DON'T TAKE IT PERSONAL (JUST ONE OF DEM DAYS)	MONICA	32	1995
DON'T TAKE MY KINDNESS FOR WEAKNESS	HEADS WITH SHAUN RYDER	60	1996
DON'T TAKE MY MIND ON A TRIP	BOY GEORGE	68	1989
DON'T TAKE NO FOR AN ANSWER	TOM ROBINSON BAND	18	1978
DON'T TALK [A]	HANK MARVIN	49	1982
DON'T TALK [B]	JON B	29	2001
DON'T TALK ABOUT LOVE	BAD BOYS INC	19	1993
DON'T TALK DIRTY TO ME	JERMAINE STEWART	61	1988
DON'T TALK JUST KISS	RIGHT SAID FRED. GUEST VOCALS: JOCELYN BROWN	3	1991
DON'T TALK TO HIM	CLIFF RICHARD & THE SHADOWS	2	1963
DON'T TALK TO ME ABOUT LOVE	ALTERED IMAGES	7	1983
DON'T TELL ME [A]	CENTRAL LINE	55	1982
DON'T TELL ME [B]	BLANCMANGE	8	1984
DON'T TELL ME [C]	VAN HALEN	27	1995
DON'T TELL ME [D]	MADONNA	4	2000
DON'T TELL ME [E]	AVRIL LAVIGNE	5	2004
DON'T TELL ME LIES	BREATHE	45	1989
DON'T TELL ME THAT IT'S OVER	AMY MacDONALD	48	2010
DON'T TELL ME YOU'RE SORRY	S CLUB 8	11	2004
DON'T TEST	JUNIOR TUCKER	54	1990
DON'T THAT BEAT ALL	ADAM FAITH	8	1962
DON'T THINK I'M NOT	KANDI	9	2000

	Peak Position	Year of Release
DON'T THINK IT (FEEL IT) LANGE FEATURING LEAH	59	2003
DON'T THINK THE WAY THEY DO SPAN	52	2004
DON'T THINK YOU'RE THE FIRST CORAL	10	2003
DON'T THROW AWAY ALL THOSE TEARDROPS FRANKIE AVALON	37	1960
DON'T THROW IT ALL AWAY GARY BENSON	20	1975
DON'T THROW YOUR LOVE AWAY SEARCHERS	1	1964
DON'T TREAT ME BAD FIREHOUSE	71	1991
DON'T TREAT ME LIKE A CHILD HELEN SHAPIRO	3	1961
DON'T TRUST ME 3OH!3	21	2009
DON'T TRY TO CHANGE ME CRICKETS	37	1963
DON'T TRY TO STOP IT ROMAN HOLLIDAY	14	1983
DON'T TURN AROUND [A] MERSEYBEATS	13	1964
DON'T TURN AROUND [B] ASWAD	1	1988
DON'T TURN AROUND [B] ACE OF BASE	5	1994
DON'T UPSET THE RHYTHM NOISETTES	2	2009
DON'T WAIT DASHBOARD CONFESSIONAL	68	2006
DON'T WAIT UP THUNDER	27	1997
DON'T WALK BIG SUPREME	58	1986
DON'T WALK AWAY [A] ELECTRIC LIGHT ORCHESTRA	21	1980
DON'T WALK AWAY [B] FOUR TOPS	16	1981
DON'T WALK AWAY [C] PAT BENATAR	42	1988
DON'T WALK AWAY [D] TONI CHILDS	53	1989
DON'T WALK AWAY [E] JADE	7	1993
DON'T WALK AWAY [E] JAVINE	16	2004
DON'T WALK AWAY TILL I TOUCH YOU ELAINE PAIGE	46	1978
DON'T WANNA BE A PLAYER JOE	16	1997
DON'T WANNA BE ALONE TRICIA PENROSE	44	2000
DON'T WANNA FALL IN LOVE JANE CHILD	22	1990
DON'T WANNA KNOW SHY FX/T POWER/DI & SKIBADEE	19	2002
DON'T WANNA LET YOU GO FIVE	9	2000
DON'T WANNA LOSE THIS FEELING DANNII MINOGUE	5	2003
DON'T WANNA LOSE YOU [A] GLORIA ESTEFAN	6	1989
DON'T WANNA LOSE YOU [B] LIONEL RICHIE	17	1996
DON'T WANNA RUN NO MORE VAGABOND	41	2009
DON'T WANNA SAY GOODNIGHT KANDIDATE	47	1978
DON'T WANT TO FORGIVE ME NOW WET WET WET	7	1995
DON'T WANT TO WAIT ANYMORE TUBES	60	1981
DON'T WANT YOU BACK ELLIE CAMPBELL	50	2001
DON'T WASTE MY TIME PAUL HARDCASTLE FEATURING CAROL KENYON	8	1986
DON'T WASTE YOUR TIME YARBOROUGH & PEOPLES	60	1984
DON'T WORRY [A] JOHNNY BRANDON	18	1955
DON'T WORRY [B] BILLY FURY WITH THE FOUR KESTRELS	40	1961
DON'T WORRY [C] KIM APPLEBY	2	1990
DON'T WORRY [D] NEWTON	61	1997
DON'T WORRY [E] APPLETON	5	2003
DON'T WORRY BABY LOS LOBOS	57	1985
DON'T WORRY BE HAPPY BOBBY McFERRIN	2	1988
DON'T YOU SECOND IMAGE	68	1983
DON'T YOU FORGET ABOUT ME SIMPLE MINDS	7	1985
DON'T YOU FORGET ABOUT ME BEST COMPANY	65	1993
DON'T YOU GET SO MAD JEFFREY OSBORNE	54	1983
DON'T YOU JUST KNOW IT AMAZULU	15	1985
DON'T YOU KNOW BUTTERSCOTCH	17	1970
DON'T YOU KNOW IT ADAM FAITH	12	1961
DON'T YOU LOVE ME [A] 49ERS	12	1990
DON'T YOU LOVE ME [B] ETERNAL	3	1997
DON'T YOU ROCK ME DADDY-O LONNIE DONEGAN	4	1957
DON'T YOU ROCK ME DADDY-O VIPERS SKIFFLE GROUP	10	1957
DON'T YOU THINK IT'S TIME MIKE BERRY WITH THE OUTLAWS	6	1963
DON'T YOU WANNA BE RELEVANT? CRIBS	39	2007
DON'T YOU WANT ME [A] HUMAN LEAGUE	1	1981
DON'T YOU WANT ME [A] FARM	18	1992
DON'T YOU WANT ME [B] JODY WATLEY	55	1987
DON'T YOU WANT ME [C] FELIX	6	1992
DON'T YOU WANT ME BABY MANDY SMITH	59	1989
DON'T YOU WORRY MADASUN	14	2000
DON'T YOU WORRY 'BOUT A THING INCOGNITO	19	1992
DOO WOP (THAT THING) LAURYN HILL	3	1998
DOOBEDOOD'NDOOBE DOOBEDOOD'NDOOBE DIANA ROSS	12	1972
DOODAH CARTOONS	7	1999
DOOMS NIGHT AZZIDO DA BASS	8	2000
DOOMSDAY EVELYN THOMAS	41	1976
DOOP DOOP	1	1994
THE DOOR TURIN BRAKES	67	2001
THE DOOR IS STILL OPEN TO MY HEART DEAN MARTIN	42	1964
DOOR #1 LEVERT SWEAT GILL	45	1998
DOORS OF YOUR HEART BEAT	33	1981
DOOT DOOT FREUR	59	1983
THE DOPE SHOW MARILYN MANSON	12	1998
DOPES TO INFINITY MONSTER MAGNET	58	1995
DOUBLE BARREL DAVE & ANSIL COLLINS	1	1971
DOUBLE DOUBLE DUTCH DOPE SMUGGLAZ	15	1999
DOUBLE DROP FIERCE GIRL	74	2004
DOUBLE DUTCH [A] FATBACK BAND	31	1977
DOUBLE DUTCH [B] MALCOLM McLAREN	3	1983
DOUBLE TROUBLE LYNYRD SKYNYRD	21	1976
DOUBLEBACK ZZ TOP	29	1990
DOVE (I'LL BE LOVING YOU) MOONY	9	2002
DOV'E L'AMORE CHER	21	1999
DOWN [A] BLINK-182	24	2004
DOWN [B] JAY SEAN FEATURING LIL WAYNE	3	2009
DOWN AND UNDER (TOGETHER) KID CRÈME FEATURING MC SHURAKANO	55	2003
DOWN AT THE DOCTOR'S DR FEELGOOD	48	1978
DOWN BOY HOLLY VALANCE	2	2002
DOWN BY THE LAZY RIVER OSMONDS	40	1972
DOWN BY THE WATER PJ HARVEY	38	1995
DOWN DEEP INSIDE (THEME FROM 'THE DEEP') DONNA SUMMER	5	1977
DOWN DOWN STATUS QUO	1	1974
DOWN DOWN DOWN GAMBAFREAKS	57	2000
DOWN FOR THE ONE BEVERLEY KNIGHT	55	1995
DOWN 4 U IRV GOTTI FEATURING ASHANTI, CHARLI BALTIMORE & VITA	4	2002
DOWN 4 WHATEVA NUTTIN' NYCE	62	1995
DOWN IN A HOLE ALICE IN CHAINS	36	1993
DOWN IN THE BOONDOCKS BILLY JOE ROYAL	38	1965
DOWN IN THE SUBWAY SOFT CELL	24	1984
DOWN IN THE TUBE STATION AT MIDNIGHT JAM	15	1978
DOWN LOW (NOBODY HAS TO KNOW) R KELLY FEATURING RONALD ISLEY	23	1996
DOWN ON THE BEACH TONIGHT DRIFTERS	7	1974
DOWN ON THE CORNER CREEDENCE CLEARWATER REVIVAL	31	1970
DOWN ON THE STREET SHAKATAK	9	1984
DOWN SO LONG JEWEL	38	1999
DOWN THAT ROAD SHARA NELSON	19	1993
DOWN THE DRAIN STAKKA BO	64	1993
DOWN THE DUSTPIPE STATUS QUO	12	1970
DOWN THE HALL FOUR SEASONS	34	1977
DOWN THE RIVER NILE JOHN LEYTON	42	1962
DOWN THE WIRE A.S.A.P.	67	1990
DOWN TO EARTH [A] CURIOSITY KILLED THE CAT	3	1987
DOWN TO EARTH [B] MONIE LOVE	31	1990
DOWN TO EARTH [C] GRACE	20	1996
DOWN TO THE SEA TIM BOOTH	68	2004
DOWN TO THE WIRE GHOST DANCE	66	1989
DOWN UNDER MEN AT WORK	1	1983
DOWN WITH THE CLIQUE AALIYAH	33	1995
DOWN WITH THE KING RUN DMC	69	1993
DOWN YONDER JOHNNY & THE HURRICANES	8	1960
DOWNHEARTED EDDIE FISHER	3	1953
DOWNING STREET KINDLING LARRIKIN LOVE	35	2006
DOWNLOAD IT CLEA	21	2003
DOWNTOWN EMMA BUNTON	3	2006
DOWNTOWN PEACHES	50	2006
DOWNTOWN [A] PETULA CLARK	2	1964
DOWNTOWN [B] ONE 2 MANY	43	1988
DOWNTOWN [C] SWV	19	1994
THE DOWNTOWN LIGHTS BLUE NILE	67	1989
DOWNTOWN TRAIN ROD STEWART	10	1990
DOWNTOWN VENUS PM DAWN	58	1995
DRACULA'S TANGO TOTO COELO	54	1982
DRAG ME DOWN BOOMTOWN RATS	50	1984
DRAGGING ME DOWN INSPIRAL CARPETS	12	1992
DRAGNET RAY ANTHONY	7	1953
DRAGNET TED HEATH	9	1953
DRAGNET ART OF NOISE	60	1987
DRAGON POWER JKD BAND	58	1978
DRAGONFLY TORNADOS	41	1963
DRAGOSTEA DIN TEI O-ZONE	3	2004
DRAGULA ROB ZOMBIE	44	1998
DRAIN THE BLOOD DISTILLERS	51	2003
DRAMA! ERASURE	4	1989
DRAMA QUEEN SWITCHES	61	2007
DRAW OF THE CARDS KIM CARNES	49	1981
(DRAWING) RINGS AROUND THE WORLD SUPER FURRY ANIMALS	28	2001
DRAWING SHAPES MORNING RUNNER	70	2005
DRE DAY DR DRE	59	1994
DREADLOCK HOLIDAY 10 C.C.	1	1978
THE DREAM [A] DREAM FREQUENCY	67	1994
DREAM [B] DIZZEE RASCAL	14	2004
DREAM A LIE UB40	10	1980
DREAM A LITTLE DREAM OF ME MAMA CASS	11	1968
DREAM A LITTLE DREAM OF ME ANITA HARRIS	33	1968
DREAM ABOUT YOU D'BORA	75	1991
DREAM ANOTHER DREAM RIALTO	39	1998
DREAM BABY ROY ORBISON	2	1962
DREAM BABY GLEN CAMPBELL	39	1971
DREAM CATCH ME NEWTON FAULKNER	7	2007
DREAM COME TRUE BRAND NEW HEAVIES FEATURING N'DEA DAVENPORT	24	1992
DREAM GIRL MARK WYNTER	27	1961
DREAM KITCHEN FRAZIER CHORUS	57	1989
DREAM LOVER BOBBY DARIN	1	1959
DREAM OF ME (BASED ON LOVE'S THEME) ORCHESTRAL MANOEUVRES IN THE DARK	24	1993
DREAM OF OLWEN SECOND CITY SOUND	43	1969
DREAM ON [A] DEPECHE MODE	6	2001
DREAM ON [B] CHRISTIAN FALK FEATURING ROBYN	29	2008
DREAM ON DREAMER BRAND NEW HEAVIES FEATURING N'DEA DAVENPORT	15	1994
DREAM ON (IS THIS A DREAM) LOVE DECADE	52	1991
DREAM SEQUENCE (ONE) PAULINE MURRAY & THE INVISIBLE GIRLS	67	1980
DREAM SOME PARADISE INTASTELLA	69	1991
DREAM SWEET DREAMS AZTEC CAMERA	67	1993

	Peak Position	Year of Release
DREAM TALK ALMA COGAN	48	1960
DREAM TO ME DARIO G	9	2001
DREAM TO SLEEP H20	17	1983
DREAM UNIVERSE DJ GARRY	36	2002
DREAMBOAT [A] ALMA COGAN	1	1955
DREAMBOAT [B] LIMMIE & THE FAMILY COOKIN'	31	1973
DREAMER [A] SUPERTRAMP	13	1975
DREAMER [A] CK & SUPREME DREAM TEAM	23	2002
DREAMER [B] JACKSONS	22	1977
THE DREAMER ALL ABOUT EVE	41	1991
DREAMER [D] COLDCUT	54	1993
DREAMER [E] LIVIN' JOY	1	1994
DREAMER [F] OZZY OSBOURNE	18	2002
DREAMIN' [A] JOHNNY BURNETTE	5	1960
DREAMIN' [B] LIVERPOOL EXPRESS	40	1977
DREAMIN' [C] CLIFF RICHARD	8	1980
DREAMIN' [D] STATUS QUO	15	1986
DREAMIN' [E] VANESSA WILLIAMS	74	1989
DREAMIN' [F] LOLEATTA HOLLOWAY	59	2000
DREAMIN' [G] AMP FIDDLER	71	2004
DREAMING [A] BLONDIE	2	1979
THE DREAMING [B] KATE BUSH	48	1982
DREAMING [C] ORCHESTRAL MANOEUVRES IN THE DARK	50	1988
DREAMING [D] GLEN GOLDSMITH	12	1988
DREAMING [E] MN8	21	1996
DREAMING [F] RUFF DRIVERZ PRESENTS ARROLA	10	1998
DREAMING [G] M PEOPLE	13	1999
DREAMING [H] BT FEATURING KIRSTY HAWKSHAW	38	2000
DREAMING [I] AURORA	24	2002
DREAMING [J] I DREAM FEATURING FRANKIE & CALVIN	19	2004
DREAMING OF ME DEPECHE MODE	57	1981
DREAMING OF YOU [A] THRILLSEEKERS	48	2002
DREAMING OF YOU [B] CORAL	13	2002
DREAMLOVER MARIAH CAREY	9	1993
DREAMS [A] FLEETWOOD MAC	24	1977
DREAMS [A] WILD COLOUR	25	1995
DREAMS [A] CORRS	6	1998
DREAMS [A] DEEP DISH FEATURING STEVIE NICKS	14	2006
DREAMS [B] GRACE SLICK	50	1980
DREAMS [C] VAN HALEN	62	1986
DREAMS [D] GABRIELLE	1	1993
DREAMS [E] CRANBERRIES	27	1994
DREAMS [F] SMOKIN' BEATS FEATURING LYN EDEN	23	1998
DREAMS [G] QUENCH	75	1996
DREAMS [H] MISS SHIVA	30	2001
DREAMS [I] KINGS OF TOMORROW	69	2003
DREAMS [K] GAME	8	2005
DREAMS CAN TELL A LIE NAT 'KING' COLE	10	1956
A DREAM'S A DREAM SOUL II SOUL	6	1990
THE DREAMS I DREAM SHADOWS	42	1966
DREAMS OF CHILDREN JAM	1	1980
DREAMS OF HEAVEN GROUND LEVEL	54	1993
DREAMS OF YOU RALPH McTELL	36	1976
DREAMS TO REMEMBER ROBERT PALMER	68	1991
DREAMSCAPE '94 TIME FREQUENCY	32	1994
DREAMTIME [A] DARYL HALL	28	1986
DREAMTIME [B] ZEE	31	1996
DREAMY DAYS ROOTS MANUVA	53	2001
DREAMY LADY T REX DISCO PARTY	30	1975
DRED BASS DEAD DRED	60	1994
DRESS YOU UP MADONNA	5	1985
DRESSED FOR SUCCESS ROXETTE	18	1989
DRIFT AWAY MICHAEL BOLTON	18	1992
DRIFTING [A] SHEILA WALSH & CLIFF RICHARD	64	1983
DRIFTING [B] MOJOLATORS FEATURING CAMILLA	52	2001
DRIFTING AWAY LANGE FEATURING SKYE	9	2002
DRIFTWOOD TRAVIS	13	1999
THE DRILL DIRT DEVILS	15	2002
DRINK THE ELIXIR SALAD	66	1995
DRINK UP THY ZIDER ADGE CUTLER & THE WURZELS	45	1967
DRINKING IN LA BRAN VAN 3000	3	1998
DRINKING SONG MARIO LANZA	13	1955
DRIP FED FRED MADNESS FEATURING IAN DURY	55	2000
DRIVE [A] CARS	4	1984
DRIVE [B] R.E.M.	11	1992
DRIVE [C] GEOFFREY WILLIAMS	52	1997
DRIVE [D] INCUBUS	40	2001
DRIVE ME CRAZY PARTIZAN	36	1997
DRIVE ON BROTHER BEYOND	39	1989
DRIVE SAFELY DARLIN' TONY CHRISTIE	35	1976
DRIVE-IN SATURDAY DAVID BOWIE	3	1973
DRIVEN BY YOU BRIAN MAY	6	1991
DRIVER'S SEAT SNIFF 'N' THE TEARS	42	1979
DRIVIN' HOME DUANE EDDY & THE REBELS	30	1961
DRIVIN' ME WILD COMMON FEATURING LILY ALLEN	56	2007
DRIVING EVERYTHING BUT THE GIRL	36	1990
DRIVING AWAY FROM HOME (JIM'S TUNE) IT'S IMMATERIAL	18	1986
DRIVING HOME FOR CHRISTMAS CHRIS REA	33	2007
DRIVING HOME FOR CHRISTMAS (EP) CHRIS REA	53	1988
DRIVING IN MY CAR MADNESS	4	1982
DRIVING IN MY CAR MAUREEN REES	49	1997
DRIVING WITH THE BRAKES ON DEL AMITRI	18	1995
DROP DEAD GORGEOUS REPUBLICA	7	1997
DROP DOWN TO EARTH PURESSENCE	56	2007
DROP IT LIKE IT'S HOT SNOOP DOGG FEATURING PHARRELL	10	2004
DROP SOME DRUMS (LOVE) TATTOO	58	2001
DROP THE BOY BROS	2	1988
DROP THE PILOT JOAN ARMATRADING	11	1983
DROP THE PRESSURE MYLO	19	2004
DROP THE ROCK (EP) D-TEK	70	1993
DROP THE WORLD LIL WAYNE FEATURING EMINEM	51	2010
DROPS OF JUPITER (TELL ME) TRAIN	10	2001
DROWNED WORLD (SUBSTITUTE FOR LOVE) MADONNA	10	1998
THE DROWNERS SUEDE	49	1992
DROWNING [A] BEAT	22	1981
DROWNING [B] BACKSTREET BOYS	4	2002
DROWNING [C] CRAZY TOWN	50	2002
DROWNING IN BERLIN MOBILES	9	1982
DROWNING THE THE SEA OF LOVE ADVENTURES	44	1988
DROWSY WITH HOPE SHAKEDOWN	46	2003
THE DRUGS DON'T WORK VERVE	1	1997
DRUMBEATS SL2	26	1992
DRUMMER MAN TONIGHT	14	1978
DRUMMIN' UP A STORM SANDY NELSON	39	1962
DRUMMING SONG FLORENCE + THE MACHINE	54	2009
DRUMS ARE MY BEAT SANDY NELSON	30	1962
THE DRUMSTRUCK (EP) N-JOI	33	1993
DRUNK ON LOVE BASIA	41	1995
DRUNKARD LOGIC FAT LADY SINGS	56	1993
DRUNKEN FOOL BURN	54	2003
DRUNKEN STARS MAMPI SWIFT	72	2004
DRY COUNTY [A] BLACKFOOT	43	1982
DRY COUNTY [B] BON JOVI	9	1994
DRY LAND MARILLION	34	1991
DRY RISER KERBDOG	60	1994
DRY YOUR EYES STREETS	1	2004
DU THE DUDEK TROPHY BOYZ	49	2005
DUALITY SLIPKNOT	15	2004
DUB BE GOOD TO ME BEATS INTERNATIONAL FEATURING LINDY LAYTON	1	1990
DUB WAR DANCE CONSPIRACY	72	1992
DUBPLATE CULTURE SOUNDSCAPE	48	1998
DUCHESS [A] STRANGLERS	14	1979
DUCHESS [A] MY LIFE STORY	39	1997
DUCHESS [B] GENESIS	46	1980
DUCK FOR THE OYSTER MALCOLM McLAREN	54	1983
DUCK TOY HAMPENBERG	30	2002
DUDE BEENIE MAN FEATURING MS THING	7	2004
DUDE DESCENDING A STAIRCASE APOLLO 440 FEATURING THE BEATNUTS	58	2003
DUDE (LOOKS LIKE A LADY) AEROSMITH	20	1987
DUEL [A] PROPAGANDA	21	1985
DUEL [B] SWERVEDRIVER	60	1993
DUELLING BANJOS 'DELIVERANCE' SOUNDTRACK	17	1973
DUI HAR MAR SUPERSTAR	46	2004
DUKE OF EARL DARTS	6	1979
DUM DUM BRENDA LEE	22	1961
DUM DUM GIRL TALK TALK	74	1984
DUMB [A] BEAUTIFUL SOUTH	16	1998
DUMB [B] 411	3	2004
DUMB WAITERS PSYCHEDELIC FURS	59	1981
DUMMY CRUSHER KERBDOG	37	1994
DUNE BUGGY PRESIDENTS OF THE UNITED STATES OF AMERICA	15	1996
DUNE SEA UNBELIEVABLE TRUTH	46	1998
DUNNO WHAT IT IS (ABOUT YOU) BEATMASTERS FEATURING ELAINE VASSELL	43	1992
DURHAM TOWN (THE LEAVIN') ROGER WHITTAKER	12	1969
DUSK TIL DAWN DANNY HOWELLS & DICK TREVOR FEATURING ERIRE	37	2004
DUST ROYWORLD	29	2008
DUST DEVIL MADNESS	64	2009
DUSTED LEFTFIELD/ROOTS MANUVA	28	1999
D. W. WASHBURN MONKEES	17	1968
D'YA WANNA GO FASTER TERRORVISION	28	2001
DYNA-MITE MUD	4	1973
DYNAMITE [A] CLIFF RICHARD & THE SHADOWS	16	1959
DYNAMITE [B] STACY LATTISAW	51	1980
DY-NA-MI-TEE MS DYNAMITE	5	2002
DYNOMITE (PART 1) TONY CAMILLO'S BAZUKA	28	1975
D'YOU KNOW WHAT I MEAN? OASIS	1	1997

E

	Peak Position	Year of Release
E DRUNKENMUNKY	41	2003
E = MC2 BIG AUDIO DYNAMITE	11	1986
E – BOW THE LETTER R.E.M.	4	1996
E SAMBA JUNIOR JACK	34	2003
E TALKING SOULWAX	27	2005
EACH AND EVERYONE EVERYTHING BUT THE GIRL	28	1984
EACH TIME E-17	2	1998
EACH TIME YOU BREAK MY HEART NICK KAMEN	5	1986
EANIE MEANY JIM NOIR	67	2006
EARDRUM BUZZ WIRE	68	1989
EARLY IN THE MORNING [A] BUDDY HOLLY	17	1958
EARLY IN THE MORNING [B] VANITY FARE	8	1969
EARLY IN THE MORNING [C] GAP BAND	55	1982
EARLY MORNING RAIN PAUL WELLER	40	2005
EARLY TO BED PONI-TAILS	26	1959

Title / Artist	Peak Position	Year of Release
EARTH ANGEL [A] CREW CUTS	4	1955
EARTH ANGEL [B] DREADZONE	51	1997
THE EARTH DIES SCREAMING UB40	10	1980
EARTH SONG MICHAEL JACKSON	1	1995
EARTHBOUND CONNOR REEVES	14	1997
THE EARTHSHAKER PAUL MASTERSON PRESENTS SUSHI	35	2002
EASE MY MIND ARRESTED DEVELOPMENT	33	1994
EASE ON BY BASS-O-MATIC	61	1990
EASE ON DOWN THE ROAD DIANA ROSS & MICHAEL JACKSON	45	1978
EASE THE PRESSURE [A] 2WO THIRD3	45	1994
EASE THE PRESSURE [B] BELOVED	43	1996
EASE YOUR MIND GALLIANO	45	1996
EASIER SAID THAN DONE [A] ESSEX	41	1963
EASIER SAID THAN DONE [B] SHAKATAK	12	1982
EASIER SAID THAN DONE [C] STARGATE	55	2002
EASIER TO LIE AQUALUNG	60	2004
EASIER TO WALK AWAY ELTON JOHN	63	1990
EAST COAST/WEST COAST KILLAS GROUP THERAPY	51	1996
EAST EASY RIDER JULIAN COPE	51	1991
EAST OF EDEN BIG COUNTRY	17	1984
EAST RIVER BRECKER BROTHERS	34	1978
EAST WEST HERMAN'S HERMITS	33	1966
EASTER MARILLION	34	1990
EASY [A] COMMODORES	9	1977
EASY [B] LOUD	67	1992
EASY [C] TERRORVISION	12	1997
EASY [D] EMILIANA TORRINI	63	2000
EASY [E] GROOVE ARMADA	31	2003
EASY [F] SUGABABES	8	2006
EASY COME EASY GO SUTHERLAND BROTHERS	50	1979
EASY EASY SCOTLAND WORLD CUP SQUAD	20	1974
EASY GOING ME ADAM FAITH	12	1961
EASY LADY SPAGNA	62	1987
EASY LIFE [A] BODYSNATCHERS	50	1980
EASY LIFE [B] CABARET VOLTAIRE	61	1990
EASY LIVIN' FASTWAY	74	1983
EASY LOVER PHILIP BAILEY (DUET WITH PHIL COLLINS)	1	1985
EASY/LUCKY/FREE BRIGHT EYES	42	2005
EASY RIDER RAIN BAND	63	2003
EASY TO SMILE SENSELESS THINGS	18	1992
EAT IT WEIRD AL YANKOVIC	36	1984
EAT ME DRINK ME LOVE ME POP WILL EAT ITSELF	17	1992
EAT MY GOAL COLLAPSED LUNG	18	1996
EAT THE RICH AEROSMITH	34	1993
EAT YOU ALIVE LIMP BIZKIT	10	2003
EAT YOUR HEART OUT PAUL HARDCASTLE	59	1984
EAT YOURSELF WHOLE KINGMAKER	15	1992
EATEN ALIVE DIANA ROSS	71	1985
EATING ME ALIVE DIANA BROWN & BARRIE K SHARPE	53	1992
EBB TIDE FRANK CHACKSFIELD	9	1954
EBB TIDE RIGHTEOUS BROTHERS	3	1966
EBENEEZER GOODE SHAMEN	1	1992
EBONY AND IVORY PAUL McCARTNEY & STEVIE WONDER	1	1982
EBONY EYES EVERLY BROTHERS	1	1961
ECHO GIRLS CAN'T CATCH	19	2010
ECHO BEACH [A] MARTHA & THE MUFFINS	10	1980
ECHO BEACH [B] TOYAH	54	1987
ECHO CHAMBER BEATS INTERNATIONAL	60	1991
ECHO MY HEART LINDY LAYTON	42	1991
ECHO ON MY MIND PART II EARTHLING	61	1995
ECHOES AROUND THE SUN PAUL WELLER	19	2008
ECHOES IN A SHALLOW BAY (EP) COCTEAU TWINS	65	1985
ECUADOR SASH! FEATURING RODRIGUEZ	2	1997
EDDIE'S GUN KOOKS	35	2005
EDDIE'S SONG SON OF DORK	10	2006
EDDY VORTEX STEVE GIBBONS BAND	56	1978
EDELWEISS VINCE HILL	2	1967
EDEN SARAH BRIGHTMAN	68	1999
EDGE OF A BROKEN HEART VIXEN	51	1988
EDGE OF DARKNESS ERIC CLAPTON FEATURING MICHAEL KAMEN	65	1986
THE EDGE OF HEAVEN WHAM!	1	1986
EDIBLE FLOWERS FINN BROTHERS	32	2005
EDIE (CIAO BABY) CULT	32	1989
ED'S FUNKY DINER (FRIDAY NIGHT, SATURDAY MORNING) IT'S IMMATERIAL	65	1986
EDWOULD LARRIKIN LOVE	49	2006
EENY MEENY SHOWSTOPPERS	33	1968
EGG RUSH FLOWERED UP	54	1991
EGO [A] ELTON JOHN	34	1978
EGO [B] SATURDAYS	9	2009
EGYPTIAN REGGAE JONATHAN RICHMAN & THE MODERN LOVERS	5	1977
EI NELLY	11	2001
EIGHT BY TEN KEN DODD	22	1964
8 DAYS A WEEK SWEET FEMALE ATTITUDE	43	2000
EIGHT MILES HIGH BYRDS	24	1966
808 BLAQUE IVORY	31	1999
EIGHTEEN FORWARD, RUSSIA!	44	2006
18 AND LIFE SKID ROW	12	1990
18 CARAT LOVE AFFAIR ASSOCIATES	21	1982
EIGHTEEN STRINGS TINMAN	9	1994
18 TIL I DIE BRYAN ADAMS	22	1997
EIGHTEEN WITH A BULLET PETE WINGFIELD	7	1975
EIGHTEEN YELLOW ROSES BOBBY DARIN	37	1963
EIGHTH DAY HAZEL O'CONNOR	5	1980
8TH WORLD WONDER KIMBERLEY LOCKE	49	2004
EIGHTIES KILLING JOKE	60	1984
80S ROMANCE BELLE STARS	71	1984
86'D SUBCIRCUS	56	1997
EINSTEIN A GO-GO LANDSCAPE	5	1981
EITHER WAY TWANG	8	2007
EL BIMBO BIMBO JET	12	1975
EL CAMINOS IN THE WEST GRANDADDY	48	2003
EL CAPITAN [A] OPM	20	2002
EL CAPITAN [B] IDLEWILD	39	2005
EL LUTE BONEY M	12	1979
EL MANANA GORILLAZ	27	2006
EL NINO AGNELLI & NELSON	21	1998
EL PARAISO RICO DEETAH	39	1999
EL PASO MARTY ROBBINS	19	1960
EL PRESIDENT DRUGSTORE	20	1998
EL SALVADOR ATHLETE	31	2003
EL SCORCHO WEEZER	50	1996
EL TRAGO (THE DRINK) 2 IN A ROOM	34	1994
EL VINO COLLAPSO BLACK LACE	42	1985
ELDORADO DRUM THEATRE	44	1987
ELEANOR PUT YOUR BOOTS ON FRANZ FERDINAND	30	2006
ELEANOR RIGBY BEATLES	1	1966
ELEANOR RIGBY RAY CHARLES	36	1968
ELECTED ALICE COOPER	4	1972
ELECTION DAY ARCADIA	7	1985
ELECTRIC LISA SCOTT-LEE	13	2005
ELECTRIC AVENUE EDDY GRANT	2	1983
ELECTRIC BARBARELLA DURAN DURAN	23	1999
ELECTRIC BLUE ICEHOUSE	53	1988
ELECTRIC BOOGALOO OLLIE & JERRY	57	1985
ELECTRIC FEEL MGMT	22	2008
ELECTRIC GUITAR FLUKE	58	1993
ELECTRIC GUITARS PREFAB SPROUT	53	1997
ELECTRIC HEAD PART 2 (THE ECSTASY) WHITE ZOMBIE	31	1996
ELECTRIC LADY GEORDIE	32	1973
ELECTRIC MAINLINE SPIRITUALIZED	49	1993
ELECTRIC MAN MANSUN	23	2000
ELECTRIC TRAINS SQUEEZE	44	1995
ELECTRIC YOUTH DEBBIE GIBSON	14	1989
ELECTRICAL STORM U2	5	2002
ELECTRICITY [A] SPIRITUALIZED	32	1997
ELECTRICITY [B] SUEDE	5	1999
ELECTRICITY [C] ELTON JOHN	4	2005
ELECTROLITE R.E.M.	29	1996
ELECTRON BLUE R.E.M.	26	2005
ELECTRONIC PLEASURE N-TRANCE	11	1996
ELEGANTLY AMERICAN: ONE NIGHT IN HEAVEN M PEOPLE	31	1994
ELEGANTLY WASTED INXS	20	1997
ELEKTRO OUTWORK FEATURING MR GEE	49	2006
ELEKTROBANK CHEMICAL BROTHERS	17	1997
ELEMENTS NEO CORTEX	67	2004
ELENI TOL & TOL	73	1990
ELENORE TURTLES	7	1968
ELEPHANT PAW (GET DOWN TO THE FUNK) PAN POSITION	55	1994
ELEPHANT STONE STONE ROSES	8	1990
ELEPHANT TANGO CYRIL STAPLETON	19	1955
THE ELEPHANT'S GRAVEYARD (GUILTY) BOOMTOWN RATS	26	1981
ELEVATE MY MIND STEREO MC'S	74	1990
ELEVATION [A] XPANSIONS	49	1990
ELEVATION [B] GTO	59	1992
ELEVATION [C] U2	3	2001
ELEVATION [D] OPEN	54	2004
ELEVATOR FLO RIDA FEATURING TIMBALAND	20	2008
ELEVATOR SONG DUBSTAR	25	1996
ELEVEN TO FLY TIN TIN OUT FEATURING WENDY PAGE	26	1999
ELISABETH SERENADE GUNTER KALLMAN CHOIR	39	1964
ELIZABETHAN REGGAE BORIS GARDINER	14	1970
ELLE DJ GREGORY	73	2003
ELMO JAMES CHAIRMEN OF THE BOARD	21	1972
ELO EP ELECTRIC LIGHT ORCHESTRA	34	1978
ELOISE BARRY RYAN	2	1968
ELOISE DAMNED	3	1986
ELSTREE BUGGLES	55	1980
ELUSIVE SCOTT MATTHEWS	56	2006
ELUSIVE BUTTERFLY BOB LIND	5	1966
ELUSIVE BUTTERFLY VAL DOONICAN	5	1966
ELVIS AIN'T DEAD SCOUTING FOR GIRLS	8	2007
THE ELVIS MEDLEY ELVIS PRESLEY	51	1985
ELYSIUM (I GO CRAZY) ULTRABEAT VERSUS SCOTT BROWN	35	2006
EMBARRASSMENT MADNESS	4	1980
EMBERS JUST JACK	17	2009
EMBRACE AGNELLI & NELSON	35	2000
EMBRACING THE SUNSHINE BT	34	1995
EMERALD CITY SEEKERS	50	1967
EMERGE FISCHERSPOONER	25	2002
EMERGENCY KOOL & THE GANG	50	1985
EMERGENCY 72 TURIN BRAKES	41	2001
EMERGENCY (DIAL 999) LOOSE ENDS	41	1984
EMERGENCY ON PLANET EARTH JAMIROQUAI	32	1993
EMILY [A] BOWLING FOR SOUP	67	2002
EMILY [B] ADAM GREEN	53	2005
EMILY [C] STEPHEN FRETWELL	42	2005
EMILY KANE ART BRUT	41	2005
EMMA HOT CHOCOLATE	3	1974
EMOTION SAMANTHA SANG	11	1978
EMOTION DESTINY'S CHILD	3	2001
EMOTIONAL CONTENT FUNK D'VOID	74	2004
EMOTIONAL RESCUE ROLLING STONES	9	1980
EMOTIONAL TIME HOTHOUSE FLOWERS	38	1993
EMOTIONS [A] BRENDA LEE	45	1961
EMOTIONS [B] MARIAH CAREY	17	1991
THE EMPEROR'S NEW CLOTHES SINEAD O'CONNOR	31	1990
EMPIRE [A] QUEENSRYCHE	61	1990

Title / Artist	Peak Position	Year of Release
EMPIRE [B] KASABIAN	9	2006
EMPIRE LINE MY LIFE STORY	58	1999
EMPIRE SONG KILLING JOKE	43	1982
EMPIRE STATE HUMAN HUMAN LEAGUE	62	1980
EMPIRE STATE OF MIND JAY-Z FEATURING ALICIA KEYS	2	2009
EMPIRE STATE OF MIND PART II ALICIA KEYS	4	2009
EMPTY AT THE END ELECTRIC SOFT PARADE	39	2001
EMPTY GARDEN ELTON JOHN	51	1982
EMPTY ROOMS GARY MOORE	23	1984
EMPTY SKIES KOSHEEN	73	2000
EMPTY SOULS MANIC STREET PREACHERS	2	2005
EMPTY WORLD DOGS D'AMOUR	61	1990
ENCHANTED LADY PASADENAS	31	1988
ENCORE CHERYL LYNN	68	1984
ENCORE TONGUE 'N' CHEEK	37	1989
ENCORE UNE FOIS SASH!	2	1997
ENCORES EP DIRE STRAITS	31	1993
END CREDITS CHASE & STATUS FEATURING PLAN B	9	2009
THE END HAS A START EDITORS	27	2007
THE END HAS NO END STROKES	27	2004
THE END IS THE BEGINNING IS THE END SMASHING PUMPKINS	10	1997
END OF A CENTURY BLUR	19	1994
THE END OF THE INNOCENCE DON HENLEY	48	1992
END OF THE LINE [A] TRAVELING WILBURYS	52	1989
END OF THE LINE [B] HONEYZ	5	1998
END OF THE LINE [C] MOHAIR	52	2005
END OF THE ROAD BOYZ II MEN	1	1992
END OF THE WORLD [A] SKEETER DAVIS	18	1963
END OF THE WORLD [A] SONIA	18	1990
THE END OF THE WORLD [B] CURE	25	2004
END OF THE WORLD [C] ASH	62	2007
THE END...OR THE BEGINNING CLASSIX NOUVEAUX	60	1982
ENDLESS DICKIE VALENTINE	19	1954
ENDLESS ART A HOUSE	46	1992
ENDLESS LOVE DIANA ROSS & LIONEL RICHIE	7	1981
ENDLESS LOVE LUTHER VANDROSS & MARIAH CAREY	3	1994
ENDLESS SLEEP MARTY WILDE	4	1958
ENDLESS SLEEP JODY REYNOLDS	66	1979
ENDLESS SUMMER NIGHTS RICHARD MARX	50	1988
ENDLESSLY [A] BROOK BENTON	28	1959
ENDLESSLY [B] JOHN FOXX	66	1983
ENDS EVERLAST	47	1999
ENEMIES FRIENDS HOPE OF THE STATES	25	2003
ENEMY MAKER DUB WAR	41	1996
THE ENEMY WITHIN THIRST	61	1991
ENERGIZE SLAMM	57	1993
ENERGY KERI HILSON	43	2009
THE ENERGY (FEEL THE VIBE) ASTRO TRAX	74	1998
ENERGY FLASH (EP) BELTRAM	52	1991
ENERGY IS EUROBEAT MAN TO MAN	43	1987
ENERVATE TRANSA	42	1998
ENGINE ENGINE NO. 9 ROGER MILLER	33	1965
ENGINE NO. 9 MIDNIGHT STAR	64	1987
ENGLAND CRAZY RIDER & TERRY VENABLES	46	2002
ENGLAND SWINGS ROGER MILLER	13	1966
ENGLAND WE'LL FLY THE FLAG ENGLAND WORLD CUP SQUAD	2	1982
ENGLAND'S IRIE BLACK GRAPE FEATURING JOE STRUMMER & KEITH ALLEN	6	1996
ENGLISH CIVIL WAR (JOHNNY COMES MARCHING HOME) CLASH	25	1979
ENGLISH COUNTRY GARDEN [A] JIMMIE RODGERS	5	1962
ENGLISH COUNTRY GARDEN [B] DANDYS	57	1998
ENGLISH SUMMER RAIN PLACEBO	23	2004
THE ENGLISH WAY FIGHTSTAR	62	2008
ENGLISHMAN IN NEW YORK STING	15	1988
ENJOY THE SILENCE DEPECHE MODE	6	1990
ENJOY THE SILENCE LACUNA COIL	41	2006
ENJOY YOURSELF [A] JACKSONS	42	1977
ENJOY YOURSELF [B] A+	5	1999
ENOLA GAY ORCHESTRAL MANOEUVRES IN THE DARK	8	1980
ENOUGH CRYIN' MARY J BLIGE FEATURING BROOK-LYNN	46	2006
ENOUGH IS ENOUGH [A] CHUMBAWAMBA & CREDIT TO THE NATION	56	1993
ENOUGH IS ENOUGH [B] Y-TRIBE FEATURING ELISABETH TROY	49	1999
ENTER SANDMAN METALLICA	5	1991
ENTER THE SCENE DJ SUPREME VS THE RHYTHM MASTERS	49	1997
ENTER YOUR FANTASY EP JOEY NEGRO	35	1992
THE ENTERTAINER MARVIN HAMLISCH	25	1974
ENTOURAGE OMARION	58	2007
ENTRY OF THE GLADIATORS NERO & THE GLADIATORS	37	1961
ENVY ASH	21	2002
THE EP ZERO B	32	1992
EP THREE HUNDRED REASONS	37	2001
EP TWO HUNDRED REASONS	47	2001
EPIC FAITH NO MORE	25	1990
EPLE ROYKSOPP	16	2003
E-PRO BECK	38	2005
EQUINOXE PART 5 JEAN-MICHEL JARRE	45	1979
EQUINOXE (PART V) SHADOWS	50	1980
ERASE/REWIND CARDIGANS	7	1999
ERASURE-ISH (A LITTLE RESPECT/STOP!) BJORN AGAIN	25	1992
ERECTION (TAKE IT TO THE TOP) CORTINA FEATURING BK & MADAM FRICTION	48	2002
ERNIE (THE FASTEST MILKMAN IN THE WEST) BENNY HILL	1	1971
EROTICA MADONNA	3	1992
ESCAPADE JANET JACKSON	17	1990
ESCAPE [A] GARY CLAIL ON-U SOUND SYSTEM	44	1991
ESCAPE [B] ENRIQUE IGLESIAS	3	2002
ESCAPE ARTISTS NEVER DIE FUNERAL FOR A FRIEND	19	2004
ESCAPE (THE PINA COLADA SONG) RUPERT HOLMES	23	1980
ESCAPING [A] ASIA BLUE	50	1992
ESCAPING [B] DINA CARROLL	3	1996
E.S.P. BEE GEES	51	1987
ESPECIALLY FOR YOU KYLIE MINOGUE & JASON DONOVAN	1	1988
ESPECIALLY FOR YOU DENISE & JOHNNY	3	1998
THE ESSENTIAL WALLY PARTY MEDLEY GAY GORDON & THE MINCE PIES	60	1986
ET LES OISEAUX CHANTAIENT (AND THE BIRDS WERE SINGING) SWEET PEOPLE	4	1980
ET MEME FRANCOISE HARDY	31	1965
ETERNAL FLAME BANGLES	1	1989
ETERNAL FLAME ATOMIC KITTEN	1	2001
ETERNAL LOVE PJ & DUNCAN	12	1994
ETERNALLY JIMMY YOUNG	8	1953
ETERNITY [A] ORION	38	2000
ETERNITY [B] ROBBIE WILLIAMS	1	2001
ETHER RADIO CHIKINKI	50	2004
ETHNIC PRAYER HAVANA	71	1993
THE ETON RIFLES JAM	3	1979
EUGINA SALT TANK	40	1996
EURODISCO BIS	37	1998
EUROPA AND THE PIRATE TWINS THOMAS DOLBY	48	1981
EUROPE (AFTER THE RAIN) JOHN FOXX	40	1981
EUROPEAN FEMALE STRANGLERS	9	1983
EUROPEAN SON JAPAN	31	1982
EVACUATE THE DANCEFLOOR CASCADA	1	2009
EVANGELINE [A] ICICLE WORKS	53	1987
EVANGELINE [B] COCTEAU TWINS	34	1993
EVAPOR 8 ALTERN 8	6	1992
EVE OF DESTRUCTION BARRY McGUIRE	3	1965
THE EVE OF THE WAR JEFF WAYNE'S WAR OF THE WORLDS	3	1978
EVE THE APPLE OF MY EYE BELL X1	65	2004
EVEN AFTER ALL FINLEY QUAYE	10	1997
EVEN BETTER THAN THE REAL THING U2	8	1992
EVEN FLOW PEARL JAM	27	1992
EVEN GOD CAN'T CHANGE THE PAST CHARLOTTE CHURCH	17	2005
EVEN IF ANDY ABRAHAM	67	2008
EVEN MORE PARTY POPS RUSS CONWAY	27	1960
EVEN NOW BOB SEGER & THE SILVER BULLET BAND	73	1983
EVEN THE BAD TIMES ARE GOOD TREMELOES	4	1967
EVEN THE NIGHTS ARE BETTER AIR SUPPLY	44	1982
EVEN THOUGH YOU BROKE MY HEART GEMINI	40	1995
EVEN THOUGH YOU'VE GONE JACKSONS	31	1978
EVENING FALLS... ENYA	20	1988
EVENING STAR JUDAS PRIEST	53	1979
EVER BLAZIN' SEAN PAUL	12	2005
EVER FALLEN IN LOVE FINE YOUNG CANNIBALS	9	1987
EVER FALLEN IN LOVE (WITH SOMEONE YOU SHOULDN'T'VE) BUZZCOCKS	12	1978
EVER FALLEN IN LOVE (WITH SOMEONE YOU SHOULDN'T'VE) VARIOUS ARTISTS (EP'S & LP'S)	28	2005
EVER REST MYSTICA	62	1998
EVER SINCE YOU SAID GOODBYE MARTY WILDE	31	1962
EVER SO LONELY MONSOON	12	1982
EVEREST SUPERNATURALS	52	1999
EVERGLADE L7	27	1992
EVERGREEN [A] HAZELL DEAN	63	1984
EVERGREEN [B] WILL YOUNG	1	2002
EVERGREEN [B] BELLE LAWRENCE	73	2002
EVERLASTING [A] NATALIE COLE	28	1988
THE EVERLASTING [B] MANIC STREET PREACHERS	11	1998
EVERLASTING LOVE [A] LOVE AFFAIR	1	1968
EVERLASTING LOVE [A] ROBERT KNIGHT	19	1969
EVERLASTING LOVE [A] REX SMITH & RACHEL SWEET	35	1981
EVERLASTING LOVE [A] SANDRA	45	1988
EVERLASTING LOVE [A] WORLDS APART	20	1993
EVERLASTING LOVE [A] GLORIA ESTEFAN	19	1995
EVERLASTING LOVE [A] CAST FROM CASUALTY	5	1998
EVERLASTING LOVE [A] JAMIE CULLUM	20	2004
EVERLASTING LOVE [B] HOWARD JONES	62	1989
EVERLONG FOO FIGHTERS	18	1997
EVERLOVIN' RICK NELSON	23	1961
EVERMORE RUBY MURRAY	3	1955
EVERY ANGEL ALL ABOUT EVE	30	1988
EVERY BEAT OF MY HEART ROD STEWART	2	1986
EVERY BEAT OF THE HEART RAILWAY CHILDREN	24	1990
EVERY BREATH OF THE WAY MELANIE	70	1983
EVERY BREATH YOU TAKE POLICE	1	1983
EVERY DAY ANTICAPPELLA	45	1992
EVERY DAY HURTS SAD CAFE	3	1979
EVERY DAY I FALL APART SUPERSTAR	66	1998
EVERY DAY I LOVE YOU BOYZONE	3	1999
EVERY DAY (I LOVE YOU MORE) JASON DONOVAN	2	1989
EVERY DAY OF MY LIFE MALCOLM VAUGHAN	5	1955
EVERY DAY OF THE WEEK JADE	19	1995

Title / Artist	Peak Position	Year of Release
EVERY DAY SHOULD BE A HOLIDAY DANDY WARHOLS	29	1998
EVERY GIRL AND BOY SPAGNA	23	1988
EVERY HEARTBEAT AMY GRANT	25	1991
EVERY KINDA PEOPLE ROBERT PALMER	43	1978
EVERY KINDA PEOPLE MINT JULEPS	58	1987
EVERY KINDA PEOPLE CHAKA DEMUS & PLIERS	47	1996
EVERY LITTLE BIT HURTS SPENCER DAVIS GROUP	41	1965
EVERY LITTLE STEP BOBBY BROWN	6	1989
EVERY LITTLE TEARDROP GALLAGHER & LYLE	32	1977
EVERY LITTLE THING JEFF LYNNE	59	1990
EVERY LITTLE THING HE DOES IS MAGIC SHAWN COLVIN	65	1994
EVERY LITTLE THING I DO SOUL FOR REAL	31	1996
EVERY LITTLE THING SHE DOES IS MAGIC POLICE	1	1981
EVERY LITTLE THING SHE DOES IS MAGIC CHAKA DEMUS & PLIERS	51	1997
EVERY LITTLE TIME POPPERS PRESENTS AURA	44	1997
EVERY LITTLE TIME ONYX FEATURING GEMMA J	66	2004
EVERY LOSER WINS NICK BERRY	1	1986
EVERY MAN MUST HAVE A DREAM LIVERPOOL EXPRESS	17	1976
EVERY MORNING [A] SUGAR RAY	10	1999
EVERY MORNING [B] BASSHUNTER	17	2009
EVERY NIGHT PHOEBE SNOW	37	1979
EVERY NITE'S A SATURDAY NIGHT WITH YOU DRIFTERS	29	1976
EVERY 1'S A WINNER HOT CHOCOLATE	12	1978
EVERY OTHER TIME LYTE FUNKIE ONES	24	2002
EVERY ROSE HAS ITS THORN POISON	13	1989
EVERY SINGLE DAY DODGY	32	1998
EVERY TIME JANET JACKSON	46	1998
EVERY TIME I FALL GINA G	52	1997
EVERY TIME I FALL IN LOVE UPSIDE DOWN	18	1996
EVERY TIME IT RAINS ACE OF BASE	22	1999
EVERY TIME YOU GO AWAY PAUL YOUNG	4	1985
EVERY TIME YOU TOUCH ME MOBY	28	1995
EVERY WAY THAT I CAN SERTAB	72	2003
EVERY WHICH WAY BUT LOOSE EDDIE RABBITT	41	1979
EVERY WOMAN KNOWS LULU	44	1994
EVERY WOMAN NEEDS LOVE STELLA BROWNE	55	2000
EVERY WORD ERCOLA FEATURING DANIELLA	47	2009
EVERY YEAR EVERY CHRISTMAS LUTHER VANDROSS	43	1995
EVERY YOU EVERY ME PLACEBO	11	1999
EVERYBODY [A] TOMMY ROE	9	1963
EVERYBODY [B] CAPPELLA	66	1991
EVERYBODY [C] ALTERN 8	58	1993
EVERYBODY [D] DJ BOBO	47	1994
EVERYBODY [E] CLOCK	6	1995
EVERYBODY [F] KINKY	71	1996
EVERYBODY [G] PROGRESS PRESENTS THE BOY WUNDA	7	1999
EVERYBODY [H] HEAR'SAY	4	2001
EVERYBODY [I] MARTIN SOLVEIG	22	2005
EVERYBODY [J] RUDENKO	24	2009
EVERYBODY (ALL OVER THE WORLD) FPI PROJECT	65	1991
EVERYBODY (BACKSTREET'S BACK) BACKSTREET BOYS	3	1997
EVERYBODY BE SOMEBODY RUFFNECK FEATURING YAVAHN	13	1995
EVERYBODY COME DOWN DELGADOS	67	2004
EVERYBODY COME ON (CAN U FEEL IT) MR REDZ VS DJ SKRIBBLE	13	2003
EVERYBODY CRIES LIBERTY X	13	2004
EVERYBODY DANCE CHIC	9	1978
EVERYBODY DANCE EVOLUTION	19	1993
EVERYBODY DANCE (THE HORN SONG) BARBARA TUCKER	28	1998
EVERYBODY EVERYBODY BLACK BOX	16	1990
(EVERYBODY) GET DANCIN' BOMBERS	37	1979
EVERYBODY GET TOGETHER DAVE CLARK FIVE	8	1970
EVERYBODY GET UP [A] FIVE	2	1998
EVERYBODY GET UP [B] CAPRICCIO	44	1999
EVERYBODY GETS A SECOND CHANCE MIKE + THE MECHANICS	56	1992
EVERYBODY GO HOME THE PARTY'S OVER CLODAGH RODGERS	47	1970
EVERYBODY GONFI-GON TWO COWBOYS	7	1994
EVERYBODY HAVE A GOOD TIME ARCHIE BELL & THE DRELLS	43	1977
EVERYBODY HERE WANTS YOU JEFF BUCKLEY	43	1998
EVERYBODY HURTS R.E.M.	7	1993
EVERYBODY HURTS HELPING HAITI	1	2010
EVERYBODY IN LOVE JLS	1	2009
EVERYBODY IN THE PLACE (EP) PRODIGY	2	1992
EVERYBODY IS A STAR POINTER SISTERS	61	1979
EVERYBODY KNOWS [A] DAVE CLARK FIVE	37	1965
EVERYBODY KNOWS [B] DAVE CLARK FIVE	2	1967
EVERYBODY KNOWS [C] FREE ASSOCIATION	74	2003
EVERYBODY KNOWS (EXCEPT YOU) DIVINE COMEDY	14	1997
EVERYBODY LETS SOMEBODY LOVE FRANK K FEATURING WISTON OFFICE	61	1991
EVERYBODY LOVES A LOVER DORIS DAY	25	1958
EVERYBODY LOVES SOMEBODY DEAN MARTIN	11	1964
EVERYBODY MOVE CATHY DENNIS	25	1991
EVERYBODY (MOVE YOUR BODY) DIVA	44	1996
EVERYBODY MUST PARTY GEORGIE PORGIE	61	1995
EVERYBODY NEEDS A 303 FATBOY SLIM	34	1997
EVERYBODY NEEDS SOMEBODY [A] BIRDLAND	44	1991
EVERYBODY NEEDS SOMEBODY [B] NICK HOWARD	64	1995
EVERYBODY NEEDS SOMEBODY TO LOVE BLUES BROTHERS	12	1990
EVERYBODY ON THE FLOOR (PUMP IT) TOKYO GHETTO PUSSY	26	1995
EVERYBODY PUMP DJ POWER	46	1992
EVERYBODY (RAP) CRIMINAL ELEMENT ORCHESTRA & WENDELL WILLIAMS	30	1990
EVERYBODY SALSA MODERN ROMANCE	12	1981
EVERYBODY SAY EVERYBODY DO LET LOOSE	29	1995
EVERYBODY THINKS THEY'RE GOING TO GET THEIRS BIS	64	1997
EVERYBODY UP! GLAM METAL DETECTIVES	29	1995
EVERYBODY WANTS HER THUNDER	36	1992
EVERYBODY WANTS ME PIGEON DETECTIVES	51	2008
EVERYBODY WANTS TO RULE THE WORLD TEARS FOR FEARS	2	1985
EVERYBODY WANTS TO RUN THE WORLD TEARS FOR FEARS	5	1986
EVERYBODY'S A ROCK STAR TALL PAUL	60	2002
EVERYBODY'S CHANGING KEANE	4	2004
EVERYBODY'S FOOL EVANESCENCE	24	2004
EVERYBODY'S FREE (TO FEEL GOOD) ROZALLA	6	1991
EVERYBODY'S FREE (TO WEAR SUNSCREEN) BAZ LUHRMANN	1	1999
EVERYBODY'S GONE SENSELESS THINGS	73	1991
EVERYBODY'S GONE TO WAR NERINA PALLOT	14	2006
EVERYBODY'S GONNA BE HAPPY KINKS	17	1965
EVERYBODY'S GOT SUMMER ATLANTIC STARR	36	1994
EVERYBODY'S GOT TO LEARN SOMETIME KORGIS	5	1980
EVERYBODY'S GOT TO LEARN SOMETIME YAZZ	56	1994
(EVERYBODY'S GOT TO LEARN SOMETIME) I NEED YOUR LOVING BABY D	3	1995
EVERYBODY'S GOTTA LEARN SOMETIME CANTAMUS GIRLS CHOIR	73	2005
EVERYBODY'S HAPPY NOWADAYS BUZZCOCKS	29	1979
EVERYBODY'S LAUGHING PHIL FEARON & GALAXY	10	1984
EVERYBODY'S SOMEBODY'S FOOL CONNIE FRANCIS	5	1960
EVERYBODY'S SOMEONE LeANN RIMES & BRIAN McFADDEN	48	2006
EVERYBODY'S TALKIN' NILSSON	23	1969
EVERYBODY'S TALKIN' BEAUTIFUL SOUTH	12	1994
EVERYBODY'S TALKIN' 'BOUT LOVE SILVER CONVENTION	25	1977
EVERYBODY'S TWISTING FRANK SINATRA	22	1962
EVERYDAY [A] MOODY BLUES	44	1965
EVERYDAY [B] DON McLEAN	38	1973
EVERYDAY [C] SLADE	3	1974
EVERYDAY [D] JAM MACHINE	68	1989
EVERYDAY [E] ORCHESTRAL MANOEUVRES IN THE DARK	59	1993
EVERYDAY [F] PHIL COLLINS	15	1994
EVERYDAY [G] INCOGNITO	23	1995
EVERYDAY [H] CRAIG McLACHLAN & THE CULPRITS	65	1995
EVERYDAY [I] AGNELLI & NELSON	17	1999
EVERYDAY [J] BON JOVI	5	2002
EVERYDAY [K] SHY FX & T-POWER FEATURING TOP CAT	75	2006
EVERYDAY [L] CAST OF HIGH SCHOOL MUSICAL 2	59	2007
EVERYDAY GIRL DJ RAP	47	1999
EVERYDAY I LOVE YOU LESS AND LESS KAISER CHIEFS	10	2005
EVERYDAY I WRITE THE BOOK ELVIS COSTELLO & THE ATTRACTIONS	28	1983
EVERYDAY IS A WINDING ROAD SHERYL CROW	12	1996
EVERYDAY IS LIKE SUNDAY MORRISSEY	9	1988
EVERYDAY LIVING WOODENTOPS	72	1986
EVERYDAY NOW TEXAS	44	1989
EVERYDAY OF MY LIFE HOUSE TRAFFIC	24	1997
EVERYDAY PEOPLE SLY & THE FAMILY STONE	36	1969
EVERYDAY PEOPLE ARETHA FRANKLIN	69	1991
EVERYDAY SUNSHINE FISHBONE	60	1992
EVERYDAY THANG MELANIE WILLIAMS	38	1994
EVERYONE I MEET IS FROM CALIFORNIA AMERICA	3	1972
EVERYONE NOSE (ALL THE GIRLS STANDING IN THE LINE FOR THE BATHROOM) N*E*R*D	41	2008
EVERYONE SAYS 'HI' DAVID BOWIE	20	2002
EVERYONE SAYS I'M PARANOID APARTMENT	67	2005
EVERYONE SAYS YOU'RE SO FRAGILE IDLEWILD	47	1998
EVERYONE'S GONE TO THE MOON JONATHAN KING	4	1965
EVERYTHING [A] JODY WATLEY	74	1990
EVERYTHING [B] KICKING BACK WITH TAXMAN	54	1990
EVERYTHING [C] UHF	46	1991
EVERYTHING [D] HYSTERIX	65	1995
EVERYTHING [E] SARAH WASHINGTON	30	1996
EVERYTHING [F] INXS	71	1997
EVERYTHING [G] MARY J BLIGE	6	1997
EVERYTHING [H] DUM DUMS	21	2000
EVERYTHING [I] FEFE DOBSON	42	2004

Title / Artist	Peak Position	Year of Release
EVERYTHING [J] ALANIS MORISSETTE	22	2004
EVERYTHING [K] MICHAEL BUBLE	38	2007
EVERYTHING A MAN COULD EVER NEED GLEN CAMPBELL	32	1970
EVERYTHING ABOUT YOU UGLY KID JOE	3	1992
EVERYTHING CHANGES TAKE THAT	1	1994
EVERYTHING COUNTS DEPECHE MODE	6	1983
EVERYTHING EVENTUALLY APPLETON	38	2003
EVERYTHING GOOD IS BAD WESTWORLD	72	1988
EVERYTHING I AM PLASTIC PENNY	6	1968
(EVERYTHING I DO) I DO IT FOR YOU BRYAN ADAMS	1	1991
(EVERYTHING I DO) I DO IT FOR YOU FATIMA MANSIONS	7	1992
(EVERYTHING I DO) I DO IT FOR YOU Q FEATURING TONY JACKSON	47	1994
EVERYTHING I HAVE IS YOURS EDDIE FISHER	8	1953
EVERYTHING I OWN BREAD	32	1972
EVERYTHING I OWN KEN BOOTHE	1	1974
EVERYTHING I OWN BOY GEORGE	1	1987
EVERYTHING I WANTED DANNII	15	1997
EVERYTHING IS ALRIGHT (UPTIGHT) CJ LEWIS	10	1994
EVERYTHING IS AVERAGE NOWADAYS KAISER CHIEFS	19	2007
EVERYTHING IS BEAUTIFUL RAY STEVENS	6	1970
EVERYTHING IS BORROWED STREETS	37	2008
EVERYTHING IS EVERYTHING [A] LAURYN HILL	19	1999
EVERYTHING IS EVERYTHING [B] PHOENIX	74	2004
EVERYTHING IS GONNA BE ALRIGHT SOUNDS OF BLACKNESS	29	1994
EVERYTHING IS GREAT INNER CIRCLE	37	1979
EVERYTHING I'VE GOT IN MY POCKET MINNIE DRIVER	34	2004
EVERYTHING MUST CHANGE PAUL YOUNG	9	1984
EVERYTHING MUST GO MANIC STREET PREACHERS	5	1996
EVERYTHING MY HEART DESIRES ADAM RICKITT	15	1999
EVERYTHING SHE WANTS WHAM!	2	1984
EVERYTHING STARTS WITH AN 'E' E-ZEE POSSEE	15	1989
EVERYTHING TO EVERYONE EVERCLEAR	41	1998
EVERYTHING WILL FLOW SUEDE	24	1999
EVERYTHING YOU NEED MADISON AVENUE	33	2001
EVERYTHING YOU WANT VERTICAL HORIZON	42	2000
EVERYTHING'L TURN OUT FINE STEALERS WHEEL	33	1973
EVERYTHING'S ALRIGHT MOJOS	9	1964
EVERYTHING'S COOL POP WILL EAT ITSELF	23	1994
EVERYTHING'S GONE GREEN NEW ORDER	38	1981
EVERYTHING'S GONNA BE ALRIGHT SWEETBOX	5	1998
EVERYTHING'S NOT YOU STONEPROOF	68	1999
EVERYTHING'S RUINED FAITH NO MORE	28	1992
EVERYTHING'S TUESDAY CHAIRMEN OF THE BOARD	12	1971
EVERYTIME [A] LUSTRAL	30	1997
EVERYTIME [B] TATYANA ALI	20	1999
EVERYTIME [C] A1	3	1999
EVERYTIME [D] BRITNEY SPEARS	1	2004
EVERYTIME I CLOSE MY EYES BABYFACE	13	1997
EVERYTIME I SEE HER (SOUND OF EDEN) ANOTHER CHANCE	62	2007
EVERYTIME I THINK OF YOU FM	73	1990
EVERYTIME WE TOUCH [A] CASCADA	2	2006
EVERYTIME WE TOUCH [B] DAVID GUETTA FEATURING CHRIS WILLIS	68	2009
EVERYTIME YOU NEED ME FRAGMA FEATURING MARIA RUBIA	3	2001
EVERYTIME YOU SLEEP DEACON BLUE	64	2001
EVERYTIME YOU TOUCH ME QFX	22	1996
EVERYWHERE [A] FLEETWOOD MAC	4	1988
EVERYWHERE [A] LNM PROJEKT FEATURING BONNIE BAILEY	38	2005
EVERYWHERE [B] MICHELLE BRANCH	18	2002
EVERYWHERE I GO [A] ISOTONIK	25	1992
EVERYWHERE I GO [B] JACKSON BROWNE	67	1994
EVERYWHERE I LOOK DARYL HALL & JOHN OATES	74	1991
EVE'S VOLCANO (COVERED IN SIN) JULIAN COPE	41	1987
EVIDENCE FAITH NO MORE	32	1995
EVIL [A] LADYTRON	44	2003
EVIL [B] INTERPOL	18	2005
EVIL HEARTED YOU YARDBIRDS	3	1965
EVIL MAN FATIMA MANSIONS	59	1992
THE EVIL THAT MEN DO IRON MAIDEN	5	1988
EVIL TWIN LOVE/HATE	59	1991
EVIL WOMAN ELECTRIC LIGHT ORCHESTRA	10	1976
EVOLUTIONDANCE PART ONE (EP) EVOLUTION	52	1994
EV'RY LITTLE BIT MILLIE SCOTT	63	1987
EV'RY TIME WE SAY GOODBYE SIMPLY RED	11	1987
EV'RYWHERE DAVID WHITFIELD	3	1955
THE EX BILLY TALENT	61	2004
EXCEEDER MASON VS PRINCESS SUPERSTAR	3	2007
EXCERPT FROM A TEENAGE OPERA KEITH WEST	2	1967
EXCITABLE AMAZULU	12	1985
EXCITED M PEOPLE	29	1992
EXCLUSIVE APOLLO PRESENTS HOUSE OF VIRGINISM	67	1996
EXCLUSIVELY YOURS MARK WYNTER	32	1961
EXCUSE SOULWAX	35	2005
EXCUSE ME BABY MAGIC LANTERNS	44	1966
EXCUSE ME MISS JAY-Z	17	2003
EXCUSE MY BROTHER MITCHELL BROTHERS	58	2005
EX-FACTOR LAURYN HILL	4	1999
EX-GIRLFRIEND NO DOUBT	23	2000
EXHALE (SHOOP SHOOP) WHITNEY HOUSTON	11	1995
EXODUS [A] BOB MARLEY & THE WAILERS	14	1977
EXODUS [B] SUNSCREEM	40	1995
EXODUS – LIVE LEVELLERS	24	1996
THE EXORCIST SCIENTIST	46	1990
EXORCIST SHADES OF RHYTHM	53	1991
EXPANDER FUTURE SOUND OF LONDON	72	1994
EXPANSIONS SCOTT GROOVES FEATURING ROY AYERS	68	1998
EXPANSIONS '86 (EXPAND YOUR MIND) CHRIS PAUL FEATURING DAVID JOSEPH	58	1986
EXPERIENCE DIANA ROSS	47	1986
EXPERIMENT IV KATE BUSH	23	1986
EXPERIMENTS WITH MICE JOHNNY DANKWORTH	7	1956
EXPLAIN THE REASONS FIRST LIGHT	65	1983
EXPLORATION OF SPACE COSMIC GATE	29	2002
EXPO 2000 KRAFTWERK	27	2000
EXPRESS [A] B.T. EXPRESS	34	1975
EXPRESS [B] DINA CARROLL	12	1993
EXPRESS YOUR FREEDOM ANTICAPPELLA	31	1995
EXPRESS YOURSELF [A] MADONNA	5	1989
EXPRESS YOURSELF [B] N.W.A.	26	1989
EXPRESS YOURSELF [C] JIMI POLO	59	1992
EXPRESSION SALT-N-PEPA	23	1990
EXPRESSLY (EP) EDWYN COLLINS	42	1994
EXPRESSO BONGO EP CLIFF RICHARD & THE SHADOWS	14	1960
EXTACY SHADES OF RHYTHM	16	1991
EXTENDED PLAY EP BRYAN FERRY	7	1976
THE EXTENDED PLEASURE OF DANCE (EP) 808 STATE	56	1990
EXTERMINATE! SNAP! FEATURING NIKI HARIS	2	1993
EXTRAVAGANZA JAMIE FOXX FEATURING KANYE WEST	43	2006
EXTREME WAYS MOBY	39	2002
EXTREMIS HAL FEATURING GILLIAN ANDERSON	23	1997
EYE BEE M COMMANDER TOM	75	2000
EYE FOR AN EYE UNKLE	31	2003
EYE HATE U ARTIST FORMERLY KNOWN AS PRINCE (AFKAP)	20	1995
EYE KNOW DE LA SOUL	14	1989
EYE LEVEL SIMON PARK ORCHESTRA	1	1972
EYE OF THE TIGER SURVIVOR	1	1982
EYE OF THE TIGER FRANK BRUNO	28	1995
EYE TALK FASHION	69	1984
EYE TO EYE CHAKA KHAN	16	1985
EYE WONDER APPLES	75	1991
EYEBALL (EYEBALL PAUL'S THEME) SUNBURST	48	2000
EYES DON'T LIE TRUCE	20	1998
THE EYES HAVE IT KAREL FIALKA	52	1980
EYES OF A STRANGER QUEENSRYCHE	59	1989
EYES OF BLUE PAUL CARRACK	40	1996
EYES OF SORROW A GUY CALLED GERALD	52	1989
THE EYES OF TRUTH ENIGMA	21	1994
EYES ON YOU JAY SEAN FEATURING RISHI RICH PROJECT	6	2004
EYES THAT SEE IN THE DARK KENNY ROGERS	61	1983
EYES WITHOUT A FACE BILLY IDOL	18	1984
EZ PASS HAR MAR SUPERSTAR	59	2003
EZY WOLFSBANE	68	1991

F

Title / Artist	Peak Position	Year of Release
FA FA FA FA FA (SAD SONG) OTIS REDDING	23	1966
FABLE ROBERT MILES	7	1996
FABRICATED LUNACY TERRIS	62	2001
FABULOUS [A] CHARLIE GRACIE	8	1957
FABULOUS [B] JAHEIM	41	2003
FABULOUS [C] SHARPAY	64	2007
THE FACE AND WHY NOT?	13	1990
FACE DROP SEAN KINGSTON	56	2009
FACE FOR THE RADIO VIEW	69	2007
FACE THE STRANGE EP THERAPY?	18	1993
FACE TO FACE SIOUXSIE & THE BANSHEES	21	1992
FACES 2 UNLIMITED	8	1993
THE FACES (EP) FACES	41	1977
FACT OF LIFE [A] OUI 3	38	1994
FACTS + FIGURES HUGH CORNWELL	61	1987
THE FACTS OF LIFE [A] DANNY MADDEN	72	1990
THE FACTS OF LIFE [B] BLACK BOX RECORDER	20	2000
FACTS OF LOVE CLIMIE FISHER	50	1989
FADE [A] PARIS ANGELS	70	1991
FADE [B] SOLU MUSIC FEATURING KIMBLEE	18	2006
FADE INTO YOU MAZZY STAR	48	1994
FADE TO GREY VISAGE	8	1981
FADED BEN HARPER	54	1998
FADER DRUGSTORE	72	1995
FADING LIKE A FLOWER ROXETTE	12	1991
FADING LIKE A FLOWER DANCING DJS VS ROXETTE	18	2005
FAILURE [A] SKINNY	31	1998
FAILURE [B] KINGS OF CONVENIENCE	63	2001
FAILURE'S NOT FLATTERING NEW FOUND GLORY	67	2004
FAINT LINKIN PARK	15	2003
A FAIR AFFAIR (JE T'AIME) MISTY OLDLAND	49	1994
FAIR BLOWS THE WIND FOR FRANCE PELE	62	1992
FAIR FIGHT DJ ZINC	72	2002

Title / Artist	Peak Position	Year of Release
FAIRGROUND SIMPLY RED	1	1995
FAIRPLAY SOUL II SOUL FEATURING ROSE WINDROSS	63	1988
FAIRWEATHER FRIEND SYMPOSIUM	25	1997
FAIRYTALE [A] DANA	13	1976
FAIRYTALE [B] ALEXANDER RYBAK	10	2009
FAIRYTALE OF NEW YORK POGUES FEATURING KIRSTY MacCOLL	5	1987
FAIT ACCOMPLI CURVE	22	1992
FAITH [A] GEORGE MICHAEL	2	1987
FAITH [B] WEE PAPA GIRL RAPPERS	60	1988
FAITH CAN MOVE MOUNTAINS JOHNNIE RAY & THE FOUR LADS	7	1952
FAITH CAN MOVE MOUNTAINS NAT 'KING' COLE	10	1953
FAITH CAN MOVE MOUNTAINS JIMMY YOUNG	11	1953
FAITH HEALER RECOIL	60	1992
FAITH IN PEOPLE HONEYMOON MACHINE	64	2005
FAITH (IN THE POWER OF LOVE) ROZALLA	11	1991
FAITH OF THE HEART ROD STEWART	60	1999
FAITHFUL GO WEST	13	1992
THE FAITHFUL HUSSAR TED HEATH	18	1956
THE FAITHFUL HUSSAR LOUIS ARMSTRONG WITH HIS ALL-STARS	27	1956
THE FAITHFUL HUSSAR (DON'T CRY MY LOVE) VERA LYNN	29	1957
FAITHFULNESS SKIN	64	2003
FAITHLESS SCRITTI POLITTI	56	1982
FAKE [A] ALEXANDER O'NEAL	16	1987
FAKE [B] SIMPLY RED	21	2003
FAKE FUR URUSEI YATSURA	40	1997
FAKE PLASTIC TREES RADIOHEAD	20	1995
THE FAKE SOUND OF PROGRESS LOSTPROPHETS	21	2002
FAKER AUDIOWEB	70	1997
FALCON RAH BAND	35	1980
FALIING IN LOVE AGAIN TECHNO TWINS	70	1982
THE FALL [A] MINISTRY	53	1996
THE FALL [B] WAY OUT WEST	61	2000
FALL AT YOUR FEET CROWDED HOUSE	17	1991
FALL AT YOUR FEET CM2 FEATURING LISA LAW	66	2002
FALL BACK DOWN RANCID	42	2003
FALL BEHIND ME DONNAS	55	2004
FALL DOWN (SPIRIT OF LOVE) TRAMAINE	60	1985
FALL EP RIDE	34	1990
FALL FROM GRACE ESKIMOS & EGYPT	51	1993
FALL IN LOVE WITH ME [A] EARTH, WIND & FIRE	47	1983
FALL IN LOVE WITH ME [B] BOOTH & THE BAD ANGEL	57	1998
FALL IN LOVE WITH YOU CLIFF RICHARD	2	1960
FALL OUT POLICE	47	1979
FALL TO LOVE DIESEL PARK WEST	48	1992
FALL TO PIECES VELVET REVOLVER	32	2004
THE FALL VS 2003 FALL	64	2002
FALLEN SARAH McLACHLAN	50	2004
THE FALLEN FRANZ FERDINAND	14	2006
FALLEN ANGEL [A] FRANKIE VALLI	11	1976
FALLEN ANGEL [B] POISON	59	1988
FALLEN ANGEL [C] TRACI LORDS	72	1995
FALLEN ANGEL [D] ELBOW	19	2003
FALLEN ANGELS BUFFY SAINTE-MARIE	57	1992
FALLIN' [A] CONNIE FRANCIS	20	1958
FALLIN' [B] TEENAGE FANCLUB & DE LA SOUL	59	1994
FALLIN' [C] ALICIA KEYS	3	2001
FALLIN' [D] UN-CUT	63	2003
FALLIN' [E] SADIE AMA	68	2007
FALLIN' IN LOVE HAMILTON, JOE FRANK & REYNOLDS	33	1975
FALLING [A] ROY ORBISON	9	1963
FALLING [B] JULEE CRUISE	7	1990
FALLING [C] CATHY DENNIS	32	1993
FALLING [D] ALISON MOYET	42	1993
FALLING [E] ANT & DEC	14	1997
FALLING [F] BOOM!	11	2001
FALLING [G] LIQUID STATE FEATURING MARCELLA WOODS	60	2002
FALLING [H] McALMONT & BUTLER	23	2002
FALLING ANGELS RIDING (MUTINY) DAVID ESSEX	29	1985
FALLING APART AT THE SEAMS MARMALADE	9	1976
FALLING AWAY FROM ME KORN	24	2000
FALLING DOWN [A] DURAN DURAN	52	2007
FALLING DOWN [B] OASIS	10	2009
FALLING IN AND OUT OF LOVE FEMME FATALE	69	1989
FALLING IN LOVE [A] SURFACE	67	1983
FALLING IN LOVE [B] SYBIL	68	1986
FALLING IN LOVE [C] LA BOUCHE	43	1995
FALLING IN LOVE AGAIN [A] LONDONBEAT	60	1989
FALLING IN LOVE AGAIN [B] EAGLE-EYE CHERRY	8	1998
FALLING IN LOVE (IS HARD ON THE KNEES) AEROSMITH	22	1997
FALLING INTO YOU CELINE DION	10	1996
FALLING OUT OF REACH GUILLEMOTS	49	2008
FALLING STARS SUNSET STRIPPERS	3	2005
FALLING TO PIECES FAITH NO MORE	41	1990
FALSE ALARM BRONX	73	2004
FALTER HUNDRED REASONS	38	2002
FAME [A] DAVID BOWIE	17	1975
FAME [B] IRENE CARA	1	1982
FAME [B] NATURI NAUGHTON	33	2009
FAMILIAR FEELING MOLOKO	10	2003
FAMILIUS HORRIBILUS POP WILL EAT ITSELF	27	1993
FAMILY AFFAIR [A] SLY & THE FAMILY STONE	15	1972
FAMILY AFFAIR [A] B.E.F. FEATURING LALAH HATHAWAY	37	1991
FAMILY AFFAIR [A] SHABBA RANKS FEATURING PATRA & TERRY & MONICA	18	1993
FAMILY AFFAIR [B] MARY J BLIGE	8	2001
FAMILY MAN [A] MIKE OLDFIELD FEATURING MAGGIE REILLY	45	1982
FAMILY MAN [A] DARYL HALL & JOHN OATES	15	1983
FAMILY MAN [A] FLEETWOOD MAC	54	1987
FAMILY MAN [B] ROACHFORD	25	1989
FAMILY OF MAN FARM	58	1990
FAMILY PORTRAIT P!NK	11	2002
FAMINE SINEAD O'CONNOR	51	1995
FAMOUS LAST WORDS MY CHEMICAL ROMANCE	8	2007
FAN MAIL DICKIES	57	1980
FAN THE FLAME BARBARA PENNINGTON	62	1985
FANCY PANTS KENNY	4	1975
FAN'DABI'DOZI KRANKIES	46	1981
FANFARE FOR THE COMMON MAN EMERSON, LAKE & PALMER	2	1977
FANLIGHT FANNY CLINTON FORD	22	1962
FANS KINGS OF LEON	13	2007
FANTASTIC DAY HAIRCUT 100	9	1982
FANTASTIC VOYAGE COOLIO	41	1994
FANTASY [A] EARTH, WIND & FIRE	14	1978
FANTASY [A] BLACK BOX	5	1990
FANTASY [B] GERARD KENNY	34	1980
FANTASY [C] FANTASY UFO	56	1990
FANTASY [D] TEN CITY	45	1993
FANTASY [E] MARIAH CAREY	4	1995
FANTASY [F] LEVELLERS	16	1995
FANTASY [G] APPLETON	2	2002
FANTASY ISLAND [A] TIGHT FIT	5	1982
FANTASY ISLAND [B] M PEOPLE	33	1997
FANTASY REAL GALAXY FEATURING PHIL FEARON	41	1983
FAR LONGPIGS	37	1996
FAR ABOVE THE CLOUDS MIKE OLDFIELD	53	1999
FAR AND AWAY AIDA	58	2000
FAR AWAY [A] SHIRLEY BASSEY	24	1962
FAR AWAY [B] NICKELBACK	40	2006
FAR AWAY EYES ROLLING STONES	3	1978
FAR FAR AWAY SLADE	2	1974
FAR FROM HOME [A] LEVELLERS	71	1991
(FAR FROM) HOME [B] TIGA	65	2006
FAR FROM OVER FRANK STALLONE	68	1983
FAR GONE AND OUT JESUS & MARY CHAIN	23	1992
FAR OUT [A] SON'Z OF A LOOP DA LOOP ERA	36	1992
FAR OUT [B] DEEJAY PUNK-ROC	43	1998
FARAWAY PLACES BACHELORS	36	1963
FAREWELL ANGELINA JOAN BAEZ	35	1966
FAREWELL – BRING IT ON HOME TO ME ROD STEWART	7	1974
FAREWELL IS A LONELY SOUND JIMMY RUFFIN	8	1970
FAREWELL MR SORROW ALL ABOUT EVE	36	1991
FAREWELL MY SUMMER LOVE MICHAEL JACKSON	7	1984
FAREWELL MY SUMMER LOVE CHAOS	55	1992
FAREWELL TO THE FAIRGROUND WHITE LIES	33	2009
FAREWELL TO THE MOON YORK	37	2000
FAREWELL TO TWILIGHT SYMPOSIUM	25	1997
FARMER BILL'S COWMAN (I WAS KAISER BILL'S BATMAN) WURZELS	32	1977
FARON YOUNG PREFAB SPROUT	74	1985
FAR-OUT SON OF LUNG & THE RAMBLINGS OF A MADMAN FUTURE SOUND OF LONDON	22	1995
FASCINATED [A] LISA B	35	1993
FASCINATED [B] RAVEN MAIZE	37	2002
FASCINATING RHYTHM BASS-O-MATIC	9	1990
FASCINATION ALPHABEAT	6	2008
FASHION DAVID BOWIE	5	1980
FASHION '98 GLAMMA KID	49	1998
FASHION CRISIS HITS NEW YORK FRANK & WALTERS	42	1993
FASSY HOLE RONI SIZE	60	2004
FAST AS YOU CAN FIONA APPLE	33	2000
FAST BOY BLUETONES	25	2003
FAST CAR [A] TRACY CHAPMAN	5	1988
FAST CAR [B] DILLINJA	56	2003
FAST FOOD SONG FAST FOOD ROCKERS	2	2003
FASTEN YOUR SEATBELT PENDULUM & FRESH FEATURING SPYDA	60	2005
FASTER MANIC STREET PREACHERS	16	1994
FASTER KILL PUSSYCAT PAUL OAKENFOLD FEATURING BRITTANY MURPHY	7	2006
FASTER THAN THE SPEED OF NIGHT BONNIE TYLER	43	1983
FASTER THE CHASE INME	31	2004
FASTLOVE GEORGE MICHAEL	1	1996
FAT BASTARD (EP) MEDWAY	69	2000
FAT BLACK HEART PELE	75	1993
FAT BOTTOMED GIRLS QUEEN	11	1978
FAT LIP SUM 41	8	2001
FAT NECK BLACK GRAPE	10	1996
FATAL HESITATION CHRIS DE BURGH	44	1986
FATHER [A] CHRISTIANS	55	1992
FATHER [B] LL COOL J	10	1998
FATHER AND DAUGHTER PAUL SIMON	31	2006
FATHER AND SON BOYZONE	2	1995
FATHER AND SON RONAN KEATING & YUSUF	2	2005
FATHER CHRISTMAS DO NOT TOUCH ME GOODIES	7	1974
FATHER FIGURE GEORGE MICHAEL	11	1988
FATTIE BUM BUM CARL MALCOLM	8	1975
FATTIE BUM BUM DIVERSIONS	34	1975
FAVOURITE SHIRTS (BOY MEETS GIRL) HAIRCUT 100	4	1981
FAVOURITE THINGS BIG BROVAZ	2	2003

Title / Artist	Peak Position	Year of Release
FBI SHADOWS	6	1961
FE' REAL MAXI PRIEST FEATURING APACHE INDIAN	33	1992
F.E.A.R. IAN BROWN	13	2001
THE FEAR LILY ALLEN	1	2009
FEAR LOVES THIS PLACE JULIAN COPE	42	1992
FEAR OF THE DARK [A] GORDON GILTRAP BAND	58	1979
FEAR OF THE DARK (LIVE) [B] IRON MAIDEN	8	1993
FEAR SATAN MOGWAI	57	1998
FEAR, THE MINDKILLER EON	63	1991
FEARLESS BRAVERY	43	2005
FED UP HOUSE OF PAIN	68	1996
FEDORA (I'LL BE YOUR DAWG) CARAMBA	56	1983
FEE FI FO FUM CANDY GIRLS FEATURING SWEET PUSSY PAULINE	23	1995
FEED MY FRANKENSTEIN ALICE COOPER	27	1992
FEED THE FEELING PERCEPTION	58	1992
FEED THE TREE BELLY	32	1993
FEED YOUR ADDICTION EASTERN LANE	72	2003
FEEDING TIME LOOK	50	1981
FEEL [A] RUTH JOY	67	1992
FEEL [B] HOUSE OF LOVE	45	1992
FEEL [C] ROBBIE WILLIAMS	4	2002
FEEL EVERY BEAT ELECTRONIC	39	1991
FEEL FREE SOUL II SOUL FEATURING DO'REEN	64	1988
FEEL GOOD [A] PHATS & SMALL	7	1999
FEEL GOOD [B] MADASUN	29	2000
FEEL GOOD INC GORILLAZ	2	2005
FEEL GOOD TIME P!NK FEATURING WILLIAM ORBIT	3	2003
FEEL IT [A] HI-LUX	41	1995
FEEL IT [B] CAROL BAILEY	41	1995
FEEL IT [C] NENEH CHERRY	68	1997
FEEL IT [D] TAMPERER FEATURING MAYA	1	1998
FEEL IT [E] INAYA DAY	51	2000
FEEL IT BOY BEENIE MAN FEATURING JANET JACKSON	9	2002
FEEL IT WITH ME ULTRABEAT	57	2005
FEEL LIKE CALLING HOME MR BIG	35	1977
FEEL LIKE CHANGE BLACK	56	1991
FEEL LIKE MAKING LOVE [A] ROBERTA FLACK	34	1974
FEEL LIKE MAKIN' LOVE [A] GEORGE BENSON	28	1983
FEEL LIKE MAKIN' LOVE [B] BAD COMPANY	20	1975
FEEL LIKE MAKING LOVE [B] PAULINE HENRY	12	1993
FEEL LIKE SINGIN' [A] SANDY B	60	1993
FEEL LIKE SINGING [B] TAK TIX	33	1996
FEEL ME BLANCMANGE	46	1982
FEEL ME FLOW NAUGHTY BY NATURE	23	1995
FEEL MY BODY FRANK'O MOIRAGHI FEATURING AMNESIA	39	1996
FEEL NO PAIN SADE	56	1992
FEEL SO FINE JOHNNY PRESTON	18	1960
FEEL SO GOOD [A] MA$E	10	1997
FEEL SO GOOD [B] JON THE DENTIST VS OLLIE JAYE	72	2000
FEEL SO HIGH DES'REE	13	1991
FEEL SO REAL [A] STEVE ARRINGTON	5	1985
FEEL SO REAL [B] DREAM FREQUENCY FEATURING DEBBIE SHARP	23	1992
FEEL SURREAL FREEFALL FEATURING PSYCHOTROPIC	63	1991
FEEL THA VIBE THAT KID CHRIS	52	1997
FEEL THE BEAT [A] CAMISRA	32	1998
FEEL THE BEAT [B] DARUDE	5	2000
FEEL THE DRUM (EP) PARKS & WILSON	71	2000
FEEL THE DRUMS NATIVE	46	2001
FEEL THE HEAT RONI SIZE	55	2002
FEEL THE MUSIC GURU	34	1995
FEEL THE NEED [A] LEIF GARRETT	38	1979
FEEL THE NEED [A] G NATION FEATURING ROSIE	58	1997
FEEL THE NEED [B] JT TAYLOR	57	1991
FEEL THE NEED [C] WEIRD SCIENCE	62	2000
FEEL THE NEED IN ME DETROIT EMERALDS	4	1973
FEEL THE NEED IN ME FORREST	17	1983
FEEL THE NEED IN ME SHAKIN' STEVENS	26	1988
FEEL THE PAIN DINOSAUR JR	25	1994
FEEL THE RAINDROPS ADVENTURES	58	1985
FEEL THE REAL DAVID BENDETH	44	1979
FEEL THE RHYTHM [A] JAZZI P	51	1990
FEEL THE RHYTHM [B] TERRORIZE	69	1992
FEEL THE RHYTHM [C] JINNY	74	1993
FEEL THE SAME TRIPLE X	32	1999
FEEL THE SUNSHINE ALEX REECE	26	1995
FEEL THE VIBE (TIL THE MORNING COMES) AXWELL	16	2005
FEEL TOGETHER BEN MACKLIN FEATURING TIGER LILY	71	2007
FEEL WHAT YOU WANT KRISTINE W	33	1994
FEELIN' LA'S	43	1991
FEELIN' ALRIGHT E.Y.C.	16	1993
THE FEELIN (CLAP YOUR HANDS) RHYTHMATIC JUNKIES	67	1999
FEELIN' FINE ULTRABEAT	12	2003
FEELIN' INSIDE BOBBY BROWN	40	1997
FEELIN' ME THERESE	61	2007
FEELIN' SO GOOD JENNIFER LOPEZ FEATURING BIG PUN & FAT JOE	15	2000
FEELIN' THE SAME WAY NORAH JONES	72	2002
FEELIN' U SHY FX & T-POWER FEATURING KELE LE ROC	34	2003
FEELIN' WAY TOO DAMN GOOD NICKELBACK	39	2004
FEELIN' YOU ALI	63	1998
THE FEELING [A] URBAN HYPE	67	1992
THE FEELING [B] TIN TIN OUT FEATURING SWEET TEE	32	1994
FEELING A MOMENT FEEDER	13	2005
FEELING FOR YOU CASSIUS	16	1999
FEELING GOOD NINA SIMONE	40	1994
FEELING GOOD HUFF & HERB	31	1997
FEELING GOOD MUSE	24	2001
FEELING IT TOO 3 JAYS	17	1999
FEELING SO REAL MOBY	30	1994
FEELING THE LOVE REACTOR	56	2004
FEELING THIS BLINK-182	15	2003
FEELING THIS WAY CONDUCTOR & THE COWBOY	35	2000
FEELINGS MORRIS ALBERT	4	1975
FEELINGS OF FOREVER TIFFANY	52	1988
FEELS GOOD (DON'T WORRY BOUT A THING) NAUGHTY BY NATURE FEATURING 3LW	44	2002
FEELS JUST LIKE IT SHOULD JAMIROQUAI	8	2005
(FEELS LIKE) HEAVEN [A] FICTION FACTORY	6	1984
FEELS LIKE HEAVEN [B] URBAN COOKIE COLLECTIVE	5	1993
FEELS LIKE HOME MECK FEATURING DINO	39	2007
FEELS LIKE I'M IN LOVE KELLY MARIE	1	1980
FEELS LIKE THE FIRST TIME [A] FOREIGNER	39	1978
FEELS LIKE THE FIRST TIME [B] SINITTA	45	1986
FEELS LIKE THE RIGHT TIME SHAKATAK	41	1980
FEELS SO GOOD [A] VAN HALEN	63	1989
FEELS SO GOOD [B] XSCAPE	34	1995
FEELS SO GOOD [C] ZERO VU FEATURING LORNA B	69	1997
FEELS SO GOOD [D] MELANIE B	5	2001
FEELS SO REAL (WON'T LET GO) PATRICE RUSHEN	51	1984
FEELS SO RIGHT VICTOR SIMONELLI PRESENTS SOLUTION	63	1996
FEENIN' JODECI	18	1994
FEET UP GUY MITCHELL	2	1952
FELICITY ORANGE JUICE	63	1982
FELL IN LOVE WITH A BOY JOSS STONE	18	2004
FELL IN LOVE WITH A GIRL WHITE STRIPES	21	2002
FELL ON BLACK DAYS SOUNDGARDEN	24	1995
FEMALE INTUITION MAI TAI	54	1986
FEMALE OF THE SPECIES SPACE	14	1996
FERGUS SINGS THE BLUES DEACON BLUE	14	1989
FERNANDO ABBA	1	1976
FERRIS WHEEL EVERLY BROTHERS	22	1964
FERRY ACROSS THE MERSEY GERRY & THE PACEMAKERS	8	1964
FERRY 'CROSS THE MERSEY CHRISTIANS, HOLLY JOHNSON, PAUL McCARTNEY, GERRY MARSDEN & STOCK AITKEN WATERMAN	1	1989
FESTIVAL TIME SAN REMO STRINGS	39	1971
FEUER FREI RAMMSTEIN	35	2002
FEVA LAS VEGAS N-DUBZ	57	2007
FEVER [A] PEGGY LEE	5	1958
FEVER [A] HELEN SHAPIRO	38	1964
FEVER [A] McCOYS	44	1965
FEVER [A] MADONNA	6	1993
FEVER [B] S-J	46	1997
FEVER [C] STARSAILOR	18	2001
FEVER CALLED LOVE RHC	65	1992
FEVER FOR THE FLAVA HOT ACTION COP	41	2003
FEVER PITCH THE EP PRETENDERS, LA'S, ORLANDO, NICK HORNBY	65	1997
FICTION OF LIFE CHINA DRUM	65	1997
FIDELITY REGINA SPEKTOR	45	2007
FIELD OF DREAMS FLIP & FILL FEATURING JO JAMES	28	2003
FIELDS OF ANFIELD ROAD LIVERPOOL COLLECTIVE/KOP CHOIR	14	2009
FIELDS OF FIRE (400 MILES) BIG COUNTRY	10	1983
FIELDS OF GOLD STING	16	1993
THE FIELDS OF LOVE ATB FEATURING YORK	16	2001
FIESTA [A] POGUES	24	1988
FIESTA [B] R KELLY FEATURING JAY-Z	23	2001
!FIESTA FATAL! B-TRIBE	64	1993
FIFTEEN FEET OF PURE WHITE SNOW NICK CAVE & THE BAD SEEDS	52	2001
15 MINUTES YEAH YOU'S	36	2009
15 MINUTES OF FAME SHEEP ON DRUGS	44	1993
15 STEPS (EP) MONKEY MAFIA	67	1997
15 WAYS FALL	65	1994
15 YEARS (EP) LEVELLERS	11	1992
5TH ANNIVERSARY EP JUDGE DREAD	31	1977
A FIFTH OF BEETHOVEN WALTER MURPHY & THE BIG APPLE BAND	28	1976
50:50:00 LEMAR	5	2003
51ST STATE NEW MODEL ARMY	71	1986
50FT QUEENIE PJ HARVEY	27	1993
54-66 (WAS MY NUMBER) ASWAD	70	1984
FIFTY GRAND FOR CHRISTMAS PAUL HOLT	35	2004
59TH STREET BRIDGE SONG (FEELING GROOVY) HARPERS BIZARRE	34	1967
57 BIFFY CLYRO	61	2002
57 CHANNELS (AND NOTHIN' ON) BRUCE SPRINGSTEEN	32	1992
50 TO A POUND PADDINGTONS	32	2005
50 WAYS TO LEAVE YOUR LOVER PAUL SIMON	23	1976
FIFTY-FOUR SEA LEVEL	63	1979
FIGARO BROTHERHOOD OF MAN	1	1978
THE FIGHT MARTY WILDE	47	1960
FIGHT McKOY	54	1993
FIGHT FOR OURSELVES SPANDAU BALLET	15	1986
FIGHT FOR THIS LOVE CHERYL COLE	1	2009
FIGHT FOR YOUR RIGHT (TO PARTY) NYCC	14	1998
FIGHT MUSIC D12	11	2001
THE FIGHT SONG MARILYN MANSON	24	2001
FIGHT TEST FLAMING LIPS	28	2003

Title / Artist	Peak Position	Year of Release
FIGHT THE POWER PUBLIC ENEMY	29	1989
FIGHT THE YOUTH FISHBONE	60	1992
FIGHTER CHRISTINA AGUILERA	3	2003
FIGHTING FIT GENE	22	1996
FIGURE IT OUT LIL' CHRIS	57	2007
FIGURE OF 8 GRID	50	1992
FIGURE OF EIGHT PAUL McCARTNEY	42	1989
FIJI ATLANTIS VS AVATAR	52	2000
FILL HER UP GENE	36	1999
FILL ME IN CRAIG DAVID	1	2000
FILL MY LITTLE WORLD FEELING	10	2006
FILLING UP WITH HEAVEN HUMAN LEAGUE	36	1995
A FILM FOR THE FUTURE IDLEWILD	53	1998
FILM MAKER COOPER TEMPLE CLAUSE	20	2002
FILMSTAR SUEDE	9	1997
FILTHY SAINT ETIENNE	39	1991
FILTHY/GORGEOUS SCISSOR SISTERS	5	2005
THE FINAL ARREARS MULL HISTORICAL SOCIETY	32	2003
THE FINAL COUNTDOWN EUROPE	1	1986
FINALLY [A] CE CE PENISTON	2	1991
FINALLY [B] KINGS OF TOMORROW FEATURING JULIE McKNIGHT	24	2001
FINALLY FOUND HONEYZ	4	1998
FINCHLEY CENTRAL NEW VAUDEVILLE BAND	11	1967
FIND A WAY [A] COLDCUT FEATURING QUEEN LATIFAH	52	1990
FIND A WAY [B] A TRIBE CALLED QUEST	41	1998
FIND 'EM, FOOL 'EM, FORGET 'EM S-EXPRESS	43	1992
FIND ME (ODYSSEY TO ANYOONA) JAM & SPOON FEATURING PLAVKA	22	1994
FIND MY LOVE FAIRGROUND ATTRACTION	7	1988
FIND MY WAY BACK HOME NASHVILLE TEENS	34	1965
FIND THE ANSWER WITHIN BOO RADLEYS	37	1995
FIND THE COLOUR FEEDER	24	2003
FIND THE RIVER R.E.M.	54	1993
FIND THE TIME [A] FIVE STAR	7	1986
FIND THE TIME (PART ONE) [B] QUADROPHONIA	41	1991
FIND THE TIME [C] GET CAPE. WEAR CAPE. FLY.	33	2008
FINDERS KEEPERS [A] CHAIRMEN OF THE BOARD	21	1973
FINDERS KEEPERS [B] YOU ME AT SIX	33	2009
FINDING OUT TRUE LOVE IS BLIND LOUIS XIV	57	2005
FINE DAY [A] ROLF HARRIS	24	2000
FINE DAY [B] KIRSTY HAWKSHAW	62	2002
FINE LINE PAUL McCARTNEY	20	2005
FINE TIME [A] NEW ORDER	11	1988
FINE TIME [B] YAZZ	9	1989
FINER NIGHTMARES ON WAX	63	1999
FINER FEELINGS KYLIE MINOGUE	11	1992
THE FINEST S.O.S. BAND	17	1986
THE FINEST TRUCE	54	1995
FINEST DREAMS RICHARD X FEATURING KELIS	8	2003
FINEST WORKSONG R.E.M.	50	1988
FINETIME CAST	17	1995
FINGER OF SUSPICION DICKIE VALENTINE WITH THE STARGAZERS	1	1954
FINGERS AND THUMBS (COLD SUMMER'S DAY) ERASURE	20	1995
FINGERS OF LOVE CROWDED HOUSE	25	1994
FINGS AIN'T WOT THEY USED T'BE MAX BYGRAVES	5	1960
FINGS AIN'T WOT THEY USED TO BE RUSS CONWAY	47	1960
FINISHED SYMPHONY HYBRID	58	1999
FIRE [A] CRAZY WORLD OF ARTHUR BROWN	1	1968
FIRE [B] POINTER SISTERS	34	1979
FIRE [B] BRUCE SPRINGSTEEN	54	1987
FIRE [C] U2	35	1981
FIRE [D] SLY & ROBBIE	60	1987
FIRE [E] PRODIGY	11	1992
FIRE [F] PRIZNA FEATURING DEMOLITION MAN	33	1995
FIRE [G] SCOOTER	45	1997
FIRE [H] BUSTA RHYMES	60	2000
FIRE [I] MOUSSE T FEATURING EMMA LANFORD	58	2002
FIRE [J] LETHAL BIZZLE	34	2005
FIRE [K] FERRY CORSTEN	40	2006
FIRE [L] KASABIAN	3	2009
FIRE AND RAIN JAMES TAYLOR	42	1970
FIRE BRIGADE MOVE	3	1968
FIRE BURNING SEAN KINGSTON	12	2009
FIRE DEPARTMENT BE YOUR OWN PET	59	2005
FIRE DOWN BELOW JERI SOUTHERN	22	1957
FIRE DOWN BELOW SHIRLEY BASSEY	30	1957
FIRE IN MY HEART SUPER FURRY ANIMALS	25	1999
FIRE ISLAND FIRE ISLAND	66	1992
FIRE OF LOVE JUNGLE HIGH WITH BLUE PEARL	71	1993
FIRE UP THE SHOESAW LIONROCK	43	1996
FIRE WOMAN CULT	15	1989
FIRE WORKS SIOUXSIE & THE BANSHEES	22	1982
FIREBALL [A] DON SPENCER	32	1963
FIREBALL [B] DEEP PURPLE	15	1971
FIRED UP [A] ELEVATORMAN	44	1995
FIRED UP! [B] FUNKY GREEN DOGS	17	1997
FIREFLIES OWL CITY	2	2010
FIREFLY INME	43	2002
FIREPILE (EP) THROWING MUSES	46	1992
FIRES BURNING RUN TINGS	58	1992
FIRESTARTER PRODIGY	1	1996
FIREWIRE COSMIC GATE	9	2001
FIREWORKS ROXETTE	30	1994
FIREWORKS EP EMBRACE	34	1997
FIRM BIZZ FIRM FEATURING DAWN ROBINSON	18	1997
FIRST ATHEIST TABERNACLE CHOIR SPITTING IMAGE	22	1986
FIRST BOY IN THIS TOWN (LOVE SICK) SCRITTI POLITTI	63	1988
FIRST CUT IS THE DEEPEST PP ARNOLD	18	1967
FIRST CUT IS THE DEEPEST ROD STEWART	1	1977
FIRST CUT IS THE DEEPEST SHERYL CROW	37	2003
FIRST DATE BLINK-182	31	2001
FIRST DAY FUTUREHEADS	58	2003
THE FIRST DAY (HORIZON) MAN WITH NO NAME	72	1998
FIRST DAY OF MY LIFE [A] RASMUS	50	2004
FIRST DAY OF MY LIFE [B] BRIGHT EYES	37	2005
FIRST IMPRESSIONS IMPRESSIONS	16	1975
FIRST IT GIVETH QUEENS OF THE STONE AGE	33	2003
THE FIRST THE LAST THE ETERNITY (TIL THE END) SNAP! FEATURING SUMMER	15	1995
FIRST LOVE MACCABEES	40	2006
1ST MAN IN SPACE ALL SEEING I	28	1999
THE FIRST MAN YOU REMEMBER MICHAEL BALL & DIANA MORRISON	68	1989
THE FIRST NIGHT MONICA	6	1998
FIRST OF MAY BEE GEES	6	1969
1ST OF THA MONTH BONE THUGS-N-HARMONY	32	1995
FIRST OF THE GANG TO DIE MORRISSEY	6	2004
THE FIRST PICTURE OF YOU LOTUS EATERS	15	1983
FIRST TASTE OF LOVE BEN E KING	27	1961
FIRST THING IN THE MORNING KIKI DEE	32	1977
THE FIRST TIME [A] ADAM FAITH & THE ROULETTES	5	1963
THE FIRST TIME [B] ROBIN BECK	1	1988
THE FIRST TIME [C] SURFACE	60	1991
FIRST TIME [D] SUNBLOCK	9	2006
FIRST TIME EVER JOANNA LAW	67	1990
THE FIRST TIME EVER I SAW YOUR FACE ROBERTA FLACK	14	1972
THE FIRST TIME EVER I SAW YOUR FACE CELINE DION	19	2000
THE FIRST TIME EVER I SAW YOUR FACE LEONA LEWIS	73	2007
FIRST WE TAKE MANHATTAN JENNIFER WARNES	74	1987
FISH OUT OF WATER ONE MINUTE SILENCE	56	2001
FISHERMAN'S BLUES WATERBOYS	32	1989
FISHING FOR A DREAM TURIN BRAKES	32	2005
FIT BUT YOU KNOW IT STREETS	4	2004
FIVE COLOURS IN HER HAIR McFLY	1	2004
THE $5.98 EP – GARAGE DAYS REVISITED METALLICA	27	1987
FIVE FATHOMS EVERYTHING BUT THE GIRL	27	1999
5.15 WHO	20	1973
555 DELAKOTA	42	1999
555 FOR FILMSTARS DIVE DIVE	48	2005
5-4-3-2-1 MANFRED MANN	5	1964
FIVE GET OVER EXCITED HOUSEMARTINS	11	1987
505 ARCTIC MONKEYS	74	2007
500 (SHAKE BABY SHAKE) LUSH	21	1996
FIVE LITTLE FINGERS FRANKIE McBRIDE	19	1967
FIVE LIVE EP GEORGE MICHAEL & QUEEN WITH LISA STANSFIELD	1	1993
5 MILE (THESE ARE THE DAYS) TURIN BRAKES	31	2003
FIVE MILES OUT MIKE OLDFIELD FEATURING MAGGIE REILLY	43	1982
5 MILES TO EMPTY BROWNSTONE	12	1997
FIVE MINUTES [A] STRANGLERS	11	1978
5 MINUTES [B] LIL' MO FEATURING MISSY 'MISDEMEANOR' ELLIOTT	72	1998
5 O'CLOCK NONCHALANT	44	1996
5 O'CLOCK WORLD JULIAN COPE	42	1989
5 REBECCAS VIEW	57	2008
5-7-0-5 CITY BOY	8	1978
5, 6, 7, 8 STEPS	14	1997
5 STEPS DRU HILL	22	1997
5000 MINUTES OF PAIN MINUTEMAN	75	2002
5 YEAR'S TIME NOAH & THE WHALE	7	2008
FIX BLACKSTREET	7	1997
FIX MY SINK DJ SNEAK FEATURING BEAR WHO?	26	2003
FIX UP LOOK SHARP DIZZEE RASCAL	17	2003
FIX YOU COLDPLAY	4	2005
FIXATION ANDY LING	55	2000
FIXER VENT 414	71	1996
FLAGPOLE SITTA HARVEY DANGER	57	1998
FLAMBOYANT PET SHOP BOYS	12	2004
THE FLAME [A] ARCADIA	58	1986
FLAME [A] SEBADOH	30	1999
THE FLAME [B] FINE YOUNG CANNIBALS	17	1996
FLAME [B] BELL X1	65	2006
THE FLAME STILL BURNS JIMMY NAIL WITH STRANGE FRUIT	47	1998
THE FLAME TREES OF THIKA VIDEO SYMPHONIC	42	1981
FLAMES OF PARADISE JENNIFER RUSH & ELTON JOHN	59	1987
FLAMING JUNE BT	19	1997
FLAMING SWORD CARE	48	1983
FLAP YOUR WINGS NELLY	1	2004
FLASH [A] QUEEN	10	1980
FLASH [A] QUEEN & VANGUARD	15	2003
FLASH [B] BBE	5	1997
FLASH [C] BK & NICK SENTIENCE	67	2001
FLASH [D] GRIFTERS	63	1999
FLASH BACK [B] CALVIN HARRIS	18	2009
FLASHBACK [A] IMAGINATION	16	1981

Title / Artist	Peak Position	Year of Release
FLASHBACK JACK ADAMSKI	46	1990
FLASHDANCE DEEP DISH	3	2004
FLASHDANCE...WHAT A FEELING BJORN AGAIN	65	1993
FLASHDANCE...WHAT A FEELING IRENE CARA	2	1983
THE FLASHER MISTURA FEATURING LLOYD MICHELS	23	1976
FLASHING LIGHTS KANYE WEST FEATURING DWELE	48	2008
FLAT BEAT MR OIZO	1	1999
FLATHEAD FRATELLIS	67	2007
FLATLINERS NEBULA II	54	1992
FLAVA [A] PETER ANDRE	1	1996
FLAVA [B] IMAJIN	64	2000
FLAVA IN YOUR EAR CRAIG MACK	57	1994
FLAVOR OF THE WEAK AMERICAN HI-FI	31	2001
FLAVOUR OF THE OLD SCHOOL BEVERLEY KNIGHT	33	1995
FLAWLESS ONES	7	2001
FLAWLESS (GO TO THE CITY) GEORGE MICHAEL	8	2004
FLEE FLY FLO FE-M@IL	46	2000
FLESH A SPLIT SECOND	68	1991
FLESH JAN JOHNSTON	36	2001
FLESH FOR FANTASY BILLY IDOL	54	1984
FLESH OF MY FLESH ORANGE JUICE	41	1983
FLETCH THEME HAROLD FALTERMEYER	74	1985
FLEX DIZZEE RASCAL	23	2007
FLIGHT OF ICARUS IRON MAIDEN	11	1983
FLIGHT 643 DJ TIESTO	56	2001
FLIP JESSE GREEN	26	1977
FLIP REVERSE BLAZIN' SQUAD	2	2003
THE FLIPSIDE MOLOKO	53	1998
FLIRT JONATHAN KING	22	1972
FLIRTATION WALTZ WINIFRED ATWELL	10	1953
F.L.M. MEL & KIM	7	1987
FLOAT ON [A] FLOATERS	1	1977
FLOAT ON [B] MODEST MOUSE	46	2004
FLOATATION GRID	60	1990
FLOATING TERRA FIRMA	64	1996
FLOATING IN THE WIND HUDSON-FORD	35	1974
FLOBBADANCE BILL & BEN	23	2002
FLOETIC FLOETRY	73	2003
FLOODLIT WORLD ULTRASOUND	39	1999
THE FLOOR JOHNNY GILL	53	1993
FLOOR SPACE OUR HOUSE	52	1996
FLOOR-ESSENCE MAN WITH NO NAME	68	1995
THE FLORAL DANCE BRIGHOUSE & RASTRICK BRASS BAND	2	1977
FLORAL DANCE TERRY WOGAN	21	1978
FLORIBUNDA MOTHER'S PRIDE	42	1998
FLOWER DUET JONATHAN PETERS PRESENTS LUMINAIRE	75	1999
FLOWER DUET (FROM LAKME) MADY MESPLE & DANIELLE MILLET WITH THE PARIS OPERACOMIQUE ORCHESTRA CONDUCTED BY ALAIN LOMBARD	47	1985
FLOWER OF SCOTLAND SCOTTISH RUGBY TEAM WITH RONNIE BROWNE	73	1990
FLOWER OF THE WEST RUNRIG	43	1991
FLOWERS [A] TITIYO	71	1990
FLOWERS [B] SWEET FEMALE ATTITUDE	2	2000
FLOWERS IN DECEMBER MAZZY STAR	40	1996
FLOWERS IN THE RAIN MOVE	2	1967
FLOWERS IN THE WINDOW TRAVIS	18	2002
FLOWERS OF ROMANCE PUBLIC IMAGE LTD	24	1981
FLOWERS ON THE WALL STATLER BROTHERS	38	1966
FLOWERZ ARMAND VAN HELDEN FEATURING ROLAND CLARK	18	1999
FLOWTATION VINCENT DE MOOR	54	1997
FLOY JOY SUPREMES	9	1972
FLUORESCENT ADOLESCENT ARCTIC MONKEYS	5	2007
FLUX BLOC PARTY	8	2007
THE FLY U2	1	1991
FLY [A] SUGAR RAY	58	1998
FLY [B] POB FEATURING DJ PATRICK REID	74	1999
FLY [C] MARK JOSEPH	28	2003
FLY [D] MATT GOSS	31	2004
FLY [E] HILARY DUFF	20	2006
FLY AWAY [A] HADDAWAY	20	1995
FLY AWAY [B] LENNY KRAVITZ	1	1999
FLY AWAY [C] VINCENT DE MOOR	30	2001
FLY AWAY [D] HONEY RYDER	31	2009
FLY AWAY (BYE BYE) EYES CREAM	53	1999
FLY BI TEEBONE FEATURING MC KIE & MC SPARKS	43	2000
FLY BY II BLUE	6	2002
FLY GIRL QUEEN LATIFAH	67	1991
FLY LIFE BASEMENT JAXX	19	1997
FLY LIKE AN EAGLE SEAL	13	1997
FLY ME AWAY GOLDFRAPP	26	2006
FLY ON THE WALL MILEY CYRUS	16	2009
FLY ON THE WINGS OF LOVE XTM & DJ CHUCKY PRESENTS ANNIA	8	2003
FLY ROBIN FLY SILVER CONVENTION	28	1975
FLY TO THE ANGELS SLAUGHTER	55	1991
FLY TOO HIGH JANIS IAN	44	1979
FLY WITH ME COLOURSOUND	49	2002
FLYING [A] CAST	4	1996
FLYING [B] BRYAN ADAMS	39	2004
FLYING ELVIS LEILANI	73	2000
FLYING HIGH [A] COMMODORES	37	1978
FLYING HIGH [B] FREEEZ	35	1981
FLYING HIGH [C] CAPTAIN HOLLYWOOD PROJECT	58	1995
FLYING MACHINE CLIFF RICHARD	37	1971
FLYING SAUCER WEDDING PRESENT	22	1992
THE FLYING SONG PQM FEATURING CICA	68	2000
FLYING THE FLAG (FOR YOU) SCOOCH	5	2007
FLYING WITHOUT WINGS WESTLIFE	1	1999
FLYSWATER EELS	55	2000
FM (NO STATIC AT ALL) STEELY DAN	49	1978
FOE-DEE-O-DEE RUBETTES	15	1975
FOG ON THE TYNE (REVISITED) GAZZA & LINDISFARNE	2	1990
FOGGY MOUNTAIN BREAKDOWN LESTER FLATT & EARL SCRUGGS	39	1967
FOGHORN A	63	1998
FOLDING STARS BIFFY CLYRO	18	2007
THE FOLK SINGER TOMMY ROE	4	1963
FOLLOW DA LEADER NIGEL & MARVIN	5	2002
FOLLOW ME [A] JT TAYLOR	59	1992
FOLLOW ME [B] ALY-US	43	1992
FOLLOW ME [C] ATOMIC KITTEN	20	2000
FOLLOW ME [D] UNCLE KRACKER	3	2001
FOLLOW ME HOME SUGABABES	32	2006
FOLLOW THAT DREAM EP ELVIS PRESLEY	34	1962
FOLLOW THE LEADER ERIC B & RAKIM	21	1988
FOLLOW THE LEADERS KILLING JOKE	55	1981
FOLLOW THE LIGHT SUB FOCUS	38	2009
FOLLOW THE RULES LIVIN' JOY	9	1996
FOLLOW YOU DOWN GIN BLOSSOMS	30	1996
FOLLOW YOU FOLLOW ME GENESIS	7	1978
FOLLOW YOU FOLLOW ME SONNY JONES FEATURING TARA CHASE	42	2000
FOLLOWED THE WAVES AUF DER MAUR	35	2004
FOLLOWING BANGLES	55	1987
THE FOOD CHRISTMAS EP VARIOUS ARTISTS (EP'S & LP'S)	63	1989
FOOD FOR THOUGHT [A] BARRON KNIGHTS	46	1979
FOOD FOR THOUGHT [B] UB40	4	1980
FOOL [A] ELVIS PRESLEY	15	1973
FOOL [B] AL MATTHEWS	16	1975
FOOL [C] MANSUN	28	2001
FOOL AGAIN WESTLIFE	1	2000
A FOOL AM I CILLA BLACK	13	1966
FOOL FOR LOVE RUSSELL	52	2000
FOOL FOR YOUR LOVING WHITESNAKE	13	1980
FOOL (IF YOU THINK IT'S OVER) CHRIS REA	30	1978
FOOL IF YOU THINK IT'S OVER ELKIE BROOKS	17	1982
A FOOL NEVER LEARNS ANDY WILLIAMS	40	1964
FOOL NO MORE S CLUB 8	4	2003
FOOL NUMBER ONE BRENDA LEE	38	1961
THE FOOL ON THE HILL SHIRLEY BASSEY	48	1971
A FOOL SUCH AS I ELVIS PRESLEY	1	1959
FOOL TO CRY ROLLING STONES	6	1976
FOOLED AROUND AND FELL IN LOVE ELVIN BISHOP	34	1976
FOOLED BY A SMILE SWING OUT SISTER	43	1987
FOOLIN' YOURSELF PAUL HARDCASTLE	51	1986
FOOLISH [A] ASHANTI	4	2002
FOOLISH [B] TYLER JAMES	16	2005
FOOLISH BEAT DEBBIE GIBSON	9	1988
FOOLISH LITTLE GIRL SHIRELLES	38	1963
FOOL'S GOLD STONE ROSES	8	1989
FOOL'S PARADISE MELI'SA MORGAN	41	1986
FOOLS RUSH IN BROOK BENTON	50	1961
FOOLS RUSH IN RICK NELSON	12	1963
FOOT OF THE MOUNTAIN A-HA	66	2009
FOOT STOMPIN' MUSIC HAMILTON BOHANNON	23	1975
FOOT TAPPER SHADOWS	1	1963
FOOTLOOSE KENNY LOGGINS	6	1984
FOOTPRINT DISCO CITIZENS	34	1997
FOOTPRINTS IN THE SAND LEONA LEWIS	2	2007
FOOTPRINTS IN THE SNOW JOHNNY DUNCAN & THE BLUE GRASS BOYS	27	1957
FOOTSEE WIGAN'S CHOSEN FEW	9	1975
FOOTSTEPS [A] STEVE LAWRENCE	4	1960
FOOTSTEPS [A] RONNIE CARROLL	36	1960
FOOTSTEPS [A] SHOWADDYWADDY	31	1981
FOOTSTEPS [B] STILTSKIN	34	1994
FOOTSTEPS [C] DANIEL O'DONNELL	25	1996
FOOTSTEPS FOLLOWING ME FRANCES NERO	17	1991
FOR A FEW DOLLARS MORE SMOKIE	17	1978
FOR A FRIEND COMMUNARDS	28	1988
FOR A LIFETIME ASCENSION FEATURING ERIN LORDAN	45	2002
FOR A PENNY PAT BOONE	19	1959
FOR ALL THAT YOU WANT GARY BARLOW	24	1999
FOR ALL THE COWS FOO FIGHTERS	28	1995
FOR ALL TIME CATHERINE ZETA JONES	36	1992
FOR ALL WE KNOW SHIRLEY BASSEY	6	1971
FOR ALL WE KNOW CARPENTERS	18	1971
FOR ALL WE KNOW NICKI FRENCH	42	1995
FOR AMERICA RED BOX	10	1986
FOR AN ANGEL PAUL VAN DYK	28	1998
FOR BRITAIN ONLY ALICE COOPER	66	1982
(FOR GOD'S SAKE) GIVE MORE POWER TO THE PEOPLE CHI-LITES	32	1971
FOR HER LIGHT FIELDS OF THE NEPHILIM	54	1990
FOR LOVE (EP) LUSH	35	1992
FOR LOVERS WOLFMAN FEATURING PETE DOHERTY	7	2004
FOR MAMA MATT MONRO	23	1964
FOR OLD TIME'S SAKE MILLICAN & NESBITT	38	1974
FOR ONCE IN MY LIFE STEVIE WONDER	3	1968
FOR ONCE IN MY LIFE DOROTHY SQUIRES	24	1969
FOR REAL TRICKY	45	1999
FOR REASONS UNKNOWN KILLERS	53	2007
FOR SPACIOUS LIES NORMAN COOK FEATURING LESTER	48	1989
FOR SURE SCOOCH	15	2000
FOR THE DEAD GENE	14	1996
FOR THE GOOD TIMES PERRY COMO	7	1973

Title / Artist	Peak Position	Year of Release
FOR THOSE ABOUT TO ROCK (WE SALUTE YOU) AC/DC	15	1982
FOR TOMORROW BLUR	28	1993
FOR WHAT IT'S WORTH [A] OUI 3	26	1993
FOR WHAT IT'S WORTH [B] CARDIGANS	31	2003
FOR WHAT YOU DREAM OF BEDROCK FEATURING KYO	25	1996
FOR WHOM THE BELL TOLLS [A] SIMON DUPREE & THE BIG SOUND	43	1968
FOR WHOM THE BELL TOLLS [B] BEE GEES	4	1993
FOR YOU [A] RICK NELSON	14	1964
FOR YOU [B] FARMERS BOYS	66	1983
FOR YOU [C] SNOWY WHITE	65	1985
FOR YOU [D] ELECTRONIC	16	1996
FOR YOU [E] STAIND	55	2002
FOR YOU FOR LOVE AVERAGE WHITE BAND	46	1980
FOR YOU I WILL MONICA	27	1997
FOR YOUR BABIES SIMPLY RED	9	1992
FOR YOUR BLUE EYES ONLY TONY HADLEY	67	1992
FOR YOUR EYES ONLY SHEENA EASTON	8	1981
FOR YOUR LOVE [A] YARDBIRDS	3	1965
FOR YOUR LOVE [B] STEVIE WONDER	23	1995
FORBIDDEN CITY ELECTRONIC	14	1996
FORBIDDEN COLOURS DAVID SYLVIAN & RYUICHI SAKAMOTO	16	1983
FORBIDDEN FRUIT PAUL VAN DYK	69	1997
FORBIDDEN ZONE BEDROCK	71	1997
FORCA NELLY FURTADO	40	2004
THE FORCE BEHIND THE POWER DIANA ROSS	27	1992
FOREIGN SAND ROGER TAYLOR & YOSHIKI	26	1994
FORERUNNER NATURAL BORN GROOVES	64	1996
A FOREST CURE	31	1980
FOREST FIRE LLOYD COLE & THE COMMOTIONS	41	1984
FOREVER [A] ROY WOOD	8	1973
FOREVER [B] KISS	65	1990
FOREVER [C] DAMAGE	6	1996
FOREVER [D] CHARLATANS	12	1999
FOREVER [E] TINA COUSINS	45	1999
FOREVER [F] DEE DEE	12	2002
FOREVER [G] N-TRANCE	6	2002
FOREVER [H] TRINITY-X	19	2002
FOREVER [I] CHRIS BROWN	4	2008
FOREVER [J] DRAKE FEATURING KANYE WEST, LIL WAYNE & EMINEM	42	2009
FOREVER AND A DAY [A] BROTHERS IN RHYTHM PRESENT CHARVONI	51	1994
FOREVER AND A DAY [B] STATE ONE	62	2003
FOREVER AND EVER SLIK	1	1976
FOREVER AND EVER, AMEN RANDY TRAVIS	55	1988
FOREVER AND FOR ALWAYS SHANIA TWAIN	6	2003
FOREVER AS ONE VENGABOYS	28	2001
FOREVER AUTUMN JUSTIN HAYWARD	5	1978
FOREVER CAME TODAY DIANA ROSS & THE SUPREMES	25	1968
FOREVER FAILURE PARADISE LOST	66	1995
FOREVER FREE W.A.S.P.	25	1989
FOREVER GIRL OTT	24	1997
FOREVER IN BLUE JEANS NEIL DIAMOND	16	1979
FOREVER IN LOVE KENNY G	47	1993
FOREVER IS OVER SATURDAYS	2	2009
FOREVER J TERRY HALL	67	1994
A FOREVER KIND OF LOVE BOBBY VEE	13	1962
(FOREVER) LIVE AND DIE ORCHESTRAL MANOEUVRES IN THE DARK	11	1986
FOREVER LOST MAGIC NUMBERS	15	2005
FOREVER LOVE GARY BARLOW	1	1996
FOREVER MAN ERIC CLAPTON	51	1985
FOREVER MAN (HOW MANY TIMES) BEATCHUGGERS FEATURING ERIC CLAPTON	26	2000
FOREVER MORE [A] PUFF JOHNSON	29	1997
FOREVER MORE [B] MOLOKO	17	2003

Title / Artist	Peak Position	Year of Release
FOREVER NOW LEVEL 42	19	1994
FOREVER REELING KINESIS	65	2003
FOREVER TOGETHER RAVEN MAIZE	67	1989
FOREVER YOUNG [A] ROD STEWART	57	1988
FOREVER YOUNG [B] INTERACTIVE	28	1996
FOREVER YOUNG [C] 4 VINI FEATURING ELISABETH TROY	75	2002
FOREVER YOUR GIRL PAULA ABDUL	24	1989
FOREVERGREEN FINITRIBE	51	1992
FORGET ABOUT THE WORLD GABRIELLE	23	1996
FORGET ABOUT TOMORROW FEEDER	12	2003
FORGET ABOUT YOU MOTORS	13	1978
FORGET HIM BOBBY RYDELL	13	1963
FORGET HIM BILLY FURY	59	1983
FORGET I WAS A G WHITEHEAD BROTHERS	40	1995
FORGET ME KNOTS RONI SIZE	61	2003
FORGET-ME-NOT [A] VERA LYNN	5	1952
FORGET ME NOT [B] EDEN KANE	3	1962
FORGET ME NOT [C] MARTHA REEVES & THE VANDELLAS	11	1971
FORGET ME NOTS PATRICE RUSHEN	8	1982
FORGET ME NOTS TONGUE 'N' CHEEK	26	1991
FORGET MYSELF ELBOW	22	2005
FORGIVE ME [A] LYNDEN DAVID HALL	30	2000
FORGIVE ME [B] LEONA LEWIS	5	2000
FORGIVEN (I FEEL YOUR LOVE) SPACE BROTHERS	27	1997
FORGIVENESS [A] ENGINEERS	48	2005
FORGIVENESS [B] LEONA LEWIS	46	2007
FORGOT ABOUT DRE DR DRE FEATURING EMINEM	7	2000
FORGOTTEN DREAMS LEROY ANDERSON & HIS POPS CONCERT ORCHESTRA	24	1957
FORGOTTEN DREAMS CYRIL STAPLETON	27	1957
FORGOTTEN TOWN CHRISTIANS	22	1987
FORMED A BAND ART BRUT	52	2004
FORMULAE JJ72	28	2002
FORSAKEN DREAMS DILLINJA	71	2004
FORT WORTH JAIL LONNIE DONEGAN	14	1959
FORTRESS AROUND YOUR HEART STING	49	1985
FORTRESS EUROPE ASIAN DUB FOUNDATION	57	2003
FORTUNE FADED RED HOT CHILI PEPPERS	11	2003
FORTUNES OF WAR FISH	67	1994
48 CRASH SUZI QUATRO	3	1973
45 RPM POPPY FIELDS	28	2004
40 MILES CONGRESS	26	1991
FORTY MILES OF BAD ROAD DUANE EDDY & THE REBELS	11	1959
49 PERCENT ROYKSOPP	55	2005
40 YEARS PAUL HARDCASTLE	53	1988
FORWARD THE REVOLUTION SPIRAL TRIBE	70	1992
FOUND A CURE ULTRA NATE	6	1998
FOUND LOVE DOUBLE DEE FEATURING DANY	33	1990
FOUND OUT ABOUT YOU GIN BLOSSOMS	40	1994
FOUND OUT TOO LATE 999	69	1979
FOUND THAT SOUL MANIC STREET PREACHERS	9	2001
FOUND YOU [A] DODGY	19	1997
FOUND YOU [B] ROSS COPPERMAN	68	2007
FOUNDATION BEENIE MAN AND THE TAXI GANG	69	1998
FOUNDATIONS KATE NASH	2	2007
FOUNTAIN O' YOUTH CANDYLAND	72	1991
4 AM FOREVER LOSTPROPHETS	34	2007
FOUR BACHARACH AND DAVID SONGS EP DEACON BLUE	2	1990
FOUR BIG SPEAKERS WHALE FEATURING BUS 75	69	1998
4 EVER VERONICAS	17	2009
FOUR FROM TOYAH EP TOYAH	4	1981
4 IN THE MORNING GWEN STEFANI	22	2007
FOUR KICKS KINGS OF LEON	24	2005

Title / Artist	Peak Position	Year of Release
FOUR LETTER WORD KIM WILDE	6	1988
FOUR LITTLE HEELS BRIAN HYLAND	29	1960
FOUR LITTLE HEELS AVONS	45	1960
FOUR MINUTE WARNING MARK OWEN	4	2003
4 MINUTES MADONNA FEATURING JUSTIN TIMBERLAKE	1	2008
4 MORE DE LA SOUL FEATURING ZHANE	52	1997
FOUR MORE FROM TOYAH EP TOYAH	14	1981
4 MY PEOPLE MISSY ELLIOTT	5	2002
4 PAGE LETTER AALIYAH	24	1997
THE 4 PLAYS EPS R KELLY	23	1995
FOUR SEASONS IN ONE DAY CROWDED HOUSE	26	1992
4 SEASONS OF LONELINESS BOYZ II MEN	10	1997
FOUR STRONG WINDS NEIL YOUNG	57	1979
FOUR TO THE FLOOR STARSAILOR	24	2004
FOUR WINDS BRIGHT EYES	57	2007
4 WORDS (TO CHOKE UPON) BULLET FOR MY VALENTINE	40	2005
FOURPLAY (EP) VARIOUS ARTISTS (EP'S & LP'S)	45	1992
FOURTEEN FORWARD, RUSSIA!	74	2005
14 HOURS TO SAVE THE EARTH TOMSKI	42	1998
FOURTH RENDEZ-VOUS JEAN-MICHEL JARRE	65	1986
FOX FORCE FIVE CHRIS & JAMES	71	1995
FOX ON THE RUN [A] MANFRED MANN	5	1969
FOX ON THE RUN [B] SWEET	2	1975
FOXHOLE TELEVISION	36	1978
FOXTROT UNIFORM CHARLIE KILO BLOODHOUND GANG	47	2005
FOXY FOXY MOTT THE HOOPLE	33	1974
'FRAGGLE ROCK' THEME FRAGGLES	33	1984
FRAGILE STING	70	1988
FRAGILE JULIO IGLESIAS	53	1994
FRAGILE THING BIG COUNTRY FEATURING EDDI READER	69	1999
FRANCESCA – THE MADDENING GLARE SPECIAL NEEDS	69	2004
THE FRANK SONATA LONGPIGS	57	1999
FRANKENSTEIN EDGAR WINTER GROUP	18	1973
FRANKIE SISTER SLEDGE	1	1985
FRANKIE AND JOHNNY MR ACKER BILK & HIS PARAMOUNT JAZZ BAND	42	1962
FRANKIE AND JOHNNY SAM COOKE	30	1963
FRANKIE AND JOHNNY ELVIS PRESLEY	21	1966
FRANTIC METALLICA	16	2003
FREAK [A] BRUCE FOXTON	23	1983
FREAK [B] SILVERCHAIR	34	1997
FREAK [C] STRANGELOVE	43	1997
FREAK IT! STUDIO 45	36	1999
FREAK LIKE ME ADINA HOWARD	33	1995
FREAK LIKE ME TRU FAITH & DUB CONSPIRACY	12	2000
FREAK LIKE ME SUGABABES	1	2002
FREAK ME SILK	46	1993
FREAK ME ANOTHER LEVEL	1	1998
FREAK MODE REELISTS	16	2002
FREAK ON STONEBRIDGE VS ULTRA NATE	37	2005
FREAK ON A LEASH KORN	24	1999
FREAKIN' IT WILL SMITH	15	2000
FREAKIN' OUT GRAHAM COXON	37	2004
FREAKIN' YOU JUNGLE BROTHERS	70	2000
FREAKS LIVE	60	1997
THE FREAKS COME OUT CEVIN FISHER'S BIG BREAK	34	1998
FREAKS (LIVE) MARILLION	24	1988
FREAKY BE BEAUTIFUL MOIST	47	1995
FREAKYTIME POINT BREAK	13	2000
THE FRED EP VARIOUS ARTISTS (EP'S & LP'S)	26	1992
FREDDY KREUGER REUBEN	53	2004
FREDERICK PATTI SMITH GROUP	63	1979
FREE [A] DENIECE WILLIAMS	1	1977
FREE [B] CURIOSITY KILLED THE CAT	56	1987

Title / Artist	Peak Position	Year of Release
FREE [C] WILL DOWNING	58	1988
FREE [D] STEVIE WONDER	49	1989
FREE [E] DJ QUICKSILVER	7	1997
FREE [F] ULTRA NATE	4	1997
FREE [G] JOHN 'OO' FLEMING	61	2000
FREE [H] VAST	55	2000
FREE [I] CLAIRE FREELAND	44	2001
FREE [J] MYA	11	2001
FREE [K] ESTELLE	15	2004
FREE AS A BIRD BEATLES	2	1995
FREE AT LAST SIMON	36	2001
FREE BIRD LYNYRD SKYNYRD	21	1976
FREE (C'MON) CATCH	70	1990
FREE ELECTRIC BAND ALBERT HAMMOND	19	1973
FREE EP FREE	11	1978
FREE FALLIN' TOM PETTY	64	1989
FREE, GAY AND HAPPY COMING OUT CREW	50	1995
FREE HUEY BOO RADLEYS	54	1998
FREE (LET IT BE) STUART	41	2003
FREE LOVE JULIET ROBERTS	25	1993
FREE ME [A] ROGER DALTREY	39	1980
FREE ME [B] CAST	7	1997
FREE ME [C] EMMA BUNTON	5	2003
FREE MY NAME OCEAN COLOUR SCENE	23	2005
FREE 'N' EASY ALMIGHTY	35	1991
FREE RANGE FALL	40	1992
FREE SALUTE LITTLE BARRIE	73	2005
FREE SATPAL RAM ASIAN DUB FOUNDATION	56	1998
FREE SPIRIT KIM APPLEBY	51	1994
THE FREE STYLE MEGA-MIX BOBBY BROWN	14	1990
FREE THINGS FOR POOR PEOPLE INFADELS	52	2008
FREE TO DECIDE CRANBERRIES	33	1996
FREE TO FALL DEBBIE HARRY	46	1987
FREE TO LOVE AGAIN SUZETTE CHARLES	58	1993
FREE WORLD KIRSTY MacCOLL	43	1989
FREE YOUR BODY PRAGA KHAN FEATURING JADE 4 U	39	1992
FREE YOUR MIND [A] EN VOGUE	16	1992
FREE YOUR MIND [B] SPACE BABY	55	1995
FREE YOURSELF UNTOUCHABLES	26	1985
FREE/SAIL ON CHANTE MOORE	69	1995
FREEBASE TALL PAUL	43	2000
FREED FROM DESIRE GALA	2	1997
FREEDOM [A] WHAM!	1	1984
FREEDOM [B] ALICE COOPER	50	1988
FREEDOM [C] GEORGE MICHAEL	28	1990
FREEDOM [C] ROBBIE WILLIAMS	2	1996
FREEDOM [D] A HOMEBOY, A HIPPIE & A FUNKI DREDD	68	1990
FREEDOM [E] LONDON BOYS	54	1991
FREEDOM [F] MICHELLE GAYLE	16	1995
FREEDOM [G] SHIVA	18	1995
FREEDOM [H] ROBERT MILES FEATURING KATHY SLEDGE	15	1997
FREEDOM [I] ERASURE	27	2000
FREEDOM [J] QFX	36	2003
FREEDOM COME FREEDOM GO FORTUNES	6	1971
FREEDOM (EP) QFX	41	1995
FREEDOM FIGHTERS MUSIC	15	2004
FREEDOM GOT AN A.K. DA LENCH MOB	51	1993
FREEDOM (MAKE IT FUNKY) BLACK MAGIC	41	1996
FREEDOM OVERSPILL STEVE WINWOOD	69	1986
FREEDOM'S PRISONER STEVE HARLEY	58	1979
FREEEK! GEORGE MICHAEL	7	2002
FREEFLOATING GARY CLARK	50	1993
FREEK 'N YOU JODECI	17	1995
FREEK U BON GARCON	42	2005
FREELOADER DRIFTWOOD	32	2003
FREELOVE DEPECHE MODE	19	2001
FREESTYLER BOMFUNK MC'S	2	2000
FREET TATA BOX INHIBITORS	67	2001
FREEWAY OF LOVE ARETHA FRANKLIN	51	1985
FREEWHEEL BURNIN' JUDAS PRIEST	42	1984

Title / Artist	Peak Position	Year of Release
THE FREEZE [A] SPANDAU BALLET	17	1981
FREEZE [B] T-PAIN FEATURING CHRIS BROWN	62	2008
FREEZE THE ATLANTIC CABLE	44	1997
FREEZE-FRAME J GEILS BAND	27	1982
FREIGHT TRAIN CHARLES McDEVITT SKIFFLE GROUP FEATURING NANCY WHISKEY	5	1957
FRENCH DISCO STEREOLAB	75	1994
FRENCH FOREIGN LEGION FRANK SINATRA	18	1959
FRENCH KISS LIL' LOUIS	2	1989
FRENCH KISSES JENTINA	20	2004
FRENCH KISSIN' IN THE USA DEBBIE HARRY	8	1986
FREQUENCY ALTERN 8	41	1992
FRESH [A] KOOL & THE GANG	11	1984
FRESH! [B] GINA G	6	1997
FRIDAY DANIEL BEDINGFIELD	28	2003
FRIDAY 13TH (EP) DAMNED	50	1981
FRIDAY I'M IN LOVE CURE	6	1992
FRIDAY NIGHT McFLY	3	2006
FRIDAY NIGHT (LIVE VERSION) KIDS FROM *'FAME'*	13	1983
FRIDAY ON MY MIND EASYBEATS	6	1966
FRIDAY ON MY MIND GARY MOORE	26	1987
FRIDAY STREET PAUL WELLER	21	1997
FRIDAY'S ANGELS GENERATION X	62	1979
FRIDAY'S CHILD WILL YOUNG	4	2004
FRIED MY LITTLE BRAINS KILLS	55	2003
A FRIEND KRS ONE	66	1997
FRIEND OF MINE KELLY PRICE	25	1998
FRIEND OF THE NIGHT MOGWAI	38	2006
FRIEND OR FOE [A] ADAM ANT	9	1982
FRIEND OR FOE [B] T.A.T.U.	48	2006
FRIENDLY PERSUASION PAT BOONE	3	1956
FRIENDLY PERSUASION FOUR ACES FEATURING AL ALBERTS	29	1957
FRIENDLY PRESSURE JHELISA	75	1995
FRIENDS [A] BEACH BOYS	25	1968
FRIENDS [B] ARRIVAL	8	1970
FRIENDS [C] SHALAMAR	12	1982
FRIENDS [D] AMII STEWART	12	1985
FRIENDS [E] JODY WATLEY WITH ERIC B & RAKIM	21	1989
FRIENDS [F] TIGER	72	1998
THE FRIENDS AGAIN EP FRIENDS AGAIN	59	1984
FRIENDS AND NEIGHBOURS BILLY COTTON & HIS BAND, VOCALS BY THE BANDITS	3	1954
FRIENDS FOREVER THUNDERBUGS	5	1999
FRIENDS IN LOW PLACES GARTH BROOKS	36	1995
FRIENDS WILL BE FRIENDS QUEEN	14	1986
FRIENDSHIP SABRINA JOHNSTON	58	1991
FRIGGIN' IN THE RIGGIN' SEX PISTOLS	3	1979
FRIGHTENED CITY SHADOWS	3	1961
THE FROG PRINCESS DIVINE COMEDY	15	1996
FROGGY MIX JAMES BROWN	50	1985
FROGGY STYLE NUTTIN' NYCE	68	1995
FROM A DISTANCE BETTE MIDLER	6	1990
FROM A DISTANCE CLIFF RICHARD	11	1990
FROM A JACK TO A KING NED MILLER	2	1963
FROM A LOVER TO A FRIEND PAUL McCARTNEY	45	2001
FROM A TO H AND BACK AGAIN SHEEP ON DRUGS	40	1993
FROM A WINDOW [A] BILLY J KRAMER & THE DAKOTAS	10	1964
FROM A WINDOW [B] NORTHERN UPROAR	17	1996
FROM DESPAIR TO WHERE MANIC STREET PREACHERS	25	1993
FROM EAST TO WEST VOYAGE	13	1978
FROM HEAD TO TOE ELVIS COSTELLO	43	1982
FROM HERE TO ETERNITY [A] GIORGIO	16	1977
FROM HERE TO ETERNITY [B] IRON MAIDEN	21	1992
FROM HERE TO ETERNITY [C] MICHAEL BALL	36	1994
FROM HERE TO THERE TO YOU HANK LOCKLIN	44	1962

Title / Artist	Peak Position	Year of Release
FROM ME TO YOU BEATLES	1	1963
FROM NEW YORK TO LA PATSY GALLANT	6	1977
FROM NOW ON JAKI GRAHAM	73	1989
FROM OUT OF NOWHERE FAITH NO MORE	23	1990
FROM PARIS TO BERLIN INFERNAL	2	2006
FROM RUSH HOUR WITH LOVE REPUBLICA	20	1998
FROM RUSSIA WITH LOVE [A] MATT MONRO	20	1963
FROM RUSSIA WITH LOVE [A] JOHN BARRY ORCHESTRA	39	1963
FROM RUSSIA WITH LOVE [B] MATT DAREY PRESENTS DSP	40	2000
FROM THA CHUUUCH TO DA PALACE SNOOP DOGG	27	2002
FROM THE BEGINNING NEW RHODES	64	2005
FROM THE BENCH AT BELVIDERE BOO RADLEYS	24	1995
FROM THE BOTTOM OF MY HEART MOODY BLUES	22	1965
FROM THE FIRE FIELDS OF THE NEPHILIM	62	2002
FROM THE FLOORBOARDS UP PAUL WELLER	6	2005
FROM THE GHETTO DREAD FLIMSTONE & THE NEW TONE AGE FAMILY	66	1991
FROM THE HEART ANOTHER LEVEL	6	1999
FROM THE HIP (EP) LLOYD COLE & THE COMMOTIONS	59	1988
FROM THE UNDERWORLD HERD	6	1967
FROM THIS DAY MACHINE HEAD	74	1999
FROM THIS MOMENT ON SHANIA TWAIN	9	1998
FROM YESTERDAY THIRTY SECONDS TO MARS	37	2008
FRONTIER PSYCHIATRIST AVALANCHES	18	2001
FRONTIN' PHARRELL WILLIAMS FEATURING JAY-Z	6	2003
FRONTIN' JAMIE CULLUM	12	2004
FRONTLINE CAPTAIN	62	2006
FROSTY THE SNOWMAN COCTEAU TWINS	58	1993
FROZEN MADONNA	1	1998
FROZEN HEART FM	64	1987
FROZEN METAL HEAD (EP) BEASTIE BOYS	55	1992
FROZEN ORANGE JUICE PETER SARSTEDT	10	1969
FRQUENCY RHYTHMATIC	62	1990
FUCK FOREVER BABYSHAMBLES	4	2005
F**K IT (I DON'T WANT YOU BACK) EAMON	1	2004
FUCK IT UP TOWERS OF LONDON	46	2005
***K THE MILLENNIUM 2K	28	1997
FUEL METALLICA	31	1998
FU-GEE-LA FUGEES	21	1996
FUGITIVE MOTEL ELBOW	44	2003
FULL METAL JACKET (I WANNA BE YOUR DRILL INSTRUCTOR) ABIGAIL MEAD & NIGEL GOULDING	2	1987
THE FULL MONTY-MONSTER MIX VARIOUS ARTISTS (EP'S & LP'S)	62	1998
FULL MOON BRANDY	15	2002
FULL OF LIFE (HAPPY NOW) WONDER STUFF	28	1993
FULL TERM LOVE MONIE LOVE	34	1992
FULL TIME JOB DORIS DAY & JOHNNIE RAY	11	1953
FUN DA MOB FEATURING JOCELYN BROWN	33	1998
FUN DAY STEVIE WONDER	63	1991
FUN FOR ME MOLOKO	36	1996
FUN FUN FUN STATUS QUO WITH THE BEACH BOYS	24	1996
THE FUN LOVIN' CRIMINAL FUN LOVIN' CRIMINALS	26	1996
THE FUNERAL OF HEARTS H.I.M.	15	2004
FUNERAL PYRE JAM	4	1981
THE FUNERAL (SEPTEMBER 25TH, 1977) THULI DUMAKUDE	75	1988
FUNGI MAMA (BEBOPAFUNKADISCOLYPSO) TOM BROWNE	58	1982
FUNHOUSE P!NK	29	2009
FUNK & DRIVE ELEVATORMAN	37	1995
FUNK DAT SAGAT	25	1993

Title / Artist	Peak Position	Year of Release
FUNK ON AH ROLL JAMES BROWN	40	1999
THE FUNK PHENOMENA ARMAND VAN HELDEN	38	1997
FUNK THEORY ROKOTTO	49	1978
FUNKATARIUM JUMP	56	1997
FUNKDAFIED DA BRAT	65	1994
FUNKIN' FOR JAMAICA (NY) TOM BROWNE	10	1980
FUNKY BROADWAY WILSON PICKETT	43	1967
FUNKY COLD MEDINA TONE LOC	13	1989
FUNKY DORY RACHEL STEVENS	26	2003
FUNKY GIBBON GOODIES	4	1975
FUNKY GUITAR TC 1992	40	1992
FUNKY JAM PRIMAL SCREAM	7	1994
FUNKY LOVE KAVANA	32	1998
FUNKY LOVE VIBRATIONS BASS-O-MATIC	71	1991
FUNKY MOPED JASPER CARROTT	5	1975
FUNKY MUSIC UTAH SAINTS	23	2000
FUNKY NASSAU BEGINNING OF THE END	31	1974
FUNKY SENSATION LADIES CHOICE	41	1986
FUNKY STREET ARTHUR CONLEY	46	1968
FUNKY TOWN LIPPS INC	2	1980
FUNKY TOWN PSEUDO ECHO	8	1987
FUNKY WEEKEND STYLISTICS	10	1976
FUNNY ALL OVER VERNONS GIRLS	31	1963
FUNNY BREAK (ONE IS ENOUGH) ORBITAL	21	2001
FUNNY FAMILIAR FORGOTTEN FEELINGS TOM JONES	7	1967
FUNNY FUNNY SWEET	13	1971
FUNNY HOW AIRHEAD	57	1991
FUNNY HOW LOVE CAN BE IVY LEAGUE	8	1965
FUNNY HOW LOVE IS FINE YOUNG CANNIBALS	58	1986
FUNNY HOW TIME FLIES (WHEN YOU'RE HAVING FUN) JANET JACKSON	59	1987
FUNNY HOW TIME SLIPS AWAY DOROTHY MOORE	38	1976
FUNNY LITTLE FROG BELLE & SEBASTIAN	13	2006
FUNNY WAY OF LAUGHIN' BURL IVES	29	1962
FUNTIME BOY GEORGE	45	1995
F.U.R.B. (F U RIGHT BACK) FRANKEE	1	2004
FURIOUS ANGELS ROB DOUGAN	42	1998
FURNITURE FUGAZI	61	2001
FURNITURE MUSIC BILL NELSON'S RED NOISE	59	1979
FURTHER LONGVIEW	24	2003
THE FURTHER ADVENTURES OF THE NORTH VARIOUS ARTISTS (EP'S & LP'S)	64	1990
FURY PRINCE	60	2006
FUTURE HALO VARGA	67	2000
FUTURE LOVE PRESENCE	66	1999
FUTURE LOVE EP SEAL	12	1991
FUTURE MANAGEMENT ROGER TAYLOR	49	1981
THE FUTURE MUSIC (EP) LIQUID	59	1992
THE FUTURE OF THE FUTURE (STAY GOLD) DEEP DISH WITH EBTG	31	1998
FUTURE SHOCK HERBIE HANCOCK	54	1984
FUTURE SOUND (EP) PHUTURE ASSASSINS	64	1992
THE FUTURE'S SO BRIGHT I GOTTA WEAR SHADES TIMBUK 3	21	1987
FUZION PESHAY FEATURING CO-ORDINATE	41	2002
THE F-WORD BABYBIRD	35	2000
FX A GUY CALLED GERALD	52	1989

G

Title / Artist	Peak Position	Year of Release
GABRIEL ROY DAVIS, JR FEATURING PEVEN EVERETT	22	1997
GAINESVILLE ROCK CITY LESS THAN JAKE	57	2001
GAL WINE CHAKA DEMUS & PLIERS	20	1994
GAL WITH THE YALLER SHOES MICHAEL HOLLIDAY	13	1956
GALAXIA MOONMAN FEATURING CHANTAL	50	2000
GALAXIE BLIND MELON	37	1995
GALAXY WAR	14	1978
GALAXY OF LOVE CROWN HEIGHTS AFFAIR	24	1978
GALLOPING HOME LONDON STRING CHORALE	31	1974
GALLOWS POLE JIMMY PAGE & ROBERT PLANT	35	1994
GALVANIZE CHEMICAL BROTHERS	3	2005
GALVESTON GLEN CAMPBELL	14	1969
GALVESTON BAY LONNIE HILL	51	1986
THE GALWAY GIRL SHARON SHANNON & STEVE EARLE	67	2008
GAMBLER MADONNA	4	1985
THE GAMBLER KENNY ROGERS	22	2007
GAMBLIN' BAR ROOM BLUES SENSATIONAL ALEX HARVEY BAND	38	1975
GAMBLIN' MAN LONNIE DONEGAN	1	1957
THE GAME [A] ECHO & THE BUNNYMEN	28	1987
THE GAME [B] NICHOLA HOLT	72	2000
GAME BOY KWS	1	1992
THE GAME IS WON LUCIE SILVAS	38	2005
GAME OF LOVE [A] WAYNE FONTANA & THE MINDBENDERS	2	1965
GAME OF LOVE [B] TONY HADLEY	72	1993
THE GAME OF LOVE [C] SANTANA FEATURING MICHELLE BRANCH	16	2002
GAME ON CATATONIA	33	1998
GAME OVER SCARFACE	34	1997
GAMEMASTER LOST TRIBE	24	1999
GAMES NEW KIDS ON THE BLOCK	14	1991
GAMES PEOPLE PLAY JOE SOUTH	6	1969
GAMES PEOPLE PLAY INNER CIRCLE	67	1994
GAMES THAT LOVERS PLAY DONALD PEERS	46	1966
THE GAMES WE PLAY ANDREAS JOHNSON	41	2000
GAMES WITHOUT FRONTIERS PETER GABRIEL	4	1980
(THE GANG THAT SANG) HEART OF MY HEART MAX BYGRAVES	7	1954
GANGSTA, GANGSTA N.W.A.	70	1990
GANGSTA LOVIN' EVE FEATURING ALICIA KEYS	6	2002
GANGSTA WALK COOLIO FEATURING SNOOP DOGG	67	2006
GANGSTA'S PARADISE COOLIO FEATURING LV	1	1995
GANGSTA'S PARADISE LV	24	1995
GANGSTER OF THE GROOVE HEATWAVE	19	1981
GANGSTER TRIPPIN FATBOY SLIM	3	1998
GANGSTERS SPECIAL A.K.A.	6	1979
GANGSTERS AND THUGS TRANSPLANTS	35	2005
GARAGE CORRUPTED CRU FEATURING MC NEAT	59	2002
GARAGE GIRLS LONYO FEATURING MC ONYX STONE	39	2001
GARDEN OF DELIGHT MISSION	49	1986
THE GARDEN OF EDEN FRANKIE VAUGHAN	1	1957
GARDEN OF EDEN DICK JAMES	14	1957
GARDEN OF EDEN GARY MILLER	14	1957
THE GARDEN OF EDEN JOE VALINO	23	1957
GARDEN PARTY RICK NELSON	41	1972
GARDEN PARTY [A] MEZZOFORTE	17	1983
GARDEN PARTY [B] MARILLION	16	1983
GARY GILMORE'S EYES ADVERTS	18	1977
GARY GLITTER (EP) GARY GLITTER	57	1980
THE GAS FACE 3RD BASS	71	1990
GASOLINA DADDY YANKEE	5	2005
GASOLINE ALLEY ELKIE BROOKS	52	1983
GASOLINE ALLEY BRED HOLLIES	14	1970
GATECRASHING LIVING IN A BOX	36	1989
GATHER IN THE MUSHROOMS BENNY HILL	12	1961
GAUDETE STEELEYE SPAN	14	1973
GAVE IT ALL AWAY BOYZONE	9	2010
GAY BAR ELECTRIC SIX	5	2003
GAY BOYFRIEND HAZZARDS	67	2003
THE GAY CAVALIEROS (THE STORY SO FAR) STEVE WRIGHT	61	1984
GAYE CLIFFORD T WARD	8	1973
GBI TOWA TEI FEATURING KYLIE MINOGUE	63	1998
GEE BABY PETER SHELLEY	4	1974
GEE BUT IT'S LONELY PAT BOONE	30	1958
GEE WHIZ IT'S YOU CLIFF RICHARD	4	1961
GEEK STINK BREATH GREEN DAY	16	1995
GENERAL PUBLIC GENERAL PUBLIC	60	1984
GENERALS AND MAJORS XTC	32	1980
GENERATION SEX DIVINE COMEDY	19	1998
GENERATIONS INSPIRAL CARPETS	28	1992
GENERATIONS OF LOVE JESUS LOVES YOU	35	1991
GENERATOR HOLLOWAYS	14	2006
GENETIC ENGINEERING ORCHESTRAL MANOEUVRES IN THE DARK	20	1983
GENIE BROOKLYN BRONX & QUEENS	40	1985
GENIE IN A BOTTLE CHRISTINA AGUILERA	1	1999
GENIE IN A BOTTLE SPEEDWAY	10	2003
GENIE WITH THE LIGHT BROWN LAMP SHADOWS	17	1964
GENIUS PITCHSHIFTER	71	1998
GENIUS MOVE THAT PETROL EMOTION	65	1987
GENIUS OF LOVER TOM TOM CLUB	65	1981
GENO DEXY'S MIDNIGHT RUNNERS	1	1980
THE GENTLE ART OF CHOKING MY VITRIOL	39	2002
GENTLE ON MY MIND DEAN MARTIN	2	1969
GENTLEMAN WHO FELL MILLA	65	1994
A GENTLEMAN'S EXCUSE ME FISH	30	1990
GENTLEMEN TAKE POLAROIDS JAPAN	60	1980
GEORDIE BOYS (GAZZA RAP) GAZZA	31	1990
GEORDIE IN WONDERLAND WILDHEARTS	31	1995
GEORGE BEST – A TRIBUTE BRIAN KENNEDY & PETER CORRY	4	2006
GEORGIA ON MY MIND RAY CHARLES	24	1960
GEORGINA BAILEY NOOSHA FOX	31	1977
GEORGY GIRL SEEKERS	3	1967
GEORGY PORGY [A] CHARME	68	1984
GEORGY PORGY [B] ERIC BENET FEATURING FAITH EVANS	28	1999
GEPETTO BELLY	49	1993
GERALDINE GLASVEGAS	16	2008
GERM FREE ADOLESCENCE X-RAY SPEX	19	1978
GERONIMO SHADOWS	11	1963
GERTCHA CHAS & DAVE	20	1979
GESUNDHEIT HYSTERICS	44	1981
(GET A) GRIP (ON YOURSELF) STRANGLERS	33	1977
GET A LIFE [A] SOUL II SOUL	3	1989
GET A LIFE [B] JULIAN LENNON	56	1992
GET A LIFE [C] FREESTYLERS	66	2004
GET A LITTLE FREAKY WITH ME AARON HALL	66	1993
GET ALONG WITH YOU KELIS	51	2000
GET ANOTHER LOVE CHANTAL CURTIS	51	1979
GET AWAY GEORGIE FAME & THE BLUE FLAMES	1	1966
GET BACK [A] BEATLES WITH BILLY PRESTON	1	1969
GET BACK [A] ROD STEWART	11	1976
GET BACK [B] MOTHER	73	1994
GET BUSY [A] MR LEE	41	1989
GET BUSY [B] SEAN PAUL	4	2003
GET CARTER ROY BUDD	68	1999
GET DANCING DISCO TEX & THE SEX-O-LETTES	8	1974
GET DOWN [A] GILBERT O'SULLIVAN	1	1973
GET DOWN [B] GENE CHANDLER	11	1979
GET DOWN [C] M-D-EMM	55	1992
GET DOWN [D] CRAIG MACK	54	1995
GET DOWN [E] JUNGLE BROTHERS	52	1999
GET DOWN [F] FLEET	71	2005
GET DOWN [G] GROOVE ARMADA FEATURING STUSH	9	2007

Title / Artist	Peak Position	Year of Release
GET DOWN AND GET WITH IT SLADE	16	1971
GET DOWN ON IT KOOL & THE GANG	3	1981
GET DOWN ON IT LOUCHIE LOU & MICHIE ONE	58	1995
GET DOWN SATURDAY NIGHT OLIVER CHEATHAM	38	1983
GET DOWN TONIGHT KC & THE SUNSHINE BAND	21	1975
GET DOWN (YOU'RE THE ONE FOR ME) BACKSTREET BOYS	14	1996
GET 'EM OFF TOKYO DRAGONS	75	2004
GET FREE VINES	24	2002
GET GET DOWN PAUL JOHNSON	5	1999
GET HERE OLETA ADAMS	4	1991
GET HERE Q FEATURING TRACY ACKERMAN	37	1993
GET HIGHER BLACK GRAPE	24	1997
GET IN THE SWING SPARKS	27	1975
GET INTO IT TONY SCOTT	63	1990
GET INTO THE MUSIC DJ'S RULE FEATURING KAREN BROWN	65	1996
GET INTO YOU DANNII MINOGUE	36	1994
GET INVOLVED RAPHAEL SAADIQ & Q-TIP	36	1999
GET IT [A] DARTS	10	1979
GET IT [B] STEVIE WONDER & MICHAEL JACKSON	37	1988
GET IT ON [A] T REX	1	1971
GET IT ON [A] POWER STATION	22	1985
GET IT ON [A] BUS STOP FEATURING T REX	59	2000
GET IT ON [B] KINGDOM COME	75	1988
GET IT ON [C] INTENSO PROJECT/LISA SCOTT-LEE	23	2004
GET IT ON THE FLOOR DMX FEATURING SWIZZ BEATZ	34	2004
GET IT ON TONITE MONTELL JORDAN	15	2000
GET IT POPPIN' FAT JOE FEATURING NELLY	34	2005
GET IT RIGHT [A] ARETHA FRANKLIN	74	1983
GET IT RIGHT [B] JOE FAGIN	53	1986
GET IT RIGHT NEXT TIME GERRY RAFFERTY	30	1979
GET IT SHAWTY LLOYD	72	2007
GET IT TOGETHER [A] CRISPY & COMPANY	21	1975
GET IT TOGETHER [B] BEASTIE BOYS	19	1994
GET IT TOGETHER [C] SEAL	25	2003
GET IT UP RM PROJECT	49	1999
GET IT UP FOR LOVE DAVID CASSIDY	11	1975
GET IT UP FOR LOVE TATA VEGA	52	1979
GET IT UP FOR LOVE LUCIANA	55	1994
GET IT UP (THE FEELING) ULTRA NATE	51	2001
GET IT WHILE IT'S HOT NODESHA	55	2003
GET IT WHILE YOU CAN OLYMPIC RUNNERS	35	1978
GET LOOSE [A] EVELYN 'CHAMPAGNE' KING	45	1983
GET LOOSE [B] L.A. MIX PERFORMED BY JAZZI P	25	1989
GET LOOSE [C] D4	64	2002
GET LOST EDEN KANE	10	1961
GET LOW LIL JON & THE EAST SIDE BOYZ	10	2005
GET LUCKY JERMAINE STEWART	13	1988
GET ME DINOSAUR JR	44	1992
GET ME HOME FOXY BROWN FEATURING BLACKSTREET	11	1997
GET ME OFF BASEMENT JAXX	22	2002
GET ME OUT NEW MODEL ARMY	34	1990
GET ME OUTTA HERE JET	37	2005
GET ME TO THE WORLD ON TIME ELECTRIC PRUNES	42	1967
GET MYSELF ARRESTED GOMEZ	45	1998
GET MYSELF INTO IT RAPTURE	36	2006
GET NO BETTER CASSIDY FEATURING MASHONDA	24	2004
GET OFF DANDY WARHOLS	34	2000
GET OFF OF MY CLOUD ROLLING STONES	1	1965
GET OFF THIS CRACKER	41	1994
GET OFF YOUR HIGH HORSE ROLLO GOES CAMPING	43	1994
GET ON IT PHOEBE ONE	38	1999
GET ON THE BUS DESTINY'S CHILD FEATURING TIMBALAND	15	1999
GET ON THE DANCE FLOOR ROB BASE & DJ E-Z ROCK	14	1989
GET ON THE FUNK TRAIN MUNICH MACHINE	41	1977
GET ON UP [A] JAZZY DEE	53	1983
GET ON UP [B] JODECI	20	1996
GET ON UP, GET ON DOWN ROY AYERS	41	1978
GET ON YOUR BOOTS U2	12	2009
GET ON YOUR FEET GLORIA ESTEFAN	23	1989
GET OUT [A] HAROLD MELVIN & THE BLUENOTES	35	1975
GET OUT [B] BUSTA RHYMES	57	2000
GET OUT [C] FELON	31	2002
GET OUT OF MY LIFE WOMAN LEE DORSEY	22	1966
GET OUT OF MYSELF REDD KROSS	63	1997
GET OUT OF THIS HOUSE SHAWN COLVIN	70	1997
GET OUT YOUR LAZY BED MATT BIANCO	15	1984
GET OUTTA MY DREAMS GET INTO MY CAR BILLY OCEAN	3	1988
GET OVER IT [A] OK GO	21	2003
GET OVER IT [B] GUILLEMOTS	20	2008
GET OVER YOU [A] UNDERTONES	57	1979
GET OVER YOU [B] SOPHIE ELLIS-BEXTOR	3	2002
GET READY [A] TEMPTATIONS	10	1969
GET READY [A] CAROL HITCHCOCK	56	1987
GET READY! [B] ROACHFORD	22	1991
GET READY [C] MA$E FEATURING BLACKSTREET	32	1999
GET READY FOR LOVE NICK CAVE & THE BAD SEEDS	62	2005
GET READY FOR THIS 2 UNLIMITED	2	1991
GET REAL PAUL RUTHERFORD	47	1988
GET RIGHT JENNIFER LOPEZ	1	2005
GET SEXY SUGABABES	2	2009
GET SHAKY IAN CAREY PROJECT	9	2009
GET SOME THERAPY STEVE WRIGHT & THE SISTERS OF SOUL	75	1983
GET THAT LOVE THOMPSON TWINS	66	1987
GET THE BALANCE RIGHT DEPECHE MODE	13	1983
GET THE FUNK OUT EXTREME	19	1991
GET THE GIRL! KILL THE BADDIES! POP WILL EAT ITSELF	9	1993
GET THE KEYS AND GO LLAMA FARMERS	74	1999
GET THE MESSAGE ELECTRONIC	8	1991
GET THE PARTY STARTED P!NK	2	2002
GET THE PARTY STARTED SHIRLEY BASSEY	47	2007
GET THROUGH MARK JOSEPH	38	2003
GET TOGETHER [A] WONDER STUFF	33	1989
GET TOGETHER [B] MADONNA	7	2006
GET TOUGH KLEEER	49	1981
GET UP [A] J.A.L.N. BAND	53	1978
GET UP [B] BLACKOUT	67	2001
GET UP [C] BEVERLEY KNIGHT	17	2001
GET UP [D] 50 CENT	24	2009
GET UP AND BOOGIE [A] SILVER CONVENTION	7	1976
GET UP AND BOOGIE [B] FREDDIE JAMES	54	1979
GET UP AND MOVE HARVEY	24	2002
GET UP (BEFORE THE NIGHT IS OVER) TECHNOTRONIC FEATURING YA KID K	2	1990
GET UP (EVERYBODY) BYRON STINGILY	14	1997
GET UP! GET INSANE! STRETCH 'N' VERN PRESENTS MADDOG	6	1997
GET UP I FEEL LIKE BEING A SEX MACHINE JAMES BROWN	32	1970
GET UP OFFA THAT THING JAMES BROWN	22	1976
GET UP ON THE DANCE FLOOR GEORGE SAMPSON	30	2008
GET UP STAND UP [A] PHUNKY PHANTOM	27	1998
GET UP STAND UP [B] STELLAR PROJECT FEATURING BRANDI EMMA	14	2004
GET UP SUNSHINE SREET BIZARRE INC	45	1996
GET UR FREAK ON MISSY ELLIOTT	4	2001
GET WILD NEW POWER GENERATION	19	1995
GET YOUR BODY ADAMSKI FEATURING NINA HAGEN	68	1992
GET YOUR FEET OUT OF MY SHOES BOOTHILL FOOT-TAPPERS	64	1984
GET YOUR HANDS OFF MY MAN! JUNIOR VASQUEZ	22	1995
GET YOUR HANDS OFF MY WOMAN DARKNESS	43	2003
GET YOUR LOVE BACK THREE DEGREES	34	1974
GET YOUR NUMBER MARIAH CAREY	9	2005
GET YOUR WAY JAMIE CULLUM	44	2005
GET YOURSELF TOGETHER YOUNG DISCIPLES	65	1990
GET-A-WAY [A] MAXX	4	1994
GETAWAY [B] MUSIC	26	2002
GETAWAY [C] TEXAS	6	2005
GETO HEAVEN COMMON FEATURING MACY GRAY	48	2001
GETS ME THROUGH OZZY OSBOURNE	18	2002
GETT OFF PRINCE & THE NEW POWER GENERATION	4	1991
GETTIN' IN THE WAY JILL SCOTT	30	2000
GETTIN' JIGGY WIT IT WILL SMITH	3	1998
GETTIN' READY FOR LOVE DIANA ROSS	23	1977
GETTING A DRAG LYNSEY DE PAUL	18	1972
GETTING AWAY WITH IT [A] ELECTRONIC	12	1989
GETTING AWAY WITH IT [B] EGG	58	1999
GETTING AWAY WITH IT (ALL MESSED UP) JAMES	22	2001
GETTING AWAY WITH MURDER PAPA ROACH	45	2004
GETTING BETTER SHED SEVEN	14	1996
GETTING CLOSER [A] WINGS	60	1979
GETTING CLOSER [B] HAYWOODE	67	1985
GETTING' ENOUGH LIL' CHRIS	17	2006
GETTING INTO SOMETHING ALISON MOYET	51	1994
GETTING' INTO U W.O.S.P.	48	2001
GETTING' IT RIGHT ALISON LIMERICK	57	1992
GETTING MIGHTY CROWDED BETTY EVERETT	29	1965
GETTING' MONEY JUNIOR M.A.F.I.A.	63	1996
GETTING OVER YOU ANDY WILLIAMS	35	1974
GETTING UP PIGBAG	61	1982
GETTO JAM DOMINO	33	1994
GHANDARA GODIEGO	56	1980
GHETTO RHYTHM MASTERS FEATURING JOE WATSON	71	2002
GHETTO CHILD DETROIT SPINNERS	7	1973
GHETTO DAY CRYSTAL WATERS	40	1994
GHETTO GIRL SIMPLY RED	34	1998
GHETTO GOSPEL 2PAC FEATURING ELTON JOHN	1	2005
GHETTO HEAVEN FAMILY STAND	10	1990
GHETTO MUSICK OUTKAST	55	2003
GHETTO ROMANCE DAMAGE	7	2000
GHETTO STORY CHAM	62	2006
GHETTO SUPERSTAR (THAT IS WHAT YOU ARE) PRAS MICHEL FEATURING ODB & MYA	2	1998
G.H.E.T.T.O.U.T. CHANGING FACES	10	1997
THE GHOST AT NUMBER ONE JELLYFISH	43	1993
GHOST DANCER ADDRISI BROTHERS	57	1979
GHOST HOUSE HOUSE ENGINEERS	69	1987
GHOST IN YOU PSYCHEDELIC FURS	68	1984
THE GHOST OF LOVE [A] TAVARES	29	1978
GHOST OF LOVE [B] FICTION FACTORY	64	1984
THE GHOST OF TOM JOAD BRUCE SPRINGSTEEN	26	1996

Title / Artist	Peak Position	Year of Release
THE GHOST OF YOU MY CHEMICAL ROMANCE	27	2005
GHOST TOWN SPECIALS	1	1981
GHOSTBUSTERS [A] RAY PARKER, JR	2	1984
GHOSTBUSTERS [B] RUN DMC	65	1989
GHOSTDANCING SIMPLE MINDS	13	1986
GHOSTFACED KILLER DEAD 60S	25	2005
GHOSTS [A] JAPAN	5	1982
GHOSTS [B] MICHAEL JACKSON	5	1997
GHOSTS [C] TENTH PLANET	59	2001
GHOSTS [D] DIRTY VEGAS	31	2002
GHOSTS 'N' STUFF DEADMAU5 FEATURING ROB SWIRE	12	2009
GIA DESPINA VANDI	63	2004
GIDDY STRATOSPHERES LONG BLONDES	37	2007
GIDDY-UP 2 IN A ROOM	74	1996
GIDDY-UP-A-DING-DONG FREDDIE BELL & THE BELLBOYS	4	1956
THE GIFT [A] INXS	11	1993
THE GIFT [B] DANIEL O'DONNELL	46	1994
THE GIFT [C] WAY OUT WEST/MISS JOANNA LAW	15	1996
THE GIFT OF CHRISTMAS CHILDLINERS	9	1995
GIGANTOR DICKIES	72	1980
GIGI BILLY ECKSTINE	8	1959
GIGOLO DAMNED	29	1987
GILLY GILLY OSSENFEFFER KATZENELLEN BOGEN BY THE SEA MAX BYGRAVES	7	1954
GIMME A CALL TOMMY REILLY	14	2009
GIMME ALL YOUR LOVIN' [A] ZZ TOP	10	1983
GIMME ALL YOUR LOVIN' [B] KYM MAZELLE & JOCELYN BROWN	22	1994
GIMME DAT BANANA BLACK GORILLA	29	1977
GIMME DAT DING PIPKINS	6	1970
GIMME GIMME GIMME (A MAN AFTER MIDNIGHT) ABBA	3	1979
GIMME GIMME GOOD LOVIN' CRAZY ELEPHANT	12	1969
GIMME HOPE JO'ANNA EDDY GRANT	7	1988
GIMME LITTLE SIGN BRENTON WOOD	8	1967
GIMME LITTLE SIGN DANIELLE BRISEBOIS	75	1995
GIMME LOVE ALEXIA	17	1998
GIMME LUV (EENIE MEENIE MINY MO) DAVID MORALES & THE BAD YARD CLUB	37	1993
GIMME MORE BRITNEY SPEARS	3	2007
GIMME SHELTER (EP) VARIOUS ARTISTS (EP'S & LP'S)	23	1993
GIMME SOME BRENDON	14	1977
GIMME SOME PAT & MICK	53	1991
GIMME SOME LOVE GINA G	25	1997
GIMME SOME LOVIN' THUNDER	36	1990
GIMME SOME LOVING SPENCER DAVIS GROUP	2	1966
GIMME SOME MORE BUSTA RHYMES	5	1999
GIMME THAT BODY Q-TEE	40	1996
GIMME THAT REMIX CHRIS BROWN FEATURING LIL' WAYNE	23	2006
GIMME THE LIGHT SEAN PAUL	5	2002
GIMME THE SUNSHINE CURIOSITY	73	1993
GIMME YOUR LOVIN' ATLANTIC STARR	66	1978
GIMMIX! PLAY LOUD JOHN COOPER CLARKE	39	1979
GIN AND JUICE SNOOP DOGGY DOGG	39	1994
GIN GAN GOOLIE SCAFFOLD	38	1969
GIN HOUSE BLUES AMEN CORNER	12	1967
GIN SOAKED BOY DIVINE COMEDY	38	1999
GINCHY BERT WEEDON	35	1961
GINGER DAVID DEVANT & HIS SPIRIT WIFE	54	1997
GINGERBREAD FRANKIE AVALON	30	1958
GINNY COME LATELY BRIAN HYLAND	5	1962
GIRL [A] ST LOUIS UNION	11	1966
GIRL [A] TRUTH	27	1966
GIRL [B] DESTINY'S CHILD	6	2005
GIRL [C] BECK	45	2005

Title / Artist	Peak Position	Year of Release
GIRL ALL THE BAD GUYS WANT BOWLING FOR SOUP	8	2002
THE GIRL CAN'T HELP IT LITTLE RICHARD	9	1957
THE GIRL CAN'T HELP IT DARTS	6	1977
GIRL CRAZY HOT CHOCOLATE	7	1982
GIRL DON'T COME SANDIE SHAW	3	1964
THE GIRL FROM IPANEMA STAN GETZ & JOAO GILBERTO	29	1964
THE GIRL FROM IPANEMA ASTRUD GILBERTO	55	1984
GIRL FROM MARS ASH	11	1995
THE GIRL I LOVE HAMFATTER	71	2008
A GIRL I ONCE KNEW NORTHERN UPROAR	63	1997
THE GIRL I USED TO KNOW BROTHER BEYOND	48	1991
GIRL I'M GONNA MISS YOU MILLI VANILLI	2	1989
GIRL IN THE MOON DARIUS	21	2003
GIRL IN THE WOOD FRANKIE LAINE	11	1953
THE GIRL IS MINE MICHAEL JACKSON & PAUL McCARTNEY	8	1982
GIRL IS ON MY MIND BLACK KEYS	62	2004
GIRL (IT'S ALL I HAVE) SHY	60	1980
GIRL I'VE BEEN HURT SNOW	48	1993
A GIRL LIKE YOU [A] CLIFF RICHARD & THE SHADOWS	3	1961
A GIRL LIKE YOU [B] YOUNG RASCALS	37	1967
A GIRL LIKE YOU [C] EDWYN COLLINS	4	1995
GIRL OF MY BEST FRIEND ELVIS PRESLEY	9	1976
GIRL OF MY BEST FRIEND BRYAN FERRY	57	1993
GIRL OF MY DREAMS TONY BRENT	16	1958
GIRL OF MY DREAMS GERRY MONROE	43	1972
GIRL ON TV LYTE FUNKIE ONES	6	2000
GIRL POWER SHAMPOO	25	1996
THE GIRL SANG THE BLUES EVERLY BROTHERS	25	1963
GIRL TALK TLC	30	2002
GIRL TO GIRL 49ERS	31	1990
GIRL TONITE TWISTA FEATURING TREY SONGZ	47	2005
GIRL U FOR ME SILK	67	1993
GIRL U WANT ROBERT PALMER	57	1994
THE GIRL WITH THE LONELIEST EYES HOUSE OF LOVE	58	1991
GIRL YOU KNOW IT'S TRUE MILLI VANILLI	3	1988
GIRL YOU KNOW IT'S TRUE KEITH 'N' SHANE	36	2000
GIRL, YOU'LL BE A WOMAN SOON URGE OVERKILL	61	1994
GIRL YOU'RE SO TOGETHER MICHAEL JACKSON	33	1984
GIRL/BOY (EP) APHEX TWIN	64	1996
GIRLFIGHT BROOKE VALENTINE	35	2005
GIRLFRIEND [A] MICHAEL JACKSON	41	1980
GIRLFRIEND [B] PEBBLES	8	1988
GIRLFRIEND [C] BILLIE	1	1998
GIRLFRIEND [D] *NSYNC FEATURING NELLY	2	2002
GIRLFRIEND [E] ALICIA KEYS	24	2002
GIRLFRIEND [F] B2K	10	2003
GIRLFRIEND [G] DARKNESS	39	2006
GIRLFRIEND [H] AVRIL LAVIGNE	2	2007
GIRLFRIEND IN A COMA SMITHS	13	1987
GIRLFRIEND/BOYFRIEND BLACKSTREET FEATURING JANET	11	1999
GIRLFRIEND'S STORY GEMMA FOX FEATURING MC LYTE	38	2004
GIRLIE PEDDLERS	34	1970
GIRLIE GIRLIE SOPHIA GEORGE	7	1985
GIRLS [A] JOHNNY BURNETTE	37	1961
GIRLS [B] MOMENTS & WHATNAUTS	3	1975
GIRLS [B] POWERCUT FEATURING NUBIAN PRINZ	50	1991
GIRLS [C] BEASTIE BOYS	34	1987
GIRLS [D] PRODIGY	19	2004
GIRLS [E] CAM'RON FEATURING MONA LISA	25	2005
GIRLS [F] BEENIE FEATURING AKON	47	2006

Title / Artist	Peak Position	Year of Release
THE GIRLS [G] CALVIN HARRIS	3	2007
GIRLS [H] SUGABABES	3	2008
THE GIRL'S A FREAK DJ TOUCHE	65	2004
GIRLS AIN'T NOTHING BUT TROUBLE DJ JAZZY JEFF & THE FRESH PRINCE	21	1986
GIRLS AND BOYS [A] PRINCE & THE REVOLUTION	11	1986
GIRLS AND BOYS [B] BLUR	5	1994
GIRLS + BOYS [C] HED BOYS	21	1994
GIRLS AND BOYS [D] GOOD CHARLOTTE	6	2003
GIRLS AND BOYS IN LOVE RUMBLE STRIPS	64	2007
GIRLS ARE MORE FUN RAY PARKER, JR	46	1986
GIRLS ARE OUT TO GET YOU FASCINATIONS	32	1971
GIRLS BEST FRIEND DATSUNS	71	2004
GIRLS CAN GET IT DR HOOK	40	1980
GIRLS DEM SUGAR BEENIE MAN FEATURING MYA	13	2001
GIRLS GIRLS GIRLS [A] STEVE LAWRENCE	49	1960
GIRLS GIRLS GIRLS [B] FOURMOST	33	1966
GIRLS GIRLS GIRLS [C] SAILOR	7	1976
GIRLS GIRLS GIRLS [D] KANDIDATE	34	1979
GIRLS GIRLS GIRLS [E] MOTLEY CRUE	26	1987
GIRLS GIRLS GIRLS [F] JAY-Z	11	2002
GIRLS JUST WANNA HAVE FUN LOLLY	14	2000
GIRLS JUST WANT TO HAVE FUN CYNDI LAUPER	2	1984
GIRL'S LIFE GIRLFRIEND	68	1993
GIRLS LIKE US B-15 PROJECT FEATURING CHRISSY D	7	2000
GIRLS NIGHT OUT ALDA	20	1998
GIRL'S NOT GREY AFI	22	2003
THE GIRLS OF SUMMER (EP) ARAB STRAP	74	1997
GIRLS ON FILM DURAN DURAN	5	1981
GIRLS ON MY MIND FATBACK	69	1985
GIRLS ON TOP GIRL THING	25	2000
GIRLS' SCHOOL WINGS	1	1977
GIRLS TALK DAVE EDMUNDS	4	1979
GIRLS WHO PLAY GUITARS MAXIMO PARK	31	2007
GIRLSHAPEDLOVEDRUG GOMEZ	66	2006
GIT DOWN CENOGINERZ	75	2002
GIT DOWN (SHAKE YOUR THANG) GAYE BYKERS ON ACID	54	1987
GIT ON UP DJ 'FAST' EDDIE FEATURING SUNDANCE	49	1989
GITTIN' FUNKY KID 'N' PLAY	55	1988
GIV ME LUV ALCATRAZ	12	1996
GIVE A LITTLE BIT SUPERTRAMP	29	1977
GIVE A LITTLE LOVE [A] BAY CITY ROLLERS	1	1975
GIVE A LITTLE LOVE [B] ASWAD	11	1988
GIVE A LITTLE LOVE [C] DANIEL O'DONNELL	7	1998
GIVE A LITTLE LOVE [D] INVISIBLE MAN	48	1999
GIVE A LITTLE LOVE BACK TO THE WORLD EMMA	33	1990
GIVE AND TAKE [A] PIONEERS	35	1972
GIVE AND TAKE [B] BRASS CONSTRUCTION	62	1985
GIVE GIVE GIVE TOMMY STEELE	28	1959
GIVE GIVE GIVE ME MORE MORE MORE WONDER STUFF	72	1988
GIVE HER MY LOVE JOHNSTON BROTHERS	27	1957
GIVE HER WHAT SHE WANTS FRANKIE OLIVER	58	1997
GIVE IN TO ME MICHAEL JACKSON	2	1993
GIVE IRELAND BACK TO THE IRISH WINGS	16	1972
GIVE IT X-PRESS 2 FEATURING KURT WAGNER	33	2005
GIVE IT ALL AWAY WORLD PARTY	43	1993
GIVE IT AWAY [A] RED HOT CHILI PEPPERS	9	1994
GIVE IT AWAY [B] DEEPEST BLUE	9	2004
GIVE IT SOME EMOTION TRACIE	24	1983
GIVE IT TO ME [A] TROGGS	12	1967
GIVE IT TO ME [B] BAM BAM	65	1988
GIVE IT TO ME [C] TIMBALAND FEATURING NELLY FURTADO & JUSTIN TIMBERLAKE	1	2007
GIVE IT 2 ME [D] MADONNA	7	2008

Title / Artist	Peak Position	Year of Release
GIVE IT TO ME BABY RICK JAMES	47	1981
GIVE IT TO ME NOW KENNY	38	1973
GIVE IT TO ME RIGHT MELANIE FIONA	41	2009
GIVE IT TO YOU [A] MARTHA WASH	37	1993
GIVE IT TO YOU [B] JORDAN KNIGHT	5	1999
GIVE IT UP [A] KC & THE SUNSHINE BAND	1	1983
GIVE IT UP [A] CUT 'N' MOVE	61	1993
GIVE IT UP [B] TALK TALK	59	1986
GIVE IT UP [C] HOTHOUSE FLOWERS	30	1990
GIVE IT UP [D] WILSON PHILLIPS	36	1992
GIVE IT UP [E] GOODMEN	5	1993
GIVE IT UP [F] PUBLIC ENEMY	18	1994
GIVE IT UP [G] SELENA VS X MEN	61	2001
GIVE IT UP TURN IT LOOSE EN VOGUE	22	1993
GIVE ME A LITTLE MORE TIME GABRIELLE	5	1996
GIVE ME A REASON [A] CORRS	27	2001
GIVE ME A REASON [B] TONY DE VIT FEATURING NIKI MAK	53	2003
GIVE ME A REASON [C] TRIPLE EIGHT	9	2003
GIVE ME ALL YOUR LOVE [A] WHITESNAKE	18	1988
GIVE ME ALL YOUR LOVE [B] MAGIC AFFAIR	30	1994
GIVE ME AN INCH HAZEL O'CONNOR	41	1980
GIVE ME BACK ME BRAIN DUFFO	60	1979
GIVE ME BACK MY HEART DOLLAR	4	1982
GIVE ME BACK MY MAN B-52's	61	1980
GIVE ME FIRE GBH	69	1982
GIVE ME JUST A LITTLE MORE TIME CHAIRMEN OF THE BOARD	3	1970
GIVE ME JUST A LITTLE MORE TIME KYLIE MINOGUE	2	1992
GIVE ME JUST ONE MORE NIGHT (UNA NOCHE) 98o	61	2000
GIVE ME LIFE MR V	40	1994
GIVE ME LOVE [A] DIDDY	23	1994
GIVE ME LOVE [B] DJ DADO VS MICHELLE WEEKS	59	1998
GIVE ME LOVE (GIVE ME PEACE ON EARTH) GEORGE HARRISON	8	1973
GIVE ME MORE TIME [A] NICOLE	75	1982
GIVE ME MORE TIME [B] WHITESNAKE	29	1984
GIVE ME ONE MORE CHANCE [A] DONALD PEERS	36	1972
GIVE ME ONE MORE CHANCE [B] LUKE GOSS & THE BAND OF THIEVES	68	1993
GIVE ME RHYTHM BLACK CONNECTION	32	1998
GIVE ME SOME KINDA MAGIC DOLLAR	34	1982
GIVE ME SOME MORE DJ GERT	50	2001
GIVE ME STRENGTH JON OF THE PLEASED WIMMIN	30	1996
GIVE ME THE NIGHT GEORGE BENSON	7	1980
GIVE ME THE NIGHT MIRAGE FEATURING ROY GAYLE	49	1984
GIVE ME THE NIGHT RANDY CRAWFORD	60	1997
GIVE ME THE NIGHT XAVIER	65	2005
GIVE ME THE REASON LUTHER VANDROSS	26	1986
GIVE ME TIME DUSTY SPRINGFIELD	24	1967
GIVE ME TONIGHT SHANNON	24	1984
GIVE ME WHAT I WANT KIDS IN GLASS HOUSES	62	2008
GIVE ME YOU MARY J BLIGE	19	2000
GIVE ME YOUR BODY CHIPPENDALES	28	1992
GIVE ME YOUR HEART TONIGHT SHAKIN' STEVENS	11	1982
GIVE ME YOUR LOVE [A] REEF	44	2003
GIVE ME YOUR LOVE [B] XTM & DJ CHUCKY PRESENTS ANNIA	28	2005
GIVE ME YOUR WORD TENNESSEE ERNIE FORD	6	1953
GIVE ME YOUR WORD BILLY FURY	27	1966
GIVE MYSELF TO LOVE FRANCIS ROSSI OF STATUS QUO	42	1996
GIVE PEACE A CHANCE PLASTIC ONO BAND	2	1969
GIVE U ONE 4 CHRISTMAS HOT PANTZ	64	2005
GIVE UP THE FUNK (LET'S DANCE) B.T. EXPRESS	52	1980
GIVE YOU DJAIMIN	45	1992
GIVE YOU ALL THE LOVE MISHKA	34	1999
GIVEN TO FLY PEARL JAM	12	1998
GIVEN UP MIRRORBALL	12	1999
GIVES YOU HELL ALL-AMERICAN REJECTS	18	2009
GIVIN' IT UP INCOGNITO	43	1993
GIVIN' UP GIVIN' IN THREE DEGREES	12	1978
GIVING HIM SOMETHING HE CAN FEEL EN VOGUE	16	1992
GIVING IN ADEMA	62	2002
GIVING IT ALL AWAY ROGER DALTREY	5	1973
GIVING IT BACK PHIL HURTT	36	1978
GIVING UP GIVING IN SHEENA EASTON	54	2000
GIVING YOU THE BENEFIT PEBBLES	73	1990
GIVING YOU THE BEST THAT I GOT ANITA BAKER	55	1988
GIVING YOU UP KYLIE MINOGUE	6	2005
G.L.A.D. KIM APPLEBY	10	1991
GLAD ALL OVER DAVE CLARK FIVE	1	1963
GLAD ALL OVER CRYSTAL PALACE	50	1990
GLAD IT'S ALL OVER CAPTAIN SENSIBLE	6	1984
GLAM LISA B	49	1993
GLAM RAID SPACE RAIDERS	68	1998
GLAM ROCK COPS CARTER-THE UNSTOPPABLE SEX MACHINE	24	1994
GLAM SLAM PRINCE	29	1988
GLAMOROUS FERGIE FEATURING LUDACRIS	6	2007
GLASGOW RANGERS (NINE IN A ROW) RANGERS FC	54	1997
A GLASS OF CHAMPAGNE SAILOR	2	1975
GLASTONBURY SONG WATERBOYS	29	1993
GLENDORA PERRY COMO	18	1956
GLENDORA GLEN MASON	28	1956
GLENN MILLER MEDLEY JOHN ANDERSON BIG BAND	61	1985
GLITTER AND TRAUMA BIFFY CLYRO	21	2004
GLITTERBALL [A] SIMPLE MINDS	18	1998
GLITTERBALL [B] FC KAHUNA	64	2002
GLITTERING PRIZE SIMPLE MINDS	16	1982
GLOBAL LOVE HIGH CONTRAST	68	2002
GLOBETROTTER TORNADOS	5	1963
GLORIA [A] JONATHAN KING	65	1979
GLORIA [A] LAURA BRANIGAN	6	1983
GLORIA [B] U2	55	1981
GLORIA [C] VAN MORRISON & JOHN LEE HOOKER	31	1993
GLORIOUS [A] ANDREAS JOHNSON	4	2000
GLORIOUS [B] CAPTAIN	30	2006
GLORIOUS [C] NATALIE IMBRUGLIA	23	2007
A GLORIOUS DAY EMBRACE	28	2005
GLORY BOX PORTISHEAD	13	1995
GLORY DAYS [A] BRUCE SPRINGSTEEN	17	1985
GLORY DAYS [B] JUST JACK	32	2007
GLORY GLORY MAN. UNITED MANCHESTER UNITED FOOTBALL CLUB	13	1983
GLORY OF LOVE PETER CETERA	3	1986
GLORY OF THE 80'S TORI AMOS	46	1999
GLORYLAND DARYL HALL & THE SOUNDS OF BLACKNESS	36	1994
GLOVES HORRORS	34	2007
GLOW SPANDAU BALLET	10	1981
GLOW OF LOVE CHANGE	14	1980
GLOW WORM MILLS BROTHERS	10	1953
GO [A] SCOTT FITZGERALD	52	1988
GO [B] MOBY	10	1991
GO [C] JOCASTA	50	1997
GO [D] HANSON	44	2007
GO AWAY [A] GLORIA ESTEFAN	13	1993
GO AWAY [B] HONEYCRACK	41	1996
GO AWAY LITTLE GIRL MARK WYNTER	6	1962
GO (BEFORE YOU BREAK MY HEART) GIGLIOLA CINQUETTI	8	1974
GO BUDDY GO STRANGLERS	8	1977
GO CUT CREATOR GO LL COOL J	66	1987
GO DEEP JANET JACKSON	13	1998
GO DEH YAKA (GO TO THE TOP) MONYAKA	14	1983
GO ENGLAND ENGLAND BOYS	26	2002
GO FOR IT! COVENTRY CITY CUP FINAL SQUAD	61	1987
GO FOR IT (HEART AND SOUL) ROCKY V FEATURING JOEY B ELLIS & TYNETTA HARE	20	1991
GO FOR THE HEART SOX	47	1995
GO GO GO CHUCK BERRY	38	1963
GO GONE ESTELLE	32	2005
GO HOME STEVIE WONDER	67	1985
GO INTO THE LIGHT IAN McNABB	66	1994
GO LET IT OUT OASIS	1	2000
GO MR SUNSHINE REMI NICOLE	57	2007
GO NORTH RICHARD BARNES	38	1970
GO NOW MOODY BLUES	1	1964
GO ON BY ALMA COGAN	16	1955
GO ON GIRL ROXANNE SHANTE	55	1988
GO ON MOVE REEL 2 REAL FEATURING THE MAD STUNTMAN	7	1994
GO TECHNO 2 HOUSE	65	1992
GO THE DISTANCE MICHAEL BOLTON	14	1997
GO TO SLEEP RADIOHEAD	12	2003
GO WEST VILLAGE PEOPLE	15	1979
GO WEST PET SHOP BOYS	2	1993
GO WILD IN THE COUNTRY BOW WOW WOW	7	1982
GO WITH THE FLOW [A] LOOP DA LOOP	47	1997
GO WITH THE FLOW [B] QUEENS OF THE STONE AGE	21	2003
GO YOUR OWN WAY FLEETWOOD MAC	38	1977
GOD TORI AMOS	44	1994
GOD GAVE ROCK AND ROLL TO YOU ARGENT	18	1973
GOD GAVE ROCK AND ROLL TO YOU II KISS	4	1992
GOD IS A DJ [A] FAITHLESS	6	1998
GOD IS A DJ [B] P!NK	11	2004
GOD KILLED THE QUEEN LOUIS XIV	68	2005
GOD KNOWS MANDO DIAO	64	2005
GOD LEAD YOUR SOUL SLEEPY JACKSON	69	2006
GOD OF ABRAHAM MNO	66	1991
GOD ONLY KNOWS BEACH BOYS	2	1966
GOD ONLY KNOWS DIESEL PARK WEST	57	1992
GOD PUT A SMILE ON YOUR FACE RONSON FEATURING DAPTONE HORNS	63	2007
GOD SAVE THE QUEEN SEX PISTOLS	2	1977
GOD! SHOW ME MAGIC SUPER FURRY ANIMALS	33	1996
GOD THANK YOU WOMAN CULTURE CLUB	1	1986
GODDESS ON A HIWAY MERCURY REV	26	1998
GODHEAD NITZER EBB	52	1992
GODHOPPING DOGS DIE IN HOT CARS	24	2004
GODLESS DANDY WARHOLS	66	2001
GOD'S CHILD BIG BANG THEORY	51	2002
GOD'S GONNA PUNISH YOU TYMES	41	1976
GOD'S GREAT BANANA SKIN CHRIS REA	31	1992
GOD'S HOME MOVIE HORSE	56	1993
GOD'S KITCHEN BLANCMANGE	65	1982
GOD'S MISTAKE TEARS FOR FEARS	61	1996
GODSPEED BT	54	1998
GODSTAR PSYCHIC TV	67	1986
GODZILLA CREATURES	53	2003
GO-GO DANCER WEDDING PRESENT	20	1992
GOIN' DOWN MELANIE C	4	1999
GOIN' PLACES JACKSONS	26	1977
GOIN' TO THE BANK COMMODORES	43	1986
GOIN' TO VEGAS JIMMY RAY	49	1998
GOING ALL THE WAY ALLSTARS	19	2002
GOING BACK DUSTY SPRINGFIELD	10	1966

Title	Artist	Peak Position	Year of Release
GOING BACK TO CALI	LL COOL J	37	1988
GOING BACK TO MY HOME TOWN	HAL PAIGE & THE WHALERS	50	1960
GOING BACK TO MY ROOTS	ODYSSEY	4	1981
GOING BACK TO MY ROOTS	FPI PROJECT	9	1989
GOING DOWN THE ROAD	ROY WOOD	13	1974
GOING DOWN TO LIVERPOOL	BANGLES	56	1986
GOING DOWN TOWN TONIGHT	STATUS QUO	20	1984
GOING FOR GOLD	SHED SEVEN	8	1996
GOING FOR THE ONE	YES	24	1977
GOING HOME [A]	OSMONDS	4	1973
GOING HOME [B]	TYRREL CORPORATION	58	1992
GOING HOME (THEME OF 'LOCAL HERO')	MARK KNOPFLER	56	1983
GOING IN WITH MY EYES OPEN	DAVID SOUL	2	1977
GOING LEFT RIGHT	DEPARTMENT S	55	1981
GOING MISSING	MAXIMO PARK	20	2005
GOING NOWHERE	GABRIELLE	9	1993
GOING OUT	SUPERGRASS	5	1996
GOING OUT OF MY HEAD [A]	DODIE WEST	39	1965
GOING OUT OF MY HEAD [B]	FATBOY SLIM	57	1997
GOING OUT WITH GOD	KINKY MACHINE	74	1993
GOING ROUND	D'BORA	40	1995
GOING THROUGH THE MOTIONS	HOT CHOCOLATE	53	1979
GOING TO A GO-GO	MIRACLES	44	1966
GOING TO A GO-GO	SHARONETTES	46	1975
GOING TO A GO GO	ROLLING STONES	26	1982
GOING TO A TOWN	RUFUS WAINWRIGHT	54	2007
GOING UNDER	EVANESCENCE	8	2003
GOING UNDERGROUND	JAM	1	1980
GOING UNDERGROUND	BUFFALO TOM	6	1999
GOING UP THE COUNTRY	CANNED HEAT	19	1969
GOLD [A]	JOHN STEWART	43	1979
GOLD [B]	SPANDAU BALLET	2	1983
GOLD [C]	EAST 17	28	1992
GOLD [D]	ARTIST FORMERLY KNOWN AS PRINCE (AFKAP)	10	1995
GOLD [E]	BEVERLEY KNIGHT	27	2002
GOLD DIGGER [A]	KANYE WEST FEATURING JAMIE FOXX	2	2005
GOLD DIGGER [A]	GLEE CAST	44	2010
GOLD DIGGER [B]	DOLLY ROCKERS	46	2009
GOLD LION	YEAH YEAH YEAHS	53	2006
GOLDEN	JILL SCOTT	59	2004
GOLDEN AGE OF ROCK AND ROLL	MOTT THE HOOPLE	16	1974
GOLDEN BROWN	STRANGLERS	2	1982
GOLDEN BROWN	KALEEF	22	1996
GOLDEN BROWN	OMAR	37	1997
GOLDEN DAYS	BUCKS FIZZ	42	1984
GOLDEN GATE BRIDGE	OCEAN COLOUR SCENE	40	2004
GOLDEN GAZE	IAN BROWN	29	2000
GOLDEN GREEN	WONDER STUFF	33	1989
GOLDEN GUN	SUEDE	14	2003
THE GOLDEN LADY	THREE DEGREES	56	1979
GOLDEN LIGHTS	TWINKLE	21	1965
THE GOLDEN PATH	CHEMICAL BROTHERS FEATURING THE FLAMING LIPS	17	2003
GOLDEN RETRIEVER	SUPER FURRY ANIMALS	13	2003
GOLDEN SKANS	KLAXONS	7	2007
GOLDEN SKIN	SILVER SUN	32	1997
GOLDEN SLUMBERS	TRASH	35	1969
GOLDEN TOUCH	RAZORLIGHT	9	2004
GOLDEN YEARS	DAVID BOWIE	8	1975
GOLDEN YEARS	LOOSE ENDS	59	1985
THE GOLDEN YEARS EP	MOTORHEAD	8	1980
GOLDENBALLS (MR BECKHAM TO YOU)	BELL & SPURLING	25	2002
GOLDENBOOK	FAMILY CAT	42	1994
GOLDENEYE	TINA TURNER	10	1995
GOLDFINGER [A]	SHIRLEY BASSEY	21	1964
GOLDFINGER [B]	ASH	5	1996
GOLDRUSH	YELLO	54	1986
GONE [A]	SHIRLEY BASSEY	36	1964
GONE [B]	DAVID HOLMES	75	1996
GONE [C]	CURE	60	1996
GONE [D]	*NSYNC	24	2001
GONE AWAY	OFFSPRING	42	1997
GONE DEAD TRAIN	NAZARETH	49	1978
GONE GONE GONE [A]	EVERLY BROTHERS	36	1964
GONE GONE GONE [B]	JOHNNY MATHIS	15	1979
GONE TILL NOVEMBER	WYCLEF JEAN	3	1998
GONE TOO SOON	MICHAEL JACKSON	33	1993
GONE UP IN FLAMES	MORNING RUNNER	39	2005
GONNA BE MINE	ADDICTIVE FEATURING T2	47	2008
GONNA BUILD A MOUNTAIN	MATT MONRO	44	1961
GONNA BUILD A MOUNTAIN	SAMMY DAVIS, JR	26	1962
GONNA CAPTURE YOUR HEART	BLUE	18	1977
GONNA CATCH YOU	LONNIE GORDON	32	1991
GONNA CATCH YOU	BARKIN BROTHERS FEATURING JOHNNIE FIORI	51	2000
GONNA FLY NOW (THEME FROM ROCKY)	BILL CONTI	52	2007
GONNA GET ALONG WITHOUT YA NOW	PATIENCE & PRUDENCE	22	1957
GONNA GET ALONG WITHOUT YA NOW	TRINI LOPEZ	41	1967
GONNA GET ALONG WITHOUT YOU NOW	VIOLA WILLS	8	1979
GONNA GIVE HER ALL THE LOVE I'VE GOT	JIMMY RUFFIN	26	1967
GONNA MAKE YOU A STAR	DAVID ESSEX	1	1974
GONNA MAKE YOU AN OFFER YOU CAN'T REFUSE	JIMMY HELMS	8	1973
GONNA MAKE YOU BLUSH	PAPERDOLLS	65	1998
GONNA MAKE YOU SWEAT (EVERYBODY DANCE NOW)	C & C MUSIC FACTORY (FEATURING FREEDOM WILLIAMS)	3	1990
GONNA WORK IT OUT	HI-GATE	25	2001
GOO GOO BARABAJAGAL (LOVE IS HOT)	DONOVAN WITH THE JEFF BECK GROUP	12	1969
GOOD AS GOLD	BEAUTIFUL SOUTH	23	1994
THE GOOD THE BAD THE UGLY	HUGO MONTENEGRO	1	1968
GOOD BEAT	DEEE-LITE	53	1991
GOOD BOYS	BLONDIE	12	2003
GOOD DANCERS	SLEEPY JACKSON	71	2003
GOOD DAY	SEAN MAGUIRE	12	1996
GOOD ENOUGH [A]	BOBBY BROWN	41	1992
GOOD ENOUGH [B]	DODGY	4	1996
GOOD ENOUGH FOR YOU	FREEFALLER	21	2005
GOOD ENOUGH (LA VACHE)	MILK INC	23	1998
GOOD EVENING FRIENDS	FRANKIE LAINE & JOHNNIE RAY	25	1957
GOOD EVENING PHILADELPHIA	RICKY ROSS	58	1996
GOOD FEELING	REEF	24	1995
GOOD FOR ME	AMY GRANT	60	1992
GOOD FORTUNE	PJ HARVEY	41	2000
GOOD FRIEND	PARIS RED	61	1992
GOOD FRUIT	HEFNER	50	2000
GOOD GIRLS	JOE	29	1998
GOOD GIRLS DON'T	KNACK	66	1979
GOOD GIRLS GO BAD	COBRA STARSHIP	17	2009
GOOD GOD [A]	KORN	25	1997
GOOD GOD [B]	JFK	71	2001
GOOD GOLLY MISS MOLLY	LITTLE RICHARD	8	1958
GOOD GOLLY MISS MOLLY	JERRY LEE LEWIS	31	1963
GOOD GOLLY MISS MOLLY	SWINGING BLUE JEANS	11	1964
GOOD GOOD FEELING	ERIC & THE GOOD GOOD FEELING	73	1989
GOOD GRIEF CHRISTINA	CHICORY TIP	17	1973
A GOOD HEART	FEARGAL SHARKEY	1	1985
A GOOD IDEA	SUGAR	65	1992
GOOD IS GOOD	SHERYL CROW	75	2005
THE GOOD LIFE [A]	TONY BENNETT	27	1963
GOOD LIFE [B]	INNER CITY	4	1988
GOOD LIFE [C]	E.V.E.	39	1995
THE GOOD LIFE [D]	NEW POWER GENERATION	15	1995
GOOD LIFE [E]	KANYE WEST FEATURING T-PAIN	23	2007
GOOD LOVE	MELI'SA MORGAN	59	1988
GOOD LOVE CAN NEVER DIE	ALVIN STARDUST	11	1975
GOOD LOVE REAL LOVE	D'BORA	58	1996
GOOD LOVER	D-INFLUENCE	46	1992
GOOD LOVIN'	REGINA BELLE	73	1989
GOOD LOVIN' AIN'T EASY TO COME BY	MARVIN GAYE & TAMMI TERRELL	26	1969
GOOD LOVIN' GONE BAD	BAD COMPANY	31	1975
GOOD LUCK	BASEMENT JAXX FEATURING LISA KEKAULA	12	2003
GOOD LUCK CHARM	ELVIS PRESLEY	1	1962
GOOD MORNING	LEAPY LEE	29	1970
GOOD MORNING BRITAIN	AZTEC CAMERA & MICK JONES	19	1990
GOOD MORNING FREEDOM	BLUE MINK	10	1970
GOOD MORNING JUDGE	10 C.C.	5	1977
GOOD MORNING LITTLE SCHOOLGIRL	YARDBIRDS	44	1964
GOOD MORNING STARSHINE	OLIVER	6	1969
GOOD MORNING SUNSHINE	AQUA	18	1998
GOOD OLD ARSENAL	ARSENAL FC FIRST TEAM SQUAD	16	1971
GOOD OLD ROCK 'N ROLL	DAVE CLARK FIVE	7	1969
THE GOOD ONES	KILLS	23	2005
GOOD PEOPLE	JACK JOHNSON	50	2005
GOOD REASON	SEAFOOD	65	2004
GOOD RHYMES	DA CLICK	14	1999
GOOD ROCKIN' TONIGHT	MONTROSE	71	1980
GOOD SIGN	EMILIA	54	1999
GOOD SONG	BLUR	22	2003
GOOD SOULS	STARSAILOR	12	2001
GOOD STUFF [A]	B-52's	21	1992
GOOD STUFF [B]	KELIS	19	2000
GOOD STUFF [C]	CLOR	50	2005
GOOD SWEET LOVIN'	LOUCHIE LOU & MICHIE ONE	34	1996
A GOOD THING	SAINT ETIENNE	70	2005
GOOD THING [A]	FINE YOUNG CANNIBALS	7	1989
GOOD THING [B]	ETERNAL	8	1996
GOOD THING GOING	YAZZ	53	1996
GOOD THING GOING	SID OWEN	14	2000
GOOD THING GOING (WE'VE GOT A GOOD THING GOING)	SUGAR MINOTT	4	1981
GOOD THINGS	RIVAL SCHOOLS	74	2002
GOOD TIME [A]	PERAN	37	2002
GOOD TIME [B]	A	23	2003
GOOD TIME BABY	BOBBY RYDELL	42	1961
GOOD TIMES [A]	ERIC BURDON & THE ANIMALS	20	1967
GOOD TIMES [B]	CHIC	5	1979
GOOD TIMES [C]	MATT BIANCO	55	1988
GOOD TIMES [D]	REID	55	1989
GOOD TIMES [E]	JIMMY BARNES & INXS	18	1991
GOOD TIMES [F]	EDIE BRICKELL	40	1994
GOOD TIMES [G]	ED CASE & SKIN	49	2002
GOOD TIMES [H]	DREAM FREQUENCY	67	1994
GOOD TIMES (BETTER TIMES)	CLIFF RICHARD	12	1969
GOOD TIMES GONNA COME	AQUALUNG	71	2002
GOOD TIMIN'	JIMMY JONES	1	1960
GOOD TO BE ALIVE	DJ RAP	36	1998
GOOD TO GO LOVER	GWEN GUTHRIE	37	1987

Title	Artist	Peak Position	Year of Release
GOOD TRADITION	TANITA TIKARAM	10	1988
GOOD 2 GO	TRIPLE EIGHT	42	2005
GOOD VIBRATIONS [A]	BEACH BOYS	1	1966
GOOD VIBRATIONS [A]	PSYCHIC TV	65	1986
GOOD VIBRATIONS [A]	BRIAN WILSON	30	2004
GOOD VIBRATIONS [B]	MARKY MARK & THE FUNKY BUNCH FEATURING LOLEATTA HOLLOWAY	14	1991
GOOD VIBRATIONS [C]	BROTHERS LIKE OUTLAW FEATURING ALISON EVELYN	74	1993
GOOD WEEKEND	ART BRUT	56	2005
A GOOD YEAR FOR THE ROSES	ELVIS COSTELLO & THE ATTRACTIONS	6	1981
GOODBYE [A]	MARY HOPKIN	2	1969
A GOODBYE [B]	CAMEO	65	1986
GOODBYE [C]	SUNDAYS	27	1992
GOODBYE [D]	AIR SUPPLY	66	1993
GOODBYE [E]	SPICE GIRLS	1	1998
GOODBYE [F]	DEF LEPPARD	54	1999
GOODBYE [G]	CORAL	21	2002
GOODBYE BABY AND AMEN	LULU	40	1994
GOODBYE BLUEBIRD	WAYNE FONTANA	49	1966
GOODBYE CIVILIAN	SKIDS	52	1980
GOODBYE CRUEL WORLD [A]	JAMES DARREN	28	1961
GOODBYE CRUEL WORLD [B]	SHAKESPEAR'S SISTER	32	1991
GOODBYE GIRL [A]	SQUEEZE	63	1978
GOODBYE GIRL [B]	GO WEST	25	1985
GOODBYE HEARTBREAK	LIGHTHOUSE FAMILY	14	1996
GOODBYE IS JUST ANOTHER WORD	NEW SEEKERS	36	1973
GOODBYE JIMMY GOODBYE	RUBY MURRAY	10	1959
GOODBYE MR A	HOOSIERS	4	2007
GOODBYE MR MACKENZIE	GOODBYE MR MACKENZIE	62	1988
GOODBYE MY LOVE [A]	SEARCHERS	4	1965
GOODBYE MY LOVE [B]	GLITTER BAND	2	1975
GOODBYE MY LOVER	JAMES BLUNT	9	2006
GOODBYE NOTHING TO SAY	JAVELLS FEATURING NOSMO KING	26	1974
GOODBYE SAM HELLO SAMANTHA	CLIFF RICHARD	6	1970
GOODBYE STRANGER [A]	SUPERTRAMP	57	1979
GOODBYE STRANGER [B]	PEPSI & SHIRLIE	9	1987
GOODBYE TO LOVE	CARPENTERS	9	1972
GOODBYE TO LOVE AGAIN	MAXI PRIEST	57	1988
GOODBYE TONIGHT	LOSTPROPHETS	42	2004
GOODBYE YELLOW BRICK ROAD	ELTON JOHN	6	1973
GOODBYE-EE [A]	PETER COOK & DUDLEY MOORE	18	1965
GOODBYE-EE [B]	14-18	33	1975
GOODBYE'S (THE SADDEST WORD)	CELINE DION	38	2002
GOODGROOVE	DEREK B	16	1988
GOODIES	CIARA FEATURING PETEY PABLO	1	2005
GOODNESS GRACIOUS ME	PETER SELLERS & SOPHIA LOREN	4	1960
GOODNIGHT [A]	ROY ORBISON	14	1965
GOODNIGHT [B]	BABYBIRD	28	1996
GOODNIGHT AND GO	IMOGEN HEAP	56	2006
GOODNIGHT GIRL	WET WET WET	1	1992
GOODNIGHT GOODNIGHT	HOT HOT HEAT	36	2005
GOODNIGHT MIDNIGHT	CLODAGH RODGERS	4	1969
GOODNIGHT MRS. FLINTSTONE	PILTDOWN MEN	18	1961
GOODNIGHT MOON	SHIVAREE	63	2001
GOODNIGHT SAIGON	BILLY JOEL	29	1984
GOODNIGHT SWEET PRINCE	MR ACKER BILK & HIS PARAMOUNT JAZZ BAND	50	1960
GOODNIGHT TONIGHT	WINGS	5	1979
GOODWILL CITY	GOODBYE MR MACKENZIE	49	1989
GOODY GOODY	FRANKIE LYMON & THE TEENAGERS	24	1957
GOODY TWO SHOES	ADAM ANT	1	1982
GOODYBYE BAD TIMES	GIORGIO MORODER & PHIL OAKEY	44	1985
GOOGLE EYE	NASHVILLE TEENS	10	1964
GORECKI	LAMB	30	1997
GORGEOUS	GENE LOVES JEZEBEL	68	1987
GOSP	LWS	65	1994
GOSPEL OAK EP	SINEAD O'CONNOR	28	1997
GOSSIP CALYPSO	BERNARD CRIBBINS	25	1962
GOSSIP FOLKS	MISSY ELLIOTT FEATURING LUDACRIS	9	2003
GOT 'TIL IT'S GONE	JANET FEATURING Q-TIP & JONI	6	1997
GOT A FEELING	PATRICK JUVET	34	1978
GOT A GIRL	FOUR PREPS	28	1960
GOT A LITTLE HEARTACHE	ALVIN STARDUST	55	1985
GOT A LOT O' LIVIN' TO DO	ELVIS PRESLEY	17	1957
GOT A LOVE FOR YOU	JOMANDA	43	1991
GOT A MATCH	RUSS CONWAY	30	1958
GOT FUNK	FUNK JUNKEEZ	57	1998
GOT IT AT THE DELMAR	SENSELESS THINGS	50	1991
GOT LOVE TO KILL	JULIETTE & THE LICKS	56	2005
GOT ME A FEELING	MISTY OLDLAND	59	1993
GOT MY MIND MADE UP	INSTANT FUNK	46	1979
GOT MY MIND SET ON YOU	GEORGE HARRISON	2	1987
GOT MY MOJO WORKING	JIMMY SMITH	48	1966
GOT MYSELF TOGETHER	BUCKETHEADS	12	1996
GOT NO BRAINS	BAD MANNERS	44	1982
GOT NONE	ROBERT POST	42	2005
GOT SOME TEETH	OBIE TRICE	8	2003
GOT THE FEELIN'	FIVE	3	1998
GOT THE LIFE	KORN	23	1998
GOT THE TIME	ANTHRAX	16	1991
GOT TO BE CERTAIN	KYLIE MINOGUE	2	1988
GOT TO BE REAL	ERIK	42	1994
GOT TO BE THERE	MICHAEL JACKSON	5	1972
GOT TO GET	ROB 'N' RAZ FEATURING LEILA K	8	1989
GOT TO GET IT [A]	CULTURE BEAT	4	1993
GOT TO GET IT [B]	SISQO	14	2000
GOT TO GET UP	AFRIKA BAMBAATAA	22	1998
GOT TO GET YOU BACK	KYM MAZELLE	29	1989
GOT TO GET YOU INTO MY LIFE	CLIFF BENNETT & THE REBEL ROUSERS	6	1966
GOT TO GET YOU INTO MY LIFE	EARTH, WIND & FIRE	33	1978
GOT TO GIVE IT UP	MARVIN GAYE	7	1977
GOT TO GIVE IT UP	AALIYAH	37	1996
GOT TO GIVE ME LOVE	DANA DAWSON	27	1995
GOT TO HAVE YOUR LOVE	MANTRONIX FEATURING WONDRESS	4	1990
GOT TO HAVE YOUR LOVE	LIBERTY X	2	2002
GOT TO KEEP ON	COOKIE CREW	17	1989
GOT TO LOVE SOMEBODY	SISTER SLEDGE	34	1980
GOT TO RELEASE	SATURATED SOUL FEATURING MISS BUNTY	56	2004
GOT UR SELF A	NAS	30	2002
GOT YOU	PHAROAHE MONCH	27	2001
GOT YOU ON MY MIND	TONY BRENT	12	1953
GOT YOUR MONEY	OL' DIRTY BASTARD FEATURING KELIS	11	2000
GOTHAM CITY	R KELLY	9	1997
GOTTA BE A SIN	ADAM ANT	48	1995
GOTTA BE SOMEBODY	NICKELBACK	20	2008
GOTTA BE YOU	3T: RAP BY HERBIE	10	1997
GOTTA CATCH 'EM ALL	50 GRIND FEATURING POKEMON ALLSTARS	57	2001
GOTTA GET A DATE	FRANK IFIELD	49	1960
GOTTA GET AWAY	OFFSPRING	43	1995
GOTTA GET IT RIGHT	LENA FIAGBE	20	1993
GOTTA GET LOOSE	MR & MRS SMITH	70	1996
GOTTA GET THRU THIS	DANIEL BEDINGFIELD	1	2001
GOTTA GET YOU HOME TONIGHT	EUGENE WILDE	18	1984
GOTTA GETCHA	JERMAINE DUPRI	54	2005
GOTTA GO HOME	BONEY M	12	1979
GOTTA GO MY OWN WAY	GABRIELLA & TROY	40	2007
GOTTA HAVE HOPE	BLACKOUT	46	1999
GOTTA HAVE RAIN	MAX BYGRAVES	28	1958
GOTTA HAVE SOMETHING IN THE BANK FRANK	FRANKIE VAUGHAN & THE KAYE SISTERS	8	1957
GOTTA KEEP PUSHIN'	Z FACTOR	47	1998
GOTTA KNOW (YOUR NAME)	MALAIKA	68	1993
GOTTA LOTTA LOVE	ICE-T	24	1994
GOTTA...MOVIN' ON UP	PM DAWN FEATURING KY-MANI	68	1998
GOTTA PULL MYSELF TOGETHER	NOLANS	9	1980
GOTTA SEE BABY TONIGHT	MR ACKER BILK & HIS PARAMOUNT JAZZ BAND	24	1962
GOTTA SEE JANE	R DEAN TAYLOR	17	1968
GOTTA TELL YOU	SAMANTHA MUMBA	2	2000
GOTTA WORK	AMERIE	21	2007
GOURYELLA	GOURYELLA	15	1999
GOVINDA [A]	RADHA KRISHNA TEMPLE	23	1970
GOVINDA [B]	KULA SHAKER	7	1996
GRACE [A]	BAND AKA	41	1982
GRACE [B]	SUPERGRASS	13	2002
GRACE [C]	SIMON WEBBE	36	2007
GRACE [D]	WILL YOUNG	33	2008
GRACE KELLY	MIKA	1	2007
GRACEADELICA	DARK STAR	25	2000
GRACELAND	BIBLE	51	1989
GRAFFITI	MAXIMO PARK	15	2005
GRANADA	FRANKIE LAINE	9	1954
GRANADA	FRANK SINATRA	15	1961
GRAND COOLIE DAM	LONNIE DONEGAN	6	1958
GRAND PIANO	MIXMASTER	9	1989
GRAND UNIFICATION (PART 1)	FIGHTSTAR	20	2005
GRANDAD	CLIVE DUNN	1	1970
GRANDMA'S PARTY	PAUL NICHOLAS	9	1976
GRANDPA'S PARTY	MONIE LOVE	16	1989
GRANITE	PENDULUM	29	2007
GRANITE ST.A.T.U.E	SALAD	50	1995
GRAPEVYNE	BROWNSTONE	16	1995
GRATEFUL WHEN YOU'RE DEAD – JERRY WAS THERE	KULA SHAKER	35	1996
THE GRAVE AND THE CONSTANT	FUN LOVIN' CRIMINALS	72	1996
GRAVEL PIT	WU-TANG CLAN	6	2000
GRAVITATE TO ME	THE THE	63	1989
GRAVITY [A]	JAMES BROWN	65	1986
GRAVITY [B]	EMBRACE	7	2004
GRAVITY [C]	PIXIE LOTT	20	2010
GRAVITY'S RAINBOW	KLAXONS	35	2007
GREASE	FRANKIE VALLI	3	1978
GREASE	CRAIG McLACHLAN	44	1993
GREASE MEGAMIX	FRANKIE VALLI, JOHN TRAVOLTA & OLIVIA NEWTON-JOHN	47	1990
GREASED LIGHTNIN'	JOHN TRAVOLTA	11	1978
GREAT BALLS OF FIRE	JERRY LEE LEWIS	1	1957
GREAT BALLS OF FIRE	TINY TIM	45	1969
THE GREAT BEYOND	R.E.M.	3	2000
GREAT DJ	TING TINGS	33	2008
THE GREAT ESCAPE [A]	ENGLAND SUPPORTERS' BAND	26	1998
THE GREAT ESCAPE [B]	WE ARE SCIENTISTS	37	2005
THE GREAT ESCAPE [C]	MORNING RUNNER	56	2006
THE GREAT ESCAPE [D]	BOYS LIKE GIRLS	72	2008
GREAT GOSH A'MIGHTY (IT'S A MATTER OF TIME)	LITTLE RICHARD	62	1986
THE GREAT PRETENDER	PLATTERS	5	1956

Title / Artist	Peak Position	Year of Release
THE GREAT PRETENDER JIMMY PARKINSON	9	1956
THE GREAT PRETENDER FREDDIE MERCURY	4	1987
THE GREAT ROCK 'N' ROLL SWINDLE SEX PISTOLS	21	1979
THE GREAT SNOWMAN BOB LUMAN	49	1961
THE GREAT SONG OF INDIFFERENCE BOB GELDOF	15	1990
THE GREAT TEST HUNDRED REASONS	29	2003
GREAT THINGS ECHOBELLY	13	1995
THE GREAT TRAIN ROBBERY BLACK UHURU	62	1986
GREATER LOVE SOUNDMAN & DON LLOYDIE WITH ELISABETH TROY	49	1995
THE GREATEST COCKNEY RIPOFF COCKNEY REJECTS	21	1980
GREATEST DAY [A] BEVERLEY KNIGHT	14	1999
GREATEST DAY [B] TAKE THAT	1	2008
THE GREATEST FLAME RUNRIG	30	1993
THE GREATEST HIGH HURRICANE #1	43	1999
THE GREATEST LOVE OF ALL GEORGE BENSON	27	1977
GREATEST LOVE OF ALL WHITNEY HOUSTON	8	1986
THE GREATEST LOVE YOU'LL NEVER KNOW LUTRICIA McNEAL	17	1998
THE GREATEST ROMANCE EVER SOLD ARTIST	65	2000
THE GREATEST SHOW ON EARTH STRANGELOVE	36	1997
THE GREATNESS AND PERFECTION OF LOVE JULIAN COPE	52	1984
GREECE THREE DRIVES	12	1999
GREECE 2000 THREE DRIVES	12	1998
GREED LAURENT GARNIER	36	2000
GREEDY FLY BUSH	22	1997
THE GREEDY UGLY PEOPLE HEFNER	64	2000
GREEN AND GREY NEW MODEL ARMY	37	1989
THE GREEN DOOR FRANKIE VAUGHAN	2	1956
THE GREEN DOOR JIM LOWE	8	1956
GREEN DOOR GLEN MASON	24	1956
GREEN DOOR SHAKIN' STEVENS	1	1981
GREEN FIELDS [A] BEVERLEY SISTERS	29	1960
GREEN FIELDS [A] UNIT FOUR PLUS TWO	48	1964
GREEN FIELDS [B] GOOD, THE BAD & THE QUEEN	51	2007
GREEN GREEN GRASS OF HOME TOM JONES	1	1966
GREEN GREEN GRASS OF HOME ELVIS PRESLEY	29	1975
GREEN GREEN GRASS OF HOME KATHERINE JENKINS	62	2006
GREEN JEANS FLEE-REKKERS	23	1960
THE GREEN LEAVES OF SUMMER KENNY BALL & HIS JAZZMEN	7	1962
GREEN LIGHT [A] CLIFF RICHARD	57	1979
GREEN LIGHT [B] JOHN LEGEND FEATURING ANDRE 3000	35	2008
GREEN LIGHT FREEMASONS EP BEYONCE	12	2007
THE GREEN MAN SHUT UP & DANCE	43	1992
THE GREEN MANALISHI (WITH THE TWO-PRONG CROWN) FLEETWOOD MAC	10	1970
GREEN ONIONS BOOKER T & THE MG's	7	1979
GREEN RIVER CREEDENCE CLEARWATER REVIVAL	19	1969
GREEN SHIRT ELVIS COSTELLO	68	1985
GREEN STREET GREEN NEW VAUDEVILLE BAND	37	1967
GREEN TAMBOURINE LEMON PIPERS	7	1968
GREEN TAMBOURINE SUNDRAGON	50	1968
GREEN TINTED SIXTIES MIND MR BIG	72	1992
GREENBACK DOLLAR CHARLES McDEVITT SKIFFLE GROUP FEATURING NANCY WHISKEY	28	1957
GREENBANK DRIVE CHRISTIANS	63	1990
GREENFIELDS BROTHERS FOUR	40	1960
GREETINGS TO THE NEW BRUNETTE BILLY BRAGG WITH JOHNNY MARR & KIRSTY MacCOLL	58	1986
GREY DAY MADNESS	4	1981
GRIEF NEVER GROWS OLD ONE WORLD PROJECT	4	2005
GRILLZ NELLY FEATURING PAUL WALL, ALI & GIPP	24	2006
GRIMLY FIENDISH DAMNED	21	1985
GRIND ALICE IN CHAINS	23	1995
GRIND WITH ME PRETTY RICKY	26	2005
GRIP LIKE A VICE GO! TEAM	57	2007
GRITTY SHAKER DAVID HOLMES	53	1997
THE GROOVE RODNEY FRANKLIN	7	1980
GROOVE BABY GROOVE (EP) STARGAZERS	56	1982
GROOVE IS IN THE HEART DEEE-LITE	2	1990
THE GROOVE LINE HEATWAVE	12	1978
GROOVE MACHINE MARVIN & TAMARA	11	1999
GROOVE OF LOVE E.V.E.	30	1994
GROOVE THANG ZHANE	34	1994
GROOVE TO MOVE CHANNEL X	67	1991
GROOVEBIRD NATURAL BORN GROOVES	21	1997
GROOVEJET (IF THIS AIN'T LOVE) SPILLER	1	2000
GROOVELINE BLOCKSTER	18	1999
THE GROOVER T REX	4	1973
GROOVIN' [A] YOUNG RASCALS	8	1967
GROOVIN' [A] PATO BANTON & THE REGGAE REVOLUTION	14	1996
GROOVIN' [B] WAR	43	1985
GROOVIN' IN THE MIDNIGHT MAXI PRIEST	50	1992
GROOVIN' (THAT'S WHAT WE'RE DOIN') S.O.S. BAND	72	1983
GROOVIN' WITH MR. BLOE MR BLOE	2	1970
GROOVIN' (YOU'RE THE BEST THING STYLE COUNCIL	5	1984
GROOVY BABY MICROBE	29	1969
GROOVY BEAT D.O.P.	54	1996
GROOVY FEELING FLUKE	45	1993
A GROOVY KIND OF LOVE MINDBENDERS	2	1966
A GROOVY KIND OF LOVE LES GRAY	32	1977
A GROOVY KIND OF LOVE PHIL COLLINS	1	1988
THE GROOVY THANG MINIMAL FUNK 2	65	1998
GROOVY TRAIN FARM	6	1990
GROUND LEVEL STEREO MC'S	19	1993
THE GROUNDBREAKER FALLACY & FUSION	47	2002
GROUNDED MY VITRIOL	29	2001
GROUNDS FOR DIVORCE ELBOW	19	2008
GROUPIE GIRL TONY JOE WHITE	22	1970
GROW KUBB	18	2006
GROWING ON ME DARKNESS	11	2003
GROWN AND SEXY CHAMILLIONAIRE	35	2006
THE GRUDGE MORTIIS	51	2004
G.T.O. SINITTA	15	1987
GUAGLIONE PEREZ 'PREZ' PRADO & HIS ORCHESTRA	2	1994
GUANTANAMERA SANDPIPERS	7	1966
GUANTANAMERA WYCLEF JEAN & THE REFUGEE ALLSTARS	25	1997
GUANTANAMO OUTLANDISH	31	2003
GUARANTEED LEVEL 42	17	1991
GUARDIAN ANGEL NINO DE ANGELO	57	1984
GUARDIANS OF THE LAND GEORGE BOWYER	33	1998
GUDBUY T' JANE SLADE	2	1972
GUDVIBE TINMAN	49	1995
GUERRILLA FUNK PARIS	38	1995
GUERRILLA RADIO RAGE AGAINST THE MACHINE	32	1999
GUESS I WAS A FOOL ANOTHER LEVEL	5	1998
GUESS WHO'S BACK RAKIM	32	1997
GUESS YOU DIDN'T LOVE ME TERRI WALKER	60	2003
GUIDING STAR CAST	9	1997
GUILTY [A] JIM REEVES	29	1963
GUILTY [B] PEARLS	10	1974
GUILTY [C] MIKE OLDFIELD	22	1979
GUILTY [D] BARBRA STREISAND & BARRY GIBB	34	1981
GUILTY [E] CLASSIX NOUVEAUX	43	1981
GUILTY [F] PAUL HARDCASTLE	55	1984
GUILTY [G] YARBOROUGH & PEOPLES	53	1986
GUILTY [H] BLUE	2	2003
GUILTY [I] RASMUS	15	2004
GUILTY [J] DE SOUZA FEATURING SHENA	46	2007
GUILTY CONSCIENCE EMINEM FEATURING DR DRE	5	1999
GUILTY OF LOVE WHITESNAKE	31	1983
GUITAR BOOGIE SHUFFLE BERT WEEDON	10	1959
GUITAR MAN [A] ELVIS PRESLEY	19	1968
THE GUITAR MAN [B] BREAD	16	1972
GUITAR TANGO SHADOWS	4	1962
GUITARRA G BANDA SONORA	50	2001
GUN LAW KANE GANG	53	1985
GUNMAN 187 LOCKDOWN	16	1997
GUNS AT DAWN DJ BARON FEATURING PENDULUM	71	2005
GUNS DON'T KILL PEOPLE RAPPERS DO GOLDIE LOOKIN CHAIN	3	2004
GUNS FOR HIRE AC/DC	37	1983
GUNS OF NAVARONE SKATALITES	36	1967
GUNSLINGER FRANKIE LAINE	50	1961
GUNZ AND PIANOZ BASS BOYZ	74	1996
GURNEY SLADE MAX HARRIS	11	1960
THE GUSH RAGING SPEEDHORN	47	2001
GYM AND TONIC SPACEDUST	1	1998
GYPSY FLEETWOOD MAC	46	1982
GYPSY BEAT PACKABEATS	49	1961
GYPSY BOY, GYPSY GIRL SHARADA HOUSE GANG	52	1997
GYPSY EYES JIMI HENDRIX EXPERIENCE	35	1971
GYPSY ROAD CINDERELLA	54	1988
GYPSY ROAD HOG SLADE	48	1977
GYPSY ROVER HIGHWAYMEN	41	1961
GYPSY WOMAN BRIAN HYLAND	42	1971
GYPSY WOMAN (LA DA DEE) CRYSTAL WATERS	2	1991
GYPSYS TRAMPS AND THIEVES CHER	4	1971

H

Title / Artist	Peak Position	Year of Release
HA CHA CHA (FUNKTION) BRASS CONSTRUCTION	37	1977
HA HA SAID THE CLOWN MANFRED MANN	4	1967
HAD ENOUGH ENEMY	4	2007
HAD TO BE CLIFF RICHARD & OLIVIA NEWTON-JOHN	22	1995
HAIL CAESAR AC/DC	56	1996
HAIL HAIL ROCK 'N' ROLL GARLAND JEFFREYS	72	1992
HAIL MARY MAKAVELI	43	1998
HAITIAN DIVORCE STEELY DAN	17	1976
HALE BOPP DER DRITTE RAUM	75	1999
HALEY'S GOLDEN MEDLEY BILL HALEY & HIS COMETS	50	1981
HALF A BOY HALF A MAN NICK LOWE	53	1984
HALF A HEART H & CLAIRE	8	2002
HALF A MINUTE MATT BIANCO	23	1984
HALF AS MUCH ROSEMARY CLOONEY	3	1952
HALF LIGHT ATHLETE	16	2005
HALF MAN HALF MACHINE GOLDIE LOOKIN CHAIN	32	2004
HALF OF MY HEART EMILE FORD	42	1961
HALF ON A BABY R KELLY	16	1998

Title / Artist	Peak Position	Year of Release
HALF THE DAY'S GONE AND WE HAVEN'T EARNT A PENNY KENNY LYNCH	50	1983
HALF THE MAN JAMIROQUAI	15	1994
HALF THE WORLD BELINDA CARLISLE	35	1992
HALFWAY AROUND THE WORLD A*TEENS	30	2001
HALFWAY DOWN THE STAIRS MUPPETS	7	1977
HALFWAY HOTEL VOYAGER	33	1979
HALFWAY TO HEAVEN EUROPE	42	1992
HALFWAY TO PARADISE BILLY FURY	3	1961
HALFWAY UP HALFWAY DOWN DENNIS BROWN	56	1982
HALLELUIAH MAN LOVE & MONEY	63	1988
HALLELUJAH [A] MILK & HONEY FEATURING GALI ATARI	5	1979
HALLELUJAH [B] JEFF BUCKLEY	2	2007
HALLELUJAH [B] KATE VOEGELE	53	2008
HALLELUJAH [B] ALEXANDRA BURKE	1	2008
HALLELUJAH [B] LEONARD COHEN	36	2008
HALLELUJAH '92 INNER CITY	22	1992
HALLELUJAH DAY JACKSON 5	20	1973
HALLELUJAH FREEDOM JUNIOR CAMPBELL	10	1972
HALLELUJAH I LOVE HER SO EDDIE COCHRAN	22	1960
HALLELUJAH I LOVE HER SO DICK JORDAN	47	1960
HALLO SPACEBOY DAVID BOWIE	12	1996
HALLOWED BE THY NAME (LIVE) IRON MAIDEN	9	1993
HALLS OF ILLUSION INSANE CLOWN POSSE	56	1998
HALO [A] TEXAS	10	1997
HALO [B] SOIL	74	2002
HALO [C] BEYONCE	4	2009
HALO [C] GLEE CAST	9	2010
(HAMMER HAMMER) THEY PUT ME IN THE MIX MC HAMMER	20	1991
HAMMER HORROR KATE BUSH	44	1978
HAMMER TO FALL QUEEN	13	1984
HAMMER TO THE HEART TAMPERER FEATURING MAYA	6	2000
HAND A HANDKERCHIEF TO HELEN SUSAN MAUGHAN	41	1963
HAND HELD IN BLACK AND WHITE DOLLAR	19	1981
HAND IN GLOVE SANDIE SHAW	27	1984
HAND IN HAND GRACE	38	1997
HAND IN MY POCKET ALANIS MORISSETTE	26	1995
HAND IN YOUR HEAD MONEY MARK	40	1998
HAND OF THE DEAD BODY SCARFACE FEATURING ICE CUBE	41	1995
HAND ON MY HEART SHRIEKBACK	52	1984
HAND ON YOUR HEART KYLIE MINOGUE	1	1989
HAND ON YOUR HEART JOSE GONZALEZ	29	2006
THE HAND THAT FEEDS NINE INCH NAILS	7	2005
HANDBAGS AND GLADRAGS CHRIS FARLOWE	33	1967
HANDBAGS AND GLADRAGS STEREOPHONICS	4	2001
HANDFUL OF PROMISES BIG FUN	21	1990
HANDFUL OF SONGS TOMMY STEELE & THE STEELMEN	5	1957
HANDLE ME ROBYN	17	2007
HANDLE WITH CARE TRAVELING WILBURYS	21	1988
HANDLEBARS FLOBOTS	14	2008
HANDS [A] JEWEL	35	1998
HANDS [B] RACONTEURS	29	2006
HANDS ACROSS THE OCEAN MISSION	28	1990
HANDS AROUND MY THROAT DEATH IN VEGAS	36	2002
HANDS CLEAN ALANIS MORISSETTE	12	2002
HANDS DOWN DASHBOARD CONFESSIONAL	60	2003
HANDS OFF – SHE'S MINE BEAT	9	1980
HANDS TO HEAVEN BREATHE	4	1988
HANDS UP [A] CLUBZONE	50	1994
HANDS UP [B] TREVOR & SIMON	12	2000
HANDS UP [C] LLOYD BANK$ FEATURING 50 CENT	43	2006
HANDS UP [D] OUT OF OFFICE	52	2007
HANDS UP (4 LOVERS) RIGHT SAID FRED	60	1993
HANDS UP (GIVE ME YOUR HEART) OTTAWAN	3	1981
HANDS UP! HANDS UP! ZIG & ZAG	21	1995
HANDY MAN JIMMY JONES	3	1960
HANDY MAN DEL SHANNON	36	1964
HANG 'EM HIGH HUGO MONTENEGRO	50	1969
HANG IN LONG ENOUGH PHIL COLLINS	34	1990
HANG ME UP TO DRY COLD WAR KIDS	57	2007
HANG MYSELF ON YOU CANDYSKINS	65	1997
HANG ON IN THERE BABY JOHNNY BRISTOL	3	1974
HANG ON IN THERE BABY CURIOSITY	3	1992
HANG ON NOW KAJAGOOGOO	13	1983
HANG ON SLOOPY McCOYS	5	1965
HANG ON SLOOPY SANDPIPERS	32	1976
HANG ON TO A DREAM TIM HARDIN	50	1967
HANG ON TO YOUR LOVE JASON DONOVAN	8	1990
HANG TOGETHER ODYSSEY	36	1981
HANG UP ANDY ABRAHAM	63	2006
HANG YOUR HEAD DEACON BLUE	21	1993
HANGAR 18 MEGADETH	26	1991
HANGIN' CHIC	64	1983
HANGIN' AROUND BIG BROVAZ	57	2006
HANGIN' ON A STRING (CONTEMPLATING) LOOSE ENDS	13	1985
HANGIN' OUT KOOL & THE GANG	52	1980
HANGIN' TOUGH NEW KIDS ON THE BLOCK	1	1989
HANGING AROUND [A] HAZEL O'CONNOR	45	1981
HANGING AROUND [B] ME ME ME	19	1996
HANGING AROUND [C] CARDIGANS	17	1999
HANGING AROUND [D] GEMMA HAYES	62	2002
HANGING AROUND [E] POLYPHONIC SPREE	39	2002
HANGING AROUND WITH THE BIG BOYS BLOOMSBURY SET	56	1983
HANGING BY A MOMENT LIFEHOUSE	25	2001
HANGING GARDEN CURE	34	1982
HANGING ON THE TELEPHONE BLONDIE	5	1978
HANGINAROUND COUNTING CROWS	46	1999
HANGOVER BETTY BOO	50	1993
HANKY PANKY [A] TOMMY JAMES & THE SHONDELLS	38	1966
HANKY PANKY [B] MADONNA	2	1990
HANNA HANNA CHINA CRISIS	44	1984
HANNAH WE KNOW TINY DANCERS	33	2007
HAPPENIN' ALL OVER AGAIN LONNIE GORDON	4	1990
HAPPENIN' ALL OVER AGAIN TRACY SHAW	46	1998
THE HAPPENING SUPREMES	6	1967
HAPPENINGS TEN YEARS TIME AGO YARDBIRDS	43	1966
HAPPINESS [A] KEN DODD	31	1964
HAPPINESS [B] SERIOUS ROPE PRESENTS SHARON DEE CLARK	54	1993
HAPPINESS [C] ROGER TAYLOR	32	1994
HAPPINESS [D] PIZZAMAN	19	1995
HAPPINESS [E] KAMASUTRA FEATURING JOCELYN BROWN	45	1997
HAPPINESS [F] SOUND DE-ZIGN	19	2001
HAPPINESS [G] ORSON	27	2006
HAPPINESS [H] GOLDFRAPP	25	2008
HAPPINESS HAPPENING LOST WITNESS	18	1999
HAPPINESS IS JUST AROUND THE BEND CUBA GOODING	72	1983
HAPPINESS IS ME AND YOU GILBERT O'SULLIVAN	19	1974
HAPPINESS (MY VISION IS CLEAR) BINI & MARTINI	53	2000
HAPPY [A] SURFACE	56	1987
HAPPY [A] MN8	8	1995
HAPPY [A] PAULINE HENRY	46	1996
HAPPY [B] NED'S ATOMIC DUSTBIN	16	1991
HAPPY [C] TRAVIS	38	1997
HAPPY [D] LIGHTHOUSE FAMILY	51	2002
HAPPY [E] ASHANTI	13	2002
HAPPY [F] MAX SEDGLEY	30	2004
HAPPY [G] LEONA LEWIS	2	2009
HAPPY ANNIVERSARY [A] JOAN REGAN	29	1960
HAPPY ANNIVERSARY [B] SLIM WHITMAN	14	1974
HAPPY AS ANNIE LARRIKIN LOVE	32	2006
HAPPY BIRTHDAY [A] STEVIE WONDER	2	1981
HAPPY BIRTHDAY [B] ALTERED IMAGES	2	1981
HAPPY BIRTHDAY [C] TECHNOHEAD	18	1996
HAPPY BIRTHDAY REVOLUTION LEVELLERS	57	2000
HAPPY BIRTHDAY SWEET SIXTEEN NEIL SEDAKA	3	1961
HAPPY BIZZNESS ROACH MOTEL	75	1994
HAPPY BUSMAN FRANK & WALTERS	49	1992
HAPPY DAY BLINK	57	1994
HAPPY DAYS [A] PRATT & McCLAIN WITH BROTHERLOVE	31	1977
HAPPY DAYS [B] SWEET MERCY FEATURING JOE ROBERTS	63	1996
HAPPY DAYS [C] PJ	57	1997
HAPPY DAYS AND LONELY NIGHTS RUBY MURRAY	6	1955
HAPPY DAYS AND LONELY NIGHTS FRANKIE VAUGHAN	12	1955
HAPPY DAYS AND LONELY NIGHTS SUZI MILLER & THE JOHNSTON BROTHERS	14	1955
HAPPY ENDING [A] JOE JACKSON	58	1984
HAPPY ENDING [B] MIKA	7	2007
HAPPY ENDINGS (GIVE YOURSELF A PINCH) LIONEL BART	68	1989
HAPPY EVER AFTER JULIA FORDHAM	27	1988
HAPPY FEELING HAMILTON BOHANNON	49	1975
HAPPY GO LUCKY ME GEORGE FORMBY	40	1960
HAPPY GUITAR TOMMY STEELE	20	1958
HAPPY HEART ANDY WILLIAMS	19	1969
HAPPY HOME 2PAC	17	1998
HAPPY HOUR HOUSEMARTINS	3	1986
HAPPY HOUSE SIOUXSIE & THE BANSHEES	17	1980
HAPPY JACK WHO	3	1966
HAPPY JUST TO BE WITH YOU MICHELLE GAYLE	11	1995
HAPPY (LOVE THEME FROM 'LADY SINGS THE BLUES') MICHAEL JACKSON	52	1983
THE HAPPY MAN THOMAS LANG	67	1988
HAPPY NATION ACE OF BASE	40	1993
HAPPY PEOPLE [A] STATIC REVENGER	23	2001
HAPPY PEOPLE [B] R KELLY	6	2004
H.A.P.P.Y. RADIO EDWIN STARR	9	1979
H-A-P-P-Y RADIO MICHAELA	62	1989
HAPPY SHOPPER 60FT DOLLS	38	1996
THE HAPPY SONG OTIS REDDING	24	1968
HAPPY TALK CAPTAIN SENSIBLE	1	1982
HAPPY TO BE ON AN ISLAND IN THE SUN DEMIS ROUSSOS	5	1975
HAPPY TO MAKE YOUR ACQUAINTANCE SAMMY DAVIS, JR & CARMEN McRAE	46	1960
HAPPY TOGETHER TURTLES	12	1967
HAPPY TOGETHER JASON DONOVAN	10	1991
HAPPY UP HERE ROYKSOPP	44	2009
HAPPY WANDERER OBERKIRCHEN CHILDREN'S CHOIR	2	1954
HAPPY WANDERER STARGAZERS	12	1954
HAPPY WHEN IT RAINS JESUS & MARY CHAIN	25	1987
THE HAPPY WHISTLER DON ROBERTSON	8	1956
THE HAPPY WHISTLER CYRIL STAPLETON ORCHESTRA FEATURING DESMOND LANE, PENNY WHISTLE	22	1956

Title / Artist	Peak Position	Year of Release
HAPPY XMAS (WAR IS OVER) JOHN & YOKO & THE PLASTIC ONO BAND WITH THE HARLEM COMMUNITY CHOIR	2	1972
HAPPY XMAS (WAR IS OVER) IDOLS	5	2003
HARBOUR LIGHTS PLATTERS	11	1960
HARD RIHANNA FEATURING YOUNG JEEZY	42	2010
HARD AS A ROCK AC/DC	33	1995
HARD BEAT EP 19 VARIOUS ARTISTS (EP'S & LP'S)	71	2001
A HARD DAY'S NIGHT BEATLES	1	1964
A HARD DAY'S NIGHT PETER SELLERS	14	1965
HARD HABIT TO BREAK CHICAGO	8	1984
HARD HEADED WOMAN ELVIS PRESLEY	2	1958
HARD HEARTED HANNAH TEMPERANCE SEVEN	28	1961
HARD HOUSE MUSIC MELT FEATURING LITTLE MS MARCIE	59	2000
HARD KNOCK LIFE (GHETTO ANTHEM) JAY-Z	2	1998
A HARD RAIN'S GONNA FALL BRYAN FERRY	10	1973
HARD ROAD BLACK SABBATH	33	1978
HARD ROCK HALLELUJAH LORDI	25	2006
THE HARD TIMES RESEARCH	73	2006
HARD TIMES COME EASY RICHIE SAMBORA	37	1998
HARD TO BEAT HARD-FI	9	2005
HARD TO EXPLAIN STROKES	16	2001
HARD TO HANDLE OTIS REDDING	15	1968
HARD TO HANDLE BLACK CROWES	39	1990
HARD TO MAKE A STAND SHERYL CROW	22	1997
HARD TO SAY I'M SORRY CHICAGO	4	1982
HARD TO SAY I'M SORRY AZ YET FEATURING PETER CETERA	7	1997
HARD TO SAY I'M SORRY AQUAGEN	33	2003
HARD UP AWESOME 3	55	1990
THE HARD WAY NASHVILLE TEENS	45	1966
THE HARDCORE EP HYPNOTIST	68	1991
HARDCORE HEAVEN DJ SEDUCTION	26	1992
HARDCORE HIP HOUSE TYREE	70	1989
HARDCORE – THE FINAL CONFLICT HARDCORE RHYTHM TEAM	69	1992
HARDCORE UPROAR TOGETHER	12	1990
HARDCORE WILL NEVER DIE Q-BASS	64	1992
HARDEN MY HEART QUATERFLASH	49	1982
HARDER KOSHEEN	53	2002
HARDER BETTER FASTER STRONGER DAFT PUNK	25	2001
THE HARDER I TRY BROTHER BEYOND	2	1988
THE HARDER THEY COME [A] ROCKER'S REVENGE	30	1983
THE HARDER THEY COME [A] MADNESS	44	1992
THE HARDER THEY COME [B] PAUL OAKENFOLD	38	2003
HARDER TO BREATHE MAROON 5	13	2004
THE HARDEST BUTTON TO BUTTON WHITE STRIPES	23	2003
HARDEST PART IS THE NIGHT BON JOVI	68	1985
THE HARDEST THING 980	29	2000
HARDROCK HERBIE HANCOCK	65	1984
HARDTRANCE ACPERIENCE HARDFLOOR	56	1992
HARE KRISHNA MANTRA RADHA KRISHNA TEMPLE	12	1969
HARLEM DESIRE LONDON BOYS	17	1989
HARLEM SHUFFLE BOB & EARL	7	1969
HARLEM SHUFFLE ROLLING STONES	13	1986
HARLEQUIN – THE BEAUTY AND THE BEAST SVEN VATH	72	1994
HARMONIC GENERATOR DATSUNS	33	2003
HARMONICA MAN BRAVADO	37	1994
HARMONY TC 1993	51	1993
HARMONY IN MY HEAD BUZZCOCKS	32	1979
HARMOUR LOVE SYREETA	32	1975
HARPER VALLEY P.T.A. JEANNIE C RILEY	12	1968
HARROWDOWN HILL THOM YORKE	23	2006
HARVEST FOR THE WORLD ISLEY BROTHERS	10	1976
HARVEST FOR THE WORLD CHRISTIANS	8	1988
HARVEST FOR THE WORLD TERRY HUNTER	48	1997
HARVEST MOON NEIL YOUNG	36	1993
HARVEST OF LOVE BENNY HILL	20	1963
HARVESTER OF SORROW METALLICA	20	1988
HARVEY NICKS MITCHELL BROTHERS FEATURING SWAY	62	2005
HAS IT COME TO THIS STREETS	18	2001
HASH PIPE WEEZER	21	2001
HASTA LA VISTA SYLVIA	38	1975
HATE (I REALLY DON'T LIKE YOU) PLAIN WHITE T'S	53	2008
HATE IT OR LOVE IT GAME FEATURING 50 CENT	4	2005
HATE ME NOW NAS FEATURING PUFF DADDY	14	1999
THE HATE SONG RAGING SPEEDHORN	69	2002
HATE THAT I LOVE YOU RIHANNA FEATURING NE-YO	15	2007
HATE TO SAY I TOLD YOU SO HIVES	23	2002
HATERS SO SOLID CREW PRESENTS MR SHABZ	8	2002
HATS OFF TO LARRY DEL SHANNON	6	1961
HAUNTED POGUES	42	1986
HAUNTED SHANE MacGOWAN & SINEAD O'CONNOR	30	1995
HAUNTED BY YOU GENE	32	1995
HAVA NAGILA SPOTNICKS	13	1963
HAVE A CHEEKY CHRISTMAS CHEEKY GIRLS	10	2003
HAVE A DRINK ON ME LONNIE DONEGAN	8	1961
HAVE A GOOD FOREVER COOLNOTES	73	1985
HAVE A LITTLE FAITH JOE COCKER	67	1995
HAVE A NICE DAY [A] ROXANNE SHANTE	58	1987
HAVE A NICE DAY [B] STEREOPHONICS	5	2001
HAVE A NICE DAY [C] BON JOVI	6	2005
HAVE FUN, GO MAD! BLAIR	37	1995
HAVE FUN GO MAD TWEENIES	20	2002
HAVE I BEEN A FOOL JACK PENATE	73	2007
HAVE I STAYED TOO LONG SONNY & CHER	42	1966
HAVE I THE RIGHT HONEYCOMBS	1	1964
HAVE I THE RIGHT DEAD END KIDS	6	1977
HAVE I TOLD YOU LATELY VAN MORRISON	74	1989
HAVE I TOLD YOU LATELY ROD STEWART	5	1993
HAVE I TOLD YOU LATELY THAT I LOVE YOU CHIEFTAINS WITH VAN MORRISON	71	1995
HAVE IT ALL FOO FIGHTERS	37	2003
HAVE LOST IT (EP) TEENAGE FANCLUB	53	1995
HAVE LOVE WILL TRAVEL (EP) CRAZYHEAD	68	1989
HAVE MERCY YAZZ	42	1994
HAVE PITY ON THE BOY PAUL & BARRY RYAN	18	1966
HAVE YOU EVER? [A] BRANDY	13	1998
HAVE YOU EVER [B] S CLUB 7	1	2001
HAVE YOU EVER BEEN IN LOVE LEO SAYER	10	1982
HAVE YOU EVER BEEN MELLOW (EP) PARTY ANIMALS	43	1996
HAVE YOU EVER HAD IT BLUE STYLE COUNCIL	14	1986
HAVE YOU EVER LOVED SOMEBODY [A] PAUL & BARRY RYAN	49	1966
HAVE YOU EVER LOVED SOMEBODY [B] SEARCHERS	48	1966
HAVE YOU EVER LOVED SOMEBODY [C] FREDDIE JACKSON	33	1987
HAVE YOU EVER NEEDED SOMEONE SO BAD DEF LEPPARD	16	1992
HAVE YOU EVER REALLY LOVED A WOMAN? BRYAN ADAMS	4	1995
HAVE YOU EVER SEEN THE RAIN CREEDENCE CLEARWATER REVIVAL	36	1971
HAVE YOU EVER SEEN THE RAIN BONNIE TYLER	47	1983
HAVE YOU EVER SEEN THE RAIN? JEEVAS	70	2004
HAVE YOU MADE UP YOUR MIND PAUL WELLER	47	2008
HAVE YOU SEEN HER CHI-LITES	3	1972
HAVE YOU SEEN HER MC HAMMER	8	1990
HAVE YOU SEEN YOUR MOTHER BABY STANDING IN THE SHADOW ROLLING STONES	5	1966
HAVEN'T MET YOU YET MICHAEL BUBLE	5	2009
HAVEN'T SEEN YOU PERFUME	71	1996
HAVEN'T STOPPED DANCING YET GONZALEZ	15	1979
HAVEN'T YOU HEARD PATRICE RUSHEN	62	1980
HAVIN' A GOOD TIME SOUVERNANCE	63	2002
HAVING A PARTY OSMONDS	28	1975
HAWAII TATTOO WAIKIKIS	41	1965
HAWAIIAN WEDDING SONG JULIE ROGERS	31	1965
HAWKEYE FRANKIE LAINE	7	1955
HAYFEVER TRASH CAN SINATRAS	61	1993
HAYLING FC KAHUNA	49	2003
HAZARD RICHARD MARX	3	1992
HAZEL LOOP DA LOOP	20	1999
HAZELL MAGGIE BELL	37	1978
HAZIN' & PHAZIN' CHOO CHOO PROJECT	21	2000
HAZY EYES FIGHTSTAR	47	2006
HAZY SHADE OF WINTER BANGLES	11	1988
A HAZY SHADE OF WINTER SIMON & GARFUNKEL	30	1991
HE AIN'T HEAVY, HE'S MY BROTHER HOLLIES	1	1969
HE AIN'T HEAVY, HE'S MY BROTHER BILL MEDLEY	25	1988
HE AIN'T NO COMPETITION BROTHER BEYOND	6	1988
HE DOESN'T LOVE YOU LIKE I DO NICK HEYWARD	58	1993
HE DON'T LOVE YOU HUMAN NATURE	18	2001
HE GOT GAME PUBLIC ENEMY FEATURING STEPHEN STILLS	16	1998
HE GOT WHAT HE WANTED (BUT HE LOST WHAT HE HAD) LITTLE RICHARD	38	1962
HE IS SAILING JON & VANGELIS	61	1983
HE KNOWS YOU KNOW MARILLION	35	1983
HE LOVES U NOT DREAM	17	2001
HE REMINDS ME RANDY CRAWFORD	65	1983
HE SAID HE LOVED ME REVEREND & THE MAKERS	16	2007
HE THINKS HE'LL KEEP HER MARY CHAPIN CARPENTER	71	1993
HE WAS BEAUTIFUL (CAVATINA) (THE THEME FROM 'THE DEER HUNTER') IRIS WILLIAMS	18	1979
HE WASN'T AVRIL LAVIGNE	23	2005
HE WASN'T MAN ENOUGH TONI BRAXTON	5	2000
HEAD JULIAN COPE	57	1991
HEAD ABOVE WATER CLIVE GRIFFIN	60	1989
HEAD LIKE A HOLE NINE INCH NAILS	45	1991
HEAD ON JESUS & MARY CHAIN	57	1989
HEAD ON COLLISION NEW FOUND GLORY	64	2002
HEAD OVER FEET ALANIS MORISSETTE	7	1996
HEAD OVER HEELS [A] ABBA	25	1982
HEAD OVER HEELS [B] TEARS FOR FEARS	12	1985
HEAD OVER HEELS [C] NICK HAVERSON	48	1993
HEAD OVER HEELS [D] ALLURE FEATURING NAS	18	1997
HEAD OVER HEELS IN LOVE KEVIN KEEGAN	31	1979
HEAD TO TOE (EP) BREEDERS	68	1994
HEADACHE FRANK BLACK	53	1994
HEADING FOR A BREAKDOWN SOUNDTRACK OF OUR LIVES	70	2005
HEADING WEST CYNDI LAUPER	68	1989
HEADLESS CROSS BLACK SABBATH	62	1989
HEADLIGHTS ON PARADE BLUE NILE	72	1990
HEADLINE NEWS EDWIN STARR	39	1966
HEADLINE NEWS WILLIAM BELL	70	1986
HEADLINES MIDNIGHT STAR	16	1986
HEADLINES (FRIENDSHIP NEVER ENDS) SPICE GIRLS	11	2007

Title / Artist	Peak Position	Year of Release
HEADLOCK IMOGEN HEAP	74	2006
HEADLONG QUEEN	14	1991
HEADS DOWN NO NONSENSE MINDLESS BOOGIE ALBERTO Y LOST TRIOS PARANOIAS	47	1978
HEADS HIGH MR VEGAS	16	1998
HEADS SHOULDERS KNEEZ AND TOEZ KIG	18	2009
HEADSPRUNG LL COOL J	25	2004
HEADZ UP GEORGE SAMPSON	30	2008
HEAL THE PAIN GEORGE MICHAEL	31	1991
HEAL (THE SEPARATION) SHAMEN	31	1996
HEAL THE WORLD MICHAEL JACKSON	2	1992
THE HEALING GAME VAN MORRISON	46	1997
HEALING HANDS ELTON JOHN	45	1989
HEALING LOVE CLIFF RICHARD	19	1993
HEAR ME CALLING 2WO THIRD3	48	1994
HEAR MY CALL ALISON LIMERICK	73	1992
HEAR MY NAME ARMAND VAN HELDEN	34	2004
HEAR THE DRUMMER (GET WICKED) CHAD JACKSON	3	1990
HEAR YOU CALLING AURORA	17	1999
HEARD 'EM SAY KANYE WEST FEATURING ADAM LEVINE	22	2005
HEARD IT ALL BEFORE SUNSHINE ANDERSON	9	2001
HEARSAY '89 ALEXANDER O'NEAL	56	1989
HEART [A] MAX BYGRAVES	14	1957
HEART [A] JOHNSTON BROTHERS	23	1957
HEART [B] RITA PAVONE	27	1967
HEART [C] PET SHOP BOYS	1	1988
HEART [D] GARY NUMAN	43	1991
HEART [E] SERAPHIM SUITE	45	2004
HEART AND SOUL [A] JAN & DEAN	24	1961
HEART AND SOUL [B] EXILE	54	1981
HEART AND SOUL [C] T'PAU	4	1987
HEART AND SOUL [D] NO SWEAT	64	1990
HEART AND SOUL [E] CILLA BLACK WITH DUSTY SPRINGFIELD	75	1993
HEART AND SOUL [F] TSD	69	1996
HEART AND SOUL (EP) HUEY LEWIS & THE NEWS	61	1985
THE HEART ASKS PLEASURE FIRST MICHAEL NYMAN	60	1994
HEART ATTACK OLIVIA NEWTON-JOHN	46	1982
HEART ATTACK AND VINE SREAMIN' JAY HAWKINS	42	1993
HEART (DON'T CHANGE MY MIND) DIANA ROSS	31	1993
HEART FAILED (IN THE BACK OF A TAXI) SAINT ETIENNE	50	2000
HEART FULL OF SOUL YARDBIRDS	2	1965
HEART GO BOOM APOLLO FOUR FORTY	57	1999
HEART IN A CAGE STROKES	25	2006
HEART LIKE A WHEEL [A] HUMAN LEAGUE	29	1990
HEART LIKE A WHEEL [B] CORRS	68	2005
THE HEART NEVER LIES McFLY	3	2007
THE HEART OF A MAN FRANKIE VAUGHAN	5	1959
HEART OF A SINGLE GIRL GEORGE CHAKIRIS	49	1960
THE HEART OF A TEENAGE GIRL CRAIG DOUGLAS	10	1960
HEART OF ASIA WATERGATE	3	2000
HEART OF GLASS BLONDIE	1	1979
HEART OF GLASS ASSOCIATES	56	1988
HEART OF GOLD [A] NEIL YOUNG	10	1972
HEART OF GOLD [B] JOHNNY HATES JAZZ	19	1988
HEART OF GOLD [C] FORCE & STYLES FEATURING KELLY LLORENNA	55	1998
HEART OF GOLD [C] KELLY LLORENNA	19	2002
HEART OF LOTHIAN MARILLION	29	1985
THE HEART OF ROCK AND ROLL HUEY LEWIS & THE NEWS	49	1986
HEART OF SOUL CULT	51	1992
HEART OF STONE [A] KENNY	11	1973
HEART OF STONE [B] SUZI QUATRO	60	1982
HEART OF STONE [C] BUCKS FIZZ	50	1988
HEART OF STONE [C] CHER	43	1990
HEART OF STONE [D] DAVE STEWART	36	1994
HEART OF THE SUN RED BOX	71	1987
HEART OF THE WORLD BIG COUNTRY	50	1990
HEART ON MY SLEEVE GALLAGHER & LYLE	6	1976
HEART OVER MIND KIM WILDE	34	1992
HEART (STOP BEATING IN TIME) LEO SAYER	22	1982
HEART USER CLIFF RICHARD	46	1985
HEARTACHE [A] ROY ORBISON	44	1968
HEARTACHE [B] GENE LOVES JEZEBEL	71	1986
HEARTACHE [C] PEPSI & SHIRLIE	2	1987
HEARTACHE ALL OVER THE WORLD ELTON JOHN	45	1986
HEARTACHE AVENUE MAISONETTES	7	1982
HEARTACHE TONIGHT EAGLES	40	1979
HEARTACHES PATSY CLINE	31	1962
HEARTACHES VINCE HILL	28	1966
HEARTACHES BY THE NUMBER GUY MITCHELL	5	1959
HEARTBEAT [A] RUBY MURRAY	3	1954
HEARTBEAT [B] BUDDY HOLLY	30	1959
HEARTBEAT [B] ENGLAND SISTERS	33	1960
HEARTBEAT [B] SHOWADDYWADDY	7	1975
HEARTBEAT [B] NICK BERRY	2	1992
HEARTBEAT [B] HEARTBEAT COUNTRY	75	1994
HEARTBEAT [C] SAMMY HAGAR	67	1980
HEARTBEAT [D] TIPPA IRIE	59	1986
HEARTBEAT [E] DON JOHNSON	46	1986
HEARTBEAT [F] SEDUCTION	75	1990
HEARTBEAT [G] GRID	72	1992
HEARTBEAT [H] JIMMY SOMERVILLE	24	1995
HEARTBEAT [I] KRS ONE	66	1997
HEARTBEAT [J] STEPS	1	1998
HEARTBEAT [K] ANNIE	50	2005
HEARTBEAT [L] SCOUTING FOR GIRLS	10	2008
HEARTBEAT [M] NNEKA	20	2009
A HEARTBEAT AWAY McGANNS	42	1999
HEARTBEAT (TAINAI KAIKI II) RETURNING TO THE WOMB DAVID SYLVIAN/RYUICHI SAKAMOTO FEATURING INGRID CHAVEZ	58	1992
HEARTBEATS JOSE GONZALEZ	9	2006
HEARTBEATZ STYLES & BREEZE FEATURING KAREN DANZIG	16	2005
HEARTBREAK MRS WOOD FEATURING EVE GALLAGHER	44	1996
HEARTBREAK HOTEL [A] ELVIS PRESLEY	2	1956
HEARTBREAK HOTEL [A] STAN FREBERG & HIS SKIFFLE GROUP	24	1956
HEARTBREAK HOTEL [B] JACKSONS	44	1980
HEARTBREAK HOTEL [C] WHITNEY HOUSTON FEATURING FAITH EVANS & KELLY PRICE	26	2000
HEARTBREAK (MAKE ME A DANCER) FREEMASONS FEATURING SOPHIE ELLIS-BEXTOR	13	2009
HEARTBREAK RADIO ROY ORBISON	36	1992
HEARTBREAK STATION CINDERELLA	63	1991
HEARTBREAK STROLL RAVEONETTES	49	2003
HEARTBREAKER [A] DIONNE WARWICK	2	1982
HEARTBREAKER [B] MUSICAL YOUTH	44	1983
HEARTBREAKER [C] COLOR ME BADD	58	1992
HEARTBREAKER [D] MARIAH CAREY FEATURING JAY-Z	5	1999
HEARTBREAKER [E] GLITTERATI	45	2005
HEARTBREAKER [F] WILL.I.AM FEATURING CHERYL COLE	4	2008
HEARTBREAKER [G] MSTKRFT	50	2009
HEARTBROKE AND BUSTED MAGNUM	49	1990
HEARTBROKEN T2 FEATURING JODIE	2	2007
HEARTHAMMER (EP) RUNRIG	25	1991
HEARTLAND THE THE	29	1986
HEARTLESS KANYE WEST	10	2008
THE HEARTLESS CREW THEME HEARTLESS CREW	21	2002
HEARTLIGHT NEIL DIAMOND	47	1982
HEARTLINE ROBIN GEORGE	68	1985
HEARTS BURST INTO FIRE BULLET FOR MY VALENTINE	66	2008
THE HEART'S FILTHY LESSON DAVID BOWIE	35	1995
THE HEART'S LONE DESIRE MATTHEW MARSDEN	13	1998
HEARTS ON FIRE [A] SAM HARRIS	67	1985
HEARTS ON FIRE [B] BRYAN ADAMS	57	1987
HEART-SHAPED BOX NIRVANA	5	1993
HEART-SHAPED GLASSES MARILYN MANSON	19	2007
HEARTSONG GORDON GILTRAP	21	1978
HEARTSPARK DOLLARSIGN EVERCLEAR	48	1996
THE HEAT IS ON [A] AGNETHA FALTSKOG	35	1983
THE HEAT IS ON [B] GLENN FREY	12	1985
HEAT IT UP WEE PAPA GIRL RAPPERS FEATURING TWO MEN & A DRUM MACHINE	21	1988
HEAT OF THE BEAT ROY AYERS & WAYNE HENDERSON	43	1979
HEAT OF THE MOMENT ASIA	46	1982
HEAT OF THE NIGHT BRYAN ADAMS	50	1987
HEATER SAMIM	12	2007
HEATHER HONEY TOMMY ROE	24	1969
HEATSEEKER AC/DC	12	1988
HEAVEN [A] PSYCHEDELIC FURS	29	1984
HEAVEN [B] BRYAN ADAMS	38	1985
HEAVEN [B] DJ SAMMY & YANOU FEATURING DO	1	2002
HEAVEN [C] TWO PEOPLE	63	1987
HEAVEN [D] CHIMES	24	1989
HEAVEN [E] CHRIS REA	57	1991
HEAVEN [F] TIGERTAILZ	71	1991
HEAVEN [G] WHYCLIFFE	56	1993
HEAVEN [H] FITS OF GLOOM	47	1994
HEAVEN [I] SOLO (US)	35	1996
HEAVEN [J] SARAH WASHINGTON	28	1996
HEAVEN [K] KINANE	49	1998
HEAVEN & EARTH [A] RED	41	2001
HEAVEN AND EARTH [B] POP!	14	2004
HEAVEN AND HELL, THIRD MOVEMENT (THEME FROM THE BBC-TV SERIES 'THE COSMOS) VANGELIS	48	1981
HEAVEN BESIDE YOU ALICE IN CHAINS	35	1996
HEAVEN CAN WAIT PAUL YOUNG	71	1990
HEAVEN FOR EVERYONE QUEEN	2	1995
HEAVEN GIVE ME WORDS PROPAGANDA	36	1990
HEAVEN HELP LENNY KRAVITZ	20	1993
HEAVEN HELP ME DEON ESTUS	41	1989
HEAVEN HELP MY HEART TINA ARENA	25	1995
HEAVEN HELP US ALL STEVIE WONDER	29	1970
THE HEAVEN I NEED THREE DEGREES	42	1985
HEAVEN IN MY HANDS LEVEL 42	12	1988
HEAVEN IS DEF LEPPARD	13	1993
HEAVEN IS A HALFPIPE OPM	4	2001
HEAVEN IS A PLACE ON EARTH BELINDA CARLISLE	1	1987
HEAVEN IS A PLACE ON EARTH SODA CLUB FEATURING HANNAH ALETHA	13	2003
HEAVEN IS CLOSER (FEELS LIKE HEAVEN) DARIO G	39	2003
HEAVEN IS HERE JULIE FELIX	22	1970
HEAVEN IS IN THE BACK SEAT OF MY CADILLAC HOT CHOCOLATE	25	1976
HEAVEN IS MY WOMAN'S LOVE VAL DOONICAN	34	1973
HEAVEN IS WAITING DANSE SOCIETY	60	1983
HEAVEN KNOWS [A] DONNA SUMMER	34	1979
HEAVEN KNOWS [B] JAKI GRAHAM	59	1985
HEAVEN KNOWS [B] LALAH HATHAWAY	66	1990

Title / Artist	Peak Position	Year of Release
HEAVEN KNOWS [C] ROBERT PLANT	33	1988
HEAVEN KNOWS [D] COOL DOWN ZONE	52	1990
HEAVEN KNOWS [E] LUTHER VANDROSS	34	1993
HEAVEN KNOWS [F] SQUEEZE	27	1996
HEAVEN KNOWS – DEEP DEEP DOWN ANGEL MORAES	72	1996
HEAVEN KNOWS I'M MISERABLE NOW SMITHS	10	1984
HEAVEN MUST BE MISSING AN ANGEL TAVARES	4	1976
HEAVEN MUST BE MISSING AN ANGEL WORLDS APART	29	1993
HEAVEN MUST HAVE SENT YOU ELGINS	3	1971
HEAVEN MUST HAVE SENT YOU BACK TO ME CICERO	70	1992
HEAVEN ON EARTH SPELLBOUND	73	1997
HEAVEN ON THE 7TH FLOOR PAUL NICHOLAS	40	1977
HEAVEN OR HELL STRANGLERS	46	1992
HEAVEN SCENT BEDROCK	35	1999
HEAVEN SENT [A] PAUL HAIG	74	1983
HEAVEN SENT [B] INXS	31	1992
HEAVEN SENT [C] M1	72	2003
HEAVEN WILL COME SPACE BROTHERS	25	1999
HEAVENLY SHOWADDYWADDY	34	1975
HEAVEN'S EARTH DELERIUM	44	2000
HEAVEN'S HERE HOLLY JOHNSON	62	1989
HEAVEN'S ON FIRE KISS	43	1984
HEAVEN'S WHAT I FEEL GLORIA ESTEFAN	17	1998
HEAVY CROSS GOSSIP	37	2009
HEAVY FUEL DIRE STRAITS	55	1991
HEAVY MAKES YOU HAPPY BOBBY BLOOM	31	1971
HEAVY ON MY HEART ANASTACIA	21	2005
HEAVY VIBES MONTANA SEXTET	59	1983
HEAVYWEIGHT CHAMPION OF THE WORLD REVEREND & THE MAKERS	8	2007
HEDONISM (JUST BECAUSE YOU FEEL GOOD) SKUNK ANANSIE	13	1997
THE HEINRICH MANEUVER INTERPOL	31	2007
HELEN WHEELS PAUL McCARTNEY & WINGS	12	1973
HELENA MY CHEMICAL ROMANCE	20	2005
HELICOPTER BLOC PARTY	26	2004
HELICOPTER TUNE DEEP BLUE	68	1994
HELIOPOLIS BY NIGHT ABERFELDY	66	2004
HELIUM DALLAS SUPERSTARS	64	2003
THE HELL EP TRICKY VS THE GRAVEDIGGAZ	12	1995
HELL HATH NO FURY FRANKIE LAINE	28	1956
HE'LL HAVE TO GO JIM REEVES	12	1960
HE'LL HAVE TO GO BRYAN FERRY	63	1989
HE'LL HAVE TO STAY JEANNE BLACK	41	1960
HELL RAISER SWEET	2	1973
THE HELL SONG SUM 41	35	2003
HELL YEAH GINUWINE	27	2003
HELLA GOOD NO DOUBT	12	2002
HELLBOUND TYGERS OF PAN TANG	48	1981
HELLO [A] LIONEL RICHIE	1	1984
HELLO [A] JHAY PALMER FEATURING MC IMAGE	69	2002
HELLO [B] BELOVED	19	1990
HELLO AGAIN NEIL DIAMOND	51	1981
HELLO AMERICA DEF LEPPARD	45	1980
HELLO BUDDY TREMELOES	32	1971
HELLO DARLIN' FUZZ TOWNSHEND	51	1997
HELLO DARLING TIPPA IRIE	22	1986
HELLO DOLLY LOUIS ARMSTRONG	4	1964
HELLO DOLLY FRANKIE VAUGHAN	18	1964
HELLO DOLLY KENNY BALL & HIS JAZZMEN	30	1964
HELLO DOLLY FRANK SINATRA WITH COUNT BASIE	47	1964
HELLO DOLLY BACHELORS	38	1966
HELLO GOODBYE BEATLES	1	1967
HELLO HAPPINESS DRIFTERS	12	1976
HELLO HEARTACHE GOODBYE LOVE LITTLE PEGGY MARCH	29	1963
HELLO! HELLO! I'M BACK AGAIN GARY GLITTER	2	1973
HELLO HONKY TONKS (ROCK YOUR BODY) PIZZAMAN	41	1996
HELLO HOW ARE YOU EASYBEATS	20	1968
HELLO HURRAY ALICE COOPER	6	1973
HELLO I AM YOUR HEART BETTE BRIGHT	50	1980
HELLO I LOVE YOU DOORS	15	1968
HELLO JOSEPHINE WAYNE FONTANA & THE MINDBENDERS	46	1963
HELLO LITTLE GIRL FOURMOST	9	1963
HELLO MARY LOU (GOODBYE HEART) RICKY NELSON	2	1961
HELLO MUDDAH HELLO FADDAH ALLAN SHERMAN	14	1963
HELLO STRANGER YVONNE ELLIMAN	26	1977
HELLO SUMMERTIME BOBBY GOLDSBORO	14	1974
HELLO SUNSHINE SUPER FURRY ANIMALS	31	2003
HELLO SUZIE AMEN CORNER	4	1969
HELLO THIS IS JOANNIE (THE TELEPHONE ANSWERING MACHINE SONG) PAUL EVANS	6	1978
HELLO TIGER URUSEI YATSURA	63	1998
HELLO (TURN YOUR RADIO ON) SHAKESPEAR'S SISTER	14	1992
HELLO WORLD [A] TREMELOES	14	1969
HELLO WORLD [B] SEA FRUIT	59	1999
HELLO YOUNG LOVERS PAUL ANKA	44	1960
HELLO? IS THIS THING ON? !!!	74	2004
HELLRAISER ANNE SAVAGE	74	2003
HELL'S PARTY GLAM	42	1993
HELP! BEATLES	1	1965
HELP TINA TURNER	40	1984
HELP! BANANARAMA/LA NA NEE NEE NOO NOO	3	1989
HELP (EP) VARIOUS ARTISTS (EP'S & LP'S)	51	1995
HELP, GET ME SOME HELP! OTTAWAN	49	1981
HELP I'M A FISH LITTLE TREES	11	2001
HELP IT ALONG CLIFF RICHARD	29	1973
HELP ME [A] TIMO MAAS FEATURING KELIS	65	2002
HELP ME [B] NICK CARTER	17	2002
HELP ME FIND A WAY TO YOUR HEART DARYL HALL	70	1994
HELP ME GIRL ERIC BURDON & THE ANIMALS	14	1966
HELP ME MAKE IT HUFF & PUFF	31	1996
HELP ME MAKE IT THROUGH THE NIGHT GLADYS KNIGHT & THE PIPS	11	1972
HELP ME MAKE IT THROUGH THE NIGHT JOHN HOLT	6	1974
HELP ME MAMA LEMONESCENT	36	2003
HELP ME RHONDA BEACH BOYS	27	1965
HELP MY FRIEND SLO-MOSHUN	52	1994
HELP THE AGED PULP	8	1997
HELP YOURSELF [A] TOM JONES	5	1968
HELP YOURSELF [A] TONY FERRINO	42	1996
HELP YOURSELF [B] JULIAN LENNON	53	1991
HELP YOURSELF [C] AMY WINEHOUSE	46	2004
HELPLESS TRACEY ULLMAN	61	1984
HELULE HELULE TREMELOES	14	1968
HELYOM HALIB CAPPELLA	11	1989
HENRIETTA FRATELLIS	19	2006
HENRY LEE NICK CAVE & THE BAD SEEDS & PJ HARVEY	36	1996
HENRY VIII SUITE (EP) EARLY MUSIC CONSORT DIRECTED BY DAVID MUNROW	49	1971
HER GUY	58	1991
HER ROYAL MAJESTY JAMES DARREN	36	1962
HERCULEAN GOOD, THE BAD & THE QUEEN	22	2006
HERCULES FRANKIE VAUGHAN	42	1962
HERE LUSCIOUS JACKSON	59	1995
HERE AND NOW [A] LUTHER VANDROSS	43	1990
HERE AND NOW [B] DEL AMITRI	21	1995
HERE AND NOW [C] STEPS	4	2001
HERE COME THE GIRLS ERNIE K-DOE	43	2007
HERE COME THE GOOD TIMES A HOUSE	37	1994
HERE COME THE NICE SMALL FACES	12	1967
HERE COMES MY BABY TREMELOES	4	1967
HERE COMES SUMMER JERRY KELLER	1	1959
HERE COMES SUMMER DAVE CLARK FIVE	44	1970
HERE COMES THAT FEELING BRENDA LEE	5	1962
HERE COMES THAT SOUND SIMON HARRIS	38	1988
HERE COMES THE BIG RUSH ECHOBELLY	56	1997
HERE COMES THE HAMMER MC HAMMER	15	1991
HERE COMES THE HOTSTEPPER INI KAMOZE	4	1995
HERE COMES THE JUDGE [A] SHORTY LONG	30	1968
HERE COMES THE JUDGE [B] PIGMEAT MARKHAM	19	1968
HERE COMES THE MAN BOOM BOOM BOOM	74	1986
HERE COMES THE NIGHT [A] LULU	50	1964
HERE COMES THE NIGHT [A] THEM	2	1965
HERE COMES THE NIGHT [B] BEACH BOYS	37	1979
HERE COMES THE PAIN LEE HASLAM	71	2004
HERE COMES THE RAIN AGAIN EURYTHMICS	8	1984
HERE COMES THE RUMOUR MILL YOUNG KNIVES	36	2006
HERE COMES THE STAR HERMAN'S HERMITS	33	1969
HERE COMES THE SUMMER UNDERTONES	34	1979
HERE COMES THE SUN STEVE HARLEY	10	1976
HERE COMES THE WAR NEW MODEL ARMY	25	1993
HERE COMES YOUR MAN PIXIES	54	1989
HERE 4 ONE BLAZIN' SQUAD	6	2004
HERE I AM [A] BRYAN ADAMS	5	2002
HERE I AM [B] EXPLOSION	75	2005
HERE I AM (COME AND TAKE ME) UB40	46	1990
HERE I COME BARRINGTON LEVY	41	1985
HERE I COME (SING DJ) TALISMAN P MEETS BARRINGTON LEVY	37	2001
HERE I GO 2 UNLIMITED	22	1995
HERE I GO AGAIN [A] HOLLIES	4	1964
HERE I GO AGAIN [B] ARCHIE BELL & THE DRELLS	11	1972
HERE I GO AGAIN [C] GUYS & DOLLS	33	1975
HERE I GO AGAIN [D] TWIGGY	17	1976
HERE I GO AGAIN [E] WHITESNAKE	9	1982
HERE I GO AGAIN [E] FRASH	69	1995
HERE I GO AGAIN [F] MARIO	11	2005
HERE I GO IMPOSSIBLE AGAIN ERASURE	25	2005
HERE I STAND [A] MILLTOWN BROTHERS	41	1991
HERE I STAND [B] BITTY McLEAN	10	1994
HERE IN MY HEART AL MARTINO	1	1952
HERE (IN YOUR ARMS) HELLOGOOODBYE	4	2007
HERE IS THE NEWS ELECTRIC LIGHT ORCHESTRA	24	1982
HERE IT COMES DOVES	73	1999
HERE IT COMES AGAIN [A] FORTUNES	4	1965
HERE IT COMES AGAIN [B] BLACK	70	1991
HERE IT COMES AGAIN [C] MELANIE C	7	2003
HERE IT GOES AGAIN OK GO	36	2006
HERE SHE COMES AGAIN STANDS	25	2004
HERE THERE AND EVERYWHERE EMMYLOU HARRIS	30	1976
HERE TO STAY [A] NEW ORDER	15	2002
HERE TO STAY [B] KORN	12	2002
HERE WE ARE GLORIA ESTEFAN	23	1990
HERE WE COME TIMBALAND/MISSY ELLIOTT & MAGOO	43	1999
HERE WE GO [A] EVERTON FC	14	1985
HERE WE GO [B] C & C MUSIC FACTORY (FEATURING FREEDOM WILLIAMS)	20	1991
HERE WE GO [C] STAKKA BO	13	1993
HERE WE GO [D] ARAB STRAP	48	1998
HERE WE GO [E] FREESTYLERS	45	1999

Title / Artist	Peak Position	Year of Release
HERE WE GO [F] TRINA FEATURING KELLY ROWLAND	15	2006
HERE WE GO AGAIN [A] RAY CHARLES	38	1967
HERE WE GO AGAIN [B] PORTRAIT	37	1993
HERE WE GO AGAIN [C] A HOMEBOY, A HIPPIE & A FUNKI DREDD	57	1994
HERE WE GO AGAIN [D] ARETHA FRANKLIN	68	1998
HERE WE GO ROCK 'N' ROLL SPIDER	57	1984
HERE WE GO ROUND THE MULBERRY BUSH TRAFFIC	8	1967
HERE WITH ME DIDO	4	2001
HERE YOU COME AGAIN DOLLY PARTON	75	1984
HERE'S MY A RAPINATION FEATURING CAROL KENYON	69	1993
HERE'S THE GOOD NEWS PAUL WELLER	21	2005
HERE'S TO LOVE (AULD LANG SYNE) JOHN CHRISTIE	24	1977
HERE'S WHERE THE STORY ENDS TIN TIN OUT FEATURING SHELLEY NELSON	7	1998
HERMANN LOVES PAULINE SUPER FURRY ANIMALS	26	1997
HERNANDO'S HIDEAWAY JOHNSTON BROTHERS	1	1955
HERNANDO'S HIDEAWAY JOHNNIE RAY	11	1955
HERO [A] DAVID CROSBY FEATURING PHIL COLLINS	56	1993
HERO [B] MARIAH CAREY	7	1993
HERO [B] X FACTOR FINALISTS	1	2008
HERO [C] ENRIQUE IGLESIAS	1	2002
HERO [D] CHAD KROEGER FEATURING JOSEY SCOTT	4	2002
HERO [E] NAS FEATURING KERI HILSON	70	2008
HERO OF THE DAY METALLICA	17	1996
HEROES [A] DAVID BOWIE	24	1977
HEROES [B] RONI SIZE/REPRAZENT	31	1997
THE HEROES [C] SHED SEVEN	18	1998
HEROES AND VILLAINS BEACH BOYS	8	1967
HERSHAM BOYS SHAM 69	6	1979
HE'S A PIRATE KLAUS BADELT	40	2006
HE'S A REBEL CRYSTALS	19	1962
HE'S A SAINT, HE'S A SINNER MIQUEL BROWN	68	1984
HE'S BACK (THE MAN BEHIND THE MASK) ALICE COOPER	61	1986
HE'S FIT LOVE BITES	48	2006
HE'S GONNA STEP ON YOU AGAIN JOHN KONGOS	4	1971
HE'S GOT NO LOVE SEARCHERS	12	1965
HE'S GOT THE WHOLE WORLD IN HIS HANDS LAURIE LONDON	12	1957
HE'S IN TOWN ROCKIN' BERRIES	3	1964
HE'S MINE MOKENSTEF	70	1995
HE'S MISSTRA KNOW IT ALL STEVIE WONDER	10	1974
HE'S OLD ENOUGH TO KNOW BETTER BROOK BROTHERS	37	1962
HE'S ON THE PHONE SAINT ETIENNE FEATURING ETIENNE DAHO	11	1995
HE'S SO FINE CHIFFONS	16	1963
HE'S THE GREATEST DANCER SISTER SLEDGE	6	1979
HE'S THE ONE BILLIE DAVIS	40	1963
HEWLETT'S DAUGHTER GRANDADDY	71	2000
HEXAGRAM DEFTONES	68	2003
HEY! JULIO IGLESIAS	31	1983
HEY AMERICA JAMES BROWN	47	1971
HEY! BABY [A] BRUCE CHANNEL	2	1962
HEY BABY [A] DJ OTZI	1	2001
HEY BABY [B] NO DOUBT	2	2002
HEY BOY HEY GIRL CHEMICAL BROTHERS	3	1999
HEY CHILD EAST 17	3	1997
HEY DJ WORLD'S FAMOUS SUPREME TEAM	52	1984
HEY DJ LIGHTER SHADE OF BROWN	33	1994
HEY DJ I CAN'T DANCE TO THAT MUSIC YOU'RE PLAYING BEATMASTERS FEATURING BETTY BOO	7	1989
HEY DJ! (PLAY THAT SONG) N-TYCE	20	1997
HEY DUDE KULA SHAKER	2	1996
HEY GIRL [A] SMALL FACES	10	1966
HEY GIRL [B] EXPRESSOS	60	1980
HEY GIRL [C] DELAYS	40	2003
HEY GIRL DON'T BOTHER ME TAMS	1	1971
HEY GOD BON JOVI	13	1996
HEY GOOD LOOKIN' BO DIDDLEY	39	1965
HEY GOOD LOOKING TOMMY ZANG	45	1961
HEY JEALOUSY GIN BLOSSOMS	24	1994
HEY JOE [A] FRANKIE LAINE	1	1953
HEY JOE [B] JIMI HENDRIX	6	1967
HEY JUDE BEATLES	1	1968
HEY JUDE WILSON PICKETT	16	1969
HEY JULIE FOUNTAINS OF WAYNE	57	2004
HEY JUPITER TORI AMOS	20	1996
HEY KID MATT WILLIS	11	2006
HEY LITTLE GIRL [A] DEL SHANNON	2	1962
HEY LITTLE GIRL [B] ICEHOUSE	17	1983
HEY LITTLE GIRL [C] MATHIAS WARE FEATURING ROB TAYLOR	42	2002
HEY LORD DON'T ASK ME QUESTIONS GRAHAM PARKER	32	1978
HEY LOVE KING SUN-D'MOET	66	1987
HEY LOVER LL COOL J FEATURING BOYZ II MEN	17	1996
HEY! LUCIANI FALL	59	1986
HEY MA CAM'RON FEATURING JUELZ SANTANA	8	2003
HEY MAMA [A] FRANKIE VAUGHAN	21	1963
HEY MAMA [B] JOE BROWN	33	1973
HEY MAMA [C] BLACK EYED PEAS	6	2004
HEY MAN (NOW YOU'RE REALLY LIVING) EELS	45	2005
HEY MANHATTAN PREFAB SPROUT	72	1988
HEY MATTHEW KAREL FIALKA	9	1987
HEY MISS PAYNE CHEQUERS	32	1976
HEY MR CHRISTMAS SHOWADDYWADDY	13	1974
HEY MR DJ [A] ZHANE	26	1993
HEY MR DJ [B] OPEN ARMS FEATURING ROWETTA	62	1996
HEY MR DJ [C] VAN MORRISON	58	2002
HEY MR DREAM MAKER CLIFF RICHARD	31	1976
HEY MISTER HEARTACHE KIM WILDE	31	1988
HEY MR MUSIC MAN PETERS & LEE	16	1976
HEY MUSIC LOVER S-EXPRESS	6	1989
HEY NOW (GIRLS JUST WANT TO HAVE FUN) CYNDI LAUPER	4	1994
HEY NOW (MEAN MUGGIN') XZIBIT	9	2005
HEY NOW NOW SWIRL 360	61	1998
HEY PAPA! ALEX CARTANA	34	2004
HEY! PARADISE FLICKMAN	69	2001
HEY PAULA PAUL & PAULA	8	1963
HEY ROCK AND ROLL SHOWADDYWADDY	2	1974
HEY SCENESTERS! CRIBS	27	2005
HEY SENORITA WAR	40	1978
HEY SEXY LADY SHAGGY FEATURING BRIAN AND TONY GOLD	10	2002
HEY STOOPID ALICE COOPER	21	1991
HEY THERE ROSEMARY CLOONEY	4	1955
HEY THERE JOHNNIE RAY	5	1955
HEY THERE LITA ROZA	17	1955
HEY THERE SAMMY DAVIS, JR	19	1955
HEY THERE DELILAH PLAIN WHITE T'S	2	2007
(HEY THERE) LONELY GIRL EDDIE HOLMAN	4	1974
HEY THERE LONELY GIRL BIG FUN	62	1990
HEY VENUS THAT PETROL EMOTION	49	1990
HEY WHATEVER WESTLIFE	4	2003
HEY! WHAT'S YOUR NAME BABY JUNE	75	1992
HEY WILLY HOLLIES	22	1971
HEY YA! OUTKAST	3	2003
HEY YOU [A] TOMMY STEELE	28	1957
HEY YOU [B] QUIREBOYS	14	1990
(HEY YOU) THE ROCKSTEADY CREW ROCKSTEADY CREW	6	1983
HEYKENS SERANADE PIPES & DRUMS & MILITARY BAND OF THE ROYAL SCOTS DRAGOON GUARDS	30	1972
HI DE HI, HI DE HO KOOL & THE GANG	29	1982
HI DE HI (HOLIDAY ROCK) PAUL SHANE & THE YELLOWCOATS	36	1981
HI DE HO K7 & THE SWING KIDS	17	1994
HI FIDELITY [A] ELVIS COSTELLO & THE ATTRACTIONS	30	1980
HI-FIDELITY [B] KIDS FROM FAME FEATURING VALERIE LANDSBERG	5	1982
HI HI HAZEL GENO WASHINGTON & THE RAM JAM BAND	45	1966
HI HI HAZEL TROGGS	42	1967
HI HI HI WINGS	5	1972
HI HO SILVER JIM DIAMOND	5	1986
HI! HOW YA DOIN'? KENNY G	70	1984
HI LILI HI LO ALAN PRICE SET	11	1966
HI TENSION HI TENSION	13	1978
HIBERNACULUM MIKE OLDFIELD	47	1994
HIDDEN AGENDA CRAIG DAVID	10	2003
HIDDEN PLACE BJORK	21	2001
HIDE TWEN2Y 4 SE7EN	42	2004
HIDE AND SEEK [A] MARTY WILDE	47	1961
HIDE AND SEEK [B] HOWARD JONES	12	1984
HIDE U KOSHEEN	6	2000
HIDE YOUR HEART KISS	59	1989
HIDE-A-WAY NU SOUL FEATURING KELI RICH	27	1996
HIDEAWAY [A] DAVE DEE, DOZY, BEAKY, MICK & TICH	10	1966
HIDEAWAY [B] DE'LACY	9	1995
HIDEAWAY [C] DELAYS	35	2006
HIDING ALL THE STARS CHICANE	42	2009
HIGH [A] CURE	8	1992
HIGH [B] HYPER GO GO	30	1992
HIGH [C] FEEDER	24	1997
HIGH [D] PROPHETS OF SOUND	73	1998
HIGH [E] LIGHTHOUSE FAMILY	4	1998
HIGH [F] JAMES BLUNT	16	2005
HIGH AGAIN (HIGH ON EMOTION) THOMAS FALKE	55	2005
HIGH & DRY RADIOHEAD	17	1995
HIGH AS A KITE ONE TRIBE FEATURING ROGER	55	1995
HIGH CLASS BABY CLIFF RICHARD & THE DRIFTERS	7	1958
HIGH ENERGY EVELYN THOMAS	5	1984
HIGH 5 PALLADIUM	44	2007
HIGH FLY JOHN MILES	17	1975
HIGH HEAD BLUES BLACK CROWES	25	1995
HIGH HOPES [A] FRANK SINATRA	6	1959
HIGH HOPES [B] PINK FLOYD	26	1994
HIGH HORSE EVELYN KING	55	1986
HIGH IN THE SKY AMEN CORNER	6	1968
HIGH LIFE MODERN ROMANCE	8	1983
HIGH NOON [A] FRANKIE LAINE	7	1952
HIGH NOON [B] DJ SHADOW	22	1997
HIGH NOON [C] SERIOUS DANGER	54	1998
HIGH ON A HAPPY VIBE URBAN COOKIE COLLECTIVE	31	1994
HIGH ON EMOTION CHRIS DE BURGH	44	1984
HIGH ROLLERS ICE-T	63	1989
HIGH SCHOOL CONFIDENTIAL JERRY LEE LEWIS	12	1959
HIGH SCHOOL NEVER ENDS BOWLING FOR SOUP	40	2007
HIGH TIME PAUL JONES	4	1966
HIGH TIMES JAMIROQUAI	20	1997

Peak Position / Year of Release

HIGH VOLTAGE JOHNNY & THE HURRICANES 24 1961
HIGH VOLTAGE (LIVE VERSION) AC/DC 48 1980
HIGH VOLTAGE/POINTS OF AUTHORITY LINKIN PARK 9 2002
HIGHER [A] CREED 47 2000
HIGHER [B] DAVID MORALES & ALBERT CABRERA PRESENT MOCA FEATURING DEANNA 41 2000
HIGHER AND HIGHER UNATION 42 1993
HIGHER (FEEL IT) ERICK 'MORE' MORILLO PRESENTS RAW 74 1995
HIGHER GROUND [A] STEVIE WONDER 29 1973
HIGHER GROUND [A] RED HOT CHILI PEPPERS 54 1990
HIGHER GROUND [B] GUN 48 1992
HIGHER GROUND [C] UB40 8 1993
HIGHER GROUND [D] SASHA WITH SAM MOLLISON 19 1994
HIGHER LOVE STEVE WINWOOD 13 1986
A HIGHER PLACE PEYTON 68 2004
HIGHER STATE OF CONSCIOUSNESS '96 REMIXES WINK 7 1996
HIGHER THAN HEAVEN [A] AGE OF CHANCE 53 1990
HIGHER THAN HEAVEN [B] KELLE BRYAN 14 1999
HIGHER THAN REASON UNBELIEVABLE TRUTH 38 1998
HIGHER THAN THE SUN PRIMAL SCREAM 40 1991
HIGHLIFE CYPRESS HILL 35 2000
HIGHLY EVOLVED VINES 32 2002
HIGHLY INFLAMMABLE X-RAY SPEX 45 1979
HIGHLY STRUNG SPANDAU BALLET 15 1984
HIGHNESS ENVY & OTHER SINS 65 2008
HIGHRISE TOWN LANTERNS 50 1999
HIGHWAY 5 BLESSING 30 1991
HIGHWAY CODE MASTER SINGERS 25 1966
THE HIGHWAY SONG NANCY SINATRA 21 1969
HIGHWAY TO HELL (LIVE) AC/DC 56 1979
HIGHWAYS OF MY LIFE ISLEY BROTHERS 25 1974
HIGHWIRE [A] LINDA CARR & THE LOVE SQUAD 15 1975
HIGHWIRE [B] ROLLING STONES 29 1991
HI-HEEL SNEAKERS TOMMY TUCKER 23 1964
HI-HO SILVER LINING JEFF BECK 14 1967
HI-LILI HI-LO RICHARD CHAMBERLAIN 20 1963
HILLBILLY ROCK HILLBILLY ROLL WOOLPACKERS 5 1996
HIM [A] RUPERT HOLMES 31 1980
HIM [B] SARAH BRIGHTMAN & THE LONDON PHILHARMONIC 55 1983
THE HINDU TIMES OASIS 1 2002
HIP HOP DEAD PREZ 41 2000
HIP HOP, BE BOP (DON'T STOP) MAN PARRISH 41 1983
HIP HOP DON'T YA DROP HONKY 70 1996
HIP HOP HOORAY NAUGHTY BY NATURE 20 1993
HIP HOP IS DEAD NAS FEATURING WILL I AM 35 2007
HIP HOP POLICE CHAMILLIONAIRE FEATURING SLICK RICK 50 2007
HIP HOUSE DJ 'FAST' EDDIE 47 1989
HIP HOUSIN' X-PRESS 2 FEATURING LO-PRO 55 1994
HIP TO BE SQUARE HUEY LEWIS & THE NEWS 41 1986
HIP TO HIP V 5 2004
HIP TODAY EXTREME 44 1995
HIPPY CHICK SOHO 8 1990
HIPPY HIPPY SHAKE SWINGING BLUE JEANS 2 1963
HIPPY HIPPY SHAKE GEORGIA SATELLITES 63 1989
HIPS DON'T LIE SHAKIRA FEATURING WYCLEF JEAN 1 2006
HIS GIRL GUESS WHO 45 1967
HISTORY [A] MAI TAI 8 1985
HISTORY [B] VERVE 24 1995
HISTORY [C] MICHAEL JACKSON 5 1997
HISTORY [D] FUNERAL FOR A FRIEND 21 2005
HISTORY MAKER DELIRIOUS? 4 2010
HISTORY NEVER REPEATS SPLIT ENZ 63 1981
HISTORY OF THE WORLD (PART 1) DAMNED 51 1980
HISTORY REPEATING PROPELLERHEADS & SHIRLEY BASSEY 19 1997
HIT [A] SUGARCUBES 17 1992
HIT [B] WANNADIES 20 1997
HIT 'EM HIGH (THE MONSTARS' ANTHEM) B REAL/BUSTA RHYMES/COOLIO/LL COOL J/ METHOD MAN 8 1997
HIT 'EM WIT DA HEE MISSY 'MISDEMEANOR' ELLIOTT 25 1998
HIT AND MISS JOHN BARRY SEVEN 10 1960
HIT AND RUN [A] GIRLSCHOOL 32 1981
HIT AND RUN [B] TOTAL CONTRAST 41 1985
HIT BY LOVE CE CE PENISTON 33 1994
HIT 'EM UP STYLE (OOPS) BLU CANTRELL 12 2001
HIT IT BEAT 70 1981
HIT ME OFF NEW EDITION 20 1996
HIT ME WITH YOUR RHYTHM STICK IAN DURY & THE BLOCKHEADS 1 1978
HIT OR MISS (WAITED TOO LONG) NEW FOUND GLORY 58 2001
HIT THAT OFFSPRING 11 2004
HIT THAT PERFECT BEAT BRONSKI BEAT 3 1985
HIT THE FREEWAY TONI BRAXTON FEATURING LOON 29 2003
HIT THE GROUND DARLING BUDS 27 1989
HIT THE GROUND RUNNING TIM FINN 50 1993
HIT THE NORTH FALL 57 1987
HIT THE ROAD JACK RAY CHARLES 6 1961
HITCHIN' A RIDE [A] VANITY FARE 16 1969
HITCHIN' A RIDE [A] SINITTA 24 1990
HITCHIN' A RIDE [B] GREEN DAY 25 1997
HI-TEK MAMPI SWIFT 72 2004
HITMIX (OFFICIAL BOOTLEG MEGA-MIX) ALEXANDER O'NEAL 19 1989
HITS MEDLEY GIPSY KINGS 53 1994
HITSVILLE UK CLASH 56 1981
HOBART PAVING SAINT ETIENNE 23 1993
HOBO HUMPIN' SLOBO BABE WHALE 15 1994
HOCUS POCUS FOCUS 20 1973
HOEDOWN THROWDOWN MILEY CYRUS 18 2009
HOGWASH FARM (THE DIESEL HANDS EP) DAWN OF THE REPLICANTS 65 1998
HOKEY COKEY JUDGE DREAD 64 1978
HOKEY COKEY SNOWMEN 18 1981
HOKEY COKEY BLACK LACE 31 1985
THE HOKEY COKEY CAPTAIN SENSIBLE 71 1994
HOKOYO ORANGE JUICE 60 1982
HOKUS POKUS INSANE CLOWN POSSE 53 1998
HOLD BACK THE NIGHT TRAMMPS 5 1975
HOLD BACK THE NIGHT KWS FEATURES GUEST VOCAL FROM THE TRAMMPS 30 1992
HOLD BACK THE RIVER WET WET WET 31 1990
HOLD BACK TOMORROW MIKI & GRIFF 26 1959
HOLD IT STEPHEN 'TIN TIN' DUFFY 55 1983
HOLD IT, DON'T DROP IT JENNIFER LOPEZ 72 2008
HOLD IT DOWN [A] SENSELESS THINGS 19 1992
HOLD IT DOWN [B] 2 BAD MICE 48 1992
HOLD ME [A] TEDDY PENDERGRASS & WHITNEY HOUSTON 44 1986
HOLD ME [B] PJ PROBY 3 1964
HOLD ME [B] BA ROBERTSON & MAGGIE BELL 11 1981
HOLD ME [C] SAVAGE GARDEN 16 2000
HOLD ME CLOSE DAVID ESSEX 1 1975
HOLD ME IN YOUR ARMS RICK ASTLEY 10 1989
HOLD ME NOW [A] THOMPSON TWINS 4 1983
HOLD ME NOW [B] JOHNNY LOGAN 2 1987
HOLD ME NOW [C] POLYPHONIC SPREE 72 2004
HOLD ME THRILL ME KISS ME MURIEL SMITH 3 1953
HOLD ME THRILL ME KISS ME GLORIA ESTEFAN 11 1994
HOLD ME, THRILL ME, KISS ME, KILL ME U2 2 1995
HOLD ME TIGHT JOHNNY NASH 5 1968
HOLD ME TIGHTER IN THE RAIN BILLY GRIFFIN 17 1983
HOLD MY BODY TIGHT EAST 17 12 1995
HOLD MY HAND [A] DON CORNELL 1 1954
HOLD MY HAND [B] KEN DODD 44 1981
HOLD MY HAND [C] HOOTIE & THE BLOWFISH 50 1995
HOLD ON [A] STREETBAND 18 1978
HOLD ON [B] EN VOGUE 5 1990
HOLD ON [C] WILSON PHILLIPS 6 1990
HOLD ON [D] CB MILTON 62 1995
HOLD ON [E] HAPPY CLAPPERS 27 1995
HOLD ON [F] JOSE NUNEZ FEATURING OCTAHVIA 44 1999
HOLD ON [G] GOOD CHARLOTTE 34 2003
HOLD ON [H] KT TUNSTALL 21 2007
HOLD ON [I] LAZEE FEATURING NEVERSTORE 46 2009
HOLD ON [J] MICHAEL BUBLE 72 2009
HOLD ON (EP) ANN NESBY 75 1997
HOLD ON ME PHIXX 10 2003
HOLD ON MY HEART GENESIS 16 1992
HOLD ON TIGHT [A] ELECTRIC LIGHT ORCHESTRA 4 1981
HOLD ON TIGHT [B] SAMANTHA FOX 26 1986
HOLD ON TO LOVE [A] PETER SKELLERN 14 1975
HOLD ON TO LOVE [B] GARY MOORE 65 1984
HOLD ON TO ME MJ COLE FEATURING ELISABETH TROY 35 2000
HOLD ON TO MY LOVE JIMMY RUFFIN 7 1980
HOLD ON TO OUR LOVE JAMES FOX 13 2004
HOLD ON TO THE NIGHTS RICHARD MARX 60 1990
HOLD ON TO WHAT YOU'VE GOT EVELYN KING 47 1988
HOLD ON TO YOUR FRIENDS MORRISSEY 47 1994
HOLD THAT SUCKER DOWN OT QUARTET 24 1994
HOLD THE HEART BIG COUNTRY 55 1986
HOLD THE LINE TOTO 14 1979
HOLD TIGHT [A] DAVE DEE, DOZY, BEAKY, MICK & TICH 4 1966
HOLD TIGHT [B] LIVERPOOL EXPRESS 46 1976
HOLD YOU DOWN JENNIFER LOPEZ FEATURING FAT JOE 6 2005
HOLD YOU TIGHT TARA KEMP 69 1991
HOLD YOUR HEAD UP ARGENT 5 1972
HOLD YOUR HEAD UP HIGH BORIS DLUGOSCH PRESENTS BOOM 23 1997
HOLD YOUR HORSES BABE CELI BEE & THE BUZZY BUNCH 72 1978
HOLDIN' ON TONY RALLO & THE MIDNIGHT BAND 34 1980
HOLDING BACK THE YEARS SIMPLY RED 2 1985
HOLDING ON [A] BEVERLEY CRAVEN 32 1991
HOLDING ON [B] CLOCK 66 1993
HOLDING ON [C] DJ MANTA 47 1999
HOLDING ON [D] HEATHER SMALL 58 2000
HOLDING ON FOR YOU LIBERTY X 5 2002
HOLDING ON 4 U CLOCK 27 1996
HOLDING ON TO NOTHING AGNELLI & NELSON FEATURING AUREUS 41 2004
HOLDING ON TO YOU TERENCE TRENT D'ARBY 20 1995
HOLDING ON (WHEN LOVE IS GONE) LTD 70 1978
HOLDING OUT FOR A HERO BONNIE TYLER 2 1985
HOLE HEARTED EXTREME 12 1991
HOLE IN MY HEART ALPHABEAT 29 2010
HOLE IN MY SHOE TRAFFIC 2 1967
HOLE IN MY SHOE NEIL 2 1984
HOLE IN MY SOUL AEROSMITH 29 1997

Title / Artist	Peak Position	Year of Release
HOLE IN THE BUCKET [A] HARRY BELAFONTE & ODETTA	32	1961
HOLE IN THE BUCKET [B] SPEARHEAD	55	1995
HOLE IN THE EARTH DEFTONES	69	2006
HOLE IN THE GROUND BERNARD CRIBBINS	9	1962
HOLE IN THE HEAD SUGABABES	1	2003
HOLE IN THE ICE NEIL FINN	43	2001
HOLE IN THE WORLD EAGLES	69	2003
HOLIDAE INN CHINGY	35	2004
HOLIDAY [A] MADONNA	2	1984
HOLIDAY [A] MAD'HOUSE	24	2002
HOLIDAY [B] GREEN DAY	11	2005
HOLIDAY [C] DIZZEE RASCAL FEATURING CHROME	1	2009
HOLIDAY 80 (DOUBLE SINGLE) HUMAN LEAGUE	46	1980
HOLIDAY RAP MC MIKER 'G' & DEEJAY SVEN	6	1986
HOLIDAYS IN THE SUN SEX PISTOLS	8	1977
HOLLABACK GIRL GWEN STEFANI	8	2005
HOLLER [A] GINUWINE	13	1998
HOLLER [B] SPICE GIRLS	1	2000
HOLLIEDAZE (MEDLEY) HOLLIES	28	1981
THE HOLLOW A PERFECT CIRCLE	72	2000
HOLLOW HEART BIRDLAND	70	1989
THE HOLLOW MAN MARILLION	30	1994
HOLLY HOLY UB40	31	1998
HOLLYWOOD [A] BOZ SCAGGS	33	1977
HOLLYWOOD [B] MADONNA	2	2003
HOLLYWOOD [C] MARINA AND THE DIAMONDS	12	2010
HOLLYWOOD (DOWN ON YOUR LUCK) THIN LIZZY	53	1982
HOLLYWOOD NIGHTS BOB SEGER & THE SILVER BULLET BAND	42	1978
HOLLYWOOD TEASE GIRL	50	1980
THE HOLY CITY MOIRA ANDERSON	43	1969
HOLY COW LEE DORSEY	6	1966
HOLY DAYS ZOE	72	1992
HOLY DIVER DIO	72	1983
HOLY JOE HAYSI FANTAYZEE	51	1982
THE HOLY RIVER ARTIST	19	1997
HOLY ROLLER NAZARETH	36	1975
HOLY ROLLER NOVACAINE KINGS OF LEON	53	2003
HOLY SMOKE IRON MAIDEN	3	1990
HOLY WARS...THE PUNISHMENT DUE MEGADETH	24	1990
HOMBURG PROCOL HARUM	6	1967
HOME [A] PUBLIC IMAGE LTD	75	1986
HOME [B] GOD MACHINE	65	1993
HOME [C] DEPECHE MODE	23	1997
HOME [C] COAST 2 COAST FEATURING DISCOVERY	44	2001
HOME [D] CHAKRA	46	1997
HOME [E] SHERYL CROW	25	1997
HOME [F] JULIE McKNIGHT	61	2002
HOME [G] BONE THUGS-N-HARMONY FEATURING PHIL COLLINS	19	2003
HOME [H] SIMPLY RED	40	2004
HOME [I] MICHAEL BUBLE	31	2005
HOME [I] WESTLIFE	3	2007
HOME [J] SIMPLE MINDS	41	2005
HOME [K] ROOSTER	33	2006
HOME ALONE R KELLY FEATURING KEITH MURRAY	17	1998
HOME AND AWAY KAREN BODDINGTON & MARK WILLIAMS	73	1989
HOME AND DRY PET SHOP BOYS	14	2002
HOME FOR CHRISTMAS DAY RED CAR AND THE BLUE CAR	44	1991
HOME IS WHERE THE HEART IS GLADYS KNIGHT & THE PIPS	35	1977
HOME LOVIN' MAN ANDY WILLIAMS	7	1970
HOME OF THE BRAVE JODY MILLER	49	1965
HOME SWEET HOME MOTLEY CRUE	37	1986
HOMECOMING KANYE WEST FEATURING CHRIS MARTIN	9	2008
HOMELY GIRL CHI-LITES	5	1974
HOMELY GIRL UB40	6	1989
HOMETOWN GLORY ADELE	19	2008
HOMETOWN UNICORN SUPER FURRY ANIMALS	47	1996
HOMEWARD BOUND SIMON & GARFUNKEL	9	1966
HOMEWARD BOUND QUIET FIVE	44	1966
HOMICIDE 999	40	1978
HOMICIDE SHADES OF RHYTHM	53	1991
HOMING WALTZ VERA LYNN	9	1952
HOMO SAPIENS COOPER TEMPLE CLAUSE	36	2006
HOMOPHOBIC ASSHOLE SENSELESS THINGS	52	1992
HONALOOCHIE BOOGIE MOTT THE HOOPLE	12	1973
HONDY (NO ACCESS) HONDY	26	1997
HONEST I DO DANNY STORM	42	1962
HONEST I DO LOVE YOU CANDI STATON	48	1978
HONEST MEN ELECTRIC LIGHT ORCHESTRA PART 2	60	1991
HONESTLY ZWAN	28	2003
HONESTY ALEX PARKS	56	2006
HONEY [A] BOBBY GOLDSBORO	2	1968
HONEY [B] MARIAH CAREY	3	1997
HONEY [C] MOBY	33	1998
HONEY [D] BILLIE RAY MARTIN	54	1999
HONEY [E] R KELLY & JAY-Z	35	2002
HONEY BE GOOD BIBLE	54	1989
HONEY CHILE [A] FATS DOMINO	29	1957
HONEY CHILE [B] MARTHA REEVES & THE VANDELLAS	30	1968
HONEY COME BACK GLEN CAMPBELL	4	1970
HONEY HONEY SWEET DREAMS	10	1974
HONEY HONEY ORIGINAL CAST RECORDING	69	2008
HONEY I GEORGE McCRAE	33	1976
HONEY I NEED PRETTY THINGS	13	1965
HONEY I'M LOST DOOLEYS	24	1979
HONEY TO THE BEE BILLIE	3	1999
HONEYCOMB JIMMIE RODGERS	30	1957
THE HONEYDRIPPER JETS	58	1982
THE HONEYMOON SONG MANUEL & HIS MUSIC OF THE MOUNTAINS	22	1959
THE HONEYTHIEF HIPSWAY	17	1986
HONG KONG GARDEN SIOUXSIE & THE BANSHEES	7	1978
HONKY CAT ELTON JOHN	31	1972
THE HONKY DOODLE DAY EP HONKY	61	1993
HONKY TONK TRAIN BLUES KEITH EMERSON	21	1976
HONKY TONK WOMEN ROLLING STONES	1	1969
HONKY TONK WOMEN POGUES	56	1992
HOOCHIE BOOTY ULTIMATE KAOS	17	1995
HOODED FRESH BC	74	2004
HOODIE LADY SOVEREIGN	44	2005
HOOKED 99TH FLOOR ELEVATORS FEATURING TONY DE VIT	28	1995
HOOKED ON A FEELING JONATHAN KING	23	1971
HOOKED ON CAN-CAN ROYAL PHILHARMONIC ORCHESTRA ARRANGED & CONDUCTED BY LOUIS CLARK	47	1981
HOOKED ON CLASSICS ROYAL PHILHARMONIC ORCHESTRA ARRANGED & CONDUCTED BY LOUIS CLARK	2	1981
HOOKED ON LOVE DEAD OR ALIVE	69	1987
HOOKED ON YOU [A] SYDNEY YOUNGBLOOD	72	1991
HOOKED ON YOU [B] VOLATILE AGENTS FEATURING SIMONE BENN	54	2001
HOOKS IN YOU MARILLION	30	1989
HOOLIGAN EMBRACE	18	1999
HOOLIGAN 69 RAGGA TWINS	56	1991
HOOLIGAN'S HOLIDAY MOTLEY CRUE	36	1994
HOORAY HOORAY (IT'S A CHEEKY HOLIDAY) CHEEKY GIRLS	3	2003
HOORAY HOORAY IT'S A HOLI-HOLIDAY BONEY M	3	1979
HOOTIN' NIGEL GEE	57	2001
HOOTS MON LORD ROCKINGHAM'S XI	1	1958
HOOVERS & HORNS FERGIE & BK	57	2000
HOOVERVILLE (THEY PROMISED US THE WORLD) CHRISTIANS	21	1987
THE HOP THEATRE OF HATE	70	1982
HOPE [A] SHAGGY	19	2001
HOPE [B] TWISTA FEATURING FAITH EVANS	25	2005
HOPE AND WAIT ORION TOO	46	2002
HOPE (I WISH YOU'D BELIEVE ME) WAH!	37	1983
HOPE IN A HOPELESS WORLD PAUL YOUNG	42	1993
HOPE (NEVER GIVE UP) LOVELAND FEATURING RACHEL McFARLANE	37	1994
HOPE OF DELIVERANCE PAUL McCARTNEY	18	1993
HOPE ST LEVELLERS	12	1995
HOPE THERE'S SOMEONE ANTONY & THE JOHNSONS	44	2005
HOPELESS DIONNE FARRIS	42	1997
HOPELESSLY RICK ASTLEY	33	1993
HOPELESSLY DEVOTED TO YOU OLIVIA NEWTON-JOHN	2	1978
HOPELESSLY DEVOTED TO YOU SONIA	61	1994
HOPES & FEARS WILL YOUNG	65	2009
HOPPIPOLLA SIGUR ROS	24	2005
THE HORN TRACK EGYPTIAN EMPIRE	61	1992
HORNY [A] MARK MORRISON	5	1996
HORNY [B] MOUSSE T VERSUS HOT 'N' JUICY	2	1998
HORNY AS A DANDY MOUSSE T VS DANDY WARHOLS	17	2006
HORNY AS FUNK SOAPY	35	1996
HORNY HORNS PERFECT PHASE	21	1999
HORROR HEAD (EP) CURVE	31	1992
HORSE SPLODGENESSABOUNDS	26	1980
HORSE AND CARRIAGE CAM'RON FEATURING MA$E	12	1998
HORSE WITH NO NAME AMERICA	3	1972
HORSEMEN BEES	41	2004
HORSEPOWER RAVESIGNAL III	61	1991
HOSANNAS FROM THE BASEMENTS OF HELL KILLING JOKE	72	2006
HOSPITAL FOOD DAVID GRAY	34	2005
HOSTAGE IN A FROCK CECIL	68	1997
HOT [A] IDEAL	49	1994
HOT [B] AVRIL LAVIGNE	30	2007
HOT [C] INNA	6	2010
HOT & WET (BELIEVE IT) TZANT	36	1996
HOT BLOODED FOREIGNER	42	1978
HOT BOYZ MISSY MISDEMEANOR ELLIOTT FEATURING NAS, EVE & Q-TIP	18	2000
HOT DIGGITY PERRY COMO	4	1956
HOT DIGGITY MICHAEL HOLLIDAY	14	1956
HOT DIGGITY STARGAZERS	28	1956
HOT DOG SHAKIN' STEVENS	24	1980
HOT FUN 7TH HEAVEN	47	1985
HOT HOT HOT [A] ARROW	38	1984
HOT HOT HOT [A] PAT & MICK	47	1993
HOT HOT HOT!!! [B] CURE	45	1988
HOT IN HERRE NELLY	4	2002
HOT IN HERRE TIGA	46	2003
HOT IN THE CITY BILLY IDOL	13	1982
HOT KISS JULIETTE & THE LICKS	50	2006
HOT LIKE FIRE [A] AALIYAH	30	1997
HOT LIKE FIRE [B] DJ AMS & KHIZA FEATURING BINNS & TAFARI	72	2005
HOT LOVE [A] T REX	1	1971
HOT LOVE [B] DAVID ESSEX	57	1980
HOT LOVE [C] KELLY MARIE	22	1981
HOT LOVE [D] FIVE STAR	68	1990
HOT LOVE NOW WONDER STUFF	19	1994

Title / Artist	Peak Position	Year of Release
HOT N COLD KATY PERRY	4	2008
HOT PEPPER FLOYD CRAMER	46	1962
HOT ROCKIN' JUDAS PRIEST	60	1981
(HOT ST) COUNTRY GRAMMAR** NELLY	7	2000
HOT SHOT [A] BARRY BLUE	23	1974
HOT SHOT [B] KAREN YOUNG	34	1978
HOT SHOT [C] CLIFF RICHARD	46	1979
HOT SHOT TOTTENHAM TOTTENHAM HOTSPUR FA CUP FINAL SQUAD	18	1987
HOT SPOT FOXY BROWN	31	1999
HOT STUFF DONNA SUMMER	11	1979
HOT STUFF ARSENAL FC	9	1998
HOT STUFF (LET'S DANCE) CRAIG DAVID	7	2007
HOT SUMMER SALSA JIVE BUNNY & THE MASTERMIXERS	43	1991
HOT TODDY TED HEATH	6	1953
HOT TRACKS EP NAZARETH	15	1977
HOT VALVES EP BE BOP DELUXE	36	1976
HOT WATER LEVEL 42	18	1984
HOTEL CASSIDY FEATURING R KELLY	3	2004
HOTEL CALIFORNIA EAGLES	8	1977
HOTEL CALIFORNIA JAM ON THE MUTHA	62	1990
HOTEL ILLNESS BLACK CROWES	47	1992
HOTEL LOUNGE (BE THE DEATH OF ME) dEUS	55	1995
HOTEL ROOM RICHARD HAWLEY	64	2006
HOTEL ROOM SERVICE PITBULL	9	2009
HOTEL YORBA WHITE STRIPES	26	2001
HOTLEGS ROD STEWART	5	1978
HOTLINE TO HEAVEN BANANARAMA	58	1984
HOTNESS DYNAMITE MC & ORIGIN UNKNOWN	66	2003
HOUND DOG ELVIS PRESLEY	2	1956
HOUND DOG MAN FABIAN	46	1960
HOUNDS OF LOVE KATE BUSH	18	1986
HOUNDS OF LOVE FUTUREHEADS	8	2005
HOURGLASS SQUEEZE	16	1987
HOUSE ARREST KRUSH	3	1987
HOUSE ENGERY REVENGE CAPPELLA	73	1989
HOUSE FLY TRICKY DISCO	55	1991
A HOUSE IN THE COUNTRY PRETTY THINGS	50	1966
THE HOUSE IS HAUNTED (BY THE ECHO OF YOUR LAST GOODBYE) MARC ALMOND	55	1986
THE HOUSE IS MINE HYPNOTIST	65	1991
HOUSE IS NOT A HOME CHARLES & EDDIE	29	1993
HOUSE MUSIC EDDIE AMADOR	37	1998
HOUSE NATION HOUSEMASTER BOYZ & THE RUDE BOY OF HOUSE	8	1987
HOUSE OF BROKEN LOVE GREAT WHITE	44	1990
HOUSE OF FIRE ALICE COOPER	65	1989
HOUSE OF FUN MADNESS	1	1982
HOUSE OF GOD DHS	72	2002
HOUSE OF JEALOUS LOVERS RAPTURE	27	2003
HOUSE OF JOY VICKI SUE ROBINSON	48	1997
HOUSE OF LOVE [A] EAST 17	10	1992
HOUSE OF LOVE [B] RuPAUL	40	1993
HOUSE OF LOVE [C] SKIN	45	1994
HOUSE OF LOVE [D] AMY GRANT WITH VINCE GILL	46	1995
HOUSE OF LOVE (IN MY HOUSE) SMOOTH TOUCH	58	1994
HOUSE OF THE BLUE DANUBE MALCOLM McLAREN & THE BOOTZILLA ORCHESTRA	73	1989
THE HOUSE OF THE RISING SUN ANIMALS	1	1964
HOUSE OF THE RISING SUN FRIJID PINK	4	1970
HOUSE OF THE RISING SUN RAGE	41	1993
HOUSE ON FIRE [A] BOOMTOWN RATS	24	1982
HOUSE ON FIRE [B] ARKARNA	33	1997
HOUSE PARTY AT BOOTHY'S LITTLE MAN TATE	29	2006
HOUSE SOME MORE LOCK 'N' LOAD	45	2001
THE HOUSE THAT JACK BUILT [A] ALAN PRICE SET	4	1967

Title / Artist	Peak Position	Year of Release
THE HOUSE THAT JACK BUILT [B] TRACIE	9	1983
A HOUSE WITH LOVE IN IT VERA LYNN	17	1956
HOUSECALL SHABBA RANKS FEATURING MAXI PRIEST	8	1991
HOUSES IN MOTION TALKING HEADS	50	1981
HOW ABOUT THAT ADAM FAITH	4	1960
HOW AM I SUPPOSED TO LIVE WITHOUT YOU MICHAEL BOLTON	3	1990
HOW BIZARRE OMC	5	1996
HOW 'BOUT I LOVE YOU MORE MULL HISTORICAL SOCIETY	37	2004
HOW 'BOUT US CHAMPAIGN	5	1981
HOW 'BOUT US LULU	46	1993
HOW CAN I BE SURE DUSTY SPRINGFIELD	36	1970
HOW CAN I BE SURE DAVID CASSIDY	1	1972
HOW CAN I BE SURE? DARREN DAY	71	1998
HOW CAN I FALL BREATHE	48	1988
HOW CAN I FORGET YOU ELISA FIORILLO	50	1988
HOW CAN I KEEP FROM SINGING ENYA	32	1991
HOW CAN I LOVE YOU MORE M PEOPLE	8	1991
HOW CAN I MEET HER EVERLY BROTHERS	12	1962
HOW CAN I TELL HER FOURMOST	33	1964
HOW CAN THIS BE LOVE ANDREW GOLD	19	1978
HOW CAN WE BE LOVERS MICHAEL BOLTON	10	1990
HOW CAN WE EASE THE PAIN MAXI PRIEST FEATURING BERES HAMMOND	41	1988
HOW CAN YOU EXPECT ME TO BE TAKEN SERIOUSLY PET SHOP BOYS	4	1991
HOW CAN YOU TELL SANDIE SHAW	21	1965
HOW CAN YOU TELL ME IT'S OVER LORRAINE CATO	46	1993
HOW COME? [A] RONNIE LANE & SLIM CHANCE	11	1974
HOW COME [B] YOUSSOU N'DOUR & CANIBUS	52	1998
HOW COME [C] D12	4	2004
HOW COME, HOW LONG BABYFACE FEATURING STEVIE WONDER	10	1997
HOW COME IT NEVER RAINS DOGS D'AMOUR	44	1989
HOW COME YOU DON'T CALL ME ALICIA KEYS	26	2002
HOW COULD AN ANGEL BREAK MY HEART TONI BRAXTON WITH KENNY G	22	1997
HOW COULD I? (INSECURITY) ROACHFORD	34	1998
HOW COULD THIS GO WRONG EXILE	67	1979
HOW COULD WE DARE TO BE WRONG COLIN BLUNSTONE	45	1973
(HOW COULD YOU) BRING HIM HOME EAMON	61	2007
HOW DEEP IS YOUR LOVE PORTRAIT	41	1995
HOW DEEP IS YOUR LOVE [A] BEE GEES	3	1977
HOW DEEP IS YOUR LOVE [A] TAKE THAT	1	1996
HOW DEEP IS YOUR LOVE [B] DRU HILL FEATURING REDMAN	9	1998
HOW DID IT EVER COME TO THIS? EASYWORLD	50	2004
HOW DID YOU KNOW KURTIS MANTRONIK PRESENTS CHAMONIX	16	2003
HOW DO I BREATHE MARIO	21	2007
HOW DO I KNOW? MARLO	56	1999
HOW DO I LIVE TRISHA YEARWOOD	66	1997
HOW DO I LIVE LeANN RIMES	7	1998
HOW DO I SAY GOODBYE D-RAIL	63	2005
HOW DO YOU DO [A] AL HUDSON	57	1978
HOW DO YOU DO! [B] ROXETTE	13	1992
HOW DO YOU DO IT? GERRY & THE PACEMAKERS	1	1963
HOW DO YOU KNOW IT'S LOVE TERESA BREWER	21	1960
HOW DO YOU LIKE IT KEITH SWEAT	71	1994
HOW DO YOU SAY…LOVE DEEE-LITE	52	1991

Title / Artist	Peak Position	Year of Release
HOW DO YOU SPEAK TO AN ANGEL DEAN MARTIN	15	1954
HOW DO YOU WANT IT? 2PAC FEATURING K-CI & JOJO	17	1996
HOW DO YOU WANT ME TO LOVE YOU? 911	10	1998
HOW DOES IT FEEL [A] SLADE	15	1975
HOW DOES IT FEEL [B] ELECTROSET	27	1992
HOW DOES IT FEEL [C] WANNADIES	53	1996
(HOW DOES IT FEEL TO BE) ON TOP OF THE WORLD ENGLAND UNITED	9	1998
HOW DOES IT FEEL TO FEEL RIDE	58	1994
HOW DOES THAT GRAB YOU DARLIN' NANCY SINATRA	19	1966
HOW GEE BLACK MACHINE	17	1994
HOW HIGH CHARLATANS	6	1997
HOW HIGH THE MOON ELLA FITZGERALD	46	1960
HOW HIGH THE MOON GLORIA GAYNOR	33	1976
HOW HOW YELLO	59	1994
HOW I WANNA BE LOVED DANA DAWSON	42	1996
HOW I'M COMIN' LL COOL J	37	1993
HOW IT IS BIOHAZARD	62	1994
HOW IT SHOULD BE INSPIRAL CARPETS	49	1993
HOW LONG ACE	20	1974
HOW LONG ROD STEWART	41	1982
HOW LONG YAZZ & ASWAD	31	1993
HOW LONG? PAUL CARRACK	32	1996
HOW LONG DO I GET RAISSA	47	2000
HOW LONG HAS IT BEEN JIM REEVES	45	1965
HOW LONG'S A TEAR TAKE TO DRY? BEAUTIFUL SOUTH	12	1999
HOW LOW LUDACRIS	67	2010
HOW LUCKY YOU ARE SKIN	32	1996
HOW MANY LIES SPANDAU BALLET	34	1987
HOW MANY TEARS BOBBY VEE	10	1961
HOW MANY TEARS CAN YOU HIDE SHAKIN' STEVENS	47	1988
HOW MANY TIMES BROTHER BEYOND	62	1987
HOW MEN ARE AZTEC CAMERA	25	1988
HOW MUCH I FEEL ALIBI	58	1998
(HOW MUCH IS) THAT DOGGIE IN THE WINDOW LITA ROZA	1	1953
(HOW MUCH IS) THAT DOGGIE IN THE WINDOW PATTI PAGE	9	1953
HOW MUCH LOVE [A] LEO SAYER	10	1977
HOW MUCH LOVE [B] VIXEN	35	1990
HOW MUSIC CAME ABOUT (BOP B DA B DA DA) GAP BAND	61	1987
HOW RUDE SHE WAS TOWERS OF LONDON	30	2005
HOW SHE THREW IT ALL AWAY (EP) STYLE COUNCIL	41	1988
HOW SOON HENRY MANCINI	10	1964
HOW SOON IS NOW SMITHS	16	1985
HOW SOON IS NOW INNER SANCTUM	75	1998
HOW SOON IS NOW HUNDRED REASONS	47	2004
HOW SOON WE FORGET COLONEL ABRAMS	75	1987
HOW SWEET IT IS MARVIN GAYE	49	1964
HOW SWEET IT IS JUNIOR WALKER & THE ALL-STARS	22	1966
HOW THE HEART BEHAVES WAS (NOT WAS)	53	1990
HOW TO BE A MILLIONAIRE ABC	49	1984
HOW TO BE DEAD SNOW PATROL	39	2004
HOW TO FALL IN LOVE PART 1 BEE GEES	30	1994
HOW TO SAVE A LIFE FRAY	4	2007
HOW TO WIN YOUR LOVE ENGELBERT HUMPERDINCK	59	2000
HOW U LIKE BASS NORMAN BASS	17	2001
HOW WAS IT FOR YOU JAMES	32	1990
HOW WE DO GAME FEATURING 50 CENT	5	2005
HOW WE DO IT (ROUND OUR WAY) LLOYD FEATURING LUDACRIS	75	2008
HOW WILL I KNOW WHITNEY HOUSTON	5	1986
HOW WILL I KNOW (WHO YOU ARE) JESSICA	47	1999

Title / Artist	Peak Position	Year of Release
HOW WONDERFUL TO KNOW PEARL CARR & TEDDY JOHNSON	23	1961
HOW WONDERFUL YOU ARE GORDON HASKELL	2	2002
HOW WOULD U FEEL DAVID MORALES FEATURING LEA LORIEN	71	2004
HOW YOU GONNA ACT LIKE THAT TYRESE	30	2003
HOW YOU GONNA SEE ME NOW ALICE COOPER	61	1978
HOW YOU REMIND ME NICKELBACK	4	2002
HOWARD'S WAY SIMON MAY ORCHESTRA	21	1985
HOW'D I DO DAT BENTLEY RHYTHM ACE	57	2000
HOW'S IT GOING TO BE THIRD EYE BLIND	51	1998
HOW'S YOUR EVENING SO FAR JOSH WINK & LIL LOUIS	23	2000
HOWZAT SHERBET	4	1976
HUBBLE BUBBLE TOIL AND TROUBLE MANFRED MANN	11	1964
HUDSON STREET AGNELLI & NELSON	29	2000
HUG MY SOUL SAINT ETIENNE	32	1994
HUMAN [A] HUMAN LEAGUE	8	1986
HUMAN [B] PRETENDERS	33	1999
HUMAN [C] KILLERS	3	2008
HUMAN BEHAVIOUR BJORK	36	1993
HUMAN BEING BETA BAND	57	2001
HUMAN BEINGS SEAL	50	1998
HUMAN NATURE MICHAEL JACKSON	62	2009
HUMAN NATURE [A] GARY CLAIL ON-U SOUND SYSTEM	10	1991
HUMAN NATURE [B] MADONNA	8	1995
HUMAN RACING NIK KERSHAW	19	1984
HUMAN TOUCH [A] RICK SPRINGFIELD	23	1984
HUMAN TOUCH [B] BRUCE SPRINGSTEEN	11	1992
HUMAN WORK OF ART MAXI PRIEST	71	1990
HUMAN WORK OF ART CLIFF RICHARD	24	1993
HUMANISTIC KAWALA	68	2000
HUMANITY REBEL MC FEATURING LINCOLM THOMPSON	62	1992
HUMMING BIRD FRANKIE LAINE	16	1955
HUMP DE BUMP RED HOT CHILI PEPPERS	41	2007
HUMPIN' GAP BAND	36	1981
HUMPIN' AROUND BOBBY BROWN	8	1992
101 DAM-NATIONS SCARLET PARTY	44	1982
HUNDRED MILE HIGH CITY OCEAN COLOUR SCENE	4	1997
100MPH EL PRESIDENTE	37	2005
A HUNDRED POUNDS OF CLAY CRAIG DOUGLAS	9	1961
HUNG UP [A] PAUL WELLER	11	1994
HUNG UP [B] MADONNA	1	2005
HUNGAH KARYN WHITE	69	1994
THE HUNGER DISTILLERS	48	2004
HUNGER STRIKE TEMPLE OF THE DOG	51	1992
HUNGRY KOSHEEN	13	2002
HUNGRY EYES EYEOPENER	16	2004
HUNGRY FOR HEAVEN DIO	56	1985
HUNGRY FOR LOVE JOHNNY KIDD & THE PIRATES	20	1963
HUNGRY HEART BRUCE SPRINGSTEEN	28	1980
HUNGRY LIKE THE WOLF DURAN DURAN	5	1982
HUNT BARRY RYAN	34	1969
HUNTER [A] BJORK	44	1998
HUNTER [B] DIDO	17	2001
HUNTING FOR WITCHES BLOC PARTY	22	2007
HUNTING HIGH AND LOW A-HA	5	1988
HURDY GURDY MAN DONOVAN	4	1968
HURRICANE [A] BOB DYLAN	43	1976
HURRICANE [B] WARM JETS	34	1998
HURRICANE [C] ATHLETE	31	2007
HURRICANE JANE BLACK KIDS	36	2008
HURRY HOME WAVELENGTH	17	1982
HURRY UP AND WAIT STEREOPHONICS	11	1999
HURRY UP ENGLAND – THE PEOPLE'S ANTHEM SHAM 69 & THE SPECIAL ASSEMBLY	10	2006
HURRY UP HARRY SHAM 69	10	1978
HURT [A] MANHATTANS	4	1976
HURT [A] ELVIS PRESLEY	37	1976
HURT [B] JOHNNY CASH	42	2003
HURT [C] CHRISTINA AGUILERA	11	2006
HURT BY LOVE INEZ FOXX	40	1964
HURT ME SO BAD LULU	42	1999
HURT SO GOOD SUSAN CADOGAN	4	1975
HURT SO GOOD JIMMY SOMERVILLE	15	1995
HURTFUL ERIK HASSLE	59	2010
HURTING KIND (I'VE GOT MY EYES ON YOU) ROBERT PLANT	45	1990
HUSAN BHANGRA KNIGHTS VS HUSAN	7	2003
HUSBAND FLUFFY	58	1996
HUSH [A] DEEP PURPLE	62	1988
HUSH [A] KULA SHAKER	2	1997
HUSH [B] LL COOL J FEATURING 7 AURELIUS	3	2005
HUSH BOY BASEMENT JAXX	27	2006
HUSH HUSH PUSSYCAT DOLLS	17	2009
HUSH NOT A WORD TO MARY JOHN ROWLES	12	1968
THE HUSTLE VAN McCOY WITH THE SOUL CITY SYMPHONY	3	1975
HUSTLE! (TO THE MUSIC...) FUNKY WORM	13	1988
HUSTLER'S AMBITION 50 CENT	13	2006
HYBRID EAT STATIC	41	1997
HYMN [A] ULTRAVOX	11	1982
HYMN [B] MOBY	31	1994
HYMN [C] ULTRAMARINE FEATURING DAVID McALMONT	65	1996
HYMN TO HER PRETENDERS	8	1986
HYMNE A L'AMOUR ELAINE PAIGE	68	1995
HYPE! HYPE! SLK	22	2005
HYPER MUSIC MUSE	24	2001
HYPERACTIVE THOMAS DOLBY	17	1984
HYPERBALLAD BJORK	8	1996
HYPERREAL SHAMEN	29	1991
HYPNOSIS MUD	16	1973
HYPNOTIC ST-8 ALTERN 8	16	1992
HYPNOTIC TANGO MASTER BLASTER	64	2004
HYPNOTISED [A] CABARET VOLTAIRE	66	1989
HYPNOTISED [B] SIMPLE MINDS	18	1995
HYPNOTISED [C] PAUL OAKENFOLD	57	2003
HYPNOTISING KID CRÈME FEATURING CHARLISE	31	2003
HYPNOTIZE [A] SCRITTI POLITTI	68	1984
HYPNOTIZE [B] D-INFLUENCE	33	1997
HYPNOTIZE [C] NOTORIOUS B.I.G.	10	1997
HYPNOTIZE [D] SYSTEM OF A DOWN	48	2005
HYPNOTIZED PLIES FEATURING AKON	66	2008
HYPNOTIZIN' WINX	35	1996
HYPOCRITE [A] LUSH	52	1994
HYPOCRITE [B] SPECIALS	66	1996
HYSTERIA [A] DEF LEPPARD	26	1987
HYSTERIA [B] MUSE	17	2003

I

Title / Artist	Peak Position	Year of Release
I [A] PETEY PABLO	51	2002
I [B] JOY ZIPPER	73	2005
I ADORE MI AMOR COLOR ME BADD	44	1991
I ADORE YOU CARON WHEELER	59	1992
I AIN'T GOIN' OUT LIKE THAT CYPRESS HILL	15	1993
I AIN'T GONNA CRY LITTLE ANGELS	26	1991
I AIN'T GONNA STAND FOR IT STEVIE WONDER	10	1981
I AIN'T GOT TIME ANYMORE CLIFF RICHARD	21	1970
I AIN'T LOSING ANY SLEEP SUNSHINE UNDERGROUND	47	2006
I AIN'T LYIN' GEORGE McCRAE	12	1975
I AIN'T MAD AT CHA 2PAC FEATURING K-CI & JOJO	13	1996
I AIN'T NEW TA THIS ICE-T	62	1993
I AIN'T SAYING MY GOODBYES TOM VEK	45	2005
I ALMOST FELT LIKE CRYING CRAIG McLACHLAN & CHECK 1-2	50	1990
I ALMOST LOST MY MIND PAT BOONE	14	1956
I ALONE LIVE	48	1995
I AM [A] CHAKRA	24	1997
I AM [B] SUGGS	38	1998
I AM [C] MARY J BLIGE	34	2010
I AM A CIDER DRINKER 2007 WURZELS FEATURING TONY BLACKBURN	57	2007
I AM A CIDER DRINKER (PALOMA BLANCA) WURZELS	3	1976
I AM A ROCK SIMON & GARFUNKEL	17	1966
I AM BLESSED ETERNAL	7	1995
I AM DOWN SALT-N-PEPA	41	1988
I AM I QUEENSRYCHE	40	1995
I AM, I FEEL ALISHA'S ATTIC	14	1996
I AM (I'M ME) TWISTED SISTER	18	1983
I AM IN LOVE WITH THE WORLD CHICKEN SHED	15	1997
I AM LV LV	64	1996
I AM MINE PEARL JAM	26	2002
I AM NOT MY HAIR INDIA.ARIE	65	2006
I AM ONE [A] SMASHING PUMPKINS	73	1992
I AM ONE [B] W.A.S.P.	56	1992
I AM THE BEAT LOOK	6	1981
I AM THE BLACK GOLD OF THE SUN NUYORICAN SOUL FEATURING JOCELYN BROWN	31	1997
I AM THE LAW ANTHRAX	32	1987
I AM THE MOB CATATONIA	40	1997
I AM THE MUSIC HEAR ME! MILLIONAIRE HIPPIES	52	1993
I AM THE MUSIC MAN BLACK LACE	52	1989
I AM THE NEWS OCEAN COLOUR SCENE	31	2000
I AM THE ONE CRACKOUT	72	2002
I AM THE RESURRECTION STONE ROSES	33	1992
I AM THE SUN DARK STAR	31	2000
I AM WHAT I AM [A] GREYHOUND	20	1972
I AM WHAT I AM [B] GLORIA GAYNOR	13	1984
I AM WHAT I AM [C] MARK OWEN	29	1997
I AM...I SAID NEIL DIAMOND	4	1971
I AN'T MOVIN' DES'REE	44	1994
I APOLOGISE PJ PROBY	11	1965
I BE THE PROPHET STARVING SOULS	66	1995
I BEG YOUR PARDON KON KAN	5	1989
I BEGIN TO WONDER DANNII MINOGUE	2	2003
I BELIEVE [A] FRANKIE LAINE	1	1953
I BELIEVE [A] DAVID WHITFIELD	49	1960
I BELIEVE [A] BACHELORS	2	1964
I BELIEVE [A] ROBSON GREEN & JEROME FLYNN	1	1995
I BELIEVE [B] EMF	6	1991
I BELIEVE [C] REESE PROJECT	74	1992
I BELIEVE [D] BON JOVI	11	1993
I BELIEVE [E] ROBERT PLANT	64	1993
I BELIEVE [F] MARCELLA DETROIT	11	1994
I BELIEVE [G] SOUNDS OF BLACKNESS	17	1994
I BELIEVE [H] BLESSID UNION OF SOULS	29	1995
I BELIEVE [I] HAPPY CLAPPERS	7	1995
I BELIEVE [J] BOOTH & THE BAD ANGEL	25	1996
I BELIEVE [K] ABSOLUTE FEATURING SUZANNE PALMER	38	1997
I BELIEVE [L] LANGE FEATURING SARAH DWYER	68	1999
I BELIEVE [M] JAMESTOWN FEATURING JOCELYN BROWN	62	1999

Title / Artist	Peak Position	Year of Release
I BELIEVE [N] STEPHEN GATELY	11	2000
I BELIEVE (A SOULFUL RECORDING) TEARS FOR FEARS	23	1985
I BELIEVE I CAN FLY R KELLY	1	1997
I BELIEVE I'M GONNA LOVE YOU FRANK SINATRA	34	1975
I BELIEVE IN A THING CALLED LOVE DARKNESS	2	2003
I BELIEVE IN CHRISTMAS TWEENIES	9	2001
I BELIEVE IN FATHER CHRISTMAS GREG LAKE	2	1975
I BELIEVE (IN LOVE) [A] HOT CHOCOLATE	8	1971
I BELIEVE IN LOVE [B] COOPER	50	2002
I BELIEVE IN MIRACLES JACKSON SISTERS	72	1987
I BELIEVE IN MIRACLES PASADENAS	34	1992
I BELIEVE IN THE SPIRIT TIM BURGESS	44	2003
I BELIEVE IN YOU [A] OUR TRIBE	42	1993
I BELIEVE IN YOU [A] AMP FIDDLER	72	2004
I BELIEVE IN YOU [B] KYLIE MINOGUE	2	2004
I BELIEVE IN YOU AND ME WHITNEY HOUSTON	16	1997
I BELIEVE MY HEART DUNCAN JAMES & KEEDIE	2	2004
I BELIEVE YOU DOROTHY MOORE	20	1977
I BELONG KATHY KIRBY	36	1965
I BELONG TO YOU [A] WHITNEY HOUSTON	54	1991
I BELONG TO YOU [B] GINA G	6	1996
I BELONG TO YOU [C] LENNY KRAVITZ	75	1998
I BET YOU LOOK GOOD ON THE DANCEFLOOR ARCTIC MONKEYS	1	2005
I BREATHE AGAIN ADAM RICKITT	5	1999
I BRUISE EASILY NATASHA BEDINGFIELD	12	2005
I CALL IT LOVE LIONEL RICHIE	45	2006
I CALL YOUR NAME A-HA	44	1990
I CALLED U LIL' LOUIS	16	1990
I CAN NAS	19	2003
I CAN BE TAIO CRUZ	18	2008
I CAN BUY YOU A CAMP	46	2001
I CAN CALL YOU PORTRAIT	61	1995
I CAN CAST A SPELL DISCO TEX PRESENTS CLOUDBURST	35	2001
I CAN CLIMB MOUNTAINS HELL IS FOR HEROES	41	2002
I CAN DANCE [A] BRIAN POOLE & THE TREMELOES	21	1963
I CAN DANCE [B] DJ 'FAST' EDDIE	47	1989
I CAN DO IT RUBETTES	7	1975
I CAN DO THIS MONIE LOVE	37	1989
I CAN DREAM SKUNK ANANSIE	41	1995
I CAN DREAM ABOUT YOU DAN HARTMAN	12	1985
I CAN DRIVE SHAKESPEAR'S SISTER	30	1996
I CAN FEEL IT SILENCERS	62	1993
I CAN FEEL YOU ANASTACIA	67	2008
I CAN HEAR MUSIC BEACH BOYS	10	1969
I CAN HEAR THE GRASS GROW MOVE	5	1967
I CAN HEAR VOICES/CANED AND UNABLE HI-GATE	12	2000
I CAN HEAR YOUR HEARTBEAT CHRIS REA	60	1983
I CAN HELP BILLY SWAN	6	1974
I CAN HELP ELVIS PRESLEY	30	1983
I CAN LOVE YOU LIKE THAT ALL-4-ONE	33	1995
I CAN MAKE IT BETTER [A] WHISPERS	44	1981
I CAN MAKE IT BETTER [B] LUTHER VANDROSS	44	1996
I CAN MAKE YOU FEEL GOOD SHALAMAR	7	1982
I CAN MAKE YOU FEEL GOOD KAVANA	8	1997
I CAN MAKE YOU FEEL LIKE MAXX	56	1995
I CAN ONLY DISAPPOINT U MANSUN	8	2000
I CAN PROVE IT TONY ETORIA	21	1977
I CAN PROVE IT PHIL FEARON	8	1986
I CAN SEE CLEARLY DEBORAH HARRY	23	1993
I CAN SEE CLEARLY NOW JOHNNY NASH	5	1972
I CAN SEE CLEARLY NOW HOTHOUSE FLOWERS	23	1990
I CAN SEE CLEARLY NOW JIMMY CLIFF	23	1994
I CAN SEE FOR MILES WHO	10	1967
I CAN SEE HER NOW DRAMATIS	57	1982
I CAN SEE IT BLANCMANGE	71	1986
I CAN SING A RAINBOW – LOVE IS BLUE (MEDLEY) DELLS	15	1969
I CAN TAKE OR LEAVE YOUR LOVING HERMAN'S HERMITS	11	1968
I CAN TRANSFORM YA CHRIS BROWN FEATURING LIL' WAYNE	26	2009
I CANNOT GIVE YOU MY LOVE CLIFF RICHARD	13	2005
I CAN'T ASK FOR ANY MORE THAN YOU CLIFF RICHARD	17	1976
I CAN'T BE WITH YOU CRANBERRIES	23	1995
I CAN'T BELIEVE YOU'RE GONE WEBB BROTHERS	69	2001
I CAN'T BREAK DOWN SINEAD QUINN	2	2003
I CAN'T COME DOWN EMBRACE	54	2006
I CAN'T CONTROL MYSELF TROGGS	2	1966
I CAN'T DANCE GENESIS	7	1992
I CAN'T DECIDE SCISSOR SISTERS	64	2007
I CAN'T DENY IT ROD STEWART	26	2001
I CAN'T EXPLAIN WHO	8	1965
I CAN'T FACE THE WORLD LEMON TREES	52	1993
(I CAN'T GET ME NO) SATISFACTION DEVO	41	1978
I CAN'T GET NEXT TO YOU TEMPTATIONS	13	1970
(I CAN'T GET NO) SATISFACTION ROLLING STONES	1	1965
(I CAN'T GET NO) SATISFACTION BUBBLEROCK	29	1974
I CAN'T GET NO SLEEP MASTERS AT WORK PRESENT INDIA	44	1995
I CAN'T GET YOU OUT OF MY MIND YVONNE ELLIMAN	17	1977
I CAN'T GO FOR THAT (NO CAN DO) DARYL HALL & JOHN OATES	8	1982
(I CAN'T HELP) FALLING IN LOVE WITH YOU UB40	1	1993
I CAN'T HELP IT [A] JOHNNY TILLOTSON	41	1962
I CAN'T HELP IT [B] JUNIOR	53	1982
I CAN'T HELP IT [C] BANANARAMA	20	1988
I CAN'T HELP MYSELF [A] FOUR TOPS	10	1965
I CAN'T HELP MYSELF [A] DONNIE ELBERT	11	1972
I CAN'T HELP MYSELF [B] ORANGE JUICE	42	1982
I CAN'T HELP MYSELF [C] JOEY LAWRENCE	27	1993
I CAN'T HELP MYSELF [D] JULIA FORDHAM	62	1994
I CAN'T HELP MYSELF [E] LUCID	7	1998
I CAN'T IMAGINE THE WORLD WITHOUT ME ECHOBELLY	39	1994
I CAN'T LEAVE YOU ALONE GEORGE McCRAE	9	1974
I CAN'T LEAVE YOU ALONE TRACIE YOUNG	60	1985
I CAN'T LET GO [A] HOLLIES	2	1966
I CAN'T LET GO [B] MARTI WEBB	65	1987
I CAN'T LET MAGGIE GO HONEYBUS	8	1968
I CAN'T LET YOU GO IAN VAN DAHL	20	2003
I CAN'T LET YOU GO [A] HAYWOODE	50	1984
I CAN'T LET YOU GO [B] 52ND STREET	57	1986
I CAN'T LET YOU GO [C] MACK VIBE FEATURING JACQUELINE	53	1995
I CAN'T LIVE A DREAM OSMONDS	37	1976
I CAN'T MAKE A MISTAKE MC LYTE	46	1998
I CAN'T MAKE IT SMALL FACES	26	1967
I CAN'T MAKE IT ALONE PJ PROBY	37	1966
I CAN'T MAKE IT ALONE MARIA McKEE	74	1993
I CAN'T MAKE YOU LOVE ME [A] BONNIE RAITT	50	1991
I CAN'T MAKE YOU LOVE ME [B] GEORGE MICHAEL	3	1997
I CAN'T READ DAVID BOWIE	73	1998
I CAN'T READ YOU DANIEL BEDINGFIELD	6	2003
I CAN'T SAY GOODBYE KIM WILDE	51	1990
I CAN'T SAY GOODBYE TO YOU HELEN REDDY	43	1981
I CAN'T SEE NICOLE RAY	55	1998
I CAN'T SLEEP BABY (IF I) R KELLY	1	2000
I CAN'T STAND IT [A] SPENCER DAVIS GROUP	47	1964
I CAN'T STAND IT [B] TWENTY 4 SEVEN FEATURING CAPTAIN HOLLYWOOD	7	1990
I CAN'T STAND MY BABY REZILLOS	71	1979
I CAN'T STAND THE RAIN ANN PEEBLES	41	1974
I CAN'T STAND THE RAIN ERUPTION FEATURING PRECIOUS WILSON	5	1978
I CAN'T STAND THE RAIN TINA TURNER	57	1985
I CAN'T STAND UP FOR FALLING DOWN ELVIS COSTELLO & THE ATTRACTIONS	4	1980
I CAN'T STOP [A] OSMONDS	12	1974
I CAN'T STOP [B] GARY NUMAN	27	1986
I CAN'T STOP [C] SANDY RIVERA	58	2003
I CAN'T STOP LOVIN' YOU (THOUGH I TRY) LEO SAYER	6	1978
I CAN'T STOP LOVING YOU RAY CHARLES	1	1962
I CAN'T STOP THIS FEELING I'VE GOT RAZORLIGHT	44	2007
I CAN'T TAKE THE POWER OFF-SHORE	7	1991
I CAN'T TELL A WALTZ FROM A TANGO ALMA COGAN	6	1954
I CAN'T TELL THE BOTTOM FROM THE TOP HOLLIES	7	1970
I CAN'T TELL YOU WHY BROWNSTONE	27	1995
I CAN'T TURN AROUND JM SILK	62	1986
I CAN'T TURN AWAY SAVANNA	61	1981
I CAN'T TURN YOU LOOSE OTIS REDDING	29	1966
I CAN'T WAIT [A] STEVIE NICKS	47	1986
I CAN'T WAIT [B] NU SHOOZ	2	1986
I CAN'T WAIT [B] LADIES FIRST	19	2002
I CAN'T WAIT ANYMORE SAXON	71	1988
I CARE SOUL II SOUL	17	1995
I CAUGHT YOU OUT REBECCA DE RUVO	72	1994
I CHANGED MY MIND KEYSHIA COLE	48	2006
I CHOOSE LIFE KEISHA WHITE	63	2006
I CLOSE MY EYES AND COUNT TO TEN DUSTY SPRINGFIELD	4	1968
I COME FROM ANOTHER PLANET, BABY JULIAN COPE	34	1996
I CONFESS BEAT	54	1982
I COULD BE AN ANGLE EIGHTIES MATCHBOX B-LINE DISASTER	35	2004
I COULD BE HAPPY ALTERED IMAGES	7	1981
I COULD BE SO GOOD FOR YOU DENNIS WATERMAN WITH THE DENNIS WATERMAN BAND	3	1980
I COULD BE THE ONE STACIE ORRICO	34	2004
I COULD EASILY FALL CLIFF RICHARD & THE SHADOWS	6	1964
I COULD FALL IN LOVE WITH YOU ERASURE	21	2007
I COULD HAVE BEEN A DREAMER DIO	69	1987
I COULD NEVER LOVE ANOTHER TEMPTATIONS	47	1968
I COULD NEVER MISS YOU (MORE THAN I DO) LULU	62	1981
I COULD NEVER TAKE THE PLACE OF YOUR MAN PRINCE	29	1987
I COULD NOT LOVE YOU MORE BEE GEES	14	1997
I COULD SING OF YOUR LOVE FOREVER DELIRIOUS?	40	2001
I COULDN'T LIVE WITHOUT YOUR LOVE PETULA CLARK	6	1966
I COUNT THE TEARS DRIFTERS	28	1961
I CRIED FOR YOU [A] RICKY STEVENS	34	1961
I CRIED FOR YOU [B] KATIE MELUA	35	2005
I DECIDED SOLANGE	27	2008
I DID WHAT I DID FOR MARIA TONY CHRISTIE	2	1971

	Peak Position	Year of Release
I DIDN'T KNOW I LOVED YOU (TILL I SAW YOU ROCK 'N' ROLL) GARY GLITTER	4	1972
I DIDN'T KNOW I LOVED YOU (TILL I SAW YOU ROCK 'N' ROLL) ROCK GODDESS	57	1984
I DIDN'T KNOW I WAS LOOKING FOR LOVE (EP) EVERYTHING BUT THE GIRL	72	1993
I DIDN'T KNOW MY OWN STRENGTH WHITNEY HOUSTON	44	2009
I DIDN'T MEAN IT STATUS QUO	21	1994
I DIDN'T MEAN TO HURT YOU ROCKIN' BERRIES	43	1964
I DIDN'T MEAN TO TURN YOU ON ROBERT PALMER	9	1986
I DIDN'T WANT TO NEED YOU HEART	47	1990
I DIE: YOU DIE GARY NUMAN	6	1980
I DIG YOU BABY MARVIN RAINWATER	19	1958
I DISAPPEAR METALLICA	35	2000
I DO JAMELIA	36	1999
I DO I DO I DO I DO I DO ABBA	38	1975
I DO NOT HOOK UP KELLY CLARKSON	36	2009
I DO WHAT I DO...THEME FOR '9 1/2 WEEKS' JOHN TAYLOR	42	1986
I DON'T BELIEVE IN 'IF' ANYMORE ROGER WHITTAKER	8	1970
I DON'T BELIEVE IN MIRACLES [A] COLIN BLUNSTONE	31	1972
I DON'T BELIEVE IN MIRACLES [B] SINITTA	22	1988
I DON'T BELIEVE YOU P!NK	62	2009
I DON'T BLAME YOU AT ALL SMOKEY ROBINSON & THE MIRACLES	11	1971
I DON'T CARE [A] LIBERACE	28	1956
I DON'T CARE [B] LOS BRAVOS	16	1966
I DON'T CARE [C] SHAKESPEAR'S SISTER	7	1992
I DON'T CARE [D] TONY DE VIT	65	2002
I DON'T CARE [E] FALL OUT BOY	33	2008
I DON'T CARE IF THE SUN DON'T SHINE ELVIS PRESLEY	23	1956
I DON'T DANCE CHAD & RYAN	57	2007
I DON'T EVEN KNOW IF I SHOULD CALL YOU BABY SOUL FAMILY SENSATION	49	1991
I DON'T EVER WANT TO SEE YOU AGAIN UNCLE SAM	30	1998
I DON'T FEEL LIKE DANCIN' SCISSOR SISTERS	1	2006
I DON'T KNOW [A] RUTH	66	1997
I DON'T KNOW [B] HONEYZ	28	2001
I DON'T KNOW ANYBODY ELSE BLACK BOX	4	1990
I DON'T KNOW HOW TO LOVE HIM PETULA CLARK	47	1972
I DON'T KNOW HOW TO LOVE HIM YVONNE ELLIMAN	47	1972
I DON'T KNOW IF IT'S RIGHT EVELYN 'CHAMPAGNE' KING	67	1979
I DON'T KNOW WHAT IT IS RUFUS WAINWRIGHT	74	2004
I DON'T KNOW WHAT IT IS BUT I LOVE IT CHRIS REA	65	1984
I DON'T KNOW WHAT YOU WANT BUT I CAN'T GIVE IT TO YOU PET SHOP BOYS	15	1999
I DON'T KNOW WHERE IT COMES FROM RIDE	46	1994
I DON'T KNOW WHY [A] EDEN KANE	7	1962
I DON'T KNOW WHY [B] SHAWN COLVIN	52	1993
I DON'T KNOW WHY [C] ANDY & DAVID WILLIAMS	37	1973
(I DON'T KNOW WHY) BUT I DO CLARENCE 'FROGMAN' HENRY	3	1961
I DON'T KNOW WHY I LOVE YOU HOUSE OF LOVE	41	1989
I DON'T LIKE MONDAYS BOOMTOWN RATS	1	1979
I DON'T LOVE YOU MY CHEMICAL ROMANCE	13	2007
I DON'T LOVE YOU ANYMORE QUIREBOYS	24	1990
I DON'T LOVE YOU BUT I THINK I LIKE YOU GILBERT O'SULLIVAN	14	1975
I DON'T MIND BUZZCOCKS	55	1978
I DON'T MIND AT ALL BOURGEOIS TAGG	35	1988
I DON'T NEED A MAN PUSSYCAT DOLLS	7	2006
I DON'T NEED ANYTHING SANDIE SHAW	50	1967
I DON'T NEED NO DOCTOR (LIVE) W.A.S.P.	31	1987
I DON'T NEED TO TELL HER LURKERS	49	1978
I DON'T REALLY CARE K-GEE	22	2000
I DON'T REMEMBER PETER GABRIEL	62	1983
I DON'T SMOKE DJ DEE KLINE	11	2000
I DON'T THINK SO DINOSAUR JR	67	1995
I DON'T THINK THAT MAN SHOULD SLEEP ALONE RAY PARKER JR	13	1987
I DON'T WANNA BE A STAR CORONA	22	1995
I DON'T WANNA DANCE EDDY GRANT	1	1982
I DON'T WANNA FIGHT TINA TURNER	7	1993
I DON'T WANNA GET HURT DONNA SUMMER	7	1989
I DON'T WANNA GO ON WITH YOU LIKE THAT ELTON JOHN	30	1988
(I DON'T WANNA GO TO) CHELSEA ELVIS COSTELLO & THE ATTRACTIONS	16	1978
I DON'T WANNA KNOW [A] MARIO WINANS FEATURING ENYA & P DIDDY	1	2004
I DON'T WANNA KNOW [B] NEW FOUND GLORY	48	2005
I DON'T WANNA LOSE AT LOVE TANITA TIKARAM	73	1998
I DON'T WANNA LOSE YOU [A] KANDIDATE	11	1979
I DON'T WANNA LOSE YOU [B] TINA TURNER	8	1989
I DON'T WANNA PLAY HOUSE TAMMY WYNETTE	37	1976
I DON'T WANNA TAKE THIS PAIN DANNII MINOGUE	40	1992
I DON'T WANNA TO LOSE YOUR LOVE EMOTIONS	40	1977
I DON'T WANT A LOVER TEXAS	8	1989
I DON'T WANT CONTROL OF YOU TEENAGE FANCLUB	43	1997
I DON'T WANT NOBODY (TELLIN' ME WHAT TO DO) CHERIE AMORE	33	2000
I DON'T WANT OUR LOVING TO DIE HERD	5	1968
I DON'T WANT TO TONI BRAXTON	9	1997
I DON'T WANT TO BE GAVIN DEGRAW	38	2005
I DON'T WANT TO BE A FREAK (BUT I CAN'T HELP MYSELF) DYNASTY	20	1979
I DON'T WANT TO BE A HERO JOHNNY HATES JAZZ	11	1987
I DON'T WANT TO GO ON WITHOUT YOU MOODY BLUES	33	1965
I DON'T WANT TO HURT YOU (EVERY SINGLE TIME) FRANK BLACK	63	1996
I DON'T WANT TO KNOW DONNAS	55	2005
I DON'T WANT TO LOSE MY WAY DREAMCATCHER	14	2002
I DON'T WANT TO MISS A THING AEROSMITH	4	1998
I DON'T WANT TO PUT A HOLD ON YOU BERNI FLINT	3	1977
I DON'T WANT TO TALK ABOUT IT ROD STEWART	1	1977
I DON'T WANT TO TALK ABOUT IT EVERYTHING BUT THE GIRL	3	1988
I DON'T WANT TO WAIT PAULA COLE	43	1998
I DON'T WANT YOUR LOVE DURAN DURAN	14	1988
I DREAM TILT	69	1995
I DREAMED BEVERLEY SISTERS	24	1957
I DREAMED A DREAM PATTI LUPONE	45	2009
I DREAMED A DREAM SUSAN BOYLE	37	2009
I DROVE ALL NIGHT CYNDI LAUPER	7	1989
I DROVE ALL NIGHT ROY ORBISON	7	1992
I EAT CANNIBALS PART 1 TOTO COELO	8	1982
I ENJOY BEING A GIRL PAT SUZUKI	49	1960
I FEEL A CRY COMING ON HANK LOCKLIN	29	1966
I FEEL DIVINE S-J	30	1998
I FEEL FINE BEATLES	1	1964
I FEEL FINE WET WET WET	30	1990
I FEEL FOR YOU [A] CHAKA KHAN	1	1984
I FEEL FOR YOU [B] BOB SINCLAR	9	2000
I FEEL FREE CREAM	11	1966
I FEEL GOOD THINGS FOR YOU DADDY'S FAVOURITE	44	1998
I FEEL IT [A] MOBY	38	1993
I FEEL IT [B] LORRAINE	29	2006
I FEEL JUST LIKE A CHILD DEVENDRA BANHART	68	2005
I FEEL LIKE BUDDY HOLLY ALVIN STARDUST	7	1984
I FEEL LIKE WALKIN' IN THE RAIN MILLIE JACKSON	55	1984
I FEEL LOVE [A] DONNA SUMMER	1	1977
I FEEL LOVE [A] MESSIAH FEATURING PRECIOUS WILSON	19	1992
I FEEL LOVE [A] VANESSA-MAE	41	1997
I FEEL LOVE [B] CRW	15	2000
I FEEL LOVE COMIN' ON FELICE TAYLOR	11	1967
I FEEL LOVE COMIN' ON DANA	66	1982
I FEEL LOVE (MEDLEY) BRONSKI BEAT & MARC ALMOND	3	1985
I FEEL LOVED DEPECHE MODE	12	2001
I FEEL SO BOX CAR RACER	41	2002
I FEEL SO BAD ELVIS PRESLEY	4	1961
I FEEL SO FINE KMC FEATURING DAHNY	33	2002
I FEEL SOMETHING IN THE AIR CHER	43	1966
I FEEL STEREO DINO LENNY	60	2002
I FEEL THE EARTH MOVE MARTIKA	7	1989
I FEEL YOU [A] LOVE DECADE	34	1992
I FEEL YOU [B] DEPECHE MODE	8	1993
I FEEL YOU [C] PETER ANDRE	1	1996
I FINALLY FOUND SOMEONE BARBRA STREISAND & BRYAN ADAMS	10	1997
I FORGOT [A] COOLNOTES	63	1984
I FORGOT [B] LIONEL RICHIE	34	2001
I FOUGHT THE LAW BOBBY FULLER FOUR	33	1966
I FOUGHT THE LAW CLASH	29	1988
I FOUGHT THE LLOYDS OYSTAR	25	2008
I FOUND HEAVEN TAKE THAT	15	1992
I FOUND LOVE [A] DARLENE DAVIS	55	1987
I FOUND LOVE [B] LONE JUSTICE	45	1987
I FOUND LOVE [C] C & C MUSIC FACTORY FEATURING ZELMA DAVIS	26	1995
I FOUND LOVIN' FATBACK	7	1984
I FOUND LOVIN' STEVE WALSH	9	1987
I FOUND OUT [A] CHRISTIANS	56	1990
I FOUND OUT [B] PIGEON DETECTIVES	39	2006
I FOUND OUT THE HARD WAY FOUR PENNIES	14	1964
I FOUND SOMEONE [A] CHER	5	1987
I FOUND SOMEONE [B] BILLY & SARAH GAINES	48	1997
I FOUND SUNSHINE CHI-LITES	35	1974
I FOUND U AXWELL FEATURING MAX C	6	2007
I (FRIDAY NIGHT) DUBSTAR	37	2000
I GAVE IT UP (WHEN I FELL IN LOVE) LUTHER VANDROSS	28	1988
I GAVE MY EYES TO STEVIE WONDER MILLION DEAD	72	2004
I GAVE YOU EVERYTHING CODE RED	50	1996
I GAVE YOU MY HEART (DIDN'T I) HOT CHOCOLATE	13	1984
I GET A KICK OUT OF YOU GARY SHEARSTON	7	1974
I GET A LITTLE SENTIMENTAL OVER YOU NEW SEEKERS	5	1974
I GET ALONG PET SHOP BOYS	18	2002
I GET AROUND BEACH BOYS	7	1964
I GET IT IN 50 CENT	75	2009

Title	Artist	Peak Position	Year of Release
I GET LIFTED	BARBARA TUCKER	33	1994
I GET LONELY	JANET JACKSON	5	1998
I GET SO EXCITED	EQUALS	44	1968
I GET THE SWEETEST FEELING	JACKIE WILSON	3	1972
I GET THE SWEETEST FEELING	LIZ McCLARNON	5	2006
I GET WEAK	BELINDA CARLISLE	10	1988
I GIVE	TAKE 5	70	1998
I GIVE IT ALL TO YOU	MARY KIANI	35	1995
I GIVE YOU MY HEART	MR PRESIDENT	52	1997
I GO APE	NEIL SEDAKA	9	1959
I GO TO EXTREMES	BILLY JOEL	70	1990
I GO TO PIECES (EVERYTIME)	GERRI GRANGER	50	1978
I GO TO SLEEP	PRETENDERS	7	1981
I GO WILD	ROLLING STONES	29	1995
I GOT 5 ON IT	LUNIZ	3	1996
I GOT A FEELING	RICKY NELSON	27	1958
I GOT A GIRL	LOU BEGA	55	1999
I GOT A LITTLE SONG	OFF-SHORE	64	1991
I GOT A MAN	POSITIVE K	43	1993
I GOT DA FEELIN'	SWEET TEE	31	1988
I GOT IT FROM MY MAMA	WILL.I.AM	38	2007
I GOT IT GOIN' ON [A]	TONE LOC	55	1989
I GOT IT GOIN' ON [B]	US3 FEATURING KOBIE POWELL & RAHSAAN	52	1994
I GOT MINE	MOTORHEAD	46	1983
I GOT MY EDUCATION	UNCANNY ALLIANCE	39	1992
I GOT RHYTHM	HAPPENINGS	28	1967
I GOT SOMEBODY ELSE	CHANGING FACES	42	1997
I GOT SOUL	YOUNG SOUL REBELS	10	2009
I GOT STUNG	ELVIS PRESLEY	1	1959
I GOT THE MUSIC IN ME	KIKI DEE BAND	19	1974
I GOT THE VIBRATION/A POSITIVE VIBRATION	BLACK BOX	21	1996
I GOT THIS FEELING	BABY BUMPS	22	2000
I GOT TO SING	J.A.L.N. BAND	40	1977
I GOT YOU [A]	SPLIT ENZ	12	1980
I GOT YOU [B]	LEONA LEWIS	14	2010
I GOT YOU BABE	SONNY & CHER	1	1965
I GOT YOU BABE	UB40 FEATURING CHRISSIE HYNDE	1	1985
I GOT YOU BABE	CHER WITH BEAVIS & BUTT-HEAD	35	1994
I GOT YOU BABE	AVID MERRION/DAVINA McCALL/PATSY KENSIT	5	2005
I GOT YOU (I FEEL GOOD)	JAMES BROWN & THE FAMOUS FLAMES	29	1966
I GOTTA FEELING	BLACK EYED PEAS	1	2009
I GUESS I'LL ALWAYS LOVE YOU	ISLEY BROTHERS	45	1966
I GUESS THAT'S WHY THEY CALL IT THE BLUES	ELTON JOHN	5	1983
I HAD TOO MUCH TO DREAM LAST NIGHT	ELECTRIC PRUNES	49	1967
I HATE MYSELF FOR LOVING YOU	JOAN JETT & THE BLACKHEARTS	46	1988
I HATE…PEOPLE	ANTI-NOWHERE LEAGUE	46	1982
I HATE ROCK 'N' ROLL	JESUS & MARY CHAIN	61	1995
I HATE THIS PART	PUSSYCAT DOLLS	12	2008
I HAVE A DREAM	ABBA	2	1979
I HAVE A DREAM	WESTLIFE	1	1999
I HAVE FORGIVEN JESUS	MORRISSEY	10	2005
I HAVE NOTHING	WHITNEY HOUSTON	3	1993
I HAVE PEACE	STRIKE	17	1997
I HAVEN'T STOPPED DANCING YET	PAT & MICK	9	1989
I HEAR A SYMPHONY	SUPREMES	39	1966
I HEAR TALK	BUCKS FIZZ	34	1985
I HEAR YOU KNOCKING	DAVE EDMUNDS	1	1970
I HEAR YOU NOW	JON & VANGELIS	8	1980
I HEAR YOUR NAME	INCOGNITO	42	1995
I HEARD A HEART BREAK LAST NIGHT	JIM REEVES	38	1967
I HEARD A RUMOUR	BANANARAMA	14	1987
I HEARD IT THROUGH THE GRAPEVINE	GLADYS KNIGHT & THE PIPS	47	1967
I HEARD IT THROUGH THE GRAPEVINE	MARVIN GAYE	1	1969
I HEARD IT THROUGH THE GRAPEVINE	SLITS	60	1979
I HONESTLY LOVE YOU	OLIVIA NEWTON-JOHN	22	1974
I HOPE YOU DANCE	LEE ANN WOMACK	40	2001
I HOPE YOU DANCE	RONAN KEATING	2	2004
I IMAGINE	MARY KIANI	35	1995
I JUST CALLED TO SAY I LOVE YOU	STEVIE WONDER	1	1984
I JUST CAN'T BE HAPPY TODAY	DAMNED	46	1979
I JUST CAN'T (FORGIVE AND FORGET)	BLUE ZOO	60	1983
I JUST CAN'T GET ENOUGH	HERD & FITZ FEATURING ABIGAIL BAILEY	11	2005
I JUST CAN'T HELP BELIEVING	ELVIS PRESLEY	6	1971
I JUST CAN'T STOP LOVING YOU	MICHAEL JACKSON	1	1987
(I JUST) DIED IN YOUR ARMS	CUTTING CREW	4	1986
I JUST DIED IN YOUR ARMS	RESOURCE	42	2003
I JUST DON'T HAVE THE HEART	CLIFF RICHARD	3	1989
I JUST DON'T KNOW WHAT TO DO WITH MYSELF	DUSTY SPRINGFIELD	3	1964
I JUST DON'T KNOW WHAT TO DO WITH MYSELF	WHITE STRIPES	13	2003
I JUST FALL IN LOVE AGAIN	ANNE MURRAY	58	1979
I JUST GO FOR YOU	JIMMY JONES	35	1960
I JUST HAD TO HEAR YOUR VOICE	OLETA ADAMS	42	1993
I JUST KEEP THINKING ABOUT YOU BABY	TATA VEGA	52	1979
I JUST NEED MYSELF	OCEAN COLOUR SCENE	13	2003
(I JUST WANNA) B WITH U	TRANSVISION VAMP	30	1991
I JUST WANNA BE LOVED	CULTURE CLUB	31	1998
I JUST WANNA BE YOUR EVERYTHING	ANDY GIBB	26	1977
I JUST WANNA KNOW	TAIO CRUZ	29	2006
I JUST WANNA LIVE	GOOD CHARLOTTE	9	2005
I JUST WANNA LOVE U (GIVE IT TO ME)	JAY-Z	17	2000
I JUST WANNA (SPEND SOME TIME WITH YOU)	ALTON EDWARDS	20	1982
I JUST WANT TO DANCE WITH YOU	DANIEL O'DONNELL	20	1992
I JUST WANT TO MAKE LOVE TO YOU	ETTA JAMES	5	1996
I JUST WANT TO SEE THE BOY HAPPY	MORRISSEY	16	2006
I JUST WANT YOU	OZZY OSBOURNE	43	1996
I KEEP FORGETTIN'	MICHAEL McDONALD	43	1986
I KEEP RINGING MY BABY	SOUL BROTHERS	43	1965
I KISS YOUR LIPS	TOKYO GHETTO PUSSY	55	1996
I KISSED A GIRL	KATY PERRY	1	2008
I KISSED A GIRL	NICKI BLISS	50	2008
I KNEW I LOVED YOU	SAVAGE GARDEN	10	1999
I KNEW THE BRIDE	DAVE EDMUNDS	26	1977
I KNEW YOU WERE WAITING (FOR ME)	ARETHA FRANKLIN & GEORGE MICHAEL	1	1987
I KNOW [A]	PERRY COMO	13	1959
I KNOW [B]	PAUL KING	59	1987
I KNOW [C]	BLUR	48	1990
I KNOW [D]	NEW ATLANTIC	12	1992
I KNOW [E]	DIONNE FARRIS	41	1995
I KNOW A PLACE [A]	PETULA CLARK	17	1965
I KNOW A PLACE [B]	KIM ENGLISH	52	1995
I KNOW ENOUGH (I DON'T GET ENOUGH)	THEAUDIENCE	25	1998
I KNOW HIM SO WELL	ELAINE PAIGE & BARBARA DICKSON	1	1985
I KNOW HIM SO WELL	STEPS	5	2001
(I KNOW) I'M LOSING YOU	TEMPTATIONS	19	1966
I KNOW MY LOVE	CHIEFTAINS FEATURING THE CORRS	37	1999
I KNOW THE LORD	TABERNACLE	55	1995
I KNOW THERE'S SOMETHING GOING ON	FRIDA	43	1982
I KNOW UR GIRLFRIEND HATES ME	ANNIE	54	2008
I KNOW WHAT BOYS LIKE	SHAMPOO	42	1996
I KNOW WHAT I LIKE (IN YOUR WARDROBE)	GENESIS	21	1974
I KNOW WHAT I'M HERE FOR	JAMES	22	1999
I KNOW WHAT YOU WANT	BUSTA RHYMES & MARIAH CAREY	3	2003
I KNOW WHERE I'M GOING	GEORGE HAMILTON IV	23	1958
I KNOW WHERE I'M GOING	COUNTRYMEN	45	1962
I KNOW WHERE IT'S AT	ALL SAINTS	4	1997
I KNOW YOU DON'T LOVE ME	ROACHFORD	42	1995
I KNOW YOU GOT SOUL	ERIC B & RAKIM	13	1988
I KNOW YOU WANT ME (CALLE OCHO)	PITBULL	4	2009
I KNOW YOU'RE OUT THERE SOMEWHERE	MOODY BLUES	52	1988
I LEARNED FROM THE BEST	WHITNEY HOUSTON	19	1999
I LEFT MY HEART IN SAN FRANCISCO	TONY BENNETT	25	1965
I LIFT MY CUP	GLOWORM	20	1993
I LIKE [A]	SHANICE	49	1994
I LIKE [B]	KUT KLOSE	72	1995
I LIKE [C]	MONTELL JORDAN FEATURING SLICK RICK	24	1996
I LIKE [D]	JULIET ROBERTS	17	1999
I LIKE GIRLS	HOUND DOGS	26	2006
I LIKE IT [A]	GERRY & THE PACEMAKERS	1	1963
I LIKE IT [B]	DJH FEATURING STEFY	16	1991
I LIKE IT [C]	OVERWEIGHT POOCH FEATURING CE CE PENISTON	58	1992
I LIKE IT [D]	D:REAM	26	1993
I LIKE IT [E]	JOMANDA	67	1993
I LIKE IT [F]	ANGEL MORAES	70	1997
I LIKE IT [G]	NARCOTIC THRUST	9	2004
I LIKE LOVE (I LOVE LOVE)	SOLITAIRE	57	2003
I LIKE THAT	HOUSTON	11	2004
I LIKE THE WAY [A]	DENI HINES	37	1997
I LIKE THE WAY [B]	BODYROCKERS	3	2005
I LIKE THE WAY (THE KISSING GAME)	HI-FIVE	43	1991
I LIKE THE WAY (THE KISSING GAME)	KALEEF	58	1997
I LIKE TO MOVE IT	REEL 2 REAL FEATURING THE MAD STUNTMAN	5	1994
I LIKE TO ROCK	APRIL WINE	41	1980
I LIKE (WHAT YOU'RE DOING TO ME)	YOUNG & COMPANY	20	1980
I LIKE YOU SO MUCH BETTER WHEN YOU'RE NAKED	IDA MARIA	13	2008
I LIKE YOUR KIND OF LOVE	ANDY WILLIAMS	16	1957
I LIVE FOR SPEED	STAR SPANGLES	60	2003
I LIVE FOR THE SUN	VANITY FARE	20	1968
I LIVE FOR THE WEEKEND	TRIUMPH	59	1980
I LIVE FOR YOUR LOVE	NATALIE COLE	23	1988
I LOST MY HEART TO A STARSHIP TROOPER	SARAH BRIGHTMAN & HOT GOSSIP	6	1978
I LOVE A MAN IN UNIFORM	GANG OF FOUR	65	1982
I LOVE A RAINY NIGHT	EDDIE RABBITT	53	1981
I LOVE AMERICA	PATRICK JUVET	12	1978
I LOVE BEING IN LOVE WITH YOU	ADAM FAITH & THE ROULETTES	33	1964

	Peak Position	Year of Release
I LOVE CHRISTMAS FAST FOOD ROCKERS	25	2003
I LOVE COLLEGE ASHER ROTH	26	2009
I LOVE FOOTBALL WES	75	1998
I LOVE HER PAUL & BARRY RYAN	17	1966
I LOVE HOW YOU LOVE ME JIMMY CRAWFORD	18	1961
I LOVE HOW YOU LOVE ME MAUREEN EVANS	34	1964
I LOVE HOW YOU LOVE ME PAUL & BARRY RYAN	21	1966
I LOVE I HATE NEIL ARTHUR	50	1994
I LOVE IT WHEN WE DO RONAN KEATING	5	2002
I LOVE LAKE TAHOE A	59	1999
I LOVE MEN EARTHA KITT	50	1984
I LOVE MUSIC O'JAYS	13	1976
I LOVE MUSIC ENIGMA	25	1981
I LOVE MUSIC ROZALLA	18	1994
I LOVE MY CHICK BUSTA RHYMES	8	2006
I LOVE MY DOG CAT STEVENS	28	1966
I LOVE MY RADIO (MY DEE JAY'S RADIO) TAFFY	6	1987
I LOVE ROCK 'N' ROLL JOAN JETT & THE BLACKHEARTS	4	1982
I LOVE ROCK 'N' ROLL BRITNEY SPEARS	13	2002
I LOVE SATURDAY ERASURE	20	1994
I LOVE THE NIGHTLIFE (DISCO ROUND) ALICIA BRIDGES	32	1978
I LOVE THE SOUND OF BREAKING GLASS NICK LOWE	7	1978
I LOVE THE WAY YOU LOVE MARV JOHNSON	35	1960
I LOVE THE WAY YOU LOVE ME BOYZONE	2	1998
I LOVE TO BOOGIE T REX	13	1976
I LOVE TO LOVE (BUT MY BABY LOVES TO DANCE) TINA CHARLES	1	1976
I LOVE YOU [A] CLIFF RICHARD & THE SHADOWS	1	1960
I LOVE YOU [B] DONNA SUMMER	10	1977
I LOVE YOU [C] YELLO	41	1983
I LOVE YOU [D] VANILLA ICE	45	1991
I LOVE YOU [E] FLESH & BONES	70	2002
I LOVE YOU ALWAYS FOREVER DONNA LEWIS	5	1996
I LOVE YOU ANYWAY BOYZONE	5	2008
I LOVE YOU BABY PAUL ANKA	3	1957
I LOVE YOU BABY FREDDIE & THE DREAMERS	16	1964
I LOVE YOU BECAUSE AL MARTINO	48	1963
I LOVE YOU BECAUSE JIM REEVES	5	1964
I LOVE YOU BUT RESEARCH	63	2005
I LOVE YOU 'CAUSE I HAVE TO DOGS DIE IN HOT CARS	32	2004
I LOVE YOU GOODBYE THOMAS DOLBY	36	1992
I LOVE YOU LOVE ME LOVE GARY GLITTER	1	1973
I LOVE YOU MORE THAN ROCK N ROLL THUNDER	27	2004
I LOVE YOU SO MUCH IT HURTS CHARLIE GRACIE	14	1957
(I LOVE YOU) WHEN YOU SLEEP TRACIE	59	1984
I LOVE YOU, YES I DO MERSEYBEATS	22	1965
I LOVE YOU, YES I LOVE YOU EDDY GRANT	37	1981
I LOVE YOUR SMILE SHANICE	2	1991
I LOVE YOU...STOP! RED 5	11	1997
I LUV U [A] SHUT UP & DANCE FEATURING RICHIE DAVIS & PROFESSOR T	68	1995
I LUV U [B] DIZZEE RASCAL	29	2003
I LUV U [C] ORDINARY BOYS	7	2007
I LUV U BABY ORIGINAL	2	1995
I MADE IT THROUGH THE RAIN BARRY MANILOW	37	1981
I MADE IT THROUGH THE RAIN JOHN BARROWMAN	14	2009
I MAY NEVER PASS THIS WAY AGAIN ROBERT EARL	14	1958
I MAY NEVER PASS THIS WAY AGAIN PERRY COMO	15	1958
I MAY NEVER PASS THIS WAY AGAIN RONNIE HILTON WITH THE MICHAEL SAMMES SINGERS	27	1958
I MET A GIRL SHADOWS	22	1966
I MIGHT SHAKIN' STEVENS	18	1990
I MIGHT BE CRYING TANITA TIKARAM	64	1995
I MIGHT BE LYING EDDIE & THE HOT RODS	44	1977
I MISS YOU [A] HADDAWAY	9	1993
I MISS YOU [B] 4 OF US	62	1993
I MISS YOU [C] BJORK	36	1997
I MISS YOU [D] DARREN HAYES	20	2002
I MISS YOU [E] BLINK-182	8	2004
I MISS YOU [F] BASSHUNTER	32	2008
I MISS YOU BABY MARV JOHNSON	25	1969
I MISSED AGAIN PHIL COLLINS	14	1981
I MISSED THE BUS KRIS KROSS	57	1992
I MUST BE IN LOVE RUTLES	39	1978
I MUST BE SEEING THINGS GENE PITNEY	6	1965
I MUST STAND ICE-T	23	1996
I NEED MEREDITH BROOKS	28	1997
I NEED A GIRL GROUNDED	43	2005
I NEED A GIRL (PART ONE) P DIDDY FEATURING USHER & LOON	4	2002
I NEED A MAN [A] MAN TO MAN	43	1987
I NEED A MAN [B] EURYTHMICS	26	1988
I NEED A MAN [C] LI KWAN	51	1994
I NEED A MIRACLE [A] COCO	39	1997
I NEED A MIRACLE [B] CASCADA	8	2007
I NEED ANOTHER (EP) DODGY	67	1993
I NEED DIRECTION TEENAGE FANCLUB	48	2000
I NEED IT JOHNNY 'GUITAR' WATSON	35	1976
I NEED LOVE [A] LL COOL J	8	1987
I NEED LOVE [B] OLIVIA NEWTON-JOHN	75	1992
I NEED SOME FINE WINE AND YOU, YOU NEED TO BE NICER CARDIGANS	59	2005
I NEED SOMEBODY LOVELAND FEATURING RACHEL McFARLANE	21	1995
I NEED SOMETHING NEWTON FAULKNER	70	2008
I NEED THE KEY MINIMAL CHIC FEATURING MATT GOSS	54	2004
I NEED TO BE IN LOVE CARPENTERS	36	1976
I NEED TO KNOW MARC ANTHONY	28	1999
I NEED YOU [A] JOE DOLAN	43	1977
I NEED YOU [B] POINTER SISTERS	25	1984
I NEED YOU [C] B.V.S.M.P.	3	1988
I NEED YOU [D] DEUCE	10	1995
I NEED YOU [E] NIKITA WARREN	48	1996
I NEED YOU [F] 3T	3	1996
I NEED YOU [G] WIRELESS	68	1997
I NEED YOU [H] LEANN RIMES	13	2001
I NEED YOU [I] DAVE GAHAN	27	2003
I NEED YOU [J] STANDS	39	2003
I NEED YOU [K] N-DUBZ	5	2009
I NEED YOU NOW [A] EDDIE FISHER	13	1954
I NEED YOU NOW [B] SINNAMON	70	1996
I NEED YOU NOW [C] AGNES	40	2009
I NEED YOU TONIGHT JUNIOR M.A.F.I.A. FEATURING AALIYAH	66	1996
I NEED YOUR LOVE TONIGHT ELVIS PRESLEY	1	1959
I NEED YOUR LOVIN' [A] TEENA MARIE	28	1980
I NEED YOUR LOVIN' [A] CURIOSITY	47	1992
I NEED YOUR LOVIN' [B] ALYSON WILLIAMS	8	1989
I NEED YOUR LOVIN' (LIKE THE SUNSHINE) MARC ET CLAUDE	12	2000
I NEED YOUR LOVING HUMAN LEAGUE	72	1986
I NEVER FELT LIKE THIS BEFORE MICA PARIS	15	1993
I NEVER GO OUT IN THE RAIN HIGH SOCIETY	53	1980
I NEVER KNEW ROGER SANCHEZ	24	2000
I NEVER LOVED YOU ANYWAY CORRS	43	1997
I NEVER WANT AN EASY LIFE IF ME AND HE WERE EVER TO GET THERE CHARLATANS	38	1994
I ONLY HAVE EYES FOR YOU ART GARFUNKEL	1	1975
I ONLY LIVE TO LOVE YOU CILLA BLACK	26	1967
I ONLY WANNA BE WITH YOU [A] BAY CITY ROLLERS	4	1976
I ONLY WANNA BE WITH YOU [A] SAMANTHA FOX	16	1989
I ONLY WANT TO BE WITH YOU [A] DUSTY SPRINGFIELD	4	1963
I ONLY WANT TO BE WITH YOU [A] TOURISTS	4	1979
I ONLY WANT TO BE WITH YOU [B] BARRY WHITE	36	1995
I OWE YOU NOTHING BROS	1	1988
I OWE YOU ONE SHALAMAR	13	1980
I PREDICT A RIOT KAISER CHIEFS	9	2004
I PRETEND DES O'CONNOR	1	1968
I PROMISE STACIE ORRICO	22	2004
I PROMISE YOU (GET READY) SAMANTHA FOX	58	1987
I PROMISED MYSELF NICK KAMEN	50	1990
I PRONOUNCE YOU MADNESS	44	1988
I PUT A SPELL ON YOU NINA SIMONE	28	1965
I PUT A SPELL ON YOU ALAN PRICE SET	9	1966
I PUT A SPELL ON YOU BRYAN FERRY	18	1993
I PUT A SPELL ON YOU SONIQUE	8	1998
I QUIT [A] BROS	4	1988
I QUIT [B] HEPBURN	8	1999
I RAN A FLOCK OF SEAGULLS	43	1982
I REALLY DIDN'T MEAN IT LUTHER VANDROSS	16	1987
I RECALL A GYPSY WOMAN DON WILLIAMS	13	1976
I REFUSE HUE & CRY	47	1988
I REFUSE (WHAT YOU WANT) SOMORE FEATURING DAMON TRUEITT	21	1998
I REMEMBER [A] COOLIO	73	1994
I REMEMBER [B] DEADMAU5 & KASKADE	14	2009
I REMEMBER ELVIS PRESLEY (THE KING IS DEAD) DANNY MIRROR	4	1977
I REMEMBER YESTERDAY DONNA SUMMER	14	1977
I REMEMBER YOU [A] FRANK IFIELD	1	1962
I REMEMBER YOU [B] SKID ROW	36	1990
I ROCK TOM NOVY	55	2000
I SAID I LOVE YOU RAUL MALO	57	2002
I SAID NEVER AGAIN (BUT HERE WE ARE) RACHEL STEVENS	12	2005
I SAID PIG ON FRIDAY EASTERN LANE	65	2004
I SAVED THE WORLD TODAY EURYTHMICS	11	1999
I SAW HER AGAIN MAMAS & THE PAPAS	11	1966
I SAW HER STANDING THERE ELTON JOHN BAND FEATURING JOHN LENNON & THE MUSCLE SHOALS HORNS	40	1981
I SAW HIM STANDING THERE TIFFANY	8	1988
I SAW LINDA YESTERDAY DOUG SHELDON	36	1963
I SAW MOMMY KISSING SANTA CLAUS JIMMY BOYD	3	1953
I SAW MOMMY KISSING SANTA CLAUS BEVERLEY SISTERS	6	1953
I SAW MOMMY KISSING SANTA CLAUS BILLY COTTON & HIS BAND, VOCALS BY THE MILL GIRLS & THE BANDITS	11	1953
I SAW THE LIGHT [A] TODD RUNDGREN	36	1973
I SAW THE LIGHT [B] THE THE	31	1995
I SAY A LITTLE PRAYER DIANA KING	17	1997
I SAY A LITTLE PRAYER FOR YOU ARETHA FRANKLIN	4	1968
I SAY NOTHING VOICE OF THE BEEHIVE	22	1987
I SAY YEAH SECCHI FEATURING ORLANDO JOHNSON	46	1991
I SCARE MYSELF THOMAS DOLBY	46	1984
I SECOND THAT EMOTION SMOKEY ROBINSON & THE MIRACLES	27	1968
I SECOND THAT EMOTION DIANA ROSS & THE SUPREMES & THE TEMPTATIONS	18	1969
I SECOND THAT EMOTION JAPAN	9	1982

	Peak Position	Year of Release
I SECOND THAT EMOTION ALYSON WILLIAMS WITH CHUCK STANLEY	44	1989
I SEE A STAR MOUTH & MACNEAL	8	1974
I SEE GIRLS (CRAZY) STUDIO B/ROMEO & HARRY BROOKS	12	2003
I SEE ONLY YOU NOOTROPIC	42	1996
I SEE THE MOON STARGAZERS	1	1954
I SEE YOU BABY GROOVE ARMADA FEATURING GRAM'MA FUNK	11	1999
I SEE YOU YOU SEE ME MAGIC NUMBERS	20	2006
I SEE YOUR SMILE GLORIA ESTEFAN	48	1993
I SEEN A MAN DIE SCARFACE	55	1995
I SHALL BE RELEASED TREMELOES	29	1968
I SHALL BE THERE B*WITCHED FEATURING LADYSMITH BLACK MAMBAZO	13	1999
I SHALL OVERCOME HARD-FI	36	2008
I SHOT THE SHERIFF ERIC CLAPTON	9	1974
I SHOT THE SHERIFF LIGHT OF THE WORLD	40	1981
I SHOT THE SHERIFF WARREN G	2	1997
I SHOT THE SHERIFF BOB MARLEY & THE WAILERS	67	2005
I SHOULD BE SO LUCKY KYLIE MINOGUE	1	1988
I SHOULD CARE FRANK IFIELD	33	1964
I SHOULD HAVE CHEATED KEYSHIA COLE	48	2006
I SHOULD HAVE KNOWN BETTER [A] NATURALS	24	1964
I SHOULD HAVE KNOWN BETTER [B] JIM DIAMOND	1	1984
I SHOULDA LOVED YA NARADA MICHAEL WALDEN	8	1980
I SHOULD'VE KNOWN AIMEE MANN	45	1993
I SINGS MARY MARY	32	2000
I SLEEP ALONE AT NIGHT JIM DIAMOND	72	1985
I SPEAKA DA LINGO BLACK LACE	49	1985
I SPECIALIZE IN LOVE SHARON BROWN	38	1982
I SPECIALIZE IN LOVE ARIZONA FEATURING ZEITIA	74	1994
I SPECIALIZE IN LOVE ARIZONA FEATURING ZEITIA	74	1994
I SPY GET CAPE. WEAR CAPE. FLY.	37	2007
I SPY FOR THE FBI JAMO THOMAS	44	1969
I SPY FOR THE FBI UNTOUCHABLES	59	1985
I STAND ACCUSED MERSEYBEATS	38	1966
I STAND ALONE E-MOTION	60	1996
I STARTED A JOKE FAITH NO MORE	49	1998
I STARTED SOMETHING I COULDN'T FINISH SMITHS	23	1987
I STILL BELIEVE [A] RONNIE HILTON	3	1954
I STILL BELIEVE [B] MARIAH CAREY	16	1999
I STILL BELIEVE IN YOU CLIFF RICHARD	7	1992
I STILL HAVEN'T FOUND WHAT I'M LOOKING FOR U2	6	1987
I STILL LOVE YOU ALL KENNY BALL & HIS JAZZMEN	24	1961
I STILL REMEMBER GARY NUMAN	74	1986
I STILL REMEMBER BLOC PARTY	20	2007
I STILL THINK ABOUT YOU DANGER DANGER	46	1992
I STILL THINK OF YOU UTAH SAINTS	32	1994
I SURRENDER [A] RAINBOW	3	1981
I SURRENDER [B] ROSIE GAINES	39	1997
I SURRENDER [C] DAVID SYLVIAN	40	1999
I SURRENDER (TO THE SPIRIT OF THE NIGHT) SAMANTHA FOX	25	1987
I SURRENDER TO YOUR LOVE BY ALL MEANS	65	1988
I SWEAR ALL-4-ONE	2	1994
I TALK TO THE TREES CLINT EASTWOOD	18	1970
I TALK TO THE WIND OPUS III	52	1992
I THANK YOU [A] SAM & DAVE	34	1968
I THANK YOU [B] ADEVA	17	1989
I THINK I LOVE YOU PARTRIDGE FAMILY STARRING SHIRLEY JONES FEATURING DAVID CASSIDY	18	1971
I THINK I LOVE YOU VOICE OF THE BEEHIVE	25	1991
I THINK I LOVE YOU KACI	10	2002
I THINK I WANT TO DANCE WITH YOU RUMPLE-STILTS-SKIN	51	1983
I THINK I'M IN LOVE SPIRITUALIZED	27	1998
I THINK I'M IN LOVE WITH YOU JESSICA SIMPSON	15	2000
I THINK I'M PARANOID GARBAGE	9	1998
I THINK IT'S GOING TO RAIN UB40	6	1980
I THINK OF YOU [A] MERSEYBEATS	5	1964
I THINK OF YOU [B] PERRY COMO	14	1971
I THINK OF YOU [C] DETROIT EMERALDS	27	1973
I THINK OF YOU [D] BRYAN POWELL	61	1993
I THINK THEY LIKE ME DEM FRANCHIZE BOYZ	66	2006
I THINK WE'RE ALONE NOW TIFFANY	1	1988
I THINK WE'RE ALONE NOW PASCAL FEATURING KAREN PARRY	23	2002
I THINK WE'RE ALONE NOW GIRLS ALOUD	4	2006
I THOUGHT I MEANT THE WORLD TO YOU ALYSHA WARREN	40	1995
I THOUGHT IT TOOK A LITTLE TIME DIANA ROSS	32	1976
I THOUGHT IT WAS OVER FEELING	9	2008
I THOUGHT IT WAS YOU [A] HERBIE HANCOCK	15	1978
I THOUGHT IT WAS YOU [A] SEX-O-SONIQUE	32	1997
I THOUGHT IT WAS YOU [B] JULIA FORDHAM	45	1991
I THREW IT ALL AWAY BOB DYLAN	30	1969
I TOLD YOU SO [A] JIMMY JONES	33	1961
I TOLD YOU SO [B] OCEAN COLOUR SCENE	34	2007
I TOUCH MYSELF DIVINYLS	10	1991
I TOUCH MYSELF FHM HIGH STREET HONEYS	34	2007
I TRIED BONE THUGS-N-HARMONY FEATURING AKON	69	2007
I TRY [A] MACY GRAY	6	1999
I TRY [B] TALIB KWELI FEATURING MARY J BLIGE	59	2004
I TURN TO YOU [A] CHRISTINA AGUILERA	19	2000
I TURN TO YOU [B] MELANIE C	1	2000
I UNDERSTAND G-CLEFS	17	1961
I UNDERSTAND FREDDIE & THE DREAMERS	5	1964
I UNDERSTAND IT IDLEWILD	32	2005
I WALK THE EARTH VOICE OF THE BEEHIVE	42	1988
I WANNA BE A FLINTSTONE SCREAMING BLUE MESSIAHS	28	1988
I WANNA BE A HIPPY TECHNOHEAD	6	1996
I WANNA BE A WINNER BROWN SAUCE	15	1981
I WANNA BE ADORED STONE ROSES	20	1991
I WANNA BE DOWN BRANDY	36	1994
I WANNA BE FREE MINTY	67	1999
I WANNA BE FREE (TO BE WITH HIM) SCARLET	21	1995
I WANNA BE IN LOVE AGAIN BEIJING SPRING	43	1993
I WANNA BE LOVED [A] RICKY NELSON	30	1960
I WANNA BE LOVED [B] ELVIS COSTELLO	25	1984
I WANNA BE THE ONLY ONE ETERNAL FEATURING BEBE WINANS	1	1997
I WANNA BE U CHOCOLATE PUMA	6	2001
I WANNA BE WITH YOU MANDY MOORE	21	2000
I WANNA BE WITH YOU [A] COFFEE	57	1980
I WANNA BE WITH YOU [B] MAZE FEATURING FRANKIE BEVERLY	55	1986
I WANNA BE YOUR LADY HINDA HICKS	14	1998
I WANNA BE YOUR LOVER PRINCE	41	1980
I WANNA BE YOUR MAN [A] ROLLING STONES	12	1963
I WANNA BE YOUR MAN [A] REZILLOS	71	1979
I WANNA BE YOUR MAN [B] CHAKA DEMUS & PLIERS	19	1994
I WANNA BE YOUR MAN [C] IRONIK	35	2008
I WANNA DANCE WIT CHOO DISCO TEX & THE SEX-O-LETTES FEATURING SIR MONTI ROCK III	6	1975
I WANNA DANCE WITH SOMEBODY FLIP & FILL	13	2002
I WANNA DANCE WITH SOMEBODY (WHO LOVES ME) WHITNEY HOUSTON	1	1987
I WANNA DO IT WITH YOU BARRY MANILOW	8	1982
I WANNA GET NEXT TO YOU ROSE ROYCE	14	1977
(I WANNA GIVE YOU) DEVOTION NOMAD FEATURING MC MIKEE FREEDOM	2	1991
I WANNA GO BACK NEW SEEKERS	25	1977
I WANNA GO HOME LONNIE DONEGAN	5	1960
I WANNA GO WHERE THE PEOPLE GO WILDHEARTS	16	1995
I WANNA HAVE SOME FUN SAMANTHA FOX	63	1989
I WANNA HAVE YOUR BABIES NATASHA BEDINGFIELD	7	2007
I WANNA HOLD ON TO YOU MICA PARIS	27	1993
I WANNA HOLD YOU McFLY	3	2005
I WANNA HOLD YOUR HAND DOLLAR	9	1979
I WANNA KNOW [A] STACCATO	65	1996
I WANNA KNOW [B] JOE	37	2001
I WANNA KNOW [C] BLUESKINS	56	2004
(I WANNA KNOW) WHY SINCLAIR	58	1994
(I WANNA) LOVE MY LIFE AWAY GENE PITNEY	26	1961
I WANNA LOVE YOU AKON FEATURING SNOOP DOGGY DOGG	3	2007
I WANNA LOVE YOU [A] JADE	13	1993
I WANNA LOVE YOU [B] SOLID HARMONIE	20	1998
I WANNA LOVE YOU FOREVER JESSICA SIMPSON	7	2000
I WANNA MAKE YOU FEEL GOOD SYSTEM	73	1984
I WANNA 1-2-1 WITH YOU SOLID GOLD CHARTBUSTERS	62	1999
I WANNA SEX YOU UP COLOR ME BADD	1	1991
I WANNA SING SABRINA JOHNSTON	46	1992
I WANNA STAY HERE MIKI & GRIFF	23	1963
I WANNA STAY HOME JELLYFISH	59	1991
I WANNA STAY WITH YOU GALLAGHER & LYLE	6	1976
I WANNA STAY WITH YOU UNDERCOVER	28	1993
I WANNA THANK YOU ANGIE STONE FEATURING SNOOP DOGG	31	2004
I WANT AN ALIEN FOR CHRISTMAS FOUNTAINS OF WAYNE	36	1997
I WANT CANDY BRIAN POOLE & THE TREMELOES	25	1965
I WANT CANDY BOW WOW WOW	9	1982
I WANT CANDY CANDY GIRLS FEATURING VALERIE MALCOLM	30	1996
I WANT CANDY AARON CARTER	31	2000
I WANT CANDY MELANIE C	24	2007
I WANT HER KEITH SWEAT	26	1988
I WANT IT CHANELLE HAYES	63	2008
I WANT IT ALL QUEEN	3	1989
I WANT IT THAT WAY BACKSTREET BOYS	1	1999
I WANT LOVE ELTON JOHN	9	2001
I WANT MORE [A] CAN	26	1976
I WANT MORE [B] FAITHLESS	22	2004
I WANT OUT HELLOWEEN	69	1988
I WANT OUT (I CAN'T BELIEVE) HARRY 'CHOO CHOO' ROMERO	51	2001
I WANT THAT MAN DEBORAH HARRY	13	1989
I WANT THE WORLD 2WO THIRD3	20	1994
I WANT TO BE ALONE 2WO THIRD3	29	1994
(I WANT TO BE) ELECTED MR BEAN & SMEAR CAMPAIGN FEATURING BRUCE DICKINSON	9	1992
I WANT TO BE FREE TOYAH	8	1981
I WANT TO BE STRAIGHT IAN DURY & THE BLOCKHEADS	22	1980
I WANT TO BE THERE WHEN YOU COME ECHO & THE BUNNYMEN	30	1997
I WANT TO BE WANTED BRENDA LEE	31	1960
I WANT TO BE YOUR MAN ROGER	61	1987

	Peak Position	Year of Release
I WANT TO BE YOUR PROPERTY BLUE MERCEDES	23	1987
I WANT TO BREAK FREE QUEEN	3	1984
I WANT TO GIVE PERRY COMO	31	1974
I WANT TO GO WITH YOU EDDY ARNOLD	46	1966
I WANT TO HEAR IT FROM YOU GO WEST	43	1987
I WANT TO HOLD YOUR HAND BEATLES	1	1963
(I WANT TO) KILL SOMEBODY S*M*A*S*H	26	1994
I WANT TO KNOW WHAT LOVE IS FOREIGNER	1	1984
I WANT TO KNOW WHAT LOVE IS TERRI SYMON	54	1995
I WANT TO KNOW WHAT LOVE IS MARIAH CAREY	19	2009
I WANT TO LIVE GRACE	30	1995
I WANT TO STAY HERE STEVE (Lawrence) & EYDIE (Gorme)	3	1963
I WANT TO THANK YOU ROBIN S	48	1994
I WANT TO TOUCH YOU CATHERINE WHEEL	35	1992
I WANT TO WAKE UP WITH YOU BORIS GARDINER	1	1986
I WANT TO WALK YOU HOME FATS DOMINO	14	1959
I WANT U ROSIE GAINES	70	1995
I WANT YOU [A] BOB DYLAN	16	1966
I WANT YOU [A] SOPHIE B HAWKINS	49	1993
I WANT YOU [B] GARY LOW	52	1983
I WANT YOU [C] UTAH SAINTS	25	1993
I WANT YOU [D] JULIET ROBERTS	28	1994
I WANT YOU [E] SECRET LIFE	70	1994
I WANT YOU [F] SALAD	60	1996
I WANT YOU [G] INSPIRAL CARPETS FEATURING MARK E SMITH	18	1994
I WANT YOU [H] SAVAGE GARDEN	11	1997
I WANT YOU [I] Z2 VOCAL BY ALISON RIVERS	61	2000
I WANT YOU [J] CZR FEATURING DELANO	57	2000
I WANT YOU [K] JANET JACKSON	14	2004
I WANT YOU (ALL TONIGHT) CURTIS HAIRSTON	44	1983
I WANT YOU BACK [A] JACKSON 5	2	1970
I WANT YOU BACK [A] CLEOPATRA	4	1998
I WANT YOU BACK [B] BANANARAMA	5	1988
I WANT YOU BACK [C] MELANIE B FEATURING MISSY 'MISDEMEANOR' ELLIOTT	1	1998
I WANT YOU BACK [D] *NSYNC	5	1997
I WANT YOU BACK [E] X-PRESS 2	50	2002
I WANT YOU FOR MYSELF ANOTHER LEVEL/ GHOSTFACE KILLAH	2	1999
I WANT YOU (FOREVER) DJ CARL COX	23	1991
I WANT YOU I NEED YOU I LOVE YOU ELVIS PRESLEY	14	1956
I WANT YOU NEAR ME TINA TURNER	22	1992
I WANT YOU SO HARD (BOY'S BAD NEWS) EAGLES OF DEATH METAL	73	2006
I WANT YOU TO BE MY BABY BILLIE DAVIS	33	1968
I WANT YOU TO STAY MAXIMO PARK	21	2006
I WANT YOU TO WANT ME [A] CHEAP TRICK	29	1979
I WANT YOU TO WANT ME [B] SOLID HARMONIE	16	1998
I WANT YOUR LOVE [A] CHIC	4	1979
I WANT YOUR LOVE [A] ROGER SANCHEZ PRESENTS TWILIGHT	31	1999
I WANT YOUR LOVE [B] TRANSVISION VAMP	5	1988
I WANT YOUR LOVE [C] ATOMIC KITTEN	10	2000
I WANT YOUR LOVIN' (JUST A LITTLE BIT) CURTIS HAIRSTON	13	1985
I WANT YOUR SEX GEORGE MICHAEL	3	1987
I WANT YOUR SOUL ARMAND VAN HELDEN	19	2007
I WAS A KING EDDIE MURPHY FEATURING SHABBA RANKS	64	1993
I WAS BORN ON CHRISTMAS DAY SAINT ETIENNE CO STARRING TIM BURGESS	37	1993
I WAS BORN TO BE ME TOM JONES	61	1988
I WAS BORN TO LOVE YOU FREDDIE MERCURY	11	1985
I WAS BROUGHT TO MY SENSES STING	31	1996
I WAS KAISER BILL'S BATMAN WHISTLING JACK SMITH	5	1967
I WAS MADE FOR DANCIN' LEIF GARRETT	4	1979
I WAS MADE FOR LOVIN' YOU KISS	50	1979
I WAS MADE TO LOVE HER STEVIE WONDER	5	1967
I WAS MADE TO LOVE YOU LORRAINE CATO	41	1996
I WAS ONLY JOKING ROD STEWART	5	1978
I WAS RIGHT AND YOU WERE WRONG DEACON BLUE	32	1994
I WAS THE ONE ELVIS PRESLEY	45	1996
I WAS TIRED OF BEING ALONE PATRICE RUSHEN	39	1982
I WASN'T BUILT TO GET UP SUPERNATURALS	25	1998
I WEAR MY SKIN ONE MINUTE SILENCE	44	2003
I (WHO HAVE NOTHING) SHIRLEY BASSEY	6	1963
I (WHO HAVE NOTHING) TOM JONES	16	1970
I (WHO HAVE NOTHING) SYLVESTER	46	1979
I WILL BILLY FURY	14	1964
I WILL RUBY WINTERS	4	1977
I WILL ALWAYS LOVE YOU WHITNEY HOUSTON	1	1992
I WILL ALWAYS LOVE YOU SARAH WASHINGTON	12	1993
I WILL ALWAYS LOVE YOU RIK WALLER	6	2002
I WILL BE HERE TIESTO & SNEAKY SOUNDSYSTEM	44	2009
I WILL BE RELEASED UP YER RONSON FEATURING MARY PEARCE	32	1997
I WILL BE WITH YOU T'PAU	14	1988
I WILL BE YOUR GIRLFRIEND DUBSTAR	28	1998
I WILL COME TO YOU HANSON	5	1997
I WILL DRINK THE WINE FRANK SINATRA	16	1971
I WILL FOLLOW UNA MAS	55	2002
I WILL FOLLOW YOU INTO THE DARK DEATH CAB FOR CUTIE	66	2006
I WILL GO WITH YOU (CON TE PARTIRO) DONNA SUMMER	44	1999
I WILL LOVE AGAIN LARA FABIAN	63	2000
I WILL LOVE YOU ALL MY LIFE FOSTER & ALLEN	49	1983
I WILL LOVE YOU (EV'RY TIME WHEN WE ARE GONE) FUREYS	54	1982
I WILL REMEMBER TOTO	64	1995
I WILL RETURN SPRINGWATER	5	1971
I WILL SURVIVE [A] ARRIVAL	16	1970
I WILL SURVIVE [B] GLORIA GAYNOR	1	1979
I WILL SURVIVE [B] BILLIE JO SPEARS	47	1979
I WILL SURVIVE [B] CHANTAY SAVAGE	12	1996
I WILL SURVIVE [B] DIANA ROSS	14	1996
I WILL SURVIVE [B] CAKE	29	1997
I WILL WAIT HOOTIE & THE BLOWFISH	57	1998
I WILL WAIT FOR YOU TINY DANCERS	36	2007
I WISH [A] STEVIE WONDER	5	1976
I WISH [B] GABRIELLE	26	1993
I WISH [C] SKEE-LO	15	1995
I WISH [D] R KELLY	12	2000
I WISH [E] MINI VIVA	73	2009
I WISH HE DIDN'T TRUST ME SO MUCH BOBBY WOMACK	64	1985
I WISH I COULD SHIMMY LIKE MY SISTER KATE OLYMPICS	40	1961
I WISH I KNEW HOW IT WOULD FEEL SHARLENE HECTOR WITH THE NEW INSPIRATIONAL CHOIR	28	2004
(I WISH I KNEW HOW IT WOULD FEEL TO BE) FREE/ONE LIGHTHOUSE FAMILY	6	2001
I WISH I WAS A GIRL VIOLENT DELIGHT	25	2003
I WISH I WAS A PUNK ROCKER SANDI THOM	1	2005
I WISH I WAS JAMES BOND SCOUTING FOR GIRLS	40	2008
I WISH I WAS YOU NEW RHODES	63	2004
I WISH IT COULD BE A WOMBLING CHRISTMAS WOMBLES FEATURING ROY WOOD	22	2000
I WISH IT COULD BE CHRISTMAS EVERY DAY WIZZARD	4	1973
I WISH IT COULD BE CHRISTMAS EVERYDAY ROY WOOD BIG BAND	59	1995
I WISH IT WASN'T TRUE SUPATONIC	69	2004
I WISH IT WOULD RAIN TEMPTATIONS	45	1968
I WISH IT WOULD RAIN FACES	8	1973
I WISH IT WOULD RAIN DOWN PHIL COLLINS	7	1990
I WISH U HEAVEN PRINCE	24	1988
I WISH YOU LOVE PAUL YOUNG	33	1997
I WISH YOU WOULD JOCELYN BROWN	51	1984
I WONDER [A] DICKIE VALENTINE	4	1955
I WONDER [A] JANE FROMAN	14	1955
I WONDER [B] BRENDA LEE	14	1963
I WONDER [C] CRYSTALS	36	1964
I WONDER HOW SHINING	58	2002
I WONDER IF HEAVEN GOT A GHETTO 2PAC	21	1998
I WONDER IF I TAKE YOU HOME LISA LISA & CULT JAM WITH FULL FORCE	12	1985
I WONDER WHO'S KISSING HER NOW EMILE FORD	43	1962
I WONDER WHY [A] SHOWADDYWADDY	2	1978
I WONDER WHY [B] CURTIS STIGERS	5	1992
I WONDER WHY HE'S THE GREATEST DJ TONY TOUCH FEATURING TOTAL	68	2000
I WON'T BACK DOWN TOM PETTY	28	1989
I WON'T BLEED FOR YOU CLIMIE FISHER	35	1988
I WON'T CHANGE YOU SOPHIE ELLIS-BEXTOR	9	2004
I WON'T CLOSE MY EYES UB40	32	1982
I WON'T COME IN WHILE HE'S THERE JIM REEVES	12	1967
I WON'T CRY GLEN GOLDSMITH	34	1987
I WON'T FEEL BAD SIMPLY RED	68	1988
I WON'T FORGET YOU JIM REEVES	3	1964
I WON'T HOLD YOU BACK TOTO	37	1983
I WON'T LAST A DAY WITHOUT YOU CARPENTERS	9	1972
I WON'T LET THE SUN GO DOWN ON ME NIK KERSHAW	2	1983
I WON'T LET YOU DOWN PhD	3	1982
I WON'T LET YOU DOWN W.I.P. FEATURING EMMIE	53	2002
I WON'T MENTION IT AGAIN RUBY WINTERS	45	1978
I WON'T RUN AWAY ALVIN STARDUST	7	1984
I WOULD DIE 4 U PRINCE & THE REVOLUTION	58	1984
I WOULD DIE 4 U SPACE COWBOY	55	2002
I WOULD DO FOR YOU UB40	45	1989
I WOULD FIX YOU KENICKIE	36	1998
I WOULD NEVER BLUE NILE	52	2004
I WOULDN'T BELIEVE YOUR RADIO STEREOPHONICS	11	1999
I WOULDN'T LIE YARBOROUGH & PEOPLES	61	1986
I WOULDN'T NORMALLY DO THIS KIND OF THING PET SHOP BOYS	13	1993
I WOULDN'T TRADE YOU FOR THE WORLD BACHELORS	4	1964
I WOULDN'T WANNA HAPPEN TO YOU EMBRACE	23	2000
I WRITE SINS NOT TRAGEDIES PANIC! AT THE DISCO	25	2006
I WRITE THE SONGS DAVID CASSIDY	11	1975
I WROTE YOU A SONG MISTY OLDLAND	73	1994
IBIZA MAXIMA FEATURING LILY	55	1993
ICE BOX OMARION	14	2007
ICE CREAM NEW YOUNG PONY CLUB	40	2007
ICE CREAM GUERILLA WOLFMAN	60	2005
THE ICE CREAM MAN TORNADOS	18	1963

	Peak Position	Year of Release
ICE HOCKEY HAIR SUPER FURRY ANIMALS	12	1998
ICE ICE BABY VANILLA ICE	1	1990
ICE IN THE SUN STATUS QUO	8	1968
ICE RAIN ALEX WHITCOMBE & BIG C	44	1998
ICEBLINK LUCK COCTEAU TWINS	38	1990
ICH BIN EIN AUSLANDER POP WILL EAT ITSELF	28	1994
ICH WILL RAMMSTEIN	30	2002
ICING ON THE CAKE STEPHEN 'TIN TIN' DUFFY	14	1985
ICKY THUMP WHITE STRIPES	2	2007
I'D BE SURPRISINGLY GOOD FOR YOU LINDA LEWIS	40	1979
I'D COME FOR YOU NICKELBACK	67	2009
I'D DIE WITHOUT YOU PM DAWN	30	1992
I'D DO ANYTHING MIKE PRESTON	23	1960
I'D DO ANYTHING FOR LOVE (BUT I WON'T DO THAT) MEAT LOAF	1	1993
I'D LIE FOR YOU (AND THAT'S THE TRUTH) MEAT LOAF	2	1995
I'D LIKE TO TEACH THE WORLD TO SING NO WAY SIS	27	1996
I'D LIKE TO TEACH THE WORLD TO SING DEMI HOLBORN	27	2002
I'D LIKE TO TEACH THE WORLD TO SING (IN PERFECT HARMONY) NEW SEEKERS	1	1971
I'D LOVE YOU TO WANT ME LOBO	5	1974
I'D NEVER FIND ANOTHER YOU BILLY FURY	5	1961
I'D RATHER DANCE WITH YOU KINGS OF CONVENIENCE	60	2004
I'D RATHER GO BLIND CHICKEN SHACK	14	1969
I'D RATHER GO BLIND RUBY TURNER	24	1987
I'D RATHER GO BLIND SYDNEY YOUNGBLOOD	44	1990
I'D RATHER JACK REYNOLDS GIRLS	8	1989
I'D REALLY LOVE TO SEE YOU TONIGHT ENGLAND DAN & JOHN FORD COLEY	26	1976
I'D WAIT FOR LIFE TAKE THAT	17	2007
THE IDEAL HEIGHT BIFFY CLYRO	46	2003
IDEAL WORLD CHRISTIANS	14	1987
IDENTITY X-RAY SPEX	24	1978
IDIOTS AT THE WHEEL EP. KINGMAKER	30	1992
IDLE GOSSIP PERRY COMO	3	1954
IDLE ON PARADE EP ANTHONY NEWLEY	13	1959
IDOL AMANDA GHOST	63	2000
THE IDOL [A] W.A.S.P.	41	1992
THE IDOL [B] MARC ALMOND	44	1995
IEYA TOYAH	48	1982
IF [A] TELLY SAVALAS	1	1975
IF [A] YIN & YAN	25	1975
IF [A] JOHN ALFORD	24	1996
IF [A] DOLLY PARTON	73	2002
IF [B] JANET JACKSON	14	1993
IF... [C] BLUETONES	13	1998
IF A MAN ANSWERS BOBBY DARIN	24	1962
IF ANYONE FINDS THIS I LOVE YOU RUBY MURRAY WITH ANNE WARREN	4	1955
IF DREAMS CAME TRUE PAT BOONE	16	1958
IF EVER 3RD STOREE	53	1999
IF EVERY DAY WAS LIKE CHRISTMAS ELVIS PRESLEY	9	1966
IF EVERYBODY LOOKED THE SAME GROOVE ARMADA	25	1999
IF EYE LOVE U 2 NIGHT MAYTE	67	1995
IF GOD WILL SEND HIS ANGELS U2	12	1997
IF HE TELLS YOU ADAM FAITH & THE ROULETTES	25	1964
IF I AIN'T GOT YOU ALICIA KEYS	18	2004
IF I CAN DREAM ELVIS PRESLEY	11	1969
IF I CAN DREAM (EP) MICHAEL BALL	51	1992
IF I CAN'T 50 CENT/G-UNIT	10	2004
IF I CAN'T CHANGE YOUR MIND SUGAR	30	1993
IF I CAN'T HAVE YOU YVONNE ELLIMAN	4	1978
IF I CAN'T HAVE YOU KIM WILDE	12	1993
IF I COULD [A] DAVID ESSEX	13	1975
IF I COULD [B] HUNDRED REASONS	19	2002
IF I COULD BUILD MY WHOLE WORLD AROUND YOU MARVIN GAYE & TAMMI TERRELL	41	1968
IF I COULD (EL CONDOR PASA) JULIE FELIX	19	1970
IF I COULD FLY GRACE	29	1996
IF I COULD GIVE YOU ALL MY LOVE COUNTING CROWS	50	2003
IF I COULD GO ANGIE MARTINEZ FEATURING LIL' MO & SACARIO	61	2003
IF I COULD ONLY MAKE YOU CARE MIKE BERRY	37	1980
IF I COULD ONLY SAY GOODBYE DAVID HASSELHOFF	35	1993
IF I COULD TALK I'D TELL YOU LEMONHEADS	39	1996
IF I COULD TURN BACK THE HANDS OF TIME R KELLY	2	1999
IF I COULD TURN BACK TIME CHER	6	1989
IF I DIDN'T CARE DAVID CASSIDY	9	1974
IF I DIE TOMORROW MOTLEY CRUE	63	2005
IF I EVER FALL IN LOVE SHAI	36	1993
IF I EVER FEEL BETTER PHOENIX	65	2001
IF I EVER LOSE MY FAITH IN YOU STING	14	1993
IF I FALL ALICE MARTINEAU	45	2002
IF I GIVE MY HEART TO YOU JOAN REGAN	3	1954
IF I GIVE MY HEART TO YOU DORIS DAY WITH THE MELLOMEN	4	1954
IF I GIVE YOU MY NUMBER PJ & DUNCAN	15	1994
IF I HAD A HAMMER TRINI LOPEZ	4	1963
IF I HAD EYES JACK JOHNSON	60	2008
IF I HAD NO LOOT TONY TONI TONE	44	1993
IF I HAD WORDS SCOTT FITZGERALD & YVONNE KEELEY & THE ST THOMAS MORE SCHOOL CHOIR	3	1978
IF I HAD YOU KORGIS	13	1979
IF I HAVE TO GO AWAY JIGSAW	36	1977
IF I HAVE TO STAND ALONE LONNIE GORDON	68	1990
IF I KNEW THEN WHAT I KNOW NOW VAL DOONICAN	14	1968
IF I LET YOU GO WESTLIFE	1	1999
IF I LOVE U 2 NITE MICA PARIS	43	1991
IF I LOVE YA THEN I NEED YA IF I NEED YA THEN I WANT YOU AROUND EARTHA KITT	43	1994
IF I LOVED YOU RICHARD ANTHONY	18	1964
IF I NEEDED SOMEONE HOLLIES	20	1965
IF I NEVER KNEW YOU (LOVE THEME FROM 'POCAHONTAS') JON SECADA & SHANICE	51	1995
IF I NEVER SEE YOU AGAIN WET WET WET	3	1997
IF I NEVER SEE YOUR FACE AGAIN MAROON 5 FEATURING RIHANNA	28	2008
IF I ONLY HAD TIME JOHN ROWLES	3	1968
IF I ONLY KNEW TOM JONES	11	1994
IF I REMEMBER BENZ	59	1997
IF I RULED THE WORLD [A] HARRY SECOMBE	18	1963
IF I RULED THE WORLD [A] TONY BENNETT	40	1965
IF I RULED THE WORLD [B] KURTIS BLOW	24	1986
IF I RULED THE WORLD [B] NAS	12	1996
IF I SAID YOU HAD A BEAUTIFUL BODY WOULD YOU HOLD IT AGAINST ME BELLAMY BROTHERS	3	1979
IF I SAY YES FIVE STAR	15	1986
IF I SHOULD FALL FROM GRACE WITH GOD POGUES	58	1988
IF I SHOULD LOVE AGAIN BARRY MANILOW	66	1982
IF I SURVIVE HYBRID FEATURING JULEE CRUISE	52	1999
IF I THOUGHT YOU'D EVER CHANGE YOUR MIND CILLA BLACK	20	1969
IF I THOUGHT YOU'D EVER CHANGE YOUR MIND AGNETHA FALTSKOG	11	2004
IF I TOLD YOU THAT WHITNEY HOUSTON & GEORGE MICHAEL	9	2000
IF I WAS [A] MIDGE URE	1	1985
IF I WAS [B] ASWAD	58	1995
IF I WAS A RIVER TINA ARENA	43	1998
IF I WAS YOUR GIRLFRIEND PRINCE	20	1987
IF I WERE A BOY BEYONCE	1	2008
IF I WERE A CARPENTER BOBBY DARIN	9	1966
IF I WERE A CARPENTER FOUR TOPS	7	1968
IF I WERE A CARPENTER ROBERT PLANT	63	1993
IF I WERE A RICH MAN TOPOL	9	1967
IF I WERE YOU [A] k.d. lang	53	1995
IF I WERE YOU [B] CANDEE JAY	14	2004
IF I'M NOT YOUR LOVER AL B SURE! FEATURING SLICK RICK	54	1989
IF IT DON'T FIT DON'T FORCE IT KELLEE PATTERSON	44	1978
IF IT HAPPENS AGAIN UB40	9	1984
IF IT MAKES YOU HAPPY SHERYL CROW	9	1996
IF IT WASN'T FOR THE REASON THAT I LOVE YOU MIKI ANTHONY	27	1973
IF IT'S ALRIGHT WITH YOU BABY KORGIS	56	1980
IF IT'S LOVE THAT YOU WANT DONNY OSMOND	70	1988
IF IT'S LOVIN' THAT YOU WANT RIHANNA	11	2005
IF LEAVING ME IS EASY PHIL COLLINS	17	1981
IF LIFE IS LIKE A LOVE BANK I WANT AN OVERDRAFT WILDHEARTS	31	1995
IF LOOKS COULD KILL TRANSVISION VAMP	41	1991
IF LOVE WAS A TRAIN MICHELLE SHOCKED	63	1989
IF LOVE WAS LIKE GUITARS IAN McNABB	67	1993
IF LOVING YOU IS WRONG (I DON'T WANT TO BE RIGHT) ROD STEWART	23	1980
IF MADONNA CALLS JUNIOR VASQUEZ	24	1996
IF MY FRIENDS COULD SEE ME NOW LINDA CLIFFORD	50	1978
IF NOT FOR YOU OLIVIA NEWTON-JOHN	7	1971
IF NOT YOU DR HOOK	5	1976
IF ONLY [A] HANSON	15	2000
IF ONLY [B] KT TUNSTALL	45	2008
IF ONLY I COULD SYDNEY YOUNGBLOOD	3	1989
IF ONLY I COULD LIVE MY LIFE AGAIN JANE MORGAN	27	1959
IF ONLY TOMORROW RONNIE CARROLL	33	1962
(IF PARADISE IS) HALF AS NICE AMEN CORNER	1	1969
IF – READ TO FAURE'S 'PAVANE' DES LYNAM FEATURING WIMBLEDON CHORAL SOCIETY	45	1998
IF SHE KNEW LEMAR	14	2008
IF SHE KNEW WHAT SHE WANTS BANGLES	31	1986
IF SHE SHOULD COME TO YOU ANTHONY NEWLEY	4	1960
IF 60S WERE 90S BEAUTIFUL PEOPLE	74	1994
IF THAT WERE ME MELANIE C	18	2000
IF THAT'S OK WITH YOU SHAYNE WARD	2	2007
IF THAT'S YOUR BOYFIEND (HE WASN'T LAST NIGHT) ME'SHELL NDEGEOCELLO	74	1994
IF THE KIDS ARE UNITED SHAM 69	9	1978
IF THE RIVER CAN BEND ELTON JOHN	32	1998
IF THE WHOLE WORLD STOPPED LOVING VAL DOONICAN	3	1967
IF THERE WAS A MAN PRETENDERS FOR 007	49	1987
IF THERE'S ANY JUSTICE LEMAR	3	2004
IF THIS IS IT [A] HUEY LEWIS & THE NEWS	39	1984
IF THIS IS IT [B] NEWTON FAULKNER	56	2009
IF THIS IS LOVE [A] JJ	55	1991
IF THIS IS LOVE [B] JEANIE TRACY	73	1994
IF THIS IS LOVE [C] SATURDAYS	8	2008
IF THIS ISN'T LOVE JENNIFER HUDSON	37	2009
IF TODAY WAS YOUR LAST DAY NICKELBACK	64	2009
IF TOMORROW NEVER COMES RONAN KEATING	1	2002

	Peak Position	Year of Release
IF U WANT ME MICHAEL WOODS FEATURING IMOGEN BAILEY	46	2003
IF WE EVER MEET AGAIN TIMBALAND FEATURING KATY PERRY	3	2010
IF WE FALL IN LOVE TONIGHT ROD STEWART	58	1996
IF WE HOLD ON TOGETHER DIANA ROSS	11	1992
IF WE TRY KAREN RAMIREZ	23	1998
IF WE WERE LOVERS GLORIA ESTEFAN	40	1993
IF YA GETTING' DOWN FIVE	2	1999
IF YOU ASKED ME TO CELINE DION	57	1992
IF YOU BELIEVE JOHNNIE RAY	7	1955
IF YOU BUY THIS RECORD YOU LIFE WILL BE TAMPERER FEATURING MAYA	3	1998
IF YOU C JORDAN SOMETHING CORPORATE	68	2003
IF YOU CAN WANT SMOKEY ROBINSON & THE MIRACLES	50	1968
IF YOU CAN'T DO IT WHEN YOU'RE YOUNG, WHEN CAN YOU DO IT? THEAUDIENCE	48	1998
IF YOU CAN'T GIVE ME LOVE SUZI QUATRO	4	1978
IF YOU CAN'T SAY NO LENNY KRAVITZ	48	1998
IF YOU CAN'T STAND THE HEAT BUCKS FIZZ	10	1982
IF YOU CARED KIM APPLEBY	44	1991
IF YOU COME BACK BLUE	1	2001
IF YOU COME TO ME ATOMIC KITTEN	3	2003
IF YOU COULD READ MY MIND GORDON LIGHTFOOT	30	1971
IF YOU COULD READ MY MIND STARS ON 54	23	1998
IF YOU COULD SEE ME NOW SHAKATAK	49	1983
IF YOU DON'T KNOW ME BY NOW HAROLD MELVIN & THE BLUENOTES	9	1973
IF YOU DON'T KNOW ME BY NOW SIMPLY RED	2	1989
IF YOU DON'T LOVE ME PREFAB SPROUT	33	1992
IF YOU DON'T WANT ME TO DESTROY YOU SUPER FURRY ANIMALS	18	1996
IF YOU DON'T WANT MY LOVE ROBERT JOHN	42	1968
IF YOU EVER EAST 17 FEATURING GABRIELLE	2	1996
IF YOU EVER LEAVE ME BARBRA STREISAND/ VINCE GILL	26	1999
IF YOU FEEL IT THELMA HOUSTON	48	1981
IF YOU GO JON SECADA	39	1994
IF YOU GO AWAY [A] TERRY JACKS	8	1974
IF YOU GO AWAY [B] NEW KIDS ON THE BLOCK	9	1991
IF YOU GOT THE MONEY JAMIE T	13	2006
IF YOU GOTTA GO GO NOW MANFRED MANN	2	1965
IF YOU GOTTA MAKE A FOOL OF SOMEBODY FREDDIE & THE DREAMERS	3	1963
IF YOU HAD MY LOVE JENNIFER LOPEZ	4	1999
IF YOU HAVE TO GO GENEVA	69	2000
IF YOU KNEW SOUSA (AND FRIENDS) ROYAL PHILHARMONIC ORCHESTRA ARRANGED & CONDUCTED BY LOUIS CLARK	71	1982
IF YOU KNOW WHAT I MEAN NEIL DIAMOND	35	1976
IF YOU LEAVE ORCHESTRAL MANOEUVRES IN THE DARK	48	1986
IF YOU LEAVE ME NOW CHICAGO	1	1976
IF YOU LEAVE ME NOW UPSIDE DOWN	27	1996
IF YOU LEAVE ME NOW SYSTEM PRESENTS KERRI B	55	2003
IF YOU LET ME STAY TERENCE TRENT D'ARBY	7	1987
IF YOU LOVE HER DICK EMERY	32	1969
IF YOU LOVE ME [A] MARY HOPKIN	32	1976
IF YOU LOVE ME [B] BROWNSTONE	8	1995
IF YOU LOVE SOMEBODY SET THEM FREE STING	26	1985
IF YOU ONLY LET ME IN MN8	6	1995
IF YOU REALLY CARED GABRIELLE	15	1996
IF YOU REALLY LOVE ME STEVIE WONDER	20	1972
IF YOU REALLY WANNA KNOW MARC DORSEY	58	1999
IF YOU REALLY WANT TO MEAT LOAF	59	1983
IF YOU REMEMBER ME CHRIS THOMPSON	42	1979
IF YOU SEEK AMY BRITNEY SPEARS	20	2009
IF YOU SHOULD NEED A FRIEND FIRE ISLAND FEATURING MARK ANTHONI	51	1995
IF YOU TALK IN YOUR SLEEP ELVIS PRESLEY	40	1974
IF YOU THINK YOU KNOW HOW TO LOVE ME SMOKEY	3	1975
(IF YOU THINK YOU'RE) GROOVY PP ARNOLD	41	1968
IF YOU TOLERATE THIS YOUR CHILDREN WILL BE NEXT MANIC STREET PREACHERS	1	1998
IF YOU WALK AWAY PETER COX	24	1997
IF YOU WANNA BE HAPPY JIMMY SOUL	39	1963
IF YOU WANNA BE HAPPY ROCKY SHARPE & THE REPLAYS	46	1983
IF YOU WANNA PARTY MOLELLA FEATURING THE OUTHERE BROTHERS	9	1995
IF YOU WANT LUCIANA	47	1994
IF YOU WANT ME HINDA HICKS	25	1998
IF YOU WANT MY LOVE CHEAP TRICK	57	1982
IF YOU WANT MY LOVIN' EVELYN KING	43	1981
IF YOU WERE A SAILBOAT KATIE MELUA	23	2007
IF YOU WERE HERE TONIGHT ALEXANDER O'NEAL	13	1986
IF YOU WERE HERE TONIGHT MATT GOSS	23	1996
IF YOU WERE MINE MARCOS HERNANDEZ	41	2006
IF YOU WERE MINE MARY EDDY ARNOLD	49	1966
IF YOU WERE THE ONLY BOY IN THE WORLD STEVIE MARSH	24	1959
IF YOU WERE WITH ME NOW KYLIE MINOGUE & KEITH WASHINGTON	4	1991
IF YOU'LL BE MINE BABYBIRD	28	1998
IF YOUR GIRL ONLY KNEW AALIYAH	15	1996
IF YOUR HEART ISN'T IN IT ATLANTIC STARR	48	1986
IF YOU'RE GONE MATCHBOX 20	50	2001
IF YOU'RE LOOKING FOR A WAY OUT ODYSSEY	6	1980
IF YOU'RE NOT THE ONE DANIEL BEDINGFIELD	1	2002
IF YOU'RE READY (COME GO WITH ME) STAPLE SINGERS	34	1974
IF YOU'RE READY (COME GO WITH ME) RUBY TURNER FEATURING JONATHAN BUTLER	30	1986
IF YOU'RE THINKING OF ME DODGY	11	1996
IGGIN' ME CHICO DeBARGE	50	1998
IGNITION R KELLY	1	2003
IGNORANCE [A] OCEANIC FEATURING SIOBHAN MAHER	72	1992
IGNORANCE [B] PARAMORE	14	2009
IGUANA MAURO PICOTTO	33	2000
III WISHES TERRORVISION	42	1999
IKO IKO DIXIE CUPS	23	1965
IKO IKO NATASHA	10	1982
IKO IKO BELLE STARS	35	1982
IL ADORE BOY GEORGE	50	1995
IL EST NE LE DIVIN ENFANT SIOUXSIE & THE BANSHEES	49	1982
IL NOSTRO CONCERTO UMBERTO BINDI	47	1960
IL SILENZIO NINI ROSSO	8	1965
I'LL ALWAYS BE AROUND C & C MUSIC FACTORY	42	1995
I'LL ALWAYS BE IN LOVE WITH YOU MICHAEL HOLLIDAY	27	1958
I'LL ALWAYS LOVE MY MAMA INTRUDERS	32	1974
I'LL ALWAYS LOVE YOU TAYLOR DAYNE	41	1988
I'LL BE FOXY BROWN FEATURING JAY-Z	9	1997
(I'LL BE A) FREAK FOR YOU ROYALLE DELITE	45	1985
I'LL BE AROUND TERRI WELLS	17	1984
I'LL BE AROUND RAPPIN' 4-TAY FEATURING THE SPINNERS	30	1995
I'LL BE BACK ARNEE & THE TERMINATORS	5	1991
I'LL BE GOOD RENE & ANGELA	22	1985
I'LL BE GOOD TO YOU QUINCY JONES FEATURING RAY CHARLES & CHAKA KHAN	21	1990
I'LL BE HOME PAT BOONE	1	1956
I'LL BE HOME THIS CHRISTMAS SHAKIN' STEVENS	34	1991
I'LL BE LOVING YOU (FOREVER) NEW KIDS ON THE BLOCK	5	1990
I'LL BE MISSING YOU PUFF DADDY & FAITH EVANS	1	1997
I'LL BE OK McFLY	1	2005
I'LL BE READY SUNBLOCK	4	2006
I'LL BE SATISFIED SHAKIN' STEVENS	10	1982
I'LL BE THERE [A] GERRY & THE PACEMAKERS	15	1965
I'LL BE THERE [B] JACKIE TRENT	38	1969
I'LL BE THERE [C] JACKSON 5	4	1970
I'LL BE THERE [C] MARIAH CAREY	2	1992
I'LL BE THERE [D] INNOCENCE	26	1992
I'LL BE THERE [E] 99TH FLOOR ELEVATORS FEATURING TONY DE VIT	37	1996
I'LL BE THERE [F] EMMA	7	2004
I'LL BE THERE FOR YOU [A] BON JOVI	18	1989
I'LL BE THERE FOR YOU [B] REMBRANDTS	3	1995
I'LL BE THERE FOR YOU [C] SOLID HARMONIE	18	1998
I'LL BE THERE FOR YOU (DOYA DODODO DOYA) HOUSE OF VIRGINISM	29	1993
I'LL BE THERE FOR YOU-YOU'RE ALL I NEED TO GET BY METHOD MAN/MARY J BLIGE	10	1995
I'LL BE WAITING [A] CLIVE GRIFFIN	56	1991
I'LL BE WAITING [B] FULL INTENTION PRESENTS SHENA	44	2001
I'LL BE WITH YOU IN APPLE BLOSSOM TIME ROSEMARY JUNE	14	1959
I'LL BE YOUR ANGEL KIRA	9	2003
I'LL BE YOUR BABY TONIGHT ROBERT PALMER & UB40	6	1990
I'LL BE YOUR BABY TONIGHT NORAH JONES	67	2003
I'LL BE YOUR EVERYTHING TOMMY PAGE	53	1990
I'LL BE YOUR FRIEND ROBERT OWENS	25	1991
I'LL BE YOUR SHELTER TAYLOR DAYNE	43	1990
I'LL COME RUNNIN' JUICE	48	1998
I'LL COME RUNNING CLIFF RICHARD	26	1967
I'LL COME WHEN YOU CALL RUBY MURRAY	6	1955
I'LL CRY FOR YOU EUROPE	28	1992
I'LL CUT YOUR TAIL OFF JOHN LEYTON	36	1963
I'LL DO ANYTHING – TO MAKE YOU MINE HOLLOWAY & CO	58	1999
I'LL DO ANYTHING YOU WANT ME TO BARRY WHITE	20	1975
I'LL DO YA WHALE	53	1995
I'LL FIND MY WAY HOME JON & VANGELIS	6	1981
I'LL FIND YOU [A] DAVID WHITFIELD	27	1957
I'LL FIND YOU [B] MICHELLE GAYLE	26	1994
I'LL FLY FOR YOU SPANDAU BALLET	9	1984
I'LL GET BY CONNIE FRANCIS	19	1958
I'LL GET BY SHIRLEY BASSEY	10	1961
I'LL GIVE YOU THE EARTH (TOUS LES BATEAUX, TOUS LES OISEAUX) KEITH MICHELL	30	1971
I'LL GO CRAZY IF I DON'T GO CRAZY TONIGHT U2	32	2009
I'LL GO ON HOPING DES O'CONNOR	30	1970
I'LL GO WHERE YOUR MUSIC TAKES ME JIMMY JAMES & THE VAGABONDS	23	1976
I'LL GO WHERE YOUR MUSIC TAKES ME TINA CHARLES	27	1978
I'LL HOUSE YOU RICHIE RICH MEETS THE JUNGLE BROTHERS	22	1988
I'LL KEEP ON LOVING YOU PRINCESS	16	1986

	Peak Position	Year of Release
I'LL KEEP YOU SATISFIED BILLY J. KRAMER & THE DAKOTAS	4	1963
I'LL KEEP YOUR DREAMS ALIVE GEORGE BENSON & PATTI AUSTIN	68	1992
I'LL LOVE YOU FOREVER TODAY CLIFF RICHARD	27	1968
I'LL MAKE LOVE TO YOU BOYZ II MEN	5	1994
I'LL MANAGE SOMEHOW MENSWEAR	49	1995
I'LL MEET YOU AT MIDNIGHT SMOKIE	11	1976
I'LL NEVER BREAK YOUR HEART BACKSTREET BOYS	8	1995
I'LL NEVER FALL IN LOVE AGAIN [A] JOHNNIE RAY	26	1959
I'LL NEVER FALL IN LOVE AGAIN [B] TOM JONES	2	1967
I'LL NEVER FALL IN LOVE AGAIN [C] BOBBIE GENTRY	1	1969
I'LL NEVER FIND ANOTHER YOU SEEKERS	1	1965
I'LL NEVER GET OVER YOU [A] JOHNNY KIDD & THE PIRATES	4	1963
I'LL NEVER GET OVER YOU [B] EVERLY BROTHERS	35	1965
I'LL NEVER GET OVER YOU (GETTING OVER ME) EXPOSE	75	1993
I'LL NEVER LOVE THIS WAY AGAIN DIONNE WARWICK	62	1983
I'LL NEVER QUITE GET OVER YOU BILLY FURY	35	1966
I'LL NEVER STOP *NSYNC	13	2000
I'LL NEVER STOP LOVING YOU DORIS DAY	17	1955
I'LL PICK A ROSE FOR MY ROSE MARV JOHNSON	10	1969
I'LL PUT YOU TOGETHER AGAIN HOT CHOCOLATE	13	1978
I'LL REMEMBER MADONNA	7	1994
I'LL REMEMBER TONIGHT PAT BOONE	18	1959
I'LL SAIL THIS SHIP ALONE BEAUTIFUL SOUTH	31	1989
I'LL SAY FOREVER MY LOVE JIMMY RUFFIN	7	1970
I'LL SEE IT THROUGH TEXAS	40	2003
I'LL SEE YOU ALONG THE WAY RICK CLARKE	63	1988
I'LL SEE YOU AROUND SILVER SUN	26	1998
I'LL SEE YOU IN MY DREAMS PAT BOONE	27	1962
I'LL SET YOU FREE BANGLES	74	1989
I'LL SLEEP WHEN I'M DEAD BON JOVI	17	1993
I'LL STAND BY YOU PRETENDERS	10	1994
I'LL STAND BY YOU GIRLS ALOUD	1	2004
I'LL STAY BY YOU KENNY LYNCH	29	1965
I'LL STAY SINGLE JERRY LORDAN	26	1960
I'LL STEP DOWN GARRY MILLS	39	1961
I'LL STICK AROUND FOO FIGHTERS	18	1995
I'LL STOP AT NOTHING SANDIE SHAW	4	1965
I'LL TAKE THE RAIN R.E.M.	44	2001
I'LL TAKE YOU HOME DRIFTERS	37	1963
I'LL TAKE YOU HOME CLIFF BENNETT & THE REBEL ROUSERS	42	1965
I'LL TAKE YOU HOME AGAIN KATHLEEN SLIM WHITMAN	7	1957
I'LL TAKE YOU THERE STAPLE SINGERS	30	1972
I'LL TAKE YOU THERE GENERAL PUBLIC	73	1994
I'LL TRY ANYTHING DUSTY SPRINGFIELD	13	1967
I'LL WAIT TAYLOR DAYNE	29	1994
I'LL WALK WITH GOD MARIO LANZA	18	1955
ILLEGAL SHAKIRA FEATURING CARLOS SANTANA	34	2006
ILLEGAL ALIEN GENESIS	46	1984
ILLEGAL ATTACKS IAN BROWN FEATURING SINEAD O'CONNOR	16	2007
ILLEGAL GUNSHOT RAGGA TWINS	51	1990
ILLUMINATIONS SWANS WAY	57	1984
ILLUSIONS CYPRESS HILL	23	1996
ILOVEROCKNROLL JESUS & MARY CHAIN	38	1998
I'M A BELIEVER MONKEES	1	1967
I'M A BELIEVER ROBERT WYATT	29	1974
I'M A BELIEVER EMF/REEVES & MORTIMER	3	1995
I'M A BETTER MAN (FOR HAVING LOVED YOU) ENGELBERT HUMPERDINCK	15	1969
I'M A BITCH OLGA	68	1994
I'M A BOY WHO	2	1966
I'M A CLOWN DAVID CASSIDY	3	1973
I'M A CUCKOO BELLE & SEBASTIAN	14	2004
I'M A DISCO DANCER CHRISTOPHER JUST	69	1997
I'M A DOUN FOR LACK O' JOHNNIE (A LITTLE SCOTTISH FANTASY) VANESSA-MAE	28	1996
(I'M A) DREAMER B B & Q BAND	35	1986
I'M A FLIRT R KELLY FEATURING TI & T-PAIN	18	2007
I'M A FOOL SLIM WHITMAN	16	1956
I'M A FOOL TO CARE JOE BARRY	49	1961
I'M A GOOD MAN MARTIN SOLVEIG	57	2004
I'M A LITTLE CHRISTMAS CRACKER BOUNCING CZECKS	72	1984
I'M A MAN SPENCER DAVIS GROUP	9	1967
I'M A MAN CHICAGO	8	1970
I'M A MAN NOT A BOY [A] CHESNEY HAWKES	27	1991
I'M A MAN NOT A BOY [B] NORTH & SOUTH	7	1997
I'M A MAN – YE KE YE KE (MEDLEY) CLUBHOUSE	69	1989
I'M A MESSAGE IDLEWILD	41	1998
I'M A MIDNIGHT MOVER WILSON PICKETT	38	1968
I'M A MOODY GUY SHANE FENTON & THE FENTONES	22	1961
I'M A RAT TOWERS OF LONDON	46	2007
(I'M A) ROAD RUNNER JUNIOR WALKER & THE ALL-STARS	12	1969
I'M A SLAVE 4 U BRITNEY SPEARS	4	2001
I'M A SUCKER FOR YOUR LOVE TEENA MARIE, CO-LEAD VOCALS RICK JAMES	43	1979
I'M A TIGER LULU	9	1968
I'M A WONDERFUL THING, BABY KID CREOLE & THE COCONUTS	4	1982
I'M ALIVE [A] HOLLIES	1	1965
I'M ALIVE [B] ELECTRIC LIGHT ORCHESTRA	20	1980
I'M ALIVE [C] CUT 'N' MOVE	49	1995
I'M ALIVE [D] SEAL	4	1994
I'M ALIVE [E] STRETCH 'N' VERN PRESENT MADDOG	17	1996
I'M ALIVE [F] CELINE DION	17	2002
I'M ALL ABOUT YOU DJ LUCK & MC NEAT FEATURING ARI GOLD	18	2001
I'M ALL OVER IT JAMIE CULLUM	55	2009
I'M ALL YOU NEED SAMANTHA FOX	41	1986
I'M ALREADY THERE WESTLIFE	62	2007
I'M ALRIGHT [A] YOUNG STEVE & THE AFTERNOON BOYS	40	1982
I'M ALRIGHT [B] KATHERINE E	41	1991
(I'M ALWAYS TOUCHED BY YOUR) PRESENCE DEAR BLONDIE	10	1978
I'M AN UPSTART ANGELIC UPSTARTS	31	1979
I'M BACK FOR MORE LULU & BOBBY WOMACK	27	1993
I'M BAD LL COOL J	71	1987
I'M BLUE 5,6,7,8'S	71	2004
I'M BORN AGAIN BONEY M	35	1979
I'M BROKEN PANTERA	19	1994
I'M CHILLIN' KURTIS BLOW	64	1986
I'M COMIN' HARDCORE M.A.N.I.C.	60	1992
I'M COMING HOME TOM JONES	2	1967
I'M COMING HOME CINDY TRINI LOPEZ	28	1966
I'M COMING OUT DIANA ROSS	13	1980
I'M COMING WITH YA MATT GOSS	22	2003
I'M COUNTING ON YOU PETULA CLARK	41	1962
I'M CRYING ANIMALS	8	1964
I'M DOIN' FINE DAY ONE	68	1999
I'M DOING FINE JASON DONOVAN	22	1990
I'M DOING FINE NOW NEW YORK CITY	20	1973
I'M DOING FINE NOW PASADENAS	4	1992
I'M EASY FAITH NO MORE	3	1993
I'M EVERY WOMAN CHAKA KHAN	8	1978
I'M EVERY WOMAN WHITNEY HOUSTON	4	1993
I'M FALLING BLUEBELLS	62	1984
I'M FOR REAL NIGHTMARES ON WAX	38	1990
I'M FOREVER BLOWING BUBBLES WEST HAM UNITED CUP SQUAD	31	1975
I'M FOREVER BLOWING BUBBLES COCKNEY REJECTS	35	1980
I'M FREE [A] ROGER DALTREY	13	1973
I'M FREE [B] SOUP DRAGONS FEATURING JUNIOR REID	5	1990
I'M FREE [C] JON SECADA	50	1993
I'M FROM FURTHER NORTH THAN YOU WEDDING PRESENT	34	2005
I'M GLAD JENNIFER LOPEZ	11	2003
I'M GOIN' DOWN MARY J BLIGE	12	1995
I'M GOING ALL THE WAY SOUNDS OF BLACKNESS	14	1993
I'M GOING HOME (TO SEE MY BABY) GENE VINCENT	36	1961
I'M GOING SLIGHTLY MAD QUEEN	22	1991
I'M GONE DIANA ROSS	36	1995
I'M GONNA BE (500 MILES) PROCLAIMERS	11	1988
(I'M GONNA BE) 500 MILES PROCLAIMERS FEATURING BRIAN POTTER & ANDY PIPKIN	1	2007
I'M GONNA BE A COUNTRY GIRL AGAIN BUFFY SAINTE-MARIE	34	1972
I'M GONNA BE ALRIGHT JENNIFER LOPEZ FEATURING NAS	3	2002
I'M GONNA BE STRONG GENE PITNEY	2	1964
I'M GONNA BE STRONG CYNDI LAUPER	37	1995
I'M GONNA BE WARM THIS WINTER CONNIE FRANCIS	48	1962
I'M GONNA CHANGE EVERYTHING JIM REEVES	42	1962
(I'M GONNA) CRY MYSELF BLIND PRIMAL SCREAM	49	1994
I'M GONNA GET MARRIED LLOYD PRICE	23	1959
I'M GONNA GET ME A GUN CAT STEVENS	6	1967
I'M GONNA GET THERE SOMEHOW VAL DOONICAN	25	1965
I'M GONNA GET YA BABY BLACK CONNECTION	62	1998
I'M GONNA GET YOU BIZARRE INC FEATURING ANGIE BROWN	3	1992
I'M GONNA GET YOU SUCKA GAP BAND	63	1989
I'M GONNA GETCHA GOOD! SHANIA TWAIN	4	2002
I'M GONNA KNOCK ON YOUR DOOR EDDIE HODGES	37	1961
I'M GONNA KNOCK ON YOUR DOOR LITTLE JIMMY OSMOND	11	1974
I'M GONNA LOVE HER FOR BOTH OF US MEAT LOAF	62	1981
I'M GONNA LOVE YOU FOREVER CROWN HEIGHTS AFFAIR	47	1978
I'M GONNA LOVE YOU JUST A LITTLE BIT MORE BABY BARRY WHITE	23	1973
I'M GONNA MAKE YOU LOVE ME DIANA ROSS & THE SUPREMES & THE TEMPTATIONS	3	1969
I'M GONNA MAKE YOU MINE [A] LOU CHRISTIE	2	1969
I'M GONNA MAKE YOU MINE [B] TANYA BLOUNT	69	1994
I'M GONNA MISS YOU FOREVER AARON CARTER	24	1998
I'M GONNA RUN AWAY FROM YOU TAMI LYNN	4	1971
I'M GONNA SIT DOWN AND WRITE MYSELF A LETTER BARRY MANILOW	36	1982
I'M GONNA SIT RIGHT DOWN AND WRITE MYSELF A LETTER BILLY WILLIAMS	22	1957

	Peak Position	Year of Release
I'M GONNA SOOTHE YOU MARIA McKEE	35	1993
I'M GONNA TEAR YOUR PLAYHOUSE DOWN PAUL YOUNG	9	1984
I'M IN A DIFFERENT WORLD FOUR TOPS	27	1968
I'M IN A PHILLY MOOD DARYL HALL	52	1993
I'M IN FAVOUR OF FRIENDSHIP FIVE SMITH BROTHERS	20	1955
I'M IN HEAVEN [A] JASON NEVINS PRESENTS UKNY FEATURING HOLLY JAMES	9	2003
I'M IN HEAVEN [B] N-TRANCE	46	2004
I'M IN IT FOR LOVE DONNY OSMOND	70	1987
I'M IN LOVE [A] FOURMOST	17	1964
I'M IN LOVE [B] EVELYN KING	27	1981
I'M IN LOVE [C] RUBY TURNER	57	1986
I'M IN LOVE [D] LILLO THOMAS	54	1987
I'M IN LOVE [E] STARPARTY	26	2000
I'M IN LOVE [F] AUDIO BULLYS	27	2005
I'M IN LOVE AGAIN [A] FATS DOMINO	12	1956
I'M IN LOVE AGAIN [B] SAD CAFE	40	1981
I'M IN LOVE (AND I LOVE THE FEELING) ROSE ROYCE	51	1979
I'M IN LOVE WITH A GERMAN FILM STAR PASSIONS	25	1981
I'M IN LOVE WITH THE GIRL ON A CERTAIN MANCHESTER VIRGIN MEGASTORE CHECKOUT DESK FRESHIES	54	1981
I'M IN LUV JOE	22	1994
I'M IN THE HOUSE STEVE AOKI FEATURING ZUPER BLAHQ	29	2010
I'M IN THE MOOD CE CE PENISTON	16	1994
I'M IN THE MOOD FOR DANCING NOLANS	3	1980
I'M IN THE MOOD FOR LOVE LORD TANAMO	58	1990
I'M IN THE MOOD FOR LOVE JOOLS HOLLAND & JAMIROQUAI	29	2001
I'M IN YOU PETER FRAMPTON	41	1977
I'M INTO SOMETHING GOOD HERMAN'S HERMITS	1	1964
I'M JUST A BABY LOUISE CORDET	13	1962
I'M JUST A SINGER (IN A ROCK 'N' ROLL BAND) MOODY BLUES	36	1973
I'M JUST YOUR PUPPET ON A ... (STRING) LONDONBEAT	55	1995
I'M LEAVIN' [A] ELVIS PRESLEY	23	1971
I'M LEAVING [B] LODGER	40	1998
I'M LEAVIN' [C] OUTSIDAZ FEATURING RAH DIGGA	41	2002
I'M LEAVING IT (ALL) UP TO YOU DONNY & MARIE OSMOND	2	1974
I'M LEAVING IT UP TO YOU DALE & GRACE	42	1964
I'M LEFT YOU'RE RIGHT SHE'S GONE ELVIS PRESLEY	21	1958
I'M LIKE A BIRD NELLY FURTADO	5	2001
I'M LIVING IN SHAME DIANA ROSS & THE SUPREMES	14	1969
I'M LONELY HOLLIS P MONROE	51	1999
I'M LOOKING FOR THE ONE (TO BE WITH ME) JAZZY JEFF & THE FRESH PRINCE	24	1993
I'M LOOKING OUT THE WINDOW CLIFF RICHARD & THE SHADOWS	2	1962
I'M LOST WITHOUT YOU BILLY FURY	16	1965
I'M LUCKY JOAN ARMATRADING	46	1981
I'M MANDY FLY ME 10 C.C.	6	1976
I'M NEVER GIVING UP SWEET DREAMS	21	1983
IM NIN'ALU OFRA HAZA	15	1988
I'M NO ANGEL MARCELLA DETROIT	33	1994
I'M NO REBEL VIEW FROM THE HILL	59	1987
I'M NOT A FOOL COCKNEY REJECTS	65	1979
I'M NOT A GIRL NOT YET A WOMAN BRITNEY SPEARS	2	2002
I'M NOT A TEENAGE DELINQUENT FRANKIE LYMON & THE TEENAGERS	12	1957
I'M NOT ALONE CALVIN HARRIS	1	2009
I'M NOT ANYBODY'S GIRL KACI	55	2003
I'M NOT ASHAMED BIG COUNTRY	69	1995
I'M NOT FEELING YOU YVETTE MICHELLE	36	1997
I'M NOT GIVING YOU UP GLORIA ESTEFAN	28	1996
I'M NOT GONNA LET YOU (GET THE BEST OF ME) COLONEL ABRAMS	24	1986
I'M NOT GONNA TEACH YOUR BOYFRIEND HOW TO DANCE WITH YOU BLACK KIDS	11	2008
I'M NOT IN LOVE 10 C.C.	1	1975
I'M NOT IN LOVE JOHNNY LOGAN	51	1987
I'M NOT IN LOVE WILL TO POWER	29	1991
I'M NOT IN LOVE FUN LOVIN' CRIMINALS	12	1997
I'M NOT MAD ALEX GARDNER	44	2010
I'M NOT MISSING YOU STACIE ORRICO	22	2006
I'M NOT OKAY (I PROMISE) MY CHEMICAL ROMANCE	19	2005
I'M NOT PERFECT (BUT I'M PERFECT FOR YOU) GRACE JONES	56	1986
I'M NOT READY KEITH SWEAT	53	1999
I'M NOT SATISFIED FINE YOUNG CANNIBALS	46	1990
I'M NOT SCARED EIGHTH WONDER	7	1988
I'M NOT SHY FRANK	40	2006
I'M NOT SORRY PIGEON DETECTIVES	12	2007
I'M NOT THE MAN I USED TO BE FINE YOUNG CANNIBALS	20	1989
I'M NOT TO BLAME ALIBI	51	1997
(I'M NOT YOUR) STEPPING STONE SEX PISTOLS	21	1980
I'M NOT YOUR TOY LA ROUX	27	2009
I'M ON AUTOMATIC SHARPE & NUMAN	44	1989
I'M ON FIRE [A] 5000 VOLTS	4	1975
I'M ON FIRE [B] BRUCE SPRINGSTEEN	5	1985
I'M ON MY WAY [A] DEAN PARRISH	38	1975
I'M ON MY WAY [B] PROCLAIMERS	43	1989
I'M ON MY WAY [C] BETTY BOO	44	1992
I'M ON MY WAY TO A BETTER PLACE CHAIRMEN OF THE BOARD	30	1972
I'M ONLY SLEEPING SUGGS	7	1995
I'M OUT OF YOUR LIFE ARNIE'S LOVE	67	1983
I'M OUTSTANDING SHAQUILLE O'NEAL	70	1994
I'M OUTTA LOVE ANASTACIA	6	2000
I'M OUTTA TIME OASIS	12	2008
I'M OVER YOU MARTINE McCUTCHEON	2	2000
I'M QUALIFIED TO SATISFY BARRY WHITE	37	1977
I'M RAVING SCOOTER	33	1996
I'M READY [A] CAVEMAN	65	1991
I'M READY [B] SIZE 9	52	1995
I'M READY [C] BRYAN ADAMS	20	1998
I'M READY FOR LOVE MARTHA REEVES & THE VANDELLAS	22	1966
I'M REAL [A] JAMES BROWN FEATURING FULL FORCE	31	1988
I'M REAL [B] JENNIFER LOPEZ FEATURING JA RULE	4	2001
I'M REALLY HOT MISSY ELLIOTT	22	2004
I'M RIFFIN (ENGLISH RASTA) MC DUKE	75	1989
I'M RIGHT HERE SAMANTHA MUMBA	5	2002
I'M RUSHING BUMP	45	1992
I'M SHAKIN' ROONEY	73	2004
I'M SHY MARY ELLEN (I'M SHY) BOB WALLIS & HIS STORYVILLE JAZZ BAND	44	1961
I'M SICK OF YOU GOODBYE MR MACKENZIE	49	1989
I'M SO BEAUTIFUL DIVINE	52	1984
I'M SO CRAZY [A] KC & THE SUNSHINE BAND	34	1975
I'M SO CRAZY [B] PAR-T-ONE VS INXS	19	2001
I'M SO EXCITED POINTER SISTERS	11	1984
I'M SO GLAD I'M STANDING HERE TODAY CRUSADERS, FEATURED VOCALIST JOE COCKER	61	1981
I'M SO HAPPY [A] LIGHT OF THE WORLD	35	1981
I'M SO HAPPY [B] JULIA & COMPANY	56	1985
I'M SO HAPPY [C] WALTER BEASLEY	70	1988
I'M SO HAPPY I CAN'T STOP CRYING STING	54	1996
I'M SO IN LOVE ALYSHA WARREN	61	1994
I'M SO INTO YOU SWV	17	1993
I'M SO LONELY CAST	14	1997
I'M SO PAID AKON FEATURING LIL WAYNE	59	2008
I'M SORRY [A] PLATTERS	18	1957
I'M SORRY [B] BRENDA LEE	12	1960
I'M SORRY [C] HOTHOUSE FLOWERS	53	1988
I'M SORRY I MADE YOU CRY CONNIE FRANCIS	11	1958
I'M SPRUNG T-PAIN	30	2006
I'M STANDING (HIGHER) X-STATIC	41	1995
I'M STARTING TO GO STEADY JOHNNY PRESTON	49	1960
I'M STILL GONNA NEED YOU OSMONDS	32	1975
I'M STILL IN LOVE WITH YOU [A] AL GREEN	35	1972
I'M STILL IN LOVE WITH YOU [B] SEAN PAUL FEATURING SASHA	6	2003
I'M STILL STANDING ELTON JOHN	4	1983
I'M STILL WAITING DIANA ROSS	1	1971
I'M STILL WAITING COURTNEY PINE FEATURING CARROLL THOMPSON	66	1990
I'M STILL WAITING ANGELHEART FEATURING ALETIA BOURNE	74	1997
I'M STONE IN LOVE WITH YOU STYLISTICS	9	1972
I'M STONE IN LOVE WITH YOU JOHNNY MATHIS	10	1975
I'M TELLIN' YOU CHUBBY CHUNKS FEATURING KIM RUFFIN	61	1999
I'M TELLING YOU NOW FREDDIE & THE DREAMERS	2	1963
I'M THAT TYPE OF GUY LL COOL J	43	1989
I'M THE FACE HIGH NUMBERS	49	1980
I'M THE LEADER OF THE GANG HULK HOGAN WITH GREEN JELLY	25	1993
I'M THE LEADER OF THE GANG (I AM) GARY GLITTER	1	1973
I'M THE LONELY ONE CLIFF RICHARD & THE SHADOWS	8	1964
I'M THE MAN ANTHRAX	20	1987
I'M THE ONE GERRY & THE PACEMAKERS	2	1964
I'M THE ONE FOR YOU ADEVA	51	1992
I'M THE ONE YOU NEED JODY WATLEY	50	1992
I'M THE URBAN SPACEMAN BONZO DOG DOO-DAH BAND	5	1968
I'M THROWING MY ARMS AROUND PARIS MORRISSEY	21	2009
I'M TIRED OF GETTING PUSHED AROUND TWO MEN, A DRUM MACHINE & A TRUMPET	18	1988
I'M TOO SCARED STEVEN DANTE	34	1988
I'M TOO SEXY RIGHT SAID FRED	2	1991
I'M WAKING UP TO US BELLE & SEBASTIAN	39	2001
I'M WALKIN' FATS DOMINO	19	1957
I'M WALKING BACKWARDS FOR CHRISTMAS GOONS	4	1956
I'M WALKING BEHIND YOU EDDIE FISHER WITH SALLY SWEETLAND (SOPRANO)	1	1953
I'M WALKING BEHIND YOU DOROTHY SQUIRES	12	1953
I'M WITH STUPID PET SHOP BOYS	8	2006
I'M WITH YOU AVRIL LAVIGNE	7	2003
I'M WONDERING STEVIE WONDER	22	1967
I'M YOUR ANGEL CELINE DION & R KELLY	3	1998
I'M YOUR BABY TONIGHT WHITNEY HOUSTON	5	1990
I'M YOUR BOOGIE MAN KC & THE SUNSHINE BAND	41	1977
I'M YOUR MAN [A] BLUE ZOO	55	1982
I'M YOUR MAN [B] WHAM!	1	1985
I'M YOUR MAN [B] LISA MOORISH	24	1995
I'M YOUR MAN [B] SHANE RICHIE	2	2003
I'M YOUR PUPPET JAMES & BOBBY PURIFY	12	1976
I'M YOUR TOY ELVIS COSTELLO & THE ATTRACTIONS WITH THE ROYAL PHILHARMONIC ORCHESTRA	51	1982

	Peak Position	Year of Release
I'M YOURS JASON MRAZ	11	2008
IMAGE HANK LEVINE	45	1961
IMAGE OF A GIRL MARK WYNTER	11	1960
IMAGE OF A GIRL NELSON KEENE	37	1960
IMAGE OF YOU RED SNAPPER	60	1998
IMAGINATION [A] ROCKY SHARPE & THE REPLAYS	39	1979
IMAGINATION [B] BELOUIS SOME	17	1985
IMAGINATION [C] JON THE DENTIST VS OLLIE JAYE	72	1999
IMAGINE [A] JOHN LENNON	1	1975
IMAGINE [A] RANDY CRAWFORD	60	1982
IMAGINE [A] GLEE CAST	57	2010
IMAGINE [B] SHOLA AMA	24	2000
IMAGINE ME IMAGINE YOU FOX	15	1975
IMITATION OF LIFE [A] BILLIE RAY MARTIN	29	1996
IMITATION OF LIFE [B] R.E.M.	6	2001
IMMACULATE FOOLS IMMACULATE FOOLS	51	1985
IMMORTALITY CELINE DION WITH THE BEE GEES	5	1998
IMPERIAL WIZARD DAVID ESSEX	32	1979
THE IMPORTANCE OF BEING IDLE OASIS	1	2005
IMPORTANCE OF YOUR LOVE VINCE HILL	32	1968
IMPOSSIBLE [A] CAPTAIN HOLLYWOOD PROJECT	29	1994
IMPOSSIBLE [B] CHARLATANS	15	2000
IMPOSSIBLE [C] DANIEL MERRIWEATHER	67	2009
THE IMPOSSIBLE DREAM CARTER-THE UNSTOPPABLE SEX MACHINE	21	1992
IMPOSSIBLE LOVE UB40	47	1990
THE IMPRESSION THAT I GET MIGHTY MIGHTY BOSSTONES	12	1998
THE IMPRESSIONS EP SOLAR STONE	75	1998
IMPULSIVE WILSON PHILLIPS	42	1990
IN 4 CHOONS LATER ROZALLA	50	1992
IN A BIG COUNTRY BIG COUNTRY	17	1983
IN A BROKEN DREAM PYTHON LEE JACKSON	3	1972
IN A BROKEN DREAM THUNDER	26	1995
IN A CAGE (ON PROZAC) MY RED CELL	61	2004
IN A DARK PLACE GARY NUMAN	63	2006
IN A DREAM LONGVIEW	38	2004
IN A FUNNY WAY MERCURY REV	28	2005
IN A GOLDEN COACH BILLY COTTON & HIS BAND, VOCALS BY DOREEN STEPHENS	3	1953
IN A GOLDEN COACH DICKIE VALENTINE	7	1953
IN A LIFETIME CLANNAD FEATURING BONO	17	1985
IN A LITTLE SPANISH TOWN BING CROSBY	22	1956
IN A PERSIAN MARKET SAMMY DAVIS, JR	28	1956
IN A ROOM DODGY	12	1996
IN A STATE [A] 2 FOR JOY	61	1990
IN A STATE [B] UNKLE	44	2003
IN A WORD OR 2 MONIE LOVE	33	1993
IN ALL THE RIGHT PLACES LISA STANSFIELD	8	1993
IN AND OUT [A] WILLIE HUTCH	51	1982
IN AND OUT [B] 3RD EDGE	15	2002
IN AND OUT [C] SPEEDWAY	31	2004
IN AND OUT OF LOVE [A] DIANA ROSS & THE SUPREMES	13	1967
IN AND OUT OF LOVE [B] IMAGINATION	16	1981
IN AND OUT OF MY LIFE [A] TONJA DANTZLER	66	1994
IN AND OUT OF MY LIFE [B] A.T.F.C. PRESENTS ONEPHATDEEVA	11	1999
IN BETWEEN DAYS CURE	15	1985
THE IN BETWEENIES GOODIES	7	1974
IN BLOOM NIRVANA	28	1992
THE IN CROWD DOBIE GRAY	25	1965
THE IN CROWD BRYAN FERRY	13	1974
IN DA CLUB 50 CENT	3	2003
IN DE GHETTO DAVID MORALES & THE BAD YARD CLUB FEATURING CRYSTAL WATERS & DELTA	35	1996
IN DEMAND TEXAS	6	2000
IN DREAMS ROY ORBISON	6	1963
IN DULCE DECORUM DAMNED	72	1987
IN DULCE JUBILO MIKE OLDFIELD	4	1975
IN FOR A PENNY SLADE	11	1975
IN FOR THE KILL LA ROUX	2	2009
IN GOD'S COUNTRY (IMPORT) U2	48	1987
IN IT FOR LOVE RICHIE SAMBORA	58	1998
IN IT FOR THE MONEY CLIENT	51	2004
IN LIVERPOOL SUZANNE VEGA	52	1992
IN LOVE [A] MICHAEL HOLLIDAY	26	1958
IN LOVE [B] DATSUNS	25	2002
IN LOVE [C] LISA MAFFIA	13	2003
IN LOVE WITH LOVE DEBBIE HARRY	45	1987
IN LOVE WITH THE FAMILIAR WIRELESS	69	1998
IN MY ARMS [A] ERASURE	13	1997
IN MY ARMS [B] MYLO	13	2005
IN MY ARMS [C] KYLIE MINOGUE	10	2008
IN MY BED [A] DRU HILL	16	1997
IN MY BED [B] AMY WINEHOUSE	60	2004
IN MY CHAIR STATUS QUO	21	1970
IN MY DEFENCE FREDDIE MERCURY	8	1992
IN MY DREAMS [A] WILL DOWNING	34	1988
IN MY DREAMS [B] JOHNNA	66	1996
IN MY EYES MILK INC	9	2002
IN MY HEAD [A] QUEENS OF THE STONE AGE	44	2005
IN MY HEAD [B] JASON DERULO	1	2010
IN MY HEART [A] TEXAS	74	1991
IN MY HEART [B] ETHAN	49	2005
IN MY LIFE [A] SOULED OUT	75	1992
IN MY LIFE [B] KIM WILDE	54	1993
IN MY LIFE [C] JOSE NUNEZ FEATURING OCTAHVIA	56	1998
IN MY LIFE [D] RYZE	46	2002
IN MY LIFE [E] OZZY OSBOURNE	63	2005
IN MY MIND MILKY	48	2002
IN MY OWN TIME FAMILY	4	1971
IN MY PLACE COLDPLAY	2	2002
IN MY STREET CHORDS	50	1980
IN MY WORLD ANTHRAX	29	1990
IN OLD LISBON FRANK CHACKSFIELD	15	1956
IN ONE EAR CAGE THE ELEPHANT	51	2008
IN OUR LIFETIME TEXAS	4	1999
IN PRIVATE DUSTY SPRINGFIELD	14	1989
IN PUBLIC KELIS FEATURING NAS	17	2005
IN PURSUIT BOXER REBELLION	57	2004
IN SPIRIT DILEMMA	42	1996
IN SUMMER BILLY FURY	5	1963
IN THE AIR TONIGHT PHIL COLLINS	2	1981
IN THE AIR TONIGHT LIL' KIM FEATURING PHIL COLLINS	26	2001
IN THE ARMS OF LOVE [A] ANDY WILLIAMS	33	1966
IN THE ARMS OF LOVE [B] CATHERINE ZETA JONES	72	1995
IN THE ARMY NOW STATUS QUO	2	1986
IN THE AYER FLO RIDA FEATURING WILL.I.AM	29	2008
IN THE BACK OF MY MIND FLEETWOOD MAC	58	1990
IN THE BAD BAD OLD DAYS FOUNDATIONS	8	1969
IN THE BEGINNING [A] FRANKIE LAINE	20	1955
IN THE BEGINNING [B] E.Y.C.	41	1995
IN THE BEGINNING [C] ROGER GOODE FEATURING TASHA BAXTER	33	2002
IN THE BELLY OF A SHARK GALLOWS	56	2007
IN THE BEST POSSIBLE TASTE (PART 2) KINGMAKER	41	1995
IN THE BLEAK MID WINTER NEVADA	71	1983
IN THE BOTTLE C.O.D.	54	1983
IN THE BROWNIES BILLY CONNOLLY	38	1979
IN THE BUSH MUSIQUE	16	1978
IN THE CAULDRON OF LOVE ICICLE WORKS	53	1984
IN THE CHAPEL IN THE MOONLIGHT BACHELORS	27	1965
IN THE CITY [A] JAM	21	1977
IN THE CITY [B] LAHAYNA	33	2007
IN THE CLOSET MICHAEL JACKSON	8	1992
IN THE CLOUDS ALL ABOUT EVE	47	1987
(IN THE) COLD LIGHT OF DAY GENE PITNEY	38	1967
IN THE COUNTRY CLIFF RICHARD	6	1966
IN THE COUNTRY FARMERS BOYS	44	1984
IN THE END LINKIN PARK	8	2001
IN THE EVENING SHERYL LEE RALPH	64	1985
IN THE FOREST BABY O	46	1980
IN THE FUTURE WHEN ALL'S WELL MORRISSEY	17	2006
IN THE GHETTO ELVIS PRESLEY	2	1969
IN THE GHETTO BEATS INTERNATIONAL	44	1991
IN THE GRIND DILLINJA	71	2004
IN THE HALL OF THE MOUNTAIN KING NERO & THE GLADIATORS	48	1961
IN THE HEAT OF A PASSIONATE MOMENT PRINCESS	74	1986
IN THE HEAT OF THE NIGHT [A] DIAMOND HEAD	67	1982
IN THE HEAT OF THE NIGHT [B] IMAGINATION	22	1982
IN THE HEAT OF THE NIGHT [C] STAR PILOTS	21	2009
IN THE HOUSE CLOCK	23	1995
IN THE MEANTIME [A] GEORGIE FAME & THE BLUE FLAMES	22	1965
IN THE MEANTIME [B] SPACEHOG	29	1996
IN THE MIDDLE [A] ALEXANDER O'NEAL	32	1993
IN THE MIDDLE [B] SUGABABES	8	2004
IN THE MIDDLE OF A DARK DARK NIGHT GUY MITCHELL	25	1957
IN THE MIDDLE OF AN ISLAND KING BROTHERS	19	1957
IN THE MIDDLE OF NOWHERE DUSTY SPRINGFIELD	8	1965
IN THE MIDDLE OF THE HOUSE ALMA COGAN	20	1956
IN THE MIDDLE OF THE HOUSE JIMMY PARKINSON	26	1956
IN THE MIDDLE OF THE HOUSE JOHNSTON BROTHERS	27	1956
IN THE MIDDLE OF THE NIGHT MAGIC AFFAIR	38	1994
IN THE MIDNIGHT HOUR WILSON PICKETT	12	1965
IN THE MOOD ERNIE FIELDS	13	1959
IN THE MOOD GLENN MILLER	12	1976
IN THE MOOD SOUND 9418	46	1976
IN THE MOOD RAY STEVENS	31	1977
IN THE MORNING [A] CORAL	6	2005
IN THE MORNING [B] RAZORLIGHT	3	2006
IN THE NAME OF LOVE [A] SHARON REDD	31	1983
IN THE NAME OF LOVE [B] SWAN LAKE	53	1988
IN THE NAME OF LOVE '88 THOMPSON TWINS	46	1988
IN THE NAME OF THE FATHER [A] BONO & GAVIN FRIDAY	46	1994
IN THE NAME OF THE FATHER [B] BLACK GRAPE	8	1995
IN THE NAVY VILLAGE PEOPLE	2	1979
IN THE NIGHT BARBARA DICKSON	48	1980
IN THE ONES YOU LOVE DIANA ROSS	34	1996
IN THE REALM OF THE SENSES BASS-O-MATIC	66	1990
IN THE SHADOWS RASMUS	3	2004
IN THE SHAPE OF A HEART JACKSON BROWNE	66	1986
IN THE SPRINGTIME MAXI PRIEST	54	1986
IN THE STILL OF THE NITE (I'LL REMEMBER) BOYZ II MEN	27	1993
IN THE STONE EARTH, WIND & FIRE	53	1980
IN THE SUMMERTIME MUNGO JERRY	1	1970
IN THE SUMMERTIME SHAGGY FEATURING RAYVON	5	1995

	Peak Position	Year of Release
IN THE SUMMERTIME JUNGLE BOYS	72	2004
IN THE THICK OF IT BRENDA RUSSELL	51	1980
IN THE VALLEY MIDNIGHT OIL	60	1993
IN THE WAITING LINE ZERO 7	47	2001
IN THE YEAR 2525 (EXORDIUM AND TERMINUS) ZAGER & EVANS	1	1969
IN THESE ARMS BON JOVI	9	1993
IN THIS CITY IGLU & HARTLY	5	2008
IN THIS HOME ON ICE CLAP YOUR HANDS SAY YEAH	68	2006
IN THIS WORLD MOBY	35	2002
IN THOUGHTS OF YOU BILLY FURY	9	1965
IN TOO DEEP [A] DEAD OR ALIVE	14	1985
IN TOO DEEP [B] GENESIS	19	1986
IN TOO DEEP [C] BELINDA CARLISLE	6	1996
IN TOO DEEP [D] SUM 41	13	2001
IN WALKED LOVE LOUISE	17	1996
IN YER FACE 808 STATE	9	1991
IN YOUR ARMS (RESCUE ME) NU GENERATION	8	2000
IN YOUR BONES FIRE ISLAND	66	1992
IN YOUR CAR [A] COOLNOTES	13	1985
IN YOUR CAR [B] KENICKIE	24	1997
IN YOUR CARE TASMIN ARCHER	16	1993
IN YOUR DANCE E-LUSTRIOUS	69	1994
IN YOUR EYES [A] GEORGE BENSON	7	1983
IN YOUR EYES [B] NIAMH KAVANAGH	24	1993
IN YOUR EYES [C] KYLIE MINOGUE	3	2002
IN YOUR HANDS REDD SQUARE FEATURING TIFF LACEY	64	2002
IN YOUR ROOM [A] BANGLES	35	1988
IN YOUR ROOM [B] DEPECHE MODE	8	1994
IN YOUR WILDEST DREAMS TINA TURNER FEATURING BARRY WHITE	32	1996
IN YOUR WORLD MUSE	13	2002
IN ZAIRE [A] JOHNNY WAKELIN	4	1976
IN ZAIRE [B] AFRICAN BUSINESS	73	1990
INBETWEENER SLEEPER	16	1995
THE INCIDENTALS ALISHA'S ATTIC	13	1998
INCOMMUNICADO MARILLION	6	1987
INCOMPLETE [A] SISQO	13	2000
INCOMPLETE [B] BACKSTREET BOYS	8	2005
INCONSOLABLE BACKSTREET BOYS	24	2007
INCREDIBLE [A] M-BEAT FEATURING GENERAL LEVY	8	1994
INCREDIBLE [B] KEITH MURRAY FEATURING LL COOL J	52	1998
INCREDIBLE [C] SHAPESHIFTERS	12	2006
INCREDIBLE (WHAT I MEANT TO SAY) DARIUS	9	2003
INDEPENDENCE LULU	11	1993
INDEPENDENCE DAY COMSAT ANGELS	71	1984
INDEPENDENT LOVE SONG SCARLET	12	1995
INDEPENDENT WOMEN PART 1 DESTINY'S CHILD	1	2000
INDESCRIBABLY BLUE ELVIS PRESLEY	21	1967
INDESTRUCTIBLE [A] FOUR TOPS FEATURING SMOKEY ROBINSON	30	1989
INDESTRUCTIBLE [B] ALISHA'S ATTIC	12	1997
INDIAN LOVE CALL SLIM WHITMAN	7	1955
INDIAN LOVE CALL KARL DENVER	32	1963
INDIAN LOVE CALL RAY STEVENS	34	1975
INDIAN RESERVATION DON FARDON	3	1970
INDIAN RESERVATION 999	51	1981
INDIAN ROPE CHARLATANS	57	1991
INDIAN SUMMER [A] BELLE STARS	52	1983
INDIAN SUMMER [B] MANIC STREET PREACHERS	22	2007
INDIANA FREDDY CANNON	42	1960
INDIANA WANTS ME R. DEAN TAYLOR	2	1971
INDIANS ANTHRAX	44	1987
INDICA MOVIN' MELODIES	62	1996
INDIE-YARN TRICKBABY	47	1996
INDIGO MOLOKO	51	2000
INDUSTRIAL STRENGTH (EP) KROKUS	62	1981
INERTIATIC ESP MARS VOLTA	42	2003
INFATUATION ROD STEWART	27	1984
INFECTED [A] THE THE	48	1986
INFECTED [B] BARTHEZZ	25	2002
INFERNO SOUVLAKI	24	1997
INFIDELITY SIMPLY RED	31	1987
INFILTRATE 202 ALTERN 8	28	1991
INFINITE DREAMS IRON MAIDEN	6	1989
INFINITY GURU JOSH	3	1990
INFO-FREAKO JESUS JONES	42	1989
INFORMER SNOW	2	1993
INFRA-RED PLACEBO	42	2006
INHALE STONE SOUR	63	2003
INHERIT THE WIND WILTON FELDER	39	1980
INJECTED WITH A POISON PRAGA KHAN FEATURING JADE 4 U	39	1992
THE INK IN THE WELL DAVID SYLVIAN	36	1984
INKANYEZI NEZAZI (THE STAR AND THE WISEMAN) LADYSMITH BLACK MAMBAZO	33	1997
INNA CITY MAMMA NENEH CHERRY	31	1989
INNAMORATA DEAN MARTIN	21	1956
INNER CITY LIFE GOLDIE PRESENTS METALHEADS	39	1994
INNER LIFE DECOY AND ROY	45	2003
INNER SMILE TEXAS	6	2001
INNOCENT [A] ADDIS BLACK WIDOW	42	1996
INNOCENT [B] STEREOPHONICS	54	2009
INNOCENT EYES DELTA GOODREM	9	2003
INNOCENT MAN MARK MORRISON FEATURING DMX	46	2006
INNOCENT X THERAPY?	53	1995
INNOCENTE (FALLING IN LOVE) DELERIUM FEATURING LEIGH NASH	32	2001
INNUENDO QUEEN	1	1991
INSANE [A] TEXAS FEATURING THE WU TANG CLAN	4	1998
INSANE [B] DARK MONKS	62	2002
INSANE IN THE BRAIN CYPRESS HILL	21	1993
INSANE IN THE BRAIN JASON NEVINS VERSUS CYPRESS HILL	19	1999
INSANIA PETER ANDRE	3	2004
INSANITY OCEANIC	3	1991
INSATIABLE [A] DARREN HAYES	8	2002
INSATIABLE [B] THICK D	35	2002
INSENSITIVE JANN ARDEN	40	1996
INSIDE STILTSKIN	1	1994
INSIDE A DREAM JANE WIEDLIN	64	1988
INSIDE AMERICA JUGGY JONES	39	1976
INSIDE – LOOKING OUT ANIMALS	12	1966
INSIDE LOOKING OUT GRAND FUNK RAILROAD	40	1971
INSIDE LOVE (SO PERSONAL) GEORGE BENSON	57	1983
INSIDE OF LOVE NADA SURF	73	2003
INSIDE OUT [A] ODYSSEY	3	1982
INSIDE OUT [B] MIGHTY LEMON DROPS	74	1988
INSIDE OUT [C] GUN	57	1989
INSIDE OUT [D] SHARA NELSON	34	1994
INSIDE OUT [E] CULTURE BEAT	32	1996
INSIDE OUTSIDE CLASSIX NOUVEAUX	45	1981
INSIDE THAT I CRIED CE CE PENISTON	42	1992
INSIDE YOUR DREAMS U96	44	1994
INSOMNIA [A] FAITHLESS	3	1995
INSOMNIA [B] FEEDER	22	1999
INSOMNIA [C] CRAIG DAVID	43	2008
INSOMNIAC ECHOBELLY	47	1994
INSPECTOR GADGET KARTOON KREW	58	1985
INSPECTOR MORSE THEME BARRINGTON PHELOUNG	61	1993
INSPIRATION STRIKE	27	1996
INSSOMNIAK DJPC	62	1991
INSTANT KARMA LENNON, ONO & THE PLASTIC ONO BAND	5	1970
INSTANT REPLAY DAN HARTMAN	8	1978
INSTANT REPLAY YELL!	10	1990
INSTANT REPLAY GAMBAFREAKS FEATURING PACO RIVAZ	57	1998
INSTANT STREET dEUS	49	1997
INSTINCT CROWDED HOUSE	12	1996
INSTINCTION SPANDAU BALLET	10	1982
INSTINCTUAL IMAGINATION	62	1988
INSTRUMENTS OF DARKNESS (ALL OF US ARE ONE PEOPLE) ART OF NOISE	45	1992
INTACT NED'S ATOMIC DUSTBIN	36	1992
INTENSIFY WAY OUT WEST	46	2001
INTERCEPTOR EAT STATIC	44	1997
INTERESTING DRUG MORRISSEY	9	1989
INTERGALACTIC BEASTIE BOYS	5	1998
INTERLUDE MORRISSEY & SIOUXSIE	25	1994
INTERNAL EXILE FISH	37	1991
INTERNATIONAL BRASS CONSTRUCTION	70	1984
INTERNATIONAL BRIGHT YOUNG THING JESUS JONES	7	1991
INTERNATIONAL JET SET SPECIALS	6	1980
THE INTERNATIONAL LANGUAGE OF SCREAMING SUPER FURRY ANIMALS	24	1997
INTERNATIONAL RESCUE FUZZBOX	11	1989
INTERSTATE 5 WEDDING PRESENT	62	2004
INTERSTATE LOVE SONG STONE TEMPLE PILOTS	53	1994
INTERVENTION LAVINE HUDSON	57	1988
INTO A SWAN SIOUXSIE	59	2007
INTO DUST MAZZY STAR	71	2009
INTO MY ARMS NICK CAVE & THE BAD SEEDS	53	1997
INTO MY WORLD AUDIOWEB	42	1996
INTO OBLIVION (REUNION) FUNERAL FOR A FRIEND	16	2007
INTO SPACE PLAYTHING	48	2001
INTO THE BLUE [A] MISSION	32	1990
INTO THE BLUE [B] MOBY	34	1995
INTO THE BLUE [C] GENEVA	26	1997
INTO THE FIRE THIRTEEN SENSES	35	2004
INTO THE FUTURE NEW ATLANTIC FEATURING LINDA WRIGHT	70	1992
INTO THE GROOVE MADONNA	1	1985
INTO THE MOTION COOLNOTES	66	1986
INTO THE NIGHT LOVE INC	39	2004
INTO THE SUN WEEKEND PLAYERS	42	2002
INTO THE VALLEY SKIDS	10	1979
INTO TOMORROW PAUL WELLER MOVEMENT	36	1991
INTO YOU FABOLOUS FEATURING TAMIA	18	2003
INTO YOUR ARMS LEMONHEADS	14	1993
INTO YOUR EYES ARMAND VAN HELDEN	48	2005
INTO YOUR HEAD HONEYMOON MACHINE	66	2005
INTO YOUR HEART 6 BY SIX	51	1996
INTOXICATION REACT 2 RHYTHM	73	1997
INTRO ALAN BRAXE & FRED FALKE	35	2000
INTUITION [A] LINX	7	1981
INTUITION [B] JEWEL	52	2003
INVADERS MUST DIE PRODIGY	49	2009
INVALID LITTER DEPT AT THE DRIVE-IN	50	2001
INVINCIBLE MUSE	21	2007
INVINCIBLE (THEME FROM 'THE LEGEND OF BILLIE JEAN') PAT BENATAR	53	1985
INVISIBLE [A] ALISON MOYET	21	1984
INVISIBLE [B] PUBLIC DEMAND	41	1997
INVISIBLE [C] TILT	20	1999
INVISIBLE [D] D-SIDE	7	2003
INVISIBLE BALLOON MIDGET	66	1998
INVISIBLE GIRL MINNIE DRIVER	68	2005
THE INVISIBLE MAN [A] QUEEN	12	1989
INVISIBLE MAN [B] 980	66	1997
INVISIBLE SUN POLICE	2	1981
INVISIBLE TOUCH GENESIS	7	1986

Title	Artist	Peak Position	Year of Release
INVITATIONS	SHAKATAK	24	1982
I.O.I.O.	BEE GEES	49	1970
I.O.U. [A]	JANE KENNAWAY & STRANGE BEHAVIOUR	65	1981
I.O.U. [B]	FREEEZ	2	1983
IOU [C]	BILL TARMEY	55	1994
IOU LOVE	SIX BY SEVEN	48	2002
IRE FEELINGS (SKANGA)	RUPIE EDWARDS	9	1974
IRENE	PHOTOS	56	1980
IRIE	LUCK & NEAT	31	2002
IRIS	GOO GOO DOLLS	26	1998
IRIS	RONAN KEATING	15	2006
IRISH BLOOD ENGLISH HEART	MORRISSEY	3	2004
IRISH BLUE	FLIP & FILL FEATURING JUNIOR	20	2003
THE IRISH KEEP GATE-CRASHING	THRILLS	48	2005
THE IRISH ROVER	POGUES & THE DUBLINERS	8	1987
IRISH SON	BRIAN McFADDEN	6	2004
IRON	MEGA CITY FOUR	48	1993
IRON FIST	MOTORHEAD	29	1982
IRON HORSE	CHRISTIE	47	1972
IRON LION ZION	BOB MARLEY & THE WAILERS	5	1992
IRONIC	ALANIS MORISSETTE	11	1996
IRREPLACEABLE	BEYONCE	4	2006
IRRESISTIBLE [A]	CATHY DENNIS	24	1992
IRRESISTIBLE [B]	CORRS	20	2000
IRRESISTIBLE [C]	JESSICA SIMPSON	11	2001
IS	SMALLER	55	1997
IS A BLUE BIRD BLUE	CONWAY TWITTY	43	1960
IS IT A CRIME	SADE	49	1986
IS IT A DREAM	CLASSIX NOUVEAUX	11	1982
IS IT A DREAM	DAMNED	34	1985
IS IT A SIN?	DEEPEST BLUE	24	2004
IS IT ANY WONDER	KEANE	3	2006
IS IT BECAUSE	HONEYCOMBS	38	1964
IS IT COS I'M COOL?	MOUSSE T FEATURING EMMA LANFORD	9	2004
IS IT GOOD TO YOU	HEAVY D & THE BOYZ	46	1991
IS IT GOOD TO YOU	TEDDY RILEY FEATURING TAMMY LUCAS	53	1992
IS IT JUST ME?	DARKNESS	8	2006
IS IT LIKE TODAY	WORLD PARTY	19	1993
IS IT LOVE	BASEMENT BOYS PRESENT ULTRA NATE	71	1991
IS IT LOVE YOU'RE AFTER	ROSE ROYCE	13	1979
IS IT LOVE?	CHILI HI FLY	37	2000
IS IT REALLY OVER	JIM REEVES	17	1965
IS IT TRUE [A]	BRENDA LEE	17	1964
IS IT TRUE [B]	YOHANNA	49	2009
IS IT YOU	CASSIE	52	2008
IS NOTHING SACRED	MEAT LOAF FEATURING PATTI RUSSO	15	1999
IS SHE REALLY GOING OUT WITH HIM?	JOE JACKSON	13	1979
IS THAT LOVE	SQUEEZE	35	1981
IS THAT YOUR FINAL ANSWER? (WHO WANTS TO BE A MILLIONAIRE – THE SINGLE)	AMOURE	33	2000
IS THERE ANY LOVE IN YOUR HEART	LENNY KRAVITZ	52	1993
IS THERE ANYBODY OUT THERE	BASSHEADS	5	1991
IS THERE ANYBODY THERE	SCORPIONS	39	1979
IS THERE SOMEONE OUT THERE?	CODE RED	34	1997
IS THERE SOMETHING I SHOULD KNOW	DURAN DURAN	1	1983
IS THERE SOMETHING I SHOULD KNOW	ALLSTARS	12	2001
IS THIS A DREAM?	LOVE DECADE	39	1996
IS THIS A LOVE THING	RAYDIO	27	1978
IS THIS CHRISTMAS?	WOMBATS	49	2008
IS THIS LOVE [A]	BOB MARLEY & THE WAILERS	9	1978
IS THIS LOVE [C]	WHITESNAKE	9	1987
IS THIS LOVE [D]	CLAP YOUR HANDS SAY YEAH	74	2005
IS THIS LOVE? [B]	ALISON MOYET	3	1986
IS THIS THE WAY TO AMARILLO	TONY CHRISTIE	18	1971
IS THIS THE WAY TO AMARILLO (SANTA'S)	SANTA	30	2006
(IS THIS THE WAY TO) AMARILLO?	TONY CHRISTIE FEATURING PETER KAY	1	2005
(IS THIS THE WAY TO) THE WORLD CUP?	TONY CHRISTIE	8	2006
IS THIS WHAT I GET FOR LOVING YOU	MARIANNE FAITHFULL	43	1967
IS VIC THERE?	DEPARTMENT S	22	1981
IS YOUR LOVE IN VAIN	BOB DYLAN	56	1978
IS YOUR LOVE STRONG ENOUGH	BRYAN FERRY	22	1986
ISLAND GIRL	ELTON JOHN	14	1975
ISLAND HEAD EP	INSPIRAL CARPETS	21	1990
ISLAND IN THE SUN [A]	HARRY BELAFONTE	3	1957
ISLAND IN THE SUN [A]	RIGHTEOUS BROTHERS	24	1966
ISLAND IN THE SUN [B]	WEEZER	31	2001
ISLAND OF DREAMS	SPRINGFIELDS	5	1962
ISLAND OF LOST SOULS	BLONDIE	11	1982
ISLANDS IN THE STREAM	KENNY ROGERS & DOLLY PARTON	7	1983
ISLANDS IN THE STREAM	VANESSA JENKINS & BRYN WEST FEATURING TOM JONES & ROBIN GIBB	1	2009
ISLE OF INNISFREE	BING CROSBY	3	1952
ISMS	DOG EAT DOG	43	1996
ISN'T IT A WONDER	BOYZONE	2	1997
ISN'T IT AMAZING	HOTHOUSE FLOWERS	46	1993
ISN'T IT MIDNIGHT	FLEETWOOD MAC	60	1988
ISN'T IT TIME	BABYS	45	1978
ISN'T LIFE STRANGE	MOODY BLUES	13	1972
ISN'T SHE LOVELY	DAVID PARTON	4	1977
ISOBEL	BJORK	23	1995
ISRAEL	SIOUXSIE & THE BANSHEES	41	1980
ISRAELITES	DESMOND DEKKER & THE ACES	1	1969
ISSUES	SATURDAYS	4	2008
ISTANBUL	FRANKIE VAUGHAN WITH THE PETER KNIGHT SINGERS	11	1954
ISTANBUL (NOT CONSTANTINOPLE)	THEY MIGHT BE GIANTS	61	1990
IT AIN'T A CRIME	HOUSE OF PAIN	37	1994
IT AIN'T ENOUGH	DREEM TEEM VERSUS ARTFUL DODGER	20	2001
IT AIN'T FAIR	EDWIN STARR	56	1985
IT AIN'T GONNA BE ME	C.J. BOLLAND	35	1999
IT AIN'T HARD TO TELL	NAS	64	1994
IT AIN'T ME, BABE	JOHNNY CASH	28	1965
IT AIN'T NECESSARILY SO	BRONSKI BEAT	16	1984
IT AIN'T OVER TIL IT'S OVER	LENNY KRAVITZ	11	1991
IT AIN'T WHAT YOU DO IT'S THE WAY THAT YOU DO IT	FUN BOY THREE & BANANARAMA	4	1982
IT BEGAN IN AFRICA	URBAN ALL STARS	64	1988
IT BEGAN IN AFRIKA	CHEMICAL BROTHERS	8	2001
IT CAN'T BE RIGHT	2PLAY FEATURING RAGHAV & NAILA BOSS	8	2004
IT COULD HAPPEN TO YOU	ROBERT PALMER	71	1989
IT DIDN'T MATTER	STYLE COUNCIL	9	1987
IT DOESN'T HAVE TO BE	ERASURE	12	1987
IT DOESN'T HAVE TO BE THIS WAY	BLOW MONKEYS	5	1987
IT DOESN'T MATTER	WYCLEF JEAN FEATURING THE ROCK & MELKY SEDECK	3	2000
IT DOESN'T MATTER ANYMORE [A]	BUDDY HOLLY	1	1959
IT DOESN'T MATTER ANYMORE [B]	PURESSENCE	47	1998
IT DOESN'T OFTEN SNOW AT CHRISTMAS	PET SHOP BOYS	40	2009
IT DOESN'T REALLY MATTER	ZAPP	57	1986
IT DON'T COME EASY	RINGO STARR	4	1971
IT ENDED ON AN OILY STAGE	BRITISH SEA POWER	18	2005
IT ENDS TONIGHT	ALL-AMERICAN REJECTS	66	2006
IT FE DONE	SUPERCAT	66	1992
IT FEELS SO GOOD	SONIQUE	1	1998
IT HAD TO BE YOU	HARRY CONNICK JR	32	1991
IT HURTS	ANGELS & AIRWAVES	59	2006
IT HURTS SO MUCH	JIM REEVES	8	1965
IT HURTS TO BE IN LOVE	GENE PITNEY	36	1964
IT IS JAZZ	TINGO TANGO	68	1990
IT IS TIME TO GET FUNKY	D MOB FEATURING LRS	9	1989
IT ISN'T, IT WASN'T, IT AIN'T NEVER GONNA BE	ARETHA FRANKLIN & WHITNEY HOUSTON	29	1989
IT ISN'T RIGHT	PLATTERS	23	1957
IT JUST WON'T DO	TIM DELUXE FEATURING SAM OBERNIK	14	2002
IT KEEPS RAININ	FATS DOMINO	49	1961
IT KEEP'S RAININ' (TEARS FROM MY EYES)	BITTY McLEAN	2	1993
IT KEEPS RIGHT ON A HURTIN'	JOHNNY TILLOTSON	31	1962
IT LOOKS LIKE YOU	EVAN DANDO	68	2003
IT MAKES ME WONDER	BRUCE FOXTON	74	1984
IT MAKES YOU FEEL LIKE DANCIN'	ROSE ROYCE	16	1978
IT MAY BE WINTER OUTSIDE (BUT IN MY HEART IT'S SPRING)	LOVE UNLIMITED	11	1975
IT MEANS NOTHING	STEREOPHONICS	12	2007
IT MEK	DESMOND DEKKER	7	1969
IT MIGHT AS WELL RAIN UNTIL SEPTEMBER	CAROLE KING	3	1962
IT MUST BE HIM (SEUL SUR SON ETOILE)	VIKKI CARR	2	1967
IT MUST BE LOVE [A]	LABI SIFFRE	14	1971
IT MUST BE LOVE [A]	MADNESS	4	1981
IT MUST BE LOVE [B]	ROBIN S	37	1997
IT MUST BE LOVE [C]	MERO	33	2000
IT MUST BE SANTA	JOAN REGAN	42	1961
IT MUST HAVE BEEN LOVE [A]	MAGNUM	33	1988
IT MUST HAVE BEEN LOVE [B]	ROXETTE	3	1990
IT NEVER RAINS (IN SOUTHERN CALIFORNIA)	TONY! TONI! TONE!	69	1991
IT ONLY TAKES A MINUTE	ONE HUNDRED TON & A FEATHER	9	1976
IT ONLY TAKES A MINUTE	TAVARES	46	1986
IT ONLY TAKES A MINUTE	TAKE THAT	7	1992
IT ONLY TOOK A MINUTE	JOE BROWN & THE BRUVVERS	6	1962
IT OUGHTA SELL A MILLION	LYN PAUL	37	1975
IT SEEMS TO HANG ON	ASHFORD & SIMPSON	48	1978
IT SEEMS TO HANG ON	KWS	58	1994
IT SHOULD HAVE BEEN ME	YVONNE FAIR	5	1976
IT SHOULD'VE BEEN ME	ADEVA	48	1991
IT STARTED ALL OVER AGAIN	BRENDA LEE	15	1962
IT STARTED WITH A KISS	HOT CHOCOLATE	5	1982
IT SURE BRINGS OUT THE LOVE IN YOUR EYES	DAVID SOUL	12	1978
IT TAKES ALL NIGHT LONG	GARY GLITTER	25	1977
IT TAKES MORE	MS DYNAMITE	7	2002
IT TAKES SCOOP	FATMAN SCOOP FEATURING THE CROOKLYN CLAN	9	2004
IT TAKES TWO [A]	MARVIN GAYE & KIM WESTON	16	1967
IT TAKES TWO [A]	ROD STEWART & TINA TURNER	5	1990
IT TAKES TWO [B]	ROB BASE & DJ E-Z ROCK	24	1988

	Peak Position	Year of Release
IT TAKES TWO BABY LIZ KERSHAW, BRUNO BROOKES, JIVE BUNNY & LONDONBEAT	53	1989
IT TAKES TWO TO TANGO RICHARD MYHILL	17	1978
IT WAS A GOOD DAY ICE CUBE	27	1993
IT WAS EASIER TO HURT HER WAYNE FONTANA	36	1965
IT WASN'T ME SHAGGY	1	2001
IT WILL BE ALRIGHT ODYSSEY	43	1981
IT WILL BE YOU PAUL YOUNG	34	1994
IT WILL COME IN TIME BILLY PRESTON & SYREETA	47	1980
IT WILL MAKE ME CRAZY FELIX	11	1992
IT WON'T BE LONG ALISON MOYET	50	1991
IT WON'T SEEM LIKE CHRISTMAS (WITHOUT YOU) ELVIS PRESLEY	13	1979
THE ITALIAN THEME CYRIL STAPLETON	18	1956
ITALO HOUSE MIX ROCOCO	54	1989
ITCHYCOO PARK SMALL FACES	3	1967
ITCHYCOO PARK M PEOPLE	11	1995
IT'LL BE ME CLIFF RICHARD & THE SHADOWS	2	1962
IT'S A BEAUTIFUL THING OCEAN COLOUR SCENE	12	1998
IT'S A BETTER THAN GOOD TIME GLADYS KNIGHT & THE PIPS	59	1978
IT'S A DISCO NIGHT (ROCK DON'T STOP) ISLEY BROTHERS	14	1979
IT'S A FINE DAY OPUS III	5	1992
IT'S A FINE DAY MISS JANE	62	1999
IT'S A GAME BAY CITY ROLLERS	16	1977
IT'S A GAS WEDDING PRESENT	71	1994
IT'S A GIRL THING MY LIFE STORY	37	1999
IT'S A GOOD LIFE CEVIN FISHER FEATURING RAMONA KELLY	54	2001
IT'S A HARD LIFE QUEEN	6	1984
IT'S A HEARTACHE BONNIE TYLER	4	1977
IT'S A HIT WE ARE SCIENTISTS	29	2006
IT'S A LONG WAY TO THE TOP (IF YOU WANNA ROCK 'N' ROLL) AC/DC	55	1980
IT'S A LOVE THING WHISPERS	9	1981
IT'S A LOVING THING C.B. MILTON	34	1994
IT'S A MAN'S MAN'S MAN'S WORLD JAMES BROWN & THE FAMOUS FLAMES	13	1966
IT'S A MAN'S MAN'S MAN'S WORLD BRILLIANT	58	1985
IT'S A MAN'S MAN'S MAN'S WORLD JEANIE TRACY & BOBBY WOMACK	73	1995
IT'S A MIRACLE CULTURE CLUB	4	1984
IT'S A MISTAKE MEN AT WORK	33	1983
IT'S A PARTY [A] BUSTA RHYMES FEATURING ZHANE	23	1996
IT'S A PARTY [B] BOUNTY KILLER	65	1999
IT'S A RAGGY WALTZ DAVE BRUBECK QUARTET	36	1962
IT'S A RAINBOW RAINBOW (GEORGE & ZIPPY)	15	2002
IT'S A RAINY DAY ICE MC	73	1995
IT'S A SHAME [A] MOTOWN SPINNERS	20	1970
IT'S A SHAME [B] KRIS KROSS	31	1992
IT'S A SHAME ABOUT RAY LEMONHEADS	31	1992
IT'S A SHAME (MY SISTER) MONIE LOVE FEATURING TRUE IMAGE	12	1990
IT'S A SIN PET SHOP BOYS	1	1987
IT'S A SIN TO TELL A LIE GERRY MONROE	13	1971
IT'S A TRIP (TUNE IN, TURN ON, DROP OUT) CHILDREN OF THE NIGHT	52	1988
IT'S ABOUT TIME [A] LEMONHEADS	57	1993
IT'S ABOUT TIME [B] ONE NIGHT ONLY	37	2008
IT'S ABOUT TIME YOU WERE MINE THUNDERBUGS	43	1999
IT'S ALL ABOUT THE BENJAMINS PUFF DADDY & THE FAMILY	18	1998
IT'S ALL ABOUT U [A] SWV	36	1996
IT'S ALL ABOUT YOU [B] JUSTIN	34	1999
IT'S ALL ABOUT YOU (NOT ABOUT ME) TRACIE SPENCER	65	1999
IT'S ALL BEEN DONE BEFORE BARENAKED LADIES	28	1999
IT'S ALL COMING BACK TO ME NOW PANDORA'S BOX	51	1989
IT'S ALL COMING BACK TO ME NOW CELINE DION	3	1996
IT'S ALL COMING BACK TO ME NOW MEAT LOAF FEATURING MARION RAVEN	6	2006
IT'S ALL GONE CHRIS REA	69	1986
IT'S ALL GOOD [A] HAMMER	52	1994
IT'S ALL GOOD [B] DA MOB FEATURING JOCELYN BROWN	54	1999
IT'S ALL GRAVY ROMEO FEATURING CHRISTINA MILIAN	9	2002
IT'S ALL IN THE GAME TOMMY EDWARDS	1	1958
IT'S ALL IN THE GAME CLIFF RICHARD	2	1963
IT'S ALL IN THE GAME FOUR TOPS	5	1970
IT'S ALL OVER CLIFF RICHARD	9	1967
IT'S ALL OVER NOW [A] SHANE FENTON & THE FENTONES	29	1962
IT'S ALL OVER NOW [B] ROLLING STONES	1	1964
IT'S ALL OVER NOW BABY BLUE JOAN BAEZ	22	1965
IT'S ALL OVER NOW BABY BLUE MILLTOWN BROTHERS	48	1993
IT'S ALL RIGHT STERLING VOID	53	1989
IT'S ALL THE WAY LIVE (NOW) COOLIO	34	1996
IT'S ALL TRUE [A] LEMONHEADS	61	1996
IT'S ALL TRUE [B] TRACEY THORN	75	2007
IT'S ALL UP TO YOU JIM CAPALDI	27	1974
IT'S ALL VAIN MAGNOLIA	55	2004
IT'S ALL YOURS MC LYTE FEATURING GINA THOMPSON	36	1998
IT'S ALMOST TOMORROW DREAMWEAVERS	1	1956
IT'S ALMOST TOMORROW MARK WYNTER	12	1963
IT'S ALRIGHT [A] SHO NUFF	53	1980
IT'S ALRIGHT [B] PET SHOP BOYS	5	1989
IT'S ALRIGHT [B] HYPER GO GO	49	1994
IT'S ALRIGHT [C] EAST 17	3	1993
IT'S ALRIGHT [D] BRYAN POWELL	73	1993
IT'S ALRIGHT [E] DENI HINES	35	1997
IT'S ALRIGHT [F] ECHO & THE BUNNYMEN	41	2001
IT'S ALRIGHT (BABY'S COMING BACK) EURYTHMICS	12	1986
IT'S ALRIGHT, I FEEL IT! NUYORICAN SOUL FEATURING JOCELYN BROWN	26	1997
IT'S ALRIGHT NOW BELOVED	48	1990
IT'S AN OPEN SECRET JOY STRINGS	32	1964
IT'S BEEN A WHILE STAIND	15	2001
IT'S BEEN NICE EVERLY BROTHERS	26	1963
IT'S BEEN SO LONG GEORGE McCRAE	4	1975
IT'S BEGINNING TO LOOK A LOT LIKE CHRISTMAS PERRY COMO	47	2007
IT'S BETTER TO HAVE (AND DON'T NEED) DON COVAY	29	1974
IT'S CALLED A HEART DEPECHE MODE	18	1985
IT'S CHICO TIME CHICO	1	2006
IT'S CHRISTMAS TIME STATUS QUO	40	2008
IT'S DIFFERENT FOR GIRLS JOE JACKSON	5	1980
IT'S ECSTASY WHEN YOU LAY DOWN NEXT TO ME BARRY WHITE	40	1977
IT'S FOR YOU CILLA BLACK	7	1964
IT'S FOUR IN THE MORNING FARON YOUNG	3	1972
IT'S GETTING BETTER MAMA CASS	8	1969
IT'S GOING DOWN X-ECUTIONERS	7	2002
IT'S GOING TO HAPPEN! UNDERTONES	18	1981
IT'S GONNA BE A COLD COLD CHRISTMAS DANA	4	1975
IT'S GONNA BE A LOVELY DAY S.O.U.L. S.Y.S.T.E.M. INTRODUCING MICHELLE VISAGE	17	1993
IT'S GONNA BE (A LOVELY DAY) BRANCACCIO & AISHER	40	2002
IT'S GONNA BE ALL RIGHT GERRY & THE PACEMAKERS	24	1964
IT'S GONNA BE ALRIGHT RUBY TURNER	57	1990
IT'S GONNA BE ALRIGHT PUSSY 2000	70	2001
IT'S GONNA BE ME *NSYNC	9	2000
IT'S GONNA BE MY WAY PRECIOUS	27	2000
IT'S GOOD NEWS WEEK HEDGEHOPPERS ANONYMOUS	5	1965
IT'S GREAT WHEN WE'RE TOGETHER FINLEY QUAYE	29	1997
IT'S GRIM UP NORTH JUSTIFIED ANCIENTS OF MU MU	10	1991
IT'S GROWING TEMPTATIONS	45	1965
IT'S HAPPENIN' PLUS ONE FEATURING SIRRON	40	1990
IT'S HARD SOMETIMES FRANKIE KNUCKLES	67	1991
IT'S HARD TO BE HUMBLE MAC DAVIS	27	1980
IT'S HERE KIM WILDE	42	1990
IT'S IMPOSSIBLE PERRY COMO	4	1971
IT'S IN EVERY ONE OF US CLIFF RICHARD	45	1985
IT'S IN HIS KISS BETTY EVERETT	34	1968
IT'S IN HIS KISS LINDA LEWIS	6	1975
IT'S IN OUR HANDS BJORK	37	2002
IT'S IN YOUR EYES PHIL COLLINS	30	1996
IT'S JURASSIC SOUL CITY ORCHESTRA	70	1993
IT'S JUST A FEELING TERRORIZE	47	1992
IT'S JUST PORN MUM TRUCKS	35	2002
(IT'S JUST) THE WAY THAT YOU LOVE ME PAULA ABDUL	74	1989
IT'S LATE RICKY NELSON	3	1959
IT'S LATE SHAKIN' STEVENS	11	1983
(IT'S LIKE A) SAD OLD KINDA MOVIE PICKETTYWITCH	16	1970
IT'S LIKE THAT [A] RUN DMC VERSUS JASON NEVINS	1	1998
IT'S LIKE THAT [B] MARIAH CAREY	4	2005
IT'S LIKE THAT Y'ALL SWEET TEE	31	1988
IT'S LOVE KEN DODD	36	1966
IT'S LOVE THAT REALLY COUNTS MERSEYBEATS	24	1963
IT'S LOVE (TRIPPIN') GOLDTRIX PRESENTS ANDREA BROWN	6	2002
IT'S LULU BOO RADLEYS	25	1995
IT'S ME ALICE COOPER	34	1994
IT'S MY HOUSE DIANA ROSS	32	1979
IT'S MY HOUSE STORM	36	1979
IT'S MY LIFE GLEE CAST	14	2010
IT'S MY LIFE [A] ANIMALS	7	1965
IT'S MY LIFE [B] TALK TALK	13	1984
IT'S MY LIFE [B] NO DOUBT	17	2003
IT'S MY LIFE [B] LIQUID PEOPLE VS TALK TALK	64	2003
IT'S MY LIFE [C] DR ALBAN	2	1992
IT'S MY LIFE [D] BON JOVI	3	2000
IT'S MY LIFE [D] GLEE CAST	14	2010
IT'S MY PARTY [A] LESLEY GORE	9	1963
IT'S MY PARTY [A] DAVE STEWART WITH BARBARA GASKIN	1	1981
IT'S MY PARTY [B] CHAKA KHAN	71	1989
IT'S MY TIME [A] EVERLY BROTHERS	39	1968
IT'S MY TIME [B] JADE EWEN	27	2009
IT'S MY TURN [A] DIANA ROSS	16	1981
IT'S MY TURN [B] ANGELIC	11	2000
IT'S NATURE'S WAY (NO PROBLEM) DOLLAR	58	1988
IT'S NEVER TOO LATE DIANA ROSS	41	1982
IT'S NICE TO GO TRAV'LING FRANK SINATRA	48	1960
IT'S NO GOOD DEPECHE MODE	5	1997
IT'S NOT A LOVE THING GEOFFREY WILLIAMS	63	1992
IT'S NOT ABOUT YOU SCOUTING FOR GIRLS	31	2007
IT'S NOT OVER YET KLAXONS	13	2007
IT'S NOT RIGHT BUT IT'S OKAY WHITNEY HOUSTON	3	1999
IT'S NOT THAT EASY LEMAR	7	2006

	Peak Position	Year of Release
IT'S NOT THE END OF THE WORLD? [A] SUPER FURRY ANIMALS	30	2002
IT'S NOT THE END OF THE WORLD [B] LOSTPROPHETS	16	2009
IT'S NOT UNUSUAL TOM JONES	1	1965
IT'S NOW OR NEVER ELVIS PRESLEY	1	1960
IT'S OH SO QUIET BJORK	4	1995
IT'S OK [A] DELIRIOUS?	18	2000
IT'S OK [B] ATOMIC KITTEN	3	2002
IT'S OKAY [A] DES'REE	69	2003
IT'S OKAY [B] GAME FEATURING JUNIOR REID	26	2006
IT'S ON [A] FLOWERED UP	38	1990
IT'S ON [B] NAUGHTY BY NATURE	48	1993
IT'S ON YOU (SCAN ME) EUROGROOVE	25	1995
IT'S ONE OF THOSE NIGHTS (YES LOVE) PARTRIDGE FAMILY STARRING SHIRLEY JONES FEATURING DAVID CASSIDY	11	1972
IT'S ONLY LOVE [A] TONY BLACKBURN	40	1969
IT'S ONLY LOVE [A] ELVIS PRESLEY	3	1980
IT'S ONLY LOVE [B] GARY U.S. BONDS	43	1981
IT'S ONLY LOVE [C] BRYAN ADAMS & TINA TURNER	29	1985
IT'S ONLY LOVE [D] SIMPLY RED	13	1989
IT'S ONLY MAKE BELIEVE CONWAY TWITTY	1	1958
IT'S ONLY MAKE BELIEVE BILLY FURY	10	1964
IT'S ONLY MAKE BELIEVE GLEN CAMPBELL	4	1970
IT'S ONLY MAKE BELIEVE CHILD	10	1978
IT'S ONLY NATURAL CROWDED HOUSE	24	1992
IT'S ONLY PAIN KATIE MELUA	41	2006
IT'S ONLY ROCK 'N' ROLL VARIOUS ARTISTS (EP'S & LP'S)	19	1999
IT'S ONLY ROCK AND ROLL ROLLING STONES	10	1974
IT'S ONLY US ROBBIE WILLIAMS	1	1999
IT'S ONLY YOU (MEIN SCHMERZ LENE LOVICH	68	1982
IT'S 'ORRIBLE BEING IN LOVE (WHEN YOU'RE 8½) CLAIRE & FRIENDS	13	1986
IT'S OVER [A] ROY ORBISON	1	1964
IT'S OVER [B] FUNK MASTERS	8	1983
IT'S OVER [B] CLOCK	10	1997
IT'S OVER [C] LEVEL 42	10	1987
IT'S OVER [D] RIMES FEATURING SHAILA PROSPERE	51	1999
IT'S OVER [E] KURUPT	21	2001
IT'S OVER (DISTORTION) PIANOHEADZ	39	1998
IT'S OVER LOVE TODD TERRY PRESENTS SHANNON	16	1997
IT'S OVER NOW [A] ULTRA NATE	62	1989
IT'S OVER NOW [B] DEBORAH COX	49	1999
IT'S OVER NOW [B] BIG ANG FEATURING SIOBHAN	29	2005
IT'S OVER NOW [C] 112	22	2001
IT'S PARTY TIME AGAIN GEORGE VAN DUSEN	43	1988
IT'S PROBABLY ME STING WITH ERIC CLAPTON	30	1992
IT'S RAINING [A] DARTS	2	1978
IT'S RAINING [B] SHAKIN' STEVENS	10	1981
IT'S RAINING AGAIN SUPERTRAMP FEATURING VOCALS BY ROGER HODGSON	26	1982
IT'S RAINING MEN WEATHER GIRLS	2	1983
IT'S RAINING MEN MARTHA WASH	56	2000
IT'S RAINING MEN GERI HALLIWELL	1	2001
IT'S RAINING MEN...THE SEQUEL MARTHA WASH FEATURING RuPAUL	21	1998
IT'S SO EASY ANDY WILLIAMS	13	1970
IT'S SO HIGH MATT FRETTON	50	1983
IT'S SO NICE (TO HAVE YOU HOME) NEW SEEKERS	44	1976
IT'S STILL ROCK AND ROLL TO ME BILLY JOEL	14	1980
IT'S STILL YOU MICHAEL BALL	58	1991
IT'S SUMMERTIME (LET IT GET INTO YOU) SMOOTH	46	1995
IT'S TEMPTATION SHEER ELEGANCE	41	1976
IT'S THE END OF THE WORLD AS WE KNOW IT R.E.M.	39	1991
IT'S THE LITTLE THINGS WE DO ZUTONS	47	2006
IT'S THE MOST WONDERFUL TIME OF THE YEAR ANDY WILLIAMS	21	2007
IT'S THE SAME OLD SONG FOUR TOPS	34	1965
IT'S THE SAME OLD SONG WEATHERMEN	19	1971
IT'S THE SAME OLD SONG KC & THE SUNSHINE BAND	47	1978
IT'S THE WAY YOU MAKE ME FEEL STEPS	2	2001
IT'S TIME [A] ELVIS COSTELLO & THE ATTRACTIONS	58	1996
IT'S TIME [B] FERRY CORSTEN	51	2004
IT'S TIME FOR LOVE CHI-LITES	5	1975
IT'S TIME TO CRY PAUL ANKA	28	1960
IT'S TOO LATE [A] CAROLE KING	6	1971
IT'S TOO LATE [A] QUARTZ INTRODUCING DINA CARROLL	8	1991
IT'S TOO LATE [B] LUCIE SILVAS	62	2000
IT'S TOO LATE NOW [A] SWINGING BLUE JEANS	30	1963
IT'S TOO LATE NOW [B] LONG JOHN BALDRY	21	1969
IT'S TOO SOON TO KNOW PAT BOONE	7	1958
IT'S TRICKY RUN DMC	16	1987
IT'S TRICKY 2003 RUN DMC FEATURING JACKNIFE LEE	20	2003
IT'S TRUE QUEEN PEN	24	1998
IT'S UP TO YOU RICK NELSON	22	1963
IT'S UP TO YOU PETULA EDISON LIGHTHOUSE	49	1971
IT'S UP TO YOU (SHINING THROUGH) LAYO & BUSHWACKA!	25	2003
IT'S WHAT WE'RE ALL ABOUT SUM 41	32	2002
IT'S WHAT'S UPFRONT THAT COUNTS YOSH PRESENTS LOVEDEEJAY AKEMI	31	1995
IT'S WONDERFUL (TO BE LOVED BY YOU) JIMMY RUFFIN	6	1970
IT'S WRITTEN IN THE STARS PAUL WELLER	7	2002
IT'S WRITTEN ON YOUR BODY RONNIE BOND	52	1980
IT'S YER MONEY I'M AFTER BABY WONDER STUFF	40	1988
IT'S YOU [A] FREDDIE STARR	9	1974
IT'S YOU [B] MANHATTANS	43	1977
IT'S YOU [C] EMF	23	1992
IT'S YOUR DAY TODAY PJ PROBY	32	1968
IT'S YOUR DESTINY ELECTRA	51	1989
IT'S YOUR LIFE SMOKIE	5	1977
IT'S YOUR THING ISLEY BROTHERS	30	1969
IT'S YOUR TIME ARTHUR BAKER FEATURING SHIRLEY LEWIS	64	1989
IT'S YOURS JON CUTLER FEATURING E-MAN	38	2002
IT'S...IT'S...THE SWEET MIX SWEET	45	1985
ITSY BITSY TEENY WEENY YELLOW POLKA DOT BIKINI BRIAN HYLAND	8	1960
ITSY BITSY TEENY WEENY YELLOW POLKA DOT BIKINI BOMBALURINA FEATURING TIMMY MALLETT	1	1990
ITZA TRUMPET THING MONTANO VS THE TRUMPET MAN	46	1999
I'VE BEEN A BAD BAD BOY PAUL JONES	5	1967
I'VE BEEN AROUND THE WORLD MARTI PELLOW	28	2001
I'VE BEEN DRINKING JEFF BECK & ROD STEWART	27	1973
I'VE BEEN HURT GUY DARRELL	12	1973
I'VE BEEN IN LOVE BEFORE CUTTING CREW	24	1986
I'VE BEEN LONELY FOR SO LONG FREDERICK KNIGHT	22	1972
I'VE BEEN LOSING YOU A-HA	8	1986
I'VE BEEN THINKING ABOUT YOU LONDONBEAT	2	1990
I'VE BEEN TO A MARVELOUS PARTY DIVINE COMEDY	28	1998
I'VE BEEN WAITING STEREO NATION	53	1996
I'VE BEEN WATCHIN' JOE PUBLIC	75	1992
I'VE BEEN WRONG BEFORE CILLA BLACK	17	1965
I'VE DONE EVERYTHING FOR YOU SAMMY HAGAR	36	1980
I'VE FOUND LOVE AGAIN RICHARD CARTRIDGE	50	2004
I'VE GOT A LIFE EURYTHMICS	14	2005
I'VE GOT A LITTLE PUPPY SMURFS	4	1996
I'VE GOT A LITTLE SOMETHING FOR YOU MN8	2	1995
I'VE GOT A THING ABOUT YOU BABY ELVIS PRESLEY	33	1974
I'VE GOT MINE UB40	45	1983
I'VE GOT NEWS FOR YOU FEARGAL SHARKEY	12	1991
I'VE GOT NOTHING CHARTJACKERS	36	2009
I'VE GOT SOMETHING TO SAY REEF	15	1999
I'VE GOT THIS FEELING MAVERICKS	27	1998
I'VE GOT TO LEARN TO SAY NO RICHARD 'DIMPLES' FIELDS	56	1982
I'VE GOT TO MOVE CALVIN RICHARDSON	74	2004
I'VE GOT YOU MARTINE McCUTCHEON	6	1999
I'VE GOT YOU ON MY MIND DORIAN GRAY	36	1968
I'VE GOT YOU ON MY MIND WHITE PLAINS	17	1970
I'VE GOT YOU UNDER MY SKIN FOUR SEASONS WITH FRANKIE VALLI	12	1966
I'VE GOT YOU UNDER MY SKIN NENEH CHERRY	25	1990
I'VE GOT YOU UNDER MY SKIN FRANK SINATRA WITH BONO	4	1993
(I'VE GOT YOUR) PLEASURE CONTROL SIMON HARRIS FEATURING LONNIE GORDON	60	1989
I'VE GOTTA GET A MESSAGE TO YOU BEE GEES	1	1968
I'VE HAD ENOUGH [A] WINGS	42	1978
I'VE HAD ENOUGH [A] IVAN MATIAS	69	1996
I'VE HAD ENOUGH [B] EARTH, WIND & FIRE	29	1982
I'VE HAD ENOUGH [C] HILLMAN MINX	72	1998
(I'VE HAD) THE TIME OF MY LIFE BILL MEDLEY & JENNIFER WARNES	6	1987
I'VE JUST BEGUN TO LOVE YOU DYNASTY	51	1980
I'VE LOST YOU ELVIS PRESLEY	9	1970
I'VE NEVER BEEN IN LOVE SUZI QUATRO	56	1980
I'VE NEVER BEEN TO ME CHARLENE	1	1982
I'VE PASSED THIS WAY BEFORE JIMMY RUFFIN	29	1967
I'VE SEEN THE WORD BLANCMANGE	65	1982
I'VE TOLD EVERY LITTLE STAR LINDA SCOTT	7	1961
I'VE WAITED SO LONG ANTHONY NEWLEY	3	1959
IVORY SKIN UP	48	1991
IVORY TOWER THREE KAYES	20	1956
IZ U NELLY	36	2003
IZZO (H.O.V.A.) JAY-Z	21	2001

J

	Peak Position	Year of Release
JACK AND DIANE JOHN COUGAR	25	1982
JACK AND JILL RAYDIO	11	1978
JACK AND JILL PARTY PETE BURNS	75	2004
JACK IN THE BOX [A] CLODAGH RODGERS	4	1971
JACK IN THE BOX [B] MOMENTS	7	1977
JACK LE FREAK CHIC	19	1987
JACK MIX II MIRAGE	4	1987
JACK MIX III MIRAGE	4	1987
JACK MIX IV MIRAGE	8	1987

Title	Artist	Peak Position	Year of Release
JACK MIX VII	MIRAGE	50	1988
JACK O' DIAMONDS	LONNIE DONEGAN	14	1957
JACK TALKING	DAVE STEWART & THE SPIRITUAL COWBOYS	69	1990
THE JACK THAT HOUSE BUILT	JACK 'N' CHILL	6	1987
JACK THE GROOVE	RAZE	20	1987
JACK THE RIPPER [A]	LL COOL J	37	1988
JACK THE RIPPER [B]	NICK CAVE & THE BAD SEEDS	68	1992
JACK TO THE SOUND OF THE UNDERGROUND	HITHOUSE	14	1988
JACK YOUR BODY	STEVE 'SILK' HURLEY	1	1987
JACKET HANGS	BLUE AEROPLANES	72	1990
JACKIE	SCOTT WALKER	22	1967
JACKIE WILSON SAID	KEVIN ROWLAND & DEXY'S MIDNIGHT RUNNERS	5	1982
JACKIE'S RACING	WHITEOUT	72	1995
JACK'S HEROES	POGUES & THE DUBLINERS	63	1990
JACKSON	NANCY SINATRA & LEE HAZLEWOOD	11	1967
JACKY	MARC ALMOND	17	1991
JACQUELINE [A]	BOBBY HELMS WITH THE ANITA KERR SINGERS	20	1958
JACQUELINE [B]	CORAL	44	2007
JACQUES DERRIDA	SCRITTI POLITTI	43	1982
JACQUES YOUR BODY (MAKE ME SWEAT)	LES RYTHMES DIGITALES	9	1999
JA-DA	JOHNNY & THE HURRICANES	14	1961
JADED [A]	GREEN DAY	28	1996
JADED [B]	AEROSMITH	13	2001
JAGGED END	MICHAEL COURTNEY	64	2002
JAGUAR	DJ ROLANDO AKA AZTEC MYSTIC	43	2000
JAI HO! (YOU ARE MY DESTINY)	AR RAHMAN & PUSSYCAT DOLLS FEATURING NICOLE SCHERZINGER	3	2009
JAIL HOUSE RAP	FAT BOYS	63	1985
JAILBIRD	PRIMAL SCREAM	29	1994
JAILBREAK [A]	THIN LIZZY	31	1976
JAILBREAK [B]	PARADOX	66	1990
JAILHOUSE ROCK	ELVIS PRESLEY	1	1958
JAILHOUSE ROCK EP	ELVIS PRESLEY	18	1958
JAM	MICHAEL JACKSON	13	1992
THE JAM EP	A TRIBE CALLED QUEST	61	1997
JAM IT JAM	SHE ROCKERS	58	1990
JAM J	JAMES	24	1994
JAM JAM JAM (ALL NIGHT LONG)	PEOPLE'S CHOICE	40	1978
JAM ON REVENGE (THE WIKKI WIKKI SONG)	NEWCLEUS	44	1983
JAM SIDE DOWN	STATUS QUO	17	2002
JAMAICAN IN NEW YORK	SHINEHEAD	30	1993
JAMBALAYA	JO STAFFORD	11	1952
JAMBALAYA	FATS DOMINO	41	1962
JAMBALAYA (ON THE BAYOU)	CARPENTERS	12	1974
JAMBOREE	NAUGHTY BY NATURE FEATURING ZHANE	51	1999
THE JAMES BOND THEME	JOHN BARRY ORCHESTRA	13	1962
JAMES BOND THEME	MOBY	8	1997
JAMES DEAN (I WANNA KNOW)	DANIEL BEDINGFIELD	4	2002
JAMES HAS KITTENS	BLU PETER	70	1998
JAMMIN'	BOB MARLEY FEATURING MC LYTE	42	2000
JAMMIN' IN AMERICA	GAP BAND	64	1984
JAMMING	BOB MARLEY & THE WAILERS	9	1977
JANA	KILLING JOKE	54	1995
JANE [A]	JEFFERSON STARSHIP	21	1980
JANE [B]	PERFECT DAY	68	1989
JANE FALLS DOWN	MODERN	35	2005
JANEIRO	SOLID SESSIONS	47	2002
JANIE, DON'T TAKE YOUR LOVE TO TOWN	JON BON JOVI	13	1997
JANIE JONES (STRUMMERVILLE)	BABYSHAMBLES & FRIENDS	17	2006
JANUARY	PILOT	1	1975
JANUARY FEBRUARY	BARBARA DICKSON	11	1980
JAPANESE BOY	ANEKA	1	1981
JARROW SONG	ALAN PRICE	6	1974
JAWS	LALO SCHIFRIN	14	1976
JAYOU	JURASSIC 5	56	1998
JAZZ CARNIVAL	AZYMUTH	19	1980
JAZZ IT UP	REEL 2 REAL	7	1996
JAZZ RAP	KIM CARNEGIE	73	1991
JAZZ THING	GANG STARR	66	1990
JAZZIN' THE WAY YOU KNOW	JAZZY M	47	2000
JCB SONG	NIZLOPI	1	2005
JE NE SAIS PAS POURQUOI	KYLIE MINOGUE	2	1988
JE SUIS MUSIC	CERRONE	39	1979
JE T'AIME (ALLO ALLO)	RENE & YVETTE	57	1986
JE T'AIME (MOI NON PLUS)	JUDGE DREAD	9	1975
JE T'AIME...MOI NON PLUS	JANE BIRKIN & SERGE GAINSBOURG	1	1969
JE VOULAIS TE DIRE (QUE JE T'ATTENDS)	MANHATTAN TRANSFER	40	1978
JEALOUS AGAIN	BLACK CROWES	70	1991
JEALOUS GUY	ROXY MUSIC	1	1981
JEALOUS GUY	JOHN LENNON	65	1985
JEALOUS HEART	CADETS WITH EILEEN READ	42	1965
JEALOUS HEART	CONNIE FRANCIS	44	1966
JEALOUS LOVE [A]	JO BOXERS	72	1983
JEALOUS LOVE [B]	HAZELL DEAN	63	1984
JEALOUS MIND	ALVIN STARDUST	1	1974
JEALOUSY [A]	BILLY FURY	2	1961
JEALOUSY [B]	AMII STEWART	58	1979
JEALOUSY [C]	ADVENTURES OF STEVIE V	58	1991
JEALOUSY [D]	PET SHOP BOYS	12	1991
JEALOUSY [E]	OCTOPUS	59	1996
JEALOUSY [F]	MARTIN SOLVEIG	62	2006
THE JEAN GENIE	DAVID BOWIE	2	1972
JEAN THE BIRDMAN	DAVID SYLVIAN & ROBERT FRIPP	68	1993
JEANETTE	BEAT	45	1982
JEANNIE	DANNY WILLIAMS	14	1962
JEANNIE, JEANNIE, JEANNIE	EDDIE COCHRAN	31	1961
JEANNY	FALCO	68	1986
JEANS ON	DAVID DUNDAS	3	1976
JEDI WANNABE	BELLATRIX	65	2000
JEEPSTER	T REX	2	1971
JEEPSTER	POLECATS	53	1981
JELLYHEAD	CRUSH	50	1996
JENNIFER ECCLES	HOLLIES	7	1968
JENNIFER JUNIPER	DONOVAN	5	1968
JENNIFER JUNIPER	SINGING CORNER MEETS DONOVAN	68	1990
JENNIFER SHE SAID	LLOYD COLE & THE COMMOTIONS	31	1988
JENNY	STELLASTARR*	46	2003
JENNY DON'T BE HASTY	PAOLO NUTINI	20	2006
JENNY FROM THE BLOCK	JENNIFER LOPEZ	3	2002
JENNY JENNY	LITTLE RICHARD	11	1957
JENNY ONDIOLINE	STEREOLAB	75	1994
JENNY TAKE A RIDE	MITCH RYDER & THE DETROIT WHEELS	33	1966
JENNY WREN	PAUL McCARTNEY	22	2005
JEOPARDY	GREG KIHN BAND	63	1983
JEREMY	PEARL JAM	15	1992
JERICHO [A]	SIMPLY RED	53	1986
JERICHO [B]	PRODIGY	11	1992
JERK IT OUT	CAESARS	8	2003
JERUSALEM [A]	FALL	69	1988
JERUSALEM [A]	FAT LES 2000	10	2000
JERUSALEM [A]	KEEDIE & THE ENGLAND CRICKET TEAM	19	2005
JERUSALEM [B]	HERB ALPERT & THE TIJUANA BRASS	42	1970
JESAMINE	CASUALS	2	1968
JESSE HOLD ON	B*WITCHED	4	1999
JESSICA [A]	JOSHUA KADISON	15	1994
JESSICA [B]	ADAM GREEN	63	2004
JESSICA [C]	ELLIOT MINOR	19	2007
JESSIE'S GIRL	RICK SPRINGFIELD	43	1984
JESUS	CLIFF RICHARD	35	1972
JESUS CHRIST	LONGPIGS	61	1995
JESUS CHRIST POSE	SOUNDGARDEN	30	1992
JESUS HAIRDO	CHARLATANS	48	1994
JESUS HE KNOWS ME	GENESIS	20	1992
JESUS OF SUBURBIA	GREEN DAY	17	2005
JESUS SAYS	ASH	15	1998
JESUS TO A CHILD	GEORGE MICHAEL	1	1996
JESUS WALKS	KANYE WEST	16	2004
JET	PAUL McCARTNEY & WINGS	7	1974
JET CITY WOMAN	QUEENSRYCHE	39	1991
JET-STAR	TEKNOO TOO	56	1991
JETSTREAM	NEW ORDER FEATURING ANA MANTRONIC	20	2005
JEWEL	CRANES	29	1993
JEZEBEL	MARTY WILDE	19	1962
JEZEBEL	SHAKIN' STEVENS	58	1989
JIBARO	ELECTRA	54	1988
JIG A JIG	EAST OF EDEN	7	1971
JIGGA JIGGA	SCOOTER	48	2004
JIGGY	CLIPZ	71	2004
JIGSAW FALLING INTO PLACE	RADIOHEAD	30	2008
JILTED JOHN	JILTED JOHN	4	1978
JIMMIE JONES	VAPORS	44	1981
JIMMY [A]	PURPLE HEARTS	60	1980
JIMMY [B]	MIA	66	2007
JIMMY JIMMY	UNDERTONES	16	1979
JIMMY LEE	ARETHA FRANKLIN	46	1987
JIMMY MACK	MARTHA REEVES & THE VANDELLAS	21	1967
JIMMY OLSEN'S BLUES	SPIN DOCTORS	40	1993
JIMMY UNKNOWN	LITA ROZA	15	1956
JIMMY'S GIRL	JOHNNY TILLOTSON	43	1961
JINGLE BELL ROCK	MAX BYGRAVES	7	1959
JINGLE BELL ROCK	CHUBBY CHECKER & BOBBY RYDELL	40	1962
JINGLE BELLS	JUDGE DREAD	64	1978
JINGLE BELLS	CRAZY FROG	5	2005
JINGLE BELLS (BASS)	BASSHUNTER	35	2008
JINGLE BELLS LAUGHING ALL THE WAY	HYSTERICS	44	1981
JINGO	CANDIDO	55	1981
JINGO	JELLYBEAN	12	1987
JINGO	F.K.W.	30	1994
JITTERBUGGIN'	HEATWAVE	34	1981
JIVE TALKIN'	BEE GEES	5	1975
JIVE TALKIN'	BOOGIE BOX HIGH	7	1987
JJ TRIBUTE	ASHA	38	1995
JOAN OF ARC	ORCHESTRAL MANOEUVRES IN THE DARK	5	1981
JOANNA [A]	SCOTT WALKER	7	1968
JOANNA [B]	KOOL & THE GANG	2	1984
JOANNA [C]	MRS WOOD	34	1995
JOCELYN SQUARE	LOVE & MONEY	51	1989
JOCK MIX 1	MAD JOCKS FEATURING JOCKMASTER B.A.	46	1987
JOCKO HOMO	DEVO	62	1978
JODY	JERMAINE STEWART	50	1986
JOE	INSPIRAL CARPETS	37	1995
JOE LE TAXI	VANESSA PARADIS	3	1988
JOE LOUIS	JOHN SQUIRE	43	2002
JOE 90 (THEME)	BARRY GRAY ORCHESTRA WITH PETER BECKETT – KEYBOARDS	53	1986
JOGI	PANJABI MC FEATURING JAY-Z	25	2003
JOHN AND JULIE	EDDIE CALVERT	6	1955

	Peak Position	Year of Release
JOHN I'M ONLY DANCING DAVID BOWIE	12	1972
JOHN I'M ONLY DANCING POLECATS	35	1981
JOHN KETLEY (IS A WEATHERMAN) TRIBE OF TOFFS	21	1988
JOHN THE REVELATOR DEPECHE MODE	18	2006
JOHN WAYNE IS BIG LEGGY HAYSI FANTAYZEE	11	1982
JOHNNY AND MARY ROBERT PALMER	44	1980
JOHNNY ANGEL PATTI LYNN	37	1962
JOHNNY ANGEL SHELLEY FABARES	41	1962
JOHNNY B. GOODE JIMI HENDRIX	35	1972
JOHNNY B GOODE PETE TOSH	48	1983
JOHNNY B. GOODE JUDAS PRIEST	64	1988
JOHNNY CASH SONS & DAUGHTERS	68	2004
JOHNNY COME HOME FINE YOUNG CANNIBALS	8	1985
JOHNNY COME LATELY STEVE EARLE	75	1988
JOHNNY DAY ROLF HARRIS	44	1963
JOHNNY FRIENDLY JO BOXERS	31	1983
JOHNNY GET ANGRY CAROL DEENE	32	1962
JOHNNY JOHNNY PREFAB SPROUT	64	1986
JOHNNY MATHIS' FEET AMERICAN MUSIC CLUB	58	1993
JOHNNY PANIC AND THE BIBLE OF DREAMS JOHNNY PANIC & THE BIBLE OF DREAMS	70	1991
JOHNNY REGGAE PIGLETS	3	1971
JOHNNY REMEMBER ME JOHN LEYTON	1	1961
JOHNNY REMEMBER ME METEORS	66	1983
JOHNNY ROCCO MARTY WILDE	30	1960
JOHNNY THE HORSE MADNESS	44	1999
JOHNNY WILL PAT BOONE	4	1961
JOIN IN AND SING AGAIN JOHNSTON BROTHERS	9	1955
JOIN IN AND SING (NO. 3) JOHNSTON BROTHERS	24	1956
JOIN ME LIGHTFORCE	53	2000
JOIN OUR CLUB SAINT ETIENNE	21	1992
JOIN THE PARTY HONKY	28	1977
JOIN TOGETHER WHO	9	1972
JOINING YOU ALANIS MORISSETTE	28	1999
JOINTS & JAMS BLACK EYED PEAS	53	1998
JOJO ACTION MR PRESIDENT	73	1998
JOKE (I'M LAUGHING) EDDI READER	42	1994
THE JOKE ISN'T FUNNY ANYMORE SMITHS	49	1985
THE JOKER STEVE MILLER BAND	1	1990
THE JOKER FATBOY SLIM	32	2005
JOKER & THE THIEF WOLFMOTHER	64	2006
THE JOKER (THE WIGAN JOKER) ALLNIGHT BAND	50	1979
JOLE BLON GARY U.S. BONDS	51	1981
JOLENE DOLLY PARTON	7	1976
JOLENE STRAWBERRY SWITCHBLADE	53	1985
JOLENE – LIVE UNDER BLACKPOOL LIGHTS WHITE STRIPES	16	2004
JONAH BREATHE	60	1988
JONATHAN DAVID BELLE & SEBASTIAN	31	2001
THE JONES' TEMPTATIONS	69	1992
JONES VS JONES KOOL & THE GANG	17	1981
JONESTOWN MIND ALMIGHTY	26	1995
JONNY SNIPER ENTER SHIKARI	75	2007
JOOK GAL ELEPHANT MAN	41	2004
JORDAN: THE EP PREFAB SPROUT	35	1991
JOSE AND HIS AMAZING TECHNICOLOR OVERCOAT MARIO ROSENSTOCK	45	2006
JOSEPH MEGA REMIX JASON DONOVAN & ORIGINAL LONDON CAST FEATURING LINZI HATELY, DAVID EASTER & JOHNNY AMOBI	13	1991
JOSEPHINE [A] CHRIS REA	67	1985
JOSEPHINE [B] TERRORVISION	23	1998
JOSEY DEEP BLUE SOMETHING	27	1996
JOURNEY [A] DUNCAN BROWNE	23	1972
THE JOURNEY [A] CITIZEN CANED	41	2001
THE JOURNEY [B] 911	3	1997

	Peak Position	Year of Release
THE JOURNEY [C] AMSTERDAM	32	2005
THE JOURNEY CONTINUES MARK BROWN FEATURING SARAH CRACKNELL	11	2008
JOURNEY TO THE MOON BIDDU ORCHESTRA	41	1978
JOURNEY TO THE PAST AALIYAH	22	1998
JOY [A] BAND AKA	24	1983
JOY [B] TEDDY PENDERGRASS	58	1988
JOY [C] SOUL II SOUL	4	1992
JOY [D] STAXX FEATURING CAROL LEEMING	14	1993
JOY [E] 7669	60	1994
JOY [F] BLACKSTREET	56	1995
JOY [G] DENI HINES	47	1998
JOY [H] KATHY BROWN	63	1999
JOY! [I] GAY DAD	22	1999
JOY [J] MARK RYDER	34	2001
JOY AND HAPPINESS STABBS	65	1994
JOY AND HEARTBREAK MOVEMENT 98 FEATURING CARROLL THOMPSON	27	1990
JOY AND PAIN [A] DONNA ALLEN	10	1989
JOY AND PAIN [A] ROB BASE & DJ E-Z ROCK	47	1989
JOY AND PAIN [A] MAZE	57	1989
JOY AND PAIN [B] ANGELLE	43	2002
(JOY) I KNOW IT ODYSSEY	51	1985
JOY OF LIVING [A] CLIFF (Richard) & HANK (Marvin)	25	1970
JOY OF LIVING [B] OUI 3	55	1995
JOY TO THE WORLD THREE DOG NIGHT	24	1971
JOYBRINGER MANFRED MANN'S EARTH BAND	9	1973
JOYENERGIZER JOY KITIKONTI	57	2001
JOYRIDE ROXETTE	4	1991
JOYRIDER (YOU'RE PLAYING WITH FIRE) COLOUR GIRL	51	2000
JOYS OF CHRISTMAS CHRIS REA	67	1987
JOYS OF LIFE DAVID JOSEPH	61	1984
JUDGE FUDGE HAPPY MONDAYS	24	1991
JUDGEMENT DAY MS DYNAMITE	25	2005
THE JUDGEMENT IS THE MIRROR DALI'S CAR	66	1984
JUDY PIPETTES	46	2006
JUDY IN DISGUISE (WITH GLASSES) JOHN FRED & THE PLAYBOY BAND	3	1968
JUDY OVER THE RAINBOW ORANGE	73	1994
JUDY SAYS (KNOCK YOU IN THE HEAD) VIBRATORS	70	1978
JUDY TEEN COCKNEY REBEL	5	1974
JUGGERNAUTS ENTER SHIKARI	28	2009
JUGGLING RAGGA TWINS	71	1991
JUICEBOX STROKES	5	2005
JUICY WRECKS-N-EFFECT	29	1990
JUICY NOTORIOUS B.I.G.	72	1994
JUICY FRUIT MTUME	34	1983
A JUICY RED APPLE SKIN UP	32	1992
JUKE BOX BABY PERRY COMO	22	1956
JUKE BOX GYPSY LINDISFARNE	56	1978
JUKE BOX HERO FOREIGNER	48	1981
JUKE BOX JIVE RUBETTES	3	1974
JULIA [A] EURYTHMICS	44	1985
JULIA [B] CHRIS REA	18	1993
JULIA [C] SILVER SUN	51	1997
JULIA SAYS WET WET WET	3	1995
JULIE ANN KENNY	10	1975
JULIE DO YA LOVE ME WHITE PLAINS	8	1970
JULIE DO YA LOVE ME BOBBY SHERMAN	28	1970
JULIE (EP) LEVELLERS	17	1994
JULIE OCEAN UNDERTONES	41	1981
JULIET FOUR PENNIES	1	1964
JULIET (KEEP THAT IN MIND) THEA GILMORE	35	2003
JULY [A] OCEAN COLOUR SCENE	31	2000
JULY [B] NATTY	53	2008
JUMBO [A] BEE GEES	25	1968
JUMBO [B] UNDERWORLD	21	1999
JUMP [A] VAN HALEN	7	1984
JUMP [A] BUS STOP	23	1999

	Peak Position	Year of Release
JUMP [B] AZTEC CAMERA	34	1984
JUMP [C] KRIS KROSS	2	1992
JUMP! [D] MOVEMENT	57	1992
JUMP [E] GIRLS ALOUD	2	2003
JUMP [F] FADERS	21	2005
JUMP [G] FUN DMENTAL 03	44	2006
JUMP [H] MADONNA	9	2006
JUMP [I] FLO RIDA FEATURING NELLY FURTADO	21	2009
JUMP AROUND HOUSE OF PAIN	8	1992
JUMP BACK (SET ME FREE) DHAR BRAXTON	32	1986
JUMP DOWN B*WITCHED	16	2000
JUMP (FOR MY LOVE) POINTER SISTERS	6	1984
JUMP IN MY CAR DAVID HASSELHOFF	3	2006
JUMP IN THE POOL FRIENDLY FIRES	57	2009
JUMP JIVE AN' WAIL BRIAN SETZER ORCHESTRA	34	1999
JUMP N' SHOUT BASEMENT JAXX	12	1999
THE JUMP OFF LIL' KIM FEATURING MR CHEEKS	16	2003
JUMP ON DEMAND SPUNGE	39	2002
JUMP START NATALIE COLE	36	1987
JUMP THAT ROCK SCOOTER VS STATUS QUO	57	2008
JUMP THE GUN THREE DEGREES	48	1979
JUMP THEY SAY DAVID BOWIE	9	1993
JUMP TO IT ARETHA FRANKLIN	42	1982
JUMP TO MY BEAT WILDCHILD	30	1996
JUMP TO MY LOVE INCOGNITO	29	1996
JUMP TO THE BEAT STACY LATTISAW	3	1980
JUMP TO THE BEAT DANNII MINOGUE	8	1991
JUMP UP JUST 4 JOKES FEATURING M.C.R.B.	67	2002
JUMPIN' LIBERTY X	6	2003
JUMPIN' JACK FLASH ROLLING STONES	1	1968
JUMPIN' JACK FLASH ARETHA FRANKLIN	58	1986
JUMPIN' JIVE JOE JACKSON'S JUMPIN' JIVE	43	1981
JUMPIN' JUMPIN' DESTINY'S CHILD	5	2000
JUMPING ALL OVER THE WORLD SCOOTER	28	2008
JUNE AFTERNOON ROXETTE	52	1996
JUNE JULY APARTMENT	67	2005
JUNEAU FUNERAL FOR A FRIEND	19	2003
JUNGLE BILL YELLO	61	1992
THE JUNGLE BOOK GROOVE JUNGLE BOOK	14	1993
JUNGLE BROTHER JUNGLE BROTHERS	18	1997
JUNGLE FEVER CHAKACHAS	29	1972
JUNGLE HIGH JUNO REACTOR	45	1997
JUNGLE ROCK HANK MIZELL	3	1976
JUNGLE ROCK JUNGLE BOYS	30	2004
JUNGLIST DRUMSOUND/SIMON BASSLINE SMITH	67	2003
JUNIOR'S FARM PAUL McCARTNEY & WINGS	16	1974
JUNKIES EASYWORLD	40	2003
JUPITER EARTH, WIND & FIRE	41	1978
JUS 1 KISS BASEMENT JAXX	23	2001
JUS' A RASCAL DIZZEE RASCAL	30	2003
JUS' COME COOL JACK	44	1996
JUS' REACH (RECYCLED) GALLIANO	66	1992
JUST [A] RADIOHEAD	19	1995
JUST [A] MARK RONSON FEATURING ALEX GREENWALD	36	2006
JUST [B] JAMIE SCOTT	29	2004
JUST A DAY FEEDER	12	2001
JUST A DAY AWAY BARCLAY JAMES HARVEST	68	1983
JUST A DREAM [A] NENA	70	1984
JUST A DREAM [B] DONNA DE LORY	71	1993
JUST A FEELING BAD MANNERS	13	1981
JUST A FEW THINGS THAT I AIN'T BEAUTIFUL SOUTH	30	2003
JUST A FRIEND [A] BIZ MARKIE	55	1990
JUST A FRIEND [B] MARIO	18	2003
JUST A GIRL NO DOUBT	3	1996
JUST A GROOVE NOMAD	16	1991
JUST A LIL BIT 50 CENT	10	2005
JUST A LITTLE LIBERTY X	1	2002

Title	Artist	Peak Position	Year of Release
JUST A LITTLE BIT [A]	UNDERTAKERS	49	1964
JUST A LITTLE BIT [B]	MUTYA BUENA	65	2007
JUST A LITTLE BIT BETTER	HERMAN'S HERMITS	15	1965
JUST A LITTLE BIT OF LOVE	REBEKAH RYAN	51	1996
JUST A LITTLE BIT TOO LATE	WAYNE FONTANA & THE MINDBENDERS	20	1965
JUST A LITTLE GIRL	AMY STUDT	14	2002
JUST A LITTLE MISUNDERSTANDING	CONTOURS	31	1970
JUST A LITTLE MORE	DELUXE	74	1989
JUST A LITTLE MORE LOVE	DAVID GUETTA FEATURING CHRIS WILLIS	19	2003
JUST A LITTLE TOO MUCH	RICKY NELSON	11	1959
JUST A LITTLE WHILE	JANET JACKSON	15	2004
JUST A MAN	MARK MORRISON	48	2004
JUST A MIRAGE	JELLYBEAN FEATURING ADELE BERTEI	13	1988
JUST A RIDE	JEM	16	2005
JUST A SHADOW	BIG COUNTRY	26	1985
JUST A SMILE	PILOT	31	1975
JUST A STEP FROM HEAVEN	ETERNAL	8	1994
JUST A TOUCH	KEITH SWEAT	35	1996
JUST A TOUCH OF LOVE	SLAVE	64	1980
JUST A TOUCH OF LOVE EVERYDAY	C & C MUSIC FACTORY FEATURING ZELMA DAVIS	31	1991
JUST AN ILLUSION	IMAGINATION	2	1982
JUST ANOTHER BROKEN HEART	SHEENA EASTON	33	1981
JUST ANOTHER DAY [A]	JON SECADA	5	1992
JUST ANOTHER DAY [B]	JONATHAN WILKES	24	2001
JUST ANOTHER DREAM	CATHY DENNIS	13	1991
JUST ANOTHER GROOVE	MIGHTY DUB KATZ	43	1996
JUST ANOTHER ILLUSION	HURRICANE #1	35	1997
JUST ANOTHER NIGHT	MICK JAGGER	32	1985
JUST AROUND THE HILL	SASH!	8	2000
JUST AS LONG AS YOU ARE THERE	VANESSA PARADIS	57	1993
JUST AS MUCH AS EVER	NAT 'KING' COLE	18	1960
JUST BE	TIESTO FEATURING KIRSTY HAWKSHAW	43	2004
JUST BE DUB TO ME	REVELATION	36	2003
JUST BE GOOD TO ME	S.O.S. BAND	13	1984
JUST BE TONIGHT	BBG	45	1997
JUST BECAUSE	JANE'S ADDICTION	14	2003
JUST BEFORE YOU LEAVE	DEL AMITRI	37	2002
JUST BETWEEN YOU AND ME	APRIL WINE	52	1981
JUST BORN	JIM DALE	27	1958
JUST CALL	SHERRICK	23	1987
JUST CALL ME	GOOD GIRLS	75	1993
JUST CAN'T GET ENOUGH [A]	DEPECHE MODE	8	1981
JUST CAN'T GET ENOUGH [A]	SATURDAYS	2	2009
JUST CAN'T GET ENOUGH [B]	TRANSFORMER 2	45	1996
JUST CAN'T GET ENOUGH [C]	HARRY 'CHOO CHOO' ROMERO PRESENTS INAYA DAY	39	1999
JUST CAN'T GET ENOUGH (NO NO NO NO)	EYE TO EYE FEATURING TAKA BOOM	36	2001
JUST CAN'T GIVE YOU UP	MYSTIC MERLIN	20	1980
JUST CAN'T STAND IT	MATT BIANCO	66	1986
JUST CAN'T WAIT (SATURDAY)	100% FEATURING JENNIFER JOHN	28	2005
JUST CHECKIN'	BEAUTIFUL SOUTH	59	2000
JUST CRUISIN'	WILL SMITH	23	1997
JUST DANCE	LADY GAGA	1	2009
JUST DANCE	LADY GAGA FEATURING COLBY O'DONIS & AKON	62	2010
JUST DON'T WANT TO BE LONELY	MAIN INGREDIENT	27	1974
JUST DON'T WANT TO BE LONELY	FREDDIE McGREGOR	9	1987
JUST FADE AWAY	STIFF LITTLE FINGERS	47	1981
JUST FINE	MARY J BLIGE	16	2008
JUST FOR KICKS	MIKE SARNE	22	1963
JUST FOR MONEY	PAUL HARDCASTLE	19	1985
JUST FOR OLD TIME'S SAKE	FOSTER & ALLEN	47	1984
JUST FOR ONE DAY (HEROES)	DAVID GUETTA VS DAVID BOWIE	73	2003
JUST FOR TONIGHT	ONE NIGHT ONLY	9	2008
JUST FOR YOU [A]	FREDDIE & THE DREAMERS	41	1964
JUST FOR YOU [B]	GLITTER BAND	10	1974
JUST FOR YOU [C]	ALAN PRICE	32	1978
JUST FOR YOU [D]	M PEOPLE	8	1997
JUST FOR YOU [E]	LIONEL RICHIE	20	2004
JUST FRIENDS	NINE BLACK ALPS	52	2005
JUST FUCK	TOM NEVILLE	60	2004
JUST GET UP AND DANCE	AFRIKA BAMBAATAA	45	1991
JUST GETS BETTER	TJR FEATURING XAVIER	28	1987
JUST GIVE THE DJ A BREAK	DYNAMIX II FEATURING TOO TOUGH TEE	50	1987
JUST GO	LIONEL RICHIE	52	2009
JUST GOOD FRIENDS	FISH FEATURING SAM BROWN	63	1995
JUST GOT LUCKY	JO BOXERS	7	1983
JUST GOT PAID	JOHNNY KEMP	68	1988
JUST HOLD ON	TOPLOADER	20	2000
JUST IN CASE	JAHEIM	34	2001
JUST IN LUST	WILDHEARTS	28	1995
JUST IN TIME	RAW SILK	49	1983
JUST KEEP IT UP	DEE CLARK	26	1959
JUST KEEP ME MOVING	k.d. lang	59	1993
JUST KEEP ROCKIN'	DOUBLE TROUBLE & THE REBEL MC	11	1989
JUST KICK	COHEN VS DELUXE	70	2004
JUST KICKIN' IT	XSCAPE	49	1993
JUST LET ME DO MY THING	SINE	33	1978
JUST LIKE A MAN	DEL AMITRI	25	1992
JUST LIKE A PILL	P!NK	1	2002
JUST LIKE A WOMAN	MANFRED MANN	10	1966
JUST LIKE ANYONE	SOUL ASYLUM	52	1995
JUST LIKE BRUCE LEE	KILLCITY	63	2004
JUST LIKE EDDIE	HEINZ	5	1963
JUST LIKE FRED ASTAIRE	JAMES	17	1999
JUST LIKE HEAVEN	CURE	29	1987
JUST LIKE HEAVEN	KATIE MELUA	35	2005
JUST LIKE HONEY	JESUS & MARY CHAIN	45	1985
JUST LIKE JESSE JAMES	CHER	11	1990
JUST LIKE PARADISE	DAVID LEE ROTH	27	1988
(JUST LIKE) STARTING OVER	JOHN LENNON	1	1980
JUST LISTEN TO MY HEART	SPOTNICKS	36	1963
JUST LOOKIN' [A]	CHARLATANS	32	1995
JUST LOOKING [B]	STEREOPHONICS	4	1999
JUST LOSE IT	EMINEM	1	2004
JUST LOVING YOU	ANITA HARRIS	6	1967
(JUST) ME AND YOU	NEW VISION	23	2000
JUST MELLOW	RUTHLESS RAP ASSASSINS	75	1990
JUST MY IMAGINATION	McGANNS	59	1998
JUST MY IMAGINATION (RUNNING AWAY WITH ME)	TEMPTATIONS	8	1971
JUST MY SOUL RESPONDING	SMOKEY ROBINSON	35	1974
JUST ONE LOOK [A]	HOLLIES	2	1964
JUST ONE LOOK [B]	FAITH, HOPE & CHARITY	38	1976
JUST ONE MORE KISS	RENEE & RENATO	48	1983
JUST ONE MORE NIGHT	YELLOW DOG	8	1978
JUST ONE SMILE	GENE PITNEY	8	1966
JUST OUT OF REACH (OF MY TWO EMPTY ARMS)	KEN DODD	29	1972
JUST OUTSIDE OF HEAVEN	H20	38	1983
JUST PLAY MUSIC	BIG AUDIO DYNAMITE	51	1988
JUST PLAYIN'	JT PLAYAZ	30	1997
JUST PUT YOUR HAND IN MINE	SPACE COWBOY	71	2003
JUST RIGHT	SOUL II SOUL	38	1992
JUST ROUND	A VERY GOOD FRIEND OF MINE	55	1999
JUST SAY NO	GRANGE HILL CAST	5	1986
JUST SAY YES	SNOW PATROL	15	2009
JUST SAY YOU LOVE ME	MALACHI	49	2003
JUST SEVEN NUMBERS (CAN STRAIGHTEN OUT MY LIFE)	FOUR TOPS	36	1971
JUST SHOW ME HOW TO LOVE YOU	SARAH BRIGHTMAN & THE LSO FEATURING JOSE CURA	54	1997
JUST SO YOU KNOW	AMERICAN HEAD CHARGE	52	2002
JUST STAND UP!	ARTISTS STAND UP TO CANCER	26	2008
JUST TAH LET U KNOW	EAZY-E	30	1996
JUST TAKE MY HEART	MR BIG	26	1992
JUST THE ONE	LEVELLERS, SPECIAL GUEST JOE STRUMMER	12	1995
JUST THE TWO OF US	GROVER WASHINGTON, JR	34	1981
JUST THE TWO OF US	WILL SMITH	2	1998
JUST THE WAY	ALFONZO HUNTER	38	1997
JUST THE WAY I'M FEELING	FEEDER	10	2003
JUST THE WAY IT IS	LISA MOORISH	42	1995
JUST THE WAY YOU ARE [A]	BARRY WHITE	12	1978
JUST THE WAY YOU ARE [A]	BILLY JOEL	19	1978
JUST THE WAY YOU ARE [B]	MILKY	8	2002
JUST THE WAY YOU LIKE IT	S.O.S. BAND	32	1984
JUST THIRTEEN	LURKERS	66	1979
JUST THIS SIDE OF LOVE	MALANDRA BURROWS	11	1990
JUST TO BE CLOSE TO YOU	COMMODORES	62	1978
JUST TO SEE HER	SMOKEY ROBINSON	52	1987
JUST WALK IN MY SHOES	GLADYS KNIGHT & THE PIPS	35	1972
JUST WALKIN' IN THE RAIN	JOHNNIE RAY	1	1956
JUST WANNA KNOW	MAXI PRIEST	33	1992
JUST WANNA TOUCH ME	FIDELFATTI FEATURING RONETTE	65	1990
JUST WANT TO LIVE	OPEN	52	2004
JUST WANT YOU TO KNOW	BACKSTREET BOYS	8	2005
JUST WAVE HELLO	CHARLOTTE CHURCH	34	1999
JUST WHAT I ALWAYS WANTED	MARI WILSON	8	1982
JUST WHAT I NEEDED	CARS	17	1979
JUST WHEN I NEEDED YOU MOST	RANDY VANWARMER	8	1979
JUST WHEN I NEEDED YOU MOST	BARBARA JONES	31	1981
JUST WHEN YOU'RE THINKING THINGS OVER	CHARLATANS	12	1995
JUST WHO IS THE FIVE O'CLOCK HERO	JAM	8	1982
JUSTIFIED AND ANCIENT	KLF, GUEST VOCALS TAMMY WYNETTE	2	1991
JUSTIFY MY LOVE	MADONNA	2	1990
JUSTIFY THE RAIN	COSMIC ROUGH RIDERS	39	2003
JUXTAPOZED WITH U	SUPER FURRY ANIMALS	14	2001

K

Title	Artist	Peak Position	Year of Release
KA-CHING	SHANIA TWAIN	8	2003
KALEIDOSCOPE SKIES	JAM & SPOON FEATURING PLAVKA	48	1997
KAMICHI	HELL IS FOR HEROES	72	2004
KAMIKAZE	KING ADORA	68	2003
KANSAS CITY	LITTLE RICHARD	26	1959
KANSAS CITY	TRINI LOPEZ	35	1963
KANSAS CITY STAR	ROGER MILLER	48	1965
KARA KARA	NEW WORLD	17	1971
KARAOKE QUEEN	CATATONIA	36	1999
KARAOKE SOUL	TOM McRAE	48	2003

Title	Artist	Peak Position	Year of Release
KARMA CHAMELEON	CULTURE CLUB	4	1983
KARMA HOTEL	SPOOKS	15	2001
KARMA POLICE	RADIOHEAD	8	1997
KARMACOMA	MASSIVE ATTACK	28	1995
KARMADROME	POP WILL EAT ITSELF	17	1992
KATE	BEN FOLDS FIVE	39	1997
KATE BUSH ON STAGE EP	KATE BUSH	10	1979
KATHLEEN	ROACHFORD	43	1989
KATHLEEN (EP)	TINDERSTICKS	61	1994
KAYLEIGH	MARILLION	2	1985
KEEEP YOUR BODY WORKING	KLEEER	51	1979
KEEP A KNOCKIN'	LITTLE RICHARD	21	1957
KEEP AN OPEN MIND	CAPTAIN	53	2008
KEEP AWAY FROM OTHER GIRLS	HELEN SHAPIRO	40	1962
KEEP COMING BACK	RICHARD MARX	55	1991
KEEP CONTROL	SONO	66	2001
KEEP DOIN' IT	SHOWDOWN	41	1977
KEEP EACH OTHER WARM	BUCKS FIZZ	45	1986
(KEEP FEELING) FASCINATION	HUMAN LEAGUE	2	1983
KEEP FISHIN'	WEEZER	29	2002
KEEP GIVIN' ME YOUR LOVE	CE CE PENISTON	36	1994
KEEP GIVING ME LOVE [A]	D TRAIN	65	1983
KEEP GIVING ME LOVE [B]	BOMB THE BASS	62	1992
KEEP HOLDING ON	GLEE CAST	47	2010
KEEP HOPE ALIVE [A]	SERIAL DIVA	57	1997
KEEP HOPE ALIVE [B]	CRYSTAL METHOD	71	1998
KEEP IN TOUCH	FREEEZ	49	1980
KEEP IN TOUCH (BODY TO BODY)	SHADES OF LOVE	64	1995
KEEP IT COMIN' (DANCE TILL YOU CAN'T DANCE NO MORE)	C & C MUSIC FACTORY FEATURING UNIQUE & DEBORAH COOPER	34	1992
KEEP IT COMIN' LOVE	KC & THE SUNSHINE BAND	31	1976
KEEP IT DARK	GENESIS	33	1981
KEEP IT ON	HANNAH JONES	67	1993
KEEP IT OUT OF SIGHT	PAUL & BARRY RYAN	30	1967
KEEP IT TO YOURSELF	REUBEN	62	2005
KEEP IT TOGETHER	DAVID GRANT	56	1990
KEEP IT UP	SHARADA HOUSE GANG	36	1995
KEEP LOVE NEW	BETTY WRIGHT	71	1989
KEEP LOVE TOGETHER	LOVE TO INFINITY	38	1995
KEEP LOVE TOGETHER	SODA CLUB FEATURING ANDREA ANATOLA	31	2003
KEEP ME A SECRET	AINSLIE HENDERSON	5	2003
KEEP ME FROM THE COLD	CURTIS STIGERS	57	1995
KEEP ME IN MIND	BOY GEORGE	29	1987
KEEP ON [A]	BRUCE CHANNEL	12	1968
KEEP ON [B]	CABARET VOLTAIRE	55	1990
KEEP ON BELIEVING	GRAND PRIX	75	1982
KEEP ON BURNING	EDWYN COLLINS	45	1996
KEEP ON DANCIN'	GARY'S GANG	8	1979
KEEP ON DANCIN' (LET'S GO)	PERPETUAL MOTION	12	1998
KEEP ON DANCING	BAY CITY ROLLERS	9	1971
KEEP ON JAMMIN'	WILLIE HUTCH	73	1985
KEEP ON JUMPIN'	LISA MARIE EXPERIENCE	7	1996
KEEP ON JUMPIN'	TODD TERRY FEATURING MARTHA WASH & JOCELYN BROWN	8	1996
KEEP ON JUMPIN'	CORENELL & LISA MARIE EXPERIENCE	37	2007
KEEP ON KEEPIN' ON [A]	REDSKINS	43	1984
KEEP ON LOVING YOU	REO SPEEDWAGON	7	1981
KEEP ON MOVIN' [A]	SOUL II SOUL FEATURING CARON WHEELER	5	1989
KEEP ON MOVIN' [C]	FIVE	1	1999
KEEP ON MOVING [B]	BOB MARLEY & THE WAILERS	17	1995
KEEP ON PUMPIN' IT	VISIONMASTERS WITH TONY KING & KYLIE MINOGUE	49	1991
KEEP ON PUSHING OUR LOVE	NIGHTCRAWLERS FEATURING JOHN REID & ALYSHA WARREN	30	1996
KEEP ON RUNNIN' (TILL YOU BURN)	UK SUBS	41	1981
KEEP ON RUNNING	SPENCER DAVIS GROUP	1	1965
KEEP ON RUNNING	JOHN ALFORD	24	1996
(KEEP ON) SHINING	LOVELAND FEATURING RACHEL McFARLANE	37	1994
KEEP ON TRUCKIN'	EDDIE KENDRICKS	18	1973
KEEP ON WALKIN'	CE CE PENISTON	10	1992
KEEP ON, KEEPIN' ON [B]	MC LYTE FEATURING XSCAPE	27	1996
KEEP PUSHIN' [A]	CLOCK	7	1995
KEEP PUSHIN' [B]	BORIS DLUGOSCH PRESENTS BOOOM!	41	1996
KEEP PUSHIN' ON	YETI	57	2005
KEEP REACHING OUT FOR LOVE	LINER	49	1979
KEEP SEARCHIN' (WE'LL FOLLOW THE SUN)	DEL SHANNON	3	1965
KEEP STEPPIN'	OMAR	57	1994
KEEP TALKING	PINK FLOYD	26	1994
KEEP THE CAR RUNNING	ARCADE FIRE	56	2007
KEEP THE CUSTOMER SATISFIED	MARSHA HUNT	41	1970
KEEP THE FAITH	BON JOVI	5	1992
KEEP THE FIRE BURNIN'	DAN HARTMAN STARRING LOLEATTA HOLLOWAY	49	1995
KEEP THE FIRES BURNING	CLOCK	36	1994
KEEP THE HOME FIRES BURNING	BLUETONES	13	2000
KEEP THE MUSIC STRONG	BIZARRE INC	33	1996
KEEP THEIR HEADS RINGIN'	DR DRE	25	1995
KEEP THIS FIRE BURNING	BEVERLEY KNIGHT	16	2005
KEEP THIS FREQUENCY CLEAR	DTI	73	1988
KEEP US TOGETHER	STARSAILOR	47	2006
KEEP WARM	JINNY	11	1991
KEEP WHAT YA GOT	IAN BROWN	18	2004
KEEP YOUR EYE ON ME	HERB ALPERT	19	1987
KEEP YOUR HANDS OFF MY BABY	LITTLE EVA	30	1963
KEEP YOUR HANDS OFF MY GIRL	GOOD CHARLOTTE	23	2007
KEEP YOUR HANDS TO YOURSELF	GEORGIA SATELLITES	69	1987
KEEP YOUR HEAD UP	GIRLS CAN'T CATCH	26	2009
KEEP YOUR LOVE	PARTIZAN FEATURING NATALIE ROBB	53	1997
KEEP YOUR WORRIES	GURU'S JAZZAMATAZZ FEATURING ANGIE STONE	57	2000
KEEPER OF THE CASTLE	FOUR TOPS	18	1972
KEEPIN' LOVE NEW	HOWARD JOHNSON	45	1982
KEEPIN' THE FAITH	DE LA SOUL	50	1991
KEEPING A RENDEZVIUS	BUDGIE	71	1981
KEEPING SECRETS	SWITCH	61	1984
KEEPING THE DREAM ALIVE	FREIHEIT	14	1988
KEEPS GETTIN' BETTER	CHRISTINA AGUILERA	14	2008
KEEPS IN ME IN WONDERLAND	STEVE MILLER BAND	52	1982
KEINE LUST	RAMMSTEIN	35	2005
KELLY	WAYNE GIBSON	48	1964
KELLY WATCH THE STARS	AIR	18	1998
KELLY'S HEROES	BLACK GRAPE	17	1995
KENNEDY	WEDDING PRESENT	33	1989
KENTUCKY RAIN	ELVIS PRESLEY	21	1970
KERNKRAFT 400	ZOMBIE NATION	2	2000
KERRY KERRY	CINERAMA	71	1998
THE KETCHUP SONG (ASEREJE)	LAS KETCHUP	1	2002
KEVIN CARTER	MANIC STREET PREACHERS	9	1996
KEWPIE DOLL	PERRY COMO	9	1958
KEWPIE DOLL	FRANKIE VAUGHAN	10	1958
THE KEY [A]	SENSER	47	1993
THE KEY [B]	MATT GOSS	40	1995
KEY LARGO	BERTIE HIGGINS	60	1982
THE KEY THE SECRET	URBAN COOKIE COLLECTIVE	2	1993
KEY TO MY LIFE	BOYZONE	3	1995
A KICK I N THE MOUTH	REUBEN	58	2005
KICK IN THE EYE	BAUHAUS	59	1981
KICK IN THE EYE (EP)	BAUHAUS	45	1982
KICK IT [A]	NITZER EBB	56	1995
KICK IT [B]	REGGAE BOYZ	59	1998
KICK IT [C]	PEACHES FEATURING IGGY POP	39	2003
KICK IT IN	SIMPLE MINDS	15	1989
KICK PUSH	LUPE FIASCO	27	2006
KICKIN' HARD	KLUBBHEADS	36	1998
KICKIN' IN THE BEAT	PAMELA FERNANDEZ	43	1994
KICKING MY HEART AROUND	BLACK CROWES	55	1998
KICKING UP DUST	LITTLE ANGELS	46	1990
KICKING UP THE LEAVES	MARK WYNTER	24	1960
KID	PRETENDERS	33	1979
KID 2000	HYBRID FEATURING CHRISSIE HYNDE	32	2000
KIDDIO	BROOK BENTON	41	1960
KIDS [A]	ROBBIE WILLIAMS & KYLIE MINOGUE	2	2000
KIDS [B]	MGMT	16	2008
THE KIDS ARE ALRIGHT	WHO	41	1966
THE KIDS ARE BACK	TWISTED SISTER	32	1983
THE KIDS ARE SICK AGAIN	MAXIMO PARK	50	2009
THE KIDS AREN'T ALRIGHT	OFFSPRING	11	1999
KIDS IN AMERICA	KIM WILDE	2	1981
THE KID'S LAST FIGHT	FRANKIE LAINE	3	1954
KIDS OF THE CENTURY	HELLOWEEN	56	1991
KIDS ON THE STREET	ANGELIC UPSTARTS	57	1981
KIDS WITH GUNS	GORILLAZ	27	2006
KIKI RIRI BOOM	SHAFT	62	2001
THE KILL	THIRTY SECONDS TO MARS	28	2007
KILL ALL HIPPIES	PRIMAL SCREAM	24	2000
KILL 100	X-PRESS 2	59	2006
KILL THE DIRECTOR	WOMBATS	35	2007
KILL THE KING	RAINBOW	41	1977
KILL THE POOR	DEAD KENNEDYS	49	1980
KILL YOUR OWN	HUNDRED REASONS	48	2006
KILL YOUR TELEVISION	NED'S ATOMIC DUSTBIN	53	1990
KILLA	CHERISH FEATURING YUNG JOC	52	2008
KILLAMANGIRO	BABYSHAMBLES	8	2004
KILLED BY DEATH	MOTORHEAD	51	1984
KILLER	ADAMSKI	1	1990
KILLER	ATB	4	2000
KILLER (EP)	SEAL	8	1991
KILLER ON THE LOOSE	THIN LIZZY	10	1980
KILLER QUEEN	QUEEN	2	1974
KILLERS LIVE EP	THIN LIZZY	19	1981
KILLIN' TIME	TINA COUSINS	15	1999
KILLING IN THE NAME	RAGE AGAINST THE MACHINE	1	1993
THE KILLING JAR	SIOUXSIE & THE BANSHEES	41	1988
KILLING LONELINESS	H.I.M.	26	2006
KILLING ME SOFTLY	FUGEES	1	1996
KILLING ME SOFTLY WITH HIS SONG	ROBERTA FLACK	6	1973
THE KILLING MOON	ECHO & THE BUNNYMEN	9	1984
THE KILLING OF GEORGIE	ROD STEWART	2	1976
A KIND OF CHRISTMAS CARD	MORTEN HARKET	53	1995
A KIND OF MAGIC	QUEEN	3	1986
KINDA LOVE	DARIUS	8	2004
KINDA NEW	SPEKTRUM	70	2004
KINETIC	GOLDEN GIRLS	38	1998
KING	UB40	4	1980

THE KING AND QUEEN OF AMERICA EURYTHMICS 29 1990
KING CREOLE ELVIS PRESLEY 2 1958
KING FOR A DAY [A] THOMPSON TWINS 22 1985
KING FOR A DAY [B] JAMIROQUAI 20 1999
KING IN A CATHOLIC STYLE (WAKE UP) CHINA CRISIS 19 1985
THE KING IS DEAD GO WEST 67 1987
THE KING IS HALF UNDRESSED JELLYFISH 39 1991
THE KING IS HERE/THE 900 NUMBER 45 KING 60 1989
KING KONG TERRY LIGHTFOOT & HIS NEW ORLEANS JAZZMEN 29 1961
KING MIDAS IN REVERSE HOLLIES 18 1967
KING OF CLOWNS NEIL SEDAKA 23 1962
KING OF DREAMS DEEP PURPLE 70 1990
KING OF EMOTION BIG COUNTRY 16 1988
KING OF KINGS EZZ RECO & THE LAUNCHERS WITH BOSIE GRANT 44 1964
THE KING OF KISSINGDOM MY LIFE STORY 35 1997
KING OF LOVE DAVE EDMUNDS 68 1990
KING OF MISERY HONEYCRACK 32 1996
KING OF MY CASTLE WAMDUE PROJECT 1 1999
KING OF NEW YORK FUN LOVIN' CRIMINALS 28 1997
KING OF PAIN POLICE 17 1984
THE KING OF ROCK 'N' ROLL PREFAB SPROUT 7 1988
KING OF SNAKE UNDERWORLD 17 1999
KING OF SORROW SADE 59 2001
KING OF THE COPS BILLY HOWARD 6 1975
KING OF THE DANCEHALL BEENIE MAN 14 2004
KING OF THE KERB ECHOBELLY 25 1995
KING OF THE MOUNTAIN KATE BUSH 4 2005
KING OF THE NEW YORK STREET DION 74 1989
KING OF THE ROAD ROGER MILLER 1 1965
KING OF THE ROAD (EP) PROCLAIMERS 9 1990
KING OF THE RODEO KINGS OF LEON 41 2005
KING OF THE RUMBLING SPIRES TYRANNOSAURUS REX 44 1969
THE KING OF WISHFUL THINKING GO WEST 18 1990
KING ROCKER GENERATION X 11 1979
KING WITHOUT A CROWN ABC 44 1987
KINGDOM ULTRAMARINE 46 1993
KINGDOM DAVE GAHAN 44 2007
KINGDOM OF DOOM GOOD, THE BAD & THE QUEEN 20 2007
KINGDOM OF RUST DOVES 28 2009
KINGS AND QUEENS [A] KILLING JOKE 58 1985
KINGS AND QUEENS [B] THIRTY SECONDS TO MARS 28 2009
KING'S CALL PHIL LYNOTT 35 1980
KINGS OF THE WILD FRONTIER ADAM & THE ANTS 2 1980
KINGSTON TOWN UB40 4 1990
KINKY AFRO HAPPY MONDAYS 5 1990
KINKY BOOTS PATRICK MACNEE & HONOR BLACKMAN 5 1990
KINKY LOVE PALE SAINTS 72 1991
KISS [A] DEAN MARTIN 5 1953
KISS [B] PRINCE & THE REVOLUTION 6 1986
KISS [B] AGE OF CHANCE 50 1987
KISS [B] ART OF NOISE FEATURING TOM JONES 5 1988
KISS AND SAY GOODBYE MANHATTANS 4 1976
KISS AND SAY GOODBYE UB40 19 2005
KISS AND TELL [A] BRYAN FERRY 41 1988
KISS AND TELL [B] BROWNSTONE 21 1997
KISS AND TELL [C] YOU ME AT SIX 42 2009
KISS FROM A ROSE SEAL 4 1994
KISS KISS [A] HOLLY VALENCE 1 2002
KISS KISS [B] CHRIS BROWN FEATURING T-PAIN 38 2007
KISS LIKE ETHER CLAUDIA BRUCKEN 63 1991
KISS ME [A] STEPHEN 'TIN TIN' DUFFY 4 1985
KISS ME [B] SIXPENCE NONE THE RICHER 4 1999
KISS ME ANOTHER GEORGIA GIBBS 24 1956
KISS ME DEADLY LITA FORD 75 1988
KISS ME GOODBYE PETULA CLARK 50 1968
KISS ME HONEY HONEY KISS ME SHIRLEY BASSEY 3 1958
KISS ME QUICK ELVIS PRESLEY 14 1963
KISS ME THRU THE PHONE SOULJA BOY TELL'EM FEATURING SAMMIE 6 2009
KISS MY EYES BOB SINCLAR 67 2003
THE KISS OF DAWN H.I.M. 59 2007
KISS OF LIFE [A] SADE 44 1993
KISS OF LIFE [B] SUPERGRASS 23 2004
KISS OF LIFE [C] FRIENDLY FIRES 30 2009
KISS ON MY LIST DARYL HALL & JOHN OATES 33 1980
KISS ON THE LIPS DUALERS 21 2004
KISS THAT FROG PETER GABRIEL 46 1993
KISS THE BRIDE ELTON JOHN 20 1983
KISS THE DIRT (FALLING DOWN THE MOUNTAIN) INXS 54 1986
KISS THE GIRL PETER ANDRE 9 1998
KISS THE RAIN BILLIE MYERS 4 1998
KISS THEM FOR ME SIOUXSIE & THE BANSHEES 32 1991
KISS THIS THING GOODBYE DEL AMITRI 43 1989
KISS (WHEN THE SUN DON'T SHINE) VENGABOYS 3 1999
KISS WITH A FIST FLORENCE + THE MACHINE 51 2008
KISS YOU ALL OVER EXILE 6 1978
KISS YOU ALL OVER NO MERCY 16 1997
KISS YOU OFF SCISSOR SISTERS 43 2007
KISSES IN THE MOONLIGHT GEORGE BENSON 60 1986
KISSES ON THE WIND NENEH CHERRY 20 1989
KISSES SWEETER THAN WINE JIMMIE RODGERS 7 1957
KISSES SWEETER THAN WINE FRANKIE VAUGHAN 8 1957
KISSIN' COUSINS ELVIS PRESLEY 10 1964
KISSIN' IN THE BACK ROW OF THE MOVIES DRIFTERS 2 1974
KISSIN' YOU TOTAL 29 1996
KISSING A FOOL GEORGE MICHAEL 18 1988
KISSING GATE SAM BROWN 23 1990
KISSING WITH CONFIDENCE WILL POWERS 17 1983
KITE NICK HEYWARD 44 1993
KITES SIMON DUPREE & THE BIG SOUND 9 1967
KITSCH BARRY RYAN 37 1970
KITTY CAT STEVENS 47 1967
KLACTOVEESEDSTEIN BLUE RONDO A LA TURK 50 1982
KLUB KOLLABORATIONS BK 43 2003
KLUBHOPPING KLUBBHEADS 10 1996
KNEE DEEP AND DOWN RAIN BAND 56 2003
KNEE DEEP IN THE BLUES GUY MITCHELL 3 1957
KNEE DEEP IN THE BLUES TOMMY STEELE & THE STEELMEN 15 1957
KNIFE EDGE ALARM 43 1986
KNIGHTS OF CYDONIA MUSE 10 2006
KNIVES OUT RADIOHEAD 13 2001
KNOCK KNOCK WHO'S THERE MARY HOPKIN 2 1970
KNOCK ME OUT GARY'S GANG 45 1982
KNOCK ON WOOD EDDIE FLOYD 19 1967
KNOCK ON WOOD OTIS REDDING & CARLA THOMAS 35 1967
KNOCK ON WOOD DAVID BOWIE 10 1974
KNOCK ON WOOD AMII STEWART 6 1979
KNOCK OUT TRIPLE EIGHT 8 2003
KNOCK THREE TIMES DAWN 1 1971
KNOCK YOU DOWN KERI HILSON FEATURING KENYE WEST & NE-YO 6 2009
KNOCKDOWN ALESHA 45 2006
KNOCKED IT OFF BA ROBERTSON 8 1979
KNOCKED OUT PAULA ABDUL 21 1990
KNOCKIN' ON HEAVEN'S DOOR BOB DYLAN 14 1973
KNOCKIN' ON HEAVEN'S DOOR ERIC CLAPTON 38 1975
KNOCKIN' ON HEAVEN'S DOOR GUNS N' ROSES 2 1992
KNOCKIN' ON HEAVEN'S DOOR DUNBLANE 1 1996
KNOCKING AT YOUR BACK DOOR DEEP PURPLE 68 1985
KNOCKS ME OFF MY FEET DONELL JONES 58 1997
KNOW BY NOW ROBERT PALMER 25 1994
KNOW YOU WANNA 3RD EDGE 17 2003
KNOW YOUR ENEMY GREEN DAY 21 2009
KNOW YOUR RIGHTS CLASH 43 1982
KNOWING ME KNOWING YOU ABBA 1 1977
KO SMUJJI 43 2004
KOKOMO [A] BEACH BOYS 25 1988
KOKOMO [B] ADAM GREEN 63 2004
KOMMOTION DUANE EDDY & THE REBELS 13 1960
KOMODO (SAVE A SOUL) MAURO PICOTTO 13 2001
KON-TIKI SHADOWS 1 1961
KOOCHIE RYDER FREAKY REALISTIC 52 1993
KOOCHY ARMAND VAN HELDEN 4 2000
KOOKIE KOOKIE (LEND ME YOUR COMB) EDWARD BYRNES & CONNIE STEVENS 27 1960
KOOKIE LITTLE PARADISE FRANKIE VAUGHAN 31 1960
KOOL IN THE KAFTAN BA ROBERTSON 17 1980
KOOTCHI NENEH CHERRY 38 1996
KOREAN BODEGA FUN LOVIN' CRIMINALS 15 1999
KOWALSKI PRIMAL SCREAM 8 1997
KRAFTY NEW ORDER 8 2005
KRUPA APOLLO 440 23 1996
KU KLUX KHAN STEEL PULSE 41 1978
KUMBAYA SANDPIPERS 38 1969
KUNG FU ASH 57 1995
KUNG FU FIGHTING CARL DOUGLAS 1 1974
KUNG FU FIGHTING BUS STOP FEATURING CARL DOUGLAS 8 1998
KUNG-FU 187 LOCKDOWN 9 1998
KUT IT RED EYE 62 1994
KYRIE MR MISTER 11 1986
KYRILA (EP) DEMIS ROUSSOS 33 1977

L

L WELLS FRANZ FERDINAND 14 2006
LA [A] MARC ET CLAUDE 28 1998
LA [B] AMY MacDONALD 48 2007
LA BAMBA LOS LOBOS 1 1987
LA BAMBA RITCHIE VALENS 49 1987
LA BOOGA ROOGA SURPRISE SISTERS 38 1976
LA BREEZE SIMIAN 55 2003
LA CAMISA NEGRA JUANES 32 2006
L.A. CONNECTION RAINBOW 40 1978
LA DEE DAH JACKIE DENNIS 4 1958
LA DERNIERE VALSE MIREILLE MATHIEU 26 1967
LA DONNA E MOBILE JOSE CARRERAS, PLACIDO DOMINGO & LUCIANO PAVAROTTI 21 1994
LA FEMME ACCIDENT ORCHESTRAL MANOEUVRES IN THE DARK 42 1985
LA FOLIE STRANGLERS 47 1982
LA ISLA BONITA MADONNA 1 1987
LA LA LA [A] MASSIEL 35 1968
LA LA LA [B] NAILA BOSS 65 2004

	Peak Position	Year of Release
LA LA LA HEY HEY OUTHERE BROTHERS	7	1995
LA LA LAND [A] GREEN VELVET	29	2002
LA LA LAND [B] DEMI LOVATO	35	2009
LA LA (MEANS I LOVE YOU) SWING OUT SISTER	37	1994
LA LUNA [A] BELINDA CARLISLE	38	1989
LA LUNA [B] MOVIN' MELODIES PRODUCTION	64	1994
LA MER (BEYOND THE SEA) BOBBY DARIN	8	1960
LA MOUCHE CASSIUS	53	1999
LA MUSICA RUFF DRIVERZ PRESENTS ARROLA	14	1999
LA PLUME DE MA TANTE HUGO & LUIGI	29	1959
LA PRIMAVERA SASH!	3	1998
LA RITOURNELLE SEBASTIEN TELLIER	66	2005
THE L.A. RUN CARVELLS	31	1977
LA SERENISSIMA DNA	34	1990
LA SERENISSIMA (THEME FROM 'VENICE IN PERIL') RONDO VENEZIANO	58	1983
LA TODAY ALEX GOLD FEATURING PHILIP OAKEY	68	2003
LA TRISTESSE DURERA (SCREAM TO A SIGH) MANIC STREET PREACHERS	22	1993
A LA VIE, A L'AMOUR JAKIE QUARTZ	55	1989
LA VIE EN ROSE GRACE JONES	12	1986
L.A. WOMAN BILLY IDOL	70	1990
LA YENKA JOHNNY & CHARLEY	49	1965
LABELLED WITH LOVE SQUEEZE	4	1981
LABELS OF LOVE FERGIE	56	2008
LABOUR OF LOVE HUE & CRY	6	1987
THE LABYRINTH MOOGWAI	68	2001
LACKEY OTHERS	21	2005
LA-DI-DA SAD CAFE	41	1980
LADIES MANTRONIX	55	1986
THE LADIES' BRAS JONNY TRUNK & WISBEY	27	2007
LADIES MAN D4	41	2003
LADIES NIGHT KOOL & THE GANG	9	1979
LADIES NIGHT ATOMIC KITTEN FEATURING KOOL & THE GANG	8	2003
LADY [A] WHISPERS	55	1980
LADY [B] KENNY ROGERS	12	1980
LADY [C] D'ANGELO	21	1996
LADY BARBARA PETER NOONE & HERMAN'S HERMITS	13	1970
LADY D'ARBANVILLE CAT STEVENS	8	1970
LADY ELEANOR LINDISFARNE	3	1972
LADY GODIVA PETER & GORDON	16	1966
LADY (HEAR ME TONIGHT) MODJO	1	2000
THE LADY IN RED CHRIS DE BURGH	1	1986
LADY IS A TRAMP BUDDY GRECO	26	1960
LADY JANE DAVID GARRICK	28	1966
LADY JANE TONY MERRICK	49	1966
LADY LADY MARK JOSEPH	36	2005
LADY LET IT LIE FISH	46	1994
LADY LINE PAINTER JANE BELLE & SEBASTIAN	41	1997
LADY LOVE BUG CLODAGH RODGERS	28	1971
LADY LOVE ME (ONE MORE TIME) GEORGE BENSON	11	1983
LADY LUCK [A] LLOYD PRICE	45	1960
LADY LUCK [B] ROD STEWART	56	1995
LADY LYNDA BEACH BOYS	6	1979
LADY MADONNA BEATLES	1	1968
LADY MARMALADE ALL SAINTS	1	1998
LADY MARMALADE CHRISTINA AGUILERA/LIL' KIM/MYA/PINK	1	2001
LADY MARMALADE (VOULEZ-VOUS COUCHER AVEC MOI CE SOIR) LABELLE	17	1975
LADY OF THE SEA (HEAR HER CALLING) SETH LAKEMAN	52	2006
LADY ROSE MUNGO JERRY	5	1971
LADY SHINE (SHINE ON) THS – THE HORN SECTION	54	1984
LADY WILLPOWER UNION GAP FEATURING GARY PUCKETT	5	1968
LADY WRITER DIRE STRAITS	51	1979
LADY (YOU BRING ME UP) COMMODORES	56	1980
LADY (YOU BRING ME UP) SIMPLY SMOOTH	70	1998
LADYBIRD NANCY SINATRA & LEE HAZLEWOOD	47	1967
THE LADYBOY IS MINE STUNTMASTERZ	10	2001
LADYFINGERS LUSCIOUS JACKSON	43	1999
LADYFLASH GO! TEAM	26	2004
LADYKILLERS LUSH	22	1996
LADYSHAVE GUSGUS	64	1999
LAFFY TAFFY D4L	29	2006
LAGARTIJA NICK BAUHAUS	44	1983
LAID JAMES	25	1993
LAID SO LOW (TEARS ROLL DOWN) TEARS FOR FEARS	17	1992
LAILA TAZ & STEREO NATION	44	2001
LAKINI'S JUICE LIVE	29	1997
LALA ASHLEE SIMPSON	11	2005
LA-LA MEANS I LOVE YOU DELFONICS	19	1971
LAMBADA KAOMA	4	1989
LAMBORGHINI SHUT UP & DANCE	55	1990
LAMENT ULTRAVOX	22	1984
LAMPLIGHT DAVID ESSEX	7	1973
LANA ROY ORBISON	15	1966
LAND OF 1000 DANCES WILSON PICKETT	22	1966
LAND OF A MILLION DRUMS OUTKAST FEATURING KILLER MIKE & S BROWN	46	2002
LAND OF A THOUSAND WORDS SCISSOR SISTERS	19	2006
LAND OF CONFUSION GENESIS	14	1986
LAND OF HOPE AND GLORY EX PISTOLS	69	1985
THE LAND OF MAKE BELIEVE BUCKS FIZZ	1	1981
THE LAND OF MAKE BELIEVE ALLSTARS	9	2002
THE LAND OF RING DANG DO KING KURT	67	1987
LAND OF THE LIVING [A] KRISTINE W	57	1996
LAND OF THE LIVING [B] MILK INC	18	2002
LANDSLIDE [A] OLIVIA NEWTON-JOHN	18	1982
LANDSLIDE [B] HARMONIX	28	1996
LANDSLIDE [C] SPIN CITY	30	2000
LANDSLIDE [D] DIXIE CHICKS	55	2003
LANDSLIDE OF LOVE TRANSVISION VAMP	14	1989
THE LANE ICE-T	18	1996
THE LANGUAGE OF LOVE JOHN D LOUDERMILK	13	1962
LANGUAGE OF VIOLENCE DISPOSABLE HEROES OF HIPHOPRISY	68	1992
LAP OF LUXURY JETHRO TULL	70	1984
LAPDANCE N*E*R*D FEATURING LEE HARVEY & VITA	20	2001
LARGER THAN LIFE BACKSTREET BOYS	5	1999
LAS PALABRAS DE AMOR QUEEN	17	1982
LAS VEGAS TONY CHRISTIE	21	1971
LASER LOVE [A] T REX	41	1976
LASER LOVE [B] AFTER THE FIRE	62	1979
THE LAST BEAT OF MY HEART SIOUXSIE & THE BANSHEES	44	1988
LAST CHANCE CHINA DRUM	60	1996
LAST CHRISTMAS WHAM!	2	1984
LAST CHRISTMAS WHIGFIELD	21	1995
LAST CHRISTMAS ALIEN VOICES FEATURING THE THREE DEGREES	54	1998
LAST CHRISTMAS CRAZY FROG	16	2006
LAST CUP OF SORROW FAITH NO MORE	51	1997
LAST DANCE DONNA SUMMER	51	1978
LAST DAY SILVER SUN	48	1997
LAST DROP KEVIN LYTTLE	22	2004
THE LAST FAREWELL ROGER WHITTAKER	2	1975
THE LAST FAREWELL SHIP'S COMPANY & ROYAL MARINE BAND OF HMS ARK ROYAL	46	1978
THE LAST FAREWELL ELVIS PRESLEY	48	1984
LAST FILM KISSING THE PINK	19	1983
LAST GOODBYE [A] JEFF BUCKLEY	54	1995
LAST GOODBYE [B] ATOMIC KITTEN	2	2002
LAST GOODBYE [C] AVENUE	50	2008
LAST HORIZON BRIAN MAY	51	1993
THE LAST KISS [A] DAVID CASSIDY	6	1985
LAST KISS [B] PEARL JAM	42	1999
LAST NIGHT P DIDDY FEATURING KEYSHIA COLE	14	2007
LAST NIGHT [A] MERSEYBEATS	40	1964
LAST NIGHT [B] KID 'N' PLAY	71	1987
LAST NIGHT [C] AZ YET	21	1997
LAST NIGHT [C] STROKES	14	2001
LAST NIGHT [D] GLORIA GAYNOR	67	2000
LAST NIGHT A DJ BLEW MY MIND FAB FOR FEATURING ROBERT OWENS	34	2003
LAST NIGHT A DJ SAVED MY LIFE INDEEP	13	1983
LAST NIGHT A DJ SAVED MY LIFE COLD JAM FEATURING GRACE	64	1990
LAST NIGHT A DJ SAVED MY LIFE SYLK 130	33	1998
LAST NIGHT A DJ SAVED MY LIFE (BIG LOVE) SEAMUS HAJI	13	2004
LAST NIGHT ANOTHER SOLDIER ANGELIC UPSTARTS	51	1980
LAST NIGHT AT DANCELAND RANDY CRAWFORD	61	1980
LAST NIGHT I DREAMT THAT SOMEBODY LOVED ME SMITHS	30	1987
LAST NIGHT IN SOHO DAVE DEE, DOZY, BEAKY, MICK & TICH	8	1968
LAST NIGHT ON EARTH U2	10	1997
LAST NIGHT ON THE BACK PORCH ALMA COGAN	27	1959
LAST NIGHT WAS MADE FOR LOVE BILLY FURY	4	1962
LAST NITE VITAMIN C	70	2003
LAST OF THE ENGLISH ROSES PETE DOHERTY	67	2009
LAST OF THE FAMOUS INTERNATIONAL PLAYBOYS MORRISSEY	6	1989
LAST ONE STANDING GIRL THING	8	2000
LAST PLANE (ONE WAY TICKET) CLINT EASTWOOD & GENERAL SAINT	51	1984
LAST REQUEST PAOLO NUTINI	5	2006
LAST RESORT [A] PAPA ROACH	3	2001
THE LAST RESORT [B] DEAD 60S	24	2005
LAST RHYTHM LAST RHYTHM	62	1996
THE LAST SONG [A] ELTON JOHN	21	1992
THE LAST SONG [B] ALL-AMERICAN REJECTS	69	2003
LAST STOP THIS TOWN EELS	23	1998
LAST SUMMER LOSTPROPHETS	13	2004
LAST THING ON MY MIND [A] BANANARAMA	71	1992
LAST THING ON MY MIND [A] STEPS	6	1998
LAST THING ON MY MIND [B] RONAN KEATING & LeANN RIMES	5	2004
THE LAST TIME [A] ROLLING STONES	1	1965
THE LAST TIME [A] WHO	44	1967
THE LAST TIME [B] PARADISE LOST	60	1995
LAST TIME FOREVER SQUEEZE	45	1985
LAST TIME I SAW HIM DIANA ROSS	35	1974
LAST TO KNOW P!NK	21	2004
LAST TRAIN HOME LOSTPROPHETS	8	2004
LAST TRAIN TO CLARKSVILLE MONKEES	23	1967
LAST TRAIN TO LONDON ELECTRIC LIGHT ORCHESTRA	8	1979
LAST TRAIN TO SAN FERNANDO JOHNNY DUNCAN & THE BLUE GRASS BOYS	2	1957
LAST TRAIN TO TRANCENTRAL KLF FEATURING THE CHILDREN OF THE REVOLUTION	2	1991
THE LAST WALTZ ENGELBERT HUMPERDINCK	1	1967
LATE AT NIGHT FUTURESHOCK	73	2003
LATE IN THE DAY SUPERGRASS	18	1997

	Peak Position	Year of Release
LATE IN THE EVENING PAUL SIMON	58	1980
LATELY [A] STEVIE WONDER	3	1981
LATELY [A] RUDY GRANT	58	1981
LATELY [B] SKUNK ANANSIE	33	1999
LATELY [C] DIVINE	52	1999
LATELY [C] SAMANTHA MUMBA	6	2001
LATELY [D] LISA SCOTT-LEE	6	2003
LATELY [E] JON B	68	2005
THE LATIN THEME CARL COX	52	1998
LATIN THING LATIN THING	41	1996
LATINO HOUSE MIRAGE	70	1989
LAUGH AT ME SONNY	9	1965
THE LAUGHING GNOME DAVID BOWIE	6	1973
LAUGHTER IN THE RAIN NEIL SEDAKA	15	1974
THE LAUNCH DJ JEAN	2	1999
LAUNDROMAT NIVEA	33	2003
LAURA [A] NICK HEYWARD	45	1985
LAURA [B] JIMMY NAIL	58	1992
LAURA [C] NEK	59	1998
LAURA [D] SCISSOR SISTERS	12	2003
LAUREL AND HARDY EQUALS	35	1968
LAVA SILVER SUN	35	1996
LAVENDER MARILLION	5	1985
LAW OF THE LAND TEMPTATIONS	41	1973
LAW UNTO MYSELF KONKRETE	60	2001
LAWDY MISS CLAWDY ELVIS PRESLEY	15	1957
LAWNCHAIRS OUR DAUGHTER'S WEDDING	49	1981
LAY ALL YOUR LOVE ON ME ABBA	7	1981
LAY BACK IN THE ARMS OF SOMEONE SMOKIE	12	1977
LAY DOWN STRAWBS	12	1972
LAY DOWN SALLY ERIC CLAPTON	39	1978
LAY DOWN THE LAW SWITCHES	51	2007
LAY DOWN YOUR ARMS [A] ANNE SHELTON	1	1956
LAY DOWN YOUR ARMS [B] BELINDA CARLISLE	27	1993
LAY LADY LAY BOB DYLAN	5	1969
LAY LOVE ON YOU LUISA FERNANDEZ	31	1978
LAY YOUR HANDS SIMON WEBBE	4	2005
LAY YOUR HANDS ON ME [A] THOMPSON TWINS	13	1984
LAY YOUR HANDS ON ME [B] BON JOVI	18	1989
LAY YOUR LOVE ON ME [A] RACEY	3	1978
LAY YOUR LOVE ON ME [B] ROACHFORD	36	1994
LAY YOUR LOVE ON ME [C] BWO	69	2008
LAYLA DEREK & THE DOMINOES	4	1972
LAYLA (ACOUSTIC) ERIC CLAPTON	45	1992
LAZARUS BOO RADLEYS	50	1994
LAZER BEAM SUPER FURRY ANIMALS	28	2005
LAZY [A] SUEDE	9	1997
LAZY [B] X-PRESS 2	2	2002
LAZY BONES JONATHAN KING	23	1971
LAZY DAYS ROBBIE WILLIAMS	8	1997
LAZY LOVER SUPERNATURALS	34	1996
LAZY RIVER BOBBY DARIN	2	1961
LAZY SUNDAY SMALL FACES	2	1968
LAZYITIS – ONE ARMED BOXER HAPPY MONDAYS & KARL DENVER	46	1990
LDN LILY ALLEN	6	2006
LE DISC JOCKEY ENCORE	12	1998
LE FREAK CHIC	7	1978
LE VOIE LE SOLEIL SUBLIMINAL CUTS	23	1994
LEADER OF THE PACK SHANGRI-LAS	3	1965
LEADER OF THE PACK TWISTED SISTER	47	1986
LEADER OF THE PACK JOAN COLLINS FAN CLUB	60	1988
LEADERS OF THE FREE WORLD ELBOW	53	2005
LEAFY MYSTERIES PAUL WELLER	23	2002
LEAN BACK TERROR SQUAD FEATURING FAT JOE & REMY	24	2004
LEAN ON ME BILL WITHERS	18	1972
LEAN ON ME MUD	7	1976
LEAN ON ME CLUB NOUVEAU	3	1987
LEAN ON ME MICHAEL BOLTON	14	1994
LEAN ON ME GLEE CAST	43	2010
LEAN ON ME (AH-LI-AYO) RED BOX	3	1985
LEAN ON ME I WON'T FALL OVER CARTER-THE UNSTOPPABLE SEX MACHINE	16	1993
LEAN ON ME (WITH THE FAMILY) 2-4 FAMILY	69	1999
LEAN ON YOU CLIFF RICHARD	17	1989
LEAN PERIOD ORANGE JUICE	74	1984
LEAP OF FAITH BRUCE SPRINGSTEEN	46	1992
LEAP UP AND DOWN (WAVE YOUR KNICKERS IN THE AIR) ST CECILIA	12	1971
LEARN CHINESE JIN	59	2005
LEARN TO FLY FOO FIGHTERS	21	1999
LEARNIN' THE BLUES FRANK SINATRA	2	1955
LEARNIN' THE GAME BUDDY HOLLY	36	1960
LEARNING TO BREATHE NERINA PALLOT	70	2007
LEARNING TO FLY [A] TOM PETTY & THE HEARTBREAKERS	46	1991
LEARNING TO FLY [B] MOTHER'S PRIDE	54	1999
THE LEATHER SEA GARY NUMAN VS ADE FENTON	72	2007
LEAVE A LIGHT ON BELINDA CARLISLE	4	1989
LEAVE A LITTLE LOVE LULU	8	1965
LEAVE A TENDER MOMENT ALONE BILLY JOEL	29	1984
LEAVE BEFORE THE LIGHTS COME ON ARCTIC MONKEYS	4	2006
LEAVE 'EM SOMETHING TO DESIRE SPRINKLER	45	1998
LEAVE (GET OUT) JOJO	2	2004
LEAVE HOME CHEMICAL BROTHERS	17	1995
LEAVE IN SILENCE DEPECHE MODE	18	1982
LEAVE IT [A] MIKE McGEAR	36	1974
LEAVE IT [B] YES	56	1984
LEAVE IT ALONE LIVING COLOUR	34	1993
LEAVE IT UP TO ME AARON CARTER	22	2002
LEAVE ME ALONE MICHAEL JACKSON	2	1989
LEAVE ME ALONE (I'M LONELY) P!NK	34	2007
LEAVE RIGHT NOW WILL YOUNG	1	2003
LEAVE THEM ALL BEHIND RIDE	9	1992
LEAVIN' [A] TONY RICH PROJECT	52	1996
LEAVIN' [B] SHELBY LYNNE	73	2000
LEAVIN' [C] JESSE McCARTNEY	48	2008
LEAVIN' ON A JET PLANE PETER, PAUL & MARY	2	1970
LEAVING HERE BIRDS	45	1965
LEAVING LAS VEGAS SHERYL CROW	66	1994
LEAVING ME NOW LEVEL 42	15	1985
LEAVING NEW YORK R.E.M.	5	2004
LEAVING ON A JET PLANE CHANTAL KREVIAZUK	59	1999
LEAVING ON THE MIDNIGHT TRAIN NICK STRAKER BAND	61	1980
THE LEAVING SONG PART 2 AFI	43	2003
THE LEBANON HUMAN LEAGUE	11	1984
LEEDS LEEDS LEEDS LEEDS UNITED FC	54	1992
LEEDS UNITED LEEDS UNITED FC	10	1972
LEFT HOPE OF THE STATES	63	2006
LEFT BANK WINIFRED ATWELL	14	1956
LEFT BEHIND SLIPKNOT	24	2001
LEFT MY HEART IN TOKYO MINI VIVA	7	2009
LEFT OF CENTER SUZANNE VEGA FEATURING JOE JACKSON	32	1986
LEFT OUTSIDE ALONE ANASTACIA	3	2004
LEFT TO MY OWN DEVICES PET SHOP BOYS	4	1988
LEGACY [A] MAD COBRA FEATURING RICHIE STEPHENS	64	1993
THE LEGACY [B] PUSH	22	2001
LEGACY EP MANSUN	7	1998
LEGACY (SHOW ME LOVE) [A] SPACE BROTHERS	31	1999
LEGACY (SHOW ME LOVE) [B] BELLE & SEBASTIAN	15	2000
A LEGAL MATTER WHO	32	1966
LEGEND OF A COWGIRL IMANI COPPOLA	32	1998
LEGEND OF THE GOLDEN SNAKE DEPTH CHARGE	75	1995
THE LEGEND OF XANADU DAVE DEE, DOZY, BEAKY, MICK & TICH	1	1968
LEGENDS OF THE DARK BLACK – PART 2 WILDCHILD	34	1995
LEGGO SKANGA RUPIE EDWARDS	32	1975
LEGS [A] ART OF NOISE	69	1985
LEGS [B] ZZ TOP	16	1985
LEMMINGS SFX	51	1993
LEMON TREE FOOL'S GARDEN	26	1996
LENINGRAD BILLY JOEL	53	1989
LENNY SUPERGRASS	10	1995
LENNY AND TERENCE CARTER-THE UNSTOPPABLE SEX MACHINE	40	1993
LENNY VALENTINO AUTEURS	41	1993
LEONARD NIMOY FREAKY REALISTIC	71	1993
LEROY WHEATUS	22	2002
LES ARTISTES SANTOGOLD	27	2008
LES BICYCLETTES DE BELSIZE ENGELBERT HUMPERDINCK	5	1968
LES FLEUR 4 HERO	53	2001
L'ESPERANZA [A] SVEN VATH	63	1993
L'ESPERANZA [B] AIRSCAPE	33	1999
LESS TALK MORE ACTION TIM DELUXE	45	2003
LESSON ONE RUSS CONWAY	21	1962
LESSONS IN LOVE [A] ALLISONS	30	1962
LESSONS IN LOVE [B] LEVEL 42	3	1986
LESSONS LEARNT FROM ROCK I TO ROCKY III CORNERSHOP	37	2002
LET A BOY CRY GALA	11	1997
LET A GOOD THING GO GEMMA HAYES	54	2002
LET 'EM IN WINGS	2	1976
LET 'EM IN BILLY PAUL	26	1977
LET 'EM IN SHINEHEAD	70	1993
LET FOREVER BE CHEMICAL BROTHERS	9	1999
LET GO WITH THE FLOW BEAUTIFUL SOUTH	47	2003
LET HER CRY HOOTIE & THE BLOWFISH	75	1995
LET HER DOWN EASY TERENCE TRENT D'ARBY	18	1993
LET HER FALL THEN JERICO	65	1987
LET HER FEEL IT SIMPLICIOUS	34	1984
LET HER GO STRAWBERRY SWITCHBLADE	59	1985
LET IT ALL BLOW DAZZ BAND	12	1984
LET IT ALL HANG OUT JONATHAN KING	26	1970
LET IT BE BEATLES	2	1970
LET IT BE FERRY AID	1	1987
LET IT BE ME EVERLY BROTHERS	13	1960
LET IT BE ME JUSTIN	15	2000
LET IT BE WITH YOU BELOUIS SOME	53	1987
LET IT FLOW SPIRITUALIZED ELECTRIC MAINLINE	30	1995
LET IT GO [A] BRIT & ALEX	75	2008
LET IT GO [B] WILL YOUNG	58	2009
LET IT LAST CARLEEN ANDERSON	16	1995
LET IT LIVE HAVEN	72	2001
LET IT LOOSE LEMON TREES	55	1993
LET IT RAIN [A] UFO	62	1982
LET IT RAIN [B] EAST 17	10	1995
LET IT RAIN [C] 4 STRINGS	49	2003
LET IT REIGN INNER CITY	51	1991
LET IT RIDE TODD TERRY PROJECT	58	1999
LET IT ROCK [A] CHUCK BERRY	6	1963
LET IT ROCK [A] ROLLING STONES	2	1971
LET IT ROCK [B] KEVIN RUDOLF FEATURING LIL'WAYNE	5	2008
LET IT ROLL RAZE PRESENTS DOUG LAZY	27	1989
LET IT SLIDE [A] MUDHONEY	60	1991
LET IT SLIDE [B] ARIEL	57	1993
LET IT SWING BOBBYSOCKS	44	1985
LET LOVE BE THE LEADER FM	71	1987

	Peak Position	Year of Release
LET LOVE BE YOUR ENERGY ROBBIE WILLIAMS	10	2001
LET LOVE LEAD THE WAY SPICE GIRLS	1	2000
LET LOVE RULE LENNY KRAVITZ	39	1990
LET LOVE SHINE AMOS	31	1995
LET LOVE SPEAK UP ITSELF BEAUTIFUL SOUTH	51	1991
LET ME BE BLACK DIAMOND	56	1994
LET ME BE THE NUMBER 1 (LOVE OF YOUR LIFE) DOOLEY SILVERSPOON	44	1976
LET ME BE THE ONE [A] SHADOWS	12	1975
LET ME BE THE ONE [B] FIVE STAR	18	1985
LET ME BE THE ONE [C] BLESSID UNION OF SOULS	74	1996
LET ME BE THE ONE [D] MINT CONDITION	63	1997
LET ME BE THE ONE [E] CLIFF RICHARD	29	2002
LET ME BE YOUR FANTASY BABY D	1	1994
(LET ME BE YOUR) TEDDY BEAR ELVIS PRESLEY	3	1957
LET ME BE YOUR UNDERWEAR CLUB 69	33	1992
LET ME BE YOUR WINGS BARRY MANILOW & DEBRA BYRD	73	1994
LET ME BE YOURS FIVE STAR	51	1988
LET ME BLOW YA MIND EVE FEATURING GWEN STEFANI	4	2001
LET ME CLEAR MY THROAT DJ KOOL	8	1997
LET ME COME ON HOME OTIS REDDING	48	1967
LET ME CRY ON YOUR SHOULDER KEN DODD	11	1967
LET ME DOWN EASY STRANGLERS	48	1985
LET ME ENTERTAIN YOU ROBBIE WILLIAMS	3	1998
LET ME FLY DARREN STYLES/MARK BREEZE	59	2003
LET ME GO HEAVEN 17	41	1982
LET ME GO HOME ALL ABOUT EVE	52	2004
LET ME GO LOVER DEAN MARTIN	3	1955
LET ME GO LOVER RUBY MURRAY	5	1955
LET ME GO LOVER TERESA BREWER WITH THE LANCERS	9	1955
LET ME GO LOVER JOAN WEBER	16	1955
LET ME GO LOVER KATHY KIRBY	10	1964
LET ME HEAR YOU SAY 'OLE OLE' OUTHERE BROTHERS	18	1997
LET ME HOLD YOU BOW WOW FEATURING OMARION	27	2005
LET ME IN [A] OSMONDS	2	1973
LET ME IN [A] OTT	12	1997
LET ME IN [B] YOUNG BUCK	62	2004
LET ME INTRODUCE YOU TO THE FAMILY STRANGLERS	42	1981
LET ME KISS YOU MORRISSEY	8	2004
LET ME KISS YOU NANCY SINATRA	46	2004
LET ME KNOW [A] JUNIOR	53	1982
LET ME KNOW [B] MAXI PRIEST	49	1987
LET ME KNOW [C] ROISIN MURPHY	28	2007
LET ME KNOW (I HAVE THE RIGHT) GLORIA GAYNOR	32	1979
LET ME LET GO FAITH HILL	72	1999
LET ME LIVE QUEEN	9	1996
LET ME LOVE YOU MARIO	2	2005
LET ME LOVE YOU FOR TONIGHT KARIYA	44	1989
LET ME MOVE ON GENE	69	2005
LET ME OUT BEN'S BROTHER	38	2007
LET ME RIDE DR DRE	31	1994
LET ME ROCK YOU KANDIDATE	58	1980
LET ME SEE MORCHEEBA	46	1998
LET ME SHOW YOU [A] K-KLASS	13	1993
LET ME SHOW YOU [B] CAMISRA	5	1998
LET ME SHOW YOU [C] TONY MOMRELLE	67	1998
LET ME TAKE YOU THERE BETTY BOO	12	1992
LET ME TALK EARTH, WIND & FIRE	29	1980
LET ME THINK ABOUT IT IDA CORR & FEDDE LE GRAND	2	2007
LET ME TRY AGAIN TAMMY JONES	5	1975
LET ME WAKE UP IN YOUR ARMS LULU	51	1993
LET MY LOVE OPEN YOUR DOOR PETE TOWNSHEND	46	1980
LET MY NAME BE SORROW MARY HOPKIN	46	1971
LET MY PEOPLE GO (PART 1) WINANS	71	1985
LET MY PEOPLE GO-GO RAINMAKERS	18	1987
LET ROBESON SING MANIC STREET PREACHERS	19	2001
LET SOMEBODY LOVE YOU KENI BURKE	59	1981
LET THE BASS KICK 2 FOR JOY	67	1991
LET THE BASS KICK IN MIAMI GIRL CHUCKIE & LMFAO	9	2009
LET THE BEAT CONTROL YOUR BODY 2 UNLIMITED	6	1994
LET THE BEAT HIT 'EM LISA LISA & CULT JAM	17	1991
LET THE BEAT HIT 'EM SHENA	28	1997
LET THE BEAT HIT 'EM PART 2 LISA LISA & CULT JAM	49	1991
LET THE BEATS ROLL TIM DELUXE FEATURING SIMON FRANKS	71	2007
LET THE DAY BEGIN CALL	42	1989
LET THE DRUMS SPEAK MIGHTY DUB KATZ	73	2002
LET THE FLAME BURN BRIGHTER GRAHAM KENDRICK	55	1989
LET THE FREAK BIG RON	57	2000
LET THE GOOD TIMES ROLL SHEEP ON DRUGS	56	1994
LET THE HAPPINESS IN DAVID SYLVIAN	66	1987
LET THE HEALING BEGIN JOE COCKER	32	1994
LET THE HEARTACHES BEGIN LONG JOHN BALDRY	1	1967
LET THE LITTLE GIRL DANCE BILLY BLAND	15	1960
LET THE LOVE Q-TEX	30	1996
LET THE MUSIC HEAL YOUR SOUL BRAVO ALL STARS	36	1998
LET THE MUSIC (LIFT YOU UP) LOVELAND FEATURING RACHEL McFARLANE VS DARLENE LEWIS	16	1994
LET THE MUSIC MOVE U RAZE	57	1987
LET THE MUSIC PLAY [A] BARRY WHITE	9	1976
LET THE MUSIC PLAY [B] CHARLES EARLAND	46	1978
LET THE MUSIC PLAY [C] SHANNON	14	1984
LET THE MUSIC PLAY [C] MARY KIANI	19	1996
LET THE MUSIC PLAY [C] BBG FEATURING ERIN	46	1996
LET THE MUSIC TAKE CONTROL JM SILK	47	1987
LET THE MUSIC USE YOU NIGHTWRITERS	51	1992
LET THE PEOPLE KNOW TOPLOADER	52	1999
LET THE RHYTHM MOVE YOU SHARADA HOUSE GANG	50	1996
LET THE RHYTHM PUMP DOUG LAZY	45	1989
LET THE SUNSHINE IN PEDDLERS	50	1965
LET THE SUNSHINE IN MILK & SUGAR FEATURING LIZZY PATTINSON	18	2003
LET THE WATER RUN DOWN PJ PROBY	19	1965
LET THE YOUNG GIRL DO WHAT SHE WANTS TO IAN McNABB	38	2005
LET THEM ALL TALK ELVIS COSTELLO	59	1983
LET THERE BE DRUMS SANDY NELSON	3	1961
LET THERE BE HOUSE DESKEE	52	1990
LET THERE BE LIGHT MIKE OLDFIELD	51	1995
LET THERE BE LOVE [A] NAT 'KING' COLE WITH GEORGE SHEARING	11	1962
LET THERE BE LOVE [B] SIMPLE MINDS	6	1991
LET THERE BE LOVE [C] OASIS	2	2005
LET THERE BE PEACE ON EARTH (LET IT BEGIN WITH ME) MICHAEL WARD	15	1973
LET THERE BE ROCK ONSLAUGHT	50	1989
LET THIS BE A PRAYER ROLLO GOES SPIRITUAL WITH PAULINE TAYLOR	26	1996
LET THIS FEELING SIMONE ANGEL	60	1993
LET TRUE LOVE BEGIN NAT 'KING' COLE	29	1961
LET U GO ATB	34	2001
LET YOUR BODY GO TOM WILSON	60	1996
LET YOUR BODY GO DOWNTOWN MARTYN FORD	38	1977
LET YOUR HEAD GO VICTORIA BECKHAM	3	2004
LET YOUR HEART DANCE SECRET AFFAIR	32	1979
LET YOUR LOVE FLOW BELLAMY BROTHERS	7	1976
LET YOUR SOUL BE YOUR PILOT STING	15	1996
LET YOUR YEAH BE YEAH PIONEERS	5	1971
LET YOUR YEAH BE YEAH ALI CAMPBELL	25	1995
LET YOURSELF GO [A] T-CONNECTION	52	1978
LET YOURSELF GO [B] SYBIL	32	1987
LETHAL INDUSTRY DJ TIESTO	25	2002
LETITGO PRINCE	30	1994
LET'S SARAH VAUGHAN	37	1961
LET'S ALL CHANT MICHAEL ZAGER BAND	8	1978
LET'S ALL CHANT PAT & MICK	11	1988
LET'S ALL CHANT GUSTO	21	1996
(LET'S ALL GO BACK) DISCO NIGHTS JAZZ & THE BROTHERS GRIMM	57	1988
LET'S ALL (GO TO THE FIRE DANCES) KILLING JOKE	51	1983
LET'S ALL GO TOGETHER MARION	37	1995
LET'S ALL SING LIKE THE BIRDIES SING TWEETS	44	1981
LET'S BE FRIENDS JOHNNY NASH	42	1975
LET'S BE LOVERS TONIGHT SHERRICK	63	1987
LET'S CALL IT LOVE LISA STANSFIELD	48	2001
LET'S CALL IT QUITS SLADE	11	1976
LET'S CELEBRATE NEW YORK SKYY	67	1982
LET'S CLEAN UP THE GHETTO PHILADELPHIA INTERNATIONAL ALL-STARS	34	1977
LET'S DANCE [A] CHRIS MONTEZ	2	1962
LET'S DANCE [A] BRUNO & LIZ & THE RADIO 1 POSSE	54	1990
LET'S DANCE [B] BOMBERS	58	1979
LET'S DANCE [C] DAVID BOWIE	1	1983
LET'S DANCE [C] HI_TACK	38	2007
LET'S DANCE [D] CHRIS REA	12	1987
LET'S DANCE [D] MIDDLESBROUGH FC FEATURING BOB MORTIMER & CHRIS REA	44	1997
LET'S DANCE [E] FIVE	1	2001
LET'S DANCE TO JOY DIVISION WOMBATS	15	2007
LET'S DO IT AGAIN [A] GEORGE BENSON	56	1988
LET'S DO IT AGAIN [B] LYNDEN DAVID HALL	69	2000
LET'S DO ROCK STEADY BODYSNATCHERS	22	1980
LET'S DO THE LATIN HUSTLE M & O BAND	16	1976
LET'S DO THE LATIN HUSTLE EDDIE DRENNON & B.B.S. UNLIMITED	20	1976
LET'S FACE THE MUSIC AND DANCE NAT 'KING' COLE	30	1994
LET'S FLY AWAY VOYAGE	38	1979
LET'S FUNK TONIGHT BLUE FEATHERS	50	1982
LET'S GET BACK TO BED...BOY SARAH CONNOR FEATURING TQ	16	2001
LET'S GET BLOWN SNOOP DOGG FEATURING PHARRELL	13	2005
LET'S GET BRUTAL NITRO DELUXE	24	1988
LET'S GET DOWN [A] ISOTONIK	25	1992
LET'S GET DOWN [B] MARK MORRISON	39	1995
LET'S GET DOWN [C] TONY TONI TONE FEATURING DJ QUIK	33	1997
LET'S GET DOWN [D] JT PLAYAZ	64	1998
LET'S GET DOWN [E] SPACEDUST	20	1999
LET'S GET DOWN [F] SUPAFLY VS FISHBOWL	22	2005
LET'S GET EXCITED ALESHA DIXON	13	2009
LET'S GET FUNKTIFIED BOILING POINT	41	1978
LET'S GET HAPPY MASS ORDER	45	1992
LET'S GET ILL P DIDDY FEATURING KELIS	25	2003
LET'S GET IT ON [A] MARVIN GAYE	31	1973
LET'S GET IT ON [B] SHABBA RANKS	22	1995
LET'S GET IT ON [C] BIG BOSS STYLUS PRESENTS RED VENOM	72	1999

Title	Artist	Peak Position	Year of Release
LET'S GET IT STARTED	BLACK EYED PEAS	11	2004
LET'S GET IT UP	AC/DC	13	1982
LET'S GET MARRIED	PROCLAIMERS	21	1994
LET'S GET READY TO RHUMBLE	PJ & DUNCAN	9	1994
LET'S GET ROCKED	DEF LEPPARD	2	1992
LET'S GET SANDY	BE YOUR OWN PET	51	2006
LET'S GET SERIOUS	JERMAINE JACKSON	8	1980
LET'S GET TATTOOS	CARTER – THE UNSTOPPABLE SEX MACHINE	30	1994
LET'S GET THIS PARTY STARTED	ZENA	69	2003
LET'S GET THIS STRAIGHT (FROM THE START)	KEVIN ROWLAND & DEXY'S MIDNIGHT RUNNERS	17	1982
LET'S GET TOGETHER [A]	HAYLEY MILLS	17	1961
LET'S GET TOGETHER [B]	ALEXANDER O'NEAL	38	1996
LET'S GET TOGETHER AGAIN [A]	BIG BEN BANJO BAND	18	1955
LET'S GET TOGETHER AGAIN [B]	GLITTER BAND	8	1974
LET'S GET TOGETHER (IN OUR MINDS)	GORKY'S ZYGOTIC MYNCI	43	1998
LET'S GET TOGETHER NO. 1	BIG BEN BANJO BAND	6	1954
LET'S GET TOGETHER (SO GROOVY NOW)	KRUSH PERSPECTIVE	61	1993
LET'S GET TOGETHER (TONITE)	STEVE WALSH	74	1987
LET'S GO [A]	ROUTERS	32	1963
LET'S GO [B]	CARS	51	1979
LET'S GO [C]	VARDIS	59	1980
LET'S GO [D]	TRICK DADDY FEATURING TWISTA & LIL' JON	26	2005
LET'S GO ALL THE WAY	SLY FOX	3	1986
LET'S GO CRAZY	PRINCE & THE REVOLUTION	7	1985
LET'S GO DISCO	REAL THING	39	1978
LET'S GO ROUND AGAIN	LOUISE	10	1997
LET'S GO ROUND AGAIN PART 1	AVERAGE WHITE BAND	12	1980
LET'S GO ROUND THERE	DARLING BUDS	49	1989
LET'S GO STEADY AGAIN	NEIL SEDAKA	42	1963
LET'S GO TO BED	CURE	44	1982
LET'S GO TO SAN FRANCISCO	FLOWERPOT MEN	4	1967
LET'S GO TOGETHER	CHANGE	37	1985
LET'S GROOVE [A]	EARTH, WIND & FIRE	3	1981
LET'S GROOVE [A]	PHAT 'N' PHUNKY	61	1997
LET'S GROOVE [B]	GEORGE MOREL FEATURING HEATHER WILDMAN	42	1996
LET'S HANG ON	FOUR SEASONS WITH THE SOUND OF FRANKIE VALLI	4	1965
LET'S HANG ON	BANDWAGON	36	1969
LET'S HANG ON	DARTS	11	1980
LET'S HANG ON	BARRY MANILOW	12	1981
LET'S HANG ON	SHOOTING PARTY	66	1990
LET'S HAVE A BALL	WINIFRED ATWELL	4	1957
LET'S HAVE A DING DONG	WINIFRED ATWELL	3	1955
LET'S HAVE A PARTY [A]	WINIFRED ATWELL	2	1953
LET'S HAVE A PARTY [B]	WANDA JACKSON	32	1960
LET'S HAVE A QUIET NIGHT IN	DAVID SOUL	8	1977
LET'S HAVE ANOTHER PARTY	WINIFRED ATWELL	1	1954
LET'S HEAR IT FOR THE BOY	DENIECE WILLIAMS	2	1984
LET'S JUMP THE BROOMSTICK	BRENDA LEE	12	1961
LET'S JUMP THE BROOMSTICK	COAST TO COAST	28	1981
LET'S KILL MUSIC	COOPER TEMPLE CLAUSE	41	2001
LET'S LIVE IT UP (NITE PEOPLE)	DAVID JOSEPH	26	1983
LET'S LOVE DANCE TONIGHT	GARY'S GANG	49	1979
LET'S MAKE A BABY	BILLY PAUL	30	1976
LET'S MAKE A NIGHT TO REMEMBER	BRYAN ADAMS	10	1996
LET'S MAKE LOVE AND LISTEN TO DEATH FROM ABOVE	CSS	39	2007
LET'S PARTY	JIVE BUNNY & THE MASTERMIXERS	1	1989
LET'S PLAY HOUSE	KRAZE	71	1989
LET'S PRETEND	LULU	11	1967
LET'S PUSH IT [A]	INNOCENCE	25	1990
LET'S PUSH IT [B]	NIGHTCRAWLERS FEATURING JOHN REID	23	1996
LET'S PUSH THINGS FORWARD	STREETS	30	2002
LET'S PUT IT ALL TOGETHER	STYLISTICS	9	1974
LET'S RIDE [A]	MONTELL JORDAN FEATURING MASTER P & SILKK THE SHOCKER	25	1998
LET'S RIDE [B]	GAME	42	2007
LET'S ROCK	E-TRAX	60	2001
LET'S ROCK 'N' ROLL	WINIFRED ATWELL	24	1957
LET'S SEE ACTION	WHO	16	1971
LET'S SLIP AWAY	CLEO LAINE	42	1960
LET'S SPEND THE NIGHT TOGETHER	ROLLING STONES	3	1967
LET'S SPEND THE NIGHT TOGETHER	MASH!	66	1995
LET'S START AGAIN	BLAZIN' SQUAD	51	2009
LET'S START OVER	PAMELA FERNANDEZ	59	1995
LET'S START THE DANCE	HAMILTON BOHANNON	56	1978
LET'S START TO DANCE AGAIN	HAMILTON BOHANNON	49	1982
LET'S STAY HOME TONIGHT	JOE	29	2002
LET'S STAY TOGETHER	AL GREEN	7	1972
LET'S STAY TOGETHER	TINA TURNER	6	1983
LET'S STAY TOGETHER	BOBBY M FEATURING JEAN CARN	53	1983
LET'S STAY TOGETHER	PASADENAS	22	1992
LET'S STICK TOGETHER	BRYAN FERRY	4	1976
LET'S SWING AGAIN	JIVE BUNNY & THE MASTERMIXERS	19	1990
LET'S TALK ABOUT LOVE	HELEN SHAPIRO	23	1962
LET'S TALK ABOUT SEX	SALT-N-PEPA FEATURING PSYCHOTROPIC	2	1991
LET'S TALK ABOUT SHHH	ONE WAY FEATURING AL HUDSON	64	1985
LET'S THINK ABOUT LIVING	BOB LUMAN	6	1960
LET'S TRY AGAIN	NEW KIDS ON THE BLOCK	8	1990
LET'S TURKEY TROT	LITTLE EVA	13	1963
LET'S TWIST AGAIN	CHUBBY CHECKER	2	1961
LET'S TWIST AGAIN	JOHN ASHER	14	1975
LET'S WAIT AWHILE	JANET JACKSON	3	1987
LET'S WALK THATA-WAY	DORIS DAY & JOHNNIE RAY	4	1953
LET'S WHIP IT UP (YOU GO GIRL)	SLEAZESISTERS WITH VIKKI SHEPARD	46	1996
LET'S WOMBLE TO THE PARTY TONIGHT	WOMBLES	34	1975
LET'S WORK	MICK JAGGER	31	1987
LET'S WORK IT OUT	RAGHAV FEATURING JAHAZIEL	15	2004
LET'S WORK TOGETHER	CANNED HEAT	2	1970
THE LETTER [A]	LONG & THE SHORT	35	1964
THE LETTER [B]	BOX TOPS	5	1967
THE LETTER [B]	MINDBENDERS	42	1967
THE LETTER [B]	JOE COCKER	39	1970
THE LETTER [B]	AMII STEWART	39	1980
THE LETTER [C]	PJ HARVEY	28	2004
LETTER FROM AMERICA	PROCLAIMERS	3	1987
LETTER FULL OF TEARS	BILLY FURY	32	1962
LETTER TO A SOLDIER	BARBARA LYON	27	1956
A LETTER TO ELSIE	CURE	28	1992
LETTER TO LUCILLE	TOM JONES	31	1973
A LETTER TO YOU	SHAKIN' STEVENS	10	1984
LETTER 2 MY UNBORN	2PAC	21	2001
LETTERS TO YOU	FINCH	39	2003
LETTIN' YA MIND GO	DESERT	74	2001
LETTING GO	WINGS	41	1975
LETTING THE CABLES SLEEP	BUSH	51	2000
LEVI STUBBS TEARS	BILLY BRAGG	29	1986
LFO	LFO	12	1990
LIAR [A]	GRAHAM BONNET	51	1981
LIAR [B]	ROLLINS BAND	27	1994
LIAR LIAR	CREDIT TO THE NATION	60	1995
LIARS' BAR	BEAUTIFUL SOUTH	43	1997
LIBERATE	LEE HASLAM	71	2004
LIBERATION [A]	LIBERATION	28	1992
LIBERATION [B]	PET SHOP BOYS	14	1994
LIBERATION [C]	LIPPY LOU	57	1995
LIBERATION (TEMPTATION – FLY LIKE AN EAGLE)	MATT DAREY PRESENTS MASH UP	19	1999
LIBERATOR	SPEAR OF DESTINY	67	1984
LIBERIAN GIRL	MICHAEL JACKSON	13	1989
THE LIBERTINE	PATRICK WOLF	67	2005
LIBERTY TOWN	PERFECT DAY	58	1989
LIBIAMO	JOSE CARRERAS, PLACIDO DOMINGO & LUCIANO PAVAROTTI	21	1994
LICENCE TO KILL	GLADYS KNIGHT	6	1989
LICK A SHOT	CYPRESS HILL	20	1994
LICK A SMURP FOR CHRISTMAS (ALL FALL DOWN)	FATHER ABRAPHART & THE SMURPS	58	1978
LICK IT	20 FINGERS FEATURING ROULA	48	1995
LICK IT UP	KISS	31	1983
LIDO SHUFFLE	BOZ SCAGGS	13	1977
LIE TO ME	BON JOVI	10	1995
LIES [A]	STATUS QUO	11	1980
LIES [B]	THOMPSON TWINS	67	1982
LIES [C]	JONATHAN BUTLER	18	1987
LIES [D]	EN VOGUE	44	1990
LIES [E]	EMF	28	1991
LIES [F]	McFLY	4	2008
LIES IN YOUR EYES	SWEET	35	1976
LIFE [A]	HADDAWAY	6	1993
LIFE [B]	BLAIR	44	1996
LIFE [C]	DES'REE	8	1998
THE LIFE [D]	STYLES & PHAROAHE MONCH	50	2002
LIFE AIN'T EASY	CLEOPATRA	4	1998
LIFE AT A TOP PEOPLE'S HEALTH FARM	STYLE COUNCIL	28	1988
LIFE BECOMING A LANDSLIDE	MANIC STREET PREACHERS	36	1994
LIFE BEGINS AT THE HOP	XTC	54	1979
LIFE FOR RENT	DIDO	8	2003
LIFE GOES ON [A]	GEORGIE PORGIE	54	2000
LIFE GOES ON [B]	LeANN RIMES	11	2002
LIFE GOT COLD	GIRLS ALOUD	3	2003
LIFE IN A DAY [A]	SIMPLE MINDS	62	1979
LIFE IN A DAY [B]	I AM KLOOT	43	2003
LIFE IN A NORTHERN TOWN	DREAM ACADEMY	15	1985
LIFE IN MONO	MONO	60	1998
LIFE IN ONE DAY	HOWARD JONES	14	1985
LIFE IN TECHNICOLOR II	COLDPLAY	28	2009
LIFE IN TOKYO	JAPAN	28	1982
LIFE IS A FLOWER	ACE OF BASE	5	1998
LIFE IS A HIGHWAY	TOM COCHRANE	62	1992
LIFE IS A LONG SONG	JETHRO TULL	11	1971
LIFE IS A MINESTRONE	10 C.C.	7	1975
LIFE IS A ROCK (BUT THE RADIO ROLLED ME)	REUNION	33	1974
LIFE IS A ROLLERCOASTER	RONAN KEATING	1	2000
LIFE IS FOR LIVING	BARCLAY JAMES HARVEST	61	1980
LIFE IS SWEET	CHEMICAL BROTHERS	25	1995
LIFE IS TOO SHORT GIRL	SHEER ELEGANCE	9	1976
A LIFE LESS ORDINARY	ASH	10	1997

Title / Artist	Peak Position	Year of Release
LIFE, LOVE AND HAPPINESS BRIAN KENNEDY	27	1996
LIFE LOVE AND UNITY DREADZONE	56	1996
THE LIFE OF RILEY LIGHTNING SEEDS	28	1992
LIFE OF SURPRISES PREFAB SPROUT	24	1993
LIFE ON MARS DAVID BOWIE	3	1973
LIFE ON YOUR OWN HUMAN LEAGUE	16	1984
LIFE STORY ANGIE STONE	22	2000
LIFE SUPPORTING MACHINE THESE ANIMAL MEN	62	1997
LIFE WILL BE THE DEATH OF ME ORDINARY BOYS	50	2005
LIFE WITH YOU PROCLAIMERS	58	2007
LIFEBOAT TERRY NEASON	72	1994
THE LIFEBOAT PARTY KID CREOLE & THE COCONUTS	49	1983
LIFEFORMS FUTURE SOUND OF LONDON	14	1994
LIFELINE SPANDAU BALLET	7	1982
LIFE'S A CINCH MUNDY	75	1996
LIFE'S A TREAT SHAUN THE SHEEP	20	2007
LIFE'S BEEN GOOD JOE WALSH	14	1978
LIFE'S JUST A BALLGAME WOMACK & WOMACK	32	1988
LIFE'S TOO SHORT [A] HOLE IN ONE	36	1997
LIFE'S TOO SHORT [B] LIGHTNING SEEDS	27	1999
LIFE'S WHAT YOU MAKE IT TALK TALK	16	1986
LIFESAVER GURU	61	1996
LIFESTYLES OF THE RICH AND FAMOUS GOOD CHARLOTTE	8	2003
LIFETIME LOVE JOYCE SIMS	34	1987
LIFETIME PILING UP TALKING HEADS	50	1992
LIFETIMES SLAM FEATURING TYRONE PALMER	61	2001
LIFT 808 STATE	38	1991
LIFT EVERY VOICE (TAKE ME AWAY) MASS ORDER	35	1992
LIFT IT HIGH (ALL ABOUT BELIEF) 1999 MANCHESTER UNITED SQUAD	11	1999
LIFT ME UP [A] HOWARD JONES	52	1992
LIFT ME UP [B] RED 5	26	1997
LIFT ME UP [C] GERI HALLIWELL	1	1999
LIFT ME UP [C] REEL	39	2001
LIFT ME UP [D] MOBY	18	2005
LIFTED LIGHTHOUSE FAMILY	4	1995
LIFTING ME HIGHER GEMS FOR JEM	28	1995
THE LIGHT [A] COMMON	56	2000
LIGHT [B] PHAROAHE MONCH	72	2000
THE LIGHT [C] MICHELLE WEEKS	69	2003
LIGHT A CANDLE DANIEL O'DONNELL	23	2000
LIGHT A RAINBOW TUKAN	38	2001
LIGHT AIRCRAFT ON FIRE AUTEURS	58	1996
LIGHT AND DAY POLYPHONIC SPREE	40	2003
THE LIGHT COMES FROM WITHIN LINDA McCARTNEY	56	1999
LIGHT EMITTING ELECTRICAL WAVE THESE ANIMAL MEN	72	1997
LIGHT FLIGHT PENTANGLE	43	1970
LIGHT IN YOUR EYES SHERYL CROW	73	2004
LIGHT MY FIRE [A] JOSE FELICIANO	6	1968
LIGHT MY FIRE [A] DOORS	7	1968
LIGHT MY FIRE [A] MIKE FLOWERS POPS	39	1996
LIGHT MY FIRE [A] UB40	63	2000
LIGHT MY FIRE [A] WILL YOUNG	1	2002
LIGHT MY FIRE [B] CLUBHOUSE FEATURING CARL	7	1993
LIGHT MY FIRE/137 DISCO HEAVEN (MEDLEY) AMII STEWART	7	1979
(LIGHT OF EXPERIENCE) DOINA DE JALE GHEORGHE ZAMFIR	4	1976
LIGHT OF LOVE T REX	22	1974
LIGHT OF MY LIFE LOUISE	8	1995
LIGHT OF THE WORLD KIM APPLEBY	41	1993
LIGHT UP THE FIRE PARCHMENT	31	1972
LIGHT UP THE NIGHT BROTHERS JOHNSON	47	1980
LIGHT UP THE WORLD FOR CHRISTMAS LAMPIES	48	2001
LIGHT YEARS PEARL JAM	52	2000
LIGHT YOUR ASS ON FIRE BUSTA RHYMES FEATURING PHARRELL	62	2003
THE LIGHTER DJ SS	63	2002
LIGHTERS UP LIL' KIM	12	2005
LIGHTNIN' STRIKES LOU CHRISTIE	11	1966
LIGHTNING ZOE	37	1991
LIGHTNING BLUE EYES SECRET MACHINES	57	2006
LIGHTNING CRASHES LIVE	33	1996
LIGHTNING FLASH BROTHERHOOD OF MAN	67	1982
LIGHTNING STRIKES OZZY OSBOURNE	72	1986
THE LIGHTNING TREE SETTLERS	36	1971
LIGHTS AND SOUNDS YELLOWCARD	59	2006
LIGHTS OF CINCINNATI SCOTT WALKER	13	1969
LIGHTS OUT LISA MARIE PRESLEY	16	2003
LIKE A BABY LEN BARRY	10	1966
LIKE A BOY CIARA	16	2007
LIKE A BUTTERFLY MAC & KATIE KISSOON	18	1975
LIKE A CAT CRW FEATURING VERONIKA	57	2002
LIKE A CHILD JULIE ROGERS	20	1964
LIKE A CHILD AGAIN MISSION	30	1992
LIKE A FEATHER NIKKA COSTA	53	2001
LIKE A HURRICANE MISSION	49	1986
LIKE A MOTORWAY SAINT ETIENNE	47	1994
LIKE A PLAYA LA GANZ	75	1996
LIKE A PRAYER MADONNA	1	1989
LIKE A PRAYER MAD'HOUSE	3	2002
LIKE A ROLLING STONE BOB DYLAN	4	1965
LIKE A ROLLING STONE ROLLING STONES	12	1995
LIKE A ROSE A1	6	2000
LIKE A SATELLITE (EP) THUNDER	28	1993
LIKE A STAR CORINNE BAILEY RAE	32	2005
LIKE A VIRGIN MADONNA	3	1984
LIKE A WOMAN TONY RICH PROJECT	27	1996
LIKE A YO-YO SABRINA	72	1989
LIKE AN ANIMAL GLOVE	52	1983
LIKE AN OLD TIME MOVIE VOICE OF SCOTT McKENZIE	50	1967
LIKE CLOCKWORK BOOMTOWN RATS	6	1978
LIKE DREAMERS DO [A] APPLEJACKS	20	1964
LIKE DREAMERS DO [B] MICA PARIS FEATURING COURTNEY PINE	26	1988
LIKE FLAMES BERLIN	47	1987
LIKE GLUE SEAN PAUL	3	2003
LIKE I DO [A] MAUREEN EVANS	3	1962
LIKE I DO [B] FOR REAL	45	1997
LIKE I LIKE IT AURRA	43	1985
LIKE I LOVE YOU JUSTIN TIMBERLAKE	2	2002
LIKE IT OR LEAVE IT CHIKINKI	65	2004
LIKE I'VE NEVER BEEN GONE BILLY FURY	3	1963
LIKE LOVERS DO LLOYD COLE	24	1995
LIKE MARVIN GAYE SAID (WHAT'S GOING ON) SPEECH	35	1996
LIKE PRINCES DO DIESEL PARK WEST	58	1989
LIKE SISTER AND BROTHER DRIFTERS	7	1973
LIKE STRANGERS EVERLY BROTHERS	11	1960
LIKE THE SUN RYANDAN	69	2007
LIKE THIS KELLY ROWLAND FEATURING EVE	4	2007
LIKE THIS AND LIKE THAT [A] MONICA	33	1996
LIKE THIS AND LIKE THAT [B] LaKIESHA BERRI	54	1997
LIKE THIS LIKE THAT [A] MAURO PICOTTO	21	2001
LIKE THIS LIKE THAT [B] SE:SA FEATURING SHARON PHILLIPS	63	2007
LIKE TO GET TO KNOW YOU WELL HOWARD JONES	4	1984
LIKE TOY SOLDIERS EMINEM	1	2005
LIKE WE USED TO BE GEORGIE FAME & THE BLUE FLAMES	33	1965
LIKE WHAT TOMMI	12	2003
LIKE YOU BOW WOW FEATURING CIARA	17	2006
LIKE YOU'LL NEVER SEE ME AGAIN ALICIA KEYS	53	2008
A LIL' AIN'T ENOUGH DAVID LEE ROTH	32	1991
LIL' BIG MAN OMERO MUMBA	42	2002
LIL' DEVIL CULT	11	1987
LIL' DUB CHEFIN' SPACE MONKEYZ VS GORILLAZ	73	2002
LIL' RED RIDING HOOD SAM THE SHAM & THE PHARAOHS	46	1966
LIL' RED RIDING HOOD 999	59	1981
LIL STAR KELIS FEATURING CEE LO	3	2007
LILAC WINE ELKIE BROOKS	16	1978
LILIAN DEPECHE MODE	18	2006
LILY THE PINK SCAFFOLD	1	1968
LILY WAS HERE DAVID A STEWART FEATURING CANDY DULFER	6	1990
LIMBO ROCK CHUBBY CHECKER	32	1962
LINDA LU JOHNNY KIDD & THE PIRATES	47	1961
THE LINE LISA STANSFIELD	64	1997
LINE DANCE PARTY WOOLPACKERS	25	1997
LINE UP ELASTICA	20	1994
LINES PLANETS	36	1979
LINGER CRANBERRIES	14	1993
LION RIP DUKE SPIRIT	25	2005
THE LION SLEEPS TONIGHT (WIMOWEH) TOKENS	11	1961
THE LION SLEEPS TONIGHT DAVE NEWMAN	34	1972
THE LION SLEEPS TONIGHT TIGHT FIT	1	1982
LIONROCK LIONROCK	63	1992
THE LION'S MOUTH KAJAGOOGOO	25	1984
LIP GLOSS PULP	50	1993
LIP SERVICE (EP) WET WET WET	15	1992
LIP UP FATTY BAD MANNERS	15	1980
LIPS LIKE SUGAR ECHO & THE BUNNYMEN	36	1987
LIPSMACKIN' ROCK 'N' ROLLIN' PETER BLAKE	40	1977
LIPSTICK [A] ROCKET FROM THE CRYPT	64	1998
LIPSTICK [B] ALESHA	14	2006
LIPSTICK ON YOUR COLLAR CONNIE FRANCIS	3	1959
LIPSTICK POWDER AND PAINT SHAKIN' STEVENS	11	1985
LIQUID COOL APOLLO 440	35	1994
LIQUID DREAMS O-TOWN	3	2001
LIQUID LIPS BLUETONES	25	2003
LIQUID LIVES HADOUKEN	36	2007
THE LIQUIDATOR HARRY J ALL STARS	9	1969
LISTEN [A] URBAN SPECIES FEATURING MC SOLAAR	47	1994
LISTEN [B] BEYONCE	8	2007
LISTEN EP STIFF LITTLE FINGERS	33	1982
LISTEN LIKE THIEVES INXS	46	1986
LISTEN LIKE THIEVES WAS (NOT WAS)	58	1992
LISTEN LITTLE GIRL KEITH KELLY	47	1960
LISTEN TO ME [A] BUDDY HOLLY	16	1958
LISTEN TO ME [B] HOLLIES	11	1968
LISTEN TO THE MUSIC DOOBIE BROTHERS	29	1974
LISTEN TO THE OCEAN NINA & FREDERIK	46	1960
LISTEN TO THE RADIO: ATMOSPHERICS TOM ROBINSON	39	1983
LISTEN TO THE RHYTHM K3M	71	1992
LISTEN TO THE RHYTHM FLOW GTO	72	1991
LISTEN TO WHAT THE MAN SAID WINGS	6	1975
LISTEN TO YOUR FATHER FEARGAL SHARKEY	23	1984
LISTEN TO YOUR HEART [A] ROXETTE	6	1989
LISTEN TO YOUR HEART [A] DHT FEATURING EDMEE	7	2005
LISTEN TO YOUR HEART [B] SONIA	10	1989
LISTEN UP GOSSIP	39	2007
LITHIUM NIRVANA	11	1992
LITHIUM EVANESCENCE	32	2007
LITTLE ARITHMETICS dEUS	44	1996
LITTLE ARROWS LEAPY LEE	2	1968

	Peak Position	Year of Release
LITTLE BABY NOTHING MANIC STREET PREACHERS	29	1992
LITTLE BAND OF GOLD JAMES GILREATH	29	1963
LITTLE BERNADETTE HARRY BELAFONTE	16	1958
LITTLE BIRD ANNIE LENNOX	3	1993
A LITTLE BIT ROSIE RIBBONS	19	2003
A LITTLE BIT FURTHER AWAY KOKOMO	45	1982
A LITTLE BIT ME A LITTLE BIT YOU MONKEES	3	1967
A LITTLE BIT MORE [A] DR HOOK	2	1976
A LITTLE BIT MORE [A] 911	1	1999
A LITTLE BIT MORE [B] KYM SIMS	30	1992
A LITTLE BIT OF ACTION NADIA	27	2004
LITTLE BIT OF HEAVEN LISA STANSFIELD	32	1993
LITTLE BIT OF LOVE FREE	13	1972
LITTLE BIT OF LOVIN' KELE LE ROC	8	1998
A LITTLE BIT OF LUCK DJ LUCK & MC NEAT	9	1999
A LITTLE BIT OF SNOW HOWARD JONES	70	1987
A LITTLE BIT OF SOAP SHOWADDYWADDY	5	1978
A LITTLE BITTY TEAR BURL IVES	9	1962
LITTLE BITTY TEAR MIKI & GRIFF	16	1962
LITTLE BLACK BOOK [A] JIMMY DEAN	33	1962
LITTLE BLACK BOOK [B] BELINDA CARLISLE	28	1992
LITTLE BLUE BIRD VINCE HILL	42	1969
A LITTLE BOOGIE WOOGIE IN THE BACK OF MY MIND GARY GLITTER	31	1977
A LITTLE BOOGIE WOOGIE (IN THE BACK OF MY MIND) SHAKIN' STEVENS	12	1987
LITTLE BOY LOST MICHAEL HOLLIDAY	50	1960
LITTLE BOY SAD JOHNNY BURNETTE	12	1961
LITTLE BRITAIN DREADZONE	20	1996
LITTLE BROTHER BLUE PEARL	31	1990
LITTLE BROWN JUG GLENN MILLER	12	1976
LITTLE BY LITTLE [A] DUSTY SPRINGFIELD	17	1966
LITTLE BY LITTLE [B] OASIS	2	2002
LITTLE CHILD DES'REE	69	1994
LITTLE CHILDREN BILLY J KRAMER & THE DAKOTAS	1	1964
LITTLE CHRISTINE DICK JORDAN	39	1960
LITTLE DARLIN' [A] DIAMONDS	3	1957
LITTLE DARLIN' [B] MARVIN GAYE	50	1966
LITTLE DARLING RUBETTES	30	1975
LITTLE DEREK SWAY	38	2006
LITTLE DEVIL NEIL SEDAKA	9	1961
LITTLE DISCOURAGE IDLEWILD	24	1999
LITTLE DOES SHE KNOW KURSAAL FLYERS	14	1976
LITTLE DONKEY BEVERLEY SISTERS	14	1959
LITTLE DONKEY GRACIE FIELDS	21	1959
LITTLE DONKEY NINA & FREDERIK	3	1960
LITTLE DROPS OF SILVER GERRY MONROE	37	1971
LITTLE DRUMMER BOY BEVERLEY SISTERS	6	1959
LITTLE DRUMMER BOY HARRY SIMEONE CHORALE	13	1959
LITTLE DRUMMER BOY MICHAEL FLANDERS	20	1959
LITTLE DRUMMER BOY PIPES & DRUMS & MILITARY BAND OF THE ROYAL SCOTS DRAGOON GUARDS	13	1972
LITTLE DRUMMER BOY/PEACE ON EARTH BANDAGED	3	2008
LITTLE DRUMMER BOY (REMIX) RuPAUL	61	1994
LITTLE 15 (IMPORT) DEPECHE MODE	60	1988
LITTLE FLUFFY CLOUDS ORB	10	1993
LITTLE GIRL [A] MARTY WILDE	16	1960
LITTLE GIRL [B] TROGGS	37	1968
LITTLE GIRL [C] BANNED	36	1977
LITTLE GIRL LOST ICICLE WORKS	59	1988
LITTLE GREEN APPLES ROGER MILLER	19	1968
LITTLE HOUSE OF SAVAGES WALKMEN	72	2004
A LITTLE IN LOVE CLIFF RICHARD	15	1981
LITTLE JEANNIE ELTON JOHN	33	1980
LITTLE L JAMIROQUAI	5	2001
LITTLE LADY ANEKA	50	1981
A LITTLE LESS CONVERSATION ELVIS VS JXL	1	2002
A LITTLE LESS 16 CANDLES, A LITTLE MORE 'TOUCH ME' FALL OUT BOY	38	2006
LITTLE LIES FLEETWOOD MAC	5	1987
LITTLE LION MAN MUMFORD & SONS	24	2009
LITTLE LOST SOMETIMES ALMIGHTY	42	1991
LITTLE LOVE LIL' LOVE	34	2005
A LITTLE LOVE AND UNDERSTANDING GILBERT BECAUD	10	1975
A LITTLE LOVE A LITTLE KISS KARL DENVER	19	1962
A LITTLE LOVIN' [A] NEIL SEDAKA	34	1974
A LITTLE LOVING [B] FOURMOST	6	1964
LITTLE MAN SONNY & CHER	4	1966
LITTLE MIRACLES (HAPPEN EVERY DAY) LUTHER VANDROSS	28	1993
LITTLE MISS CAN'T BE WRONG SPIN DOCTORS	23	1993
LITTLE MISS LONELY HELEN SHAPIRO	8	1962
LITTLE MISS PERFECT SUMMER MATTHEWS	32	2004
A LITTLE MORE LOVE OLIVIA NEWTON-JOHN	4	1978
A LITTLE PEACE NICOLE	1	1982
LITTLE PIECE OF LEATHER DONNIE ELBERT	27	1972
LITTLE PINK STARS RADISH	32	1997
LITTLE RED CORVETTE PRINCE & THE REVOLUTION	2	1983
LITTLE RED MONKEY FRANK CHACKSFIELD'S TUNESMITHS, FEATURING JACK JORDAN – CLAVIOLINE	10	1953
LITTLE RED ROOSTER ROLLING STONES	1	1964
A LITTLE RESPECT ERASURE	4	1988
A LITTLE RESPECT WHEATUS	3	2001
LITTLE RHYMES MERCURY REV	51	2002
A LITTLE SAMBA UGLY DUCKLING	70	2001
LITTLE SERENADE EDDIE CALVERT	28	1958
THE LITTLE SHOEMAKER PETULA CLARK	7	1954
LITTLE SISTER [A] ELVIS PRESLEY	1	1961
LITTLE SISTER [B] QUEENS OF THE STONE AGE	18	2005
A LITTLE SOUL PULP	22	1998
LITTLE STAR [A] ELEGANTS	25	1958
LITTLE STAR [B] MADONNA	6	1998
LITTLE THINGS [A] DAVE BERRY	5	1965
LITTLE THINGS [B] INDIA.ARIE	62	2003
LITTLE THINGS MEAN A LOT KITTY KALLEN	1	1954
LITTLE THINGS MEAN A LOT ALMA COGAN	11	1954
LITTLE THOUGHT BLOC PARTY	38	2004
A LITTLE TIME BEAUTIFUL SOUTH	1	1990
LITTLE TOWN CLIFF RICHARD	11	1982
LITTLE TOWN FLIRT DEL SHANNON	4	1963
LITTLE TRAIN MAX BYGRAVES	28	1958
LITTLE WHITE BERRY ROY CASTLE	40	1960
LITTLE WHITE BULL TOMMY STEELE	6	1959
LITTLE WHITE LIES STATUS QUO	47	1999
LITTLE WILLY SWEET	4	1972
LITTLE WONDER DAVID BOWIE	14	1997
A LITTLE YOU FREDDIE & THE DREAMERS	26	1965
LITTLEST THINGS LILY ALLEN	21	2006
LIVE AND LEARN JOE PUBLIC	43	1992
LIVE AND LET DIE WINGS	9	1973
LIVE AND LET DIE GUNS N' ROSES	5	1991
LIVE ANIMAL (F**K LIKE A BEAST) W.A.S.P.	61	1988
LIVE ANOTHER LIFE PLASTIC BOY FEATURING ROZALLA	55	2003
LIVE AT TFI FRIDAY EP STING	53	1996
LIVE AT THE MARQUEE (EP) EDDIE & THE HOT RODS	43	1976
LIVE (EP) BARCLAY JAMES HARVEST	49	1977
THE LIVE EP GARY NUMAN	27	1985
LIVE FOR LOVING YOU GLORIA ESTEFAN	33	1991
LIVE FOR THE ONE I LOVE TINA ARENA	63	2000
LIVE FOREVER OASIS	10	1994
LIVE IN A HIDING PLACE IDLEWILD	26	2002
LIVE IN MANCHESTER (PARTS 1 + 2) N-JOI	12	1992
LIVE IN THE SKY DAVE CLARK FIVE	39	1968
LIVE IN TROUBLE BARRON KNIGHTS	7	1977
LIVE IS LIFE OPUS	6	1985
LIVE IS LIFE HERMES HOUSE BAND & DJ OTZI	50	2002
LIVE IT UP MENTAL AS ANYTHING	3	1987
LIVE LIKE HORSES ELTON JOHN & LUCIANO PAVAROTTI	9	1996
LIVE MY LIFE BOY GEORGE	62	1988
LIVE OR DIE DILLINJA	53	2002
LIVE THE DREAM CAST	7	1997
LIVE TO TELL MADONNA	2	1986
LIVE TOGETHER LISA STANSFIELD	10	1990
LIVE TWICE DARIUS	7	2005
LIVE WITH ME MASSIVE ATTACK	17	2006
LIVE YOUR LIFE TI FEATURING RIHANNA	2	2008
LIVE YOUR LIFE BE FREE BELINDA CARLISLE	12	1991
LIVELY LONNIE DONEGAN	13	1960
LIVERPOOL (ANTHEM) LIVERPOOL FC	54	1983
LIVERPOOL LOU SCAFFOLD	7	1974
LIVERPOOL (WE'RE NEVER GONNA...) LIVERPOOL FC	54	1983
LIVIN' IN THE LIGHT CARON WHEELER	14	1990
LIVIN' IN THIS WORLD GURU	61	1996
LIVIN' IT UP [A] NORTHERN UPROAR	24	1996
LIVIN' IT UP [B] JA RULE FEATURING CASE	5	2001
LIVIN' IT UP (FRIDAY NIGHT) BELL & JAMES	59	1979
LIVIN' LA VIDA LOCA RICKY MARTIN	1	1999
LIVIN' LOVIN' DOLL CLIFF RICHARD	20	1959
LIVIN' ON A PRAYER BON JOVI	4	1986
LIVIN' ON THE EDGE AEROSMITH	19	1993
LIVIN' ON THE EDGE OF THE NIGHT IGGY POP	51	1990
LIVIN' THING ELECTRIC LIGHT ORCHESTRA	4	1976
LIVIN' THING BEAUTIFUL SOUTH	24	2004
LIVING AFTER MIDNIGHT JUDAS PRIEST	12	1980
LIVING BY NUMBERS NEW MUSIK	13	1980
THE LIVING DAYLIGHTS A-HA	5	1987
LIVING DOLL CLIFF RICHARD & THE DRIFTERS	1	1959
LIVING DOLL CLIFF RICHARD & THE YOUNG ONES FEATURING HANK B MARVIN	1	1986
THE LIVING DREAM SUNDANCE	56	1999
LIVING FOR THE CITY STEVIE WONDER	15	1974
LIVING FOR THE CITY GILLAN	50	1982
LIVING FOR THE WEEKEND HARD-FI	15	2005
LIVING FOR YOU SONNY & CHER	44	1966
LIVING IN A BOX LIVING IN A BOX	5	1987
LIVING IN A BOX BOBBY WOMACK	70	1987
LIVING IN A FANTASY URBAN HYPE	57	1993
LIVING IN A WORLD (TURNED UPSIDE DOWN) PRIVATE LIVES	53	1984
LIVING IN AMERICA JAMES BROWN	5	1986
LIVING IN ANOTHER WORLD TALK TALK	48	1986
LIVING IN DANGER ACE OF BASE	18	1995
LIVING IN HARMONY CLIFF RICHARD	12	1972
LIVING IN SIN BON JOVI	35	1989
LIVING IN THE PAST [A] JETHRO TULL	3	1969
LIVING IN THE PAST [B] DRUM THEATRE	67	1986
LIVING IN THE ROSE (THE BALLADS EP) NEW MODEL ARMY	51	1993
LIVING IN THE (SLIGHTLY MORE RECENT) PAST JETHRO TULL	32	1993
LIVING IN THE SUNSHINE CLUBHOUSE FEATURING CARL	21	1994
LIVING IN THE UK SHAKATAK	52	1981
LIVING IS A PROBLEM BECAUSE EVERYTHING DIES BIFFY CLYRO	19	2007
LIVING NEXT DOOR TO ALICE SMOKIE	5	1976
LIVING NEXT DOOR TO ALICE (WHO THE F**K IS ALICE) SMOKIE FEATURING ROY CHUBBY BROWN	3	1995
LIVING ON AN ISLAND STATUS QUO	16	1979
LIVING ON MY OWN FREDDIE MERCURY	1	1985
LIVING ON THE CEILING BLANCMANGE	7	1982

	Peak Position	Year of Release
LIVING ON THE FRONT LINE EDDY GRANT	11	1979
LIVING ON VIDEO TRANS-X	9	1985
LIVING THE DREAM MILLION DEAD	60	2005
THE LIVING TREE SHIRLEY BASSEY	37	2007
LIVING WITH THE HUMAN MACHINES STRANGELOVE	53	1996
THE LIVING YEARS MIKE + THE MECHANICS	2	1989
LIZARD (GONNA GET YOU) MAURO PICOTTO	27	1999
LK (CAROLINA CAROL BELA) DJ MARKY & XRS FEATURING STAMINA MC	17	2002
L-L-LUCY MUD	10	1975
LO MISMO QUE YO (IF ONLY) ALEX CUBA BAND FEATURING RON SEXSMITH	52	2004
LOADED [A] PRIMAL SCREAM	16	1990
LOADED [B] RICKY MARTIN	19	2001
LOADED GUN DEAD 60S	28	2005
LOADSAMONEY (DOIN' UP THE HOUSE) HARRY ENFIELD	4	1988
LOBSTER & SCRIMP TIMBALAND FEATURING JAY-Z	48	1999
LOCAL BOY RIFLES	36	2005
LOCAL BOY IN THE PHOTOGRAPH STEREOPHONICS	14	1997
LOC'ED AFTER DARK TONE LOC	21	1989
LOCH LOMOND RUNRIG & THE TARTAN ARMY	9	2007
LOCK AND LOAD BOB SEGER & THE SILVER BULLET BAND	57	1996
LOCK UP YA DAUGHTERS NOISE NEXT DOOR	12	2004
LOCK UP YOUR DAUGHTERS SLADE	29	1981
LOCKED OUT CROWDED HOUSE	12	1994
LOCKED UP AKON	5	2004
LOCO FUN LOVIN' CRIMINALS	5	2001
LOCO IN ACAPULCO FOUR TOPS	7	1988
THE LOCO-MOTION [A] LITTLE EVA	2	1962
LOCO-MOTION [A] VERNONS GIRLS	47	1962
THE LOCOMOTION [A] DAVE STEWART WITH BARBARA GASKIN	70	1986
THE LOCO-MOTION [A] KYLIE MINOGUE	2	1988
LOCOMOTION [B] ORCHESTRAL MANOEUVRES IN THE DARK	5	1984
L.O.D. (LOVE ON DELIVERY) BILLY OCEAN	19	1976
THE LODGERS STYLE COUNCIL	13	1985
THE LOGICAL SONG SUPERTRAMP	7	1979
THE LOGICAL SONG SCOOTER	2	2002
L'OISEAU ET L'ENFANT MARIE MYRIAM	42	1977
LOLA KINKS	2	1970
LOLA ANDY TAYLOR	60	1990
LOLA STARS AND STRIPES STILLS	39	2004
LOLA'S THEME SHAPESHIFTERS	1	2004
LOLLIPOP [A] MUDLARKS	2	1958
LOLLIPOP [A] CHORDETTES	6	1958
LOLLIPOP [B] DADA FEATURING SANDY RIVERA & TRIX	18	2007
LOLLIPOP [C] MIKA	59	2007
LOLLIPOP [D] LIL' WAYNE	26	2008
LOLLY LOLLY WENDY & LISA	64	1989
LONDINIUM CATATONIA	20	1999
LONDON BOYS T REX	40	1976
LONDON BRIDGE FERGIE	3	2006
LONDON CALLING CLASH	11	1979
LONDON GIRLS CHAS & DAVE	63	1983
LONDON KID JEAN-MICHEL JARRE FEATURING HANK MARVIN	52	1989
LONDON NIGHTS LONDON BOYS	2	1989
A LONDON THING SCOTT GARCIA FEATURING MC STYLES	29	1997
LONDON TIMES RADIO HEART FEATURING GARY NUMAN	48	1987
LONDON TONIGHT COLLAPSED LUNG	31	1996
LONDON TOWN [A] WINGS	60	1978
LONDON TOWN [B] LIGHT OF THE WORLD	41	1980
LONDON TOWN [C] BUCKS FIZZ	34	1983
LONDON TOWN [D] JDS	49	1998
LONDON X-PRESS X-PRESS 2	59	1993
LONDON'S BRILLIANT WENDY JAMES	62	1993
LONDON'S BRILLIANT PARADE ELVIS COSTELLO & THE ATTRACTIONS	48	1994
LONDRES STRUTT SMELLS LIKE HEAVEN	57	1993
THE LONE RANGER QUANTUM JUMP	5	1979
LONE RIDER JOHN LEYTON	40	1962
THE LONELIEST MAN IN THE WORLD TOURISTS	32	1979
LONELINESS [A] DES O'CONNOR	18	1969
LONELINESS [B] TOMCRAFT	1	2003
LONELINESS [C] ED HARCOURT	59	2005
LONELINESS IS GONE NINE YARDS	70	1998
LONELY [A] EDDIE COCHRAN	41	1960
LONELY [B] MR ACKER BILK WITH THE LEON YOUNG STRING CHORALE	14	1962
LONELY [C] PETER ANDRE	6	1997
LONELY [D] AKON	1	2005
LONELY AT THE TOP ORDINARY BOYS	10	2006
LONELY BALLERINA MANTOVANI	16	1955
LONELY BOY [A] PAUL ANKA	3	1959
LONELY BOY [B] ANDREW GOLD	11	1977
LONELY BOY LONELY GUITAR DUANE EDDY & THE REBELETTES	35	1963
THE LONELY BULL TIJUANA BRASS	22	1963
LONELY BUOY JOE LEAN & THE JING JANG JONG	43	2008
LONELY CITY JOHN LEYTON	14	1962
LONELY, CRYIN', ONLY THERAPY?	32	1998
LONELY DAYS BEE GEES	33	1970
LONELY DAYS, LONELY NIGHTS DON DOWNING	32	1973
LONELY (HAVE WE LOST OUR LOVE) LANCE ELLINGTON	57	1993
LONELY HEART UFO	41	1981
LONELY HEARTS STILL BEAT THE SAME RESEARCH	50	2006
LONELY MAN THEME CLIFF ADAMS	39	1960
LONELY NIGHT MAGNUM	70	1986
LONELY NO MORE ROB THOMAS	11	2005
THE LONELY ONE ALICE DEEJAY	16	2000
LONELY PUP (IN A CHRISTMAS SHOP) ADAM FAITH	4	1960
LONELY STREET CLARENCE 'FROGMAN' HENRY	42	1961
LONELY SYMPHONY FRANCES RUFFELLE	25	1994
LONELY TEENAGER DION	47	1961
LONELY THIS CHRISTMAS MUD	1	1974
LONELY TOGETHER BARRY MANILOW	21	1980
THE LONER GARY MOORE	53	1987
LONESOME ADAM FAITH	12	1962
LONESOME DAY BRUCE SPRINGSTEEN	39	2002
LONESOME NUMBER ONE DON GIBSON	47	1962
LONESOME (SI TU VOIS MA MERE) CHRIS BARBER FEATURING MONTY SUNSHINE	27	1959
LONESOME TRAVELLER LONNIE DONEGAN	28	1958
LONG AFTER TONIGHT IS ALL OVER JIMMY RADLCIFFE	40	1965
LONG AND LASTING LOVE (ONCE IN A LIFETIME) GLENN MEDEIROS	42	1988
THE LONG AND WINDING ROAD RAY MORGAN	32	1970
THE LONG AND WINDING ROAD WILL YOUNG & GARETH GATES	1	2002
LONG AS I CAN SEE THE LIGHT CREEDENCE CLEARWATER REVIVAL	20	1970
LONG AS I CAN SEE THE LIGHT MONKEY MAFIA	51	1998
LONG BLACK VEIL STRANGLERS	51	2004
LONG COOL WOMAN IN A BLACK DRESS HOLLIES	32	1972
A LONG DECEMBER COUNTING CROWS	62	1996
LONG DISTANCE TURIN BRAKES	22	2002
THE LONG GOODBYE RONAN KEATING	3	2003
LONG HAIRED LOVER FROM LIVERPOOL LITTLE JIMMY OSMOND	1	1972
LONG HOT SUMMER [A] STYLE COUNCIL	3	1983
LONG HOT SUMMER [B] GIRLS ALOUD	7	2005
LONG HOT SUMMER NIGHT JT TAYLOR	63	1991
LONG LEGGED GIRL (WITH THE SHORT DRESS ON) ELVIS PRESLEY	49	1967
LONG LEGGED WOMAN DRESSED IN BLACK MUNGO JERRY	13	1974
LONG LIVE LOVE [A] SANDIE SHAW	1	1965
LONG LIVE LOVE [A] NICK BERRY	47	1992
LONG LIVE LOVE [B] OLIVIA NEWTON-JOHN	11	1974
LONG LIVE ROCK WHO	48	1979
LONG LIVE ROCK 'N' ROLL RAINBOW	33	1978
LONG LIVE THE QUEEN FRANK TURNER	65	2008
LONG LIVE THE UK MUSIC SCENE HELEN LOVE	65	1998
LONG LONG WAY TO GO DEF LEPPARD	40	2003
LONG LOST LOVER THREE DEGREES	40	1975
LONG MAY YOU RUN (LIVE) NEIL YOUNG	71	1993
LONG NIGHT CORRS	31	2004
LONG ROAD TO RUIN FOO FIGHTERS	35	2007
THE LONG RUN EAGLES	66	1979
LONG SHOT KICK DE BUCKET PIONEERS	21	1969
LONG TALL GLASSES LEO SAYER	4	1974
LONG TALL SALLY PAT BOONE	18	1956
LONG TALL SALLY LITTLE RICHARD	3	1957
LONG TERM LOVERS OF PAIN (EP) HUE & CRY	48	1991
LONG TIME ARROW	30	1985
LONG TIME COMING [A] BUMP & FLEX	73	1998
LONG TIME COMING [B] DELAYS	16	2004
LONG TIME GONE GALLIANO	15	1994
LONG TRAIN RUNNIN' DOOBIE BROTHERS	7	1993
LONG TRAIN RUNNING BANANARAMA	30	1991
A LONG WALK JILL SCOTT	54	2001
LONG WAY ROOTJOOSE	68	1997
LONG WAY AROUND EAGLE-EYE CHERRY FEATURING NENEH CHERRY	48	2000
LONG WAY FROM HOME WHITESNAKE	55	1979
LONG WAY SOUTH JJ72	68	2000
LONG WAY TO GO STEVIE NICKS	60	1989
LONG WAY 2 GO CASSIE	12	2006
LONG WHITE CAR HIPSWAY	55	1986
LONGER DAN FOGELBERG	59	1980
THE LONGEST DAY 24	56	2005
THE LONGEST TIME BILLY JOEL	25	1984
LONGTIME BOY NINA & FREDERIK	43	1961
LONGVIEW GREEN DAY	30	1995
LONNIE DONEGAN SHOWCASE (LP) LONNIE DONEGAN	26	1956
LONNIE'S SKIFFLE PARTY LONNIE DONEGAN	23	1958
LOO-BE-LOO CHUCKS	22	1963
THE LOOK ROXETTE	7	1989
LOOK AROUND VINCE HILL	12	1971
LOOK AT ME GERI HALLIWELL	2	1999
LOOK AT ME (I'M IN LOVE) MOMENTS	42	1975
LOOK AT ME NOW JESSY	29	2003
LOOK AT THAT GIRL GUY MITCHELL	1	1953
LOOK AT US NORTHERN HEIGHTZ	29	2004
LOOK AT YOURSELF DAVID McALMONT	40	1997
LOOK AWAY BIG COUNTRY	7	1986
LOOK BEFORE YOU LEAP DAVE CLARK FIVE	50	1966
LOOK BUT DON'T TOUCH (EP) SKIN	33	1994
LOOK FOR A STAR GARRY MILLS	7	1960
LOOK FOR ME CHIPMUNK FEATURING TALAY RILEY	7	2009
LOOK FOR THE WOMAN DAN LE SAC VS SCROOBIUS PIP	72	2008

Title	Artist	Peak Position	Year of Release
LOOK HOMEWARD ANGEL	JOHNNIE RAY	7	1957
LOOK INTO MY EYES	BONE THUGS-N-HARMONY	16	1997
LOOK MAMA	HOWARD JONES	10	1985
LOOK ME IN THE HEART	TINA TURNER	31	1990
LOOK OF LOVE [A]	GLADYS KNIGHT & THE PIPS	21	1973
THE LOOK OF LOVE [A]	T-EMPO	71	1996
THE LOOK OF LOVE [B]	ABC	4	1982
THE LOOK OF LOVE [C]	MADONNA	9	1987
LOOK ON THE FLOOR (HYPNOTIC TANGO)	BANANARAMA	26	2005
LOOK OUT SUNSHINE!	FRATELLIS	70	2008
LOOK THROUGH ANY WINDOW	HOLLIES	4	1965
LOOK THROUGH MY EYES	PHIL COLLINS	61	2003
LOOK UP TO THE LIGHT	EVOLUTION	55	1995
LOOK WHAT YOU DONE FOR ME	AL GREEN	44	1972
LOOK WHAT YOU STARTED	TEMPTATIONS	63	1988
LOOK WHAT YOU'VE DONE	JET	28	2004
LOOK WHO IT IS	HELEN SHAPIRO	47	1963
LOOK WHO'S DANCING	ZIGGY MARLEY & THE MELODY MAKERS	65	1989
LOOK WHO'S PERFECT NOW	TRANSISTER	56	1998
LOOK WHO'S TALKING	DR ALBAN	55	1994
LOOK WOT YOU DUN	SLADE	4	1972
LOOKIN' AT YOU	WARREN G FEATURING TOI	60	2002
LOOKIN' THROUGH THE WINDOWS	JACKSON 5	9	1972
LOOKING AFTER NO. 1	BOOMTOWN RATS	11	1977
LOOKING AS YOU ARE	EMBRACE	11	2005
LOOKING AT MIDNIGHT	IMAGINATION	29	1983
LOOKING FOR A LOVE	JOYCE SIMS	39	1989
LOOKING FOR A NEW LOVE	JODY WATLEY	13	1987
LOOKING FOR A PLACE	MANIA	29	2004
LOOKING FOR A SONG	BIG AUDIO	68	1994
LOOKING FOR ATLANTIS	PREFAB SPROUT	51	1990
LOOKING FOR CLUES	ROBERT PALMER	33	1980
LOOKING FOR LEWIS AND CLARK	LONG RYDERS	59	1985
LOOKING FOR LINDA	HUE & CRY	15	1989
LOOKING FOR LOVE	KAREN RAMIREZ	8	1998
LOOKING FOR LOVE TONIGHT	FAT LARRY'S BAND	46	1979
LOOKING FOR THE SUMMER	CHRIS REA	49	1991
LOOKING HIGH HIGH HIGH	BRYAN JOHNSON	20	1960
LOOKING THROUGH PATIENT EYES	PM DAWN	11	1993
LOOKING THROUGH THE EYES OF LOVE	GENE PITNEY	3	1965
LOOKING THROUGH THE EYES OF LOVE	PARTRIDGE FAMILY STARRING DAVID CASSIDY	9	1973
LOOKING THROUGH YOUR EYES	LeANN RIMES	38	1998
LOOKING UP	MICHELLE GAYLE	11	1993
LOOKS LIKE I'M IN LOVE AGAIN	KEY WEST FEATURING ERIK	46	1993
LOOKS LOOKS LOOKS	SPARKS	26	1975
LOOP DI LOVE	SHAG	4	1972
LOOP-DE-LOOP	FRANKIE VAUGHAN	5	1963
LOOPS OF FURY EP	CHEMICAL BROTHERS	13	1996
LOOPS OF INFINITY	COSMIC BABY	70	1994
LOOPZILLA	GEORGE CLINTON	57	1982
LOOSE	THERAPY?	25	1995
LOOSE CANNON	KILLING JOKE	25	2003
LOOSE FIT	HAPPY MONDAYS	17	1991
LOOSEN YOUR HOLD	SOUTH	73	2003
LOPEZ	808 STATE	20	1997
LORD DON'T SLOW ME DOWN	OASIS	10	2007
LORDS OF THE NEW CHURCH	TASMIN ARCHER	26	1993
LORELEI	LONNIE DONEGAN	10	1960
LORRAINE	BAD MANNERS	21	1980
LOS AMERICANOS	ESPIRITU	45	1993
LOS ANGELES IS BURNING	BAD RELIGION	67	2004
LOSE CONTROL [A]	JAMES	38	1990
LOSE CONTROL [B]	MISSY ELLIOTT	7	2005
LOSE IT	SUPERGRASS	75	1995
LOSE MY BREATH	DESTINY'S CHILD	2	2004
LOSE YOURSELF	EMINEM	1	2002
LOSER [A]	BECK	15	1994
LOSER [B]	THUNDER	48	2003
LOSING A FRIEND	NYLON	29	2006
LOSING GRIP	AVRIL LAVIGNE	22	2003
LOSING MY GRIP	SAMSON	63	1982
LOSING MY MIND	LIZA MINNELLI	6	1989
LOSING MY RELIGION	R.E.M.	19	1991
LOSING YOU [A]	BRENDA LEE	10	1963
LOSING YOU [B]	DUSTY SPRINGFIELD	9	1964
LOST [A]	MICHAEL BUBLE	19	2007
LOST [B]	COLDPLAY	55	2008
LOST AGAIN	YELLO	73	1983
LOST AND FOUND [A]	D*NOTE	59	1997
LOST & FOUND [B]	FEEDER	12	2006
THE LOST ART OF KEEPING A SECRET	QUEENS OF THE STONE AGE	31	2000
LOST CAT	CATATONIA	41	1996
LOST FOR WORDS	RONAN KEATING	9	2003
LOST IN A MELODY	DELAYS	28	2004
LOST IN AMERICA	ALICE COOPER	22	1994
LOST IN EMOTION [A]	LISA LISA & CULT JAM	58	1987
LOST IN EMOTION [B]	JOHN 'OO' FLEMING	74	1999
LOST IN FRANCE	BONNIE TYLER	9	1976
LOST IN LOVE [A]	UP YER RONSON FEATURING MARY PEARCE	27	1995
LOST IN LOVE [B]	LEGEND B	45	1997
LOST IN MUSIC [A]	SISTER SLEDGE	4	1979
LOST IN MUSIC [B]	STEREO MC'S	46	1991
LOST IN SPACE [A]	APOLLO FOUR FORTY	4	1998
LOST IN SPACE [B]	ELECTRASY	60	1998
LOST IN SPACE [C]	LIGHTHOUSE FAMILY	6	1998
LOST IN THE PLOT	DEARS	49	2004
LOST IN THE TRANSLATION	PACIFICA	54	1999
LOST IN YOU [A]	ROD STEWART	21	1988
LOST IN YOU [B]	GARTH BROOKS	70	1999
LOST IN YOUR EYES	DEBBIE GIBSON	34	1989
LOST IN YOUR LOVE	TONY HADLEY	42	1992
LOST JOHN	LONNIE DONEGAN	2	1956
LOST MYSELF	LONGPIGS	22	1996
LOST WEEKEND	LLOYD COLE & THE COMMOTIONS	17	1985
LOST WITHOUT EACH OTHER	HANSON	39	2005
LOST WITHOUT U	ROBIN THICKE	11	2007
LOST WITHOUT YOU [A]	JAYN HANNA	44	1997
LOST WITHOUT YOU [B]	DELTA GOODREM	4	2003
LOST WITHOUT YOUR LOVE	BREAD	27	1977
LOST YOU SOMEWHERE	CHICANE	35	1997
A LOT OF LOVE	MARTI PELLOW	59	2003
LOTTERY WINNERS ON ACID	CRIMEA	31	2006
LOTUS	R.E.M.	26	1998
LOUIE LOUIE	KINGSMEN	26	1964
LOUIE LOUIE	MOTORHEAD	68	1978
LOUIE LOUIE	FAT BOYS	46	1988
LOUIE LOUIE	THREE AMIGOS	15	1999
LOUIS QUATORZE	BOW WOW WOW	66	1982
LOUISE [A]	PHIL EVERLY	47	1982
LOUISE [B]	HUMAN LEAGUE	13	1984
LOUNGER	DOGS DIE IN HOT CARS	43	2004
LOUNGIN	LL COOL J	7	1996
L.O.V.E.	AL GREEN	24	1975
LOVE	JOHN LENNON	41	1982
LOVE	JIMMY NAIL	33	1995
LOVE ACTION (I BELIEVE IN LOVE)	HUMAN LEAGUE	3	1981
LOVE AIN'T GONNA WAIT FOR YOU	S CLUB	2	2003
LOVE AIN'T HERE ANYMORE	TAKE THAT	3	1994
LOVE AIN'T NO STRANGER	WHITESNAKE	44	1985
LOVE ALL DAY	NICK HEYWARD	31	1984
LOVE ALL THE HURT AWAY	ARETHA FRANKLIN & GEORGE BENSON	49	1981
LOVE AND AFFECTION	JOAN ARMATRADING	10	1976
LOVE AND AFFECTION	SINITTA	62	1990
LOVE AND AFFECTION	MR PINK PRESENTS THE PROGRAM	22	2002
LOVE AND ANGER	KATE BUSH	38	1990
LOVE AND DESIRE (PART 1)	ARPEGGIO	63	1979
LOVE & DEVOTION	(MC SAR &) THE REAL McCOY	11	1995
LOVE AND HAPPINESS (YEMAYA Y OCHUN)	RIVER OCEAN FEATURING INDIA	50	1994
LOVE AND KISSES	DANNII MINOGUE	8	1991
LOVE AND LONELINESS	MOTORS	58	1980
LOVE AND MARRIAGE	FRANK SINATRA	3	1956
LOVE AND MONEY	LOVE & MONEY	68	1987
LOVE AND PAIN [A]	CARLTON	56	1991
LOVE & PAIN [B]	CLOR	48	2005
LOVE AND PRIDE	KING	2	1985
LOVE AND REGRET	DEACON BLUE	28	1989
LOVE AND TEARS	NAOMI CAMPBELL	40	1994
LOVE AND UNDERSTANDING	CHER	10	1991
LOVE ANYWAY	MIKE SCOTT	50	1997
LOVE AT FIRST SIGHT [A]	KYLIE MINOGUE	2	2002
LOVE @ 1ST SIGHT [B]	MARY J BLIGE FEATURING METHOD MAN	18	2003
LOVE AT FIRST SIGHT (JE T'AIME...MOI NON PLUS)	SOUNDS NICE	18	1969
LOVE ATTACK	SHAKIN' STEVENS	28	1989
LOVE BALLAD	GEORGE BENSON	29	1979
LOVE BE MY LOVER (PLAYA SOL)	NOVACANE VS NO ONE DRIVING	69	2002
LOVE BITES	DEF LEPPARD	11	1988
LOVE BLONDE	KIM WILDE	23	1983
LOVE BOMB BABY	TIGERTAILZ	75	1989
LOVE BREAKDOWN	ROZALLA	65	1992
LOVE BUG	RAMSEY & FEN FEATURING LYNSEY MOORE	75	2000
LOVE BUG – SWEETS FOR MY SWEET (MEDLEY)	TINA CHARLES	26	1977
LOVE BURNS	BLACK REBEL MOTORCYCLE CLUB	37	2002
LOVE CAN BUILD A BRIDGE	CHILDREN FOR RWANDA	57	1994
LOVE CAN BUILD A BRIDGE	CHER, CHRISSIE HYNDE & NENEH CHERRY WITH ERIC CLAPTON	1	1995
LOVE CAN MOVE MOUNTAINS	CELINE DION	46	1992
LOVE CAN'T TURN AROUND	FARLEY 'JACKMASTER' FUNK	10	1986
LOVE CAN'T TURN AROUND	HEAVY WEATHER	56	1996
THE LOVE CATS	CURE	7	1983
LOVE CHANGES EVERYTHING [A]	CLIMIE FISHER	2	1987
LOVE CHANGES EVERYTHING [B]	MICHAEL BALL	2	1989
LOVE CHILD [A]	DIANA ROSS & THE SUPREMES	15	1968
LOVE CHILD [B]	GOODBYE MR MACKENZIE	52	1990
LOVE CITY GROOVE	LOVE CITY GROOVE	7	1995
LOVE COME DOWN [A]	EVELYN KING	7	1982
LOVE COME DOWN [A]	ALISON LIMERICK	36	1994
LOVE COME DOWN [B]	EVE GALLAGHER	57	1990
LOVE COME HOME	OUR TRIBE WITH FRANKE PHAROAH & KRISTINE W	73	1994
LOVE COME RESCUE ME	LOVESTATION	42	1995
LOVE COMES	BANANARAMA	44	2009
LOVE COMES AGAIN	TIESTO FEATURING BT	30	2004
LOVE COMES QUICKLY	PET SHOP BOYS	19	1986

	Peak Position	Year of Release
LOVE COMES TO MIND CHIMES	49	1990
LOVE COMMANDMENTS GISELE JACKSON	54	1997
LOVE CONQUERS ALL [A] DEEP PURPLE	57	1991
LOVE CONQUERS ALL [B] ABC	47	1991
LOVE DANCE VISION	74	1983
LOVE DETECTIVE ARAB STRAP	66	2001
LOVE DISCO STYLE EROTIC DRUM BAND	47	1979
LOVE DOESN'T HAVE TO HURT ATOMIC KITTEN	4	2003
LOVE DON'T COME EASY ALARM	48	1990
LOVE DON'T COST A THING JENNIFER LOPEZ	1	2001
LOVE DON'T LET ME GO DAVID GUETTA FEATURING CHRIS WILLIS	46	2002
LOVE DON'T LET ME GO (WALKING AWAY) DAVID GUETTA VS THE EGG	3	2006
LOVE DON'T LIVE URBAN BLUES PROJECT PRESENTS MICHAEL PROCTER	55	1996
LOVE DON'T LIVE HERE ANYMORE ROSE ROYCE	2	1978
LOVE DON'T LIVE HERE ANYMORE JIMMY NAIL	3	1985
LOVE DON'T LIVE HERE ANYMORE DOUBLE TROUBLE FEATURING JANETTE SEWELL & CARL BROWN	21	1990
LOVE DON'T LOVE YOU EN VOGUE	64	1993
LOVE ENOUGH FOR TWO PRIMA DONNA	48	1980
LOVE ENUFF SOUL II SOUL	12	1995
LOVE ETC PET SHOP BOYS	14	2009
LOVE EVICTION QUARTZ LOCK FEATURING LONNIE GORDON	32	1995
LOVE FOOLOSOPHY JAMIROQUAI	14	2002
LOVE FOR LIFE LISA MOORISH	37	1996
THE LOVE GAME MUDLARKS	30	1959
LOVE GAMES [A] DRIFTERS	33	1975
LOVE GAMES [B] LEVEL 42	38	1981
LOVE GAMES [C] BELLE & THE DEVOTIONS	11	1984
LOVE GENERATION BOB SINCLAR FEATURING GARY NESTA PINE	12	2005
LOVE GLOVE VISAGE	54	1984
LOVE GROOVE (GROOVE WITH YOU) SMOOTH	46	1996
LOVE GROWS (WHERE MY ROSEMARY GOES) EDISON LIGHTHOUSE	1	1970
LOVE GUARANTEED DAMAGE	7	1997
LOVE HANGOVER [A] DIANA ROSS	10	1976
LOVE HANGOVER [A] ASSOCIATES	21	1982
LOVE HANGOVER [A] PAULINE HENRY	37	1995
LOVE HANGOVER [B] SCARLET	54	1995
LOVE HAS COME AGAIN HUMAN MOVEMENT FEATURING SOPHIE MOLET	53	2001
LOVE HAS COME AROUND DONALD BYRD	41	1981
LOVE HAS FOUND ITS WAY DENNIS BROWN	47	1982
LOVE HAS GONE DAVE ARMSTRONG & REDROCHE FEATURING H-BOOGIE	43	2008
LOVE HAS PASSED AWAY SUPERNATURALS	38	1997
LOVE HER WALKER BROTHERS	20	1965
LOVE HERE I COME BAD BOYS INC	26	1994
LOVE HIT ME MAXINE NIGHTINGALE	11	1977
LOVE HOUSE SAMANTHA FOX	32	1988
LOVE HOW YOU FEEL SHARON REDD	39	1983
LOVE HURTS [A] JIM CAPALDI	4	1975
LOVE HURTS [A] CHER	43	1991
LOVE HURTS [B] PETER POLYCARPOU	26	1993
THE LOVE I LOST HAROLD MELVIN & THE BLUENOTES	21	1974
THE LOVE I LOST WEST END FEATURING SYBIL	3	1993
LOVE IN A PEACEFUL WORLD LEVEL 42	31	1994
LOVE IN A TRASHCAN RAVEONETTES	26	2005
LOVE IN AN ELEVATOR AEROSMITH	13	1989
LOVE IN ANGER ARMOURY SHOW	63	1987
LOVE IN C MINOR CERRONE	31	1977
LOVE IN ITSELF.2 DEPECHE MODE	21	1983
LOVE IN THE FIRST DEGREE BANANARAMA	3	1987
LOVE IN THE KEY OF C BELINDA CARLISLE	20	1996
LOVE IN THE NATURAL WAY KIM WILDE	32	1989
LOVE IN THE SUN GLITTER BAND	15	1975
LOVE IN THIS CLUB USHER FEATURING YOUNG JEEZY	4	2008
THE LOVE IN YOUR EYES VICKY LEANDROS	40	1973
THE LOVE IN YOUR EYES DANIEL O'DONNELL	47	1993
LOVE INFINITY SILVER CITY	62	1993
LOVE INJECTION TRUSSEL	43	1980
LOVE INSIDE SHARON FORRESTER	50	1995
LOVE IS...[A] VIKKI	49	1985
LOVE IS [B] ALANNAH MYLES	61	1990
LOVE IS A BATTLEFIELD PAT BENATAR	17	1984
LOVE IS A BEAUTIFUL THING AL GREEN	56	1993
LOVE IS A DESERTER KILLS	44	2005
LOVE IS A GOLDEN RING FRANKIE LAINE	19	1957
LOVE IS A HURRICANE BOYZONE	72	2010
LOVE IS A KILLER VIXEN	41	1990
LOVE IS A LOSING GAME AMY WINEHOUSE	46	2007
LOVE IS A MANY SPLENDOURED THING FOUR ACES FEATURING AL ALBERTS	2	1955
LOVE IS A STRANGER EURYTHMICS	6	1982
LOVE IS A WONDERFUL COLOUR ICICLE WORKS	15	1984
LOVE IS A WONDERFUL THING MICHAEL BOLTON	23	1991
LOVE IS ALL [A] MALCOLM ROBERTS	12	1969
LOVE IS ALL [A] ENGELBERT HUMPERDINCK	44	1973
LOVE IS ALL [B] RAPTURE	38	2004
LOVE IS ALL AROUND [A] TROGGS	5	1967
LOVE IS ALL AROUND [A] WET WET WET	1	1994
LOVE IS ALL AROUND [B] DJ BOBO	49	1995
LOVE IS ALL IS ALRIGHT UB40	29	1982
LOVE IS ALL THAT MATTERS HUMAN LEAGUE	41	1988
LOVE IS ALL WE NEED MARY J BLIGE	15	1997
LOVE IS AN ARROW ABERFELDY	60	2005
LOVE IS AN UNFAMILIAR NAME DUKE SPIRIT	33	2005
LOVE IS BLUE [A] JEFF BECK	23	1968
LOVE IS BLUE [B] EDWARD BALL	59	1997
LOVE IS BLUE (L'AMOUR EST BLEU) [A] PAUL MAURIAT	12	1968
LOVE IS CONTAGIOUS TAJA SEVELLE	7	1988
LOVE IS DEAD BRETT ANDERSON	42	2007
LOVE IS EVERYWHERE CICERO	19	1992
LOVE IS FOREVER BILLY OCEAN	34	1987
LOVE IS GONE DAVID GUETTA	9	2007
LOVE IS HERE AND NOW YOU'RE GONE SUPREMES	17	1967
LOVE IS HOLY KIM WILDE	16	1992
LOVE IS IN CONTROL (FINGER ON THE TRIGGER) DONNA SUMMER	18	1982
LOVE IS IN THE AIR JOHN PAUL YOUNG	5	1978
LOVE IS IN THE AIR MILK & SUGAR/JOHN PAUL YOUNG	25	2002
LOVE IS IN YOUR EYES LEMON TREES	75	1992
LOVE IS JUST THE GREAT PRETENDER ANIMAL NIGHTLIFE	28	1985
LOVE IS LIFE HOT CHOCOLATE	6	1970
LOVE IS LIKE A VIOLIN KEN DODD	8	1960
LOVE IS LIKE OXYGEN SWEET	9	1978
LOVE IS LOVE BARRY RYAN	25	1969
LOVE IS NOISE VERVE	4	2008
LOVE IS NOT A GAME J MAJIK FEATURING KATHY BROWN	34	2001
LOVE IS ON THE ONE XAVIER	53	1982
LOVE IS ON THE WAY LUTHER VANDROSS	38	1993
LOVE IS ONLY A FEELING DARKNESS	5	2004
LOVE IS SO EASY STARGARD	45	1978
LOVE IS SO NICE URBAN SOUL	75	1998
LOVE IS STRANGE EVERLY BROTHERS	11	1965
LOVE IS STRONG ROLLING STONES	14	1994
LOVE IS STRONGER THAN DEATH THE THE	39	1993
LOVE IS STRONGER THAN PRIDE SADE	44	1988
LOVE IS THE ANSWER ENGLAND DAN & JOHN FORD COLEY	45	1979
LOVE IS THE ART LIVING IN A BOX	45	1988
LOVE IS THE DRUG ROXY MUSIC	2	1975
LOVE IS THE DRUG GRACE JONES	35	1986
LOVE IS THE GOD MARIA NAYLER	65	1998
LOVE IS THE GUN BLUE MERCEDES	46	1988
LOVE IS THE ICON BARRY WHITE	20	1995
LOVE IS THE KEY CHARLATANS	16	2001
LOVE IS THE LAW SEAHORSES	3	1997
LOVE IS THE MESSAGE LOVE INCORPORATED FEATURING MC NOISE	59	1991
LOVE IS THE SEVENTH WAVE STING	41	1985
LOVE IS THE SLUG WE'VE GOT A FUZZBOX & WE'RE GONNA USE IT	31	1986
LOVE IS THE SWEETEST THING PETER SKELLERN FEATURING GRIMETHORPE COLLIERY BAND	60	1978
(LOVE IS) THE TENDER TRAP FRANK SINATRA	2	1956
LOVE IS WAR BRILLIANT	64	1986
LOVE IT WHEN YOU CALL FEELING	18	2006
LOVE IZ ERICK SERMON	72	2003
LOVE KILLS [A] FREDDIE MERCURY	10	1984
LOVE KILLS [B] JOE STRUMMER	69	1986
LOVE KISSES AND HEARTACHES MAUREEN EVANS	44	1960
LOVE LADY DAMAGE	33	1997
LOVE LETTER MARC ALMOND	68	1985
LOVE LETTERS [A] KETTY LESTER	4	1962
LOVE LETTERS [A] ELVIS PRESLEY	6	1966
LOVE LETTERS [A] ALISON MOYET	4	1987
LOVE LETTERS [B] ALI	63	1998
LOVE LETTERS IN THE SAND PAT BOONE	2	1957
LOVE LETTERS IN THE SAND VINCE HILL	23	1967
LOVE LIES LOST HELEN TERRY	34	1984
LOVE LIGHT IN FLIGHT STEVIE WONDER	44	1984
LOVE LIKE A FOUNTAIN IAN BROWN	23	1999
LOVE LIKE A MAN TEN YEARS AFTER	3	1970
LOVE LIKE A RIVER CLIMIE FISHER	22	1989
LOVE LIKE A ROCKET BOB GELDOF	61	1987
LOVE LIKE BLOOD KILLING JOKE	16	1985
LOVE LIKE THIS [A] FAITH EVANS	24	1998
LOVE LIKE THIS [B] NATASHA BEDINGFIELD FEATURING SEAN KINGSTON	20	2008
LOVE LIKE YOU AND ME GARY GLITTER	10	1975
A LOVE LIKE YOURS IKE & TINA TURNER	16	1966
LOVE LOCKDOWN KANYE WEST	8	2008
L.O.V.E...LOVE ORANGE JUICE	65	1981
LOVE LOVE LOVE BOBBY HEBB	32	1972
LOVE, LOVE, LOVE – HERE I COME ROLLO GOES MYSTIC	32	1995
LOVE LOVES TO LOVE LOVE LULU	32	1967
LOVE MACHINE [A] ELVIS PRESLEY	38	1967
LOVE MACHINE (PART 1) [B] MIRACLES	3	1976
LOVE MACHINE [C] GIRLS ALOUD	2	2004
LOVE MADE ME VIXEN	36	1989
LOVE MAKES NO SENSE ALEXANDER O'NEAL	26	1993
LOVE MAKES THE WORLD GO ROUND [A] PERRY COMO	6	1958
LOVE MAKES THE WORLD GO ROUND [A] JETS	21	1982
LOVE MAKES THE WORLD GO ROUND [B] DON-E	18	1992
LOVE MAN OTIS REDDING	43	1969
LOVE ME [A] DIANA ROSS	38	1974
LOVE ME [B] YVONNE ELLIMAN	6	1976
LOVE ME [B] MARTINE McCUTCHEON	6	1999
LOVE ME [C] PATRIC	54	1994
LOVE ME [D] JUSTIN BIEBER	71	2010
LOVE ME AND LEAVE ME SEAHORSES	16	1997

Title	Artist	Peak Position	Year of Release
LOVE ME AS THOUGH THERE WERE NO TOMORROW	NAT 'KING' COLE	11	1956
LOVE ME BABY	SUSAN CADOGAN	22	1975
LOVE ME DO	BEATLES	4	1962
LOVE ME FOR A REASON	OSMONDS	1	1974
LOVE ME FOR A REASON	BOYZONE	2	1994
LOVE ME FOREVER	MARION RYAN	5	1958
LOVE ME FOREVER	EYDIE GORME	21	1958
LOVE ME FOREVER	FOUR ESQUIRES	23	1958
LOVE ME LIKE A LOVER	TINA CHARLES	31	1976
LOVE ME LIKE I LOVE YOU	BAY CITY ROLLERS	4	1976
LOVE ME LIKE THIS	REAL TO REEL	68	1984
LOVE ME LIKE YOU	MAGIC NUMBERS	12	2005
LOVE ME LOVE MY DOG	PETER SHELLEY	3	1975
LOVE ME NOW [A]	BRIANA CORRIGAN	48	1996
LOVE ME NOW [B]	SECRET KNOWLEDGE	66	1996
LOVE ME OR HATE ME	LADY SOVEREIGN	26	2007
LOVE ME OR LEAVE ME	SAMMY DAVIS, JR	8	1955
LOVE ME OR LEAVE ME	DORIS DAY	20	1955
LOVE ME RIGHT NOW	ROSE ROYCE	60	1985
LOVE ME RIGHT (OH SHEILA)	ANGEL CITY FEATURING LARA McALLEN	11	2003
LOVE ME TENDER	ELVIS PRESLEY	11	1956
LOVE ME TENDER	RICHARD CHAMBERLAIN	15	1962
LOVE ME TENDER	ROLAND RAT SUPERSTAR	32	1984
LOVE ME THE RIGHT WAY	RAPINATION & KYM MAZELLE	22	1993
LOVE ME TO SLEEP	HOT CHOCOLATE	50	1980
LOVE ME TONIGHT [A]	TOM JONES	9	1969
LOVE ME TONIGHT [B]	TREVOR WALTERS	27	1981
LOVE ME WARM AND TENDER	PAUL ANKA	19	1962
LOVE ME WITH ALL YOUR HEART	KARL DENVER	37	1964
LOVE MEETING LOVE	LEVEL 42	61	1980
LOVE MISSILE F1-11	SIGUE SIGUE SPUTNIK	3	1986
LOVE MOVES IN MYSTERIOUS WAYS	JULIA FORDHAM	19	1992
LOVE MY WAY	PSYCHEDELIC FURS	42	1982
LOVE NEEDS NO DISGUISE	GARY NUMAN & DRAMATIS	33	1981
LOVE NEVER DIES...	BELINDA CARLISLE	54	1988
LOVE OF A LIFETIME [A]	CHAKA KHAN	52	1986
LOVE OF A LIFETIME [B]	HONEYZ	9	1999
LOVE OF MY LIFE [A]	DOOLEYS	9	1977
LOVE OF MY LIFE [B]	QUEEN	63	1979
THE LOVE OF RICHARD NIXON	MANIC STREET PREACHERS	2	2004
LOVE OF THE COMMON PEOPLE	NICKY THOMAS	9	1970
LOVE OF THE COMMON PEOPLE	PAUL YOUNG	2	1983
LOVE OF THE LOVED	CILLA BLACK	35	1963
LOVE OH LOVE	LIONEL RICHIE	52	1992
LOVE ON A FARMBOY'S WAGES	XTC	50	1983
LOVE ON A MOUNTAIN TOP	ROBERT KNIGHT	10	1973
LOVE ON A MOUNTAIN TOP	SINITTA	20	1989
LOVE ON A SUMMER NIGHT	McCRARYS	52	1982
LOVE ON LOVE	E-ZEE POSSEE	59	1990
LOVE ON LOVE	CANDI STATON	27	1999
LOVE ON MY MIND	FREEMASONS FEATURING AMANDA WILSON	11	2005
LOVE ON THE LINE [A]	BARCLAY JAMES HARVEST	63	1980
LOVE ON THE LINE [B]	BLAZIN' SQUAD	6	2002
LOVE ON THE NORTHERN LINE	NORTHERN LINE	15	2000
LOVE ON THE ROCKS	NEIL DIAMOND	17	1980
LOVE ON THE RUN	CHICANE FEATURING PETER CUNNAH	33	2003
LOVE ON THE SIDE	BROKEN ENGLISH	69	1987
LOVE ON YOUR SIDE	THOMPSON TWINS	9	1983
LOVE OR MONEY [A]	BLACKWELLS	46	1961
LOVE OR MONEY [A]	JIMMY CRAWFORD	49	1961

Title	Artist	Peak Position	Year of Release
LOVE OR MONEY [A]	BILLY FURY	57	1982
LOVE OR MONEY [B]	SAMMY HAGAR	67	1980
LOVE OR NOTHING	DIANA BROWN & BARRIE K SHARPE	71	1991
LOVE OVER GOLD (LIVE)	DIRE STRAITS	50	1984
LOVE OVERBOARD	GLADYS KNIGHT & THE PIPS	42	1988
LOVE PAINS	HAZELL DEAN	48	1989
LOVE PAINS	LIZA MINNELLI	41	1990
THE LOVE PARADE	DREAM ACADEMY	68	1985
LOVE PATROL	DOOLEYS	29	1980
LOVE, PEACE & GREASE	BT	41	1997
LOVE, PEACE & NAPPINESS	LOST BOYZ	57	1997
LOVE PEACE AND UNDERSTANDING	DREAM FREQUENCY	71	1991
LOVE PLUS ONE	HAIRCUT 100	3	1982
LOVE POTION NO. 9	TYGERS OF PAN TANG	45	1982
LOVE POWER	DIONNE WARWICK & JEFFREY OSBORNE	63	1987
LOVE PROFUSION	MADONNA	11	2003
LOVE REACTION	DIVINE	65	1983
LOVE REALLY HURTS WITHOUT YOU	BILLY OCEAN	2	1976
LOVE REARS ITS UGLY HEAD	LIVING COLOUR	12	1991
LOVE REMOVAL MACHINE	CULT	18	1987
LOVE RENDEZVOUS	M PEOPLE	32	1995
LOVE RESURRECTION	ALISON MOYET	10	1984
LOVE RESURRECTION	D'LUX	58	1996
LOVE REVOLUTION	PHIXX	13	2004
LOVE ROLLERCOASTER	RED HOT CHILI PEPPERS	7	1997
LOVE RULES	WEST END	44	1995
THE LOVE SCENE	JOE	22	1997
LOVE SCENES	BEVERLEY CRAVEN	34	1993
LOVE SEE NO COLOUR	FARM	35	1991
LOVE SENSATION	911	21	1996
LOVE SENSATION '06	LOLEATTA HOLLOWAY	37	2006
LOVE SENSATION 2006	EDDIE THONEICK & KURD MAVERICK	39	2006
LOVE SEX MAGIC	CIARA FEATURING JUSTIN TIMBERLAKE	5	2009
LOVE SHACK	B-52's	2	1990
LOVE SHADOW	FASHION	51	1982
LOVE SHINE	RHYTHM SOURCE	74	1995
LOVE SHINE A LIGHT	KATRINA & THE WAVES	3	1997
LOVE SHINES THROUGH	CHAKRA	67	1999
LOVE SHOULD BE A CRIME	O-TOWN	38	2002
LOVE SHOULDA BROUGHT YOU HOME	TONI BRAXTON	33	1994
LOVE SHY	KRISTINE BLOND	22	1998
LOVE SHY	PLATNUM	12	2008
LOVE SICK	BOB DYLAN	64	1998
LOVE SITUATION	MARK FISHER FEATURING DOTTY GREEN	59	1985
LOVE SLAVE	WEDDING PRESENT	17	1992
LOVE SNEAKIN' UP ON YOU	BONNIE RAITT	69	1994
A LOVE SO BEAUTIFUL	MICHAEL BOLTON	27	1995
LOVE SO BRIGHT	MARK SHAW	54	1990
LOVE SO RIGHT	BEE GEES	41	1976
LOVE SO STRONG	SECRET LIFE	37	1993
LOVE SONG [A]	DAMNED	20	1979
LOVE SONG [B]	SIMPLE MINDS	6	1981
LOVE SONG [C]	UTAH SAINTS	37	2000
LOVE SONG [D]	SARA BAREILLES	4	2008
LOVE SONG FOR A VAMPIRE	ANNIE LENNOX	3	1993
LOVE SONGS ARE BACK AGAIN (MEDLEY)	BAND OF GOLD	24	1984
THE LOVE SONGS EP	DANIEL O'DONNELL	27	1997
LOVE SPREADS	STONE ROSES	2	1994
LOVE STEALS US FROM LONELINESS	IDLEWILD	16	2005
LOVE STIMULATION	HUMATE	18	1999

Title	Artist	Peak Position	Year of Release
LOVE STORY [A]	JETHRO TULL	29	1969
LOVE STORY [B]	LAYO & BUSHWACKA!	8	2002
LOVE STORY [C]	TAYLOR SWIFT	2	2009
LOVE STRAIN	KYM MAZELLE	52	1989
A LOVE SUPREME	WILL DOWNING	14	1988
LOVE TAKE OVER	FIVE STAR	25	1985
LOVE TAKES TIME	MARIAH CAREY	37	1990
LOVE THE LIFE	JTQ WITH NOEL McKOY	34	1993
LOVE THE ONE YOU'RE WITH	STEPHEN STILLS	37	1971
LOVE THE ONE YOU'RE WITH	BUCKS FIZZ	47	1986
LOVE THE ONE YOU'RE WITH	LUTHER VANDROSS	31	1994
LOVE THEM	EAMON FEATURING GHOSTFACE	27	2004
LOVE THEME FROM 'A STAR IS BORN' (EVERGREEN)	BARBRA STREISAND	3	1977
LOVE THEME FROM SPARTACUS	TERRY CALLIER	57	1998
LOVE THEME FROM THE GODFATHER	ANDY WILLIAMS	42	1972
LOVE THEME FROM 'THE THORN BIRDS'	JUAN MARTIN	10	1984
LOVE THING [A]	PASADENAS	22	1990
LOVE THING [B]	TINA TURNER	29	1992
LOVE THING [C]	EVOLUTION	32	1993
LOVE...THY WILL BE DONE	MARTIKA	9	1991
LOVE TIMES LOVE	HEAVY PETTIN'	69	1984
LOVE TO HATE YOU	ERASURE	4	1991
LOVE II LOVE	DAMAGE	12	1996
LOVE TO LOVE YOU	CORRS	62	1997
LOVE TO LOVE YOU BABY	DONNA SUMMER	4	1976
LOVE TO SEE YOU CRY	ENRIQUE IGLESIAS	12	2002
LOVE TO STAY	ALTERED IMAGES	46	1983
LOVE TODAY	MIKA	6	2007
LOVE TOGETHER	L.A. MIX FEATURING KEVIN HENRY	66	1989
LOVE TOUCH	ROD STEWART	27	1986
LOVE TOWN	BOOKER NEWBURY III	6	1983
LOVE TRAIN [A]	O'JAYS	9	1973
LOVE TRAIN [B]	HOLLY JOHNSON	4	1989
LOVE TRAIN [C]	WOLFMOTHER	62	2006
LOVE TRIAL	KELLY MARIE	51	1981
LOVE, TRUTH AND HONESTY	BANANARAMA	23	1988
LOVE U 4 LIFE	JODECI	23	1995
LOVE U MORE	SUNSCREEM	23	1992
LOVE UNLIMITED	FUN LOVIN' CRIMINALS	18	1998
LOVE WALKED IN	THUNDER	21	1991
LOVE WARS	WOMACK & WOMACK	14	1984
LOVE WASHES OVER	ART OF TRANCE	60	2002
LOVE WHAT YOU DO	DIVINE COMEDY	26	2001
LOVE WILL COME	TOMSKI FEATURING JAN JOHNSTON	31	2000
LOVE WILL COME THROUGH	TRAVIS	28	2004
LOVE WILL CONQUER ALL	LIONEL RICHIE	45	1986
LOVE WILL FIND A WAY [A]	DAVID GRANT	24	1983
LOVE WILL FIND A WAY [B]	YES	73	1987
LOVE WILL FIND A WAY [C]	DELIRIOUS?	55	2008
LOVE WILL KEEP US ALIVE	EAGLES	52	1996
LOVE WILL KEEP US TOGETHER	CAPTAIN & TENNILLE	32	1975
LOVE WILL KEEP US TOGETHER	JTQ FEATURING ALISON LIMERICK	63	1995
LOVE WILL LEAD YOU BACK	TAYLOR DAYNE	69	1990
LOVE WILL MAKE YOU FAIL IN SCHOOL	ROCKY SHARPE & THE REPLAYS FEATURING THE TOP LINERS	60	1979
LOVE WILL NEVER DO (WITHOUT YOU)	JANET JACKSON	34	1990
LOVE WILL SAVE THE DAY	WHITNEY HOUSTON	10	1988
LOVE WILL SET YOU FREE (JAMBE MYTH)	STARCHASER	24	2002
LOVE WILL TEAR US APART	JOY DIVISION	13	1980

	Peak Position	Year of Release
LOVE WILL TEAR US APART HONEYROOT	70	2005
LOVE WON'T LET ME WAIT MAJOR HARRIS	37	1975
LOVE WON'T WAIT GARY BARLOW	1	1997
LOVE WORTH DYING FOR THUNDER	60	1997
A LOVE WORTH WAITING FOR SHAKIN' STEVENS	2	1984
LOVE X LOVE GEORGE BENSON	10	1980
LOVE YA UNKLEJAM	54	2007
LOVE YOU ALL MY LIFETIME CHAKA KHAN	49	1992
LOVE YOU ANYWAY DE NADA	15	2001
LOVE YOU BETTER MACCABEES	36	2009
LOVE YOU DOWN READY FOR THE WORLD	60	1987
LOVE YOU INSIDE OUT BEE GEES	13	1979
LOVE YOU LIKE MAD VS	7	2004
LOVE YOU MORE BUZZCOCKS	34	1978
THE LOVE YOU SAVE JACKSON 5	7	1970
LOVE YOU SOME MORE CEVIN FISHER FEATURING SHEILA SMITH	60	2001
LOVE YOU TOO MUCH HOUSE OF LOVE	73	2005
LOVE YOUR MONEY DAISY CHAINSAW	26	1992
LOVE YOUR SEXY...!! BYKER GROOOVE!	48	1994
LOVE ZONE BILLY OCEAN	49	1986
LOVEBIRDS DODGY	65	1993
LOVEDRIVE SCORPIONS	69	1979
LOVEFOOL CARDIGANS	2	1996
LOVEGAME LADY GAGA	19	2009
LOVELIGHT ROBBIE WILLIAMS	8	2006
LOVELIGHT (RIDE ON A LOVE TRAIN) JAYN HANNA	42	1996
LOVELY BUBBA SPARXXX	24	2002
LOVELY DAUGHTER MERZ	60	1999
LOVELY DAY BILL WITHERS	4	1978
LOVELY DAZE JAZZY JEFF & FRESH PRINCE	37	1998
LOVELY MONEY DAMNED	42	1982
LOVELY ONE JACKSONS	29	1980
LOVELY THING REGGAE PHILHARMONIC ORCHESTRA	71	1990
LOVENEST WEDDING PRESENT	58	1991
LOVER [A] JOE ROBERTS	22	1994
LOVER [B] DAN REED NETWORK	45	1990
LOVER [C] RACHEL McFARLANE	36	1998
LOVER COME BACK TO ME DEAD OR ALIVE	11	1985
THE LOVER IN ME SHEENA EASTON	15	1989
THE LOVER IN YOU SUGARHILL GANG	54	1982
LOVER LOVER LOVER IAN McCULLOCH	47	1992
LOVER PLEASE VERNONS GIRLS	16	1962
A LOVER SPURNED MARC ALMOND	29	1990
THE LOVER THAT YOU ARE PULSE FEATURING ANTOINETTE ROBERSON	22	1996
LOVERBOY [A] BILLY OCEAN	15	1985
LOVERBOY [B] CHAIRMEN OF THE BOARD FEATURING GENERAL JOHNSON	56	1986
LOVERBOY [C] MARIAH CAREY	12	2001
LOVERIDE NUANCE FEATURING VIKKI LOVE	59	1985
THE LOVERS [A] ALEXANDER O'NEAL	28	1988
LOVERS [B] TEARS	24	2005
LOVERS & FRIENDS LIL JON & THE EAST SIDE BOYZ	10	2005
THE LOVERS ARE LOSING KEANE	52	2008
A LOVER'S CONCERTO TOYS	5	1965
A LOVERS HOLIDAY CHANGE	14	1980
LOVER'S LANE GEORGIO	54	1988
LOVERS OF THE WORLD UNITE DAVID & JONATHAN	7	1966
THE LOVERS WE WERE MICHAEL BALL	63	1994
LOVE'S A GAME MAGIC NUMBERS	24	2005
LOVE'S A LOADED GUN ALICE COOPER	38	1991
LOVE'S A PRIMA DONNA STEVE HARLEY	41	1976
LOVE'S ABOUT TO CHANGE MY HEART DONNA SUMMER	20	1989
LOVE'S BEEN GOOD TO ME FRANK SINATRA	8	1969
LOVE'S COMIN' AT YA MELBA MOORE	15	1982
LOVE'S CRASHING WAVES DIFFORD & TILBROOK	57	1984
LOVE'S DIVINE SEAL	68	2003
LOVE'S EASY TEARS COCTEAU TWINS	53	1986
LOVE'S GONNA GET YOU [A] UK PLAYERS	52	1983
LOVE'S GONNA GET YOU [B] JOCELYN BROWN	70	1986
LOVE'S GOT A HOLD ON MY HEART STEPS	2	1999
LOVE'S GOT ME LOOSE ENDS	40	1990
LOVE'S GOT ME ON A TRIP SO HIGH LONI CLARK	59	1994
LOVE'S GOTTA HOLD ON ME [A] DOLLAR	4	1979
LOVE'S GOTTA HOLD ON ME [B] ZOO EXPERIENCE FEATURING DESTRY	66	1992
LOVE'S GREAT ADVENTURE ULTRAVOX	12	1984
LOVE'S JUST A BROKEN HEART CILLA BLACK	5	1966
LOVE'S MADE A FOOL OF YOU CRICKETS	26	1959
LOVE'S MADE A FOOL OF YOU BUDDY HOLLY	39	1964
LOVE'S MADE A FOOL OF YOU MATCHBOX	63	1981
LOVES ME LIKE A ROCK PAUL SIMON	39	1973
LOVE'S ON EVERY CORNER DANNII MINOGUE	44	1992
LOVE'S SUCH A WONDERFUL THING REAL THING	33	1977
LOVE'S SWEET EXILE MANIC STREET PREACHERS	26	1991
LOVE'S TAKEN OVER CHANTE MOORE	54	1993
LOVE'S THEME LOVE UNLIMITED ORCHESTRA	10	1974
LOVE'S UNKIND DONNA SUMMER	3	1977
LOVE'S UNKIND SOPHIE LAWRENCE	21	1991
LOVESICK [A] GANG STARR	50	1991
LOVESICK [B] UNDERCOVER FEATURING JOHN MATTHEWS	62	1993
LOVESICK BLUES FRANK IFIELD	1	1962
LOVESONG CURE	18	1989
LOVESTONED I THINK SHE KNOWS JUSTIN TIMBERLAKE	11	2007
LOVESTRUCK MADNESS	10	1999
LOVETOWN PETER GABRIEL	49	1994
LOVEY DOVEY TONY TERRY	44	1988
LOVIN' CRW	49	2000
LOVIN' EACH DAY RONAN KEATING	2	2001
LOVIN' IS EASY HEAR'SAY	6	2002
LOVIN' (LET ME LOVE YOU) APACHE INDIAN	53	1997
LOVIN' LIVIN' AND GIVIN' DIANA ROSS	54	1978
LOVIN' ON THE SIDE REID	71	1989
LOVIN' THINGS MARMALADE	6	1968
LOVIN' UP A STORM JERRY LEE LEWIS	28	1959
LOVIN' YOU [A] SHANICE	54	1992
LOVIN' YOU [A] UBM	46	1998
LOVIN' YOU [B] POKER PETS FEATURING NATE JAMES	43	2005
LOVIN' YOU MORE STEVE MAC VS MOSQUITO FEATURING STEVE SMITH	73	2005
LOVIN' YOU YOU SPARKLE	65	1999
LOVING AND FREE KIKI DEE	13	1976
LOVING ARMS ELVIS PRESLEY	47	1981
LOVING EVERY MINUTE LIGHTHOUSE FAMILY	20	1996
LOVING JUST FOR FUN KELLY MARIE	21	1980
THE LOVING KIND GIRLS ALOUD	10	2008
LOVING ON THE LOSING SIDE TOMMY HUNT	28	1976
LOVING THE ALIEN DAVID BOWIE	19	1985
LOVING THE ALIEN SCUMFROG VS BOWIE	41	2002
LOVING YOU [A] ELVIS PRESLEY	24	1957
LOVING YOU [B] MINNIE RIPERTON	2	1975
LOVING YOU [B] MASSIVO FEATURING TRACY	25	1990
LOVING YOU '03 [B] MARC ET CLAUDE	37	2003
LOVING YOU [C] DONALD BYRD	41	1983
LOVING YOU [D] CHRIS REA	65	1982
LOVING YOU [E] FEARGAL SHARKEY	26	1985
LOVING YOU AGAIN CHRIS REA	47	1987
LOVING YOU AIN'T EASY PAGLIARO	31	1972
LOVING YOU HAS MADE ME BANANAS GUY MARKS	25	1978
LOVING YOU IS SWEETER THAN EVER FOUR TOPS	21	1966
LOVING YOU IS SWEETER THAN EVER NICK KAMEN	16	1987
LOVING YOU MORE BT FEATURING VINCENT COVELLO	14	1995
LOVING YOU (OLE OLE OLE) BRIAN HARVEY & THE REFUGEE CREW	20	2001
LOVING YOU'S A DIRTY JOB BUT SOMEBODY'S GOTTA DO IT BONNIE TYLER, GUEST VOALS TODD RUNDGREN	73	1985
LOW [A] CRACKER	43	1994
LOW [B] FOO FIGHTERS	21	2003
LOW [C] KELLY CLARKSON	35	2003
LOW [D] FLO RIDA FEATURING T-PAIN	2	2008
LOW C SUPERGRASS	52	2005
LOW FIVE SNEAKER PIMPS	39	1999
LOW LIFE IN HIGH PLACES THUNDER	22	1992
LOW RIDER WAR	12	1976
LOWDOWN [A] BOZ SCAGGS	28	1976
LOWDOWN [A] HINDSIGHT	62	1987
LOWDOWN [B] ELECTRAFIXION	54	1995
LOWRIDER CYPRESS HILL	33	2001
THE LOYALISER FATIMA MANSIONS	58	1994
LSD (EP) KAOTIC CHEMISTRY	68	1992
LSF KASABIAN	10	2004
LSI SHAMEN	6	1992
LUCAS WITH THE LID OFF LUCAS	37	1994
LUCHINI AKA (THIS IS IT) CAMP LO	74	1997
LUCILLE [A] LITTLE RICHARD	10	1957
LUCILLE [A] EVERLY BROTHERS	4	1960
LUCILLE [B] KENNY ROGERS	1	1977
LUCKY BRITNEY SPEARS	5	2000
LUCKY 7 MEGAMIX UK MIXMASTERS	43	1991
LUCKY DEVIL FRANK IFIELD	22	1960
LUCKY DEVIL CARL DOBKINS, JR	44	1960
LUCKY FIVE RUSS CONWAY	14	1960
LUCKY LIKE THAT CLEA	55	2006
LUCKY LIPS CLIFF RICHARD	4	1963
LUCKY LOVE ACE OF BASE	20	1995
LUCKY LUCKY ME MARVIN GAYE	67	1994
LUCKY MAN VERVE	7	1997
LUCKY NUMBER LENE LOVICH	3	1979
THE LUCKY ONE LAURA BRANIGAN	56	1984
LUCKY ONE AMY GRANT	60	1994
LUCKY PRESSURE RONI SIZE/REPRAZENT	58	2001
LUCKY STAR [A] MADONNA	14	1984
LUCKY STAR [B] SUPERFUNK FEATURING RON CARROLL	42	2000
LUCKY STAR [C] BASEMENT JAXX FEATURING DIZZEE RASCAL	23	2002
LUCKY STARS DEAN FRIEDMAN	3	1978
LUCKY TOWN (LIVE) BRUCE SPRINGSTEEN	48	1993
LUCKY YOU LIGHTNING SEEDS	15	1994
LUCRETIA MY REFLECTION SISTERS OF MERCY	20	1988
LUCY [A] HABIT	56	1988
LUCY [B] JEALOUSY	30	2006
LUCY IN THE SKY WITH DIAMONDS ELTON JOHN	10	1974
LUDI DREAM WARRIORS	39	1991
LUKA SUZANNE VEGA	23	1987
LULLABY [A] CURE	5	1989
LULLABY [B] SHAWN MULLINS	9	1999
LULLABY [C] MELANIE B	13	2001
LULLABY [D] STARSAILOR	36	2001
LULLABY [E] LEMAR	5	2003
LULLABY OF BROADWAY WINIFRED SHAW	42	1976
LULLABY OF THE LEAVES VENTURES	43	1961
LUMBERED LONNIE DONEGAN	6	1961

	Peak Position	Year of Release
LUMP PRESIDENTS OF THE UNITED STATES OF AMERICA	15	1996
LUMP IN MY THROAT DEPARTURE	30	2005
THE LUNATICS (HAVE TAKEN OVER THE ASYLUM) FUN BOY THREE	20	1981
LUNCH OR DINNER SUNSHINE ANDERSON	57	2001
LUSH ORBITAL	43	1993
LUST FOR LIFE IGGY POP	26	1996
LUTON AIRPORT CATS UK	22	1979
LUV DA SUNSHINE INTENSO PROJECT	22	2002
LUV DUP HIGH FIDELITY	70	1998
LUV 4 LUV ROBIN S	11	1993
LUV IS COOL SYSTEM OF LIFE	63	2004
LUV ME LUV ME SHAGGY	5	2001
LUV U BETTER LL COOL J	7	2002
LUV'D UP CRUSH	45	1996
LUVSTRUCK SOUTHSIDE SPINNERS	9	2000
LUVSTUFF SAGAT	71	1994
LUXURIOUS GWEN STEFANI	44	2005
L'VIA L'VIAQUEZ MARS VOLTA	53	2005
LYDIA DEAN FRIEDMAN	31	1978
LYIN' EYES EAGLES	23	1975
LYING IS THE MOST FUN A GIRL CAN HAVE PANIC! AT THE DISCO	39	2006
LYLA OASIS	1	2005
LYRIC ZWAN	44	2003
LYRIC ON MY LIP TALI	39	2002

M

	Peak Position	Year of Release
MA BAKER BONEY M	2	1977
MA HE'S MAKING EYES AT ME JOHNNY OTIS & HIS ORCHESTRA WITH MARIE ADAMS & THE THREE TONS OF JOY	2	1957
MA HE'S MAKING EYES AT ME LENA ZAVARONI	10	1974
MA I DON'T LOVE HER CLIPSE FEATURING FAITH EVANS	38	2003
MA SAYS PA SAYS DORIS DAY & JOHNNIE RAY	12	1953
MA SOLITUDA CATHERINE WHEEL	53	1998
MACARENA LOS DEL RIO	2	1996
MACARENA LOS DEL MAR FEATURING WIL VELOZ	43	1996
MACARENA LOS DEL CHIPMUNKS	65	1996
MACARTHUR PARK RICHARD HARRIS	4	1968
MACARTHUR PARK DONNA SUMMER	5	1978
MACDONALD'S CAVE PILTDOWN MEN	14	1960
MACH 5 PRESIDENTS OF THE UNITED STATES OF AMERICA	29	1996
MACHINE YEAH YEAH YEAH	18	2002
MACHINE + SOUL GARY NUMAN	72	1992
MACHINE GUN [A] COMMODORES	20	1974
MACHINE GUN [B] PORTISHEAD	52	2008
MACHINE SAYS YES FC KAHUNA	58	2002
MACHINEHEAD BUSH	48	1996
MACHINERY SHEENA EASTON	38	1982
MACHINES BIFFY CLYRO	29	2007
MACK THE KNIFE BOBBY DARIN	1	1959
MACK THE KNIFE LOUIS ARMSTRONG WITH HIS ALL-STARS	24	1959
MACK THE KNIFE ELLA FITZGERALD	19	1960
MACK THE KNIFE KING KURT	55	1984
MACUSHLA BERNIE NOLAN	38	2004
MAD NE-YO	19	2008
MAD ABOUT THE BOY DINAH WASHINGTON	41	1992
MAD ABOUT YOU [A] BRUCE RUFFIN	9	1972
MAD ABOUT YOU [B] BELINDA CARLISLE	67	1988
MAD ABOUT YOU [C] STING	56	1991
MAD DOG ELASTICA	44	2000
MAD EYED SCREAMER CREATURES	24	1981
MAD IF YA DON'T GAYLE & GILLIAN	75	1993
MAD LOVE (EP) LUSH	55	1990
MAD PASSIONATE LOVE BERNARD BRESSLAW	6	1958
MAD WORLD TEARS FOR FEARS	3	1982
MAD WORLD MICHAEL ANDREWS FEATURING GARY JULES	1	2003
MADAGASCAR ART OF TRANCE	41	1998
MADAM BUTTERFLY (UN BEL DI VEDREMO) MALCOLM McLAREN	13	1984
MADAME HELGA STEREOPHONICS	4	2003
MADCHESTER RAVE ON EP HAPPY MONDAYS	19	1989
MADE FOR LOVIN' YOU ANASTACIA	27	2001
MADE IN ENGLAND ELTON JOHN	18	1995
MADE IN HEAVEN FREDDIE MERCURY	57	1985
MADE IN TWO MINUTES BUG KAN & PLASTIC JAM FEATURING PATTI LOW & DOOGIE	64	1991
MADE IT BACK BEVERLEY KNIGHT FEATURING REDMAN	19	1998
MADE IT LAST HIGH CONTRAST	74	2004
MADE OF STONE STONE ROSES	20	1990
MADE TO LOVE (GIRLS GIRLS GIRLS) EDDIE HODGES	37	1962
MADE UP STORIES GO:AUDIO	33	2008
MADE YOU ADAM FAITH	5	1960
MADE YOU LOOK NAS	27	2003
MADE-UP LOVE SONG #43 GUILLEMOTS	23	2006
THE MADISON RAY ELLINGTON	36	1962
MADLY IN LOVE BROS	14	1990
MADNESS (IS ALL IN THE MIND) MADNESS	8	1983
MADNESS THING LEILANI	19	1999
MAGGIE FOSTER & ALLEN	27	1983
MAGGIE MAY ROD STEWART	1	1971
MAGGIE'S FARM BOB DYLAN	22	1965
MAGGIE'S FARM SPECIALS	4	1980
MAGGIE'S FARM (LIVE) TIN MACHINE	48	1989
MAGGIE'S LAST PARTY V.I.M.	68	1991
MAGIC [A] PILOT	11	1974
MAGIC [B] OLIVIA NEWTON-JOHN	32	1980
MAGIC [C] SASHA WITH SAM MOLLISON	32	1994
MAGIC [D] D-INFLUENCE	45	1997
MAGIC [E] NICK DRAKE	32	2004
MAGIC BUS WHO	26	1968
MAGIC CARPET RIDE MIGHTY DUB KATZ	24	1997
MAGIC FLY SPACE	2	1977
MAGIC FLY MINIMALISTIX	36	2003
THE MAGIC FRIEND 2 UNLIMITED	11	1992
MAGIC HOUR [A] HALO JAMES	59	1990
MAGIC HOUR [B] CAST	28	1999
THE MAGIC IS THERE DANIEL O'DONNELL	16	1998
MAGIC MANDRAKE SARR BAND	68	1978
MAGIC MIND EARTH, WIND & FIRE	54	1978
MAGIC MOMENTS PERRY COMO	1	1958
MAGIC MOMENTS RONNIE HILTON	22	1958
THE MAGIC NUMBER DE LA SOUL	7	1989
THE MAGIC PIPER (OF LOVE) EDWYN COLLINS	32	1997
THE MAGIC POSITION PATRICK WOLF	69	2007
MAGIC ROUNDABOUT JASPER CARROTT	5	1975
MAGIC SMILE ROSIE VELA	27	1987
MAGIC STYLE BADMAN	61	1991
MAGIC TOUCH [A] ODYSSEY	41	1982
MAGIC TOUCH [B] ROSE ROYCE	43	1984
MAGIC TOUCH [C] LOOSE ENDS	16	1985
MAGICAL BUCKS FIZZ	57	1985
MAGICAL MYSTERY TOUR (DOUBLE EP) BEATLES	2	1967
MAGICAL SPIEL BARRY RYAN	49	1970
MAGICK KLAXONS	29	2006
MAGIC'S BACK (THEME FROM 'THE GHOSTS OF OXFORD STREET') MALCOLM McLAREN FEATURING ALISON LIMERICK	42	1991
MAGIC'S WAND WHODINI	47	1982
MAGIC'S WAND (THE WHODINI ELECTRIC EP) WHODINI	63	1984
THE MAGNIFICENT AGENT OO	65	1998
MAGNIFICENT U2	42	2009
THE MAGNIFICENT SEVEN [A] AL CAIOLA	34	1961
THE MAGNIFICENT SEVEN [A] JOHN BARRY SEVEN	45	1961
THE MAGNIFICENT SEVEN [B] CLASH	34	1981
THE MAGNIFICENT 7 [B] SCOOBIE	58	2001
MAGNUM (DOUBLE SINGLE) MAGNUM	47	1980
MAH NA MAH NA PIERO UMILIANI	8	1977
MAID OF ORLEANS (THE WALTZ JOAN OF ARC) ORCHESTRAL MANOEUVRES IN THE DARK	4	1982
MAIDEN JAPAN IRON MAIDEN	43	1981
MAIDS WHEN YOU'RE YOUNG NEVER WED AN OLD MAN DUBLINERS	43	1967
THE MAIGRET THEME JOE LOSS ORCHESTRA	20	1962
THE MAIN ATTRACTION PAT BOONE	12	1962
MAIN OFFENDER HIVES	24	2002
MAIN THEME FROM 'THE THORNBIRDS' HENRY MANCINI	23	1984
MAIN TITLE THEME FROM 'MAN WITH THE GOLDEN ARM' BILLY MAY	9	1956
MAIN TITLE THEME FROM 'MAN WITH THE GOLDEN ARM' JET HARRIS	12	1962
MAINSTREAM THEA GILMORE	50	2003
MAIS OUI KING BROTHERS	16	1960
THE MAJESTY OF ROCK SPINAL TAP	61	1992
MAJOR TOM (COMING HOME) PETER SCHILLING	42	1984
MAJORCA PETULA CLARK	12	1955
MAKE A DAFT NOISE FOR CHRISTMAS GOODIES	20	1975
MAKE A FAMILY GARY CLARK	70	1993
MAKE A MOVE ON ME [A] OLIVIA NEWTON-JOHN	43	1982
MAKE A MOVE ON ME [B] JOEY NEGRO	11	2006
MAKE BELIEVE IT'S YOUR FIRST TIME CARPENTERS	60	1983
MAKE HER MINE NAT 'KING' COLE	11	1954
MAKE HER SAY KID CUDI FEATURING KANYE WEST, COMMON & LADY GAGA	67	2009
MAKE IT A PARTY WINIFRED ATWELL	7	1956
MAKE IT CLAP BUSTA RHYMES FEATURING SPLIFF STAR	16	2003
MAKE IT EASY SHYSTIE	59	2004
MAKE IT EASY ON YOURSELF WALKER BROTHERS	1	1965
MAKE IT GOOD A1	11	2002
MAKE IT HAPPEN MARIAH CAREY	17	1992
MAKE IT HOT [A] NICOLE FEATURING MISSY 'MISDEMEANOR' ELLIOTT	22	1998
MAKE IT HOT [B] VS	29	2004
MAKE IT LAST [A] SKIPWORTH & TURNER	60	1989
MAKE IT LAST [B] EMBRACE	35	2001
MAKE IT MINE SHAMEN	42	1990
MAKE IT ON MY OWN ALISON LIMERICK	16	1992
MAKE IT REAL SCORPIONS	72	1980
MAKE IT RIGHT CHRISTIAN FALK FEATURING DEMETREUS	22	2000
MAKE IT SOON TONY BRENT	9	1953
MAKE IT TONIGHT WET WET WET	37	1991
MAKE IT UP WITH LOVE ATL	21	2004
MAKE IT WITH YOU [A] BREAD	5	1970
MAKE IT WITH YOU [A] PASADENAS	20	1992
MAKE IT WITH YOU [A] LET LOOSE	7	1996
MAKE IT WITH YOU [B] UNIVERSAL	33	1997
MAKE LOVE EASY FREDDIE JACKSON	70	1994

Title	Artist	Peak Position	Year of Release
MAKE LOVE LIKE A MAN	DEF LEPPARD	12	1992
MAKE LOVE TO ME [A]	JO STAFFORD	8	1954
MAKE LOVE TO ME [A]	JOHN LEYTON & THE LeROYS	49	1964
MAKE LOVE TO ME [B]	JILL FRANCIS	70	1993
MAKE LUV	ROOM 5 FEATURING OLIVER CHEATHAM	1	2003
MAKE ME	JANET JACKSON	73	2009
MAKE ME AN ISLAND	JOE DOLAN	3	1969
MAKE ME BAD	KORN	25	2000
MAKE ME LAUGH	ANTHRAX	26	1988
MAKE ME SMILE (COME UP AND SEE ME)	STEVE HARLEY & COCKNEY REBEL	1	1975
MAKE ME SMILE (COME UP AND SEE ME)	ERASURE	14	2003
MAKE ME WANNA SCREAM	BLU CANTRELL	24	2003
MAKE MY BODY ROCK	JOMANDA	44	1989
MAKE MY DAY	BUJU BANTON	72	1993
MAKE MY HEART FLY	PROCLAIMERS	63	1988
MAKE MY LOVE	SHAWN CHRISTOPHER	57	1994
MAKE SOMEONE HAPPY	JIMMY DURANTE	69	1996
MAKE THAT MOVE	SHALAMAR	30	1981
MAKE THE DEAL	OCEAN COLOUR SCENE	35	2003
MAKE THE WORLD GO AWAY	EDDY ARNOLD	8	1966
MAKE THE WORLD GO AWAY	DONNY & MARIE OSMOND	18	1975
MAKE THE WORLD GO ROUND	SANDY B	20	1996
MAKE THINGS RIGHT	LEMON JELLY	33	2005
MAKE UP YOUR MIND	BASS JUMPERS	44	1999
MAKE WAY FOR NODDY	NODDY	29	2003
MAKE WAY FOR THE INDIAN	APACHE INDIAN & TIM DOG	29	1995
MAKE YOU FEEL MY LOVE	ADELE	26	2008
MAKE YOU HAPPY	LEVELLERS	38	2005
MAKE YOURS A HAPPY HOME	GLADYS KNIGHT & THE PIPS	35	1976
MAKEDAMN SURE	TAKING BACK SUNDAY	36	2006
MAKES ME LOVE YOU	ECLIPSE	25	1999
MAKES ME WANNA DIE	TRICKY	29	1997
MAKES ME WONDER	MAROON 5	2	2007
MAKIN' HAPPY	CRYSTAL WATERS	18	1991
MAKIN' IT	DAVID NAUGHTON	44	1979
MAKIN' LOVE	FLOYD ROBINSON	9	1959
MAKIN' OUT	MARK OWEN	30	2004
MAKIN' WHOOPEE	RAY CHARLES	42	1965
MAKING LOVE (OUT OF NOTHING AT ALL)	BONNIE TYLER	45	1996
MAKING PLANS FOR NIGEL	XTC	17	1979
MAKING THE MOST OF	DODGY WITH THE KICK HORNS	22	1995
MAKING TIME	CREATION	49	1966
MAKING UP AGAIN	GOLDIE	7	1978
MAKING YOUR MIND UP	BUCKS FIZZ	1	1981
MALE STRIPPER	MAN 2 MAN MEET MAN PARRISH	4	1986
MALIBU	HOLE	22	1999
MALT AND BARLEY BLUES	McGUINNESS FLINT	5	1971
MAMA [A]	DAVID WHITFIELD	12	1955
MAMA [A]	CONNIE FRANCIS	2	1960
MAMA [B]	DAVE BERRY	5	1966
MAMA [C]	GENESIS	4	1983
MAMA [D]	KIM APPLEBY	19	1991
MAMA [E]	SPICE GIRLS	1	1997
MAMA AFRICA	AKON	47	2007
MAMA DO	PIXIE LOTT	1	2009
MAMA GAVE BIRTH TO THE SOUL CHILDREN	QUEEN LATIFAH + DE LA SOUL	14	1991
MAMA I'M COMING HOME	OZZY OSBOURNE	46	1991
MAMA (LOVES A CRACKHEAD)	PLAN B	41	2006
MAMA NEVER TOLD ME	SISTER SLEDGE	20	1975
MAMA SAID [A]	CARLEEN ANDERSON	26	1994
MAMA SAID [B]	METALLICA	19	1996
MAMA SAID [C]	DIONNE BROMFIELD	43	2009
MAMA SAID KNOCK YOU OUT	LL COOL J	41	1990
MAMA TOLD ME NOT TO COME	THREE DOG NIGHT	3	1970
MAMA TOLD ME NOT TO COME	TOM JONES & STEREOPHONICS	4	2000
MAMA USED TO SAY	JUNIOR	7	1982
MAMA USED TO SAY	AZURE	56	1998
MAMA WEER ALL CRAZEE NOW	SLADE	1	1972
MAMA – WHO DA MAN?	RICHARD BLACKWOOD	3	2000
MA-MA-MA-BELLE	ELECTRIC LIGHT ORCHESTRA	22	1974
MAMA'S BOY	SUZI QUATRO	34	1980
MAMA'S PEARL	JACKSON 5	25	1971
MAMBO ITALIANO	ROSEMARY CLOONEY WITH THE MELLOMEN	1	1954
MAMBO ITALIANO	DEAN MARTIN	14	1955
MAMBO ITALIANO	SHAFT	12	2000
MAMBO NO 5 (A LITTLE BIT OF...)	LOU BEGA	1	1999
MAMBO NO 5	BOB THE BUILDER	1	2001
MAMBO ROCK	BILL HALEY & HIS COMETS	14	1955
MAMMA MIA	ABBA	1	1975
MAMMA MIA	A*TEENS	12	1999
MAMMOTH	INTERPOL	44	2007
MAMMY BLUE	ROGER WHITTAKER	31	1971
MAMOUNA	BRYAN FERRY	57	1995
MAMY BLUE	LOS POP TOPS	35	1971
MAN	ROSEMARY CLOONEY	7	1954
MAN BEHIND THE MUSIC	QUEEN PEN	38	1998
THE MAN DON'T GIVE A FUCK	SUPER FURRY ANIMALS	16	1996
THE MAN FROM LARAMIE	JIMMY YOUNG	1	1955
THE MAN FROM LARAMIE	AL MARTINO	19	1955
MAN FROM MADRID	TONY OSBORNE SOUND FEATURING JOANNE BROWN	50	1961
MAN FROM NAZARETH	JOHN PAUL JOANS	25	1971
MAN! I FEEL LIKE A WOMAN	SHANIA TWAIN	3	1999
MAN I HATE YOUR BAND	LITTLE MAN TATE	26	2006
THE MAN I LOVE	KATE BUSH & LARRY ADLER	27	1994
THE MAN IN BLACK	COZY POWELL	18	1974
MAN IN THE MIRROR	MICHAEL JACKSON	2	1988
MAN IN THE MOON	CSILLA	69	1996
MAN LIKE ME	NO REASON	53	2004
A MAN NEEDS TO BE TOLD	CHARLATANS	31	2001
MAN OF MYSTERY	SHADOWS	5	1960
MAN OF STEEL	MEAT LOAF	21	2003
MAN OF THE WORLD	FLEETWOOD MAC	2	1969
MAN ON FIRE [A]	FRANKIE VAUGHAN	6	1957
MAN ON FIRE [B]	ROGER TAYLOR	66	1984
MAN ON THE CORNER	GENESIS	41	1982
MAN ON THE EDGE	IRON MAIDEN	10	1995
MAN ON THE MOON	R.E.M.	18	1992
MAN OUT OF TIME	ELVIS COSTELLO	58	1982
MAN SHORTAGE	LOVINDEER	69	1986
THE MAN THAT GOT AWAY	JUDY GARLAND	18	1955
MAN TO MAN	HOT CHOCOLATE	14	1976
THE MAN WHO CAN'T BE MOVED	SCRIPT	2	2008
THE MAN WHO PLAYS THE MANDOLINO	DEAN MARTIN	21	1957
THE MAN WHO SOLD THE WORLD	LULU	3	1974
THE MAN WHO SOLD THE WORLD (LIVE)	DAVID BOWIE	39	1995
THE MAN WHO TOLD EVERYTHING	DOVES	32	2000
MAN WITH THE CHILD IN HIS EYES	KATE BUSH	6	1978
MAN WITH THE RED FACE	LAURENT GARNIER	36	2000
A MAN WITHOUT LOVE	KENNETH McKELLAR	30	1966
A MAN WITHOUT LOVE	ENGELBERT HUMPERDINCK	2	1968
MANCHESTER	BEAUTIFUL SOUTH	41	2006
MANCHESTER UNITED	MANCHESTER UNITED FC	50	1976
MANCHILD	NENEH CHERRY	5	1989
MANDINKA	SINEAD O'CONNOR	17	1988
MANDOLIN RAIN	BRUCE HORNSBY & THE RANGE	70	1987
MANDOLINS IN THE MOONLIGHT	PERRY COMO	13	1958
MANDY [A]	EDDIE CALVERT	9	1958
MANDY [B]	BARRY MANILOW	11	1975
MANDY [B]	WESTLIFE	1	2003
MANEATER [A]	DARYL HALL & JOHN OATES	6	1982
MANEATER [B]	NELLY FURTADO	1	2006
MANGOS	ROSEMARY CLOONEY	17	1957
MANHATTAN SKYLINE	A-HA	13	1987
MANHATTAN SPIRITUAL	REG OWEN	20	1959
MANIAC	MICHAEL SEMBELLO	43	1983
MANIC MINDS	MANIX	63	1991
MANIC MONDAY	BANGLES	2	1986
MANILA	SEELENLUFT FEATURING MICHAEL SMITH	70	2003
MANN GEGEN MANN	RAMMSTEIN	59	2006
MANNEQUIN	KIDS FROM FAME FEATURING GENE ANTHONY RAY	50	1982
MANNISH BOY	MUDDY WATERS	51	1988
MAN-SIZE	PJ HARVEY	42	1993
MANSIZE ROOSTER	SUPERGRASS	20	1995
MANTRA FOR A STATE MIND	S-EXPRESS	21	1989
MANY OF HORROR (WHEN WE COLLIDE)	BIFFY CLYRO	20	2010
MANY RIVERS TO CROSS	UB40	16	1983
MANY RIVERS TO CROSS	CHER	37	1993
MANY TEARS AGO	CONNIE FRANCIS	12	1961
MANY TOO MANY	GENESIS	43	1978
MANY WEATHERS APART	MERZ	48	1999
MAP OF THE PROBLEMATIQUE	MUSE	18	2007
MAPS	YEAH YEAH YEAH	37	2003
MARBLE BREAKS IRON BENDS	PETER FENTON	46	1966
MARBLEHEAD JOHNSON	BLUETONES	7	1996
MARBLES	BLACK GRAPE	46	1998
MARCH OF THE MODS	JOE LOSS ORCHESTRA	31	1964
MARCH OF THE PIGS	NINE INCH NAILS	45	1994
MARCH OF THE SIAMESE CHILDREN	KENNY BALL & HIS JAZZMEN	4	1962
MARCHETA	KARL DENVER	8	1961
MARGATE	CHAS & DAVE	46	1982
MARGIE	FATS DOMINO	18	1959
MARGO	BILLY FURY	28	1959
MARGUERITA TIME	STATUS QUO	3	1983
MARIA [A]	PJ PROBY	8	1965
MARIA	US5	38	2006
MARIA [B]	BLONDIE	1	1999
MARIA ELENA [A]	LOS INDIOS TABAJARAS	5	1963
MARIA ELENA [B]	GENE PITNEY	25	1969
MARIA (I LIKE IT LOUD)	SCOOTER VS MARC ACARDIPANE & DICK RULES	16	2003
MARIA MARIA	SANTANA FEATURING THE PRODUCT G&B	6	2000
MARIANA	GIBSON BROTHERS	11	1980
MARIANNE [A]	HILLTOPPERS	20	1957
MARIANNE [B]	CLIFF RICHARD	22	1968
MARIE	BACHELORS	9	1965
MARIE CELESTE	POLECATS	53	1981
MARIE MARIE	SHAKIN' STEVENS	19	1980
(MARIE'S THE NAME) HIS LATEST FLAME	ELVIS PRESLEY	1	1961
MARJORINE	JOE COCKER	48	1968
MARKET SQUARE HEROES	MARILLION	53	1982
MARLENE ON THE WALL	SUZANNE VEGA	21	1986
MAROC 7	SHADOWS	24	1967

	Peak Position	Year of Release
MARQUEE MOON TELEVISION	30	1977
MARQUIS LINOLEUM	73	1997
MARRAKESH EXPRESS CROSBY STILLS & NASH	17	1969
MARRIED MEN BONNIE TYLER	35	1979
MARRY ME MIKE PRESTON	14	1961
MARTA BACHELORS	20	1967
MARTA'S SONG DEEP FOREST	26	1995
MARTELL CRIBS	39	2005
MARTHA'S HARBOUR ALL ABOUT EVE	10	1988
MARTIAN HOP ROCKY SHARPE & THE REPLAYS	55	1980
MARTIKA'S KITCHEN MARTIKA	17	1991
MARTYR DEPECHE MODE	13	2006
MARVELLOUS LIGHTNING SEEDS	24	1995
MARVIN MARVIN THE PARANOID ANDROID	53	1981
MARY [A] SUPERGRASS	36	1999
MARY [B] SCISSOR SISTERS	14	2004
MARY ANN BLACK LACE	42	1979
MARY ANNE SHADOWS	17	1965
MARY HAD A LITTLE BOY SNAP!	8	1990
MARY HAD A LITTLE LAMB WINGS	9	1972
MARY JANE [A] DEL SHANNON	35	1964
MARY JANE [B] MEGADETH	46	1988
MARY JANE [C] SPIN DOCTORS	55	1994
MARY JANE (ALL NIGHT LONG) MARY J BLIGE	17	1995
MARY JANE'S LAST DANCE TOM PETTY	52	1994
MARY OF THE FOURTH FORM BOOMTOWN RATS	15	1977
MARY'S BOY CHILD HARRY BELAFONTE	1	1957
MARY'S BOY CHILD NINA & FREDERIK	26	1959
MARY'S BOY CHILD – OH MY LORD BONEY M	1	1978
MARY'S PRAYER DANNY WILSON	3	1987
MAS QUE MANCADA RONALDO'S REVENGE	37	1998
MAS QUE NADA ECHOBEATZ	10	1998
MAS QUE NADA TAMBA TRIO	34	1998
MAS QUE NADA COLOUR GIRL FEATURING PSG	57	2001
MAS QUE NADA SERGIO MENDES & THE BLACK EYED PEAS	6	2006
MASH IT UP MDM	66	2001
MASQUERADE [A] SKIDS	14	1979
MASQUERADE [B] EVELYN THOMAS	60	1984
MASQUERADE [C] FALL	69	1998
MASQUERADE [D] GERIDEAU	63	1998
MASS DESTRUCTION FAITHLESS	7	2004
MASSACHUSETTS BEE GEES	1	1967
THE MASSES AGAINST THE CLASSES MANIC STREET PREACHERS	1	2000
MASSIVE ATTACK EP MASSIVE ATTACK	27	1992
MASTER AND SERVANT DEPECHE MODE	9	1984
THE MASTER HAS COME BACK DAMIAN 'JR GONG' MARLEY	74	2005
MASTERBLASTER 2000 DJ LUCK & MC NEAT FEATURING JJ	5	2000
MASTERBLASTER (JAMMIN') STEVIE WONDER	2	1980
THE MASTERPLAN DIANA BROWN & BARRIE K SHARPE	39	1990
MATADOR JEFF WAYNE	57	1982
MATCHSTALK MEN AND MATCHSTALK CATS AND DOGS BRIAN & MICHAEL	1	1978
MATED DAVID GRANT & JAKI GRAHAM	20	1985
MATERIAL GIRL MADONNA	3	1985
MATHAR INDIAN VIBES	52	1994
MATHEMATICS CHERRY GHOST	57	2007
MATINEE FRANZ FERDINAND	8	2004
A MATTER OF FACT INNOCENCE	37	1990
MATTER OF TIME NINE YARDS	59	1999
A MATTER OF TRUST BILLY JOEL	52	1986
MATTERS AT ALL KIDS IN GLASS HOUSES	65	2010
MATTHEW AND SON CAT STEVENS	2	1967
MATT'S MOOD MATT BIANCO	44	1984
MATT'S MOOD BREEKOUT KREW	51	1984
MAX DON'T HAVE SEX WITH YOUR EX E-ROTIC	45	1995
THE MAXI PRIEST EP MAXI PRIEST	62	1991
MAXIMUM (EP) DREADZONE	56	1995
MAXIMUM OVERDRIVE 2 UNLIMITED	15	1993
MAY EACH DAY ANDY WILLIAMS	19	1966
MAY I HAVE THE NEXT DREAM WITH YOU MALCOLM ROBERTS	8	1968
MAY IT BE ENYA	50	2002
MAY THE SUN SHINE NAZARETH	22	1979
MAY YOU ALWAYS JOAN REGAN	9	1959
MAY YOU ALWAYS McGUIRE SISTERS	15	1959
MAYBE [A] THOM PACE	14	1979
MAYBE [B] ENRIQUE IGLESIAS	12	2002
MAYBE [C] EMMA	6	2003
MAYBE [D] N*E*R*D	25	2004
MAYBE [E] JAY SEAN	19	2008
MAYBE BABY CRICKETS	4	1958
MAYBE I KNOW LESLEY GORE	20	1964
MAYBE I KNOW SEASHELLS	32	1972
MAYBE I'M AMAZED WINGS	28	1977
MAYBE I'M AMAZED CARLEEN ANDERSON	24	1998
MAYBE I'M DEAD MONEY MARK	45	1998
MAYBE LOVE STEVIE NICKS	42	1994
MAYBE THAT'S WHAT IT TAKES ALEX PARKS	3	2003
MAYBE TOMORROW [A] BILLY FURY	18	1959
MAYBE TOMORROW [B] CHORDS	40	1980
MAYBE TOMORROW [C] UB40	14	1987
MAYBE TOMORROW [D] STEREOPHONICS	3	2003
MAYBE (WE SHOULD CALL IT A DAY) HAZELL DEAN	15	1988
MAYOR OF SIMPLETON XTC	46	1989
ME AGAINST THE MUSIC BRITNEY SPEARS FEATURING MADONNA	2	2003
ME AND BABY BROTHER WAR	21	1976
ME AND JULIO DOWN BY THE SCHOOLYARD PAUL SIMON	15	1972
ME AND MRS JONES BILLY PAUL	12	1973
ME AND MRS JONES FREDDIE JACKSON	32	1992
ME AND MR SANCHEZ BLUE RONDO A LA TURK	40	1981
ME AND MY GIRL (NIGHT-CLUBBING) DAVID ESSEX	13	1982
ME AND MY IMAGINATION SOPHIE ELLIS-BEXTOR	23	2007
ME AND MY LIFE TREMELOES	4	1970
ME AND MY SHADOW FRANK SINATRA & SAMMY DAVIS, JR	20	1962
ME AND MY TEDDY BEAR SIR TERRY WOGAN & ALED JONES	27	2009
ME AND THE FARMER HOUSEMARTINS	15	1987
ME & U CASSIE	6	2006
ME AND YOU AND A DOG NAMED BOO LOBO	4	1971
ME AND YOU VERSUS THE WORLD SPACE	9	1996
ME. IN TIME CHARLATANS	28	1991
ME ISRAELITES CHOPS-EMC + EXTENSIVE	60	1992
ME JULIE ALI G & SHAGGY	2	2002
ME LOVE SEAN KINGSTON	32	2007
ME MYSELF AND I [A] DE LA SOUL	22	1989
ME, MYSELF & I [B] BEYONCE	11	2004
ME MYSELF AND I [B] DARREN HAYES	59	2007
ME MYSELF I JOAN ARMATRADING	21	1980
ME NO POP I KID CREOLE & THE COCONUTS PRESENTS COATI MUNDI	32	1981
ME OR YOU? KILLING JOKE	57	1983
ME PLUS ONE KASABIAN	22	2007
ME THE PEACEFUL HEART LULU	9	1968
MEA CULPA PART II ENIGMA	55	1991
MEAN GIRL STATUS QUO	20	1973
MEAN MAN W.A.S.P.	21	1989
MEAN MEAN MAN WANDA JACKSON	40	1961
MEAN STREAK [A] CLIFF RICHARD	10	1959
MEAN STREAK [B] Y&T	41	1983
MEAN TO ME SHAYE COGAN	40	1960
MEAN WOMAN BLUES ROY ORBISON	3	1963
THE MEANING OF CHRISTMAS BORIS GARDINER	69	1986
THE MEANING OF LOVE [A] DEPECHE MODE	12	1982
THE MEANING OF LOVE [B] MICHELLE	16	2004
MEANT TO LIVE SWITCHFOOT	29	2004
MEANTIME FUTUREHEADS	49	2004
MEASURE OF A MAN SAM & MARK	19	2004
MEAT PIE SAUSAGE ROLL GRANDAD ROBERTS & HIS SON ELVIS	67	1998
MECCA CHEETAHS	36	1964
MECHANICAL WONDER OCEAN COLOUR SCENE	49	2001
THE MEDAL SONG CULTURE CLUB	32	1984
MEDICATION SPIRITUALIZED	55	1992
MEDICINE SHOW BIG AUDIO DYNAMITE	29	1986
THE MEDICINE SONG STEPHANIE MILLS	29	1984
MEDS PLACEBO FEATURING ALISON MOSSHART	35	2006
MEET EL PRESIDENTE DURAN DURAN	24	1987
MEET HER AT THE LOVE PARADE DA HOOL	11	1998
MEET ME HALFWAY BLACK EYED PEAS	1	2009
MEET ME ON THE CORNER [A] MAX BYGRAVES	2	1955
MEET ME ON THE CORNER [B] LINDISFARNE	5	1972
(MEET) THE FLINTSTONES BC-52's	3	1994
MEGABLAST BOMB THE BASS FEATURING MERLIN & ANTONIA	6	1988
MEGACHIC – CHIC MEDLEY CHIC	58	1990
MEGALOMANIA PELE	73	1992
MEGAMIX [A] TECHNOTRONIC	6	1990
MEGAMIX [B] CRYSTAL WATERS	39	1992
MEGAMIX [C] CORONA	36	1997
MEGAREX MARC BOLAN & T REX	72	1985
MEGLOMANIAC INCUBUS	23	2004
MEIN TEIL (IMPORT) RAMMSTEIN	61	2004
MEISO DJ KRUSH	52	1996
MELANCHOLY ROSE MARC ALMOND	71	1987
MELLOW DOUBT TEENAGE FANCLUB	34	1995
MELLOW MELLOW RIGHT ON LOWRELL	37	1979
MELLOW YELLOW DONOVAN	8	1967
THE MELOD-EP DODGY	53	1994
MELODY OF LOVE INK SPOTS	10	1955
MELODY OF LOVE (WANNA BE LOVED) DONNA SUMMER	21	1994
MELT [A] SIOUXSIE & THE BANSHEES	49	1982
MELT [B] MELANIE C	27	2003
THE MELTING MOON VHS OR BETA	63	2005
MELTING POT BLUE MINK	3	1969
MEMO FROM TURNER MICK JAGGER	32	1970
MEMORIES [A] PUBLIC IMAGE LTD	60	1979
MEMORIES [B] MIKE BERRY	55	1981
MEMORIES [C] BEVERLEY CRAVEN	68	1991
MEMORIES [D] DAVID GUETTA FEATURING KID CUDI	30	2010
MEMORIES ARE MADE OF THIS DEAN MARTIN	1	1956
MEMORIES ARE MADE OF THIS DAVE KING FEATURING THE KEYNOTES	5	1956
MEMORIES ARE MADE OF THIS VAL DOONICAN	11	1967
MEMORY ELAINE PAIGE	6	1981
MEMORY BARBRA STREISAND	34	1982
MEMORY LANE CHOONG FAMILY	57	2006
THE MEMORY REMAINS METALLICA	13	1997
MEMORY: THEME FROM THE MUSICAL 'CATS' ALED JONES	42	1985
MEMPHIS LONNIE MACK	47	1979
MEMPHIS TENNESSEE CHUCK BERRY	6	1963

Title	Artist	Peak Position	Year of Release
MEMPHIS TENNESSEE	DAVE BERRY & THE CRUISERS	19	1963
MEN IN BLACK [A]	FRANK BLACK	37	1996
MEN IN BLACK [B]	WILL SMITH	1	1997
MEN'S NEEDS	CRIBS	17	2007
MENTAL	MANIC MC's FEATURING SARA CARLSON	30	1989
MENTAL PICTURE	JON SECADA	44	1995
MENTASM	SECOND PHASE	48	1991
MERCEDES BENZ	SWAY	53	2009
MERCEDES BOY	PEBBLES	42	1988
MERCI CHERI	VINCE HILL	36	1966
MERCURY [A]	LOWGOLD	48	2001
MERCURY [B]	BLOC PARTY	16	2008
MERCURY AND SOLACE	BT	38	1999
MERCURY SUMMER	FIGHTSTAR	46	2009
MERCY	DUFFY	1	2008
MERCY ME	ALKALINE TRIO	30	2005
MERCY MERCY ME – I WANT YOU	ROBERT PALMER	9	1991
MERKINBALL EP	PEARL JAM	25	1995
MERMAIDS	PAUL WELLER	30	1997
MERRY CHRISTMAS DARLING	CARPENTERS	25	1972
MERRY CHRISTMAS EVERYONE	SHAKIN' STEVENS	1	1985
MERRY GENTLE POPS	BARRON KNIGHTS WITH DUKE D'MOND	9	1965
A MERRY JINGLE	GREEDIES	28	1980
THE MERRY PLOUGHBOY	DERMOT O'BRIEN	46	1966
MERRY XMAS EVERYBODY	SLADE	1	1973
MERRY XMAS EVERYBODY	METAL GURUS	55	1990
MERRY XMAS EVERYBODY	TONY CHRISTIE	49	2005
MERRY X-MESS	ROTTERDAM TERMINATION SOURCE	73	1993
MERRYMAKING AT MY PLACE	CALVIN HARRIS	43	2007
MERSEYBEAT	IAN McNABB	74	1996
MESCALITO	SOURMASH	73	2000
MESMERISE	CHAPTERHOUSE	60	1991
MESMERIZE	JA RULE FEATURING ASHANTI	12	2003
MESMERIZED	FAITH EVANS	48	2005
A MESS OF BLUES	ELVIS PRESLEY	2	1960
A MESS OF THE BLUES	STATUS QUO	15	1983
THE MESSAGE [A]	GRANDMASTER FLASH & THE FURIOUS FIVE	8	1982
THE MESSAGE [B]	49ERS	68	1992
MESSAGE IN A BOTTLE	POLICE	1	1979
MESSAGE IN A BOTTLE	DANCE FLOOR VIRUS	49	1995
MESSAGE IN A BOTTLE	T FACTORY	51	2002
MESSAGE IN THE BOX	WORLD PARTY	39	1990
THE MESSAGE IS LOVE	ARTHUR BAKER & THE BACKSTREET DISCIPLES FEATURING AL GREEN	38	1989
MESSAGE OF LOVE [A]	PRETENDERS	11	1981
MESSAGE OF LOVE [B]	LOVEHAPPY	37	1995
MESSAGE TO MARTHA	LOU JOHNSON	36	1964
MESSAGE TO MARTHA (KENTUCKY BLUEBIRD)	ADAM FAITH	12	1964
A MESSAGE TO YOU RUDY	SPECIALS (FEATURING RICO)	10	1979
A MESSAGE TO YOUR HEART	SAMANTHA JANUS	30	1991
MESSAGE II (SURVIVAL)	MELLE MEL & DUKE BOOTEE	74	1983
MESSAGE UNDERSTOOD	SANDIE SHAW	6	1965
MESSAGES	ORCHESTRAL MANOEUVRES IN THE DARK	13	1980
MESSAGES FROM THE STARS	RAH BAND	42	1983
MESSED UP	BEAT UP	62	2004
MESSIN'	LADIES FIRST	30	2001
METAFORCE	ART OF NOISE	53	1999
METAL GURU	T REX	1	1972
METAL HEALTH	QUIET RIOT	45	1983
METAL MICKEY	SUEDE	17	1992
METEOR MAN	DEE D. JACKSON	48	1978
METHOD OF MODERN LOVE [A]	DARYL HALL & JOHN OATES	21	1985
METHOD OF MODERN LOVE [B]	SAINT ETIENNE	56	2009
METROPOLIS	OLIVER LIEB presents SMOKED	72	2000
METROSOUND	ADAM F & J MAJIK	54	2002
MEXICALI ROSE	KARL DENVER	8	1961
THE MEXICAN	FENTONES	41	1962
MEXICAN GIRL	SMOKIE	19	1978
MEXICAN RADIO	WALL OF VOODOO	64	1983
MEXICAN WAVE	KERBDOG	49	1997
MEXICO	LONG JOHN BALDRY	15	1968
MF FROM HELL	DATSUNS	55	2003
MFEO	KAVANA	8	1997
MI CHICO LATINO	GERI HALLIWELL	1	1999
MI TIERRA	GLORIA ESTEFAN	36	1993
MIAMI	WILL SMITH	3	1998
MIAMI HIT MIX	GLORIA ESTEFAN	8	1992
MIAMI VICE THEME	JAN HAMMER	5	1985
MICHAEL [A]	HIGHWAYMEN	1	1961
MICHAEL [A]	GENO WASHINGTON & THE RAM JAM BAND	39	1967
MICHAEL [B]	FRANZ FERDINAND	17	2004
MICHAEL AND THE SLIPPER TREE	EQUALS	24	1969
MICHAEL CAINE	MADNESS	11	1984
MICHAEL JACKSON	MITCHELL BROTHERS	65	2007
MICHAEL JACKSON MEDLEY	ASHAYE	45	1983
MICHAEL ROW THE BOAT	LONNIE DONEGAN	6	1961
MICHELLE	OVERLANDERS	1	1966
MICHELLE	DAVID & JONATHAN	11	1966
MICHIKO	SULTANS OF PING	43	1993
MICKEY	TONI BASIL	2	1982
MICKEY	LOLLY	4	1999
MICRO KID	LEVEL 42	37	1983
THE MICROPHONE FIEND	ERIC B & RAKIM	74	1988
MICROWAVED	PITCHSHIFTER	54	1998
MIDAS TOUCH	MIDNIGHT STAR	8	1986
THE MIDDLE	JIMMY EAT WORLD	26	2002
MIDDLE OF NOWHERE	HOT HOT HEAT	47	2005
MIDDLE OF THE NIGHT	BROTHERHOOD OF MAN	41	1978
MIDDLEMAN	TERRORVISION	25	1994
MIDLIFE CRISIS	FAITH NO MORE	10	1992
MIDNIGHT [A]	PAUL ANKA	26	1958
MIDNIGHT [B]	UN-CUT	26	2003
MIDNIGHT AT THE LOST AND FOUND	MEAT LOAF	17	1983
MIDNIGHT AT THE OASIS	MARIA MULDAUR	21	1974
MIDNIGHT AT THE OASIS	BRAND NEW HEAVIES FEATURING N'DEA DAVENPORT	13	1994
MIDNIGHT BLUE	LOUISE TUCKER	59	1983
MIDNIGHT COWBOY	MIDNIGHT COWBOY SOUNDTRACK	47	1980
MIDNIGHT FLYER	NAT 'KING' COLE	23	1959
MIDNIGHT GROOVIN'	LIGHT OF THE WORLD	72	1979
MIDNIGHT IN A PERFECT WORLD	DJ SHADOW	54	1996
MIDNIGHT IN CHELSEA	JON BON JOVI	4	1997
MIDNIGHT IN MOSCOW	KENNY BALL & HIS JAZZMEN	2	1961
MIDNIGHT RIDER	PAUL DAVIDSON	10	1976
MIDNIGHT SHIFT	BUDDY HOLLY	26	1959
MIDNIGHT SUMMER DREAM	STRANGLERS	35	1983
MIDNIGHT TO SIX MAN	PRETTY THINGS	46	1966
MIDNIGHT TRAIN TO GEORGIA	GLADYS KNIGHT & THE PIPS	10	1976
MIDNITE	D-INFLUENCE	58	1995
MIDNITE DYNAMOS	MATCHBOX	14	1980
MIDNITE SPECIAL	PAUL EVANS	41	1960
MIDSUMMER MADNESS (EP)	RHYTHM SECTION	66	1992
MIG29	MIG29	62	1992
MIGHT BE STARS	WANNADIES	51	1995
THE MIGHTY HIGH	REVIVAL 3000	47	1997
MIGHTY JOE	SHOCKING BLUE	43	1970
MIGHTY POWER OF LOVE	TAVARES	25	1977
MIGHTY QUINN	MANFRED MANN	1	1968
MIGRAINE SKANK	GRACIOUS K	53	2009
MIKE OLDFIELD'S SINGLE (THEME FROM TUBULAR BELLS)	MIKE OLDFIELD	31	1974
MILES AWAY [A]	JOHN FOXX	51	1980
MILES AWAY [B]	WINGER	56	1991
MILES AWAY [C]	MADONNA	39	2008
MILES FROM HOME	PESHAY	75	1998
MILK	GARBAGE FEATURING TRICKY	10	1996
MILK AND ALCOHOL	DR FEELGOOD	9	1979
MILKMAN'S SON	UGLY KID JOE	39	1995
MILKSHAKE	KELIS	2	2003
MILKY WAY	SHEER ELEGANCE	18	1976
THE MILL HILL SELF HATE CLUB	EDWARD BALL	57	1996
MILLENNIUM [A]	KILLING JOKE	34	1994
MILLENNIUM [B]	ROBBIE WILLIAMS	1	1998
MILLENNIUM CHIMES	BIG BEN	53	2000
THE MILLENNIUM PRAYER	CLIFF RICHARD	1	1999
MILLION DOLLAR BILL	WHITNEY HOUSTON	5	2009
MILLION DOLLAR LOVE	DUB WAR	73	1997
MILLION DRUMS	TONY SHEVETON	49	1964
A MILLION LOVE SONGS	TAKE THAT	7	1992
MILLION MILES AWAY	OFFSPRING	21	2001
MILLION SUNS	OOBERMAN	43	1999
A MILLION WAYS	OK GO	43	2006
MILLIONAIRE	KELIS FEATURING ANDRE 3000	3	2004
MILLIONAIRE SWEEPER	KENICKIE	60	1996
MILLIONS LIKE US	PURPLE HEARTS	57	1979
MILLY MOLLY MANDY	GLYN POOLE	35	1973
MILORD	EDITH PIAF	24	1960
MILORD	FRANKIE VAUGHAN	34	1960
MIND	FARM	31	1991
MIND ADVENTURES	DES'REE	43	1992
MIND BLOWIN'	SMOOTH	36	1995
MIND BLOWING DECISIONS	HEATWAVE	9	1978
MIND BODY SOUL	FANTASY UFO FEATURING JAY GROOVE	50	1991
MIND GAMES	JOHN LENNON	26	1973
MIND OF A TOY	VISAGE	13	1981
A MIND OF ITS OWN	VICTORIA BECKHAM	6	2002
THE MIND OF LOVE	k.d. lang	72	1993
THE MIND OF THE MACHINE	N-TRANCE	15	1997
MIND OVER MONEY	TURIN BRAKES	31	2001
MIND TRICK	JAMIE CULLUM	32	2005
MIND UP TONIGHT	MELBA MOORE	22	1983
MINDCIRCUS	WAY OUT WEST FEATURING TRICIA LEE	39	2002
MINDLESS BOOGIE	HOT CHOCOLATE	46	1979
MINDSTREAM	MEAT BEAT MANIFESTO	55	1993
MINE	EVERYTHING BUT THE GIRL	58	1984
MINE ALL MINE	CA$HFLOW	15	1986
MINE TO GIVE	PHOTEK FEATURING ROBERT OWENS	44	2001
MINEFIELD	I-LEVEL	52	1983
MINERVA	DEFTONES	15	2003
MINIMAL	PET SHOP BOYS	19	2006
MINISTRY OF LOVE	HYSTERIC EGO	39	1997
MINISTRY OF MAYHEM	NOISE NEXT DOOR	12	2004
MINNIE THE MOOCHER	REGGAE PHILHARMONIC ORCHESTRA	35	1988
MINORITY	GREEN DAY	18	2000
MINORITY OF ONE	JOHNNY PANIC	60	2005
MINT CAR	CURE	31	1996
MINUETTO ALLEGRETTO	WOMBLES	16	1974
MINUTE BY MINUTE	DOOBIE BROTHERS	47	1979

	Peak Position	Year of Release
A MINUTE OF YOUR TIME TOM JONES	14	1968
THE MINUTE YOU'RE GONE CLIFF RICHARD	1	1965
THE MIRACLE [A] QUEEN	21	1989
MIRACLE [B] JON BON JOVI	29	1990
MIRACLE [C] OLIVE	41	1997
THE MIRACLE [D] CLIFF RICHARD	23	1999
A MIRACLE [E] HIDDEN CAMERAS	70	2003
MIRACLE GOODNIGHT DAVID BOWIE	40	1993
THE MIRACLE OF LOVE EURYTHMICS	23	1986
THE MIRACLE OF YOU DANNY WILLIAMS	41	1961
MIRACLES [A] GARY NUMAN	49	1985
MIRACLES [B] PET SHOP BOYS	10	2003
MIRROR IN THE BATHROOM BEAT	4	1980
MIRROR KISSERS CRIBS	27	2005
MIRROR MAN HUMAN LEAGUE	2	1982
MIRROR MIRROR [A] PINKERTON'S ASSORTED COLOURS	9	1966
MIRROR MIRROR [B] DIANA ROSS	36	1982
MIRROR MIRROR (MON AMOUR) DOLLAR	4	1981
MIRRORS SALLY OLDFIELD	19	1978
MISERERE ZUCCHERO WITH LUCIANO PAVAROTTI	15	1992
MISERY [A] SOUL ASYLUM	30	1995
MISERY [B] MOFFATTS	47	1999
MISERY BUSINESS PARAMORE	17	2007
MISFIT [A] CURIOSITY KILLED THE CAT	7	1987
MISFIT [B] AMY STUDT	6	2003
MISGUIDED DYVERSE	71	2004
MISIRLOU (THE THEME TO THE MOTION PICTURE 'PULP FICTION') SPAGHETTI SURFERS	55	1995
MISLED [A] KOOL & THE GANG	28	1985
MISLED [B] QUIREBOYS	37	1990
MISLED [C] CELINE DION	15	1995
MISS AMERICA BIG DISH	37	1991
MISS CALIFORNIA DANTE THOMAS FEATURING PRAS	25	2001
MISS CHATELAINE k.d. lang	68	1993
MISS FAT BOOTY – PART II MOS DEF FEATURING GHOSTFACE KILLAH	64	2000
MISS HIT AND RUN BARRY BLUE	26	1974
MISS INDEPENDENT [A] KELLY CLARKSON	6	2003
MISS INDEPENDENT [B] NE-YO	6	2008
MISS LUCIFER PRIMAL SCREAM	25	2002
MISS MODULAR STEREOLAB	60	1997
MISS MURDER AFI	44	2006
MISS PARKER [A] BENZ	35	1996
MISS PARKER [B] MORGAN	74	1999
MISS PERFECT ABS FEATURING NODESHA	5	2003
MISS SARAJEVO PASSENGERS	6	1995
MISS THE GIRL CREATURES	21	1983
MISS WORLD HOLE	64	1994
MISS YOU [A] JIMMY YOUNG	15	1963
MISS YOU [B] ROLLING STONES	3	1978
MISS YOU LIKE CRAZY NATALIE COLE	2	1989
MISS YOU MUCH JANET JACKSON	22	1989
MISS YOU NIGHTS CLIFF RICHARD	15	1976
MISS YOU NIGHTS WESTLIFE	3	2003
MIS-SHAPES PULP	2	1995
MISSING [A] TERRY HALL	75	1989
MISSING [B] EVERYTHING BUT THE GIRL	3	1994
MISSING WORDS SELECTER	23	1980
MISSING YOU [A] CHRIS DE BURGH	3	1988
MISSING YOU [B] JOHN WAITE	9	1984
MISSING YOU [B] TINA TURNER	12	1996
MISSING YOU [C] SOUL II SOUL FEATURING KYM MAZELLE	22	1990
MISSING YOU [D] MARY J BLIGE	19	1997
MISSING YOU [E] LUCY CARR	28	2003
MISSING YOU NOW MICHAEL BOLTON FEATURING KENNY G	28	1992
MISSION OF LOVE JASON DONOVAN	26	1992
MISSIONARY MAN EURYTHMICS	31	1987

	Peak Position	Year of Release
MISSISSIPPI PUSSYCAT	1	1976
MRS HOOVER CANDYSKINS	65	1996
MRS MILLS' MEDLEY MRS MILLS	18	1961
MRS MILLS PARTY MEDLEY MRS MILLS	50	1964
MRS. ROBINSON SIMON & GARFUNKEL	4	1968
MRS ROBINSON LEMONHEADS	19	1992
MRS. ROBINSON (EP) SIMON & GARFUNKEL	9	1969
MRS WASHINGTON GIGOLO AUNTS	74	1994
MISSY MISSY PAUL & BARRY RYAN	43	1966
MISTAKE STEPHANIE McINTOSH	47	2007
MISTAKES AND REGRETS ...AND YOU WILL KNOW US BY THE TRAIL OF THE DEAD	69	2000
MR ALIBI MARIA WILLSON	43	2003
MR BACHELOR LOOSE ENDS	50	1988
MR BASS MAN JOHNNY CYMBAL	24	1963
MR BIG STUFF HEAVY D. & THE BOYZ	61	1986
MR BIG STUFF QUEEN LATIFAH, SHADES & FREE	31	1997
MR BLOBBY MR BLOBBY	1	1993
MR BLUE MIKE PRESTON	12	1959
MR BLUE DAVID MacBETH	18	1959
MR BLUE SKY ELECTRIC LIGHT ORCHESTRA	6	1978
MR BRIGHTSIDE KILLERS	10	2004
MR CABDRIVER LENNY KRAVITZ	58	1990
MR CROWLEY OZZY OSBOURNE'S BLIZZARD OF OZ	46	1980
MR CUSTER CHARLIE DRAKE	12	1960
MR DEVIL BIG TIME CHARLIE FEATURING SOOZY Q	39	2000
MR DJ [A] CONCEPT	27	1985
MR DJ [B] BLACKOUT	19	2001
MR DJ [C] CHARLEAN DANCE	51	2007
MR E'S BEAUTIFUL BLUES EELS	11	2000
MR FIXIT ROOTJOOSE	54	1997
MR FRIDAY NIGHT LISA MOORISH	24	1996
MR GUDER CARPENTERS	12	1974
MR GUITAR BERT WEEDON	47	1961
MR HANKEY THE CHRISTMAS POO MR HANKEY	4	1999
MISTER JONES [A] OUT OF MY HAIR	73	1995
MR JONES [B] COUNTING CROWS	28	1994
MR KIRK'S NIGHTMARE 4 HERO	73	1990
MR LEE DIANA ROSS	58	1988
MR LOVERMAN SHABBA RANKS	3	1992
MR MANIC AND SISTER COOL SHAKATAK	56	1987
MISTER MENTAL EIGHTIES MATCHBOX B-LINE DISASTER	25	2004
MR PHARMACIST FALL	75	1986
MISTER PORTER MICKIE MOST	45	1963
MR PRESIDENT D, B, M & T	33	1970
MR RAFFLES (MAN IT WAS MEAN) STEVE HARLEY & COCKNEY REBEL	13	1975
MR ROCK & ROLL AMY MacDONALD	12	2007
MR SANDMAN DICKIE VALENTINE	5	1954
MR SANDMAN CHORDETTES	11	1954
MR SANDMAN FOUR ACES FEATURING AL ALBERTS	9	1955
MR SANDMAN MAX BYGRAVES	16	1955
MR SECOND CLASS SPENCER DAVIS GROUP	35	1968
MR SLEAZE STOCK AITKEN WATERMAN	3	1987
MR SOFT COCKNEY REBEL	8	1974
MR SOLITAIRE ANIMAL NIGHTLIFE	25	1984
MR SUCCESS FRANK SINATRA	25	1958
MR TAMBOURINE MAN BYRDS	1	1965
MR TELEPHONE MAN NEW EDITION	19	1985
MR VAIN CULTURE BEAT	1	1993
MR WENDAL ARRESTED DEVELOPMENT	4	1993
MR WONDERFUL PEGGY LEE	5	1957
MR WRITER STEREOPHONICS	5	2001
MR ZERO KEITH RELF	50	1966
MISTI BLU AMILLIONSONS	39	2002
MISTLETOE AND WINE CLIFF RICHARD	1	1988
MISTRESS MABEL FRATELLIS	23	2008

	Peak Position	Year of Release
MISTY JOHNNY MATHIS	12	1960
MISTY RAY STEVENS	2	1975
MISTY BLUE DOROTHY MOORE	5	1976
MISTY MORNING, ALBERT BRIDGE POGUES	41	1989
MISUNDERSTANDING GENESIS	42	1980
MISUNDERSTOOD [A] BON JOVI	21	2002
MISUNDERSTOOD [B] ROBBIE WILLIAMS	8	2004
MISUNDERSTOOD MAN CLIFF RICHARD	19	1995
MITCH BISCUIT BOY	75	2001
MITTAGEISEN (METAL POSTCARD) SIOUXSIE & THE BANSHEES	47	1979
MIX IT UP DAN REED NETWORK	49	1991
MIXED BIZNESS BECK	34	2000
MIXED EMOTIONS ROLLING STONES	36	1989
MIXED TRUTH RAGGA TWINS	65	1992
MIXED UP WORLD SOPHIE ELLIS-BEXTOR	7	2003
MIYAKO HIEAWAY MARION	45	1998
MJB DA MVP MARY J BLIGE	33	2006
M'LADY SLY & THE FAMILY STONE	32	1968
MMM MMM MMM MMM CRASH TEST DUMMIES	2	1994
MMMBOP HANSON	1	1997
MO' FIRE BAD COMPANY UK/RAWHILL CRU	24	2003
MO MONEY MO PROBLEMS NOTORIOUS B.I.G. FEATURING PUFF DADDY & MA$E	10	1997
MOAN AND GROAN MARK MORRISON	7	1997
MOANIN' CHRIS FARLOWE	46	1967
MOB RULES BLACK SABBATH	46	1981
MOBILE RAY BURNS	4	1955
MOBSCENE MARILYN MANSON	13	2003
MOCKIN' BIRD HILL MIGIL FIVE	10	1964
MOCKINGBIRD [A] INEZ & CHARLIE FOXX	33	1969
MOCKINGBIRD [A] CARLY SIMON & JAMES TAYLOR	34	1974
MOCKINGBIRD [A] BELLE STARS	51	1982
MOCKINGBIRD [B] EMINEM	4	2005
THE MODEL KRAFTWERK	1	1981
MODEL LIFE CHOCOLATE MONDAY	61	2005
MODELS FOR THE PROGRAMME HELL IS FOR HEROES	56	2005
MODERN AGE STROKES	68	2001
MODERN ART ART BRUT	49	2004
MODERN FEELING IKARA COLT	61	2004
MODERN GIRL [A] SHEENA EASTON	8	1980
MODERN GIRL [B] MEAT LOAF	17	1984
MODERN LOVE DAVID BOWIE	2	1983
MODERN ROMANCE (I WANT TO FALL IN LOVE AGAIN) FRANCIS ROSSI & BERNARD FROST	54	1985
MODERN WAY KAISER CHIEFS	11	2005
A MODERN WAY OF LETTING GO IDLEWILD	28	2003
THE MODERN WORLD JAM	36	1977
MODUS OPERANDI PHOTEK	66	1998
MOI...LOLITA ALIZEE	9	2002
MOIRA JANE'S CAFE DEFINITION OF SOUND	34	1992
MOLLIE'S SONG BEVERLEY CRAVEN	61	1993
MOLLY CARRIE	56	1998
MOLLY'S CHAMBERS KINGS OF LEON	23	2003
A MOMENT LIKE THIS LEONA LEWIS	1	2006
MOMENT OF MY LIFE BOBBY D'AMBROSIO FEATURING MICHELLE WEEKS	23	1997
MOMENTS IN LOVE/BEAT BOX ART OF NOISE	51	1985
MOMENTS IN SOUL JT & THE BIG FAMILY	7	1990
MOMENTS OF PLEASURE KATE BUSH	26	1993
MON AMI GIRESSE	61	2001
MON AMOUR TOKYO PIZZICATO FIVE	72	1997
MONA CRAIG McLACHLAN & CHECK 1-2	2	1990
MONA LISA CONWAY TWITTY	5	1959
MONDAY MONDAY MAMAS & THE PAPAS	3	1966
MONDAY MORNING CANDYSKINS	34	1997
MONDAY MORNING 5:19 RIALTO	37	1997
MONEY [A] BERN ELLIOTT & THE FENMEN	14	1963

	Peak Position	Year of Release
MONEY [A] FLYING LIZARDS	5	1979
MONEY [A] BACKBEAT BAND	48	1994
MONEY [B] SKIN	18	1994
MONEY [C] CHARLI BALTIMORE	12	1998
MONEY [D] DAN REED NETWORK	45	1990
MONEY [E] JAMELIA FEATURING BEENIE MAN	5	2000
(MONEY CAN'T) BUY ME LOVE BLACKSTREET	18	1997
MONEY DON'T MATTER 2 NIGHT PRINCE & THE NEW POWER GENERATION	19	1992
MONEY (EVERYBODY LOVES HER) GUN	73	1989
MONEY FOR NOTHING DIRE STRAITS	4	1985
MONEY GO ROUND (PART 1) STYLE COUNCIL	11	1983
MONEY GREED TRICKY	25	1998
MONEY HONEY BAY CITY ROLLERS	3	1975
MONEY IN MY POCKET DENNIS BROWN	14	1979
MONEY LOVE NENEH CHERRY	23	1992
MONEY MONEY MONEY ABBA	3	1976
MONEY THAT'S YOUR PROBLEM TONIGHT	66	1978
MONEY TO BURN RICHARD ASHCROFT	17	2000
MONEY'S TOO TIGHT TO MENTION VALENTINE BROTHERS	73	1983
MONEY'S TOO TIGHT TO MENTION SIMPLY RED	13	1985
MONEYTALKS AC/DC	36	1990
MONIE IN THE MIDDLE MONIE LOVE	46	1990
THE MONKEES RAMPAGE	51	1995
THE MONKEES EP MONKEES	33	1980
MONKEY [A] GEORGE MICHAEL	13	1988
MONKEY [B] SHAFT	61	1992
MONKEY BUSINESS [A] SKID ROW	19	1991
MONKEY BUSINESS [B] DANGER DANGER	42	1992
MONKEY CHOP DAN-I	30	1979
MONKEY GONE TO HEAVEN PIXIES	60	1989
MONKEY MAN MAYTALS	47	1970
MONKEY MAN GENERAL LEVY	75	1993
MONKEY SPANNER DAVE & ANSIL COLLINS	7	1971
MONKEY WAH RADICAL ROB	67	1992
MONKEY WRENCH FOO FIGHTERS	12	1997
MONO COURTNEY LOVE	41	2004
MONOCULTURE SOFT CELL	52	2002
MONSIEUR DUPONT SANDIE SHAW	6	1969
MONSTER [A] L7	33	1992
MONSTER [B] LIQUID PEOPLE VS SIMPLE MINDS	67	2002
MONSTER [C] AUTOMATIC	4	2006
MONSTER D] LADY GAGA	68	2009
MONSTER HOSPITAL METRIC	55	2006
MONSTER MASH BOBBY 'BORIS' PICKETT & THE CRYPT-KICKERS	3	1973
MONSTERS FUNERAL FOR A FRIEND	36	2005
MONSTERS AND ANGELS VOICE OF THE BEEHIVE	17	1991
MONTEGO BAY BOBBY BLOOM	3	1970
MONTEGO BAY FREDDIE NOTE & THE RUDIES	45	1970
MONTEGO BAY SUGAR CANE	54	1978
MONTEGO BAY AMAZULU	16	1986
MONTREAL WEDDING PRESENT	40	1997
MONTREAUX EP SIMPLY RED	11	1992
MONTUNO GLORIA ESTEFAN	55	1993
MONY MONY TOMMY JAMES & THE SHONDELLS	1	1968
MONY MONY BILLY IDOL	7	1987
MONY MONY AMAZULU	38	1987
MONY MONY STATUS QUO	48	2000
THE MOOD CLUB FIRSTBORN	69	1999
MOODSWINGS MY VITRIOL	39	2002
MOODSWINGS (TO COME AT ME LIKE THAT) CHARLOTTE CHURCH	14	2006
MOODY BLUE ELVIS PRESLEY	6	1977
MOODY PLACES NORTHSIDE	32	1990
MOODY RIVER PAT BOONE	18	1961
MOOG ERUPTION DIGITAL ORGASM	62	1992
MOON VIRUS	36	1997
MOON HOP DERRICK MORGAN	49	1970
MOON OVER BOURBON STREET STING	44	1986
MOON RIVER DANNY WILLIAMS	1	1961
MOON RIVER HENRY MANCINI	44	1961
MOON RIVER GREYHOUND	12	1972
MOON SHADOW CAT STEVENS	22	1971
MOON TALK PERRY COMO	17	1958
MOONCHILD FIELDS OF THE NEPHILIM	28	1988
MOONGLOW MORRIS STOLOFF	7	1956
MOONGLOW SOUNDS ORCHESTRAL	43	1965
MOONLIGHT AND MUZAK M	33	1979
MOONLIGHT & ROSES JIM REEVES	34	1971
MOONLIGHT GAMBLER FRANKIE LAINE	13	1956
MOONLIGHT SERENADE GLENN MILLER	12	1954
MOONLIGHT SHADOW MIKE OLDFIELD FEATURING MAGGIE REILLY	4	1983
MOONLIGHTING LEO SAYER	2	1975
'MOONLIGHTING' THEME AL JARREAU	8	1987
MOONSHINE SALLY MUD	10	1975
MOR BLUR	15	1997
MORE [A] JIMMY YOUNG	4	1956
MORE [A] PERRY COMO	10	1956
MORE [B] SISTERS OF MERCY	14	1990
MORE… [C] HIGH	67	1991
MORE AND MORE [A] ANDY WILLIAMS	45	1967
MORE AND MORE [B] CAPTAIN HOLLYWOOD PROJECT	23	1993
MORE & MORE [C] SPOILED & ZIGO	31	2000
MORE & MORE [D] JOE FEATURING G UNIT	12	2004
MORE AND MORE PARTY POPS RUSS CONWAY	5	1959
MORE BEATS & PIECES COLDCUT	37	1997
MORE GOOD OLD ROCK 'N ROLL DAVE CLARK FIVE	34	1970
MORE HUMAN THAN HUMAN WHITE ZOMBIE	51	1995
THE MORE I GET THE MORE I WANT KWS FEATURING TEDDY PENDERGRASS	35	1994
THE MORE I SEE (THE LESS I BELIEVE) FUN BOY THREE	68	1983
THE MORE I SEE YOU CHRIS MONTEZ	3	1966
THE MORE I SEE YOU JOY MARSHALL	34	1966
THE MORE I SEE YOU BARBARA WINDSOR & MIKE REID	46	1999
MORE LIFE IN A TRAMP'S VEST STEREOPHONICS	33	1997
MORE LIKE THE MOVIES DR HOOK	14	1978
MORE LOVE [A] FEARGAL SHARKEY	44	1988
MORE LOVE [B] NEXT OF KIN	33	1999
MORE MONEY FOR YOU AND ME (MEDLEY) FOUR PREPS	39	1961
MORE MORE MORE [A] ANDREA TRUE CONNECTION	5	1976
MORE MORE MORE [A] BANANARAMA	24	1993
MORE MORE MORE [A] RACHEL STEVENS	3	2004
MORE, MORE, MORE [B] CARMEL	23	1984
MORE PARTY POPS RUSS CONWAY	10	1958
MORE THAN A FEELING BOSTON	22	1977
MORE THAN A LOVER BONNIE TYLER	27	1977
MORE THAN A WOMAN [A] TAVARES	7	1978
MORE THAN A WOMAN [A] 911	2	1998
MORE THAN A WOMAN [B] AALIYAH	1	2002
MORE THAN EVER (COME PRIMA) MALCOLM VAUGHAN WITH THE MICHAEL SAMMES SINGERS	5	1958
MORE THAN EVER (COME PRIMA) ROBERT EARL	26	1958
MORE THAN I CAN BEAR MATT BIANCO	50	1985
MORE THAN I CAN SAY CRICKETS	42	1960
MORE THAN I CAN SAY BOBBY VEE	4	1961
MORE THAN I CAN SAY LEO SAYER	2	1980
MORE THAN I NEEDED TO KNOW SCOOCH	5	2000
MORE THAN IN LOVE KATE ROBBINS & BEYOND	2	1981
MORE THAN LIKELY PM DAWN FEATURING BOY GEORGE	40	1993
MORE THAN LOVE [A] KEN DODD	14	1966
MORE THAN LOVE [B] WET WET WET	19	1992
MORE THAN ONE KIND OF LOVE JOAN ARMATRADING	75	1990
MORE THAN PHYSICAL BANANARAMA	41	1986
MORE THAN THAT BACKSTREET BOYS	12	2001
MORE THAN THIS [A] ROXY MUSIC	6	1982
MORE THAN THIS [A] EMMIE	5	1999
MORE THAN THIS [B] PETER GABRIEL	47	2002
MORE THAN US EP TRAVIS	16	1998
MORE THAN WORDS EXTREME	2	1991
MORE THAN YOU KNOW MARTIKA	15	1990
THE MORE THEY KNOCK, THE MORE I LOVE YOU GLORIA D BROWN	57	1985
MORE TO LIFE CLIFF RICHARD	23	1991
MORE TO LOVE VOLCANO	32	1994
MORE TO THIS WORLD BAD BOYS INC	8	1994
THE MORE YOU IGNORE ME THE CLOSER I GET MORRISSEY	8	1994
THE MORE YOU LIVE, THE MORE YOU LOVE A FLOCK OF SEAGULLS	26	1984
MORGEN IVO ROBIC	23	1959
MORNIN' AL JARREAU	28	1983
MORNING [A] VAL DOONICAN	12	1971
MORNING [B] WET WET WET	16	1996
MORNING AFTER DARK TIMBALAND FEATURING SO SHY & NELLY FURTADO	6	2009
THE MORNING AFTER (FREE AT LAST) STRIKE	38	1995
MORNING AFTERGLOW ELECTRASY	19	1998
MORNING ALWAYS COMES TOO SOON BRAD CARTER	48	2004
MORNING DANCE SPYRO GYRA	17	1979
MORNING GLORY JAMES & BOBBY PURIFY	27	1976
MORNING HAS BROKEN CAT STEVENS	9	1972
MORNING HAS BROKEN NEIL DIAMOND	36	1992
MORNING HAS BROKEN DANIEL O'DONNELL	32	2000
MORNING OF OUR LIVES MODERN LOVERS	29	1978
THE MORNING PAPERS PRINCE & THE NEW POWER GENERATION	52	1993
MORNING SIDE OF THE MOUNTAIN DONNY & MARIE OSMOND	5	1975
MORNING SUN ROBBIE WILLIAMS	45	2010
MORNING WONDER EARLIES	67	2004
MORNINGLIGHT TEAM DEEP	42	1997
MORNINGTOWN RIDE SEEKERS	2	1966
MORRIS BROWN OUTKAST	43	2006
THE MOST BEAUTIFUL GIRL CHARLIE RICH	2	1974
THE MOST BEAUTIFUL GIRL IN THE WORLD PRINCE	1	1994
MOST GIRLS P!NK	5	2000
MOST HIGH PAGE & PLANT	26	1998
MOST LIKELY YOU GO YOUR OWN WAY BOB DYLAN	51	2007
MOST PRECIOUS LOVE BLAZE PRESENTS UDA FEATURING BARBARA TUCKER	17	2005
THE MOST TIRING DAY CECIL	69	1998
MOTHER [A] DANZIG	62	1994
MOTHER [B] M FACTOR	18	2002
MOTHER AND CHILD REUNION PAUL SIMON	5	1972
MOTHER DAWN BLUE PEARL	50	1992
MOTHER FIXATION MINUTEMAN	45	2003
MOTHER NATURE AND FATHER TIME NAT 'KING' COLE	7	1953
MOTHER OF MINE NEIL REID	2	1972
MOTHER UNIVERSE SOUP DRAGONS	26	1990
MOTHER-IN-LAW ERNIE K-DOE	29	1961
MOTHERLAND-A-FRI-CA TRIBAL HOUSE	57	1990

	Peak Position	Year of Release
MOTHERLESS CHILD ERIC CLAPTON	63	1994
MOTHER'S TALK TEARS FOR FEARS	14	1984
MOTHERSHIP RECONNECTION SCOTT GROOVES FEATURING PARLIAMENT/FUNKADELIC	55	1998
THE MOTION OF LOVE GENE LOVES JEZEBEL	56	1987
MOTIVATION SUM 41	21	2002
THE MOTIVE (LIVING WITHOUT YOU) THEN JERICO	18	1987
MOTIVELESS CRIME SOUTH	72	2004
MOTOR BIKING CHRIS SPEDDING	14	1975
MOTORBIKE BEAT REVILLOS	45	1980
MOTORBIKE TO HEAVEN SALAD	42	1995
MOTORCYCLE RUMBLE STRIPS	46	2007
MOTORCYCLE EMPTINESS MANIC STREET PREACHERS	17	1992
MOTORCYCLE MICHAEL JO ANN CAMPBELL	41	1961
MOTORCYCLE RIDER ICICLE WORKS	73	1990
MOTORHEAD LIVE MOTORHEAD	6	1981
MOTORMANIA ROMAN HOLLIDAY	40	1983
MOTORTOWN KANE GANG	45	1987
THE MOTOWN SONG ROD STEWART	10	1991
MOTOWNPHILLY BOYZ II MEN	23	1992
MOULDY OLD DOUGH LIEUTENANT PIGEON	1	1972
MOUNTAIN GREENERY MEL TORME	4	1956
MOUNTAIN OF LOVE KENNY LYNCH	33	1960
MOUNTAINS [A] PRINCE & THE REVOLUTION	45	1986
MOUNTAINS [B] BIFFY CLYRO	5	2008
THE MOUNTAIN'S HIGH DICK & DEEDEE	37	1961
MOUSE IN A HOLE HEAVY STEREO	53	1996
MOUTH MERRIL BAINBRIDGE	51	1996
MOUTH FOR WAR PANTERA	73	1992
MOUTHWASH KATE NASH	23	2007
MOVE [A] INSPIRAL CARPETS	49	1989
MOVE [B] MOBY	21	1993
MOVE ALONG ALL-AMERICAN REJECTS	42	2006
MOVE ANY MOUNTAIN SHAMEN	4	1991
MOVE AWAY CULTURE CLUB	1	1986
MOVE AWAY JIMMY BLUE DEL AMITRI	36	1990
MOVE BABY MOVE SARTORELLO	56	1996
MOVE CLOSER PHYLLIS NELSON	1	1985
MOVE CLOSER TOM JONES	49	1989
MOVE IN A LITTLE CLOSER HARMONY GRASS	24	1969
MOVE IN MY DIRECTION BANANARAMA	14	2005
MOVE IN STEREO (LIV ULLMAN ON DRUMS) DO ME BAD THINGS	49	2005
MOVE IT CLIFF RICHARD & THE DRIFTERS	2	1958
MOVE IT BABY SIMON SCOTT	37	1964
MOVE IT LIKE THIS BAHA MEN	16	2002
MOVE IT UP CAPPELLA	16	1994
MOVE MANIA SASH! FEATURING SHANNON	8	1998
MOVE ME NO MOUNTAIN SOUL II SOUL, LEAD VOCALS KOFI	31	1992
MOVE MOVE MOVE (THE RED TRIBE) MANCHESTER UNITED FC	6	1996
MOVE NOW MARK B FEATURING TOMMY EVANS	61	2004
MOVE ON DAVID JORDAN	60	2008
MOVE ON BABY CAPPELLA	7	1994
MOVE ON UP CURTIS MAYFIELD	12	1971
MOVE ON UP SUE CHALONER	64	1993
MOVE ON UP TRICKSTER	19	1998
MOVE OVER DARLING DORIS DAY	8	1964
MOVE OVER DARLING TRACEY ULLMAN	8	1983
MOVE RIGHT OUT RICK ASTLEY	58	1991
MOVE THAT BODY [A] TECHNOTRONIC FEATURING REGGIE	12	1991
MOVE THAT BODY [B] NUSH	46	1995
MOVE THE CROWD ERIC B & RAKIM	53	1988
MOVE THIS MOUNTAIN SOPHIE ELLIS-BEXTOR	3	2002
MOVE TO MEMPHIS A-HA	47	1991
MOVE YA BODY NINA SKY	6	2004
MOVE YOUR ASS SCOOTER	23	1995
MOVE YOUR BODY [A] GENE FARROW & GF BAND	33	1978
MOVE YOUR BODY [B] TYREE FEATURING JMD	72	1989
MOVE YOUR BODY [C] XPANSIONS	7	1991
MOVE YOUR BODY [D] ANTICAPPELLA FEATURING MC FIXX IT	21	1994
MOVE YOUR BODY [E] EUROGROOVE	29	1995
MOVE YOUR BODY [F] RUFFNECK FEATURING YAVAHN	60	1996
MOVE YOUR BODY [G] EIFFEL 65	3	2000
MOVE YOUR FEET [A] M-D-EMM	67	1992
MOVE YOUR FEET [B] JUNIOR SENIOR	3	2003
MOVE YOUR FEET TO THE RHYTHM OF THE BEAT HITHOUSE	69	1989
MOVE YOUR LOVE DJH FEATURING STEFY	73	1991
MOVEMENT LCD SOUNDSYSTEM	52	2004
MOVIE STAR HARPO	24	1976
MOVIES [A] HOTHOUSE FLOWERS	68	1990
MOVIES [B] ALIEN ANT FARM	5	2001
MOVIESTAR STEREOPHONICS	5	2004
MOVIN' [A] BRASS CONSTRUCTION	23	1976
MOVIN' [A] 400 BLOWS	54	1985
MOVIN' [B] MARATHON	36	1992
MOVIN' [C] MONE	48	1996
MOVIN' ON [A] BANANARAMA	24	1992
MOVIN' ON [B] APACHE INDIAN	48	1993
MOVIN' ON [C] DEBBIE PENDER	41	1998
MOVIN' ON [D] PROSPECT PARK/CAROLYN HARDING	55	1998
MOVIN' OUT (ANTHONY'S SONG) BILLY JOEL	35	1978
MOVIN' THRU YOUR SYSTEM JARK PRONGO	58	1999
MOVIN TOO FAST ARTFUL DODGER & ROMINA JOHNSON	2	2000
MOVING SUPERGRASS	9	1999
MOVING IN THE RIGHT DIRECTION PASADENAS	49	1992
MOVING MOUNTAINS USHER	25	2008
MOVING ON [A] DREADZONE	58	1997
MOVING ON [B] TAIO CRUZ	26	2007
MOVING ON UP M PEOPLE	2	1993
MOVING ON UP (ON THE RIGHT SIDE) BEVERLEY KNIGHT	42	1996
MOVING PICTURES CRIBS	38	2007
MOVING TO BLACKWATER REUBEN	59	2004
MOVING TO CALIFORNIA STRAW	50	1999
MOVING TO NEW YORK WOMBATS	13	2008
MOVING TOO FAST SUPAFLY INC	23	2006
MOVING UP MOVING ON MOZAIC	62	1996
MOZART 40 SOVEREIGN COLLECTION	27	1971
MOZART SYMPHONY NO. 40 IN G MINOR K550 1ST MOVEMENT (ALLEGRO MOLTO) WALDO DE LOS RIOS	5	1971
MRS OFFICER LIL WAYNE, BOBBY VALENTINO, KIDD KIDD	57	2008
MS GRACE TYMES	1	1974
MS JACKSON OUTKAST	2	2001
MUCH AGAINST EVERYONE'S ADVICE SOULWAX	56	2000
MUCH LOVE SHOLA AMA	17	1998
MUCHO MACHO TOTO COELO	8	1982
(MUCHO MAMBO) SWAY SHAFT	2	1999
MUCK IT OUT FARMERS BOYS	48	1983
MUDDY WATER BLUES PAUL RODGERS	45	1994
MUHAMMAD ALI FAITHLESS	29	2001
MULDER AND SCULLY CATATONIA	3	1998
MULE (CHANT NO. 2) BEGGAR & CO	37	1981
MULE SKINNER BLUES FENDERMEN	32	1960
MULE SKINNER BLUES RUSTY DRAPER	39	1960
MULE TRAIN FRANK IFIELD	22	1963
MULL OF KINTYRE WINGS	1	1977
MULTIPLICATION BOBBY DARIN	5	1961
MULTIPLICATION SHOWADDYWADDY	39	1981
MULTIPLY XZIBIT	39	2002
MUM'S GONE TO ICELAND BENNETT	34	1997
MUNDAYA (THE BOY) TIM DELUXE FEATURING SHAHIN BADAR	61	2004
MUNDIAN TO BACH KE PANJABI MC	5	2003
MUNICH EDITORS	10	2005
THE MUPPET SHOW MUSIC HALL EP MUPPETS	19	1977
MURDER ON THE DANCEFLOOR SOPHIE ELLIS-BEXTOR	2	2001
MURDER SHE WROTE [A] TAIRRIE B	71	1990
MURDER SHE WROTE [B] CHAKA DEMUS & PLIERS	27	1994
MURDERATION EBONY DUBSTERS	59	2004
MURPHY AND THE BRICKS NOEL MURPHY	57	1987
MURPHY'S LAW CHERI	13	1982
MUSAK TRISCO	28	2001
MUSCLE CAR MYLO FEATURING FREEFORM FIVE	38	2006
MUSCLE DEEP THEN JERICO	48	1987
MUSCLE MUSEUM MUSE	25	1999
MUSCLEBOUND SPANDAU BALLET	10	1981
MUSCLES DIANA ROSS	15	1982
MUSIC [A] JOHN MILES	3	1976
MUSIC [A] FARGETTA & ANNE-MARIE SMITH	34	1993
MUSIC [B] ONE WAY FEATURING AL HUDSON	56	1979
MUSIC [C] FR DAVID	71	1983
MUSIC PART 1 [D] D TRAIN	23	1983
MUSIC [E] OMAR	53	1992
MUSIC [F] MADONNA	1	2000
MUSIC [G] ERICK SERMON FEATURING MARVIN GAYE	36	2001
MUSIC AND LIGHTS IMAGINATION	5	1982
MUSIC AND YOU [A] SAL SOLO WITH THE LONDON COMMUNITY GOSPEL CHOIR	52	1985
MUSIC AND YOU [B] ROOM 5 FEATURING OLIVER CHEATHAM	38	2003
MUSIC FOR CHAMELEONS GARY NUMAN	19	1982
MUSIC GETS THE BEST OF ME SOPHIE ELLIS-BEXTOR	14	2002
THE MUSIC I LIKE ALEXIA	31	1998
MUSIC IN MY MIND ADAM F	27	1998
THE MUSIC IN YOU MONOBOY FEATURING DELORES	50	2001
MUSIC IS A PASSION ATLANTIC OCEAN	59	1994
MUSIC IS LIFE DIRT DEVILS	53	2003
THE MUSIC IS MOVING FARGETTA	74	1996
MUSIC IS MOVING CORTINA	42	2001
MUSIC IS MY RADAR BLUR	10	2000
MUSIC IS POWER RICHARD ASHCROFT	20	2006
MUSIC IS THE ANSWER (DANCING' & PRANCIN') DANNY TENAGLIA & CELEDA	36	1998
MUSIC MAKES ME HIGH LOST BOYZ	42	1996
MUSIC MAKES YOU FEEL LIKE DANCING BRASS CONSTRUCTION	39	1980
MUSIC MAKES YOU LOSE CONTROL LES RYTHMES DIGITALES	69	1998
MUSIC MATTERS FAITHLESS FEATURING CASS FOX	38	2007
THE MUSIC OF GOODBYE (LOVE THEME FROM 'OUT OF AFRICA') AL JARREAU	75	1986
MUSIC OF MY HEART *NSYNC & GLORIA ESTEFAN	34	2000
THE MUSIC OF THE NIGHT MICHAEL CRAWFORD	7	1987
THE MUSIC OF THE NIGHT BARBRA STREISAND (DUET WITH MICHAEL CRAWFORD)	54	1994
THE MUSIC OF TORVILL AND DEAN EP RICHARD HARTLEY/MICHAEL REED ORCHESTRA	9	1984

Title / Artist	Peak Position	Year of Release
MUSIC POWER PORNO	72	2006
MUSIC REVOLUTION SCUMFROG	46	2003
MUSIC SAVED MY LIFE CEVIN FISHER	67	1999
MUSIC SOUNDS BETTER WITH YOU STARDUST	2	1998
MUSIC STOP RAILWAY CHILDREN	66	1990
MUSIC TAKES YOU BLAME	48	1992
THE MUSIC THAT WE HEAR (MOOG ISLAND) MORCHEEBA	47	1997
MUSIC TO WATCH GIRLS BY ANDY WILLIAMS	9	1967
MUSICAL FREEDOM (MOVING ON UP) PAUL SIMPSON FEATURING ADEVA	22	1989
MUSICAL MELODY UNIQUE 3	29	1990
THE MUSIC'S GOT ME BASS BUMPERS	25	1994
THE MUSIC'S GOT ME BROOKLYN BOUNCE	67	1998
THE MUSIC'S NO GOOD WITHOUT YOU CHER	8	2001
MUSIQUE DAFT PUNK	7	1997
MUSKRAT EVERLY BROTHERS	20	1961
MUSKRAT RAMBLE FREDDY CANNON	32	1961
MUST BE LOVE FYA FEATURING SMUJJI	13	2004
MUST BE MADISON JOE LOSS ORCHESTRA	20	1962
MUST BE SANTA TOMMY STEELE	40	1960
MUST BE SANTA BOB DYLAN	41	2010
MUST BE THE MUSIC [A] HYSTERIX	40	1994
MUST BE THE MUSIC [B] JOEY NEGRO FEATURING TAKA BOOM	8	2000
MUST BEE THE MUSIC KING BEE FEATURING MICHELE	44	1991
MUST GET OUT MAROON 5	39	2005
A MUST TO AVOID HERMAN'S HERMITS	6	1965
MUSTAFA CHA CHA CHA STAIFFI & HIS MUSTAFAS	43	1964
MUSTANG SALLY WILSON PICKETT	28	1966
MUSTANG SALLY COMMITMENTS	63	1991
MUSTAPHA BOB AZZAM	23	1960
MUTANTS IN MEGA CITY ONE FINK BROTHERS	50	1985
MUTATIONS EP ORBITAL	24	1992
MUTUAL ATTRACTION CHANGE	60	1985
MUTUALLY ASSURED DESTRUCTION GILLAN	32	1981
MUZIKIZUM X-PRESS 2	52	2001
MY 16TH APOLOGY (EP) SHAKESPEAR'S SISTER	61	1993
MY ADIDAS RUN DMC	62	1986
MY AFFAIR KIRSTY MacCOLL	56	1991
MY ALL MARIAH CAREY	4	1998
MY ANGEL ROCK GODDESS	64	1983
MY APOCALYPSE METALLICA	51	2008
MY ARMS KEEP MISSING YOU RICK ASTLEY	2	1987
MY BABY LIL' ROMEO	67	2001
MY BABY JUST CARES FOR ME NINA SIMONE	5	1987
MY BABY LEFT ME DAVE BERRY & THE CRUISERS	37	1964
MY BABY LEFT ME ELVIS PRESLEY	18	2007
MY BABY LEFT ME – THAT'S ALL RIGHT (MEDLEY) SLADE	32	1977
MY BABY LOVES LOVIN' WHITE PLAINS	9	1970
MY BAG LLOYD COLE & THE COMMOTIONS	46	1987
MY BAND D12	2	2004
MY BEAT BLAZE FEATURING PALMER BROWN	53	2001
MY BEATBOX DEEJAY PUNK-ROC	43	1998
MY BEAUTIFUL FRIEND CHARLATANS	31	1999
MY BEST FRIEND'S GIRL CARS	3	1978
MY BLUE HEAVEN FRANK SINATRA	33	1961
MY BODY LEVERT SWEAT GILL	21	1998
MY BONNIE TONY SHERIDAN & THE BEATLES	48	1963
MY BOO USHER	5	2004
MY BOOK BEAUTIFUL SOUTH	43	1990
MY BOOMERANG WON'T COME BACK CHARLIE DRAKE	14	1961
MY BOY ELVIS PRESLEY	5	1974
MY BOY FLAT TOP FRANKIE VAUGHAN	20	1956
MY BOY LOLLIPOP MILLIE	2	1964
MY BOYFRIEND'S BACK ANGELS	50	1963
MY BRAVE FACE PAUL McCARTNEY	18	1989
MY BROTHER JAKE FREE	4	1971
MY CAMERA NEVER LIES BUCKS FIZZ	1	1982
MY CHERIE AMOUR STEVIE WONDER	4	1969
MY CHILD CONNIE FRANCIS	26	1965
MY CIRCUITBOARD CITY WOMBATS	69	2009
MY COCO STELLASTARR*	73	2004
MY COO-CO-CHOO ALVIN STARDUST	2	1973
MY COUNTRY MIDNIGHT OIL	66	1993
MY CULTURE 1 GIANT LEAP FEATURING MAXI JAZZ & ROBBIE WILLIAMS	9	2002
MY CUTIE CUTIE SHAKIN' STEVENS	75	1990
MY DEFINITION OF A BOOMBASTIC JAZZ STYLE DREAM WARRIORS	13	1990
MY DELIRIUM LADYHAWKE	33	2008
MY DESIRE AMIRA	20	1997
MY DESTINY [A] LIONEL RICHIE	7	1992
MY DESTINY [B] DELINQUENT FEATURING K-CAT	19	2008
MY DING-A-LING CHUCK BERRY	1	1972
MY DIXIE DARLING LONNIE DONEGAN	10	1957
MY DJ (PUMP IT UP SOME) RICHIE RICH	74	1988
MY DOCS KISS AMC	66	1990
MY DOORBELL WHITE STRIPES	10	2005
MY DRUG CHERRYFALLS	71	2005
MY DRUG BUDDY LEMONHEADS	44	1993
MY DYING MACHINE GARY NUMAN	66	1984
MY EGYPTIAN LOVER SPACE COWBOY FEATURING NADIA OH	45	2007
MY EVER CHANGING MOODS STYLE COUNCIL	5	1984
MY EYES TRAVIS	60	2007
MY EYES ADORED YOU FRANKIE VALLI	5	1975
MY FAMILY DEPENDS ON ME SIMONE	75	1991
MY FATHER'S EYES ERIC CLAPTON	33	1998
MY FATHER'S SHOES LEVEL 42	55	1992
MY FATHER'S SON CONNOR REEVES	12	1997
MY FAVORITE MISTAKE SHERYL CROW	9	1998
MY FAVOURITE GAME CARDIGANS	14	1998
MY FAVOURITE WASTE OF TIME OWEN PAUL	3	1986
MY FEELING JUNIOR JACK	31	2000
MY FEET KEEP DANCING CHIC	21	1979
MY FIRST NIGHT WITHOUT YOU CYNDI LAUPER	53	1989
MY FOOLISH FRIEND TALK TALK	57	1983
MY FORBIDDEN LOVER CHIC	15	1979
MY FORBIDDEN LOVER ROMINA JOHNSON FEATURING LUCI MARTIN & NORMA JEAN	59	2000
MY FREND STAN SLADE	2	1973
MY FRIEND [A] FRANKIE LAINE	3	1954
MY FRIEND [B] ROY ORBISON	35	1969
MY FRIEND [C] GROOVE ARMADA	36	2001
MY FRIEND JACK SMOKE	45	1967
MY FRIEND JACK BONEY M	57	1980
MY FRIEND THE SEA PETULA CLARK	7	1961
MY FRIENDS [A] RED HOT CHILI PEPPERS	29	1995
MY FRIENDS [B] STEREOPHONICS	32	2007
MY FRIENDS OVER YOU NEW FOUND GLORY	30	2002
MY GENERATION [A] WHO	2	1965
MY GENERATION [A] ZIMMERS	26	2007
MY GENERATION [B] LIMP BIZKIT	15	2000
MY GENERATION [C] BILLIAM	23	2008
MY GETAWAY TIONNE 'T-BOZ' WATKINS	44	2001
MY GIRL [A] TEMPTATIONS	2	1965
MY GIRL [A] OTIS REDDING	11	1965
MY GIRL [A] WHISPERS	26	1980
MY GIRL [B] MADNESS	3	1980
MY GIRL [C] ROD STEWART	32	1981
MY GIRL BILL JIM STAFFORD	20	1974
MY GIRL JOSEPHINE FATS DOMINO	32	1961
MY GIRL JOSEPHINE SUPERCAT FEATURING JACK RADICS	22	1995
MY GIRL LOLLIPOP (MY BOY LOLLIPOP) BAD MANNERS	9	1982
MY GIRL LOVES ME SHALAMAR	45	1985
MY GIRL MY GIRL WARREN STACEY	26	2002
MY GUY [A] MARY WELLS	5	1964
MY GUY [B] TRACEY ULLMAN	23	1984
MY GUY – MY GIRL (MEDLEY) AMII STEWART & JOHNNY BRISTOL	39	1980
MY GUY – MY GIRL (MEDLEY) AMII STEWART & DEON ESTUS	63	1986
MY HAND OVER MY HEART MARC ALMOND	33	1992
MY HAPPINESS CONNIE FRANCIS	4	1959
MY HAPPY ENDING AVRIL LAVIGNE	5	2004
MY HEAD'S IN MISSISSIPPI ZZ TOP	37	1991
MY HEART GENE VINCENT	16	1960
MY HEART CAN'T TELL YOU NO ROD STEWART	49	1989
MY HEART GOES BANG (GET ME TO THE DOCTOR) DEAD OR ALIVE	23	1985
MY HEART GOES BOOM FRENCH AFFAIR	44	2000
MY HEART HAS A MIND OF ITS OWN CONNIE FRANCIS	3	1960
MY HEART THE BEAT D-SHAKE	42	1991
MY HEART WILL GO ON CELINE DION	1	1998
MY HEART'S BEATING WILD (TIC TAC TIC TAC) GIBSON BROTHERS	56	1983
MY HEART'S SYMPHONY GARY LEWIS & THE PLAYBOYS	36	1975
MY HERO FOO FIGHTERS	21	1998
MY HOMETOWN BRUCE SPRINGSTEEN	9	1985
MY HOUSE TERRORVISION	29	1994
MY HOUSE IS YOUR HOUSE MAXTREME	66	2002
MY HUMPS BLACK EYED PEAS	3	2005
MY IMMORTAL EVANESCENCE	7	2003
MY IRON LUNG RADIOHEAD	24	1994
MY JAMAICAN GUY GRACE JONES	56	1983
MY KIND OF GIRL MATT MONRO	5	1961
MY KIND OF GIRL FRANK SINATRA WITH COUNT BASIE	35	1963
MY KINDA LIFE CLIFF RICHARD	15	1977
MY KINGDOM FUTURE SOUND OF LONDON	13	1996
MY LAST NIGHT WITH YOU ARROWS	25	1975
MY LIFE [A] BILLY JOEL	12	1978
MY LIFE [B] CHANEL	39	2006
MY LIFE [C] GAME FEATURING LIL WAYNE	34	2008
MY LIFE IS IN YOUR HANDS MELTDOWN	44	1996
MY LIFE WOULD SUCK WITHOUT YOU KELLY CLARKSON	1	2009
MY LIFE WOULD SUCK WITHOUT YOU GLEE CAST	53	2010
MY LITTLE BABY MIKE BERRY WITH THE OUTLAWS	34	1963
MY LITTLE BROTHER ART BRUT	49	2004
MY LITTLE CORNER OF THE WORLD ANITA BRYANT	48	1960
MY LITTLE GIRL [A] CRICKETS	17	1963
MY LITTLE GIRL [B] AUTUMN	37	1971
MY LITTLE LADY TREMELOES	6	1968
MY LITTLE ONE MARMALADE	15	1971
MY LOVE [A] PETULA CLARK	4	1966
MY LOVE [B] PAUL McCARTNEY & WINGS	9	1973
MY LOVE [C] LIONEL RICHIE	70	1983
MY LOVE [D] JULIO IGLESIAS FEATURING STEVIE WONDER	5	1988
MY LOVE [E] LONDON BOYS	46	1989
MY LOVE [F] MARY J BLIGE	29	1994
MY LOVE [G] KELE LE ROC	8	1999
MY LOVE [H] WESTLIFE	1	2000
MY LOVE [I] KLUSTER FEATURING RON CARROLL	73	2001

Title / Artist	Peak Position	Year of Release
MY LOVE [J] JUSTIN TIMBERLAKE FEATURING TI	2	2006
MY LOVE AND DEVOTION DORIS DAY	10	1952
MY LOVE AND DEVOTION MATT MONRO	29	1962
MY LOVE FOR YOU JOHNNY MATHIS	9	1960
MY LOVE IS A FIRE DONNY OSMOND	64	1991
MY LOVE IS ALWAYS SAFFRON HILL FEATURING BEN ONONO	28	2003
MY LOVE IS DEEP SARA PARKER	22	1997
MY LOVE IS FOR REAL PAULA ABDUL FEATURING OFFRA HAZA	28	1995
MY LOVE IS FOR REAL STRIKE	35	1996
MY LOVE IS GUARANTEED SYBIL	42	1987
MY LOVE IS LIKE...WO! MYA	33	2003
MY LOVE IS MAGIC BAS NOIR	73	1989
MY LOVE IS SO RAW ALYSON WILLIAMS FEATURING NIKKI D	34	1989
MY LOVE IS THE SHHH! SOMETHIN' FOR THE PEOPLE FEATURING TRINA & TAMARA	64	1998
MY LOVE IS WAITING MARVIN GAYE	34	1983
MY LOVE IS YOUR LOVE WHITNEY HOUSTON	2	1999
MY LOVE LIFE MORRISSEY	29	1991
MY LOVER'S PRAYER OTIS REDDING	37	1966
MY LOVER'S PRAYER ALISTAIR GRIFFIN	5	2004
MY LOVIN' EN VOGUE	4	1992
MY MAGIC MAN ROCHELLE	27	1986
MY MAMMY HAPPENINGS	34	1967
MY MAN JADE EWEN	35	2009
MY MAN A SWEET MAN MILLIE JACKSON	50	1972
MY MAN AND ME LYNSEY DE PAUL	40	1975
MY MARIE ENGELBERT HUMPERDINCK	31	1970
MY MATE PAUL DAVID HOLMES	39	1998
MY MELANCHOLY BABY TOMMY EDWARDS	29	1959
MY MELANCHOLY BABY CHAS & DAVE	51	1983
MY MIND'S EYE SMALL FACES	4	1966
MY MUM IS ONE IN A MILLION CHILDREN OF TANSLEY SCHOOL	27	1981
MY MY MY ARMAND VAN HELDEN	15	2004
MY NAME McLEAN	10	2010
MY NAME IS EMINEM	2	1999
MY NAME IS JACK MANFRED MANN	8	1968
MY NAME IS NOT SUSAN WHITNEY HOUSTON	29	1991
MY NAME IS PRINCE PRINCE & THE NEW POWER GENERATION	7	1992
MY NECK MY BACK (LICK IT) KHIA	4	2004
MY NEIGHBOUR'S HOUSE BLUETONES	68	2006
MY OH MY [A] SAD CAFE	14	1980
MY OH MY [B] SLADE	2	1983
MY OH MY [C] AQUA	6	1998
MY OLD MAN'S A DUSTMAN LONNIE DONEGAN	1	1960
MY OLD PIANO DIANA ROSS	5	1980
MY ONE SIN NAT 'KING' COLE	17	1955
MY ONE TEMPTATION MICA PARIS	7	1988
MY ONE TRUE FRIEND BETTE MIDLER	58	1998
MY ONLY LOVE BOB SINCLAR FEATURING LEE A GENESIS	56	1999
MY OWN SUMMER (SHOVE IT) DEFTONES	29	1998
MY OWN TRUE LOVE DANNY WILLIAMS	45	1963
MY OWN WAY DURAN DURAN	14	1981
MY OWN WORST ENEMY LIT	16	1999
MY PATCH JIM NOIR	65	2006
MY PEACE OF HEAVEN TEN CITY	63	1992
MY PERFECT COUSIN UNDERTONES	9	1980
MY PERSONAL POSSESSION NAT 'KING' COLE & THE FOUR KNIGHTS	21	1957
MY PHILOSOPHY BOOGIE DOWN PRODUCTIONS	69	1988
MY PLACE NELLY	1	2004
MY PLAGUE SLIPKNOT	43	2002
MY PRAYER PLATTERS	4	1956
MY PRAYER GERRY MONROE	9	1970
MY PREROGATIVE BOBBY BROWN	6	1988
MY PREROGATIVE BRITNEY SPEARS	3	2004
MY PRETTY ONE CLIFF RICHARD	6	1987
MY PUPPET PAL TIGER	62	1996
MY RECOVERY INJECTION BIFFY CLYRO	24	2004
MY REMEDY HINDA HICKS	61	2000
MY RESISTANCE IS LOW ROBIN SARSTEDT	3	1976
MY RISING STAR NORTHSIDE	50	1990
MY SACRIFICE CREED	18	2002
MY SALT HEART HUE & CRY	47	1991
MY SENTIMENTAL FRIEND HERMAN'S HERMITS	2	1969
MY SEPTEMBER LOVE DAVID WHITFIELD	3	1956
MY SHARONA KNACK	6	1979
MY SHIP IS COMING IN WALKER BROTHERS	3	1965
MY SIDE OF THE BED SUSANNA HOFFS	44	1991
MY SIMPLE HEART THREE DEGREES	9	1979
MY SISTER JULIANA HATFIELD THREE	71	1993
MY SON JOHN DAVID WHITFIELD	22	1956
MY SON MY SON VERA LYNN WITH FRANK WEIR, HIS SAXOPHONE, HIS ORCHESTRA & CHORUS	1	1954
MY SOUL PLEADS FOR YOU SIMON WEBBE	45	2007
MY SPECIAL ANGEL MALCOLM VAUGHAN	3	1957
MY SPECIAL ANGEL BOBBY HELMS WITH THE ANITA KERR SINGERS	22	1957
MY SPECIAL CHILD SINEAD O'CONNOR	42	1991
MY SPECIAL DREAM SHIRLEY BASSEY	32	1964
MY SPIRIT TILT	61	1997
MY STAR IAN BROWN	5	1998
MY SUNDAY BABY DALE SISTERS	36	1961
MY SUPERSTAR DIMESTARS	72	2001
MY SWEET JANE G.U.N.	51	1997
MY SWEET LORD GEORGE HARRISON	1	1971
MY SWEET ROSALIE BROTHERHOOD OF MAN	30	1976
MY TELEPHONE COLDCUT	52	1989
MY TIME [A] SOUVLAKI	63	1998
MY TIME [B] DUTCH FEATURING CRYSTAL WATERS	22	2003
MY TOOT TOOT DENISE LA SALLE	6	1985
MY TOWN GLASS TIGER	33	1991
MY TRUE LOVE JACK SCOTT	9	1958
MY UKELELE MAX BYGRAVES	19	1959
MY UNFINISHED SYMPHONY DAVID WHITFIELD	29	1956
MY UNKNOWN LOVE COUNT INDIGO	59	1996
MY VISION JAKATTA FEATURING SEAL	6	2002
MY WAY [A] EDDIE COCHRAN	23	1963
MY WAY [B] FRANK SINATRA	5	1969
MY WAY [B] DOROTHY SQUIRES	25	1970
MY WAY [B] ELVIS PRESLEY	9	1977
MY WAY [B] SEX PISTOLS	7	1978
MY WAY [B] SHANE MacGOWAN	29	1996
MY WAY [C] LIMP BIZKIT	6	2001
MY WAY OF GIVING IN CHRIS FARLOWE	48	1967
MY WAY OF THINKING UB40	6	1980
MY WEAKNESS IS NONE OF YOUR BUSINESS EMBRACE	9	1998
MY WHITE BICYCLE NAZARETH	14	1975
MY WOMAN'S MAN DAVE DEE	42	1970
MY WORLD [A] CUPID'S INSPIRATION	33	1968
MY WORLD [B] BEE GEES	16	1972
MY WORLD [C] SECRET AFFAIR	16	1980
MY WORLD OF BLUE KARL DENVER	29	1964
MYFANWY DAVID ESSEX	41	1987
MYKONOS FLEET FOXES	53	2009
MYMYMY ARMAND VAN HELDEN FEATURING TARA	12	2006
MYSTERIES OF LOVE L.A. MIX	46	1991
MYSTERIES OF THE WORLD MFSB	41	1981
MYSTERIOUS GIRL PETER ANDRE FEATURING BUBBLER RANX	1	1995
MYSTERIOUS TIMES SASH! FEATURING TINA COUSINS	2	1998
MYSTERIOUS WAYS U2	13	1991
MYSTERY [A] DIO	34	1984
MYSTERY [B] MYSTERY	56	2001
THE MYSTERY [C] DOUG WALKER	36	2008
MYSTERY GIRL [A] JESS CONRAD	18	1961
MYSTERY GIRL [B] DUKES	47	1981
MYSTERY LADY BILLY OCEAN	49	1985
MYSTERY LAND Y-TRAXX FEATURING NEVE	70	2003
MYSTERY LAND (EP) Y-TRAXX	63	1997
MYSTERY SONG STATUS QUO	11	1976
MYSTERY TRAIN ELVIS PRESLEY	25	1957
MYSTICAL MACHINE GUN KULA SHAKER	14	1999
MYSTIFY INXS	14	1989
MYZSTERIOUS MIZSTER JONES SLADE	50	1985

N

Title / Artist	Peak Position	Year of Release
N DEY SAY NELLY	6	2005
NA NA HEY HEY KISS HIM GOODBYE STEAM	9	1970
NA NA HEY HEY KISS HIM GOODBYE BANANARAMA	5	1983
NA NA IS THE SADDEST WORD STYLISTICS	5	1975
NA NA NA COZY POWELL	10	1974
NACHNA ONDA NEI TIGERSTYLE	62	2008
NADINE (IS IT YOU) CHUCK BERRY	27	1964
NAGASAKI BADGER DISCO CITIZENS	56	1998
NAILS IN MY FEET CROWDED HOUSE	22	1993
NAIROBI TOMMY STEELE	3	1958
NAIVE KOOKS	5	2006
NAIVE SONG MIRWAIS	50	2000
NAKASAKI EP (I NEED A LOVER TONIGHT) KEN DOH	7	1996
NAKED [A] REEF	11	1995
NAKED [B] LOUISE	5	1996
NAKED AND SACRED CHYNNA PHILLIPS	62	1996
NAKED AND SACRED MARIA NAYLER	32	1998
NAKED EYE LUSCIOUS JACKSON	25	1997
NAKED IN THE RAIN BLUE PEARL	4	1990
NAKED LOVE (JUST SAY YOU WANT ME) QUARTZ & DINA CARROLL	39	1991
NAKED WITHOUT YOU ROACHFORD	53	1998
NAME AND NUMBER CURIOSITY	14	1989
THE NAME OF THE GAME ABBA	1	1977
THE NAMELESS ONE WENDY JAMES	34	1993
NANCY BOY PLACEBO	4	1997
A NANNY IN MANHATTAN LILYS	16	1998
NAPOLEON WOLFMAN	44	2004
NAPPY LOVE GOODIES	21	1975
NARCO TOURISTS SLAM VS UNKLE	66	2001
NARCOTIC INFLUENCE EMPIRION	64	1996
NASHVILLE BOOGIE BERT WEEDON	29	1959
NASHVILLE CATS LOVIN' SPOONFUL	26	1967
NASTRADAMUS NAS	24	2000
NASTY JANET JACKSON	19	1986
NASTY BREAKS CLIPZ	72	2005
NASTY GIRL [A] INAYA DAY	9	2005
NASTY GIRL [B] NOTORIOUS B.I.G. FEATURING DIDDY, NELLY, JAGGED EDGE AND AVERY STORM	1	2006
NASTY GIRLS T.W.A.	51	1995
NATALIE'S PARTY SHACK	63	1999
NATHAN JONES SUPREMES	5	1971
NATHAN JONES BANANARAMA	15	1988
NATIONAL EXPRESS DIVINE COMEDY	8	1999
NATIVE BOY (UPTOWN) ANIMAL NIGHTLIFE	60	1983
NATIVE LAND EVERYTHING BUT THE GIRL	73	1984
NATIVE NEW YORKER ODYSSEY	5	1978
NATIVE NEW YORKER BLACK BOX	46	1997

Title / Artist	Peak Position	Year of Release
NATURAL [A] BRYAN POWELL	73	1993
NATURAL [B] PETER ANDRE	6	1997
NATURAL [C] S CLUB 7	3	2000
NATURAL BLUES MOBY	11	2000
NATURAL BORN BUGIE HUMBLE PIE	4	1969
NATURAL BORN KILLAZ DR DRE & ICE CUBE	45	1995
NATURAL HIGH [A] BLOODSTONE	40	1973
NATURAL HIGH [B] BITTY McLEAN	63	1996
NATURAL LIFE NATURAL LIFE	47	1992
NATURAL ONE FOLK IMPLOSION	45	1996
NATURAL SINNER FAIR WEATHER	6	1970
NATURAL THING INNOCENCE	16	1990
NATURAL WORLD RODEO JONES	75	1993
NATURE BOY [A] BOBBY DARIN	24	1961
NATURE BOY [A] GEORGE BENSON	26	1977
NATURE BOY [A] CENTRAL LINE	21	1983
NATURE BOY [B] NICK CAVE & THE BAD SEEDS	37	2004
NATURE OF LOVE WATERFRONT	63	1989
NATURE'S LAW EMBRACE	2	2006
NATURE'S TIME FOR LOVE JOE BROWN & THE BRUVVERS	26	1963
NAUGHTY CHRISTMAS (GOBLIN IN THE OFFICE) FAT LES	21	1998
NAUGHTY GIRL [A] HOLLY VALANCE	16	2002
NAUGHTY GIRL [B] BEYONCE	10	2004
NAUGHTY GIRLS SAMANTHA FOX FEATURING FULL FORCE	31	1988
NAUGHTY LADY OF SHADY LANE DEAN MARTIN	5	1955
NAUGHTY LADY OF SHADY LANE AMES BROTHERS	6	1955
NAUGHTY NAUGHTY JOHN PARR	58	1986
NAUGHTY NAUGHTY NAUGHTY JOY SARNEY	26	1977
THE NAUGHTY NORTH & THE SEXY SOUTH E-MOTION	17	1996
NAZIS ROGER TAYLOR	22	1994
NEANDERTHAL MAN HOTLEGS	2	1970
NEAR TO ME TEENAGE FANCLUB & JAD FAIR	68	2002
NEAR WILD HEAVEN R.E.M.	27	1991
NEAR YOU MIGIL FIVE	31	1964
NEARER THAN HEAVEN DELAYS	21	2004
NEARLY LOST YOU SCREAMING TREES	50	1993
NECESSARY EVIL BODY COUNT	45	1994
NEED GOOD LOVE TUFF JAM	44	1998
NEED TO FEEL LOVED REFLEKT FEATURING DELLINE BASS	14	2005
NEED YOU TONIGHT INXS	2	1987
NEED YOUR LOVE SO BAD FLEETWOOD MAC	31	1968
NEED YOUR LOVE SO BAD GARY MOORE	48	1995
NEEDIN' U DAVID MORALES PRESENTS THE FACE	8	1998
NEEDIN' YOU II DAVID MORALES PRESENTS THE FACE FEATURING JULIET ROBERTS	11	2001
THE NEEDLE AND THE DAMAGE DONE NEIL YOUNG	75	1993
NEEDLES AND PINS SEARCHERS	1	1964
NEEDLES AND PINS SMOKIE	10	1977
NEGASONIC TEENAGE WARHEAD MONSTER MAGNET	49	1995
NEGATIVE MANSUN	27	1998
NEGOTIATE WITH LOVE RACHEL STEVENS	10	2005
NEHEMIAH HOPE OF THE STATES	30	2004
NEIGHBOUR UGLY KID JOE	28	1992
NEIGHBOURHOOD #2 (LAIKA) ARCADE FIRE	30	2005
NEIGHBOURHOOD [A] SPACE	11	1996
NEIGHBOURHOOD [B] ZED BIAS	25	2000
NEIL JUNG TEENAGE FANCLUB	62	1995
NEITHER ONE OF US GLADYS KNIGHT & THE PIPS	31	1973
NELLIE THE ELEPHANT TOY DOLLS	4	1984
NELSON MANDELA SPECIAL A.K.A.	9	1984
NE-NE-NA-NA-NA-NA-NU-NU BAD MANNERS	28	1980
NEON KNIGHTS BLACK SABBATH	22	1980
NEON LIGHTS KRAFTWERK	53	1978
NEPTUNE INME	46	2003
NERVOUS MATT BIANCO	59	1989
NERVOUS BREAKDOWN [A] CARLEEN ANDERSON	27	1994
NERVOUS BREAKDOWN [B] SHRINK	42	1998
NERVOUS SHAKEDOWN AC/DC	35	1984
NERVOUS WRECK RADIO STARS	39	1978
NESSAJA SCOOTER	4	2002
NESSUN DORMA LUCIANNO PAVAROTTI	2	1990
NESSUN DORMA FROM 'TURANDOT' LUIS COBOS FEATURING PLACIDO DOMINGO	59	1990
NETHERWORLD LSG	63	1997
NEUROTICA CUD	37	1994
NEUTRON DANCE POINTER SISTERS	31	1985
NEVER [A] HEART	8	1988
NEVER [B] HOUSE OF LOVE	41	1989
NEVER [C] JOMANDA	40	1993
NEVER [D] ELECTRAFIXION	58	1995
NEVER 'AD NOTHIN' ANGELIC UPSTARTS	52	1979
NEVER AGAIN KELLY CLARKSON	9	2007
NEVER AGAIN [A] DISCHARGE	64	1981
NEVER AGAIN [B] MISSION	34	1992
NEVER AGAIN [C] JC 001	67	1993
NEVER AGAIN [D] HAPPY CLAPPERS	49	1996
NEVER AGAIN [E] NICKELBACK	30	2002
NEVER AGAIN (THE DAYS TIME ERASED) CLASSIX NOUVEAUX	44	1981
NEVER BE ANYONE ELSE BUT YOU RICKY NELSON	14	1959
NEVER BE LONELY FEELING	9	2006
NEVER BE THE SAME AGAIN MELANIE C & LISA 'LEFT EYE' LOPES	1	2000
NEVER BE YOUR WOMAN NAUGHTY BOY PRESENTS WILEY FEATURING EMELI SANDE	8	2010
NEVER BEFORE DEEP PURPLE	35	1972
NEVER CAN SAY GOODBYE JACKSON 5	33	1971
NEVER CAN SAY GOODBYE GLORIA GAYNOR	2	1974
NEVER CAN SAY GOODBYE COMMUNARDS	4	1987
NEVER CAN SAY GOODBYE YAZZ	61	1997
NEVER CAN TELL I KAMANCHI	69	2003
NEVER DO A TANGO WITH AN ESKIMO ALMA COGAN	6	1955
NEVER DO YOU WRONG STEPHANIE MILLS	57	1993
NEVER DONE NOTHING LIKE THAT BEFORE SUPERGRASS	75	2002
NEVER ENDING HALO	56	2002
NEVER ENDING DREAM CASCADA	46	2007
NEVER ENDING SONG OF LOVE NEW SEEKERS	2	1971
NEVER ENDING STORY LIMAHL	4	1984
NEVER ENOUGH [A] JESUS JONES	42	1989
NEVER ENOUGH [B] CURE	13	1990
NEVER ENOUGH [C] BORIS DLUGOSCH FEATURING ROISIN MURPHY	16	2001
NEVER ENOUGH [D] OPEN	53	2004
NEVER EVER ALL SAINTS	1	1997
NEVER FELT LIKE THIS BEFORE SHAZNAY LEWIS	8	2004
NEVER FELT THIS WAY HI-LUX	58	1995
NEVER FORGET TAKE THAT	1	1995
NEVER FORGET YOU NOISETTES	20	2009
NEVER FOUND A LOVE LIKE THIS BEFORE UPSIDE DOWN	19	1996
NEVER GIVE UP MONIE LOVE	41	1993
NEVER GIVE UP ON A GOOD THING GEORGE BENSON	14	1982
NEVER GIVE YOU UP SHARON REDD	20	1982
NEVER GOIN' DOWN ADAMSKI FEATURING JIMI POLO	51	1991
NEVER GOING NOWHERE BLUETONES	40	2003
NEVER GONNA BE THE SAME [A] DANNY WILSON	69	1989
NEVER GONNA BE THE SAME [B] SEAN PAUL	22	2006
NEVER GONNA CHANGE MY MIND JOEY LAWRENCE	49	1998
NEVER GONNA COME BACK DOWN BT	51	2001
NEVER GONNA CRY AGAIN EURYTHMICS	63	1981
NEVER GONNA FALL IN LOVE AGAIN DANA	31	1976
NEVER GONNA GIVE YOU UP [A] MUSICAL YOUTH	6	1983
NEVER GONNA GIVE YOU UP [B] RICK ASTLEY	1	1987
NEVER GONNA (GIVE YOU UP) [B] F.K.W.	48	1993
NEVER GONNA GIVE YOU UP (WON'T LET YOU BE) PATRICE RUSHEN	66	1981
NEVER GONNA LEAVE YOUR SIDE DANIEL BEDINGFIELD	1	2003
NEVER GONNA LET YOU GO [A] SERGIO MENDES	45	1983
NEVER GONNA LET YOU GO [B] TINA MOORE	7	1997
NEVER GOODBYE KARL DENVER	9	1962
NEVER HAD A DREAM COME TRUE [A] STEVIE WONDER	6	1970
NEVER HAD A DREAM COME TRUE [B] S CLUB 7	1	2000
NEVER HAD IT SO GOOD TAKE 5	34	1999
NEVER IN A MILLION YEARS BOOMTOWN RATS	62	1981
NEVER KNEW LOVE [A] RICK ASTLEY	70	1991
NEVER KNEW LOVE [B] OLETA ADAMS	22	1995
NEVER KNEW LOVE [C] NIGHTCRAWLERS	59	1999
NEVER KNEW LOVE [D] STELLA BROWNE	42	2002
NEVER KNEW LOVE LIKE THIS ALEXANDER O'NEAL FEATURING CHERRELLE	26	1988
NEVER KNEW LOVE LIKE THIS PAULINE HENRY FEATURING WAYNE MARSHALL	40	1996
NEVER KNEW LOVE LIKE THIS BEFORE STEPHANIE MILLS	4	1980
NEVER LEAVE YOU TINCHY STRYDER FEATURING AMELLE	1	2009
NEVER LEAVE YOU (UH OOOH UH OOOH) LUMIDEE	2	2003
NEVER LET GO [A] JOHN BARRY ORCHESTRA	49	1960
NEVER LET GO [B] HYPER GO GO	45	1993
NEVER LET GO [C] CLIFF RICHARD	32	1993
NEVER LET HER SLIP AWAY ANDREW GOLD	5	1978
NEVER LET HER SLIP AWAY TREVOR WALTERS	73	1984
NEVER LET HER SLIP AWAY UNDERCOVER	5	1992
NEVER LET ME DOWN DAVID BOWIE	34	1987
NEVER LET ME DOWN AGAIN DEPECHE MODE	22	1987
NEVER LET YOU DOWN HONEYZ	7	1999
NEVER LET YOU GO NKOTB	42	1994
NEVER LOOK BACK DUMONDE	36	2001
NEVER LOSE YOUR SENSE OF WONDER YETI	36	2005
NEVER LOST HIS HARDCORE NRG	59	1997
NEVER LOST THAT FEELING SWERVEDRIVER	62	1992
NEVER MEANT TO HURT YOU GOOD SHOES	34	2007
NEVER MIND CLIFF RICHARD	21	1959
NEVER MIND THE PRESENTS BARRON KNIGHTS	17	1980
NEVER MISS A BEAT KAISER CHIEFS	5	2008
NEVER MISS THE WATER CHAKA KHAN FEATURING ME'SHELL NDEGEOCELLO	59	1997
NEVER MY LOVE SUGAR MINOTT	52	1981
NEVER NEVER [A] ASSEMBLY	4	1983
NEVER NEVER [B] WARM JETS	37	1998
NEVER NEVER GONNA GIVE YA UP BARRY WHITE	14	1974
NEVER NEVER GONNA GIVE YOU UP LISA STANSFIELD	25	1997
NEVER NEVER LOVE SIMPLY RED	18	1996

Title / Artist	Peak Position	Year of Release
NEVER NEVER NEVER SHIRLEY BASSEY	8	1973
NEVER ON SUNDAY DON COSTA	27	1960
NEVER ON SUNDAY MANUEL & HIS MUSIC OF THE MOUNTAINS	29	1960
NEVER ON SUNDAY LYNN CORNELL	30	1960
NEVER ON SUNDAY MAKADOPOULOS & HIS GREEK SERENADERS	36	1960
NEVER ON SUNDAY CHAQUITO	50	1960
NEVER (PAST TENSE) ROC PROJECT FEATURING TINA ARENA	42	2003
NEVER REALLY WAS MARIO WINANS FEATURING LIL' FLIP	44	2004
NEVER SAW A MIRACLE CURTIS STIGERS	34	1992
NEVER SAY DIE BLACK SABBATH	21	1978
NEVER SAY DIE (GIVE A LITTLE BIT MORE) CLIFF RICHARD	15	1983
NEVER SAY GOODBYE BON JOVI	21	1987
NEVER STOP [A] ECHO & THE BUNNYMEN	15	1983
NEVER STOP [B] BRAND NEW HEAVIES FEATURING N'DEA DAVENPORT	43	1991
NEVER SURRENDER SAXON	18	1981
NEVER TAKE ME ALIVE SPEAR OF DESTINY	14	1987
NEVER TEAR US APART INXS	24	1988
NEVER THERE CAKE	66	1999
NEVER TOO FAR MARIAH CAREY FEATURING MYSTIKAL	32	2002
NEVER TOO LATE KYLIE MINOGUE	4	1989
NEVER TOO MUCH LUTHER VANDROSS	13	1983
NEVER TRUST A STRANGER KIM WILDE	7	1988
NEVER TURN AWAY ORCHESTRAL MANOEUVRES IN THE DARK	70	1984
NEVER TURN YOUR BACK ON MOTHER EARTH SPARKS	13	1974
NEVER UNDERSTAND JESUS & MARY CHAIN	47	1985
NEVER WANNA SAY SOUNDBWOY ENT	18	2006
NEVER WENT TO CHURCH STREETS	20	2006
NEVER WIN FISCHERSPOONER	55	2005
NEVERTHELESS FRANKIE VAUGHAN	29	1968
NEVERTHELESS EVE GRAHAM & THE NEW SEEKERS	34	1973
NEW NO DOUBT	30	1999
NEW AMSTERDAM ELVIS COSTELLO & THE ATTRACTIONS	36	1980
NEW ANGER GARY NUMAN	46	1988
NEW BEGINNING [A] STEPHEN GATELY	3	2000
NEW BEGINNING [B] PRECIOUS	50	2000
NEW BEGINNING (MAMBA SEYRA) BUCKS FIZZ	8	1986
NEW BIRD REEF	73	1999
NEW BORN MUSE	12	2001
NEW DAWN PROPHETS OF SOUND	51	2002
A NEW DAY [A] KILLING JOKE	56	1984
NEW DAY [B] WYCLEF JEAN FEATURING BONO	23	1999
NEW DAY [C] SHAPESHIFTERS	72	2007
A NEW DAY HAS COME CELINE DION	7	2002
NEW DIMENSIONS IMAGINATION	56	1983
NEW DIRECTION [A] FREAKPOWER	60	1996
NEW DIRECTION [B] S CLUB JUNIORS	2	2002
NEW DIVIDE LINKIN PARK	19	2009
NEW EMOTION TIME FREQUENCY	36	1993
A NEW ENGLAND KIRSTY MacCOLL	7	1985
A NEW FASHION BILL WYMAN	37	1982
A NEW FLAME SIMPLY RED	17	1989
NEW GENERATION SUEDE	21	1995
NEW GUITAR IN TOWN LURKERS	72	1979
NEW HOME NEW LIFE ALARM	45	2004
NEW HORIZON JOHN PARR VERSUS TOMMYKNOCKERS	43	2006
NEW IDEAS DYKEENIES	54	2007
NEW IN TOWN LITTLE BOOTS	13	2009
NEW KICKS JOHANN	54	1996
NEW KID IN TOWN EAGLES	20	1977
NEW KIND OF MEDICINE ULTRA NATE	14	1998
NEW LIFE DEPECHE MODE	11	1981
NEW LIVE AND RARE EP DEEP PURPLE	31	1977
NEW LIVE AND RARE II (EP) DEEP PURPLE	45	1978
NEW LIVE AND RARE VOLUME 3 EP DEEP PURPLE	48	1980
NEW MISTAKE JELLYFISH	55	1993
NEW MOON ON MONDAY DURAN DURAN	9	1984
NEW ORLEANS U.S. BONDS	16	1961
NEW ORLEANS BERN ELLIOTT & THE FENMEN	24	1964
NEW ORLEANS HARLEY QUINNE	19	1972
NEW ORLEANS GILLAN	17	1981
NEW POLICY ONE TERRORVISION	42	1993
THE NEW POLLUTION BECK	14	1997
NEW POWER GENERATION PRINCE	26	1990
NEW SENSATION INXS	25	1988
NEW SHOES PAOLO NUTINI	21	2007
NEW SONG HOWARD JONES	3	1983
NEW SOUL YAEL NAIM	30	2008
A NEW SOUTH WALES ALARM FEATURING THE MORRISTON ORPHEUS MALE VOICE CHOIR	31	1989
NEW THING FROM LONDON TOWN SHARPE & NUMAN	52	1986
NEW TOY LENE LOVICH	53	1981
NEW WAY, NEW LIFE ASIAN DUB FOUNDATION	49	2000
NEW WORLD IN THE MORNING ROGER WHITTAKER	17	1970
NEW WORLD MAN RUSH	36	1982
NEW YEAR SUGABABES	12	2000
NEW YEARS DAY U2	10	1983
NEW YEARS DUB MUSIQUE VS U2	15	2001
NEW YORK PALOMA FAITH	15	2009
NEW YORK AFTERNOON MONDO KANE	70	1986
NEW YORK CITY T REX	15	1975
NEW YORK CITY BOY PET SHOP BOYS	14	1999
NEW YORK CITY COPS STROKES	16	2001
NEW YORK EYES NICOLE WITH TIMMY THOMAS	41	1985
NEW YORK GROOVE HELLO	9	1975
NEW YORK MINING DISASTER 1941 BEE GEES	12	1967
NEW YORK, NEW YORK GERARD KENNY	43	1996
NEW YORK NEW YORK [B] RYAN ADAMS	53	2001
NEW YORK NEW YORK [C] MOBY FEATURING DEBBIE HARRY	43	2006
NEW YORK UNDERCOVER 4-TRACK EP VARIOUS ARTISTS (EP'S & LP'S)	39	1978
NEWBORN ELBOW	42	2001
NEWBORN FRIEND SEAL	45	1994
NEWGRANGE CLANNAD	65	1983
THE NEWS CARBON/SILICON	59	2007
NEWS AT TEN VAPORS	44	1980
NEWS OF THE WORLD JAM	27	1978
NEXT BEST SUPERSTAR MELANIE C	10	2005
THE NEXT BIG THING JESUS JONES	49	1997
NEXT DOOR TO AN ANGEL NEIL SEDAKA	29	1962
THE NEXT EPISODE DR DRE FEATURING SNOOP DOGGY DOGG	3	2001
NEXT LEVEL ILS	75	2002
NEXT LIFETIME ERYKAH BADU	30	1997
NEXT PLANE HOME DANIEL POWTER	70	2008
THE NEXT TIME CLIFF RICHARD & THE SHADOWS	1	1962
NEXT TIME YOU FALL IN LOVE REVA RICE & GREG ELLIS	59	1993
NEXT TO YOU ASWAD	24	1990
NEXT YEAR FOO FIGHTERS	42	2000
NHS (EP) DJ DOC SCOTT	64	1992
NIALL QUINN'S DISCO PANTS A LOVE SUPREME	59	1999
NICE AND SLOW [A] JESSE GREEN	17	1976
NICE AND SLOW [B] USHER	24	1998
NICE GUY EDDIE SLEEPER	10	1996
NICE IN NICE STRANGLERS	30	1986
NICE LEGS SHAME ABOUT HER FACE MONKS	19	1979
NICE 'N' EASY FRANK SINATRA	15	1960
NICE 'N' SLEAZY STRANGLERS	18	1978
NICE 'N' SLOW FREDDIE JACKSON	56	1988
NICE ONE CYRIL COCKEREL CHORUS	14	1973
NICE WEATHER FOR DUCKS LEMON JELLY	16	2003
THE NIGHT [A] FRANKIE VALLI & THE FOUR SEASONS	7	1975
THE NIGHT [A] INTASTELLA	60	1995
THE NIGHT [A] SOFT CELL	39	2003
THE NIGHT [B] SCOOTER	16	2003
A NIGHT AT DADDY GEE'S SHOWADDYWADDY	39	1979
A NIGHT AT THE APOLLO LIVE! DARYL HALL & JOHN OATES FEATURING DAVID RUFFIN & EDDIE KENDRICK	58	1985
NIGHT BIRDS SHAKATAK	9	1982
NIGHT BOAT TO CAIRO MADNESS	56	1993
THE NIGHT CHICAGO DIED PAPER LACE	3	1974
NIGHT CRAWLER JUDAS PRIEST	63	1993
NIGHT DANCING JOE FARRELL	57	1978
THE NIGHT THE EARTH CRIED GRAVEDIGGAZ	44	1998
NIGHT FEVER [A] FATBACK BAND	38	1976
NIGHT FEVER [B] BEE GEES	1	1978
NIGHT FEVER [B] CAROL DOUGLAS	66	1978
NIGHT FEVER [B] ADAM GARCIA	15	1998
THE NIGHT FEVER MEGAMIX UK MIXMASTERS	23	1991
NIGHT GAMES GRAHAM BONNET	6	1981
THE NIGHT HAS A THOUSAND EYES BOBBY VEE	3	1963
NIGHT IN MOTION CUBIC 22	15	1991
NIGHT IN MY VEINS PRETENDERS	25	1994
A NIGHT IN NEW YORK ELBOW BONES & THE RACKETEERS	33	1984
THE NIGHT IS YOUNG GARY MILLER	29	1961
NIGHT LADIES CRUSADERS	55	1984
NIGHT LIFE DAVID LEE ROTH	72	1994
NIGHT LINE RANDY CRAWFORD	51	1983
NIGHT MOVES BOB SEGER & THE SILVER BULLET BAND	45	1995
NIGHT NURSE SLY & ROBBIE FEATURING SIMPLY RED	14	1997
NIGHT OF FEAR MOVE	2	1967
NIGHT OF THE LIVING BASEHEADS PUBLIC ENEMY	63	1988
NIGHT OF THE LONG GRASS TROGGS	17	1967
NIGHT OF THE VAMPIRE MOONTREKKERS	50	1961
NIGHT ON FIRE VHS OR BETA	69	2005
NIGHT OWL GERRY RAFFERTY	5	1979
NIGHT PORTER JAPAN	29	1982
THE NIGHT THEY DROVE OLD DIXIE DOWN JOAN BAEZ	6	1971
A NIGHT TO REMEMBER SHALAMAR	5	1982
NIGHT TO REMEMBER 911	38	1996
A NIGHT TO REMEMBER LIBERTY X	6	2005
NIGHT TRAIN [A] BUDDY MORROW	12	1953
NIGHT TRAIN [B] VISAGE	12	1982
NIGHT VISION HELL IS FOR HEROES	38	2002
THE NIGHT THE WINE THE ROSES LIQUID GOLD	32	1980
THE NIGHT YOU MURDERED LOVE ABC	31	1987
NIGHTBIRD CONVERT	39	1992
THE NIGHTFLY BLANK & JONES	55	2000
NIGHTLIFE KENICKIE	27	1997
NIGHTMARE [A] GILLAN	36	1981
NIGHTMARE [B] SAXON	50	1983
NIGHTMARE [C] KID UNKNOWN	64	1992

Title / Artist	Peak Position	Year of Release
NIGHTMARE [D] BRAINBUG	11	1997
NIGHTMARES A FLOCK OF SEAGULLS	53	1983
NIGHTRAIN GUNS N' ROSES	17	1988
NIGHTS IN WHITE SATIN MOODY BLUES	9	1969
NIGHTS IN WHITE SATIN DICKIES	39	1979
NIGHTS IN WHITE SATIN ELKIE BROOKS	33	1982
NIGHTS OF PLEASURE LOOSE ENDS	42	1986
NIGHTS ON BROADWAY CANDI STATON	6	1977
NIGHTS OVER EGYPT INCOGNITO	56	1999
NIGHTSHIFT COMMODORES	3	1985
NIGHTSWIMMING R.E.M.	27	1993
NIGHTTRAIN PUBLIC ENEMY	55	1992
THE NIGHTTRAIN KADOC	14	1996
NIKITA ELTON JOHN	3	1985
NIKKE DOES IT BETTER NIKKE? NICOLE!	73	1991
NIMBUS 808 STATE	59	1992
NINE FORWARD, RUSSIA!	40	2006
9 A.M. (THE COMFORT ZONE) LONDONBEAT	19	1988
9 CRIMES DAMIEN RICE	29	2006
911 WYCLEF FEATURING MARY J BLIGE	9	2000
911 IS A JOKE PUBLIC ENEMY	41	1990
900 DEGREES IAN POOLEY	57	2001
NINE IN THE AFTERNOON PANIC AT THE DISCO	13	2008
NINE MILLION BICYCLES KATIE MELUA	5	2005
9PM (TILL I COME) ATB	1	1999
977 PRETENDERS	66	1994
NINE TIMES OUT OF TEN CLIFF RICHARD & THE SHADOWS	3	1960
9 TO 5 [A] SHEENA EASTON	3	1980
9 TO 5 [B] DOLLY PARTON	47	1981
9 TO 5 [C] LADY SOVEREIGN	33	2005
NINE 2FIVE [D] ORDINARY BOYS FEATURING LADY SOVEREIGN	6	2006
NINE WAYS JDS	47	1997
19 [A] PAUL HARDCASTLE	1	1985
NINETEEN [B] FORWARD, RUSSIA!	67	2006
1985 BOWLING FOR SOUP	35	2004
1980 ESTELLE	14	2004
1999 [A] PRINCE & THE REVOLUTION	2	1983
1999 [B] BINARY FINARY	11	1998
1979 SMASHING PUMPKINS	16	1996
1973 JAMES BLUNT	4	2007
NINETEEN63 NEW ORDER	21	1995
1962 GRASS-SHOW	53	1997
19/2000 GORILLAZ	6	2001
NINETEENTH NERVOUS BREAKDOWN ROLLING STONES	2	1966
90S GIRL BLACKGIRL	23	1994
98.6 KEITH	24	1967
98.6 BYSTANDERS	45	1967
95 – NASTY W.A.S.P.	70	1986
99.5 CAROL LYNN TOWNES	47	1984
99.9O F SUZANNE VEGA	46	1992
99 PROBLEMS JAY-Z	12	2004
99 RED BALLOONS NENA	1	1984
96 TEARS ? (QUESTION MARK) & THE MYSTERIANS	37	1966
96 TEARS STRANGLERS	17	1990
92 DEGREES POP WILL EAT ITSELF	23	1990
92 TOUR (EP) MOTORHEAD	63	1992
NINETY-NINE WAYS TAB HUNTER	5	1957
NIPPLE TO THE BOTTLE GRACE JONES	50	1982
NITE AND DAY AL B SURE!	44	1988
NITE AND FOG MERCURY REV	47	2001
NITE CLUB SPECIALS (FEATURING RICO)	10	1979
NITE LIFE KIM ENGLISH	35	1994
NITE NITE KANO FEATURING MIKE SKINNER & LEO THE LION	25	2005
NI-TEN-ICHI-RYU (TWO SWORDS TECHNIQUE) PHOTEK	37	1997
NITRO PALE X	74	2001
N-N-NINETEEN NOT OUT COMMENTATORS	13	1985
NO CHUCK D	55	1996
NO AIR JORDIN SPARKS FEATURING CHRIS BROWN	3	2008
NO AIR GLEE CAST	52	2010
NO ALIBIS ERIC CLAPTON	53	1990
NO ARMS CAN EVER HOLD YOU BACHELORS	7	1964
NO BIG DEAL OVACAST & BECKY MEASURES	67	2007
NO BLUE SKIES LLOYD COLE	42	1990
NO CAN DO SUGABABES	23	2009
NO CHANCE (NO CHARGE) BILLY CONNOLLY	24	1976
NO CHARGE JJ BARRIE	1	1976
NO CHEAP THRILL SUZANNE VEGA	40	1997
NO CHRISTMAS WEDDING PRESENT	25	1992
NO CLASS MOTORHEAD	61	1979
NO CLAUSE 28 BOY GEORGE	57	1988
NO CONVERSATION VIEW FROM THE HILL	58	1986
NO DIGGITY BLACKSTREET FEATURING DR DRE	9	1996
NO DISTANCE LEFT TO RUN BLUR	14	1999
NO DOUBT [A] 702	59	1997
NO DOUBT [B] IMAJIN	42	1999
NO DOUBT ABOUT IT HOT CHOCOLATE	2	1980
NO DREAM IMPOSSIBLE LINDSAY	32	2001
NO EDUCATION NO FUTURE (FK THE CURFEW)** MOGWAI	68	1998
NO EMOTION IDLEWILD	36	2007
NO ESCAPIN' THIS BEATNUTS	47	2001
NO FACE, NO NAME, NO NUMBER TRAFFIC	40	1968
NO FEAR RASMUS	43	2005
NO FLOW LISA ROXANNE	18	2001
NO FOOL (FOR LOVE) HAZELL DEAN	41	1985
NO FRONTS DOG EAT DOG	9	1995
NO GETTING OVER YOU PARIS	49	1982
NO GOOD DA FOOL	38	1999
NO GOOD ADVICE GIRLS ALOUD	2	2003
NO GOOD FOR ME [A] BRUCE WAYNE	70	1998
NO GOOD 4 ME [B] OXIDE & NEUTRINO FEATURING MEGAMAN	6	2000
NO GOOD (START THE DANCE) PRODIGY	4	1994
NO GOODBYES [A] CURTIS MAYFIELD	65	1978
NO GOODBYES [B] SUBWAYS	27	2005
NO GOVERNMENT NICOLETTE	67	1995
NO HIDING PLACE KEN MACKINTOSH	45	1960
NO HONESTLY LYNSEY DE PAUL	7	1974
NO LAUGHING IN HEAVEN GILLAN	31	1981
NO LETTING GO WAYNE WONDER	3	2003
NO LIES S.O.S. BAND	64	1987
NO LIMIT 2 UNLIMITED	1	1993
NO LIMITS BAKSHELF DOG	51	2002
NO LOVE JOAN ARMATRADING	50	1982
NO MAN'S LAND [A] GERARD KENNY	56	1985
NO MAN'S LAND [B] BILLY JOEL	50	1994
NO MAN'S LAND [C] BEVERLEY KNIGHT	43	2007
(NO MATTER HOW HIGH I GET) I'LL STILL BE LOOKIN' UP TO YOU WILTON FELDER FEATURING BOBBY WOMACK & INTRODUCING ALLTRINA GRAYSON	63	1985
NO MATTER HOW I TRY GILBERT O'SULLIVAN	5	1971
NO MATTER WHAT [A] BADFINGER	5	1971
NO MATTER WHAT [B] BOYZONE	1	1998
NO MATTER WHAT I DO WILL MELLOR	23	1998
NO MATTER WHAT SIGN YOU ARE DIANA ROSS & THE SUPREMES	37	1969
NO MATTER WHAT THEY SAY LIL' KIM	35	2000
NO MATTER WHAT YOU DO BENNY BENASSI PRESENTS THE BIZ	40	2004
NO MEMORY SCARLET FANTASTIC	24	1987
NO MERCY STRANGLERS	37	1984
NO MILK TODAY HERMAN'S HERMITS	7	1966
NO MORE [A] McGUIRE SISTERS	20	1955
NO MORE [B] UNIQUE 3	74	1991
NO MORE [C] RUFF ENDZ	11	2000
NO MORE [D] A1	6	2001
NO MORE [E] RONI SIZE FEATURING BEVERLEY KNIGHT	26	2005
NO MORE [F] JAMELIA	43	2007
NO MORE AFFAIRS TINDERSTICKS	58	1995
NO MORE ALCOHOL SUGGS FEATURING LOUCHIE LOU & MICHIE ONE	24	1996
NO MORE (BABY I'MA DO RIGHT) 3LW	6	2001
NO MORE DRAMA MARY J BLIGE	9	2002
NO MORE HEROES STRANGLERS	8	1977
NO MORE (I CAN'T STAND IT) MAXX	8	1994
NO MORE 'I LOVE YOUS' ANNIE LENNOX	2	1995
NO MORE 'I LOVE YOU'S LOVER SPEAKS	58	1986
NO MORE LIES SHARPE & NUMAN	34	1988
NO MORE LONELY NIGHTS (BALLAD) PAUL McCARTNEY	2	1984
(NO MORE) LOVE AT YOUR CONVENIENCE ALICE COOPER	44	1977
NO MORE MR. NICE GUY ALICE COOPER	10	1973
NO MORE MR. NICE GUY MEGADETH	13	1990
NO MORE RAINY DAYS FREE SPIRIT	68	1995
NO MORE RUNNING AWAY AIR TRAFFIC	45	2007
NO MORE TALK DUBSTAR	20	1997
NO MORE TEARS [A] HOLLYWOOD BEYOND	47	1986
NO MORE TEARS [B] JAKI GRAHAM	60	1988
NO MORE TEARS [C] OZZY OSBOURNE	32	1991
NO MORE TEARS (ENOUGH IS ENOUGH) DONNA SUMMER & BARBRA STREISAND	3	1979
NO MORE TEARS (ENOUGH IS ENOUGH) KYM MAZELLE & JOCELYN BROWN	13	1994
NO MORE THE FOOL ELKIE BROOKS	5	1986
NO MORE TOMORROWS PAUL JOHNSON	67	1989
NO MORE TURNING BACK GITTA	54	2000
NO MULE'S FOOL FAMILY	29	1969
NO NEED ALFIE	66	2004
NO NO JOE SILVER CONVENTION	41	1976
NO NO NO [A] NANCY NOVA	63	1982
NO NO NO [B] DESTINY'S CHILD FEATURING WYCLEF JEAN	5	1998
NO NO NO [C] MANIJAMA FEATURING MUKUPA & LIL' T	66	2003
NO, NOT NOW HOT HOT HEAT	38	2003
NO ONE [A] RAY CHARLES	35	1963
NO ONE [B] 2 UNLIMITED	17	1994
NO ONE [C] ALICIA KEYS	6	2007
NO ONE BUT YOU BILLY ECKSTINE	3	1954
NO ONE CAN MARILLION	26	1991
NO ONE CAN BREAK A HEART LIKE YOU DAVE CLARK FIVE	28	1968
NO ONE CAN LOVE YOU MORE THAN ME KYM MAZELLE	62	1991
NO ONE CAN MAKE MY SUNSHINE SMILE EVERLY BROTHERS	11	1962
NO ONE CAN STOP US NOW CHELSEA FC	23	1994
NO ONE ELSE COMES CLOSE JOE	41	1998
NO ONE GETS THE PRIZE DIANA ROSS	59	1979
NO ONE IS INNOCENT SEX PISTOLS, PUNK PRAYER BY RONALD BIGGS	7	1978
NO ONE IS TO BLAME HOWARD JONES	16	1986
NO ONE KNOWS QUEENS OF THE STONE AGE	15	2002
NO ONE KNOWS MARK RONSON	66	2007
NO ONE LIKE YOU SCORPIONS	64	1982
NO ONE SPEAKS GENEVA	32	1996
NO ONE TO CRY TO RAY CHARLES	38	1964
NO ONE WILL EVER KNOW FRANK IFIELD	25	1966
NO ONE'S DRIVING DAVE CLARKE	37	1996
NO ORDINARY LOVE SADE	14	1992
NO ORDINARY MORNING/HALCYON CHICANE	28	2000
NO OTHER BABY BOBBY HELMS	30	1958
NO OTHER BABY PAUL McCARTNEY	42	1999
NO OTHER LOVE RONNIE HILTON	1	1956
NO OTHER LOVE JOHNSTON BROTHERS	22	1956

Title / Artist	Peak Position	Year of Release
NO OTHER LOVE EDMUND HOCKRIDGE	24	1956
NO OTHER ONE TAIO CRUZ	42	2009
NO PANTIES TRINA	45	2002
NO PARTICULAR PLACE TO GO CHUCK BERRY	3	1964
NO PIGEONS SPORTY THIEVZ	21	1999
NO PLACE TO HIDE KORN	26	1996
NO PROMISES [A] ICEHOUSE	72	1986
NO PROMISES [B] SHAYNE WARD	2	2006
NO PUSSY BLUES GRINDERMAN	64	2007
NO RAIN BLIND MELON	17	1993
NO REGRETS [A] SHIRLEY BASSEY	39	1965
NO REGRETS [B] WALKER BROTHERS	7	1976
NO REGRETS [B] MIDGE URE	9	1982
NO REGRETS [C] ROBBIE WILLIAMS	4	1998
NO RELIGION VAN MORRISON	54	1995
NO REST NEW MODEL ARMY	28	1985
NO SCRUBS TLC	3	1999
NO SELF CONTROL PETER GABRIEL	33	1980
NO SELL OUT MALCOLM X	60	1984
NO SLEEP NO NEED EP VAULTS	70	2004
NO SLEEP TILL BROOKLYN BEASTIE BOYS	14	1987
NO SLEEP TONIGHT [A] FADERS	13	2005
NO SLEEP TONIGHT [B] ENTER SHIKARI	63	2009
NO SON OF MINE GENESIS	6	1991
NO STONE UNTURNED TRUTH	66	1984
NO STRESS CYCLEFLY	68	2002
NO SUBSTITUTE LOVE ESTELLE	30	2008
NO SUCH THING JOHN MAYER	42	2003
NO SUPERSTAR REMADY	75	2010
NO SURPRISES RADIOHEAD	4	1998
NO SURRENDER DEUCE	29	1996
NO SURVIVORS GBH	63	1982
NO SWEAT '98 NORTH & SOUTH	29	1998
NO TENGO DINERO LOS UMBRELLOS	33	1998
NO TIME LIL' KIM FEATURING PUFF DADDY	45	1997
NO TIME FOR TEARS ENEMY	16	2009
NO TIME TO BE 21 ADVERTS	34	1978
NO TIME TO CRY SISTERS OF MERCY	63	1985
NO TIME TO PLAY GURU FEATURING D C LEE	25	1993
NO TOMORROW ORSON	1	2006
NO TREND KOOPA	71	2005
NO U HANG UP/IF THAT'S OKAY WITH YOU SHAYNE WARD	2	2007
NO WAY FREAKPOWER	29	1998
NO WAY BACK FOO FIGHTERS	64	2006
NO WAY NO WAY VANILLA	14	1997
NO WAY OUT FRANCESCO ZAPPALA	69	1992
NO WOMAN NO CRY BOB MARLEY & THE WAILERS	8	1975
NO WOMAN NO CRY LONDONBEAT	64	1991
NO WOMAN NO CRY FUGEES	2	1996
NO WORRIES SIMON WEBBE	4	2005
NO WOW KILLS	53	2005
NO YOU DIDN'T, NO YOU DON'T COURTEENERS	35	2008
NO YOU GIRLS FRANZ FERDINAND	22	2009
THE NOBODIES MARILYN MANSON	34	2001
NOBODY [A] TONI BASIL	52	1982
NOBODY [B] TONGUE 'N' CHEEK	59	1990
NOBODY [C] SHARA NELSON	49	1994
NOBODY [D] KEITH SWEAT FEATURING ATHENA CAGE	30	1997
NOBODY BETTER TINA MOORE	20	1998
NOBODY BUT YOU GLADYS KNIGHT & THE PIPS	34	1977
NOBODY (CAN LOVE ME) TONGUE IN CHEEK	41	1988
NOBODY DOES IT BETTER CARLY SIMON	7	1977
NOBODY ELSE [A] NICK KAMEN	47	1987
NOBODY ELSE [B] TYRESE	59	1999
NOBODY I KNOW PETER & GORDON	10	1964
NOBODY KNOWS [A] NIK KERSHAW	44	1986
NOBODY KNOWS [B] TONY RICH PROJECT	4	1996

Title / Artist	Peak Position	Year of Release
NOBODY KNOWS [C] P!NK	27	2006
NOBODY MADE ME RANDY EDELMAN	60	1982
NOBODY MOVE NOBODY GET HURT WE ARE SCIENTISTS	21	2005
NOBODY NEEDS YOUR LOVE GENE PITNEY	2	1966
NOBODY TOLD ME JOHN LENNON	6	1984
NOBODY WANTS TO BE LONELY RICKY MARTIN WITH CHRISTINA AGUILERA	4	2001
NOBODY WINS ELTON JOHN	42	1981
NOBODY'S BUSINESS [A] H20 FEATURING BILLIE	19	1996
NOBODY'S BUSINESS [B] PEACE BY PIECE	50	1998
NOBODY'S CHILD KAREN YOUNG	6	1969
NOBODY'S CHILD TRAVELING WILBURYS	44	1990
NOBODY'S DARLIN' BUT MINE FRANK IFIELD	4	1963
NOBODY'S DIARY YAZOO	3	1983
NOBODY'S FOOL [A] JIM REEVES	32	1970
NOBODY'S FOOL [B] HAIRCUT 100	9	1982
NOBODY'S HERO STIFF LITTLE FINGERS	36	1980
NOBODY'S HOME AVRIL LAVIGNE	24	2004
NOBODY'S SUPPOSED TO BE HERE DEBORAH COX	55	1999
NOBODY'S TWISTING YOUR ARM WEDDING PRESENT	46	1988
NOCTURNE T99	33	1991
NOMANSLAND (DAVID'S SONG) DJ SAKIN & FRIENDS	14	1999
NOMZAMO (ONE PEOPLE ONE CAUSE) LATIN QUARTER	73	1987
NON HO L'ETA PER AMARTI GIGLIOLA CINQUETTI	17	1964
NON STOP WHITEY	67	2005
NONE OF YOUR BUSINESS SALT-N-PEPA	19	1994
(NONSTOPOPERATION) DUST JUNKYS	47	1997
NOOKIE JAMESY P	14	2005
NO-ONE BUT YOU [B] QUEEN	13	1998
NO-ONE DRIVING (DOUBLE SINGLE) JOHN FOXX	32	1980
NORA MALONE TERESA BREWER	26	1957
NORMAN CAROL DEENE	24	1962
NORMAN BATES LANDSCAPE	40	1981
NORMAN 3 TEENAGE FANCLUB	50	1993
NORTH AMERICAN SCUM LCD SOUNDSYSTEM	40	2007
NORTH COUNTRY BOY CHARLATANS	4	1997
NORTH, SOUTH, EAST, WEST MARVIN & TAMARA	38	2000
NORTH TO ALASKA JOHNNY HORTON	23	1961
NORTHERN LIGHTS [A] RENAISSANCE	10	1978
NORTHERN LITES [B] SUPER FURRY ANIMALS	11	1999
NORTHERN STAR MELANIE C	4	1999
NOT A DRY EYE IN THE HOUSE MEAT LOAF	7	1996
NOT A JOB ELBOW	26	2004
NOT A MINUTE TOO SOON VIXEN	37	1991
NOT ABOUT US GENESIS	66	1998
NOT ALONE BERNARD BUTLER	27	1998
NOT ANYONE BLACK BOX	31	1995
NOT AS A STRANGER FRANK SINATRA	18	1955
NOT AT ALL STATUS QUO	50	1989
NOT ENOUGH MELANIE WILLIAMS	65	1994
NOT ENOUGH LOVE IN THE WORLD CHER	31	1996
NOT EVEN GONNA TRIP HONEYZ	24	2000
NOT EVERYONE NINE BLACK ALPS	31	2005
NOT FADE AWAY ROLLING STONES	3	1964
NOT FAIR LILY ALLEN	5	2009
NOT FOR ALL THE LOVE IN THE WORLD THRILLS	39	2004
NOT FOR YOU PEARL JAM	34	1995
NOT GON' CRY MARY J BLIGE	39	1996
NOT GONNA GET US t.A.T.u.	7	2003
NOT IF YOU WERE THE LAST JUNKIE ON EARTH DANDY WARHOLS	13	1998
NOT IN LOVE ENRIQUE FEATURING KELIS	5	2004

Title / Artist	Peak Position	Year of Release
NOT ME NOT I DELTA GOODREM	18	2003
NOT NINETEEN FOREVER COURTEENERS	19	2008
NOT NOW BLINK-182	30	2005
NOT NOW JOHN PINK FLOYD	30	1983
NOT OVER YET GRACE	6	1995
NOT OVER YOU YET DIANA ROSS	9	1999
NOT READY TO MAKE NICE DIXIE CHICKS	70	2006
NOT RESPONSIBLE TOM JONES	18	1966
NOT SLEEPING AROUND NED'S ATOMIC DUSTBIN	19	1992
NOT SO MANIC NOW DUBSTAR	18	1996
NOT SUCH AN INNOCENT GIRL VICTORIA BECKHAM	6	2001
NOT THAT KIND ANASTACIA	11	2001
NOT THE GIRL YOU THINK YOU ARE CROWDED HOUSE	20	1996
(NOT THE) GREATEST RAPPER 1000 CLOWNS	23	1999
NOT TODAY MARY J BLIGE FEATURING EVE	40	2003
NOT TONIGHT LIL' KIM	11	1997
NOT TOO LATE FOR LOVE BEVERLEY KNIGHT	31	2004
NOT TOO LITTLE NOT TOO MUCH CHRIS SANDFORD	17	1963
NOT UNTIL NEXT TIME JIM REEVES	13	1965
NOT WHERE IT'S AT DEL AMITRI	21	1997
NOTGONNACHANGE SWING OUT SISTER	49	1992
NOTHIN' NORE	11	2002
NOTHIN' AT ALL HEART	38	1988
NOTHIN' BETTER TO DO LeANN RIMES	48	2007
NOTHIN' BUT A GOOD TIME POISON	35	1988
NOTHIN' BUT A PARTY TRUCE	71	1997
NOTHIN' MY LOVE CAN'T FIX JOEY LAWRENCE	13	1993
NOTHIN' PERSONAL DUST JUNKYS	62	1998
(NOTHIN' SERIOUS) JUST BUGGIN' WHISTLE	7	1986
NOTHIN' (THAT COMPARES 2 U) JACKSONS	33	1989
NOTHIN' TO DO MICHAEL HOLLIDAY	20	1956
NOTHING [A] FRAZIER CHORUS	51	1990
NOTHING [B] FLUFFY	52	1996
NOTHING [C] A	9	2002
NOTHING [D] HOLDEN & THOMPSON	51	2003
NOTHING AS IT SEEMS PEARL JAM	22	2000
NOTHING AT ALL LUKE SLATER	70	2002
NOTHING 'BOUT ME STING	32	1994
NOTHING BUT GREEN LIGHTS TOM VEK	59	2005
NOTHING BUT LOVE OPTIMYSTIC	37	1994
NOTHING BUT YOU PAUL VAN DYK FEATURING HEMSTOCK	14	2003
NOTHING CAN CHANGE THIS LOVE BITTY McLEAN	55	1995
NOTHING CAN DIVIDE US JASON DONOVAN	5	1988
NOTHING CAN STOP ME GENE CHANDLER	41	1968
NOTHING CAN STOP US SAINT ETIENNE	54	1991
NOTHING CHANGES AROUND HERE THRILLS	40	2007
NOTHING COMES EASY SANDIE SHAW	14	1966
NOTHING COMPARES 2 U SINEAD O'CONNOR	1	1990
NOTHING COMPARES 2 U MXM	68	1990
NOTHING ELSE MATTERS METALLICA	6	1992
NOTHING EVER HAPPENS DEL AMITRI	11	1990
NOTHING FAILS MADONNA	11	2003
NOTHING HAS BEEN PROVED DUSTY SPRINGFIELD	16	1989
NOTHING HAS BEEN PROVED STRINGS OF LOVE	59	1990
NOTHING HURTS LIKE LOVE DANIEL BEDINGFIELD	3	2004
NOTHING IN MY WAY KEANE	19	2006
NOTHING IN PARTICULAR BROTHERHOOD	55	1996
NOTHING IN THIS WORLD PARIS HILTON	55	2006
NOTHING IS FOREVER ULTRACYNIC	47	1992
NOTHING IS REAL BUT THE GIRL BLONDIE	26	1999

Title / Artist	Peak Position	Year of Release
NOTHING LASTS FOREVER ECHO & THE BUNNYMEN	8	1997
NOTHING LEFT ORBITAL	32	1999
NOTHING LEFT TOULOUSE SAD CAFE	62	1980
NOTHING LESS THAN BRILLIANT SANDIE SHAW	66	1994
NOTHING NATURAL LUSH	43	1991
NOTHING REALLY MATTERS MADONNA	7	1999
NOTHING RHYMED GILBERT O'SULLIVAN	8	1970
NOTHING SACRED – A SONG FOR KIRSTY RUSSELL WATSON	17	2002
NOTHING TO DECLARE LAPTOP	74	1999
NOTHING TO FEAR CHRIS REA	16	1992
NOTHING TO LOSE [A] UK	67	1979
NOTHING TO LOSE [B] S-EXPRESS	32	1990
NOTHING WITHOUT ME MANCHILD	40	2001
NOTHING WRONG WITH YOU FINN BROTHERS	31	2004
NOTHING'S GONNA CHANGE MY LOVE FOR YOU GLENN MEDEIROS	1	1988
NOTHING'S GONNA CHANGE YOUR MIND BADLY DRAWN BOY	38	2006
NOTHING'S GONNA STOP ME NOW SAMANTHA FOX	8	1987
NOTHING'S GONNA STOP US NOW STARSHIP	1	1987
NOTHIN'S GONNA CHANGE LABI SIFFRE	52	1987
NOTORIOUS DURAN DURAN	7	1986
NOTORIOUS B.I.G. NOTORIOUS B.I.G. FEATURING PUFF DADDY	16	2000
NOVELTY WAVES BIOSPHERE	51	1995
NOVEMBER RAIN GUNS N' ROSES	4	1992
NOVEMBER SPAWNED A MONSTER MORRISSEY	12	1990
NOVOCAINE FOR THE SOUL EELS	10	1997
NOW [A] AL MARTINO	3	1953
NOW [B] VAL DOONICAN	43	1968
NOW [C] DEF LEPPARD	23	2002
NOW ALWAYS AND FOREVER GAY DAD	41	2001
NOW AND FOREVER RICHARD MARX	13	1994
NOW I KNOW WHAT MADE OTIS BLUE PAUL YOUNG	14	1993
NOW I'M HERE QUEEN	11	1975
NOW I'M THAT CHICK LIVVI FRANC FEATURING PITBULL	40	2009
NOW IS THE TIME JIMMY JAMES & THE VAGABONDS	5	1976
NOW IS TOMORROW DEFINITION OF SOUND	46	1991
NOW IT'S GONE CHORDS	63	1979
NOW IT'S ON GRANDADDY	23	2003
NOW I'VE FOUND YOU SEAN MAGUIRE	22	1995
NOW OR NEVER [A] TOM NOVY FEATURING LIMA	64	2001
NOW OR NEVER [B] CAST OF HIGH SCHOOL MUSICAL 3	41	2008
NOW THAT I OWN THE BBC SPARKS	60	1996
NOW THAT THE MAGIC HAS GONE JOE COCKER	28	1992
NOW THAT WE FOUND LOVE HEAVY D. & THE BOYZ	2	1991
NOW THAT WE'VE FOUND LOVE THIRD WORLD	10	1978
NOW THAT YOU GOT IT GWEN STEFANI	59	2007
NOW THAT YOU LOVE ME ALICE BAND	44	2002
NOW THAT YOU'VE GONE MIKE + THE MECHANICS	35	1999
NOW THEY'LL SLEEP BELLY	28	1995
NOW THOSE DAYS ARE GONE BUCKS FIZZ	8	1982
NOW WE ARE FREE GLADIATOR FEATURING IZZY	19	2004
NOW WE'RE THRU POETS	31	1964
NOW YOU'RE GONE [A] BLACK	66	1989
NOW YOU'RE GONE [B] WHITESNAKE	31	1990
NOW YOU'RE GONE [C] BASSHUNTER FEATURING DJ MENTAL THEO'S BAZZHEADZ	1	2008
NOW YOU'RE IN HEAVEN JULIAN LENNON	59	1989
NOWHERE [A] THERAPY?	18	1994
NOWHERE [B] LONGVIEW	72	2003
NOWHERE AGAIN SECRET MACHINES	49	2004
NOWHERE FAST MEAT LOAF	67	1984
NOWHERE GIRL B-MOVIE	67	1982
NOWHERE LAND CLUBHOUSE FEATURING CARL	56	1995
NOWHERE MAN THREE GOOD REASONS	47	1966
NOWHERE TO RUN MARTHA REEVES & THE VANDELLAS	26	1962
NOWHERE TO RUN 2000 NU GENERATION	66	2000
N-R-G ADAMSKI	12	1990
NU FLOW BIG BROVAZ	3	2002
NUCLEAR RYAN ADAMS	37	2002
NUCLEAR DEVICE (THE WIZARD OF AUS) STRANGLERS	36	1979
NUCLEAR HOLIDAY 3 COLOURS RED	22	1997
NUDE RADIOHEAD	21	2008
NUFF VIBES EP APACHE INDIAN	5	1993
NUMB [A] LINKIN PARK	14	2003
NUMB [B] PET SHOP BOYS	23	2006
NUMB [C] HONEY RYDER	32	2008
NUMB/ENCORE JAY-Z VS LINKIN PARK	14	2004
#9 DREAM JOHN LENNON	23	1975
THE NUMBER OF THE BEAST IRON MAIDEN	3	1982
NUMBER ONE [A] E.Y.C.	27	1994
NUMBER ONE [B] A	47	1998
NUMBER 1 [C] TWEENIES	5	2000
NUMBER ONE [D] PLAYGROUP	66	2001
NUMBER 1 [E] EBONY DUBSTERS	58	2004
NUMBER ONE [F] JOHN LEGEND	62	2005
NUMBER 1 [G] GOLDFRAPP	9	2005
NUMBER ONE [H] PHARRELL FEATURING KANYE WEST	31	2006
NUMBER 1 [I] TINCHY STRYDER FEATURING N-DUBZ	1	2009
NUMBER ONE BLIND VERUCA SALT	68	1995
NUMBER ONE DEE JAY GOODY GOODY	55	1978
NUMBER ONE DOMINATOR TOP	67	1991
NUMBER ONE ENEMY DAISY DARES YOU FEATURING CHIPMUNK	13	2010
NO. 1 RAT FAN ROLAND RAT SUPERSTAR	72	1985
THE NUMBER ONE SONG IN HEAVEN SPARKS	14	1979
NUMBER ONE SPOT LUDACRIS	30	2005
NUMBERS SOFT CELL	25	1983
NUMERO UNO STARLIGHT	9	1989
NUNC DIMITTIS PAUL PHEONIX	56	1979
NURSERY RHYMES ICEBERG SLIMM	37	2000
NURTURE LFO	47	1991
NUT ROCKER B. BUMBLE & THE STINGERS	1	1962
NUTBUSH CITY LIMITS IKE & TINA TURNER	4	1973
NUTBUSH CITY LIMITS TINA TURNER	23	1991
NUTHIN' BUT A 'G' THANG DR DRE	31	1994
NW5 MADNESS	24	2008
N.WO MINISTRY	49	1992
NYC BEAT ARMAND VAN HELDEN	22	2007
N.Y.C. (CAN YOU BELIEVE THIS CITY) CHARLES & EDDIE	33	1993
NYC (THERE'S NO NEED TO STOP) CHARLATANS	53	2006

O

Title / Artist	Peak Position	Year of Release
O OMARION	47	2005
O BABY SIOUXSIE & THE BANSHEES	34	1995
O L'AMOUR DOLLAR	7	1988
O' MY FATHER HAD A RABBIT RAY MOORE	24	1986
O SUPERMAN LAURIE ANDERSON	2	1981
03 BONNIE AND CLYDE JAY-Z FEATURING BEYONCE KNOWLES	2	2003
OAKLAND STROKE TONY! TONI! TONE!	50	1990
OBJECT OF MY DESIRE DANA RAYNE	7	2005
OBJECTION (TANGO) SHAKIRA	17	2002
OBJECTS IN THE REAR VIEW MIRROR MAY APPEAR CLOSER THAN THEY ARE MEAT LOAF	26	1994
OB-LA-DI OB-LA-DA MARMALADE	1	1968
OB-LA-DI OB-LA-DA BEDROCKS	20	1968
OBLIVION TERRORVISION	21	1994
OBLIVION (HEAD IN THE CLOUDS) (EP) MANIX	43	1992
OBLIVIOUS AZTEC CAMERA	18	1983
THE OBOE SONG CLERGY	50	2002
OBSESSED [A] 999	71	1981
OBSESSED [B] MARIAH CAREY	52	2009
OBSESSION [A] REG OWEN	43	1960
OBSESSION [B] ANIMOTION	5	1985
OBSESSION [C] ARMY OF LOVERS	67	1991
OBSESSION [D] ULTRA-SONIC	75	1994
OBSESSION [E] TIESTO & JUNKIE XL	56	2002
OBSESSION (NO ES AMOR) FRANKIE J	38	2005
OBSESSION (SI ES AMOR) 3RD WISH	15	2004
OBSESSIONS SUEDE	29	2002
OBSTACLE 1 INTERPOL	41	2002
OBVIOUS WESTLIFE	3	2004
THE OBVIOUS CHILD PAUL SIMON	15	1990
OBVIOUSLY McFLY	1	2004
OCEAN AVENUE YELLOWCARD	65	2004
OCEAN BLUE ABC	51	1986
OCEAN DEEP CLIFF RICHARD	27	1984
OCEAN DRIVE LIGHTHOUSE FAMILY	11	1995
OCEAN OF ETERNITY FUTURE BREEZE	46	2002
OCEAN PIE SHED SEVEN	33	1994
OCEAN SPRAY MANIC STREET PREACHERS	15	2001
OCTOBER SWIMMER JJ72	29	2000
ODE TO BILLY JOE BOBBIE GENTRY	13	1967
ODE TO BOY ALISON MOYET	59	1994
ODE TO JOY (FROM BEETHOVEN'S SYMPHONY NO 9) BBC CONCERT ORCHESTRA/BBC SYMPHONY CHORUS/ STEPHEN JACKSON	36	1996
ODE TO MY FAMILY CRANBERRIES	26	1994
THE ODYSSEY DRUMSOUND/SIMON BASSLINE SMITH	66	2004
OF COURSE I'M LYING YELLO	23	1989
OF COURSE YOU CAN SPEARHEAD	74	1994
OFF ON HOLIDAY SUGGS	7	1995
OFF ON YOUR OWN (GIRL) AL B SURE!	70	1988
OFF THE HOOK [A] JODY WATLEY	51	1998
OFF THE HOOK [B] CSS	43	2007
OFF THE WALL MICHAEL JACKSON	7	1979
OFF THE WALL WISD'ME	33	2000
OFF 2 WORK DIZZEE RASCAL	44	2005
OFFICE BOY BONDE DO ROLE	75	2007
THE OFFICIAL BBC CHILDREN IN NEED MEDLEY PETER KAY'S ANIMATED ALL STAR BAND	1	2009
OFFICIAL SECRETS M	64	1980
OFFSHORE CHICANE	14	1996
OFFSHORE BANKING BUSINESS MEMBERS	31	1979
OH CIARA FEATURING LUDACRIS	4	2005
OH AFRICA AKON	56	2010
OH BABE WHAT WOULD YOU SAY? HURRICANE SMITH	4	1972
OH BABY RHIANNA	18	2002
OH BABY I... ETERNAL	4	1994
(OH BABY MINE) I GET SO LONELY FOUR KNIGHTS	5	1954

Title	Artist	Peak Position	Year of Release
OH BOY [A]	CRICKETS	3	1957
OH BOY [A]	MUD	1	1975
OH BOY [A]	FABULOUS BAKER BOYS	34	1997
OH BOY [B]	CAM'RON FEATURING JUELZ SANTANA	13	2002
OH BOY (THE MOOD I'M IN)	BROTHERHOOD OF MAN	8	1977
OH CAROL [A]	NEIL SEDAKA	3	1959
OH CAROL! [A]	CLINT EASTWOOD & GENERAL SAINT	54	1994
OH CAROL [B]	SMOKIE	5	1978
OH CAROLINA	SHAGGY	1	1993
OH DIANE	FLEETWOOD MAC	9	1983
OH FATHER	MADONNA	16	1996
OH GIRL	CHI-LITES	5	1972
OH GIRL	PAUL YOUNG	25	1990
OH HAPPY DAY [A]	JOHNSTON BROTHERS	4	1953
OH HAPPY DAY [B]	EDWIN HAWKINS SINGERS FEATURING DOROTHY COMBS MORRISON	2	1969
OH HOW I MISS YOU	BACHELORS	30	1967
OH JIM	GAY DAD	47	1999
OH JULIE	SHAKIN' STEVENS	1	1982
OH LA LA LA	2 EIVISSA	13	1997
OH L'AMOUR	ERASURE	13	2003
OH LONESOME ME	CRAIG DOUGLAS	15	1962
OH LORI	ALESSI	8	1977
OH LOUISE	JUNIOR	74	1985
OH MANDY	SPINTO BAND	54	2006
OH ME OH MY (I'M A FOOL FOR YOU BABY)	LULU	47	1969
OH MEIN PAPA	EDDIE CALVERT	1	1953
OH MILLWALL	MILLWALL FC	41	2004
OH MY GOD [A]	A TRIBE CALLED QUEST	68	1994
OH MY GOD [B]	KAISER CHIEFS	6	2004
OH MY GOD [B]	MARK RONSON FEATURING LILY ALLEN	8	2007
OH MY GOSH	BASEMENT JAXX	8	2005
OH MY PAPA	EDDIE FISHER	9	1954
OH NO [A]	COMMODORES	44	1981
OH NO [B]	MOS DEF/NATE DOGG/ PHAROAHE MONCH	24	2001
OH NO NOT MY BABY	MANFRED MANN	11	1965
OH NO NOT MY BABY	ROD STEWART	6	1973
OH NO NOT MY BABY	CHER	33	1992
OH NO WON'T DO	CUD	49	1991
OH OH, I'M FALLING IN LOVE AGAIN	JIMMIE RODGERS	18	1958
OH PATTI (DON'T FEEL SORRY FOR LOVERBOY)	SCRITTI POLITTI	13	1988
OH, PEOPLE	PATTI LABELLE	26	1986
OH PRETTY WOMAN	ROY ORBISON	1	1964
OH PRETTY WOMAN	GARY MOORE FEATURING ALBERT KING	48	1990
OH ROMEO	MINDY McCREADY	41	1998
OH SHEILA	READY FOR THE WORLD	50	1985
OH STACEY (LOOK WHAT YOU'VE DONE!)	ZUTONS	24	2006
OH THE GUILT	NIRVANA	12	1993
OH WELL	FLEETWOOD MAC	2	1969
OH WELL	OH WELL	28	1989
OH WHAT A CIRCUS	DAVID ESSEX	3	1978
OH! WHAT A DAY	CRAIG DOUGLAS	43	1960
OH WHAT A FEELING	CHANGE	56	1985
OH! WHAT A GIRL!	SIMPLY RED	57	2006
OH WHAT A NIGHT	CLOCK	13	1996
OH WHAT A SHAME	ROY WOOD	13	1975
OH! WHAT A WORLD	SISTER BLISS WITH COLETTE	40	1995
OH WORLD	PAUL RUTHERFORD	61	1989
OH YEAH! [A]	BILL WITHERS	60	1985
OH YEAH [B]	ASH	6	1996
OH YEAH [C]	CAPRICE	24	1999
OH YEAH [D]	FOXY BROWN	27	2001
OH YEAH [E]	SUBWAYS	25	2005
OH YEAH, BABY	DWEEB	70	1997
OH YEAH (ON THE RADIO)	ROXY MUSIC	5	1980
OH YES! YOU'RE BEAUTIFUL	GARY GLITTER	2	1974
OH YOU PRETTY THING	PETER NOONE	12	1971
OH YOU WANT MORE	TY FEATURING ROOTS MANUVA	65	2004
OHIO	UTAH SAINTS	42	1995
OI	PLATINUM 45 FEATURING MORE FIRE CREW	8	2002
OK	BIG BROVAZ	7	2003
O.K. FRED	ERROL DUNKLEY	11	1979
O.K.?	JULIE COVINGTON, RULA LENSKA, CHARLOTTE CORNWELL & SUE JONES-DAVIES	10	1977
OKAY!	DAVE DEE, DOZY, BEAKY, MICK & TICH	4	1967
OL' MACDONALD	FRANK SINATRA	11	1960
OL' RAG BLUES	STATUS QUO	9	1983
OLD [A]	KEVIN ROWLAND & DEXY'S MIDNIGHT RUNNERS	17	1982
OLD [B]	MACHINE HEAD	43	1995
OLD AND WISE	ALAN PARSONS PROJECT	74	1983
OLD BEFORE I DIE	ROBBIE WILLIAMS	2	1997
THE OLD FASHIONED WAY	CHARLES AZNAVOUR	38	1973
OLD FLAMES	FOSTER & ALLEN	51	1982
OLD FOLKS	A	54	1999
OLD HABITS DIE HARD	MICK JAGGER & DAVE STEWART	45	2004
THE OLD MAN AND THE ANGEL	IT BITES	72	1987
OLD MAN AND ME (WHEN I GET TO HEAVEN)	HOOTIE & THE BLOWFISH	57	1996
OLD OAKEN BUCKET	TOMMY SANDS	25	1960
THE OLD PAYOLA ROLL BLUES	STAN FREBERG WITH JESSIE WHITE	40	1960
OLD PIANO RAG	DICKIE VALENTINE	15	1955
OLD POP IN AN OAK	REDNEX	12	1995
OLD RED EYES IS BACK	BEAUTIFUL SOUTH	22	1992
OLD RIVERS	WALTER BRENNAN	38	1962
THE OLD RUGGED CROSS	ETHNA CAMPBELL	33	1976
OLD SHEP	CLINTON FORD	27	1959
OLD SIAM SIR	WINGS	35	1979
OLD SMOKEY	JOHNNY & THE HURRICANES	24	1961
THE OLD SONGS	BARRY MANILOW	48	1981
OLD TIME'S SAKE	EMINEM	61	2009
OLD TOWN	CORRS	68	2005
OLDER	GEORGE MICHAEL	3	1997
OLDEST SWINGER IN TOWN	FRED WEDLOCK	6	1981
OLE OLA (MULHER BRASILEIRA)	ROD STEWART FEATURING THE SCOTTISH WORLD CUP FOOTBALL SQUAD	4	1978
OLIVE TREE	JUDITH DURHAM	33	1967
OLIVER'S ARMY	ELVIS COSTELLO & THE ATTRACTIONS	2	1979
OLYMPIAN	GENE	18	1995
OLYMPIC	808 STATE	10	1990
THE OMD REMIXES	ORCHESTRAL MANOEUVRES IN THE DARK	56	1998
OMEN [A]	ORBITAL	46	1990
THE OMEN [B]	PROGRAM 2 BELTRAM	53	1991
OMEN [C]	PRODIGY	4	2009
OMEN III	MAGIC AFFAIR	17	1994
OMG	USHER FEATURING WILL.I.AM	8	2010
ON	APHEX TWIN	32	1993
ON A CAROUSEL	HOLLIES	4	1967
ON A CROWDED STREET	BARBARA PENNINGTON	57	1985
ON A DAY LIKE TODAY	BRYAN ADAMS	13	1998
ON A GOOD THING	C-SIXTY FOUR	54	2005
ON A LITTLE STREET IN SINGAPORE	MANHATTAN TRANSFER	20	1978
ON A MISSION [A]	ALOOF	64	1992
ON A MISSION [B]	GABRIELLA CILMI	9	2010
ON A NIGHT LIKE THIS	KYLIE MINOGUE	2	2000
ON A NOOSE	TOWERS OF LONDON	32	2005
ON A RAGGA TIP	SL2	2	1992
ON A ROPE	ROCKET FROM THE CRYPT	12	1996
ON A SATURDAY NIGHT	TERRY DACTYL & THE DINOSAURS	45	1973
ON A SLOW BOAT TO CHINA	EMILE FORD & THE CHECKMATES	3	1960
ON A SUNDAY [A]	NICK HEYWARD	52	1983
ON A SUN-DAY [B]	BENZ	73	1997
ON AND ON [A]	ASWAD	25	1989
ON AND ON [B]	LONGPIGS	16	1996
ON & ON [C]	ERYKAH BADU	12	1997
ON BENDED KNEE	BOYZ II MEN	20	1994
ON CALL	KINGS OF LEON	18	2007
ON EVERY STREET	DIRE STRAITS	42	1992
ON FIRE [A]	T-CONNECTION	16	1978
ON FIRE [B]	TONE LOC	13	1989
ON FIRE [C]	LLOYD BANK$	19	2004
ON HER MAJESTY'S SECRET SERVICE	PROPELLERHEADS & DAVID ARNOLD	7	1997
ON HORSEBACK	MIKE OLDFIELD	4	1975
ON MOTHER KELLY'S DOORSTEP	DANNY LA RUE	33	1968
ON MY KNEES	411 FEATURING GHOSTFACE KILLAH	4	2004
ON MY MIND	FUTURESHOCK FEATURING BEN ONONO	51	2003
ON MY OWN [A]	PATTI LABELLE & MICHAEL McDONALD	2	1986
ON MY OWN [B]	CRAIG McLACHLAN	59	1992
ON MY OWN [B]	GLEE CAST	73	2010
ON MY OWN [C]	PEACH	69	1998
ON MY RADIO	SELECTER	8	1979
ON MY WAY [A]	MR FINGERS	71	1992
ON MY WAY [B]	MIKE KOGLIN FEATURING BEATRICE	28	1999
ON MY WAY HOME	ENYA	26	1996
ON MY WORD	CLIFF RICHARD	12	1965
ON OUR OWN (FROM GHOSTBUSTERS II)	BOBBY BROWN	4	1989
ON POINT	HOUSE OF PAIN	19	1994
ON SILENT WINGS	TINA TURNER	13	1996
ON STANDBY	SHED SEVEN	12	1996
ON THE BEACH [A]	CLIFF RICHARD & THE SHADOWS	7	1964
ON THE BEACH [B]	CHRIS REA	12	1986
ON THE BEACH [B]	YORK	4	2000
ON THE BEAT	BB & Q BAND	41	1981
ON THE BIBLE	DEUCE	13	1995
ON THE DANCEFLOOR	DJ DISCIPLE	67	1994
ON THE HORIZON	MELANIE C	14	2003
ON THE INSIDE (THEME FROM 'PRISONER CELL BLOCK H')	LYNNE HAMILTON	3	1989
ON THE LEVEL	YOMANDA	28	2000
ON THE MOVE	BARTHEZZ	18	2001
ON THE NIGHT	PAT & MICK	11	1988
ON THE ONE	LUKK FEATURING FELICIA COLLINS	72	1985
ON THE RADIO	DONNA SUMMER	32	1980
ON THE RADIO	MARTINE McCUTCHEON	7	2001
ON THE RADIO	REGINA SPEKTOR	60	2006
...ON THE RADIO (REMEMBER THE DAYS)	NELLY FURTADO	18	2002
ON THE REBOUND	FLOYD CRAMER	1	1961
ON THE ROAD AGAIN	CANNED HEAT	8	1968
ON THE ROPES (EP)	WONDER STUFF	10	1993
ON THE ROSE	TIGER	57	1997
ON THE RUN [A]	DE BOS	51	1997
ON THE RUN [B]	OMC	56	1997
ON THE RUN [C]	BIG TIME CHARLIE	22	1999
ON THE RUN [D]	TILLMANN UHRMACHER	16	2002

Title	Artist	Peak Position	Year of Release
ON THE RUN [E]	CRESCENT	49	2002
ON THE STREET WHERE YOU LIVE	VIC DAMONE	1	1958
ON THE STREET WHERE YOU LIVE	DAVID WHITFIELD	16	1958
ON THE TOP OF THE WORLD	DIVA SURPRISE FEATURING GEORGIA JONES	29	1998
ON THE TRAIL	PRIME MOVERS	74	1986
ON THE TURNING AWAY	PINK FLOYD	55	1987
ON THE VERGE OF SOMETHING WONDERFUL	DARREN HAYES	20	2007
ON THE WINGS OF A NIGHTINGALE	EVERLY BROTHERS	41	1984
ON THE WINGS OF LOVE	JEFFREY OSBORNE	11	1984
ON WITH THE MOTLEY	HARRY SECOMBE	16	1955
ON YA WAY	HELICOPTER	32	1994
ON YOUR OWN [A]	VERVE	28	1995
ON YOUR OWN [B]	BLUR	5	1997
ONCE	GENEVEVE	43	1966
ONCE AGAIN [A]	CUD	45	1992
1NCE AGAIN [B]	A TRIBE CALLED QUEST	34	1996
ONCE AND NEVER AGAIN	LONG BLONDES	30	2006
ONCE AROUND THE BLOCK	BADLY DRAWN BOY	27	1999
ONCE AROUND THE SUN	CAPRICE	24	2001
ONCE BITTEN TWICE SHY [A]	IAN HUNTER	14	1975
ONCE BITTEN TWICE SHY [B]	VESTA WILLIAMS	14	1987
ONCE I HAD A SWEETHEART	PENTANGLE	46	1969
ONCE IN A LIFETIME	TALKING HEADS	14	1981
ONCE IN A WHILE	BLACK VELVETS	75	2005
ONCE IN EVERY LIFETIME	KEN DODD	28	1961
ONCE MORE	ORB	38	2001
ONCE THERE WAS A TIME	TOM JONES	18	1966
ONCE UPON A CHRISTMAS SONG	GERALDINE	5	2008
ONCE UPON A DREAM	BILLY FURY	7	1962
ONCE UPON A LONG AGO	PAUL McCARTNEY	10	1987
ONCE UPON A TIME [A]	MARVIN GAYE & MARY WELLS	50	1964
ONCE UPON A TIME [B]	TOM JONES	32	1965
ONCE UPON A TIME [C]	POGUES	66	1994
ONCE UPON A TIME IN AMERICA	JEEVAS	61	2003
ONCE YOU'VE TASTED LOVE	TAKE THAT	47	1992
ONE [A]	METALLICA	13	1989
ONE [B]	BEE GEES	71	1989
ONE [C]	U2	7	1992
ONE [C]	MICA PARIS	29	1995
ONE [C]	MARY J BLIGE & U2	2	2006
THE ONE [D]	ELTON JOHN	10	1992
ONE [E]	BUSTA RHYMES FEATURING ERYKAH BADU	23	1998
THE ONE [F]	BACKSTREET BOYS	8	2000
THE ONE [G]	DEE DEE	28	2003
THE ONE [H]	CASSIUS HENRY FEATURING FREEWAY	56	2004
THE ONE [I]	UPPER STREET	35	2006
THE ONE [J]	KYLIE MINOGUE	36	2008
ONE & ONE	ROBERT MILES FEATURING MARIA NAYLER	3	1996
ONE AND ONE IS ONE	MEDICINE HEAD	3	1973
THE ONE AND ONLY [A]	GLADYS KNIGHT & THE PIPS	32	1978
THE ONE AND ONLY [B]	CHESNEY HAWKES	1	1991
ONE ARMED SCISSOR	AT THE DRIVE-IN	64	2000
ONE BETTER DAY	MADNESS	17	1984
ONE BETTER WORLD	ABC	32	1989
ONE BIG FAMILY EP	EMBRACE	21	1997
ONE BROKEN HEART FOR SALE	ELVIS PRESLEY	12	1963
ONE BY ONE	CHER	7	1996
ONE CALL AWAY	CHINGY FEATURING J WEAV	26	2004
ONE COOL REMOVE	SHAWN COLVIN WITH MARY CHAPIN CARPENTER	40	1995
ONE DANCE WON'T DO	AUDREY HALL	20	1986
ONE DAY [A]	TYRREL CORPORATION	59	1992
ONE DAY [B]	D MOB	41	1994
ONE DAY AT A TIME [A]	LENA MARTELL	1	1979
ONE DAY AT A TIME [B]	ALICE BAND	52	2001
ONE DAY I'LL FLY AWAY	RANDY CRAWFORD	2	1980
ONE DAY IN YOUR LIFE [A]	MICHAEL JACKSON	1	1981
ONE DAY IN YOUR LIFE [B]	ANASTACIA	11	2002
ONE DAY LIKE THIS	ELBOW	35	2008
ONE DRINK TOO MANY	SAILOR	35	1977
ONE EP	MANSUN	37	1996
ONE FINE DAY [A]	CHIFFONS	29	1963
ONE FINE DAY [B]	OPERABABES	54	2002
ONE FINE DAY [C]	JAKATTA	39	2003
ONE FINE MORNING	TOMMY HUNT	44	1976
ONE FOOT IN THE GRAVE	ERIC IDLE FEATURING RICHARD WILSON	50	1994
THE ONE FOR ME	JOE	34	1994
ONE FOR SORROW	STEPS	2	1998
ONE FOR THE BRISTOL CITY	BRISTOL CITY & THE WURZELS	66	2007
ONE FOR THE MOCKINGBIRD	CUTTING CREW	52	1987
ONE FOR THE MONEY	HORACE BROWN	12	1996
ONE FOR THE RADIO	McFLY	2	2008
ONE FOR YOU ONE FOR ME	JONATHAN KING	29	1978
ONE FOR YOU ONE FOR ME	LA BIONDA	54	1978
ONE GIANT LOVE	CUD	52	1994
ONE GIFT OF LOVE	DEAR JON	68	1995
ONE GOODBYE IN TEN	SHARA NELSON	21	1993
ONE GREAT THING	BIG COUNTRY	19	1986
ONE HEADLIGHT	WALLFLOWERS	54	1997
ONE HEART	CELINE DION	27	2003
ONE HEART BETWEEN TWO	DAVE BERRY	41	1964
ONE HELLO	RANDY CRAWFORD	48	1982
ONE HORSE TOWN	THRILLS	18	2003
101	SHEENA EASTON	54	1989
100 MILES AND RUNNIN'	N.W.A.	38	1990
100%	SONIC YOUTH	28	1992
100%	MARY KIANI	23	1997
100% PURE LOVE	CRYSTAL WATERS	15	1994
THE ONE I GAVE MY HEART TO	AALIYAH	30	1997
THE ONE I LOVE [A]	R.E.M.	16	1987
THE ONE I LOVE [B]	DAVID GRAY	8	2005
ONE IN A MILLION	AALIYAH	15	1997
ONE IN TEN	UB40	7	1981
ONE IN TEN	808 STATE Vs UB40	17	1992
ONE INCH ROCK	TYRANNOSAURUS REX	7	1968
ONE KISS FROM HEAVEN	LOUISE	9	1996
ONE LAST BREATH/BULLETS	CREED	47	2002
ONE LAST KISS	J GEILS BAND	74	1979
ONE LAST LOVE SONG	BEAUTIFUL SOUTH	14	1994
ONE LESS LONELY GIRL	JUSTIN BIEBER	62	2010
ONE LIFE STAND	HOT CHIP	41	2010
ONE LOVE [A]	ATLANTIC STARR	58	1985
ONE LOVE [B]	PAT BENATAR	59	1989
ONE LOVE [C]	STONE ROSES	4	1990
ONE LOVE [D]	DR ALBAN	45	1992
ONE LOVE [E]	PRODIGY	8	1993
ONE LOVE [F]	BLUE	3	2002
ONE LOVE [G]	DAVID GUETTA FEATURING ESTELLE	46	2009
ONE LOVE FAMILY	LIQUID	14	1995
ONE LOVE IN MY LIFETIME	INNOCENCE	40	1992
ONE LOVE – PEOPLE GET READY	BOB MARLEY & THE WAILERS	5	1984
ONE LOVER AT A TIME	ATLANTIC STARR	57	1987
ONE LOVER (DON'T STOP THE SHOW)	FORREST	67	1983
ONE MAN	CHANELLE	16	1989
ONE MAN ARMY	OUR LADY PEACE	70	2000
ONE MAN BAND	LEO SAYER	6	1974
ONE MAN IN MY HEART	HUMAN LEAGUE	13	1995
ONE MAN WOMAN	SHEENA EASTON	14	1980
ONE MAN'S BITCH	PHOEBE ONE	59	1998
ONE MIND, TWO HEARTS	PARADISE	42	1983
ONE MINUTE MAN	MISSY ELLIOTT FEATURING LUDACRIS	10	2001
ONE MIRROR TO MANY	BLACK CROWES	51	1996
ONE MOMENT IN TIME	WHITNEY HOUSTON	1	1988
ONE MORE	HAZIZA	75	2001
ONE MORE CHANCE [A]	DIANA ROSS	49	1981
ONE MORE CHANCE [B]	MAXI PRIEST	40	1993
ONE MORE CHANCE [C]	E.Y.C.	25	1994
ONE MORE CHANCE [D]	MADONNA	11	1995
ONE MORE CHANCE [E]	ONE	31	1997
ONE MORE CHANCE [F]	MICHAEL JACKSON	5	2003
ONE MORE CHANCE [G]	BLOC PARTY	15	2009
ONE MORE CHANCE/STAY WITH ME	NOTORIOUS B.I.G.	34	1997
ONE MORE DANCE	ESTHER & ABI OFARIM	13	1968
ONE MORE GOOD NIGHT WITH THE BOYS	TASMIN ARCHER	45	1996
ONE MORE NIGHT	PHIL COLLINS	4	1985
ONE MORE NIGHT ALONE	FRIDAY HILL	13	2006
ONE MORE RIVER	LUCIANA	67	1994
ONE MORE SATURDAY NIGHT	MATCHBOX	63	1982
ONE MORE SUNRISE (MORGEN)	DICKIE VALENTINE	14	1959
ONE MORE TIME [A]	WHYCLIFFE	72	1994
ONE MORE TIME [B]	DAFT PUNK	2	2000
ONE MORE TRY [A]	GEORGE MICHAEL	8	1988
ONE MORE TRY [B]	KRISTINE W	41	1996
ONE NATION	MASQUERADE	54	1986
ONE NATION UNDER A GROOVE (PART 1)	FUNKADELIC	9	1978
ONE NIGHT	ELVIS PRESLEY	1	1959
ONE NIGHT	MUD	32	1975
ONE NIGHT IN BANGKOK	MURRAY HEAD	12	1984
ONE NIGHT IN HEAVEN	M PEOPLE	6	1993
ONE NIGHT STAND [A]	LET LOOSE	12	1995
ONE NIGHT STAND [B]	ALOOF	30	1996
ONE NIGHT STAND [C]	MIS-TEEQ	5	2001
ONE NINE FOR SANTA	FOGWELL FLAX & THE ANKLEBITERS FROM FREHOLD JUNIOR SCHOOL	68	1981
10538 OVERTURE	ELECTRIC LIGHT ORCHESTRA	9	1972
ONE OF THE LIVING	TINA TURNER	55	1985
ONE OF THE LUCKY ONES	JOAN REGAN	47	1960
ONE OF THE PEOPLE	ADAMSKI'S THING	56	1998
ONE OF THESE DAYS	AMBASSADOR	67	2000
ONE OF THESE NIGHTS	EAGLES	23	1975
ONE OF THOSE NIGHTS	BUCKS FIZZ	20	1981
ONE OF US [A]	ABBA	3	1981
ONE OF US [B]	JOAN OSBORNE	6	1996
ONE OF US [C]	HELL IS FOR HEROES	71	2004
ONE OF US MUST KNOW (SOONER OR LATER)	BOB DYLAN	33	1966
ONE ON ONE	DARYL HALL & JOHN OATES	63	1983
ONE PERFECT SUNRISE	ORBITAL	29	2004
ONE PIECE AT A TIME	JOHNNY CASH WITH THE TENNESSEE THREE	32	1976
ONE PURE THOUGHT	HOT CHIP	53	2008
ONE REASON WHY	CRAIG McLACHLAN	29	1992
ONE ROAD	LOVE AFFAIR	16	1969
ONE RULE FOR YOU	AFTER THE FIRE	40	1979
ONE SHINING MOMENT	DIANA ROSS	10	1992
ONE SHOT [A]	BROTHERHOOD	55	1996
ONE SHOT [B]	JLS	6	2010
ONE SLIP	PINK FLOYD	50	1988
ONE SMALL DAY	ULTRAVOX	27	1984

Title / Artist	Peak Position	Year of Release
ONE STEP KILLAH PRIEST	45	1998
ONE STEP AHEAD NIK KERSHAW	55	1989
ONE STEP AT A TIME JORDIN SPARKS	16	2009
ONE STEP AWAY TAVARES	16	1977
ONE STEP BEYOND MADNESS	7	1979
ONE STEP CLOSER [A] LINKIN PARK	24	2001
ONE STEP CLOSER [B] S CLUB JUNIORS	2	2002
ONE STEP CLOSER (TO LOVE) GEORGE McCRAE	57	1984
ONE STEP FURTHER BARDO	2	1982
ONE STEP OUT OF TIME MICHAEL BALL	20	1992
ONE STEP TOO FAR FAITHLESS FEATURING DIDO	6	2002
ONE SWEET DAY MARIAH CAREY & BOYZ II MEN	6	1995
1 THING AMERIE	4	2005
1000% FATIMA MANSIONS	61	1992
1000 YEARS (JUST LEAVE ME NOW) JUPITER ACE FEATURING SHEENA	51	2005
138 TREK DJ ZINC	27	2000
ONE TIME JUSTIN BIEBER	11	2010
ONE TO ANOTHER CHARLATANS	3	1996
THE ONE TO CRY ESCORTS	49	1964
1 TO 1 RELIGION BOMB THE BASS FEATURING CARLTON	53	1995
THE ONE TO SING THE BLUES MOTORHEAD	45	1991
ONE TONGUE HOTHOUSE FLOWERS	45	1993
ONE TOUCH 365	60	2006
ONE TRUE WOMAN YAZZ	60	1992
1 2 STEP CIARA FEATURING MISSY ELLIOTT	3	2005
1-2-3 [A] LEN BARRY	3	1965
1-2-3 [B] PROFESSIONALS	43	1980
1-2-3 [C] GLORIA ESTEFAN & MIAMI SOUND MACHINE	9	1988
1-2-3 [D] CHIMES	60	1989
ONE, TWO, THREE [E] DINA CARROLL	16	1998
1234 [A] MRS WOOD	54	1998
1234 [B] FEIST	8	2007
1-2-3-4 GET WITH THE WICKED RICHARD BLACKWOOD	10	2000
1,2,3,4 (SUMPIN' NEW) COOLIO	13	1996
1-2-3 O'LEARY DES O'CONNOR	4	1968
ONE VISION QUEEN	7	1985
ONE VOICE BILL TARMEY	16	1993
ONE WAY LEVELLERS	33	1991
ONE WAY LOVE CLIFF BENNETT & THE REBEL ROUSERS	9	1964
ONE WAY MIRROR KINESIS	71	2003
ONE WAY OUT REID	66	1988
ONE WAY TICKET [A] ERUPTION	9	1979
ONE WAY TICKET [B] DARKNESS	8	2005
ONE WEEK BARENAKED LADIES	5	1999
ONE WILD NIGHT BON JOVI	10	2001
ONE WISH [A] SHYSTIE	40	2004
ONE WISH [B] RAY J	13	2005
ONE WOMAN JADE	22	1993
ONE WORD KELLY OSBOURNE	9	2005
THE ONE-OFF SONG FOR THE SUMMER KOOPA	21	2007
THE ONES YOU LOVE RICK ASTLEY	48	1993
ONION SONG MARVIN GAYE & TAMMI TERRELL	9	1969
ONLY [A] ANTHRAX	36	1993
ONLY [B] NINE INCH NAILS	20	2005
ONLY A BOY TIM BURGESS	54	2003
ONLY CRYING KEITH MARSHALL	12	1981
THE ONLY EXCEPTION PARAMORE	57	2010
THE ONLY FLAME IN TOWN ELVIS COSTELLO	71	1984
ONLY FOOLS (NEVER FALL IN LOVE) SONIA	10	1991
ONLY FOR A WHILE TOPLOADER	19	2001
ONLY FOR LOVE LIMAHL	16	1983
ONLY HAPPY WHEN IT RAINS GARBAGE	29	1995
ONLY HUMAN DINA CARROLL	33	1996
ONLY IF... ENYA	43	1997
ONLY IN MY DREAMS DEBBIE GIBSON	11	1987
THE ONLY LIVING BOY IN NEW CROSS CARTER-THE UNSTOPPABLE SEX MACHINE	7	1992
THE ONLY LIVING BOY IN NEW YORK (EP) EVERYTHING BUT THE GIRL	42	1993
ONLY LOVE NANA MOUSKOURI	2	1986
ONLY LOVE CAN BREAK YOUR HEART ELKIE BROOKS	43	1978
ONLY LOVE CAN BREAK YOUR HEART MINT JULEPS	62	1986
ONLY LOVE CAN BREAK YOUR HEART SAINT ETIENNE	39	1991
ONLY LOVE REMAINS PAUL McCARTNEY	34	1986
ONLY LOVING DOES IT GUYS & DOLLS	42	1978
ONLY MAN AUDIO BULLYS	44	2010
THE ONLY MAN ON THE ISLAND TOMMY STEELE	16	1958
THE ONLY MAN ON THE ISLAND VIC DAMONE	24	1958
ONLY ME HYPERLOGIC	35	1995
THE ONLY ONE [A] TRANSVISION VAMP	15	1989
THE ONLY ONE [B] GUN	29	1995
ONLY ONE [C] PETER ANDRE	16	1996
THE ONLY ONE [D] THUNDER	31	1998
THE ONLY ONE [E] CURE	48	2008
THE ONLY ONE I KNOW CHARLATANS	9	1990
ONLY ONE ROAD CELINE DION	8	1995
ONLY ONE WOMAN MARBLES	5	1968
ONLY ONE WORD PROPAGANDA	71	1990
ONLY ONE WORD COMES TO MIND BIFFY CLYRO	27	2005
THE ONLY RHYME THAT BITES MC TUNES VERSUS 808 STATE	10	1990
ONLY SAW TODAY – INSTANT KARMA AMOS	48	1994
ONLY SIXTEEN CRAIG DOUGLAS	1	1959
ONLY SIXTEEN SAM COOKE	23	1959
ONLY SIXTEEN AL SAXON	24	1959
ONLY TENDER LOVE DEACON BLUE	22	1993
ONLY THE HEARTACHES HOUSTON WELLS	22	1963
ONLY THE LONELY [A] ROY ORBISON	1	1960
ONLY THE LONELY [A] PRELUDE	55	1982
ONLY THE LONELY [B] T'PAU	28	1989
ONLY THE LOOT CAN MAKE ME HAPPY R KELLY	24	2000
ONLY THE MOMENT MARC ALMOND	45	1989
ONLY THE ONES WE LOVE TANITA TIKARAM	69	1991
ONLY THE STRONG SURVIVE BILLY PAUL	33	1977
ONLY THE STRONG SURVIVE DJ KRUSH	71	1996
ONLY THE STRONGEST WILL SURVIVE HURRICANE #1	19	1998
ONLY THE WOMEN KNOW SIX CHIX	72	2000
THE ONLY THING THAT LOOKS GOOD ON ME IS YOU BRYAN ADAMS	6	1996
ONLY THIS MOMENT ROYKSOPP	33	2005
ONLY TIME ENYA	32	2000
ONLY TIME WILL TELL [A] ASIA	54	1982
ONLY TIME WILL TELL [B] TEN CITY	63	1992
ONLY TO BE WITH YOU ROACHFORD	21	1994
ONLY U ASHANTI	2	2005
ONLY WANNA KNOW U COS URE FAMOUS OXIDE & NEUTRINO	12	2001
THE ONLY WAY IS UP YAZZ & THE PLASTIC POPULATION	1	1988
THE ONLY WAY OUT CLIFF RICHARD	10	1982
ONLY WHEN I LOSE MYSELF DEPECHE MODE	17	1998
ONLY WHEN I SLEEP CORRS	58	1997
ONLY WHEN YOU LEAVE SPANDAU BALLET	3	1984
ONLY WITH YOU CAPTAIN HOLLYWOOD PROJECT	61	1993
ONLY WOMEN BLEED JULIE COVINGTON	12	1977
ONLY YESTERDAY CARPENTERS	7	1975
ONLY YOU [A] HILLTOPPERS	3	1956
ONLY YOU [A] PLATTERS	5	1956
ONLY YOU [A] MARK WYNTER	38	1964
ONLY YOU [A] JEFF COLLINS	40	1972
ONLY YOU [A] RINGO STARR	28	1974
ONLY YOU (AND YOU ALONE) [A] CHILD	33	1979
ONLY YOU [A] JOHN ALFORD	9	1996
ONLY YOU [B] TEDDY PENDERGRASS	41	1978
ONLY YOU [C] YAZOO	2	1982
ONLY YOU [C] FLYING PICKETS	1	1983
ONLY YOU [D] PRAISE	4	1991
ONLY YOU [E] PORTISHEAD	35	1998
ONLY YOU [F] CASINO	72	1999
ONLY YOU CAN FOX	3	1975
ONLY YOU CAN ROCK ME UFO	50	1978
ONLY YOUR LOVE BANANARAMA	27	1990
ONWARD CHRISTIAN SOLDIERS HARRY SIMEONE CHORALE	35	1960
OO...AH...CANTONA OO LA LA	64	1992
007 MUSICAL YOUTH	26	1983
007 (SHANTY TOWN) DESMOND DEKKER & THE ACES	14	1967
OOCHIE WALLY QB FINEST FEATURING NAS & BRAVEHEARTS	30	2001
OOCHY KOOCHY (F.U. BABY YEAH YEAH) BABY FORD	58	1988
OO-EEH BABY STONEBRIDGE McGUINNESS	54	1979
OOH! AAH! CANTONA 1300 DRUMS FEATURING THE UNJUSTIFIED ANCIENTS OF MU	11	1996
OOH AAH (G-SPOT) WAYNE MARSHALL	29	1994
OOH AAH...JUST A LITTLE BIT GINA G	1	1996
OOH-AH-AA (I FEEL IT) E.Y.C.	33	1995
OOH BABY GILBERT O'SULLIVAN	18	1973
OOH BOY ROSE ROYCE	46	1980
OOH I DO LYNSEY DE PAUL	25	1974
OOH I LIKE IT JONNY L	73	1993
OOH LA KOOKS	20	2006
OOH! LA! LA! [A] JOE 'MR PIANO' HENDERSON	44	1960
OOH LA LA [B] COOLIO	14	1997
OOH LA LA [C] ROD STEWART	16	1998
OOH LA LA [D] WISEGUYS	2	1998
OOH LA LA [E] GOLDFRAPP	4	2005
OOH LA LA LA RED RAW FEATURING 007	59	1995
OOH LA LA LA (LET'S GO DANCIN') KOOL & THE GANG	6	1982
OOH MY SOUL LITTLE RICHARD	22	1958
OOH STICK YOU! DAPHNE & CELESTE	8	2000
OOH TO BE AH KAJAGOOGOO	7	1983
OOH-WAKKA-DOO-WAKKA-DAY GILBERT O'SULLIVAN	8	1972
OOH WEE MARK RONSON	15	2003
OOH! WHAT A LIFE GIBSON BROTHERS	10	1979
OOHHH BABY VIDA SIMPSON	70	1995
O-O-O ADRENALIN M.O.D.	49	1988
OOO LA LA LA TEENA MARIE	74	1988
OOOH DE LA SOUL FEATURING REDMAN	29	2000
OOOIE, OOOIE, OOOIE PRICKLY HEAT	57	1998
OOOPS 808 STATE FEATURING BJORK	42	1991
OOOPS UP SNAP!	5	1990
OOPS!...I DID IT AGAIN BRITNEY SPEARS	1	2000
OOPS (OH MY) TWEET	5	2002
OOPS UPSIDE YOUR HEAD GAP BAND	6	1980
OOPS UPSIDE YOUR HEAD DJ CASPER FEATURING THE GAP BAND	16	2004
OOPSY DAISY CHIPMUNK	1	2009
OPAL MANTRA THERAPY?	13	1993
OPEN ARMS [A] MARIAH CAREY	4	1996
OPEN ARMS [B] WILT	59	2000
OPEN ARMS [C] TINA TURNER	25	2004
OPEN HEART ZOO MARTIN GRECH	68	2002
OPEN ROAD [A] GARY BARLOW	7	1997
OPEN ROAD [B] BRYAN ADAMS	21	2004

Title	Artist	Peak Position	Year of Release
OPEN ROADS	CERYS MATTHEWS	53	2006
OPEN SESAME	LEILA K	23	1993
OPEN UP [A]	MUNGO JERRY	21	1972
OPEN UP [B]	LEFTFIELD LYDON	13	1993
OPEN UP THE RED BOX	SIMPLY RED	61	1986
OPEN UP YOUR HEART	JOAN & RUSTY REGAN	19	1955
OPEN YOUR EYES [A]	BLACK BOX	48	1991
OPEN YOUR EYES [B]	GOLDFINGER	75	2002
OPEN YOUR EYES [C]	SNOW PATROL	26	2007
OPEN YOUR HEART [A]	HUMAN LEAGUE	6	1981
OPEN YOUR HEART [B]	M PEOPLE	9	1995
OPEN YOUR HEART [C]	MADONNA	4	1986
OPEN YOUR MIND [A]	808 STATE	38	1991
OPEN YOUR MIND [B]	USURA	7	1993
OPEN YOUR MIND (LET ME IN)	REAL PEOPLE	70	1991
OPEN YOUR WINDOW	REVEREND & THE MAKERS	65	2007
THE OPERA HOUSE	JACK E MAKOSSA	48	1987
THE OPERA SONG (BRAVE NEW WORLD)	JURGEN VRIES FEATURING CMC	3	2003
OPERAA HOUSE	WORLD'S FAMOUS SUPREME TEAM SHOW	75	1990
OPERATION BLADE (BASS IN THE PLACE)	PUBLIC DOMAIN FEATURING CHUCK D	5	2000
OPERATOR [A]	MIDNIGHT STAR	66	1985
OPERATOR [B]	LITTLE RICHARD	67	1986
OPIUM SCUMBAGZ	OLAV BASOSKI	56	2000
O.P.P.	NAUGHTY BY NATURE	35	1991
OPPORTUNITIES (LET'S MAKE LOTS OF MONEY)	PET SHOP BOYS	11	1986
THE OPPOSITE OF ADULTS	CHIDDY BANG	12	2010
OPPOSITES ATTRACT	PAULA ABDUL & THE WILD PAIR	2	1990
OPTIMISTIC	SOUNDS OF BLACKNESS	28	1992
OPUS 40	MERCURY REV	31	1999
OPUS 17 (DON'T YOU WORRY 'BOUT ME)	FOUR SEASONS WITH FRANKIE VALLI	20	1966
ORANGE BLOSSOM SPECIAL	SPOTNICKS	29	1962
ORANGE CRUSH	R.E.M.	28	1989
THE ORANGE THEME	CYGNUS X	43	2000
ORCHARD ROAD	LEO SAYER	16	1983
ORCHESTRAL MANOEUVRES IN THE DARKNESS EP	DIFF'RENT DARKNESS	66	2003
ORDINARY ANGEL	HUE & CRY	42	1988
ORDINARY DAY [A]	CURIOSITY KILLED THE CAT	11	1987
ORDINARY DAY [B]	VANESSA CARLTON	53	2002
ORDINARY GIRL	ALISON MOYET	43	1987
ORDINARY LIVES	BEE GEES	54	1989
ORDINARY PEOPLE	JOHN LEGEND	27	2005
ORDINARY WORLD	DURAN DURAN	6	1993
ORDINARY WORLD	AURORA FEATURING NAIMEE COLEMAN	5	2000
ORIGINAL	LEFTFIELD FEATURING TONI HALLIDAY	18	1995
ORIGINAL BIRD DANCE	ELECTRONICAS	22	1981
ORIGINAL NUTTAH	UK APACHI WITH SHY FX	39	1994
ORIGINAL PRANKSTER	OFFSPRING	6	2000
ORIGINAL SIN	ELTON JOHN	39	2002
ORIGINAL SIN (THEME FROM 'THE SHADOW')	TAYLOR DAYNE	63	1995
ORINOCO FLOW	ENYA	1	1988
ORLANDO DAWN	LIQUID	53	2000
ORPHEUS	ASH	13	2004
ORVILLE'S SONG	KEITH HARRIS & ORVILLE	4	1982
OSCAR	SHACK	67	2000
OSSIE'S DREAM (SPURS ARE ON THEIR WAY TO WEMBLEY)	TOTTENHAM HOTSPUR FA CUP FINAL SQUAD	5	1981
THE OTHER MAN'S GRASS	PETULA CLARK	20	1967
THE OTHER SIDE [A]	AEROSMITH	46	1990
THE OTHER SIDE [B]	DAVID GRAY	35	2002
THE OTHER SIDE [C]	PAUL VAN DYK FEATURING WAYNE JACKSON	58	2005
THE OTHER SIDE [D]	PENDULUM	54	2008
THE OTHER SIDE OF LOVE	YAZOO	13	1982
THE OTHER SIDE OF ME	ANDY WILLIAMS	42	1976
THE OTHER SIDE OF SUMMER	ELVIS COSTELLO	43	1991
THE OTHER SIDE OF THE SUN	JANIS IAN	44	1980
OTHER SIDE OF THE WORLD	KT TUNSTALL	13	2005
THE OTHER SIDE OF YOU	MIGHTY LEMON DROPS	67	1986
THE OTHER WOMAN, THE OTHER MAN	GERARD KENNY	69	1984
OTHERNESS (EP)	COCTEAU TWINS	59	1995
OTHERSIDE [A]	RED HOT CHILI PEPPERS	33	2000
THE OTHERSIDE [B]	BREAKS CO-OP	43	2006
OTHERWISE	MORCHEEBA	64	2002
OUCH	N-DUBZ	22	2008
OUIJA BOARD OUIJA BOARD	MORRISSEY	18	1989
OUR DAY WILL COME	RUBY & THE ROMANTICS	38	1963
OUR FAVOURITE MELODIES	CRAIG DOUGLAS	9	1962
OUR FRANK	MORRISSEY	26	1991
OUR GOAL	ARSENAL FC	46	2000
OUR HOUSE	MADNESS	5	1982
OUR HOUSE IS DADLESS	KID BRITISH	63	2009
OUR KIND OF LOVE	HANNAH	41	2000
OUR LAST SONG TOGETHER	NEIL SEDAKA	31	1973
OUR LIPS ARE SEALED	GO-GOS	47	1982
OUR LIPS ARE SEALED	FUN BOY THREE	7	1983
OUR LIVES	CALLING	13	2004
OUR LOVE	ELKIE BROOKS	43	1982
(OUR LOVE) DON'T THROW IT ALL AWAY	ANDY GIBB	32	1979
OUR RADIO ROCKS	PJ & DUNCAN	15	1995
OUR TRUTH	LACUNA COIL	40	2006
OUR VELOCITY	MAXIMO PARK	9	2007
OUR WORLD	BLUE MINK	17	1970
OUT COME THE FREAKS	WAS (NOT WAS)	41	1984
OUT COME THE FREAKS (AGAIN)	WAS (NOT WAS)	44	1988
OUT DEMONS OUT	EDGAR BROUGHTON BAND	39	1970
OUT HERE ON MY OWN	IRENE CARA	58	1982
OUT IN THE DARK	LURKERS	72	1979
OUT IN THE FIELDS	GARY MOORE & PHIL LYNOTT	5	1985
OUT IS THROUGH	ALANIS MORISSETTE	56	2004
OUT OF BREATH	RONI SIZE FEATURING RAHZEL	44	2004
OUT OF CONTROL [A]	ANGELIC UPSTARTS	58	1980
OUT OF CONTROL [B]	ROLLING STONES	51	1998
OUT OF CONTROL [C]	CHEMICAL BROTHERS	21	1999
OUT OF CONTROL (BACK FOR MORE)	DARUDE	13	2001
OUT OF HAND	MIGHTY LEMON DROPS	66	1987
OUT OF MY HEAD	MARRADONA	38	1994
OUT OF MY HEART	BBMAK	36	2002
OUT OF MY MIND [A]	JOHNNY TILLOTSON	34	1963
OUT OF MY MIND [B]	DURAN DURAN	21	1997
OUT OF OUR MINDS	CRACKOUT	63	2003
OUT OF REACH [A]	VICE SQUAD	68	1982
OUT OF REACH [B]	PRIMITIVES	25	1988
OUT OF REACH [C]	GABRIELLE	4	2001
OUT OF SEASON	ALMIGHTY	41	1993
OUT OF SIGHT [A]	BABYBIRD	58	2000
OUT OF SIGHT [B]	SPIRITUALIZED	65	2001
OUT OF SIGHT, OUT OF MIND	LEVEL 42	41	1983
OUT OF SPACE	PRODIGY	5	1992
OUT OF TEARS	ROLLING STONES	36	1994
OUT OF THE BLUE [A]	DEBBIE GIBSON	19	1988
OUT OF THE BLUE [B]	SYSTEM F	14	1999
OUT OF THE BLUE [C]	DELTA GOODREM	9	2004
OUT OF THE QUESTION	MUMM RA	45	2006
OUT OF THE SILENT PLANET	IRON MAIDEN	20	2000
OUT OF THE SINKING	PAUL WELLER	16	1994
OUT OF THE STORM	INCOGNITO	57	1996
OUT OF THE VOID	GRASS-SHOW	75	1997
OUT OF THIS WORLD	TONY HATCH	50	1962
OUT OF TIME [A]	CHRIS FARLOWE	1	1966
OUT OF TIME [A]	DAN McCAFFERTY	41	1975
OUT OF TIME [A]	ROLLING STONES	45	1975
OUT OF TIME [B]	BLUR	5	2003
OUT OF TOUCH	DARYL HALL & JOHN OATES	48	1984
OUT OF TOUCH	UNITING NATIONS	7	2004
OUT OF TOWN	MAX BYGRAVES	18	1956
OUT OF YOUR MIND	TRUE STEPPERS & DANE BOWERS FEATURING VICTORIA BECKHAM	2	2000
OUT ON THE FLOOR	DOBIE GRAY	42	1975
OUT THERE [A]	DINOSAUR, JR	44	1993
OUT THERE [B]	FRIENDS OF MATTHEW	61	1999
OUT THERE [C]	PENDULUM	34	2005
OUT WITH HER	BLOW MONKEYS	30	1987
OUTA SPACE	BILLY PRESTON	44	1972
OUTDOOR MINER	WIRE	51	1979
OUTERSPACE GIRL	BELOVED	38	1993
OUTLAW	OLIVE	14	1997
OUTLINES	CLOR	43	2005
OUTRAGEOUS	STIX 'N' STONED	39	1996
OUTSHINED	SOUNDGARDEN	50	1992
OUTSIDE [A]	OMAR	43	1994
OUTSIDE [B]	GEORGE MICHAEL	2	1998
OUTSIDE [C]	STAIND	33	2001
OUT-SIDE [D]	BETA BAND	54	2004
OUTSIDE IN THE RAIN	GWEN GUTHRIE	37	1987
OUTSIDE MY WINDOW	STEVIE WONDER	52	1980
OUTSIDE OF HEAVEN	EDDIE FISHER	1	1953
OUTSIDE YOUR DOOR	STANDS	49	2004
OUTSIDE YOUR ROOM (EP)	SLOWDIVE	69	1993
OUTSPOKEN – PART 1	BEN WATT FEATURING ESTELLE	74	2005
OUTSTANDING	GAP BAND	68	1983
OUTSTANDING	KENNY THOMAS	12	1991
OUTSTANDING	ANDY COLE	68	1999
OUTTA CONTROL	50 CENT FEATURING MOBB DEEP	7	2005
OUTTA HERE	ESMEE DENTERS	7	2009
OUTTA MY HEAD (AY YA YA)	ASHLEE SIMPSON	24	2008
OUTTA SPACE	MELLOW TRAX	41	2000
OUTTATHAWAY	VINES	20	2002
OVER [A]	PORTISHEAD	25	1997
OVER [B]	LINDSAY LOHAN	27	2005
OVER AND OVER [A]	DAVE CLARK FIVE	45	1965
OVER AND OVER [B]	JAMES BOYS	39	1973
OVER AND OVER [C]	SHALAMAR	23	1983
OVER & OVER [D]	PLUX FEATURING GEORGIA JONES	33	1996
OVER AND OVER [E]	PUFF JOHNSON	20	1997
OVER AND OVER [F]	NELLY FEATURING TIM McGRAW	1	2005
OVER AND OVER [G]	TURIN BRAKES	62	2005
OVER AND OVER [H]	HOT CHIP	27	2006
OVER MY HEAD	LIT	37	2000
OVER MY HEAD (CABLE CAR)	FRAY	19	2007
OVER MY SHOULDER [A]	MIKE + THE MECHANICS	12	1995
OVER MY SHOULDER [B]	I AM KLOOT	38	2005
OVER RISING	CHARLATANS	15	1991
OVER THE BARRICADE	MESH-29	35	2007
OVER THE EDGE	ALMIGHTY	38	1993
OVER THE HILLS AND FAR AWAY	GARY MOORE	20	1986
OVER THE RAINBOW	SAM HARRIS	67	1985
OVER THE RAINBOW	EVA CASSIDY	42	2001

Title / Artist	Peak Position	Year of Release
OVER THE RAINBOW – YOU BELONG TO ME (MEDLEY) MATCHBOX	15	1980
OVER THE RIVER BITTY McLEAN	27	1995
OVER THE SEA JESSE RAE	65	1985
OVER THE WEEKEND NICK HEYWARD	43	1986
OVER THERE BABE TEAM	45	2002
OVER THERE (I DON'T CARE) HOUSE OF PAIN	20	1995
OVER TO YOU JOHN (HERE WE GO AGAIN) JIVE BUNNY & THE MASTERMIXERS	28	1991
OVER UNDER SIDEWAYS DOWN YARDBIRDS	10	1966
OVER YOU [A] FREDDIE & THE DREAMERS	13	1964
OVER YOU [B] ROXY MUSIC	5	1980
OVER YOU [C] RAY PARKER, JR	65	1988
OVER YOU [D] JUSTIN	11	1999
OVER YOU [E] WARREN CLARKE FEATURING KATHY BROWN	42	2001
OVER YOU [F] MICKY MODELLE V JESSY	35	2006
OVERCOME TRICKY	34	1995
OVERDRIVE DJ SANDY VS HOUSETRAP	32	2000
OVERJOYED STEVIE WONDER	17	1986
OVERKILL [A] MOTORHEAD	39	1979
OVERKILL [B] MEN AT WORK	21	1983
OVERLOAD [A] SUGABABES	6	2000
OVERLOAD [B] VOODOO & SERANO	30	2003
OVERNIGHT CELEBRITY TWISTA	16	2004
OVERPROTECTED BRITNEY SPEARS	4	2002
OVERRATED SIOBHAN DONAGHY	19	2003
OVERRATED (EVERYTHING IS) LESS THAN JAKE	61	2006
OVERTHROWN LIBIDO	53	1998
OVERTIME LEVEL 42	62	1991
OWNER OF A LONELY HEART YES	28	1983
OWNER OF A LONELY HEART MAX GRAHAM VS YES	9	2005
OXBOW LAKES ORB	38	1995
OXFORD COMMA VAMPIRE WEEKEND	38	2008
OXYGEN [A] BLAGGERS I.T.A.	51	1993
OXYGEN [B] JJ72	23	2000
OXYGEN [C] WILLY MASON	23	2005
OXYGENE 8 JEAN-MICHEL JARRE	17	1997
OXYGENE PART IV JEAN-MICHEL JARRE	4	1977
OXYGENE 10 JEAN-MICHEL JARRE	21	1997
OYE GLORIA ESTEFAN	33	1998
OYE COMO VA TITO PUENTE Jr & THE LATIN RHYTHM FEATURING TITO PUENTE, INDIA & CALI ALEMAN	36	1996
OYE MI CANTO (HEAR MY VOICE) GLORIA ESTEFAN	16	1989

P

Title / Artist	Peak Position	Year of Release
P MACHINERY PROPAGANDA	50	1985
PABLO RUSS CONWAY	45	1961
PACIFIC 808 STATE	10	1989
PACIFIC MELODY AIRSCAPE	27	1997
PACK OF WOLVES NIGHTBREED	45	2004
PACK UP YOUR SORROWS JOAN BAEZ	50	1966
PACKET OF PEACE LIONROCK	32	1993
PACKJAMMED (WITH THE PARTY POSSE) STOCK AITKEN WATERMAN	41	1987
PAC-MAN [A] POWERPILL	43	1992
PACMAN [B] ED RUSH & OPTICAL/UNIVERSAL	61	2002
PAC'S LIFE 2PAC FEATURING TI & ASHANTI	21	2007
THE PADDLE DJ TOUCHE	65	2004
PADDY'S REVENGE STEVE MAC	17	2008
PAGAN POETRY BJORK	38	2001
PAID IN FULL ERIC B & RAKIM	15	1987
PAID MY DUES ANASTACIA	14	2001
PAIN [A] BETTY WRIGHT	42	1986
PAIN [B] JIMMY EAT WORLD	38	2004
THE PAIN INSIDE COSMIC ROUGH RIDERS	36	2001
PAIN KILLER TURIN BRAKES	5	2003
A PAIN THAT I'M USED TO DEPECHE MODE	15	2005
PAINKILLER JUDAS PRIEST	74	1990
PAINT A PICTURE MAN WITH NO NAME FEATURING HANNAH	42	1996
PAINT IT, BLACK ROLLING STONES	1	1966
PAINT IT BLACK MODETTES	42	1980
PAINT ME DOWN SPANDAU BALLET	30	1981
PAINT THE SILENCE SOUTH	69	2001
PAINT THE TOWN RED DELIRIOUS?	56	2005
PAINT YOUR TARGET FIGHTSTAR	9	2005
PAINTED MOON SILENCERS	57	1988
PAINTER MAN CREATION	36	1966
PAINTER MAN BONEY M	10	1979
A PAIR OF BROWN EYES POGUES	72	1985
PAISLEY PARK PRINCE & THE REVOLUTION	18	1985
PAL OF MY CRADLE DAYS ANN BREEN	69	1983
PALE BLUE EYES PAUL QUINN & EDWYYN COLLINS	72	1984
PALE MOVIE SAINT ETIENNE	28	1994
PALE RED JERRY BURNS	64	1992
PALE SHELTER TEARS FOR FEARS	5	1983
PALISADES PARK FREDDY CANNON	20	1962
PALLADIO ESCALA	39	2009
PALOMA BLANCA GEORGE BAKER SELECTION	10	1975
PAMELA PAMELA WAYNE FONTANA	11	1966
PANAMA VAN HALEN	61	1984
THE PANDEMONIUM SINGLE KILLING JOKE	28	1994
PANDORA'S BOX [A] PROCOL HARUM	16	1975
PANDORA'S BOX [B] ORCHESTRAL MANOEUVRES IN THE DARK	7	1991
PANDORA'S KISS LOUISE	5	2003
PANIC SMITHS	11	1986
PANIC ATTACK PADDINGTONS	25	2005
PANIC ON MADDER ROSE	65	1994
PANINARO '95 PET SHOP BOYS	15	1995
PANIS ANGELICUS ANTHONY WAY	55	1995
PANTHER PARTY MAD MOSES	50	1997
PAPA CAN YOU HEAR ME N-DUBZ	19	2008
PAPA DON'T PREACH MADONNA	1	1986
PAPA DON'T PREACH KELLY OSBOURNE	3	2002
PAPA LOVES MAMA JOAN REGAN	29	1960
PAPA LOVES MAMBO PERRY COMO	16	1954
PAPA OOM MOW MOW SHARONETTES	26	1975
PAPA OOM MOW MOW GARY GLITTER	38	1975
PAPA WAS A ROLLIN' STONE TEMPTATIONS	14	1973
PAPA WAS A ROLLING STONE WAS (NOT WAS)	12	1990
PAPARAZZI LADY GAGA	4	2009
PAPA'S GOT A BRAND NEW BAG JAMES BROWN & THE FAMOUS FLAMES	25	1965
PAPA'S GOT A BRAND NEW PIGBAG PIGBAG	3	1982
PAPA'S GOT A BRAND NEW PIGBAG SILENT UNDERDOG	73	1985
PAPER DOLL [A] WINDSOR DAVIES & DON ESTELLE	41	1975
PAPER DOLL [B] PM DAWN	49	1991
PAPER HOUSE FOOLPROOF	53	2004
PAPER PLANE STATUS QUO	8	1973
PAPER PLANES MIA	19	2008
PAPER ROSES KAYE SISTERS	7	1960
PAPER ROSES ANITA BRYANT	24	1960
PAPER ROSES MAUREEN EVANS	40	1960
PAPER ROSES MARIE OSMOND	2	1973
PAPER SUN TRAFFIC	5	1967
PAPER TIGER SUE THOMPSON	30	1965
PAPERBACK WRITER BEATLES	1	1966
PAPERCUT LINKIN PARK	14	2001
PAPERFACES FEEDER	41	1999
PAPILLON [A] N-JOI	70	1994
PAPILLON [B] EDITORS	23	2009
PAPUA NEW GUINEA FUTURE SOUND OF LONDON	22	1992
PARA MI MOTIVATION	71	2001
PARACHUTE CHERYL COLE	5	2009
PARADE WHITE & TORCH	54	1982
PARADISE [A] FRANK IFIELD	26	1965
PARADISE [B] STRANGLERS	48	1983
PARADISE [C] BLACK	38	1988
PARADISE [D] SADE	29	1988
PARADISE [E] BIRDLAND	70	1989
PARADISE [F] DIANA ROSS	61	1989
PARADISE [G] RALPH FRIDGE	68	1999
PARADISE [H] KACI	11	2001
PARADISE [I] LL COOL J FEATURING AMERIE	18	2003
PARADISE BIRD AMII STEWART	39	1980
PARADISE CITY GUNS N' ROSES	6	1989
PARADISE CITY N-TRANCE	28	1998
PARADISE LOST HERD	15	1968
PARADISE SKIES MAX WEBSTER	43	1979
PARALLEL WORLDS ELLIOT MINOR	22	2007
PARALYSED ELVIS PRESLEY	8	1957
PARANOID [A] BLACK SABBATH	4	1970
PARANOID [A] DICKIES	45	1979
PARANOID [B] JONAS BROTHERS	56	2009
PARANOID ANDROID RADIOHEAD	3	1997
PARANOIMIA ART OF NOISE FEATURING MAX HEADROOM	12	1986
PARDON ME INCUBUS	61	2000
PARIS BY AIR TYGERS OF PAN TANG	63	1982
PARIS IS BURNING LADYHAWKE	47	2008
PARIS IS ONE DAY AWAY MOOD	42	1982
PARIS MATCH STYLE COUNCIL	3	1983
PARISIENNE GIRL INCOGNITO	73	1980
PARISIENNE WALKWAYS GARY MOORE	8	1979
PARKLIFE BLUR	10	1994
PART OF THE PROCESS MORCHEEBA	38	1998
PART OF THE UNION STRAWBS	2	1973
PART TIME LOVE [A] GLADYS KNIGHT & THE PIPS	30	1975
PART TIME LOVE [B] ELTON JOHN	15	1978
PARTAY FEELING B-CREW	45	1997
PART-TIME LOVER STEVIE WONDER	3	1985
PARTY [A] ELVIS PRESLEY	2	1957
THE PARTY [B] KRAZE	29	1988
THE PARTY AIN'T OVER YET STATUS QUO	11	2005
PARTY ALL NIGHT [A] KREUZ	75	1995
PARTY ALL NIGHT [B] MYTOWN	22	1999
PARTY CRASHERS RADIO 4	75	2004
PARTY DOLL BUDDY KNOX	29	1957
PARTY DOLL JETS	72	1984
PARTY FEARS TWO ASSOCIATES	9	1982
PARTY FOR TWO SHANIA TWAIN & MARK McGRATH	10	2004
PARTY FOUR (EP) MAD JOCKS FEATURING JOCKMASTER B.A.	57	1993
PARTY FREAK CA$HFLOW	15	1986
PARTY HARD [A] PULP	29	1998
PARTY HARD [B] ANDREW WK	19	2001
PARTY IN PARIS UK SUBS	37	1980
PARTY IN THE USA MILEY CYRUS	11	2009
PARTY LIGHTS GAP BAND	30	1980
PARTY PARTY ELVIS COSTELLO & THE ATTRACTIONS WITH THE ROYAL HORN GUARDS	48	1982
PARTY PEOPLE NELLY & FERGIE	14	2008
PARTY PEOPLE (LIVE YOUR LIFE BE FREE) PIANOMAN	43	1997
PARTY PEOPLE...FRIDAY NIGHT 911	5	1997
PARTY POPS RUSS CONWAY	24	1957
PARTY STARTER WILL SMITH	19	2005
PARTY TIME FATBACK BAND	41	1976
PARTY TIME (THE GO-GO EDIT) KURTIS BLOW	67	1985

Title / Artist	Peak Position	Year of Release
PARTY UP THE WORLD D:REAM	20	1995
PARTY ZONE DAFFY DUCK FEATURING THE GROOVE GANG	58	1991
PARTYLINE BRASS CONSTRUCTION	56	1984
PARTYMAN PRINCE	14	1989
THE PARTY'S JUST BEGUN CHEETAH GIRLS	53	2007
THE PARTY'S OVER LONNIE DONEGAN	9	1962
PASADENA TEMPERANCE SEVEN	4	1961
PASILDA AFRO MEDUSA	31	2000
PASS & MOVE (IT'S THE LIVERPOOL GROOVE) LIVERPOOL FC & THE BOOT ROOM BOYS	4	1996
PASS IT ON [A] BITTY McLEAN	35	1993
PASS IT ON [B] CORAL	5	2003
PASS OUT TINIE TEMPAH	1	2010
PASS THAT DUTCH MISSY ELLIOTT	10	2003
PASS THE COURVOISIER – PART II BUSTA RHYMES, P DIDDY & PHARRELL	16	2002
PASS THE DUTCHIE MUSICAL YOUTH	1	1982
PASS THE MIC BEASTIE BOYS	47	1992
PASS THE VIBES DEFINITION OF SOUND	23	1995
A PASSAGE TO BANGKOK RUSH	41	1981
PASSCHENDAELE GOODBOOKS	73	2007
THE PASSENGER SIOUXSIE & THE BANSHEES	41	1987
THE PASSENGER IGGY POP	22	1998
PASSENGERS ELTON JOHN	5	1984
PASSIN' ME BY PHARCYDE	55	1993
PASSING BREEZE RUSS CONWAY	16	1960
PASSING STRANGERS [A] BILLY ECKSTINE & SARAH VAUGHAN	20	1957
PASSING STRANGERS [A] JOE LONGTHORNE & LIZ DAWN	34	1994
PASSING STRANGERS [B] ULTRAVOX	57	1980
P.A.S.S.I.O.N. RHYTHM SYNDICATE	58	1991
PASSION [A] ROD STEWART	17	1980
PASSION [B] GAT DECOR	6	1992
PASSION [C] JON OF THE PLEASED WIMMIN	27	1995
PASSION [D] AMEN! UK	15	1997
PASSION IN DARK ROOMS MOOD	74	1982
PASSION KILLER ONE THE JUGGLER	71	1983
THE PASSION OF LOVERS BAUHAUS	56	1981
PASSION RULES THE GAME SCORPIONS	74	1989
PASSIONATE FRIEND TEARDROP EXPLODES	25	1981
PAST, PRESENT AND FUTURE CINDY & THE SAFFRONS	56	1983
PAST THE MISSION TORI AMOS	31	1994
PATCHES CLARENCE CARTER	2	1970
PATHS ROBERT MILES FEATURING NINA MIRANDA	74	2001
PATHS OF PARADISE JOHNNIE RAY	20	1955
PATHWAY TO THE MOON MN8	25	1996
PATIENCE [A] GUNS N' ROSES	10	1989
PATIENCE [B] NERINA PALLOT	61	2001
PATIENCE [C] TAKE THAT	1	2006
PATIENCE OF ANGELS EDDI READER	33	1994
PATIO SONG GORKY'S ZYGOTIC MYNCI	41	1996
PATRICIA PEREZ 'PREZ' PRADO & HIS ORCHESTRA	8	1958
PATT (PARTY ALL THE TIME) SHARAM	8	2006
THE PAY OFF (AMOI DE PAYER) KENNY BALL & HIS JAZZMEN	23	1962
PAY TO THE PIPER CHAIRMEN OF THE BOARD	34	1971
THE PAYBACK MIX JAMES BROWN	12	1988
PAYBACK TIME DYSFUNCTIONAL PSYCHEDELIC WALTONS	48	2003
PAYING THE PRICE OF LOVE BEE GEES	23	1993
PCP MANIC STREET PREACHERS	16	1994
PE 2000 PUFF DADDY FEATURING HURRICANE G	13	1999
PEACE [A] SABRINA JOHNSTON	8	1991
PEACE [B] DEPECHE MODE	57	2009
PEACE AND JOY SOUNDSTATION	62	1995
PEACE & QUIET RIFLES	48	2006
PEACE IN OUR TIME [A] IMPOSTER	48	1984
PEACE IN OUR TIME [B] BIG COUNTRY	39	1989
PEACE IN OUR TIME [C] CLIFF RICHARD	8	1993
PEACE IN THE WORLD DON-E	41	1992
PEACE ON EARTH HI TENSION	8	1978
PEACE ON EARTH/LITTLE DRUMMER BOY DAVID BOWIE & BING CROSBY	3	1982
PEACE + LOVEISM SON'Z OF A LOOP DA LOOP ERA	60	1992
PEACE THROUGHOUT THE WORLD MAXI PRIEST FEATURING JAZZIE B	41	1990
PEACEFUL GEORGIE FAME	16	1969
PEACH PRINCE	14	1993
PEACHES [A] STRANGLERS	8	1977
PEACHES [B] DARTS	66	1980
PEACHES [C] PRESIDENTS OF THE UNITED STATES OF AMERICA	8	1996
PEACHES [D] PINK GREASE	44	2005
PEACHES AND CREAM 112	32	2001
PEACOCK SUIT PAUL WELLER	5	1996
PEAKIN' BLEACHIN'	32	2000
PEARL CHAPTERHOUSE	67	1991
PEARL IN THE SHELL HOWARD JONES	7	1984
PEARL RIVER THREE 'N' ONE PRESENTS JOHNNY SHAKER FEATURING SERIAL DIVA	32	1999
PEARL'S A SINGER ELKIE BROOKS	8	1977
PEARL'S GIRL UNDERWORLD	22	1996
PEARLY-DEWDROPS' DROPS COCTEAU TWINS	29	1984
PEEK-A-BOO [A] NEW VAUDEVILLE BAND FEATURING TRISTRAM	7	1967
PEEK-A-BOO [B] STYLISTICS	35	1973
PEEK-A-BOO [C] SIOUXSIE & THE BANSHEES	16	1988
THE PEEL SESSIONS (1ST JUNE 1982) NEW ORDER	54	1986
PEGGY SUE BUDDY HOLLY	6	1957
PEGGY SUE GOT MARRIED BUDDY HOLLY	13	1959
PENCIL FULL OF LEAD PAOLO NUTINI	17	2009
PENNIES FROM HEAVEN INNER CITY	24	1992
PENNY AND ME HANSON	10	2005
PENNY ARCADE ROY ORBISON	27	1969
PENNY LANE BEATLES	2	1967
PENNY LOVER LIONEL RICHIE	18	1984
PENTHOUSE AND PAVEMENT HEAVEN 17	54	1981
PEOPLE [A] TYMES	16	1969
PEOPLE [B] INTASTELLA	74	1991
PEOPLE [C] ALFIE	53	2003
PEOPLE ARE PEOPLE DEPECHE MODE	4	1984
PEOPLE ARE STILL HAVING SEX LaTOUR	15	1991
PEOPLE ARE STRANGE ECHO & THE BUNNYMEN	29	1988
PEOPLE EVERYDAY ARRESTED DEVELOPMENT	2	1992
PEOPLE GET READY JEFF BECK & ROD STEWART	49	1992
PEOPLE GET READY ROD STEWART	45	1993
PEOPLE GET REAL SAINT ETIENNE	21	1992
PEOPLE HELP THE PEOPLE CHERRY GHOST	27	2007
PEOPLE HOLD ON COLDCUT FEATURING LISA STANSFIELD	11	1989
PEOPLE HOLD ON LISA STANSFIELD VS THE DIRTY ROTTEN SCOUNDRELS	4	1997
PEOPLE IN THA MIDDLE SPEARHEAD	49	1995
PEOPLE LIKE YOU PEOPLE LIKE ME GLITTER BAND	5	1976
PEOPLE OF LOVE AMEN! UK	36	1997
PEOPLE OF THE SUN RAGE AGAINST THE MACHINE	26	1996
PEPE DUANE EDDY & THE REBELS	2	1961
PEPE RUSS CONWAY	19	1961
PEPPER BUTTHOLE SURFERS	59	1996
PEPPER BOX PEPPERS	6	1974
PEPPERMINT TWIST DANNY PEPPERMINT & THE JUMPING JACKS	26	1962
PEPPERMINT TWIST JOEY DEE & THE STARLITERS	33	1962
PER SEMPRE AMORE (FOREVER IN LOVE) LOLLY	11	2000
PERFECT [A] FAIRGROUND ATTRACTION	1	1988
PERFECT [B] LIGHTNING SEEDS	18	1995
PERFECT [C] PJ & DUNCAN	16	1995
PERFECT [D] SMASHING PUMPKINS	24	1998
PERFECT BLISS BELLEFIRE	18	2001
PERFECT DAY [A] EMF	27	1995
PERFECT DAY [B] DURAN DURAN	28	1995
PERFECT DAY [B] KIRSTY MacCOLL & EVAN DANDO	75	1995
PERFECT DAY [B] VARIOUS ARTISTS (EP'S & LP'S)	1	1997
PERFECT DAY [C] SKIN	33	1996
A PERFECT DAY ELISE PJ HARVEY	25	1998
THE PERFECT DRUG NINE INCH NAILS	43	1997
PERFECT GENTLEMAN WYCLEF JEAN	4	2001
THE PERFECT KISS NEW ORDER	46	1985
PERFECT LOVE SIMPLY RED	30	2005
PERFECT LOVESONG DIVINE COMEDY	42	2001
PERFECT MOMENT MARTINE McCUTCHEON	1	1999
PERFECT MOTION SUNSCREEM	18	1992
PERFECT PLACE VOICE OF THE BEEHIVE	37	1992
PERFECT SKIN LLOYD COLE & THE COMMOTIONS	26	1984
PERFECT STRANGERS DEEP PURPLE	48	1985
PERFECT 10 BEAUTIFUL SOUTH	2	1998
PERFECT TIMING KIKI DEE	66	1981
PERFECT WAY SCRITTI POLITTI	48	1985
PERFECT WORLD HUEY LEWIS & THE NEWS	48	1988
THE PERFECT YEAR DINA CARROLL	5	1993
PERFECTION DANNII MINOGUE & SOUL SEEKERZ	11	2005
PERFIDIA VENTURES	4	1960
PERFUME PARIS ANGELS	55	1991
PERFUMED GARDEN RAH BAND	45	1982
PERHAPS LOVE PLACIDO DOMINGO WITH JOHN DENVER	46	1981
PERMANENT YEARS EAGLE-EYE CHERRY	43	1999
PERPETUAL DAWN ORB	18	1991
PERRY MASON OZZY OSBOURNE	23	1995
PERSEVERANCE TERRORVISION	5	1996
PERSONAL FEELING AUDIOWEB	65	1998
PERSONAL JESUS DEPECHE MODE	13	1989
PERSONAL JESUS JOHNNY CASH	42	2003
PERSONAL JESUS MARILYN MANSON	13	2004
PERSONAL TOUCH ERROL BROWN	25	1987
PERSONALITY [A] ANTHONY NEWLEY	6	1959
PERSONALITY [A] LLOYD PRICE	9	1959
PERSONALITY [A] LENA ZAVARONI	33	1974
PERSONALITY [B] EUGENE WILDE	34	1985
PER-SO-NAL-LY WIGAN'S OVATION	38	1975
PERSUASION TIM FINN	43	1993
A PESSIMIST IS NEVER DISAPPOINTED THEAUDIENCE	27	1998
PETAL WUBBLE-U	55	1998
PETER AND THE WOLF CLYDE VALLEY STOMPERS	25	1962
PETER GUNN ART OF NOISE FEATURING DUANE EDDY	8	1986
PETER GUNN THEME DUANE EDDY & THE REBELS	6	1959
PETER PIPER RUN DMC	62	1986
PETITE FLEUR CHRIS BARBER'S JAZZ BAND	3	1959
PETS PORNO FOR PYROS	53	1993
PHANTOM LIMB SHINS	42	2007
THE PHANTOM OF THE OPERA SARAH BRIGHTMAN & STEVE HARLEY	7	1986
PHASED (EP) ALL ABOUT EVE	38	1992
PHAT BEACH (I'LL BE READY) NAUGHTY BOY	36	2006
PHAT GIRLS IGNORANTS	59	1993

Title / Artist	Peak Position	Year of Release
PHATT BASS WARP BROTHERS VERSUS AQUAGEN	9	2000
PHENOMENON LL COOL J	9	1997
PHEW WOW FARMERS BOYS	59	1984
PHILADELPHIA NEIL YOUNG	62	1994
PHILADELPHIA FREEDOM ELTON JOHN BAND	12	1975
PHOBIA FLOWERED UP	75	1990
PHONE HOME JONNY CHINGAS	43	1983
PHOREVER PEOPLE SHAMEN	5	1992
PHOTOGRAPH [A] RINGO STARR	8	1973
PHOTOGRAPH [B] DEF LEPPARD	66	1983
PHOTOGRAPH [C] NICKELBACK	18	2005
PHOTOGRAPH OF MARY TREY LORENZ	38	1993
THE PHOTOS ON MY WALL GOOD SHOES	48	2007
PHUTURE 2000 CARL COX	40	1999
PHYSICAL OLIVIA NEWTON-JOHN	7	1981
PIANISSIMO KEN DODD	21	1962
PIANO IN THE DARK BRENDA RUSSELL	23	1988
PIANO LOCO DJ LUCK & MC NEAT	12	2001
PIANO MEDLEY NO. 114 CHARLIE KUNZ	16	1954
PIANO PARTY WINIFRED ATWELL	10	1959
PICCADILLY PALARE MORRISSEY	18	1990
PICK A BALE OF COTTON LONNIE DONEGAN	11	1962
PICK A PART THAT'S NEW STEREOPHONICS	4	1999
PICK ME UP I'LL DANCE MELBA MOORE	48	1979
PICK UP THE PIECES [A] HUDSON-FORD	8	1973
PICK UP THE PIECES [B] AVERAGE WHITE BAND	6	1975
PICKIN' A CHICKEN EVE BOSWELL	9	1955
PICKNEY GAL DESMOND DEKKER & THE ACES	42	1970
PICNIC IN THE SUMMERTIME DEEE-LITE	43	1994
A PICTURE OF YOU [A] JOE BROWN & THE BRUVVERS	2	1962
PICTURE OF YOU [B] BOYZONE	2	1997
PICTURE THIS BLONDIE	12	1978
PICTURES IN THE DARK MIKE OLDFIELD FEATURING ALED JONES, ANITA HEGERLAND & BARRY PALMER	50	1985
PICTURES OF LILY WHO	4	1967
PICTURES OF MATCHSTICK MEN STATUS QUO	7	1968
PICTURES OF YOU CURE	24	1990
PIE JESU SARAH BRIGHTMAN & PAUL MILES-KINGSTON	3	1985
PIECE BY PIECE KENNY THOMAS	36	1993
PIECE OF ME BRITNEY SPEARS	2	2007
PIECE OF MY HEART SAMMY HAGAR	67	1982
PIECE OF MY HEART SHAGGY FEATURING MARSHA	7	1997
PIECE OF MY HEART BEVERLEY KNIGHT	16	2006
PIECE OF THE ACTION [A] BUCKS FIZZ	12	1981
PIECE OF THE ACTION [B] MEAT LOAF	47	1985
PIECES [A] MY VITRIOL	56	2000
PIECES [B] CHASE & STATUS	70	2008
THE PIECES DON'T FIT ANYMORE JAMES MORRISON	30	2006
PIECES OF A DREAM [A] INCOGNITO	35	1994
PIECES OF A DREAM [B] ANASTACIA	48	2005
PIECES OF ICE DIANA ROSS	46	1983
PIECES OF ME ASHLEE SIMPSON	4	2004
PIED PIPER CRISPIAN ST. PETERS	5	1966
PIED PIPER BOB & MARCIA	11	1971
PIED PIPER (THE BEEJE) STEVE RACE	29	1963
PIES WILEY	45	2004
PIHA IAN POOLEY & MAGIK J	53	2002
PILGRIMAGE SOURMASH	73	2000
PILLOW TALK SYLVIA	14	1973
PILLS AND SOAP IMPOSTER	16	1983
PILOT OF THE AIRWAVES CHARLIE DORE	66	1979
PILOTS GOLDFRAPP	68	2001
PILTDOWN RIDES AGAIN PILTDOWN MEN	14	1961
PIMP 50 CENT	5	2003
PIN YEAH YEAH YEAH	26	2003
PINBALL BRIAN PROTHEROE	22	1974
PINBALL WIZARD WHO	4	1969
PINBALL WIZARD ELTON JOHN	7	1976
PINBALL WIZARD – SEE ME FEEL ME (MEDLEY) NEW SEEKERS	16	1973
PINCUSHION ZZ TOP	15	1994
PINEAPPLE HEAD CROWDED HOUSE	27	1994
PING PONG STEREOLAB	45	1994
PINK AEROSMITH	13	1997
PINK CADILLAC NATALIE COLE	5	1988
PINK CHAMPAGNE [A] SHAKIN' STEVENS	59	1990
PINK CHAMPAGNE [B] RHYTHM ETERNITY	72	1992
PINK FLOWER DAISY CHAINSAW	65	1992
THE PINK GREASE PINK GREASE	75	2004
THE PINK PARKER EP GRAHAM PARKER & THE RUMOUR	24	1977
PINK SQUARES IWASACUBSCOUT	71	2008
PINK SUNSHINE FUZZBOX	14	1989
PINKY BLUE ALTERED IMAGES	35	1982
THE PIONEERS BLOC PARTY	18	2005
PIPELINE CHANTAYS	16	1963
PIPELINE BRUCE JOHNSTON	33	1977
PIPES OF PEACE PAUL McCARTNEY	1	1983
PIRANHA TRIPPING DAISY	72	1996
PISSING IN THE WIND BADLY DRAWN BOY	22	2001
PISTOL PACKIN' MAMA GENE VINCENT	15	1960
PISTOL WHIP JOSHUA RYAN	29	2001
PITCHIN' (IN EVERY DIRECTION) HI-GATE	6	2000
PJANOO ERIC PRYDZ	2	2008
A PLACE CALLED HOME PJ HARVEY	43	2001
A PLACE IN THE SUN [A] SHADOWS	24	1966
A PLACE IN THE SUN [B] STEVIE WONDER	20	1967
PLACE IN YOUR HEART NAZARETH	70	1978
PLACE YOUR HANDS REEF	6	1996
PLACES TILT	64	1997
PLACES THAT BELONG TO YOU BARBRA STREISAND	17	1992
PLAN A DANDY WARHOLS	66	2003
PLAN B DEXY'S MIDNIGHT RUNNERS	58	1981
PLAN 9 808 STATE	50	1993
PLAN OF MY OWN DEEYAH	37	2005
PLANET CARAVAN PANTERA	26	1994
PLANET CLAIRE B-52's	12	1986
THE PLANET DANCE (MOVE YA BODY) LIQUID OXYGEN	56	1990
PLANET E K.C. FLIGHTT	48	1989
PLANET EARTH DURAN DURAN	12	1981
PLANET GIRL ZODIAC MINDWARP & THE LOVE REACTION	63	1988
PLANET LOVE DJ QUICKSILVER	12	1998
THE PLANET OF LOVE CARL COX	44	1993
PLANET OF SOUND PIXIES	27	1991
PLANET ROCK AFRIKA BAMBAATAA & THE SONIC SOUL FORCE	53	1982
PLANET ROCK PAUL OAKENFOLD PRESENTS AFRIKA BAMBAATAA	47	2001
PLANET ROCK/FUNKY PLANET POWERS THAT BE	63	2003
PLANET TELEX RADIOHEAD	17	1995
PLANET VIOLET NALIN I.N.C.	51	1998
PLANETARY SIT-IN (EVERY GIRL HAS YOUR NAME) JULIAN COPE	34	1996
THE PLASTIC AGE BUGGLES	16	1980
PLASTIC DREAMS JAYDEE	18	1997
PLASTIC MAN KINKS	31	1969
PLATINUM BLONDE PRELUDE	45	1980
PLATINUM POP THIS YEAR'S BLONDE	46	1981
PLAY JENNIFER LOPEZ	3	2001
PLAY DEAD BJORK & DAVID ARNOLD	12	1993
PLAY EP RIDE	32	1990
PLAY IT COOL SUPER FURRY ANIMALS	27	1997
PLAY ME LIKE YOU PLAY YOUR GUITAR DUANE EDDY & THE REBELETTES	9	1975
PLAY MY MUSIC JONAS BROTHERS	57	2008
PLAY THAT FUNKY MUSIC WILD CHERRY	7	1976
PLAY THAT FUNKY MUSIC THUNDER	39	1991
PLAY THAT FUNKY MUSIC VANILLA ICE	10	1998
PLAY THE GAME QUEEN	14	1980
PLAY THE HITS HAL	38	2005
PLAY TO WIN HEAVEN 17	46	1981
PLAYA HATA LUNIZ	20	1996
PLAYA NO MO' LINA	46	2001
PLAYAS GON' PLAY 3LW	21	2001
PLAYA'S ONLY R KELLY FEATURING GAME	33	2005
PLAYAZ CLUB RAPPIN' 4-TAY	63	1995
PLAYED A LIVE (THE BONGO SONG) SAFRI DUO	6	2001
PLAYGROUND [A] ANITA HARRIS	46	1967
PLAYGROUND [B] FUN DMENTAL 03	44	2006
PLAYGROUND LOVE AIR	25	2000
PLAYGROUND SUPERSTAR HAPPY MONDAYS	51	2005
PLAYGROUND TWIST SIOUXSIE & THE BANSHEES	28	1979
PLAYING WITH FIRE N-DUBZ FEATURING MR HUDSON	14	2009
PLAYING WITH KNIVES BIZARRE INC	4	1991
PLAYING WITH THE BOY TECHNICIAN 2	70	1992
PLAYTHING LINX	48	1982
PLAYTIME RONI SIZE	53	2002
PLEASANT VALLEY SUNDAY MONKEES	11	1967
PLEASE [A] ELTON JOHN	33	1996
PLEASE [B] U2	7	1997
PLEASE [C] ROBIN GIBB	23	2003
PLEASE BE CRUEL INSPIRAL CARPETS	50	1991
PLEASE COME HOME FOR CHRISTMAS EAGLES	30	1978
PLEASE COME HOME FOR CHRISTMAS BON JOVI	7	1994
PLEASE DON'T ASK ABOUT BARBARA BOBBY VEE	29	1962
PLEASE DON'T BE SCARED BARRY MANILOW	35	1989
PLEASE DON'T FALL IN LOVE CLIFF RICHARD	7	1983
PLEASE DON'T GO [A] DONALD PEERS	3	1968
PLEASE DON'T GO [B] KC & THE SUNSHINE BAND	3	1979
PLEASE DON'T GO [B] KWS	1	1992
PLEASE DON'T GO [B] DOUBLE YOU?	41	1992
PLEASE DON'T GO [C] NO MERCY	4	1997
PLEASE DON'T LEAVE ME P!NK	12	2009
PLEASE DON'T MAKE ME CRY UB40	10	1983
PLEASE DON'T STOP THE RAIN JAMES MORRISON	33	2009
PLEASE DON'T TEASE CLIFF RICHARD & THE SHADOWS	1	1960
PLEASE DON'T TOUCH JOHNNY KIDD	25	1959
PLEASE DON'T TURN ME ON ARTFUL DODGER FEATURING LIFFORD	4	2000
PLEASE FORGIVE ME [A] BRYAN ADAMS	2	1993
PLEASE FORGIVE ME [B] DAVID GRAY	18	1999
PLEASE HELP ME I'M FALLING HANK LOCKLIN	9	1960
PLEASE MR. POSTMAN CARPENTERS	2	1975
PLEASE MR POSTMAN BACKBEAT BAND	69	1994
PLEASE, PLEASE McFLY	1	2006
PLEASE PLEASE ME BEATLES	2	1963
PLEASE PLEASE ME DAVID CASSIDY	16	1974
PLEASE PLEASE PLEASE SHOUT OUT LOUDS	53	2006
PLEASE RELEASE ME MIKE FLOWERS POPS	39	1996
PLEASE SAVE ME SUNSCREEM VS PUSH	36	2001
PLEASE SIR MARTYN JOSEPH	45	1993
PLEASE STAND UP BRITISH SEA POWER	34	2005
PLEASE STAY [A] CRYIN' SHAMES	26	1966
PLEASE STAY [B] KYLIE MINOGUE	10	2000

Title / Artist	Peak Position	Year of Release
PLEASE TELL HIM I SAID HELLO DANA	8	1975
PLEASE (YOU GOT THAT...) INXS	50	1993
PLEASE YOURSELF BIG SUPREME	64	1987
PLEASURE BOYS VISAGE	44	1982
PLEASURE DOME SOUL II SOUL	51	1997
PLEASURE FROM THE BASS TIGA	57	2004
PLEASURE LOVE DE FUNK FEATURING F45	49	1999
PLEASURE PRINCIPLE JANET JACKSON	24	1987
PLENTY GOOD LOVIN' CONNIE FRANCIS	18	1959
PLOWED SPONGE	74	1995
PLUG IN BABY MUSE	11	2001
PLUG IT IN BASEMENT JAXX FEATURING JC CHASEZ	22	2004
PLUG ME IN (TO THE CENTRAL LOVE LINE) SCARLET FANTASTIC	67	1988
PLUG MYSELF IN D.O.S.E. FEATURING MARK E SMITH	50	1996
PLUS ECHELON	57	2004
PLUSH STONE TEMPLE PILOTS	23	1993
THE POACHER RONNIE LANE & SLIM CHANCE	36	1974
POCKET CALCULATOR KRAFTWERK	39	1981
POD TENACIOUS D	51	2006
POEMS NEARLY GOD	28	1996
POETRY IN MOTION JOHNNY TILLOTSON	1	1960
POGUETRY IN MOTION EP POGUES	29	1986
POING ROTTERDAM TERMINATION SOURCE	27	1992
POINT OF NO RETURN [A] NU SHOOZ	48	1986
POINT OF NO RETURN [B] CENTORY	67	1994
POINT OF VIEW [A] MATUMBI	35	1979
POINT OF VIEW [B] DB BOULEVARD	3	2002
POISON [A] ALICE COOPER	2	1989
POISON [B] BELL BIV DEVOE	19	1990
POISON [C] PRODIGY	15	1995
POISON [D] BARDOT	45	2001
POISON [E] GROOVE COVERAGE	32	2005
POISON ARROW ABC	6	1982
POISON HEART RAMONES	69	1992
POISON IVY COASTERS	15	1959
POISON IVY PARAMOUNTS	35	1964
POISON IVY LAMBRETTAS	7	1980
POISON STREET NEW MODEL ARMY	64	1987
POKER FACE LADY GAGA	1	2009
POLARIS ASH	32	2007
POLICE AND THIEVES JUNIOR MURVIN	23	1980
POLICE OFFICER SMILEY CULTURE	12	1984
POLICE ON MY BACK LETHAL BIZZLE	37	2007
POLICE STATE T-POWER	63	1996
POLICEMAN SKANK...(THE STORY OF MY LIFE) AUDIOWEB	21	1998
POLICY OF TRUTH DEPECHE MODE	16	1990
THE POLITICS OF DANCING RE-FLEX	28	1984
POLK SALAD ANNIE ELVIS PRESLEY	23	1973
POLYESTERDAY GUSGUS	55	1998
PON DE REPLAY RIHANNA	2	2005
PON DE RIVER, PON DE BANK ELEPHANT MAN	29	2003
PONY GINUWINE	16	1997
PONY TIME CHUBBY CHECKER	27	1961
POODLE ROCKIN' GORKY'S ZYGOTIC MYNCI	52	2000
POOL HALL RICHARD FACES	8	1973
POOR JENNY EVERLY BROTHERS	14	1959
POOR LENO ROYKSOPP	38	2001
POOR LITTLE FOOL RICKY NELSON	4	1958
POOR MAN'S SON ROCKIN' BERRIES	5	1965
POOR ME ADAM FAITH	1	1960
POOR MISGUIDED FOOL STARSAILOR	23	2002
POOR PEOPLE OF PARIS WINIFRED ATWELL	1	1956
POP *NSYNC	9	2001
POP COP GYRES	71	1996
POP GO THE WORKERS BARRON KNIGHTS WITH DUKE D'MOND	5	1965
POP GOES MY LOVE FREEEZ	26	1983
POP GOES THE WEASEL [A] ANTHONY NEWLEY	12	1961
POP GOES THE WEASEL [B] 3RD BASS	64	1991
POP IS DEAD RADIOHEAD	42	1993
POP LIFE PRINCE & THE REVOLUTION	60	1985
POP MUZIK M	2	1979
POP MUZIK ALL SYSTEMS GO	63	1988
THE POP SINGER'S FEAR OF THE POLLEN COUNT DIVINE COMEDY	17	1999
POP THAT BOOTY MARQUES HOUSTON FEATURING JERMAINE	23	2004
POP YA COLLAR USHER	2	2001
POPCORN HOT BUTTER	5	1972
POPCORN CRAZY FROG	12	2005
POPCORN LOVE NEW EDITION	43	1983
POPPA JOE SWEET	11	1972
POPPA PICCOLINO DIANA DECKER	2	1953
POPPED! FOOL BOONA	52	1999
POPPIHOLLA CHICANE	7	2009
POPS WE LOVE YOU DIANA ROSS, MARVIN GAYE, SMOKEY ROBINSON & STEVIE WONDER	66	1979
POPSCENE BLUR	32	1992
POP!ULAR DARREN HAYES	12	2004
PORCELAIN MOBY	5	2000
PORK AND BEANS WEEZER	33	2008
PORNOGRAPHY CLIENT	22	2005
PORT AU PRINCE WINIFRED ATWELL & FRANK CHACKSFIELD	18	1956
PORTRAIT OF MY LOVE MATT MONRO	3	1960
PORTSMOUTH MIKE OLDFIELD	3	1976
PORTUGUESE WASHERWOMAN JOE 'FINGERS' CARR	20	1956
POSITIVE BLEEDING URGE OVERKILL	67	1993
POSITIVE EDUCATION SLAM	44	2001
POSITIVE TENSION BLOC PARTY	5	2005
POSITIVELY FOURTH STREET BOB DYLAN	8	1965
POSITIVITY [A] SUEDE	16	2002
POSITIVITY [B] STEVIE WONDER FEATURING AISHA MORRIS	54	2005
POSSE (I NEED YOU ON THE FLOOR) SCOOTER	15	2002
POSSESSED VEGAS	32	1992
POSSESSION TRANSFER	54	2001
POSSIBLY MAYBE BJORK	13	1996
POST MODERN SLEAZE SNEAKER PIMPS	22	1997
POSTCARD FROM HEAVEN LIGHTHOUSE FAMILY	24	1999
POSTMAN PAT KEN BARRIE	44	1982
POTENTIAL BREAK UP SONG ALY & AJ	22	2007
POUNDCAKE VAN HALEN	74	1991
POUNDING DOVES	21	2002
POUR LE MONDE CROWDED HOUSE	51	2007
POUR SOME SUGAR ON ME DEF LEPPARD	18	1987
POW (FORWARD) LETHAL BIZZLE	11	2005
POW WOW WOW FONTANA FEATURING DARRYL D'BONNEAU	62	2001
POWDER BLUE ELBOW	41	2001
THE POWER [A] SNAP!	1	1990
POWER [B] NU COLOURS	40	1992
THE POWER [C] MONIE LOVE	33	1993
POWER AND THE GLORY SAXON	32	1983
THE POWER IS YOURS REDSKINS	59	1986
THE POWER '96 SNAP! FEATURING EINSTEIN	42	1996
POWER OF A WOMAN ETERNAL	5	1995
THE POWER (OF ALL THE LOVE IN THE WORLD) D:REAM	40	1995
P.OWER OF A.MERICAN N.ATIVES DANCE 2 TRANCE	25	1993
THE POWER (OF BHANGRA) SNAP! VS MOTIVO	34	2003
THE POWER OF GOODBYE MADONNA	6	1998
THE POWER OF LOVE [A] FRANKIE GOES TO HOLLYWOOD	1	1984
THE POWER OF LOVE [B] JENNIFER RUSH	1	1985
THE POWER OF LOVE [B] CELINE DION	4	1994
THE POWER OF LOVE [B] FITS OF GLOOM FEATURING LIZZY MACK	49	1994
THE POWER OF LOVE [C] HUEY LEWIS & THE NEWS	9	1985
POWER OF LOVE [D] DEEE-LITE	25	1990
THE POWER OF LOVE [E] Q-TEX	49	1994
THE POWER OF LOVE [F] HOLLY JOHNSON	56	1999
POWER OF LOVE-LOVE POWER LUTHER VANDROSS	31	1991
POWER OUT ARCADE FIRE	26	2005
POWER RANGERS MIGHTY MORPH'N POWER RANGERS	3	1994
POWER TO ALL OUR FRIENDS CLIFF RICHARD	4	1973
POWER TO THE PEOPLE JOHN LENNON & THE PLASTIC ONO BAND	7	1971
THE POWER ZONE TIME FREQUENCY	17	1993
POWERLESS (SAY WHAT YOU WANT) NELLY FURTADO	13	2003
POWERSIGN (ONLY YOUR LOVE) PKA	70	1992
POWERTRIP MONSTER MAGNET	39	1999
PRACTICE WHAT YOU PREACH BARRY WHITE	20	1995
PRAISE INNER CITY	59	1992
PRAISE YOU FATBOY SLIM	1	1999
PRANCE ON EDDIE HENDERSON	44	1978
PRANGIN' OUT STREETS FEATURING PETE DOHERTY	25	2006
PRAY [A] MC HAMMER	8	1990
PRAY [B] TAKE THAT	1	1993
PRAY [C] TINA COUSINS	20	1998
PRAY [D] LASGO	17	2002
PRAY [E] SYNTAX	28	2003
PRAY FOR LOVE LOVE TO INFINITY	69	1996
PRAYER DISTURBED	31	2002
THE PRAYER BLOC PARTY	4	2007
PRAYER FOR THE DYING SEAL	14	1994
PRAYER FOR YOU TEXAS	73	1989
A PRAYER TO THE MUSIC MARCO POLO	65	1995
PRAYER TOWER PARADISE ORGANISATION	70	1993
PRAYING FOR TIME GEORGE MICHAEL	6	1990
PREACHER MAN BANANARAMA	20	1991
PREACHER PREACHER ANIMAL NIGHTLIFE	67	1985
PRECIOUS [A] JAM	1	1982
PRECIOUS [B] ANNIE LENNOX	23	1992
PRECIOUS [C] DEPECHE MODE	4	2005
PRECIOUS HEART TALL PAUL VS INXS	14	2001
PRECIOUS ILLUSIONS ALANIS MORISSETTE	53	2002
PRECIOUS LIFE CRW PRESENTS VERONIKA	57	2002
PRECIOUS TIME VAN MORRISON	36	1999
PRECIOUS TIME MACCABEES	49	2007
PREDICTABLE GOOD CHARLOTTE	12	2004
PREGNANT FOR THE LAST TIME MORRISSEY	25	1991
PREPARE TO LAND SUPERNATURALS	48	1997
PRESENCE OF LOVE (LAUGHERNE) ALARM	44	1988
PRESS PAUL McCARTNEY	25	1986
PRESSURE [A] SUNSCREEM	60	1992
PRESSURE [B] BILLY OCEAN	55	1993
PRESSURE [C] DRIZABONE	33	1994
PRESSURE COOKER G CLUB PRESENTS BANDA SONORA	46	2002
PRESSURE DROP IZZY STADLIN'	45	1992
PRESSURE ON ROGER TAYLOR	45	1998
THE PRESSURE PART 1 SOUNDS OF BLACKNESS	46	1991
PRESSURE POINT ZUTONS	19	2004
PRESSURE US SUNSCREEM	19	1993
PRETEND NAT 'KING' COLE	2	1953
PRETEND ALVIN STARDUST	4	1981
PRETEND BEST FRIEND TERRORVISION	25	1994

	Peak Position	Year of Release
PRETEND WE'RE DEAD L7	21	1992
THE PRETENDER FOO FIGHTERS	8	2007
PRETENDER GOT MY HEART ALISHA'S ATTIC	43	2001
PRETENDERS TO THE THRONE BEAUTIFUL SOUTH	18	1995
PRETTIEST EYES BEAUTIFUL SOUTH	37	1994
PRETTY AMAZING GRACE NEIL DIAMOND	49	2008
PRETTY BLUE EYES CRAIG DOUGLAS	4	1960
PRETTY BROWN EYES JIM REEVES	33	1968
PRETTY DEEP TANYA DONELLY	55	1997
PRETTY FLAMINGO MANFRED MANN	1	1966
PRETTY FLY (FOR A WHITE GUY) OFFSPRING	1	1999
PRETTY GOOD YEAR TORI AMOS	7	1994
PRETTY GREEN EYES ULTRABEAT	2	2003
PRETTY IN PINK PSYCHEDELIC FURS	18	1981
PRETTY JENNY JESS CONRAD	50	1962
PRETTY LADY SAVANA	48	2004
PRETTY LITTLE ANGEL EYES CURTIS LEE	47	1961
PRETTY LITTLE ANGEL EYES SHOWADDYWADDY	5	1978
PRETTY LITTLE BLACK EYED SUSIE GUY MITCHELL	2	1953
PRETTY NOOSE SOUNDGARDEN	14	1996
PRETTY PAPER ROY ORBISON	6	1964
PRETTY THING BO DIDDLEY	34	1963
PRETTY VACANT SEX PISTOLS	6	1977
PRETTY WOMAN JUICY LUCY	44	1970
THE PRICE OF LOVE EVERLY BROTHERS	2	1965
THE PRICE OF LOVE (REMIX) BRYAN FERRY	49	1989
PRICE TO PAY STAIND	36	2003
PRICE YOU PAY QUESTIONS	56	1983
PRIDE (IN THE NAME OF LOVE) U2	3	1984
PRIDE (IN THE NAME OF LOVE) CLIVILLES & COLE	15	1992
PRIDE'S PARANOIA FUTURESHOCK	60	2003
PRIMAL SCREAM MOTLEY CRUE	32	1991
PRIMARY CURE	43	1981
PRIMARY INSTINCT SENSELESS THINGS	41	1993
PRIMARY RHYMING MC TUNES	67	1990
PRIME MOVER ZODIAC MINDWARP & THE LOVE REACTION	18	1987
PRIME MOVER RUSH	43	1988
PRIME TIME [A] TUBES	34	1979
PRIME TIME [B] HAIRCUT 100	46	1983
PRIME TIME [C] MTUME	57	1984
PRIMITIVE (THE WAY I TREAT YOU) AMBULANCE LTD	72	2005
PRIMROSE LANE DICKIE PRIDE	28	1959
THE PRINCE MADNESS	16	1979
A PRINCE AMONG ISLANDS EP CAPERCAILLIE	39	1992
PRINCE CHARMING ADAM & THE ANTS	1	1981
PRINCE HARRY SOHO DOLLS	57	2004
PRINCE IGOR RHAPSODY FEATURING WARREN G & SISSEL	15	1998
PRINCE OF DARKNESS BOW WOW WOW	58	1981
PRINCE OF PEACE GALLIANO	47	1992
PRINCES OF THE NIGHT BLAST FEATURING VDC	40	1994
PRINCESS IN RAGS GENE PITNEY	9	1965
PRINCESS OF THE NIGHT SAXON	57	1981
PRINCIPAL'S OFFICE YOUNG MC	54	1990
PRINCIPLES OF LUST ENIGMA	59	1991
THE PRISONER FAB FEATURING MC NUMBER 6	56	1990
PRISONER ALL BLUE	73	1999
PRISONER OF LOVE [A] MILLIE SCOTT	52	1986
PRISONER OF LOVE [B] SPEAR OF DESTINY	59	1984
A PRISONER OF THE PAST PREFAB SPROUT	30	1997
PRIVATE DANCER TINA TURNER	26	1984
PRIVATE EMOTION RICKY MARTIN FEATURING MEJA	9	2000
PRIVATE EYE ALKALINE TRIO	51	2002
PRIVATE EYES DARYL HALL & JOHN OATES	32	1982
PRIVATE INVESTIGATIONS DIRE STRAITS	2	1982
PRIVATE LIFE GRACE JONES	17	1980
PRIVATE NUMBER JUDY CLAY & WILLIAM BELL	8	1968
PRIVATE NUMBER 911	3	1999
PRIVATE PARTY WALLY JUMP, JR & THE CRIMINAL ELEMENT ORCHESTRA	57	1988
PRIVILEGE (SET ME FREE) PATTI SMITH GROUP	72	1978
PRIX CHOC REMIXES ETIENNE DE CRECY	60	1998
PRIZE OF GOLD JOAN REGAN	6	1955
PROBABLY A ROBBERY RENEGADE SOUNDWAVE	38	1990
PROBLEM IS DUB PISTOLS FEATURING TERRY HALL	66	2003
PROBLEMS EVERLY BROTHERS	6	1959
PROCESS OF ELMINATION ERIC GABLE	63	1994
PROCESSED BEATS KASABIAN	17	2004
PROCESSION NEW ORDER	38	1981
PRODIGAL BLUES BILLY IDOL	47	1990
PRODIGAL SON STEEL PULSE	35	1978
PRODUCT OF THE WORKING CLASS LITTLE ANGELS	40	1991
PROFESSIONAL WIDOW (IT'S GOT TO BE BIG) TORI AMOS	1	1996
PROFIT IN PEACE OCEAN COLOUR SCENE	13	1999
PROFOUNDLY IN LOVE WITH PANDORA IAN & THE BLOCKHEADS	45	1985
PROFOUNDLY YOURS HUE & CRY	74	1992
PRO-GEN SHAMEN	4	1990
THE PROGRAM DAVID MORALES	66	1993
PROMISCUOUS NELLY FURTADO FEATURING TIMBALAND	3	2006
A PROMISE ECHO & THE BUNNYMEN	49	1981
PROMISE DELIRIOUS?	20	1997
THE PROMISE [A] ARCADIA	37	1986
THE PROMISE [B] WHEN IN ROME	58	1989
THE PROMISE [C] MICHAEL NYMAN	60	1994
THE PROMISE [D] ESSENCE	27	1998
THE PROMISE [E] GIRLS ALOUD	1	2008
PROMISE ME BEVERLEY CRAVEN	3	1991
THE PROMISE OF A NEW DAY PAULA ABDUL	52	1991
THE PROMISE YOU MADE COCK ROBIN	28	1986
PROMISED LAND [A] CHUCK BERRY	26	1965
PROMISED LAND [A] ELVIS PRESLEY	9	1975
PROMISED LAND [B] STYLE COUNCIL	27	1989
PROMISED LAND [B] JOE SMOOTH	56	1989
PROMISED YOU A MIRACLE SIMPLE MINDS	13	1982
PROMISES [A] KEN DODD	6	1966
PROMISES [B] ERIC CLAPTON	37	1978
PROMISES [C] BUZZCOCKS	20	1978
PROMISES [D] BASIA	48	1988
PROMISES [E] TAKE THAT	38	1991
PROMISES [F] PARIS RED	59	1993
PROMISES [G] DEF LEPPARD	41	1999
PROMISES [H] CRANBERRIES	13	1999
PROMISES PROMISES COOPER TEMPLE CLAUSE	19	2003
PROPANE NIGHTMARES PENDULUM	9	2008
PROPER CRIMBO BO SELECTA	4	2003
PROPER EDUCATION ERIC PRYDZ VS FLOYD	2	2007
PROPHASE TRANSA	65	1997
THE PROPHET CJ BOLLAND	19	1997
PROTECT YOUR MIND (FOR THE LOVE OF A PRINCESS) DJ SAKIN & FRIENDS	4	1999
PROTECTION MASSIVE ATTACK FEATURING TRACEY THORN	14	1995
PROUD HEATHER SMALL	16	2000
PROUD MARY CREEDENCE CLEARWATER REVIVAL	8	1969
PROUD MARY CHECKMATES LTD	30	1969
THE PROUD ONE OSMONDS	5	1975
PROUD TO FALL IAN McCULLOCH	51	1989
PROVE IT TELEVISION	25	1977
PROVE YOUR LOVE TAYLOR DAYNE	8	1988
PROVIDER N*E*R*D	20	2003
PSYCHE ROCK PIERRE HENRY	58	1997
PSYCHEDELIC SHACK TEMPTATIONS	33	1970
PSYCHO THEE UNSTRUNG	41	2005
PSYCHO BASE SHADES OF RHYTHM	57	1997
PSYCHONAUT FIELDS OF THE NEPHILIM	35	1989
PSYCHOSIS SAFARI EIGHTIES MATCHBOX B-LINE DISASTER	26	2002
PSYCHOSOCIAL SLIPKNOT	67	2008
PSYKO FUNK BOO-YAA T.R.I.B.E.	43	1990
A PUB WITH NO BEER SLIM DUSTY	3	1959
A PUBLIC AFFAIR JESSICA SIMPSON	20	2007
PUBLIC ENEMY NO 1 HYPO PSYCHO	53	2004
PUBLIC IMAGE PUBLIC IMAGE LTD	9	1978
PUCKWUDGIE CHARLIE DRAKE	47	1972
PUFF (UP IN SMOKE) KENNY LYNCH	33	1962
PULL SHAPES PIPETTES	26	2006
PULL THE WIRES FROM THE WALL DELGADOS	69	1998
PULL UP TO THE BUMPER GRACE JONES	12	1981
PULL UP TO THE BUMPER PATRA	50	1995
PULLIN' ME BACK CHINGY FEATURING TYRESE	44	2006
PULLING MUSSELS (FROM THE SHELL) SQUEEZE	44	1980
PULLING PUNCHES DAVID SYLVIAN	56	1984
PULSAR 2002 MAURO PICOTTO	35	2002
PULS(T)AR BEN LIEBRAND	68	1990
PULVERTURM NIELS VAN GOGH	75	1999
PUMP IT BLACK EYED PEAS	3	2006
PUMP IT UP [A] ELVIS COSTELLO & THE ATTRACTIONS	24	1978
PUMP IT UP [B] JOE BUDDEN	13	2003
PUMP IT UP [C] DANZEL	11	2004
PUMP ME UP GRANDMASTER MELLE MEL & THE FURIOUS FIVE	45	1985
PUMP UP LONDON MR LEE	64	1988
PUMP UP THE BITTER STARTURN ON 45 (PINTS)	12	1988
PUMP UP THE JAM TECHNOTRONIC FEATURING FELLY	2	1989
PUMP UP THE JAM DONS FEATURING TECHNOTRONIC	22	2005
PUMP UP THE VOLUME M/A/R/R/S	1	1987
PUMP UP THE VOLUME GREED FEATURING RICARDO DA FORCE	51	1995
PUMPIN' NOVY VERSUS ENIAC	19	2000
PUMPING ON YOUR STEREO SUPERGRASS	11	1999
PUMPKIN TRICKY	26	1995
PUMPKIN SOUP KATE NASH	23	2007
PUMPS AMY WINEHOUSE	69	2004
PUNCH AND JUDY MARILLION	29	1984
PUNK [A] FERRY CORSTEN	29	2002
A PUNK [B] VAMPIRE WEEKEND	55	2008
PUNK ROCK 101 BOWLING FOR SOUP	43	2003
PUNK ROCK PRINCESS SOMETHING CORPORATE	33	2003
PUNKA KENICKIE	38	1996
PUNKY REGGAE PARTY BOB MARLEY & THE WAILERS	9	1977
PUPPET MAN TOM JONES	49	1971
PUPPET ON A STRING SANDIE SHAW	1	1967
PUPPY LOVE PAUL ANKA	33	1960
PUPPY LOVE DONNY OSMOND	1	1972
PUPPY LOVE S CLUB JUNIORS	6	2002
THE PUPPY SONG DAVID CASSIDY	1	1973
PURE [A] LIGHTNING SEEDS	16	1989
PURE [B] GTO	57	1990
PURE [C] 3 COLOURS RED	28	1997
PURE AND SIMPLE HEAR'SAY	1	2001
PURE MASSACRE SILVERCHAIR	71	1995

Title / Artist	Peak Position	Year of Release
PURE MORNING PLACEBO	4	1998
PURE PLEASURE DIGITAL EXCITATION	37	1992
PURE PLEASURE SEEKER MOLOKO	21	2000
PURE SHORES ALL SAINTS	1	2000
PURELY BY COINCIDENCE SWEET SENSATION	11	1975
PURGATORY IRON MAIDEN	52	1981
PURITY NEW MODEL ARMY	61	1990
PURPLE HAZE [A] JIMI HENDRIX EXPERIENCE	3	1967
PURPLE HAZE [B] GROOVE ARMADA	36	2002
PURPLE HEATHER ROD STEWART WITH THE SCOTTISH EURO '96 SQUAD	16	1996
PURPLE LOVE BALLOON CUD	27	1992
PURPLE MEDLEY PRINCE	33	1995
PURPLE PEOPLE EATER SHEB WOOLEY	12	1958
PURPLE PEOPLE EATER JACKIE DENNIS	29	1958
PURPLE PILLS D12	2	2001
PURPLE RAIN PRINCE & THE REVOLUTION	8	1984
PUSH [A] MOIST	20	1994
PUSH [B] MATCHBOX 20	38	1998
THE PUSH (FAR FROM HERE) PAUL JACKSON & STEVE SMITH	51	2004
PUSH IT [A] SALT-N-PEPA	2	1988
PUSH IT [B] GARBAGE	9	1998
PUSH IT ALL ASIDE ALISHA'S ATTIC	24	2001
PUSH IT ALONG PAUL WELLER	28	2008
PUSH THE BEAT MIRAGE	67	1988
PUSH THE BEAT/BAUHAUS CAPPELLA	60	1988
PUSH THE BUTTON SUGABABES	1	2005
PUSH THE FEELING ON NIGHTCRAWLERS	3	1994
PUSH THE GHOST TWANG	63	2007
PUSH UP FREESTYLERS	22	2004
PUSH UPSTAIRS UNDERWORLD	12	1999
THE PUSHBIKE SONG MIXTURES	2	1971
PUSHER SHAPESHIFTERS	56	2007
PUSHIN' ME OUT D-SIDE	21	2004
PUSHING THE SENSES FEEDER	30	2005
PUSS JESUS LIZARD	12	1993
PUSS 'N' BOOTS ADAM ANT	5	1983
PUSSYCAT MULU	50	1997
PUSSYOLE (OLD SKOOL) DIZZEE RASCAL	22	2007
PUT A LIGHT IN THE WINDOW KING BROTHERS	25	1958
PUT A LITTLE LOVE IN YOUR HEART DAVE CLARK FIVE	31	1969
PUT A LITTLE LOVE IN YOUR HEART ANNIE LENNOX & AL GREEN	28	1988
PUT EM HIGH STONEBRIDGE	6	2004
PUT EM' IN THEIR PLACE MOBB DEEP	75	2006
PUT HIM OUT MS DYNAMITE	19	2002
PUT HIM OUT OF YOUR MIND DR FEELGOOD	73	1979
PUT IT THERE PAUL McCARTNEY	32	1990
PUT MY ARMS AROUND YOU KEVIN KITCHEN	64	1985
PUT OUR HEADS TOGETHER O'JAYS	45	1983
PUT THE LIGHT ON WET WET WET	56	1991
PUT THE MESSAGE IN THE BOX BRIAN KENNEDY	37	1997
PUT THE NEEDLE ON IT DANNII MINOGUE	7	2002
PUT THE NEEDLE TO THE RECORD CRIMINAL ELEMENT ORCHESTRA	63	1987
PUT THE SUN BACK CORAL	64	2008
PUT YOU IN YOUR PLACE SUNSHINE UNDERGROUND	39	2006
PUT YOU ON THE GAME GAME	46	2005
PUT YOUR ARMS AROUND ME [A] TEXAS	10	1997
PUT YOUR ARMS AROUND ME [B] NATURAL	32	2002
PUT YOUR FAITH IN ME ALISON LIMERICK	42	1997
PUT YOUR HANDS TOGETHER D MOB FEATURING NUFF JUICE	7	1990
PUT YOUR HANDS UP REFLEX FEATURING MC VIPER	72	2001
PUT YOUR HANDS UP FOR DETROIT FEDDE LE GRAND	1	2006
PUT YOUR HANDS WHERE MY EYES COULD SEE BUSTA RHYMES	16	1997
PUT YOUR HANDZ UP WHOOLIGANZ	53	1994
PUT YOUR HEAD ON MY SHOULDER PAUL ANKA	7	1959
PUT YOUR LOVE IN ME HOT CHOCOLATE	10	1977
PUT YOUR MONEY WHERE YOUR MOUTH IS ROSE ROYCE	44	1977
PUT YOUR MONEY WHERE YOUR MOUTH IS JET	23	2006
PUT YOUR RECORDS ON CORINNE BAILEY RAE	2	2006
PUT YOURSELF IN MY PLACE [A] ISLEY BROTHERS	13	1969
PUT YOURSELF IN MY PLACE [A] ELGINS	28	1971
PUT YOURSELF IN MY PLACE [B] KYLIE MINOGUE	11	1994
PUTTING ON THE STYLE LONNIE DONEGAN	1	1957
PYJAMARAMA ROXY MUSIC	10	1973
PYRAMID SONG RADIOHEAD	5	2001
P.Y.T. (PRETTY YOUNG THING) MICHAEL JACKSON	11	1984

Q

Title / Artist	Peak Position	Year of Release
QUADROPHONIA QUADROPHONIA	14	1991
QUANDO M'INNAMORO (A MAN WITHOUT LOVE) SANDPIPERS	33	1968
QUANDO QUANDO QUANDO PAT BOONE	41	1962
QUANDO QUANDO QUANDO ENGELBERT HUMPERDINCK	40	1999
THE QUARTER MOON V.I.P.'S	55	1980
QUARTER TO THREE U.S. BONDS	7	1961
QUE SERA CHRIS REA	73	1988
QUE SERA MI VIDA (IF YOU SHOULD GO) GIBSON BROTHERS	5	1979
QUE SERA SERA GENO WASHINGTON & THE RAM JAM BAND	43	1966
QUE SERA SERA HERMES HOUSE BAND	53	2002
QUE TAL AMERICA TWO MAN SOUND	46	1979
QUEEN FOR TONIGHT HELEN SHAPIRO	33	1963
QUEEN JANE KINGMAKER	29	1993
QUEEN OF CLUBS KC & THE SUNSHINE BAND	7	1974
QUEEN OF HEARTS [A] DAVE EDMUNDS	11	1979
QUEEN OF HEARTS [B] CHARLOTTE	54	1994
QUEEN OF MY HEART WESTLIFE	1	2001
QUEEN OF MY SOUL AVERAGE WHITE BAND	23	1976
QUEEN OF NEW ORLEANS JON BON JOVI	10	1997
THE QUEEN OF 1964 NEIL SEDAKA	35	1975
THE QUEEN OF OUTER SPACE WEDDING PRESENT	23	1992
QUEEN OF RAIN ROXETTE	28	1992
QUEEN OF THE HOP BOBBY DARIN	24	1959
QUEEN OF THE NEW YEAR DEACON BLUE	21	1990
QUEEN OF THE NIGHT WHITNEY HOUSTON	14	1993
QUEEN OF THE RAPPING SCENE (NOTHING EVER GOES THE WAY YOU PLAN) MODERN ROMANCE	37	1982
THE QUEEN'S BIRTHDAY SONG ST JOHN'S COLLEGE SCHOOL CHOIR & THE BAND OF THE GRENADIER GUARDS	40	1986
QUEEN'S FIRST EP QUEEN	17	1977
QUEER GARBAGE	13	1995
THE QUEST BRYN CHRISTOPHER	45	2008
QUESTION [A] MOODY BLUES	2	1970
THE QUESTION [B] SEVEN GRAND HOUSING AUTHORITY	70	1993
QUESTION [C] SYSTEM OF A DOWN	41	2005
THE QUESTION IS WHAT IS THE QUESTION SCOOTER	49	2008
QUESTION OF FAITH LIGHTHOUSE FAMILY	21	1998
A QUESTION OF LUST DEPECHE MODE	28	1986
A QUESTION OF TIME DEPECHE MODE	17	1986
QUESTIONS AND ANSWERS [A] SHAM 69	18	1979
QUESTIONS AND ANSWERS [B] BIFFY CLYRO	26	2003
QUESTIONS I CAN'T ANSWER HEINZ	39	1964
QUESTIONS (MUST BE ASKED) DAVID FORBES	57	2001
QUICK JOEY SMALL (RUN JOEY RUN) KASENETZ-KATZ SINGING ORCHESTRAL CIRCUS	19	1968
QUIEREME MUCHO (YOURS) JULIO IGLESIAS	3	1982
QUIET LIFE JAPAN	19	1981
THE QUIET THINGS THAT NO ONE EVER KNOWS BRAND NEW	39	2004
QUIT PLAYING GAMES (WITH MY HEART) BACKSTREET BOYS	2	1997
QUIT THIS TOWN EDDIE & THE HOT RODS	36	1978
QUITE A PARTY FIREBALLS	29	1961
QUITE RIGHTLY SO PROCOL HARUM	50	1968
QUOTE GOODBYE QUOTE CAROLYNE MAS	71	1980
QUOTH POLYGON WINDOW	49	1993

R

Title / Artist	Peak Position	Year of Release
R 'N' B GOLDIE LOOKIN CHAIN	26	2005
R TO THE A CJ LEWIS	34	1995
R U READY SALT-N-PEPA	24	1997
R U SLEEPING INDO	31	1998
RABBIT CHAS & DAVE	8	1980
RABBIT HEART (RAISE IT UP) FLORENCE + THE MACHINE	12	2009
THE RACE [A] YELLO	7	1988
RACE [B] TIGER	37	1996
RACE [C] LEAVES	66	2002
RACE FOR THE PRIZE FLAMING LIPS	39	1999
THE RACE IS ON [A] SUZI QUATRO	43	1978
THE RACE IS ON [B] DAVE EDMUNDS & THE STRAY CATS	34	1981
RACE WITH THE DEVIL [A] GENE VINCENT	28	1956
RACE WITH THE DEVIL [B] GUN	8	1968
RACE WITH THE DEVIL [B] GIRLSCHOOL	49	1980
RACHEL AL MARTINO	10	1953
RACHMANINOFF'S 18TH VARIATION ON A THEME BY PAGANINI (THE STORY OF THREE LOVES) WINIFRED ATWELL	9	1954
RACING GREEN HIGH CONTRAST	73	2004
THE RACING RATS EDITORS	26	2007
RACIST FRIENDS SPECIAL A.K.A.	60	1983
RADANCER MARMALADE	6	1972
RADAR BRITNEY SPEARS	46	2009
RADAR LOVE GOLDEN EARRING	7	1973
RADAR LOVE OH WELL	65	1990
RADIATION VIBE FOUNTAINS OF WAYNE	32	1997
RADICAL YOUR LOVER LITTLE ANGELS FEATURING THE BIG BAD HORNS	34	1990
RADICCIO EP ORBITAL	37	1992
RADIO [A] SHAKY FEATURING ROGER TAYLOR	37	1992
RADIO [B] TEENAGE FANCLUB	31	1993
RADIO [C] CORRS	18	1999
RADIO [D] CLIENT	68	2004
RADIO [E] ROBBIE WILLIAMS	1	2004
RADIO [F] LUDES	68	2004
RADIO AFRICA LATIN QUARTER	19	1986
RADIO DISCO WILT	56	2000
RADIO 4 UK THEME ROYAL BALLET SINFONIA & GAVIN SUTHERLAND	29	2006

Title / Artist	Peak Position	Year of Release
RADIO GA GA QUEEN	2	1984
RADIO GAGA ELECTRIC SIX	21	2005
RADIO HEAD TALKING HEADS	52	1987
RADIO HEART [A] RADIO HEART FEATURING GARY NUMAN	35	1987
RADIO HEART [B] FUTUREHEADS	65	2008
RADIO MUSICOLA NIK KERSHAW	43	1986
RADIO NO 1 AIR	31	2001
RADIO ON RICKY ROSS	35	1996
RADIO RADIO ELVIS COSTELLO & THE ATTRACTIONS	29	1978
RADIO ROMANCE TIFFANY	13	1988
RADIO SONG R.E.M.	28	1991
RADIO WALL OF SOUND SLADE	21	1991
RADIO WAVES ROGER WATERS	74	1987
RADIOACTIVE GENE SIMMONS	41	1979
RADIOACTIVITY KRAFTWERK	43	1991
RAG DOLL [A] FOUR SEASONS WITH THE SOUND OF FRANKIE VALLI	2	1964
RAG DOLL [B] AEROSMITH	42	1990
RAG MAMA RAG BAND	16	1970
RAGAMUFFIN MAN MANFRED MANN	8	1969
RAGE HARD FRANKIE GOES TO HOLLYWOOD	4	1986
RAGE TO LOVE KIM WILDE	19	1985
RAGGA HOUSE (ALL NIGHT LONG) SIMON HARRIS FEATURING DADDY FREDDY	56	1990
RAGGAMUFFIN GIRL APACHE INDIAN FEATURING FRANKIE PAUL	31	1995
RAGING COSMIC GATE	48	2003
RAGING EP BEYOND	68	1991
RAGS TO RICHES DAVID WHITFIELD	3	1953
RAGS TO RICHES ELVIS PRESLEY	9	1971
RAGTIME COWBOY JOE DAVID SEVILLE & THE CHIPMUNKS	11	1959
RAIN [A] BRUCE RUFFIN	19	1971
RAIN [B] STATUS QUO	7	1976
RAIN [C] CULT	17	1985
THE RAIN [D] ORAN 'JUICE' JONES	4	1986
RAIN [E] MADONNA	7	1993
RAIN [F] GROOVE CORPORATION	71	1994
RAIN [G] MIKA	72	2009
RAIN AND TEARS APHRODITE'S CHILD	29	1968
RAIN DOWN LOVE FREEMASONS FEATURING SIEDAH GARRETT	12	2007
RAIN DOWN ON ME KANE	38	2004
RAIN FALL DOWN ROLLING STONES	33	2005
RAIN FALLS FRANKIE KNUCKLES FEATURING LISA MICHAELIS	48	1992
RAIN FOREST [A] BIDDU ORCHESTRA	39	1976
RAIN FOREST [B] PAUL HARDCASTLE	41	1984
RAIN IN THE SUMMERTIME ALARM	18	1987
RAIN KING COUNTING CROWS	49	1994
RAIN ON ME ASHANTI	19	2003
RAIN ON YOUR PARADE DUFFY	15	2008
RAIN OR SHINE FIVE STAR	2	1986
RAIN RAIN RAIN FRANKIE LAINE & THE FOUR LADS	8	1954
RAIN SHOWERS SIZZLA	51	1999
THE RAIN (SUPA DUPA FLY) MISSY 'MISDEMEANOR' ELLIOTT	16	1997
RAINBOW [A] MARMALADE	3	1970
RAINBOW [B] PETERS & LEE	17	1974
RAINBOW CHASER NIRVANA	34	1968
RAINBOW CHILD DAN REED NETWORK	60	1990
RAINBOW COUNTRY BOB MARLEY VERSUS FUNKSTAR DELUXE	11	2000
RAINBOW IN THE DARK DIO	46	1983
RAINBOW LAKE WENDY & LISA	70	1990
RAINBOW PEOPLE MANIX	57	1992
RAINBOW (SAMPLE FREE) SOLO	59	1991
RAINBOW THEME SAXON	66	1980
RAINBOW VALLEY LOVE AFFAIR	5	1968
RAINBOWS (EP) TERRY HALL	62	1995

Title / Artist	Peak Position	Year of Release
RAINBOWS OF COLOUR GROOVERIDER	40	1998
RAINCLOUD LIGHTHOUSE FAMILY	6	1997
THE RAINDANCE DARE	62	1989
RAINDROPS [A] STUNT	51	2006
RAINDROPS [B] BASEMENT JAXX	21	2009
RAINDROPS (ENCORE UNE FOIS) SASH! FEATURING STUNT	9	2008
RAINDROPS KEEP FALLIN' ON MY HEAD BOBBIE GENTRY	40	1970
RAINDROPS KEEP FALLING ON MY HEAD SACHA DISTEL	10	1970
RAINDROPS KEEP FALLING ON MY HEAD BJ THOMAS	38	1970
RAININ' THROUGH MY SUNSHINE REAL THING	40	1978
RAINING ALL OVER THE WORLD ADVENTURES	68	1992
RAINING IN MY HEART LEO SAYER	21	1978
RAINMAKER [A] SPARKLEHORSE	61	1996
RAINMAKER [B] IRON MAIDEN	13	2003
RAINY DAY WOMEN NOS. 12 & 35 BOB DYLAN	7	1966
RAINY DAYS AND MONDAYS CARPENTERS	63	1993
RAINY DAYZ MARY J BLIGE FEATURING JA RULE	17	2002
RAINY NIGHT IN GEORGIA RANDY CRAWFORD	18	1981
A RAINY NIGHT IN SOHO POGUES	67	1991
RAISE HYPER GO GO	36	1994
RAISE YOUR HAND EDDIE FLOYD	42	1967
RAISE YOUR HANDS [A] REEL 2 REAL FEATURING THE MAD STUNTMAN	14	1994
RAISE YOUR HANDS [B] BIG ROOM GIRL FEATURING DARRYL PANDY	40	1999
RAISED ON ROCK ELVIS PRESLEY	36	1973
RAM GOAT LIVER PLUTO SHERVINGTON	43	1976
RAMA LAMA DING DONG ROCKY SHARPE & THE REPLAYS	17	1979
RAMBLIN' ROSE NAT 'KING' COLE	5	1962
RAM-BUNK-SHUSH VENTURES	45	1961
RAME SNAP! FEATURING RUKMANI	50	1996
RAMONA BACHELORS	4	1964
RANDOM LADY SOVEREIGN	73	2005
RANDY BLUE MINK	9	1973
RANKING FULL STOP BEAT	6	1979
RAOUL AUTOMATIC	30	2006
RAOUL AND THE KINGS OF SPAIN TEARS FOR FEARS	31	1995
RAP DIS OXIDE & NEUTRINO	12	2001
RAP SCHOLAR DAS EFX FEATURING REDMAN	42	1998
RAP SUMMARY BIG DADDY KANE	52	1989
RAP SUPERSTAR/ROCK SUPERSTAR CYPRESS HILL	13	2000
RAP YOUR LOVE SET THE TONE	67	1983
RAPE ME NIRVANA	32	1993
RAPID HOPE LOSS DASHBOARD CONFESSIONAL	75	2004
RAPP PAYBACK (WHERE IZ MOSES?) JAMES BROWN	39	1981
RAPPAZ R N DAINJA KRS ONE	47	1996
RAPPER'S DELIGHT SUGARHILL GANG	3	1979
RAPTURE [A] BLONDIE	5	1981
RAPTURE [B] IIO	2	2001
RARE, PRECIOUS AND GONE MIKE SCOTT	74	1998
THE RASCAL KING MIGHTY MIGHTY BOSSTONES	63	1998
RASPBERRY BERET PRINCE & THE REVOLUTION	25	1985
RASPUTIN BONEY M	2	1978
THE RAT WALKMEN	45	2004
RAT IN MI KITCHEN UB40	12	1987
RAT RACE SPECIALS	5	1980
RAT RAPPING ROLAND RAT SUPERSTAR	14	1983

Title / Artist	Peak Position	Year of Release
RAT TRAP BOOMTOWN RATS	1	1978
RATAMAHATTA SEPULTURA	23	1996
RATHER BE VERVE	56	2008
THE RATTLER GOODBYE MR MACKENZIE	37	1989
RATTLESNAKES LLOYD COLE & THE COMMOTIONS	65	1984
RAUNCHY BILL JUSTIS	11	1958
RAUNCHY KEN MACKINTOSH	19	1958
RAVE ALERT PRAGA KHAN	52	1992
THE RAVE DIGGER MC LETHAL	66	1992
RAVE GENERATOR TOXIC TWO	13	1992
RAVE ON BUDDY HOLLY	5	1958
RAVEL'S PAVANE POUR UNE INFANTE DEFUNTE WILLIAM ORBIT	31	2000
RAVING I'M RAVING SHUT UP & DANCE FEATURING PETER BOUNCER	2	1992
RAW [A] SPANDAU BALLET	47	1988
RAW [B] ALARM	51	1991
RAW [C] MELKY SEDECK	50	1999
RAW POWER APOLLO FOUR FORTY	32	1997
RAWHIDE FRANKIE LAINE	6	1959
RAY OF LIGHT MADONNA	2	1998
RAYS OF THE RISING SUN DENISE JOHNSON	45	1994
RAYS OF THE RISING SUN MOZAIC	32	1996
RAZOR'S EDGE MEAT LOAF	41	1984
RAZZAMATAZZ QUINCY JONES FEATURING PATTI AUSTIN	11	1981
RAZZLE DAZZLE [A] BILL HALEY & HIS COMETS	13	1956
RAZZLE DAZZLE [B] HEATWAVE	43	1979
RE:EVOLUTION SHAMEN WITH TERENCE McKENNA	18	1993
REACH [A] JUDY CHEEKS	17	1994
REACH [B] LIL MO' YIN YANG	28	1996
REACH [C] GLORIA ESTEFAN	15	1996
REACH [D] S CLUB 7	2	2000
REACH 4 THE MELODY VICTORIA WILSON JAMES	72	1997
REACH FOR THE STARS SHIRLEY BASSEY	1	1961
REACH OUT MIDFIELD GENERAL FEATURING LINDA LEWIS	61	2000
REACH OUT AND TOUCH DIANA ROSS	33	1970
REACH OUT FOR ME DIONNE WARWICK	23	1964
REACH OUT I'LL BE THERE FOUR TOPS	1	1966
REACH OUT I'LL BE THERE GLORIA GAYNOR	14	1975
REACH OUT I'LL BE THERE MICHAEL BOLTON	37	1993
REACH UP TONEY LEE	64	1983
(REACH UP FOR THE) SUNRISE DURAN DURAN	5	2004
REACH UP (PAPA'S GOT A BRAND NEW PIG BAG) PERFECTO ALLSTARZ	6	1995
REACHIN' [A] PHASE II	70	1989
REACHIN' [B] HOUSE OF VIRGINISM	35	1994
REACHING FOR THE BEST EXCITERS	31	1975
REACHING FOR THE WORLD HAROLD MELVIN & THE BLUENOTES	48	1977
REACHOUT DJ ZINC	73	2002
REACT ERICK SERMON FEATURING REDMAN	14	2002
REACTOR PARTY SHITDISCO	73	2006
READ 'EM AND WEEP BARRY MANILOW	17	1983
READ MY LIPS [A] DSK	46	1991
READ MY LIPS [B] ALEX PARTY	28	1996
READ MY LIPS (ENOUGH IS ENOUGH) JIMMY SOMERVILLE	26	1990
READ MY MIND CONNOR REEVES	19	1998
READ MY MIND KILLERS	15	2007
READY BRUCE WAYNE	44	1997
READY AN' WILLING (SWEET SATISFACTION) WHITESNAKE	43	1980
READY FOR A NEW DAY TODD TERRY FEATURING MARTHA WASH	20	1998
READY FOR LOVE [A] JIMMY JONES	46	1960
READY FOR LOVE [B] GARY MOORE	56	1989

Title	Artist	Peak Position	Year of Release
READY FOR THE FLOOR	HOT CHIP	6	2008
READY FOR THE WEEKEND	CALVIN HARRIS	3	2009
READY OR NOT [A]	LIGHTNING SEEDS	20	1996
READY OR NOT [B]	FUGEES	1	1996
READY OR NOT [B]	COURSE	5	1997
READY OR NOT [C]	DJ DADO & SIMONE JAY	51	1999
READY OR NOT [D]	A1	3	1999
READY OR NOT HERE I COME	DELFONICS	41	1971
READY STEADY GO [A]	GENERATION X	47	1978
READY STEADY GO [B]	PAUL OAKENFOLD	16	2002
READY STEADY WHO (EP)	WHO	58	1983
READY TO GO	REPUBLICA	13	1996
READY TO RECEIVE	ANIMALHOUSE	61	2000
READY TO RUN	DIXIE CHICKS	53	1999
READY WILLING AND ABLE	DORIS DAY	7	1955
READY2WEAR	FELIX DA HOUSECAT	62	2005
REAL [A]	DONNA ALLEN	34	1995
REAL [B]	PLUMB	41	2004
REAL A LIE	AUF DER MAUR	33	2004
REAL COOL WORLD	DAVID BOWIE	53	1992
REAL EMOTION	REID	65	1989
REAL FASHION REGGAE STYLE	CAREY JOHNSON	19	1987
REAL GIRL	MUTYA BUENA	2	2007
REAL GONE KID	DEACON BLUE	8	1988
REAL GOOD	DOUBLE SIX	66	1998
REAL GOOD TIME	ALDA	7	1998
REAL GREAT BRITAIN	ASIAN DUB FOUNDATION	41	2000
REAL LIFE [A]	SIMPLE MINDS	34	1991
REAL LIFE [B]	BON JOVI	21	1999
THE REAL LIFE [C]	RAVEN MAIZE	12	2001
REAL LOVE [A]	RUBY MURRAY	18	1958
REAL LOVE [B]	JODY WATLEY	31	1989
REAL LOVE [C]	DRIZABONE	16	1991
REAL LOVE [D]	DARE	67	1991
REAL LOVE [D]	TIME FREQUENCY	8	1992
REAL LOVE [E]	MARY J BLIGE	26	1992
REAL LOVE [F]	BEATLES	4	1996
THE REAL ME	W.A.S.P.	23	1989
A REAL MOTHER FOR YA	JOHNNY 'GUITAR' WATSON	44	1977
REAL PEOPLE	APACHE INDIAN	66	1997
REAL REAL REAL	JESUS JONES	19	1990
THE REAL SLIM SHADY	EMINEM	1	2000
THE REAL THING [A]	JELLYBEAN FEATURING STEVEN DANTE	13	1987
THE REAL THING [B]	BROTHERS JOHNSON	50	1981
THE REAL THING [C]	ABC	68	1989
THE REAL THING [D]	TONY DI BART	1	1994
THE REAL THING [E]	LISA STANSFIELD	9	1997
THE REAL THING [F]	2 UNLIMITED	6	1994
REAL THINGS	JAVINE	4	2003
REAL TO ME	BRIAN McFADDEN	1	2004
REAL VIBRATION	EXPRESS OF SOUND	45	1996
REAL WILD CHILD (WILD ONE)	IGGY POP	10	1987
THE REAL WILD HOUSE	RAUL ORELLANA	29	1989
REAL WORLD	D-SIDE	9	2003
REALITY USED TO BE A GOOD FRIEND OF MINE	PM DAWN	29	1992
REALLY DOE	ICE CUBE	66	1993
REALLY FREE	JOHN OTWAY & WILD WILLY BARRETT	27	1977
REALLY SAYING SOMETHING	BANANARAMA WITH FUN BOY THREE	5	1982
REAP THE WILD WIND	ULTRAVOX	12	1982
REASON	IAN VAN DAHL	8	2002
THE REASON [A]	CELINE DION	11	1997
THE REASON [B]	HOOBASTANK	12	2004
REASON FOR LIVING	RODDY FRAME	45	1998
REASON TO BELIEVE	ROD STEWART	1	1971
REASON TO LIVE	KISS	33	1987
REASONS [A]	KLESHAY	33	1998
REASONS [B]	UB40/HUNTERZ/DHOL BLASTERS	75	2005
REASONS TO BE CHEERFUL (PART 3)	IAN DURY & THE BLOCKHEADS	3	1979
REBEL MUSIC	REBEL MC	53	1990
REBEL NEVER GETS OLD	DAVID BOWIE	47	2004
REBEL REBEL	DAVID BOWIE	5	1974
REBEL ROUSER	DUANE EDDY & THE REBELS	19	1958
REBEL RUN	TOYAH	24	1983
REBEL WITHOUT A PAUSE	PUBLIC ENEMY	37	1987
REBEL WOMAN	DNA FEATURING JAZZI P	42	1991
REBEL YELL	BILLY IDOL	6	1984
REBEL YELL	SCOOTER	30	1996
REBELLION (LIES)	ARCADE FIRE	19	2005
REBIRTH OF SLICK (COOL LIKE DAT)	DIGABLE PLANETS	67	1993
RECIPE FOR LOVE	HARRY CONNICK, JR	32	1991
RECKLESS	AFRIKA BAMBAATAA FEATURING UB40 & FAMILY	17	1988
RECKLESS GIRL	BEGINERZ	28	2002
RECKONER	RADIOHEAD	74	2008
RECONNECTION (EP)	ZERO B	54	1993
RECOVER	AUTOMATIC	25	2006
RECOVER YOUR SOUL	ELTON JOHN	16	1998
RECOVERY	FONTELLA BASS	32	1966
RED [A]	ELBOW	36	2001
RED [B]	DANIEL MERRIWEATHER	5	2009
RED ALERT	BASEMENT JAXX	5	1999
RED BALLOON	DAVE CLARK FIVE	7	1968
RED BLOODED WOMAN	KYLIE MINOGUE	5	2004
RED DRESS [A]	ALVIN STARDUST	7	1974
RED DRESS [B]	SUGABABES	4	2006
RED FLAG	BILLY TALENT	49	2006
RED FRAME WHITE LIGHT	ORCHESTRAL MANOEUVRES IN THE DARK	67	1980
RED GUITAR	DAVID SYLVIAN	17	1984
RED HOT [A]	PRINCESS	58	1987
RED HOT [B]	VANESSA-MAE	37	1995
RED LETTER DAY	PET SHOP BOYS	9	1997
RED LIGHT GREEN LIGHT	MITCHELL TOROK	29	1957
RED LIGHT GREEN LIGHT EP	WILDHEARTS	30	1996
RED LIGHT SPECIAL	TLC	18	1995
RED LIGHT SPELLS DANGER	BILLY OCEAN	2	1977
RED RAIN	PETER GABRIEL	46	1987
RED RED WINE	JIMMY JAMES & THE VAGABONDS	36	1968
RED RED WINE	TONY TRIBE	46	1969
RED RED WINE	UB40	1	1983
RED RIVER ROCK	JOHNNY & THE HURRICANES	3	1959
RED SAILS IN THE SUNSET	FATS DOMINO	34	1963
THE RED SHOES	KATE BUSH	21	1994
RED SKIES [A]	FIXX	57	1982
RED SKIES [B]	SAMSON	65	1983
RED SKY	STATUS QUO	19	1986
THE RED STROKES	GARTH BROOKS	13	1994
RED SUN RISING	LOST WITNESS	22	1999
RED THREE, THUNDER/STORM	DAVE CLARKE	45	1995
THE RED, THE WHITE, THE BLUE	HOPE OF THE STATES	15	2004
REDEFINE	SOIL	68	2004
REDEMPTION SONG	JOE STRUMMER & THE MESCALEROS	46	2003
REDNECK WOMAN	GRETCHEN WILSON	42	2004
REDONDO BEACH	MORRISSEY	11	2005
REDUNDANT	GREEN DAY	27	1998
REELIN' AND ROCKIN'	DAVE CLARK FIVE	24	1965
REELIN' AND ROCKIN'	CHUCK BERRY	18	1973
REELING	PASADENAS	75	1990
REET PETITE (THE SWEETEST GIRL IN TOWN)	JACKIE WILSON	1	1957
REET PETITE	DARTS	51	1979
REET PETITE	PINKY & PERKY	47	1993
REFLECT	THREE 'N' ONE	66	1997
REFLECTION	VANESSA-MAE	53	1998
REFLECTIONS	DIANA ROSS & THE SUPREMES	5	1967
REFLECTIONS OF MY LIFE	MARMALADE	3	1969
THE REFLEX	DURAN DURAN	1	1984
REFUGEES	TEARS	9	2005
REFUSE-RESIST	SEPULTURA	51	1994
REGGAE FOR IT NOW	BILL LOVELADY	12	1979
REGGAE LIKE IT USED TO BE	PAUL NICHOLAS	17	1976
REGGAE MUSIC	UB40	28	1994
REGGAE TUNE	ANDY FAIRWEATHER-LOW	10	1974
REGINA	SUGARCUBES	55	1989
REGRET	NEW ORDER	4	1993
REGULATE	WARREN G & NATE DOGG	5	1994
REHAB [A]	AMY WINEHOUSE	7	2006
REHAB [A]	GLEE CAST	62	2010
REHAB [B]	RIHANNA	16	2008
REIGN	UNKLE FEATURING IAN BROWN	40	2004
REIGNS	JA RULE	9	2003
REILLY	OLYMPIC ORCHESTRA	26	1983
RELAX [A]	FRANKIE GOES TO HOLLYWOOD	1	1983
RELAX [B]	CRYSTAL WATERS	37	1995
RELAX [C]	DEETAH	11	1998
RELAX TAKE IT EASY	MIKA	18	2007
RELAY	WHO	21	1973
RELEASE [A]	AFRO CELT SOUND SYSTEM	71	2000
RELEASE [B]	MEDWAY	67	2001
RELEASE ME [A]	ENGELBERT HUMPERDINCK	1	1967
RELEASE ME [B]	WILSON PHILLIPS	36	1990
RELEASE ME [C]	LAURA	47	2007
RELEASE ME [D]	AGNES	3	2009
RELEASE THE PRESSURE	LEFTFIELD	13	1996
RELEASE YO' SELF [A]	METHOD MAN	46	1995
RELEASE YO SELF [B]	TRANSATLANTIC SOUL	43	1997
RELIGHT MY FIRE	TAKE THAT FEATURING LULU	1	1993
RELIGION	FRONT 242	46	1993
RELOAD	PPK	39	2002
REMAIN	KUBB	45	2005
REMEDY [A]	BLACK CROWES	24	1992
REMEDY [B]	LITTLE BOOTS	6	2009
REMEMBER [A]	ROCK CANDY	32	1971
REMEMBER [B]	JIMI HENDRIX EXPERIENCE	35	1971
REMEMBER [C]	BT	27	1998
REMEMBER [D]	DISTURBED	56	2002
REMEMBER I LOVE YOU	JIM DIAMOND	42	1985
REMEMBER ME [A]	DIANA ROSS	7	1971
REMEMBER ME [B]	CLIFF RICHARD	35	1987
REMEMBER ME [C]	BLUE BOY	8	1997
REMEMBER ME [D]	JORIO	54	2001
REMEMBER ME [E]	BRITISH SEA POWER	30	2003
REMEMBER ME [F]	ZUTONS	39	2004
REMEMBER ME [G]	KANO	71	2005
REMEMBER ME [H]	TI FEATURING MARY J BLIGE	34	2009
REMEMBER ME THIS WAY	GARY GLITTER	3	1974
REMEMBER ME WITH LOVE	GLORIA ESTEFAN	22	1991
REMEMBER (SHA-LA-LA)	BAY CITY ROLLERS	6	1974
REMEMBER THE DAY	INNOCENCE	56	1991
(REMEMBER THE DAYS OF THE) OLD SCHOOL YARD	CAT STEVENS	44	1977
REMEMBER THE RAIN	BOB LIND	46	1966
REMEMBER THE TIME	MICHAEL JACKSON	3	1992
REMEMBER THEN	SHOWADDYWADDY	17	1979
REMEMBER (WALKIN' IN THE SAND)	SHANGRI-LAS	14	1964
REMEMBER WHEN	PLATTERS	25	1959
REMEMBER YESTERDAY	JOHN MILES	32	1976
REMEMBER YOU'RE A WOMBLE	WOMBLES	3	1974
REMEMBER YOU'RE MINE	PAT BOONE	5	1957
REMEMBERANCE DAY	B-MOVIE	61	1981

Title / Artist	Peak Position	Year of Release
REMEMBERESE STILLS	75	2003
REMEMBERING CHRISTMAS EXETER BRAMDEAN BOYS' CHOIR	46	1993
REMEMBERING THE FIRST TIME SIMPLY RED	22	1995
REMIND ME ROYKSOPP	21	2002
REMINDING ME (OF SEF) COMMON FEATURING CHANTAY SAVAGE	59	1997
REMINISCE [A] MARY J BLIGE	31	1993
REMINISCE [B] BLAZIN' SQUAD	8	2003
REMINISCING BUDDY HOLLY	17	1962
REMIXES – VOLUME 2 ED RUSH & OPTICAL	69	2004
REMOTE CONTROL BEASTIE BOYS	21	1999
RENAISSANCE M PEOPLE	5	1994
RENDEZVOUS [A] TINA CHARLES	27	1977
RENDEZVOUS [B] TYGERS OF PAN TANG	49	1982
RENDEZVOUS [C] CRAIG DAVID	8	2001
RENDEZ-VOUS 98 JEAN-MICHEL JARRE & APOLLO 440	12	1998
RENDEZ-VU BASEMENT JAXX	4	1999
RENE DMC (DEVASTATING MACHO CHARISMA) RENE & YVETTE	57	1986
RENEGADE CAVALCADE ASH	33	2004
RENEGADE MASTER WILDCHILD	3	1995
RENEGADE SNARES OMNI TRIO	61	2003
RENEGADE SOUNDWAVE RENEGADE SOUNDWAVE	64	1994
RENEGADES OF FUNK AFRIKA BAMBAATAA & THE SONIC SOUL FORCE	30	1984
RENT PET SHOP BOYS	8	1987
RENTA SANTA CHRIS HILL	10	1975
RENTED ROOMS TINDERSTICKS	56	1997
RE-OFFENDER TRAVIS	7	2003
REPEAT MANIC STREET PREACHERS	26	1991
REPEATED LOVE A.T.G.O.C.	38	1998
REPEATED OFFENDER RIFLES	26	2006
REPLAY IYAZ	1	2010
REPORT TO THE DANCEFLOOR ENERGISE	69	1991
REPRESENT SOUL II SOUL	39	1997
REPTILLA STROKES	17	2004
REPUBLICAN PARTY REPTILE (EP) BIG COUNTRY	37	1991
REPUTATION DUSTY SPRINGFIELD	38	1990
REPUTATIONS (JUST BE GOOD TO ME) ANDREA GRANT	75	1998
REQUEST & LINE BLACK EYED PEAS FEATURING MACY GRAY	31	2001
REQUEST LINE ZHANE	22	1997
REQUIEM [A] SLIK	24	1976
REQUIEM [B] LONDON BOYS	4	1988
RE-REWIND THE CROWD SAY BO SELECTA ARTFUL DODGER FEATURING CRAIG DAVID	2	1999
RESCUE ECHO & THE BUNNYMEN	62	1980
RESCUE ME [A] FONTELLA BASS	11	1965
RESCUE ME [B] ALARM	48	1987
RESCUE ME [C] MADONNA	3	1991
RESCUE ME [D] BELL BOOK & CANDLE	63	1998
RESCUE ME [E] SUNKIDS FEATURING CHANCE	50	1999
RESCUE ME [F] ULTRA	8	1999
RESISTANCE MUSE	38	2010
RESOLVE FOO FIGHTERS	32	2005
RESPECT [A] ARETHA FRANKLIN	10	1967
RESPECT [A] REAL ROXANNE	71	1988
RESPECT [A] ADEVA	17	1989
RESPECT [B] SUB SUB	49	1994
RESPECT [C] JUDY CHEEKS	23	1995
RESPECT YOURSELF KANE GANG	21	1984
RESPECT YOURSELF BRUCE WILLIS	7	1987
RESPECT YOURSELF ROBERT PALMER	45	1995
RESPECTABLE [A] ROLLING STONES	23	1978
RESPECTABLE [B] MEL & KIM	1	1987
RESPECTABLE [B] GIRLS@PLAY	29	2001
REST AND PLAY EP ORBITAL	33	2002
REST IN PEACE EXTREME	13	1992
REST OF MY LOVE URBAN COOKIE COLLECTIVE	67	1995
REST OF THE NIGHT NATALIE COLE	56	1989
RESTLESS [A] JOHNNY KIDD & THE PIRATES	22	1960
RESTLESS [B] GILLAN	25	1982
RESTLESS [C] STATUS QUO	39	1994
RESTLESS [D] JX	22	2004
RESTLESS DAYS (SHE CRIES OUT LOUD) AND WHY NOT?	38	1989
RESTLESS (I KNOW YOU KNOW) NEJA	47	1998
RESURRECTION [A] BRIAN MAY WITH COZY POWELL	23	1993
RESURRECTION [B] PPK	3	2001
RESURRECTION JOE CULT	74	1984
RESURRECTION SHUFFLE ASHTON, GARDNER & DYKE	3	1971
RETOX FATBOY SLIM	73	2002
RETREAT [A] HELL IS FOR HEROES	39	2003
RETREAT [B] RAKES	24	2005
RETURN OF DJANGO UPSETTERS	5	1969
THE RETURN OF EVIL BILL CLINIC	70	2000
THE RETURN OF NOTHING SANDSTORM	54	2000
THE RETURN OF PAN WATERBOYS	24	1993
RETURN OF THE ELECTRIC WARRIOR (EP) MARC BOLAN & T REX	50	1981
RETURN OF THE LOS PALMAS SEVEN MADNESS	7	1981
RETURN OF THE MACK MARK MORRISON	1	1996
RETURN OF THE RED BARON ROYAL GUARDSMEN	37	1967
RETURN THE FAVOUR KERI HILSON FEATURING TIMBALAND	19	2009
THE RETURN (TIME TO SAY GOODBYE) DJ VISAGE FEATURING CLARISSA	58	2000
RETURN TO BRIXTON CLASH	57	1990
RETURN TO INNOCENCE ENIGMA	3	1994
RETURN TO ME DEAN MARTIN	2	1958
RETURN TO REALITY ANTARCTICA	53	2000
RETURN TO SENDER ELVIS PRESLEY	1	1962
REUNITED PEACHES & HERB	4	1979
REVEILLE ROCK JOHNNY & THE HURRICANES	14	1959
REVELATION ELECTRIQUE BOUTIQUE	37	2000
REVELRY KINGS OF LEON	29	2009
REVERENCE [A] JESUS & MARY CHAIN	10	1992
REVERENCE [B] FAITHLESS	10	1997
REVEREND BLACK GRAPE BLACK GRAPE	9	1995
REVIVAL [A] CHRIS BARBER'S JAZZ BAND	43	1962
REVIVAL [B] EURYTHMICS	26	1989
REVIVAL [C] MARTINE GIRAULT	37	1992
REVOL MANIC STREET PREACHERS	22	1994
REVOLT INTO STYLE BILL NELSON'S RED NOISE	69	1979
REVOLUTION [A] CULT	30	1985
REVOLUTION [B] THOMPSON TWINS	56	1985
REVOLUTION [C] ARRESTED DEVELOPMENT	4	1993
REVOLUTION [D] COLDCUT	67	2001
REVOLUTION [E] BK	42	2002
REVOLUTION BABY TRANSVISION VAMP	30	1988
REVOLUTION (IN THE SUMMERTIME) COSMIC ROUGH RIDERS	35	2001
REVOLUTION 909 DAFT PUNK	47	1998
REVOLUTION OVER THE PHONE MARDOUS	74	2005
REVOLUTIONS JEAN-MICHEL JARRE	52	1988
REVOLUTIONS (EP) SHARKEY	53	1997
REVOLVING DOOR CRAZY TOWN	23	2001
REWARD TEARDROP EXPLODES	6	1981
REWIND [A] CELETIA	29	1998
REWIND [B] PRECIOUS	11	2000
REWIND [C] STEREOPHONICS	17	2005
REWIND [D] PAOLO NUTINI	27	2006
REWIND (FIND A WAY) BEVERLEY KNIGHT	40	1998
RHAPSODY FOUR SEASONS	37	1977
RHAPSODY IN THE RAIN LOU CHRISTIE	37	1966
RHIANNON FLEETWOOD MAC	46	1978
RHINESTONE COWBOY GLEN CAMPBELL	4	1975
RHINESTONE COWBOY (GIDDY UP GIDDY UP) RIKKI & DAZ FEATURING GLEN CAMPBELL	12	2002
THE RHYME KEITH MURRAY	59	1996
THE RHYTHM CLOCK	28	1994
RHYTHM & BLUES ALIBI GOMEZ	18	1999
RHYTHM AND GREENS SHADOWS	22	1964
RHYTHM BANDITS JUNIOR SENIOR	22	2003
THE RHYTHM DIVINE YELLO FEATURING SHIRLEY BASSEY	54	1987
RHYTHM DIVINE ENRIQUE IGLESIAS	45	1999
RHYTHM IS A DANCER SNAP!	1	1992
RHYTHM IS A MYSTERY K-KLASS	3	1991
RHYTHM IS GONNA GET YOU GLORIA ESTEFAN & MIAMI SOUND MACHINE	16	1988
RHYTHM NATION JANET JACKSON	23	1989
RHYTHM OF LIFE OLETA ADAMS	38	1990
RHYTHM OF LOVE SCORPIONS	59	1988
RHYTHM OF MY HEART ROD STEWART	3	1991
RHYTHM OF MY HEART RUNRIG	24	1996
RHYTHM OF THE BEAST NICKO McBRAIN	72	1991
RHYTHM OF THE JUNGLE QUICK	41	1982
RHYTHM OF THE NIGHT [A] DeBARGE	4	1985
THE RHYTHM OF THE NIGHT [B] CORONA	2	1994
RHYTHM OF THE NIGHT [C] POWERHOUSE	38	1997
RHYTHM OF THE RAIN CASCADES	5	1963
RHYTHM OF THE RAIN JASON DONOVAN	9	1990
RHYTHM TAKES CONTROL UNIQUE 3 FEATURING KARIN	41	1990
RHYTHM TALK JOCKO	56	1980
RIBBON IN THE SKY STEVIE WONDER	45	1982
RICE IS NICE LEMON PIPERS	41	1968
RICH AH GETTING RICHER REBEL MC INTRODUCING LITTLE T	48	1992
RICH AND STRANGE CUD	24	1992
RICH GIRL GWEN STEFANI FEATURING EVE	4	2005
RICH IN PARADISE FPI PROJECT	9	1989
RICH KIDS RICH KIDS	24	1978
RICH MAN POOR MAN JIMMY YOUNG	25	1956
RICHARD III SUPERGRASS	2	1997
RICOCHET [A] JOAN REGAN & THE SQUADRONAIRES	8	1953
RICOCHET [B] B B & Q BAND	71	1987
RICOCHET [C] FAITH NO MORE	27	1995
RIDDIM US3 FEATURING TUKKA YOOT	34	1993
THE RIDDLE [A] NIK KERSHAW	3	1984
RIDDLE [B] EN VOGUE	33	2000
RIDDLE ME UB40	59	1984
RIDE [A] ANA ANN	24	2002
RIDE [B] VINES	25	2004
RIDE [C] DYNAMITE MC	54	2004
RIDE A ROCKET LITHIUM & SONYA MADAN	40	1997
RIDE A WHITE HORSE [B] GOLDFRAPP	15	2006
RIDE A WHITE SWAN T REX	2	1970
RIDE A WILD HORSE [A] DEE CLARK	16	1975
RIDE AWAY ROY ORBISON	34	1965
RIDE (EP) RIDE	71	1990
RIDE IT [A] GERI HALLIWELL	4	2004
RIDE IT [B] JAY SEAN	11	2008
RIDE LIKE THE WIND CHRISTOPHER CROSS	69	1980
RIDE LIKE THE WIND SAXON	52	1988
RIDE LIKE THE WIND EAST SIDE BEAT	3	1991
RIDE MY SEE-SAW MOODY BLUES	42	1968
RIDE ON BABY CHRIS FARLOWE	31	1966
RIDE ON THE RHYTHM LITTLE LOUIE & MARC ANTHONY	36	1991
RIDE ON TIME BLACK BOX	1	1989
RIDE THE BULLET ARMY OF LOVERS	67	1992
RIDE THE GROOVE PLAYERS ASSOCIATION	42	1979

Title	Artist	Peak Position	Year of Release
RIDE THE LOVE TRAIN	LIGHT OF THE WORLD	49	1981
RIDE THE RHYTHM	Z FACTOR	52	2001
RIDE THE STORM [A]	AKABU FEATURING LINDA CLIFFORD	69	2001
RIDE THE STORM [B]	SIMON WEBBE	36	2007
RIDE THE TIGER	BOO RADLEYS	38	1997
RIDE WID US	SO SOLID CREW	19	2002
RIDE WIT ME	NELLY FEATURING CITY SPUD	3	2001
RIDE WIT U	JOE FEATURING G UNIT	12	2004
RIDE-O-ROCKET	BROTHERS JOHNSON	50	1978
RIDERS IN THE SKY	RAMRODS	8	1961
RIDERS IN THE SKY	SHADOWS	12	1980
RIDERS ON THE STORM	DOORS	22	1971
RIDERS ON THE STORM	ANNABEL LAMB	27	1983
RIDICULOUS THOUGHTS	CRANBERRIES	20	1995
RIDIN'	CHAMILLIONAIRE FEATURING KRAYZIE BONE	2	2006
RIDIN' SOLO	JASON DERULO	44	2010
RIDING ON A TRAIN	PASADENAS	13	1988
RIDING ON THE WINGS	MOTIV 8	44	2005
RIDING WITH THE ANGELS	SAMSON	55	1981
RIGHT ABOUT NOW	MOUSSE T FEATURING EMMA LANFORD	28	2004
RIGHT AND EXACT	CHRISSY WARD	59	1995
RIGHT BACK WHERE WE STARTED FROM	MAXINE NIGHTINGALE	8	1975
RIGHT BACK WHERE WE STARTED FROM	SINITTA	4	1989
RIGHT BEFORE MY EYES	PATTI DAY	69	1989
RIGHT BEFORE MY EYES	N 'N' G FEATURING KALLAGHAN	12	2000
RIGHT BESIDE YOU	SOPHIE B HAWKINS	13	1994
RIGHT BETWEEN THE EYES	WAX	60	1986
RIGHT BY YOUR SIDE	EURYTHMICS	10	1983
THE RIGHT COMBINATION	SEIKO & DONNIE WAHLBERG	44	1990
THE RIGHT DECISION	JESUS JONES	36	1993
RIGHT HERE [A]	SWV	3	1993
RIGHT HERE [B]	ULTIMATE KAOS	18	1995
RIGHT HERE RIGHT NOW [A]	JESUS JONES	31	1990
RIGHT HERE RIGHT NOW [B]	DISCO CITIZENS	40	1995
RIGHT HERE RIGHT NOW [C]	FIERCE	25	1999
RIGHT HERE RIGHT NOW [D]	FATBOY SLIM	2	1999
RIGHT HERE WAITING	RICHARD MARX	2	1989
RIGHT IN THE NIGHT (FALL IN LOVE WITH MUSIC)	JAM & SPOON FEATURING PLAVKA	10	1994
RIGHT IN THE SOCKET	SHALAMAR	44	1980
THE RIGHT KINDA LOVER	PATTI LABELLE	50	1994
RIGHT NEXT DOOR (BECAUSE OF ME)	ROBERT CRAY BAND	50	1987
RIGHT NOW [A]	CREATURES	14	1983
RIGHT NOW [B]	AIRHEAD	50	1992
RIGHT NOW [C]	ATOMIC KITTEN	10	1999
RIGHT NOW [D]	AKON	6	2008
RIGHT ON	SILICONE SOUL	15	2001
RIGHT ON TRACK	BREAKFAST CLUB	54	1987
RIGHT ROUND	FLO RIDA	1	2009
RIGHT SAID FRED	BERNARD CRIBBINS	10	1962
THE RIGHT STUFF [A]	BRYAN FERRY	37	1987
THE RIGHT STUFF [B]	VANESSA WILLIAMS	62	1988
RIGHT STUFF [C]	LC ANDERSON VS PSYCHO RADIO	45	2003
THE RIGHT THING	SIMPLY RED	11	1987
THE RIGHT THING TO DO	CARLY SIMON	17	1973
THE RIGHT THING TO SAY	NAT 'KING' COLE	42	1962
RIGHT THURR	CHINGY	17	2003
THE RIGHT TIME	ULTRA	28	1998
RIGHT TO BE WRONG	JOSS STONE	29	2004
THE RIGHT TO LOVE	DAVID WHITFIELD	30	1958
THE RIGHT WAY	PETER ANDRE	14	2004
RIGHT WHERE YOU WANT ME	JESSE McCARTNEY	54	2006
RIKKI DON'T LOSE THAT NUMBER	STEELY DAN	58	1979
RIKKI DON'T LOSE THAT NUMBER	TOM ROBINSON	58	1984
RING	ALEXIA	48	2003
RING A DING GIRL	RONNIE CARROLL	46	1962
RING DING DING [A]	PONDLIFE	11	2005
RING DING DING [B]	LOC	58	2005
RING MY BELL [A]	ANITA WARD	1	1979
RING MY BELL [A]	DJ JAZZY JEFF & THE FRESH PRINCE	37	1991
RING MY BELL [B]	MONIE LOVE Vs ADEVA	20	1991
RING OF BRIGHT WATER	VAL DOONICAN	48	1969
RING OF FIRE [A]	DUANE EDDY & THE REBELS	17	1961
RING OF FIRE [B]	ERIC BURDON & THE ANIMALS	35	1969
RING OF ICE	JENNIFER RUSH	14	1985
RING OUT SOLSTICE BELLS (EP)	JETHRO TULL	28	1976
RING RING [A]	ABBA	32	1974
RING RING [B]	DOLLAR	61	1982
RING RING RING	AARON SOUL	14	2001
RING RING RING (HA HA HEY)	DE LA SOUL	10	1991
RING THE BELLS	JAMES	37	1992
RINGO	LORNE GREENE	22	1964
RIO [A]	MICHAEL NESMITH	28	1977
RIO [B]	DURAN DURAN	9	1982
RIOT RADIO	DEAD 60S	30	2004
RIP	GARY NUMAN	29	2002
RIP IT UP [A]	BILL HALEY & HIS COMETS	4	1956
RIP IT UP [A]	LITTLE RICHARD	30	1956
RIP IT UP [A]	ELVIS PRESLEY	27	1957
RIP IT UP [B]	ORANGE JUICE	8	1983
RIP IT UP [C]	RAZORLIGHT	20	2003
RIPGROOVE	DOUBLE 99	14	1997
RIPPED IN 2 MINUTES	A VS B	49	1998
RIPPIN KITTIN	GOLDEN BOY WITH MISS KITTIN	67	2002
RISE [A]	HERB ALPERT	13	1979
RISE [B]	PUBLIC IMAGE LTD	11	1986
RISE [C]	ZION TRAIN	61	1996
RISE [D]	EDDIE AMADOR	19	2000
RISE [E]	GABRIELLE	1	2000
RISE [F]	SOUL PROVIDERS FEATURING MICHELLE SHELLERS	59	2001
RISE & FALL	CRAIG DAVID & STING	2	2003
THE RISE AND FALL OF FLINGEL BUNT	SHADOWS	5	1964
RISE AND SHINE	CARDIGANS	29	1996
RISE 'IN	STEVE LAWLER	50	2000
RISE OF THE EAGLES	EIGHTIES MATCHBOX B-LINE DISASTER	40	2004
RISE TO THE OCCASION	CLIMIE FISHER	10	1987
RISE UP [A]	JAMAICA UNITED	54	1998
RISE UP [B]	YVES LAROCK	13	2007
RISIN' TO THE TOP	KENI BURKE	70	1992
RISING SIGN	HURRICANE #1	47	1998
RISING SUN [A]	MEDICINE HEAD	11	1973
RISING SUN [B]	FARM	48	1992
RISINGSON	MASSIVE ATTACK	11	1997
THE RITUAL	EBONY DUBSTERS	58	2004
THE RIVER [A]	BRUCE SPRINGSTEEN	35	1981
THE RIVER [B]	KING TRIGGER	57	1982
THE RIVER [C]	TOTAL CONTRAST	44	1986
THE RIVER [D]	BEAUTIFUL SOUTH	59	2000
THE RIVER [E]	BREED 77	39	2004
RIVER BELOW	BILLY TALENT	70	2004
RIVER DEEP MOUNTAIN HIGH	IKE & TINA TURNER	3	1966
RIVER DEEP MOUNTAIN HIGH	SUPREMES & THE FOUR TOPS	11	1971
THE RIVER (LE COLLINE SONO IN FIORO)	KEN DODD	3	1965
RIVER MAN	NICK DRAKE	48	2004
THE RIVER OF DREAMS	BILLY JOEL	3	1993
RIVER OF PAIN	THUNDER	31	1995
RIVER STAY 'WAY FROM MY DOOR	FRANK SINATRA	18	1960
THE RIVERBOAT SONG	OCEAN COLOUR SCENE	15	1996
RIVERDANCE	BILL WHELAN FEATURING ANUNA & THE RTE CONCERT ORCHESTRA	9	1994
RIVERS OF BABYLON	BONEY M	1	1978
THE RIVERS OF BELIEF	ENIGMA	68	1992
THE RIVER'S RUN DRY	VINCE HILL	41	1962
RIVERSIDE (LET'S GO)	SIDNEY SAMSON FEATURING WIZARD SLEEVE	2	2010
ROACHES	TRANCESETTERS	55	2000
THE ROAD	FRANK TURNER	62	2009
THE ROAD LEADS WHERE IT'S LED	SECRET MACHINES	56	2005
ROAD RAGE	CATATONIA	5	1998
THE ROAD TO HELL (PART 2)	CHRIS REA	10	1989
THE ROAD TO MANDALAY	ROBBIE WILLIAMS	1	2001
ROAD TO NOWHERE	TALKING HEADS	6	1985
ROAD TO OUR DREAM	T'PAU	42	1988
THE ROAD TO PARADISE	BHOYS FROM PARADISE	46	2004
ROAD TO YOUR SOUL	ALL ABOUT EVE	37	1989
ROAD TRIPPIN'	RED HOT CHILI PEPPERS	30	2001
ROADBLOCK	STOCK AITKEN WATERMAN	13	1987
ROADHOUSE MEDLEY (ANNIVERSARY WALTZ PART 25)	STATUS QUO	21	1992
ROADRUNNER	JONATHAN RICHMAN & THE MODERN LOVERS	11	1977
ROAM	B-52's	17	1990
ROBERT DE NIRO'S WAITING	BANANARAMA	3	1984
ROBIN HOOD	GARY MILLER	10	1956
ROBIN HOOD	DICK JAMES	29	1956
ROBIN (THE HOODED MAN)	CLANNAD	42	1984
ROBIN'S RETURN	NEVILLE DICKIE	33	1969
ROBOT	TORNADOS	17	1963
ROBOT MAN	CONNIE FRANCIS	2	1960
ROBOT ROCK	DAFT PUNK	32	2005
ROBOT WARS (ANDROID LOVE)	SIR KILLALOT VS ROBO BABE	51	2000
THE ROBOTS	KRAFTWERK	20	1991
ROC YA BODY (MIC CHECK 1 2)	MVP	5	2005
ROCCO	DEATH IN VEGAS	51	1997
ROCHDALE COWBOY	MIKE HARDING	22	1975
ROC-IN-IT	DEEJAY PUNK-ROC VS ONYX	59	1999
THE ROCK [A]	ALARM FEATURING THE MORRISTON ORPHEUS MALE VOICE CHOIR	31	1989
THE ROCK [B]	DELAKOTA	60	1998
THE ROCK [C]	PUNX	59	2002
ROCK A HULA BABY	ELVIS PRESLEY	1	1962
ROCK AND A HARD PLACE	ROLLING STONES	63	1989
ROCK AND ROLL DREAMS COME THROUGH	MEAT LOAF	11	1994
ROCK AND ROLL IS DEAD	LENNY KRAVITZ	22	1995
ROCK AND ROLL (IS GONNA SET THE NIGHT ON FIRE)	PRETTY BOY FLOYD	75	1990
ROCK AND ROLL MUSIC	BEACH BOYS	36	1976
ROCK AND ROLL (PARTS 1 & 2)	GARY GLITTER	2	1972
ROCK & ROLL QUEEN	SUBWAYS	22	2005
ROCK AND ROLL SUICIDE	DAVID BOWIE	22	1974
ROCK AND ROLL WALTZ	KAY STARR	1	1956
ROCK AROUND THE CLOCK	BILL HALEY & HIS COMETS	1	1955
ROCK AROUND THE CLOCK	TELEX	34	1979
ROCK AROUND THE CLOCK	TEN POLE TUDOR	63	1979

	Peak Position	Year of Release
ROCK BOTTOM [A] LYNSEY DE PAUL & MIKE MORAN	19	1977
ROCK BOTTOM [B] BABYFACE	50	1994
ROCK DA FUNKY BEATS PUBLIC DOMAIN FEATURING CHUCK D	19	2001
ROCK DA HOUSE TALL PAUL	12	1997
ROCK DJ ROBBIE WILLIAMS	1	2000
ROCK HARD SUZI QUATRO	68	1980
R.O.C.K. IN THE USA JOHN COUGAR MELLENCAMP	67	1986
ROCK IS DEAD MARILYN MANSON	23	1999
ROCK ISLAND LINE LONNIE DONEGAN	8	1956
ROCK ISLAND LINE STAN FREBERG & HIS SKIFFLE GROUP	24	1956
ROCK IT SUB FOCUS	38	2009
ROCK LOBSTER B-52's	12	1979
ROCK ME AMADEUS FALCO	1	1986
ROCK ME BABY [A] DAVID CASSIDY	11	1972
ROCK ME BABY [B] JOHNNY NASH	47	1985
ROCK ME BABY [C] BABY ROOTS	71	1992
ROCK ME GENTLY ANDY KIM	2	1974
ROCK ME GOOD UNIVERSAL	19	1997
ROCK ME STEADY DJ PROFESSOR	49	1992
ROCK ME TONIGHT (FOR OLD TIME'S SAKE) FREDDIE JACKSON	18	1986
ROCK MY HEART HADDAWAY	9	1994
ROCK MY WORLD FIVE STAR	28	1988
ROCK 'N ME STEVE MILLER BAND	11	1976
ROCK 'N' ROLL [A] STATUS QUO	8	1981
ROCK 'N' ROLL [B] JOHN McENROE & PAT CASH WITH THE FULL METAL RACKETS	66	1991
ROCK 'N' ROLL AIN'T NOISE POLLUTION AC/DC	15	1980
ROCK 'N' ROLL CHILDREN DIO	26	1985
ROCK 'N' ROLL DAMNATION AC/DC	24	1978
ROCK 'N' ROLL DANCE PARTY JIVE BUNNY & THE MASTERMIXERS	48	1991
ROCK 'N' ROLL (DOLE) J PAC	51	1995
ROCK 'N' ROLL DREAMS COME THROUGH JIM STEINMAN, VOCALS BY RORY DODD	52	1981
ROCK 'N' ROLL GYPSY SAXON	72	1986
ROCK 'N' ROLL HIGH SCHOOL RAMONES	67	1979
ROCK 'N ROLL (I GAVE YOU THE BEST YEARS OF MY LIFE) KEVIN JOHNSON	23	1975
ROCK 'N' ROLL IS KING ELECTRIC LIGHT ORCHESTRA	13	1983
ROCK 'N' ROLL LADY SHOWADDYWADDY	15	1974
ROCK 'N' ROLL LIES RAZORLIGHT	56	2003
ROCK 'N' ROLL MERCENARIES MEAT LOAF FEATURING JOHN PARR	31	1986
ROCK 'N' ROLL NIGGER BIRDLAND	47	1990
ROCK 'N' ROLL OUTLAW ROSE TATTOO	60	1981
ROCK 'N' ROLL STAGE SHOW (LP) BILL HALEY & HIS COMETS	30	1956
ROCK 'N' ROLL WINTER WIZZARD	6	1974
ROCK N ROLLER KANO	44	2009
ROCK OF AGES DEF LEPPARD	41	1983
ROCK ON DAVID ESSEX	3	1973
ROCK ON BROTHER CHEQUERS	21	1975
THE ROCK SHOW BLINK-182	14	2001
ROCK STAR N*E*R*D	15	2002
ROCK STEADY [A] WHISPERS	38	1987
ROCK STEADY [B] BONNIE RAITT & BRYAN ADAMS	50	1995
ROCK STEADY [C] ALL SAINTS	3	2006
ROCK THAT BODY BLACK EYED PEAS	11	2010
ROCK THE BELLS KADOC	34	1997
ROCK THE BOAT [A] HUES CORPORATION	6	1974
ROCK THE BOAT [A] FORREST	4	1983
ROCK THE BOAT [A] DELAGE	63	1990
ROCK THE BOAT [B] AALIYAH	12	2002
ROCK THE CASBAH CLASH	15	1982
ROCK THE DISCOTEK RAMP	49	1996
ROCK THE FUNKY BEAT NATURAL BORN CHILLERS	30	1997
ROCK THE HOUSE [A] SOURCE FEATURING NICOLE	63	1992
ROCK THE HOUSE [B] GORILLAZ	18	2001
ROCK THE JOINT BILL HALEY & HIS COMETS	20	1957
ROCK THE MIDNIGHT DAVID GRANT	46	1983
ROCK THE NIGHT EUROPE	12	1987
ROCK THIS PARTY (EVERYBODY DANCE NOW) BOB SINCLAR & CUTEE B	3	2006
ROCK THIS TOWN STRAY CATS	9	1981
ROCK 'TIL YOU DROP STATUS QUO	38	1992
ROCK 2 HOUSE X-PRESS 2 FEATURING LO-PRO	55	1994
ROCK WIT U (AWWW BABY) ASHANTI	7	2003
ROCK WIT'CHA BOBBY BROWN	33	1989
ROCK WITH THE CAVEMAN TOMMY STEELE & THE STEELMEN	13	1956
ROCK WITH YOU MICHAEL JACKSON	7	1980
ROCK WITH YOU D-INFLUENCE	30	1998
ROCK YOUR BABY GEORGE McCRAE	1	1974
ROCK YOUR BABY KWS	8	1992
ROCK YOUR BODY [A] CLOCK	30	1998
ROCK YOUR BODY [B] JUSTIN TIMBERLAKE	2	2003
ROCK YOUR BODY ROCK FERRY CORSTEN	11	2004
ROCK-A-BEATIN' BOOGIE BILL HALEY & HIS COMETS	4	1955
ROCK-A-BILLY GUY MITCHELL	1	1957
ROCKABILLY BOB COLUMBO FEATURING OOE	59	1999
ROCKABILLY GUY POLECATS	35	1981
ROCKABILLY REBEL MATCHBOX	18	1979
ROCK-A-BYE YOUR BABY (WITH A DIXIE MELODY) JERRY LEWIS	12	1957
ROCK-A-DOODLE-DOO LINDA LEWIS	15	1973
THE ROCKAFELLER SKANK FATBOY SLIM	6	1998
ROCKALL MEZZOFORTE	75	1983
ROCKARIA! ELECTRIC LIGHT ORCHESTRA	9	1977
ROCKER ALTER EGO	32	2004
ROCKET [A] MUD	6	1974
ROCKET [B] DEF LEPPARD	15	1989
ROCKET [C] EL PRESIDENTE	48	2005
ROCKET [D] GOLDFRAPP	47	2010
ROCKET (A NATURAL GAMBLER) BRAUND REYNOLDS	27	2005
ROCKET MAN [A] SPOTNICKS	38	1962
ROCKET MAN [B] ELTON JOHN	2	1972
ROCKET MAN (I THINK IT'S GOING TO BE A LONG LONG TIME) [B] KATE BUSH	12	1991
ROCKET RIDE FELIX DA HOUSECAT	55	2004
ROCKET 2 U JETS	69	1988
ROCKFERRY DUFFY	45	2008
ROCKIN' ALL OVER THE WORLD STATUS QUO	3	1977
ROCKIN' ALONE (IN AN OLD ROCKIN' CHAIR) MIKI & GRIFF	44	1960
ROCKIN' AROUND THE CHRISTMAS TREE BRENDA LEE	6	1962
ROCKIN' AROUND THE CHRISTMAS TREE JETS	62	1983
ROCKIN' AROUND THE CHRISTMAS TREE MEL & KIM	3	1987
ROCKIN' BACK INSIDE MY HEART JULEE CRUISE	66	1991
ROCKIN' CHAIR MAGNUM	27	1990
ROCKIN' FOR MYSELF MOTIV 8	18	1993
ROCKIN' GOOD CHRISTMAS ROY 'CHUBBY' BROWN	51	1996
A ROCKIN' GOOD WAY SHAKY & BONNIE	5	1984
ROCKIN' ME PROFESSOR	56	1994
ROCKIN' MY BODY 49ERS FEATURING ANN-MARIE SMITH	31	1995
ROCKIN' OVER THE BEAT TECHNOTRONIC FEATURING YA KID K	9	1990
ROCKIN' RED WING SAMMY MASTERS	36	1960
ROCKIN' ROBIN BOBBY DAY	29	1958
ROCKIN' ROBIN MICHAEL JACKSON	3	1972
ROCKIN' ROBIN LOLLY	10	1999
ROCKIN' ROLL BABY STYLISTICS	6	1974
ROCKIN' SOUL HUES CORPORATION	24	1974
ROCKIN' THE SUBURBS BEN FOLDS	53	2001
ROCKIN' THROUGH THE RYE BILL HALEY & HIS COMETS	3	1956
ROCKIN' TO THE MUSIC BLACK BOX	39	1993
ROCKIN' TO THE RHYTHM CONVERT	42	1993
ROCKIN' WITH RITA (HEAD TO TOE) VINDALOO SUMMER SPECIAL	56	1986
ROCKING GOOSE JOHNNY & THE HURRICANES	3	1960
ROCKING MUSIC MARTIN SOLVEIG	35	2004
ROCKIT HERBIE HANCOCK	8	1983
ROCKS PRIMAL SCREAM	7	1994
ROCKS ROD STEWART	55	1998
ROCKS ON THE ROAD JETHRO TULL	47	1992
ROCKSTAR [A] BIZARRE	17	2005
ROCKSTAR [B] NICKELBACK	2	2007
ROCKY AUSTIN ROBERTS	22	1975
ROCKY MOUNTAIN EP JOE WALSH	39	1977
THE RODEO SONG GARRY LEE & SHOWDOWN	44	1993
RODRIGO'S GUITAR CONCERTO DE ARANJUEZ (THEME FROM 2ND MOVEMENT) MANUEL & HIS MUSIC OF THE MOUNTAINS	3	1976
ROFO'S THEME ROFO	44	1992
ROK DA HOUSE [A] BEATMASTERS FEATURING THE COOKIE CREW	5	1988
ROK DA HOUSE [B] VINYLGROOVER & THE RED HED	72	2001
ROK THE NATION ROB 'N' RAZ FEATURING LEILA K	41	1990
ROLL AWAY DUSTY SPRINGFIELD	68	1995
ROLL AWAY THE STONE MOTT THE HOOPLE	8	1973
ROLL CALL LIL JON & THE EAST SIDE BOYZ	38	2005
ROLL ON MIS-TEEQ	7	2002
ROLL ON DOWN THE HIGHWAY BACHMAN-TURNER OVERDRIVE	22	1975
ROLL OVER BEETHOVEN ELECTRIC LIGHT ORCHESTRA	6	1973
ROLL OVER LAY DOWN STATUS QUO	9	1975
ROLL THE BONES RUSH	49	1992
ROLL TO ME DEL AMITRI	22	1995
ROLL WID US AKALA	72	2005
ROLL WITH IT [A] STEVE WINWOOD	53	1988
ROLL WITH IT [B] OASIS	2	1995
A ROLLER SKATING JAM NAMED 'SATURDAYS' DE LA SOUL	22	1991
ROLLERBLADE NICK HEYWARD	37	1996
ROLLERBLADE MOVIN' MELODIES	71	1997
ROLLERCOASTER [A] GRID	19	1994
ROLLERCOASTER [B] NORTHERN UPROAR	41	1995
ROLLERCOASTER [C] B*WITCHED	1	1998
ROLLERCOASTER (EP) JESUS & MARY CHAIN	46	1990
ROLLERCOASTER (EP) EVERYTHING BUT THE GIRL	65	1994
ROLLIN' LIMP BIZKIT	1	2001
ROLLIN' HOME STATUS QUO	9	1986
ROLLIN' IN MY 5.0 VANILLA ICE	27	1991
ROLLIN' ON CIRRUS	62	1978
ROLLIN' STONE DAVID ESSEX	5	1975
ROLLOUT (MY BUSINESS) LUDACRIS	20	2002
ROLLOVER DJ JET	34	2003
ROLODEX PROPAGANDA AT THE DRIVE-IN	54	2000
ROMAN P PSYCHIC TV	65	1986

	Peak Position	Year of Release
ROMANCE (LET YOUR HEART GO) DAVID CASSIDY	54	1985
ROMANCING THE STONE EDDY GRANT	52	1984
ROMANTIC KARYN WHITE	23	1991
ROMANTIC RIGHTS DEATH FROM ABOVE 1979	57	2004
ROMANTIC TYPE PIGEON DETECTIVES	19	2007
ROMANTICA JANE MORGAN	39	1960
ROME WASN'T BUILT IN A DAY MORCHEEBA	34	2000
ROMEO [A] PETULA CLARK	3	1961
ROMEO [B] MR BIG	4	1977
ROMEO [C] BASEMENT JAXX	6	2001
ROMEO AND JULIET DIRE STRAITS	8	1981
ROMEO DUNN ROMEO	3	2002
ROMEO ME SLEEPER	39	1997
ROMEO WHERE'S JULIET COLLAGE	46	1985
RONDO KENNY BALL & HIS JAZZMEN	24	1963
RONI BOBBY BROWN	21	1989
ROOBARB AND CUSTARD SHAFT	7	1991
ROOF IS ON FIRE WESTBAM	58	1998
ROOF TOP SINGING NEW WORLD	50	1973
ROOFTOPS (A LIBERATION BROADCAST) LOSTPROPHETS	8	2006
ROOM AT THE TOP ADAM ANT	13	1990
ROOM ELEVEN DAISY CHAINSAW	65	1992
ROOM IN BROOKLYN JOHN SQUIRE	44	2004
ROOM IN YOUR HEART LIVING IN A BOX	5	1989
ROOM ON THE 3RD FLOOR McFLY	5	2004
ROOMS ON FIRE STEVIE NICKS	16	1989
THE ROOT OF ALL EVIL BEAUTIFUL SOUTH	50	2001
ROOTLESS TREE DAMIEN RICE	50	2007
ROOTS SPUNGE	52	2002
ROOTS BLOODY ROOTS SEPULTURA	19	1996
ROSALIE – COWGIRLS' SONG (MEDLEY) THIN LIZZY	20	1978
ROSALYN PRETTY THINGS	41	1964
ROSANNA TOTO	12	1983
THE ROSE [A] MICHAEL BALL	42	1995
THE ROSE [A] HEATHER PEACE	56	2000
THE ROSE [A] WESTLIFE	1	2006
ROSE [B] FEELING	38	2007
ROSE GARDEN LYNN ANDERSON	3	1971
ROSE GARDEN NEW WORLD	15	1971
A ROSE HAS TO DIE DOOLEYS	11	1978
A ROSE IS STILL A ROSE ARETHA FRANKLIN	22	1998
ROSE MARIE SLIM WHITMAN	1	1955
ROSE ROUGE ST GERMAIN	54	2001
ROSEABILITY IDLEWILD	38	2000
ROSES [A] HAYWOODE	11	1985
ROSES [A] RHYTHM-N-BASS	56	1992
ROSES [B] dEUS	56	1997
ROSES [C] OUTKAST	4	2004
ROSES ARE RED [A] RONNIE CARROLL	3	1962
ROSES ARE RED [B] MAC BAND FEATURING THE McCAMPBELL BROTHERS	8	1988
ROSES ARE RED (MY LOVE) BOBBY VINTON	15	1962
ROSES FOR THE DEAD FUNERAL FOR A FRIEND	39	2006
ROSES IN THE HOSPITAL MANIC STREET PREACHERS	15	1993
ROSES OF PICARDY VINCE HILL	13	1967
ROSETTA FAME & PRICE TOGETHER	11	1971
ROSIE [A] DON PARTRIDGE	4	1968
ROSIE [B] JOAN ARMATRADING	49	1980
ROTATION HERB ALPERT	46	1980
ROTTERDAM BEAUTIFUL SOUTH	6	1996
ROUGH BOY ZZ TOP	23	1986
ROUGH BOYS [A] PETE TOWNSHEND	39	1980
ROUGH BOYS [B] NORTHERN UPROAR	41	1995
ROUGH JUSTICE [A] BANANARAMA	23	1984
ROUGH JUSTICE [B] ROLLING STONES	15	2005
ROUGH WITH THE SMOOTH SHARA NELSON	30	1995
ROUGHNECK (EP) PROJECT 1	49	1992
ROULETTE RUSS CONWAY	1	1959
ROUND AND ROUND [A] JIMMY YOUNG	30	1957
ROUND AND ROUND [B] SPANDAU BALLET	18	1984
ROUND AND ROUND [C] JAKI GRAHAM	9	1985
ROUND AND ROUND [D] NEW ORDER	21	1989
ROUND & ROUND [E] HI-TEK FEATURING JONELL	73	2001
ROUND EVERY CORNER PETULA CLARK	43	1965
ROUND HERE [A] COUNTING CROWS	70	1994
ROUND HERE [B] GEORGE MICHAEL	32	2004
ROUND OF BLUES SHAWN COLVIN	73	1994
ROUND ROUND SUGABABES	1	2002
THE ROUSSOS PHENOMENON EP DEMIS ROUSSOS	1	1976
ROUTINE CHECK MITCHELL BROTHERS/ KANO/THE STREETS	42	2005
ROXANNE POLICE	12	1979
ROYAL EVENT RUSS CONWAY	15	1959
ROYAL MILE GERRY RAFFERTY	67	1980
ROY'S KEEN MORRISSEY	42	1997
R.R. EXPRESS ROSE ROYCE	52	1981
RSVP [A] FIVE STAR	45	1985
RSVP [B] JASON DONOVAN	17	1991
RSVP [C] POP WILL EAT ITSELF	27	1993
RUB A DUB DUB EQUALS	34	1970
RUB-A-DUB DOUBLE TROUBLE	66	1991
RUBBER BALL BOBBY VEE	4	1961
RUBBER BALL MARTY WILDE	9	1961
RUBBER BALL AVONS	30	1961
RUBBER BULLETS 10 C.C.	1	1973
RUBBER LOVER MARMADUKE DUKE	12	2009
RUBBERBAND GIRL KATE BUSH	12	1993
THE RUBBERBAND MAN DETROIT SPINNERS	16	1976
RUBBERBANDMAN YELLO	58	1991
RUBBERNECKIN' ELVIS PRESLEY	5	2003
RUBBISH CARTER-THE UNSTOPPABLE SEX MACHINE	14	1992
THE RUBETTES AUTEURS	66	1999
RUBY KAISER CHIEFS	1	2007
RUBY ANN MARTY ROBBINS	24	1963
RUBY DON'T TAKE YOUR LOVE TO TOWN KENNY ROGERS & THE FIRST EDITION	2	1969
RUBY RED [A] SLADE	51	1982
RUBY RED [B] MARC ALMOND	47	1986
RUBY TUESDAY ROLLING STONES	3	1967
RUBY TUESDAY MELANIE	9	1970
RUBY TUESDAY ROD STEWART	11	1993
RUDD IKARA COLT	72	2002
RUDE BOY RIHANNA	2	2010
RUDE BOY ROCK LIONROCK	20	1998
RUDE BUOYS OUTA JAIL SPECIALS	5	1980
RUDEBOX ROBBIE WILLIAMS	4	2006
RUDI GOT MARRIED LAUREL AITKEN & THE UNITONE	60	1980
RUDI'S IN LOVE LOCOMOTIVE	25	1968
RUDY'S ROCK BILL HALEY & HIS COMETS	26	1956
RUFF IN THE JUNGLE BIZNESS PRODIGY	5	1992
RUFF MIX WONDER DOGS	31	1982
RUFFNECK MC LYTE	67	1994
RUGGED AND MEAN, BUTCH AND ON SCREEN PEE BEE SQUAD	52	1985
RUINED IN A DAY NEW ORDER	22	1993
RULE THE WORLD TAKE THAT	2	2007
RULES AND REGULATIONS WE'VE GOT A FUZZBOX & WE'RE GONNA USE IT	41	1986
RULES OF THE GAME BUCKS FIZZ	57	1983
RUMBLE IN THE JUNGLE FUGEES	3	1997
RUMORS TIMEX SOCIAL CLUB	13	1986
RUMOUR HAS IT DONNA SUMMER	19	1978
RUMOURS [A] HOT CHOCOLATE	44	1973
RUMOURS [B] AWESOME	58	1997
RUMOURS [C] DAMAGE	22	2000
RUMP SHAKER WRECKS-N-EFFECT	24	1992
RUN [A] SANDIE SHAW	32	1966
RUN [B] SPIRITUALIZED	59	1991
RUN [C] LIGHTHOUSE FAMILY	30	2002
RUN [D] SNOW PATROL	5	2004
RUN [D] LEONA LEWIS	1	2008
RUN [D] AMERITZ	52	2008
RUN [E] GNARLS BARKLEY	32	2008
RUN [F] AMY MacDONALD	75	2008
RUN AWAY [A] 10 C.C.	50	1982
RUN AWAY [B] (MC SAR &) THE REAL McCOY	6	1995
RUN AWAY (I WANNA BE WITH U) NIVEA	48	2002
RUN BABY RUN [A] NEWBEATS	10	1971
RUN, BABY, RUN [B] SHERYL CROW	24	1995
RUN BACK CARL DOUGLAS	25	1977
RUN FOR COVER SUGABABES	13	2001
RUN FOR HOME LINDISFARNE	10	1978
RUN FOR YOUR LIFE [A] BUCKS FIZZ	14	1983
RUN FOR YOUR LIFE [B] NORTHERN LINE	18	1999
RUN FROM LOVE JIMMY SOMERVILLE	52	1991
RUN IT! CHRIS BROWN FEATURING JUELZ SANTANA	2	2006
RUN ON MOBY	33	1999
RUN RUDOLPH RUN CHUCK BERRY	36	1963
RUN RUN AWAY SLADE	7	1984
RUN RUN RUN [A] JO JO GUNNE	6	1972
RUN RUN RUN [B] PHOENIX	66	2004
RUN SILENT SHAKESPEAR'S SISTER	54	1989
RUN THE SHOW KAT DELUNA FEATURING BUSTA RHYMES	41	2008
RUN THIS TOWN JAY-Z FEATURING RIHANNA AND KANYE WEST	1	2009
RUN TO HIM BOBBY VEE	6	1961
RUN TO ME BEE GEES	9	1972
RUN TO MY LOVIN' ARMS BILLY FURY	25	1965
RUN TO THE DOOR CLINTON FORD	25	1967
RUN TO THE HILLS IRON MAIDEN	7	1982
RUN TO THE SUN ERASURE	6	1994
RUN TO YOU [A] BRYAN ADAMS	11	1985
RUN TO YOU [A] RAGE	3	1992
RUN TO YOU [B] WHITNEY HOUSTON	15	1993
RUN TO YOU [C] ROXETTE	27	1994
RUN 2 NEW ORDER	49	1989
RUNAGROUND JAMES	29	1998
RUNAROUND MARTHA WASH	49	1993
RUNAROUND SUE DION	11	1961
RUNAROUND SUE DOUG SHELDON	36	1961
RUNAROUND SUE RACEY	13	1980
RUNAWAY [A] DEL SHANNON	1	1961
THE RUNAWAY [B] ELKIE BROOKS	50	1979
RUNAWAY [C] DEEE-LITE	45	1992
RUNAWAY [D] JANET JACKSON	6	1995
RUNAWAY [E] CORRS	2	1996
RUNAWAY [F] E'VOKE	30	1995
RUNAWAY [G] NUYORICAN SOUL FEATURING INDIA	24	1997
RUNAWAY [H] JAMIROQUAI	18	2006
RUNAWAY BOYS STRAY CATS	9	1980
RUNAWAY GIRL STERLING VOID	53	1989
RUNAWAY HORSES BELINDA CARLISLE	40	1990
RUNAWAY LOVE EN VOGUE	36	1993
RUNAWAY LOVE LUDACRIS FEATURING MARY J. BLIGE	52	2007
RUNAWAY SKIES CELETIA	66	1998
RUNAWAY TRAIN [A] ELTON JOHN & ERIC CLAPTON	31	1992
RUNAWAY TRAIN [B] SOUL ASYLUM	7	1993
THE RUNNER THREE DEGREES	10	1979
RUNNIN [A] BASSTOY	62	2000
RUNNIN' [B] BASS BUMPERS	68	1993
RUNNIN' [C] 2PAC & THE NOTORIOUS B.I.G.	15	1998
RUNNIN' [D] PHARCYDE	36	1996
RUNNIN' [E] MARK PICCHIOTTI PRESENTS BASSTOY	13	2002

Title / Artist	Peak Position	Year of Release
RUNNIN' [F] DOMAN & GOODING	56	2009
RUNNIN' AWAY SLY & THE FAMILY STONE	17	1972
RUNNIN' AWAY NICOLE	69	1996
RUNNIN' DOWN A DREAM TOM PETTY	55	1989
RUNNIN' (DYIN' TO LIVE) 2PAC & THE NOTORIOUS B.I.G.	17	2004
RUNNIN' FOR THE RED LIGHT (I GOTTA LIFE) MEAT LOAF	21	1996
RUNNIN' WITH THE DEVIL VAN HALEN	52	1980
RUNNING ALL OVER THE WORLD STATUS QUO	17	1988
RUNNING AROUND TOWN BILLIE RAY MARTIN	29	1995
RUNNING BEAR JOHNNY PRESTON	1	1960
RUNNING FREE IRON MAIDEN	19	1980
RUNNING FROM PARADISE DARYL HALL & JOHN OATES	41	1980
RUNNING IN THE FAMILY LEVEL 42	6	1987
RUNNING OUT OF TIME DIGITAL ORGASM	16	1991
RUNNING SCARED ROY ORBISON	9	1961
RUNNING UP THAT HILL KATE BUSH	3	1985
RUNNING UP THAT HILL PLACEBO	44	2007
RUNNING WITH THE NIGHT LIONEL RICHIE	9	1984
RUN'S HOUSE RUN DMC	37	1988
RUPERT JACKIE LEE	14	1971
THE RUSH [A] LUTHER VANDROSS	53	1992
RUSH [B] FREAKPOWER	62	1994
RUSH [C] KLESHAY	19	1999
RUSH HOUR [A] JANE WIEDLIN	12	1988
RUSH HOUR [A] JOYRIDER	22	1996
RUSH HOUR [B] BAD COMPANY	59	2002
RUSH RUSH PAULA ABDUL	6	1989
RUSH SONG A	35	2005
RUSHES DARIUS	5	2002
RUSHING LONI CLARK	37	1993
RUSSIAN ROULETTE RIHANNA	2	2009
RUSSIANS STING	12	1985
RUST ECHO & THE BUNNYMEN	22	1999
RUSTY CAGE SOUNDGARDEN	41	1992

S

Title / Artist	Peak Position	Year of Release
S CLUB PARTY S CLUB 7	2	1999
SABOTAGE BEASTIE BOYS	19	1994
SABRE DANCE LOVE SCULPTURE	5	1968
SACRAMENTO MIDDLE OF THE ROAD	23	1972
SACRED CYCLES PETER LAZONBY	49	2000
SACRED TRUST ONE TRUE VOICE	2	2002
THE SACREMENT H.I.M.	23	2003
SACRIFICE ELTON JOHN	1	1989
SAD AND LONELY SECRET MACHINES	38	2005
SAD BUT TRUE METALLICA	20	1993
SAD EYES ROBERT JOHN	31	1979
SAD MOVIES (MAKE ME CRY) CAROL DEENE	44	1961
SAD MOVIES (MAKE ME CRY) SUE THOMPSON	46	1965
SAD SONGS (SAY SO MUCH) ELTON JOHN	7	1984
SAD SWEET DREAMER SWEET SENSATION	1	1974
SADDLE UP DAVID CHRISTIE	9	1982
SADIE'S SHAWL FRANK CORDELL	29	1956
SADNESS PART 1 ENIGMA	1	1990
SAFARI (EP) BREEDERS	69	1992
SAFE FROM HARM [A] MASSIVE ATTACK	25	1991
SAFE FROM HARM [B] NARCOTIC THRUST	24	2002
THE SAFETY DANCE MEN WITHOUT HATS	6	1983
SAFFRON EASTERN LANE	55	2004
SAID I LOVED YOU BUT I LIED MICHAEL BOLTON	15	1993
SAID IT ALL TAKE THAT	48	2009
SAID SHE WAS A DANCER JETHRO TULL	55	1988
SAIL AWAY [A] LITTLE ANGELS	45	1993
SAIL AWAY [B] URBAN COOKIE COLLECTIVE	18	1994
SAIL AWAY [C] DAVID GRAY	26	2001
SAIL ON COMMODORES	8	1979
SAILING [A] ROD STEWART	1	1975
SAILING [B] CHRISTOPHER CROSS	48	1981
SAILING OFF THE EDGE OF THE WORLD STRAW	52	2001
SAILING ON THE SEVEN SEAS ORCHESTRAL MANOEUVRES IN THE DARK	3	1991
SAILOR PETULA CLARK	1	1961
SAILOR ANNE SHELTON	10	1961
SAILORTOWN ENERGY ORCHARD	73	1990
THE SAINT [A] THOMPSON TWINS	53	1992
THE SAINT [B] ORBITAL	3	1997
ST ANGER METALLICA	9	2003
ST ELMO'S FIRE (MAN IN MOTION) JOHN PARR	6	1985
SAINT OF ME ROLLING STONES	26	1998
ST PETERSBURG SUPERGRASS	22	2005
ST TERESA JOAN OSBORNE	33	1996
ST. THERESE OF THE ROSES MALCOLM VAUGHAN	3	1956
ST VALENTINE'S DAY MASSACRE EP MOTORHEAD & GIRLSCHOOL	5	1981
THE SAINTS ARE COMING SKIDS	48	1978
THE SAINTS ARE COMING U2 & GREEN DAY	2	2006
THE SAINTS ROCK 'N' ROLL BILL HALEY & HIS COMETS	5	1956
SALE OF THE CENTURY SLEEPER	10	1996
SALLY [A] GERRY MONROE	4	1970
SALLY [B] CARMEL	60	1986
SALLY [C] KERBDOG	69	1996
SALLY ANN JOE BROWN & THE BRUVVERS	28	1963
SALLY CINNAMON STONE ROSES	46	1990
SALLY DON'T YOU GRIEVE LONNIE DONEGAN	11	1958
SALLY MACLENNANE POGUES	51	1985
SALMON DANCE CHEMICAL BROTHERS	27	2007
SAL'S GOT A SUGAR LIP LONNIE DONEGAN	13	1959
SALSA HOUSE RICHIE RICH	50	1989
SALSOUL NUGGET (IF U WANNA) M&S PRESENTS GIRL NEXT DOOR	6	2001
SALT IN THE WOUND CARPET BOMBERS FOR PEACE	67	2003
SALT SWEAT SUGAR JIMMY EAT WORLD	60	2001
THE SALT WOUND ROUTINE THIRTEEN SENSES	45	2005
SALTWATER [A] JULIAN LENNON	6	1991
SALTWATER [B] CHICANE FEATURING MAIRE BRENNAN OF CLANNAD	6	1999
SALTY DYLAN RHYMES FEATURING K ELLIS	70	2005
SALTY DOG PROCOL HARUM	44	1969
SALVA MEA (SAVE ME) FAITHLESS	9	1995
SALVATION CRANBERRIES	13	1996
SAM [A] KEITH WEST	38	1967
SAM [B] OLIVIA NEWTON-JOHN	6	1977
SAMANTHA KENNY BALL & HIS JAZZMEN	13	1961
SAMBA DE JANIERO BELLINI	8	1997
SAMBA MAGIC SUMMER DAZE	61	1996
SAMBA PA TI SANTANA	27	1974
SAMBUCA WIDEBOYS FEATURING DENNIS G	15	2001
SAME GIRL R KELLY & USHER	26	2007
SAME JEANS VIEW	3	2007
SAME MAN TILL WEST & DJ DELICIOUS	36	2006
SAME MISTAKE JAMES BLUNT	57	2007
SAME OLD BRAND NEW YOU A1	1	2000
THE SAME OLD SCENE ROXY MUSIC	12	1980
SAME OLD STORY ULTRAVOX	31	1986
SAME PICTURE GOLDRUSH	64	2002
SAME SONG DIGITAL UNDERGROUND	52	1991
SAME TEMPO CHANGING FACES	53	1998
SAME THING IN REVERSE BOY GEORGE	56	1995
SAMSON AND DELILAH [A] MIDDLE OF THE ROAD	26	1972
SAMSON AND DELILAH [B] BAD MANNERS	58	1982
SAN ANTONIO ROSE FLOYD CRAMER	36	1961
SAN BERNADINO CHRISTIE	7	1970
SAN DAMIANO (HEART AND SOUL) SAL SOLO	15	1985
SAN FRANCISCAN NIGHTS ERIC BURDON & THE ANIMALS	7	1967
SAN FRANCISCO (BE SURE TO WEAR SOME FLOWERS IN YOUR HAIR) SCOTT McKENZIE	1	1967
SAN FRANCISCO DAYS CHRIS ISAAK	62	1993
SAN FRANCISCO (YOU'VE GOT ME) VILLAGE PEOPLE	45	1977
SAN MIGUEL LONNIE DONEGAN	19	1959
SAN MIGUEL KINGSTON TRIO	29	1959
SANCTIFIED LADY MARVIN GAYE	51	1985
SANCTIFY YOURSELF SIMPLE MINDS	10	1986
SANCTIMONIOUS HALO	44	2002
SANCTUARY [A] IRON MAIDEN	29	1980
SANCTUARY [B] NEW MUSIK	31	1980
SANCTUARY [C] DEJURE	62	2003
SANCTUS (MISSA LUBA) TROUBADOURS DU ROI BAUDOUIN	28	1969
SAND IN MY SHOES DIDO	29	2004
SANDBLASTED (EP) SWERVEDRIVER	67	1991
SANDCASTLES BOMB THE BASS FEATURING BERNARD FOWLER	54	1995
SANDMAN BLUE BOY	25	1997
SANDS OF TIME KALEEF	26	1998
SANDSTORM [A] CAST	8	1996
SANDSTORM [B] DARUDE	3	2000
SANDWICHES DETROIT GRAND PU BAHS	29	2000
SANDY JOHN TRAVOLTA	2	1978
SANITY KILLING JOKE	70	1986
SANTA BRING MY BABY BACK TO ME ELVIS PRESLEY	7	1957
SANTA CLAUS IS BACK IN TOWN ELVIS PRESLEY	41	1980
SANTA CLAUS IS COMIN' TO TOWN CARPENTERS	37	1975
SANTA CLAUS IS COMIN' TO TOWN BRUCE SPRINGSTEEN	9	1985
SANTA CLAUS IS COMING TO TOWN JACKSON 5	43	1972
SANTA CLAUS IS COMING TO TOWN BJORN AGAIN	55	1992
SANTA CLAUS IS ON THE DOLE SPITTING IMAGE	22	1986
SANTA CRUZ (YOU'RE NOT THAT FAR) THRILLS	33	2003
SANTA MARIA TATJANA	40	1996
SANTA MARIA DJ MILANO FEATURING SAMANTHA FOX	31	1998
SANTA MONICA (WATCH THE WORLD DIE) EVERCLEAR	40	1996
SANTA'S LIST CLIFF RICHARD	5	2003
SANTO NATALE DAVID WHITFIELD	2	1954
SARA [A] FLEETWOOD MAC	37	1980
SARA [B] STARSHIP	66	1986
SARAH THIN LIZZY	24	1979
SARTORIAL ELOQUENCE ELTON JOHN	44	1980
SAT IN YOUR LAP KATE BUSH	11	1981
SATAN ORBITAL	3	1991
SATAN REJECTED MY SOUL MORRISSEY	39	1998
THE SATCH EP JOE SATRIANI	53	1993
SATELLITE [A] HOOTERS	22	1987
SATELLITE [B] BELOVED	19	1996
SATELLITE [C] OCEANLAB	19	2004
SATELLITE KID DOGS D'AMOUR	26	1989
SATELLITE OF LOVE 04 LOU REED	10	2004
SATIN SHEETS BELLAMY BROTHERS	43	1976

Title / Artist	Peak Position	Year of Release
SATISFACTION [A] OTIS REDDING	33	1966
SATISFACTION [A] ARETHA FRANKLIN	37	1967
SATISFACTION [A] VANILLA ICE	22	1991
SATISFACTION [B] WENDY & LISA	27	1989
SATISFACTION [C] EVE	20	2003
SATISFACTION [D] BENNY BENASSI PRESENTS THE BIZ	2	2003
SATISFACTION GUARANTEED (OR TAKE YOUR LOVE BACK) HAROLD MELVIN & THE BLUENOTES	32	1974
SATISFIED RICHARD MARX	52	1989
SATISFIED (TAKE ME HIGHER) H20	66	1997
SATISFY MY LOVE [A] EXOTERIX	62	1994
SATISFY MY LOVE [B] SABRINA JOHNSTON	62	1994
SATISFY MY LOVE [C] PESHAY VERSUS FLYTRONIX	67	2002
SATISFY MY SOUL BOB MARLEY & THE WAILERS	21	1978
SATISFY YOU PUFF DADDY FEATURING R KELLY	8	2000
SATURDAY [A] JOEY NEGRO FEATURING TAKA BOOM	41	2000
SATURDAY [B] OMAR	43	1994
SATURDAY [C] EAST 57TH STREET FEATURING DONNAL ALLEN	29	1997
SATURDAY GIGS MOTT THE HOOPLE	41	1974
SATURDAY LOVE CHERRELLE WITH ALEXANDER O'NEAL	6	1985
SATURDAY LOVE ILLEGAL MOTION FEATURING SIMONE CHAPMAN	67	1993
SATURDAY NIGHT [A] T-CONNECTION	41	1979
SATURDAY NIGHT [B] BLUE NILE	50	1991
SATURDAY NIGHT [C] WHIGFIELD	1	1994
SATURDAY NIGHT [C] SINDY	70	1996
SATURDAY NIGHT [D] SUEDE	6	1997
SATURDAY NIGHT [E] UD PROJECT	19	2004
SATURDAY NIGHT AT THE MOVIES DRIFTERS	3	1972
SATURDAY NIGHT AT THE MOVIES ROBSON & JEROME	1	1996
SATURDAY NIGHT (BENEATH THE PLASTIC PALM TREES) LEYTON BUZZARDS	53	1979
SATURDAY NIGHT PARTY (READ MY LIPS) ALEX PARTY	29	1993
SATURDAY NIGHT SUNDAY MORNING T-EMPO	19	1994
SATURDAY NIGHT'S ALRIGHT FOR FIGHTING ELTON JOHN	7	1973
SATURDAY NITE [A] EARTH, WIND & FIRE	17	1977
SATURDAY NITE [B] BRAND NEW HEAVIES	35	1999
SATURDAY NITE AT THE DUCK POND COUGARS	33	1963
SATURDAY (OOOH OOOH) LUDACRIS	31	2002
SATURDAY SUPERHOUSE BIFFY CLYRO	13	2007
SATURDAY'S NOT WHAT IT USED TO BE KINGMAKER	63	1993
SATURN 5 INSPIRAL CARPETS	20	1994
THE SAVAGE SHADOWS	10	1961
SAVANNA DANCE DEEP FOREST	28	1994
SAVE A LITTLE BIT GLEN GOLDSMITH	73	1988
SAVE A PRAYER DURAN DURAN	2	1982
SAVE A PRAYER 56K FEATURING BEJAY	46	2003
SAVE IT FOR LATER BEAT	47	1982
SAVE IT 'TIL THE MOURNING AFTER SHUT UP & DANCE	25	1995
SAVE ME [A] DAVE DEE, DOZY, BEAKY, MICK & TICH	3	1966
SAVE ME [B] SILVER CONVENTION	30	1975
SAVE ME [C] QUEEN	11	1980
SAVE ME [D] FLEETWOOD MAC	53	1990
SAVE ME [E] BIG COUNTRY	41	1990
SAVE ME [F] EMBRACE	29	2000
SAVE ME [G] MEEKER	60	2000
SAVE ME [H] REMY ZERO	55	2002
SAVE ME [I] DARREN STYLES	70	2007
SAVE MYSELF WILLY MASON	42	2007
SAVE OUR LOVE ETERNAL	8	1994
SAVE THE BEST FOR LAST VANESSA WILLIAMS	3	1992
SAVE THE CHILDREN MARVIN GAYE	41	1971
SAVE THE LAST DANCE FOR ME DRIFTERS	2	1960
SAVE THE LAST DANCE FOR ME BEN E. KING	69	1987
SAVE THE LAST DANCE FOR ME GENERAL SAINT FEATURING DON CAMPBELL	75	1994
SAVE THE LIES (GOOD TO ME) GABRIELLA CILMI	33	2008
SAVE THE WORLD GET THE GIRL KING BLUES	68	2009
SAVE TONIGHT EAGLE-EYE CHERRY	6	1998
SAVE UP ALL YOUR TEARS CHER	37	1991
SAVE US [A] PHILIP JAP	53	1982
SAVE US [B] FEEDER	34	2006
SAVE YOUR KISSES FOR ME BROTHERHOOD OF MAN	1	1976
SAVE YOUR LOVE RENEE & RENATO	1	1982
SAVE YOUR LOVE (FOR NUMBER 1) RENE & ANGELA FEATURING KURTIS BLOW	66	1985
SAVE YOURSELF SPEEDWAY	10	2003
SAVED [A] MR ROY	24	1995
SAVED [B] OCTOPUS	40	1996
SAVED BY THE BELL ROBIN GIBB	2	1969
SAVED MY LIFE LIL' LOUIS & THE WORLD	74	1992
SAVING ALL MY LOVE FOR YOU WHITNEY HOUSTON	1	1985
SAVING FOREVER FOR YOU SHANICE	42	1993
SAVING MY FACE KT TUNSTALL	50	2007
SAVIOUR'S DAY CLIFF RICHARD	1	1990
SAXUALITY CANDY DULFER	60	1990
SAXY LADY QUIVVER	56	1994
SAY CREATURES	72	1999
SAY A LITTLE PRAYER BOMB THE BASS FEATURING MAUREEN	10	1988
SAY A PRAYER TAYLOR DAYNE	58	1995
SAY (ALL I NEED) ONEREPUBLIC	51	2008
SAY CHEESE (SMILE PLEASE) FAST FOOD ROCKERS	10	2003
SAY GOODBYE S CLUB	2	2003
SAY, HAS ANYBODY SEEN MY SWEET GYPSY ROSE DAWN FEATURING TONY ORLANDO	12	1973
SAY HELLO DEEP DISH	14	2005
SAY HELLO TO THE ANGELS INTERPOL	65	2003
SAY HELLO WAVE GOODBYE SOFT CELL	3	1982
SAY HELLO WAVE GOODBYE DAVID GRAY	26	2002
SAY HOW I FEEL RHIAN BENSON	27	2004
SAY I CHRISTINA MILIAN FEATURING YOUNG JEEZY	4	2006
SAY I WON'T BE THERE SPRINGFIELDS	5	1963
SAY...IF YOU FEEL ALRIGHT CRYSTAL WATERS	45	1997
SAY I'M YOUR NO. 1 PRINCESS	7	1985
SAY IT [A] ABC	42	1992
SAY IT [B] MARIA RUBIA	40	2001
SAY IT [C] BOOTY LUV	16	2009
SAY IT AGAIN [A] JERMAINE STEWART	7	1988
SAY IT AGAIN [B] PRECIOUS	6	1999
SAY IT AIN'T SO WEEZER	37	1995
SAY IT ISN'T SO [A] DARYL HALL & JOHN OATES	69	1983
SAY IT ISN'T SO [B] BON JOVI	10	2000
SAY IT ISN'T SO [C] GARETH GATES	4	2003
SAY IT ONCE ULTRA	16	1998
SAY IT RIGHT NELLY FURTADO	10	2007
SAY IT WITH FLOWERS DOROTHY SQUIRES & RUSS CONWAY	23	1961
SAY IT WITH PRIDE SCOTLAND WORLD CUP SQUAD	45	1990
SAY IT'S OVER N-DUBZ	40	2010
SAY JUST WORDS PARADISE LOST	53	1997
SAY MY NAME [A] ZEE	36	1997
SAY MY NAME [B] DESTINY'S CHILD	3	2000
SAY NO GO DE LA SOUL	18	1989
SAY NOTHIN' OMAR	29	1997
SAY SAY SAY PAUL McCARTNEY & MICHAEL JACKSON	2	1983
SAY SAY SAY (WAITING 4 U) HI_TACK	4	2006
SAY SOMETHIN' MARIAH CAREY	27	2006
SAY SOMETHING [A] JAMES	24	1994
SAY SOMETHING [B] HAVEN	24	2002
SAY SOMETHING ANYWAY BELLEFIRE	26	2004
SAY THAT YOU'RE HERE FRAGMA	25	2001
SAY WHAT! X-PRESS 2	32	1993
SAY WHAT YOU WANT TEXAS	3	1997
SAY WHEN LENE LOVICH	19	1979
SAY WONDERFUL THINGS RONNIE CARROLL	6	1963
SAY YEAH [A] LIMIT	17	1985
SAY YEAH [B] BULLETPROOF	40	2001
SAY YES BLOOD ARM	52	2005
SAY YOU DO ULTRA	11	1998
SAY YOU DON'T MIND COLIN BLUNSTONE	15	1972
SAY YOU LOVE ME [A] FLEETWOOD MAC	40	1976
SAY YOU LOVE ME [B] SIMPLY RED	7	1998
SAY YOU LOVE ME [C] JOHNSON	56	1999
SAY YOU REALLY WANT ME KIM WILDE	29	1987
SAY YOU, SAY ME LIONEL RICHIE	8	1985
SAY YOU WILL FOREIGNER	71	1987
SAY YOU'LL BE MINE [A] AMY GRANT	41	1994
SAY YOU'LL BE MINE [B] STEPS	4	1999
SAY YOU'LL BE MINE [C] QFX	34	1999
SAY YOU'LL BE THERE SPICE GIRLS	1	1996
SAY YOU'LL STAY UNTIL TOMORROW TOM JONES	40	1977
SAY YOU'RE MINE AGAIN JUNE HUTTON & AXEL STORDAHL & THE BOYS NEXT DOOR	6	1953
(SAY) YOU'RE MY GIRL ROY ORBISON	23	1965
SAY YOU'RE WRONG JULIAN LENNON	75	1985
SCALES OF JUSTICE LIVING IN A BOX	30	1987
SCANDAL QUEEN	25	1989
SCANDALOUS [A] CLICK	54	1996
SCANDALOUS [B] MIS-TEEQ	2	2003
SCAR TISSUE RED HOT CHILI PEPPERS	15	1999
SCARECROW SUB FOCUS	60	2005
SCARED SLACKER	36	1997
SCARLET ALL ABOUT EVE	34	1990
SCARLET RIBBONS HARRY BELAFONTE	18	1957
SCARLETT O'HARA JET HARRIS & TONY MEEHAN	2	1963
SCARS WITNESS	71	1999
SCARY MONSTERS (AND SUPER CREEPS) DAVID BOWIE	20	1981
SCARY MOVIES BAD MEETS EVIL FEATURING EMINEM & ROYCE DA 5'9"	63	2001
THE SCARY-GO-ROUND EP JELLYFISH	49	1991
SCATMAN (SKI-BA-BOP-BA-DOP-BOP) SCATMAN JOHN	3	1995
SCATMAN'S WORLD SCATMAN JOHN	10	1995
SCATTER & SWING LIONROCK	54	1998
SCATTERLINGS OF AFRICA JULUKA	44	1983
SCATTERLINGS OF AFRICA JOHNNY CLEGG & SAVUKA	75	1987
SCHEME EUGENE RED LIGHT COMPANY	69	2008
SCHEMING MAXIM	53	2000
SCHMOO SPOOKY	72	1993
SCHNAPPI SCHNAPPI	32	2005
SCHONEBERG MARMION	53	1996
SCHOOL DAY CHUCK BERRY	24	1957
SCHOOL DAY (RING! RING! GOES THE BELL) DON LANG & HIS FRANTIC FIVE	26	1957
SCHOOL LOVE BARRY BLUE	11	1974
SCHOOL OF ROCK SCHOOL OF ROCK	51	2004
SCHOOL'S OUT ALICE COOPER	1	1972

Title / Artist	Peak Position	Year of Release
SCHOOL'S OUT DAPHNE & CELESTE	12	2000
SCHOOLTIME CHRONICLE SMILEY CULTURE	59	1986
SCHTEEVE YOURCODENAMEIS:MILO	58	2004
SCIENCE OF SILENCE RICHARD ASHCROFT	14	2002
THE SCIENTIST COLDPLAY	10	2002
SCOOBY DOO [A] DWEEB	63	1997
SCOOBY DOO [B] J MAJIK & WICKAMAN	67	2004
SCOOBY SNACKS FUN LOVIN' CRIMINALS	22	1996
SCOPE PARIS ANGELS	75	1990
SCORCHIO SASHA/EMERSON	23	2000
SCORPIO RISING DEATH IN VEGAS FEATURING LIAM GALLAGHER	14	2002
SCOTCH ON THE ROCKS BAND OF THE BLACK WATCH	8	1975
SCOTLAND BE GOOD TARTAN ARMY	54	1998
SCOTLAND FOREVER SIDNEY DEVINE	48	1978
SCOTLAND SCOTLAND JASON SCOTLAND TRINIDAD & TOBAGO TARTAN ARMY	30	2006
SCOTS MACHINE VOYAGE	13	1978
SCOTTISH RAIN SILENCERS	71	1989
A SCOTTISH SOLDIER ANDY STEWART	19	1961
SCRAMBLED EGGS RONI SIZE	57	2002
THE SCRATCH SURFACE NOISE	26	1980
SCREAM [A] DISCO ANTHEM	47	1994
SCREAM [B] MICHAEL JACKSON & JANET JACKSON	3	1995
SCREAM [C] NUT	43	1997
SCREAM [D] TIMBALAND FEATURING KERI HILSON & NICOLE SCHERZINGER	12	2008
SCREAM AIM FIRE BULLET FOR MY VALENTINE	34	2008
SCREAM IF YOU WANNA GO FASTER GERI HALLIWELL	8	2001
SCREAM (PRIMAL SCREAM) MANTRONIX	46	1987
SCREAM UNTIL YOU LIKE IT W.A.S.P.	32	1987
THE SCREAMER YOSH PRESENTS LOVEDEEJAY AKEMI	38	1996
SCULLERY CLIFFORD T WARD	37	1974
SE A VIDA E (THAT'S THE WAY LIFE IS) PET SHOP BOYS	8	1996
SEA OF BLUE TECHNATION	56	2001
SEA OF HEARTBREAK DON GIBSON	14	1961
SEA OF LOVE MARTY WILDE	3	1959
SEA OF LOVE HONEYDRIPPERS	56	1985
SEA OF TROUBLE CORD	50	2006
SEA SPRAY PAUL WELLER	59	2008
SEAGULL RAINBOW COTTAGE	33	1976
THE SEAGULL'S NAME WAS NELSON PETER E BENNETT WITH THE CO-OPERATION CHOIR	45	1970
SEAL MY FATE BELLY	35	1995
SEAL OUR FATE GLORIA ESTEFAN	24	1991
SEALED WITH A KISS BRIAN HYLAND	3	1962
SEALED WITH A KISS JASON DONOVAN	1	1989
SEANCE NEBULA II	55	1992
SEARCH AND DESTORY DICTATORS	49	1977
SEARCH FOR THE HERO M PEOPLE	9	1995
SEARCHIN' COASTERS	30	1957
SEARCHIN' HOLLIES	12	1963
SEARCHIN' FOR MY RIZLA RATPACK	58	1992
SEARCHIN' (I GOTTA FIND A MAN) HAZELL DEAN	6	1984
SEARCHIN' MY SOUL VONDA SHEPARD	10	1998
SEARCHING [A] CHANGE	11	1980
SEARCHING [B] CHINA BLACK	4	1994
SEARCHING [C] JAMIE SCOTT	33	2005
SEARCHING FOR A SOUL CONNOR REEVES	28	1998
SEARCHING FOR THE GOLDEN EYE MOTIV 8 & KYM MAZELLE	40	1995
SEASIDE ORDINARY BOYS	27	2004
SEASIDE SHUFFLE TERRY DACTYL & THE DINOSAURS	2	1972
SEASON NO. 5 BEDLAM AGO GO	57	1998
SEASONS IN THE ABYSS SLAYER	51	1991
SEASONS IN THE SUN TERRY JACKS	1	1974
SEASONS IN THE SUN WESTLIFE	1	1999
SEASONS OF GOLD GIDEA PARK	28	1981
SEASONSTREAM (EP) THOUSAND YARD STARE	65	1991
SEATTLE PUBLIC IMAGE LTD	47	1987
2ND AMENDMENT EASYWORLD	42	2003
SECOND CHANCE [A] PHILLIP LEO	57	1994
SECOND CHANCE [B] SHINEDOWN	74	2009
SECOND HAND ROSE BARBRA STREISAND	14	1966
THE SECOND LINE CLINIC	56	2000
SECOND, MINUTE OR HOUR JACK PENATE	17	2007
SECOND NATURE [A] DAN HARTMAN	66	1985
SECOND NATURE [B] ELECTRONIC	35	1997
SECOND ROUND KO CANIBUS	35	1998
THE SECOND SUMMER OF LOVE DANNY WILSON	23	1989
THE SECOND TIME KIM WILDE	29	1984
THE SECOND TIME AROUND SHALAMAR	45	1979
THE SECOND TIME (THEME FROM 'BILITIS') ELAINE PAIGE	69	1987
SECRET [A] ORCHESTRAL MANOEUVRES IN THE DARK	34	1985
SECRET [B] MADONNA	5	1994
SECRET AGENT MAN – JAMES BOND IS BACK BRUCE WILLIS	43	1987
SECRET COMBINATION [A] RANDY CRAWFORD	48	1981
SECRET COMBINATION [B] KALOMOIRA	71	2008
SECRET GARDEN [A] T'PAU	18	1988
SECRET GARDEN [B] QUINCY JONES FEATURING AL B SURE!, JAMES INGRAM, EL DeBARGE & BARRY WHITE	67	1990
SECRET GARDEN [C] BRUCE SPRINGSTEEN	17	1995
SECRET HEART TIGHT FIT	41	1982
SECRET KISS CORAL	25	2003
SECRET LOVE [A] DORIS DAY	1	1954
SECRET LOVE [A] KATHY KIRBY	4	1963
SECRET LOVE [A] DANIEL O'DONNELL & MARY DUFF	28	1995
SECRET LOVE [B] BEE GEES	5	1991
SECRET LOVE [C] DANNI'ELLE GAHA	41	1993
SECRET LOVE [D] SHAH	69	1998
SECRET LOVE [E] KELLY PRICE	26	1999
SECRET LOVERS ATLANTIC STARR	10	1986
SECRET MESSAGES ELECTRIC LIGHT ORCHESTRA	48	1983
SECRET RENDEZVOUS [A] RENE & ANGELA	54	1985
SECRET RENDEZVOUS [B] KARYN WHITE	22	1989
SECRET SMILE SEMISONIC	13	1999
SECRET STAR HOUSE OF ZEKKARIYAS AKA WOMACK & WOMACK	46	1994
SECRET SUNDAY LOVER ALI LOVE	45	2007
THE SECRET VAMPIRE SOUNDTRACK EP BIS	25	1996
SECRETLY SKUNK ANANSIE	16	1999
SECRETS [A] SUTHERLAND BROTHERS & QUIVER	35	1976
SECRETS [B] FIAT LUX	65	1984
SECRETS [C] PRIMITIVES	49	1989
SECRETS [D] SUNSCREEM	36	1996
SECRETS [E] ETERNAL	9	1996
SECRETS [F] MUTINY UK	47	2001
SECRETS IN THE STREET NILS LOFGREN	53	1985
SECRETS (OF SUCCESS) COOKIE CREW FEATURING DANNY D	53	1991
SECRETS OF THE HEART CHESNEY HAWKES	57	1991
THE SECRETS THAT YOU KEEP MUD	3	1975
THE SEDUCTION (LOVE THEME) JAMES LAST BAND	48	1980
SEE A BRIGHTER DAY JTQ WITH NOEL McKOY	49	1993
SEE EMILY PLAY PINK FLOYD	6	1967
SEE IT IN A BOY'S EYES JAMELIA	5	2004
SEE IT LIKE A BABY MARILLION	45	2007
SEE JUNGLE (JUNGLE BOY) BOW WOW WOW	45	1982
SEE LINE WOMAN '99 SONGSTRESS	64	1999
SEE ME LUTHER VANDROSS	60	1987
SEE MY BABY JIVE WIZZARD	1	1973
SEE MY FRIEND KINKS	10	1965
SEE THAT GLOW THIS ISLAND EARTH	47	1985
SEE THE DAY DEE C LEE	3	1985
SEE THE DAY GIRLS ALOUD	9	2006
SEE THE LIGHT PARADISE	73	2005
SEE THE LIGHTS SIMPLE MINDS	20	1991
SEE THE STAR DELIRIOUS?	16	1999
SEE THOSE EYES ALTERED IMAGES	11	1982
SEE THRU IT APHRODITE FEATURING WILDFLOWER	68	2002
SEE WANT MUST HAVE BLUE MERCEDES	57	1988
SEE YA ATOMIC KITTEN	6	2000
SEE YOU DEPECHE MODE	6	1982
SEE YOU AGAIN MILEY CYRUS	11	2008
SEE YOU LATER REGENTS	55	1980
SEE YOU LATER ALLIGATOR BILL HALEY & HIS COMETS	7	1956
THE SEED (2.0) ROOTS FEATURING CODY CHESTNUTT	33	2003
SEEING THINGS BLACK CROWES	72	1991
THE SEEKER WHO	19	1970
SEEMS FINE CONCRETES	52	2004
SEEN THE LIGHT SUPERGRASS	22	2003
SEETHER VERUCA SALT	61	1994
SEIZE THE DAY F.K.W.	45	1993
SELA LIONEL RICHIE	43	1987
SELECTA (URBAN HEROES) JAMESON & VIPER	51	2002
SELF! FUZZBOX	24	1989
SELF CONTROL LAURA BRANIGAN	5	1984
SELF CONTROL INFERNAL	18	2006
SELF DESTRUCTION STOP THE VIOLENCE	75	1989
SELF ESTEEM OFFSPRING	37	1995
SELF SUICIDE GOLDIE LOOKIN CHAIN	32	2004
SELFISH OTHER TWO	46	1993
SELFISH JEAN TRAVIS	30	2007
SELFISH WAYS DOGS	45	2005
SELLING JESUS SKUNK ANANSIE	46	1995
SELLING THE DRAMA LIVE	30	1995
SEMI-CHARMED LIFE THIRD EYE BLIND	33	1997
SEMI-DETACHED SUBURBAN MR JAMES MANFRED MANN	2	1966
SEND HIS LOVE TO ME PJ HARVEY	34	1995
SEND IN THE BOYS MILBURN	22	2006
SEND IN THE CLOWNS JUDY COLLINS	6	1975
SEND ME AN ANGEL [A] BLACKFOOT	66	1983
SEND ME AN ANGEL [B] SCORPIONS	27	1991
SEND ME THE PILLOW YOU DREAM ON JOHNNY TILLOTSON	21	1962
SEND MY HEART ADVENTURES	62	1984
SEND ONE YOUR LOVE STEVIE WONDER	52	1979
SEND YOUR LOVE STING	30	2003
SENDING OUT AN S.O.S. RETTA YOUNG	28	1975
SENORITA JUSTIN TIMBERLAKE	13	2003
SENSATION ELECTROSET	69	1995
SENSATIONAL MICHELLE GAYLE	14	1997
SENSE LIGHTNING SEEDS	31	1992
SENSE TERRY HALL	54	1994
SENSE OF DANGER PRESENCE FEATURING SHARA NELSON	61	1998
SENSES WORKING OVERTIME XTC	10	1982
SENSITIVITY [A] RALPH TRESVANT	18	1991
SENSITIVITY [B] SHAPESHIFTERS & CHIC	40	2006
SENSITIZE THAT PETROL EMOTION	55	1991
SENSUAL SEDUCTION SNOOP DOGG	24	2008
SENSUAL SOPHIS-TI-CAT/THE PLAYER CARL COX	25	1996

	Peak Position	Year of Release
THE SENSUAL WORLD KATE BUSH	12	1989
SENSUALITY LOVESTATION	16	1998
SENTIMENTAL [A] ALEXANDER O'NEAL	53	1992
SENTIMENTAL [B] DEBORAH COX	34	1995
SENTIMENTAL [C] KYM MARSH	35	2003
SENTIMENTAL FOOL LLOYD COLE	73	1995
SENTINEL MIKE OLDFIELD	10	1992
SENZA UNA DONNA (WITHOUT A WOMAN) ZUCCHERO & PAUL YOUNG	4	1991
SEPARATE LIVES PHIL COLLINS & MARILYN MARTIN	4	1985
SEPARATE TABLES CHRIS DE BURGH	30	1992
SEPARATE WAYS GARY MOORE	59	1992
SEPTEMBER EARTH, WIND & FIRE	3	1978
SEPTEMBER IN THE RAIN DINAH WASHINGTON	35	1961
SEPTEMBER SONG IAN McCULLOCH	51	1984
SERENADE [A] MARIO LANZA	15	1955
SERENADE [B] SLIM WHITMAN	8	1956
SERENADE [B] MARIO LANZA	25	1956
SERENADE [C] SHADES	75	1997
SERENATA SARAH VAUGHAN	37	1961
SERENITY ARMIN VAN BUUREN	72	2005
SERENITY IN MURDER SLAYER	50	1995
SERIOUS [A] BILLY GRIFFIN	64	1984
SERIOUS [B] SERIOUS INTENTION	51	1986
SERIOUS [C] DEJA	75	1987
SERIOUS [D] DONNA ALLEN	8	1987
SERIOUS [E] DURAN DURAN	48	1990
SERIOUS [F] MAXWELL D	38	2001
SERIOUS [G] POP!	16	2005
SERIOUS MIX MIRAGE	42	1987
SERPENTS KISS MISSION	70	1986
SESAME'S TREET SMART E'S	2	1992
SET ADRIFT ON A MEMORY BLISS PM DAWN	3	1991
SET FIRE TO ME WILLIE COLON	41	1986
SET IN STONE BEDROCK	71	1997
SET IT OFF [A] HARLEQUIN 4S/BUNKER KRU	55	1988
SET IT OFF [B] PEACHES	36	2002
SET ME FREE [A] KINKS	9	1965
SET ME FREE [B] JAKI GRAHAM	7	1986
SET ME FREE [C] BRIT PACK	41	2000
SET ME FREE [C] LORENZ	35	2006
SET THE FIRE TO THE THIRD BAR SNOW PATROL FEATURING MARTHA WAINWRIGHT	18	2006
SET THE RECORD STRAIGHT REEF	19	2000
SET THE TONE NATE JAMES	69	2005
SET THEM FREE ASWAD	70	1988
THE SET UP (YOU DON'T KNOW) OBIE TRICE FEATURING NATE DOGG	32	2004
SET YOU FREE N-TRANCE FEATURING KELLY LLORENNA	2	1994
SET YOUR LOVING FREE LISA STANSFIELD	28	1992
SETTING SUN CHEMICAL BROTHERS	1	1996
SETTLE DOWN [A] LILLO THOMAS	66	1985
SETTLE DOWN [B] UNBELIEVABLE TRUTH	46	1998
7 [A] PRINCE & THE NEW POWER GENERATION	27	1992
SEVEN [B] DAVID BOWIE	32	2000
SEVEN AND SEVEN IS (LIVE) ALICE COOPER	62	1982
SEVEN CITIES SOLAR STONE	39	1999
7 COLOURS LOST WITNESS	28	2000
SEVEN DAFFODILS MOJOS	30	1964
SEVEN DAFFODILS CHEROKEES	33	1964
SEVEN DAYS [A] ANNE SHELTON	20	1956
SEVEN DAYS [B] STING	25	1993
SEVEN DAYS [C] MARY J BLIGE FEATURING GEORGE BENSON	22	1998
7 DAYS [D] CRAIG DAVID	1	2000
SEVEN DAYS AND ONE WEEK BBE	3	1996
SEVEN DAYS IN SUNNY JUNE JAMIROQUAI	14	2005
SEVEN DAYS IN THE SUN FEEDER	14	2001

	Peak Position	Year of Release
SEVEN DRUNKEN NIGHTS DUBLINERS	7	1967
SEVEN (EP) JAMES	46	1992
747 KENT	61	1999
747 (STRANGERS IN THE NIGHT) SAXON	13	1980
SEVEN LITTLE GIRLS SITTING IN THE BACK SEAT AVONS	3	1959
SEVEN LITTLE GIRLS SITTING IN THE BACK SEAT PAUL EVANS & THE CURLS	25	1959
SEVEN LITTLE GIRLS SITTING IN THE BACKSEAT BOMBALURINA	18	1990
SEVEN LONELY DAYS GISELE MacKENZIE	6	1953
7 NATION ARMY WHITE STRIPES	7	2003
7 O'CLOCK QUIREBOYS	36	1989
SEVEN O'CLOCK NEWS SIMON & GARFUNKEL	30	1991
SEVEN ROOMS OF GLOOM FOUR TOPS	12	1967
SEVEN SEAS ECHO & THE BUNNYMEN	16	1984
SEVEN SEAS OF RHYE QUEEN	10	1974
7 SECONDS YOUSSOU N'DOUR (FEATURING NENEH CHERRY)	3	1994
7:7 EXPANSION SYSTEM 7	39	1993
7-6-5-4-3-2-1 (BLOW YOUR WHISTLE) RIMSHOTS	26	1975
SEVEN TEARS GOOMBAY DANCE BAND	1	1982
7 THINGS MILEY CYRUS	25	2008
7000 DOLLARS AND YOU STYLISTICS	24	1977
7 WAYS TO LOVE COLA BOY	8	1991
7 WEEKS INME	36	2005
SEVEN WONDERS FLEETWOOD MAC	56	1987
7 YEAR BITCH SLADE	60	1985
SEVEN YEARS IN TIBET DAVID BOWIE	61	1997
7TEEN REGENTS	11	1980
17 YOURCODENAMEIS:MILO	65	2005
SEVENTEEN [A] BOYD BENNETT & HIS ROCKETS	16	1955
SEVENTEEN [A] FRANKIE VAUGHAN	18	1955
SEVENTEEN [B] LET LOOSE	11	1994
SEVENTEEN [C] LADYTRON	68	2002
17 AGAIN EURYTHMICS	27	2000
SEVENTH SON GEORGIE FAME	25	1969
78 STONE WOBBLE GOMEZ	44	1998
'74-'75 CONNELLS	14	1995
77 STRINGS KURTIS MANTRONIK PRESENTS CHAMONIX	71	2002
76 TROMBONES KING BROTHERS	19	1961
SEVERINA MISSION	25	1987
SEWN FEELING	7	2006
SEX [A] SLEAZESISTERS WITH VIKKI SHEPARD	53	1995
SEX [B] ROBBIE RIVERA FEATURING BILLY PAUL	55	2002
SEX [C] GA GAS	71	2005
SEX AND CANDY MARCY PLAYGROUND	29	1998
SEX AS A WEAPON PAT BENATAR	67	1986
SEX BOMB TOM JONES & MOUSSE T	3	2000
SEX DRUGS AND ROCKS THROUGH YOUR WINDOW AGENT BLUE	71	2004
SEX IS NOT THE ENEMY GARBAGE	24	2005
SEX LIFE GEOFFREY WILLIAMS	71	1997
SEX ME R KELLY & PUBLIC ANNOUNCEMENT	75	1993
THE SEX OF IT KID CREOLE & THE COCONUTS	29	1990
SEX ON FIRE KINGS OF LEON	1	2008
SEX ON THE BEACH T-SPOON	2	1998
SEX ON THE STREETS PIZZAMAN	23	1995
SEX OVER THE PHONE VILLAGE PEOPLE	59	1985
SEX TALK (LIVE) T'PAU	23	1988
SEX TYPE THING STONE TEMPLE PILOTS	55	1993
SEXCRIME (NINETEEN EIGHTY FOUR) EURYTHMICS	4	1984
SEXED UP ROBBIE WILLIAMS	10	2003
SEXIEST MAN IN JAMAICA MINT ROYALE	20	2002
SEXOMATIC BAR-KAYS	51	1985
SEXUAL [A] MARIA ROWE	67	1995

	Peak Position	Year of Release
SEXUAL [B] AMBER	34	2000
SEXUAL GUARANTEE ALCAZAR	30	2002
(SEXUAL) HEALING MARVIN GAYE	4	1982
SEXUAL HEALING ALIBI VS ROCKEFELLER	34	2007
SEXUAL REVOLUTION MACY GRAY	45	2001
SEXUALITY BILLY BRAGG	27	1991
SEXX LAWS BECK	27	1999
SEXY MFSB	37	1975
SEXY BITCH GG	60	2009
SEXY BOY AIR	13	1998
SEXY CAN I RAY J FEATURING YUNG BERG	66	2008
SEXY CHICK DAVID GUETTA FEATURING AKON	1	2009
SEXY CINDERELLA LYNDEN DAVID HALL	17	1997
SEXY CREAM SLICK	47	1979
SEXY EYES DR HOOK	4	1980
SEXY EYES – REMIXES WHIGFIELD	68	1998
SEXY GIRL LILLO THOMAS	23	1987
SEXY IN LATIN LITTLE MAN TATE	20	2007
SEXY LOVE NE-YO	5	2006
SEXY MF PRINCE & THE NEW POWER GENERATION	4	1992
SEXY! NO NO NO GIRLS ALOUD	5	2007
SEXYBACK JUSTIN TIMBERLAKE	1	2006
SGT PEPPER'S LONELY HEARTS CLUB BAND – WITH A LITTLE HELP FROM MY FRIENDS BEATLES	63	1978
SGT ROCK (IS GOING TO HELP ME) XTC	16	1981
SHA LA LA MANFRED MANN	3	1964
SHA LA LA LA LEE SMALL FACES	3	1966
SHA LA LA LA LEE PLASTIC BERTRAND	39	1978
SHA LA LA MEANS I LOVE YOU BARRY WHITE	55	1979
SHACKLES (PRAISE YOU) MARY MARY	5	2000
SHADDAP YOU FACE JOE DOLCE MUSIC THEATRE	1	1981
SHADES OF BLUE (EP) THE THE	54	1991
SHADES OF GREEN MISSION	49	1992
SHADES OF PARANOIMIA ART OF NOISE	53	1992
SHADES OF SUMMER RODEO JONES	59	1993
SHADES (THEME FROM THE CROWN PAINT TELEVISION COMMERCIAL) UNITED KINGDOM SYMPHONY	68	1985
SHADOW DANCING ANDY GIBB	42	1978
THE SHADOW OF LOVE DAMNED	25	1985
SHADOW OF THE DAY LINKIN PARK	46	2007
SHADOWS BREED 77	42	2005
SHADOWS OF THE NIGHT PAT BENATAR	50	1985
SHADOWTIME SIOUXSIE & THE BANSHEES	57	1991
SHADY LADY GENE PITNEY	29	1970
SHADY LANE PAVEMENT	40	1997
SHAFT VAN TWIST	57	1985
SHAKABOOM! HUNTER FEATURING RUBY TURNER	64	1995
SHAKALAKA BABY PREEYA KALIDAS	38	2002
SHAKE [A] OTIS REDDING	28	1967
SHAKE [B] ANDREW RIDGELEY	58	1990
SHAKE [C] YING YANG TWINS FEATURING PITBULL	49	2006
SHAKE A LEG ROLL DEEP	24	2005
SHAKE! (HOW ABOUT A SAMPLING GENE) GENE AND JIM ARE INTO SHAKES	68	1988
SHAKE IT METRO STATION	6	2009
SHAKE IT BABY DJD PRESENTS HYDRAULIC DOGS	56	2002
SHAKE IT DOWN MUD	12	1976
SHAKE IT (MOVE A LITTLE CLOSER) LEE CABRERA FEATURING ALEX CARTANA	16	2003
SHAKE IT (NO TE MUEVAS TANTO) LEE-CABRERA	58	2003
SHAKE IT OFF MARIAH CAREY	9	2005
SHAKE ME I RATTLE KAYE SISTERS	27	1958
SHAKE RATTLE AND ROLL BILL HALEY & HIS COMETS	4	1954

Title	Artist	Peak Position	Year of Release
(SHAKE SHAKE SHAKE) SHAKE YOUR BOOTY	KC & THE SUNSHINE BAND	22	1976
SHAKE THE DISEASE	DEPECHE MODE	18	1985
SHAKE THIS MOUNTAIN	HORSE	52	1993
SHAKE UR BODY	SHY FX & T POWER FEATURING DI	7	2002
SHAKE (WHAT YA MAMA GAVE YA)	GENERAL LEVY VS ZEUS	51	2004
SHAKE YA ASS	MYSTIKAL	30	2000
SHAKE YA BODY	N-TRANCE	37	2000
SHAKE YA SHIMMY	PORN KINGS VERSUS FLIP & FILL	28	2003
SHAKE YA TAILFEATHER	NELLY, P DIDDY & MURPHY LEE	10	2003
SHAKE YOU DOWN	GREGORY ABBOTT	6	1986
SHAKE YOUR BODY (DOWN TO THE GROUND)	JACKSONS	4	1979
SHAKE YOUR BODY (DOWN TO THE GROUND)	FULL INTENTION	34	1997
SHAKE YOUR BON-BON	RICKY MARTIN	12	1999
SHAKE YOUR FOUNDATIONS	AC/DC	24	1986
SHAKE YOUR GROOVE THING	PEACHES & HERB	26	1979
SHAKE YOUR HEAD	WAS (NOT WAS)	4	1992
SHAKE YOUR LOVE	DEBBIE GIBSON	7	1988
SHAKE YOUR RUMP TO THE FUNK	BAR-KAYS	41	1977
SHAKE YOUR THANG (IT'S YOUR THING)	SALT-N-PEPA FEATURING E.U.	22	1988
SHAKERMAKER	OASIS	11	1994
SHAKESPEARE'S SISTER	SMITHS	26	1985
SHAKESPEARE'S WAY WITH WORDS	ONE TRUE VOICE	10	2003
SHAKIN' ALL OVER	JOHNNY KIDD & THE PIRATES	1	1960
SHAKIN' LIKE A LEAF	STRANGLERS	58	1987
THE SHAKIN' STEVENS EP	SHAKIN' STEVENS	2	1982
SHAKING THE TREE	YOUSSOU N'DOUR & PETER GABRIEL	57	1989
SHAKING THE TREE	PETER GABRIEL	57	1990
SHAKTI (THE MEANING OF WITHIN)	MONSOON	41	1982
SHALALA LALA	VENGABOYS	5	2000
SHA-LA-LA (MAKES ME HAPPY)	AL GREEN	20	1974
SHALL WE TAKE A TRIP	NORTHSIDE	50	1990
SHAME [A]	ALAN PRICE SET	45	1967
SHAME [B]	EVELYN 'CHAMPAGNE' KING	39	1978
SHAME [B]	ALTERN 8 VS EVELYN KING	74	1992
SHAME [B]	ZHANE	66	1995
SHAME [B]	RUFF DRIVERZ	51	1998
SHAME [C]	ORCHESTRAL MANOEUVRES IN THE DARK	52	1987
SHAME [D]	EURYTHMICS	41	1987
SHAME [E]	PJ HARVEY	45	2004
SHAME & SCANDAL	MADNESS	38	2005
SHAME AND SCANDAL IN THE FAMILY	LANCE PERCIVAL	37	1965
SHAME ON ME	ALEXANDER O'NEAL	71	1991
SHAME ON YOU	GUN	33	1990
SHAME SHAME SHAME [A]	JIMMY REED	45	1964
SHAME SHAME SHAME [B]	SHIRLEY & COMPANY	6	1975
SHAME SHAME SHAME [B]	SINITTA	28	1992
SHAMELESS	GARTH BROOKS	71	1992
SHAMROCKS AND SHENIGANS	HOUSE OF PAIN	23	1993
SHANG-A-LANG	BAY CITY ROLLERS	2	1974
SHANGHAI'D IN SHANGHAI	NAZARETH	41	1974
SHANGRI-LA	RUTLES	68	1996
SHANNON	HENRY GROSS	32	1976
SHANTE	MASS PRODUCTION	59	1980
SHAPE	SUGABABES	11	2003
SHAPE OF MY HEART [A]	STING	57	1993
SHAPE OF MY HEART [B]	BACKSTREET BOYS	4	2000
THE SHAPE OF THINGS TO COME	HEADBOYS	45	1979
THE SHAPE YOU'RE IN	ERIC CLAPTON	75	1983
SHAPES OF THINGS	YARDBIRDS	3	1966
SHAPES THAT GO TOGETHER	A-HA	27	1994
SHARE MY LIFE	INNER CITY	62	1994
SHARE THE FALL	RONI SIZE/REPRAZENT	37	1997
SHARE THE NIGHT	WORLD PREMIERE	64	1984
SHARE YOUR LOVE (NO DIGGITY)	PASSION	62	1997
SHARING THE NIGHT TOGETHER	DR HOOK	43	1980
SHARING YOU	BOBBY VEE	10	1962
SHARK	THROWING MUSES	53	1996
SHARK IN THE WATER	VV BROWN	34	2009
SHARP AS A KNIFE	BRANDON COOKE FEATURING ROXANNE SHANTE	45	1988
SHARP DRESSED MAN	ZZ TOP	22	1983
SHATTER	FEEDER	11	2005
SHATTERED DREAMS	JOHNNY HATES JAZZ	5	1987
SHATTERED GLASS	DTOX	75	1992
SHAWTY GET LOOSE	LIL' MAMA FEATURING CHRIS BROWN & T-PAIN	57	2008
SHAZAM!	DUANE EDDY & THE REBELS	4	1960
SH-BOOM	CREW CUTS	12	1954
SH-BOOM	STAN FREBERG WITH THE TOADS	15	1954
SH-BOOM (LIFE COULD BE A DREAM)	DARTS	48	1980
SHE [A]	CHARLES AZNAVOUR	1	1974
SHE [A]	ELVIS COSTELLO	19	1999
SHE [B]	VEGAS	43	1992
SHE AIN'T WORTH IT	GLENN MEDEIROS FEATURING BOBBY BROWN	12	1990
SHE BANGS	RICKY MARTIN	3	2000
SHE BANGS THE DRUMS	STONE ROSES	34	1989
SHE BELIEVES IN ME [A]	KENNY ROGERS	42	1979
SHE BELIEVES (IN ME) [B]	RONAN KEATING	2	2004
SHE BLINDED ME WITH SCIENCE	THOMAS DOLBY	49	1982
SHE BOP	CYNDI LAUPER	46	1984
SHE CAME HOME FOR CHRISTMAS	MEW	55	2003
SHE CAN ROCK IT	POWER STATION	63	1996
SHE COMES FROM THE RAIN	WEATHER PROPHETS	62	1987
SHE COMES IN THE FALL	INSPIRAL CARPETS	27	1990
SHE CRIES YOUR NAME	BETH ORTON	40	1997
SHE DON'T FOOL ME	STATUS QUO	36	1982
SHE DON'T LET NOBODY	CHAKA DEMUS & PLIERS	4	1993
SHE DRIVES ME CRAZY	FINE YOUNG CANNIBALS	5	1989
SHE DROVE ME TO DAYTIME TELEVISION	FUNERAL FOR A FRIEND	20	2003
SHE GOT GAME	TYMES 4	40	2001
SHE GOT ME ON	PAUL JOHNSON	70	2005
SHE HATES ME	PUDDLE OF MUDD	14	2002
SHE HITS ME	4 OF US	35	1993
SHE HOLDS THE KEY	SECRET LIFE	63	1994
SHE IS BEAUTIFUL	ANDREW WK	55	2002
SHE IS LOVE	OASIS	2	2002
SHE IS SUFFERING	MANIC STREET PREACHERS	25	1994
SHE KISSED ME	TERENCE TRENT D'ARBY	16	1993
SHE KISSED ME (IT FELT LIKE A HIT)	SPIRITUALIZED	38	2003
SHE KNOWS	BALAAM AND THE ANGEL	70	1986
SHE LEFT ME	GO:AUDIO	41	2008
SHE LEFT ME ON FRIDAY	SHED SEVEN	11	1998
SHE LOVED LIKE DIAMOND	SPANDAU BALLET	49	1982
SHE LOVES ME NOT	PAPA ROACH	14	2002
SHE LOVES YOU	BEATLES	1	1963
SHE MAKES MY DAY	ROBERT PALMER	6	1988
SHE MAKES MY NOSE BLEED	MANSUN	9	1997
SHE MEANS NOTHING TO ME	PHIL EVERLY & CLIFF RICHARD	9	1983
SHE MIGHT	NOISE NEXT DOOR	27	2005
SHE MOVES IN HER OWN WAY	KOOKS	7	2006
SHE MOVES (LALALA)	KARAJA	42	2002
SHE NEEDS LOVE	WAYNE FONTANA & THE MINDBENDERS	32	1965
SHE SAID [D]	PLAN B	3	2010
SHE SAID [A]	LONGPIGS	16	1995
SHE SAID [B]	PHARCYDE	51	1996
SHE SAID [C]	JON SPENCER BLUES EXPLOSION	58	2002
SHE SELLS	BANDERAS	41	1991
SHE SELLS SANCTUARY	CULT	15	1985
SHE SHE LITTLE SHEILA	GENE VINCENT	22	1961
SHE SOLD ME MAGIC	LOU CHRISTIE	25	1969
SHE TALKS TO ANGELS	BLACK CROWES	70	1991
SHE USED TO BE MINE	SPIN DOCTORS	55	1996
SHE WAITS FOR ME	PROTOCOL	65	2005
SHE WANTS TO DANCE WITH ME	RICK ASTLEY	6	1988
SHE WANTS TO MOVE	NERD	12	2004
SHE WANTS YOU	BILLIE	3	1998
SHE WAS HOT	ROLLING STONES	42	1984
SHE WEARS MY RING	SOLOMON KING	3	1968
SHE WEARS RED FEATHERS	GUY MITCHELL	1	1953
SHE WILL BE LOVED	MAROON 5	4	2004
SHE WILL HAVE HER WAY	NEIL FINN	26	1998
SHE WOLF	SHAKIRA	4	2009
SHE WON'T TALK TO ME	LUTHER VANDROSS	34	1989
SHE WORKS HARD FOR THE MONEY	DONNA SUMMER	25	1983
SHED A TEAR	WET WET WET	22	1993
SHED MY SKIN	D*NOTE	73	2002
SHE'D RATHER BE WITH ME	TURTLES	4	1967
SHEELA-NA-GIG	PJ HARVEY	69	1992
SHEENA IS A PUNK ROCKER	RAMONES	22	1977
SHEEP	HOUSEMARTINS	56	1986
THE SHEFFIELD GRINDER	TONY CAPSTICK & THE CARLTON MAIN/FRICKLEY COLLIERY BAND	3	1981
SHEFFIELD SONG	SUPERNATURALS	45	1998
SHEILA [A]	TOMMY ROE	3	1962
SHEILA [B]	JAMIE T	15	2006
SHEILA TAKE A BOW	SMITHS	10	1987
SHELLSHOCK	NEW ORDER	28	1986
SHELTER	BRAND NEW HEAVIES	31	1998
SHELTER ME [A]	CINDERELLA	55	1990
SHELTER ME [B]	CIRCUIT	44	1991
THE SHEPHERD'S SONG	TONY OSBORNE SOUND	46	1973
SHERIFF FATMAN	CARTER-THE UNSTOPPABLE SEX MACHINE	23	1991
SHERRI DON'T FAIL ME NOW	STATUS QUO	38	1994
SHERRY	FOUR SEASONS	8	1962
SHERRY	ADRIAN BAKER	10	1975
SHE'S A BAD MAMA JAMA (SHE'S BUILT, SHE'S STACKED)	CARL CARLTON	34	1981
SHE'S A GIRL AND I'M A MAN	LLOYD COLE	55	1991
SHE'S A GOOD GIRL	SLEEPER	28	1997
SHE'S A GROOVY FREAK	REAL THING	52	1980
SHE'S A LADY	TOM JONES	13	1971
SHE'S A LITTLE ANGEL	LITTLE ANGELS	21	1990
SHE'S A MYSTERY TO ME	ROY ORBISON	27	1989
SHE'S A RAINBOW	WORLD OF TWIST	62	1992
SHE'S A RIVER	SIMPLE MINDS	9	1995
SHE'S A STAR	JAMES	9	1997
SHE'S A SUPERSTAR	VERVE	66	1992
SHE'S A VISION	ALL EYES	65	2004
SHE'S A WIND UP	DR FEELGOOD	34	1977
SHE'S A WOMAN	SCRITTI POLITTI FEATURING SHABBA RANKS	20	1991

Title	Artist	Peak Position	Year of Release
SHE'S ABOUT A MOVER	SIR DOUGLAS QUINTET	15	1965
SHE'S ALL ON MY MIND	WET WET WET	17	1995
SHE'S ALRIGHT	BITTY McLEAN	53	1996
SHE'S ALWAYS A WOMAN	BILLY JOEL	53	1986
SHE'S ATTRACTED TO	YOUNG KNIVES	38	2006
SHE'S CRAFTY	BEASTIE BOYS	34	1987
SHE'S EVERY WOMAN	GARTH BROOKS	55	1996
SHE'S GONE [A]	BUDDY KNOX	45	1962
SHE'S GONE [B]	DARYL HALL & JOHN OATES	42	1976
SHE'S GONE [B]	MATTHEW MARSDEN FEATURING DESTINY'S CHILD	24	1998
SHE'S GONNA BREAK SOON	LESS THAN JAKE	39	2003
SHE'S GONNA WIN	BILBO	42	1978
SHE'S GOT A REASON	DOGS	36	2005
SHE'S GOT CLAWS	GARY NUMAN	6	1981
SHE'S GOT ISSUES	OFFSPRING	41	1999
SHE'S GOT IT	LITTLE RICHARD	15	1957
SHE'S GOT ME DANCING	TOMMY SPARKS	22	2009
SHE'S GOT ME GOING CRAZY	2 IN A ROOM	54	1991
SHE'S GOT SOUL	JAMESTOWN FEATURING JOCELYN BROWN	57	1991
SHE'S GOT STANDARDS	RIFLES	32	2006
SHE'S GOT THAT VIBE	R KELLY	3	1992
SHE'S GOT YOU	PATSY CLINE	43	1962
SHE'S GOT YOU HIGH	MUMM RA	41	2007
SHE'S IN FASHION	SUEDE	13	1999
SHE'S IN LOVE WITH YOU	SUZI QUATRO	11	1979
SHE'S IN PARTIES	BAUHAUS	26	1983
SHE'S LEAVING HOME	BILLY BRAGG WITH CARA TIVEY	1	1988
SHE'S LIKE A STAR	TAIO CRUZ	20	2008
SHE'S LIKE THE WIND	PATRICK SWAYZE FEATURING WENDY FRASER	17	1988
SHE'S LOST YOU	ZEPHYRS	48	1965
SHE'S MADONNA	ROBBIE WILLIAMS & PET SHOP BOYS	16	2007
SHE'S MINE	CAMEO	35	1987
SHE'S MY EVERYTHING	FREEFALLER	36	2005
SHE'S MY MACHINE	DAVID LEE ROTH	64	1994
SHE'S MY MAN	SCISSOR SISTERS	29	2007
SHE'S NEW TO YOU	SUSAN MAUGHAN	45	1963
SHE'S NOT LEAVING	RESEARCH	73	2004
SHE'S NOT THERE	ZOMBIES	12	1964
SHE'S NOT THERE	NEIL MacARTHUR	34	1969
SHE'S NOT THERE	SANTANA	11	1977
SHE'S NOT THERE/KICKS EP	UK SUBS	36	1979
SHE'S NOT YOU	ELVIS PRESLEY	1	1962
SHE'S ON FIRE [A]	TRAIN	49	2002
SHE'S ON FIRE [B]	CUBAN HEELS	72	2005
SHE'S ON IT	BEASTIE BOYS	10	1987
SHE'S OUT OF MY LIFE	MICHAEL JACKSON	3	1980
SHE'S PLAYING HARD TO GET	HI-FIVE	55	1992
(SHE'S) SEXY AND 17	STRAY CATS	29	1983
SHE'S SO BEAUTIFUL	CLIFF RICHARD	17	1985
SHE'S SO COLD	ROLLING STONES	33	1980
SHE'S SO FINE	THUNDER	34	1990
SHE'S SO HIGH [A]	BLUR	48	1990
SHE'S SO HIGH [B]	TAL BACHMAN	30	1999
SHE'S SO HIGH [B]	KURT NILSEN	25	2004
SHE'S SO LOVELY	SCOUTING FOR GIRLS	7	2007
SHE'S SO MODERN	BOOMTOWN RATS	12	1978
SHE'S STRANGE	CAMEO	22	1984
SHE'S THE MASTER OF THE GAME	RICHARD JON SMITH	63	1983
SHE'S THE ONE [A]	JAMES BROWN	45	1988
SHE'S THE ONE [B]	ROBBIE WILLIAMS	1	1999
SHIFTER	TIMO MAAS FEATURING MC CHICKABOO	38	2002
SHIFTING WHISPERING SANDS	BILLY VAUGHN ORCHESTRA & CHORUS, NARRATION BY KEN NORDINE	20	1956
SHIFTING WHISPERING SANDS (PARTS 1 & 2)	EAMONN ANDREWS WITH RON GOODWIN & HIS ORCHESTRA	18	1956
SHIMMY SHAKE	740 BOYZ	54	1995
SHINDIG	SHADOWS	6	1963
SHINE [A]	JOE BROWN	33	1961
SHINE [B]	MOTORHEAD	59	1983
SHINE [C]	SLOWDIVE	52	1991
SHINE [D]	ASWAD	5	1994
SHINE [E]	MOLLY HALF HEAD	73	1995
SHINE [F]	SPACE BROTHERS	18	1997
SHINE [G]	MONTROSE AVENUE	58	1998
SHINE [H]	LOVEFREEKZ	6	2005
SHINE [I]	LUTHER VANDROSS	50	2006
SHINE [I]	BOOTY LUV	10	2007
SHINE [J]	TAKE THAT	1	2007
SHINE A LITTLE LOVE	ELECTRIC LIGHT ORCHESTRA	6	1979
SHINE EYE	RAGGA TWINS FEATURING JUNIOR REID	63	1992
SHINE EYE GAL	SHABBA RANKS (FEATURING MYKAL ROSE)	46	1995
SHINE IT ALL AROUND	ROBERT PLANT & THE STRANGE SENSATION	32	2005
SHINE LIKE A STAR	BERRI	20	1995
SHINE ON [A]	HOUSE OF LOVE	20	1990
SHINE ON [B]	DEGREES OF MOTION FEATURING BITI	8	1992
SHINE ON [C]	SCOTT & LEON	34	2001
SHINE ON [D]	KOOKS	25	2008
SHINE ON ME	LOVESTATION FEATURING LISA HUNT	71	1993
SHINE ON SILVER SUN	STRAWBS	34	1973
SHINE SO HARD (EP)	ECHO & THE BUNNYMEN	37	1981
SHINE (SOMEONE WHO NEEDS ME)	MONACO	55	1997
SHINED ON ME	PRAISE CATS FEATURING ANDREA LOVE	24	2002
SHINING [A]	DOUBLE DEE	58	2003
SHINING [B]	KRISTIAN LEONTIOU	13	2004
SHINING LIGHT	ASH	8	2001
SHINING LIGHT	ANNIE LENNOX	39	2009
SHINING ROAD	CRANES	57	1994
SHINING STAR	MANHATTANS	45	1980
SHINING STAR (EP)	INXS	27	1991
SHINOBI VS DRAGON NINJA	LOSTPROPHETS	41	2001
SHINY DISCO BALLS	WHO DA FUNK FEATURING JESSICA EVE	15	2002
SHINY HAPPY PEOPLE	R.E.M.	6	1991
SHINY SHINY	HAYSI FANTAYZEE	16	1983
SHIP AHOY	MARXMAN	64	1993
SHIP OF FOOLS [A]	WORLD PARTY	42	1987
SHIP OF FOOLS [B]	ERASURE	6	1988
SHIPBUILDING [A]	ROBERT WYATT	35	1983
SHIPBUILDING [B]	TASMIN ARCHER	40	1994
SHIPS IN THE NIGHT	BE BOP DELUXE	23	1976
SHIPS (WHERE WERE YOU)	BIG COUNTRY	29	1993
SHIPWRECKED	GENESIS	54	1997
SHIRALEE	TOMMY STEELE	11	1957
SHIRLEY	SHAKIN' STEVENS	6	1982
SHIT ON YOU	D12	10	2001
SHIVER [A]	GEORGE BENSON	19	1986
SHIVER [B]	S-J	59	1998
SHIVER [C]	COLDPLAY	35	2000
SHIVER [D]	NATALIE IMBRUGLIA	8	2005
SHIVERING SAND	MEGA CITY FOUR	35	1992
SHIVERS	ARMIN VAN BUUREN	72	2005
SHO' YOU RIGHT	BARRY WHITE	14	1987
SHOCK HORROR	VIEW	64	2009
THE SHOCK OF THE LIGHTNING	OASIS	3	2008
SHOCK THE MONKEY	PETER GABRIEL	58	1982
SHOCK TO THE SYSTEM	BILLY IDOL	30	1993
SHOCK YOUR MAMA	DEBBIE GIBSON	74	1993
SHOCKAHOLIC	KINKY MACHINE	70	1993
SHOCKED	KYLIE MINOGUE	6	1991
SHOES	REPARATA	43	1975
SHOO BE DOO BE DOO DA DAY	STEVIE WONDER	46	1968
SHOO DOO FU FU OOH	LENNY WILLIAMS	38	1977
SHOOP	SALT-N-PEPA	13	1993
THE SHOOP SHOOP SONG (IT'S IN HIS KISS)	CHER	1	1991
SHOORAH SHOORAH	BETTY WRIGHT	27	1975
SHOOT ALL THE CLOWNS	BRUCE DICKINSON	37	1994
SHOOT ME DOWN	BOY KILL BOY	63	2006
SHOOT ME (WITH YOUR LOVE) [A]	TASHA THOMAS	59	1979
SHOOT ME WITH YOUR LOVE [B]	D:REAM	7	1995
SHOOT SHOOT	UFO	48	1979
SHOOT THE DOG	GEORGE MICHAEL	12	2002
SHOOT THE RUNNER	KASABIAN	17	2006
SHOOT YOUR GUN	22-20'S	30	2004
SHOOTING FROM MY HEART	BIG BAM BOO	61	1989
SHOOTING FROM THE HEART	CLIFF RICHARD	51	1984
SHOOTING STAR [A]	DOLLAR	14	1978
SHOOTING STAR [A]	BOYZONE	2	1997
SHOOTING STAR [B]	FLIP & FILL	3	2002
SHOOTING STAR [C]	DEEPEST BLUE	57	2004
SHOOTING STAR [D]	AIR TRAFFIC	30	2007
SHOPLIFTERS OF THE WORLD UNITE	SMITHS	12	1987
SHOPPING	SUPERSISTER	36	2001
SHORLEY WALL	OOBERMAN	47	2000
SHORT CUT TO SOMEWHERE	FISH & TONY BANKS	75	1986
SHORT DICK MAN	20 FINGERS FEATURING GILLETTE	21	1994
SHORT FAT FANNIE	LARRY WILLIAMS	21	1957
SHORT SHORT MAN	20 FINGERS FEATURING GILLETTE	11	1995
SHORT SKIRT LONG JACKET	CAKE	63	2001
SHORT'NIN' BREAD	TONY CROMBIE & HIS ROCKETS	25	1956
SHORT'NIN' BREAD	VISCOUNTS	16	1960
SHORTSHARPSHOCK EP	THERAPY?	9	1993
SHORTY	WANNADIES	41	1997
SHORTY (GOT HER EYES ON ME)	DONELL JONES	19	2000
SHORTY (YOU KEEP PLAYIN' WITH MY MIND)	IMAJIN FEATURING KEITH MURRAY	22	1998
SHOT BY BOTH SIDES	MAGAZINE	41	1978
SHOT DOWN	NINE BLACK ALPS	25	2005
SHOT DOWN IN THE NIGHT	HAWKWIND	59	1980
SHOT IN THE DARK [A]	OZZY OSBOURNE	20	1986
SHOT IN THE DARK [B]	DJ HYPE	63	1993
SHOT OF POISON	LITA FORD	63	1992
SHOT OF RHYTHM AND BLUES	JOHNNY KIDD & THE PIRATES	48	1963
SHOT SHOT	GOMEZ	28	2002
SHOT YOU DOWN	AUDIO BULLYS FEATURING NANCY SINATRA	3	2005
SHOTGUN WEDDING	ROY C	6	1966
SHOTGUN WEDDING	ROD STEWART	21	1993
SHOULD I DO IT?	POINTER SISTERS	50	1981
SHOULD I EVER (FALL IN LOVE)	NIGHTCRAWLERS	34	1996
SHOULD I STAY	GABRIELLE	13	2000
SHOULD I STAY OR SHOULD I GO	CLASH	1	1982
SHOULDA WOULDA COULDA	BEVERLEY KNIGHT	10	2002
SHOULDER HOLSTER	MORCHEEBA	53	1997
SHOULDN'T DO THAT	KAJA	63	1985

	Peak Position	Year of Release
SHOULDN'T LET THE SIDE DOWN HOGGBOY	74	2002
SHOULD'VE KNOWN BETTER RICHARD MARX	50	1988
SHOUT [A] LULU & THE LUVVERS	7	1964
SHOUT (IT OUT) [A] LOUCHIE LOU & MICHIE ONE	7	1993
SHOUT [B] TEARS FOR FEARS	4	1984
SHOUT [C] ANT & DEC	10	1997
SHOUT SHOUT (KNOCK YOURSELF OUT) ROCKY SHARPE & THE REPLAYS	19	1982
SHOUT TO THE TOP STYLE COUNCIL	7	1984
SHOUT TO THE TOP FIRE ISLAND FEATURING LOLEATTA HOLLOWAY	23	1998
SHOUTING FOR THE GUNNERS ARSENAL FA CUP SQUAD FEATURING TIPPA IRIE & PETER HUNNIGALE	34	1993
THE SHOUTY TRACK LEMON JELLY	21	2005
THE SHOW [A] DOUG E FRESH & THE GET FRESH CREW	7	1985
THE SHOW [B] GIRLS ALOUD	2	2004
THE SHOW [C] LENKA	33	2009
SHOW A LITTLE LOVE ULTIMATE KAOS	23	1995
SHOW ME [A] DEXY'S MIDNIGHT RUNNERS	16	1981
SHOW ME [B] LINDY LAYTON	47	1993
SHOW ME [C] ULTRA NATE	62	1994
SHOW ME [D] DANA DAWSON	28	1996
SHOW ME A SIGN KONTAKT	19	2003
SHOW ME GIRL HERMAN'S HERMITS	19	1964
SHOW ME HEAVEN MARIA McKEE	1	1990
SHOW ME HEAVEN TINA ARENA	29	1995
SHOW ME HEAVEN CHIMIRA	70	1997
SHOW ME HEAVEN SAINT FEATURING SUZANNA DEE	36	2003
SHOW ME LOVE [A] ROBIN S	6	1993
SHOW ME LOVE [A] STEVE ANGELLO & LAIDBACK LUKE FEATURING ROBIN S	11	2009
SHOW ME LOVE [B] ROBYN	8	1998
SHOW ME LOVE [C] INDIEN	69	2003
SHOW ME MARY CATHERINE WHEEL	62	1993
SHOW ME THE MEANING OF BEING LONELY BACKSTREET BOYS	3	2000
SHOW ME THE MONEY ARCHITECHS	20	2001
SHOW ME THE WAY [A] PETER FRAMPTON	10	1976
SHOW ME THE WAY [B] OSMOND BOYS	60	1992
SHOW ME WHAT I'M LOOKING AT CAROLINA LIAR	31	2009
SHOW ME WHAT YOU GOT JAY-Z	38	2006
SHOW ME YOUR MONKEY PERCY FILTH	72	2003
SHOW ME YOUR SOUL P DIDDY, LENNY KRAVITZ, PHARRELL WILLIAMS & LOON	35	2004
SHOW ME YOU'RE A WOMAN MUD	8	1975
THE SHOW MUST GO ON [A] LEO SAYER	2	1973
THE SHOW MUST GO ON [B] QUEEN	16	1991
THE SHOW (THEME FROM 'CONNIE') REBECCA STORM	22	1985
SHOW YOU THE WAY TO GO JACKSONS	1	1977
SHOW YOU THE WAY TO GO DANNII MINOGUE	30	1992
SHOW YOUR HAND SUPER FURRY ANIMALS	46	2007
SHOWDOWN [A] ELECTRIC LIGHT ORCHESTRA	12	1973
SHOWDOWN [B] JODY LEI	34	2003
SHOWER YOUR LOVE KULA SHAKER	14	1999
SHOWING OUT (GET FRESH AT THE WEEKEND) MEL & KIM	3	1986
SHOWROOM DUMMIES KRAFTWERK	25	1982
THE SHUFFLE VAN McCOY	4	1977
SHUGGIE LOVE MONKEY BARS/GABRIELLE WIDMAN	61	2004
SHUT 'EM DOWN PUBLIC ENEMY	21	1992
SHUT IT DOWN PITBULL FEATURING AKON	33	2010
SHUT UP [A] MADNESS	7	1981

	Peak Position	Year of Release
SHUT UP [B] KELLY OSBOURNE	12	2003
SHUT UP [C] BLACK EYED PEAS	2	2003
SHUT UP [D] SIMPLE PLAN	44	2005
SHUT UP AND DANCE AEROSMITH	24	1994
SHUT UP AND DRIVE RIHANNA	5	2007
SHUT UP AND FORGET ABOUT IT DANE	9	2001
SHUT UP AND KISS ME MARY CHAPIN CARPENTER	35	1995
SHUT UP AND LET ME GO TING TINGS	6	2008
SHUT UP (AND SLEEP WITH ME) SIN WITH SEBASTIAN	44	1995
SHUT YOUR MOUTH [A] MADE IN LONDON	74	2000
SHUT YOUR MOUTH [B] GARBAGE	20	2002
SHUTDOWN PITCHSHIFTER	66	2002
SHY BOY BANANARAMA	4	1982
SHY GIRL MARK WYNTER	28	1963
SHY GUY DIANA KING	2	1995
SHY GUY ASWAD	62	2002
(SI SI) JE SUIS UN ROCK STAR BILL WYMAN	14	1981
SI TU DOIS PARTIR FAIRPORT CONVENTION	21	1969
SIC TRANSIT GLORIA GLORY FADES BRAND NEW	37	2004
SICK AND TIRED [A] FATS DOMINO	26	1958
SICK & TIRED [B] CARDIGANS	34	1995
SICK AND TIRED [C] ANASTACIA	4	2004
SICK MAN BLUES GOODIES	4	1975
SICK OF DRUGS WILDHEARTS	14	1996
SICK OF GOODBYES SPARKLEHORSE	57	1998
SICK OF IT PRIMITIVES	24	1989
SIDE TRAVIS	14	2001
SIDE BY SIDE KAY STARR	7	1953
SIDE SADDLE RUSS CONWAY	1	1959
SIDE SHOW [A] CHANTER SISTERS	43	1976
SIDE SHOW [B] WENDY & LISA	49	1988
SIDE STREETS SAINT ETIENNE	36	2005
THE SIDEBOARD SONG (GOT MY BEER IN THE SIDEBOARD HERE) CHAS & DAVE	55	1979
SIDESHOW BARRY BIGGS	3	1976
SIDEWALK TALK JELLYBEAN FEATURING CATHERINE BUCHANAN	47	1986
SIDEWALKING JESUS & MARY CHAIN	30	1988
THE SIDEWINDER SLEEPS TONITE R.E.M.	17	1993
SIGHT FOR SORE EYES M PEOPLE	6	1994
THE SIGN ACE OF BASE	2	1994
SIGN O' THE TIMES PRINCE	10	1987
A SIGN OF THE TIMES [A] PETULA CLARK	49	1966
SIGN OF THE TIMES [B] BRYAN FERRY	37	1978
SIGN OF THE TIMES [C] BELLE STARS	3	1983
SIGN OF THE TIMES [D] GRANDMASTER FLASH	72	1985
SIGN YOUR NAME TERENCE TRENT D'ARBY	2	1988
SIGNAL [A] JD AKA DREADY	64	2003
SIGNAL [B] FRESH	58	2003
SIGNAL FIRE SNOW PATROL	4	2007
SIGNALS OVER THE AIR THURSDAY	62	2003
THE SIGNATURE TUNE OF 'THE ARMY GAME' MICHAEL MEDWIN, BERNARD BRESSLAW, ALFIE BASS & LESLIE FYSON	5	1958
SIGNED SEALED DELIVERED I'M YOURS STEVIE WONDER	15	1970
SIGNED SEALED DELIVERED (I'M YOURS) BOYSTOWN GANG	50	1982
SIGNED SEALED DELIVERED I'M YOURS BLUE FEATURING STEVIE WONDER & ANGIE STONE	11	2003
SIGNS [A] TESLA	70	1991
SIGNS…[B] BLAMELESS	49	1996
SIGNS [C] DJ BADMARSH & SHRI FEATURING UK APACHE	63	2001
SIGNS [D] SNOOP DOGG FEATURING CHARLIE WILSON & JUSTIN TIMBERLAKE	2	2005
THE SILENCE [A] MIKE KOGLIN	20	1998

	Peak Position	Year of Release
SILENCE [B] DELERIUM FEATURING SARAH McLACHLAN	3	1999
SILENCE [C] TAIKO	72	2002
SILENCE [D] GOMEZ	41	2004
SILENCE IS EASY STARSAILOR	9	2003
SILENCE IS GOLDEN TREMELOES	1	1967
SILENCE WHEN YOU'RE BURNING HAPPYLIFE	73	2004
SILENT ALL THESE YEARS TORI AMOS	26	1991
SILENT LUCIDITY QUEENSRYCHE	18	1991
SILENT NIGHT BING CROSBY	8	1952
SILENT NIGHT DICKIES	47	1978
SILENT NIGHT BROS	2	1988
SILENT NIGHT SIMON & GARFUNKEL	30	1991
SILENT NIGHT SINEAD O'CONNOR	60	1991
SILENT RUNNING (ON DANGEROUS GROUND) MIKE + THE MECHANICS	21	1986
SILENT SCREAM RICHARD MARX	32	1994
SILENT SIGH BADLY DRAWN BOY	16	2002
SILENT TO THE DARK II ELECTRIC SOFT PARADE	23	2002
SILENT VOICE INNOCENCE	37	1990
SILENT WORDS JAN JOHNSTON	57	2001
SILENTLY BAD MINDED PRESSURE DROP	53	1998
SILHOUETTES HERMAN'S HERMITS	3	1965
SILHOUETTES CLIFF RICHARD	10	1990
SILK PYJAMAS THOMAS DOLBY	62	1992
SILLY GAMES JANET KAY	2	1979
SILLY GAMES LINDY LAYTON FEATURING JANET KAY	22	1990
SILLY LOVE 10 C.C.	24	1974
SILLY LOVE SONGS WINGS	2	1976
SILLY THING SEX PISTOLS	6	1979
SILVER [A] ECHO & THE BUNNYMEN	30	1984
SILVER [B] MOIST	50	1995
SILVER [C] HUNDRED REASONS	15	2002
SILVER AND GOLD [A] A.S.A.P.	60	1989
SILVER & GOLD [B] SWAY FEATURING AKON	61	2009
SILVER BELLS SIR TERRY WOGAN & ALED JONES	27	2009
SILVER DREAM MACHINE (PART 1) DAVID ESSEX	4	1980
SILVER LADY DAVID SOUL	1	1977
SILVER LINING STIFF LITTLE FINGERS	68	1981
SILVER MACHINE HAWKWIND	3	1972
SILVER SCREEN SHOWER SCENE FELIX DA HOUSECAT	39	2001
SILVER SHADOW ATLANTIC STARR	41	1985
SILVER SHORTS WEDDING PRESENT	14	1992
SILVER STAR FOUR SEASONS	3	1976
SILVER THUNDERBIRD MARC COHN	54	1991
SILVERMAC WESTWORLD	42	1987
SILVERY RAIN CLIFF RICHARD	27	1971
SIMBA GROOVE HI POWER	73	1990
SIMON SAYS [A] 1910 FRUITGUM CO.	2	1968
SIMON SAYS [B] PHAROAHE MONCH	24	2000
SIMON SMITH AND HIS AMAZING DANCING BEAR ALAN PRICE SET	4	1967
SIMON TEMPLAR SPLODGENESSABOUNDS	7	1980
SIMPLE AS THAT HUEY LEWIS & THE NEWS	47	1987
SIMPLE GAME FOUR TOPS	3	1971
SIMPLE KIND OF LIFE NO DOUBT	69	2000
SIMPLE LIFE ELTON JOHN	44	1993
SIMPLE SIMON (YOU GOTTA REGARD) MANTRONIX	72	1988
SIMPLE SINCERITY RADISH	50	1997
THE SIMPLE THINGS [A] JOE COCKER	17	1994
SIMPLE THINGS [B] SAW DOCTORS	56	1997
THE SIMPLE TRUTH (A CHILD IS BORN) CHRIS DE BURGH	36	1987
SIMPLY IRRESISTABLE ROBERT PALMER	44	1988
THE SIMPSONS THEME GREEN DAY	19	2007
SIN NINE INCH NAILS	35	1991

Title / Artist	Peak Position	Year of Release
SIN SIN SIN ROBBIE WILLIAMS	22	2006
SINBAD QUEST SYSTEM 7	74	1993
SINCE DAY ONE TEENA MARIE	69	1990
SINCE I DON'T HAVE YOU ART GARFUNKEL	38	1979
SINCE I DON'T HAVE YOU GUNS N' ROSES	10	1994
SINCE I LEFT YOU AVALANCHES	16	2001
SINCE I MET YOU BABY GARY MOORE & B.B. KING	59	1992
SINCE I MET YOU LADY UB40 FEATURING LADY SAW	40	2001
SINCE I TOLD YOU IT'S OVER STEREOPHONICS	16	2003
SINCE U BEEN GONE KELLY CLARKSON	5	2005
SINCE YESTERDAY STRAWBERRY SWITCHBLADE	5	1985
SINCE YOU'RE GONE CARS	37	1982
SINCE YOU'VE BEEN GONE [A] ARETHA FRANKLIN	47	1968
SINCE YOU'VE BEEN GONE [B] RAINBOW	6	1979
SINCERE MJ COLE	13	1998
SINCERELY McGUIRE SISTERS	14	1955
SINFUL PETE WYLIE	13	1986
SING TRAVIS	3	2001
SING A HAPPY SONG [A] GEORGE McCRAE	38	1975
SING A HAPPY SONG [B] O'JAYS	39	1979
SING A LITTLE SONG DESMOND DEKKER & THE ACES	16	1975
SING-A-LONG A	57	1998
SING A LONG SHANKS & BIGFOOT	12	2000
SING A SONG BYRON STINGILY	38	1997
SING A SONG (BREAK IT DOWN) MANTRONIX	61	1988
SING A SONG OF FREEDOM CLIFF RICHARD	13	1971
SING AND SHOUT SECOND IMAGE	53	1984
SING BABY SING STYLISTICS	3	1975
SING DON'T SPEAK BLACKFOOT SUE	36	1973
SING FOR ABSOLUTION MUSE	16	2004
SING FOR EVER ST PHILIPS CHOIR	49	1987
SING FOR THE MOMENT EMINEM	6	2003
SING HALLELUJAH! DR ALBAN	16	1993
SING IT AGAIN WITH JOE JOE 'MR PIANO' HENDERSON	18	1955
SING IT BACK MOLOKO	4	1999
SING IT FOR ENGLAND YOUNG STANLEY	58	2006
SING IT OUT HOPE OF THE STATES	39	2006
SING IT (THE HALLELUJAH SONG) MOZAIC	14	1995
SING IT TO YOU (DEE-DOOB-DEE-DOO) LAVINIA JONES	45	1995
SING IT WITH JOE JOE 'MR PIANO' HENDERSON	14	1955
SING LIKE AN ANGEL JERRY LORDAN	36	1960
SING LITTLE BIRDIE PEARL CARR & TEDDY JOHNSON	12	1959
SING ME BROTHERS	8	1977
SING ME AN OLD FASHIONED SONG BILLIE JO SPEARS	34	1976
SING (OOH-EE-OOH) VIVIENNE McKONE	47	1992
SING OUR OWN SONG UB40	5	1986
SING SING GAZ	60	1979
SING UP FOR THE CHAMPIONS REDS UNITED	12	1997
SING YOUR LIFE MORRISSEY	33	1991
SINGALONG-A-SANTA SANTA CLAUS & THE CHRISTMAS TREES	19	1982
SINGALONG-A-SANTA AGAIN SANTA CLAUS & THE CHRISTMAS TREES	39	1983
THE SINGER SANG HIS SONG BEE GEES	25	1968
SINGIN' IN THE RAIN MINT ROYALE	1	2005
SINGIN' IN THE RAIN PART 1 SHEILA B DEVOTION	11	1978
THE SINGING DOGS (MEDLEY) DON CHARLES PRESENTS THE SINGING DOGS	13	1955
SINGING IN MY SLEEP SEMISONIC	39	2000
SINGING THE BLUES GUY MITCHELL	1	1956
SINGING THE BLUES TOMMY STEELE & THE STEELMEN	1	1956
SINGING THE BLUES DAVE EDMUNDS	28	1980
SINGING THE BLUES DANIEL O'DONNELL	23	1994
SINGING THE BLUES CLIFF RICHARD & THE SHADOWS	40	2009
THE SINGLE [A] RISE	70	1994
SINGLE [B] EVERYTHING BUT THE GIRL	20	1996
SINGLE [C] PET SHOP BOYS	14	1996
SINGLE [D] NATASHA BEDINGFIELD	3	2004
SINGLE AGAIN FIERY FURNACES	49	2004
SINGLE GIRL [A] SANDY POSEY	15	1967
SINGLE GIRL [B] LUSH	21	1996
SINGLE LADIES (PUT A RING ON IT) BEYONCE	7	2008
SINGLE LIFE CAMEO	15	1985
THE SINGLES 1981-83 BAUHAUS	52	1983
SINK A SHIP KAISER CHIEFS	9	2005
SINK THE BISMARK DON LANG	43	1960
SINK TO THE BOTTOM FOUNTAINS OF WAYNE	42	1997
SINNER NEIL FINN	39	1998
SINS OF THE FAMILY PF SLOAN	38	1965
SIPPIN' SODA GUY MITCHELL	11	1954
SIR DANCEALOT OLYMPIC RUNNERS	35	1979
SIR DUKE STEVIE WONDER	2	1977
SIREN SOUNDS RONI SIZE	67	2003
SIRENS DIZZEE RASCAL	20	2007
SISSYNECK BECK	30	1997
SISTA SISTA BEVERLEY KNIGHT	31	1999
SISTER [A] BROS	10	1989
SISTER [B] SISTER 2 SISTER	18	2000
SISTER DEW dEUS	62	1999
SISTER FRICTION HAYSI FANTAYZEE	62	1983
SISTER HAVANA URGE OVERKILL	58	1993
SISTER JANE NEW WORLD	9	1972
SISTER MOON TRANSVISION VAMP	41	1988
SISTER OF MERCY THOMPSON TWINS	11	1984
SISTER PAIN ELECTRAFIXION	27	1996
SISTER ROSETTA (CAPTURE THE SPIRIT) NOISETTES	63	2007
SISTER SAVIOUR RAPTURE	51	2003
SISTER SISTER SISTER BLISS	34	2000
SISTER SURPRISE GARY NUMAN	32	1983
SISTERS ARE DOING IT FOR THEMSELVES EURYTHMICS & ARETHA FRANKLIN	9	1985
THE SISTERS EP PULP	19	1994
SIT AND WAIT SYDNEY YOUNGBLOOD	16	1989
SIT DOWN JAMES	2	1991
SIT DOWN AND CRY ERROL DUNKLEY	52	1980
THE SIT SONG BARRON KNIGHTS	44	1980
SITTIN' ON A FENCE TWICE AS MUCH	25	1966
(SITTIN' ON) THE DOCK OF THE BAY OTIS REDDING	3	1968
SITTIN' UP IN MY ROOM BRANDY	30	1996
SITTING AT HOME HONEYCRACK	32	1995
SITTING DOWN HERE LENE MARLIN	5	2000
SITTING IN THE PARK GEORGIE FAME & THE BLUE FLAMES	12	1967
SITTING ON TOP OF THE WORLD LIVERPOOL FC	50	1986
SITTING, WAITING, WISHING JACK JOHNSON	65	2006
SITUATION YAZOO	14	1990
SIX MANSUN	16	1999
SIX DAYS DJ SHADOW	28	2002
SIX FEET DEEP (EP) GRAVEDIGGAZ	64	1995
643 (LOVE'S ON FIRE) DJ TIESTO FEATURING SUZANNE PALMER	36	2002
SIX MILLION STEPS (WEST RUNS SOUTH) RAHNI HARRIS & F.L.O.	43	1978
6 OF 1 THING CRAIG DAVID	39	2008
SIX PACK POLICE	17	1980
THE SIX TEENS SWEET	9	1974
634-5789 WILSON PICKETT	36	1966
6 UNDERGROUND SNEAKER PIMPS	9	1996
SIXTEEN MUSICAL YOUTH	23	1984
16 BARS STYLISTICS	7	1976
SIXTEEN REASONS CONNIE STEVENS	9	1960
SIXTEEN TONS FRANKIE LAINE	10	1956
SIXTEEN TONS TENNESSEE ERNIE FORD	49	1956
THE SIXTH SENSE VARIOUS ARTISTS (MONTAGES)	49	1990
THE 6TH SENSE COMMON	56	2000
68 GUNS ALARM	17	1983
SIXTY MILE SMILE 3 COLOURS RED	20	1997
60 MILES AND HOUR NEW ORDER	29	2001
SIXTY MINUTE MAN TRAMMPS	40	1975
69 POLICE DAVID HOLMES	53	2000
THE SIZE OF A COW WONDER STUFF	5	1991
SK8ER BOI AVRIL LAVIGNE	8	2002
SKA DJ ZINC	54	2004
SKA TRAIN BEATMASTERS FEATURING BETTY BOO	7	1989
SKAT STRUT MC SKAT KAT & THE STRAY MOB	64	1991
SKATEAWAY DIRE STRAITS	37	1981
SKELETON BOY FRIENDLY FIRES	48	2009
SKELETONS STEVIE WONDER	59	1987
SKIFFLE SESSION EP LONNIE DONEGAN	20	1956
SKIING IN THE SNOW WIGAN'S OVATION	12	1975
SKIN CHARLOTTE	56	1999
SKIN DEEP [A] DUKE ELLINGTON	7	1954
SKIN DEEP [A] TED HEATH	9	1954
SKIN DEEP [B] STRANGLERS	15	1984
SKIN DEEP [C] NATASHA THOMAS	54	2006
THE SKIN GAME GARY NUMAN	68	1992
SKIN O' MY TEETH MEGADETH	13	1992
SKIN ON SKIN GRACE	21	1996
SKIN TRADE DURAN DURAN	22	1987
THE SKIN UP (EP) SKIN	67	1993
SKINHEAD MOONSTOMP SYMARIP	54	1980
SKINNY LO-RIDER FEATURING CUMBERBATCH	44	2006
SKIP A BEAT BARRATT WAUGH	56	2003
SKIP TO MY LU LISA LISA	34	1994
SKIP TO THE END FUTUREHEADS	24	2006
SKUNK FUNK GALLIANO	41	1992
SKWEEZE ME PLEEZE ME SLADE	1	1973
SKY SONIQUE	2	2000
A SKY BLUE SHIRT AND A RAINBOW TIE NORMAN BROOKS	17	1954
SKY HIGH JIGSAW	9	1975
SKY HIGH NEWTON	56	1995
SKY PILOT ERIC BURDON & THE ANIMALS	40	1968
SKY PLUS NYLON MOON	43	1996
SKY STARTS FALLING DOVES	45	2005
SKYDIVE (I FEEL WONDERFUL) FREEFALL FEATURING JAN JOHNSTON	35	1998
THE SKYE BOAT SONG ROGER WHITTAKER & DES O'CONNOR	10	1986
SKYLARK MICHAEL HOLLIDAY	39	1960
SKY'S THE LIMIT NOTORIOUS B.I.G. FEATURING 112	35	1998
SKYWRITER JACKSON 5	25	1973
SLADE LIVE AT READING '80 (EP) SLADE	44	1980
SLAIN BY ELF URUSEI YATSURA	64	1998
SLAIN THE TRUTH (AT THE ROADHOUSE) BASEMENT	48	2003
SLAM [A] HUMANOID	54	1989
SLAM [B] ONYX	31	1993
SLAM [C] PENDULUM	34	2005
SLAM DUNK (DA FUNK) FIVE	10	1997
SLAM JAM WWF SUPERSTARS	4	1992
SLANG DEF LEPPARD	17	1996
SLAP AND TICKLE SQUEEZE	24	1979

	Peak Position	Year of Release
SLASH DOT DASH FATBOY SLIM	12	2004
SLASH 'N' BURN MANIC STREET PREACHERS	20	1992
SLAVE NEW WORLD SEPULTURA	46	1994
SLAVE TO LOVE BRYAN FERRY	10	1985
SLAVE TO THE GRIND SKID ROW	43	1991
SLAVE TO THE RHYTHM GRACE JONES	12	1985
SLAVE TO THE VIBE AFTERSHOCK	11	1993
SLAVE TO THE WAGE PLACEBO	19	2000
SLAVES NO MORE BLOW MONKEYS FEATURING SYLVIA TELLA	73	1989
SLEAZY BED TRACK BLUETONES	35	1998
SLEDGEHAMMER PETER GABRIEL	4	1986
SLEDGER PORN KINGS	71	2001
SLEEP [A] MARION	17	1995
SLEEP [B] CONJURE ONE	42	2003
SLEEP [C] TEXAS	6	2006
SLEEP ALONE WONDER STUFF	43	1991
SLEEP FREAK HEAVY STEREO	46	1995
SLEEP NOW IN THE FIRE RAGE AGAINST THE MACHINE	43	2000
SLEEP ON THE LEFT SIDE CORNERSHOP	23	1998
SLEEP TALK [A] ALYSON WILLIAMS	17	1989
SLEEP TALK [B] A.T.F.C. FEATURING LISA MILLETT	33	2002
SLEEP WALK SANTO & JOHNNY	22	1959
SLEEP WELL TONIGHT GENE	36	1994
SLEEP WHEN I'M DEAD CURE	68	2008
SLEEP WITH ME BIRDLAND	32	1990
SLEEPER AUDIOWEB	50	1995
SLEEPIN' ON THE JOB GILLAN	55	1980
SLEEPING AWAKE P.O.D.	42	2003
SLEEPING BAG ZZ TOP	27	1985
SLEEPING IN MENSWEAR	24	1995
SLEEPING IN MY CAR ROXETTE	14	1994
SLEEPING SATELLITE TASMIN ARCHER	1	1992
SLEEPING WITH THE LIGHT ON BUSTED	3	2003
SLEEPING WITH THE LIGHTS ON CURTIS STIGERS	53	1992
SLEEPING WITH VICTOR LYNDEN DAVID HALL	49	2000
SLEEPWALK ULTRAVOX	29	1980
SLEEPWALKERS MODEY LEMON	71	2005
SLEEPWALKING MARIA LAWSON	20	2006
SLEEPY JOE HERMAN'S HERMITS	12	1968
SLEEPY SHORES JOHNNY PEARSON	8	1971
SLEIGH RIDE S CLUB JUNIORS	6	2002
SLICE OF DA PIE MONIE LOVE	29	2000
SLID FLUKE	59	1993
SLIDE [A] RAH BAND	50	1981
SLIDE [B] GOO GOO DOLLS	43	1999
SLIDE ALONG SIDE SHIFTY	29	2004
SLIDLING IAN McCULLOCH	61	2003
SLIGHT RETURN BLUETONES	2	1996
THE SLIGHTEST TOUCH FIVE STAR	4	1987
SLIP AND DIP COFFEE	57	1980
SLIP AND SLIDE MEDICINE HEAD	22	1974
(SLIP & SLIDE) SUICIDE KOSHEEN	50	2001
SLIP SLIDIN' AWAY PAUL SIMON	36	1977
SLIP YOUR DISC TO THIS HEATWAVE	15	1977
SLIPPERY PEOPLE TALKING HEADS	68	1984
SLIPPERY SLOPES CLIPZ	72	2005
SLIPPIN' DMX	30	1999
SLIPPING AWAY [A] DAVE EDMUNDS	60	1983
SLIPPING AWAY [B] MANSUN	55	2004
SLIPPING AWAY [C] MOBY	53	2006
SLITHER VELVET REVOLVER	35	2004
SLOGANS BOB MARLEY & THE WAILERS	45	2005
SLOOP JOHN B BEACH BOYS	2	1966
SLOPPY HEART FRAZIER CHORUS	73	1989
SLOW KYLIE MINOGUE	1	2003
SLOW AND SEXY SHABBA RANKS FEATURING JOHNNY GILL	17	1992
SLOW DOWN [A] JOHN MILES	10	1977
SLOW DOWN [B] LOOSE ENDS	27	1986
SLOW DOWN [C] BOBBY VALENTINO	4	2005
SLOW EMOTION REPLAY THE THE	35	1993
SLOW FLOW BRAXTONS	26	1997
SLOW HANDS INTERPOL	36	2004
SLOW IT DOWN EAST 17	13	1993
SLOW JAMZ TWISTA	3	2004
SLOW MOTION ULTRAVOX	33	1981
SLOW RIVERS ELTON JOHN & CLIFF RICHARD	44	1986
SLOW TRAIN TO DAWN THE THE	64	1987
SLOW TRAIN TO PARADISE TAVARES	62	1978
SLOW TWISTIN' CHUBBY CHECKER	23	1962
SLOWDIVE SIOUXSIE & THE BANSHEES	41	1982
SLOWHAND POINTER SISTERS	10	1981
SLY MASSIVE ATTACK	24	1994
SMACK MY BITCH UP PRODIGY	8	1997
SMACK THAT AKON FEATURING EMINEM	1	2006
SMALL ADS SMALL ADS	63	1981
SMALL BIT OF LOVE SAW DOCTORS	24	1994
SMALL BLUE THING SUZANNE VEGA	65	1986
SMALL SAD SAM PHIL McLEAN	34	1962
SMALL TOWN JOHN COUGAR MELLENCAMP	53	1986
SMALL TOWN BOY UK	74	1996
A SMALL VICTORY FAITH NO MORE	29	1992
SMALLTOWN BOY BRONSKI BEAT	3	1984
SMALLTOWN CREED KANE GANG	60	1984
SMARTY PANTS FIRST CHOICE	9	1973
SMASH IT UP DAMNED	35	1979
SMASH SUMTHIN' ADAM F FEATURING REDMAN	47	2001
S.M.D.U. BROCK LANDARS	49	1998
SMELLS LIKE NIRVANA WEIRD AL YANKOVIC	58	1992
SMELLS LIKE TEEN SPIRIT NIRVANA	7	1991
SMELLS LIKE TEEN SPIRIT ABIGAIL	29	1994
SMILE MICHAEL JACKSON	74	2009
SMILE [A] NAT 'KING' COLE	2	1954
SMILE [A] ROBERT DOWNEY, JR	68	1993
SMILE [B] PUSSYCAT	24	1977
THE SMILE [C] DAVID ESSEX	52	1983
SMILE [D] AUDREY HALL	14	1986
SMILE [E] ASWAD FEATURING SWEETIE IRIE	53	1990
SMILE [F] SUPERNATURALS	23	1997
SMILE [G] LONESTAR	55	2000
SMILE [H] FUTURE BREEZE	67	2001
SMILE [I] MONROE	60	2004
SMILE [J] DAVID GILMOUR	72	2006
SMILE [K] LILY ALLEN	1	2006
A SMILE IN A WHISPER FAIRGROUND ATTRACTION	75	1988
SMILE LIKE YOU MEAN IT KILLERS	11	2005
SMILE TO SHINE BAZ	58	2002
SMILER HEAVY STEREO	46	1995
SMILEY FACES GNARLS BARKLEY	10	2006
SMILIN' BRYN CHRISTOPHER	31	2008
THE SMILING FACE BURN	72	2002
SMOKE NATALIE IMBRUGLIA	5	1998
SMOKE GETS IN YOUR EYES PLATTERS	1	1959
SMOKE GETS IN YOUR EYES BLUE HAZE	32	1972
SMOKE GETS IN YOUR EYES BRYAN FERRY	17	1974
SMOKE GETS IN YOUR EYES JOHN ALFORD	13	1996
SMOKE IT DANDY WARHOLS	59	2005
SMOKE MACHINE X-PRESS 2	43	2001
SMOKE ON THE WATER DEEP PURPLE	21	1977
SMOKE ON THE WATER ROCK AID ARMENIA	39	1989
SMOKEBELCH II SABRES OF PARADISE	55	1993
SMOKERS OUTSIDE THE HOSPITAL DOORS EDITORS	7	2007
SMOKESTACK LIGHTNIN' HOWLIN' WOLF	42	1964
SMOKEY BLUES AWAY A NEW GENERATION	38	1968
SMOKIN' IN THE BOYS' ROOM MOTLEY CRUE	51	1985
SMOKIN' IN THE BOYS' ROOM BROWNSVILLE STATION	27	1974
SMOKIN' ME OUT WARREN G FEATURING RONALD ISLEY	14	1997
SMOOTH SANTANA FEATURING ROB THOMAS	3	1999
SMOOTH CRIMINAL MICHAEL JACKSON	8	1988
SMOOTH CRIMINAL ALIEN ANT FARM	3	2001
SMOOTH OPERATOR SADE	19	1984
SMOOTHER OPERATOR BIG DADDY KANE	65	1989
SMOOTHIN' GROOVIN' INGRAM	56	1983
SMOULDER KING ADORA	62	2000
SMUGGLER'S BLUES GLENN FREY	22	1985
THE SMURF TYRONE BRUNSON	52	1982
THE SMURF SONG FATHER ABRAHAM & THE SMURFS	2	1978
THE SNAKE [A] AL WILSON	41	1975
SNAKE [B] R KELLY FEATURING BIG TIGGER	10	2003
SNAKE BITE (EP) DAVID COVERDALE'S WHITESNAKE	61	1978
SNAKE IN THE GRASS DAVE DEE, DOZY, BEAKY, MICK & TICH	23	1969
SNAP MEGAMIX SNAP!	10	1991
SNAP YOUR FINGAZ KUMARA	70	2000
SNAPPED IT KRUST	58	2002
SNAPPINESS BBG FEATURING DINA TAYLOR	28	1990
SNAPSHOT 3 RONI SIZE	61	2003
SNEAKIN' SUSPICION DR FEELGOOD	47	1977
SNEAKING OUT THE BACK DOOR MATT BIANCO	44	1984
SNITCH OBIE TRICE FEATURING AKON	44	2006
SNOBBERY AND DECAY ACT	60	1987
SNOOKER LOOPY MATCHROOM MOB WITH CHAS & DAVE	6	1986
SNOOP DOGG SNOOP DOGG	13	2001
SNOOP'S UPSIDE YA HEAD SNOOP DOGGY DOGG FEATURING CHARLIE WILSON	12	1996
SNOOPY VS THE RED BARON ROYAL GUARDSMEN	8	1967
SNOOPY VS. THE RED BARON HOTSHOTS	4	1973
SNOT RAP KENNY EVERETT	9	1983
SNOW [A] ORN	61	1997
SNOW [B] JJ72	21	2001
SNOW COACH RUSS CONWAY	7	1959
SNOW (HEY HO) RED HOT CHILI PEPPERS	16	2006
SNOWBIRD ANNE MURRAY	23	1970
SNOWBOUND FOR CHRISTMAS DICKIE VALENTINE	28	1957
SNOWDEN DOVES	17	2005
THE SNOWS OF NEW YORK CHRIS DE BURGH	60	1995
SO ALIVE RYAN ADAMS	21	2004
SO AMAZING LUTHER VANDROSS	33	1987
SO BEAUTIFUL [A] URBAN COOKIE COLLECTIVE	68	1995
SO BEAUTIFUL [B] CHRIS DE BURGH	29	1997
SO BEAUTIFUL [C] DJ INNOCENCE FEATURING ALEX CHARLES	51	2002
SO BEAUTIFUL [D] DARREN HAYES	15	2005
SO CALLED FRIEND TEXAS	30	1993
SO CLOSE [A] DIANA ROSS	43	1983
SO CLOSE [B] HALL & OATES	69	1990
SO CLOSE [C] DINA CARROLL	20	1992
SO CLOSE TO LOVE WENDY MOTEN	35	1994
SO COLD THE NIGHT COMMUNARDS	8	1986
SO CONFUSED 2PLAY FEATURING RAGHAV & JUCXI	6	2004
SO DAMN BEAUTIFUL POLOROID	28	2003
SO DAMN COOL UGLY KID JOE	44	1992
SO DEEP REESE PROJECT	54	1993
SO DEEP IS THE NIGHT KEN DODD	31	1964
SO DO I KENNY BALL & HIS JAZZMEN	14	1962
SO EASY ROYKSOPP	21	2002
SO EMOTIONAL WHITNEY HOUSTON	5	1987
SO FAR AWAY DIRE STRAITS	20	1985

	Peak Position	Year of Release
SO FINE [A] HOWARD JOHNSON	45	1982
SO FINE [B] KINANE	63	1998
SO FINE [C] SEAN PAUL	25	2009
SO FRESH SO CLEAN OUTKAST	16	2001
SO GOOD [A] ROY ORBISON	32	1967
SO GOOD [B] ETERNAL	13	1994
SO GOOD [C] BOYZONE	3	1995
SO GOOD [D] JULIET ROBERTS	15	1998
SO GOOD [E] RACHEL STEVENS	10	2005
SO GOOD [F] BRATZ ROCK ANGELZ	23	2005
SO GOOD SO RIGHT BRENDA RUSSELL	51	1980
SO GOOD TO BE BACK HOME AGAIN TOURISTS	8	1980
SO GOOD (TO COME HOME TO) IVAN MATAIS	69	1996
SO GRIMEY SO SOLID CREW	62	2004
SO GROOVY WENDELL WILLIAMS	74	1991
SO HARD PET SHOP BOYS	4	1990
SO HELP ME GIRL GARY BARLOW	11	1997
SO HERE I AM UB40	25	1982
SO HERE WE ARE BLOC PARTY	5	2005
SO HOT JC	74	1998
SO HUMAN LADY SOVEREIGN	38	2009
SO I BEGIN GALLEON	36	2002
SO IN LOVE ORCHESTRAL MANOEUVRES IN THE DARK	27	1985
SO IN LOVE (THE REAL DEAL) JUDY CHEEKS	27	1993
SO IN LOVE WITH YOU [A] FREDDY BRECK	44	1974
SO IN LOVE WITH YOU [B] SPEAR OF DESTINY	36	1988
SO IN LOVE WITH YOU [C] TEXAS	28	1994
SO IN LOVE WITH YOU [D] DUKE	22	1996
SO INTO YOU [A] MICHAEL WATFORD	53	1994
SO INTO YOU [B] WILDHEARTS	22	2003
SO IT WILL ALWAYS BE EVERLY BROTHERS	23	1963
SO LITTLE TIME ARKARNA	46	1997
SO LONELY [A] POLICE	6	1980
SO LONELY [B] JAKATTA	8	2002
SO LONG [A] FISCHER-Z	72	1980
SO LONG [B] FIERCE	15	1999
SO LONG [C] WILLY MASON	45	2005
SO LONG BABY DEL SHANNON	10	1961
SO LOW OCEAN COLOUR SCENE	34	1999
SO MACHO SINITTA	2	1986
SO MANY TIMES GADJO FEATURING ALEXANDRA PRINCE	22	2005
SO MANY WAYS [A] BRAXTONS	32	1997
SO MANY WAYS [B] ELLIE CAMPBELL	26	1999
SO MUCH IN LOVE [A] TYMES	21	1963
SO MUCH IN LOVE [A] ALL-4-ONE	49	1994
SO MUCH IN LOVE [B] MIGHTY AVENGERS	46	1964
SO MUCH LOVE TONY BLACKBURN	31	1968
SO MUCH LOVE TO GIVE [A] THOMAS BANGALTER & DJ FALCON	71	2003
SO MUCH LOVE TO GIVE [B] FREELOADERS FEATURING THE REAL THING	9	2005
SO MUCH TROUBLE IN THE WORLD BOB MARLEY & THE WAILERS	56	1979
SO NATURAL LISA STANSFIELD	15	1993
SO NEAR TO CHRISTMAS ALVIN STARDUST	29	1984
SO NOT OVER YOU SIMPLY RED	34	2007
SO PURE [A] BABY D	3	1996
SO PURE [B] ALANIS MORISSETTE	38	1999
SO REAL [A] LOVE DECADE	14	1991
SO REAL [B] HARRY	53	2002
SO RIGHT RAILWAY CHILDREN	68	1990
SO RIGHT K-KLASS	20	1992
SO ROTTEN BLAK TWANG FEATURING JAHMALI	48	2002
SO SAD THE SONG GLADYS KNIGHT & THE PIPS	20	1976
SO SAD (TO WATCH GOOD LOVE GO BAD) EVERLY BROTHERS	4	1960
SO SAYS I SHINS	73	2004
SO SEDUCTIVE TONY YAYO FEATURING 50 CENT	28	2005
SO SEXY TWISTA FEATURING R KELLY	28	2004
SO SICK NE-YO	1	2006
SO SORRY I SAID LIZA MINNELLI	62	1989
SO STRONG BEN SHAW FEATURING ADELE HOLNESS	72	2001
SO TELL ME WHY POISON	25	1991
SO THE STORY GOES LIVING IN A BOX FEATURING BOBBY WOMACK	34	1987
SO THIS IS ROMANCE LINX	15	1981
SO TIRED [A] FRANKIE VAUGHAN	21	1967
SO TIRED [B] OZZY OSBOURNE	20	1984
SO TIRED OF BEING ALONE SYBIL	53	1996
SO UNDER PRESSURE DANNII MINOGUE	20	2006
SO WATCHA GONNA DO NOW PUBLIC ENEMY	50	1995
SO WHAT [A] GILBERT O'SULLIVAN	70	1990
SO WHAT! [B] RONNY JORDAN	32	1992
SO WHAT [C] FIELD MOB FEATURING CIARA	56	2006
SO WHAT [D] P!NK	1	2008
SO WHAT IF I DAMAGE	12	2001
SO WHAT THE FUSS STEVIE WONDER	19	2005
SO WHY SO SAD MANIC STREET PREACHERS	8	2001
SO YESTERDAY HILARY DUFF	9	2003
SO YOU KNOW INME	33	2005
SO YOU WIN AGAIN HOT CHOCOLATE	1	1977
SO YOU'D LIKE TO SAVE THE WORLD LLOYD COLE	72	1993
SO YOUNG [A] SUEDE	22	1993
SO YOUNG [B] CORRS	6	1998
SOAK UP THE SUN SHERYL CROW	16	2002
SOAPBOX LITTLE ANGELS	33	1993
SOBER [A] DRUGSTORE	68	1998
SOBER [B] JENNIFER PAIGE	68	1999
SOBER [C] P!NK	9	2009
SOC IT TO ME BADFELLAS FEATURING CK	55	2003
SOCK IT 2 ME MISSY 'MISDEMEANOR' ELLIOTT	33	1997
SODA POP AVID MERRION/DAVINA McCALL/ PATSY KENSIT	5	2005
SOFA SONG KOOKS	28	2005
SOFT AS YOUR FACE SOUP DRAGONS	66	1987
SOFT LIKE ME SAINT ETIENNE	40	2003
SOFT TOP HARD SHOULDER CHRIS REA	53	1993
SOFTLY AS I LEAVE YOU MATT MONRO	10	1962
SOFTLY SOFTLY [A] RUBY MURRAY	1	1955
SOFTLY SOFTLY [B] EQUALS	48	1968
SOFTLY WHISPERING I LOVE YOU CONGREGATION	4	1971
SOFTLY WHISPERING I LOVE YOU PAUL YOUNG	21	1990
SOLACE OF YOU LIVING COLOUR	33	1991
SOLD BOY GEORGE	24	1987
SOLD ME DOWN THE RIVER ALARM	43	1989
SOLD MY ROCK 'N' ROLL (GAVE IT FOR FUNKY SOUL) LINDA & THE FUNKY BOYS	36	1976
SOLD OUT EP REEL BIG FISH	62	2002
SOLDIER DESTINY'S CHILD FEATURING TI & LIL' WAYNE	4	2005
SOLDIER BLUE BUFFY SAINTE-MARIE	7	1971
SOLDIER BOY SHIRELLES	23	1962
SOLDIER BOY CHEETAHS	39	1965
SOLDIER GIRL POLYPHONIC SPREE	26	2003
SOLDIER OF LOVE DONNY OSMOND	29	1988
A SOLDIER'S CHRISTMAS LETTER SOLDIERS	65	2009
SOLDIER'S SONG HOLLIES	58	1980
SOLEX (CLOSE TO THE EDGE) MICHAEL WOODS	52	2003
SOLEY SOLEY MIDDLE OF THE ROAD	5	1971
SOLID ASHFORD & SIMPSON	3	1985
SOLID BOND IN YOUR HEART STYLE COUNCIL	11	1983
SOLID GOLD EASY ACTION T REX	2	1972
SOLID ROCK (LIVE) DIRE STRAITS	50	1984
SOLID WOOD ALISON MOYET	44	1995
SOLITAIRE ANDY WILLIAMS	4	1974
SOLITAIRE CARPENTERS	32	1975
SOLITARY MAN H.I.M.	9	2004
SOLOMON BITES THE WORM BLUETONES	10	1998
SOLSBURY HILL PETER GABRIEL	13	1977
SOLSBURY HILL ERASURE	10	2002
(SOLUTION TO) THE PROBLEM MASQUERADE	64	1986
SOLVED UNBELIEVABLE TRUTH	39	1998
SOME BEAUTIFUL JACK WILD	46	1970
SOME CANDY TALKING JESUS & MARY CHAIN	13	1986
SOME FANTASTIC PLACE SQUEEZE	73	1993
SOME FINER DAY ALL ABOUT EVE	57	1992
SOME GIRLS [A] RACEY	2	1979
SOME GIRLS [B] ULTIMATE KAOS	9	1994
SOME GIRLS [C] JC CHASEZ	13	2004
SOME GIRLS [D] RACHEL STEVENS	2	2004
SOME GUYS HAVE ALL THE LUCK ROBERT PALMER	16	1982
SOME GUYS HAVE ALL THE LUCK ROD STEWART	15	1984
SOME GUYS HAVE ALL THE LUCK MAXI PRIEST	12	1987
SOME JUSTICE URBAN SHAKEDOWN FEATURING MICKY FINN	23	1992
SOME KIND OF A SUMMER DAVID CASSIDY	3	1973
SOME KIND OF BLISS KYLIE MINOGUE	22	1997
SOME KIND OF FRIEND BARRY MANILOW	48	1983
SOME KIND OF HEAVEN BBG	65	1990
SOME KIND OF WONDERFUL BLOW MONKEYS	67	1987
SOME KINDA EARTHQUAKE DUANE EDDY & THE REBELS	12	1959
SOME KINDA FUN CHRIS MONTEZ	10	1963
SOME KINDA RUSH BOOTY LUV	19	2007
SOME LIE 4 LOVE L.A. GUNS	61	1991
SOME LIKE IT HOT POWER STATION	14	1985
SOME MIGHT SAY OASIS	1	1995
SOME MIGHT SAY SUPERNOVA	55	1996
SOME MIGHT SAY DE-CODE FEATURING BEVERLI SKEETE	69	1996
SOME OF YOUR LOVIN' DUSTY SPRINGFIELD	8	1965
SOME OLD GIRL PADDINGTONS	47	2004
SOME OTHER GUY BIG THREE	37	1963
SOME OTHER SUCKER'S PARADE DEL AMITRI	46	1997
SOME PEOPLE [A] CAROL DEENE	25	1962
SOME PEOPLE [B] BELOUIS SOME	33	1986
SOME PEOPLE [C] PAUL YOUNG	56	1986
SOME PEOPLE [D] CLIFF RICHARD	3	1987
SOME PEOPLE SAY TERRORVISION	22	1995
SOME SAY KRISTIAN LEONTIOU	54	2004
SOME THINGS YOU NEVER GET USED TO DIANA ROSS & THE SUPREMES	34	1968
SOME VELVET MORING PRIMAL SCREAM	44	2003
SOMEBODY [A] STARGAZERS	20	1955
SOMEBODY [B] JUNIOR	64	1984
SOMEBODY [C] DEPECHE MODE	16	1984
SOMEBODY [D] BRYAN ADAMS	35	1985
SOMEBODY [E] BRILLIANT	67	1986
SOMEBODY [F] SHORTIE VS BLACK LEGEND	37	2001
SOMEBODY ELSE'S GIRL BILLY FURY	18	1963
SOMEBODY ELSE'S GUY JOCELYN BROWN	13	1984
SOMEBODY ELSE'S GUY LOUCHIE LOU & MICHIE ONE	54	1993
SOMEBODY ELSE'S GUY CE CE PENISTON	13	1998
SOMEBODY HELP ME SPENCER DAVIS GROUP	1	1966

	Peak Position	Year of Release
(SOMEBODY) HELP ME OUT BEGGAR & CO	15	1981
SOMEBODY IN THE HOUSE SAY YEAH! 2 IN A ROOM	66	1989
SOMEBODY LIKE YOU ELATE	38	1997
SOMEBODY LOVES YOU NIK KERSHAW	70	1999
SOMEBODY PUT SOMETHING IN MY DRINK RAMONES	69	1986
SOMEBODY STOLE MY GAL JOHNNIE RAY	6	1953
SOMEBODY TO LOVE [A] BRAD NEWMAN	47	1962
SOMEBODY TO LOVE [A] JETS	56	1982
SOMEBODY TO LOVE [B] QUEEN	2	1976
SOMEBODY TO LOVE [B] GLEE CAST	26	2010
SOMEBODY TO LOVE [C] BOOGIE PIMPS	3	2003
SOMEBODY TO SHOVE SOUL ASYLUM	32	1993
SOMEBODY TOLD ME KILLERS	3	2004
SOMEBODY'S BABY PAT BENATAR	48	1993
SOMEBODY'S WATCHING ME ROCKWELL	6	1984
SOMEBODY'S WATCHING ME BEATFREAKZ	3	2006
SOMEDAY [A] RICKY NELSON	9	1958
SOMEDAY [B] GAP BAND	17	1984
SOMEDAY [C] GLASS TIGER	66	1987
SOMEDAY [D] MARIAH CAREY	38	1991
SOMEDAY [D] REZONANCE Q	29	2003
SOMEDAY [E] M PEOPLE WITH HEATHER SMALL	38	1992
SOMEDAY [F] EDDY	49	1994
SOMEDAY [G] LOVE TO INFINITY	75	1995
SOMEDAY [H] ETERNAL	4	1996
SOMEDAY [I] CHARLOTTE	74	1999
SOMEDAY [J] STROKES	27	2002
SOMEDAY [K] NICKELBACK	6	2003
SOMEDAY I'LL BE SATURDAY NIGHT BON JOVI	7	1995
SOMEDAY I'LL FIND YOU SHOLA AMA & CRAIG ARMSTRONG	28	1998
SOMEDAY (I'M COMING BACK) LISA STANSFIELD	10	1992
SOMEDAY MAN MONKEES	47	1969
SOMEDAY ONE DAY SEEKERS	11	1966
SOMEDAY WE'LL BE TOGETHER DIANA ROSS & THE SUPREMES	13	1969
SOMEDAY WE'LL KNOW NEW RADICALS	48	1999
SOMEDAY WE'RE GONNA LOVE AGAIN SEARCHERS	11	1964
SOMEDAY (YOU'LL BE SORRY) KENNY BALL & HIS JAZZMEN	28	1961
SOMEDAY (YOU'LL COME RUNNING) FM	64	1989
SOMEDAY (YOU'LL WANT ME TO WANT YOU) JODIE SANDS	14	1958
SOMEHOW SOMEWHERE DEEP SENSATION	74	2004
SOMEONE [A] JOHNNY MATHIS	6	1959
SOMEONE [B] ASCENSION	43	1997
SOMEONE [C] SWV FEATURING PUFF DADDY	34	1997
SOMEONE ALWAYS GETS THERE FIRST BENNETT	69	1997
SOMEONE BELONGING TO SOMEONE BEE GEES	49	1983
SOMEONE ELSE NOT ME DURAN DURAN	53	2000
SOMEONE ELSE'S BABY ADAM FAITH	2	1960
SOMEONE ELSE'S ROSES JOAN REGAN	5	1954
SOMEONE LIKE ME ATOMIC KITTEN	8	2004
SOMEONE LIKE YOU [A] DINA CARROLL	38	2001
SOMEONE LIKE YOU [B] RUSSELL WATSON & FAYE TOZER	10	2002
SOMEONE LOVES YOU HONEY LUTRICIA McNEAL	9	1998
SOMEONE MUST HAVE HURT YOU A LOT FRANKIE VAUGHAN	46	1965
SOMEONE ON YOUR MIND JIMMY YOUNG	13	1955
SOMEONE SAVED MY LIFE TONIGHT ELTON JOHN	22	1975
SOMEONE SHOULD TELL HER MAVERICKS	45	1999
SOMEONE SHOULD TELL YOU LEMAR	21	2006
SOMEONE SOMEONE BRIAN POOLE & THE TREMELOES	2	1964
SOMEONE SOMEWHERE WANNADIES	38	1996
SOMEONE SOMEWHERE (IN SUMMERTIME) SIMPLE MINDS	36	1982
SOMEONE THERE FOR ME RICHARD BLACKWOOD	23	2000
SOMEONE TO CALL MY LOVER JANET JACKSON	11	2001
SOMEONE TO HOLD TREY LORENZ	65	1992
SOMEONE TO LOVE [A] SEAN MAGUIRE	14	1994
SOMEONE TO LOVE [B] EAST 17	16	1996
SOMEONE TO SOMEBODY FEARGAL SHARKEY	64	1986
SOMEONE'S DAUGHTER BETH ORTON	49	1997
SOMEONE'S LOOKING AT YOU BOOMTOWN RATS	4	1980
SOMEONE'S TAKEN MARIA AWAY ADAM FAITH	34	1965
SOMERSAULT ZERO 7 FEATURING SIA	56	2004
SOMETHIN' ELSE EDDIE COCHRAN	22	1959
SOMETHIN' 4 DA HONEYZ MONTELL JORDAN	15	1995
SOMETHIN' IS GOIN' ON CLIFF RICHARD	9	2004
SOMETHIN' STUPID NANCY SINATRA & FRANK SINATRA	1	1967
SOMETHIN' STUPID ALI & KIBIBI CAMPBELL	30	1995
SOMETHIN' STUPID ROBBIE WILLIAMS & NICOLE KIDMAN	1	2001
SOMETHING [A] GEORGIE FAME & THE BLUE FLAMES	23	1965
SOMETHING [B] BEATLES	4	1969
SOMETHING [B] SHIRLEY BASSEY	4	1970
SOMETHING [C] LASGO	4	2002
SOMETHING ABOUT THE MUSIC DA SLAMMIN' PHROGZ	53	2000
SOMETHING ABOUT THE WAY YOU LOOK TONIGHT ELTON JOHN	1	1997
SOMETHING ABOUT YOU [A] LEVEL 42	6	1985
SOMETHING ABOUT YOU [B] MR ROY	49	1994
SOMETHING ABOUT YOU [C] NEW EDITION	16	1997
SOMETHING ABOUT YOU [D] JAMELIA	9	2006
SOMETHING BEAUTIFUL ROBBIE WILLIAMS	3	2003
SOMETHING BEAUTIFUL REMAINS TINA TURNER	27	1996
SOMETHING BETTER BEGINNING HONEYCOMBS	39	1965
SOMETHING BETTER CHANGE STRANGLERS	9	1977
SOMETHING 'BOUT YOU BABY I LIKE TOM JONES	36	1974
SOMETHING 'BOUT YOU BABY I LIKE STATUS QUO	9	1981
SOMETHING CHANGED PULP	10	1996
SOMETHING DEEP INSIDE BILLIE PIPER	4	2000
SOMETHING DIFFERENT SHAGGY FEATURING WAYNE WONDER	21	1996
SOMETHING ELSE [A] SEX PISTOLS	3	1979
SOMETHING ELSE [B] AGENT BLUE	59	2004
SOMETHING FOR THE GIRL WITH EVERYTHING SPARKS	17	1975
SOMETHING FOR THE PAIN BON JOVI	8	1995
SOMETHING FOR THE WEEKEND [A] DIVINE COMEDY	14	1996
SOMETHING 4 THE WEEKEND [B] SUPER FURRY ANIMALS	18	1996
SOMETHING FOR THE WEEKEND [C] FRED & ROXY	36	2000
SOMETHING GOIN' ON TODD TERRY FEATURING MARTHA WASH & JOCELYN BROWN	5	1997
SOMETHING GOOD UTAH SAINTS	4	1992
SOMETHING GOT ME STARTED SIMPLY RED	11	1991
SOMETHING HAPPENED ON THE WAY TO HEAVEN PHIL COLLINS	15	1990
SOMETHING HERE IN MY HEART (KEEPS A-TELLIN' ME NO) PAPER DOLLS	11	1968
SOMETHING IN COMMON BOBBY BROWN & WHITNEY HOUSTON	16	1994
SOMETHING IN MY HOUSE DEAD OR ALIVE	12	1987
SOMETHING IN THE AIR THUNDERCLAP NEWMAN	1	1969
SOMETHING IN THE AIR FISH	51	1992
SOMETHING IN THE AIR TOM PETTY	53	1993
SOMETHING IN THE AIR HAYLEY SANDERSON	61	2006
SOMETHING IN YOUR EYES [A] BELL BIV DEVOE	60	1993
SOMETHING IN YOUR EYES [B] ED CASE	38	2000
SOMETHING INSIDE OF ME CORAL	41	2005
(SOMETHING INSIDE) SO STRONG LABI SIFFRE	4	1987
SOMETHING INSIDE SO STRONG MICHAEL BALL	40	1996
SOMETHING INSIDE (SO STRONG) RIK WALLER	25	2002
SOMETHING IS SQUEEZING MY SKULL MORRISSEY	46	2009
SOMETHING JUST AIN'T RIGHT KEITH SWEAT	55	1988
SOMETHING KINDA OOOOH GIRLS ALOUD	3	2006
SOMETHING MISSING PETULA CLARK	44	1961
SOMETHING OLD, SOMETHING NEW FANTASTICS	9	1971
SOMETHING ON MY MIND CHRIS ANDREWS	41	1966
SOMETHING ON YOUR MIND MYNC PROJECT FEATURING ABIGAIL BAILEY	71	2006
SOMETHING OUTA NOTHING LETITIA DEAN & PAUL MEDFORD	12	1986
SOMETHING SO GOOD RAILWAY CHILDREN	57	1991
SOMETHING SO REAL (CHINHEADS THEME) LOVE DECREE	61	1989
SOMETHING SO RIGHT ANNIE LENNOX FEATURING PAUL SIMON	44	1995
SOMETHING SPECIAL [A] STEVE HARVEY	46	1983
SOMETHING SPECIAL [B] NOMAD	73	1991
SOMETHING STUPID CORONATION STREET CAST: AMANDA BARRIE & JOHNNIE BRIGGS	35	1995
SOMETHING TELLS ME (SOMETHING IS GONNA HAPPEN TONIGHT) CILLA BLACK	3	1971
SOMETHING THAT I SAID RUTS	29	1979
SOMETHING THAT YOU SAID BANGLES	38	2003
SOMETHING TO BELIEVE IN [A] POISON	35	1990
SOMETHING TO BELIEVE IN [B] RAMONES	69	1986
SOMETHING TO DO DEPECHE MODE	75	2004
SOMETHING TO MISS SENSELESS THINGS	57	1995
SOMETHING TO TALK ABOUT BADLY DRAWN BOY	28	2002
SOMETHING WILD RARE	57	1996
SOMETHING WORTHWHILE GUN	39	1995
SOMETHING YOU GOT AND WHY NOT?	39	1990
SOMETHING'S BEEN MAKING ME BLUE SMOKIE	17	1976
SOMETHING'S BURNING KENNY ROGERS & THE FIRST EDITION	8	1970
SOMETHING'S COOKIN' IN THE KITCHEN DANA	44	1979
SOMETHING'S GOIN' ON [A] MYSTIC 3	63	2000
SOMETHING'S GOING ON [B] A	51	2002
SOMETHING'S GOTTA GIVE SAMMY DAVIS, JR	11	1955
SOMETHING'S GOTTEN HOLD OF MY HEART GENE PITNEY	5	1967
SOMETHING'S GOTTEN HOLD OF MY HEART MARC ALMOND FEATURING SPECIAL GUEST STAR GENE PITNEY	1	1989

	Peak Position	Year of Release
SOMETHING'S HAPPENING HERMAN'S HERMITS	6	1968
SOMETHING'S JUMPIN' IN YOUR SHIRT MALCOLM McLAREN & THE BOOTZILLA ORCHESTRA FEATURING LISA MARIE	29	1989
SOMETHING'S MISSING CHORDS	55	1980
SOMETIME AROUND MIDNIGHT AIRBORNE TOXIC EVENT	33	2009
SOMETIMES [A] ERASURE	2	1986
SOMETIMES [B] MAX Q	53	1990
SOMETIMES [C] JAMES	18	1993
SOMETIMES [D] BRAND NEW HEAVIES	11	1997
SOMETIMES [E] TIN TIN OUT FEATURING SHELLEY NELSON	20	1998
SOMETIMES [F] LES RYTHMES DIGITALES FEATURING NIK KERSHAW	56	1999
SOMETIMES [G] BRITNEY SPEARS	3	1999
SOMETIMES [H] ASH	21	2001
SOMETIMES ALWAYS JESUS & MARY CHAIN	22	1994
SOMETIMES I MISS YOU SO MUCH PM DAWN	58	1996
SOMETIMES IT HURTS TINDERSTICKS	60	2003
SOMETIMES (IT SNOWS IN APRIL) AMAR	48	2000
SOMETIMES IT'S A BITCH STEVIE NICKS	40	1991
SOMETIMES LOVE JUST AIN'T ENOUGH PATTY SMYTH WITH DON HENLEY	22	1992
SOMETIMES (THEME FROM 'CHAMPIONS') ELAINE PAIGE	72	1984
SOMETIMES WHEN WE TOUCH DAN HILL	13	1978
SOMETIMES WHEN WE TOUCH NEWTON	32	1997
SOMETIMES YOU CAN'T MAKE IT ON YOUR OWN U2	1	2005
SOMEWHERE [A] PJ PROBY	6	1964
SOMEWHERE [A] PET SHOP BOYS	9	1997
SOMEWHERE [B] EFUA	42	1993
SOMEWHERE ACROSS FOREVER STELLASTARR	61	2003
SOMEWHERE ALONG THE WAY NAT 'KING' COLE	3	1952
SOMEWHERE DOWN THE CRAZY RIVER ROBBIE ROBERTSON	15	1988
SOMEWHERE ELSE [A] CHINA DRUM	74	1997
SOMEWHERE ELSE [B] RAZORLIGHT	2	2005
SOMEWHERE I BELONG LINKIN PARK	10	2003
SOMEWHERE IN AMERICA (THERE'S A STREET NAMED AFTER MY DAD) WAS (NOT WAS)	57	1992
SOMEWHERE IN MY HEART AZTEC CAMERA	3	1988
SOMEWHERE IN THE COUNTRY GENE PITNEY	19	1968
SOMEWHERE IN THE NIGHT BARRY MANILOW	42	1978
SOMEWHERE MY LOVE MIKE SAMMES SINGERS	14	1966
SOMEWHERE MY LOVE MANUEL & HIS MUSIC OF THE MOUNTAINS	42	1966
SOMEWHERE ONLY WE KNOW KEANE	3	2004
SOMEWHERE OUT THERE LINDA RONSTADT & JAMES INGRAM	8	1987
SOMEWHERE OVER THE RAINBOW CLIFF RICHARD	11	2001
SOMEWHERE OVER THE RAINBOW ISRAEL KAMAKAWIWO'OLE	46	2007
SOMEWHERE SOMEBODY FIVE STAR	23	1987
SOMEWHERE SOMEHOW WET WET WET	7	1995
SON OF A GUN JX	6	1994
SON OF A GUN (BETCHA THINK THIS SONG IS ABOUT YOU) JANET JACKSON FEATURING CARLY SIMON	13	2001
SON OF A PREACHER MAN DUSTY SPRINGFIELD	9	1968
SON OF HICKORY HOLLER'S TRAMP OC SMITH	2	1968
SON OF MARY HARRY BELAFONTE	18	1958
SON OF MY FATHER CHICORY TIP	1	1972
SON OF SAM ELLIOTT SMITH	55	2000
SON OF THREE BREEDERS	72	2002
SON THIS IS SHE JOHN LEYTON	15	1962
SONG 4 MUTYA (OUT OF CONTROL) GROOVE ARMADA	8	2007
SONG AWAY HOCKEY	49	2009
(SONG FOR A) FUTURE GENERATION B-52's	63	1983
SONG FOR GUY ELTON JOHN	4	1978
SONG FOR LOVE EXTREME	12	1992
A SONG FOR LOVERS [A] RICHARD ASHCROFT	3	2000
SONG 4 LOVERS [B] LIBERTY X	5	2005
A SONG FOR MAMA BOYZ II MEN	34	1997
A SONG FOR SHELTER FATBOY SLIM	30	2001
SONG FOR WHOEVER BEAUTIFUL SOUTH	2	1989
SONG FOR YOU MICHAEL BUBLE	45	2005
THE SONG FROM MOULIN ROUGE MANTOVANI	1	1953
SONG FROM THE EDGE OF THE WORLD SIOUXSIE & THE BANSHEES	59	1987
SONG OF DREAMS BECKY TAYLOR	60	2001
SONG OF JOY MIGUEL RIOS	16	1970
SONG OF LIFE LEFTFIELD	59	1992
SONG OF MEXICO TONY MEEHAN COMBO	39	1964
THE SONG OF MY LIFE PETULA CLARK	32	1971
SONG OF THE DREAMER JOHNNIE RAY	10	1955
SONG SUNG BLUE NEIL DIAMOND	14	1972
THE SONG THAT I SING (THEME FROM 'WE'LL MEET AGAIN') STUTZ BEARCATS & THE DENIS KING ORCHESTRA	36	1982
SONG TO THE SIREN THIS MORTAL COIL	66	1983
SONG 2 BLUR	2	1997
SONGBIRD [A] KENNY G	22	1987
SONGBIRD [B] OASIS	3	2003
SONGBIRD [C] EVA CASSIDY	56	2009
SONGS FOR CHRISTMAS '87 EP MINI POPS	39	1988
SONGS FOR SWINGING LOVERS (LP) FRANK SINATRA	12	1956
SONIC BOOM BOY WESTWORLD	11	1987
SONIC BOOM (LIFE'S TOO SHORT) QUO VADIS	49	2000
SONIC EMPIRE MEMBERS OF MAYDAY	59	2002
SONNET (IMPORT) VERVE	74	1998
SONS AND DAUGHTERS' THEME KERRI & MICK	68	1984
SONS OF THE STAGE WORLD OF TWIST	47	1991
SOON MY BLOODY VALENTINE	41	1990
SOON BE DONE SHAGGY	46	1993
SOONER OR LATER [A] LARRY GRAHAM	54	1982
SOONER OR LATER [B] DUNCAN JAMES	35	2006
SOOPA HOOPZ SOOPA HOOPZ FEATURING QPR MASSIVE	54	2004
SOOTHE ME SAM & DAVE	35	1967
SOPHIA NERINA PALLOT	32	2006
SORRENTO MOON (I REMEMBER) TINA ARENA	22	1996
SORROW [A] MERSEYS	4	1966
SORROW [B] DAVID BOWIE	3	1973
SORRY [A] BEN ADAMS	18	2005
SORRY [B] PADDINGTONS	41	2005
SORRY [C] MADONNA	1	2006
SORRY [D] MADNESS	23	2007
SORRY BLAME IT ON ME AKON	22	2007
SORRY BUT I'M GONNA HAVE TO PASS COASTERS	41	1994
SORRY DOESN'T ALWAYS MAKE IT RIGHT DIANA ROSS	23	1975
SORRY FOR YOU RONI SIZE	61	2003
SORRY (I DIDN'T KNOW) MONSTA BOY FEATURING DENZIE	25	2000
SORRY (I RAN ALL THE WAY HOME) IMPALAS	28	1959
SORRY I'M A LADY BACCARA	8	1978
SORRY ROBBIE BERT WEEDON	28	1960
SORRY SEEMS TO BE THE HARDEST WORD ELTON JOHN	11	1976
SORRY SEEMS TO BE THE HARDEST WORD BLUE FEATURING ELTON JOHN	1	2002
THE SORRY SUITOR DIVE DIVE	54	2005
SORRY SUZANNE HOLLIES	3	1969
SORRY'S NOT GOOD ENOUGH McFLY	3	2006
SORTED FOR ES & WIZZ PULP	2	1995
A SORTA FAIRYTALE TORI AMOS	41	2002
S.O.S. [A] ABBA	6	1975
S.O.S. [B] ABC	39	1984
SOS [C] RIHANNA	2	2006
SOS [D] A-STUDIO FEATURING POLINA	64	2006
SOS [E] JONAS BROTHERS	13	2008
THE SOS EP SHAMEN	14	1993
SOS (LET THE MUSIC PLAY) JORDIN SPARKS	13	2009
SOS (MESSAGE IN A BOTTLE) FILTERFUNK	60	2006
SOUL BEAT CALLING I KAMANCHI	69	2003
SOUL BOSSA NOVA COOL, THE FAB & THE GROOVY PRESENT QUINCY JONES	47	1998
THE SOUL CAGES STING	57	1991
SOUL CHA CHA VAN McCOY	34	1977
SOUL CITY WALK ARCHIE BELL & THE DRELLS	13	1976
SOUL CLAP '69 BOOKER T & THE MG's	35	1969
SOUL COAXING RAYMOND LEFEVRE	46	1968
SOUL DEEP BOX TOPS	22	1969
SOUL DEEP GARY U.S. BONDS	59	1982
SOUL DEEP (PART 1) COUNCIL COLLECTIVE	24	1984
SOUL DRACULA HOT BLOOD	32	1976
SOUL FINGER BAR-KAYS	33	1967
SOUL FREEDOM – FREE YOUR SOUL DEGREES OF MOTION FEATURING BITI	64	1992
SOUL HEAVEN GOODFELLAS FEATURING LISA MILLETT	27	2001
SOUL INSIDE SOFT CELL	16	1983
SOUL INSPIRATION SIMON CLIMIE	60	1992
SOUL LIMBO BOOKER T & THE MG's	30	1969
SOUL LOVE BLESSING	73	1994
SOUL LOVE – SOUL MAN WOMACK & WOMACK	58	1986
SOUL MAN SAM & DAVE	24	1967
SOUL MAN SAM MOORE & LOU REED	30	1987
SOUL OF MY SOUL MICHAEL BOLTON	32	1994
THE SOUL OF MY SUIT T REX	42	1977
SOUL PASSING THROUGH SOUL TOYAH	57	1985
SOUL PROVIDER MICHAEL BOLTON	35	1996
SOUL SEARCHIN' TIME TRAMMPS	42	1976
SOUL SERENADE WILLIE MITCHELL	43	1968
SOUL SISTER BROWN SUGAR SAM & DAVE	15	1969
SOUL SOUND SUGABABES	30	2001
SOUL SURVIVOR YOUNG JEEZY FEATURING AKON	16	2006
SOUL TRAIN SWANS WAY	20	1984
SOULJACKER PART 1 EELS	30	2001
SOULMATE WEE PAPA GIRL RAPPERS	45	1988
SOULMATE NATASHA BEDINGFIELD	7	2007
SOULS RICK SPRINGFIELD	23	1984
SOUL'S ON FIRE TRACIE	73	1984
THE SOULSHAKER MAX LINEN	55	2001
SOUND [A] JAMES	9	1991
THE SOUND [B] X-PRESS 2	38	1996
SOUND ADVICE RONI SIZE	61	2002
SOUND AND VISION DAVID BOWIE	3	1977
SOUND BWOY BURIAL GANT	67	1997
SOUND CLASH (CHAMPION SOUND) KICK SQUAD	59	1990
THE SOUND OF BAMBOO FLICKMAN	11	2000
THE SOUND OF BLUE JFK	55	2002
SOUND OF CONFUSION SECRET AFFAIR	45	1980
THE SOUND OF THE CROWD HUMAN LEAGUE	12	1981

	Peak Position	Year of Release
THE SOUND OF CRYING PREFAB SPROUT	23	1992
SOUND OF DRUMS KULA SHAKER	3	1998
THE SOUND OF EDEN SHADES OF RHYTHM	35	1991
SOUND OF EDEN CASINO	52	1997
SOUND OF FREEDOM BOB SINCLAR, CUTEE B & DOLLARMAN	14	2007
THE SOUND OF MUSIC DAYTON	75	1983
THE SOUND OF MUSIK FALCO	61	1986
THE SOUND OF OH YEAH TOMBA VIRA	51	2001
THE SOUND OF SILENCE BACHELORS	3	1966
SOUND OF SOUNDS/PING ONE DOWN GOMEZ	48	2002
SOUND OF SPEED (EP) JESUS & MARY CHAIN	30	1993
THE SOUND OF THE SUBURBS MEMBERS	12	1979
SOUND OF THE UNDERGROUND GIRLS ALOUD	1	2002
THE SOUND OF VIOLENCE CASSIUS	49	2002
THE SOUND OF YOUR CRY ELVIS PRESLEY	59	1982
SOUND SYSTEM [A] STEEL PULSE	71	1979
SOUND SYSTEM [B] DRUM CLUB	62	1993
SOUND YOUR FUNKY HORN KC & THE SUNSHINE BAND	17	1974
SOUNDS OF EDEN (EVERYTIME I SEE THE) DEEP COVER	63	2002
SOUNDS OF WICKEDNESS TZANT	11	1998
SOUR TIMES PORTISHEAD	13	1994
SOUTH AFRICAN MAN HAMILTON BOHANNON	22	1975
SOUTH MANZ DILLINJA	53	2002
SOUTH OF THE BORDER ROBBIE WILLIAMS	14	1997
SOUTH OF THE RIVER MICA PARIS	50	1990
SOUTH PACIFIC DJ ZINC	62	2004
SOUTHAMPTON BOYS RED 'N' WHITE MACHINES	16	2003
SOUTHERN COMFORT BERNI FLINT	48	1977
SOUTHERN FREEEZ FREEEZ	8	1981
SOUTHERN NIGHTS GLEN CAMPBELL	28	1977
SOUTHERN SUN PAUL OAKENFOLD	16	2002
SOUTHSIDE DAVE CLARKE	34	1996
SOUVENIR ORCHESTRAL MANOEUVRES IN THE DARK	3	1981
SOUVENIRS VOYAGE	56	1978
SOWETO [A] MALCOLM McLAREN & THE McLARENETTES	32	1983
SOWETO [B] JEFFREY OSBORNE	44	1986
SOWING THE SEEDS OF HATRED CREDIT TO THE NATION	72	1994
SOWING THE SEEDS OF LOVE TEARS FOR FEARS	5	1989
SPACE [A] NEW MODEL ARMY	39	1991
SPACE [B] SLIPMATT	41	2003
SPACE AGE LOVE SONG A FLOCK OF SEAGULLS	34	1982
SPACE BASS SLICK	16	1979
THE SPACE BETWEEN DAVE MATTHEWS BAND	35	2001
SPACE COWBOY JAMIROQUAI	17	1994
SPACE JAM QUAD CITY DJS	57	1997
THE SPACE JUNGLE ADAMSKI	7	1990
SPACE LORD MONSTER MAGNET	45	1999
SPACE OASIS BILLIE RAY MARTIN	66	1996
SPACE ODDITY DAVID BOWIE	1	1969
SPACE RIDER SHAUN ESCOFFERY	52	2001
SPACE STATION NO. 5 [A] SAMMY HAGAR	52	1979
SPACE STATION NO. 5 [B] MONTROSE	71	1980
SPACE WALK LEMON JELLY	36	2002
SPACED INVADER HATIRAS FEATURING SLARTA JOHN	14	2001
SPACEHOPPER BAD COMPANY	56	2002
SPACEMAN [A] 4 NON BLONDES	53	1993
SPACEMAN [B] BABYLON ZOO	1	1996
SPACEMAN [C] KILLERS	57	2009

	Peak Position	Year of Release
A SPACEMAN CAME TRAVELLING CHRIS DE BURGH	40	1986
SPACER SHEILA & B. DEVOTION	18	1979
SPANISH CRAIG DAVID	8	2003
SPANISH DANCE TROUPE GORKY'S ZYGOTIC MYNCI	47	1999
SPANISH EYES AL MARTINO	5	1970
SPANISH FLEA HERB ALPERT & THE TIJUANA BRASS	3	1965
SPANISH HARLEM JIMMY JUSTICE	20	1962
SPANISH HARLEM SOUNDS INCORPORATED	35	1964
SPANISH HARLEM ARETHA FRANKLIN	14	1971
SPANISH HORSES AZTEC CAMERA	52	1992
SPANISH STROLL MINK DE VILLE	20	1977
SPANISH WINE CHRIS WHITE	37	1976
SPARE PARTS BRUCE SPRINGSTEEN	32	1988
SPARK TORI AMOS	16	1998
SPARKLE MY LIFE STORY	34	1996
SPARKLE OF MY EYES UB40	40	2001
SPARKS ROYKSOPP	41	2003
SPARKY'S DREAM TEENAGE FANCLUB	40	1995
THE SPARROW RAMBLERS (FROM THE ABBEY HEY JUNIOR SCHOOL)	11	1979
THE SPARTANS SOUNDS INCORPORATED	30	1964
SPEAK LIKE A CHILD STYLE COUNCIL	4	1983
SPEAK TO ME PRETTY BRENDA LEE	3	1962
SPEAK TO ME SOMEONE GENE	30	1997
SPEAKEASY SHED SEVEN	24	1994
SPECIAL [A] GARBAGE	15	1998
SPECIAL [B] MEW	46	2005
THE SPECIAL A.K.A. LIVE! EP SPECIAL A.K.A.	1	1980
SPECIAL BREW BAD MANNERS	3	1980
SPECIAL CASES MASSIVE ATTACK	15	2003
SPECIAL F/X WHISPERS	69	1987
SPECIAL KIND OF LOVE DINA CARROLL	16	1992
SPECIAL KIND OF LOVER NU COLOURS	38	1996
SPECIAL KIND OF SOMETHING KAVANA	13	1998
SPECIAL NEEDS PLACEBO	27	2003
SPECIAL 2003 LEE-CABRERA	45	2003
SPECIAL WAY RIVER CITY PEOPLE	44	1991
THE SPECIAL YEARS VAL DOONICAN	7	1965
SPECTACULAR GRAHAM COXON	32	2004
THE SPECTRE OF LOVE STRANGLERS	57	2006
SPEECHLESS [A] D-SIDE	9	2003
SPEECHLESS [B] MISH MASH	16	2006
SPEED BILLY IDOL	47	1994
SPEED AT THE SOUND OF LONELINESS ALABAMA 3	72	1997
SPEED (CAN YOU FEEL IT?) AZZIDO DA BASS FEATURING ROLAND CLARK	68	2002
SPEED OF SOUND COLDPLAY	2	2005
SPEED UP FUNKERMAN	55	2008
SPEED YOUR LOVE TO ME SIMPLE MINDS	20	1984
SPEEDWELL SAINT ETIENNE	54	1991
SPEEDY GONZALES PAT BOONE	2	1962
THE SPELL! [A] FUNKY WORM	61	1988
THE SPELL [B] ALPHABEAT	20	2009
SPELLBOUND SIOUXSIE & THE BANSHEES	22	1981
SPEND SOME TIME BRAND NEW HEAVIES FEATURING N'DEA DAVENPORT	26	1994
SPEND THE DAY URBAN COOKIE COLLECTIVE	59	1995
SPEND THE NIGHT [A] COOLNOTES	11	1985
SPEND THE NIGHT [B] DANNY J LEWIS	29	1998
SPENDING MY TIME ROXETTE	22	1991
SPICE OF LIFE MANHATTAN TRANSFER	19	1984
SPICE UP YOUR LIFE SPICE GIRLS	1	1997
SPIDER PIG SIMPSONS	23	2007
SPIDERS MOBY	50	2005
SPIDERS AND SNAKES JIM STAFFORD	14	1974
SPIDER'S WEB KATIE MELUA	52	2006
SPIDERWEBS NO DOUBT	16	1997
SPIES LIKE US PAUL McCARTNEY	13	1985
SPIKEE UNDERWORLD	63	1993

	Peak Position	Year of Release
SPILLER FROM RIO (DO IT EASY) LAGUNA	40	1997
SPIN SPIN SUGAR SNEAKER PIMPS	21	1997
SPIN THAT WHEEL (TURTLES GET REAL) HI-TEK 3 FEATURING YA KID K	15	1990
SPIN THE BLACK CIRCLE PEARL JAM	10	1994
SPIN THE WHEEL BELLEFIRE	67	2004
SPINDRIFT (EP) THOUSAND YARD STARE	58	1992
SPINNIN' AND SPINNIN' SYREETA	49	1974
SPINNIN' WHEELS CRESCENT	61	2002
SPINNING CLARKESVILLE	72	2004
SPINNING AROUND KYLIE MINOGUE	1	2000
SPINNING ROCK BOOGIE HANK C BURNETTE	21	1976
SPINNING THE WHEEL GEORGE MICHAEL	2	1996
SPIRAL SCRATCH EP BUZZCOCKS	31	1979
SPIRAL SYMPHONY SCIENTIST	74	1991
SPIRALING KEANE	23	2008
SPIRIT [A] BAUHAUS	42	1982
SPIRIT [B] WAYNE MARSHALL	58	1995
SPIRIT [C] SOUNDS OF BLACKNESS FEATURING CRAIG MACK	35	1997
SPIRIT BODY AND SOUL NOLAN SISTERS	34	1979
SPIRIT IN THE SKY NORMAN GREENBAUM	34	1970
SPIRIT IN THE SKY DOCTOR & THE MEDICS	1	1986
SPIRIT IN THE SKY GARETH GATES FEATURING THE KUMARS	1	2003
SPIRIT INSIDE SPIRITS	39	1995
THE SPIRIT IS WILLING PETER STRAKER & THE HANDS OF DR TELENY	40	1972
SPIRIT OF RADIO RUSH	13	1980
SPIRIT OF '76 ALARM	22	1986
SPIRITS (HAVING FLOWN) BEE GEES	16	1980
SPIRITS IN THE MATERIAL WORLD POLICE	12	1981
SPIRITS IN THE MATERIAL WORLD PATO BANTON WITH STING	36	1996
SPIRITUAL HIGH (STATE OF INDEPENDENCE) MOODSWINGS FEATURING CHRISSIE HYNDE	66	1991
SPIRITUAL LOVE URBAN SPECIES	35	1994
SPIRITUAL THANG ERIC BENET	62	1997
SPIRITUALIZED FINLEY QUAYE	26	2000
SPIT IN THE RAIN DEL AMITRI	21	1990
SPIT IT OUT [A] SLIPKNOT	28	2000
SPIT IT OUT [B] BRENDAN BENSON	75	2005
SPIT YOUR GAME NOTORIOUS B.I.G.	64	2006
SPITTING GAMES SNOW PATROL	23	2003
SPLIFFHEAD RAGGA TWINS	51	1990
SPLISH SPLASH CHARLIE DRAKE	7	1958
SPLISH SPLASH BOBBY DARIN	18	1958
SPLITTING THE ATOM MASSIVE ATTACK	64	2009
SPOILED JOSS STONE	32	2005
SPOOKY [A] CLASSICS IV	46	1968
SPOOKY [A] ATLANTA RHYTHM SECTION	48	1979
SPOOKY [B] NEW ORDER	22	1993
SPOONMAN SOUNDGARDEN	20	1994
SPOT THE PIGEON EP GENESIS	14	1977
SPOTLIGHT [A] JENNIFER HUDSON	11	2008
SPOTLIGHT [B] GUCCI MANE FEATURING USHER	46	2010
SPREAD A LITTLE HAPPINESS STING	16	1982
SPREAD LOVE FIGHT CLUB FEATURING LAURENT KONRAD	70	2004
SPREAD YOUR LOVE BLACK REBEL MOTORCYCLE CLUB	27	2002
SPREAD YOUR WINGS QUEEN	34	1978
SPRING IN MY STEP NU MATIC	58	1992
SPRINGTIME FOR THE WORLD BLOW MONKEYS	69	1990
SPUTNIK STYLUS TROUBLE	63	2001
SPY IN THE HOUSE OF LOVE WAS (NOT WAS)	21	1987
SPYBREAK! PROPELLERHEADS	40	1997
SPYCATCHER J MAJIK & WICKAMAN	67	2004

Title	Artist	Peak Position	Year of Release
SQUARES	BETA BAND	42	2002
SQUEEZE BOX	WHO	10	1976
SQUIRT	FLUKE	46	1997
SS PAPARAZZI	STOCK AITKEN WATERMAN	68	1988
S-S-S-SINGLE BED	FOX	4	1976
SSSST (LISTEN)	JONAH	25	2000
ST.A.T.U.ESQUE	SLEEPER	17	1996
STATUS ROCK	HEADBANGERS	60	1981
STABBED IN THE BACK	MIND OF KANE	64	1991
STACCATO'S THEME	ELMER BERNSTEIN	4	1959
STACY'S MUM	FOUNTAINS OF WAYNE	11	2004
STAGE ONE	SPACE MANOEUVRES	25	2000
STAGES	ZZ TOP	43	1986
STAGGER LEE	LLOYD PRICE	7	1959
STAINSBY GIRLS	CHRIS REA	26	1985
THE STAIRCASE (MYSTERY)	SIOUXSIE & THE BANSHEES	24	1979
STAIRWAY OF LOVE	MICHAEL HOLLIDAY	3	1958
STAIRWAY OF LOVE	TERRY DENE	16	1958
STAIRWAY TO HEAVEN [A]	NEIL SEDAKA	8	1960
STAIRWAY TO HEAVEN [B]	FAR CORPORATION	8	1985
STAIRWAY TO HEAVEN [B]	DREAD ZEPPELIN	62	1991
STAIRWAY TO HEAVEN [B]	ROLF HARRIS	7	1993
STAIRWAY TO HEAVEN [B]	LED ZEPPELIN	37	2007
STAKES IS HIGH	DE LA SOUL	55	1996
STAKKER HUMANOID	HUMANOID	17	1988
STALEMATE	MAC BAND FEATURING THE McCAMPBELL BROTHERS	40	1988
STAMP!	JEREMY HEALY & AMOS	11	1996
STAN	EMINEM	1	2000
STAN BOWLES	OTHERS	36	2004
STAND [A]	R.E.M.	48	1989
STAND [B]	POISON	25	1993
STAND ABOVE ME	ORCHESTRAL MANOEUVRES IN THE DARK	21	1993
STAND AND DELIVER	ADAM & THE ANTS	1	1981
STAND AND FIGHT	PACK FEATURING NIGEL BENN	61	1990
STAND BACK	LINUS LOVES FEATURING SAM OBERNIK	31	2003
STAND BY	ROMAN HOLLIDAY	61	1983
STAND BY LOVE	SIMPLE MINDS	13	1991
STAND BY ME [A]	BEN E KING	1	1961
STAND BY ME [A]	KENNY LYNCH	39	1964
STAND BY ME [A]	JOHN LENNON	30	1975
STAND BY ME [A]	4 THE CAUSE	12	1998
STAND BY ME [B]	OASIS	2	1997
STAND BY ME [C]	SHAYNE WARD	14	2006
STAND BY MY WOMAN	LENNY KRAVITZ	55	1991
STAND BY YOUR MAN	TAMMY WYNETTE	1	1975
STAND CLEAR	ADAM F FEATURING M.O.P.	43	2001
STAND DOWN MARGARET (DUB)	BEAT	22	1980
STAND INSIDE YOUR LOVE	SMASHING PUMPKINS	23	2000
STAND OR FALL	FIXX	54	1982
STAND TOUGH	POINT BREAK	7	2000
STAND UP [A]	DAVID LEE ROTH	72	1988
STAND UP [B]	LOLEATTA HOLLOWAY	68	1994
STAND UP [C]	THUNDER	23	1995
STAND UP [D]	LOVE TRIBE	23	1996
STAND UP [E]	LUDACRIS	14	2003
STAND UP [F]	DEAD 60S	54	2007
STAND UP FOR YOUR LOVE RIGHTS	YAZZ	2	1988
STAND UP JAMROCK	BOB MARLEY & THE WAILERS	56	2005
STAND UP TALL	DIZZEE RASCAL	10	2004
STANDING	SILVIO ECOMO	70	2000
STANDING HERE	CREATURES	53	1989
STANDING HERE ALL ALONE	MICHELLE	69	1996
STANDING IN THE NEED OF LOVE	RIVER CITY PEOPLE	36	1992
STANDING IN THE ROAD	BLACKFOOT SUE	4	1972

Title	Artist	Peak Position	Year of Release
STANDING IN THE SHADOW	WHITESNAKE	62	1984
STANDING IN THE SHADOWS OF LOVE	FOUR TOPS	6	1967
STANDING IN THE WAY OF CONTROL	GOSSIP	7	2006
STANDING NEXT TO ME	LAST SHADOW PUPPETS	30	2008
STANDING ON MY OWN AGAIN	GRAHAM COXON	20	2006
STANDING ON THE CORNER	KING BROTHERS	4	1960
STANDING ON THE CORNER	FOUR LADS	34	1960
STANDING ON THE INSIDE	NEIL SEDAKA	26	1973
STANDING ON THE TOP (PART 1)	TEMPTATIONS FEATURING RICK JAMES	53	1982
STANDING ON THE VERGE (OF GETTING IT ON)	PLATINUM HOOK	72	1978
STANDING OUTSIDE A BROKEN PHONE BOOTH WITH MONEY IN MY HAND	PRIMITIVE RADIO GODS	74	1996
STANDING OUTSIDE THE FIRE	GARTH BROOKS	28	1994
STANDING TOGETHER – WORLD CUP 2006	SIGNAL 1 & SIGNAL 2	67	2006
STANDING WATCHING	CHERRYFALLS	64	2004
STANLEY (HERE I AM)	AIRHEADZ	36	2001
STAN'S WORLD CUP SONG	STAN BOARDMAN	15	2006
STAR [A]	STEALERS WHEEL	25	1974
STAR [B]	EARTH, WIND & FIRE	16	1979
STAR [C]	NAZARETH	54	1979
STAR [D]	KIKI DEE	13	1981
STAR [E]	SECOND IMAGE	60	1982
STAR [F]	ERASURE	11	1990
STAR [G]	D:REAM	26	1993
STAR [H]	CULT	65	1995
STAR [I]	BRYAN ADAMS	13	1996
STAR [J]	PRIMAL SCREAM	16	1997
THE STAR AND THE WISEMAN	LADYSMITH BLACK MAMBAZO	63	1998
STAR CATCHING GIRL	BROTHER BROWN FEATURING FRANK'EE	51	2001
STAR CHASERS	4 HERO	41	1998
STAR FLEET	BRIAN MAY & FRIENDS	65	1983
STAR GIRL	McFLY	1	2006
STAR GUITAR	CHEMICAL BROTHERS	8	2002
STAR ON A TV SHOW	STYLISTICS	12	1975
STAR PEOPLE '97	GEORGE MICHAEL	2	1997
STAR SIGN	TEENAGE FANCLUB	44	1991
STAR 69	FATBOY SLIM	10	2001
STAR TO FALL	CABIN CREW	4	2005
STAR TREKKIN'	FIRM	1	1987
STAR WARS THEME – CANTINA BAND	MECO	7	1977
STARBRIGHT	JOHNNY MATHIS	47	1960
STARBUCKS	A	20	2002
STARCHILD	LEVEL 42	47	1981
STARCROSSED	ASH	22	2004
STARDATE 1990	DAN REED NETWORK	39	1990
STARDUST [A]	BILLY WARD	13	1957
STARDUST [A]	NAT 'KING' COLE	24	1957
STARDUST [B]	DAVID ESSEX	7	1974
STARDUST [B]	MARTIN L GORE	44	2003
STARDUST [C]	MENSWEAR	16	1995
STARGAZER	SIOUXSIE & THE BANSHEES	64	1995
STARING AT THE RUDE BOIS	GALLOWS	31	2007
STARING AT THE RUDE BOYS	RUTS	22	1980
STARING AT THE SUN [A]	U2	3	1997
STARING AT THE SUN [B]	ROOSTER	5	2005
STARLIGHT	MUSE	13	2006
STARLIGHT [A]	DESIDERIO	57	2000
STARLIGHT [B]	SUPERMEN LOVERS FEATURING MANI HOFFMAN	2	2001
STARLITE	YOUNG HEART ATTACK	69	2004

Title	Artist	Peak Position	Year of Release
STARLOVERS	GUSGUS	62	1999
STARMAKER	KIDS FROM *'FAME'*	3	1982
STARMAN	DAVID BOWIE	10	1972
STARMAN	CULTURE CLUB	7	1999
STARRY EYED [A]	MICHAEL HOLLIDAY	1	1960
STARRY EYED [B]	ELLIE GOULDING	4	2010
STARRY EYED SURPRISE	PAUL OAKENFOLD	6	2002
A STARRY NIGHT	JOY STRINGS	35	1964
STARS [A]	SYLVESTER	47	1979
STARS [A]	FELIX	29	1993
STARS [B]	HEAR 'N AID	26	1986
STARS [C]	SIMPLY RED	8	1991
STARS [D]	CHINA BLACK	19	1994
STARS [E]	DUBSTAR	15	1995
STARS [F]	ROXETTE	56	1999
STARS [G]	MORJAC FEATURING RAZ CONWAY	38	2003
STARS AND STRIPES FOREVER	MR ACKER BILK & HIS PARAMOUNT JAZZ BAND	22	1961
STARS ARE BLIND	PARIS HILTON	5	2006
STARS ON 45	STARSOUND	2	1981
STARS ON 45 VOLUME 2	STARSOUND	2	1981
STARS ON 45 VOLUME 3	STARSOUND	17	1981
STARS ON STEVIE	STARSOUND	14	1982
STARS OVER 45	CHAS & DAVE	21	1981
STARS OVER CLOUGHANOVER	SAW DOCTORS	69	2005
STARS SHINE IN YOUR EYES	RONNIE HILTON	13	1955
STARSHIP	ICEBERG SLIMM FEATURING COREE	73	2004
STARSHIP TROOPERS	UNITED CITIZEN FEDERATION FEATURING SARAH BRIGHTMAN	58	1998
STARSKY & HUTCH – THE THEME	ANDY G'S STARSKY & HUTCH ALL STARS	51	1998
STARSTRUKK	30H!3 FEATURING KATY PERRY	3	2009
START	JAM	1	1980
START A BRAND NEW LIFE (SAVE ME)	BASSHEADS	49	1993
START AGAIN [A]	TEENAGE FANCLUB	54	1997
START AGAIN [B]	MONTROSE AVENUE	59	1998
START CHOPPIN	DINOSAUR, JR	20	1993
START ME UP [A]	ROLLING STONES	7	1981
START ME UP [B]	SALT-N-PEPA	39	1992
START MOVIN'	TERRY DENE	15	1957
START MOVIN'	SAL MINEO	16	1957
START TALKING LOVE	MAGNUM	22	1988
START THE COMMOTION	WISEGUYS	47	1998
STARTING AGAIN	SECOND IMAGE	65	1985
STARTING OVER AGAIN	NATALIE COLE	56	1989
STARTING TOGETHER	SU POLLARD	2	1986
STARTOUCHERS	DIGITAL ORGASM	31	1992
STARTRAX CLUB DISCO	STARTRAX	18	1981
STARTURN ON 45 (PINTS)	STARTURN ON 45 (PINTS)	45	1981
STARVATION	STARVATION	33	1985
STARZ IN THEIR EYES	JUST JACK	2	2007
STATE OF INDEPENDENCE	DONNA SUMMER	14	1982
STATE OF INDEPENDENCE	JON & VANGELIS	67	1984
STATE OF LOVE	IMAGINATION	67	1984
STATE OF MIND [A]	FISH	32	1989
STATE OF MIND [B]	HOLLY VALANCE	8	2003
STATE OF SHOCK	JACKSONS, LEAD VOCALS MICK JAGGER & MICHAEL JACKSON	14	1984
STATE OF THE NATION	NEW ORDER	30	1986
STAY [A]	MAURICE WILLIAMS & THE ZODIACS	14	1961
STAY [A]	HOLLIES	8	1963
STAY [A]	JACKSON BROWNE	12	1978
STAY [A]	DREAMHOUSE	62	1995
STAY [B]	BARRY MANILOW FEATURING KEVIN DiSIMONE & JAMES JOLIS	23	1982
STAY [C]	SHAKESPEAR'S SISTER	1	1992
STAY [D]	KENNY THOMAS	22	1993
STAY [E]	ETERNAL	4	1993
STAY [F]	60FT DOLLS	48	1996

	Peak Position	Year of Release
STAY [G] 18 WHEELER	59	1997
STAY [H] SASH! FEATURING LA TREC	2	1997
STAY [I] BERNARD BUTLER	12	1998
STAY [J] MICA PARIS	40	1998
STAY [K] STEPHEN GATELY	13	2001
STAY [L] ROB TISSERA, VINYLGROOVER & THE RED HED	61	2004
STAY [M] SIMPLY RED	36	2007
STAY [N] JAY SEAN	59	2008
STAY A LITTLE WHILE, CHILD LOOSE ENDS	52	1986
STAY A WHILE RAKIM	53	1998
STAY ANOTHER DAY EAST 17	1	1994
STAY AWAY BABY JANE CHESNEY HAWKES	74	2002
STAY AWAY FROM ME STAR SPANGLES	52	2003
STAY AWHILE DUSTY SPRINGFIELD	13	1964
STAY BEAUTIFUL MANIC STREET PREACHERS	40	1991
STAY (FARAWAY, SO CLOSE) U2	4	1993
STAY FLY THREE 6 MAFIA	33	2006
STAY FOREVER JOEY LAWRENCE	41	1993
STAY GOLD DEEP DISH	41	1996
STAY (I MISSED YOU) LISA LOEB & NINE STORIES	6	1994
STAY IN THE SUN KENICKIE	43	1998
STAY ON THESE ROADS A-HA	5	1988
STAY OUT OF MY LIFE FIVE STAR	9	1987
STAY RIGHT HERE AKIN	60	1997
STAY THE NIGHT GHOSTS	25	2007
STAY THE SAME [A] BENT	59	2003
STAY THE SAME [B] GABRIELLE	20	2004
STAY THIS WAY BRAND NEW HEAVIES FEATURING N'DEA DAVENPORT	40	1992
STAY TOGETHER [A] SUEDE	3	1994
STAY TOGETHER [B] BARBARA TUCKER	46	1995
STAY (TONIGHT) ISHA-D	28	1995
STAY TOO LONG PLAN B	9	2010
STAY WHERE YOU ARE AMBULANCE LTD	67	2005
STAY WITH ME [A] FACES	6	1972
STAY WITH ME [A] McFLY	18	2008
STAY WITH ME [B] BLUE MINK	11	1972
STAY WITH ME [C] EIGHTH WONDER	65	1985
STAY WITH ME [D] MISSION	30	1986
STAY WITH ME [E] JOHN O'KANE	41	1992
STAY WITH ME [F] ERASURE	15	1995
STAY WITH ME [G] ULTRA HIGH	36	1995
STAY WITH ME [H] RICHIE RICH & ESERA TUAOLO	58	1997
STAY WITH ME [I] ANGELIC	36	2001
STAY WITH ME [J] IRONIK	5	2008
STAY WITH ME BABY WALKER BROTHERS	26	1967
STAY WITH ME BABY DAVID ESSEX	45	1978
STAY WITH ME BABY RUBY TURNER	39	1994
STAY WITH ME (BABY) REBECCA WHEATLEY	10	2000
STAY WITH ME HEARTACHE WET WET WET	30	1990
STAY WITH ME TILL DAWN JUDIE TZUKE	16	1979
STAY WITH ME TILL DAWN LUCID	25	1999
STAY WITH ME TONIGHT [A] JEFFREY OSBORNE	18	1984
STAY WITH ME TONIGHT [B] HUMAN LEAGUE	40	1996
STAY WITH YOU [A] LEMON JELLY	31	2004
STAY WITH YOU [B] GOO GOO DOLLS	39	2006
STAY YOUNG ULTRASOUND	30	1998
STAYIN' ALIVE BEE GEES	4	1978
STAYIN' ALIVE RICHARD ACE	66	1978
STAYIN' ALIVE N-TRANCE FEATURING RICARDO DA FORCE	2	1995
STAYING ALIVE 95 FEVER FEATURING TIPPA IRIE	48	1995
STAYING FAT BLOC PARTY	51	2004
STAYING IN BOBBY VEE	4	1961
STAYING OUT FOR THE SUMMER DODGY	19	1994
STAYING TOGETHER DEBBIE GIBSON	53	1988
STEADY AS SHE GOES RACONTEURS	4	2006
STEAL MY SUNSHINE LEN	8	1999
STEAL YOUR FIRE GUN	24	1992
STEAL YOUR LOVE AWAY GEMINI	37	1996
STEALTH WAY OUT WEST FEATURING KIRSTY HAWKSHAW	67	2002
STEAM [A] PETER GABRIEL	10	1993
STEAM [B] EAST 17	7	1994
STEAMY WINDOWS TINA TURNER	13	1990
STEEL BARS MICHAEL BOLTON	17	1992
A STEEL GUITAR AND A GLASS OF WINE PAUL ANKA	41	1962
STEELO 702	41	1996
STELLIFY IAN BROWN	31	2009
STEM DJ SHADOW	74	1996
STEP BACK IN TIME KYLIE MINOGUE	4	1990
STEP BY STEP [A] STEVE PERRY	41	1960
STEP BY STEP [B] JOE SIMON	14	1973
STEP BY STEP [C] TAFFY	59	1987
STEP BY STEP [D] NEW KIDS ON THE BLOCK	2	1990
STEP BY STEP [E] WHITNEY HOUSTON	13	1996
STEP IN THE NAME OF LOVE R KELLY	14	2003
A STEP IN THE RIGHT DIRECTION TRUTH	32	1983
STEP INSIDE LOVE CILLA BLACK	8	1968
STEP INTO A DREAM WHITE PLAINS	21	1973
STEP INTO A WORLD (RAPTURE'S DELIGHT) KRS ONE	24	1997
STEP INTO CHRISTMAS ELTON JOHN	24	1973
STEP INTO MY OFFICE BABY BELLE & SEBASTIAN	32	2003
STEP INTO MY WORLD HURRICANE #1	19	1997
STEP INTO THE BREEZE SPIRITUALIZED	75	1990
STEP IT UP STEREO MC'S	12	1992
STEP OFF JUNIOR GISCOMBE	63	1990
STEP OFF (PART 1) GRANDMASTER MELLE MEL & THE FURIOUS FIVE	8	1984
STEP ON HAPPY MONDAYS	5	1990
STEP ON MY OLD SIZE NINES STEREOPHONICS	16	2001
STEP RIGHT UP JAKI GRAHAM	15	1986
STEP TO ME (DO ME) MANTRONIX	59	1991
STEPPIN' OUT [A] KOOL & THE GANG	12	1981
STEPPIN' OUT [B] JOE JACKSON	6	1983
STEPPIN STONES DJ ZINC	62	2004
STEPPING STONE [A] FARM	58	1990
STEPPING STONE [A] PJ & DUNCAN	11	1996
STEPPING STONE [B] DUFFY	21	2008
STEP-TWO-THREE-FOUR STRICT INSTRUCTOR	49	1998
STEREO PAVEMENT	48	1997
STEREOTYPE SPECIALS	6	1980
STEREOTYPES BLUR	7	1996
STEVE MCQUEEN [A] SHERYL CROW	44	2002
STEVE MCQUEEN [B] AUTOMATIC	16	2008
STEWBALL LONNIE DONEGAN	27	1956
STICK IT OUT RIGHT SAID FRED & FRIENDS	4	1993
STICK TO THE STATUS QUO CAST OF *HIGH SCHOOL MUSICAL*	74	2007
STICKS AND STONES CUD	68	1994
STICKS N STONES JAMIE T	15	2009
STICKWITU PUSSYCAT DOLLS	1	2005
STICKY WEDDING PRESENT	17	1992
STIFF UPPER LIP AC/DC	65	2000
STILL [A] KARL DENVER	13	1963
STILL [A] KEN DODD	35	1963
STILL [B] COMMODORES	4	1979
STILL [C] MACY GRAY	18	2000
STILL A FRIEND OF MINE INCOGNITO	47	1993
STILL A THRILL SYBIL	55	1997
STILL BE LOVIN' YOU DAMAGE	11	2001
STILL BELIEVE SHOLA AMA	26	1999
STILL DRE DR DRE FEATURING SNOOP DOGGY DOGG	6	2000
STILL FEEL THE RAIN STEX	63	1991
STILL FIGURING OUT ELLIOT MINOR	17	2008
STILL GOT THE BLUES (FOR YOU) GARY MOORE	31	1990
STILL HAVEN'T FOUND WHAT I'M LOOKING FOR CHIMES	6	1990
STILL I'M SAD YARDBIRDS	3	1965
STILL IN LOVE [A] GO WEST	43	1993
STILL IN LOVE [B] LIONEL RICHIE	66	1996
STILL IN LOVE SONG STILLS	45	2004
A STILL LIFE LESS THAN JAKE	61	2006
STILL OF THE NIGHT WHITESNAKE	16	1987
STILL ON YOUR SIDE BBMAK	8	2001
STILL THE SAME SLADE	73	1987
STILL TOO YOUNG TO REMEMBER IT BITES	60	1989
STILL WAITING SUM 41	16	2002
STILL WATER (LOVE) FOUR TOPS	10	1970
STILL WATERS (RUN DEEP) BEE GEES	18	1997
STILLNESS IN TIME JAMIROQUAI	9	1995
STILLNESS OF HEART LENNY KRAVITZ	44	2002
THE STING RAGTIMERS	31	1974
STING ME BLACK CROWES	42	1992
STING ME RED (YOU THINK YOU'RE SO) WHO DA FUNK FEATURING TERRA DEVA	32	2003
STINGRAY SHADOWS	19	1965
THE STINGRAY MEGAMIX FAB FEATURING AQUA MARINA	66	1990
STINKIN THINKIN HAPPY MONDAYS	31	1992
STIR IT UP JOHNNY NASH	13	1972
STITCHES DYKEENIES	61	2007
STOLE KELLY ROWLAND	2	2002
STOLEN JAY SEAN	4	2004
STOLEN CAR BETH ORTON	34	1999
STOLEN CAR (TAKE ME DANCING) STING	60	2004
STOMP [A] BROTHERS JOHNSON	6	1980
STOMP [A] QUINCY JONES FEATURING MELLE MEL, COOLIO, YO-YO, SHAQUILLE O'NEAL & THE LUNIZ	28	1996
STOMP [B] GOD'S PROPERTY	60	1997
STOMP [C] STEPS	1	2000
STONE BY STONE CATATONIA	19	2001
STONE COLD RAINBOW	34	1982
STONE COLD SOBER PALOMA FAITH	17	2009
STONE LOVE KOOL & THE GANG	45	1987
STONED IN LOVE CHICANE FEATURING TOM JONES	7	2006
STONED LOVE SUPREMES	3	1971
STONEY END BARBRA STREISAND	27	1971
STONEY GROUND GUYS & DOLLS	38	1976
THE STONK HALE & PACE & THE STONKERS	1	1991
STOOD ON GOLD GORKY'S ZYGOTIC MYNCI	65	2001
STOOD UP RICKY NELSON	27	1958
STOOL PIGEON KID CREOLE & THE COCONUTS	7	1982
STOP [A] SAM BROWN	4	1988
STOP [B] SPICE GIRLS	2	1998
STOP [C] BLACK REBEL MOTORCYCLE CLUB	19	2003
STOP [D] JAMELIA	9	2004
STOP AND GO DAVID GRANT	19	1983
STOP AND STARE ONEREPUBLIC	4	2008
STOP BAJON...PRIMAVERA TULLIO DE PISCOPO	58	1987
STOP BREAKING MY HEART INNER CIRCLE	50	1979
STOP BY RAHSAAN PATTERSON	50	1997
STOP CRYING YOUR HEART OUT OASIS	2	2002
STOP CRYING YOUR HEART OUT LEONA LEWIS	29	2009
STOP DRAGGIN' MY HEART AROUND STEVIE NICKS WITH TOM PETTY & THE HEARTBREAKERS	50	1981
STOP (EP) MEGA CITY FOUR	36	1992
STOP FEELING SORRY FOR YOURSELF ADAM FAITH	23	1965
STOP HER ON SIGHT (SOS) EDWIN STARR	11	1966
STOP IN THE NAME OF LOVE SUPREMES	7	1965

	Peak Position	Year of Release
STOP KNOCKING THE WALLS DOWN RICKY	32	2005
STOP LISTENING TANITA TIKARAM	67	1998
STOP LIVING THE LIE DAVID SNEDDON	1	2003
STOP LOOK AND LISTEN [A] WAYNE FONTANA & THE MINDBENDERS	37	1964
STOP LOOK AND LISTEN [B] DONNA SUMMER	57	1984
STOP LOOK LISTEN (TO YOUR HEART) DIANA ROSS & MARVIN GAYE	25	1974
STOP LOVING ME LOVING YOU DARYL HALL	30	1994
STOP ME MARK RONSON FEATURING DANIEL MERRIWEATHER	2	2007
STOP ME (IF YOU'VE HEARD IT ALL BEFORE) BILLY OCEAN	12	1976
STOP MY HEAD EVAN DANDO	38	2003
STOP PLAYING WITH MY MIND BARBARA TUCKER FEATURING DARYL D'BONNEAU	17	2000
STOP SIGN ABS	10	2003
STOP STARTING TO START STOPPING (EP) D.O.P.	58	1996
STOP STOP STOP HOLLIES	2	1966
STOP THAT GIRL CHRIS ANDREWS	36	1966
STOP THE CAVALRY JONA LEWIE	3	1980
STOP THE ROCK APOLLO FOUR FORTY	10	1999
STOP THE VIOLENCE BOOGIE DOWN PRODUCTIONS	69	1988
STOP THE WAR NOW EDWIN STARR	33	1971
STOP THE WORLD EXTREME	22	1992
STOP THIS CRAZY THING COLDCUT FEATURING JUNIOR REID & THE AHEAD OF OUR TIME ORCHESTRA	21	1988
STOP TO LOVE LUTHER VANDROSS	24	1987
STOP YOUR CRYING SPIRITUALIZED	18	2001
STOP YOUR SOBBING PRETENDERS	34	1979
STORIES [A] IZIT	52	1989
STORIES [B] THERAPY?	14	1995
STORIES [C] HOLIDAY PLAN	58	2004
STORIES OF JOHNNY MARC ALMOND	23	1985
THE STORM [A] WORLD OF TWIST	42	1990
STORM [B] SPACE KITTENS	58	1996
STORM [C] VANESSA-MAE	54	1997
STORM [D] STORM	32	1998
STORM ANIMAL STORM	21	2000
STORM IN A TEACUP FORTUNES	7	1972
THE STORM IS OVER R KELLY	18	2001
STORMS IN AFRICA (PART II) ENYA	41	1989
STORMTROOPER IN DRAG PAUL GARDINER	49	1981
STORMY IN THE NORTHA KARMA IN THE SOUTH WILDHEARTS	17	2003
STORMY WEATHER ECHO & THE BUNNYMEN	55	2005
THE STORY OF THE BLUES [A] WAH!	3	1983
THE STORY OF LOVE OTT	11	1998
THE STORY OF MY LIFE [A] MICHAEL HOLLIDAY	1	1958
STORY OF MY LIFE [A] GARY MILLER	14	1958
THE STORY OF MY LIFE [A] DAVE KING	20	1958
THE STORY OF MY LIFE [A] ALMA COGAN	25	1958
THE STORY OF MY LIFE [B] KRISTIAN LEONTIOU	9	2004
STORY OF MY LOVE CONWAY TWITTY	30	1959
STORY OF THE BLUES [B] GARY MOORE	40	1992
THE STORY OF TINA AL MARTINO	10	1954
STORY OF TINA RONNIE HARRIS	12	1954
STOWAWAY BARBARA LYON	12	1955
STRAIGHT AHEAD [A] KOOL & THE GANG	15	1983
STRAIGHT AHEAD [B] TUBE & BERGER FEATURING CHRISSIE HYNDE	29	2004
STRAIGHT AT YER HEAD LIONROCK	33	1996
STRAIGHT FROM THE HEART [A] BRYAN ADAMS	51	1986
STRAIGHT FROM THE HEART [B] DOOLALLY	9	1998
STRAIGHT LINES NEW MUSIK	53	1979
STRAIGHT OUT OF THE JUNGLE JUNGLE BROTHERS	72	1989
STRAIGHT THROUGH MY HEART BACKSTREET BOYS	72	2009
STRAIGHT TO HELL CLASH	17	1982
STRAIGHT TO MY FEET HAMMER FEATURING DEION SAUNDERS	57	1995
STRAIGHT TO THE HEART REAL THING	71	1986
STRAIGHT TO YOU NICK CAVE & THE BAD SEEDS	68	1992
STRAIGHT UP [A] PAULA ABDUL	3	1989
STRAIGHT UP [B] CHANTE MOORE	11	2001
STRAIGHT UP NO BENDS BRIAN HARVEY	26	2001
STRAIGHTEN OUT STRANGLERS	9	1977
STRANDED [A] HEART	60	1990
STRANDED [B] DEEP DISH	60	1997
STRANDED [C] LUTRICIA McNEAL	3	1998
STRANDED (HAITI MON AMOUR) JAY-Z FEATURING BONO, THE EDGE & RIHANNA	41	2010
STRANGE WET WET WET	13	1997
STRANGE AND BEAUTIFUL AQUALUNG	7	2002
STRANGE BAND FAMILY	11	1970
STRANGE BREW CREAM	17	1967
STRANGE CURRENCIES R.E.M.	9	1995
STRANGE GLUE CATATONIA	11	1998
STRANGE KIND OF LOVE LOVE & MONEY	45	1989
STRANGE KIND OF WOMAN DEEP PURPLE	8	1971
STRANGE LADY IN TOWN FRANKIE LAINE	6	1955
STRANGE LITTLE GIRL [A] SAD CAFE	32	1980
STRANGE LITTLE GIRL [B] STRANGLERS	7	1982
STRANGE LOVE PHIXX	19	2005
STRANGE MAGIC ELECTRIC LIGHT ORCHESTRA	38	1976
STRANGE RELATIONSHIP DARREN HAYES	15	2002
STRANGE TOWN JAM	15	1979
STRANGE WAY ALL ABOUT EVE	51	1991
STRANGE WORLD [A] KE	73	1996
STRANGE WORLD [B] PUSH	21	2001
STRANGELOVE DEPECHE MODE	16	1987
THE STRANGER SHADOWS	5	1960
STRANGER SHAKATAK	43	1982
STRANGER IN A STRANGE LAND IRON MAIDEN	22	1986
STRANGER IN MOSCOW MICHAEL JACKSON	4	1996
STRANGER IN PARADISE TONY BENNETT	1	1955
STRANGER IN PARADISE FOUR ACES	6	1955
STRANGER IN PARADISE TONY MARTIN	6	1955
STRANGER IN PARADISE EDDIE CALVERT	14	1955
STRANGER IN PARADISE BING CROSBY	17	1955
STRANGER IN PARADISE DON CORNELL	19	1955
STRANGER IN TOWN DEL SHANNON	40	1965
A STRANGER ON HOME GROUND FAITH BROTHERS	69	1985
STRANGER ON THE SHORE MR ACKER BILK WITH THE LEON YOUNG STRING CHORALE	2	1961
STRANGER ON THE SHORE ANDY WILLIAMS	30	1962
STRANGER ON THE SHORE OF LOVE STEVIE WONDER	55	1987
STRANGER THINGS ABC	57	1997
STRANGERS IN OUR TOWN SPEAR OF DESTINY	49	1987
STRANGERS IN THE NIGHT FRANK SINATRA	1	1966
STRANGERS WHEN WE MEET DAVID BOWIE	39	1995
THE STRANGEST PARTY (THESE ARE THE TIMES) INXS	15	1994
THE STRANGEST THING '97 GEORGE MICHAEL	2	1997
STRANGLEHOLD UK SUBS	26	1979
STRASBOURG RAKES	57	2004
STRATEGIC HAMLETS URUSEI YATSURA	38	1997
STRAW DOGS STIFF LITTLE FINGERS	44	1979
STRAWBERRY NICOLA RENEE	55	1998
STRAWBERRY BLONDE (THE BAND PLAYED ON) FRANK D'RONE	24	1960
STRAWBERRY FAIR ANTHONY NEWLEY	3	1960
STRAWBERRY FIELDS FOREVER BEATLES	32	1967
STRAWBERRY FIELDS FOREVER CANDY FLIP	3	1990
STRAWBERRY KISSES NIKKI WEBSTER	64	2002
STRAWBERRY LETTER 23 BROTHERS JOHNSON	35	1977
STRAY CAT STRUT STRAY CATS	11	1981
THE STREAK RAY STEVENS	1	1974
STREAMLINE TRAIN VIPERS SKIFFLE GROUP	23	1957
STREET CAFE ICEHOUSE	62	1983
A STREET CALLED HOPE GENE PITNEY	37	1970
STREET DANCE BREAK MACHINE	3	1984
STREET DREAMS NAS	12	1997
STREET FIGHTER II WORLD WARRIOR	70	1994
STREET FIGHTING MAN ROLLING STONES	21	1971
STREET GANG A.R.E. WEAPONS	72	2001
STREET LIFE [A] ROXY MUSIC	9	1973
STREET LIFE [B] CRUSADERS	5	1979
STREET LIFE [C] BEENIE MAN	13	2003
STREET OF DREAMS RAINBOW	52	1983
STREET SPIRIT (FADE OUT) RADIOHEAD	5	1996
STREET TUFF DOUBLE TROUBLE & THE REBEL MC	3	1989
STREETCAR FUNERAL FOR A FRIEND	15	2005
STREETPLAYER (MECHANIK) FASHION	46	1982
THE STREETS WC FEATURING SNOOP DOGG & NATE DOGG	48	2003
STREETS OF LONDON RALPH McTELL	2	1974
STREETS OF LONDON ANTI-NOWHERE LEAGUE	48	1982
STREETS OF LOVE ROLLING STONES	15	2005
STREETS OF PHILADELPHIA BRUCE SPRINGSTEEN	2	1994
STREETWALKIN' SHAKATAK	38	1982
STRENGTH ALARM	40	1985
STRENGTH IN NUMBERS MUSIC	38	2008
STRENGTH TO STRENGTH HUE & CRY	46	1987
STRESS BLAGGERS I.T.A.	56	1993
STRESSED OUT A TRIBE CALLED QUEST FEATURING FAITH EVANS & RAPHAEL SAADIQ	33	1996
STRETCHIN' OUT GAYLE ADAMS	64	1980
STRICT MACHINE GOLDFRAPP	20	2003
STRICTLY BUSINESS KURTIS MANTRONIK VS EPMD	43	1998
STRICTLY ELVIS EP ELVIS PRESLEY	26	1960
STRICTLY HARDCORE GOLD BLADE	64	1997
STRICTLY SOCIAL RONI SIZE	70	2004
STRIKE IT DUB WAR	70	1995
STRIKE IT UP BLACK BOX	16	1991
STRIKE ME PINK DEBORAH HARRY	46	1993
STRINGS KRISTIN HERSH	60	1994
STRINGS FOR YASMIN TIN TIN OUT	31	1997
STRINGS OF LIFE RHYTHIM IS RHYTHIM	74	1989
STRINGS OF LIFE PLANK 15	60	2002
STRINGS OF LIFE (STRONGER ON MY OWN) SOUL CENTRAL FEATURING KATHY BROWN	6	2005
STRIP [A] ADAM ANT	41	1983
STRIP [B] PINK GREASE	36	2005
STRIPPED DEPECHE MODE	15	1986
THE STROKE BILLY SQUIER	52	1981
STROKE YOU UP CHANGING FACES	43	1994
STROLLIN' PRINCE & THE NEW POWER GENERATION	4	1992
STROLLIN' ON MAXI PRIEST	32	1986
STRONG [A] LIQUID	15	1998
STRONG [B] ROBBIE WILLIAMS	4	1999
STRONG AGAIN N-DUBZ	24	2009
STRONG ARM OF THE LAW SAXON	63	1980
STRONG AS STEEL FIVE STAR	16	1987
STRONG ENOUGH [A] SHERYL CROW	33	1995

	Peak Position	Year of Release
STRONG ENOUGH [B] CHER	5	1999
STRONG IN LOVE CHICANE FEATURING MASON	32	1998
STRONG LOVE SPENCER DAVIS GROUP	44	1965
STRONGER KANYE WEST	1	2007
STRONGER [A] GARY BARLOW	16	1999
STRONGER [B] BRITNEY SPEARS	7	2000
STRONGER [C] SUGABABES	7	2002
STRONGER THAN ME AMY WINEHOUSE	71	2003
STRONGER THAN THAT CLIFF RICHARD	14	1990
STRONGER TOGETHER [A] SHANNON	46	1985
STRONGER TOGETHER [B] SYBIL	41	1993
STRUMMIN' CHAS & DAVE WITH ROCKNEY	52	1978
STRUMPET MY LIFE STORY	27	1997
STRUNG OUT [A] WENDY & LISA	44	1990
STRUNG OUT [B] DOT ALLISON	67	2002
STRUT YOUR FUNKY STUFF FRANTIQUE	10	1979
THE STRUTT BAMBOO	36	1998
STRYDERMAN TINCHY STRYDER	74	2008
STUCK [A] NED'S ATOMIC DUSTBIN	64	1995
STUCK [B] STACIE ORRICO	9	2003
STUCK IN A GROOVE PURETONE	26	2003
STUCK IN A MOMENT YOU CAN'T GET OUT OF U2	2	2001
STUCK IN THE MIDDLE [A] DANNI'ELLE GAHA	68	1992
STUCK IN THE MIDDLE [B] CLEA	23	2004
STUCK IN THE MIDDLE WITH YOU STEALERS WHEEL	8	1973
STUCK IN THE MIDDLE WITH YOU LOUISE	4	2001
STUCK ON U [A] PJ & DUNCAN	12	1995
STUCK ON YOU [B] ELVIS PRESLEY	3	1960
STUCK ON YOU [C] TREVOR WALTERS	9	1984
STUCK ON YOU [C] LIONEL RICHIE	12	1984
STUCK WITH EACH OTHER SHONTELLE FEATURING AKON	23	2009
STUCK WITH ME GREEN DAY	24	1996
STUCK WITH YOU HUEY LEWIS & THE NEWS	12	1986
STUFF LIKE THAT QUINCY JONES	34	1978
STUMBLE AND FALL RAZORLIGHT	27	2004
STUMBLIN' IN SUZI QUATRO & CHRIS NORMAN	41	1978
STUNT 101 G UNIT	25	2003
STUNTMAN ALFIE	51	2003
STUPID CUPID CONNIE FRANCIS	1	1958
STUPID GIRL GARBAGE	4	1996
STUPID GIRLS P!NK	4	2006
STUPID KID [A] SULTANS OF PING FC	67	1992
STUPID KID [B] ALKALINE TRIO	53	2002
THE STUPID ONES BLUESKINS	61	2004
STUPID QUESTION NEW MODEL ARMY	31	1989
STUPID THING AIMEE MANN	47	1993
STUPIDISCO JUNIOR JACK	26	2004
STUTTER JOE FEATURING MYSTIKAL	7	2001
STUTTER RAP (NO SLEEP 'TIL BEDTIME) MORRIS MINOR & THE MAJORS	4	1988
STUTTERING (KISS ME AGAIN) BEN'S BROTHER	41	2008
STYLE [A] ORBITAL	13	1999
STYLE [B] MIS-TEEQ	13	2003
SUB-CULTURE NEW ORDER	63	1985
SUBDIVISIONS RUSH	53	1982
SUBHUMAN GARBAGE	50	1995
SUBMARINES DJ FRESH	73	2004
SUBPLATES VOLUME 1 (EP) VARIOUS ARTISTS (EP'S & LP'S)	69	1993
SUBSTITUTE [A] WHO	5	1966
SUBSTITUTE [B] CLOUT	2	1978
SUBSTITUTE [C] LIQUID GOLD	8	1980
SUBTERRANEAN HOMESICK BLUES BOB DYLAN	9	1965
SUBURBAN KNIGHTS HARD-FI	7	2007
SUBURBAN ROCK 'N' ROLL SPACE	67	2004
SUBURBIA PET SHOP BOYS	8	1986
SUCCESS [A] SIGUE SIGUE SPUTNIK	31	1988
SUCCESS [B] DANNII MINOGUE	11	1991
SUCCESS HAS MADE A FAILURE OF OUR HOME SINEAD O'CONNOR	18	1992
SUCH A FEELING BIZARRE INC	13	1991
SUCH A FOOL 22-20'S	29	2005
SUCH A GOOD FEELIN' MISS BEHAVIN'	62	2002
SUCH A GOOD FEELING BROTHERS IN RHYTHM	64	1991
SUCH A NIGHT JOHNNIE RAY	1	1954
SUCH A NIGHT ELVIS PRESLEY	13	1964
SUCH A PHANTASY TIME FREQUENCY	25	1994
SUCH A SHAME TALK TALK	49	1984
SUCK YOU DRY MUDHONEY	65	1992
SUCKER DJ DIMPLES D	17	1990
SUCKERPUNCH WILDHEARTS	38	1994
SUCU SUCU LAURIE JOHNSON ORCHESTRA	9	1961
SUCU SUCU NINA & FREDERIK	23	1961
SUCU SUCU TED HEATH	36	1961
SUCU SUCU PING PING & AL VERLANE	41	1961
SUCU SUCU JOE LOSS ORCHESTRA	48	1961
SUDDENLY [A] OLIVIA NEWTON-JOHN & CLIFF RICHARD	15	1980
SUDDENLY [B] BILLY OCEAN	4	1985
SUDDENLY [C] ANGRY ANDERSON	3	1988
SUDDENLY [D] SEAN MAGUIRE	18	1995
SUDDENLY [E] LeANN RIMES	47	2003
SUDDENLY I SEE KT TUNSTALL	12	2005
SUDDENLY THERE'S A VALLEY PETULA CLARK	7	1955
SUDDENLY THERE'S A VALLEY JO STAFFORD	12	1955
SUDDENLY THERE'S A VALLEY LEE LAWRENCE WITH RAY MARTIN & HIS ORCHESTRA	14	1955
SUDDENLY YOU LOVE ME TREMELOES	6	1968
SUEDEHEAD MORRISSEY	5	1988
SUENO LATINO SUENO LATINO FEATURING CAROLINA DAMAS	47	2000
SUE'S GOTTA BE MINE DEL SHANNON	21	1963
SUFFER NEVER FINN	29	1995
SUFFER THE CHILDREN TEARS FOR FEARS	52	1985
SUFFER WELL DEPECHE MODE	12	2006
THE SUFFERING COHEED AND CAMBRIA	60	2006
SUFFOCATE [A] FEEDER	37	1998
SUFFOCATE [B] KING ADORA	39	2001
SUFFOCATING UNDER WORDS OF SORROW BULLET FOR MY VALENTINE	37	2005
SUGA FLO RIDA	19	2009
SUGAH RUBY AMANFU	32	2003
SUGAR LADYTRON	45	2005
SUGAR AND SPICE SEARCHERS	2	1963
SUGAR BABY LOVE RUBETTES	1	1974
SUGAR BEE CANNED HEAT	49	1970
SUGAR BOX THEN JERICO	22	1989
SUGAR BRIDGE (IT WILL STAND) BLUEBELLS	11	1983
SUGAR CANDY KISSES MAC & KATIE KISSOON	3	1975
SUGAR COATED ICEBERG LIGHTNING SEEDS	12	1997
SUGAR DADDY SECRET KNOWLEDGE	75	1996
SUGAR DOLL JETS	55	1981
SUGAR FOR THE SOUL STEVE BALSAMO	32	2002
SUGAR FREE JUICY	45	1986
SUGAR FREE PAULINE HENRY	57	1995
SUGAR (GIMME SOME) TRICK DADDY	61	2005
SUGAR HONEY ICE TEA GOODFELLAZ	25	1997
SUGAR IS SWEETER C J BOLLAND	11	1996
SUGAR KANE SONIC YOUTH	26	1993
SUGAR ME LYNSEY DE PAUL	5	1972
SUGAR MICE MARILLION	22	1987
SUGAR MOON PAT BOONE	6	1958
SUGAR RUSH MAN WITH NO NAME	55	1996
SUGAR SHACK [A] JIMMY GILMER & THE FIREBALLS	45	1963
SUGAR SHACK [B] SEB	61	1995
SUGAR SUGAR ARCHIES	1	1969
SUGAR SUGAR SAKKARIN	12	1971
SUGAR SUGAR DUKE BAYSEE	30	1994
SUGAR TOWN NANCY SINATRA	8	1967
SUGAR WE'RE GOIN' DOWN FALL OUT BOY	8	2006
SUGARBUSH DORIS DAY & FRANKIE LAINE	8	1952
SUGARHILL AZ	67	1996
SUGARMAN FREE ASSOCIATION	53	2003
SUGARTIME McGUIRE SISTERS	14	1958
SUGARTIME ALMA COGAN	16	1958
SUGARTIME JIM DALE	25	1958
SUICIDE BLONDE INXS	11	1990
SUKIYAKI KYU SAKAMOTO	6	1963
SUKIYAKI KENNY BALL & HIS JAZZMEN	10	1963
SULKY GIRL ELVIS COSTELLO & THE ATTRACTIONS	22	1994
SULTANA TITANIC	5	1971
SULTANS OF SWING DIRE STRAITS	8	1979
SUMAHAMA BEACH BOYS	45	1979
SUMATRAN ELECTRIC SOFT PARADE	65	2001
SUMERLAND (DREAMED) FIELDS OF THE NEPHILIM	37	1990
SUMMER CHARLOTTE HATHERLEY	31	2004
SUMMER BREEZE ISLEY BROTHERS	16	1974
SUMMER BREEZE GEOFFREY WILLIAMS	56	1992
SUMMER BUNNIES R KELLY	23	1994
SUMMER EDITION NUKLEUZ DJs	59	2003
SUMMER '89 CALIFORNIA SUNSHINE	56	1997
SUMMER FUN BARRACUDAS	37	1980
SUMMER GIRLS LYTE FUNKIE ONES	16	1999
SUMMER GONNA COME AGAIN SUPERSISTER	51	2001
SUMMER HOLIDAY CLIFF RICHARD & THE SHADOWS	1	1963
SUMMER HOLIDAY KEVIN THE GERBIL	50	1984
SUMMER HOLIDAY (EP) ZZ TOP	51	1985
SUMMER HOLIDAY MEDLEY DARREN DAY	17	1996
SUMMER IN SIAM POGUES	64	1990
SUMMER IN SPACE COSMOS	49	1999
SUMMER IN THE CITY LOVIN' SPOONFUL	8	1966
THE SUMMER IS MAGIC EXOTICA FEATURING ITSY FOSTER	68	1995
SUMMER IS OVER FRANK IFIELD	25	1964
SUMMER JAM UD PROJECT	14	2003
SUMMER MADNESS KOOL & THE GANG	17	1981
SUMMER MOVED ON A-HA	33	2000
SUMMER NIGHT CITY ABBA	5	1978
SUMMER NIGHTS [A] MARIANNE FAITHFULL	10	1965
SUMMER NIGHTS [B] JOHN TRAVOLTA & OLIVIA NEWTON-JOHN	1	1978
SUMMER OF '42 BIDDU ORCHESTRA	14	1975
SUMMER OF '69 BRYAN ADAMS	42	1985
SUMMER OF LOVE (COMME CI COMME CA) [A] LONYO – COMME CI COMME CA	8	2000
SUMMER OF LOVE [B] STEPS	5	2000
SUMMER OF MY LIFE SIMON MAY	7	1976
THE SUMMER OF SEVENTEENTH DOLL WINIFRED ATWELL	24	1959
SUMMER ON THE UNDERGROUND A	72	1998
SUMMER RAIN BELINDA CARLISLE	23	1991
SUMMER SET MR ACKER BILK & HIS PARAMOUNT JAZZ BAND	5	1960
SUMMER SON TEXAS	5	1999
SUMMER SONG BEDAZZLED	73	1992
SUMMER SUNSHINE CORRS	6	2004
SUMMER (THE FIRST TIME) BOBBY GOLDSBORO	9	1973
SUMMER WIND FRANK SINATRA	36	1966
SUMMERLANDS BEIJING SPRING	53	1993

	Peak Position	Year of Release
SUMMERLOVE SENSATION BAY CITY ROLLERS	3	1974
SUMMER'S MAGIC MARK SUMMERS	27	1991
SUMMER'S OVER RIALTO	60	1998
SUMMERSAULT TASTE XPERIENCE FEATURING NATASHA PEARL	66	1999
SUMMERTIME [A] AL MARTINO	49	1960
SUMMERTIME [A] MARCELS	46	1961
SUMMERTIME [A] BILLY STEWART	39	1966
SUMMERTIME [A] FUN BOY THREE	18	1982
SUMMERTIME [B] DJ JAZZY JEFF & THE FRESH PRINCE	8	1991
SUMMERTIME [C] SUNDAYS	15	1997
SUMMERTIME [D] ANOTHER LEVEL FEATURING TQ	7	1999
SUMMERTIME [E] NEW KIDS ON THE BLOCK	34	2008
SUMMERTIME [F] WILEY	45	2008
SUMMERTIME BLUES EDDIE COCHRAN	18	1958
SUMMERTIME BLUES WHO	38	1970
SUMMERTIME CITY MIKE BATT WITH THE NEW EDITION	4	1975
SUMMERTIME HEALING EUSEBE	32	1995
SUMMERTIME OF OUR LIVES A1	5	1999
SUMTHIN' SUMTHIN' THE MANTRA MAXWELL	27	1997
SUN [A] VIRUS	62	1995
SUN [B] JOHN LYDON	42	1997
SUN [C] SLUSNIK LUNA	40	2001
THE SUN AIN'T GONNA SHINE ANYMORE WALKER BROTHERS	1	1966
THE SUN AIN'T GONNA SHINE ANYMORE CHER	26	1996
THE SUN ALWAYS SHINES ON TV A-HA	1	1985
THE SUN ALWAYS SHINES ON TV DIVA	53	1995
THE SUN AND THE RAIN MADNESS	5	1983
SUN ARISE ROLF HARRIS	3	1962
SUN CITY ARTISTS UNITED AGAINST APARTHEID	21	1985
THE SUN DOES RISE JAH WOBBLE'S INVADERS OF THE HEART	41	1994
THE SUN DOESN'T SHINE BEATS INTERNATIONAL	66	1991
THE SUN GOES DOWN [A] THIN LIZZY	52	1983
SUN GOES DOWN [B] DAVID JORDAN	4	2008
THE SUN GOES DOWN (LIVING IT UP) LEVEL 42	10	1983
THE SUN HAS COME YOUR WAY SAM & MARK	1	2004
SUN HITS THE SKY SUPERGRASS	10	1997
SUN IS SHINING [A] TECHNIQUE	64	1999
SUN IS SHINING [B] BOB MARLEY VERSUS FUNKSTAR DE LUXE	3	1999
THE SUN IS SHINING (DOWN ON ME) DT8 PROJECT	17	2004
SUN KING CULT	39	1989
THE SUN MACHINE E-ZEE POSSEE	62	1990
SUN OF JAMAICA GOOMBAY DANCE BAND	50	1982
THE SUN RISING BELOVED	26	1989
SUN SHINING DOWN CIRCA FEATURING DESTRY	70	1999
SUN STREET KATRINA & THE WAVES	22	1986
SUN WORSHIPPERS (POSITIVE THINKING) DIANA BROWN & BARRIE K. SHARPE	61	1990
SUNBURN [A] GRAHAM GOULDMAN	52	1979
SUNBURN [B] MICHELLE COLLINS	28	1999
SUNBURN [C] MUSE	22	2000
SUNCHYME DARIO G	2	1997
SUNDANCE SUNDANCE	33	1997
SUNDAY [A] BUSTER	49	1976
SUNDAY [B] SONIC YOUTH	72	1998
SUNDAY GIRL [A] BLONDIE	1	1979
SUNDAY GIRL [B] ERASURE	33	2007
SUNDAY MORNING [A] NO DOUBT	50	1997
SUNDAY MORNING [B] MAROON 5	27	2004
SUNDAY MORNING CALL OASIS	4	2000
SUNDAY MORNINGS VANESSA PARADIS	49	1993
SUNDAY SHINING FINLEY QUAYE	16	1997
SUNDAY SHOUTIN' JOHNNY CORPORATE	45	2000
SUNDAY SUNDAY BLUR	26	1993
SUNDOWN [A] GORDON LIGHTFOOT	33	1974
SUNDOWN [A] ELWOOD	72	2000
SUNDOWN [B] S CLUB 8	4	2003
SUNFLOWER PAUL WELLER	16	1993
SUNGLASSES TRACEY ULLMAN	18	1984
SUNGLASSES AT NIGHT [A] TIGA & ZYNTHERIUS	25	2002
SUNGLASSES AT NIGHT [B] SKEPTA	64	2009
SUNLIGHT DJ SAMMY	8	2003
SUNMACHINE DARIO G	17	1998
SUNNY [A] BOBBY HEBB	12	1966
SUNNY [A] GEORGIE FAME	13	1966
SUNNY [A] CHER	32	1966
SUNNY [A] BONEY M	3	1976
SUNNY [A] BOOGIE PIMPS	10	2004
SUNNY [B] MORRISSEY	42	1995
SUNNY AFTERNOON KINKS	1	1966
SUNNY CAME HOME SHAWN COLVIN	29	1998
SUNNY DAY PIGBAG	53	1981
SUNNY HONEY GIRL CLIFF RICHARD	19	1971
SUNRISE [A] MOVEMENT 98 FEATURING CARROLL THOMPSON	58	1990
SUNRISE [B] GOLDENSCAN	52	2000
SUNRISE [C] PULP	23	2001
SUNRISE [D] SIMPLY RED	7	2003
SUNRISE [E] NORAH JONES	30	2004
SUNRISE [F] ANGEL CITY	9	2005
SUNRISE (HERE I AM) RATTY	51	2001
SUNSET NITIN SAWHNEY FEATURING ESKA	65	2001
SUNSET AND BABYLON W.A.S.P.	38	1993
SUNSET (BIRD OF PREY) FATBOY SLIM	9	2000
SUNSET BOULEVARD MICHAEL BALL	72	1993
SUNSET NOW HEAVEN 17	24	1984
SUNSET ON IBIZA THREE DRIVES ON A VINYL	44	2001
SUNSET PEOPLE DONNA SUMMER	46	1980
SUNSHINE [A] WARREN MILLS	74	1985
SUNSHINE [B] UMBOZA	14	1996
SUNSHINE [C] JAY-Z FEATURING BABYFACE & FOXY	25	1997
SUNSHINE [D] GABRIELLE	9	1999
SUNSHINE [E] ALEXANDER O'NEAL	72	1989
SUNSHINE [F] YOMANDA	16	2000
SUNSHINE [G] GARETH GATES	3	2003
SUNSHINE [H] HOLIDAY PLAN	58	2004
SUNSHINE [I] TWISTA	3	2004
SUNSHINE [J] LIL' FLIP	14	2004
THE SUNSHINE AFTER THE RAIN NEW ATLANTIC/U4EA FEATURING BERRI	26	1994
THE SUNSHINE AFTER THE RAIN BERRI	4	1995
SUNSHINE AFTER THE RAIN ELKIE BROOKS	10	1977
SUNSHINE & HAPPINESS DARRYL PANDY/NERIO'S DUBWORK	68	1999
SUNSHINE AND LOVE HAPPY MONDAYS	62	1992
SUNSHINE DAY OSIBISA	17	1976
SUNSHINE DAY CLOCK	58	1999
SUNSHINE GIRL HERMAN'S HERMITS	8	1968
SUNSHINE IN THE RAIN BWO	69	2008
THE SUNSHINE OF LOVE LOUIS ARMSTRONG	41	1968
SUNSHINE OF YOUR LOVE CREAM	25	1968
THE SUNSHINE OF YOUR SMILE MIKE BERRY	9	1980
SUNSHINE ON A RAINY DAY ZOE	4	1990
SUNSHINE ON A RAINY DAY REAL & RICHARDSON FEATURING JOBABE	69	2003
SUNSHINE ON LEITH PROCLAIMERS	41	1988
SUNSHINE PLAYROOM JULIAN COPE	64	1983
SUNSHINE SUPERMAN DONOVAN	2	1966
SUNSTORM HURLEY & TODD	38	2000
SUNSTROKE CHICANE	21	1997
SUNTAN STAN	40	1993
SUPAFLY FUGATIVE	48	2010
SUPER BOWL SUNDAE OZOMATLI	68	1999
SUPER DUPER LOVE (ARE YOU DIGGIN ON ME) JOSS STONE	18	2004
SUPER GRAN BILLY CONNOLLY	32	1985
SUPER LOVE WIGAN'S OVATION	41	1975
SUPER MASSIVE BLACK HOLE MUSE	4	2006
SUPER POPOID GROOVE WIN	63	1987
SUPER TROUPER ABBA	1	1980
SUPER TROUPER A*TEENS	21	1999
SUPER WOMBLE WOMBLES	20	1975
SUPERBAD SUPERSLICK REDHEAD KINGPIN & THE FBI	68	1989
SUPERCHANNEL ALARM MMVI	24	2006
SUPERFLY 1990 CURTIS MAYFIELD & ICE-T	48	1990
SUPERFLY GUY S-EXPRESS	5	1988
SUPERFREAK BEATFREAKZ	7	2006
SUPERFREAKON MISSY ELLIOTT	72	2001
SUPERGIRL GRAHAM BONNEY	19	1966
SUPERHERO REEF	55	2000
SUPERHUMAN CHRIS BROWN FEATURING KERI HILSON	32	2008
SUPERHUMAN TOUCH ATHLETE	71	2009
SUPERMAN STEREOPHONICS	13	2005
SUPERMAN (GIOCA JOUER) BLACK LACE	9	1983
SUPERMAN (IT'S NOT EASY) FIVE FOR FIGHTING	48	2002
SUPERMAN'S BIG SISTER IAN DURY & THE BLOCKHEADS	51	1980
SUPERMARIOLAND AMBASSADORS OF FUNK FEATURING MC MARIO	8	1992
SUPERMARKET SWEEP (WILL YOU DANCE WITH ME) BAR CODES FEATURING ALISON BROWN	72	1994
SUPERMODEL (YOU BETTER WORK) RuPAUL	39	1993
SUPERNATURAL KIM ENGLISH	50	1997
SUPERNATURAL GIVER KINKY MACHINE	70	1993
SUPERNATURAL SUPERSERIOUS R.E.M.	54	2008
SUPERNATURAL THING FREELAND	65	2004
SUPERNATURE [A] CERRONE	8	1978
SUPERNATURE [B] BARON & FRESH	59	2005
SUPERNOVA [A] FIVE THIRTY	75	1991
SUPERNOVA [B] MR HUDSON & KANYE WEST	2	2009
SUPERSHIP GEORGE 'BAD' BENSON	30	1975
SUPERSONIC [A] HWA FEATURING SONIC THE HEDGEHOG	33	1992
SUPERSONIC [B] OASIS	31	1994
SUPERSONIC [C] JAMIROQUAI	22	1999
SUPERSONIC ROCKET SHIP KINKS	16	1972
SUPERSTAR [A] CARPENTERS	18	1971
SUPERSTAR [A] SONIC YOUTH	45	1994
SUPERSTAR [B] MURRAY HEAD	47	1972
SUPERSTAR [C] LYDIA MURDOCK	14	1983
SUPERSTAR [D] NOVY VERSUS ENIAC	32	1998
SUPERSTAR [E] SUPERSTAR	49	1998
SUPERSTAR [F] ONES	45	2003
SUPERSTAR [G] JAMELIA	3	2003
SUPERSTAR [H] LUPE FIASCO FEATURING MATTHEW SANTOS	4	2008
SUPERSTAR (REMEMBER HOW YOU GOT WHERE YOU ARE) TEMPTATIONS	32	1972
SUPERSTAR TRADESMAN VIEW	15	2006
SUPERSTITION STEVIE WONDER	11	1973
SUPERSTITION – GOOD TIMES (MEDLEY) CLUBHOUSE	59	1983
SUPERSTITIOUS EUROPE	34	1988
SUPERSTRING CYGNUS X	33	2001
SUPERSTYLIN' GROOVE ARMADA	12	2001
SUPERWOMAN KARYN WHITE	11	1989

	Peak Position	Year of Release
SUPPORT THE TOON – IT'S YOUR DUTY (EP) MUNGO JERRY & TOON TRAVELLERS	57	1999
SUPREME ROBBIE WILLIAMS	4	2000
THE SUPREME EP SINITTA	49	1993
SURE TAKE THAT	1	1994
SURE FEELS GOOD ULTRABEAT VERSUS DARREN STYLES	52	2007
SURE SHOT BEASTIE BOYS	27	1994
SURE THING DARLING BUDS	71	1992
SURF CITY JAN & DEAN	26	1963
SURFIN BIRD TRASHMEN	50	2009
SURFIN' USA BEACH BOYS	34	1963
SURFIN' USA AARON CARTER	18	1998
SURPRISE BIZARRE INC	21	1996
SURPRISE SURPRISE CENTRAL LINE	48	1983
SURRENDER [A] ELVIS PRESLEY	1	1961
SURRENDER [B] DIANA ROSS	10	1971
SURRENDER [C] SWING OUT SISTER	7	1987
SURRENDER [D] ROGER TAYLOR	38	1999
SURRENDER [E] LASGO	24	2004
SURRENDER YOUR LOVE [A] NIGHTCRAWLERS	7	1995
SURRENDER (YOUR LOVE) [B] JAVINE	15	2003
SURROUND YOURSELF WITH SORROW CILLA BLACK	3	1969
SURVIVAL CAR FOUNTAINS OF WAYNE	53	1997
SURVIVALISM NINE INCH NAILS	29	2007
SURVIVE DAVID BOWIE	28	2000
SURVIVOR DESTINY'S CHILD	1	2001
SUSANNA ART COMPANY	12	1984
SUSANNAH'S STILL ALIVE DAVE DAVIES	20	1967
SUSAN'S HOUSE EELS	9	1997
SUSIE DARLIN' ROBIN LUKE	23	1958
SUSIE DARLIN' TOMMY ROE	37	1962
SUSPICION TERRY STAFFORD	31	1964
SUSPICION ELVIS PRESLEY	9	1977
SUSPICIOUS CHARACTER BLOOD ARM	62	2006
SUSPICIOUS MINDS ELVIS PRESLEY	2	1969
SUSPICIOUS MINDS CANDI STATON	31	1982
SUSPICIOUS MINDS FINE YOUNG CANNIBALS	8	1986
SUSPICIOUS MINDS GARETH GATES	1	2002
SUSSUDIO PHIL COLLINS	12	1985
SUZANNE BEWARE OF THE DEVIL DANDY LIVINGSTONE	14	1972
SUZIE BOY KILL BOY	17	2006
SVEN SVEN SVEN BELL & SPURLING	7	2001
SW LIVE EP PETER GABRIEL	39	1994
SWAGGA LIKE US JAY-Z FEATURING KANYE WEST & LIL WAYNE	33	2008
SWALLOW MY PRIDE RAMONES	49	1977
SWALLOWED BUSH	7	1997
SWAMP THING GRID	3	1994
SWAN LAKE CATS	48	1979
SWASTIKA EYES PRIMAL SCREAM	22	1999
SWAY [A] DEAN MARTIN	6	1954
SWAY [A] BOBBY RYDELL	12	1960
SWAY [B] STRANGELOVE	47	1996
SWAY [C] KOOKS	41	2008
SWEAR IT AGAIN WESTLIFE	1	1999
SWEARIN' TO GOD FRANKIE VALLI	31	1975
SWEAT USURA	29	1993
SWEAT (A LA LA LA LA LONG) INNER CIRCLE	3	1992
SWEAT IN A BULLET SIMPLE MINDS	52	1981
SWEATING BULLETS MEGADETH	26	1993
SWEDISH RHAPSODY MANTOVANI	2	1953
SWEDISH RHAPSODY RAY MARTIN	4	1953
SWEET ABOUT ME GABRIELLA CILMI	6	2008
SWEET AND LOW DEBORAH HARRY	57	1990
SWEET BABY MACY GRAY FEATURING ERYKAH BADU	23	2001
SWEET BIRD OF TRUTH THE THE	55	1987
SWEET CAROLINE NEIL DIAMOND	8	1971
SWEET CAROLINE GLEE CAST	59	2010
SWEET CATATONIA CATATONIA	61	1996
SWEET CHEATIN' RITA ALVIN STARDUST	37	1975
SWEET CHILD O' MINE GUNS N' ROSES	6	1988
SWEET CHILD O' MINE SHERYL CROW	30	1999
SWEET CHILD O' MINE TAKEN BY TREES	23	2009
SWEET DANGER ANGELWITCH	75	1980
SWEET DISPOSITION TEMPER TRAP	6	2009
SWEET DREAM JETHRO TULL	7	1969
SWEET DREAMS BEYONCE	5	2009
SWEET DREAMS [A] DAVE SAMPSON	29	1960
SWEET DREAMS [B] DJ SCOTT FEATURING LORNA B	37	1995
SWEET DREAMS [B] SWING FEATURING DR ALBAN	59	1995
SWEET DREAMS [C] TOMMY McLAIN	49	1966
SWEET DREAMS [C] ROY BUCHANAN	40	1973
SWEET DREAMS [C] ELVIS COSTELLO	42	1981
SWEET DREAMS [D] LA BOUCHE	44	1994
SWEET DREAMS (ARE MADE OF THIS) EURYTHMICS	2	1983
SWEET DREAMS MY LA EX RACHEL STEVENS	2	2003
SWEET EMOTION AEROSMITH	74	1994
THE SWEET ESCAPE GWEN STEFANI FEATURING AKON	2	2007
SWEET FREEDOM [A] MICHAEL McDONALD	12	1986
SWEET FREEDOM [A] SAFRI DUO FEATURING MICHAEL McDONALD	54	2002
SWEET FREEDOM [B] POSITIVE GANG	34	1993
SWEET FREEDOM PART 2 POSITIVE GANG	67	1993
SWEET HARMONY [A] LIQUID	14	1992
SWEET HARMONY [A] DANNY BYRD FEATURING LIQUID	64	2010
SWEET HARMONY [B] BELOVED	8	1993
SWEET HEART CONTRACT MAGAZINE	54	1980
SWEET HITCH-HIKER CREEDENCE CLEARWATER REVIVAL	36	1971
SWEET HOME ALABAMA LYNYRD SKYNYRD	21	1976
SWEET ILLUSION JUNIOR CAMPBELL	15	1973
SWEET IMPOSSIBLE YOU BRENDA LEE	28	1963
SWEET INSPIRATION JOHNNY JOHNSON & THE BANDWAGON	10	1970
SWEET INVISIBILITY HUE & CRY	55	1989
SWEET JOHNNY GORKY'S ZYGOTIC MYNCI	60	1998
SWEET LADY TYRESE	55	1999
SWEET LADY LUCK WHITESNAKE	25	1994
SWEET LEAF MAGOO:MOGWAI	60	1998
SWEET LIES [A] ROBERT PALMER	58	1988
SWEET LIES [B] ELLIE CAMPBELL	42	1999
SWEET LIKE CHOCOLATE SHANKS & BIGFOOT	1	1999
SWEET LIPS MONACO	18	1997
SWEET LITTLE MYSTERY WET WET WET	5	1987
SWEET LITTLE ROCK 'N' ROLLER SHOWADDYWADDY	15	1979
SWEET LITTLE SIXTEEN CHUCK BERRY	16	1958
SWEET LITTLE SIXTEEN JERRY LEE LEWIS	38	1962
SWEET LOVE [A] COMMODORES	32	1977
SWEET LOVE [B] ANITA BAKER	13	1986
SWEET LOVE [B] M-BEAT FEATURING NAZLYN	18	1994
SWEET LOVE 2K [B] FIERCE	3	2000
SWEET LUI-LOUISE IRONHORSE	64	1979
SWEET LULLABY DEEP FOREST	10	1994
SWEET MEMORY BELLE STARS	22	1983
SWEET MUSIC SHOWADDYWADDY	14	1975
SWEET N SOUR JON SPENCER BLUES EXPLOSION	66	2002
SWEET NOTHINS SEARCHERS	48	1963
SWEET NOTHIN'S BRENDA LEE	4	1960
SWEET OLD-FASHIONED GIRL TERESA BREWER	3	1956
SWEET PEA MANFRED MANN	36	1967
SWEET PEA, MY SWEET PEA PAUL WELLER	44	2000
SWEET POTATO PIE DOMINO	42	1994
SWEET REVENGE SPOOKS	67	2001
SWEET REVIVAL (KEEP IT COMIN') SHADES OF RHYTHM	61	1993
SWEET SENSATION [A] MELODIANS	41	1970
SWEET SENSATION [B] SHADES OF RHYTHM	54	1991
SWEET SENSATION [C] SHABOOM	64	1999
SWEET SENSUAL LOVE BIG MOUNTAIN	51	1994
SWEET SHOP AVENGERZ BIS	46	1997
SWEET SISTER PEACE BY PIECE	46	1996
SWEET SIXTEEN BILLY IDOL	17	1987
SWEET SMELL OF SUCCESS STRANGLERS	65	1990
SWEET SOMEBODY SHANNON	25	1984
SWEET SOUL MUSIC ARTHUR CONLEY	7	1967
SWEET SOUL SENSATIONS LIGHTNING SEEDS	67	2000
SWEET SOUL SISTER CULT	42	1990
SWEET STUFF GUY MITCHELL	25	1957
SWEET SUBURBIA SKIDS	70	1978
SWEET SURRENDER [A] ROD STEWART	23	1983
SWEET SURRENDER [B] WET WET WET	6	1989
SWEET SWEET SMILE CARPENTERS	40	1978
SWEET TALKIN' GUY CHIFFONS	4	1966
SWEET TALKIN' WOMAN ELECTRIC LIGHT ORCHESTRA	6	1978
SWEET THANG JONESTOWN	49	1998
SWEET THING MICK JAGGER	24	1993
SWEET TOXIC LOVE JESUS LOVES YOU	65	1992
SWEET UNDERSTANDING LOVE FOUR TOPS	29	1973
SWEET WILLIAM MILLIE	30	1964
SWEETER THAN THE MIDNIGHT RAIN LUKE GOSS & THE BAND OF THIEVES	52	1993
SWEETER THAN WINE DIONNE RAKEEM	46	2001
SWEETER THAN YOU RICKY NELSON	19	1959
SWEETEST CHILD MARIA McKEE	45	1992
SWEETEST DAY OF MAY JOE T VANNELLI PROJECT	45	1995
THE SWEETEST DAYS VANESSA WILLIAMS	41	1995
THE SWEETEST GIRL SCRITTI POLITTI	64	1981
SWEETEST GIRL MADNESS	35	1986
SWEETEST GIRL (DOLLAR BILL) WYCLEF JEAN FEATURING AKON, LIL WAYNE & NIIA	66	2007
SWEETEST SMILE BLACK	8	1987
THE SWEETEST SURRENDER FACTORY OF UNLIMITED RHYTHM	59	1996
SWEETEST SWEETEST JERMAINE JACKSON	52	1984
THE SWEETEST TABOO SADE	31	1985
SWEETEST THING [A] GENE LOVES JEZEBEL	75	1986
THE SWEETEST THING [B] REFUGEE ALLSTARS FEATURING LAURYN HILL	18	1997
SWEETEST THING [C] U2	3	1998
SWEETHEART ENGELBERT HUMPERDINCK	22	1970
SWEETIE PIE EDDIE COCHRAN	38	1960
SWEETNESS [A] MICHELLE GAYLE	4	1994
SWEETNESS [B] XSTASIA	65	2001
SWEETNESS [C] JIMMY EAT WORLD	38	2002
SWEETNESS AND LIGHT LUSH	47	1990
SWEETS WORLD OF TWIST	58	1991
SWEETS FOR MY SWEET SEARCHERS	1	1963
SWEETS FOR MY SWEET CJ LEWIS	3	1994
SWEETSMOKE MR SCRUFF	75	2002
SWEETY REEF	46	1999
SWIM FISHBONE	54	1993
SWIMMING HORSES SIOUXSIE & THE BANSHEES	28	1984
SWING LOW UB40 FEATURING UNITED COLOURS OF SOUND	15	2003
SWING LOW '99 RUSSELL WATSON	38	1999
SWING LOW (RUN WITH THE BALL) UNION FEATURING THE ENGLAND WORLD CUP SQUAD	16	1991
SWING LOW SWEET CHARIOT ERIC CLAPTON	19	1975

	Peak Position	Year of Release
SWING LOW SWEET CHARIOT LADYSMITH BLACK MAMBAZO FEATURING CHINA BLACK	15	1995
SWING MY HIPS (SEX DANCE) LEMONESCENT	48	2002
SWING MY WAY KP & ENVYI	14	1998
SWING SWING ALL-AMERICAN REJECTS	13	2003
SWING THAT HAMMER MIKE COTTON'S JAZZMEN	36	1963
SWING THE MOOD JIVE BUNNY & THE MASTERMIXERS	1	1989
SWING YOUR DADDY JIM GILSTRAP	4	1975
SWINGIN' LIGHT OF THE WORLD	45	1979
SWINGIN' LOW OUTLAWS	46	1961
SWINGIN' SHEPHERD BLUES TED HEATH	3	1958
SWINGIN' SHEPHERD BLUES ELLA FITZGERALD	15	1958
SWINGIN' SHEPHERD BLUES MOE KOFFMAN QUARTETTE	23	1958
SWINGING IN THE RAIN NORMAN VAUGHAN	34	1962
SWINGING ON A STAR BIG DEE IRWIN	7	1963
SWINGING SCHOOL BOBBY RYDELL	44	1960
SWINGS & ROUNDABOUTS RONI SIZE	57	2002
SWISS MAID DEL SHANNON	2	1962
SWITCH [A] BENELUX & NANCY DEE	52	1979
SWITCH [B] SENSER	39	1994
SWITCH [C] HOWIE B	62	1997
SWITCH [D] PESHAY	59	1999
THE SWITCH [E] PLANET FUNK	52	2003
SWITCH [F] WILL SMITH	4	2005
SWITCH IT ON WILL YOUNG	5	2005
SWITCHED ON SWING KINGS OF SWING ORCHESTRA	48	1982
SWOON MISSION	73	1995
SWORDS OF A THOUSAND MEN TEN POLE TUDOR	10	1981
SYLVIA FOCUS	4	1973
SYLVIA'S MOTHER DR HOOK & THE MEDICINE SHOW	2	1972
SYLVIE SAINT ETIENNE	12	1998
SYMMETRY C BRAINCHILD	31	1999
SYMPATHY [A] RARE BIRD	27	1970
SYMPATHY [B] MARILLION	17	1992
SYMPATHY FOR THE DEVIL GUNS N' ROSES	9	1995
SYMPATHY FOR THE DEVIL ROLLING STONES	14	2003
SYMPHONY DONELL RUSH	66	1992
SYMPHONY OF DESTRUCTION MEGADETH	15	1992
SYNAESTHESIA (FLY AWAY) THRILLSEEKERS FEATURING SHERYL DEANE	28	2001
SYNCHRONICITY II POLICE	17	1983
SYNERGY TRANCESETTERS	72	2001
SYNTH & STRINGS YOMANDA	8	1999
SYSTEM ADDICT FIVE STAR	3	1986
SYSTEM CHECK BROCKIE/ED SOLO	68	2004
SYSTEM OF SURVIVAL EARTH, WIND & FIRE	54	1987
SZIGET (WE GET WRECKED) HAMFATTER	54	2007

T

	Peak Position	Year of Release
T-SHIRT SHONTELLE	6	2009
T-10/THE TENTH PLANET DISTORTED MINDS	43	2003
THE TABLE BEAUTIFUL SOUTH	47	1999
TABOO GLAMMA KID FEATURING SHOLA AMA	10	1999
TACKY LOVE SONG CREDIT TO THE NATION	60	1998
TAHITI DAVID ESSEX	8	1983
TAINTED LOVE SOFT CELL	1	1981
TAINTED LOVE IMPEDANCE	54	1989
TAINTED LOVE ICON	51	1996
TAINTED LOVE MARILYN MANSON	5	2002
TAINTED LOVE RICHARD GREY	52	2007
TAKE COLOUR FIELD	70	1984
TAKE A BOW [A] MADONNA	16	1994
TAKE A BOW [B] RIHANNA	1	2008
TAKE A BOW [B] GLEE CAST	36	2010
TAKE A CHANCE MAGIC NUMBERS	16	2006
TAKE A CHANCE ON ME ABBA	1	1978
TAKE A CHANCE WITH ME ROXY MUSIC	26	1982
TAKE A FREE FALL DANCE 2 TRANCE	36	1993
TAKE A HEART SORROWS	21	1965
(TAKE A LITTLE) PIECE OF MY HEART ERMA FRANKLIN	9	1992
TAKE A LITTLE TIME (DOUBLE SINGLE) GARY MOORE	75	1987
TAKE A LOOK LEVEL 42	32	1988
TAKE A LOOK AROUND [A] TEMPTATIONS	13	1972
TAKE A LOOK AROUND [B] LIMP BIZKIT	3	2000
TAKE A LOOK AT YOURSELF COVERDALE PAGE	43	1993
TAKE A MESSAGE TO MARY EVERLY BROTHERS	20	1959
TAKE A PICTURE FILTER	25	2000
TAKE A REST GANG STARR	63	1991
TAKE A RUN AT THE SUN DINOSAUR, JR	53	1997
TAKE A TOKE C & C MUSIC FACTORY FEATURING MARTHA WASH	26	1995
TAKE BACK THE CITY SNOW PATROL	6	2008
TAKE CALIFORNIA PROPELLERHEADS	69	1996
TAKE CARE OF YOURSELF LEVEL 42	39	1989
TAKE CONTROL AMERIE	10	2007
TAKE CONTROL [A] STATE OF MIND	46	1998
TAKE CONTROL [B] JAIMESON FEATURING ANGEL BLU & CK	16	2004
TAKE CONTROL OF THE PARTY BG THE PRINCE OF RAP	71	1992
TAKE DOWN THE UNION JACK BILLY BRAGG & THE BLOKES	22	2002
TAKE FIVE [A] DAVE BRUBECK QUARTET	6	1961
TAKE 5 [B] NORTHSIDE	40	1991
TAKE 4 (EP) MIKE OLDFIELD	72	1978
TAKE GOOD CARE OF HER ADAM WADE	38	1961
TAKE GOOD CARE OF MY BABY BOBBY VEE	3	1961
TAKE GOOD CARE OF MY BABY SMOKIE	34	1980
TAKE GOOD CARE OF MY HEART MICHAELA	66	1990
TAKE GOOD CARE OF YOURSELF THREE DEGREES	9	1975
TAKE HER BACK PIGEON DETECTIVES	20	2007
TAKE IT FLOWERED UP	34	1991
TAKE IT AND RUN BANDITS	32	2003
TAKE IT AWAY [A] PAUL McCARTNEY	15	1982
TAKE IT AWAY [B] USED	44	2005
TAKE IT BACK PINK FLOYD	23	1994
TAKE IT (CLOSING TIME) TOM NOVY & LIMA	31	2006
TAKE IT EASY [A] LET LOOSE	25	1996
TAKE IT EASY [B] MINT ROYALE	66	2000
TAKE IT EASY [C] 3SL	11	2002
TAKE IT EASY ON ME A HOUSE	55	1992
TAKE IT FROM ME [A] ROGER CHRISTIAN	63	1989
TAKE IT FROM ME [B] GIRLFRIEND	47	1993
TAKE IT OFF DONNAS	38	2003
TAKE IT ON THE RUN REO SPEEDWAGON	19	1981
TAKE IT OR LEAVE IT SEARCHERS	31	1966
TAKE IT SATCH EP LOUIS ARMSTRONG WITH HIS ALL-STARS	29	1956
TAKE IT TO THE LIMIT EAGLES	12	1976
TAKE IT TO THE STREETS RAMPAGE FEATURING BILLY LAWRENCE	58	1997
TAKE IT TO THE TOP [A] KOOL & THE GANG	15	1981
TAKE IT TO THE TOP [B] CLOUD	72	1981
TAKE ME DREAM FREQUENCY	39	1992
TAKE ME AWAY [A] TRUE FAITH WITH FINAL CUT	51	1991
TAKE ME AWAY [A] CAPPELLA FEATURING LOLEATTA HOLLOWAY	25	1992
TAKE ME AWAY [B] D:REAM	18	1994
TAKE ME AWAY [C] CULTURE BEAT	51	1996
TAKE ME AWAY [D] STONEBRIDGE FEATURING THERESE	9	2005
TAKE ME AWAY [E] HAJI & EMANUEL	73	2006
TAKE ME AWAY (I'LL FOLLOW YOU) BAD BOYS INC	15	1994
TAKE ME AWAY INTO THE NIGHT 4 STRINGS	15	2002
TAKE ME AWAY (PARADISE) MIX FACTORY	51	1993
TAKE ME BACK [A] RHYTHMATIC	71	1990
TAKE ME BACK [B] TINCHY STRYDER	3	2009
TAKE ME BACK TO LOVE AGAIN KATHY SLEDGE	62	1992
TAKE ME BACK TO YOUR HOUSE BASEMENT JAXX	42	2006
TAKE ME BAK 'OME SLADE	1	1972
TAKE ME BY THE HAND SUBMERGE FEATURING JAN JOHNSTON	28	1997
TAKE ME DOWN TO THE RIVER SKIN	26	1995
TAKE ME FOR A LITTLE WHILE COVERDALE PAGE	29	1993
TAKE ME FOR WHAT I'M WORTH SEARCHERS	20	1965
TAKE ME GIRL I'M READY JUNIOR WALKER & THE ALL-STARS	16	1973
TAKE ME HIGH CLIFF RICHARD	27	1973
TAKE ME HIGHER [A] R.A.F.	59	1994
TAKE ME HIGHER [B] DIANA ROSS	32	1995
TAKE ME HIGHER [C] GEORGIE PORGIE	61	1996
TAKE ME HOME [A] PHIL COLLINS	19	1985
TAKE ME HOME [B] JOE COCKER FEATURING BEKKA BRAMLETT	41	1994
TAKE ME HOME COUNTRY ROADS OLIVIA NEWTON-JOHN	15	1973
TAKE ME HOME – MUTINY SOPHIE ELLIS-BEXTOR	2	2001
TAKE ME HOME (WOMBLE 'TIL I DIE) EVERSTRONG	73	2005
TAKE ME I'M YOURS SQUEEZE	19	1978
TAKE ME IN YOUR ARMS DOOBIE BROTHERS	29	1975
TAKE ME IN YOUR ARMS AND LOVE ME GLADYS KNIGHT & THE PIPS	13	1967
TAKE ME IN YOUR ARMS AND LOVE ME SCRITTI POLITTI & SWEETIE IRIE	47	1991
TAKE ME NOW TAMMY PAYNE	55	1991
TAKE ME OUT FRANZ FERDINAND	3	2004
TAKE ME OVER McKAY	65	2003
TAKE ME THERE BLACKSTREET & MYA FEATURING MA$E & BLINKY BLINK	7	1998
TAKE ME TO HEAVEN BABY D	15	1996
TAKE ME TO THE CLOUDS ABOVE LMC VS U2	1	2004
TAKE ME TO THE HOSPITAL PRODIGY	38	2009
TAKE ME TO THE MARDI GRAS PAUL SIMON	7	1973
TAKE ME TO THE NEXT PHASE ISLEY BROTHERS	50	1978
TAKE ME TO YOUR HEART RICK ASTLEY	8	1988
TAKE ME TO YOUR HEART AGAIN VINCE HILL	13	1966
TAKE ME TO YOUR HEAVEN CHARLOTTE NILSSON	20	1999
TAKE ME UP [A] SOUNDSOURCE	61	1992
TAKE ME UP [B] SONIC SURFERS FEATURING JOCELYN BROWN	61	1993
TAKE ME WITH YOU [A] PRINCE & THE REVOLUTION	7	1985
TAKE ME WITH YOU [B] COSMOS	32	2002
TAKE MY ADVICE KYM SIMS	13	1992
TAKE MY BREATH AWAY (LOVE THEME FROM 'TOP GUN') [A] BERLIN	1	1986
TAKE MY BREATH AWAY [A] SODA CLUB FEATURING HANNAH ALETHA	16	2002
TAKE MY BREATH AWAY [B] EMMA BUNTON	5	2001

	Peak Position	Year of Release
TAKE MY HAND JURGEN VRIES FEATURING ANDREA BRITTON	23	2004
TAKE MY HEART AL MARTINO	9	1952
TAKE MY HEART (YOU CAN HAVE IT IF YOU WANT IT) KOOL & THE GANG	29	1982
TAKE MY SCARS MACHINE HEAD	73	1997
TAKE MY TIME SHEENA EASTON	44	1981
TAKE OFF SOME TIME NEW ATLANTIC	64	1993
TAKE ON ME A-HA	2	1985
TAKE ON ME A1	1	2000
TAKE ON THE WORLD JUDAS PRIEST	14	1979
THE TAKE OVER THE BREAKS OVER FALL OUT BOY	48	2007
TAKE THAT WILEY & CHEW FU	20	2010
TAKE THAT LOOK OFF YOUR FACE MARTI WEBB	3	1980
TAKE THAT SITUATION NICK HEYWARD	11	1983
TAKE THAT TO THE BANK SHALAMAR	20	1979
TAKE THE BOX AMY WINEHOUSE	57	2004
TAKE THE LONG ROAD AND WALK IT MUSIC	14	2002
TAKE THE LONG WAY HOME FAITHLESS	15	1998
TAKE THESE CHAINS FROM MY HEART RAY CHARLES	5	1963
TAKE THIS HEART RICHARD MARX	13	1992
TAKE THIS TIME SEAN MAGUIRE	27	1994
TAKE TO THE MOUNTAINS RICHARD BARNES	35	1970
TAKE YOU OUT LUTHER VANDROSS	59	2001
TAKE YOU THERE [A] RONNI SIMON	58	1995
TAKE YOU THERE [B] SEAN KINGSTON	47	2008
TAKE YOUR MAMA SCISSOR SISTERS	17	2004
TAKE YOUR MAMA FOR A RIDE LULU	37	1975
TAKE YOUR PARTNER BY THE HAND HOWIE B FEATURING ROBBIE ROBERTSON	74	1998
TAKE YOUR SHOES OFF CHEEKY GIRLS	3	2003
TAKE YOUR TIME [A] HIGH	56	1990
TAKE YOUR TIME [B] MANTRONIX FEATURING WONDRESS	10	1990
TAKE YOUR TIME [C] LOVE BITE	56	2000
TAKE YOUR TIME (DO IT RIGHT) PART 1 S.O.S. BAND	51	1980
TAKEN FOR GRANTED SIA	10	2000
TAKES A LITTLE TIME TOTAL CONTRAST	17	1985
TAKES TWO TO TANGO LOUIS ARMSTRONG	6	1952
TAKIN' A CHANCE ON YOU DOLLAR	62	1980
TAKIN' BACK MY LOVE ENRIQUE IGLESIAS FEATURING CIARA	12	2009
TAKIN' HOLD SAM LA MORE	70	2003
TAKING CHANCES CELINE DION	40	2007
TAKING OFF CURE	39	2004
TAKING ON THE WORLD GUN	50	1990
TAKING THE VEIL DAVID SYLVIAN	53	1986
TALES FROM A DANCEOGRAPHIC OCEAN (EP) JAM & SPOON	49	1992
TALES FROM THE HARD SIDE BIOHAZARD	47	1994
TALES OF THE HOOD TUBBY T	47	2002
TALK COLDPLAY	10	2006
TALK ABOUT IT IN THE MORNING MARTYN JOSEPH	43	1995
TALK ABOUT OUR LOVE BRANDY FEATURING KANYE WEST	6	2004
TALK BACK DOUBLE TROUBLE FEATURING JANETTE SEWELL	71	1990
TALK DIRTY TO ME POISON	67	1987
TALK OF THE TOWN PRETENDERS	8	1980
TALK SHOWS ON MUTE INCUBUS	43	2004
TALK TALK TALK TALK	23	1982
TALK TALK TALK ORDINARY BOYS	17	2004
TALK TO ME [A] THIRD WORLD	56	1979
TALK TO ME [B] STEVIE NICKS	68	1986
TALK TO ME [C] ANITA BAKER	68	1990
TALK TO ME [D] 60FT DOLLS	37	1996
TALK YOU DOWN SCRIPT	47	2009
TALKIN' ALL THAT JAZZ STETSASONIC	54	1988
TALKING IN YOUR SLEEP [A] CRYSTAL GAYLE	11	1978
TALKING IN YOUR SLEEP [A] MARTINE McCUTCHEON	6	1999
TALKING IN YOUR SLEEP [B] BUCKS FIZZ	15	1984
TALKING LOUD AND CLEAR ORCHESTRAL MANOEUVRES IN THE DARK	11	1984
TALKING OF LOVE ANITA DOBSON	43	1987
TALKING WITH MYSELF ELECTRIBE 101	23	1990
TALL DARK STRANGER ROSE BRENNAN	31	1961
TALL 'N' HANDSOME OUTRAGE	51	1995
TALLAHASSEE LASSIE TOMMY STEELE	16	1959
TALLAHASSEE LASSIE FREDDY CANNON	17	1959
TALLYMAN JEFF BECK	30	1967
TALONS BLOC PARTY	39	2008
TALULA TORI AMOS	22	1996
TAMBOURINE EVE	19	2007
TAMMY DEBBIE REYNOLDS	2	1957
TAM-TAM POUR L'ETHIOPE STARVATION	33	1985
TANGERINE FEEDER	60	1997
TANGO IN MONO EXPRESSOS	70	1981
TANSY ALEX WELSH	45	1961
TANTALISE (WO WO EE YEH YEH) JIMMY THE HOOVER	18	1983
TAP THE BOTTLE YOUNG BLACK TEENAGERS	39	1994
TAP TURNS ON THE WATER C.C.S.	5	1971
TAPE LOOP MORCHEEBA	42	1996
TARANTINO'S NEW STAR NORTH & SOUTH	18	1997
TARANTULA SMASHING PUMPKINS	59	2007
TARANTULA [A] FAITHLESS	29	2002
TARANTULA [B] PENDULUM & FRESH FEATURING SPYDA	60	2005
TARA'S THEME SPIRO & WIX	29	1996
TARA'S THEME FROM 'GONE WITH THE WIND' ROSE OF ROMANCE ORCHESTRA	71	1982
TARGET EMBRACE	29	2006
TARRED & FEATHERED (WHAT A BAD BOY) DOGS	64	2005
TARZAN BOY BALTIMORA	3	1985
TASTE IN MEN PLACEBO	16	2000
TASTE IT INXS	21	1992
A TASTE OF AGGRO BARRON KNIGHTS	3	1978
TASTE OF BITTER LOVE GLADYS KNIGHT & THE PIPS	35	1980
A TASTE OF HONEY MR ACKER BILK WITH THE LEON YOUNG STRING CHORALE	16	1963
THE TASTE OF INK USED	52	2003
THE TASTE OF YOUR TEARS KING	11	1985
TASTE THE LAST GIRL SONS & DAUGHTERS	75	2005
TASTE THE PAIN RED HOT CHILI PEPPERS	29	1990
TASTE YOU AUF DER MAUR	51	2004
TASTE YOUR LOVE HORACE BROWN	58	1995
TASTY FISH OTHER TWO	41	1991
TASTY LOVE FREDDIE JACKSON	73	1986
TATTOO [A] MIKE OLDFIELD	33	1992
TATTOO [B] JORDIN SPARKS	24	2008
TATTOOED MILLIONAIRE BRUCE DICKINSON	18	1990
TATTVA KULA SHAKER	4	1996
TAVERN IN THE TOWN TERRY LIGHTFOOT & HIS NEW ORLEANS JAZZMEN	49	1962
TAXI J BLACKFOOT	48	1984
TAXLOSS MANSUN	15	1997
TCHAIKOVSKY ONE SECOND CITY SOUND	22	1966
TE AMO SULTANA	57	1994
TEA FOR TWO CHA CHA TOMMY DORSEY ORCHESTRA STARRING WARREN COVINGTON	3	1958
TEACH ME TO TWIST CHUBBY CHECKER & BOBBY RYDELL	45	1962
TEACH ME TONIGHT DE CASTRO SISTERS	20	1955
TEACH YOU TO ROCK TONY CROMBIE & HIS ROCKETS	25	1956
TEACHER [A] JETHRO TULL	4	1970
TEACHER [B] I-LEVEL	56	1983
THE TEACHER [C] BIG COUNTRY	28	1986
TEACHER TEACHER JOHNNY MATHIS	27	1958
TEAR AWAY DROWNING POOL	65	2002
TEAR DOWN THE WALLS NO SWEAT	61	1991
A TEAR FELL TERESA BREWER	2	1956
TEAR ME APART SUZI QUATRO	27	1977
TEAR OFF YOUR OWN HEAD ELVIS COSTELLO	58	2002
TEAR SOUP QUESTIONS	66	1983
TEAR YOU DOWN BROOKES BROTHERS	56	2008
TEARDROP [A] SANTO & JOHNNY	50	1960
TEARDROP [B] MASSIVE ATTACK	10	1998
TEARDROP [B] NEWTON FAULKNER	57	2007
TEARDROP CITY MONKEES	44	1969
TEARDROPS [A] SHAKIN' STEVENS	5	1984
TEARDROPS [B] WOMACK & WOMACK	3	1988
TEARDROPS [B] LOVESTATION	14	1998
TEARDROPS [C] 411	23	2004
TEARDROPS ON MY GUITAR TAYLOR SWIFT	51	2009
TEARIN' UP MY HEART *NSYNC	9	1997
TEARING ROLLINS BAND	54	1992
TEARING US APART ERIC CLAPTON & TINA TURNER	56	1987
TEARS [A] DANNY WILLIAMS	22	1962
TEARS [B] KEN DODD	1	1965
TEARS [C] FRANKIE KNUCKLES PRESENTS SATOSHI TOMIIE	50	1989
TEARS [C] NU COLOURS	55	1992
TEARS ARE FALLING KISS	57	1985
TEARS ARE NOT ENOUGH ABC	19	1981
TEARS DON'T FALL BULLET FOR MY VALENTINE	37	2006
TEARS DON'T LIE MARK' OH	24	1995
TEARS DRY ON THEIR OWN AMY WINEHOUSE	16	2007
TEARS FROM A WILLOW OOBERMAN	63	1999
TEARS FROM HEAVEN HEARTBEAT	32	1987
TEARS FROM THE MOON CONJURE ONE	42	2003
THE TEARS I CRIED GLITTER BAND	8	1975
TEARS IN HEAVEN ERIC CLAPTON	5	1992
TEARS IN HEAVEN CHOIRBOYS	22	2005
TEARS IN THE RAIN N-TRANCE	53	1998
TEARS IN THE WIND CHICKEN SHACK	29	1969
TEARS OF A CLOWN SMOKEY ROBINSON & THE MIRACLES	1	1970
TEARS OF A CLOWN BEAT	6	1979
TEARS OF THE DRAGON BRUCE DICKINSON	28	1994
TEARS ON MY PILLOW [A] JOHNNY NASH	1	1975
TEARS ON MY PILLOW [B] KYLIE MINOGUE	1	1990
TEARS ON THE TELEPHONE [A] CLAUDE FRANCOIS	35	1976
TEARS ON THE TELEPHONE [B] HOT CHOCOLATE	37	1983
TEARS RUN RINGS MARC ALMOND	26	1988
TEARS WON'T WASH AWAY MY HEARTACHE KEN DODD	22	1969
TEARY EYED MISSY ELLIOTT	47	2005
TEASE ME [A] KEITH KELLY	27	1960
TEASE ME [B] CHAKA DEMUS & PLIERS	3	1993
TEASER GEORGE BENSON	45	1987
TECHNARCHY CYBERSONIK	73	1990
TECHNO FUNK LOST	75	1991
TECHNO TRANCE D-SHAKE	20	1990
TECHNOCAT TECHNOCAT FEATURING TOM WILSON	33	1995
TECHNOLOGIC DAFT PUNK	40	2005
TEDDY BEAR [A] RED SOVINE	4	1981
TEDDY BEAR [B] BOOKER NEWBURY III	44	1983
TEDDY BEAR'S LAST RIDE DIANA WILLIAMS	54	1981
TEDDY PICKER ARCTIC MONKEYS	20	2007
TEEN ANGEL MARK DINNING	37	1960
TEEN BEAT SANDY NELSON	9	1959
TEENAGE UK SUBS	32	1980
TEENAGE ANGST PLACEBO	30	1996

Title / Artist	Peak Position	Year of Release
TEENAGE DEPRESSION EDDIE & THE HOT RODS	35	1976
TEENAGE DIRTBAG WHEATUS	2	2001
TEENAGE DREAM MARC BOLAN & T REX	13	1974
TEENAGE IDOL RICK NELSON	39	1962
TEENAGE KICKS UNDERTONES	31	1978
TEENAGE LAMENT '74 ALICE COOPER	12	1974
TEENAGE LIFE DAZ SAMPSON	8	2006
TEENAGE PUNKS SULTANS OF PING	49	1993
TEENAGE RAMPAGE SWEET	2	1974
TEENAGE SCREAMERS TOKYO DRAGONS	61	2004
TEENAGE SENSATION CREDIT TO THE NATION	24	1994
TEENAGE TURTLES BACK TO THE PLANET	52	1993
TEENAGE WARNING ANGELIC UPSTARTS	29	1979
A TEENAGER IN LOVE MARTY WILDE	2	1959
A TEENAGER IN LOVE CRAIG DOUGLAS	13	1959
A TEENAGER IN LOVE DION & THE BELMONTS	28	1959
TEENAGERS MY CHEMICAL ROMANCE	9	2007
TEENSVILLE CHET ATKINS	46	1960
TEETHGRINDER THERAPY?	30	1992
TELEFUNKIN' N-TYCE	16	1998
TELEGRAM SAM T REX	1	1972
TELEGRAPH ORCHESTRAL MANOEUVRES IN THE DARK	42	1983
TELEPHONE LADY GAGA FEATURING BEYONCE	1	2009
THE TELEPHONE ALWAYS RINGS FUN BOY THREE	17	1982
TELEPHONE LINE ELECTRIC LIGHT ORCHESTRA	8	1977
TELEPHONE MAN MERI WILSON	6	1977
TELEPHONE OPERATOR PETE SHELLEY	66	1983
TELEPHONE THING FALL	58	1990
TELEPORT MAN WITH NO NAME	55	1996
TELETUBBIES SAY EH-OH! TELETUBBIES	1	1997
TELEVATORS MARS VOLTA	41	2004
TELEVISION THE DRUG OF THE NATION DISPOSABLE HEROES OF HIPHOPRISY	44	1992
TELL HER ABOUT IT BILLY JOEL	4	1983
TELL HER I'M NOT HOME IKE & TINA TURNER	48	1966
TELL HER NO ZOMBIES	42	1965
TELL HER THIS DEL AMITRI	32	1995
TELL HIM [A] BILLIE DAVIS	10	1963
TELL HIM [A] EXCITERS	46	1963
TELL HIM [A] HELLO	6	1974
TELL HIM [A] QUENTIN & ASH	25	1996
TELL HIM [B] BARBRA STREISAND & CELINE DION	3	1997
TELL IT LIKE IT T-I-IS B-52's	61	1992
TELL IT ON THE MOUNTAIN PETER, PAUL & MARY	33	1964
TELL IT TO MY FACE KEITH	50	1967
TELL IT TO MY HEART TAYLOR DAYNE	3	1988
TELL IT TO MY HEART Q-CLUB	28	1996
TELL IT TO MY HEART KELLY LLORENNA	9	2002
TELL IT TO THE RAIN FOUR SEASONS WITH FRANKIE VALLI	37	1967
TELL LAURA I LOVE HER RICKY VALENCE	1	1960
TELL ME [A] NICK KAMEN	40	1988
TELL ME [B] GROOVE THEORY	31	1995
TELL ME [C] DRU HILL	30	1997
TELL ME [D] BILLIE MYERS	28	1998
TELL ME [E] MELANIE B	4	2000
TELL ME [F] BOBBY VALENTINO	38	2005
TELL ME [G] P DIDDY FEATURING CHRISTINA AGUILERA	8	2006
TELL ME A STORY FRANKIE LAINE & JIMMY BOYD	5	1953
TELL ME BABY RED HOT CHILI PEPPERS	16	2006
TELL ME 'BOUT IT JOSS STONE	28	2007
TELL ME DO U WANNA GINUWINE	16	1997
TELL ME (HOW IT FEELS) 52ND STREET	54	1985
TELL ME I'M NOT DREAMING TITIYO	45	1994
TELL ME IS IT TRUE UB40	14	1997
TELL ME IT'S NOT OVER STARSAILOR	73	2009
TELL ME IT'S REAL K-CI & JOJO	16	1999
TELL ME MA SHAM ROCK	13	1998
TELL ME ON A SUNDAY MARTI WEBB	67	1980
TELL ME THAT YOU LOVE ME PAUL ANKA	25	1957
TELL ME THE WAY CAPPELLA	17	1995
TELL ME THERE'S A HEAVEN CHRIS REA	24	1990
TELL ME TOMORROW [A] SMOKEY ROBINSON	51	1982
TELL ME TOMORROW [B] PRINCESS	34	1986
TELL ME WHAT HE SAID HELEN SHAPIRO	2	1962
TELL ME WHAT IT'S WORTH LIGHTSPEED CHAMPION	72	2008
TELL ME WHAT YOU SEE VON BONDIES	43	2004
TELL ME WHAT YOU WANT [A] JIMMY RUFFIN	39	1974
TELL ME WHAT YOU WANT [B] LOOSE ENDS	74	1984
TELL ME WHAT YOU WANT [C] BLU PETER	70	1998
TELL ME WHAT YOU WANT ME TO DO TEVIN CAMPBELL	63	1992
TELL ME WHEN [A] APPLEJACKS	7	1964
TELL ME WHEN [B] HUMAN LEAGUE	6	1995
TELL ME WHEN THE FEVER ENDED ELECTRIBE 101	32	1989
TELL ME WHERE IT HURTS GARBAGE	50	2007
TELL ME WHERE YOU'RE GOING SILJE	55	1990
TELL ME WHY [A] ELVIS PRESLEY	15	1965
TELL ME WHY [B] ALVIN STARDUST	16	1974
TELL ME WHY [C] MUSICAL YOUTH	33	1983
TELL ME WHY [D] BOBBY WOMACK	60	1984
TELL ME WHY [E] THIS WAY UP	72	1987
TELL ME WHY [F] GENESIS	40	1993
TELL ME WHY [G] DECLAN FEATURING THE YOUNG VOICES CHOIR	29	2002
TELL ME WHY [H] SUPERMODE	13	2006
TELL ME WHY (THE RIDDLE) PAUL VAN DYK FEATURING SAINT ETIENNE	7	2000
TELL THAT GIRL TO SHUT UP TRANSVISION VAMP	45	1988
TELL THE CHILDREN SHAM 69	45	1980
TELLIN' STORIES CHARLATANS	16	1997
TELSTAR TORNADOS	1	1962
TEMMA HARBOUR MARY HOPKIN	6	1970
TEMPERATURE SEAN PAUL	11	2006
TEMPERATURE RISING PKA	68	1991
TEMPERAMENTAL EVERYTHING BUT THE GIRL	72	2000
TEMPERTEMPER GOLDIE	13	1998
TEMPLE OF DOOM DJ FRESH	60	2003
TEMPLE OF DREAMS [A] MESSIAH	20	1992
TEMPLE OF DREAMS [B] FUTURE BREEZE	21	2002
TEMPLE OF LOVE SISTERS OF MERCY	3	1992
TEMPO FIESTA (PARTY TIME) ITTY BITTY BOOZY WOOZY	34	1995
TEMPORARY BEAUTY GRAHAM PARKER & THE RUMOUR	50	1982
TEMPTATION [A] EVERLY BROTHERS	1	1961
TEMPTATION [B] NEW ORDER	29	1982
TEMPTATION [C] HEAVEN 17	2	1983
TEMPTATION [D] JOAN ARMATRADING	65	1985
TEMPTATION [E] WET WET WET	12	1988
TEMPTED SQUEEZE	41	1981
TEMPTED TO TOUCH RUPEE	44	2004
10AM AUTOMATIC BLACK KEYS	66	2004
10 IN 01 MEMBERS OF MAYDAY	31	2001
TEN MILES HIGH LITTLE ANGELS	18	1994
10 SECOND BIONIC MAN KINKY MACHINE	66	1994
TEN STOREY LOVE SONG STONE ROSES	11	1995
TEN TEN PAOLO NUTINI	51	2010
TEN THOUSAND MILES MICHAEL HOLLIDAY	24	1956
TEN THOUSAND NIGHT ALPHABEAT	16	2008
10 X 10 808 STATE	67	1993
TEN TO TWENTY SNEAKER PIMPS	56	1999
10 YEARS ASLEEP KINGMAKER	15	1993
TEN YEARS TIME GABRIELLE	43	2004
TENDENCY BATTLE	37	2006
TENDER [A] BLUR	2	1999
TENDER [B] FEEDER	11	2005
TENDER HANDS CHRIS DE BURGH	43	1989
TENDER HEART LIONEL RICHIE	29	2001
TENDER LOVE FORCE MDs	23	1986
TENDER LOVE KENNY THOMAS	26	1991
TENDERLY NAT 'KING' COLE	10	1954
TENDERNESS DIANA ROSS	73	1982
TENNESSEE ARRESTED DEVELOPMENT	18	1992
TENNESSEE WIG WALK BONNIE LOU	4	1954
TENSHI GOURYELLA	45	2000
TEQUILA [A] CHAMPS	5	1958
TEQUILA [A] TED HEATH	21	1958
TEQUILA [A] NO WAY JOSE	47	1985
TEQUILA [B] TERRORVISION	2	1999
TEQUILA SUNRISE CYPRESS HILL	23	1998
TERESA JOE DOLAN	20	1969
TERRA FIRMA YOUNG KNIVES	43	2007
TERRITORY SEPULTURA	66	1993
TERRY TWINKLE	4	1964
TERRY'S THEME FROM 'LIMELIGHT' FRANK CHACKSFIELD	2	1953
TERRY'S THEME FROM 'LIMELIGHT' RON GOODWIN	3	1953
TESLA GIRLS ORCHESTRAL MANOEUVRES IN THE DARK	21	1984
THE TEST CHEMICAL BROTHERS	14	2002
TEST OF TIME [A] WILL DOWNING	67	1989
TEST OF TIME [B] CRESCENT	60	2002
TEST THE THEORY AUDIOWEB	56	1999
TESTAMENT 4 CHUBBY CHUNKS VOLUME II	52	1994
TESTIFY [A] M PEOPLE	12	1998
TESTIFY [B] BYRON STINGILY	48	1998
TETRIS DOCTOR SPIN	6	1992
TEXAS CHRIS REA	69	1990
TEXAS COWBOYS GRID	17	1993
THA CROSSROADS BONE THUGS-N-HARMONY	8	1996
THA DOGGFATHER SNOOP DOGGY DOGG	36	1998
THA HORNS OF JERICHO DJ SUPREME	29	1998
THA WILD STYLE DJ SUPREME	24	1996
THANK ABBA FOR THE MUSIC VARIOUS ARTISTS (EP'S & LP'S)	4	1999
THANK GOD I FOUND YOU MARIAH CAREY FEATURING JOE & 980	10	2000
THANK GOD IT'S CHRISTMAS QUEEN	21	1984
THANK GOD IT'S FRIDAY R KELLY	14	1996
THANK U ALANIS MORISSETTE	5	1998
THANK U VERY MUCH SCAFFOLD	4	1967
THANK YOU [A] PALE FOUNTAINS	48	1982
THANK YOU [B] BOYZ II MEN	26	1995
THANK YOU [C] DIDO	3	2001
THANK YOU [D] JAMELIA	2	2004
THANK YOU BABY! SHANIA TWAIN	11	2003
THANK YOU FOR A GOOD YEAR ALEXANDER O'NEAL	30	1988
THANK YOU FOR A LIFETIME CLIFF RICHARD	3	2008
THANK YOU FOR BEING A FRIEND ANDREW GOLD	42	1978
THANK YOU FOR HEARING ME SINEAD O'CONNOR	13	1994
THANK YOU FOR LOVING ME BON JOVI	12	2000
THANK YOU FOR THE MUSIC ABBA	33	1983
THANK YOU FOR THE PARTY DUKES	53	1982
THANK YOU FOR THE VENOM MY CHEMICAL ROMANCE	71	2005
THANK YOU MY LOVE IMAGINATION	22	1985
THANK YOU WORLD WORLD PARTY	68	1991

Title / Artist	Peak Position	Year of Release
THANKS A LOT BRENDA LEE	41	1965
THANKS FOR MY CHILD CHERYL PEPSII RILEY	75	1989
THANKS FOR SAVING MY LIFE BILLY PAUL	33	1974
THANKS FOR THE MEMORY (WHAM BAM THANK YOU MAM) SLADE	7	1975
THANKS FOR THE NIGHT DAMNED	43	1984
THANKYOU WHOEVER YOU ARE MARILLION	15	2007
THAT CERTAIN SMILE MIDGE URE	28	1985
THAT DAY NATALIE IMBRUGLIA	11	2001
THAT DON'T IMPRESS ME MUCH SHANIA TWAIN	3	1999
THAT EXTRA MILE RICKY	50	2004
THAT FEELING DJ CHUS PRESENTS GROOVE FOUNDATION	65	2002
THAT GIRL [A] STEVIE WONDER	39	1982
THAT GIRL [B] MAXI PRIEST/SHAGGY	15	1996
THAT GIRL [C] McFLY	3	2004
THAT GIRL BELONGS TO YESTERDAY GENE PITNEY	7	1964
THAT GIRL (GROOVY SITUATION) FREDDIE McGREGOR	47	1987
THAT GOLDEN RULE BIFFY CLYRO	10	2009
THAT GREAT LOVE SOUND RAVEONETTES	34	2003
THAT KISS COURTEENERS	36	2008
THAT LADY ISLEY BROTHERS	14	1973
THAT LOOK DE'LACY	19	1996
THAT LOOK IN YOUR EYE ALI CAMPBELL	5	1995
THAT LOVING FEELING CICERO	46	1992
THAT LUCKY OLD SUN VELVETS	46	1961
THAT MAN (HE'S ALL MINE) INNER CITY	42	1990
THAT MAN WILL NOT HANG McLUSKY	71	2004
THAT MEANS A LOT PJ PROBY	30	1965
THAT NOISE ANTHONY NEWLEY	34	1962
THAT OLD BLACK MAGIC SAMMY DAVIS, JR	16	1955
THAT OLD PAIR OF JEANS FATBOY SLIM	39	2006
THAT OLE DEVIL CALLED LOVE ALISON MOYET	2	1985
THAT SAME OLD FEELING PICKETTYWITCH	5	1970
THAT SOUND MICHAEL MOOG	32	1999
THAT SOUNDS GOOD TO ME JIVE BUNNY & THE MASTERMIXERS	4	1990
THAT THING YOU DO! WONDERS	22	1997
THAT WAS MY VEIL JOHN PARISH & POLLY JEAN HARVEY	75	1996
THAT WAS THEN BUT THIS IS NOW ABC	18	1983
THAT WAS THEN, THIS IS NOW MONKEES	68	1986
THAT WAS YESTERDAY FOREIGNER	28	1985
THAT WOMAN'S GOT ME DRINKING SHANE MacGOWAN & THE POPES	34	1994
THAT ZIPPER TRACK DJ DAN PRESENTS NEEDLE DAMAGE	53	2001
THAT'LL BE THE DAY CRICKETS	1	1957
THAT'LL BE THE DAY EVERLY BROTHERS	30	1965
THAT'LL DO NICELY BAD MANNERS	49	1983
THAT'S ALL GENESIS	16	1983
THAT'S ALL RIGHT ELVIS PRESLEY	3	2004
THAT'S AMORE DEAN MARTIN	2	1954
THAT'S ENTERTAINMENT JAM	21	1981
THAT'S HOW A LOVE SONG WAS BORN RAY BURNS WITH THE CORONETS	14	1955
THAT'S HOW GOOD YOUR LOVE IS IL PADRINOS FEATURING JOCELYN BROWN	54	2002
THAT'S HOW I FEEL ABOUT YOU LONDONBEAT	69	1992
THAT'S HOW I'M LIVIN' ICE-T	21	1993
THAT'S HOW I'M LIVING TONI SCOTT	48	1989
THAT'S HOW PEOPLE GROW UP MORRISSEY	14	2008
THAT'S HOW STRONG MY LOVE IS IN CROWD	48	1965
THAT'S JUST THE WAY IT IS PHIL COLLINS	26	1990
THAT'S LIFE FRANK SINATRA	44	1966
THAT'S LIVIN' ALRIGHT JOE FAGIN	3	1984
THAT'S LOVE BILLY FURY WITH THE FOUR JAYS	19	1960
THAT'S LOVE, THAT IS BLANCMANGE	33	1983
THAT'S MORE LIKE IT SKYLARK	62	2004
THAT'S MY DOLL FRANKIE VAUGHAN	28	1959
THAT'S MY GOAL SHAYNE WARD	1	2005
THAT'S MY HOME MR ACKER BILK & HIS PARAMOUNT JAZZ BAND	7	1961
THAT'S NICE NEIL CHRISTIAN	14	1966
THAT'S NO WAY TO TELL A LIE JAMES DEAN BRADFIELD	18	2006
THAT'S NOT MY NAME TING TINGS	1	2008
THAT'S RIGHT DEEP RIVER BOYS	29	1956
THAT'S THAT S**** SNOOP DOGG FEATURING R KELLY	38	2006
THAT'S THE WAY HONEYCOMBS	12	1965
THAT'S THE WAY GOD PLANNED IT BILLY PRESTON	11	1969
THAT'S THE WAY (I LIKE IT) KC & THE SUNSHINE BAND	4	1975
THAT'S THE WAY (I LIKE IT) DEAD OR ALIVE	22	1984
THAT'S THE WAY (I LIKE IT) CLOCK	11	1998
THAT'S THE WAY I WANNA ROCK 'N' ROLL AC/DC	22	1988
THAT'S THE WAY IT FEELS TWO NATIONS	74	1987
THAT'S THE WAY IT IS [A] MEL & KIM	10	1988
THAT'S THE WAY IT IS [B] CELINE DION	12	1999
THAT'S THE WAY LOVE GOES [A] CHARLES DICKENS	37	1965
THAT'S THE WAY LOVE GOES [B] YOUNG MC	65	1991
THAT'S THE WAY LOVE GOES [C] JANET JACKSON	2	1993
THAT'S THE WAY LOVE IS [A] TEN CITY	8	1989
THAT'S THE WAY LOVE IS [A] VOLCANO WITH SAM CARTWRIGHT	72	1995
THAT'S THE WAY LOVE IS [A] BYRON STINGILY	32	2000
THAT'S THE WAY LOVE IS [B] BOBBY BROWN	56	1993
THAT'S THE WAY OF THE WORLD D MOB WITH CATHY DENNIS	48	1990
THAT'S THE WAY THE MONEY GOES M	45	1980
THAT'S THE WAY YOU DO IT PURPLE KINGS	26	1994
THAT'S WHAT FRIENDS ARE FOR [A] DENIECE WILLIAMS	8	1977
THAT'S WHAT FRIENDS ARE FOR [B] DIONNE WARWICK & FRIENDS FEATURING ELTON JOHN, STEVIE WONDER & GLADYS KNIGHT	16	1985
THAT'S WHAT I LIKE JIVE BUNNY & THE MASTERMIXERS	1	1989
THAT'S WHAT I THINK CYNDI LAUPER	31	1993
THAT'S WHAT I WANT MARAUDERS	43	1963
THAT'S WHAT I WANT TO BE NEIL REID	45	1972
THAT'S WHAT LIFE IS ALL ABOUT BING CROSBY	41	1975
THAT'S WHAT LOVE CAN DO TOUTES LES FILLES	44	1999
THAT'S WHAT LOVE IS FOR AMY GRANT	60	1991
THAT'S WHAT LOVE WILL DO JOE BROWN & THE BRUVVERS	3	1963
THAT'S WHAT YOU GET PARAMORE	55	2008
THAT'S WHEN I REACH FOR MY REVOLVER MOBY	50	1996
THAT'S WHEN I THINK OF YOU 1927	46	1989
THAT'S WHEN THE MUSIC TAKES ME NEIL SEDAKA	18	1973
THAT'S WHERE MY MIND GOES SLAMM	68	1994
THAT'S WHERE THE HAPPY PEOPLE GO TRAMMPS	35	1976
THAT'S WHY I LIE RAY J	71	1998
THAT'S WHY I'M CRYING IVY LEAGUE	22	1965
THAT'S WHY WE LOSE CONTROL YOUNG OFFENDERS	60	1998
THAT'S YOU NAT 'KING' COLE	10	1960
THE WAY LOVE GOES LEMAR	8	2010
THEIR WAY LITTL'ANS FEATURING PETER DOHERTY	22	2005
THEM BONES ALICE IN CHAINS	26	1993
THEM GIRLS THEM GIRLS ZIG & ZAG	5	1994
THEM THANGS 50 CENT/G-UNIT	10	2004
THEM THERE EYES EMILE FORD	18	1960
THE THEME [A] UNIQUE 3	61	1989
THEME [B] SABRES OF PARADISE	56	1994
THE THEME [C] DREEM TEEM	34	1997
THE THEME [D] TRACEY LEE	51	1997
THE THEME [E] JURGEN VRIES	13	2002
THEME FOR A DREAM CLIFF RICHARD	3	1961
THEME FOR YOUNG LOVERS SHADOWS	12	1964
THEME FROM 'A SUMMER PLACE' PERCY FAITH	2	1960
THEME FROM 'A SUMMER PLACE' NORRIE PARAMOUR	36	1960
THEME FROM 'CADE'S COUNTY' HENRY MANCINI	42	1972
THEME FROM 'CHEERS' GARY PORTNOY	58	1984
THEME FROM 'COME SEPTEMBER' BOBBY DARIN ORCHESTRA	50	1961
THEME FROM 'DIXIE' DUANE EDDY & THE REBELS	7	1961
THEME FROM 'DR KILDARE' JOHNNIE SPENCE	15	1962
THEME FROM 'DR KILDARE' (THREE STARS WILL SHINE TONIGHT) RICHARD CHAMBERLAIN	12	1962
THEME FROM 'E.T. (THE EXTRA-TERRESTRIAL)' JOHN WILLIAMS	17	1982
THEME FROM 'EXODUS' FERRANTE & TEICHER	6	1961
THEME FROM 'EXODUS' SEMPRINI	25	1961
THEME FROM 'GUTBUSTER' BENTLEY RHYTHM ACE	29	2000
THEME FROM 'HARRY'S GAME' CLANNAD	5	1982
THEME FROM 'HILL STREET BLUES' MIKE POST FEATURING LARRY CARLTON	25	1982
THEME FROM 'JURASSIC PARK' JOHN WILLIAMS	45	1993
THEME FROM 'M*A*S*H' (SUICIDE IS PAINLESS) MASH	1	1980
THEME FROM 'MAHOGANY' (DO YOU KNOW WHERE YOU'RE GOING TO) DIANA ROSS	5	1976
THEME FROM 'M.A.S.H.' (SUICIDE IS PAINLESS) MANIC STREET PREACHERS	7	1992
THEME FROM 'MISSION: IMPOSSIBLE' ADAM CLAYTON & LARRY MULLEN	7	1996
THEME FROM 'NEW YORK, NEW YORK' FRANK SINATRA	4	1980
THEME FROM 'PICNIC' MORRIS STOLOFF	7	1956
THEME FROM 'P.O.P.' PERFECTLY ORDINARY PEOPLE	61	1988
THEME FROM 'RANDALL & HOPKIRK (DECEASED)' NINA PERSSON & DAVID ARNOLD	49	2000
THEME FROM S-EXPRESS S-EXPRESS	1	1988
THEME FROM 'SHAFT' ISAAC HAYES	4	1971
THE THEME FROM 'SHAFT' EDDY & THE SOUL BAND	13	1985
THEME FROM 'SPARTA FC' FALL	66	2004
THEME FROM 'SUPERMAN' (MAIN TITLE) LONDON SYMPHONY ORCHESTRA	32	1979
THEME FROM 'THE APARTMENT' FERRANTE & TEICHER	44	1960
THEME FROM 'THE DEER HUNTER' (CAVATINA) SHADOWS	9	1979
THEME FROM THE FILM 'THE LEGION'S LAST PATROL' KEN THORNE	4	1963

Title / Artist	Peak Position	Year of Release
THEME FROM 'THE HONG KONG BEAT' RICHARD DENTON & MARTIN COOK	25	1978
THEME FROM 'THE ONEDIN LINE' VIENNA PHILHARMONIC ORCHESTRA	15	1971
THE THEME FROM 'THE PERSUADERS' JOHN BARRY ORCHESTRA	13	1971
THEME FROM 'THE PROFESSIONALS' LAURIE JOHNSON'S LONDON BIG BAND	36	1997
THEME FROM 'THE THREEPENNY OPERA' LOUIS ARMSTRONG WITH HIS ALL-STARS	8	1956
THEME FROM 'THE THREEPENNY OPERA' BILLY VAUGHN	12	1956
THEME FROM 'THE THREEPENNY OPERA' DICK HYMAN TRIO	9	1956
THEME FROM 'THE TRAVELLING MAN' DUNCAN BROWNE	68	1984
THEME FROM 'TURNPIKE' (EP) dEUS	68	1996
THEME FROM 'VIETNAM' (CANON IN D) ORCHESTRE DE CHAMBRE JEAN-FRANCOIS PAILLARD	61	1988
THEME FROM 'WHICH WAY IS UP' STARGARD	19	1978
THEME FROM 'Z CARS' NORRIE PARAMOUR	33	1962
THEME FROM 'Z-CARS' JOHNNY KEATING	8	1962
THEME ONE COZY POWELL	62	1979
THEME TO 'ST TRINIAN'S' GIRLS ALOUD	51	2008
THEN CHARLATANS	12	1990
THEN CAME YOU DIONNE WARWICK & THE DETROIT SPINNERS	29	1974
THEN CAME YOU JUNIOR GISCOMBE	32	1992
THEN HE KISSED ME CRYSTALS	2	1963
THEN I FEEL GOOD KATHERINE E	56	1992
THEN I KISSED HER BEACH BOYS	4	1967
THEN YOU CAN TELL ME GOODBYE CASINOS	28	1967
THEN YOU TURN AWAY ORCHESTRAL MANOEUVRES IN THE DARK	50	1991
THERE AIN'T NOTHIN' LIKE THE LOVE MONTAGE	64	1997
THERE AIN'T NOTHING LIKE SHAGGIN' TAMS	21	1987
THERE ARE MORE QUESTIONS THAN ANSWERS JOHNNY NASH	9	1972
THERE ARE MORE SNAKES THAN LADDERS CAPTAIN SENSIBLE	57	1984
THERE BUT FOR FORTUNE JOAN BAEZ	8	1965
THERE BUT FOR THE GRACE OF GOD FIRE ISLAND FEATURING LOVE NELSON	32	1994
THERE BY THE GRACE OF GOD MANIC STREET PREACHERS	6	2002
THERE GOES MY EVERYTHING ENGELBERT HUMPERDINCK	2	1967
THERE GOES MY EVERYTHING ELVIS PRESLEY	6	1971
THERE GOES MY FIRST LOVE DRIFTERS	3	1975
THERE GOES THAT SONG AGAIN GARY MILLER	29	1961
THERE GOES THE FEAR DOVES	3	2002
THERE GOES THE NEIGHBORHOOD SHERYL CROW	19	1998
THERE I GO VIKKI CARR	50	1967
THERE I GO AGAIN POWER OF DREAMS	65	1992
THERE IS A LIGHT THAT NEVER GOES OUT SMITHS	25	1992
THERE IS A LIGHT THAT NEVER GOES OUT MORRISSEY	11	2005
THERE IS A MOUNTAIN DONOVAN	8	1967
THERE IS A STAR PHARAO	43	1995
THERE IS ALWAYS SOMETHING THERE TO REMIND ME HOUSEMARTINS	35	1988
THERE IS NO LOVE BETWEEN US ANYMORE POP WILL EAT ITSELF	66	1988
THERE IT GO (THE WHISTLE SONG) JUELZ SANTANA	47	2006
THERE IT IS SHALAMAR	5	1982
THERE I'VE SAID IT AGAIN AL SAXON	48	1961
THERE I'VE SAID IT AGAIN BOBBY VINTON	34	1964
THERE MUST BE A REASON FRANKIE LAINE	9	1954
THERE MUST BE A WAY JONI JAMES	24	1959
THERE MUST BE A WAY FRANKIE VAUGHAN	7	1967
THERE MUST BE AN ANGEL (PLAYING WITH MY HEART) EURYTHMICS	1	1985
THERE MUST BE THOUSANDS QUADS	66	1979
THERE SHE GOES [A] LA'S	13	1989
THERE SHE GOES [B] SIXPENCE NONE THE RICHER	14	1999
THERE SHE GOES AGAIN QUIREBOYS	37	1990
THERE SHE GOES MY BEAUTIFUL WORLD NICK CAVE & THE BAD SEEDS	45	2004
THERE THERE RADIOHEAD	4	2003
THERE THERE MY DEAR DEXY'S MIDNIGHT RUNNERS	7	1980
THERE WILL NEVER BE ANOTHER TONIGHT BRYAN ADAMS	32	1991
THERE WILL NEVER BE ANOTHER YOU [A] CHRIS MONTEZ	37	1966
THERE WILL NEVER BE ANOTHER YOU [B] JIMMY RUFFIN	68	1985
THERE WON'T BE MANY COMING HOME ROY ORBISON	12	1966
THERE YOU GO P!NK	6	2000
THERE YOU'LL BE FAITH HILL	3	2001
(THERE'LL BE BLUEBIRDS OVER) WHITE CLIFFS OF DOVER ROBSON GREEN & JEROME FLYNN	1	1995
THERE'LL BE SAD SONGS (TO MAKE YOU CRY) BILLY OCEAN	12	1986
THERE'S A BRAND NEW WORLD FIVE STAR	61	1988
THERE'S A GHOST IN MY HOUSE R DEAN TAYLOR	3	1974
THERE'S A GHOST IN MY HOUSE FALL	30	1987
THERE'S A GOLDMINE IN THE SKY PAT BOONE	5	1957
THERE'S A GUY WORKS DOWN THE CHIPSHOP SWEARS HE'S ELVIS KIRSTY MacCOLL	14	1981
THERE'S A HEARTACHE FOLLOWING ME JIM REEVES	6	1964
THERE'S A KIND OF HUSH HERMAN'S HERMITS	7	1967
THERE'S A KIND OF HUSH (ALL OVER THE WORLD) CARPENTERS	22	1976
THERE'S A SILENCE ELECTRIC SOFT PARADE	52	2001
THERE'S A STAR ASH	13	2002
THERE'S A WHOLE LOT OF LOVING GUYS & DOLLS	2	1975
THERE'S ALWAYS ROOM ON THE BROOM LIARS	74	2004
(THERE'S) ALWAYS SOMETHING THERE TO REMIND ME SANDIE SHAW	1	1964
THERE'S GONNA BE A SHOWDOWN ARCHIE BELL & THE DRELLS	36	1973
THERE'S GOT TO BE A WAY MARIAH CAREY	54	1991
THERE'S GOTTA BE MORE TO LIFE STACIE ORRICO	12	2003
THERE'S MORE TO LOVE COMMUNARDS	20	1988
THERE'S NO LIVING WITHOUT YOU WILL DOWNING	67	1993
THERE'S NO ONE QUITE LIKE GRANDMA ST WINIFRED'S SCHOOL CHOIR	1	1980
THERE'S NO OTHER WAY BLUR	8	1991
THERE'S NOTHING BETTER THAN LOVE LUTHER VANDROSS, DUET WITH GREGORY HINES	72	1988
THERE'S NOTHING I WON'T DO JX	4	1996
THERE'S NOTHING LIKE THIS OMAR	14	1991
THERE'S SOMETHING WRONG IN PARADISE KID CREOLE & THE COCONUTS	35	1983
THERE'S THE GIRL HEART	34	1987
THERE'S YOUR TROUBLE DIXIE CHICKS	26	1999
THESE ARE DAYS 10,000 MANIACS	58	1992
THESE ARE THE DAYS [A] O-TOWN	36	2003
THESE ARE THE DAYS [B] JAMIE CULLUM	12	2004
THESE ARE THE DAYS OF OUR LIVES QUEEN	1	1991
THESE ARE THE TIMES DRU HILL	4	1999
THESE ARMS OF MINE PROCLAIMERS	51	1994
THESE BOOTS ARE MADE FOR WALKIN' NANCY SINATRA	1	1966
THESE BOOTS ARE MADE FOR WALKIN' BILLY RAY CYRUS	63	1992
THESE BOOTS ARE MADE FOR WALKIN' JESSICA SIMPSON	4	2005
THESE DAYS BON JOVI	7	1996
THESE DREAMS HEART	8	1986
THESE EARLY DAYS EVERYTHING BUT THE GIRL	75	1988
THESE THINGS ARE WORTH FIGHTING FOR GARY CLAIL ON-U SOUND SYSTEM	45	1993
THESE THINGS WILL KEEP ME LOVING YOU VELVELETTES	34	1971
THESE WOODEN IDEAS IDLEWILD	32	2000
THESE WORDS NATASHA BEDINGFIELD	1	2004
THEY JEM	6	2005
THEY ALL LAUGHED FRANK SINATRA	41	1999
(THEY CALL HER) LA BAMBA CRICKETS	21	1964
THEY DON'T CARE ABOUT US MICHAEL JACKSON	4	1996
THEY DON'T KNOW [A] TRACEY ULLMAN	2	1983
THEY DON'T KNOW [B] JON B	32	1998
THEY DON'T KNOW [C] SO SOLID CREW	3	2001
THEY GLUED YOUR HEAD ON UPSIDE DOWN BELLRAYS	75	2002
(THEY LONG TO BE) CLOSE TO YOU CARPENTERS	6	1970
(THEY LONG TO BE) CLOSE TO YOU GWEN GUTHRIE	25	1986
THEY SAY IT'S GONNA RAIN HAZELL DEAN	58	1985
THEY SHOOT HORSES DON'T THEY RACING CARS	14	1977
THEY WILL KILL US ALL (WITHOUT MERCY) BRONX	65	2004
THEY'RE COMING TO TAKE ME AWAY HA-HAAA! NAPOLEON XIV	4	1966
THEY'RE HERE EMF	29	1992
THIEVES IN THE TEMPLE PRINCE	7	1990
THIEVES LIKE US NEW ORDER	18	1984
THIGHS HIGH (GRIP YOUR HIPS AND MOVE) TOM BROWNE	45	1980
THIN LINE BETWEEN LOVE AND HATE PRETENDERS	49	1984
THE THIN WALL ULTRAVOX	14	1981
A THING CALLED LOVE JOHNNY CASH WITH THE EVANGEL TEMPLE CHOIR	4	1972
THE THING I LIKE AALIYAH	33	1995
THINGS [A] BOBBY DARIN	2	1962
THE THINGS [B] AUDIOBULLYS	22	2003
THINGS CAN ONLY GET BETTER [A] HOWARD JONES	6	1985
THINGS CAN ONLY GET BETTER [B] D:REAM	1	1993
THINGS FALL APART SERAFIN	49	2003
THINGS GET BETTER EDDIE FLOYD	31	1967
THINGS HAVE CHANGED BOB DYLAN	58	2000
THINGS I'VE SEEN SPOOKS	6	2001
THE THINGS THE LONELY DO AMAZULU	43	1986
THINGS THAT ARE RUNRIG	40	1995
THINGS THAT GO BUMP IN THE NIGHT ALLSTARS	12	2001

Title / Artist	Peak Position	Year of Release
THINGS THAT MAKE YOU GO HMMM C & C MUSIC FACTORY (FEATURING FREEDOM WILLIAMS)	4	1991
THINGS WE DO FOR LOVE [A] 10 C.C.	6	1976
THINGS WE DO FOR LOVE [B] HORACE BROWN	27	1996
THINGS WILL GO MY WAY CALLING	34	2004
THINK [A] CHRIS FARLOWE	37	1966
THINK [B] BRENDA LEE	26	1964
THINK [C] ARETHA FRANKLIN	26	1968
THINK ABOUT... DJH FEATURING STEFY	22	1991
THINK ABOUT ME ARTFUL DODGER FEATURING MICHELLE ESCOFFERY	11	2001
THINK ABOUT THAT DANDY LIVINGSTONE	26	1973
THINK ABOUT THE WAY (BOM DIGI DIGI BOM...) ICE MC	42	1994
THINK ABOUT YOUR CHILDREN MARY HOPKIN	19	1970
THINK FOR A MINUTE HOUSEMARTINS	18	1986
THINK I'M GONNA FALL IN LOVE WITH YOU DOOLEYS	13	1977
THINK IT ALL OVER SANDIE SHAW	42	1969
THINK IT OVER CRICKETS	11	1958
(THINK OF ME) WHEREVER YOU ARE KEN DODD	21	1975
THINK OF YOU [A] USHER	70	1995
THINK OF YOU [B] WHIGFIELD	7	1995
THINK SOMETIMES ABOUT ME SANDIE SHAW	32	1966
THINK TWICE CELINE DION	1	1994
THINKIN' ABOUT YOUR BODY BOBBY McFERRIN	46	1988
THINKIN' AIN'T FOR ME PAUL JONES	32	1967
THINKING ABOUT TOMORROW BETH ORTON	57	2003
THINKING ABOUT YOUR BODY 2 MAD	43	1991
THINKING ABOUT YOUR LOVE [A] SKIPWORTH & TURNER	24	1985
THINKING ABOUT YOUR LOVE [A] PHILLIP LEO	64	1995
THINKING ABOUT YOUR LOVE [B] KENNY THOMAS	4	1991
THINKING IT OVER LIBERTY	5	2001
THINKING OF YOU [A] SISTER SLEDGE	11	1984
THINKING OF YOU [A] MAUREEN	11	1990
THINKING OF YOU [A] CURTIS LYNCH, JR FEATURING KELE LE ROC & RED RAT	70	2000
THINKING OF YOU [A] PAUL WELLER	18	2004
THINKING OF YOU [B] COLOUR FIELD	12	1985
THINKING OF YOU [C] HANSON	23	1998
THINKING OF YOU [D] STATUS QUO	21	2004
THINKING OF YOU [E] KATY PERRY	27	2009
THINKING OF YOU BABY DAVE CLARK FIVE	26	1964
THINKING OVER DANA GLOVER	38	2003
THIRD FINGER, LEFT HAND PEARLS	31	1972
THE THIRD MAN SHADOWS	44	1981
THIRD RAIL SQUEEZE	39	1993
THIRTEEN FORWARD, RUSSIA!	74	2005
13 STEPS LEAD DOWN ELVIS COSTELLO & THE ATTRACTIONS	59	1994
THE 13TH CURE	15	1996
13TH DISCIPLE FIVE THIRTY	67	1991
30TH CENTURY MAN CATHERINE WHEEL	47	1993
36D BEAUTIFUL SOUTH	46	1992
THIRTY THREE SMASHING PUMPKINS	21	1996
THIS AIN'T A LOVE SONG [A] BON JOVI	6	1995
THIS AIN'T A LOVE SONG [B] SCOUTING FOR GIRLS	1	2010
THIS AIN'T A SCENE IT'S AN ARMS RACE FALL OUT BOY	2	2007
THIS AND THAT TOM JONES	44	1966
THIS BEAT IS MINE VICKY D	42	1982
THIS BEAT IS TECHNOTRONIC TECHNOTRONIC FEATURING MC ERIC	14	1990
THIS BOY [A] JUSTIN	34	1998
THIS BOY [B] TOM BAXTER	65	2004
THIS BRUTAL HOUSE NITRO DELUXE	47	1987
THIS CAN BE REAL CANDY FLIP	60	1990
THIS CHARMING MAN SMITHS	8	1983
THIS CORROSION SISTERS OF MERCY	7	1987
THIS COWBOY SONG STING FEATURING PATO BANTON	15	1995
THIS DAY SHOULD LAST FOREVER OCEAN COLOUR SCENE	53	2005
THIS DJ WARREN G	12	1994
THIS DOOR SWINGS BOTH WAYS HERMAN'S HERMITS	18	1966
THIS FEELIN' [A] FRANK HOOKER & POSITIVE PEOPLE	48	1980
THIS FEELING [B] PURESSENCE	33	1998
THIS FLIGHT TONIGHT NAZARETH	11	1973
THIS GARDEN LEVELLERS	12	1993
THIS GENERATION ROACHFORD	38	1994
THIS GOLDEN RING FORTUNES	15	1966
THIS GROOVE VICTORIA BECKHAM	3	2004
THIS GUY'S IN LOVE WITH YOU HERB ALPERT	3	1968
THIS HERE GIRAFFE FLAMING LIPS	72	1996
THIS HOUSE [A] TRACIE SPENCER	65	1991
THIS HOUSE [B] ALISON MOYET	40	1991
THIS HOUSE IS NOT A HOME REMBRANDTS	58	1996
THIS HOUSE (IS WHERE YOUR LOVE STANDS) BIG SOUND AUTHORITY	21	1985
THIS I PROMISE YOU *NSYNC	21	2000
THIS I SWEAR [A] RICHARD DARBYSHIRE	50	1993
THIS I SWEAR [B] KIM WILDE	46	1996
THIS IS A CALL FOO FIGHTERS	5	1995
THIS IS A REBEL SONG SINEAD O'CONNOR	60	1997
THIS IS A SONG MAGIC NUMBERS	36	2007
THIS IS A WARNING/SUPER DJ DILLINJA	47	2003
THIS IS AN EMERGENCY PIGEON DETECTIVES	14	2008
THIS IS ENGLAND CLASH	24	1985
THIS IS FOR REAL DAVID DEVANT & HIS SPIRIT WIFE	61	1997
THIS IS FOR THE LOVER IN YOU BABYFACE	12	1996
THIS IS FOR THE POOR OTHERS	42	2004
THIS IS GOODBYE LUCY CARR	41	2003
THIS IS HARDCORE PULP	12	1998
THIS IS HOW A HEART BREAKS ROB THOMAS	67	2005
THIS IS HOW IT FEELS INSPIRAL CARPETS	14	1990
THIS IS HOW WE DO IT MONTELL JORDAN	11	1995
THIS IS HOW WE DO IT MIS-TEEQ	7	2002
THIS IS HOW WE PARTY S.O.A.P.	36	1998
THIS IS IT! [A] ADAM FAITH	5	1961
THIS IS IT [B] MELBA MOORE	9	1976
THIS IS IT [B] DANNII MINOGUE	10	1993
THIS IS IT [C] DAN HARTMAN	17	1979
THIS IS IT [D] 4MANDU	45	1995
THIS IS IT [E] STATE OF MIND	30	1998
THIS IS IT (YOUR SOUL) HOTHOUSE FLOWERS	67	1993
THIS IS LOVE [A] GARY NUMAN	28	1986
THIS IS LOVE [B] GEORGE HARRISON	55	1988
THIS IS LOVE [C] PJ HARVEY	41	2001
THIS IS ME [A] CLIMIE FISHER	22	1988
THIS IS ME [B] SAW DOCTORS	31	2002
THIS IS ME [C] DEMI LOVATO & JOE JONAS	33	2008
THIS IS MINE HEAVEN 17	23	1984
THIS IS MUSIC VERVE	35	1995
THIS IS MY HOLLYWOOD 3 COLOURS RED	48	1997
THIS IS MY LIFE EARTHA KITT	73	1986
THIS IS MY NIGHT CHAKA KHAN	14	1985
THIS IS MY SONG PETULA CLARK	1	1967
THIS IS MY SONG HARRY SECOMBE	2	1967
THIS IS MY SOUND DJ SHOG	40	2002
THIS IS MY TIME 3 COLOURS RED	36	1999
THIS IS NOT A LOVE SONG PUBLIC IMAGE LTD	5	1983
THIS IS NOT A SONG FRANK & WALTERS	46	1992
THIS IS NOT AMERICA DAVID BOWIE & THE PAT METHENY GROUP	14	1985
THIS IS NOT REAL LOVE GEORGE MICHAEL & MUTYA	15	2006
THIS IS OUR SONG CODE RED	59	1996
THIS IS RADIO CLASH CLASH	47	1981
THIS IS SKA LONGSY D'S HOUSE SOUND	56	1989
THIS IS THE DAY THE THE	71	1983
THIS IS THE GIRL KANO FEATURING CRAIG DAVID	18	2007
THIS IS THE LAST TIME KEANE	18	2004
THIS IS THE LIFE AMY MacDONALD	28	2007
THIS IS THE NEW SHIT MARILYN MANSON	29	2003
THIS IS THE PLACE ZEITIA MASSIAH	62	1994
THIS IS THE RIGHT TIME LISA STANSFIELD	13	1989
THIS IS THE SOUND OF YOUTH THESE ANIMAL MEN	72	1994
THIS IS THE STORY OF MY LIFE (BABY) WIZZARD	34	1974
THIS IS THE WAY [A] BRUCE FOXTON	56	1983
THIS IS THE WAY [B] DANNII MINOGUE	27	1993
THIS IS THE WAY [C] F.K.W.	63	1994
THIS IS THE WAY [D] E-TYPE	53	1995
THIS IS THE WORLD CALLING BOB GELDOF	25	1986
THIS IS THE WORLD WE LIVE IN ALCAZAR	15	2004
THIS IS TOMORROW BRYAN FERRY	9	1977
THIS IS WAR THIRTY SECONDS TO MARS	59	2010
THIS IS WHAT WE DO CRACKOUT	65	2004
THIS IS WHERE I CAME IN BEE GEES	18	2001
THIS IS WHY I'M HOT MIMS	18	2007
THIS IS YOUR LAND SIMPLE MINDS	13	1989
THIS IS YOUR LIFE [A] BLOW MONKEYS	32	1988
THIS IS YOUR LIFE [B] BANDERAS	16	1991
THIS IS YOUR LIFE [C] DUST BROTHERS	60	1999
THIS IS YOUR NIGHT [A] HEAVY D & THE BOYZ	30	1994
THIS IS YOUR NIGHT [B] ANOTHERSIDE	41	2003
THIS IZ REAL SHYHEIM	61	1996
THIS KIND OF LOVE PHIL FEARON & GALAXY	70	1985
THIS KISS FAITH HILL	13	1998
THIS LITTLE BIRD MARIANNE FAITHFULL	6	1965
THIS LITTLE BIRD NASHVILLE TEENS	38	1965
THIS LITTLE GIRL GARY U.S. BONDS	43	1981
THIS LOVE [A] LeANN RIMES	54	2004
THIS LOVE [B] MAROON 5	3	2004
THIS LOVE AFFAIR STEFAN DENNIS	67	1989
THIS LOVE I HAVE FOR YOU LANCE FORTUNE	26	1960
THIS MONDAY MORNING FEELING TITO SIMON	45	1975
THIS MORNING NORTHERN UPROAR	17	1996
THIS MUST BE LOVE LITTLE MAN TATE	33	2007
THIS MUST BE THE PLACE TALKING HEADS	51	1984
THIS NEW YEAR CLIFF RICHARD	30	1992
THIS OLD HEART OF MINE ISLEY BROTHERS	3	1966
THIS OLD HEART OF MINE ROD STEWART	4	1975
THIS OLD SKIN BEAUTIFUL SOUTH	43	2004
THIS OLD TOWN PAUL WELLER & GRAHAM COXON	39	2007
THIS OLE HOUSE ROSEMARY CLOONEY	1	1954
THIS OLE HOUSE BILLIE ANTHONY	4	1954
THIS OLE HOUSE SHAKIN' STEVENS	1	1981
THIS ONE PAUL McCARTNEY	18	1989
THIS ONE'S FOR THE CHILDREN NEW KIDS ON THE BLOCK	9	1990
THIS ONE'S FOR YOU ED HARCOURT	41	2004
THIS PARTY SUCKS! FUSED	64	1999
THIS PERFECT DAY SAINTS	34	1977
THIS PICTURE PLACEBO	23	2003

Title / Artist	Peak Position	Year of Release
THIS PLANET'S ON FIRE SAMMY HAGAR	52	1979
THIS SONG IS ABOUT YOU ENEMY	41	2008
THIS STRANGE EFFECT DAVE BERRY	37	1965
THIS SUMMER SQUEEZE	32	1995
THIS TIME [A] TROY SHONDELL	22	1961
THIS TIME [B] BRYAN ADAMS	41	1986
THIS TIME [C] DINA CARROLL	23	1993
THIS TIME [D] MICHELLE SWEENEY	57	1994
THIS TIME [E] JUDY CHEEKS	23	1995
THIS TIME [F] CURTIS STIGERS	28	1995
THIS TIME [G] STARSAILOR	24	2006
THIS TIME AROUND PHATS & SMALL	15	2001
THIS TIME BABY JACKIE MOORE	49	1979
THIS TIME I FOUND LOVE ROZALLA	33	1994
THIS TIME I KNOW IT'S FOR REAL DONNA SUMMER	3	1989
THIS TIME I KNOW IT'S FOR REAL KELLY LLORENNA	14	2004
THIS TIME (I'M GONNA TRY IT MY WAY) DJ SHADOW	54	2007
THIS TIME (LIVE) WET WET WET	38	1993
THIS TIME OF YEAR RUNRIG	38	1995
THIS TIME (WE'LL GET IT RIGHT) ENGLAND WORLD CUP SQUAD	2	1982
THIS TOWN AIN'T BIG ENOUGH FOR THE BOTH OF US SPARKS	2	1974
THIS TOWN AIN'T BIG ENOUGH FOR THE BOTH OF US BRITISH WHALE	6	2005
THIS TRAIN DON'T STOP THERE ANYMORE ELTON JOHN	24	2002
THIS USED TO BE MY PLAYGROUND MADONNA	3	1992
THIS WAITING HEART CHRIS DE BURGH	59	1989
THIS WAY DILATED PEOPLES	35	2004
THIS WHEEL'S ON FIRE [A] JULIE DRISCOLL, BRIAN AUGER & THE TRINITY	5	1968
THIS WHEEL'S ON FIRE [B] SIOUXSIE & THE BANSHEES	14	1987
THIS WILL BE NATALIE COLE	32	1975
THIS WILL BE OUR YEAR BEAUTIFUL SOUTH	36	2005
THIS WOMAN'S WORK KATE BUSH	25	1989
THIS WORLD IS NOT MY HOME JIM REEVES	22	1965
THIS WORLD OF WATER NEW MUSIK	31	1980
THIS WRECKAGE GARY NUMAN	20	1980
THIS YEAR'S LOVE DAVID GRAY	20	2001
THNKS FR TH MMRS FALL OUT BOY	12	2007
THOIA THONG R KELLY	14	2003
THONG SONG SISQO	3	2000
THE THORN EP SIOUXSIE & THE BANSHEES	47	1984
THORN IN MY SIDE EURYTHMICS	5	1986
THOSE FIRST IMPRESSIONS ASSOCIATES	43	1984
THOSE SIMPLE THINGS RIGHT SAID FRED	29	1992
THOSE WERE THE DAYS MARY HOPKIN	1	1968
THOU SHALT ALWAYS KILL DAN LE SAC VS SCROOBIUS PIP	34	2007
THOU SHALT NOT STEAL FREDDIE & THE DREAMERS	44	1965
THOUGHT I'D DIED AND GONE TO HEAVEN BRYAN ADAMS	8	1992
THE THOUGHT OF IT LOUIE LOUIE	34	1992
THOUGHT U WERE THE ONE FOR ME JOEY B ELLIS	58	1991
THOUGHTLESS KORN	37	2002
A THOUSAND MILES VANESSA CARLTON	6	2002
A THOUSAND STARS BILLY FURY	14	1961
A THOUSAND TREES STEREOPHONICS	22	1997
THREE [A] WEDDING PRESENT	14	1992
3 [B] BRITNEY SPEARS	7	2009
3AM [A] MATCHBOX 20	64	1998
3AM [B] BOBBY BLANCO & MIKKI MOTO	70	2004
3AM [C] BUSTED	1	2004
3AM [D] EMINEM	56	2009
3AM ETERNAL KLF FEATURING THE CHILDREN OF THE REVOLUTION	1	1991
THREE BABIES SINEAD O'CONNOR	42	1990
THE THREE BELLS BROWNS	6	1959
THREE BELLS BRIAN POOLE & THE TREMELOES	17	1965
THE THREE BELLS DANIEL O'DONNELL	71	1993
THE THREE BELLS (THE JIMMY BROWN SONG) COMPAGNONS DE LA CHANSON	21	1959
THREE COINS IN THE FOUNTAIN FRANK SINATRA	1	1954
THREE COINS IN THE FOUNTAIN FOUR ACES FEATURING AL ALBERTS	5	1954
THREE EP MANSUN	19	1996
3 FEET TALL I AM KLOOT	46	2003
3 IS FAMILY DANA DAWSON	9	1995
3 LIBRAS A PERFECT CIRCLE	49	2001
THREE LIONS (THE OFFICIAL SONG OF THE ENGLAND FOOTBALL TEAM) BADDIEL & SKINNER & LIGHTNING SEEDS	1	1996
THREE LITTLE BIRDS BOB MARLEY & THE WAILERS	17	1980
THREE LITTLE PIGS GREEN JELLY	5	1993
THREE LITTLE WORDS (I LOVE YOU) APPLEJACKS	23	1964
3 MCS AND 1 DJ BEASTIE BOYS	21	1999
THREE MINUTE HERO SELECTER	16	1980
THREE NIGHTS A WEEK FATS DOMINO	45	1960
THREE RING CIRCUS BARRY BIGGS	22	1977
3..6..9 SECONDS OF LIGHT BELLE & SEBASTIAN	32	1997
3 SONGS EP WEDDING PRESENT	25	1990
THREE STARS RUBY WRIGHT	19	1959
THREE STEPS TO HEAVEN EDDIE COCHRAN	1	1960
THREE STEPS TO HEAVEN SHOWADDYWADDY	2	1975
3345 BLACK VELVETS	34	2005
THREE TIMES A LADY COMMODORES	1	1978
THREE TIMES A MAYBE K CREATIVE	58	1992
3 X 3 EP GENESIS	10	1982
3 WORDS CHERYL COLE FEATURING WILL.I.AM	4	2009
3'S & 7'S QUEENS OF THE STONE AGE	19	2007
THREESOME FENIX TX	66	2002
3IL (THRILL) SOUL U*NIQUE	66	2000
THRILL HAS GONE TEXAS	60	1989
THRILL ME [A] SIMPLY RED	33	1992
THRILL ME [B] JUNIOR JACK	29	2002
THRILLER MICHAEL JACKSON	10	1983
THROUGH KINGS OF TOMORROW	74	2003
THROUGH THE BARRICADES SPANDAU BALLET	6	1986
THROUGH THE GATE ARTIFICIAL INTELLIGENCE	73	2004
THROUGH THE PAIN (SHE TOLD ME) P DIDDY FEATURING MARIO WINANS	50	2007
THROUGH THE RAIN MARIAH CAREY	8	2002
THROUGH THE ROOF CUD	44	1992
THROUGH THE STORM ARETHA FRANKLIN & ELTON JOHN	41	1989
THROUGH THE WIRE KANYE WEST	9	2004
THROUGH THE YEARS [A] GARY GLITTER	49	1992
THROUGH THE YEARS [B] CILLA BLACK	54	1993
THROW AWAY THE KEY LINX	21	1981
THROW DOWN A LINE CLIFF RICHARD & HANK MARVIN	7	1969
THROW THESE GUNS AWAY DUNBLANE	1	1996
THROW YA GUNZ ONYX	34	1993
THROW YOUR HANDS UP LV	24	1995
THROW YOUR SET IN THE AIR CYPRESS HILL	15	1995
THROWING IT ALL AWAY GENESIS	22	1987
THROWING MY BABY OUT WITH THE BATHWATER TEN POLE TUDOR	10	1981
THROWN AWAY STRANGLERS	42	1981
THRU KINGS OF TOMORROW FEATURING HAZE	55	2005
THRU THE GLASS THIRTEEN SENSES	18	2005
THRU' THESE WALLS PHIL COLLINS	56	1982
THUG LOVIN' JA RULE FEATURING BOBBY BROWN	15	2002
THUGZ MANSION 2PAC	24	2003
THUNDER [A] PRINCE & THE NEW POWER GENERATION	28	1992
THUNDER [B] EAST 17	4	1995
THUNDER AND LIGHTNING THIN LIZZY	39	1983
THUNDER IN MY HEART LEO SAYER	22	1977
THUNDER IN MY HEART AGAIN MECK FEATURING LEO SAYER	1	2006
THUNDER IN THE MOUNTAINS TOYAH	4	1981
THUNDERBALL TOM JONES	35	1966
THUNDERBIRDS [A] BARRY GRAY ORCHESTRA	61	1981
THUNDERBIRDS [B] BUSTED	1	2004
THUNDERBIRDS ARE GO FAB FEATURING MC PARKER	5	1990
THUNDERDOME MESSIAH	29	1993
THUNDERSTRUCK AC/DC	13	1990
THURSDAY'S CHILD DAVID BOWIE	16	1999
THUS SPAKE ZARATHUSTRA PHILHARMONIA ORCHESTRA, CONDUCTOR LORIN MAAZEL	33	1969
TI AMO GINA G	11	1997
TIC, TIC TAC CHILLI FEATURING CARRAPICHO	59	1997
TIC TOC KLEA	61	2002
TICK TICK BOOM HIVES	41	2007
TICK TOCK LEMAR	45	2007
TICKET OUTTA LOSERVILLE SON OF DORK	3	2005
TICKET TO RIDE BEATLES	1	1965
TICKET TO THE MOON ELECTRIC LIGHT ORCHESTRA	24	1982
THE TIDE IS HIGH BLONDIE	1	1980
THE TIDE IS HIGH (GET THE FEELING) ATOMIC KITTEN	1	2002
THE TIDE IS TURNING (AFTER LIVE AID) ROGER WATERS	54	1987
THE TIDE THAT LEFT AND NEVER CAME BACK VEILS	63	2004
TIE A YELLOW RIBBON ROUND THE OLD OAK TREE DAWN FEATURING TONY ORLANDO	1	1973
TIE ME KANGAROO DOWN SPORT ROLF HARRIS	9	1960
TIE YOUR MOTHER DOWN QUEEN	13	1977
TIED TO THE 90'S TRAVIS	30	1997
TIED UP YELLO	60	1988
TIED UP TOO TIGHT HARD-FI	15	2005
TIGER BABY SILVER CONVENTION	41	1976
TIGER FEET MUD	1	1974
TIGHTEN UP – I JUST CAN'T STOP DANCING WALLY JUMP, JR & THE CRIMINAL ELEMENT ORCHESTRA	24	1987
TIJUANA TAXI HERB ALPERT & THE TIJUANA BRASS	37	1966
TIK TOK KE$HA	5	2009
TIL I HEAR IT FROM YOU GIN BLOSSOMS	39	1996
('TIL) I KISSED YOU EVERLY BROTHERS	2	1959
...TIL THE COPS COME KNOCKIN' MAXWELL	63	1996
TIL THE DAY EASYWORLD	27	2004
TIL THE END HAVEN	28	2002
TILL TONY BENNETT	35	1961
TILL DOROTHY SQUIRES	25	1970
TILL TOM JONES	2	1971
TILL I CAN'T TAKE LOVE NO MORE EDDY GRANT	42	1983
TILL I COLLAPSE EMINEM	73	2009
TILL I GET MY WAY BLACK KEYS	62	2004

Title / Artist	Peak Position	Year of Release
TILL I LOVED YOU PLACIDO DOMINGO & JENNIFER RUSH	24	1989
TILL I LOVED YOU (LOVE THEME FROM 'GOYA') BARBRA STREISAND & DON JOHNSON	16	1988
TILL TEARS DO US PART HEAVENS CRY	68	2001
TILL THE END OF THE DAY KINKS	8	1965
TILL THERE WAS YOU PEGGY LEE	30	1961
TILL WE MEET AGAIN [A] INNER CITY	47	1991
TILL WE MEET AGAIN [B] PUSH	46	2000
TILL YOU COME BACK TO ME LEO SAYER	51	1983
TILT YA HEAD BACK NELLY & CHRISTINA AGUILERA	5	2004
TILTED SUGAR	48	1993
TIME [A] CRAIG DOUGLAS	9	1961
TIME [B] LIGHT OF THE WORLD	35	1981
TIME [C] FRIDA & BA ROBERTSON	45	1983
TIME [D] FREDDIE MERCURY	32	1986
TIME [E] KIM WILDE	71	1990
TIME [F] SUPERGRASS	2	1995
TIME [G] MARION	29	1996
TIME AFTER TIME [A] CYNDI LAUPER	3	1984
TIME AFTER TIME [A] HYPERSTATE	71	1993
TIME AFTER TIME [A] CHANGING FACES	35	1998
TIME AFTER TIME [A] DISTANT SOUNDZ	20	2002
TIME AFTER TIME [A] NOVASPACE	29	2003
TIME AFTER TIME [B] BELOVED	46	1990
TIME AFTER TIME [C] ELLIOT MINOR	47	2008
TIME ALONE WILL TELL MALCOLM ROBERTS	45	1967
TIME AND CHANCE COLOR ME BADD	62	1993
A TIME AND PLACE MIKE + THE MECHANICS	58	1991
TIME AND THE RIVER NAT 'KING' COLE	23	1960
TIME AND TIDE BASIA	61	1988
TIME AND TIME AGAIN PAPA ROACH	54	2002
TIME BOMB [A] 808 STATE	59	1992
TIME BOMB [B] RANCID	56	1995
TIME (CLOCK OF THE HEART) CULTURE CLUB	3	1982
TIME DRAGS BY CLIFF RICHARD	10	1966
TIME FOR ACTION SECRET AFFAIR	13	1979
TIME FOR DELIVERANCE DO ME BAD THINGS	57	2004
TIME FOR HEROES LIBERTINES	20	2003
TIME FOR LIVING ASSOCIATION	23	1968
TIME FOR LOVE KIM ENGLISH	48	1995
TIME FOR THE REVOLUTION 10 REVOLUTIONS	59	2003
THE TIME HAS COME ADAM FAITH	4	1961
THE TIME HAS COME PP ARNOLD	47	1967
TIME HAS TAKEN ITS TOLL ON YOU CRAZYHEAD	65	1988
THE TIME IN BETWEEN CLIFF RICHARD & THE SHADOWS	22	1965
TIME IS MY EVERYTHING IAN BROWN	15	2005
THE TIME IS NOW MOLOKO	2	2000
TIME IS ON MY SIDE ROLLING STONES	62	1982
TIME IS RUNNING OUT MUSE	8	2003
TIME IS TIGHT BOOKER T & THE MG's	4	1969
A TIME LIKE THIS HAYWOODE	48	1983
TIME LOVE AND TENDERNESS MICHAEL BOLTON	28	1991
TIME OF MY LIFE [A] TOPLOADER	18	2002
THE TIME OF MY LIFE [B] DAVID COOK	61	2008
TIME OF OUR LIVES ALISON LIMERICK	36	1994
TIME OF YOUR LIFE (GOOD RIDDANCE) GREEN DAY	11	1998
TIME SELLER SPENCER DAVIS GROUP	30	1967
TIME STAND STILL RUSH WITH AIMEE MANN	42	1987
TIME TO BURN STORM	3	2000
TIME TO GET BACK HYSTERIC EGO	50	1999
TIME TO GET UP LIQUID	46	1993
TIME TO GROW LEMAR	9	2005
TIME TO MAKE THE FLOOR BURN VARIOUS ARTISTS (MONTAGES)	16	1990
TIME TO MAKE YOU MINE LISA STANSFIELD	14	1992
TIME TO MOVE ON SPARKLE	40	1998
TIME TO PRETEND MGMT	35	2008
TIME TO SAY GOODBYE SARAH BRIGHTMAN/ANDREA BOCELLI	2	1997
TIME TO WASTE ALKALINE TRIO	32	2005
THE TIME WARP 2 DAMIAN	7	1987
TIME WILL CRAWL DAVID BOWIE	33	1987
TIMEBOMB CHUMBAWAMBA	59	1993
TIMELESS DANIEL O'DONNELL & MARY DUFF	32	1996
TIMELESS (KEEP ON MOVIN') RON VAN DEN BEUKEN	65	2004
TIMELESS MELODY LA'S	57	1990
TIMES LIKE THESE FOO FIGHTERS	12	2002
TIMES OF OUR LIVES PAUL VAN DYK FEATURING VEGA 4	28	2003
THE TIMES THEY ARE A-CHANGIN' PETER, PAUL & MARY	44	1964
TIMES THEY ARE A-CHANGIN' BOB DYLAN	9	1965
THE TIMES THEY ARE A-CHANGIN' IAN CAMPBELL FOLK GROUP	42	1965
THE TIMEWARP CAST OF THE NEW ROCKY HORROR SHOW	57	1998
TIN MACHINE TIN MACHINE	48	1989
TIN SOLDIER SMALL FACES	9	1967
TIN SOLDIERS STIFF LITTLE FINGERS	36	1980
TINA MARIE PERRY COMO	24	1955
TINGLE THAT PETROL EMOTION	49	1991
TINSEL TOWN RONNY JORDAN	64	1994
TINSELTOWN TO THE BOOGIEDOWN SCRITTI POLITTI	46	1999
TINY CHILDREN TEARDROP EXPLODES	44	1982
TINY DANCER MARCO DEMARK FEATURING CASEY BARNES	54	2008
TINY DANCER (HOLD ME CLOSER) IRONIK FEATURING CHIPMUNK & ELTON JOHN	3	2009
TINY DYNAMITE (EP) COCTEAU TWINS	52	1985
TINY MACHINE DARLING BUDS	60	1990
TIPP CITY AMPS	61	1995
THE TIPS OF MY FINGERS DES O'CONNOR	15	1970
TIPSY J-KWON	4	2004
TIRED OF BEING ALONE AL GREEN	4	1971
TIRED OF BEING ALONE TEXAS	19	1992
TIRED OF BEING SORRY ENRIQUE IGLESIAS	20	2007
TIRED OF ENGLAND DIRTY PRETTY THINGS	54	2008
TIRED OF TOEIN' THE LINE ROCKY BURNETTE	58	1979
TIRED OF WAITING FOR YOU KINKS	1	1965
TISHBITE COCTEAU TWINS	34	1996
TKO LE TIGRE	50	2005
TNT FOR THE BRAIN ENIGMA	60	1997
TO A BRIGHTER DAY (O' HAPPY DAY) BEAT SYSTEM	70	1993
TO ALL THE GIRLS I'VE LOVED BEFORE JULIO IGLESIAS & WILLIE NELSON	17	1984
TO BE A LOVER BILLY IDOL	22	1986
TO BE FREE EMILIANA TORRINI	44	2001
TO BE IN LOVE MAW PRESENTS INDIA	23	1999
TO BE LOVED MALCOLM VAUGHAN WITH THE MICHAEL SAMMES SINGERS	14	1958
TO BE LOVED JACKIE WILSON	23	1958
TO BE OR NOT TO BE BA ROBERTSON	9	1980
TO BE OR NOT TO BE (THE HITLER RAP) MEL BROOKS	12	1984
TO BE REBORN BOY GEORGE	13	1987
TO BE WITH YOU MR BIG	3	1992
TO BE WITH YOU AGAIN LEVEL 42	10	1987
TO CUT A LONG STORY SHORT SPANDAU BALLET	5	1980
TO DIE A VIRGIN DIVINE COMEDY	67	2006
TO DIE FOR LUKE GALLIANA	42	2001
TO EARTH WITH LOVE GAY DAD	10	1999
TO FRANCE MIKE OLDFIELD FEATURING MAGGIE REILLY	48	1984
TO GET DOWN (ROCK THING) TIMO MAAS	14	2002
TO HAVE AND TO HOLD CATHERINE STOCK	17	1986
TO HERE KNOWS WHEN MY BLOODY VALENTINE	29	1991
TO KNOW HIM IS TO LOVE HIM TEDDY BEARS	2	1958
TO KNOW SOMEONE DEEPLY IS TO KNOW SOMEONE SOFTLY TERENCE TRENT D'ARBY	55	1990
TO KNOW YOU IS TO LOVE YOU PETER & GORDON	5	1965
TO LIVE AND DIE IN LA MAKAVELI	10	1997
TO LOSE MY LIFE WHITE LIES	34	2009
TO LOVE A WOMAN LIONEL RICHIE FEATURING ENRIQUE IGLESIAS	19	2003
TO LOVE AGAIN ALESHA DIXON	15	2009
TO LOVE ONCE AGAIN SOLID HARMONIE	55	1998
TO LOVE SOMEBODY BEE GEES	41	1967
TO LOVE SOMEBODY NINA SIMONE	5	1969
TO LOVE SOMEBODY JIMMY SOMERVILLE	8	1990
TO LOVE SOMEBODY MICHAEL BOLTON	16	1992
TO MAKE A BIG MAN CRY PJ PROBY	34	1966
TO THE BEAT OF THE DRUM (LA LUNA) ETHICS	13	1995
TO THE BIRDS SUEDE	49	1992
TO THE CLUB SPANKOX	69	2004
TO THE END BLUR	16	1994
TO THE LIMIT TONY DE VIT	44	1995
TO THE MOON AND BACK SAVAGE GARDEN	3	1997
TO THE WORLD O.R.G.A.N.	33	1998
TO WHOM IT CONCERNS CHRIS ANDREWS	13	1965
TO WIN JUST ONCE SAW DOCTORS	14	1996
TO YOU I BELONG B*WITCHED	1	1998
TO YOU I BESTOW MUNDY	60	1996
TOAST STREETBAND	18	1978
TOAST OF LOVE THREE DEGREES	36	1976
TOBACCO ROAD NASHVILLE TEENS	6	1964
TOCA ME FRAGMA	11	1999
TOCA'S MIRACLE FRAGMA	1	2000
TOCCATA SKY	5	1980
TOCCATA & FUGUE VANESSA-MAE	16	1995
TODAY [A] SANDIE SHAW	27	1968
TODAY [B] TALK TALK	14	1982
TODAY [C] SMASHING PUMPKINS	44	1993
TODAY [D] MELANIE BROWN	41	2005
TODAY FOREVER RIDE	14	1990
TODAY THE SUN'S ON US SOPHIE ELLIS-BEXTOR	64	2007
TODAY WAS A FAIRYTALE TAYLOR SWIFT	57	2010
TODAY'S THE DAY SEAN MAGUIRE	27	1997
TODAY'S YOUR LUCKY DAY HAROLD MELVIN & THE BLUENOTES FEATURING NIKKO	66	1984
TOGETHER [A] CONNIE FRANCIS	6	1961
TOGETHER [A] PJ PROBY	8	1964
TOGETHER [B] O.C. SMITH	25	1977
TOGETHER [C] DANNY CAMPBELL & SASHA	57	1993
TOGETHER [D] ARTIFICIAL FUNK FEATURING NELLIE ETTISON	40	2003
TOGETHER AGAIN [A] RAY CHARLES	48	1966
TOGETHER AGAIN [B] JANET JACKSON	4	1997
TOGETHER FOREVER RICK ASTLEY	2	1988
TOGETHER IN ELECTRIC DREAMS GIORGIO MORODER & PHIL OAKEY	3	1984
TOGETHER WE ARE BEAUTIFUL STEVE ALLAN	67	1979
TOGETHER WE ARE BEAUTIFUL FERN KINNEY	1	1980
TOGETHERNESS MIKE PRESTON	41	1960
TOKOLOSHE MAN JOHN KONGOS	4	1971
TOKYO CLASSIX NOUVEAUX	67	1981
TOKYO JOE BRYAN FERRY	15	1977
TOKYO MELODY HELMUT ZACHARIAS	9	1964
TOKYO STEALTH FIGHTER DAVE ANGEL	58	1997

Title / Artist	Peak Position	Year of Release
TOKYO STORM WARNING ELVIS COSTELLO	73	1986
TOLEDO ELVIS COSTELLO/BURT BACHARACH	72	1999
TOM DOOLEY LONNIE DONEGAN	3	1958
TOM DOOLEY KINGSTON TRIO	5	1958
TOM HARK ELIAS & HIS ZIGZAG JIVE FLUTES	2	1958
TOM HARK TED HEATH	24	1958
TOM HARK PIRANHAS	6	1980
TOM HARK (WE WANT FALMER) SEAGULLS SKA	17	2005
TOM JONES INTERNATIONAL TOM JONES	31	2002
TOM PILLIBI JACQUELINE BOYER	33	1960
TOM SAWYER RUSH	25	1981
TOM THE MODEL BETH GIBBONS & RUSTIN MAN	70	2003
TOM THE PEEPER ACT ONE	40	1974
TOM TRAUBERT'S BLUES (WALTZING MATILDA) ROD STEWART	6	1992
TOMB OF MEMORIES PAUL YOUNG	16	1985
TOMBOY PERRY COMO	10	1959
TOMMY GUN CLASH	19	1978
TOMMY SHOTS YOUNG HEART ATTACK	54	2004
TOMORROW [A] JOHNNY BRANDON & THE PHANTOMS	8	1955
TOMORROW [B] SANDIE SHAW	9	1966
TOMORROW [C] COMMUNARDS	23	1987
TOMORROW [D] TONGUE 'N' CHEEK	20	1990
TOMORROW [E] SILVERCHAIR	59	1995
TOMORROW [F] JAMES	12	1997
TOMORROW [G] DUMONDE	60	2001
TOMORROW COMES TODAY GORILLAZ	33	2002
TOMORROW NEVER DIES SHERYL CROW	12	1997
TOMORROW NIGHT ATOMIC ROOSTER	11	1971
TOMORROW PEOPLE ZIGGY MARLEY & THE MELODY MAKERS	22	1988
TOMORROW RISING CLIFF RICHARD	29	1973
TOMORROW ROBINS WILL SING STEVIE WONDER	71	1995
TOMORROW TOMORROW BEE GEES	23	1969
TOMORROW'S CLOWN MARTY WILDE	33	1961
TOMORROW'S GIRLS [A] UK SUBS	28	1979
TOMORROW'S GIRLS [B] DONALD FAGEN	46	1993
TOMORROW'S (JUST ANOTHER DAY) MADNESS	8	1983
TOM'S DINER SUZANNE VEGA	58	1987
TOM'S DINER DNA FEATURING SUZANNE VEGA	2	1990
TOM'S PARTY T-SPOON	27	1999
TOM-TOM TURNAROUND NEW WORLD	6	1971
TONES OF HOME BLIND MELON	62	1993
TONGUE R.E.M.	13	1995
TONGUE TIED CAT	17	1993
TONIGHT [A] SHIRLEY BASSEY	21	1962
TONIGHT [B] MOVE	11	1971
TONIGHT [C] RUBETTES	12	1974
TONIGHT [D] ZAINE GRIFF	54	1980
TONIGHT [E] MODETTES	68	1981
TONIGHT [F] STEVE HARVEY	63	1983
TONIGHT [G] KOOL & THE GANG	2	1984
TONIGHT [H] BOOMTOWN RATS	73	1984
TONIGHT [I] DAVID BOWIE	53	1984
TONIGHT [J] NEW KIDS ON THE BLOCK	3	1990
TONIGHT [K] DEF LEPPARD	34	1993
TONIGHT [L] BAD COMPANY	56	2002
TONIGHT [M] WESTLIFE	3	2003
TONIGHT [N] JAY SEAN	23	2009
TONIGHT (COULD BE THE NIGHT) VELVETS	50	1961
TONIGHT I CELEBRATE MY LOVE PEABO BRYSON & ROBERTA FLACK	2	1983
TONIGHT I'M ALL RIGHT NARADA MICHAEL WALDEN	34	1980
TONIGHT I'M FREE PJ & DUNCAN	62	1993
TONIGHT I'M GONNA LET GO SYLEENA JOHNSON	38	2002
TONIGHT I'M GONNA LOVE YOU ALL OVER FOUR TOPS	43	1982
TONIGHT I'M YOURS (DON'T HURT ME) ROD STEWART	8	1981
TONIGHT IN TOKYO SANDIE SHAW	21	1967
TONIGHT IS WHAT IT MEANS TO BE YOUNG JIM STEINMAN & FIRE INC	67	1984
TONIGHT THE STREETS ARE OURS RICHARD HAWLEY	40	2007
TONIGHT TONIGHT SMASHING PUMPKINS	7	1996
TONIGHT TONIGHT TONIGHT GENESIS	18	1987
TONIGHT YOU BELONG TO ME PATIENCE & PRUDENCE	28	1956
TONIGHT'S THE NIGHT [A] ROD STEWART	5	1976
TONIGHT'S THE NIGHT [B] GINA G	57	2006
TONIGHT'S TODAY JACK PENATE	23	2009
TONITE [A] SUPERCAR	15	1999
TONITE [B] PHATS & SMALL	11	1999
TOO BAD NICKELBACK	9	2002
TOO BEAUTIFUL TO LAST ENGELBERT HUMPERDINCK	14	1972
TOO BIG SUZI QUATRO	14	1974
TOO BLIND TO SEE IT KYM SIMS	5	1991
TOO BUSY THINKING ABOUT MY BABY MARVIN GAYE	5	1969
TOO BUSY THINKING 'BOUT MY BABY MARDI GRAS	19	1972
TOO BUSY THINKING ABOUT MY BABY STEPS	2	2001
TOO CLOSE NEXT	24	1998
TOO CLOSE BLUE	1	2001
TOO COLD ROOTS MANUVA	39	2005
TOO DRUNK TO FUCK DEAD KENNEDYS	36	1981
TOO FAR GONE LISA SCOTT-LEE	11	2003
TOO GONE, TOO LONG EN VOGUE	20	1997
TOO GOOD LITTLE TONY	19	1960
TOO GOOD TO BE FORGOTTEN CHI-LITES	10	1974
TOO GOOD TO BE FORGOTTEN AMAZULU	5	1986
TOO GOOD TO BE TRUE TOM PETTY & THE HEARTBREAKERS	34	1992
TOO HARD TO BE FREE AMEN	72	2001
TOO HOT [A] KOOL & THE GANG	23	1980
TOO HOT [A] COOLIO	9	1996
TOO HOT [B] FUN LOVIN' CRIMINALS	61	2003
TOO HOT [C] FYA	49	2004
TOO HOT TO HANDLE HEATWAVE	15	1977
TOO HOT TO TROT COMMODORES	38	1978
TOO LATE JUNIOR	20	1982
TOO LATE FOR GOODBYES JULIAN LENNON	6	1984
TOO LATE TO SAY GOODBYE RICHARD MARX	38	1990
TOO LATE TOO LATE MR HUDSON & THE LIBRARY	53	2007
TOO LATE, TOO SOON JON SECADA	43	1997
TOO LITTLE TOO LATE JOJO	4	2007
TOO LOST IN YOU SUGABABES	10	2003
TOO MANY BEAUTIFUL GIRLS CLINTON FORD	48	1961
TOO MANY BROKEN HEARTS JASON DONOVAN	1	1989
TOO MANY DJ'S SOULWAX	40	2000
TOO MANY FISH FRANKIE KNUCKLES FEATURING ADEVA	34	1995
TOO MANY GAMES MAZE FEATURING FRANKIE BEVERLY	36	1985
TOO MANY MC'S/LET ME CLEAR MY THROAT PUBLIC DOMAIN	34	2002
TOO MANY PEOPLE [A] PAULINE HENRY	38	1993
TOO MANY PEOPLE [B] WET WET WET	46	2007
TOO MANY RIVERS BRENDA LEE	22	1965
TOO MANY TEARS DAVID COVERDALE & WHITESNAKE	46	1997
TOO MANY WALLS CATHY DENNIS	17	1991
TOO MUCH [A] ELVIS PRESLEY	6	1957
TOO MUCH [B] BROS	2	1989
TOO MUCH [C] SPICE GIRLS	1	1997
TOO MUCH FOR ONE HEART MICHAEL BARRYMORE	25	1995
TOO MUCH HEAVEN BEE GEES	3	1978
TOO MUCH INFORMATION DURAN DURAN	35	1993
TOO MUCH KISSING SENSELESS THINGS	69	1993
TOO MUCH LOVE WILL KILL YOU BRIAN MAY	5	1992
TOO MUCH LOVE WILL KILL YOU QUEEN	15	1996
TOO MUCH TEQUILA CHAMPS	49	1960
TOO MUCH TOO LITTLE TOO LATE JOHNNY MATHIS & DENIECE WILLIAMS	3	1978
TOO MUCH TOO LITTLE TOO LATE SILVER SUN	20	1998
TOO MUCH TOO YOUNG LITTLE ANGELS	22	1992
TOO MUCH TROUBLE LIMAHL	64	1984
TOO NICE TO TALK TO BEAT	7	1980
TOO REAL LEVELLERS	46	1998
TOO RIGHT TO BE WRONG CARTER TWINS	61	1997
TOO RISKY JIM DAVIDSON	52	1980
TOO SHY KAJAGOOGOO	1	1983
TOO SOON TO KNOW ROY ORBISON	3	1966
TOO TIRED GARY MOORE	71	1990
TOO WICKED (EP) ASWAD	61	1991
TOO YOUNG BILL FORBES	29	1960
TOO YOUNG DONNY OSMOND	5	1972
TOO YOUNG TO DIE JAMIROQUAI	10	1993
TOO YOUNG TO GO STEADY NAT 'KING' COLE	8	1956
TOOFUNKY GEORGE MICHAEL	4	1992
TOOK MY LOVE BIZARRE INC FEATURING ANGIE BROWN	19	1993
TOOK THE LAST TRAIN DAVID GATES	50	1978
TOOTHPASTE KISSES MACCABEES	70	2008
TOP O' THE MORNING TO YA HOUSE OF PAIN	8	1993
TOP OF THE POPS REZILLOS	17	1978
TOP OF THE STAIRS SKEE-LO	38	1996
TOP OF THE WORLD [A] CARPENTERS	5	1973
TOP OF THE WORLD [B] VAN HALEN	63	1991
TOP OF THE WORLD [C] BRANDY FEATURING MA$E	2	1998
TOP OF THE WORLD [D] WILDHEARTS	26	2003
TOP OF THE WORLD (OLÉ OLÉ OLÉ) CHUMBAWAMBA	21	1998
TOP TEEN BABY GARRY MILLS	24	1960
TOPKNOT CORNERSHOP	53	2004
TOPSY (PARTS 1 AND 2) COZY COLE	29	1958
TORCH SOFT CELL	2	1982
TORERO JULIUS LAROSA	15	1958
TORERO – CHA CHA CHA RENATO CAROSONE & HIS SEXTET	25	1958
TORN [A] NATALIE IMBRUGLIA	2	1997
TORN [B] LeTOYA	35	2006
TORN BETWEEN TWO LOVERS MARY MacGREGOR	4	1977
TORN ON THE PLATFORM JACK PENATE	7	2007
TORTURE [A] JACKSONS	26	1984
TORTURE [B] KING	23	1986
TOSH FLUKE	32	1995
TOSS IT UP MAKAVELI	15	1997
TOSSING AND TURNING [A] IVY LEAGUE	3	1965
TOSSING AND TURNING [B] WINDJAMMER	18	1984
TOSSING AND TURNING [C] CHAKKA BOOM BANG	57	1996
TOTAL CONFUSION A HOMEBOY, A HIPPIE & A FUNKI DREDD	56	1990
TOTAL ECLIPSE OF THE HEART BONNIE TYLER	1	1983
TOTAL ECLIPSE OF THE HEART NICKI FRENCH	5	1994
TOTAL ECLIPSE OF THE HEART JAN WAYNE	28	2003

Title	Artist	Peak Position	Year of Release
TOTAL ERASURE	PHILIP JAP	41	1982
THE TOTAL MIX	BLACK BOX	12	1990
TOTTENHAM TOTTENHAM	TOTTENHAM HOTSPUR FA CUP FINAL SQUAD	19	1982
TOUCH [A]	LORI & THE CHAMELEONS	70	1979
THE TOUCH [B]	KIM WILDE	56	1984
TOUCH [C]	AMERIE	19	2005
TOUCH BY TOUCH	DIANA ROSS	47	1984
TOUCH IT [A]	MONIFAH	29	1999
TOUCH IT [B]	BUSTA RHYMES	6	2006
TOUCH ME	CASS FOX	52	2006
TOUCH ME [A]	49ERS	3	1989
TOUCH ME [B]	RUI DA SILVA FEATURING CASSANDRA	1	2001
TOUCH ME [C]	ANGEL CITY	18	2004
TOUCH ME (ALL NIGHT LONG)	CATHY DENNIS	5	1991
TOUCH ME (I WANT YOUR BODY)	SAMANTHA FOX	3	1986
TOUCH ME IN THE MORNING	DIANA ROSS	9	1973
TOUCH ME LIKE THAT	DANNII MINOGUE VS JASON NEVINS	48	2007
TOUCH ME TEASE ME [A]	CASE FEATURING FOXXY BROWN	26	1996
TOUCH ME TEASE ME [B]	3SL	16	2002
TOUCH ME TOUCH ME	DAVE DEE, DOZY, BEAKY, MICK & TICH	13	1967
TOUCH ME WITH YOUR LOVE	BETH ORTON	60	1997
TOUCH MY BODY	MARIAH CAREY	6	2008
TOUCH MY FIRE	JAVINE	18	2005
TOUCH MYSELF	T-BOZ	48	1996
A TOUCH OF EVIL	JUDAS PRIEST	58	1991
A TOUCH OF LOVE	CLEOPATRA	24	1999
A TOUCH OF VELVET A STING OF BRASS	RON GRAINER ORCHESTRA	60	1978
TOUCH THE SKY [A]	29 PALMS	51	2002
TOUCH THE SKY [B]	KANYE WEST FEATURING LUPE FIASCO	6	2006
A TOUCH TOO MUCH	ARROWS	8	1974
TOUCH TOO MUCH	AC/DC	29	1980
TOUCH YOU	KATOI	70	2003
TOUCHED BY GOD	KATCHA	57	1999
TOUCHED BY THE HAND OF CICCIOLINA	POP WILL EAT ITSELF	28	1990
TOUCHED BY THE HAND OF GOD	NEW ORDER	20	1987
TOUCHY!	A-HA	11	1988
TOUGHER THAN THE REST	BRUCE SPRINGSTEEN	13	1988
TOUR DE FRANCE	KRAFTWERK	20	1983
TOURIST	ATHLETE	43	2005
TOURNIQUET [A]	MARILYN MANSON	28	1997
TOURNIQUET [B]	HEADSWIM	30	1998
TOUS LES GARCONS ET LES FILLES	FRANCOISE HARDY	36	1964
TOWER OF STRENGTH [A]	FRANKIE VAUGHAN	1	1961
TOWER OF STRENGTH [A]	GENE McDANIELS	49	1961
TOWER OF STRENGTH [B]	MISSION	12	1988
TOWER OF STRENGTH [C]	SKIN	19	1994
TOWERS OF LONDON	XTC	31	1980
TOWN	NORTHERN UPROAR	48	1996
A TOWN CALLED HYPOCRISY	LOSTPROPHETS	23	2006
A TOWN CALLED MALICE	JAM	1	1982
TOWN CLOWNS	BLAMELESS	56	1995
TOWN CRIER	CRAIG DOUGLAS	36	1963
TOWN OF PLENTY	ELTON JOHN	74	1988
TOWN TO TOWN	MICRODISNEY	55	1987
TOWN WITHOUT PITY	GENE PITNEY	32	1962
TOWN WITHOUT PITY	EDDI READER	26	1996
TOXIC	BRITNEY SPEARS	1	2004
TOXIC GIRL	KINGS OF CONVENIENCE	44	2001
TOXICITY	SYSTEM OF A DOWN	25	2002
TOXYGENE	ORB	4	1997
TOY	CASUALS	30	1968
TOY BALLOONS	RUSS CONWAY	7	1961
TOY BOY	SINITTA	4	1987
TOY SOLDIERS	MARTIKA	5	1989
TOYS FOR BOYS	MARION	57	1995
TRACEY IN MY ROOM	EBTG VERSUS SOUL VISION	34	2001
TRACIE	LEVEL 42	25	1989
TRACKIN'	BILLY CRAWFORD	32	2003
TRACKS OF MY TEARS	SMOKEY ROBINSON & THE MIRACLES	9	1969
TRACKS OF MY TEARS	LINDA RONSTADT	42	1976
TRACKS OF MY TEARS	COLIN BLUNSTONE	60	1982
TRACKS OF MY TEARS	GO WEST	16	1993
TRACY	CUFF LINKS	4	1969
TRADE (EP) (DISC 2)	VARIOUS ARTISTS (EP'S & LP'S)	75	1998
TRAFFIC [A]	STEREOPHONICS	20	1997
TRAFFIC [B]	TIESTO	48	2003
TRAGEDY [A]	ARGENT	34	1972
TRAGEDY [B]	BEE GEES	1	1979
TRAGEDY [B]	STEPS	1	1998
TRAGEDY AND MYSTERY	CHINA CRISIS	46	1983
TRAGIC COMIC	EXTREME	15	1993
THE TRAIL OF THE LONESOME PINE	LAUREL & HARDY WITH THE AVALON BOYS FEATURING CHILL WILLS	2	1975
TRAIL OF TEARS	DOGS D'AMOUR	47	1989
TRAILER LOAD A GIRLS	SHABBA RANKS	63	1991
TRAIN [A]	SISTERS OF MERCY	46	1984
TRAIN [B]	GOLDFRAPP	23	2003
THE TRAIN IS COMING	SHAGGY FEATURING WAYNE WONDER	21	1996
THE TRAIN IS COMING	UB40	30	1999
TRAIN OF CONSEQUENCES	MEGADETH	22	1995
TRAIN OF LOVE	ALMA COGAN	27	1960
TRAIN OF THOUGHT [A]	A-HA	8	1986
TRAIN OF THOUGHT [B]	ESCRIMA	36	1995
TRAIN ON A TRACK	KELLY ROWLAND	20	2003
TRAIN TO SKAVILLE	ETHIOPIANS	40	1967
TRAIN TOUR TO RAINBOW CITY	PYRAMIDS	35	1967
TRAINS AND BOATS AND PLANES	BURT BACHARACH	4	1965
TRAINS AND BOATS AND PLANES	BILLY J KRAMER & THE DAKOTAS	12	1965
TRAINS TO BRAZIL	GUILLEMOTS	36	2006
TRAMBONE	KREW-KATS	33	1961
TRAMP [A]	OTIS REDDING & CARLA THOMAS	18	1967
TRAMP [B]	SALT-N-PEPA	2	1988
TRAMPOLENE	JULIAN COPE	31	1987
TRAMPS AND THIEVES	QUIREBOYS	41	1992
TRANCESCRIPT	HARDFLOOR	72	1993
TRANQUILIZE	KILLERS	13	2007
TRANQUILLIZER	GENEVA	24	1997
TRANSAMAZONIA	SHAMEN	28	1995
TRANSATLANTIC	ROACH MOTEL	73	1993
TRANSFER AFFECTION	A FLOCK OF SEAGULLS	38	1983
TRANSISTOR RADIO	BENNY HILL	24	1961
TRANSMISSION [A]	GAY DAD	58	2001
TRANSMISSION [B]	VIOLENT DELIGHT	64	2003
TRANSONIC	WIRED	73	1999
TRANSYLVANIA	McFLY	1	2007
TRANZ EURO XPRESS	X-PRESS 2	45	1996
TRANZY STATE OF MIND	PUSH	31	2002
TRAPPED [A]	COLONEL ABRAMS	3	1985
TRAPPED [B]	GUYVER	72	2003
TRASH [A]	ROXY MUSIC	40	1979
TRASH [B]	SUEDE	3	1996
TRASHED	SKIN	30	2003
THE TRAVELLER	SPEAR OF DESTINY	44	1987
TRAVELLERS TUNE	OCEAN COLOUR SCENE	5	1997
TRAVELLIN' BAND	CREEDENCE CLEARWATER REVIVAL	8	1970
TRAVELLIN' HOME	VERA LYNN	20	1957
TRAVELLIN' LIGHT	CLIFF RICHARD & THE SHADOWS	1	1959
TRAVELLIN' MAN	RICKY NELSON	2	1961
TRAVELLING LIGHT	TINDERSTICKS	51	1995
TRAVELLING MAN	STUDIO 2	40	1998
TREASON (IT'S JUST A STORY)	TEARDROP EXPLODES	18	1981
TREASURE OF LOVE	CLYDE McPHATTER	27	1956
TREAT 'EM RIGHT	CHUBB ROCK	67	1991
TREAT HER LIKE A LADY [A]	TEMPTATIONS	12	1984
TREAT HER LIKE A LADY [B]	CELINE DION	29	1999
TREAT HER LIKE A LADY [C]	JOE	60	2000
TREAT HER RIGHT	ROY HEAD	30	1965
TREAT INFAMY	REST ASSURED	14	1998
TREAT ME GOOD	YAZZ	20	1990
TREAT ME LIKE A LADY [A]	FIVE STAR	54	1990
TREAT ME LIKE A LADY [B]	ZOE BIRKETT	12	2003
TREAT ME RIGHT	ADEVA	62	1990
TREATY	YOTHU YINDI	72	1992
TREBLE CHANCE	JOE 'MR PIANO' HENDERSON	28	1959
TREE FROG	HOPE A.D.	73	1994
THE TREES	PULP	23	2001
TREMBLE	MARC ET CLAUDE	29	2002
TREMELO SONG (EP)	CHARLATANS	44	1992
THE TRIAL OF HISSING SID	KEITH MICHELL, CAPTAIN BEAKY & HIS BAND	53	1980
TRIALS OF LIFE	KALEEF	75	1997
TRIBAL BASE	REBEL MC FEATURING TENOR FLY & BARRINGTON LEVY	20	1991
TRIBAL DANCE	2 UNLIMITED	4	1993
TRIBULATIONS	LCD SOUNDSYSTEM	59	2005
TRIBUTE (RIGHT ON)	PASADENAS	5	1988
TRIBUTE TO A KING	WILLIAM BELL	31	1968
TRIBUTE TO BUDDY HOLLY	MIKE BERRY WITH THE OUTLAWS	24	1961
TRIBUTE TO JIM REEVES	LARRY CUNNINGHAM & THE MIGHTY AVONS	40	1965
TRIBUTE TO JINKY	JIMMY JOHNSTONE, JIM KERR, SIMPLE MINDS & LAURA MCGHEE	28	2006
TRIBUTE TO OUR ANCESTORS	RUBBADUBB	56	1998
TRICK ME	KELIS	2	2004
A TRICK OF THE LIGHT	TRIFFIDS	73	1988
TRICK OF THE NIGHT	BANANARAMA	32	1987
TRICKY DISCO	TRICKY DISCO	14	1990
TRICKY KID	TRICKY	28	1997
TRIGGER HIPPIE	MORCHEEBA	40	1996
TRIGGER INSIDE	THERAPY?	22	1994
TRINI TRAX	TRINI LOPEZ	59	1981
TRIP II THE MOON	ACEN	38	1992
A TRIP TO TRUMPTON	URBAN HYPE	6	1992
TRIPLE TROUBLE	BEASTIE BOYS	37	2004
TRIPPIN' [A]	MARK MORRISON	8	1996
TRIPPIN' [B]	ORIS JAY PRESENTS DELSENA	42	2002
TRIPPIN' ON SUNSHINE	PIZZAMAN	18	1994
TRIPPIN' ON YOU	CAHILL FEATURING NIKKI BELLE	25	2008
TRIPPIN' ON YOUR LOVE [A]	A WAY OF LIFE	55	1990
TRIPPIN' ON YOUR LOVE [B]	KENNY THOMAS	17	1993
TRIPPING	ROBBIE WILLIAMS	2	2005
TRIPPY	ARAB STRAP	48	1998
TRIPWIRE	LIONROCK	44	1994
TRIUMPH [A]	WU-TANG CLAN FEATURING CAPPADONNA	46	1997
TRIUMPH [B]	HISS	53	2003
TRIUMPH OF A HEART	BJORK	31	2005
TRIXSTAR	BLAK TWANG FEATURING ESTELLE	54	2002
TROCADERO	SHOWADDYWADDY	32	1976

Title / Artist	Peak Position	Year of Release
THE TROOPER IRON MAIDEN	5	1983
TROPIC ISLAND HUM PAUL McCARTNEY	21	2004
TROPICAL ICE-LAND FIERY FURNACES	52	2004
TROPICAL SOUNDCLASH DJ GREGORY	59	2002
TROPICALIA BECK	39	1998
T.R.O.U.B.L.E. ELVIS PRESLEY	31	1975
TROUBLE [A] GILLAN	14	1980
TROUBLE [B] LINDSEY BUCKINGHAM	31	1982
TROUBLE [C] HEAVEN 17	51	1987
TROUBLE [D] SHAMPOO	11	1994
TROUBLE [E] COLDPLAY	10	2000
TROUBLE [F] CYPRESS HILL	33	2001
TROUBLE [G] P!NK	7	2003
TROUBLE [G] SHAKIN' STEVENS	20	2005
TROUBLE [H] RAY LAMONTAGNE	25	2006
TROUBLE BOYS THIN LIZZY	53	1981
TROUBLE IN PARADISE AL JARREAU	36	1983
TROUBLE IS MY MIDDLE NAME BROOK BROTHERS	38	1963
TROUBLE IS MY MIDDLE NAME FOUR PENNIES	32	1966
TROUBLE SLEEPING CORINNE BAILEY RAE	40	2006
TROUBLE TOWN MARTIN STEPHENSON & THE DAINTEES	58	1987
THE TROUBLE WITH HARRY ALFI & HARRY	15	1956
THE TROUBLE WITH LOVE IS KELLY CLARKSON	35	2003
TROUBLED GIRL KAREN RAMIREZ	50	1998
TROY (THE PHOENIX FROM THE FLAME) SINEAD O'CONNOR	48	2002
TRUCK ON SIMPLE KID	38	2004
TRUCK ON (TYKE) T REX	12	1973
TRUDIE JOE 'MR PIANO' HENDERSON	14	1958
TRUE [A] SPANDAU BALLET	1	1983
TRUE [B] JAIMESON FEATURING ANGEL BLU	4	2003
TRUE BLUE MADONNA	1	1986
TRUE COLORS [A] CYNDI LAUPER	12	1986
TRUE COLORS [A] GLEE CAST	35	2010
TRUE COLOURS [A] PHIL COLLINS	26	1998
TRUE COLOURS [B] GO WEST	48	1986
TRUE DEVOTION SAMANTHA FOX	62	1987
TRUE FAITH NEW ORDER	4	1987
TRUE LOVE [A] TERRY LIGHTFOOT & HIS NEW ORLEANS JAZZMEN	33	1961
TRUE LOVE [A] RICHARD CHAMBERLAIN	30	1963
TRUE LOVE [A] BING CROSBY & GRACE KELLY	4	1983
TRUE LOVE [A] SHAKIN' STEVENS	23	1988
TRUE LOVE [A] ELTON JOHN & KIKI DEE	2	1993
TRUE LOVE [B] CHIMES	48	1990
TRUE LOVE FOR EVER MORE BACHELORS	34	1965
TRUE LOVE NEVER DIES FLIP AND FULL FEATURING KELLY LLORENNA	7	2001
TRUE LOVE WAYS BUDDY HOLLY	25	1960
TRUE LOVE WAYS PETER & GORDON	2	1965
TRUE LOVE WAYS CLIFF RICHARD WITH THE LONDON PHILHARMONIC ORCHESTRA	8	1983
TRUE LOVE WAYS DAVID ESSEX & CATHERINE ZETA JONES	38	1994
TRUE LOVE WILL FIND YOU IN THE END SPECTRUM	70	1992
TRUE NATURE JANE'S ADDICTION	41	2003
TRUE SKOOL COLDCUT FEATURING ROOTS MANUVA	61	2006
TRUE SPIRIT CARLEEN ANDERSON	24	1994
TRUE STEP TONIGHT TRUE STEPPERS FEATURING BRIAN HARVEY	25	2000
TRUE (THE FAGGOT IS YOU) MOREL	64	2000
TRUE TO FORM HYBRID FEATURING PETER HOOK	59	2003
TRUE TO US VANILLA	36	1998
TRUE TO YOUR HEART 980 FEATURING STEVIE WONDER	51	1998
TRUGANINI MIDNIGHT OIL	29	1993

Title / Artist	Peak Position	Year of Release
TRULY [A] LIONEL RICHIE	6	1982
TRULY [A] STEVEN HOUGHTON	23	1998
TRULY [B] HINDA HICKS	31	1998
TRULY [C] PESHAY FEATURING KYM MAZELLE	55	2000
TRULY [D] DELERIUM	54	2004
TRULY MADLY DEEPLY [A] SAVAGE GARDEN	4	1998
TRULY MADLY DEEPLY [A] CASCADA	4	2006
TRULY MADLY DEEPLY [B] DUALERS	23	2005
TRULY ONE ORIGIN UNKNOWN	53	2002
TRUST [A] BROTHER BEYOND	53	1990
TRUST [B] NED'S ATOMIC DUSTBIN	21	1991
TRUST ME GURU FEATURING N'DEA DAVENPORT	34	1993
TRUST ME TO OPEN MY MOUTH SQUEEZE	72	1987
THE TRUTH [A] COLONEL ABRAMS	53	1985
THE TRUTH [B] REAL PEOPLE	41	1991
THE TRUTH IS NO WORDS MUSIC	18	2003
TRUTH OR DARE SHIRLEY MURDOCK	60	1986
TRY [A] BROS	27	1991
TRY [B] IAN VAN DAHL	15	2002
TRY [C] NELLY FURTADO	15	2004
TRY A LITTLE KINDNESS GLEN CAMPBELL	45	1970
TRY A LITTLE TENDERNESS OTIS REDDING	46	1967
TRY AGAIN AALIYAH	5	2000
TRY AGAIN TODAY CHARLATANS	24	2004
TRY HONESTY BILLY TALENT	68	2003
TRY JAH LOVE THIRD WORLD	47	1982
TRY ME OUT CORONA	6	1995
TRY MY WORLD GEORGIE FAME	37	1967
TRY SLEEPING WITH A BROKEN HEART ALICIA KEYS	71	2010
TRY TO UNDERSTAND LULU	25	1965
TRY TRY TRY [A] JULIAN COPE	24	1995
TRY TRY TRY [B] SMASHING PUMPKINS	73	2000
TRYIN' HILLTOPPERS	30	1956
TRYIN' TO GET THE FEELING AGAIN CARPENTERS	44	1994
TRYING TO FORGET JIM REEVES	33	1967
TRYING TO GET TO YOU ELVIS PRESLEY	16	1957
TRYOUTS FOR THE HUMAN RACE SPARKS	45	1979
TSOP (THE SOUND OF PHILADELPHIA) MFSB FEATURING THE THREE DEGREES	22	1974
TSUNAMI MANIC STREET PREACHERS	11	1999
TU AMOR KACI	24	2001
TU M'AIMES ENCORE (TO LOVE ME AGAIN) CELINE DION	7	1995
TUBTHUMPING CHUMBAWAMBA	2	1997
TUBULAR BELLS CHAMPS BOYS	41	1976
TUCH ME FONDA RAE	49	1984
TUESDAY AFTERNOON JENNIFER BROWN	57	1999
TUESDAY MORNING POGUES	18	1993
TUESDAY SUNSHINE QUESTIONS	46	1984
TUFF ACT TO FOLLOW MN8	15	1996
TUG OF WAR PAUL McCARTNEY	53	1982
TULANE STEVE GIBBONS BAND	12	1977
TULIPS BLOC PARTY	38	2004
TULIPS FROM AMSTERDAM MAX BYGRAVES	3	1958
TUM BIN JIYA BALLY SAGOO	21	1997
TUMBLE AND FALL FEEDER	5	2005
TUMBLING DICE ROLLING STONES	5	1972
TUMBLING TUMBLEWEEDS SLIM WHITMAN	19	1956
THE TUNE SUGGS	33	1995
TUNED TO A DIFFERENT STATION DOGS	29	2005
TUNES SPLITS THE ATOM MC TUNES VERSUS 808 STATE	18	1990
TUNNEL OF LOVE [A] DIRE STRAITS	54	1981
TUNNEL OF LOVE [B] FUN BOY THREE	10	1983
TUNNEL OF LOVE [C] BRUCE SPRINGSTEEN	45	1987
TURN [A] TRAVIS	8	1999
TURN [B] FEEDER	27	2001
TURN AROUND [A] FAB!	59	1998
TURN AROUND [B] PHATS & SMALL	2	1999

Title / Artist	Peak Position	Year of Release
TURN AROUND AND COUNT 2 TEN DEAD OR ALIVE	70	1988
TURN BACK THE CLOCK JOHNNY HATES JAZZ	12	1987
TURN BACK TIME AQUA	1	1998
TURN DA LIGHTS OFF TWEET FEATURING MISSY ELLIOTT	29	2005
TURN INTO YEAH YEAH YEAHS	54	2006
TURN IT AROUND ALENA	14	1999
TURN IT AROUND 4 STRINGS	50	2004
TURN IT DOWN SWEET	41	1974
TURN IT INTO LOVE HAZELL DEAN	21	1988
TURN IT ON LEVEL 42	57	1981
TURN IT ON AGAIN GENESIS	8	1980
TURN IT UP [A] CONWAY BROTHERS	11	1985
TURN IT UP [B] RICHIE RICH	48	1988
TURN IT UP [C] TECHNOTRONIC FEATURING MELISSA & EINSTEIN	42	1990
TURN IT UP [D] PETER ANDRE	64	1995
TURN IT UP [E] RAJA NEE	42	1995
TURN IT UP [F] FEELING	67	2008
TURN IT UP (SAY YEAH) DJ DUKE	31	1994
TURN IT UP/FIRE IT UP BUSTA RHYMES	2	1998
TURN ME LOOSE WALLY JUMP, JR & THE CRIMINAL ELEMENT ORCHESTRA	60	1987
TURN ME ON RMXCRW FEATURING EBON-E PLUS AMBUSH	52	2003
TURN ME ON [A] DANNY TENAGLIA FEATURING LIZ TORRES	53	1999
TURN ME ON [B] KEVIN LYTTLE	2	2003
TURN ME ON TURN ME OFF HONEY BANE	37	1981
TURN ME OUT (TURN TO SUGAR) PRAXIS FEATURING KATHY BROWN	35	1995
TURN OFF MILLTOWN BROTHERS	55	1993
TURN OFF THE LIGHT NELLY FURTADO	4	2001
TURN ON THE NIGHT KISS	41	1988
TURN ON, TUNE IN, COP OUT FREAKPOWER	3	1993
TURN THE BEAT AROUND GLORIA ESTEFAN	21	1994
TURN THE LIGHTS OUT WHEN YOU LEAVE ELTON JOHN	32	2005
TURN THE MUSIC UP PLAYERS ASSOCIATION	8	1979
TURN THE MUSIC UP CHRIS PAUL	73	1988
TURN THE TIDE SYLVER	56	2002
TURN THIS THING AROUND EL PRESIDENTE	39	2006
TURN TO GOLD DAVID AUSTIN	68	1984
TURN TO STONE ELECTRIC LIGHT ORCHESTRA	18	1977
TURN! TURN! TURN! (TO EVERYTHING THERE IS A SEASON) BYRDS	26	1965
TURN UP THE BASS TYREE FEATURING KOOL ROCK STEADY	12	1989
TURN UP THE NIGHT BLACK SABBATH	37	1982
TURN UP THE POWER N-TRANCE	23	1994
TURN UP THE SOUND LISA PIN-UP	60	2002
TURN YOUR BACK ON ME KAJAGOOGOO	47	1984
TURN YOUR CAR AROUND LEE RYAN	12	2005
TURN YOUR LIGHTS DOWN LOW BOB MARLEY FEATURING LAURYN HILL	15	1999
TURN YOUR LOVE AROUND GEORGE BENSON	29	1981
TURN YOUR LOVE AROUND TONY DI BART	66	1996
TURN YOUR RADIO ON RAY STEVENS	33	1972
TURNED AWAY AUDIOBULLYS	22	2003
TURNING AWAY SHAKIN' STEVENS	15	1986
TURNING JAPANESE VAPORS	3	1980
TURNING THE TOWN RED ELVIS COSTELLO	25	1984
TURQUOISE [A] DONOVAN	30	1965
TURQUOISE [B] CIRCULATION	64	2001
TURTLE POWER PARTNERS IN KRYME	1	1990
TURTLE RHAPSODY ORCHESTRA ON THE HALF SHELL	36	1990
TUSH GHOSTFACE FEATURING MISSY ELLIOTT	34	2004
TUSK FLEETWOOD MAC	6	1979

Title / Artist	Peak Position	Year of Release
TUTTI FRUTTI LITTLE RICHARD	29	1957
TUXEDO JUNCTION MANHATTAN TRANSFER	24	1976
TV FLYING LIZARDS	43	1980
TV CRIMES BLACK SABBATH	33	1992
TV DINNERS ZZ TOP	67	1984
TV SAVAGE BOW WOW WOW	45	1982
TV TAN WILDHEARTS	53	1993
TVC 15 DAVID BOWIE	33	1976
TWANGLING THREE FINGERS IN A BOX MIKE	40	1994
TWEEDLE DEE FRANKIE VAUGHAN	17	1955
TWEEDLE DEE GEORGIA GIBBS	20	1955
TWEEDLE DEE LITTLE JIMMY OSMOND	4	1973
TWEEDLE DEE TWEEDLE DUM MIDDLE OF THE ROAD	2	1971
THE TWELFTH OF NEVER CLIFF RICHARD	8	1964
THE TWELFTH OF NEVER DONNY OSMOND	1	1973
THE TWELFTH OF NEVER ELVIS PRESLEY	21	1995
THE TWELFTH OF NEVER CARTER TWINS	61	1997
TWELFTH STREET RAG BERT WEEDON	47	1960
TWELVE FORWARD, RUSSIA!	36	2006
12:51 STROKES	7	2003
12 REASONS WHY I LOVE HER MY LIFE STORY	32	1996
TWELVE STEPS TO LOVE BRIAN POOLE & THE TREMELOES	32	1964
20TH CENTURY BRAD	64	1993
20TH CENTURY BOY T REX	3	1973
20 DEGREES JONNY L	66	1998
21ST CENTURY WEEKEND PLAYERS	22	2001
21ST CENTURY CHRISTMAS CLIFF RICHARD	2	2006
21ST CENTURY (DIGITAL BOY) BAD RELIGION	41	1995
21ST CENTURY GIRLS 21ST CENTURY GIRLS	16	1999
25 MILES EDWIN STARR	36	1969
25 MILES 2001 THREE AMIGOS	30	2001
25 OR 6 TO 4 CHICAGO	7	1970
TWENTY FOREPLAY JANET JACKSON	22	1996
24 HOURS [A] BETTY BOO	25	1990
24 HOURS [B] AGENT SUMO	44	2001
TWENTY FOUR HOURS [C] ATHLETE	42	2005
24 HOURS A DAY NOMAD	61	1992
TWENTY FOUR HOURS FROM TULSA GENE PITNEY	5	1963
24 HOURS FROM YOU NEXT OF KIN	13	1999
24/7 [A] 3T	11	1996
24/7 [B] FIXATE	42	2001
24-7-365 CHARLES & EDDIE	38	1995
24 SYCAMORE GENE PITNEY	34	1973
20 HZ (NEW FREQUENCIES) CAPRICORN	73	1997
29 PALMS ROBERT PLANT	21	1993
21 PADDINGTONS	47	2004
21 QUESTIONS 50 CENT FEATURING NATE DOGG	6	2003
21 SECONDS SO SOLID CREW	1	2001
£20 TO GET IN SHUT UP & DANCE	56	1990
20 SECONDS TO COMPLY SILVER BULLET	11	1989
TWENTY TINY FINGERS STARGAZERS	4	1955
TWENTY TINY FINGERS ALMA COGAN	17	1955
TWENTY TINY FINGERS CORONETS	20	1955
20/20 GEORGE BENSON	29	1985
22 LILY ALLEN	14	2009
22 DAYS 22-20'S	34	2004
22 DREAMS PAUL WELLER	59	2008
22 GRAND JOB RAKES	39	2005
22 – THE DEATH OF ALL THE ROMANCE DEARS	53	2005
TWENTY WILD HORSES STATUS QUO	53	1999
TWENTY YEARS PLACEBO	18	2004
TWENTY-FIRST CENTURY BOY SIGUE SIGUE SPUTNIK	20	1986
21ST CENTURY LIFE SAM SPARRO	44	2008

Title / Artist	Peak Position	Year of Release
TWENTYFOURSEVEN [C] ARTFUL DODGER FEATURING MELANIE BLATT	6	2001
TWENTY-TWENTY SURGERY TAKING BACK SUNDAY	60	2006
TWICE AS HARD BLACK CROWES	47	1991
TWILIGHT ELECTRIC LIGHT ORCHESTRA	30	1981
TWILIGHT CAFE SUSAN FASSBENDER	21	1981
TWILIGHT TIME PLATTERS	3	1958
TWILIGHT WORLD SWING OUT SISTER	32	1987
TWILIGHT ZONE [A] IRON MAIDEN	31	1981
TWILIGHT ZONE [B] 2 UNLIMITED	2	1992
TWILIGHT ZONE – TWILIGHT TONE (MEDLEY) MANHATTAN TRANSFER	25	1980
TWILIGHTS LAST GLEAMING HIGH CONTRAST	74	2004
TWIN EARTH MONSTER MAGNET	67	1993
TWINKIE LEE GARY WALKER	26	1966
TWINKLE WHIPPING BOY	55	1996
TWINKLE TOES ROY ORBISON	29	1966
TWINKLE TWINKLE (I'M NOT A STAR) JAZZY JEFF & THE FRESH PRINCE	62	1994
TWINLIGHTS (EP) COCTEAU TWINS	59	1995
THE TWIST [A] CHUBBY CHECKER	2	1960
TWIST [B] GOLDFRAPP	31	2003
TWIST AND SHOUT [A] BRIAN POOLE & THE TREMELOES	4	1963
TWIST AND SHOUT [A] ISLEY BROTHERS	42	1963
TWIST AND SHOUT [A] SALT-N-PEPA	4	1988
TWIST AND SHOUT [A] CHAKA DEMUS & PLIERS FEATURING JACK RADICS & TAXI GANG	1	1993
TWIST AND SHOUT [B] DEACON BLUE	10	1991
TWIST 'EM OUT DILLINJA FEATURING SKIBADEE	35	2002
TWIST IN MY SOBRIETY TANITA TIKARAM	22	1988
TWIST OF FATE [A] OLIVIA NEWTON-JOHN	57	1983
TWIST OF FATE [B] SIOBHAN DONAGHY	52	2003
TWIST (ROUND 'N' ROUND) CHILL FAC-TORR	37	1983
TWIST TWIST CHAKACHAS	48	1962
THE TWIST (YO, TWIST) FAT BOYS & CHUBBY CHECKER	2	1988
TWISTED KEITH SWEAT	39	1996
TWISTED (EVERYDAY HURTS) SKUNK ANANSIE	26	1996
TWISTED TRANSISTOR KORN	27	2005
THE TWISTER VIPER	55	1998
TWISTERELLA RIDE	36	1992
TWISTIN' THE NIGHT AWAY SAM COOKE	6	1962
TWISTIN' THE NIGHT AWAY DIVINE	47	1985
TWISTING BY THE POOL DIRE STRAITS	14	1983
'TWIXT TWELVE AND TWENTY PAT BOONE	18	1959
2 BECOME 1 SPICE GIRLS	1	1996
TWO CAN PLAY THAT GAME BOBBY BROWN	3	1994
2 DEEP GANG STARR	67	1992
TWO DIFFERENT WORLDS RONNIE HILTON	13	1956
TWO DOORS DOWN MYSTERY JETS	24	2008
TWO EP MANSUN	32	1996
2 FACED LOUISE	3	2000
TWO FATT GUITARS (REVISITED) DIRECKT	36	1994
2-4-6-8 MOTORWAY TOM ROBINSON BAND	5	1977
TWO HEARTS [A] CLIFF RICHARD	34	1988
TWO HEARTS [B] PHIL COLLINS	6	1988
TWO HEARTS [C] STEPHANIE MILLS FEATURING TEDDY PENDERGRASS	49	1981
2 HEARTS [D] KYLIE MINOGUE	4	2007
TWO HEARTS BEAT AS ONE U2	18	1983
TWO HEARTS TOGETHER ORANGE JUICE	60	1982
TWO IN A MILLION [A] MICA PARIS	51	1993
TWO IN A MILLION [B] S CLUB 7	2	1999
TWO KINDS OF TEARDROPS DEL SHANNON	5	1963
TWO LEFT FEET HOLLOWAYS	33	2006
2 LEGIT 2 QUIT HAMMER	60	1991
TWO LITTLE BOYS ROLF HARRIS	1	1969

Title / Artist	Peak Position	Year of Release
TWO LITTLE BOYS SPLODGENESSABOUNDS	26	1980
TWO LITTLE BOYS FRON MALE VOICE CHOIR	57	2008
2 LITTLE BOYS/NEVER SAY DIE 2005 MONKEY HANGERZ	24	2005
TWO LOVERS TWANG	34	2007
2 MINUTES TO MIDNIGHT IRON MAIDEN	11	1984
TWO MONTHS OFF UNDERWORLD	12	2002
TWO MORE YEARS BLOC PARTY	7	2005
THE TWO OF US MAC & KATIE KISSOON	46	1976
TWO OUT OF THREE AIN'T BAD MEAT LOAF	32	1978
TWO PAINTINGS AND A DRUM CARL COX	24	1996
TWO PEOPLE [A] TINA TURNER	43	1986
2 PEOPLE [B] JEAN JACQUES SMOOTHIE	12	2001
TWO PINTS OF LAGER AND A PACKET OF CRISPS PLEASE SPLODGENESSABOUNDS	7	1980
2 + 2 = 5 RADIOHEAD	15	2003
TWO PRINCES SPIN DOCTORS	3	1993
2 REMIXES BY AFX AFX	69	2001
TWO SILHOUETTES DEL SHANNON	23	1963
2 STEP ROCK BANDITS	35	2003
TWO STEPS BEHIND DEF LEPPARD	32	1993
TWO STREETS VAL DOONICAN	39	1967
2 THE RHYTHM SOUND FACTORY	72	1993
2000 MILES PRETENDERS	15	1983
2, 3, GO WEDDING PRESENT	67	1996
2 TIMES ANN LEE	2	1999
TWO TIMING TOUCH AND BROKEN BONES HIVES	44	2004
THE TWO TONE EP VARIOUS ARTISTS (EP'S & LP'S)	30	1993
TWO TRIBES FRANKIE GOES TO HOLLYWOOD	1	1984
2V231 ANTICAPPELLA	24	1991
2-WAY RAYVON	67	2002
2 WAY STREET MISSJONES	49	1998
TWO WORLDS COLLIDE INSPIRAL CARPETS	32	1992
TWO WRONGS (DON'T MAKE A RIGHT) WYCLEF JEAN FEATURING CLAUDETTE ORTIZ	14	2002
TWYFORD DOWN GALLIANO	37	1994
TYPE LIVING COLOUR	75	1990
TYPICAL! FRAZIER CHORUS	53	1989
TYPICAL AMERICAN GOATS	53	1993
TYPICAL GIRLS SLITS	60	1979
TYPICAL MALE TINA TURNER	33	1986
TYPICAL ME KANO	22	2005

Title / Artist	Peak Position	Year of Release
U LONI CLARK	28	1994
U & ME CAPPELLA	10	1994
U & UR HAND P!NK	10	2006
U BLOW MY MIND BLACKSTREET	39	1995
U CAN'T TOUCH THIS MC HAMMER	3	1990
U CAN'T TOUCH THIS CRAZY FROG	5	2005
U DON'T HAVE TO SAY U LOVE ME MASH!	37	1994
U DON'T KNOW ME BASEMENT JAXX FEATURING LISA KEKAULA	26	2005
U FOUND OUT HANDBAGGERS	55	1996
U GIRLS (LOOK SO SEXY) NUSH	15	1994
U GOT 2 KNOW CAPPELLA	6	1993
U GOT 2 LET THE MUSIC CAPPELLA	2	1993
U GOT IT BAD USHER	5	2001
U GOT ME PARA BEATS FEATURING CARMEN REECE	59	2005
U GOT THE LOOK PRINCE	11	1987
U (I GOT THE FEELING) DJ SCOT PROJECT	66	1996
U KNOW WHAT'S UP DONELL JONES	2	2000
U KNOW Y MOGUAI	62	2003
U KRAZY KATZ PJ & DUNCAN	15	1995

Title / Artist	Peak Position	Year of Release
U MAKE ME WANNA BLUE	4	2003
U + ME = LOVE FUNKY WORM	46	1989
U R THE BEST THING D:REAM	4	1992
U REMIND ME USHER	3	2001
U SEXY THING CLOCK	11	1997
U SHINE ON MATT DAREY & MARCELLA WOODS	34	2002
U16 GIRLS TRAVIS	40	1997
U SURE DO STRIKE	4	1994
U TURN USHER	16	2002
U WILL KNOW BMU	23	1995
UBIK TIMO MAAS FEATURING MARTIN BETTINGHAUS	33	2000
UFO SNEAKY SOUND SYSTEM	52	2008
UGLY [A] DAPHNE & CELESTE	18	2000
UGLY [B] BUBBA SPARXXX	7	2001
UGLY [C] SUGABABES	3	2005
UGLY DUCKLING MIKE REID	10	1975
UH HUH B2K	31	2002
UH HUH OH YEH PAUL WELLER	18	1992
UH LA LA LA ALEXIA	10	1998
UH OH (I'M BACK) LETHAL BIZZLE	47	2005
UH UH NO NO CASUAL SEX CARRIE McDOWELL	68	1987
UHF UHF	46	1991
UHH IN YOU SNOW	67	1993
UH-UH OOH OOH LOOK OUT (HERE IT COMES) ROBERTA FLACK	72	1989
UK BLAK CARON WHEELER	40	1990
UK-USA ESKIMOS & EGYPT	52	1993
'ULLO JOHN GOT A NEW MOTOR? ALEXEI SAYLE	15	1984
THE ULTIMATE FUNKY CHOAD FEATURING NICK SKITZ	51	1998
THE ULTIMATE HIGH TIME FREQUENCY	17	1993
THE ULTIMATE SIN OZZY OSBOURNE	72	1986
ULTIMATE TRUNK FUNK EP BRAND NEW HEAVIES FEATURING N'DEA DAVENPORT	19	1992
ULTRA FLAVA HELLER & FARLEY PROJECT	22	1996
ULTRA STIMULATION FINLEY QUAYE	51	1998
ULTRAFUNKULA ARMAND VAN HELDEN	46	1997
ULTRA-OBSCENE BREAKBEAT ERA	48	1999
ULTRAVIOLET [A] McFLY	9	2005
ULTRAVIOLET [B] STIFF DYLANS	41	2008
ULYSSES FRANZ FERDINAND	20	2009
UM UM UM UM UM UM WAYNE FONTANA & THE MINDBENDERS	5	1964
UM UM UM UM UM UM MAJOR LANCE	40	1964
UMBRELLA [A] RIHANNA FEATURING JAY-Z	1	2007
UMBRELLA [B] MANIC STREET PREACHERS	47	2008
UMI SAYS MOS DEF	60	2000
UN BANC, UN ABRE, UNE RUE SEVERINE	9	1971
(UN, DOS, TRES) MARIA RICKY MARTIN	6	1997
UNA PALOMA BLANCA JONATHAN KING	5	1975
UNBEARABLE WONDER STUFF	16	1994
UNBELIEVABLE [A] EMF	3	1990
UNBELIEVABLE [B] SKIN	18	1994
UNBELIEVABLE [C] LISA LASHES	63	2000
UNBELIEVABLE [D] CRAIG DAVID	18	2006
UN-BREAK MY HEART TONI BRAXTON	2	1996
UNBREAKABLE WESTLIFE	1	2002
UNCERTAIN SMILE THE THE	68	1982
UNCHAIN MY HEART JOE COCKER	46	1987
UNCHAINED MELODY JIMMY YOUNG	1	1955
UNCHAINED MELODY AL HIBBLER	2	1955
UNCHAINED MELODY LES BAXTER	10	1955
UNCHAINED MELODY LIBERACE	20	1955
UNCHAINED MELODY JIMMY YOUNG WITH THE MICHAEL SAMMES SINGERS	43	1964
UNCHAINED MELODY RIGHTEOUS BROTHERS	1	1965
UNCHAINED MELODY LEO SAYER	54	1986
UNCHAINED MELODY ROBSON GREEN & JEROME FLYNN	1	1995
UNCHAINED MELODY GARETH GATES	1	2002
UNCLE JOHN FROM JAMAICA VENGABOYS	6	2000
UNCLE SAM MADNESS	21	1985
UNCONDITIONAL [A] BRAVERY	49	2005
UNCONDITIONAL [B] PETER ANDRE	50	2009
UNCONDITIONAL LOVE [A] DONNA SUMMER	14	1983
UNCONDITIONAL LOVE [B] SUSANNA HOFFS	65	1991
UNDECIDED YOUSSOU N'DOUR	53	1995
UNDER A RAGING MOON ROGER DALTREY	43	1986
UNDER ATTACK ABBA	26	1982
(UNDER HER) SPELL HUGH CORNWALL	62	2005
UNDER MY THUMB WHO	44	1967
UNDER MY THUMB WAYNE GIBSON	17	1974
UNDER MY WHEELS ALICE COOPER	66	1982
UNDER NEW MANAGEMENT BARRON KNIGHTS WITH DUKE D'MOND	15	1966
UNDER ONE ROOF RUBETTES	40	1976
UNDER PRESSURE QUEEN & DAVID BOWIE	1	1981
UNDER PRESSURE (ICE ICE BABY) JEDWARD FEATURING VANILLA ICE	2	2010
UNDER THE BOARDWALK DRIFTERS	45	1964
UNDER THE BOARDWALK TOM TOM CLUB	22	1982
UNDER THE BOARDWALK BRUCE WILLIS	2	1987
UNDER THE BRIDGE RED HOT CHILI PEPPERS	13	1992
UNDER THE BRIDGE ALL SAINTS	1	1998
UNDER THE BRIDGES OF PARIS DEAN MARTIN	6	1955
UNDER THE BRIDGES OF PARIS EARTHA KITT	7	1955
UNDER THE COVERS EP HARRY	43	2003
UNDER THE GOD TIN MACHINE	51	1989
UNDER THE GUN SISTERS OF MERCY	19	1993
UNDER THE MOON OF LOVE SHOWADDYWADDY	1	1976
UNDER THE SHEETS ELLIE GOULDING	53	2009
UNDER THE THUMB AMY STUDT	10	2003
UNDER THE TREE WATER BABIES	27	2005
UNDER THE WATER BROTHER BROWN FEATURING FRANK'EE	18	1999
UNDER THE WEATHER KT TUNSTALL	39	2005
UNDER YOUR SPELL RONNY JORDAN	72	1993
UNDER YOUR THUMB GODLEY & CREME	3	1981
UNDERCOVER GEMMA HAYES	63	2006
UNDERCOVER ANARCHIST SILVER BULLET	33	1991
UNDERCOVER ANGEL ALAN O'DAY	43	1977
UNDERCOVER LOVER SMOOTH	41	1996
UNDERCOVER OF THE NIGHT ROLLING STONES	11	1983
UNDERDOG [A] KASABIAN	32	2009
UNDERDOG [B] YOU ME AT SIX	49	2010
UNDERDOG (SAVE ME) TURIN BRAKES	39	2001
UNDERDOSE INME	66	2002
UNDERGROUND [A] DAVID BOWIE	21	1986
UNDERGROUND [B] BEN FOLDS FIVE	37	1996
UNDERGROUND [C] RHYTHM MASTERS	50	2001
UNDERLOVE MELBA MOORE	60	1983
UNDERNEATH IT ALL NO DOUBT	18	2002
UNDERNEATH THE BLANKET GO GILBERT O'SULLIVAN	40	1971
UNDERNEATH YOUR CLOTHES SHAKIRA	3	2002
UNDERPASS JOHN FOXX	31	1980
UNDERSTAND THIS GROOVE FRANKE	60	1992
UNDERSTANDING JANE ICICLE WORKS	52	1986
UNDERWATER [A] HARRY THUMANN	41	1981
UNDERWATER [B] DELERIUM FEATURING RANI	33	2001
UNDERWATER LOVE SMOKE CITY	4	1997
UNDERWEAR GOES INSIDE THE PANTS LAZY B	30	2006
UNDISCLOSED DESIRES MUSE	49	2009
UNDISCOVERED JAMES MORRISON	63	2007
UNDIVIDED LOVE LOUISE	5	1996
UNDONE – THE SWEATER SONG WEEZER	35	1995
UNDRESSED WHITE TOWN	57	1997
UNEMPLOYED IN SUMMERTIME EMILIANA TORRINI	63	2000
UNEXPLAINED GRAVEDIGGAZ	48	1998
UNEXPLAINED EP EMF	18	1992
UNFAITHFUL RIHANNA	2	2006
UNFINISHED SYMPATHY MASSIVE	13	1991
UNFORGETTABLE NATALIE COLE WITH NAT 'KING' COLE	19	1991
THE UNFORGETTABLE FIRE U2	6	1985
UNFORGIVABLE SINNER LENE MARLIN	13	2000
THE UNFORGIVEN [A] METALLICA	15	1991
UNFORGIVEN [B] D:REAM	29	1993
THE UNFORGIVEN II METALLICA	15	1998
UNHOLY KISS	26	1992
UNIFORM INSPIRAL CARPETS	51	1994
UNIFORMS (CORPS D'ESPRIT) PETE TOWNSHEND	48	1982
UNINTENDED MUSE	20	2000
UNINVITED FREEMASONS FEATURING BAILEY TZUKE	8	2007
UNINVITED GUEST MARILLION	53	1989
UNION CITY BLUES BLONDIE	13	1979
UNION OF THE SNAKE DURAN DURAN	3	1983
UNITED JUDAS PRIEST	26	1980
UNITED CALYPSO '98 REDS UNITED	33	1998
UNITED COLOURS BEST SHOT	64	1994
UNITED NATIONS OF HOUSE – VOLUME 1 VARIOUS ARTISTS (EP'S & LP'S)	71	2005
UNITED STATES OF WHATEVER LIAM LYNCH	10	2002
UNITED (WE LOVE YOU) MANCHESTER UNITED & THE CHAMPIONS	37	1993
UNITED WE STAND BROTHERHOOD OF MAN	10	1970
UNITY UNITY	64	1991
U.N.I.T.Y. QUEEN LATIFAH	74	1994
UNITY (PART 1 – THE THIRD COMING) AFRIKA BAMBAATAA & JAMES BROWN	49	1984
UNIVERSAL NATE JAMES	72	2005
UNIVERSAL [A] SMALL FACES	16	1968
UNIVERSAL [B] ORCHESTRAL MANOEUVRES IN THE DARK	55	1996
THE UNIVERSAL [C] BLUR	5	1995
UNIVERSAL HEART-BEAT JULIANA HATFIELD	65	1995
UNIVERSAL MUSIC METEOR SEVEN	71	2002
UNIVERSAL NATION PUSH	35	1999
UNIVERSALLY SPEAKING RED HOT CHILI PEPPERS	27	2003
THE UNKNOWN MARK B & BLADE	49	2001
UNLEASH THE DRAGON SISQO	6	2000
UNLOCK THE FUNK LOCKSMITH	42	1980
THE UNNAMED FEELING METALLICA	42	2004
UNO MUSE	73	1999
UNO MAS DANIEL O'DONNELL	25	1999
UNPLAYED PIANO DAMIEN RICE & LISA HANNIGAN	24	2005
UNPREDICTABLE JAMIE FOXX FEATURING LUDACRIS	16	2006
UNPRETTY TLC	6	1999
UNSAFE BUILDING 1990 ALARM	54	1990
UNSATISFIED NINE BLACK ALPS	30	2005
UNSKINNY BOP POISON	15	1990
UNSQUARE DANCE DAVE BRUBECK QUARTET	14	1962
UNSTABLE ADEMA	46	2003
THE UNSUNG HEROES OF HIP HOP SUBSONIC	63	1991
UNTIL IT SLEEPS METALLICA	5	1996
UNTIL IT'S TIME FOR YOU TO GO FOUR PENNIES	19	1965
UNTIL IT'S TIME FOR YOU TO GO ELVIS PRESLEY	5	1972

Title	Artist	Peak Position	Year of Release
UNTIL MY DYING DAY	UB40	15	1995
UNTIL THE DAY	FUNKY GREEN DOGS	75	1998
UNTIL THE DAY I DIE	STORY OF THE YEAR	62	2004
UNTIL THE END OF TIME	2PAC	4	2001
UNTIL THE NIGHT	BILLY JOEL	50	1979
UNTIL THE TIME IS THROUGH	FIVE	2	1998
UNTIL YOU COME BACK (THAT'S WHAT I'M GONNA DO)	MIKI HOWARD	67	1990
UNTIL YOU COME BACK TO ME	ADEVA	45	1992
UNTIL YOU COME BACK TO ME (THAT'S WHAT I'M GONNA DO)	ARETHA FRANKLIN	26	1974
UNTIL YOU FIND OUT	NED'S ATOMIC DUSTBIN	51	1990
UNTIL YOU LOVED ME	MOFFATTS	36	1999
UNTIL YOU SUFFER SOME (FIRE AND ICE)	POISON	32	1993
UNTOUCHABLE [A]	RIALTO	20	1998
UNTOUCHABLE [B]	GIRLS ALOUD	11	2009
UNTOUCHED	VERONICAS	8	2009
UNWRITTEN	NATASHA BEDINGFIELD	6	2004
UP! [A]	SHANIA TWAIN	21	2003
UP [B]	SATURDAYS	5	2008
UP ABOVE MY HEAD I HEAR MUSIC IN THE AIR	FRANKIE LAINE & JOHNNIE RAY	25	1957
UP AGAINST THE WALL	TOM ROBINSON BAND	33	1978
UP ALL NIGHT [A]	SLAUGHTER	62	1990
UP ALL NIGHT [B]	MATT WILLIS	7	2006
UP ALL NIGHT [C]	YOUNG KNIVES	45	2008
UP ALL NIGHT [D]	TAKE THAT	14	2009
UP ALL NIGHT/TAKE CONTROL	JOHN B	58	2002
UP AND DOWN [A]	HIGH	53	1990
UP AND DOWN [B]	VENGABOYS	4	1998
UP AND DOWN [C]	BOYSTEROUS	53	2003
UP AND DOWN [D]	SCENT	23	2004
UP AROUND THE BEND	CREEDENCE CLEARWATER REVIVAL	3	1970
UP AROUND THE BEND	HANOI ROCKS	61	1984
UP AT THE LAKE	CHARLATANS	23	2004
UP IN A PUFF OF SMOKE	POLLY BROWN	43	1974
UP MIDDLE FINGER	OXIDE & NEUTRINO	7	2001
UP ON THE CATWALK	SIMPLE MINDS	27	1984
UP ON THE DOWN SIDE	OCEAN COLOUR SCENE	19	2001
UP ON THE ROOF	KENNY LYNCH	10	1962
UP ON THE ROOF	JULIE GRANT	33	1963
UP ON THE ROOF	ROBSON GREEN & JEROME FLYNN	1	1995
UP ROCKING BEATS	BOMFUNK MC'S	11	2000
UP TEMPO	TRONIKHOUSE	68	1992
UP THE BRACKET	LIBERTINES	29	2002
UP THE HILL BACKWARDS	DAVID BOWIE	32	1981
UP THE JUNCTION	SQUEEZE	2	1979
UP THE LADDER TO THE ROOF	SUPREMES	6	1970
UP THE POOL	JETHRO TULL	11	1971
UP TO NO GOOD	PORN KINGS	28	1996
UP TO THE WILDSTYLE	PORN KINGS VERSUS DJ SUPREME	10	1999
UP TOWN TOP RANKING	ALTHEA & DONNA	1	1977
UP, UP AND AWAY	JOHNNY MANN SINGERS	6	1967
UP WHERE WE BELONG	JOE COCKER & JENNIFER WARNES	7	1983
UP WITH THE COCK	JUDGE DREAD	49	1978
UP WITH THE PEOPLE	LAMBCHOP	66	2000
UPFIELD	BILLY BRAGG	46	1996
UPRISING [A]	ARTIFICIAL INTELLIGENCE	73	2004
UPRISING [B]	MUSE	9	2009
UPROCK	ROCKSTEADY CREW	64	1984
UPS AND DOWN	SNOOP DOGG	36	2005
UPSIDE DOWN [A]	DIANA ROSS	2	1980
UPSIDE DOWN [B]	A*TEENS	10	2001
UPSIDE DOWN [C]	JACK JOHNSON	30	2006
UPSIDE DOWN [C]	PALOMA FAITH	55	2010
UPTIGHT [A]	STEVIE WONDER	14	1966
UPTIGHT [B]	SHARA NELSON	19	1994
UPTOWN DOWNTOWN	FULL INTENTION	61	1996
UPTOWN FESTIVAL	SHALAMAR	30	1977
UPTOWN GIRL	BILLY JOEL	1	1983
UPTOWN GIRL	WESTLIFE	1	2001
UPTOWN TOP RANKING	ALI & FRAZIER	33	1993
UPTOWN UPTEMPO WOMAN	RANDY EDELMAN	25	1976
URBAN CITY GIRL	BENZ	31	1996
URBAN GUERRILLA	HAWKWIND	39	1973
URBAN PRESSURE	GRIM NORTHERN SOCIAL	60	2003
URBAN TRAIN	DJ TIESTO	22	2001
THE URGE [A]	FREDDY CANNON	18	1960
URGE [B]	WILDHEARTS	26	1997
URGENT	FOREIGNER	45	1981
URGENTLY IN LOVE	BILLY CRAWFORD	48	1998
US AGAINST THE WORLD	WESTLIFE	8	2008
U.S. MALE	ELVIS PRESLEY	15	1968
USA	WWF SUPERSTARS FEATURING HACKSAW JIM DUGGAN	71	1993
USE IT UP AND WEAR IT OUT	ODYSSEY	1	1980
USE IT UP AND WEAR IT OUT	PAT & MICK	22	1990
USE SOMEBODY	KINGS OF LEON	2	2008
USE SOMEBODY	PIXIE LOTT	52	2009
USED FOR GLUE	RIVAL SCHOOLS	42	2002
USED TA BE MY GIRL	O'JAYS	12	1978
USED TO LOVE U	JOHN LEGEND	29	2005
USELESS	DEPECHE MODE	28	1997
USELESS (I DON'T NEED YOU NOW)	KYM MAZELLE	48	1988
UTOPIA	GOLDFRAPP	62	2001
UTOPIA (WHERE I WANT TO BE)	STEREO STAR FEATURING MIA J	66	2005

V

Title	Artist	Peak Position	Year of Release
V THIRTEEN	BIG AUDIO DYNAMITE	49	1987
VACATION	CONNIE FRANCIS	10	1962
VADO VIA	DRUPI	17	1973
VAGABONDS	NEW MODEL ARMY	37	1989
VALENTINE [A]	T'PAU	9	1988
VALENTINE [B]	DELAYS	23	2006
VALENTINO	CONNIE FRANCIS	27	1960
VALERIE [A]	STEVE WINWOOD	19	1982
VALERIE [B]	ZUTONS	9	2006
VALERIE [C]	MARK RONSON FEATURING AMY WINEHOUSE	2	2007
VALERIE [C]	AMY WINEHOUSE	37	2007
VALLERI	MONKEES	12	1968
VALLEY OF TEARS	FATS DOMINO	25	1957
VALLEY OF TEARS	BUDDY HOLLY	12	1961
VALLEY OF THE DOLLS	DIONNE WARWICK	28	1968
VALLEY OF THE DOLLS	GENERATION X	23	1979
VALLEY OF THE SHADOWS	ORIGIN UNKNOWN	60	1996
THE VALLEY ROAD	BRUCE HORNSBY & THE RANGE	44	1988
VALOTTE	JULIAN LENNON	55	1984
VAMOS A LA PLAYA	RIGHEIRA	53	1983
VAMP	OUTLANDER	51	1991
VAMPIRE RACECOURSE	SLEEPY JACKSON	50	2003
VANESSA	TED HEATH	11	1953
VANILLA RADIO	WILDHEARTS	26	2002
VANITY KILLS	ABC	70	1985
VAPORIZER	LUPINE HOWL	68	2000
VAPORS	SNOOP DOGGY DOGG	18	1997
VASOLINE	STONE TEMPLE PILOTS	48	1994
VAVOOM!	MAN WITH NO NAME	43	1998
VAYA CON DIOS	LES PAUL & MARY FORD	7	1953
VAYA CON DOS	MILLICAN & NESBITT	20	1973
VEGAS [A]	SLEEPER	33	1995
VEGAS [B]	AGNELLI & NELSON	48	2001
VEGAS TWO TIMES	STEREOPHONICS	23	2002
VEHICLE	IDES OF MARCH	31	1970
VELCRO FLY	ZZ TOP	54	1986
VELOURIA	PIXIES	28	1990
VELVET MOODS	JOHAN GIELEN PRESENTS ABNEA	74	2001
VENCEREMOS – WE WILL WIN	WORKING WEEK	64	1984
VENI VIDI VICI	RONNIE HILTON	12	1954
VENTOLIN	APHEX TWIN	49	1995
VENTURA HIGHWAY	AMERICA	43	1972
VENUS [A]	FRANKIE AVALON	16	1959
VENUS [A]	DICKIE VALENTINE	20	1959
VENUS [B]	SHOCKING BLUE	8	1970
VENUS [B]	BANANARAMA	8	1986
VENUS [B]	DON PABLO'S ANIMALS	4	1990
VENUS AND MARS	JO BREEZER	27	2001
VENUS AS A BOY	BJORK	29	1993
VENUS IN BLUE JEANS	MARK WYNTER	4	1962
VENUS IN FURS (LIVE)	VELVET UNDERGROUND	71	1994
VERDI	MAURO PICOTTO	74	2001
VERMILION	SLIPKNOT	31	2004
VERNON'S WONDERLAND	VERNON'S WONDERLAND	59	1996
VERONICA [A]	ELVIS COSTELLO	31	1989
VERONICA [B]	SULTANS OF PING FC	69	1992
VERSION OF ME	THOUSAND YARD STARE	57	1993
VERTIGO	U2	1	2004
VERY BEST FRIEND	PROUD MARY	75	2001
VERY METAL NOISE POLLUTION (EP)	POP WILL EAT ITSELF	45	1989
A VERY PRECIOUS LOVE	DORIS DAY	16	1958
THE VERY THOUGHT OF YOU	TONY BENNETT	21	1965
THE VERY THOUGHT OF YOU	NATALIE COLE	71	1992
VESSEL	ED RUSH & OPTICAL/UNIVERSAL	61	2002
VIBE	ZHANE	67	1994
VIBEOLOGY	PAULA ABDUL	19	1992
VIBRATOR	TERENCE TRENT D'ARBY	57	1995
VICE	RAZORLIGHT	18	2004
VICIOUS CIRCLES	POLTERGEIST	32	1996
VICIOUS CIRCLES	VICIOUS CIRCLES	68	2000
VICTIM OF LOVE [A]	ERASURE	7	1987
VICTIM OF LOVE [B]	BRYAN ADAMS	68	1987
VICTIMS	CULTURE CLUB	3	1983
VICTIMS OF SUCCESS	DOGS D'AMOUR	36	1990
VICTORIA	KINKS	33	1970
VICTORIA	FALL	35	1988
VICTORY	KOOL & THE GANG	30	1987
VIDEO	INDIA.ARIE	32	2001
VIDEO KILLED THE RADIO STAR	BUGGLES	1	1979
VIDEO KILLED THE RADIO STAR	PRESIDENTS OF THE UNITED STATES OF AMERICA	52	1998
VIDEO KILLED THE RADIO STAR	DRAGONHEART	74	2004
VIDEO PHONE	BEYONCE FEATURING LADY GAGA	58	2010
VIDEOTHEQUE	DOLLAR	17	1982
VIENNA	ULTRAVOX	2	1981
VIENNA CALLING	FALCO	10	1986
VIETNAM	JIMMY CLIFF	46	1970
VIEW FROM A BRIDGE	KIM WILDE	16	1982
A VIEW TO A KILL	DURAN DURAN	2	1985
VILLAGE OF ST BERNADETTE	ANNE SHELTON	27	1959
VINCENT	DON McLEAN	1	1972
VINDALOO	FAT LES	2	1998
VIOLA	MOOGWAI	55	2000
VIOLAINE	COCTEAU TWINS	56	1996

Title / Artist	Peak Position	Year of Release
VIOLENCE OF SUMMER (LOVE'S TAKING OVER) DURAN DURAN	20	1990
VIOLENTLY (EP) HUE & CRY	21	1989
VIOLENTLY HAPPY BJORK	13	1994
VIOLET [A] SEAL	39	1992
VIOLET [B] HOLE	17	1995
VIOLET HILL COLDPLAY	8	2008
VIP JUNGLE BROTHERS	33	1999
VIRGIN MARY LONNIE DONEGAN	27	1960
VIRGINIA PLAIN ROXY MUSIC	4	1972
VIRGINIA PLAIN SLAMM	60	1993
VIRTUAL INSANITY JAMIROQUAI	3	1996
VIRTUALITY VBIRDS	21	2003
VIRUS [A] IRON MAIDEN	16	1996
VIRUS [B] MUTINY UK	42	2001
VISAGE VISAGE	21	1981
THE VISION MARIO PIU PRESENTS DJ ARABESQUE	16	2001
VISION INCISION LO FIDELITY ALLSTARS	30	1998
VISION OF LOVE MARIAH CAREY	9	1990
VISION OF YOU BELINDA CARLISLE	41	1990
VISIONARY REDD KROSS	75	1994
VISIONS [A] CLIFF RICHARD	7	1966
VISIONS [B] LENA FIAGBE	48	1994
VISIONS IN BLUE ULTRAVOX	15	1983
VISIONS OF CHINA JAPAN	32	1981
VISIONS OF PARADISE MICK JAGGER	43	2002
VISIONS OF YOU JAH WOBBLE'S INVADERS OF THE HEART	35	1992
VITAL SIGNS RUSH	41	1981
VITO SATAN CAMPAG VELOCET	75	2000
VIVA BOBBY JOE EQUALS	6	1969
VIVA EL FULHAM TONY REES & THE COTTAGERS	46	1975
VIVA ENGLAND UNDERCOVER	49	2004
VIVA FOREVER SPICE GIRLS	1	1998
VIVA LA MEGABABES SHAMPOO	27	1994
VIVA LA RADIO LOLLY	6	1999
VIVA LA VIDA COLDPLAY	1	2008
VIVA LAS VEGAS ELVIS PRESLEY	15	1964
VIVA LAS VEGAS ZZ TOP	10	1992
VIVE LE ROCK ADAM ANT	50	1985
VIVID ELECTRONIC	17	1999
VIVRANT THING Q-TIP	39	2000
VOGUE MADONNA	1	1990
THE VOICE [A] ULTRAVOX	16	1981
THE VOICE [B] EIMEAR QUINN	40	1996
VOICE IN THE WILDERNESS CLIFF RICHARD	2	1960
VOICE OF FREEDOM FREEDOM WILLIAMS	62	1993
VOICE OF THE SIREN IRRITANT	70	2007
THE VOICE WITHIN CHRISTINA AGUILERA	9	2003
VOICES [A] ANN LEE	27	2000
VOICES [B] DARIO G	37	2000
VOICES [C] BEDROCK	44	2000
VOICES [D] DISTURBED	52	2001
VOICES [E] KC FLIGHTT VS FUNKY JUNCTION	59	2001
VOICES IN THE SKY MOODY BLUES	27	1968
VOID EXOTERIX	58	1993
VOLARE DEAN MARTIN	2	1958
VOLARE DOMENICO MODUGNO	10	1958
VOLARE MARINO MARINI & HIS QUARTET	13	1958
VOLARE CHARLIE DRAKE	28	1958
VOLARE BOBBY RYDELL	22	1960
VOLCANO DAMIEN RICE	29	2005
VOLCANO GIRLS VERUCA SALT	56	1997
VOLUME 1 (WHAT YOU WANT WHAT YOU NEED) INDUSTRY STANDARD	34	1998
VOODOO WARRIOR	37	2001
VOODOO CHILD ROGUE TRADERS	3	2006
VOODOO CHILE JIMI HENDRIX EXPERIENCE	1	1970
VOODOO LOVE LEE-CABRERA	58	2004
VOODOO PEOPLE PRODIGY	13	1994
VOODOO RAY A GUY CALLED GERALD	12	1989
VOODOO VOODOO DEN HEGARTY	73	1979
VOULEZ-VOUS ABBA	3	1979
THE VOW TOYAH	50	1983
VOYAGE VOYAGE DESIRELESS	5	1987
VOYAGER PENDULUM	46	2004
VOYEUR KIM CARNES	68	1982
VULNERABLE ROXETTE	44	1995

W

Title / Artist	Peak Position	Year of Release
WACK ASS MF RHYTHMKILLAZ	32	2001
WADE IN THE WATER RAMSEY LEWIS	31	1972
WAGES DAY DEACON BLUE	18	1989
THE WAGON DINOSAUR, JR	49	1991
WAIL JON SPENCER BLUES EXPLOSION	66	1997
WAIT ROBERT HOWARD & KYM MAZELLE	7	1989
WAIT A MINUTE RAY J FEATURING LIL' KIM	54	2001
WAIT AND BLEED SLIPKNOT	27	2000
WAIT FOR ME MALCOLM VAUGHAN	13	1959
WAIT FOR ME DARLING JOAN REGAN & THE JOHNSTON BROTHERS	18	1954
WAIT FOR ME MARIANNE MARMALADE	30	1968
WAIT (THE WHISPER SONG) YING YANG TWINS	47	2005
WAIT UNTIL MIDNIGHT YELLOW DOG	54	1978
WAIT UNTIL TONIGHT (MY LOVE) GALAXY FEATURING PHIL FEARON	20	1983
WAIT YOUR TURN RIHANNA	45	2009
WAITIN' FOR A SUPERMAN FLAMING LIPS	73	1999
WAITING [A] STYLE COUNCIL	52	1987
WAITING [B] GREEN DAY	34	2001
THE WAITING 18 AMEN	61	2001
WAITING FOR A GIRL LIKE YOU FOREIGNER	8	1981
WAITING FOR A STAR TO FALL BOY MEETS GIRL	9	1988
WAITING FOR A TRAIN FLASH & THE PAN	7	1983
WAITING FOR AN ALIBI THIN LIZZY	9	1979
WAITING FOR THAT DAY GEORGE MICHAEL	23	1990
(WAITING FOR) THE GHOST TRAIN MADNESS	18	1986
WAITING FOR THE GREAT LEAP FORWARDS BILLY BRAGG	52	1988
WAITING FOR THE LOVEBOAT ASSOCIATES	53	1984
WAITING FOR THE NIGHT SAXON	66	1986
WAITING FOR THE SIRENS' CALL NEW ORDER	21	2005
WAITING FOR THE SUMMER DELIRIOUS?	26	2001
WAITING FOR THE SUN RUFF DRIVERZ	37	1999
WAITING FOR TONIGHT JENNIFER LOPEZ	5	1999
WAITING 4 PETER GELDERBLOM	29	2007
WAITING GAME COOPER TEMPLE CLAUSE	41	2007
WAITING HOPEFULLY D*NOTE	46	1997
WAITING IN VAIN BOB MARLEY & THE WAILERS	27	1977
WAITING IN VAIN LEE RITENOUR & MAXI PRIEST	65	1993
WAITING IN VAIN ANNIE LENNOX	31	1995
WAITING ON A FRIEND ROLLING STONES	50	1981
WAKE IN THE CITY IKARA COLT	55	2004
WAKE ME UP GIRLS ALOUD	4	2005
WAKE ME UP BEFORE YOU GO GO WHAM!	1	1984
WAKE ME UP BEFORE YOU GO GO TEAM DEC	64	2009
WAKE ME UP WHEN SEPTEMBER ENDS GREEN DAY	8	2005
WAKE UP [A] DANSE SOCIETY	61	1983
WAKE UP [B] LOSTPROPHETS	18	2004
WAKE UP [C] HILARY DUFF	7	2005
WAKE UP [D] ARCADE FIRE	29	2005
WAKE UP AND SCRATCH ME SULTANS OF PING	50	1994
WAKE UP BOO! BOO RADLEYS	9	1995
WAKE UP CALL MAROON 5	33	2007
WAKE UP DEAD MEGADETH	65	1987
WAKE UP EVERYBODY HAROLD MELVIN & THE BLUENOTES	23	1976
WAKE UP LITTLE SUSIE EVERLY BROTHERS	2	1957
WAKE UP LITTLE SUSIE KING BROTHERS	22	1957
WAKE UP SUSAN DETROIT SPINNERS	29	1977
WAKING UP ELASTICA	13	1995
WAKING UP IN VEGAS KATY PERRY	19	2009
WAKING WITH A STRANGER TYRREL CORPORATION	59	1992
WALHALLA GOURYELLA	27	1999
THE WALK [A] INMATES	36	1980
THE WALK [B] CURE	12	1983
WALK [C] PANTERA	35	1993
WALK AWAY [A] SHANE FENTON & THE FENTONES	38	1962
WALK AWAY [B] MATT MONRO	4	1964
WALK AWAY [C] SISTERS OF MERCY	45	1984
WALK AWAY [D] JOYCE SIMS	24	1988
WALK AWAY [F] FRANZ FERDINAND	13	2005
WALK AWAY [G] KELLY CLARKSON	21	2006
WALK AWAY [H] FUNERAL FOR A FRIEND	40	2007
WALK AWAY FROM LOVE DAVID RUFFIN	10	1976
WALK AWAY RENEE FOUR TOPS	3	1967
WALK DON'T RUN VENTURES	8	1960
WALK DON'T RUN JOHN BARRY SEVEN	11	1960
WALK/DON'T WALK MY LIFE STORY	48	2000
WALK HAND IN HAND TONY MARTIN	2	1956
WALK HAND IN HAND RONNIE CARROLL	13	1956
WALK HAND IN HAND JIMMY PARKINSON	26	1956
WALK HAND IN HAND GERRY & THE PACEMAKERS	29	1965
WALK IDIOT WALK HIVES	13	2004
WALK IN LOVE MANHATTAN TRANSFER	12	1978
A WALK IN THE BLACK FOREST HORST JANKOWSKI	3	1965
A WALK IN THE DARK WHITEY	67	2005
WALK IN THE NIGHT JUNIOR WALKER & THE ALL-STARS	16	1972
WALK IN THE NIGHT PAUL HARDCASTLE	54	1988
A WALK IN THE PARK NICK STRAKER BAND	20	1980
WALK INTO THE SUN DIRTY VEGAS	54	2004
WALK INTO THE WIND VEGAS	65	1993
WALK LIKE A CHAMPION KALIPHZ FEATURING PRINCE NASEEM	23	1996
WALK LIKE A MAN FOUR SEASONS	12	1963
WALK LIKE A MAN DIVINE	23	1985
WALK LIKE A PANTHER '98 ALL SEEING I FEATURING TONY CHRISTIE	10	1999
WALK LIKE AN EGYPTIAN BANGLES	3	1986
WALK OF LIFE [A] DIRE STRAITS	2	1986
WALK OF LIFE [B] BILLIE PIPER	25	2000
WALK ON [A] ROY ORBISON	39	1968
WALK ON [B] U2	5	2001
WALK ON AIR T'PAU	62	1991
WALK ON BY [A] LEROY VAN DYKE	5	1962
WALK ON BY [B] DIONNE WARWICK	9	1964
WALK ON BY [B] STRANGLERS	21	1978
WALK ON BY [B] AVERAGE WHITE BAND	46	1979
WALK ON BY [B] D TRAIN	44	1982
WALK ON BY [B] SYBIL	6	1990
WALK ON BY [B] GABRIELLE	7	1997
WALK ON GILDED SPLINTERS MARSHA HUNT	46	1969
WALK ON THE WILD SIDE LOU REED	10	1973
WALK ON THE WILD SIDE JAMIE J MORGAN	27	1990
WALK ON THE WILD SIDE BEAT SYSTEM	63	1990
WALK ON WATER MILK INC	10	2002
WALK OUT TO WINTER AZTEC CAMERA	64	1983

Title / Artist	Peak Position	Year of Release
WALK RIGHT BACK EVERLY BROTHERS	1	1961
WALK RIGHT BACK PERRY COMO	33	1973
WALK RIGHT IN ROOFTOP SINGERS	10	1963
WALK RIGHT NOW JACKSONS	7	1981
WALK TALL VAL DOONICAN	3	1964
WALK THE DINOSAUR WAS (NOT WAS)	10	1987
WALK...(THE DOG) LIKE AN EGYPTIAN JODE FEATURING YO-HANS	48	1998
WALK THIS LAND E-Z ROLLERS	18	1999
WALK THIS WAY RUN DMC	8	1986
WALK THIS WAY SUGABABES VS GIRLS ALOUD	1	2007
WALK THIS WORLD HEATHER NOVA	69	1995
WALK THROUGH THE FIRE PETER GABRIEL	69	1984
WALK THROUGH THE WORLD MARC COHN	37	1993
WALK WITH FAITH IN YOUR HEART BACHELORS	21	1966
WALK WITH ME SEEKERS	10	1966
WALK WITH ME MY ANGEL DON CHARLES	39	1962
WALK WITH ME TALK WITH ME DARLING FOUR TOPS	32	1972
WALKAWAY CAST	9	1996
WALKED OUTTA HEAVEN JAGGED EDGE	21	2004
WALKIE TALKIE MAN STERIOGRAM	19	2004
WALKIN' C.C.S.	7	1971
WALKIN' BACK TO HAPPINESS HELEN SHAPIRO	1	1961
WALKIN' IN THE RAIN WITH THE ONE I LOVE LOVE UNLIMITED	14	1972
A WALKIN' MIRACLE LIMMIE & THE FAMILY COOKIN'	6	1974
WALKIN' ON SHEER BRONZE FEATURING LISA MILLETT	63	1994
WALKIN' ON THE SUN SMASH MOUTH	19	1997
WALKIN' ON UP DJ PROF-X-OR	64	1997
WALKIN' TALL [A] FRANKIE VAUGHAN	28	1959
WALKIN' TALL [B] ADAM FAITH	23	1963
WALKIN' THE DOG DENNISONS	36	1964
WALKIN' THE LINE BRASS CONSTRUCTION	47	1983
WALKIN' TO MISSOURI TONY BRENT	7	1952
WALKING AFTER YOU FOO FIGHTERS	20	1998
WALKING ALONE RICHARD ANTHONY	37	1963
WALKING AWAY [A] CRAIG DAVID	3	2000
WALKING AWAY [B] EGG VERSUS DAVID GUETTA	56	2006
WALKING BY MYSELF GARY MOORE	48	1990
WALKING DEAD PURESSENCE	40	2002
WALKING DOWN MADISON KIRSTY MacCOLL	23	1991
WALKING DOWN YOUR STREET BANGLES	16	1987
WALKING IN MEMPHIS MARC COHN	22	1991
WALKING IN MEMPHIS CHER	11	1995
WALKING IN MY SHOES DEPECHE MODE	14	1993
WALKING IN MY SLEEP ROGER DALTREY	56	1984
WALKING IN RHYTHM BLACKBYRDS	23	1975
WALKING IN THE AIR ALED JONES	5	1985
WALKING IN THE AIR PETER AUTY & THE SINFONIA OF LONDON	37	1985
WALKING IN THE AIR DIGITAL DREAM BABY	49	1991
WALKING IN THE NAME FUNKSTAR DE LUXE VS TERRY MAXX	42	2000
WALKING IN THE RAIN [A] WALKER BROTHERS	26	1967
WALKING IN THE RAIN [A] PARTRIDGE FAMILY STARRING DAVID CASSIDY	10	1973
WALKING IN THE RAIN [B] MODERN ROMANCE	7	1983
WALKING IN THE SUN TRAVIS	20	2004
WALKING IN THE SUNSHINE BAD MANNERS	10	1981
WALKING INTO SUNSHINE CENTRAL LINE	42	1981
WALKING MY BABY BACK HOME JOHNNIE RAY	12	1952
WALKING MY CAT NAMED DOG NORMA TANEGA	22	1966
WALKING ON A DREAM EMPIRE OF THE SUN	64	2009
WALKING ON AIR [A] FRAZIER CHORUS	60	1991
WALKING ON AIR [B] BAD BOYS INC	24	1993
WALKING ON BROKEN GLASS ANNIE LENNOX	8	1992
WALKING ON ICE RIVER CITY PEOPLE	62	1990
WALKING ON SUNSHINE [A] ROCKER'S REVENGE FEATURING DONNIE CALVIN	4	1982
WALKING ON SUNSHINE [A] EDDY GRANT	57	1989
WALKING ON SUNSHINE [A] KRUSH	71	1992
WALKING ON SUNSHINE [B] KATRINA & THE WAVES	8	1985
WALKING ON SUNSHINE [B] GLEE CAST	9	2010
WALKING ON THE CHINESE WALL PHILIP BAILEY	34	1985
WALKING ON THE MILKY WAY ORCHESTRAL MANOEUVRES IN THE DARK	17	1996
WALKING ON THE MOON POLICE	1	1979
WALKING ON THIN ICE YOKO ONO	35	1981
WALKING ON WATER MADASUN	14	2000
WALKING SHADE BILLY CORGAN	74	2005
WALKING THE FLOOR OVER YOU PAT BOONE	39	1960
WALKING TO NEW ORLEANS FATS DOMINO	19	1960
WALKING WITH THEE CLINIC	65	2002
WALKING WOUNDED EVERYTHING BUT THE GIRL	6	1996
WALL STREET SHUFFLE 10 C.C.	10	1974
WALL TO WALL CHRIS BROWN	75	2007
WALLFLOWER MEGA CITY FOUR	69	1993
WALLS COME TUMBLING DOWN! STYLE COUNCIL	6	1985
THE WALLS FELL DOWN MARBLES	28	1969
WALTZ #2 (XO) ELLIOTT SMITH	52	1998
WALTZ AWAY DREAMING TOBY BOURKE/ GEORGE MICHAEL	10	1997
WALTZ DARLING MALCOLM McLAREN & THE BOOTZILLA ORCHESTRA	31	1989
WALTZING ALONG JAMES	23	1997
WAM BAM [A] HANDLEY FAMILY	30	1973
WAM BAM [B] NT GANG	71	1988
THE WAND FLAMING LIPS	41	2006
THE WANDERER [A] DION	10	1962
THE WANDERER [A] STATUS QUO	7	1984
THE WANDERER [B] DONNA SUMMER	48	1980
WANDERIN' EYES CHARLIE GRACIE	6	1957
WANDERIN' EYES FRANKIE VAUGHAN	6	1957
THE WANDERING DRAGON SHADES OF RHYTHM	55	1994
WANDERLUST [A] DELAYS	28	2004
WANDERLUST [B] R.E.M.	27	2005
WAND'RIN' STAR LEE MARVIN	1	1970
WANNA BE STARTIN' SOMETHING MICHAEL JACKSON	8	1983
WANNA BE THAT WAY IKARA COLT	49	2004
WANNA BE WITH YOU JINNY	30	1995
WANNA BE YOUR LOVER GAYLE & GILLIAN	62	1994
WANNA DROP A HOUSE (ON THAT BITCH) URBAN DISCHARGE FEATURING SHE	51	1996
WANNA GET TO KNOW YA G UNIT	27	2004
WANNA GET UP 2 UNLIMITED	38	1998
WANNA MAKE YOU GO...UUH! THOSE 2 GIRLS	74	1994
WANNABE SPICE GIRLS	1	1996
WANNABE GANGSTER WHEATUS	22	2002
WANT LOVE HYSTERIC EGO	28	1996
WANT YOU BAD OFFSPRING	15	2001
WANTED [A] AL MARTINO	4	1954
WANTED [A] PERRY COMO	4	1954
WANTED [B] DOOLEYS	3	1979
WANTED [C] STYLE COUNCIL	20	1987
WANTED [D] HALO JAMES	45	1989
WANTED [E] PRINCESS IVORI	69	1990
WANTED DEAD OR ALIVE [A] BON JOVI	13	1987
WANTED DEAD OR ALIVE [B] 2PAC & SNOOP DOGGY DOGG	16	1997
WANTED IT ALL CLAYTOWN TROUPE	74	1992
WAP-BAM-BOOGIE MATT BIANCO	11	1988
WAR [A] EDWIN STARR	3	1970
WAR [A] BRUCE SPRINGSTEEN	18	1986
WAR [B] UGLY RUMOURS	21	2007
WAR BABIES SIMPLE MINDS	43	1998
WAR BABY TOM ROBINSON	6	1983
WAR CHILD BLONDIE	39	1982
WAR LORD SHADOWS	18	1965
WAR OF NERVES ALL SAINTS	7	1998
WAR OF THE WORLDS GET CAPE. WEAR CAPE. FLY.	39	2006
WAR PARTY EDDY GRANT	42	1983
THE WAR SONG CULTURE CLUB	2	1984
WAR STORIES STARJETS	51	1979
WARFAIR CLAWFINGER	54	1994
WARHEAD UK SUBS	30	1980
WARLOCK BLACK RIOT	68	1988
WARM AND TENDER LOVE PERCY SLEDGE	34	1966
WARM IT UP KRIS KROSS	16	1992
WARM LOVE BEATMASTERS FEATURING CLAUDIA FONTAINE	51	1989
WARM MACHINE BUSH	45	2000
WARM SUMMER DAZE VYBE	60	1995
WARM THIS WINTER GABRIELLA CILMI	22	2008
WARM WET CIRCLES MARILLION	22	1987
WARMED OVER KISSES BRIAN HYLAND	28	1962
WARNING [A] ADEVA	17	1989
WARNING [B] AKA	43	1996
WARNING [C] FREESTYLERS FEATURING NAVIGATOR	68	1998
WARNING [D] GREEN DAY	27	2000
WARNING SIGN NICK HEYWARD	25	1984
WARPAINT BROOK BROTHERS	5	1961
WARPED RED HOT CHILI PEPPERS	31	1995
WARRIOR [A] MC WILDSKI	49	1990
WARRIOR [B] DANCE 2 TRANCE	56	1995
WARRIOR [C] WARRIOR	19	2000
WARRIOR GROOVE DSM	68	1985
WARRIOR SOUND PRESSURE DROP	72	2001
WARRIORS [A] GARY NUMAN	20	1983
WARRIORS [B] ASWAD	33	1994
WARRIOR'S DANCE PRODIGY	13	2009
WARRIORS (OF THE WASTELAND) FRANKIE GOES TO HOLLYWOOD	19	1986
WARWICK AVENUE DUFFY	3	2008
WAS IT WORTH IT PET SHOP BOYS	24	1991
WAS THAT ALL IT WAS KYM MAZELLE	33	1990
WAS THAT YOU SPEAR OF DESTINY	55	1987
WASH IN THE RAIN BEES	31	2004
WASH YOUR FACE IN MY SINK DREAM WARRIORS	16	1990
WASHOUT FALLOUT TRUST	75	2006
WASSUUP DA MUTTZ	11	2000
WASTE A MOMENT FIGHTSTAR	29	2006
WASTED DEF LEPPARD	61	1979
WASTED SMALLER	72	1996
WASTED IN AMERICA LOVE/HATE	38	1992
WASTED LITTLE DJS VIEW	15	2006
WASTED TIME [A] SKID ROW	20	1991
WASTED TIME [B] KINGS OF LEON	51	2003
WASTED YEARS IRON MAIDEN	18	1986
WASTELAND MISSION	11	1987
WASTELANDS MIDGE URE	46	1986
WASTER REEF	56	2003
WASTING MY TIME [A] DEFAULT	73	2003
WASTING MY TIME [B] KOSHEEN	49	2003
WATCH ME LABI SIFFRE	29	1972

Title / Artist	Peak Position	Year of Release
WATCH OUT [A] BRANDI WELLS	74	1982
WATCH OUT [B] FERRY CORSTEN	57	2006
WATCH OUT [C] ALEX GAUDINO FEATURING SHENA	16	2008
WATCH THE MIRACLE START PAULINE HENRY	54	1994
WATCH THE SUN COME UP EXAMPLE	19	2009
WATCH THE SUNRISE AXWELL FEATURING STEVE EDWARDS	70	2006
WATCH WHAT YOU SAY GURU FEATURING CHAKA KHAN	28	1995
WATCHA GONNA DO KEISHA WHITE	53	2004
WATCHA GONNA DO WITH MY LOVIN' INNER CITY	12	1989
WATCHDOGS UB40	39	1987
A WATCHER'S POINT OF VIEW PM DAWN	36	1991
WATCHIN' FREEMASONS FEATURING AMANDA WILSON	19	2006
WATCHING THOMPSON TWINS	33	1983
WATCHING CARS GO BY FELIX DA HOUSECAT	49	2004
WATCHING THE DETECTIVES ELVIS COSTELLO	15	1977
WATCHING THE RIVER FLOW BOB DYLAN	24	1971
WATCHING THE WHEELS JOHN LENNON	30	1981
WATCHING THE WILDLIFE FRANKIE GOES TO HOLLYWOOD	28	1987
WATCHING THE WORLD GO BY MAXI PRIEST	36	1996
WATCHING WINDOWS RONI SIZE/ REPRAZENT	28	1998
WATCHING XANADU MULL HISTORICAL SOCIETY	36	2002
WATCHING YOU [A] ETHER	74	1998
WATCHING YOU [B] ROGUE TRADERS	33	2006
WATCHING YOU WATCHING ME DAVID GRANT	10	1983
WATER [A] GENO WASHINGTON & THE RAM JAM BAND	39	1966
WATER [B] MARTIKA	59	1990
WATER FROM A VINE LEAF WILLIAM ORBIT	59	1993
THE WATER IS OVER MY HEAD ROCKIN' BERRIES	43	1996
THE WATER MARGIN GODIEGO	37	1977
THE WATER MARGIN PETE MAC, JR	37	1977
WATER ON GLASS KIM WILDE	11	1981
WATER RUNS DRY BOYZ II MEN	24	1995
WATER WATER TOMMY STEELE & THE STEELMEN	5	1957
WATER WAVE MARK VAN DALE WITH ENRICO	71	1998
WATERFALL [A] WENDY & LISA	66	1987
WATERFALL [B] STONE ROSES	27	1992
WATERFALL [C] ATLANTIC OCEAN	21	1994
WATERFALLS [A] PAUL McCARTNEY	9	1980
WATERFALLS [B] TLC	4	1995
WATERFRONT SIMPLE MINDS	13	1983
WATERLOO [A] STONEWALL JACKSON	24	1959
WATERLOO [B] ABBA	1	1974
WATERLOO [B] DOCTOR & THE MEDICS FEATURING ROY WOOD	45	1986
WATERLOO SUNSET KINKS	2	1967
WATERLOO SUNSET CATHY DENNIS	11	1997
WATERMAN OLAV BASOSKI FEATURING MICHIE ONE	45	2005
WATERY, DOMESTIC (EP) PAVEMENT	58	1992
THE WAVE COSMIC GATE	48	2003
THE WAVE OF THE FUTURE QUADROPHONIA	40	1991
WAVES BLANCMANGE	19	1983
WAVING FLAGS BRITISH SEA POWER	31	2008
WAVY GRAVY SASHA	64	2002
WAX THE VAN LOLA	65	1987
THE WAY [A] FUNKY GREEN DOGS	43	1997
THE WAY [B] GLOBAL COMMUNICATION	51	1997
THE WAY [C] FASTBALL	21	1998
THE WAY [D] DANIEL BEDINGFIELD	41	2005
WAY AWAY YELLOWCARD	63	2004
WAY BACK HOME JUNIOR WALKER & THE ALL-STARS	35	1973
WAY BEHIND ME PRIMITIVES	36	1988
WAY DOWN ELVIS PRESLEY	1	1977
WAY DOWN NOW WORLD PARTY	66	1990
WAY DOWN YONDER IN NEW ORLEANS FREDDY CANNON	3	1960
THE WAY DREAMS ARE DANIEL O'DONNELL	18	1999
THE WAY I AM EMINEM	8	2000
THE WAY I ARE TIMBALAND FEATURING DOE & KERI HILSON	1	2007
THE WAY I FEEL [A] LEMON TREES	62	1992
THE WAY I FEEL [B] ROACHFORD	20	1997
THE WAY I FEEL ABOUT YOU KARYN WHITE	65	1992
THE WAY I WALK JACK SCOTT	30	1959
THE WAY I WANT TO TOUCH YOU CAPTAIN & TENNILLE	28	1976
WAY IN MY BRAIN SL2	26	1991
THE WAY IT GOES STATUS QUO	39	1999
THE WAY IT IS BRUCE HORNSBY & THE RANGE	15	1986
THE WAY IT IS CHAMELEON	34	1996
THE WAY IT USED TO BE ENGELBERT HUMPERDINCK	3	1969
THE WAY IT WAS/REDHEAD BARON	71	2004
THE WAY IT'S GOIN' DOWN (T.W.I.S.M. FOR LIFE) SHAQUILLE O'NEAL	62	1998
A WAY OF LIFE [A] FAMILY DOGG	6	1969
WAY OF LIFE [B] DAVE CLARKE	59	2003
WAY OF THE WORLD [A] CHEAP TRICK	73	1980
WAY OF THE WORLD [B] TINA TURNER	13	1991
THE WAY (PUT YOUR HAND IN MY HAND) DIVINE INSPIRATION	5	2002
THE WAY SHE LOVES ME RICHARD MARX	38	1994
THE WAY THAT YOU FEEL ADEVA	54	1997
THE WAY THAT YOU LOVE ME VANESSA WILLIAMS	52	1995
THE WAY TO YOUR LOVE HEAR'SAY	1	2001
THE WAY WE WERE BARBRA STREISAND	31	1974
THE WAY WE WERE – TRY TO REMEMBER GLADYS KNIGHT & THE PIPS	4	1975
THE WAY YOU ARE TEARS FOR FEARS	24	1983
THE WAY YOU DO THE THINGS YOU DO UB40	49	1991
THE WAY YOU LIKE IT ADEMA	61	2002
THE WAY YOU LOOK TONIGHT LETTERMEN	36	1961
THE WAY YOU LOOK TONIGHT DENNY SEYTON & THE SABRES	48	1964
THE WAY YOU LOOK TONIGHT EDWARD WOODWARD	42	1971
THE WAY YOU LOVE ME [A] KARYN WHITE	42	1988
THE WAY YOU LOVE ME [B] FAITH HILL	15	2001
THE WAY YOU MAKE ME FEEL [A] MICHAEL JACKSON	3	1987
THE WAY YOU MAKE ME FEEL [B] RONAN KEATING	6	2000
THE WAY YOU MOVE OUTKAST FEATURING SLEEPY BROWN	7	2004
THE WAY YOU USED TO SMILE RESEARCH	66	2005
THE WAY YOU WORK IT E.Y.C.	14	1994
WAYDOWN CATHERINE WHEEL	67	1995
WAYS OF LOVE CLAYTOWN TROUPE	57	1990
WAYUH (PEOPLE DON'T DANCE NO MORE) RAPTURE	65	2006
WAYWARD WIND TEX RITTER	8	1956
WAYWARD WIND GOGI GRANT	9	1956
WAYWARD WIND JIMMY YOUNG	27	1956
THE WAYWARD WIND FRANK IFIELD	1	1963
WE ALL FOLLOW MAN. UNITED MANCHESTER UNITED FC	10	1985
WE ALL SLEEP ALONE CHER	47	1988
WE ALL STAND TOGETHER PAUL McCARTNEY & THE FROG CHORUS	3	1984
WE ALMOST GOT IT TOGETHER TANITA TIKARAM	52	1990
WE APOLOGISE FOR NOTHING FIGHTSTAR	63	2007
WE ARE ANA JOHNSSON	8	2004
WE ARE ALIVE PAUL VAN DYK	15	2000
WE ARE ALL MADE OF STARS MOBY	11	2002
WE ARE ALL ON DRUGS WEEZER	47	2005
WE ARE BACK LFO	47	1991
WE ARE DA CLICK DA CLICK	38	1999
WE ARE DETECTIVE THOMPSON TWINS	7	1983
WE ARE EACH OTHER BEAUTIFUL SOUTH	30	1992
WE ARE E-MALE E-MALE	44	1998
WE ARE ENGLAND RICKY	54	2006
WE ARE FAMILY SISTER SLEDGE	5	1979
WE ARE GLASS GARY NUMAN	5	1980
WE ARE GOING ON DOWN DEADLY SINS	45	1994
WE ARE GOLDEN MIKA	4	2009
WE ARE I. E. LENNIE DE ICE	61	1999
WE ARE IN LOVE [A] ADAM FAITH & THE ROULETTES	11	1963
WE ARE IN LOVE [B] HARRY CONNICK, JR	62	1991
WE ARE LOVE DJ ERIC	37	1999
WE ARE NOT ALONE FRANKIE VAUGHAN	11	1958
WE ARE RAVING – THE ANTHEM SLIPSTREEM	18	1992
WE ARE THE BAND MORE	59	1981
WE ARE THE CHAMPIONS QUEEN	2	1977
WE ARE THE CHAMPIONS HANK MARVIN FEATURING BRIAN MAY	66	1992
WE ARE THE CHAMPIONS CRAZY FROG	11	2006
WE ARE THE FIRM COCKNEY REJECTS	54	1980
WE ARE THE PEOPLE [A] FEEDER	25	2008
WE ARE THE PEOPLE [B] EMPIRE OF THE SUN	14	2009
WE ARE THE PIGS SUEDE	18	1994
WE ARE THE WORLD USA FOR AFRICA	1	1985
WE ARE THE WORLD 25 FOR HAITI ARTISTS FOR HAITI	50	2010
WE ARE YOUR FRIENDS JUSTICE VERSUS SIMIAN	20	2006
WE BE BURNIN' SEAN PAUL	2	2005
WE BELONG PAT BENATAR	22	1985
WE BELONG IN THIS WORLD TOGETHER STEREO MC'S	59	2001
WE BELONG TOGETHER MARIAH CAREY	2	2005
WE BREAK THE DAWN MICHELLE WILLIAMS	47	2008
WE BUILT THIS CITY STARSHIP	12	1985
WE CALL IT ACIEED D MOB FEATURING GARY HAISMAN	3	1988
WE CAME TO DANCE ULTRAVOX	18	1983
WE CAN LeANN RIMES	27	2003
WE CAN BE BRAVE AGAIN ARMOURY SHOW	66	1985
WE CAN BE STRONG WILLY MASON	52	2007
WE CAN DO ANYTHING COCKNEY REJECTS	65	1980
WE CAN DO IT (EP) LIVERPOOL FC	15	1977
WE CAN GET DOWN MYRON	74	1997
WE CAN MAKE IT MONE	64	1995
WE CAN MAKE IT HAPPEN PRINCE CHARLES & THE CITY BEAT BAND	56	1986
WE CAN WORK IT OUT [A] BEATLES	1	1965
WE CAN WORK IT OUT [A] STEVIE WONDER	27	1971
WE CAN WORK IT OUT [A] FOUR SEASONS	34	1976
WE CAN WORK IT OUT [B] BRASS CONSTRUCTION	70	1983
WE CARE A LOT FAITH NO MORE	53	1988
WE CLOSE OUR EYES GO WEST	5	1985
WE CLOSE OUR EYES GROOVE CUTTERS	33	2005
WE COME 1 FAITHLESS	3	2001
WE COME TO PARTY N-TYCE	12	1997
WE COULD BE KINGS GENE	17	1997
WE COULD BE TOGETHER DEBBIE GIBSON	22	1989
WE CRY SCRIPT	15	2008
WE DANCED TOGETHER RAKES	38	2007

Title / Artist	Peak Position	Year of Release
WE DIDN'T START THE FIRE BILLY JOEL	7	1989
WE DO IT R & J STONE	5	1976
WE DON'T CARE AUDIOBULLYS	15	2002
WE DON'T CARE AKON	61	2009
WE DON'T HAVE TO... JERMAINE STEWART	2	1986
WE DON'T HAVE TO TAKE OUR CLOTHES OFF DA PLAYAZ VS CLEA	35	2005
WE DON'T HAVE TO TAKE OUR CLOTHES OFF LIL' CHRIS	63	2007
WE DON'T NEED A REASON DARE	52	1991
WE DON'T NEED ANOTHER HERO (THUNDERDOME) TINA TURNER	3	1985
WE DON'T NEED NOBODY ELSE WHIPPING BOY	51	1995
(WE DON'T NEED THIS) FASCIST GROOVE THANG HEAVEN 17	40	1981
WE DON'T TALK ANYMORE CLIFF RICHARD	1	1979
WE DON'T WORK FOR FREE GRANDMASTER MELLE MEL & THE FURIOUS FIVE	45	1984
WE FIT TOGETHER O-TOWN	20	2001
WE GOT A LOVE THANG CE CE PENISTON	6	1992
WE GOT IT IMMATURE FEATURING SMOOTH	26	1996
WE GOT LOVE ALMA COGAN	26	1959
WE GOT OUR OWN THANG HEAVY D. & THE BOYZ	69	1989
WE GOT THE FUNK POSITIVE FORCE	18	1980
WE GOT THE GROOVE PLAYERS ASSOCIATION	61	1980
WE GOT THE LOVE [A] TOUCH OF SOUL	46	1990
WE GOT THE LOVE [B] LINDY LAYTON	38	1993
WE GOT THE LOVE [B] ERIK	55	1994
WE GOT THE LOVE [C] TRI	61	1995
WE GOTTA DO IT DJ PROFESSOR FEATURING FRANCESCO ZAPPALA	57	1991
WE GOTTA GET OUT OF THIS PLACE ANIMALS	2	1965
WE GOTTA GET OUT OF THIS PLACE ANGELIC UPSTARTS	65	1980
WE GOTTA LOVE KYM SIMS	58	1996
WE HATE IT WHEN OUR FRIENDS BECOME SUCCESSFUL MORRISSEY	17	1992
WE HAVE A DREAM SCOTLAND WORLD CUP SQUAD	5	1982
WE HAVE A DREAM PUDSEY'S BEAUTIFUL DREAMERS WITH THE TARTAN ARMY	40	2008
WE HAVE ALL THE TIME IN THE WORLD LOUIS ARMSTRONG	3	1994
WE HAVE EXPLOSIVE FUTURE SOUND OF LONDON	12	1997
WE HAVEN'T TURNED AROUND GOMEZ	38	1999
WE JUST BE DREAMIN' BLAZIN' SQUAD	3	2003
WE JUST WANNA PARTY WITH YOU SNOOP DOGGY DOGG FEATURING JD	21	1997
WE KILL THE WORLD (DON'T KILL THE WORLD) BONEY M	39	1981
WE KNOW SOMETHING YOU DON'T KNOW DJ FORMAT FEATURING CHALI 2NA & AKIL	73	2003
WE LAUGHED ROSETTA LIFE FEATURING BILLY BRAGG	11	2005
WE LET THE STARS GO PREFAB SPROUT	50	1990
WE LIKE TO PARTY (THE VENGABUS) VENGABOYS	3	1999
WE LOVE EACH OTHER CHARLIE RICH	37	1975
WE LOVE YOU [A] ROLLING STONES	8	1967
WE LOVE YOU [B] ORCHESTRAL MANOEUVRES IN THE DARK	54	1986
WE LOVE YOU [C] MENSWEAR	22	1996
WE LUV U GRAND THEFT AUDIO	70	2001
WE MADE IT BUSTA RHYMES FEATURING LINKIN PARK	10	2008
WE MADE YOU EMINEM	4	2009
WE NEED A RESOLUTION AALIYAH FEATURING TIMBALAND	20	2001
WE NEED LOVE CASHMERE	52	1985
WE R ONE SAME DIFFERENCE	13	2008
WE RIDE RIHANNA	17	2006
WE ROCK DIO	42	1984
WE RUN THIS MISSY ELLIOTT	38	2006
WE SAIL ON THE STORMY WATERS GARY CLARK	34	1993
WE SHALL OVERCOME JOAN BAEZ	26	1965
WE SHOULD BE TOGETHER CLIFF RICHARD	10	1991
WE SHOULDN'T HOLD HANDS IN THE DARK L.A. MIX	69	1991
WE TAKE MYSTERY (TO BED) GARY NUMAN	9	1982
WE THUGGIN' FAT JOE	48	2002
WE TRYING TO STAY ALIVE WYCLEF JEAN & THE REFUGEE ALLSTARS	13	1997
WE USED TO BE FRIENDS DANDY WARHOLS	18	2003
WE WAIT AND WE WONDER PHIL COLLINS	45	1994
WE WALK TING TINGS	58	2009
WE WALKED IN LOVE DOLLAR	61	1986
WE WANNA THANK YOU (THE THINGS YOU DO) BIG BROVAZ	17	2004
(WE WANT) THE SAME THING BELINDA CARLISLE	6	1990
WE WANT YOUR SOUL FREELAND	35	2003
WE WEREN'T BORN TO FOLLOW BON JOVI	25	2009
WE WILL GILBERT O'SULLIVAN	16	1971
WE WILL MAKE LOVE RUSS HAMILTON	2	1957
WE WILL MEET AGAIN OLETA ADAMS	51	1996
WE WILL NEVER BE THIS YOUNG AGAIN DANNY WILLIAMS	44	1961
WE WILL ROCK YOU FIVE & QUEEN	1	2000
WE WILL SURVIVE WARP BROTHERS	19	2001
WEAK [A] SWV	33	1993
WEAK [B] SKUNK ANANSIE	20	1996
WEAK BECOME HEROES STREETS	27	2002
WEAK IN THE PRESENCE OF BEAUTY ALISON MOYET	6	1987
WEAK SPOT EVELYN THOMAS	26	1976
THE WEAKNESS IN ME KEISHA WHITE	17	2006
WEAPON OF CHOICE BLACK REBEL MOTORCYCLE CLUB	35	2007
WEAR MY HAT PHIL COLLINS	43	1997
WEAR MY KISS SUGABABES	7	2010
WEAR MY RING AROUND YOUR NECK ELVIS PRESLEY	3	1958
WEAR YOU TO THE BALL UB40	35	1990
WEAR YOUR LOVE LIKE HEAVEN DEFINITION OF SOUND	17	1991
WEARING MY ROLEX WILEY	2	2008
WEATHER FORECAST MASTER SINGERS	45	1966
WEATHER WITH YOU CROWDED HOUSE	7	1992
WEAVE YOUR SPELL LEVEL 42	43	1982
THE WEAVER (EP) PAUL WELLER	18	1993
THE WEDDING [A] JULIE ROGERS	3	1964
THE WEDDING [B] CLIFF RICHARD FEATURING HELEN HOBSON	40	1996
WEDDING BELL BLUES FIFTH DIMENSION	16	1970
WEDDING BELLS [A] EDDIE FISHER	5	1955
WEDDING BELLS [B] GODLEY & CREME	7	1981
WEDDING RING RUSS HAMILTON	20	1957
WEDNESDAY WEEK UNDERTONES	11	1980
WEE RULE WEE PAPA GIRL RAPPERS	6	1988
WEE TOM LORD ROCKINGHAM'S XI	16	1959
WEEK IN WEEK OUT ORDINARY BOYS	36	2004
WEEKEND [A] EDDIE COCHRAN	15	1961
WEEKEND [B] MICK JACKSON	38	1979
WEEKEND [C] CLASS ACTION FEATURING CHRIS WILTSHIRE	49	1983
WEEKEND [C] TODD TERRY PROJECT	28	1988
WEEKEND [D] BAD HABIT BOYS	41	2000
WEEKEND [E] SCOOTER	12	2003
THE WEEKEND [F] MICHAEL GRAY	7	2004
WEEKEND GIRL S.O.S. BAND	51	1984
THE WEEKEND HAS LANDED MINKY	70	1999
WEEKEND WITHOUT MAKEUP LONG BLONDES	28	2006
WEEKENDER FLOWERED UP	20	1992
WEEKENDS AND BLEAK DAYS (HOT SUMMER) YOUNG KNIVES	35	2006
THE WEIGHT BAND	21	1968
WEIGHT FOR THE BASS UNIQUE 3	29	1990
WEIGHT OF THE WORLD [A] RINGO STARR	74	1992
WEIGHT OF THE WORLD [B] LEMAR	31	2009
WEIGHTLESS WET WET WET	10	2008
WEIRD [A] REEF	19	1995
WEIRD [B] HANSON	19	1998
WEIRDO CHARLATANS	19	1992
WELCOME GINO LATINO	17	1990
WELCOME BACK MA$E	29	2004
WELCOME HOME PETERS & LEE	1	1973
WELCOME HOME BABY BROOK BROTHERS	33	1962
WELCOME TO CHICAGO EP GENE FARRIS	74	2003
WELCOME TO JAMROCK DAMIAN 'JR GONG' MARLEY	13	2005
WELCOME TO MY LIFE SIMPLE PLAN	49	2005
WELCOME TO MY TRUTH ANASTACIA	25	2004
WELCOME TO MY WORLD JIM REEVES	6	1963
WELCOME TO OUR WORLD (OF MERRY MUSIC) MASS PRODUCTION	44	1977
WELCOME TO PARADISE GREEN DAY	20	1994
WELCOME TO THE BLACK PARADE MY CHEMICAL ROMANCE	1	2006
WELCOME TO THE CHEAP SEATS (EP) WONDER STUFF	8	1992
(WELCOME) TO THE DANCE DES MITCHELL	5	2000
WELCOME TO THE FUTURE SHIMMON & WOOLFSON	69	1998
WELCOME TO THE JUNGLE GUNS N' ROSES	24	1987
WELCOME TO THE PLEASURE DOME FRANKIE GOES TO HOLLYWOOD	2	1985
WELCOME TO THE REAL WORLD GUN	43	1992
WELCOME TO THE TERRORDOME PUBLIC ENEMY	18	1990
WELCOME TO TOMORROW SNAP! FEATURING SUMMER	6	1994
WELCOME TO WHEREVER YOU ARE BON JOVI	19	2006
WELL ALL RIGHT SANTANA	53	1978
WE'LL BE RIGHT BACK STEINSKI & MASS MEDIA	63	1987
WE'LL BE TOGETHER STING	41	1987
WE'LL BE WITH YOU POTTERS	34	1972
WE'LL BRING THE HOUSE DOWN SLADE	10	1981
WELL DID YOU EVAH! DEBORAH HARRY & IGGY POP	42	1991
WE'LL FIND OUR DAY STEPHANIE DE SYKES	17	1975
WE'LL GATHER LILACS – ALL MY LOVING (MEDLEY) SIMON MAY	49	1977
WELL I ASK YOU EDEN KANE	1	1961
WE'LL LIVE AND DIE IN THESE TOWNS ENEMY	21	2007
WE'LL SING IN THE SUNSHINE LANCASTRIANS	44	1964
WE'RE ALL ALONE RITA COOLIDGE	6	1977
WE'RE ALL GOING TO DIE MALCOLM MIDDLETON	31	2007
WE'RE ALL IN LOVE BLACK REBEL MOTORCYCLE CLUB	45	2003
WE'RE ALL IN THIS TOGETHER CAST OF HIGH SCHOOL MUSICAL	40	2006
WE'RE ALMOST THERE MICHAEL JACKSON	46	1981
WE'RE COMIN' AT YA QUARTZ FEATURING STEPZ	65	1990
WE'RE COMING OVER MR SMASH & FRIENDS FEATURING THE ENGLAND SUPPORTERS' BAND	67	2002

Title	Artist	Peak Position	Year of Release
WE'RE ENGLAND (TOM HARK)	TALKSPORT ALLSTARS	37	2006
WE'RE GOING OUT	YOUNGER YOUNGER 28'S	61	1999
WE'RE GOING TO IBIZA!	VENGABOYS	1	1999
WE'RE GOING TO MISS YOU	JAMES	48	1999
WE'RE GONNA DO IT AGAIN	MANCHESTER UNITED FEATURING STRYKER	6	1995
WE'RE GONNA GO FISHIN'	HANK LOCKLIN	18	1962
WE'RE IN THIS LOVE TOGETHER	AL JARREAU	55	1981
WE'RE IN THIS TOGETHER [A]	SIMPLY RED	11	1996
WE'RE IN THIS TOGETHER [B]	NINE INCH NAILS	39	1999
WE'RE NOT ALONE	HHC	44	1997
WE'RE NOT GONNA SLEEP TONIGHT	EMMA BUNTON	20	2001
WE'RE NOT GONNA TAKE IT	TWISTED SISTER	58	1984
WE'RE ON THE BALL	ANT & DEC	3	2002
WE'RE ONLY YOUNG ONCE	AVONS	45	1960
WE'RE REALLY SAYING SOMETHING	BUFFALO G	17	2000
WE'RE THROUGH	HOLLIES	7	1964
WEST END GIRLS	PET SHOP BOYS	1	1985
WEST END GIRLS	EAST 17	11	1993
WEST END PAD	CATHY DENNIS	25	1996
WEST OF ZANZIBAR	ANTHONY STEEL & THE RADIO REVELLERS	11	1954
WEST ONE (SHINE ON ME)	RUTS	43	1980
WESTERN MOVIES	OLYMPICS	12	1958
WESTSIDE [A]	TQ	4	1999
WESTSIDE [B]	ATHLETE	42	2003
WET DREAM	MAX ROMEO	10	1969
WET MY WHISTLE	MIDNIGHT STAR	60	1987
WE'VE GOT IT GOIN' ON	BACKSTREET BOYS	3	1995
WE'VE GOT THE JUICE	DEREK B	56	1988
WE'VE GOT THE WHOLE WORLD AT OUR FEET	ENGLAND WORLD CUP SQUAD	66	1986
WE'VE GOT THE WHOLE WORLD IN OUR HANDS	NOTTINGHAM FOREST FC & PAPER LACE	24	1978
WE'VE GOT TO LIVE TOGETHER	R.A.F.	34	1992
WE'VE GOT TO WORK IT OUT	BEL CANTO	65	1995
WE'VE GOT TONIGHT	BOB SEGER & THE SILVER BULLET BAND	22	1979
WE'VE GOT TONIGHT	KENNY ROGERS & SHEENA EASTON	28	1983
WE'VE GOT TONIGHT	ELKIE BROOKS	69	1987
WE'VE GOT TONIGHT	RONAN KEATING FEATURING LULU	4	2002
WE'VE HAD ENOUGH	ALKALINE TRIO	50	2003
WE'VE ONLY JUST BEGUN	CARPENTERS	28	1971
WE'VE ONLY JUST BEGUN	BITTY McLEAN	23	1995
WFL	HAPPY MONDAYS	68	1989
WHADDA U WANT (FROM ME)	FRANKIE KNUCKLES FEATURING ADEVA	36	1995
WHADDA WE LIKE?	ROUND SOUND PRESENTS ONYX STONE & MC MALIBU	69	2002
WHAM BAM	CANDY GIRLS FEATURING SWEET PUSSY PAULINE	20	1996
WHAM RAP	WHAM!	8	1983
WHAT	SOFT CELL	3	1982
WHAT A BEAUTIFUL DAY	LEVELLERS	13	1997
WHAT A CRAZY WORLD WE'RE LIVING IN	JOE BROWN & THE BRUVVERS	37	1962
WHAT A DIFFERENCE A DAY MAKES	ESTHER PHILLIPS	6	1975
WHAT A FOOL BELIEVES	DOOBIE BROTHERS	31	1979
WHAT A FOOL BELIEVES	ARETHA FRANKLIN	46	1980
WHAT A FOOL BELIEVES	PETER COX	39	1998
WHAT A GIRL WANTS	CHRISTINA AGUILERA	3	2000
WHAT A LOVELY DANCE	HAL	36	2005
WHAT A MOUTH	TOMMY STEELE	5	1960
WHAT A NIGHT	CITY BOY	39	1978
WHAT A PARTY	FATS DOMINO	43	1961
WHAT A WASTE	IAN DURY & THE BLOCKHEADS	9	1978
WHAT A WASTER	LIBERTINES	37	2002
WHAT A WOMAN IN LOVE WON'T DO	SANDY POSEY	48	1967
WHAT A WONDERFUL WORLD [A]	LOUIS ARMSTRONG	1	1968
WHAT A WONDERFUL WORLD [A]	NICK CAVE & SHANE McGOWAN	72	1992
WHAT A WONDERFUL WORLD [A]	CLIFF RICHARD	11	2001
WHAT A WONDERFUL WORLD [A]	EVA CASSIDY & KATIE MELUA	1	2007
(WHAT A) WONDERFUL WORLD [B]	JOHNNY NASH	25	1976
WHAT A WONDERFUL WORLD [C]	AXWELL & BOB SINCLAR FEATURING RON CARROLL	48	2008
WHAT ABOUT LOVE	HEART	14	1988
WHAT ABOUT ME	CRIBS	75	2004
WHAT ABOUT NOW	DAUGHTRY	11	2009
WHAT ABOUT NOW	WESTLIFE	2	2009
WHAT ABOUT THIS LOVE	MR FINGERS	74	1990
WHAT ABOUT US [A]	POINT BREAK	24	2000
WHAT ABOUT US [B]	BRANDY	4	2002
WHAT ABOUT YOUR FRIENDS	TLC	59	1992
WHAT AM I FIGHTING FOR	UNKLEJAM	16	2007
WHAT AM I GONNA DO [A]	EMILE FORD & THE CHECKMATES	33	1961
WHAT AM I GONNA DO [B]	ROD STEWART	3	1983
WHAT AM I GONNA DO WITH YOU	BARRY WHITE	5	1975
WHAT AM I TO YOU	KENNY LYNCH	37	1964
WHAT ARE WE GONNA DO ABOUT IT?	MERCY MERCY	59	1985
WHAT ARE WE GONNA GET 'ER INDOORS	DENNIS WATERMAN & GEORGE COLE	21	1983
WHAT ARE YOU DOING SUNDAY	DAWN FEATURING TONY ORLANDO	3	1971
WHAT ARE YOU UNDER	DEFINITION OF SOUND	68	1992
WHAT BECAME OF THE LIKELY LADS	LIBERTINES	9	2004
WHAT BECOMES OF THE BROKENHEARTED	JIMMY RUFFIN	4	1966
WHAT BECOMES OF THE BROKENHEARTED	DAVE STEWART. GUEST VOCALS: COLIN BLUNSTONE	13	1981
WHAT BECOMES OF THE BROKENHEARTED	ROBSON GREEN & JEROME FLYNN	1	1996
WHAT CAN I DO	CORRS	3	1998
WHAT CAN I SAY	BOZ SCAGGS	10	1977
(WHAT CAN I SAY) TO MAKE YOU LOVE ME	ALEXANDER O'NEAL	27	1988
WHAT CAN YOU DO FOR ME [A]	UTAH SAINTS	10	1991
WHAT CAN YOU DO 4 ME? [B]	LISA LASHES	52	2003
WHAT CAR	CLIFF RICHARD	12	2005
WHAT DID I DO TO YOU (EP)	LISA STANSFIELD	25	1990
WHAT DIFFERENCE DOES IT MAKE	SMITHS	12	1984
WHAT DO I DO	PHIL FEARON & GALAXY	5	1984
WHAT DO I DO NOW?	SLEEPER	14	1995
WHAT DO I GET	BUZZCOCKS	37	1978
WHAT DO I HAVE TO DO	KYLIE MINOGUE	6	1991
WHAT DO YA SAY	CHUBBY CHECKER	37	1963
WHAT DO YOU WANT [A]	ADAM FAITH	1	1959
WHAT DO YOU WANT? [B]	MORILLO FEATURING TERRA DEVA	61	2005
WHAT DO YOU WANT FROM ME? [A]	MONACO	11	1997
WHAT DO YOU WANT FROM ME? [B]	CASCADA	51	2008
WHAT DO YOU WANT TO MAKE THOSE EYES AT ME FOR	EMILE FORD & THE CHECKMATES	1	1959
WHAT DO YOU WANT TO MAKE THOSE EYES AT ME FOR	SHAKIN' STEVENS	5	1987
WHAT DOES IT FEEL LIKE?	FELIX DA HOUSECAT	66	2002
WHAT DOES IT TAKE	THEN JERICO	33	1989
WHAT DOES IT TAKE (TO WIN YOUR LOVE)	JUNIOR WALKER & THE ALL-STARS	13	1969
WHAT DOES IT TAKE (TO WIN YOUR LOVE)	KENNY G	64	1986
WHAT DOES YOUR SOUL LOOK LIKE (PART 1)	DJ SHADOW	54	1995
WHAT ELSE IS THERE?	ROYKSOPP	32	2005
WHAT EVER HAPPENED TO OLD FASHIONED LOVE	DANIEL O'DONNELL	21	1993
WHAT GOD WANTS PART 1	ROGER WATERS	35	1992
WHAT GOES AROUND [A]	BITTY McLEAN	36	1994
WHAT GOES AROUND [B]	LUCIANA	67	1994
WHAT GOES AROUND COMES AROUND [A]	BOB MARLEY & THE WAILERS	42	1996
WHAT GOES AROUND COMES AROUND [B]	JUSTIN TIMBERLAKE	4	2007
WHAT GOES ON	BRYAN FERRY	67	1978
WHAT GOOD AM I	CILLA BLACK	24	1967
WHAT HAPPENED TO THE MUSIC	JOEY NEGRO	51	1993
WHAT HAPPENS TOMORROW	DURAN DURAN	11	2005
WHAT HAVE I DONE TO DESERVE THIS	PET SHOP BOYS & DUSTY SPRINGFIELD	2	1987
WHAT HAVE THEY DONE TO MY SONG MA	NEW SEEKERS	44	1970
WHAT HAVE THEY DONE TO MY SONG MA	MELANIE	39	1971
WHAT HAVE THEY DONE TO THE RAIN	SEARCHERS	13	1964
WHAT HAVE YOU DONE FOR ME LATELY	JANET JACKSON	3	1986
WHAT HAVE YOU DONE (IS THIS ALL)	ONE TRIBE FEATURING GEM	52	1992
WHAT HOPE HAVE I	SPHINX	43	1995
WHAT HURTS THE MOST [A]	JO O'MEARA	13	2005
WHAT HURTS THE MOST [B]	CASCADA	10	2007
WHAT I AM	EDIE BRICKELL & THE NEW BOHEMIANS	31	1989
WHAT I AM	TIN TIN OUT FEATURING EMMA BUNTON	2	1999
WHAT I CAN DO FOR YOU	SHERYL CROW	43	1995
WHAT I DO BEST	ROBIN S	43	1993
WHAT I GO TO SCHOOL FOR	BUSTED	3	2002
WHAT I GOT	SUBLIME	71	1997
WHAT I GOT IS WHAT YOU NEED	UNIQUE	27	1983
WHAT I LIKE MOST ABOUT YOU IS YOUR GIRLFRIEND	SPECIAL A.K.A.	51	1984
WHAT I MEAN	MODJO	59	2001
WHAT I MISS THE MOST	ALOOF	70	1998
WHAT I REALLY WANT FOR CHRISTMAS	BRIAN WILSON	66	2005
WHAT I SAW	KINGS OF LEON	22	2003
WHAT I WANT	BOB SINCLAR PRESENTS FIREBALL	52	2008
WHAT IF… [A]	LIGHTNING SEEDS	14	1996
WHAT IF [B]	KATE WINSLET	6	2001
WHAT IF A WOMAN	JOE	53	2002
WHAT IF I'M RIGHT	SANDI THOM	22	2006
WHAT IN THE WORLD	NU COLOURS	57	1993
WHAT IN THE WORLD'S COME OVER YOU	JACK SCOTT	11	1960
WHAT IN THE WORLD'S COME OVER YOU	ROCKIN' BERRIES	23	1965

Title / Artist	Peak Position	Year of Release
WHAT IN THE WORLD'S COME OVER YOU TAM WHITE	36	1975
WHAT IS A MAN FOUR TOPS	16	1969
WHAT IS HOUSE (EP) LFO	62	1992
WHAT IS LIFE [A] OLIVIA NEWTON-JOHN	16	1972
WHAT IS LIFE [A] SHAWN MULLINS	62	1999
WHAT IS LIFE? [B] BLACK UHURU	56	1984
WHAT IS LOVE [A] HOWARD JONES	2	1983
WHAT IS LOVE [B] DEEE-LITE	2	1990
WHAT IS LOVE [C] HADDAWAY	2	1993
WHAT IS THE PROBLEM? GRAFITI	37	2003
WHAT IS THIS THING CALLED LOVE ALEXANDER O'NEAL	53	1991
WHAT IS TRUTH JOHNNY CASH	21	1970
WHAT IT FEELS LIKE FOR A GIRL MADONNA	7	2001
WHAT IT IS [A] GARNET MIMMS & TRUCKIN' CO	44	1977
WHAT IT IS [B] FREDDY FRESH	63	1999
WHAT IT'S LIKE EVERLAST	34	1999
WHAT I'VE DONE LINKIN PARK	6	2007
WHAT I'VE GOT IN MIND BILLIE JO SPEARS	4	1976
WHAT KIND OF FOOL ALL ABOUT EVE	29	1988
WHAT KIND OF FOOL AM I? ANTHONY NEWLEY	36	1961
WHAT KIND OF FOOL AM I? SAMMY DAVIS, JR	26	1962
WHAT KIND OF FOOL AM I? SHIRLEY BASSEY	47	1963
WHAT KIND OF FOOL (HEARD IT ALL BEFORE) KYLIE MINOGUE	14	1992
WHAT KIND OF MAN WOULD I BE MINT CONDITION	38	1997
WHAT KINDA BOY YOU LOOKING FOR (GIRL) HOT CHOCOLATE	10	1983
WHAT MADE MILWAUKEE FAMOUS (HAS MADE A LOSER OUT OF ME) ROD STEWART	4	1972
WHAT MAKES A GIRL FIERCE FIERCE GIRL	52	2005
WHAT MAKES A MAN WESTLIFE	2	2000
WHAT MAKES A MAN A MAN (LIVE) MARC ALMOND	60	1993
WHAT MAKES YOU CRY PROCLAIMERS	38	1994
WHAT MORE DO YOU WANT FRANKIE VAUGHAN	25	1960
WHAT MY HEART WANTS TO SAY GARETH GATES	5	2002
WHAT NOW ADAM FAITH WITH JOHNNY KEATING & HIS ORCHESTRA	31	1963
WHAT NOW MY LOVE SHIRLEY BASSEY	5	1962
WHAT NOW MY LOVE SONNY & CHER	13	1966
WHAT PLANET YOU ON BODYROX FEATURING LUCIANA	54	2008
WHAT PRESENCE? ORANGE JUICE	47	1984
WHAT THE HELL TOKYO DRAGONS	59	2005
WHAT THE WORLD IS WAITING FOR STONE ROSES	8	1989
WHAT THEY DO ROOTS	49	1997
WHAT TIME IS IT [A] SPIN DOCTORS	56	1993
WHAT TIME IS IT? [A] DUST JUNKYS	39	1998
WHAT TIME IS IT [B] CAST OF HIGH SCHOOL MUSICAL 2	20	2007
WHAT TIME IS LOVE (LIVE AT TRANCENTRAL) KLF FEATURING THE CHILDREN OF THE REVOLUTION	5	1990
WHAT TO DO BUDDY HOLLY	27	1961
WHAT TOOK YOU SO LONG [A] EMMA BUNTON	1	2001
WHAT TOOK YOU SO LONG [B] COURTEENERS	20	2008
WHAT U DO COLOURS FEATURING EMMANUEL & ESKA	51	1999
WHAT U GON' DO LIL JON & THE EAST SIDE BOYZ	38	2005
WHAT 'U' WAITIN' '4' JUNGLE BROTHERS	35	1990
WHAT WAS HER NAME DAVE CLARKE FEATURING CHICKS ON SPEED	50	2004
WHAT WE DO KRAY TWINZ FEATURING TWISTA & LETHAL B	23	2005
WHAT? WHAT YOU GOT? LITTLE MAN TATE	40	2006
WHAT WILL BE WILL BE (DESTINY) DIVINE INSPIRATION	55	2003
WHAT WILL I DO WITHOUT YOU LENE LOVICH	58	1980
WHAT WILL MARY SAY JOHNNY MATHIS	49	1963
WHAT WILL YOU DO (WHEN THE MONEY GOES) MILBURN	44	2007
WHAT WOULD HAPPEN MEREDITH BROOKS	49	1998
WHAT WOULD I BE VAL DOONICAN	2	1966
WHAT WOULD STEVE DO MUMM RA	40	2007
WHAT WOULD WE DO DSK	46	1991
WHAT WOULD YOU DO CITY HIGH	3	2001
WHAT WOULD YOU DO IF...? CODE RED	55	1998
WHAT YA GOT 4 ME SIGNUM	70	1998
WHAT YA LOOKIN' AT CROW	60	2001
WHAT YOU COULD'VE WON MILBURN	66	2006
WHAT YOU DO BIG BASS VS MICHELLE NARINE	67	2000
WHAT YOU DO (PLAYING WITH STONES) BIG BASS VS MICHELLE NARINE	27	2007
WHAT YOU DO TO ME (EP) TEENAGE FANCLUB	31	1992
WHAT YOU GET HUNDRED REASONS	30	2004
WHAT YOU GET IS WHAT YOU SEE TINA TURNER	30	1987
WHAT YOU GONNA DO ABOUT IT TOTAL CONTRAST	63	1986
WHAT YOU GOT ABS	4	2002
WHAT YOU LOKK FOR SAM BEETON	41	2008
WHAT YOU NEED [A] INXS	51	1986
WHAT YOU NEED [B] POWERHOUSE FEATURING DUANE HARDEN	13	1999
WHAT YOU NEED IS SINEAD QUINN	19	2003
WHAT YOU NEED (TONIGHT) NU CIRCLES FEATURING EMMA B	46	2003
WHAT YOU SAY LIGHTNING SEEDS	41	1997
WHAT YOU SEE IS WHAT YOU GET GLEN GOLDSMITH	33	1988
WHAT YOU THINK OF THAT MEMPHIS BLEEK FEATURING JAY-Z	58	1999
WHAT YOU WAITING FOR [A] STARGARD	39	1978
WHAT YOU WAITING FOR [B] GWEN STEFANI	4	2004
WHAT YOU WANT [A] XPANSIONS FEATURING DALE JOYNER	55	1991
WHAT YOU WANT [B] FUTURE FORCE	47	1996
WHAT YOU WANT [C] MA$E FEATURING TOTAL	15	1998
WHAT YOU WON'T DO FOR LOVE GO WEST	15	1993
WHAT YOUR BOYFRIEND SAID LITTLE MAN TATE	60	2008
WHAT YOU'RE MADE OF LUCIE SILVAS	7	2004
WHAT YOU'RE MISSING K-KLASS	24	1994
WHAT YOU'RE PROPOSING STATUS QUO	2	1980
WHATCHA GONE DO? LINK	48	1998
WHAT'CHA GONNA DO [A] SHABBA RANKS FEATURING QUEEN LATIFAH	21	1993
WHAT'CHA GONNA DO [B] ETERNAL	16	1999
WHATCHA GONNA DO ABOUT IT DORIS TROY	37	1964
WHATCHA GONNA DO ABOUT IT SMALL FACES	14	1965
WHATCHA GONNA DO NOW CHRIS ANDREWS	40	1966
WHATCHA SAY JASON DERULO	3	2009
WHATCHA THINK ABOUT THAT PUSSYCAT DOLLS	9	2009
WHATCHULOOKINAT WHITNEY HOUSTON	13	2002
WHAT'D I SAY JERRY LEE LEWIS	10	1961
WHAT'D YOU COME HERE FOR? TRINA & TAMARA	46	1999
WHATEVER [A] OASIS	3	1994
WHATEVER [B] EN VOGUE	14	1997
WHATEVER [C] IDEAL US FEATURING LIL' MO	31	2000
WHATEVER GETS YOU THROUGH THE NIGHT JOHN LENNON WITH THE PLASTIC ONO NUCLEAR BAND	36	1974
WHATEVER HAPPENED TO COREY HAIM? THRILLS	22	2004
WHATEVER HAPPENED TO MY ROCK AND ROLL BLACK REBEL MOTORCYCLE CLUB	46	2002
WHATEVER HAPPENED TO YOU ('LIKELY LADS' THEME) HIGHLY LIKELY	35	1973
WHATEVER I DO (WHEREVER I GO) HAZELL DEAN	4	1984
WHATEVER IT TAKES [A] OLYMPIC RUNNERS	61	1978
WHATEVER IT TAKES [B] LEONA LEWIS	61	2007
WHATEVER LOLA WANTS ALMA COGAN	26	1957
WHATEVER MAKES YOU HAPPY TEN CITY	60	1990
WHATEVER U WANT CHRISTINA MILIAN FEATURING JOE BUDDEN	9	2004
WHATEVER WILL BE WILL BE DORIS DAY	1	1956
WHATEVER YOU LIKE TI	47	2008
WHATEVER YOU NEED TINA TURNER	27	2000
WHATEVER YOU WANT [A] STATUS QUO	4	1979
WHATEVER YOU WANT [B] TINA TURNER	23	1996
WHAT'LL I DO JANET JACKSON	9	1995
WHAT'S A GIRL TO DO SISTER 2 SISTER	61	2000
WHAT'S ANOTHER YEAR JOHNNY LOGAN	1	1980
WHAT'S GOIN' DOWN HONKY	49	1996
WHAT'S GOING ON [A] MEKON FEATURING ROXANNE SHANTE	43	2000
WHAT'S GOING ON [B] CYNDI LAUPER	57	1987
WHAT'S GOING ON [B] MUSIC RELIEF '94	70	1994
WHAT'S GOING ON [B] ARTISTS AGAINST AIDS WORLDWIDE	6	2001
WHAT'S GOING ON [C] WOOKIE	45	2000
WHAT'S HAPPENIN' METHOD MAN FEATURING BUSTA RHYMES	17	2004
WHAT'S HIDEOUS DO ME BAD THINGS	33	2005
WHAT'S IN A KISS? GILBERT O'SULLIVAN	19	1980
WHAT'S IN A WORD CHRISTIANS	33	1992
WHAT'S IN THE BOX? (SEE WHATCHA GOT) BOO RADLEYS	25	1996
WHAT'S IT ALL ABOUT RUN DMC	48	1990
WHAT'S IT GONNA BE?! [A] BUSTA RHYMES FEATURING JANET	6	1999
WHAT'S IT GONNA BE [B] H TWO O FEATURING PLATNUM	2	2008
WHAT'S IT LIKE TO BE BEAUTIFUL LENA FIAGBE	52	1994
WHAT'S LEFT OF ME NICK LACHEY	47	2007
WHAT'S LOVE GOT TO DO WITH IT TINA TURNER	3	1984
WHAT'S LOVE GOT TO DO WITH IT WARREN G FEATURING ADINA HOWARD	2	1996
WHAT'S LUV FAT JOE FEATURING ASHANTI	4	2002
WHAT'S MY AGE AGAIN? BLINK-182	17	1999
WHAT'S MY NAME? SNOOP DOGGY DOGG	20	1993
WHAT'S NEW PUSSYCAT TOM JONES	11	1965
WHAT'S ON YOUR MIND GEORGE BENSON	45	1981
WHAT'S SO DIFFERENT? GINUWINE	10	1999
WHAT'S THAT TUNE (DOO-DOO-DOO-DOO-DOO-DOO-DOO-DOO-DOO-DOO) DOROTHY	31	1995
WHAT'S THE COLOUR OF MONEY? HOLLYWOOD BEYOND	7	1986
WHAT'S THE FREQUENCY, KENNETH R.E.M.	9	1994
WHAT'S THE POINT WE'VE GOT A FUZZBOX & WE'RE GONNA USE IT	51	1987
WHAT'S UP 4 NON BLONDES	2	1993
WHAT'S UP DJ MIKO	6	1994

Title / Artist	Peak Position	Year of Release
WHAT'S UP WITH THAT ZZ TOP	58	1996
(WHAT'S WRONG WITH) DREAMING RIVER CITY PEOPLE	40	1989
WHAT'S WRONG WITH THIS PICTURE CHESNEY HAWKES	63	1993
WHAT'S YOUR DAMAGE? TEST ICICLES	31	2006
WHAT'S YOUR FANTASY LUDACRIS	19	2001
WHAT'S YOUR FLAVA CRAIG DAVID	8	2002
WHAT'S YOUR NAME [A] CHICORY TIP	13	1972
WHAT'S YOUR NAME WHAT'S YOUR NUMBER ANDREA TRUE CONNECTION	34	1978
WHAT'S YOUR NAME? [B] ANGEL LEE	39	2000
WHAT'S YOUR NUMBER? CYPRESS HILL	44	2004
WHAT'S YOUR PROBLEM? BLANCMANGE	40	1985
WHAT'S YOUR SIGN DES'REE	19	1998
WHAT'S YOUR SIGN GIRL BARRY BIGGS	55	1979
WHATTA MAN SALT-N-PEPA WITH EN VOGUE	7	1994
WHAZZUP TRUE PARTY	13	2000
THE WHEEL SPEAR OF DESTINY	59	1983
WHEEL OF FORTUNE ACE OF BASE	20	1993
WHEELS [A] STRING-A-LONGS	8	1961
WHEELS [B] FOO FIGHTERS	22	2009
WHEELS AIN'T COMING DOWN SLADE	60	1981
WHEELS CHA CHA JOE LOSS ORCHESTRA	21	1961
WHEELS OF STEEL SAXON	20	1980
THE WHEELS ON THE BUS MAD DONNA	17	2002
WHEN [A] KALIN TWINS	1	1958
WHEN [A] SHOWADDYWADDY	3	1977
WHEN [B] SUNSCREEM	47	1995
WHEN [C] SHANIA TWAIN	18	1998
WHEN A CHILD IS BORN (SOLEADO) JOHNNY MATHIS	1	1976
WHEN A CHILD IS BORN JOHNNY MATHIS & GLADYS KNIGHT	74	1981
WHEN A HEART BEATS NIK KERSHAW	27	1985
WHEN A MAN LOVES A WOMAN [A] PERCY SLEDGE	2	1966
WHEN A MAN LOVES A WOMAN [A] MICHAEL BOLTON	8	1991
WHEN A MAN LOVES A WOMAN [B] JODY WATLEY	33	1994
WHEN A WOMAN GABRIELLE	6	2000
WHEN A WOMAN'S FED UP R KELLY	24	2000
WHEN AM I GONNA MAKE A LIVING SADE	36	1984
WHEN BOUZOUKIS PLAYED VICKY LEANDROS	44	1973
WHEN BOYS TALK INDEEP	67	1983
WHEN CAN I SEE YOU BABYFACE	35	1994
WHEN CHILDREN RULE THE WORLD RED HILL CHILDREN	40	1996
WHEN DID YOUR HEART GO MISSING? ROONEY	45	2007
WHEN DO I GET TO SING 'MY WAY' SPARKS	32	1994
WHEN DOVES CRY PRINCE	4	1984
WHEN DOVES CRY GINUWINE	10	1997
WHEN DREAMS TURN TO DUST CATHY DENNIS	43	1997
WHEN FOREVER HAS GONE DEMIS ROUSSOS	2	1976
WHEN HE SHINES SHEENA EASTON	12	1981
WHEN HEROES GO DOWN SUZANNE VEGA	58	1993
WHEN I ARGUE I SEE SHAPES IDLEWILD	19	1999
WHEN I CALL YOUR NAME MARY KIANI	18	1995
WHEN I COME AROUND GREEN DAY	27	1995
WHEN I COME HOME SPENCER DAVIS GROUP	12	1966
WHEN I DREAM [A] TEARDROP EXPLODES	47	1980
WHEN I DREAM [B] CAROL KIDD FEATURING TERRY WAITE	58	1992
WHEN I FALL IN LOVE [A] NAT 'KING' COLE	2	1957
WHEN I FALL IN LOVE [A] DONNY OSMOND	4	1973
WHEN I FALL IN LOVE [A] RICK ASTLEY	2	1987
WHEN I FALL IN LOVE [B] ANT & DEC	12	1996
WHEN I GET HOME SEARCHERS	35	1965
WHEN I GROW UP [A] MICHELLE SHOCKED	67	1989
WHEN I GROW UP [B] GARBAGE	9	1999
WHEN I GROW UP [C] PUSSYCAT DOLLS	3	2008
WHEN I GROW UP TO BE A MAN BEACH BOYS	27	1964
WHEN I KISS YOU (I HEAR CHARLIE PARKER) SPARKS	36	1995
WHEN I LEAVE THE WORLD BEHIND ROSE MARIE	63	1983
WHEN I LOOK INTO YOUR EYES [A] FIREHOUSE	65	1992
WHEN I LOOK INTO YOUR EYES [B] MAXEE	55	2001
WHEN I LOST YOU SARAH WHATMORE	6	2002
WHEN I NEED YOU LEO SAYER	1	1977
WHEN I NEED YOU WILL MELLOR	5	1998
WHEN I NEED YOU CLIFF RICHARD	38	2007
WHEN I SAID GOODBYE STEPS	5	2000
WHEN I SEE YOU MACY GRAY	26	2003
WHEN I SEE YOU SMILE BAD ENGLISH	61	1989
WHEN I THINK OF YOU [A] JANET JACKSON	10	1986
WHEN I THINK OF YOU [B] KENNY THOMAS	27	1995
WHEN I THINK OF YOU [C] CHRIS DE BURGH	59	1999
WHEN I THINK OF YOU [D] LEE RYAN	15	2006
WHEN I WAS YOUNG [A] ERIC BURDON & THE ANIMALS	45	1967
WHEN I WAS YOUNG [B] RIVER CITY PEOPLE	62	1991
WHEN I'M ALONE RIFLES	64	2005
WHEN I'M AWAY FROM YOU FRANKIE MILLER	42	1979
WHEN I'M BACK ON MY FEET AGAIN MICHAEL BOLTON	44	1990
WHEN I'M CLEANING WINDOWS (TURNED OUT NICE AGAIN) 2 IN A TENT	25	1994
WHEN I'M DEAD AND GONE McGUINNESS FLINT	2	1970
WHEN I'M GONE [A] EMINEM	5	2006
WHEN I'M GONE [B] SIMPLE PLAN	26	2008
WHEN I'M GOOD AND READY SYBIL	5	1993
WHEN I'M SIXTY FOUR KENNY BALL & HIS JAZZMEN	43	1967
WHEN IT'S LOVE VAN HALEN	28	1988
WHEN IT'S OVER SUGAR RAY	32	2001
WHEN IT'S TIME TO ROCK UFO	70	1983
WHEN JOHNNY COMES MARCHING HOME ADAM FAITH	5	1960
WHEN JULIE COMES AROUND CUFF LINKS	10	1970
WHEN LOVE & HATE COLLIDE DEF LEPPARD	2	1995
WHEN LOVE BREAKS DOWN PREFAB SPROUT	25	1985
WHEN LOVE COMES ALONG MATT MONRO	46	1962
WHEN LOVE COMES CALLING PAUL JOHNSON	52	1987
WHEN LOVE COMES ROUND AGAIN (L'ARCA DI NOE) KEN DODD	19	1971
WHEN LOVE COMES TO TOWN U2 FEATURING B.B. KING	6	1989
WHEN LOVE TAKES OVER DAVID GUETTA FEATURING KELLY ROWLAND	1	2009
WHEN LOVE TAKES OVER AIRI L	22	2009
WHEN LOVE TAKES OVER YOU DONNA SUMMER	72	1989
WHEN MEXICO GAVE UP THE RHUMBA MITCHELL TOROK	6	1956
WHEN MY BABY SCOOCH	29	1999
WHEN MY LITTLE GIRL IS SMILING CRAIG DOUGLAS	9	1962
WHEN MY LITTLE GIRL IS SMILING JIMMY JUSTICE	9	1962
WHEN MY LITTLE GIRL IS SMILING DRIFTERS	31	1962
WHEN ONLY LOVE WILL DO RICHARD DARBYSHIRE	54	1994
WHEN ROCK 'N ROLL CAME TO TRINIDAD NAT 'KING' COLE	28	1957
WHEN SHE WAS MY GIRL FOUR TOPS	3	1981
WHEN SMOKEY SINGS ABC	11	1987
WHEN THE BOYS TALK ABOUT THE GIRLS VALERIE CARR	29	1958
WHEN THE DAWN BREAKS NARCOTIC THRUST	28	2005
WHEN THE FINGERS POINT CHRISTIANS	34	1987
WHEN THE GIRL IN YOUR ARMS IS THE GIRL IN YOUR HEART CLIFF RICHARD	3	1961
WHEN THE GOING GETS TOUGH BOYZONE	1	1999
WHEN THE GOING GETS TOUGH, THE TOUGH GET GOING BILLY OCEAN	1	1986
WHEN THE HEARTACHE IS OVER TINA TURNER	10	1999
WHEN THE HOODOO COMES DIESEL PARK WEST	62	1989
WHEN THE LAST TIME CLIPSE	41	2003
WHEN THE LIGHTS GO DOWN ARMAND VAN HELDEN	70	2005
WHEN THE LIGHTS GO OUT FIVE	4	1998
WHEN THE MORNING COMES LOVE DECADE	69	1993
WHEN THE MORNING SUN DRIES THE DEW QUIET FIVE	45	1965
WHEN THE NIGHT COMES JOE COCKER	61	1990
WHEN THE NIGHT FEELS MY SONG BEDOUIN SOUNDCLASH	24	2005
WHEN THE RAIN BEGINS TO FALL JERMAINE JACKSON & PIA ZADORA	68	1984
WHEN THE SH.. GOES DOWN CYPRESS HILL	19	1993
WHEN THE SUMMERTIME IS OVER JACKIE TRENT	39	1965
WHEN THE SUN COMES SHINING THRU' LONG JOHN BALDRY	29	1968
WHEN THE SUN GOES DOWN [A] DJ FRESH FEATURING ADAM F	68	2004
WHEN THE SUN GOES DOWN [B] ARCTIC MONKEYS	1	2006
WHEN THE TIGERS BROKE FREE PINK FLOYD	39	1982
WHEN THE WIND BLOWS DAVID BOWIE	44	1986
WHEN THE WORLD IS RUNNING DOWN DIFFERENT GEAR VERSUS THE POLICE	28	2000
WHEN THE YEAR ENDS IN 1 TOTTENHAM HOTSPUR FA CUP FINAL SQUAD	44	1991
WHEN THIS RIVER ROLLS OVER YOU STANDS	32	2003
WHEN TOMORROW COMES EURYTHMICS	30	1986
WHEN TWO WORLDS COLLIDE JIM REEVES	17	1969
WHEN TWO WORLDS DRIFT APART CLIFF RICHARD	46	1977
WHEN WE ARE FAR FROM HOME ENGLAND WORLD CUP SQUAD	66	1986
WHEN WE ARE GONE FALLOUT TRUST	73	2005
WHEN WE ARE TOGETHER TEXAS	12	1999
WHEN WE DANCE STING	9	1994
WHEN WE WAS FAB GEORGE HARRISON	25	1988
WHEN WE WERE YOUNG [A] SOLOMON KING	21	1968
WHEN WE WERE YOUNG [B] BUCKS FIZZ	10	1983
WHEN WE WERE YOUNG [C] WHIPPING BOY	46	1996
WHEN WE WERE YOUNG [D] HUMAN NATURE	43	2001
WHEN WILL I BE FAMOUS BROS	2	1988
WHEN WILL I BE LOVED EVERLY BROTHERS	4	1960
WHEN WILL I SEE YOU AGAIN THREE DEGREES	1	1974
WHEN WILL I SEE YOU AGAIN BROTHER BEYOND	43	1989
WHEN WILL I SEE YOU AGAIN SHEILA FERGUSON	60	1994
WHEN WILL I SEE YOUR FACE AGAIN JAMIE SCOTT & THE TOWN	41	2007
WHEN WILL THE GOOD APPLES FALL SEEKERS	11	1967

Title	Artist	Peak Position	Year of Release
WHEN WILL YOU BE MINE	AVERAGE WHITE BAND	49	1979
WHEN WILL YOU MAKE MY TELEPHONE RING	DEACON BLUE	34	1988
WHEN WILL YOU SAY I LOVE YOU	BILLY FURY	3	1963
WHEN YOU ARE A KING	WHITE PLAINS	13	1971
WHEN YOU ASK ABOUT LOVE	CRICKETS	27	1960
WHEN YOU ASK ABOUT LOVE	MATCHBOX	4	1980
WHEN YOU BELIEVE	MARIAH CAREY & WHITNEY HOUSTON	4	1998
WHEN YOU BELIEVE	LEON JACKSON	1	2007
WHEN YOU COME BACK TO ME	JASON DONOVAN	2	1989
WHEN YOU GET RIGHT DOWN TO IT	RONNIE DYSON	34	1971
(WHEN YOU GONNA) GIVE IT UP TO ME	SEAN PAUL FEATURING KEYSHIA COLE	31	2006
WHEN YOU GONNA LEARN	JAMIROQUAI	28	1992
WHEN YOU KISS ME	SHANIA TWAIN	21	2003
WHEN YOU LOOK AT ME	CHRISTINA MILIAN	3	2002
WHEN YOU LOOK ME IN THE EYES	JONAS BROTHERS	30	2008
WHEN YOU LOSE THE ONE YOU LOVE	DAVID WHITFIELD WITH CHORUS & MANTOVANI & HIS ORCHESTRA	7	1955
WHEN YOU MADE THE MOUNTAIN	OPUS III	71	1994
WHEN YOU SAY NOTHING AT ALL	RONAN KEATING	1	1999
(WHEN YOU SAY YOU LOVE SOMEBODY) IN THE HEART	KOOL & THE GANG	7	1984
WHEN YOU SLEEP	LONGVIEW	74	2002
WHEN YOU TELL ME THAT YOU LOVE ME	DIANA ROSS	2	1991
WHEN YOU TELL ME THAT YOU LOVE ME	WESTLIFE FEATURING DIANA ROSS	2	2005
WHEN YOU TOUCH ME	FREEMASONS FEATURING KATHERINE ELLIS	23	2008
WHEN YOU WALK IN THE ROOM	SEARCHERS	3	1964
WHEN YOU WALK IN THE ROOM	CHILD	38	1978
WHEN YOU WALK IN THE ROOM	PAUL CARRACK	48	1987
WHEN YOU WALK IN THE ROOM	STATUS QUO	34	1995
WHEN YOU WALK IN THE ROOM	AGNETHA FALTSKOG	34	2004
WHEN YOU WASN'T FAMOUS	STREETS	8	2006
WHEN YOU WERE SWEET SIXTEEN	FUREYS WITH DAVEY ARTHUR	14	1981
WHEN YOU WERE YOUNG [A]	DEL AMITRI	20	1993
WHEN YOU WERE YOUNG [B]	KILLERS	2	2006
WHEN YOUR 'EX' WANTS YOU BACK	SURFACE	52	1984
WHEN YOUR HEART STOPS BEATING	PLUS 44	47	2007
WHEN YOUR OLD WEDDING RING WAS NEW	JIMMY ROSELLI	51	1983
WHEN YOU'RE GONE [A]	BRYAN ADAMS FEATURING MELANIE C	3	1998
WHEN YOU'RE GONE [B]	SORAYA VIVIAN	59	2002
WHEN YOU'RE GONE [C]	AVRIL LAVIGNE	3	2007
WHEN YOU'RE IN LOVE WITH A BEAUTIFUL WOMAN	DR HOOK	1	1979
WHEN YOU'RE NUMBER 1	GENE CHANDLER	43	1979
WHEN YOU'RE YOUNG	JAM	17	1979
WHEN YOU'RE YOUNG AND IN LOVE	MARVELETTES	13	1967
WHEN YOU'RE YOUNG AND IN LOVE	FLYING PICKETS	7	1984
WHENEVER GOD SHINES HIS LIGHT	VAN MORRISON WITH CLIFF RICHARD	20	1989
WHENEVER I SAY YOUR NAME	STING & MARY J BLIGE	60	2003
WHENEVER I STOP	MIKE + THE MECHANICS	73	1999
WHENEVER WHEREVER	SHAKIRA	2	2002
WHENEVER YOU NEED ME	T'PAU	16	1991
WHENEVER YOU NEED SOMEBODY	RICK ASTLEY	3	1987
WHENEVER YOU NEED SOMEONE	BAD BOYS INC	26	1993
WHENEVER YOU WANT MY LOVE	REAL THING	18	1978
WHENEVER YOU'RE NEAR	CHER	72	1993
WHENEVER YOU'RE READY	FIVE STAR	11	1987
WHERE ARE THEY NOW?	GENE	22	1997
WHERE ARE YOU [A]	KAVANA	26	1996
WHERE ARE YOU [B]	IMAANI	15	1998
WHERE ARE YOU BABY	BETTY BOO	3	1990
WHERE ARE YOU GOING TO MY LOVE	BROTHERHOOD OF MAN	22	1970
WHERE ARE YOU NOW (MY LOVE)	JACKIE TRENT	1	1965
WHERE ARE YOU NOW?	GENERATOR	60	1999
WHERE CAN I FIND LOVE	LIVIN' JOY	12	1997
WHERE DID ALL THE GOOD TIMES GO	DONNY OSMOND	18	1974
WHERE DID ALL THE LOVE GO	KASABIAN	30	2009
WHERE DID I GO WRONG	UB40	26	1988
WHERE DID OUR LOVE GO	SUPREMES	3	1964
WHERE DID OUR LOVE GO	DONNIE ELBERT	8	1972
WHERE DID OUR LOVE GO	MANHATTAN TRANSFER	40	1978
WHERE DID OUR LOVE GO	TRICIA PENROSE	71	1996
WHERE DID WE GO WRONG	LIQUID GOLD	56	1982
WHERE DID YOUR HEART GO	WHAM!	1	1986
WHERE DO BROKEN HEARTS GO	WHITNEY HOUSTON	14	1988
(WHERE DO I BEGIN) LOVE STORY	ANDY WILLIAMS	4	1971
(WHERE DO I BEGIN) LOVE STORY	SHIRLEY BASSEY	34	1971
WHERE DO I STAND?	MONTROSE AVENUE	38	1998
WHERE DO U WANT ME TO PUT IT	SOLO (US)	45	1996
WHERE DO WE GO	TEN CITY	60	1989
WHERE DO WE GO FROM HERE	CLIFF RICHARD	60	1982
WHERE DO YOU GO	NO MERCY	2	1997
WHERE DO YOU GO TO MY LOVELY	PETER SARSTEDT	1	1969
WHERE DOES MY HEART BEAT NOW	CELINE DION	72	1993
WHERE DOES TIME GO	JULIA FORDHAM	41	1989
WHERE EAGLES FLY	CRYSTAL PALACE	50	1990
WHERE HAS ALL THE LOVE GONE	YAZZ	16	1989
WHERE HAS ALL THE LOVE GONE	MAUREEN	51	1991
WHERE HAS LOVE GONE	HOLLY JOHNSON	73	1990
WHERE HAVE ALL THE COWBOYS GONE?	PAULA COLE	15	1997
WHERE HAVE YOU BEEN TONIGHT?	SHED SEVEN	23	1995
WHERE I FIND MY HEAVEN	GIGOLO AUNTS	29	1995
WHERE I WANNA BE	SHADE SHEIST FEATURING NATE DOGG & KURUPT	14	2001
WHERE I'M HEADED	LENE MARLIN	31	2001
WHERE IN THE WORLD [A]	SWING OUT SISTER	47	1989
WHERE IN THE WORLD [B]	BBM	57	1994
WHERE IS MY MAN	EARTHA KITT	36	1984
WHERE IS THE FEELING?	KYLIE MINOGUE	16	1995
WHERE IS THE LOVE [A]	ROBERTA FLACK & DONNY HATHAWAY	29	1972
WHERE IS THE LOVE [A]	MICA PARIS & WILL DOWNING	19	1989
WHERE IS THE LOVE [B]	BETTY WRIGHT	25	1975
WHERE IS THE LOVE [B]	ADEVA	54	1997
WHERE IS THE LOVE [C]	BLACK EYED PEAS	1	2003
WHERE IS THE LOVE (WE USED TO KNOW)	DELEGATION	22	1977
WHERE IS TOMORROW	CILLA BLACK	39	1968
WHERE IT'S AT	BECK	35	1996
WHERE LOVE LIVES	ALISON LIMERICK	9	1991
WHERE MY GIRLS AT?	702	22	1999
WHERE THE ACTION IS	WESTWORLD	54	1987
WHERE THE BOYS ARE	CONNIE FRANCIS	5	1961
WHERE THE HEART IS	SOFT CELL	21	1982
WHERE THE HOOD AT?	DMX	16	2003
WHERE THE POOR BOYS DANCE	LULU	24	2000
WHERE THE ROSE IS SOWN	BIG COUNTRY	29	1984
WHERE THE STORY ENDS	BLAZIN' SQUAD	8	2003
WHERE THE STREETS HAVE NO NAME	U2	4	1987
WHERE THE STREETS HAVE NO NAME – CAN'T TAKE MY EYES OFF YOU	PET SHOP BOYS	4	1991
WHERE THE WILD ROSES GROW	NICK CAVE & KYLIE MINOGUE	11	1995
WHERE THE WINDS BLOW	FRANKIE LAINE	2	1953
WHERE WE BELONG	LOSTPROPHETS	32	2010
WHERE WERE YOU	ADULT NET	66	1989
WHERE WERE YOU HIDING WHEN THE STORM BROKE	ALARM	22	1984
WHERE WERE YOU (ON OUR WEDDING DAY)?	LLOYD PRICE	15	1959
WHERE WILL THE DIMPLE BE	ROSEMARY CLOONEY WITH THE MELLOMEN	6	1955
WHERE WILL YOU BE	SUE NICHOLLS	17	1968
WHERE YOU ARE	RAHSAAN PATTERSON	55	1998
WHERE YOU GONNA BE TONIGHT?	WILLIE COLLINS	46	1986
WHERE'S JACK THE RIPPER	GROOVERIDER	61	1999
WHERE'S ME JUMPER	SULTANS OF PING FC	67	1992
WHERE'S MY	ADAM F FEATURING LIL' MO	37	2002
WHERE'S ROMEO	CA VA CA VA	49	1982
WHERE'S THE LOVE	HANSON	4	1997
WHERE'S THE PARTY AT	JAGGED EDGE FEATURING NELLY	25	2001
WHERE'S THE PLEASURE	PROTOCOL	27	2006
WHERE'S YOUR HEAD AT	BASEMENT JAXX	9	2001
WHERE'S YOUR LOVE	CRAIG DAVID FEATURNG TINCHY STRYDER	58	2008
WHERE'S YOUR LOVE BEEN	HELIOCENTRIC WORLD	71	1995
WHEREVER I LAY MY HAT (THAT'S MY HOME)	PAUL YOUNG	1	1983
WHEREVER I MAY ROAM	METALLICA	25	1992
WHEREVER WOULD I BE	DUSTY SPRINGFIELD & DARYL HALL	44	1995
WHEREVER YOU ARE	NEIL FINN	32	2001
WHEREVER YOU WILL GO	CALLING	3	2002
WHICH WAY SHOULD I JUMP	MILLTOWN BROTHERS	38	1991
WHICH WAY YOU GOIN' BILLY	POPPY FAMILY	7	1970
WHIGGLE IN LINE	BLACK DUCK	33	1994
WHILE I LIVE	KENNY DAMON	48	1966
WHILE YOU SEE A CHANCE	STEVE WINWOOD	45	1981
WHINE AND GRINE	PRINCE BUSTER	21	1998
WHIP IT	DEVO	51	1980
WHIPLASH	JFK	47	2002
WHIPPIN' PICCADILLY	GOMEZ	35	1998
WHISKEY IN THE JAR	THIN LIZZY	6	1973
WHISKEY IN THE JAR	POGUES & THE DUBLINERS	63	1990
WHISKEY IN THE JAR	METALLICA	29	1999
THE WHISPER	SELECTER	36	1980
WHISPER A PRAYER	MICA PARIS	65	1993
WHISPER YOUR NAME	HUMAN NATURE	53	1997
WHISPERING	BACHELORS	18	1963
WHISPERING	NINO TEMPO & APRIL STEVENS	20	1964

Title / Artist	Peak Position	Year of Release
WHISPERING GRASS WINDSOR DAVIES & DON ESTELLE	1	1975
WHISPERING HOPE JIM REEVES	50	1961
WHISPERING YOUR NAME ALISON MOYET	18	1994
WHISPERS [A] ELTON JOHN	47	1990
WHISPERS [B] IAN BROWN	33	2002
WHISTLE DOWN THE WIND NICK HEYWARD	13	1983
WHISTLE DOWN THE WIND TINA ARENA	24	1998
WHISTLE FOR THE CHOIR FRATELLIS	9	2006
THE WHISTLE SONG FRANKIE KNUCKLES	17	1991
THE WHISTLE SONG (BLOW MY WHISTLE BITCH) DJ ALIGATOR PROJECT	5	2000
THE WHISTLER HONKY	41	1994
WHITE BIRD VANESSA-MAE	66	2001
WHITE BOY WITH A FEATHER JASON DOWNS FEATURING MILK	19	2001
WHITE BOYS AND HEROES GARY NUMAN	20	1982
WHITE CHRISTMAS MANTOVANI	6	1952
WHITE CHRISTMAS PAT BOONE	29	1957
WHITE CHRISTMAS FREDDIE STARR	41	1975
WHITE CHRISTMAS BING CROSBY	5	1977
WHITE CHRISTMAS DARTS	48	1980
WHITE CHRISTMAS JIM DAVIDSON	52	1980
WHITE CHRISTMAS KEITH HARRIS & ORVILLE	40	1986
WHITE CHRISTMAS MAX BYGRAVES	71	1989
WHITE CLIFFS OF DOVER MR ACKER BILK & HIS PARAMOUNT JAZZ BAND	30	1960
WHITE CLIFFS OF DOVER RIGHTEOUS BROTHERS	21	1966
WHITE COATS (EP) NEW MODEL ARMY	50	1987
THE WHITE COLLAR BOY BELLE & SEBASTIAN	45	2006
WHITE FLAG DIDO	2	2003
THE WHITE HARE SETH LAKEMAN	47	2006
WHITE HORSE TAYLOR SWIFT	60	2009
WHITE HORSES JACKY	10	1968
WHITE LIE FOREIGNER	58	1994
WHITE LIES MR HUDSON	20	2009
WHITE LIGHT, WHITE HEAT DAVID BOWIE	46	1983
WHITE LIGHTNING FALL	56	1990
WHITE LINES (DON'T DO IT) DURAN DURAN FEATURING MELLE MEL & GRANDMASTER FLASH & THE FURIOUS FIVE	17	1995
WHITE LINES (DON'T DON'T DO IT) GRANDMASTER FLASH & MELLE MEL	7	1984
WHITE LOVE ONE DOVE	43	1993
(WHITE MAN) IN HAMMERSMITH PALAIS CLASH	32	1978
WHITE NO SUGAR CLINT BOON EXPERIENCE	61	1999
WHITE ONE IS EVIL ELLIOT MINOR	27	2007
WHITE PUNKS ON DOPE TUBES	28	1977
WHITE RIBBON DAY DELIRIOUS?	41	1997
WHITE RIOT CLASH	38	1977
WHITE ROOM CREAM	28	1969
WHITE RUSSIAN GALAXY CRIMEA	51	2006
WHITE SILVER SANDS BILL BLACK'S COMBO	50	1960
WHITE SKIES SUNSCREEM	25	1996
A WHITE SPORT COAT TERRY DENE	18	1957
A WHITE SPORT COAT (AND A PINK CARNATION) KING BROTHERS	6	1957
WHITE WEDDING BILLY IDOL	6	1985
WHITE WEDDING MURDERDOLLS	24	2003
A WHITER SHADE OF PALE PROCOL HARUM	1	1967
A WHITER SHADE OF PALE MUNICH MACHINE INTRODUCING CHRIS BENNETT	42	1978
A WHITER SHADE OF PALE ANNIE LENNOX	16	1995
WHO? ED CASE & SWEETIE IRIE	29	2001
WHO AM I [A] ADAM FAITH	5	1961
WHO AM I [B] BEENIE MAN	10	1998
WHO AM I [C] WILL YOUNG	11	2006
WHO ARE WE RONNIE HILTON	6	1956
WHO ARE WE VERA LYNN	30	1956
WHO ARE YOU WHO	18	1978
WHO CAN I RUN TO XSCAPE	31	1996
WHO CAN IT BE NOW? MEN AT WORK	45	1982
WHO CAN MAKE ME FEEL GOOD BASSHEADS	38	1992
WHO CARES GNARLS BARKLEY	60	2006
WHO COMES TO BOOGIE LITTLE BENNY & THE MASTERS	33	1985
WHO COULD BE BLUER JERRY LORDAN	16	1960
WHO DO U LOVE DEBORAH COX	31	1996
WHO DO YOU LOVE [A] JUICY LUCY	14	1970
WHO DO YOU LOVE? [B] INTRUDERS	65	1984
WHO DO YOU LOVE [C] JOSE PADILLA FEATURING ANGELA JOHN	59	1998
WHO DO YOU LOVE NOW (STRINGER) RIVA FEATURING DANNII MINOGUE	3	2001
WHO DO YOU THINK YOU ARE [A] CANDLEWICK GREEN	21	1974
WHO DO YOU THINK YOU ARE [B] KIM WILDE	49	1992
WHO DO YOU THINK YOU ARE [C] SAINT ETIENNE	23	1993
WHO DO YOU THINK YOU ARE [D] SPICE GIRLS	1	1997
WHO DO YOU THINK YOU ARE KIDDING JURGEN KLINSMANN TONEDEF ALLSTARS	13	2006
WHO DO YOU WANT FOR YOUR LOVE ICICLE WORKS	54	1986
WHO FEELS LOVE? OASIS	4	2000
WHO FOUND WHO JELLYBEAN FEATURING ELISA FIORILLO	10	1987
WHO GETS THE LOVE STATUS QUO	34	1988
WHO INVITED YOU DONNAS	61	2003
WHO IS IT [A] MANTRONIX	40	1987
WHO IS IT [B] MICHAEL JACKSON	10	1992
WHO IS IT [C] BJORK	26	2004
WHO IS SHE 2 U BRANDY	50	2005
WHO KEEPS CHANGING YOUR MIND SOUTH ST. PLAYER	49	2000
WHO KILLED BAMBI TEN POLE TUDOR	24	1979
WHO KNEW P!NK	5	2006
WHO LET IN THE RAIN CYNDI LAUPER	32	1994
WHO LET THE DOGS OUT BAHA MEN	2	2000
WHO LOVES YOU FOUR SEASONS	6	1975
WHO MADE WHO AC/DC	16	1986
WHO NEEDS ENEMIES COOPER TEMPLE CLAUSE	22	2002
WHO NEEDS LOVE LIKE THAT ERASURE	10	1985
WHO PAYS THE FERRYMAN YANNIS MARKOPOULOS	11	1977
WHO PAYS THE PIPER GARY CLAIL ON-U SOUND SYSTEM	31	1992
WHO PUT THE BOMP VISCOUNTS	21	1961
WHO PUT THE BOMP (IN THE BOMP-A-BOMP-A-BOMP) SHOWADDYWADDY	37	1982
WHO PUT THE LIGHTS OUT DANA	14	1971
WHO SAID (STUCK IN THE UK) PLANET FUNK	36	2003
WHO SAYS YOU CAN'T GO HOME BON JOVI	5	2006
WHO THE HELL ARE YOU MADISON AVENUE	10	2000
WHO TOLD YOU RONI SIZE/REPRAZENT	17	2000
WHO WANTS THE WORLD STRANGLERS	39	1980
WHO WANTS TO BE THE DISCO KING WONDER STUFF	28	1989
WHO WANTS TO LIVE FOREVER QUEEN	24	1986
WHO WANTS TO LIVE FOREVER SARAH BRIGHTMAN	45	1997
WHO WAS IT HURRICANE SMITH	23	1972
WHO WE BE DMX	34	2001
WHO WEARS THESE SHOES ELTON JOHN	50	1984
WHO WERE YOU WITH IN THE MOONLIGHT DOLLAR	14	1979
WHO WHAT WHEN WHERE WHY MANHATTAN TRANSFER	49	1978
WHO WHERE WHY JESUS JONES	21	1991
WHO WILL SAVE YOUR SOUL JEWEL	52	1997
WHO WILL YOU RUN TO HEART	30	1987
WHO YOU ARE PEARL JAM	18	1996
WHO YOU LOOKING AT SALFORD JETS	72	1980
WHO YOU WIT JAY-Z	65	1997
WHOA [A] BLACK ROB	44	2000
WHOA [B] LIL' KIM	43	2006
WHO'D HAVE KNOWN LILY ALLEN	39	2009
WHO'D SHE COO OHIO PLAYERS	43	1976
WHODUNNIT TAVARES	5	1977
WHOLE AGAIN ATOMIC KITTEN	1	2001
WHOLE LOTTA HISTORY GIRLS ALOUD	6	2006
WHOLE LOTTA LOVE C.C.S.	13	1970
WHOLE LOTTA LOVE GOLDBUG	3	1996
WHOLE LOTTA LOVE LED ZEPPELIN	21	1997
WHOLE LOTTA ROSIE AC/DC	36	1980
WHOLE LOTTA SHAKIN' GOIN' ON JERRY LEE LEWIS	8	1957
WHOLE LOTTA TROUBLE STEVIE NICKS	62	1989
WHOLE LOTTA WOMAN MARVIN RAINWATER	1	1958
WHOLE NEW WORLD [A] IT BITES	54	1986
A WHOLE NEW WORLD (ALADDIN'S THEME) [B] PEABO BRYSON & REGINA BELLE	12	1993
A WHOLE NEW WORLD [B] KATIE PRICE & PETER ANDRE	12	2006
THE WHOLE OF THE MOON WATERBOYS	3	1985
THE WHOLE OF THE MOON LITTLE CAESAR	68	1990
THE WHOLE TOWN'S LAUGHING AT ME TEDDY PENDERGRASS	44	1977
THE WHOLE WORLD OUTKAST FEATURING KILLER MIKE	19	2002
THE WHOLE WORLD LOST ITS HEAD GO-GOS	29	1995
WHOOMP! (THERE IT IS) TAG TEAM	34	1994
WHOOMP THERE IT IS BM DUBS PRESENT MR RUMBLE	32	2001
WHOOMPH! (THERE IT IS) CLOCK	4	1995
WHOOPS NOW JANET JACKSON	9	1995
WHOOPSIE DAISY TERRI WALKER	41	2005
WHOOSH WHOOSH	72	1997
WHO'S AFRAID OF THE BIG BAD LOVE WILD WEEKEND	70	1990
WHO'S AFRAID OF THE BIG BAD NOISE? AGE OF CHANCE	65	1987
WHO'S COMING ROUND 5050	54	2001
WHO'S CRYING NOW JOURNEY	46	1982
WHO'S DAVID BUSTED	1	2004
WHO'S GONNA FIND ME CORAL	25	2007
WHO'S GONNA LOVE ME IMPERIALS	17	1978
WHO'S GONNA RIDE YOUR WILD HORSES U2	14	1992
WHO'S GONNA ROCK YOU NOLANS	12	1980
WHO'S GOT A MATCH BIFFY CLYRO	27	2008
WHO'S IN THE HOUSE BEATMASTERS FEATURING MERLIN	8	1989
WHO'S IN THE STRAWBERRY PATCH WITH SALLY TONY ORLAND & DAWN	37	1974
WHO'S JOHNNY ('SHORT CIRCUIT' THEME) EL DeBARGE	60	1986
WHO'S LEAVING WHO HAZELL DEAN	4	1988
WHO'S LOVIN' YOU JACKSON 5	36	2009
WHO'S LOVING MY BABY SHOLA AMA	13	1997
WHO'S SORRY NOW JOHNNIE RAY	17	1956
WHO'S SORRY NOW CONNIE FRANCIS	1	1958
WHO'S THAT GIRL? [A] EURYTHMICS	3	1983
WHO'S THAT GIRL [B] FLYING PICKETS	71	1984
WHO'S THAT GIRL [C] MADONNA	1	1987
WHO'S THAT GIRL [D] EVE	6	2001
WHO'S THAT GIRL [E] ROBYN	26	2008
WHO'S THAT GIRL (SHE'S GOT IT) A FLOCK OF SEAGULLS	66	1985
WHO'S THAT MIX THIS YEAR'S BLONDE	62	1987
WHO'S THE BAD MAN DEE PATTEN	42	1999

Title / Artist	Peak Position	Year of Release
WHO'S THE DADDY LOVEBUG	35	2003
WHO'S THE DARKMAN DARKMAN	46	1994
WHO'S THE MACK MARK MORRISON	13	1997
WHO'S THE MAN HOUSE OF PAIN	23	1993
WHO'S ZOOMIN' WHO ARETHA FRANKLIN	11	1986
WHOSE FIST IS THIS ANYWAY EP PRONG	58	1992
WHOSE LAW (IS IT ANYWAY) GURU JOSH	26	1990
WHOSE PROBLEM? MOTELS	42	1980
WHY [A] ANTHONY NEWLEY	1	1960
WHY [A] FRANKIE AVALON	20	1960
WHY [A] DONNY OSMOND	3	1972
WHY [B] ROGER WHITTAKER	47	1971
WHY [C] CARLY SIMON	10	1982
WHY [C] GLAMMA KID	10	1999
WHY? [D] BRONSKI BEAT	6	1984
WHY [E] ANNIE LENNOX	5	1992
WHY [E] DJ SAMMY	7	2005
WHY [F] D MOB WITH CATHY DENNIS	23	1994
WHY [G] RICARDO DA FORCE	58	1996
WHY [H] 3T FEATURING MICHAEL JACKSON	2	1996
WHY [I] MIS-TEEQ	8	2001
WHY [J] AGENT SUMO	40	2002
WHY [K] GABRIELLE	42	2007
WHY ARE PEOPLE GRUDGEFUL FALL	43	1993
WHY ARE YOU BEING SO REASONABLE NOW WEDDING PRESENT	42	1988
WHY ARE YOU LOOKING GRAVE? MEW	53	2006
WHY BABY WHY PAT BOONE	17	1957
WHY BELIEVE IN YOU TEXAS	66	1991
WHY CAN'T I BE YOU [A] CURE	21	1987
WHY CAN'T I BE YOU? [B] SHED SEVEN	23	2003
WHY CAN'T I WAKE UP WITH YOU TAKE THAT	2	1993
WHY CAN'T THIS BE LOVE VAN HALEN	8	1986
WHY CAN'T WE BE LOVERS HOLLAND-DOZIER FEATURING LAMONT DOZIER	29	1972
WHY CAN'T WE LIVE TOGETHER TIMMY THOMAS	12	1973
WHY CAN'T YOU CLARENCE 'FROGMAN' HENRY	42	1961
WHY CAN'T YOU FREE SOME TIME ARMAND VAN HELDEN	34	2001
WHY DID YA TONY DI BART	46	1995
WHY DID YOU DO IT STRETCH	16	1975
WHY DIDN'T YOU CALL ME MACY GRAY	38	2000
WHY DO FOOLS FALL IN LOVE TEENAGERS FEATURING FRANKIE LYMON	1	1956
WHY DO FOOLS FALL IN LOVE ALMA COGAN	22	1956
WHY DO FOOLS FALL IN LOVE DIANA ROSS	4	1981
WHY DO I ALWAYS GET IT WRONG LIVE REPORT	73	1989
WHY DO I DO TYLER JAMES	25	2004
WHY DO LOVERS BREAK EACH OTHER'S HEARTS SHOWADDYWADDY	22	1980
WHY DO YOU KEEP ON RUNNING BOY STINX	49	2001
WHY DO YOU LOVE ME GARBAGE	7	2005
WHY DOES A MAN HAVE TO BE STRONG PAUL YOUNG	63	1987
WHY DOES IT ALWAYS RAIN ON ME TRAVIS	10	1999
WHY DOES MY HEART FEEL SO BAD MOBY	16	1999
WHY DON'T THEY UNDERSTAND GEORGE HAMILTON IV	22	1958
WHY DON'T WE FALL IN LOVE AMERIE FEATURING LUDACRIS	40	2002
WHY DON'T WE TRY AGAIN BRIAN MAY	44	1998
WHY DON'T YOU [A] RAGE	44	1993
WHY DON'T YOU [B] GRAMOPHONEDZIE	12	2010
WHY DON'T YOU BELIEVE ME JONI JAMES	11	1953
WHY DON'T YOU DANCE WITH ME FUTURE BREEZE	50	1997
WHY DON'T YOU DO IT FOR ME 22-20'S	41	2004
WHY DON'T YOU GET A JOB OFFSPRING	2	1999
WHY DON'T YOU TAKE ME ONE DOVE	30	1994
WHY D'YA LIE TO ME SPIDER	65	1983
WHY GO? FAITHLESS FEATURING ESTELLE	49	2005
WHY (LOOKING BACK) HEARTLESS CREW	50	2003
WHY ME [A] LINDA MARTIN	59	1992
WHY ME [B] A HOUSE	52	1994
WHY ME [C] PJ & DUNCAN	27	1994
WHY ME [D] ASHER D	43	2002
WHY (MUST WE FALL IN LOVE) DIANA ROSS & THE SUPREMES & THE TEMPTATIONS	31	1970
WHY MUST WE WAIT UNTIL TONIGHT TINA TURNER	16	1993
WHY NOT NOW MATT MONRO	24	1961
WHY NOT TONIGHT MOJOS	25	1964
WHY OH WHY SPEARHEAD	45	1997
WHY OH WHY OH WHY GILBERT O'SULLIVAN	6	1973
WHY SHE'S A GIRL FROM THE CHAINSTORE BUZZCOCKS	61	1980
WHY SHOULD I BOB MARLEY & THE WAILERS	42	1992
WHY SHOULD I BE LONELY TONY BRENT	24	1959
WHY SHOULD I CRY NONA HENDRYX	60	1987
WHY SHOULD I LOVE YOU DES'REE	44	1992
WHY WHY BYE BYE BOB LUMAN	46	1960
WHY WHY WHY DEJA VU	57	1994
WHY WON'T YOU GIVE ME YOUR LOVE ZUTONS	9	2006
WHY YOU FOLLOW ME ERIC BENET	48	2000
WHY YOU TREAT ME SO BAD SHAGGY FEATURING GRAND PUBA	11	1996
WHY YOU WANNA TI	22	2006
WHY'D YOU LIE TO ME ANASTACIA	25	2002
WHY'S EVERYBODY ALWAYS PICKIN' ON ME? BLOODHOUND GANG	56	1997
WIBBLING RIVALRY (INTERVIEWS WITH NOEL AND LIAM GALLAGHER) OAS*S	52	1995
WICHITA LINEMAN GLEN CAMPBELL	7	1969
WICKED ICE CUBE	62	1993
WICKED GAME CHRIS ISAAK	10	1990
WICKED LOVE OCEANIC	25	1991
WICKED SOUL KUBB	25	2005
WICKED WAYS BLOW MONKEYS	60	1986
WICKEDEST SOUND REBEL MC FEATURING TENOR FLY	43	1991
THE WICKER MAN IRON MAIDEN	9	2000
WICKY WACKY HOUSE PARTY TEAM	55	1985
WIDE AWAKE TWANG	15	2007
WIDE AWAKE IN A DREAM BARRY BIGGS	44	1981
WIDE BOY NIK KERSHAW	9	1985
WIDE EYED AND LEGLESS ANDY FAIRWEATHER-LOW	6	1975
WIDE EYED ANGEL ORIGIN	73	2000
WIDE OPEN SKY GOLDRUSH	70	2002
WIDE OPEN SPACE MANSUN	15	1996
WIDE PRAIRIE LINDA McCARTNEY	74	1998
THE WIDOW MARS VOLTA	20	2005
WIFEY NEXT	19	2000
WIG WAM BAM BLACK LACE	63	1986
WIG WAM BAM DAMIAN	49	1989
WIGGLE IT 2 IN A ROOM	3	1991
WIGGLY WORLD MR JACK	32	1997
WIGWAM WIGWAM	60	2006
WIG-WAM BAM SWEET	4	1972
WIKKA WRAP EVASIONS	20	1981
WILD 2NITE SHAGGY	61	2005
THE WILD AMERICA (EP) IGGY POP	63	1993
WILD AND WONDERFUL ALMIGHTY	50	1990
WILD AS ANGELS EP LEVELLERS	34	2002
WILD BLUE YONDER PAUL WELLER	22	2006
WILD BOYS DURAN DURAN	2	1984
WILD BOYS PHIXX	12	2004
WILD CAT GENE VINCENT	21	1956
WILD CHILD [A] W.A.S.P.	71	1986
WILD CHILD [B] ENYA	72	2001
WILD DANCES RUSLANA	47	2004
WILD FLOWER CULT	24	1987
WILD FRONTIER GARY MOORE	35	1987
WILD HEARTED SON CULT	40	1991
WILD HEARTED WOMAN ALL ABOUT EVE	33	1988
WILD HONEY BEACH BOYS	29	1967
WILD HORSES SUSAN BOYLE	9	2009
WILD IN THE COUNTRY ELVIS PRESLEY	4	1961
WILD IS THE WIND DAVID BOWIE	24	1981
WILD LOVE MUNGO JERRY	32	1973
WILD LUV ROACH MOTEL	75	1994
WILD 'N FREE REDNEX	55	1995
WILD NIGHT JOHN MELLENCAMP FEATURING ME'SHELL NDEGEOCELLO	34	1994
WILD ONE [A] BOBBY RYDELL	7	1960
THE WILD ONE [B] SUZI QUATRO	7	1974
THE WILD ONES SUEDE	18	1994
WILD SIDE MOTLEY CRUE	23	1988
WILD SIDE OF LIFE TOMMY QUICKLY & THE REMO FOUR	33	1964
WILD SIDE OF LIFE STATUS QUO	9	1976
THE WILD SON VEILS	74	2004
WILD SURF ASH	31	1998
WILD THING [A] TROGGS	2	1966
WILD THING [A] GOODIES	21	1975
WILD THING [B] TONE LOC	21	1989
WILD WEST HERO ELECTRIC LIGHT ORCHESTRA	6	1978
WILD WILD LIFE TALKING HEADS	43	1986
WILD WILD WEST [A] WILL SMITH FEATURING DRU HILL	2	1999
WILD WILD WEST [B] GET READY	65	1995
WILD WIND JOHN LEYTON	2	1961
WILD WOMEN DO NATALIE COLE	16	1990
WILD WOOD PAUL WELLER	14	1993
WILD WORLD JIMMY CLIFF	8	1970
WILD WORLD MAXI PRIEST	5	1988
WILD WORLD MR BIG	59	1993
WILD WORLD CAT STEVENS	52	2007
WILDERNESS JURGEN VRIES FEATURING SHENA	20	2003
WILDEST DREAMS IRON MAIDEN	6	2003
WILDLIFE (EP) GIRLSCHOOL	58	1982
WILDSIDE MARKY MARK & THE FUNKY BUNCH	42	1991
WILE OUT ZINC FEATURING MS DYNAMITE	38	2010
WILFRED THE WEASEL KEITH MICHELL	5	1980
WILL I EVER ALICE DEEJAY	7	2000
WILL I WHAT MIKE SARNE WITH BILLIE DAVIS	18	1962
WILL I? IAN VAN DAHL	5	2001
WILL SHE ALWAYS BE WAITING BLUEBELLS	72	1983
WILL THE WOLF SURVIVE LOS LOBOS	57	1985
WILL 2K WILL SMITH	2	1999
WILL WE BE LOVERS DEACON BLUE	31	1993
WILL YOU [A] HAZEL O'CONNOR	8	1981
WILL YOU [B] P.O.D.	68	2004
WILL YOU BE MY BABY INFINITI FEATURING GRAND PUBA	53	1996
WILL YOU BE THERE MICHAEL JACKSON	9	1993
WILL YOU BE THERE (IN THE MORNING) HEART	19	1993
WILL YOU BE WITH ME MARIA NAYLER	65	1998
WILL YOU LOVE ME TOMORROW SHIRELLES	4	1961
WILL YOU LOVE ME TOMORROW MELANIE	37	1974
WILL YOU LOVE ME TOMORROW BRYAN FERRY	23	1993
WILL YOU MARRY ME PAULA ABDUL	73	1992
WILL YOU SATISFY? CHERRELLE	57	1986
WILL YOU WAIT FOR ME KAVANA	29	1999
WILLIAM OTHERS	29	2005
WILLIAM, IT WAS REALLY NOTHING SMITHS	17	1984
WILLIE CAN ALMA COGAN WITH DESMOND LANE – PENNY WHISTLE	13	1956
WILLIE CAN BEVERLEY SISTERS	23	1956

Title / Artist	Peak Position	Year of Release
WILLING TO FORGIVE ARETHA FRANKLIN	17	1994
WILLINGLY MALCOLM VAUGHAN	13	1959
WILLOW TREE IVY LEAGUE	50	1966
WILMOT SABRES OF PARADISE	36	1994
WIMMIN' ASHLEY HAMILTON	27	2003
WIMOWEH KARL DENVER	4	1962
(WIN PLACE OR SHOW) SHE'S A WINNER INTRUDERS	14	1974
WINCHESTER CATHEDRAL NEW VAUDEVILLE BAND	4	1966
THE WIND PJ HARVEY	29	1999
THE WIND BENEATH MY WINGS LEE GREENWOOD	49	1984
WIND BENEATH MY WINGS BETTE MIDLER	5	1989
WIND BENEATH MY WINGS BILL TARMEY	40	1994
WIND BENEATH MY WINGS STEVEN HOUGHTON	3	1997
THE WIND CRIES MARY JIMI HENDRIX EXPERIENCE	6	1967
WIND IT UP GWEN STEFANI	3	2006
WIND IT UP (REWOUND) PRODIGY	11	1993
WIND ME UP (LET ME GO) CLIFF RICHARD	2	1965
WIND OF CHANGE SCORPIONS	2	1991
WIND THE BOBBIN UP JO JINGLES	21	2004
A WINDMILL IN OLD AMSTERDAM RONNIE HILTON	23	1965
WINDMILLS OF YOUR MIND NOEL HARRISON	8	1969
WINDOW IN THE SKIES U2	4	2007
WINDOW PANE (EP) REAL PEOPLE	60	1991
WINDOW SHOPPER 50 CENT	11	2005
WINDOW SHOPPING R. DEAN TAYLOR	36	1974
WINDOWLICKER APHEX TWIN	16	1999
WINDOWS '98 SIL	58	1998
WINDPOWER THOMAS DOLBY	31	1982
THE WINDSOR WALTZ VERA LYNN	11	1953
WINDSWEPT BRYAN FERRY	46	1985
WINGDINGS SUGARCOMA	57	2002
WINGS OF A BUTTERFLY H.I.M.	10	2005
WINGS OF A DOVE MADNESS	2	1983
WINGS OF LOVE BONE	55	1994
WINKER'S SONG (MISPRINT) IVOR BIGGUN & THE RED NOSE BURGLARS	22	1978
THE WINKLE MAN JUDGE DREAD	35	1976
THE WINNER [A] HEARTBEAT	70	1988
THE WINNER [B] COOLIO	53	1997
THE WINNER TAKES IT ALL ABBA	1	1980
THE WINNER'S SONG GERALDINE	2	2008
WINNING DAYS VINES	42	2004
WINTER [A] LOVE & MONEY	52	1991
WINTER [B] TORI AMOS	25	1992
WINTER [C] SPECIAL NEEDS	69	2004
WINTER [D] DT8 PROJECT FEATURING ANDREA BRITTON	35	2005
WINTER [E] CORD	34	2006
WINTER CEREMONY (TOR-CHENEY-NAHANA) SACRED SPIRIT	45	1996
WINTER IN JULY BOMB THE BASS	7	1991
WINTER MELODY DONNA SUMMER	27	1977
WINTER SONG CHRIS REA	27	1991
A WINTER STORY ALED JONES	51	1986
WINTER WINDS MUMFORD & SONS	44	2009
WINTER WONDERLAND JOHNNY MATHIS	17	1958
WINTER WONDERLAND COCTEAU TWINS	58	1993
WINTER WORLD OF LOVE ENGELBERT HUMPERDINCK	7	1969
A WINTER'S TALE [A] DAVID ESSEX	2	1982
A WINTER'S TALE [B] QUEEN	6	1995
WIPE OUT SURFARIS	5	1963
WIPEOUT FAT BOYS & THE BEACH BOYS	2	1987
WIPE OUT ANIMAL	38	1994
WIPE THE NEEDLE RAGGA TWINS	71	1991
WIRE TO WIRE RAZORLIGHT	5	2008
WIRED FOR SOUND CLIFF RICHARD	4	1981
WIRES ATHLETE	4	2005
WISDOM OF A FOOL NORMAN WISDOM	13	1957
THE WISDOM OF A FOOL RONNIE CARROLL	20	1957
WISE UP! SUCKER POP WILL EAT ITSELF	41	1989
WISEMEN JAMES BLUNT	23	2005
WISER TIME BLACK CROWES	34	1995
WISH SOUL II SOUL	24	1993
A WISH AWAY WONDER STUFF	43	1988
WISH I JEM	24	2005
WISH I COULD FLY ROXETTE	11	1999
WISH I DIDN'T MISS YOU ANGIE STONE	30	2002
WISH I HAD AN ANGEL NIGHTWISH	60	2004
WISH I WAS SKINNY BOO RADLEYS	75	1993
WISH I WERE YOU ALISHA'S ATTIC	29	1999
WISH THE WORLD AWAY AMERICAN MUSIC CLUB	46	1994
WISH YOU WERE HERE [A] EDDIE FISHER	8	1953
WISH YOU WERE HERE [B] FIRST LIGHT	71	1984
WISH YOU WERE HERE [C] ALOOF	43	1996
WISH YOU WERE HERE [D] WYCLEF JEAN	28	2001
WISH YOU WERE HERE [E] INCUBUS	27	2002
WISHES HUMAN NATURE	44	1997
WISHFUL THINKING CHINA CRISIS	9	1984
WISHIN' AND HOPIN' MERSEYBEATS	13	1964
WISHING BUDDY HOLLY	10	1963
WISHING I WAS HERE NATALIE IMBRUGLIA	19	1998
WISHING I WAS LUCKY WET WET WET	6	1987
WISHING (IF I HAD A PHOTOGRAPH OF YOU) A FLOCK OF SEAGULLS	10	1982
WISHING ON A STAR ROSE ROYCE	3	1978
WISHING ON A STAR FRESH 4 FEATURING LIZZ E	10	1989
WISHING ON A STAR COVER GIRLS	38	1992
WISHING ON A STAR 88.3 FEATURING LISA MAY	61	1995
WISHING ON A STAR JAY-Z FEATURING GWEN DICKEY	13	1998
WISHING ON A STAR PAUL WELLER	11	2004
WISHING WELL [A] FREE	7	1973
WISHING WELL [B] TERENCE TRENT D'ARBY	4	1987
THE WISHING WELL [C] G.O.S.H.	22	1988
WISHING YOU WERE HERE ALISON MOYET	72	1991
WISHING YOU WERE SOMEHOW HERE AGAIN SARAH BRIGHTMAN	7	1987
WISHLIST PEARL JAM	30	1998
THE WITCH RATTLES	8	1970
WITCH DOCTOR DON LANG & HIS FRANTIC FIVE	5	1958
WITCH DOCTOR DAVID SEVILLE	11	1958
WITCH DOCTOR CARTOONS	2	1999
THE WITCH QUEEN OF NEW ORLEANS REDBONE	2	1971
WITCHCRAFT FRANK SINATRA	12	1958
WITCHCRAFT ROBERT PALMER	50	1992
WITCHES' BREW JANIE JONES	46	1966
THE WITCH'S PROMISE JETHRO TULL	4	1970
WITH A GIRL LIKE YOU TROGGS	1	1966
WITH A LITTLE HELP FROM MY FRIENDS YOUNG IDEA	10	1967
WITH A LITTLE HELP FROM MY FRIENDS JOE BROWN	32	1967
WITH A LITTLE HELP FROM MY FRIENDS JOE COCKER	1	1968
WITH A LITTLE HELP FROM MY FRIENDS WET WET WET	1	1988
WITH A LITTLE HELP FROM MY FRIENDS SAM & MARK	1	2004
WITH A LITTLE LOVE SAM BROWN	44	1990
WITH A LITTLE LUCK WINGS	5	1978
WITH ALL MY HEART PETULA CLARK	4	1957
WITH ARMS WIDE OPEN CREED	13	2001
WITH EVERY BEAT OF MY HEART TAYLOR DAYNE	53	1989
WITH EVERY HEARTBEAT [A] FIVE STAR	49	1989
WITH EVERY HEARTBEAT [B] ROBYN WITH KLEERUP	1	2007
WITH GOD ON OUR SIDE NEVILLE BROTHERS	47	1989
WITH LOVE HILARY DUFF	29	2007
WITH ME DESTINY'S CHILD	19	1998
WITH MY OWN EYES SASH!	10	2000
WITH ONE LOOK BARBRA STREISAND	30	1993
WITH OR WITHOUT YOU U2	4	1987
WITH OR WITHOUT YOU MARY KIANI	46	1997
WITH PEN IN HAND VIKKI CARR	39	1969
WITH THE EYES OF A CHILD CLIFF RICHARD	20	1969
WITH THE WIND AND THE RAIN IN YOUR HAIR PAT BOONE	21	1959
WITH THESE HANDS SHIRLEY BASSEY	38	1960
WITH THESE HANDS TOM JONES	13	1965
WITH YOU [A] JESSICA SIMPSON	7	2004
WITH YOU [B] SUBWAYS	29	2005
WITH YOU [C] CHRIS BROWN	8	2008
WITH YOU I'M BORN AGAIN BILLY PRESTON & SYREETA	2	1980
WITH YOUR LOVE MALCOLM VAUGHAN	18	1956
WITHOUT A DOUBT BLACK SHEEP	60	1994
WITHOUT HER HERB ALPERT & THE TIJUANA BRASS	36	1969
WITHOUT LOVE [A] DONNA LEWIS	39	1997
WITHOUT LOVE [B] DINA CARROLL	13	1999
WITHOUT LOVE (THERE IS NOTHING) TOM JONES	10	1969
WITHOUT ME EMINEM	1	2002
WITHOUT YOU [A] MATT MONRO	37	1965
WITHOUT YOU [B] NILSSON	1	1972
WITHOUT YOU [B] MARIAH CAREY	1	1994
WITHOUT YOU [C] MOTLEY CRUE	39	1990
WITHOUT YOU [D] LUCY PEARL	51	2001
WITHOUT YOU [E] EL PRESIDENTE	30	2005
WITHOUT YOU [F] FEELING	53	2008
WITHOUT YOU (ONE AND ONE) LINDY LAYTON	71	1991
WITHOUT YOUR LOVE ROGER DALTREY	55	1980
WITNESS (1 HOPE) ROOTS MANUVA	45	2001
WITNESS (EP) ANN NESBY	42	1996
WITNESS FOR THE WORLD CRY BEFORE DAWN	67	1989
THE WIZARD PAUL HARDCASTLE	15	1986
WIZARDS OF THE SONIC WESTBAM	32	1995
WIZZY WOW BLACKSTREET	37	2003
WOE IS ME HELEN SHAPIRO	35	1963
W.O.L.D. HARRY CHAPIN	34	1974
WOLF [A] SHY FX	60	2002
THE WOLF [B] DAVE CLARKE	66	2002
WOMAN [A] JOSE FERRER	7	1954
WOMAN [B] PETER & GORDON	28	1966
WOMAN [C] JOHN LENNON	1	1981
WOMAN [D] ANTI-NOWHERE LEAGUE	72	1982
WOMAN [E] NENEH CHERRY	9	1996
WOMAN [F] WOLFMOTHER	31	2006
WOMAN FROM LIBERIA JIMMIE RODGERS	18	1958
THE WOMAN I LOVE HOLLIES	42	1993
WOMAN IN CHAINS TEARS FOR FEARS	26	1989
WOMAN IN CHAINS TEARS FOR FEARS FEATURING OLETA ADAMS	57	1992
A WOMAN IN LOVE [A] FRANKIE LAINE	1	1956
WOMAN IN LOVE [A] FOUR ACES FEATURING AL ALBERTS	19	1956
WOMAN IN LOVE [A] RONNIE HILTON	30	1956
WOMAN IN LOVE [B] THREE DEGREES	3	1979
WOMAN IN LOVE [C] BARBRA STREISAND	1	1980
WOMAN IN LOVE [C] LIZ McCLARNON	5	2006
WOMAN IN LOVE [D] REBEKAH RYAN	64	1997
THE WOMAN IN ME [A] DONNA SUMMER	62	1983

Title / Artist	Peak Position	Year of Release
THE WOMAN IN ME [B] KINANE	73	1996
WOMAN IN ME [C] CARLEEN ANDERSON	74	1998
WOMAN IN WINTER SKIDS	49	1980
WOMAN OF MINE DEAN FRIEDMAN	52	1978
WOMAN OF PRINCIPLE TROUBLE FUNK	65	1987
WOMAN TO WOMAN BEVERLEY CRAVEN	40	1991
WOMAN TROUBLE ARTFUL DODGER FEATURING ROBBIE CRAIG & CRAIG DAVID	6	2000
WOMAN WOMAN GARY PUCKETT AND THE UNION GAP	48	1968
WOMANIZER BRITNEY SPEARS	3	2008
WOMANKIND LITTLE ANGELS	12	1993
A WOMAN'S PLACE GILBERT O'SULLIVAN	42	1974
A WOMAN'S STORY MARC ALMOND & THE WILLING SINNERS	41	1986
WOMAN'S WORLD JAGS	75	1980
A WOMAN'S WORTH ALICIA KEYS	18	2002
WOMBLING MERRY CHRISTMAS WOMBLES	2	1974
THE WOMBLING SONG WOMBLES	4	1974
WOMBLING WHITE TIE AND TAILS WOMBLES	22	1975
WOMEN BEAT THEIR MEN JUNIOR CARTIER	70	1999
WOMEN IN UNIFORM SKYHOOKS	73	1979
WOMEN IN UNIFORM IRON MAIDEN	35	1980
WOMEN OF IRELAND MIKE OLDFIELD	70	1997
WON BETA BAND	30	2001
WONDER EMBRACE	14	2001
THE WONDER OF LOVE LOVELAND FEATURING RACHEL McFARLANE	53	1995
THE WONDER OF YOU RONNIE HILTON	22	1959
THE WONDER OF YOU RAY PETERSON	23	1959
THE WONDER OF YOU ELVIS PRESLEY	1	1970
WONDERBOY [A] KINKS	36	1968
WONDERBOY [B] TENACIOUS D	21	2002
WONDERFUL [A] MARI WILSON	47	1983
WONDERFUL [B] RUNRIG	29	1993
WONDERFUL [C] ADAM ANT	32	1995
WONDERFUL [D] EVERCLEAR	36	2000
WONDERFUL [E] BRIAN WILSON	29	2004
WONDERFUL [F] JA RULE FEATURING R KELLY & ASHANTI	1	2004
WONDERFUL [G] GARY GO	25	2009
WONDERFUL CHRISTMAS TIME PAUL McCARTNEY	6	1979
WONDERFUL COPENHAGEN DANNY KAYE	5	1953
WONDERFUL DREAM ANNE-MARIE DAVID	13	1973
WONDERFUL EXCUSE FAMILY CAT	48	1994
WONDERFUL LAND SHADOWS	1	1962
WONDERFUL LIFE BLACK	8	1986
WONDERFUL LIFE TJ DAVIS	42	2001
WONDERFUL LIFE TINA COUSINS	58	2005
WONDERFUL NIGHT FATBOY SLIM	51	2004
THE WONDERFUL SECRET OF LOVE ROBERT EARL	17	1959
WONDERFUL THINGS FRANKIE VAUGHAN	22	1958
A WONDERFUL TIME UP THERE PAT BOONE	2	1958
A WONDERFUL TIME UP THERE ALVIN STARDUST	56	1981
WONDERFUL TONIGHT DAMAGE	3	1997
WONDERFUL TONIGHT (LIVE) ERIC CLAPTON	30	1991
WONDERFUL WONDERFUL RONNIE HILTON	27	1957
WONDERFUL WONDERFUL GARY MILLER	29	1957
WONDERFUL WORLD [A] SAM COOKE	2	1960
WONDERFUL WORLD [A] HERMAN'S HERMITS	7	1965
WONDERFUL WORLD [B] WORLDS APART	51	1993
WONDERFUL WORLD [C] JAMES MORRISON	8	2006
WONDERFUL WORLD BEAUTIFUL PEOPLE JIMMY CLIFF	6	1969
WONDERFUL WORLD OF THE YOUNG DANNY WILLIAMS	8	1962
WONDERING DIRTY PRETTY THINGS	34	2006
WONDERING WHY MJ COLE	30	2003

Title / Artist	Peak Position	Year of Release
WONDERLAND [A] COMMODORES	40	1980
WONDERLAND [B] BIG COUNTRY	8	1984
WONDERLAND [C] PAUL YOUNG	24	1986
WONDERLAND [D] 911	13	1999
WONDERLAND [E] PSYCHEDELIC WALTONS FEATURING ROISIN MURPHY	37	2002
WONDERMAN RIGHT SAID FRED	55	1994
WONDEROUS STORIES YES	7	1977
WONDERWALL MIKE FLOWERS POPS	2	1995
WONDERWALL OASIS	2	1995
WONDERWALL DE-CODE FEATURING BEVERLI SKEETE	69	1996
WONDERWALL RYAN ADAMS	27	2004
WONDROUS PLACE BILLY FURY	25	1960
WON'T GET FOOLED AGAIN WHO	9	1971
WON'T GIVE IN FINN BROTHERS	26	2004
WON'T GO HOME WITHOUT YOU MAROON 5	44	2007
WON'T GO QUIETLY EXAMPLE	6	2007
WON'T LET THIS FEELING GO SUNDANCE	40	2000
WON'T SOMEBODY DANCE WITH ME LYNSEY DE PAUL	14	1973
WON'T STOP LOVING YOU A CERTAIN RATIO	55	1990
WON'T TAKE IT LYING DOWN HONEYZ	7	2000
WON'T TALK ABOUT IT NORMAN COOK FEATURING BILLY BRAGG	29	1989
WON'T TALK ABOUT IT BEATS INTERNATIONAL	9	1990
WON'T YOU HOLD MY HAND NOW KING	24	1985
WON'T YOU SAY CHRISTIAN FRY	48	1999
WOO HOO 5,6,7,8'S	28	2004
WOOD BEEZ (PRAY LIKE ARETHA FRANKLIN) SCRITTI POLITTI	10	1984
WOODEN HEART ELVIS PRESLEY	1	1961
WOODPECKERS FROM SPACE VIDEO KIDS	72	1985
WOODSTOCK MATTHEWS' SOUTHERN COMFORT	1	1970
WOO-HAH!! GOT YOU ALL IN CHECK BUSTA RHYMES	8	1996
WOOLY BULLY SAM THE SHAM & THE PHARAOHS	11	1965
WOPBABALUBOP FUNKDOOBIEST	37	1993
THE WORD DOPE SMUGGLAZ	62	1998
THE WORD GIRL SCRITTI POLITTI FEATURING RANKING ANN	6	1985
A WORD IN YOUR EAR ALFIE	66	2002
THE WORD IS LOVE (SAY THE WORD) VOICES OF LIFE	26	1998
WORD IS OUT KYLIE MINOGUE	16	1991
WORD LOVE RHIANNA	41	2002
WORD OF MOUTH MIKE + THE MECHANICS	13	1991
WORD PERFECT KRS ONE	70	1997
WORD UP CAMEO	3	1986
WORD UP GUN	8	1994
WORD UP MELANIE G	14	1999
WORDS [A] ALLISONS	34	1961
WORDS [B] BEE GEES	8	1968
WORDS [B] RITA COOLIDGE	25	1978
WORDS [B] BOYZONE	1	1996
WORDS [C] FR DAVID	2	1983
WORDS [D] CHRISTIANS	18	1989
WORDS [E] PAUL VAN DYK FEATURING TONI HALLIDAY	54	1997
WORDS ARE NOT ENOUGH STEPS	5	2001
WORDS JUST GET IN THE WAY RICHARD ASHCROFT	40	2006
WORDS OF LOVE MAMAS & THE PAPAS	47	1967
WORDS THAT SAY MEGA CITY FOUR	66	1991
WORDS WITH THE SHAMEN DAVID SYLVIAN	72	1985
WORDY RAPPINGHOOD TOM TOM CLUB	7	1981
WORDY RAPPINGHOOD CHICKS ON SPEED	66	2004
WORK CIARA FEATURING MISSY ELLIOTT	52	2009
WORK [A] TECHNOTRONIC FEATURING REGGIE	40	1991

Title / Artist	Peak Position	Year of Release
WORK [B] BARRINGTON LEVY	65	1994
WORK [C] JIMMY EAT WORLD	49	2005
WORK [D] KELLY ROWLAND	4	2008
WORK [E] SATURDAYS	22	2009
WORK ALL DAY BARRY BIGGS	38	1976
WORK IT [A] MISSY ELLIOTT	6	2002
WORK IT [B] NELLY FEATURING JUSTIN TIMBERLAKE	7	2003
WORK IT OUT [A] SHIVA	36	1995
WORK IT OUT [B] DEF LEPPARD	22	1996
WORK IT OUT [C] BEYONCE	7	2002
WORK IT TO THE BONE LNR	64	1989
WORK IT UP SLEAZE SISTERS	74	1998
WORK MI BODY MONKEY MAFIA FEATURING PATRA	75	1996
W.O.R.K. (N.O. NAH NO NO MY DADDY DON'T) BOW WOW WOW	62	1981
WORK REST AND PLAY (EP) MADNESS	6	1980
WORK THAT BODY DIANA ROSS	7	1982
WORK THAT MAGIC DONNA SUMMER	74	1991
WORK THAT SUCKER TO DEATH XAVIER	53	1982
WORK WORK WORK (PUB CLUB SLEEP) RAKES	28	2005
WORKAHOLIC 2 UNLIMITED	4	1992
THE WORKER FISCHER-Z	53	1979
WORKIN' FOR THE MAN ROY ORBISON	50	1962
WORKIN' OVERTIME DIANA ROSS	32	1989
WORKIN' UP A SWEAT FULL CIRCLE	41	1987
WORKING FOR THE YANKEE DOLLAR SKIDS	20	1979
WORKING IN A GOLDMINE AZTEC CAMERA	31	1988
WORKING IN THE COALMINE LEE DORSEY	8	1966
WORKING MAN RITA MacNEIL	11	1990
WORKING MOTHER MARTYN JOSEPH	65	1992
WORKING MY WAY BACK TO YOU FOUR SEASONS WITH FRANKIE VALLI	50	1966
WORKING MY WAY BACK TO YOU – FORGIVE ME GIRL (MEDLEY) DETROIT SPINNERS	1	1980
WORKING ON A BUILDING OF LOVE CHAIRMEN OF THE BOARD	20	1972
WORKING ON IT CHRIS REA	53	1989
WORKING WITH FIRE AND STEEL CHINA CRISIS	48	1983
WORLD BEE GEES	9	1967
THE WORLD NICK HEYWARD	47	1995
WORLD AT YOUR FEET EMBRACE	3	2006
WORLD CUP '98 – PAVANE WIMBLEDON CHORAL SOCIETY	26	1998
WORLD DESTRUCTION TIME ZONE	44	1985
WORLD FILLED WITH LOVE CRAIG DAVID	15	2003
WORLD GO ROUND BUSTA RHYMES FEATURING ESTELLE	66	2009
WORLD, HOLD ON (CHILDREN OF THE SKY) BOB SINCLAR FEATURING STEVE EDWARDS	9	2006
WORLD IN MOTION ENGLANDNEWORDER	1	1990
THE WORLD IN MY ARMS NAT 'KING' COLE	36	1961
WORLD IN MY EYES DEPECHE MODE	17	1990
THE WORLD IN MY HANDS SNAP! FEATURING SUMMER	44	1995
WORLD IN UNION KIRI TE KANAWA	4	1991
WORLD IN UNION SHIRLEY BASSEY/BRYN TERFEL	35	1999
WORLD IN UNION '95 LADYSMITH BLACK MAMBAZO FEATURING PJ POWERS	47	1995
WORLD IN YOUR HANDS CULTURE BEAT	52	1994
THE WORLD IS A GHETTO GETO BOYS FEATURING FLAJ	49	1996
THE WORLD IS FLAT ECHOBELLY	31	1997
THE WORLD IS MINE [A] MALCOLM VAUGHAN	29	1957
THE WORLD IS MINE [B] ICE CUBE	60	1997
THE WORLD IS MINE [C] DAVID GUETTA FEATURING JD DAVIS	49	2005
THE WORLD IS NOT ENOUGH GARBAGE	11	1999

Title	Artist	Peak Position	Year of Release
THE WORLD IS OUTSIDE	GHOSTS	35	2007
THE WORLD IS STONE	CYNDI LAUPER	15	1992
THE WORLD IS WHAT YOU MAKE IT	PAUL BRADY	67	1996
WORLD LOOKING IN	MORCHEEBA	48	2001
WORLD OF BROKEN HEARTS	AMEN CORNER	24	1967
WORLD OF GOOD	SAW DOCTORS	15	1996
A WORLD OF OUR OWN [A]	SEEKERS	3	1965
WORLD OF OUR OWN [B]	WESTLIFE	1	2002
WORLD ON FIRE	SARAH McLACHLAN	72	2004
THE WORLD OUTSIDE	FOUR ACES	18	1959
THE WORLD OUTSIDE	RONNIE HILTON WITH THE MICHAEL SAMMES SINGERS	18	1959
THE WORLD OUTSIDE	RUSS CONWAY	24	1959
WORLD OUTSIDE YOUR WINDOW	TANITA TIKARAM	58	1989
THE WORLD SHE KNOWS	DMAC	33	2002
THE WORLD SHOULD REVOLVE AROUND ME	LITTLE JACKIE	14	2008
WORLD SHUT YOUR MOUTH	JULIAN COPE	19	1986
WORLD (THE PRICE OF LOVE)	NEW ORDER	13	1993
THE WORLD TONIGHT	PAUL McCARTNEY	23	1997
THE WORLD WE KNEW	FRANK SINATRA	33	1967
A WORLD WITHOUT HEROES	KISS	55	1982
A WORLD WITHOUT LOVE	PETER & GORDON	1	1964
WORLD WITHOUT YOU	BELINDA CARLISLE	34	1988
WORLDS APART	CACTUS WORLD NEWS	58	1986
THE WORLD'S GREATEST	R KELLY	4	2002
WORLD'S ON FIRE	BREED 77	43	2004
WORRIED ABOUT RAY	HOOSIERS	5	2007
WORRY ABOUT IT LATER	FUTUREHEADS	52	2006
WORRY ABOUT THE WIND	HAL	53	2004
WORST COMES TO WORST	DILATED PEOPLES	29	2002
WORZEL SONG	JON PERTWEE	33	1980
WOT	CAPTAIN SENSIBLE	26	1982
WOT DO U CALL IT?	WILEY	31	2004
WOT'S IT TO YA	ROBBIE NEVIL	43	1987
WOULD	ALICE IN CHAINS	19	1993
WOULD I LIE TO YOU [A]	WHITESNAKE	37	1981
WOULD I LIE TO YOU? [B]	EURYTHMICS	17	1985
WOULD I LIE TO YOU [C]	CHARLES & EDDIE	1	1992
WOULD YOU BE HAPPIER	CORRS	14	2001
WOULD YOU...?	TOUCH & GO	3	1998
WOULDN'T CHANGE A THING [A]	KYLIE MINOGUE	2	1989
WOULDN'T CHANGE A THING [B]	HAVEN	57	2004
WOULDN'T IT BE GOOD	NIK KERSHAW	4	1984
WOULDN'T IT BE NICE	BEACH BOYS	58	1990
WOULDN'T YOU	N-DUBZ	64	2009
WOULDN'T YOU LOVE TO LOVE ME	TAJA SEVELLE	59	1988
WOW [A]	KATE BUSH	14	1979
WOW [B]	KYLIE MINOGUE	5	2007
WOW AND FLUTTER	STEREOLAB	70	1994
WOW WOW – NA NA	GRAND PLAZ	41	1990
WOZ NOT WOZ	ERIC PRYDZ & STEVE ANGELLO	55	2004
WRAP HER UP	ELTON JOHN	12	1985
WRAP ME UP	ALEX PARTY	17	1995
WRAP MY BODY TIGHT	JOHNNY GILL	57	1991
WRAP MY WORDS AROUND YOU	DANIEL BEDINGFIELD	12	2005
WRAP YOUR ARMS AROUND ME	AGNETHA FALTSKOG	44	1983
WRAPPED AROUND HER	JOAN ARMATRADING	56	1992
WRAPPED AROUND YOUR FINGER	POLICE	7	1983
WRAPPING PAPER	CREAM	34	1966
WRATH CHILD	IRON MAIDEN	31	1981
WRATH OF KANE	BIG DADDY KANE	52	1989
THE WRECK OF THE EDMUND FITZGERALD	GORDON LIGHTFOOT	40	1977
WRECK OF THE ANTOINETTE	DAVE DEE, DOZY, BEAKY, MICK & TICH	14	1968
THE WRECKONING	BOOMKAT	37	2003
WRECKX SHOP	WRECKX-N-EFFECT FEATURING APACHE INDIAN	26	1994
WRENCH	ALMIGHTY	26	1994
WRESTLEMANIA	WWF SUPERSTARS	14	1993
WRITER'S BLOCK	JUST JACK	74	2007
WRITING ON THE WALL	TOMMY STEELE	30	1961
WRITING TO REACH YOU	TRAVIS	14	1999
WRITTEN IN THE STARS	ELTON JOHN & LeANN RIMES	10	1999
WRITTEN ON THE WIND	ROGER DALTREY	46	1977
WRONG [A]	EVERYTHING BUT THE GIRL	8	1996
WRONG [B]	DEPECHE MODE	24	2009
WRONG IMPRESSION	NATALIE IMBRUGLIA	10	2002
WRONG NUMBER	CURE	62	1997
WRONG OR RIGHT	SABRE FEATURING PREZIDENT BROWN	71	1995
WUNDERBAR	TEN POLE TUDOR	34	1981
WUTHERING HEIGHTS	KATE BUSH	1	1978

X

Title	Artist	Peak Position	Year of Release
X [A]	XZIBIT FEATURING SNOOP DOGG	14	2001
X [B]	WARRIOR	64	2003
X [C]	LIBERTY X	47	2006
THE X FILES	MARK SNOW	2	1996
X GON GIVE IT TO YA	DMX	6	2003
X-RATED	DJ NATION	52	2004
X RAY FOLLOW ME	SPACE FROG	70	2002
X Y & ZEE	POP WILL EAT ITSELF	15	1991
XANADU	OLIVIA NEWTON-JOHN & ELECTRIC LIGHT ORCHESTRA	1	1980
XANADU	SHARLEEN SPITERI	71	2010
X-FILES	DJ DADO	8	1996
XMAS PARTY	SNOWMEN	44	1982
X-MAS TIME	DJ OTZI	51	2001
XPAND YA MIND (EXPANSIONS)	WAG YA TAIL	49	1992
XPRESS YOURSELF	FAMILY FOUNDATION	42	1992
X-RAY	SUB FOCUS	60	2005
XX SEX	WE'VE GOT A FUZZBOX & WE'RE GONNA USE IT	41	1986

Y

Title	Artist	Peak Position	Year of Release
Y CONTROL	YEAH YEAH YEAH	29	2004
Y (HOW DEEP IS YOUR LOVE)	DJ SCOT PROJECT	57	1998
Y VIVA ESPANA	SYLVIA	4	1974
Y VIVA SUSPENDERS	JUDGE DREAD	27	1976
YA DON'T SEE THE SIGNS	MARK B & BLADE	23	2001
YA MAMA	FATBOY SLIM	30	2001
YA PLAYIN YASELF	JERU THE DAMAJA	67	1996
YA YA TWIST	PETULA CLARK	14	1962
YAAH	D-SHAKE	20	1990
YABBA DABBA DOO	DARKMAN	37	1994
YAH MO B THERE	JAMES INGRAM WITH MICHAEL McDONALD	12	1984
YAHHH!	SOULJA BOY TELL'EM FEATURING ARAB	49	2008
YAKETY YAK	COASTERS	12	1958
YEAH [A]	AUDIOWEB	73	1996
YEAH [B]	WANNADIES	56	2000
YEAH [C]	USHER FEATURING LIL' JON & LUDACRIS	1	2004
YEAH! BUDDY	ROYAL HOUSE	35	1989
YEAH YEAH	BODYROX FEATURING LUCIANA	2	2006
THE YEAH YEAH YEAH SONG	FLAMING LIPS	16	2006
YEAH YEAH YEAH YEAH YEAH [A]	POGUES	43	1988
YEAH YEAH YEAH YEAH YEAH [B]	WEDDING PRESENT	51	1994
YEAR OF DECISION	THREE DEGREES	13	1974
YEAR OF THE CAT	AL STEWART	31	1977
YEAR OF THE RAT	BADLY DRAWN BOY	38	2004
YEAR 3000	BUSTED	2	2003
YEARNING FOR YOUR LOVE	GAP BAND	47	1981
YEARS FROM NOW	DR HOOK	47	1980
YEARS GO BY	STAN CAMPBELL	65	1987
YEARS LATER	CACTUS WORLD NEWS	59	1986
YEARS MAY COME, YEARS MAY GO	HERMAN'S HERMITS	7	1970
YEBO	ART OF NOISE	63	1989
YEH YEH	GEORGIE FAME & THE BLUE FLAMES	1	1964
YEH YEH	MATT BIANCO	13	1985
YEH YEH YEH	MELANIE C	27	2003
YEHA-NOHA (WISHES OF HAPPINESS AND PROSPERITY)	SACRED SPIRIT	37	1995
YEKE YEKE	MORY KANTE	25	1988
YELLOW	COLDPLAY	4	2000
YELLOW PEARL	PHILIP LYNOTT	14	1981
YELLOW RIVER	CHRISTIE	1	1970
YELLOW ROSE OF TEXAS	MITCH MILLER	2	1955
YELLOW ROSE OF TEXAS	GARY MILLER	13	1955
YELLOW ROSE OF TEXAS	RONNIE HILTON	15	1955
YELLOW SUBMARINE	BEATLES	1	1966
YEOVIL TRUE	YEOVIL TOWN FC	36	2004
YEP	DUANE EDDY & THE REBELS	17	1959
YER OLD	REEF	21	1997
YES [A]	MERRY CLAYTON	70	1988
YES [B]	McALMONT & BUTLER	8	1995
YES I DO	SHAKIN' STEVENS	60	1990
YES I WILL	HOLLIES	9	1965
YES MY DARLING DAUGHTER	EYDIE GORME	10	1962
YES SIR I CAN BOOGIE	BACCARA	1	1977
YES TONIGHT JOSEPHINE	JOHNNIE RAY	1	1957
YES TONIGHT JOSEPHINE	JETS	25	1981
YESTERDAY	MATT MONRO	8	1965
YESTERDAY	MARIANNE FAITHFULL	36	1965
YESTERDAY	RAY CHARLES	44	1967
YESTERDAY	BEATLES	8	1976
YESTERDAY	WET WET WET	4	1997
YESTERDAY HAS GONE	CUPID'S INSPIRATION	4	1968
YESTERDAY HAS GONE	PJ PROBY & MARC ALMOND FEATURING THE MY LIFE STORY ORCHESTRA	58	1996
YESTERDAY MAN	CHRIS ANDREWS	3	1965
YESTERDAY ONCE MORE	CARPENTERS	2	1973
YESTERDAY ONCE MORE	REDD KROSS	45	1994
YESTERDAY TODAY	OCEAN COLOUR SCENE	49	1991
YESTERDAY WENT TOO SOON	FEEDER	20	1999
YESTERDAY WHEN I WAS MAD	PET SHOP BOYS	13	1994
YESTERDAYS	GUNS N' ROSES	8	1992
YESTERDAY'S DREAMS	FOUR TOPS	23	1968
YESTERDAY'S GONE	CHAD STUART & JEREMY CLYDE	37	1963
YESTERDAY'S MEN	MADNESS	18	1985
YESTER-ME YESTER-YOU YESTERDAY	STEVIE WONDER	2	1969
YET ANOTHER DAY	ARMIN VAN BUUREN FEATURING RAY WILSON	70	2003
YIM	JEZ & CHOOPIE	36	1998
YING TONG SONG	GOONS	3	1956
YIPPIE I OH	BARNDANCE BOYS	32	2003
Y.M.C.A.	VILLAGE PEOPLE	1	1978
YO! (EXCUSE ME MISS)	CHRIS BROWN	13	2006
YO! SWEETNESS	MC HAMMER	16	1991
YO YO GET FUNKY	DJ 'FAST' EDDIE	54	1989

Title / Artist	Peak Position	Year of Release
THE YODELLING SONG FRANK IFIELD FEATURING THE BACKROOM BOYS	40	1991
YOSHIMI BATTLES THE PINK ROBOTS PART 1 FLAMING LIPS	18	2003
YOU [A] BANDWAGON	34	1969
YOU [B] GEORGE HARRISON	38	1975
YOU [C] RANDY EDELMAN	49	1977
YOU [D] TEN SHARP	1	1992
YOU [E] BONNIE RAITT	31	1994
YOU [F] STAXX FEATURING CAROL LEEMING	50	1995
YOU [G] POINT BREAK	14	2000
YOU [H] S CLUB 7	2	2002
YOU [I] SHAZNAY LEWIS	56	2004
YOU [J] THEE UNSTRUNG	59	2004
YOU [K] LLOYD FEATURING LIL WAYNE	45	2007
YOU AIN'T GOIN' NOWHERE BYRDS	45	1968
YOU AIN'T LIVIN' TILL YOU'RE LOVIN' MARVIN GAYE & TAMMI TERRELL	21	1969
YOU AIN'T REALLY DOWN STATUS IV	56	1983
YOU AIN'T SEEN NOTHIN' YET BACHMAN-TURNER OVERDRIVE	2	1974
YOU AIN'T SEEN NOTHIN' YET BUS STOP FEATURING RANDY BACHMAN	22	1998
YOU ALL DAT BAHA MEN: GUEST VOCAL IMANI COPPOLA	14	2001
YOU ALWAYS HURT THE ONE YOU LOVE CONNIE FRANCIS	13	1958
YOU ALWAYS HURT THE ONE YOU LOVE CLARENCE 'FROGMAN' HENRY	6	1961
YOU AND I [A] RICK JAMES	46	1978
YOU AND I [B] WILL YOUNG	2	2002
YOU & I [C] GRAHAM COXON	39	2006
YOU AND I [D] MEDINA	39	2009
YOU AND I WILL NEVER SEE THINGS EYE TO EYE KINGMAKER	33	1995
YOU AND ME [A] LINER	44	1979
YOU AND ME [B] DJ SEDUCTION	26	1992
YOU AND ME [C] LISA B	39	1994
YOU AND ME [D] EASYWORLD	57	2002
YOU AND ME [E] UNITING NATIONS	15	2005
YOU AND ME [F] ONE NIGHT ONLY	46	2007
YOU & ME SONG WANNADIES	18	1996
YOU AND ME TONIGHT [A] AURRA	12	1986
YOU AND ME (TONIGHT) [B] ALISTAIR GRIFFIN	18	2004
YOU AND YOUR HEART SO BLUE BUCKS FIZZ	43	1985
YOU ANGEL YOU MANFRED MANN'S EARTH BAND	54	1979
YOU ARE LIONEL RICHIE	43	1983
YOU ARE ALIVE FRAGMA	4	2001
YOU ARE AWFUL DICK EMERY	43	1973
YOU ARE BEAUTIFUL JOHNNY MATHIS	38	1960
YOU ARE EVERYTHING PEARLS	41	1973
YOU ARE EVERYTHING DIANA ROSS & MARVIN GAYE	5	1974
YOU ARE EVERYTHING MELANIE WILLIAMS & JOE ROBERTS	28	1995
YOU ARE IN MY SYSTEM ROBERT PALMER	53	1983
YOU ARE MY DESTINY PAUL ANKA	6	1958
YOU ARE MY FIRST LOVE RUBY MURRAY	16	1956
YOU ARE MY HIGH DEMON VS HEARTBREAKER	70	2001
YOU ARE MY LADY FREDDIE JACKSON	49	1985
YOU ARE MY LOVE LIVERPOOL EXPRESS	11	1976
YOU ARE MY MELODY CHANGE	48	1984
YOU ARE MY SISTER ANTONY & THE JOHNSONS	39	2005
YOU ARE MY WORLD COMMUNARDS	21	1985
YOU ARE NOT ALONE MICHAEL JACKSON	1	1995
YOU ARE NOT ALONE X FACTOR FINALISTS	1	2009
YOU ARE SOMEBODY FULL INTENTION	75	1998
YOU ARE THE GENERATION THAT BOUGHT MORE SHOES AND YOU GET WHAT YOU DESERVE JOHNNY BOY	50	2004
YOU ARE THE MUSIC IN ME CAST OF HIGH SCHOOL MUSICAL 2	26	2007
YOU ARE THE ONE A-HA	13	1988
YOU ARE THE SUNSHINE OF MY LIFE STEVIE WONDER	7	1973
YOU ARE THE UNIVERSE BRAND NEW HEAVIES	21	1997
YOU ARE THE WAY PRIMITIVES	58	1991
YOU ARE THE WEAKEST LINK ECHOBASS	53	2001
YOU BE ILLIN' RUN DMC	42	1987
YOU BELONG IN ROCK 'N' ROLL TIN MACHINE	33	1991
YOU BELONG TO ME [A] JO STAFFORD	1	1952
YOU BELONG TO ME [B] GARY GLITTER	40	1976
YOU BELONG TO ME [C] JX	17	1995
YOU BELONG TO ME [D] MICHAEL MOOG	62	2001
YOU BELONG WITH ME TAYLOR SWIFT	30	2009
YOU BET YOUR LOVE HERBIE HANCOCK	18	1979
YOU BETTER MOUNT RUSHMORE PRESENTS THE KNACK	53	1999
YOU BETTER COME HOME PETULA CLARK	44	1965
YOU BETTER NOT WASTE MY TIME N-DUBZ	26	2007
YOU BETTER YOU BET WHO	9	1981
YOU BLOW ME AWAY ROBERT PALMER	38	1994
YOU BRING ME DOWN BLOOD RED SHOES	64	2008
YOU BRING ME JOY [A] MEECHIE	74	1995
YOU BRING ME JOY [B] RHYTHM FACTOR	53	1995
YOU BRING ME UP K-CI & JOJO	21	1997
YOU BRING ON THE SUN LONDONBEAT	32	1992
YOU BROKE MY HEART LOVE BITES	13	2005
YOU CAME KIM WILDE	3	1988
YOU CAME YOU SAW YOU CONQUERED PEARLS	32	1972
YOU CAN CALL ME AL PAUL SIMON	4	1986
YOU CAN COUNT ON ME JAKI GRAHAM	62	1995
YOU CAN DANCE (IF YOU WANT TO) GO GO LORENZO & THE DAVIS PINCKNEY PROJECT	46	1986
YOU CAN DO IT [A] AL HUDSON & THE PARTNERS	15	1979
YOU CAN DO IT [B] ICE CUBE FEATURING MACK 10 & MS TOI	2	2004
YOU CAN DO MAGIC [A] LIMMIE & THE FAMILY COOKIN'	3	1973
YOU CAN DO MAGIC [B] AMERICA	59	1982
YOU CAN GET IT MAXX	21	1994
YOU CAN GET IT IF YOU REALLY WANT DESMOND DEKKER	2	1970
YOU CAN GO YOUR OWN WAY CHRIS REA	28	1994
YOU CAN HAVE HIM DIONNE WARWICK	37	1965
YOU CAN HAVE IT ALL [A] GEORGE McCRAE	23	1975
YOU CAN HAVE IT ALL [B] EVE GALLAGHER	43	1995
YOU CAN HAVE IT (TAKE MY HEART) ROBERT PALMER	66	1983
YOU CAN LEAVE ME NOW HOTHOUSE FLOWERS	65	1998
YOU CAN MAKE ME DANCE SING OR ANYTHING (EVEN TAKE THE DOG FOR A WALK, MEND A FUSE, FOLD AWAY THE IRONING BOARD, OR ANY OTHER DOMESTIC SHORTCOMINGS) ROD STEWART & THE FACES	12	1974
YOU CAN NEVER STOP ME LOVING YOU KENNY LYNCH	10	1963
YOU CAN TALK TO ME SEAHORSES	15	1997
YOU CAN WIN IF YOU WANT MODERN TALKING	70	1985
YOU CAN'T BE TRUE TO TWO DAVE KING FEATURING THE KEYNOTES	11	1956
YOU CAN'T BLAME LOVE THOMAS & TAYLOR	53	1986
YOU CAN'T CHANGE ME ROGER SANCHEZ FEATURING ARMAND VAN HELDEN AND N'DEA DAVENPORT	25	2001
YOU CAN'T FOOL ME DENNIS MYSTERY JETS	41	2005
YOU CAN'T GO HOME AGAIN DJ SHADOW	30	2002
YOU CAN'T HAVE IT ALL ASH	16	2007
YOU CAN'T HIDE (YOUR LOVE FROM ME) DAVID JOSEPH	13	1983
YOU CAN'T HURRY LOVE [A] SUPREMES	3	1966
YOU CAN'T HURRY LOVE [A] PHIL COLLINS	1	1982
YOU CAN'T HURRY LOVE [B] CONCRETES	55	2004
YOU CAN'T RUN FROM LOVE MAXINE SINGLETON	57	1983
YOU CAN'T SIT DOWN PHIL UPCHURCH COMBO	39	1966
YOU CAN'T STEAL MY LOVE MANDO DIAO	73	2005
YOU CAN'T STOP ROCK 'N' ROLL TWISTED SISTER	43	1983
YOU CANT STOP THE BEAT (HAIRSPRAY) NIKKI BLONSKY, ZAC EFRON & AMANDA BYNES	71	2007
YOU CAN'T STOP THE REIGN SHAQUILLE O'NEAL	40	1997
YOU CAUGHT MY EYE JUDY BOUCHER	18	1987
YOU COME FROM EARTH LENA	69	1993
YOU COME THROUGH PJ HARVEY	41	2004
YOU COULD BE MINE GUNS N' ROSES	3	1991
YOU COULD BE MY EVERYTHING MIKEY GRAHAM	62	2001
YOU COULD HAVE BEEN A LADY HOT CHOCOLATE	22	1971
YOU COULD HAVE BEEN WITH ME SHEENA EASTON	54	1981
YOU DID CUT ME CHINA CRISIS	54	1985
YOU DIDN'T EXPECT THAT BILLY CRAWFORD	35	2003
YOU DISAPPEAR FROM VIEW TEARDROP EXPLODES	41	1983
YOU DO McALMONT & BUTLER	17	1995
YOU DO SOMETHING TO ME [A] PAUL WELLER	9	1995
YOU DO SOMETHING TO ME [B] DUM DUMS	27	2000
YOU DON'T BELIEVE ME STRAY CATS	57	1981
YOU DON'T BRING ME FLOWERS BARBRA (Streisand) & NEIL (Diamond)	5	1978
YOU DON'T CARE ABOUT US PLACEBO	5	1998
YOU DON'T FOOL ME – THE REMIXES QUEEN	17	1996
YOU DON'T HAVE TO BE A BABY TO CRY CARAVELLES	6	1963
YOU DON'T HAVE TO BE A STAR (TO BE IN MY SHOW) MARILYN McCOO & BILLY DAVIS, JR	7	1977
YOU DON'T HAVE TO BE IN THE ARMY TO FIGHT IN THE WAR MUNGO JERRY	13	1971
YOU DON'T HAVE TO GO CHI-LITES	3	1976
YOU DON'T HAVE TO SAY YOU LOVE ME DUSTY SPRINGFIELD	1	1966
YOU DON'T HAVE TO SAY YOU LOVE ME ELVIS PRESLEY	9	1971
YOU DON'T HAVE TO SAY YOU LOVE ME GUYS & DOLLS	5	1976
YOU DON'T HAVE TO SAY YOU LOVE ME DENISE WELCH	23	1995
YOU DON'T HAVE TO WORRY MARY J BLIGE	36	1993
YOU DON'T KNOW [A] HELEN SHAPIRO	1	1961
YOU DON'T KNOW [B] BERLIN	39	1987
YOU DON'T KNOW [C] CYNDI LAUPER	27	1997
YOU DON'T KNOW [D] MASS SYNDICATE FEATURING SU SU BOBIEN	71	1998
YOU DON'T KNOW [E] 702	36	1999
YOU DON'T KNOW [F] 50 CENT	32	2007
(YOU DON'T KNOW) HOW GLAD I AM KIKI DEE BAND	33	1975

Title / Artist	Peak Position	Year of Release
YOU DON'T KNOW ME [A] RAY CHARLES	9	1962
YOU DON'T KNOW ME [B] ARMAND VAN HELDEN FEATURING DUANE HARDEN	1	1999
YOU DON'T KNOW MY NAME ALICIA KEYS	19	2003
YOU DON'T KNOW NOTHIN' FOR REAL	54	1995
YOU DON'T KNOW (OH-OH-OH) SERIOUS INTENTION	75	1985
YOU DON'T KNOW WHAT LOVE IS WHITE STRIPES	18	2007
YOU DON'T KNOW WHAT YOU'VE GOT RAL DONNER	25	1961
YOU DON'T LOVE ME [A] GARY WALKER	26	1966
YOU DON'T LOVE ME [B] MARILYN	40	1984
YOU DON'T LOVE ME [C] JAGGED EDGE	66	1990
YOU DON'T LOVE ME [D] KOOKS	12	2006
YOU DON'T LOVE ME (NO NO NO) DAWN PENN	3	1994
YOU DON'T MISS YOUR WATER CRAIG DAVID	43	2004
YOU DON'T NEED A REASON PHIL FEARON & GALAXY	42	1985
YOU DON'T NEED SOMEONE NEW LOTUS EATERS	53	1983
YOU DON'T OWE ME A THING JOHNNIE RAY	12	1957
YOU DON'T UNDERSTAND HOUSE OF LOVE	46	1992
YOU DON'T UNDERSTAND ME ROXETTE	42	1996
YOU DREAMER BIG COUNTRY	68	1995
YOU DRIVE ME CRAZY [A] SHAKIN' STEVENS	2	1981
(YOU DRIVE ME) CRAZY [B] BRITNEY SPEARS	5	1999
YOU DRIVE ME CRAZY [B] SUGARCOMA	57	2002
YOU DROVE ME TO IT HELL IS FOR HEROES	28	2002
YOU (EP) FIVE THIRTY	72	1991
YOU FOUND ME FRAY	35	2009
YOU GAVE ME LOVE CROWN HEIGHTS AFFAIR	10	1980
YOU GAVE ME SOMEBODY TO LOVE MANFRED MANN	36	1966
YOU GET THE BEST FROM ME (SAY SAY SAY) ALICIA MYERS	58	1984
YOU GET WHAT YOU GIVE NEW RADICALS	5	1999
YOU GET WHAT YOU GIVE LMC FEATURING RACHEL McFARLANE	30	2006
YOU GIVE LOVE A BAD NAME BON JOVI	14	1986
YOU GIVE ME SOMETHING JAMIROQUAI	16	2001
YOU GIVE ME SOMETHING JAMES MORRISON	5	2006
YOU GO TO MY HEAD BRYAN FERRY	33	1975
YOU GONNA WANT ME TIGA	64	2005
YOU GOT IT ROY ORBISON	3	1989
YOU GOT IT (THE RIGHT STUFF) NEW KIDS ON THE BLOCK	1	1989
YOU GOT ME [A] CHRISTIAN FRY	45	1998
YOU GOT ME [B] ROOTS FEATURING ERYKAH BADU	31	1999
YOU GOT ME BURNING PESHAY FEATURING CO-ORDINATE	41	2002
(YOU GOT ME) BURNING UP CEVIN FISHER FEATURING LOLEATTA HOLLOWAY	14	1999
YOU GOT ME ROCKING ROLLING STONES	23	1994
YOU GOT ME RUNNING LENNY WILLIAMS	67	1978
YOU GOT NOTHING ON ME GLITTERATI	36	2005
YOU GOT SOUL JOHNNY NASH	6	1969
YOU GOT THE DIRTEE LOVE FLORENCE + THE MACHINE FEATURING DIZZEE RASCAL	2	2010
YOU GOT THE FLOOR ARTHUR ADAMS	38	1981
YOU GOT THE LOVE [A] SOURCE FEATURING CANDI STATON	4	1991
YOU GOT THE LOVE [A] SOLITAIRE	63	2005
YOU'VE GOT THE LOVE [A] FLORENCE + THE MACHINE	13	2009
YOU GOT THE LOVE [B] T2 FEATURING ROBIN S	62	1997
YOU GOT THE POWER [A] WAR	58	1982
YOU GOT THE POWER [B] QFX	33	1996
YOU GOT THE STYLE ATHLETE	37	2002
YOU GOT TO BE THERE KADOC	45	1996
YOU GOT WHAT IT TAKES MARV JOHNSON	7	1960
YOU GOT WHAT IT TAKES JOHNNY KIDD & THE PIRATES	25	1960
YOU GOT WHAT IT TAKES DAVE CLARK FIVE	28	1967
YOU GOT WHAT IT TAKES SHOWADDYWADDY	2	1977
YOU GOTTA BE DES'REE	10	1994
YOU GOTTA BE A HUSTLER IF YOU WANNA GET ON SUE WILKINSON	25	1980
YOU GOTTA BELIEVE MARKY MARK & THE FUNKY BUNCH	54	1992
(YOU GOTTA) FIGHT FOR YOUR RIGHT TO PARTY BEASTIE BOYS	11	1987
YOU GOTTA HAVE LOVE IN YOUR HEART SUPREMES & THE FOUR TOPS	25	1971
YOU GOTTA LOVE SOMEONE ELTON JOHN	33	1990
YOU GOTTA STOP ELVIS PRESLEY	38	1967
(YOU GOTTA WALK) DON'T LOOK BACK PETE TOSH	43	1978
YOU HAD ME JOSS STONE	9	2004
YOU HAVE MARC ALMOND	57	1984
YOU HAVE BEEN LOVED GEORGE MICHAEL	2	1997
YOU HAVE KILLED ME MORRISSEY	3	2006
YOU HAVE PLACED A CHILL IN MY HEART EURYTHMICS	16	1988
YOU HAVEN'T DONE NOTHIN' STEVIE WONDER	30	1974
YOU HELD THE WORLD IN YOUR ARMS IDLEWILD	9	2002
YOU JUST MIGHT SEE ME CRY OUR KID	2	1976
YOU KEEP IT ALL IN BEAUTIFUL SOUTH	8	1989
YOU KEEP ME HANGIN' ON [A] SUPREMES	8	1966
YOU KEEP ME HANGIN' ON [A] VANILLA FUDGE	18	1967
YOU KEEP ME HANGIN' ON [A] KIM WILDE	2	1986
(YOU KEEP ME) HANGIN' ON [B] CLIFF RICHARD	13	1974
YOU KEEP ME HANGIN' ON – STOP IN THE NAME OF LOVE (MEDLEY) RONI HILL	36	1977
YOU KEEP RUNNING AWAY FOUR TOPS	26	1967
YOU KNOW HOW TO LOVE ME PHYLLIS HYMAN	47	1980
YOU KNOW HOW WE DO IT ICE CUBE	41	1994
YOU KNOW I LOVE YOU...DON'T YOU HOWARD JONES	43	1986
YOU KNOW I'M NO GOOD AMY WINEHOUSE	18	2007
YOU KNOW ME ROBBIE WILLIAMS	6	2009
YOU KNOW ME BETTER ROISIN MURPHY	47	2008
YOU KNOW MY NAME CHRIS CORNELL	7	2006
YOU KNOW THAT I LOVE YOU DONELL JONES	41	2002
YOU KNOW WHAT I MEAN VERNONS GIRLS	16	1962
(YOU KNOW) YOU CAN DO IT CENTRAL LINE	67	1981
YOU KNOWS I LOVES YOU GOLDIE LOOKIN CHAIN	22	2005
YOU LAY SO EASY ON MY MIND ANDY WILLIAMS	32	1975
YOU LEARN ALANIS MORISSETTE	24	1996
YOU LET YOUR HEART GO TOO FAST SPIN DOCTORS	66	1994
YOU LIED TO ME CATHY DENNIS	34	1992
YOU LIFT ME UP REBEKAH RYAN	26	1996
YOU LIGHT MY FIRE SHEILA B. DEVOTION	44	1978
YOU LIGHT UP MY LIFE DEBBY BOONE	48	1977
YOU LIKE ME DON'T YOU JERMAINE JACKSON	41	1981
YOU LITTLE FOOL ELVIS COSTELLO	52	1982
YOU LITTLE THIEF FEARGAL SHARKEY	5	1986
YOU LITTLE TRUSTMAKER TYMES	18	1974
YOU LOOK SO FINE GARBAGE	19	1999
YOU LOVE US MANIC STREET PREACHERS	16	1991
YOU LOVE YOU SUBCIRCUS	61	1997
YOU MADE ME BELIEVE IN MAGIC BAY CITY ROLLERS	34	1977
YOU MADE ME LOVE YOU NAT 'KING' COLE	22	1959
YOU MADE ME THE THIEF OF YOUR HEART SINEAD O'CONNOR	42	1994
YOU MAKE IT HEAVEN TERRI WELLS	53	1983
YOU MAKE IT MOVE DAVE DEE, DOZY, BEAKY, MICK & TICH	26	1966
YOU MAKE IT REAL JAMES MORRISON	7	2008
YOU MAKE LOVING FUN FLEETWOOD MAC	45	1977
YOU MAKE ME FEEL BRAND NEW STYLISTICS	2	1974
YOU MAKE ME FEEL BRAND NEW SIMPLY RED	7	2003
(YOU MAKE ME FEEL LIKE A) NATURAL WOMAN MARY J BLIGE	23	1995
YOU MAKE ME FEEL LIKE DANCING LEO SAYER	2	1976
YOU MAKE ME FEEL LIKE DANCING GROOVE GENERATION FEATURING LEO SAYER	32	1998
YOU MAKE ME FEEL (MIGHTY REAL) SYLVESTER	8	1978
YOU MAKE ME FEEL (MIGHTY REAL) JIMMY SOMERVILLE	5	1990
YOU MAKE ME FEEL MIGHTY REAL DREAM FREQUENCY	65	1994
YOU MAKE ME FEEL (MIGHTY REAL) BYRON STINGILY	13	1998
YOU MAKE ME GO OOH KRISTINE BLOND	35	2002
YOU MAKE ME SICK P!NK	9	2001
YOU MAKE ME WANNA... USHER	1	1998
YOU MAKE ME WANT TO SCREAM DANDYS	71	1998
YOU MAKE ME WORK CAMEO	74	1988
YOU MAKE NO BONES ALFIE	61	2001
YOU ME AND US ALMA COGAN	18	1957
YOU MEAN EVERYTHING TO ME NEIL SEDAKA	45	1960
YOU MEAN THE WORLD TO ME TONI BRAXTON	30	1994
YOU MIGHT NEED SOMEBODY RANDY CRAWFORD	11	1981
YOU MIGHT NEED SOMEBODY SHOLA AMA	4	1997
YOU MUST BE PREPARED TO DREAM IAN McNABB	54	1994
YOU MUST GO ON BERNARD BUTLER	44	1999
YOU MUST HAVE BEEN A BEAUTIFUL BABY BOBBY DARIN	10	1961
YOU MUST LOVE ME MADONNA	10	1996
YOU MY LOVE FRANK SINATRA	13	1955
YOU NEED HANDS MAX BYGRAVES	3	1958
YOU NEED LOVE LIKE I DO TOM JONES & HEATHER SMALL	24	2000
YOU NEED WHEELS MERTON PARKAS	40	1979
YOU NEEDED ME ANNE MURRAY	22	1979
YOU NEEDED ME BOYZONE	1	1999
YOU NEVER CAN TELL CHUCK BERRY	23	1964
YOU NEVER DONE IT LIKE THAT CAPTAIN & TENNILLE	63	1978
YOU NEVER KNOW MARLY	23	2004
YOU NEVER KNOW WHAT YOU'VE GOT ME & YOU FEATURING WE THE PEOPLE BAND	31	1979
YOU NEVER LOVE THE SAME WAY TWICE ROZALLA	16	1994
YOU ON MY MIND SWING OUT SISTER	28	1989
YOU ONLY LIVE TWICE NANCY SINATRA	11	1967
YOU ONLY TELL ME YOU LOVE ME WHEN YOU'RE DRUNK PET SHOP BOYS	8	2000
YOU ONLY YOU RITA PAVONE	21	1967
YOU OUGHTA KNOW ALANIS MORISSETTE	22	1995
YOU OVERDID IT DOLL COURTEENERS	28	2010
YOU OWE IT ALL TO ME TEXAS	39	1993
YOU PLAYED YOURSELF ICE-T	64	1990
YOU + ME TECHNIQUE	56	1999

Title / Artist	Peak Position	Year of Release
YOU + ME = LOVE UNDISPUTED TRUTH	43	1977
YOU PUT ME IN HEAVEN WITH YOUR TOUCH RHYTHM OF LIFE	24	2000
YOU RAISE ME UP DANIEL O'DONNELL	22	2003
YOU RAISE ME UP WESTLIFE	1	2005
YOU RAISE ME UP JOSH GROBAN	74	2007
YOU REALLY GOT ME KINKS	1	1964
YOU REMIND ME MARY J BLIGE	48	1993
YOU REMIND ME OF SOMETHING R KELLY	24	1995
YOU ROCK MY WORLD MICHAEL JACKSON	2	2001
YOU SAID NO BUSTED	1	2003
(YOU SAID) YOU'D GIMME SOME MORE KC & THE SUNSHINE BAND	41	1983
YOU SCARE ME TO DEATH MARC BOLAN & T REX	51	1981
YOU SEE THE TROUBLE WITH ME BARRY WHITE	2	1976
YOU SEE THE TROUBLE WITH ME BLACK LEGEND	1	2000
YOU SEND ME SAM COOKE	29	1958
YOU SEND ME ROD STEWART	7	1974
YOU SENT ME FLYING AMY WINEHOUSE	60	2004
YOU SEXY DANCER ROCKFORD FILES	34	1995
YOU SEXY SUGAR PLUM (BUT I LIKE IT) RODGER COLLINS	22	1976
YOU SEXY THING HOT CHOCOLATE	2	1975
YOU SEXY THING T-SHIRT	63	1997
YOU SHOOK ME ALL NIGHT LONG AC/DC	38	1980
YOU SHOULD BE... BLOCKSTER	3	1999
YOU SHOULD BE DANCING BEE GEES	5	1976
YOU SHOULD BE MINE BRIAN McKNIGHT FEATURING MA$E	36	1998
YOU SHOULD HAVE KNOWN LAURA WHITE	32	2009
YOU SHOULD HAVE KNOWN BETTER TC CURTIS	50	1985
YOU SHOULD READILY KNOW PIRATES FEATURING ENYA, SHOLA AMA, NAILA BOSS & ISHANI	8	2004
YOU SHOWED ME SALT-N-PEPA	15	1991
YOU SHOWED ME LIGHTNING SEEDS	8	1997
YOU SPIN ME ROUND (LIKE A RECORD) DEAD OR ALIVE	1	1985
YOU STILL TOUCH ME STING	27	1996
YOU STOLE THE SUN FROM MY HEART MANIC STREET PREACHERS	5	1999
YOU STOOD UP V	12	2004
YOU SURE LOOK GOOD TO ME PHYLLIS HYMAN	56	1981
YOU SURROUND ME ERASURE	15	1989
YOU TAKE ME AWAY REEL	31	2002
YOU TAKE ME UP THOMPSON TWINS	2	1984
YOU TAKE MY BREATH AWAY [A] SUREAL	15	2000
YOU TAKE MY BREATH AWAY [B] EVA CASSIDY	54	2003
YOU TAKE MY HEART AWAY DE ETTA LITTLE & NELSON PIGFORD	35	1977
YOU TALK BABYSHAMBLES	54	2007
YOU TALK TOO MUCH SULTANS OF PING FC	26	1993
YOU THINK YOU OWN ME HINDA HICKS	19	1998
YOU THINK YOU'RE A MAN DIVINE	16	1984
YOU TO ME ARE EVERYTHING REAL THING	1	1976
YOU TO ME ARE EVERYTHING SONIA	13	1991
YOU TO ME ARE EVERYTHING SEAN MAGUIRE	16	1995
YOU TOOK THE WORDS RIGHT OUT OF MY MOUTH MEAT LOAF	33	1978
YOU TRIP ME UP JESUS & MARY CHAIN	55	1985
YOU USED TO HOLD ME [A] SCOTT & LEON	19	2000
YOU USED TO HOLD ME [B] CALVIN HARRIS	27	2010
YOU USED TO HOLD ME SO TIGHT THELMA HOUSTON	49	1984
YOU USED TO LOVE ME FAITH EVANS	42	1995
YOU USED TO SALSA RICHIE RICH FEATURING RALPHI ROSARIO	52	1991
YOU WANNA KNOW THUNDER	49	1999
YOU WANT IT YOU GOT IT DETROIT EMERALDS	12	1973
YOU WANT THIS JANET JACKSON	14	1994
(YOU WANT TO) MAKE A MEMORY BON JOVI	33	2007
YOU WEAR IT WELL [A] ROD STEWART	1	1972
YOU WEAR IT WELL [B] EL DeBARGE WITH DeBARGE	54	1985
YOU WERE ALWAYS THE ONE CRIBS	66	2004
(YOU WERE MADE FOR) ALL MY LOVE JACKIE WILSON	33	1960
YOU WERE MADE FOR ME FREDDIE & THE DREAMERS	3	1963
YOU WERE MEANT FOR ME JEWEL	32	1997
YOU WERE ON MY MIND CRISPIAN ST PETERS	2	1966
YOU WERE RIGHT BADLY DRAWN BOY	9	2002
YOU WERE THE LAST LAUGH DANDY WARHOLS	34	2003
YOU WERE THERE HEINZ	26	1964
YOU WEREN'T IN LOVE WITH ME BILLY FIELD	67	1982
YOU WEREN'T THERE LENE MARLIN	59	2003
YOU WILL RISE SWEETBACK	64	1997
YOU WILL YOU WON'T ZUTONS	22	2004
YOU WIN AGAIN BEE GEES	1	1987
YOU WOKE UP MY NEIGHBOURHOOD BILLY BRAGG	54	1991
YOU WON'T BE LEAVING HERMAN'S HERMITS	20	1966
YOU WON'T FIND ANOTHER FOOL LIKE ME NEW SEEKERS	1	1973
YOU WON'T FORGET ABOUT ME DANNII MINOGUE VS FLOWER POWER	7	2004
YOU WON'T SEE ME CRY WILSON PHILLIPS	18	1992
YOU WOT? DJ Q FEATURING MC BONEZ	50	2008
YOU WOULDN'T KNOW LOVE CHER	55	1990
YOU YOU ROMEO SHIRLEY BASSEY	29	1957
YOU YOU YOU ALVIN STARDUST	6	1974
YOU'LL ALWAYS BE A FRIEND HOT CHOCOLATE	23	1972
YOU'LL ALWAYS FIND ME IN THE KITCHEN AT PARTIES JONA LEWIE	16	1980
YOU'LL ANSWER TO ME CLEO LAINE	5	1961
YOU'LL BE IN MY HEART PHIL COLLINS	17	1999
YOU'LL BE MINE (PARTY TIME) GLORIA ESTEFAN	18	1996
YOU'LL BE SORRY STEPS	4	2001
YOU'LL COME 'ROUND STATUS QUO	14	2004
YOU'LL NEVER BE ALONE ANASTACIA	31	2002
YOU'LL NEVER BE SO WRONG HOT CHOCOLATE	52	1981
YOU'LL NEVER FIND ANOTHER LOVE LIKE MINE LOU RAWLS	10	1976
YOU'LL NEVER GET TO HEAVEN DIONNE WARWICK	20	1964
YOU'LL NEVER GET TO HEAVEN EP STYLISTICS	24	1976
YOU'LL NEVER KNOW [A] SHIRLEY BASSEY	6	1961
YOU'LL NEVER KNOW [B] HI GLOSS	12	1981
YOU'LL NEVER KNOW WHAT YOU'RE MISSING REAL THING	16	1977
YOU'LL NEVER KNOW WHAT YOU'RE MISSING ('TIL YOU TRY) EMILE FORD & THE CHECKMATES	12	1960
YOU'LL NEVER NEVER KNOW PLATTERS	23	1957
YOU'LL NEVER STOP ME LOVING YOU SONIA	1	1989
YOU'LL NEVER WALK ALONE GERRY & THE PACEMAKERS	1	1963
YOU'LL NEVER WALK ALONE ELVIS PRESLEY	44	1968
YOU'LL NEVER WALK ALONE CROWD	1	1985
YOU'LL NEVER WALK ALONE ROBSON & JEROME	1	1996
YOU'LL NEVER WALK ALONE CARRERAS/ DOMINGO/PAVAROTTI WITH MEHTA	35	1998
YOU'LL SEE MADONNA	5	1995
YOUNG AGAIN SHINING	52	2002
YOUNG AMERICANS DAVID BOWIE	18	1975
YOUNG AMERICANS TALKING DAVID VAN DAY	43	1983
YOUNG AND FOOLISH RONNIE HILTON	17	1955
YOUNG AND FOOLISH EDMUND HOCKRIDGE	10	1956
YOUNG AND FOOLISH DEAN MARTIN	20	1956
THE YOUNG AND THE HOPELESS GOOD CHARLOTTE	34	2003
YOUNG AT HEART [A] FRANK SINATRA	12	1954
YOUNG AT HEART [B] BLUEBELLS	1	1984
YOUNG BLOOD UFO	36	1980
YOUNG BOY PAUL McCARTNEY	19	1997
YOUNG DISCIPLES (EP) YOUNG DISCIPLES	48	1992
YOUNG EMOTIONS RICKY NELSON	48	1960
YOUNG FOLKS PETER BJORN & JOHN FEATURING BERGSMAN	13	2006
YOUNG FOREVER JAY-Z FEATURING MR HUDSON	10	2009
YOUNG, FREE AND SINGLE SUNFIRE	20	1983
YOUNG FREE AND SINGLE URBNRI	34	2008
YOUNG FRESH N' NEW KELIS	32	2001
YOUNG GIFTED AND BLACK BOB & MARCIA	5	1970
YOUNG GIRL UNION GAP FEATURING GARY PUCKETT	1	1968
YOUNG GIRL DARREN DAY	42	1994
YOUNG GIRL JOE LONGTHORNE	61	1994
YOUNG GIRL GLEE CAST	62	2010
YOUNG GIRLS & HAPPY ENDINGS GORKY'S ZYGOTIC MYNCI	49	1997
YOUNG GODS LITTLE ANGELS	34	1991
YOUNG GUNS (GO FOR IT) WHAM!	3	1982
YOUNG HEARTS KINGS OF TOMORROW	45	2002
YOUNG HEARTS KUJAY DADA	41	2003
YOUNG HEARTS RUN FREE CANDI STATON	2	1976
YOUNG HEARTS RUN FREE KYM MAZELLE	20	1997
YOUNG LIVERS ROCKET FROM THE CRYPT	67	1996
YOUNG LOVE [A] TAB HUNTER	1	1957
YOUNG LOVE [A] SONNY JAMES	11	1957
YOUNG LOVE [A] DONNY OSMOND	1	1973
YOUNG LOVE [B] MYSTERY JETS	34	2008
YOUNG LOVERS PAUL & PAULA	9	1963
THE YOUNG MC SUPERFUNK	62	2000
THE YOUNG NEW MEXICAN PUPPETEER TOM JONES	6	1972
THE YOUNG OFFENDER'S MUM CARTER–THE UNSTOPPABLE SEX MACHINE	34	1995
THE YOUNG ONES CLIFF RICHARD & THE SHADOWS	1	1962
YOUNG PARISIANS ADAM & THE ANTS	9	1981
YOUNG SOUL REBELS MICA PARIS	61	1991
YOUNG TURKS ROD STEWART	11	1981
YOUNG WORLD RICKY NELSON	19	1962
YOUNGER GIRL CRITTERS	38	1966
THE YOUNGEST WAS THE MOST LOVED MORRISSEY	14	2006
YOUR BABY AIN'T YOUR BABY ANYMORE PAUL DA VINCI	20	1974
YOUR BABY'S GONE SURFIN' DUANE EDDY & THE REBELETTES	49	1963
YOUR BODY [A] TOM NOVY FEATURING MICHAEL MARSHALL	10	2005
YOUR BODY [B] PRETTY RICKY	37	2006
YOUR BODY'S CALLIN' R KELLY	19	1994
YOUR CARESS (ALL I NEED) DJ FLAVOURS	19	1997
YOUR CASSETTE PET BOW WOW WOW	58	1980
YOUR CHEATING HEART RAY CHARLES	13	1962

Title / Artist	Peak Position	Year of Release
YOUR CHRISTMAS WISH SMURFS	8	1996
YOUR DREAM ADRIAN GURVITZ	61	1982
YOUR DRESS JOHN FOXX	61	1983
YOUR EARS SHOULD BE BURNING NOW MARTI WEBB	61	1980
YOUR EYES [A] SIMPLY RED	26	2000
YOUR EYES [B] RIK ROK FEATURING SHAGGY	57	2004
YOUR FACE SLACKER	33	1997
YOUR FASCINATION GARY NUMAN	46	1985
YOUR FAVOURITE THING SUGAR	40	1994
YOUR GAME WILL YOUNG	3	2004
YOUR GENERATION GENERATION X	36	1977
YOUR GHOST KRISTIN HERSH	45	1994
YOUR HONOUR PLUTO	19	1982
YOUR HURTIN' KIND OF LOVE DUSTY SPRINGFIELD	37	1965
YOUR KISS IS SWEET SYREETA	12	1975
YOUR KISSES ARE CHARITY CULTURE CLUB	25	1999
YOUR KISSES ARE WASTED ON ME PIPETTES	35	2006
YOUR LATEST TRICK DIRE STRAITS	26	1986
YOUR LOSS MY GAIN OMAR	47	1992
YOUR LOVE [A] HIPSWAY	66	1989
YOUR LOVE [B] FRANKIE KNUCKLES	59	1989
YOUR LOVE [C] DIANA ROSS	14	1993
YOUR LOVE [D] INNER CITY	28	1996
YOUR LOVE ALONE IS NOT ENOUGH MANIC STREET PREACHERS	2	2007
YOUR LOVE GETS SWEETER FINLEY QUAYE	16	1998
(YOUR LOVE HAS LIFTED ME) HIGHER AND HIGHER RITA COOLIDGE	48	1977
YOUR LOVE IS A 187 WHITEHEAD BROTHERS	32	1995
YOUR LOVE IS A LIE SIMPLE PLAN	63	2008
YOUR LOVE IS CALLING EVOLUTION	60	1996
YOUR LOVE IS KING SADE	6	1984
YOUR LOVE IS LIFTING ME NOMAD	60	1992
YOUR LOVE IS MY DRUG KE$HA	63	2010
(YOUR LOVE KEEPS LIFTING ME) HIGHER AND HIGHER JACKIE WILSON	11	1969
YOUR LOVE TAKES ME HIGHER BELOVED	39	1990
YOUR LOVING ARMS BILLIE RAY MARTIN	6	1994
YOUR LUCKY DAY IN HELL EELS	35	1997
YOUR MA SAID YOU CRIED IN YOUR SLEEP LAST NIGHT DOUG SHELDON	29	1962
YOUR MAGIC PUT A SPELL ON ME LJ JOHNSON	27	1976
YOUR MAMA DON'T DANCE POISON	13	1989
YOUR MAMA WON'T LIKE ME SUZI QUATRO	31	1975
YOUR MIRROR SIMPLY RED	17	1992
YOUR MISSUS IS A NUTTER GOLDIE LOOKIN CHAIN	14	2005
YOUR MOTHER'S GOT A PENIS GOLDIE LOOKIN CHAIN	14	2004
YOUR MUSIC INTENSO PROJECT FEATURING LAURA JAYE	32	2003
YOUR NEW CUCKOO CARDIGANS	35	1997
YOUR OWN RELIGION ALFIE	61	2005
YOUR OWN SPECIAL WAY GENESIS	43	1977
YOUR PAINTED SMILE BRYAN FERRY	52	1994
YOUR PERSONAL TOUCH EVELYN KING	37	1985
YOUR PLACE OR MINE CHOCOLATE MONDAY	49	2005
YOUR SECRET LOVE LUTHER VANDROSS	14	1996
YOUR SMILE OCTOPUS	42	1996
YOUR SONG ELTON JOHN	7	1971
YOUR SONG BILLY PAUL	37	1977
YOUR SONG ROD STEWART	41	1992
YOUR SONG ELTON JOHN & ALESSANDRO SAFINA	4	2002
YOUR SWAYING ARMS DEACON BLUE	23	1991
YOUR TENDER LOOK JOE BROWN & THE BRUVVERS	31	1962
YOUR TIME HASN'T COME YET BABY ELVIS PRESLEY	22	1968
YOUR TIME IS GONNA COME DREAD ZEPPELIN	59	1990
YOUR TOWN DEACON BLUE	14	1992
YOUR WOMAN WHITE TOWN	1	1997
YOUR WOMAN TYLER JAMES	60	2005
YOU'RE A BETTER MAN THAN I SHAM 69	49	1979
YOU'RE A LADY PETER SKELLERN	3	1972
YOU'RE A STAR AQUARIAN DREAM	67	1979
YOU'RE A SUPERSTAR LOVE INC	7	2002
YOU'RE ALL I HAVE SNOW PATROL	7	2006
YOU'RE ALL I NEED MOTLEY CRUE	23	1988
YOU'RE ALL I NEED TO GET BY MARVIN GAYE & TAMMI TERRELL	19	1968
YOU'RE ALL I NEED TO GET BY JOHNNY MATHIS & DENIECE WILLIAMS	45	1978
YOU'RE ALL THAT MATTERS TO ME CURTIS STIGERS	6	1992
YOU'RE BEAUTIFUL JAMES BLUNT	1	2005
YOU'RE BREAKIN' MY HEART KEELY SMITH	14	1965
YOU'RE DRIVING ME CRAZY TEMPERANCE SEVEN	1	1961
YOU'RE EVERYTHING TO ME BORIS GARDINER	11	1986
(YOU'RE) FABULOUS BABE KENNY WILLIAMS	35	1977
YOU'RE FREE YOMANDA	22	2003
YOU'RE FREE TO GO JIM REEVES	48	1972
YOU'RE GONE MARILLION	7	2004
YOU'RE GONNA GET NEXT TO ME BO KIRKLAND & RUTH DAVIS	12	1977
YOU'RE GONNA LOSE US CRIBS	30	2005
YOU'RE GONNA MISS ME TURNTABLE ORCHESTRA	52	1989
YOU'RE GORGEOUS BABYBIRD	3	1996
(YOU'RE) HAVING MY BABY PAUL ANKA FEATURING ODIA COATES	6	1974
YOU'RE HISTORY SHAKESPEAR'S SISTER	7	1989
YOU'RE IN A BAD WAY SAINT ETIENNE	12	1993
YOU'RE IN LOVE WILSON PHILLIPS	29	1991
YOU'RE IN MY HEART [A] ROD STEWART	3	1977
YOU'RE IN MY HEART [B] DAVID ESSEX	59	1983
YOU'RE INVITED (BUT YOUR FRIEND CAN'T COME) VINCE NEIL	63	1992
YOU'RE LOOKING HOT TONIGHT BARRY MANILOW	47	1983
YOU'RE LYING LINX	15	1980
YOU'RE MAKIN ME HIGH TONI BRAXTON	7	1996
YOU'RE MORE THAN A NUMBER IN MY LITTLE RED BOOK DRIFTERS	5	1976
YOU'RE MOVING OUT TODAY CAROLE BAYER SAGER	6	1977
YOU'RE MY ANGEL MIKEY GRAHAM	13	2000
YOU'RE MY BEST FRIEND [A] QUEEN	7	1976
YOU'RE MY BEST FRIEND [B] DON WILLIAMS	35	1976
YOU'RE MY EVERYTHING [A] TEMPTATIONS	26	1967
YOU'RE MY EVERYTHING [B] MAX BYGRAVES	34	1969
YOU'RE MY EVERYTHING [C] LEE GARRETT	15	1976
YOU'RE MY EVERYTHING [C] EAST SIDE BEAT	65	1993
YOU'RE MY GIRL ROCKIN' BERRIES	40	1965
YOU'RE MY HEART, YOU'RE MY SOUL MODERN TALKING	56	1985
YOU'RE MY LAST CHANCE 52ND STREET	49	1986
YOU'RE MY LIFE BARRY BIGGS	36	1977
YOU'RE MY MATE RIGHT SAID FRED	18	2001
YOU'RE MY NUMBER ONE S CLUB 7	2	1999
(YOU'RE MY ONE AND ONLY) TRUE LOVE ANN-MARIE SMITH	46	1995
(YOU'RE MY) SOUL AND INSPIRATION RIGHTEOUS BROTHERS	15	1966
YOU'RE MY WORLD [A] CILLA BLACK	1	1964
YOU'RE MY WORLD [B] NICK HEYWARD	67	1988
YOU'RE NEVER TOO YOUNG COOLNOTES	42	1984
YOU'RE NO GOOD SWINGING BLUE JEANS	3	1964
YOU'RE NO GOOD ASWAD	35	1995
YOU'RE NOT ALONE [A] OLIVE	1	1997
YOU'RE NOT ALONE [B] EMBRACE	14	2000
YOU'RE NOT ALONE [C] ENEMY	18	2007
YOU'RE NOT ALONE [D] TINCHY STRYDER	14	2009
YOU'RE NOT HERE TYRREL CORPORATION	42	1994
YOU'RE OK [A] OTTAWAN	56	1980
YOU'RE OK [B] k.d. lang	44	1996
YOU'RE ONE IMPERIAL TEEN	69	1996
(YOU'RE PUTTIN') A RUSH ON ME STEPHANIE MILLS	62	1987
YOU'RE READY NOW FRANKIE VALLI	11	1971
YOU'RE SHINING STYLES & BREEZE	19	2004
YOU'RE SINGING OUR LOVE SONG TO SOMEBODY ELSE JERRY WALLACE	46	1960
YOU'RE SIXTEEN JOHNNY BURNETTE	3	1961
YOU'RE SIXTEEN RINGO STARR	4	1974
YOU'RE SO PRETTY WE'RE SO PRETTY CHARLATANS	56	2006
YOU'RE SO RIGHT FOR ME [A] EASTSIDE CONNECTION	44	1978
YOU'RE SO RIGHT FOR ME [B] ROOSTER	14	2005
YOU'RE SO VAIN CARLY SIMON	3	1972
YOU'RE SPEAKING MY LANGUAGE JULIETTE & THE LICKS	35	2005
YOU'RE STILL THE ONE SHANIA TWAIN	10	1998
YOU'RE SUCH A GOOD LOOKING WOMAN JOE DOLAN	17	1970
(YOU'RE THE) DEVIL IN DISGUISE ELVIS PRESLEY	1	1963
YOU'RE THE FIRST THE LAST MY EVERYTHING BARRY WHITE	1	1974
YOU'RE THE FIRST THE LAST MY EVERYTHING HOWARD BROWN	13	2005
YOU'RE THE GREATEST LOVER JONATHAN KING	67	1979
YOU'RE THE INSPIRATION CHICAGO	14	1985
YOU'RE THE ONE [A] KATHY KIRBY	17	1964
YOU'RE THE ONE [B] PETULA CLARK	23	1965
YOU'RE THE ONE [C] BANG	74	1989
YOU'RE THE ONE [D] SWV	13	1996
YOU'RE THE ONE FOR ME D TRAIN	15	1982
YOU'RE THE ONE FOR ME – DAYBREAK – AM PAUL HARDCASTLE	41	1984
YOU'RE THE ONE FOR ME, FATTY MORRISSEY	19	1992
YOU'RE THE ONE I LOVE SHOLA AMA	3	1997
YOU'RE THE ONE THAT I WANT JOHN TRAVOLTA & OLIVIA NEWTON-JOHN	1	1978
YOU'RE THE ONE THAT I WANT HYLDA BAKER & ARTHUR MULLARD	22	1978
YOU'RE THE ONE THAT I WANT CRAIG McLACHLAN & DEBBIE GIBSON	13	1993
YOU'RE THE ONLY GOOD THING JIM REEVES	17	1961
YOU'RE THE ONLY ONE VAL DOONICAN	37	1968
YOU'RE THE REASON WAMDUE PROJECT	39	2000
YOU'RE THE REASON WHY RUBETTES	28	1976
YOU'RE THE STAR ROD STEWART	19	1995
YOU'RE THE STORM CARDIGANS	74	2003
YOU'RE THE STORY OF MY LIFE JUDY CHEEKS	30	1995
YOU'RE THE TOP CHA AL SAXON	17	1959
YOU'RE THE VOICE JOHN FARNHAM	6	1987
YOU'RE THE VOICE HEART	56	1991
YOU'RE THE WORLD TO ME DAVID GRAY	53	2007
YOU'RE WALKING ELECTRIBE 101	50	1990
YOURS DIONNE WARWICK	66	1983
YOURS FATALLY BIG BROVAZ	15	2004
YOURS UNTIL TOMORROW GENE PITNEY	34	1968
YOUTH AGAINST FASCISM SONIC YOUTH	52	1992
YOUTH GONE WILD SKID ROW	22	1989
YOUTH OF NATION ON FIRE BILL NELSON	73	1981
YOUTH OF THE NATION P.O.D.	36	2002
YOUTH OF TODAY MUSICAL YOUTH	13	1982

	Peak Position	Year of Release
YOU'VE BEEN DOING ME WRONG DELEGATION	49	1977
YOU'VE BEEN GONE CROWN HEIGHTS AFFAIR	44	1980
YOU'VE COME BACK PJ PROBY	25	1966
YOU'VE GIVEN ME SOMETHING THAT I CAN'T GIVE BACK NEW RHODES	38	2005
YOU'VE GOT A FRIEND JAMES TAYLOR	4	1971
YOU'VE GOT A FRIEND BIG FUN & SONIA FEATURING GARY BARNACLE	14	1990
YOU'VE GOT A FRIEND BRAND NEW HEAVIES	9	1997
YOU'VE GOT A FRIEND McFLY	1	2005
YOU'VE GOT A LOT TO ANSWER FOR CATATONIA	35	1996
YOU'VE GOT ANOTHER THING COMIN' JUDAS PRIEST	66	1982
YOU'VE GOT IT SIMPLY RED	46	1989
YOU'VE GOT IT BAD OCEAN COLOUR SCENE	7	1996
YOU'VE GOT LOVE BUDDY HOLLY & THE CRICKETS	40	1964
YOU'VE GOT ME DANGLING ON A STRING CHAIRMEN OF THE BOARD	5	1970
YOU'VE GOT ME THINKING BELOVED	23	1993
YOU'VE GOT MY NUMBER (WHY DON'T YOU USE IT) UNDERTONES	32	1979
YOU'VE GOT THAT SOMETHIN' ROBYN	54	1996
YOU'VE GOT TO CHOOSE DARLING BUDS	45	1989
YOU'VE GOT TO GIVE ME ROOM OLETA ADAMS	49	1991
YOU'VE GOT TO HIDE YOUR LOVE AWAY SILKIE	28	1965
YOU'VE GOT YOUR TROUBLES FORTUNES	2	1965
YOU'VE LOST THAT LOVIN' FEELIN' RIGHTEOUS BROTHERS	1	1965
YOU'VE LOST THAT LOVIN' FEELIN' CILLA BLACK	2	1965
YOU'VE LOST THAT LOVIN' FEELIN' TELLY SAVALAS	47	1975
YOU'VE LOST THAT LOVIN' FEELIN' DARYL HALL & JOHN OATES	55	1980
YOU'VE MADE ME SO VERY HAPPY BLOOD SWEAT & TEARS	35	1969
YOU'VE NEVER BEEN IN LOVE LIKE THIS BEFORE UNIT FOUR PLUS TWO	14	1965
YOU'VE NOT CHANGED SANDIE SHAW	18	1967
YOU'VE SAID ENOUGH CENTRAL LINE	58	1982
YOYO BOY ALBERTA	48	1998
YUM YUM (GIMME SOME) FATBACK BAND	40	1975
YUMMY YUMMY YUMMY OHIO EXPRESS	5	1968

Z

	Peak Position	Year of Release
ZABADAK! DAVE DEE, DOZY, BEAKY, MICK & TICH	3	1967
ZAMBESI LOU BUSCH	2	1956
ZAMBESI EDDIE CALVERT	13	1956
ZAMBESI PIRANHAS FEATURING BORING BOB GROVER	17	1982
ZEPHYR ELECTRAFIXION	47	1994
THE ZEPHYR SONG RED HOT CHILI PEPPERS	11	2002
ZERO YEAH YEAH YEAHS	49	2009
ZEROES AND ONES JESUS JONES	30	1993
ZEROTONINE JUNKIE XL	63	2000
ZEROX ADAM & THE ANTS	45	1981
ZEROXED ZERO ZERO	71	1991
ZIGGY STARDUST BAUHAUS	15	1982
ZING A LITTLE ZONG BING CROSBY & JANE WYMAN	10	1952
ZING WENT THE STRINGS OF MY HEART TRAMMPS	29	1974
ZION YOUTH DREADZONE	49	1995
ZIP GUN BOOGIE T REX	41	1974

45 RPM

EP Index

45 RPM

KEY TO INDEX ENTRIES

Album Title | Artist/Group | Peak Position | Year of Release

	Peak Position	Year of Release
A BA NI BI IZHAR COHEN & ALPHABETA	20	1978
'A' BOMB IN WARDOUR STREET JAM	1	1978
A9 ARIEL	28	2000
THE A TEAM MIKE POST	45	1984
A&E GOLDFRAPP	10	2008
AAAH D YAAA GOATS	53	1993
AARON'S PARTY (COME GET IT) AARON CARTER	51	2000
ABACAB GENESIS	9	1981
ABACUS (WHEN I FALL IN LOVE) AXUS	62	1998
ABANDON [A] DARE	71	1989
ABANDON [B] THAT PETROL EMOTION	73	1990
ABANDON SHIP BLAGGERS I.T.A.	48	1994
ABBA-ESQUE EP ERASURE	1	1992
THE ABBEY ROAD EP SPIRITUALIZED	39	1998
ABC JACKSON 5	8	1970

A

A

Title	Artist	Peak Position	Year of Release
ACKER NO. 1	MR ACKER BILK	6	1961
ACKER NO. 2	MR ACKER BILK	11	1962
ACKER'S AWAY	MR ACKER BILK	16	1960
ADAM FAITH NO. 1	ADAM FAITH	12	1962
ADAM NO. 1	ADAM FAITH	4	1961
ADAM NO. 3	ADAM FAITH	19	1961
ADAM'S HIT PARADE	ADAM FAITH	1	1960
ADAM'S LATEST HITS	ADAM FAITH	20	1963
AIN'T GONNA KISS YOU	SEARCHERS	1	1963
ALL ALONE AM I	BRENDA LEE	8	1963
ALL MY LOVING	BEATLES	1	1964
ALL THE WAY	FRANK SINATRA	6	1961
AMERICA	TRINI LOPEZ	16	1964
ANDY SINGS	ANDY STEWART	3	1961
ANDY STEWART SINGS	ANDY STEWART	12	1962
ANDY WILLIAMS FAVOURITES	ANDY WILLIAMS	3	1965
ANDY WILLIAMS FAVOURITES VOLUME 2	ANDY WILLIAMS	17	1965
ANDY'S NEWEST HITS	ANDY WILLIAMS	6	1967
ANIMAL TRACKS	ANIMALS	7	1966
THE ANIMALS ARE BACK	ANIMALS	8	1965
THE ANIMALS IS HERE	ANIMALS	3	1965
ANOTHER SIX	RUSS CONWAY	12	1960
ANYONE WHO HAD A HEART	CILLA BLACK	5	1964
AS LONG AS HE NEEDS ME	SHIRLEY BASSEY	3	1961
AS WAS	MANFRED MANN	4	1966
AT THE CAVERN	BIG THREE	6	1963
AT YOUR REQUEST VOLUME 2	HARRY SECOMBE	17	1960

B

Title	Artist	Peak Position	Year of Release
BACHELORS	BACHELORS	5	1964
BACHELORS' HITS	BACHELORS	1	1964
BACHELORS' HITS VOLUME 2	BACHELORS	9	1966
BACHELORS VOLUME 2	BACHELORS	7	1964
BACKSTAGE	GENE PITNEY	6	1966
BAND OF THIEVES	MR ACKER BILK	6	1962
BARBER'S BEST VOLUME 1	CHRIS BARBER'S JAZZ BAND	11	1960
BART FOR BART'S SAKE	LIONEL BART	20	1960
BBC TV'S SONG FOR EUROPE	KATHY KIRBY	9	1965
THE BEACH BOYS HITS	BEACH BOYS	1	1966
BEATLE CRACKER MUSIC	ARTHUR WILKINSON ORCHESTRA	7	1966
THE BEATLES (NO. 1)	BEATLES	2	1963
BEATLES FOR SALE	BEATLES	1	1965
BEATLES FOR SALE (NO. 2)	BEATLES	5	1965
THE BEATLES' HITS	BEATLES	1	1963
THE BEATLES' MILLION SELLERS	BEATLES	1	1965
BECAUSE THEY'RE YOUNG	DUANE EDDY	17	1961
BELAFONTE AT CHRISTMAS TIME	HARRY BELAFONTE	18	1961
BERN ELLIOTT AND THE FENMEN	BERN ELLIOTT AND THE FENMEN	10	1964
THE BEST OF BENNETT	TONY BENNETT	2	1967
THE BEST OF CHUCK BERRY	CHUCK BERRY	5	1964
THE BEST OF SELLERS	PETER SELLERS	15	1960
THE BEST OF SELLERS NO. 2	PETER SELLERS	8	1960
THE BEVS FOR CHRISTMAS	BEVERLEY SISTERS	11	1960
BILLY FURY AND THE TORNADOS	BILLY FURY AND THE TORNADOS	2	1963
BILLY FURY HITS	BILLY FURY	8	1962
THE BLACK AND WHITE MINSTREL SHOW	GEORGE MITCHELL MINSTRELS	1	1962
BLOWIN' IN THE WIND	PETER, PAUL & MARY	13	1964
BOB DYLAN	BOB DYLAN	3	1965
BOBBY VEE NO. 1	BOBBY VEE	19	1961
BOBBY VEE'S BIGGEST HITS	BOBBY VEE	16	1963
THE BOYS	SHADOWS	1	1962
BRUBECK IN EUROPE	DAVE BRUBECK	15	1960
BUDDY HOLLY NO. 1	BUDDY HOLLY	18	1961
BUMBLE BEE	SEARCHERS	1	1965
THE BUTTON-DOWN MIND OF BOB NEWHART VOLUME 1	BOB NEWHART	2	1961
THE BUTTON-DOWN MIND STRIKES BACK	BOB NEWHART	20	1962
BY A SLEEPY LAGOON	KARL DENVER	2	1962
BY APPOINTMENT	PETER COOK & DUDLEY MOORE	18	1966

C

Title	Artist	Peak Position	Year of Release
CAN I GET IT FROM YOU	DAVE BERRY	12	1965
CAROUSEL NO. 1	ORIGINAL FILM SOUNDTRACK	12	1960
C'EST FAB	FRANCOISE HARDY	5	1964
C'EST FRANCOISE	FRANCOISE HARDY	18	1964
CHRISTMAS AT HOME WITH NINA & FREDERIK	NINA & FREDERIK	2	1961
CHRISTMAS CARD FROM JIM REEVES	JIM REEVES	3	1966
CHRISTMAS WITH PINKY AND PERKY	PINKY & PERKY	16	1961
CHRISTMAS WITH THE MINSTRELS	GEORGE MITCHELL MINSTRELS	4	1961
CHUCK AND BO	CHUCK BERRY & BO DIDDLEY	6	1963
CHUCK AND BO VOLUME 2	CHUCK BERRY & BO DIDDLEY	15	1963
CHUCK AND BO VOLUME 3	CHUCK BERRY & BO DIDDLEY	12	1964
CHUCK BERRY	CHUCK BERRY	7	1963
CILLA'S HITS	CILLA BLACK	6	1966
CLARINET JAMBOREE	MR ACKER BILK & TERRY LIGHTFOOT	19	1961
CLARINET JAMBOREE	TERRY LIGHTFOOT'S NEW ORLEANS JAZZMEN	19	1961
CLIFF RICHARD NO. 2	CLIFF RICHARD & THE SHADOWS	19	1962
CLIFF SINGS 'DON'T TALK TO HIM'	CLIFF RICHARD & THE SHADOWS	15	1964
CLIFF SINGS NO. 1	CLIFF RICHARD & THE SHADOWS	4	1960
CLIFF SINGS NO. 2	CLIFF RICHARD & THE SHADOWS	3	1960
CLIFF SINGS NO. 3	CLIFF RICHARD	2	1960
CLIFF'S HIT PARADE	CLIFF RICHARD & THE SHADOWS	4	1962
CLIFF'S HITS FROM 'ALADDIN AND HIS WONDERFUL LAMP'	CLIFF RICHARD & THE SHADOWS	20	1965
CLIFF'S LUCKY LIPS	CLIFF RICHARD & THE SHADOWS	17	1963
CLIFF'S SILVER DISCS	CLIFF RICHARD & THE SHADOWS	1	1960
C'MON EVERYBODY	EDDIE COCHRAN	2	1960
COME DANCE WITH ME NO. 1	FRANK SINATRA	11	1960
COME DANCE WITH ME NO. 2	FRANK SINATRA	13	1960
COME FLY WITH ME (PART 4)	FRANK SINATRA	10	1960

D

Title	Artist	Peak Position	Year of Release
DA DOO RON RON	CRYSTALS	18	1964
DANCE ON WITH THE SHADOWS	SHADOWS	16	1963
DANCE WITH JIMMY SHAND NO. 2	JIMMY SHAND & HIS BAND	15	1962
DANCE WITH THE SHADOWS	SHADOWS	20	1964
DANCE WITH THE SHADOWS NO. 3	SHADOWS	16	1965
DANCING PARTY	CHUBBY CHECKER	17	1963
DANCING TIME FOR LATINS	JOE LOSS & HIS ORCHESTRA	17	1961
THE DAVE CLARK FIVE	DAVE CLARK FIVE	3	1964
DECK OF CARDS	TEX RITTER	19	1962
DECK OF CARDS	WINK MARTINDALE	11	1963
DEDICATED KINKS	KINKS	7	1966
DEL SHANNON	DEL SHANNON	14	1962
DEL SHANNON NO. 2	DEL SHANNON	9	1963
DID YOU EVER HAVE TO MAKE UP YOUR MIND	LOVIN' SPOONFUL	3	1966
DIDDYNESS	KEN DODD	8	1967
DODDY AND THE DIDDY MEN	KEN DODD	4	1965
DONOVAN, VOLUME ONE	DONOVAN	12	1966
DON'T BLAME ME	FRANK IFIELD	19	1964
DON'T LET THE SUN CATCH YOU CRYING	GERRY & THE PACEMAKERS	15	1964
DON'T MAKE ME OVER	DIONNE WARWICK	13	1964
DON'T THINK TWICE, IT'S ALRIGHT	JOAN BAEZ	10	1965
DOONICAN'S IRISH STEW	VAL DOONICAN	4	1966
DOWNTOWN	PETULA CLARK	12	1965
DREAM	CLIFF RICHARD & THE SHADOWS	3	1961
DREAMS OF OLWEN	MANTOVANI & HIS ORCHESTRA	17	1960
DUSTY	DUSTY SPRINGFIELD	3	1964
DUSTY IN NEW YORK	DUSTY SPRINGFIELD	13	1965
DYNAMIC SHIRLEY BASSEY	SHIRLEY BASSEY	15	1964

E

Title	Artist	Peak Position	Year of Release
EASY COME EASY GO (OST)	ELVIS PRESLEY	1	1967
EIGHT MILES HIGH	BYRDS	8	1966
1812 OVERTURE	PAUL VAN KEMPEN	11	1960
EINE KLEINE BEATLE MUSIC	BAROCK AND ROLL ENSEMBLE	4	1965
ELLA SINGS IRVING BERLIN	ELLA FITZGERALD	17	1960
ELVIS FOR YOU VOLUME 1	ELVIS PRESLEY	11	1964
ELVIS FOR YOU VOLUME 2	ELVIS PRESLEY	18	1964
ELVIS SINGS CHRISTMAS SONGS	ELVIS PRESLEY	16	1960
EMILE	EMILE FORD AND THE CHECKMATES	1	1960
EN FRANCAIS	BARBRA STREISAND	10	1966
THE EVERLY BROTHERS	EVERLY BROTHERS	15	1960
THE EVERLY BROTHERS – NO. 4	EVERLY BROTHERS	8	1960
THE EVERLY BROTHERS – NO. 5	EVERLY BROTHERS	7	1960
THE EVERLY BROTHERS – NO. 6	EVERLY BROTHERS	20	1962
EXCERPTS FROM THE DESERT SONG	DAVID WHITFIELD	16	1962
EXODUS AND OTHER THEMES	MANTOVANI & HIS ORCHESTRA	3	1961
EXPRESSO BONGO (OST)	CLIFF RICHARD & THE SHADOWS	1	1960

Title	Artist	Peak Position	Year of Release
EXTRACTS FROM THE ALBUM 'A HARD DAY'S NIGHT'	BEATLES	8	1965
EXTRACTS FROM THE FILM 'A HARD DAY'S NIGHT'	BEATLES	1	1964

F

Title	Artist	Peak Position	Year of Release
FABULOUS MISS BASSEY	SHIRLEY BASSEY	5	1960
FABULOUS MISS BASSEY NO. 2	SHIRLEY BASSEY	15	1961
THE FACTS OF LIFE FROM STEPTOE AND SON	WILFRED BRAMBELL & HARRY H CORBETT	4	1963
FARLOWE IN THE MIDNIGHT HOUR	CHRIS FARLOWE	6	1966
FATS FOR FAME	GEORGIE FAME	15	1965
FATS WALLER	FATS WALLER	14	1960
FIRST DELIVERY	ALLAN SMETHURST	7	1966
FIRST LADY OF RECORD	CONNIE FRANCIS	7	1961
FIVE BY FIVE	ROLLING STONES	1	1964
FIVE YARDBIRDS	YARDBIRDS	5	1965
FOLLOW THAT DREAM (OST)	ELVIS PRESLEY	1	1962
FOLLOW THAT GIRL	ORIGINAL LONDON STAGE CAST SOUNDTRACK	19	1960
FOOT TAPPING WITH THE SHADOWS	SHADOWS	7	1963
A FOREVER KIND OF LOVE	BOBBY VEE	14	1963
FOUR BY THE BEACH BOYS	BEACH BOYS	11	1964
FOUR HITS	JOHNNY MATHIS	17	1961
FOUR HITS AND A MISTER	MR ACKER BILK	2	1962
FOUR MORE	CRICKETS	7	1960
FOUR SHOW HITS	JOHNNY MATHIS	17	1961
THE FOUR TOPS	FOUR TOPS	2	1966
FOUR TOPS HITS	FOUR TOPS	1	1967
FOURMOST SOUND	FOURMOST	15	1964
FRANK IFIELD'S HITS	FRANK IFIELD	1	1962
FROM THE HEART VOLUME 1	JIM REEVES	4	1964
FROM THE HEART VOLUME 2	JIM REEVES	14	1964
FUN, FUN, FUN	BEACH BOYS	19	1964

G

Title	Artist	Peak Position	Year of Release
THE GAME OF LOVE	WAYNE FONTANA AND THE MINDBENDERS	19	1965
GEORGIE FAME	GEORGIE FAME	2	1967
GETAWAY	GEORGIE FAME	7	1966
GO AWAY FROM MY WORLD	MARIANNE FAITHFULL	4	1965
GOD ONLY KNOWS	BEACH BOYS	3	1966
GOLDEN HITS OF THE HARRY SIMEONE CHORALE	HARRY SIMEONE CHORALE	8	1961
GOT LIVE IF YOU WANT IT	ROLLING STONES	1	1965
THE GREAT CARUSO	MARIO LANZA	16	1960
GREEN SHADES OF VAL DOONICAN	VAL DOONICAN	1	1965
GROOVIN' WITH MANFRED MANN	MANFRED MANN	3	1964
GUITAR GENIUS	CHET ATKINS	19	1963

H

Title	Artist	Peak Position	Year of Release
HANDEL'S ARIAS	KENNETH McKELLAR	9	1960
A HARD RAIN'S GONNA FALL	JOAN BAEZ	7	1966
HEARTACHES	CONNIE FRANCIS	14	1961
HEARTBEAT	BUDDY HOLLY	13	1961
HELEN	HELEN SHAPIRO	1	1961
HELEN'S HIT PARADSE	HELEN SHAPIRO	1	1962
HERMANIA	HERMAN'S HERMITS	19	1965
HERMAN'S HERMITS HITS	HERMAN'S HERMITS	10	1965
HI!	GENO WASHINGTON & THE RAM JAM BAND	7	1967
HITS	EDEN KANE	12	1962
HITS FROM 'SUMMER HOLIDAY'	CLIFF RICHARD & THE SHADOWS	4	1963
HITS FROM THE SEEKERS	SEEKERS	1	1966
HITS FROM 'THE YOUNG ONES'	CLIFF RICHARD & THE SHADOWS	1	1962
THE HITS OF CHER	CHER	10	1966
THE HITS OF THE DAVE CLARK FIVE	DAVE CLARK FIVE	20	1965
HOLIDAY CARNIVAL	CLIFF RICHARD & THE SHADOWS	1	1963
THE HOLLIES	HOLLIES	6	1964
HOUSE AT POOH CORNER	IAN CARMICHAEL	10	1961
HOW DO YOU LIKE IT?	GERRY & THE PACEMAKERS	2	1963
HUNGRY FOR LOVE	SEARCHERS	4	1964

I

Title	Artist	Peak Position	Year of Release
I AM A ROCK	SIMON AND GARFUNKEL	4	1966
I CAN'T LET GO	HOLLIES	9	1966
I CAN'T STOP LOVING YOU	RAY CHARLES	10	1963
I NEED YOU	WALKER BROTHERS	1	1966
I ONLY WANT TO BE WITH YOU	DUSTY SPRINGFIELD	8	1964
I THINK OF YOU	MERSEYBEATS	8	1964
IF YOU GOTTA MAKE A FOOL OF SOMEBODY	FREDDIE & THE DREAMERS	8	1963
I'M ALIVE	HOLLIES	5	1965
I'M THE ONE	GERRY & THE PACEMAKERS	11	1964
IN CONCERT	PETE SEEGER	18	1964
IN DREAMS	ROY ORBISON	6	1963
IN SEARCH OF THE CASTAWAYS (OST)	MAURICE CHEVALIER & HAYLEY MILLS	18	1963
IN THE WIND VOLUME 1	PETER, PAUL & MARY	12	1965
INDIAN LOVE CALL	JEANETTE MacDONALD & NELSON EDDY	12	1960
INSTRUMENTAL ASYLUM	MANFRED MANN	3	1966
IT'S FOR YOU	CILLA BLACK	12	1964
IT'S LOVE	JOHNNY MATHIS	20	1961
IT'S LOVE THAT REALLY COUNTS	DIONNE WARWICK	18	1964
IT'S OVER	ROY ORBISON	3	1964
IT'S SO EASY	CRICKETS	18	1962
IT'S THE TEMPTATIONS	TEMPTATIONS	8	1967
I'VE GOT A CRUSH ON YOU	FRANK SINATRA	14	1960

J

Title	Artist	Peak Position	Year of Release
JAILHOUSE ROCK (OST)	ELVIS PRESLEY	14	1961
JAZZ SEBASTIAN BACH	SWINGLE SINGERS	11	1964
JAZZ SEBASTIAN BACH VOLUME 2	SWINGLE SINGERS	18	1965
JERRY LEE LEWIS – NO. 4	JERRY LEE LEWIS	13	1962
JERRY LEE LEWIS – NO. 5	JERRY LEE LEWIS	14	1962
JET AND TONY	JET HARRIS & TONY MEEHAN	3	1963
JOE BROWN HIT PARADE	JOE BROWN	20	1963
THE JOHN BARRY SOUND	JOHN BARRY 7 + 4	4	1961
JOHN LEYTON	JOHN LEYTON	11	1962
JOURNEY TO THE CENTRE OF THE EARTH	PAT BOONE	8	1960
JUG BAND MUSIC	LOVIN' SPOONFUL	8	1966
JUST FOR FUN	BOBBY VEE & THE CRICKETS	1	1963
JUST FOR YOU	PETER AND GORDON	20	1964
JUST ONE LOOK	HOLLIES	10	1964
JUST ONE MORE CHANCE	FRANK IFIELD	5	1963

K

Title	Artist	Peak Position	Year of Release
KARL DENVER HITS	KARL DENVER	7	1962
KATHY KIRBY VOLUME 2	KATHY KIRBY	20	1964
KENNETH MCKELLAR NO. 2	KENNETH McKELLAR	13	1960
KENNETH MCKELLAR SINGS HANDEL	KENNETH McKELLAR	12	1960
KENNY BALL'S HIT PARADE	KENNY BALL & HIS JAZZMEN	5	1962
KENNY'S BIG FOUR	KENNY BALL & HIS JAZZMEN	3	1961
KID GALAHAD (OST)	ELVIS PRESLEY	1	1962
THE KING AND I	ORIGINAL FILM SOUNDTRACK	12	1960
KING OF THE TWIST	CHUBBY CHECKER	3	1962
KINKSIZE HITS	KINKS	3	1965
KINKSIZE SESSION	KINKS	1	1964
KOOKIE	ED BYRNES	20	1961
KWYET KINKS	KINKS	1	1965

L

Title	Artist	Peak Position	Year of Release
THE LADY IS A TRAMP	FRANK SINATRA	7	1960
LAND OF MY FATHERS	HARRY SECOMBE	8	1960
LAND OF SONG	IVOR EMMANUEL	13	1961
THE LATE, GREAT BUDDY HOLLY	BUDDY HOLLY	4	1960
LATIN STYLE	JOE LOSS & HIS ORCHESTRA	19	1962
LAWRENCE OF ARABIA VOLUME 1	LONDON PHILHARMONIC ORCHESTRA	13	1964
LAWRENCE OF ARABIA VOLUME 2	LONDON PHILHARMONIC ORCHESTRA	18	1965
LISTEN TO CLIFF NO. 1	CLIFF RICHARD & THE SHADOWS	17	1961
LISTEN TO ME	BUDDY HOLLY	12	1962
LITTLE PIECES OF HANCOCK	TONY HANCOCK	6	1962
LIVE IT UP	HEINZ	12	1964
LIVING WITH JAY AND THE AMERICANS	JAY & THE AMERICANS	10	1966
THE LONELY ONE	DUANE EDDY	16	1961
LONG TALL SALLY	BEATLES	1	1964
LOOK INTO MY EYES, MARIA	CLIFF RICHARD	15	1965
LOOS OF ENGLAND	DAVE DEE, DOZY, BEAKY, MICK AND TICH	8	1967
LOS SHADOWS	SHADOWS	4	1963
LOVE IN LAS VEGAS (OST)	ELVIS PRESLEY	3	1964
LOVE IS THE THING	NAT 'KING' COLE	2	1960
LOVE SONGS	CLIFF RICHARD	4	1963

M

Title	Artist	Peak Position	Year of Release
MACHINES	MANFRED MANN	1	1966
MADEMOISELLE DUSTY	DUSTY SPRINGFIELD	17	1965

Title / Artist	Peak Position	Year of Release
MAGGIE MAY JUDY GARLAND	18	1964
MANTOVANI'S BIG FOUR MANTOVANI & HIS ORCHESTRA	6	1960
ME AND MY SHADOWS NO. 1 CLIFF RICHARD & THE SHADOWS	5	1961
ME AND MY SHADOWS NO. 2 CLIFF RICHARD & THE SHADOWS	8	1961
ME AND MY SHADOWS NO. 3 CLIFF RICHARD & THE SHADOWS	6	1961
MEAN AS HELL – BALLADS FROM THE TRUE WEST JOHNNY CASH	8	1966
MEET MISTER MATHIS JOHNNY MATHIS	18	1960
MEET THE DAKOTAS DAKOTAS	19	1963
MERRY CHRISTMAS PART 1 BING CROSBY	9	1960
A MESSAGE TO MARTHA – FROM ADAM ADAM FAITH	17	1965
MIREILLE MATHIEU MIREILLE MATHIEU	9	1967
MR ACKER BILK REQUESTS VOLUME 2 MR ACKER BILK	11	1960
THE MOJOS MOJOS	12	1964
MOODS OF ELLA ELLA FITZGERALD	17	1960
THE MOODY BLUES MOODY BLUES	12	1965
MORE HITS FROM HELEN HELEN SHAPIRO	12	1962
MORE OF FRANK IFIELD'S HITS FRANK IFIELD	4	1963
MORE PARTY POPS RUSS CONWAY	7	1960
MORE SOUNDS FROM THE TORNADOS TORNADOS	8	1963
MORNINGTOWN RIDE SEEKERS	1	1967
MOST HAPPY FELLA EDMUND HOCKRIDGE	8	1960
MOVING PETER, PAUL & MARY	16	1964
MR ACKER BILK MARCHES ON MR ACKER BILK	12	1960
MR ACKER BILK SINGS MR ACKER BILK	15	1960
MR TAMBOURINE MAN BOB DYLAN	4	1966
MRS BROWN YOU'VE GOT A LOVELY DAUGHTER HERMAN'S HERMITS	3	1965
MUSIC FROM THE SOUNDTRACK 'HOLD ON' HERMAN'S HERMITS	4	1966
THE MUSIC MAN EDMUND HOCKRIDGE	20	1961
THE MUSICK TEMPERANCE SEVEN	2	1961
MY CONCERTO FOR YOU NO. 2 RUSS CONWAY	11	1961
MY FAIR LADY NO. 4 ORIGINAL BROADWAY STAGE CAST SOUNDTRACK	20	1960
MY MAN BARBRA STREISAND	8	1966

N

Title / Artist	Peak Position	Year of Release
NEVER ON SUNDAY ORIGINAL FILM SOUNDTRACK	8	1961
NEVER TO BE FORGOTTEN EDDIE COCHRAN	18	1963
NINA & FREDERIK NO. 1 NINA & FREDERIK	13	1960
NINA & FREDERIK NO. 2 NINA & FREDERIK	8	1960
NINA & FREDERIK NO. 3 NINA & FREDERIK	8	1960
NINA & FREDERIK VOLUME 1 NINA & FREDERIK	2	1960
NINA & FREDERIK VOLUME 2 NINA & FREDERIK	3	1960
NO LIVING WITHOUT LOVING MANFRED MANN	1	1965
NOBODY'S CHILD ALEXANDER BROTHERS	20	1966
NOWHERE MAN BEATLES	4	1966

Title / Artist	Peak Position	Year of Release
OH PRETTY WOMAN ROY ORBISON	9	1965
OLIVER ORIGINAL LONDON STAGE CAST SOUNDTRACK	5	1961
ON STAGE MERSEYBEATS	2	1964
ON STAGE TOM JONES	3	1965
ON THE AIR SPOTNICKS	2	1963
THE ONE IN THE MIDDLE MANFRED MANN	1	1965
ONE TOO MANY MORNINGS BOB DYLAN	8	1966
ONLY THE LONELY ROY ORBISON	15	1963
ORIGINALS FROM MARVIN GAYE MARVIN GAYE	3	1967
OUR GRACIE SINGS COMEDY SONGS GRACIE FIELDS	16	1960
OUT OF THE SHADOWS SHADOWS	3	1963
OUT OF THE SHADOWS NO. 2 SHADOWS	20	1963
OVER YOU FREDDIE AND THE DREAMERS	17	1964

P

Title / Artist	Peak Position	Year of Release
PJ PROBY PJ PROBY	13	1965
PADDY ROBERTS STRIKES AGAIN PADDY ROBERTS	1	1960
PEACE IN THE VALLEY ELVIS PRESLEY	12	1961
PEPE DUANE EDDY	10	1961
PETER, PAUL & MARY PETER, PAUL & MARY	3	1963
PHONETIC PUNCTUATION VICTOR BORGE	15	1961
PILLOW TALK DORIS DAY	11	1960
THE PINK PANTHER HENRY MANCINI	14	1964
PLANET SUITE – MARS & JUPITER BBC SYMPHONY ORCHESTRA	14	1960
PLAY IT COOL BILLY FURY	2	1962
PLEASE FRANK IFIELD	18	1964
THE PRETTY THINGS PRETTY THINGS	6	1964
PRIVILEGE PAUL JONES	1	1967

R

Title / Artist	Peak Position	Year of Release
R&B WITH BOOKER T VOL. 2 BOOKER T AND THE MG'S	19	1965
RACE WITH THE DEVIL GENE VINCENT	19	1962
RAININ' IN MY HEART PRETTY THINGS	12	1965
RAVE ON BUDDY HOLLY	9	1961
READY STEADY WHO WHO	1	1966
REVISITED EARTHA KITT	18	1962
RHYTHM AND BLUES AT THE FLAMINGO GEORGIE FAME	8	1965
RHYTHM AND GREENS (OST) SHADOWS	8	1964
RICHARD ANTHONY RICHARD ANTHONY	18	1964
ROAD TO THE ISLES KENNETH McKELLAR	8	1960
ROCKING HORSE COWBOY RUSS CONWAY	12	1960
ROLF HARRIS AND SHAMUS O'SHEAN THE LEPRACHAUN ROLF HARRIS	9	1966
THE ROLLING STONES ROLLING STONES	1	1964
ROSE MARIE (SELECTION) DAVID WHITFIELD	15	1961
ROY ORBISON'S STAGE SHOW HITS ROY ORBISON	10	1965

S

Title / Artist	Peak Position	Year of Release
SACRED SONGS HARRY SECOMBE	9	1960
SACRED SONGS VOLUME 2 HARRY SECOMBE	15	1960
SALAD DAYS ORIGINAL LONDON STAGE CAST SOUNDTRACK	19	1960
SAMMY DAVIS, JR IMPERSONATING SAMMY DAVIS, JR	18	1963
SCARLET RIBBONS HARRY BELAFONTE	18	1960
SEARCHERS '65 SEARCHERS	15	1965
SEARCHERS PLAY THE SYSTEM SEARCHERS	4	1964
THE SEEKERS SEEKERS	1	1965
SEVEN AGES OF ACKER MR ACKER BILK	6	1960
SEVEN AGES OF ACKER VOLUME 2 MR ACKER BILK	9	1961
SEVEN BRIDES FOR SEVEN BROTHERS ORIGINAL FILM SOUNDTRACK	9	1960
SEVEN BRIDES FOR SEVEN BROTHERS VOLUME 2 ORIGINAL FILM SOUNDTRACK	18	1961
THE SHADOWS SHADOWS	1	1961
THE SHADOWS NO. 2 SHADOWS	12	1962
THE SHADOWS NO. 3 SHADOWS	13	1962
THE SHADOWS TO THE FORE SHADOWS	1	1961
SHAKE WITH THE SWINGING BLUE JEANS SWINGING BLUE JEANS	13	1964
SHAKIN' ALL OVER JOHNNY KIDD & THE PIRATES	11	1961
SHINDIG WITH THE SHADOWS SHADOWS	9	1963
SHIRLEY & LEE SHIRLEY & LEE	16	1960
SHIRLEY NO 2 SHIRLEY BASSEY	15	1961
SHOW SOUVENIRS HARRY SECOMBE	18	1962
SILVER DAGGER AND OTHER THINGS JOAN BAEZ	3	1965
SINCERELY BOBBY VEE	8	1962
THE SINGING POSTMAN ALLAN SMETHURST	20	1965
SINGS CHRISTMAS CAROLS MARIO LANZA	10	1960
SITTIN' & THINKIN' SPENCER DAVIS GROUP	3	1966
SMOOTH SARAH SARAH VAUGHAN	11	1960
SOLO JOHN – SOLO SCOTT WALKER BROTHERS	4	1966
SOME PEOPLE ORIGINAL FILM SOUNDTRACK	2	1962
SOMETHIN' ELSE EDDIE COCHRAN	6	1960
SOMEWHERE MATT MONRO	19	1965
SOMEWHERE PJ PROBY	19	1965
SONG FOR EUROPE MATT MONRO	16	1964
THE SONG IS YOU FRANK SINATRA	19	1960
SONGS FOR SWINGIN' LOVERS NO. 1 FRANK SINATRA	20	1960
SONGS FROM THE FILM 'WHAT A CRAZY WORLD' FREDDIE & THE DREAMERS	15	1964
SONGS FROM THE FROST REPORT JULIE FELIX	5	1966
SONGS TO WARM THE HEART JIM REEVES	12	1962
SONGS TO WARM THE HEART VOLUME 2 JIM REEVES	9	1964
THE SOUND OF MUSIC PETULA CLARK	4	1961
THE SOUND OF MUSIC ORIGINAL BROADWAY STAGE CAST SOUNDTRACK	13	1961
THE SOUND OF MUSIC ORIGINAL LONDON STAGE CAST SOUNDTRACK	19	1962
THE SOUND OF THE TORNADOS TORNADOS	2	1962
SOUTH PACIFIC MARY MARTIN	20	1960
SOUTH PACIFIC NO. 1 ORIGINAL FILM SOUNDTRACK	1	1960
SPEAK TO ME GENTLY BRENDA LEE	18	1962
SPIN WITH THE PENNIES FOUR PENNIES	6	1964
SPOTLIGHT ON THE SHADOWS SHADOWS	1	1962
THE SPOTNICKS IN PARIS SPOTNICKS	17	1963
SPURS GO MARCHING ON TOTTENHAM HOTSPUR FA CUP SQUAD	6	1967
STACCATO ELMER BERNSTEIN	6	1960
STARRING SAMMY DAVIS, VOLUME 1 SAMMY DAVIS, JR	20	1960
STILL KEN DODD	18	1964
STRICTLY ELVIS ELVIS PRESLEY	1	1960
STRICTLY FOR GROWN UPS PADDY ROBERTS	1	1960
STRICTLY PRIMA LOUIS PRIMA	12	1960
THE STUDENT PRINCE MARIO LANZA	8	1960

Title	Artist	Peak Position	Year of Release
SUCH A NIGHT	ELVIS PRESLEY	4	1960
SUNDAY NIGHT AT THE LONDON PALLADIUM	ROBERT HORTON	7	1960
THE SUPREMES HITS	SUPREMES	6	1965
SWEETS FOR MY SWEET	SEARCHERS	5	1963
SWINGING WITH THE INCREDIBLE JIMMY SMITH	JIMMY SMITH	10	1966

T

Title	Artist	Peak Position	Year of Release
TAKE FIVE	DAVE BRUBECK	4	1961
TAKE FOUR	CLIFF RICHARD & THE SHADOWS	4	1965
TAKE THESE CHAINS FROM MY HEART	RAY CHARLES	16	1963
TAUBER FAVOURITES	HARRY SECOMBE	18	1962
A TEENAGER SINGS THE BLUES	HELEN SHAPIRO	15	1962
TELL ME	HOWLIN' WOLF	16	1964
TELL THE BOYS	SANDIE SHAW	4	1967
TELSTAR	TORNADOS	4	1963
TEMPERANCE SEVEN	TEMPERANCE SEVEN	3	1961
THE TEMPTATIONS	TEMPTATIONS	18	1965
TENDERLY	NAT 'KING' COLE	9	1961
THAT GIRL BELONGS TO YESTERDAY	GENE PITNEY	13	1965
THAT'S ALL	BOBBY DARIN	6	1960
THE BILLY J KRAMER HITS	BILLY J KRAMER WITH THE DAKOTAS	8	1963
THEM	THEM	5	1965
THEME MUSIC FROM 'INSPECTOR MAIGRET'	RON GRAINER ORCHESTRA	13	1962
THEMES FROM 'ALADDIN & HIS WONDERFUL LAMP'	SHADOWS	14	1965
(THERE'S) ALWAYS SOMETHING THERE TO REMIND ME	SANDIE SHAW	9	1965
THIS IS MIKI & GRIFF	MIKI & GRIFF	2	1960
THIS IS MY SONG	PETULA CLARK	6	1967
THOSE BRILLIANT SHADOWS	SHADOWS	6	1964
THOSE TALENTED SHADOWS	SHADOWS	9	1966
THREE WHEELS ON MY WAGON	NEW CHRISTY MINSTRELS	5	1966
THUNDERBIRDS ARE GO (OST)	SHADOWS	6	1966
TICKLE ME (OST)	ELVIS PRESLEY	3	1965
TICKLE ME VOLUME 2 (OST)	ELVIS PRESLEY	8	1965
TILL	TONY BENNETT	7	1966
TIME TO CELEBRATE NO. 2	RUSS CONWAY	17	1960
THE TIMES THEY ARE A-CHANGIN'	BYRDS	15	1966
TOMMY THE TOREADOR (OST)	TOMMY STEELE	4	1960
TONY'S HITS	ANTHONY NEWLEY	6	1960
TOP SIX	ANONYMOUS COVER VERSIONS	10	1964
TOP SIX VOLUME 2	ANONYMOUS COVER VERSIONS	10	1964
TOP SIX VOLUME 3	ANONYMOUS COVER VERSIONS	16	1964
TOP TEN RECORD CLUB	ANONYMOUS COVER VERSIONS	17	1964
TOP TEN RECORD NO. 3	ANONYMOUS COVER VERSIONS	15	1963
TOP TEN RECORD NO. 7	ANONYMOUS COVER VERSIONS	16	1963
TOP TEN RECORD NO. 9	ANONYMOUS COVER VERSIONS	17	1964
TORNADO ROCK	TORNADOS	7	1963
TOUCH OF GOLD	ELVIS PRESLEY	8	1960
TOUCH OF GOLD VOLUME 2	ELVIS PRESLEY	10	1960
A TRIBUTE TO BUDDY HOLLY	MIKE BERRY	17	1963
TRINI LOPEZ AT PJ'S	TRINI LOPEZ	11	1963
TROGGS TOPS	TROGGS	8	1967
TWANGY	DUANE EDDY	4	1960
TWENTY FOUR HOURS FROM TULSA	GENE PITNEY	7	1964
TWIST AND SHOUT	BEATLES	1	1963

U

Title	Artist	Peak Position	Year of Release
UM, UM, UM, UM, UM, UM	WAYNE FONTANA & THE MINDBENDERS	7	1964
UNFORGETTABLE	NAT 'KING' COLE	2	1960
UNIT FOUR PLUS TWO	UNIT FOUR PLUS TWO	11	1965
THE UNIVERSAL SOLDIER	DONOVAN	1	1965

Title	Artist	Peak Position	Year of Release
THE VENTURES	VENTURES	20	1961
VIVA IFIELD	FRANK IFIELD	11	1963

W

Title	Artist	Peak Position	Year of Release
THE WAGES OF SIN	WILFRED BRAMBELL & HARRY H CORBETT	10	1963
WALKIN' ALONE	RICHARD ANTHONY	6	1964
THE WAYS OF LOVE	TOMMY EDWARDS	15	1960
WELCOME TO MY WORLD	JIM REEVES	6	1964
WEST SIDE STORY	ORIGINAL BROADWAY STAGE CAST SOUNDTRACK	5	1962
WEST SIDE STORY	ORIGINAL BROADWAY STAGE CAST SOUNDTRACK	15	1963
WESTERN FAVOURITES	FRANKIE LAINE	7	1961
WHEN JOANNA LOVED ME	TONY BENNETT	5	1965
WHEN YOU WALK IN THE ROOM	SEARCHERS	12	1965
WHITE CHRISTMAS	NINA & FREDERIK	11	1962
WILD WEEKEND	DAVE CLARK FIVE	10	1965
WITH A SONG IN MY HEART	ELLA FITZGERALD	10	1960
WITH GOD ON OUR SIDE	JOAN BAEZ	1	1966
THE WONDERFUL LAND OF THE SHADOWS	SHADOWS	6	1962
WONDERFUL LIFE	CLIFF RICHARD & THE SHADOWS	3	1964

Title	Artist	Peak Position	Year of Release
YANKEE DOODLE DONEGAN	LONNIE DONEGAN	8	1960
YEP!	DUANE EDDY	16	1960
YESTERDAY	BEATLES	1	1966
YOU PUT THE HURT ON ME	SPENCER DAVIS GROUP	4	1965
YOU'LL NEVER WALK ALONE	PERRY COMO	20	1960
YOU'LL NEVER WALK ALONE	GERRY & THE PACEMAKERS	8	1964
YOU'RE BREAKIN' ME UP	LEE DORSEY	7	1966